RACEHORSE RECORD FLAT 2010

A-Z GUIDE TO HORSES THAT RAN DURING THE 2009 SEASON

Editor	**Ashley Rumney**
Comments by	**David Bellingham, Mark Brown, Steffan Edwards, Walter Glynn, Keith Hewitt, Richard Lowther, Lee McKenzie, David Orton, Ashley Rumney, David Toft, Ronald Wood, Richard Young**
Raceform Ratings	**Paul Curtis, Simon Turner, Sam Walker**
Speed Figures	**David Bellingham**
Development	**Phillip Lamphee, Dan Dipol**

Published in 2009 by Raceform Ltd,
Compton, Newbury, Berkshire, RG20 6NL

A catalogue record for this book is available from the British Library

ISBN 978-1-906820-23-7

Printed in the UK by CPI William Clowes Ltd Beccles NR34 7TL

CONTENTS

Full details of all Raceform services and publications are available from
Raceform, Sanders Road, Wellingborough, Northants NN8 4BX.
Tel: 01933 304858 • Fax: 01933 270300
Email: shop@racingpost.com

Cover Photo: Conduit (Ryan Moore) wins the
King George VI and Queen Elizabeth Stakes at Ascot

INTRODUCTION

Raceform's Racehorse Record has been designed not only as an historical reference, but also as a guide to the future, with the aim being to provide factual information about individual horses that ran under Flat Racing Rules in Britain during the 2009 season, and also to pinpoint conditions that are likely to prove conducive to future success.

For full season's results and ratings, refer to *The Form Book Flat Annual for 2010*.

The horses are listed in alphabetical order.

KEY TO HORSE RECORDS

Vortex

101 (109) (111) **113**

9-y-o b g Danehill (USA)-Roupala (USA) (Vaguely Noble)

Miss Gay Kelleway Coriolis Partnership

Placings:045301/2601160/11111001302421 4P/251011300220/25 652004311/310202303000561-30604000504 **(4089)**

2008: 8^{3}SD, 8^{0}FT, 8^{6}FT, 7^{0}G, 8^{4}SD, 7^{0}SD, 7^{0}G, 7^{0}F, 7^{5}F, 7^{0}GF, 8^{4}SD,

	Starts	1st	2nd	3rd	Win & Pl
Career Total (Turf)	**42**	**4**	**6**	**4**	**152718**
Career Total (AW)	**36**	**13**	**4**	**4**	**181450**

109	12/07	Ling	7f	(0-100)H	STD	£9971
108	2/07	Ndas	7f110y	(90-105)H	GD	£33673
108	12/06	Ling	7f		STD	£6232
101	12/06	Ling	1m		STD	£5505
115	6/05	NmkJ	7f		GD	£29000
111	5/05	NmkR	7f	(0-105)H	G-F	£12045
116	4/05	Ling	7f		STD	£6043
105	9/04	Taby	1m		FST	£11646
	5/04	Jage	1m120y		FST	£46583
104	3/04	Wolv	1m100y	B(0-105)H	SS	£20300
93	2/04	Wolv	1m100y	D(0-85)H	SLW	£4108
89	2/04	Wolv	1m100y	D(0-85)H	SS	£4085
82	1/04	Ling	1m	D(0-80)H	STD	£4199
82	1/04	Wolv	1m100y	D(0-80)H	STD	£4065
86	7/03	Wolv	7f	E(0-70)	STD	£3526
77	7/03	Nott	1m54y	E(0-70)	FRM	£3604
70	12/02	Ling	7f	D	STD	£3640

Total win prize-money £208227

Going (Turf): Sf: 0-0 GS: 0-2 **Gd: 2-15** GF: 1-22 Fm: 1-3
Distance: 5f/6f: 0-1 **7f-8f: 11-64** 9f-13f: 6-13 14f+: 0-0
Track : **LH: 14-39** RH: 0-4 **Tight: 11-25** Gall: 1-9
Aids: Bl: 0-4 Vi: 0-3 Tstrap: 0-0 Ckp: 0-0
Best Rating: **116** 4/05 Ling 7f stand

Very useful; stays 1m, but possibly better at 7f; acts best on a fast surface and Polytrack; has worn blinkers, eyeshield, tongue tie and visor.

Name of horse, plus country of origin suffix in brackets

Master Split Second speed rating on left, Raceform rating on right (All-Weather ratings in brackets)

Age, colour, sex and pedigree. The sire's name is followed by the dam's name, then the dam's sire's name in brackets

Trainer's name in bold (plus date of transfer and previous trainer's name if the horse changed stables during the season), followed by the owner's name

Complete list of the horse's placings, starting with its first recorded race. Turf outings are in roman type and All-Weather/Dirt outings in bold type. A slash '/' or dash '-' indicates a change of season. This is followed in brackets by the Raceform number of the last race in the Form Book in which the horse competed

2008 season's record, broken down into race types followed by career record

Career wins, showing (left to right) winning Raceform rating, date of win (month/year), course, distance, race conditions and type, going, win prize money

Career going record (wins-runs),best figures in bold

Career distance record

Career track type record

Career aids record for the season (blinkers, visor, tongue strap)

Best Raceform rating achieved during the season, followed by the relevant date, course, distance, going and race type

Raceform master comment on selected horses only.

RACING POST RATINGS

Racing Post Ratings for each horse are listed after the Starting Price and indicate the actual level of performance attained in that race. The figure in the back index represents the BEST public form that Raceform's Handicappers still believe the horse capable of reproducing.

To use the ratings constructively in determining those horses best-in in future events, the following procedure should be followed:

(i) In races where all runners are the same age and are set to carry the same weight, no calculations are necessary. The horse with the highest rating is best-in.

(ii) In races where all runners are the same age but are set to carry different weights, add one point to the Raceform Rating for every pound less than 10 stone to be carried; deduct one point for every pound more than 10 stone.

For example,

Horse	Adjustment Age & Weight	RR from 10st	base rating	Adjusted rating
Hyperides	3-10-1	-1	78	77
Midas	3-9-13	+1	80	81
Tehran	3-9-7	+7	71	78
Happy Landing	3-8-11	+17	60	77

Therefore Midas is top-rated (best-in)

(iii) In races concerning horses of different ages the procedure in example (ii) should again be followed, but reference must also be made to the Official Scale of Weight-For-Age.

For example,

12 furlongs July 20th

Horse	Age & Weight	Adjusted from 10st	RR base rating	Adjusted rating	W-F-A deduct	Final rating
Pride Of India	5-10-0	0	90	90	Nil	90
Barnes Park	4-9-9	+5	83	88	Nil	88
Masked Light	3-9-4	+10	85	95	-12	83
Stokes	4-8-7	+21	73	94	Nil	94

Therefore Stokes is top-rated (best-in)

(A 3-y-o is deemed 12lb less mature than a 4-y-o or older horse on 20th July over 12f. Therefore, the deduction of 12 points is necessary.)

The following symbols are used in conjunction with the ratings:

++	almost certain to prove better
+	likely to prove better
d	disappointing (has run well below best recently)
?	form hard to evaluate
t	tentative rating based on race-time rating mayprove unreliable

TOP RATED HORSES

THAT RACED IN BRITAIN IN 2009

Horse	Rating
Sea The Stars (IRE)	138
Rip Van Winkle (IRE)	132
Goldikova (IRE)	131
Fame And Glory	131
Gladiatorus (USA)	129
Mastercraftsman (IRE)	129
Conduit (IRE)	127
Scenic Blast (AUS)	127
Paco Boy (IRE)	126
Yeats (IRE)	125
Youmzain (IRE)	125
Aqlaam	125
Twice Over	125
Tartan Bearer (IRE)	125
Zacinto	125
Ask	124
Vision D'Etat (FR)	124
Kingsgate Native (IRE)	123
Fleeting Spirit (IRE)	123
Casual Conquest (IRE)	123
Main Aim	123
Never On Sunday (FR)	123
Delegator	123
Sariska	123
St Nicholas Abbey (IRE)	123
Presvis	122
Famous Name	122
Bronze Cannon (USA)	122
Mawatheeq (USA)	122
Gitano Hernando	122
Geordieland (FR)	121
Cesare	121
Borderlescott	121
Takeover Target (AUS)	121

The Official Scale of Weight, Age & Distance (Flat)

The following scale should only be used in conjunction with the Official ratings published in this book. Use of any other scale will introduce errors into calculations. The allowances are expressed as the number of pounds that is deemed the average horse in each group falls short of maturity at different dates and distances.

Dist		Jan		Feb		Mar		Apr		May		Jun		Jul		Aug		Sep		Cct		Nov		Dec	
(fur)	Age	1-15	16-31	1-14	15-28	1-15	16-31	1-15	16-30	1-15	16-31	1-15	16-30	1-15	16-31	1-15	16-31	1-15	16-30	1-15	16-31	1-15	16-30	1-15	16-31
5	2	-	-	-	-	-	47	44	41	38	36	34	32	30	28	26	24	22	20	19	18	17	17	16	16
	3	15	15	14	14	13	12	11	10	9	8	7	6	5	4	3	2	1	1	-	-	-	-	-	-
6	2	-	-	-	-	-	-	-	-	44	41	38	36	33	31	28	26	24	22	21	20	19	18	17	17
	3	16	16	15	15	14	13	12	11	10	9	8	7	6	5	4	3	2	2	1	1	-	-	-	-
7	2	-	-	-	-	-	-	-	-	-	-	-	-	38	35	32	30	27	25	23	22	21	20	19	19
	3	18	18	17	17	16	15	14	13	12	11	10	9	8	7	6	5	4	3	2	2	1	1	-	-
8	2	-	-	-	-	-	-	-	-	-	-	-	-	-	-	37	34	31	28	26	24	23	22	21	20
	3	20	20	19	19	18	17	15	14	13	12	11	10	9	8	7	6	5	4	3	3	2	2	1	1
9	3	22	22	21	21	20	19	17	15	14	13	12	11	10	9	8	7	6	5	4	4	3	3	2	2
	4	1	1	-	-	-	-	-	-	-	-	-	-	-	-	-	-	-	-	-	-	-	-	-	-
10	3	23	23	22	22	21	20	19	17	15	14	13	12	11	10	9	8	7	6	5	5	4	4	3	3
	4	2	2	1	1	-	-	-	-	-	-	-	-	-	-	-	-	-	-	-	-	-	-	-	-
11	3	24	24	23	23	22	21	20	19	17	15	14	13	12	11	10	9	8	7	6	6	5	5	4	4
	4	3	3	2	2	1	1	-	-	-	-	-	-	-	-	-	-	-	-	-	-	-	-	-	-
12	3	25	25	24	24	23	22	21	20	19	17	15	14	13	12	11	10	9	8	7	7	6	6	5	5
	4	4	4	3	3	2	2	1	1	-	-	-	-	-	-	-	-	-	-	-	-	-	-	-	-
13	3	26	26	25	25	24	23	22	21	20	19	17	15	14	13	12	11	10	9	8	8	7	7	6	6
	4	5	5	4	4	3	3	2	1	-	-	-	-	-	-	-	-	-	-	-	-	-	-	-	-
14	3	27	27	26	26	25	24	23	22	21	20	19	17	15	14	13	12	11	10	9	9	8	8	7	7
	4	6	6	5	5	4	4	3	2	1	-	-	-	-	-	-	-	-	-	-	-	-	-	-	-
15	3	28	28	27	27	26	25	24	23	22	21	20	19	17	15	14	13	12	11	10	9	8	8	7	7
	4	6	6	5	5	4	4	3	3	2	1	-	-	-	-	-	-	-	-	-	-	-	-	-	-
16	3	29	29	28	28	27	26	25	24	23	22	21	20	19	17	15	14	13	12	11	10	9	9	8	8
	4	7	7	6	6	5	5	4	4	3	2	1	-	-	-	-	-	-	-	-	-	-	-	-	-
18	3	31	31	30	30	29	28	27	26	25	24	23	22	21	20	18	16	14	13	12	11	10	10	9	9
	4	8	8	7	7	6	6	5	5	4	3	2	1	-	-	-	-	-	-	-	-	-	-	-	-
20	3	33	33	32	32	31	30	29	28	27	26	25	24	23	22	20	18	16	14	13	12	11	11	10	10
	4	9	9	8	8	7	7	6	6	5	4	3	2	1	-	-	-	-	-	-	-	-	-	-	-

REVIEW OF THE SEASON

by Richard Lowther

Two thousand and ten will be remembered as the year of Sea The Stars. The three-year-old colt, trained on the Curragh by John Oxx and ridden every time by veteran Michael Kinane, won all six of his races, each at the top level and over distances ranging from a mile to a mile and a half. By general consensus he was one of the all-time greats.

The year had its sadness too, never more so than in early September when apprentice jockeys Jamie Kyne and Jan Wilson died in a fire in Malton. The apprentice jockeys' championship, won by Freddie Tylicki, was renamed in honour of the two young riders.

Punters got the turf season off to a flying start when Expresso Star was a decisive winner of the William Hill Lincoln at Doncaster on March 28. The John Gosden-trained gelding had been the ante-post favourite since the market opened in January and landed a big gamble.

The first recognised Guineas trials were held at Newmarket's Craven meeting on April 15-16. Luca Cumani's Fantasia won the Leslie Harrison Memorial Nell Gwyn Stakes by seven lengths under Frankie Dettori, but was ruled out of the 1000 Guineas as her owner George Strawbridge already had the warm favourite Rainbow View. The Banshahousestables.com Craven Stakes was won easily by Delegator, from the Brian Meehan yard. The colt had been a massive springer in the Guineas market following a sparkling gallop.

The trials at Newbury on April 18 did not look like having much effect on the Guineas markets. Mick Channon's Lahaleeb beat Super Sleuth a head in the Dubai Duty Free Fred Darling Stakes, with Sariska an eyecatching fourth. The Bathwick Tyres Greenham Stakes went to Vocalised from the yard of Jim Bolger, who had won the previous year's Guineas with New Approach.

Sea The Stars took his first steps on the road to greatness with a victory in the Stanjames.com 2000 Guineas at Newmarket on May 2. The son of Cape Cross, who had endured an interrupted preparation for the Classic, went off at 8/1, but beat the favourite Delegator by a comfortable length and a half. Jim Bolger's Gan Amhras was third (Vocalised was an absentee), ahead of the Aidan O'Brien pair Rip Van Winkle and Mastercraftsman. The following afternoon's Stanjames.com 1000 Guineas appeared at the mercy of Rainbow View, who had been the outstanding 2-y-o of her year and went off at 8/11. She could manage only fifth, though, behind 20/1 winner Ghanaati who was trained by Barry Hills and ridden by his son Richard. Cuis Ghaire, from the Bolger yard, was second, a place ahead of Super Sleuth. The well-bred Ghanaati was making her turf debut, having run in a couple of Kempton maidens at two.

Hills, father and son, and owner Hamdan Al Maktoum treamed up again at Chester three days later to land the Totesport.com Chester Cup with Daraahem. The big chestnut was Hills senior's fourth win in this historic race, and his 150th winner at Chester. Aidan O'Brien saddled the first two in the next day's Virgin Money Chester Vase, but there was a surprise outcome. Colm O'Donoghue made all aboard 25/1 shot Golden Sword, winning by two lengths from the favourite Masterofthehorse, who was given a lot to do by rider Johnny Murtagh.

Murtagh was below par again on the final day of Chester's meeting when partnering the Irish Derby winner Frozen Fire in a three-runner Betchronicle.com Ormonde Stakes. The race was a complete farce, the runners barely breaking into a trot for the first three-quarters of a mile. When the sprint to the line finally developed, Frozen Fire was quickly beaten, finishing last of three behind Buccellati, the mount of William Buick, and Scintillo.

Frozen Fire's trainer Aidan O'Brien enjoyed a happier time the following weekend when landing a pair of Derby trials. Age Of Aquarius and Murtagh took the

Totesport.com Derby Trial at Lingfield despite running green, and the next day Fame And Glory, ridden by Seamie Heffernan, was an impressive five-length winner of the Derrinstown Stud Derby Trial at Leopardstown.

Lingfield's Oaks Trial was won in clear-cut style by the favourite Midday, from the Henry Cecil yard, and at York on May 13 there was another taking trial for the fillies' Classic when Sariska and Jamie Spencer landed the Tattersalls Musidora Stakes in decisive fashion.

Spencer must have had high hopes of winning the next day's York feature, the Totesport.com Dante Stakes, aboard the Racing Post Trophy winner Crowded House, but Brian Meehan's colt was to run rather flat, finishing only eighth of ten. The race was another triumph for the Ballydoyle team, with Black Bear Island and Colm O'Donoghue holding Johnny Murtagh's mount, the favourite Freemantle, by a head.

There was a tight finish to the Group 1 Juddmonte Lockinge Stakes at Newbury on May 16. The John Gosden-trained Virtual, ridden by Jimmy Fortune, got up on the line to pip Alexandros and Frankie Dettori by a nose, with Twice Over half a length away in third. The result might have been different had Dettori not had his whip knocked out of his hand with a furlong to run.

Mastercraftsman's win in the Boylesports.com Irish 2000 Guineas at the Curragh on May 23 gave trainer Aidan O'Brien his ninth consecutive Irish Classic and provided Sea The Stars' Guineas form with an early boost. O'Brien's Classic run ended the next day when Again, trained by David Wachman, took the Irish 1000 Guineas by a neck from Lahaleeb. This was the first victory in the race for Johnny Murtagh, who had also partnered Mastercraftsman.

The 9/4 favourite Sariska obliged in the Investec Oaks at Epsom on June 5, but only by a head from Midday. The winner, trained by Michael Bell, had to survive a lengthy stewards' enquiry, after which her rider Jamie Spencer picked up a five-day ban for careless riding which ruled him out of part of Royal Ascot. One of those affected in a rough race was Rainbow View, who finished well held in fourth.

Earlier in the day there was a three-day photo finish in the Investec Coronation Cup, with two noses separating the first three home, Ask, Youmzain and Look Here. Ask, ridden by Ryan Moore for Sir Michael Stoute, was supplementing his win in the Yorkshire Cup in May.

A small field of 12 turned out for the Investec Derby, eight of them trained in Ireland including six from Ballydoyle. Johnny Murtagh chose to ride Rip Van Winkle, but it was another of the Aidan O'Brien squad, Fame And Glory under Seamie Heffernan, who went off favourite. In the event neither was able to trouble Sea The Stars, the 11/4 shot winning by a comfortable length and three quarters to become the first horse since Nashwan 20 years earlier to land both the Guineas and the Derby. The next four home were all trained by O'Brien, Fame And Glory finishing second followed by Masterofthehorse, Rip Van Winkle and Golden Sword. Crowded House did best of the British quartet in sixth, a place ahead of Age Of Aquarius, with another O'Brien trial winner Black Bear Island in tenth. Sea The Stars' performance was not extravagant, but it was one of sheer class.

Chantilly's Prix du Jockey Club on June 7 went to Le Havre, trained by Jean-Claude Rouget who was on his way to the French championship. The colt injured himself shortly afterwards and did not race again.

The five-day Royal Ascot meeting opened with three consecutive Group 1 events. The first of them, the Queen Anne Stakes, was won in commanding style by Paco Boy, trained by Richard Hannon and ridden by his son-in-law Richard Hughes. Despite his win, the colt's stamina for a mile was still the subject of considerable debate. The King's Stand Stakes produced a strong field of international sprinters. Scenic Blast, successful by three-quarters of a length from Fleeting Spirit, was a fourth Australian-trained winner of this event in the last seven years. He was the first runner/ride in Britain for trainer Danny Morton and jockey Steven Arnold.

Mastercraftsman secured his second top-level win of the year when successful in the St James's Palace Stakes. The admirably tough grey, who rallied to deny Delegator by a neck, was winning away from the Curragh for the first time.

Richard Hannon and Richard Hughes enjoyed further first-day success when Canford Cliffs was a brilliant six-length winner of the Coventry Stakes. Hughes went on to ride a treble aboard Judgethemoment in the Ascot Stakes. History was made in the final race on day one, the Windsor Castle Stakes. Strike The Tiger, trained by Wesley Ward and ridden by John Velasquez, became the first-ever winner on the Flat in Britain to be trained in the USA.

There was a blanket finish to day's two feature race, the Group 1 Prince Of Wales's Stakes. Victory went to the Eric Libaud-trained Vision D'Etat, the previous year's French Derby winner, with Tartan Bearer, Never On Sunday and Twice Over not beaten far.

The Royal Hunt Cup went to the runner that had dominated the market, Forgotten Voice. Trained by Jeremy Noseda and ridden by Johnny Murtagh, the 4/1 favourite was a comfortable winner, looking a potential Group horse in a handicap.

History-maker Wesley Ward enjoyed further success when Jealous Again and John Velasquez took the Queen Mary Stakes by five lengths. The filly was subsequently snapped up by Godolphin.

Ascot's third day belonged to the magnificent Yeats, who brought the house down when winning the Gold Cup for the fourth consecutive year. Johnny Murtagh's mount, who beat Patkai by three and a half lengths, was the first four-time winner in the 207-year history of the famous race.

Father Time, ridden by Eddie Ahern, was a clear-cut winner of the King Edward VII Stakes on day four of the meeting. This was Henry Cecil's 71st winner at the Royal meeting, but his first since 2002.

The 1000 Guineas winner Ghanaati and Richard Hills followed up easily in the Coronation Stakes, establishing herself as the best miling filly of her age in Europe. The winners of the French and Irish Guineas, Elusive Wave and Again, were among those she beat. Ghanaati's trainer Barry Hills doubled up with Giganticus in the Buckingham Palace Handicap, in the hands of son Michael.

There was a surprise outcome to the Group 1 Golden Jubilee Stakes, the highlight of Ascot's final day. The race went to 20/1 shot Art Connoisseur, who had been without a win since the Coventry Stakes a year earlier. A neck ahead of the Wesley Ward-trained Cannonball, Art Connoisseur was ridden for trainer Michael Bell by Tom Queally, replacing the suspended Jamie Spencer. Hayley Turner would have been in line to take the mount had she not been stood down following a head injury. At one time she had been set to miss the whole season, but following a successful appeal she returned to action in July.

The last, and longest, race of the meeting, the Queen Alexandra Stakes, went to the Nicky Henderson-trained Caracciola. At the age of twelve, the gelding was the oldest ever Royal Ascot winner, and earlier in the season had become the oldest Listed-race winner when successful at York.

Aidan O'Brien saddled a record seventh winner of the Dubai Duty Free Irish Derby when Fame And Glory was an easy five-length scorer at the Curragh on June 28. O'Brien was also responsible for the second and fourth, Golden Sword and Masterofthehorse, in a field which for the first time since 1957 lacked an overseas runner. Sea The Stars was declared, but was pulled out because of the yielding ground. Instead, Sea The Stars waited until Sandown on July 4 and the Coral-Eclipse. The dual Classic hero duly landed the odds but had to dig deep to repel Rip Van Winkle, with Conduit in third. On a hot day the excitement became all too much for the winning owner Christopher Tsui, and he fainted after the race.

There was some excellent racing at Newmarket's July Festival. On the first day the brilliant French mare Goldikova was a comfortable half-length winner over Heaven Sent in the Group 1 Etihad Airways Falmouth Stakes. Trained by Freddie Head and ridden by Olivier Peslier, she was winning her fourth race at the top level.

The highlight of the three days, the Darley July Cup, was a controversial race. It was won by Fleeting Spirit, ridden by Tom Queally, but the filly hung badly to her left near the finish before veering right, hampering runner-up Main Aim and fifth-placed King's Apostle. Three Royal Ascot winners were beaten, Paco Boy a never-nearer fourth but Scenic Blast and Art Connoisseur finishing down the field.

Oaks heroine Sariska followed up in the Irish equivalent at the Curragh on July 12. In a race run in heavy ground, the evens favourite won by a ludicrously easy three lengths from Roses In The Snow, with Midday third.

The first Flat fixture at Ffos Las, the new course in west Wales, was on July 21. Barry and Michael Hills teamed up to take the opening race with juvenile filly Our Dream Queen.

Sir Michael Stoute enjoyed a personal triumph when he sent out the first three home in Ascot's King George VI and Queen Elizabeth Stakes on July 25. Conduit and Ryan Moore beat Tartan Bearer by a length and a three-quarters, with Ask back in third. The first and second both carried the colours of the Ballymacoll Stud, and the result effectively clinched a tenth trainers' championship for Stoute. There was an odd postscript to the race when it emerged that death threats had been issued to Conduit by a man who stood to owe a gambling syndicate £50,000 if the chestnut won the big race.

The Glorious Goodwood meeting straddled the end of July and beginning of August. On day one the speedy two-year-old Monsieur Chevalier made it six wins from seven starts with a last-to-first surge in the Betfair Molecomb Stakes. His trainer Richard Hannon was to land another top Goodwood two-year-old event, the Richmond Stakes, with Dick Turpin later in the week.

Day two's highlight, the BGC Sussex Stakes, provided Rip Van Winkle with his first Group 1 success of the season, the 6/4 favourite accounting for Paco Boy and Ghanaati under Johnny Murtagh. Aidan O'Brien had gone down to the start in order to check over Rip Van Winkle, the colt having been troubled by a recurring hoof problem.

The Audi King George Stakes on the third day went to Kingsgate Native, who had returned to training after proving infertile at stud. Now owned by the Cheveley Park Stud and trained by Sir Michael Stoute, the colt was an impressive winner over Total Gallery.

Goodwood's final day was misty and murky with limited visibility. The conditions were no problem to Midday, who was a good winner of the Blue Square Nassau Stakes at the main expense of Rainbow View.

The Bluesquare.com Stewards' Cup produced its usual cavalry charge, but when they emerged from the gloom it was 14/1 shot Genki who showed in front. The winner was ridden by Steve Drowne for trainer Roger Charlton.

A Richard Hughes treble helped the Irish team to an easy win in the Shergar Cup at Ascot on August 8. The jockey scored aboard Polly's Mark, We'll Come and Press The Button.

York's Ebor meeting took place on August 18-21, and the first day was blessed with an appearance from Sea The Stars in the Juddmonte International Stakes. Sent off at 1/4, he raced somewhat lazily but still broke the track record in proving much too good for Mastercraftsman, his only real rival. There were no home-based runners in a field of just four, the other pair being pacemakers for Mastercraftsman who finished over 30 lengths adrift.

Earlier in the afternoon Monitor Closely advertised his St Leger credentials by taking the Ladbrokes Great Voltigeur Stakes from Mastery and Father Time. Peter Chapple-Hyam's colt, the outsider of the seven at 28/1, was stepping up to 1m4f for the first time.

The historic Irish Thoroughbred Marketing Gimcrack Stakes saw an emphatic winner in Showcasing from the stable of John Gosden. The favourite was two lengths too strong for Taajub, with Monsieur Chevalier back in third.

Aidan O'Brien's Changingoftheguard started a warm favourite for the Totesport

Ebor, but the three-year-old found one too good in the form of Sesenta. The mare, trained in Ireland by Willie Mullins, was a first winner in Britain for apprentice Gary Carroll.

Sariska started a warm favourite for the Darley Yorkshire Oaks on the third day, but she went down by three parts of a length to Jimmy Fortune's mount Dar Re Mi, trained by John Gosden. Sariska was the sixth Oaks winner to be beaten in the York race since 1997, but it turned out that she had been heavily in season.

Borderlescott landed the Coolmore Nunthorpe Stakes for the second time, but his win the previous year was at Newmarket as the Ebor meeting had been a washout. This time Robin Bastiman's flagbearer won by a neck from Benbaun with two-year-old Radiohead third and Kingsgate Native back in sixth.

The Prix Morny at Deauville on August 23 was one of the top juvenile races of the season, although the five runners were separated by only around a length at the line. Victory went to Arcano, from the filly Special Duty with Canford Cliffs close up in third. Arcano, trained by Brian Meehan, had been bought by Hamdan Al Maktoum since winning the July Stakes at Newmarket on his previous start.

Delegator, twice runner-up in Group 1s earlier in the season, was a cosy winner of the Group 2 Totesport Celebration Mile at Goodwood on August 29. However the colt, by this stage with Godolphin, subsequently tested positive for a prohibited substance and was disqualified, the race being awarded to runner-up Zacinto.

Six-times Champion jockey Kieren Fallon, whose career was almost wrecked by race-fixing allegations and a drugs ban, returned to action at the beginning of September after nearly two years out of the saddle. Our Kes at Wolverhampton on September 5 was his first winner and there were signs during the autumn that all Fallon's old ability and hunger remained.

The Betfred Sprint Cup at Haydock on September 5 saw a surprise winner when Regal Parade, trained by David Nicholls, proved too strong in the latter stages for favourite Fleeting Spirit. This was a first Grade 1 victory for jockey Adrian Nicholls, the trainer's son.

Racing in his home country for the only time during the season, Sea The Stars maintained his flawless record with victory in the Irish Champion Stakes at Leopardstown on September 5. Too good for old rivals Fame And Glory and Mastercraftsman, this was his fifth Group 1 of the campaign and his best performance yet.

Earlier in the day Rainbow View gained a deserved first Group 1 win of the year, in the Coolmore Fusaichi Pegasus Matron Stakes. John Gosden's filly, wearing cheekpieces for the first time, beat Heaven Sent and Again.

As always there was some interesting racing at Doncaster's St Leger meeting from September 9-12. The DFS Doncaster Cup looked a fine opportunity for Geordieland, but the enigmatic grey could finish only third behind Askar Tau and Darley Sun. The winner, trained by Marcus Tregoning, was adding to his Lonsdale Cup win at York the previous month.

The DFS Champagne Stakes on the final day went to the Godolphin representative Poet's Voice under Frankie Dettori. The favourite scored at the chief expense of Aidan O'Brien's Viscount Nelson.

Saeed Bin Suroor had two runners in the Ladbrokes St Leger and it was Dettori's mount Kite Wood, winner of the Geoffrey Freer Stakes at Newbury, who was the punters' choice at 9/4 favourite. He ran well, but was beaten three-quarters of a length into second by his stablemate Mastery, a 14/1 shot ridden by Ted Durcan. Monitor Closely was third, a place ahead of Father Time. This was Godolphin's sixth St Leger but their first British Classic since Rule Of Law won the Leger in 2004.

The Irish Field St Leger at the Curragh went off just 20 minutes later than the Doncaster version. It saw another Classic win for John Oxx, this time with the Aga Khan's progressive four-year-old Alandi, who beat Clowance half a length. The runner-up had not been seen on a racecourse since finishing fourth in the 2008 Oaks.

There was controversy at Longchamp's Arc trials meeting on September 13. Dar Re Mi beat the hot favourite Stacelita, the French Oaks winner, by a short neck in the Prix Vermeille, only to be demoted to fifth by the stewards for causing interference to the fourth home. Dar Re Mi's owner Lady Lloyd-Webber lodged an appeal, but the result stood.

On the same card Andre Fabre's Cavalryman was a cosy winner of the Prix Niel, while Spanish Moon took the Prix Foy from Vision D'Etat. Spanish Moon, trained by Sir Michael Stoute, was banned from running in Britain due to his misbehaviour at the stalls.

The William Hill Ayr Gold Cup on September 19 went to the Clive Cox-trained, Frankie Dettori-ridden Jimmy Styles, who beat Barney McGrew by a head with Knot In Wood third. The latter's trainer Richard Fahey and jockey Brian McHugh had already won the inaugural Bronze Cup at Ayr with Baldemar and the Silver Cup with Kaldoun Kingdom.

A select field of four turned out for the Sony Queen Elizabeth II Stakes at Ascot on September 26. The odds-on favourite Rip Van Winkle comfortably added another Group 1 to the Sussex Stakes, with Zacinto second and Delegator third. Prix du Moulin winner Aqlaam was last of the quartet.

The other Group 1 on Ascot's card, the Meon Valley Stud Fillies' Mile, was won by Hibaayeb and jockey Neil Callan. The Clive Brittain-trained winner was the only maiden in the line-up.

There was another brace of Group 1 juvenile races at Newmarket on October 2. A high-quality renewal of the Electrolux Cheveley Park Stakes was won in taking style by Special Duty, trained in France by Criquette Head-Maarek, and the filly looked a worthy ante-post favourite for the 1000 Guineas. Thirty-five minutes later the unbeaten Awzaan, trained by Mark Johnston, proved too strong for Radiohead, Showcasing and Poet's Voice in an intriguing Shadwell Middle Park Stakes.

Ghanaati looked to have been found a good opportunity in the next day's Kingdom of Bahrain Sun Chariot Stakes, but the Guineas winner was beaten by 16/1-shot Sahpresa, a first winner in Britain for French trainer Rod Collet.

Later on the Newmarket card there was a fine finish to the Totesport.com Cambridgeshire, with Supaseus making all and holding off Tartan Gigha by a nose. This was the biggest career win to date for jockey Travis Block.

Sea The Stars rounded off a stellar career in the Prix de l'Arc de Triomphe at Longchamp on October 4. The 4/6 favourite overcame trouble in running under a fine ride by Michael Kinane to score in imperious fashion from Youmzain, who was runner-up for the third year in succession. Cavalryman was third, ahead of Conduit, Dar Re Mi and Fame And Glory. The Breeders' Cup Classic was under consideration for Sea The Stars, but it was announced shortly after the Arc that this brilliant colt had run his last race and would be retired to stud in Ireland.

The British continued their domination of France's top sprint, the Prix de l'Abbaye. Cross-channel raiders filled the first four positions, victory going to Total Gallery from the Stan Moore stable who beat Fleeting Spirit by a neck. Borderlescott was back in sixth.

Otherwise Arc day was a triumph for the Aga Khan, who won four Group 1 races with Rosanara (Prix Marcel Boussac), Siyouni (Prix Jean-Luc Lagardere), Shalanaya (Prix de l'Opera) and Alandi (Prix du Cadran). Yeats was retired after finishing third in the last-named race.

A piece of history was made at Warwick's meeting on October 5. Victory for the two-year-old Comedy Hall gave trainer Mark Johnston his 200th winner of the calendar year, the first time a Flat trainer had achieved this feat.

Newmarket staged an excellent Champions Day fixture on October 17. The main event, the Emirates Airline Champion Stakes, saw a popular winner in the Henry Cecil-trained Twice Over. Another success at the top level for jockey Tom Queally, Twice Over won by half a length and a length from Mawatheeq and Sariska, with Fame And Glory a disappointing sixth.

Aidan O'Brien sent out a 1-2 in the Jumeirah Dewhurst Stakes, with Beethoven and Ryan Moore, sent off at 33/1, holding off 20/1 chance Fencing Master. The Ballydoyle first string Steinbeck was fourth.

Darley Sun became the first three-year-old to land the Totesport.com Cesarewitch since 1998 when justifying favouritism against 31 opponents. Ridden by apprentice Andrea Atzeni, Darley Sun was the biggest training success so far for David Simcock.

St Nicholas Abbey, trained by Aidan O'Brien and ridden by Johnny Murtagh, was a brilliant winner of the Racing Post Trophy at Doncaster on October 24. Following his three-length victory the colt immediately became ante-post favourite for both the 2000 Guineas and Derby.

European runners enjoyed a very successful time of it at the two-day Breeders' Cup held at Santa Anita, California. They won six races in all, with Man Of Iron for Aidan O'Brien in the Marathon and Midday for Henry Cecil in the Filly & Mare Turf scoring on day one.

On the second day John Gosden was on target with Pounced in the Juvenile Turf before Goldikova was an impressive winner of the Mile, a race she had also won the year before. Another horse gaining back-to-back wins at the meeting was Conduit, who had Dar Re Mi and Spanish Moon back in third and fourth when landing his second Turf.

There was a brilliant winner of the Breeders' Cup Classic when Zenyatta, taking on males for the first time, stetched her unbeaten record to 14. Twice Over was a highly creditable third but Rip Van Winkle finished only tenth, a place behind Kentucky Derby winner Mine That Bird. Zenyatta was beaten in the vote for Horse of the Year by another brillliant unbeaten filly, Rachel Alexandra.

Michael Kinane, who played such an important role in Sea The Stars's success, announced his retirement at the end of the year at the age of 50. The Irishman rode numerous big-race winners in a career lasting 34 years.

Vincent O'Brien, perhaps the twentieth century's most successful trainer, died in June at the age of 92. O'Brien, who began his career as a highly successful jumps trainer before moving to Ballydoyle and concentrating on the Flat, sent out many champions under both codes.

A Big Sky Brewing (USA)

88(107) (78)66

5-y-o b g Arch (USA)-Runalpharun (USA) (Thunder Rumble (USA))

T D Barron Trevor Boanas

Placings:0/015460/0126630252301**5**-**26000000300** (7729)

2009: 7^{2}SD, 7^{6}SD, 7^{0}F, 7^{0}GF, 7^{0}SF, 6^{0}SD, 6^{0}SD, 5^{0}SD, 7^{3}SD, 6^{0}SD, 7^{0}SD,

	Starts	1st	2nd	3rd	Win & Pl
Career Total (Turf)	18	1	1	2	5491
Career Total (AW)	14	2	3	1	7206

74	9/08	Wolv	7f32y	(0-65)H	STD	£2388
66	4/08	Wolv	7f32y	(0-55)H	STD	£2047
63	4/07	Pont	6f		G-F	£3886

Total win prize-money £8321

Going (Turf): Sf: 0-2 GS: 0-5 Gd: 0-3 **GF: 1-7** Fm: 0-1
Distance: 5f/6f: 1-9 **7f-8f: 2-21** 9f-13f: 0-2 14f+: 0-0
Track : **LH: 3-19** RH: 0-8 **Tight: 2-17** Gall: 0-1
Aids: **Bl: 2-17** Vi: 0-0 Tstrap: 0-0 Ckp: 0-0
Best Rating: **78** 1/09 Wolv 7f32y stand

Modest; effective at around 7f; acts on fast ground and on Polytrack; has worn blinkers.

A Chailin Mo Chroi (IRE)

83(96) (42)42

4-y-o ch f Daggers Drawn (USA)-Clangigi (IRE) (Paris House)

Aidan Anthony Howard (T G McCourt 7/8) Nicholas Bennett

Placings:0066-0000 (7751)

2009: 14^{0}Y, 12^{0}GF, 9^{0}SF, 13^{0}SD,

	Starts	1st	2nd	3rd	Win & Pl
Career Total (Turf)	5	0	0	0	
Career Total (AW)	3	0	0	0	

Going (Turf): **Sf: 0-0 GS: 0-0 Gd: 0-1 GF: 0-1 Fm: 0-0**
Distance: 5f/6f: 0-0 7f-8f: 0-1 9f-13f: 0-5 14f+: 0-2
Track : LH: 0-4 RH: 0-3 Tight: 0-3 Gall: 0-0
Aids: Bl: 0-2 Vi: 0-1 Tstrap: 0-2 Ckp: 0-2
Best Rating: **42** 9/08 Dund 1m4f stand

A Dream Come True

88(98) (68)64

4-y-o b f Where Or When (IRE)-Katy Ivory (IRE) (Night Shift (USA))

D K Ivory Dean Ivory

Placings:0450/**5**11**5**0-000 (5195)

2009: 8^{0}G, 10^{0}GS, 10^{0}SD,

	Starts	1st	2nd	3rd	Win & Pl
Career Total (Turf)	4	0	0	0	0
Career Total (AW)	8	2	0	0	3829

68	2/08	Wolv	1m1f103y	(0-60)H	STD	£2047
68	2/08	Ling	1m2f	(0-65)H	STD	£1781

Total win prize-money £3829

Going (Turf): **Sf: 0-0 GS: 0-2 Gd: 0-2 GF: 0-0 Fm: 0-0**
Distance: 5f/6f: 0-0 7f-8f: 0-5 **9f-13f: 2-7** 14f+: 0-0
Track : **LH: 2-6** RH: 0-5 **Tight: 2-7** Gall: 0-0
Aids: Bl: 0-0 Vi: 0-0 Tstrap: 0-0 Ckp: 0-0
Best Rating: **68** 2/08 Wolv 1m1f103y stand

Modest; stays 1m2f and acts on Polytrack.

A Lot Of Red (IRE)

94 49

3-y-o b c Barathea (IRE)-A Lot Of Kir (IRE) (Selkirk (USA))

P J O'Gorman T Mohan

Placings:0600050 (6390)

2009: 8^{0}GF, 6^{6}GF, 5^{0}S, 7^{0}GF, 6^{0}GF, 8^{5}GF, 8^{0}GF,

	Starts	1st	2nd	3rd	Win & Pl
Career Total (Turf)	7	0	0	0	0

Going (Turf): **Sf: 0-1 GS: 0-0 Gd: 0-0 GF: 0-6 Fm: 0-0**
Distance: 5f/6f: 0-3 7f-8f: 0-2 9f-13f: 0-2 14f+: 0-0
Track : LH: 0-2 RH: 0-0 Tight: 0-0 Gall: 0-1
Aids: Bl: 0-2 Vi: 0-0 Tstrap: 0-0 Ckp: 0-0
Best Rating: **49** 9/09 Wwck 1m22y gd-fm

A One (IRE)

86(91) (43)55

10-y-o b g Alzao (USA)-Anita's Contessa (IRE) (Anita's Prince)

Mrs H J Manners (H J Manners 14/9) Mrs H J Manners

Placings:6324550/00041500**2**0**1**0/300000/4311101150000/050350300/00/00000/00033100-0000 (7332)

2009: 8^{0}GF, 9^{0}GF, 7^{0}GF, 12^{0}SD,

	Starts	1st	2nd	3rd	Win & Pl
Career Total (Turf)	58	8	2	7	39007
Career Total (AW)	8	0	0	0	0

55	8/08	Wind	1m3f135y	G-S	£2047
89	7/04	Wind	1m2f7yE(0-75)H	G-F	£3620
84	7/04	Sand	1m2f7yE(0-75)H	G-F	£5060
77	7/04	Wind	1m2f7yD(0-85)H	G-F	£5525
75	6/04	Wind	1m67y C(0-90)H	G-F	£9303
61	6/04	Chep	7f16y F	G-F	£3164
67	10/02	Leic	7f9y G(0-60)H	G-S	£2401
71	6/02	Chep	7f16y F	SFT	£2478

Total win prize-money £33599

Going (Turf): Sf: 1-3 GS: 2-11 Gd: 0-9 **GF: 5-32** Fm: 0-3
Distance: 5f/6f: 0-8 7f-8f: 3-27 **9f-13f: 5-31** 14f+: 0-0
Track : LH: 0-23 **RH: 4-15 Tight: 4-21** Gall: 0-7
Aids: Bl: 0-0 Vi: 0-0 Tstrap: 0-0 Ckp: 0-0
Best Rating: **89** 7/04 Wind 1m2f7y gd-fm

Modest; effective at up to 1m2f; acts well on easy ground, but has won on good to firm; front-runner.

A P Ling

81(82) (54)31

2-y-o b f Antonius Pius (USA)-Spain (Polar Falcon (USA))

C N Kellett Dachel Stud

Placings:005 (7630)

2009: 8^{0}S, 8^{0}S, 7^{5}SD,

	Starts	1st	2nd	3rd	Win & Pl
Career Total (Turf)	2	0	0	0	
Career Total (AW)	1	0	0	0	0

Going (Turf): **Sf: 0-2 GS: 0-0 Gd: 0-0 GF: 0-0 Fm: 0-0**
Distance: 5f/6f: 0-0 7f-8f: 0-1 9f-13f: 0-2 14f+: 0-0
Track : LH: 0-3 RH: 0-0 Tight: 0-1 Gall: 0-0
Aids: Bl: 0-0 Vi: 0-0 Tstrap: 0-0 Ckp: 0-0
Best Rating: **54** 12/09 Wolv 7f32y stand

A Pocketful Of Rye (IRE)

93(95) (68)66

2-y-o b f Acclamation-Rye (IRE) (Charnwood Forest (IRE))

J A Osborne Morsethehorse Syndicate

Placings:5260 (7003)

2009: 6^{5}SD, 7^{2}GF, 8^{6}SS, 8^{0}SD,

	Starts	1st	2nd	3rd	Win & Pl
Career Total (Turf)	1	0	1	0	1542
Career Total (AW)	3	0	0	0	0

Going (Turf): **Sf: 0-0 GS: 0-0 Gd: 0-0 GF: 0-1 Fm: 0-0**
Distance: 5f/6f: 0-1 7f-8f: 0-2 9f-13f: 0-1 14f+: 0-0
Track : LH: 0-3 RH: 0-1 Tight: 0-3 Gall: 0-0
Aids: Bl: 0-0 Vi: 0-0 Tstrap: 0-0 Ckp: 0-0
Best Rating: **68** 10/09 Ling 1m std-slw

Modest; effective over 6f-7f; acts on fast ground.

A Touch Of Luck

79 39

2-y-o b g Lucky Story (USA)-Optimise (IRE) (Danehill (USA))

T D Easterby www.realityracingsyndicate.co.uk II

Placings:040 (2231)

2009: 5^{0}GF, 5^{4}GS, 6^{0}GS,

	Starts	1st	2nd	3rd	Win & Pl
Career Total (Turf)	3	0	0	0	241

Going (Turf): **Sf: 0-0 GS: 0-2 Gd: 0-0 GF: 0-1 Fm: 0-0**
Distance: 5f/6f: 0-3 7f-8f: 0-0 9f-13f: 0-0 14f+: 0-0
Track : LH: 0-0 RH: 0-0 Tight: 0-0 Gall: 0-0
Aids: Bl: 0-0 Vi: 0-0 Tstrap: 0-0 Ckp: 0-0
Best Rating: **39** 5/09 Newc 5f gd-sft

A Valley Away (IRE)

(97) (46)

5-y-o ch m City On A Hill (USA)-Sharkiyah (IRE) (Polish Precedent (USA))

Jane Chapple-Hyam The Tunworth Beaters

Placings:50-40 (0116)

2009: 11^{4}SS, 11^{0}SD,

	Starts	1st	2nd	3rd	Win & Pl
Career Total (Turf)	0	0	0	0	
Career Total (AW)	4	0	0	0	0

Going (Turf): **Sf: 0-0 GS: 0-0 Gd: 0-0 GF: 0-0 Fm: 0-0**
Distance: 5f/6f: 0-0 7f-8f: 0-0 9f-13f: 0-3 14f+: 0-1
Track : LH: 0-2 RH: 0-2 Tight: 0-0 Gall: 0-1
Aids: Bl: 0-0 Vi: 0-0 Tstrap: 0-0 Ckp: 0-0
Best Rating: **46** 11/08 Kemp 1m4f stand

A Wish For You

(93) (70)68

4-y-o ch f Tumbleweed Ridge-Peperonata (IRE) (Cyrano De Bergerac)

D K Ivory Lesley Ivory And Cynthia Smith

Placings:003300325421/3400000-0 (0108)

2009: 5^{0}SD,

	Starts	1st	2nd	3rd	Win & Pl
Career Total (Turf)	6	0	0	2	900

Career Total (AW)	14	1	2	2	4463

69 12/07 Wolv 5f20y STD £2388
Total win prize-money £2389

Going (Turf): Sf: 0-0 GS: 0-2 Gd: 0-1 GF: 0-3 Fm: 0-0
Distance: **5f/6f: 1-20** 7f-8f: 0-0 9f-13f: 0-0 14f+: 0-0
Track : **LH: 1-13** RH: 0-2 **Tight: 1-10** Gall: 0-2
Aids: Bl: 0-2 Vi: 0-0 Tstrap: 1-5 Ckp: 1-5
Best Rating: 70 12/07 Sthl 5f stand

Modest filly; effective over 5f; acts on sand; has worn cheekpieces.

Aahaygirl (IRE)

99(97) (58)**82**

3-y-o b f Choisir (AUS)-Siem Reap (USA) (El Gran Senor (USA))
K R Burke Mogeely Stud & Mrs Maura Gittins

Placings:24023260-0335236 **(3305)**
2009: 5⁰SD, **6**³SD, 6³G, 6⁵GS, 6²GF, 6³GS, 7⁶GF,

	Starts	1st	2nd	3rd	Win & Pl
Career Total (Turf)	13	0	4	3	8635
Career Total (AW)	2	0	0	1	403

Going (Turf): Sf: 0-2 GS: 0-3 Gd: 0-2 GF: 0-4 Fm: 0-1
Distance: 5f/6f: 0-10 7f-8f: 0-5 9f-13f: 0-0 14f+: 0-0
Track : LH: 0-5 RH: 0-0 Tight: 0-3 Gall: 0-0
Aids: Bl: 0-2 Vi: 0-1 Tstrap: 0-0 Ckp: 0-0
Best Rating: 82 8/08 Ches 6f18y good

Modest; effective over 5f-7f; acts on fast and easy ground; has worn blinkers and a visor.

Aahaygran (USA)

84 **60**

3-y-o b f Gulch (USA)-Boundless Beauty (USA) (Copelan (USA))
K R Burke Mogeely Stud & Mrs Maura Gittins

Placings:50-6 **(1047)**
2009: 7⁶G,

	Starts	1st	2nd	3rd	Win & Pl
Career Total (Turf)	3	0	0	0	0

Going (Turf): Sf: 0-0 GS: 0-0 Gd: 0-2 GF: 0-1 Fm: 0-0
Distance: 5f/6f: 0-1 7f-8f: 0-2 9f-13f: 0-0 14f+: 0-0
Track : LH: 0-0 RH: 0-0 Tight: 0-0 Gall: 0-0
Aids: Bl: 0-0 Vi: 0-0 Tstrap: 0-0 Ckp: 0-0
Best Rating: 60 7/08 Donc 7f good

Aaim To Prosper (IRE)

107(102) (79)**92**

5-y-o br g Val Royal (FR)-Bint Al Balad (IRE) (Ahonoora)
B J Meehan (M R Channon 21/8) CGA Racing Partnership 2

Placings:43212220/0446101301 **(7151)**
2009: 12⁰GS, 12⁴G, 14⁴G, **16**⁶SD, 16¹GS, 21⁰G, 16¹GS, 16³GF, 18⁰G, 16¹G,

	Starts	1st	2nd	3rd	Win & Pl
Career Total (Turf)	15	3	3	2	42546
Career Total (AW)	3	1	1	0	6915

92 10/09 NmkR 2m (0-90)H GD £7771
88 8/09 Asct 2m (0-100)H G-S £17230
86 7/09 Newb 2m (0-80)H G-S £4857
73 9/06 Wolv 1m141y STD £3886
Total win prize-money £33745

Going (Turf): Sf: 0-1 **GS: 2-3** Gd: 1-10 GF: 0-1 Fm: 0-0
Distance: 5f/6f: 0-0 7f-8f: 0-2 9f-13f: 1-8 **14f+: 3-8**
Track : LH: 2-7 RH: 2-7 Tight: 1-6 **Gall: 2-5**
Aids: Bl: 0-1 **Vi: 2-4** Tstrap: 0-0 Ckp: 0-0
Best Rating: 96 11/06 StCl 1m2f good

Useful, stays 2m; acts on good or softer ground and Polytrack; has worn a visor.

Aajel (USA)

107 (77)**102**

5-y-o gr g Aljabr (USA)-Awtaan (USA) (Arazi (USA))
M P Tregoning Hamdan Al Maktoum

Placings:16331/1 **(5481)**
2009: 16¹GF,

	Starts	1st	2nd	3rd	Win & Pl
Career Total (Turf)	4	2	0	2	22492
Career Total (AW)	2	1	0	0	3071

102 8/09 Yarm 2m (0-95)H G-F £7569
99 9/07 Yarm 1m6f17y (0-100)H G-F £12464
71 2/07 Ling 1m2f STD £3071
Total win prize-money £23105

Going (Turf): Sf: 0-0 GS: 0-0 Gd: 0-1 **GF: 2-2** Fm: 0-1
Distance: 5f/6f: 0-0 7f-8f: 0-0 9f-13f: 1-4 **14f+: 2-2**
Track : **LH: 3-5** RH: 0-1 **Tight: 3-5** Gall: 0-0
Aids: Bl: 0-0 Vi: 0-0 Tstrap: 0-0 Ckp: 0-0
Best Rating: 102 8/09 Yarm 2m gd-fm

Very useful; stays 2m; acts on fast ground; goes on Polytrack.

Aakef (IRE)

91 **89**

3-y-o b g Exceed And Excel (AUS)-Bush Baby (Zamindar (USA))
M A Jarvis Hamdan Al Maktoum

Placings:2010-100 **(6240)**
2009: 5¹G, 6⁰GF, 6⁰G,

	Starts	1st	2nd	3rd	Win & Pl
Career Total (Turf)	7	2	1	0	15415

89 4/09 Yarm 5f43y (0-90)H GD £10281
78 8/08 Yarm 6f3y GD £3784
Total win prize-money £14066

Going (Turf): Sf: 0-0 GS: 0-0 **Gd: 2-4** GF: 0-3 Fm: 0-0
Distance: 5f/6f: 1-5 7f-8f: 1-2 9f-13f: 0-0 14f+: 0-0
Track : LH: 0-1 RH: 0-0 Tight: 0-1 Gall: 0-0
Aids: Bl: 0-0 Vi: 0-0 Tstrap: 0-0 Ckp: 0-0
Best Rating: 89 4/09 Yarm 5f43y good

Useful; effective over 5-6f; suited by good and faster ground.

Aalsmeer

101 **93**

2-y-o b f Invincible Spirit (IRE)-Flower Market (Cadeaux Genereux)
E S McMahon J C Fretwell

Placings:322230 **(6660)**
2009: 5³GF, 5²GS, 5²GS, 6²GS, 5³G, 5⁰GS,

	Starts	1st	2nd	3rd	Win & Pl
Career Total (Turf)	6	0	3	2	13510

Going (Turf): Sf: 0-0 GS: 0-4 Gd: 0-1 GF: 0-1 Fm: 0-0
Distance: 5f/6f: 0-6 7f-8f: 0-0 9f-13f: 0-0 14f+: 0-0
Track : LH: 0-1 RH: 0-0 Tight: 0-0 Gall: 0-0
Aids: Bl: 0-0 Vi: 0-0 Tstrap: 0-0 Ckp: 0-0
Best Rating: 93 5/09 York 5f gd-sft

Very useful; Listed placed; effective over 5f; acts on good ground.

Aalya (IRE)

86 **54**

2-y-o b f Peintre Celebre (USA)-Weqaar (USA) (Red Ransom (USA))
J L Dunlop Hamdan Al Maktoum

Placings:6 **(5547)**
2009: 8⁶GF,

	Starts	1st	2nd	3rd	Win & Pl
Career Total (Turf)	1	0	0	0	0

Going (Turf): Sf: 0-0 GS: 0-0 Gd: 0-0 GF: 0-1 Fm: 0-0
Distance: 5f/6f: 0-0 7f-8f: 0-0 9f-13f: 0-1 14f+: 0-0
Track : LH: 0-0 RH: 0-1 Tight: 0-0 Gall: 0-0
Aids: Bl: 0-0 Vi: 0-0 Tstrap: 0-0 Ckp: 0-0
Best Rating: 54 9/09 Leic 1m60y gd-fm

Aaman (IRE)

96(95) (57)**61**

3-y-o gr c Dubai Destination (USA)-Amellnaa (IRE) (Sadler's Wells (USA))
E F Vaughan Mohammed Rashid

Placings:60-002130 **(6188)**
2009: 8⁰G, 12⁰HY, 11²F, 16¹G, 16³SD, 15⁰GF,

	Starts	1st	2nd	3rd	Win & Pl
Career Total (Turf)	5	1	1	0	4182
Career Total (AW)	3	0	0	1	385

61 8/09 Gdwd 2m (0-70)H GD £3238
Total win prize-money £3238

Going (Turf): Sf: 0-1 GS: 0-0 **Gd: 1-2** GF: 0-1 Fm: 0-1
Distance: 5f/6f: 0-2 7f-8f: 0-0 9f-13f: 0-3 **14f+: 1-3**
Track : LH: 0-5 **RH: 1-3 Tight: 1-2** Gall: 0-1
Aids: Bl: 0-0 Vi: 0-0 Tstrap: 0-0 Ckp: 0-0
Best Rating: 61 8/09 Gdwd 2m good

Moderate; stays 2m; acts on good/fast ground.

Aasifa (USA)

72 **37**

3-y-o b f Diesis-Lady's Truth (USA) (Riverman (USA))
C E Brittain Saeed Manana

Placings:0 **(2178)**
2009: 9⁰G,

	Starts	1st	2nd	3rd	Win & Pl
Career Total (Turf)	1	0	0	0	

Going (Turf): Sf: 0-0 GS: 0-0 Gd: 0-1 GF: 0-0 Fm: 0-0
Distance: 5f/6f: 0-0 7f-8f: 0-0 9f-13f: 0-1 14f+: 0-0
Track : LH: 0-0 RH: 0-1 Tight: 0-1 Gall: 0-0
Aids: Bl: 0-0 Vi: 0-0 Tstrap: 0-0 Ckp: 0-0
Best Rating: 37 5/09 Gdwd 1m1f192y good

Aattash (IRE)

96(95) (69)**73**

2-y-o b c Clodovil (IRE)-Mothers Footprints (IRE) (Maelstrom Lake)
M R Channon Sheikh Ahmed Al Maktoum

Placings:0345350 **(6901)**

2009: 6^{0}GF, 6^{3}GF, 7^{4}G, 8^{5}SD, 8^{3}GF, 8^{5}GF, 8^{0}GF,

	Starts	1st	2nd	3rd	Win & Pl
Career Total (Turf)	6	0	0	2	1276
Career Total (AW)	1	0	0	0	0

Going (Turf): Sf: 0-0 GS: 0-0 Gd: 0-1 GF: 0-5 Fm: 0-0
Distance: 5f/6f: 0-2 7f-8f: 0-3 9f-13f: 0-2 14f+: 0-0
Track : LH: 0-3 RH: 0-2 Tight: 0-2 Gall: 0-0
Aids: Bl: 0-0 Vi: 0-1 Tstrap: 0-0 Ckp: 0-0
Best Rating: 73 9/09 Gdwd 1m gd-fm

Fair; stays 1m; acts on fast ground; sure to win a race.

Abandagold (IRE)

95 **72**

2-y-o b f Orpen (USA)-Rainbow Java (IRE) (Fairy King (USA))
P D Evans (A B Haynes 9/6) Bathwick Gold Partnership

Placings:64212 **(3589)**
2009: 5^{6}GF, 6^{4}GS, 6^{2}GF, 7^{1}GF, 7^{2}GF,

	Starts	1st	2nd	3rd	Win & Pl
Career Total (Turf)	5	1	2	0	6167

68 6/09 Ches 7f2y G-F £4047
Total win prize-money £4047

Going (Turf): Sf: 0-0 GS: 0-1 Gd: 0-0 **GF: 1-4** Fm: 0-0
Distance: 5f/6f: 0-3 **7f-8f: 1-2** 9f-13f: 0-0 14f+: 0-0
Track : **LH: 1-2** RH: 0-0 **Tight: 1-1** Gall: 0-0
Aids: Bl: 0-0 Vi: 0-0 Tstrap: 0-0 Ckp: 0-0
Best Rating: 72 7/09 Wwck 7f26y gd-fm

Modest; effective over 6-7f; acts on fast ground.

Abayaan

(98) (71)

3-y-o gr c Sadler's Wells (USA)-Showdown (Darshaan)
Jane Chapple-Hyam Mrs Jane Chapple-Hyam

Placings:1 **(7780)**
2009: 11^{1}SD,

	Starts	1st	2nd	3rd	Win & Pl
Career Total (Turf)	0	0	0	0	
Career Total (AW)	1	1	0	0	2730

71 12/09 Sthl 1m3f STD £2729
Total win prize-money £2730

Going (Turf): Sf: 0-0 GS: 0-0 Gd: 0-0 GF: 0-0 Fm: 0-0
Distance: 5f/6f: 0-0 7f-8f: 0-0 **9f-13f: 1-1** 14f+: 0-0
Track : **LH: 1-1** RH: 0-0 Tight: 0-0 Gall: 0-0
Aids: Bl: 0-0 Vi: 0-0 Tstrap: 0-0 Ckp: 0-0
Best Rating: 71 12/09 Sthl 1m3f stand

Fair; stays 1m3f and acts on Fibresand.

Abbashinko

84(95) (55)**24**

3-y-o b f Shinko Forest (IRE)-Abbaleva (Shaddad (USA))
Tom Dascombe Keith Gannon

Placings:403 **(7107)**
2009: 7^{4}SD, 6^{0}GF, 6^{3}SD,

	Starts	1st	2nd	3rd	Win & Pl
Career Total (Turf)	1	0	0	0	
Career Total (AW)	2	0	0	1	385

Going (Turf): Sf: 0-0 GS: 0-0 Gd: 0-0 GF: 0-1 Fm: 0-0
Distance: 5f/6f: 0-2 7f-8f: 0-1 9f-13f: 0-0 14f+: 0-0
Track : LH: 0-1 RH: 0-1 Tight: 0-1 Gall: 0-0
Aids: Bl: 0-0 Vi: 0-0 Tstrap: 0-0 Ckp: 0-0
Best Rating: 55 9/09 Wolv 7f32y stand

Moderate; acts on Polytrack

Abbey Express

62 **52**

4-y-o b g Bahamian Bounty-Glimpse (Night Shift (USA))
M A Barnes Abbadis Racing Club

Placings:06600/0-0 **(4897)**
2009: 8^{0}GS,

	Starts	1st	2nd	3rd	Win & Pl
Career Total (Turf)	7	0	0	0	0

Going (Turf): Sf: 0-0 GS: 0-1 Gd: 0-4 GF: 0-1 Fm: 0-1
Distance: 5f/6f: 0-3 7f-8f: 0-2 9f-13f: 0-2 14f+: 0-0
Track : LH: 0-1 RH: 0-2 Tight: 0-1 Gall: 0-1
Aids: Bl: 0-1 Vi: 0-0 Tstrap: 0-0 Ckp: 0-0
Best Rating: 52 7/07 Ayr 6f good

Abbey Steps (IRE)

102 **58**

3-y-o b g Choisir (AUS)-Hello Mary (IRE) (Dolphin Street (FR))
T D Easterby Miss Betty Duxbury

Placings:63305-44000 **(3727)**
2009: 5^{4}GF, 6^{4}GS, 6^{0}GF, 5^{0}GF, 7^{0}G,

	Starts	1st	2nd	3rd	Win & Pl
Career Total (Turf)	10	0	0	2	1175

Going (Turf): Sf: 0-0 GS: 0-3 Gd: 0-2 GF: 0-4 Fm: 0-1
Distance: 5f/6f: 0-9 7f-8f: 0-1 9f-13f: 0-0 14f+: 0-0
Track : LH: 0-2 RH: 0-2 Tight: 0-1 Gall: 0-1
Aids: Bl: 0-5 Vi: 0-0 Tstrap: 0-0 Ckp: 0-0
Best Rating: 58 8/08 Ripn 6f gd-sft

Modest-looking sort; handles ease in the ground.

Abbeygate

80(100) (53)**8**

8-y-o b g Unfuwain (USA)-Ayunli (Chief Singer)
T Keddy Mrs H Keddy

Placings:006/00000000/1214155/004651040032535/4604 0302/2524600-00050 **(4880)**
2009: 8^{0}SD, 9^{0}SD, 10^{0}SD, 8^{5}SD, 10^{0}GS,

	Starts	1st	2nd	3rd	Win & Pl
Career Total (Turf)	8	0	0	0	
Career Total (AW)	45	4	5	3	13576

54 4/06 Wolv 1m1f103y (0-45) STD £1535
57 11/05 Sthl 1m (0-60)H STD £2971
59 3/05 Sthl 7f (0-50) STD £2954
52 2/05 Sthl 1m (0-55)H STD £2923
Total win prize-money £10385

Going (Turf): Sf: 0-2 GS: 0-3 Gd: 0-2 GF: 0-1 Fm: 0-0
Distance: 5f/6f: 0-0 **7f-8f: 3-16** 9f-13f: 1-34 14f+: 0-3
Track : **LH: 4-41** RH: 0-10 **Tight: 1-25** Gall: 0-0
Aids: Bl: 0-3 Vi: 0-0 Tstrap: 1-15 Ckp: 1-15
Best Rating: 59 3/05 Sthl 7f stand

Moderate; stays 1m4f, but has only won over shorter; acts on Fibresand and Polytrack.

Abbi Jicaro

89 **49**

2-y-o b f Passing Glance-Makeover (Priolo (USA))
Mrs L Williamson G D Kendrick

Placings:446400 **(6821)**

2009: 6^{4}GF, 7^{4}GF, 7^{6}G, 6^{4}S, 5^{0}GF, 8^{0}GF,

	Starts	1st	2nd	3rd	Win & Pl
Career Total (Turf)	6	0	0	0	517

Going (Turf): Sf: 0-1 GS: 0-0 Gd: 0-1 GF: 0-4 Fm: 0-0
Distance: 5f/6f: 0-3 7f-8f: 0-3 9f-13f: 0-0 14f+: 0-0
Track : LH: 0-2 RH: 0-0 Tight: 0-1 Gall: 0-1
Aids: Bl: 0-0 Vi: 0-0 Tstrap: 0-0 Ckp: 0-0
Best Rating: 49 6/09 Wind 6f gd-fm

Moderate form at up to 7f on fast ground.

Abbondanza (IRE)

108(118) (112)**104**

6-y-o b g Cape Cross (IRE)-Ninth Wonder (USA) (Forty Niner (USA))
I Semple Belstane Park Racing & Gordon Leckie

Placings:36/100/601**641110/26**15202**313-4211**140600 **(6487)**
2009: 7^{4}SD, 8^{2}SD, 8^{1}SD, 7^{1}SD, 7^{1}SD, 8^{4}GF, 7^{0}GF, 7^{6}GF, 6^{0}G, 7^{0}GF,

	Starts	1st	2nd	3rd	Win & Pl
Career Total (Turf)	18	3	2	1	21303
Career Total (AW)	16	7	2	2	61377

112 5/09 Ling 7f (0-105)H STD £12952
109 3/09 Ling 7f (0-100)H STD £12952
105 3/09 Ling 1m (0-100)H STD £11656
94 12/08 Wolv 1m141y (0-85)H STD £5180
82 5/08 Muss 1m GD £5180
92 12/07 Wolv 1m141y (0-85)H STD £4857
83 11/07 Wolv 1m141y (0-75)H STD £2968
79 11/07 Wolv 1m141y (0-70)H STD £3076
75 8/07 Ayr 1m (0-80)H G-F £5829
79 5/06 Newc 1m2f32y G-F £3238
Total win prize-money £67895

Going (Turf): Sf: 0-3 GS: 0-2 Gd: 1-3 **GF: 2-10** Fm: 0-0
Distance: 5f/6f: 0-1 7f-8f: 5-14 9f-13f: 5-19 14f+: 0-0
Track : **LH: 9-23** RH: 1-9 **Tight: 8-19** Gall: 1-7
Aids: Bl: 0-0 Vi: 0-1 Tstrap: 9-26 Ckp: 9-26
Best Rating: 112 5/09 Ling 7f stand

Smart; effective over 7f-1m2f; acts on fast ground; suited by Polytrack; has worn cheekpieces.

Abhainn (IRE)

101(91) (67)**65**

3-y-o ch g Hawk Wing (USA)-Grannys Reluctance (IRE) (Anita's Prince)
B Palling H Perkins

Placings:504650306-040633011 **(6362)**
2009: 8^{0}SD, 7^{4}SD, 7^{0}SD, 6^{6}F, 5^{3}GF, 6^{3}G, 5^{0}GF, 6^{1}GS, 6^{1}GF,

	Starts	1st	2nd	3rd	Win & Pl
Career Total (Turf)	9	2	0	2	4671
Career Total (AW)	9	0	0	1	302

65 9/09 Wwck 6f (0-65)H G-F £1942
57 9/09 Chep 6f16y (0-60)H G-S £2137
Total win prize-money £4080

Going (Turf): Sf: 0-1 **GS: 1-1** Gd: 0-2 **GF: 1-4** Fm: 0-1
Distance: 5f/6f: 1-10 7f-8f: 1-7 9f-13f: 0-1 14f+: 0-0
Track : **LH: 1-13** RH: 0-0 Tight: 0-9 Gall: 0-2
Aids: Bl: 0-0 Vi: 0-1 Tstrap: 0-1 Ckp: 0-1
Best Rating: 67 7/08 Wolv 5f216y stand

Plating class; stays 7f; acts on good and eay ground and Polytrack.

Abhar (USA)

(86) (51)

2-y-o b c Essence Of Dubai (USA)-Jocey's Dance (USA) (Seattle Dancer (USA))

J R Best John Fletcher

Placings:06 **(7571)**

2009: 7^{0}SD, 6^{6}SD,

	Starts	1st	2nd	3rd	Win & Pl
Career Total (Turf)	0	0	0	0	
Career Total (AW)	2	0	0	0	0

Going (Turf): **Sf: 0-0 GS: 0-0 Gd: 0-0 GF: 0-0 Fm: 0-0**
Distance: 5f/6f: 0-1 7f-8f: 0-1 9f-13f: 0-0 14f+: 0-0
Track : LH: 0-1 RH: 0-1 Tight: 0-1 Gall: 0-0
Aids: Bl: 0-0 Vi: 0-0 Tstrap: 0-0 Ckp: 0-0
Best Rating: **51** 11/09 Ling 6f stand

Abigails Angel

75(92) (54)14

2-y-o b f Olden Times-Make Ready (Beveled (USA))

B R Johnson Tann Racing

Placings:003 **(7482)**

2009: 8^{0}SD, 7^{0}G, 8^{3}SD,

	Starts	1st	2nd	3rd	Win & Pl
Career Total (Turf)	1	0	0	0	
Career Total (AW)	2	0	0	1	292

Going (Turf): **Sf: 0-0 GS: 0-0 Gd: 0-1 GF: 0-0 Fm: 0-0**
Distance: 5f/6f: 0-0 7f-8f: 0-3 9f-13f: 0-0 14f+: 0-0
Track : LH: 0-2 RH: 0-1 Tight: 0-1 Gall: 0-0
Aids: Bl: 0-0 Vi: 0-0 Tstrap: 0-0 Ckp: 0-0
Best Rating: **54** 11/09 Ling 1m stand

Moderate; effective over 1m; acts on Polytrack.

Ability N Delivery

(104) (73)69

4-y-o gr g Kyllachy-Tryptonic (FR) (Baryshnikov (AUS))

Michael J Browne Michael J Browne

Placings:5500-000102122 **(7554)**

2009: 6^{0}SH, 5^{0}S, **5^{0}SD**, 5^{1}G, 5^{0}YS, 5^{2}Y, 5^{1}HY, 6^{2}GY, 5^{2}SD,

	Starts	1st	2nd	3rd	Win & Pl
Career Total (Turf)	11	2	2	0	12563
Career Total (AW)	2	0	1	0	806
69 8/09 Bell 5f	(47-65)H	HVY	£5031		
64 7/09 Bell 5f	(47-65)H	GD	£5031		

Total win prize-money £10064

Going (Turf): **Sf: 1-4** GS: 0-0 **Gd: 1-2** GF: 0-0 Fm: 0-0
Distance: **5f/6f: 2-13** 7f-8f: 0-0 9f-13f: 0-0 14f+: 0-0
Track : **LH: 2-9** RH: 0-0 Tight: 0-1 Gall: 0-0
Aids: Bl: 0-1 Vi: 0-0 Tstrap: 2-6 Ckp: 2-6
Best Rating: **73** 11/09 Ling 5f stand

Able Dara

100(89) (46)46

6-y-o b g Lahib (USA)-Nishara (Nishapour (FR))

N Bycroft N Bycroft

Placings:650005006-000000 **(4972)**

2009: 8^{0}GF, 14^{0}GF, 16^{0}G, 9^{0}G, 12^{0}GF, 11^{0}GF,

	Starts	1st	2nd	3rd	Win & Pl
Career Total (Turf)	10	0	0	0	0
Career Total (AW)	5	0	0	0	0

Going (Turf): **Sf: 0-0 GS: 0-1 Gd: 0-3 GF: 0-6 Fm: 0-0**
Distance: 5f/6f: 0-0 7f-8f: 0-2 9f-13f: 0-7 14f+: 0-6
Track : LH: 0-10 RH: 0-5 Tight: 0-6 Gall: 0-1
Aids: Bl: 0-3 Vi: 0-0 Tstrap: 0-2 Ckp: 0-2
Best Rating: **46** 6/08 Rdcr 1m6f19y gd-fm

Plating class; stays 2m.

Able Master (IRE)

109 111

3-y-o b g Elusive City (USA)-Foresta Verde (USA) (Green Forest (USA))

B Smart Ron Hull

Placings:113500-420331255 **(7292)**

2009: 5^{4}GF, 6^{2}GS, 6^{0}GF, 6^{3}G, 6^{3}GF, 6^{1}GS, 7^{2}GF, 7^{5}GS, 6^{5}S,

	Starts	1st	2nd	3rd	Win & Pl
Career Total (Turf)	15	3	2	3	47834
111 9/09 York 6f	(0-100)H	G-S	£11656		
81 5/08 Bevl 5f		G-F	£9346		
83 5/08 Ripn 5f		GD	£3238		

Total win prize-money £24242

Going (Turf): Sf: 0-2 **GS: 1-5 Gd: 1-3 GF: 1-5** Fm: 0-0
Distance: **5f/6f: 3-10** 7f-8f: 0-5 9f-13f: 0-0 14f+: 0-0
Track : LH: 0-1 RH: 0-0 Tight: 0-1 Gall: 0-0
Aids: Bl: 0-0 Vi: 0-0 Tstrap: 0-0 Ckp: 0-0
Best Rating: **111** 9/09 York 6f gd-sft

Smart; Listed placed; effective over 5f-6f; acts on good and fast ground.

Aboukir

91(98) (70)63

3-y-o b g Almutawakel-Conquestadora (Hernando (FR))

P F I Cole The Fairy Story Partnership

Placings:1-060300 **(4734)**

2009: 11^{0}G, 8^{6}GF, 9^{0}GF, 8^{3}SD, 8^{0}GS, 9^{0}GS,

	Starts	1st	2nd	3rd	Win & Pl
Career Total (Turf)	5	0	0	0	0
Career Total (AW)	2	1	0	1	3610
70 11/08 Sthl 1m		STD	£3207		

Total win prize-money £3207

Going (Turf): **Sf: 0-0 GS: 0-2 Gd: 0-1 GF: 0-2 Fm: 0-0**
Distance: 5f/6f: 0-0 **7f-8f: 1-3** 9f-13f: 0-4 14f+: 0-0
Track : **LH: 1-3** RH: 0-3 Tight: 0-2 Gall: 0-0
Aids: Bl: 0-0 Vi: 0-0 Tstrap: 0-0 Ckp: 0-0
Best Rating: **70** 11/08 Sthl 1m stand

Son of Almutawakel and half-brother to Traphalgar, a three-time winner on the all-weather; dam won over 2m; big, scopey sort; effective over 1m; acts on Fibresand.

Above Average (IRE)

105 108

3-y-o b c High Chaparral (IRE)-Crystal Valkyrie (IRE) (Danehill (USA))

B W Hills J Hanson

Placings:05-21003503 **(6854)**

2009: 10^{2}G, 10^{1}G, 12^{0}GF, 12^{0}GF, 13^{3}G, 12^{5}GF, 14^{0}GF, 16^{3}G,

	Starts	1st	2nd	3rd	Win & Pl
Career Total (Turf)	10	1	1	2	52250
101 4/09 Sand 1m2f7y		GD	£36900		

Total win prize-money £36901

Going (Turf): Sf: 0-0 GS: 0-0 **Gd: 1-5** GF: 0-5 Fm: 0-0
Distance: 5f/6f: 0-0 7f-8f: 0-2 **9f-13f: 1-6** 14f+: 0-2
Track : LH: 0-4 **RH: 1-4** Tight: 0-1 Gall: 0-6
Aids: Bl: 0-0 Vi: 0-0 Tstrap: 0-0 Ckp: 0-0
Best Rating: **108** 10/09 NmkR 2m good

Smart; winner in Group 3 company; effective at 1m4f-2m and acts on good ground.

Above Limits (IRE)

109(103) (75)99

2-y-o b f Exceed And Excel (AUS)-Cin Isa Luv (USA) (Private Account (USA))

Tom Dascombe Findlay & Bloom

Placings:3160336 **(6660)**

2009: 5^{3}SD, 5^{1}GF, 6^{6}GF, 5^{0}GS, 5^{3}GF, 5^{3}GF, 5^{6}GS,

	Starts	1st	2nd	3rd	Win & Pl
Career Total (Turf)	6	1	0	2	17259
Career Total (AW)	1	0	0	1	626
82 5/09 Sand 5f6y		G-F	£5180		

Total win prize-money £5181

Going (Turf): Sf: 0-0 GS: 0-2 Gd: 0-0 **GF: 1-4** Fm: 0-0
Distance: **5f/6f: 1-7** 7f-8f: 0-0 9f-13f: 0-0 14f+: 0-0
Track : LH: 0-1 RH: 0-0 Tight: 0-1 Gall: 0-0
Aids: Bl: 0-0 Vi: 0-0 Tstrap: 0-0 Ckp: 0-0
Best Rating: **99** 9/09 Donc 5f gd-fm

Useful; Listed placed; stays 5f; acts on fast ground and on Polytrack.

Abraham Lincoln (IRE)

109(103) (97)109

5-y-o b h Danehill (USA)-Moon Drop (Dominion)

D Nicholls Dr Marwan Koukash

Placings:52/4101/0200000-5623003 **(3524)**

2009: 6^{5}SD, 5^{6}S, 6^{2}G, 6^{3}S, 6^{0}GF, 6^{0}G, 6^{3}GF,

	Starts	1st	2nd	3rd	Win & Pl
Career Total (Turf)	18	1	3	2	33749
Career Total (AW)	2	1	0	0	9957
95 10/07 Dund 6f		STD	£9677		
99 9/07 Curr 6f		G-F	£13195		

Total win prize-money £22873

Going (Turf): Sf: 0-5 GS: 0-1 Gd: 0-4 **GF: 1-5** Fm: 0-1
Distance: **5f/6f: 2-20** 7f-8f: 0-0 9f-13f: 0-0 14f+: 0-0
Track : LH: 0-3 RH: 0-1 Tight: 0-2 Gall: 0-0
Aids: Bl: 0-0 Vi: 0-0 Tstrap: 0-0 Ckp: 0-0
Best Rating: **109** 5/08 Curr 6f firm

Very useful; Group placed; effective over 6f; acts on most ground and on Polytrack.

Abriachan

98(87) (67)79

2-y-o b c Celtic Swing-Cape Finisterre (IRE) (Cape Cross (IRE))

M G Quinlan Thomas Mann

Placings:310 **(5692)**

2009: 7^{3}SD, 7^{1}GF, 7^{0}GS,

	Starts	1st	2nd	3rd	Win & Pl
Career Total (Turf)	2	1	0	0	2730
Career Total (AW)	1	0	0	1	530
79 8/09 Folk 7f		G-F	£2729		

Total win prize-money £2730

Going (Turf): Sf: 0-0 GS: 0-1 Gd: 0-0 **GF: 1-1** Fm: 0-0
Distance: 5f/6f: 0-0 **7f-8f: 1-3** 9f-13f: 0-0 14f+: 0-0
Track : LH: 0-2 RH: 0-0 Tight: 0-1 Gall: 0-1
Aids: Bl: 0-0 Vi: 0-0 Tstrap: 0-0 Ckp: 0-0
Best Rating: 79 8/09 Folk 7f gd-fm

Modest; stays 7f; acts on Polytrack; should improve.

Absa Lutte (IRE)

98(106) (78)**64**
6-y-o b m Darnay-Zenana (IRE) (Lucky Guest)
Patrick Morris (Miss Gay Kelleway 3/11) D & D Coatings Ltd

Placings:0060020/30305405**4**53**2315**-020**630311**21 **(7738)**
2009: 10^0S, 6^2S, 7^0SH, **6**^{6}SD, **6**^{3}SD, 7^0GF, **5**^{3}SD, **5**^{1}SD, **6**^{1}SD, 5^2S, **6**^{1}SD,

	Starts	1st	2nd	3rd	Win & Pl
Career Total (Turf)	22	0	3	3	4789
Career Total (AW)	11	4	1	3	11857

78 12/09 Kemp 6f (0-70)H STD £2266
73 10/09 Kemp 6f (0-70) STD £2047
74 10/09 Kemp 5f (0-70) STD £2047
74 11/08 Wolv 5f216y (0-65)H STD £2729
Total win prize-money £9091

Going (Turf): **Sf: 0-6 GS: 0-1 Gd: 0-3 GF: 0-3 Fm: 0-2**
Distance: **5f/6f: 4-18** 7f-8f: 0-12 9f-13f: 0-3 14f+: 0-0
Track : LH: 1-13 **RH: 3-10 Tight: 1-4** Gall: 0-0
Aids: Bl: 0-0 Vi: 0-0 Tstrap: 0-0 Ckp: 0-0
Best Rating: 78 12/09 Kemp 6f stand

Modest; effective over 5f-7f; acts on fast ground; goes on Polytrack; has worn a tongue tie.

Absher (IRE)

76(75) (40)**33**
2-y-o b c Noverre (USA)-Turn To Vodka (FR) (Polish Precedent (USA))
Patrick Morris Haif Mohammed Al-Ghatani

Placings:50 **(1358)**
2009: 5^5SD, 5^0GF,

	Starts	1st	2nd	3rd	Win & Pl
Career Total (Turf)	1	0	0	0	
Career Total (AW)	1	0	0	0	0

Going (Turf): **Sf: 0-0 GS: 0-0 Gd: 0-0 GF: 0-1 Fm: 0-0**
Distance: 5f/6f: 0-2 7f-8f: 0-0 9f-13f: 0-0 14f+: 0-0
Track : LH: 0-1 RH: 0-0 Tight: 0-1 Gall: 0-0
Aids: Bl: 0-0 Vi: 0-0 Tstrap: 0-0 Ckp: 0-0
Best Rating: 40 4/09 Wolv 5f20y stand

Absinthe (IRE)

93(104) (81)**83**
3-y-o b g King's Best (USA)-Triple Try (IRE) (Sadler's Wells (USA))
W R Swinburn P W Harris

Placings:53-322 **(5997)**
2009: 8^3GF, 10^2SD, 10^2GS,

	Starts	1st	2nd	3rd	Win & Pl
Career Total (Turf)	3	0	1	2	2571
Career Total (AW)	2	0	1	0	771

Going (Turf): **Sf: 0-0 GS: 0-2 Gd: 0-0 GF: 0-1 Fm: 0-0**
Distance: 5f/6f: 0-0 7f-8f: 0-2 9f-13f: 0-3 14f+: 0-0
Track : LH: 0-0 RH: 0-4 Tight: 0-1 Gall: 0-0
Aids: Bl: 0-0 Vi: 0-0 Tstrap: 0-0 Ckp: 0-0

Best Rating: 83 9/09 Sand 1m2f7y gd-sft

Fair; acts on fast and on easy ground and Polytrack; stays 1m2f.

Absolut Power (GER)

109(106) (85)**85**
8-y-o ch g Acatenango (GER)-All Our Dreams (Caerleon (USA))
J A Geake Kimpton Down Racing Club

Placings:215310/**565**2-04645 **(6622)**
2009: 16^0GF, 16^4GS, 21^6G, 16^4GF, 16^5G,

	Starts	1st	2nd	3rd	Win & Pl
Career Total (Turf)	13	2	2	1	38112
Career Total (AW)	2	0	0	0	419

8/04 Badn 1m4f SFT £19014
5/04 Siro 1m3f GD £8802
Total win prize-money £27817

Going (Turf): **Sf: 1-2** GS: 0-2 **Gd: 1-7** GF: 0-2 Fm: 0-0
Distance: 5f/6f: 0-0 7f-8f: 0-0 **9f-13f: 2-5** 14f+: 0-10
Track : **LH: 1-6** RH: 0-6 Tight: 0-3 Gall: 0-3
Aids: Bl: 0-0 Vi: 0-5 Tstrap: 0-0 Ckp: 0-0
Best Rating: 95 8/04 Colo 1m3f good

Useful; stays 2m; acts on easy ground; has worn visor.

Absolute Music (USA)

106 **98**
2-y-o b/br f Consolidator (USA)-Allegro Lady (USA) (Souvenir Copy (USA))
R M H Cowell Khalifa Dasmal

Placings:210420132 **(7230a)**
2009: 5^2GF, 5^1GF, 6^0GF, 5^4G, 5^2VS, 5^0GF, 5^1GS, 6^3VS, 7^2HO,

	Starts	1st	2nd	3rd	Win & Pl
Career Total (Turf)	9	2	3	1	51568

83 9/09 Ripn 5f G-S £6542
72 5/09 Leic 5f2y G-F £3238
Total win prize-money £9781

Going (Turf): Sf: 0-0 **GS: 1-1** Gd: 0-1 **GF: 1-4** Fm: 0-0
Distance: **5f/6f: 2-8** 7f-8f: 0-1 9f-13f: 0-0 14f+: 0-0
Track : LH: 0-0 RH: 0-0 Tight: 0-0 Gall: 0-0
Aids: Bl: 0-0 Vi: 0-0 Tstrap: 0-0 Ckp: 0-0
Best Rating: 98 11/09 MsnL 7f holding

Useful; effective at 5f; acts on any ground.

Abstract Folly (IRE)

100(102) (59)**72**
7-y-o b g Rossini (USA)-Cochiti (Kris)
J D Bethell Craig Monty

Placings:44/506360452100**26/6**0501504**154/0**51336/0410 036**0**-45420**5** **(7598)**
2009: 16^4G, 15^5GF, 14^4GF, 14^2GF, 15^0S, **16**^{5}SD,

	Starts	1st	2nd	3rd	Win & Pl
Career Total (Turf)	38	4	2	4	19345
Career Total (AW)	9	1	1	0	3807

70 7/08 Rdcr 1m6f19y (0-70)H G-F £4533
70 8/07 Rdcr 1m6f19y (0-65)H FRM £1943
67 9/06 Wolv 1m4f50y (0-60)H STD £2730
60 7/06 Catt 1m3f214y (0-65)H FRM £3412
63 9/05 Carl 7f200y (0-55)H G-F £2984
Total win prize-money £15604

Going (Turf): Sf: 0-2 GS: 0-3 Gd: 0-9 **GF: 2-21 Fm: 2-3**
Distance: 5f/6f: 0-0 7f-8f: 1-7 9f-13f: 2-20 14f+: 2-20
Track : **LH: 4-34** RH: 1-12 **Tight: 4-33** Gall: 0-2
Aids: **Bl: 1-11** Vi: 0-0 Tstrap: 0-0 Ckp: 0-0
Best Rating: 74 8/07 Thsk 2m gd-fm

Modest; stays 2m; acts on firm ground; has worn blinkers.

Abu Derby (IRE)

97(92) (72)**64**
3-y-o b g Fath (USA)-Solas Abu (IRE) (Red Sunset)
J G Given One Stop Partnership

Placings:4446**22-366404405** **(6880)**
2009: **6**^{3}SS, **5**^{6}SD, 6^6GF, **6**^{4}SD, **5**^{0}SD, 6^4G, **6**^{4}SD, **6**^{0}SD, 7^5SD,

	Starts	1st	2nd	3rd	Win & Pl
Career Total (Turf)	6	0	0	0	572
Career Total (AW)	9	0	2	1	2015

Going (Turf): **Sf: 0-1 GS: 0-0 Gd: 0-2 GF: 0-2 Fm: 0-1**
Distance: 5f/6f: 0-12 7f-8f: 0-3 9f-13f: 0-0 14f+: 0-0
Track : LH: 0-7 RH: 0-2 Tight: 0-0 Gall: 0-2
Aids: Bl: 0-1 Vi: 0-0 Tstrap: 0-0 Ckp: 0-0
Best Rating: 72 12/08 Sthl 6f stand

Modest; effective over 6f and acts on Fibresand.

Abu Dubai (IRE)

87(95) (65)**43**
3-y-o b f Kheleyf (USA)-Boudica (IRE) (Alhaarth (IRE))
A M Hales (C A Dwyer 5/6) Gary P Martin

Placings:05622505 **(2681)**
2009: **6**^{0}SD, **7**^{5}SD, **7**^{6}SD, **8**^{2}SD, **9**^{2}SD, **8**^{5}SD, 8^0GF, **9**^{5}SD,

	Starts	1st	2nd	3rd	Win & Pl
Career Total (Turf)	1	0	0	0	
Career Total (AW)	7	0	2	0	1572

Going (Turf): **Sf: 0-0 GS: 0-0 Gd: 0-0 GF: 0-1 Fm: 0-0**
Distance: 5f/6f: 0-1 7f-8f: 0-3 9f-13f: 0-4 14f+: 0-0
Track : LH: 0-7 RH: 0-0 Tight: 0-7 Gall: 0-0
Aids: Bl: 0-0 Vi: 0-0 Tstrap: 0-0 Ckp: 0-0
Best Rating: 65 4/09 Wolv 1m141y stand

Modest; effective over 1m1f; acts on Polytrack.

Abulharith

99(93) (59)**68**
3-y-o b g Medicean-Limuru (Salse (USA))
M J Scudamore (R A Harris 23/10) The Yes No Wait Sorries

Placings:6**0**-60502303**0** **(6804)**
2009: 9^6GF, 11^0GF, 11^5G, 10^0G, 11^2G, **11**^{3}SD, 9^0GF, 9^3GF, 9^0SD,

	Starts	1st	2nd	3rd	Win & Pl
Career Total (Turf)	8	0	1	1	867
Career Total (AW)	3	0	0	1	302

Going (Turf): **Sf: 0-0 GS: 0-1 Gd: 0-3 GF: 0-4 Fm: 0-0**
Distance: 5f/6f: 0-0 7f-8f: 0-2 9f-13f: 0-9 14f+: 0-0
Track : LH: 0-4 RH: 0-5 Tight: 0-5 Gall: 0-0
Aids: Bl: 0-0 Vi: 0-0 Tstrap: 0-0 Ckp: 0-0
Best Rating: 68 4/09 Leic 1m1f218y gd-fm

Modest; stays 1m4f; acts on good ground.

Academy Gigsnreels (USA)

(85) (61)67

4-y-o b/br g Rahy (USA)-Eloquent Minister (USA) (Deputy Minister (CAN))

Seamus Fahey (Eoin Griffin 20/9) Hickey Hughes Partnership

Placings:3020-5004 (7779)

2009: 17^5SW, 14^0YS, 12^0SD, 12^4SD,

	Starts	1st	2nd	3rd	Win & Pl
Career Total (Turf)	4	0	1	1	1988
Career Total (AW)	4	0	0	0	0

Going (Turf): Sf: 0-0 GS: 0-0 Gd: 0-2 GF: 0-1 Fm: 0-0
Distance: 5f/6f: 0-0 7f-8f: 0-0 9f-13f: 0-5 14f+: 0-3
Track : LH: 0-5 RH: 0-3 Tight: 0-0 Gall: 0-0
Aids: Bl: 0-1 Vi: 0-0 Tstrap: 0-0 Ckp: 0-0
Best Rating: 67 7/08 Tipp 1m1f good

Academy Of War (USA)

81(90) (43)48

3-y-o b/br g Royal Academy (USA)-Lover Come Back (USA) (Dynaformer (USA))

J M Bradley E A Hayward

Placings:6-00050 (5286)

2009: 6^0GF, 6^0GF, 6^0GS, 8^5SD, 12^0GF,

	Starts	1st	2nd	3rd	Win & Pl
Career Total (Turf)	5	0	0	0	0
Career Total (AW)	1	0	0	0	0

Going (Turf): Sf: 0-0 GS: 0-2 Gd: 0-0 GF: 0-3 Fm: 0-0
Distance: 5f/6f: 0-2 7f-8f: 0-3 9f-13f: 0-1 14f+: 0-0
Track : LH: 0-2 RH: 0-1 Tight: 0-2 Gall: 0-1
Aids: Bl: 0-0 Vi: 0-0 Tstrap: 0-0 Ckp: 0-0
Best Rating: 48 10/08 Leic 5f218y gd-sft

Accede

100(101) (90)85

3-y-o b f Acclamation-Here To Me (Muhtarram (USA))

J G Portman Mrs D Joly

Placings:310-000225**0**06 (7366)

2009: 8^0GF, 7^0GS, 9^0GF, 10^2GF, 10^2S, 10^5G, 10^0G, 8^0SD, 10^6SD,

	Starts	1st	2nd	3rd	Win & Pl
Career Total (Turf)	10	1	2	1	7412
Career Total (AW)	2	0	0	0	0

77 5/08 Newb 6f8y SFT £3885

Total win prize-money £3886

Going (Turf): Sf: 1-2 GS: 0-2 Gd: 0-3 GF: 0-3 Fm: 0-0
Distance: 5f/6f: 0-1 **7f-8f: 1-5** 9f-13f: 0-6 14f+: 0-0
Track : LH: 0-7 RH: 0-2 Tight: 0-3 Gall: 0-3
Aids: Bl: 0-0 Vi: 0-0 Tstrap: 0-0 Ckp: 0-0
Best Rating: 90 10/09 Ling 1m stand

Fair; effective over 6f; acts on soft ground.

Acclaben (IRE)

89 54

3-y-o b g Acclamation-Jour De Grace (SWE) (Steve's Friend (USA))

G A Swinbank Adrian Butler

Placings:0066-55 (3684)

2009: 8^5GF, 8^5GS,

	Starts	1st	2nd	3rd	Win & Pl
Career Total (Turf)	6	0	0	0	0

Going (Turf): Sf: 0-0 GS: 0-2 Gd: 0-2 GF: 0-2 Fm: 0-0
Distance: 5f/6f: 0-3 7f-8f: 0-2 9f-13f: 0-1 14f+: 0-0
Track : LH: 0-1 RH: 0-1 Tight: 0-1 Gall: 0-0
Aids: Bl: 0-0 Vi: 0-0 Tstrap: 0-0 Ckp: 0-0
Best Rating: 54 6/09 Pont 1m4y gd-fm

Acclaim To Fame (IRE)

96 46

3-y-o b g Acclamation-Khafaya (Unfuwain (USA))

A P Jarvis (K R Burke 20/7) Mr & Mrs Halsall

Placings:00-0466 (4943)

2009: 12^0GF, 10^4G, 11^6G, 10^6GF,

	Starts	1st	2nd	3rd	Win & Pl
Career Total (Turf)	6	0	0	0	0

Going (Turf): Sf: 0-1 GS: 0-1 Gd: 0-2 GF: 0-2 Fm: 0-0
Distance: 5f/6f: 0-1 7f-8f: 0-1 9f-13f: 0-4 14f+: 0-0
Track : LH: 0-4 RH: 0-0 Tight: 0-2 Gall: 0-2
Aids: Bl: 0-0 Vi: 0-0 Tstrap: 0-0 Ckp: 0-0
Best Rating: 46 8/09 Newc 1m2f32y gd-fm

Moderate; stays 1m2f; acts on a sound surface.

Acclaimed (IRE)

(107) (99)105

4-y-o b g Hawk Wing (USA)-Park Charger (Tirol)

John Joseph Hanlon (J Noseda 26/9) The Acclaimed Partnership

Placings:14-56 (6290)

2009: 8^5SD, 10^6SD,

	Starts	1st	2nd	3rd	Win & Pl
Career Total (Turf)	2	1	0	0	3290
Career Total (AW)	2	0	0	0	420

88 8/08 Wind 1m67y G-S £2729

Total win prize-money £2730

Going (Turf): Sf: 0-0 **GS: 1-1** Gd: 0-1 GF: 0-0 Fm: 0-0
Distance: 5f/6f: 0-0 7f-8f: 0-0 **9f-13f: 1-4** 14f+: 0-0
Track : LH: 0-2 **RH: 1-2 Tight: 1-2** Gall: 0-1
Aids: Bl: 0-0 Vi: 0-0 Tstrap: 0-0 Ckp: 0-0
Best Rating: 105 9/08 Newb 1m1f good

Useful prospect; effective over 1m; acts on soft ground.

Accompanist

(100) (68)62

6-y-o b g Pivotal-Abscond (USA) (Unbridled (USA))

T G McCourt Mrs P McCourt

Placings:0222401/000600**2346**/060553330-4060**624315** (7785)

2009: 10^4SH, 11^0Y, 12^6GY, 12^0Y, 12^6SD, 10^2SD, 10^4SD, 10^3SD, 10^1SD, 13^5SD,

	Starts	1st	2nd	3rd	Win & Pl
Career Total (Turf)	22	1	3	2	9096
Career Total (AW)	14	1	2	3	11948

68 11/09 Dund 1m2f150y (50-70)H STD £5702
78 10/06 Wind 1m67y G-S £3238

Total win prize-money £8941

Going (Turf): Sf: 0-3 **GS: 1-2** Gd: 0-4 GF: 0-7 Fm: 0-0
Distance: 5f/6f: 0-0 7f-8f: 0-3 **9f-13f: 2-31** 14f+: 0-2
Track : **LH: 1-18 RH: 1-14 Tight: 1-4** Gall: 0-0
Aids: Bl: 1-23 Vi: 0-3 Tstrap: 1-4 Ckp: 1-4
Best Rating: 82 8/06 Hayd 1m2f120y gd-fm

Fair; effective over 1m-1m 2f; acts on good ground.

According To Pete

95(95) (71)71

8-y-o b g Accordion-Magic Bloom (Full Of Hope)

J M Jefferson P Nelson

Placings:003/30/54-00 (6676)

2009: 17^0G, 18^0G,

	Starts	1st	2nd	3rd	Win & Pl
Career Total (Turf)	8	0	0	2	1494
Career Total (AW)	1	0	0	0	0

Going (Turf): Sf: 0-2 GS: 0-1 Gd: 0-4 GF: 0-1 Fm: 0-0
Distance: 5f/6f: 0-0 7f-8f: 0-0 9f-13f: 0-4 14f+: 0-5
Track : LH: 0-8 RH: 0-1 Tight: 0-1 Gall: 0-3
Aids: Bl: 0-0 Vi: 0-0 Tstrap: 0-0 Ckp: 0-0
Best Rating: 79 10/07 York 1m4f good

Fair; very useful chaser; stays 1m6f; acts with ease in the ground.

Accountable

80(71) (21)47

2-y-o b c Avonbridge-Fair Compton (Compton Place)

B G Powell Mrs P Jubert

Placings:50 (5571)

2009: 6^5GF, 6^0SD,

	Starts	1st	2nd	3rd	Win & Pl
Career Total (Turf)	1	0	0	0	0
Career Total (AW)	1	0	0	0	

Going (Turf): Sf: 0-0 GS: 0-0 Gd: 0-0 GF: 0-1 Fm: 0-0
Distance: 5f/6f: 0-2 7f-8f: 0-0 9f-13f: 0-0 14f+: 0-0
Track : LH: 0-0 RH: 0-1 Tight: 0-0 Gall: 0-1
Aids: Bl: 0-0 Vi: 0-0 Tstrap: 0-0 Ckp: 0-0
Best Rating: 47 8/09 Wind 6f gd-fm

Accumulation (UAE)

80(72) (20)21

3-y-o ch f Halling (USA)-Roseate (USA) (Mt. Livermore (USA))

M W Easterby A G Black

Placings:000-50 (5442)

2009: 8^5GF, 14^0GF,

	Starts	1st	2nd	3rd	Win & Pl
Career Total (Turf)	4	0	0	0	0
Career Total (AW)	1	0	0	0	

Going (Turf): Sf: 0-1 GS: 0-1 Gd: 0-0 GF: 0-2 Fm: 0-0
Distance: 5f/6f: 0-0 7f-8f: 0-2 9f-13f: 0-2 14f+: 0-1
Track : LH: 0-3 RH: 0-0 Tight: 0-3 Gall: 0-0
Aids: Bl: 0-1 Vi: 0-0 Tstrap: 0-0 Ckp: 0-0
Best Rating: 21 8/08 Rdcr 7f gd-sft

Ace Club

(94) (57)**23**

8-y-o ch g Indian Rocket-Presently (Cadeaux Genereux)
Garry Moss Brooklands Racing

Placings:21/50042000000/620000000000021030/400006 43000563041/010501/00600050-5600 **(1412)**
2009: 5^{5}SD, 5^{6}SD, 5^{0}SD, 5^{0}SD,

	Starts	1st	2nd	3rd	Win & Pl
Career Total (Turf)	17	1	2	0	6006
Career Total (AW)	49	4	2	3	9303

57	12/07	Wolv	5f20y	(0-55)H	STD	£2047
55	2/07	Sthl	6f	(0-50)H	SS	£2047
54	12/06	Sthl	6f	(0-45)	STD	£1706
51	11/05	Sthl	6f	(0-40)	STD	£1450
66	9/03	Muss	5f	D	GD	£3406

Total win prize-money £10658

Going (Turf): Sf: 0-3 GS: 0-1 **Gd: 1-3** GF: 0-9 Fm: 0-1
Distance: **5f/6f: 5-52** 7f-8f: 0-13 9f-13f: 0-1 14f+: 0-0
Track : **LH: 4-46** RH: 0-5 **Tight: 1-16** Gall: 0-2
Aids: **Bl: 4-38** Vi: 0-3 Tstrap: 0-1 Ckp: 0-1
Best Rating: **70** 9/03 Pont 5f gd-fm

Moderate; effective from 5f-7f; acts on decent ground and sand; has worn blinkers and a visor.

Ace Of Hearts

107(116) (105)**106**

10-y-o b g Magic Ring (IRE)-Lonely Heart (Midyan (USA))
C F Wall Archangels 1

Placings:41321400/0320025362/050211100300/0603110 105/0020262000/056012360/422242-**522**010**2** **(7810)**
2009: 8^{5}SD, 10^{2}SD, 8^{2}SD, 8^{0}GF, 8^{1}GF, 8^{0}G, 8^{2}SD,

	Starts	1st	2nd	3rd	Win & Pl
Career Total (Turf)	66	9	13	6	232764
Career Total (AW)	6	1	3	0	17642

106	5/09	NmkR	1m	(0-95)H	G-F	£9714
98	8/07	Gdwd	1m1f	(0-90)H	G-F	£9715
108	8/05	Wind	1m67y	(0-100)H	G-F	£13483
104	7/05	Sand	1m14y	H	G-F	£58000
98	6/05	Ripn	1m1f	(0-100)H	G-F	£12119
98	6/04	Pont	1m4y	B(0-105)H	G-F	£12093
97	6/04	Donc	1m	D(0-85)H	FRM	£5736
90	5/04	NmkR	1m	D(0-80)	G-F	£6747
83	7/02	Newb	1m	D(0-85)H	G-F	£5564
76	4/02	Wolv	7f	F	STD	£2345

Total win prize-money £135519

Going (Turf): Sf: 0-6 GS: 0-12 Gd: 0-15 **GF: 8-32** Fm: 1-1
Distance: 5f/6f: 0-0 7f-8f: 5-33 9f-13f: 5-39 14f+: 0-0
Track : LH: 2-16 **RH: 4-28 Tight: 4-22** Gall: 0-5
Aids: Bl: 0-0 Vi: 0-0 Tstrap: 0-0 Ckp: 0-0
Best Rating: **108** 7/06 Sand 1m14y gd-fm

Very useful; effective from 1m-1m1f; handles most ground; goes on Polytrack; likes to race prominently.

Ace Of Spies (IRE)

100(95) (75)**66**

4-y-o br g Machiavellian (USA)-Nadia (Nashwan (USA))
G A Harker A S Ward

Placings:03/2434000042205-632120606505 **(6221)**
2009: 7^{6}GF, 8^{3}GF, 7^{2}GF, 6^{1}GF, 7^{2}GF, 8^{0}GF, 5^{6}GF, 7^{0}F, 6^{6}GF, 7^{5}G, 7^{0}GF, 6^{5}GF,

	Starts	1st	2nd	3rd	Win & Pl
Career Total (Turf)	22	1	4	2	6164
Career Total (AW)	5	0	1	1	1454

60	4/09	Newc	6f	(0-52)H	G-F	£2320

Total win prize-money £2320

Going (Turf): Sf: 0-2 GS: 0-1 Gd: 0-4 **GF: 1-14** Fm: 0-1
Distance: **5f/6f: 1-4** 7f-8f: 0-14 9f-13f: 0-9 14f+: 0-0
Track : LH: 0-12 RH: 0-12 Tight: 0-14 Gall: 0-1
Aids: Bl: 0-0 Vi: 0-2 Tstrap: 1-8 Ckp: 1-8
Best Rating: **75** 12/07 Wolv 1m141y stand

Moderate; effective at around 6f-1m; acts on good and fast ground; goes on Polytrack; has worn cheekpieces and a visor.

Achak (IRE)

81 (85)**91**

3-y-o b g Invincible Spirit (IRE)-She's So Lovely (Distant Relative)
G M Lyons Sean Jones

Placings:3510-401 **(5042a)**
2009: 7^{4}SD, 7^{0}G, 5^{1}SD,

	Starts	1st	2nd	3rd	Win & Pl
Career Total (Turf)	4	0	0	1	1338
Career Total (AW)	3	2	0	0	18149

85	8/09	Dund	5f	STD	£11404
75	9/08	Dund	6f	STD	£6097

Total win prize-money £17502

Going (Turf): **Sf: 0-1 GS: 0-0 Gd: 0-2 GF: 0-1 Fm: 0-0**
Distance: **5f/6f: 2-3** 7f-8f: 0-4 9f-13f: 0-0 14f+: 0-0
Track : **LH: 2-6** RH: 0-0 Tight: 0-0 Gall: 0-0
Aids: Bl: 0-1 Vi: 0-0 Tstrap: 0-0 Ckp: 0-0
Best Rating: **91** 7/08 Leop 7f good

Achieved

58

6-y-o b g Lahib (USA)-Equity's Darling (IRE) (Law Society (USA))
D C O'Brien Mrs V O'Brien

Placings:0 **(2981)**
2009: 10^{0}GF,

	Starts	1st	2nd	3rd	Win & Pl
Career Total (Turf)	1	0	0	0	

Going (Turf): **Sf: 0-0 GS: 0-0 Gd: 0-0 GF: 0-1 Fm: 0-0**
Distance: 5f/6f: 0-0 7f-8f: 0-0 9f-13f: 0-1 14f+: 0-0
Track : LH: 0-0 RH: 0-1 Tight: 0-1 Gall: 0-0
Aids: Bl: 0-0 Vi: 0-0 Tstrap: 0-0 Ckp: 0-0
Best Rating:

Achromatic

96(97) (58)**53**

3-y-o gr g Green Desert (USA)-Pericardia (Petong)
W R Swinburn The Grey Masters

Placings:000-40402 **(7755)**
2009: 8^{4}CF, 8^{0}GF, 8^{4}SD, 9^{0}SD, 8^{2}SD,

	Starts	1st	2nd	3rd	Win & Pl
Career Total (Turf)	5	0	0	0	192
Career Total (AW)	3	0	1	0	605

Going (Turf): **Sf: 0-1 GS: 0-0 Gd: 0-1 GF: 0-3 Fm: 0-0**
Distance: 5f/6f: 0-0 7f-8f: 0-3 9f-13f: 0-5 14f+: 0-0
Track : LH: 0-4 RH: 0-2 Tight: 0-3 Gall: 0-0
Aids: Bl: 0-0 Vi: 0-2 Tstrap: 0-0 Ckp: 0-0
Best Rating: **58** 12/09 Wolv 1m141y stand

Moderate; effective at around 1m; acts on Polytrack.

Acol

73 **28**

2-y-o ch g Domedriver (IRE)-Bridge Pal (First Trump)
A G Foster Miss E G Macgregor

Placings:000 **(7167)**
2009: 7^{0}G, 8^{0}GS, 7^{0}S,

	Starts	1st	2nd	3rd	Win & Pl
Career Total (Turf)	3	0	0	0	

Going (Turf): **Sf: 0-1 GS: 0-1 Gd: 0-1 GF: 0-0 Fm: 0-0**
Distance: 5f/6f: 0-0 7f-8f: 0-3 9f-13f: 0-0 14f+: 0-0
Track : LH: 0-3 RH: 0-0 Tight: 0-0 Gall: 0-1
Aids: Bl: 0-0 Vi: 0-0 Tstrap: 0-0 Ckp: 0-0
Best Rating: **28** 9/09 Ayr 7f50y good

Acquainted

74 **43**

2-y-o b f Shamardal (USA)-Love Everlasting (Pursuit Of Love)
M L W Bell Mr & Mrs G Middlebrook

Placings:0 **(7183)**
2009: 7^{0}G,

	Starts	1st	2nd	3rd	Win & Pl
Career Total (Turf)	1	0	0	0	

Going (Turf): **Sf: 0-0 GS: 0-0 Gd: 0-1 GF: 0-0 Fm: 0-0**
Distance: 5f/6f: 0-0 7f-8f: 0-1 9f-13f: 0-0 14f+: 0-0
Track : LH: 0-0 RH: 0-0 Tight: 0-0 Gall: 0-0
Aids: Bl: 0-0 Vi: 0-0 Tstrap: 0-0 Ckp: 0-0
Best Rating: **43** 10/09 NmkR 7f good

Acquavella

98 **66**

3-y-o b f Danehill Dancer (IRE)-Oh So Well (IRE) (Sadler's Wells (USA))
R A Fahey Dr Anne J F Gillespie

Placings:330530 **(6538)**
2009: 8^{3}GF, 11^{3}GF, 10^{0}S, 10^{5}GF, 11^{3}G, 12^{0}GF,

	Starts	1st	2nd	3rd	Win & Pl
Career Total (Turf)	6	0	0	3	1252

Going (Turf): **Sf: 0-1 GS: 0-0 Gd: 0-1 GF: 0-4 Fm: 0-0**
Distance: 5f/6f: 0-0 7f-8f: 0-0 9f-13f: 0-6 14f+: 0-0
Track : LH: 0-3 RH: 0-3 Tight: 0-4 Gall: 0-1
Aids: Bl: 0-0 Vi: 0-0 Tstrap: 0-0 Ckp: 0-0
Best Rating: **66** 9/09 Haml 1m3f16y good

Fair; stays 1m3f and acts on fast ground.

Acquaviva

78 **23**

2-y-o ch f Medicean-Amazing Bay (Mazilier (USA))
Eve Johnson Houghton David Herbert

Placings:00 **(3633)**
2009: 6^{0}GF, 5^{0}G,

	Starts	1st	2nd	3rd	Win & Pl
Career Total (Turf)	2	0	0	0	

Going (Turf): **Sf: 0-0 GS: 0-0 Gd: 0-1 GF: 0-1 Fm: 0-0**
Distance: 5f/6f: 0-1 7f-8f: 0-1 9f-13f: 0-0 14f+: 0-0
Track : LH: 0-0 RH: 0-0 Tight: 0-0 Gall: 0-0
Aids: Bl: 0-0 Vi: 0-0 Tstrap: 0-0 Ckp: 0-0
Best Rating: **23** 6/09 Newb 6f8y gd-fm

Acquiesced (IRE)

101(90) (64)81

3-y-o b f Refuse To Bend (IRE)-North East Bay (USA) (Prospect Bay (CAN))

R Hannon Mrs J Wood

Placings:221405-025 (2079)

2009: 7^{0}SD, 7^{2}GF, 7^{5}GS,

	Starts	1st	2nd	3rd	Win & Pl
Career Total (Turf)	8	1	3	0	13957
Career Total (AW)	1	0	0	0	

76 8/08 Wind 6f G-S £5569

Total win prize-money £5569

Going (Turf): Sf: 0-0 **GS: 1-2** Gd: 0-1 GF: 0-5 Fm: 0-0
Distance: **5f/6f: 1-3** 7f-8f: 0-6 9f-13f: 0-0 14f+: 0-0
Track : LH: 0-1 RH: 0-1 Tight: 0-1 **Gall: 1-1**
Aids: Bl: 0-0 Vi: 0-0 Tstrap: 0-0 Ckp: 0-0
Best Rating: **81** 5/09 Ling 7f gd-fm

Useful; effective over 6f; acts on fast ground.

Acquisition

113(99) (65)93

3-y-o b f Dansili-Quota (Rainbow Quest (USA))

H R A Cecil K Abdulla

Placings:4111130 (7131)

2009: 10^{4}GF, 11^{1}GF, 12^{1}G, 12^{1}G, 14^{1}S, 12^{3}GF, 13^{0}SD,

	Starts	1st	2nd	3rd	Win & Pl
Career Total (Turf)	6	4	0	1	24434
Career Total (AW)	1	0	0	0	

91 9/09 Hayd 1m6f (0-90)H SFT £9714
87 8/09 Sals 1m4f (0-85)H GD £4857
77 7/09 Ripn 1m4f10y (0-80)H GD £5180
62 6/09 Leic 1m3f183y G-F £3238

Total win prize-money £22990

Going (Turf): Sf: 1-1 GS: 0-0 **Gd: 2-2** GF: 1-3 Fm: 0-0
Distance: 5f/6f: 0-0 7f-8f: 0-0 **9f-13f: 3-6** 14f+: 1-1
Track : LH: 1-2 **RH: 3-5 Tight: 2-5** Gall: 0-0
Aids: Bl: 0-0 Vi: 0-0 Tstrap: 0-0 Ckp: 0-0
Best Rating: **93** 10/09 Gdwd 1m4f gd-fm

Useful; stays 1m6f; acts on fast ground.

Acropolis (IRE)

(105) (75)101

8-y-o b g Sadler's Wells (USA)-Dedicated Lady (IRE) (Pennine Walk)

B G Powell (Mrs J L Le Brocq 28/11) Mrs J L Le Brocq

Placings:0163/14/2345/00/5340030/33326302-36U406256 (7888)

2009: 16^{3}SD, 14^{6}GF, 12^{U}GS, 12^{4}GS, 12^{0}F, 13^{6}SF, 12^{2}SD, 11^{5}SD, 12^{6}SD,

	Starts	1st	2nd	3rd	Win & Pl
Career Total (Turf)	30	2	2	8	155264
Career Total (AW)	6	0	2	1	1693

107 9/04 Leop 1m2f G-F £27507
77 9/03 Gway 1m100y G-Y £8441

Total win prize-money £35949

Going (Turf): Sf: 0-4 GS: 0-6 Gd: 0-6 **GF: 1-9** Fm: 0-1
Distance: 5f/6f: 0-0 7f-8f: 0-3 **9f-13f: 2-23** 14f+: 0-10
Track : **LH: 1-18** RH: 0-15 Tight: 0-13 Gall: 0-7
Aids: Bl: 0-1 Vi: 0-12 Tstrap: 0-2 Ckp: 0-2
Best Rating: **123** 10/04 Lonc 1m4f good

Modest; effective at 1m4f-2m; effective on most ground; has worn cheekpieces, a tongue tie, blinkers and a visor.

Across The Sands

(102) (57)

3-y-o b c Oasis Dream-Well Beyond (IRE) (Don't Forget Me)

C N Kellett G C Chipman & R Charlesworth

Placings:030540 (7838)

2009: 5^{0}SD, 5^{3}SD, 5^{0}SD, 5^{5}SD, 5^{4}SD, 5^{0}SS,

	Starts	1st	2nd	3rd	Win & Pl
Career Total (Turf)	0	0	0	0	
Career Total (AW)	6	0	0	1	403

Going (Turf): Sf: 0-0 GS: 0-0 Gd: 0-0 GF: 0-0 Fm: 0-0
Distance: 5f/6f: 0-6 7f-8f: 0-0 9f-13f: 0-0 14f+: 0-0
Track : LH: 0-5 RH: 0-0 Tight: 0-5 Gall: 0-0
Aids: Bl: 0-0 Vi: 0-0 Tstrap: 0-0 Ckp: 0-0
Best Rating: **57** 11/09 Ling 5f stand

Modest; effective over 5f; acts on Polytrack.

Across The Sea (USA)

80 52

2-y-o gr/ro g Giant's Causeway (USA)-Trust Your Heart (USA) (Relaunch (USA))

T P Tate Mrs Fitri Hay

Placings:0 (6382)

2009: 8^{0}GF,

	Starts	1st	2nd	3rd	Win & Pl
Career Total (Turf)	1	0	0	0	

Going (Turf): Sf: 0-0 GS: 0-0 Gd: 0-0 GF: 0-1 Fm: 0-0
Distance: 5f/6f: 0-0 7f-8f: 0-1 9f-13f: 0-0 14f+: 0-0
Track : LH: 0-1 RH: 0-0 Tight: 0-0 Gall: 0-1
Aids: Bl: 0-0 Vi: 0-0 Tstrap: 0-0 Ckp: 0-0
Best Rating: **52** 9/09 Newc 1m gd-fm

Acrosstheuniverse (USA)

(90) (60)

3-y-o b/br f Forestry (USA)-Belong To Lassie (USA) (Belong To Me (USA))

J R Gask Horses First Racing Limited

Placings:4-35 (6641)

2009: 5^{3}SD, 5^{5}SD,

	Starts	1st	2nd	3rd	Win & Pl
Career Total (Turf)	0	0	0	0	
Career Total (AW)	3	0	0	1	403

Going (Turf): Sf: 0-0 GS: 0-0 Gd: 0-0 GF: 0-0 Fm: 0-0
Distance: 5f/6f: 0-3 7f-8f: 0-0 9f-13f: 0-0 14f+: 0-0
Track : LH: 0-3 RH: 0-0 Tight: 0-3 Gall: 0-0
Aids: Bl: 0-0 Vi: 0-0 Tstrap: 0-0 Ckp: 0-0
Best Rating: **60** 1/09 Ling 5f stand

Fair; suited by 5f and acts on Polytrack.

Acrostic

114(102) (99)107

4-y-o ch g Tobougg (IRE)-Royal Dream (Ardkinglass)

L M Cumani L Marinopoulos

Placings:53122-44163 (5200)

2009: 8^{4}GF, 8^{4}G, 8^{1}G, 8^{6}G, 8^{3}GF,

	Starts	1st	2nd	3rd	Win & Pl
Career Total (Turf)	8	2	1	2	75213
Career Total (AW)	2	0	1	0	2239

106 7/09 Sand 1m14y H GD £62310
80 6/08 Nott 1m75y G-F £2428

Total win prize-money £64738

Going (Turf): Sf: 0-0 GS: 0-1 **Gd: 1-4 GF: 1-3** Fm: 0-0
Distance: 5f/6f: 0-0 7f-8f: 0-6 **9f-13f: 2-4** 14f+: 0-0
Track : LH: 1-5 RH: 1-4 Tight: 0-3 Gall: 0-3
Aids: Bl: 0-0 Vi: 0-0 Tstrap: 0-0 Ckp: 0-0
Best Rating: **107** 8/09 York 1m gd-fm

Smart; effective at 1m; acts on most ground and on Polytrack.

Act Green

99(92) (76)76

3-y-o ch f Haafhd-Roaring Twenties (Halling (USA))

M L W Bell W J Gredley

Placings:051-362503 (4720)

2009: 10^{3}G, 8^{6}GF, 8^{2}GF, 8^{5}S, 6^{0}G, 8^{3}G,

	Starts	1st	2nd	3rd	Win & Pl
Career Total (Turf)	7	0	1	2	4316
Career Total (AW)	2	1	0	0	5181

76 10/08 GrLe 1m STD £5180

Total win prize-money £5181

Going (Turf): Sf: 0-1 GS: 0-0 Gd: 0-4 GF: 0-2 Fm: 0-0
Distance: 5f/6f: 0-1 **7f-8f: 1-5** 9f-13f: 0-3 14f+: 0-0
Track : **LH: 1-4** RH: 0-1 Tight: 0-1 **Gall: 1-1**
Aids: Bl: 0-0 Vi: 0-2 Tstrap: 0-0 Ckp: 0-0
Best Rating: **76** 6/09 Thsk 1m gd-fm

Fair; stays 1m; acts on Polytrack; has worn a visor.

Act Of Kalanisi (IRE)

99 88

3-y-o b g Kalanisi (IRE)-Act Of The Pace (IRE) (King's Theatre (IRE))

M Johnston Mrs Joan Keaney

Placings:51216 (5909)

2009: 11^{5}G, 11^{1}G, 12^{2}GF, 15^{1}GF, 12^{6}GF,

	Starts	1st	2nd	3rd	Win & Pl
Career Total (Turf)	5	2	1	0	10704

88 7/09 Ches 1m7f195y (0-85)H G-F £5828
81 6/09 Catt 1m3f214y GD £3238

Total win prize-money £9066

Going (Turf): Sf: 0-0 GS: 0-0 **Gd: 1-2 GF: 1-3** Fm: 0-0
Distance: 5f/6f: 0-0 7f-8f: 0-0 9f-13f: 1-4 14f+: 1-1
Track : **LH: 2-4** RH: 0-1 **Tight: 2-4** Gall: 0-1
Aids: Bl: 0-0 Vi: 0-0 Tstrap: 0-0 Ckp: 0-0
Best Rating: **88** 7/09 Ches 1m7f195y gd-fm

Fair; stays 1m4f and acts on fast ground.

Act Three

95(92) (52)72

5-y-o br m Beat Hollow-Rada's Daughter (Robellino (USA))

Mouse Hamilton-Fairley Runs In The Family

Placings:560/02203-30360 (6584)

2009: 13^{3}GS, 13^{0}GF, 13^{3}GF, 14^{6}GF, 12^{0}SD,

	Starts	1st	2nd	3rd	Win & Pl
Career Total (Turf)	12	0	2	3	3246
Career Total (AW)	1	0	0	0	

Going (Turf): Sf: 0-4 GS: 0-3 Gd: 0-1 GF: 0-4 Fm: 0-0
Distance: 5f/6f: 0-0 7f-8f: 0-0 9f-13f: 0-6 14f+: 0-7
Track : LH: 0-7 RH: 0-6 Tight: 0-8 Gall: 0-4
Aids: Bl: 0-0 Vi: 0-0 Tstrap: 0-0 Ckp: 0-0
Best Rating: 72 8/08 Sals 1m6f21y gd-sft

Modest; effective over 1m5f; acts on soft ground.

Actabou

88 **68**

4-y-o b g Tobougg (IRE)-Carreamia (Weldnaas (USA))
F P Murtagh Famous Five Racing

Placings:020/050100-0460U06 **(5147)**
2009: 9^{0}GF, 8^{4}GF, 6^{6}GF, 6^{0}G, 5^{U}G, 7^{0}G, 5^{6}GS,

	Starts	1st	2nd	3rd	Win & Pl
Career Total (Turf)	**16**	**1**	**1**	**0**	**3137**

68 6/08 Rdcr 6f (0-70)H G-F £2331
Total win prize-money £2331

Going (Turf): Sf: 0-1 GS: 0-2 Gd: 0-5 **GF: 1-8** Fm: 0-0
Distance: **5f/6f: 1-8** 7f-8f: 0-6 9f-13f: 0-2 14f+: 0-0
Track : LH: 0-1 RH: 0-4 Tight: 0-2 Gall: 0-0
Aids: Bl: 0-3 Vi: 0-0 Tstrap: 0-0 Ckp: 0 0
Best Rating: 74 9/07 Thsk 6f gd-fm

Modest sort; effective over 6f.

Acting Elegant

90(72) (19)**52**

2-y-o b f Needwood Blade-Diamond Vanessa (IRE) (Distinctly North (USA))
P D Evans Miss D L Wisbey & R J Viney

Placings:6354000 **(6589)**
2009: 5^{6}GF, 6^{3}GF, 6^{5}GF, 6^{4}G, 5^{0}SF, 7^{0}GF, 6^{0}GS,

	Starts	1st	2nd	3rd	Win & Pl
Career Total (Turf)	**6**	**0**	**0**	**1**	**447**
Career Total (AW)	**1**	**0**	**0**	**0**	

Going (Turf): Sf: 0-0 GS: 0-1 Gd: 0-1 GF: 0-4 Fm: 0-0
Distance: 5f/6f: 0-3 7f-8f: 0-4 9f-13f: 0-0 14f+: 0-0
Track : LH: 0-2 RH: 0-0 Tight: 0-1 Gall: 0-1
Aids: Bl: 0-0 Vi: 0-0 Tstrap: 0-0 Ckp: 0-0
Best Rating: 52 7/09 Yarm 6f3y good

Plating-class; stays 6f; acts on good ground.

Action Girl

96(97) (58)**61**

4-y-o gr f Act One-Mohican Girl (Dancing Brave (USA))
R M H Cowell Bottisham Heath Stud

Placings:6400006 **(7732)**
2009: 10^{6}GF, 8^{4}G, 9^{0}GS, 9^{0}GF, 10^{0}SD, 8^{0}SD, 12^{6}SD,

	Starts	1st	2nd	3rd	Win & Pl
Career Total (Turf)	**4**	**0**	**0**	**0**	**0**
Career Total (AW)	**3**	**0**	**0**	**0**	**0**

Going (Turf): Sf: 0-0 GS: 0-1 Gd: 0-1 GF: 0-2 Fm: 0-0
Distance: 5f/6f: 0-0 7f-8f: 0-1 9f-13f: 0-6 14f+: 0-0
Track : LH: 0-4 RH: 0-3 Tight: 0-6 Gall: 0-0
Aids: Bl: 0-0 Vi: 0-0 Tstrap: 0-3 Ckp: 0-3
Best Rating: 61 7/09 Wind 1m67y good

Action Impact (ARG)

(106) (87)**72**

5-y-o b g Bernstein (USA)-Valeur (ARG) (Lode (USA))
G L Moore T Bowley

Placings:166/602151102133-6261 **(3734)**
2009: 10^{6}SD, 12^{2}SD, 12^{6}SD, 11^{1}SD,

	Starts	1st	2nd	3rd	Win & Pl
Career Total (Turf)	**5**	**2**	**1**	**0**	**4734**
Career Total (AW)	**14**	**4**	**2**	**2**	**15111**

87 7/09 Kemp 1m3f (0-80)H STD £4727
81 11/08 GrLe 1m2f (0-75)H STD £2590
72 8/08 Ling 1m2f (0-65)H GD £2047
69 8/08 Ling 1m2f (0-62)H STD £2047
66 8/08 Ling 1m2f (0-55)H STD £2047
10/07 Muni 1m2f SFT £1722
Total win prize-money £15181

Going (Turf): Sf: 1-3 GS: 0-0 **Gd: 1-2** GF: 0-0 Fm: 0-0
Distance: 5f/6f: 0-0 7f-8f: 0-2 **9f-13f: 6-17** 14f+: 0-0
Track : **LH: 4-12** RH: 1-2 **Tight: 3-8** Gall: 1-4
Aids: Bl: 0-1 Vi: 0-0 Tstrap: 0-0 Ckp: 0-0
Best Rating: 87 7/09 Kemp 1m3f stand

Fair; effective over 1m2f-1m4f; acts on good and softer ground and on Polytrack.

Activate

98 **71**

2-y-o b g Motivator-Princess Manila (CAN) (Manila (USA))
M L W Bell Highclere Thoroughbred Racing Tudor Min

Placings:062 **(6965)**
2009: 7^{0}GS, 8^{6}G, 7^{2}G,

	Starts	1st	2nd	3rd	Win & Pl
Career Total (Turf)	**3**	**0**	**1**	**0**	**1633**

Going (Turf): Sf: 0-0 GS: 0-1 Gd: 0-2 GF: 0-0 Fm: 0-0
Distance: 5f/6f: 0-0 7f-8f: 0-2 9f-13f: 0-1 14f+: 0-0
Track : LH: 0-1 RH: 0-0 Tight: 0-0 Gall: 0-0
Aids: Bl: 0-0 Vi: 0-0 Tstrap: 0-0 Ckp: 0-0
Best Rating: 71 10/09 Brig 7f214y good

Active Asset (IRE)

92(101) (62)**75**

7-y-o ch g Sinndar (IRE)-Sacristy (Godswalk (USA))
J A Glover Brian Morton

Placings:2120/50061653346246356/01030313300020/31 06234006440**5045/6051-0600530** **(7847)**
2009: 8^{0}G, 9^{6}GF, 9^{0}G, 10^{0}GF, 12^{5}SD, 12^{3}SD, 12^{0}SD,

	Starts	1st	2nd	3rd	Win & Pl
Career Total (Turf)	**52**	**5**	**5**	**8**	**54504**
Career Total (AW)	**11**	**1**	**0**	**2**	**8869**

75 5/08 Bevl 1m1f207y (0-70)H G-F £2654
76 3/07 Ling 1m4f STD £7478
87 7/06 Newc 1m2f32y (0-85)H G-F £6232
84 4/06 Hayd 1m2f120y (0-85)H GD £6477
81 6/05 Gdwd 1m1f192y (0-85)H GD £7410
73 7/04 Yarm 7f3y F G-F £2961
Total win prize-money £33213

Going (Turf): Sf: 0-5 GS: 0-5 Gd: 2-15 **GF: 3-26** Fm: 0-1
Distance: 5f/6f: 0-0 7f-8f: 1-4 **9f-13f: 5-59** 14f+: 0-0
Track : **LH: 3-32** RH: 2-24 **Tight: 2-27** Gall: 1-14
Aids: Bl: 0-0 Vi: 0-0 Tstrap: 0-0 Ckp: 0-0
Best Rating: 91 8/07 NmkJ 1m2f gd-fm

Modest; stays 1m4f; acts on good or faster ground; also goes on Polytrack.

Actodos (IRE)

(104) (74)**86**

5-y-o ro g Act One-Really Gifted (IRE) (Cadeaux Genereux)
B R Millman G D C Jewell

Placings:462/1330/**003** **(6258)**
2009: 16^{0}SD, 12^{0}SD, 13^{3}SD,

	Starts	1st	2nd	3rd	Win & Pl
Career Total (Turf)	**6**	**0**	**1**	**2**	**3949**
Career Total (AW)	**4**	**1**	**0**	**1**	**3724**

82 4/07 Sthl 1m4f STD £2968
Total win prize-money £2969

Going (Turf): Sf: 0-0 GS: 0-4 Gd: 0-1 GF: 0-1 Fm: 0-0
Distance: 5f/6f: 0-0 7f-8f: 0-3 **9f-13f: 1-3** 14f+: 0-4
Track : **LH: 1-3** RH: 0-4 Tight: 0-2 Gall: 0-1
Aids: Bl: 0-0 Vi: 0-0 Tstrap: 0-0 Ckp: 0-0
Best Rating: 86 5/07 Ches 1m4f66y gd-fm

Fair; stays 1m6f; acts fast and on easy ground; also goes on Fibresand and Polytrack.

Actress Annie

(86) (34)**34**

4-y-o gr f Act One-Kembla (Known Fact (USA))
Mike Murphy M Murphy

Placings:0600-0 **(0061)**
2009: 8^{0}SD,

	Starts	1st	2nd	3rd	Win & Pl
Career Total (Turf)	**1**	**0**	**0**	**0**	
Career Total (AW)	**4**	**0**	**0**	**0**	**0**

Going (Turf): Sf: 0-0 GS: 0-0 Gd: 0-1 GF: 0-0 Fm: 0-0
Distance: 5f/6f: 0-0 7f-8f: 0-3 9f-13f: 0-2 14f+: 0-0
Track : LH: 0-2 RH: 0-3 Tight: 0-1 Gall: 0-1
Aids: Bl: 0-0 Vi: 0-0 Tstrap: 0-0 Ckp: 0-0
Best Rating: 34 10/08 Kemp 1m stand

Actuality

(100) (50)**68**

7-y-o b g So Factual (USA)-Cottage Maid (Inchinor)
J Balding George Doyle

Placings:0535012/03/000000/300-00 **(0405)**
2009: 7^{0}SD, 8^{0}SD,

	Starts	1st	2nd	3rd	Win & Pl
Career Total (Turf)	**10**	**0**	**0**	**1**	**607**
Career Total (AW)	**10**	**1**	**1**	**2**	**4986**

79 11/05 Wolv 7f32y STD £3044
Total win prize-money £3044

Going (Turf): Sf: 0-0 GS: 0-0 Gd: 0-7 GF: 0-3 Fm: 0-0
Distance: 5f/6f: 0-0 **7f-8f: 1-17** 9f-13f: 0-3 14f+: 0-0
Track : **LH: 1-10** RH: 0-6 **Tight: 1-5** Gall: 0-0
Aids: Bl: 0-0 Vi: 0-0 Tstrap: 0-1 Ckp: 0-1
Best Rating: 82 12/05 Ling 1m stand

Acuzio

(29) (59)**67**

8-y-o b g Mon Tresor-Veni Vici (IRE) (Namaqualand (USA))
S Wynne Steve Wynne

Placings:66040050/246032202456/05132541654033/224 44335/0 **(7649)**
2009: 16^{0}SD,

	Starts	1st	2nd	3rd	Win & Pl
Career Total (Turf)	**40**	**2**	**6**	**6**	**17455**

	Starts	1st	2nd	3rd	Win & Pl
Career Total (AW)	3	0	1	0	746

60 7/06 Wwck 1m4f134y (0-60)H GD £2730
57 6/06 Muss 1m4f (0-65)H G-F £3238
Total win prize-money £5969

Going (Turf): Sf: 0-4 GS: 0-6 **Gd: 1-10 GF: 1-17** Fm: 0-3
Distance: 5f/6f: 0-0 7f-8f: 0-3 **9f-13f: 2-34** 14f+: 0-6
Track : LH: 1-36 RH: 1-6 **Tight: 1-22** Gall: 0-0
Aids: Bl: 0-3 Vi: 0-0 Tstrap: 1-3 Ckp: 1-3
Best Rating: 67 8/07 Ches 1m4f66y gd-fm

Modest; stays 1m4f; acts on the Polytrack and on quick and easy ground on turf; has worn a tongue-strap/cheek-pieces/blinkers.

Ada River

104(102) (56)**102**
4-y-o b f Dansili-Miss Meltemi (IRE) (Miswaki Tern (USA))
A M Balding G B Russell

Placings:6/1420-2200 (7588)
2009: 8^{2}GF, 8^{2}GS, 8^{0}G, 8^{0}SD,

	Starts	1st	2nd	3rd	Win & Pl
Career Total (Turf)	7	0	3	0	27435
Career Total (AW)	2	1	0	0	2457

82 4/08 Kemp 1m STD £2456
Total win prize-money £2457

Going (Turf): **Sf: 0-0 GS: 0-1 Gd: 0-4 GF: 0-2 Fm: 0-0**
Distance: 5f/6f: 0-0 **7f-8f: 1-4** 9f-13f: 0-5 14f+: 0-0
Track : LH: 0-1 **RH: 1-6** Tight: 0-0 Gall: 0-2
Aids: Bl: 0-0 Vi: 0-0 Tstrap: 0-0 Ckp: 0-0
Best Rating: 102 9/09 Sand 1m14y gd-sft

Smart; placed in Listed company; stays 1m2f but suited by 1m; acts on good ground and on Polytrack.

Adab (IRE)

69 **54**
4-y-o b g Invincible Spirit (IRE)-Acate (IRE) (Classic Music (USA))
Miss Tracy Waggott H Conlon

Placings:2/300-0000 (5946)
2009: 7^{0}GF, 5^{0}GF, 6^{0}G, 5^{0}G,

	Starts	1st	2nd	3rd	Win & Pl
Career Total (Turf)	8	0	1	1	1662

Going (Turf): **Sf: 0-0 GS: 0-2 Gd: 0-3 GF: 0-3 Fm: 0-0**
Distance: 5f/6f: 0-5 7f-8f: 0-3 9f-13f: 0-0 14f+: 0-0
Track : LH: 0-2 RH: 0-1 Tight: 0-1 Gall: 0-1
Aids: Bl: 0-0 Vi: 0-1 Tstrap: 0-1 Ckp: 0-1
Best Rating: 67 5/07 Ling 5f good

Adage

91(109) (61)**57**
6-y-o b m Vettori (IRE)-Aymara (Darshaan)
David Pinder Ms L Burns

Placings:003/06000653/0512610166/644033330662-5460300040 (7751)
2009: 16^{5}SD, 13^{4}SD, 16^{6}G, 16^{0}G, 16^{3}SD, 13^{0}SF, 16^{0}SD, 16^{0}SD, 16^{4}SD, 13^{0}SD,

	Starts	1st	2nd	3rd	Win & Pl
Career Total (Turf)	18	0	1	2	1857
Career Total (AW)	25	3	1	5	9757

65 9/07 Wolv 1m5f194y (0-65)H STD £2047
65 7/07 Wolv 1m5f194y (0-65)H STD £2388
64 5/07 Wolv 1m5f194y (0-65)H STD £2730
Total win prize-money £7167

Going (Turf): **Sf: 0-2 GS: 0-3 Gd: 0-4 GF: 0-9 Fm: 0-0**
Distance: 5f/6f: 0-0 7f-8f: 0-2 9f-13f: 0-14 **14f+: 3-27**
Track : **LH: 3-28** RH: 0-13 **Tight: 3-24** Gall: 0-3
Aids: Bl: 0-3 Vi: 0-0 Tstrap: 0-6 Ckp: 0-6
Best Rating: 67 9/05 Carl 7f200y gd-fm

Moderate; stays 2m; acts on Polytrack; goes well at Wolverhampton; has worn a tongue tie.

Adam De Beaulieu (USA)

(73) (17)
2-y-o b g Broken Vow (USA)-Gambling Champ (USA) (Fabulous Champ (USA))
P C Haslam S A B Dinsmore

Placings:0 (7637)
2009: 5^{0}SD,

	Starts	1st	2nd	3rd	Win & Pl
Career Total (Turf)	0	0	0	0	
Career Total (AW)	1	0	0	0	

Going (Turf): **Sf: 0-0 GS: 0-0 Gd: 0-0 GF: 0-0 Fm: 0-0**
Distance: 5f/6f: 0-1 7f-8f: 0-0 9f-13f: 0-0 14f+: 0-0
Track : LH: 0-0 RH: 0-0 Tight: 0-0 Gall: 0-0
Aids: Bl: 0-0 Vi: 0-0 Tstrap: 0-0 Ckp: 0-0
Best Rating: 17 12/09 Sthl 5f stand

Adare (GER)

(77) (19)**55**
6-y-o b g Saddlers' Hall (IRE)-Aughamore Beauty (IRE) (Dara Monarch)
R Brotherton Millend Racing Club

Placings:6/0 (0978)
2009: 12^{0}SD,

	Starts	1st	2nd	3rd	Win & Pl
Career Total (Turf)	1	0	0	0	0
Career Total (AW)	1	0	0	0	

Going (Turf): **Sf: 0-0 GS: 0-0 Gd: 0-1 GF: 0-0 Fm: 0-0**
Distance: 5f/6f: 0-0 7f-8f: 0-0 9f-13f: 0-2 14f+: 0-0
Track : LH: 0-2 RH: 0-0 Tight: 0-1 Gall: 0-0
Aids: Bl: 0-0 Vi: 0-0 Tstrap: 0-0 Ckp: 0-0
Best Rating: 55 5/07 Rdcr 1m2f good

Addahab (USA)

72(99) (64)**65**
2-y-o b f Rock Hard Ten (USA)-Compassionate (USA) (Housebuster (USA))
Saeed Bin Suroor Godolphin

Placings:51 (7140)
2009: 8^{5}GS, 8^{1}SD,

	Starts	1st	2nd	3rd	Win & Pl
Career Total (Turf)	1	0	0	0	0
Career Total (AW)	1	1	0	0	3562

64 10/09 Wolv 1m141y STD £3561
Total win prize-money £3562

Going (Turf): **Sf: 0-0 GS: 0-1 Gd: 0-0 GF: 0-0 Fm: 0-0**
Distance: 5f/6f: 0-0 7f-8f: 0-1 **9f-13f: 1-1** 14f+: 0-0
Track : **LH: 1-2** RH: 0-0 **Tight: 1-1** Gall: 0-1
Aids: Bl: 0-0 Vi: 0-0 Tstrap: 1-1 Ckp: 1-1
Best Rating: 65 10/09 Newc 1m gd-sft

Modest; stays 1m; acts on Polytrack and easy ground.

Addictive Dream (IRE)

(82) (47)
2-y-o ch g Kheleyf (USA)-Nottambula (IRE) (Thatching)
W R Swinburn Caveat Emptor Partnership

Placings:0 (5778)
2009: 6^{0}SD,

	Starts	1st	2nd	3rd	Win & Pl
Career Total (Turf)	0	0	0	0	
Career Total (AW)	1	0	0	0	

Going (Turf): **Sf: 0-0 GS: 0-0 Gd: 0-0 GF: 0-0 Fm: 0-0**
Distance: 5f/6f: 0-1 7f-8f: 0-0 9f-13f: 0-0 14f+: 0-0
Track : LH: 0-0 RH: 0-1 Tight: 0-0 Gall: 0-0
Aids: Bl: 0-0 Vi: 0-0 Tstrap: 0-0 Ckp: 0-0
Best Rating: 47 9/09 Kemp 6f stand

Addiena

89(84) (34)**70**
5-y-o b m Golan (IRE)-Nurse Goodbody (USA) (Personal Hope (USA))
B Palling Wayne Devine

Placings:46301-60500 (7495)
2009: 12^{6}G, 12^{0}SD, 8^{5}GF, 8^{0}HY, 12^{0}SD,

	Starts	1st	2nd	3rd	Win & Pl
Career Total (Turf)	8	1	0	1	3806
Career Total (AW)	2	0	0	0	

70 8/08 Chep 1m14y (0-75)H SFT £3238
Total win prize-money £3238

Going (Turf): **Sf: 1-4** GS: 0-0 Gd: 0-1 GF: 0-3 Fm: 0-0
Distance: 5f/6f: 0-0 7f-8f: 0-0 **9f-13f: 1-10** 14f+: 0-0
Track : LH: 0-5 RH: 0-0 Tight: 0-2 Gall: 0-0
Aids: Bl: 0-0 Vi: 0-0 Tstrap: 0-0 Ckp: 0-0
Best Rating: 70 8/08 Chep 1m14y soft

Moderate; effective at 1m; acts on fast ground.

Addikt (IRE)

99 (70)**84**
4-y-o b c Diktat-Frond (Alzao (USA))
G A Harker Good Breed Limited

Placings:06534/4611400-440000 (6760)
2009: 8^{4}GS, 8^{4}GF, 9^{0}G, 8^{0}S, 8^{0}GF, 9^{0}G,

	Starts	1st	2nd	3rd	Win & Pl
Career Total (Turf)	16	2	0	0	8119
Career Total (AW)	2	0	0	1	845

84 7/08 Donc 1m2f60y (0-70)H GD £3412
78 7/08 Nott 1m2f50y (0-70)H G-S £3561
Total win prize-money £6974

Going (Turf): Sf: 0-3 **GS: 1-5 Gd: 1-4** GF: 0-4 Fm: 0-0
Distance: 5f/6f: 0-1 7f-8f: 0-4 **9f-13f: 2-13** 14f+: 0-0
Track : **LH: 2-8** RH: 0-8 Tight: 0-6 **Gall: 1-3**
Aids: Bl: 0-0 Vi: 0-0 Tstrap: 0-0 Ckp: 0-0
Best Rating: 84 7/08 Donc 1m2f60y good

Useful; stays 1m2f; acts on good and easy ground; also goes on Polytrack.

Addison De Witt

100 **66**
3-y-o ch g Where Or When (IRE)-Star Entry (In The Wings)
Micky Hammond Peter J Davies

Placings:000-0240442123 (5952)

2009: 8^{0}GF, 12^{2}F, 12^{4}GF, 14^{0}GF, 12^{4}F, 12^{4}GF, 11^{2}GS, 10^{1}GF, 11^{2}GS, 14^{3}GF,

	Starts	1st	2nd	3rd	Win & Pl
Career Total (Turf)	13	1	3	1	5890

58 8/09 Newc 1m2f32y (0-65)H G-F £2331
Total win prize-money £2331

Going (Turf): Sf: 0-1 GS: 0-4 Gd: 0-0 **GF: 1-6** Fm: 0-2
Distance: 5f/6f: 0-1 7f-8f: 0-3 **9f-13f: 1-7** 14f+: 0-2
Track : **LH: 1-8** RH: 0-5 Tight: 0-10 **Gall: 1-1**
Aids: Bl: 0-0 **Vi: 1-4** Tstrap: 0-1 Ckp: 0-1
Best Rating: **66** 9/09 Rdcr 1m6f19y gd-fm

Modest; effective over 1m4f; acts on fast ground; has worn a visor.

Addwaitya

105(99) (82)82
4-y-o br g Xaar-Three White Sox (Most Welcome)
Mrs L J Mongan (C F Wall 19/10) Mrs P J Sheen

Placings:006/0201036-31625250 **(7684)**
2009: 9^{3}GF, 9^{1}GF, 8^{6}GS, 8^{2}G, 9^{5}GF, 10^{2}GF, 10^{5}SD, 10^{0}SD,

	Starts	1st	2nd	3rd	Win & Pl
Career Total (Turf)	13	2	3	2	10985
Career Total (AW)	5	0	0	0	0

78 6/09 Gdwd 1m1f (0-70)H G-F £3123
77 6/08 Gdwd 1m1f192y (0-70)H G-F £3238
Total win prize-money £6361

Going (Turf): Sf: 0-2 GS: 0-2 Gd: 0-2 **GF: 2-7** Fm: 0-0
Distance: 5f/6f: 0-1 7f-8f: 0-5 **9f-13f: 2-12** 14f+: 0-0
Track : LH: 0-6 **RH: 2-9 Tight: 2-8** Gall: 0-1
Aids: Bl: 0-0 Vi: 0-0 Tstrap: 0-2 Ckp: 0-2
Best Rating: **82** 12/09 Ling 1m2f stand

Fair; stays 1m2f and acts on fast ground.

Adele Blanc Sec (FR)

96(94) (83)75
2-y-o b f Marchand De Sable (USA)-Plead (FR) (Bering)
Tom Dascombe The Trial Partnership

Placings:21 **(5368)**
2009: 6^{2}GF, 6^{1}SD,

	Starts	1st	2nd	3rd	Win & Pl
Career Total (Turf)	1	0	1	0	1657
Career Total (AW)	1	1	0	0	2047

83 8/09 Ling 6f STD £2047
Total win prize-money £2047

Going (Turf): **Sf: 0-0 GS: 0-0 Gd: 0-0 GF: 0-1 Fm: 0-0**
Distance: **5f/6f: 1-2** 7f-8f: 0-0 9f-13f: 0-0 14f+: 0-0
Track : **LH: 1-1** RH: 0-0 **Tight: 1-1** Gall: 0-1
Aids: Bl: 0-0 Vi: 0-0 Tstrap: 0-0 Ckp: 0-0
Best Rating: **83** 8/09 Ling 6f stand

Very useful; effective over 6f; acts on fast ground; goes on Polytrack.

Admin (IRE)

92(99) (82)75
2-y-o ch g Namid-Night Rhapsody (IRE) (Mujtahid (USA))
R M Beckett The Anagram Partnership

Placings:352231 **(6700)**
2009: 5^{3}G, 6^{5}GS, 5^{2}G, 5^{2}SD, 5^{3}SD, 5^{1}SS,

	Starts	1st	2nd	3rd	Win & Pl
Career Total (Turf)	3	0	1	1	1349
Career Total (AW)	3	1	1	1	5165

71 10/09 Ling 5f SS £3238
Total win prize-money £3238

Going (Turf): **Sf: 0-0 GS: 0-1 Gd: 0-2 GF: 0-0 Fm: 0-0**
Distance: **5f/6f: 1-6** 7f-8f: 0-0 9f-13f: 0-0 14f+: 0-0
Track : **LH: 1-4** RH: 0-0 **Tight: 1-3** Gall: 0-0
Aids: Bl: 0-0 Vi: 0-0 Tstrap: 0-0 Ckp: 0-0
Best Rating: **82** 8/09 Ling 5f stand

Fair; effective over 5f; acts on good ground; goes on Polytrack.

Admirable Duchess

94 69
2-y-o gr f Compton Place-Smart Hostess (Most Welcome)
D J S Ffrench Davis Brian W Taylor

Placings:53450 **(6418)**
2009: 6^{5}GF, 6^{3}GF, 5^{4}GF, 5^{5}F, 6^{0}GF,

	Starts	1st	2nd	3rd	Win & Pl
Career Total (Turf)	5	0	0	1	983

Going (Turf): **Sf: 0-0 GS: 0-0 Gd: 0-0 GF: 0-4 Fm: 0-1**
Distance: 5f/6f: 0-4 7f-8f: 0-1 9f-13f: 0-0 14f+: 0-0
Track : LH: 0-1 RH: 0-0 Tight: 0-0 Gall: 0-1
Aids: Bl: 0-0 Vi: 0-0 Tstrap: 0-0 Ckp: 0-0
Best Rating: **69** 7/09 Sals 6f gd-fm

Admirable Duque (IRE)

101(103) (76)76
3-y-o b g Selkirk (USA)-Stunning (USA) (Nureyev (USA))
D J S Ffrench Davis Brian W Taylor

Placings:03600-310050000010 **(7476)**
2009: 11^{3}GF, 12^{1}GF, 12^{0}GF, 14^{0}GF, 11^{5}C, 14^{0}GF, 14^{0}G, 13^{0}GF, 12^{0}GS, 12^{0}SD, 12^{1}SD, 12^{0}SD,

	Starts	1st	2nd	3rd	Win & Pl
Career Total (Turf)	14	1	0	2	3368
Career Total (AW)	3	1	0	0	2388

76 10/09 Wolv 1m4f50y (0-65)H STD £2388
76 5/09 Wwck 1m4f134y (0-70)H G-F £2914
Total win prize-money £5302

Going (Turf): Sf: 0-0 GS: 0-1 Gd: 0-6 **GF: 1-7** Fm: 0-0
Distance: 5f/6f: 0-0 7f-8f: 0-4 **9f-13f: 2-9** 14f+: 0-4
Track : **LH: 2-4** RH: 0-8 **Tight: 1-6** Gall: 0-2
Aids: Bl: 0-2 Vi: 0-0 Tstrap: 1-2 Ckp: 1-2
Best Rating: **76** 10/09 Wolv 1m4f50y stand

Fair; stays 1m4f; acts on good and fast ground.

Admiral (IRE)

88 39
8-y-o b g Alhaarth (IRE)-Coast Is Clear (IRE) (Rainbow Quest (USA))
S Parr Chris Roper & Willie McKay

Placings:64/01310/50/160/0/400000 **(3023)**
2009: 12^{4}GF, 14^{0}G, 12^{0}GF, 16^{0}G, 15^{0}GF, 12^{0}G,

	Starts	1st	2nd	3rd	Win & Pl
Career Total (Turf)	19	3	0	1	116205

92 5/06 Ches 2m2f147y H G-F £74784
90 6/04 Asct 1m4f B(0-105)H G-F £29000
84 5/04 Gdwd 1m4f C(0-95)H G-F £9486
Total win prize-money £113271

Going (Turf): Sf: 0-0 GS: 0-2 Gd: 0-7 **GF: 3-10** Fm: 0-0
Distance: 5f/6f: 0-0 7f-8f: 0-2 **9f-13f: 2-9** 14f+: 1-8
Track : LH: 1-8 **RH: 2-9 Tight: 2-8** Gall: 1-5
Aids: Bl: 0-1 Vi: 0-0 Tstrap: 0-1 Ckp: 0-1
Best Rating: **94** 5/06 Asct 2m gd-sft

Admiral Arry

78(81) (30)14
4-y-o ch g Compton Admiral-Loreto Rose (Lahib (USA))
J M Bradley Ray Styles

Placings:00-006 **(2537)**
2009: 7^{0}G, 5^{0}GF, 9^{6}GF,

	Starts	1st	2nd	3rd	Win & Pl
Career Total (Turf)	3	0	0	0	0
Career Total (AW)	2	0	0	0	

Going (Turf): **Sf: 0-0 GS: 0-0 Gd: 0-1 GF: 0-2 Fm: 0-0**
Distance: 5f/6f: 0-1 7f-8f: 0-2 9f-13f: 0-2 14f+: 0-0
Track : LH: 0-2 RH: 0-2 Tight: 0-0 Gall: 0-2
Aids: Bl: 0-0 Vi: 0-1 Tstrap: 0-1 Ckp: 0-1
Best Rating: **30** 9/08 GrLe 1m stand

Admiral Bond (IRE)

84(103) (69)69
4-y-o ch g Titus Livius (FR)-Where's Charlotte (Sure Blade (USA))
G R Oldroyd R C Bond

Placings:536020065201-255250050566 **(7838)**
2009: 5^{2}SD, 5^{5}SD, 5^{5}SD, 5^{2}SF, 5^{5}SD, 6^{0}GF, 5^{0}SD, 5^{5}SD, 5^{0}SD, 5^{5}GF, 5^{6}SD, 5^{6}SS,

	Starts	1st	2nd	3rd	Win & Pl
Career Total (Turf)	10	0	1	1	1912
Career Total (AW)	14	1	3	0	4504

66 12/08 Sthl 5f STD £2388
Total win prize-money £2388

Going (Turf): **Sf: 0-0 GS: 0-3 Gd: 0-3 GF: 0-4 Fm: 0-0**
Distance: **5f/6f: 1-24** 7f-8f: 0-0 9f-13f: 0-0 14f+: 0-0
Track : LH: 0-13 RH: 0-0 Tight: 0-11 Gall: 0-2
Aids: Bl: 0-2 Vi: 0-3 Tstrap: 1-14 Ckp: 1-14
Best Rating: **69** 1/09 Wolv 5f20y stand

Moderate sprinter; handles good and easy ground and Polytrack; has worn blinkers/visor and cheekpieces.

Admiral Breese

76(85) (55)40
2-y-o b g Halling (USA)-Covet (Polish Precedent (USA))
R Hollinshead Lodge Hyson Delnevo And Breese Racing

Placings:033 **(7781)**
2009: 8^{0}S, 7^{3}SD, 7^{3}SD,

	Starts	1st	2nd	3rd	Win & Pl
Career Total (Turf)	1	0	0	0	
Career Total (AW)	2	0	0	2	688

Going (Turf): **Sf: 0-1 GS: 0-0 Gd: 0-0 GF: 0-0 Fm: 0-0**
Distance: 5f/6f: 0-0 7f-8f: 0-2 9f-13f: 0-1 14f+: 0-0
Track : LH: 0-3 RH: 0-0 Tight: 0-0 Gall: 0-0
Aids: Bl: 0-0 Vi: 0-0 Tstrap: 0-0 Ckp: 0-0
Best Rating: **55** 11/09 Sthl 7f stand

Admiral Cochrane (IRE)

93(96) (73)64
2-y-o b c Noverre (USA)-Michelle Hicks (Ballad Rock)

W Jarvis Dr J Walker

Placings:64033213 (7824)
2009: 6^{6}S, 5^{4}G, 5^{0}GF, 6^{3}SD, 6^{3}SD, 7^{2}SD, 5^{1}SD, 7^{3}SD,

	Starts	1st	2nd	3rd	Win & Pl
Career Total (Turf)	3	0	0	0	241
Career Total (AW)	5	1	1	3	3983

70 12/09 Wolv 5f216y (0-65) STD £2388
Total win prize-money £2388

Going (Turf): Sf: 0-1 GS: 0-0 Gd: 0-1 GF: 0-1 Fm: 0-0
Distance: **5f/6f: 1-6** 7f-8f: 0-2 9f-13f: 0-0 14f+: 0-0
Track : **LH: 1-2** RH: 0-3 **Tight: 1-1** Gall: 0-0
Aids: Bl: 0-0 Vi: 0-0 Tstrap: 0-0 Ckp: 0-0
Best Rating: **73** 12/09 Kemp 7f stand

Modest; stays 7f; acts on Fibresand and Polytrack.

Admiral Dundas (IRE)

106(102) (84)**90**
4-y-o b g Noverre (USA)-Brandish (Warning)
W Jarvis Dr J Walker

Placings:5/160115256-0200641560 (7014)
2009: 8^{0}GF, 8^{2}GS, 8^{0}G, 10^{0}G, 9^{6}G, 10^{4}G, 9^{1}G, 9^{5}SD, 9^{6}S, 10^{0}GS,

	Starts	1st	2nd	3rd	Win & Pl
Career Total (Turf)	16	3	2	0	18588
Career Total (AW)	4	1	0	0	2034

84 9/09 Haml 1m1f36y GD £5180
85 8/08 Pont 1m4y (0-75)H GD £3885
75 7/08 NmkJ 1m (0-75)H G-F £3885
74 1/08 Ling 1m STD £1845
Total win prize-money £14799

Going (Turf): Sf: 0-2 GS: 0-2 **Gd: 2-9** GF: 1-3 Fm: 0-0
Distance: 5f/6f: 0-0 7f-8f: 2-6 9f-13f: 2-14 14f+: 0-0
Track : **LH: 2-8** RH: 1-8 **Tight: 2-6** Gall: 0-3
Aids: Bl: 0-1 Vi: 0-0 Tstrap: 0-1 Ckp: 0-1
Best Rating: **90** 8/08 Sand 1m14y good

Useful; effective over 1m; acts on most ground and on Polytrack.

Admiral Of The Dee (IRE)

71 **28**
3-y-o b g Catcher In The Rye (IRE)-Grandmette (IRE) (Grand Lodge (USA))
Patrick Morris Chester Racing Club Ltd

Placings:6 (3237)
2009: 7^{6}GF,

	Starts	1st	2nd	3rd	Win & Pl
Career Total (Turf)	1	0	0	0	0

Going (Turf): Sf: 0-0 GS: 0-0 Gd: 0-0 GF: 0-1 Fm: 0-0
Distance: 5f/6f: 0-0 7f-8f: 0-1 9f-13f: 0-0 14f+: 0-0
Track : LH: 0-0 RH: 0-1 Tight: 0-0 Gall: 0-0
Aids: Bl: 0-0 Vi: 0-0 Tstrap: 0-0 Ckp: 0-0
Best Rating: **28** 6/09 Bevl 7f100y gd-fm

Admiral Sandhoe (USA)

96(99) (70)**75**
3-y-o ch g Diesis-Dancing Sea (USA) (Storm Cat (USA))
Mrs A J Perrett Martin & Valerie Slade

Placings:653335-0200460 (5429)
2009: 8^{0}GS, 7^{2}GF, 8^{0}SD, 7^{0}GF, 7^{4}SD, 7^{6}GF, 7^{0}G,

	Starts	1st	2nd	3rd	Win & Pl
Career Total (Turf)	11	0	1	3	2573
Career Total (AW)	2	0	0	0	0

Going (Turf): Sf: 0-0 GS: 0-3 Gd: 0-1 GF: 0-7 Fm: 0-0
Distance: 5f/6f: 0-2 7f-8f: 0-9 9f-13f: 0-2 14f+: 0-0
Track : LH: 0-4 RH: 0-4 Tight: 0-3 Gall: 0-0
Aids: Bl: 0-0 Vi: 0-0 Tstrap: 0-0 Ckp: 0-0
Best Rating: **75** 8/08 Sals 6f gd-sft

Modest; stays 7f; acts on most ground and on Polytrack.

Admirals Way

(100) (61)**65**
4-y-o ch g Observatory (USA)-Dockage (CAN) (Riverman (USA))
C N Kellett J E Titley

Placings:00/00240621206342546-040140 (1080)
2009: 8^{0}SD, 7^{4}SD, 7^{0}SD, 7^{1}SD, 5^{4}SD, 8^{0}SD,

	Starts	1st	2nd	3rd	Win & Pl
Career Total (Turf)	8	1	3	0	6482
Career Total (AW)	17	1	1	1	2954

61 3/09 Kemp 7f (0-60)H STD £2047
64 5/08 Yarm 7f3y (0-60)H GD £1942
Total win prize-money £3990

Going (Turf): Sf: 0-3 GS: 0-1 **Gd: 1-3** GF: 0-1 Fm: 0-0
Distance: 5f/6f: 0-6 **7f-8f: 2-17** 9f-13f: 0-2 14f+: 0-0
Track : LH: 0-13 **RH: 1-6** Tight: 0-9 Gall: 0-4
Aids: Bl: 0-0 Vi: 0-0 Tstrap: 0-0 Ckp: 0-0
Best Rating: **65** 6/08 Leic 7f9y gd-fm

Modest; stays 1m1f; acts on Polytrack and good ground on turf; does not look that genuine.

Admire The View (IRE)

105 **90**
2-y-o ch f Dubawi (IRE)-Miss Honorine (IRE) (Highest Honor (FR))
D R Lanigan Saif Ali & Saeed H Altayer

Placings:010 (4795)
2009: 6^{0}GF, 7^{1}G, 7^{0}G,

	Starts	1st	2nd	3rd	Win & Pl
Career Total (Turf)	3	1	0	0	5666

90 7/09 Thsk 7f GD £5666
Total win prize-money £5666

Going (Turf): Sf: 0-0 GS: 0-0 **Gd: 1-2** GF: 0-1 Fm: 0-0
Distance: 5f/6f: 0-0 **7f-8f: 1-3** 9f-13f: 0-0 14f+: 0-0
Track : **LH: 1-1** RH: 0-0 **Tight: 1-1** Gall: 0-0
Aids: Bl: 0-0 Vi: 0-0 Tstrap: 0-0 Ckp: 0-0
Best Rating: **90** 7/09 Thsk 7f good

55,000gns half-sister to a winning juvenile over 6f, had shown promise on her debut and scored easily next time; stays 7f; acts on good ground.

Adnams

97(86) (47)**66**
3-y-o b g Nayef (USA)-Bedford Joy (GER) (Big Shuffle (USA))
C F Wall M Tilbrook

Placings:55060 (5782)
2009: 8^{5}GF, 10^{5}GF, 10^{0}GF, 11^{6}GS, 11^{0}SD,

	Starts	1st	2nd	3rd	Win & Pl
Career Total (Turf)	4	0	0	0	103
Career Total (AW)	1	0	0	0	

Going (Turf): Sf: 0-0 GS: 0-1 Gd: 0-0 GF: 0-3 Fm: 0-0
Distance: 5f/6f: 0-0 7f-8f: 0-1 9f-13f: 0-4 14f+: 0-0
Track : LH: 0-2 RH: 0-2 Tight: 0-3 Gall: 0-0
Aids: Bl: 0-0 Vi: 0-0 Tstrap: 0-0 Ckp: 0-0
Best Rating: **66** 6/09 NmkJ 1m gd-fm

Minor promise on debut over 1m on fast ground.

Adoring (IRE)

101 **82**
3-y-o b f One Cool Cat (USA)-Refined (IRE) (Statoblest)
W J Haggas Highclere Thoroughbred Racing (Gimcrack)

Placings:156 (5030)
2009: 7^{1}GF, 7^{5}G, 8^{6}GF,

	Starts	1st	2nd	3rd	Win & Pl
Career Total (Turf)	3	1	0	0	5181

82 5/09 NmkR 7f G-F £5180
Total win prize-money £5181

Going (Turf): Sf: 0-0 GS: 0-0 Gd: 0-1 **GF: 1-2** Fm: 0-0
Distance: 5f/6f: 0-0 **7f-8f: 1-3** 9f-13f: 0-0 14f+: 0-0
Track : LH: 0-0 RH: 0-0 Tight: 0-0 Gall: 0-0
Aids: Bl: 0-0 Vi: 0-0 Tstrap: 0-0 Ckp: 0-0
Best Rating: **82** 7/09 NmkJ 7f good

Useful; effective at 7f; acts on fast ground.

Adorn

92(101) (86)**104**
3-y-o b f Kyllachy-Red Tiara (USA) (Mr Prospector (USA))
J Noseda Cheveley Park Stud

Placings:414-5000 (5069)
2009: 6^{5}HY, 5^{0}G, 6^{0}S, 6^{0}GF,

	Starts	1st	2nd	3rd	Win & Pl
Career Total (Turf)	6	0	0	0	14228
Career Total (AW)	1	1	0	0	5181

86 9/08 Kemp 6f STD £5180
Total win prize-money £5181

Going (Turf): Sf: 0-2 GS: 0-0 Gd: 0-1 GF: 0-3 Fm: 0-0
Distance: **5f/6f: 1-7** 7f-8f: 0-0 9f-13f: 0-0 14f+: 0-0
Track : LH: 0-1 **RH: 1-1** Tight: 0-0 Gall: 0-0
Aids: Bl: 0-0 Vi: 0-0 Tstrap: 0-0 Ckp: 0-0
Best Rating: **104** 10/08 NmkR 6f gd-fm

Smart; stays 6f; effective on fast ground and on Polytrack; likes to race prominently.

Adozen Dreams

83(94) (54)**61**
3-y-o b f Monsieur Bond (IRE)-Chicago Bond (USA) (Real Quiet (USA))
N Bycroft N Bycroft

Placings:604156040-0000000 (6488)
2009: 5^{0}GF, 5^{0}G, 5^{0}G, 6^{0}GF, 5^{0}GF, 8^{0}GF, 10^{0}GF,

	Starts	1st	2nd	3rd	Win & Pl
Career Total (Turf)	12	1	0	0	265
Career Total (AW)	4	0	0	0	289

Going (Turf): Sf: 0-1 **GS: 1-1** Gd: 0-3 GF: 0-7 Fm: 0-0
Distance: **5f/6f: 1-14** 7f-8f: 0-0 9f-13f: 0-2 14f+: 0-0
Track : LH: 0-4 RH: 0-2 Tight: 0-3 Gall: 0-2
Aids: Bl: 0-0 Vi: 0-0 Tstrap: 0-3 Ckp: 0-3
Best Rating: **61** 7/08 Muss 5f gd-sft

Modest; suited by 5f and easy ground.

Advanced

111(101) (96)109

6-y-o b g Night Shift (USA)-Wonderful World (GER) (Dashing Blade)

K A Ryan T Doherty and McHeen

Placings:12010/3232/5002014520/05542200004-213604301440 **(7232a)**

2009: 6²GF, 6¹F, 5³G, 6⁶GF, 6⁰S, 7⁴G, 6³GF, 6⁰G, 7¹G, 7⁴GF, 7⁴GS, 6⁰HO,

	Starts	1st	2nd	3rd	Win & Pl
Career Total (Turf)	**39**	**5**	**7**	**4**	**275590**
Career Total (AW)	**3**	**0**	**1**	**0**	**8990**

109 9/09 Asct 7f H GD £93465
105 4/09 Pont 6f (0-100)H FRM £11215
119 9/07 Ayr 6f H G-S £75407
98 9/05 Sals 6f GD £9512
82 7/05 Wind 6f G-F £3757
Total win prize-money £193357

Going (Turf): Sf: 0-7 GS: 1-6 **Gd: 2-13** GF: 1-9 Fm: 1-2
Distance: **5f/6f: 4-31** 7f-8f: 1-11 9f-13f: 0-0 14f+: 0-0
Track : **LH: 1-6** RH: 0-1 Tight: 0-0 **Gall: 1-4**
Aids: Bl: 0-1 Vi: 0-0 Tstrap: 0-1 Ckp: 0-1
Best Rating: **119** 9/07 Ayr 6f gd-sft

Smart; winner of the 2007 Ayr Gold Cup; placed in Group and Listed company; effective at 5f-7f; acts on most ground; has worn a tongue tie and cheekpieces; likes to race prominently.

Adventure Story

98 74

2-y-o ch f Bold Edge-Birthday Venture (Soviet Star (USA))

R Hannon Lady Whent

Placings:6221 **(7288)**

2009: 6⁶G, 5²G, 5²GF, 6¹S,

	Starts	1st	2nd	3rd	Win & Pl
Career Total (Turf)	**4**	**1**	**2**	**0**	**7729**

74 11/09 Donc 6f SFT £6152
Total win prize-money £6152

Going (Turf): **Sf: 1-1** GS: 0-0 Gd: 0-2 GF: 0-1 Fm: 0-0
Distance: **5f/6f: 1-3** 7f-8f: 0-1 9f-13f: 0-0 14f+: 0-0
Track : LH: 0-0 RH: 0-0 Tight: 0-0 Gall: 0-1
Aids: Bl: 0-0 Vi: 0-0 Tstrap: 0-0 Ckp: 0-0
Best Rating: **74** 11/09 Donc 6f soft

Fair; effective at 6f; acts on fast and soft ground.

Adversane

(90) (32)39

5-y-o ch g Alhaarth (IRE)-Cragreen (Green Desert (USA))

A J Liddderdale Miss Lauren Meek

Placings:006/26300/000 **(0871)**

2009: 12⁰SD, 12⁰SD, 12⁰SD,

	Starts	1st	2nd	3rd	Win & Pl
Career Total (Turf)	**6**	**0**	**0**	**1**	**530**
Career Total (AW)	**5**	**0**	**1**	**0**	**705**

Going (Turf): **Sf: 0-3 GS: 0-1 Gd: 0-1 GF: 0-1 Fm: 0-0**
Distance: 5f/6f: 0-0 7f-8f: 0-3 9f-13f: 0-5 14f+: 0-3
Track : LH: 0-6 RH: 0-3 Tight: 0-4 Gall: 0-1
Aids: Bl: 0-0 Vi: 0-1 Tstrap: 0-1 Ckp: 0-1
Best Rating: **71** 6/07 Gdwd 1m6f gd-fm

Advertise

100 71

3-y-o br g Passing Glance-Averami (Averti (IRE))

A M Balding Kingsclere Racing CLub

Placings:610-652404 **(6790)**

2009: 7⁶GF, 7⁵GF, 7²GF, 7⁴GF, 7⁰GF, 6⁴G,

	Starts	1st	2nd	3rd	Win & Pl
Career Total (Turf)	**9**	**1**	**1**	**0**	**4587**

71 8/08 Wwck 7f26y SFT £2914
Total win prize-money £2914

Going (Turf): **Sf: 1-2** GS: 0-0 Gd: 0-1 GF: 0-6 Fm: 0-0
Distance: 5f/6f: 0-1 **7f-8f: 1-8** 9f-13f: 0-0 14f+: 0-0
Track : **LH: 1-5** RH: 0-1 Tight: 0-2 Gall: 0-0
Aids: Bl: 0-0 Vi: 0-0 Tstrap: 0-0 Ckp: 0-0
Best Rating: **71** 8/08 Wwck 7f26y soft

Modest; effective over 7f; acts on fast and soft ground.

Advertisement (USA)

92(96) (72)81

2-y-o b/br c Mr Greeley (USA)-Banner (USA) (A.P. Indy (USA))

J Noseda M Barber, Tom Ludt & Winstar Farm

Placings:43 **(4790)**

2009: 6⁴GF, 8³SD,

	Starts	1st	2nd	3rd	Win & Pl
Career Total (Turf)	**1**	**0**	**0**	**0**	**481**
Career Total (AW)	**1**	**0**	**0**	**1**	**403**

Going (Turf): **Sf: 0-0 GS: 0-0 Gd: 0-0 GF: 0-1 Fm: 0-0**
Distance: 5f/6f: 0-1 7f-8f: 0-1 9f-13f: 0-0 14f+: 0-0
Track : LH: 0-1 RH: 0-0 Tight: 0-1 Gall: 0-0
Aids: Bl: 0-0 Vi: 0-0 Tstrap: 0-0 Ckp: 0-0
Best Rating: **81** 7/09 Asct 6f gd-fm

Advisor (FR)

101 85

3-y-o gr g Anabaa (USA)-Armilina (FR) (Linamix (FR))

P F Nicholls (M L W Bell 6/8) The Royal Ascot Racing Club

Placings:65-5164426 **(4709)**

2009: 8⁵G, 8¹GS, 9⁶G, 9⁴G, 10⁴G, 12²S, 11⁶GS,

	Starts	1st	2nd	3rd	Win & Pl
Career Total (Turf)	**9**	**1**	**1**	**0**	**5599**

80 4/09 Wind 1m67y (0-75)H G-S £3070
Total win prize-money £3071

Going (Turf): Sf: 0-3 **GS: 1-2** Gd: 0-4 GF: 0-0 Fm: 0-0
Distance: 5f/6f: 0-0 7f-8f: 0-0 **9f-13f: 1-9** 14f+: 0-0
Track : LH: 0-5 **RH: 1-3 Tight: 1-4** Gall: 0-1
Aids: Bl: 0-0 Vi: 0-0 Tstrap: 0-0 Ckp: 0-0
Best Rating: **85** 8/09 Donc 1m4f soft

Fair; stays 1m and acts on easy ground.

Aegean (USA)

81 (100)71

2-y-o b f Northern Afleet (USA)-Apt To Star (USA) (Aptitude (USA))

Wesley A Ward Steven Michael Bell

Placings:110 **(3086)**

2009: 4¹FT, 5¹SD, 6⁰GF,

	Starts	1st	2nd	3rd	Win & Pl
Career Total (Turf)	**1**	**0**	**0**	**0**	
Career Total (AW)	**2**	**2**	**0**	**0**	**66024**

100 4/09 Chur 5f STD £47079
90 4/09 Keen 4f110y FST £18944
Total win prize-money £66024

Going (Turf): **Sf: 0-0 GS: 0-0 Gd: 0-0 GF: 0-1 Fm: 0-0**
Distance: **5f/6f: 1-2** 7f-8f: 0-0 9f-13f: 0-0 14f+: 0-0
Track : LH: 0-0 RH: 0-0 Tight: 0-0 Gall: 0-0
Aids: **Bl: 2-3** Vi: 0-0 Tstrap: 0-0 Ckp: 0-0
Best Rating: **100** 4/09 Chur 5f stand

Grade 3 winner in the US; effective over 5f; acts on dirt.

Aegean Dancer

105(97) (105)102

7-y-o b g Piccolo-Aegean Flame (Anshan)

B Smart Pinnacle Piccolo Partnership

Placings:2221/0345022141/13010242014/02600000-200 **(5132)**

2009: 5²GF, 5⁰G, 5⁰GF,

	Starts	1st	2nd	3rd	Win & Pl
Career Total (Turf)	**30**	**4**	**9**	**1**	**64366**
Career Total (AW)	**6**	**2**	**0**	**1**	**11698**

105 11/07 Wolv 5f20y (0-95)H STD £7124
94 6/07 Muss 5f (0-105)H GD £31160
89 4/07 Thsk 5f (0-80)H G-F £5181
85 8/06 Carl 5f (0-80)H G-F £6477
77 7/06 Carl 5f (0-70)H FRM £3238
59 12/05 Sthl 6f STD £3309
Total win prize-money £56493

Going (Turf): Sf: 0-0 GS: 0-1 Gd: 1-9 **GF: 2-17** Fm: 1-3
Distance: **5f/6f: 6-35** 7f-8f: 0-1 9f-13f: 0-0 14f+: 0-0
Track : LH: 2-3 RH: 2-2 Tight: 1-1 **Gall: 2-2**
Aids: Bl: 0-0 Vi: 0-0 Tstrap: 0-0 Ckp: 0-0
Best Rating: **105** 11/07 Wolv 5f20y stand

Useful; effective at 5f-6f; acts on good and faster ground and on sand; likes to race prominently.

Aegean Destiny

100(89) (60)65

2-y-o b f Beat Hollow-Starlist (Observatory (USA))

R A Harris (R Hannon 24/9) P Nurcombe

Placings:6031200540 **(7788)**

2009: 5⁶GF, 6⁰GF, 5³G, 7¹GF, 8²G, 7⁰SD, 8⁰SD, 8⁵SD, 7⁴SF, 8⁰SD,

	Starts	1st	2nd	3rd	Win & Pl
Career Total (Turf)	**5**	**1**	**1**	**1**	**3195**
Career Total (AW)	**5**	**0**	**0**	**0**	**0**

65 9/09 Leic 7f9y G-F £1942
Total win prize-money £1943

Going (Turf): Sf: 0-0 GS: 0-0 Gd: 0-2 **GF: 1-3** Fm: 0-0
Distance: 5f/6f: 0-3 **7f-8f: 1-6** 9f-13f: 0-1 14f+: 0-0
Track : LH: 0-6 RH: 0-1 Tight: 0-3 Gall: 0-3
Aids: Bl: 0-0 Vi: 0-0 Tstrap: 0-0 Ckp: 0-0
Best Rating: **65** 9/09 Leic 7f9y gd-fm

Modest; stays 1m; acts on good and faster ground; handles Polytrack.

Aegean King

91(92) (50)55

3-y-o b g Falbrav (IRE)-Aegean Dream (IRE) (Royal Academy (USA))

M Wigham Theobalds Stud & Partners

Placings:6653 **(3611)**

2009: 5⁶SD, 5⁶GF, 5⁵GF, 5³GF,

	Starts	1st	2nd	3rd	Win & Pl
Career Total (Turf)	3	0	0	1	433
Career Total (AW)	1	0	0	0	0

Going (Turf): Sf: 0-0 GS: 0-0 Gd: 0-0 GF: 0-3 Fm: 0-0
Distance: 5f/6f: 0-4 7f-8f: 0-0 9f-13f: 0-0 14f+: 0-0
Track : LH: 0-0 RH: 0-1 Tight: 0-0 Gall: 0-0
Aids: Bl: 0-0 Vi: 0-0 Tstrap: 0-0 Ckp: 0-0
Best Rating: 55 5/09 Muss 5f gd-fm

Moderate sprinter; best at 5f on fast ground.

Aegean Pride

87(97) (62)**62**
4-y-o b f Sakhee (USA)-Aegean Dream (IRE) (Royal Academy (USA))
A Berry A B Parr

Placings:03**50046-600000** **(2812)**
2009: 7^{0}SD, 8^{0}SD, 7^{0}SD, 7^{0}GF, 7^{0}GS, 6^{0}GF,

	Starts	1st	2nd	3rd	Win & Pl
Career Total (Turf)	6	0	0	1	578
Career Total (AW)	7	0	0	0	0

Going (Turf): Sf: 0-0 GS: 0-3 Gd: 0-0 GF: 0-3 Fm: 0-0
Distance: 5f/6f: 0-0 7f-8f: 0-11 9f-13f: 0-2 14f+: 0-0
Track : LH: 0-6 RH: 0-3 Tight: 0-6 Gall: 0-0
Aids: Bl: 0-0 Vi: 0-0 Tstrap: 0-0 Ckp: 0-0
Best Rating: 62 9/08 Kemp 7f stand

Modest; best at around 7f on easy ground; handles Polytrack.

Aegean Prince

87(106) (86)**86**
5-y-o b g Dr Fong (USA)-Dizzydaisy (Sharpo)
P Howling (P J Hobbs 18/3) Theobalds Stud

Placings:301/20003650/026533165001-260000 **(6636)**
2009: 14^{2}GF, **12^{6}SD**, 12^{0}G, **11^{0}SD**, 14^{0}G, 13^{0}SD,

	Starts	1st	2nd	3rd	Win & Pl
Career Total (Turf)	21	1	3	4	14627
Career Total (AW)	8	2	0	0	7318
86	12/08	Ling	1m4f	(0-85)H	STD £4727
86	7/08	Wind	1m3f135y	(0-80)H	SFT £5375
76	10/06	Ling	7f		STD £2590

Total win prize-money £12693

Going (Turf): Sf: 1-4 GS: 0-3 Gd: 0-9 GF: 0-5 Fm: 0-0
Distance: 5f/6f: 0-1 7f-8f: 1-3 **9f-13f: 2-22** 14f+: 0-3
Track : LH: 2-11 RH: 0-14 **Tight: 3-14** Gall: 0-4
Aids: Bl: 0-1 Vi: 0-0 Tstrap: 0-3 Ckp: 0-3
Best Rating: 86 12/08 Ling 1m4f stand

Fair; effective up to 1m6f; acts on most ground on turf; goes on Polytrack; has worn blinkers and cheekpieces.

Aegean Rose

79(94) (52)**23**
4-y-o br f Superior Premium-Lady Sabina (Bairn (USA))
M Blanshard Mrs Lesley Bowtell

Placings:040000 **(1967)**
2009: 8^{0}SD, 8^{4}SD, 8^{0}SD, 10^{0}GF, 12^{0}SD, 10^{0}SD,

	Starts	1st	2nd	3rd	Win & Pl
Career Total (Turf)	1	0	0	0	
Career Total (AW)	5	0	0	0	192

Going (Turf): Sf: 0-0 GS: 0-0 Gd: 0-0 GF: 0-1 Fm: 0-0
Distance: 5f/6f: 0-0 7f-8f: 0-2 9f-13f: 0-4 14f+: 0-0
Track : LH: 0-4 RH: 0-2 Tight: 0-3 Gall: 0-0
Aids: Bl: 0-0 Vi: 0-0 Tstrap: 0-0 Ckp: 0-0
Best Rating: 52 3/09 Kemp 1m stand

Aegean Shadow

100(87) (43)**65**
3-y-o ch f Sakhee (USA)-Noble View (USA) (Distant View (USA))
M Wigham Theobalds Stud 2

Placings:10 **(5806)**
2009: 5^{1}S, 8^{0}SD,

	Starts	1st	2nd	3rd	Win & Pl
Career Total (Turf)	1	1	0	0	2914
Career Total (AW)	1	0	0	0	
65	7/09	Leic	5f218y		SFT £2914

Total win prize-money £2914

Going (Turf): Sf: 1-1 GS: 0-0 Gd: 0-0 GF: 0-0 Fm: 0-0
Distance: 5f/6f: 1-1 7f-8f: 0-1 9f-13f: 0-0 14f+: 0-0
Track : LH: 0-0 RH: 0-1 Tight: 0-0 Gall: 0-0
Aids: Bl: 0-0 Vi: 0-0 Tstrap: 0-0 Ckp: 0-0
Best Rating: 65 7/09 Leic 5f218y soft

Modest; effective at 6f; acts on soft ground.

Aerodynamic (IRE)

93 **78**
2-y-o b c Oratorio (IRE)-Willowbridge (IRE) (Entrepreneur)
Pat Eddery Mrs Gay Smith

Placings:16 **(3138)**
2009: 6^{1}G, 7^{6}GF,

	Starts	1st	2nd	3rd	Win & Pl
Career Total (Turf)	2	1	0	0	4561
78	6/09	Nott	6f15y		GD £3885

Total win prize-money £3886

Going (Turf): Sf: 0-0 GS: 0-0 **Gd: 1-1** GF: 0-1 Fm: 0-0
Distance: 5f/6f: 0-0 **7f-8f: 1-2** 9f-13f: 0-0 14f+: 0-0
Track : LH: 0-0 RH: 0-0 Tight: 0-0 Gall: 0-0
Aids: Bl: 0-0 Vi: 0-0 Tstrap: 0-0 Ckp: 0-0
Best Rating: 78 6/09 Nott 6f15y good

Useful; effective at 6f; acts on good ground.

Aeroplane

94(110) (109)**97**
6-y-o b h Danehill Dancer (IRE)-Anita At Dawn (IRE) (Anita's Prince)
P D Evans (Ian Williams 25/11) R Piff

Placings:2/14010/0/0306000321-1433601162 **(7827)**
2009: **7^{1}SD**, **6^{4}SD**, **7^{3}SD**, **7^{3}SD**, **7^{6}SD**, **7^{0}GF**, **7^{1}SD**, **7^{1}SD**, **7^{6}SD**, **8^{2}SD**,

	Starts	1st	2nd	3rd	Win & Pl
Career Total (Turf)	14	2	1	1	20594
Career Total (AW)	13	4	2	3	41910
90	11/09	Ling	7f		STD £1978
102	9/09	Wolv	7f32y		STD £2914
108	1/09	Kemp	7f	(0-100)H	STD £11215
107	12/08	Ling	7f	(0-100)H	STD £11656
110	9/06	Sthl	7f		GD £8724
97	4/06	NmkR	7f		GD £5181

Total win prize-money £41673

Going (Turf): Sf: 0-1 GS: 0-3 **Gd: 2-6** GF: 0-4 Fm: 0-0
Distance: 5f/6f: 0-6 **7f-8f: 6-21** 9f-13f: 0-0 14f+: 0-0
Track : LH: 4-11 RH: 1-5 **Tight: 4-9** Gall: 0-2
Aids: Bl: 0-0 Vi: 0-0 Tstrap: 0-4 Ckp: 0-4
Best Rating: 110 9/06 Sthl 7f good

Smart; effective at around 7f-1m; acts on good ground; goes on Polytrack; difficult ride; has worn cheekpieces.

Aestival

47(84) (44)**29**
3-y-o b g Falbrav (IRE)-Summer Night (Nashwan (USA))
Sir Mark Prescott Lady Katharine Watts

Placings:060-0 **(6910)**
2009: 10^{0}G,

	Starts	1st	2nd	3rd	Win & Pl
Career Total (Turf)	3	0	0	0	0
Career Total (AW)	1	0	0	0	

Going (Turf): Sf: 0-1 GS: 0-1 Gd: 0-1 GF: 0-0 Fm: 0-0
Distance: 5f/6f: 0-3 7f-8f: 0-0 9f-13f: 0-1 14f+: 0-0
Track : LH: 0-2 RH: 0-1 Tight: 0-2 Gall: 0-0
Aids: Bl: 0-0 Vi: 0-0 Tstrap: 0-0 Ckp: 0-0
Best Rating: 44 10/08 Ling 6f stand

Aetos

91 **61**
2-y-o b c Royal Applause-Hagwah (USA) (Dancing Brave (USA))
M P Tregoning Sir Alex Ferguson & Sotirios Hassiakos

Placings:4 **(4410)**
2009: 6^{4}G,

	Starts	1st	2nd	3rd	Win & Pl
Career Total (Turf)	1	0	0	0	962

Going (Turf): Sf: 0-0 GS: 0-0 Gd: 0-1 GF: 0-0 Fm: 0-0
Distance: 5f/6f: 0-1 7f-8f: 0-0 9f-13f: 0-0 14f+: 0-0
Track : LH: 0-0 RH: 0-0 Tight: 0-0 Gall: 0-0
Aids: Bl: 0-0 Vi: 0-0 Tstrap: 0-0 Ckp: 0-0
Best Rating: 61 7/09 Gdwd 6f good

Affirmable

85 **55**
2-y-o b f Doyen (IRE)-Bella Bellisimo (IRE) (Alzao (USA))
J W Hills Longview Stud & Bloodstock Ltd

Placings:6 **(5000)**
2009: 7^{6}G,

	Starts	1st	2nd	3rd	Win & Pl
Career Total (Turf)	1	0	0	0	0

Going (Turf): Sf: 0-0 GS: 0-0 Gd: 0-1 GF: 0-0 Fm: 0-0
Distance: 5f/6f: 0-0 7f-8f: 0-1 9f-13f: 0-0 14f+: 0-0
Track : LH: 0-0 RH: 0-0 Tight: 0-0 Gall: 0-0
Aids: Bl: 0-0 Vi: 0-0 Tstrap: 0-0 Ckp: 0-0
Best Rating: 55 8/09 NmkJ 7f good

Affirmatively

98(101) (69)**52**
4-y-o b f Diktat-Circlet (Lion Cavern (USA))
A W Carroll Let's Give It A Go Racing

Placings:01400/**3550000060-0043200305**00 **(4204)**
2009: 6^{0}SD, 7^{0}SD, 5^{4}SD, 5^{3}SD, 5^{2}SD, 5^{0}SD, 5^{0}F, 5^{3}GF, 5^{0}GF, 5^{5}G, 5^{0}GF, 5^{0}SD,

	Starts	1st	2nd	3rd	Win & Pl
Career Total (Turf)	11	1	0	1	4874

	Starts	1st	2nd	3rd	Win & Pl
Career Total (AW)	16	0	1	2	1168

67 4/07 Wind 5f10y G-F £3238

Total win prize-money £3239

Going (Turf): Sf: 0-0 GS: 0-3 Gd: 0-2 **GF: 1-5** Fm: 0-1

Distance: **5f/6f: 1-21** 7f-8f: 0-6 9f-13f: 0-0 14f+: 0-0

Track : LH: 0-14 RH: 0-4 Tight: 0-10 **Gall: 1-2**

Aids: Bl: 0-8 Vi: 0-0 Tstrap: 0-1 Ckp: 0-1

Best Rating: 69 1/08 Ling 7f stand

Moderate; effective at around 5f-7f; acts on fast ground; also goes on Polytrack.

Affluent

101(103) (81)**94**

3-y-o b f Oasis Dream-Valencia (Kenmare (FR))

R Charlton K Abdulla

Placings:1-231554 **(5245)**

2009: 5^{2}SD, 5^{3}GF, 5^{1}G, 5^{5}GF, 5^{5}G, 5^{4}F,

	Starts	1st	2nd	3rd	Win & Pl
Career Total (Turf)	6	2	0	1	11206
Career Total (AW)	1	0	1	0	1612

94 5/09 Wind 5f10y (0-85)H GD £5180

73 10/08 Nott 5f13y HVY £2914

Total win prize-money £8095

Going (Turf): **Sf: 1-1** GS: 0-0 **Gd: 1-2** GF: 0-2 Fm: 0-1

Distance: **5f/6f: 2-7** 7f-8f: 0-0 9f-13f: 0-0 14f+: 0-0

Track : LH: 0-1 RH: 0-1 Tight: 0-0 **Gall: 1-2**

Aids: Bl: 0-0 Vi: 0-0 Tstrap: 0-0 Ckp: 0-0

Best Rating: 94 5/09 Wind 5f10y good

Fair; effective over 5f; acts on good and heavy ground and on Polytrack.

Aflaam (IRE)

102(97) (72)**86**

4-y-o br g Dubai Destination (USA)-Arjuzah (IRE) (Ahonoora)

R A Harris (P Howling 26/10) The Circle Bloodstock I Limited

Placings:31-0040530000 **(7699)**

2009: 8^{0}SD, 7^{0}GF, 8^{4}GF, 7^{0}SF, 7^{5}G, 8^{3}GF, 8^{0}GF, 7^{0}SD, 10^{0}SD, 10^{0}SD,

	Starts	1st	2nd	3rd	Win & Pl
Career Total (Turf)	7	1	0	2	7127
Career Total (AW)	5	0	0	0	

86 8/08 Thsk 1m G-S £5634

Total win prize-money £5634

Going (Turf): Sf: 0-0 **GS: 1-1** Gd: 0-1 GF: 0-5 Fm: 0-0

Distance: 5f/6f: 0-0 **7f-8f: 1-9** 9f-13f: 0-3 14f+: 0-0

Track : **LH: 1-2** RH: 0-5 **Tight: 1-3** Gall: 0-0

Aids: Bl: 0-0 Vi: 0-0 Tstrap: 0-0 Ckp: 0-0

Best Rating: 86 8/08 Thsk 1m gd-sft

Closely related to top-class sprinter Malhub; stays 1m; acts on fast ground.

Africa's Star (IRE)

97(90) (59)**67**

3-y-o br f Johannesburg (USA)-Grable (IRE) (Sadler's Wells (USA))

M Dods K Knox

Placings:64044-030400 **(5621)**

2009: 6^{0}GF, 5^{3}GF, 5^{0}GF, 5^{4}GF, 5^{0}G, 7^{0}S,

	Starts	1st	2nd	3rd	Win & Pl
Career Total (Turf)	9	0	0	1	770
Career Total (AW)	2	0	0	0	289

Going (Turf): **Sf: 0-1 GS: 0-1 Gd: 0-1 GF: 0-5 Fm: 0-1**

Distance: 5f/6f: 0-8 7f-8f: 0-3 9f-13f: 0-0 14f+: 0-0

Track : LH: 0-2 RH: 0-0 Tight: 0-2 Gall: 0-0

Aids: Bl: 0-1 Vi: 0-0 Tstrap: 0-1 Ckp: 0-1

Best Rating: 67 6/08 NmkJ 7f firm

African Art (USA)

108(94) (71)**89**

3-y-o ch c Johannesburg (USA)-Perovskia (USA) (Stravinsky (USA))

B J Meehan Matthew Green & Sangster Family

Placings:4-140530 **(7027)**

2009: 8^{1}GF, 8^{4}GF, 8^{0}GF, 8^{5}GF, 8^{3}GF, 7^{0}SD,

	Starts	1st	2nd	3rd	Win & Pl
Career Total (Turf)	6	1	0	1	5718
Career Total (AW)	1	0	0	0	

85 4/09 Hayd 1m30y G-F £3238

Total win prize-money £3238

Going (Turf): Sf: 0-0 GS: 0-1 Gd: 0-0 **GF: 1-5** Fm: 0-0

Distance: 5f/6f: 0-0 7f-8f: 0-5 **9f-13f: 1-2** 14f+: 0-0

Track : **LH: 1-3** RH: 0-1 Tight: 0-0 Gall: 0-0

Aids: Bl: 0-0 Vi: 0-0 Tstrap: 0-0 Ckp: 0-0

Best Rating: 89 10/09 Pont 1m4y gd-fm

Useful; stays 1m; acts on fast ground.

African Cheetah

104(103) (84)**80**

3-y-o ch c Pivotal-Miss Queen (USA) (Miswaki (USA))

R Hollinshead (M Johnston 19/10) Ray Robinson

Placings:3631443561 **(7672)**

2009: 7^{3}GF, 7^{6}GF, 8^{3}G, 10^{1}GS, 10^{4}GS, 9^{4}GF, 12^{3}GF, 11^{5}G, 10^{6}GF, 8^{1}SD,

	Starts	1st	2nd	3rd	Win & Pl
Career Total (Turf)	9	1	0	3	5374
Career Total (AW)	1	1	0	0	3238

84 12/09 Wolv 1m141y (0-75)H STD £3238

71 5/09 Newc 1m2f32y G-S £2719

Total win prize-money £5958

Going (Turf): Sf: 0-0 **GS: 1-2** Gd: 0-2 GF: 0-5 Fm: 0-0

Distance: 5f/6f: 0-0 7f-8f: 0-2 **9f-13f: 2-8** 14f+: 0-0

Track : **LH: 2-7** RH: 0-2 Tight: 1-4 Gall: 1-2

Aids: Bl: 0-0 Vi: 0-0 Tstrap: 0-0 Ckp: 0-0

Best Rating: 84 12/09 Wolv 1m141y stand

Fair; effective over 1m2f; acts on easy ground.

African Rose

111 **116**

4-y-o ch f Observatory (USA)-New Orchid (USA) (Quest For Fame)

Mme C Head-Maarek K Abdulla

Placings:2133/314210-460 **(4837a)**

2009: 5^{4}G, 6^{6}GF, 6^{0}GS,

	Starts	1st	2nd	3rd	Win & Pl
Career Total (Turf)	13	3	2	3	210118

115 9/08 Donc 6f SFT £93670

105 5/08 Lonc 7f GD £20221

101 8/07 Claf 7f SFT £7094

Total win prize-money £120987

Going (Turf): **Sf: 2-4** GS: 0-2 Gd: 1-5 GF: 0-1 Fm: 0-0

Distance: 5f/6f: 1-4 **7f-8f: 2-9** 9f-13f: 0-0 14f+: 0-0

Track : LH: 0-1 **RH: 1-8** Tight: 0-0 Gall: 0-0

Aids: Bl: 0-0 Vi: 0-0 Tstrap: 0-0 Ckp: 0-0

Best Rating: 116 8/08 Deau 6f110y soft

Group class; runner-up in the 2008 Prix Maurice De Gheest and winner of the Group 1 Sprint Cup at Doncaster; effective at around 6f-7f; acts on good or softer ground.

After The Show

95(104) (69)**78**

8-y-o b g Royal Applause-Tango Teaser (Shareef Dancer (USA))

Rae Guest Miss L Thompson

Placings:604051/60602000/**1241**/263622600**4**/063405340 3/3550111340**052-2300000404** **(7808)**

2009: 5^{2}SD, 5^{3}SD, 5^{0}SD, 5^{0}HY, 5^{0}SD, 5^{0}S, 6^{0}SD, 6^{4}SD, 6^{0}SD, 5^{4}SD,

	Starts	1st	2nd	3rd	Win & Pl
Career Total (Turf)	29	4	2	3	18808
Career Total (AW)	32	2	5	4	14883

80 4/08 Wind 5f10y (0-80)H G-S £4533

76 4/08 Sthl 6f (0-60)H GD £1774

76 3/08 Wwck 5f110y (0-75)H G-S £3071

73 12/05 Ling 5f (0-70)H STD £3031

75 10/05 Sthl 5f (0-70)H STD £3376

71 10/03 Yarm 5f43y D(0-85) SFT £3929

Total win prize-money £19714

Going (Turf): Sf: 1-11 **GS: 2-9** Gd: 1-6 GF: 0-3 Fm: 0-0

Distance: **5f/6f: 6-55** 7f-8f: 0-6 9f-13f: 0-0 14f+: 0-0

Track : **LH: 3-23** RH: 0-9 Tight: 1-16 Gall: 1-6

Aids: Bl: 0-1 Vi: 0-0 Tstrap: 0-3 Ckp: 0-3

Best Rating: 82 8/06 NmkJ 5f soft

Moderate; effective over 5f-6f; acts on soft ground; also goes on sand.

Afton View (IRE)

(99) (64)**64**

4-y-o gr g Clodovil (IRE)-Moonlight Partner (IRE) (Red Sunset)

S Parr Willie McKay

Placings:656043/**55**050002304**3050-5602200** **(0792)**

2009: 8^{5}SD, 6^{6}SD, 5^{0}SD, 6^{2}SD, 6^{2}SS, 8^{0}SD, 8^{0}SD,

	Starts	1st	2nd	3rd	Win & Pl
Career Total (Turf)	11	0	1	1	1090
Career Total (AW)	17	0	2	2	1864

Going (Turf): **Sf: 0-2 GS: 0-1 Gd: 0-2 GF: 0-6 Fm: 0-0**

Distance: 5f/6f: 0-11 7f-8f: 0-13 9f-13f: 0-4 14f+: 0-0

Track : LH: 0-19 RH: 0-5 Tight: 0-14 Gall: 0-1

Aids: Bl: 0-2 Vi: 0-0 Tstrap: 0-4 Ckp: 0-4

Best Rating: 64 12/07 Wolv 7f32y stand

Moderate; effective over 6f-7f; acts on fast ground; goes on Polytrack; has worn cheekpieces.

Again (IRE)

110 **114**

3-y-o b f Danehill Dancer (IRE)-Cumbres (FR) (Kahyasi)

David Wachman M Tabor & Mrs John Magnier

Placings:01110-1030 **(6525a)**

2009: 8^{1}HY, 8^{0}GF, 8^{3}GY, 10^{0}G,

	Starts	1st	2nd	3rd	Win & Pl
Career Total (Turf)	9	4	0	1	429098

114 5/09 Curr 1m HVY £217961

110 8/08 Curr 7f SFT £123970

107 8/08 Leop 7f HVY £59742

82 7/08 Curr 1m G-F £8637
Total win prize-money £410313

Going (Turf): **Sf: 3-4** GS: 0-1 Gd: 0-1 GF: 1-2 Fm: 0-0
Distance: 5f/6f: 0-0 **7f-8f: 4-8** 9f-13f: 0-1 14f+: 0-0
Track : LH: 1-2 **RH: 2-5** Tight: 0-0 **Gall: 2-3**
Aids: Bl: 0-0 Vi: 0-0 Tstrap: 0-1 Ckp: 0-1
Best Rating: **114** 5/09 Curr 1m heavy

High class; Irish trained; winner of the Group 2 Debutante Stakes and Group 1 Moyglare Stud Stakes; stays 1m; acts on any ground.

Against The Rules

(84) (45)**55**
3-y-o b g Diktat-Bella Bellisimo (IRE) (Alzao (USA))
J A R Toller M Barber

Placings:050000-0 **(5574)**
2009: 8^{0}SD,

	Starts	1st	2nd	3rd	Win & Pl
Career Total (Turf)	3	0	0	0	0
Career Total (AW)	4	0	0	0	

Going (Turf): **Sf: 0-0 GS: 0-1 Gd: 0-0 GF: 0-2 Fm: 0-0**
Distance: 5f/6f: 0-1 7f-8f: 0-5 9f-13f: 0-1 14f+: 0-0
Track : LH: 0-1 RH: 0-3 Tight: 0-0 Gall: 0-1
Aids: Bl: 0-0 Vi: 0-0 Tstrap: 0-2 Ckp: 0-2
Best Rating: **55** 7/08 NmkJ 7f gd-fm

Moderate gelding; stays 7f; acts on fast ground.

Agapanthus (GER)

95(100) (75)**88**
4-y-o b g Tiger Hill (IRE)-Astilbe (GER) (Monsun (GER))
B J Curley Curley Leisure

Placings:1/40000040-160006 **(7248)**
2009: 10^{1}G, 10^{6}GS, 9^{0}S, 9^{0}G, 10^{0}GS, 10^{6}HY,

	Starts	1st	2nd	3rd	Win & Pl
Career Total (Turf)	10	2	0	0	5552
Career Total (AW)	5	0	0	0	0

77 4/09 Yarm 1m2f21y (0-75)H GD £2978
10/07 Brem 7f GD £2027
Total win prize-money £5006

Going (Turf): Sf: 0-3 GS: 0-2 **Gd: 2-5** GF: 0-0 Fm: 0-0
Distance: 5f/6f: 0-0 7f-8f: 1-1 9f-13f: 1-14 14f+: 0-0
Track : **LH: 1-6** RH: 0-7 **Tight: 1-2** Gall: 0-2
Aids: Bl: 0-0 Vi: 0-0 Tstrap: 0-3 Ckp: 0-3
Best Rating: **88** 6/08 Colo 1m3f good

Modest; effective over 1m2f; acts on good ground; has worn cheekpieces.

Age Of Aquarius (IRE)

115 (83)**118**
3-y-o b c Galileo (IRE)-Clara Bow (FR) (Top Ville)
A P O'Brien Mrs Magnier/Tabor/Smith/Mordukhovitch

Placings:14-102 **(3970a)**
2009: 11^{1}GF, 12^{0}G, 12^{2}GS,

	Starts	1st	2nd	3rd	Win & Pl
Career Total (Turf)	4	1	1	0	180562
Career Total (AW)	1	1	0	0	6097

108 5/09 Ling 1m3f106y G-F £36900
83 9/08 Dund 1m STD £6097
Total win prize-money £42998

Going (Turf): Sf: 0-1 GS: 0-1 Gd: 0-1 **GF: 1-1** Fm: 0-0
Distance: 5f/6f: 0-0 7f-8f: 1-1 9f-13f: 1-4 14f+: 0-0
Track : **LH: 2-4** RH: 0-1 **Tight: 1-2** Gall: 0-0
Aids: Bl: 0-0 Vi: 0-0 Tstrap: 0-0 Ckp: 0-0
Best Rating: **118** 7/09 Lonc 1m4f gd-sft

Smart; Irish-trained; landed Lingfield Derby trial in May; stays 1m4f, acts on soft ground and on Polytrack.

Age Of Couture

86 **50**
3-y-o ch f Hold That Tiger (USA)-Three Wishes (Sadler's Wells (USA))
W Jarvis Plantation Stud

Placings:60-0 **(2664)**
2009: 7^{0}GF,

	Starts	1st	2nd	3rd	Win & Pl
Career Total (Turf)	3	0	0	0	0

Going (Turf): **Sf: 0-1 GS: 0-0 Gd: 0-0 GF: 0-2 Fm: 0-0**
Distance: 5f/6f: 0-0 7f-8f: 0-3 9f-13f: 0-0 14f+: 0-0
Track : LH: 0-0 RH: 0-1 Tight: 0-0 Gall: 0-0
Aids: Bl: 0-0 Vi: 0-0 Tstrap: 0-0 Ckp: 0-0
Best Rating: **50** 6/09 Donc 7f gd-fm

Age Of Reason (UAE)

105(104) (107)**113**
4-y-o b g Halling (USA)-Time Changes (USA) (Danzig (USA))
Saeed Bin Suroor Godolphin

Placings:1/130040-31125342 **(7237)**
2009: 12^{3}GS, 12^{1}GF, 12^{1}G, 12^{2}G, 12^{5}G, 13^{3}GF, 11^{4}GF, 12^{2}SD,

	Starts	1st	2nd	3rd	Win & Pl
Career Total (Turf)	12	2	1	3	372559
Career Total (AW)	3	2	1	0	15085

2/09 Dohr 1m4f GD £197917
109 1/09 Ndas 1m4f (100-110)H G-F £72916
95 1/08 Wolv 1m141y (0-85)H STD £4533
88 12/07 Ling 1m STD £1943
Total win prize-money £277311

Going (Turf): Sf: 0-1 GS: 0-2 **Gd: 1-3 GF: 1-4** Fm: 0-2
Distance: 5f/6f: 0-0 7f-8f: 1-1 **9f-13f: 3-12** 14f+: 0-2
Track : **LH: 3-6** RH: 0-6 **Tight: 2-4** Gall: 1-6
Aids: Bl: 0-0 Vi: 0-0 Tstrap: 0-0 Ckp: 0-0
Best Rating: **113** 6/09 Siro 1m4f good

Smart; winner in UAE and Group-placed on the continent; stays 1m4f; acts on good/fast ground and on Polytrack; likes to race prominently.

Ageebah

(100) (68)**63**
3-y-o b f Acclamation-Flag (Selkirk (USA))
C E Brittain Saeed Manana

Placings:6505-215 **(0782)**
2009: 8^{2}SD, 8^{1}SD, 7^{5}SD,

	Starts	1st	2nd	3rd	Win & Pl
Career Total (Turf)	2	0	0	0	0
Career Total (AW)	5	1	1	0	3447

68 2/09 Kemp 1m (0-70)H STD £2590
Total win prize-money £2590

Going (Turf): **Sf: 0-0 GS: 0-1 Gd: 0-1 GF: 0-0 Fm: 0-0**
Distance: 5f/6f: 0-3 **7f-8f: 1-4** 9f-13f: 0-0 14f+: 0-0
Track : LH: 0-3 **RH: 1-2** Tight: 0-3 Gall: 0-1
Aids: Bl: 0-0 Vi: 0-0 Tstrap: 0-0 Ckp: 0-0
Best Rating: **68** 2/09 Kemp 1m stand

Modest; stays 1m; acts on easy ground and on Polytrack.

Agent Archie (USA)

85 **70**
2-y-o b c Smart Strike (CAN)-Dans La Ville (CHI) (Winning (USA))
J R Best D Gorton

Placings:61 **(6200)**
2009: 7^{6}GS, 9^{1}G,

	Starts	1st	2nd	3rd	Win & Pl
Career Total (Turf)	2	1	0	0	4695

70 9/09 Gdwd 1m1f GD £4695
Total win prize-money £4695

Going (Turf): Sf: 0-0 GS: 0-1 **Gd: 1-1** GF: 0-0 Fm: 0-0
Distance: 5f/6f: 0-0 7f-8f: 0-1 **9f-13f: 1-1** 14f+: 0-0
Track : LH: 0-0 **RH: 1-1 Tight: 1-1** Gall: 0-0
Aids: Bl: 0-0 Vi: 0-0 Tstrap: 0-0 Ckp: 0-0
Best Rating: **70** 9/09 Gdwd 1m1f good

Fair; stays 1m1f; acts on good ground.

Agent Boo

92(88) (59)**65**
2-y-o b c Monsieur Bond (IRE)-Silca Boo (Efisio)
E S McMahon Mr & Mrs E R Smith

Placings:0563016 **(6345)**
2009: 5^{0}GF, 5^{5}GF, 5^{6}SD, 5^{3}SF, 7^{0}SD, 6^{1}S, 5^{6}SD,

	Starts	1st	2nd	3rd	Win & Pl
Career Total (Turf)	3	1	0	0	2914
Career Total (AW)	4	0	0	1	454

65 8/09 Ayr 6f (0-65) SFT £2914
Total win prize-money £2914

Going (Turf): **Sf: 1-1** GS: 0-0 Gd: 0-0 GF: 0-2 Fm: 0-0
Distance: **5f/6f: 1-6** 7f-8f: 0-1 9f-13f: 0-0 14f+: 0-0
Track : LH: 0-3 RH: 0-0 Tight: 0-2 Gall: 0-0
Aids: **Bl: 1-2** Vi: 0-0 Tstrap: 0-0 Ckp: 0-0
Best Rating: **65** 8/09 Ayr 6f soft

Modest; suited by 6f and soft ground; has worn blinkers.

Agent Stone (IRE)

100 **74**
3-y-o ch g Night Shift (USA)-Just One Smile (IRE) (Desert Prince (IRE))
D Nicholls The Untouchable Partnership

Placings:035-016 **(2028)**
2009: 5^{0}GF, 6^{1}G, 6^{6}G,

	Starts	1st	2nd	3rd	Win & Pl
Career Total (Turf)	6	1	0	1	4008

74 5/09 Donc 6f GD £3238
Total win prize-money £3238

Going (Turf): Sf: 0-0 GS: 0-1 **Gd: 1-2** GF: 0-3 Fm: 0-0
Distance: **5f/6f: 1-4** 7f-8f: 0-2 9f-13f: 0-0 14f+: 0-0
Track : LH: 0-3 RH: 0-1 Tight: 0-2 Gall: 0-0
Aids: Bl: 0-0 **Vi: 1-2** Tstrap: 0-0 Ckp: 0-0
Best Rating: **74** 5/09 Donc 6f good

Fair; stays 6f; acts on good ground; has worn tongue tie.

Agente Parmigiano (IRE)

102(101) (97)91

3-y-o ch c Captain Rio-Kama's Wheel (Magic Ring (IRE))

G A Butler Fawzi Abdulla Nass

Placings:261540-043645430 **(6815)**

2009: 9^{0}SD, 8^{4}SD, 6^{3}GS, 7^{6}G, 7^{4}GF, 7^{5}GF, 7^{4}SD, 7^{3}GF, 7^{0}G,

	Starts	1st	2nd	3rd	Win & Pl
Career Total (Turf)	11	1	1	2	9913
Career Total (AW)	4	0	0	0	3268

87 6/08 Yarm 6f3y G-F £2137

Total win prize-money £2137

Going (Turf): Sf: 0-1 GS: 0-1 Gd: 0-2 **GF: 1-7** Fm: 0-0
Distance: 5f/6f: 0-4 **7f-8f: 1-10** 9f-13f: 0-1 14f+: 0-0
Track : LH: 0-4 RH: 0-2 Tight: 0-4 Gall: 0-0
Aids: Bl: 0-0 Vi: 0-0 Tstrap: 0-1 Ckp: 0-1
Best Rating: 97 8/09 Kemp 7f stand

Useful; effective at up to 1m; acts on fast ground and Polytrack; has worn cheekpieces and a tongue tie.

Agente Romano (USA)

102(101) (72)72

4-y-o br c Street Cry (IRE)-Dixie Bay (USA) (Dixieland Band (USA))

Evan Williams (G A Butler 16/7) Mrs Janet Davies

Placings:26/30023-650252 **(4021)**

2009: 10^{6}GF, 14^{5}GF, 13^{0}GF, 13^{2}GF, 12^{5}GF, 11^{2}GF,

	Starts	1st	2nd	3rd	Win & Pl
Career Total (Turf)	8	0	3	0	4047
Career Total (AW)	5	0	1	2	1586

Going (Turf): Sf: 0-0 GS: 0-0 Gd: 0-1 GF: 0-7 Fm: 0-0
Distance: 5f/6f: 0-0 7f-8f: 0-3 9f-13f: 0-8 14f+: 0-2
Track : LH: 0-9 RH: 0-4 Tight: 0-6 Gall: 0-5
Aids: Bl: 0-3 Vi: 0-0 Tstrap: 0-0 Ckp: 0-0
Best Rating: 72 6/09 NmkJ 1m5f gd-fm

Modest; stays 1m5f; acts on Polytrack and fast turf; has worn blinkers.

Aggbag

102(103) (60)60

5-y-o b g Fath (USA)-Emaura (Dominion)

Miss M E Rowland (J Mackie 26/6) Miss M E Rowland

Placings:5033300100543U3/30500020/16413643005-543224040123300 **(6256)**

2009: 8^{5}SD, 7^{4}SD, 7^{3}SD, 7^{2}SD, 7^{2}SD, 7^{4}F, 7^{0}SD, 8^{4}F, 8^{0}GF, 8^{1}G, 8^{2}GF, 7^{3}G, 8^{3}SD, 8^{0}SF, 8^{0}SD,

	Starts	1st	2nd	3rd	Win & Pl
Career Total (Turf)	13	1	1	3	4138
Career Total (AW)	36	3	3	8	11404

59 6/09 Wwck 1m22y (0-60)H GD £2047
61 2/08 Wolv 7f32y (0-52)H STD £1774
59 1/08 Wolv 7f32y (0-52)H STD £1774
60 8/06 Wolv 5f216y STD £3238

Total win prize-money £8836

Going (Turf): Sf: 0-0 GS: 0-1 **Gd: 1-7** GF: 0-2 Fm: 0-3
Distance: 5f/6f: 1-17 **7f-8f: 2-25** 9f-13f: 1-7 14f+: 0-0
Track : **LH: 4-39** RH: 0-2 **Tight: 3-27** Gall: 0-1
Aids: Bl: 0-0 Vi: 0-0 Tstrap: 0-2 Ckp: 0-2
Best Rating: 61 2/08 Wolv 7f32y stand

Moderate; effective at around 7f-1m; acts on good ground; goes on Fibresand and Polytrack.

Agglestone Rock

94(104) (67)71

4-y-o b g Josr Algarhoud (IRE)-Royalty (IRE) (Fairy King (USA))

P A Kirby Geoff Kirby Basil Holian Michael Buckley

Placings:0036/5434-31002 **(7084)**

2009: 16^{3}SD, 13^{1}SD, 10^{0}GS, 16^{0}S, 15^{2}S,

	Starts	1st	2nd	3rd	Win & Pl
Career Total (Turf)	5	0	1	0	867
Career Total (AW)	8	1	0	3	3912

67 2/09 Ling 1m5f (0-75)H STD £2729

Total win prize-money £2730

Going (Turf): Sf: 0-2 GS: 0-3 Gd: 0-0 GF: 0-0 Fm: 0-0
Distance: 5f/6f: 0-0 7f-8f: 0-5 **9f-13f: 1-5** 14f+: 0-3
Track : **LH: 1-10** RH: 0-2 **Tight: 1-9** Gall: 0-2
Aids: Bl: 0-0 Vi: 0-0 Tstrap: 0-0 Ckp: 0-0
Best Rating: 71 10/09 Catt 1m7f177y soft

Fair; stays 2m; acts on soft ground.

Aggravation

104(103) (72)78

7-y-o b g Sure Blade (USA)-Confection (Formidable (USA))

C Grant (D R C Elsworth 5/10) Gareth Cheshire

Placings:000031/30306000010263200030/021023051103400 4/60011405634363/030534020-33050360 **(6547)**

2009: 8^{3}GF, 8^{3}SD, 8^{0}G, 8^{5}GF, 8^{0}GF, 8^{3}GF, 8^{6}S, 8^{0}G,

	Starts	1st	2nd	3rd	Win & Pl
Career Total (Turf)	44	4	3	8	22520
Career Total (AW)	28	3	2	7	16073

77 6/07 Wind 1m67y (0-75)H G-F £3238
77 5/07 NmkR 1m (0-75)H G-F £3886
77 6/06 Wind 1m67y (0-75)H G-F £3238
74 6/06 Wind 1m67y (0-75)H G-F £3238
72 3/06 Ling 1m (0-65)H STD £2730
70 7/05 Ling 1m STD £4173
65 12/04 Ling 6f STD £4095

Total win prize-money £24601

Going (Turf): Sf: 0-5 GS: 0-5 Gd: 0-7 **GF: 4-24** Fm: 0-3
Distance: 5f/6f: 1-7 7f-8f: 3-42 9f-13f: 3-23 14f+: 0-0
Track : LH: 3-38 RH: 3-15 **Tight: 6-42** Gall: 0-1
Aids: Bl: 0-0 **Vi: 1-3** Tstrap: 0-0 Ckp: 0-0
Best Rating: 78 6/08 Wind 1m67y gd-fm

Fair; effective at around 1m; acts well on fast ground; also goes on Polytrack.

Agilete

105(112) (84)87

7-y-o b g Piccolo-Ingerence (FR) (Akarad (FR))

J Pearce S & M Supplies (Aylsham) Ltd

Placings:03350/5253334050/00000300540363120255/53540334/121140211301004 **(7583)**

2009: 9^{1}SD, 9^{2}SD, 9^{1}SD, 9^{1}SD, 10^{4}G, 8^{0}SD, 10^{2}G, 10^{1}G, 10^{1}GS, 11^{3}G, 10^{0}GF, 10^{1}GF, 10^{0}GS, 8^{0}SF, 9^{4}SF,

	Starts	1st	2nd	3rd	Win & Pl
Career Total (Turf)	38	3	4	9	26824
Career Total (AW)	21	4	1	3	9790

87 9/09 Yarm 1m2f21y (0-90)H G-F £7477
81 8/09 Hayd 1m2f95y (0-70)H G-S £3238
76 7/09 Sand 1m2f7y (0-70)H GD £3238
73 3/09 Wolv 1m1f103y (0-65)H STD £2047
67 2/09 Wolv 1m1f103y (0-65)H STD £2047
63 1/09 Wolv 1m1f103y (0-45) STD £1364
58 9/06 Wolv 1m4f50y (0-55)H SF £2388

Total win prize-money £21801

Going (Turf): Sf: 0-2 **GS: 1-6 Gd: 1-8 GF: 1-19** Fm: 0-3
Distance: 5f/6f: 0-7 7f-8f: 0-12 **9f-13f: 7-39** 14f+: 0-1
Track : **LH: 6-47** RH: 1-6 **Tight: 5-29** Gall: 0-3
Aids: Bl: 0-1 Vi: 0-0 Tstrap: 0-2 Ckp: 0-2
Best Rating: 87 9/09 Yarm 1m2f21y gd-fm

Useful; effective at up to 1m4f; acts on most ground and on Polytrack.

Agnes Love

76(100) (64)27

3-y-o gr f Piccolo-Erracht (Emarati (USA))

J Akehurst David S M Caplin

Placings:00005136335-06251300 **(7518)**

2009: 5^{0}GF, 5^{6}F, 5^{2}SD, 5^{5}SD, 5^{1}SD, 6^{3}SD, 6^{0}SD, 6^{0}SD,

	Starts	1st	2nd	3rd	Win & Pl
Career Total (Turf)	7	0	0	0	0
Career Total (AW)	12	2	1	4	7634

64 8/09 Kemp 5f (0-70)H STD £2590
58 9/08 Kemp 5f (0-65) STD £2047

Total win prize-money £4637

Going (Turf): Sf: 0-2 GS: 0-0 Gd: 0-1 GF: 0-3 Fm: 0-1
Distance: **5f/6f: 2-19** 7f-8f: 0-0 9f-13f: 0-0 14f+: 0-0
Track : LH: 0-9 **RH: 2-5** Tight: 0-6 Gall: 0-1
Aids: Bl: 0-0 Vi: 0-0 Tstrap: 0-0 Ckp: 0-0
Best Rating: 64 9/09 Ling 6f stand

Modest; suited by 5f and acts on Polytrack.

Agony And Ecstasy

96(95) (77)78

2-y-o ch f Captain Rio-Agony Aunt (Formidable (USA))

R M Beckett Miss Rachel Tregaskes

Placings:651513 **(7267)**

2009: 6^{6}G, 7^{5}GF, 7^{1}S, 8^{5}SD, 8^{1}GS, 8^{3}SD,

	Starts	1st	2nd	3rd	Win & Pl
Career Total (Turf)	4	2	0	0	4436
Career Total (AW)	2	0	0	1	915

78 10/09 Wind 1m67y (0-75) G-S £2388
69 8/09 Ling 7f140y SFT £2047

Total win prize-money £4435

Going (Turf): Sf: 1-1 GS: 1-1 Gd: 0-1 GF: 0-1 Fm: 0-0
Distance: 5f/6f: 0-1 7f-8f: 1-4 9f-13f: 1-1 14f+: 0-0
Track : LH: 0-2 **RH: 1-2 Tight: 1-1** Gall: 0-0
Aids: Bl: 0-0 Vi: 0-0 Tstrap: 0-1 Ckp: 0-1
Best Rating: 78 10/09 Wind 1m67y gd-sft

Fair; effective over 1m; acts on soft ground.

Agricultural

82 30

3-y-o b c Daylami (IRE)-Rustic (IRE) (Grand Lodge (USA))

Mrs L B Normile Mrs Jennifer Carnaby

Placings:60 **(4014)**

2009: 9^{6}G, 11^{0}GF,

	Starts	1st	2nd	3rd	Win & Pl
Career Total (Turf)	2	0	0	0	0

Going (Turf): Sf: 0-0 GS: 0-0 Gd: 0-1 GF: 0-1 Fm: 0-0
Distance: 5f/6f: 0-0 7f-8f: 0-0 9f-13f: 0-2 14f+: 0-0
Track : LH: 0-0 RH: 0-2 Tight: 0-2 Gall: 0-0
Aids: Bl: 0-0 Vi: 0-0 Tstrap: 0-0 Ckp: 0-0
Best Rating: 30 7/09 Haml 1m3f16y gd-fm

Ahla Wasahl

108(106) (105)101

3-y-o br f Dubai Destination (USA)-In Full Cry (USA) (Seattle Slew (USA))

D M Simcock Sultan Ali

Placings:513060-250412 (7132)

2009: 8^{2}GF, 8^{5}GS, 7^{0}GF, 8^{4}GF, 8^{1}G, 8^{2}SD,

	Starts	1st	2nd	3rd	Win & Pl
Career Total (Turf)	10	1	1	1	44627
Career Total (AW)	2	1	1	0	12494

101 9/09 Asct 1m (0-110)H GD £22708
76 6/08 Kemp 6f STD £3885
Total win prize-money £26594

Going (Turf): Sf: 0-0 GS: 0-5 **Gd: 1-1** GF: 0-4 Fm: 0-0
Distance: 5f/6f: 1-3 7f-8f: 1-8 9f-13f: 0-1 14f+: 0-0
Track : LH: 0-3 **RH: 2-4** Tight: 0-1 **Gall: 1-3**
Aids: Bl: 0-0 Vi: 0-0 Tstrap: 0-0 Ckp: 0-0
Best Rating: **105** 10/09 Ling 1m stand

Smart; Listed winner; stays 1m; acts on fast and easy ground; goes on Polytrack.

Ahlawy (IRE)

104(110) (96)83

6-y-o gr g Green Desert (USA)-On Call (Alleged (USA))

F Sheridan Dr Franco Moretti

Placings:U4166/00044652114200/06505563323-113110622 (5186)

2009: 9^{1}SD, 9^{1}SD, 12^{3}SD, 9^{1}SD, 9^{1}SD, 10^{0}SD, 10^{6}GF, 10^{2}G, 10^{2}GF,

	Starts	1st	2nd	3rd	Win & Pl
Career Total (Turf)	28	3	4	1	18086
Career Total (AW)	11	4	1	3	14591

96 4/09 Wolv 1m1f103y (0-85)H STD £5180
89 3/09 Wolv 1m1f103y STD £2047
84 1/09 Wolv 1m1f103y (0-75)H STD £2590
64 1/09 Wolv 1m1f103y STD £2047
86 8/07 Rdcr 1m2f (0-75)H G-F £2717
73 8/07 Ripn 1m1f170y (0-85)H G-F £5047
77 5/06 Yarm 7f3y GD £3238
Total win prize-money £22868

Going (Turf): Sf: 0-5 GS: 0-5 Gd: 1-7 **GF: 2-11** Fm: 0-0
Distance: 5f/6f: 0-0 7f-8f: 1-4 **9f-13f: 6-34** 14f+: 0-1
Track : **LH: 5-29** RH: 1-8 **Tight: 6-17** Gall: 0-8
Aids: **Bl: 4-13** Vi: 0-0 Tstrap: 0-0 Ckp: 0-0
Best Rating: **96** 4/09 Wolv 1m1f103y stand

Useful; effective over 1m2f; acts on fast ground and on Polytrack; has worn blinkers and a tongue tie.

Ahmedy (IRE)

81(95) (77)34

6-y-o b g Polish Precedent (USA)-Nawaji (USA) (Trempolino (USA))

J J Quinn Exors Of The Late Lady Anne Bentinck

Placings:216/34004340105/10 (7020)

2009: 12^{1}SF, 10^{0}GS,

	Starts	1st	2nd	3rd	Win & Pl
Career Total (Turf)	13	2	1	1	11767
Career Total (AW)	3	1	0	1	4404

77 10/09 Wolv 1m4f50y (0-70)H SF £3238
77 9/06 Folk 1m1f149y (0-75)H G-F £4533
64 7/05 Rdcr 7f G-F £4140
Total win prize-money £11913

Going (Turf): Sf: 0-0 GS: 0-1 Gd: 0-4 **GF: 2-8** Fm: 0-0
Distance: 5f/6f: 0-0 7f-8f: 1-5 **9f-13f: 2-11** 14f+: 0-0
Track : LH: 1-5 RH: 1-8 **Tight: 2-5** Gall: 0-4
Aids: Bl: 0-0 Vi: 0-0 Tstrap: 0-0 Ckp: 0-0
Best Rating: **81** 7/06 NmkJ 1m2f gd-fm

Fair sort; stays ten furlongs and acts on fast ground.

Ahwahnee

(83) (43)

2-y-o ch f Compton Place-Tahara (IRE) (Caerleon (USA))

R M Beckett C J Harper

Placings:0 (6971)

2009: 5^{0}SD,

	Starts	1st	2nd	3rd	Win & Pl
Career Total (Turf)	0	0	0	0	
Career Total (AW)	1	0	0	0	

Going (Turf): **Sf: 0-0 GS: 0-0 Gd: 0-0 GF: 0-0 Fm: 0-0**
Distance: 5f/6f: 0-1 7f-8f: 0-0 9f-13f: 0-0 14f+: 0-0
Track : LH: 0-0 RH: 0-1 Tight: 0-0 Gall: 0-0
Aids: Bl: 0-0 Vi: 0-0 Tstrap: 0-0 Ckp: 0-0
Best Rating: **43** 10/09 Kemp 5f stand

Ailsa Carmel (IRE)

96 76

2-y-o b f Antonius Pius (USA)-Dancing Duchess (IRE) (Danehill Dancer (IRE))

M R Channon Mrs M Findlay

Placings:361124 (3430)

2009: 5^{3}G, 5^{6}GF, 5^{1}G, 5^{1}GF, 6^{2}GF, 5^{4}GF,

	Starts	1st	2nd	3rd	Win & Pl
Career Total (Turf)	6	2	1	1	9365

76 6/09 Carl 5f193y G-F £2729
71 6/09 Brig 5f213y GD £3565
Total win prize-money £6295

Going (Turf): Sf: 0-0 GS: 0-0 **Gd: 1-2 GF: 1-4** Fm: 0-0
Distance: **5f/6f: 2-6** 7f-8f: 0-0 9f-13f: 0-0 14f+: 0-0
Track : LH: 1-1 RH: 1-1 Tight: 0-0 Gall: 0-1
Aids: Bl: 0-0 Vi: 0-0 Tstrap: 0-0 Ckp: 0-0
Best Rating: **76** 6/09 Newc 6f gd-fm

Ailsa Craig (IRE)

98(99) (66)72

3-y-o b f Chevalier (IRE)-Sharplaw Destiny (IRE) (Petardia)

E W Tuer (R Hannon 28/9) E Tuer

Placings:560-632251306 (7423)

2009: 7^{6}GF, 6^{3}G, 6^{2}GF, 7^{2}GF, 7^{5}S, 8^{1}GF, 8^{3}GS, 7^{0}GF, 8^{6}SD,

	Starts	1st	2nd	3rd	Win & Pl
Career Total (Turf)	11	1	2	2	5507
Career Total (AW)	1	0	0	0	0

72 8/09 Bath 1m5y (0-70)H G-F £2849
Total win prize-money £2849

Going (Turf): Sf: 0-3 GS: 0-1 Gd: 0-1 **GF: 1-6** Fm: 0-0
Distance: 5f/6f: 0-2 7f-8f: 0-9 **9f-13f: 1-1** 14f+: 0-0
Track : **LH: 1-4** RH: 0-2 **Tight: 1-1** Gall: 0-1
Aids: Bl: 0-0 Vi: 0-0 Tstrap: 0-1 Ckp: 0-1
Best Rating: **72** 8/09 Bath 1m5y gd-fm

Modest; effective at 6f-1m and acts on fast ground; has worn cheekpieces.

Aim To Achieve (IRE)

99(97) (70)78

3-y-o b f Galileo (IRE)-Sabander Bay (USA) (Lear Fan (USA))

B W Hills Jack Hanson & Sir Alex Ferguson

Placings:0-413 (4095)

2009: 8^{4}G, 8^{1}SD, 8^{3}G,

	Starts	1st	2nd	3rd	Win & Pl
Career Total (Turf)	3	0	0	1	2352
Career Total (AW)	1	1	0	0	4857

70 6/09 Kemp 1m STD £4857
Total win prize-money £4857

Going (Turf): **Sf: 0-0 GS: 0-0 Gd: 0-3 GF: 0-0 Fm: 0-0**
Distance: 5f/6f: 0-0 **7f-8f: 1-4** 9f-13f: 0-0 14f+: 0-0
Track : LH: 0-2 **RH: 1-1** Tight: 0-0 Gall: 0-2
Aids: Bl: 0-0 Vi: 0-0 Tstrap: 0-0 Ckp: 0-0
Best Rating: **78** 7/09 NmkJ 1m good

Fair; stays 1m and acts on Polytrack and good ground on turf.

Aimeeskeepingfa ith

77(82) (49)50

2-y-o b f Beckett (IRE)-Keeping The Faith (IRE) (Ajraas (USA))

M R Channon Mrs Patricia Wilson

Placings:000 (6069)

2009: 6^{0}S, 6^{0}GF, 5^{0}SD,

	Starts	1st	2nd	3rd	Win & Pl
Career Total (Turf)	2	0	0	0	
Career Total (AW)	1	0	0	0	

Going (Turf): **Sf: 0-1 GS: 0-0 Gd: 0-0 GF: 0-1 Fm: 0-0**
Distance: 5f/6f: 0-2 7f-8f: 0-1 9f-13f: 0-0 14f+: 0-0
Track : LH: 0-2 RH: 0-0 Tight: 0-2 Gall: 0-0
Aids: Bl: 0-0 Vi: 0-0 Tstrap: 0-0 Ckp: 0-0
Best Rating: **50** 9/09 Epsm 6f gd-fm

Ain't Talkin'

(100) (53)49

3-y-o ch c Zaha (CAN)-Royal Ivy (Mujtahid (USA))

M J Attwater Canisbay Bloodstock

Placings:00000400-1 (0267)

2009: 7^{1}SD,

	Starts	1st	2nd	3rd	Win & Pl
Career Total (Turf)	4	0	0	0	
Career Total (AW)	5	1	0	0	2167

53 1/09 Ling 7f (0-60)H STD £2047
Total win prize-money £2047

Going (Turf): **Sf: 0-1 GS: 0-0 Gd: 0-2 GF: 0-1 Fm: 0-0**
Distance: 5f/6f: 0-2 **7f-8f: 1-6** 9f-13f: 0-1 14f+: 0-0
Track : **LH: 1-3** RH: 0-4 **Tight: 1-2** Gall: 0-0
Aids: Bl: 0-0 Vi: 0-0 Tstrap: 0-0 Ckp: 0-0
Best Rating: **53** 1/09 Ling 7f stand

Aine (IRE)

103 102

4-y-o ch f Danehill Dancer (IRE)-Antinnaz (IRE) (Thatching)

T Stack Mrs T Stack

Placings:112002-40016350 (5815a)
2009: 5^{4}Y, 6^{0}HY, 6^{0}GF, 6^{1}S, 6^{6}HY, 5^{3}S, 5^{5}HY, 7^{0}HY,

	Starts	1st	2nd	3rd	Win & Pl
Career Total (Turf)	14	3	2	1	67692

102	7/09	Fair	6f		SFT	£26861
100	4/08	Navn	5f182y	(60-100)H	G-Y	£11966
82	4/08	Tipp	5f		HVY	£9573

Total win prize-money £48403

Going (Turf): **Sf: 2-8** GS. 0-0 Gd: 0-1 GF: 0-1 Fm: 0-0
Distance: **5f/6f: 3-12** 7f-8f: 0-2 9f-13f: 0-0 14f+: 0-0
Track : **LH: 2-7** RH: 1-1 Tight: 0-0 Gall: 0-0
Aids: Bl: 0-1 Vi: 0-0 Tstrap: 0-0 Ckp: 0-0
Best Rating: **102** 7/09 Fair 6f soft

Smart filly; effective at 5f-6f; raced only on an easy surface.

Aine's Delight (IRE)

103(70) (17)67
3-y-o b f King's Best (USA)-Gentle Thoughts (Darshaan)
Andrew Turnell Dave Murray, Joe Mallon & Peter Ross

Placings:00-0014041 (6910)
2009: 8^{0}F, 8^{0}F, 8^{1}G, 7^{4}G, 8^{0}G, 8^{4}GF, 10^{1}G,

	Starts	1st	2nd	3rd	Win & Pl
Career Total (Turf)	8	2	0	0	5293
Career Total (AW)	1	0	0	0	0

67	10/09	Wind	1m2f7y	(0-65)H	GD	£2047
66	6/09	Sals	1m	(0-60)H	GD	£3043

Total win prize-money £5091

Going (Turf): Sf: 0-0 GS: 0-1 **Gd: 2-4** GF: 0-1 Fm: 0-2
Distance: 5f/6f: 0-1 7f-8f: 1-4 9f-13f: 1-4 14f+: 0-0
Track : LH: 0-3 **RH: 1-2 Tight: 1-2** Gall: 0-1
Aids: Bl: 0-0 Vi: 0-0 Tstrap: 0-0 Ckp: 0-0
Best Rating: **67** 10/09 Wind 1m2f7y good

Modest; effective over 1m; acts on good ground.

Ainia

103(92) (52)81
4-y-o b f Alhaarth (IRE)-Vayavaig (Damister (USA))
D M Simcock Mrs Julia Annable

Placings:5422452-216600 (6886a)
2009: 8^{2}G, 9^{1}GF, 8^{6}GS, 12^{6}G, 9^{0}GF, 8^{0}S,

	Starts	1st	2nd	3rd	Win & Pl
Career Total (Turf)	12	1	4	0	10641
Career Total (AW)	1	0	0	0	0

80	6/09	Muss	1m1f	(0-85)H	G-F	£5828

Total win prize-money £5828

Going (Turf): Sf: 0-4 GS: 0-3 Gd: 0-3 **GF: 1-2** Fm: 0-0
Distance: 5f/6f: 0-0 7f-8f: 0-5 **9f-13f: 1-8** 14f+: 0-0
Track : LH: 0-4 **RH: 1-6 Tight: 1-4** Gall: 0-3
Aids: Bl: 0-0 Vi: 0-0 Tstrap: 0-0 Ckp: 0-0
Best Rating: **81** 8/09 Gdwd 1m1f192y gd-fm

Fair; effective at 1m-1m2f; acts on fast but goes well on easy ground.

Aintgottaname

(73) (32)
2-y-o b f Trade Fair-Emouna (Cadeaux Genereux)
M J McGrath A Morris

Placings:000 (7624)
2009: 7^{0}SD, 8^{0}SD, 8^{0}SD,

	Starts	1st	2nd	3rd	Win & Pl
Career Total (Turf)	0	0	0	0	
Career Total (AW)	3	0	0	0	

Going (Turf): **Sf: 0-0 GS: 0-0 Gd: 0-0 GF: 0-0 Fm: 0-0**
Distance: 5f/6f: 0-0 7f-8f: 0-3 9f-13f: 0-0 14f+: 0-0
Track : LH: 0-2 RH: 0-1 Tight: 0-2 Gall: 0-0
Aids: Bl: 0-0 Vi: 0-0 Tstrap: 0-0 Ckp: 0-0
Best Rating: **32** 12/09 Ling 1m stand

Ainthegorgeous

73 30
2-y-o b c Dr Fong (USA)-Free Spirit (IRE) (Caerleon (USA))
P T Midgley Anthony D Copley

Placings:000 (5519)
2009: 7^{0}GF, 7^{0}G, 6^{0}G,

	Starts	1st	2nd	3rd	Win & Pl
Career Total (Turf)	3	0	0	0	

Going (Turf): **Sf: 0-0 GS: 0-0 Gd: 0-2 GF: 0-1 Fm: 0-0**
Distance: 5f/6f: 0-1 7f-8f: 0-2 9f-13f: 0-0 14f+: 0-0
Track : LH: 0-0 RH: 0-2 Tight: 0-0 Gall: 0-0
Aids: Bl: 0-0 Vi: 0-0 Tstrap: 0-0 Ckp: 0-0
Best Rating: **30** 8/09 Bevl 7f100y good

Aintwogrand (IRE)

87(81) (40)53
2-y-o b f Acclamation-Rebel Clan (IRE) (Tagula (IRE))
M R Channon Billy Parish

Placings:65655 (4747)
2009: 5^{6}F, 6^{5}G, 5^{6}GF, 6^{5}G, 6^{5}SD,

	Starts	1st	2nd	3rd	Win & Pl
Career Total (Turf)	4	0	0	0	0
Career Total (AW)	1	0	0	0	0

Going (Turf): **Sf: 0-0 GS: 0-0 Gd: 0-2 GF: 0-1 Fm: 0-1**
Distance: 5f/6f: 0-4 7f-8f: 0-1 9f-13f: 0-0 14f+: 0-0
Track : LH: 0-2 RH: 0-0 Tight: 0-1 Gall: 0-1
Aids: Bl: 0-0 Vi: 0-0 Tstrap: 0-0 Ckp: 0-0
Best Rating: **53** 6/09 Gdwd 6f good

Plating-class; stays 6f; acts on a sound surface.

Air Chief Marshal (IRE)

103 110
2-y-o b c Danehill Dancer (IRE)-Hawala (IRE) (Warning)
A P O'Brien Mrs John Magnier

Placings:2130622454 (7072a)
2009: 6^{2}GY, 7^{1}HY, 5^{3}HY, 6^{0}GF, 6^{6}SH, 6^{2}HY, 6^{2}HY, 7^{4}SH, 6^{5}G, 7^{4}Y,

	Starts	1st	2nd	3rd	Win & Pl
Career Total (Turf)	10	1	3	1	112768

86	5/09	Gowr	7f	HVY	£10733

Total win prize-money £10734

Going (Turf): **Sf: 1-4** GS: 0-0 Gd: 0-1 GF: 0-1 Fm: 0-0
Distance: 5f/6f: 0-6 **7f-8f: 1-4** 9f-13f: 0-0 14f+: 0-0
Track : LH: 0-2 **RH: 1-1** Tight: 0-0 Gall: 0-0
Aids: Bl: 0-0 Vi: 0-0 Tstrap: 0-0 Ckp: 0-0
Best Rating: **110** 9/09 Curr 7f sft-hvy

Smart; Group placed; effective at 5-7f; handles heavy ground.

Air Lion (USA)

(93) (59)
3-y-o b g Lion Heart (USA)-Swigert (USA) (Fusaichi Pegasus (USA))
R M H Cowell Atlantic Thoroughbreds

Placings:236 (4174)
2009: 5^{2}SD, 5^{3}SD, 5^{6}SD,

	Starts	1st	2nd	3rd	Win & Pl
Career Total (Turf)	0	0	0	0	
Career Total (AW)	3	0	1	1	1191

Going (Turf): **Sf: 0-0 GS: 0-0 Gd: 0-0 GF: 0-0 Fm: 0-0**
Distance: 5f/6f: 0-3 7f-8f: 0-0 9f-13f: 0-0 14f+: 0-0
Track : LH: 0-0 RH: 0-0 Tight: 0-0 Gall: 0-0
Aids: Bl: 0-0 Vi: 0-0 Tstrap: 0-0 Ckp: 0-0
Best Rating: **59** 2/09 Sthl 5f stand

Modest; suited by 5f and acts on Fibresand.

Air Maze

98(100) (75)76
3-y-o b f Dansili-Begueule (FR) (Bering)
Sir Mark Prescott Plantation Stud

Placings:22113230 (6560)
2009: 7^{2}SD, 8^{2}SD, 9^{1}SF, 10^{1}G, 10^{3}G, 12^{2}GS, 13^{3}SD, 11^{0}G,

	Starts	1st	2nd	3rd	Win & Pl
Career Total (Turf)	4	1	1	1	4261
Career Total (AW)	4	1	2	1	4705

70	7/09	Bath	1m2f46y	(0-70)H	GD	£2719
70	2/09	Wolv	1m1f103y		SF	£2729

Total win prize-money £5450

Going (Turf): Sf: 0-0 GS: 0-1 **Gd: 1-3** GF: 0-0 Fm: 0-0
Distance: 5f/6f: 0-0 7f-8f: 0-2 **9f-13f: 2-5** 14f+: 0-1
Track : **LH: 2-8** RH: 0-0 **Tight: 2-6** Gall: 0-1
Aids: Bl: 0-0 Vi: 0-0 Tstrap: 0-0 Ckp: 0-0
Best Rating: **76** 9/09 Epsm 1m4f10y gd-sft

Fair; stays 1m2f; acts on good ground and on sand.

Ajaan

108 108
5-y-o br h Machiavellian (USA)-Alakananda (Hernando (FR))
H R A Cecil Niarchos Family

Placings:51/043114/115000-2045 (6851)
2009: 18^{2}GF, 16^{0}S, 14^{4}S, 18^{5}G,

	Starts	1st	2nd	3rd	Win & Pl
Career Total (Turf)	18	5	1	1	92603

108	5/08	NmkR	1m6f	(0-105)H	G-S	£24924
106	5/08	NmkR	1m4f	(0-100)H	GD	£12952
94	8/07	NmkJ	1m6f175y	(0-95)H	SFT	£9067
96	8/07	Pont	1m4f8y	(0-90)H	FRM	£9348
80	10/06	Wind	1m67y		SFT	£4533

Total win prize-money £60826

Going (Turf): **Sf: 2-5** GS: 1-3 Gd: 1-4 GF: 0-5 Fm: 1-1
Distance: 5f/6f: 0-0 7f-8f: 0-1 **9f-13f: 3-7** 14f+: 2-10
Track : LH: 1-7 **RH: 4-10** Tight: 1-5 **Gall: 3-8**
Aids: **Bl: 4-13** Vi: 0-0 Tstrap: 0-0 Ckp: 0-0
Best Rating: **108** 5/08 NmkR 1m6f gd-sft

Very useful; stays 2m2f; acts on any ground; wears blinkers.

Ajara (IRE)

(95) (69)
3-y-o b f Elusive City (USA)-My-Lorraine (IRE) (Mac's Imp (USA))

N J Vaughan Butt Scholes

Placings:41-0 (0276)
2009: 7⁰SD,

	Starts	1st	2nd	3rd	Win & Pl
Career Total (Turf)	0	0	0	0	
Career Total (AW)	3	1	0	0	3238

69 12/08 Wolv 7f32y STD £3238
Total win prize-money £3238

Going (Turf): **Sf: 0-0 GS: 0-0 Gd: 0-0 GF: 0-0 Fm: 0-0**
Distance: 5f/6f: 0-0 **7f-8f: 1-3** 9f-13f: 0-0 14f+: 0-0
Track : **LH: 1-3** RH: 0-0 **Tight: 1-3** Gall: 0-0
Aids: Bl: 0-0 Vi: 0-0 Tstrap: 0-0 Ckp: 0-0
Best Rating: **69** 12/08 Wolv 7f32y stand

Fair; stays 7f and should stay 1m; acts on Polytrack; should improve.

Ajara Boy

78(69) (16)**36**
2-y-o ch c Avonbridge-Cultural Role (Night Shift (USA))
Tom Dascombe (N J Vaughan 3/7) Butt Scholes

Placings:0660 (6858)
2009: 6⁰G, 6⁶GF, 5⁶SS, 8⁰SD,

	Starts	1st	2nd	3rd	Win & Pl
Career Total (Turf)	2	0	0	0	0
Career Total (AW)	2	0	0	0	0

Going (Turf): **Sf: 0-0 GS: 0-0 Gd: 0-1 GF: 0-1 Fm: 0-0**
Distance: 5f/6f: 0-3 7f-8f: 0-0 9f-13f: 0-1 14f+: 0-0
Track : LH: 0-3 RH: 0-0 Tight: 0-2 Gall: 0-0
Aids: Bl: 0-0 Vi: 0-1 Tstrap: 0-0 Ckp: 0-0
Best Rating: **36** 9/09 Pont 6f gd-fm

Ajhar (USA)

109(112) (107)**106**
5-y-o b g Diesis-Min Alhawa (USA) (Riverman (USA))
M P Tregoning Hamdan Al Maktoum

Placings:222/122/01346-01 (5004)
2009: 10⁰SD, 10¹G,

	Starts	1st	2nd	3rd	Win & Pl
Career Total (Turf)	9	2	5	1	36897
Career Total (AW)	4	1	0	0	10165

106 8/09 NmkJ 1m2f GD £12462
107 9/08 Kemp 1m3f (0-95)H STD £7477
88 5/07 Newb 1m2f6y G-S £6477
Total win prize-money £26416

Going (Turf): Sf: 0-3 **GS: 1-2 Gd: 1-4** GF: 0-0 Fm: 0-0
Distance: 5f/6f: 0-0 7f-8f: 0-2 **9f-13f: 3-11** 14f+: 0-0
Track : LH: 1-5 **RH: 2-7** Tight: 0-1 **Gall: 2-6**
Aids: Bl: 0-0 Vi: 0-0 Tstrap: 0-0 Ckp: 0-0
Best Rating: **107** 11/08 Ling 1m2f stand

Smart; stays 1m3f; acts on good and softer ground and Polytrack.

Ajigolo

102(110) (55)**99**
6-y-o ch g Piccolo-Ajig Dancer (Niniski (USA))
N Wilson Mrs Maureen Eason

Placings:0105413162/00000/540126006004511040/10245 5061000500-0000000000 (7478)
2009: 6⁰GF, 5⁰GF, 5⁰GF, 6⁰S, 6⁰G, 6⁰GS, 6⁰GF, 6⁰G, 6⁰SD, 6⁰SD,

	Starts	1st	2nd	3rd	Win & Pl
Career Total (Turf)	42	4	1	1	76151
Career Total (AW)	16	4	2	0	38847

99 5/08 NmkR 6f (0-100)H GD £11656
100 2/08 Ling 5f (0-100)H STD £9971
100 10/07 Wolv 5f216y (0-85)H STD £4857
93 10/07 Ling 6f (0-85)H STD £5181
104 3/07 Wolv 5f216y (0-100)H STD £11658
107 9/05 Badn 6f GD £35461
91 7/05 Donc 6f G-F £4784
88 5/05 Sals 5f G-F £4751
Total win prize-money £88324

Going (Turf): Sf: 0-1 GS: 0-3 **Gd: 2-20 GF: 2-18** Fm: 0-0
Distance: **5f/6f: 8-52** 7f-8f: 0-6 9f-13f: 0-0 14f+: 0-0
Track : **LH: 5-19** RH: 0-3 **Tight: 4-15** Gall: 0-0
Aids: Bl: 0-1 Vi: 0-2 Tstrap: 0-0 Ckp: 0-0
Best Rating: **107** 10/05 Sals 5f good

Useful; best over 6f; acts on fast ground and on Polytrack.

Ajjaadd (USA)

(100) (78)**67**
3-y-o b g Elusive Quality (USA)-Millstream (USA) (Dayjur (USA))
T E Powell Lol Pratt

Placings:643-22 (7686)
2009: 5²SD, 6²SD,

	Starts	1st	2nd	3rd	Win & Pl
Career Total (Turf)	1	0	0	0	0
Career Total (AW)	4	0	2	1	2482

Going (Turf): **Sf: 0-0 GS: 0-0 Gd: 0-0 GF: 0-1 Fm: 0-0**
Distance: 5f/6f: 0-3 7f-8f: 0-2 9f-13f: 0-0 14f+: 0-0
Track : LH: 0-3 RH: 0-1 Tight: 0-3 Gall: 0-0
Aids: Bl: 0-0 Vi: 0-0 Tstrap: 0-0 Ckp: 0-0
Best Rating: **78** 11/08 Ling 7f stand

Fair; effective at up to 7f and acts on Polytrack.

Ajool (USA)

86 **69**
2-y-o ch f Aljabr (USA)-Tamgeed (USA) (Woodman (USA))
B W Hills Hamdan Al Maktoum

Placings:5 (7182)
2009: 7⁵G,

	Starts	1st	2nd	3rd	Win & Pl
Career Total (Turf)	1	0	0	0	0

Going (Turf): **Sf: 0-0 GS: 0-0 Gd: 0-1 GF: 0-0 Fm: 0-0**
Distance: 5f/6f: 0-0 7f-8f: 0-1 9f-13f: 0-0 14f+: 0-0
Track : LH: 0-0 RH: 0-0 Tight: 0-0 Gall: 0-0
Aids: Bl: 0-0 Vi: 0-0 Tstrap: 0-0 Ckp: 0-0
Best Rating: **69** 10/09 NmkR 7f good

Akabar

88 **51**
3-y-o b g Piccolo-Fredora (Inchinor)
R M Beckett Mrs Carolyn Thornton Roberts

Placings:0460 (4905)
2009: 6⁰G, 6⁴GF, 6⁶GF, 6⁰GF,

	Starts	1st	2nd	3rd	Win & Pl
Career Total (Turf)	4	0	0	0	0

Going (Turf): **Sf: 0-0 GS: 0-0 Gd: 0-1 GF: 0-3 Fm: 0-0**
Distance: 5f/6f: 0-3 7f-8f: 0-1 9f-13f: 0-0 14f+: 0-0
Track : LH: 0-1 RH: 0-0 Tight: 0-0 Gall: 0-1
Aids: Bl: 0-1 Vi: 0-0 Tstrap: 0-0 Ckp: 0-0
Best Rating: **51** 7/09 Sals 6f gd-fm

Akamon

(89) (67)
2-y-o ch f Monsun (GER)-Akanta (GER) (Wolfhound (USA))
E A L Dunlop Mrs J Ellis & Lady Derby

Placings:62 (7276)
2009: 6⁶SD, 7²SD,

	Starts	1st	2nd	3rd	Win & Pl
Career Total (Turf)	0	0	0	0	
Career Total (AW)	2	0	1	0	964

Going (Turf): **Sf: 0-0 GS: 0-0 Gd: 0-0 GF: 0-0 Fm: 0-0**
Distance: 5f/6f: 0-1 7f-8f: 0-1 9f-13f: 0-0 14f+: 0-0
Track : LH: 0-1 RH: 0-1 Tight: 0-1 Gall: 0-0
Aids: Bl: 0-0 Vi: 0-0 Tstrap: 0-0 Ckp: 0-0
Best Rating: **67** 11/09 Wolv 7f32y stand

Akash (IRE)

(90) (36)**36**
9-y-o b g Dr Devious (IRE)-Akilara (IRE) (Kahyasi)
K M Prendergast Wye Diamonds

Placings:502114/05220/120000/0000/0/0/00 (0300)
2009: 12⁰SD, 14⁰SD,

	Starts	1st	2nd	3rd	Win & Pl
Career Total (Turf)	21	3	4	0	37537
Career Total (AW)	4	0	0	0	

96 4/04 Pont 1m2f6yC(0-90) SFT £9210
84 9/02 Rosc 7f G-Y £6349
85 8/02 Leop 1m GD £7975
Total win prize-money £23535

Going (Turf): **Sf: 1-7** GS: 0-3 **Gd: 1-6** GF: 0-1 Fm: 0-1
Distance: 5f/6f: 0-1 **7f-8f: 2-4** 9f-13f: 1-18 14f+: 0-2
Track : **LH: 2-11** RH: 0-7 Tight: 0-3 Gall: 0-1
Aids: **Bl: 1-3** Vi: 0-0 Tstrap: 0-0 Ckp: 0-0
Best Rating: **96** 4/04 Pont 1m2f6y soft

Akbabend

110(103) (87)**89**
3-y-o b g Refuse To Bend (IRE)-Akdariya (IRE) (Shirley Heights)
M Johnston Markus Graff

Placings:043-205213 (7066)
2009: 9²GF, 9⁰GS, 10⁵GS, 11²GF, 12¹SD, 12³SD,

	Starts	1st	2nd	3rd	Win & Pl
Career Total (Turf)	6	0	2	0	2191
Career Total (AW)	3	1	0	2	6395

86 10/09 Wolv 1m4f50y (0-85)H STD £5046
Total win prize-money £5046

Going (Turf): **Sf: 0-1 GS: 0-2 Gd: 0-1 GF: 0-2 Fm: 0-0**
Distance: 5f/6f: 0-0 7f-8f: 0-2 **9f-13f: 1-7** 14f+: 0-0
Track : **LH: 1-5** RH: 0-3 **Tight: 1-5** Gall: 0-1
Aids: Bl: 0-0 Vi: 0-0 Tstrap: 0-0 Ckp: 0-0
Best Rating: **89** 8/09 Catt 1m3f214y gd-fm

Fair; stays 1m4f and acts on fast ground.

Akhenaten

108(101) (93)**98**
3-y-o b c High Chaparral (IRE)-Lady Adnil (IRE) (Stravinsky (USA))
M R Channon Box 41

Placings:631454-1006224003310 (6270)
2009: 8¹SD, 9⁰SD, 10⁰GS, 8⁶GF, 6²GF, 6²GF, 7⁴G, 6⁰G, 6⁰G, 7³GS, 7³GF, 7¹GF, 7⁰G,

	Starts	1st	2nd	3rd	Win & Pl
Career Total (Turf)	17	2	2	3	42770
Career Total (AW)	2	1	0	0	4985

98 9/09 Donc 7f (0-100)H G-F £12462
93 3/09 Wolv 1m141y STD £4984
79 9/08 Ches 7f2y G-S £5504
Total win prize-money £22952

Going (Turf): Sf: 0-0 **GS: 1-5** Gd: 0-6 **GF: 1-6** Fm: 0-0
Distance: 5f/6f: 0-4 **7f-8f: 2-12** 9f-13f: 1-3 14f+: 0-0
Track : **LH: 2-5** RH: 0-3 **Tight: 2-4** Gall: 0-2
Aids: Bl: 0-0 Vi: 0-0 Tstrap: 0-0 Ckp: 0-0
Best Rating: **98** 9/09 Donc 7f gd-fm

Very useful; effective over 7f-1m; acts on fast and easy ground; goes on Polytrack.

Akmal

112 **109**

3-y-o ch g Selkirk (USA)-Ayun (USA) (Swain (IRE))
J L Dunlop Hamdan Al Maktoum

Placings:060-23112151111 **(6854)**
2009: 9^{2}GF, 12^{3}GF, 11^{1}G, 12^{1}F, 12^{2}GF, 14^{1}G, 12^{5}G, 14^{1}GF, 14^{1}GF, 14^{1}GF, 16^{1}G,

	Starts	1st	2nd	3rd	Win & Pl
Career Total (Turf)	14	7	2	1	125714

106 10/09 NmkR 2m GD £36900
109 10/09 NmkR 1m6f G-F £22708
106 9/09 Yarm 1m6f17y (0-100)H G-F £12462
105 8/09 York 1m6f (0-105)H G-F £32380
98 7/09 York 1m6f (0-95)H GD £7641
89 6/09 Thsk 1m4f (0-85)H FRM £5569
74 5/09 Ling 1m3f106y GD £2729
Total win prize-money £120392

Going (Turf): Sf: 0-1 GS: 0-0 **Gd: 3-6 GF: 3-6** Fm: 1-1
Distance: 5f/6f: 0-0 7f-8f: 0-2 9f-13f: 2-7 **14f+: 5-5**
Track : **LH: 5-7** RH: 2-6 Tight: 3-5 **Gall: 4-6**
Aids: Bl: 0-1 Vi: 0-0 Tstrap: 0-0 Ckp: 0-0
Best Rating: **109** 10/09 NmkR 1m6f gd-fm

Smart; winner of the Group 3 Jockey Club Cup; stays 2m; acts on good and faster ground; has worn blinkers.

Akram (IRE)

94 **63**

7-y-o b g Night Shift (USA)-Akdariya (IRE) (Shirley Heights)
Jonjo O'Neill John P McManus

Placings:4311/5/0060400/05 **(6369)**
2009: 8^{0}GF, 10^{5}GF,

	Starts	1st	2nd	3rd	Win & Pl
Career Total (Turf)	14	2	0	1	17659

98 7/05 Gway 1m100y (60-90)H G-F £9234
76 7/05 Tipp 1m1f G-F £6125
Total win prize-money £15360

Going (Turf): Sf: 0-2 GS: 0-0 Gd: 0-3 **GF: 2-9** Fm: 0-0
Distance: 5f/6f: 0-0 7f-8f: 0-4 **9f-13f: 2-10** 14f+: 0-0
Track : LH: 0-7 **RH: 1-4** Tight: 0-2 Gall: 0-0
Aids: Bl: 0-0 Vi: 0-0 Tstrap: 0-1 Ckp: 0-1
Best Rating: **98** 7/05 Gway 1m100y gd-fm

Useful performer; best over a mile on fast ground.

Aktia (IRE)

94(87) (63)**68**

2-y-o b f Danehill Dancer (IRE)-La Gandilie (FR) (Highest Honor (FR))
L M Cumani Mrs M Marinopoulos

Placings:603 **(7430)**
2009: 8^{6}GF, 8^{0}GF, 7^{3}SD,

	Starts	1st	2nd	3rd	Win & Pl
Career Total (Turf)	2	0	0	0	0
Career Total (AW)	1	0	0	1	626

Going (Turf): **Sf: 0-0 GS: 0-0 Gd: 0-0 GF: 0-2 Fm: 0-0**
Distance: 5f/6f: 0-0 7f-8f: 0-1 9f-13f: 0-2 14f+: 0-0
Track : LH: 0-1 RH: 0-1 Tight: 0-0 Gall: 0-0
Aids: Bl: 0-0 Vi: 0-0 Tstrap: 0-0 Ckp: 0-0
Best Rating: **68** 9/09 Hayd 1m30y gd-fm

Akubra (IRE)

(74) (26)

2-y-o b f One Cool Cat (USA)-Dreaming Waters (Groom Dancer (USA))
Norma Twomey R H Sawyer & Mrs Norma Twomey

Placings:00 **(7736)**
2009: 6^{0}SD, 6^{0}SD,

	Starts	1st	2nd	3rd	Win & Pl
Career Total (Turf)	0	0	0	0	
Career Total (AW)	2	0	0	0	

Going (Turf): **Sf: 0-0 GS: 0-0 Gd: 0-0 GF: 0-0 Fm: 0-0**
Distance: 5f/6f: 0-2 7f-8f: 0-0 9f-13f: 0-0 14f+: 0-0
Track : LH: 0-0 RH: 0-2 Tight: 0-0 Gall: 0-0
Aids: Bl: 0-0 Vi: 0-0 Tstrap: 0-0 Ckp: 0-0
Best Rating: **26** 9/09 Kemp 6f stand

Akula (IRE)

83 **66**

2-y-o ch c Soviet Star (USA)-Danielli (IRE) (Danehill (USA))
M H Tompkins Jay Three Racing

Placings:300 **(6066)**
2009: 7^{3}S, 7^{0}S, 8^{0}GF,

	Starts	1st	2nd	3rd	Win & Pl
Career Total (Turf)	3	0	0	1	566

Going (Turf): **Sf: 0-2 GS: 0-0 Gd: 0-0 GF: 0-1 Fm: 0-0**
Distance: 5f/6f: 0-0 7f-8f: 0-3 9f-13f: 0-0 14f+: 0-0
Track : LH: 0-0 RH: 0-1 Tight: 0-0 Gall: 0-0
Aids: Bl: 0-0 Vi: 0-0 Tstrap: 0-0 Ckp: 0-0
Best Rating: **66** 7/09 Yarm 7f3y soft

Al Adham

86 **54**

2-y-o b c Dansili-Miss Meggy (Pivotal)
M bin Shafya (Saeed Bin Suroor 3/8) Sheikh Mansoor bin Mohammed al Maktoum

Placings:600
2009: 6^{6}GF, 6^{0}G, 6^{0}FT,

	Starts	1st	2nd	3rd	Win & Pl
Career Total (Turf)	2	0	0	0	0
Career Total (AW)	1	0	0	0	

Going (Turf): **Sf: 0-0 GS: 0-0 Gd: 0-1 GF: 0-1 Fm: 0-0**
Distance: 5f/6f: 0-3 7f-8f: 0-0 9f-13f: 0-0 14f+: 0-0
Track : LH: 0-1 RH: 0-0 Tight: 0-1 Gall: 0-0
Aids: Bl: 0-0 Vi: 0-0 Tstrap: 0-0 Ckp: 0-0
Best Rating: **54** 7/09 Epsm 6f gd-fm

Al Azy (IRE)

101(99) (61)**66**

4-y-o b c Nayef (USA)-Nasheed (USA) (Riverman (USA))
Gerard Keane (D M Simcock 2/7) Eoin Carroll

Placings:6564/3400-**5003**0101600 **(6130a)**
2009: **12**^{5}SD, **10**^{0}SD, **9**^{0}SD, **16**^{3}SD, 15^{0}GF, 14^{1}GF, 12^{0}GF, 11^{1}GF, 12^{6}GF, 14^{0}HY, 14^{0}G,

	Starts	1st	2nd	3rd	Win & Pl
Career Total (Turf)	15	2	0	1	5505
Career Total (AW)	4	0	0	1	302

61 7/09 Yarm 1m3f101y (0-65)H G-F £1942
56 5/09 Yarm 1m6f17y (0-70)H G-F £2719
Total win prize-money £4663

Going (Turf): Sf: 0-2 GS: 0-3 Gd: 0-3 **GF: 2-7** Fm: 0-0
Distance: 5f/6f: 0-0 7f-8f: 0-2 9f-13f: 1-12 14f+: 1-5
Track : **LH: 2-11** RH: 0-8 **Tight: 2-9** Gall: 0-0
Aids: Bl: 0-2 Vi: 0-0 Tstrap: 0-0 Ckp: 0-0
Best Rating: **69** 10/07 Bath 1m2f46y gd-sft

Moderate; effective over 1m4f-2m; acts on fast ground and Polytrack.

Al Barq (IRE)

77 **46**

2-y-o ch f Traditionally (USA)-Prayer (IRE) (Rainbow Quest (USA))
Miss D Mountain Miss Debbie Mountain

Placings:000 **(5519)**
2009: 6^{0}G, 7^{0}G, 6^{0}G,

	Starts	1st	2nd	3rd	Win & Pl
Career Total (Turf)	3	0	0	0	

Going (Turf): **Sf: 0-0 GS: 0-0 Gd: 0-3 GF: 0-0 Fm: 0-0**
Distance: 5f/6f: 0-2 7f-8f: 0-1 9f-13f: 0-0 14f+: 0-0
Track : LH: 0-0 RH: 0-0 Tight: 0-0 Gall: 0-0
Aids: Bl: 0-0 Vi: 0-0 Tstrap: 0-0 Ckp: 0-0
Best Rating: **46** 7/09 NmkJ 6f good

Al Dafa (USA)

91 **65**

2-y-o ch c Kingmambo (USA)-Crimson Conquest (USA) (Diesis)
Saeed Bin Suroor Godolphin

Placings:40 **(5966)**
2009: 6^{4}GF, 7^{0}GS,

	Starts	1st	2nd	3rd	Win & Pl
Career Total (Turf)	2	0	0	0	265

Going (Turf): **Sf: 0-0 GS: 0-1 Gd: 0-0 GF: 0-1 Fm: 0-0**
Distance: 5f/6f: 0-1 7f-8f: 0-1 9f-13f: 0-0 14f+: 0-0
Track : LH: 0-0 RH: 0-0 Tight: 0-0 Gall: 0-0
Aids: Bl: 0-0 Vi: 0-0 Tstrap: 0-0 Ckp: 0-0
Best Rating: **65** 8/09 Ling 6f gd-fm

Al Ghazal (USA)

101 **100**

2-y-o b c Motivator-Mansfield Park (Green Desert (USA))
Saeed Bin Suroor Godolphin

Placings:3110 **(7017)**
2009: 6^{3}GF, 7^{1}G, 9^{1}GF, 8^{0}GS,

	Starts	1st	2nd	3rd	Win & Pl
Career Total (Turf)	4	2	0	1	10670

92 10/09 Leic 1m1f218y G-F £6854

83 8/09 Sand 7f16y GD £3238

Total win prize-money £10092

Going (Turf): Sf: 0-0 GS: 0-1 Gd: 1-1 GF: 1-2 Fm: 0-0
Distance: 5f/6f: 0-1 7f-8f: 1-2 9f-13f: 1-1 14f+: 0-0
Track : LH: 0-0 RH: 2-2 Tight: 0-0 Gall: 0-1
Aids: Bl: 0-0 Vi: 0-0 Tstrap: 0-0 Ckp: 0-0
Best Rating: 100 10/09 Donc 1m gd-sft

Very useful; stays 1m2f; acts on good/fast ground.

Al Gillani (IRE)

84(113) (92)61

4-y-o b g Monashee Mountain (USA)-Whisper Dawn (IRE) (Fasliyev (USA))

J R Boyle The Paddock Space Partnership

Placings:50020111-1062 **(4870)**

2009: 6^{1}SD, 6^{0}SD, 6^{6}G, 6^{2}SD,

	Starts	1st	2nd	3rd	Win & Pl
Career Total (Turf)	3	0	0	0	0
Career Total (AW)	9	4	2	0	16080

92 3/09 Kemp 6f (0-80)H STD £4727
85 9/08 GrLe 6f (0-75)H STD £4209
79 9/08 Kemp 6f (0-60)H STD £2047
73 9/08 GrLe 6f STD £2590

Total win prize-money £13573

Going (Turf): Sf: 0-0 GS: 0-1 Gd: 0-1 GF: 0-1 Fm: 0-0
Distance: 5f/6f: 4-10 7f-8f: 0-2 9f-13f: 0-0 14f+: 0-0
Track : LH: 2-5 RH: 2-4 Tight: 0-3 Gall: 2-2
Aids: Bl: 0-0 Vi: 0-0 Tstrap: 0-0 Ckp: 0-0
Best Rating: 92 3/09 Kemp 6f stand

Useful; effective over 6f; acts on Polytrack.

Al Jaadl

91 61

2-y-o b f Shamardal (USA)-Three Wishes (Sadler's Wells (USA))

W Jarvis Abdullah Saeed Belhab

Placings:5 **(6567)**

2009: 7^{5}GF,

	Starts	1st	2nd	3rd	Win & Pl
Career Total (Turf)	1	0	0	0	0

Going (Turf): Sf: 0-0 GS: 0-0 Gd: 0-0 GF: 0-1 Fm: 0-0
Distance: 5f/6f: 0-0 7f-8f: 0-1 9f-13f: 0-0 14f+: 0-0
Track : LH: 0-0 RH: 0-0 Tight: 0-0 Gall: 0-0
Aids: Bl: 0-0 Vi: 0-0 Tstrap: 0-0 Ckp: 0-0
Best Rating: 61 10/09 Leic 7f9y gd-fm

Al Jathaab (USA)

(86) (66)

4-y-o gr g Aljabr (USA)-Al Ihsas (IRE) (Danehill (USA))

M Wigham Mrs Roxanne Simms

Placings:053 **(0800)**

2009: 8^{0}SD, 8^{5}SD, 8^{3}SD,

	Starts	1st	2nd	3rd	Win & Pl
Career Total (Turf)	0	0	0	0	
Career Total (AW)	3	0	0	1	385

Going (Turf): Sf: 0-0 GS: 0-0 Gd: 0-0 GF: 0-0 Fm: 0-0
Distance: 5f/6f: 0-0 7f-8f: 0-2 9f-13f: 0-1 14f+: 0-0
Track : LH: 0-1 RH: 0-2 Tight: 0-1 Gall: 0-0
Aids: Bl: 0-0 Vi: 0-0 Tstrap: 0-0 Ckp: 0-0
Best Rating: 66 3/09 Kemp 1m stand

Al Joza

84(89) (64)61

2-y-o b f Dubawi (IRE)-Avila (Ajdal (USA))

C E Brittain Saeed Manana

Placings:400 **(6477)**

2009: 6^{4}SD, 8^{0}GF, 7^{0}GF,

	Starts	1st	2nd	3rd	Win & Pl
Career Total (Turf)	2	0	0	0	
Career Total (AW)	1	0	0	0	289

Going (Turf): Sf: 0-0 GS: 0-0 Gd: 0-0 GF: 0-2 Fm: 0-0
Distance: 5f/6f: 0-1 7f-8f: 0-2 9f-13f: 0-0 14f+: 0-0
Track : LH: 0-0 RH: 0-1 Tight: 0-0 Gall: 0-0
Aids: Bl: 0-0 Vi: 0-0 Tstrap: 0-0 Ckp: 0-0
Best Rating: 64 7/09 Kemp 6f stand

Half-sister to several winners from 7f to 2m; modest form to date.

Al Khaleej (IRE)

104(108) (107)112

5-y-o b g Sakhee (USA)-Mood Swings (IRE) (Shirley Heights)

E A L Dunlop Mayoof Sultan

Placings:015/2130/12-00 **(4796)**

2009: 6^{0}G, 7^{0}G,

	Starts	1st	2nd	3rd	Win & Pl
Career Total (Turf)	8	1	2	1	36629
Career Total (AW)	3	2	0	0	12036

107 4/08 Kemp 7f (0-90)H STD £6854
92 7/07 NmkJ 1m (0-100)H GD £12464
76 7/06 Wolv 5f216y STD £5181

Total win prize-money £24500

Going (Turf): Sf: 0-2 GS: 0-0 Gd: 1-5 GF: 0-1 Fm: 0-0
Distance: 5f/6f: 1-3 7f-8f: 2-7 9f-13f: 0-1 14f+: 0-0
Track : LH: 1-2 RH: 1-2 Tight: 1-3 Gall: 0-0
Aids: Bl: 0-0 Vi: 0-0 Tstrap: 0-0 Ckp: 0-0
Best Rating: 112 5/08 Asct 7f gd-fm

Smart; runner-up in the 2008 Victoria Cup, but missed the rest of that season; effective over 7f-1m1f; acts on good and faster ground and on Polytrack.

Al Khawarezmi

74 36

2-y-o b c Shamardal (USA)-Mrs Ting (USA) (Lyphard (USA))

M Johnston Sheikh Hamdan Bin Mohammed Al Maktoum

Placings:00 **(6754)**

2009: 6^{0}S, 7^{0}G,

	Starts	1st	2nd	3rd	Win & Pl
Career Total (Turf)	2	0	0	0	

Going (Turf): Sf: 0-1 GS: 0-0 Gd: 0-1 GF: 0-0 Fm: 0-0
Distance: 5f/6f: 0-1 7f-8f: 0-1 9f-13f: 0-0 14f+: 0-0
Track : LH: 0-0 RH: 0-0 Tight: 0-0 Gall: 0-0
Aids: Bl: 0-0 Vi: 0-0 Tstrap: 0-0 Ckp: 0-0
Best Rating: 36 10/09 Leic 7f9y good

Al Khimiya (IRE)

95(100) (74)70

2-y-o b f Van Nistelrooy (USA)-Golden Flyer (FR) (Machiavellian (USA))

S Woodman (S A Callaghan 12/10) Al Khimiya Partnership

Placings:0236413141 **(7824)**

2009: 6^{0}SD, 7^{2}GF, 7^{3}GF, 7^{6}GF, 7^{4}SD, 7^{1}SD, 8^{3}SD, 8^{1}SD, 8^{4}SD, 7^{1}SD,

	Starts	1st	2nd	3rd	Win & Pl
Career Total (Turf)	3	0	1	1	1675
Career Total (AW)	7	3	0	1	7958

74 12/09 Kemp 7f (0-75) STD £2590
58 10/09 Kemp 1m STD £2590
68 9/09 Kemp 7f STD £2047

Total win prize-money £7227

Going (Turf): Sf: 0-0 GS: 0-0 Gd: 0-0 GF: 0-3 Fm: 0-0
Distance: 5f/6f: 0-1 7f-8f: 3-8 9f-13f: 0-1 14f+: 0-0
Track : LH: 0-6 RH: 3-3 Tight: 0-5 Gall: 0-0
Aids: Bl: 0-0 Vi: 0-0 Tstrap: 0-0 Ckp: 0-0
Best Rating: 74 12/09 Kemp 7f stand

Fair; effective over 7f-1m; acts on fast ground; goes on Polytrack.

Al Mugtareb (IRE)

96(91) (70)73

3-y-o b c Acclamation-Billie Bailey (USA) (Mister Baileys)

M Johnston Hamdan Al Maktoum

Placings:453-10250500 **(5340)**

2009: 5^{1}GF, 7^{0}GF, 6^{2}GF, 6^{5}G, 7^{0}GF, 7^{5}GF, 8^{0}G, 7^{0}GS,

	Starts	1st	2nd	3rd	Win & Pl
Career Total (Turf)	10	1	1	0	4578
Career Total (AW)	1	0	0	1	578

68 4/09 Catt 5f212y G-F £2266

Total win prize-money £2267

Going (Turf): Sf: 0-0 GS: 0-1 Gd: 0-3 GF: 1-6 Fm: 0-0
Distance: 5f/6f: 1-3 7f-8f: 0-8 9f-13f: 0-0 14f+: 0-0
Track : LH: 1-3 RH: 0-1 Tight: 1-3 Gall: 0-0
Aids: Bl: 0-1 Vi: 0-0 Tstrap: 0-0 Ckp: 0-0
Best Rating: 73 5/09 Haml 6f5y gd-fm

Fair; effective over 6-7f; acts on fast ground and on Polytrack.

Al Muheer (IRE)

112(113) (104)110

4-y-o b c Diktat-Dominion Rose (USA) (Spinning World (USA))

C E Brittain Saeed Manana

Placings:3332152/20520005500-4611305520100 **(6270)**

2009: 8^{4}SD, 10^{6}SD, 8^{1}SD, 7^{1}SD, 7^{3}SD, 7^{0}SD, 7^{5}SD, 7^{5}GF, 7^{2}GF, 7^{0}GF, 7^{1}G, 7^{0}GF, 7^{0}G,

	Starts	1st	2nd	3rd	Win & Pl
Career Total (Turf)	19	2	4	3	123222
Career Total (AW)	12	2	1	1	22648

110 7/09 Asct 7f H GD £93465
102 3/09 Wolv 7f32y (0-95)H STD £9462
99 2/09 Ling 1m STD £7771
92 8/07 Ling 7f140y G-F £2730

Total win prize-money £113428

Going (Turf): Sf: 0-0 GS: 0-3 Gd: 1-4 GF: 1-12 Fm: 0-0
Distance: 5f/6f: 0-6 7f-8f: 4-23 9f-13f: 0-2 14f+: 0-0
Track : LH: 2-7 RH: 0-6 Tight: 2-7 Gall: 0-0
Aids: Bl: 3-10 Vi: 0-0 Tstrap: 0-2 Ckp: 0-2
Best Rating: 110 7/09 Asct 7f good

Smart; Listed placed; effective over 7f-1m; acts on most ground; goes on Polytrack; has worn blinkers, cheekpieces and a tongue tie.

Al Mukaala (IRE)

(88) (57)**67**

3-y-o ch g Cadeaux Genereux-Crescent Moon (Mr Prospector (USA))
B N Pollock Mrs Nicola Pollock

Placings:045000-0 **(0808)**
2009: 8^{0}SD,

	Starts	1st	2nd	3rd	Win & Pl
Career Total (Turf)	4	0	0	0	289
Career Total (AW)	3	0	0	0	

Going (Turf): **Sf: 0-1 GS: 0-0 Gd: 0-2 GF: 0-0 Fm: 0-1**
Distance: 5f/6f: 0-4 7f-8f: 0-3 9f-13f: 0-0 14f+: 0-0
Track : LH: 0-2 RH: 0-1 Tight: 0-0 Gall: 0-1
Aids: Bl: 0-0 Vi: 0-0 Tstrap: 0-0 Ckp: 0-0
Best Rating: **67** 7/08 Donc 6f good

Modest; effective at 6f; acts on good ground.

Al Naouwee (USA)

91(92) (61)**80**

2-y-o b/br c Forest Camp (USA)-Dancehall Deelites (CAN) (Afternoon Deelites (USA))
B Smart A M A Al Shorafa

Placings:3240 **(7016)**
2009: 7^{3}GF, 7^{2}GF, 7^{4}SD, 6^{0}GS,

	Starts	1st	2nd	3rd	Win & Pl
Career Total (Turf)	3	0	1	1	1638
Career Total (AW)	1	0	0	0	289

Going (Turf): **Sf: 0-0 GS: 0-1 Gd: 0-0 GF: 0-2 Fm: 0-0**
Distance: 5f/6f: 0-1 7f-8f: 0-3 9f-13f: 0-0 14f+: 0-0
Track : LH: 0-1 RH: 0-0 Tight: 0-1 Gall: 0-0
Aids: Bl: 0-0 Vi: 0-0 Tstrap: 0-0 Ckp: 0-0
Best Rating: **80** 8/09 Rdcr 7f gd-fm

Fair; stays 7f; acts on fast ground and Polytrack.

Al Qasi (IRE)

107 (85)**114**

6-y-o b h Elnadim (USA)-Delisha (Salse (USA))
P W Chapple-Hyam Ziad A Galadari

Placings:611211/6021520/2020233-6400 **(6848)**
2009: 7^{6}G, 7^{4}S, 6^{0}GS, 7^{0}G,

	Starts	1st	2nd	3rd	Win & Pl
Career Total (Turf)	23	4	6	2	155846
Career Total (AW)	1	1	0	0	3239

120	8/07	Curr	6f		SH	£32939
112	9/06	Asct	6f	(0-100)H	G-S	£15580
109	8/06	Ripn	6f	(0-85)H	SFT	£6309
87	7/06	York	6f	(0-80)H	G-F	£6477
85	7/06	Ling	6f		STD	£3238

Total win prize-money £64544

Going (Turf): **Sf: 1-4 GS: 1-7** Gd: 0-8 **GF: 1-2** Fm: 0-0
Distance: **5f/6f: 5-11** 7f-8f: 0-13 9f-13f: 0-0 14f+: 0-0
Track : **LH: 1-2** RH: 0-2 **Tight: 1-1** Gall: 0-0
Aids: Bl: 0-0 Vi: 0-0 Tstrap: 0-0 Ckp: 0-0
Best Rating: **120** 8/07 Curr 6f sft-hvy

Smart; winner in Group 3 company and Group 2 placed; effective over 6f-7f; best with give in the ground and acts on Polytrack.

Al Qeddaaf (IRE)

101(104) (84)**83**

3-y-o b g Alhaarth (IRE)-Just Special (Cadeaux Genereux)
D McCain Jnr (W J Haggas 22/10) T G Leslie

Placings:02-51003 **(6973)**
2009: 6^{5}G, 8^{1}S, 8^{0}GF, 10^{0}SD, 10^{3}SD,

	Starts	1st	2nd	3rd	Win & Pl
Career Total (Turf)	5	1	1	0	3710
Career Total (AW)	2	0	0	1	703

83	6/09	Yarm	1m3y	(0-65)H	SFT	£2072

Total win prize-money £2072

Going (Turf): **Sf: 1-2** GS: 0-0 Gd: 0-2 GF: 0-1 Fm: 0-0
Distance: 5f/6f: 0-3 7f-8f: 0-1 **9f-13f: 1-3** 14f+: 0-0
Track : LH: 0-1 RH: 0-2 Tight: 0-0 Gall: 0-0
Aids: Bl: 0-0 Vi: 0-0 Tstrap: 0-0 Ckp: 0-0
Best Rating: **84** 10/09 Kemp 1m2f stand

Fair; stays 1m2f; acts on soft ground; goes on Polytrack.

Al Rayanah

99(100) (60)**60**

6-y-o b m Almushtarak (IRE)-Desert Bloom (FR) (Last Tycoon)
G Prodromou Faisal Al-Nassar

Placings:625/01555420134524354/0062060003235/4203 0136346200-26054046 **(7152)**
2009: 8^{2}GF, 8^{6}G, 8^{0}S, 8^{5}SD, 8^{4}G, 8^{0}GF, 8^{4}GF, 8^{6}SD,

	Starts	1st	2nd	3rd	Win & Pl
Career Total (Turf)	38	2	4	5	11781
Career Total (AW)	17	1	4	2	7130

57	7/08	Yarm	1m3y	(0-70)H	G-F	£2719
55	7/06	Nott	1m54y		G-F	£2730
61	2/06	Sthl	1m		STD	£3238

Total win prize-money £8689

Going (Turf): Sf: 0-7 GS: 0-10 Gd: 0-6 **GF: 2-12** Fm: 0-3
Distance: 5f/6f: 0-1 **7f-8f: 1-22 9f-13f: 2-32** 14f+: 0-0
Track : **LH: 2-22** RH: 0-4 Tight: 0-12 Gall: 0-0
Aids: Bl: 0-2 Vi: 0-0 Tstrap: 1-15 Ckp: 1-15
Best Rating: **68** 10/06 Leic 7f9y soft

Moderate; effective over 7f-1m; acts on Fibresand and Polytrack; has worn cheekpieces.

Al Sabaheya

101(102) (81)**85**

3-y-o b f Kheleyf (USA)-Baalbek (Barathea (IRE))
C E Brittain Saeed Manana

Placings:13-052055046033 **(6778)**
2009: 8^{0}SD, 10^{5}GF, 8^{2}GF, 8^{0}G, 7^{5}G, 8^{5}GF, 7^{0}G, 7^{4}GS, 7^{6}SD, 9^{0}GF, 7^{3}GS, 8^{3}SS,

	Starts	1st	2nd	3rd	Win & Pl
Career Total (Turf)	11	1	1	2	7634
Career Total (AW)	3	0	0	1	403

74	8/08	Brig	6f209y	G-S	£3561

Total win prize-money £3562

Going (Turf): Sf: 0-0 **GS: 1-3** Gd: 0-4 GF: 0-4 Fm: 0-0
Distance: 5f/6f: 0-0 **7f-8f: 1-10** 9f-13f: 0-4 14f+: 0-0
Track : **LH: 1-4** RH: 0-5 Tight: 0-4 Gall: 0-0
Aids: Bl: 0-4 Vi: 0-0 Tstrap: 0-0 Ckp: 0-0
Best Rating: **85** 9/08 Newb 7f good

Fair; effective over 1m and acts on most ground; has worn blinkers.

Al Shababiya (IRE)

(90) (67)

2-y-o b f Dubawi (IRE)-Multaka (USA) (Gone West (USA))
D M Simcock Ahmad Al Shaikh

Placings:02 **(7816)**
2009: 8^{0}SD, 8^{2}SD,

	Starts	1st	2nd	3rd	Win & Pl
Career Total (Turf)	0	0	0	0	
Career Total (AW)	2	0	1	0	771

Going (Turf): **Sf: 0-0 GS: 0-0 Gd: 0-0 GF: 0-0 Fm: 0-0**
Distance: 5f/6f: 0-0 7f-8f: 0-1 9f-13f: 0-1 14f+: 0-0
Track : LH: 0-2 RH: 0-0 Tight: 0-2 Gall: 0-0
Aids: Bl: 0-0 Vi: 0-0 Tstrap: 0-0 Ckp: 0-0
Best Rating: **67** 12/09 Wolv 1m141y stand

Modest; stays 1m; acts on Polytrack.

Al Wasef (USA)

99 **73**

4-y-o b g Danzig (USA)-Widady (USA) (Gone West (USA))
J S Goldie Frank Brady

Placings:2046-005306 **(3857)**
2009: 7^{0}GS, 6^{0}GS, 7^{5}GF, 7^{3}G, 8^{0}GF, 8^{6}GF,

	Starts	1st	2nd	3rd	Win & Pl
Career Total (Turf)	10	0	1	1	1931

Going (Turf): **Sf: 0-0 GS: 0-3 Gd: 0-3 GF: 0-4 Fm: 0-0**
Distance: 5f/6f: 0-1 7f-8f: 0-7 9f-13f: 0-2 14f+: 0-0
Track : LH: 0-4 RH: 0-4 Tight: 0-4 Gall: 0-1
Aids: Bl: 0-0 Vi: 0-0 Tstrap: 0-0 Ckp: 0-0
Best Rating: **73** 6/08 York 1m good

Fair; suited by a mile; acts on good and soft ground.

Al Zaeem

71(82) (47)**49**

2-y-o b c Mujahid (USA)-Tycho's Star (Mystiko (USA))
Miss D Mountain Miss Debbie Mountain

Placings:050 **(6431)**
2009: 7^{0}GS, 8^{5}GF, 8^{0}SD,

	Starts	1st	2nd	3rd	Win & Pl
Career Total (Turf)	2	0	0	0	0
Career Total (AW)	1	0	0	0	

Going (Turf): **Sf: 0-0 GS: 0-1 Gd: 0-0 GF: 0-1 Fm: 0-0**
Distance: 5f/6f: 0-0 7f-8f: 0-1 9f-13f: 0-2 14f+: 0-0
Track : LH: 0-1 RH: 0-1 Tight: 0-2 Gall: 0-0
Aids: Bl: 0-0 Vi: 0-2 Tstrap: 0-0 Ckp: 0-0
Best Rating: **49** 8/09 Wind 1m67y gd-fm

Al Zir (USA)

98 **109**

2-y-o b c Medaglia D'Oro (USA)-Bayou Plans (USA) (Bayou Hebert (USA))
Saeed Bin Suroor Godolphin

Placings:113 **(7017)**
2009: 7^{1}GS, 7^{1}GF, 8^{3}GS,

	Starts	1st	2nd	3rd	Win & Pl
Career Total (Turf)	3	2	0	1	37625

107	9/09	Donc	7f	G-F	£10904
93	8/09	NmkJ	7f	G-S	£5180

Total win prize-money £16085

Going (Turf): Sf: 0-0 **GS: 1-2** Gd: 0-0 **GF: 1-1** Fm: 0-0
Distance: 5f/6f: 0-0 **7f-8f: 2-3** 9f-13f: 0-0 14f+: 0-0
Track : LH: 0-0 RH: 0-0 Tight: 0-0 Gall: 0-0
Aids: Bl: 0-0 Vi: 0-0 Tstrap: 0-0 Ckp: 0-0
Best Rating: **109** 10/09 Donc 1m gd-sft

Smart; cost $1.6m; third in the Group 1 Racing Post Trophy at two; stays 1m and acts on most ground.

Alacity (IRE)

99 61

3-y-o b f Elusive City (USA)-Minamala (IRE) (Desert King (IRE))
N Bycroft Mrs J Dickinson

Placings:00-364063652 **(7241)**
2009: 6^{3}F, 7^{6}GF, 8^{4}G, 6^{0}G, 7^{6}S, 5^{3}GF, 6^{6}GF, 5^{5}S, 5^{2}S,

	Starts	1st	2nd	3rd	Win & Pl
Career Total (Turf)	11	0	1	2	1763

Going (Turf): **Sf: 0-4 GS: 0-0 Gd: 0-3 GF: 0-3 Fm: 0-1**
Distance: 5f/6f: 0-6 7f-8f: 0-5 9f-13f: 0-0 14f+: 0-0
Track : LH: 0-3 RH: 0-0 Tight: 0-2 Gall: 0-1
Aids: Bl: 0-0 Vi: 0-0 Tstrap: 0-0 Ckp: 0-0
Best Rating: **61** 11/09 Nott 5f13y soft

Moderate; effective at 5f; acts on most ground on turf.

Alainmaar (FR)

108 110

3-y-o b g Johar (USA)-Lady Elgar (IRE) (Sadler's Wells (USA))
M A Jarvis Hamdan Al Maktoum

Placings:211 **(6453)**
2009: 8^{2}GF, 10^{1}GF, 10^{1}GF,

	Starts	1st	2nd	3rd	Win & Pl
Career Total (Turf)	3	2	1	0	17242
110 10/09 NmkR 1m2f	(0-100)H		G-F		£12462
99 9/09 Pont 1m2f6y			G-F		£3238

Total win prize-money £15700

Going (Turf): Sf: 0-0 GS: 0-0 Gd: 0-0 **GF: 2-3** Fm: 0-0
Distance: 5f/6f: 0-0 7f-8f: 0-1 **9f-13f: 2-2** 14f+: 0-0
Track : **LH: 1-1** RH: 0-0 Tight: 0-0 Gall: 0-0
Aids: Bl: 0-0 Vi: 0-0 Tstrap: 0-0 Ckp: 0-0
Best Rating: **110** 10/09 NmkR 1m2f gd-fm

Smart; stays 1m2f; acts on fast ground.

Alan Devonshire

93(16) 99

4-y-o br g Mtoto-Missed Again (High Top)
M H Tompkins Russell Trew Ltd

Placings:361223/404600-00000000 **(7057)**
2009: 7^{0}GF, 8^{0}GF, 10^{0}G, 9^{0}S, 7^{0}SD, 6^{0}GS, 8^{0}GF, 7^{0}GF,

	Starts	1st	2nd	3rd	Win & Pl
Career Total (Turf)	19	1	2	2	17769
Career Total (AW)	1	0	0	0	
78 8/07 Newc 7f			GD		£2839

Total win prize-money £2839

Going (Turf): Sf: 0-2 GS: 0-2 **Gd: 1-6** GF: 0-9 Fm: 0-0
Distance: 5f/6f: 0-0 **7f-8f: 1-11** 9f-13f: 0-9 14f+: 0-0
Track : LH: 0-8 RH: 0-4 Tight: 0-8 Gall: 0-1
Aids: Bl: 0-0 Vi: 0-0 Tstrap: 0-0 Ckp: 0-0
Best Rating: **99** 5/08 Ling 1m3f106y gd-fm

Very useful; Listed placed; best at around 1m; acts on good and faster ground.

Alanbrooke

111 106

3-y-o gr c Hernando (FR)-Alouette (Darshaan)
M Johnston Sheikh Hamdan Bin Mohammed Al Maktoum

Placings:51-260112623203 **(7117)**
2009: 11^{2}GS, 12^{6}G, 12^{0}GS, 14^{1}G, 16^{1}G, 16^{2}G, 12^{6}GS, 14^{2}GF, 14^{3}S, 18^{2}GF, 18^{0}G, 16^{3}GS,

	Starts	1st	2nd	3rd	Win & Pl
Career Total (Turf)	14	3	4	2	50542
100 7/09 Asct 2m	(0-95)H		GD		£7477
94 7/09 Sand 1m6f	(0-85)H		GD		£6476
67 10/08 Nott 1m75y			SFT		£2914

Total win prize-money £16867

Going (Turf): Sf: 1-2 GS: 0-4 **Gd: 2-6** GF: 0-2 Fm: 0-0
Distance: 5f/6f: 0-0 7f-8f: 0-0 9f-13f: 1-6 **14f+: 2-8**
Track : LH: 1-4 **RH: 2-10** Tight: 0-3 **Gall: 1-7**
Aids: **Bl: 2-9** Vi: 0-0 Tstrap: 0-0 Ckp: 0-0
Best Rating: **106** 9/09 NmkR 2m2f gd-fm

Very useful; stays 2m2f; acts on any ground; has worn blinkers.

Alannah (IRE)

97(79) (38)43

4-y-o b f Alhaarth (IRE)-Aljeeza (Halling (USA))
Mrs P N Dutfield Mrs Nerys Dutfield

Placings:0006/00-040 **(6758)**
2009: 10^{0}G, 11^{4}G, 11^{0}G,

	Starts	1st	2nd	3rd	Win & Pl
Career Total (Turf)	6	0	0	0	144
Career Total (AW)	3	0	0	0	0

Going (Turf): **Sf: 0-0 GS: 0-1 Gd: 0-3 GF: 0-2 Fm: 0-0**
Distance: 5f/6f: 0-1 7f-8f: 0-2 9f-13f: 0-5 14f+: 0-1
Track : LH: 0-6 RH: 0-2 Tight: 0-6 Gall: 0-0
Aids: Bl: 0-0 Vi: 0-0 Tstrap: 0-0 Ckp: 0-0
Best Rating: **43** 8/09 Bath 1m3f144y good

Plating-class; stays 1m3f plus; acts on good ground.

Alarazi (IRE)

101(105) (99)110

5-y-o b g Spectrum (IRE)-Alaya (IRE) (Ela-Mana-Mou)
T G Mills Johnny Eddis

Placings:16/42225326-50303 **(4794)**
2009: 10^{5}SD, 8^{0}S, 10^{3}SD, 10^{0}GF, 10^{3}G,

	Starts	1st	2nd	3rd	Win & Pl
Career Total (Turf)	13	1	4	2	58556
Career Total (AW)	2	0	0	1	2376
73 3/07 Curr 1m			HVY		£8797

Total win prize-money £8797

Going (Turf): **Sf: 1-5** GS: 0-0 Gd: 0-2 GF: 0-1 Fm: 0-0
Distance: 5f/6f: 0-0 **7f-8f: 1-5** 9f-13f: 0-9 14f+: 0-1
Track : LH: 0-4 **RH: 1-10** Tight: 0-1 **Gall: 1-4**
Aids: Bl: 0-7 Vi: 0-0 Tstrap: 0-0 Ckp: 0-0
Best Rating: **110** 5/08 Curr 1m2f gd-yld

Very useful; ex-Irish; stays 1m2f but appears to get further; acts on soft ground; has worn blinkers.

Alazeyab (USA)

115 106

3-y-o b c El Prado (IRE)-Itnab (Green Desert (USA))
M A Jarvis Hamdan Al Maktoum

Placings:613-50100240 **(6480)**
2009: 10^{5}GF, 10^{0}S, 10^{1}G, 10^{0}GF, 9^{0}G, 8^{2}GF, 8^{4}GF, 9^{0}GF,

	Starts	1st	2nd	3rd	Win & Pl
Career Total (Turf)	11	2	1	1	30639
104 6/09 NmkJ 1m2f	(0-100)H		GD		£12952
84 9/08 Newb 7f			GD		£5504

Total win prize-money £18457

Going (Turf): Sf: 0-1 GS: 0-1 **Gd: 2-4** GF: 0-5 Fm: 0-0
Distance: 5f/6f: 0-0 7f-8f: 1-5 9f-13f: 1-6 14f+: 0-0
Track : LH: 0-3 **RH: 1-3** Tight: 0-1 **Gall: 1-4**
Aids: Bl: 0-0 Vi: 0-0 Tstrap: 0-0 Ckp: 0-0
Best Rating: **106** 9/09 Donc 1m gd-fm

Smart; stays 1m2f; acts on good ground; has worn a tongue tie; likes to race prominently.

Albaasha (IRE)

97(94) (61)68

3-y-o ch c Lemon Drop Kid (USA)-Cozy Maria (USA) (Cozzene (USA))
Sir Michael Stoute Hamdan Al Maktoum

Placings:6-55256 **(3674)**
2009: 10^{5}GF, 9^{5}GS, 12^{2}GF, **16^{5}SD**, 11^{6}F,

	Starts	1st	2nd	3rd	Win & Pl
Career Total (Turf)	4	0	1	0	1253
Career Total (AW)	2	0	0	0	0

Going (Turf): **Sf: 0-0 GS: 0-1 Gd: 0-0 GF: 0-2 Fm: 0-1**
Distance: 5f/6f: 0-0 7f-8f: 0-1 9f-13f: 0-4 14f+: 0-1
Track : LH: 0-4 RH: 0-2 Tight: 0-3 Gall: 0-1
Aids: Bl: 0-0 Vi: 0-3 Tstrap: 0-0 Ckp: 0-0
Best Rating: **68** 6/09 Donc 1m4f gd-fm

Moderate; stays 1m4f; acts on fast ground.

Albacocca

72(82) (47)35

2-y-o gr f With Approval (CAN)-Ballymac Girl (Niniski (USA))
Sir Mark Prescott Miss K Rausing

Placings:000 **(6284)**
2009: 8^{0}SD, 8^{0}SD, 8^{0}GF,

	Starts	1st	2nd	3rd	Win & Pl
Career Total (Turf)	1	0	0	0	
Career Total (AW)	2	0	0	0	

Going (Turf): **Sf: 0-0 GS: 0-0 Gd: 0-0 GF: 0-1 Fm: 0-0**
Distance: 5f/6f: 0-0 7f-8f: 0-1 9f-13f: 0-2 14f+: 0-0
Track : LH: 0-2 RH: 0-1 Tight: 0-1 Gall: 0-0
Aids: Bl: 0-0 Vi: 0-0 Tstrap: 0-0 Ckp: 0-0
Best Rating: **47** 9/09 Wolv 1m141y stand

Albaher

89 79

3-y-o b c Oasis Dream-Dance Sequence (USA) (Mr Prospector (USA))
J L Dunlop Hamdan Al Maktoum

Placings:1-4000 **(6680)**
2009: 8^{4}G, 8^{0}GF, 8^{0}G, 10^{0}G,

	Starts	1st	2nd	3rd	Win & Pl
Career Total (Turf)	5	1	0	0	7036
79 7/08 Asct 6f			G-F		£6476

Total win prize-money £6476

Going (Turf): Sf: 0-0 GS: 0-0 Gd: 0-3 **GF: 1-2** Fm: 0-0
Distance: **5f/6f: 1-1** 7f-8f: 0-1 9f-13f: 0-3 14f+: 0-0
Track : LH: 0-1 RH: 0-2 Tight: 0-0 Gall: 0-1

Aids: Bl: 0-0 Vi: 0-0 Tstrap: 0-0 Ckp: 0-0
Best Rating: **79** 7/08 Asct 6f gd-fm

Cost 150,000gns; half-brother to dual 5f juvenile winner Dance On, dual winning sprinter Hornpipe, and Sequential, a dual winner over middle distances; dam won the Lowther Stakes; winner on debut over 6f; acts on fast ground.

Albaqaa

110(108) (95)**100**
4-y-o ch g Medicean-Basbousate Nadia (Wolfhound (USA))
R A Fahey Mrs Josephine Tattersall

Placings:020566/1214052510-**53423** (3873)
2009: 11^{5}SD, 10^{3}GF, 10^{4}GF, 8^{2}G, 10^{3}GF,

	Starts	1st	2nd	3rd	Win & Pl
Career Total (Turf)	20	3	4	2	65620
Career Total (AW)	1	0	0	0	932

92 9/08 Ches 1m2f75y (0-100)H G-F £21185
86 4/08 Bevl 7f100y (0-90)H G-S £6799
85 3/08 Rdcr 1m1f G-S £2331
Total win prize-money £30317

Going (Turf): Sf: 0-4 **GS: 2-7** Gd: 0-4 GF: 1-5 Fm: 0-0
Distance: 5f/6f: 0-1 7f-8f: 1-9 **9f-13f: 2-11** 14f+: 0-0
Track : **LH: 2-9** RH: 1-5 **Tight: 2-3** Gall: 0-5
Aids: Bl: 0-0 Vi: 0-1 Tstrap: 0-0 Ckp: 0-0
Best Rating: **100** 6/09 York 1m208y good

Very useful; stays 1m2f and acts on most ground; has worn a visor; can pull hard.

Albaseet (IRE)

98(93) (75)**70**
3-y-o b g Desert Style (IRE)-Double Eight (IRE) (Common Grounds)
M P Tregoning Hamdan Al Maktoum

Placings:46422-**3** (5110)
2009: 6^{3}GF,

	Starts	1st	2nd	3rd	Win & Pl
Career Total (Turf)	4	0	0	1	1011
Career Total (AW)	2	0	2	0	2216

Going (Turf): **Sf: 0-2 GS: 0-1 Gd: 0-0 GF: 0-1 Fm: 0-0**
Distance: 5f/6f: 0-5 7f-8f: 0-1 9f-13f: 0-0 14f+: 0-0
Track : LH: 0-2 RH: 0-1 Tight: 0-1 Gall: 0-0
Aids: Bl: 0-0 Vi: 0-0 Tstrap: 0-0 Ckp: 0-0
Best Rating: **75** 11/08 Kemp 6f stand

Fair; effective at 5f-6f; acts on Polytrack.

Albeed

88 **60**
2-y-o b f Tiger Hill (IRE)-Ayun (USA) (Swain (IRE))
J L Dunlop Hamdan Al Maktoum

Placings:000 (6992)
2009: 7^{0}G, 7^{0}GF, 8^{0}GS,

	Starts	1st	2nd	3rd	Win & Pl
Career Total (Turf)	3	0	0	0	

Going (Turf): **Sf: 0-0 GS: 0-1 Gd: 0-1 GF: 0-1 Fm: 0-0**
Distance: 5f/6f: 0-0 7f-8f: 0-3 9f-13f: 0-0 14f+: 0-0
Track : LH: 0-2 RH: 0-0 Tight: 0-0 Gall: 0-1
Aids: Bl: 0-0 Vi: 0-0 Tstrap: 0-0 Ckp: 0-0
Best Rating: **60** 10/09 Donc 1m gd-sft

Albero Di Giuda (IRE)

84(96) (57)**27**
4-y-o b f Clodovil (IRE)-All Away (IRE) (Glow (USA))
F Sheridan Jon Owen

Placings:56212333431/213113103421-**460353050** (7877)
2009: 5^{4}SD, 7^{6}SD, 7^{0}SD, 5^{3}SD, 5^{5}SD, 5^{3}SD, 7^{0}GF, 5^{5}SD, 7^{0}SD,

	Starts	1st	2nd	3rd	Win & Pl
Career Total (Turf)	11	1	2	4	10901
Career Total (AW)	21	6	2	5	20925

9/08 Tagl 5f STD £2206
5/08 Capa 7f H GD £4412
4/08 Capa 6f STD £2574
3/08 Capa 6f H STD £2941
1/08 Capa 6f STD £1838
12/07 Capa 6f STD £1689
6/07 Capa 7f110y STD £3378
Total win prize-money £19038

Going (Turf): Sf: 0-3 GS: 0-0 **Gd: 1-7** GF: 0-1 Fm: 0-0
Distance: **5f/6f: 5-18** 7f-8f: 2-14 9f-13f: 0-0 14f+: 0-0
Track : LH: 0-6 RH: 0-0 Tight: 0-6 Gall: 0-0
Aids: Bl: 0-0 Vi: 0-0 Tstrap: 0-1 Ckp: 0-1
Best Rating: **57** 2/09 Wolv 7f32y stand

Modest; effective over 5f-7f; acts on Fibresand and handles Polytrack; has worn a tongue tie.

Albertine Rose

93(99) (72)**87**
3-y-o gr f Namid-Barathiki (Barathea (IRE))
W R Muir Mr & Mrs G Middlebrook

Placings:302231-**000** (4601)
2009: 5^{0}G, 5^{0}S, 5^{0}G,

	Starts	1st	2nd	3rd	Win & Pl
Career Total (Turf)	7	0	1	2	4917
Career Total (AW)	2	1	1	0	3877

72 11/08 Wolv 5f216y STD £3070
Total win prize-money £3071

Going (Turf): **Sf: 0-2 GS: 0-2 Gd: 0-2 GF: 0-1 Fm: 0-0**
Distance: **5f/6f: 1-9** 7f-8f: 0-0 9f-13f: 0-0 14f+: 0-0
Track : **LH: 1-3** RH: 0-0 **Tight: 1-2** Gall: 0-2
Aids: Bl: 0-0 Vi: 0-0 Tstrap: 0-0 Ckp: 0-0
Best Rating: **87** 10/08 NmkR 6f gd-sft

Useful; Listed placed; stays 6f; acts on most ground and on Polytrack.

Alberts Story (USA)

(101) (62)**61**
5-y-o b g Tale Of The Cat (USA)-Hazino (USA) (Hazaam (USA))
R A Fahey Mr & Mrs G Calder

Placings:450/50102455/0300003-**430** (0493)
2009: 10^{4}SD, 12^{3}SD, 12^{0}SD,

	Starts	1st	2nd	3rd	Win & Pl
Career Total (Turf)	15	1	1	1	4826
Career Total (AW)	6	0	0	2	726

56 7/07 Carl 7f200y (0-70)H G-F £2817
Total win prize-money £2817

Going (Turf): Sf: 0-1 GS: 0-0 Gd: 0-4 **GF: 1-9** Fm: 0-1
Distance: 5f/6f: 0-3 **7f-8f: 1-3** 9f-13f: 0-15 14f+: 0-0
Track : LH: 0-12 **RH: 1-8** Tight: 0-9 Gall: 0-0
Aids: Bl: 0-1 Vi: 0-0 Tstrap: 0-3 Ckp: 0-3
Best Rating: **62** 10/07 Wolv 1m1f103y stand

Moderate performer; stays 1m2f; acts on fast ground and Polytrack.

Albiera (IRE)

66(89) (41)**7**
4-y-o b f Xaar-Madam Waajib (IRE) (Waajib)
H Morrison Mrs M C Keogh

Placings:0000 (7658)
2009: 8^{0}GS, 9^{0}SD, 9^{0}SD, 12^{0}SD,

	Starts	1st	2nd	3rd	Win & Pl
Career Total (Turf)	1	0	0	0	
Career Total (AW)	3	0	0	0	

Going (Turf): **Sf: 0-0 GS: 0-1 Gd: 0-0 GF: 0-0 Fm: 0-0**
Distance: 5f/6f: 0-0 7f-8f: 0-0 9f-13f: 0-4 14f+: 0-0
Track : LH: 0-3 RH: 0-1 Tight: 0-4 Gall: 0-0
Aids: Bl: 0-0 Vi: 0-0 Tstrap: 0-0 Ckp: 0-0
Best Rating: **41** 10/09 Wolv 1m1f103y stand

Alcalde

107 **95**
3-y-o b g Hernando (FR)-Alexandrine (IRE) (Nashwan (USA))
M Johnston Sheikh Hamdan Bin Mohammed Al Maktoum

Placings:11-**0200163** (7018)
2009: 12^{0}S, 12^{2}GF, 14^{0}GF, 10^{0}GF, 10^{1}GF, 10^{6}S, 12^{3}GS,

	Starts	1st	2nd	3rd	Win & Pl
Career Total (Turf)	9	3	1	1	21985

93 10/09 Wwck 1m2f188y (0-95)H G-F £9714
83 10/08 Leic 1m1f218y SFT £6854
83 9/08 Brig 7f214y SFT £2719
Total win prize-money £19288

Going (Turf): **Sf: 2-4** GS: 0-1 Gd: 0-0 GF: 1-4 Fm: 0-0
Distance: 5f/6f: 0-0 7f-8f: 1-1 **9f-13f: 2-7** 14f+: 0-1
Track : **LH: 2-7** RH: 1-2 Tight: 0-0 Gall: 0-5
Aids: Bl: 0-1 Vi: 0-0 Tstrap: 0-0 Ckp: 0-0
Best Rating: **95** 10/09 Donc 1m4f gd-sft

Useful; winner of both his starts at two; stays at least 1m2f; handles soft ground.

Aldaado (IRE)

100 **78**
3-y-o b g Alhaarth (IRE)-Zobaida (IRE) (Green Desert (USA))
M Dods A Wynn-Williams, D Graham, D Neale

Placings:04311530 (6680)
2009: 8^{0}GF, 10^{4}GS, 7^{3}GF, 8^{1}GF, 8^{1}GF, 8^{5}GF, 8^{3}G, 10^{0}G,

	Starts	1st	2nd	3rd	Win & Pl
Career Total (Turf)	8	2	0	2	4644

78 6/09 Haml 1m65y (0-70)H G-F £3238
Total win prize-money £3238

Going (Turf): Sf: 0-0 GS: 0-1 Gd: 0-2 **GF: 2-5** Fm: 0-0
Distance: 5f/6f: 0-0 7f-8f: 0-2 **9f-13f: 2-6** 14f+: 0-0
Track : LH: 0-3 **RH: 2-5 Tight: 1-2** Gall: 0-2
Aids: Bl: 0-0 Vi: 0-0 Tstrap: 0-0 Ckp: 0-0
Best Rating: **78** 6/09 Haml 1m65y gd-fm

Fair; stays 1m; acts on any ground.

Alderbed

89(89) (44)**46**
3-y-o b g Bahri (USA)-Tanasie (Cadeaux Genereux)

George Baker Park Cottage Racing & Willie Carson

Placings:000005-66 **(3054)**
2009: 11^{6}G, 9^{6}GF,

	Starts	1st	2nd	3rd	Win & Pl
Career Total (Turf)	5	0	0	0	0
Career Total (AW)	3	0	0	0	0

Going (Turf): **Sf: 0-0 GS: 0-0 Gd: 0-2 GF: 0-3 Fm: 0-0**
Distance: 5f/6f: 0-3 7f-8f: 0-1 9f-13f: 0-4 14f+: 0-0
Track : LH: 0-3 RH: 0-1 Tight: 0-3 Gall: 0-2
Aids: Bl: 0-1 Vi: 0-2 Tstrap: 0-0 Ckp: 0-0
Best Rating: **46** 6/08 Wind 6f gd-fm

Aldermoor (USA)

108 **98**
3-y-o b g Tale Of The Cat (USA)-Notting Hill (BRZ) (Jules (USA))
S C Williams Phil & Frances Kendall

Placings:121-400000100 **(7294)**
2009: 6^{4}GF, 5^{0}G, 6^{0}GF, 6^{0}G, 6^{0}GF, 6^{0}GS, 7^{1}GF, 6^{0}G, 7^{0}S,

	Starts	1st	2nd	3rd	Win & Pl
Career Total (Turf)	12	3	1	0	23743

94 10/09 NmkR 7f (0-100)H G-F £12462
98 9/08 Ches 5f16y G-F £6476
86 7/08 Catt 5f212y G-F £2590
Total win prize-money £21528

Going (Turf): Sf: 0-1 GS: 0-1 Gd: 0-4 **GF: 3-6** Fm: 0-0
Distance: **5f/6f: 2-10** 7f-8f: 1-2 9f-13f: 0-0 14f+: 0-0
Track : **LH: 2-2** RH: 0-0 **Tight: 2-2** Gall: 0-0
Aids: Bl: 0-0 Vi: 0-0 Tstrap: 0-0 Ckp: 0-0
Best Rating: **98** 9/08 Ches 5f16y gd-fm

Useful; effective over 5f-7f; acts on good and faster ground; has worn a tongue tie.

Aldiruos (IRE)

(94) (59)
9-y-o ch g Bigstone (IRE)-Ball Cat (FR) (Cricket Ball (USA))
A W Carroll Aramis Racing Syndicate

Placings:014/**5**0 **(0485)**
2009: 16^{5}SD, 13^{0}SD,

	Starts	1st	2nd	3rd	Win & Pl
Career Total (Turf)	3	1	0	0	7403
Career Total (AW)	2	0	0	0	0

4/03 Lonc 1m4f SFT £6169
Total win prize-money £6169

Going (Turf): **Sf: 1-1** GS: 0-0 Gd: 0-2 GF: 0-0 Fm: 0-0
Distance: 5f/6f: 0-0 7f-8f: 0-0 **9f-13f: 1-4** 14f+: 0-1
Track : LH: 0-1 **RH: 1-2** Tight: 0-1 Gall: 0-0
Aids: Bl: 0-1 Vi: 0-0 Tstrap: 0-0 Ckp: 0-0
Best Rating: **59** 1/09 Kemp 2m stand

Aldorable

86(71) (19)**59**
2-y-o ch f Starcraft (NZ)-Aldora (Magic Ring (IRE))
R A Teal Back 4 More Partnership

Placings:0440 **(6775)**
2009: 7^{0}SD, 6^{4}GF, 6^{4}GF, 6^{0}SD,

	Starts	1st	2nd	3rd	Win & Pl
Career Total (Turf)	2	0	0	0	625
Career Total (AW)	2	0	0	0	

Going (Turf): **Sf: 0-0 GS: 0-0 Gd: 0-0 GF: 0-2 Fm: 0-0**
Distance: 5f/6f: 0-3 7f-8f: 0-1 9f-13f: 0-0 14f+: 0-0
Track : LH: 0-1 RH: 0-2 Tight: 0-1 Gall: 0-0
Aids: Bl: 0-0 Vi: 0-0 Tstrap: 0-0 Ckp: 0-0
Best Rating: **59** 10/09 NmkR 6f gd-fm

Aleatricis

104 (31)**88**
4-y-o br/gr g Kingmambo (USA)-Alba Stella (Nashwan (USA))
J J Quinn Exors Of The Late Lady Anne Bentinck

Placings:000/55111112-221430 **(6115)**
2009: 12^{2}GF, 12^{2}GF, 12^{1}G, 13^{4}GF, 15^{3}GF, 18^{0}GF,

	Starts	1st	2nd	3rd	Win & Pl
Career Total (Turf)	14	6	3	1	21949
Career Total (AW)	3	0	0	0	

86 5/09 Pont 1m4f8y (0-85)H GD £5180
75 7/08 Folk 1m4f (0-65)H G-F £2047
72 7/08 Yarm 1m3f101y (0-65)H G-F £1942
69 7/08 Haml 1m3f16y (0-65)H GD £2266
74 7/08 Ayr 1m2f (0-65)H GD £2590
55 7/08 Haml 1m4f17y (0-65)H GD £2266
Total win prize-money £16295

Going (Turf): Sf: 0-0 GS: 0-1 **Gd: 4-5** GF: 2-8 Fm: 0-0
Distance: 5f/6f: 0-0 7f-8f: 0-4 **9f-13f: 6-10** 14f+: 0-3
Track : LH: 3-9 RH: 3-8 **Tight: 4-12** Gall: 0-1
Aids: Bl: 0-1 Vi: 0-0 Tstrap: 0-0 Ckp: 0-0
Best Rating: **88** 7/09 Ches 1m7f195y gd-fm

Useful; stays 1m4f; acts on most ground; has worn blinkers.

Aleqa

58
2-y-o b f Oasis Dream-Vanishing Point (USA) (Caller I.D. (USA))
C F Wall Ms Aida Fustoq

Placings:0 **(6615)**
2009: 6^{0}G,

	Starts	1st	2nd	3rd	Win & Pl
Career Total (Turf)	1	0	0	0	

Going (Turf): **Sf: 0-0 GS: 0-0 Gd: 0-1 GF: 0-0 Fm: 0-0**
Distance: 5f/6f: 0-0 7f-8f: 0-1 9f-13f: 0-0 14f+: 0-0
Track : LH: 0-0 RH: 0-0 Tight: 0-0 Gall: 0-0
Aids: Bl: 0-0 Vi: 0-0 Tstrap: 0-0 Ckp: 0-0

Aleron (IRE)

101 (14)**69**
11-y-o b g Sadler's Wells (USA)-High Hawk (Shirley Heights)
J J Quinn Grahame Liles

Placings:502/42**001**200**661**/**5164**2123**3000033434**/212043 520/36/**0146660**/30/3543-0253 **(5554)**
2009: 15^{0}GF, 15^{2}GF, 16^{5}G, 16^{3}GS,

	Starts	1st	2nd	3rd	Win & Pl
Career Total (Turf)	50	5	9	11	52487
Career Total (AW)	10	1	0	0	4274

78 5/06 Haml 1m3f16y (0-75)H G-F £5505
78 5/04 Newc 1m2f32yE(0-65) HVY £3744
78 4/03 Muss 1m6f E(0-70)H G-F £4046
67 2/03 Sthl 1m4f E(0-75)H SLW £3347
68 11/02 Catt 1m5f175yE(0-70)H G-S £3932
4/02 Ndas 7f110y (20-50)H GD £5607
Total win prize-money £26183

Going (Turf): Sf: 1-6 GS: 1-12 Gd: 1-13 **GF: 2-18** Fm: 0-1
Distance: 5f/6f: 0-0 7f-8f: 1-5 **9f-13f: 3-36** 14f+: 2-19
Track : **LH: 4-41** RH: 2-14 **Tight: 3-32** Gall: 2-10
Aids: Bl: 0-0 Vi: 1-9 Tstrap: 2-20 Ckp: 2-20
Best Rating: **87** 5/03 Haml 1m5f9y gd-sft

Modest; stays 1m6f; acts on any ground; usually wears cheekpieces.

Alessano

103(99) (73)**86**
7-y-o ch g Hernando (FR)-Alessandra (Generous (IRE))
G L Moore D J Deer

Placings:1/465432315/04111432/**5**/505P **(6734)**
2009: 14^{5}GF, 16^{0}G, 12^{5}SD, 14^{P}S,

	Starts	1st	2nd	3rd	Win & Pl
Career Total (Turf)	17	4	2	3	42816
Career Total (AW)	6	1	0	0	5015

96 8/06 NmkJ 1m6f175y (0-95)H SFT £8420
86 7/06 Sand 1m6f (0-80)H G-F £6477
83 7/06 Wind 1m3f135y (0-80)H G-F £6477
82 10/05 Gdwd 1m3f (0-85)H GD £5928
68 12/04 Ling 1m STD £4085
Total win prize-money £31387

Going (Turf): Sf: 1-5 GS: 0-4 Gd: 1-3 **GF: 2-5** Fm: 0-0
Distance: 5f/6f: 0-0 7f-8f: 1-1 9f-13f: 2-16 14f+: 2-6
Track : LH: 1-7 **RH: 3-13 Tight: 3-12** Gall: 1-6
Aids: **Bl: 4-15** Vi: 0-0 Tstrap: 0-1 Ckp: 0-1
Best Rating: **99** 10/06 NmkR 1m4f gd-sft

Useful performer; stays 1m6f; acts on fast ground and Polytrack; has worn blinkers; likes to race prominently.

Alexander Family (IRE)

(92) (66)**57**
3-y-o b f Danetime (IRE)-Villa Nova (IRE) (Petardia)
E F Vaughan Noel O'Callaghan

Placings:000-15 **(0542)**
2009: 7^{1}SD, 7^{5}SD,

	Starts	1st	2nd	3rd	Win & Pl
Career Total (Turf)	3	0	0	0	
Career Total (AW)	2	1	0	0	2047

66 1/09 Wolv 7f32y (0-60)H STD £2047
Total win prize-money £2047

Going (Turf): **Sf: 0-1 GS: 0-0 Gd: 0-1 GF: 0-0 Fm: 0-0**
Distance: 5f/6f: 0-2 **7f-8f: 1-3** 9f-13f: 0-0 14f+: 0-0
Track : **LH: 1-1** RH: 0-3 **Tight: 1-1** Gall: 0-0
Aids: Bl: 0-0 Vi: 0-0 Tstrap: 0-0 Ckp: 0-0
Best Rating: **66** 1/09 Wolv 7f32y stand

Modest; ex-Irish; effective over 7f; acts on Polytrack.

Alexander Gulch (USA)

95(100) (85)**83**
3-y-o b g Thunder Gulch (USA)-Lovely Later (USA) (Green Dancer (USA))
K A Ryan Noel O'Callaghan

Placings:013-225 **(1019)**
2009: 8^{2}SD, 10^{2}SD, 10^{5}G,

	Starts	1st	2nd	3rd	Win & Pl
Career Total (Turf)	3	1	0	0	5181
Career Total (AW)	3	0	2	1	3468

83 8/08 Pont 6f GD £5180
Total win prize-money £5181

Going (Turf): Sf: 0-0 GS: 0-0 **Gd: 1-2** GF: 0-1 Fm: 0-0
Distance: **5f/6f: 1-2** 7f-8f: 0-2 9f-13f: 0-2 14f+: 0-0

Track : LH: 1-5 RH: 0-0 Tight: 0-2 Gall: 0-1
Aids: Bl: 0-0 Vi: 0-0 Tstrap: 0-2 Ckp: 0-2
Best Rating: **85** 3/09 Ling 1m2f stand

Useful; stays 1m; acts on good ground and on Polyrack; has worn cheekpieces.

Alexander Guru

(103) (69)**65**
5-y-o ch g Ishiguru (USA)-Superspring (Superlative)
M Blanshard M Blanshard

Placings:2002430/15053322540405-005 **(0577)**
2009: 9^{0}SD, 8^{0}SD, 9^{5}SD,

	Starts	1st	2nd	3rd	Win & Pl
Career Total (Turf)	3	0	0	1	403
Career Total (AW)	21	1	4	2	5472

69 1/08 Wolv 1m1f103y (0-65)H STD £2047
Total win prize-money £2048

Going (Turf): **Sf: 0-0 GS: 0-2 Gd: 0-0 GF: 0-1 Fm: 0-0**
Distance: 5f/6f: 0-0 7f-8f: 0-4 **9f-13f: 1-20** 14f+: 0-0
Track : **LH: 1-12** RH: 0-11 **Tight: 1-12** Gall: 0-1
Aids: Bl: 0-0 Vi: 0-0 Tstrap: 0-0 Ckp: 0-0
Best Rating: **69** 6/08 Kemp 1m4f stand

Modest; stays 1m4f but effective at shorter; acts on Polytrack.

Alexander Loyalty (IRE)

93(87) (43)**64**
3-y-o b f Invincible Spirit (IRE)-Nassma (IRE) (Sadler's Wells (USA))
E F Vaughan Noel O'Callaghan

Placings:06-0005 **(3427)**
2009: 5^{0}SD, 6^{0}GF, 7^{0}SD, 8^{5}GF,

	Starts	1st	2nd	3rd	Win & Pl
Career Total (Turf)	4	0	0	0	0
Career Total (AW)	2	0	0	0	

Going (Turf): **Sf: 0-2 GS: 0-0 Gd: 0-0 GF: 0-2 Fm: 0-0**
Distance: 5f/6f: 0-2 7f-8f: 0-3 9f-13f: 0-1 14f+: 0-0
Track : LH: 0-1 RH: 0-3 Tight: 0-1 Gall: 0-0
Aids: Bl: 0-0 Vi: 0-1 Tstrap: 0-0 Ckp: 0-0
Best Rating: **64** 11/08 Leop 7f soft

Alexandros

112 **119**
4-y-o ch c Kingmambo (USA)-Arlette (IRE) (King Of Kings (IRE))
Saeed Bin Suroor Godolphin

Placings:21113/42020313-11302010 **(7746a)**
2009: 8^{1}G, 8^{1}GF, 8^{3}G, 8^{0}Y, 8^{2}S, 8^{0}GF, 8^{1}S, 8^{0}G,

	Starts	1st	2nd	3rd	Win & Pl
Career Total (Turf)	21	7	4	4	652242

114 11/09 Nott 1m75y SFT £15577
116 2/09 Ndas 1m194y (95-115)H G-F £62500
114 1/09 Ndas 1m (95-110)H GD £50000
112 10/08 Bath 1m5y GD £7569
111 7/07 Deau 6f SFT £27027
101 7/07 Lonc 7f G-S £17568
92 6/07 StCl 7f G-S £9459
Total win prize-money £189702

Going (Turf): **Sf: 2-5 GS: 2-5 Gd: 2-6** GF: 1-4 Fm: 0-0
Distance: 5f/6f: 1-3 7f-8f: 3-12 9f-13f: 3-6 14f+: 0-0
Track : **LH: 5-9** RH: 2-7 Tight: 1-3 **Gall: 2-4**

Aids: Bl: 0-0 Vi: 0-0 Tstrap: 0-0 Ckp: 0-0
Best Rating: **119** 5/09 Newb 1m soft

Group class; ex-French; winner in Group 3 company and close second in the 2009 Lockinge; stays 1m; acts on most ground on turf.

Alf Tupper

(98) (73)**53**
6-y-o b g Atraf-Silvery (Petong)
John J Walsh (Adrian McGuinness 15/5) Curb Your Enthusiasm Syndicate

Placings:000/4000/0000620040/5003503324400512-4130000 **(6128a)**
2009: 9^{4}SD, 8^{1}SD, 8^{3}SD, 8^{0}SD, 8^{0}SD, 12^{0}S, 8^{0}G,

	Starts	1st	2nd	3rd	Win & Pl
Career Total (Turf)	30	0	2	2	4124
Career Total (AW)	11	2	1	2	5988

73 1/09 Wolv 1m141y (0-60)H STD £2047
56 12/08 Wolv 1m141y (0-58)H STD £2047
Total win prize-money £4094

Going (Turf): **Sf: 0-4 GS: 0-2 Gd: 0-6 GF: 0-9 Fm: 0-3**
Distance: 5f/6f: 0-0 7f-8f: 0-18 **9f-13f: 2-23** 14f+: 0-0
Track : **LH: 2-26** RH: 0-12 **Tight: 2-6** Gall: 0-0
Aids: Bl: 0-1 Vi: 0-0 Tstrap: 0-0 Ckp: 0-0
Best Rating: **73** 1/09 Wolv 1m141y stand

Moderate; effective from 1m-1m2f; acts on fast and easy ground; goes on Polytrack.

Alfalasteeni

70 **22**
2-y-o ch g Kyllachy-Mrs Nash (Night Shift (USA))
Ian Williams Dr Marwan Koukash

Placings:0060 **(4547)**
2009: 6^{0}S, 5^{0}G, 6^{6}S, 5^{0}GS,

	Starts	1st	2nd	3rd	Win & Pl
Career Total (Turf)	4	0	0	0	0

Going (Turf): **Sf: 0-2 GS: 0-1 Gd: 0-1 GF: 0-0 Fm: 0-0**
Distance: 5f/6f: 0-4 7f-8f: 0-0 9f-13f: 0-0 14f+: 0-0
Track : LH: 0-0 RH: 0-0 Tight: 0-0 Gall: 0-0
Aids: Bl: 0-1 Vi: 0-0 Tstrap: 0-0 Ckp: 0-0
Best Rating: **22** 7/09 Hayd 6f soft

Alfalevva

85(96) (57)**46**
2-y-o b g Piccolo-Evanesce (Lujain (USA))
M R Channon Lord Ilsley Racing (The Dell Days)

Placings:0060420 **(7474)**
2009: 5^{0}S, 6^{0}GF, 6^{6}F, 6^{0}GF, **8^{4}SD**, 9^{2}SD, 10^{0}SD,

	Starts	1st	2nd	3rd	Win & Pl
Career Total (Turf)	4	0	0	0	0
Career Total (AW)	3	0	1	0	898

Going (Turf): **Sf: 0-1 GS: 0-0 Gd: 0-0 GF: 0-2 Fm: 0-1**
Distance: 5f/6f: 0-2 7f-8f: 0-3 9f-13f: 0-2 14f+: 0-0
Track : LH: 0-3 RH: 0-2 Tight: 0-1 Gall: 0-1
Aids: Bl: 0-0 Vi: 0-0 Tstrap: 0-0 Ckp: 0-0
Best Rating: **57** 10/09 Wolv 1m1f103y stand

Alfathaa

109 **105**
4-y-o b g Nayef (USA)-Arctic Char (Polar Falcon (USA))

W J Haggas Hamdan Al Maktoum

Placings:315/06206-5556620 **(6480)**
2009: 8^{5}GF, 8^{5}G, 9^{5}G, 8^{6}GF, 10^{6}G, 8^{2}GF, 9^{0}GF,

	Starts	1st	2nd	3rd	Win & Pl
Career Total (Turf)	15	1	2	1	24753

90 9/07 Newb 1m G-F £6477
Total win prize-money £6477

Going (Turf): Sf: 0-1 GS: 0-2 Gd: 0-5 **GF: 1-7** Fm: 0-0
Distance: 5f/6f: 0-0 **7f-8f: 1-9** 9f-13f: 0-6 14f+: 0-0
Track : LH: 0-3 RH: 0-5 Tight: 0-1 Gall: 0-5
Aids: Bl: 0-3 Vi: 0-0 Tstrap: 0-2 Ckp: 0-2
Best Rating: **105** 9/09 Asct 1m gd-fm

Smart; effective over 1m, should get further; acts on fast and easy ground; has worn blinkers and cheekpieces.

Alfie Flits

103 (96)**104**
7-y-o b g Machiavellian (USA)-Elhilmeya (IRE) (Unfuwain (USA))
G A Swinbank Mrs J Porter & R H Hall

Placings:121301/05263/36304-0 **(4781)**
2009: 10^{0}G,

	Starts	1st	2nd	3rd	Win & Pl
Career Total (Turf)	16	3	2	4	70876
Career Total (AW)	1	0	0	0	

118 11/06 Wind 1m3f135y G-S £16595
113 6/06 Pont 1m4f8y G-F £19631
98 5/06 Thsk 1m4f HVY £5181
Total win prize-money £41410

Going (Turf): **Sf: 1-5 GS: 1-2** Gd: 0-3 **GF: 1-5** Fm: 0-0
Distance: 5f/6f: 0-0 7f-8f: 0-0 **9f-13f: 3-14** 14f+: 0-3
Track : **LH: 2-12** RH: 0-4 **Tight: 2-5** Gall: 0-2
Aids: Bl: 0-0 Vi: 0-0 Tstrap: 0-0 Ckp: 0-0
Best Rating: **118** 11/06 Wind 1m3f135y gd-sft

Smart; Listed winner and Group placed; useful hurdler; effective at up to 1m6f and acts on any ground.

Alfie Lee (IRE)

84 (3)**50**
12-y-o ch g Case Law-Nordic Living (IRE) (Nordico (USA))
D A Nolan Miss M McFadyen-Murray

Placings:54100/005005/00000400/000000060/000000400/040/0600005000/000/00000500/00004030-50 **(3445)**
2009: 5^{5}GF, 5^{0}GF,

	Starts	1st	2nd	3rd	Win & Pl
Career Total (Turf)	65	1	0	1	6815
Career Total (AW)	6	0	0	0	292

81 5/99 Gdwd 5f D GD £4123
Total win prize-money £4124

Going (Turf): Sf: 0-5 GS: 0-8 **Gd: 1-19** GF: 0-30 Fm: 0-3
Distance: **5f/6f: 1-63** 7f-8f: 0-8 9f-13f: 0-0 14f+: 0-0
Track : LH: 0-7 RH: 0-1 Tight: 0-3 Gall: 0-2
Aids: Bl: 0-4 Vi: 0-1 Tstrap: 0-16 Ckp: 0-16
Best Rating: **89** 6/00 Sand 5f6y gd-fm

Selling grade; suited by 5f and fast ground; usually tongue tied; has worn blinkers; cheekpieces and an eyeshield.

Alfie Tupper (IRE)

93(103) (78)**67**
6-y-o ch g Soviet Star (USA)-Walnut Lady (Forzando)
J R Boyle Epsom Equine Spa Partnership

Placings:1/33U600/0000613243214/2024P1061413-00000 (7664)
2009: 10^{0}G, 10^{0}SD, 10^{0}GF, 10^{0}SD, 8^{0}SD,

	Starts	1st	2nd	3rd	Win & Pl
Career Total (Turf)	15	2	0	2	8772
Career Total (AW)	22	4	4	3	15537

78	10/08	Wolv	1m141y	(0-70)H	STD	£3238
77	9/08	Wolv	1m141y	(0-70)H	STD	£3885
67	7/08	Sand	1m2f7y	(0-70)H	G-F	£3238
76	12/07	Wolv	1m1f103y	(0-60)H	STD	£2047
62	9/07	Wolv	1m1f103y	(0-55)	STD	£2047
76	8/05	Wwck	7f26y		G-F	£3250

Total win prize-money £17708

Going (Turf): Sf: 0-1 GS: 0-1 Gd: 0-4 **GF: 2-9** Fm: 0-0
Distance: 5f/6f: 0-2 7f-8f: 1-10 **9f-13f: 5-25** 14f+: 0-0
Track : **LH: 5-21** RH: 1-10 **Tight: 4-17** Gall: 0-4
Aids: Bl: 0-0 Vi: 0-0 Tstrap: 0-0 Ckp: 0-0
Best Rating: **88** 8/06 Sals 1m gd-fm

Fair; stays 1m4f; acts on fast ground; also goes on Polytrack.

Alfies Express

(89) (53)
5-y-o br g My Best Valentine-Ali Rose (Cigar)
S Curran (F E Sutherland 22/9) Miss H P J Scheffers

Placings:000 (7549)
2009: 9^{0}SD, 12^{0}SD, 12^{0}SD,

	Starts	1st	2nd	3rd	Win & Pl
Career Total (Turf)	0	0	0	0	
Career Total (AW)	3	0	0	0	

Going (Turf): **Sf: 0-0 GS: 0-0 Gd: 0-0 GF: 0-0 Fm: 0-0**
Distance: 5f/6f: 0-0 7f-8f: 0-0 9f-13f: 0-3 14f+: 0-0
Track : LH: 0-3 RH: 0-0 Tight: 0-3 Gall: 0-0
Aids: Bl: 0-0 Vi: 0-0 Tstrap: 0-0 Ckp: 0-0
Best Rating: **53** 11/09 Ling 1m4f stand

Alfonso The Wise (IRE)

77 44
2-y-o b c Galileo (IRE)-Dalawara (IRE) (Top Ville)
J Noseda M Tabor, Mrs J Magnier & D Smith

Placings:0 (6620)
2009: 8^{0}G,

	Starts	1st	2nd	3rd	Win & Pl
Career Total (Turf)	1	0	0	0	

Going (Turf): **Sf: 0-0 GS: 0-0 Gd: 0-1 GF: 0-0 Fm: 0-0**
Distance: 5f/6f: 0-0 7f-8f: 0-1 9f-13f: 0-0 14f+: 0-0
Track : LH: 0-0 RH: 0-0 Tight: 0-0 Gall: 0-0
Aids: Bl: 0-0 Vi: 0-0 Tstrap: 0-0 Ckp: 0-0
Best Rating: **44** 10/09 Newb 1m good

Alfred Nobel (IRE)

105 (98)113
2-y-o b c Danehill Dancer (IRE)-Glinting Desert (IRE) (Desert Prince (IRE))
A P O'Brien D Smith, Mrs J Magnier, M Tabor

Placings:23111650 (7307a)
2009: 5^{2}Y, 6^{3}HY, 7^{1}G, 6^{1}GY, 6^{1}HY, 7^{6}SH, 7^{5}GF, 8^{0}FT,

	Starts	1st	2nd	3rd	Win & Pl
Career Total (Turf)	7	3	1	1	239257
Career Total (AW)	1	0	0	0	

113	7/09	Curr	6f	HVY	£126747
107	6/09	Curr	6f	G-Y	£69902
88	5/09	Leop	7f	GD	£11740

Total win prize-money £208391

Going (Turf): **Sf: 1-2** GS: 0-0 **Gd: 1-1** GF: 0-1 Fm: 0-0
Distance: **5f/6f: 2-4** 7f-8f: 1-3 9f-13f: 0-1 14f+: 0-0
Track : **LH: 1-3** RH: 0-0 Tight: 0-0 Gall: 0-0
Aids: Bl: 0-0 Vi: 0-0 Tstrap: 0-0 Ckp: 0-0
Best Rating: **113** 7/09 Curr 6f heavy

Group class; winner of the Group 1 Phoenix Stakes; stays 7f; acts on testing and fast ground.

Alfredtheordinary

(105) (65)58
4-y-o b g Hunting Lion (IRE)-Solmorin (Fraam)
M R Channon M Channon

Placings:0464005031/6500300225500-012600 (7650)
2009: 10^{0}SD, 8^{1}SD, 8^{2}SD, 8^{6}SD, 8^{0}SD, 8^{0}SD,

	Starts	1st	2nd	3rd	Win & Pl
Career Total (Turf)	14	0	1	1	1289
Career Total (AW)	15	2	2	1	5482

64	3/09	Ling	1m	(0-55)H	STD	£2047
65	11/07	Kemp	1m	(0-60)	STD	£1706

Total win prize-money £3753

Going (Turf): **Sf: 0-2 GS: 0-1 Gd: 0-4 GF: 0-4 Fm: 0-3**
Distance: 5f/6f: 0-3 **7f-8f: 2-11** 9f-13f: 0-15 14f+: 0-0
Track : LH: 1-20 RH: 1-5 **Tight: 1-14** Gall: 0-5
Aids: Bl: 0-0 Vi: 0-0 Tstrap: 0-0 Ckp: 0-0
Best Rating: **65** 3/09 Ling 1m stand

Moderate gelding; stays 1m; acts on fast ground and on Polytrack.

Alfresco

105(117) (91)83
5-y-o b g Mtoto-Maureena (IRE) (Grand Lodge (USA))
J R Best Mrs A M Riney

Placings:00/6211006030014421/25312000000244022200 0-6351200000400 (7603)
2009: 8^{6}SD, 7^{3}SD, 8^{5}SD, 6^{1}GF, 6^{2}GF, 5^{0}G, 5^{0}GS, 6^{0}G, 6^{0}SD, 8^{0}GF, 7^{4}SS, 7^{0}SD, 8^{0}SD,

	Starts	1st	2nd	3rd	Win & Pl
Career Total (Turf)	22	1	5	0	8455
Career Total (AW)	30	5	4	3	31813

83	5/09	Gdwd	6f	(0-80)H	G-F	£4857
101	2/08	Ling	1m	(0-95)H	STD	£6800
90	12/07	Ling	1m	(0-85)H	STD	£4857
84	9/07	Kemp	7f	(0-80)H	STD	£4728
82	4/07	Ling	1m	(0-75)H	STD	£2914
72	3/07	Ling	1m	(0-75)H	STD	£3071

Total win prize-money £27230

Going (Turf): Sf: 0-3 GS: 0-3 Gd: 0-3 **GF: 1-11** Fm: 0-2
Distance: 5f/6f: 1-13 **7f-8f: 5-30** 9f-13f: 0-9 14f+: 0-0
Track : **LH: 4-22** RH: 1-15 **Tight: 4-22** Gall: 0-5
Aids: **Bl: 6-35** Vi: 0-8 Tstrap: 0-2 Ckp: 0-2
Best Rating: **101** 2/08 Ling 1m stand

Useful on sand, fair on turf; effective at 6f-1m; acts on Polytrack and fast turf; has worn blinkers a visor and cheek-pieces.

Alhaque (USA)

99(95) (70)83
3-y-o ch g Galileo (IRE)-Safeen (USA) (Storm Cat (USA))
W J Haggas (P W Chapple-Hyam 14/5) Saleh Al Homaizi & Imad Al Sagar

Placings:225-30622 (6417)
2009: 11^{3}GF, 10^{0}GF, 10^{6}G, 12^{2}SD, 14^{2}GF,

	Starts	1st	2nd	3rd	Win & Pl
Career Total (Turf)	7	0	3	1	5203
Career Total (AW)	1	0	1	0	771

Going (Turf): **Sf: 0-0 GS: 0-0 Gd: 0-2 GF: 0-5 Fm: 0-0**
Distance: 5f/6f: 0-0 7f-8f: 0-3 9f-13f: 0-4 14f+: 0-1
Track : LH: 0-1 RH: 0-3 Tight: 0-1 Gall: 0-0
Aids: Bl: 0-0 Vi: 0-0 Tstrap: 0-0 Ckp: 0-0
Best Rating: **83** 10/08 NmkR 1m gd-fm

Fair; effective over 7f-1m; acts on fast ground.

Alhena (IRE)

84 54
2-y-o b f Alhaarth (IRE)-Mail Boat (Formidable (USA))
K A Ryan Thomas Doherty

Placings:00 (6284)
2009: 6^{0}GF, 8^{0}GF,

	Starts	1st	2nd	3rd	Win & Pl
Career Total (Turf)	2	0	0	0	

Going (Turf): **Sf: 0-0 GS: 0-0 Gd: 0-0 GF: 0-2 Fm: 0-0**
Distance: 5f/6f: 0-1 7f-8f: 0-0 9f-13f: 0-1 14f+: 0-0
Track : LH: 0-1 RH: 0-0 Tight: 0-0 Gall: 0-0
Aids: Bl: 0-0 Vi: 0-0 Tstrap: 0-0 Ckp: 0-0
Best Rating: **54** 9/09 Rdcr 6f gd-fm

Alicante

107 78
3-y-o gr f Pivotal-Alba Stella (Nashwan (USA))
Sir Mark Prescott Miss K Rausing

Placings:060-51106 (5912)
2009: 8^{5}GF, 11^{1}G, 11^{1}GS, 12^{0}G, 12^{6}GF,

	Starts	1st	2nd	3rd	Win & Pl
Career Total (Turf)	8	2	0	0	4339

78	7/09	Yarm	1m3f101y	(0-65)H	G-S	£2072
71	7/09	Haml	1m3f16y	(0-65)H	GD	£2266

Total win prize-money £4339

Going (Turf): Sf: 0-1 **GS: 1-2 Gd: 1-2** GF: 0-3 Fm: 0-0
Distance: 5f/6f: 0-3 7f-8f: 0-1 **9f-13f: 2-4** 14f+: 0-0
Track : LH: 1-3 RH: 1-2 **Tight: 2-5** Gall: 0-0
Aids: Bl: 0-0 Vi: 0-0 Tstrap: 0-0 Ckp: 0-0
Best Rating: **78** 7/09 Yarm 1m3f101y gd-sft

Modest; stays 1m3f and acts on good ground.

Alice Alleyne (IRE)

101(99) (77)77
2-y-o b f Oasis Dream-Vas Y Carla (USA) (Gone West (USA))
Sir Michael Stoute Plantation Stud

Placings:221 (6436)
2009: 6^{2}SD, 6^{2}GF, 7^{1}SD,

	Starts	1st	2nd	3rd	Win & Pl
Career Total (Turf)	1	0	1	0	1510
Career Total (AW)	2	1	1	0	5103

77	10/09	Wolv	7f32y	STD £3561

Total win prize-money £3562

Going (Turf): **Sf: 0-0 GS: 0-0 Gd: 0-0 GF: 0-1 Fm: 0-0**
Distance: 5f/6f: 0-1 **7f-8f: 1-2** 9f-13f: 0-0 14f+: 0-0

Track : LH: **1-1** RH: 0-1 **Tight: 1-1** Gall: 0-0
Aids: Bl: 0-0 Vi: 0-0 Tstrap: 0-0 Ckp: 0-0
Best Rating: 77 10/09 Wolv 7f32y stand

Modest; should prove suited by 7f; acts on Polytrack; should improve.

Alice Cullen

80 **55**
2-y-o b f Bertolini (USA)-Albavilla (Spectrum (IRE))
W R Swinburn Pendley Farm

Placings:0 **(7182)**
2009: 7^{0}G,

	Starts	1st	2nd	3rd	Win & Pl
Career Total (Turf)	1	0	0	0	

Going (Turf): Sf: 0-0 GS: 0-0 Gd: 0-1 GF: 0-0 Fm: 0-0
Distance: 5f/6f: 0-0 7f-8f: 0-1 9f-13f: 0-0 14f+: 0-0
Track : LH: 0-0 RH: 0-0 Tight: 0-0 Gall: 0-0
Aids: Bl: 0-0 Vi: 0-0 Tstrap: 0-0 Ckp: 0-0
Best Rating: 55 10/09 NmkR 7f good

Alimarr (IRE)

(88) (60)**53**
3-y-o ch f Noverre (USA)-Tiger Desert (GER) (Desert King (IRE))
S Parr Willie McKay

Placings:065560-5056 **(0684)**
2009: 5^{5}SD, 8^{0}SD, 5^{5}SD, 7^{6}SD,

	Starts	1st	2nd	3rd	Win & Pl
Career Total (Turf)	2	0	0	0	0
Career Total (AW)	8	0	0	0	147

Going (Turf): Sf: 0-1 GS: 0-0 Gd: 0-1 GF: 0-0 Fm: 0-0
Distance: 5f/6f: 0-3 7f-8f: 0-6 9f-13f: 0-1 14f+: 0-0
Track : LH: 0-6 RH: 0-0 Tight: 0-1 Gall: 0-2
Aids: Bl: 0-1 Vi: 0-0 Tstrap: 0-3 Ckp: 0-3
Best Rating: 60 11/08 GrLe 1m stand

Alinghi (IRE)

(86) (60)
2-y-o b f Oratorio (IRE)-The Stick (Singspiel (IRE))
R Hannon Lord Roborough

Placings:5 **(6942)**
2009: 6^{5}SD,

	Starts	1st	2nd	3rd	Win & Pl
Career Total (Turf)	0	0	0	0	
Career Total (AW)	1	0	0	0	0

Going (Turf): Sf: 0-0 GS: 0-0 Gd: 0-0 GF: 0-0 Fm: 0-0
Distance: 5f/6f: 0-1 7f-8f: 0-0 9f-13f: 0-0 14f+: 0-0
Track : LH: 0-0 RH: 0-1 Tight: 0-0 Gall: 0-0
Aids: Bl: 0-0 Vi: 0-0 Tstrap: 0-0 Ckp: 0-0
Best Rating: 60 10/09 Kemp 6f stand

Alis Aquilae (IRE)

93 **63**
3-y-o b g Captain Rio-Garnock Academy (USA) (Royal Academy (USA))
T J Etherington R Hogton R Bradley Training at Woldhouse

Placings:50 **(3003)**
2009: 6^{5}GF, 5^{0}GF,

	Starts	1st	2nd	3rd	Win & Pl
Career Total (Turf)	2	0	0	0	0

Going (Turf): Sf: 0-0 GS: 0-0 Gd: 0-0 GF: 0-2 Fm: 0-0
Distance: 5f/6f: 0-1 7f-8f: 0-1 9f-13f: 0-0 14f+: 0-0
Track : LH: 0-0 RH: 0-0 Tight: 0-0 Gall: 0-0
Aids: Bl: 0-0 Vi: 0-0 Tstrap: 0-0 Ckp: 0-0
Best Rating: 63 5/09 Nott 6f15y gd-fm

Alittlemoreflair

99(97) (62)**48**
3-y-o ch f Grape Tree Road-Native Flair (Be My Native (USA))
J Pearce Lady Green

Placings:04503000305 **(6037)**
2009: 8^{0}SD, 9^{4}SD, 12^{5}SD, 12^{0}SD, 12^{3}SD, 12^{0}GF, 14^{0}S, 12^{0}SD, 12^{3}G, 16^{0}GF, 16^{5}GF,

	Starts	1st	2nd	3rd	Win & Pl
Career Total (Turf)	5	0	0	1	578
Career Total (AW)	6	0	0	1	302

Going (Turf): Sf: 0-1 GS: 0-0 Gd: 0-1 GF: 0-3 Fm: 0-0
Distance: 5f/6f: 0-0 7f-8f: 0-1 9f-13f: 0-7 14f+: 0-3
Track : LH: 0 6 RH: 0 5 Tight: 0-7 Gall: 0-1
Aids: Bl: 0-0 Vi: 0-3 Tstrap: 0-0 Ckp: 0-0
Best Rating: 62 4/09 Kemp 1m4f stand

Modest; effective over 1m1f; acts on Polytrack.

Aliybee (IRE)

(82) (56)
3-y-o b f Barathea (IRE)-Aliyshan (IRE) (Darshaan)
E J O'Neill Miss A H Marshall

Placings:04-0 **(0138)**
2009: 9^{0}SD,

	Starts	1st	2nd	3rd	Win & Pl
Career Total (Turf)	0	0	0	0	
Career Total (AW)	3	0	0	0	0

Going (Turf): Sf: 0-0 GS: 0-0 Gd: 0-0 GF: 0-0 Fm: 0-0
Distance: 5f/6f: 0-0 7f-8f: 0-2 9f-13f: 0-1 14f+: 0-0
Track : LH: 0-3 RH: 0-0 Tight: 0-1 Gall: 0-0
Aids: Bl: 0-0 Vi: 0-0 Tstrap: 0-0 Ckp: 0-0
Best Rating: 56 12/08 Dund 7f stand

Alkhafif

44(81) (32)**93**
3-y-o b g Royal Applause-My First Romance (Danehill (USA))
E A L Dunlop Hamdan Al Maktoum

Placings:1-00 **(5766)**
2009: 8^{0}SD, 7^{0}GF,

	Starts	1st	2nd	3rd	Win & Pl
Career Total (Turf)	2	1	0	0	4533
Career Total (AW)	1	0	0	0	

93 5/08 NmkR 6f FRM £4533
Total win prize-money £4533

Going (Turf): Sf: 0-0 GS: 0-0 Gd: 0-0 GF: 0-1 **Fm: 1-1**
Distance: 5f/6f: 1-1 7f-8f: 0-2 9f-13f: 0-0 14f+: 0-0
Track : LH: 0-0 RH: 0-1 Tight: 0-0 Gall: 0-0
Aids: Bl: 0-0 Vi: 0-0 Tstrap: 0-0 Ckp: 0-0
Best Rating: 93 5/08 NmkR 6f firm

Useful; half-brother to four winners including Romantic Myth and Romantic Liaison; suited by 6f and fast ground.

Alkhataaf (USA)

81 **43**
2-y-o b c Green Desert (USA)-Elrafa Ah (USA) (Storm Cat (USA))
J L Dunlop Hamdan Al Maktoum

Placings:0 **(6054)**
2009: 6^{0}GF,

	Starts	1st	2nd	3rd	Win & Pl
Career Total (Turf)	1	0	0	0	

Going (Turf): Sf: 0-0 GS: 0-0 Gd: 0-0 GF: 0-1 Fm: 0-0
Distance: 5f/6f: 0-0 7f-8f: 0-1 9f-13f: 0-0 14f+: 0-0
Track : LH: 0-0 RH: 0-0 Tight: 0-0 Gall: 0-0
Aids: Bl: 0-0 Vi: 0-0 Tstrap: 0-0 Ckp: 0-0
Best Rating: 43 9/09 Newb 6f8y gd-fm

All About You (IRE)

101(98) (74)**86**
3-y-o b g Mind Games-Expectation (IRE) (Night Shift (USA))
P Howling (W J Haggas 24/10) Andrew Baker

Placings:21-304504**3**60 **(7534)**
2009: 6^{3}F, 7^{0}G, 7^{4}G, 8^{5}GF, 8^{0}S, 7^{4}GF, 8^{3}GF, 7^{6}SD, 6^{0}SD,

	Starts	1st	2nd	3rd	Win & Pl
Career Total (Turf)	9	1	1	2	8353
Career Total (AW)	2	0	0	0	0

86 10/08 Wind 6f GD £3561
Total win prize-money £3562

Going (Turf): Sf: 0-1 GS: 0-0 **Gd: 1-4** GF: 0-3 Fm: 0-1
Distance: 5f/6f: 1-2 7f-8f: 0-8 9f-13f: 0-1 14f+: 0-0
Track : LH: 0-3 RH: 0-3 Tight: 0-1 **Gall: 1-1**
Aids: Bl: 0-4 Vi: 0-0 Tstrap: 0-0 Ckp: 0-0
Best Rating: 86 10/08 Wind 6f good

Fair; effective over 6f; acts on good ground; has worn blinkers.

All For You (IRE)

101(98) (68)**75**
3-y-o b f High Chaparral (IRE)-Quatre Saisons (FR) (Homme De Loi (IRE))
M Botti Lucky Seven Stable

Placings:5-0213503 **(6455)**
2009: 8^{0}G, 8^{2}G, 7^{1}GF, 7^{3}GF, 7^{5}G, 7^{0}SD, 7^{3}SD,

	Starts	1st	2nd	3rd	Win & Pl
Career Total (Turf)	5	1	1	1	5020
Career Total (AW)	3	0	0	1	433

71 6/09 Ling 7f (0-75)H G-F £3238
Total win prize-money £3238

Going (Turf): Sf: 0-0 GS: 0-0 Gd: 0-3 **GF: 1-2** Fm: 0-0
Distance: 5f/6f: 0-0 **7f-8f: 1-7** 9f-13f: 0-1 14f+: 0-0
Track : LH: 0-5 RH: 0-2 Tight: 0-3 Gall: 0-0
Aids: Bl: 0-0 Vi: 0-0 Tstrap: 0-2 Ckp: 0-2
Best Rating: 75 7/09 Wwck 7f26y gd-fm

Fair; effective over 7f; acts on fast ground; has worn cheekpieces.

All Guns Firing (IRE)

104(86) (43)78

3-y-o b g High Chaparral (IRE)-Lili Cup (FR) (Fabulous Dancer (USA))

D Carroll (M A Jarvis 24/7) Miss A Muir

Placings:03-0364 **(7780)**

2009: 10^{0}G, 14^{3}G, 12^{6}G, 11^{4}SD,

	Starts	1st	2nd	3rd	Win & Pl
Career Total (Turf)	5	0	0	2	1782
Career Total (AW)	1	0	0	0	0

Going (Turf): **Sf: 0-0 GS: 0-1 Gd: 0-4 GF: 0-0 Fm: 0-0**
Distance: 5f/6f: 0-0 7f-8f: 0-1 9f-13f: 0-4 14f+: 0-1
Track : LH: 0-2 RH: 0-3 Tight: 0-1 Gall: 0-0
Aids: Bl: 0-0 Vi: 0-0 Tstrap: 0-0 Ckp: 0-0
Best Rating: **78** 7/09 Sand 1m6f good

Fair; stays 1m6f and acts on soft ground; has worn a tongue tie.

All In The Red (IRE)

101(106) (73)75

4-y-o ch g Redback-Light-Flight (IRE) (Brief Truce (USA))

A Crook (B N Pollock 5/3) Paul Fowlie & the timemaster.co.uk

Placings:53/62143225100444-113010502030B03 **(4434)**

2009: 8^{1}SD, 8^{1}SD, 8^{3}SD, 10^{0}G, 10^{1}GF, 8^{0}SD, 11^{5}SD, 12^{0}GF, 10^{2}S, 10^{0}G, 11^{3}GF, 11^{0}GF, 10^{B}GF, 10^{0}G, 10^{3}GF,

	Starts	1st	2nd	3rd	Win & Pl
Career Total (Turf)	18	2	3	3	8743
Career Total (AW)	13	3	1	2	9419

75 4/09 Nott 1m2f50y (0-70)H G-F £2590
68 2/09 Kemp 1m (0-70) STD £2729
70 2/09 Sthl 1m STD £2047
66 9/08 Leic 7f9y GD £1942
72 4/08 GrLe 6f STD £2590
Total win prize-money £11900

Going (Turf): Sf: 0-2 GS: 0-2 **Gd: 1-6 GF: 1-8** Fm: 0-0
Distance: 5f/6f: 1-4 **7f-8f: 3-13** 9f-13f: 1-14 14f+: 0-0
Track : **LH: 3-20** RH: 1-5 Tight: 0-4 **Gall: 1-6**
Aids: Bl: 0-3 Vi: 0-2 Tstrap: 4-16 Ckp: 4-16
Best Rating: **75** 5/09 Hayd 1m2f95y soft

Fair; stays 1m2f; acts on most ground; goes on sand; has worn blinkers and cheekpieces.

All Moving Parts (USA)

90 58

2-y-o b/br g Forest Camp (USA)-Smooth Player (USA) (Bertrando (USA))

J S Wainwright Charles Wentworth

Placings:0066 **(6923)**

2009: 6^{0}GF, 6^{0}GS, 8^{6}GS, 8^{6}GF,

	Starts	1st	2nd	3rd	Win & Pl
Career Total (Turf)	4	0	0	0	0

Going (Turf): **Sf: 0-0 GS: 0-2 Gd: 0-0 GF: 0-2 Fm: 0-0**
Distance: 5f/6f: 0-2 7f-8f: 0-0 9f-13f: 0-2 14f+: 0-0
Track : LH: 0-1 RH: 0-0 Tight: 0-0 Gall: 0-0
Aids: Bl: 0-0 Vi: 0-0 Tstrap: 0-0 Ckp: 0-0
Best Rating: **58** 9/09 Ayr 6f gd-sft

All Of Me (IRE)

(99) (63)46

5-y-o b g Xaar-Silk Point (IRE) (Barathea (IRE))

Paul W Flynn (Mark L Fagan 8/9) Patrick G Walsh

Placings:0421/16000/0000050 **(7729)**

2009: 6^{0}GF, 7^{0}S, 8^{0}YS, 6^{0}S, 7^{0}SD, 7^{5}SD, 7^{0}SD,

	Starts	1st	2nd	3rd	Win & Pl
Career Total (Turf)	8	0	0	0	
Career Total (AW)	8	2	1	0	10011

85 4/07 Wolv 7f32y (0-80)H STD £4728
79 12/06 Wolv 7f32y STD £3886
Total win prize-money £8614

Going (Turf): **Sf: 0-4 GS: 0-0 Gd: 0-2 GF: 0-1 Fm: 0-0**
Distance: 5f/6f: 0-2 **7f-8f: 2-9** 9f-13f: 0-5 14f+: 0-0
Track : **LH: 2-12** RH: 0-3 **Tight: 2-8** Gall: 0-0
Aids: Bl: 0-3 Vi: 0-0 Tstrap: 0-2 Ckp: 0-2
Best Rating: **85** 4/07 Wolv 7f32y stand

Fair performer; gets 7f; acts on Polytrack; has worn a tongue-tie/cheekpieces.

All Right Now

(78) (35)

2-y-o b c Night Shift (USA)-Cookie Cutter (IRE) (Fasliyev (USA))

S Kirk Patrick Wilmott

Placings:0 **(7859)**

2009: 7^{0}SD,

	Starts	1st	2nd	3rd	Win & Pl
Career Total (Turf)	0	0	0	0	
Career Total (AW)	1	0	0	0	

Going (Turf): **Sf: 0-0 GS: 0-0 Gd: 0-0 GF: 0-0 Fm: 0-0**
Distance: 5f/6f: 0-0 7f-8f: 0-1 9f-13f: 0-0 14f+: 0-0
Track : LH: 0-1 RH: 0-0 Tight: 0-1 Gall: 0-0
Aids: Bl: 0-0 Vi: 0-0 Tstrap: 0-0 Ckp: 0-0
Best Rating: **35** 12/09 Wolv 7f32y stand

All Spin (IRE)

98(100) (65)69

3-y-o ch g Spinning World (USA)-Mad Annie (USA) (Anabaa (USA))

A P Jarvis Mrs Ann Jarvis

Placings:00426036-64340F **(5517)**

2009: 5^{6}GF, 7^{4}G, 6^{3}SD, 5^{4}GF, 5^{0}GF, 5^{F}GF,

	Starts	1st	2nd	3rd	Win & Pl
Career Total (Turf)	9	0	1	0	2137
Career Total (AW)	5	0	0	2	1049

Going (Turf): **Sf: 0-0 GS: 0-1 Gd: 0-2 GF: 0-6 Fm: 0-0**
Distance: 5f/6f: 0-12 7f-8f: 0-2 9f-13f: 0-0 14f+: 0-0
Track : LH: 0-2 RH: 0-3 Tight: 0-2 Gall: 0-1
Aids: Bl: 0-0 Vi: 0-1 Tstrap: 0-0 Ckp: 0-0
Best Rating: **69** 9/08 Hayd 6f gd-fm

Modest; stays 6f; acts on fast ground and on Polytrack.

All The Aces (IRE)

111(111) (113)114

4-y-o b g Spartacus (IRE)-Lili Cup (FR) (Fabulous Dancer (USA))

M A Jarvis A D Spence

Placings:321/124-215256 **(7031)**

2009: 13^{2}S, 12^{1}G, 12^{5}G, 12^{2}SD, 14^{5}S, 12^{6}S,

	Starts	1st	2nd	3rd	Win & Pl
Career Total (Turf)	10	2	3	1	78146
Career Total (AW)	2	1	1	0	17227

114 6/09 NmkJ 1m4f GD £22708
102 4/08 Leic 1m3f183y (0-95)H G-S £9346
79 10/07 Ling 1m2f STD £3238
Total win prize-money £35294

Going (Turf): Sf: 0-4 **GS: 1-1 Gd: 1-2** GF: 0-2 Fm: 0-1
Distance: 5f/6f: 0-0 7f-8f: 0-1 **9f-13f: 3-9** 14f+: 0-2
Track : LH: 1-6 **RH: 2-6** Tight: 1-2 Gall: 1-5
Aids: Bl: 0-0 Vi: 0-0 Tstrap: 0-0 Ckp: 0-0
Best Rating: **114** 6/09 NmkJ 1m4f good

Smart; Listed winner and Group placed; stays 1m5f; acts on most ground and on Polytrack; likes to race prominently.

All The Nines (IRE)

99(99) (72)86

3-y-o b f Elusive City (USA)-Sagaing (Machiavellian (USA))

Mrs D J Sanderson R J Budge

Placings:0-61115600 **(4507)**

2009: 7^{6}SD, 6^{1}SD, 6^{1}GF, 6^{1}GF, 6^{5}GF, 6^{6}GF, 6^{0}SD, 6^{0}G,

	Starts	1st	2nd	3rd	Win & Pl
Career Total (Turf)	6	2	0	0	14099
Career Total (AW)	3	1	0	0	4094

86 5/09 Haml 6f5y (0-80)H G-F £7447
79 5/09 Haml 6f5y (0-80)H G-F £6476
72 4/09 Sthl 6f STD £4094
Total win prize-money £18017

Going (Turf): Sf: 0-0 GS: 0-0 Gd: 0-2 **GF: 2-4** Fm: 0-0
Distance: 5f/6f: 1-6 **7f-8f: 2-3** 9f-13f: 0-0 14f+: 0-0
Track : **LH: 1-4** RH: 0-0 Tight: 0-1 Gall: 0-0
Aids: Bl: 0-0 Vi: 0-0 Tstrap: 0-0 Ckp: 0-0
Best Rating: **86** 5/09 Haml 6f5y gd-fm

Fair; effective over 6f; acts on fast ground; goes on Fibresand.

All You Need (IRE)

91(102) (67)58

5-y-o b g Iron Mask (USA)-Choice Pickings (IRE) (Among Men (USA))

R Hollinshead N Chapman

Placings:320/001062030/0652300400005-0510061506406 **(7460)**

2009: 7^{0}SD, 8^{5}SD, 5^{1}SD, 5^{0}SD, 7^{0}GF, 6^{6}SD, 5^{1}GF, 6^{5}GF, 8^{0}G, 6^{6}G, 5^{4}SD, 8^{0}SD, 5^{6}SD,

	Starts	1st	2nd	3rd	Win & Pl
Career Total (Turf)	15	1	1	1	4900
Career Total (AW)	23	2	2	2	6279

58 6/09 Leic 5f218y G-F £1942
60 2/09 Wolv 5f216y (0-45) STD £1364
76 7/07 Wolv 5f216y STD £2388
Total win prize-money £5697

Going (Turf): Sf: 0-2 GS: 0-0 Gd: 0-4 **GF: 1-9** Fm: 0-0
Distance: **5f/6f: 3-23** 7f-8f: 0-11 9f-13f: 0-4 14f+: 0-0
Track : **LH: 2-24** RH: 0-2 **Tight: 2-22** Gall: 0-0
Aids: Bl: 0-1 Vi: 0-3 Tstrap: 2-16 Ckp: 2-16
Best Rating: **81** 7/06 York 6f gd-fm

Moderate; suited by 6f-7f; acts on fast ground; also goes on Polytrack; has worn cheekpieces.

Allanit (GER)

(98) (72)**103**

5-y-o b g Tiger Hill (IRE)-Astilbe (GER) (Monsun (GER))

B J Curley (A P Stringer 14/1) Curley Leisure

Placings:3/1300/331561000**0-0000** **(5227)**

2009: 12^{0}SD, 10^{0}SD, 10^{0}SD, 12^{0}SF,

	Starts	1st	2nd	3rd	Win & Pl
Career Total (Turf)	**14**	**3**	**0**	**4**	**19211**
Career Total (AW)	**5**	**0**	**0**	**0**	

Date	Course	Distance	Going	Prize
8/08	Duss	1m2f110y	GD	£8823
5/08	Badn	1m2f	GD	£2941
4/07	Hanv	1m2f	GD	£2027

Total win prize-money £13792

Going (Turf): Sf: 0-5 GS: 0-1 **Gd: 3-8** GF: 0-0 Fm: 0-0
Distance: 5f/6f: 0-0 7f-8f: 0-2 **9f-13f: 3-17** 14f+: 0-0
Track : LH: 0-7 RH: 0-4 Tight: 0-2 Gall: 0-2
Aids: Bl: 0-0 Vi: 0-0 Tstrap: 0-0 Ckp: 0-0
Best Rating: **103** 6/08 Dort 1m2f good

Smart; ex-German trained; stays 1m2f; acts on good and softer ground.

Allannah Abu

(83) (51)

2-y-o b f Dubawi (IRE)-Alexandrine (IRE) (Nashwan (USA))

Sir Mark Prescott Ennistown Stud

Placings:000 **(7135)**

2009: 7^{0}SD, 7^{0}SS, 7^{0}SD,

	Starts	1st	2nd	3rd	Win & Pl
Career Total (Turf)	**0**	**0**	**0**	**0**	
Career Total (AW)	**3**	**0**	**0**	**0**	

Going (Turf): **Sf: 0-0 GS: 0-0 Gd: 0-0 GF: 0-0 Fm: 0-0**
Distance: 5f/6f: 0-0 7f-8f: 0-3 9f-13f: 0-0 14f+: 0-0
Track : LH: 0-2 RH: 0-1 Tight: 0-2 Gall: 0-0
Aids: Bl: 0-0 Vi: 0-0 Tstrap: 0-0 Ckp: 0-0
Best Rating: **51** 10/09 Ling 7f std-slw

Allexes (IRE)

89(92) (45)**57**

3-y-o b/br f Exceed And Excel (AUS)-Lizanne (USA) (Theatrical)

J R Boyle The Allexes Partnership

Placings:00-000**000** **(6289)**

2009: 8^{0}GF, 7^{0}GF, 6^{0}G, 7^{0}SD, 7^{0}SD, 10^{0}SD,

	Starts	1st	2nd	3rd	Win & Pl
Career Total (Turf)	**5**	**0**	**0**	**0**	
Career Total (AW)	**3**	**0**	**0**	**0**	

Going (Turf): **Sf: 0-1 GS: 0-1 Gd: 0-1 GF: 0-2 Fm: 0-0**
Distance: 5f/6f: 0-1 7f-8f: 0-6 9f-13f: 0-1 14f+: 0-0
Track : LH: 0-1 RH: 0-3 Tight: 0-1 Gall: 0-0
Aids: Bl: 0-0 Vi: 0-0 Tstrap: 0-1 Ckp: 0-1
Best Rating: **57** 6/09 Gdwd 1m gd-fm

Allez Frank (GER)

86(87) (57)**59**

8-y-o b g Macanal (USA)-Agua Clara (GER) (Roi Dagobert)

A E Jones Jim White

Placings:00/21204/6112156/01052110/**130-3** **(4263)**

2009: 12^{3}S,

	Starts	1st	2nd	3rd	Win & Pl
Career Total (Turf)	**23**	**7**	**4**	**1**	**43497**
Career Total (AW)	**3**	**1**	**0**	**1**	**1763**

Date	Course	Distance	Going	Prize
2/08	Neus	1m3f110y	STD	£1470
9/06	Siro	1m3f	HVY	£7327
9/06	Siro	1m4f	GD	£6379
6/06	Amie	1m6f110y	GD	£6896
7/05	Kref	1m3f165y	GD	£3333
5/05	Siro	1m3f	GD	£8865
5/05	Brem	1m4f	GD	£2127
9/04	Badn	1m1f	SFT	£3169

Total win prize-money £39570

Going (Turf): Sf: 2-9 GS: 0-0 **Gd: 5-14** GF: 0-0 Fm: 0-0
Distance: 5f/6f: 0-0 7f-8f: 0-2 **9f-13f: 7-22** 14f+: 1-2
Track : **LH: 1-4** RH: 0-1 Tight: 0-2 Gall: 0-0
Aids: **Bl: 2-4** Vi: 0-0 Tstrap: 0-0 Ckp: 0-0
Best Rating: **59** 7/09 Chep 1m4f23y soft

Moderate; multiple winner on the continent; stays 1m4f; acts on good and softer ground and on sand.

Allformary

100(92) (64)**78**

3-y-o b f Tobougg (IRE)-Bollin Rita (Rambo Dancer (CAN))

B Smart Alan D Crombie

Placings:21-300551200 **(6847)**

2009: 8^{3}GF, 8^{0}GS, 7^{0}GF, 8^{5}SD, 10^{5}G, 8^{1}S, 8^{2}G, 8^{0}SD, 7^{0}G,

	Starts	1st	2nd	3rd	Win & Pl
Career Total (Turf)	**9**	**2**	**2**	**1**	**10355**
Career Total (AW)	**2**	**0**	**0**	**0**	**0**

Rating	Date	Course	Distance	Race	Going	Prize
71	9/09	Thsk	1m	(0-70)H	SFT	£4274
69	10/08	Newc	7f		HVY	£3561

Total win prize-money £7836

Going (Turf): **Sf: 2-3** GS: 0-1 Gd: 0-3 GF: 0-2 Fm: 0-0
Distance: 5f/6f: 0-0 **7f-8f: 2-9** 9f-13f: 0-2 14f+: 0-0
Track : **LH: 1-8** RH: 0-0 **Tight: 1-2** Gall: 0-1
Aids: Bl: 0-0 Vi: 0-0 Tstrap: 0-0 Ckp: 0-0
Best Rating: **78** 9/09 Ayr 1m good

Fair; stays 1m; handles most ground on turf.

Allied Powers (IRE)

110(101) (70)**113**

4-y-o b c Invincible Spirit (IRE)-Always Friendly (High Line)

M L W Bell David Fish And Edward Ware

Placings:0/**36311143210-0102320** **(6873a)**

2009: 10^{0}G, 12^{1}G, 10^{0}G, 10^{2}G, 12^{3}HY, 10^{2}GY, 12^{0}F,

	Starts	1st	2nd	3rd	Win & Pl
Career Total (Turf)	**17**	**5**	**3**	**3**	**101005**
Career Total (AW)	**2**	**0**	**0**	**1**	**363**

Rating	Date	Course	Distance	Race	Going	Prize
112	5/09	Haml	1m4f17y	(0-110)H	GD	£23843
105	9/08	Ayr	1m2f	(0-100)H	HVY	£12952
97	5/08	Newb	1m3f5y	(0-80)H	GD	£5504
92	5/08	Ches	1m4f66y	(0-95)H	GD	£10037
91	4/08	Pont	1m4f8y	(0-75)H	HVY	£3238

Total win prize-money £55576

Going (Turf): Sf: 2-5 GS: 0-3 **Gd: 3-7** GF: 0-0 Fm: 0-1
Distance: 5f/6f: 0-0 7f-8f: 0-1 **9f-13f: 5-17** 14f+: 0-1
Track : **LH: 4-14** RH: 1-5 **Tight: 2-4** Gall: 1-4
Aids: Bl: 0-0 Vi: 0-0 Tstrap: 0-0 Ckp: 0-0
Best Rating: **113** 7/09 York 1m2f88y good

Smart; stays 1m6f but effective at 1m2f; acts on good and softer ground.

Alloro

(83) (23)**51**

5-y-o ch g Auction House (USA)-Minette (Bishop Of Cashel)

A Kirtley A Kirtley

Placings:04000/540005000/**5-00** **(0174)**

2009: 8^{0}SD, 8^{0}SD,

	Starts	1st	2nd	3rd	Win & Pl
Career Total (Turf)	**13**	**0**	**0**	**0**	**587**
Career Total (AW)	**4**	**0**	**0**	**0**	**0**

Going (Turf): **Sf: 0-3 GS: 0-3 Gd: 0-2 GF: 0-5 Fm: 0-0**
Distance: 5f/6f: 0-3 7f-8f: 0-10 9f-13f: 0-3 14f+: 0-1
Track : LH: 0-8 RH: 0-4 Tight: 0-2 Gall: 0-1
Aids: Bl: 0-0 Vi: 0-0 Tstrap: 0-1 Ckp: 0-1
Best Rating: **63** 5/06 Gdwd 6f soft

Almadaa

73(85) (66)**38**

2-y-o b c Exceed And Excel (AUS)-Masaader (USA) (Wild Again (USA))

E A L Dunlop Hamdan Al Maktoum

Placings:0340 **(6643)**

2009: 6^{0}G, 6^{3}SD, 6^{4}SD, 6^{0}G,

	Starts	1st	2nd	3rd	Win & Pl
Career Total (Turf)	**2**	**0**	**0**	**0**	
Career Total (AW)	**2**	**0**	**0**	**1**	**353**

Going (Turf): **Sf: 0-0 GS: 0-0 Gd: 0-2 GF: 0-0 Fm: 0-0**
Distance: 5f/6f: 0-4 7f-8f: 0-0 9f-13f: 0-0 14f+: 0-0
Track : LH: 0-2 RH: 0-0 Tight: 0-2 Gall: 0-0
Aids: Bl: 0-0 Vi: 0-0 Tstrap: 0-0 Ckp: 0-0
Best Rating: **66** 8/09 Ling 6f stand

Fair; stays 6f; acts on fast ground and Polytrack.

Almahaza (IRE)

(104) (72)**56**

5-y-o b g Alzao (USA)-Morna's Moment (USA) (Timeless Moment (USA))

A J Chamberlain G B Heffaran

Placings:0000002123/01014024042 **(7784)**

2009: 8^{0}SD, 8^{1}SD, 10^{0}SD, 8^{1}SD, 10^{4}SD, 13^{0}SD, 8^{2}SD, 12^{4}SD, 10^{0}SD, 8^{4}SD, 8^{2}SD,

	Starts	1st	2nd	3rd	Win & Pl
Career Total (Turf)	**6**	**1**	**0**	**0**	**2817**
Career Total (AW)	**15**	**2**	**4**	**1**	**6815**

Rating	Date	Course	Distance	Race	Going	Prize
63	3/09	Sthl	1m	(0-60)H	STD	£2047
61	2/09	Sthl	1m	(0-52)H	STD	£2047
55	10/07	Wind	1m2f7y		GD	£2817

Total win prize-money £6911

Going (Turf): Sf: 0-0 GS: 0-3 **Gd: 1-2** GF: 0-1 Fm: 0-0
Distance: 5f/6f: 0-0 **7f-8f: 2-6** 9f-13f: 1-13 14f+: 0-2
Track : **LH: 2-13** RH: 1-8 **Tight: 1-12** Gall: 0-0
Aids: **Bl: 1-7** Vi: 0-0 Tstrap: 0-2 Ckp: 0-2
Best Rating: **72** 12/09 Sthl 1m stand

Modest; effective over 1m-1m2f; acts on good ground and on sand.

Almamia

(89) (47)**68**

4-y-o b f Hernando (FR)-Alborada (Alzao (USA))

Sir Mark Prescott Miss K Rausing

Placings:333/6 (0178)
2009: 12^{6}SD,

	Starts	1st	2nd	3rd	Win & Pl
Career Total (Turf)	2	0	0	2	1156
Career Total (AW)	2	0	0	1	302

Going (Turf): Sf: 0-1 GS: 0-0 Gd: 0-0 GF: 0-1 Fm: 0-0
Distance: 5f/6f: 0-0 7f-8f: 0-1 9f-13f: 0-3 14f+: 0-0
Track: LH: 0-4 RH: 0-0 Tight: 0-1 Gall: 0-0
Aids: Bl: 0-0 Vi: 0-0 Tstrap: 0-0 Ckp: 0-0
Best Rating: 68 10/07 Nott 1m54y gd-fm

Fair form in maidens; acts on fast and in soft ground; will stay 1m2f; likely to win a race.

Almatlaie (USA)

(86) (33)35
3-y-o b f Elusive Quality (USA)-Hachiyah (IRE) (Generous (IRE))
J W Unett John Malone

Placings:0-60 (5882)
2009: 5^{6}SD, 5^{0}SD,

	Starts	1st	2nd	3rd	Win & Pl
Career Total (Turf)	1	0	0	0	
Career Total (AW)	2	0	0	0	0

Going (Turf): Sf: 0-0 GS: 0-0 Gd: 0-0 GF: 0-0 Fm: 0-0
Distance: 5f/6f: 0-3 7f-8f: 0-0 9f-13f: 0-0 14f+: 0-0
Track: LH: 0-2 RH: 0-1 Tight: 0-2 Gall: 0-0
Aids: Bl: 0-0 Vi: 0-0 Tstrap: 0-0 Ckp: 0-0
Best Rating: 35 10/08 Fair 6f sft-hvy

Almaty Express

92(112) (86)58
7-y-o b g Almaty (IRE)-Express Girl (Sylvan Express)
J R Weymes Highmoor Racing & Miss K Buckle

Placings:300341/0566024160000012/200133500006532/1 12120005064/113013333051600060-50110000000606 (7819)
2009: 5^{5}SD, 5^{0}SD, 5^{1}SD, 5^{1}SD, 5^{0}SD, 5^{0}G, 5^{0}SD, 5^{0}GF, 5^{0}SD, 5^{0}SD, 5^{0}SD, 5^{6}SD, 5^{0}SD, 5^{6}SD,

	Starts	1st	2nd	3rd	Win & Pl
Career Total (Turf)	25	1	1	2	5487
Career Total (AW)	56	12	5	8	49496

86 4/09 Wolv 5f20y (0-85)H STD £5180
82 3/09 Wolv 5f20y (0-80)H STD £5504
90 5/08 GrLe 5f (0-85)H STD £4533
85 2/08 Wolv 5f20y (0-75)H STD £2730
80 1/08 Wolv 5f20y (0-65)H STD £2047
77 1/08 Wolv 5f20y (0-65)H STD £1774
82 2/07 Wolv 5f20y (0-75)H STD £3071
81 1/07 Wolv 5f20y (0-70)H STD £3071
79 1/07 Wolv 5f20y (0-70)H STD £3238
69 2/06 Wolv 5f20y (0-75)H STD £3238
64 11/05 Wolv 5f20y (0-60)H STD £2867
64 8/05 Wolv 5f20y (0-70)H STD £3408
55 7/04 Catt 5f G G-F £2891
Total win prize-money £43560

Going (Turf): Sf: 0-4 GS: 0-1 Gd: 0-10 GF: 1-9 Fm: 0-1
Distance: 5f/6f: 13-81 7f-8f: 0-0 9f-13f: 0-0 14f+: 0-0
Track: LH: 12-59 RH: 0-3 Tight: 11-51 Gall: 1-7
Aids: Bl: 11-62 Vi: 0-0 Tstrap: 1-8 Ckp: 1-8
Best Rating: 90 5/08 GrLe 5f stand

Modest; best over 5f and acts on Polytrack; very effective from the front; goes well at Wolverhampton; usually wears blinkers.

Almazar

91(80) (57)55
3-y-o b g Green Desert (USA)-Zaqrah (USA) (Silver Hawk (USA))
J L Dunlop Hamdan Al Maktoum

Placings:000-55 (2417)
2009: 8^{5}GF, 7^{5}G,

	Starts	1st	2nd	3rd	Win & Pl
Career Total (Turf)	4	0	0	0	0
Career Total (AW)	1	0	0	0	

Going (Turf): Sf: 0-1 GS: 0-0 Gd: 0-1 GF: 0-2 Fm: 0-0
Distance: 5f/6f: 0-1 7f-8f: 0-3 9f-13f: 0-1 14f+: 0-0
Track: LH: 0-2 RH: 0-0 Tight: 0-1 Gall: 0-0
Aids: Bl: 0-0 Vi: 0-0 Tstrap: 0-0 Ckp: 0-0
Best Rating: 57 9/08 Ling 7f stand

Almiqdaad

115 105
3-y-o b c Haafhd-Etizaaz (USA) (Diesis)
M A Jarvis Hamdan Al Maktoum

Placings:415-5010 (6480)
2009: 10^{5}GS, 10^{0}GF, 10^{1}GF, 9^{0}GF,

	Starts	1st	2nd	3rd	Win & Pl
Career Total (Turf)	7	2	0	0	72044

105 9/09 Newb 1m2f6y (0-105)H G-F £62310
87 8/08 NmkJ 1m GD £5180
Total win prize-money £67491

Going (Turf): Sf: 0-0 GS: 0-1 Gd: 1-2 GF: 1-4 Fm: 0-0
Distance: 5f/6f: 0-0 7f-8f: 1-3 9f-13f: 1-4 14f+: 0-0
Track: LH: 1-1 RH: 0-3 Tight: 0-0 Gall: 1-3
Aids: Bl: 0-0 Vi: 0-0 Tstrap: 0-0 Ckp: 0-0
Best Rating: 105 9/09 Newb 1m2f6y gd-fm

Very useful; stays 1m2f; acts on good and fast ground.

Almora Guru

(93) (52)60
5-y-o b m Ishiguru (USA)-Princess Almora (Pivotal)
W M Brisbourne J W Jenkins

Placings:00456260/30102500006530/00-005544 (1037)
2009: 8^{0}SD, 8^{0}SD, 8^{5}SD, 8^{5}SF, 7^{4}SD, 8^{4}SD,

	Starts	1st	2nd	3rd	Win & Pl
Career Total (Turf)	18	1	2	1	4387
Career Total (AW)	12	0	0	1	302

57 4/07 Yarm 6f3y (0-65)H G-F £1943
Total win prize-money £1943

Going (Turf): Sf: 0-1 GS: 0-1 Gd: 0-5 GF: 1-11 Fm: 0-0
Distance: 5f/6f: 0-17 7f-8f: 1-6 9f-13f: 0-7 14f+: 0-0
Track: LH: 0-13 RH: 0-3 Tight: 0-11 Gall: 0-0
Aids: Bl: 0-0 Vi: 0-0 Tstrap: 0-1 Ckp: 0-1
Best Rating: 60 5/07 Rdcr 6f good

Plater; stays 1m; acts on Polytrack.

Almost Married (IRE)

88 (54)65
5-y-o b g Indian Ridge-Shining Hour (USA) (Red Ransom (USA))
J S Goldie Jim Goldie Racing Club

Placings:40/40010236-000 (6413)
2009: 5^{0}GF, 6^{0}GF, 6^{0}GF,

	Starts	1st	2nd	3rd	Win & Pl
Career Total (Turf)	11	1	1	1	5966
Career Total (AW)	2	0	0	0	192

65 8/08 Ayr 6f (0-70)H G-S £3885
Total win prize-money £3886

Going (Turf): Sf: 0-4 GS: 1-1 Gd: 0-3 GF: 0-3 Fm: 0-0
Distance: 5f/6f: 1-11 7f-8f: 0-2 9f-13f: 0-0 14f+: 0-0
Track: LH: 0-2 RH: 0-1 Tight: 0-2 Gall: 0-0
Aids: Bl: 0-0 Vi: 0-0 Tstrap: 0-0 Ckp: 0-0
Best Rating: 65 8/08 Ayr 6f gd-sft

Moderate; effective over 6f; acts on easy ground.

Almowj

84(98) (41)38
6-y-o b g Fasliyev (USA)-Tiriana (Common Grounds)
G H Jones G H Jones

Placings:5305/06500260006065/205/6040-000 (4220)
2009: 10^{0}G, 8^{0}G, 10^{0}G,

	Starts	1st	2nd	3rd	Win & Pl
Career Total (Turf)	12	0	0	1	866
Career Total (AW)	16	0	2	0	1191

Going (Turf): Sf: 0-0 GS: 0-0 Gd: 0-7 GF: 0-4 Fm: 0-1
Distance: 5f/6f: 0-3 7f-8f: 0-16 9f-13f: 0-9 14f+: 0-0
Track: LH: 0-17 RH: 0-5 Tight: 0-12 Gall: 0-0
Aids: Bl: 0-3 Vi: 0-0 Tstrap: 0-3 Ckp: 0-3
Best Rating: 62 9/05 Pont 6f good

Almuktahem

106(107) (88)86
3-y-o b c Green Desert (USA)-Nasanice (IRE) (Nashwan (USA))
Sir Michael Stoute Hamdan Al Maktoum

Placings:5421303 (5648)
2009: 7^{5}GS, 7^{4}GF, 8^{2}GF, 9^{1}GF, 10^{3}GS, 10^{0}GF, 10^{3}SD,

	Starts	1st	2nd	3rd	Win & Pl
Career Total (Turf)	6	1	1	1	4969
Career Total (AW)	1	0	0	1	1156

83 7/09 Ling 1m1f G-F £2729
Total win prize-money £2730

Going (Turf): Sf: 0-0 GS: 0-2 Gd: 0-0 GF: 1-4 Fm: 0-0
Distance: 5f/6f: 0-0 7f-8f: 0-2 9f-13f: 1-5 14f+: 0-0
Track: LH: 1-3 RH: 0-2 Tight: 1-3 Gall: 0-0
Aids: Bl: 0-0 Vi: 1-4 Tstrap: 0-0 Ckp: 0-0
Best Rating: 88 9/09 Ling 1m2f stand

Fair; stays 1m1f and acts on most ground; has worn a visor.

Almuntaser (IRE)

94 57
2-y-o b g Celtic Swing-Fire Reply (IRE) (Royal Academy (USA))
Ian Williams Dr Marwan Koukash

Placings:405050 (6905)
2009: 5^{4}GF, 6^{0}G, 6^{5}S, 6^{0}GF, 6^{5}GS, 6^{0}G,

	Starts	1st	2nd	3rd	Win & Pl
Career Total (Turf)	6	0	0	0	349

Going (Turf): Sf: 0-1 GS: 0-1 Gd: 0-2 GF: 0-2 Fm: 0-0
Distance: 5f/6f: 0-5 7f-8f: 0-1 9f-13f: 0-0 14f+: 0-0
Track: LH: 0-0 RH: 0-0 Tight: 0-0 Gall: 0-2
Aids: Bl: 0-2 Vi: 0-0 Tstrap: 0-0 Ckp: 0-0
Best Rating: 57 6/09 Wind 5f10y gd-fm

Almutaham (USA)

85 **52**

2-y-o b/br c Dynaformer (USA)-Forest Lady (USA) (Woodman (USA))

J L Dunlop Hamdan Al Maktoum

Placings:00 **(5499)**

2009: 7^{0}G, 8^{0}G,

	Starts	1st	2nd	3rd	Win & Pl
Career Total (Turf)	2	0	0	0	

Going (Turf): Sf: 0-0 GS: 0-0 Gd: 0-2 GF: 0-0 Fm: 0-0
Distance: 5f/6f: 0-0 7f-8f: 0-1 9f-13f: 0-1 14f+: 0-0
Track : LH: 0-0 RH: 0-0 Tight: 0-0 Gall: 0-0
Aids: Bl: 0-0 Vi: 0-0 Tstrap: 0-0 Ckp: 0-0
Best Rating: 52 8/09 Chep 1m14y good

Almutawaazin

57

3-y-o b g Nayef (USA)-Crown Water (USA) (Chief's Crown (USA))

M P Tregoning Hamdan Al Maktoum

Placings:0-00 **(1809)**

2009: 8^{0}S, 12^{0}GF,

	Starts	1st	2nd	3rd	Win & Pl
Career Total (Turf)	3	0	0	0	

Going (Turf): Sf: 0-1 GS: 0-1 Gd: 0-0 GF: 0-1 Fm: 0-0
Distance: 5f/6f: 0-0 7f-8f: 0-2 9f-13f: 0-1 14f+: 0-0
Track : LH: 0-0 RH: 0-1 Tight: 0-1 Gall: 0-0
Aids: Bl: 0-0 Vi: 0-0 Tstrap: 0-0 Ckp: 0-0

Alnadana (IRE)

109 **112**

4-y-o gr f Danehill Dancer (IRE)-Alnamara (FR) (Linamix (FR))

A De Royer-Dupre H H Aga Khan

Placings:12/554213-252120 **(6479)**

2009: 8^{2}S, 8^{5}S, 8^{2}G, 8^{1}GS, 9^{2}G, 8^{0}GF,

	Starts	1st	2nd	3rd	Win & Pl
Career Total (Turf)	14	3	5	1	228312

112	7/09	MsnL	1m		G-S	£38835
103	7/08	MsnL	1m		GD	£20221
87	8/07	Deau	1m		GD	£7095

Total win prize-money £66151

Going (Turf): Sf: 0-4 GS: 1-4 Gd: 2-5 GF: 0-1 Fm: 0-0
Distance: 5f/6f: 0-0 7f-8f: 3-11 9f-13f: 0-3 14f+: 0-0
Track : LH: 0-5 RH: 1-4 Tight: 0-1 Gall: 0-0
Aids: Bl: 0-0 Vi: 0-0 Tstrap: 0-0 Ckp: 0-0
Best Rating: 112 8/09 Arlt 1m1f110y good

Smart French filly; effective at 1m on good and easy ground.

Alnwick

109(105) (83)**83**

5-y-o b g Kylian (USA)-Cebwob (Rock City)

P D Cundell Entre Nous and P D Cundell

Placings:0000/4262653/13262141-30244042513043 **(7151)**

2009: 16^{3}SD, 16^{0}SD, 16^{2}SD, 16^{4}SD, 16^{4}GF, 14^{0}G, 16^{4}SD, 16^{2}GS, 21^{5}G, 16^{1}SD, 14^{3}G, 16^{0}GF, 16^{4}SD, 16^{3}G,

	Starts	1st	2nd	3rd	Win & Pl
Career Total (Turf)	14	2	1	3	14827
Career Total (AW)	19	2	5	2	13724

83	8/09	Kemp	2m	(0-85)H	STD	£4727
78	7/08	Newb	2m	(0-80)H	GD	£5180
77	6/08	Wwck	1m6f213y	(0-75)H	FRM	£3238
71	1/08	Kemp	2m	(0-65)H	STD	£2047

Total win prize-money £15194

Going (Turf): Sf: 0-0 GS: 0-1 Gd: 1-8 GF: 0-4 Fm: 1-1
Distance: 5f/6f: 0-1 7f-8f: 0-3 9f-13f: 0-4 14f+: 4-25
Track : LH: 2-14 RH: 2-18 Tight: 0-12 Gall: 0-2
Aids: Bl: 0-0 Vi: 0-0 Tstrap: 0-1 Ckp: 0-1
Best Rating: 83 10/09 NmkR 2m good

Fair; stays 2m; acts on firm and soft ground; goes on Polytrack; has worn cheekpieces.

Along The Nile

83 **53**

7-y-o b g Desert Prince (IRE)-Golden Fortune (Forzando)

K G Reveley William Hoey

Placings:03600460/0426531101/2010002020/020005/00-000 **(7248)**

2009: 10^{0}GF, 10^{0}GF, 10^{0}HY,

	Starts	1st	2nd	3rd	Win & Pl
Career Total (Turf)	39	4	5	2	42314

87	6/06	Newc	1m3y	(0-85)H	G-F	£6232
82	8/05	Pont	1m4y	(0-90)H	GD	£9340
74	7/05	Hayd	1m30y	(0-70)H	G-F	£5319
68	6/05	Pont	1m4y	(0-75)H	G-F	£5018

Total win prize-money £25910

Going (Turf): Sf: 0-6 GS: 0-6 Gd: 1-8 GF: 3-16 Fm: 0-3
Distance: 5f/6f: 0-4 7f-8f: 0-9 9f-13f: 4-26 14f+: 0-0
Track : LH: 3-23 RH: 0-7 Tight: 0-4 Gall: 0-5
Aids: Bl: 0-0 Vi: 0-0 Tstrap: 0-1 Ckp: 0-1
Best Rating: 91 9/06 Pont 1m2f6y gd-fm

Useful performer; stays 1m2f and acts on a fast surface; has worn a tongue tie; often held up; likes Pontefract.

Alotago (IRE)

81(73) (19)**46**

2-y-o ch f Tagula (IRE)-Batool (USA) (Bahri (USA))

D Nicholls Ian W Glenton

Placings:0600 **(6639)**

2009: 7^{0}G, 7^{6}GF, 8^{0}GS, 8^{0}SD,

	Starts	1st	2nd	3rd	Win & Pl
Career Total (Turf)	3	0	0	0	0
Career Total (AW)	1	0	0	0	

Going (Turf): Sf: 0-0 GS: 0-1 Gd: 0-1 GF: 0-1 Fm: 0-0
Distance: 5f/6f: 0-0 7f-8f: 0-3 9f-13f: 0-1 14f+: 0-0
Track : LH: 0-2 RH: 0-2 Tight: 0-1 Gall: 0-0
Aids: Bl: 0-0 Vi: 0-0 Tstrap: 0-0 Ckp: 0-0
Best Rating: 46 8/09 Bevl 7f100y gd-fm

Alpen Glen

111(96) (71)**97**

3-y-o ch f Halling (USA)-Anne D'Autriche (IRE) (Rainbow Quest (USA))

M Johnston Sheikh Hamdan Bin Mohammed Al Maktoum

Placings:1160050 **(7720)**

2009: 12^{1}GF, 10^{1}GF, 10^{6}G, 9^{0}G, 9^{0}GF, 10^{5}SD, 12^{0}SD,

	Starts	1st	2nd	3rd	Win & Pl
Career Total (Turf)	5	2	0	0	13163
Career Total (AW)	2	0	0	0	419

97	6/09	Ches	1m2f75y	(0-95)H	G-F	£9714
87	6/09	Chep	1m4f23y		G-F	£3238

Total win prize-money £12952

Going (Turf): Sf: 0-0 GS: 0-0 Gd: 0-2 GF: 2-3 Fm: 0-0
Distance: 5f/6f: 0-0 7f-8f: 0-0 9f-13f: 2-7 14f+: 0-0
Track : LH: 2-4 RH: 0-3 Tight: 1-4 Gall: 0-0
Aids: Bl: 0-0 Vi: 0-0 Tstrap: 0-0 Ckp: 0-0
Best Rating: 97 6/09 Ches 1m2f75y gd-fm

Very useful; stays 1m4f; acts on fast ground.

Alpes Maritimes

97(111) (92)**63**

5-y-o b g Danehill Dancer (IRE)-Miss Riviera (Kris)

G L Moore R A Green

Placings:0524/30533344211/2000-055630 **(3024)**

2009: 10^{0}SD, 10^{5}SD, 10^{5}SD, 10^{6}GF, 10^{3}SD, 10^{0}SD,

	Starts	1st	2nd	3rd	Win & Pl
Career Total (Turf)	14	0	1	4	5219
Career Total (AW)	11	2	2	1	11536

86	12/07	Ling	1m2f	(0-80)H	STD	£4605
75	11/07	Ling	1m2f		STD	£2817

Total win prize-money £7423

Going (Turf): Sf: 0-2 GS: 0-1 Gd: 0-4 GF: 0-7 Fm: 0-0
Distance: 5f/6f: 0-0 7f-8f: 0-9 9f-13f: 2-16 14f+: 0-0
Track : LH: 2-16 RH: 0-4 Tight: 2-11 Gall: 0-3
Aids: Bl: 0-0 Vi: 0-0 Tstrap: 0-5 Ckp: 0-5
Best Rating: 92 1/08 Ling 1m2f stand

Useful; effective over 7f-1m2f; acts on fast ground; also goes on Polytrack; has worn cheekpieces.

Alpha Tauri (USA)

101(85) (51)**77**

3-y-o b c Aldebaran (USA)-Seven Moons (JPN) (Sunday Silence (USA))

H R A Cecil Niarchos Family

Placings:66-2000 **(4786)**

2009: 7^{2}GF, 6^{0}GF, 6^{0}S, 6^{0}G,

	Starts	1st	2nd	3rd	Win & Pl
Career Total (Turf)	5	0	1	0	907
Career Total (AW)	1	0	0	0	0

Going (Turf): Sf: 0-1 GS: 0-0 Gd: 0-2 GF: 0-2 Fm: 0-0
Distance: 5f/6f: 0-3 7f-8f: 0-3 9f-13f: 0-0 14f+: 0-0
Track : LH: 0-2 RH: 0-0 Tight: 0-0 Gall: 0-1
Aids: Bl: 0-1 Vi: 0-0 Tstrap: 0-0 Ckp: 0-0
Best Rating: 77 4/09 Wwck 7f26y gd-fm

Alpha Vega (IRE)

81(94) (65)**49**

3-y-o b f Marju (IRE)-Szabo (IRE) (Anabaa (USA))

J R Fanshawe Lael Stable

Placings:043 **(7590)**

2009: 8^{0}G, 11^{4}SD, 12^{3}SD,

	Starts	1st	2nd	3rd	Win & Pl
Career Total (Turf)	1	0	0	0	
Career Total (AW)	2	0	0	1	578

Going (Turf): Sf: 0-0 GS: 0-0 Gd: 0-1 GF: 0-0 Fm: 0-0
Distance: 5f/6f: 0-0 7f-8f: 0-0 9f-13f: 0-3 14f+: 0-0
Track : LH: 0-1 RH: 0-2 Tight: 0-0 Gall: 0-0
Aids: Bl: 0-0 Vi: 0-2 Tstrap: 0-0 Ckp: 0-0

Best Rating: 65 10/09 Kemp 1m3f stand

Modest; stays 1m4f and acts on Polytrack; has worn a visor.

Alphacino

93(83) (46)66

2-y-o b g Hunting Lion (IRE)-Fading Away (Fraam)

P C Haslam (M R Channon 22/7) The Mount Racing Club

Placings:43255421500 **(7597)**

2009: 5^4G, 5^3SD, 6^2G, 6^5F, 7^5S, 7^4GF, 7^2S, 7^1G, 7^5G, 7^0GF, 8^0SD,

	Starts	1st	2nd	3rd	Win & Pl
Career Total (Turf)	9	1	2	0	6005
Career Total (AW)	2	0	0	1	454

66 7/09 Thsk 7f GD £4338

Total win prize-money £4339

Going (Turf): Sf: 0-2 GS: 0-0 **Gd: 1-4** GF: 0-2 Fm: 0-1
Distance: 5f/6f: 0-3 **7f-8f: 1-7** 9f-13f: 0-1 14f+: 0-0
Track : **LH: 1-4** RH: 0-2 **Tight: 1-4** Gall: 0-0
Aids: Bl: 0-0 Vi: 0-0 Tstrap: 1-4 Ckp: 1-4
Best Rating: 66 7/09 Thsk 7f good

Modest; effective at 7f; handles easy ground; has worn cheekpieces.

Alpine Rose (FR)

116 116

4-y-o gr f Linamix (FR)-Fragrant Hill (Shirley Heights)

A De Royer-Dupre Ecurie Des Monceaux

Placings:511335-312140 **(6850)**

2009: 10^3G, 10^1GS, 12^2S, 10^1G, 10^4G, 10^0G,

	Starts	1st	2nd	3rd	Win & Pl
Career Total (Turf)	12	4	1	3	355168

116 8/09 Deau 1m2f GD £138689
107 5/09 StCl 1m2f110y G-S £71942
7/08 Claf 1m3f SFT £10661
84 6/08 Chan 1m2f110y GD £8088

Total win prize-money £229381

Going (Turf): Sf: 1-2 GS: 1-2 **Gd: 2-7** GF: 0-0 Fm: 0-0
Distance: 5f/6f: 0-0 7f-8f: 0-0 **9f-13f: 4-12** 14f+: 0-0
Track : LH: 1-4 **RH: 2-5** Tight: 0-0 Gall: 0-0
Aids: Bl: 0-0 Vi: 0-0 Tstrap: 0-0 Ckp: 0-0
Best Rating: 116 8/09 Deau 1m2f good

Group-class; winner of the Group 1 Prix Jean Romanet in 2009; effective at 1m2f-1m4f; acts well on easy ground.

Alqaahir (USA)

89(105) (74)76

7-y-o b h Swain (IRE)-Crafty Example (USA) (Crafty Prospector (USA))

Lee Smyth Leslie Lavery

Placings:3/240660021-0001106 **(7672)**

2009: 8^0G, 7^0GY, 7^0S, 8^1SD, 8^1SD, 8^0SD, 8^6SD,

	Starts	1st	2nd	3rd	Win & Pl
Career Total (Turf)	9	0	1	1	1849
Career Total (AW)	8	3	1	0	10678

74 10/09 Wolv 1m141y (0-70)H STD £3238
72 10/09 Wolv 1m141y (0-70)H STD £3561
71 12/08 Kemp 7f (0-70)H STD £2914

Total win prize-money £9714

Going (Turf): Sf: 0-3 GS: 0-0 Gd: 0-3 GF: 0-2 Fm: 0-0
Distance: 5f/6f: 0-0 7f-8f: 1-8 **9f-13f: 2-9** 14f+: 0-0
Track : **LH: 2-11** RH: 1-3 **Tight: 2-7** Gall: 0-0
Aids: Bl: 0-0 Vi: 0-0 Tstrap: 0-0 Ckp: 0-0
Best Rating: 76 6/08 Rdcr 1m2f gd-fm

Modest; stays 1m plus; acts on soft ground; goes on Polytrack.

Alqaffay (IRE)

102(101) (76)79

4-y-o b c King's Best (USA)-Spirit Of Tara (IRE) (Sadler's Wells (USA))

J H M Gosden Hamdan Al Maktoum

Placings:03-23322 **(5773)**

2009: 9^2G, 12^3GS, 10^3GF, 9^2G, 10^2GF,

	Starts	1st	2nd	3rd	Win & Pl
Career Total (Turf)	5	0	3	2	4143
Career Total (AW)	2	0	0	1	578

Going (Turf): Sf: 0-0 GS: 0-1 Gd: 0-2 GF: 0-2 Fm: 0-0
Distance: 5f/6f: 0-0 7f-8f: 0-1 9f-13f: 0-6 14f+: 0-0
Track : LH: 0-4 RH: 0-3 Tight: 0-4 Gall: 0-1
Aids: Bl: 0-0 Vi: 0-0 Tstrap: 0-0 Ckp: 0-0
Best Rating: 79 6/09 Sals 1m1f198y good

Fair; effective over 1m2f; acts on fast and easy ground.

Alrafid (IRE)

(98) (63)

10-y-o ch g Halling (USA)-Ginger Tree (USA) (Dayjur (USA))

G L Moore G L Moore

Placings:02/1/0001062**2426**/05620060/0/**245** **(0393)**

2009: 16^2SD, 12^4SD, 13^5SD,

	Starts	1st	2nd	3rd	Win & Pl
Career Total (Turf)	19	2	4	0	29693
Career Total (AW)	7	0	2	0	2989

82 8/03 Gdwd 1m1f D(0-80)H GD £11017
79 4/02 Ripn 1m D G-F £4322

Total win prize-money £15341

Going (Turf): Sf: 0-3 GS: 0-0 **Gd: 1-9 GF: 1-7** Fm: 0-0
Distance: 5f/6f: 0-1 7f-8f: 1-7 9f-13f: 1-17 14f+: 0-1
Track : LH: 0-11 **RH: 2-12 Tight: 2-14** Gall: 0-4
Aids: Bl: 0-3 Vi: 0-0 Tstrap: 0-0 Ckp: 0-0
Best Rating: 93 12/03 Ling 1m2f stand

Fair; acts on fast, soft ground and Polytrack; effective at up to 2m; usually held up; has worn blinkers.

Alrasm (IRE)

100 92

2-y-o b g Acclamation-New Deal (Rainbow Quest (USA))

M A Jarvis Hamdan Al Maktoum

Placings:21002 **(6993)**

2009: 6^2G, 6^1GF, 6^0GF, 6^0GF, 8^2GS,

	Starts	1st	2nd	3rd	Win & Pl
Career Total (Turf)	5	1	2	0	7643

87 5/09 Donc 6f G-F £3885

Total win prize-money £3886

Going (Turf): Sf: 0-0 GS: 0-1 Gd: 0-1 **GF: 1-3** Fm: 0-0
Distance: **5f/6f: 1-3** 7f-8f: 0-2 9f-13f: 0-0 14f+: 0-0
Track : LH: 0-1 RH: 0-0 Tight: 0-0 Gall: 0-1
Aids: Bl: 0-0 Vi: 0-0 Tstrap: 0-0 Ckp: 0-0
Best Rating: 92 10/09 Donc 1m gd-sft

Useful; effective at 6f on fast ground.

Alsace Lorraine (IRE)

107 96

4-y-o b f Giant's Causeway (USA)-Mer De Corail (IRE) (Sadler's Wells (USA))

J R Fanshawe Merry Fox Stud Limited

Placings:246-112142 **(6267)**

2009: 8^1G, 8^1GF, 8^2GF, 9^1G, 9^4GF, 8^2G,

	Starts	1st	2nd	3rd	Win & Pl
Career Total (Turf)	9	3	3	0	36352

92 7/09 Gdwd 1m1f (0-100)H GD £12462
89 6/09 Donc 1m (0-80)H G-F £6476
77 4/09 Yarm 1m3y (0-75)H GD £3238

Total win prize-money £22176

Going (Turf): Sf: 0-0 GS: 0-0 **Gd: 2-4** GF: 1-5 Fm: 0-0
Distance: 5f/6f: 0-0 7f-8f: 1-4 **9f-13f: 2-5** 14f+: 0-0
Track : LH: 0-2 **RH: 1-3 Tight: 1-2** Gall: 0-1
Aids: Bl: 0-0 Vi: 0-0 Tstrap: 0-0 Ckp: 0-0
Best Rating: 96 9/09 Asct 1m good

Useful; effective over 1m; acts on fast ground.

Alsadaa (USA)

(108) (82)77

6-y-o b g Kingmambo (USA)-Aljawza (USA) (Riverman (USA))

Mrs L J Mongan Mrs P J Sheen

Placings:3/640/00**100**030503/12-60 **(5802)**

2009: 11^6SD, 12^0GF,

	Starts	1st	2nd	3rd	Win & Pl
Career Total (Turf)	13	1	0	3	7988
Career Total (AW)	6	1	1	0	4689

77 9/08 Asct 1m4f (0-80)H GD £6002
69 4/07 Sthl 7f (0-70)H STD £3071

Total win prize-money £9073

Going (Turf): Sf: 0-3 GS: 0-1 **Gd: 1-3** GF: 0-6 Fm: 0-0
Distance: 5f/6f: 0-0 7f-8f: 1-8 9f-13f: 1-11 14f+: 0-0
Track : LH: 1-11 RH: 1-3 Tight: 0-6 **Gall: 1-1**
Aids: Bl: 0-0 Vi: 0-0 Tstrap: 0-0 Ckp: 0-0
Best Rating: 82 2/09 Kemp 1m3f stand

Fair; effective over 7f-1m4f; acts on fast ground; also goes on Fibresand.

Alsahil (USA)

98(99) (77)78

3-y-o ch c Diesis-Tayibah (IRE) (Sadler's Wells (USA))

Micky Hammond (M P Tregoning 8/4) R D Bickenson

Placings:3-16 **(7769)**

2009: 7^1G, 8^6SD,

	Starts	1st	2nd	3rd	Win & Pl
Career Total (Turf)	1	1	0	0	3238
Career Total (AW)	2	0	0	1	626

78 4/09 Brig 7f214y GD £3238

Total win prize-money £3238

Going (Turf): Sf: 0-0 GS: 0-0 **Gd: 1-1** GF: 0-0 Fm: 0-0
Distance: 5f/6f: 0-0 **7f-8f: 1-3** 9f-13f: 0-0 14f+: 0-0
Track : **LH: 1-1** RH: 0-2 Tight: 0-0 Gall: 0-0
Aids: Bl: 0-0 Vi: 0-0 Tstrap: 0-0 Ckp: 0-0
Best Rating: 78 4/09 Brig 7f214y good

Fair; effective over 1m; acts on good ground.

Alseraaj (USA)

(97) (53)71

4-y-o ch f El Prado (IRE)-Barzah (IRE) (Darshaan)

Ian Williams Dr Marwan Koukash

Placings:6/0050050-**003** **(1122)**

2009: 8^0SD, 12^0SD, 10^3SD,

	Starts	1st	2nd	3rd	Win & Pl
Career Total (Turf)	8	0	0	0	0
Career Total (AW)	3	0	0	1	302

Going (Turf): **Sf: 0-2 GS: 0-1 Gd: 0-2 GF: 0-3 Fm: 0-0**
Distance: 5f/6f: 0-0 7f-8f: 0-4 9f-13f: 0-7 14f+: 0-0
Track : LH: 0-8 RH: 0-0 Tight: 0-4 Gall: 0-0
Aids: Bl: 0-0 Vi: 0-0 Tstrap: 0-0 Ckp: 0-0
Best Rating: **71** 6/08 Nott 1m2f50y gd-fm

Moderate; stays 1m2f and acts on Polytrack.

Alsufooh (USA)

88 **56**
2-y-o ch f Haafhd-Dufoof (USA) (Kingmambo (USA))
M Johnston Hamdan Al Maktoum

Placings:55 **(7167)**
2009: 7^5G, 7^5S,

	Starts	1st	2nd	3rd	Win & Pl
Career Total (Turf)	2	0	0	0	0

Going (Turf): **Sf: 0-1 GS: 0-0 Gd: 0-1 GF: 0-0 Fm: 0-0**
Distance: 5f/6f: 0-0 7f-8f: 0-2 9f-13f: 0-0 14f+: 0-0
Track : LH: 0-2 RH: 0-0 Tight: 0-1 Gall: 0-0
Aids: Bl: 0-0 Vi: 0-0 Tstrap: 0-0 Ckp: 0-0
Best Rating: **56** 10/09 Catt 7f good

Alternative Choice (USA)

(93) (62)
3-y-o b g Grand Slam (USA)-Northern Fleet (USA) (Afleet (CAN))
N P Littmoden A A Goodman

Placings:00-52 **(1036)**
2009: 7^5SD, 8^2SD,

	Starts	1st	2nd	3rd	Win & Pl
Career Total (Turf)	0	0	0	0	
Career Total (AW)	4	0	1	0	605

Going (Turf): **Sf: 0-0 GS: 0-0 Gd: 0-0 GF: 0-0 Fm: 0-0**
Distance: 5f/6f: 0-0 7f-8f: 0-4 9f-13f: 0-0 14f+: 0-0
Track : LH: 0-2 RH: 0-2 Tight: 0-2 Gall: 0-0
Aids: Bl: 0-0 Vi: 0-0 Tstrap: 0-0 Ckp: 0-0
Best Rating: **62** 10/08 Kemp 7f stand

Moderate; effective over 1m; acts on Polytrack.

Althabea

84(59) **46**
2-y-o b c Avonbridge-Mandolin (IRE) (Sabrehill (USA))
Ian Williams Dr Marwan Koukash

Placings:06000 **(6906)**
2009: 7^0SD, 5^6GF, 7^0G, 6^0GS, 6^0G,

	Starts	1st	2nd	3rd	Win & Pl
Career Total (Turf)	4	0	0	0	0
Career Total (AW)	1	0	0	0	

Going (Turf): **Sf: 0-0 GS: 0-1 Gd: 0-2 GF: 0-1 Fm: 0-0**
Distance: 5f/6f: 0-2 7f-8f: 0-3 9f-13f: 0-0 14f+: 0-0
Track : LH: 0-2 RH: 0-0 Tight: 0-1 Gall: 0-1
Aids: Bl: 0-1 Vi: 0-0 Tstrap: 0-0 Ckp: 0-0
Best Rating: **46** 7/09 Leic 5f2y gd-fm

Improved on debut when dropped to a seller; effective over 5f on fast ground.

Altilhar (USA)

(107) (83)**83**
6-y-o b g Dynaformer (USA)-Al Desima (Emperor Jones (USA))
G L Moore H R Hunt

Placings:0031/00002114/500/4-4 **(0511)**
2009: 16^4SD,

	Starts	1st	2nd	3rd	Win & Pl
Career Total (Turf)	11	2	1	0	9948
Career Total (AW)	6	1	0	1	5911
83 9/06 Sand	1m2f7y (0-80)H			G-F	£5505
81 8/06 Brig	1m1f209y (0-70)H			G-F	£3238
73 10/05 Ling	7f			STD	£4563

Total win prize-money £13307

Going (Turf): Sf: 0-1 GS: 0-1 Gd: 0-2 **GF: 2-7** Fm: 0-0
Distance: 5f/6f: 0-0 7f-8f: 1-4 **9f-13f: 2-11** 14f+: 0-2
Track : **LH: 2-9** RH: 1-5 **Tight: 1-9** Gall: 0-2
Aids: **Bl: 2-6** Vi: 0-0 Tstrap: 0-0 Ckp: 0-0
Best Rating: **86** 3/07 Ling 1m4f stand

Useful colt; stays 1m2f; acts on Polytrack and fast ground on turf; usually wears blinkers.

Altimatum (USA)

94(96) (64)**74**
3-y-o ch c Rahy (USA)-Aldiza (USA) (Storm Cat (USA))
P F I Cole D S Lee

Placings:60-200446 **(7671)**
2009: 7^2F, 8^0GF, 8^0SD, 8^4G, 12^4SD, 8^6SD,

	Starts	1st	2nd	3rd	Win & Pl
Career Total (Turf)	5	0	1	0	1298
Career Total (AW)	3	0	0	0	192

Going (Turf): **Sf: 0-1 GS: 0-0 Gd: 0-1 GF: 0-2 Fm: 0-1**
Distance: 5f/6f: 0-0 7f-8f: 0-4 9f-13f: 0-4 14f+: 0-0
Track : LH: 0-3 RH: 0-3 Tight: 0-1 Gall: 0 0
Aids: Bl: 0-2 Vi: 0-0 Tstrap: 0-0 Ckp: 0-0
Best Rating: **74** 7/09 Brig 7f214y firm

Fair; stays 1m and acts on fast ground.

Alto Singer (IRE)

(92) (36)**61**
4-y-o b f Alhaarth (IRE)-Sonatina (Distant Relative)
L A Dace N A Dunger

Placings:0/4060-00 **(0513)**
2009: 8^0SD, 8^0SD,

	Starts	1st	2nd	3rd	Win & Pl
Career Total (Turf)	5	0	0	0	0
Career Total (AW)	2	0	0	0	

Going (Turf): **Sf: 0-2 GS: 0-1 Gd: 0-0 GF: 0-2 Fm: 0-0**
Distance: 5f/6f: 0-3 7f-8f: 0-3 9f-13f: 0-1 14f+: 0-0
Track : LH: 0-3 RH: 0-2 Tight: 0-2 Gall: 0-1
Aids: Bl: 0-0 Vi: 0-0 Tstrap: 0-1 Ckp: 0-1
Best Rating: **61** 7/08 Wind 1m67y soft

Altos Reales

96(103) (57)**48**
5-y-o b m Mark Of Esteem (IRE)-Karsiyaka (IRE) (Kahyasi)
M J Scudamore (J G Given 27/8) F K Jennings

Placings:0000600414332/613004-0005200210 **(7840)**
2009: 9^0SD, 11^0SD, 11^0SD, 12^5GS, 11^2SD, 10^0GF, 11^0SD, 14^2SD, 12^1SD, 12^0SS,

	Starts	1st	2nd	3rd	Win & Pl
Career Total (Turf)	6	0	0	0	0
Career Total (AW)	23	3	3	3	8764
53 12/09 Wolv	1m4f50y (0-60)H			STD	£2047
62 2/08 Kemp	1m3f (0-60)H			STD	£2047
59 11/07 Kemp	1m3f (0-65)H			STD	£2047

Total win prize-money £6143

Going (Turf): **Sf: 0-0 GS: 0-1 Gd: 0-3 GF: 0-2 Fm: 0-0**
Distance: 5f/6f: 0-1 7f-8f: 0-2 **9f-13f: 3-24** 14f+: 0-2
Track : LH: 1-21 **RH: 2-7 Tight: 1-15** Gall: 0-2
Aids: Bl: 0-0 Vi: 0-0 Tstrap: 0-0 Ckp: 0-0
Best Rating: **62** 2/08 Kemp 1m3f stand

Moderate; stays 1m3f; acts easy ground and on sand.

Alubari

(87) (51)
2-y-o b c Tiger Hill (IRE)-Why So Silent (Mill Reef (USA))
W R Swinburn P W Harris

Placings:6 **(7050)**
2009: 7^6SD,

	Starts	1st	2nd	3rd	Win & Pl
Career Total (Turf)	0	0	0	0	
Career Total (AW)	1	0	0	0	0

Going (Turf): **Sf: 0-0 GS: 0-0 Gd: 0-0 GF: 0-0 Fm: 0-0**
Distance: 5f/6f: 0-0 7f-8f: 0-1 9f-13f: 0-0 14f+: 0-0
Track : LH: 0-0 RH: 0-1 Tight: 0-0 Gall: 0-0
Aids: Bl: 0-0 Vi: 0-0 Tstrap: 0-0 Ckp: 0-0
Best Rating: **51** 10/09 Kemp 7f stand

Alucica

(101) (62)**50**
6-y-o b m Celtic Swing-Acicula (IRE) (Night Shift (USA))
D Shaw Shakespeare Racing

Placings:0/00002040310/54614500010300-0350 **(0494)**
2009: 8^0SS, 8^3SD, 7^5SD, 10^0SD,

	Starts	1st	2nd	3rd	Win & Pl
Career Total (Turf)	6	0	0	1	304
Career Total (AW)	25	3	1	2	7233
61 7/08 Kemp	1m (0-58)H			STD	£2047
56 3/08 Kemp	7f (0-52)H			STD	£2047
51 6/07 Ling	7f (0-65)H			STD	£2047

Total win prize-money £6143

Going (Turf): **Sf: 0-0 GS: 0-1 Gd: 0-4 GF: 0-1 Fm: 0-0**
Distance: 5f/6f: 0-9 **7f-8f: 3-20** 9f-13f: 0-2 14f+: 0-0
Track : LH: 1-14 **RH: 2-12 Tight: 1-12** Gall: 0-0
Aids: Bl: 0-0 **Vi: 3-27** Tstrap: 0-0 Ckp: 0-0
Best Rating: **62** 10/08 Kemp 1m stand

Moderate; effective over 6f-1m; acts on good ground and on Polytrack; has worn various headgear.

Alvee (IRE)

99(94) (63)**62**
4-y-o br f Key Of Luck (USA)-Alleluia (Caerleon (USA))
J R Fanshawe Merry Fox Stud Limited

Placings:643-000 **(6025)**
2009: 16^0G, 14^0G, 13^0SD,

	Starts	1st	2nd	3rd	Win & Pl
Career Total (Turf)	4	0	0	0	202
Career Total (AW)	2	0	0	1	703

Going (Turf): **Sf: 0-1 GS: 0-1 Gd: 0-2 GF: 0-0 Fm: 0-0**

Distance: 5f/6f: 0-0 7f-8f: 0-0 9f-13f: 0-3 14f+: 0-3
Track : LH: 0-5 RH: 0-1 Tight: 0-3 Gall: 0-1
Aids: Bl: 0-0 Vi: 0-1 Tstrap: 0-0 Ckp: 0-0
Best Rating: 63 9/08 Kemp 1m4f stand

Modest half-sister to top-class stayer Allegretto; stays 1m4f; acts on Polytrack.

Alwaary (USA)

115(92) (75)120
3-y-o b c Dynaformer (USA)-Tabrir (IRE) (Unfuwain (USA))
J H M Gosden Hamdan Al Maktoum

Placings:31-41246 (5134)
2009: 11^4GF, 11^1G, 12^2G, 12^4G, 12^6GF,

	Starts	1st	2nd	3rd	Win & Pl
Career Total (Turf)	6	2	1	0	106465
Career Total (AW)	1	0	0	1	770

106 5/09 Gdwd 1m3f GD £22708
85 9/08 Yarm 1m3y GD £5046
Total win prize-money £27754

Going (Turf): Sf: 0-0 GS: 0-0 **Gd: 2-4** GF: 0-2 Fm: 0-0
Distance: 5f/6f: 0-0 7f-8f: 0-1 **9f-13f: 2-6** 14f+: 0-0
Track : LH: 0-2 **RH: 1-4 Tight: 1-2** Gall: 0-3
Aids: Bl: 0-0 Vi: 0-0 Tstrap: 0-0 Ckp: 0-0
Best Rating: 120 7/09 Asct 1m4f good

Listed class but probably up to Group class; effective at 1m4f and acts on good ground.

Alwarqaa

69 34
2-y-o b f Oasis Dream-Al Sifaat (Unfuwain (USA))
B W Hills Hamdan Al Maktoum

Placings:0 (7183)
2009: 7^0G,

	Starts	1st	2nd	3rd	Win & Pl
Career Total (Turf)	1	0	0	0	

Going (Turf): Sf: 0-0 GS: 0-0 Gd: 0-1 GF: 0-0 Fm: 0-0
Distance: 5f/6f: 0-0 7f-8f: 0-1 9f-13f: 0-0 14f+: 0-0
Track : LH: 0-0 RH: 0-0 Tight: 0-0 Gall: 0-0
Aids: Bl: 0-0 Vi: 0-0 Tstrap: 0-0 Ckp: 0-0
Best Rating: 34 10/09 NmkR 7f good

Always Best

94 (59)55
5-y-o b g Best Of The Bests (IRE)-Come To The Point (Pursuit Of Love)
R Allan Wares Scott-Watson Fraser Dickson

Placings:U01002330/15050254505004**2**/00031600-340P60 (5732)
2009: 13^3GF, 15^4GF, 12^0GS, 13^PG, 12^6S, 12^0GS,

	Starts	1st	2nd	3rd	Win & Pl
Career Total (Turf)	32	3	2	4	15093
Career Total (AW)	6	0	1	0	771

55 8/08 Ayr 1m5f13y (0-65)H SFT £2914
63 4/07 Catt 1m3f214y (0-75)H G-F £3238
65 7/06 Leic 7f9y G-F £4533
Total win prize-money £10687

Going (Turf): Sf: 1-6 GS: 0-5 Gd: 0-8 **GF: 2-11** Fm: 0-2
Distance: 5f/6f: 0-0 7f-8f: 1-6 9f-13f: 1-24 14f+: 1-8
Track : **LH: 2-25** RH: 0-10 **Tight: 1-21** Gall: 0-3
Aids: Bl: 0-2 Vi: 0-3 Tstrap: 0-2 Ckp: 0-2
Best Rating: 69 10/06 Wind 1m67y gd-sft

Moderate; stays 1m4f; acts on fast and easy ground.

Always Bold (IRE)

107(106) (93)94
4-y-o ch g King's Best (USA)-Tarakana (USA) (Shahrastani (USA))
D McCain Jnr T G Leslie

Placings:321001106331000-0203 (4769)
2009: 20^0GF, 15^2G, 21^0G, 16^3GS,

	Starts	1st	2nd	3rd	Win & Pl
Career Total (Turf)	14	3	1	1	28816
Career Total (AW)	5	1	1	3	6296

94 9/08 Haml 1m5f9y (0-95)H SFT £10592
93 7/08 NmkJ 1m6f175y (0-85)H G-F £6476
93 7/08 Haml 1m5f9y (0-85)H GD £7447
81 2/08 Wolv 1m4f50y STD £2457
Total win prize-money £26973

Going (Turf): Sf: 1-1 GS: 0-3 **Gd: 1-5 GF: 1-5** Fm: 0-0
Distance: 5f/6f: 0-0 7f-8f: 0-0 9f-13f: 1-6 **14f+: 3-13**
Track : LH: 1-7 **RH: 3-12 Tight: 3-8** Gall: 1-8
Aids: Bl: 0-0 Vi: 0-0 Tstrap: 0-0 Ckp: 0-0
Best Rating: 94 9/08 Haml 1m5f9y soft

Useful; stays at least 2m; acts on most ground on turf; goes on Polytrack.

Always Certain (USA)

(99) (68)70
4-y-o ch g Giant's Causeway (USA)-Mining Missharriet (USA) (Mining (USA))
P G Murphy J Cooper

Placings:66/**2**40010004000-650 (0743)
2009: 12^6SD, 16^5SD, 14^0SD,

	Starts	1st	2nd	3rd	Win & Pl
Career Total (Turf)	7	1	0	0	3562
Career Total (AW)	10	0	1	0	1131

70 6/08 Ches 1m2f75y (0-70)H G-F £3561
Total win prize-money £3562

Going (Turf): Sf: 0-1 GS: 0-1 Gd: 0-2 **GF: 1-3** Fm: 0-0
Distance: 5f/6f: 0-1 7f-8f: 0-5 **9f-13f: 1-9** 14f+: 0-2
Track : **LH: 1-10** RH: 0-5 **Tight: 1-8** Gall: 0-1
Aids: Bl: 0-0 Vi: 0-0 Tstrap: 0-0 Ckp: 0-0
Best Rating: 70 6/08 Ches 1m2f75y gd-fm

Moderate; effective over 1m2f; acts on Polytrack and on fast ground on turf.

Always Dazzling

94 62
2-y-o ch f Cadeaux Genereux-Woodlass (USA) (Woodman (USA))
M Johnston Always Trying Partnership VII

Placings:2 (3910)
2009: 6^2GF,

	Starts	1st	2nd	3rd	Win & Pl
Career Total (Turf)	1	0	1	0	867

Going (Turf): Sf: 0-0 GS: 0-0 Gd: 0-0 GF: 0-1 Fm: 0-0
Distance: 5f/6f: 0-1 7f-8f: 0-0 9f-13f: 0-0 14f+: 0-0
Track : LH: 0-0 RH: 0-0 Tight: 0-0 Gall: 0-0
Aids: Bl: 0-0 Vi: 0-0 Tstrap: 0-0 Ckp: 0-0
Best Rating: 62 7/09 Ayr 6f gd-fm

Always De One

88(82) (40)57
2-y-o b f Fruits Of Love (USA)-Yes Virginia (USA) (Roanoke (USA))
M Johnston Always Trying Partnership VII

Placings:0400 (7597)
2009: 7^0GF, 7^4GF, 8^0GF, 8^0SD,

	Starts	1st	2nd	3rd	Win & Pl
Career Total (Turf)	3	0	0	0	385
Career Total (AW)	1	0	0	0	

Going (Turf): Sf: 0-0 GS: 0-0 Gd: 0-0 GF: 0-3 Fm: 0-0
Distance: 5f/6f: 0-0 7f-8f: 0-3 9f-13f: 0-1 14f+: 0-0
Track : LH: 0-1 RH: 0-1 Tight: 0-1 Gall: 0-0
Aids: Bl: 0-0 Vi: 0-0 Tstrap: 0-0 Ckp: 0-0
Best Rating: 57 10/09 Rdcr 1m gd-fm

Always Dixie (IRE)

84(87) (60)50
2-y-o b f Lucky Story (USA)-Jerre Jo Glanville (USA) (Skywalker (USA))
M Johnston Always Trying Partnership VII

Placings:3500 (7887)
2009: 5^3GF, 7^5SD, 7^0SD, 7^0SD,

	Starts	1st	2nd	3rd	Win & Pl
Career Total (Turf)	1	0	0	1	578
Career Total (AW)	3	0	0	0	0

Going (Turf): Sf: 0-0 GS: 0-0 Gd: 0-0 GF: 0-1 Fm: 0-0
Distance: 5f/6f: 0-1 7f-8f: 0-3 9f-13f: 0-0 14f+: 0-0
Track : LH: 0-3 RH: 0-0 Tight: 0-2 Gall: 0-0
Aids: Bl: 0-0 Vi: 0-0 Tstrap: 0-0 Ckp: 0-0
Best Rating: 60 12/09 Wolv 7f32y stand

Moderate half-sister to Parkview Love; promise on debut over 5f on fast ground well beaten on Fibresand on next run in December.

Always Engaged

(82) (24)
4-y-o b f Compton Place-Good Standing (USA) (Distant View (USA))
J R Norton J R Norton Ltd

Placings:0-06 (0380)
2009: 6^0SS, 5^6SD,

	Starts	1st	2nd	3rd	Win & Pl
Career Total (Turf)	0	0	0	0	
Career Total (AW)	3	0	0	0	0

Going (Turf): Sf: 0-0 GS: 0-0 Gd: 0-0 GF: 0-0 Fm: 0-0
Distance: 5f/6f: 0-2 7f-8f: 0-1 9f-13f: 0-0 14f+: 0-0
Track : LH: 0-2 RH: 0-0 Tight: 0-0 Gall: 0-0
Aids: Bl: 0-0 Vi: 0-0 Tstrap: 0-0 Ckp: 0-0
Best Rating: 24 1/09 Sthl 6f std-slw

Always Roses

73(82) (33)30
2-y-o ch f Generous (IRE)-Arcady (Slip Anchor)
C C Bealby J H Henderson

Placings:050 (7450)
2009: 10^0GF, 8^5SD, 8^0SD,

	Starts	1st	2nd	3rd	Win & Pl
Career Total (Turf)	1	0	0	0	
Career Total (AW)	2	0	0	0	0

Going (Turf): Sf: 0-0 GS: 0-0 Gd: 0-0 GF: 0-1 Fm: 0-0
Distance: 5f/6f: 0-0 7f-8f: 0-2 9f-13f: 0-1 14f+: 0-0
Track: LH: 0-2 RH: 0-1 Tight: 0-0 Gall: 0-0
Aids: Bl: 0-0 Vi: 0-0 Tstrap: 0-0 Ckp: 0-0
Best Rating: 33 11/09 Sthl 1m stand

Always The Sun

93(98) (59)50
3-y-o b f Intikhab (USA)-Dane Dancing (IRE) (Danehill (USA))
P Leech Miss C Elbrow

Placings:600-0U54005656 (7652)
2009: 8⁰SD, 7ᵁSD, 9⁵GF, 6⁴G, 6⁰G, 6⁰G, 8⁵SD, 7⁶SD, 7⁵SD, 8⁶SD,

	Starts	1st	2nd	3rd	Win & Pl
Career Total (Turf)	4	0	0	0	144
Career Total (AW)	9	0	0	0	138

Going (Turf): Sf: 0-0 GS: 0-0 Gd: 0-3 GF: 0-1 Fm: 0-0
Distance: 5f/6f: 0-3 7f-8f: 0-8 9f-13f: 0-2 14f+: 0-0
Track: LH: 0-9 RH: 0-1 Tight: 0-5 Gall: 0-2
Aids: Bl: 0-0 Vi: 0-0 Tstrap: 0-8 Ckp: 0-8
Best Rating: 59 11/09 Kemp 7f stand

Moderate; stays 7f; acts on Polytrack; has worn cheek-pieces.

Alyarf (USA)

107 109
3-y-o b c Dixie Union (USA)-Tabheej (IRE) (Mujtahid (USA))
B W Hills Hamdan Al Maktoum

Placings:01-41 (2278)
2009: 8⁴GF, 7¹GF,

	Starts	1st	2nd	3rd	Win & Pl
Career Total (Turf)	4	2	0	0	30084
109 5/09 NmkR 7f			G-F		£22708
98 9/08 Hayd 6f			G-F		£3885

Total win prize-money £26594

Going (Turf): Sf: 0-0 GS: 0-1 Gd: 0-0 **GF: 2-3** Fm: 0-0
Distance: 5f/6f: 1-2 7f-8f: 1-2 9f-13f: 0-0 14f+: 0-0
Track: LH: 0-0 RH: 0-0 Tight: 0-0 Gall: 0-0
Aids: Bl: 0-0 Vi: 0-0 Tstrap: 0-0 Ckp: 0-0
Best Rating: 109 5/09 NmkR 7f gd-fm

Smart; Listed winner; effective at 6f-1m; acts on fast ground.

Alyseve

81(79) (19)33
4-y-o b f Averti (IRE)-Leen (Distant Relative)
Mrs C A Dunnett Ron Spore

Placings:000-00606 (3245)
2009: 6⁰G, 7⁰GF, 5⁶G, 5⁰GF, 9⁶GF,

	Starts	1st	2nd	3rd	Win & Pl
Career Total (Turf)	6	0	0	0	0
Career Total (AW)	2	0	0	0	

Going (Turf): Sf: 0-1 GS: 0-0 Gd: 0-2 GF: 0-3 Fm: 0-0
Distance: 5f/6f: 0-3 7f-8f: 0-3 9f-13f: 0-2 14f+: 0-0
Track: LH: 0-5 RH: 0-0 Tight: 0-2 Gall: 0-1

Aids: Bl: 0-0 Vi: 0-0 Tstrap: 0-3 Ckp: 0-3
Best Rating: 33 5/09 Catt 5f212y good

Am I Blue

99(96) (48)65
3-y-o b f Dubai Destination (USA)-Seal Indigo (IRE) (Glenstal (USA))
Tim Vaughan (H J L Dunlop 5/10) David Lovell

Placings:6-4000025 (6543)
2009: 10⁴GF, 9⁰SD, 14⁰G, 11⁰GS, 12⁰SD, 15²GF, 14⁵GF,

	Starts	1st	2nd	3rd	Win & Pl
Career Total (Turf)	6	0	1	0	797
Career Total (AW)	2	0	0	0	

Going (Turf): Sf: 0-0 GS: 0-2 Gd: 0-1 GF: 0-3 Fm: 0-0
Distance: 5f/6f: 0-0 7f-8f: 0-0 9f-13f: 0-5 14f+: 0-3
Track: LH: 0-6 RH: 0-2 Tight: 0-7 Gall: 0-0
Aids: Bl: 0-1 Vi: 0-0 Tstrap: 0-0 Ckp: 0-0
Best Rating: 65 4/09 Bath 1m2f46y gd-fm

Amanda Carter

107 92
6-y-o b m Tobougg (IRE)-Al Guswa (Shernazar)
R A Fahey Mrs Janis Macpherson

Placings:00/0126106/012016150-3054066155 (7018)
2009: 10³G, 12⁰G, 10⁵GF, 10⁴GF, 9⁰G, 12⁶GF, 16⁶GS, 13¹G, 13⁵GF, 12⁵GS,

	Starts	1st	2nd	3rd		Win & Pl
Career Total (Turf)	28	6	2	1		41645
92 9/09 Ayr	1m5f13y	(0-90)H			GD	£11527
89 7/08 Newc	1m2f32y	(0-80)H			G-F	£7447
84 7/08 Hayd	1m3f200y	(0-80)H			GD	£5504
71 5/08 Donc	1m4f	(0-70)H			G-F	£3238
71 7/07 Newc	1m2f32y	(0-80)H			GD	£6477
63 6/07 Carl	1m1f61y	(0-70)H			GD	£2817

Total win prize-money £37011

Going (Turf): Sf: 0-1 GS: 0-5 **Gd: 4-9** GF: 2-13 Fm: 0-0
Distance: 5f/6f: 0-0 7f-8f: 0-2 **9f-13f: 5-22** 14f+: 1-4
Track: **LH: 5-21** RH: 1-7 Tight: 0-8 **Gall: 3-10**
Aids: Bl: 0-0 Vi: 0-0 Tstrap: 0-0 Ckp: 0-0
Best Rating: 92 9/09 Ayr 1m5f13y good

Useful; stays 1m5f; acts on good and fast ground.

Amanjena

105(94) (86)95
4-y-o b f Beat Hollow-Placement (Kris)
A M Balding Mrs M E Wates

Placings:63/016021-6500 (6239)
2009: 10⁶GS, 10⁵GF, 10⁰GF, 10⁰G,

	Starts	1st	2nd	3rd		Win & Pl
Career Total (Turf)	11	1	1	1		15099
Career Total (AW)	1	1	0	0		2590
95 9/08 Asct	1m2f	(0-90)			G-F	£11215
86 4/08 Kemp	1m2f	(0-75)H			STD	£2590

Total win prize-money £13806

Going (Turf): Sf: 0-1 GS: 0-1 Gd: 0-2 **GF: 1-7** Fm: 0-0
Distance: 5f/6f: 0-0 7f-8f: 0-2 **9f-13f: 2-10** 14f+: 0-0
Track: LH: 0-6 **RH: 2-4** Tight: 0-4 **Gall: 1-4**
Aids: Bl: 0-0 Vi: 0-0 Tstrap: 0-0 Ckp: 0-0
Best Rating: 95 9/08 Asct 1m2f gd-fm

Useful; suited by 1m2f; acts on fast ground and on Polytrack.

Amarillo Slim (IRE)

82(88) (37)13
5-y-o b g Danehill Dancer (IRE)-Jungle Story (IRE) (Alzao (USA))
S Curran Micky Power

Placings:00030/000/00-0 (2634)
2009: 11⁰GF,

	Starts	1st	2nd	3rd	Win & Pl
Career Total (Turf)	9	0	0	1	612
Career Total (AW)	2	0	0	0	

Going (Turf): Sf: 0-2 GS: 0-0 Gd: 0-2 GF: 0-2 Fm: 0-0
Distance: 5f/6f: 0-1 7f-8f: 0-6 9f-13f: 0-4 14f+: 0-0
Track: LH: 0-8 RH: 0-1 Tight: 0-2 Gall: 0-0
Aids: Bl: 0-1 Vi: 0-0 Tstrap: 0-0 Ckp: 0-0
Best Rating: 71 10/06 Navn 5f yld-sft

Amary (IRE)

96 81
2-y-o b f Acclamation-Amistad (GER) (Winged Love (IRE))
C E Brittain Saeed Manana

Placings:1206 (6447)
2009: 6¹GF, 6²G, 6⁰G, 7⁶GF,

	Starts	1st	2nd	3rd	Win & Pl
Career Total (Turf)	4	1	1	0	9451
78 5/09 Newc 6f			G-F		£4921

Total win prize-money £4922

Going (Turf): Sf: 0-0 GS: 0-0 Gd: 0-2 **GF: 1-2** Fm: 0-0
Distance: **5f/6f: 1-3** 7f-8f: 0-1 9f-13f: 0-0 14f+: 0-0
Track: LH: 0-0 RH: 0-0 Tight: 0-0 Gall: 0-0
Aids: Bl: 0-0 Vi: 0-0 Tstrap: 0-0 Ckp: 0-0
Best Rating: 81 7/09 NmkJ 6f good

Useful; effective over 6f; acts on good and faster ground.

Amatara (IRE)

(90) (30)38
3-y-o b f Indian Haven-Mother's Hope (IRE) (Idris (IRE))
B G Powell B McNamee, P Webb, R Vaughan

Placings:0400-000 (1183)
2009: 8⁰SD, 8⁰SD, 10⁰SD,

	Starts	1st	2nd	3rd	Win & Pl
Career Total (Turf)	3	0	0	0	385
Career Total (AW)	4	0	0	0	

Going (Turf): Sf: 0-2 GS: 0-0 Gd: 0-0 GF: 0-1 Fm: 0-0
Distance: 5f/6f: 0-1 7f-8f: 0-4 9f-13f: 0-2 14f+: 0-0
Track: LH: 0-1 RH: 0-4 Tight: 0-0 Gall: 0-0
Aids: Bl: 0-0 Vi: 0-0 Tstrap: 0-1 Ckp: 0-1
Best Rating: 38 9/08 Leic 1m60y heavy

Amazing Blue Sky

104(98) (63)77
3-y-o b g Barathea (IRE)-Azure Lake (USA) (Lac Ouimet (USA))
Mrs R A Carr David W Chapman

Placings:0400145-033262005200231131 (4715)
2009: 9⁰SF, 8³SD, 11³SD, 8²SD, 11⁶GF, 11²SD, 8⁰GS, 8⁰GF, 12⁵SD, 10²G, 8⁰G, 12⁰GF, 10²G, 8³GS, 10¹GS, 10¹G, 9³GF, 10¹GS,

	Starts	1st	2nd	3rd	Win & Pl
Career Total (Turf)	13	3	2	2	16952
Career Total (AW)	12	1	2	2	5718

77 8/09 Sand 1m2f7y (0-90)H G-S £7771
73 7/09 Donc 1m2f60y (0-70)H GD £3238
71 7/09 Donc 1m2f60y (0-70)H G-S £3412
63 12/08 Wolv 1m1f103y STD £3238
Total win prize-money £17659

Going (Turf): Sf: 0-0 **GS: 2-4** Gd: 1-5 GF: 0-4 Fm: 0-0
Distance: 5f/6f: 0-0 7f-8f: 0-7 **9f-13f: 4-18** 14f+: 0-0
Track : **LH: 3-18** RH: 1-6 Tight: 1-9 **Gall: 2-2**
Aids: Bl: 0-6 Vi: 0-0 Tstrap: 0-0 Ckp: 0-0
Best Rating: 77 8/09 Sand 1m2f7y gd-sft

Moderate; stays 1m2f; acts on Fibresand and Polytrack and good ground on turf.

Amazing King (IRE)

101(99) (68)74
5-y-o b g King Charlemagne (USA)-Kraemer (USA) (Lyphard (USA))
P A Kirby The New Venture Partnership

Placings:0656/03045/041-061220 **(6768)**
2009: 9^{0}G, 12^{6}GF, 11^{1}G, 11^{2}GS, 12^{2}GF, 12^{0}GS,

	Starts	1st	2nd	3rd	Win & Pl
Career Total (Turf)	14	1	2	1	3921
Career Total (AW)	4	1	0	0	2605

68 7/09 Yarm 1m3f101y (0-60)H GD £2072
68 11/08 Wolv 1m4f50y (0-55)H STD £2388
Total win prize-money £4460

Going (Turf): Sf: 0-1 GS: 0-4 **Gd: 1-5** GF: 0-4 Fm: 0-0
Distance: 5f/6f: 0-1 7f-8f: 0-8 **9f-13f: 2-9** 14f+: 0-0
Track : **LH: 2-8** RH: 0-8 **Tight: 2-7** Gall: 0-1
Aids: Bl: 0-0 Vi: 0-0 Tstrap: 0-0 Ckp: 0-0
Best Rating: 74 8/09 Muss 1m4f100y gd-fm

Modest; stays 1m4f; acts on fast ground.

Amazing Memories (IRE)

70 16
3-y-o b c Barathea (IRE)-Early Memory (USA) (Devil's Bag (USA))
John A Harris Triumph 8 International

Placings:0-0 **(6573)**
2009: 7^{0}GF,

	Starts	1st	2nd	3rd	Win & Pl
Career Total (Turf)	2	0	0	0	

Going (Turf): Sf: 0-1 GS: 0-0 Gd: 0-0 GF: 0-1 Fm: 0-0
Distance: 5f/6f: 0-0 7f-8f: 0-2 9f-13f: 0-0 14f+: 0-0
Track : LH: 0-0 RH: 0-1 Tight: 0-0 Gall: 0-0
Aids: Bl: 0-0 Vi: 0-0 Tstrap: 0-0 Ckp: 0-0
Best Rating: 16 10/09 Leic 7f9y gd-fm

Amazing Tiger (GER)

103(104) (85)73
3-y-o b c Tiger Hill (IRE)-Allure (GER) (Konigsstuhl (GER))
M Johnston Sheikh Hamdan Bin Mohammed Al Maktoum

Placings:510620 **(6846)**
2009: 10^{5}G, 8^{1}GF, 12^{0}SD, 8^{6}GF, 8^{2}SS, 7^{0}G,

	Starts	1st	2nd	3rd	Win & Pl
Career Total (Turf)	4	1	0	0	2267
Career Total (AW)	2	0	1	0	806

73 6/09 Muss 1m G-F £2266
Total win prize-money £2267

Going (Turf): Sf: 0-0 GS: 0-0 Gd: 0-2 **GF: 1-2** Fm: 0-0
Distance: 5f/6f: 0-0 **7f-8f: 1-3** 9f-13f: 0-3 14f+: 0-0
Track : LH: 0-4 **RH: 1-2 Tight: 1-4** Gall: 0-1
Aids: Bl: 0-0 Vi: 0-0 Tstrap: 0-0 Ckp: 0-0
Best Rating: 85 10/09 Ling 1m std-slw

Fair; stays 1m2f; acts on a sound surface and on Polytrack.

Amazing Valour (IRE)

7-y-o b g Sinndar (IRE)-Flabbergasted (IRE) (Sadler's Wells (USA))
P Bowen Gwilym J Morris

Placings:200/500/0 **(4168)**
2009: 16^{0}G,

	Starts	1st	2nd	3rd	Win & Pl
Career Total (Turf)	7	0	1	0	1716

Going (Turf): Sf: 0-1 GS: 0-0 Gd: 0-2 GF: 0-2 Fm: 0-2
Distance: 5f/6f: 0-0 7f-8f: 0-0 9f-13f: 0-5 14f+: 0-2
Track : LH: 0-6 RH: 0-1 Tight: 0-0 Gall: 0-1
Aids: Bl: 0-2 Vi: 0-0 Tstrap: 0-0 Ckp: 0-0
Best Rating: 69 6/05 Bell 1m6f good

Amber Glow

5-y-o ch m Tumbleweed Ridge-Sweet Victoria (IRE) (Mukaddamah (USA))
A Berry B J Forber

Placings:PP **(7221)**
2009: 10^{P}GF, 11^{P}S,

	Starts	1st	2nd	3rd	Win & Pl
Career Total (Turf)	2	0	0	0	

Going (Turf): Sf: 0-1 GS: 0-0 Gd: 0-0 GF: 0-1 Fm: 0-0
Distance: 5f/6f: 0-0 7f-8f: 0-0 9f-13f: 0-2 14f+: 0-0
Track : LH: 0-2 RH: 0-0 Tight: 0-2 Gall: 0-0
Aids: Bl: 0-0 Vi: 0-0 Tstrap: 0-0 Ckp: 0-0

Amber Moon

83(99) (60)49
4-y-o ch m Singspiel (IRE)-Merewood (USA) (Woodman (USA))
Miss A Stokell (J A Osborne 10/3) Ms Caron Stokell

Placings:0064-22433115605000 (3717)
2009: 7^{2}SD, 7^{2}SD, 8^{4}SD, 8^{3}SD, 8^{3}SD, 8^{1}SF, 8^{1}SD, 9^{5}SD, 8^{6}SD, 10^{0}GF, 8^{5}SD, 7^{0}GF, 8^{0}G, 8^{0}SD,

	Starts	1st	2nd	3rd	Win & Pl
Career Total (Turf)	3	0	0	0	149
Career Total (AW)	15	2	2	2	5695

54 3/09 Sthl 1m (0-55) STD £1706
60 3/09 Wolv 1m141y (0-50)H SF £2388
Total win prize-money £4094

Going (Turf): Sf: 0-0 GS: 0-0 Gd: 0-1 GF: 0-2 Fm: 0-0
Distance: 5f/6f: 0-0 7f-8f: 1-8 9f-13f: 1-10 14f+: 0-0
Track : **LH: 2-16** RH: 0-2 **Tight: 1-8** Gall: 0-0
Aids: **Bl: 2-15** Vi: 0-0 Tstrap: 0-0 Ckp: 0-0
Best Rating: 60 3/09 Wolv 1m141y std-fst

Moderate; effective over 7f-1m and acts on sand; has worn blinkers.

Amber Ridge

102(95) (41)56
4-y-o b g Tumbleweed Ridge-Amber Brown (Thowra (FR))
B P J Baugh Saddle Up Racing

Placings:00654/000000-006030220000 (5179)
2009: 8^{0}SD, 9^{0}SD, 9^{6}SD, 10^{0}GF, 8^{3}GF, 8^{0}GS, 8^{2}GF, 8^{2}GF, 8^{0}GF, 8^{0}G, 8^{0}G, 8^{0}G,

	Starts	1st	2nd	3rd	Win & Pl
Career Total (Turf)	16	0	2	1	2649
Career Total (AW)	7	0	0	0	0

Going (Turf): Sf: 0-2 GS: 0-3 Gd: 0-6 GF: 0-5 Fm: 0-0
Distance: 5f/6f: 0-4 7f-8f: 0-8 9f-13f: 0-11 14f+: 0-0
Track : LH: 0-12 RH: 0-0 Tight: 0-7 Gall: 0-2
Aids: Bl: 0-0 Vi: 0-1 Tstrap: 0-3 Ckp: 0-3
Best Rating: 56 6/09 NmkJ 1m gd-fm

Moderate; effective over 1m; acts on fast ground.

Amber Sunset

97(96) (64)78
3-y-o b f Monsieur Bond (IRE)-Quantum Lady (Mujadil (USA))
J Jay David J Orchard

Placings:40432401140-00000405 (7861)
2009: 7^{0}GF, 7^{0}G, 7^{0}G, 7^{0}SD, 7^{0}SD, 7^{4}SS, 8^{0}SS, 7^{5}SD,

	Starts	1st	2nd	3rd	Win & Pl
Career Total (Turf)	12	2	1	1	15740
Career Total (AW)	7	0	0	0	409

78 10/08 Catt 7f (0-85) G-S £3885
75 10/08 Wwck 7f26y SFT £2914
Total win prize-money £6800

Going (Turf): Sf: 1-2 GS: 1-3 Gd: 0-4 GF: 0-2 Fm: 0-1
Distance: 5f/6f: 0-7 **7f-8f: 2-12** 9f-13f: 0-0 14f+: 0-0
Track : **LH: 2-10** RH: 0-2 **Tight: 1-6** Gall: 0-0
Aids: Bl: 0-0 Vi: 0-0 Tstrap: 0-0 Ckp: 0-0
Best Rating: 78 10/08 Catt 7f gd-sft

Fair; effective over 5f-7f; acts on most ground; goes on Polytrack.

Ambitious Choice (IRE)

91 (24)43
3-y-o b f Choisir (AUS)-Alexander Ambition (IRE) (Entrepreneur)
Muredach Kelly Mrs E Dolan

Placings:000000 **(5941)**
2009: 5^{0}Y, 7^{0}GF, 6^{0}GF, 5^{0}SD, 7^{0}HY, 7^{0}G,

	Starts	1st	2nd	3rd	Win & Pl
Career Total (Turf)	5	0	0	0	
Career Total (AW)	1	0	0	0	

Going (Turf): Sf: 0-1 GS: 0-0 Gd: 0-1 GF: 0-2 Fm: 0-0
Distance: 5f/6f: 0-3 7f-8f: 0-3 9f-13f: 0-0 14f+: 0-0
Track : LH: 0-2 RH: 0-4 Tight: 0-1 Gall: 0-0
Aids: Bl: 0-0 Vi: 0-0 Tstrap: 0-2 Ckp: 0-2
Best Rating: 43 6/09 Rosc 7f gd-fm

Ambrogina

79(94) (60)47
2-y-o b f Osorio (GER)-Oh Bej Oh Bej (IRE) (Distinctly North (USA))

M Botti Immobiliare Casa Paola SRL

Placings:502 (7792)
2009: 6^{5}HY, 7^{0}SD, 8^{2}SS,

	Starts	1st	2nd	3rd	Win & Pl
Career Total (Turf)	1	0	0	0	0
Career Total (AW)	2	0	1	0	806

Going (Turf): **Sf: 0-1 GS: 0-0 Gd: 0-0 GF: 0-0 Fm: 0-0**
Distance: 5f/6f: 0-1 7f-8f: 0-2 9f-13f: 0-0 14f+: 0-0
Track : LH: 0-1 RH: 0-1 Tight: 0-0 Gall: 0-0
Aids: Bl: 0-0 Vi: 0-0 Tstrap: 0-0 Ckp: 0-0
Best Rating: **60** 12/09 Sthl 1m std-slw

Modest; effective over 1m; acts on Fibresand.

Ambrose Princess (IRE)

103(101) (60)**63**
4-y-o b f Chevalier (IRE)-Mark One (Mark Of Esteem (IRE))
M J Scudamore The Yes No Wait Sorries

Placings:0601**41065030**/0110222533-21 (4301)
2009: 16^{2}G, 16^{1}G,

	Starts	1st	2nd	3rd	Win & Pl
Career Total (Turf)	15	4	4	1	13119
Career Total (AW)	9	1	0	2	2652
62 7/09 Ling 2m (0-70)H				GD	£2729
54 7/08 Nott 1m2f50y				GD	£2388
48 7/08 Chep 7f16y				G-F	£1942
57 10/07 Wolv 7f32y				STD	£2047
57 8/07 Ripn 6f				G-F	£2730

Total win prize-money £11839

Going (Turf): Sf: 0-0 GS: 0-1 **Gd: 2-7 GF: 2-6** Fm: 0-1
Distance: 5f/6f: 1-5 **7f-8f: 2-6** 9f-13f: 1-11 14f+: 1-2
Track : **LH: 3-13** RH: 0-5 **Tight: 2-8** Gall: 0-3
Aids: Bl: 0-0 Vi: 0-0 Tstrap: 0-1 Ckp: 0-1
Best Rating: **63** 8/08 Brig 1m3f196y gd-sft

Moderate; stays 2m but effective over shorter; acts on a sound surface; also goes on Fibresand and Polytrack.

Ameeq (USA)

102(100) (75)**78**
7-y-o b/br g Silver Hawk (USA)-Haniya (IRE) (Caerleon (USA))
Dr R D P Newland (G L Moore 16/3) A P Darwell, S R Trow, C E Stedman

Placings:330/44224/11646/26/00-05023 (5068)
2009: 12^{0}SD, 16^{5}SD, 12^{0}SD, 14^{2}G, 17^{3}GF,

	Starts	1st	2nd	3rd	Win & Pl
Career Total (Turf)	16	0	3	3	8628
Career Total (AW)	6	2	1	0	12281
84 3/06 Kemp 1m2f (0-90)H				STD	£7790
69 2/06 Ling 1m2f				STD	£3238

Total win prize-money £11029

Going (Turf): **Sf: 0-1 GS: 0-1 Gd: 0-8 GF: 0-6 Fm: 0-0**
Distance: 5f/6f: 0-0 7f-8f: 0-3 **9f-13f: 2-16** 14f+: 0-3
Track : LH: 1-12 RH: 1-8 **Tight: 1-9** Gall: 0-7
Aids: Bl: 0-2 Vi: 0-0 Tstrap: 0-0 Ckp: 0-0
Best Rating: **90** 3/07 Ling 1m4f stand

Fair gelding; useful hurdler; suited by 1m2f, but stays further; acts on fast ground and Polytrack.

Ameer (IRE)

106 **100**
2-y-o b c Monsun (GER)-Ailette (Second Set (IRE))
Saeed Bin Suroor Godolphin

Placings:113 (6656a)
2009: 7^{1}G, 8^{1}GF, 8^{3}VS,

	Starts	1st	2nd	3rd	Win & Pl
Career Total (Turf)	3	2	0	1	27723
88 9/09 Newb 1m				G-F	£11215
85 8/09 NmkJ 7f				GD	£4857

Total win prize-money £16073

Going (Turf): Sf: 0-0 GS: 0-0 **Gd: 1-1 GF: 1-1** Fm: 0-0
Distance: 5f/6f: 0-0 **7f-8f: 2-3** 9f-13f: 0-0 14f+: 0-0
Track : LH: 0-1 RH: 0-0 Tight: 0-0 Gall: 0-0
Aids: Bl: 0-0 Vi: 0-0 Tstrap: 0-0 Ckp: 0-0
Best Rating: **100** 10/09 StCl 1m v soft

Useful-looking son of Monsun; holds Derby entry.

Amenable (IRE)

78(97) (77)**35**
2-y-o b g Bertolini (USA)-Graceful Air (IRE) (Danzero (AUS))
D Nicholls Turton Brown Williams Lindley

Placings:001 (6356)
2009: 5^{0}GF, 0^{0}GS, 6^{1}SD,

	Starts	1st	2nd	3rd	Win & Pl
Career Total (Turf)	2	0	0	0	
Career Total (AW)	1	1	0	0	**4094**
77 9/09 Sthl 6f				STD	£4094

Total win prize-money £4094

Going (Turf): **Sf: 0-0 GS: 0-1 Gd: 0-0 GF: 0-1 Fm: 0-0**
Distance: **5f/6f: 1-3** 7f-8f: 0-0 9f-13f: 0-0 14f+: 0-0
Track : **LH: 1-1** RH: 0-0 Tight: 0-0 Gall: 0-0
Aids: Bl: 0-0 Vi: 0-0 Tstrap: 0-0 Ckp: 0-0
Best Rating: **77** 9/09 Sthl 6f stand

Modest; suited by 6f and Fibresand.

American Agent (USA)

(90) (60)
2-y-o b c Eavesdropper (USA)-Storm Season (USA) (Storm Cat (USA))
P F I Cole Parrish Hill Partnerships

Placings:54 (7843)
2009: 7^{5}SD, 5^{4}SD,

	Starts	1st	2nd	3rd	Win & Pl
Career Total (Turf)	0	0	0	0	
Career Total (AW)	2	0	0	0	289

Going (Turf): **Sf: 0-0 GS: 0-0 Gd: 0-0 GF: 0-0 Fm: 0-0**
Distance: 5f/6f: 0-1 7f-8f: 0-1 9f-13f: 0-0 14f+: 0-0
Track : LH: 0-2 RH: 0-0 Tight: 0-2 Gall: 0-0
Aids: Bl: 0-0 Vi: 0-0 Tstrap: 0-0 Ckp: 0-0
Best Rating: **60** 12/09 Ling 7f stand

American Champ (IRE)

(74) (11)
3-y-o b g Pyrus (USA)-Sandy Fitzgerald (IRE) (Last Tycoon)
Patrick Morris Rob Lloyd Racing Limited

Placings:0 (7753)
2009: 8^{0}SD,

	Starts	1st	2nd	3rd	Win & Pl
Career Total (Turf)	0	0	0	0	
Career Total (AW)	1	0	0	0	

Going (Turf): **Sf: 0-0 GS: 0-0 Gd: 0-0 GF: 0-0 Fm: 0-0**
Distance: 5f/6f: 0-0 7f-8f: 0-0 9f-13f: 0-1 14f+: 0-0
Track : LH: 0-1 RH: 0-0 Tight: 0-1 Gall: 0-0
Aids: Bl: 0-0 Vi: 0-0 Tstrap: 0-0 Ckp: 0-0
Best Rating: **11** 12/09 Wolv 1m141y stand

American Light

(96) (76)**71**
3-y-o b g Statue Of Liberty (USA)-Break Of Dawn (USA) (Mt. Livermore (USA))
D M Simcock (J G Burns 16/10) Tick Tock Partnership

Placings:5343-0302 (7714)
2009: 6^{0}G, 5^{3}GY, 5^{0}SD, 5^{2}SD,

	Starts	1st	2nd	3rd	Win & Pl
Career Total (Turf)	3	0	0	1	586
Career Total (AW)	5	0	1	2	3508

Going (Turf): **Sf: 0-1 GS: 0-0 Gd: 0-1 GF: 0-0 Fm: 0-0**
Distance: 5f/6f: 0-8 7f-8f: 0-0 9f-13f: 0-0 14f+: 0-0
Track : LH: 0-6 RH: 0-1 Tight: 0-1 Gall: 0-0
Aids: Bl: 0-0 Vi: 0-0 Tstrap: 0-0 Ckp: 0-0
Best Rating: **76** 11/08 Dund 5f stand

Modest; best over 5f; acts on easy ground and on Polytrack.

American Spin

103(106) (82)**82**
5-y-o ch g Groom Dancer (USA)-Sea Vixen (Machiavellian (USA))
L A Dace G Collacott

Placings:3/124050 (3737)
2009: 11^{1}SD, 12^{2}SD, 12^{4}SD, 16^{0}G, 21^{5}GF, 16^{0}SD,

	Starts	1st	2nd	3rd	Win & Pl
Career Total (Turf)	3	0	0	1	1550
Career Total (AW)	4	1	1	0	3197
71 1/09 Kemp 1m3f				STD	£1978

Total win prize-money £1979

Going (Turf): **Sf: 0-1 GS: 0-0 Gd: 0-1 GF: 0-1 Fm: 0-0**
Distance: 5f/6f: 0-0 7f-8f: 0-1 **9f-13f: 1-3** 14f+: 0-3
Track : LH: 0-2 **RH: 1-4** Tight: 0-3 Gall: 0-1
Aids: Bl: 0-0 Vi: 0-0 Tstrap: 0-0 Ckp: 0-0
Best Rating: **82** 6/09 Asct 2m5f159y gd-fm

Fair; stays 1m4f; acts on Polytrack; has worn eyeshield.

Amerigo (IRE)

104 **102**
4-y-o gr g Daylami (IRE)-Geminiani (IRE) (King Of Kings (IRE))
M A Jarvis Mrs Gay Smith

Placings:0/112-50362 (5481)
2009: 18^{5}GF, 16^{0}G, 21^{3}GF, 16^{6}G, 16^{2}GF,

	Starts	1st	2nd	3rd	Win & Pl
Career Total (Turf)	9	2	2	1	31921
91 5/08 Sand 1m6f (0-85)H				G-F	£5828
85 4/08 Yarm 1m3f101y				G-F	£2914

Total win prize-money £8742

Going (Turf): Sf: 0-0 GS: 0-0 Gd: 0-2 **GF: 2-6** Fm: 0-1
Distance: 5f/6f: 0-0 7f-8f: 0-0 9f-13f: 1-2 14f+: 1-7
Track : LH: 1-5 RH: 1-4 **Tight: 1-3** Gall: 0-2
Aids: Bl: 0-0 Vi: 0-0 Tstrap: 0-0 Ckp: 0-0
Best Rating: **102** 5/09 Ches 2m2f147y gd-fm

Very useful; runner-up in 2008 Queen's Vase; stays 2m2f and acts on fast ground.

Ames Souer (IRE)

(93) (44)**34**

6-y-o b m Fayruz-Taispeain (IRE) (Petorius)

P D Evans Diamond Racing Ltd

Placings:000/60/56/1030-6 (0056)

2009: 6^{6}SD,

	Starts	1st	2nd	3rd	Win & Pl
Career Total (Turf)	5	1	0	1	1618
Career Total (AW)	7	0	0	0	0

7/08 Oste 7f GD £735

Total win prize-money £735

Going (Turf): Sf: 0-1 GS: 0-1 **Gd: 1-3** GF: 0-0 Fm: 0-0
Distance: 5f/6f: 0-8 **7f-8f: 1-4** 9f-13f: 0-0 14f+: 0-0
Track : LH: 0-5 RH: 0-1 Tight: 0-3 Gall: 0-0
Aids: Bl: 0-0 Vi: 0-0 Tstrap: 0-0 Ckp: 0-0
Best Rating: **44** 1/09 Kemp 6f stand

Modest; effective at around 1m-1m4f; acts on most ground on turf.

Amethyst Dawn (IRE)

106 **76**

3-y-o gr f Act One-A L'Aube (IRE) (Selkirk (USA))

T D Easterby D A West

Placings:03150-050523502201 (7246)

2009: 9^{0}GF, 8^{5}GF, 8^{0}F, 9^{5}GF, 12^{2}G, 12^{3}G, 14^{5}G, 12^{0}GS, 8^{2}GF, 8^{2}GF, 7^{0}GF, 8^{1}S,

	Starts	1st	2nd	3rd	Win & Pl
Career Total (Turf)	17	2	3	2	13440

73 11/09 Nott 1m75y (0-70)H SFT £3238
76 8/08 Bevl 7f100y SFT £5018

Total win prize-money £8257

Going (Turf): **Sf: 2-3** GS: 0-1 Gd: 0-5 GF: 0-7 Fm: 0-1
Distance: 5f/6f: 0-0 7f-8f: 1-7 9f-13f: 1-9 14f+: 0-1
Track : LH: 1-8 RH: 1-5 Tight: 0-3 Gall: 0-4
Aids: Bl: 0-0 Vi: 0-0 Tstrap: 0-0 Ckp: 0-0
Best Rating: **76** 8/08 Bevl 7f100y soft

Modest; effective at around 1m-1m4f; acts on most ground on turf.

Amical Risks (FR)

92(95) (65)**51**

5-y-o bl g Take Risks (FR)-Miss High (FR) (Concorde Jr (USA))

W J Musson The City Boys

Placings:0/535/526466600-403 (7085)

2009: 11^{4}G, 12^{0}G, 11^{3}S,

	Starts	1st	2nd	3rd	Win & Pl
Career Total (Turf)	11	0	0	2	1383
Career Total (AW)	5	0	1	0	605

Going (Turf): **Sf: 0-2 GS: 0-3 Gd: 0-6 GF: 0-0 Fm: 0-0**
Distance: 5f/6f: 0-0 7f-8f: 0-1 9f-13f: 0-15 14f+: 0-0
Track : LH: 0-5 RH: 0-7 Tight: 0-9 Gall: 0-1
Aids: Bl: 0-0 Vi: 0-0 Tstrap: 0-0 Ckp: 0-0
Best Rating: **65** 2/08 Kemp 1m3f stand

Plating class; French import; stays 1m4f; acts on Polytrack and soft turf.

Amir Pasha (UAE)

101(98) (58)**58**

4-y-o br g Halling (USA)-Clarinda (IRE) (Lomond (USA))

Micky Hammond J McAllister

Placings:060603-300 (3617)

2009: 16^{3}GF, 16^{0}F, 17^{0}G,

	Starts	1st	2nd	3rd	Win & Pl
Career Total (Turf)	7	0	0	1	578
Career Total (AW)	2	0	0	1	482

Going (Turf): **Sf: 0-0 GS: 0-1 Gd: 0-3 GF: 0-2 Fm: 0-1**
Distance: 5f/6f: 0-0 7f-8f: 0-0 9f-13f: 0-4 14f+: 0-5
Track : LH: 0-3 RH: 0-6 Tight: 0-6 Gall: 0-1
Aids: Bl: 0-0 Vi: 0-1 Tstrap: 0-1 Ckp: 0-1
Best Rating: **58** 4/09 Muss 2m gd-fm

Moderate; effective at around 1m5f; acts on Polytrack.

Amitola (IRE)

103 **89**

2-y-o ch f Choisir (AUS)-Emly Express (IRE) (High Estate)

T D Barron J Browne

Placings:15 (7147)

2009: 6^{1}GF, 6^{5}G,

	Starts	1st	2nd	3rd	Win & Pl
Career Total (Turf)	2	1	0	0	3721

89 10/09 Ayr 6f G-F £2914

Total win prize-money £2914

Going (Turf): Sf: 0-0 GS: 0-0 Gd: 0-1 **GF: 1-1** Fm: 0-0
Distance: **5f/6f: 1-2** 7f-8f: 0-0 9f-13f: 0-0 14f+: 0-0
Track : LH: 0-0 RH: 0-0 Tight: 0-0 Gall: 0-0
Aids: Bl: 0-0 Vi: 0-0 Tstrap: 0-0 Ckp: 0-0
Best Rating: **89** 10/09 NmkR 6f good

Useful half-sister to three winners including the one-time useful sprinter Damika; winner over 6f on fast ground.

Amjad

86 **37**

12-y-o ch g Cadeaux Genereux-Babita (Habitat)

S G West Miss Kate Milligan

Placings:5045500200**6**/**1**60430/52330/0-0 (2656)

2009: 13^{0}GF,

	Starts	1st	2nd	3rd	Win & Pl
Career Total (Turf)	16	0	1	1	1684
Career Total (AW)	8	1	1	2	4047

83 1/01 Sthl 1m E(0-70)H STD £2464

Total win prize-money £2464

Going (Turf): **Sf: 0-1 GS: 0-2 Gd: 0-5 GF: 0-8 Fm: 0-0**
Distance: 5f/6f: 0-2 **7f-8f: 1-7** 9f-13f: 0-12 14f+: 0-3
Track : **LH: 1-15** RH: 0-4 Tight: 0-5 Gall: 0-4
Aids: Bl: 0-5 Vi: 0-2 Tstrap: 0-0 Ckp: 0-0
Best Rating: **83** 1/01 Sthl 1m stand

Amno Dancer (IRE)

90(81) (59)**74**

2-y-o b g Namid-Special Dancer (Shareef Dancer (USA))

M H Tompkins David P Noblett

Placings:653050 (7333)

2009: 6^{8}SD, 6^{5}G, 6^{3}GF, 5^{0}GF, 7^{5}G, 6^{0}SD,

	Starts	1st	2nd	3rd	Win & Pl
Career Total (Turf)	4	0	0	1	566
Career Total (AW)	2	0	0	0	0

Going (Turf): **Sf: 0-0 GS: 0-0 Gd: 0-2 GF: 0-2 Fm: 0-0**
Distance: 5f/6f: 0-3 7f-8f: 0-3 9f-13f: 0-0 14f+: 0-0
Track : LH: 0-2 RH: 0-0 Tight: 0-1 Gall: 0-0
Aids: Bl: 0-0 Vi: 0-0 Tstrap: 0-0 Ckp: 0-0
Best Rating: **74** 7/09 Yarm 6f3y gd-fm

Fair; effective over 6f; acts on fast ground.

Amosite

99(98) (66)**73**

3-y-o b f Central Park (IRE)-Waterline Dancer (IRE) (Danehill Dancer (IRE))

J R Jenkins Rowley

Placings:0402306020036-40130530 (4952)

2009: 6^{4}SD, 6^{0}GF, 5^{1}GF, 5^{3}GF, 5^{0}GF, 5^{5}GF, 5^{3}GF, 5^{0}G,

	Starts	1st	2nd	3rd	Win & Pl
Career Total (Turf)	16	1	2	3	6453
Career Total (AW)	5	0	0	1	716

71 4/09 Nott 5f13y (0-70)H G-F £2590

Total win prize-money £2590

Going (Turf): Sf: 0-1 GS: 0-1 Gd: 0-4 **GF: 1-9** Fm: 0-1
Distance: **5f/6f: 1-20** 7f-8f: 0-1 9f-13f: 0-0 14f+: 0-0
Track : LH: 0-4 RH: 0-1 Tight: 0-4 Gall: 0-1
Aids: Bl: 0-2 **Vi: 1-12** Tstrap: 0-0 Ckp: 0-0
Best Rating: **73** 5/09 NmkR 5f gd-fm

Fair; effective over 5f-6f; acts on fast ground and Polytrack; has worn a visor.

Amour Propre

114 **119**

3-y-o ch c Paris House-Miss Prim (Case Law)

H Candy Simon Broke And Partners

Placings:0111-105 (5233)

2009: 5^{1}GF, 5^{0}GF, 5^{5}GF,

	Starts	1st	2nd	3rd	Win & Pl
Career Total (Turf)	7	4	0	0	79669

119 5/09 NmkR 5f G-F £36900
108 10/08 Asct 5f G-S £28385
100 7/08 Bath 5f11y FRM £4857
87 6/08 Wwck 5f G-F £3070

Total win prize-money £73214

Going (Turf): Sf: 0-1 GS: 1-1 Gd: 0-0 **GF: 2-4** Fm: 1-1
Distance: **5f/6f: 4-7** 7f-8f: 0-0 9f-13f: 0-0 14f+: 0-0
Track : **LH: 2-2** RH: 0-0 Tight: 0-0 **Gall: 1-1**
Aids: Bl: 0-0 Vi: 0-0 Tstrap: 0-0 Ckp: 0-0
Best Rating: **119** 5/09 NmkR 5f gd-fm

Group-class; winner of the Group 3 Cornwallis Stakes at two and the Group 3 Palace House Stakes at three; effective over 5f; acts on most ground, but best on quick; suited by forcing tactics.

Amouretta

54(86) (40)**24**

4-y-o b f Daylami (IRE)-Allumette (Rainbow Quest (USA))

T T Clement P Arnold

Placings:0U0/0006-0 (6188)

2009: 15^{0}GF,

	Starts	1st	2nd	3rd	Win & Pl
Career Total (Turf)	6	0	0	0	
Career Total (AW)	2	0	0	0	0

Going (Turf): Sf: 0-2 GS: 0-1 Gd: 0-1 GF: 0-2 Fm: 0-0
Distance: 5f/6f: 0-0 7f-8f: 0-2 9f-13f: 0-4 14f+: 0-2
Track : LH: 0-3 RH: 0-4 Tight: 0-3 Gall: 0-0
Aids: Bl: 0-0 Vi: 0-3 Tstrap: 0-1 Ckp: 0-1
Best Rating: 47 10/07 NmkR 1m soft

Amoureuse

74(61) **32**
2-y-o b f Needwood Blade-Good Health (Magic Ring (IRE))
I W McInnes Mrs Ann Milburn

Placings:0000 **(2575)**
2009: 5^{0}GF, 5^{0}GF, 5^{0}G, 5^{0}SD,

	Starts	1st	2nd	3rd	Win & Pl
Career Total (Turf)	3	0	0	0	
Career Total (AW)	1	0	0	0	

Going (Turf): Sf: 0-0 GS: 0-0 Gd: 0-1 GF: 0-2 Fm: 0-0
Distance: 5f/6f: 0-4 7f-8f: 0-0 9f-13f: 0-0 14f+: 0-0
Track : LH: 0-0 RH: 0-0 Tight: 0-0 Gall: 0-0
Aids: Bl: 0-0 Vi: 0-0 Tstrap: 0-1 Ckp: 0-1
Best Rating: 32 5/09 Catt 5f gd-fm

Amron Hill

(96) (52)**35**
6-y-o b g Polar Prince (IRE)-Maradata (IRE) (Shardari)
R Hollinshead Geoff Lloyd

Placings:0006550/010-33 **(0300)**
2009: 16^{3}SD, 14^{3}SD,

	Starts	1st	2nd	3rd	Win & Pl
Career Total (Turf)	1	0	0	0	
Career Total (AW)	11	1	0	2	4650
52 12/08 Sthl	1m6f	(0-70)H		STD	£4094

Total win prize-money £4094

Going (Turf): Sf: 0-1 GS: 0-0 Gd: 0-0 GF: 0-0 Fm: 0-0
Distance: 5f/6f: 0-0 7f-8f: 0-1 9f-13f: 0-7 **14f+: 1-4**
Track : **LH: 1-10** RH: 0-1 Tight: 0-7 Gall: 0-0
Aids: Bl: 0-0 Vi: 0-0 Tstrap: 0-0 Ckp: 0-0
Best Rating: 62 11/06 Wolv 1m141y stand

Amroth

98(82) (28)**56**
3-y-o b f Rock Of Gibraltar (IRE)-Gwen John (USA) (Peintre Celebre (USA))
P D Evans K J Mercer

Placings:04500 **(7154)**
2009: 10^{0}S, 11^{4}GF, 10^{5}GF, 11^{0}GS, 16^{0}SD,

	Starts	1st	2nd	3rd	Win & Pl
Career Total (Turf)	4	0	0	0	241
Career Total (AW)	1	0	0	0	

Going (Turf): Sf: 0-1 GS: 0-1 Gd: 0-0 GF: 0-2 Fm: 0-0
Distance: 5f/6f: 0-0 7f-8f: 0-0 9f-13f: 0-4 14f+: 0-1
Track : LH: 0-3 RH: 0-1 Tight: 0-3 Gall: 0-1
Aids: Bl: 0-0 Vi: 0-1 Tstrap: 0-0 Ckp: 0-0
Best Rating: 56 9/09 Leic 1m3f183y gd-fm

Amtaar

79(88) (67)**53**
2-y-o b f Nayef (USA)-Emerald Fire (Pivotal)
C E Brittain Saeed Manana

Placings:0324 **(6181)**
2009: 7^{0}GF, 7^{3}SD, 6^{2}SD, 7^{4}GF,

	Starts	1st	2nd	3rd	Win & Pl
Career Total (Turf)	2	0	0	0	0
Career Total (AW)	2	0	1	1	1552

Going (Turf): Sf: 0-0 GS: 0-0 Gd: 0-0 GF: 0-2 Fm: 0-0
Distance: 5f/6f: 0-1 7f-8f: 0-3 9f-13f: 0-0 14f+: 0-0
Track : LH: 0-1 RH: 0-2 Tight: 0-1 Gall: 0-0
Aids: Bl: 0-0 Vi: 0-0 Tstrap: 0-0 Ckp: 0-0
Best Rating: 67 8/09 Ling 6f stand

Amwell Brave

96(104) (62)**53**
8-y-o b g Pyramus (USA)-Passage Creeping (IRE) (Persian Bold)
J R Jenkins Amwell Racing

Placings:0500**345/22335050006000010/2604504503125/3320554630346043226/144546400446 2050/033634363003 0-313054500** **(6204)**
2009: 11^{3}SD, 13^{1}SD, 13^{3}SD, 12^{0}SD, 12^{5}SD, 11^{4}GF, 14^{5}SD, 13^{0}F, 12^{0}G,

	Starts	1st	2nd	3rd	Win & Pl
Career Total (Turf)	28	0	0	3	5392
Career Total (AW)	65	4	8	14	26480
57 1/09 GrLe	1m5f66y	(0-45)		STD	£1706
69 1/07 Kemp	1m4f	(0-65)H		STD	£2590
67 10/05 Ling	1m4f	(0-55)H		STD	£2655
71 11/04 Ling	1m4f			STD	£3789

Total win prize-money £10743

Going (Turf): Sf: 0-5 GS: 0-4 Gd: 0-10 GF: 0-7 Fm: 0-2
Distance: 5f/6f: 0-2 7f-8f: 0-5 **9f-13f: 3-71** 14f+: 1-15
Track : **LH: 3-61** RH: 1-27 **Tight: 2-44** Gall: 1-9
Aids: Bl: 0-0 Vi: 0-3 Tstrap: 0-0 Ckp: 0-0
Best Rating: 89 6/07 NmkJ 1m4f soft

Moderate; effective at up to 2m; acts on most ground and on sand.

Amwell House

(97) (53)**52**
4-y-o gr g Auction House (USA)-Amwell Star (USA) (Silver Buck (USA))
J R Jenkins Amwell Racing

Placings:500000/063506**464-04300** **(0802)**
2009: 8^{0}SD, 8^{4}SD, 8^{3}SD, 8^{0}SD, 8^{0}SD,

	Starts	1st	2nd	3rd	Win & Pl
Career Total (Turf)	12	0	0	1	385
Career Total (AW)	8	0	0	1	241

Going (Turf): Sf: 0-1 GS: 0-2 Gd: 0-1 GF: 0-8 Fm: 0-0
Distance: 5f/6f: 0-3 7f-8f: 0-8 9f-13f: 0-7 14f+: 0-2
Track : LH: 0-8 RH: 0-7 Tight: 0-5 Gall: 0-0
Aids: Bl: 0-0 Vi: 0-0 Tstrap: 0-0 Ckp: 0-0
Best Rating: 53 11/08 Wolv 1m4f50y stand

Plating-class performer; effective over 1m4f.

Amylyn

73 **28**
2-y-o b f Starcraft (NZ)-Skirt Around (Deploy)
J R Holt P V Thomas

Placings:0 **(7244)**
2009: 8^{0}S,

	Starts	1st	2nd	3rd	Win & Pl
Career Total (Turf)	1	0	0	0	

Going (Turf): Sf: 0-1 GS: 0-0 Gd: 0-0 GF: 0-0 Fm: 0-0
Distance: 5f/6f: 0-0 7f-8f: 0-0 9f-13f: 0-1 14f+: 0-0
Track : LH: 0-1 RH: 0-0 Tight: 0-0 Gall: 0-0
Aids: Bl: 0-0 Vi: 0-0 Tstrap: 0-0 Ckp: 0-0
Best Rating: 28 11/09 Nott 1m75y soft

An Tadh (IRE)

102 (104)**97**
6-y-o b g Halling (USA)-Tithcar (Cadeaux Genereux)
G M Lyons Vincent Gaul

Placings:5241123/0511553/20000/**0166400-1000** **(5045a)**
2009: 5^{1}SD, 5^{0}GF, 5^{0}GF, 6^{0}SD,

	Starts	1st	2nd	3rd	Win & Pl
Career Total (Turf)	25	4	3	2	99195
Career Total (AW)	5	2	0	0	22128
93 4/09 Dund	5f			STD	£12075
104 4/08 Dund	5f			STD	£10052
111 6/06 Leop	7f			G-F	£31379
106 6/06 Naas	7f			G-F	£10101
98 7/05 Gway	7f			G-F	£23085
88 7/05 Rosc	7f			Y-S	£6860

Total win prize-money £93555

Going (Turf): Sf: 0-1 GS: 0-0 Gd: 0-5 **GF: 3-11** Fm: 0-1
Distance: 5f/6f: 2-15 **7f-8f: 4-15** 9f-13f: 0-0 14f+: 0-0
Track : **LH: 4-11** RH: 2-7 Tight: 0-1 Gall: 0-1
Aids: Bl: 0-2 Vi: 0-0 Tstrap: 0-3 Ckp: 0-3
Best Rating: 111 4/07 Curr 7f gd-fm

Very useful; Irish trained; winner in Group 3 company; effective from 5f-7f; acts well on fast ground; has worn blinkers and cheekpieces; likes to race prominently.

Ana Moutabahi

(89) (70)
2-y-o b c Anabaa (USA)-Runaway Venus (USA) (Runaway Groom (CAN))
C G Cox H E Sheikh Sultan Bin Khalifa Al Nahyan

Placings:024 **(7800)**
2009: 7^{0}SD, 7^{2}SD, 7^{4}SD,

	Starts	1st	2nd	3rd	Win & Pl
Career Total (Turf)	0	0	0	0	
Career Total (AW)	3	0	1	0	1493

Going (Turf): Sf: 0-0 GS: 0-0 Gd: 0-0 GF: 0-0 Fm: 0-0
Distance: 5f/6f: 0-0 7f-8f: 0-3 9f-13f: 0-0 14f+: 0-0
Track : LH: 0-1 RH: 0-2 Tight: 0-1 Gall: 0-0
Aids: Bl: 0-0 Vi: 0-0 Tstrap: 0-0 Ckp: 0-0
Best Rating: 70 12/09 Wolv 7f32y stand

Modest; stays 7f; acts on Polytrack.

Anacot Steel (IRE)

72 **17**
4-y-o ch g Danehill Dancer (IRE)-Paper Moon (IRE) (Lake Coniston (IRE))
Patrick Morris Rob Lloyd Racing Limited

Placings:00 **(4347)**
2009: 8^{0}HY, 9^{0}G,

	Starts	1st	2nd	3rd	Win & Pl
Career Total (Turf)	2	0	0	0	

Going (Turf): Sf: 0-1 GS: 0-0 Gd: 0-1 GF: 0-0 Fm: 0-0

Distance: 5f/6f: 0-0 7f-8f: 0-0 9f-13f: 0-2 14f+: 0-0
Track : LH: 0-1 RH: 0-1 Tight: 0-0 Gall: 0-0
Aids: Bl: 0-0 Vi: 0-0 Tstrap: 0-0 Ckp: 0-0
Best Rating: 17 5/09 Hayd 1m30y heavy

Anacreon (IRE)

90(96) (76)**57**
3-y-o b g Dansili-Anbella (FR) (Common Grounds)
J H M Gosden H R H Princess Haya Of Jordan

Placings:0-2100 **(4148)**
2009: 7^{2}SD, 6^{1}SD, 10^{0}GF, 6^{0}GF,

	Starts	1st	2nd	3rd	Win & Pl
Career Total (Turf)	3	0	0	0	
Career Total (AW)	2	1	1	0	3536

76 4/09 Ling 6f STD £2729
Total win prize-money £2730

Going (Turf): **Sf: 0-0 GS: 0-1 Gd: 0-0 GF: 0-2 Fm: 0-0**
Distance: **5f/6f: 1-2** 7f-8f: 0-2 9f-13f: 0-1 14f+: 0-0
Track : **LH: 1-2** RH: 0-0 **Tight: 1-2** Gall: 0-1
Aids: Bl: 0-0 Vi: 0-0 Tstrap: 0-0 Ckp: 0-0
Best Rating: 76 4/09 Ling 6f stand

Fair; suited by 6f-7f and acts on Polytrack.

Anagram

87(94) (65)**47**
3-y-o b f Efisio-Saint Ann (USA) (Geiger Counter (USA))
W R Muir Mr & Mrs G Middlebrook

Placings:03260 **(7353)**
2009: 5^{0}G, 5^{3}SD, 7^{2}SD, 5^{6}S, 7^{0}SD,

	Starts	1st	2nd	3rd	Win & Pl
Career Total (Turf)	2	0	0	0	0
Career Total (AW)	3	0	1	1	1367

Going (Turf): **Sf: 0-1 GS: 0-0 Gd: 0-1 GF: 0-0 Fm: 0-0**
Distance: 5f/6f: 0-3 7f-8f: 0-2 9f-13f: 0-0 14f+: 0-0
Track : LH: 0-5 RH: 0-0 Tight: 0-3 Gall: 0-1
Aids: Bl: 0-4 Vi: 0-0 Tstrap: 0-0 Ckp: 0-0
Best Rating: 65 10/09 Wolv 7f32y stand

Ananda Kanda (USA)

90(83) (56)**75**
2-y-o b f Hero's Tribute (USA)-Roja (USA) (L'Enjoleur (CAN))
B Ellison Koo's Racing Club

Placings:010456 **(6011)**
2009: 5^{0}GF, 6^{1}HY, 7^{0}SD, 6^{4}GS, 8^{5}SD, 8^{6}GS,

	Starts	1st	2nd	3rd	Win & Pl
Career Total (Turf)	4	1	0	0	4126
Career Total (AW)	2	0	0	0	0

70 5/09 Hayd 6f HVY £3885
Total win prize-money £3886

Going (Turf): **Sf: 1-1** GS: 0-2 Gd: 0-0 GF: 0-1 Fm: 0-0
Distance: **5f/6f: 1-3** 7f-8f: 0-3 9f-13f: 0-0 14f+: 0-0
Track : LH: 0-2 RH: 0-1 Tight: 0-0 Gall: 0-0
Aids: Bl: 0-0 Vi: 0-0 Tstrap: 0-0 Ckp: 0-0
Best Rating: 75 7/09 Newc 6f gd-sft

Fair; effective over 6f; acts on testing ground.

Anasy (USA)

64(82) (39)
3-y-o b f Gone West (USA)-Blue Moon (FR) (Lomitas)
T Keddy Mrs V A Ward

Placings:6-000 **(6831)**
2009: 7^{0}SD, 7^{0}G, 9^{0}SF,

	Starts	1st	2nd	3rd	Win & Pl
Career Total (Turf)	1	0	0	0	
Career Total (AW)	3	0	0	0	0

Going (Turf): **Sf: 0-0 GS: 0-0 Gd: 0-1 GF: 0-0 Fm: 0-0**
Distance: 5f/6f: 0-0 7f-8f: 0-3 9f-13f: 0-1 14f+: 0-0
Track : LH: 0-3 RH: 0-0 Tight: 0-3 Gall: 0-0
Aids: Bl: 0-0 Vi: 0-0 Tstrap: 0-0 Ckp: 0-0
Best Rating: 39 10/09 Wolv 1m1f103y std-fst

Anaya

88(96) (71)**71**
2-y-o b f Tobougg (IRE)-Nacho Venture (FR) (Rainbow Quest (USA))
M R Channon Ian O'Connor Construction Ltd

Placings:00322245 **(7825)**
2009: 8^{0}G, 8^{0}GF, 8^{3}GF, 8^{2}GS, 8^{2}SD, 8^{2}SD, 8^{4}SD, 8^{5}SD,

	Starts	1st	2nd	3rd	Win & Pl
Career Total (Turf)	4	0	1	1	1734
Career Total (AW)	4	0	2	0	2120

Going (Turf): **Sf: 0-0 GS: 0-1 Gd: 0-1 GF: 0-2 Fm: 0-0**
Distance: 5f/6f: 0-0 7f-8f: 0-5 9f-13f: 0-3 14f+: 0-0
Track : LH: 0-4 RH: 0-3 Tight: 0-2 Gall: 0-1
Aids: Bl: 0-0 Vi: 0-0 Tstrap: 0-0 Ckp: 0-0
Best Rating: 71 10/09 Kemp 1m stand

Anchorage Boy (USA)

78 **56**
2-y-o b g Southern Image (USA)-Alaskan Winter (USA) (Gulch (USA))
Miss Amy Weaver Anchorage Partnership

Placings:005 **(4666)**
2009: 7^{0}G, 7^{0}G, 7^{5}G,

	Starts	1st	2nd	3rd	Win & Pl
Career Total (Turf)	3	0	0	0	0

Going (Turf): **Sf: 0-0 GS: 0-0 Gd: 0-3 GF: 0-0 Fm: 0-0**
Distance: 5f/6f: 0-0 7f-8f: 0-3 9f-13f: 0-0 14f+: 0-0
Track : LH: 0-0 RH: 0-0 Tight: 0-0 Gall: 0-0
Aids: Bl: 0-0 Vi: 0-0 Tstrap: 0-0 Ckp: 0-0
Best Rating: 56 8/09 Yarm 7f3y good

Ancien Regime (IRE)

109(110) (97)**113**
4-y-o b g King's Best (USA)-Sadalsud (IRE) (Shaadi (USA))
Saeed Bin Suroor Godolphin

Placings:142/61316-203100 **(6661)**
2009: 6^{2}S, 6^{0}GF, 6^{3}S, 6^{1}SD, 6^{0}GF, 6^{0}GS,

	Starts	1st	2nd	3rd	Win & Pl
Career Total (Turf)	13	3	2	2	94564
Career Total (AW)	1	1	0	0	12952

97 8/09 Ling 6f STD £12952
111 7/08 Sand 5f6y G-F £36900
106 5/08 NmkR 6f (0-105)H FRM £24924
84 8/07 Yarm 6f3y G-S £3562
Total win prize-money £78339

Going (Turf): Sf: 0-3 **GS: 1-2** Gd: 0-2 **GF: 1-5 Fm: 1-1**
Distance: **5f/6f: 3-12** 7f-8f: 1-2 9f-13f: 0-0 14f+: 0-0
Track : **LH: 1-1** RH: 0-0 **Tight: 1-1** Gall: 0-1
Aids: Bl: 0-0 Vi: 0-0 Tstrap: 0-0 Ckp: 0-0
Best Rating: 113 9/08 Donc 6f soft

Group class; winner in Group 3 company; effective over 5f-6f; acts on most ground; goes on Polytrack.

Ancient Cross

104(101) (73)**83**
5-y-o b g Machiavellian (USA)-Magna Graecia (IRE) (Warning)
M W Easterby P J Bown

Placings:0/254442230-6342435243121 **(6846)**
2009: 7^{6}GF, 7^{3}SD, 7^{4}GS, 7^{2}SD, 7^{4}GS, 7^{3}GF, 6^{5}G, 7^{2}G, 9^{4}GF, 8^{3}GS, 7^{1}G, 7^{2}GF, 7^{1}G,

	Starts	1st	2nd	3rd	Win & Pl
Career Total (Turf)	20	2	5	3	13280
Career Total (AW)	3	0	1	1	1310

83 10/09 Catt 7f (0-75)H GD £2914
75 9/09 Muss 7f30y (0-65)H GD £2266
Total win prize-money £5181

Going (Turf): Sf: 0-3 GS: 0-5 **Gd: 2-6** GF: 0-6 Fm: 0-0
Distance: 5f/6f: 0-3 **7f-8f: 2-17** 9f-13f: 0-3 14f+: 0-0
Track : LH: 1-11 RH: 1-5 **Tight: 2-8** Gall: 0-1
Aids: Bl: 0-5 Vi: 0-0 Tstrap: 0-0 Ckp: 0-0
Best Rating: 83 10/09 Catt 7f good

Fair; effective over 6f-1m; acts on most ground; has worn a tongue tie.

Ancient Lights

(112) (100)**89**
4-y-o b c High Chaparral (IRE)-Fascinating Hill (FR) (Danehill (USA))
H R A Cecil Ennismore Racing II

Placings:13-3 **(1642)**
2009: 10^{3}SD,

	Starts	1st	2nd	3rd	Win & Pl
Career Total (Turf)	2	1	0	1	6314
Career Total (AW)	1	0	0	1	1926

89 5/08 NmkR 1m2f G-F £5180
Total win prize-money £5181

Going (Turf): Sf: 0-0 GS: 0-0 Gd: 0-1 **GF: 1-1** Fm: 0-0
Distance: 5f/6f: 0-0 7f-8f: 0-0 **9f-13f: 1-3** 14f+: 0-0
Track : LH: 0-1 RH: 0-1 Tight: 0-1 Gall: 0-0
Aids: Bl: 0-0 Vi: 0-0 Tstrap: 0-0 Ckp: 0-0
Best Rating: 100 5/09 Ling 1m2f stand

Very useful; stays 1m2f and acts on fast ground.

Ancient Oak

53
2-y-o ch c Compton Place-Dolce Piccata (Piccolo)
H A McWilliams J Nixon

Placings:06 **(6246)**
2009: 5^{0}GF, 6^{6}GF,

	Starts	1st	2nd	3rd	Win & Pl
Career Total (Turf)	2	0	0	0	0

Going (Turf): **Sf: 0-0 GS: 0-0 Gd: 0-0 GF: 0-2 Fm: 0-0**
Distance: 5f/6f: 0-2 7f-8f: 0-0 9f-13f: 0-0 14f+: 0-0
Track : LH: 0-0 RH: 0-0 Tight: 0-0 Gall: 0-0
Aids: Bl: 0-0 Vi: 0-0 Tstrap: 0-0 Ckp: 0-0

And A Partridge

74(89) (53)**20**

3-y-o ch g Compton Place-Dunloe (IRE) (Shaadi (USA))

J A Osborne John Egan & 12 Day Partners

Placings:505 (2487)

2009: 8^{5}SD, 10^{0}GF, 12^{5}SD,

	Starts	1st	2nd	3rd	Win & Pl
Career Total (Turf)	1	0	0	0	
Career Total (AW)	2	0	0	0	0

Going (Turf): **Sf: 0-0 GS: 0-0 Gd: 0-0 GF: 0-1 Fm: 0-0**
Distance: 5f/6f: 0-0 7f-8f: 0-0 9f-13f: 0-3 14f+: 0-0
Track : LH: 0-2 RH: 0-1 Tight: 0-3 Gall: 0-0
Aids: Bl: 0-0 Vi: 0-0 Tstrap: 0-0 Ckp: 0-0
Best Rating: **53** 4/09 Wolv 1m141y stand

Andaman Sunset

(104) (77)**74**

4-y-o b c Red Ransom (USA)-Miss Amanpuri (Alzao (USA))

J L Spearing Skip Racing Limited

Placings:00242/450614-000000 (7767)

2009: 10^{0}SD, 12^{0}SD, 10^{0}SD, 9^{0}SD, 10^{0}SD, 11^{0}SD,

	Starts	1st	2nd	3rd	Win & Pl
Career Total (Turf)	9	0	2	0	3556
Career Total (AW)	8	1	0	0	4059

77 9/08 GrLe 1m2f (0-70)H STD £3885
Total win prize-money £3886

Going (Turf): **Sf: 0-3 GS: 0-1 Gd: 0-3 GF: 0-2 Fm: 0-0**
Distance: 5f/6f: 0-3 7f-8f: 0-5 **9f-13f: 1-9** 14f+: 0-0
Track : **LH: 1-7** RH: 0-3 Tight: 0-4 **Gall: 1-1**
Aids: Bl: 0-1 Vi: 0-0 Tstrap: 1-3 Ckp: 1-3
Best Rating: **84** 10/07 Newb 1m soft

Modest; stays 1m2f; acts on most ground and on Polytrack; has worn cheekpieces.

Andean Margin (IRE)

103(100) (75)**72**

3-y-o b g Giant's Causeway (USA)-Spiritual Air (Royal Applause)

M W Easterby (S A Callaghan 28/1) A Chandler & L Westwood

Placings:50040012-22230000 (6804)

2009: 8^{2}SD, 7^{2}SD, 7^{2}SD, 8^{3}GF, 7^{0}SD, 7^{0}GF, 7^{0}GF, 9^{0}SD,

	Starts	1st	2nd	3rd	Win & Pl
Career Total (Turf)	7	0	0	1	939
Career Total (AW)	9	1	4	0	5905

71 12/08 Sthl 7f (0-65) STD £2047
Total win prize-money £2047

Going (Turf): **Sf: 0-2 GS: 0-1 Gd: 0-0 GF: 0-4 Fm: 0-0**
Distance: 5f/6f: 0-0 **7f-8f: 1-12** 9f-13f: 0-4 14f+: 0-0
Track : **LH: 1-8** RH: 0-5 Tight: 0-3 Gall: 0-2
Aids: **Bl: 1-7** Vi: 0-0 Tstrap: 0-0 Ckp: 0-0
Best Rating: **75** 1/09 Ling 7f stand

Fair; stays 1m and acts on easy ground, Polytrack and Fibresand; has worn blinkers.

Andhaar

106(100) (85)**81**

3-y-o b g Bahri (USA)-Deraasaat (Nashwan (USA))

S Gollings (E A L Dunlop 1/10) P J Martin

Placings:63204-32103333 (7620)

2009: 9^{3}G, 10^{2}GF, 10^{1}SD, 10^{0}G, 9^{3}GF, 12^{3}GF, 11^{3}GF, 9^{3}SD,

	Starts	1st	2nd	3rd	Win & Pl
Career Total (Turf)	10	0	1	5	4799
Career Total (AW)	3	1	1	1	4256

76 6/09 Ling 1m2f STD £2729
Total win prize-money £2730

Going (Turf): **Sf: 0-0 GS: 0-1 Gd: 0-4 GF: 0-5 Fm: 0-0**
Distance: 5f/6f: 0-0 7f-8f: 0-4 **9f-13f: 1-9** 14f+: 0-0
Track : **LH: 1-5** RH: 0-6 **Tight: 1-8** Gall: 0-0
Aids: Bl: 0-0 Vi: 0-0 Tstrap: 0-0 Ckp: 0-0
Best Rating: **85** 12/09 Wolv 1m1f103y stand

Fair; stays 1m4f; acts on fast ground and on Polytrack.

Andina (IRE)

95 **72**

2-y-o ch f Singspiel (IRE)-Fragrant Oasis (USA) (Rahy (USA))

J W Hills Wood Hall Stud Limited

Placings:3 (2494)

2009: 6^{3}GF,

	Starts	1st	2nd	3rd	Win & Pl
Career Total (Turf)	1	0	0	1	578

Going (Turf): **Sf: 0-0 GS: 0-0 Gd: 0-0 GF: 0-1 Fm: 0-0**
Distance: 5f/6f: 0-0 7f-8f: 0-1 9f-13f: 0-0 14f+: 0-0
Track : LH: 0-0 RH: 0-0 Tight: 0-0 Gall: 0-0
Aids: Bl: 0-0 Vi: 0-0 Tstrap: 0-0 Ckp: 0-0
Best Rating: **72** 5/09 Newb 6f8y gd-fm

Andorn (GER)

100(98) (59)**84**

5-y-o b h Monsun (GER)-Anthyllis (GER) (Lycius (USA))

P A Kirby (B J Curley 25/4) Preesall Garage

Placings:61/1310/140006-032035616 (6845)

2009: 7^{0}F, 8^{3}SD, 9^{2}GF, 12^{0}GS, 11^{3}GF, 12^{5}GF, 12^{6}G, 12^{1}GF, 13^{6}G,

	Starts	1st	2nd	3rd	Win & Pl
Career Total (Turf)	17	5	1	2	24376
Career Total (AW)	4	0	0	1	302

62 9/09 Muss 1m4f100y G-F £2590
4/08 Mulh 1m SFT £1470
103 8/07 Badn 1m GD £10135
5/07 Colo 1m1f55y H GD £2702
10/06 Hopp 1m GD £2068
Total win prize-money £18968

Going (Turf): Sf: 1-4 GS: 0-1 **Gd: 3-7** GF: 1-4 Fm: 0-1
Distance: 5f/6f: 0-0 **7f-8f: 3-6** 9f-13f: 2-14 14f+: 0-1
Track : LH: 1-9 RH: 1-7 **Tight: 1-7** Gall: 0-3
Aids: Bl: 0-0 Vi: 0-0 Tstrap: 0-0 Ckp: 0-0
Best Rating: **103** 8/07 Badn 1m good

Modest; effective over 1m2f-1m4f; acts on fast ground.

Andrasta

103(90) (45)**61**

4-y-o b f Bertolini (USA)-Real Popcorn (IRE) (Jareer (USA))

S A Harris (A Berry 24/8) A B Parr

Placings:450003100520330/60303000362046334612005 0-5001000644515560060 (7427)

2009: 5^{5}SD, 6^{0}GF, 6^{0}G, 5^{1}G, 5^{0}HY, 5^{0}GF, 5^{0}GF, 6^{6}G, 6^{4}G, 6^{4}G, 5^{5}G, 5^{1}GF, 5^{5}GF, 5^{5}HY, 5^{6}GF, 5^{0}GS, 5^{0}GF, 5^{6}S, 5^{0}SD,

	Starts	1st	2nd	3rd	Win & Pl
Career Total (Turf)	45	4	2	5	16284
Career Total (AW)	13	0	1	3	1471

55 8/09 Ayr 5f (0-65)H G-F £2047
61 5/09 Haml 5f4y (0-75)H GD £3238
54 8/08 Ayr 5f (0-65)H SFT £2729
71 10/07 Catt 5f212y (0-65)H GD £2730
Total win prize-money £10745

Going (Turf): Sf: 1-9 GS: 0-6 **Gd: 2-17** GF: 1-12 Fm: 0-1
Distance: **5f/6f: 4-48** 7f-8f: 0-10 9f-13f: 0-0 14f+: 0-0
Track : **LH: 1-15** RH: 0-4 **Tight: 1-9** Gall: 0-3
Aids: Bl: 0-0 Vi: 0-0 Tstrap: 0-4 Ckp: 0-4
Best Rating: **71** 10/07 Catt 5f212y good

Moderate; suited by 5f-6f; acts on most ground and on Fibresand.

Anduril

77(100) (52)**57**

8-y-o ch g Kris-Attribute (Warning)

D Carroll (I W McInnes 19/6) John Allan Milburn

Placings:045/6036400400125/31423624210404250244/0/ 00305000001005602 3/5000006/50164000625030006 0- 05000 (7802)

2009: 8^{0}SS, 8^{5}SD, 8^{0}SD, 8^{0}G, 8^{0}SD,

	Starts	1st	2nd	3rd	Win & Pl
Career Total (Turf)	43	2	4	2	23057
Career Total (AW)	42	3	4	4	13532

57 2/08 Sthl 1m (0-50)H STD £1911
74 8/06 Ayr 1m (0-80)H G-S £6477
80 5/05 Hayd 1m30y (0-70)H GD £3762
69 2/05 Wolv 1m141y STD £2982
58 11/04 Wolv 1m141y STD £2667
Total win prize-money £17799

Going (Turf): Sf: 0-11 **GS: 1-5 Gd: 1-14** GF: 0-13 Fm: 0-0
Distance: 5f/6f: 0-1 7f-8f: 2-32 **9f-13f: 3-52** 14f+: 0-0
Track : **LH: 5-69** RH: 0-14 **Tight: 2-41** Gall: 0-2
Aids: **Bl: 3-49** Vi: 0-1 Tstrap: 1-14 Ckp: 1-14
Best Rating: **84** 9/05 Gdwd 1m good

Moderate performer; stays 1m2f; well served by a strong pace; does not look an easy ride; usually wears blinkers; acts on Fibresand.

Anessia

78(93) (55)**55**

3-y-o b f Fantastic Light (USA)-Lamarque (IRE) (Nureyev (USA))

Tom Dascombe Grant Thornton Racing Club

Placings:4500 (5988)

2009: 10^{4}SD, 10^{5}HY, 10^{0}S, 12^{0}SD,

	Starts	1st	2nd	3rd	Win & Pl
Career Total (Turf)	2	0	0	0	0
Career Total (AW)	2	0	0	0	0

Going (Turf): **Sf: 0-2 GS: 0-0 Gd: 0-0 GF: 0-0 Fm: 0-0**
Distance: 5f/6f: 0-0 7f-8f: 0-0 9f-13f: 0-4 14f+: 0-0
Track : LH: 0-3 RH: 0-1 Tight: 0-1 Gall: 0-1
Aids: Bl: 0-0 Vi: 0-0 Tstrap: 0-0 Ckp: 0-0
Best Rating: **55** 7/09 Nott 1m2f50y heavy

Moderate; stays 1m2f; acts on Polytrack.

Anfield Road

84(99) (74)**75**

4-y-o ch g Dr Fong (USA)-Mackenzie's Friend (Selkirk (USA))

L Corcoran (D R Gandolfo 25/9) The A T P Racing Partnership

Placings:0222601-0005 **(7647)**
2009: 16^{0}SD, 12^{0}SD, 12^{0}S, 12^{5}SD,

	Starts	1st	2nd	3rd	Win & Pl
Career Total (Turf)	7	0	3	0	4143
Career Total (AW)	4	1	0	0	2590

74 12/08 GrLe 1m5f66y STD £2590
Total win prize-money £2590

Going (Turf): **Sf: 0-3 GS: 0-0 Gd: 0-1 GF: 0-0 Fm: 0-0**
Distance: 5f/6f: 0-0 7f-8f: 0-1 9f-13f: 0-8 **14f+: 1-2**
Track : **LH: 1-4** RH: 0-7 Tight: 0-2 **Gall: 1-3**
Aids: Bl: 0-0 Vi: 0-1 Tstrap: 0-1 Ckp: 0-1
Best Rating: **75** 8/08 Wxfd 1m4f good

Fair; stays 1m5f; acts on good and heavy ground and Polytrack; has worn cheekpieces.

Anfield Star (IRE)

(86) (36)**59**
3-y-o b g Celtic Swing-Shenkara (IRE) (Night Shift (USA))
Patrick Morris Rob Lloyd Racing Limited

Placings:000-**600** **(7002)**
2009: 5^{6}SD, 7^{0}SD, 5^{0}SD,

	Starts	1st	2nd	3rd	Win & Pl
Career Total (Turf)	3	0	0	0	
Career Total (AW)	3	0	0	0	0

Going (Turf): **Sf: 0-1 GS: 0-0 Gd: 0-0 GF: 0-0 Fm: 0-0**
Distance: 5f/6f: 0-2 7f-8f: 0-4 9f-13f: 0-0 14f+: 0-0
Track : LH: 0-2 RH: 0-2 Tight: 0-2 Gall: 0-0
Aids: Bl: 0-1 Vi: 0-0 Tstrap: 0-0 Ckp: 0-0
Best Rating: **59** 9/08 Curr 7f yield

Angaric (IRE)

99(93) (69)**78**
6-y-o ch g Pivotal-Grannys Reluctance (IRE) (Anita's Prince)
B Smart B Smart

Placings:365000/2121220064/2260333034/30404502-031000400 **(7679)**
2009: 6^{0}SD, 5^{3}GF, 7^{1}G, 7^{0}GF, 7^{0}GF, 5^{0}GF, 5^{4}GS, 6^{0}GF, 6^{0}SD,

	Starts	1st	2nd	3rd	Win & Pl
Career Total (Turf)	36	3	6	5	26149
Career Total (AW)	7	0	1	2	2455

72 5/09 Muss 7f30y (0-65)H GD £2266
77 5/06 Bevl 7f100y (0-85)H GD £6477
70 5/06 Muss 7f30y (0-65)H G-F £3238
Total win prize-money £11983

Going (Turf): Sf: 0-2 GS: 0-4 **Gd: 2-12** GF: 1-17 Fm: 0-1
Distance: 5f/6f: 0-16 **7f-8f: 3-26** 9f-13f: 0-1 14f+: 0-0
Track : LH: 0-19 **RH: 3-12 Tight: 2-20** Gall: 0-1
Aids: Bl: 0-0 Vi: 0-0 Tstrap: 0-0 Ckp: 0-0
Best Rating: **81** 4/07 Muss 7f30y gd-fm

Modest; best at around 7f; acts on most ground and on Polytrack; has worn a tongue tie.

Angel Of Fashion (IRE)

103(90) (62)**77**
2-y-o b f Invincible Spirit (IRE)-Vanitycase (IRE) (Editor's Note (USA))
B W Hills John Sillett

Placings:0245610016 **(6541)**
2009: 5^{0}GS, 5^{2}GF, 5^{4}GF, 5^{5}GF, 6^{6}SD, 5^{1}GF, 6^{0}G, 7^{0}GS, 5^{1}GF, 6^{6}GF,

	Starts	1st	2nd	3rd	Win & Pl
Career Total (Turf)	9	2	1	0	8568
Career Total (AW)	1	0	0	0	0

77 9/09 Leic 5f218y (0-75) G-F £3238
74 7/09 Leic 5f218y G-F £3885
Total win prize-money £7124

Going (Turf): Sf: 0-0 GS: 0-2 Gd: 0-1 **GF: 2-6** Fm: 0-0
Distance: **5f/6f: 2-9** 7f-8f: 0-1 9f-13f: 0-0 14f+: 0-0
Track : LH: 0-4 RH: 0-1 Tight: 0-0 Gall: 0-1
Aids: Bl: 0-0 Vi: 0-0 Tstrap: 0-0 Ckp: 0-0
Best Rating: **77** 9/09 Leic 5f218y gd-fm

Fair; stays 6f; acts on fast ground.

Angel Rock (IRE)

107(103) (86)**89**
4-y-o b c Rock Of Gibraltar (IRE)-Nomothetis (IRE) (Law Society (USA))
M Grassi (M Botti 21/10) Tenuta Dorna Di Montaltuzzo SRL

Placings:6/10**1401**-015500 **(7312a)**
2009: 10^{0}S, 8^{1}S, 8^{5}G, 8^{5}G, 10^{0}GF, 8^{0}HY,

	Starts	1st	2nd	3rd	Win & Pl
Career Total (Turf)	10	3	0	0	19289
Career Total (AW)	3	1	0	0	5208

89 5/09 Hayd 1m30y (0-90)H SFT £9066
89 10/08 Nott 1m75y (0-85)H HVY £7447
86 8/08 GrLe 1m (0-80)H STD £4857
82 7/08 Yarm 1m2f21y G-F £2775
Total win prize-money £24146

Going (Turf): **Sf: 2-4** GS: 0-0 Gd: 0-2 GF: 1-4 Fm: 0-0
Distance: 5f/6f: 0-0 7f-8f: 1-4 **9f-13f: 3-9** 14f+: 0-0
Track : **LH: 4-9** RH: 0-3 Tight: 1-2 Gall: 1-5
Aids: Bl: 0-0 Vi: 0-0 Tstrap: 0-1 Ckp: 0-1
Best Rating: **89** 5/09 Hayd 1m30y soft

Useful; stays 1m2f; acts on any ground and on Polytrack; has worn cheekpieces.

Angel Song

96(94) (70)**65**
3-y-o b f Dansili-Something Blue (Petong)
Sir Mark Prescott Plantation Stud

Placings:13460 **(7337)**
2009: 6^{1}SD, 6^{3}SD, 7^{4}GS, 5^{6}SD, 6^{0}SD,

	Starts	1st	2nd	3rd	Win & Pl
Career Total (Turf)	1	0	0	0	385
Career Total (AW)	4	1	0	1	3452

70 1/09 Sthl 6f STD £2729
Total win prize-money £2730

Going (Turf): **Sf: 0-0 GS: 0-1 Gd: 0-0 GF: 0-0 Fm: 0-0**
Distance: **5f/6f: 1-4** 7f-8f: 0-1 9f-13f: 0-0 14f+: 0-0
Track : **LH: 1-4** RH: 0-1 Tight: 0-1 Gall: 0-0
Aids: Bl: 0-0 Vi: 0-0 Tstrap: 0-0 Ckp: 0-0
Best Rating: **70** 1/09 Sthl 6f stand

Fair; suited by 6f; acts on Fibresand.

Angel Voices (IRE)

(109) (73)**72**
6-y-o b m Tagula (IRE)-Lithe Spirit (IRE) (Dancing Dissident (USA))
K R Burke Mrs P Sahota

Placings:330/2043/535524**501**/**215230**45410**006-26600** **(1528)**
2009: 6^{2}SD, 5^{6}SD, 8^{6}SD, 6^{0}SD, 5^{0}SD,

	Starts	1st	2nd	3rd	Win & Pl
Career Total (Turf)	17	1	2	4	32256
Career Total (AW)	18	2	3	1	7332

72 8/08 Haml 6f5y (0-65)H SFT £2266
73 1/08 Kemp 7f (0-75)H STD £2590
61 12/07 Kemp 6f (0-55) STD £2047
Total win prize-money £6906

Going (Turf): **Sf: 1-4** GS: 0-5 Gd: 0-5 GF: 0-2 Fm: 0-0
Distance: 5f/6f: 1-15 **7f-8f: 2-19** 9f-13f: 0-1 14f+: 0-0
Track : LH: 0-13 **RH: 2-11** Tight: 0-10 Gall: 0-1
Aids: Bl: 0-0 Vi: 0-4 Tstrap: 3-14 Ckp: 3-14
Best Rating: **81** 9/05 Leop 7f gd-yld

Modest; effective from 6f-7f; acts on good and easier ground and on Polytrack; suited by forcing tactics; has worn various headgear.

Angel's Pursuit (IRE)

101(91) (87)**106**
2-y-o ch c Pastoral Pursuits-Midnight Angel (Machiavellian (USA))
R Hannon Malih L Al Basti

Placings:1036220120 **(6486)**
2009: 5^{1}GF, 5^{0}GF, 5^{3}G, 6^{6}G, 5^{2}G, 5^{2}G, 6^{0}SD, 6^{1}GF, 6^{2}GF, 6^{0}GF,

	Starts	1st	2nd	3rd	Win & Pl
Career Total (Turf)	9	2	3	1	49737
Career Total (AW)	1	0	0	0	

96 9/09 Donc 6f G-F £10904
90 5/09 NmkR 5f G-F £5180
Total win prize-money £16085

Going (Turf): Sf: 0-0 GS: 0-0 Gd: 0-4 **GF: 2-5** Fm: 0-0
Distance: **5f/6f: 2-9** 7f-8f: 0-1 9f-13f: 0-0 14f+: 0-0
Track : LH: 0-1 RH: 0-2 Tight: 0-0 Gall: 0-1
Aids: Bl: 0-0 Vi: 0-0 Tstrap: 0-0 Ckp: 0-0
Best Rating: **106** 9/09 Newb 6f8y gd-fm

Smart; runner-up in the 2009 Mill Reef Stakes; effective over 5f-6f; acts on good and faster ground.

Angela Jones

55
2-y-o ch f Cape Town (IRE)-Full English (Perugino (USA))
D K Ivory Recycled Products Limited

Placings:00 **(4912)**
2009: 6^{0}G, 5^{0}G,

	Starts	1st	2nd	3rd	Win & Pl
Career Total (Turf)	2	0	0	0	

Going (Turf): **Sf: 0-0 GS: 0-0 Gd: 0-2 GF: 0-0 Fm: 0-0**
Distance: 5f/6f: 0-1 7f-8f: 0-1 9f-13f: 0-0 14f+: 0-0
Track : LH: 0-0 RH: 0-0 Tight: 0-0 Gall: 0-0
Aids: Bl: 0-0 Vi: 0-0 Tstrap: 0-0 Ckp: 0-0

Angelena Ballerina (IRE)

96(95) (69)**80**
2-y-o ch f Indian Haven-Nom Francais (First Trump)
A Bailey Bridgewater Equine Ltd

Placings:424206562 **(6858)**
2009: 5^{4}GF, 6^{2}GF, 5^{4}GF, 6^{2}G, 6^{0}G, 6^{6}GS, 7^{5}SD, 6^{6}GS, 8^{2}SD,

	Starts	1st	2nd	3rd	Win & Pl
Career Total (Turf)	7	0	2	0	4741

Career Total (AW)	2	0	1	0	705

Going (Turf): Sf: 0-0 GS: 0-2 Gd: 0-2 GF: 0-3 Fm: 0-0
Distance: 5f/6f: 0-7 7f-8f: 0-1 9f-13f: 0-1 14f+: 0-0
Track : LH: 0-4 RH: 0-0 Tight: 0-3 Gall: 0-0
Aids: Bl: 0-0 Vi: 0-0 Tstrap: 0-5 Ckp: 0-5
Best Rating: 80 6/09 NmkJ 6f good

Useful; effective over 6f; acts on fast ground; has worn cheekpieces.

Angelica's Art (IRE)

84(59) **55**
3-y-o b f Marju (IRE)-Flatter (IRE) (Barathea (IRE))
B J Meehan Matthew Green & Pierre Rolin

Placings:00000 **(4650)**
2009: 7^{0}GF, 8^{0}F, 9^{0}GF, 12^{0}GF, **11^{0}SD,**

	Starts	1st	2nd	3rd	Win & Pl
Career Total (Turf)	4	0	0	0	
Career Total (AW)	1	0	0	0	

Going (Turf): Sf: 0-0 GS: 0-0 Gd: 0-0 GF: 0-3 Fm: 0-1
Distance: 5f/6f: 0-0 7f-8f: 0-1 9f-13f: 0-4 14f+: 0-0
Track : LH: 0-1 RH: 0-3 Tight: 0-2 Gall: 0-0
Aids: Bl: 0-1 Vi: 0-0 Tstrap: 0-0 Ckp: 0-0
Best Rating: 55 5/09 Nott 1m75y firm

Angelo Poliziano

96(104) (74)**74**
3-y-o ch g Medicean-Helen Sharp (Pivotal)
Mrs A Duffield Middleham Park Racing XXVIII

Placings:0-040061**454410000** **(7355)**
2009: 7^{0}GF, 6^{4}F, 7^{0}GF, 5^{0}GF, 5^{6}GF, **5^{1}SD, 5^{4}SD,** 5^{5}G, 5^{4}G, 5^{4}G, 5^{1}GF, 5^{0}GS, 5^{0}GF, **5^{0}SD, 5^{0}SD,**

	Starts	1st	2nd	3rd	Win & Pl
Career Total (Turf)	11	1	0	0	3628
Career Total (AW)	5	1	0	0	3886

74	8/09	Newc	5f	(0-75)H	G-F	£2978
74	6/09	Wolv	5f20y	(0-70)H	STD	£3885

Total win prize-money £6865

Going (Turf): Sf: 0-0 GS: 0-1 Gd: 0-3 **GF: 1-6** Fm: 0-1
Distance: 5f/6f: 2-13 7f-8f: 0-3 9f-13f: 0-0 14f+: 0-0
Track : LH: 1-7 RH: 0-1 **Tight: 1-4** Gall: 0-1
Aids: Bl: 1-4 Vi: 0-2 Tstrap: 1-4 Ckp: 1-4
Best Rating: 74 8/09 Newc 5f gd-fm

Fair; effective at 5f; has worn headgear.

Angelofthenorth

103 **53**
7-y-o b m Tomba-Dark Kristal (IRE) (Gorytus (USA))
C J Teague Michael Marsh Racing

Placings:34333010/1100045050033/66045040**0000**/0/001354-060435230 **(5008)**
2009: 6^{0}GF, 5^{0}GF, 5^{0}GF, 5^{4}G, 5^{3}GF, 5^{5}S, 5^{2}G, 5^{3}GF, 5^{0}G,

	Starts	1st	2nd	3rd	Win & Pl
Career Total (Turf)	47	4	1	9	21158
Career Total (AW)	2	0	0	0	

53	5/08	Muss	5f		G-F	£2266
76	4/05	Nott	5f13y	(0-70)H	G-S	£3478
75	3/05	Muss	5f	(0-75)H	G-S	£4007
64	9/04	Ripn	5f		G-F	£4102

Total win prize-money £13855

Going (Turf): Sf: 0-9 **GS: 2-5** Gd: 0-12 **GF: 2-20** Fm: 0-1
Distance: 5f/6f: 4-47 7f-8f: 0-2 9f-13f: 0-0 14f+: 0-0
Track : LH: 0-6 RH: 0-2 Tight: 0-4 Gall: 0-2
Aids: Bl: 0-4 Vi: 0-0 Tstrap: 0-0 Ckp: 0-0
Best Rating: 76 4/05 Nott 5f13y gd-sft

Plating-class; best over 5f and acts on most ground; has worn blinkers.

Angels And Demons (IRE)

82(78) (5)**35**
3-y-o b f Golan (IRE)-I Want You Now (IRE) (Nicolotte)
R C Guest (Garry Moss 26/7) Brooklands Racing

Placings:00050 **(6310)**
2009: 6^{0}SD, 8^{0}GS, 8^{0}G, 12^{5}G, 12^{0}GF,

	Starts	1st	2nd	3rd	Win & Pl
Career Total (Turf)	4	0	0	0	0
Career Total (AW)	1	0	0	0	

Going (Turf): Sf: 0-0 GS: 0-1 Gd: 0-2 GF: 0-1 Fm: 0-0
Distance: 5f/6f: 0-1 7f-8f: 0-0 9f-13f: 0-4 14f+: 0-0
Track : LH: 0-2 RH: 0-3 Tight: 0-2 Gall: 0-0
Aids: Bl: 0-0 Vi: 0-0 Tstrap: 0-0 Ckp: 0-0
Best Rating: 35 9/09 Muss 1m4f100y good

Angelsbemine

(72) (10)**30**
3-y-o b f Almaty (IRE)-Undercover Girl (IRE) (Barathea (IRE))
J R Norton Gary Hancock

Placings:00000-0 **(0041)**
2009: 6^{0}SS,

	Starts	1st	2nd	3rd	Win & Pl
Career Total (Turf)	2	0	0	0	
Career Total (AW)	4	0	0	0	

Going (Turf): Sf: 0-1 GS: 0-1 Gd: 0-0 GF: 0-0 Fm: 0-0
Distance: 5f/6f: 0-4 7f-8f: 0-2 9f-13f: 0-0 14f+: 0-0
Track : LH: 0-4 RH: 0-0 Tight: 0-0 Gall: 0-0
Aids: Bl: 0-0 Vi: 0-1 Tstrap: 0-0 Ckp: 0-0
Best Rating: 30 8/08 Ripn 5f gd-sft

Angie's Nap (USA)

86(95) (67)**57**
2-y-o ch f Lion Heart (USA)-Magick Top (USA) (Topsider (USA))
P S McEntee (E A L Dunlop 29/5) Eventmaker Racehorses

Placings:002006**201114653** **(7868)**
2009: 5^{0}GF, 5^{0}G, 5^{2}GF, **5^{0}SD, 5^{0}SD,** 6^{6}G, **5^{2}SD, 5^{0}SD, 5^{1}SD, 6^{1}SD, 5^{1}SD, 6^{4}SD, 5^{6}SD, 5^{5}SS, 7^{3}SS,**

	Starts	1st	2nd	3rd	Win & Pl
Career Total (Turf)	4	0	1	0	578
Career Total (AW)	11	3	1	1	9193

59	11/09	Sthl	5f		STD	£2047
67	10/09	Sthl	6f	(0-65)	STD	£2524
58	9/09	Sthl	5f	(0-70)	STD	£3412

Total win prize-money £7984

Going (Turf): Sf: 0-0 GS: 0-0 Gd: 0-2 GF: 0-2 Fm: 0-0
Distance: 5f/6f: 3-13 7f-8f: 0-2 9f-13f: 0-0 14f+: 0-0
Track : LH: 1-4 RH: 0-1 Tight: 0-1 Gall: 0-2
Aids: Bl: 0-0 Vi: 0-2 Tstrap: 3-9 Ckp: 3-9
Best Rating: 67 10/09 Sthl 6f stand

Modest; suited by 5f-6f and Fibresand; has worn cheekpieces and a visor.

Angle Of Attack (IRE)

90(101) (71)**83**
4-y-o b g Acclamation-Travel Spot Girl (Primo Dominie)
A D Brown S Pedersen

Placings:54462053136/01033550-0000600001 **(7869)**
2009: 5^{0}GF, 5^{0}GF, 5^{0}GF, 5^{0}HY, **6^{6}SD,** 5^{0}GF, 6^{0}GF, 5^{0}G, **7^{0}SD, 6^{1}SS,**

	Starts	1st	2nd	3rd	Win & Pl
Career Total (Turf)	22	1	1	4	8198
Career Total (AW)	7	2	0	0	4908

	12/09	Sthl	6f	(0-50)H	SS	£1942
83	8/08	Haml	5f4y	(0-75)H	SFT	£3238
74	10/07	Ling	5f	(0-65)	STD	£2730

Total win prize-money £7911

Going (Turf): Sf: 1-6 GS: 0-3 Gd: 0-4 GF: 0-9 Fm: 0-0
Distance: 5f/6f: 3-27 7f-8f: 0-2 9f-13f: 0-0 14f+: 0-0
Track : LH: 2-11 RH: 0-0 **Tight: 1-7** Gall: 0-0
Aids: Bl: 0-1 **Vi: 1-1** Tstrap: 0-1 Ckp: 0-1
Best Rating: 83 8/08 Haml 5f4y soft

Moderate; effective at 5f-6f; acts on good and soft ground and both AW surfaces.

Anglezarke (IRE)

109 **107**
3-y-o br f Acclamation-Welsh Mist (Damister (USA))
T D Easterby David W Armstrong

Placings:1416254-1236 **(3638)**
2009: 5^{1}G, 5^{2}G, 5^{3}GF, 5^{6}G,

	Starts	1st	2nd	3rd	Win & Pl
Career Total (Turf)	11	3	2	1	95429

97	5/09	York	5f		GD	£12952
88	7/08	York	5f	H	G-F	£7123
74	4/08	Ripn	5f		G-S	£4209

Total win prize-money £24285

Going (Turf): Sf: 0-2 **GS: 1-2 Gd: 1-5 GF: 1-2** Fm: 0-0
Distance: 5f/6f: 3-11 7f-8f: 0-0 9f-13f: 0-0 14f+: 0-0
Track : LH: 0-0 RH: 0-0 Tight: 0-0 Gall: 0-0
Aids: Bl: 0-0 Vi: 0-0 Tstrap: 0-0 Ckp: 0-0
Best Rating: 107 6/09 Asct 5f gd-fm

Smart; runner-up in the Group 2 Flying Childers in 2008; third in the 2009 King's Stand; effective over 5f-6f and acts on most ground.

Angus Newz

108 (79)**100**
6-y-o ch m Compton Place-Hickleton Lady (IRE) (Kala Shikari)
M Quinn M J Quinn

Placings:00513131343/12515010000104/6000160400521 3/3230611300511300-0435040540333560 **(6843)**
2009: 5^{0}GS, 5^{4}G, 5^{3}GF, 6^{5}GS, 6^{0}HY, 5^{4}GY, 5^{0}G, 5^{5}GF, 5^{4}S, 6^{0}G, 5^{3}GS, 5^{3}GF, 6^{3}GF, 6^{5}GF, 6^{6}GF, 5^{0}G,

	Starts	1st	2nd	3rd	Win & Pl
Career Total (Turf)	69	13	3	13	178251
Career Total (AW)	2	0	0	0	351

98	9/08	Ches	6f18y		G-S	£24978
96	9/08	Leic	5f2y		HVY	£7477
93	6/08	NmkJ	6f		G-F	£9066
96	6/08	Carl	5f	(0-85)H	SFT	£5180
95	10/07	NmkR	6f	(0-100)H	GD	£12464

96 5/07 Ripn 6f (0-95)H GD £9348
97 9/06 Haml 5f4y G-S £17034
100 6/06 Sand 5f6y G-F £15898
101 5/06 Nott 6f15y SFT £17034
91 4/06 Leic 5f218y G-S £6232
80 8/05 Wwck 5f110y G-F £3757
71 7/05 Yarm 5f43y G-S £2912
66 6/05 Hayd 6f G-F £3653
Total win prize-money £135035

Going (Turf): Sf: 3-14 **GS: 4-14** Gd: 2-15**GF: 4-25**Fm: 0-0
Distance: **5f/6f: 11-64** 7f-8f: 2-7 9f-13f: 0-0 14f+: 0-0
Track : **LH: 2-15** RH: 1-1 Tight: 1-9 Gall: 1-4
Aids: Bl: 0-0 **Vi: 7-44** Tstrap: 0-0 Ckp: 0-0
Best Rating: **101** 5/06 Nott 6f15y soft

Very useful; winner in Listed company; effective over 5f-6f; acts on most ground, but may prefer cut; suited by forcing tactics; has worn a visor.

Anhar (USA)

101 **95**
2-y-o b/br c Kingmambo (USA)-Because (IRE) (Sadler's Wells (USA))
Saeed Bin Suroor Godolphin

Placings:12 **(7184)**
2009: 8^{1}GS, 10^{2}G,

	Starts	1st	2nd	3rd	Win & Pl
Career Total (Turf)	**2**	**1**	**1**	**0**	**5527**

79 10/09 Nott 1m75y G-S £2914
Total win prize-money £2914

Going (Turf): Sf: 0-0 **GS: 1-1** Gd: 0-1 GF: 0-0 Fm: 0-0
Distance: 5f/6f: 0-0 7f-8f: 0-0 **9f-13f: 1-2** 14f+: 0-0
Track : **LH: 1-1** RH: 0-0 Tight: 0-0 Gall: 0-0
Aids: Bl: 0-0 Vi: 0-0 Tstrap: 0-0 Ckp: 0-0
Best Rating: **95** 10/09 NmkR 1m2f good

Useful; effective over 1m; acts on easy ground.

Anice Stellato (IRE)

104 **93**
3-y-o br f Dalakhani (IRE)-Summer Spice (IRE) (Key Of Luck (USA))
R M Beckett Clipper Logistics

Placings:1-50215 **(6419)**
2009: 11^{5}GF, 12^{0}GF, 10^{2}GF, 12^{1}GF, 12^{5}GF,

	Starts	1st	2nd	3rd	Win & Pl
Career Total (Turf)	**6**	**2**	**1**	**0**	**16810**

93 9/09 NmkR 1m4f (0-95)H G-F £9066
81 8/08 NmkJ 7f GD £4857
Total win prize-money £13923

Going (Turf): Sf: 0-0 GS: 0-0 **Gd: 1-1 GF: 1-5** Fm: 0-0
Distance: 5f/6f: 0-0 7f-8f: 1-1 9f-13f: 1-5 14f+: 0-0
Track : LH: 0-1 **RH: 1-4** Tight: 0-3 **Gall: 1-2**
Aids: Bl: 0-1 Vi: 0-0 Tstrap: 0-0 Ckp: 0-0
Best Rating: **93** 9/09 NmkR 1m4f gd-fm

Very useful; stays 1m4f; acts on a sound surface; has worn blinkers.

Animator

98(99) (78)**75**
4-y-o b g Act One-Robsart (IRE) (Robellino (USA))
C Grant Woodgate Family

Placings:0**5**4**1**/14061**0**3-00 **(2200)**
2009: 10^{0}F, 10^{0}S,

	Starts	1st	2nd	3rd	Win & Pl
Career Total (Turf)	**9**	**1**	**0**	**1**	**4253**
Career Total (AW)	**4**	**2**	**0**	**0**	**5505**

75 8/08 Wind 1m2f7y (0-75)H G-S £3070
78 4/08 Kemp 1m2f (0-75)H STD £2590
70 11/07 Wolv 1m141y (0-75) STD £2914
Total win prize-money £8576

Going (Turf): Sf: 0-1 **GS: 1-3** Gd: 0-1 GF: 0-3 Fm: 0-1
Distance: 5f/6f: 0-0 7f-8f: 0-2 **9f-13f: 3-11** 14f+: 0-0
Track : LH: 1-4 **RH: 2-7 Tight: 2-5** Gall: 0-1
Aids: Bl: 0-0 Vi: 0-0 Tstrap: 0-0 Ckp: 0-0
Best Rating: **78** 4/08 Kemp 1m2f stand

Fair; stays 1m2f; acts on easy ground and Polytrack.

Anita's Luck (IRE)

80 **66**
2-y-o b g Key Of Luck (USA)-Anita's Contessa (IRE) (Anita's Prince)
B Palling H Perkins

Placings:4 **(1083)**
2009: 5^{4}GF,

	Starts	1st	2nd	3rd	Win & Pl
Career Total (Turf)	**1**	**0**	**0**	**0**	**192**

Going (Turf): **Sf: 0-0 GS: 0-0 Gd: 0-0 GF: 0-1 Fm: 0-0**
Distance: 5f/6f: 0-1 7f-8f: 0-0 9f-13f: 0-0 14f+: 0-0
Track : LH: 0-0 RH: 0-0 Tight: 0-0 Gall: 0-0
Aids: Bl: 0-0 Vi: 0-0 Tstrap: 0-0 Ckp: 0-0
Best Rating: **66** 4/09 Leic 5f2y gd-fm

Anitra's Dance

67(75) (22)**32**
2-y-o b f Tobougg (IRE)-Dancemma (Emarati (USA))
P Howling Gaming Media Solutions Ltd

Placings:000 **(3925)**
2009: 6^{0}SD, 6^{0}GS, 5^{0}SF,

	Starts	1st	2nd	3rd	Win & Pl
Career Total (Turf)	**1**	**0**	**0**	**0**	
Career Total (AW)	**2**	**0**	**0**	**0**	

Going (Turf): **Sf: 0-0 GS: 0-1 Gd: 0-0 GF: 0-0 Fm: 0-0**
Distance: 5f/6f: 0-3 7f-8f: 0-0 9f-13f: 0-0 14f+: 0-0
Track : LH: 0-1 RH: 0-1 Tight: 0-1 Gall: 0-0
Aids: Bl: 0-0 Vi: 0-0 Tstrap: 0-0 Ckp: 0-0
Best Rating: **32** 6/09 NmkJ 6f gd-sft

Anjomarba (IRE)

101(97) (65)**80**
2-y-o b f Tillerman-Golden Charm (IRE) (Common Grounds)
W G M Turner Marbary Partnership

Placings:0324511104500433 **(7805)**
2009: 5^{0}G, 5^{3}GF, 5^{2}F, 5^{4}SD, 6^{5}G, 6^{1}G, 6^{1}F, 6^{1}GS, 6^{0}GF, 5^{4}G, 6^{5}GF, 6^{0}GF, 6^{0}S, 7^{4}SD, 5^{3}SD, 6^{3}SD,

	Starts	1st	2nd	3rd	Win & Pl
Career Total (Turf)	**12**	**3**	**1**	**1**	**14420**
Career Total (AW)	**4**	**0**	**0**	**2**	**1008**

80 6/09 York 6f G-S £6476
71 6/09 Thsk 6f FRM £4274
68 5/09 Yarm 6f3y GD £1942
Total win prize-money £12693

Going (Turf): Sf: 0-1 **GS: 1-1 Gd: 1-4** GF: 0-4 **Fm: 1-2**
Distance: **5f/6f: 2-14** 7f-8f: 1-2 9f-13f: 0-0 14f+: 0-0
Track : LH: 0-5 RH: 0-0 Tight: 0-4 Gall: 0-1
Aids: Bl: 0-0 Vi: 0-0 Tstrap: 0-1 Ckp: 0-1
Best Rating: **80** 6/09 York 6f gd-sft

Fair; suited by 5f-6f; acts on fast and soft ground; goes on Polytrack; has worn cheekpieces.

Anmar (USA)

(108) (111)**99**
3-y-o ch c Rahy (USA)-Ranin (Unfuwain (USA))
Saeed Bin Suroor Godolphin

Placings:120-1 **(7323)**
2009: 10^{1}SD,

	Starts	1st	2nd	3rd	Win & Pl
Career Total (Turf)	**3**	**1**	**1**	**0**	**11313**
Career Total (AW)	**1**	**1**	**0**	**0**	**7353**

111 11/09 Kemp 1m2f STD £7352
83 8/08 Sand 7f16y GD £4857
Total win prize-money £12210

Going (Turf): Sf: 0-1 GS: 0-1 **Gd: 1-1** GF: 0-0 Fm: 0-0
Distance: 5f/6f: 0-0 7f-8f: 1-3 9f-13f: 1-1 14f+: 0-0
Track : LH: 0-0 **RH: 2-4** Tight: 0-0 Gall: 0-1
Aids: Bl: 0-0 **Vi: 1-1** Tstrap: 0-0 Ckp: 0-0
Best Rating: **111** 11/09 Kemp 1m2f stand

Smart; suited by 1m2f; acts on any ground including Polytrack; has worn a visor.

Ann Birkett

89 **33**
3-y-o ch f Beat Hollow-Blue Gentian (USA) (Known Fact (USA))
Miss J Feilden J Birkett

Placings:0 **(3549)**
2009: 10^{0}GF,

	Starts	1st	2nd	3rd	Win & Pl
Career Total (Turf)	**1**	**0**	**0**	**0**	

Going (Turf): **Sf: 0-0 GS: 0-0 Gd: 0-0 GF: 0-1 Fm: 0-0**
Distance: 5f/6f: 0-0 7f-8f: 0-0 9f-13f: 0-1 14f+: 0-0
Track : LH: 0-1 RH: 0-0 Tight: 0-1 Gall: 0-0
Aids: Bl: 0-0 Vi: 0-0 Tstrap: 0-0 Ckp: 0-0
Best Rating: **33** 7/09 Yarm 1m2f21y gd-fm

Anna's Boy

86 **42**
2-y-o ch g Reel Buddy (USA)-Simianna (Bluegrass Prince (IRE))
A Berry A Underwood

Placings:063 **(6381)**
2009: 6^{0}S, 6^{6}S, 6^{3}GF,

	Starts	1st	2nd	3rd	Win & Pl
Career Total (Turf)	**3**	**0**	**0**	**1**	**751**

Going (Turf): **Sf: 0-2 GS: 0-0 Gd: 0-0 GF: 0-1 Fm: 0-0**
Distance: 5f/6f: 0-2 7f-8f: 0-1 9f-13f: 0-0 14f+: 0-0
Track : LH: 0-0 RH: 0-0 Tight: 0-0 Gall: 0-0
Aids: Bl: 0-0 Vi: 0-0 Tstrap: 0-0 Ckp: 0-0
Best Rating: **42** 9/09 Newc 6f gd-fm

Annabelle's Charm (IRE)

102(105) (77)**99**

4-y-o ch f Indian Ridge-Kylemore (IRE) (Sadler's Wells (USA))

L M Cumani Merry Fox Stud Limited

Placings:35-1531241020 **(7347a)**

2009: 10^{1}SD, 10^{5}SD, 10^{3}G, 9^{1}GF, 9^{2}G, 8^{4}GF, 8^{1}GF, 8^{0}G, 8^{2}S, 10^{0}VS,

	Starts	1st	2nd	3rd	Win & Pl
Career Total (Turf)	8	2	2	1	50704
Career Total (AW)	4	1	0	1	3133

99	8/09	Bath	1m5y	G-F	£22708
85	4/09	Folk	1m1f149y (0-80)H	G-F	£5180
77	1/09	Ling	1m2f	STD	£2729

Total win prize-money £30619

Going (Turf): Sf: 0-1 GS: 0-0 Gd: 0-3 **GF: 2-3** Fm: 0-0
Distance: 5f/6f: 0-0 7f-8f: 0-2 **9f-13f: 3-10** 14f+: 0-0
Track : **LH: 2-6** RH: 1-6 **Tight: 3-7** Gall: 0-1
Aids: Bl: 0-0 Vi: 0-0 Tstrap: 0-0 Ckp: 0-0
Best Rating: 99 10/09 Siro 1m soft

Very useful; Listed winner; effective at 1m-1m2f; acts on fast ground and on Polytrack.

Annacaboe (IRE)

21

2-y-o b f Footstepsinthesand-Alexandria (IRE) (Irish River (FR))

Mrs L C Jewell Kevin Quinn

Placings:0 **(4906)**

2009: 5^{0}G,

	Starts	1st	2nd	3rd	Win & Pl
Career Total (Turf)	1	0	0	0	

Going (Turf): Sf: 0-0 GS: 0-0 Gd: 0-1 GF: 0-0 Fm: 0-0
Distance: 5f/6f: 0-1 7f-8f: 0-0 9f-13f: 0-0 14f+: 0-0
Track : LH: 0-0 RH: 0-0 Tight: 0-0 Gall: 0-0
Aids: Bl: 0-0 Vi: 0-0 Tstrap: 0-0 Ckp: 0-0

Annambo

99(101) (66)**63**

9-y-o ch g In The Wings-Anna Matrushka (Mill Reef (USA))

Andrew Reid A S Reid

Placings:3/120100/00/0062010200/403/44121062/036043 201 **(6226)**

2009: 11^{0}GF, 14^{3}GF, 11^{6}GF, 12^{0}G, 12^{4}SD, 13^{F}, 12^{2}SD, 13^{0}SD, 12^{1}SD,

	Starts	1st	2nd	3rd	Win & Pl
Career Total (Turf)	28	4	2	4	33089
Career Total (AW)	11	2	4	0	8836

66	9/09	Kemp	1m4f	(0-60)H	STD	£2047
71	8/07	Wolv	1m4f50y		STD	£2047
82	6/07	Newb	1m5f61y	(0-75)H	G-F	£3238
82	7/05	NmkJ	1m6f175y	(0-85)H	G-F	£6097
91	7/03	Bath	1m3f144y	C(0-85) HRD		£10381
78	4/03	Thsk	1m4f	D	FRM	£5609

Total win prize-money £29422

Going (Turf): Sf: 0-2 GS: 0-1 Gd: 0-5 **GF: 2-14 Fm: 2-6**
Distance: 5f/6f: 0-0 7f-8f: 0-0 **9f-13f: 4-22** 14f+: 2-17
Track : **LH: 4-23** RH: 2-14 **Tight: 3-23** Gall: 2-13
Aids: Bl: 0-0 **Vi: 2-7** Tstrap: 0-4 Ckp: 0-4
Best Rating: 91 7/03 Bath 1m3f144y hard

Moderate; stays 2m, but effective at shorter; acts on most types of ground including Polytrack; has worn a visor and cheekpieces.

Annan Rock (IRE)

84(87) (41)**37**

3-y-o b g Statue Of Liberty (USA)-My Enigma (Rainbow Quest (USA))

W J Musson Libertys

Placings:060 **(4381)**

2009: 8^{0}SD, 8^{6}SD, 8^{0}G,

	Starts	1st	2nd	3rd	Win & Pl
Career Total (Turf)	1	0	0	0	
Career Total (AW)	2	0	0	0	0

Going (Turf): Sf: 0-0 GS: 0-0 Gd: 0-1 GF: 0-0 Fm: 0-0
Distance: 5f/6f: 0-0 7f-8f: 0-1 9f-13f: 0-2 14f+: 0-0
Track : LH: 0-2 RH: 0-1 Tight: 0-3 Gall: 0-0
Aids: Bl: 0-0 Vi: 0-0 Tstrap: 0-0 Ckp: 0-0
Best Rating: 41 7/09 Ling 1m stand

Anne Of Kiev (IRE)

(104) (87)**68**

4-y-o b f Oasis Dream-Top Flight Queen (Mark Of Esteem (IRE))

J R Gask Horses First Racing Limited

Placings:42/2212-01 **(7634)**

2009: 5^{0}SD, 5^{1}SD,

	Starts	1st	2nd	3rd	Win & Pl
Career Total (Turf)	2	0	1	0	1124
Career Total (AW)	6	2	3	0	9874

84	12/09	Wolv	5f20y	(0-75)H	STD	£3238
79	10/08	Wolv	5f20y		STD	£3070

Total win prize-money £6309

Going (Turf): Sf: 0-0 GS: 0-1 Gd: 0-1 GF: 0-0 Fm: 0-0
Distance: **5f/6f: 2-7** 7f-8f: 0-1 9f-13f: 0-0 14f+: 0-0
Track : **LH: 2-6** RH: 0-0 **Tight: 2-5** Gall: 0-1
Aids: Bl: 0-0 Vi: 0-0 Tstrap: 0-0 Ckp: 0-0
Best Rating: 87 8/08 GrLe 6f stand

Fair; effective from 5f-7f; acts on good ground and on Polytrack; has worn a tongue tie.

Annelko

71 **21**

2-y-o b c Sulamani (IRE)-Creeking (Persian Bold)

A B Haynes David Prosser

Placings:0 **(6931)**

2009: 8^{0}G,

	Starts	1st	2nd	3rd	Win & Pl
Career Total (Turf)	1	0	0	0	

Going (Turf): Sf: 0-0 GS: 0-0 Gd: 0-1 GF: 0-0 Fm: 0-0
Distance: 5f/6f: 0-0 7f-8f: 0-0 9f-13f: 0-1 14f+: 0-0
Track : LH: 0-1 RH: 0-0 Tight: 0-1 Gall: 0-0
Aids: Bl: 0-0 Vi: 0-0 Tstrap: 0-0 Ckp: 0-0
Best Rating: 21 10/09 Bath 1m5y good

Annes Rocket (IRE)

101(98) (67)**62**

4-y-o b c Fasliyev (USA)-Aguilas Perla (IRE) (Indian Ridge)

J C Fox The Cross Keys Racing Club

Placings:05541/560040-0066211U000200410 **(7051)**

2009: 8^{0}SD, 8^{0}SD, 7^{6}SD, 7^{6}SD, 6^{2}GF, 8^{1}GF, 6^{1}GF, 6^{U}G, 7^{0}F, 8^{0}GF, 7^{0}F, 7^{2}G, 7^{0}SD, 7^{0}SD, 8^{4}GF, 7^{1}SD, 7^{0}SD,

	Starts	1st	2nd	3rd	Win & Pl
Career Total (Turf)	14	2	2	0	6661
Career Total (AW)	14	2	0	0	5016

67	10/09	Kemp	7f	(0-55)H	STD	£2047
62	5/09	Brig	6f209y	(0-60)H	G-F	£2460
59	5/09	Wwck	1m22y	(0-60)H	G-F	£2047
67	12/07	Wolv	5f216y		STD	£2968

Total win prize-money £9524

Going (Turf): Sf: 0-1 GS: 0-2 Gd: 0-2 **GF: 2-7** Fm: 0-2
Distance: 5f/6f: 1-7 **7f-8f: 2-20** 9f-13f: 1-1 14f+: 0-0
Track : **LH: 3-16** RH: 1-6 **Tight: 1-9** Gall: 0-0
Aids: Bl: 0-0 Vi: 0-0 Tstrap: 0-0 Ckp: 0-0
Best Rating: 67 10/09 Kemp 7f stand

Moderate; effective over 6f-1m; acts on fast ground and on Polytrack.

Annes Sound (IRE)

90 (43)**50**

3-y-o gr f Mull Of Kintyre (USA)-Striking Sound (USA) (Rubiano (USA))

Patrick Morris Sensible Syndicate

Placings:00-00000 **(5872)**

2009: 10^{0}GF, 11^{0}GF, 10^{0}G, 10^{0}GF, 10^{0}G,

	Starts	1st	2nd	3rd	Win & Pl
Career Total (Turf)	6	0	0	0	
Career Total (AW)	1	0	0	0	

Going (Turf): Sf: 0-0 GS: 0-0 Gd: 0-2 GF: 0-3 Fm: 0-0
Distance: 5f/6f: 0-0 7f-8f: 0-2 9f-13f: 0-5 14f+: 0-0
Track : LH: 0-6 RH: 0-1 Tight: 0-3 Gall: 0-2
Aids: Bl: 0-0 Vi: 0-0 Tstrap: 0-0 Ckp: 0-0
Best Rating: 50 5/09 Ches 1m2f75y gd-fm

Annia (IRE)

90(87) (66)**74**

2-y-o b f Antonius Pius (USA)-Floosie (IRE) (Night Shift (USA))

N P Littmoden (David Marnane 14/8) Mrs Linda Francis

Placings:6000000000 **(7778)**

2009: 5^{6}SD, 5^{0}SD, 6^{0}YS, 5^{0}GF, 5^{0}SD, 5^{U}F, 6^{0}SD, 8^{0}SD, 5^{0}SD, 5^{0}SD,

	Starts	1st	2nd	3rd	Win & Pl
Career Total (Turf)	3	0	0	0	
Career Total (AW)	7	0	0	0	

Going (Turf): Sf: 0-0 GS: 0-0 Gd: 0-0 GF: 0-1 Fm: 0-1
Distance: 5f/6f: 0-9 7f-8f: 0-1 9f-13f: 0-0 14f+: 0-0
Track : LH: 0-7 RH: 0-1 Tight: 0-2 Gall: 0-1
Aids: Bl: 0-0 Vi: 0-0 Tstrap: 0-0 Ckp: 0-0
Best Rating: 74 8/09 Newb 5f34y gd-fm

Moderate sprinter; has worn a tongue tie.

Annia Galeria (IRE)

89(90) (52)**58**

2-y-o b f Antonius Pius (USA)-Jay Gee (IRE) (Second Set (IRE))

C A Dwyer (A B Haynes 20/7) S B Components Ltd & Mrs Shelley Dwyer

Placings:130**500** **(5950)**

2009: 5^{1}GF, 6^{3}G, 5^{0}SD, 5^{5}SD, 5^{0}SD, 5^{0}GF,

	Starts	1st	2nd	3rd	Win & Pl
Career Total (Turf)	3	1	0	1	2232
Career Total (AW)	3	0	0	0	0

58 7/09 Leic 5f2y G-F £1942

Total win prize-money £1943

Going (Turf): Sf: 0-0 GS: 0-0 Gd: 0-1 **GF: 1-2** Fm: 0-0
Distance: **5f/6f: 1-5** 7f-8f: 0-1 9f-13f: 0-0 14f+: 0-0
Track : LH: 0-1 RH: 0-2 Tight: 0-1 Gall: 0-0
Aids: Bl: 0-0 Vi: 0-0 Tstrap: 0-0 Ckp: 0-0
Best Rating: 58 7/09 Leic 5f2y gd-fm

Half-sister to winners, including the once very useful Collateral Damage; winner of 5f seller on fast ground.

Annibale Caro

95(96) (58)**79**

7-y-o b g Mtoto-Isabella Gonzaga (Rock Hopper)

J S Goldie Thomson & Fyffe Racing

Placings:050/3115/60/0500/**31113220-0000** **(5334)**

2009: 11^{0}GF, 10^{0}GF, 12^{0}GF, 10^{0}S,

	Starts	1st	2nd	3rd	Win & Pl
Career Total (Turf)	20	5	2	2	20667
Career Total (AW)	5	0	0	1	408

74 5/08 Newc 1m4f93y (0-60)H G-F £2590
68 5/08 Muss 1m4f (0-60)H G-F £2266
59 5/08 Catt 1m3f214y GD £2047
88 8/05 Ayr 1m2f192y (0-70)H G-F £3643
86 8/05 Carl 1m3f206y (0-80)H G-F £6886

Total win prize-money £17434

Going (Turf): Sf: 0-2 GS: 0-0 Gd: 1-8 **GF: 4-10** Fm: 0-0
Distance: 5f/6f: 0-1 7f-8f: 0-2 **9f-13f: 5-21** 14f+: 0-1
Track : **LH: 3-16** RH: 2-9 **Tight: 2-13** Gall: 1-3
Aids: Bl: 0-0 Vi: 0-0 Tstrap: 0-0 Ckp: 0-0
Best Rating: 88 8/05 Ayr 1m2f192y gd-fm

Fair; effective at around 1m4f; suited by quick ground.

Annie Go (IRE)

84(89) (49)**63**

5-y-o b m Golan (IRE)-Simple Annie (Simply Great (FR))

Aidan Anthony Howard A R Douglas

Placings:00400 **(7473a)**

2009: 10^{0}G, 14^{0}G, 16^{4}GY, 16^{0}SD, 12^{0}SD,

	Starts	1st	2nd	3rd	Win & Pl
Career Total (Turf)	3	0	0	0	338
Career Total (AW)	2	0	0	0	

Going (Turf): Sf: 0-0 GS: 0-0 Gd: 0-2 GF: 0-0 Fm: 0-0
Distance: 5f/6f: 0-0 7f-8f: 0-0 9f-13f: 0-2 14f+: 0-3
Track : LH: 0-5 RH: 0-0 Tight: 0-1 Gall: 0-0
Aids: Bl: 0-0 Vi: 0-0 Tstrap: 0-0 Ckp: 0-0
Best Rating: 63 10/09 Navn 2m gd-yld

Another Bottle (IRE)

95(98) (64)**80**

8-y-o b g Cape Cross (IRE)-Aster Aweke (IRE) (Alzao (USA))

Mrs S Leech C J Leech

Placings:033/01131/1020100/4000/005-**00540** **(2493)**

2009: 8^{0}SD, 8^{0}SD, 9^{5}GF, 12^{4}GS, 10^{0}GF,

	Starts	1st	2nd	3rd	Win & Pl
Career Total (Turf)	25	5	1	3	66611
Career Total (AW)	2	0	0	0	

105 7/05 Newb 1m (0-105)H G-F £26100
93 5/05 Ripn 1m1f170y (0-85)H G-F £6944
91 8/04 Ripn 1m C(0-100)H G-S £12272
88 7/04 Newb 1m D(0-85)H G-F £6136
84 5/04 Ayr 1m1f20y E(0-70) G-F £3594

Total win prize-money £55049

Going (Turf): Sf: 0-2 GS: 1-4 Gd: 0-7 **GF: 4-12** Fm: 0-0
Distance: 5f/6f: 0-1 **7f-8f: 3-15** 9f-13f: 2-11 14f+: 0-0
Track : LH: 1-9 **RH: 2-7 Tight: 2-7** Gall: 0-3
Aids: Bl: 0-0 Vi: 0-0 Tstrap: 0-0 Ckp: 0-0
Best Rating: 105 7/05 Newb 1m gd-fm

Useful; effective at up to 1m1f; acts on most types of ground.

Another Character (USA)

(51)

2-y-o b/br c Giant's Causeway (USA)-Mambo Halo (USA) (Southern Halo (USA))

M Blanshard Aykroyd And Sons Ltd

Placings:00 **(7400)**

2009: 8^{0}SD, 9^{0}SD,

	Starts	1st	2nd	3rd	Win & Pl
Career Total (Turf)	0	0	0	0	
Career Total (AW)	2	0	0	0	

Going (Turf): Sf: 0-0 GS: 0-0 Gd: 0-0 GF: 0-0 Fm: 0-0
Distance: 5f/6f: 0-0 7f-8f: 0-1 9f-13f: 0-1 14f+: 0-0
Track : LH: 0-1 RH: 0-1 Tight: 0-1 Gall: 0-0
Aids: Bl: 0-0 Vi: 0-0 Tstrap: 0-0 Ckp: 0-0

Another Decree

94(90) (44)**69**

4-y-o b g Diktat-Akhira (Emperor Jones (USA))

M Dods Mrs Karen S Pratt

Placings:440/016-**60530300** **(6840)**

2009: 8^{6}F, 6^{0}GS, 7^{5}G, 7^{3}GF, 7^{0}GF, 7^{3}GF, 8^{0}SD, 11^{0}G,

	Starts	1st	2nd	3rd	Win & Pl
Career Total (Turf)	13	1	0	2	4409
Career Total (AW)	1	0	0	0	

69 5/08 Pont 6f G-F £3238

Total win prize-money £3238

Going (Turf): Sf: 0-0 GS: 0-2 Gd: 0-5 **GF: 1-5** Fm: 0-1
Distance: **5f/6f: 1-6** 7f-8f: 0-6 9f-13f: 0-2 14f+: 0-0
Track : **LH: 1-6** RH: 0-0 Tight: 0-4 Gall: 0-0
Aids: Bl: 0-0 Vi: 0-0 Tstrap: 0-4 Ckp: 0-4
Best Rating: 72 10/07 NmkR 6f good

Fair; seems best at 6f; goes well on fast ground.

Another Echo

14 **22**

3-y-o b f Bahamian Bounty-Blue Nile (IRE) (Bluebird (USA))

W Storey W Storey

Placings:00-0 **(5513)**

2009: 8^{0}GF,

	Starts	1st	2nd	3rd	Win & Pl
Career Total (Turf)	3	0	0	0	

Going (Turf): Sf: 0-0 GS: 0-1 Gd: 0-0 GF: 0-2 Fm: 0-0
Distance: 5f/6f: 0-0 7f-8f: 0-2 9f-13f: 0-1 14f+: 0-0
Track : LH: 0-0 RH: 0-0 Tight: 0-0 Gall: 0-0
Aids: Bl: 0-0 Vi: 0-0 Tstrap: 0-0 Ckp: 0-0
Best Rating: 22 6/08 Haml 6f5y gd-fm

Another Genepi (USA)

(114) (71)**68**

6-y-o br m Stravinsky (USA)-Dawn Aurora (USA) (Night Shift (USA))

E J Creighton A S Reid

Placings:02/3205554/004023162433601000З/1242211040 4551453-40 **(0886)**

2009: 7^{4}SD, 7^{0}SD,

	Starts	1st	2nd	3rd	Win & Pl
Career Total (Turf)	12	0	2	2	2697
Career Total (AW)	35	6	5	4	19946

71 11/08 Sthl 7f STD £2047
83 3/08 Sthl 6f (0-65)H STD £1774
66 3/08 Wolv 5f216y STD £2331
70 1/08 Sthl 7f STD £1774
74 10/07 Wolv 7f32y (0-70)H STD £3412
76 4/07 Wolv 7f32y (0-60)H STD £2388

Total win prize-money £13731

Going (Turf): Sf: 0-0 GS: 0-0 Gd: 0-2 GF: 0-10 Fm: 0-0
Distance: 5f/6f: 2-12 **7f-8f: 4-33** 9f-13f: 0-2 14f+: 0-0
Track : **LH: 6-35** RH: 0-7 **Tight: 3-22** Gall: 0-1
Aids: **Bl: 6-31** Vi: 0-0 Tstrap: 0-2 Ckp: 0-2
Best Rating: 83 3/08 Sthl 6f stand

Modest; effective over 6f-1m; acts on a sound surface and sand; suited by forcing tactics.

Another Grand (IRE)

82(76) (37)**39**

2-y-o b g Statue Of Liberty (USA)-Fallacy (Selkirk (USA))

Mrs R A Carr David W Chapman

Placings:0F60 **(2996)**

2009: 6^{0}GS, 6^{F}GF, 5^{6}SD, 6^{0}GF,

	Starts	1st	2nd	3rd	Win & Pl
Career Total (Turf)	3	0	0	0	
Career Total (AW)	1	0	0	0	0

Going (Turf): Sf: 0-0 GS: 0-1 Gd: 0-0 GF: 0-2 Fm: 0-0
Distance: 5f/6f: 0-4 7f-8f: 0-0 9f-13f: 0-0 14f+: 0-0
Track : LH: 0-0 RH: 0-0 Tight: 0-0 Gall: 0-0
Aids: Bl: 0-0 Vi: 0-0 Tstrap: 0-0 Ckp: 0-0
Best Rating: 39 6/09 Thsk 6f gd-fm

Another Luke (IRE)

83(85) (46)48

3-y-o b c Captain Rio-Belalzao (IRE) (Alzao (USA))
T J Etherington Exors Of The Late C Hoggard

Placings:044006-00000 (6823)
2009: 8⁰F, 7⁰GF, 5⁰GF, 6⁰G, 6⁰GF,

	Starts	1st	2nd	3rd	Win & Pl
Career Total (Turf)	10	0	0	0	524
Career Total (AW)	1	0	0	0	

Going (Turf): **Sf: 0-0 GS: 0-4 Gd: 0-1 GF: 0-4 Fm: 0-1**
Distance: 5f/6f: 0-7 7f-8f: 0-4 9f-13f: 0-0 14f+: 0-0
Track : LH: 0-1 RH: 0-2 Tight: 0-2 Gall: 0-0
Aids: Bl: 0-0 Vi: 0-0 Tstrap: 0-0 Ckp: 0-0
Best Rating: 58 4/08 Newc 5f gd-sft

Another Magic Man (USA)

92(96) (71)71

2-y-o b/br c Chief Seattle (USA)-Georgia Anna (USA) (Stutz Blackhawk (USA))
J R Best Hucking Horses

Placings:05363 (7157)
2009: 7⁰GF, 7⁵SD, 7³GS, 9⁶GS, 7³SD,

	Starts	1st	2nd	3rd	Win & Pl
Career Total (Turf)	3	0	0	1	530
Career Total (AW)	2	0	0	1	403

Going (Turf): **Sf: 0-0 GS: 0-2 Gd: 0-0 GF: 0-1 Fm: 0-0**
Distance: 5f/6f: 0-0 7f-8f: 0-4 9f-13f: 0-1 14f+: 0-0
Track : LH: 0-2 RH: 0-1 Tight: 0-3 Gall: 0-0
Aids: Bl: 0-0 Vi: 0-0 Tstrap: 0-0 Ckp: 0-0
Best Rating: 71 10/09 Wolv 7f32y stand

Fair; stays 7f and acts on easy ground.

Another Socket

(98) (72)74

4-y-o b f Overbury (IRE)-Elsocko (Swing Easy (USA))
E S McMahon Mrs J McMahon

Placings:621/43003030-02 (1038)
2009: 5⁰SD, 5²SD,

	Starts	1st	2nd	3rd	Win & Pl
Career Total (Turf)	6	0	0	2	1156
Career Total (AW)	7	1	2	1	4972
69 11/07 Wolv 5f20y		STD	£2968		

Total win prize-money £2969

Going (Turf): **Sf: 0-1 GS: 0-1 Gd: 0-1 GF: 0-3 Fm: 0-0**
Distance: **5f/6f: 1-13** 7f-8f: 0-0 9f-13f: 0-0 14f+: 0-0
Track : **LH: 1-8** RH: 0-0 **Tight: 1-7** Gall: 0-1
Aids: Bl: 0-0 Vi: 0-0 Tstrap: 0-0 Ckp: 0-0
Best Rating: 74 5/08 NmkR 5f gd-fm

Fair; effective over 5f; acts on Polytrack.

Another Sold

66 14

2-y-o ch f Auction House (USA)-Countrywide Girl (IRE) (Catrail (USA))
A Berry Swanlow Stud

Placings:006 (3370)

2009: 5⁰GF, 5⁰GF, 5⁶GF,

	Starts	1st	2nd	3rd	Win & Pl
Career Total (Turf)	3	0	0	0	0

Going (Turf): **Sf: 0-0 GS: 0-0 Gd: 0-0 GF: 0-3 Fm: 0-0**
Distance: 5f/6f: 0-3 7f-8f: 0-0 9f-13f: 0-0 14f+: 0-0
Track : LH: 0-1 RH: 0-0 Tight: 0-1 Gall: 0-0
Aids: Bl: 0-0 Vi: 0-0 Tstrap: 0-0 Ckp: 0-0
Best Rating: 14 6/09 Ches 5f16y gd-fm

Another Try (IRE)

101(106) (73)70

4-y-o b g Spinning World (USA)-Mad Annie (USA) (Anabaa (USA))
A P Jarvis The Twyford Partnership

Placings:504-0011634510**2** (7813)
2009: 7⁰SD, 8⁰SD, 6¹SD, 6¹GF, 7⁶G, 7³SD, 7⁴GF, 6⁵S, 6¹GF, 6⁰SD, 7²SD,

	Starts	1st	2nd	3rd	Win & Pl
Career Total (Turf)	5	2	0	0	4667
Career Total (AW)	9	1	1	1	3277
70 10/09 Yarm 6f3y	(0-60)H	G-F	£2331		
67 6/09 Ling 6f	(0-65)H	G-F	£2047		
65 5/09 Sthl 6f	(0-55)H	STD	£2047		

Total win prize-money £6425

Going (Turf): Sf: 0-1 GS: 0-0 Gd: 0-1 **GF: 2-3** Fm: 0-0
Distance: **5f/6f: 2-4** 7f-8f: 1-10 9f-13f: 0-0 14f+: 0-0
Track : **LH: 1-6** RH: 0-4 Tight: 0-3 Gall: 0-1
Aids: Bl: 0-0 Vi: 0-0 Tstrap: 0-0 Ckp: 0-0
Best Rating: 73 12/09 Wolv 7f32y stand

Modest; effective over 6f; acts on Fibresand.

Ansells Pride (IRE)

101(102) (73)91

6-y-o b g King Charlemagne (USA)-Accounting (Sillery (USA))
B Smart Ansells Of Watford

Placings:22101/210120-000000325 (7854)
2009: 10⁰GS, 8⁰GF, 8⁰GF, 8⁰G, 8⁰GF, 8⁰SF, 8³SD, 8²SD, 8⁵SS,

	Starts	1st	2nd	3rd	Win & Pl
Career Total (Turf)	12	3	1	0	20741
Career Total (AW)	8	1	4	1	6013
90 5/08 Hayd 1m30y	(0-90)H	G-F	£8095		
91 4/08 Muss 1m	(0-85)H	SFT	£5504		
78 11/07 Muss 1m	(0-80)H	GD	£5181		
50 2/07 Kemp 1m		STD	£2047		

Total win prize-money £20830

Going (Turf): **Sf: 1-2** GS: 0-1 **Gd: 1-3 GF: 1-6** Fm: 0-0
Distance: 5f/6f: 0-0 **7f-8f: 3-10** 9f-13f: 1-10 14f+: 0-0
Track : LH: 1-12 **RH: 3-5 Tight: 2-7** Gall: 0-0
Aids: Bl: 0-0 Vi: 0-0 Tstrap: 0-0 Ckp: 0-0
Best Rating: 91 6/08 Rdcr 1m gd-fm

Modest; stays 1m; acts on most ground and on sand; effective from the front.

Ant Music (IRE)

85(85) (43)66

2-y-o b g Antonius Pius (USA)-Day Is Dawning (IRE) (Green Forest (USA))
J S Moore Phil Cunningham

Placings:64404 (7804)

2009: 5⁶GF, 6⁴G, 7⁴GF, 7⁰GF, 8⁴SD,

	Starts	1st	2nd	3rd	Win & Pl
Career Total (Turf)	4	0	0	0	678
Career Total (AW)	1	0	0	0	337

Going (Turf): **Sf: 0-0 GS: 0-0 Gd: 0-1 GF: 0-3 Fm: 0-0**
Distance: 5f/6f: 0-1 7f-8f: 0-3 9f-13f: 0-1 14f+: 0-0
Track : LH: 0-2 RH: 0-0 Tight: 0-2 Gall: 0-0
Aids: Bl: 0-0 Vi: 0-0 Tstrap: 0-0 Ckp: 0-0
Best Rating: 66 6/09 Thsk 7f gd-fm

Modest; stays 7f; acts on fast ground.

Antarctic Desert (IRE)

94 71

2-y-o b g Green Desert (USA)-Arctic Silk (Selkirk (USA))
K A Ryan Rievaulx Racing Syndicate 1

Placings:402 (6231)
2009: 7⁴S, 6⁰GS, 6²GF,

	Starts	1st	2nd	3rd	Win & Pl
Career Total (Turf)	3	0	1	0	1938

Going (Turf): **Sf: 0-1 GS: 0-1 Gd: 0-0 GF: 0-1 Fm: 0-0**
Distance: 5f/6f: 0-2 7f-8f: 0-1 9f-13f: 0-0 14f+: 0-0
Track : LH: 0-2 RH: 0-0 Tight: 0-1 Gall: 0-0
Aids: Bl: 0-0 Vi: 0-0 Tstrap: 0-0 Ckp: 0-0
Best Rating: 71 9/09 Pont 6f gd-fm

Fair; effective over 6f; acts on fast ground.

Anthemion (IRE)

93 (48)55

12-y-o ch g Night Shift (USA)-New Sensitive (Wattlefield)
Mrs J C McGregor Mrs Jean McGregor

Placings:0300/03114/40665200025/0200005313200000/50000002110640000/0000343521/503403004050**45**/052306-00 (3683)
2009: 9⁰GF, 7⁰GS,

	Starts	1st	2nd	3rd	Win & Pl
Career Total (Turf)	82	5	7	8	35500
Career Total (AW)	4	1	0	1	3197
60 8/06 Muss 1m	(0-65)H	G-F	£3412		
64 7/05 Ayr 1m	(0-70)H	GD	£4252		
64 7/05 Haml 1m1f36y	(0-70)H	G-F	£4267		
67 7/04 Haml 1m1f36y	E(0-70)H	G-F	£4322		
78 6/00 Hayd 7f30y	E(0-70)H	G-S	£3248		
78 5/00 Wolv 7f	E(0-70)H	STD	£2765		

Total win prize-money £22270

Going (Turf): Sf: 0-3 GS: 1-10 Gd: 1-19 **GF: 3-47** Fm: 0-3
Distance: 5f/6f: 0-5 **7f-8f: 4-41** 9f-13f: 2-40 14f+: 0-0
Track : LH: 3-18 RH: 3-61 **Tight: 4-56** Gall: 0-1
Aids: Bl: 0-0 Vi: 0-0 Tstrap: 0-0 Ckp: 0-0
Best Rating: 83 7/03 Ayr 1m gd-fm

Moderate; suited by around 1m; acts on most ground; likes to race prominently.

Anthology

98 87

3-y-o b c Haafhd-Annapurna (IRE) (Brief Truce (USA))
B Smart H E Sheikh Rashid Bin Mohammed

Placings:01-503 (2571)
2009: 8⁵GF, 8⁰GF, 9³GF,

	Starts	1st	2nd	3rd	Win & Pl
Career Total (Turf)	5	1	0	1	4982

87 10/08 Muss 7f30y G-S £3885
Total win prize-money £3886

Going (Turf): Sf: 0-1 **GS: 1-1** Gd: 0-0 GF: 0-3 Fm: 0-0
Distance: 5f/6f: 0-0 **7f-8f: 1-4** 9f-13f: 0-1 14f+: 0-0
Track : LH: 0-0 **RH: 1-3 Tight: 1-3** Gall: 0-0
Aids: Bl: 0-0 Vi: 0-0 Tstrap: 0-0 Ckp: 0-0
Best Rating: 87 10/08 Muss 7f30y gd-sft

Fair; stays 1m2f; acts on easy ground.

Antigua Sunrise (IRE)

107 **82**
3-y-o b f Noverre (USA)-Staff Approved (Teenoso (USA))
R A Fahey David And Jackie Knaggs

Placings:55B52-331115340 **(6138)**
2009: 7^{3}GF, 9^{3}GF, 12^{1}S, 12^{1}GF, 12^{1}GS, 14^{5}G, 10^{3}G, 9^{4}GF, 13^{0}G,

	Starts	1st	2nd	3rd	Win & Pl
Career Total (Turf)	**14**	**3**	**1**	**3**	**18510**

79 6/09 Ripn 1m4f10y (0-85)H G-S £5180
74 5/09 Bevl 1m4f16y (0-70)H G-F £2914
74 5/09 York 1m4f (0-80)H SFT £6476
Total win prize-money £14571

Going (Turf): Sf: 1-2 GS: 1-4 Gd: 0-3 **GF: 1-5** Fm: 0-0
Distance: 5f/6f: 0-2 7f-8f: 0-4 **9f-13f: 3-6** 14f+: 0-2
Track : LH: 1-7 **RH: 2-6 Tight: 2-9** Gall: 1-3
Aids: Bl: 0-0 Vi: 0-0 Tstrap: 0-0 Ckp: 0-0
Best Rating: 82 7/09 York 1m2f88y good

Fair; stays 1m4f, also effective at shorter; acts on fast and easy ground.

Antillia

(109) (76)**53**
4-y-o b f Red Ransom (USA)-Milly Of The Vally (Caerleon (USA))
C F Wall Ali Saeed

Placings:0541-03 **(0631)**
2009: 13^{0}SD, 13^{3}SD,

	Starts	1st	2nd	3rd	Win & Pl
Career Total (Turf)	**2**	**0**	**0**	**0**	**0**
Career Total (AW)	**4**	**1**	**0**	**1**	**3158**

76 12/08 Ling 1m4f (0-70)H STD £2729
Total win prize-money £2730

Going (Turf): Sf: 0-1 GS: 0-0 Gd: 0-1 GF: 0-0 Fm: 0-0
Distance: 5f/6f: 0-0 7f-8f: 0-0 **9f-13f: 1-5** 14f+: 0-1
Track : **LH: 1-5** RH: 0-1 **Tight: 1-5** Gall: 0-0
Aids: Bl: 0-0 Vi: 0-0 Tstrap: 0-0 Ckp: 0-0
Best Rating: 76 2/09 Ling 1m5f stand

Fair; stays 1m4f and acts on Polytrack.

Antinori (IRE)

110(103) (92)**103**
3-y-o b g Fasliyev (USA)-Albavilla (Spectrum (IRE))
W R Swinburn P W Harris

Placings:422-231320 **(6106)**
2009: 8^{2}SD, 10^{3}G, 10^{1}GF, 10^{3}G, 10^{2}GF, 10^{0}GF,

	Starts	1st	2nd	3rd	Win & Pl
Career Total (Turf)	**7**	**1**	**3**	**2**	**19955**
Career Total (AW)	**2**	**0**	**1**	**0**	**1647**

94 5/09 Sand 1m2f7y (0-85)H G-F £5180
Total win prize-money £5181

Going (Turf): Sf: 0-0 GS: 0-2 Gd: 0-2 **GF: 1-3** Fm: 0-0
Distance: 5f/6f: 0-0 7f-8f: 0-2 **9f-13f: 1-7** 14f+: 0-0
Track : LH: 0-4 **RH: 1-5** Tight: 0-3 Gall: 0-2
Aids: Bl: 0-0 Vi: 0-0 Tstrap: 0-2 Ckp: 0-2
Best Rating: 103 8/09 Sand 1m2f7y gd-fm

Very useful; stays 1m2f; acts on good/fast ground and on Polytrack; has worn cheekpieces.

Antipodean (UAE)

79(90) (50)**47**
3-y-o ch g Halling (USA)-Anka Britannia (USA) (Irish River (FR))
P T Midgley Jeffrey Green

Placings:3663006000 (6184)
2009: 8^{3}SD, 8^{6}SD, 11^{6}SD, 10^{3}GF, 9^{0}GF, 10^{0}G, 12^{6}GF, 10^{0}GF, 7^{0}GF, 9^{0}GF,

	Starts	1st	2nd	3rd	Win & Pl
Career Total (Turf)	**7**	**0**	**0**	**1**	**385**
Career Total (AW)	**3**	**0**	**0**	**1**	**403**

Going (Turf): Sf: 0-0 GS: 0-0 Gd: 0-1 GF: 0-6 Fm: 0-0
Distance: 5f/6f: 0-0 7f-8f: 0-3 9f-13f: 0-7 14f+: 0-0
Track : LH: 0-7 RH: 0-3 Tight: 0-3 Gall: 0-0
Aids: Bl: 0-2 Vi: 0-0 Tstrap: 0-0 Ckp: 0-0
Best Rating: 50 1/09 Sthl 1m stand

Antique Diamond (IRE)

84(66) (3)**33**
2-y-o b f Chineur (FR)-Flash And Dazzle (IRE) (Bertolini (USA))
Lucinda Featherstone D Broughton

Placings:000000 **(7157)**
2009: 6^{0}G, 5^{0}GF, 6^{0}G, 8^{0}GF, 6^{0}GF, 7^{0}SD,

	Starts	1st	2nd	3rd	Win & Pl
Career Total (Turf)	**5**	**0**	**0**	**0**	
Career Total (AW)	**1**	**0**	**0**	**0**	

Going (Turf): Sf: 0-0 GS: 0-0 Gd: 0-2 GF: 0-3 Fm: 0-0
Distance: 5f/6f: 0-3 7f-8f: 0-2 9f-13f: 0-1 14f+: 0-0
Track : LH: 0-2 RH: 0-0 Tight: 0-1 Gall: 0-0
Aids: Bl: 0-0 Vi: 0-0 Tstrap: 0-0 Ckp: 0-0
Best Rating: 33 10/09 Yarm 6f3y gd-fm

Antoella (IRE)

84(79) (40)**55**
2-y-o gr f Antonius Pius (USA)-Bella Estella (GER) (Sternkoenig (IRE))
Ian Williams Kildare Racing Club

Placings:060 **(6912)**
2009: 6^{0}GF, 7^{6}GF, 7^{0}SD,

	Starts	1st	2nd	3rd	Win & Pl
Career Total (Turf)	**2**	**0**	**0**	**0**	**0**
Career Total (AW)	**1**	**0**	**0**	**0**	

Going (Turf): Sf: 0-0 GS: 0-0 Gd: 0-0 GF: 0-2 Fm: 0-0
Distance: 5f/6f: 0-0 7f-8f: 0-3 9f-13f: 0-0 14f+: 0-0
Track : LH: 0-2 RH: 0-0 Tight: 0-1 Gall: 0-0
Aids: Bl: 0-0 Vi: 0-0 Tstrap: 0-0 Ckp: 0-0
Best Rating: 55 9/09 Wwck 7f26y gd-fm

Antoniola (IRE)

101 **83**
2-y-o b g Antonius Pius (USA)-Balliamo (IRE) (Royal Academy (USA))
T D Easterby Mrs Jennifer E Pallister

Placings:2331 **(6993)**
2009: 6^{2}GF, 6^{3}GS, 7^{3}GF, 8^{1}GS,

	Starts	1st	2nd	3rd	Win & Pl
Career Total (Turf)	**4**	**1**	**1**	**2**	**10102**

83 10/09 Donc 1m G-S £7771
Total win prize-money £7771

Going (Turf): Sf: 0-0 **GS: 1-2** Gd: 0-0 GF: 0-2 Fm: 0-0
Distance: 5f/6f: 0-2 **7f-8f: 1-2** 9f-13f: 0-0 14f+: 0-0
Track : **LH: 1-1** RH: 0-0 Tight: 0-0 **Gall: 1-1**
Aids: Bl: 0-0 Vi: 0-0 Tstrap: 0-0 Ckp: 0-0
Best Rating: 83 10/09 Donc 1m gd-sft

Useful; stays 1m; acts on easy ground but handles fast.

Antonius Moris (IRE)

95 **85**
2-y-o b c Antonius Pius (USA)-Suaad (IRE) (Fools Holme (USA))
Tom Dascombe Gary And Linnet Woodward

Placings:14032044 **(6397)**
2009: 5^{1}GF, 5^{4}GF, 5^{0}GF, 6^{3}GF, 6^{2}HY, 6^{0}S, 7^{4}GF, 6^{4}GF,

	Starts	1st	2nd	3rd	Win & Pl
Career Total (Turf)	**8**	**1**	**1**	**1**	**5957**

77 5/09 Wwck 5f110y G-F £2729
Total win prize-money £2730

Going (Turf): Sf: 0-2 GS: 0-0 Gd: 0-0 **GF: 1-6** Fm: 0-0
Distance: **5f/6f: 1-4** 7f-8f: 0-4 9f-13f: 0-0 14f+: 0-0
Track : **LH: 1-3** RH: 0-0 Tight: 0-2 Gall: 0-1
Aids: Bl: 0-0 Vi: 0-0 Tstrap: 0-0 Ckp: 0-0
Best Rating: 85 9/09 Sals 6f212y gd-fm

Fair; stays 6f and acts on fast ground; handles soft.

Antonius Park (IRE)

67 (61)**10**
2-y-o b f Antonius Pius (USA)-Special Park (USA) (Trempolino (USA))
Rodger Sweeney Mrs J B Sweeney

Placings:000060 **(7526a)**
2009: 5^{0}G, 5^{0}SD, 7^{0}SD, 8^{0}Y, 7^{6}SD, 6^{0}SD,

	Starts	1st	2nd	3rd	Win & Pl
Career Total (Turf)	**2**	**0**	**0**	**0**	
Career Total (AW)	**4**	**0**	**0**	**0**	

Going (Turf): Sf: 0-0 GS: 0-0 Gd: 0-1 GF: 0-0 Fm: 0-0
Distance: 5f/6f: 0-3 7f-8f: 0-3 9f-13f: 0-0 14f+: 0-0
Track : LH: 0-5 RH: 0-1 Tight: 0-0 Gall: 0-0
Aids: Bl: 0-0 Vi: 0-0 Tstrap: 0-0 Ckp: 0-0
Best Rating: 61 11/09 Dund 6f stand

Any Day (IRE)

94(95) (67)**70**
2-y-o b f Kheleyf (USA)-Daylight Ahead (IRE) (Tenby)
R M Beckett R Roberts

Placings:623613330 **(6827)**

2009: 5^{6}SD, 5^{2}SD, 6^{3}SD, 5^{6}G, 5^{1}SD, 5^{3}GF, 6^{3}GF, 5^{3}F, 5^{0}SF,

	Starts	1st	2nd	3rd	Win & Pl
Career Total (Turf)	4	0	0	3	1690
Career Total (AW)	5	1	1	1	4848

67 7/09 Ling 5f STD £3238

Total win prize-money £3238

Going (Turf): Sf: 0-0 GS: 0-0 Gd: 0-1 GF: 0-2 Fm: 0-1
Distance: **5f/6f: 1-9** 7f-8f: 0-0 9f-13f: 0-0 14f+: 0-0
Track : **LH: 1-7** RH: 0-0 **Tight: 1-5** Gall: 0-3
Aids: Bl: 0-0 Vi: 0-0 Tstrap: 0-0 Ckp: 0-0
Best Rating: 70 8/09 Wind 6f gd-fm

Modest; effective over 5f-6f; acts on Polytrack.

Any Given Moment (IRE)

90(87) (51)**56**
3-y-o b g Alhaarth (IRE)-Shastri (USA) (Alleged (USA))
D M Simcock Malcolm Caine

Placings:006530 **(5990)**
2009: 8^{0}SD, 8^{0}G, 8^{6}GF, 11^{5}G, 13^{3}G, 16^{0}SD,

	Starts	1st	2nd	3rd	Win & Pl
Career Total (Turf)	4	0	0	1	395
Career Total (AW)	2	0	0	0	

Going (Turf): Sf: 0-0 GS: 0-0 Gd: 0-3 GF: 0-1 Fm: 0-0
Distance: 5f/6f: 0-0 7f-8f: 0-2 9f-13f: 0-2 14f+: 0-2
Track : LH: 0-3 RH: 0-1 Tight: 0-3 Gall: 0-0
Aids: Bl: 0-0 Vi: 0-0 Tstrap: 0-0 Ckp: 0-0
Best Rating: 56 8/09 Yarm 1m3f101y good

Moderate; stays 1m5f; acts on good ground.

Any Secrets

68(71) (31)**16**
3-y-o b g Compton Place-Anyhow (IRE) (Distant Relative)
Karen George Anthony Hughes & Miss Karen George

Placings:00000 **(6611)**
2009: 8^{0}G, 8^{0}SD, 7^{0}G, 8^{0}SD, 7^{0}SD,

	Starts	1st	2nd	3rd	Win & Pl
Career Total (Turf)	2	0	0	0	
Career Total (AW)	3	0	0	0	

Going (Turf): Sf: 0-0 GS: 0-0 Gd: 0-2 GF: 0-0 Fm: 0-0
Distance: 5f/6f: 0-0 7f-8f: 0-2 9f-13f: 0-3 14f+: 0-0
Track : LH: 0-2 RH: 0-1 Tight: 0-2 Gall: 0-0
Aids: Bl: 0-0 Vi: 0-1 Tstrap: 0-1 Ckp: 0-1
Best Rating: 31 6/09 Wolv 1m141y stand

Apache Dawn

96(103) (79)**51**
5-y-o ch g Pursuit Of Love-Taza (Persian Bold)
A Sadik (G L Moore 19/3) A Sadik

Placings:623/5410602/**000262**000434-5405300 **(4170)**
2009: 10^{5}SD, 10^{4}SD, 13^{0}SD, 8^{5}F, 10^{3}G, 9^{0}GF, 11^{0}SD,

	Starts	1st	2nd	3rd	Win & Pl
Career Total (Turf)	15	1	1	1	5394
Career Total (AW)	14	0	3	2	3546

89 6/07 Newc 7f (0-75)H SFT £3886

Total win prize-money £3886

Going (Turf): Sf: 1-5 GS: 0-2 Gd: 0-3 GF: 0-4 Fm: 0-1
Distance: 5f/6f: 0-0 **7f-8f: 1-18** 9f-13f: 0-10 14f+: 0-1
Track : LH: 0-14 RH: 0-10 Tight: 0-11 Gall: 0-0
Aids: Bl: 0-4 Vi: 0-0 Tstrap: 0-0 Ckp: 0-0

Best Rating: 89 12/07 Kemp 1m stand

Moderate; stays 1m2f; acts on fast ground.

Apache Fort

76(104) (78)**75**
6-y-o b g Desert Prince (IRE)-Apogee (Shirley Heights)
T Keddy Andrew Duffield

Placings:060/01133442323013262/101664630513601024 5-0336400264050 **(6457)**
2009: 13^{0}SD, 12^{3}SD, 12^{3}SD, 13^{6}SD, 12^{4}SD, 12^{0}SD, 13^{0}SD, 12^{2}SD, 12^{6}GF, 11^{4}GF, 12^{0}SD, 16^{5}SD, 13^{0}SD,

	Starts	1st	2nd	3rd	Win & Pl
Career Total (Turf)	20	1	2	5	13044
Career Total (AW)	32	6	4	4	22799

78	10/08	Wolv	1m4f50y		STD	£3070
75	9/08	NmkR	1m4f		G-F	£6476
73	5/08	Ling	1m4f	(0-70)H	STD	£3885
74	4/08	Ling	1m4f	(0-75)H	STD	£2590
67	9/07	Ling	1m4f	(0-70)H	STD	£3238
61	1/07	Ling	1m2f	(0-58)H	STD	£1706
59	1/07	Wolv	1m4f50y	(0-45)	STD	£1911

Total win prize-money £22879

Going (Turf): Sf: 0-2 GS: 0-5 Gd: 0-5 **GF: 1-8** Fm: 0-0
Distance: 5f/6f: 0-0 7f-8f: 0-1 **9f-13f: 7-39** 14f+: 0-12
Track : **LH: 6-39** RH: 1-11 **Tight: 6-34** Gall: 1-9
Aids: **Bl: 2-21** Vi: 0-0 Tstrap: 0-0 Ckp: 0-0
Best Rating: 78 11/08 GrLe 1m6f stand

Fair; stays 1m5f; acts on fast ground; goes well on Polytrack; likes Lingfield; has worn a tongue tie and blinkers.

Apache Kid (IRE)

79 **57**
2-y-o b c Antonius Pius (USA)-She's The Tops (Shernazar)
B R Millman Karmaa Racing Limited

Placings:05 **(6200)**
2009: 7^{0}G, 9^{5}G,

	Starts	1st	2nd	3rd	Win & Pl
Career Total (Turf)	2	0	0	0	0

Going (Turf): Sf: 0-0 GS: 0-0 Gd: 0-2 GF: 0-0 Fm: 0-0
Distance: 5f/6f: 0-0 7f-8f: 0-1 9f-13f: 0-1 14f+: 0-0
Track : LH: 0-0 RH: 0-1 Tight: 0-1 Gall: 0-0
Aids: Bl: 0-0 Vi: 0-0 Tstrap: 0-0 Ckp: 0-0
Best Rating: 57 9/09 Chep 7f16y good

Apache Moon

(80) (19)
3-y-o ch g Monsieur Bond (IRE)-Mighty Squaw (Indian Ridge)
R Curtis P Hawkins

Placings:0 **(0963)**
2009: 7^{0}SD,

	Starts	1st	2nd	3rd	Win & Pl
Career Total (Turf)	0	0	0	0	
Career Total (AW)	1	0	0	0	

Going (Turf): Sf: 0-0 GS: 0-0 Gd: 0-0 GF: 0-0 Fm: 0-0
Distance: 5f/6f: 0-0 7f-8f: 0-1 9f-13f: 0-0 14f+: 0-0
Track : LH: 0-1 RH: 0-0 Tight: 0-0 Gall: 0-0
Aids: Bl: 0-0 Vi: 0-0 Tstrap: 0-0 Ckp: 0-0
Best Rating: 19 3/09 Sthl 7f stand

Apache Nation (IRE)

98(90) (42)**63**
6-y-o b g Fruits Of Love (USA)-Rachel Green (IRE) (Case Law)
M Dods Doug Graham

Placings:030/0310344041156/00000163230200/0503004 452010-0426000 **(7174)**
2009: 8^{0}G, 7^{4}GF, 8^{2}GS, 9^{6}G, 8^{0}S, 8^{0}GF, 9^{0}S,

	Starts	1st	2nd	3rd	Win & Pl
Career Total (Turf)	49	5	4	6	22718
Career Total (AW)	1	0	0	0	

63	10/08	Ayr	1m	(0-65)H	HVY	£2729
64	6/07	Ripn	1m	(0-65)H	SFT	£2590
69	9/06	Ayr	1m	(0-60)H	SFT	£2866
64	9/06	Ayr	1m	(0-70)H	G-S	£4210
64	6/06	Muss	1m1f	(0-65)H	G-F	£3238

Total win prize-money £15637

Going (Turf): Sf: 3-16 GS: 1-9 Gd: 0-12GF: 1-11 Fm: 0-1
Distance: 5f/6f: 0-2 **7f-8f: 4-29** 9f-13f: 1-19 14f+: 0-0
Track : **LH: 3-29** RH: 2-17 **Tight: 2-17** Gall: 0-2
Aids: **Bl: 1-6** Vi: 0-0 Tstrap: 0-0 Ckp: 0-0
Best Rating: 69 9/06 Ayr 1m soft

Moderate; effective at around a mile; acts on fast and soft ground.

Apache Ridge (IRE)

98 **76**
3-y-o ch g Indian Ridge-Seraphina (IRE) (Pips Pride)
K A Ryan Aidan Heeney

Placings:3-612 **(2336)**
2009: 5^{6}GS, 6^{1}GS, 5^{2}GF,

	Starts	1st	2nd	3rd	Win & Pl
Career Total (Turf)	4	1	1	1	4613

76 5/09 Haml 6f5y G-S £2590

Total win prize-money £2590

Going (Turf): Sf: 0-0 **GS: 1-2** Gd: 0-0 GF: 0-2 Fm: 0-0
Distance: 5f/6f: 0-3 **7f-8f: 1-1** 9f-13f: 0-0 14f+: 0-0
Track : LH: 0-0 RH: 0-0 Tight: 0-0 Gall: 0-0
Aids: Bl: 0-0 Vi: 0-0 Tstrap: 0-0 Ckp: 0-0
Best Rating: 76 5/09 Haml 6f5y gd-sft

Fair; stays 6f; acts on fast ground.

Apex

92(103) (74)**58**
8-y-o ch g Efisio-Royal Loft (Homing)
M Hill Martin Hill

Placings:44333030/150321000/2065005000/0054060500 30/**0635411211450532/00500** **(6365)**
2009: 8^{0}SD, 7^{0}GF, 8^{5}SD, 8^{0}SD, 8^{0}GF,

	Starts	1st	2nd	3rd	Win & Pl
Career Total (Turf)	44	5	3	6	37735
Career Total (AW)	16	1	1	2	5383

90	5/07	Bath	1m5y	(0-70)H	G-F	£3238
82	5/07	Bath	1m5y	(0-75)H	GD	£4857
68	4/07	Kemp	1m	(0-65)H	STD	£2047
61	4/07	Wwck	1m2f188y	(0-60)H	G-F	£2730
93	8/04	Newb	6f8y	D(0-80)H	G-S	£5538
79	5/04	Wwck	7f26y	D(0-80)H	SFT	£8027

Total win prize-money £26441

Going (Turf): Sf: 1-8 GS: 1-6 Gd: 1-10 **GF: 2-19** Fm: 0-1
Distance: 5f/6f: 0-22 7f-8f: 3-29 9f-13f: 3-9 14f+: 0-0
Track : **LH: 4-20** RH: 1-8 **Tight: 2-11** Gall: 0-2

Aids: Bl: 0-2 Vi: 0-0 Tstrap: 0-3 Ckp: 0-3
Best Rating: **93** 8/04 Newb 6f8y gd-sft

Fair; effective from 1m-1m2f; acts on fast ground and Polytrack.

Aphrodisia

105(103) (73)**82**

5-y-o b m Sakhee (USA)-Aegean Dream (IRE) (Royal Academy (USA))
Ian Williams bellhouseracing.com

Placings:0/0022/2360124130043-1305145 **(3627)**
2009: 8^{1}SD, 8^{3}SD, 10^{0}SD, 12^{5}SD, 10^{1}GF, 12^{4}GF, 9^{5}G,

	Starts	1st	2nd	3rd	Win & Pl
Career Total (Turf)	15	3	2	1	17796
Career Total (AW)	10	1	2	3	5583

81	4/09	Donc	1m2f60y	(0-85)H	G-F	£4857
73	1/09	Kemp	1m	(0-70)H	STD	£2590
82	6/08	NmkJ	1m	(0-85)H	G-F	£6476
72	4/08	Brig	1m1f209y	(0-65)H	GD	£2201

Total win prize-money £16125

Going (Turf): Sf: 0-2 GS: 0-0 Gd: 1-5 **GF: 2-7** Fm: 0-1
Distance: 5f/6f: 0-0 7f-8f: 2-7 9f-13f: 2-18 14f+: 0-0
Track : **LH: 2-9** RH: 1-12 Tight: 0-11 **Gall: 1-1**
Aids: Bl: 0-0 Vi: 0-0 Tstrap: 0-0 Ckp: 0-0
Best Rating: **82** 6/08 NmkJ 1m firm

Fair; stays 1m4f, but seems better suited by around 1m; acts on fast ground and on Polytrack.

Aphrodite's Rock

99 **69**

3-y-o ch f Falbrav (IRE)-Comtesse Noire (CAN) (Woodman (USA))
Miss Gay Kelleway Winterbeck Manor Stud

Placings:0-60520 **(4943)**
2009: 7^{6}GF, 7^{0}G, 6^{5}GF, 9^{2}GF, 10^{0}GF,

	Starts	1st	2nd	3rd	Win & Pl
Career Total (Turf)	6	0	1	0	806

Going (Turf): **Sf: 0-0 GS: 0-1 Gd: 0-1 GF: 0-4 Fm: 0-0**
Distance: 5f/6f: 0-1 7f-8f: 0-3 9f-13f: 0-2 14f+: 0-0
Track : LH: 0-2 RH: 0-2 Tight: 0-2 Gall: 0-1
Aids: Bl: 0-0 Vi: 0-0 Tstrap: 0-0 Ckp: 0-0
Best Rating: **69** 8/09 Folk 1m1f149y gd-fm

Moderate; effective at around a mile.

Apollo Shark (IRE)

98 **77**

4-y-o ch g Spartacus (IRE)-Shot Of Redemption (Shirley Heights)
J Howard Johnson Transcend Bloodstock LLP

Placings:4110/005010-06610 **(5409)**
2009: 7^{0}GS, 5^{6}GF, 7^{6}GF, 7^{1}G, 7^{0}G,

	Starts	1st	2nd	3rd	Win & Pl
Career Total (Turf)	15	4	0	0	14068

77	7/09	Thsk	7f	(0-70)H	GD	£4338
77	9/08	Rdcr	6f	(0-65)H	G-S	£2388
78	7/07	Muss	7f30y		GD	£3238
73	6/07	Thsk	7f		G-S	£3886

Total win prize-money £13852

Going (Turf): Sf: 0-0 **GS: 2-4 Gd: 2-9** GF: 0-2 Fm: 0-0
Distance: 5f/6f: 1-6 **7f-8f: 3-8** 9f-13f: 0-1 14f+: 0-0
Track : **LH: 2-6** RH: 1-3 **Tight: 3-7** Gall: 0-1
Aids: Bl: 0-0 Vi: 0-0 Tstrap: 0-0 Ckp: 0-0
Best Rating: **78** 7/07 Muss 7f30y good

Fair; stays 7f; acts on good and easier ground; likes to race prominently.

Apostle Of Rome (IRE)

88(88) (59)**59**

2-y-o b g Oratorio (IRE)-Novelette (Darshaan)
Tom Dascombe Christopher McHale

Placings:4066 **(6639)**
2009: 7^{4}GF, 7^{0}S, 6^{6}G, 8^{6}SD,

	Starts	1st	2nd	3rd	Win & Pl
Career Total (Turf)	3	0	0	0	241
Career Total (AW)	1	0	0	0	0

Going (Turf): **Sf: 0-1 GS: 0-0 Gd: 0-1 GF: 0-1 Fm: 0-0**
Distance: 5f/6f: 0-1 7f-8f: 0-2 9f-13f: 0-1 14f+: 0-0
Track : LH: 0-2 RH: 0-0 Tight: 0-1 Gall: 0-1
Aids: Bl: 0-0 Vi: 0-0 Tstrap: 0-0 Ckp: 0-0
Best Rating: **59** 10/09 Wolv 1m141y stand

Apotheosis

103(101) (71)**73**

4-y-o ch g Dr Fong (USA)-Carradale (Pursuit Of Love)
W R Swinburn The Converts

Placings:64-501420363 **(6288)**
2009: 8^{5}SD, 8^{0}SD, 10^{1}SD, 10^{4}GF, 10^{2}GS, 10^{0}SD, 10^{3}G, 10^{6}GF, 10^{3}SD,

	Starts	1st	2nd	3rd	Win & Pl
Career Total (Turf)	6	0	1	1	1559
Career Total (AW)	5	1	0	1	2245

71	3/09	Kemp	1m2f	(0-65)H	STD	£1942

Total win prize-money £1943

Going (Turf): **Sf: 0-0 GS: 0-2 Gd: 0-1 GF: 0-3 Fm: 0-0**
Distance: 5f/6f: 0-0 7f-8f: 0-2 **9f-13f: 1-9** 14f+: 0-0
Track : LH: 0-4 **RH: 1-6** Tight: 0-4 Gall: 0-2
Aids: Bl: 0-0 Vi: 0-0 Tstrap: 0-0 Ckp: 0-0
Best Rating: **73** 5/09 Newb 1m2f6y gd-sft

Modest; stays 1m2f; acts on Polytrack.

Appalachian Trail (IRE)

106(105) (93)**113**

8-y-o b g Indian Ridge-Karinski (USA) (Palace Music (USA))
N Wilson (I Semple 29/11) G L S Partnership

Placings:05/31204166551/50632066122/4320204310/4154002050115/0505134440-03553000130 **(7837)**
2009: 7^{0}G, 7^{3}S, 8^{5}G, 7^{5}G, 8^{3}G, 7^{0}G, 7^{0}GS, 7^{0}S, 8^{1}SD, 8^{3}SD, 7^{0}SS,

	Starts	1st	2nd	3rd	Win & Pl
Career Total (Turf)	57	8	4	6	206463
Career Total (AW)	11	2	3	2	28620

71	11/09	Wolv	1m141y		STD	£2729
113	5/08	Hayd	7f30y		GD	£18450
116	10/07	Donc	7f		GD	£9036
113	10/07	Rdcr	7f		GD	£14762
113	2/07	Ndas	6f110y	(95-110)H	GD	£36734
104	8/06	NmkJ	6f		SFT	£15898
103	8/05	Newb	7f	(0-100)H	G-F	£12493
95	12/04	Wolv	1m141y	(0-92)H	STD	£6684
94	6/04	NmkJ	1m	C(0-90)	G-F	£9841
74	4/04	Ripn	1m	D	GD	£4032

Total win prize-money £130664

Going (Turf): Sf: 1-6 GS: 0-13 **Gd: 5-20** GF: 2-17 Fm: 0-1
Distance: 5f/6f: 1-9 **7f-8f: 7-46** 9f-13f: 2-13 14f+: 0-0
Track : **LH: 4-30** RH: 1-10 **Tight: 3-11** Gall: 1-8
Aids: **Bl: 7-49** Vi: 0-1 Tstrap: 0-0 Ckp: 0-0
Best Rating: **116** 10/07 Donc 7f good

Very useful; Listed winner; effective over 6f-1m; acts on most types of ground; goes on Polytrack, but possibly best on a sound surface; regularly blinkered; usually held up.

Appeal To Reason (USA)

64

2-y-o b c Successful Appeal (USA)-Grand Mirage (USA) (Southern Halo (USA))
J R Best Findlay & Bloom

Placings:60 **(6754)**
2009: 7^{6}G, 7^{0}G,

	Starts	1st	2nd	3rd	Win & Pl
Career Total (Turf)	2	0	0	0	0

Going (Turf): **Sf: 0-0 GS: 0-0 Gd: 0-2 GF: 0-0 Fm: 0-0**
Distance: 5f/6f: 0-0 7f-8f: 0-2 9f-13f: 0-0 14f+: 0-0
Track : LH: 0-0 RH: 0-0 Tight: 0-0 Gall: 0-0
Aids: Bl: 0-0 Vi: 0-0 Tstrap: 0-0 Ckp: 0-0

Appelouse

76(95) (64)**19**

4-y-o b f Zaha (CAN)-Appelone (Emperor Jones (USA))
D W Thompson (M Dods 12/3) J A Moore

Placings:4555100 **(6074)**
2009: 8^{4}SD, 7^{5}SD, 7^{5}SD, 8^{5}SF, 8^{1}SD, 8^{0}S, 9^{0}SD,

	Starts	1st	2nd	3rd	Win & Pl
Career Total (Turf)	1	0	0	0	
Career Total (AW)	6	1	0	0	2240

64	7/09	Sthl	1m	(0-55)H	STD	£2047

Total win prize-money £2047

Going (Turf): **Sf: 0-1 GS: 0-0 Gd: 0-0 GF: 0-0 Fm: 0-0**
Distance: 5f/6f: 0-0 **7f-8f: 1-5** 9f-13f: 0-2 14f+: 0-0
Track : **LH: 1-7** RH: 0-0 Tight: 0-3 Gall: 0-0
Aids: Bl: 0-0 Vi: 0-0 Tstrap: 0-0 Ckp: 0-0
Best Rating: **64** 7/09 Sthl 1m stand

Moderate; effective over 1m; acts on Fibresand.

Applaude

106(99) (68)**80**

4-y-o b g Royal Applause-Flossy (Efisio)
R C Guest (John A Harris 25/9) Stan Wright

Placings:20062424-003501201530500 **(7851)**
2009: 8^{0}GS, 10^{0}G, 11^{3}GF, 10^{5}GS, 12^{0}G, 10^{1}G, 11^{2}SD, 12^{0}GS, 10^{1}GS, 10^{5}GF, 9^{3}G, 10^{0}HY, 12^{5}SD, 8^{0}SD, 9^{0}SD, 11^{0}SS,

	Starts	1st	2nd	3rd	Win & Pl
Career Total (Turf)	19	2	3	2	15186
Career Total (AW)	5	0	1	0	906

73	9/09	Ayr	1m2f		G-S	£6476
75	8/09	Hayd	1m2f95y		GD	£3238

Total win prize-money £9714

Going (Turf): Sf: 0-2 **GS: 1-7 Gd: 1-7** GF: 0-3 Fm: 0-0
Distance: 5f/6f: 0-0 7f-8f: 0-4 **9f-13f: 2-20** 14f+: 0-0
Track : **LH: 2-19** RH: 0-4 Tight: 0-7 Gall: 0-3
Aids: **Bl: 2-10** Vi: 0-0 Tstrap: 0-1 Ckp: 0-1
Best Rating: **80** 10/08 Rdcr 1m2f good

Fair; effective at 1m2f; handles good ground and Fibresand; has worn blinkers and an eyeshield.

Applause (IRE)

109(93) (79)98

3-y-o b f Danehill Dancer (IRE)-Sniffle (IRE) (Shernazar)

J Noseda M Tabor, D Smith & Mrs J Magnier

Placings:32-1164 (6480)

2009: 8^{1}G, 8^{1}GF, 8^{6}G, 9^{4}GF,

	Starts	1st	2nd	3rd	Win & Pl
Career Total (Turf)	4	2	0	0	15599
Career Total (AW)	2	0	1	1	2276

97 7/09 Rdcr 1m (0-85)H G-F £4857
79 7/09 Wind 1m67y GD £2729
Total win prize-money £7587

Going (Turf): Sf: 0-0 GS: 0-0 **Gd: 1-2 GF: 1-2** Fm: 0-0
Distance: 5f/6f: 0-0 7f-8f: 1-4 9f-13f: 1-2 14f+: 0-0
Track : LH: 0-1 **RH: 1-3 Tight: 1-2** Gall: 0-1
Aids: Bl: 0-0 Vi: 0-0 Tstrap: 0-0 Ckp: 0-0
Best Rating: 98 10/09 NmkR 1m1f gd-fm

Very useful; effective over 1m; acts on fast ground.

Apple Charlotte

107(104) (99)108

3-y-o b f Royal Applause-Maid Of Camelot (Caerleon (USA))

H R A Cecil De La Warr Racing

Placings:1-11203 (7132)

2009: 8^{1}GF, 10^{1}G, 10^{2}GF, 10^{0}F, 8^{3}SD,

	Starts	1st	2nd	3rd	Win & Pl
Career Total (Turf)	5	3	1	0	43650
Career Total (AW)	1	0	0	1	4308

101 5/09 Newb 1m2f6y GD £22708
102 4/09 Asct 1m G-F £7477
80 11/08 NmkR 7f G-S £4857
Total win prize-money £35042

Going (Turf): Sf: 0-0 **GS: 1-1 Gd: 1-1 GF: 1-2** Fm: 0-1
Distance: 5f/6f: 0-0 **7f-8f: 2-3** 9f-13f: 1-3 14f+: 0-0
Track : LH: 1-3 RH: 1-1 Tight: 0-1 **Gall: 2-3**
Aids: Bl: 0-0 Vi: 0-0 Tstrap: 0-0 Ckp: 0-0
Best Rating: 108 6/09 Newb 1m2f6y gd-fm

Smart; stays 1m2f; acts on fast and easy ground; goes on Polytrack.

Applesnap (IRE)

97(100) (73)76

4-y-o b f Clodovil (IRE)-Apple Brandy (USA) (Cox's Ridge (USA))

Miss Amy Weaver (J Ryan 20/4) Michael Bringloe

Placings:10/6301000061000-0050400 (4721)

2009: 6^{0}GF, 7^{0}GF, 7^{5}GF, 6^{0}G, 8^{4}SD, 8^{0}GF, 9^{0}G,

	Starts	1st	2nd	3rd	Win & Pl
Career Total (Turf)	15	2	0	0	11354
Career Total (AW)	7	1	0	1	4236

73 9/08 GrLe 6f (0-70)H STD £3561
76 6/08 Yarm 6f3y (0-70)H G-F £2428
76 5/07 Leop 6f G-F £8797
Total win prize-money £14787

Going (Turf): Sf: 0-2 GS: 0-1 Gd: 0-3 **GF: 2-9** Fm: 0-0
Distance: 5f/6f: 2-12 7f-8f: 1-9 9f-13f: 0-1 14f+: 0-0
Track : LH: 2-8 RH: 0-3 Tight: 0-3 **Gall: 1-6**
Aids: Bl: 1-4 Vi: 0-1 Tstrap: 0-5 Ckp: 0-5
Best Rating: 76 6/08 Yarm 6f3y gd-fm

Modest; ex-Irish; effective at 6f; acts on quick ground and on Polytrack; has worn cheekpieces.

Apres Ski (IRE)

82(88) (50)52

6-y-o b g Orpen (USA)-Miss Kinabalu (Shirley Heights)

J F Coupland J F Coupland

Placings:0/600041140/04000004360-0 (3174)

2009: 7^{0}GF,

	Starts	1st	2nd	3rd	Win & Pl
Career Total (Turf)	14	2	0	1	5049
Career Total (AW)	9	1	0	0	5951

71 9/06 Ling 1m (0-70)H STD £5181
67 8/06 Yarm 1m3y (0-60)H G-F £2428
62 8/06 Yarm 1m3y (0-55)H G-F £2266
Total win prize-money £9878

Going (Turf): Sf: 0-2 GS: 0-3 Gd: 0-1 **GF: 2-8** Fm: 0-0
Distance: 5f/6f: 0-5 7f-8f: 1-11 **9f-13f: 2-7** 14f+: 0-0
Track : LH: 1-14 RH: 0-4 **Tight: 1-10** Gall: 0-0
Aids: Bl: 0-0 Vi: 0-0 Tstrap: 0-0 Ckp: 0-0
Best Rating: 71 9/06 Ling 1m stand

Moderate; effective at around 6f-1m; acts on fast and easy ground; also goes on Polytrack.

April Fool

103(108) (76)79

5-y-o ch g Pivotal-Palace Affair (Pursuit Of Love)

J A Geake Miss B Swire

Placings:006/503/6413032130-651016000 (5780)

2009: 8^{6}SD, 8^{5}GS, 8^{1}F, 8^{0}GF, 8^{1}F, 8^{6}GF, 8^{0}GF, 7^{0}GF, 8^{0}SD,

	Starts	1st	2nd	3rd	Win & Pl
Career Total (Turf)	16	2	1	2	7426
Career Total (AW)	9	2	0	2	7833

79 6/09 Bath 1m5y (0-70)H FRM £2914
76 5/09 Bath 1m5y (0-70)H FRM £2719
76 10/08 Kemp 7f (0-80)H STD £5180
69 6/08 Ling 1m (0-60)H STD £2047
Total win prize-money £12862

Going (Turf): Sf: 0-2 GS: 0-3 Gd: 0-3 GF: 0-5 **Fm: 2-3**
Distance: 5f/6f: 0-1 7f-8f: 2-11 9f-13f: 2-13 14f+: 0-0
Track : LH: 3-14 RH: 1-8 **Tight: 3-15** Gall: 0-1
Aids: Bl: 0-0 **Vi: 4-20** Tstrap: 0-0 Ckp: 0-0
Best Rating: 79 6/09 Bath 1m5y firm

Modest; effective over 1m-1m2f; acts on fast ground; goes on Polytrack.

April Lady (IRE)

83(84) (32)22

3-y-o b f Tagula (IRE)-Dusty Diamond (IRE) (Royal Abjar (USA))

A Berry Alan Berry

Placings:00000 (2394)

2009: 6^{0}SS, 5^{0}SD, 6^{0}SD, 6^{0}GF, 5^{0}G,

	Starts	1st	2nd	3rd	Win & Pl
Career Total (Turf)	2	0	0	0	
Career Total (AW)	3	0	0	0	

Going (Turf): Sf: 0-0 GS: 0-0 Gd: 0-1 GF: 0-1 Fm: 0-0
Distance: 5f/6f: 0-5 7f-8f: 0-0 9f-13f: 0-0 14f+: 0-0
Track : LH: 0-3 RH: 0-0 Tight: 0-1 Gall: 0-0
Aids: Bl: 0-0 Vi: 0-0 Tstrap: 0-0 Ckp: 0-0
Best Rating: 32 2/09 Sthl 6f stand

April The Second

(86) (16)56

5-y-o b g Tomba-Little Kenny (Warning)

R J Price David Prosser & Keith Warrington

Placings:000/56-00 (7840)

2009: 11^{0}SD, 12^{0}SS,

	Starts	1st	2nd	3rd	Win & Pl
Career Total (Turf)	3	0	0	0	0
Career Total (AW)	4	0	0	0	

Going (Turf): Sf: 0-1 GS: 0-0 Gd: 0-2 GF: 0-0 Fm: 0-0
Distance: 5f/6f: 0-0 7f-8f: 0-1 9f-13f: 0-6 14f+: 0-0
Track : LH: 0-6 RH: 0-1 Tight: 0-1 Gall: 0-0
Aids: Bl: 0-0 Vi: 0-0 Tstrap: 0-0 Ckp: 0-0
Best Rating: 56 3/08 Wwck 1m2f188y soft

April's Daughter

97 57

4-y-o b f Kyllachy-April Stock (Beveled (USA))

B R Millman Eric Gadsden

Placings:64000-03040 (4640)

2009: 10^{0}G, 10^{3}GF, 11^{0}G, 10^{4}G, 11^{0}GF,

	Starts	1st	2nd	3rd	Win & Pl
Career Total (Turf)	10	0	0	1	548

Going (Turf): Sf: 0-0 GS: 0-2 Gd: 0-4 GF: 0-4 Fm: 0-0
Distance: 5f/6f: 0-0 7f-8f: 0-0 9f-13f: 0-10 14f+: 0-0
Track : LH: 0-5 RH: 0-3 Tight: 0-5 Gall: 0-1
Aids: Bl: 0-0 Vi: 0-0 Tstrap: 0-0 Ckp: 0-0
Best Rating: 57 6/08 Wind 1m2f7y gd-sft

Fair; stays 1m2f and acts on soft ground.

Apurna

81 22

4-y-o ch f Rock Of Gibraltar (IRE)-Dance Lesson (In The Wings)

John A Harris Exors Of The Late J South

Placings:00600/0 (6595)

2009: 10^{0}GS,

	Starts	1st	2nd	3rd	Win & Pl
Career Total (Turf)	6	0	0	0	

Going (Turf): Sf: 0-2 GS: 0-1 Gd: 0-1 GF: 0-2 Fm: 0-0
Distance: 5f/6f: 0-3 7f-8f: 0-2 9f-13f: 0-1 14f+: 0-0
Track : LH: 0-3 RH: 0-1 Tight: 0-0 Gall: 0-0
Aids: Bl: 0-0 Vi: 0-0 Tstrap: 0-1 Ckp: 0-1
Best Rating: 68 7/07 Tipp 5f heavy

Aqlaam

119 125

4-y-o b c Oasis Dream-Bourbonella (Rainbow Quest (USA))

W J Haggas Hamdan Al Maktoum

Placings:3/11-031214 (6271)

2009: 8^{0}S, 8^{3}GF, 8^{1}GF, 8^{2}G, 8^{1}GS, 8^{4}GF,

	Starts	1st	2nd	3rd	Win & Pl
Career Total (Turf)	9	4	1	2	503565

125 9/09 Lonc 1m G-S £221903
120 7/09 Asct 1m G-F £56770
119 6/08 Asct 7f G-F £39739
102 5/08 Newb 7f GD £5828
Total win prize-money £324240

Going (Turf): Sf: 0-1 GS: 1-2 Gd: 1-2 **GF: 2-4** Fm: 0-0
Distance: 5f/6f: 0-1 **7f-8f: 4-8** 9f-13f: 0-0 14f+: 0-0
Track : LH: 0-0 **RH: 1-3** Tight: 0-0 **Gall: 1-2**
Aids: Bl: 0-0 Vi: 0-0 Tstrap: 0-0 Ckp: 0-0
Best Rating: **125** 9/09 Lonc 1m gd-sft

Group class; winner of the 2008 Group 3 Jersey Stakes and the 2009 Group 1 Prix de Moulin; effective at 7f-1m; acts on fast and easy ground.

Aqua Vitae (IRE)

79 **51**

2-y-o ch f Camacho-Baileys Cream (Mister Baileys)
Saeed Bin Suroor Godolphin

Placings:5 **(5800)**
2009: 6^{5}GF,

	Starts	1st	2nd	3rd	Win & Pl
Career Total (Turf)	1	0	0	0	0

Going (Turf): **Sf: 0-0 GS: 0-0 Gd: 0-0 GF: 0-1 Fm: 0-0**
Distance: 5f/6f: 0-1 7f-8f: 0-0 9f-13f: 0-0 14f+: 0-0
Track : LH: 0-1 RH: 0-0 Tight: 0-1 Gall: 0-0
Aids: Bl: 0-0 Vi: 0-0 Tstrap: 0-0 Ckp: 0-0
Best Rating: **51** 9/09 Epsm 6f gd-fm

Aquapark

71(70) (25)

3-y-o b g Shinko Forest (IRE)-Waterpark (Namaqualand (USA))
R Craggs Ray Craggs

Placings:004 **(7725)**
2009: 6^{0}GF, 6^{0}GF, **12^{4}SD,**

	Starts	1st	2nd	3rd	Win & Pl
Career Total (Turf)	2	0	0	0	
Career Total (AW)	1	0	0	0	0

Going (Turf): **Sf: 0-0 GS: 0-0 Gd: 0-0 GF: 0-2 Fm: 0-0**
Distance: 5f/6f: 0-2 7f-8f: 0-0 9f-13f: 0-1 14f+: 0-0
Track : LH: 0-1 RH: 0-0 Tight: 0-0 Gall: 0-0
Aids: Bl: 0-0 Vi: 0-0 Tstrap: 0-0 Ckp: 0-0
Best Rating: **25** 12/09 Sthl 1m4f stand

Aquarian Dancer

85(94) (48)**49**

4-y-o b f Mujahid (USA)-Admonish (Warning)
Jedd O'Keeffe The Fatalists

Placings:00005/4**664-5000** **(6219)**
2009: 7^{5}SD, 8^{0}GF, 9^{0}G, 10^{0}GF,

	Starts	1st	2nd	3rd	Win & Pl
Career Total (Turf)	10	0	0	0	0
Career Total (AW)	3	0	0	0	0

Going (Turf): **Sf: 0-1 GS: 0-0 Gd: 0-4 GF: 0-5 Fm: 0-0**
Distance: 5f/6f: 0-3 7f-8f: 0-6 9f-13f: 0-4 14f+: 0-0
Track : LH: 0-8 RH: 0-3 Tight: 0-2 Gall: 0-0
Aids: Bl: 0-0 Vi: 0-0 Tstrap: 0-0 Ckp: 0-0
Best Rating: **51** 9/07 Bevl 7f100y good

Aquarian Spirit

101 **83**

2-y-o b g Fantastic Light (USA)-Notable Lady (IRE) (Victory Note (USA))
R A Fahey P S Cresswell & Mrs P A Morrison

Placings:331232 **(6088)**
2009: 7^{3}GF, 7^{3}GS, 7^{1}GS, 7^{2}G, 8^{3}GF, 8^{2}G,

	Starts	1st	2nd	3rd	Win & Pl
Career Total (Turf)	6	1	2	3	11361
75 7/09 Newc 7f			G-S	£4209	

Total win prize-money £4209

Going (Turf): Sf: 0-0 **GS: 1-2** Gd: 0-2 GF: 0-2 Fm: 0-0
Distance: 5f/6f: 0-0 **7f-8f: 1-5** 9f-13f: 0-1 14f+: 0-0
Track : LH: 0-3 RH: 0-1 Tight: 0-2 Gall: 0-0
Aids: Bl: 0-0 Vi: 0-0 Tstrap: 0-0 Ckp: 0-0
Best Rating: **83** 9/09 Ayr 1m good

Useful; stays 1m; acts on good ground.

Aquarius Star (IRE)

91 **72**

2-y-o ch f Danehill Dancer (IRE)-Easter Heroine (IRE) (Exactly Sharp (USA))
Pat Eddery Mrs Gay Smith

Placings:25 **(4817)**
2009: 7^{2}GF, 7^{5}GF,

	Starts	1st	2nd	3rd	Win & Pl
Career Total (Turf)	2	0	1	0	1156

Going (Turf): **Sf: 0-0 GS: 0-0 Gd: 0-0 GF: 0-2 Fm: 0-0**
Distance: 5f/6f: 0-0 7f-8f: 0-2 9f-13f: 0-0 14f+: 0-0
Track : LH: 0-0 RH: 0-1 Tight: 0-0 Gall: 0-0
Aids: Bl: 0-0 Vi: 0-0 Tstrap: 0-0 Ckp: 0-0
Best Rating: **72** 7/09 Bevl 7f100y gd-fm

Aqwaal (IRE)

109 **104**

3-y-o b c Red Ransom (USA)-Mubkera (IRE) (Nashwan (USA))
E A L Dunlop Hamdan Al Maktoum

Placings:031-1156 **(3780)**
2009: 10^{1}G, 10^{1}S, 12^{5}GF, 10^{6}G,

	Starts	1st	2nd	3rd	Win & Pl
Career Total (Turf)	7	3	0	1	42594
94 5/09 Newb 1m2f6y (0-105)H			SFT	£24924	
92 4/09 Sand 1m2f7y (0-90)H			GD	£7477	
77 9/08 Gdwd 1m			SFT	£4371	

Total win prize-money £36772

Going (Turf): **Sf: 2-2** GS: 0-1 Gd: 1-3 GF: 0-1 Fm: 0-0
Distance: 5f/6f: 0-0 7f-8f: 1-3 **9f-13f: 2-4** 14f+: 0-0
Track : LH: 1-1 **RH: 2-4** Tight: 0-0 **Gall: 1-3**
Aids: Bl: 0-0 Vi: 0-0 Tstrap: 0-0 Ckp: 0-0
Best Rating: **104** 7/09 NmkJ 1m2f good

Smart; stays 1m2f; acts on good and softer ground.

Aqwaas (USA)

95(93) (65)**77**

3-y-o ch f Diesis-Jinaan (USA) (Mr Prospector (USA))
Sir Michael Stoute Hamdan Al Maktoum

Placings:4-21 **(3237)**
2009: 8^{2}G, 7^{1}GF,

	Starts	1st	2nd	3rd	Win & Pl
Career Total (Turf)	2	1	1	0	3554
Career Total (AW)	1	0	0	0	0
76 6/09 Bevl 7f100y			G-F	£2590	

Total win prize-money £2590

Going (Turf): Sf: 0-0 GS: 0-0 Gd: 0-1 **GF: 1-1** Fm: 0-0
Distance: 5f/6f: 0-0 **7f-8f: 1-3** 9f-13f: 0-0 14f+: 0-0
Track : LH: 0-1 **RH: 1-2** Tight: 0-1 Gall: 0-0
Aids: Bl: 0-0 Vi: 0-0 Tstrap: 0-0 Ckp: 0-0
Best Rating: **77** 5/09 Gdwd 1m good

Fair filly; effective at around 1m; acts on good ground and Polytrack.

Arab League (IRE)

105 **69**

4-y-o b g Dubai Destination (USA)-Johnny And Clyde (USA) (Sky Classic (CAN))
R J Price Mrs P A Wallis

Placings:00/622221313 **(7124)**
2009: 8^{6}G, 10^{2}GS, 11^{2}GF, 12^{2}S, 14^{2}GF, 13^{1}G, 11^{3}GS, 16^{1}G, 16^{3}G,

	Starts	1st	2nd	3rd	Win & Pl
Career Total (Turf)	11	2	4	2	9017
68 10/09 Newb 2m (0-75)H			GD	£2590	
57 9/09 Bath 1m5f22y (0-70)H			GD	£2623	

Total win prize-money £5213

Going (Turf): Sf: 0-1 GS: 0-2 **Gd: 2-5** GF: 0-3 Fm: 0-0
Distance: 5f/6f: 0-1 7f-8f: 0-1 9f-13f: 0-5 **14f+: 2-4**
Track : **LH: 2-8** RH: 0-1 **Tight: 1-2** Gall: 0-1
Aids: Bl: 0-0 Vi: 0-0 Tstrap: 0-0 Ckp: 0-0
Best Rating: **69** 10/09 Nott 2m9y good

Modest; stays 2m; acts on fast and easy ground.

Arabian Flame (IRE)

88 **81**

3-y-o b g King's Best (USA)-Frappe (IRE) (Inchinor)
Seamus Fahey (M R Channon 18/4) Michael Allen

Placings:33-4 **(1355)**
2009: 8^{4}S,

	Starts	1st	2nd	3rd	Win & Pl
Career Total (Turf)	3	0	0	2	2118

Going (Turf): **Sf: 0-1 GS: 0-0 Gd: 0-1 GF: 0-1 Fm: 0-0**
Distance: 5f/6f: 0-0 7f-8f: 0-3 9f-13f: 0-0 14f+: 0-0
Track : LH: 0-0 RH: 0-0 Tight: 0-0 Gall: 0-0
Aids: Bl: 0-0 Vi: 0-0 Tstrap: 0-0 Ckp: 0-0
Best Rating: **81** 8/08 NmkJ 7f gd-fm

Half-brother to winners at 7f to 1m4f from the family of Footstepsinthesand; effective over 7f; acts on good ground.

Arabian Gleam

111 (89)**119**

5-y-o b h Kyllachy-Gleam Of Light (IRE) (Danehill (USA))
J Noseda Saeed Suhail

Placings:213516/50641-3031 **(6848)**
2009: 7^{3}G, 8^{0}GF, 7^{3}GF, 7^{1}G,

	Starts	1st	2nd	3rd	Win & Pl
Career Total (Turf)	13	3	0	3	252720
Career Total (AW)	2	1	1	0	4202
118 10/09 NmkR 7f			GD	£60829	
119 9/08 Donc 7f			SFT	£85155	
117 9/07 Donc 7f			G-F	£56780	
89 5/07 Ling 6f			STD	£3238	

Total win prize-money £206003

Going (Turf): **Sf: 1-1** GS: 0-2 **Gd: 1-5 GF: 1-5** Fm: 0-0

Distance: 5f/6f: 1-1 **7f-8f: 3-14** 9f-13f: 0-0 14f+: 0-0
Track : **LH: 1-3** RH: 0-2 **Tight: 1-2** Gall: 0-0
Aids: Bl: 0-0 Vi: 0-0 Tstrap: 2-5 Ckp: 2-5
Best Rating: **119** 9/08 Donc 7f soft

Group class; winner in Group 2 company; effective at 6f-7f; acts on most ground and on Polytrack; has worn cheek-pieces.

Arabian Jewel

77 **37**

2-y-o b f Kheleyf (USA)-Lady Liesel (Bin Ajwaad (IRE))
D M Simcock Saeed Manana

Placings:0 **(2490)**
2009: 6^{0}GF,

	Starts	1st	2nd	3rd	Win & Pl
Career Total (Turf)	1	0	0	0	

Going (Turf): **Sf: 0-0 GS: 0-0 Gd: 0-0 GF: 0-1 Fm: 0-0**
Distance: 5f/6f: 0-1 7f-8f: 0-0 9f-13f: 0-0 14f+: 0-0
Track : LH: 0-0 RH: 0-0 Tight: 0-0 Gall: 0-0
Aids: Bl: 0-0 Vi: 0-0 Tstrap: 0-0 Ckp: 0-0
Best Rating: **37** 5/09 Ling 6f gd-fm

Arabian Mirage

95(103) (86)**85**

3-y-o b f Oasis Dream-Bathilde (IRE) (Generous (IRE))
B J Meehan Plantation Stud

Placings:041-400 **(3746)**
2009: 7^{4}GF, 8^{0}GF, 7^{0}G,

	Starts	1st	2nd	3rd	Win & Pl
Career Total (Turf)	5	0	0	0	3851
Career Total (AW)	1	1	0	0	3886

86 11/08 Wolv 7f32y STD £3885
Total win prize-money £3886

Going (Turf): **Sf: 0-0 GS: 0-1 Gd: 0-2 GF: 0-2 Fm: 0-0**
Distance: 5f/6f: 0-0 **7f-8f: 1-6** 9f-13f: 0-0 14f+: 0-0
Track : **LH: 1-1** RH: 0-0 **Tight: 1-1** Gall: 0-0
Aids: Bl: 0-0 Vi: 0-0 Tstrap: 0-0 Ckp: 0-0
Best Rating: **86** 11/08 Wolv 7f32y stand

Half-sister to high-class stayer Tungsten Strike; fair; stays 7f; acts on Polytrack.

Arabian Moonlight

86(73) (5)**57**

3-y-o b f Barathea (IRE)-Ludynosa (USA) (Cadeaux Genereux)
E F Vaughan Saif Ali & Saeed H Altayer

Placings:0-050 **(3300)**
2009: 8^{0}GF, 10^{5}GF, 16^{0}SD,

	Starts	1st	2nd	3rd	Win & Pl
Career Total (Turf)	3	0	0	0	0
Career Total (AW)	1	0	0	0	

Going (Turf): **Sf: 0-0 GS: 0-0 Gd: 0-1 GF: 0-2 Fm: 0-0**
Distance: 5f/6f: 0-0 7f-8f: 0-1 9f-13f: 0-2 14f+: 0-1
Track : LH: 0-1 RH: 0-2 Tight: 0-2 Gall: 0-0
Aids: Bl: 0-0 Vi: 0-0 Tstrap: 0-0 Ckp: 0-0
Best Rating: **57** 4/09 Wind 1m67y gd-fm

Arabian Pearl (IRE)

97(94) (70)**79**

3-y-o b f Refuse To Bend (IRE)-Intercede (Pursuit Of Love)
P W Chapple-Hyam Arabian Shield 2004

Placings:0-0212400 **(6776)**
2009: 10^{0}GS, 8^{2}F, 7^{1}GF, 6^{2}GF, 7^{4}GF, 7^{0}SD, 7^{0}SD,

	Starts	1st	2nd	3rd	Win & Pl
Career Total (Turf)	6	1	2	0	5553
Career Total (AW)	2	0	0	0	

76 5/09 Bevl 7f100y G-F £2590
Total win prize-money £2590

Going (Turf): Sf: 0-1 GS: 0-1 Gd: 0-0 **GF: 1-3** Fm: 0-1
Distance: 5f/6f: 0-0 **7f-8f: 1-6** 9f-13f: 0-2 14f+: 0-0
Track : LH: 0-2 **RH: 1-5** Tight: 0-0 Gall: 0-1
Aids: Bl: 0-0 Vi: 0-0 Tstrap: 0-0 Ckp: 0-0
Best Rating: **79** 6/09 Carl 6f192y gd-fm

Fair; stays 1m; acts on fast ground.

Arabian Pride

91 **80**

2-y-o b g Cadeaux Genereux-Noble Peregrine (Lomond (USA))
D M Simcock Ahmad Al Shaikh

Placings:3242155 **(6063)**
2009: 6^{3}GS, 6^{2}GF, 6^{4}GF, 6^{2}G, 6^{1}GF, 6^{5}G, 7^{5}GF,

	Starts	1st	2nd	3rd	Win & Pl
Career Total (Turf)	7	1	2	1	9359

80 8/09 NmkJ 6f G-F £5180
Total win prize-money £5181

Going (Turf): Sf: 0-0 GS: 0-1 Gd: 0-2 **GF: 1-4** Fm: 0-0
Distance: **5f/6f: 1-6** 7f-8f: 0-1 9f-13f: 0-0 14f+: 0-0
Track : LH: 0-0 RH: 0-0 Tight: 0-0 Gall: 0-0
Aids: Bl: 0-0 Vi: 0-0 Tstrap: 0-0 Ckp: 0-0
Best Rating: **80** 8/09 NmkJ 6f gd-fm

Useful; suited by 6f and fast ground.

Arabian Silk (IRE)

89(86) (51)**54**

3-y-o b f Barathea (IRE)-Anthyllis (IRE) (Night Shift (USA))
D McCain Jnr (D M Simcock 22/10) P Moss & V Vyner-Brooks

Placings:0-000206 **(6969)**
2009: 8^{0}SD, 8^{0}SD, 10^{0}GS, 10^{2}G, 12^{0}SD, 11^{6}G,

	Starts	1st	2nd	3rd	Win & Pl
Career Total (Turf)	3	0	1	0	674
Career Total (AW)	4	0	0	0	

Going (Turf): **Sf: 0-0 GS: 0-1 Gd: 0-2 GF: 0-0 Fm: 0-0**
Distance: 5f/6f: 0-0 7f-8f: 0-3 9f-13f: 0-4 14f+: 0-0
Track : LH: 0-7 RH: 0-0 Tight: 0-3 Gall: 0-3
Aids: Bl: 0-0 Vi: 0-0 Tstrap: 0-0 Ckp: 0-0
Best Rating: **54** 9/09 Ffos 1m2f good

Moderate; stays 1m2f and acts on good ground.

Arabian Spirit

108(107) (96)**97**

4-y-o b g Oasis Dream-Royal Flame (IRE) (Royal Academy (USA))
E A L Dunlop P A Deal A L Deal & G Holland-Bosworth

Placings:043/525123221-420050060 **(6830)**
2009: 8^{4}SD, 8^{2}S, 7^{0}GF, 8^{0}G, 8^{5}SD, 7^{0}GS, 7^{0}G, 7^{6}SD, 8^{0}SF,

	Starts	1st	2nd	3rd	Win & Pl
Career Total (Turf)	11	1	3	1	16098
Career Total (AW)	10	1	2	1	11349

96 10/08 Kemp 1m (0-90)H STD £7477
88 7/08 Chep 7f16y (0-85)H SFT £5180
Total win prize-money £12658

Going (Turf): **Sf: 1-2** GS: 0-3 Gd: 0-4 GF: 0-2 Fm: 0-0
Distance: 5f/6f: 0-1 **7f-8f: 2-18** 9f-13f: 0-2 14f+: 0-0
Track : LH: 0-5 **RH: 1-8** Tight: 0-2 Gall: 0-1
Aids: Bl: 0-0 Vi: 0-0 Tstrap: 0-0 Ckp: 0-0
Best Rating: **97** 4/09 Newb 1m soft

Useful; effective at 7f-1m; acts on most ground and on Polytrack.

Arabian Sun

68(108) (61)**61**

5-y-o b g Singspiel (IRE)-Bright Halo (IRE) (Bigstone (IRE))
C P Morlock Simon Philip

Placings:05060404250/604031000005-00 **(3275)**
2009: 17^{0}GS, 16^{0}SD,

	Starts	1st	2nd	3rd	Win & Pl
Career Total (Turf)	8	1	0	0	2072
Career Total (AW)	17	0	1	1	1086

61 6/08 Bath 2m1f34y (0-60)H SFT £2072
Total win prize-money £2072

Going (Turf): **Sf: 1-3** GS: 0-1 Gd: 0-3 GF: 0-1 Fm: 0-0
Distance: 5f/6f: 0-0 7f-8f: 0-0 9f-13f: 0-4 **14f+: 1-21**
Track : **LH: 1-14** RH: 0-11 **Tight: 1-12** Gall: 0-2
Aids: Bl: 0-3 **Vi: 1-14** Tstrap: 0-1 Ckp: 0-1
Best Rating: **68** 10/07 Wolv 2m119y stand

Modest staying handicapper; took advantage of a soft lead when finally off the mark in slowly-run Class 6 2m1f handicap at Bath June 2008; acts on soft ground and Polytrack.

Arachnophobia (IRE)

92(104) (86)**77**

3-y-o b g Redback-La Mata (IRE) (Danehill Dancer (IRE))
Pat Eddery Pat Eddery Racing (Sharpo)

Placings:05301-31320165142 **(7181)**
2009: 5^{3}SD, 7^{1}SD, 7^{3}SD, 7^{2}SD, 6^{0}SD, 7^{1}SD, 6^{6}GS, 7^{5}SD, 7^{1}SD, 7^{4}SD, 7^{2}SD,

	Starts	1st	2nd	3rd	Win & Pl
Career Total (Turf)	5	0	0	1	578
Career Total (AW)	11	4	2	2	17018

86 9/09 Kemp 7f (0-80)H STD £4727
79 7/09 Kemp 7f (0-75)H STD £2590
75 4/09 Wolv 7f32y (0-75)H STD £3238
66 11/08 GrLe 6f (0-65) STD £2590
Total win prize-money £13145

Going (Turf): **Sf: 0-2 GS: 0-2 Gd: 0-0 GF: 0-1 Fm: 0-0**
Distance: 5f/6f: 1-8 **7f-8f: 3-8** 9f-13f: 0-0 14f+: 0-0
Track : LH: 2-4 RH: 2-7 Tight: 1-2 Gall: 1-2
Aids: Bl: 0-0 Vi: 0-0 Tstrap: 0-0 Ckp: 0-0
Best Rating: **86** 9/09 Kemp 7f stand

Fair; effective over 6f-7f; acts on easy ground; goes on Polytrack.

Aranel (IRE)

109 **97**

3-y-o ch c Hawk Wing (USA)-Antinnaz (IRE) (Thatching)

M Delcher-Sanchez Cuadra Miranda SL

Placings:15103115 **(7232a)**
2009: 8^{1}G, 8^{5}GS, 8^{1}G, 7^{0}GF, 7^{3}G, 8^{1}G, 6^{1}G, 6^{5}HO,

	Starts	1st	2nd	3rd	Win & Pl
Career Total (Turf)	8	4	0	1	59757

	10/09	Madr	6f	GD	£8737
	8/09	Sans	1m	GD	£27184
	5/09	Madr	1m	GD	£9708
	4/09	Madr	1m	GD	£5825

Total win prize-money £51456

Going (Turf): Sf: 0-0 GS: 0-1 **Gd: 4-5** GF: 0-1 Fm: 0-0
Distance: 5f/6f: 1-2 **7f-8f: 3-6** 9f-13f: 0-0 14f+: 0-0
Track : LH: 1-1 RH: 1-2 Tight: 0-0 Gall: 0-0
Aids: Bl: 0-0 Vi: 0-0 Tstrap: 0-0 Ckp: 0-0
Best Rating: **97** 11/09 MsnL 6f holding

Spanish-trained; effective over 1m on good ground.

Arashi

91(102) (71)**63**

3-y-o b g Fantastic Light (USA)-Arriving (Most Welcome)
Lucinda Featherstone Stuart Barnett

Placings:662403**2305446** **(7790)**
2009: 10^{6}GF, 8^{6}GS, 9^{2}GF, 9^{4}HY, 10^{0}F, 9^{3}SD, 8^{2}SD, 9^{3}SD, 8^{0}SD, 12^{5}SD, 12^{4}SD, 9^{4}SD, 12^{6}SD,

	Starts	1st	2nd	3rd	Win & Pl
Career Total (Turf)	5	0	1	0	1252
Career Total (AW)	8	0	1	2	1790

Going (Turf): **Sf: 0-1 GS: 0-1 Gd: 0-0 GF: 0-2 Fm: 0-1**
Distance: 5f/6f: 0-0 7f-8f: 0-0 9f-13f: 0-13 14f+: 0-0
Track : LH: 0-11 RH: 0-2 Tight: 0-10 Gall: 0-0
Aids: Bl: 0-0 Vi: 0-0 Tstrap: 0-11 Ckp: 0-11
Best Rating: **71** 9/09 Wolv 1m141y stand

Modest; stays 1m4f; acts on fast ground and Polytrack; has worn cheekpieces.

Arcano (IRE)

112 **116**

2-y-o b c Oasis Dream-Tariysha (IRE) (Daylami (IRE))
B J Meehan Hamdan Al Maktoum

Placings:111 **(5299a)**
2009: 6^{1}GF, 6^{1}G, 6^{1}G,

	Starts	1st	2nd	3rd	Win & Pl
Career Total (Turf)	3	3	0	0	244762

116	8/09	Deau	6f	GD	£194165
114	7/09	NmkJ	6f	GD	£45416
89	6/09	Newb	6f8y	G-F	£5180

Total win prize-money £244762

Going (Turf): Sf: 0-0 GS: 0-0 **Gd: 2-2** GF: 1-1 Fm: 0-0
Distance: **5f/6f: 2-2** 7f-8f: 1-1 9f-13f: 0-0 14f+: 0-0
Track : LH: 0-0 **RH: 1-1** Tight: 0-0 Gall: 0-0
Aids: Bl: 0-0 Vi: 0-0 Tstrap: 0-0 Ckp: 0-0
Best Rating: **116** 8/09 Deau 6f good

High class; winner of the July Stakes and Prix Morny; effective at 6f; acts on good, fast ground.

Arch

66 **27**

6-y-o ch g Arkadian Hero (USA)-Loriner's Lass (Saddlers' Hall (IRE))
A M Crow A M Crow

Placings:50-0 **(2943)**
2009: 12^{0}GF,

	Starts	1st	2nd	3rd	Win & Pl
Career Total (Turf)	3	0	0	0	0

Going (Turf): **Sf: 0-1 GS: 0-1 Gd: 0-0 GF: 0-1 Fm: 0-0**
Distance: 5f/6f: 0-0 7f-8f: 0-0 9f-13f: 0-3 14f+: 0-0
Track : LH: 0-1 RH: 0-2 Tight: 0-2 Gall: 0-1
Aids: Bl: 0-0 Vi: 0-0 Tstrap: 0-0 Ckp: 0-0
Best Rating: **27** 5/08 Haml 1m3f16y gd-sft

Arch Event

(85) (22)

4-y-o ch f Umistim-Arch Angel (IRE) (Archway (IRE))
A W Carroll R D Willis

Placings:00-600 **(7863)**
2009: 9^{6}SD, 7^{0}SD, 8^{0}SD,

	Starts	1st	2nd	3rd	Win & Pl
Career Total (Turf)	0	0	0	0	
Career Total (AW)	5	0	0	0	0

Going (Turf): **Sf: 0-0 GS: 0-0 Gd: 0-0 GF: 0-0 Fm: 0-0**
Distance: 5f/6f: 0-1 7f-8f: 0-2 9f-13f: 0-2 14f+: 0-0
Track : LH: 0-5 RH: 0-0 Tight: 0-5 Gall: 0-0
Aids: Bl: 0-0 Vi: 0-0 Tstrap: 0-2 Ckp: 0-2
Best Rating: **22** 11/09 Wolv 1m1f103y stand

Arch Rebel (USA)

113 (95)**107**

8-y-o b g Arch (USA)-Sheba's Step (USA) (Alysheba (USA))
Noel Meade P Garvey

Placings:36/221133/0/141262241/0333532124/505466-53 **(6093)**
2009: 10^{5}GY, 10^{3}G,

	Starts	1st	2nd	3rd	Win & Pl
Career Total (Turf)	35	6	7	8	266868
Career Total (AW)	1	0	0	0	

112	9/07	Fair	1m2f		GD	£21993
114	10/06	Leop	1m2f		SFT	£22448
113	5/06	Leop	1m		YLD	£22448
111	4/06	Curr	1m2f		Y-S	£22448
101	8/04	Curr	1m2f	(60-100)H	G-F	£12378
91	7/04	Leop	1m2f		G-Y	£7785

Total win prize-money £109501

Going (Turf): **Sf: 1-5** GS: 0-0 **Gd: 1-8 GF: 1-6** Fm: 0-2
Distance: 5f/6f: 0-1 7f-8f: 1-5 **9f-13f: 5-29** 14f+: 0-1
Track : **LH: 3-17** RH: 2-15 Tight: 0-0 Gall: 0-1
Aids: Bl: 1-3 Vi: 0-0 Tstrap: 1-13 Ckp: 1-13
Best Rating: **115** 12/07 ShTn 1m4f good

Smart; useful hurdler; stays 1m4f; acts on soft ground; often wears cheekpieces; has worn a tongue tie.

Arch Walker (IRE)

52

2-y-o ch g Choisir (AUS)-Clunie (Inchinor)
Jedd O'Keeffe A Walker

Placings:0 **(1610)**
2009: 5^{0}G,

	Starts	1st	2nd	3rd	Win & Pl
Career Total (Turf)	1	0	0	0	

Going (Turf): **Sf: 0-0 GS: 0-0 Gd: 0-1 GF: 0-0 Fm: 0-0**
Distance: 5f/6f: 0-1 7f-8f: 0-0 9f-13f: 0-0 14f+: 0-0
Track : LH: 0-1 RH: 0-0 Tight: 0-0 Gall: 0-0
Aids: Bl: 0-0 Vi: 0-0 Tstrap: 0-0 Ckp: 0-0

Archers Road (IRE)

104 **97**

2-y-o b g Titus Livius (FR)-Somoushe (IRE) (Black Minnaloushe (USA))
M R Channon John & Zoe Webster

Placings:2112221533365404 **(7016)**
2009: 5^{2}GF, 5^{1}GF, 5^{1}GF, 5^{2}GF, 5^{2}GF, 5^{2}G, 5^{1}G, 5^{5}G, 5^{3}GF, 5^{3}GS, 5^{3}G, 5^{6}GF, 5^{5}GF, 5^{4}G, 6^{0}G, 6^{4}GS,

	Starts	1st	2nd	3rd	Win & Pl
Career Total (Turf)	16	3	4	3	63874

93	5/09	Bevl	5f	GD	£9346
86	4/09	Newc	5f	G-F	£5018
89	4/09	Leic	5f2y	G-F	£2590

Total win prize-money £16956

Going (Turf): Sf: 0-0 GS: 0-2 Gd: 1-6 **GF: 2-8** Fm: 0-0
Distance: **5f/6f: 3-16** 7f-8f: 0-0 9f-13f: 0-0 14f+: 0-0
Track : LH: 0-2 RH: 0-0 Tight: 0-2 Gall: 0-1
Aids: Bl: 0-0 Vi: 0-0 Tstrap: 0-0 Ckp: 0-0
Best Rating: **97** 7/09 Gdwd 5f good

Very useful; effective over 5f and acts on fast ground but handles cut; suited by forcing tactics.

Archie Rice (USA)

100(102) (79)**91**

3-y-o b g Arch (USA)-Gold Bowl (USA) (Seeking The Gold (USA))
W Jarvis Anthony Foster

Placings:516-000500 **(6702)**
2009: 6^{0}GF, 7^{0}G, 8^{0}GF, 7^{5}GF, 8^{0}GF, 7^{0}SS,

	Starts	1st	2nd	3rd	Win & Pl
Career Total (Turf)	8	1	0	0	5856
Career Total (AW)	1	0	0	0	

84	9/08	NmkR	6f	G-F	£5180

Total win prize-money £5181

Going (Turf): Sf: 0-0 GS: 0-1 Gd: 0-1 **GF: 1-6** Fm: 0-0
Distance: **5f/6f: 1-3** 7f-8f: 0-5 9f-13f: 0-1 14f+: 0-0
Track : LH: 0-3 RH: 0-1 Tight: 0-2 Gall: 0-1
Aids: Bl: 0-0 Vi: 0-0 Tstrap: 0-0 Ckp: 0-0
Best Rating: **91** 10/08 Asct 5f gd-sft

Very useful; effective over 6f; acts on fast ground.

Archimboldo (USA)

(101) (64)**62**

6-y-o ch g Woodman (USA)-Awesome Strike (USA) (Theatrical)
T Wall The Wenlock Edge Optimists

Placings:003105/**603553663**/0/**604400-00** **(0249)**
2009: 16^{0}SD, 16^{0}SD,

	Starts	1st	2nd	3rd	Win & Pl
Career Total (Turf)	11	1	0	1	6197
Career Total (AW)	13	0	0	3	1541

80	9/05	Bath	1m5y	(0-75)	FRM	£4852

Total win prize-money £4852

Going (Turf): Sf: 0-1 GS: 0-1 Gd: 0-2 GF: 0-4 **Fm: 1-3**
Distance: 5f/6f: 0-2 7f-8f: 0-2 **9f-13f: 1-11** 14f+: 0-9

Track : LH: 1-18 RH: 0-2 Tight: 1-14 Gall: 0-0
Aids: Bl: 0-9 Vi: 0-0 Tstrap: 0-0 Ckp: 0-0
Best Rating: 80 9/05 Bath 1m5y firm

Won mile fast-ground nursery at Bath September 2005; ran best race for a while when fourth in 2m Class 6 handicap at Wolverhampton April 2008; acts on firm ground and Polytrack.

Architrave

91(97) (72)**68**

2-y-o ch g Hernando (FR)-White Palace (Shirley Heights)
Sir Mark Prescott Cheveley Park Stud

Placings:0533 **(6805)**
2009: 8^{0}G, 9^{5}GF, 8^{3}GF, 8^{3}SD,

	Starts	1st	2nd	3rd	Win & Pl
Career Total (Turf)	3	0	0	1	770
Career Total (AW)	1	0	0	1	674

Going (Turf): Sf: 0-0 GS: 0-0 Gd: 0-1 GF: 0-2 Fm: 0-0
Distance: 5f/6f: 0-0 7f-8f: 0-0 9f-13f: 0-4 14f+: 0-0
Track : LH: 0-3 RH: 0-0 Tight: 0-2 Gall: 0-0
Aids: Bl: 0-0 Vi: 0-0 Tstrap: 0-0 Ckp: 0-0
Best Rating: 72 10/09 Wolv 1m141y stand

Arcola (IRE)

101(104) (72)**74**

3-y-o ch f Nayef (USA)-Ashbilya (USA) (Nureyev (USA))
D M Simcock Ali Saeed

Placings:06-001233600 **(7476)**
2009: 8^{0}G, 8^{0}G, 9^{1}F, 9^{2}GF, 11^{3}SD, 9^{3}F, 12^{6}GF, 9^{0}SD, 12^{0}SD,

	Starts	1st	2nd	3rd	Win & Pl
Career Total (Turf)	7	1	1	1	4397
Career Total (AW)	4	0	0	1	703

74 7/09 Brig 1m1f209y (0-70)H FRM £3154
Total win prize-money £3154

Going (Turf): Sf: 0-0 GS: 0-1 Gd: 0-2 GF: 0-2 Fm: 1-2
Distance: 5f/6f: 0-0 7f-8f: 0-2 9f-13f: 1-9 14f+: 0-0
Track : LH: 1-6 RH: 0-4 Tight: 0-1 Gall: 0-2
Aids: Bl: 0-0 Vi: 0-0 Tstrap: 0-0 Ckp: 0-0
Best Rating: 74 7/09 Brig 1m1f209y gd-fm

Modest; stays 1m2f and acts on fast ground.

Arctic (IRE)

104 **111**

2-y-o gr c Shamardal (USA)-Shawanni (Shareef Dancer (USA))
Tracey Collins R A Pegum

Placings:1115 **(6450)**
2009: 5^{1}G, 5^{1}HY, 6^{1}HY, 6^{5}GF,

	Starts	1st	2nd	3rd	Win & Pl
Career Total (Turf)	4	3	0	0	88493

111 8/09 Curr 6f HVY £47402
108 7/09 Curr 5f HVY £28441
77 7/09 Bell 5f GD £7715
Total win prize-money £83560

Going (Turf): Sf: 2-2 GS: 0-0 Gd: 1-1 GF: 0-1 Fm: 0-0
Distance: 5f/6f: 3-4 7f-8f: 0-0 9f-13f: 0-0 14f+: 0-0
Track : LH: 1-1 RH: 0-0 Tight: 0-0 Gall: 0-0
Aids: Bl: 0-0 Vi: 0-0 Tstrap: 0-0 Ckp: 0-0
Best Rating: 111 8/09 Curr 6f heavy

Group-class; effective at 5-6f; handles good but acts well on testing ground.

Arctic Cape

105 **81**

4-y-o b g Cape Cross (IRE)-Arctic Air (Polar Falcon (USA))
D E Pipe (M Johnston 27/6) Mrs Christine Brown

Placings:614/40004020-6166300 **(7247)**
2009: 8^{6}F, 9^{1}GS, 9^{6}GS, 8^{6}GS, 8^{3}GF, 12^{0}S, 10^{0}S,

	Starts	1st	2nd	3rd	Win & Pl
Career Total (Turf)	18	2	1	1	12745

81 5/09 Haml 1m1f36y (0-80)H G-S £5180
83 8/07 Ayr 6f G-S £3886
Total win prize-money £9067

Going (Turf): Sf: 0-3 GS: 2-6 Gd: 0-3 GF: 0-5 Fm: 0-1
Distance: 5f/6f: 1-2 7f-8f: 0-6 9f-13f: 1-10 14f+: 0-0
Track : LH: 0-7 RH: 1-5 Tight: 1-2 Gall: 0-3
Aids: Bl: 0-2 Vi: 0-0 Tstrap: 0-0 Ckp: 0-0
Best Rating: 87 4/08 Sand 1m14y gd-sft

Fair; effective at up to 7f; acts on soft ground; likes to race prominently.

Arctic Cosmos (USA)

91(93) (72)**68**

2-y-o b c North Light (IRE)-Fifth Avenue Doll (USA) (Marquetry (USA))
J H M Gosden Ms Rachel D S Hood

Placings:44 **(6821)**
2009: 8^{4}SD, 8^{4}GF,

	Starts	1st	2nd	3rd	Win & Pl
Career Total (Turf)	1	0	0	0	0
Career Total (AW)	1	0	0	0	0

Going (Turf): Sf: 0-0 GS: 0-0 Gd: 0-0 GF: 0-1 Fm: 0-0
Distance: 5f/6f: 0-0 7f-8f: 0-2 9f-13f: 0-0 14f+: 0-0
Track : LH: 0-0 RH: 0-1 Tight: 0-0 Gall: 0-0
Aids: Bl: 0-0 Vi: 0-0 Tstrap: 0-0 Ckp: 0-0
Best Rating: 72 10/09 Kemp 1m stand

47,000gns son of North Light is a first foal of a 1m2f winner in US; promise after running green on debut; stays 1m; acts on Polytrack.

Arctic Destiny (IRE)

80 **49**

2-y-o b c Trans Island-Partytime (IRE) (Tagula (IRE))
K R Burke 3M's Syndicate

Placings:6055 **(3263)**
2009: 5^{6}GF, 6^{0}GS, 5^{5}GF, 5^{5}G,

	Starts	1st	2nd	3rd	Win & Pl
Career Total (Turf)	4	0	0	0	0

Going (Turf): Sf: 0-0 GS: 0-1 Gd: 0-1 GF: 0-2 Fm: 0-0
Distance: 5f/6f: 0-4 7f-8f: 0-0 9f-13f: 0-0 14f+: 0-0
Track : LH: 0-1 RH: 0-1 Tight: 0-1 Gall: 0-1
Aids: Bl: 0-0 Vi: 0-0 Tstrap: 0-0 Ckp: 0-0
Best Rating: 49 6/09 Ches 5f16y gd-fm

Arctic Freedom (USA)

98(94) (67)**71**

3-y-o b f War Chant (USA)-Polar Bird (Thatching)
Niall O'Callaghan (E A L Dunlop 7/7) Mrs Paul Shanahan

Placings:23-5066400 **(7449a)**
2009: 7^{5}GF, 7^{0}GF, 8^{6}SD, 7^{6}G, 6^{4}F, 8^{0}GS, 10^{0}SD,

	Starts	1st	2nd	3rd	Win & Pl
Career Total (Turf)	6	0	1	0	1778
Career Total (AW)	3	0	0	1	482

Going (Turf): Sf: 0-0 GS: 0-1 Gd: 0-1 GF: 0-3 Fm: 0-1
Distance: 5f/6f: 0-2 7f-8f: 0-4 9f-13f: 0-3 14f+: 0-0
Track : LH: 0-6 RH: 0-0 Tight: 0-1 Gall: 0-1
Aids: Bl: 0-2 Vi: 0-0 Tstrap: 0-0 Ckp: 0-0
Best Rating: 71 6/08 NmkJ 6f gd-fm

Fair; suited by 6f; acts on fast ground; goes on Polytrack.

Arctic Wings (IRE)

(92) (55)**75**

5-y-o b g In The Wings-Arctic Hunt (IRE) (Bering)
A W Carroll Paul Downing

Placings:025/416044300/600 **(7635)**
2009: 14^{6}SD, 16^{0}SD, 14^{0}SD,

	Starts	1st	2nd	3rd	Win & Pl
Career Total (Turf)	7	1	0	1	4828
Career Total (AW)	8	0	1	0	1365

75 5/07 Wind 1m3f135y (0-75)H G-S £3238
Total win prize-money £3239

Going (Turf): Sf: 0-1 GS: 1-1 Gd: 0-2 GF: 0-3 Fm: 0-0
Distance: 5f/6f: 0-0 7f-8f: 0-1 9f-13f: 1-11 14f+: 0-3
Track : LH: 0-9 RH: 0-4 Tight: 1-4 Gall: 0-2
Aids: Bl: 0-1 Vi: 0-0 Tstrap: 0-0 Ckp: 0-0
Best Rating: 75 5/07 Wind 1m3f135y gd-sft

Fair; stays 1m3f; acts on easy ground.

Ardent Prince

(105) (65)**60**

6-y-o b g Polar Prince (IRE)-Anthem Flight (USA) (Fly So Free (USA))
A J McCabe Barry M Fletcher

Placings:03/0/002000/0022020026050-01201300000060035 **(7877)**
2009: 9^{0}SD, 8^{1}SD, 7^{2}SD, 9^{0}SD, 7^{1}SD, 8^{3}SD, 8^{0}SD, 7^{0}SD, 8^{0}SD, 8^{0}SF, 8^{0}SD, 7^{0}SD, 7^{6}SD, 8^{0}SD, 7^{0}SD, 8^{3}SD, 7^{5}SD,

	Starts	1st	2nd	3rd	Win & Pl
Career Total (Turf)	6	0	1	0	674
Career Total (AW)	33	2	5	3	8297

65 2/09 Ling 7f (0-58)H STD £2047
59 1/09 Wolv 1m141y (0-55)H STD £1577
Total win prize-money £3624

Going (Turf): Sf: 0-2 GS: 0-1 Gd: 0-0 GF: 0-2 Fm: 0-1
Distance: 5f/6f: 0-0 7f-8f: 1-14 9f-13f: 1-22 14f+: 0-3
Track : LH: 2-33 RH: 0-3 Tight: 2-27 Gall: 0-1
Aids: Bl: 0-0 Vi: 0-0 Tstrap: 0-3 Ckp: 0-3
Best Rating: 65 2/09 Ling 7f stand

Moderate; effective at around 1m; acts on Polytrack.

Ardmaddy (IRE)

(102) (62)**57**

5-y-o b g Generous (IRE)-Yazmin (IRE) (Green Desert (USA))
G L Moore Blue Crocodile

Placings:55/002220/100-3105244 **(7873)**
2009: 12^{3}SD, 13^{1}SD, 12^{0}SD, 12^{5}SD, 13^{2}SD, 12^{4}SD, 16^{4}SD,

	Starts	1st	2nd	3rd	Win & Pl
Career Total (Turf)	1	0	0	0	
Career Total (AW)	17	2	4	1	7211

62	2/09	Ling	1m5f	(0-65)H	STD	£2047
63	2/08	Wolv	1m4f50y	(0-60)H	STD	£2047

Total win prize-money £4095

Going (Turf): **Sf: 0-1 GS: 0-0 Gd: 0-0 GF: 0-0 Fm: 0-0**
Distance: 5f/6f: 0-0 7f-8f: 0-4 **9f-13f: 2-13** 14f+: 0-1
Track : **LH: 2-11** RH: 0-6 **Tight: 2-11** Gall: 0-0
Aids: **Bl: 2-8** Vi: 0-0 Tstrap: 0-0 Ckp: 0-0
Best Rating: **63** 2/08 Wolv 1m4f50y stand

Moderate; effective at around 1m1f-1m4f; acts on Polytrack.

Are Can (USA)

70 **55**

3-y-o b/br c Arch (USA)-Golden Show (USA) (Theatrical)
J S Wainwright Charles Wentworth

Placings:00-00 **(4819)**
2009: 10^{0}GF, 8^{0}GF,

	Starts	1st	2nd	3rd	Win & Pl
Career Total (Turf)	4	0	0	0	

Going (Turf): **Sf: 0-0 GS: 0-0 Gd: 0-1 GF: 0-2 Fm: 0-1**
Distance: 5f/6f: 0-1 7f-8f: 0-2 9f-13f: 0-1 14f+: 0-0
Track : LH: 0-1 RH: 0-0 Tight: 0-1 Gall: 0-0
Aids: Bl: 0-0 Vi: 0-0 Tstrap: 0-2 Ckp: 0-2
Best Rating: **55** 6/08 NmkJ 7f firm

Areeda (IRE)

90 **66**

2-y-o b f Refuse To Bend (IRE)-Raindancing (IRE) (Tirol)
C E Brittain Saeed Manana

Placings:56 **(3820)**
2009: 6^{5}GF, 6^{6}GF,

	Starts	1st	2nd	3rd	Win & Pl
Career Total (Turf)	2	0	0	0	0

Going (Turf): **Sf: 0-0 GS: 0-0 Gd: 0-0 GF: 0-2 Fm: 0-0**
Distance: 5f/6f: 0-2 7f-8f: 0-0 9f-13f: 0-0 14f+: 0-0
Track : LH: 0-0 RH: 0-0 Tight: 0-0 Gall: 0-0
Aids: Bl: 0-0 Vi: 0-0 Tstrap: 0-0 Ckp: 0-0
Best Rating: **66** 7/09 NmkJ 6f gd-fm

Modest form on debut.

Areeg (IRE)

77 **40**

2-y-o b f Doyen (IRE)-Total Aloof (Groom Dancer (USA))
W Jarvis Abdullah Saeed Belhab

Placings:00 **(6363)**
2009: 7^{0}GF, 7^{0}GF,

	Starts	1st	2nd	3rd	Win & Pl
Career Total (Turf)	2	0	0	0	

Going (Turf): **Sf: 0-0 GS: 0-0 Gd: 0-0 GF: 0-2 Fm: 0-0**
Distance: 5f/6f: 0-0 7f-8f: 0-2 9f-13f: 0-0 14f+: 0-0
Track : LH: 0-1 RH: 0-0 Tight: 0-0 Gall: 0-0
Aids: Bl: 0-0 Vi: 0-0 Tstrap: 0-0 Ckp: 0-0
Best Rating: **40** 9/09 Wwck 7f26y gd-fm

Ares Choix

79 **92**

3-y-o b f Choisir (AUS)-Ares Vallis (IRE) (Caerleon (USA))
P C Haslam Mrs R J Jacobs

Placings:616635-0 **(5069)**
2009: 6^{0}GF,

	Starts	1st	2nd	3rd	Win & Pl
Career Total (Turf)	7	1	0	1	13238

80	5/08	Rdcr	6f	G-F	£3399

Total win prize-money £3400

Going (Turf): Sf: 0-1 GS: 0-1 Gd: 0-1 **GF: 1-3** Fm: 0-1
Distance: **5f/6f: 1-7** 7f-8f: 0-0 9f-13f: 0-0 14f+: 0-0
Track : LH: 0-1 RH: 0-1 Tight: 0-0 Gall: 0-0
Aids: Bl: 0-0 Vi: 0-0 Tstrap: 0-0 Ckp: 0-0
Best Rating: **92** 8/08 Deau 5f gd-sft

Very useful; stays 6f; acts on fast ground but handles cut.

Arfinnit (IRE)

88(105) (66)**63**

8-y-o b g College Chapel-Tidal Reach (USA) (Kris S (USA))
Mrs A L M King All The Kings Horses

Placings:0365163000/0306516616400024604/0**0**000400
102/**0000**/**30063**00**1**0**50146**4**00201**/**4400**00**6231**40**56006**-
20050 **(3242)**
2009: 6^{2}SD, 6^{0}SD, 5^{0}SD, 5^{5}GF, 5^{0}GF,

	Starts	1st	2nd	3rd	Win & Pl
Career Total (Turf)	57	5	3	3	20433
Career Total (AW)	31	3	2	3	9106

63	6/08	Brig	5f59y	(0-65)H	FRM	£2266
66	1/08	Kemp	6f	(0-55)H	STD	£2047
58	8/07	Wolv	5f216y	(0-50)H	STD	£2559
54	5/07	Ling	5f	(0-45)	STD	£2388
54	9/05	Brig	5f213y	(0-45)	FRM	£1547
56	6/04	Ayr	6f	E	GD	£3386
54	5/04	Ripn	6f	F	G-F	£3255
71	7/03	Ayr	6f	D	GD	£5018

Total win prize-money £22470

Going (Turf): Sf: 0-5 GS: 0-7 **Gd: 2-13** GF: 1-24 **Fm: 2-8**
Distance: **5f/6f: 8-75** 7f-8f: 0-12 9f-13f: 0-1 14f+: 0-0
Track : **LH: 4-42** RH: 1-14 **Tight: 2-17** Gall: 0-10
Aids: Bl: 0-6 **Vi: 4-33** Tstrap: 3-29 Ckp: 3-29
Best Rating: **80** 8/03 Hayd 6f gd-fm

Moderate; stays 6f; acts on most ground on turf; goes on Polytrack; usually wears headgear.

Arganil (USA)

108(111) (110)**109**

4-y-o ch g Langfuhr (CAN)-Sherona (USA) (Mr Greeley (USA))
K A Ryan The Big Moment

Placings:0/4116**11**-**11**0452**0**1**5** **(7488)**
2009: 5^{1}SD, 5^{1}SD, 6^{0}GF, 5^{4}HY, 6^{5}S, 5^{2}GS, 6^{0}G, 5^{1}SD, 6^{5}SD,

	Starts	1st	2nd	3rd	Win & Pl
Career Total (Turf)	10	2	1	0	19460
Career Total (AW)	6	5	0	0	72664

106	10/09	Dund	5f		STD	£26861
110	3/09	Ling	5f		STD	£22708
108	3/09	Sthl	5f	(0-95)H	STD	£9066
100	11/08	Wolv	5f20y	(0-95)H	STD	£7771
95	10/08	GrLe	5f	(0-85)H	STD	£5180
89	9/08	Bevl	5f	(0-75)H	SFT	£3238
85	9/08	Haml	6f5y		G-S	£3238

Total win prize-money £78064

Going (Turf): **Sf: 1-5 GS: 1-2** Gd: 0-1 GF: 0-2 Fm: 0-0
Distance: **5f/6f: 6-13** 7f-8f: 1-3 9f-13f: 0-0 14f+: 0-0
Track : **LH: 4-8** RH: 0-0 **Tight: 2-3** Gall: 1-1
Aids: Bl: 0-0 Vi: 0-0 Tstrap: 0-0 Ckp: 0-0
Best Rating: **110** 3/09 Ling 5f stand

Smart; Listed winner; effective over 5f-6f; acts on soft ground; goes on sand; likes to race prominently.

Argaum (IRE)

75(99) (71)**64**

2-y-o ch c Medicean-Poppy Carew (IRE) (Danehill (USA))
W R Swinburn P W Harris

Placings:306 **(7209)**
2009: 8^{3}SD, 8^{0}G, 7^{6}SD,

	Starts	1st	2nd	3rd	Win & Pl
Career Total (Turf)	1	0	0	0	
Career Total (AW)	2	0	0	1	794

Going (Turf): **Sf: 0-0 GS: 0-0 Gd: 0-1 GF: 0-0 Fm: 0-0**
Distance: 5f/6f: 0-0 7f-8f: 0-2 9f-13f: 0-1 14f+: 0-0
Track : LH: 0-1 RH: 0-2 Tight: 0-1 Gall: 0-0
Aids: Bl: 0-0 Vi: 0-0 Tstrap: 0-0 Ckp: 0-0
Best Rating: **71** 9/09 Kemp 1m stand

Argent Avia

87 **44**

3-y-o gr f Silver Patriarch (IRE)-Mountain Bird (Superlative)
M Brittain David J Taylor

Placings:000 **(5731)**
2009: 7^{0}GS, 9^{0}GF, 8^{0}GS,

	Starts	1st	2nd	3rd	Win & Pl
Career Total (Turf)	3	0	0	0	

Going (Turf): **Sf: 0-0 GS: 0-2 Gd: 0-0 GF: 0-1 Fm: 0-0**
Distance: 5f/6f: 0-0 7f-8f: 0-2 9f-13f: 0-1 14f+: 0-0
Track : LH: 0-2 RH: 0-1 Tight: 0-2 Gall: 0-1
Aids: Bl: 0-0 Vi: 0-0 Tstrap: 0-0 Ckp: 0-0
Best Rating: **44** 8/09 Ripn 1m1f170y gd-fm

Argentine (IRE)

103(101) (82)**84**

5-y-o b g Fasliyev (USA)-Teller (ARG) (Southern Halo (USA))
J A McShane (L Lungo 3/5) Mrs Carol Auld

Placings:341253/054046/5000303-
435144311123104000**300** **(7735)**
2009: 5^{4}SD, 5^{3}SD, 5^{5}SD, 5^{1}SD, 5^{4}SD, 5^{4}GF, 5^{3}G, 5^{1}GF, 6^{1}GF, 5^{1}GF, 5^{2}GF, 5^{3}GF, 5^{1}GF, 5^{0}G, 5^{4}GF, 6^{0}G, 5^{0}GF, 5^{3}SD, 5^{0}SD, 5^{0}SD,

	Starts	1st	2nd	3rd	Win & Pl
Career Total (Turf)	29	5	2	4	21090
Career Total (AW)	10	1	0	4	4241

84	6/09	Haml	5f4y	(0-75)H	G-F	£3238
81	6/09	Carl	5f	(0-70)H	G-F	£2914
73	6/09	Haml	6f5y	(0-60)H	G-F	£2637
65	6/09	Haml	5f4y	(0-65)H	G-F	£2388
61	3/09	Sthl	5f	(0-60)H	STD	£2047
84	7/06	Carl	5f		G-F	£3238

Total win prize-money £16463

Going (Turf): Sf: 0-2 GS: 0-3 Gd: 0-7 **GF: 5-16** Fm: 0-1
Distance: **5f/6f: 5-36** 7f-8f: 1-3 9f-13f: 0-0 14f+: 0-0
Track : LH: 0-8 **RH: 2-5** Tight: 0-8 **Gall: 2-3**
Aids: **Bl: 4-15** Vi: 0-0 Tstrap: 0-1 Ckp: 0-1
Best Rating: **84** 6/09 Haml 5f4y gd-fm

Fair; effective over 5f-6f; handles fast ground and Fibresand.

Argyll

83(86) (43)**57**

2-y-o b c Xaar-Vitesse (IRE) (Royal Academy (USA))
J Pearce Pump & Plant Services Ltd

Placings:0000000 (7661)

2009: 6^{0}GF, 6^{0}G, 7^{0}G, 7^{0}SD, 8^{0}G, 8^{0}GF, 7^{0}GF, 6^{0}SD,

	Starts	1st	2nd	3rd	Win & Pl
Career Total (Turf)	6	0	0	0	
Career Total (AW)	2	0	0	0	

Going (Turf): Sf: 0-0 GS: 0-0 Gd: 0-3 GF: 0-3 Fm: 0-0
Distance: 5f/6f: 0-3 7f-8f: 0-4 9f-13f: 0-1 14f+: 0-0
Track : LH: 0-3 RH: 0-0 Tight: 0-3 Gall: 0-1
Aids: Bl: 0-0 Vi: 0-0 Tstrap: 0-0 Ckp: 0-0
Best Rating: 57 8/09 NmkJ 7f good

Ariadnes Filly (IRE)

94(91) (63)**62**

3-y-o b f Xaar-Christaleni (Zilzal (USA))
Mrs A J Perrett Athos Christodoulou

Placings:06-500 (2827)

2009: 6^{5}GF, 5^{0}GS, 7^{0}SD,

	Starts	1st	2nd	3rd	Win & Pl
Career Total (Turf)	3	0	0	0	0
Career Total (AW)	2	0	0	0	0

Going (Turf): Sf: 0-0 GS: 0-1 Gd: 0-1 GF: 0-1 Fm: 0-0
Distance: 5f/6f: 0-2 7f-8f: 0-3 9f-13f: 0-0 14f+: 0-0
Track : LH: 0-2 RH: 0-1 Tight: 0-1 Gall: 0-1
Aids: Bl: 0-0 Vi: 0-0 Tstrap: 0-0 Ckp: 0-0
Best Rating: 63 10/08 Ling 7f stand

Ariel Bender

81 **46**

2-y-o gr g Needwood Blade-Wandering Stranger (Petong)
Peter Grayson Cannon, Grundy, Shaw, Hamill

Placings:5000660 (4327)

2009: 5^{5}GF, 5^{0}G, 5^{0}GF, 5^{0}GF, 6^{6}GF, 5^{6}S, 5^{0}G,

	Starts	1st	2nd	3rd	Win & Pl
Career Total (Turf)	7	0	0	0	0

Going (Turf): Sf: 0-1 GS: 0-0 Gd: 0-2 GF: 0-4 Fm: 0-0
Distance: 5f/6f: 0-6 7f-8f: 0-1 9f-13f: 0-0 14f+: 0-0
Track : LH: 0-2 RH: 0-0 Tight: 0-2 Gall: 0-0
Aids: Bl: 0-1 Vi: 0-0 Tstrap: 0-0 Ckp: 0-0
Best Rating: 46 6/09 Ches 5f16y gd-fm

Moderate form to date.

Arikinui

(96) (55)**38**

4-y-o b f Noverre (USA)-Off The Blocks (Salse (USA))
K R Burke Philip Richards

Placings:00-30 (0657)

2009: 8^{3}SD, 8^{0}SD,

	Starts	1st	2nd	3rd	Win & Pl
Career Total (Turf)	1	0	0	0	
Career Total (AW)	3	0	0	1	482

Going (Turf): Sf: 0-0 GS: 0-1 Gd: 0-0 GF: 0-0 Fm: 0-0
Distance: 5f/6f: 0-0 7f-8f: 0-2 9f-13f: 0-2 14f+: 0-0
Track : LH: 0-3 RH: 0-1 Tight: 0-4 Gall: 0-0
Aids: Bl: 0-0 Vi: 0-0 Tstrap: 0-0 Ckp: 0-0
Best Rating: 55 1/09 Wolv 1m141y stand

Arizona John (IRE)

105(97) (80)**86**

4-y-o b g Rahy (USA)-Preseli (IRE) (Caerleon (USA))
J Mackie (N Wilson 3/7) Derbyshire Racing

Placings:43/0610-0605013311654 (7633)

2009: 8^{0}GF, 8^{6}GF, 7^{0}GF, 7^{5}G, 6^{0}G, 8^{1}F, 7^{3}GF, 8^{3}G, 8^{1}GF, 8^{1}GF, 8^{6}GF, 8^{5}G, 8^{4}SD,

	Starts	1st	2nd	3rd	Win & Pl
Career Total (Turf)	17	4	0	3	23165
Career Total (AW)	2	0	0	0	378

81 9/09 Yarm 1m3y (0-85)H G-F £6308
79 8/09 Rdcr 1m (0-80)H G-F £5180
70 7/09 Rdcr 1m FRM £2729
86 5/08 Tipp 7f100y FRM £6605
Total win prize-money £20824

Going (Turf): Sf: 0-2 GS: 0-0 Gd: 0-5 **GF: 2-8 Fm: 2-2**
Distance: 5f/6f: 0-1 **7f-8f: 3-14** 9f-13f: 1-4 14f+: 0-0
Track : **LH: 1-6** RH: 0-5 Tight: 0-3 Gall: 0-0
Aids: **Bl: 1-3** Vi: 0-0 Tstrap: 0-0 Ckp: 0-0
Best Rating: 86 5/08 Tipp 7f100y firm

Fair; ex-Irish; best at 7f-1m; effective on fast ground; has worn blinkers.

Arjemis

100 **60**

3-y-o b f Hunting Lion (IRE)-Kungfu Kerry (Celtic Swing)
C R Wilson David Bartlett

Placings:0045210 (6103)

2009: 6^{0}GS, 5^{0}GF, 7^{4}G, 5^{5}GF, 5^{2}GF, 5^{1}GS, 7^{0}GF,

	Starts	1st	2nd	3rd	Win & Pl
Career Total (Turf)	7	1	1	0	3863

60 8/09 Catt 5f212y G-S £2914
Total win prize-money £2914

Going (Turf): Sf: 0-0 **GS: 1-2** Gd: 0-1 GF: 0-4 Fm: 0-0
Distance: **5f/6f: 1-5** 7f-8f: 0-2 9f-13f: 0-0 14f+: 0-0
Track : **LH: 1-3** RH: 0-0 **Tight: 1-3** Gall: 0-0
Aids: Bl: 0-0 Vi: 0-0 Tstrap: 0-0 Ckp: 0-0
Best Rating: 60 8/09 Catt 5f212y gd-sft

Modest; stays 7f; acts on easy ground

Arkellion

81 **48**

2-y-o b g Mark Of Esteem (IRE)-Lovellian (Machiavellian (USA))
P D Evans (A B Haynes 29/5) Bathwick Gold Partnership

Placings:0500 (5967)

2009: 6^{0}G, 7^{5}G, 6^{0}GF, 6^{0}GS,

	Starts	1st	2nd	3rd	Win & Pl
Career Total (Turf)	4	0	0	0	0

Going (Turf): Sf: 0-0 GS: 0-1 Gd: 0-2 GF: 0-1 Fm: 0-0
Distance: 5f/6f: 0-2 7f-8f: 0-2 9f-13f: 0-0 14f+: 0-0
Track : LH: 0-1 RH: 0-0 Tight: 0-1 Gall: 0-0
Aids: Bl: 0-0 Vi: 0-0 Tstrap: 0-0 Ckp: 0-0
Best Rating: 48 8/09 Ches 7f2y good

Arken Lad

90(87) (58)**63**

2-y-o b g Arakan (USA)-Object Of Vertu (FR) (Kendor (FR))
D Donovan Philip Mclaughlin

Placings:P041306 (7175)

2009: 6^{P}G, 7^{0}GF, 5^{4}SD, 6^{1}G, 7^{3}GS, 8^{0}SD, 6^{8}SD,

	Starts	1st	2nd	3rd	Win & Pl
Career Total (Turf)	4	1	0	1	2424
Career Total (AW)	3	0	0	0	0

60 7/09 Yarm 6f3y GD £1942
Total win prize-money £1943

Going (Turf): Sf: 0-0 GS: 0-1 **Gd: 1-2** GF: 0-1 Fm: 0-0
Distance: 5f/6f: 0-2 **7f-8f: 1-5** 9f-13f: 0-0 14f+: 0-0
Track : LH: 0-2 RH: 0-2 Tight: 0-2 Gall: 0-0
Aids: Bl: 0-0 Vi: 0-0 Tstrap: 1-3 Ckp: 1-3
Best Rating: 63 8/09 NmkJ 7f gd-sft

Modest; stays 6f; acts on Polytrack and good ground on turf; has worn cheekpieces.

Arlene Phillips

94(92) (48)**52**

3-y-o ch f Groom Dancer (USA)-Careful Dancer (Gorytus (USA))
R Hannon Theakston Stud Syndicate

Placings:00-03400100 (6918)

2009: 7^{0}G, 10^{3}SD, 9^{4}GS, 10^{0}GF, 14^{0}G, 10^{1}G, 12^{6}SS, 12^{0}SD,

	Starts	1st	2nd	3rd	Win & Pl
Career Total (Turf)	7	1	0	0	2459
Career Total (AW)	3	0	0	1	289

50 9/09 Ffos 1m2f (0-55)H GD £2266
Total win prize-money £2267

Going (Turf): Sf: 0-0 GS: 0-1 **Gd: 1-5** GF: 0-1 Fm: 0-0
Distance: 5f/6f: 0-0 7f-8f: 0-3 **9f-13f: 1-6** 14f+: 0-1
Track : **LH: 1-7** RH: 0-2 Tight: 0-4 **Gall: 1-1**
Aids: Bl: 0-0 Vi: 0-0 Tstrap: 0-0 Ckp: 0-0
Best Rating: 52 9/08 Wwck 7f26y good

Moderate; stays 1m2f; acts on good ground and on Polytrack.

Arlequin

94 **77**

2-y-o b c Rock Of Gibraltar (IRE)-Fairy Dance (IRE) (Zafonic (USA))
J D Bethell Dr Anne J F Gillespie

Placings:0010 (6993)

2009: 7^{0}G, 8^{0}GF, 8^{1}GF, 8^{0}GS,

	Starts	1st	2nd	3rd	Win & Pl
Career Total (Turf)	4	1	0	0	5051

77 9/09 Newc 1m G-F £5051
Total win prize-money £5051

Going (Turf): Sf: 0-0 GS: 0-1 Gd: 0-1 **GF: 1-2** Fm: 0-0
Distance: 5f/6f: 0-0 **7f-8f: 1-4** 9f-13f: 0-0 14f+: 0-0
Track : **LH: 1-3** RH: 0-0 Tight: 0-1 **Gall: 1-2**
Aids: Bl: 0-0 Vi: 0-0 Tstrap: 0-0 Ckp: 0-0
Best Rating: 77 9/09 Newc 1m gd-fm

Fair; stays 1m and acts on fast ground.

Armour

95(89) (77)**72**

2-y-o b c Azamour (IRE)-Tenable (Polish Precedent (USA))
M J Grassick Mrs S Grassick

Placings:01 (6026)

2009: 7^{0}GY, 5^{1}SD,

	Starts	1st	2nd	3rd	Win & Pl
Career Total (Turf)	1	0	0	0	
Career Total (AW)	1	1	0	0	3562

77	9/09	Wolv	5f216y	STD	£3561

Total win prize-money £3562

Going (Turf): Sf: 0-0 GS: 0-0 Gd: 0-0 GF: 0-0 Fm: 0-0
Distance: **5f/6f: 1-1** 7f-8f: 0-1 9f-13f: 0-0 14f+: 0-0
Track : **LH: 1-2** RH: 0-0 **Tight: 1-1** Gall: 0-0
Aids: Bl: 0-0 Vi: 0-0 Tstrap: 0-0 Ckp: 0-0
Best Rating: 77 9/09 Wolv 5f216y stand

Arnie Guru

85 **56**

2-y-o ch g Ishiguru (USA)-Who Goes There (Wolfhound (USA))
M J Attwater T M Jones

Placings:04 **(5722)**
2009: 7^{0}GF, 7^{4}F,

	Starts	1st	2nd	3rd	Win & Pl
Career Total (Turf)	2	0	0	0	241

Going (Turf): Sf: 0-0 GS: 0-0 Gd: 0-0 GF: 0-1 Fm: 0-1
Distance: 5f/6f: 0-0 7f-8f: 0-2 9f-13f: 0-0 14f+: 0-0
Track : LH: 0-0 RH: 0-0 Tight: 0-0 Gall: 0-0
Aids: Bl: 0-0 Vi: 0-0 Tstrap: 0-0 Ckp: 0-0
Best Rating: 56 9/09 Folk 7f firm

Aromatic

110(102) (89)**82**

3-y-o b f Medicean-Red Garland (Selkirk (USA))
J H M Gosden Cheveley Park Stud

Placings:5-11504 **(5996)**
2009: 9^{1}F, 10^{1}SD, 9^{5}GF, 10^{0}G, 8^{4}GS,

	Starts	1st	2nd	3rd	Win & Pl
Career Total (Turf)	5	1	0	0	4246
Career Total (AW)	1	1	0	0	5828
89 5/09 Ling 1m2f	(0-85)H			STD	£5828
82 5/09 Sals 1m1f198y				FRM	£3885

Total win prize-money £9714

Going (Turf): Sf: 0-0 GS: 0-1 Gd: 0-1 GF: 0-2 **Fm: 1-1**
Distance: 5f/6f: 0-0 7f-8f: 0-1 **9f-13f: 2-5** 14f+: 0-0
Track : LH: 1-2 RH: 1-3 **Tight: 2-3** Gall: 0-1
Aids: Bl: 0-1 Vi: 0-0 Tstrap: 0-0 Ckp: 0-0
Best Rating: 89 5/09 Ling 1m2f stand

Fair; stays 1m2f; acts on fast ground and Polytrack.

Aroundthebay

95(102) (86)**84**

3-y-o b f Diktat-Bayleaf (Efisio)
H J L Dunlop The Endeavour Partnership

Placings:21-10160000 **(7132)**
2009: 6^{1}SD, 7^{0}GS, 6^{1}GF, 7^{6}GF, 8^{0}G, 5^{0}SD, 7^{0}SD, 8^{0}SD,

	Starts	1st	2nd	3rd	Win & Pl
Career Total (Turf)	5	1	1	0	6728
Career Total (AW)	5	2	0	0	8613
84 6/09 Folk 6f	(0-85)H			G-F	£5180
84 3/09 Kemp 6f	(0-85)H			STD	£4727
74 10/08 Kemp 6f				STD	£3885

Total win prize-money £13794

Going (Turf): Sf: 0-0 GS: 0-1 Gd: 0-2 **GF: 1-2** Fm: 0-0
Distance: **5f/6f: 3-4** 7f-8f: 0-5 9f-13f: 0-1 14f+: 0-0
Track : LH: 0-4 **RH: 2-4** Tight: 0-2 Gall: 0-0
Aids: Bl: 0-0 Vi: 0-0 Tstrap: 0-0 Ckp: 0-0
Best Rating: 86 10/09 Ling 1m stand

Useful; effective over 6f; acts on fast ground and on Polytrack.

Arrabiata

(92) (51)**35**

4-y-o b f Piccolo-Paperweight (In The Wings)
C N Kellett Mrs N Gidleywright

Placings:0/46000000-0 **(0037)**
2009: 7^{0}SS,

	Starts	1st	2nd	3rd	Win & Pl
Career Total (Turf)	3	0	0	0	
Career Total (AW)	7	0	0	0	0

Going (Turf): Sf: 0-1 GS: 0-0 Gd: 0-0 GF: 0-2 Fm: 0-0
Distance: 5f/6f: 0-5 7f-8f: 0-4 9f-13f: 0-1 14f+: 0-0
Track : LH: 0-9 RH: 0-0 Tight: 0-5 Gall: 0-0
Aids: Bl: 0-4 Vi: 0-0 Tstrap: 0-0 Ckp: 0-0
Best Rating: 51 2/08 Wolv 5f216y stand

Arriva La Diva

100 **57**

3-y-o ch f Needwood Blade-Hillside Girl (IRE) (Tagula (IRE))
J J Quinn Allan Stennett

Placings:0-0021230 **(5626)**
2009: 6^{0}GS, 7^{0}GS, 5^{2}GF, 5^{1}G, 5^{2}GF, 5^{3}GF, 5^{0}S,

	Starts	1st	2nd	3rd	Win & Pl
Career Total (Turf)	8	1	2	1	3939
56 7/09 Ayr 5f	(0-60)H			GD	£2047

Total win prize-money £2047

Going (Turf): Sf: 0-1 GS: 0-2 **Gd: 1-2** GF: 0-3 Fm: 0-0
Distance: **5f/6f: 1-7** 7f-8f: 0-1 9f-13f: 0-0 14f+: 0-0
Track : LH: 0-0 RH: 0-0 Tight: 0-0 Gall: 0-0
Aids: Bl: 0-0 Vi: 0-0 Tstrap: 0-0 Ckp: 0-0
Best Rating: 57 8/09 Ayr 5f gd-fm

Moderate; suited by 5f and fast ground.

Arrivederla (IRE)

102(88) (63)**85**

3-y-o b f Acclamation-Alwiyda (USA) (Trempolino (USA))
H J L Dunlop William Armitage

Placings:3114 **(2696)**
2009: 7^{3}SD, 7^{1}GF, 7^{1}S, 8^{4}S,

	Starts	1st	2nd	3rd	Win & Pl
Career Total (Turf)	3	2	0	0	9096
Career Total (AW)	1	0	0	1	385
85 5/09 Hayd 7f30y	(0-80)H			SFT	£5504
76 5/09 Ling 7f				G-F	£2388

Total win prize-money £7893

Going (Turf): Sf: 1-2 GS: 0-0 Gd: 0-0 **GF: 1-1** Fm: 0-0
Distance: 5f/6f: 0-0 **7f-8f: 2-4** 9f-13f: 0-0 14f+: 0-0
Track : **LH: 1-1** RH: 0-1 Tight: 0-0 Gall: 0-0
Aids: Bl: 0-0 Vi: 0-0 Tstrap: 0-0 Ckp: 0-0
Best Rating: 85 5/09 Hayd 7f30y soft

Useful stays 7f and acts on fast and soft ground.

Arrogance

93(87) (64)**63**

3-y-o b g Josr Algarhoud (IRE)-Rise 'n Shine (Night Shift (USA))
G L Moore Mrs Charles Cyzer

Placings:0640-540 **(2479)**
2009: 9^{5}G, 9^{4}G, 11^{0}G,

	Starts	1st	2nd	3rd	Win & Pl
Career Total (Turf)	5	0	0	0	241
Career Total (AW)	2	0	0	0	265

Going (Turf): Sf: 0-0 GS: 0-1 Gd: 0-3 GF: 0-1 Fm: 0-0
Distance: 5f/6f: 0-3 7f-8f: 0-1 9f-13f: 0-3 14f+: 0-0
Track : LH: 0-2 RH: 0-4 Tight: 0-3 Gall: 0-1
Aids: Bl: 0-0 Vi: 0-0 Tstrap: 0-0 Ckp: 0-0
Best Rating: 64 9/08 Kemp 6f stand

Modest; stays 1m2f; acts on fast ground and Polytrack.

Arry's Orse

90 **69**

2-y-o b c Exceed And Excel (AUS)-Georgianna (IRE) (Petardia)
B Smart Harry Redknapp

Placings:5 **(5234)**
2009: 6^{5}GF,

	Starts	1st	2nd	3rd	Win & Pl
Career Total (Turf)	1	0	0	0	0

Going (Turf): Sf: 0-0 GS: 0-0 Gd: 0-0 GF: 0-1 Fm: 0-0
Distance: 5f/6f: 0-1 7f-8f: 0-0 9f-13f: 0-0 14f+: 0-0
Track : LH: 0-0 RH: 0-0 Tight: 0-0 Gall: 0-0
Aids: Bl: 0-0 Vi: 0-0 Tstrap: 0-0 Ckp: 0-0
Best Rating: 69 8/09 York 6f gd-fm

Art Connoisseur (IRE)

110 **120**

3-y-o b c Lucky Story (USA)-Withorwithoutyou (IRE) (Danehill (USA))
M L W Bell R A Green

Placings:11120-010000 **(6304)**
2009: 7^{0}GF, 6^{1}GF, 6^{0}GF, 5^{0}GF, 6^{0}GS, 6^{0}GF,

	Starts	1st	2nd	3rd	Win & Pl
Career Total (Turf)	11	4	1	0	385999
120 6/09 Asct 6f				G-F	£278456
115 6/08 Asct 6f				G-F	£56770
99 4/08 NmkR 5f				GD	£6476
83 4/08 Leic 5f2y				SFT	£1942

Total win prize-money £343646

Going (Turf): Sf: 1-1 GS: 0-2 Gd: 1-1 **GF: 2-7** Fm: 0-0
Distance: **5f/6f: 4-9** 7f-8f: 0-2 9f-13f: 0-0 14f+: 0-0
Track : LH: 0-0 RH: 0-0 Tight: 0-0 Gall: 0-0
Aids: Bl: 0-0 Vi: 0-0 Tstrap: 0-0 Ckp: 0-0
Best Rating: 120 6/09 Asct 6f gd-fm

High-class; winner of the Group 2 Coventry Stakes at two and the 2009 Golden Jubilee; stays 6f and acts on most ground; suited by coming from off a strong pace.

Art Deco (IRE)

(104) (103)**115**

6-y-o ch h Peintre Celebre (USA)-Sometime (IRE) (Royal Academy (USA))
C R Egerton Longmoor Holdings Ltd

Placings:12/145/6/5 **(2398)**
2009: 10^{5}SD,

	Starts	1st	2nd	3rd	Win & Pl
Career Total (Turf)	6	2	1	0	113845
Career Total (AW)	1	0	0	0	0
113 5/06 Ches 1m2f75y				G-S	£36907
80 8/05 Sand 7f16y				SFT	£4914

Total win prize-money £41821

Going (Turf): **Sf: 1-1 GS: 1-1** Gd: 0-3 GF: 0-1 Fm: 0-0
Distance: 5f/6f: 0-0 7f-8f: 1-2 9f-13f: 1-5 14f+: 0-0
Track : LH: 1-2 RH: 1-4 **Tight: 1-2** Gall: 0-0
Aids: Bl: 0-0 Vi: 0-0 Tstrap: 0-0 Ckp: 0-0
Best Rating: **115** 7/06 Lonc 1m4f good

Group class; winner of the 2006 Dee Stakes at Chester; stays 1m2f; acts on soft and quick ground.

Art Discovery (IRE)

83(91) (53)**36**
3-y-o br g Indian Haven-Lady Cinders (IRE) (Dance Of Life (USA))
M H Tompkins Miss Clare Hollest

Placings:00-200 **(6788)**
2009: 7^{2}SS, 10^{0}GS, 11^{0}G,

	Starts	1st	2nd	3rd	Win & Pl
Career Total (Turf)	2	0	0	0	
Career Total (AW)	3	0	1	0	605

Going (Turf): **Sf: 0-0 GS: 0-1 Gd: 0-1 GF: 0-0 Fm: 0-0**
Distance: 5f/6f: 0-0 7f-8f: 0-3 9f-13f: 0-2 14f+: 0-0
Track : LH: 0-5 RH: 0-0 Tight: 0-1 Gall: 0-1
Aids: Bl: 0-2 Vi: 0-0 Tstrap: 0-0 Ckp: 0-0
Best Rating: **53** 1/09 Sthl 7f std-slw

Moderate; effective over 7f; acts on Fibresand.

Art Excellence

95(95) (73)**82**
2-y-o b c Noverre (USA)-Her Ladyship (Polish Precedent (USA))
S A Callaghan Matthew Green

Placings:610 **(7030)**
2009: 7^{6}GF, 8^{1}SD, 7^{0}S,

	Starts	1st	2nd	3rd	Win & Pl
Career Total (Turf)	2	0	0	0	0
Career Total (AW)	1	1	0	0	2047
73 10/09 Kemp 1m			STD	£2047	

Total win prize-money £2047

Going (Turf): **Sf: 0-1 GS: 0-0 Gd: 0-0 GF: 0-1 Fm: 0-0**
Distance: 5f/6f: 0-0 **7f-8f: 1-3** 9f-13f: 0-0 14f+: 0-0
Track : LH: 0-0 **RH: 1-1** Tight: 0-0 Gall: 0-0
Aids: Bl: 0-0 Vi: 0-0 Tstrap: 0-0 Ckp: 0-0
Best Rating: **82** 10/09 Newb 7f soft

Fair; stays 1m and acts on Polytrack.

Art Exhibition (IRE)

76(100) (68)**46**
4-y-o ch g Captain Rio-Miss Dilletante (Primo Dominie)
B R Millman (C J Mann 11/3) John Southway & Andrew Hughes

Placings:0/00221-50 **(2163)**
2009: 12^{5}SD, 16^{0}G,

	Starts	1st	2nd	3rd	Win & Pl
Career Total (Turf)	1	0	0	0	
Career Total (AW)	7	1	2	0	3396
68 4/08 Wolv 1m4f50y (0-60)I I			STD	£2047	

Total win prize-money £2047

Going (Turf): **Sf: 0-0 GS: 0-0 Gd: 0-1 GF: 0-0 Fm: 0-0**
Distance: 5f/6f: 0-2 7f-8f: 0-1 **9f-13f: 1-4** 14f+: 0-1
Track : **LH: 1-7** RH: 0-1 **Tight: 1-4** Gall: 0-1
Aids: Bl: 0-1 Vi: 0-0 Tstrap: 0-0 Ckp: 0-0
Best Rating: **68** 4/08 Wolv 1m4f50y stand

Moderate; stays 1m4f and acts on Polytrack.

Art Fund (USA)

(94) (65)**50**
3-y-o b g Speightstown (USA)-Kew Garden (USA) (Seattle Slew (USA))
G L Moore R A Green

Placings:06501-665 **(0345)**
2009: 7^{6}SD, 6^{6}SD, 7^{5}SD,

	Starts	1st	2nd	3rd	Win & Pl
Career Total (Turf)	1	0	0	0	0
Career Total (AW)	7	1	0	0	1979
65 12/08 Ling 6f			STD	£1978	

Total win prize-money £1979

Going (Turf): **Sf: 0-0 GS: 0-1 Gd: 0-0 GF: 0-0 Fm: 0-0**
Distance: **5f/6f: 1-5** 7f-8f: 0-3 9f-13f: 0-0 14f+: 0-0
Track : **LH: 1-7** RH: 0-1 **Tight: 1-5** Gall: 0-2
Aids: Bl: 0-0 Vi: 0-0 Tstrap: 0-0 Ckp: 0-0
Best Rating: **65** 12/08 Ling 6f stand

Modest; effective over 6f on Polytrack.

Art Gallery

93(74) (42)**41**
5-y-o ch g Indian Ridge-Party Doll (Be My Guest (USA))
D W Thompson (R C Guest 27/1) Mrs Anna Kenny

Placings:050/6000/000-00300 **(6559)**
2009: 12^{0}SD, 17^{0}G, 15^{3}G, 13^{0}HY, 15^{0}G,

	Starts	1st	2nd	3rd	Win & Pl
Career Total (Turf)	10	0	0	1	302
Career Total (AW)	5	0	0	0	0

Going (Turf): **Sf: 0-2 GS: 0-1 Gd: 0-4 GF: 0-3 Fm: 0-0**
Distance: 5f/6f: 0-1 7f-8f: 0-6 9f-13f: 0-4 14f+: 0-4
Track : LH: 0-6 RH: 0-7 Tight: 0-4 Gall: 0-2
Aids: Bl: 0-6 Vi: 0-0 Tstrap: 0-1 Ckp: 0-1
Best Rating: **56** 10/06 NmkR 7f soft

Half-brother to high-class juvenile Titus Livius.

Art Jewel (IRE)

85(89) (69)**64**
2-y-o b f Bertolini (USA)-Ma N'Ieme Biche (USA) (Key To The Kingdom (USA))
S A Callaghan Matthew Green

Placings:1302 **(3719)**
2009: 5^{1}SD, 5^{3}GF, 5^{0}GS, 5^{2}SD,

	Starts	1st	2nd	3rd	Win & Pl
Career Total (Turf)	2	0	0	1	722
Career Total (AW)	2	1	1	0	4692
69 5/09 Ling 5f			STD	£3885	

Total win prize-money £3886

Going (Turf): **Sf: 0-0 GS: 0-1 Gd: 0-0 GF: 0-1 Fm: 0-0**
Distance: **5f/6f: 1-4** 7f-8f: 0-0 9f-13f: 0-0 14f+: 0-0
Track : **LH: 1-2** RH: 0-0 **Tight: 1-2** Gall: 0-1
Aids: Bl: 0-0 Vi: 0-1 Tstrap: 0-0 Ckp: 0-0
Best Rating: **69** 5/09 Ling 5f stand

Fair; half-sister to several winners from 6f to middle distances; effective over 5f; acts on Polytrack; tailflasher.

Art Machine (USA)

87(88) (67)**49**
2-y-o ch f Sky Mesa (USA)-Grazia (Sharpo)
Sir Mark Prescott Cyril Humphris

Placings:466 **(6334)**
2009: 7^{4}SD, 5^{6}SD, 6^{6}GF,

	Starts	1st	2nd	3rd	Win & Pl
Career Total (Turf)	1	0	0	0	0
Career Total (AW)	2	0	0	0	560

Going (Turf): **Sf: 0-0 GS: 0-0 Gd: 0-0 GF: 0-1 Fm: 0-0**
Distance: 5f/6f: 0-1 7f-8f: 0-2 9f-13f: 0-0 14f+: 0-0
Track : LH: 0-2 RH: 0-1 Tight: 0-1 Gall: 0-0
Aids: Bl: 0-0 Vi: 0-0 Tstrap: 0-0 Ckp: 0-0
Best Rating: **67** 9/09 Kemp 7f stand

Modest; should stay 1m; acts on Polytrack.

Art Man

(112) (92)**75**
6-y-o b g Dansili-Persuasion (Batshoof)
J D Frost (G L Moore 24/6) Mrs D Hunt

Placings:0524/645/112511100003-6604313 **(3273)**
2009: 10^{6}SD, 8^{6}SD, 8^{0}SD, 8^{4}SD, 10^{3}SD, 13^{1}SD, 12^{3}SD,

	Starts	1st	2nd	3rd	Win & Pl
Career Total (Turf)	6	0	1	0	1204
Career Total (AW)	20	6	1	3	31029
84 5/09 Ling 1m5f (0-80)H				STD	£4857
92 5/08 GrLe 1m2f (0-90)H				STD	£6623
89 5/08 GrLe 1m2f (0-85)H				STD	£4533
87 3/08 Kemp 1m3f (0-85)H				STD	£4050
82 1/08 Ling 1m2f (0-80)H				STD	£4100
69 1/08 Ling 1m2f				STD	£2331

Total win prize-money £26497

Going (Turf): **Sf: 0-1 GS: 0-1 Gd: 0-0 GF: 0-2 Fm: 0-2**
Distance: 5f/6f: 0-1 7f-8f: 0-5 **9f-13f: 6-20** 14f+: 0-0
Track : **LH: 5-15** RH: 1-9 **Tight: 3-12** Gall: 2-4
Aids: Bl: 0-0 Vi: 0-0 Tstrap: 0-0 Ckp: 0-0
Best Rating: **92** 5/08 GrLe 1m2f stand

Useful; stays 1m5f; acts on Polytrack (only wins have come on that surface); likes to come late off a strong pace.

Art Market (CAN)

(102) (66)**68**
6-y-o ch g Giant's Causeway (USA)-Fantasy Lake (USA) (Salt Lake (USA))
Miss Jo Crowley Mrs Liz Nelson

Placings:3130/040600/00006/454604-0226353 **(7479)**
2009: 8^{0}SD, 7^{2}SD, 7^{2}SD, 7^{6}SD, 7^{3}SS, 8^{5}SD, 7^{3}SD,

	Starts	1st	2nd	3rd	Win & Pl
Career Total (Turf)	15	1	0	2	12433
Career Total (AW)	13	0	2	2	2400
79 7/05 Wind 6f			G-F	£5135	

Total win prize-money £5135

Going (Turf): Sf: 0-1 GS: 0-2 Gd: 0-4 **GF: 1-8** Fm: 0-0
Distance: **5f/6f: 1-4** 7f-8f: 0-17 9f-13f: 0-7 14f+: 0-0
Track : LH: 0-11 RH: 0-7 Tight: 0-11 **Gall: 1-3**
Aids: Bl: 0-3 Vi: 0-0 Tstrap: 0-3 Ckp: 0-3
Best Rating: **98** 9/05 NmkJ 6f gd-fm

Modest; effective at around 7f; acts on fast ground and on Polytrack; has worn blinkers and a tongue-tie.

Art Scholar (IRE)

96 **90**

2-y-o b c Pyrus (USA)-Marigold (FR) (Marju (IRE))
G L Moore R A Green

Placings:120 **(6104)**
2009: 5^{1}G, 6^{2}F, 6^{0}GF,

	Starts	1st	2nd	3rd	Win & Pl
Career Total (Turf)	3	1	1	0	3747

90 8/09 Bath 5f161y GD £2590
Total win prize-money £2590

Going (Turf): Sf: 0-0 GS: 0-0 **Gd: 1-1** GF: 0-1 Fm: 0-1
Distance: **5f/6f: 1-2** 7f-8f: 0-1 9f-13f: 0-0 14f+: 0-0
Track : **LH: 1-1** RH: 0-0 Tight: 0-0 **Gall: 1-1**
Aids: Bl: 0-0 Vi: 0-0 Tstrap: 0-1 Ckp: 0-1
Best Rating: **90** 8/09 Bath 5f161y good

Oout of a half-sister to Derby runner-up The Great Gatsby; very useful; effective at around 6f; acts on good ground.

Art Summer

86 **64**

2-y-o ch f Compton Place-Karminskey Park (Sabrehill (USA))
D M Simcock Matthew Green & Associates

Placings:4323P **(6443)**
2009: 5^{4}GF, 5^{3}G, 5^{2}G, 6^{3}GF, 5^{P}SS,

	Starts	1st	2nd	3rd	Win & Pl
Career Total (Turf)	4	0	1	2	2195
Career Total (AW)	1	0	0	0	

Going (Turf): **Sf: 0-0 GS: 0-0 Gd: 0-2 GF: 0-2 Fm: 0-0**
Distance: 5f/6f: 0-5 7f-8f: 0-0 9f-13f: 0-0 14f+: 0-0
Track : LH: 0-4 RH: 0-0 Tight: 0-3 Gall: 0-1
Aids: Bl: 0-0 Vi: 0-0 Tstrap: 0-0 Ckp: 0-0
Best Rating: **64** 9/09 Epsm 6f gd-fm

Modest; effective at 5f; acts on good ground.

Art Value

100(95) (65)**55**

4-y-o ch g Barathea (IRE)-Empty Purse (Pennine Walk)
Michael Hourigan (M Wigham 6/9) Lisaleen Racing Club

Placings:030/0000-20455200 **(4640)**
2009: 9^{2}SD, 10^{0}SD, 11^{4}GF, 12^{5}GF, 14^{5}GF, 12^{2}GF, 11^{0}G, 11^{0}GF,

	Starts	1st	2nd	3rd	Win & Pl
Career Total (Turf)	11	0	1	1	1334
Career Total (AW)	4	0	1	0	578

Going (Turf): **Sf: 0-0 GS: 0-3 Gd: 0-3 GF: 0-5 Fm: 0-0**
Distance: 5f/6f: 0-0 7f-8f: 0-5 9f-13f: 0-9 14f+: 0-1
Track : LH: 0-8 RH: 0-3 Tight: 0-8 Gall: 0-0
Aids: Bl: 0-0 Vi: 0-0 Tstrap: 0-3 Ckp: 0-3
Best Rating: **73** 10/07 Leic 1m60y gd-sft

Very moderate; stays 1m4f and acts on fast ground; has worn cheekpieces.

Arte Viva (USA)

72(96) (77)**46**

2-y-o ch f Giant's Causeway (USA)-Helsinka (FR) (Pennekamp (USA))
G A Butler Fawzi Abdulla Nass

Placings:240 **(6920)**
2009: 7^{2}SD, 7^{4}SD, 8^{0}GF,

	Starts	1st	2nd	3rd	Win & Pl
Career Total (Turf)	1	0	0	0	
Career Total (AW)	2	0	1	0	2504

Going (Turf): **Sf: 0-0 GS: 0-0 Gd: 0-0 GF: 0-1 Fm: 0-0**
Distance: 5f/6f: 0-0 7f-8f: 0-2 9f-13f: 0-1 14f+: 0-0
Track : LH: 0-1 RH: 0-1 Tight: 0-1 Gall: 0-0
Aids: Bl: 0-0 Vi: 0-0 Tstrap: 0-0 Ckp: 0-0
Best Rating: **77** 9/09 Kemp 7f stand

Fair; stays 7f; acts on Polytrack; sure to improve and win races.

Artesium

83(99) (59)**48**

3-y-o ch g Haafhd-Multicolour (Rainbow Quest (USA))
Patrick Morris Alpha Gold Partnership

Placings:46043234-05001000050 **(7877)**
2009: 10^{0}GF, 7^{5}G, 7^{0}SD, 7^{0}SD, 7^{1}SD, 7^{0}SD, 8^{0}SD, 5^{0}SD, 7^{0}SD, 7^{5}SS, 7^{0}SD,

	Starts	1st	2nd	3rd	Win & Pl
Career Total (Turf)	5	0	0	0	529
Career Total (AW)	14	1	1	2	3425

59 9/09 Ling 7f (0-55)H STD £2388
Total win prize-money £2388

Going (Turf): **Sf: 0-2 GS: 0-0 Gd: 0-1 GF: 0-2 Fm: 0-0**
Distance: 5f/6f: 0-5 **7f-8f: 1-13** 9f-13f: 0-1 14f+: 0-0
Track : **LH: 1-12** RH: 0-5 **Tight: 1-8** Gall: 0-0
Aids: Bl: 0-0 Vi: 0-0 Tstrap: 0-1 Ckp: 0-1
Best Rating: **59** 9/09 Ling 7f stand

Moderate; stays 1m; acts on Polytrack and Fibresand; has worn a tongue-tie.

Arteus

103(105) (89)**79**

3-y-o b g Fantastic Light (USA)-Enchanted (Magic Ring (IRE))
Jane Chapple-Hyam Norcroft Park Stud

Placings:00P-20241001115 **(7801)**
2009: 7^{2}GF, 7^{0}S, 7^{2}GF, 7^{4}G, 7^{1}SD, 8^{0}SD, 7^{0}GF, 7^{1}GS, 7^{1}SD, 7^{1}SD, 7^{5}SD,

	Starts	1st	2nd	3rd	Win & Pl
Career Total (Turf)	8	1	2	0	5337
Career Total (AW)	6	3	0	0	9872

89 12/09 Wolv 7f32y (0-85)H STD £5046
82 11/09 Kemp 7f (0-75)H STD £2590
79 10/09 Folk 7f (0-75)H G-S £2729
72 8/09 Kemp 7f STD £2047
Total win prize-money £12413

Going (Turf): Sf: 0-1 **GS: 1-2** Gd: 0-2 GF: 0-3 Fm: 0-0
Distance: 5f/6f: 0-2 **7f-8f: 4-12** 9f-13f: 0-0 14f+: 0-0
Track : LH: 1-4 **RH: 2-4 Tight: 1-2** Gall: 0-1
Aids: **Bl: 2-3** Vi: 0-0 Tstrap: 1-2 Ckp: 1-2
Best Rating: **89** 12/09 Wolv 7f32y stand

Useful; stays 7f; acts on most ground and on Polytrack; has worn cheekpieces/blinkers.

Artful Dodger

(55)

2-y-o b c Josr Algarhoud (IRE)-Artistic Belle (IRE) (Orpen (USA))
T R Gretton Ken Tyre & Lee Tyre

Placings:0 **(7276)**
2009: 7^{0}SD,

	Starts	1st	2nd	3rd	Win & Pl
Career Total (Turf)	0	0	0	0	
Career Total (AW)	1	0	0	0	

Going (Turf): **Sf: 0-0 GS: 0-0 Gd: 0-0 GF: 0-0 Fm: 0-0**
Distance: 5f/6f: 0-0 7f-8f: 0-1 9f-13f: 0-0 14f+: 0-0
Track : LH: 0-1 RH: 0-0 Tight: 0-1 Gall: 0-0
Aids: Bl: 0-0 Vi: 0-0 Tstrap: 0-0 Ckp: 0-0

Arthur's Edge

110(108) (82)**103**

5-y-o b g Diktat-Bright Edge (Danehill Dancer (IRE))
B Palling Mrs Annabelle Mason

Placings:00/042311/210-00130502112 **(7292)**
2009: 8^{0}SD, 8^{0}GF, 7^{1}GF, 7^{3}G, 7^{0}GF, 7^{5}G, 7^{0}SD, 6^{2}G, 6^{1}GS, 5^{1}G, 6^{2}S,

	Starts	1st	2nd	3rd	Win & Pl
Career Total (Turf)	13	3	2	1	35836
Career Total (AW)	9	3	2	1	9420

94 10/09 Brig 5f213y (0-80)H GD £8831
87 10/09 Gdwd 6f (0-95)H G-S £7771
78 7/09 Chep 7f16y (0-85)H G-F £5180
82 4/08 Wolv 7f32y (0-75)H STD £3238
69 1/08 Wolv 1m141y (0-75)H STD £2457
70 11/07 Wolv 1m141y (0-55)H STD £2047
Total win prize-money £29526

Going (Turf): Sf: 0-2 **GS: 1-1 Gd: 1-6 GF: 1-4** Fm: 0-0
Distance: 5f/6f: 2-4 7f-8f: 2-10 9f-13f: 2-8 14f+: 0-0
Track : **LH: 4-10** RH: 0-3 **Tight: 3-8** Gall: 0-0
Aids: Bl: 0-0 Vi: 0-0 Tstrap: 0-0 Ckp: 0-0
Best Rating: **103** 11/09 Donc 6f soft

Useful; Listed placed; stays 1m2f, but effective over as short as 6f; acts on fast ground and on Polytrack.

Arthur's Girl

98(98) (86)**104**

4-y-o b f Hernando (FR)-Maid Of Camelot (Caerleon (USA))
J H M Gosden A E Oppenheimer

Placings:5/31240-50 **(7291)**
2009: 12^{5}G, 10^{0}S,

	Starts	1st	2nd	3rd	Win & Pl
Career Total (Turf)	6	1	1	1	40399
Career Total (AW)	2	0	0	0	0

89 5/08 Sals 1m1f198y GD £3885
Total win prize-money £3886

Going (Turf): Sf: 0-1 GS: 0-1 **Gd: 1-2** GF: 0-2 Fm: 0-0
Distance: 5f/6f: 0-1 7f-8f: 0-0 **9f-13f: 1-7** 14f+: 0-0
Track : LH: 0-4 **RH: 1-4 Tight: 1-2** Gall: 0-5
Aids: Bl: 0-0 Vi: 0-0 Tstrap: 0-0 Ckp: 0-0
Best Rating: **104** 6/08 Asct 1m4f gd-fm

Smart; runner-up in the 2008 Ribblesdale Stakes; stays 1m4f and acts on good and faster ground.

Artistic License (IRE)

104(110) (94)**94**

4-y-o b f Chevalier (IRE)-Alexander Eliott (IRE) (Night Shift (USA))
M R Channon Wood Street Syndicate IV

Placings:100/**3300322**10130-**23420641041330012400** **(7394)**
2009: 6^{2}SD, 5^{3}SD, 6^{4}SD, 5^{2}GF, 6^{0}GF, 5^{6}GF, 6^{4}GF, 6^{1}SD, 6^{0}GS, 5^{4}GF, 5^{1}F, 6^{3}GF, 6^{3}GF, 6^{0}GS, 6^{0}G, 6^{1}GF, 5^{2}F, 6^{4}GF, 6^{0}GF, 6^{0}SD,

	Starts	1st	2nd	3rd	Win & Pl
Career Total (Turf)	24	3	4	4	32888
Career Total (AW)	11	3	1	3	17841

93 8/09 Gdwd 6f (0-95)H G-F £7771
86 6/09 Bath 5f161y (0-80)H FRM £4857

94 5/09 Ling 6f (0-85)H STD £4857
89 9/08 GrLe 6f (0-85)H STD £4857
86 8/08 Ling 6f (0-75)H STD £3885
68 9/07 Folk 5f G-F £2388
Total win prize-money £28617

Going (Turf): Sf: 0-3 GS: 0-2 Gd: 0-6 **GF: 2-11** Fm: 1-2
Distance: **5f/6f: 6-31** 7f-8f: 0-4 9f-13f: 0-0 14f+: 0-0
Track : **LH: 4-13** RH: 0-5 Tight: 2-5 Gall: 2-5
Aids: Bl: 0-0 Vi: 0-0 Tstrap: 0-0 Ckp: 0-0
Best Rating: 94 9/09 Bath 5f161y firm

Useful; effective over 5f-6f; acts on fast ground and on Polytrack.

Artreju (GER)

98(101) (68)**76**
6-y-o ch g Perugino (USA)-Art Of Easter (GER) (Dashing Blade)
P Butler (G L Moore 24/7) M D Loftus

Placings:41/6560233/66020/**64**01354650**3**-**4004**00250044**0000** (7668)
2009: 8^{4}SD, **8**^{0}SD, **10**^{0}SD, **9**^{4}SD, 10^{0}GF, 9^{0}GF, 10^{2}GF, 9^{5}G, 10^{0}G, 10^{0}G, 9^{4}F, 8^{4}G, 10^{0}GF, **8**^{0}SD, **12**^{0}SD, **10**^{0}SD, **9**^{0}SD,

	Starts	1st	2nd	3rd	Win & Pl
Career Total (Turf)	28	2	3	2	22349
Career Total (AW)	14	0	0	2	1265

76 5/08 NmkR 1m2f (0-70)H G-F £3123
10/05 Kref 6f SFT £2127
Total win prize-money £5251

Going (Turf): **Sf: 1-7** GS: 0-0 Gd: 0-12 **GF: 1-7** Fm: 0-1
Distance: 5f/6f: 1-3 7f-8f: 0-11 9f-13f: 1-28 14f+: 0-0
Track : LH: 0-17 RH: 0-11 Tight: 0-13 Gall: 0-4
Aids: Bl: 0-1 Vi: 0-1 Tstrap: 0-4 Ckp: 0-4
Best Rating: 85 11/06 StCl 1m v soft

Modest; ex-German; effective at around 1m2f; acts on good and faster ground.

Arts Guild (USA)

(108) (81)**83**
4-y-o b g Theatrical-Gilded Edge (Cadeaux Genereux)
W J Musson Colin Bryce

Placings:434202**2**6-2 (5127)
2009: 9^{2}GF,

	Starts	1st	2nd	3rd	Win & Pl
Career Total (Turf)	6	0	3	1	4816
Career Total (AW)	3	0	1	0	998

Going (Turf): **Sf: 0-0 GS: 0-3 Gd: 0-1 GF: 0-2 Fm: 0-0**
Distance: 5f/6f: 0-0 7f-8f: 0-3 9f-13f: 0-6 14f+: 0-0
Track : LH: 0-4 RH: 0-3 Tight: 0-3 Gall: 0-0
Aids: Bl: 0-0 Vi: 0-0 Tstrap: 0-1 Ckp: 0-1
Best Rating: 83 8/08 Sand 1m14y gd-sft

Fair; first foal of a dam that won over 6f; stays 1m; acts on easy ground.

Artsu

105(100) (67)**83**
4-y-o b g Bahamian Bounty-War Shanty (Warrshan (USA))
M Dods F Burnside & N Riddell

Placings:410246/**5**040515044233-04224036**0** (6434)
2009: 5^{0}GF, 6^{4}GS, 5^{2}G, 5^{2}GF, 5^{4}G, 5^{0}S, 5^{3}GS, 5^{6}GF, **5**^{0}SD,

	Starts	1st	2nd	3rd	Win & Pl
Career Total (Turf)	25	2	4	3	27030
Career Total (AW)	3	0	0	0	153

82 7/08 Hayd 6f (0-85)H HVY £5504
71 6/07 Yarm 6f3y G-S £2914
Total win prize-money £8420

Going (Turf): **Sf: 1-9 GS: 1-5** Gd: 0-4 GF: 0-7 Fm: 0-0
Distance: 5f/6f: 1-21 7f-8f: 1-5 9f-13f: 0-2 14f+: 0-0
Track : LH: 0-4 RH: 0-3 Tight: 0-4 Gall: 0-1
Aids: Bl: 0-0 Vi: 0-0 Tstrap: 0-1 Ckp: 0-1
Best Rating: 83 6/09 Ayr 5f gd-fm

Fair; stays 6f; acts on soft ground but handles fast.

Arty Crafty (USA)

95(105) (82)**68**
3-y-o b f Arch (USA)-Princess Kris (Kris)
Sir Mark Prescott Mrs Sonia Rogers

Placings:000-111210 (7131)
2009: 10^{1}SD, 11^{1}G, **10**^{1}SD, **12**^{2}SD, **12**^{1}SS, **13**^{0}SD,

	Starts	1st	2nd	3rd	Win & Pl
Career Total (Turf)	1	1	0	0	2267
Career Total (AW)	8	3	1	0	7114

82 10/09 Ling 1m4f (0-60)H SS £1706
66 9/09 Kemp 1m2f (0-70)H STD £2590
68 9/09 Haml 1m3f16y (0-65)H GD £2266
54 9/09 Kemp 1m2f (0-55) STD £2047
Total win prize-money £8610

Going (Turf): Sf: 0-0 GS: 0-0 **Gd: 1-1** GF: 0-0 Fm: 0-0
Distance: 5f/6f: 0-0 7f-8f: 0-3 **9f-13f: 4-6** 14f+: 0-0
Track : LH: 1-4 **RH: 3-5 Tight: 2-5** Gall: 0-0
Aids: Bl: 0-0 Vi: 0-0 Tstrap: 0-0 Ckp: 0-0
Best Rating: 82 10/09 Ling 1m4f std-slw

Modest filly; stays 1m2f, may get further; acts on Polytrack.

Arwaah (IRE)

105 **106**
3-y-o b f Dalakhani (IRE)-Sahool (Unfuwain (USA))
M P Tregoning Hamdan Al Maktoum

Placings:5150 (7291)
2009: 8^{5}GF, 10^{1}GF, 12^{5}G, 10^{0}S,

	Starts	1st	2nd	3rd	Win & Pl
Career Total (Turf)	4	1	0	0	6208

98 8/09 Newb 1m2f6y G-F £3238
Total win prize-money £3238

Going (Turf): Sf: 0-1 GS: 0-0 Gd: 0-1 **GF: 1-2** Fm: 0-0
Distance: 5f/6f: 0-0 7f-8f: 0-1 **9f-13f: 1-3** 14f+: 0-0
Track : **LH: 1-2** RH: 0-2 Tight: 0-0 **Gall: 1-4**
Aids: Bl: 0-0 Vi: 0-0 Tstrap: 0-0 Ckp: 0-0
Best Rating: 106 10/09 NmkR 1m4f good

Very useful; stays 1m2f; acts on fast ground.

Aryacoddinme (IRE)

62
2-y-o b c Pyrus (USA)-Rainbow Pet (IRE) (Spectrum (IRE))
G A Harker John J Maguire

Placings:00 (2541)
2009: 5^{0}GF, 6^{0}F,

	Starts	1st	2nd	3rd	Win & Pl
Career Total (Turf)	2	0	0	0	

Going (Turf): **Sf: 0-0 GS: 0-0 Gd: 0-0 GF: 0-1 Fm: 0-1**
Distance: 5f/6f: 0-2 7f-8f: 0-0 9f-13f: 0-0 14f+: 0-0
Track : LH: 0-0 RH: 0-0 Tight: 0-0 Gall: 0-0
Aids: Bl: 0-0 Vi: 0-0 Tstrap: 0-0 Ckp: 0-0
Best Rating:

As Brave As You (IRE)

78(92) (51)**39**
2-y-o b g Hawk Wing (USA)-Scanno's Choice (IRE) (Pennine Walk)
B Ellison LGB, Dorothy & William Gibson

Placings:0000**436** (7597)
2009: 5^{0}G, 6^{0}GF, 7^{0}GF, 6^{0}S, **9**^{4}SD, **8**^{3}SD, **8**^{6}SD,

	Starts	1st	2nd	3rd	Win & Pl
Career Total (Turf)	4	0	0	0	
Career Total (AW)	3	0	0	1	403

Going (Turf): **Sf: 0-1 GS: 0-0 Gd: 0-1 GF: 0-2 Fm: 0-0**
Distance: 5f/6f: 0-3 7f-8f: 0-2 9f-13f: 0-2 14f+: 0-0
Track : LH: 0-3 RH: 0-0 Tight: 0-2 Gall: 0-0
Aids: Bl: 0-0 Vi: 0-0 Tstrap: 0-0 Ckp: 0-0
Best Rating: 51 10/09 Wolv 1m1f103y stand

Moderate; stays 1m; acts on Fibresand.

As You Like It (IRE)

88 (53)**55**
2-y-o b f Footstepsinthesand-Callanish (Inchinor)
John Joseph Murphy Mrs John J Murphy

Placings:00564556 (7295a)
2009: 6^{0}G, 6^{0}S, 5^{5}SD, 5^{6}GY, 6^{4}GY, 6^{5}GF, 5^{5}G, 5^{6}SD,

	Starts	1st	2nd	3rd	Win & Pl
Career Total (Turf)	6	0	0	0	418
Career Total (AW)	2	0	0	0	

Going (Turf): **Sf: 0-1 GS: 0-0 Gd: 0-2 GF: 0-1 Fm: 0-0**
Distance: 5f/6f: 0-7 7f-8f: 0-1 9f-13f: 0-0 14f+: 0-0
Track : LH: 0-2 RH: 0-2 Tight: 0-0 Gall: 0-0
Aids: Bl: 0-0 Vi: 0-0 Tstrap: 0-0 Ckp: 0-0
Best Rating: 55 10/09 Rdcr 6f gd-fm

Asaab (IRE)

83 **54**
2-y-o b f Refuse To Bend (IRE)-Shalev (GER) (Java Gold (USA))
C E Brittain Saeed Manana

Placings:60 (4047)
2009: 6^{6}GF, 6^{0}S,

	Starts	1st	2nd	3rd	Win & Pl
Career Total (Turf)	2	0	0	0	0

Going (Turf): **Sf: 0-1 GS: 0-0 Gd: 0-0 GF: 0-1 Fm: 0-0**
Distance: 5f/6f: 0-1 7f-8f: 0-1 9f-13f: 0-0 14f+: 0-0
Track : LH: 0-1 RH: 0-0 Tight: 0-0 Gall: 0-0
Aids: Bl: 0-0 Vi: 0-0 Tstrap: 0-0 Ckp: 0-0
Best Rating: 54 6/09 Pont 6f gd-fm

Asaba

47
2-y-o b f Desert Style (IRE)-Hoh Hedsor (Singspiel (IRE))
S Kirk The Flaming Sambucas

Placings:0 (3534)

2009: 6⁰GF,

	Starts	1st	2nd	3rd	Win & Pl
Career Total (Turf)	1	0	0	0	

Going (Turf): Sf: 0-0 GS: 0-0 Gd: 0-0 GF: 0-1 Fm: 0-0
Distance: 5f/6f: 0-0 7f-8f: 0-1 9f-13f: 0-0 14f+: 0-0
Track : LH: 0-0 RH: 0-0 Tight: 0-0 Gall: 0-0
Aids: Bl: 0-0 Vi: 0-0 Tstrap: 0-0 Ckp: 0-0

Asaint Needs Brass (USA)

(91) (81)83
3-y-o b/br g Lion Hearted (USA)-British Columbia (Selkirk (USA))
J R Best James D Cameron

Placings:101004-6000000 (7330)
2009: 5[6]SD, 6[0]SD, 6[0]SD, 5[0]SS, 7[0]SS, 5[0]SD, 6[0]SD,

	Starts	1st	2nd	3rd	Win & Pl
Career Total (Turf)	3	0	0	0	
Career Total (AW)	10	2	0	0	10003
81 6/08 Kemp 6f			STD	£4857	
64 3/08 Kemp 5f			STD	£4857	

Total win prize-money £9715

Going (Turf): Sf: 0-0 GS: 0-0 Gd: 0-2 GF: 0-1 Fm: 0-0
Distance: 5f/6f: 2-12 7f-8f: 0-1 9f-13f: 0-0 14f+: 0-0
Track : LH: 0-5 RH: 2-5 Tight: 0-4 Gall: 0-1
Aids: Bl: 0-0 Vi: 0-0 Tstrap: 0-0 Ckp: 0-0
Best Rating: 83 4/08 NmkR 5f good

Modest; effective at 5-6f; acts on Polytrack.

Asakusa

82(91) (48)43
3-y-o b f Royal Applause-Kiss And Don'Tell (USA) (Rahy (USA))
H R A Cecil J Shack

Placings:0-0000 (2744)
2009: 9[0]GF, 9[0]SD, 8[0]GF, 7[0]SD,

	Starts	1st	2nd	3rd	Win & Pl
Career Total (Turf)	3	0	0	0	
Career Total (AW)	2	0	0	0	

Going (Turf): Sf: 0-0 GS: 0-1 Gd: 0-0 GF: 0-2 Fm: 0-0
Distance: 5f/6f: 0-1 7f-8f: 0-1 9f-13f: 0-3 14f+: 0-0
Track : LH: 0-3 RH: 0-1 Tight: 0-2 Gall: 0-0
Aids: Bl: 0-1 Vi: 0-0 Tstrap: 0-0 Ckp: 0-0
Best Rating: 48 4/09 Wolv 1m1f103y stand

Asateer (IRE)

106 87
3-y-o b g Alhaarth (IRE)-Catatonic (Zafonic (USA))
B W Hills Hamdan Al Maktoum

Placings:44-0632 (5348)
2009: 10[0]GF, 10[6]GF, 8[3]G, 8[2]G,

	Starts	1st	2nd	3rd	Win & Pl
Career Total (Turf)	6	0	1	1	6471

Going (Turf): Sf: 0-0 GS: 0-0 Gd: 0-3 GF: 0-3 Fm: 0-0
Distance: 5f/6f: 0-0 7f-8f: 0-2 9f-13f: 0-4 14f+: 0-0
Track : LH: 0-3 RH: 0-1 Tight: 0-1 Gall: 0-0
Aids: Bl: 0-0 Vi: 0-0 Tstrap: 0-0 Ckp: 0-0
Best Rating: 87 4/09 NmkR 1m2f gd-fm

220,000gns yearling; fair form in maidens.

Ascendant

109(99) (85)96
3-y-o ch g Medicean-Ascendancy (Sadler's Wells (USA))
Sir Mark Prescott Cheveley Park Stud

Placings:533-1411 (6313)
2009: 11[1]GF, 16[4]SD, 14[1]GS, 14[1]GF,

	Starts	1st	2nd	3rd	Win & Pl
Career Total (Turf)	4	3	0	1	15796
Career Total (AW)	3	0	0	1	929
96 9/09 Muss 1m6f	(0-80)H			G-F	£6476
86 9/09 Hayd 1m6f	(0-85)H			G-S	£5504
89 8/09 Catt 1m3f214y				G-F	£3238

Total win prize-money £15219

Going (Turf): Sf: 0-1 GS: 1-1 Gd: 0-0 GF: 2-2 Fm: 0-0
Distance: 5f/6f: 0-1 7f-8f: 0-1 9f-13f: 1-2 14f+: 2-3
Track : LH: 2-4 RH: 1-3 Tight: 2-3 Gall: 0-0
Aids: Bl: 0-0 Vi: 0-0 Tstrap: 0-0 Ckp: 0-0
Best Rating: 96 9/09 Muss 1m6f gd-fm

Useful; stays 1m6f; acts on Polytrack; handles fast and easy ground on turf.

Ashalanda (FR)

108 115
3-y-o gr f Linamix (FR)-Ashaninka (USA) (Woodman (USA))
A De Royer-Dupre H H Aga Khan

Placings:11214 (7747a)
2009: 9[1]G, 12[1]S, 11[2]G, 12[1]G, 10[4]G,

	Starts	1st	2nd	3rd	Win & Pl
Career Total (Turf)	5	3	1	0	253522
115 10/09 NmkR 1m4f			GD	£56770	
104 6/09 StCl 1m4f			SFT	£71942	
6/09 Lngn 1m1f			GD	£2912	

Total win prize-money £131625

Going (Turf): Sf: 1-1 GS: 0-0 Gd: 2-4 GF: 0-0 Fm: 0-0
Distance: 5f/6f: 0-0 7f-8f: 0-0 9f-13f: 3-5 14f+: 0-0
Track : LH: 1-1 RH: 1-3 Tight: 0-0 Gall: 1-1
Aids: Bl: 0-0 Vi: 0-0 Tstrap: 0-0 Ckp: 0-0
Best Rating: 115 10/09 NmkR 1m4f good

Group-class; best at 1m4f; acts on good and soft ground.

Ashbrittle

95 64
2-y-o b g Rainbow Quest (USA)-Caesarea (GER) (Generous (IRE))
R M Beckett J L Rowsell

Placings:3 (7243)
2009: 8[3]S,

	Starts	1st	2nd	3rd	Win & Pl
Career Total (Turf)	1	0	0	1	626

Going (Turf): Sf: 0-1 GS: 0-0 Gd: 0-0 GF: 0-0 Fm: 0-0
Distance: 5f/6f: 0-0 7f-8f: 0-0 9f-13f: 0-1 14f+: 0-0
Track : LH: 0-1 RH: 0-0 Tight: 0-0 Gall: 0-0
Aids: Bl: 0-0 Vi: 0-0 Tstrap: 0-0 Ckp: 0-0
Best Rating: 64 11/09 Nott 1m75y soft

Third on debut; effective over 1m; acts on soft ground.

Ashes Summer (IRE)

95(87) (58)65
3-y-o b f Rock Of Gibraltar (IRE)-Time Ahead (Spectrum (IRE))
P R Webber Economic Security

Placings:45 (6166)
2009: 11[4]G, 12[5]SD,

	Starts	1st	2nd	3rd	Win & Pl
Career Total (Turf)	1	0	0	0	202
Career Total (AW)	1	0	0	0	0

Going (Turf): Sf: 0-0 GS: 0-0 Gd: 0-1 GF: 0-0 Fm: 0-0
Distance: 5f/6f: 0-0 7f-8f: 0-0 9f-13f: 0-2 14f+: 0-0
Track : LH: 0-1 RH: 0-1 Tight: 0-1 Gall: 0-0
Aids: Bl: 0-0 Vi: 0-0 Tstrap: 0-0 Ckp: 0-0
Best Rating: 65 9/09 Bath 1m3f144y good

Ashkalara

90 60
2-y-o b f Footstepsinthesand-Asheyana (IRE) (Soviet Star (USA))
H S Howe Roly Roper

Placings:0030 (6055)
2009: 6[0]G, 7[0]G, 6[3]GF, 7[0]GF,

	Starts	1st	2nd	3rd	Win & Pl
Career Total (Turf)	4	0	0	1	433

Going (Turf): Sf: 0-0 GS: 0-0 Gd: 0-2 GF: 0-2 Fm: 0-0
Distance: 5f/6f: 0-1 7f-8f: 0-3 9f-13f: 0-0 14f+: 0-0
Track : LH: 0-0 RH: 0-0 Tight: 0-0 Gall: 0-0
Aids: Bl: 0-0 Vi: 0-0 Tstrap: 0-0 Ckp: 0-0
Best Rating: 60 8/09 Sals 6f212y gd-fm

Out of an unraced sister to Ashkalani; modest form to date.

Ashmolian (IRE)

(97) (56)55
6-y-o b g Grand Lodge (USA)-Animatrice (USA) (Alleged (USA))
Miss Z C Davison Rags to Riches

Placings:00/044000/0043620600-530 (0546)
2009: 14[5]SD, 11[3]SD, 12[0]SD,

	Starts	1st	2nd	3rd	Win & Pl
Career Total (Turf)	12	0	1	0	1146
Career Total (AW)	9	0	0	2	542

Going (Turf): Sf: 0-4 GS: 0-3 Gd: 0-1 GF: 0-4 Fm: 0-0
Distance: 5f/6f: 0-0 7f-8f: 0-2 9f-13f: 0-12 14f+: 0-7
Track : LH: 0-11 RH: 0-8 Tight: 0-5 Gall: 0-2
Aids: Bl: 0-2 Vi: 0-0 Tstrap: 0-1 Ckp: 0-1
Best Rating: 56 3/08 Wolv 1m5f194y stand

Moderate; stays 1m7f; acts on easy ground and sand; has worn cheekpieces and blinkers.

Ashram (IRE)

112(105) (108)113
3-y-o ch g Indian Haven-Tara's Girl (IRE) (Fayruz)
Saeed Bin Suroor Godolphin

Placings:1216-02320115 (6848)
2009: 8[0]GF, 8[2]G, 7[3]GF, 7[2]S, 8[0]S, 8[1]SD, 7[1]GF, 7[5]G,

	Starts	1st	2nd	3rd	Win & Pl
Career Total (Turf)	10	3	2	1	87533
Career Total (AW)	2	1	1	0	10651
113 9/09 Newb 7f			G-F	£22708	
108 8/09 Kemp 1m			STD	£8598	
113 10/08 NmkR 7f			G-F	£34062	
87 8/08 NmkJ 7f			GD	£4533	

Total win prize-money £69902

Going (Turf): Sf: 0-2 GS: 0-0 Gd: 1-4 **GF: 2-4** Fm: 0-0
Distance: 5f/6f: 0-0 **7f-8f: 4-11** 9f-13f: 0-1 14f+: 0-0
Track : LH: 0-0 **RH: 1-4** Tight: 0-0 Gall: 0-0
Aids: Bl: 0-0 **Vi: 2-6** Tstrap: 0-0 Ckp: 0-0
Best Rating: 113 9/09 Newb 7f gd-fm

Smart; winner in Group 3 company at two; effective over 7f-1m; acts on most ground; goes on Polytrack; has worn a visor.

Asian Power (IRE)

(106) (77)**76**
4-y-o ch g Bertolini (USA)-Cynara (Imp Society (USA))
P J O'Gorman N S Yong

Placings:000500**140/41035232300430463-05** **(0243)**
2009: 6^{0}SD, 5^{5}SD,

	Starts	1st	2nd	3rd	Win & Pl
Career Total (Turf)	**8**	**0**	**1**	**0**	**2155**
Career Total (AW)	**20**	**2**	**1**	**5**	**8797**

75 2/08 Kemp 6f (0-75)H STD £2457
70 9/07 Kemp 6f (0-70) STD £2047
Total win prize-money £4505

Going (Turf): Sf: 0-1 GS: 0-0 Gd: 0-3 GF: 0-3 Fm: 0-1
Distance: 5f/6f: 2-23 7f-8f: 0-5 9f-13f: 0-0 14f+: 0-0
Track : LH: 0-11 **RH: 2-10** Tight: 0-5 Gall: 0-6
Aids: Bl: 0-0 Vi: 0-0 Tstrap: 0-0 Ckp: 0-0
Best Rating: 77 11/08 Kemp 6f stand

Modest; effective over 6f; acts on fast ground and on Polytrack.

Asian Tale (IRE)

94(93) (70)**73**
3-y-o br f Namid-Literary (Woodman (USA))
P D Evans Mrs S Clifford

Placings:3013630-**4050** **(2300)**
2009: 7^{4}SD, 7^{0}SD, 7^{5}GF, 7^{0}GF,

	Starts	1st	2nd	3rd	Win & Pl
Career Total (Turf)	**9**	**1**	**0**	**3**	**3391**
Career Total (AW)	**2**	**0**	**0**	**0**	**351**

72 5/08 Leic 5f218y G-F £2331
Total win prize-money £2331

Going (Turf): Sf: 0-0 GS: 0-4 Gd: 0-0 **GF: 1-5** Fm: 0-0
Distance: 5f/6f: 1-5 7f-8f: 0-5 9f-13f: 0-1 14f+: 0-0
Track : LH: 0-5 RH: 0-1 Tight: 0-0 Gall: 0-1
Aids: Bl: 0-0 Vi: 0-0 Tstrap: 0-0 Ckp: 0-0
Best Rating: 73 10/08 Bath 5f11y gd-sft

Fair; effective over 6f; acts on fast ground but looks better on an easy surface.

Ask

116 **124**
6-y-o b h Sadler's Wells (USA)-Request (Rainbow Quest (USA))
Sir Michael Stoute Patrick J Fahey

Placings:321024/112/15560-1131 **(7047a)**
2009: 14^{1}GS, 12^{1}G, 12^{3}G, 15^{1}S,

	Starts	1st	2nd	3rd	Win & Pl
Career Total (Turf)	**18**	**7**	**3**	**2**	**805359**

123 10/09 Lonc 1m7f110y SFT £138689
121 6/09 Epsm 1m4f10y GD £137809
121 5/09 York 1m6f G-S £79478
117 4/08 Sand 1m2f7y G-S £26681
122 9/07 Asct 1m4f G-S £28390
119 5/07 Ches 1m5f89y GD £42585
91 6/06 Chep 1m4f23y G-S £3238
Total win prize-money £456872

Going (Turf): Sf: 1-3 **GS: 4-5** Gd: 2-4 GF: 0-5 Fm: 0-1
Distance: 5f/6f: 0-0 7f-8f: 0-1 **9f-13f: 4-12** 14f+: 3-5
Track : LH: 4-8 RH: 3-9 Tight: 2-4 Gall: 2-8
Aids: Bl: 0-0 Vi: 0-0 Tstrap: 0-0 Ckp: 0-0
Best Rating: 124 7/09 Asct 1m4f good

Group class; winner of the Group 1 Coronation Cup and Prix Royal-Oak plus the Group 2 Yorkshire Cup in 2009; effective over 1m2f-1m7f; handles fast but acts well on good and soft ground; has worn a tongue-tie.

Ask Dan (IRE)

105(84) (59)**66**
3-y-o b g Refuse To Bend (IRE)-Bush Cat (USA) (Kingmambo (USA))
M Dods (B Smart 4/7) Andrew Tinkler

Placings:04**00**-400551605104240 **(6985)**
2009: 7^{4}GF, 8^{0}F, 7^{0}GF, 7^{5}GF, 7^{5}GF, 7^{1}G, 8^{6}GF, 8^{0}G, 9^{5}G, 8^{1}GS, 8^{0}GS, 8^{4}HY, 7^{2}S, 7^{4}GF, 7^{0}G,

	Starts	1st	2nd	3rd	Win & Pl
Career Total (Turf)	**17**	**2**	**1**	**0**	**5836**
Career Total (AW)	**2**	**0**	**0**	**0**	

61 8/09 Haml 1m65y G-S £2388
63 7/09 Carl 7f200y GD £2047
Total win prize-money £4435

Going (Turf): Sf: 0-2 **GS: 1-2 Gd: 1-6** GF: 0-6 Fm: 0-1
Distance: 5f/6f: 0-0 7f-8f: 1-14 9f-13f: 1-5 14f+: 0-0
Track : LH: 0-6 **RH: 2-9 Tight: 1-9** Gall: 0-0
Aids: Bl: 0-1 Vi: 0-0 Tstrap: 2-12 Ckp: 2-12
Best Rating: 66 9/09 Catt 7f soft

Moderate; effective over 7f-1m; acts on good ground; has worn cheekpieces.

Ask Frank (IRE)

94 **97**
2-y-o b g Hawk Wing (USA)-Riva Royale (Royal Applause)
G A Swinbank Frank Hanson

Placings:31 **(3613)**
2009: 6^{3}GF, 5^{1}G,

	Starts	1st	2nd	3rd	Win & Pl
Career Total (Turf)	**2**	**1**	**0**	**1**	**3168**

97 7/09 Carl 5f193y GD £2590
Total win prize-money £2590

Going (Turf): Sf: 0-0 GS: 0-0 **Gd: 1-1** GF: 0-1 Fm: 0-0
Distance: 5f/6f: 1-2 7f-8f: 0-0 9f-13f: 0-0 14f+: 0-0
Track : LH: 0-0 **RH: 1-1** Tight: 0-0 Gall: 0-0
Aids: Bl: 0-0 Vi: 0-0 Tstrap: 0-0 Ckp: 0-0
Best Rating: 97 7/09 Carl 5f193y good

Useful; effective over 5f-6f; acts on good and fast ground.

Ask Jenny (IRE)

98(102) (65)**64**
7-y-o b m Marju (IRE)-Waltzing Matilda (Mujtahid (USA))
Patrick Morris W J Crosbie

Placings:0054/000630/0000**0/0/112**0016300**55-4030**4032454040**4621155** **(7815)**
2009: 5^{4}SD, 5^{0}SD, 6^{3}SD, 5^{0}SD, 5^{4}F, 5^{0}GF, 5^{3}F, 5^{2}GS, 5^{4}GF, 6^{5}G, 5^{4}GF, 5^{0}G, 5^{4}GF, 5^{0}F, 5^{4}SD, 5^{6}SD, 5^{2}SD, 6^{1}SD, 6^{1}SD, 5^{5}SD, 5^{5}SD,

	Starts	1st	2nd	3rd	Win & Pl
Career Total (Turf)	**31**	**1**	**1**	**3**	**7479**
Career Total (AW)	**18**	**4**	**2**	**1**	**8783**

65 12/09 Ling 6f (0-60)H STD £1637
62 11/09 Ling 6f (0-60)H STD £1637
59 5/08 Tipp 5f (45-60)H FRM £4318
59 2/08 Kemp 5f STD £2047
52 1/08 Kemp 5f (0-45) STD £1295
Total win prize-money £10938

Going (Turf): Sf: 0-4 GS: 0-1 Gd: 0-6 GF: 0-8 **Fm: 1-7**
Distance: 5f/6f: 5-44 7f-8f: 0-5 9f-13f: 0-0 14f+: 0-0
Track : LH: 3-25 RH: 2-15 **Tight: 2-7** Gall: 0-2
Aids: Bl: 0-0 Vi: 0-0 Tstrap: 0-1 Ckp: 0-1
Best Rating: 65 12/09 Ling 6f stand

Modest; effective over 5f-6f; acts on Polytrack.

Ask The Oracle

(101) (68)
3-y-o ch g Where Or When (IRE)-Delphic Way (Warning)
H Morrison Miss B Swire

Placings:25340 **(7665)**
2009: 7^{2}SD, 8^{5}SD, 8^{3}SD, 10^{4}SD, 12^{0}SD,

	Starts	1st	2nd	3rd	Win & Pl
Career Total (Turf)	**0**	**0**	**0**	**0**	
Career Total (AW)	**5**	**0**	**1**	**1**	**1367**

Going (Turf): Sf: 0-0 GS: 0-0 Gd: 0-0 GF: 0-0 Fm: 0-0
Distance: 5f/6f: 0-0 7f-8f: 0-3 9f-13f: 0-2 14f+: 0-0
Track : LH: 0-3 RH: 0-2 Tight: 0-2 Gall: 0-0
Aids: Bl: 0-0 Vi: 0-0 Tstrap: 0-0 Ckp: 0-0
Best Rating: 68 11/09 Kemp 1m2f stand

Half-brother to multiple 1m-1m2f winner Parnassian; promise in maidens; stays 1m2f; acts on Polytrack.

Askar Tau (FR)

113(106) (106)**115**
4-y-o b g Montjeu (IRE)-Autriche (IRE) (Acatenango (GER))
M P Tregoning Nurlan Bizakov

Placings:00/0**2111114-01156** **(7047a)**
2009: 16^{0}G, 16^{1}GF, 18^{1}GF, 20^{5}G, 15^{6}S,

	Starts	1st	2nd	3rd	Win & Pl
Career Total (Turf)	**13**	**6**	**0**	**0**	**172810**
Career Total (AW)	**2**	**1**	**1**	**0**	**11987**

115 9/09 Donc 2m2f G-F £56770
110 8/09 York 2m88y G-F £79478
106 9/08 GrLe 2m (0-100)H STD £11215
97 8/08 NmkJ 1m6f175y (0-95)H GD £9066
84 8/08 Yarm 1m6f17y (0-75)H GD £2719
81 7/08 Sand 1m6f (0-80)H G-F £7123
72 7/08 Hayd 1m6f (0-70)H GD £3238
Total win prize-money £169612

Going (Turf): Sf: 0-3 GS: 0-0 **Gd: 3-6 GF: 3-4** Fm: 0-0
Distance: 5f/6f: 0-0 7f-8f: 0-2 9f-13f: 0-1 **14f+: 7-12**
Track : LH: 5-6 RH: 2-6 Tight: 1-2 **Gall: 4-6**
Aids: Bl: 0-0 **Vi: 2-4** Tstrap: 0-0 Ckp: 0-0
Best Rating: 115 9/09 Donc 2m2f gd-fm

Group-class; winner of the 2009 Lonsdale and Doncaster Cups; stays 2m2f; acts on good and faster ground and on Polytrack; has worn a visor.

Asmodea

(90) (58)**46**
4-y-o b f Dr Fong (USA)-Latina (IRE) (King's Theatre (IRE))
B G Powell Mrs D Topley

Placings:6/0000000-60 **(0385)**

2009: 8[6]SD, 12[0]SD,

	Starts	1st	2nd	3rd	Win & Pl
Career Total (Turf)	3	0	0	0	
Career Total (AW)	7	0	0	0	0

Going (Turf): Sf: 0-0 GS: 0-0 Gd: 0-2 GF: 0-1 Fm: 0-0
Distance: 5f/6f: 0-0 7f-8f: 0-5 9f-13f: 0-5 14f+: 0-0
Track : LH: 0-4 RH: 0-5 Tight: 0-3 Gall: 0-1
Aids: Bl: 0-0 Vi: 0-0 Tstrap: 0-0 Ckp: 0-0
Best Rating: 58 2/08 Kemp 1m stand

Aspectoflove (IRE)

111 (85)**108**
3-y-o b f Danetime (IRE)-Rose Vibert (Caerleon (USA))
John M Oxx Byerley Thoroughbred Racing

Placings:2011-4031401 **(6884a)**
2009: 6[4]GF, 7[0]Y, 7[3]G, 8[1]G, 9[4]GY, 8[0]G, 8[1]GY,

	Starts	1st	2nd	3rd	Win & Pl
Career Total (Turf)	9	2	1	1	54650
Career Total (AW)	2	2	0	0	16164

108 10/09 Naas 1m G-Y £39502
97 8/09 Leop 1m (60-90)H GD £9056
85 11/08 Dund 6f STD £9812
81 9/08 Dund 6f STD £6351
Total win prize-money £64723

Going (Turf): Sf: 0-1 GS: 0-0 **Gd: 1-3** GF: 0-1 Fm: 0-0
Distance: 5f/6f: 2-5 7f-8f: 2-5 9f-13f: 0-1 14f+: 0-0
Track : **LH: 4-5** RH: 0-3 Tight: 0-0 Gall: 0-1
Aids: Bl: 0-0 Vi: 0-0 Tstrap: 0-0 Ckp: 0-0
Best Rating: 108 10/09 Naas 1m gd-yld

Listed class; effective at around a mile but has won at 6f; acts on good ground and Polytrack.

Aspen Darlin (IRE)

109
3-y-o b f Indian Haven-Manuka Magic (IRE) (Key Of Luck (USA))
A Bailey Indian Haven Syndicate

Placings:1233051122-P **(1698)**
2009: 8[P]GF,

	Starts	1st	2nd	3rd	Win & Pl
Career Total (Turf)	11	3	3	2	139880

109 9/08 Ayr 6f HVY £45416
94 8/08 Ches 6f18y G-F £12616
76 4/08 Wwck 5f SFT £3626
Total win prize-money £61659

Going (Turf): **Sf: 2-2** GS: 0-1 Gd: 0-2 GF: 1-5 Fm: 0-1
Distance: **5f/6f: 2-8** 7f-8f: 1-3 9f-13f: 0-0 14f+: 0-0
Track : **LH: 2-3** RH: 0-0 **Tight: 1-2** Gall: 0-0
Aids: Bl: 0-0 Vi: 0-0 Tstrap: 2-5 Ckp: 2-5
Best Rating: 109 10/08 NmkR 6f gd-fm

Group class; Group 3 winner and placed at Group 1 level; effective over 5f-6f; acts on any ground; has worn cheekpieces.

Aspendale (IRE)

64 **27**
4-y-o b g Docksider (USA)-Ambria (ITY) (Final Straw)
D Carroll Yummy Mummy's Racing Club

Placings:006-0 **(2404)**
2009: 8[0]GF,

	Starts	1st	2nd	3rd	Win & Pl
Career Total (Turf)	4	0	0	0	0

Going (Turf): Sf: 0-0 GS: 0-1 Gd: 0-0 GF: 0-3 Fm: 0-0
Distance: 5f/6f: 0-1 7f-8f: 0-2 9f-13f: 0-1 14f+: 0-0
Track : LH: 0-2 RH: 0-1 Tight: 0-1 Gall: 0-1
Aids: Bl: 0-1 Vi: 0-0 Tstrap: 0-0 Ckp: 0-0
Best Rating: 27 7/08 Bevl 5f gd-sft

Aspirational (IRE)

82(101) (58)**49**
3-y-o ch g Rainbow Quest (USA)-Londonnetdotcom (IRE) (Night Shift (USA))
B Palling Derek And Jean Clee

Placings:0-06034 **(7733)**
2009: 10[0]GF, 12[6]G, 11[0]S, 9[3]SD, 12[4]SD,

	Starts	1st	2nd	3rd	Win & Pl
Career Total (Turf)	4	0	0	0	0
Career Total (AW)	2	0	0	1	252

Going (Turf): Sf: 0-2 GS: 0-0 Gd: 0-1 GF: 0-1 Fm: 0-0
Distance: 5f/6f: 0-0 7f-8f: 0-0 9f-13f: 0-6 14f+: 0-0
Track : LH: 0-6 RH: 0-0 Tight: 0-3 Gall: 0-0
Aids: Bl: 0-0 Vi: 0-0 Tstrap: 0-0 Ckp: 0-0
Best Rating: 58 11/09 Wolv 1m1f103y stand

Moderate; stays 1m2f.

Aspro Mavro (IRE)

100(97) (77)**77**
3-y-o b c Spartacus (IRE)-Alexia Reveuse (IRE) (Dr Devious (IRE))
J H M Gosden M Kerr-Dineen,Mrs C Waters & Ptnrs

Placings:0-2026 **(7287)**
2009: 8[2]SD, 8[0]SD, 8[2]G, 7[6]S,

	Starts	1st	2nd	3rd	Win & Pl
Career Total (Turf)	3	0	1	0	964
Career Total (AW)	2	0	1	0	605

Going (Turf): Sf: 0-1 GS: 0-0 Gd: 0-1 GF: 0-1 Fm: 0-0
Distance: 5f/6f: 0-0 7f-8f: 0-3 9f-13f: 0-2 14f+: 0-0
Track : LH: 0-2 RH: 0-1 Tight: 0-1 Gall: 0-0
Aids: Bl: 0-0 Vi: 0-0 Tstrap: 0-0 Ckp: 0-0
Best Rating: 77 10/09 Nott 1m75y good

Fair; effective over 1m; acts on good ground.

Asraab (IRE)

104 **82**
2-y-o b c Oasis Dream-Alexander Queen (IRE) (King's Best (USA))
Saeed Bin Suroor Godolphin

Placings:1 **(7145)**
2009: 6[1]G,

	Starts	1st	2nd	3rd	Win & Pl
Career Total (Turf)	1	1	0	0	5181

82 10/09 NmkR 6f GD £5180
Total win prize-money £5181

Going (Turf): Sf: 0-0 GS: 0-0 **Gd: 1-1** GF: 0-0 Fm: 0-0
Distance: **5f/6f: 1-1** 7f-8f: 0-0 9f-13f: 0-0 14f+: 0-0
Track : LH: 0-0 RH: 0-0 Tight: 0-0 Gall: 0-0
Aids: Bl: 0-0 Vi: 0-0 Tstrap: 0-0 Ckp: 0-0
Best Rating: 82 10/09 NmkR 6f good

Sprint-bred, out of a half-sister to Dandy Man; made winning debut over 6f on good ground.

Asrar

66 **38**
7-y-o b m King's Theatre (IRE)-Zandaka (FR) (Doyoun)
Miss Lucinda V Russell Bissett Racing

Placings:00/06035630-0 **(7170)**
2009: 15[0]S,

	Starts	1st	2nd	3rd	Win & Pl
Career Total (Turf)	11	0	0	2	1059

Going (Turf): Sf: 0-4 GS: 0-1 Gd: 0-2 GF: 0-4 Fm: 0-0
Distance: 5f/6f: 0-0 7f-8f: 0-0 9f-13f: 0-3 14f+: 0-8
Track : LH: 0-2 RH: 0-9 Tight: 0-9 Gall: 0-0
Aids: Bl: 0-0 Vi: 0-0 Tstrap: 0-1 Ckp: 0-1
Best Rating: 43 5/07 Haml 1m3f16y gd-fm

Moderate; effective at around 2m; acts on fast ground.

Assabiyya (IRE)

101 **86**
3-y-o b f Cape Cross (IRE)-Coretta (IRE) (Caerleon (USA))
Saeed Bin Suroor Godolphin

Placings:126 **(6286)**
2009: 10[1]GF, 9[2]GF, 10[6]GF,

	Starts	1st	2nd	3rd	Win & Pl
Career Total (Turf)	3	1	1	0	5620

81 8/09 Wind 1m2f7y G-F £2729
Total win prize-money £2730

Going (Turf): Sf: 0-0 GS: 0-0 Gd: 0-0 **GF: 1-3** Fm: 0-0
Distance: 5f/6f: 0-0 7f-8f: 0-0 **9f-13f: 1-3** 14f+: 0-0
Track : LH: 0-1 **RH: 1-2 Tight: 1-2** Gall: 0-0
Aids: Bl: 0-0 Vi: 0-0 Tstrap: 0-0 Ckp: 0-0
Best Rating: 86 8/09 Folk 1m1f149y gd-fm

Useful; effective over 1m2f; acts on fast ground.

Assail

69(103) (83)**6**
3-y-o b g Bertolini (USA)-Roofer (IRE) (Barathea (IRE))
H Morrison M J Watson

Placings:2-30134 **(5570)**
2009: 8[3]SD, 10[0]GF, 8[1]SD, 8[3]SD, 10[4]SD,

	Starts	1st	2nd	3rd	Win & Pl
Career Total (Turf)	1	0	0	0	
Career Total (AW)	5	1	1	2	4493

83 7/09 Kemp 1m (0-70)H STD £2590
Total win prize-money £2590

Going (Turf): Sf: 0-0 GS: 0-0 Gd: 0-0 GF: 0-1 Fm: 0-0
Distance: 5f/6f: 0-0 **7f-8f: 1-4** 9f-13f: 0-2 14f+: 0-0
Track : LH: 0-2 **RH: 1-4** Tight: 0-1 Gall: 0-0
Aids: Bl: 0-0 Vi: 0-0 Tstrap: 0-0 Ckp: 0-0
Best Rating: 83 7/09 Kemp 1m stand

Fair; effective from 1m-1m2f; acts on Fibresand and Polytrack.

Assent (IRE)

95(95) (68)**67**
3-y-o b f Kheleyf (USA)-Villafranca (IRE) (In The Wings)
B R Millman Lucky Generals Racing

Placings:04540-2644 (2321)

2009: 5^{2}SD, 7^{6}SD, 6^{4}GF, 6^{4}G,

	Starts	1st	2nd	3rd	Win & Pl
Career Total (Turf)	7	0	0	0	673
Career Total (AW)	2	0	1	0	605

Going (Turf): Sf: 0-2 GS: 0-1 Gd: 0-1 GF: 0-3 Fm: 0-0
Distance: 5f/6f: 0-6 7f-8f: 0-3 9f-13f: 0-0 14f+: 0-0
Track : LH: 0-2 RH: 0-0 Tight: 0-2 Gall: 0-2
Aids: Bl: 0-0 Vi: 0-0 Tstrap: 0-0 Ckp: 0-0
Best Rating: 68 3/09 Wolv 5f216y stand

Modest sprinter; tends to start slowly.

Asserting

104 61

3-y-o b f Reset (AUS)-Appelone (Emperor Jones (USA))
J A McShane Lothian Recycling Limited

Placings:0240-2015 (2964)

2009: 6^{2}GS, 7^{0}GF, 6^{1}F, 5^{5}GF,

	Starts	1st	2nd	3rd	Win & Pl
Career Total (Turf)	8	1	2	0	4492

59 6/09 Ayr 6f (0-60)H FRM £2266
Total win prize-money £2267

Going (Turf): Sf: 0-3 GS: 0-1 Gd: 0-1 GF: 0-2 **Fm: 1-1**
Distance: **5f/6f: 1-4** 7f-8f: 0-4 9f-13f: 0-0 14f+: 0-0
Track : LH: 0-0 RH: 0-2 Tight: 0-1 Gall: 0-0
Aids: Bl: 0-0 Vi: 0-0 Tstrap: 0-0 Ckp: 0-0
Best Rating: 61 5/09 Haml 6f5y gd-sft

Modest; effective over 6f; acts on soft and fast ground.

Asset (IRE)

114(106) (105)119

6-y-o b g Marju (IRE)-Snow Peak (Arazi (USA))
Saeed Bin Suroor Godolphin

Placings:413/102/1362625/22-41014202666 (6848)

2009: 6^{4}G, 6^{1}GF, 6^{0}G, 7^{1}GF, 7^{4}G, 6^{2}GF, 6^{0}GS, 7^{2}GF, 6^{6}GS, 6^{6}GF, 7^{6}G,

	Starts	1st	2nd	3rd	Win & Pl
Career Total (Turf)	24	4	6	2	255605
Career Total (AW)	2	1	1	0	23362

111 4/09 Leic 7f9y G-F £22708
108 2/09 Ndas 6f (95-110)H G-F £50000
121 4/07 NmkR 6f G-F £15898
106 4/06 Kemp 1m STD £15898
83 6/05 Yarm 6f3y G-F £4065
Total win prize-money £108570

Going (Turf): Sf: 0-2 GS: 0-5 Gd: 0-5 **GF: 4-12** Fm: 0-0
Distance: 5f/6f: 2-12 **7f-8f: 3-14** 9f-13f: 0-0 14f+: 0-0
Track : LH: 1-5 RH: 1-5 Tight: 0-0 **Gall: 1-4**
Aids: **Bl: 2-13** Vi: 0-2 Tstrap: 0-0 Ckp: 0-0
Best Rating: 121 4/07 NmkR 6f gd-fm

Group class; Listed winner and placed in Group company; effective over 6f-1m; acts on most ground on turf; goes on Polytrack; has worn blinkers and a visor.

Astarta (IRE)

91(90) (67)67

2-y-o b f Green Desert (USA)-Broken Romance (IRE) (Ela-Mana-Mou)
P F I Cole Litex Commerce JSC

Placings:653 (3733)

2009: 5^{6}G, 6^{5}GF, 6^{3}SD,

	Starts	1st	2nd	3rd	Win & Pl
Career Total (Turf)	2	0	0	0	123
Career Total (AW)	1	0	0	1	578

Going (Turf): Sf: 0-0 GS: 0-0 Gd: 0-1 GF: 0-1 Fm: 0-0
Distance: 5f/6f: 0-3 7f-8f: 0-0 9f-13f: 0-0 14f+: 0-0
Track : LH: 0-0 RH: 0-1 Tight: 0-0 Gall: 0-0
Aids: Bl: 0-0 Vi: 0-0 Tstrap: 0-0 Ckp: 0-0
Best Rating: 67 7/09 Kemp 6f stand

Asterrlini (IRE)

86 51

2-y-o b f Refuse To Bend (IRE)-Alithini (IRE) (Darshaan)
C E Brittain Saeed Manana

Placings:0 (6066)

2009: 8^{0}GF,

	Starts	1st	2nd	3rd	Win & Pl
Career Total (Turf)	1	0	0	0	

Going (Turf): Sf: 0-0 GS: 0-0 Gd: 0-0 GF: 0-1 Fm: 0-0
Distance: 5f/6f: 0-0 7f-8f: 0-1 9f-13f: 0-0 14f+: 0-0
Track : LH: 0-0 RH: 0-0 Tight: 0-0 Gall: 0-0
Aids: Bl: 0-0 Vi: 0-0 Tstrap: 0-0 Ckp: 0-0
Best Rating: 51 9/09 NmkR 1m gd-fm

Aston Boy

(95) (48)50

4-y-o ch g Dr Fong (USA)-Hectic Tina (Hector Protector (USA))
M Blanshard Mrs Rosemary K Wilkerson

Placings:0/000605-05 (1156)

2009: 11^{0}SD, 12^{5}SD,

	Starts	1st	2nd	3rd	Win & Pl
Career Total (Turf)	4	0	0	0	
Career Total (AW)	5	0	0	0	0

Going (Turf): Sf: 0-1 GS: 0-1 Gd: 0-1 GF: 0-1 Fm: 0-0
Distance: 5f/6f: 0-0 7f-8f: 0-1 9f-13f: 0-8 14f+: 0-0
Track : LH: 0-3 RH: 0-6 Tight: 0-4 Gall: 0-0
Aids: Bl: 0-0 Vi: 0-0 Tstrap: 0-0 Ckp: 0-0
Best Rating: 50 7/08 Wind 1m2f7y gd-fm

Aston Lad

93 49

8-y-o b g Bijou D'Inde-Fishki (Niniski (USA))
Mrs S J Humphrey (Micky Hammond 22/5) Yen Hall Farm Racing

Placings:46625050/0/51/63/444-0 (2233)

2009: 12^{0}GS,

	Starts	1st	2nd	3rd	Win & Pl
Career Total (Turf)	17	1	1	1	6005

54 10/06 Catt 1m7f177y (0-70)H SFT £3886
Total win prize-money £3886

Going (Turf): **Sf: 1-6** GS: 0-6 Gd: 0-2 GF: 0-3 Fm: 0-0
Distance: 5f/6f: 0-0 7f-8f: 0-0 9f-13f: 0-9 **14f+: 1-8**
Track : **LH: 1-13** RH: 0-4 **Tight: 1-9** Gall: 0-5
Aids: Bl: 0-0 Vi: 0-0 Tstrap: 0-0 Ckp: 0-0
Best Rating: 54 10/06 Catt 1m7f177y soft

Moderate stayer; gets two miles; winning hurdler; acts on soft ground.

Astonishment (IRE)

100(92) (76)96

2-y-o b c Desert Style (IRE)-Lucky Norwegian (IRE) (Almutawakel)
S Kirk Mrs Barbara Facchino

Placings:0242121544 (6898)

2009: 6^{0}GS, 7^{2}GF, 7^{4}GF, 7^{2}G, 7^{1}SD, 7^{2}GF, 7^{1}GF, 7^{5}GF, 6^{4}G, 8^{4}GF,

	Starts	1st	2nd	3rd	Win & Pl
Career Total (Turf)	9	1	3	0	10749
Career Total (AW)	1	1	0	0	2590

84 9/09 Gdwd 7f (0-85)H G-F £4857
76 8/09 Kemp 7f STD £2590
Total win prize-money £7447

Going (Turf): Sf: 0-0 GS: 0-1 Gd: 0-2 **GF: 1-6** Fm: 0-0
Distance: 5f/6f: 0-1 **7f-8f: 2-8** 9f-13f: 0-1 14f+: 0-0
Track : LH: 0-2 **RH: 2-3** Tight: 0-0 Gall: 0-1
Aids: Bl: 0-0 Vi: 0-0 Tstrap: 0-0 Ckp: 0-0
Best Rating: 96 10/09 Pont 1m4y gd-fm

Fair; stays 7f; acts on fast and easy ground.

Astormfromillinois (USA)

(70) (6)

6-y-o ch g Illinois Storm (USA)-Sweetannieannie (USA) (Marquetry (USA))
George Baker Miss Rebecca Curtis

Placings:0/0 (7412)

2009: 7^{0}SD,

	Starts	1st	2nd	3rd	Win & Pl
Career Total (Turf)	0	0	0	0	
Career Total (AW)	2	0	0	0	0

Going (Turf): Sf: 0-0 GS: 0-0 Gd: 0-0 GF: 0-0 Fm: 0-0
Distance: 5f/6f: 0-1 7f-8f: 0-1 9f-13f: 0-0 14f+: 0-0
Track : LH: 0-1 RH: 0-0 Tight: 0-1 Gall: 0-0
Aids: Bl: 0-0 Vi: 0-0 Tstrap: 0-0 Ckp: 0-0
Best Rating: 6 11/09 Wolv 7f32y stand

Astral Flower

(95) (64)

2-y-o b f Kalanisi (IRE)-Arum Lily (USA) (Woodman (USA))
Sir Michael Stoute K Abdulla

Placings:54 (7400)

2009: 8^{5}SD, 9^{4}SD,

	Starts	1st	2nd	3rd	Win & Pl
Career Total (Turf)	0	0	0	0	
Career Total (AW)	2	0	0	0	289

Going (Turf): Sf: 0-0 GS: 0-0 Gd: 0-0 GF: 0-0 Fm: 0-0
Distance: 5f/6f: 0-0 7f-8f: 0-1 9f-13f: 0-1 14f+: 0-0
Track : LH: 0-2 RH: 0-0 Tight: 0-2 Gall: 0-0
Aids: Bl: 0-0 Vi: 0-0 Tstrap: 0-0 Ckp: 0-0
Best Rating: 64 11/09 Wolv 1m1f103y stand

Fair; stays 1m1f; acts on Polytrack.

Astroangel

99 (69)60

5-y-o b m Groom Dancer (USA)-Nutmeg (IRE) (Lake Coniston (IRE))

M H Tompkins Mystic Meg Limited

Placings:042400300/4205204300345/4040353-04320540 (6845)
2009: 8^{0}GF, 7^{4}G, 8^{3}G, 7^{2}GF, 7^{0}F, 8^{5}GF, 8^{4}GF, 13^{0}G,

	Starts	1st	2nd	3rd	Win & Pl
Career Total (Turf)	31	0	4	5	7069
Career Total (AW)	6	0	0	1	690

Going (Turf): Sf: 0-2 GS: 0-5 Gd: 0-10 GF: 0-11 Fm: 0-3
Distance: 5f/6f: 0-7 7f-8f: 0-20 9f-13f: 0-9 14f+: 0-1
Track : LH: 0-18 RH: 0-4 Tight: 0-7 Gall: 0-0
Aids: Bl: 0-3 Vi: 0-1 Tstrap: 0-7 Ckp: 0-7
Best Rating: 69 7/06 Kemp 6f stand

Moderate; effective at around 1m; acts on fast ground and on Polytrack.

Astrobrava

94(77) (53)**55**
3-y-o ch f Falbrav (IRE)-Nutmeg (IRE) (Lake Coniston (IRE))
M H Tompkins Mystic Meg Limited

Placings:000-55360 (5328)
2009: 12^{5}GF, 9^{5}GS, 9^{3}GF, 7^{6}GF, 11^{0}SD,

	Starts	1st	2nd	3rd	Win & Pl
Career Total (Turf)	6	0	0	1	482
Career Total (AW)	2	0	0	0	

Going (Turf): Sf: 0-1 GS: 0-1 Gd: 0-1 GF: 0-3 Fm: 0-0
Distance: 5f/6f: 0-0 7f-8f: 0-3 9f-13f: 0-5 14f+: 0-0
Track : LH: 0-6 RH: 0-2 Tight: 0-1 Gall: 0-1
Aids: Bl: 0-0 Vi: 0-0 Tstrap: 0-0 Ckp: 0-0
Best Rating: 55 5/09 Bevl 1m4f16y gd-fm

Astrodiva

102(88) (48)**77**
3-y-o b f Where Or When (IRE)-Astromancer (USA) (Silver Hawk (USA))
M H Tompkins Mystic Meg Limited

Placings:5-22233342 (6766)
2009: 8^{2}G, 10^{2}G, 9^{2}G, 14^{3}G, 11^{3}G, 10^{3}GF, 12^{4}SD, 12^{2}GS,

	Starts	1st	2nd	3rd	Win & Pl
Career Total (Turf)	8	0	4	3	6159
Career Total (AW)	1	0	0	0	0

Going (Turf): Sf: 0-0 GS: 0-2 Gd: 0-5 GF: 0-1 Fm: 0-0
Distance: 5f/6f: 0-0 7f-8f: 0-0 9f-13f: 0-8 14f+: 0-1
Track : LH: 0-5 RH: 0-2 Tight: 0-3 Gall: 0-3
Aids: Bl: 0-0 Vi: 0-0 Tstrap: 0-0 Ckp: 0-0
Best Rating: 77 7/09 York 1m6f good

Fair; stays 1m2f and acts on good ground.

Astrodonna

99(104) (75)**78**
4-y-o ch f Carnival Dancer-Mega (IRE) (Petardia)
M H Tompkins Mystic Meg Limited

Placings:61/4252554646-26304621636 (7364)
2009: 8^{2}G, 8^{6}GF, 8^{3}SD, 7^{0}GF, 8^{4}GF, 8^{6}G, 8^{2}GS, 8^{1}G, 8^{6}GF, 8^{3}SS, 8^{6}SD,

	Starts	1st	2nd	3rd	Win & Pl
Career Total (Turf)	19	1	4	0	8887
Career Total (AW)	4	1	0	2	3173

78 8/09 Yarm 1m3y (0-65)H GD £1942
64 11/07 Wolv 1m141y STD £2047
Total win prize-money £3991

Going (Turf): Sf: 0-0 GS: 0-3 Gd: 1-9 GF: 0-7 Fm: 0-0
Distance: 5f/6f: 0-0 7f-8f: 0-13 9f-13f: 2-10 14f+: 0-0
Track : LH: 1-7 RH: 0-4 Tight: 1-6 Gall: 0-0
Aids: Bl: 0-0 Vi: 0-0 Tstrap: 0-0 Ckp: 0-0
Best Rating: 78 8/09 Yarm 1m3y good

Modest; stays 1m; acts on good and easier ground.

Astroleo

99(96) (54)**54**
3-y-o ch g Groom Dancer (USA)-Astrolove (IRE) (Bigstone (IRE))
M H Tompkins Mystic Meg Limited

Placings:6060-33103056 (7336)
2009: 12^{3}SD, 12^{3}GF, 14^{1}SD, 16^{0}HY, 14^{3}GF, 16^{0}SD, 16^{5}SS, 14^{6}SD,

	Starts	1st	2nd	3rd	Win & Pl
Career Total (Turf)	6	0	0	2	684
Career Total (AW)	6	1	0	1	2795

54 7/09 Sthl 1m6f (0-70)H STD £2492
Total win prize-money £2492

Going (Turf): Sf: 0-2 GS: 0-1 Gd: 0-1 GF: 0-2 Fm: 0-0
Distance: 5f/6f: 0-1 7f-8f: 0-3 9f-13f: 0-2 14f+: 1-6
Track : LH: 1-7 RH: 0-4 Tight: 0-3 Gall: 0-0
Aids: Bl: 0-0 Vi: 0-0 Tstrap: 0-0 Ckp: 0-0
Best Rating: 54 8/09 Yarm 1m6f17y gd-fm

Very moderate; stays 1m6f; acts on fast ground and Fibresand.

Astrolibra

103(97) (65)**61**
5-y-o b m Sakhee (USA)-Optimistic (Reprimand)
M H Tompkins Mystic Meg Limited

Placings:0/44003340/2312244105-40534014654 (7712)
2009: 10^{4}F, 9^{0}F, 9^{5}GF, 10^{3}G, 11^{4}F, 9^{0}GF, 11^{1}SD, 12^{4}GS, 11^{6}GS, 11^{5}SD, 12^{4}SD,

	Starts	1st	2nd	3rd	Win & Pl
Career Total (Turf)	24	2	3	3	8138
Career Total (AW)	6	1	0	1	2893

65 8/09 Sthl 1m3f (0-60)H STD £2590
60 8/08 Yarm 1m2f21y (60-92)H G-S £2072
57 6/08 Brig 1m1f209y (0-65)H G-F £1942
Total win prize-money £6605

Going (Turf): Sf: 0-2 GS: 1-4 Gd: 0-5 GF: 1-10 Fm: 0-3
Distance: 5f/6f: 0-0 7f-8f: 0-1 9f-13f: 3-29 14f+: 0-0
Track : LH: 3-23 RH: 0-6 Tight: 1-8 Gall: 0-0
Aids: Bl: 0-0 Vi: 0-0 Tstrap: 0-0 Ckp: 0-0
Best Rating: 65 8/09 Sthl 1m3f stand

Moderate; effective at up to 1m4f; acts on good ground and on Fibresand.

Astromoon

88 **59**
2-y-o b f Beat Hollow-Astromancer (USA) (Silver Hawk (USA))
M H Tompkins Mystic Meg Limited

Placings:06 (7095)
2009: 8^{0}GF, 8^{6}G,

	Starts	1st	2nd	3rd	Win & Pl
Career Total (Turf)	2	0	0	0	0

Going (Turf): Sf: 0-0 GS: 0-0 Gd: 0-1 GF: 0-1 Fm: 0-0
Distance: 5f/6f: 0-0 7f-8f: 0-1 9f-13f: 0-1 14f+: 0-0
Track : LH: 0-0 RH: 0-0 Tight: 0-0 Gall: 0-0
Aids: Bl: 0-0 Vi: 0-0 Tstrap: 0-0 Ckp: 0-0
Best Rating: 59 10/09 Yarm 1m3y good

Astronomer's Dream

72(86) (58)**57**
2-y-o ch f Galileo (IRE)-Danehill's Dream (IRE) (Danehill (USA))
E F Vaughan C G P Wyatt

Placings:0000 (7235)
2009: 7^{0}S, 7^{0}G, 7^{0}SS, 8^{0}SD,

	Starts	1st	2nd	3rd	Win & Pl
Career Total (Turf)	2	0	0	0	
Career Total (AW)	2	0	0	0	

Going (Turf): Sf: 0-1 GS: 0-0 Gd: 0-1 GF: 0-0 Fm: 0-0
Distance: 5f/6f: 0-0 7f-8f: 0-4 9f-13f: 0-0 14f+: 0-0
Track : LH: 0-1 RH: 0-1 Tight: 0-1 Gall: 0-0
Aids: Bl: 0-0 Vi: 0-0 Tstrap: 0-0 Ckp: 0-0
Best Rating: 58 10/09 Ling 7f std-slw

Astronomical (IRE)

96(97) (69)**71**
7-y-o b g Mister Baileys-Charm The Stars (Roi Danzig (USA))
R Hollinshead FWH Partnership

Placings:30/5140060/0/52002021003 (7495)
2009: 10^{5}G, 12^{2}G, 12^{0}G, 10^{0}G, 9^{2}GF, 12^{0}GS, 10^{2}GF, 10^{1}GF, 9^{0}G, 10^{0}G, 12^{3}SD,

	Starts	1st	2nd	3rd	Win & Pl
Career Total (Turf)	19	2	3	1	14378
Career Total (AW)	2	0	0	1	302

71 9/09 Nott 1m2f50y (0-70)H G-F £2637
87 5/05 Nott 1m54y (0-85)H G-F £8027
Total win prize-money £10665

Going (Turf): Sf: 0-1 GS: 0-3 Gd: 0-10 GF: 2-5 Fm: 0-0
Distance: 5f/6f: 0-0 7f-8f: 0-4 9f-13f: 2-17 14f+: 0-0
Track : LH: 2-14 RH: 0-4 Tight: 0-2 Gall: 0-6
Aids: Bl: 0-0 Vi: 0-0 Tstrap: 1-5 Ckp: 1-5
Best Rating: 87 5/05 Nott 1m54y gd-fm

Modest; stays 1m4f; acts on quick ground and on Polytrack.

Astrophysical Jet

100 **89**
2-y-o b f Dubawi (IRE)-Common Knowledge (Rainbow Quest (USA))
E S McMahon Ladas

Placings:135 (6852)
2009: 6^{1}GF, 6^{3}G, 7^{5}G,

	Starts	1st	2nd	3rd	Win & Pl
Career Total (Turf)	3	1	0	1	13091

78 8/09 Nott 6f15y G-F £3399
Total win prize-money £3400

Going (Turf): Sf: 0-0 GS: 0-0 Gd: 0-2 GF: 1-1 Fm: 0-0
Distance: 5f/6f: 0-1 7f-8f: 1-2 9f-13f: 0-0 14f+: 0-0
Track : LH: 0-0 RH: 0-0 Tight: 0-0 Gall: 0-0
Aids: Bl: 0-0 Vi: 0-0 Tstrap: 0-0 Ckp: 0-0
Best Rating: 89 10/09 NmkR 7f good

Very useful; effective at 6f; acts on good ground.

Astrovenus

85 49

2-y-o ch f Tobougg (IRE)-Astrolove (IRE) (Bigstone (IRE))
M H Tompkins Mystic Meg Limited

Placings:00 **(7096)**
2009: 6^{0}GF, 7^{0}G,

	Starts	1st	2nd	3rd	Win & Pl
Career Total (Turf)	2	0	0	0	

Going (Turf): **Sf: 0-0 GS: 0-0 Gd: 0-1 GF: 0-1 Fm: 0-0**
Distance: 5f/6f: 0-0 7f-8f: 0-2 9f-13f: 0-0 14f+: 0-0
Track : LH: 0-0 RH: 0-0 Tight: 0-0 Gall: 0-0
Aids: Bl: 0-0 Vi: 0-0 Tstrap: 0-0 Ckp: 0-0
Best Rating: **49** 10/09 Yarm 7f3y good

Aswaaq (IRE)

94 65

3-y-o b f Peintre Celebre (USA)-Hureya (USA) (Woodman (USA))
J L Dunlop Hamdan Al Maktoum

Placings:5-5 **(5435)**
2009: 8^{5}GF,

	Starts	1st	2nd	3rd	Win & Pl
Career Total (Turf)	2	0	0	0	0

Going (Turf): **Sf: 0-1 GS: 0-0 Gd: 0-0 GF: 0-1 Fm: 0-0**
Distance: 5f/6f: 0-0 7f-8f: 0-2 9f-13f: 0-0 14f+: 0-0
Track : LH: 0-0 RH: 0-0 Tight: 0-0 Gall: 0-0
Aids: Bl: 0-0 Vi: 0-0 Tstrap: 0-0 Ckp: 0-0
Best Rating: **65** 10/08 Leic 7f9y soft

At A Great Rate (USA)

103 79

3-y-o b f Arch (USA)-Glia (USA) (A.P. Indy (USA))
Dominique Sepulchre (H R A Cecil 20/8) Niarchos Family

Placings:0-1446354
2009: 10^{1}GF, 11^{4}GF, 8^{4}GF, 10^{6}S, 8^{3}G, 8^{5}GF, 10^{4}S,

	Starts	1st	2nd	3rd	Win & Pl
Career Total (Turf)	8	1	0	1	6596
59 4/09 Nott 1m2f50y				G-F	£2047

Total win prize-money £2047

Going (Turf): Sf: 0-2 GS: 0-1 Gd: 0-1 **GF: 1-4** Fm: 0-0
Distance: 5f/6f: 0-0 7f-8f: 0-2 **9f-13f: 1-6** 14f+: 0-0
Track : **LH: 1-4** RH: 0-2 Tight: 0-2 Gall: 0-1
Aids: Bl: 0-0 Vi: 0-0 Tstrap: 0-0 Ckp: 0-0
Best Rating: **79** 6/09 Nott 1m75y gd-fm

Fair; stays 1m2f; acts on fast ground.

At Wits End

(102) (75)

3-y-o b g Orpen (USA)-Pagan Princess (Mujtahid (USA))
J A R Toller George Materna

Placings:441 **(6673)**
2009: 8^{4}SD, 8^{4}SD, 9^{1}SD,

	Starts	1st	2nd	3rd	Win & Pl
Career Total (Turf)	0	0	0	0	
Career Total (AW)	3	1	0	0	2730
75 10/09 Wolv 1m1f103y				STD	£2729

Total win prize-money £2730

Going (Turf): **Sf: 0-0 GS: 0-0 Gd: 0-0 GF: 0-0 Fm: 0-0**
Distance: 5f/6f: 0-0 7f-8f: 0-0 **9f-13f: 1-3** 14f+: 0-0
Track : **LH: 1-3** RH: 0-0 **Tight: 1-3** Gall: 0-0
Aids: Bl: 0-0 Vi: 0-0 Tstrap: 0-0 Ckp: 0-0
Best Rating: **75** 10/09 Wolv 1m1f103y stand

Atabaas Allure (FR)

101(101) (82)85

3-y-o b f Alhaarth (IRE)-Atabaa (FR) (Anabaa (USA))
M Johnston Mrs R J Jacobs

Placings:52011-560300 **(5037)**
2009: 10^{5}G, 14^{6}GF, 11^{0}S, 8^{3}GF, 9^{0}G, 9^{0}GF,

	Starts	1st	2nd	3rd	Win & Pl
Career Total (Turf)	9	0	1	1	2401
Career Total (AW)	2	2	0	0	9714
82 10/08 GrLe 1m (0-85)				STD	£5504
79 9/08 Wolv 7f32y (0-75)				STD	£4209

Total win prize-money £9714

Going (Turf): **Sf: 0-2 GS: 0-1 Gd: 0-3 GF: 0-3 Fm: 0-0**
Distance: 5f/6f: 0-0 **7f-8f: 2-4** 9f-13f: 0-6 14f+: 0-1
Track : **LH: 2-4** RH: 0-6 Tight: 1-3 Gall: 1-1
Aids: Bl: 0-0 Vi: 0-0 Tstrap: 0-0 Ckp: 0-0
Best Rating: **85** 7/09 Bevl 1m100y gd-fm

Useful; stays 1m; acts on a sound surface and on Polytrack.

Atacama Crossing (IRE)

95 77

2-y-o b c Footstepsinthesand-Endure (IRE) (Green Desert (USA))
B W Hills Paul Moulton

Placings:2100 **(5762)**
2009: 6^{2}G, 5^{1}GF, 7^{0}GS, 7^{0}GF,

	Starts	1st	2nd	3rd	Win & Pl
Career Total (Turf)	4	1	1	0	4753
77 5/09 Leic 5f218y				G-F	£3885

Total win prize-money £3886

Going (Turf): Sf: 0-0 GS: 0-1 Gd: 0-1 **GF: 1-2** Fm: 0-0
Distance: **5f/6f: 1-2** 7f-8f: 0-2 9f-13f: 0-0 14f+: 0-0
Track : LH: 0-0 RH: 0-0 Tight: 0-0 Gall: 0-0
Aids: Bl: 0-0 Vi: 0-0 Tstrap: 0-0 Ckp: 0-0
Best Rating: **77** 5/09 Leic 5f218y gd-fm

Fair; effective over 6f; acts on fast ground.

Atacama Sunrise

99(104) (71)70

3-y-o b f Desert Sun-Top Of The Morning (Keen)
J Pearce Jim Furlong

Placings:54600123001 **(7776)**
2009: 10^{5}GF, 10^{4}G, 10^{6}GS, 11^{0}G, 10^{0}G, 9^{1}GF, 8^{2}SF, 8^{3}GF, 8^{0}G, 8^{0}G, 10^{1}SD,

	Starts	1st	2nd	3rd	Win & Pl
Career Total (Turf)	9	1	0	1	3259
Career Total (AW)	2	1	1	0	2684
71 12/09 Ling 1m2f (0-70)				STD	£1978
63 7/09 Yarm 1m1f (0-75)H				G-F	£2719

Total win prize-money £4699

Going (Turf): Sf: 0-0 GS: 0-1 Gd: 0-5 **GF: 1-3** Fm: 0-0
Distance: 5f/6f: 0-0 7f-8f: 0-1 **9f-13f: 2-10** 14f+: 0-0
Track : **LH: 2-6** RH: 0-2 **Tight: 2-6** Gall: 0-0
Aids: Bl: 0-0 Vi: 0-0 Tstrap: 0-1 Ckp: 0-1
Best Rating: **71** 12/09 Ling 1m2f stand

Modest; effective at around 1m2f; acts on fast ground and Polytrack.

Atakora (IRE)

87(81) (59)62

2-y-o b f King's Best (USA)-Orinoco (IRE) (Darshaan)
Mrs A J Perrett Lady Clague

Placings:006 **(6416)**
2009: 6^{0}S, 7^{0}SD, 7^{6}GF,

	Starts	1st	2nd	3rd	Win & Pl
Career Total (Turf)	2	0	0	0	0
Career Total (AW)	1	0	0	0	

Going (Turf): **Sf: 0-1 GS: 0-0 Gd: 0-0 GF: 0-1 Fm: 0-0**
Distance: 5f/6f: 0-0 7f-8f: 0-3 9f-13f: 0-0 14f+: 0-0
Track : LH: 0-0 RH: 0-2 Tight: 0-0 Gall: 0-0
Aids: Bl: 0-0 Vi: 0-0 Tstrap: 0-0 Ckp: 0-0
Best Rating: **62** 9/09 Sals 6f212y soft

Atasari (IRE)

109 109

2-y-o b f Whipper (USA)-Azra (IRE) (Danehill (USA))
J S Bolger Mrs J S Bolger

Placings:6105122 **(6852)**
2009: 5^{6}HY, 6^{1}HY, 5^{0}HY, 6^{5}SH, 8^{1}GF, 8^{2}S, 7^{2}G,

	Starts	1st	2nd	3rd	Win & Pl
Career Total (Turf)	7	2	2	0	58772
85 9/09 Gowr 1m H				G-F	£20857
78 5/09 Curr 6f				HVY	£12075

Total win prize-money £32933

Going (Turf): **Sf: 1-4** GS: 0-0 Gd: 0-1 **GF: 1-1** Fm: 0-0
Distance: 5f/6f: 1-4 7f-8f: 1-3 9f-13f: 0-0 14f+: 0-0
Track : LH: 0-0 **RH: 1-2** Tight: 0-0 Gall: 0-1
Aids: Bl: 0-0 Vi: 0-0 Tstrap: 0-0 Ckp: 0-0
Best Rating: **109** 10/09 NmkR 7f good

Very useful; effective from 7f-1m; acts on fast and soft ground.

Ateeb

98(88) (61)69

3-y-o b g Red Ransom (USA)-Design Perfection (USA) (Diesis)
M Johnston Hamdan Al Maktoum

Placings:66-5 **(1087)**
2009: 9^{5}GF,

	Starts	1st	2nd	3rd	Win & Pl
Career Total (Turf)	2	0	0	0	0
Career Total (AW)	1	0	0	0	0

Going (Turf): **Sf: 0-0 GS: 0-1 Gd: 0-0 GF: 0-1 Fm: 0-0**
Distance: 5f/6f: 0-0 7f-8f: 0-2 9f-13f: 0-1 14f+: 0-0
Track : LH: 0-1 RH: 0-1 Tight: 0-1 Gall: 0-0
Aids: Bl: 0-0 Vi: 0-0 Tstrap: 0-0 Ckp: 0-0
Best Rating: **69** 4/09 Leic 1m1f218y gd-fm

Athaakeel (IRE)

73(97) (66)6

3-y-o b f Almutawakel-Asaafeer (USA) (Dayjur (USA))
R A Harris Ridge House Stables Ltd

Placings:0100510 (7330)
2009: 5^{0}G, 5^{1}SD, 5^{0}SD, 7^{0}GF, 5^{5}SD, 6^{1}SD, 6^{0}SD,

	Starts	1st	2nd	3rd	Win & Pl
Career Total (Turf)	2	0	0	0	
Career Total (AW)	5	2	0	0	4094

64 10/09 Ling 6f STD £2047
66 6/09 Wolv 5f216y STD £2047
Total win prize-money £4094

Going (Turf): Sf: 0-0 GS: 0-0 Gd: 0-1 GF: 0-1 Fm: 0-0
Distance: 5f/6f: 2-6 7f-8f: 0-1 9f-13f: 0-0 14f+: 0-0
Track : LH: 2-4 RH: 0-1 Tight: 2-4 Gall: 0-0
Aids: Bl: 0-0 Vi: 0-0 Tstrap: 0-0 Ckp: 0-0
Best Rating: 66 6/09 Wolv 5f216y stand

Modest; suited by 6f and acts on Polytrack.

Athania (IRE)

98(101) (76)69
3-y-o ch f Fath (USA)-Xania (Mujtahid (USA))
A P Jarvis A L R Morton

Placings:0110-460361050 (6052)
2009: 6^{4}SD, 8^{6}GF, 7^{0}S, 7^{3}SD, 6^{6}GF, 7^{1}GF, 8^{0}G, 7^{5}GF, 8^{0}G,

	Starts	1st	2nd	3rd	Win & Pl
Career Total (Turf)	9	2	0	0	8865
Career Total (AW)	4	1	0	1	4622

69 7/09 Ches 7f122y (0-80)H G-F £5828
76 8/08 GrLe 6f (0-85) STD £3885
68 8/08 Sals 6f212y G-S £2914
Total win prize-money £12628

Going (Turf): Sf: 0-1 GS: 1-1 Gd: 0-2 GF: 1-5 Fm: 0-0
Distance: 5f/6f: 1-4 7f-8f: 2-9 9f-13f: 0-0 14f+: 0-0
Track : LH: 2-5 RH: 0-4 Tight: 1-1 Gall: 1-1
Aids: Bl: 0-0 Vi: 1-3 Tstrap: 0-0 Ckp: 0-0
Best Rating: 76 8/08 GrLe 6f stand

Modest; stays 7f; acts on easy ground and on Polytrack; has worn a visor.

Athboy Auction

94(94) (46)57
4-y-o b f Auction House (USA)-Thabeh (Shareef Dancer (USA))
H J Collingridge John Dover

Placings:0650050/00306-004300040 (7591)
2009: 7^{0}SD, 7^{0}GF, 6^{4}GF, 7^{3}GF, 7^{0}GF, 10^{0}GS, 7^{0}GF, 6^{4}SD, 7^{0}SD,

	Starts	1st	2nd	3rd	Win & Pl
Career Total (Turf)	13	0	0	2	880
Career Total (AW)	8	0	0	0	192

Going (Turf): Sf: 0-1 GS: 0-1 Gd: 0-2 GF: 0-9 Fm: 0-0
Distance: 5f/6f: 0-6 7f-8f: 0-14 9f-13f: 0-1 14f+: 0-0
Track : LH: 0-6 RH: 0-4 Tight: 0-3 Gall: 0-2
Aids: Bl: 0-0 Vi: 0-0 Tstrap: 0-0 Ckp: 0-0
Best Rating: 64 9/07 Sand 5f6y gd-fm

Auction House half-sister to among others multiple 7f-1m winner Melody Queen, who was later smart in the US; modest filly; seems best at 6f.

Atheer Dubai (IRE)

(105) (73)57
4-y-o b c Dubai Destination (USA)-Atheer (USA) (Lear Fan (USA))
E F Vaughan Mohammed Rashid

Placings:2004544/350300001-253 (2382)
2009: 6^{2}SD, 5^{5}SD, 6^{3}SD,

	Starts	1st	2nd	3rd	Win & Pl
Career Total (Turf)	11	0	1	0	2438
Career Total (AW)	8	1	1	3	5599

73 11/08 Ling 5f STD £3238
Total win prize-money £3238

Going (Turf): Sf: 0-0 GS: 0-0 Gd: 0-5 GF: 0-6 Fm: 0-0
Distance: 5f/6f: 1-8 7f-8f: 0-11 9f-13f: 0-0 14f+: 0-0
Track : LH: 1-10 RH: 0-1 Tight: 1-9 Gall: 0-0
Aids: Bl: 0-6 Vi: 0-0 Tstrap: 0-1 Ckp: 0-1
Best Rating: 88 6/07 Asct 6f gd-fm

Modest; effective over 5f-7f; acts on good ground and on Polytrack; has worn blinkers.

Athenian Garden (USA)

95(95) (67)59
2-y-o b f Royal Academy (USA)-Webee (USA) (Kingmambo (USA))
H R A Cecil Malih L Al Basti

Placings:64 (6965)
2009: 7^{6}SD, 7^{4}G,

	Starts	1st	2nd	3rd	Win & Pl
Career Total (Turf)	1	0	0	0	409
Career Total (AW)	1	0	0	0	0

Going (Turf): Sf: 0-0 GS: 0-0 Gd: 0-1 GF: 0-0 Fm: 0-0
Distance: 5f/6f: 0-0 7f-8f: 0-2 9f-13f: 0-0 14f+: 0-0
Track : LH: 0-2 RH: 0-0 Tight: 0-1 Gall: 0-0
Aids: Bl: 0-0 Vi: 0-0 Tstrap: 0-0 Ckp: 0-0
Best Rating: 67 10/09 Wolv 7f32y stand

Atherton (IRE)

62(74) (44)
2-y-o b c Cadeaux Genereux-Bibi Karam (IRE) (Persian Bold)
J G Given J David Abell

Placings:000 (6796)
2009: 5^{0}SD, 6^{0}SD, 6^{0}S,

	Starts	1st	2nd	3rd	Win & Pl
Career Total (Turf)	1	0	0	0	
Career Total (AW)	2	0	0	0	

Going (Turf): Sf: 0-1 GS: 0-0 Gd: 0-0 GF: 0-0 Fm: 0-0
Distance: 5f/6f: 0-2 7f-8f: 0-1 9f-13f: 0-0 14f+: 0-0
Track : LH: 0-2 RH: 0-0 Tight: 0-1 Gall: 0-0
Aids: Bl: 0-0 Vi: 0-0 Tstrap: 0-0 Ckp: 0-0
Best Rating: 44 9/09 Wolv 5f216y stand

Athlone (IRE)

100 98
5-y-o b m Montjeu (IRE)-Almi Ad (USA) (Silver Hawk (USA))
L M Cumani Allevamento Gialloblu

Placings:2/42111000/455331-06 (2974)
2009: 11^{0}G, 10^{6}GS,

	Starts	1st	2nd	3rd	Win & Pl
Career Total (Turf)	17	4	2	2	58020

96 11/08 Capa 1m2f HVY £14705
106 7/07 Siro 1m3f GD £18918
5/07 Siro 1m3f HVY £8445
5/07 Siro 1m2f GD £5067
Total win prize-money £47139

Going (Turf): Sf: 2-4 GS: 0-1 Gd: 2-10 GF: 0-2 Fm: 0-0
Distance: 5f/6f: 0-0 7f-8f: 0-0 9f-13f: 4-17 14f+: 0-0
Track : LH: 0-2 RH: 2-8 Tight: 0-0 Gall: 0-0
Aids: Bl: 0-0 Vi: 0-0 Tstrap: 0-0 Ckp: 0-0
Best Rating: 106 7/07 Siro 1m3f good

Very useful; ex-Italian-trained; stays 1m2f; acts on good or softer ground; has worn a hood.

Athwaab

93(102) (70)64
2-y-o b f Cadeaux Genereux-Ahdaaf (USA) (Bahri (USA))
M G Quinlan (E A L Dunlop 4/9) John Hanly

Placings:5001332 (7871)
2009: 5^{5}GF, 6^{0}SD, 5^{0}SD, 6^{1}SD, 6^{3}SD, 5^{3}SS, 5^{2}SD,

	Starts	1st	2nd	3rd	Win & Pl
Career Total (Turf)	1	0	0	0	0
Career Total (AW)	6	1	1	2	4355

70 9/09 Kemp 6f (0-70) STD £2266
Total win prize-money £2267

Going (Turf): Sf: 0-0 GS: 0-0 Gd: 0-0 GF: 0-1 Fm: 0-0
Distance: 5f/6f: 1-7 7f-8f: 0-0 9f-13f: 0-0 14f+: 0-0
Track : LH: 0-2 RH: 1-3 Tight: 0-1 Gall: 0-0
Aids: Bl: 0-0 Vi: 0-0 Tstrap: 0-0 Ckp: 0-0
Best Rating: 70 9/09 Kemp 6f stand

Modest; stays 6f; acts on Polytrack.

Atlaal (USA)

95 83
2-y-o ch c Speightstown (USA)-Deputy Maiden (USA) (Deputy Minister (CAN))
M A Jarvis Hamdan Al Maktoum

Placings:241 (6246)
2009: 6^{2}GF, 6^{4}GF, 6^{1}GF,

	Starts	1st	2nd	3rd	Win & Pl
Career Total (Turf)	3	1	1	0	5418

72 9/09 Hayd 6f G-F £3238
Total win prize-money £3238

Going (Turf): Sf: 0-0 GS: 0-0 Gd: 0-0 GF: 1-3 Fm: 0-0
Distance: 5f/6f: 1-2 7f-8f: 0-1 9f-13f: 0-0 14f+: 0-0
Track : LH: 0-0 RH: 0-0 Tight: 0-0 Gall: 0-0
Aids: Bl: 0-0 Vi: 0-0 Tstrap: 0-0 Ckp: 0-0
Best Rating: 83 7/09 Asct 6f gd-fm

Useful; effective over 6f; acts on fast ground.

Atlantic Beach

104 76
4-y-o ch g Kyllachy-Amused (Prince Sabo)
J Hetherton (R A Fahey 11/7) R Fell & K Everitt

Placings:64136-432460 (4783)
2009: 6^{4}GF, 6^{3}HY, 6^{2}GF, 6^{4}GF, 5^{6}GF, 6^{0}GF,

	Starts	1st	2nd	3rd	Win & Pl
Career Total (Turf)	11	1	1	2	6810

75 5/08 Ripn 6f GD £3238
Total win prize-money £3238

Going (Turf): Sf: 0-1 GS: 0-2 Gd: 1-1 GF: 0-7 Fm: 0-0
Distance: 5f/6f: 1-10 7f-8f: 0-1 9f-13f: 0-0 14f+: 0-0
Track : LH: 0-2 RH: 0-0 Tight: 0-1 Gall: 0-0
Aids: Bl: 0-1 Vi: 0-1 Tstrap: 0-0 Ckp: 0-0
Best Rating: 76 6/09 Haml 6f5y gd-fm

Modest; effective over 6f; acts on good ground.

Atlantic Gamble (IRE)

(104) (66)60

9-y-o b g Darnay-Full Traceability (IRE) (Ron's Victory (USA))

K R Burke Mrs Elaine M Burke

Placings:640/00034465/1111464515015004/05156605-0 (0081)

2009: 9^{0}SD,

	Starts	1st	2nd	3rd	Win & Pl
Career Total (Turf)	9	1	0	0	3742
Career Total (AW)	27	6	0	1	12997

59	3/08	Wolv	1m1f103y	(0-50)H	STD	£1774
66	9/07	Kemp	1m3f		STD	£2047
65	7/07	Leic	1m3f183y		SFT	£3238
69	2/07	Wolv	1m4f50y		STD	£2047
65	2/07	Wolv	1m4f50y		STD	£2047
54	1/07	Wolv	1m4f50y	(0-55)H	STD	£2047
54	1/07	Wolv	1m4f50y	(0-50)H	STD	£2388

Total win prize-money £15595

Going (Turf): **Sf: 1-2** GS: 0-1 Gd: 0-1 GF: 0-2 Fm: 0-2
Distance: 5f/6f: 0-0 7f-8f: 0-1 **9f-13f: 7-29** 14f+: 0-6
Track : **LH: 5-25** RH: 2-11 **Tight: 5-24** Gall: 0-0
Aids: Bl: 0-0 Vi: 0-0 Tstrap: 7-28 Ckp: 7-28
Best Rating: **69** 2/07 Wolv 1m4f50y stand

Modest; ex-Irish; stays at least 1m 4f; acts on Polytrack; has worn cheekpieces.

Atlantic Sport (USA)

109 111

4-y-o b c Machiavellian (USA)-Shy Lady (FR) (Kaldoun (FR))

M R Channon Mohammed Jaber

Placings:16/1231-4056 (3388)

2009: 8^{4}GF, 8^{0}S, 7^{5}G, 6^{6}S,

	Starts	1st	2nd	3rd	Win & Pl
Career Total (Turf)	10	3	1	1	50650

109	9/08	Sand	7f16y	SFT	£22708
106	7/08	Newb	7f	G-F	£7477
93	7/07	Asct	6f	G-S	£6477

Total win prize-money £36662

Going (Turf): **Sf: 1-3 GS: 1-1** Gd: 0-2 **GF: 1-4** Fm: 0-0
Distance: 5f/6f: 1-2 **7f-8f: 2-8** 9f-13f: 0-0 14f+: 0-0
Track : LH: 0-2 **RH: 1-2** Tight: 0-0 Gall: 0-1
Aids: Bl: 0-0 Vi: 0-0 Tstrap: 0-0 Ckp: 0-0
Best Rating: **111** 5/09 Hayd 7f30y good

Listed class; effective at around 7f; handles fast and soft ground.

Atlantic Story (USA)

107(114) (115)96

7-y-o b/br g Stormy Atlantic (USA)-Story Book Girl (USA) (Siberian Express (USA))

M W Easterby Matthew Green

Placings:012/0044050111/11604111/4441125014-4033645333 (6283)

2009: 8^{4}SD, 7^{0}SD, 7^{3}F, 7^{3}GF, 7^{6}G, 6^{4}GF, 6^{5}G, 6^{3}GF, 6^{3}GF, 5^{3}GF,

	Starts	1st	2nd	3rd	Win & Pl
Career Total (Turf)	22	1	2	5	21022
Career Total (AW)	19	11	0	0	75810

115	11/08	Ling	7f	(0-100)H	STD	£11527
107	3/08	Ling	7f	(0-100)H	STD	£12464
104	2/08	Ling	7f	(0-100)H	STD	£9971
97	12/07	Ling	1m	(0-100)H	STD	£9971
93	12/07	Kemp	1m	(0-85)H	STD	£4728
89	12/07	Ling	1m	(0-80)H	STD	£4605
88	2/07	Kemp	1m	(0-85)H	STD	£4728
80	1/07	Wolv	1m141y	(0-85)H	STD	£4857
76	12/06	Wolv	1m141y	(0-60)H	STD	£2730
82	11/06	Sthl	7f	(0-63)H	STD	£2730
74	11/06	Kemp	1m	(0-55)H	STD	£2388
85	8/04	Epsm	7f	D	GD	£5668

Total win prize-money £76370

Going (Turf): Sf: 0-4 GS: 0-0 **Gd: 1-7** GF: 0-10 Fm: 0-1
Distance: 5f/6f: 0-7 **7f-8f: 10-26** 9f-13f: 2-8 14f+: 0-0
Track : **LH: 9-17** RH: 3-12 **Tight: 8-16** Gall: 0-1
Aids: **Bl: 4-19** Vi: 0-0 Tstrap: 0-0 Ckp: 0-0
Best Rating: **115** 11/08 Ling 7f stand

Useful on turf; smart on sand; effective from 6f-1m; acts on most ground on turf; goes on Polytrack; has worn blinkers and a tongue tie.

Atlantis Star

103 99

2-y-o b c Cape Cross (IRE)-Ladeena (IRE) (Dubai Millennium)

Saeed Bin Suroor Godolphin

Placings:1230 (6478)

2009: 6^{1}G, 6^{2}GF, 7^{3}GF, 7^{0}GF,

	Starts	1st	2nd	3rd	Win & Pl
Career Total (Turf)	4	1	1	1	10691

88	8/09	Pont	6f	GD	£4533

Total win prize-money £4533

Going (Turf): Sf: 0-0 GS: 0-0 **Gd: 1-1** GF: 0-3 Fm: 0-0
Distance: **5f/6f: 1-1** 7f-8f: 0-3 9f-13f: 0-0 14f+: 0-0
Track : **LH: 1-2** RH: 0-1 Tight: 0-1 Gall: 0-0
Aids: Bl: 0-0 Vi: 0-0 Tstrap: 0-0 Ckp: 0-0
Best Rating: **99** 9/09 Gdwd 7f gd-fm

Very useful; by Cape Cross out of a Dubai Millennium mare and cost 200,000gns; effective at 6f-7f; acts on good/fast ground.

Atomic Twister

77 34

2-y-o b f Dubawi (IRE)-Lauren (GER) (Lightning (FR))

P F I Cole C M Budgett & R A Instone

Placings:00 (2978)

2009: 6^{0}GF, 6^{0}GF,

	Starts	1st	2nd	3rd	Win & Pl
Career Total (Turf)	2	0	0	0	

Going (Turf): **Sf: 0-0 GS: 0-0 Gd: 0-0 GF: 0-2 Fm: 0-0**
Distance: 5f/6f: 0-2 7f-8f: 0-0 9f-13f: 0-0 14f+: 0-0
Track : LH: 0-0 RH: 0-0 Tight: 0-0 Gall: 0-1
Aids: Bl: 0-0 Vi: 0-0 Tstrap: 0-0 Ckp: 0-0
Best Rating: **34** 6/09 Sals 6f gd-fm

Attainable

(97) (68)37

3-y-o b/br f Kalanisi (IRE)-Balleta (USA) (Lyphard (USA))

Mrs A J Perrett K Abdulla

Placings:62-36 (6975)

2009: 12^{3}SD, 12^{6}SD,

	Starts	1st	2nd	3rd	Win & Pl
Career Total (Turf)	1	0	0	0	0
Career Total (AW)	3	0	1	1	907

Going (Turf): **Sf: 0-1 GS: 0-0 Gd: 0-0 GF: 0-0 Fm: 0-0**
Distance: 5f/6f: 0-0 7f-8f: 0-2 9f-13f: 0-2 14f+: 0-0
Track : LH: 0-0 RH: 0-3 Tight: 0-0 Gall: 0-0
Aids: Bl: 0-0 Vi: 0-0 Tstrap: 0-0 Ckp: 0-0
Best Rating: **68** 9/08 Kemp 1m stand

Modest so far; stays 1m; acts on Polytrack.

Attorney General (IRE)

72 42

10-y-o b g Sadler's Wells (USA)-Her Ladyship (Polish Precedent (USA))

C Gordon The Morestead Breakfast Club

Placings:1160/0/0 (7036)

2009: 12^{0}S,

	Starts	1st	2nd	3rd	Win & Pl
Career Total (Turf)	6	2	0	0	9721

77	8/02	Thsk	1m4f	D(0-80)	G-S	£5967
71	7/02	Wwck	1m2f188y	D	G-F	£3753

Total win prize-money £9722

Going (Turf): Sf: 0-1 **GS: 1-1** Gd: 0-1 **GF: 1-3** Fm: 0-0
Distance: 5f/6f: 0-0 7f-8f: 0-0 **9f-13f: 2-6** 14f+: 0-0
Track : **LH: 2-3** RH: 0-2 **Tight: 1-3** Gall: 0-1
Aids: Bl: 0-0 Vi: 0-0 Tstrap: 0-0 Ckp: 0-0
Best Rating: **77** 8/02 Thsk 1m4f gd-sft

Useful; stays 1m4f and acts on most ground; usually held up; smart hurdler.

Auburn Place

(68) (16)

2-y-o ch f Compton Place-Barboukh (Night Shift (USA))

E F Vaughan Saeed Manana

Placings:0 (7106)

2009: 8^{0}SD,

	Starts	1st	2nd	3rd	Win & Pl
Career Total (Turf)	0	0	0	0	
Career Total (AW)	1	0	0	0	

Going (Turf): **Sf: 0-0 GS: 0-0 Gd: 0-0 GF: 0-0 Fm: 0-0**
Distance: 5f/6f: 0-0 7f-8f: 0-1 9f-13f: 0-0 14f+: 0-0
Track : LH: 0-0 RH: 0-1 Tight: 0-0 Gall: 0-0
Aids: Bl: 0-0 Vi: 0-0 Tstrap: 0-0 Ckp: 0-0
Best Rating: **16** 10/09 Kemp 1m stand

Auction Belle

(88) (36)48

4-y-o b f Auction House (USA)-Island Colony (USA) (Pleasant Colony (USA))

R Curtis R P Traffic Management Ltd

Placings:5-506 (0249)

2009: 12^{5}SS, 11^{0}SD, 16^{6}SD,

	Starts	1st	2nd	3rd	Win & Pl
Career Total (Turf)	1	0	0	0	0
Career Total (AW)	3	0	0	0	0

Going (Turf): **Sf: 0-0 GS: 0-1 Gd: 0-0 GF: 0-0 Fm: 0-0**
Distance: 5f/6f: 0-0 7f-8f: 0-0 9f-13f: 0-3 14f+: 0-1
Track : LH: 0-4 RH: 0-0 Tight: 0-2 Gall: 0-0
Aids: Bl: 0-0 Vi: 0-0 Tstrap: 0-0 Ckp: 0-0
Best Rating: **48** 8/08 Bath 1m3f144y gd-sft

Audacity Of Hope

104 101

2-y-o b c Red Ransom (USA)-Aliena (IRE) (Grand Lodge (USA))

P J McBride Four Winds Racing

Placings:31201143 **(7030)**

2009: 5^{3}GF, 6^{1}GF, 7^{2}GS, 7^{0}GF, 7^{1}GF, 7^{1}GF, 7^{4}GF, 7^{3}S,

	Starts	1st	2nd	3rd	Win & Pl
Career Total (Turf)	8	3	1	2	31450

93 9/09 NmkR 7f (0-95)H G-F £7771
91 9/09 Donc 7f (0-95) G-F £9714
75 6/09 Ripn 6f G-F £3238
Total win prize-money £20723

Going (Turf): Sf: 0-1 GS: 0-1 Gd: 0-0 **GF: 3-6** Fm: 0-0
Distance: 5f/6f: 1-2 **7f-8f: 2-6** 9f-13f: 0-0 14f+: 0-0
Track : LH: 0-0 RH: 0-1 Tight: 0-0 Gall: 0-0
Aids: Bl: 0-0 Vi: 0-0 Tstrap: 0-0 Ckp: 0-0
Best Rating: **101** 10/09 Newb 7f soft

Very useful; effective at 6f-7f; handles most ground; has worn a tongue tie.

Audemar (IRE)

93(105) (90)71

3-y-o ch c Exceed And Excel (AUS)-Bathe In Light (USA) (Sunshine Forever (USA))

E F Vaughan Gute Freunde Partnership

Placings:21-64104413 **(6773)**

2009: 5^{6}G, 8^{4}SD, 7^{1}SD, 7^{0}GF, 7^{4}SD, 8^{4}SD, 8^{1}SD, 8^{3}SD,

	Starts	1st	2nd	3rd	Win & Pl
Career Total (Turf)	2	0	0	0	0
Career Total (AW)	8	3	1	1	16253

90 10/09 Kemp 1m (0-80)H STD £4727
83 8/09 Kemp 7f (0-80)H STD £4727
73 10/08 GrLe 6f STD £3885
Total win prize-money £13340

Going (Turf): **Sf: 0-0 GS: 0-0 Gd: 0-1 GF: 0-1 Fm: 0-0**
Distance: 5f/6f: 1-3 **7f-8f: 2-7** 9f-13f: 0-0 14f+: 0-0
Track : LH: 1-1 **RH: 2-7** Tight: 0-0 **Gall: 1-1**
Aids: Bl: 0-0 Vi: 0-0 Tstrap: 0-0 Ckp: 0-0
Best Rating: **90** 10/09 Kemp 1m stand

Fair; effective over 7f-1m; acts on Polytrack.

Audrinna (IRE)

89 50

2-y-o b f Oratorio (IRE)-Zvezda (USA) (Nureyev (USA))

M G Quinlan Dr Angelo Macchi

Placings:02 **(3626)**

2009: 6^{0}GF, 5^{2}G,

	Starts	1st	2nd	3rd	Win & Pl
Career Total (Turf)	2	0	1	0	578

Going (Turf): **Sf: 0-0 GS: 0-0 Gd: 0-1 GF: 0-1 Fm: 0-0**
Distance: 5f/6f: 0-2 7f-8f: 0-0 9f-13f: 0-0 14f+: 0-0
Track : LH: 0-0 RH: 0-0 Tight: 0-0 Gall: 0-0
Aids: Bl: 0-0 Vi: 0-0 Tstrap: 0-0 Ckp: 0-0
Best Rating: **50** 7/09 Leic 5f218y good

Plating class; has worn a tongue tie.

August Days (IRE)

95(87) (46)56

3-y-o ch f Noverre (USA)-Vitesse (IRE) (Royal Academy (USA))

J Pearce Pump & Plant Services Ltd

Placings:6003310-6000060 **(5367)**

2009: 5^{6}GF, 5^{0}GF, 5^{0}GF, 9^{0}G, 8^{0}F, 8^{6}GS, 9^{0}F,

	Starts	1st	2nd	3rd	Win & Pl
Career Total (Turf)	12	1	0	1	2336
Career Total (AW)	2	0	0	1	302

56 8/08 Wind 5f10y G-F £2047
Total win prize-money £2047

Going (Turf): Sf: 0-0 GS: 0-2 Gd: 0-2 **GF: 1-6** Fm: 0-2
Distance: **5f/6f: 1-9** 7f-8f: 0-1 9f-13f: 0-4 14f+: 0-0
Track : LH: 0-7 RH: 0-1 Tight: 0-5 **Gall: 1-3**
Aids: Bl: 0-0 Vi: 0-0 Tstrap: 0-0 Ckp: 0-0
Best Rating: **56** 8/08 Wind 5f10y gd-fm

Moderate filly; effective at 5f; acts on fast but handles easy ground.

August Gale (USA)

(101) (83)66

4-y-o b g Storm Cat (USA)-Lady Bonanza (USA) (Seeking The Gold (USA))

M W Easterby Matthew Green

Placings:2032320000000-0 **(1039)**

2009: 7^{0}SD,

	Starts	1st	2nd	3rd	Win & Pl
Career Total (Turf)	5	0	1	1	1590
Career Total (AW)	9	0	2	1	2432

Going (Turf): **Sf: 0-1 GS: 0-1 Gd: 0-0 GF: 0-3 Fm: 0-0**
Distance: 5f/6f: 0-0 7f-8f: 0-9 9f-13f: 0-5 14f+: 0-0
Track : LH: 0-11 RH: 0-2 Tight: 0-8 Gall: 0-1
Aids: Bl: 0-2 Vi: 0-0 Tstrap: 0-0 Ckp: 0-0
Best Rating: **83** 5/08 GrLe 1m stand

Fair colt; stays 1m and acts on Polytrack.

Augusta Gold (USA)

(100) (68)68

3-y-o b c Medaglia D'Oro (USA)-Golden Gorse (USA) (His Majesty (USA))

Mme L Braem (N P Littmoden 27/3) Denvic Stables

Placings:603-52200 **(0978)**

2009: 10^{5}SD, 11^{2}SD, 12^{2}SD, 7^{0}S, 10^{0}S,

	Starts	1st	2nd	3rd	Win & Pl
Career Total (Turf)	3	0	0	0	152
Career Total (AW)	5	0	2	1	2089

Going (Turf): **Sf: 0-2 GS: 0-0 Gd: 0-1 GF: 0-0 Fm: 0-0**
Distance: 5f/6f: 0-0 7f-8f: 0-4 9f-13f: 0-4 14f+: 0-0
Track : LH: 0-4 RH: 0-3 Tight: 0-1 Gall: 0-0
Aids: Bl: 0-5 Vi: 0-0 Tstrap: 0-0 Ckp: 0-0
Best Rating: **68** 3/09 Sthl 1m4f stand

Fair; effective at around 1m4f; acts on Fibresand.

Augustus John (IRE)

83(106) (78)73

6-y-o gr g Danehill (USA)-Rizerie (FR) (Highest Honor (FR))

R Brotherton (S Parr 13/2) Arthur Clayton

Placings:05/6/2222/0003300332-33221320045322 **(7785)**

2009: 11^{3}SD, 12^{3}SD, 12^{2}SD, 12^{2}SD, 13^{1}SD, 14^{3}SD, 16^{2}SD, 16^{0}SD, 13^{0}GF, 12^{4}GF, 12^{5}SD, 12^{3}SD, 13^{2}SD, 13^{2}SD,

	Starts	1st	2nd	3rd	Win & Pl
Career Total (Turf)	8	0	1	0	2553
Career Total (AW)	23	1	9	8	12890

74 3/09 Wolv 1m5f194y (0-70)H STD £2307
Total win prize-money £2308

Going (Turf): **Sf: 0-0 GS: 0-2 Gd: 0-4 GF: 0-2 Fm: 0-0**
Distance: 5f/6f: 0-2 7f-8f: 0-4 9f-13f: 0-14 **14f+: 1-11**
Track : **LH: 1-26** RH: 0-4 **Tight: 1-18** Gall: 0-4
Aids: Bl: 0-1 Vi: 0-1 Tstrap: 0-3 Ckp: 0-3
Best Rating: **82** 2/07 Wolv 1m1f103y stand

Modest; effective up to 2m; acts on good ground; goes on sand; has worn cheekpiece and a visor.

Auld Arty (FR)

91(98) (77)72

3-y-o b/br g Dansili-Provisoire (USA) (Gone West (USA))

T G Mills Kerr & Lillie Partnership

Placings:532622-21360000 **(5283)**

2009: 6^{2}SD, 6^{1}SD, 7^{3}SD, 7^{6}SD, 6^{0}F, 7^{0}GF, 6^{0}F, 7^{0}GF,

	Starts	1st	2nd	3rd	Win & Pl
Career Total (Turf)	8	0	1	1	2023
Career Total (AW)	6	1	3	1	5675

69 1/09 Ling 6f STD £2729
Total win prize-money £2730

Going (Turf): **Sf: 0-1 GS: 0-1 Gd: 0-1 GF: 0-3 Fm: 0-2**
Distance: **5f/6f: 1-5** 7f-8f: 0-9 9f-13f: 0-0 14f+: 0-0
Track : **LH: 1-5** RH: 0-2 **Tight: 1-3** Gall: 0-2
Aids: Bl: 0-0 Vi: 0-0 Tstrap: 0-5 Ckp: 0-5
Best Rating: **77** 2/09 Kemp 7f stand

Fair; effective over 6f-7f; acts on easy ground; goes on Polytrack.

Aultcharn (FR)

95 71

2-y-o b c Kyllachy-Nuit Sans Fin (FR) (Lead On Time (USA))

B J Meehan Brimacombe,McNally,Vinciguerra,Sangster

Placings:06 **(7029)**

2009: 6^{0}G, 8^{6}S,

	Starts	1st	2nd	3rd	Win & Pl
Career Total (Turf)	2	0	0	0	0

Going (Turf): **Sf: 0-1 GS: 0-0 Gd: 0-1 GF: 0-0 Fm: 0-0**
Distance: 5f/6f: 0-0 7f-8f: 0-2 9f-13f: 0-0 14f+: 0-0
Track : LH: 0-0 RH: 0-0 Tight: 0-0 Gall: 0-0
Aids: Bl: 0-0 Vi: 0-0 Tstrap: 0-0 Ckp: 0-0
Best Rating: **71** 10/09 Newb 1m soft

Aunt Nicola

99(89) (71)82

3-y-o b f Reel Buddy (USA)-Night Gypsy (Mind Games)

M L W Bell R P B Michaelson, J Thompson & M Caine

Placings:213-4006023 **(5471)**

2009: 7^{4}GF, 6^{0}GS, 6^{0}G, 7^{6}GF, 7^{0}S, 6^{2}G, 6^{3}GF,

	Starts	1st	2nd	3rd	Win & Pl
Career Total (Turf)	9	1	1	2	9914
Career Total (AW)	1	0	1	0	524

76 6/08 Gdwd 6f G-F £3885
Total win prize-money £3886

Going (Turf): Sf: 0-1 GS: 0-1 Gd: 0-2 **GF: 1-4** Fm: 0-1
Distance: **5f/6f: 1-6** 7f-8f: 0-4 9f-13f: 0-0 14f+: 0-0
Track : LH: 0-1 RH: 0-0 Tight: 0-0 Gall: 0-0

Aids: Bl: 0-0 Vi: 0-0 Tstrap: 0-0 Ckp: 0-0
Best Rating: 82 6/08 NmkJ 6f firm

Fair; effective at 6f; acts on fast ground.

Auntie Craik

(89) (35)
5-y-o b m Cotation-Mrs Poppyford (Mistertopogigo (IRE))
S Gollings Dr L G Parry

Placings:0 (7671)
2009: 8^{0}SD,

	Starts	1st	2nd	3rd	Win & Pl
Career Total (Turf)	0	0	0	0	
Career Total (AW)	1	0	0	0	

Going (Turf): Sf: 0-0 GS: 0-0 Gd: 0-0 GF: 0-0 Fm: 0-0
Distance: 5f/6f: 0-0 7f-8f: 0-0 9f-13f: 0-1 14f+: 0-0
Track : LH: 0-1 RH: 0-0 Tight: 0-1 Gall: 0-0
Aids: Bl: 0-0 Vi: 0-0 Tstrap: 0-0 Ckp: 0-0
Best Rating: 35 12/09 Wolv 1m141y stand

Auntie Mame

102(105) (68)70
5-y-o b m Diktat-Mother Molly (USA) (Irish River (FR))
D J Coakley Finders Keepers Partnership

Placings:6/642521/11523240-31 (2517)
2009: 10^{3}GF, 11^{1}F,

	Starts	1st	2nd	3rd	Win & Pl
Career Total (Turf)	8	3	2	1	9027
Career Total (AW)	9	1	2	1	3738

70	5/09	Bath	1m3f144y	(0-65)H	FRM	£2266
63	6/08	Bath	1m2f46y	(0-70)H	GD	£2590
65	5/08	Bath	1m2f46y	(0-65)H	G-F	£2047
44	12/07	Kemp	1m3f		STD	£2047

Total win prize-money £8952

Going (Turf): Sf: 0-0 GS: 0-1 **Gd: 1-3 GF: 1-3 Fm: 1-1**
Distance: 5f/6f: 0-0 7f-8f: 0-2 **9f-13f: 4-15** 14f+: 0-0
Track : **LH: 3-9** RH: 1-6 **Tight: 3-11** Gall: 0-1
Aids: Bl: 0-0 Vi: 0-0 Tstrap: 0-0 Ckp: 0-0
Best Rating: 70 5/09 Bath 1m3f144y firm

Modest; stays 1m4f; acts on a sound surface; goes on Polytrack; has a good record at Bath.

Aunty Betty (IRE)

70 20
2-y-o b f Camacho-Jina (IRE) (Petardia)
M S Tuck Luckley Arms Partnership

Placings:0 (4851)
2009: 6^{0}GF,

	Starts	1st	2nd	3rd	Win & Pl
Career Total (Turf)	1	0	0	0	

Going (Turf): Sf: 0-0 GS: 0-0 Gd: 0-0 GF: 0-1 Fm: 0-0
Distance: 5f/6f: 0-1 7f-8f: 0-0 9f-13f: 0-0 14f+: 0-0
Track : LH: 0-0 RH: 0-0 Tight: 0-0 Gall: 0-1
Aids: Bl: 0-0 Vi: 0-0 Tstrap: 0-0 Ckp: 0-0
Best Rating: 20 8/09 Wind 6f gd-fm

Aura

(87) (39)47
4-y-o b f Barathea (IRE)-Finger Of Light (Green Desert (USA))
H J L Dunlop Barry Marsden

Placings:0/0000000-0 (0090)
2009: 11^{0}SD,

	Starts	1st	2nd	3rd	Win & Pl
Career Total (Turf)	4	0	0	0	
Career Total (AW)	5	0	0	0	

Going (Turf): Sf: 0-0 GS: 0-0 Gd: 0-3 GF: 0-1 Fm: 0-0
Distance: 5f/6f: 0-0 7f-8f: 0-3 9f-13f: 0-6 14f+: 0-0
Track : LH: 0-6 RH: 0-2 Tight: 0-2 Gall: 0-2
Aids: Bl: 0-2 Vi: 0-0 Tstrap: 0-0 Ckp: 0-0
Best Rating: 47 11/07 NmkR 7f good

Cost 115,000gns; sister to Far Hope, a smart, multiple winner over 6f to 1m in Italy, and to a winner in Greece.

Aura Of Calm (IRE)

70(82) (43)63
7-y-o ch g Grand Lodge (USA)-Penis Of Joy (IRE) (Rainbow Quest (USA))
Ronald O'Leary Mrs Ronald O'Leary

Placings:5/00000/0110/0040/000-P00 (3035)
2009: 11^{P}G, 14^{0}GF, 12^{0}GS,

	Starts	1st	2nd	3rd	Win & Pl
Career Total (Turf)	18	2	0	0	9905
Career Total (AW)	2	0	0	0	

70	9/06	Cork	1m6f	(40-70)H	FRM	£4765
70	9/06	Clon	1m4f	(40-70)H	FRM	£4765

Total win prize-money £9532

Going (Turf): Sf: 0-3 GS: 0-1 Gd: 0-4 GF: 0-5 **Fm: 2-2**
Distance: 5f/6f: 0-1 7f-8f: 0-4 9f-13f: 1-12 14f+: 1-3
Track : LH: 0-5 **RH: 2-13** Tight: 0-4 Gall: 0-1
Aids: Bl: 0-2 Vi: 0-0 Tstrap: 0-0 Ckp: 0-0
Best Rating: 70 9/06 Cork 1m6f firm

Aureate

100(105) (95)90
5-y-o ch g Jade Robbery (USA)-Anne D'Autriche (IRE) (Rainbow Quest (USA))
B Ellison The Seasiders Again

Placings:2331/36150/420530-31061210304 (7137)
2009: 12^{3}SD, 14^{1}SD, 12^{0}G, 12^{6}GF, 12^{1}SD, 12^{2}SD, 12^{1}SD, 11^{0}GF, 11^{3}S, 13^{0}G, 13^{4}SD,

	Starts	1st	2nd	3rd	Win & Pl
Career Total (Turf)	19	1	2	5	15602
Career Total (AW)	7	4	1	1	13539

72	6/09	Wolv	1m4f50y		STD	£1977
83	5/09	Sthl	1m4f		STD	£1977
95	1/09	Sthl	1m6f	(0-85)H	STD	£5180
93	6/07	Ches	1m4f66y	(0-85)H	SFT	£5505
79	11/06	Wolv	1m141y		STD	£2730

Total win prize-money £17372

Going (Turf): **Sf: 1-5** GS: 0-3 Gd: 0-7 GF: 0-4 Fm: 0-0
Distance: 5f/6f: 0-0 7f-8f: 0-3 **9f-13f: 4-17** 14f+: 1-6
Track : **LH: 5-20** RH: 0-5 **Tight: 3-14** Gall: 0-2
Aids: Bl: 0-1 Vi: 0-0 Tstrap: 0-0 Ckp: 0-0
Best Rating: 95 1/09 Sthl 1m6f stand

Fair; effective at around 1m4f; acts on most ground on turf; goes on Fibresand and Polytrack; likes to race prominently.

Aurora Lights

(61)
2-y-o ch f Fantastic Light (USA)-Sweet Revival (Claude Monet (USA))
R A Fahey R A Fahey

Placings:0 (7843)
2009: 5^{0}SD,

	Starts	1st	2nd	3rd	Win & Pl
Career Total (Turf)	0	0	0	0	
Career Total (AW)	1	0	0	0	

Going (Turf): Sf: 0-0 GS: 0-0 Gd: 0-0 GF: 0-0 Fm: 0-0
Distance: 5f/6f: 0-1 7f-8f: 0-0 9f-13f: 0-0 14f+: 0-0
Track : LH: 0-1 RH: 0-0 Tight: 0-1 Gall: 0-0
Aids: Bl: 0-0 Vi: 0-0 Tstrap: 0-0 Ckp: 0-0

Aurora Sky (IRE)

99(90) (70)75
3-y-o gr f Hawk Wing (USA)-To The Skies (USA) (Sky Classic (CAN))
J Akehurst M Chandler

Placings:23-442505 (5591)
2009: 7^{4}G, 7^{4}GF, 8^{2}G, 7^{5}GF, 8^{0}SD, 7^{5}GS,

	Starts	1st	2nd	3rd	Win & Pl
Career Total (Turf)	5	0	1	0	1438
Career Total (AW)	3	0	1	1	1638

Going (Turf): Sf: 0-0 GS: 0-1 Gd: 0-2 GF: 0-2 Fm: 0-0
Distance: 5f/6f: 0-0 7f-8f: 0-7 9f-13f: 0-1 14f+: 0-0
Track : LH: 0-3 RH: 0-3 Tight: 0-2 Gall: 0-1
Aids: Bl: 0-0 Vi: 0-0 Tstrap: 0-0 Ckp: 0-0
Best Rating: 75 7/09 Epsm 1m114y good

Aurorian (IRE)

105(105) (87)88
3-y-o b g Fantastic Light (USA)-Aurelia (Rainbow Quest (USA))
R Hannon Martin Mitchell

Placings:01426-656000541 (7628)
2009: 10^{6}GS, 10^{5}S, 10^{6}G, 8^{0}GF, 10^{0}G, 11^{0}G, 10^{5}G, 10^{4}SD, 12^{1}SD,

	Starts	1st	2nd	3rd	Win & Pl
Career Total (Turf)	11	1	0	0	5970
Career Total (AW)	3	1	1	0	7131

83	12/09	Ling	1m4f	(0-85)H	STD	£4727
81	9/08	Ling	7f		GD	£3238

Total win prize-money £7965

Going (Turf): Sf: 0-2 GS: 0-1 **Gd: 1-7** GF: 0-1 Fm: 0-0
Distance: 5f/6f: 0-0 7f-8f: 1-6 9f-13f: 1-8 14f+: 0-0
Track : **LH: 1-4** RH: 0-6 **Tight: 1-4** Gall: 0-3
Aids: Bl: 0-0 Vi: 0-0 Tstrap: 0-0 Ckp: 0-0
Best Rating: 88 5/09 Newb 1m2f6y soft

Fair; stays 1m2f; acts on good ground and on Polytrack.

Ausonius

87(101) (62)46
3-y-o b g Kyllachy-Baileys Silver (USA) (Marlin (USA))
L M Cumani Robert Tullett & Partners

Placings:00-00U2 (7022)
2009: 7^{0}GS, 6^{0}GF, 10^{U}SS, 10^{2}SD,

	Starts	1st	2nd	3rd	Win & Pl
Career Total (Turf)	4	0	0	0	

Career Total (AW)	2	0	1	0	605

Going (Turf): Sf: 0-1 GS: 0-1 Gd: 0-1 GF: 0-1 Fm: 0-0
Distance: 5f/6f: 0-0 7f-8f: 0-4 9f-13f: 0-2 14f+: 0-0
Track : LH: 0-2 RH: 0-1 Tight: 0-1 Gall: 0-0
Aids: Bl: 0-0 Vi: 0-0 Tstrap: 0-0 Ckp: 0-0
Best Rating: 62 10/09 Kemp 1m2f stand

Moderate; stays 1m2f; acts on Polytrack.

Aussie Blue (IRE)

100(95) (60)69

5-y-o b g Bahamian Bounty-Luanshya (First Trump)
R M Whitaker G F Pemberton

Placings:00/6626350332/002451000036-0000215206423000 (7236)
2009: 8^{0}GF, 8^{0}F, 8^{0}GF, 8^{0}G, 7^{2}GF, 8^{1}G, 8^{5}GF, 8^{2}G, 8^{0}S, 8^{6}GF, 7^{4}G, 8^{2}GF, 8^{3}GF, 8^{0}GF, 7^{0}SD, 8^{0}SD,

	Starts	1st	2nd	3rd	Win & Pl
Career Total (Turf)	36	2	6	4	14309
Career Total (AW)	4	0	0	1	353

65 6/09 Rdcr 1m (0-75)H GD £2590
69 6/08 Pont 1m4y (0-75)H GD £3238
Total win prize-money £5828

Going (Turf): Sf: 0-3 GS: 0-5 Gd: 2-11 GF: 0-15 Fm: 0-2
Distance: 5f/6f: 0-5 7f-8f: 1-23 9f-13f: 1-12 14f+: 0-0
Track : LH: 1-19 RH: 0-4 Tight: 0-6 Gall: 0-2
Aids: Bl: 0-4 Vi: 0-1 Tstrap: 0-1 Ckp: 0-1
Best Rating: 69 8/09 Rdcr 1m gd-fm

Modest; stays 1m; acts on fast ground; goes on Fibresand.

Australia Day (IRE)

109(107) (98)106

6-y-o gr g Key Of Luck (USA)-Atalina (FR) (Linamix (FR))
P R Webber Samantha & Emma McQuiston Partnership

Placings:35/15/600/03411022-513042 (6302)
2009: 10^{5}SD, 10^{1}G, 10^{3}G, 9^{0}G, 10^{4}G, 12^{2}GF,

	Starts	1st	2nd	3rd	Win & Pl
Career Total (Turf)	18	4	2	3	38163
Career Total (AW)	3	0	1	0	2239

104 6/09 Sand 1m2f7y (0-90)H GD £7477
102 7/08 Sand 1m2f7y (0-90)H G-F £8095
86 6/08 Wind 1m2f7y (0-80)H G-F £4533
76 5/06 Limk 1m50y G-Y £7148
Total win prize-money £27253

Going (Turf): Sf: 0-0 GS: 0-0 Gd: 1-8 GF: 2-9 Fm: 0-0
Distance: 5f/6f: 0-0 7f-8f: 0-7 9f-13f: 4-14 14f+: 0-0
Track : LH: 0-5 RH: 3-11 Tight: 1-6 Gall: 0-4
Aids: Bl: 0-0 Vi: 0-0 Tstrap: 0-0 Ckp: 0-0
Best Rating: 106 7/09 Sand 1m2f7y good

Very useful; effective at 1m2f; acts on good and faster ground and on Polytrack; front runner.

Authentic

85 49

4-y-o ch g Pivotal-Red Passion (USA) (Seeking The Gold (USA))
L M Cumani (M Gasparini 12/7) Aston House Stud

Placings:135040-40461120 (6094)
2009: 7^{4}G, 7^{0}HY, 8^{4}G, 7^{6}HY, 7^{1}GF, 7^{1}S, 7^{2}G, 8^{0}G,

	Starts	1st	2nd	3rd	Win & Pl
Career Total (Turf)	14	3	1	1	41800

6/09 Var 7f110y H SFT £14563
5/09 Siro 7f110y G-F £8755
4/08 Capa 7f110y HVY £5515
Total win prize-money £28833

Going (Turf): Sf: 2-7 GS: 0-0 Gd: 0-5 GF: 1-1 Fm: 0-0
Distance: 5f/6f: 0-1 7f-8f: 3-12 9f-13f: 0-1 14f+: 0-0
Track : LH: 0-1 RH: 0-0 Tight: 0-0 Gall: 0-0
Aids: Bl: 0-0 Vi: 0-0 Tstrap: 0-0 Ckp: 0-0
Best Rating: 49 9/09 Ayr 1m good

Autocracy

83(92) (71)55

2-y-o b c Green Desert (USA)-Imperial Bailiwick (IRE) (Imperial Frontier (USA))
W J Haggas Mr & Mrs G Middlebrook

Placings:033 (6802)
2009: 5^{0}GF, 5^{3}GS, 5^{3}SD,

	Starts	1st	2nd	3rd	Win & Pl
Career Total (Turf)	2	0	0	1	819
Career Total (AW)	1	0	0	1	530

Going (Turf): Sf: 0-0 GS: 0-1 Gd: 0-0 GF: 0-1 Fm: 0-0
Distance: 5f/6f: 0-3 7f-8f: 0-0 9f-13f: 0-0 14f+: 0-0
Track : LH: 0-1 RH: 0-0 Tight: 0-1 Gall: 0-0
Aids: Bl: 0-0 Vi: 0-0 Tstrap: 0-0 Ckp: 0-0
Best Rating: 71 10/09 Wolv 5f216y stand

Half-brother to several good winners, most notably Group 1 winner Reverence; promise on debut over 5f on fast ground.

Autumn Blades (IRE)

103(112) (86)83

4-y-o ch g Daggers Drawn (USA)-September Tide (IRE) (Thatching)
A Bailey John Stocker

Placings:440/2224113506024-4021323400033430313622332141 (7891)
2009: 7^{4}SD, 7^{0}SD, 8^{2}SD, 7^{1}SD, 7^{3}SD, 7^{2}GF, 7^{3}SD, 7^{4}GF, 7^{0}GF, 7^{0}S, 7^{0}GF, 7^{3}SF, 7^{3}GS, 7^{4}G, 7^{3}SD, 6^{0}G, 7^{3}SD, 6^{1}GF, 7^{3}SD, 8^{6}GF, 7^{2}SD, 7^{2}SD, 7^{3}SD,

	Starts	1st	2nd	3rd	Win & Pl
Career Total (Turf)	16	2	1	2	9197
Career Total (AW)	28	4	8	8	30830

12/09 Ling 7f (0-80)H STD £4727
84 12/09 Wolv 7f32y (0-85)H STD £5046
79 9/09 Brig 6f209y G-F £1942
85 3/09 Sthl 7f (0-75)H STD £2729
80 7/08 Kemp 7f (0-75)H STD £3238
49 6/08 Folk 7f G-F £2388
Total win prize-money £20072

Going (Turf): Sf: 0-1 GS: 0-1 Gd: 0-4 GF: 2-10 Fm: 0-0
Distance: 5f/6f: 0-5 7f-8f: 6-38 9f-13f: 0-1 14f+: 0-0
Track : LH: 4-20 RH: 1-11 Tight: 2-14 Gall: 0-0
Aids: Bl: 1-2 Vi: 0-1 Tstrap: 3-13 Ckp: 3-13
Best Rating: 86 12/09 Kemp 7f stand

Fair; stays 7f; handles fast ground; goes on sand; has worn blinkers and cheekpieces.

Autumn Charm

89(97) (46)44

4-y-o ch f Reel Buddy (USA)-Eurolink Cafe (Grand Lodge (USA))
Lucinda Featherstone J Roundtree

Placings:4501/41250600004-000000046 (5327)
2009: 11^{0}SD, 13^{0}SD, 14^{0}SD, 12^{0}SD, 10^{0}GS, 8^{0}GF, 11^{0}SD, 15^{4}G, 11^{6}SD,

	Starts	1st	2nd	3rd	Win & Pl
Career Total (Turf)	8	0	0	0	168
Career Total (AW)	16	2	1	0	4563

60 1/08 Sthl 7f STD £1911
54 12/07 Sthl 7f SS £2047
Total win prize-money £3959

Going (Turf): Sf: 0-2 GS: 0-2 Gd: 0-2 GF: 0-2 Fm: 0-0
Distance: 5f/6f: 0-1 7f-8f: 2-7 9f-13f: 0-13 14f+: 0-3
Track : LH: 2-19 RH: 0-4 Tight: 0-7 Gall: 0-3
Aids: Bl: 0-0 Vi: 0-2 Tstrap: 0-2 Ckp: 0-2
Best Rating: 60 1/08 Sthl 7f stand

Very moderate; stays 1m; acts on Fibresand.

Autumn Harvest

103 78

5-y-o b g Beat Hollow-Welsh Autumn (Tenby)
Jonjo O'Neill (A J McCabe 24/6) C H McGhie

Placings:6146 (2698)
2009: 12^{6}GF, 12^{1}G, 11^{4}GF, 12^{6}GS,

	Starts	1st	2nd	3rd	Win & Pl
Career Total (Turf)	4	1	0	0	4659

78 5/09 Thsk 1m4f GD £4274
Total win prize-money £4274

Going (Turf): Sf: 0-0 GS: 0-1 Gd: 1-1 GF: 0-2 Fm: 0-0
Distance: 5f/6f: 0-0 7f-8f: 0-0 9f-13f: 1-4 14f+: 0-0
Track : LH: 1-3 RH: 0-1 Tight: 1-2 Gall: 0-1
Aids: Bl: 0-0 Vi: 0-0 Tstrap: 0-0 Ckp: 0-0
Best Rating: 78 5/09 Carl 1m3f107y gd-fm

Fair; stays 1m4f and acts on good ground; bumper winner.

Autumn Morning (IRE)

97(96) (60)49

3-y-o b f Danetime (IRE)-Soviet Maid (IRE) (Soviet Star (USA))
P D Evans Mrs Sally Edwards

Placings:00205513-550254040046 (3502)
2009: 8^{5}SD, 9^{5}SD, 8^{0}SD, 9^{2}SD, 8^{5}SD, 8^{4}SD, 8^{0}SD, 8^{4}G, 8^{0}F, 8^{0}G, 8^{4}F, 7^{6}GF,

	Starts	1st	2nd	3rd	Win & Pl
Career Total (Turf)	8	0	0	0	289
Career Total (AW)	12	1	2	1	4874

57 12/08 Wolv 1m141y STD £3070
Total win prize-money £3071

Going (Turf): Sf: 0-1 GS: 0-2 Gd: 0-2 GF: 0-1 Fm: 0-2
Distance: 5f/6f: 0-5 7f-8f: 0-3 9f-13f: 1-12 14f+: 0-0
Track : LH: 1-14 RH: 0-1 Tight: 1-13 Gall: 0-2
Aids: Bl: 0-0 Vi: 0-1 Tstrap: 0-0 Ckp: 0-0
Best Rating: 60 1/09 Wolv 1m141y stand

Modest; stays at least 1m and acts on Polytrack.

Ava Doll

63(66) (14)19

2-y-o b f Statue Of Liberty (USA)-Foolish Gift (FR) (Barathea (IRE))
J R Jenkins David Bryans & Irene Hampson

Placings:000 (7388)
2009: 8^{0}G, 7^{0}G, 8^{0}SD,

	Starts	1st	2nd	3rd	Win & Pl
Career Total (Turf)	2	0	0	0	
Career Total (AW)	1	0	0	0	

Going (Turf): **Sf: 0-0 GS: 0-0 Gd: 0-2 GF: 0-0 Fm: 0-0**
Distance: 5f/6f: 0-0 7f-8f: 0-2 9f-13f: 0-1 14f+: 0-0
Track : LH: 0-1 RH: 0-0 Tight: 0-1 Gall: 0-0
Aids: Bl: 0-0 Vi: 0-0 Tstrap: 0-0 Ckp: 0-0
Best Rating: 19 10/09 NmkR 7f good

Ava's World (IRE)

89(95) (63)**33**
5-y-o b m Desert Prince (IRE)-Taibhseach (USA) (Secreto (USA))
Peter Grayson Peter Grayson Racing Clubs Limited

Placings:014006/0000/046-646 **(4621)**
2009: 5^{6}GF, 5^{4}GF, 5^{6}G,

	Starts	1st	2nd	3rd	Win & Pl
Career Total (Turf)	7	1	0	0	4536
Career Total (AW)	9	0	0	0	0

73 9/06 Catt 5f212y G-F £3886
Total win prize-money £3886

Going (Turf): Sf: 0-0 GS: 0-2 Gd: 0-2 **GF: 1-3** Fm: 0-0
Distance: **5f/6f: 1-12** 7f-8f: 0-4 9f-13f: 0-0 14f+: 0-0
Track : **LH: 1-11** RH: 0-2 **Tight: 1-11** Gall: 0-0
Aids: Bl: 0-1 Vi: 0-0 Tstrap: 0-0 Ckp: 0-0
Best Rating: 82 10/06 Catt 7f good

Modest filly who is a habitual slow starter; disappointing since winning 6f juvenile maiden at Catterick September 2006; suited by 6f or 7f on a sound surface.

Ave

108(101) (88)**109**
3-y-o b f Danehill Dancer (IRE)-Anna Amalia (IRE) (In The Wings)
Sir Michael Stoute Plantation Stud

Placings:410-312110 **(6853)**
2009: 8^{3}GF, 8^{1}S, 10^{2}G, 9^{1}GF, 9^{1}GF, 12^{0}G,

	Starts	1st	2nd	3rd	Win & Pl
Career Total (Turf)	8	3	1	1	99855
Career Total (AW)	1	1	0	0	4695

106 9/09 Gowr 1m1f100y G-F £50485
104 8/09 Sals 1m1f198y G-F £28385
100 7/09 Sals 1m (0-95)H SFT £9969
88 9/08 Kemp 7f STD £4695
Total win prize-money £93535

Going (Turf): Sf: 1-1 GS: 0-0 Gd: 0-3 **GF: 2-4** Fm: 0-0
Distance: 5f/6f: 0-0 7f-8f: 2-5 9f-13f: 2-4 14f+: 0-0
Track : LH: 0-1 **RH: 3-4 Tight: 1-1** Gall: 0-2
Aids: Bl: 0-0 Vi: 0-0 Tstrap: 0-0 Ckp: 0-0
Best Rating: 109 7/09 York 1m2f88y good

Group-class; effective from 1m-1m2f; acts on Polytrack.

Avec Moi

86(92) (48)**48**
2-y-o b f Reset (AUS)-Pardon Moi (First Trump)
Mrs C A Dunnett Christine Dunnett Racing

Placings:040050040046354 **(7514)**
2009: 5^{0}GF, 5^{4}GF, 6^{0}SD, 5^{0}GF, 5^{5}SD, 6^{0}G, 5^{0}G, 5^{4}G, 5^{0}GF, 5^{0}GF, 5^{4}SD, 6^{6}S, 6^{3}SD, 6^{5}SD, 7^{4}SD,

	Starts	1st	2nd	3rd	Win & Pl
Career Total (Turf)	9	0	0	0	414
Career Total (AW)	6	0	0	1	373

Going (Turf): **Sf: 0-1 GS: 0-0 Gd: 0-3 GF: 0-5 Fm: 0-0**
Distance: 5f/6f: 0-12 7f-8f: 0-3 9f-13f: 0-0 14f+: 0-0
Track : LH: 0-4 RH: 0-1 Tight: 0-2 Gall: 0-0
Aids: Bl: 0-0 Vi: 0-0 Tstrap: 0-0 Ckp: 0-0
Best Rating: 48 7/09 Ling 5f stand

Aven Mac (IRE)

97(67) **48**
3-y-o ch f Indian Haven-Anamara (IRE) (Fairy King (USA))
N Bycroft N Bycroft

Placings:0004020-50025650 **(7272)**
2009: 8^{5}GF, 8^{0}G, 8^{0}GF, 9^{2}G, 12^{5}GF, 12^{6}GS, 11^{5}G, 12^{0}SD,

	Starts	1st	2nd	3rd	Win & Pl
Career Total (Turf)	14	0	2	0	1590
Career Total (AW)	1	0	0	0	

Going (Turf): **Sf: 0-4 GS: 0-2 Gd: 0-4 GF: 0-4 Fm: 0-0**
Distance: 5f/6f: 0-1 7f-8f: 0-6 9f-13f: 0-8 14f+: 0-0
Track : LH: 0-6 RH: 0-5 Tight: 0-4 Gall: 0-2
Aids: Bl: 0-0 Vi: 0-0 Tstrap: 0-5 Ckp: 0-5
Best Rating: 48 9/08 Rdcr 1m gd-sft

Very moderate; stays 1m and acts on easy ground; has worn cheekpieces.

Avenuesnalleyways (IRE)

(87) (63)
2-y-o b c Bertolini (USA)-Princess Mood (GER) (Muhtarram (USA))
R M Beckett Tony Perkins & James D Cameron

Placings:0 **(5311)**
2009: 6^{0}SD,

	Starts	1st	2nd	3rd	Win & Pl
Career Total (Turf)	0	0	0	0	
Career Total (AW)	1	0	0	0	

Going (Turf): **Sf: 0-0 GS: 0-0 Gd: 0-0 GF: 0-0 Fm: 0-0**
Distance: 5f/6f: 0-1 7f-8f: 0-0 9f-13f: 0-0 14f+: 0-0
Track : LH: 0-0 RH: 0-1 Tight: 0-0 Gall: 0-0
Aids: Bl: 0-0 Vi: 0-0 Tstrap: 0-0 Ckp: 0-0
Best Rating: 63 8/09 Kemp 6f stand

Averoo

101(94) (61)**71**
4-y-o br g Averti (IRE)-Roo (Rudimentary (USA))
M D Squance M D Squance

Placings:0502/000654130-00000212140 **(7062)**
2009: 6^{0}SD, 7^{0}G, 6^{0}GF, 6^{0}G, 6^{0}S, 6^{2}GF, 6^{1}GF, 6^{2}GF, 7^{1}GF, 7^{4}SF, 7^{0}GF,

	Starts	1st	2nd	3rd	Win & Pl
Career Total (Turf)	19	3	3	1	10877
Career Total (AW)	5	0	0	0	0

67 10/09 Leic 7f9y (0-70)H G-F £2590
63 8/09 Rdcr 6f (0-55)H G-F £2388
71 6/08 Donc 6f (0-70)H GD £3238
Total win prize-money £8216

Going (Turf): Sf: 0-1 GS: 0-3 Gd: 1-6 **GF: 2-9** Fm: 0-0
Distance: **5f/6f: 2-8** 7f-8f: 1-15 9f-13f: 0-1 14f+: 0-0
Track : LH: 0-3 RH: 0-4 Tight: 0-2 Gall: 0-0
Aids: Bl. 0-0 Vi: 0-0 Tstrap: 3-12 Ckp: 3-12
Best Rating: 73 10/07 Catt 7f good

Modest; effective over 6f-1m; acts on fast ground; has worn cheekpieces.

Averroes (IRE)

101 **86**
2-y-o ch c Galileo (IRE)-Shapely (USA) (Alleged (USA))
C G Cox H E Sheikh Sultan Bin Khalifa Al Nahyan

Placings:415 **(6133a)**
2009: 7^{4}GF, 8^{1}G, 8^{5}G,

	Starts	1st	2nd	3rd	Win & Pl
Career Total (Turf)	3	1	0	0	8129

86 8/09 Chep 1m14y GD £3885
Total win prize-money £3886

Going (Turf): Sf: 0-0 GS: 0-0 **Gd: 1-2** GF: 0-1 Fm: 0-0
Distance: 5f/6f: 0-0 7f-8f: 0-2 **9f-13f: 1-1** 14f+: 0-0
Track : LH: 0-0 RH: 0-0 Tight: 0-0 Gall: 0-0
Aids: Bl: 0-0 Vi: 0-0 Tstrap: 0-0 Ckp: 0-0
Best Rating: 86 8/09 Chep 1m14y good

Avertis

103(103) (84)**84**
4-y-o b g Averti (IRE)-Double Stake (USA) (Kokand (USA))
Stef Liddiard Mrs Sally Doyle

Placings:1/13000310-330030010 **(7854)**
2009: 0^{3}GF, 0^{3}CD, 7^{0}SD, 0^{0}SD, 8^{3}SD, 8^{0}SD, 7^{0}SD, 8^{1}SD, 8^{0}SS,

	Starts	1st	2nd	3rd	Win & Pl
Career Total (Turf)	4	1	0	2	4118
Career Total (AW)	14	3	0	3	7040

82 11/08 Sthl 1m (0-75)H STD £2729
80 6/08 Yarm 1m3y (0-75)H G-F £2914
71 10/07 Kemp 7f STD £2047
Total win prize-money £7692

Going (Turf): Sf: 0-0 GS: 0-0 Gd: 0-0 **GF: 1-4** Fm: 0-0
Distance: 5f/6f: 0-0 **7f-8f: 3-12** 9f-13f: 1-6 14f+: 0-0
Track : **LH: 2-11** RH: 1-6 Tight: 0-5 Gall: 0-1
Aids: Bl: 0-1 Vi: 0-1 Tstrap: 0-1 Ckp: 0-1
Best Rating: 84 9/09 Sthl 1m stand

Fair; effective at around 1m; acts on sand; has worn a tongue-tie.

Avertitop

77 (68)**62**
4-y-o b g Averti (IRE)-Lucayan Belle (Cadeaux Genereux)
J Gallagher Adweb Ltd

Placings:62545/03-0 **(1047)**
2009: 7^{0}G,

	Starts	1st	2nd	3rd	Win & Pl
Career Total (Turf)	7	0	1	1	1252
Career Total (AW)	1	0	0	0	0

Going (Turf): **Sf: 0-0 GS: 0-0 Gd: 0-3 GF: 0-3 Fm: 0-1**
Distance: 5f/6f: 0-5 7f-8f: 0-2 9f-13f: 0-1 14f+: 0-0
Track : LH: 0-1 RH: 0-1 Tight: 0-0 Gall: 0-2
Aids: Bl: 0-0 Vi: 0-0 Tstrap: 0-0 Ckp: 0-0
Best Rating: 79 4/07 Wind 5f10y gd-fm

Fair; stays 7f; acts on fast ground.

Avertor

101 **86**
3-y-o b g Oasis Dream-Avessia (Averti (IRE))
R Charlton D J Deer

Placings:214 **(3362)**
2009: 6^{2}G, 5^{1}GS, 5^{4}GS,

	Starts	1st	2nd	3rd	Win & Pl
Career Total (Turf)	3	1	1	0	6577

76 6/09 Donc 5f G-S £5180
Total win prize-money £5181

Going (Turf): Sf: 0-0 **GS: 1-2** Gd: 0-1 GF: 0-0 Fm: 0-0
Distance: **5f/6f: 1-3** 7f-8f: 0-0 9f-13f: 0-0 14f+: 0-0
Track : LH: 0-1 RH: 0-0 Tight: 0-0 Gall: 0-0
Aids: Bl: 0-0 Vi: 0-0 Tstrap: 0-0 Ckp: 0-0
Best Rating: 86 5/09 Pont 6f good

Useful; suited by 5f-6f; acts on good ground.

Avertuoso

98 (77)**85**
5-y-o b g Averti (IRE)-First Musical (First Trump)
B Smart Pinnacle & Crossfields Racing

Placings:612602100/5350200**200**/5654000-005026 **(7119)**
2009: 5^{0}GF, 5^{0}G, 5^{5}G, 5^{0}GS, 5^{2}GF, 5^{6}GS,

	Starts	1st	2nd	3rd	Win & Pl
Career Total (Turf)	**30**	**2**	**5**	**1**	**21889**
Career Total (AW)	**2**	**0**	**0**	**0**	

92 7/06 York 5f G-F £7772
80 5/06 Muss 5f G-F £3238
Total win prize-money £11011

Going (Turf): Sf: 0-1 GS: 0-6 Gd: 0-9 **GF: 2-12** Fm: 0-2
Distance: **5f/6f: 2-31** 7f-8f: 0-1 9f-13f: 0-0 14f+: 0-0
Track : LH: 0-6 RH: 0-1 Tight: 0-3 Gall: 0-1
Aids: Bl: 0-0 Vi: 0-6 Tstrap: 0-0 Ckp: 0-0
Best Rating: 92 7/06 York 5f gd-fm

Modest; suited by 5f; acts on most ground; likes to race prominently.

Avery

(86) (18)**62**
5-y-o gr g Averti (IRE)-Bandanna (Bandmaster (USA))
R J Hodges R J Hodges

Placings:06400/**60500**/0-0 **(0104)**
2009: 7^{0}SD,

	Starts	1st	2nd	3rd	Win & Pl
Career Total (Turf)	**7**	**0**	**0**	**0**	**241**
Career Total (AW)	**5**	**0**	**0**	**0**	**0**

Going (Turf): Sf: 0-0 GS: 0-1 Gd: 0-1 GF: 0-2 Fm: 0-3
Distance: 5f/6f: 0-8 7f-8f: 0-4 9f-13f: 0-0 14f+: 0-0
Track : LH: 0-10 RH: 0-0 Tight: 0-4 Gall: 0-5
Aids: Bl: 0-1 Vi: 0-0 Tstrap: 0-0 Ckp: 0-0
Best Rating: 62 6/06 Bath 5f161y gd-fm

Aviate

(92) (76)
2-y-o b f Dansili-Emplane (USA) (Irish River (FR))
H R A Cecil K Abdulla

Placings:1 **(7450)**
2009: 8^{1}SD,

	Starts	1st	2nd	3rd	Win & Pl
Career Total (Turf)	**0**	**0**	**0**	**0**	
Career Total (AW)	**1**	**1**	**0**	**0**	**3238**

76 11/09 Kemp 1m STD £3238
Total win prize-money £3238

Going (Turf): Sf: 0-0 GS: 0-0 Gd: 0-0 GF: 0-0 Fm: 0-0
Distance: 5f/6f: 0-0 **7f-8f: 1-1** 9f-13f: 0-0 14f+: 0-0
Track : LH: 0-0 **RH: 1-1** Tight: 0-0 Gall: 0-0
Aids: Bl: 0-0 Vi: 0-0 Tstrap: 0-0 Ckp: 0-0
Best Rating: 76 11/09 Kemp 1m stand

Useful; stays 1m and acts on Polytrack.

Aviso (GER)

76(105) (76)**97**
5-y-o b g Tertullian (USA)-Akasma (GER) (Windwurf (GER))
B J Curley (A P Stringer 10/2) Curley Leisure

Placings:11134/500-**00600** **(4502)**
2009: 10^{0}SD, 8^{0}SD, 8^{6}SD, 10^{0}G, 8^{0}G,

	Starts	1st	2nd	3rd	Win & Pl
Career Total (Turf)	**9**	**3**	**0**	**1**	**87162**
Career Total (AW)	**4**	**0**	**0**	**0**	**0**

108 5/07 Colo 1m GD £67568
95 4/07 Chan 1m GD £11486
4/07 Colo 1m SFT £2027
Total win prize-money £81081

Going (Turf): Sf: 1-3 GS: 0-0 **Gd: 2-6** GF: 0-0 Fm: 0-0
Distance: 5f/6f: 0-0 **7f-8f: 3-11** 9f-13f: 0-2 14f+: 0-0
Track : LH: 0-5 **RH: 2-5** Tight: 0-1 Gall: 0-2
Aids: Bl: 0-0 Vi: 0-0 Tstrap: 0-0 Ckp: 0-0
Best Rating: 108 6/07 Hamb 1m soft

Formerly useful; won the German 2000 Guineas in 2007; best at around 1m; acts on good and soft ground.

Avitus

100 **64**
3-y-o gr g Monsieur Bond (IRE)-Top (Shirley Heights)
Micky Hammond Paul & Anne Sellars

Placings:000-32002 **(6236)**
2009: 9^{3}GF, 9^{2}F, 12^{0}GF, 12^{0}GF, 10^{2}GF,

	Starts	1st	2nd	3rd	Win & Pl
Career Total (Turf)	**8**	**0**	**2**	**1**	**2312**

Going (Turf): Sf: 0-0 GS: 0-1 Gd: 0-1 GF: 0-5 Fm: 0-1
Distance: 5f/6f: 0-2 7f-8f: 0-1 9f-13f: 0-5 14f+: 0-0
Track : LH: 0-5 RH: 0-2 Tight: 0-4 Gall: 0-0
Aids: Bl: 0-0 Vi: 0-0 Tstrap: 0-0 Ckp: 0-0
Best Rating: 64 4/09 Ripn 1m1f170y gd-fm

Moderate; effective over 1m2f; acts on fast ground.

Avoca Dancer (IRE)

101(104) (69)**65**
6-y-o ch m Compton Place-Kashra (IRE) (Dancing Dissident (USA))
Karen George (Miss Gay Kelleway 22/2) Mrs Isabel Fraser

Placings:53600/2430/000**060/2123130130205-00345003140006555** **(7052)**
2009: 7^{0}SS, 6^{0}SD, 6^{3}SD, 6^{4}SS, 6^{5}SD, 6^{0}SD, 6^{0}G, 6^{3}SD, 7^{1}GF, 7^{4}SD, 7^{0}SD, 6^{0}G, 7^{0}GS, 7^{6}GF, 7^{5}G, 7^{5}SD, 7^{5}SD,

	Starts	1st	2nd	3rd	Win & Pl
Career Total (Turf)	**20**	**2**	**1**	**2**	**7383**
Career Total (AW)	**25**	**2**	**3**	**5**	**6450**

63 6/09 Ling 7f (0-55)H G-F £2047
65 9/08 Brig 5f213y GD £1942
58 3/08 Wolv 5f216y (0-52)H STD £1774
56 1/08 Kemp 6f (0-45) STD £1365
Total win prize-money £7130

Going (Turf): Sf: 0-2 GS: 0-3 **Gd: 1-8 GF: 1-7** Fm: 0-0
Distance: **5f/6f: 3-30** 7f-8f: 1-15 9f-13f: 0-0 14f+: 0-0
Track : **LH: 2-20** RH: 1-13 **Tight: 1-13** Gall: 0-3
Aids: Bl: 0-3 Vi: 1-14 Tstrap: 1-5 Ckp: 1-5
Best Rating: 74 8/06 Curr 6f good

Modest; effective over 6f-7f; acts on fast ground; also goes on Polytrack; has worn a visor.

Avoir Choisi (IRE)

94(102) (74)**68**
3-y-o ch g Choisir (AUS)-Dolara (IRE) (Dolphin Street (FR))
N Wilson (I Semple 23/10) Gordon McDowall

Placings:4-2130060000 **(7762)**
2009: 8^{2}SD, 7^{1}SD, 8^{3}F, 7^{0}SD, 8^{0}GF, 11^{6}SD, 8^{0}G, 9^{0}SD, 7^{0}G, 7^{0}SD,

	Starts	1st	2nd	3rd	Win & Pl
Career Total (Turf)	**5**	**0**	**0**	**1**	**933**
Career Total (AW)	**6**	**1**	**1**	**0**	**3361**

74 1/09 Kemp 7f STD £2590
Total win prize-money £2590

Going (Turf): Sf: 0-1 GS: 0-0 Gd: 0-2 GF: 0-1 Fm: 0-1
Distance: 5f/6f: 0-0 **7f-8f: 1-9** 9f-13f: 0-2 14f+: 0-0
Track : LH: 0-6 **RH: 1-3** Tight: 0-2 Gall: 0-0
Aids: Bl: 0-0 Vi: 0-0 Tstrap: 0-0 Ckp: 0-0
Best Rating: 74 1/09 Kemp 7f stand

Fair; effective at a mile; handles Polytrack.

Avon Called

(62)
2-y-o b f Avonbridge-Bahawir Pour (USA) (Green Dancer (USA))
W M Brisbourne Shropshire Wolves

Placings:0 **(6461)**
2009: 8^{0}SD,

	Starts	1st	2nd	3rd	Win & Pl
Career Total (Turf)	**0**	**0**	**0**	**0**	
Career Total (AW)	**1**	**0**	**0**	**0**	

Going (Turf): Sf: 0-0 GS: 0-0 Gd: 0-0 GF: 0-0 Fm: 0-0
Distance: 5f/6f: 0-0 7f-8f: 0-0 9f-13f: 0-1 14f+: 0-0
Track : LH: 0-1 RH: 0-0 Tight: 0-1 Gall: 0-0
Aids: Bl: 0-0 Vi: 0-0 Tstrap: 0-0 Ckp: 0-0

Avon Castle

(93) (64)
2-y-o b f Avonbridge-Castellina (USA) (Danzig Connection (USA))
G L Moore D J Deer

Placings:0626 **(7886)**
2009: 5^{0}SD, 6^{6}SD, 5^{2}SD, 7^{6}SD,

	Starts	1st	2nd	3rd	Win & Pl
Career Total (Turf)	**0**	**0**	**0**	**0**	
Career Total (AW)	**4**	**0**	**1**	**0**	**806**

Going (Turf): Sf: 0-0 GS: 0-0 Gd: 0-0 GF: 0-0 Fm: 0-0
Distance: 5f/6f: 0-3 7f-8f: 0-1 9f-13f: 0-0 14f+: 0-0
Track : LH: 0-3 RH: 0-1 Tight: 0-3 Gall: 0-0
Aids: Bl: 0-0 Vi: 0-0 Tstrap: 0-0 Ckp: 0-0
Best Rating: 64 12/09 Wolv 5f216y stand

Modest; stays 6f; acts on Polytrack; should win a race.

Avon Grounds

90(71) (5)**58**
2-y-o b c Avonbridge-Good Grounds (USA) (Alleged (USA))
J M Bradley J M Bradley

Placings:0060 **(6938)**
2009: 6^{0}GF, 7^{0}GF, 7^{6}GF, 5^{0}SD,

	Starts	1st	2nd	3rd	Win & Pl
Career Total (Turf)	**3**	**0**	**0**	**0**	**0**

Career Total (AW) 1 0 0 0

Going (Turf): **Sf: 0-0 GS: 0-0 Gd: 0-0 GF: 0-3 Fm: 0-0**
Distance: 5f/6f: 0-1 7f-8f: 0-3 9f-13f: 0-0 14f+: 0-0
Track : LH: 0-1 RH: 0-1 Tight: 0-0 Gall: 0-0
Aids: Bl: 0-0 Vi: 0-0 Tstrap: 0-1 Ckp: 0-1
Best Rating: **58** 7/09 Chep 6f16y gd-fm

Avon Krystal

67(80) (47)23
2-y-o b f Avonbridge-Kryssa (Kris)
R Hannon D J Deer

Placings:0400 (5868)
2009: 6⁰GF, 5⁴HY, 6⁰SD, 8⁰G,

	Starts	1st	2nd	3rd	Win & Pl
Career Total (Turf)	3	0	0	0	202
Career Total (AW)	1	0	0	0	

Going (Turf): **Sf: 0-1 GS: 0-0 Gd: 0-1 GF: 0-1 Fm: 0-0**
Distance: 5f/6f: 0-3 7f-8f: 0-1 9f-13f: 0-0 14f+: 0-0
Track : LH: 0-1 RH: 0-1 Tight: 0-0 Gall: 0-2
Aids: Bl: 0-0 Vi: 0-0 Tstrap: 0-0 Ckp: 0-0
Best Rating: **47** 9/09 Kemp 6f stand

Avon Lady

91 69
2-y-o b f Avonbridge-Delightful Rhythm (USA) (Diesis)
J R Fanshawe Helena Springfield Ltd

Placings:61 (6786)
2009: 7⁶F, 7¹G,

	Starts	1st	2nd	3rd	Win & Pl
Career Total (Turf)	2	1	0	0	3532
69 10/09 Brig	7f214y		GD	£3532	

Total win prize-money £3532

Going (Turf): Sf: 0-0 GS: 0-0 **Gd: 1-1** GF: 0-0 Fm: 0-1
Distance: 5f/6f: 0-0 **7f-8f: 1-2** 9f-13f: 0-0 14f+: 0-0
Track : **LH: 1-1** RH: 0-0 Tight: 0-0 Gall: 0-0
Aids: Bl: 0-0 Vi: 0-0 Tstrap: 0-0 Ckp: 0-0
Best Rating: **69** 10/09 Brig 7f214y good

Fair; stays 1m and acts on good ground.

Avon River

96(79) (72)82
2-y-o ch c Avonbridge-Night Kiss (FR) (Night Shift (USA))
R Hannon Jim Horgan

Placings:01010300 (5742)
2009: 5⁰G, 5¹SD, 6⁰G, 7¹G, 7⁰G, 6³GF, 7⁰GF, 8⁰GF,

	Starts	1st	2nd	3rd	Win & Pl
Career Total (Turf)	7	1	0	1	8253
Career Total (AW)	1	1	0	0	5019
82 6/09 Donc	7f		GD	£7771	
72 5/09 Kemp	5f		STD	£5018	

Total win prize-money £12790

Going (Turf): Sf: 0-0 GS: 0-0 **Gd: 1-4** GF: 0-3 Fm: 0-0
Distance: 5f/6f: 1-3 7f-8f: 1-5 9f-13f: 0-0 14f+: 0-0
Track : LH: 0-2 **RH: 1-3** Tight: 0-1 Gall: 0-1
Aids: Bl: 0-0 Vi: 0-0 Tstrap: 0-0 Ckp: 0-0
Best Rating: **82** 6/09 Donc 7f good

Useful; stays 7f; acts on good ground and Polytrack.

Avon Rock

84 55
2-y-o b g Avonbridge-Big Pink (IRE) (Bigstone (IRE))
J W Hills D J Deer

Placings:000 (6962)
2009: 6⁰GF, 6⁰G, 6⁰G,

	Starts	1st	2nd	3rd	Win & Pl
Career Total (Turf)	3	0	0	0	

Going (Turf): **Sf: 0-0 GS: 0-0 Gd: 0-2 GF: 0-1 Fm: 0-0**
Distance: 5f/6f: 0-0 7f-8f: 0-3 9f-13f: 0-0 14f+: 0-0
Track : LH: 0-1 RH: 0-0 Tight: 0-0 Gall: 0-0
Aids: Bl: 0-0 Vi: 0-0 Tstrap: 0-0 Ckp: 0-0
Best Rating: **55** 10/09 Newb 6f110y good

Avoncreek

95(94) (45)58
5-y-o b g Tipsy Creek (USA)-Avondale Girl (IRE) (Case Law)
B P J Baugh Messrs Chrimes, Winn & Wilson

Placings:50600/**6060660**/**25400**010006-06000650 (0210)
2009: 6⁰GF, 6⁶F, 6⁰GF, 7⁰GF, 6⁰G, 5⁶GS, 6⁵GF, 6⁰GF,

	Starts	1st	2nd	3rd	Win & Pl
Career Total (Turf)	21	1	0	0	2590
Career Total (AW)	10	0	1	0	524
58 5/08 Yarm	6f3y	(0-70)H	GD	£2590	

Total win prize-money £2590

Going (Turf): Sf: 0-3 GS: 0-3 **Gd: 1-5** GF: 0-9 Fm: 0-1
Distance: 5f/6f: 0-21 **7f-8f: 1-10** 9f-13f: 0-0 14f+: 0-0
Track : LH: 0-13 RH: 0-2 Tight: 0-11 Gall: 0-0
Aids: Bl: 0-0 Vi: 0-0 Tstrap: 0-2 Ckp: 0-2
Best Rating: **58** 5/08 Yarm 6f3y good

Moderate; effective over 6f; acts on good ground; also goes on Polytrack.

Avongate

100(78) (33)78
2-y-o b g Avonbridge-Palacegate Episode (IRE) (Drumalis)
R Hannon D J Deer

Placings:00100 (7108)
2009: 5⁰GF, 5⁰G, 6¹G, 6⁰GF, 6⁰SD,

	Starts	1st	2nd	3rd	Win & Pl
Career Total (Turf)	4	1	0	0	4857
Career Total (AW)	1	0	0	0	
78 8/09 Newb	6f8y		GD	£4857	

Total win prize-money £4857

Going (Turf): Sf: 0-0 GS: 0-0 **Gd: 1-2** GF: 0-2 Fm: 0-0
Distance: 5f/6f: 0-4 **7f-8f: 1-1** 9f-13f: 0-0 14f+: 0-0
Track : LH: 0-1 RH: 0-1 Tight: 0-0 Gall: 0-1
Aids: Bl: 0-0 Vi: 0-0 Tstrap: 0-0 Ckp: 0-0
Best Rating: **78** 8/09 Newb 6f8y good

Fair; stays 6f; acts on good ground.

Avonlini

89(78) (22)42
3-y-o b f Bertolini (USA)-Avondale Girl (IRE) (Case Law)
B P J Baugh J H Chrimes

Placings:000-6000 (5614)
2009: 7⁶GF, 6⁰GF, 7⁰GF, 8⁰SD,

	Starts	1st	2nd	3rd	Win & Pl
Career Total (Turf)	6	0	0	0	0

Career Total (AW) 1 0 0 0

Going (Turf): **Sf: 0-0 GS: 0-1 Gd: 0-0 GF: 0-5 Fm: 0-0**
Distance: 5f/6f: 0-2 7f-8f: 0-4 9f-13f: 0-1 14f+: 0-0
Track : LH: 0-3 RH: 0-0 Tight: 0-2 Gall: 0-0
Aids: Bl: 0-0 Vi: 0-0 Tstrap: 0-0 Ckp: 0-0
Best Rating: **42** 7/09 Wwck 7f26y gd-fm

Avonrose

98 87
2-y-o b f Avonbridge-Loveleaves (Polar Falcon (USA))
M Johnston Around The World Partnership

Placings:01526200 (6486)
2009: 5⁰F, 6¹GF, 6⁵G, 6²F, 6⁶S, 7²G, 6⁰GF, 6⁰GF,

	Starts	1st	2nd	3rd	Win & Pl
Career Total (Turf)	8	1	2	0	8336
79 5/09 Rdcr	6f		G-F	£3691	

Total win prize-money £3691

Going (Turf): Sf: 0-1 GS: 0-0 Gd: 0-2 **GF: 1-3** Fm: 0-2
Distance: **5f/6f: 1-5** 7f-8f: 0-3 9f-13f: 0-0 14f+: 0-0
Track : LH: 0-1 RH: 0-0 Tight: 0-0 Gall: 0-0
Aids: Bl: 0-0 Vi: 0-0 Tstrap: 0-0 Ckp: 0-0
Best Rating: **87** 7/09 Hayd 6f firm

Useful; suited by 6-7f; acts on fast ground.

Avontuur (FR)

105(106) (66)75
7-y-o ch g Kabool-Ipoh (FR) (Funambule (USA))
Mrs R A Carr J M Chapman

Placings:005**0**5**2000**/4006**100**/**013403142653**4300102000 6231034-**000**132204460412030 (6984)
2009: 6⁰SD, 7⁰SD, 6⁰GF, 7¹SD, 6³G, 7²G, 5²G, 7⁰G, 6⁴G, 6⁴G, 6⁶G, 7⁰GF, 6⁴GF, 6¹GF, 6²GF, 6⁰GF, 6³G, 7⁰G,

	Starts	1st	2nd	3rd	Win & Pl
Career Total (Turf)	44	3	6	5	19621
Career Total (AW)	19	4	1	3	10129

71	8/09	Newc	6f	(0-80)H	G-F	£5361
66	6/09	Wolv	7f32y	(0-60)H	STD	£2729
67	10/08	Ayr	6f	(0-70)H	HVY	£2914
67	6/08	Carl	5f193y	(0-60)H	G-F	£2047
61	3/08	Wolv	5f216y	(0-65)H	STD	£2047
58	1/08	Wolv	5f216y	(0-50)H	STD	£1774
49	9/07	Wolv	5f216y	(0-45)	STD	£1911

Total win prize-money £18787

Going (Turf): Sf: 1-7 GS: 0-5 Gd: 0-14 **GF: 2-16** Fm: 0-2
Distance: **5f/6f: 6-32** 7f-8f: 1-24 9f-13f: 0-7 14f+: 0-0
Track : **LH: 4-30** RH: 1-13 **Tight: 4-25** Gall: 0-0
Aids: **Bl: 3-23** Vi: 0-0 Tstrap: 2-15 Ckp: 2-15
Best Rating: **75** 9/09 Rdcr 6f gd-fm

Modest; effective over 6f-7f; acts on most ground; goes on Polytrack; has worn blinkers and cheekpieces; often misses the break.

Avonvalley

94(105) (76)73
2-y-o b f Avonbridge-Piper's Ash (USA) (Royal Academy (USA))
M S Saunders Chris Scott

Placings:32210304 (5241)
2009: 5³GF, 5²G, 5²SD, 5¹GF, 5⁰GF, 5³G, 5⁰GF, 5⁴F,

	Starts	1st	2nd	3rd	Win & Pl
Career Total (Turf)	7	1	1	2	4940
Career Total (AW)	1	0	1	0	1253
71 5/09 Chep	5f16y		G-F	£2719	

Total win prize-money £2720

Going (Turf): Sf: 0-0 GS: 0-0 Gd: 0-2 **GF: 1-4** Fm: 0-1
Distance: **5f/6f: 1-8** 7f-8f: 0-0 9f-13f: 0-0 14f+: 0-0
Track : LH: 0-5 RH: 0-0 Tight: 0-1 Gall: 0-4
Aids: Bl: 0-0 Vi: 0-0 Tstrap: 0-0 Ckp: 0-0
Best Rating: **76** 5/09 Wolv 5f20y stand

Fair; suited by 5f; acts on fast ground and on Polytrack.

Avow (USA)

87(96) (66)**70**
2-y-o b g Mingun (USA)-Knoosh (USA) (Storm Bird (CAN))
J S Moore Two Bucks Stable

Placings:003053022 **(6292)**
2009: 6^{0}GS, 7^{0}GF, 7^{3}G, 7^{0}G, 7^{5}G, 6^{3}SD, 7^{0}GF, 7^{2}SD, 6^{2}SD,

	Starts	1st	2nd	3rd	Win & Pl
Career Total (Turf)	6	0	0	1	530
Career Total (AW)	3	0	2	1	1511

Going (Turf): **Sf: 0-0 GS: 0-1 Gd: 0-3 GF: 0-2 Fm: 0-0**
Distance: 5f/6f: 0-3 7f-8f: 0-6 9f-13f: 0-0 14f+: 0-0
Track : LH: 0-2 RH: 0-2 Tight: 0-2 Gall: 0-1
Aids: Bl: 0-7 Vi: 0-0 Tstrap: 0-0 Ckp: 0-0
Best Rating: **70** 7/09 Ling 7f good

Modest sprinter; has worn blinkers.

Avrilo

99(99) (58)**58**
3-y-o ch f Piccolo-Arctic High (Polar Falcon (USA))
M S Saunders Paul Nicholas

Placings:00-300420622432**4200** **(7370)**
2009: 8^{3}SD, 8^{0}G, 5^{0}F, 5^{4}GF, 5^{2}F, 6^{0}GF, 5^{6}S, 5^{2}G, 5^{2}G, 5^{4}G, 5^{3}GS, 5^{2}SD, 5^{4}SD, 5^{2}SD, 6^{0}SD, 5^{0}SD,

	Starts	1st	2nd	3rd	Win & Pl
Career Total (Turf)	10	0	3	1	3170
Career Total (AW)	8	0	2	1	1713

Going (Turf): **Sf: 0-1 GS: 0-1 Gd: 0-4 GF: 0-2 Fm: 0-2**
Distance: 5f/6f: 0-15 7f-8f: 0-2 9f-13f: 0-1 14f+: 0-0
Track : LH: 0-12 RH: 0-1 Tight: 0-6 Gall: 0-6
Aids: Bl: 0-0 Vi: 0-0 Tstrap: 0-0 Ckp: 0-0
Best Rating: **58** 10/09 Kemp 5f stand

Moderate; effective at 5f and acts on good/easy ground.

Await The Dawn (USA)

87 **93**
2-y-o b c Giant's Causeway (USA)-Valentine Band (USA) (Dixieland Band (USA))
A P O'Brien M Tabor & Mrs John Magnier

Placings:10 **(5859)**
2009: 8^{1}S, 7^{0}GF,

	Starts	1st	2nd	3rd	Win & Pl
Career Total (Turf)	2	1	0	0	10399

93 7/09 Naas 1m SFT £10398
Total win prize-money £10399

Going (Turf): **Sf: 1-1** GS: 0-0 Gd: 0-0 GF: 0-1 Fm: 0-0
Distance: 5f/6f: 0-0 **7f-8f: 1-2** 9f-13f: 0-1 14f+: 0-0
Track : **LH: 1-1** RH: 0-0 Tight: 0-0 Gall: 0-0
Aids: Bl: 0-0 Vi: 0-0 Tstrap: 0-0 Ckp: 0-0
Best Rating: **93** 7/09 Naas 1m soft

Half-brother to useful French 1m/1m1f winner Putney Bridge; winner on debut over 1m; acts on soft ground.

Awaken

95 **47**
8-y-o b m Zafonic (USA)-Dawna (Polish Precedent (USA))
Miss Tracy Waggott Miss T Waggott

Placings:00/343310/605114500/04155/000-003400 **(4944)**
2009: 9^{0}GF, 9^{0}GF, 10^{3}GF, 10^{4}F, 9^{0}GF, 10^{0}GF,

	Starts	1st	2nd	3rd	Win & Pl
Career Total (Turf)	31	4	0	4	12633

56 8/07 Rdcr 1m1f FRM £2047
61 7/06 Haml 1m3f16y G-F £2730
57 6/06 Carl 1m1f61y G-F £2730
54 9/05 Rdcr 1m2f (0-55)H GD £2716
Total win prize-money £10225

Going (Turf): Sf: 0-1 GS: 0-3 Gd: 1-5 **GF: 2-19** Fm: 1-3
Distance: 5f/6f: 0-0 7f-8f: 0-0 **9f-13f: 4-31** 14f+: 0-0
Track : LH: 2-16 RH: 2-14 **Tight: 3-12** Gall: 0-5
Aids: Bl: 0-0 Vi: 0-0 Tstrap: 0-0 Ckp: 0-0
Best Rating: **64** 7/06 Rdcr 1m1f gd-fm

Plating-class; stays 12f but effective at 9f; acts on fast ground.

Awani

85(93) (47)**44**
3-y-o b f Sakhee (USA)-Hatton Gardens (Auction Ring (USA))
E F Vaughan (Ms Caroline Hutchinson 24/5) Mrs Emma Kennedy

Placings:00306 **(6375)**
2009: 10^{0}GY, 10^{0}HY, 12^{3}SD, 11^{0}SD, 12^{6}SD,

	Starts	1st	2nd	3rd	Win & Pl
Career Total (Turf)	2	0	0	0	
Career Total (AW)	3	0	0	1	403

Going (Turf): **Sf: 0-1 GS: 0-0 Gd: 0-0 GF: 0-0 Fm: 0-0**
Distance: 5f/6f: 0-0 7f-8f: 0-0 9f-13f: 0-5 14f+: 0-0
Track : LH: 0-3 RH: 0-2 Tight: 0-1 Gall: 0-0
Aids: Bl: 0-0 Vi: 0-0 Tstrap: 0-0 Ckp: 0-0
Best Rating: **47** 8/09 Ling 1m4f stand

Awaseef (USA)

(97) (72)
2-y-o ch f Haafhd-Emtyazat (Gone West (USA))
J H M Gosden Hamdan Al Maktoum

Placings:32 **(5984)**
2009: 7^{3}SD, 8^{2}SD,

	Starts	1st	2nd	3rd	Win & Pl
Career Total (Turf)	0	0	0	0	
Career Total (AW)	2	0	1	1	1724

Going (Turf): **Sf: 0-0 GS: 0-0 Gd: 0-0 GF: 0-0 Fm: 0-0**
Distance: 5f/6f: 0-0 7f-8f: 0-2 9f-13f: 0-0 14f+: 0-0
Track : LH: 0-0 RH: 0-2 Tight: 0-0 Gall: 0-0
Aids: Bl: 0-0 Vi: 0-0 Tstrap: 0-0 Ckp: 0-0
Best Rating: **72** 9/09 Kemp 1m stand

Fair; stays 7f; acts on Polytrack.

Awatuki (IRE)

99(105) (87)**61**
6-y-o b g Distant Music (USA)-Itkan (IRE) (Marju (IRE))
J R Boyle Allen B Pope

Placings:52/**132000**5/**102**053/**5200015**-003**50** **(7775)**
2009: 10^{0}G, 9^{0}G, 9^{3}G, 10^{5}SD, 10^{0}SD,

	Starts	1st	2nd	3rd	Win & Pl
Career Total (Turf)	11	0	2	1	3103
Career Total (AW)	16	3	2	2	20439

87 11/08 GrLe 1m2f (0-80)H STD £4857
86 2/07 Kemp 1m3f (0-85)H STD £4728
78 3/06 Kemp 1m2f STD £5505
Total win prize-money £15090

Going (Turf): **Sf: 0-1 GS: 0-5 Gd: 0-3 GF: 0-1 Fm: 0-1**
Distance: 5f/6f: 0-0 7f-8f: 0-2 **9f-13f: 3-25** 14f+: 0-0
Track : LH: 1-11 **RH: 2-14** Tight: 0-10 **Gall: 1-3**
Aids: Bl: 0-0 Vi: 0-0 Tstrap: 0-0 Ckp: 0-0
Best Rating: **89** 3/07 Kemp 1m3f stand

Useful; stays 1m3f; acts on most ground on turf; goes on Polytrack.

Awe

55 **35**
5-y-o b g Muhtarram (USA)-Fleet Of Light (Spectrum (IRE))
Mrs N S Evans (Mrs K J Stephens 4/6) M Langdell

Placings:000/0 **(3207)**
2009: 8^{0}G,

	Starts	1st	2nd	3rd	Win & Pl
Career Total (Turf)	3	0	0	0	
Career Total (AW)	1	0	0	0	

Going (Turf): **Sf: 0-0 GS: 0-0 Gd: 0-1 GF: 0-2 Fm: 0-0**
Distance: 5f/6f: 0-0 7f-8f: 0-3 9f-13f: 0-1 14f+: 0-0
Track : LH: 0-1 RH: 0-0 Tight: 0-0 Gall: 0-0
Aids: Bl: 0-0 Vi: 0-0 Tstrap: 0-0 Ckp: 0-0
Best Rating: **35** 9/06 Leic 7f9y gd-fm

Awesome Act (USA)

103(92) (81)**114**
2-y-o ch c Awesome Again (CAN)-Houdini's Honey (USA) (Mr Prospector (USA))
J Noseda Mrs Susan Roy & Tom Ludt

Placings:223104 **(7304a)**
2009: 7^{2}GS, 7^{2}G, 7^{3}SD, 7^{1}GF, 7^{0}G, 8^{4}F,

	Starts	1st	2nd	3rd	Win & Pl
Career Total (Turf)	5	1	2	0	47892
Career Total (AW)	1	0	0	1	961

93 10/09 Gdwd 7f G-F £3238
Total win prize-money £3238

Going (Turf): Sf: 0-0 GS: 0-1 Gd: 0-2 **GF: 1-1** Fm: 0-1
Distance: 5f/6f: 0-0 **7f-8f: 1-6** 9f-13f: 0-0 14f+: 0-0
Track : LH: 0-1 **RH: 1-2** Tight: 0-0 Gall: 0-0
Aids: Bl: 0-0 Vi: 0-0 Tstrap: 0-0 Ckp: 0-0
Best Rating: **114** 11/09 SnAt 1m firm

Smart; stays 1m; fourth in the Breeders' Cup Juvenile Turf; acts on fast and easy ground and Polytrack.

Awesome Surprise (USA)

99(99) (72)**75**
3-y-o b f Awesome Again (CAN)-Native Roots (IRE) (Indian Ridge)
J Noseda D Brennan

Placings:4231 **(5840)**
2009: 8^{4}GF, 8^{2}GF, 7^{3}GF, 8^{1}SD,

	Starts	1st	2nd	3rd	Win & Pl
Career Total (Turf)	3	0	1	1	1769
Career Total (AW)	1	1	0	0	2730

72 9/09 Wolv 1m141y STD £2729
Total win prize-money £2730

Going (Turf): Sf: 0-0 GS: 0-0 Gd: 0-0 GF: 0-3 Fm: 0-0
Distance: 5f/6f: 0-0 7f-8f: 0-2 **9f-13f: 1-2** 14f+: 0-0
Track : **LH: 1-1** RH: 0-1 **Tight: 1-2** Gall: 0-0
Aids: Bl: 0-0 Vi: 0-0 Tstrap: 0-0 Ckp: 0-0
Best Rating: 75 8/09 Wind 1m67y gd-fm

Fair; stays 1m; acts on fast ground and on Polytrack.

Awinnersgame (IRE)

102 108
3-y-o b g Kyllachy-Polish Descent (IRE) (Danehill (USA))
J Noseda Saeed Suhail

Placings:2163116-235010 **(6661)**
2009: 7²GF, 6³G, 6⁵G, 7⁰GF, 6¹GF, 6⁰GS,

	Starts	1st	2nd	3rd	Win & Pl
Career Total (Turf)	13	4	2	2	191560

104	9/09	Yarm	6f3y	G-F	£7477
108	9/08	Donc	6f110y	SFT	£147720
94	8/08	NmkJ	7f	GF	£6176
85	5/08	Hayd	6f	GD	£3399

Total win prize-money £165073

Going (Turf): Sf: 1-1 GS: 0-1 Gd: 1-4 **GF: 2-6** Fm: 0-0
Distance: 5f/6f: 1-5 **7f-8f: 3-8** 9f-13f: 0-0 14f+: 0-0
Track : LH: 0-0 RH: 0-0 Tight: 0-0 Gall: 0-0
Aids: Bl: 0-0 Vi: 0-1 Tstrap: 0-0 Ckp: 0-0
Best Rating: 108 9/08 Donc 6f110y soft

Smart; placed in Listed company; effective at 6f-7f; acts on most ground; has worn a visor.

Awsaal

89 61
2-y-o b c Nayef (USA)-Design Perfection (USA) (Diesis)
J L Dunlop Hamdan Al Maktoum

Placings:0 **(7146)**
2009: 7⁰G,

	Starts	1st	2nd	3rd	Win & Pl
Career Total (Turf)	1	0	0	0	

Going (Turf): Sf: 0-0 GS: 0-0 Gd: 0-1 GF: 0-0 Fm: 0-0
Distance: 5f/6f: 0-0 7f-8f: 0-1 9f-13f: 0-0 14f+: 0-0
Track : LH: 0-0 RH: 0-0 Tight: 0-0 Gall: 0-0
Aids: Bl: 0-0 Vi: 0-0 Tstrap: 0-0 Ckp: 0-0
Best Rating: 61 10/09 NmkR 7f good

Awzaan

109 119
2-y-o br c Alhaarth (IRE)-Nufoos (Zafonic (USA))
M Johnston Hamdan Al Maktoum

Placings:1111 **(6450)**
2009: 6¹G, 6¹G, 6¹GF, 6¹GF,

	Starts	1st	2nd	3rd	Win & Pl
Career Total (Turf)	4	4	0	0	166370

119	10/09	NmkR	6f	G-F	£104116
113	9/09	Newb	6f8y	G-F	£45416
101	7/09	NmkJ	6f	GD	£12952
75	6/09	Haml	6f5y	GD	£3885

Total win prize-money £166370

Going (Turf): Sf: 0-0 GS: 0-0 **Gd: 2-2 GF: 2-2** Fm: 0-0
Distance: 5f/6f: 2-2 7f-8f: 2-2 9f-13f: 0-0 14f+: 0-0
Track : LH: 0-0 RH: 0-0 Tight: 0-0 Gall: 0-0

Aids: Bl: 0-0 Vi: 0-0 Tstrap: 0-0 Ckp: 0-0
Best Rating: 119 10/09 NmkR 6f gd-fm

Group class; winner of the 2009 Mill Reef and Middle Park; effective over 6f; acts on good and fast ground.

Axinit (GER)

(82) (30)3
9-y-o gr g Linamix (FR)-Assia (IRE) (Royal Academy (USA))
E J Creighton The Vixens

Placings:5052211/360/0/16/00-0 **(6210)**
2009: 12⁰SD,

	Starts	1st	2nd	3rd	Win & Pl
Career Total (Turf)	14	3	2	1	9479
Career Total (AW)	2	0	0	0	

67	4/06	Tram	1m4f	(40-60)H	GD	£3812
	11/03	Mulh	1m2f110y	H	HVY	£1753
	10/03	Colo	1m3f		SFT	£1948

Total win prize-money £7513

Going (Turf): Sf: 2-7 GS: 0-1 Gd: 1-5 GF: 0-1 Fm: 0-0
Distance: 5f/6f: 0-0 7f-8f: 0-1 **9f-13f: 3-12** 14f+: 0-3
Track : LH: 0-2 **RH: 1-4** Tight: 0-1 Gall: 0-0
Aids: Bl: 0-1 Vi: 0-0 Tstrap: 1-4 Ckp: 1-4
Best Rating: 67 4/06 Tram 1m4f good

Axiom

110 (85)109
5-y-o ch h Pivotal-Exhibitor (USA) (Royal Academy (USA))
L M Cumani DIC Racing Syndicate

Placings:430221/105015-26142 **(6270)**
2009: 8²G, 8⁶GF, 7¹G, 7⁴GF, 7²G,

	Starts	1st	2nd	3rd	Win & Pl
Career Total (Turf)	15	4	3	1	65125
Career Total (AW)	2	0	1	0	646

102	7/09	Gdwd	7f	(0-95)	GD	£12462
98	10/08	Leic	1m60y	(0-90)H	G-S	£7788
94	6/08	Donc	1m	(0-80)H	G-S	£6476
74	10/07	Leic	7f9y		SFT	£2914

Total win prize-money £29642

Going (Turf): Sf: 1-3 **GS: 2-3** Gd: 1-6 GF: 0-3 Fm: 0-0
Distance: 5f/6f: 0-0 **7f-8f: 3-13** 9f-13f: 1-4 14f+: 0-0
Track : LH: 0-3 **RH: 2-7** Tight: 0-4 Gall: 0-0
Aids: Bl: 0-0 Vi: 0-0 Tstrap: 0-0 Ckp: 0-0
Best Rating: 109 9/09 Asct 7f good

Smart; effective at 7f-1m; acts on easy ground; also goes on Polytrack.

Ay Tay Tate (IRE)

93(95) (50)68
3-y-o b g Catcher In The Rye (IRE)-Vintage Belle (IRE) (Waajib)
D Shaw (I W McInnes 18/4) Andrew Langan

Placings:6304006-000060 **(7004)**
2009: 8⁰GF, 8⁰G, 5⁰SD, 7⁰S, 9⁶SD, 9⁰SD,

	Starts	1st	2nd	3rd	Win & Pl
Career Total (Turf)	10	0	0	1	914
Career Total (AW)	3	0	0	0	0

Going (Turf): Sf: 0-2 GS: 0-1 Gd: 0-4 GF: 0-2 Fm: 0-1
Distance: 5f/6f: 0-4 7f-8f: 0-4 9f-13f: 0-5 14f+: 0-0
Track : LH: 0-9 RH: 0-0 Tight: 0-5 Gall: 0-0
Aids: Bl: 0-0 Vi: 0-1 Tstrap: 0-0 Ckp: 0-0

Best Rating: 68 5/08 Donc 6f good

Fair; suited by 6f and good ground.

Aye Aye Digby (IRE)

107 98
4-y-o b g Captain Rio-Jane Digby (IRE) (Magical Strike (USA))
H Candy Trolley Action

Placings:60135/01525405050-3126144030 **(6994)**
2009: 6³GF, 6¹G, 6²GS, 6⁶G, 6¹GS, 6⁴GF, 6⁴G, 6⁰G, 6³GS, 6⁰G,

	Starts	1st	2nd	3rd	Win & Pl
Career Total (Turf)	26	4	2	3	40542

98	7/09	NmkJ	6f	(0-90)H	G-S	£9066
95	5/09	Gdwd	6f	(0-85)H	GD	£4857
89	5/08	Nott	6f15y	(0-95)H	GD	£10361
80	8/07	Sals	6f212y		G-S	£2590

Total win prize-money £26876

Going (Turf): Sf: 0-2 **GS: 2-6 Gd: 2-10** GF: 0-8 Fm: 0-0
Distance: 5f/6f: 2-13 7f-8f: 2-12 9f-13f: 0-1 14f+: 0-0
Track : LH: 0-1 RH: 0-5 Tight: 0-1 Gall: 0-1
Aids: Bl: 0-0 Vi: 0-0 Tstrap: 0-0 Ckp: 0-0
Best Rating: 98 10/09 Gdwd 6f gd-sft

Very useful; effective over 6f-7f; acts on good and easier ground; likes to race prominently.

Aypeeyes (IRE)

97(104) (84)86
5-y-o b g King Charlemagne (USA)-Habaza (IRE) (Shernazar)
J K Price (A King 28/4) J K Price

Placings:134/00322051/10433164-401 **(1578)**
2009: 12⁴SD, 12⁰SD, 10¹G,

	Starts	1st	2nd	3rd	Win & Pl
Career Total (Turf)	13	3	2	1	22199
Career Total (AW)	9	2	0	3	9559

57	4/09	Bath	1m2f46y		GD	£1942
86	8/08	Newb	1m4f5y	(0-80)H	G-S	£13741
83	5/08	Nott	1m2f50y	(0-75)H	GD	£3238
74	9/07	Wolv	1m4f50y	(0-75)H	STD	£3071
66	10/06	Wolv	1m141y		STD	£3238

Total win prize-money £25232

Going (Turf): Sf: 0-1 GS: 1-5 **Gd: 2-4** GF: 0-2 Fm: 0-1
Distance: 5f/6f: 0-0 7f-8f: 0-0 **9f-13f: 5-22** 14f+: 0-0
Track : **LH: 5-15** RH: 0-7 **Tight: 3-14** Gall: 1-5
Aids: Bl: 0-1 **Vi: 2-5** Tstrap: 0-0 Ckp: 0-0
Best Rating: 86 8/08 Newb 1m4f5y gd-sft

Fair; stays 1m4f; acts on good and soft ground; also goes on Polytrack.

Ayrpassionata

70 36
4-y-o ch f Where Or When (IRE)-Least Said (USA) (Trempolino (USA))
I Semple Mr & Mrs Charles Villiers

Placings:66-5 **(3022)**
2009: 9⁵G,

	Starts	1st	2nd	3rd	Win & Pl
Career Total (Turf)	3	0	0	0	0

Going (Turf): Sf: 0-0 GS: 0-0 Gd: 0-1 GF: 0-2 Fm: 0-0
Distance: 5f/6f: 0-0 7f-8f: 0-1 9f-13f: 0-2 14f+: 0-0
Track : LH: 0-0 RH: 0-3 Tight: 0-3 Gall: 0-0

Aids: Bl: 0-0 Vi: 0-0 Tstrap: 0-0 Ckp: 0-0
Best Rating: **36** 6/08 Haml 1m1f36y gd-fm

Azaday (IRE)

83 **54**
2-y-o b f Azamour (IRE)-Generous Lady (Generous (IRE))
C F Wall Ms Aida Fustoq

Placings:000 **(6992)**
2009: 8^0GF, 8^0G, 8^0GS,

	Starts	1st	2nd	3rd	Win & Pl
Career Total (Turf)	3	0	0	0	

Going (Turf): **Sf: 0-0 GS: 0-1 Gd: 0-1 GF: 0-1 Fm: 0-0**
Distance: 5f/6f: 0-0 7f-8f: 0-2 9f-13f: 0-1 14f+: 0-0
Track : LH: 0-1 RH: 0-2 Tight: 0-0 Gall: 0-1
Aids: Bl: 0-0 Vi: 0-0 Tstrap: 0-0 Ckp: 0-0
Best Rating: **54** 9/09 Gdwd 1m gd-fm

Azharia

89(96) (61)**53**
3-y-o b f Oasis Dream-Presto Vento (Air Express (IRE))
R Hannon (C E Brittain 3/7) B Bull

Placings:354000500 **(7225)**
2009: 6^3SD, 7^5SD, 6^4GF, 7^0SD, 5^0GF, 6^0GF, 7^5SD, 7^0SD, 10^0SD,

	Starts	1st	2nd	3rd	Win & Pl
Career Total (Turf)	3	0	0	0	216
Career Total (AW)	6	0	0	1	403

Going (Turf): **Sf: 0-0 GS: 0-0 Gd: 0-0 GF: 0-3 Fm: 0-0**
Distance: 5f/6f: 0-4 7f-8f: 0-4 9f-13f: 0-1 14f+: 0-0
Track : LH: 0-5 RH: 0-2 Tight: 0-3 Gall: 0-0
Aids: Bl: 0-1 Vi: 0-0 Tstrap: 0-1 Ckp: 0-1
Best Rating: **61** 3/09 Kemp 7f stand

Modest; stays 6f and acts on Fibresand.

Azif

89 **73**
2-y-o ch f Where Or When (IRE)-Dance Away (Pivotal)
Miss Gay Kelleway J Ballamy,Y Mullin,R Edwards,G Kelleway

Placings:51500050 **(6185)**
2009: 5^5GF, 5^1G, 5^5GS, 5^0GF, 5^0GF, 6^0G, 6^5GF, 5^0GF,

	Starts	1st	2nd	3rd	Win & Pl
Career Total (Turf)	8	1	0	0	2730

73 4/09 Wind 5f10y GD £2729
Total win prize-money £2730

Going (Turf): Sf: 0-0 GS: 0-1 **Gd: 1-2** GF: 0-5 Fm: 0-0
Distance: **5f/6f: 1-8** 7f-8f: 0-0 9f-13f: 0-0 14f+: 0-0
Track : LH: 0-0 RH: 0-0 Tight: 0-0 **Gall: 1-2**
Aids: Bl: 0-0 Vi: 0-0 Tstrap: 0-0 Ckp: 0-0
Best Rating: **73** 4/09 Wind 5f10y good

Fair; suited by 5f; acts on good ground.

Aziz (IRE)

78(78) (36)**49**
3-y-o b c Catcher In The Rye (IRE)-Imposition (UAE) (Be My Guest (USA))
Miss D Mountain Miss Debbie Mountain

Placings:00060-0 **(1747)**
2009: 12^0GF,

	Starts	1st	2nd	3rd	Win & Pl
Career Total (Turf)	5	0	0	0	0
Career Total (AW)	1	0	0	0	

Going (Turf): **Sf: 0-2 GS: 0-1 Gd: 0-1 GF: 0-1 Fm: 0-0**
Distance: 5f/6f: 0-0 7f-8f: 0-2 9f-13f: 0-4 14f+: 0-0
Track : LH: 0-5 RH: 0-0 Tight: 0-0 Gall: 0-0
Aids: Bl: 0-3 Vi: 0-0 Tstrap: 0-0 Ckp: 0-0
Best Rating: **49** 10/08 Nott 1m75y soft

Azizi

105(93) (73)**99**
2-y-o b c Haafhd-Harayir (USA) (Gulch (USA))
W J Haggas Hamdan Al Maktoum

Placings:411214 **(6664)**
2009: 6^4GF, 7^1SD, 7^1GF, 7^2GF, 8^1GF, 8^4GS,

	Starts	1st	2nd	3rd	Win & Pl
Career Total (Turf)	5	2	1	0	23559
Career Total (AW)	1	1	0	0	2388

99 9/09 Donc 1m H G-F £12952
90 8/09 Newc 7f G-F £3784
73 7/09 Ling 7f STD £2388
Total win prize-money £19125

Going (Turf): Sf: 0-0 GS: 0-1 Gd: 0-0 **GF: 2-4** Fm: 0-0
Distance: 5f/6f: 0-0 **7f-8f: 3-6** 9f-13f: 0-0 14f+: 0-0
Track : **LH: 1-1** RH: 0-1 **Tight: 1-1** Gall: 0-1
Aids: Bl: 0-0 Vi: 0-0 Tstrap: 0-0 Ckp: 0-0
Best Rating: **99** 9/09 Donc 1m gd-fm

Very useful well bred colt; stays 1m, acts on Polytrack and fast ground.

Azlak (USA)

90 **58**
2-y-o ch c Shamardal (USA)-Nasaieb (IRE) (Fairy King (USA))
C E Brittain Saeed Manana

Placings:0066 **(5864)**
2009: 7^0G, 7^0G, 8^6G, 8^6GF,

	Starts	1st	2nd	3rd	Win & Pl
Career Total (Turf)	4	0	0	0	0

Going (Turf): **Sf: 0-0 GS: 0-0 Gd: 0-3 GF: 0-1 Fm: 0-0**
Distance: 5f/6f: 0-0 7f-8f: 0-3 9f-13f: 0-1 14f+: 0-0
Track : LH: 0-0 RH: 0-1 Tight: 0-0 Gall: 0-0
Aids: Bl: 0-0 Vi: 0-0 Tstrap: 0-0 Ckp: 0-0
Best Rating: **58** 8/09 Sand 1m14y good

Modest; stays 1m; acts on fast ground.

Azmeel

105 **101**
2-y-o b c Azamour (IRE)-Best Side (IRE) (King's Best (USA))
J H M Gosden M Al-Qatami & K M Al-Mudhaf

Placings:110 **(6319a)**
2009: 7^1G, 7^1GF, 8^0G,

	Starts	1st	2nd	3rd	Win & Pl
Career Total (Turf)	3	2	0	0	22212

101 8/09 Newb 7f G-F £17031
85 7/09 Sand 7f16y GD £5180
Total win prize-money £22212

Going (Turf): Sf: 0-0 GS: 0-0 **Gd: 1-2 GF: 1-1** Fm: 0-0
Distance: 5f/6f: 0-0 **7f-8f: 2-3** 9f-13f: 0-0 14f+: 0-0
Track : LH: 0-0 **RH: 1-2** Tight: 0-0 Gall: 0-1
Aids: Bl: 0-0 Vi: 0-0 Tstrap: 0-0 Ckp: 0-0
Best Rating: **101** 8/09 Newb 7f gd-fm

First foal of a quite useful 7f/1m winner in Ireland; winner over 7f on debut and took a Listed contest over the same trip next time; acts on good/fast ground.

Azure Mist

101(101) (71)**73**
4-y-o ch f Bahamian Bounty-Inquirendo (USA) (Roberto (USA))
M H Tompkins David P Noblett

Placings:263/50632232626332 13-3203301 **(6925)**
2009: 6^3G, 6^2G, 7^0GF, 6^3G, 7^3F, 7^0G, 7^1GF,

	Starts	1st	2nd	3rd	Win & Pl
Career Total (Turf)	16	1	4	5	7533
Career Total (AW)	10	1	3	4	6815

73 10/09 Yarm 7f3y (0-65)H G-F £2331
63 12/08 Wolv 7f32y STD £2729
Total win prize-money £5061

Going (Turf): Sf: 0-1 GS: 0-2 Gd: 0-5 **GF: 1-7** Fm: 0-1
Distance: 5f/6f: 0-2 **7f-8f: 2-17** 9f-13f: 0-7 14f+: 0-0
Track : **LH: 1-16** RH: 0-4 **Tight: 1-9** Gall: 0-4
Aids: Bl: 0-0 Vi: 0-0 Tstrap: 0-0 Ckp: 0-0
Best Rating: **73** 10/09 Yarm 7f3y gd-fm

Modest; effective at 6f-1m2f; acts on good/fast ground and on Polytrack.

Azygous

86(104) (70)**69**
6-y-o ch g Foxhound (USA)-Flag (Selkirk (USA))
M W Easterby R White & P J Sharp

Placings:11033404220/06033140634/00240000300560025/230434624610606461 0-00 **(5073)**
2009: 5^0GF, 5^0GF,

	Starts	1st	2nd	3rd	Win & Pl
Career Total (Turf)	39	2	4	5	25432
Career Total (AW)	22	3	2	3	15681

62 12/08 Ling 5f (0-60)H STD £2388
69 9/08 Folk 5f (0-60)H G-S £2590
86 7/06 Ches 5f16y (0-95)H G-F £10094
85 4/05 Ling 5f STD £7192
79 4/05 Ling 5f STD £3406
Total win prize-money £25670

Going (Turf): Sf: 0-0 **GS: 1-4** Gd: 0-12 **GF: 1-22** Fm: 0-1
Distance: **5f/6f: 5-61** 7f-8f: 0-0 9f-13f: 0-0 14f+: 0-0
Track : **LH: 4-23** RH: 0-7 **Tight: 4-14** Gall: 0-7
Aids: **Bl: 1-2** Vi: 0-2 Tstrap: 0-6 Ckp: 0-6
Best Rating: **87** 10/05 Epsm 5f good

Modest sprinter; acts on fast and easy ground; goes on Polytrack; has worn blinkers.

Azzez Life

74(67) (5)**38**
2-y-o br g Avonbridge-Glascoed (Adbass (USA))
R C Guest Shaun Taylor

Placings:00000 **(7421)**
2009: 5^0G, 6^0GF, 6^0G, 5^0GF, 6^0SD,

	Starts	1st	2nd	3rd	Win & Pl
Career Total (Turf)	4	0	0	0	
Career Total (AW)	1	0	0	0	

Going (Turf): **Sf: 0-0 GS: 0-0 Gd: 0-2 GF: 0-2 Fm: 0-0**
Distance: 5f/6f: 0-4 7f-8f: 0-1 9f-13f: 0-0 14f+: 0-0
Track : LH: 0-2 RH: 0-0 Tight: 0-0 Gall: 0-0
Aids: Bl: 0-2 Vi: 0-0 Tstrap: 0-0 Ckp: 0-0
Best Rating: **38** 8/09 Nott 6f15y gd-fm

BA Dreamflight

99(102) (59)58
4-y-o b g Noverre (USA)-Aunt Tate (Tate Gallery (USA))
H Morrison BA Racing

Placings:000/0464404361224-00300565 (5873)
2009: 12⁰SD, 12⁰SD, 10³F, 11⁰GF, 10⁰G, 9⁵GF, 10⁶SD, 10⁵G,

	Starts	1st	2nd	3rd	Win & Pl
Career Total (Turf)	14	0	1	2	1932
Career Total (AW)	10	1	1	0	2547

56 10/08 GrLe 1m2f (0-50)H STD £1942
Total win prize-money £1943

Going (Turf): **Sf: 0-3 GS: 0-1 Gd: 0-3 GF: 0-6 Fm: 0-1**
Distance: 5f/6f: 0-0 7f-8f: 0-3 **9f-13f: 1-21** 14f+: 0-0
Track : **LH: 1-15** RH: 0-8 Tight: 0-10 **Gall: 1-2**
Aids: Bl: 0-0 Vi: 0-1 Tstrap: 0-1 Ckp: 0-1
Best Rating: **59** 11/08 Sthl 1m4f stand

Moderate; stays 1m4f; acts on a sound surface; goes on Fibresand and Polytrack.

BA Globetrotter

97(91) (51)52
3-y-o ch g Needwood Blade-Generous Share (Cadeaux Genereux)
M R Channon M Channon

Placings:0000005020056-634603 (3651)
2009: 8⁶G, 5³F, 5⁴F, 5⁶GF, 7⁰GF, 6³G,

	Starts	1st	2nd	3rd	Win & Pl
Career Total (Turf)	15	0	0	2	770
Career Total (AW)	5	0	1	0	964

Going (Turf): **Sf: 0-0 GS: 0-2 Gd: 0-4 GF: 0-7 Fm: 0-2**
Distance: 5f/6f: 0-7 7f-8f: 0-7 9f-13f: 0-6 14f+: 0-0
Track : LH: 0-5 RH: 0-3 Tight: 0-3 Gall: 0-3
Aids: Bl: 0-0 Vi: 0-0 Tstrap: 0-0 Ckp: 0-0
Best Rating: **52** 9/08 Yarm 1m3y good

Moderate sprinter.

BA Jetstream

85(73) (15)53
2-y-o b g Monsieur Bond (IRE)-Merch Rhyd-Y-Grug (Sabrehill (USA))
F Jordan (M R Channon 22/7) Tony Cocum & S A Mares

Placings:60433000 (7722)
2009: 5⁶GF, 6⁰GS, 5⁴G, 6³GF, 7³S, 7⁰GF, 7⁰SD, 8⁰SD,

	Starts	1st	2nd	3rd	Win & Pl
Career Total (Turf)	6	0	0	2	736
Career Total (AW)	2	0	0	0	

Going (Turf): **Sf: 0-1 GS: 0-1 Gd: 0-1 GF: 0-3 Fm: 0-0**
Distance: 5f/6f: 0-3 7f-8f: 0-5 9f-13f: 0-0 14f+: 0-0
Track : LH: 0-2 RH: 0-1 Tight: 0-1 Gall: 0-2
Aids: Bl: 0-0 Vi: 0-0 Tstrap: 0-0 Ckp: 0-0
Best Rating: **53** 6/09 Wind 5f10y gd-fm

Baaher (USA)

103(93) (71)62
5-y-o b g War Chant (USA)-Raajiya (USA) (Gulch (USA))
J S Goldie Alf Chadwick

Placings:3/00000-2000 (6767)
2009: 13²S, 16⁰GS, 17⁰G, 16⁰GS,

	Starts	1st	2nd	3rd	Win & Pl
Career Total (Turf)	7	0	1	0	705
Career Total (AW)	3	0	0	1	454

Going (Turf): **Sf: 0-1 GS: 0-4 Gd: 0-1 GF: 0-1 Fm: 0-0**
Distance: 5f/6f: 0-0 7f-8f: 0-2 9f-13f: 0-4 14f+: 0-4
Track : LH: 0-9 RH: 0-1 Tight: 0-5 Gall: 0-2
Aids: Bl: 0-0 Vi: 0-0 Tstrap: 0-1 Ckp: 0-1
Best Rating: **71** 3/08 Wolv 1m141y stand

Moderate; stays 1m5f and acts on soft ground.

Baan (USA)

104(103) (72)70
6-y-o ch g Diesis-Madaen (USA) (Nureyev (USA))
H J Collingridge Greenstead Hall Racing Ltd

Placings:1221/6330000350/560300405632326/356233-3224361145030 (7084)
2009: 14³SD, 16²SD, 16²SD, 16⁴SD, 14³G, 12⁶SD, 16¹G, 16¹G, 16⁴G, 16⁵GS, 16⁰SD, 17³GF, 15⁰S,

	Starts	1st	2nd	3rd	Win & Pl
Career Total (Turf)	27	4	2	5	39186
Career Total (AW)	21	0	5	7	10488

70 8/09 Thsk 2m (0-65)H GD £2978
69 7/09 Yarm 2m (0-65)H GD £1942
102 10/05 Epsm 1m114y G-S £8995
91 7/05 Bevl 7f100y GD £5447
Total win prize-money £19365

Going (Turf): Sf: 0-3 GS: 1-6 **Gd: 3-10** GF: 0-8 Fm: 0-0
Distance: 5f/6f: 0-0 7f-8f: 1-4 9f-13f: 1-28 **14f+: 2-16**
Track : **LH: 3-38** RH: 1-9 **Tight: 3-28** Gall: 0-6
Aids: Bl: 0-4 Vi: 0-5 Tstrap: 0-4 Ckp: 0-4
Best Rating: **103** 4/06 Sand 1m2f7y good

Modest; stays 2m; acts on good and easy ground; handles sand.

Baarlq

90(96) (74)82
3-y-o b g Royal Applause-Second Of May (Lion Cavern (USA))
P W Chapple-Hyam Ziad A Galadari

Placings:021-00005 (6780)
2009: 8⁰GF, 7⁰S, 7⁰G, 7⁰SD, 8⁵SS,

	Starts	1st	2nd	3rd	Win & Pl
Career Total (Turf)	6	1	1	0	5243
Career Total (AW)	2	0	0	0	0

82 9/08 Wwck 7f26y GD £3412
Total win prize-money £3412

Going (Turf): Sf: 0-1 GS: 0-0 **Gd: 1-3** GF: 0-2 Fm: 0-0
Distance: 5f/6f: 0-1 **7f-8f: 1-7** 9f-13f: 0-0 14f+: 0-0
Track : **LH: 1-3** RH: 0-0 Tight: 0-2 Gall: 0-0
Aids: Bl: 0-0 Vi: 0-0 Tstrap: 0-0 Ckp: 0-0
Best Rating: **82** 9/08 Wwck 7f26y good

Runner-up on debut; effective over 7f; acts on fast ground.

Bab Al Salam (USA)

107(109) (106)99
3-y-o b c Seeking The Gold (USA)-Encandiladora (ARG) (Equalize (USA))
Saeed Bin Suroor Godolphin

Placings:1-11131 (7226)
2009: 8¹GF, 10¹SD, 10¹F, 10³GF, 10¹SD,

	Starts	1st	2nd	3rd	Win & Pl
Career Total (Turf)	3	2	0	1	18361
Career Total (AW)	3	3	0	0	22424

106 11/09 Kemp 1m2f (0-100)H STD £11091
99 9/09 Bath 1m2f46y (0-95)H FRM £8723
93 9/09 Ling 1m2f (0-90)H STD £7771
89 8/09 Sand 1m14y (0-90)H G-F £7771
77 10/08 Ling 7f STD £3561
Total win prize-money £38918

Going (Turf): Sf: 0-0 GS: 0-0 Gd: 0-0 **GF: 1-2 Fm: 1-1**
Distance: 5f/6f: 0-0 7f-8f: 1-1 **9f-13f: 4-5** 14f+: 0-0
Track : **LH: 3-3** RH: 2-2 **Tight: 3-3** Gall: 0-0
Aids: Bl: 0-0 Vi: 0-0 Tstrap: 0-0 Ckp: 0-0
Best Rating: **106** 11/09 Kemp 1m2f stand

Very useful; effective at 1m-1m2f; acts on fast ground and on Polytrack.

Bab Al Shams (IRE)

94 76
2-y-o br c Cape Cross (IRE)-Shimna (Mr Prospector (USA))
Saeed Bin Suroor Godolphin

Placings:20 (6478)
2009: 8²GF, 7⁰GF,

	Starts	1st	2nd	3rd	Win & Pl
Career Total (Turf)	2	0	1	0	1510

Going (Turf): **Sf: 0-0 GS: 0-0 Gd: 0-0 GF: 0-2 Fm: 0-0**
Distance: 5f/6f: 0-0 7f-8f: 0-1 9f-13f: 0-1 14f+: 0-0
Track : LH: 0-0 RH: 0-0 Tight: 0-0 Gall: 0-0
Aids: Bl: 0-0 Vi: 0-0 Tstrap: 0-0 Ckp: 0-0
Best Rating: **76** 9/09 Yarm 1m3y gd-fm

200,000gns half-brother to winners, including the once smart Hazeymm; effective over 1m; acts on fast ground.

Bab At The Bowster (IRE)

98 83
2-y-o b f Footstepsinthesand-Charmingly (USA) (King Of Kings (IRE))
W J Haggas Findlay & Bloom

Placings:31011 (6481)
2009: 6³G, 6¹F, 7⁰GF, 7¹GF, 7¹GF,

	Starts	1st	2nd	3rd	Win & Pl
Career Total (Turf)	5	3	0	1	32053

83 10/09 NmkR 7f G-F £18693
79 9/09 Ches 7f2y (0-95)H G-F £9146
74 8/09 Brig 6f209y FRM £3154
Total win prize-money £30994

Going (Turf): Sf: 0-0 GS: 0-0 Gd: 0-1 **GF: 2-3** Fm: 1-1
Distance: 5f/6f: 0-1 **7f-8f: 3-4** 9f-13f: 0-0 14f+: 0-0
Track : **LH: 2-2** RH: 0-1 **Tight: 1-1** Gall: 0-0
Aids: Bl: 0-0 Vi: 0-0 Tstrap: 0-0 Ckp: 0-0
Best Rating: **83** 10/09 NmkR 7f gd-fm

Useful; stays 7f; acts on fast ground.

Baba Ghanoush

(99) (47)11
7-y-o ch m Zaha (CAN)-Vrennan (Suave Dancer (USA))
M J Attwater Canisbay Bloodstock

Placings:041/5/00006/0000006-300003300 (7652)
2009: 6³SD, 6⁰SD, 8⁰SD, 8⁰SD, 7⁰SD, 8³SD, 8³SD, 8⁰SD, 8⁰SD,

	Starts	1st	2nd	3rd	Win & Pl
Career Total (Turf)	2	0	0	0	
Career Total (AW)	23	1	0	3	4337

71 12/05 Wolv 7f32y STD £3355
Total win prize-money £3355

Going (Turf): Sf: 0-0 GS: 0-0 Gd: 0-1 GF: 0-1 Fm: 0-0
Distance: 5f/6f: 0-3 **7f-8f: 1-21** 9f-13f: 0-1 14f+: 0-0
Track : LH: 1-10 RH: 0-14 Tight: 1-8 Gall: 0-1
Aids: Bl: 0-6 Vi: 0-4 Tstrap: 0-1 Ckp: 0-1
Best Rating: 71 12/05 Wolv 7f32y stand

Very moderate; stays 7f and acts on Polytrack; has worn blinkers and cheekpieces.

Babajaga (IRE)

55(70) (29)
2-y-o ch f Night Shift (USA)-Art Fair (Alzao (USA))
J M P Eustace The Macdougall Partnership

Placings:00 (4176)
2009: 6^{0}SD, 6^{0}G,

	Starts	1st	2nd	3rd	Win & Pl
Career Total (Turf)	1	0	0	0	
Career Total (AW)	1	0	0	0	

Going (Turf): Sf: 0-0 GS: 0-0 Gd: 0-1 GF: 0-0 Fm: 0-0
Distance: 5f/6f: 0-1 7f-8f: 0-1 9f-13f: 0-0 14f+: 0-0
Track : LH: 0-1 RH: 0-0 Tight: 0-1 Gall: 0-0
Aids: Bl: 0-0 Vi: 0-0 Tstrap: 0-0 Ckp: 0-0
Best Rating: 29 7/09 Ling 6f stand

Babel

(103) (68)72
4-y-o b f Xaar-Day Star (Dayjur (USA))
M Wigham R J Lorenz

Placings:53215000-006 (0896)
2009: 5^{0}SD, 5^{0}SD, 5^{6}SD,

	Starts	1st	2nd	3rd	Win & Pl
Career Total (Turf)	4	1	1	1	6195
Career Total (AW)	7	0	0	0	0

72 8/08 DRoy 5f (45-60)H YLD £4318
Total win prize-money £4319

Going (Turf): Sf: 0-0 GS: 0-0 Gd: 0-2 GF: 0-0 Fm: 0-1
Distance: **5f/6f: 1-11** 7f-8f: 0-0 9f-13f: 0-0 14f+: 0-0
Track : LH: 0-7 **RH: 1-2** Tight: 0-2 Gall: 0-0
Aids: Bl: 0-0 Vi: 0-0 Tstrap: 0-0 Ckp: 0-0
Best Rating: 72 8/08 DRoy 5f yield

Babilu

93(103) (74)65
4-y-o ch f Lomitas-Creeking (Persian Bold)
D Burchell (A G Newcombe 24/7) Mr & Mrs A J Mutch

Placings:00/320-3041 (4264)
2009: 12^{3}GS, 12^{0}GS, 11^{4}F, 16^{1}S,

	Starts	1st	2nd	3rd	Win & Pl
Career Total (Turf)	7	1	0	2	3131
Career Total (AW)	2	0	1	0	964

54 7/09 Chep 2m49y SFT £2072
Total win prize-money £2072

Going (Turf): **Sf: 1-2** GS: 0-2 Gd: 0-1 GF: 0-1 Fm: 0-1
Distance: 5f/6f: 0-2 7f-8f: 0-0 9f-13f: 0-6 **14f+: 1-1**
Track : **LH: 1-6** RH: 0-1 Tight: 0-3 Gall: 0-2
Aids: Bl: 0-0 Vi: 0-0 Tstrap: 0-0 Ckp: 0-0
Best Rating: 74 8/08 Wolv 1m4f50y stand

Modest; stays 1m4f; acts on good ground and Polytrack.

Baby Dottie

99(100) (72)69
2-y-o ch f Dr Fong (USA)-Auntie Dot Com (Tagula (IRE))
P M Phelan Tony Smith

Placings:226323 (7177)
2009: 6^{2}SD, 6^{2}G, 6^{6}G, 5^{3}SD, 7^{2}SD, 7^{3}SD,

	Starts	1st	2nd	3rd	Win & Pl
Career Total (Turf)	2	0	1	0	6956
Career Total (AW)	4	0	2	2	2181

Going (Turf): Sf: 0-0 GS: 0-0 Gd: 0-2 GF: 0-0 Fm: 0-0
Distance: 5f/6f: 0-3 7f-8f: 0-3 9f-13f: 0-0 14f+: 0-0
Track : LH: 0-2 RH: 0-2 Tight: 0-2 Gall: 0-1
Aids: Bl: 0-0 Vi: 0-0 Tstrap: 0-0 Ckp: 0-0
Best Rating: 72 7/09 Ling 6f stand

Fair; stays 7f; acts on good ground and on Polytrack.

Baby Is Here (IRE)

(77) (21)46
3-y-o br f Namid-Attymon Lill (IRE) (Marju (IRE))
D J S Ffrench Davis Miss A Jones

Placings:000-6 (7455)
2009: 12^{6}SD,

	Starts	1st	2nd	3rd	Win & Pl
Career Total (Turf)	2	0	0	0	
Career Total (AW)	2	0	0	0	0

Going (Turf): Sf: 0-1 GS: 0-1 Gd: 0-0 GF: 0-0 Fm: 0-0
Distance: 5f/6f: 0-2 7f-8f: 0-0 9f-13f: 0-2 14f+: 0-0
Track : LH: 0-2 RH: 0-2 Tight: 0-0 Gall: 0-0
Aids: Bl: 0-0 Vi: 0-0 Tstrap: 0-0 Ckp: 0-0
Best Rating: 46 10/08 Nott 1m75y soft

Baby Josr

95(98) (63)59
3-y-o br g Josr Algarhoud (IRE)-Bella Helena (Balidar)
I A Wood C R Lambourne

Placings:00030-1354002000 (6224)
2009: 5^{1}SD, 5^{3}SD, 8^{5}GS, 7^{4}G, 8^{0}S, 9^{0}GF, 7^{2}SD, 7^{0}SD, 8^{0}G, 8^{0}SD,

	Starts	1st	2nd	3rd	Win & Pl
Career Total (Turf)	8	0	0	0	154
Career Total (AW)	7	1	1	2	3377

60 3/09 Wolv 5f216y (0-60)H STD £2217
Total win prize-money £2218

Going (Turf): Sf: 0-2 GS: 0-3 Gd: 0-2 GF: 0-1 Fm: 0-0
Distance: **5f/6f: 1-6** 7f-8f: 0-5 9f-13f: 0-4 14f+: 0-0
Track : **LH: 1-7** RH: 0-3 **Tight: 1-7** Gall: 0-0
Aids: Bl: 0-0 Vi: 0-9 Tstrap: 0-0 Ckp: 0-0
Best Rating: 63 8/09 Ling 7f stand

Modest; effective over 6f-7f; acts on Polytrack.

Baby Judge (IRE)

98(87) (45)58
2-y-o ch g Captain Rio-Darling Clementine (Lion Cavern (USA))
M C Chapman (R A Harris 15/6) Roy Gowans

Placings:004055006631036040 (7791)
2009: 5^{0}G, 6^{0}GF, 5^{4}GF, 5^{0}GF, 5^{5}G, 6^{5}SD, 5^{0}SD, 6^{0}GF, 5^{6}SD, 5^{6}GS, 7^{3}GF, 7^{1}GF, 8^{0}GF, 7^{3}GF, 7^{6}S, 6^{0}SD, 5^{4}SD, 7^{0}SS,

	Starts	1st	2nd	3rd	Win & Pl
Career Total (Turf)	12	1	0	2	6132

Career Total (AW) 6 0 0 0 0
57 9/09 Yarm 7f3y (0-80) G-F £5046
Total win prize-money £5046

Going (Turf): Sf: 0-1 GS: 0-1 Gd: 0-2 **GF: 1-8** Fm: 0-0
Distance: 5f/6f: 0-12 **7f-8f: 1-5** 9f-13f: 0-1 14f+: 0-0
Track : LH: 0-5 RH: 0-0 Tight: 0-1 Gall: 0-2
Aids: Bl: 0-2 Vi: 0-0 Tstrap: 0-0 Ckp: 0-0
Best Rating: 58 7/09 Wind 5f10y good

Moderate; effective over 7f; acts on fast ground.

Baby Queen (IRE)

96(85) (40)68
3-y-o b f Royal Applause-Kissing Time (Lugana Beach)
B P J Baugh G B Hignett

Placings:050011060 (4829)
2009: 5^{0}SD, 5^{5}SF, 6^{0}GF, 5^{0}GF, 5^{1}G, 5^{1}F, 5^{0}GF, 5^{6}GS, 5^{0}G,

	Starts	1st	2nd	3rd	Win & Pl
Career Total (Turf)	7	2	0	0	4767
Career Total (AW)	2	0	0	0	0

68 6/09 Bath 5f11y (0-70)H FRM £2719
63 5/09 Nott 5f13y (0-60)H GD £2047
Total win prize-money £4767

Going (Turf): Sf: 0-0 GS: 0-1 **Gd: 1-2** GF: 0-3 **Fm: 1-1**
Distance: **5f/6f: 2-9** 7f-8f: 0-0 9f-13f: 0-0 14f+: 0-0
Track : **LH: 1-5** RH: 0-0 Tight: 0-2 **Gall: 1-2**
Aids: Bl: 0-0 Vi: 0-0 Tstrap: 0-0 Ckp: 0-0
Best Rating: 68 6/09 Bath 5f11y firm

Modest; effective over 5f; acts on good ground.

Baby Rock

93 72
4-y-o b g Selkirk (USA)-Vanishing Point (USA) (Caller I.D. (USA))
C F Wall Ms Aida Fustoq

Placings:43020-003 (5406)
2009: 6^{0}GF, 6^{0}GF, 6^{3}G,

	Starts	1st	2nd	3rd	Win & Pl
Career Total (Turf)	8	0	1	2	2160

Going (Turf): Sf: 0-0 GS: 0-3 Gd: 0-2 GF: 0-3 Fm: 0-0
Distance: 5f/6f: 0-6 7f-8f: 0-2 9f-13f: 0-0 14f+: 0-0
Track : LH: 0-2 RH: 0-0 Tight: 0-0 Gall: 0-1
Aids: Bl: 0-0 Vi: 0-0 Tstrap: 0-0 Ckp: 0-0
Best Rating: 72 8/08 Yarm 6f3y gd-sft

Modest half-brother to the stable's useful sprinter Royal Rock; best at 6f on fast ground.

Baby Strange

107(105) (94)105
5-y-o gr g Superior Premium-The Manx Touch (IRE) (Petardia)
D Shaw Market Avenue Racing Club Ltd

Placings:110412/0000264145622000-401600040030 (6944)
2009: 6^{4}SD, 6^{0}GF, 6^{1}GF, 6^{6}GF, 6^{0}GF, 6^{0}G, 7^{0}G, 5^{4}SD, 7^{0}SD, 5^{0}SD, 6^{3}SD, 7^{0}SD,

	Starts	1st	2nd	3rd	Win & Pl
Career Total (Turf)	24	5	4	0	96733
Career Total (AW)	10	0	0	1	1820

97 5/09 Newc 6f (0-90)H G-F £7569
100 5/08 Newb 6f8y (0-100)H GD £12462
110 10/06 York 6f SFT £14817
95 5/06 Asct 6f G-F £7772
85 5/06 Bath 5f11y G-S £3886
Total win prize-money £46508

Going (Turf): Sf: 1-7 GS: 1-4 Gd: 1-6 **GF: 2-7** Fm: 0-0
Distance: **5f/6f: 4-26** 7f-8f: 1-8 9f-13f: 0-0 14f+: 0-0
Track : **LH: 1-5** RH: 0-6 Tight: 0-4 **Gall: 1-1**
Aids: Bl: 0-0 Vi: 0-1 Tstrap: 0-0 Ckp: 0-0
Best Rating: **110** 10/06 York 6f soft

Very useful; effective over 5f-6f; acts on most ground; has worn a visor; likes to race prominently.

Babycakes (IRE)

81(75) (34)45
2-y-o b f Marju (IRE)-Dark Rosaleen (IRE) (Darshaan)
M L W Bell J Acheson

Placings:00 (7388)
2009: 8^{0}GS, 8^{0}SD,

	Starts	1st	2nd	3rd	Win & Pl
Career Total (Turf)	1	0	0	0	
Career Total (AW)	1	0	0	0	

Going (Turf): **Sf: 0-0 GS: 0-1 Gd: 0-0 GF: 0-0 Fm: 0-0**
Distance: 5f/6f: 0-0 7f-8f: 0-2 9f-13f: 0-0 14f+: 0-0
Track : LH: 0-2 RH: 0-0 Tight: 0-1 Gall: 0-1
Aids: Bl: 0-0 Vi: 0-0 Tstrap: 0-0 Ckp: 0-0
Best Rating: **45** 10/09 Donc 1m gd-sft

Babylonian

92 70
2-y-o b f Shamardal (USA)-Evil Empire (GER) (Acatenango (GER))
M Johnston Sheikh Hamdan Bin Mohammed Al Maktoum

Placings:325 (3820)
2009: 6^{3}GF, 6^{2}GS, 6^{5}GF,

	Starts	1st	2nd	3rd	Win & Pl
Career Total (Turf)	3	0	1	1	2428

Going (Turf): **Sf: 0-0 GS: 0-1 Gd: 0-0 GF: 0-2 Fm: 0-0**
Distance: 5f/6f: 0-3 7f-8f: 0-0 9f-13f: 0-0 14f+: 0-0
Track : LH: 0-0 RH: 0-0 Tight: 0-0 Gall: 0-0
Aids: Bl: 0-0 Vi: 0-0 Tstrap: 0-0 Ckp: 0-0
Best Rating: **70** 6/09 Donc 6f gd-sft

Fair; stays 6f and acts on good ground.

Back In The Red (IRE)

85(103) (79)69
5-y-o ch g Redback-Fureur De Vivre (IRE) (Bluebird (USA))
R A Harris Mrs Ruth M Serrell

Placings:6005150/**6451144000**1005/0554623**0041312-113140500** (3713)
2009: 5^{1}SD, 6^{1}SD, 5^{3}SD, 5^{1}SD, 6^{4}SD, 5^{0}SF, 5^{5}SD, 5^{0}F, 6^{0}SD,

	Starts	1st	2nd	3rd	Win & Pl
Career Total (Turf)	19	3	1	1	11331
Career Total (AW)	25	6	1	2	15594

79	2/09	Sthl	5f	(0-70)H	STD	£2729
73	1/09	Sthl	6f		STD	£2047
76	1/09	Sthl	5f		STD	£2047
68	12/08	Wolv	5f216y		STD	£2729
75	11/08	Kemp	6f	(0-58)H	STD	£2047
77	11/07	Wolv	5f20y	(0-75)H	STD	£2817
79	8/07	Bath	5f11y	(0-70)H	G-F	£3238
69	8/07	Leic	5f2y	(0-60)H	G-S	£2590
62	9/06	Rdcr	5f	(0-65)	G-F	£3238

Total win prize-money £23487

Going (Turf): Sf: 0-1 GS: 1-2 Gd: 0-4 **GF: 2-11** Fm: 0-1
Distance: **5f/6f: 9-44** 7f-8f: 0-0 9f-13f: 0-0 14f+: 0-0
Track : **LH: 4-24** RH: 1-5 **Tight: 2-14** Gall: 1-3
Aids: **Bl: 5-13** Vi: 0-0 Tstrap: 0-3 Ckp: 0-3
Best Rating: **79** 2/09 Sthl 5f stand

Modest; effective over 5f-6f; effective on fast ground and on sand; has worn blinkers and cheekpieces.

Back On

75(71) (22)46
2-y-o b c Reset (AUS)-Teal Flower (Pivotal)
G C Bravery Mrs Theresa Fitsall

Placings:400 (3167)
2009: 5^{4}GF, 5^{0}SD, 7^{0}GF,

	Starts	1st	2nd	3rd	Win & Pl
Career Total (Turf)	2	0	0	0	385
Career Total (AW)	1	0	0	0	

Going (Turf): **Sf: 0-0 GS: 0-0 Gd: 0-0 GF: 0-2 Fm: 0-0**
Distance: 5f/6f: 0-2 7f-8f: 0-1 9f-13f: 0-0 14f+: 0-0
Track : LH: 0-0 RH: 0-1 Tight: 0-0 Gall: 0-0
Aids: Bl: 0-0 Vi: 0-0 Tstrap: 0-0 Ckp: 0-0
Best Rating: **46** 5/09 NmkR 5f gd-fm

Back To Paris (IRE)

(93) (49)99
7-y-o b g Lil's Boy (USA)-Alisco (IRE) (Shalford (IRE))
Paul Murphy Patrick Delaney

Placings:3350/14141/0000/60/**5** (7817)
2009: 9^{5}SD,

	Starts	1st	2nd	3rd	Win & Pl
Career Total (Turf)	15	3	0	2	55375
Career Total (AW)	1	0	0	0	0

102	8/05	Leop	1m2f	H	G-F	£30010
101	6/05	Cork	1m	H	GD	£15005
87	5/05	Fair	1m1f	(60-90)H	G-F	£7351

Total win prize-money £52367

Going (Turf): Sf: 0-1 GS: 0-0 Gd: 1-4 **GF: 2-6** Fm: 0-1
Distance: 5f/6f: 0-1 7f-8f: 1-7 **9f-13f: 2-8** 14f+: 0-0
Track : LH: 1-7 **RH: 2-6** Tight: 0-1 Gall: 0-2
Aids: Bl: 0-0 Vi: 0-0 Tstrap: 0-0 Ckp: 0-0
Best Rating: **102** 8/05 Leop 1m2f gd-fm

Backlash

(108) (48)41
8-y-o b m Fraam-Mezza Luna (Distant Relative)
A W Carroll A C Pickford

Placings:0/00055156/56220000/003/40055-5000 (0601)
2009: 11^{5}SD, 12^{0}SD, 10^{0}SD, 12^{0}SD,

	Starts	1st	2nd	3rd	Win & Pl
Career Total (Turf)	8	1	0	1	1928
Career Total (AW)	21	0	2	0	421

49	10/04	Wwck	1m22y	(0-45)	G-S	£1522

Total win prize-money £1522

Going (Turf): Sf: 0-2 **GS: 1-1** Gd: 0-1 GF: 0-1 Fm: 0-3
Distance: 5f/6f: 0-4 7f-8f: 0-5 **9f-13f: 1-19** 14f+: 0-1
Track : **LH: 1-20** RH: 0-6 Tight: 0-15 Gall: 0-0
Aids: Bl: 0-1 Vi: 0-1 Tstrap: 0-1 Ckp: 0-1
Best Rating: **49** 10/04 Wwck 1m22y gd-sft

Bad Moon Rising

(92) (57)51
4-y-o ch g Piccolo-Janette Parkes (Pursuit Of Love)
J Akehurst Advance Digital Print Ltd

Placings:400/000000-20 (0802)
2009: 8^{2}SD, 8^{0}SD,

	Starts	1st	2nd	3rd	Win & Pl
Career Total (Turf)	3	0	0	0	361
Career Total (AW)	8	0	1	0	504

Going (Turf): **Sf: 0-0 GS: 0-1 Gd: 0-0 GF: 0-2 Fm: 0-0**
Distance: 5f/6f: 0-3 7f-8f: 0-7 9f-13f: 0-1 14f+: 0-0
Track : LH: 0-6 RH: 0-2 Tight: 0-5 Gall: 0-1
Aids: Bl: 0-0 Vi: 0-0 Tstrap: 0-4 Ckp: 0-4
Best Rating: **57** 11/07 Ling 7f stand

Plating class; stays 1m; acts on Polytrack.

Baddam

108 97
7-y-o b g Mujahid (USA)-Aude La Belle (FR) (Ela-Mana-Mou)
Ian Williams N Martin

Placings:4063/312110/0501155300/20200530/50001040-300420 (6115)
2009: 16^{3}GF, 20^{0}GF, 21^{0}G, 16^{4}GF, 14^{2}G, 18^{0}GF,

	Starts	1st	2nd	3rd	Win & Pl
Career Total (Turf)	42	6	4	5	181634

97	7/08	Gdwd	2m5f	(0-95)H	G-F	£31155
82	6/06	Asct	2m5f159y		G-F	£34276
104	6/06	Asct	2m4f	(0-95)H	G-F	£34276
98	8/05	NmkJ	1m6f175y	(0-95)H	G-S	£8984
86	7/05	Sand	1m6f	(0-85)H	G-F	£6906
72	5/05	Nott	1m6f15y	(0-75)H	GD	£3485

Total win prize-money £119083

Going (Turf): Sf: 0-4 GS: 1-9 Gd: 1-10 **GF: 4-18** Fm: 0-1
Distance: 5f/6f: 0-0 7f-8f: 0-3 9f-13f: 0-3 **14f+: 6-36**
Track : LH: 1-12 **RH: 5-27** Tight: 1-5 **Gall: 3-24**
Aids: Bl: 0-0 Vi: 0-1 Tstrap: 0-1 Ckp: 0-1
Best Rating: **111** 5/07 Asct 2m gd-fm

Very useful; Group placed and won twice at Royal Ascot in 2006; winning hurdler; stays 2m6f, but effective at shorter; acts on most ground.

Badge

96 70
3-y-o b g Acclamation-Be My Wish (Be My Chief (USA))
R Charlton Michael Pescod

Placings:63 (2070)
2009: 5^{6}GF, 6^{3}GS,

	Starts	1st	2nd	3rd	Win & Pl
Career Total (Turf)	2	0	0	1	482

Going (Turf): **Sf: 0-0 GS: 0-1 Gd: 0-0 GF: 0-1 Fm: 0-0**
Distance: 5f/6f: 0-2 7f-8f: 0-0 9f-13f: 0-0 14f+: 0-0
Track : LH: 0-1 RH: 0-0 Tight: 0-0 Gall: 0-1
Aids: Bl: 0-0 Vi: 0-0 Tstrap: 0-0 Ckp: 0-0
Best Rating: **70** 5/09 Donc 6f gd-sft

Fair; stays 6f and acts on easy ground.

Badge Of Honour

(102) (76)
3-y-o ch g Storming Home-Loch Katrine (Selkirk (USA))
Niall O'Callaghan (M Johnston 14/3) Kilmichael Racing Syndicate

Placings:0-2211000 (7447a)
2009: 8^{2}SD, 10^{2}SD, 8^{1}SD, 10^{1}SD, 12^{0}S, 11^{0}GY, 12^{0}SD,

	Starts	1st	2nd	3rd	Win & Pl
Career Total (Turf)	2	0	0	0	
Career Total (AW)	6	2	2	0	10818

76 3/09 Ling 1m2f (0-85)H STD £6476
74 2/09 Wolv 1m141y STD £2729
Total win prize-money £9206

Going (Turf): Sf: 0-1 GS: 0-0 Gd: 0-0 GF: 0-0 Fm: 0-0
Distance: 5f/6f: 0-0 7f-8f: 0-2 **9f-13f: 2-6** 14f+: 0-0
Track : **LH: 2-7** RH: 0-1 **Tight: 2-4** Gall: 0-0
Aids: Bl: 0-2 Vi: 0-0 Tstrap: 0-0 Ckp: 0-0
Best Rating: 76 3/09 Ling 1m2f stand

Fair; effective over 1m-1m2f; acts on Polytrack.

Badiat Alzaman (IRE)

104(106) (95)**90**
3-y-o b f Zamindar (USA)-Fair Weather (IRE) (Marju (IRE))
D M Simcock Sultan Ali

Placings:044-21500562 (7366)
2009: 7^{2}SD, 8^{1}GF, 8^{5}G, 8^{0}GF, 8^{0}GF, 9^{5}GF, 10^{6}GF, 10^{2}SD,

	Starts	1st	2nd	3rd	Win & Pl
Career Total (Turf)	7	1	0	0	6275
Career Total (AW)	4	0	2	0	3889

79 5/09 Wwck 1m22y G-F £2914
Total win prize-money £2914

Going (Turf): Sf: 0-0 GS: 0-0 Gd: 0-2 **GF: 1-5** Fm: 0-0
Distance: 5f/6f: 0-0 7f-8f: 0-6 **9f-13f: 1-5** 14f+: 0-0
Track : **LH: 1-7** RH: 0-2 Tight: 0-6 Gall: 0-1
Aids: Bl: 0-0 Vi: 0-0 Tstrap: 0-0 Ckp: 0-0
Best Rating: 95 11/09 Ling 1m2f stand

Useful; stays 1m on quick ground, also goes on Polytrack.

Badtanman

90(95) (47)**41**
3-y-o ch c Primo Valentino (IRE)-Pearls (Mon Tresor)
Peter Grayson Haldane Racing & D L Rhodes

Placings:000-643030456600006 (7510)
2009: 5^{6}SD, 5^{4}SF, 5^{3}SD, 5^{0}SD, 5^{3}SD, 5^{0}GF, 5^{4}G, 5^{5}GF, 5^{6}GF, 5^{6}G, 5^{0}SD, 5^{0}S, 5^{0}G, 7^{0}SS, 5^{6}SD,

	Starts	1st	2nd	3rd	Win & Pl
Career Total (Turf)	7	0	0	0	216
Career Total (AW)	11	0	0	2	655

Going (Turf): Sf: 0-1 GS: 0-0 Gd: 0-3 GF: 0-3 Fm: 0-0
Distance: 5f/6f: 0-16 7f-8f: 0-2 9f-13f: 0-0 14f+: 0-0
Track : LH: 0-10 RH: 0-1 Tight: 0-10 Gall: 0-0
Aids: Bl: 0-10 Vi: 0-1 Tstrap: 0-0 Ckp: 0-0
Best Rating: 47 4/09 Wolv 5f20y stand

Moderate; effective over 5f; acts on Polytrack.

Bagamoyo

101(93) (91)**86**
2-y-o b c Acclamation-Queen Of Silk (IRE) (Brief Truce (USA))
J R Fanshawe Chippenham Lodge Stud

Placings:1322 (6585)
2009: 6^{1}S, 6^{3}GF, 6^{2}GF, 6^{2}SD,

	Starts	1st	2nd	3rd	Win & Pl
Career Total (Turf)	3	1	1	1	7437
Career Total (AW)	1	0	1	0	771

82 8/09 Donc 6f SFT £4857
Total win prize-money £4857

Going (Turf): Sf: 1-1 GS: 0-0 Gd: 0-0 GF: 0-2 Fm: 0-0
Distance: 5f/6f: 1-4 7f-8f: 0-0 9f-13f: 0-0 14f+: 0-0
Track : LH: 0-1 RH: 0-1 Tight: 0-1 Gall: 0-0
Aids: Bl: 0-0 Vi: 0-0 Tstrap: 0-0 Ckp: 0-0
Best Rating: 91 10/09 Kemp 6f stand

Very useful; stays 6f; acts on most ground.

Bagber

99(106) (82)**77**
3-y-o b g Diktat-Torcross (Vettori (IRE))
P Monteith (H J L Dunlop 30/9) Allan McLuckie

Placings:453-3342243114 (6986)
2009: 8^{3}SD, 10^{3}GF, 10^{4}GF, 12^{2}GS, 10^{2}G, 12^{4}S, 11^{3}SD, 12^{1}SD, 9^{1}GF, 10^{4}G,

	Starts	1st	2nd	3rd	Win & Pl
Career Total (Turf)	10	1	2	2	6899
Career Total (AW)	3	1	0	2	2836

72 9/09 Sals 1m1f198y G-F £3238
82 8/09 Kemp 1m4f STD £2047
Total win prize-money £5285

Going (Turf): Sf: 0-2 GS: 0-2 Gd: 0-3 **GF: 1-3** Fm: 0-0
Distance: 5f/6f: 0-0 7f-8f: 0-4 **9f-13f: 2-9** 14f+: 0-0
Track : LH: 0-4 **RH: 2-6 Tight: 1-4** Gall: 0-1
Aids: Bl: 0-0 Vi: 0-0 Tstrap: 0-0 Ckp: 0-0
Best Rating: 82 8/09 Kemp 1m4f stand

Fair; stays 1m2f; acts on good and soft ground and on Polytrack.

Baggsy (IRE)

(82) (55)
2-y-o b f Statue Of Liberty (USA)-Nisibis (In The Wings)
Miss J Feilden Hoofbeats Racing Club

Placings:06 (7326)
2009: 7^{0}SD, 7^{6}SD,

	Starts	1st	2nd	3rd	Win & Pl
Career Total (Turf)	0	0	0	0	
Career Total (AW)	2	0	0	0	0

Going (Turf): Sf: 0-0 GS: 0-0 Gd: 0-0 GF: 0-0 Fm: 0-0
Distance: 5f/6f: 0-0 7f-8f: 0-2 9f-13f: 0-0 14f+: 0-0
Track : LH: 0-0 RH: 0-2 Tight: 0-0 Gall: 0-0
Aids: Bl: 0-0 Vi: 0-0 Tstrap: 0-0 Ckp: 0-0
Best Rating: 55 9/09 Kemp 7f stand

Bahama Baileys

91 **51**
4-y-o ch g Bahamian Bounty-Baileys Silver (USA) (Marlin (USA))
C A Dwyer G R Bailey Ltd (Baileys Horse Feeds)

Placings:414304064/0400-00000 (7094)
2009: 6^{0}GS, 5^{0}GF, 5^{0}GF, 8^{0}GF, 10^{0}G,

	Starts	1st	2nd	3rd	Win & Pl
Career Total (Turf)	18	1	0	1	7126

75 5/07 Newc 5f G-F £2914
Total win prize-money £2915

Going (Turf): Sf: 0-0 GS: 0-2 Gd: 0-5 **GF: 1-10** Fm: 0-1
Distance: 5f/6f: 1-11 7f-8f: 0-5 9f-13f: 0-2 14f+: 0-0
Track : LH: 0-4 RH: 0-0 Tight: 0-1 Gall: 0-1
Aids: Bl: 0-3 Vi: 0-0 Tstrap: 0-0 Ckp: 0-0
Best Rating: 75 5/07 Bevl 5f gd-fm

Bahamarama (IRE)

(96) (56)**50**
4-y-o ch f Bahamian Bounty-Cole Slaw (Absalom)
R A Harris P M Cooper

Placings:0330140005/36263136635-000 (0895)
2009: 6^{0}SS, 5^{0}SD, 5^{0}SD,

	Starts	1st	2nd	3rd	Win & Pl
Career Total (Turf)	3	0	0	1	578
Career Total (AW)	21	2	1	5	6301

56 3/08 Wolv 5f216y STD £1774
60 8/07 Wolv 5f20y STD £2047
Total win prize-money £3823

Going (Turf): Sf: 0-1 GS: 0-1 Gd: 0-0 GF: 0-1 Fm: 0-0
Distance: 5f/6f: 2-22 7f-8f: 0-2 9f-13f: 0-0 14f+: 0-0
Track : **LH: 2-20** RH: 0-0 **Tight: 2-17** Gall: 0-1
Aids: Bl: 0-0 Vi: 0-0 Tstrap: 1-10 Ckp: 1-10
Best Rating: 60 8/07 Wolv 5f20y stand

Moderate; both her wins so far have come over 5f and 6f sellers at Wolverhampton; effective over 5f; acts on Polytrack.

Bahamian Babe

103(92) (78)**93**
3-y-o ch f Bahamian Bounty-Baby Bunting (Wolfhound (USA))
M L W Bell Mrs P D Gray And H J P Farr

Placings:11104305-5010400 (6428)
2009: 5^{5}G, 5^{0}GF, 5^{1}GF, 5^{0}GF, 5^{4}G, 5^{0}GF, 6^{0}GF,

	Starts	1st	2nd	3rd	Win & Pl
Career Total (Turf)	14	3	0	1	41584
Career Total (AW)	1	1	0	0	1774

90 6/09 Leic 5f2y (0-95)H G-F £10904
93 5/08 York 5f G-F £14815
78 4/08 Thsk 5f G-S £5180
78 4/08 Sthl 5f STD £1774
Total win prize-money £32674

Going (Turf): Sf: 0-1 GS: 1-2 Gd: 0-4 **GF: 2-7** Fm: 0-0
Distance: 5f/6f: 4-15 7f-8f: 0-0 9f-13f: 0-0 14f+: 0-0
Track : LH: 0-1 RH: 0-0 Tight: 0-0 Gall: 0-1
Aids: Bl: 0-0 Vi: 0-0 Tstrap: 0-0 Ckp: 0-0
Best Rating: 93 7/08 Newb 5f34y good

Very useful; Listed winner at two; effective over 5f; acts on fast and easy ground; also goes on Fibresand.

Bahamian Ballad

97(93) (49)**54**
4-y-o ch f Bahamian Bounty-Record Time (Clantime)
J D Bethell Scotyork Partnership

Placings:0030/55504040-2400400 (6380)
2009: 5^{2}GF, 5^{4}GF, 5^{0}GF, 6^{0}G, 5^{4}G, 5^{0}GF, 5^{0}GF,

	Starts	1st	2nd	3rd	Win & Pl
Career Total (Turf)	16	0	1	1	2251
Career Total (AW)	3	0	0	0	0

Going (Turf): Sf: 0-0 GS: 0-1 Gd: 0-7 GF: 0-8 Fm: 0-0
Distance: 5f/6f: 0-19 7f-8f: 0-0 9f-13f: 0-0 14f+: 0-0
Track : LH: 0-2 RH: 0-2 Tight: 0-2 Gall: 0-2
Aids: Bl: 0-1 Vi: 0-7 Tstrap: 0-0 Ckp: 0-0
Best Rating: 68 9/07 York 5f89y gd-fm

Moderate half-sister to Moorhouse Lad; suited by 6f; acts on fast ground.

Bahamian Ballet

101 (83)**86**

7-y-o ch g Bahamian Bounty-Plie (Superlative)

E S McMahon B N Toye

Placings:310/0201352/031146003/04022000-2035250 **(5148)**

2009: 5^{2}GF, 5^{0}GF, 5^{3}GF, 5^{5}GF, 5^{2}G, 5^{5}G, 5^{0}GS,

	Starts	1st	2nd	3rd	Win & Pl
Career Total (Turf)	31	4	5	5	28139
Career Total (AW)	3	0	1	0	1542

91	7/07	Catt	5f	(0-85)H	G-S	£5181
83	6/07	Wind	5f10y	(0-75)H	GD	£3238
79	7/06	Wind	5f10y	(0-75)H	G-F	£3238
75	10/05	Wind	6f		GD	£3848

Total win prize-money £15508

Going (Turf): Sf: 0-1 GS: 1-2 **Gd: 2-12** GF: 1-16 Fm: 0-0
Distance: **5f/6f: 4-33** 7f-8f: 0-1 9f-13f: 0-0 14f+: 0-0
Track : LH: 0-8 RH: 0-1 Tight: 0-4 **Gall: 3-7**
Aids: Bl: 0-0 Vi: 0-0 Tstrap: 0-0 Ckp: 0-0
Best Rating: **91** 7/07 Catt 5f gd-sft

Fair; suited by 5f; acts on most ground; goes on Polytrack; likes to race prominently.

Bahamian Bay

(97) (53)**17**

7-y-o b m Bahamian Bounty-Moly (Inchinor)

M Brittain Northgate Lodge Racing Club

Placings:000/1044/110100/00005/2010050-030 **(0327)**

2009: 6^{0}SS, 7^{3}SD, 6^{0}SD,

	Starts	1st	2nd	3rd	Win & Pl
Career Total (Turf)	8	1	0	0	3562
Career Total (AW)	20	4	1	1	5309

53	3/08	Wolv	7f32y	(0-45)	STD	£1365
59	8/06	Bevl	5f	(0-70)H	GD	£3562
51	3/06	Sthl	5f	(0-45)	STD	£1876
48	3/05	Sthl	5f	(0-40)	STD	£1463

Total win prize-money £8267

Going (Turf): Sf: 0-0 GS: 0-3 **Gd: 1-2** GF: 0-3 Fm: 0-0
Distance: **5f/6f: 4-21** 7f-8f: 1-7 9f-13f: 0-0 14f+: 0-0
Track : **LH: 2-15** RH: 0-1 **Tight: 1-5** Gall: 0-1
Aids: Bl: 0-0 Vi: 0-2 Tstrap: 0-0 Ckp: 0-0
Best Rating: **59** 8/06 Bevl 5f good

Very moderate; stays 7f; acts on fast ground and on Polytrack; has worn a visor.

Bahamian Bliss

88(102) (67)**37**

4-y-o b f Bahamian Bounty-Fragrance (Mtoto)

J A R Toller Ms Frances Dakers

Placings:5221530-4060006 **(7592)**

2009: 6^{4}SD, 6^{0}GF, 5^{6}G, 6^{0}SD, 5^{0}SD, 5^{0}SD, 7^{6}SD,

	Starts	1st	2nd	3rd	Win & Pl
Career Total (Turf)	2	0	0	0	0
Career Total (AW)	12	1	2	1	4072

61	7/08	Ling	6f	STD	£2388

Total win prize-money £2388

Going (Turf): **Sf: 0-0 GS: 0-0 Gd: 0-1 GF: 0-1 Fm: 0-0**
Distance: **5f/6f: 1-10** 7f-8f: 0-4 9f-13f: 0-0 14f+: 0-0
Track : **LH: 1-12** RH: 0-1 **Tight: 1-11** Gall: 0-0
Aids: Bl: 0-1 Vi: 0-0 Tstrap: 0-0 Ckp: 0-0
Best Rating: **67** 4/09 Ling 6f stand

Modest; stays 7f and acts on Polytrack.

Bahamian Bolt

68 **8**

2-y-o ch g Bahamian Bounty-Feeling Blue (Missed Flight)

R Bastiman Chris Myers & Partners 2

Placings:0 **(7289)**

2009: 6^{0}S,

	Starts	1st	2nd	3rd	Win & Pl
Career Total (Turf)	1	0	0	0	-

Going (Turf): **Sf: 0-1 GS: 0-0 Gd: 0-0 GF: 0-0 Fm: 0-0**
Distance: 5f/6f: 0-1 7f-8f: 0-0 9f-13f: 0-0 14f+: 0-0
Track : LH: 0-0 RH: 0-0 Tight: 0-0 Gall: 0-0
Aids: Bl: 0-0 Vi: 0-0 Tstrap: 0-0 Ckp: 0-0
Best Rating: **8** 11/09 Donc 6f soft

Bahamian Ceilidh

95(95) (65)**76**

3-y-o ch f Bahamian Bounty-Crofters Ceilidh (Scottish Reel)

B N Pollock (Tom Dascombe 13/7) Mrs K M Lloyd

Placings:4412500-43335000000 **(6570)**

2009: 5^{4}G, 6^{3}GF, 5^{3}F, 5^{3}SD, 5^{5}GF, 5^{0}SF, 5^{0}G, 5^{0}SD, 5^{0}F, 6^{0}GF, 9^{0}GF,

	Starts	1st	2nd	3rd	Win & Pl
Career Total (Turf)	15	1	1	2	6446
Career Total (AW)	3	0	0	1	454

76	6/08	Ling	5f	G-F	£3302

Total win prize-money £3303

Going (Turf): Sf: 0-0 GS: 0-3 Gd: 0-2 **GF: 1-8** Fm: 0-2
Distance: **5f/6f: 1-17** 7f-8f: 0-0 9f-13f: 0-1 14f+: 0-0
Track : LH: 0-9 RH: 0-1 Tight: 0-4 Gall: 0-4
Aids: Bl: 0-0 Vi: 0-0 Tstrap: 0-0 Ckp: 0-0
Best Rating: **76** 6/08 Ling 5f gd-fm

Fair; effective over 5-6f; acts on fast and easy ground and Polytrack.

Bahamian Kid

98(103) (76)**76**

4-y-o b g Bahamian Bounty-Barachois Princess (USA) (Barachois (CAN))

R Hollinshead Graham Brothers Racing Partnership

Placings:502021400-0106004302 **(7845)**

2009: 7^{0}GF, 7^{1}G, 7^{0}GF, 7^{6}GF, 8^{0}GF, 7^{0}SD, 7^{4}SD, 5^{3}SD, 5^{0}SD, 7^{2}SD,

	Starts	1st	2nd	3rd	Win & Pl
Career Total (Turf)	10	1	2	0	4657
Career Total (AW)	9	1	1	1	4157

76	6/09	Wwck	7f26y	(0-70)H	GD	£2729
75	9/08	Wolv	7f32y		SF	£2388

Total win prize-money £5118

Going (Turf): Sf: 0-0 GS: 0-1 **Gd: 1-3** GF: 0-6 Fm: 0-0
Distance: 5f/6f: 0-5 **7f-8f: 2-13** 9f-13f: 0-1 14f+: 0-0
Track : **LH: 2-12** RH: 0-1 **Tight: 1-9** Gall: 0-0
Aids: Bl: 0-1 Vi: 0-2 Tstrap: 1-9 Ckp: 1-9
Best Rating: **76** 12/09 Wolv 7f32y stand

Fair; effective over 7f; acts on fast ground and on Polytrack; has worn cheekpieces, a visor and blinkers.

Bahamian Lad

95(105) (87)**76**

4-y-o b g Bahamian Bounty-Danehill Princess (IRE) (Danehill (USA))

R Hollinshead Graham Brothers Racing Partnership

Placings:2000432/010-0116503051012324 **(7875)**

2009: 8^{0}SD, 5^{1}SD, 5^{1}SD, 5^{6}SF, 5^{5}SD, 6^{0}GF, 6^{3}F, 6^{0}G, 6^{5}GF, 5^{1}SD, 5^{0}SD, 6^{1}SD, 5^{2}SD, 5^{3}SD, 6^{2}SD, 6^{4}SD,

	Starts	1st	2nd	3rd	Win & Pl
Career Total (Turf)	8	0	1	1	1843
Career Total (AW)	18	5	3	2	23309

86	10/09	Kemp	6f	(0-85)H	STD	£4727
81	9/09	Wolv	5f216y	(0-75)H	STD	£3238
81	3/09	Wolv	5f216y	(0-85)H	STD	£5180
81	2/09	Wolv	5f216y	(0-75)H	STD	£2590
75	2/08	Wolv	5f216y		STD	£2457

Total win prize-money £18193

Going (Turf): **Sf: 0-1 GS: 0-0 Gd: 0-1 GF: 0-5 Fm: 0-1**
Distance: **5f/6f: 5-24** 7f-8f: 0-2 9f-13f: 0-0 14f+: 0-0
Track : **LH: 4-15** RH: 1-4 **Tight: 4-13** Gall: 0-1
Aids: Bl: 0-0 Vi: 0-0 Tstrap: 0-0 Ckp: 0-0
Best Rating: **87** 12/09 Kemp 6f stand

Useful; stays 6f; handles fast ground; goes on Polytrack.

Bahamian Mouse (IRE)

80 **33**

3-y-o ch f Bahamian Bounty-Minnina (IRE) (In The Wings)

Andrew Turnell Mayden Stud

Placings:50 **(5789)**

2009: 6^{5}GF, 7^{0}G,

	Starts	1st	2nd	3rd	Win & Pl
Career Total (Turf)	2	0	0	0	0

Going (Turf): **Sf: 0-0 GS: 0-0 Gd: 0-1 GF: 0-1 Fm: 0-0**
Distance: 5f/6f: 0-0 7f-8f: 0-2 9f-13f: 0-0 14f+: 0-0
Track : LH: 0-0 RH: 0-0 Tight: 0-0 Gall: 0-0
Aids: Bl: 0-0 Vi: 0-0 Tstrap: 0-0 Ckp: 0-0
Best Rating: **33** 8/09 Sals 6f212y gd-fm

Bahamian Music (IRE)

96(94) (78)**81**

2-y-o b f Bahamian Bounty-Strings (Unfuwain (USA))

R A Fahey R A Fahey

Placings:31140 **(6305)**

2009: 7^{3}GF, 7^{1}GS, 7^{1}SD, 6^{4}GF, 7^{0}GF,

	Starts	1st	2nd	3rd	Win & Pl
Career Total (Turf)	4	1	0	1	6769
Career Total (AW)	1	1	0	0	4533

78	8/09	Wolv	7f32y	STD	£4533
74	7/09	Newc	7f	G-S	£4209

Total win prize-money £8742

Going (Turf): Sf: 0-0 **GS: 1-1** Gd: 0-0 GF: 0-3 Fm: 0-0
Distance: 5f/6f: 0-0 **7f-8f: 2-5** 9f-13f: 0-0 14f+: 0-0
Track : **LH: 1-2** RH: 0-0 **Tight: 1-2** Gall: 0-0
Aids: Bl: 0-0 Vi: 0-0 Tstrap: 0-0 Ckp: 0-0
Best Rating: **81** 9/09 Donc 6f110y gd-fm

Useful; stays 7f; acts on most ground and on Polytrack.

Bahamian Sun (IRE)

33

2-y-o ch g Bahamian Bounty-Firesteed (IRE) (Common Grounds)

Tom Dascombe Findlay & Bloom

Placings:00 (5787)
2009: 6^{0}S, 8^{0}G,

	Starts	1st	2nd	3rd	Win & Pl
Career Total (Turf)	2	0	0	0	

Going (Turf): **Sf: 0-1 GS: 0-0 Gd: 0-1 GF: 0-0 Fm: 0-0**
Distance: 5f/6f: 0-1 7f-8f: 0-0 9f-13f: 0-1 14f+: 0-0
Track : LH: 0-0 RH: 0-0 Tight: 0-0 Gall: 0-0
Aids: Bl: 0-0 Vi: 0-0 Tstrap: 0-0 Ckp: 0-0

Bahati (IRE)

100 82
2-y-o ch f Intikhab (USA)-Dawn Chorus (IRE) (Mukaddamah (USA))
J G Portman Prof C D Green

Placings:1046 (5797)
2009: 6^{1}GF, 7^{0}GF, 6^{4}G, 6^{6}GF,

	Starts	1st	2nd	3rd	Win & Pl
Career Total (Turf)	4	1	0	0	4848
79 5/09 Newb 6f8y		G-F	£3885		

Total win prize-money £3886

Going (Turf): Sf: 0-0 GS: 0-0 Gd: 0-1 **GF: 1-3** Fm: 0-0
Distance: 5f/6f: 0-1 **7f-8f: 1-3** 9f-13f: 0-0 14f+: 0-0
Track : LH: 0-0 RH: 0-1 Tight: 0-0 Gall: 0-0
Aids: Bl: 0-0 Vi: 0-0 Tstrap: 0-0 Ckp: 0-0
Best Rating: **82** 9/09 Donc 6f110y gd-fm

Useful; effective over 6f; acts on good/fast ground.

Baheeya

77 58
3-y-o ch f Almutawakel-My American Beauty (Wolfhound (USA))
C E Brittain Saeed Manana

Placings:0-00 (2179)
2009: 10^{0}G, 7^{0}G,

	Starts	1st	2nd	3rd	Win & Pl
Career Total (Turf)	3	0	0	0	

Going (Turf): **Sf: 0-0 GS: 0-0 Gd: 0-2 GF: 0-1 Fm: 0-0**
Distance: 5f/6f: 0-0 7f-8f: 0-2 9f-13f: 0-1 14f+: 0-0
Track : LH: 0-1 RH: 0-1 Tight: 0-0 Gall: 0-1
Aids: Bl: 0-0 Vi: 0-0 Tstrap: 0-0 Ckp: 0-0
Best Rating: **58** 5/09 Gdwd 7f good

Bahiano (IRE)

89(105) (89)81
8-y-o ch g Barathea (IRE)-Trystero (Shareef Dancer (USA))
C E Brittain C E Brittain

Placings:62/**2123**6004000**0**/45**054**063240**3**000**03**/**0**513203 0000/**3**00500000022**04**/**654**600020-500 (2243)
2009: 8^{5}SD, 8^{0}SD, 8^{0}GF,

	Starts	1st	2nd	3rd	Win & Pl
Career Total (Turf)	44	1	5	4	97022
Career Total (AW)	25	1	3	3	26951
100 2/06 Ndas 6f110y	(90-105)H	G-F	£41569		
84 2/04 Ling 7f	D	STD	£4046		

Total win prize-money £45616

Going (Turf): Sf: 0-1 GS: 0-7 Gd: 0-12 **GF: 1-22** Fm: 0-2
Distance: 5f/6f: 0-11 **7f-8f: 2-54** 9f-13f: 0-4 14f+: 0-0
Track : **LH: 2-34** RH: 0-5 Tight: 1-20 Gall: 1-12
Aids: Bl: 0-0 Vi: 0-0 Tstrap: 0-2 Ckp: 0-2
Best Rating: **108** 5/06 NmkR 6f gd-fm

Fair; formerly smart; effective from 6f-1m; acts on most ground and Polytrack; has worn cheekpieces.

Bahkov (IRE)

98(93) (59)63
3-y-o ch g Bahamian Bounty-Petrikov (IRE) (In The Wings)
Andrew Turnell (Tom Dascombe 14/7) Mayden Stud

Placings:4-54064366 (6251)
2009: 8^{5}S, 6^{4}GF, 8^{0}G, 8^{6}GF, 7^{4}GF, 6^{3}GF, 8^{6}GS, 5^{6}SD,

	Starts	1st	2nd	3rd	Win & Pl
Career Total (Turf)	7	0	0	1	950
Career Total (AW)	2	0	0	0	0

Going (Turf): **Sf: 0-1 GS: 0-1 Gd: 0-1 GF: 0-4 Fm: 0-0**
Distance: 5f/6f: 0-3 7f-8f: 0-3 9f-13f: 0-3 14f+: 0-0
Track : LH: 0-3 RH: 0-2 Tight: 0-4 Gall: 0-0
Aids: Bl: 0-0 Vi: 0-0 Tstrap: 0-0 Ckp: 0-0
Best Rating: **63** 5/09 Sals 6f gd-fm

Moderate; stays 1m; acts on fast but handles cut.

Bahrain Storm (IRE)

105 (91)100
6-y-o b g Bahhare (USA)-Dance Up A Storm (USA) (Storm Bird (CAN))
Patrick J Flynn Patrick T Sweeney

Placings:45434600356/32100/11/615035-0100 (6851)
2009: 12^{0}Y, 14^{1}SH, 10^{0}SD, 18^{0}G,

	Starts	1st	2nd	3rd	Win & Pl
Career Total (Turf)	26	4	1	4	48347
Career Total (AW)	2	1	0	0	10997
93 7/09 Gway 1m6f		SH	£13588		
100 5/08 Clon 2m	(60-90)H	FRM	£9573		
89 12/07 Dund 1m4f	(60-100)H	STD	£10996		
87 5/07 Gowr 1m4f	(50-80)H	G-F	£5836		
87 6/06 Tram 1m4f		FRM	£5718		

Total win prize-money £45715

Going (Turf): Sf: 0-2 GS: 0-0 Gd: 0-5 GF: 1-7 **Fm: 2-3**
Distance: 5f/6f: 0-1 7f-8f: 0-9 **9f-13f: 3-12** 14f+: 2-6
Track : LH: 0-7 **RH: 4-18** Tight: 0-0 Gall: 0-2
Aids: **Bl: 5-17** Vi: 0-0 Tstrap: 0-0 Ckp: 0-0
Best Rating: **100** 5/08 Leop 1m6f gd-fm

Very useful; stays 2m; acts on soft and fast ground, and on Polytrack.

Bahraj (USA)

99 67
2-y-o b/br f Key Of Luck (USA)-Alattrah (USA) (Shadeed (USA))
M Johnston Hamdan Al Maktoum

Placings:4641 (6557)
2009: 6^{4}GF, 5^{6}G, 5^{4}G, 7^{1}G,

	Starts	1st	2nd	3rd	Win & Pl
Career Total (Turf)	4	1	0	0	4669
67 10/09 Catt 7f	(0-85)H	GD	£4079		

Total win prize-money £4080

Going (Turf): Sf: 0-0 GS: 0-0 **Gd: 1-3** GF: 0-1 Fm: 0-0
Distance: 5f/6f: 0-3 **7f-8f: 1-1** 9f-13f: 0-0 14f+: 0-0
Track : **LH: 1-1** RH: 0-0 **Tight: 1-1** Gall: 0-0
Aids: Bl: 0-0 Vi: 0-0 Tstrap: 0-0 Ckp: 0-0
Best Rating: **67** 10/09 Catt 7f good

Moderate; stays 7f; acts on good ground.

Baibars (USA)

(84) (53)
2-y-o b/br c Gone West (USA)-Mombasa (USA) (Dynaformer (USA))
G A Butler Miss R Al-Attiya

Placings:0 (6943)
2009: 7^{0}SD,

	Starts	1st	2nd	3rd	Win & Pl
Career Total (Turf)	0	0	0	0	
Career Total (AW)	1	0	0	0	

Going (Turf): **Sf: 0-0 GS: 0-0 Gd: 0-0 GF: 0-0 Fm: 0-0**
Distance: 5f/6f: 0-0 7f-8f: 0-1 9f-13f: 0-0 14f+: 0-0
Track : LH: 0-0 RH: 0-1 Tight: 0-0 Gall: 0-0
Aids: Bl: 0-0 Vi: 0-0 Tstrap: 0-0 Ckp: 0-0
Best Rating: **53** 10/09 Kemp 7f stand

Baila Me (GER)

114(116) (106)110
4-y-o b f Samum (GER)-Bandeira (GER) (Law Society (USA))
Saeed Bin Suroor Godolphin

Placings:11301-2610 (7293)
2009: 10^{2}G, 12^{6}G, 13^{1}SD, 12^{0}S,

	Starts	1st	2nd	3rd	Win & Pl
Career Total (Turf)	8	3	1	1	158379
Career Total (AW)	1	1	0	0	22708
106 10/09 Ling 1m5f			STD	£22708	
110 9/08 Colo 1m4f			SFT	£73529	
104 6/08 Colo 1m3f			GD	£29412	
5/08 Chan 1m2f110y			GD	£8088	

Total win prize-money £133737

Going (Turf): Sf: 1-2 GS: 0-1 **Gd: 2-5** GF: 0-0 Fm: 0-0
Distance: 5f/6f: 0-0 7f-8f: 0-0 **9f-13f: 4-9** 14f+: 0-0
Track : LH: 1-3 **RH: 3-5 Tight: 1-1** Gall: 0-2
Aids: Bl: 0-0 Vi: 0-0 Tstrap: 0-0 Ckp: 0-0
Best Rating: **110** 9/08 Colo 1m4f soft

Group class; Group 1 winner in Germany; stays 1m5f; acts on good and easy ground; goes on Polytrack.

Baileys Cacao (IRE)

109 104
3-y-o b f Invincible Spirit (IRE)-Baileys Cream (Mister Baileys)
R Hannon William Durkan

Placings:101624-0254 (2703)
2009: 7^{0}S, 7^{2}GF, 7^{5}GF, 8^{4}G,

	Starts	1st	2nd	3rd	Win & Pl
Career Total (Turf)	10	2	2	0	251172
92 6/08 NmkJ 6f		FRM	£12489		
88 5/08 Wind 5f10y		G-F	£3626		

Total win prize-money £16116

Going (Turf): Sf: 0-2 GS: 0-0 Gd: 0-2 **GF: 1-4 Fm: 1-1**
Distance: **5f/6f: 2-3** 7f-8f: 0-6 9f-13f: 0-1 14f+: 0-0
Track : LH: 0-1 RH: 0-0 Tight: 0-1 **Gall: 1-1**
Aids: Bl: 0-0 Vi: 0-0 Tstrap: 0-0 Ckp: 0-0
Best Rating: **104** 10/08 NmkR 7f good

Smart; winner in Listed company; stays 7f; acts on fast ground; suited by forcing tactics.

Going (Turf): Sf: 0-5 GS: 1-18 Gd: 4-24 GF: 7-34 Fm: 1-9
Distance: 5f/6f: 1-3 7f-8f: 6-52 9f-13f: 7-47 14f+: 0-0

Baileys Red

78(78) (48)48

3-y-o b g Diktat-Red Ryding Hood (Wolfhound (USA))
J G Given G R Bailey Ltd (Baileys Horse Feeds)

Placings:656-00 **(3157)**
2009: 10^{0}GF, 12^{0}SD,

	Starts	1st	2nd	3rd	Win & Pl
Career Total (Turf)	3	0	0	0	0
Career Total (AW)	2	0	0	0	0

Going (Turf): **Sf: 0-1 GS: 0-0 Gd: 0-0 GF: 0-2 Fm: 0-0**
Distance: 5f/6f: 0-0 7f-8f: 0-1 9f-13f: 0-4 14f+: 0-0
Track : LH: 0-3 RH: 0-1 Tight: 0-3 Gall: 0-0
Aids: Bl: 0-0 Vi: 0-0 Tstrap: 0-0 Ckp: 0-0
Best Rating: **48** 9/08 Wolv 1m141y stand

Baileys Vision

92(49) 69

2-y-o b f Kyllachy-Southern Psychic (USA) (Alwasmi (USA))
M Johnston G R Bailey Ltd (Baileys Horse Feeds)

Placings:22040540 **(7079)**
2009: 5^{2}GF, 6^{2}G, 6^{0}GF, 6^{4}G, 7^{0}SD, 7^{5}GF, 7^{4}G, 5^{0}S,

	Starts	1st	2nd	3rd	Win & Pl
Career Total (Turf)	7	0	2	0	3559
Career Total (AW)	1	0	0	0	

Going (Turf): **Sf: 0-1 GS: 0-0 Gd: 0-3 GF: 0-3 Fm: 0-0**
Distance: 5f/6f: 0-4 7f-8f: 0-4 9f-13f: 0-0 14f+: 0-0
Track : LH: 0-4 RH: 0-0 Tight: 0-3 Gall: 0-0
Aids: Bl: 0-0 Vi: 0-2 Tstrap: 0-0 Ckp: 0-0
Best Rating: **69** 5/09 Wwck 5f110y gd-fm

Modest; effective over 6f; acts on good ground.

Bailieborough (IRE)

77(102) (64)62

10-y-o b g Charnwood Forest (IRE)-Sherannda (USA) (Trempolino (USA))
B Ellison Koo's Racing Club

Placings:0146/005620304/005025210000/06034013016 511320/52266300141411000/66350231120/0352332500 055/000205000**513-52600** **(1131)**
2009: 8^{5}SD, 8^{2}SD, 9^{6}SD, 10^{0}G, 8^{0}SD,

	Starts	1st	2nd	3rd	Win & Pl
Career Total (Turf)	90	13	11	10	96094
Career Total (AW)	12	1	1	1	3605

62 12/08 Wolv 1m1f103y (0-65)H STD £2729
91 8/06 Rdcr 1m (0-80)H GD £6477
85 8/06 Rdcr 1m (0-90)H G-F £9715
90 9/05 Pont 1m4y (0-75)H G-S £5740
85 9/05 Catt 7f (0-80)H G-F £6932
71 8/05 Newc 1m3y G-F £3080
70 8/05 Bevl 1m100y GD £3542
63 6/05 Muss 1m1f FRM £3386
74 8/04 Ayr 7f50y E G-F £3559
68 7/04 Muss 1m F G-F £3513
72 6/04 Muss 1m1f F GD £2947
70 5/04 Pont 1m4y E G-F £3731
74 8/03 Folk 7f E(0-70) G-F £3555
73 8/01 Thsk 6f D GD £4507
Total win prize-money £63421

Going (Turf): Sf: 0-5 GS: 1-18 Gd: 4-24**GF: 7-34** Fm: 1-9
Distance: 5f/6f: 1-3 7f-8f: 6-52 **9f-13f: 7-47** 14f+: 0-0

Track : **LH: 5-47** RH: 3-25 **Tight: 4-33** Gall: 0-11
Aids: Bl: 0-2 **Vi: 9-34** Tstrap: 0-2 Ckp: 0-2
Best Rating: **94** 6/07 Rdcr 1m soft

Moderate; effective at around 1m-1m2f; acts on easy ground; goes on Polytrack, but best on fast ground; has worn blinkers, a visor and cheekpieces.

Baizically (IRE)

103(85) (94)76

6-y-o ch g Galileo (IRE)-Baize (Efisio)
John Joseph Hanlon (G A Swinbank 3/8) Sean Conroy

Placings:0/14/362002/0500-0511206 **(3679)**
2009: 8^{0}G, 10^{5}S, 13^{1}GF, 14^{1}G, 12^{2}GF, 11^{0}GF, 14^{6}G,

	Starts	1st	2nd	3rd	Win & Pl
Career Total (Turf)	17	3	3	0	18338
Career Total (AW)	3	0	0	1	851

76 6/09 Muss 1m6f (0-85)H GD £6476
72 6/09 Haml 1m5f9y (0-70)H G-F £3238
85 5/06 Haml 1m1f36y G-F £3238
Total win prize-money £12953

Going (Turf): Sf: 0-1 GS: 0-0 Gd: 1-7 **GF: 2-7** Fm: 0-2
Distance: 5f/6f: 0-0 7f-8f: 0-2 9f-13f: 1-13 **14f+: 2-5**
Track : LH: 0-5 **RH: 3-14 Tight: 3-11** Gall: 0-1
Aids: Bl: 0-0 Vi: 0-0 Tstrap: 0-0 Ckp: 0-0
Best Rating: **94** 4/07 Bath 1m3f144y firm

Useful; stays 1m6f and acts on fast ground.

Bajan Parkes

104 91

6-y-o b/br g Zafonic (USA)-My Melody Parkes (Teenoso (USA))
E J Alston (C Grant 23/1) Joseph Heler

Placings:1/460/056343423105/01000200-40120045 **(7170)**
2009: 10^{4}G, 12^{0}G, 11^{1}HY, 14^{7}GS, 14^{0}GF, 12^{0}G, 11^{4}G, 15^{5}G,

	Starts	1st	2nd	3rd	Win & Pl
Career Total (Turf)	32	4	3	3	28421

83 8/09 Haml 1m3f16y (0-75)H HVY £3885
85 5/08 Carl 1m3f107y (0-80)H G-F £4533
86 9/07 Hayd 1m3f200y (0-85)H G-F £5505
87 9/05 Bath 5f161y FRM £3620
Total win prize-money £17545

Going (Turf): Sf: 1-6 GS: 0-4 Gd: 0-9 **GF: 2-12** Fm: 1-1
Distance: 5f/6f: 1-5 7f-8f: 0-2 **9f-13f: 3-19** 14f+: 0-6
Track : LH: 2-21 RH: 2-7 Tight: 1-10 Gall: 1-4
Aids: Bl: 0-0 Vi: 0-0 Tstrap: 0-1 Ckp: 0-1
Best Rating: **91** 8/08 Ayr 1m2f soft

Useful; stays 1m6f; acts on any ground; suited by forcing tactics.

Bajan Pride

100(103) (67)71

5-y-o b g Selkirk (USA)-Spry (Suave Dancer (USA))
R A Fahey R A Fahey

Placings:0302/35005112050/500-665426455 **(7784)**
2009: 11^{6}SD, 8^{6}SD, 9^{5}SD, 9^{4}SD, 8^{2}GF, 8^{6}SD, 8^{4}SD, 8^{5}SD, 8^{5}SD,

	Starts	1st	2nd	3rd	Win & Pl
Career Total (Turf)	18	1	2	2	8549
Career Total (AW)	10	1	1	0	4587

82 7/07 NmkJ 1m (0-75)H G-F £3886
78 7/07 Kcmp 1m (0-70)H STD £3238
Total win prize-money £7125

Going (Turf): Sf: 0-3 GS: 0-3 Gd: 0-5 **GF: 1-7** Fm: 0-0
Distance: 5f/6f: 0-0 **7f-8f: 2-13** 9f-13f: 0-15 14f+: 0-0

Track : LH: 0-10 **RH: 1-13** Tight: 0-12 Gall: 0-0
Aids: Bl: 0-0 Vi: 0-2 Tstrap: 0-3 Ckp: 0-3
Best Rating: **85** 8/07 Sals 1m gd-sft

Modest; effective over 1m; acts on good ground and Polytrack; has worn a visor.

Bajan Tryst (USA)

100(108) (79)87

3-y-o b/br g Speightstown (USA)-Garden Secrets (USA) (Time For A Change (USA))
K A Ryan Mrs Margaret Forsyth & Mrs R G Hillen

Placings:233-10010020 **(5799)**
2009: 5^{1}SD, 5^{0}SD, 6^{0}GF, 6^{1}G, 6^{0}GF, 5^{0}GF, 6^{2}G, 6^{0}GF,

	Starts	1st	2nd	3rd	Win & Pl
Career Total (Turf)	8	1	2	1	11818
Career Total (AW)	3	1	0	1	3307

85 7/09 Ripn 6f (0-90)H GD £8831
79 3/09 Ling 5f STD £2729
Total win prize-money £11561

Going (Turf): Sf: 0-0 GS: 0-0 **Gd: 1-4** GF: 0-4 Fm: 0-0
Distance: **5f/6f: 2-10** 7f-8f: 0-1 9f-13f: 0-0 14f+: 0-0
Track : **LH: 1-1** RH: 0-2 **Tight: 1-1** Gall: 0-0
Aids: Bl: 0-0 Vi: 0-0 Tstrap: 0-3 Ckp: 0-3
Best Rating: **87** 8/09 Ripn 6f good

Useful; effective over 5f- 6f; acts on good ground and on Polytrack.

Balaagha (USA)

109 100

3-y-o b f Mr Greeley (USA)-Echo Echo Echo (USA) (Eastern Echo (USA))
M A Jarvis Hamdan Al Maktoum

Placings:5-212226U **(6267)**
2009: 7^{2}GF, 7^{1}GF, 7^{2}G, 7^{2}G, 8^{2}G, 8^{6}GF, 8^{U}G,

	Starts	1st	2nd	3rd	Win & Pl
Career Total (Turf)	8	1	4	0	20431

76 5/09 Ches 7f2y G-F £7123
Total win prize-money £7124

Going (Turf): Sf: 0-0 GS: 0-0 Gd: 0-5 **GF: 1-3** Fm: 0-0
Distance: 5f/6f: 0-1 **7f-8f: 1-6** 9f-13f: 0-1 14f+: 0-0
Track : **LH: 1-2** RH: 0-3 **Tight: 1-2** Gall: 0-2
Aids: Bl: 0-0 Vi: 0-0 Tstrap: 0-0 Ckp: 0-0
Best Rating: **100** 7/09 Asct 1m good

Smart; effective over 7f-1m; acts on fast ground.

Balais Folly (FR)

(96) (47)53

4-y-o ch g Act One-Bhima (Polar Falcon (USA))
D Haydn Jones Five To Follow

Placings:0000060/3064453036550-000 **(7109)**
2009: 8^{0}SD, 7^{0}SS, 8^{0}SD,

	Starts	1st	2nd	3rd	Win & Pl
Career Total (Turf)	13	0	0	2	695
Career Total (AW)	10	0	0	1	302

Going (Turf): **Sf: 0-2 GS: 0-5 Gd: 0-1 GF: 0-5 Fm: 0-0**
Distance: 5f/6f: 0-0 7f-8f: 0-4 9f-13f: 0-18 14f+: 0-1
Track : LH: 0-16 RH: 0-5 Tight: 0-10 Gall: 0-0
Aids: Bl: 0-3 Vi: 0-2 Tstrap: 0-4 Ckp: 0-4
Best Rating: **54** 11/07 Wolv 1m141y stand

Moderate; effective over 1m4f; acts on Polytrack.

Balata

105(105) (76)**83**

4-y-o b g Averti (IRE)-Manila Selection (USA) (Manila (USA))

B R Millman The Links Partnership

Placings:5235/600452121-30264051612 **(6645)**

2009: 8^{3}SD, 7^{0}SD, 7^{2}GF, 7^{6}SD, 7^{4}GF, 6^{0}GF, 7^{5}SD, 7^{1}GF, 7^{6}SD, 7^{1}GF, 7^{2}G,

	Starts	1st	2nd	3rd	Win & Pl
Career Total (Turf)	13	2	3	1	13268
Career Total (AW)	11	2	2	1	8534

81 9/09 Folk 7f (0-85)H G-F £5180
80 9/09 Leic 7f9y (0-70)H G-F £2914
75 12/08 Wolv 7f32y (0-70)H STD £3238
71 12/08 Kemp 7f STD £3238
Total win prize-money £14571

Going (Turf): Sf: 0-0 GS: 0-1 Gd: 0-4 **GF: 2-7** Fm: 0-1
Distance: 5f/6f: 0-7 **7f-8f: 4-17** 9f-13f: 0-0 14f+: 0-0
Track : LH: 1-9 RH: 1-5 **Tight: 1-6** Gall: 0-5
Aids: Bl: 0-1 Vi: 0-0 Tstrap: 0-0 Ckp: 0-0
Best Rating: **83** 10/09 York 7f good

Fair; stays 7f; acts on fast ground; goes on Fibresand; has worn blinkers.

Balcarce Nov (ARG)

112(87) (55)**110**

4-y-o b c Romanov (IRE)-Rosada Fitz (ARG) (Fitzcarraldo (ARG))

T P Tate (H J Brown 28/3) Mrs Fitri Hay

Placings:13150-240415200 **(6812)**

2009: 6^{2}G, 7^{4}G, 9^{0}FT, 7^{4}S, 8^{1}G, 7^{5}GF, 8^{2}GF, 7^{0}G, 9^{0}G,

	Starts	1st	2nd	3rd	Win & Pl
Career Total (Turf)	10	2	2	0	36729
Career Total (AW)	4	1	0	1	7198

108 8/09 Hayd 1m30y (0-100)H GD £14571
9/08 Sani 7f FRM £4466
5/08 Plmo 5f FST £5684
Total win prize-money £24721

Going (Turf): Sf: 0-1 GS: 0-0 **Gd: 1-5** GF: 0-2 **Fm: 1-2**
Distance: 5f/6f: 1-2 7f-8f: 1-7 9f-13f: 1-5 14f+: 0-0
Track : **LH: 1-6** RH: 0-0 Tight: 0-0 Gall: 0-4
Aids: Bl: 0-0 Vi: 0-0 Tstrap: 0-0 Ckp: 0-0
Best Rating: **110** 9/09 Donc 1m gd-fm

Smart; formerly trained in Dubai and Argentina; stays 7f plus; acts on good/fast ground and dirt; has worn a tongue tie.

Baldemar

107 **95**

4-y-o b g Namid-Keen Melody (USA) (Sharpen Up)

R A Fahey (K R Burke 2/7) A Rhodes Haulage And P Timmins

Placings:01023/22056154-0001001000 **(6994)**

2009: 6^{0}GF, 5^{0}GF, 6^{0}GF, 6^{1}G, 6^{0}S, 6^{0}GS, 6^{1}G, 7^{0}G, 7^{0}G, 6^{0}G,

	Starts	1st	2nd	3rd	Win & Pl
Career Total (Turf)	23	4	3	1	49139

95 9/09 Ayr 6f H GD £18693
94 6/09 Epsm 6f (0-100)H GD £12462
93 8/08 Ripn 6f (0-85)H G-S £4857
74 8/07 Ripn 6f GD £3886
Total win prize-money £39898

Going (Turf): Sf: 0-4 GS: 1-3 **Gd: 3-12** GF: 0-4 Fm: 0-0
Distance: **5f/6f: 4-20** 7f-8f: 0-3 9f-13f: 0-0 14f+: 0-0
Track : **LH: 1-3** RH: 0-0 **Tight: 1-2** Gall: 0-1
Aids: Bl: 0-0 Vi: 0-0 Tstrap: 0-0 Ckp: 0-0
Best Rating: **95** 9/09 Ayr 6f good

Very useful; effective at 5f-6f; acts on good ground; likes to race prominently.

Balducci

(93) (75)

2-y-o b c Dansili-Miss Meltemi (IRE) (Miswaki Tern (USA))

A M Balding McMahon/Gorell/Pausewang/Russell

Placings:2 **(7764)**

2009: 8^{2}SD,

	Starts	1st	2nd	3rd	Win & Pl
Career Total (Turf)	0	0	0	0	
Career Total (AW)	1	0	1	0	1156

Going (Turf): **Sf: 0-0 GS: 0-0 Gd: 0-0 GF: 0-0 Fm: 0-0**
Distance: 5f/6f: 0-0 7f-8f: 0-1 9f-13f: 0-0 14f+: 0-0
Track : LH: 0-0 RH: 0-1 Tight: 0-0 Gall: 0-0
Aids: Bl: 0-0 Vi: 0-0 Tstrap: 0-0 Ckp: 0-0
Best Rating: **75** 12/09 Kemp 1m stand

Fair debut over 1m on Polytrack.

Balerno

(101) (57)**58**

10-y-o b g Machiavellian (USA)-Balabina (USA) (Nijinsky (CAN))

Mrs L J Mongan Mrs L J Mongan

Placings:06330052/400045000530 0/1304505230402125 06/001206321000304101050/00002400/020125060000/536 024100000000-20000 **(0587)**

2009: 7^{2}SD, 8^{0}SD, 5^{0}SD, 7^{0}SD, 7^{0}SD,

	Starts	1st	2nd	3rd	Win & Pl
Career Total (Turf)	46	3	5	5	17749
Career Total (AW)	54	5	6	3	18758

58 4/08 Yarm 7f3y (0-52)H G-F £1942
59 3/07 Ling 6f (0-52)H STD £1706
65 9/05 Wolv 7f32y (0-60)H STD £3012
67 8/05 Chep 7f16y (0-60) GD £3182
62 6/05 Ling 1m (0-55)H STD £3340
58 2/05 Ling 7f (0-55)H STD £2962
65 7/04 Kemp 7f E(0-70)H G-F £4280
52 1/04 Ling 1m H(0-45) STD £1645
Total win prize-money £22071

Going (Turf): Sf: 0-5 GS: 0-2 Gd: 1-11 **GF: 2-24** Fm: 0-4
Distance: 5f/6f: 1-11 **7f-8f: 7-63** 9f-13f: 0-26 14f+: 0-0
Track : **LH: 5-59** RH: 1-19 **Tight: 5-50** Gall: 1-7
Aids: Bl: 0-5 Vi: 0-1 Tstrap: 0-3 Ckp: 0-3
Best Rating: **70** 7/04 Yarm 7f3y gd-fm

Moderate; effective over 6f-1m; acts on a fast surface; goes well on Polytrack.

Balfour House

71 (1)**20**

6-y-o b g Wizard King-Tymeera (Timeless Times (USA))

D Burchell Martin and Stephen Shinton

Placings:0/0000/00/00 **(5630)**

2009: 6^{0}F, 8^{0}GS,

	Starts	1st	2nd	3rd	Win & Pl
Career Total (Turf)	5	0	0	0	
Career Total (AW)	4	0	0	0	

Going (Turf): **Sf: 0-0 GS: 0-1 Gd: 0-0 GF: 0-3 Fm: 0-1**
Distance: 5f/6f: 0-3 7f-8f: 0-3 9f-13f: 0-3 14f+: 0-0
Track : LH: 0-5 RH: 0-1 Tight: 0-2 Gall: 0-1
Aids: Bl: 0-2 Vi: 0-0 Tstrap: 0-0 Ckp: 0-0
Best Rating: **30** 2/06 Ling 6f stand

Balierus (GER)

89 **64**

2-y-o b c Singspiel (IRE)-Brighella (GER) (Lomitas)

M bin Shafya (Saeed Bin Suroor 23/10) Sheikh Majid Bin Mohammed al Maktoum

Placings:601

2009: 8^{6}GF, 8^{0}G, 6^{1}FT,

	Starts	1st	2nd	3rd	Win & Pl
Career Total (Turf)	2	0	0	0	0
Career Total (AW)	1	1	0	0	6818

12/09 Jebl 6f FST £6818
Total win prize-money £6818

Going (Turf): **Sf: 0-0 GS: 0-0 Gd: 0-1 GF: 0-1 Fm: 0-0**
Distance: **5f/6f: 1-1** 7f-8f: 0-2 9f-13f: 0-0 14f+: 0-0
Track : LH: 0-1 RH: 0-0 Tight: 0-0 Gall: 0-0
Aids: Bl: 0-0 Vi: 0-0 Tstrap: 0-0 Ckp: 0-0
Best Rating: **64** 10/09 NmkR 1m gd-fm

Baligha

91(83) (52)**52**

4-y-o ch f Alhaarth (IRE)-Najmat Jumairah (USA) (Mr Prospector (USA))

G A Swinbank The County Set Three

Placings:0505 **(2268)**

2009: 8^{0}SD, 9^{5}GF, 9^{0}G, 5^{5}G,

	Starts	1st	2nd	3rd	Win & Pl
Career Total (Turf)	3	0	0	0	0
Career Total (AW)	1	0	0	0	

Going (Turf): **Sf: 0-0 GS: 0-0 Gd: 0-2 GF: 0-1 Fm: 0-0**
Distance: 5f/6f: 0-1 7f-8f: 0-0 9f-13f: 0-3 14f+: 0-0
Track : LH: 0-2 RH: 0-2 Tight: 0-4 Gall: 0-0
Aids: Bl: 0-0 Vi: 0-0 Tstrap: 0-0 Ckp: 0-0
Best Rating: **52** 4/09 Muss 1m1f gd-fm

Baliyana (IRE)

102 **104**

3-y-o gr f Dalakhani (IRE)-Balanka (IRE) (Alzao (USA))

John M Oxx H H Aga Khan

Placings:3510-10 **(3088)**

2009: 8^{1}G, 8^{0}GF,

	Starts	1st	2nd	3rd	Win & Pl
Career Total (Turf)	6	2	0	1	61475

104 5/09 Leop 1m GD £50563
93 9/08 Leop 7f YLD £9573
Total win prize-money £60137

Going (Turf): Sf: 0-1 GS: 0-0 **Gd: 1-1** GF: 0-1 Fm: 0-0
Distance: 5f/6f: 0-1 **7f-8f: 2-5** 9f-13f: 0-0 14f+: 0-0
Track : **LH: 2-3** RH: 0-1 Tight: 0-0 Gall: 0-1
Aids: Bl: 0-0 Vi: 0-0 Tstrap: 0-0 Ckp: 0-0
Best Rating: **104** 5/09 Leop 1m good

Smart; Group 3 winner; stays 1m; acts on good and easy ground.

Ballachulish

84 **56**

2-y-o b g Kyllachy-Romantic Drama (IRE) (Primo Dominie)

H Candy Henry Candy

Placings:56000 **(6328)**
2009: 5^{5}GF, 5^{6}GF, 6^{0}G, 6^{0}GF, 5^{0}F,

	Starts	1st	2nd	3rd	Win & Pl
Career Total (Turf)	5	0	0	0	0

Going (Turf): **Sf: 0-0 GS: 0-0 Gd: 0-1 GF: 0-3 Fm: 0-1**
Distance: 5f/6f: 0-5 7f-8f: 0-0 9f-13f: 0-0 14f+: 0-0
Track : LH: 0-2 RH: 0-0 Tight: 0-0 Gall: 0-2
Aids: Bl: 0-0 Vi: 0-0 Tstrap: 0-0 Ckp: 0-0
Best Rating: **56** 7/09 Sand 5f6y gd-fm

Only minor signs of ability so far.

Ballade De La Mer

105(80) (44)**51**
3-y-o b f Ishiguru (USA)-Riviere Rouge (Forzando)
A G Foster Highland Racing 6

Placings:0060-02405 **(7118)**
2009: 10^{0}G, 11^{2}G, 12^{4}GF, 13^{0}S, 12^{5}GS,

	Starts	1st	2nd	3rd	Win & Pl
Career Total (Turf)	5	0	1	0	867
Career Total (AW)	4	0	0	0	0

Going (Turf): **Sf: 0-1 GS: 0-1 Gd: 0-2 GF: 0-1 Fm: 0-0**
Distance: 5f/6f: 0-0 7f-8f: 0-3 9f-13f: 0-5 14f+: 0-1
Track : LH: 0-6 RH: 0-3 Tight: 0-6 Gall: 0-1
Aids: Bl: 0-0 Vi: 0-0 Tstrap: 0-0 Ckp: 0-0
Best Rating: **51** 7/09 Haml 1m3f16y good

Very moderate; stays 1m3f and acts on good ground.

Ballantrae (IRE)

95 **92**
3-y-o b f Diktat-Badawi (USA) (Diesis)
M L W Bell Sheikh Marwan Al Maktoum

Placings:1010-6 **(5005)**
2009: 7^{6}G,

	Starts	1st	2nd	3rd	Win & Pl
Career Total (Turf)	5	2	0	0	13276

92 9/08 Donc 7f (0-95) SFT £9714
77 7/08 Folk 7f SFT £3561
Total win prize-money £13276

Going (Turf): **Sf: 2-2** GS: 0-1 Gd: 0-1 GF: 0-1 Fm: 0-0
Distance: 5f/6f: 0-0 **7f-8f: 2-5** 9f-13f: 0-0 14f+: 0-0
Track : LH: 0-0 RH: 0-0 Tight: 0-0 Gall: 0-0
Aids: Bl: 0-0 Vi: 0-0 Tstrap: 0-0 Ckp: 0-0
Best Rating: **92** 9/08 Donc 7f soft

Very useful; effective over 7f and acts on soft ground.

Ballarina

91 **49**
3-y-o b f Compton Place-Miss Uluwatu (IRE) (Night Shift (USA))
E J Alston Mrs P O Morris

Placings:005-66 **(2394)**
2009: 5^{6}GF, 5^{6}G,

	Starts	1st	2nd	3rd	Win & Pl
Career Total (Turf)	5	0	0	0	0

Going (Turf): **Sf: 0-0 GS: 0-1 Gd: 0-3 GF: 0-1 Fm: 0-0**
Distance: 5f/6f: 0-5 7f-8f: 0-0 9f-13f: 0-0 14f+: 0-0
Track : LH: 0-1 RH: 0-0 Tight: 0-1 Gall: 0-0
Aids: Bl: 0-0 Vi: 0-0 Tstrap: 0-0 Ckp: 0-0
Best Rating: **49** 5/09 Muss 5f gd-fm

Ballet Dancer (IRE)

92(100) (69)**74**
3-y-o b f Refuse To Bend (IRE)-Showlady (USA) (Theatrical)
M A Jarvis Sheikh Ahmed Al Maktoum

Placings:34-13400 **(4720)**
2009: 9^{1}SD, 9^{3}F, 10^{4}SD, 10^{0}G, 8^{0}G,

	Starts	1st	2nd	3rd	Win & Pl
Career Total (Turf)	4	0	0	2	1878
Career Total (AW)	3	1	0	0	3375

69 4/09 Wolv 1m1f103y STD £2729
Total win prize-money £2730

Going (Turf): **Sf: 0-0 GS: 0-0 Gd: 0-3 GF: 0-0 Fm: 0-1**
Distance: 5f/6f: 0-0 7f-8f: 0-2 **9f-13f: 1-5** 14f+: 0-0
Track : **LH: 1-4** RH: 0-2 **Tight: 1-3** Gall: 0-2
Aids: Bl: 0-0 Vi: 0-0 Tstrap: 0-0 Ckp: 0-0
Best Rating: **74** 5/09 Sals 1m1f198y firm

Fair; stays 1m1f and acts on Polytrack.

Ballinteni

104(113) (89)**100**
7-y-o b g Machiavellian (USA)-Silabteni (USA) (Nureyev (USA))
M G Quinlan (D K Ivory 4/6) David Cohen

Placings:1/04/6103264505/**2614464400-00330450** **(6812)**
2009: 10^{0}SD, 8^{0}SD, 10^{3}GF, 8^{3}GF, 8^{0}GF, 12^{4}SD, 10^{5}G, 9^{0}G,

	Starts	1st	2nd	3rd	Win & Pl
Career Total (Turf)	23	3	1	3	35532
Career Total (AW)	8	0	1	0	2859

100 5/08 Ripn 1m1f170y (0-90)H GD £9066
91 5/07 Wind 1m2f7y (0-90)H GD £8096
87 10/04 Donc 7f SFT £3542
Total win prize-money £20705

Going (Turf): Sf: 1-3 GS: 0-3 **Gd: 2-6** GF: 0-10 Fm: 0-1
Distance: 5f/6f: 0-0 7f-8f: 1-5 **9f-13f: 2-26** 14f+: 0-0
Track : LH: 0-8 **RH: 2-19 Tight: 2-10** Gall: 0-7
Aids: Bl: 0-0 Vi: 0-0 Tstrap: 0-0 Ckp: 0-0
Best Rating: **100** 5/08 Ripn 1m1f170y good

Very useful; effective from 1m-1m2f; acts on good and softer ground and on Polytrack; has worn a tongue tie.

Ballodair (IRE)

94 **80**
2-y-o b g Antonius Pius (USA)-Vision Of Dreams (Efisio)
R A Fahey Mrs H Steel

Placings:212000 **(6247)**
2009: 6^{2}G, 6^{1}G, 6^{2}G, 6^{0}S, 6^{0}GF, 6^{0}GF,

	Starts	1st	2nd	3rd	Win & Pl
Career Total (Turf)	6	1	2	0	6972

80 6/09 Thsk 6f GD £4274
Total win prize-money £4274

Going (Turf): Sf: 0-1 GS: 0-0 **Gd: 1-3** GF: 0-2 Fm: 0-0
Distance: **5f/6f: 1-4** 7f-8f: 0-2 9f-13f: 0-0 14f+: 0-0
Track : LH: 0-0 RH: 0-0 Tight: 0-0 Gall: 0-0
Aids: Bl: 0-0 Vi: 0-0 Tstrap: 0-0 Ckp: 0-0
Best Rating: **80** 6/09 Thsk 6f good

Useful; stays 6f and acts on good ground.

Ballyalla

103(76) (17)**82**
3-y-o b f Mind Games-Molly Brown (Rudimentary (USA))
R Hannon Denis J Barry

Placings:0105-5050430 **(6583)**
2009: 8^{5}GF, 7^{0}G, 6^{5}GF, 7^{0}GF, 8^{4}GF, 9^{3}GF, 10^{0}SD,

	Starts	1st	2nd	3rd	Win & Pl
Career Total (Turf)	10	1	0	1	20447
Career Total (AW)	1	0	0	0	

82 7/08 Newb 6f8y GD £5828
Total win prize-money £5828

Going (Turf): Sf: 0-1 GS: 0-0 **Gd: 1-3** GF: 0-6 Fm: 0-0
Distance: 5f/6f: 0-3 **7f-8f: 1-6** 9f-13f: 0-2 14f+: 0-0
Track : LH: 0-1 RH: 0-2 Tight: 0-2 Gall: 0-0
Aids: Bl: 0-0 Vi: 0-0 Tstrap: 0-0 Ckp: 0-0
Best Rating: **82** 7/08 Newb 6f8y good

Useful; effective at 6f; acts on good ground.

Ballycommon (USA)

85 **47**
2-y-o b g Roman Ruler (USA)-Seth's Choice (USA) (Rahy (USA))
K A Ryan F Gillespie

Placings:5 **(3910)**
2009: 6^{5}GF,

	Starts	1st	2nd	3rd	Win & Pl
Career Total (Turf)	1	0	0	0	0

Going (Turf): **Sf: 0-0 GS: 0-0 Gd: 0-0 GF: 0-1 Fm: 0-0**
Distance: 5f/6f: 0-1 7f-8f: 0-0 9f-13f: 0-0 14f+: 0-0
Track : LH: 0-0 RH: 0-0 Tight: 0-0 Gall: 0-0
Aids: Bl: 0-0 Vi: 0-0 Tstrap: 0-0 Ckp: 0-0
Best Rating: **47** 7/09 Ayr 6f gd-fm

Ballycroy Boy (IRE)

75(104) (71)**12**
4-y-o b g Captain Rio-Royal Baldini (USA) (Green Dancer (USA))
Miss M E Rowland (A Bailey 20/2) Miss M E Rowland

Placings:2010003/**133312500-3312240** **(2235)**
2009: 6^{3}SD, 7^{3}SS, 6^{1}SD, 7^{2}SD, 6^{2}SD, 7^{4}SD, 7^{0}GS,

	Starts	1st	2nd	3rd	Win & Pl
Career Total (Turf)	4	0	0	0	
Career Total (AW)	19	4	4	6	13641

69 2/09 Sthl 6f STD £2047
77 2/08 Sthl 6f SS £1774
74 1/08 Sthl 6f STD £1911
69 5/07 Sthl 5f STD £3238
Total win prize-money £8972

Going (Turf): **Sf: 0-0 GS: 0-1 Gd: 0-1 GF: 0-2 Fm: 0-0**
Distance: **5f/6f: 4-13** 7f-8f: 0-10 9f-13f: 0-0 14f+: 0-0
Track : **LH: 3-18** RH: 0-0 Tight: 0-4 Gall: 0-1
Aids: **Bl: 1-6** Vi: 0-1 Tstrap: 0-1 Ckp: 0-1
Best Rating: **77** 2/08 Sthl 6f std-slw

Modest; effective over 6f-7f; acts on soft ground; goes on Fibresand; has worn blinkers and a visor.

Ballyvonane (USA)

77(91) (46)**44**

2-y-o b c Strong Hope (USA)-Wild Light (USA) (Tabasco Cat (USA))

L A Dace M C S D Racing Partnership

Placings:4003005 **(7514)**

2009: 5^{4}GF, 6^{0}GF, 6^{0}SD, 6^{3}SD, 6^{0}SD, 6^{0}SD, 7^{5}SD,

	Starts	1st	2nd	3rd	Win & Pl
Career Total (Turf)	2	0	0	0	0
Career Total (AW)	5	0	0	1	302

Going (Turf): Sf: 0-0 GS: 0-0 Gd: 0-0 GF: 0-2 Fm: 0-0
Distance: 5f/6f: 0-6 7f-8f: 0-1 9f-13f: 0-0 14f+: 0-0
Track : LH: 0-1 RH: 0-4 Tight: 0-1 Gall: 0-1
Aids: Bl: 0-4 Vi: 0-0 Tstrap: 0-0 Ckp: 0-0
Best Rating: **46** 10/09 Kemp 6f stand

Plating-class; stays 6f; acts on Polytrack; has worn blinkers.

Balnagore

94(104) (79)**74**

5-y-o b/br g Tobougg (IRE)-Bogus Mix (IRE) (Linamix (FR))

J L Dunlop Mrs Simon Boscawen

Placings:0565/5/0600205-10**021036** **(6724)**

2009: 10^{1}SD, 10^{0}GS, 10^{0}SD, 11^{2}SD, 11^{1}SD, 11^{0}SD, 12^{3}G, 12^{6}SD,

	Starts	1st	2nd	3rd	Win & Pl
Career Total (Turf)	14	0	1	1	2093
Career Total (AW)	6	2	1	0	8725
79 8/09 Kemp	1m3f	(0-85)H		STD	£4727
74 4/09 Kemp	1m2f	(0-70)H		STD	£2590

Total win prize-money £7317

Going (Turf): **Sf: 0-4 GS: 0-5 Gd: 0-3 GF: 0-2 Fm: 0-0**
Distance: 5f/6f: 0-0 7f-8f: 0-5 **9f-13f: 2-15** 14f+: 0-0
Track : LH: 0-3 **RH: 2-12** Tight: 0-4 Gall: 0-4
Aids: Bl: 0-0 Vi: 0-0 Tstrap: 0-0 Ckp: 0-0
Best Rating: **79** 8/09 Kemp 1m3f stand

Modest; stays 1m2f; acts on most ground and Polytrack.

Balsha (USA)

80(83) (47)**52**

2-y-o ch f Mr Greeley (USA)-Carefree Cheetah (USA) (Trempolino (USA))

E A L Dunlop Hamdan Al Maktoum

Placings:006 **(7429)**

2009: 8^{0}GF, 8^{0}S, 7^{6}SD,

	Starts	1st	2nd	3rd	Win & Pl
Career Total (Turf)	2	0	0	0	
Career Total (AW)	1	0	0	0	0

Going (Turf): **Sf: 0-1 GS: 0-0 Gd: 0-0 GF: 0-1 Fm: 0-0**
Distance: 5f/6f: 0-0 7f-8f: 0-3 9f-13f: 0-0 14f+: 0-0
Track : LH: 0-0 RH: 0-1 Tight: 0-0 Gall: 0-0
Aids: Bl: 0-0 Vi: 0-0 Tstrap: 0-0 Ckp: 0-0
Best Rating: **52** 9/09 NmkR 1m gd-fm

Balthazaar's Gift (IRE)

110(86) (56)**119**

6-y-o b h Xaar-Thats Your Opinion (Last Tycoon)

C G Cox (R Simpson 28/3) H E Sheikh Sultan Bin Khalifa Al Nahyan

Placings:216011/042400/40530162304/00103020004-0310322105 **(6503a)**

2009: 6^{0}G, 6^{3}G, 6^{1}GF, 6^{0}FT, 7^{3}G, 7^{2}GF, 7^{2}G, 7^{1}GF, 8^{0}GS, 7^{5}GS,

	Starts	1st	2nd	3rd	Win & Pl
Career Total (Turf)	43	7	6	5	470933
Career Total (AW)	1	0	0	0	
119 8/09 Newb	7f			G-F	£56770
112 2/09 Ndas	6f110y	(95-110)H		G-F	£50000
110 6/08 Wind	6f			G-S	£14760
119 7/07 Asct	6f			G-S	£19873
112 11/05 MsnL	6f			G-S	£76809
106 10/05 York	6f			G-S	£15000
82 7/05 Wind	5f10y			G-S	£4823

Total win prize-money £238035

Going (Turf): Sf: 0-4 **GS: 5-11** Gd: 0-14 GF: 2-14 Fm: 0-0
Distance: **5f/6f: 5-26** 7f-8f: 2-18 9f-13f: 0-0 14f+: 0-0
Track : **LH: 1-6** RH: 0-5 Tight: 0-1 **Gall: 3-8**
Aids: Bl: 0-0 Vi: 0-2 Tstrap: 0-2 Ckp: 0-2
Best Rating: **120** 6/06 Asct 6f gd-fm

Group class; winner of the 2009 Hungerford Stakes; effective over 6-7f; acts on most ground, but ideally suited by some give; has worn cheekpieces and a visor.

Baltic Ben (USA)

81 **60**

2-y-o b g Johannesburg (USA)-Baltic Dip (IRE) (Benny The Dip (USA))

Eve Johnson Houghton Mrs C J Hue Williams & J C Nowell Smith

Placings:00 **(6728)**

2009: 8^{0}GF, 8^{0}S,

	Starts	1st	2nd	3rd	Win & Pl
Career Total (Turf)	2	0	0	0	

Going (Turf): **Sf: 0-1 GS: 0-0 Gd: 0-0 GF: 0-1 Fm: 0-0**
Distance: 5f/6f: 0-0 7f-8f: 0-2 9f-13f: 0-0 14f+: 0-0
Track : LH: 0-0 RH: 0-0 Tight: 0-0 Gall: 0-0
Aids: Bl: 0-0 Vi: 0-0 Tstrap: 0-0 Ckp: 0-0
Best Rating: **60** 9/09 Sals 1m gd-fm

Baltimore Clipper (USA)

102(90) (72)**79**

2-y-o b c Mizzen Mast (USA)-Resounding Grace (USA) (Thunder Gulch (USA))

P F I Cole Meyrick & Dunnington-Jefferson

Placings:62225 **(6728)**

2009: 7^{6}G, 7^{2}SD, 8^{2}G, 8^{2}GF, 8^{5}S,

	Starts	1st	2nd	3rd	Win & Pl
Career Total (Turf)	4	0	2	0	4818
Career Total (AW)	1	0	1	0	1060

Going (Turf): **Sf: 0-1 GS: 0-0 Gd: 0-2 GF: 0-1 Fm: 0-0**
Distance: 5f/6f: 0-0 7f-8f: 0-5 9f-13f: 0-0 14f+: 0-0
Track : LH: 0-1 RH: 0-1 Tight: 0-1 Gall: 0-0
Aids: Bl: 0-0 Vi: 0-0 Tstrap: 0-0 Ckp: 0-0
Best Rating: **79** 9/09 Donc 1m gd-fm

Fair; stays 1m; acts on a sound surface and on Polytrack.

Baltimore Jack (IRE)

103(100) (64)**76**

5-y-o b g Night Shift (USA)-Itsibitsi (IRE) (Brief Truce (USA))

T D Walford D Swales

Placings:10046404/14310640**0**0/000446620**54**-305131130 **(7014)**

2009: 7^{3}F, 5^{0}GF, 8^{5}GS, 9^{1}GF, 10^{3}GF, 10^{1}GF, 10^{1}GF, 10^{3}GF, 10^{0}GS,

	Starts	1st	2nd	3rd	Win & Pl
Career Total (Turf)	34	6	1	4	31998
Career Total (AW)	3	0	0	0	0
76 9/09 Rdcr	1m2f	(0-70)H		G-F	£2590
74 9/09 Pont	1m2f6y	(0-70)H		G-F	£3238
67 8/09 Rdcr	1m1f			G-F	£2047
82 6/07 Ayr	6f	(0-80)H		GD	£5829
84 4/07 Ripn	6f	(0-85)H		G-F	£4731
65 6/06 Ayr	6f			GD	£5181

Total win prize-money £23618

Going (Turf): Sf: 0-4 GS: 0-3 Gd: 2-7 **GF: 4-19** Fm: 0-1
Distance: 5f/6f: 3-18 7f-8f: 0-10 9f-13f: 3-9 14f+: 0-0
Track : **LH: 3-17** RH: 0-3 **Tight: 2-16** Gall: 0-1
Aids: Bl: 0-4 Vi: 0-0 Tstrap: 0-0 Ckp: 0-0
Best Rating: **84** 4/07 Ripn 6f gd-fm

Modest; stays 1m2f; acts on fast ground; has worn blinkers.

Baltimore Patriot (IRE)

96(99) (69)**63**

6-y-o b g Tiger Hill (IRE)-Berenice (Groom Dancer (USA))

R Curtis (Gerard Cully 17/9) Mrs Joanna Hughes

Placings:6022520/1021210/60320**324** **(7594)**

2009: 14^{6}G, 14^{0}GF, 17^{3}S, 14^{2}Y, 16^{0}GY, 13^{3}SD, 16^{2}SD, 13^{4}SD,

	Starts	1st	2nd	3rd	Win & Pl
Career Total (Turf)	19	3	6	1	12202
Career Total (AW)	3	0	1	1	1719
9/07 Hanv	1m2f	H	HVY	£2703	
8/07 Hanv	1m2f	H	GD	£2027	
5/07 Badn	1m1f		GD	£2027	

Total win prize-money £6757

Going (Turf): Sf: 1-5 GS: 0-0 **Gd: 2-11** GF: 0-1 Fm: 0-0
Distance: 5f/6f: 0-0 7f-8f: 0-0 **9f-13f: 3-14** 14f+: 0-8
Track : **LH: 1-10** RH: 0-0 Tight: 0-3 Gall: 0-0
Aids: Bl: 0-0 Vi: 0-0 Tstrap: 0-0 Ckp: 0-0
Best Rating: **69** 11/09 Wolv 2m119y stand

Modest; stays 2m; acts on Polytrack.

Balwearie (IRE)

63

8-y-o b g Sesaro (USA)-Eight Mile Rock (Dominion)

Miss L A Perratt Ken McGarrity

Placings:044254/606/004021234110/165204460030/3/S **(3911)**

2009: 10^{S}GF,

	Starts	1st	2nd	3rd	Win & Pl
Career Total (Turf)	35	4	4	3	23785
65 5/06 Newc	1m4f93y	(0-70)H		G-F	£4210
64 9/05 Ayr	1m5f13y	(0-55)H		SFT	£3165
58 9/05 Thsk	1m4f	(0-55)H		GD	£3757
53 7/05 Ayr	1m2f	(0-70)H		GD	£3658

Total win prize-money £14791

Going (Turf): Sf: 1-5 GS: 0-2 **Gd: 2-11** GF: 1-16 Fm: 0-1
Distance: 5f/6f: 0-5 7f-8f: 0-6 **9f-13f: 3-21** 14f+: 1-3
Track : **LH: 4-15** RH: 0-14 Tight: 1-14 Gall: 1-4
Aids: Bl: 0-0 Vi: 0-0 Tstrap: 3-23 Ckp: 3-23
Best Rating: **65** 7/06 Ayr 1m2f firm

Balzarine

80(91) (48)37
3-y-o ch f Auction House (USA)-Worsted (Whittingham (IRE))
M Blanshard G C Streatfeild

Placings:05060 **(6170)**
2009: 6^{0}GF, 8^{5}G, 8^{0}G, 8^{6}SD, 7^{0}GF,

	Starts	1st	2nd	3rd	Win & Pl
Career Total (Turf)	4	0	0	0	0
Career Total (AW)	1	0	0	0	0

Going (Turf): Sf: 0-0 GS: 0-0 Gd: 0-2 GF: 0-2 Fm: 0-0
Distance: 5f/6f: 0-0 7f-8f: 0-3 9f-13f: 0-2 14f+: 0-0
Track : LH: 0-3 RH: 0-0 Tight: 0-1 Gall: 0-0
Aids: Bl: 0-0 Vi: 0-0 Tstrap: 0-0 Ckp: 0-0
Best Rating: 48 9/09 Ling 1m stand

Ban Garda (IRE)

90 (73)54
3-y-o b f Daggers Drawn (USA)-Lifeguard (IRE) (Desert Prince (IRE))
J S Moore Coleman Bloodstock Limited

Placings:4-6 **(4854)**
2009: 8^{6}GF,

	Starts	1st	2nd	3rd	Win & Pl
Career Total (Turf)	1	0	0	0	0
Career Total (AW)	1	0	0	0	452

Going (Turf): Sf: 0-0 GS: 0-0 Gd: 0-0 GF: 0-1 Fm: 0-0
Distance: 5f/6f: 0-0 7f-8f: 0-1 9f-13f: 0-1 14f+: 0-0
Track : LH: 0-1 RH: 0-1 Tight: 0-1 Gall: 0-0
Aids: Bl: 0-0 Vi: 0-0 Tstrap: 0-0 Ckp: 0-0
Best Rating: 73 10/08 Dund 1m stand

Banana Republic (IRE)

93(91) (75)71
2-y-o ch c Danehill Dancer (IRE)-Elite Guest (IRE) (Be My Guest (USA))
P F I Cole John Manley

Placings:020 **(6548)**
2009: 7^{0}S, 8^{2}SD, 8^{0}G,

	Starts	1st	2nd	3rd	Win & Pl
Career Total (Turf)	2	0	0	0	
Career Total (AW)	1	0	1	0	1253

Going (Turf): Sf: 0-1 GS: 0-0 Gd: 0-1 GF: 0-0 Fm: 0-0
Distance: 5f/6f: 0-0 7f-8f: 0-2 9f-13f: 0-1 14f+: 0-0
Track : LH: 0-1 RH: 0-1 Tight: 0-1 Gall: 0-0
Aids: Bl: 0-0 Vi: 0-0 Tstrap: 0-0 Ckp: 0-0
Best Rating: 75 8/09 Sthl 1m stand

Fair; stays 1m and acts on Fibresand.

Banco Busto (IRE)

81(66) (13)37
2-y-o b f Chineur (FR)-Banco Solo (Distant Relative)
H S Howe Roly Roper

Placings:00 **(6567)**
2009: 7^{0}SD, 7^{0}GF,

	Starts	1st	2nd	3rd	Win & Pl
Career Total (Turf)	1	0	0	0	
Career Total (AW)	1	0	0	0	

Going (Turf): Sf: 0-0 GS: 0-0 Gd: 0-0 GF: 0-1 Fm: 0-0
Distance: 5f/6f: 0-0 7f-8f: 0-2 9f-13f: 0-0 14f+: 0-0
Track : LH: 0-0 RH: 0-1 Tight: 0-0 Gall: 0-0
Aids: Bl: 0-0 Vi: 0-0 Tstrap: 0-0 Ckp: 0-0
Best Rating: 37 10/09 Leic 7f9y gd-fm

Banda Sea (IRE)

(93) (68)61
3-y-o b c Tagula (IRE)-Non Ultra (USA) (Peintre Celebre (USA))
P J Makin J Gale M Holland D Powell R Dollar

Placings:000-240 **(7456)**
2009: 7^{2}SD, 8^{4}SD, 8^{0}SD,

	Starts	1st	2nd	3rd	Win & Pl
Career Total (Turf)	2	0	0	0	
Career Total (AW)	4	0	1	0	806

Going (Turf): Sf: 0-0 GS: 0-1 Gd: 0-0 GF: 0-1 Fm: 0-0
Distance: 5f/6f: 0-1 7f-8f: 0-5 9f-13f: 0-0 14f+: 0-0
Track : LH: 0-2 RH: 0-3 Tight: 0-2 Gall: 0-0
Aids: Bl: 0-1 Vi: 0-0 Tstrap: 0-1 Ckp: 0-1
Best Rating: 68 1/09 Ling 7f stand

Modest; effective over 7f; acts on Polytrack.

Bandama (IRE)

97(102) (74)96
6-y-o b g Green Desert (USA)-Orinoco (IRE) (Darshaan)
John Joseph Hanlon (Mrs A J Perrett 8/10) Miss Rachel O'Neill

Placings:03/3113265/4200040320/254240010-5010 **(7381a)**
2009: 10^{5}GF, 12^{0}G, 12^{1}SD, 12^{0}SD,

	Starts	1st	2nd	3rd	Win & Pl
Career Total (Turf)	27	3	4	3	62319
Career Total (AW)	5	1	1	1	4870

74	10/09	Kemp	1m4f		STD	£2047
94	10/08	NmkR	1m4f	(0-100)H	GD	£12462
93	6/06	Leic	1m1f218y	(0-85)H	G-F	£6232
85	5/06	Newb	1m2f6y		GD	£4210

Total win prize-money £24951

Going (Turf): Sf: 0-2 GS: 0-2 **Gd: 2-7** GF: 1-16 Fm: 0-0
Distance: 5f/6f: 0-0 7f-8f: 0-3 **9f-13f: 4-26** 14f+: 0-3
Track : LH: 1-9 **RH: 3-20** Tight: 0-6 **Gall: 2-17**
Aids: Bl: 0-0 Vi: 0-1 Tstrap: 0-1 Ckp: 0-1
Best Rating: 104 6/07 Kemp 1m2f stand

Useful; effective over 1m2f-1m4f; acts on fast ground; also goes on Polytrack; has worn a visor.

Bandanaman (IRE)

95(81) (43)76
3-y-o b g Danehill Dancer (IRE)-Band Of Angels (IRE) (Alzao (USA))
G A Swinbank Miss J S Peat

Placings:2540-055 **(2662)**
2009: 8^{0}SD, 9^{5}F, 8^{5}GF,

	Starts	1st	2nd	3rd	Win & Pl
Career Total (Turf)	6	0	1	0	1609
Career Total (AW)	1	0	0	0	

Going (Turf): Sf: 0-2 GS: 0-0 Gd: 0-1 GF: 0-2 Fm: 0-1
Distance: 5f/6f: 0-0 7f-8f: 0-4 9f-13f: 0-3 14f+: 0-0
Track : LH: 0-5 RH: 0-2 Tight: 0-2 Gall: 0-1
Aids: Bl: 0-0 Vi: 0-0 Tstrap: 0-0 Ckp: 0-0
Best Rating: 76 8/08 Thsk 7f soft

Fair form in maidens; stays 1m; handles soft and fast ground.

Bandear (IRE)

96(72) (31)63
2-y-o b f Royal Applause-Royals Special (IRE) (Caerleon (USA))
C E Brittain Saeed Manana

Placings:533030 **(6418)**
2009: 7^{5}SD, 7^{3}F, 6^{3}GF, 7^{0}GS, 7^{3}GF, 6^{0}GF,

	Starts	1st	2nd	3rd	Win & Pl
Career Total (Turf)	5	0	0	3	1815
Career Total (AW)	1	0	0	0	0

Going (Turf): Sf: 0-0 GS: 0-1 Gd: 0-0 GF: 0-3 Fm: 0-1
Distance: 5f/6f: 0-1 7f-8f: 0-5 9f-13f: 0-0 14f+: 0-0
Track : LH: 0-2 RH: 0-0 Tight: 0-2 Gall: 0-0
Aids: Bl: 0-0 Vi: 0-0 Tstrap: 0-0 Ckp: 0-0
Best Rating: 63 9/09 Yarm 7f3y gd-fm

Bandeau Charmer

(62)
6-y-o b m Band On The Run-Fair Enchantress (Enchantment I)
C N Kellett Heartland Thoroughbreds

Placings:6 **(3951)**
2009: 12^{6}SD,

	Starts	1st	2nd	3rd	Win & Pl
Career Total (Turf)	0	0	0	0	
Career Total (AW)	1	0	0	0	0

Going (Turf): Sf: 0-0 GS: 0-0 Gd: 0-0 GF: 0-0 Fm: 0-0
Distance: 5f/6f: 0-0 7f-8f: 0-0 9f-13f: 0-1 14f+: 0-0
Track : LH: 0-1 RH: 0-0 Tight: 0-0 Gall: 0-0
Aids: Bl: 0-0 Vi: 0-0 Tstrap: 0-0 Ckp: 0-0

Bandstand

(97) (63)
3-y-o b g Royal Applause-Incise (Dr Fong (USA))
B Smart Crossfields Racing

Placings:2 **(7853)**
2009: 6^{2}SS,

	Starts	1st	2nd	3rd	Win & Pl
Career Total (Turf)	0	0	0	0	
Career Total (AW)	1	0	1	0	806

Going (Turf): Sf: 0-0 GS: 0-0 Gd: 0-0 GF: 0-0 Fm: 0-0
Distance: 5f/6f: 0-1 7f-8f: 0-0 9f-13f: 0-0 14f+: 0-0
Track : LH: 0-1 RH: 0-0 Tight: 0-0 Gall: 0-0
Aids: Bl: 0-0 Vi: 0-0 Tstrap: 0-0 Ckp: 0-0
Best Rating: 63 12/09 Sthl 6f std-slw

From a decent family of sprinters and 7f performers; promise on belated debut over 6f on Fibresand.

Banged Up Abroad (IRE)

(58)
2-y-o b c Royal Applause-Annette Vallon (IRE) (Efisio)
M G Quinlan Mrs J Quinlan

Placings:0 (5778)
2009: 6⁰SD,

	Starts	1st	2nd	3rd	Win & Pl
Career Total (Turf)	0	0	0	0	
Career Total (AW)	1	0	0	0	

Going (Turf): Sf: 0-0 GS: 0-0 Gd: 0-0 GF: 0-0 Fm: 0-0
Distance: 5f/6f: 0-1 7f-8f: 0-0 9f-13f: 0-0 14f+: 0-0
Track : LH: 0-0 RH: 0-1 Tight: 0-0 Gall: 0-0
Aids: Bl: 0-0 Vi: 0-0 Tstrap: 0-0 Ckp: 0-0

Bankable (IRE)

112 121
5-y-o b h Medicean-Dance To The Top (Sadler's Wells (USA))
G L Moore (M F De Kock 17/5) Ramzan Kadyrov

Placings:011/115222226-15321 (5995)
2009: 8¹GF, 8⁵G, 10³G, 10²GF, 8¹GS,

	Starts	1st	2nd	3rd	Win & Pl
Career Total (Turf)	17	6	6	1	473646

109	9/09	Sand	1m14y		G-S	£22708
118	2/09	Ndas	1m194y	(100-119)H	G-F	£72916
115	5/08	Gdwd	1m		SFT	£17031
101	4/08	Asct	1m	(0-85)H	SFT	£7123
96	9/07	Asct	1m	(0-85)H	G-S	£6477
81	9/07	Newc	1m		G-F	£3785

Total win prize-money £130042

Going (Turf): **Sf: 2-4 GS: 2-4** Gd: 0-4 **GF: 2-5** Fm: 0-0
Distance: 5f/6f: 0-0 **7f-8f: 4-9** 9f-13f: 2-8 14f+: 0-0
Track : LH: 2-5 RH: 2-5 Tight: 0-2 **Gall: 2-4**
Aids: Bl: 0-0 Vi: 0-0 Tstrap: 0-0 Ckp: 0-0
Best Rating: **121** 8/08 Gdwd 1m gd-sft

Group class; winner in Listed company; effective over 1m-1m2f; acts on most ground.

Banks And Braes

92 72
2-y-o b c Red Ransom (USA)-Bonnie Doon (IRE) (Grand Lodge (USA))
R Hannon The Queen

Placings:3540 (6736)
2009: 6³G, 7⁵GF, 8⁴GF, 8⁰GS,

	Starts	1st	2nd	3rd	Win & Pl
Career Total (Turf)	4	0	0	1	914

Going (Turf): Sf: 0-0 GS: 0-1 Gd: 0-1 GF: 0-2 Fm: 0-0
Distance: 5f/6f: 0-0 7f-8f: 0-3 9f-13f: 0-1 14f+: 0-0
Track : LH: 0-1 RH: 0-2 Tight: 0-2 Gall: 0-0
Aids: Bl: 0-0 Vi: 0-0 Tstrap: 0-0 Ckp: 0-0
Best Rating: **72** 9/09 Gdwd 1m gd-fm

Bantu

73(107) (66)1
4-y-o b/br f Cape Cross (IRE)-Lalindi (IRE) (Cadeaux Genereux)
J H M Gosden H R H Princess Haya Of Jordan

Placings:02-000 (5718)
2009: 12⁰GF, 11⁰SD, 11⁰G,

	Starts	1st	2nd	3rd	Win & Pl
Career Total (Turf)	2	0	0	0	
Career Total (AW)	3	0	1	0	806

Going (Turf): Sf: 0-0 GS: 0-0 Gd: 0-1 GF: 0-1 Fm: 0-0
Distance: 5f/6f: 0-0 7f-8f: 0-0 9f-13f: 0-5 14f+: 0-0
Track : LH: 0-4 RH: 0-1 Tight: 0-3 Gall: 0-0
Aids: Bl: 0-1 Vi: 0-1 Tstrap: 0-0 Ckp: 0-0
Best Rating: **66** 11/08 Ling 1m2f stand

Baoli

83(78) (38)55
2-y-o b f Dansili-Thorntoun Piccolo (Groom Dancer (USA))
R Hannon A P Patey

Placings:0000 (7389)
2009: 6⁰G, 7⁰GF, 8⁰S, 7⁰SD,

	Starts	1st	2nd	3rd	Win & Pl
Career Total (Turf)	3	0	0	0	
Career Total (AW)	1	0	0	0	

Going (Turf): Sf: 0-1 GS: 0-0 Gd: 0-1 GF: 0-1 Fm: 0-0
Distance: 5f/6f: 0-1 7f-8f: 0-3 9f-13f: 0-0 14f+: 0-0
Track : LH: 0-1 RH: 0-0 Tight: 0-1 Gall: 0-0
Aids: Bl: 0-0 Vi: 0-0 Tstrap: 0-0 Ckp: 0-0
Best Rating: **55** 9/09 Newb 7f gd-fm

Bar Blu (IRE)

58
4-y-o b f Mull Of Kintyre (USA)-Ruwy (Soviet Star (USA))
G A Swinbank B Harker & Mrs V McGee

Placings:0 (3862)
2009: 8⁰GF,

	Starts	1st	2nd	3rd	Win & Pl
Career Total (Turf)	1	0	0	0	

Going (Turf): Sf: 0-0 GS: 0-0 Gd: 0-0 GF: 0-1 Fm: 0-0
Distance: 5f/6f: 0-0 7f-8f: 0-0 9f-13f: 0-1 14f+: 0-0
Track : LH: 0-1 RH: 0-0 Tight: 0-0 Gall: 0-0
Aids: Bl: 0-0 Vi: 0-0 Tstrap: 0-0 Ckp: 0-0

Baraconti (IRE)

94(85) (59)67
2-y-o b g Barathea (IRE)-Continuous (IRE) (Darshaan)
R A Fahey Morebrooke Racing Partnership I

Placings:50 (6672)
2009: 7⁵GF, 8⁰SD,

	Starts	1st	2nd	3rd	Win & Pl
Career Total (Turf)	1	0	0	0	0
Career Total (AW)	1	0	0	0	

Going (Turf): Sf: 0-0 GS: 0-0 Gd: 0-0 GF: 0-1 Fm: 0-0
Distance: 5f/6f: 0-0 7f-8f: 0-1 9f-13f: 0-1 14f+: 0-0
Track : LH: 0-1 RH: 0-0 Tight: 0-1 Gall: 0-0
Aids: Bl: 0-0 Vi: 0-0 Tstrap: 0-0 Ckp: 0-0
Best Rating: **67** 9/09 Rdcr 7f gd-fm

Barafundle Boy

72(79) (33)40
2-y-o b g Deportivo-Barawin (FR) (Fijar Tango (FR))
J J Bridger Mrs Liz Gardner

Placings:00000 (7429)
2009: 6⁰GF, 7⁰GF, 6⁰GS, 7⁰SD, 7⁰SD,

	Starts	1st	2nd	3rd	Win & Pl
Career Total (Turf)	3	0	0	0	
Career Total (AW)	2	0	0	0	

Going (Turf): Sf: 0-0 GS: 0-1 Gd: 0-0 GF: 0-2 Fm: 0-0
Distance: 5f/6f: 0-2 7f-8f: 0-3 9f-13f: 0-0 14f+: 0-0
Track : LH: 0-0 RH: 0-2 Tight: 0-0 Gall: 0-0
Aids: Bl: 0-0 Vi: 0-0 Tstrap: 0-0 Ckp: 0-0
Best Rating: **40** 9/09 Newb 7f gd-fm

Baralaka

(90) (67)
2-y-o ch g Barathea (IRE)-Shakalaka Baby (Nashwan (USA))
Sir Mark Prescott Mrs S L Warman

Placings:050 (6629)
2009: 6⁰SD, 6⁵SD, 7⁰SS,

	Starts	1st	2nd	3rd	Win & Pl
Career Total (Turf)	0	0	0	0	
Career Total (AW)	3	0	0	0	0

Going (Turf): Sf: 0-0 GS: 0-0 Gd: 0-0 GF: 0-0 Fm: 0-0
Distance: 5f/6f: 0-2 7f-8f: 0-1 9f-13f: 0-0 14f+: 0-0
Track : LH: 0-1 RH: 0-2 Tight: 0-1 Gall: 0-0
Aids: Bl: 0-0 Vi: 0-0 Tstrap: 0-0 Ckp: 0-0
Best Rating: **67** 9/09 Kemp 6f stand

Barastar

79 57
2-y-o b g Sampower Star-Barachois Princess (USA) (Barachois (CAN))
J R Boyle racingclub.co.uk

Placings:005 (3767)
2009: 6⁰GS, 7⁰G, 6⁵G,

	Starts	1st	2nd	3rd	Win & Pl
Career Total (Turf)	3	0	0	0	0

Going (Turf): Sf: 0-0 GS: 0-1 Gd: 0-2 GF: 0-0 Fm: 0-0
Distance: 5f/6f: 0-2 7f-8f: 0-1 9f-13f: 0-0 14f+: 0-0
Track : LH: 0-1 RH: 0-1 Tight: 0-1 Gall: 0-1
Aids: Bl: 0-0 Vi: 0-0 Tstrap: 0-0 Ckp: 0-0
Best Rating: **57** 7/09 Sand 7f16y good

Barataria

100(105) (78)76
7-y-o ch g Barathea (IRE)-Aethra (USA) (Trempolino (USA))
R Bastiman Coal Trade Partnership

Placings:030/000020/0103000/60302213-3262001000 (6987)
2009: 8³SD, 8²SD, 8⁶SD, 8²SD, 8⁰HY, 7⁰G, 8¹G, 8⁰GF, 8⁰GF, 9⁰G,

	Starts	1st	2nd	3rd	Win & Pl
Career Total (Turf)	26	2	1	3	5751
Career Total (AW)	8	1	4	2	5340

76	7/09	Yarm	1m3y	(0-65)H	GD	£1873
75	12/08	Sthl	1m	(0-62)H	STD	£2047
62	6/07	Catt	7f	(0-60)	G-F	£2047

Total win prize-money £5969

Going (Turf): Sf: 0-5 GS: 0-3 **Gd: 1-10 GF: 1-8** Fm: 0-0

Distance: 5f/6f: 0-0 **7f-8f: 2-23** 9f-13f: 1-11 14f+: 0-0
Track : **LH: 2-21** RH: 0-9 **Tight: 1-10** Gall: 0-0
Aids: Bl: 0-0 Vi: 0-0 Tstrap: 0-0 Ckp: 0-0
Best Rating: 78 4/09 Sthl 1m stand

Modest; effective over 7f-1m; acts on good/fast ground; goes on Fibresand.

Barathea's Acclaim

(87) (48)
3-y-o b f Acclamation-Missbarathea (IRE) (Barathea (IRE))
P R Hedger P C F Racing Ltd

Placings:0500 **(7195)**
2009: 7^{0}SD, 8^{5}SD, 8^{0}SD, 9^{0}SD,

	Starts	1st	2nd	3rd	Win & Pl
Career Total (Turf)	0	0	0	0	
Career Total (AW)	4	0	0	0	0

Going (Turf): Sf: 0-0 GS: 0-0 Gd: 0-0 GF: 0-0 Fm: 0-0
Distance: 5f/6f: 0-0 7f-8f: 0-2 9f-13f: 0-2 14f+: 0-0
Track : LH: 0-2 RH: 0-2 Tight: 0-2 Gall: 0-0
Aids: Bl: 0-0 Vi: 0-0 Tstrap: 0-1 Ckp: 0-1
Best Rating: 48 9/09 Wolv 1m141y stand

Barawin (IRE)

(90) (81)**79**
4-y-o ch f Hawk Wing (USA)-Cosabawn (IRE) (Barathea (IRE))
K R Burke M J Halligan

Placings:010/440-40 **(0226)**
2009: 13^{4}SD, 12^{0}SD,

	Starts	1st	2nd	3rd	Win & Pl
Career Total (Turf)	4	1	0	0	3291
Career Total (AW)	4	0	0	0	529

77 9/07 Hayd 1m30y SFT £2590
Total win prize-money £2591

Going (Turf): Sf: 1-2 GS: 0-0 Gd: 0-1 GF: 0-1 Fm: 0-0
Distance: 5f/6f: 0-1 7f-8f: 0-1 **9f-13f: 1-4** 14f+: 0-2
Track : **LH: 1-6** RH: 0-1 Tight: 0-1 Gall: 0-2
Aids: Bl: 0-2 Vi: 0-0 Tstrap: 0-0 Ckp: 0-0
Best Rating: 81 11/08 Wolv 1m5f194y stand

Useful; effective over 1m5f; acts on soft ground; handles Polytrack.

Barbarian

99(96) (71)**73**
3-y-o b g Noverre (USA)-Love In The Mist (USA) (Silver Hawk (USA))
A D Brown (B W Hills 26/6) Frank Reay

Placings:402-22052605624 **(7863)**
2009: 8^{2}SD, 8^{2}GS, 8^{0}GF, 8^{5}SD, 8^{2}GS, 8^{6}GS, 8^{0}G, 11^{5}SD, 8^{6}SD, 8^{2}SD, 8^{4}SD,

	Starts	1st	2nd	3rd	Win & Pl
Career Total (Turf)	7	0	2	0	2352
Career Total (AW)	7	0	3	0	2492

Going (Turf): Sf: 0-0 GS: 0-3 Gd: 0-2 GF: 0-2 Fm: 0-0
Distance: 5f/6f: 0-1 7f-8f: 0-6 9f-13f: 0-7 14f+: 0-0
Track : LH: 0-9 RH: 0-2 Tight: 0-7 Gall: 0-1
Aids: Bl: 0 1 Vi: 0 2 Tstrap: 0-1 Ckp: 0-1
Best Rating: 73 4/09 Wind 1m67y gd-sft

Fair; effective over 7f-1m; acts on Polytrack; has worn cheekpieces/visor.

Barbee (IRE)

85(86) (59)**75**
3-y-o ch f Night Shift (USA)-Barbizou (FR) (Selkirk (USA))
E A L Dunlop Ballygallon Stud Limited

Placings:33106000-00 **(2827)**
2009: 7^{0}GF, 7^{0}SD,

	Starts	1st	2nd	3rd	Win & Pl
Career Total (Turf)	7	1	0	1	5339
Career Total (AW)	3	0	0	1	433

75 5/08 Newc 6f G-F £4857
Total win prize-money £4857

Going (Turf): Sf: 0-0 GS: 0-0 Gd: 0-1 **GF: 1-5** Fm: 0-1
Distance: **5f/6f: 1-7** 7f-8f: 0-3 9f-13f: 0-0 14f+: 0-0
Track : LH: 0-3 RH: 0-1 Tight: 0-0 Gall: 0-2
Aids: Bl: 0-1 Vi: 0-0 Tstrap: 0-0 Ckp: 0-0
Best Rating: 75 5/08 Newc 6f gd-fm

Fair; effective at 6f; acts on fast ground and Polytrack.

Barbeito

84(92) (40)**38**
3-y-o b f Zaha (CAN)-Tinta (Robellino (USA))
M D Squance Houghton Bloodstock

Placings:6004450-60 **(3005)**
2009: 7^{6}SD, 9^{0}G,

	Starts	1st	2nd	3rd	Win & Pl
Career Total (Turf)	3	0	0	0	0
Career Total (AW)	6	0	0	0	0

Going (Turf): Sf: 0-2 GS: 0-0 Gd: 0-1 GF: 0-0 Fm: 0-0
Distance: 5f/6f: 0-0 7f-8f: 0-6 9f-13f: 0-3 14f+: 0-0
Track : LH: 0-7 RH: 0-1 Tight: 0-2 Gall: 0-1
Aids: Bl: 0-0 Vi: 0-2 Tstrap: 0-0 Ckp: 0-0
Best Rating: 40 11/08 Sthl 7f stand

Barbirolli

101(96) (60)**59**
7-y-o b g Machiavellian (USA)-Blushing Barada (USA) (Blushing Groom (FR))
W B Stone (W M Brisbourne 21/8) Miss Caroline Scott

Placings:0/46365551**3**4000**56**/3504254130**5053**/**4**266036000/04433354**63-6**10**1**4636334506125 **(7847)**
2009: 12^{6}SD, 12^{1}GF, 12^{0}SD, 12^{1}SD, 10^{4}F, 11^{6}GF, 11^{3}GF, 12^{6}GS, 12^{3}G, 11^{3}GF, 12^{4}GF, 11^{5}GS, 11^{0}S, 11^{6}GF, 12^{1}G, 12^{2}GF, 12^{5}SD,

	Starts	1st	2nd	3rd	Win & Pl
Career Total (Turf)	52	4	3	10	31435
Career Total (AW)	15	1	0	3	3902

51 8/09 Bevl 1m4f16y (0-60)H GD £2428
60 5/09 Wolv 1m4f50y (0-55)H STD £2307
55 4/09 Folk 1m4f (0-60)H G-F £2047
71 9/06 Haml 1m1f36y H G-S £9715
74 7/05 Ches 1m2f75y (0-70)H GD £5573
Total win prize-money £22073

Going (Turf): Sf: 0-5 GS: 1-8 **Gd: 2-14** GF: 1-24 Fm: 0-1
Distance: 5f/6f: 0-0 7f-8f: 0-1 **9f-13f: 5-66** 14f+: 0-0
Track : LH: 2-49 **RH: 3-17 Tight: 5-44** Gall: 0-6
Aids: Bl: 0-1 Vi: 0-2 Tstrap: 0-0 Ckp: 0-0
Best Rating: 74 7/05 Ches 1m2f75y good

Moderate; stays 1m4f; acts on good and softer ground and on Polytrack; has worn a visor and blinkers.

Barcode

(93) (53)**57**
3-y-o b f Tobougg (IRE)-Truly Madly Deeply (Most Welcome)
R Hannon A J Ilsley & G Battocchi

Placings:0000014503-200 **(0943)**
2009: 8^{2}SD, 9^{0}SF, 10^{0}SD,

	Starts	1st	2nd	3rd	Win & Pl
Career Total (Turf)	5	1	0	0	2720
Career Total (AW)	8	0	1	1	1008

54 8/08 Bath 5f11y GD £2719
Total win prize-money £2720

Going (Turf): Sf: 0-0 GS: 0-1 **Gd: 1-1** GF: 0-3 Fm: 0-0
Distance: **5f/6f: 1-3** 7f-8f: 0-5 9f-13f: 0-5 14f+: 0-0
Track : **LH: 1-6** RH: 0-4 Tight: 0-4 **Gall: 1-1**
Aids: Bl: 0-1 Vi: 0-0 Tstrap: 0-0 Ckp: 0-0
Best Rating: 57 6/08 Newb 6f8y gd-fm

Moderate; suited by 1m; acts on Polytrack and on good ground.

Bari Bay

94(94) (51)**53**
3-y-o b f Bahri (USA)-Sea Nymph (IRE) (Spectrum (IRE))
J W Mullins (R M Beckett 8/6) Seamus Mullins

Placings:0-00024345 **(5812)**
2009: 7^{0}SD, 7^{0}GF, 10^{0}SD, 12^{2}SD, 11^{4}G, 11^{3}GS, 16^{4}GF, 16^{5}SD,

	Starts	1st	2nd	3rd	Win & Pl
Career Total (Turf)	4	0	0	1	385
Career Total (AW)	5	0	1	0	605

Going (Turf): Sf: 0-0 GS: 0-1 Gd: 0-1 GF: 0-2 Fm: 0-0
Distance: 5f/6f: 0-0 7f-8f: 0-3 9f-13f: 0-4 14f+: 0-2
Track : LH: 0-6 RH: 0-2 Tight: 0-5 Gall: 0-0
Aids: Bl: 0-2 Vi: 0-0 Tstrap: 0-1 Ckp: 0-1
Best Rating: 53 8/09 Brig 1m3f196y gd-sft

Bariolo (FR)

(103) (66)**72**
5-y-o b g Priolo (USA)-La Bardane (FR) (Marignan (USA))
Noel T Chance Neil Campbell & Noel Chance Racing Club

Placings:0035036341006**4/60** **(0734)**
2009: 12^{6}SD, 13^{0}SD,

	Starts	1st	2nd	3rd	Win & Pl
Career Total (Turf)	10	1	0	1	9763
Career Total (AW)	6	0	0	2	6013

8/07 Claf 1m1f H VS £7094
Total win prize-money £7095

Going (Turf): Sf: 0-5 GS: 0-1 Gd: 0-2 GF: 0-1 Fm: 0-0
Distance: 5f/6f: 0-0 7f-8f: 0-2 **9f-13f: 1-13** 14f+: 0-1
Track : LH: 0-3 RH: 0-2 Tight: 0-2 Gall: 0-0
Aids: Bl: 0-6 Vi: 0-0 Tstrap: 0-0 Ckp: 0-0
Best Rating: 74 7/07 Deau 1m1f110y stand

Barlaman (USA)

(93) (74)
2-y-o ch c Langfuhr (CAN)-Party Circuit (USA) (Kingmambo (USA))
Saeed Bin Suroor Godolphin

Placings:43232 **(6802)**
2009: 6^{4}SD, 6^{3}SD, 5^{2}SD, 5^{3}SD, 5^{2}SD,

	Starts	1st	2nd	3rd	Win & Pl
Career Total (Turf)	0	0	0	0	
Career Total (AW)	5	0	2	2	3516

Going (Turf): Sf: 0-0 GS: 0-0 Gd: 0-0 GF: 0-0 Fm: 0-0

Distance: 5f/6f: 0-5 7f-8f: 0-0 9f-13f: 0-0 14f+: 0-0
Track : LH: 0-3 RH: 0-2 Tight: 0-3 Gall: 0-0
Aids: Bl: 0-0 Vi: 0-0 Tstrap: 0-0 Ckp: 0-0
Best Rating: 74 9/09 Wolv 5f216y stand

Fair; stays 6f; acts on Polytrack; has worn a tongue tie.

Barley Bree (IRE)

95 **40**

4-y-o ch f Danehill Dancer (IRE)-Aunty Mary (Common Grounds)
Mrs A Duffield Evelyn Duchess Of Sutherland

Placings:0-0060 (4929)
2009: 5^{0}GF, 5^{0}GF, 5^{6}G, 5^{0}G,

	Starts	1st	2nd	3rd	Win & Pl
Career Total (Turf)	5	0	0	0	0

Going (Turf): Sf: 0-0 GS: 0-1 Gd: 0-2 GF: 0-2 Fm: 0-0
Distance: 5f/6f: 0-5 7f-8f: 0-0 9f-13f: 0-0 14f+: 0-0
Track : LH: 0-0 RH: 0-0 Tight: 0-0 Gall: 0-0
Aids: Bl: 0-0 Vi: 0-0 Tstrap: 0-0 Ckp: 0-0
Best Rating: 40 9/08 Rdcr 6f gd-sft

Barliffey (IRE)

109(102) (78)**78**

4-y-o b g Bahri (USA)-Kildare Lady (IRE) (Indian Ridge)
D J Coakley Barliffey Racing

Placings:6224/3540231-4254303 (7360)
2009: 10^{4}GF, 10^{2}GF, 10^{5}GF, 8^{4}G, 8^{3}GF, 8^{0}GF, 9^{3}SD,

	Starts	1st	2nd	3rd	Win & Pl
Career Total (Turf)	13	0	4	1	7279
Career Total (AW)	5	1	0	3	4367

74 10/08 Wolv 1m1f103y STD £2729
Total win prize-money £2730

Going (Turf): Sf: 0-0 GS: 0-0 Gd: 0-2 GF: 0-10 Fm: 0-1
Distance: 5f/6f: 0-0 7f-8f: 0-9 9f-13f: 1-9 14f+: 0-0
Track : LH: 1-8 RH: 0-5 Tight: 1-5 Gall: 0-1
Aids: Bl: 0-0 Vi: 1-10 Tstrap: 0-0 Ckp: 0-0
Best Rating: 78 9/09 Gdwd 1m gd-fm

Fair; effective at 7f-1m2f; acts on fast ground; handles Polytrack.

Barndeh (IRE)

96(91) (56)**53**

6-y-o b g Marju (IRE)-Sweetest Thing (IRE) (Prince Rupert (FR))
Lee Smyth Mrs Caroline Jordan/Conor Daly

Placings:000/3230/0500400/0662-06400 (4861)
2009: 7^{0}SD, 10^{6}SD, 9^{4}G, 10^{0}GF, 9^{0}SD,

	Starts	1st	2nd	3rd	Win & Pl
Career Total (Turf)	19	0	1	2	3361
Career Total (AW)	4	0	1	0	1006

Going (Turf): Sf: 0-2 GS: 0-1 Gd: 0-6 GF: 0-4 Fm: 0-0
Distance: 5f/6f: 0-0 7f-8f: 0-8 9f-13f: 0-15 14f+: 0-0
Track : LH: 0-12 RH: 0-9 Tight: 0-1 Gall: 0-1
Aids: Bl: 0-3 Vi: 0-0 Tstrap: 0-8 Ckp: 0-8
Best Rating: 77 6/06 Leic 1m1f218y gd-fm

Modest performer; effective over a mile; acts on fast ground; has worn cheekpieces.

Barnes Bridge

62(65)

4-y-o ch g Zaha (CAN)-Mo Stopher (Sharpo)
M J Attwater Canisbay Bloodstock

Placings:00 (4205)
2009: 9^{0}GF, 12^{0}SD,

	Starts	1st	2nd	3rd	Win & Pl
Career Total (Turf)	1	0	0	0	
Career Total (AW)	1	0	0	0	

Going (Turf): Sf: 0-0 GS: 0-0 Gd: 0-0 GF: 0-1 Fm: 0-0
Distance: 5f/6f: 0-0 7f-8f: 0-0 9f-13f: 0-2 14f+: 0-0
Track : LH: 0-2 RH: 0-0 Tight: 0-2 Gall: 0-0
Aids: Bl: 0-0 Vi: 0-0 Tstrap: 0-0 Ckp: 0-0

Barney McGrew (IRE)

110(102) (101)**112**

6-y-o b g Mark Of Esteem (IRE)-Success Story (Sharrood (USA))
M Dods Andrew Tinkler

Placings:01/322551201610/00010400252-522020102 (6091)
2009: 6^{5}GF, 6^{2}GF, 6^{2}S, 6^{0}G, 6^{2}G, 6^{0}S, 5^{1}GF, 5^{0}GF, 6^{2}G,

	Starts	1st	2nd	3rd	Win & Pl
Career Total (Turf)	27	4	7	0	104433
Career Total (AW)	7	2	2	1	14648

108 8/09 York 5f89y H G-F £25904
99 5/08 Newc 6f (0-90)H G-F £6938
101 10/07 Ling 6f (0-90)H STD £8101
92 8/07 NmkJ 6f (0-85)H GD £5181
84 6/07 Gdwd 7f (0-85)H G-F £6800
75 12/06 Wolv 7f32y STD £3238
Total win prize-money £56167

Going (Turf): Sf: 0-4 GS: 0-3 Gd: 1-10 GF: 3-10 Fm: 0-0
Distance: 5f/6f: 4-21 7f-8f: 2-12 9f-13f: 0-1 14f+: 0-0
Track : LH: 2-6 RH: 1-2 Tight: 2-6 Gall: 0-1
Aids: Bl: 0-0 Vi: 0-0 Tstrap: 0-0 Ckp: 0-0
Best Rating: 112 9/09 Ayr 6f good

Smart; effective over 5f-7f; acts on good and faster ground and on Polytrack; usually held up.

Barnezet (GR)

(104) (76)**68**

3-y-o b f Invincible Spirit (IRE)-Le Meridien (IRE) (Magical Wonder (USA))
J Pearce (R Hannon 7/3) Killarney Glen

Placings:5625454233-110 (7682)
2009: 5^{1}SD, 5^{1}SD, 5^{0}SD,

	Starts	1st	2nd	3rd	Win & Pl
Career Total (Turf)	6	0	1	0	1493
Career Total (AW)	7	2	1	2	7695

65 3/09 Wolv 5f20y STD £3238
76 1/09 Ling 5f (0-70)H STD £2900
Total win prize-money £6138

Going (Turf): Sf: 0-0 GS: 0-1 Gd: 0-1 GF: 0-4 Fm: 0-0
Distance: 5f/6f: 2-13 7f-8f: 0-9 9f-13f: 0-0 14f+: 0-0
Track : LH: 2-6 RH: 0-2 Tight: 2-4 Gall: 0-6
Aids: Bl: 0-0 Vi: 0-0 Tstrap: 0-0 Ckp: 0-0
Best Rating: 76 1/09 Ling 5f stand

Fair; effective at 5f; acts on fast ground; goes on Polytrack.

Barodine

99(102) (61)**59**

6-y-o ch g Barathea (IRE)-Granted (FR) (Cadeaux Genereux)
R J Hodges The Gardens Entertainments Ltd

Placings:42/2135600/0/00-5405216455543320222000 (7750)
2009: 9^{5}SD, 12^{4}SD, 16^{0}SD, 10^{5}SD, 9^{2}SD, 9^{1}SD, 9^{6}SD, 8^{4}SD, 9^{5}GF, 8^{5}GF, 8^{5}SD, 9^{4}GF, 8^{3}G, 8^{3}SD, 13^{2}SF, 12^{0}S, 11^{2}GS, 13^{2}F, 13^{0}SD, 12^{0}SD, 13^{0}SD,

	Starts	1st	2nd	3rd	Win & Pl
Career Total (Turf)	17	1	4	2	13235
Career Total (AW)	16	1	2	1	4202

59 3/09 Wolv 1m1f103y (0-55)H STD £2388
79 5/06 Wwck 1m2f188y GD £5505
Total win prize-money £7893

Going (Turf): Sf: 0-3 GS: 0-4 Gd: 1-2 GF: 0-7 Fm: 0-1
Distance: 5f/6f: 0-0 7f-8f: 0-3 9f-13f: 2-25 14f+: 0-5
Track : LH: 2-25 RH: 0-4 Tight: 1-19 Gall: 0-0
Aids: Bl: 0-4 Vi: 0-0 Tstrap: 0-0 Ckp: 0-0
Best Rating: 88 6/06 Hayd 1m3f200y gd-fm

Moderate; stays 1m5f; acts on good ground; goes on Polytrack; has worn blinkers and a tongue tie.

Baron De'L (IRE)

105 (78)**104**

6-y-o ch g In The Wings-Lightstorm (IRE) (Darshaan)
Edward P Harty Dobbins Syndicate

Placings:032/04335220/4003004611106/60004011-140000 (5894a)
2009: 10^{1}Y, 13^{4}S, 10^{0}GF, 9^{0}Y, 14^{0}S, 10^{0}S,

	Starts	1st	2nd	3rd	Win & Pl
Career Total (Turf)	36	6	3	4	125242
Career Total (AW)	2	0	0	0	

104 4/09 Curr 1m2f YLD £28441
102 9/08 Curr 1m2f H SH £26327
93 8/08 Curr 1m2f (60-100)H SFT £12924
95 9/07 Curr 1m2f H G-F £25292
87 9/07 Curr 1m2f (60-100)H GD £12096
80 8/07 Curr 1m2f (50-90)H SH £8797
Total win prize-money £113878

Going (Turf): Sf: 1-9 GS: 0-0 Gd: 1-5 GF: 1-6 Fm: 0-1
Distance: 5f/6f: 0-0 7f-8f: 0-3 9f-13f: 6-31 14f+: 0-4
Track : LH: 0-12 RH: 6-24 Tight: 0-0 Gall: 0-1
Aids: Bl: 6-25 Vi: 0-0 Tstrap: 0-0 Ckp: 0-0
Best Rating: 104 4/09 Curr 1m2f yield

Smart; best at 1m2f; acts on most ground; has worn blinkers.

Baron Otto (IRE)

91(88) (49)**73**

3-y-o b g Anabaa (USA)-Marie Laurencin (Peintre Celebre (USA))
W J Haggas A E Oppenheimer

Placings:54-540 (3009)
2009: 8^{5}GF, 9^{4}SD, 7^{0}G,

	Starts	1st	2nd	3rd	Win & Pl
Career Total (Turf)	4	0	0	0	216
Career Total (AW)	1	0	0	0	0

Going (Turf): Sf: 0-1 GS: 0-0 Gd: 0-2 GF: 0-1 Fm: 0-0
Distance: 5f/6f: 0-0 7f-8f: 0-4 9f-13f: 0-1 14f+: 0-0
Track : LH: 0-2 RH: 0-0 Tight: 0-1 Gall: 0-0
Aids: Bl: 0-2 Vi: 0-0 Tstrap: 0-0 Ckp: 0-0
Best Rating: 73 9/08 Newb 7f good

Baronovici (IRE)

97 **59**

4-y-o b g Namid-Allegrina (IRE) (Barathea (IRE))

D W Barker David T J Metcalfe

Placings:2210/600006020-5360 **(1924)**

2009: 7^{5}GF, 7^{3}F, 7^{6}G, 6^{0}F,

	Starts	1st	2nd	3rd	Win & Pl
Career Total (Turf)	**17**	**1**	**3**	**1**	**9957**

72 7/07 Wind 6f GD £5181

Total win prize-money £5182

Going (Turf): Sf: 0-5 GS: 0-1 **Gd: 1-7** GF: 0-2 Fm: 0-2
Distance: **5f/6f: 1-9** 7f-8f: 0-8 9f-13f: 0-0 14f+: 0-0
Track : LH: 0-3 RH: 0-1 Tight: 0-4 **Gall: 1-2**
Aids: Bl: 0-0 Vi: 0-3 Tstrap: 0-2 Ckp: 0-2
Best Rating: **73** 7/07 Chep 6f16y heavy

Modest; effective over 6f; acts on most ground; likes to race prominently; has worn a visor and cheekpieces.

Barons Spy (IRE)

109 (84)**93**

8-y-o b g Danzero (AUS)-Princess Accord (USA) (D'Accord (USA))

R J Price Barry Veasey

Placings:00/42032/00002010/6502313221336/220502130 00/1414040050-045012304466 **(6540)**

2009: 7^{0}GF, 6^{4}S, 7^{5}GF, 7^{0}GS, 6^{1}GF, 6^{2}GF, 6^{3}G, 7^{0}GF, 7^{4}G, 6^{4}GS, 6^{6}GF, 6^{6}GF,

	Starts	1st	2nd	3rd	Win & Pl
Career Total (Turf)	**55**	**6**	**10**	**7**	**62097**
Career Total (AW)	**6**	**1**	**0**	**0**	**2922**

93 6/09 Wwck 6f (0-90)H G-F £7771
93 6/08 Ches 7f2y (0-85)H GD £5180
88 6/08 Bath 5f161y (0-85)H SFT £4209
84 9/07 Wwck 6f (0-85)H G-F £6477
75 8/06 Leic 7f9y (0-80)H G-S £7790
69 7/06 Nott 1m54y (0-75)H FRM £3886
60 12/05 Wolv 1m141y(0-55)H STD £2922

Total win prize-money £38236

Going (Turf): Sf: 1-7 GS: 1-6 Gd: 1-16 **GF: 2-20** Fm: 1-6
Distance: **5f/6f: 3-9** 7f-8f: 2-29 9f-13f: 2-23 14f+: 0-0
Track : **LH: 6-35** RH: 0-8 **Tight: 2-15** Gall: 1-1
Aids: Bl: 0-0 Vi: 0-0 Tstrap: 0-0 Ckp: 0-0
Best Rating: **93** 8/09 Wwck 7f26y good

Useful; effective from 6f-1m; acts on most ground and on Polytrack; usually held up.

Barony (IRE)

(73)

3-y-o ch g Swift Gulliver (IRE)-Musical Flyer (IRE) (Prince Of Birds (USA))

Lee Smyth Loughcraig Racing Syndicate

Placings:0 **(7863)**

2009: 8^{0}SD,

	Starts	1st	2nd	3rd	Win & Pl
Career Total (Turf)	**0**	**0**	**0**	**0**	
Career Total (AW)	**1**	**0**	**0**	**0**	

Going (Turf): **Sf: 0-0 GS: 0-0 Gd: 0-0 GF: 0-0 Fm: 0-0**
Distance: 5f/6f: 0-0 7f-8f: 0-0 9f-13f: 0-1 14f+: 0-0
Track : LH: 0-1 RH: 0-0 Tight: 0-1 Gall: 0-0
Aids: Bl: 0-0 Vi: 0-0 Tstrap: 0-0 Ckp: 0-0

Barq (IRE)

(91) (68)

2-y-o br c Green Desert (USA)-Zaeema (Zafonic (USA))

Saeed Bin Suroor Godolphin

Placings:3 **(7376)**

2009: 7^{3}SD,

	Starts	1st	2nd	3rd	Win & Pl
Career Total (Turf)	**0**	**0**	**0**	**0**	
Career Total (AW)	**1**	**0**	**0**	**1**	**482**

Going (Turf): **Sf: 0-0 GS: 0-0 Gd: 0-0 GF: 0-0 Fm: 0-0**
Distance: 5f/6f: 0-0 7f-8f: 0-1 9f-13f: 0-0 14f+: 0-0
Track : LH: 0-1 RH: 0-0 Tight: 0-1 Gall: 0-0
Aids: Bl: 0-0 Vi: 0-0 Tstrap: 0-0 Ckp: 0-0
Best Rating: **68** 11/09 Wolv 7f32y stand

Barraland

88(99) (67)**77**

4-y-o b g Compton Place-Dance Land (IRE) (Nordance (USA))

J S Goldie John Breslin

Placings:43100220044045/3106045424514005-00 **(3149)**

2009: 5^{0}G, 5^{0}GF,

	Starts	1st	2nd	3rd	Win & Pl
Career Total (Turf)	**31**	**3**	**3**	**1**	**15303**
Career Total (AW)	**1**	**0**	**0**	**1**	**614**

76 8/08 Folk 5f (0-75)H G-F £2590
77 3/08 Muss 5f (0-75)H GD £3238
73 5/07 Ling 5f GD £3562

Total win prize-money £9391

Going (Turf): Sf: 0-3 GS: 0-3 **Gd: 2-11** GF: 1-13 Fm: 0-1
Distance: **5f/6f: 3-32** 7f-8f: 0-0 9f-13f: 0-0 14f+: 0-0
Track : LH: 0-11 RH: 0-0 Tight: 0-3 Gall: 0-9
Aids: Bl: 0-0 Vi: 0-1 Tstrap: 0-0 Ckp: 0-0
Best Rating: **77** 3/08 Muss 5f good

Modest, has a poor strike rate; yet to win beyond 5f; acts on good/fast ground; has been tried in a visor.

Barreq (USA)

(94) (79)

2-y-o b c Proud Citizen (USA)-The Wrong Face (USA) (Marlin (USA))

B Smart A M A Al Shorafa

Placings:23 **(7800)**

2009: 7^{2}SD, 7^{3}SD,

	Starts	1st	2nd	3rd	Win & Pl
Career Total (Turf)	**0**	**0**	**0**	**0**	
Career Total (AW)	**2**	**0**	**1**	**1**	**1445**

Going (Turf): **Sf: 0-0 GS: 0-0 Gd: 0-0 GF: 0-0 Fm: 0-0**
Distance: 5f/6f: 0-0 7f-8f: 0-2 9f-13f: 0-0 14f+: 0-0
Track : LH: 0-2 RH: 0-0 Tight: 0-2 Gall: 0-0
Aids: Bl: 0-0 Vi: 0-0 Tstrap: 0-0 Ckp: 0-0
Best Rating: **79** 12/09 Wolv 7f32y stand

Fair; stays 7f; acts on Polytrack.

Barricado (FR)

106(104) (74)**87**

4-y-o b g Anabaa (USA)-Aube D'Irlande (FR) (Selkirk (USA))

P Monfort (E J O'Neill 29/8) G Augustin-Normand

Placings:3/224335-251540160

2009: 7^{2}GF, 8^{5}SD, 7^{1}GF, 8^{5}G, 8^{4}S, 8^{0}S, 8^{1}G, 7^{6}GS, 8^{0}GS,

	Starts	1st	2nd	3rd	Win & Pl
Career Total (Turf)	**14**	**2**	**2**	**3**	**25093**
Career Total (AW)	**2**	**0**	**1**	**0**	**1108**

86 8/09 Claf 1m GD £8738
84 5/09 Newc 7f (0-80)H G-F £4792

Total win prize-money £13530

Going (Turf): Sf: 0-3 GS: 0-4 **Gd: 1-5 GF: 1-2** Fm: 0-0
Distance: 5f/6f: 0-0 **7f-8f: 2-12** 9f-13f: 0-4 14f+: 0-0
Track : LH: 0-8 **RH: 1-3** Tight: 0-5 Gall: 0-0
Aids: Bl: 0-2 Vi: 0-1 Tstrap: 0-1 Ckp: 0-1
Best Rating: **87** 7/09 Vich 1m soft

Fair; stays 1m2f but effective at 7f; acts on good ground and on Polytrack; has worn blinkers and a visor; does not look straightforward.

Barshiba (IRE)

115 (84)**114**

5-y-o ch m Barathea (IRE)-Dashiba (Dashing Blade)

D R C Elsworth J C Smith

Placings:2/150124006/3006226461-43511440 **(6850)**

2009: 9^{4}GF, 9^{3}GF, 12^{5}GF, 11^{1}GF, 12^{1}G, 9^{4}S, 12^{4}GF, 10^{0}G,

	Starts	1st	2nd	3rd	Win & Pl
Career Total (Turf)	**26**	**4**	**3**	**2**	**239296**
Career Total (AW)	**2**	**1**	**1**	**0**	**4131**

114 7/09 NmkJ 1m4f GD £22708
110 7/09 Hayd 1m3f200y G-F £56770
106 10/08 NmkR 1m2f GD £24978
107 6/07 Asct 1m (0-110)H G-F £31229
84 2/07 Ling 1m STD £3071

Total win prize-money £138757

Going (Turf): Sf: 0-2 GS: 0-4 **Gd: 2-7 GF: 2-13** Fm: 0-0
Distance: 5f/6f: 0-0 7f-8f: 2-14 **9f-13f: 3-14** 14f+: 0-0
Track : **LH: 2-6** RH: 1-10 Tight: 1-5 Gall: 1-5
Aids: Bl: 0-0 Vi: 0-0 Tstrap: 0-0 Ckp: 0-0
Best Rating: **114** 8/09 York 1m4f gd-fm

Smart; winner of the Group 2 Lancashire Oaks in 2009 and a Listed winner; partially sighted in one eye; effective at 1m-1m4f; acts on a sound surface, but handles cut; can be a keen sort.

Barter

89 **57**

3-y-o ch f Daylami (IRE)-Souk (IRE) (Ahonoora)

L M Cumani Fittocks Stud

Placings:000 **(2763)**

2009: 8^{0}F, 9^{0}G, 9^{0}GF,

	Starts	1st	2nd	3rd	Win & Pl
Career Total (Turf)	**3**	**0**	**0**	**0**	

Going (Turf): **Sf: 0-0 GS: 0-0 Gd: 0-1 GF: 0-1 Fm: 0-1**
Distance: 5f/6f: 0-0 7f-8f: 0-0 9f-13f: 0-3 14f+: 0-0
Track : LH: 0-1 RH: 0-2 Tight: 0-2 Gall: 0-0
Aids: Bl: 0-0 Vi: 0-0 Tstrap: 0-0 Ckp: 0-0
Best Rating: **57** 5/09 Nott 1m75y firm

Bartica (IRE)

(99) (70)**62**

3-y-o b c Tagula (IRE)-More Risk (IRE) (Fayruz)

R Hannon R Hannon

Placings:4540534-012 **(1429)**

2009: 8^{0}SD, 8^{1}SD, 8^{2}SD,

	Starts	1st	2nd	3rd	Win & Pl
Career Total (Turf)	**3**	**0**	**0**	**0**	**722**

	Starts	1st	2nd	3rd	Win & Pl
Career Total (AW)	7	1	1	1	3017

67 2/09 Ling 1m STD £1978
Total win prize-money £1979

Going (Turf): Sf: 0-0 GS: 0-1 Gd: 0-1 GF: 0-1 Fm: 0-0
Distance: 5f/6f: 0-4 7f-8f: 1-6 9f-13f: 0-0 14f+: 0-0
Track : LH: 1-4 RH: 0-3 Tight: 1-4 Gall: 0-2
Aids: Bl: 1-2 Vi: 0-0 Tstrap: 0-1 Ckp: 0-1
Best Rating: 70 4/09 Kemp 1m stand

Modest form to date; stays 7f; acts on Polytrack.

Barton Chancer

54(68) (34)
2-y-o b f Dubai Destination (USA)-Lloc (Absalom)
W G M Turner E Vickery

Placings:056 (2457)
2009: 5^{0}G, 5^{5}SD, 5^{6}GF,

	Starts	1st	2nd	3rd	Win & Pl
Career Total (Turf)	2	0	0	0	0
Career Total (AW)	1	0	0	0	0

Going (Turf): Sf: 0-0 GS: 0-0 Gd: 0-1 GF: 0-1 Fm: 0-0
Distance: 5f/6f: 0-3 7f-8f: 0-0 9f-13f: 0-0 14f+: 0-0
Track : LH: 0-1 RH: 0-0 Tight: 0-1 Gall: 0-1
Aids: Bl: 0-0 Vi: 0-0 Tstrap: 0-0 Ckp: 0-0
Best Rating: 34 5/09 Ling 5f stand

Barton Sands (IRE)

90(110) (63)43
12-y-o b g Tenby-Hetty Green (Bay Express)
Andrew Reid A S Reid

Placings:21260/005/004000402/0460100/112444/0251201
43310312400042/13664200P000/214/3263-5000 (2182)
2009: 10^{5}SD, 9^{0}SD, 10^{0}SD, 11^{0}G,

	Starts	1st	2nd	3rd	Win & Pl
Career Total (Turf)	38	5	5	1	26718
Career Total (AW)	36	5	6	5	19379

59 12/07 Ling 1m4f (0-45) STD £1706
64 1/06 Ling 1m STD £2388
77 5/05 NmkR 1m (0-75)H G-F £4352
66 4/05 Ling 1m2f STD £2618
64 2/05 Ling 1m2f STD £2611
68 2/05 Ling 1m2f (0-65) STD £3396
73 8/04 Yarm 1m2f21y F(0-60) G-F £3031
53 4/04 Wwck 1m2f188y H GD £1582
58 8/03 Wwck 1m2f188y G G-F £3318
82 5/00 Haml 1m1f36y E FRM £2808
Total win prize-money £27811

Going (Turf): Sf: 0-5 GS: 0-2 Gd: 1-9 GF: 3-20 Fm: 1-2
Distance: 5f/6f: 0-0 7f-8f: 2-6 9f-13f: 8-67 14f+: 0-1
Track : LH: 8-52 RH: 1-16 Tight: 7-47 Gall: 0-7
Aids: Bl: 0-1 Vi: 2-4 Tstrap: 0-0 Ckp: 0-0
Best Rating: 96 9/00 NmkR 1m2f good

Moderate; stays 1m4f, but effective over shorter; best on fast ground; also goes on Polytrack; wears a tongue tie.

Barwell Bridge

104(109) (92)96
3-y-o b g Red Ransom (USA)-Sentimental Value (USA) (Diesis)
W J Greatrex (S Kirk 27/9) Mrs T Brown

Placings:0253-22121304040 (6302)
2009: 10^{2}SD, 9^{2}SD, 10^{1}SD, 9^{2}GF, 10^{1}GF, 12^{3}GF, 12^{0}G, 12^{4}GS, 14^{0}GF, 12^{4}SD, 12^{0}GF,

	Starts	1st	2nd	3rd	Win & Pl
Career Total (Turf)	8	1	1	1	14739
Career Total (AW)	7	1	3	1	9345

90 5/09 York 1m2f88y (0-85)H G-F £6476
84 1/09 Kemp 1m2f (0-85)H STD £4727
Total win prize-money £11203

Going (Turf): Sf: 0-0 GS: 0-1 Gd: 0-1 GF: 1-6 Fm: 0-0
Distance: 5f/6f: 0-1 7f-8f: 0-2 9f-13f: 2-11 14f+: 0-1
Track : LH: 1-7 RH: 1-7 Tight: 0-6 Gall: 1-6
Aids: Bl: 0-0 Vi: 0-0 Tstrap: 0-0 Ckp: 0-0
Best Rating: 96 8/09 Asct 1m4f gd-sft

Useful; effective at 1m2f-1m4f; acts on fast and easy ground and on Polytrack.

Barynya

98 76
3-y-o ch f Pivotal-Russian Rhythm (USA) (Kingmambo (USA))
Sir Michael Stoute Cheveley Park Stud

Placings:332 (3876)
2009: 7^{3}GS, 8^{3}F, 7^{2}GF,

	Starts	1st	2nd	3rd	Win & Pl
Career Total (Turf)	3	0	1	2	3054

Going (Turf): Sf: 0-0 GS: 0-1 Gd: 0-0 GF: 0-1 Fm: 0-1
Distance: 5f/6f: 0-0 7f-8f: 0-2 9f-13f: 0-1 14f+: 0-0
Track : LH: 0-2 RH: 0-0 Tight: 0-0 Gall: 0-1
Aids: Bl: 0-0 Vi: 0-0 Tstrap: 0-0 Ckp: 0-0
Best Rating: 76 7/09 York 7f gd-fm

First foal of Russian Rhythm; stays 1m; acts on fast and easy ground.

Barzan (IRE)

94 84
2-y-o ch c Danehill Dancer (IRE)-Le Montrachet (Nashwan (USA))
Tom Dascombe M A Al-Attiyah

Placings:31500 (6478)
2009: 6^{3}G, 5^{1}GF, 6^{5}G, 7^{0}GS, 7^{0}GF,

	Starts	1st	2nd	3rd	Win & Pl
Career Total (Turf)	5	1	0	1	5314

71 5/09 Brig 5f213y G-F £3784
Total win prize-money £3785

Going (Turf): Sf: 0-0 GS: 0-1 Gd: 0-2 GF: 1-2 Fm: 0-0
Distance: 5f/6f: 1-2 7f-8f: 0-3 9f-13f: 0-0 14f+: 0-0
Track : LH: 1-2 RH: 0-1 Tight: 0-1 Gall: 0-0
Aids: Bl: 0-0 Vi: 0-0 Tstrap: 0-0 Ckp: 0-0
Best Rating: 84 6/09 Epsm 6f good

Useful; stays 6f and acts on fast ground.

Basalt (IRE)

(103) (84)86
5-y-o b g Rock Of Gibraltar (IRE)-Sniffle (IRE) (Shernazar)
T J Pitt Kelly, O'Donnell, Dower & Kelman

Placings:03/0/116002603-26 (7573)
2009: 16^{2}SD, 13^{6}SD,

	Starts	1st	2nd	3rd	Win & Pl
Career Total (Turf)	9	0	1	2	4228
Career Total (AW)	5	2	1	0	6565

91 2/08 Wolv 1m4f50y (0-75)H STD £2457
72 2/08 Sthl 1m4f STD £2457
Total win prize-money £4914

Going (Turf): Sf: 0-2 GS: 0-1 Gd: 0-2 GF: 0-3 Fm: 0-0
Distance: 5f/6f: 0-0 7f-8f: 0-3 9f-13f: 2-5 14f+: 0-6
Track : LH: 2-9 RH: 0-4 Tight: 1-5 Gall: 0-5
Aids: Bl: 0-0 Vi: 0-0 Tstrap: 0-0 Ckp: 0-0
Best Rating: 91 2/08 Wolv 1m4f50y stand

Useful; ex-Coolmore; stays 2m; acts on good ground; also goes on sand.

Basaltico (IRE)

106 113
5-y-o b h Shantou (USA)-Sfilza (Indian Ridge)
L M Cumani (H J Brown 26/2) Scuderia Siba-Antezzate SRL

Placings:33153014/111215-003604200 (7215a)
2009: 10^{0}G, 13^{0}GF, 16^{3}GF, 12^{6}G, 13^{0}GF, 13^{4}GF, 14^{2}S, 12^{0}G, 16^{0}GS,

	Starts	1st	2nd	3rd	Win & Pl
Career Total (Turf)	23	6	2	4	121572

106 10/08 Nant 1m4f VS £22058
6/08 Siro 1m4f H G-F £17500
5/08 Casc 1m3f H SFT £25312
3/08 Siro 1m1f H GD £9375
10/07 Siro 1m1f SFT £4307
5/07 Siro 1m1f GD £4550
Total win prize-money £83105

Going (Turf): Sf: 2-6 GS: 0-2 Gd: 2-9 GF: 1-5 Fm: 0-0
Distance: 5f/6f: 0-0 7f-8f: 0-1 9f-13f: 6-16 14f+: 0-6
Track : LH: 1-5 RH: 0-4 Tight: 0-3 Gall: 0-2
Aids: Bl: 0-0 Vi: 0-0 Tstrap: 0-0 Ckp: 0-0
Best Rating: 113 9/08 Siro 1m3f good

Listed class; ex-Italian; best at around 1m4f; acts on most types of ground; has worn a tongue tie.

Baskerville

74 (66)69
6-y-o b g Foxhound (USA)-Miss Up N Go (Gorytus (USA))
Mrs L Williamson The Castle Bend Syndicate

Placings:42/11661/000/0340-0 (4561)
2009: 12^{0}G,

	Starts	1st	2nd	3rd	Win & Pl
Career Total (Turf)	14	3	1	1	22560
Career Total (AW)	1	0	0	0	

95 10/06 Nott 1m1f213y (0-90)H SFT £8096
86 5/06 Nott 1m54y (0-85)H SFT £6477
69 4/06 Wwck 7f26y GD £3562
Total win prize-money £18135

Going (Turf): Sf: 2-5 GS: 0-0 Gd: 1-6 GF: 0-1 Fm: 0-1
Distance: 5f/6f: 0-0 7f-8f: 1-5 9f-13f: 2-8 14f+: 0-2
Track : LH: 3-8 RH: 0-2 Tight: 0-1 Gall: 0-1
Aids: Bl: 0-0 Vi: 0-0 Tstrap: 0-0 Ckp: 0-0
Best Rating: 95 10/06 Nott 1m1f213y soft

Useful colt; effective over seven furlongs and a mile; acts on good and soft ground.

Basle

(99) (73)
2-y-o b f Trade Fair-Gibaltarik (IRE) (Jareer (USA))
Miss Gay Kelleway Raymond Tooth

Placings:21 (7190)
2009: 6^{2}SD, 5^{1}SD,

	Starts	1st	2nd	3rd	Win & Pl
Career Total (Turf)	0	0	0	0	
Career Total (AW)	2	1	1	0	4263

64 10/09 Wolv 5f216y STD £2914
Total win prize-money £2914

Going (Turf): **Sf: 0-0 GS: 0-0 Gd: 0-0 GF: 0-0 Fm: 0-0**
Distance: **5f/6f: 1-2** 7f-8f: 0-0 9f-13f: 0-0 14f+: 0-0
Track : **LH: 1-1** RH: 0-1 **Tight: 1-1** Gall: 0-0
Aids: Bl: 0-0 Vi: 0-0 Tstrap: 0-0 Ckp: 0-0
Best Rating: **73** 10/09 Kemp 6f stand

Fair; effective over 6f; acts on Polytrack.

Basque Beauty

89 **96**

4-y-o b f Nayef (USA)-River Cara (USA) (Irish River (FR))
W J Haggas Mr & Mrs Neil Weekes

Placings:3/1000-00 **(3116)**
2009: 8^{0}GF, 7^{0}GF,

	Starts	1st	2nd	3rd	Win & Pl
Career Total (Turf)	**7**	**1**	**0**	**1**	**7150**
92 7/08 Asct 1m			G-F	£6476	

Total win prize-money £6476

Going (Turf): Sf: 0-1 GS: 0-1 Gd: 0-2 **GF: 1-3** Fm: 0-0
Distance: 5f/6f: 0-0 **7f-8f: 1-5** 9f-13f: 0-2 14f+: 0-0
Track : LH: 0-1 RH: 0-2 Tight: 0-2 Gall: 0-1
Aids: Bl: 0-0 Vi: 0-0 Tstrap: 0-0 Ckp: 0-0
Best Rating: **96** 8/08 Sals 1m1f198y gd-sft

Very useful; stays 1m; acts on fast and soft ground.

Basra (IRE)

100(109) (88)**88**

6-y-o b g Soviet Star (USA)-Azra (IRE) (Danehill (USA))
Miss Jo Crowley Mrs Liz Nelson

Placings:4155/00402600/0540206**6022/3661355**2005-12455562 **(7607)**
2009: 10^{1}SD, 10^{2}SD, 10^{4}SD, 10^{5}GF, 10^{5}GF, 9^{5}GF, 10^{6}GF, 10^{2}SD,

	Starts	1st	2nd	3rd	Win & Pl
Career Total (Turf)	**25**	**1**	**3**	**0**	**13999**
Career Total (AW)	**16**	**2**	**4**	**2**	**19829**
87 1/09 Ling 1m2f	(0-80)H		STD	£4857	
88 4/08 GrLe 1m2f	(0-90)H		STD	£6938	
79 8/05 Tipp 7f100y			YLD	£6370	

Total win prize-money £18167

Going (Turf): **Sf: 0-1 GS: 0-0 Gd: 0-5 GF: 0-13 Fm: 0-0**
Distance: 5f/6f: 0-2 7f-8f: 1-13 **9f-13f: 2-26** 14f+: 0-0
Track : **LH: 2-24** RH: 0-12 Tight: 1-17 Gall: 1-7
Aids: Bl: 0-3 Vi: 0-0 Tstrap: 0-3 Ckp: 0-3
Best Rating: **94** 2/08 Ling 1m2f stand

Fir; effective over 1m-1m2f; acts on fast ground; also goes on Polytrack.

Bassinet (USA)

94(110) (83)**80**

5-y-o b m Stravinsky (USA)-Berceau (USA) (Alleged (USA))
J A R Toller John Drew

Placings:265330/**453332215030-51002000** **(6634)**
2009: 12^{5}SD, 12^{1}SD, 12^{0}SD, 12^{0}SD, 13^{2}SD, 12^{0}G, 13^{0}GF, 12^{0}SS,

	Starts	1st	2nd	3rd	Win & Pl
Career Total (Turf)	**12**	**1**	**3**	**2**	**13246**
Career Total (AW)	**14**	**1**	**1**	**4**	**7547**
83 3/09 Ling 1m4f	(0-75)H		STD	£3885	
80 6/08 NmkJ 1m4f	(0-75)H		G-F	£3885	

Total win prize-money £7772

Going (Turf): Sf: 0 2 GS: 0 2 Gd: 0 4 **GF: 1-3** Fm: 0-0
Distance: 5f/6f: 0-0 7f-8f: 0-3 **9f-13f: 2-21** 14f+: 0-2
Track : LH: 1-11 RH: 1-11 Tight: 1-9 Gall: 1-4
Aids: Bl: 0-0 Vi: 0-0 Tstrap: 0-0 Ckp: 0-0
Best Rating: **83** 3/09 Ling 1m4f stand

Fair; ex-French; stays 1m5f; acts on easy ground; also goes on Polytrack.

Batchworth Blaise

99(98) (60)**60**

6-y-o b g Little Jim-Batchworth Dancer (Ballacashtal (CAN))
E A Wheeler Astrod TA Austin Stroud & Co

Placings:0006**0/0000240503/305550**1532001020**0**-600405000**3013** **(7691)**
2009: 7^{6}SD, 7^{0}SD, 6^{0}GF, 6^{4}GF, 7^{0}GF, 8^{5}GF, 7^{0}G, 6^{0}F, 7^{0}G, 8^{3}GF, 7^{0}SD, 8^{1}SD, 7^{3}SD,

	Starts	1st	2nd	3rd	Win & Pl
Career Total (Turf)	**27**	**2**	**3**	**2**	**8813**
Career Total (AW)	**18**	**1**	**0**	**3**	**2944**
53 12/09 Ling 1m	(0-55)H		STD	£2047	
60 8/08 Gdwd 7f	(0-70)H		G-S	£3238	
56 5/08 Brig 6f209y	(0-60)H		G-F	£1942	

Total win prize-money £7228

Going (Turf): Sf: 0-0 **GS: 1-2** Gd: 0-11 **GF: 1-12** Fm: 0-2
Distance: 5f/6f: 0-6 **7f-8f: 3-37** 9f-13f: 0-2 14f+: 0-0
Track : **LH: 2-18** RH: 1-13 **Tight: 1-10** Gall: 0-2
Aids: Bl: 0-6 Vi: 0-0 Tstrap: 0-0 Ckp: 0-0
Best Rating: **60** 1/09 Kemp 7f stand

Moderate; effective at around 7f-1m; acts on easy ground; goes on Polytrack.

Bateau Bleu

95(90) (59)**62**

2-y-o b g Auction House (USA)-Fresh Look (IRE) (Alzao (USA))
P C Haslam Mrs S Mason, R Stipetic

Placings:00014 **(6639)**
2009: 5^{0}GF, 6^{0}GS, 7^{0}GF, 10^{1}GF, 8^{4}SD,

	Starts	1st	2nd	3rd	Win & Pl
Career Total (Turf)	**4**	**1**	**0**	**0**	**2590**
Career Total (AW)	**1**	**0**	**0**	**0**	**0**
62 9/09 Nott 1m2f50y	(0-75)		G-F	£2590	

Total win prize-money £2590

Going (Turf): Sf: 0-0 GS: 0-1 Gd: 0-0 **GF: 1-3** Fm: 0-0
Distance: 5f/6f: 0-2 7f-8f: 0-1 **9f-13f: 1-2** 14f+: 0-0
Track : **LH: 1-3** RH: 0-0 Tight: 0-2 Gall: 0-0
Aids: Bl: 0-0 **Vi: 1-2** Tstrap: 0-0 Ckp: 0-0
Best Rating: **62** 9/09 Nott 1m2f50y gd-fm

Modest; stays 1m2f; acts on fast ground.

Bateleur

104(105) (57)**74**

5-y-o b g Fraam-Search Party (Rainbow Quest (USA))
M R Channon Dave and Gill Hedley

Placings:01011/60633640/0540060004-**6625**0226123312404500 **(5955)**
2009: 6^{6}SD, 6^{6}SD, 6^{2}SD, 6^{5}SD, 6^{0}GF, 6^{2}F, 6^{2}GF, 6^{6}G, 6^{1}GF, 6^{2}GF, 6^{3}GF, 6^{3}G, 5^{1}F, 6^{2}GS, 5^{4}GF, 6^{0}GF, 6^{4}GF, 5^{5}GF, 6^{0}G, 6^{0}GF,

	Starts	1st	2nd	3rd	Win & Pl
Career Total (Turf)	**37**	**5**	**4**	**4**	**27562**
Career Total (AW)	**6**	**0**	**1**	**0**	**749**
72 6/09 Bath 5f161y	(0-75)H		FRM	£2719	
71 6/09 Folk 6f	(0-70)H		G-F	£3070	
83 9/06 NmkR 6f			G-F	£8420	
73 9/06 Nott 6f15y	(0-75)		GD	£3886	
64 7/06 Bath 5f161y			FRM	£2590	

Total win prize-money £20688

Going (Turf): Sf: 0-0 GS: 0-5 Gd: 1-9 **GF: 2-19 Fm: 2-4**
Distance: **5f/6f: 4-35** 7f-8f: 1-8 9f-13f: 0-0 14f+: 0-0
Track : **LH: 2-12** RH: 0-3 Tight: 0-4 **Gall: 2-8**
Aids: Bl: 0-0 Vi: 0-8 Tstrap: 0-0 Ckp: 0-0
Best Rating: **83** 9/06 NmkR 6f gd-fm

Moderate; effective at around 6f; acts on good and faster ground; goes on Polytrack; has worn a visor.

Batgirl

70 **33**

2-y-o ch f Mark Of Esteem (IRE)-Serriera (FR) (Highest Honor (FR))
John Berry Tony Fordham

Placings:00 **(7182)**
2009: 7^{0}G, 7^{0}G,

	Starts	1st	2nd	3rd	Win & Pl
Career Total (Turf)	**2**	**0**	**0**	**0**	

Going (Turf): **Sf: 0-0 GS: 0-0 Gd: 0-2 GF: 0-0 Fm: 0-0**
Distance: 5f/6f: 0-0 7f-8f: 0-2 9f-13f: 0-0 14f+: 0-0
Track : LH: 0-1 RH: 0-0 Tight: 0-0 Gall: 0-1
Aids: Bl: 0-0 Vi: 0-0 Tstrap: 0-0 Ckp: 0-0
Best Rating: **33** 10/09 NmkR 7f good

Bathwick Gino

86(91) (55)**55**

2-y-o b g Alamshar (IRE)-Rockstine (IRE) (Ballad Rock)
P D Evans (A B Haynes 11/6) Bathwick Gold Partnership

Placings:6406**4550** **(6345)**
2009: 5^{6}GF, 5^{4}GF, 7^{0}S, 5^{6}G, 7^{4}SD, 7^{5}SD, 5^{5}SD, 5^{0}SD,

	Starts	1st	2nd	3rd	Win & Pl
Career Total (Turf)	**4**	**0**	**0**	**0**	**144**
Career Total (AW)	**4**	**0**	**0**	**0**	**241**

Going (Turf): **Sf: 0-1 GS: 0-0 Gd: 0-1 GF: 0-2 Fm: 0-0**
Distance: 5f/6f: 0-5 7f-8f: 0-3 9f-13f: 0-0 14f+: 0-0
Track : LH: 0-6 RH: 0-0 Tight: 0-4 Gall: 0-1
Aids: Bl: 0-0 Vi: 0-2 Tstrap: 0-0 Ckp: 0-0
Best Rating: **55** 9/09 Wolv 5f216y stand

Modest; stays 6f; acts on Polytrack.

Bathwick Gold (IRE)

92 **73**

2-y-o b c Noverre (USA)-Taalluf (USA) (Hansel (USA))
P D Evans Bathwick Gold Partnership

Placings:0100 **(7290)**
2009: 6^{0}GF, 5^{1}GF, 6^{0}GF, 6^{0}S,

	Starts	1st	2nd	3rd	Win & Pl
Career Total (Turf)	**4**	**1**	**0**	**0**	**3400**
73 9/09 Leic 5f218y			G-F	£3399	

Total win prize-money £3400

Going (Turf): Sf: 0-1 GS: 0-0 Gd: 0-0 **GF: 1-3** Fm: 0-0
Distance: **5f/6f: 1-4** 7f-8f: 0-0 9f-13f: 0-0 14f+: 0-0
Track : LH: 0-0 RH: 0-0 Tight: 0-0 Gall: 0-0
Aids: Bl: 0-0 Vi: 0-0 Tstrap: 0-0 Ckp: 0-0
Best Rating: **73** 9/09 Leic 5f218y gd-fm

Fair; effective over 6f; acts on fast ground.

Bathwick Man

98(96) (52)**57**

4-y-o b g Mark Of Esteem (IRE)-Local Abbey (IRE) (Primo Dominie)

D E Pipe Mrs S Clifford

Placings:030/0000-3**20** **(5885)**

2009: 12^{3}HY, **16**^{2}SD, **16**^{0}SD,

	Starts	1st	2nd	3rd	Win & Pl
Career Total (Turf)	8	0	0	2	711
Career Total (AW)	2	0	1	0	771

Going (Turf): **Sf: 0-1 GS: 0-1 Gd: 0-2 GF: 0-4 Fm: 0-0**
Distance: 5f/6f: 0-0 7f-8f: 0-5 9f-13f: 0-3 14f+: 0-2
Track : LH: 0-2 RH: 0-2 Tight: 0-1 Gall: 0-0
Aids: Bl: 0-0 Vi: 0-1 Tstrap: 0-3 Ckp: 0-3
Best Rating: **62** 9/07 Ling 7f gd-fm

Bathwick Pursuit

90(88) (54)**37**

3-y-o b g Pursuit Of Love-Society Rose (Saddlers' Hall (IRE))

D E Pipe (P D Evans 13/7) W Clifford

Placings:0-05650 **(3919)**

2009: 10^{0}S, 7^{5}F, 12^{6}SD, 7^{5}F, 11^{0}G,

	Starts	1st	2nd	3rd	Win & Pl
Career Total (Turf)	4	0	0	0	0
Career Total (AW)	2	0	0	0	0

Going (Turf): **Sf: 0-1 GS: 0-0 Gd: 0-1 GF: 0-0 Fm: 0-2**
Distance: 5f/6f: 0-0 7f-8f: 0-3 9f-13f: 0-3 14f+: 0-0
Track : LH: 0-4 RH: 0-1 Tight: 0-2 Gall: 0-2
Aids: Bl: 0-0 Vi: 0-0 Tstrap: 0-0 Ckp: 0-0
Best Rating: **54** 11/08 GrLe 1m stand

Bathwick Xaara

99(86) (60)**69**

2-y-o br f Xaar-Anapola (GER) (Polish Precedent (USA))

J G Portman Mrs S Clifford

Placings:4430**660** **(6775)**

2009: 6^{4}GF, 6^{4}GF, 6^{3}GF, 6^{0}G, 7^{6}SD, 5^{6}GF, **6**^{0}SD,

	Starts	1st	2nd	3rd	Win & Pl
Career Total (Turf)	5	0	0	1	1251
Career Total (AW)	2	0	0	0	0

Going (Turf): **Sf: 0-0 GS: 0-0 Gd: 0-1 GF: 0-4 Fm: 0-0**
Distance: 5f/6f: 0-3 7f-8f: 0-4 9f-13f: 0-0 14f+: 0-0
Track : LH: 0-0 RH: 0-2 Tight: 0-0 Gall: 0-0
Aids: Bl: 0-0 Vi: 0-0 Tstrap: 0-0 Ckp: 0-0
Best Rating: **69** 6/09 Newb 6f8y gd-fm

Modest; stays 7f and acts on fast ground.

Battimoore (IRE)

98(95) (52)**52**

3-y-o b f Beckett (IRE)-Silver Spoon (IRE) (College Chapel)

I W McInnes (Daniel Mark Loughnane 13/11) Ivy House Racing

Placings:6**6**0-2020**50640** **(7787)**

2009: 6^{2}S, 7^{0}GF, 6^{2}G, 7^{0}HY, **5**^{5}SD, **5**^{0}SD, **6**^{6}SD, **7**^{4}SD, **7**^{0}SD,

	Starts	1st	2nd	3rd	Win & Pl
Career Total (Turf)	6	0	2	0	2001
Career Total (AW)	6	0	0	0	0

Going (Turf): **Sf: 0-3 GS: 0-0 Gd: 0-1 GF: 0-2 Fm: 0-0**
Distance: 5f/6f: 0-7 7f-8f: 0-5 9f-13f: 0-0 14f+: 0-0
Track : LH: 0-6 RH: 0-5 Tight: 0-5 Gall: 0-0
Aids: Bl: 0-0 Vi: 0-0 Tstrap: 0-0 Ckp: 0-0
Best Rating: **52** 12/09 Kemp 7f stand

Battle

100(91) (61)**74**

3-y-o gr g Compton Place-Molly Moon (IRE) (Primo Dominie)

H Morrison Mr&MrsHScott-Barrett,Ben&SirMartynArbib

Placings:535-40314 **(6387)**

2009: 6^{4}GF, 6^{0}GF, 5^{3}G, 5^{1}GS, 5^{4}GF,

	Starts	1st	2nd	3rd	Win & Pl
Career Total (Turf)	7	1	0	2	4003
Career Total (AW)	1	0	0	0	0

73 8/09 Bath 5f11y (0-70)H G-S £2655
Total win prize-money £2655

Going (Turf): Sf: 0-0 **GS: 1-2** Gd: 0-2 GF: 0-3 Fm: 0-0
Distance: **5f/6f: 1-7** 7f-8f: 0-1 9f-13f: 0-0 14f+: 0-0
Track : **LH: 1-4** RH: 0-0 Tight: 0-1 **Gall: 1-3**
Aids: Bl: 0-0 Vi: 0-0 Tstrap: 0-0 Ckp: 0-0
Best Rating: **74** 9/09 Nott 5f13y gd-fm

Modest; stays 6f; acts on good and easy ground and on Polytrack.

Battle Honour

87 **58**

2-y-o b g Mark Of Esteem (IRE)-Proserpine (Robellino (USA))

H Candy The Earl Cadogan

Placings:0 **(7146)**

2009: 7^{0}G,

	Starts	1st	2nd	3rd	Win & Pl
Career Total (Turf)	1	0	0	0	

Going (Turf): **Sf: 0-0 GS: 0-0 Gd: 0-1 GF: 0-0 Fm: 0-0**
Distance: 5f/6f: 0-0 7f-8f: 0-1 9f-13f: 0-0 14f+: 0-0
Track : LH: 0-0 RH: 0-0 Tight: 0-0 Gall: 0-0
Aids: Bl: 0-0 Vi: 0-0 Tstrap: 0-0 Ckp: 0-0
Best Rating: **58** 10/09 NmkR 7f good

Battle Paint (USA)

107(104) (106)**100**

5-y-o b h Tale Of The Cat (USA)-Black Speck (USA) (Arch (USA))

J H M Gosden Cheveley Park Stud

Placings:112/204/100-30 **(5232)**

2009: 6^{3}SD, 7^{0}GF,

	Starts	1st	2nd	3rd	Win & Pl
Career Total (Turf)	10	3	2	0	98673
Career Total (AW)	1	0	0	1	1120

100 8/08 Donc 6f GD £9346
98 9/06 Lonc 7f GD £11379
88 8/06 Deau 6f110y G-S £6552
Total win prize-money £27278

Going (Turf): Sf: 0-0 GS: 1-2 **Gd: 2-6** GF: 0-2 Fm: 0-0
Distance: 5f/6f: 1-3 **7f-8f: 2-8** 9f-13f: 0-0 14f+: 0-0
Track : LH: 0-1 **RH: 2-6** Tight: 0-0 Gall: 0-1
Aids: Bl: 0-0 Vi: 0-0 Tstrap: 0-0 Ckp: 0-0
Best Rating: **116** 10/06 Lonc 7f good

Smart; ex-French; Group placed; effective over 6f-1m; acts on good and easier ground.

Battle Planner (USA)

102(96) (84)**86**

3-y-o b c War Chant (USA)-The Administrator (USA) (Afleet (CAN))

I Semple (M Johnston 3/7) Gordon McDowall

Placings:1-52034 **(6671)**

2009: 10^{5}GF, 12^{2}G, 10^{0}S, 12^{3}GF, **13**^{4}SD,

	Starts	1st	2nd	3rd	Win & Pl
Career Total (Turf)	4	0	1	1	2216
Career Total (AW)	2	1	0	0	2425

84 12/08 Sthl 1m STD £2047
Total win prize-money £2047

Going (Turf): **Sf: 0-1 GS: 0-0 Gd: 0-1 GF: 0-2 Fm: 0-0**
Distance: 5f/6f: 0-0 **7f-8f: 1-1** 9f-13f: 0-4 14f+: 0-1
Track : **LH: 1-4** RH: 0-2 Tight: 0-2 Gall: 0-1
Aids: Bl: 0-0 Vi: 0-0 Tstrap: 0-2 Ckp: 0-2
Best Rating: **86** 7/09 Donc 1m4f good

Useful; effective over 1m4f; acts on Fibresand.

Battle Royal (IRE)

97 **62**

3-y-o b c Refuse To Bend (IRE)-Style Of Life (USA) (The Minstrel (CAN))

B Smart H E Sheikh Rashid Bin Mohammed

Placings:45-4440 **(6411)**

2009: 7^{4}G, 8^{4}G, 7^{4}GF, 8^{0}GF,

	Starts	1st	2nd	3rd	Win & Pl
Career Total (Turf)	6	0	0	0	1183

Going (Turf): **Sf: 0-1 GS: 0-0 Gd: 0-3 GF: 0-2 Fm: 0-0**
Distance: 5f/6f: 0-0 7f-8f: 0-4 9f-13f: 0-2 14f+: 0-0
Track : LH: 0-3 RH: 0-1 Tight: 0-2 Gall: 0-0
Aids: Bl: 0-0 Vi: 0-0 Tstrap: 0-0 Ckp: 0-0
Best Rating: **62** 10/08 Rdcr 7f good

Modest 200,000gns half-brother to eight winners, including Grey Swallow, stays 1m; acts on a sound surface.

Battle Study (IRE)

83(83) (49)**66**

2-y-o b/br g Fath (USA)-Osprey Point (IRE) (Entrepreneur)

A J McCabe Sale Of The Century

Placings:426 **(7376)**

2009: 8^{4}G, 7^{2}GF, 7^{6}SD,

	Starts	1st	2nd	3rd	Win & Pl
Career Total (Turf)	2	0	1	0	1505
Career Total (AW)	1	0	0	0	0

Going (Turf): **Sf: 0-0 GS: 0-0 Gd: 0-1 GF: 0-1 Fm: 0-0**
Distance: 5f/6f: 0-0 7f-8f: 0-3 9f-13f: 0-0 14f+: 0-0
Track : LH: 0-2 RH: 0-1 Tight: 0-2 Gall: 0-0
Aids: Bl: 0-0 Vi: 0-0 Tstrap: 0-1 Ckp: 0-1
Best Rating: **66** 9/09 Bevl 7f100y gd-fm

Battlemaiden (IRE)

95(96) (74)75

2-y-o br f Shamardal (USA)-Kirk (Selkirk (USA))

Saeed Bin Suroor Godolphin

Placings:64226 (6418)

2009: 6^{6}G, 7^{4}G, 6^{2}GF, 6^{2}SD, 6^{6}GF,

	Starts	1st	2nd	3rd	Win & Pl
Career Total (Turf)	4	0	1	0	1645
Career Total (AW)	1	0	1	0	1060

Going (Turf): Sf: 0-0 GS: 0-0 Gd: 0-2 GF: 0-2 Fm: 0-0
Distance: 5f/6f: 0-3 7f-8f: 0-2 9f-13f: 0-0 14f+: 0-0
Track : LH: 0-0 RH: 0-1 Tight: 0-0 Gall: 0-0
Aids: Bl: 0-0 Vi: 0-0 Tstrap: 0-0 Ckp: 0-0
Best Rating: 75 8/09 Yarm 6f3y gd-fm

Fair; effective at 6f; acts onfast ground.

Battling Lil (IRE)

(92) (50)56

5-y-o b m Daggers Drawn (USA)-Salva (Grand Lodge (USA))

J L Spearing T N Siviter

Placings:006005-0 (0211)

2009: 8^{0}SD,

	Starts	1st	2nd	3rd	Win & Pl
Career Total (Turf)	4	0	0	0	0
Career Total (AW)	3	0	0	0	0

Going (Turf): Sf: 0-0 GS: 0-2 Gd: 0-1 GF: 0-1 Fm: 0-0
Distance: 5f/6f: 0-1 7f-8f: 0-3 9f-13f: 0-3 14f+: 0-0
Track : LH: 0-4 RH: 0-2 Tight: 0-0 Gall: 0-1
Aids: Bl: 0-1 Vi: 0-0 Tstrap: 0-0 Ckp: 0-0
Best Rating: 56 5/08 Yarm 1m3y good

Baunagain (IRE)

106(103) (81)92

4-y-o b g No Excuse Needed-Manuka Honey (Mystiko (USA))

P W Chapple-Hyam P Ransley

Placings:0/31421535540-216000036 (7891)

2009: 6^{2}GF, 6^{1}GF, 6^{6}G, 5^{0}SD, 6^{0}SD, 5^{0}SD, 5^{0}SD, 7^{3}SD, 7^{6}SD,

	Starts	1st	2nd	3rd	Win & Pl
Career Total (Turf)	9	1	2	1	9526
Career Total (AW)	12	2	0	2	8540

92 7/09 Wwck 6f (0-85)H G-F £6231
84 5/08 GrLe 6f (0-85)H STD £4533
76 3/08 Sthl 6f STD £2457
Total win prize-money £13221

Going (Turf): Sf: 0-0 GS: 0-4 Gd: 0-2 GF: 1-3 Fm: 0-0
Distance: 5f/6f: 3-16 7f-8f: 0-5 9f-13f: 0-0 14f+: 0-0
Track : LH: 3-10 RH: 0-3 Tight: 0-6 Gall: 1-1
Aids: Bl: 0-0 Vi: 0-0 Tstrap: 0-0 Ckp: 0-0
Best Rating: 92 7/09 Wwck 6f gd-fm

Fair; effective over 6f-7f; acts on fast and easy ground; goes on sand.

Bavarian Nordic (USA)

102(98) (86)81

4-y-o b g Barathea (IRE)-Dubai Diamond (Octagonal (NZ))

Mrs A Duffield Six Iron Partnership

Placings:05522/0406461116-55653420 (6648)

2009: 9^{5}GS, 12^{5}S, 10^{6}GS, 12^{5}G, 9^{3}G, 8^{4}SD, 11^{2}S, 10^{0}G,

	Starts	1st	2nd	3rd	Win & Pl
Career Total (Turf)	20	2	3	1	9820
Career Total (AW)	3	1	0	0	4113

86 10/08 Sthl 1m4f (0-75)H STD £3412
81 10/08 Newc 1m2f32y (0-70)H HVY £2914
73 9/08 Rdcr 1m2f (0-70)H G-S £2590
Total win prize-money £8916

Going (Turf): Sf: 1-5 GS: 1-6 Gd: 0-7 GF: 0-2 Fm: 0-0
Distance: 5f/6f: 0-0 7f-8f: 0-6 9f-13f: 3-17 14f+: 0-0
Track : LH: 3-14 RH: 0-7 Tight: 1-9 Gall: 1-5
Aids: Bl: 0-0 Vi: 0-0 Tstrap: 0-0 Ckp: 0-0
Best Rating: 86 10/08 Sthl 1m4f stand

Fair; stays 1m4f; acts on soft ground and on Fibresand.

Bavarica

96(110) (72)71

7-y-o b m Dansili-Blue Gentian (USA) (Known Fact (USA))

Miss J Feilden Miss J Feilden

Placings:065300/2520142340123332/6220523145200/34042424350553552-1323051633002353100322 3 (7752)

2009: 8^{1}SD, 10^{3}SD, 10^{2}SD, 10^{3}SD, 8^{0}SD, 8^{5}SD, 8^{1}SD, 8^{6}SD, 10^{3}SD, 9^{3}G, 10^{0}SD, 10^{0}GF, 9^{2}GF, 9^{3}GF, 8^{5}GF, 9^{3}GF, 10^{1}G, 10^{0}G, 10^{0}GF, 10^{3}GF, 8^{2}SD, 9^{2}SD, 9^{3}SD,

	Starts	1st	2nd	3rd	Win & Pl
Career Total (Turf)	30	2	5	6	16607
Career Total (AW)	45	4	11	11	28011

71 7/09 NmkJ 1m2f (0-70)H GD £3123
72 2/09 Ling 1m (0-75)H STD £2590
67 1/09 Ling 1m (0-75)H STD £2900
79 6/07 Newb 1m2f6y (0-70)H G-F £3435
66 10/06 Wolv 1m141y (0-70)H SF £3886
66 3/06 Ling 1m2f (0-60)H STD £2388
Total win prize-money £18323

Going (Turf): Sf: 0-2 GS: 0-2 Gd: 1-6 GF: 1-18 Fm: 0-2
Distance: 5f/6f: 0-0 7f-8f: 2-16 9f-13f: 4-59 14f+: 0-0
Track : LH: 5-59 RH: 1-9 Tight: 4-39 Gall: 2-10
Aids: Bl: 0-0 Vi: 0-0 Tstrap: 0-0 Ckp: 0-0
Best Rating: 79 6/07 Newb 1m2f6y gd-fm

Modest; stays 1m2f; acts on most ground; goes on Polytrack.

Bawaardi (IRE)

98(103) (80)76

3-y-o b g Acclamation-Global Trend (Bluebird (USA))

R A Fahey (J H M Gosden 12/10) The Matthewman One Partnership

Placings:2-166322 (7812)

2009: 7^{1}GS, 6^{6}S, 7^{6}SD, 8^{3}SD, 8^{2}SD, 8^{2}SD,

	Starts	1st	2nd	3rd	Win & Pl
Career Total (Turf)	3	1	1	0	4657
Career Total (AW)	4	0	2	1	3304

69 9/09 Ling 7f G-S £2729
Total win prize-money £2730

Going (Turf): Sf: 0-1 GS: 1-1 Gd: 0-0 GF: 0-1 Fm: 0-0
Distance: 5f/6f: 0-1 7f-8f: 1-4 9f-13f: 0-2 14f+: 0-0
Track : LH: 0-3 RH: 0-1 Tight: 0-3 Gall: 0-0
Aids: Bl: 0-0 Vi: 0-0 Tstrap: 0-0 Ckp: 0-0
Best Rating: 80 12/09 Kemp 1m stand

Fair; stays 1m and acts on easy ground and on Polytrack.

Bawadi (USA)

102(104) (88)87

3-y-o b/br c Medaglia D'Oro (USA)-Chartreuse (CAN) (Danzatore (CAN))

Saeed Bin Suroor Godolphin

Placings:140 (6239)

2009: 10^{1}SD, 12^{4}SD, 10^{0}G,

	Starts	1st	2nd	3rd	Win & Pl
Career Total (Turf)	1	0	0	0	
Career Total (AW)	2	1	0	0	5279

85 8/09 Kemp 1m2f STD £4727
Total win prize-money £4727

Going (Turf): Sf: 0-0 GS: 0-0 Gd: 0-1 GF: 0-0 Fm: 0-0
Distance: 5f/6f: 0-0 7f-8f: 0-0 9f-13f: 1-3 14f+: 0-0
Track : LH: 0-0 RH: 1-3 Tight: 0-0 Gall: 0-1
Aids: Bl: 0-0 Vi: 0-0 Tstrap: 0-0 Ckp: 0-0
Best Rating: 88 8/09 Kemp 1m4f stand

Useful; stays 1m2f and acts on Polytrack.

Bawdsey Bank

72 21

3-y-o b g Tipsy Creek (USA)-Busy (IRE) (In The Wings)

John A Harris Miss Vivian Pratt

Placings:00 (7126)

2009: 7^{0}GF, 8^{0}G,

	Starts	1st	2nd	3rd	Win & Pl
Career Total (Turf)	2	0	0	0	

Going (Turf): Sf: 0-0 GS: 0-0 Gd: 0-1 GF: 0-1 Fm: 0-0
Distance: 5f/6f: 0-0 7f-8f: 0-1 9f-13f: 0-1 14f+: 0-0
Track : LH: 0-1 RH: 0-0 Tight: 0-0 Gall: 0-0
Aids: Bl: 0-0 Vi: 0-0 Tstrap: 0-0 Ckp: 0-0
Best Rating: 21 10/09 Leic 7f9y gd-fm

Bay Knight (IRE)

80(95) (87)81

3-y-o b c Johannesburg (USA)-Sabeline (IRE) (Caerleon (USA))

W McCreery Iona Equine Syndicate

Placings:001006110 (7445a)

2009: 7^{0}Y, 6^{0}GF, 5^{1}YS, 5^{0}S, 7^{0}HY, 6^{6}S, 7^{1}SD, 6^{1}SD, 7^{0}SD,

	Starts	1st	2nd	3rd	Win & Pl
Career Total (Turf)	6	1	0	0	5702
Career Total (AW)	3	2	0	0	18316

87 11/09 Dund 6f H STD £13588
86 10/09 Kemp 7f (0-85)H STD £4727
81 7/09 Tipp 5f Y-S £5702
Total win prize-money £24018

Going (Turf): Sf: 0-3 GS: 0-0 Gd: 0-0 GF: 0-1 Fm: 0-0
Distance: 5f/6f: 2-4 7f-8f: 1-5 9f-13f: 0-0 14f+: 0-0
Track : LH: 2-7 RH: 1-1 Tight: 0-0 Gall: 0-0
Aids: Bl: 0-0 Vi: 0-0 Tstrap: 0-0 Ckp: 0-0
Best Rating: 87 11/09 Dund 6f stand

Bayberry King (USA)

(57) (47)52

6-y-o b g Lear Fan (USA)-Myrtle (Batshoof)

Mrs A M Thorpe Don Jenkins

Placings:455/0050/0 (0131)

2009: 8^{0}SD,

	Starts	1st	2nd	3rd	Win & Pl
Career Total (Turf)	6	0	0	0	233
Career Total (AW)	2	0	0	0	216

Going (Turf): **Sf: 0-1 GS: 0-1 Gd: 0-2 GF: 0-2 Fm: 0-0**
Distance: 5f/6f: 0-2 7f-8f: 0-3 9f-13f: 0-3 14f+: 0-0
Track : LH: 0-4 RH: 0-3 Tight: 0-4 Gall: 0-1
Aids: Bl: 0-0 Vi: 0-0 Tstrap: 0-0 Ckp: 0-0
Best Rating: **52** 8/06 Thsk 1m good

Baybshambles (IRE)

102 **77**

5-y-o b g Compton Admiral-Payvashooz (Ballacashtal (CAN))
R E Barr Miss S Haykin

Placings:000/603166543016/131631020-02552100400 **(6489)**
2009: 5^{0}GF, 5^{2}GF, 5^{5}GF, 5^{5}GS, 5^{2}GF, 5^{1}GF, 5^{0}G, 5^{0}G, 5^{4}GF, 5^{0}G, 5^{0}GF,

	Starts	1st	2nd	3rd	Win & Pl
Career Total (Turf)	35	6	3	4	27717

77	7/09	Bevl	5f	(0-85)H	G-F	£6476
76	7/08	Thsk	5f	(0-85)H	G-F	£5569
75	5/08	Bevl	5f	(0-70)H	G-F	£2590
65	4/08	Ripn	5f	(0-70)H	G-S	£2914
63	10/07	Catt	5f	(0-55)H	GD	£2730
54	6/07	Rdcr	5f	(0-60)H	SFT	£2047

Total win prize-money £22327

Going (Turf): Sf: 1-4 GS: 1-6 Gd: 1-10 **GF: 3-14** Fm: 0-1
Distance: **5f/6f: 6-34** 7f-8f: 0-1 9f-13f: 0-0 14f+: 0-0
Track : LH: 0-2 RH: 0-0 Tight: 0-2 Gall: 0-0
Aids: Bl: 0-0 Vi: 0-0 Tstrap: 0-0 Ckp: 0-0
Best Rating: **77** 7/09 Bevl 5f gd-fm

Modest; effective over 5f and 6f; acts on soft ground.

Baycat (IRE)

89 **92**

3-y-o b g One Cool Cat (USA)-Greta D'Argent (IRE) (Great Commotion (USA))
J G Portman A S B Portman

Placings:11006-000 **(2329)**
2009: 7^{0}GS, 6^{0}G, 8^{0}GF,

	Starts	1st	2nd	3rd	Win & Pl
Career Total (Turf)	8	2	0	0	12059

92	4/08	Asct	5f	G-S	£6231
74	4/08	Newb	5f34y	G-S	£5828

Total win prize-money £12059

Going (Turf): Sf: 0-0 **GS: 2-4** Gd: 0-1 GF: 0-3 Fm: 0-0
Distance: **5f/6f: 2-5** 7f-8f: 0-3 9f-13f: 0-0 14f+: 0-0
Track : LH: 0-0 RH: 0-2 Tight: 0-0 Gall: 0-1
Aids: Bl: 0-0 Vi: 0-0 Tstrap: 0-0 Ckp: 0-0
Best Rating: **92** 4/08 Asct 5f gd-sft

Very useful; effective over 5f and acts on easy ground.

Baylini

99(116) (97)**90**

5-y-o gr m Bertolini (USA)-Bay Of Plenty (FR) (Octagonal (NZ))
Ms J S Doyle Mrs R S Doyle

Placings:32132/30055531/1423066402005-2330204052406 **(7574)**
2009: 10^{2}SD, 10^{3}SD, 10^{3}SD, 8^{0}SD, 12^{2}SD, 10^{0}SD, 11^{4}SD, 12^{0}GF, 12^{5}GF, 10^{2}GF, 10^{4}G, 10^{0}GF, 10^{6}SD,

	Starts	1st	2nd	3rd	Win & Pl
Career Total (Turf)	17	0	2	1	6809
Career Total (AW)	22	3	5	6	44431

99	1/08	Ling	1m2f	(0-85)H	STD	£4100
85	11/07	Ling	1m2f	(0-90)H	STD	£8724
77	10/06	Ling	7f		STD	£3886

Total win prize-money £16712

Going (Turf): **Sf: 0-0 GS: 0-4 Gd: 0-3 GF: 0-10 Fm: 0-0**
Distance: 5f/6f: 0-2 7f-8f: 1-10 **9f-13f: 2-27** 14f+: 0-0
Track : **LH: 3-23** RH: 0-10 **Tight: 3-21** Gall: 0-5
Aids: Bl: 0-0 Vi: 0-0 Tstrap: 0-0 Ckp: 0-0
Best Rating: **102** 3/08 Ling 1m2f stand

Fair; Listed placed; stays 1m4f; acts on Polytrack; probably not as good on turf.

Bazart

81(102) (76)**83**

7-y-o b g Highest Honor (FR)-Summer Exhibition (Royal Academy (USA))
B J Llewellyn Alex James

Placings:2140/10/00000/**66032**230-6 **(3423)**
2009: 14^{6}G,

	Starts	1st	2nd	3rd	Win & Pl
Career Total (Turf)	15	2	3	1	33752
Career Total (AW)	5	0	0	1	385

80	4/06	Lonc	1m110y	HVY	£10000
97	4/05	Lonc	1m	VS	£10993

Total win prize-money £20993

Going (Turf): **Sf: 1-4** GS: 0-1 Gd: 0-5 GF: 0-4 Fm: 0-0
Distance: 5f/6f: 0-0 7f-8f: 1-4 9f-13f: 1-13 14f+: 0-3
Track : LH: 0-12 RH: 0-2 Tight: 0-8 Gall: 0-4
Aids: Bl: 0-0 Vi: 0-0 Tstrap: 0-1 Ckp: 0-1
Best Rating: **98** 5/07 Ches 1m2f75y gd-fm

Fair; ex-French; stays 1m4f; acts on fast and heavy ground.

Baze Mac

83 **29**

2-y-o b f Needwood Blade-Miss Maisey (IRE) (Entrepreneur)
N Bycroft Mrs C M Whatley

Placings:0000 **(7242)**
2009: 5^{0}G, 6^{0}G, 5^{0}G, 5^{0}S,

	Starts	1st	2nd	3rd	Win & Pl
Career Total (Turf)	4	0	0	0	

Going (Turf): **Sf: 0-1 GS: 0-0 Gd: 0-3 GF: 0-0 Fm: 0-0**
Distance: 5f/6f: 0-4 7f-8f: 0-0 9f-13f: 0-0 14f+: 0-0
Track : LH: 0-0 RH: 0-0 Tight: 0-0 Gall: 0-0
Aids: Bl: 0-1 Vi: 0-0 Tstrap: 0-0 Ckp: 0-0
Best Rating: **29** 8/09 Thsk 5f good

Needwood Blade second foal of an unraced half-sister to a 6f winner.

Bazergan (IRE)

108(114) (96)**94**

4-y-o b g Machiavellian (USA)-Lunda (IRE) (Soviet Star (USA))
C E Brittain Saeed Manana

Placings:0345/103-**35005**31650 **(6106)**
2009: 8^{3}SD, 11^{5}SD, 11^{0}SD, 12^{0}G, 9^{5}GF, 10^{3}GF, 9^{1}G, 10^{6}GF, 10^{5}G, 10^{0}GF,

	Starts	1st	2nd	3rd	Win & Pl
Career Total (Turf)	13	2	0	2	19529
Career Total (AW)	4	0	0	2	3366

93	8/09	Bevl	1m1f207y(0-90)H		GD	£7641
81	8/08	Sals	1m1f198y		G-F	£3885

Total win prize-money £11528

Going (Turf): Sf: 0-1 GS: 0-0 **Gd: 1-5 GF: 1-7** Fm: 0-0
Distance: 5f/6f: 0-0 7f-8f: 0-5 **9f-13f: 2-12** 14f+: 0-0
Track : LH: 0-8 **RH: 2-5 Tight: 1-5** Gall: 0-3
Aids: Bl: 0-1 Vi: 0-0 Tstrap: 2-12 Ckp: 2-12
Best Rating: **103** 10/07 NmkR 7f good

Very useful; effective over 7f-1m2f; acts on fast ground and on Polytrack; often wears tongue tie and cheekpieces.

Bazsharani

94(85) (46)**67**

2-y-o bl f Auction House (USA)-Ewenny (Warrshan (USA))
P D Evans Barry McCabe

Placings:4256000 **(6590)**
2009: 5^{4}GF, 5^{2}GF, 6^{5}GF, 5^{6}GF, 6^{0}SD, 5^{0}F, 6^{0}GS,

	Starts	1st	2nd	3rd	Win & Pl
Career Total (Turf)	6	0	1	0	1950
Career Total (AW)	1	0	0	0	

Going (Turf): **Sf: 0-0 GS: 0-1 Gd: 0-0 GF: 0-4 Fm: 0-1**
Distance: 5f/6f: 0-5 7f-8f: 0-2 9f-13f: 0-0 14f+: 0-0
Track : LH: 0-4 RH: 0-0 Tight: 0-3 Gall: 0-1
Aids: Bl: 0-0 Vi: 0-0 Tstrap: 0-0 Ckp: 0-0
Best Rating: **67** 6/09 Ches 5f16y gd-fm

Be A Devil

73(101) (78)**33**

2-y-o ch c Dubai Destination (USA)-Devil's Imp (IRE) (Cadeaux Genereux)
W R Muir Foursome Thoroughbreds

Placings:065102322 **(7804)**
2009: 5^{0}GF, 5^{6}SD, 7^{5}SD, 7^{1}SF, 8^{0}SD, 7^{2}SD, 7^{3}SD, 7^{2}SD, 8^{2}SD,

	Starts	1st	2nd	3rd	Win & Pl
Career Total (Turf)	1	0	0	0	
Career Total (AW)	8	1	3	1	6575

73	10/09	Wolv	7f32y	(0-70)	SF	£2914

Total win prize-money £2914

Going (Turf): **Sf: 0-0 GS: 0-0 Gd: 0-0 GF: 0-1 Fm: 0-0**
Distance: 5f/6f: 0-2 **7f-8f: 1-5** 9f-13f: 0-2 14f+: 0-0
Track : **LH: 1-7** RH: 0-1 **Tight: 1-7** Gall: 0-1
Aids: Bl: 0-0 Vi: 0-0 Tstrap: 0-0 Ckp: 0-0
Best Rating: **78** 12/09 Wolv 1m141y stand

Fair; stays 1m; acts on Polytrack.

Be Grateful (IRE)

93(89) (49)**54**

2-y-o b/br f Efisio-Dwingeloo (IRE) (Dancing Dissident (USA))
H Morrison Mrs G C Maxwell & Partners

Placings:5560 **(7389)**
2009: 5^{5}GF, 5^{5}SD, 5^{6}G, 7^{0}SD,

	Starts	1st	2nd	3rd	Win & Pl
Career Total (Turf)	2	0	0	0	0
Career Total (AW)	2	0	0	0	0

Going (Turf): **Sf: 0-0 GS: 0-0 Gd: 0-1 GF: 0-1 Fm: 0-0**
Distance: 5f/6f: 0-3 7f-8f: 0-1 9f-13f: 0-0 14f+: 0-0
Track : LH: 0-3 RH: 0-0 Tight: 0-2 Gall: 0-1
Aids: Bl: 0-0 Vi: 0-0 Tstrap: 0-0 Ckp: 0-0
Best Rating: **54** 10/09 Bath 5f11y good

Be Invincible (IRE)

93 83

2-y-o b c Invincible Spirit (IRE)-Lupulina (CAN) (Saratoga Six (USA))

B W Hills A L R Morton & John C Grant

Placings:130 (7013)

2009: 5^{1}GF, 6^{3}G, 7^{0}GS,

	Starts	1st	2nd	3rd	Win & Pl
Career Total (Turf)	3	1	0	1	4129

76 4/09 Wind 5f10y G-F £2729

Total win prize-money £2730

Going (Turf): Sf: 0-0 GS: 0-1 Gd: 0-1 **GF: 1-1** Fm: 0-0
Distance: **5f/6f: 1-2** 7f-8f: 0-1 9f-13f: 0-0 14f+: 0-0
Track : LH: 0-1 RH: 0-0 Tight: 0-0 **Gall: 1-1**
Aids: Bl: 0-0 Vi: 0-0 Tstrap: 0-0 Ckp: 0-0
Best Rating: **83** 5/09 Pont 6f good

Fair; suited by 5f and fast ground.

Be Kind

86(90) (41)45

3-y-o b f Generous (IRE)-Aquavita (Kalaglow)

Karen George Miss Karen George

Placings:0600 (6859)

2009: 8^{0}GF, 12^{6}SD, 12^{0}SD, 16^{0}SD,

	Starts	1st	2nd	3rd	Win & Pl
Career Total (Turf)	1	0	0	0	
Career Total (AW)	3	0	0	0	0

Going (Turf): **Sf: 0-0 GS: 0-0 Gd: 0-0 GF: 0-1 Fm: 0-0**
Distance: 5f/6f: 0-0 7f-8f: 0-0 9f-13f: 0-3 14f+: 0-1
Track : LH: 0-1 RH: 0-3 Tight: 0-2 Gall: 0-0
Aids: Bl: 0-0 Vi: 0-0 Tstrap: 0-1 Ckp: 0-1
Best Rating: **45** 8/09 Wind 1m67y gd-fm

Bea Menace (USA)

104(105) (90)83

3-y-o b f Mizzen Mast (USA)-Questonia (Rainbow Quest (USA))

P F I Cole The Comic Strip Heroes

Placings:234-02505123115 (7181)

2009: 7^{0}GS, 7^{2}GF, 6^{5}SD, 6^{0}GF, 7^{5}G, 7^{1}F, 7^{2}GF, 7^{3}GF, 8^{1}GF, 7^{1}SD, 7^{5}SD,

	Starts	1st	2nd	3rd	Win & Pl
Career Total (Turf)	10	2	3	2	10587
Career Total (AW)	4	1	0	0	4872

90 10/09 Kemp 7f (0-85)H STD £4727
83 10/09 Pont 1m4y G-F £5180
73 7/09 Folk 7f (0-65)H FRM £2047

Total win prize-money £11955

Going (Turf): Sf: 0-1 GS: 0-1 Gd: 0-1 **GF: 1-6 Fm: 1-1**
Distance: 5f/6f: 0-2 **7f-8f: 2-11** 9f-13f: 1-1 14f+: 0-0
Track : LH: 1-4 RH: 1-2 Tight: 0-2 Gall: 0-0
Aids: **Bl: 1-3** Vi: 0-0 Tstrap: 0-0 Ckp: 0-0
Best Rating: **90** 10/09 Kemp 7f stand

Useful; effective over 7f; acts on fast ground and Polytrack.

Beach Boy (IRE)

69(76) (26)30

2-y-o ch c Pearl Of Love (IRE)-Mermaid Beach (Slew O'Gold (USA))

S Wynne MIss Gillian Milner

Placings:0000 (4018)

2009: 5^{0}SD, 5^{0}SD, 7^{0}SD, 5^{0}GF,

	Starts	1st	2nd	3rd	Win & Pl
Career Total (Turf)	1	0	0	0	
Career Total (AW)	3	0	0	0	

Going (Turf): **Sf: 0-0 GS: 0-0 Gd: 0-0 GF: 0-1 Fm: 0-0**
Distance: 5f/6f: 0-3 7f-8f: 0-1 9f-13f: 0-0 14f+: 0-0
Track : LH: 0-2 RH: 0-0 Tight: 0-2 Gall: 0-0
Aids: Bl: 0-0 Vi: 0-0 Tstrap: 0-0 Ckp: 0-0
Best Rating: **30** 7/09 Leic 5f2y gd-fm

Beacon Lodge (IRE)

113 117

4-y-o b c Clodovil (IRE)-Royal House (FR) (Royal Academy (USA))

C G Cox Mr And Mrs P Hargreaves

Placings:211/64-0121635 (6505a)

2009: 6^{0}GF, 7^{1}G, 7^{2}G, 8^{1}GS, 8^{6}G, 8^{3}G, 8^{5}GS,

	Starts	1st	2nd	3rd	Win & Pl
Career Total (Turf)	12	4	2	1	127723

117 6/09 Chan 1m G-S £38835
115 5/09 Hayd 7f30y GD £22708
106 10/07 Newb 7f SFT £21008
92 10/07 Newb 6f110y G-S £5829

Total win prize-money £88381

Going (Turf): Sf: 1-2 **GS: 2-3** Gd: 1-5 GF: 0-2 Fm: 0-0
Distance: 5f/6f: 0-3 **7f-8f: 4-9** 9f-13f: 0-0 14f+: 0-0
Track : LH: 1-2 RH: 1-3 Tight: 0-0 Gall: 0-0
Aids: Bl: 0-0 Vi: 0-0 Tstrap: 0-0 Ckp: 0-0
Best Rating: **117** 6/09 Chan 1m gd-sft

Smart; Group 3 winner; stays 1m; acts on most ground.

Bear Tobouggie

91 58

2-y-o b f Tobougg (IRE)-Brave Bear (Bold Edge)

G A Swinbank The Three Bears

Placings:0 (7288)

2009: 6^{0}S,

	Starts	1st	2nd	3rd	Win & Pl
Career Total (Turf)	1	0	0	0	

Going (Turf): **Sf: 0-1 GS: 0-0 Gd: 0-0 GF: 0-0 Fm: 0-0**
Distance: 5f/6f: 0-1 7f-8f: 0-0 9f-13f: 0-0 14f+: 0-0
Track : LH: 0-0 RH: 0-0 Tight: 0-0 Gall: 0-0
Aids: Bl: 0-0 Vi: 0-0 Tstrap: 0-0 Ckp: 0-0
Best Rating: **58** 11/09 Donc 6f soft

Beat Baby (IRE)

89 65

2-y-o ch g Johannesburg (USA)-Najiya (Nashwan (USA))

J Howard Johnson J Howard Johnson

Placings:00 (5234)

2009: 6^{0}GF, 6^{0}GF,

	Starts	1st	2nd	3rd	Win & Pl
Career Total (Turf)	2	0	0	0	

Going (Turf): **Sf: 0-0 GS: 0-0 Gd: 0-0 GF: 0-2 Fm: 0-0**
Distance: 5f/6f: 0-2 7f-8f: 0-0 9f-13f: 0-0 14f+: 0-0
Track : LH: 0-0 RH: 0-0 Tight: 0-0 Gall: 0-0
Aids: Bl: 0-0 Vi: 0-0 Tstrap: 0-0 Ckp: 0-0
Best Rating: **65** 8/09 York 6f gd-fm

Beat Companion

90(97) (69)59

3-y-o ch c Beat Hollow-Comanche Companion (Commanche Run)

P Howling S J Simmons

Placings:004 (4789)

2009: 10^{0}SD, 8^{0}S, 10^{4}SD,

	Starts	1st	2nd	3rd	Win & Pl
Career Total (Turf)	1	0	0	0	
Career Total (AW)	2	0	0	0	0

Going (Turf): **Sf: 0-1 GS: 0-0 Gd: 0-0 GF: 0-0 Fm: 0-0**
Distance: 5f/6f: 0-0 7f-8f: 0-1 9f-13f: 0-2 14f+: 0-0
Track : LH: 0-2 RH: 0-0 Tight: 0-2 Gall: 0-0
Aids: Bl: 0-0 Vi: 0-0 Tstrap: 0-0 Ckp: 0-0
Best Rating: **69** 8/09 Ling 1m2f stand

Beat Faster

89(83) (53)48

3-y-o b f Beat Hollow-Supersonic (Shirley Heights)

J G Given C G Rowles Nicholson

Placings:66-550 (7324)

2009: 8^{5}GF, 8^{5}SD, 12^{0}SD,

	Starts	1st	2nd	3rd	Win & Pl
Career Total (Turf)	1	0	0	0	0
Career Total (AW)	4	0	0	0	0

Going (Turf): **Sf: 0-0 GS: 0-0 Gd: 0-0 GF: 0-1 Fm: 0-0**
Distance: 5f/6f: 0-0 7f-8f: 0-3 9f-13f: 0-2 14f+: 0-0
Track : LH: 0-4 RH: 0-1 Tight: 0-0 Gall: 0-1
Aids: Bl: 0-0 Vi: 0-0 Tstrap: 0-0 Ckp: 0-0
Best Rating: **53** 12/08 GrLe 1m stand

Beat Seven

99 102

3-y-o ch f Beat Hollow-Twenty Seven (IRE) (Efisio)

Miss Gay Kelleway Winterbeck Manor Stud & Y Mullin

Placings:4104204-005 (3641)

2009: 10^{0}GF, 8^{0}GF, 8^{5}G,

	Starts	1st	2nd	3rd	Win & Pl
Career Total (Turf)	10	1	1	0	22300

77 4/08 Wind 5f10y G-F £2729

Total win prize-money £2730

Going (Turf): Sf: 0-0 GS: 0-2 Gd: 0-3 **GF: 1-5** Fm: 0-0
Distance: **5f/6f: 1-3** 7f-8f: 0-5 9f-13f: 0-2 14f+: 0-0
Track : LH: 0-1 RH: 0-3 Tight: 0-0 **Gall: 1-3**
Aids: Bl: 0-0 Vi: 0-0 Tstrap: 0-0 Ckp: 0-0
Best Rating: **102** 9/08 Asct 1m good

Smart; Listed placed; effective at up to 1m and acts on fast ground.

Beat Surrender (FR)

90 (90)96

2-y-o b c Bertolini (USA)-Waking Redhead (USA) (Miswaki (USA))

G M Lyons Sean Jones

Placings:10461 (6883a)
2009: 6^{1}GY, 7^{0}GF, 6^{4}HY, **6^{6}SD**, 6^{1}GY,

	Starts	1st	2nd	3rd	Win & Pl
Career Total (Turf)	4	2	0	0	53106
Career Total (AW)	1	0	0	0	

96 10/09 Naas 6f G-Y £40450
81 7/09 Naas 6f G-Y £10398
Total win prize-money £50849

Going (Turf): **Sf: 0-1 GS: 0-0 Gd: 0-0 GF: 0-1 Fm: 0-0**
Distance: **5f/6f: 2-4** 7f-8f: 0-1 9f-13f: 0-0 14f+: 0-0
Track : **LH: 2-4** RH: 0-0 Tight: 0-0 Gall: 0-1
Aids: **Bl: 1-1** Vi: 0-0 Tstrap: 0-0 Ckp: 0-0
Best Rating: **96** 10/09 Naas 6f gd-yld

Useful winner on debut; effective over 6f; acts on easy ground.

Beat The Bell

93(110) (98)**75**
4-y-o b g Beat All (USA)-Bella Beguine (Komaite (USA))
J A Osborne (A Bailey 8/1) D J P Turner

Placings:0451620211142444-5403660 (7613)
2009: **6^{5}SD**, 6^{4}GF, 7^{0}GF, **6^{3}SS**, **7^{6}SD**, **6^{6}SD**, **6^{0}SD**,

	Starts	1st	2nd	3rd	Win & Pl
Career Total (Turf)	9	1	2	0	6358
Career Total (AW)	14	3	1	1	24119

96 10/08 GrLe 6f (0-95)H STD £7477
95 10/08 Wolv 5f216y (0-75)H STD £3238
81 10/08 GrLe 6f (0-80)H STD £4857
72 6/08 Ches 6f18y GD £3238
Total win prize-money £18810

Going (Turf): Sf: 0-0 GS: 0-2 **Gd: 1-2** GF: 0-5 Fm: 0-0
Distance: **5f/6f: 3-17** 7f-8f: 1-6 9f-13f: 0-0 14f+: 0-0
Track : **LH: 4-13** RH: 0-3 Tight: 2-8 Gall: 2-4
Aids: Bl: 0-0 Vi: 0-0 Tstrap: 0-1 Ckp: 0-1
Best Rating: **98** 11/08 Kemp 6f stand

Useful; effective at 6f; acts on fast and easy ground; goes on Polytrack.

Beat The Devil

86 **57**
3-y-o ch g Nayef (USA)-Proud Titania (IRE) (Fairy King (USA))
T R George Frankie Roberts & Sharon Nelson

Placings:5 (4798)
2009: 12^{5}G,

	Starts	1st	2nd	3rd	Win & Pl
Career Total (Turf)	1	0	0	0	0

Going (Turf): **Sf: 0-0 GS: 0-0 Gd: 0-1 GF: 0-0 Fm: 0-0**
Distance: 5f/6f: 0-0 7f-8f: 0-0 9f-13f: 0-1 14f+: 0-0
Track : LH: 0-0 RH: 0-1 Tight: 0-0 Gall: 0-1
Aids: Bl: 0-0 Vi: 0-0 Tstrap: 0-0 Ckp: 0-0
Best Rating: **57** 8/09 NmkJ 1m4f good

Beat The Odds

(97) (41)**88**
5-y-o b g Beat Hollow-Biodotis (Warning)
F Sheridan (V Caruso 5/2) Frank Sheridan

Placings:00002/612020141001-514 (0825)
2009: 10^{5}HY, 10^{1}HY, **10^{4}SD**,

	Starts	1st	2nd	3rd	Win & Pl
Career Total (Turf)	19	5	3	0	16081
Career Total (AW)	1	0	0	0	0

2/09 Pisa 1m2f HVY £2427
12/08 Gros 1m3f H SH £2205
9/08 Casc 1m2f H GD £2941
8/08 Gros 1m3f H GD £2205
3/08 Siro 1m6f H GD £2573
Total win prize-money £12354

Going (Turf): Sf: 1-5 GS: 0-1 **Gd: 3-9** GF: 0-1 Fm: 0-0
Distance: 5f/6f: 0-0 7f-8f: 0-0 **9f-13f: 4-18** 14f+: 1-2
Track : LH: 0-1 RH: 0-1 Tight: 0-1 Gall: 0-0
Aids: Bl: 0-0 Vi: 0-0 Tstrap: 2-4 Ckp: 2-4
Best Rating: **41** 3/09 Ling 1m2f stand

Beat The Rush

95 **74**
2-y-o b g Tobougg (IRE)-Rush Hour (IRE) (Night Shift (USA))
Miss J A Camacho Axom (XX)

Placings:2561 (6901)
2009: 7^{2}GS, 7^{5}GF, 8^{6}G, 8^{1}GF,

	Starts	1st	2nd	3rd	Win & Pl
Career Total (Turf)	4	1	1	0	4167

74 10/09 Pont 1m4y (0-75) G-F £2914
Total win prize-money £2914

Going (Turf): Sf: 0-0 GS: 0-1 Gd: 0-1 **GF: 1-2** Fm: 0-0
Distance: 5f/6f: 0-0 7f-8f: 0-3 **9f-13f: 1-1** 14f+: 0-0
Track : **LH: 1-2** RH: 0-0 Tight: 0-1 Gall: 0-0
Aids: Bl: 0-0 Vi: 0-0 Tstrap: 0-0 Ckp: 0-0
Best Rating: **74** 10/09 Pont 1m4y gd-fm

Fair; stays 1m; acts on fast ground.

Beat The Shower

94(97) (46)**62**
3-y-o b g Beat Hollow-Crimson Shower (Dowsing (USA))
P D Niven Mrs Kate Young

Placings:6005136 (7425)
2009: 7^{6}G, 8^{0}G, **11^{0}SD**, 14^{5}GF, 11^{1}S, 13^{3}S, **12^{6}SD**,

	Starts	1st	2nd	3rd	Win & Pl
Career Total (Turf)	5	1	0	1	2481
Career Total (AW)	2	0	0	0	0

57 10/09 Catt 1m3f214y (0-60)H SFT £2047
Total win prize-money £2047

Going (Turf): **Sf: 1-2** GS: 0-0 Gd: 0-2 GF: 0-1 Fm: 0-0
Distance: 5f/6f: 0-0 7f-8f: 0-2 **9f-13f: 1-3** 14f+: 0-2
Track : **LH: 1-7** RH: 0-0 **Tight: 1-5** Gall: 0-0
Aids: Bl: 0-0 Vi: 0-0 Tstrap: 0-0 Ckp: 0-0
Best Rating: **62** 11/09 Catt 1m5f175y soft

Moderate; stays 1m5f; acts on soft ground.

Beau Fighter

105(86) (50)**80**
4-y-o b g Tobougg (IRE)-Belle De Jour (Exit To Nowhere (USA))
C F Wall P G Kingston And P T Kingston

Placings:004-1643 (7020)
2009: 10^{1}GS, 9^{6}GF, 11^{4}G, 10^{3}GS,

	Starts	1st	2nd	3rd	Win & Pl
Career Total (Turf)	6	1	0	1	4369
Career Total (AW)	1	0	0	0	

80 5/09 Newb 1m2f6y (0-70)H G-S £3238
Total win prize-money £3238

Going (Turf): Sf: 0-0 **GS: 1-2** Gd: 0-1 GF: 0-3 Fm: 0-0
Distance: 5f/6f: 0-0 7f-8f: 0-0 **9f-13f: 1-7** 14f+: 0-0
Track : **LH: 1-4** RH: 0-3 Tight: 0-3 **Gall: 1-3**
Aids: Bl: 0-0 Vi: 0-0 Tstrap: 0-0 Ckp: 0-0
Best Rating: **80** 5/09 Newb 1m2f6y gd-sft

Fair; effective at 1m2f; suited by easy ground.

Beau Jazz

(90) (44)**31**
8-y-o br g Merdon Melody-Ichor (Primo Dominie)
W De Best-Turner W De Best-Turner

Placings:000360056/5306000000/000/00006400/0/06-060 (7394)
2009: 7^{0}SD, 6^{6}SD, 6^{0}SD,

	Starts	1st	2nd	3rd	Win & Pl
Career Total (Turf)	18	0	0	1	1435
Career Total (AW)	18	0	0	1	658

Going (Turf): **Sf: 0-0 GS: 0-3 Gd: 0-3 GF: 0-11 Fm: 0-1**
Distance: 5f/6f: 0-26 7f-8f: 0-8 9f-13f: 0-2 14f+: 0-0
Track : LH: 0-21 RH: 0-4 Tight: 0-14 Gall: 0-6
Aids: Bl: 0-0 Vi: 0-0 Tstrap: 0-4 Ckp: 0-4
Best Rating: **67** 10/03 York 6f3y gd-fm

Beaubrav

101(95) (69)**63**
3-y-o b g Falbrav (IRE)-Wavy Up (IRE) (Brustolon)
M Madgwick (P W D'Arcy 23/8) The B B Partnership

Placings:060-2426325 (5286)
2009: **10^{2}SD**, 12^{4}GF, 9^{2}G, 10^{6}GF, 10^{3}G, 9^{2}GS, 12^{5}GF,

	Starts	1st	2nd	3rd	Win & Pl
Career Total (Turf)	8	0	2	1	2060
Career Total (AW)	2	0	1	0	605

Going (Turf): **Sf: 0-0 GS: 0-1 Gd: 0-4 GF: 0-3 Fm: 0-0**
Distance: 5f/6f: 0-0 7f-8f: 0-3 9f-13f: 0-7 14f+: 0-0
Track : LH: 0-4 RH: 0-5 Tight: 0-4 Gall: 0-1
Aids: Bl: 0-0 Vi: 0-0 Tstrap: 0-0 Ckp: 0-0
Best Rating: **69** 4/09 Kemp 1m2f stand

Modest maiden; stays 1m2f; acts on good ground.

Beauchamp Unique

82(61) **21**
6-y-o b m Compton Admiral-Beauchamp Jade (Kalaglow)
E J Cooper Cumberland Lodge Racing & Leisure Co Ltd

Placings:001/355300/000 (4344)
2009: **12^{0}SD**, 13^{0}GF, 7^{0}G,

	Starts	1st	2nd	3rd	Win & Pl
Career Total (Turf)	8	0	0	1	353
Career Total (AW)	4	1	0	1	1905

63 12/05 Ling 7f STD £1423
Total win prize-money £1423

Going (Turf): **Sf: 0-1 GS: 0-1 Gd: 0-1 GF: 0-4 Fm: 0-1**
Distance: 5f/6f: 0-0 **7f-8f: 1-4** 9f-13f: 0-6 14f+: 0-2
Track : **LH: 1-7** RH: 0-3 **Tight: 1-9** Gall: 0-0
Aids: Bl: 0-1 Vi: 0-0 Tstrap: 0-1 Ckp: 0-1
Best Rating: **69** 1/06 Ling 1m2f stand

Beauchamp Viceroy

98(108) (98)**84**
5-y-o ch g Compton Admiral-Compton Astoria (USA) (Lion Cavern (USA))

G A Butler Erik Penser

Placings:21402121/500/5040540-566410604214 (7489)

2009: 12^{5}SD, 10^{6}SD, 8^{6}GF, 8^{4}SD, 8^{1}SD, 7^{0}GF, 8^{6}SD, 8^{0}SD, 7^{4}SD, 7^{2}SF, 8^{1}SD, 10^{4}SD,

	Starts	1st	2nd	3rd	Win & Pl
Career Total (Turf)	8	0	0	0	337
Career Total (AW)	22	5	4	0	33172

88	10/09	Kemp	1m	(0-80)H	STD	£4727
88	7/09	Wolv	1m141y		STD	£2047
91	12/06	Wolv	7f32y	(0-95)	STD	£7124
81	12/06	Wolv	5f216y		STD	£4533
73	8/06	Wolv	5f216y		STD	£3238

Total win prize-money £21672

Going (Turf): **Sf: 0-1 GS: 0-0 Gd: 0-4 GF: 0-3 Fm: 0-0**
Distance: 5f/6f: 2-5 7f-8f: 2-16 9f-13f: 1-9 14f+: 0-0
Track : **LH: 4-19** RH: 1-6 **Tight: 4-16** Gall: 0-2
Aids: Bl: 1-3 Vi: 0-0 Tstrap: 1-6 Ckp: 1-6
Best Rating: 98 11/09 Ling 1m2f stand

Very useful; stays 1m and acts well on Polytrack; has worn blinkers, cheekpieces and a tongue tie; suited by forcing tactics.

Beauchamp Viking

94(79) (45)**42**

5-y-o b g Compton Admiral-Beauchamp Jade (Kalaglow)
S C Burrough Mrs Maureen Emery

Placings:05/0-050 (2912)
2009: 8^{0}GF, 10^{5}F, 10^{0}F,

	Starts	1st	2nd	3rd	Win & Pl
Career Total (Turf)	4	0	0	0	0
Career Total (AW)	2	0	0	0	0

Going (Turf): **Sf: 0-0 GS: 0-1 Gd: 0-0 GF: 0-1 Fm: 0-2**
Distance: 5f/6f: 0-0 7f-8f: 0-1 9f-13f: 0-5 14f+: 0-0
Track : LH: 0-4 RH: 0-2 Tight: 0-3 Gall: 0-1
Aids: Bl: 0-0 Vi: 0-0 Tstrap: 0-0 Ckp: 0-0
Best Rating: 55 5/07 Newb 1m2f6y gd-sft

Beauchamp Wizard

95(100) (77)**73**

4-y-o b c Compton Admiral-Compton Astoria (USA) (Lion Cavern (USA))
G A Butler Erik Penser

Placings:34/21-502 (6454)
2009: 9^{5}GF, 7^{0}SD, 10^{2}GF,

	Starts	1st	2nd	3rd	Win & Pl
Career Total (Turf)	4	0	2	1	1493
Career Total (AW)	3	1	0	0	2264

77	8/08	Kemp	7f	STD	£2047

Total win prize-money £2047

Going (Turf): **Sf: 0-0 GS: 0-0 Gd: 0-0 GF: 0-3 Fm: 0-1**
Distance: 5f/6f: 0-1 **7f-8f: 1-4** 9f-13f: 0-2 14f+: 0-0
Track : LH: 0-1 **RH: 1-4** Tight: 0-2 Gall: 0-0
Aids: Bl: 0-0 Vi: 0-0 Tstrap: 0-0 Ckp: 0-0
Best Rating: 77 8/08 Kemp 7f stand

Fair; effective at 7f and should stay 1m; acts on firm ground and Polytrack; has worn a tongue tie.

Beauchamp Wonder

99(93) (61)**71**

4-y-o b f Compton Admiral-Beauchamp Jade (Kalaglow)
G A Butler Erik Penser

Placings:243-23 (4053)
2009: 17^{2}G, 11^{3}S,

	Starts	1st	2nd	3rd	Win & Pl
Career Total (Turf)	4	0	1	2	2000
Career Total (AW)	1	0	1	0	674

Going (Turf): **Sf: 0-1 GS: 0-0 Gd: 0-1 GF: 0-2 Fm: 0-0**
Distance: 5f/6f: 0-0 7f-8f: 0-0 9f-13f: 0-4 14f+: 0-1
Track : LH: 0-4 RH: 0-1 Tight: 0-2 Gall: 0-3
Aids: Bl: 0-0 Vi: 0-0 Tstrap: 0-0 Ckp: 0-0
Best Rating: 71 7/09 Carl 2m1f52y good

Modest; stays 2m1f; acts on most ground.

Beauchamp Xenia

102(94) (58)**69**

3-y-o b f Compton Admiral-Beauchamp Jade (Kalaglow)
H Candy Erik Penser

Placings:0-0536 (5430)
2009: 10^{0}GS, 12^{5}GF, 12^{3}SD, 16^{6}G,

	Starts	1st	2nd	3rd	Win & Pl
Career Total (Turf)	4	0	0	0	0
Career Total (AW)	1	0	0	1	385

Going (Turf): **Sf: 0-0 GS: 0-2 Gd: 0-1 GF: 0-1 Fm: 0-0**
Distance: 5f/6f: 0-0 7f-8f: 0-1 9f-13f: 0-3 14f+: 0-1
Track : LH: 0-0 RH: 0-4 Tight: 0-2 Gall: 0-1
Aids: Bl: 0-0 Vi: 0-0 Tstrap: 0-0 Ckp: 0-0
Best Rating: 69 5/09 NmkR 1m4f gd-fm

Modest; stays 2m; acts on a sound surface on turf and Polytrack.

Beauchamp Xerxes

108(109) (103)**104**

3-y-o ch c Compton Admiral-Compton Astoria (USA) (Lion Cavern (USA))
G A Butler Erik Penser

Placings:4420012430 (7489)
2009: 8^{4}GF, 10^{4}GF, 11^{2}G, 12^{0}GF, 10^{0}G, 8^{1}GF, 9^{2}GF, 10^{4}SD, 12^{3}SD, 10^{0}SD,

	Starts	1st	2nd	3rd	Win & Pl
Career Total (Turf)	7	1	2	0	14587
Career Total (AW)	3	0	0	1	4859

85	8/09	Wind	1m67y	G-F	£2729

Total win prize-money £2730

Going (Turf): Sf: 0-0 GS: 0-0 Gd: 0-2 **GF: 1-5** Fm: 0-0
Distance: 5f/6f: 0-0 7f-8f: 0-1 **9f-13f: 1-9** 14f+: 0-0
Track : LH: 0-3 **RH: 1-6 Tight: 1-4** Gall: 0-3
Aids: Bl: 0-0 Vi: 0-0 Tstrap: 0-0 Ckp: 0-0
Best Rating: 104 9/09 Newb 1m1f gd-fm

Smart; Listed placed; effective over 1m-1m4f; acts on good and faster ground and on Polytrack.

Beauchamp Xiara

105(91) (69)**71**

3-y-o b f Compton Admiral-Beauchamp Buzz (High Top)
H Candy Erik Penser

Placings:0-420 (6698)
2009: 9^{4}F, 12^{2}SD, 12^{0}GS,

	Starts	1st	2nd	3rd	Win & Pl
Career Total (Turf)	3	0	0	0	289
Career Total (AW)	1	0	1	0	1407

Going (Turf): **Sf: 0-0 GS: 0-2 Gd: 0-0 GF: 0-0 Fm: 0-1**
Distance: 5f/6f: 0-0 7f-8f: 0-1 9f-13f: 0-3 14f+: 0-0
Track : LH: 0-0 RH: 0-3 Tight: 0-2 Gall: 0-0
Aids: Bl: 0-0 Vi: 0-0 Tstrap: 0-0 Ckp: 0-0
Best Rating: 71 5/09 Sals 1m1f198y firm

Modest; stays 1m2f; acts on fast ground.

Beauchamp Yeoman

79 **40**

2-y-o b g Compton Admiral-One Way Street (Habitat)
H Candy Erik Penser

Placings:0 (7146)
2009: 7^{0}G,

	Starts	1st	2nd	3rd	Win & Pl
Career Total (Turf)	1	0	0	0	

Going (Turf): **Sf: 0-0 GS: 0-0 Gd: 0-1 GF: 0-0 Fm: 0-0**
Distance: 5f/6f: 0-0 7f-8f: 0-1 9f-13f: 0-0 14f+: 0-0
Track : LH: 0-0 RH: 0-0 Tight: 0-0 Gall: 0-0
Aids: Bl: 0-0 Vi: 0-0 Tstrap: 0-0 Ckp: 0-0
Best Rating: 40 10/09 NmkR 7f good

Beauchamp Yorker

88 **85**

2-y-o ch c Compton Admiral-Compton Astoria (USA) (Lion Cavern (USA))
H Candy Erik Penser

Placings:1 (6108)
2009: 7^{1}GF,

	Starts	1st	2nd	3rd	Win & Pl
Career Total (Turf)	1	1	0	0	5181

85	9/09	Newb	7f	G-F	£5180

Total win prize-money £5181

Going (Turf): Sf: 0-0 GS: 0-0 Gd: 0-0 **GF: 1-1** Fm: 0-0
Distance: 5f/6f: 0-0 **7f-8f: 1-1** 9f-13f: 0-0 14f+: 0-0
Track : LH: 0-0 RH: 0-0 Tight: 0-0 Gall: 0-0
Aids: Bl: 0-0 Vi: 0-0 Tstrap: 0-0 Ckp: 0-0
Best Rating: 85 9/09 Newb 7f gd-fm

Winner on debut; effective over 7f; acts on fast ground.

Beaumont Boy

92(77) **54**

5-y-o b g Foxhound (USA)-Play The Game (Mummy's Game)
J A McShane Lothian Recycling Limited

Placings:6550/04023050/0454060-436430 (3105)
2009: 9^{4}GF, 9^{3}F, 9^{6}G, 8^{4}GF, 9^{3}GF, 7^{0}GF,

	Starts	1st	2nd	3rd	Win & Pl
Career Total (Turf)	24	0	1	3	2330
Career Total (AW)	1	0	0	0	

Going (Turf): **Sf: 0-2 GS: 0-4 Gd: 0-8 GF: 0-8 Fm: 0-2**
Distance: 5f/6f: 0-8 7f-8f: 0-7 9f-13f: 0-10 14f+: 0-0
Track : LH: 0-7 RH: 0-10 Tight: 0-10 Gall: 0-0
Aids: Bl: 0-7 Vi: 0-0 Tstrap: 0-6 Ckp: 0-6
Best Rating: **57** 8/06 Thsk 5f gd-sft

Moderate sort; effective at 7f; has worn cheekpieces and blinkers.

Beaumont Princess (IRE)

71 **7**
3-y-o b f Elusive City (USA)-Pantera Piceno (IRE) (College Chapel)
G A Swinbank G Stephenson

Placings:0 **(2439)**
2009: 6^{0}GF,

	Starts	1st	2nd	3rd	Win & Pl
Career Total (Turf)	1	0	0	0	

Going (Turf): **Sf: 0-0 GS: 0-0 Gd: 0-0 GF: 0-1 Fm: 0-0**
Distance: 5f/6f: 0-0 7f-8f: 0-1 9f-13f: 0-0 14f+: 0-0
Track : LH: 0-0 RH: 0-0 Tight: 0-0 Gall: 0-0
Aids: Bl: 0-0 Vi: 0-0 Tstrap: 0-0 Ckp: 0-0
Best Rating: **7** 5/09 Haml 6f5y gd-fm

Beaumont's Party (IRE)

98(95) (70)**69**
2-y-o b c High Chaparral (IRE)-Miss Champagne (FR) (Bering)
R Hannon Thurloe Thoroughbreds XXV

Placings:645 **(7145)**
2009: 7^{6}GF, 7^{4}SS, 6^{5}G,

	Starts	1st	2nd	3rd	Win & Pl
Career Total (Turf)	2	0	0	0	0
Career Total (AW)	1	0	0	0	265

Going (Turf): **Sf: 0-0 GS: 0-0 Gd: 0-1 GF: 0-1 Fm: 0-0**
Distance: 5f/6f: 0-1 7f-8f: 0-2 9f-13f: 0-0 14f+: 0-0
Track : LH: 0-1 RH: 0-0 Tight: 0-1 Gall: 0-0
Aids: Bl: 0-0 Vi: 0-0 Tstrap: 0-0 Ckp: 0-0
Best Rating: **70** 10/09 Ling 7f std-slw

Beautiful Breeze (IRE)

103 **81**
3-y-o ch g Tobougg (IRE)-Khayrat (IRE) (Polar Falcon (USA))
M Johnston Crone Stud Farms Ltd

Placings:31505-41051 **(3504)**
2009: 7^{4}GF, 7^{1}GF, 7^{0}GF, 8^{5}GF, 8^{1}GF,

	Starts	1st	2nd	3rd	Win & Pl
Career Total (Turf)	10	3	0	1	13053

81 7/09 Chep 1m14y (0-75)H G-F £3561
79 5/09 Wwck 7f26y (0-75)H G-F £2914
73 8/08 Bevl 7f100y G-S £5018
Total win prize-money £11495

Going (Turf): Sf: 0-1 GS: 1-2 Gd: 0-0 **GF: 2-7** Fm: 0-0
Distance: 5f/6f: 0-1 **7f-8f: 2-8** 9f-13f: 1-1 14f+: 0-0
Track : LH: 1-4 RH: 1-3 Tight: 0-2 Gall: 0-0
Aids: Bl: 0-0 Vi: 0-0 Tstrap: 0-0 Ckp: 0-0
Best Rating: **81** 7/09 Chep 1m14y gd-fm

Useful; effective at 7f; acts on easy and fast ground.

Beautiful Filly

87(101) (73)**62**
3-y-o b f Oasis Dream-Royal Alchemist (USA) (Royal Academy (USA))
D M Simcock Dr Ali Ridha

Placings:03-10020340140 **(7487)**
2009: 6^{1}SD, 7^{0}GS, 6^{0}SD, 6^{2}SD, 6^{0}SD, 7^{3}SD, 7^{4}SD, 8^{0}F, 7^{1}SD, 7^{4}SD, 8^{0}SD,

	Starts	1st	2nd	3rd	Win & Pl
Career Total (Turf)	2	0	0	0	
Career Total (AW)	11	2	1	2	10868

71 10/09 Wolv 7f32y (0-85)H STD £5046
60 4/09 Ling 6f STD £2590
Total win prize-money £7636

Going (Turf): **Sf: 0-0 GS: 0-1 Gd: 0-0 GF: 0-0 Fm: 0-1**
Distance: 5f/6f: 1-6 7f-8f: 1-6 9f-13f: 0-1 14f+: 0-0
Track : **LH: 2-8** RH: 0-4 **Tight: 2-7** Gall: 0-1
Aids: **Bl: 1-7** Vi: 0-0 Tstrap: 0-0 Ckp: 0-0
Best Rating: **73** 6/09 Kemp 6f stand

Fair; effective over 7f; acts on Polytrack; has worn blinkers.

Beautiful Lady (IRE)

86(92) (67)**74**
4-y-o b f Peintre Celebre (USA)-Puteri Wentworth (Sadler's Wells (USA))
P F I Cole H R H Sultan Ahmad Shah

Placings:245310000-50 **(2123)**
2009: 12^{5}GS, 13^{0}GS,

	Starts	1st	2nd	3rd	Win & Pl
Career Total (Turf)	6	1	0	1	4743
Career Total (AW)	5	0	1	0	963

74 8/08 Thsk 1m4f (0-70)H G-S £4338
Total win prize-money £4339

Going (Turf): Sf: 0-1 **GS: 1-3** Gd: 0-1 GF: 0-0 Fm: 0-1
Distance: 5f/6f: 0-0 7f-8f: 0-0 **9f-13f: 1-8** 14f+: 0-3
Track : **LH: 1-8** RH: 0-2 **Tight: 1-5** Gall: 0-2
Aids: Bl: 0-1 Vi: 0-0 Tstrap: 0-0 Ckp: 0-0
Best Rating: **74** 8/08 Thsk 1m4f gd-sft

Fair; stays 1m4f; acts on Polytrack and easy ground on turf.

Beaux Yeux

88(96) (55)**39**
3-y-o b f Cadeaux Genereux-Cloud Hill (Danehill (USA))
Miss A Stokell (P T Midgley 14/9) Ms Caron Stokell

Placings:0-533430000 **(7270)**
2009: 6^{5}SS, 6^{3}SD, 5^{3}SD, 6^{4}SD, 6^{3}SD, 5^{0}GS, 7^{0}S, 7^{0}GF, 6^{0}SD,

	Starts	1st	2nd	3rd	Win & Pl
Career Total (Turf)	3	0	0	0	
Career Total (AW)	7	0	0	3	1260

Going (Turf): **Sf: 0-1 GS: 0-1 Gd: 0-0 GF: 0-1 Fm: 0-0**
Distance: 5f/6f: 0-7 7f-8f: 0-3 9f-13f: 0-0 14f+: 0-0
Track : LH: 0-7 RH: 0-1 Tight: 0-1 Gall: 0-0
Aids: Bl: 0-0 Vi: 0-0 Tstrap: 0-1 Ckp: 0-1
Best Rating: **55** 3/09 Sthl 6f stand

Moderate; suited by 6f and Fibresand.

Beaver Patrol (IRE)

108 (109)**109**
7-y-o ch g Tagula (IRE)-Erne Project (IRE) (Project Manager)
Eve Johnson Houghton G C Stevens

Placings:1321062155/4055000564163/**3**01042000**65**/1560552142/334000200330-00104000000 **(5874)**
2009: 6^{0}G, 6^{0}GF, 6^{1}GF, 6^{0}GF, 7^{4}GF, 7^{0}GF, 6^{0}GF, 7^{0}GF, 6^{0}S, 6^{0}GF, 7^{0}GF,

	Starts	1st	2nd	3rd	Win & Pl
Career Total (Turf)	63	8	5	6	329854
Career Total (AW)	4	0	1	1	9611

104 2/09 Ndas 6f G-F £41666
108 9/07 Newb 6f8y (0-95)H G-F £7124
99 5/07 NmkR 6f H G-F £31160
100 6/06 Epsm 6f (0-100)H G-F £24928
98 9/05 Gdwd 6f (0-85)H G-F £6139
100 8/04 Curr 6f G-F £103521
96 5/04 Kemp 6f C G-F £7290
82 4/04 Wind 5f10y D G-S £3425
Total win prize-money £225257

Going (Turf): Sf: 0-8 GS: 1-10 Gd: 0-16 **GF: 7-29** Fm: 0-0
Distance: **5f/6f: 7-40** 7f-8f: 1-24 9f-13f: 0-3 14f+: 0-0
Track : **LH: 2-16** RH: 0-8 Tight: 1-8 **Gall: 2-15**
Aids: Bl: 1-5 Vi: 1-20 Tstrap: 0-0 Ckp: 0-0
Best Rating: **109** 6/08 Asct 6f gd-fm

Very useful; effective over 6f; probably best on fast ground; has worn blinkers; usually wears a visor/blinkers.

Bebenine (IRE)

91(88) (63)**63**
2-y-o b f Antonius Pius (USA)-Lady Fonic (Zafonic (USA))
Patrick Morris Boodles - Mario & Lisa

Placings:4406 **(2147)**
2009: 5^{4}SD, 5^{4}GF, 5^{0}GF, 5^{6}G,

	Starts	1st	2nd	3rd	Win & Pl
Career Total (Turf)	3	0	0	0	289
Career Total (AW)	1	0	0	0	216

Going (Turf): **Sf: 0-0 GS: 0-0 Gd: 0-1 GF: 0-2 Fm: 0-0**
Distance: 5f/6f: 0-4 7f-8f: 0-0 9f-13f: 0-0 14f+: 0-0
Track : LH: 0-2 RH: 0-0 Tight: 0-2 Gall: 0-0
Aids: Bl: 0-0 Vi: 0-0 Tstrap: 0-0 Ckp: 0-0
Best Rating: **63** 4/09 Ripn 5f gd-fm

Modest; acts on Polytrack.

Bebopalula (IRE)

92 **69**
2-y-o gr f Galileo (IRE)-Pearl Bright (FR) (Kaldoun (FR))
B W Hills Phil Cunningham

Placings:6 **(6992)**
2009: 8^{6}GS,

	Starts	1st	2nd	3rd	Win & Pl
Career Total (Turf)	1	0	0	0	0

Going (Turf): **Sf: 0-0 GS: 0-1 Gd: 0-0 GF: 0-0 Fm: 0-0**
Distance: 5f/6f: 0-0 7f-8f: 0-1 9f-13f: 0-0 14f+: 0-0
Track : LH: 0-1 RH: 0-0 Tight: 0-0 Gall: 0-1
Aids: Bl: 0-0 Vi: 0-0 Tstrap: 0-0 Ckp: 0-0
Best Rating: **69** 10/09 Donc 1m gd-sft

Becausewecan (USA)

109(106) (87)**94**

3-y-o b g Giant's Causeway (USA)-Belle Sultane (USA) (Seattle Slew (USA))

M Johnston Douglas Livingston

Placings:2035300011-2163421 **(6816)**

2009: 8^{2}SD, 12^{1}GS, 11^{6}GF, 12^{3}G, 11^{4}G, 12^{2}SD, 12^{1}G,

	Starts	1st	2nd	3rd	Win & Pl
Career Total (Turf)	**14**	**3**	**1**	**3**	**29292**
Career Total (AW)	**3**	**1**	**2**	**0**	**7533**

94	10/09	NmkR	1m4f	(0-105)H	GD	£11215
84	6/09	NmkJ	1m4f	(0-80)H	G-S	£5828
75	11/08	GrLe	1m	(0-75)	STD	£3885
69	11/08	Ayr	7f50y	(0-75)	HVY	£3885

Total win prize-money £24816

Going (Turf): **Sf: 1-5 GS: 1-2 Gd: 1-5** GF: 0-2 Fm: 0-0
Distance: 5f/6f: 0-4 7f-8f: 2-7 9f-13f: 2-6 14f+: 0-0
Track : LH: 2-5 RH: 2-5 Tight: 0-2 **Gall: 3-3**
Aids: Bl: 0-0 Vi: 0-0 Tstrap: 0-0 Ckp: 0-0
Best Rating: 94 10/09 NmkR 1m4f good

Useful; effective up to 1m4f; acts on fast and soft ground, goes on Fibresand and Polytrack.

Beckenham's Secret

95(95) (46)**52**

5-y-o b g Foxhound (USA)-Berliese (IRE) (High Estate)

A W Carroll Allan Jones & Mrs J J G & H Reynolds

Placings:61300406/0604**0000**5206/50200630**00**-05300**5**0030 **(2912)**

2009: 7^{0}SD, 8^{5}SD, 8^{3}SD, 8^{0}SD, 8^{0}SD, 7^{5}SD, 5^{0}GF, 9^{0}GF, 12^{3}GF, 10^{0}F,

	Starts	1st	2nd	3rd	Win & Pl
Career Total (Turf)	**22**	**0**	**2**	**3**	**3748**
Career Total (AW)	**18**	**1**	**0**	**1**	**5434**

71	4/06	Kemp	5f	STD	£5181

Total win prize-money £5182

Going (Turf): Sf: 0-1 GS: 0-2 Gd: 0-3 GF: 0-13 Fm: 0-3
Distance: 5f/6f: 1-7 7f-8f: 0-15 9f-13f: 0-17 14f+: 0-1
Track : LH: 0-22 **RH: 1-13** Tight: 0-19 Gall: 0-3
Aids: Bl: 0-3 Vi: 0-2 Tstrap: 0-0 Ckp: 0-0
Best Rating: 73 7/06 Wind 6f gd-fm

Plating-class gelding; stays 1m4f; acts on most ground and Polytrack; has worn blinkers.

Beckermet (IRE)

109(103) (93)**114**

7-y-o b g Second Empire (IRE)-Razida (IRE) (Last Tycoon)

R F Fisher Great Head House Taylor Nash Edwards

Placings:3112110405/4430220410030/36000020420035**0**/000623320000151562/400**3**0045360320-05000200**250** **(7558)**

2009: 7^{0}SD, 6^{5}G, 7^{0}GF, 6^{0}GF, 6^{0}GF, 6^{2}G, 6^{0}GF, 7^{0}G, 7^{2}SD, 6^{5}SD, 7^{0}SD,

	Starts	1st	2nd	3rd	Win & Pl
Career Total (Turf)	**75**	**7**	**10**	**10**	**204809**
Career Total (AW)	**6**	**0**	**1**	**0**	**2587**

114	9/07	Gdwd	6f		G-F	£15898
114	8/07	NmkJ	6f		SFT	£15330
112	7/05	Newb	6f8y		G-F	£16240
101	7/04	Ches	5f16y	B	GD	£10300
102	6/04	Ches	5f16y	D	GD	£4621
82	6/04	Thsk	5f	D	G-F	£4290
73	5/04	Hayd	5f	E	G-F	£3692

Total win prize-money £70374

Going (Turf): Sf: 1-5 GS: 0-7 Gd: 2-29 **GF: 4-30** Fm: 0-3
Distance: 5f/6f: 6-53 7f-8f: 1-28 9f-13f: 0-0 14f+: 0-0
Track : LH: 2-26 RH: 0-2 **Tight: 2-13** Gall: 0-11
Aids: Bl: 0-0 Vi: 0-0 Tstrap: 0-0 Ckp: 0-0
Best Rating: 114 5/08 York 6f gd-fm

Useful; Listed winner and Group placed; effective over 5f-7f; acts on fast and soft ground; suited by forcing tactics.

Becky Quick (IRE)

49(69)

4-y-o b f Fantastic Light (USA)-Private Bluff (USA) (Pine Bluff (USA))

Bruce Hellier J W Barrett

Placings:6/0-000 **(5163)**

2009: 8^{0}G, 6^{0}SD, 6^{0}S,

	Starts	1st	2nd	3rd	Win & Pl
Career Total (Turf)	**4**	**0**	**0**	**0**	**0**
Career Total (AW)	**1**	**0**	**0**	**0**	

Going (Turf): Sf: 0-1 GS: 0-2 Gd: 0-1 GF: 0-0 Fm: 0-0
Distance: 5f/6f: 0-2 7f-8f: 0-2 9f-13f: 0-1 14f+: 0-0
Track : LH: 0-2 RH: 0-0 Tight: 0-0 Gall: 0-0
Aids: Bl: 0-2 Vi: 0-0 Tstrap: 0-0 Ckp: 0-0

Becuille (IRE)

95(107) (76)**73**

4-y-o b f Redback-Danz Danz (Efisio)

B J Meehan Ms Susan McKeon

Placings:04336/00020000-50130010030 **(7360)**

2009: 8^{5}SD, 9^{0}SD, 9^{1}SD, 10^{3}SD, 10^{0}GF, 8^{0}GS, 9^{1}S, 9^{0}GF, 9^{0}SD, 9^{3}SD, 9^{0}SD,

	Starts	1st	2nd	3rd	Win & Pl
Career Total (Turf)	**14**	**1**	**1**	**1**	**5521**
Career Total (AW)	**10**	**1**	**0**	**3**	**4797**

73	7/09	Yarm	1m1f	(0-70)H	SFT	£2719
71	4/09	Wolv	1m1f103y	(0-75)H	STD	£3238

Total win prize-money £5958

Going (Turf): Sf: 1-3 GS: 0-1 Gd: 0-1 GF: 0-6 Fm: 0-2
Distance: 5f/6f: 0-1 7f-8f: 0-13 **9f-13f: 2-10** 14f+: 0-0
Track : LH: 2-15 RH: 0-6 **Tight: 2-9** Gall: 0-2
Aids: Bl: 1-5 Vi: 0-0 Tstrap: 0-0 Ckp: 0-0
Best Rating: 76 10/09 Wolv 1m1f103y stand

Modest; stays 1m2f; handles soft ground and Polytrack; has worn blinkers.

Bed Fellow (IRE)

100(80) (65)**70**

5-y-o b g Trans Island-Moonlight Partner (IRE) (Red Sunset)

P Monteith (T D Barron 9/5) The Cattlemen

Placings:0640115/430000030/5606040004040400-0535202 **(7113)**

2009: 8^{0}F, 12^{5}G, 12^{3}GF, 12^{5}S, 9^{2}G, 9^{0}GF, 9^{2}GS,

	Starts	1st	2nd	3rd	Win & Pl
Career Total (Turf)	**31**	**2**	**2**	**2**	**14167**
Career Total (AW)	**8**	**0**	**0**	**1**	**1657**

81	10/06	Newb	1m	(0-85)	HVY	£6477
72	10/06	Wind	1m67y	(0-75)	SFT	£3238

Total win prize-money £9716

Going (Turf): Sf: 2-7 GS: 0-4 Gd: 0-14 GF: 0-5 Fm: 0-1
Distance: 5f/6f: 0-0 7f-8f: 1-13 9f-13f: 1-24 14f+: 0-2
Track : LH: 0-11 **RH: 1-22 Tight: 1-15** Gall: 0-5
Aids: Bl: 0-0 Vi: 0-1 Tstrap: 0-1 Ckp: 0-1
Best Rating: 86 4/07 Kemp 1m stand

Modest; stays 1m2f; acts in soft ground and on Polytrack.

Bedarra Boy

98(100) (49)**52**

3-y-o ch g Needwood Blade-Roonah Quay (IRE) (Soviet Lad (USA))

D W P Arbuthnot P M Claydon

Placings:0063003 **(6188)**

2009: 8^{0}SD, 6^{0}GF, 9^{6}F, 10^{3}GF, 11^{0}SD, 12^{0}GF, 15^{3}GF,

	Starts	1st	2nd	3rd	Win & Pl
Career Total (Turf)	**5**	**0**	**0**	**2**	**605**
Career Total (AW)	**2**	**0**	**0**	**0**	

Going (Turf): Sf: 0-0 GS: 0-0 Gd: 0-0 GF: 0-4 Fm: 0-1
Distance: 5f/6f: 0-0 7f-8f: 0-2 9f-13f: 0-4 14f+: 0-1
Track : LH: 0-3 RH: 0-3 Tight: 0-4 Gall: 0-0
Aids: Bl: 0-0 Vi: 0-0 Tstrap: 0-0 Ckp: 0-0
Best Rating: 52 7/09 Ling 1m2f gd-fm

Moderate; stays 1m2f and acts on fast ground.

Bedloe's Island (IRE)

104(84) (34)**74**

4-y-o b g Statue Of Liberty (USA)-Scenaria (IRE) (Scenic)

N Bycroft J G Lumsden & M F Hogan

Placings:060-14232 **(6220)**

2009: 5^{1}GF, 5^{4}G, 5^{2}G, 5^{3}GS, 5^{2}GF,

	Starts	1st	2nd	3rd	Win & Pl
Career Total (Turf)	**7**	**1**	**2**	**1**	**6082**
Career Total (AW)	**1**	**0**	**0**	**0**	

68	6/09	Rdcr	5f	(0-70)H	G-F	£2590

Total win prize-money £2590

Going (Turf): Sf: 0-0 GS: 0-2 Gd: 0-2 **GF: 1-3** Fm: 0-0
Distance: 5f/6f: 1-7 7f-8f: 0-1 9f-13f: 0-0 14f+: 0-0
Track : LH: 0-2 RH: 0-1 Tight: 0-2 Gall: 0-1
Aids: Bl: 0-0 Vi: 0-0 Tstrap: 0-0 Ckp: 0-0
Best Rating: 74 8/09 Bevl 5f good

Fair; effective at 5f; handles fast and easy ground.

Bedouin Blue (IRE)

(103) (71)**66**

6-y-o b g Desert Style (IRE)-Society Fair (FR) (Always Fair (USA))

A J Lidderdale Miss Lauren Meek

Placings:520/3114/62/12-0300 **(0972)**

2009: 11^{0}SD, 12^{3}SD, 12^{0}SD, 13^{0}SD,

	Starts	1st	2nd	3rd	Win & Pl
Career Total (Turf)	**7**	**2**	**2**	**1**	**8106**
Career Total (AW)	**8**	**1**	**1**	**1**	**4145**

66	3/08	Rdcr	1m2f		G-S	£1684
70	7/06	Wolv	1m4f50y	(0-75)H	STD	£3238
74	4/06	Rdcr	1m2f	(0-70)H	G-F	£3238

Total win prize-money £8162

Going (Turf): Sf: 0-2 **GS: 1-1** Gd: 0-2 **GF: 1-2** Fm: 0-0
Distance: 5f/6f: 0-0 7f-8f: 0-2 **9f-13f: 3-12** 14f+: 0-1
Track : LH: 3-12 RH: 0-2 **Tight: 3-9** Gall: 0-0
Aids: Bl: 1-4 Vi: 0-0 Tstrap: 0-3 Ckp: 0-3
Best Rating: 77 8/06 Ripn 1m4f10y heavy

Fair gelding; stays 1m4f; acts with give in the ground and on Polytrack.

Bedouin Style (IRE)

57

3-y-o b g Desert Style (IRE)-Samaritan Woman (IRE) (Priolo (USA))

Mrs A M Thorpe Mrs T Brown

Placings:0 **(2323)**

2009: 12^{0}G,

	Starts	1st	2nd	3rd	Win & Pl
Career Total (Turf)	1	0	0	0	

Going (Turf): Sf: 0-0 GS: 0-0 Gd: 0-1 GF: 0-0 Fm: 0-0
Distance: 5f/6f: 0-0 7f-8f: 0-0 9f-13f: 0-1 14f+: 0-0
Track : LH: 0-1 RH: 0-0 Tight: 0-0 Gall: 0-0
Aids: Bl: 0-0 Vi: 0-0 Tstrap: 0-0 Ckp: 0-0

Bee Sting

69(108) (96)**93**

5-y-o b g Selkirk (USA)-Desert Lynx (IRE) (Green Desert (USA))

Mrs L Williamson D Goulding

Placings:051/010653-0 **(1798)**

2009: 10^{0}GF,

	Starts	1st	2nd	3rd	Win & Pl
Career Total (Turf)	9	2	0	0	16217
Career Total (AW)	1	0	0	1	1120

93 8/08 NmkJ 1m2f (0-90)H G-F £10361
84 6/07 Ches 1m2f75y SFT £5505
Total win prize-money £15867

Going (Turf): Sf: 1-3 GS: 0-1 Gd: 0-1 GF: 1-4 Fm: 0-0
Distance: 5f/6f: 0-0 7f-8f: 0-1 9f-13f: 2-9 14f+: 0-0
Track : LH: 1-3 RH: 1-6 Tight: 1-3 Gall: 1-4
Aids: Bl: 0-1 Vi: 0-1 Tstrap: 0-2 Ckp: 0-2
Best Rating: 96 10/08 Kemp 1m4f stand

Useful; suited by 1m2f-1m4f; acts on any ground, including Polytrack; has worn cheekpieces.

Bee Stinger

(106) (81)**89**

7-y-o b g Almaty (IRE)-Nest Egg (Prince Sabo)

P R Hedger (B G Powell 5/12) P C F Racing Ltd

Placings:03224/5305030/11351010002/0304054/1552010 0000-00441420216 **(7776)**

2009: 9^{0}SD, 8^{0}SD, 10^{4}SD, 10^{4}SD, 8^{1}SD, 8^{4}SD, 10^{2}SD, 8^{0}SD, 12^{2}SD, 12^{1}SD, 10^{6}SD,

	Starts	1st	2nd	3rd	Win & Pl
Career Total (Turf)	19	3	2	4	43297
Career Total (AW)	33	5	4	1	22224

71 12/09 Wolv 1m4f50y STD £2729
81 3/09 Ling 1m (0-70)H STD £2900
88 3/08 Wolv 1m1f103y (0-80)H STD £4857
85 1/08 Ling 1m (0-75)H STD £2590
88 9/06 Folk 7f (0-80)H G-F £7772
89 8/06 Brig 7f214y (0-80)H FRM £21812
83 7/06 Wind 1m67y (0-90)H G-F £8724
83 5/06 Ling 1m (0-70)H STD £3238
Total win prize-money £54627

Going (Turf): Sf: 0-0 GS: 0-0 Gd: 0-4 GF: 2-14 Fm: 1-1
Distance: 5f/6f: 0-8 7f-8f: 5-27 9f-13f: 3-17 14f+: 0-0
Track : LH: 6-29 RH: 1-10 Tight: 6-29 Gall: 0-1
Aids: Bl: 1-6 Vi: 0-7 Tstrap: 0-1 Ckp: 0-1
Best Rating: 89 8/06 Brig 7f214y firm

Fair; effective at around 1m-1m4f; acts on fast ground; goes on Polytrack; has worn headgear.

Bees River (IRE)

92(95) (63)**71**

3-y-o b f Acclamation-Notley Park (Wolfhound (USA))

A P Jarvis Ambrose Turnbull

Placings:3U52236-3550403040 **(6379)**

2009: 5^{3}GF, 5^{5}SD, 5^{5}G, 6^{0}F, 5^{4}F, 6^{0}GS, 5^{3}F, 5^{0}GF, 5^{4}GS, 5^{0}GF,

	Starts	1st	2nd	3rd	Win & Pl
Career Total (Turf)	14	0	1	4	3766
Career Total (AW)	3	0	1	0	1156

Going (Turf): Sf: 0-3 GS: 0-2 Gd: 0-2 GF: 0-4 Fm: 0-3
Distance: 5f/6f: 0-17 7f-8f: 0-0 9f-13f: 0-0 14f+: 0-0
Track : LH: 0-8 RH: 0-0 Tight: 0-1 Gall: 0-5
Aids: Bl: 0-0 Vi: 0-4 Tstrap: 0-0 Ckp: 0-0
Best Rating: 71 5/08 Donc 5f gd-fm

Modest; effective over 5f and acts on most ground.

Beethoven (IRE)

112 (111)**118**

2-y-o b c Oratorio (IRE)-Queen Titi (IRE) (Sadler's Wells (USA))

A P O'Brien M Tabor, D Smith & Mrs John Magnier

Placings:32435134616 **(7307a)**

2009: 6^{3}G, 6^{2}GF, 7^{4}GF, 6^{3}SH, 6^{5}HY, 6^{1}G, 7^{3}SH, 6^{4}G, 7^{6}G, 7^{1}G, 8^{6}FT,

	Starts	1st	2nd	3rd	Win & Pl
Career Total (Turf)	10	2	1	3	295122
Career Total (AW)	1	0	0	0	0

118 10/09 NmkR 7f GD £180159
85 8/09 Leop 6f GD £11740
Total win prize-money £191900

Going (Turf): Sf: 0-1 GS: 0-0 Gd: 2-5 GF: 0-2 Fm: 0-0
Distance: 5f/6f: 1-5 7f-8f: 1-5 9f-13f: 0-1 14f+: 0-0
Track : LH: 1-3 RH: 0-1 Tight: 0-0 Gall: 0-0
Aids: Bl: 0-0 Vi: 1-2 Tstrap: 0-0 Ckp: 0-0
Best Rating: 118 10/09 NmkR 7f good

Group class; surprise winner of the Dewhurst Stakes in 2009; effective over 6-7f; handles good or softer ground; has worn a visor.

Before The War (USA)

(89) (56)

2-y-o ch c El Corredor (USA)-Adrenalin Running (USA) (A.P. Indy (USA))

L M Cumani R J Baines

Placings:05 **(7580)**

2009: 7^{0}SD, 7^{5}SF,

	Starts	1st	2nd	3rd	Win & Pl
Career Total (Turf)	0	0	0	0	
Career Total (AW)	2	0	0	0	0

Going (Turf): Sf: 0-0 GS: 0-0 Gd: 0-0 GF: 0-0 Fm: 0-0
Distance: 5f/6f: 0-0 7f-8f: 0-2 9f-13f: 0-0 14f+: 0-0
Track : LH: 0-1 RH: 0-1 Tight: 0-1 Gall: 0-0
Aids: Bl: 0-0 Vi: 0-0 Tstrap: 0-0 Ckp: 0-0
Best Rating: 56 11/09 Wolv 7f32y std-fst

Moderate form so far; handles Polytrack.

Befortyfour

100(107) (102)**109**

4-y-o b g Kyllachy-Ivania (First Trump)

M A Jarvis M F Bailey

Placings:20/11123-5 **(4059)**

2009: 5^{5}S,

	Starts	1st	2nd	3rd	Win & Pl
Career Total (Turf)	6	1	2	1	15177
Career Total (AW)	2	2	0	0	8955

109 6/08 Leic 5f2y (0-95)H G-F £8723
102 5/08 GrLe 5f (0-95)H STD £6623
86 4/08 Ling 5f STD £2331
Total win prize-money £17677

Going (Turf): Sf: 0-2 GS: 0-0 Gd: 0-0 GF: 1-4 Fm: 0-0
Distance: 5f/6f: 3-8 7f-8f: 0-0 9f-13f: 0-0 14f+: 0-0
Track : LH: 2-2 RH: 0-0 Tight: 1-1 Gall: 1-1
Aids: Bl: 0-0 Vi: 0-0 Tstrap: 0-0 Ckp: 0-0
Best Rating: 109 6/08 Leic 5f2y gd-fm

Smart; suited by 5f, acts on fast ground and on Polytrack; likes to race prominently.

Behind Blue Eyes

82(71) **46**

3-y-o b g Kyllachy-Mamoura (IRE) (Lomond (USA))

Karen George Adrian Parr & Karen George

Placings:000 **(1579)**

2009: 8^{0}SD, 7^{0}G, 10^{0}G,

	Starts	1st	2nd	3rd	Win & Pl
Career Total (Turf)	2	0	0	0	
Career Total (AW)	1	0	0	0	

Going (Turf): Sf: 0-0 GS: 0-0 Gd: 0-2 GF: 0-0 Fm: 0-0
Distance: 5f/6f: 0-0 7f-8f: 0-1 9f-13f: 0-2 14f+: 0-0
Track : LH: 0-2 RH: 0-0 Tight: 0-2 Gall: 0-0
Aids: Bl: 0-0 Vi: 0-1 Tstrap: 0-1 Ckp: 0-1
Best Rating: 46 4/09 Folk 7f good

Bel Cantor

106(107) (85)**95**

6-y-o b h Largesse-Palmstead Belle (IRE) (Wolfhound (USA))

W J H Ratcliffe W J H Ratcliffe

Placings:2433402300043/3210003561116/00503062126350163/2136530353051214000-060030100420002020001240 **(7758)**

2009: 6^{0}GF, 6^{6}F, 6^{0}G, 6^{0}GF, 6^{3}GF, 6^{0}G, 6^{1}SD, 6^{0}SD, 6^{0}G, 6^{4}G, 6^{2}GF, 6^{0}SD, 6^{0}GF, 6^{0}G, 5^{2}GF, 6^{0}G, 6^{2}GF, 6^{0}GF, 5^{0}G, 5^{1}SD, 5^{2}SD, 5^{4}SD, 5^{0}SD,

	Starts	1st	2nd	3rd	Win & Pl
Career Total (Turf)	62	7	9	10	75467
Career Total (AW)	20	3	2	4	14663

85 11/09 Sthl 5f (0-75)H STD £4921
84 7/09 Kemp 6f (0-75)H STD £2590
95 8/08 Ripn 6f (0-100)H GD £12462
86 7/08 Pont 6f (0-90)H G-F £9346
80 2/08 Wolv 5f216y (0-70)H STD £2331
86 10/07 Catt 7f (0-85)H GD £4857
83 7/07 Pont 6f (0-90)H G-S £8101
85 10/06 Nott 6f15y (0-70)H HVY £3238
83 10/06 Nott 6f15y (0-75)H SFT £3238
72 5/06 Pont 6f G-S £5181
Total win prize-money £56273

Going (Turf): Sf: 2-10 GS: 2-10 Gd: 2-17 GF: 1-19 Fm: 0-6
Distance: 5f/6f: 7-72 7f-8f: 3-10 9f-13f: 0-0 14f+: 0-0
Track : LH: 5-35 RH: 1-4 Tight: 2-18 Gall: 0-2

Aids: Bl: 0-0 Vi: 0-0 Tstrap: 5-43 Ckp: 5-43
Best Rating: **95** 8/08 Ripn 6f good

Fair; effective over 5f-7f; acts on any ground and on sand; often wears cheekpieces; likes to race prominently.

Belated Silver (IRE)

95(100) (74)**72**
3-y-o gr/ro g Clodovil (IRE)-Premier Place (USA) (Out Of Place (USA))
Tom Dascombe Findlay & Bloom

Placings:054216-443613 **(3577)**
2009: 7^{4}SD, 8^{4}F, 7^{3}SD, 7^{6}S, **5^{1}SD**, 6^{3}GF,

	Starts	1st	2nd	3rd	Win & Pl
Career Total (Turf)	7	0	1	1	2147
Career Total (AW)	5	2	0	1	7614

74 6/09 Wolv 5f216y STD £2914
73 11/08 Ling 7f (0-75) STD £3885
Total win prize-money £6800

Going (Turf): **Sf: 0-3 GS: 0-0 Gd: 0-2 GF: 0-1 Fm: 0-1**
Distance: 5f/6f: 1-3 7f-8f: 1-9 9f-13f: 0-0 14f+: 0-0
Track : **LH: 2-9** RH: 0-0 **Tight: 2-5** Gall: 0-1
Aids: Bl: 0-0 Vi: 0-0 Tstrap: 0-0 Ckp: 0-0
Best Rating: **74** 6/09 Wolv 5f216y stand

Fair; stays 7f and acts on Polytrack.

Belgooree

(64) (16)
2-y-o b f Haafhd-Ziggy Zaggy (Diktat)
J G Given J Ellis

Placings:0 **(7630)**
2009: 7^{0}SD,

	Starts	1st	2nd	3rd	Win & Pl
Career Total (Turf)	0	0	0	0	
Career Total (AW)	1	0	0	0	

Going (Turf): **Sf: 0-0 GS: 0-0 Gd: 0-0 GF: 0-0 Fm: 0-0**
Distance: 5f/6f: 0-0 7f-8f: 0-1 9f-13f: 0-0 14f+: 0-0
Track : LH: 0-1 RH: 0-0 Tight: 0-1 Gall: 0-0
Aids: Bl: 0-0 Vi: 0-0 Tstrap: 0-0 Ckp: 0-0
Best Rating: **16** 12/09 Wolv 7f32y stand

Belinsky (IRE)

88(91) (71)**69**
2-y-o b c Compton Place-Westwood (FR) (Anabaa (USA))
S A Callaghan Michael Tabor

Placings:36341 **(5583)**
2009: 5^{3}GF, 6^{6}GF, 5^{3}SD, 6^{4}SD, **6^{1}SD**,

	Starts	1st	2nd	3rd	Win & Pl
Career Total (Turf)	2	0	0	1	698
Career Total (AW)	3	1	0	1	2625

64 9/09 Ling 6f STD £2047
Total win prize-money £2047

Going (Turf): **Sf: 0-0 GS: 0-0 Gd: 0-0 GF: 0-2 Fm: 0-0**
Distance: **5f/6f: 1-5** 7f-8f: 0-0 9f-13f: 0-0 14f+: 0-0
Track : **LH: 1-2** RH: 0-0 **Tight: 1-1** Gall: 0-2
Aids: Bl: 0-0 Vi: 0-0 Tstrap: 0-0 Ckp: 0-0
Best Rating: **71** 7/09 Sthl 5f stand

Fair; suited by 5f; acts on fast ground, Polytrack and Fibresand.

Bell Island

98(111) (83)**83**
5-y-o b g Dansili-Thermal Spring (Zafonic (USA))
Lady Herries L G Lazarus

Placings:2534550/4105640-01154465140 **(7695)**
2009: 10^{0}SD, 13^{1}SD, 13^{1}SD, 16^{5}SD, 13^{4}GF, 14^{4}G, 13^{6}GF, 11^{5}GF, 13^{1}SS, 13^{4}SD, 12^{0}SD,

	Starts	1st	2nd	3rd	Win & Pl
Career Total (Turf)	14	1	1	1	13010
Career Total (AW)	11	3	0	0	11083

75 10/09 Ling 1m5f (0-75)H SS £3238
81 3/09 Ling 1m5f (0-75)H STD £2900
83 2/09 Ling 1m5f (0-70)H STD £2900
83 6/08 Brig 1m3f196y G-F £2525
Total win prize-money £11564

Going (Turf): Sf: 0-3 GS: 0-2 Gd. 0-4 **GF: 1-5** Fm: 0-0
Distance: 5f/6f: 0-0 7f-8f: 0-0 **9f-13f: 4-19** 14f+: 0-6
Track : **LH: 4-11** RH: 0-9 **Tight: 3-9** Gall: 0-5
Aids: Bl: 0-2 **Vi: 3-10** Tstrap: 0-2 Ckp: 0-2
Best Rating: **91** 5/07 Chan 1m2f gd-sft

Fair; stays 1m5f; acts on Polytrack; has worn cheekpieces and a visor.

Bell's Ocean (USA)

94(93) (67)**75**
2-y-o b f Proud Citizen (USA)-Golden Train (USA) (Slew O'Gold (USA))
J Ryan Ocean Trailers Ltd

Placings:251060033500 **(6905)**
2009: 5^{2}GF, 6^{5}GF, **6^{1}GF**, 6^{0}GF, 7^{6}GF, 6^{0}G, 6^{0}GF, 6^{3}SD, 6^{3}GS, 6^{5}SD, 6^{0}G, 6^{0}G,

	Starts	1st	2nd	3rd	Win & Pl
Career Total (Turf)	10	1	1	1	6722
Career Total (AW)	2	0	0	1	337

75 5/09 NmkR 6f G-F £5180
Total win prize-money £5181

Going (Turf): Sf: 0-0 GS: 0-1 Gd: 0-3 **GF: 1-6** Fm: 0-0
Distance: **5f/6f: 1-11** 7f-8f: 0-1 9f-13f: 0-0 14f+: 0-0
Track : LH: 0-0 RH: 0-2 Tight: 0-0 Gall: 0-3
Aids: Bl: 0-0 Vi: 0-0 Tstrap: 0-0 Ckp: 0-0
Best Rating: **75** 5/09 NmkR 6f gd-fm

Fair; effective over 6f; acts on most ground.

Bella Charlie (IRE)

(78) (61)
2-y-o b c Pyrus (USA)-Beseeching (IRE) (Hamas (IRE))
M G Quinlan The Chicken On A Chain Partnership

Placings:066 **(7864)**
2009: 7^{0}SD, 7^{6}SD, 6^{6}SS,

	Starts	1st	2nd	3rd	Win & Pl
Career Total (Turf)	0	0	0	0	
Career Total (AW)	3	0	0	0	0

Going (Turf): **Sf: 0-0 GS: 0-0 Gd: 0-0 GF: 0-0 Fm: 0-0**
Distance: 5f/6f: 0-1 7f-8f: 0-2 9f-13f: 0-0 14f+: 0-0
Track : LH: 0-1 RH: 0-2 Tight: 0-0 Gall: 0-0
Aids: Bl: 0-0 Vi: 0-0 Tstrap: 0-0 Ckp: 0-0
Best Rating: **61** 11/09 Kemp 7f stand

Bella Fighetta

74(88) (38)**11**
3-y-o b f Bertolini (USA)-My Girl (Mon Tresor)
Ms J S Doyle John H Sissons

Placings:06650 **(7629)**
2009: 10^{0}S, 8^{6}SD, 7^{6}SD, 6^{5}SD, 5^{0}SD,

	Starts	1st	2nd	3rd	Win & Pl
Career Total (Turf)	1	0	0	0	
Career Total (AW)	4	0	0	0	0

Going (Turf): **Sf: 0-1 GS: 0-0 Gd: 0-0 GF: 0-0 Fm: 0-0**
Distance: 5f/6f: 0-2 7f-8f: 0-2 9f-13f: 0-1 14f+: 0-0
Track : LH: 0-3 RH: 0-2 Tight: 0-2 Gall: 0-0
Aids: Bl: 0-1 Vi: 0-0 Tstrap: 0-1 Ckp: 0-1
Best Rating: **38** 11/09 Kemp 6f stand

Bella Medici

(99) (60)**68**
4-y-o ch f Medicean-Missouri (Charnwood Forest (IRE))
P G Murphy Miss J Collison

Placings:01020R60-0 **(0502)**
2009: 16^{0}SD,

	Starts	1st	2nd	3rd	Win & Pl
Career Total (Turf)	7	1	1	0	2521
Career Total (AW)	2	0	0	0	

54 7/08 Yarm 1m2f21y G-F £1942
Total win prize-money £1943

Going (Turf): Sf: 0-0 GS: 0-1 Gd: 0-4 **GF: 1-2** Fm: 0-0
Distance: 5f/6f: 0-0 7f-8f: 0-0 **9f-13f: 1-7** 14f+: 0-2
Track : **LH: 1-5** RH: 0-4 **Tight: 1-5** Gall: 0-2
Aids: Bl: 0-0 Vi: 0-0 Tstrap: 0-0 Ckp: 0-0
Best Rating: **68** 8/08 Yarm 1m3f101y gd-sft

Moderate; effective at 1m 4f; acts on fast and easy ground.

Bella Rowena

85 **70**
3-y-o b f Kyllachy-Luxurious (USA) (Lyphard (USA))
A M Balding Horses for Causes

Placings:646-00 **(3387)**
2009: 7^{0}GF, 7^{0}GF,

	Starts	1st	2nd	3rd	Win & Pl
Career Total (Turf)	5	0	0	0	962

Going (Turf): **Sf: 0-1 GS: 0-1 Gd: 0-0 GF: 0-3 Fm: 0-0**
Distance: 5f/6f: 0-2 7f-8f: 0-3 9f-13f: 0-0 14f+: 0-0
Track : LH: 0-1 RH: 0-1 Tight: 0-1 Gall: 0-0
Aids: Bl: 0-0 Vi: 0-0 Tstrap: 0-0 Ckp: 0-0
Best Rating: **70** 7/08 Gdwd 7f gd-fm

Bella Swan

99 **88**
2-y-o ch f Leporello (IRE)-Lydia Maria (Dancing Brave (USA))
W R Swinburn Pendley Farm

Placings:32154 **(6447)**
2009: 6^{3}GF, 5^{2}GF, **6^{1}GF**, 7^{5}G, 7^{4}GF,

	Starts	1st	2nd	3rd	Win & Pl
Career Total (Turf)	5	1	1	1	15671

85 7/09 NmkJ 6f G-F £9714
Total win prize-money £9714

Going (Turf): Sf: 0-0 GS: 0-0 Gd: 0-1 **GF: 1-4** Fm: 0-0

Distance: **5f/6f: 1-3** 7f-8f: 0-2 9f-13f: 0-0 14f+: 0-0
Track : LH: 0-0 RH: 0-1 Tight: 0-0 Gall: 0-0
Aids: Bl: 0-0 Vi: 0-0 Tstrap: 0-0 Ckp: 0-0
Best Rating: 88 10/09 NmkR 7f gd-fm

Useful; effective over 6f; acts on fast ground.

Bellaharry (IRE)

78(75) (24)**37**
2-y-o b f Lucky Story (USA)-Saharan Song (IRE) (Singspiel (IRE))
Matthew Salaman (M Salaman 31/8) Mrs P G Lewin & D Grieve

Placings:060 (7120)
2009: 8^{0}G, 7^{6}SD, 8^{0}GF,

	Starts	1st	2nd	3rd	Win & Pl
Career Total (Turf)	2	0	0	0	
Career Total (AW)	1	0	0	0	0

Going (Turf): Sf: 0-0 GS: 0-0 Gd: 0-1 GF: 0-1 Fm: 0-0
Distance: 5f/6f: 0-0 7f-8f: 0-1 9f-13f: 0-2 14f+: 0-0
Track : LH: 0-2 RH: 0-0 Tight: 0-1 Gall: 0-0
Aids: Bl: 0-0 Vi: 0-0 Tstrap: 0-0 Ckp: 0-0
Best Rating: 37 8/09 Chep 1m14y good

Belle Bellino (FR)

87 **64**
4-y-o b f Robellino (USA)-Hoh Chi Min (Efisio)
R M Beckett Terry Cooper

Placings:000/45010-60 (1591)
2009: 5^{6}GF, 5^{0}GS,

	Starts	1st	2nd	3rd	Win & Pl
Career Total (Turf)	10	1	0	0	2831
64 9/08 Bath 5f161y			SFT	£2590	

Total win prize-money £2590

Going (Turf): Sf: 1-2 GS: 0-4 Gd: 0-1 GF: 0-2 Fm: 0-1
Distance: **5f/6f: 1-8** 7f-8f: 0-2 9f-13f: 0-0 14f+: 0-0
Track : **LH: 1-2** RH: 0-0 Tight: 0-0 **Gall: 1-3**
Aids: Bl: 0-0 Vi: 0-0 Tstrap: 0-0 Ckp: 0-0
Best Rating: 65 7/07 Gdwd 6f gd-sft

Modest filly; stays 6f; acts on good ground.

Belle Des Airs (IRE)

105 **90**
3-y-o ch f Dr Fong (USA)-Belle Reine (King Of Kings (IRE))
R M Beckett Mrs M E Slade

Placings:6120-4225312 (5918)
2009: 7^{4}GS, 6^{2}G, 7^{2}S, 6^{5}GS, 7^{3}G, 7^{1}GF, 7^{2}GF,

	Starts	1st	2nd	3rd	Win & Pl
Career Total (Turf)	11	2	4	1	19860
89 9/09 Epsm 7f	(0-85)H			G-F	£6476
73 7/08 Leic 5f218y				G-F	£3885

Total win prize-money £10362

Going (Turf): Sf: 0-2 GS: 0-3 Gd: 0-3 **GF: 2-3** Fm: 0-0
Distance: 5f/6f: 1-4 7f-8f: 1-7 9f-13f: 0-0 14f+: 0-0
Track : **LH: 1-1** RH: 0-1 **Tight: 1-1** Gall: 0-0
Aids: Bl: 0-0 Vi: 0-0 Tstrap: 0-0 Ckp: 0-0
Best Rating: 90 9/09 Gdwd 7f gd-fm

Useful; effective over 6-7f; acts on fast and easy ground.

Belle Eponine

91(81) (54)**59**
2-y-o b f Fraam-Red Ryding Hood (Wolfhound (USA))
E J O'Neill Mrs P A L Butler

Placings:601000 (6960a)
2009: 5^{6}GF, 6^{0}GF, 7^{1}GF, 7^{0}SD, 7^{0}G, 9^{0}SD,

	Starts	1st	2nd	3rd	Win & Pl
Career Total (Turf)	4	1	0	0	1943
Career Total (AW)	2	0	0	0	
59 6/09 Rdcr 7f			G-F	£1942	

Total win prize-money £1943

Going (Turf): Sf: 0-0 GS: 0-0 Gd: 0-1 **GF: 1-3** Fm: 0-0
Distance: 5f/6f: 0-2 **7f-8f: 1-3** 9f-13f: 0-1 14f+: 0-0
Track : LH: 0-1 RH: 0-0 Tight: 0-0 Gall: 0-0
Aids: Bl: 0-0 Vi: 0-0 Tstrap: 0-0 Ckp: 0-0
Best Rating: 59 6/09 Rdcr 7f gd-fm

Moderate filly; stays 7f; acts on fast ground.

Belle Noverre (IRE)

95(99) (79)**76**
5-y-o b m Noverre (USA)-Belle Etoile (FR) (Lead On Time (USA))
Shaun Harley (J S Bolger 15/6) Lough Derg Syndicate

Placings:0040301/12022306060-000**450046** (7399)
2009: 6^{0}YS, 9^{0}GF, 10^{0}G, 8^{4}GF, 6^{5}SD, 8^{0}SD, 7^{0}G, 10^{4}SD, 9^{6}SD,

	Starts	1st	2nd	3rd	Win & Pl
Career Total (Turf)	20	0	3	2	11397
Career Total (AW)	7	2	0	0	10576
73 4/08 Dund 7f	(50-75)H			STD	£5334
71 11/07 Dund 1m	(50-70)H			STD	£4902

Total win prize-money £10237

Going (Turf): Sf: 0-1 GS: 0-0 Gd: 0-6 GF: 0-6 Fm: 0-1
Distance: 5f/6f: 0-3 **7f-8f: 2-14** 9f-13f: 0-10 14f+: 0-0
Track : **LH: 1-11** RH: 0-9 Tight: 0-2 Gall: 0-1
Aids: Bl: 0-0 Vi: 0-0 Tstrap: 0-13 Ckp: 0-13
Best Rating: 84 6/08 Leop 1m gd-fm

Belle Park

86(90) (51)**33**
2-y-o b f Hamairi (IRE)-Cape Siren (Warning)
Karen George Eastington Racing Club

Placings:0000 (7661)
2009: 5^{0}SD, 5^{0}G, 8^{0}SD, 6^{0}SD,

	Starts	1st	2nd	3rd	Win & Pl
Career Total (Turf)	1	0	0	0	
Career Total (AW)	3	0	0	0	

Going (Turf): Sf: 0-0 GS: 0-0 Gd: 0-1 GF: 0-0 Fm: 0-0
Distance: 5f/6f: 0-3 7f-8f: 0-1 9f-13f: 0-0 14f+: 0-0
Track : LH: 0-2 RH: 0-2 Tight: 0-1 Gall: 0-1
Aids: Bl: 0-0 Vi: 0-0 Tstrap: 0-0 Ckp: 0-0
Best Rating: 51 11/09 Kemp 1m stand

Belle Zorro

(84) (52)
2-y-o br f Dr Fong (USA)-Special Beat (Bustino)
M L W Bell Vega Group

Placings:000 (6627)
2009: 8^{0}SD, 8^{0}SD, 7^{0}SS,

	Starts	1st	2nd	3rd	Win & Pl
Career Total (Turf)	0	0	0	0	
Career Total (AW)	3	0	0	0	

Going (Turf): Sf: 0-0 GS: 0-0 Gd: 0-0 GF: 0-0 Fm: 0-0
Distance: 5f/6f: 0-0 7f-8f: 0-3 9f-13f: 0-0 14f+: 0-0
Track : LH: 0-1 RH: 0-2 Tight: 0-1 Gall: 0-0
Aids: Bl: 0-0 Vi: 0-0 Tstrap: 0-0 Ckp: 0-0
Best Rating: 52 9/09 Kemp 1m stand

Belles Beau

(79) (43)
2-y-o b f Fraam-Victory Flip (IRE) (Victory Note (USA))
R Hollinshead Tim Leadbeater

Placings:0 (7800)
2009: 7^{0}SD,

	Starts	1st	2nd	3rd	Win & Pl
Career Total (Turf)	0	0	0	0	
Career Total (AW)	1	0	0	0	

Going (Turf): Sf: 0-0 GS: 0-0 Gd: 0-0 GF: 0-0 Fm: 0-0
Distance: 5f/6f: 0-0 7f-8f: 0-1 9f-13f: 0-0 14f+: 0-0
Track : LH: 0-1 RH: 0-0 Tight: 0-1 Gall: 0-0
Aids: Bl: 0-0 Vi: 0-0 Tstrap: 0-0 Ckp: 0-0
Best Rating: 43 12/09 Wolv 7f32y stand

Bellini Rose (IRE)

(94) (65)
2-y-o b f Bertolini (USA)-Prospectress (USA) (Mining (USA))
Tom Dascombe Five Horses Ltd

Placings:14 (7251)
2009: 5^{1}SS, 7^{4}SD,

	Starts	1st	2nd	3rd	Win & Pl
Career Total (Turf)	0	0	0	0	
Career Total (AW)	2	1	0	0	3018
65 10/09 Ling 5f			SS	£2729	

Total win prize-money £2730

Going (Turf): Sf: 0-0 GS: 0-0 Gd: 0-0 GF: 0-0 Fm: 0-0
Distance: **5f/6f: 1-1** 7f-8f: 0-1 9f-13f: 0-0 14f+: 0-0
Track : **LH: 1-2** RH: 0-0 **Tight: 1-2** Gall: 0-0
Aids: Bl: 0-0 Vi: 0-0 Tstrap: 0-0 Ckp: 0-0
Best Rating: 65 10/09 Ling 5f std-slw

Modest; effective at 5f on Polytrack.

Bellomi (IRE)

86(99) (75)**94**
4-y-o gr g Lemon Drop Kid (USA)-Reina Blanca (Darshaan)
A G Juckes Whispering Winds

Placings:22210/061010040-00 (2149)
2009: 7^{0}GF, 8^{0}G,

	Starts	1st	2nd	3rd	Win & Pl
Career Total (Turf)	12	3	3	0	26160
Career Total (AW)	4	0	0	0	0
85 8/08 NmkJ 7f				GD	£3885
94 6/08 Epsm 7f	(0-100)H			GD	£12462
83 9/07 Ches 7f2y				G-F	£5505

Total win prize-money £21853

Going (Turf): Sf: 0-0 GS: 0-1 **Gd: 2-5** GF: 1-6 Fm: 0-0
Distance: 5f/6f: 0-2 **7f-8f: 3-13** 9f-13f: 0-1 14f+: 0-0
Track : **LH: 2-8** RH: 0-2 **Tight: 2-5** Gall: 0-0
Aids: Bl: 0-0 Vi: 0-0 Tstrap: 0-1 Ckp: 0-1
Best Rating: 94 6/08 Epsm 7f good

Below Zero (IRE)

92 93

2-y-o b c Shamardal (USA)-Chilly Start (IRE) (Caerleon (USA))

M Johnston Sheikh Hamdan Bin Mohammed Al Maktoum

Placings:31 **(2649)**

2009: 6^{3}G, 5^{1}F,

	Starts	1st	2nd	3rd	Win & Pl
Career Total (Turf)	2	1	0	1	4632

93 6/09 Bath 5f161y FRM £3885

Total win prize-money £3886

Going (Turf): Sf: 0-0 GS: 0-0 Gd: 0-1 GF: 0-0 **Fm: 1-1**
Distance: **5f/6f: 1-2** 7f-8f: 0-0 9f-13f: 0-0 14f+: 0-0
Track : **LH: 1-1** RH: 0-0 Tight: 0-0 **Gall: 1-1**
Aids: Bl: 0-0 Vi: 0-0 Tstrap: 0-0 Ckp: 0-0
Best Rating: **93** 6/09 Bath 5f161y firm

Useful juvenile; effective at 6f; handles firm ground.

Ben

(97) (64)58

4-y-o b g Bertolini (USA)-Bold Byzantium (Bold Arrangement)

P G Murphy Mrs Dianne Murphy

Placings:4423353266330/40310250004-0000 **(1038)**

2009: 5^{0}SD, 6^{0}SD, 5^{0}SD, 5^{0}SD,

	Starts	1st	2nd	3rd	Win & Pl
Career Total (Turf)	13	0	3	3	4794
Career Total (AW)	15	1	0	3	4005

56 4/08 Kemp 5f STD £2456

Total win prize-money £2457

Going (Turf): Sf: 0-1 **GS: 0-1** Gd: 0-3 **GF: 0-6 Fm: 0-2**
Distance: **5f/6f: 1-28** 7f-8f: 0-0 9f-13f: 0-0 14f+: 0-0
Track : LH: 0-16 **RH: 1-4** Tight: 0-10 Gall: 0-1
Aids: Bl: 0-2 **Vi: 1-10** Tstrap: 0-0 Ckp: 0-0
Best Rating: **73** 7/07 Sand 5f6y good

Modest; effective over 5f; acts on fast and easy ground; also goes on Polytrack.

Ben Bacchus (IRE)

92(102) (57)39

7-y-o b g Bahhare (USA)-Bodfaridistinction (IRE) (Distinctly North (USA))

P W Hiatt Exors of the Late John Hedges

Placings:050/0500030/2000/0213050S0403-1550600366 **(3594)**

2009: 12^{1}SD, 12^{5}SD, 13^{5}SD, 12^{0}SD, 11^{6}SD, 12^{0}GS, 11^{0}GF, 11^{3}GF, 12^{6}SD, 12^{6}GF,

	Starts	1st	2nd	3rd	Win & Pl
Career Total (Turf)	15	0	0	2	930
Career Total (AW)	21	2	2	2	6017

57 1/09 Kemp 1m4f (0-55)H STD £3043
55 2/08 Kemp 1m4f (0-45) STD £1365

Total win prize-money £4409

Going (Turf): **Sf: 0-2 GS: 0-5 Gd: 0-2 GF: 0-6 Fm: 0-0**
Distance: 5f/6f: 0-0 7f-8f: 0-3 **9f-13f: 2-27** 14f+: 0-6
Track : LH: 0-25 **RH: 2-10** Tight: 0-15 Gall: 0-2
Aids: Bl: 0-5 Vi: 0-0 Tstrap: 0-0 Ckp: 0-0
Best Rating: **57** 1/09 Kemp 1m4f stand

Moderate; stays 1m5f; acts on fast ground and on Polytrack.

Ben Chorley

104 (23)98

5-y-o gr g Inchinor-Arantxa (Sharpo)

D R Lanigan Diamond Racing Ltd

Placings:01/0/111-50 **(3873)**

2009: 8^{5}GF, 10^{0}GF,

	Starts	1st	2nd	3rd	Win & Pl
Career Total (Turf)	7	4	0	0	19875
Career Total (AW)	1	0	0	0	

98 6/08 Ripn 1m1f (0-90)H SFT £8723
90 5/08 Newb 1m (0-80)H SFT £5504
85 4/08 Pont 1m4y (0-75)H G-S £3238
73 9/06 Newc 7f GD £1943

Total win prize-money £19409

Going (Turf): **Sf: 2-2** GS: 1-1 Gd: 1-2 GF: 0-2 Fm: 0-0
Distance: 5f/6f: 0-1 7f-8f: 2-3 9f-13f: 2-4 14f+: 0-0
Track : LH: 1-3 RH: 1-1 **Tight: 1-1** Gall: 0-1
Aids: Bl: 0-0 Vi: 0-0 Tstrap: 0-0 Ckp: 0-0
Best Rating: **98** 6/08 Ripn 1m1f soft

Very useful; effective over 1m-1m1f; suited by good and softer ground; likes to race prominently.

Ben's Dream (IRE)

102(97) (48)73

3-y-o br g Kyllachy-Kelso Magic (USA) (Distant View (USA))

A M Balding Alan Halsall

Placings:0422-550414003 **(6739)**

2009: 6^{5}SD, 5^{5}GF, 6^{0}F, 5^{4}G, 6^{1}G, 6^{4}GF, 6^{0}GS, 6^{0}SD, 6^{3}GS,

	Starts	1st	2nd	3rd	Win & Pl
Career Total (Turf)	11	1	2	1	10055
Career Total (AW)	2	0	0	0	0

70 7/09 Wwck 6f (0-80)H GD £6476

Total win prize-money £6476

Going (Turf): Sf: 0-1 GS: 0-3 **Gd: 1-3** GF: 0-3 Fm: 0-1
Distance: **5f/6f: 1-13** 7f-8f: 0-0 9f-13f: 0-0 14f+: 0-0
Track : **LH: 1-2** RH: 0-2 Tight: 0-0 Gall: 0-4
Aids: Bl: 0-0 Vi: 0-0 Tstrap: 0-1 Ckp: 0-1
Best Rating: **73** 7/09 Wind 6f gd-fm

Fair; effective over 5-6f; acts on fast and easy ground.

Benandonner (USA)

107(110) (102)103

6-y-o ch g Giant's Causeway (USA)-Cape Verdi (IRE) (Caerleon (USA))

Mike Murphy (R A Fahey 7/12) Phil Woods

Placings:6423232120/2303316500/212260003-40201400032314 **(7827)**

2009: 7^{4}SD, 8^{0}GF, 7^{2}SD, 8^{0}S, 8^{1}GF, 7^{4}S, 7^{0}GF, 8^{0}G, 8^{0}G, 8^{3}GF, 8^{2}G, 8^{3}SD, 7^{1}SD, 8^{4}SD,

	Starts	1st	2nd	3rd	Win & Pl
Career Total (Turf)	32	3	6	6	67870
Career Total (AW)	11	2	4	2	23583

79 12/09 Ling 7f STD £1978
103 6/09 Ripn 1m (0-95)H G-F £8831
98 4/08 Sthl 1m (0-100)H STD £10361
98 8/07 Asct 1m (0-100)H G-F £17234
83 9/06 Nott 1m1f213y (0-75)H GD £3238

Total win prize-money £41645

Going (Turf): Sf: 0-7 GS: 0-3 Gd: 1-9 **GF: 2-12** Fm: 0-0
Distance: 5f/6f: 0-2 **7f-8f: 4-24** 9f-13f: 1-17 14f+: 0-0
Track : **LH: 3-19** RH: 2-11 **Tight: 2-12** Gall: 1-7
Aids: Bl: 0-0 Vi: 0-0 Tstrap: 0-0 Ckp: 0-0
Best Rating: **106** 4/08 Newb 1m soft

Very useful; effective over 7f-1m; acts on most ground; goes on sand; suited by forcing tactics.

Benayoun

91(97) (57)44

5-y-o b g Inchinor-Sosumi (Be My Chief (USA))

B J Llewellyn Gethyn Mills

Placings:0516/04053-6 **(2609)**

2009: 12^{6}GF,

	Starts	1st	2nd	3rd	Win & Pl
Career Total (Turf)	4	1	0	0	2389
Career Total (AW)	6	0	0	1	262

55 10/06 Nott 1m54y SFT £2388

Total win prize-money £2389

Going (Turf): **Sf: 1-2** GS: 0-1 Gd: 0-0 GF: 0-1 Fm: 0-0
Distance: 5f/6f: 0-1 7f-8f: 0-5 **9f-13f: 1-4** 14f+: 0-0
Track : **LH: 1-6** RH: 0-2 Tight: 0-4 Gall: 0-0
Aids: Bl: 0-2 Vi: 0-0 Tstrap: 0-0 Ckp: 0-0
Best Rating: **57** 11/06 Kemp 1m stand

Moderate performer; effective over a mile; acts on soft ground.

Benbaun (IRE)

116 120

8-y-o b g Stravinsky (USA)-Escape To Victory (Salse (USA))

K A Ryan Ransley, Birks, Hillen

Placings:04016120/1012132/20151206/2222153/101110/5020563-0231244 **(6522a)**

2009: 5^{0}Y, 5^{2}G, 5^{3}G, 5^{1}GY, 5^{2}GF, 5^{4}G, 5^{4}G,

	Starts	1st	2nd	3rd	Win & Pl
Career Total (Turf)	50	13	12	4	811693

114 6/09 Curr 5f G-Y £40825
124 10/07 Lonc 5f G-S £96520
123 9/07 Curr 6f G-F £32939
123 9/07 Curr 5f GD £32939
119 5/07 Curr 6f G-F £35135
119 8/06 Curr 5f GD £33620
117 9/05 Curr 5f GD £34574
117 6/05 Curr 5f G-F £46170
99 6/04 Sand 5f6y C G-F £9048
98 5/04 Thsk 5f C(0-100)H G-F £9821
90 5/04 Hayd 6f D(0-85)H GD £5791
82 9/03 Rdcr 5f E(0-75) FRM £3234
62 8/03 Chep 5f16y D H G-F £5040

Total win prize-money £385660

Going (Turf): Sf: 0-4 GS: 1-2 Gd: 4-14 **GF: 6-22** Fm: 1-3
Distance: **5f/6f: 13-45** 7f-8f: 0-5 9f-13f: 0-0 14f+: 0-0
Track : LH: 0-5 RH: 0-3 Tight: 0-2 Gall: 0-0
Aids: **Bl: 7-16** Vi: 5-28 Tstrap: 0-0 Ckp: 0-0
Best Rating: **124** 10/07 Lonc 5f gd-sft

Group class; winner of 2007 Prix de l'Abbaye; runner-up in the 2009 Nunthorpe; effective over 5f-6f; acts best on fast ground, but handles soft; usually wears headgear; has a fantastic record at the Curragh.

Bencoolen (IRE)

106(90) (52)99

4-y-o b g Daylami (IRE)-Jakarta (IRE) (Machiavellian (USA))

D Nicholls Eamon Maher

Placings:510/5551001-203000130 **(6480)**

2009: 8^{2}GF, 10^{0}G, 8^{3}GF, 10^{0}GF, 8^{0}G, 8^{0}G, 9^{1}S, 8^{3}GS, 9^{0}GF,

	Starts	1st	2nd	3rd	Win & Pl
Career Total (Turf)	18	4	1	2	29779
Career Total (AW)	1	0	0	0	

99 8/09 Gdwd 1m1f (0-90)H SFT £12952
93 10/08 NmkR 1m2f (0-85)H G-F £0
88 7/08 Wwck 1m2f188y (0-85)H GD £6476
79 8/07 Chep 1m14y G-F £3562
Total win prize-money £22990

Going (Turf): Sf: 1-1 GS: 0-3 Gd: 1-7 **GF: 2-7** Fm: 0-0
Distance: 5f/6f: 0-0 7f-8f: 0-5 **9f-13f: 4-14** 14f+: 0-0
Track : LH: 1-8 RH: 1-6 **Tight: 1-8** Gall: 0-2
Aids: Bl: 0-0 Vi: 0-1 Tstrap: 1-2 Ckp: 1-2
Best Rating: **99** 8/09 Gdwd 1m1f soft

Very useful; stays 1m2f; acts on fast and soft ground; has worn cheekpieces and a visor.

Bended Knee

99 80
3-y-o b f Refuse To Bend (IRE)-Flavian (Catrail (USA))
H Candy Major M G Wyatt

Placings:2231 **(7189)**
2009: 8^{2}F, 7^{2}G, 6^{3}G, 7^{1}G,

	Starts	1st	2nd	3rd	Win & Pl
Career Total (Turf)	4	1	2	1	7155

80 10/09 NmkR 7f (0-85)H GD £5180
Total win prize-money £5181

Going (Turf): Sf: 0-0 GS: 0-0 **Gd: 1-3** GF: 0-0 Fm: 0-1
Distance: 5f/6f: 0-1 **7f-8f: 1-2** 9f-13f: 0-1 14f+: 0-0
Track : LH: 0-1 RH: 0-0 Tight: 0-1 Gall: 0-1
Aids: Bl: 0-0 Vi: 0-0 Tstrap: 0-0 Ckp: 0-0
Best Rating: **80** 10/09 NmkR 7f good

Modest; effective over 6f-1m; acts on good and fast ground.

Benedict Spirit (IRE)

102(107) (78)75
4-y-o b g Invincible Spirit (IRE)-Kathy Caerleon (IRE) (Caerleon (USA))
D Burchell (M H Tompkins 30/5) Jason Tucker

Placings:03/410401-15322220**2**04340 **(7668)**
2009: 12^{1}SS, 14^{5}SD, 12^{3}SD, 12^{2}SD, 12^{2}SD, 9^{2}G, 9^{2}GF, 10^{0}S, 12^{2}GF, 9^{0}SD, 12^{4}SD, 12^{3}SD, 11^{4}SD, 9^{0}SD,

	Starts	1st	2nd	3rd	Win & Pl
Career Total (Turf)	7	0	3	0	4258
Career Total (AW)	15	3	2	3	12651

74 1/09 Sthl 1m4f (0-70)H SS £2729
76 12/08 Sthl 1m3f (0-70)H STD £2729
74 1/08 Sthl 1m STD £2457
Total win prize-money £7917

Going (Turf): **Sf: 0-1 GS: 0-0 Gd: 0-3 GF: 0-3 Fm: 0-0**
Distance: 5f/6f: 0-0 7f-8f: 1-4 **9f-13f: 2-17** 14f+: 0-1
Track : **LH: 3-19** RH: 0-1 Tight: 0-6 Gall: 0-4
Aids: Bl: 0-0 Vi: 0-0 Tstrap: 0-3 Ckp: 0-3
Best Rating: **78** 11/09 Sthl 1m4f stand

Fair; stays 1m4f; acts on good ground; goes on Fibresand; has worn cheekpieces.

Benedicte (IRE)

105 91
3-y-o b f Galileo (IRE)-Rachelle (IRE) (Mark Of Esteem (IRE))
M Botti The Great Partnership

Placings:6100 **(7291)**
2009: 10^{6}GF, 10^{1}GF, 10^{0}G, 10^{0}S,

	Starts	1st	2nd	3rd	Win & Pl
Career Total (Turf)	4	1	0	0	5828

67 9/09 Ches 1m2f75y G-F £5828
Total win prize-money £5828

Going (Turf): Sf: 0-1 GS: 0-0 Gd: 0-1 **GF: 1-2** Fm: 0-0
Distance: 5f/6f: 0-0 7f-8f: 0-0 **9f-13f: 1-4** 14f+: 0-0
Track : **LH: 1-3** RH: 0-0 **Tight: 1-1** Gall: 0-2
Aids: Bl: 0-0 Vi: 0-0 Tstrap: 0-0 Ckp: 0-0
Best Rating: **91** 10/09 NmkR 1m2f good

Modest; stays 1m2f; acts on fast ground.

Benetti (IRE)

64 43
3-y-o ch g Kheleyf (USA)-Assigh Lady (IRE) (Great Commotion (USA))
M Madgwick Collingwood Investment Properties Ltd

Placings:00430-00 **(2651)**
2009: 6^{0}F, 5^{0}F,

	Starts	1st	2nd	3rd	Win & Pl
Career Total (Turf)	7	0	0	1	443

Going (Turf): **Sf: 0-0 GS: 0-1 Gd: 0-0 GF: 0-2 Fm: 0-4**
Distance: 5f/6f: 0-3 7f-8f: 0-4 9f-13f: 0-0 14f+: 0-0
Track : LH: 0-3 RH: 0-0 Tight: 0-0 Gall: 0-2
Aids: Bl: 0-0 Vi: 0-1 Tstrap: 0-0 Ckp: 0-0
Best Rating: **43** 8/08 NmkJ 7f gd-sft

Benfleet Boy

93(88) (54)79
5-y-o gr g Fasliyev (USA)-Nicely (IRE) (Bustino)
B G Powell Miss J Semple

Placings:41/10430002-20 **(7036)**
2009: 12^{2}GF, 12^{0}S,

	Starts	1st	2nd	3rd	Win & Pl
Career Total (Turf)	10	1	2	1	7700
Career Total (AW)	2	1	0	0	4534

83 4/08 Folk 7f (0-75)H SFT £2590
83 9/06 Kemp 7f STD £4533
Total win prize-money £7124

Going (Turf): **Sf: 1-3** GS: 0-1 Gd: 0-2 GF: 0-4 Fm: 0-0
Distance: 5f/6f: 0-1 **7f-8f: 2-4** 9f-13f: 0-7 14f+: 0-0
Track : LH: 0-4 **RH: 1-6** Tight: 0-1 Gall: 0-3
Aids: Bl: 0-0 Vi: 0-0 Tstrap: 0-0 Ckp: 0-0
Best Rating: **83** 4/08 Folk 7f soft

Fair; stays 1m2f; acts on Polytrack and on soft ground.

Bengal Tiger

87(102) (85)61
3-y-o ch g Tagula (IRE)-Floriana (Selkirk (USA))
A M Balding Kingsclere Racing CLub

Placings:0621 **(5987)**
2009: 8^{0}GF, 8^{6}GF, 12^{2}SD, 12^{1}SD,

	Starts	1st	2nd	3rd	Win & Pl
Career Total (Turf)	2	0	0	0	0
Career Total (AW)	2	1	1	0	2652

85 9/09 Kemp 1m4f STD £2047
Total win prize-money £2047

Going (Turf): **Sf: 0-0 GS: 0-0 Gd: 0-0 GF: 0-2 Fm: 0-0**
Distance: 5f/6f: 0-0 7f-8f: 0-1 **9f-13f: 1-3** 14f+: 0-0
Track : LH: 0-0 **RH: 1-3** Tight: 0-0 Gall: 0-0
Aids: Bl: 0-0 Vi: 0-0 Tstrap: 0-0 Ckp: 0-0
Best Rating: **85** 9/09 Kemp 1m4f stand

Fair; stays 1m4f; acts well on Polytrack.

Bengers Lass (USA)

75(87) (36)1
3-y-o ch f Orientate (USA)-Wiedniu (USA) (Danzig Connection (USA))
R Curtis R P Phillips

Placings:0005 **(7590)**
2009: 10^{0}SD, 8^{0}GS, 10^{0}G, 12^{5}SD,

	Starts	1st	2nd	3rd	Win & Pl
Career Total (Turf)	2	0	0	0	
Career Total (AW)	2	0	0	0	0

Going (Turf): **Sf: 0-0 GS: 0-1 Gd: 0-1 GF: 0-0 Fm: 0-0**
Distance: 5f/6f: 0-0 7f-8f: 0-0 9f-13f: 0-4 14f+: 0-0
Track : LH: 0-1 RH: 0-3 Tight: 0-2 Gall: 0-0
Aids: Bl: 0-0 Vi: 0-0 Tstrap: 0-0 Ckp: 0-0
Best Rating: **36** 11/09 Kemp 1m4f stand

Benhego

(103) (92)76
4-y-o ch g Act One-Sadaka (USA) (Kingmambo (USA))
G L Moore Findlay & Bloom

Placings:50001621**0**50-**114** **(1007)**
2009: 16^{1}SD, 16^{1}SD, 16^{4}SD,

	Starts	1st	2nd	3rd	Win & Pl
Career Total (Turf)	8	1	1	0	3394
Career Total (AW)	6	3	0	0	14440

85 3/09 Ling 2m (0-85)H STD £5180
83 2/09 Kemp 2m (0-85)H STD £5828
92 8/08 GrLe 2m (0-75)H STD £2590
68 7/08 Yarm 1m6f17y (0-70)H G-F £2719
Total win prize-money £16319

Going (Turf): Sf: 0-0 GS: 0-2 Gd: 0-1 **GF: 1-5** Fm: 0-0
Distance: 5f/6f: 0-0 7f-8f: 0-3 9f-13f: 0-1 **14f+: 4-10**
Track : **LH: 3-9** RH: 1-3 **Tight: 2-6** Gall: 1-3
Aids: Bl: 0-0 Vi: 0-0 Tstrap: 0-0 Ckp: 0-0
Best Rating: **92** 3/09 Kemp 2m stand

Useful; stays 2m; acts on fast ground and on Polytrack.

Benitez Bond

87(95) (58)39
4-y-o ch g Bahamian Bounty-Triple Tricks (IRE) (Royal Academy (USA))
G R Oldroyd R C Bond

Placings:0/6-02606 **(5617)**
2009: 8^{0}G, 8^{2}SD, 8^{6}GF, 9^{0}SD, 9^{6}SD,

	Starts	1st	2nd	3rd	Win & Pl
Career Total (Turf)	4	0	0	0	0
Career Total (AW)	3	0	1	0	605

Going (Turf): **Sf: 0-1 GS: 0-0 Gd: 0-1 GF: 0-2 Fm: 0-0**
Distance: 5f/6f: 0-1 7f-8f: 0-2 9f-13f: 0-4 14f+: 0-0
Track : LH: 0-4 RH: 0-0 Tight: 0-2 Gall: 0-0
Aids: Bl: 0-0 Vi: 0-0 Tstrap: 0-0 Ckp: 0-0
Best Rating: **58** 7/09 Sthl 1m stand

Moderate; effective over 1m; acts on Fibresand.

Benllech

106(111) (101)99
5-y-o b g Lujain (USA)-Four Legs Good (IRE) (Be My Guest (USA))

D M Simcock Mohammed Al Shafar

Placings:02500444**2211**/06**4**00**41**/**11212151**1-0400022 **(3318)**
2009: 6[0]GF, 6[4]GF, 7[0]SD, 6[0]SD, 6[0]G, 6[2]GF, 6[2]GF,

	Starts	1st	2nd	3rd	Win & Pl
Career Total (Turf)	16	0	4	0	13222
Career Total (AW)	19	9	3	0	46594

101	11/08	Kemp	6f	(0-100)H	STD	£11215
96	9/08	Ling	6f	(0-95)H	STD	£7477
92	3/08	Kemp	6f	(0-95)H	STD	£6543
86	2/08	Ling	6f	(0-80)H	STD	£4100
82	1/08	Ling	6f	(0-75)H	STD	£2590
76	1/08	Ling	6f	(0-75)H	STD	£2590
75	12/07	Ling	6f		STD	£1943
86	12/06	Wolv	7f32y		STD	£3886
70	11/06	Kemp	7f		STD	£2266

Total win prize-money £42616

Going (Turf): **Sf: 0-1 GS: 0-2 Gd: 0-4 GF: 0-8 Fm: 0-1**
Distance: **5f/6f: 7-23** 7f-8f: 2-12 9f-13f: 0-0 14f+: 0-0
Track : **LH: 6-22** RH: 3-7 **Tight: 6-13** Gall: 0-6
Aids: Bl: 0-0 Vi: 0-0 Tstrap: 0-0 Ckp: 0-0
Best Rating: **101** 11/08 Kemp 6f stand

Very useful; effective at around 6f-7f; acts on a sound surface but probably at his best on Polytrack.

Bennelong

87(104) (81)**82**

3-y-o b g Bahamian Bounty-Bundle Up (USA) (Miner's Mark (USA))
G L Moore (R M Beckett 21/10) M&R Refurbishments Ltd

Placings:33-526431235 **(7769)**
2009: 8[5]S, 8[2]SD, 8[6]SD, 8[4]G, 7[3]GF, 8[1]SD, 8[2]SD, 8[3]SD, 8[5]SD,

	Starts	1st	2nd	3rd	Win & Pl
Career Total (Turf)	5	0	0	3	1974
Career Total (AW)	6	1	2	1	4974

76	10/09	Sthl	1m	STD	£2729

Total win prize-money £2730

Going (Turf): **Sf: 0-1 GS: 0-1 Gd: 0-2 GF: 0-1 Fm: 0-0**
Distance: 5f/6f: 0-1 **7f-8f: 1-10** 9f-13f: 0-0 14f+: 0-0
Track : **LH: 1-3** RH: 0-5 Tight: 0-1 Gall: 0-0
Aids: Bl: 0-0 Vi: 0-0 Tstrap: 1-2 Ckp: 1-2
Best Rating: **82** 9/08 Newb 6f8y good

Fair; effective over 1m; acts on good and easier ground and on Polytrack; has worn cheekpieces.

Benny The Bear

89 **62**

2-y-o ch g Rambling Bear-Mitchelland (Namaqualand (USA))
James Moffatt R R Whitton

Placings:34 **(5157)**
2009: 6[3]GF, 6[4]S,

	Starts	1st	2nd	3rd	Win & Pl
Career Total (Turf)	2	0	0	1	674

Going (Turf): **Sf: 0-1 GS: 0-0 Gd: 0-0 GF: 0-1 Fm: 0-0**
Distance: 5f/6f: 0-1 7f-8f: 0-1 9f-13f: 0-0 14f+: 0-0
Track : LH: 0-0 RH: 0-0 Tight: 0-0 Gall: 0-0
Aids: Bl: 0-0 Vi: 0-0 Tstrap: 0-0 Ckp: 0-0
Best Rating: **62** 8/09 Newc 6f gd-fm

Benozzo Gozzoli

90(93) (51)**62**

3-y-o ch g Medicean-Star Precision (Shavian)
H Morrison Miss B Swire

Placings:60400004410 **(7255)**
2009: 8[6]SD, 8[0]SD, 8[4]SD, 9[0]GS, 8[0]SD, 8[0]GF, 8[0]GS, 10[4]G, 16[4]SS, 16[1]G, 16[0]SD,

	Starts	1st	2nd	3rd	Win & Pl
Career Total (Turf)	5	1	0	0	2216
Career Total (AW)	6	0	0	0	0

62	10/09	Nott	2m9y	(0-65)H	GD	£2047

Total win prize-money £2047

Going (Turf): Sf: 0-0 GS: 0-2 **Gd: 1-2** GF: 0-1 Fm: 0-0
Distance: 5f/6f: 0-0 7f-8f: 0-3 9f-13f: 0-5 **14f+: 1-3**
Track : **LH: 1-8** RH: 0-2 Tight: 0-5 Gall: 0-1
Aids: Bl: 0-0 Vi: 0-0 Tstrap: 0-0 Ckp: 0-0
Best Rating: **62** 10/09 Nott 2m9y good

Modest; stays 2m; acts on easy ground.

Benrish (IRE)

87 **73**

2-y-o b c Refuse To Bend (IRE)-Miss Trish (IRE) (Danetime (IRE))
X Nakkachdji (B Smart 20/7) Prime Equestrian SARL

Placings:2234
2009: 6[2]GF, 6[2]G, 7[3]G, 7[4]HO,

	Starts	1st	2nd	3rd	Win & Pl
Career Total (Turf)	4	0	2	1	8961

Going (Turf): **Sf: 0-0 GS: 0-0 Gd: 0-2 GF: 0-1 Fm: 0-0**
Distance: 5f/6f: 0-2 7f-8f: 0-2 9f-13f: 0-0 14f+: 0-0
Track : LH: 0-0 RH: 0-0 Tight: 0-0 Gall: 0-0
Aids: Bl: 0-0 Vi: 0-0 Tstrap: 0-0 Ckp: 0-0
Best Rating: **73** 10/09 MsnL 7f good

Bentley

97(104) (69)**62**

5-y-o b g Piccolo-April Lee (Superpower)
J G Given Danethorpe Racing Partnership

Placings:066006**5**666**4**/32**1**4**11**6624405500032/22250046 3220421432003-0060005140 **(7876)**
2009: 7[0]F, **5[0]SD**, 7[6]G, 8[0]G, 5[0]GS, 6[0]GF, 7[5]SD, 5[1]SD, 5[4]SD, 7[0]SD,

	Starts	1st	2nd	3rd	Win & Pl
Career Total (Turf)	18	0	2	0	1664
Career Total (AW)	43	5	8	5	19982

65	12/09	Wolv	5f216y		STD	£2047
68	6/08	Wolv	7f32y	(0-60)H	STD	£2388
69	2/07	Wolv	5f20y	(0-65)H	SS	£2388
70	2/07	Sthl	5f	(0-60)H	STD	£2388
56	1/07	Wolv	5f216y	(0-60)H	STD	£2388

Total win prize-money £11602

Going (Turf): **Sf: 0-3 GS: 0-5 Gd: 0-6 GF: 0-3 Fm: 0-1**
Distance: **5f/6f: 4-46** 7f-8f: 1-14 9f-13f: 0-1 14f+: 0-0
Track : **LH: 4-34** RH: 0-8 **Tight: 4-28** Gall: 0-1
Aids: Bl: 0-0 **Vi: 3-43** Tstrap: 0-0 Ckp: 0-0
Best Rating: **70** 2/07 Sthl 5f stand

Moderate; effective over 5f-7f; acts on most ground on turf; goes on Fibresand and Polytrack.

Bentley Brook (IRE)

(110) (85)**51**

7-y-o ch g Singspiel (IRE)-Gay Bentley (USA) (Riverman (USA))
R Curtis John Wardle

Placings:225/221305300/065600445/504511/2313102153-5646140 **(7867)**
2009: 12[5]SD, 16[6]SD, 12[4]SD, 16[6]SD, 16[1]SD, 14[4]SD, 14[0]SS,

	Starts	1st	2nd	3rd	Win & Pl
Career Total (Turf)	12	1	2	2	9096
Career Total (AW)	32	6	4	3	27783

80	11/09	Wolv	2m119y	(0-75)H	STD	£3885
90	5/08	Sthl	1m3f	(0-80)H	STD	£4921
89	2/08	Sthl	1m6f	(0-75)H	SS	£2593
82	2/08	Sthl	1m3f	(0-75)H	STD	£2593
70	12/07	Sthl	1m4f	(0-75)H	STD	£2968
72	12/07	Sthl	1m4f	(0-70)H	SS	£2968
79	5/05	Chep	1m14y		GD	£3458

Total win prize-money £23392

Going (Turf): Sf: 0-2 GS: 0-2 **Gd: 1-3** GF: 0-5 Fm: 0-0
Distance: 5f/6f: 0-2 7f-8f: 0-4 **9f-13f: 5-27** 14f+: 2-11
Track : **LH: 6-33** RH: 0-9 **Tight: 1-18** Gall: 0-4
Aids: Bl: 0-3 Vi: 0-0 Tstrap: 0-0 Ckp: 0-0
Best Rating: **90** 5/08 Sthl 1m3f stand

Fair; stays 2m; acts on easy ground; goes on Fibresand and Polytrack; has worn blinkers and a tongue tie.

Berberi

38

3-y-o ch c Bertolini (USA)-Bird Of Prey (IRE) (Last Tycoon)
A G Newcombe W I Bloomfield

Placings:0 **(1508)**
2009: 8[0]GF,

	Starts	1st	2nd	3rd	Win & Pl
Career Total (Turf)	1	0	0	0	

Going (Turf): **Sf: 0-0 GS: 0-0 Gd: 0-0 GF: 0-1 Fm: 0-0**
Distance: 5f/6f: 0-0 7f-8f: 0-0 9f-13f: 0-1 14f+: 0-0
Track : LH: 0-1 RH: 0-0 Tight: 0-0 Gall: 0-0
Aids: Bl: 0-0 Vi: 0-0 Tstrap: 0-0 Ckp: 0-0

Berbice (IRE)

99(103) (93)**95**

4-y-o gr g Acclamation-Pearl Bright (FR) (Kaldoun (FR))
S Donohoe Mrs Samantha Donohoe

Placings:341432/03005506500-00500622215 **(7054)**
2009: 5[0]S, 7[0]HY, 6[5]GF, 7[0]Y, 6[0]S, 6[6]GF, 6[2]F, 7[2]SD, 8[2]SD, 7[1]SD, 8[5]SD,

	Starts	1st	2nd	3rd	Win & Pl
Career Total (Turf)	21	1	2	2	39462
Career Total (AW)	7	1	2	1	5114

79	10/09	Kemp	7f	(0-75)H	STD	£2590
82	6/07	Gdwd	6f		GD	£5019

Total win prize-money £7610

Going (Turf): Sf: 0-4 GS: 0-3 **Gd: 1-7** GF: 0-4 Fm: 0-2
Distance: 5f/6f: 1-13 7f-8f: 1-15 9f-13f: 0-0 14f+: 0-0
Track : LH: 0-7 **RH: 1-6** Tight: 0-1 Gall: 0-1
Aids: **Bl: 1-3** Vi: 0-0 Tstrap: 0-3 Ckp: 0-3
Best Rating: **105** 9/07 Newb 6f8y gd-fm

Fair; placed in Group company as a juvenile; effective over 6f-7f; acts on good ground; goes on Polytrack; has worn a tongue tie and blinkers.

Bere Davis (FR)

103(93) (61)**80**

4-y-o gr g Verglas (IRE)-Zerelda (Exhibitioner)
M A Barnes (P D Evans 5/10) J G White

Placings:105/02364554260-2331054260030454 **(6987)**

2009: 7^{2}G, 8^{3}F, 8^{3}GF, 8^{1}GF, 7^{0}GF, 7^{5}GF, 7^{4}GF, 8^{2}GF, 7^{6}GF, 8^{0}GF, 7^{0}GF, 7^{3}G, 7^{0}G, 8^{4}GF, 8^{5}GF, 9^{4}G,

	Starts	1st	2nd	3rd	Win & Pl
Career Total (Turf)	29	2	4	4	17392
Career Total (AW)	1	0	0	0	

79 5/09 Thsk 1m (0-75)H G-F £4274
73 6/07 Hayd 6f G-F £3238
Total win prize-money £7513

Going (Turf): Sf: 0-2 GS: 0-2 Gd: 0-8 **GF: 2-16** Fm: 0-1
Distance: 5f/6f: 1-3 7f-8f: 1-18 9f-13f: 0-9 14f+: 0-0
Track : **LH: 1-13** RH: 0-5 **Tight: 1-7** Gall: 0-0
Aids: Bl: 0-1 Vi: 0-1 Tstrap: 0-1 Ckp: 0-1
Best Rating: **82** 5/08 Chep 1m14y good

Fair; effective over 1m; acts on good ground.

Beresford Lady

(89) (47)**48**
5-y-o b m Presidium-Coney Hills (Beverley Boy)
A D Brown Mrs Susan Johnson

Placings:0405660/60000-6 **(0080)**
2009: 8^{6}SD,

	Starts	1st	2nd	3rd	Win & Pl
Career Total (Turf)	5	0	0	0	277
Career Total (AW)	8	0	0	0	0

Going (Turf): **Sf: 0-1 GS: 0-2 Gd: 0-2 GF: 0-0 Fm: 0-0**
Distance: 5f/6f: 0-0 7f-8f: 0-4 9f-13f: 0-9 14f+: 0-0
Track : LH: 0-10 RH: 0-3 Tight: 0-6 Gall: 0-1
Aids: Bl: 0-0 Vi: 0-0 Tstrap: 0-2 Ckp: 0-2
Best Rating: **48** 10/08 Newc 1m2f32y heavy

Bergonzi (IRE)

105 (78)**81**
5-y-o ch g Indian Ridge-Lady Windley (Baillamont (USA))
J Howard Johnson Transcend Bloodstock LLP

Placings:052/12216032/00-56301265 **(6822)**
2009: 13^{5}GF, 9^{6}GF, 11^{3}GF, 12^{0}GF, 15^{1}G, 13^{2}G, 16^{6}GF, 14^{5}GF,

	Starts	1st	2nd	3rd	Win & Pl
Career Total (Turf)	19	3	4	2	27208
Career Total (AW)	2	0	1	0	1156

77 7/09 Catt 1m7f177y (0-85)H GD £5180
87 5/07 Wind 1m3f135y (0-85)H GD £6477
73 4/07 Leic 1m1f218y G-F £4533
Total win prize-money £16192

Going (Turf): Sf: 0-1 GS: 0-3 **Gd: 2-5** GF: 1-10 Fm: 0-0
Distance: 5f/6f: 0-0 7f-8f: 0-2 **9f-13f: 2-14** 14f+: 1-5
Track : LH: 1-11 RH: 1-8 **Tight: 2-13** Gall: 0-3
Aids: Bl: 0-0 Vi: 0-1 Tstrap: 0-1 Ckp: 0-1
Best Rating: **91** 9/07 Gdwd 1m3f gd-sft

Useful; stays 2m; suited by a sound surface; has worn a visor.

Bering De Lauriere (FR)

(85) (37)
6-y-o ch g Evening World (FR)-Shenedova (FR) (Hellios (USA))
B G Powell B G Powell

Placings:04 **(0516)**
2009: 13^{0}SD, 12^{4}SD,

	Starts	1st	2nd	3rd	Win & Pl
Career Total (Turf)	0	0	0	0	
Career Total (AW)	2	0	0	0	0

Going (Turf): **Sf: 0-0 GS: 0-0 Gd: 0-0 GF: 0-0 Fm: 0-0**
Distance: 5f/6f: 0-0 7f-8f: 0-0 9f-13f: 0-2 14f+: 0-0
Track : LH: 0-2 RH: 0-0 Tight: 0-1 Gall: 0-0
Aids: Bl: 0-0 Vi: 0-0 Tstrap: 0-0 Ckp: 0-0
Best Rating: **37** 2/09 Ling 1m5f stand

Berkalani (IRE)

79 **12**
3-y-o b f Ashkalani (IRE)-Berkeley Hall (Saddlers' Hall (IRE))
P D Evans Richard Edwards Gwynne Williams

Placings:00 **(6934)**
2009: 7^{0}GS, 10^{0}G,

	Starts	1st	2nd	3rd	Win & Pl
Career Total (Turf)	2	0	0	0	

Going (Turf): **Sf: 0-0 GS: 0-1 Gd: 0-1 GF: 0-0 Fm: 0-0**
Distance: 5f/6f: 0-0 7f-8f: 0-1 9f-13f: 0-1 14f+: 0-0
Track : LH: 0-1 RH: 0-0 Tight: 0-1 Gall: 0-0
Aids: Bl: 0-0 Vi: 0-0 Tstrap: 0-0 Ckp: 0-0
Best Rating: **12** 10/09 Bath 1m2f46y good

Berling (IRE)

95 **72**
2-y-o gr c Montjeu (IRE)-Danaskaya (IRE) (Danehill (USA))
J L Dunlop Benny Andersson

Placings:653 **(6697)**
2009: 8^{6}G, 8^{5}GF, 9^{3}GS,

	Starts	1st	2nd	3rd	Win & Pl
Career Total (Turf)	3	0	0	1	770

Going (Turf): **Sf: 0-0 GS: 0-1 Gd: 0-1 GF: 0-1 Fm: 0-0**
Distance: 5f/6f: 0-0 7f-8f: 0-2 9f-13f: 0-1 14f+: 0-0
Track : LH: 0-0 RH: 0-2 Tight: 0-1 Gall: 0-0
Aids: Bl: 0-0 Vi: 0-0 Tstrap: 0-0 Ckp: 0-0
Best Rating: **72** 10/09 Gdwd 1m1f gd-sft

Fair; stays 1m1f; acts on easy ground.

Bermacha

89(97) (63)**69**
4-y-o ch f Bertolini (USA)-Machaera (Machiavellian (USA))
J E Long Essex Racing Club

Placings:50643221/305000-05000 **(7422)**
2009: 8^{0}SD, 8^{5}SD, 9^{0}GF, 8^{0}G, 8^{0}SD,

	Starts	1st	2nd	3rd	Win & Pl
Career Total (Turf)	7	0	0	1	722
Career Total (AW)	12	1	2	1	4801

74 10/07 Wolv 1m141y STD £2817
Total win prize-money £2817

Going (Turf): **Sf: 0-1 GS: 0-0 Gd: 0-2 GF: 0-4 Fm: 0-0**
Distance: 5f/6f: 0-4 7f-8f: 0-8 **9f-13f: 1-7** 14f+: 0-0
Track : **LH: 1-12** RH: 0-3 **Tight: 1-8** Gall: 0-2
Aids: Bl: 0-0 Vi: 0-0 Tstrap: 0-0 Ckp: 0-0
Best Rating: **74** 10/07 Wolv 1m141y stand

Fair; stays 1m; acts on Polytrack.

Bermondsey Bob (IRE)

96(64) (14)**72**
3-y-o b g Trans Island-Tread Softly (IRE) (Roi Danzig (USA))
J L Spearing A A Campbell

Placings:001060-000045150 **(6739)**
2009: 6^{0}GF, 6^{0}F, 7^{0}GF, 8^{0}GF, 7^{4}G, 5^{5}GF, 6^{1}GS, 5^{5}GF, 6^{0}GS,

	Starts	1st	2nd	3rd	Win & Pl
Career Total (Turf)	14	2	0	0	5375
Career Total (AW)	1	0	0	0	

55 9/09 Chep 6f16y (0-60)H G-S £2137
72 8/08 Sals 6f G-F £3238
Total win prize-money £5375

Going (Turf): Sf: 0-0 **GS: 1-5** Gd: 0-2 **GF: 1-6** Fm: 0-1
Distance: 5f/6f: 1-8 7f-8f: 1-6 9f-13f: 0-1 14f+: 0-0
Track : LH: 0-3 RH: 0-1 Tight: 0-2 Gall: 0-2
Aids: Bl: 0-0 Vi: 0-0 Tstrap: 0-1 Ckp: 0-1
Best Rating: **72** 8/08 Sals 6f gd-fm

Modest; effective at 6f; acts on fast and easy ground.

Bermondsey Girl

97(99) (67)**73**
3-y-o b f Bertolini (USA)-Upend (Main Reef)
C F Wall Whatton Manor Stud & Ne'er Do Wells II

Placings:5061003 **(6925)**
2009: 7^{5}GS, 8^{0}G, 7^{6}G, 7^{1}G, 7^{0}SD, 7^{0}SD, 7^{3}GF,

	Starts	1st	2nd	3rd	Win & Pl
Career Total (Turf)	5	1	0	1	3076
Career Total (AW)	2	0	0	0	

73 7/09 Ling 7f (0-70)H GD £2729
Total win prize-money £2730

Going (Turf): Sf: 0-0 GS: 0-1 **Gd: 1-3** GF: 0-1 Fm: 0-0
Distance: 5f/6f: 0-0 **7f-8f: 1-7** 9f-13f: 0-0 14f+: 0-0
Track : LH: 0-2 RH: 0-1 Tight: 0-2 Gall: 0-0
Aids: Bl: 0-0 Vi: 0-0 Tstrap: 0-0 Ckp: 0-0
Best Rating: **73** 7/09 Ling 7f good

Modest; effective over 7f; acts on good ground.

Bernabeu (IRE)

93(102) (64)**54**
7-y-o b g Mark Of Esteem (IRE)-Snow Ballet (IRE) (Sadler's Wells (USA))
S Curran G Peck & Tony Scarff (MBII)

Placings:040/0000/**30112**/0440-**524455505** **(7549)**
2009: 12^{5}SD, 12^{2}SD, 12^{4}SD, 12^{4}SD, 12^{5}SD, 13^{5}SD, 11^{5}G, 12^{0}SD, 12^{5}SD,

	Starts	1st	2nd	3rd	Win & Pl
Career Total (Turf)	9	0	0	0	465
Career Total (AW)	16	2	2	1	6334

56 12/07 Wolv 1m4f50y (0-55)H STD £2047
53 11/07 Ling 1m2f (0-45) STD £2047
Total win prize-money £4096

Going (Turf): **Sf: 0-2 GS: 0-0 Gd: 0-1 GF: 0-3 Fm: 0-0**
Distance: 5f/6f: 0-0 7f-8f: 0-7 **9f-13f: 2-17** 14f+: 0-1
Track : **LH: 2-16** RH: 0-4 **Tight: 2-9** Gall: 0-0
Aids: Bl: 0-1 Vi: 0-0 Tstrap: 0-0 Ckp: 0-0
Best Rating: **64** 2/09 Kemp 1m4f stand

Moderate; ex Irish; effective at around 1m2f-1m4f; acts on Polytrack.

Bernie The Bolt (IRE)

113(85) (50)**102**
3-y-o br g Milan-Chaparral Lady (IRE) (Broken Hearted)
A M Balding B P McGuire

Placings:00-5333131 **(6115)**

2009: 10^{5}GF, 12^{3}G, 14^{3}G, 16^{3}G, 14^{1}GS, 14^{3}GF, 18^{1}GF,

	Starts	1st	2nd	3rd	Win & Pl
Career Total (Turf)	8	2	0	4	35315
Career Total (AW)	1	0	0	0	

102 9/09 NmkR 2m2f (0-105)H G-F £25904
85 8/09 Ling 1m6f G-S £2590
Total win prize-money £28494

Going (Turf): Sf: 0-1 **GS: 1-1** Gd: 0-3 **GF: 1-3** Fm: 0-0
Distance: 5f/6f: 0-0 7f-8f: 0-1 9f-13f: 0-3 **14f+: 2-5**
Track : LH: 1-5 RH: 1-4 Tight: 1-3 Gall: 1-4
Aids: Bl: 0-0 Vi: 0-0 Tstrap: 0-0 Ckp: 0-0
Best Rating: **102** 9/09 NmkR 2m2f gd-fm

Fair; stays 1m6f; acts on easy ground.

Bernix

89(91) (51)**32**
7-y-o gr g Linamix (FR)-Bernique (USA) (Affirmed (USA))
N Tinkler Danum Racing

Placings:63250/00400006 **(7761)**
2009: 12^{0}GS, 10^{0}GF, 8^{4}SD, 11^{0}SD, 8^{0}G, 9^{0}GF, 8^{0}SD, 11^{6}SD,

	Starts	1st	2nd	3rd	Win & Pl
Career Total (Turf)	9	0	1	1	1638
Career Total (AW)	4	0	0	0	0

Going (Turf): **Sf: 0-0 GS: 0-1 Gd: 0-3 GF: 0-5 Fm: 0-0**
Distance: 5f/6f: 0-0 7f-8f: 0-2 9f-13f: 0-11 14f+: 0-0
Track : LH: 0-10 RH: 0-3 Tight: 0-3 Gall: 0-2
Aids: Bl: 0-0 Vi: 0-0 Tstrap: 0-4 Ckp: 0-4
Best Rating: **71** 5/07 Thsk 1m4f gd-fm

Berriedale

103(77) (14)**54**
3-y-o ch f Fraam-Carradale (Pursuit Of Love)
Mrs A Duffield Evelyn Duchess Of Sutherland

Placings:00-5016400 **(4755)**
2009: 10^{5}GF, 11^{0}SD, 12^{1}GF, 14^{6}GF, 12^{4}GF, 11^{0}GS, 12^{0}GF,

	Starts	1st	2nd	3rd	Win & Pl
Career Total (Turf)	8	1	0	0	2254
Career Total (AW)	1	0	0	0	

54 5/09 Bevl 1m4f16y (0-55) G-F £2013
Total win prize-money £2013

Going (Turf): Sf: 0-0 GS: 0-1 Gd: 0-2 **GF: 1-5** Fm: 0-0
Distance: 5f/6f: 0-0 7f-8f: 0-2 **9f-13f: 1-6** 14f+: 0-1
Track : LH: 0-4 **RH: 1-3 Tight: 1-3** Gall: 0-0
Aids: Bl: 0-0 Vi: 0-0 Tstrap: 0-0 Ckp: 0-0
Best Rating: **54** 5/09 Bevl 1m4f16y gd-fm

Moderate; stays 1m4f; acts on a sound surface.

Berrymead

95(96) (51)**61**
4-y-o br f Killer Instinct-Mill End Quest (King's Signet (USA))
Miss A Stokell Ms Caron Stokell

Placings:445660/10060065-00600300601564056005**50** **(7839)**
2009: 6^{0}SS, 6^{0}SD, 5^{6}SD, 8^{0}SF, 8^{0}SD, 5^{3}GF, 6^{0}GF, 5^{0}G, 5^{6}F, 5^{0}F, 5^{1}G, 5^{5}GF, 5^{6}F, 5^{4}GF, 7^{0}G, 5^{5}GS, 5^{6}G, 5^{0}GF, 5^{0}S, 5^{5}SD, 5^{5}SD, 5^{0}SS,

	Starts	1st	2nd	3rd	Win & Pl
Career Total (Turf)	22	2	0	1	5224
Career Total (AW)	14	0	0	0	241

61 6/09 Brig 5f59y (0-60)H GD £2590
63 4/08 Sthl 6f (0-60)H GD £1774
Total win prize-money £4364

Going (Turf): Sf: 0-1 GS: 0-4 **Gd: 2-7** GF: 0-7 Fm: 0-3
Distance: **5f/6f: 2-30** 7f-8f: 0-5 9f-13f: 0-1 14f+: 0-0
Track : **LH: 2-22** RH: 0-0 Tight: 0-5 Gall: 0-3
Aids: Bl: 0-6 Vi: 0-0 Tstrap: 0-1 Ckp: 0-1
Best Rating: **63** 4/08 Sthl 6f good

Very moderate; best over 5f-6f; acts on a sound surface; has worn blinkers.

Berrynarbor

97(91) (35)**57**
4-y-o b f Tobougg (IRE)-River Art (USA) (Irish River (FR))
A G Newcombe Mrs Jayne Bramhill

Placings:6001/4236-0060 **(7658)**
2009: 12^{0}SD, 11^{0}G, 10^{6}G, 12^{0}SD,

	Starts	1st	2nd	3rd	Win & Pl
Career Total (Turf)	8	0	1	1	990
Career Total (AW)	4	1	0	0	2048

62 11/07 Wolv 7f32y STD £2047
Total win prize-money £2048

Going (Turf): **Sf: 0-1 GS: 0-1 Gd: 0-5 GF: 0-1 Fm: 0-0**
Distance: 5f/6f: 0-1 **7f-8f: 1-3** 9f-13f: 0-7 14f+: 0-1
Track : **LH: 1-10** RH: 0-1 **Tight: 1-6** Gall: 0-1
Aids: Bl: 0-0 Vi: 0-0 Tstrap: 0-0 Ckp: 0-0
Best Rating: **62** 11/07 Wolv 7f32y stand

Moderate; stays at least 1m3f; acts on a sound surface; also goes on Polytrack.

Bert's Memory

101(102) (55)**55**
5-y-o b m Bertolini (USA)-Meg's Memory (IRE) (Superlative)
Jennie Candlish Ms Jennie Candlish

Placings:63053344**523**/000106**065**/1026306-24050 **(6097)**
2009: 12^{2}GF, 11^{4}S, 12^{0}HY, 9^{5}GF, 13^{0}GF,

	Starts	1st	2nd	3rd	Win & Pl
Career Total (Turf)	20	1	2	3	6172
Career Total (AW)	12	1	1	2	2914

49 3/08 Sthl 1m (0-45) STD £1295
59 10/07 Leic 7f9y (0-60)H G-S £2590
Total win prize-money £3886

Going (Turf): Sf: 0-6 **GS: 1-4** Gd: 0-4 GF: 0-5 Fm: 0-1
Distance: 5f/6f: 0-4 **7f-8f: 2-19** 9f-13f: 0-8 14f+: 0-1
Track : **LH: 1-22** RH: 0-3 Tight: 0-11 Gall: 0-0
Aids: Bl: 0-5 Vi: 0-0 Tstrap: 2-12 Ckp: 2-12
Best Rating: **66** 10/06 Catt 5f212y good

Moderate; effective at around 1m; acts on good ground; goes on Fibresand.

Bertbrand

100(103) (69)**75**
4-y-o b g Bertolini (USA)-Mi Amor (IRE) (Alzao (USA))
I W McInnes (D Flood 13/7) Barrie Kirby

Placings:00446**1**/0440**51**00000000-200**514**000**2**006 **(7727)**
2009: 5^{2}SD, 6^{0}SD, 6^{0}SD, 5^{5}SD, 5^{1}SD, 5^{4}SD, 5^{0}SF, 5^{0}SD, 5^{0}GF, 5^{2}S, 5^{0}S, 5^{0}SD, 7^{6}SD,

	Starts	1st	2nd	3rd	Win & Pl
Career Total (Turf)	9	0	1	0	605
Career Total (AW)	24	3	1	0	8709

66 6/09 Wolv 5f20y STD £2047
69 6/08 Wolv 5f216y STD £2914
75 1/08 Wolv 5f216y (0-70)H STD £2730
Total win prize-money £7691

Going (Turf): **Sf: 0-3 GS: 0-2 Gd: 0-2 GF: 0-2 Fm: 0-0**
Distance: **5f/6f: 3-25** 7f-8f: 0-7 9f-13f: 0-1 14f+: 0-0
Track : **LH: 3-21** RH: 0-4 **Tight: 3-17** Gall: 0-1
Aids: Bl: 0-8 Vi: 0-0 Tstrap: 1-5 Ckp: 1-5
Best Rating: **75** 7/08 Ches 7f2y good

Moderate; suited by 5f-6f; acts on sand and soft turf; has worn blinkers and cheekpieces.

Bertie Bacon

61
3-y-o b g Bertolini (USA)-Streaky (IRE) (Danetime (IRE))
W G M Turner Graham Brown

Placings:0 **(5367)**
2009: 9^{0}F,

	Starts	1st	2nd	3rd	Win & Pl
Career Total (Turf)	1	0	0	0	

Going (Turf): **Sf: 0-0 GS: 0-0 Gd: 0-0 GF: 0-0 Fm: 0-1**
Distance: 5f/6f: 0-0 7f-8f: 0-0 9f-13f: 0-1 14f+: 0-0
Track : LH: 0-1 RH: 0-0 Tight: 0-1 Gall: 0-0
Aids: Bl: 0-0 Vi: 0-0 Tstrap: 0-1 Ckp: 0-1

Bertie Black

41
2-y-o b g Bertolini (USA)-Bella Chica (IRE) (Bigstone (IRE))
N Tinkler Mrs Janis Macpherson

Placings:0 **(2100)**
2009: 6^{0}GS,

	Starts	1st	2nd	3rd	Win & Pl
Career Total (Turf)	1	0	0	0	

Going (Turf): **Sf: 0-0 GS: 0-1 Gd: 0-0 GF: 0-0 Fm: 0-0**
Distance: 5f/6f: 0-1 7f-8f: 0-0 9f-13f: 0-0 14f+: 0-0
Track : LH: 0-0 RH: 0-0 Tight: 0-0 Gall: 0-0
Aids: Bl: 0-0 Vi: 0-1 Tstrap: 0-0 Ckp: 0-0

Bertie Boo

(67) **52**
4-y-o b g Where Or When (IRE)-Lucy Boo (Singspiel (IRE))
G J Smith P Voce

Placings:0000-0 **(1777)**
2009: 8^{0}SD,

	Starts	1st	2nd	3rd	Win & Pl
Career Total (Turf)	3	0	0	0	
Career Total (AW)	2	0	0	0	

Going (Turf): **Sf: 0-0 GS: 0-2 Gd: 0-1 GF: 0-0 Fm: 0-0**
Distance: 5f/6f: 0-0 7f-8f: 0-1 9f-13f: 0-3 14f+: 0-1
Track : LH: 0-4 RH: 0-1 Tight: 0-2 Gall: 0-2
Aids: Bl: 0-0 Vi: 0-0 Tstrap: 0-0 Ckp: 0-0
Best Rating: **52** 8/08 Catt 1m3f214y gd-sft

Bertie Buckle (IRE)

(87) (49)
2-y-o b g Bertolini (USA)-Buckle (IRE) (Common Grounds)
J R Gask The Bertie Buckle Syndicate

Placings:060 **(7736)**

2009: 5^{0}SD, 5^{6}SD, 6^{0}SD,

	Starts	1st	2nd	3rd	Win & Pl
Career Total (Turf)	0	0	0	0	
Career Total (AW)	3	0	0	0	0

Going (Turf): Sf: 0-0 GS: 0-0 Gd: 0-0 GF: 0-0 Fm: 0-0
Distance: 5f/6f: 0-3 7f-8f: 0-0 9f-13f: 0-0 14f+: 0-0
Track : LH: 0-2 RH: 0-1 Tight: 0-2 Gall: 0-0
Aids: Bl: 0-0 Vi: 0-0 Tstrap: 0-0 Ckp: 0-0
Best Rating: 49 12/09 Kemp 6f stand

Bertie Smalls

94(85) (55)**51**

3-y-o b g Xaar-Largo (IRE) (Selkirk (USA))
M H Tompkins The Grass Partnership

Placings:000-003 **(3005)**
2009: 10^{0}GF, 11^{0}G, 9^{3}G,

	Starts	1st	2nd	3rd	Win & Pl
Career Total (Turf)	4	0	0	1	289
Career Total (AW)	2	0	0	0	

Going (Turf): Sf: 0-0 GS: 0-1 Gd: 0-2 GF: 0-1 Fm: 0-0
Distance: 5f/6f: 0-0 7f-8f: 0-3 9f-13f: 0-3 14f+: 0-0
Track : LH: 0-3 RH: 0-1 Tight: 0-3 Gall: 0-0
Aids: Bl: 0-1 Vi: 0-0 Tstrap: 0-0 Ckp: 0-0
Best Rating: 55 9/08 Ling 1m stand

Bertie Southstreet

105(106) (73)**78**

6-y-o b/br g Bertolini (USA)-Salvezza (IRE) (Superpower)
Karen George (J R Boyle 13/7) Adrian Parr & Karen George

Placings:34441/4006/**502060**/**546005145046052-360513050114142** **(7645)**
2009: 5^{3}SD, 6^{6}SD, 7^{0}SD, 6^{5}SD, 6^{1}GF, 6^{3}GF, 5^{0}G, 6^{5}SD, 5^{0}G, 5^{1}SD, 5^{1}SD, 5^{4}SD, 5^{1}SD, 5^{4}SD, 5^{2}SD,

	Starts	1st	2nd	3rd	Win & Pl
Career Total (Turf)	22	3	0	2	13767
Career Total (AW)	23	3	3	1	10873

73	10/09	Wolv	5f20y		STD	£2388
72	9/09	Wolv	5f216y	(0-70)H	STD	£2729
70	8/09	Wolv	5f216y	(0-60)H	STD	£2388
71	6/09	Folk	6f		G-F	£2047
78	6/08	Newb	5f34y	(0-70)H	G-F	£3238
67	7/05	Carl	5f		FRM	£3435

Total win prize-money £16226

Going (Turf): Sf: 0-2 GS: 0-1 Gd: 0-4 **GF: 2-13** Fm: 1-2
Distance: **5f/6f: 6-38** 7f-8f: 0-7 9f-13f: 0-0 14f+: 0-0
Track : **LH: 3-22** RH: 1-3 **Tight: 3-19** Gall: 1-8
Aids: Bl: 1-11 **Vi: 3-6** Tstrap: 1-6 Ckp: 1-6
Best Rating: 81 7/06 Wind 6f gd-fm

Modest sprinter; acts on most ground; goes on Polytrack; has worn blinkers, visor and cheekpieces.

Bertie Vista

97(99) (59)**66**

4-y-o b g Bertolini (USA)-Off Camera (Efisio)
T D Easterby Three Jolly Farmers

Placings:06/04336053233-0504345**5**03 **(6823)**
2009: 8^{0}F, 6^{5}SD, 7^{0}GF, 7^{4}GF, 7^{3}SD, 7^{4}G, 7^{5}G, 5^{5}SD, 7^{0}GF, 6^{3}GF,

	Starts	1st	2nd	3rd	Win & Pl
Career Total (Turf)	20	0	1	6	3363
Career Total (AW)	3	0	0	1	353

Going (Turf): Sf: 0-1 GS: 0-4 Gd: 0-7 GF: 0-7 Fm: 0-1
Distance: 5f/6f: 0-10 7f-8f: 0-13 9f-13f: 0-0 14f+: 0-0
Track : LH: 0-9 RH: 0-2 Tight: 0-7 Gall: 0-0
Aids: Bl: 0-10 Vi: 0-0 Tstrap: 0-2 Ckp: 0-2
Best Rating: 66 9/08 Catt 7f gd-sft

Modest; stays 7f acts on good and easier ground.

Bertie's Birthday (IRE)

84 **44**

3-y-o b f Elnadim (USA)-Goldfinch (Zilzal (USA))
Jonjo O'Neill Paolo C Garavelli

Placings:60 **(2496)**
2009: 7^{6}F, 6^{0}GF,

	Starts	1st	2nd	3rd	Win & Pl
Career Total (Turf)	2	0	0	0	0

Going (Turf): Sf: 0-0 GS: 0-0 Gd: 0-0 GF: 0-1 Fm: 0-1
Distance: 5f/6f: 0-0 7f-8f: 0-2 9f-13f: 0-0 14f+: 0-0
Track : LH: 0-1 RH: 0-0 Tight: 0-0 Gall: 0-0
Aids: Bl: 0-0 Vi: 0-0 Tstrap: 0-0 Ckp: 0-0
Best Rating: 44 5/09 Wwck 7f26y firm

Bertoliver

105(107) (85)**101**

5-y-o b g Bertolini (USA)-Calcavella (Pursuit Of Love)
S C Williams (Tom Dascombe 5/9) Mrs A Shone

Placings:0460102/611050636/01300604665-0003220100**543** **(7872)**
2009: 5^{0}G, 5^{0}GF, 5^{0}HY, 5^{3}GF, 5^{2}GF, 5^{2}GF, 5^{0}G, 5^{1}GF, 5^{0}GS, 5^{0}GS, 5^{5}SD, 6^{4}SD, 5^{3}SD,

	Starts	1st	2nd	3rd	Win & Pl
Career Total (Turf)	30	5	3	2	51053
Career Total (AW)	10	0	0	2	2549

90	8/09	Ches	5f16y	(0-85)H	G-F	£5828
101	5/08	Ches	5f16y	(0-100)H	GD	£13246
89	6/07	Sand	5f6y	(0-85)H	GD	£5181
84	5/07	Wind	5f10y	(0-85)H	GD	£6477
74	9/06	NmkR	6f		G-F	£4533

Total win prize-money £35268

Going (Turf): Sf: 0-2 GS: 0-5 **Gd: 3-11** GF: 2-12 Fm: 0-0
Distance: **5f/6f: 5-39** 7f-8f: 0-1 9f-13f: 0-0 14f+: 0-0
Track : **LH: 2-12** RH: 0-3 **Tight: 2-11** Gall: 1-6
Aids: Bl: 0-0 Vi: 0-0 Tstrap: 0-0 Ckp: 0-0
Best Rating: 101 5/08 Ches 5f16y good

Useful; best over 5f; acts on most types of ground and on Polytrack; suited by forcing tactics.

Bespoke Boy

98(105) (61)**70**

4-y-o b g Acclamation-Milly Fleur (Primo Dominie)
Mrs N S Evans (P C Haslam 26/3) Running Dragon Racing 2

Placings:12006/000060-400060 **(4263)**
2009: 10^{4}SD, 8^{0}SD, 9^{0}SD, 10^{0}G, 12^{6}GF, 12^{0}S,

	Starts	1st	2nd	3rd	Win & Pl
Career Total (Turf)	13	1	1	0	9558
Career Total (AW)	4	0	0	0	144

79	5/07	Ripn	6f	GD	£2914

Total win prize-money £2915

Going (Turf): Sf: 0-1 GS: 0-2 **Gd: 1-7** GF: 0-3 Fm: 0-0
Distance: **5f/6f: 1-9** 7f-8f: 0-3 9f-13f: 0-5 14f+: 0-0
Track : LH: 0-10 RH: 0-0 Tight: 0-5 Gall: 0-1
Aids: Bl: 0-0 Vi: 0-0 Tstrap: 0-1 Ckp: 0-1
Best Rating: 97 6/07 Epsm 6f good

Moderate; effective over 6f; acts on good ground.

Bessie Lou (IRE)

92(92) (53)**73**

3-y-o b f Montjeu (IRE)-Almond Mousse (FR) (Exit To Nowhere (USA))
K A Ryan Highbank Syndicate

Placings:44-2600006 **(6807)**
2009: 8^{2}GS, 10^{6}GF, 10^{0}G, 8^{0}S, 10^{0}GF, 8^{0}G, 12^{6}SD,

	Starts	1st	2nd	3rd	Win & Pl
Career Total (Turf)	8	0	1	0	1661
Career Total (AW)	1	0	0	0	0

Going (Turf): Sf: 0-2 GS: 0-1 Gd: 0-2 GF: 0-3 Fm: 0-0
Distance: 5f/6f: 0-0 7f-8f: 0-3 9f-13f: 0-6 14f+: 0-0
Track : LH: 0-7 RH: 0-1 Tight: 0-4 Gall: 0-1
Aids: Bl: 0-0 Vi: 0-0 Tstrap: 0-1 Ckp: 0-1
Best Rating: 73 5/09 Hayd 1m30y gd-sft

Fair; ability in maidens over 1m on fast and easy ground.

Best Bidder (USA)

92(69) (41)**72**

3-y-o b/br f Mr Greeley (USA)-Party Stripes (USA) (Candy Stripes (USA))
Patrick Morris Rob Lloyd Racing Limited

Placings:500-000000 **(3482)**
2009: 7^{0}SD, 8^{0}GF, 10^{0}G, 12^{0}GF, 11^{0}G, 12^{0}GF,

	Starts	1st	2nd	3rd	Win & Pl
Career Total (Turf)	8	0	0	0	0
Career Total (AW)	1	0	0	0	

Going (Turf): Sf: 0-0 GS: 0-2 Gd: 0-2 GF: 0-3 Fm: 0-0
Distance: 5f/6f: 0-0 7f-8f: 0-3 9f-13f: 0-6 14f+: 0-0
Track : LH: 0-5 RH: 0-3 Tight: 0-5 Gall: 0-0
Aids: Bl: 0-0 Vi: 0-0 Tstrap: 0-0 Ckp: 0-0
Best Rating: 72 9/08 Curr 7f yield

Best In Class

97(105) (80)**71**

3-y-o gr g Best Of The Bests (IRE)-Third Party (Terimon)
S C Williams (Tom Dascombe 2/9) Mrs A Shone

Placings:6-21400614010 **(7684)**
2009: 8^{2}SD, 8^{1}SD, 8^{4}GS, 10^{0}GF, 9^{0}G, 8^{6}GF, 7^{1}SD, 8^{4}SD, 8^{0}SD, 10^{1}SD, 10^{0}SD,

	Starts	1st	2nd	3rd	Win & Pl
Career Total (Turf)	4	0	0	0	0
Career Total (AW)	8	3	1	0	9556

80	11/09	Kemp	1m2f	(0-75)H	STD	£2590
74	7/09	Ling	7f	(0-70)H	STD	£2729
66	2/09	Kemp	1m		STD	£3238

Total win prize-money £8558

Going (Turf): Sf: 0-0 GS: 0-1 Gd: 0-1 GF: 0-2 Fm: 0-0
Distance: 5f/6f: 0-1 **7f-8f: 2-5** 9f-13f: 1-6 14f+: 0-0
Track : LH: 1-3 **RH: 2-9 Tight: 1-6** Gall: 0-1
Aids: Bl: 0-0 Vi: 0-0 Tstrap: 0-0 Ckp: 0-0
Best Rating: 80 11/09 Kemp 1m2f stand

Fair; stays 1m and acts on Polytrack.

Best Intent

77 49

2-y-o ch f King's Best (USA)-Hydro Calido (USA) (Nureyev (USA))

M A Jarvis Lordship Stud

Placings:0 (7182)

2009: 7^{0}G,

	Starts	1st	2nd	3rd	Win & Pl
Career Total (Turf)	1	0	0	0	

Going (Turf): Sf: 0-0 GS: 0-0 Gd: 0-1 GF: 0-0 Fm: 0-0
Distance: 5f/6f: 0-0 7f-8f: 0-1 9f-13f: 0-0 14f+: 0-0
Track : LH: 0-0 RH: 0-0 Tight: 0-0 Gall: 0-0
Aids: Bl: 0-0 Vi: 0-0 Tstrap: 0-0 Ckp: 0-0
Best Rating: 49 10/09 NmkR 7f good

Best One

100(108) (77)85

5-y-o ch g Best Of The Bests (IRE)-Nasaieb (IRE) (Fairy King (USA))

R A Harris The Govin Partnership

Placings:00334336/044311243422300-050036060000510003154 (7889)

2009: 5^{0}GF, 5^{5}GF, 5^{0}GF, 5^{0}F, 5^{3}F, 5^{6}GF, 5^{0}SD, 5^{6}SD, 5^{0}F, 5^{0}G, 6^{0}G, 5^{5}GF, 5^{1}SD, 7^{0}SD, 5^{0}SD, 5^{0}SD, 5^{3}SD, 5^{1}SD, 5^{5}SS, 5^{4}SD,

	Starts	1st	2nd	3rd	Win & Pl
Career Total (Turf)	24	1	3	6	11016
Career Total (AW)	19	3	0	3	7798

61 12/09 Sthl 5f (0-55)H STD £1706
58 10/09 Kemp 5f (0-50)H STD £2047
79 5/08 Brig 5f59y (0-75)H G-F £2525
67 3/08 Ling 6f STD £2047
Total win prize-money £8327

Going (Turf): Sf: 0-3 GS: 0-2 Gd: 0-5 GF: 1-10 Fm: 0-4
Distance: 5f/6f: 4-32 7f-8f: 0-9 9f-13f: 0-2 14f+: 0-0
Track : LH: 2-28 RH: 1-2 Tight: 1-17 Gall: 0-4
Aids: Bl: 1-13 Vi: 1-7 Tstrap: 0-7 Ckp: 0-7
Best Rating: 85 9/08 Leic 5f2y good

Moderate; effective at 5f-6f; acts on most ground; also goes on Polytrack and Fibresand; has worn a visor, cheekpieces, blinkers and a tongue tie.

Best Prospect (IRE)

102(98) (87)94

7-y-o b g Orpen (USA)-Bright Prospect (USA) (Miswaki (USA))

M Dods D Neale

Placings:31223435/05014062014/0006002130/1000401-40003025 (5334)

2009: 11^{4}SD, 10^{0}GS, 10^{0}GF, 8^{0}G, 10^{3}S, 10^{0}GS, 10^{2}HY, 10^{5}S,

	Starts	1st	2nd	3rd	Win & Pl
Career Total (Turf)	42	6	5	5	72127
Career Total (AW)	2	0	0	0	890

94 10/08 Yarm 1m2f21y (0-85)H SFT £4857
99 3/08 Donc 1m2f60y (0-85)H SFT £4533
91 9/07 Hayd 1m2f120y (0-85)H SFT £5181
100 10/06 Newb 1m2f6y (0-95)H HVY £8724
87 7/06 NmkJ 1m4f (0-90)H G-F £9715
83 5/05 Newc 1m2f32y GD £3360
Total win prize-money £36374

Going (Turf): Sf: 4-15 GS: 0-8 Gd: 1-11 GF: 1-8 Fm: 0-0
Distance: 5f/6f: 0-0 7f-8f: 0-1 9f-13f: 6-43 14f+: 0-0
Track : LH: 5-33 RH: 1-10 Tight: 1-8 Gall: 4-14
Aids: Bl: 0-0 Vi: 0-0 Tstrap: 0-0 Ckp: 0-0
Best Rating: 101 11/06 Wind 1m2f7y gd-sft

Useful; suited by 1m2f-1m4f; acts on most ground; has worn a tongue tie.

Best Shot

(63)

3-y-o b f Xaar-Xaymara (USA) (Sanglamore (USA))

B W Hills K Abdulla

Placings:0 (1605)

2009: 8^{0}SD,

	Starts	1st	2nd	3rd	Win & Pl
Career Total (Turf)	0	0	0	0	
Career Total (AW)	1	0	0	0	

Going (Turf): Sf: 0-0 GS: 0-0 Gd: 0-0 GF: 0-0 Fm: 0-0
Distance: 5f/6f: 0-0 7f-8f: 0-1 9f-13f: 0-0 14f+: 0-0
Track : LH: 0-0 RH: 0-1 Tight: 0-0 Gall: 0-0
Aids: Bl: 0-0 Vi: 0-0 Tstrap: 0-0 Ckp: 0-0

Best Show (IRE)

85 59

2-y-o b c King's Best (USA)-Showering (Danehill (USA))

Mrs A J Perrett John E Bodie

Placings:6P (5722)

2009: 7^{6}G, 7^{P}F,

	Starts	1st	2nd	3rd	Win & Pl
Career Total (Turf)	2	0	0	0	0

Going (Turf): Sf: 0-0 GS: 0-0 Gd: 0-1 GF: 0-0 Fm: 0-1
Distance: 5f/6f: 0-0 7f-8f: 0-2 9f-13f: 0-0 14f+: 0-0
Track : LH: 0-0 RH: 0-0 Tight: 0-0 Gall: 0-0
Aids: Bl: 0-0 Vi: 0-0 Tstrap: 0-0 Ckp: 0-0
Best Rating: 59 8/09 NmkJ 7f good

Best Trip (IRE)

75 29

2-y-o b g Whipper (USA)-Tereed Elhawa (Cadeaux Genereux)

R C Guest P J Duffen & P Brown

Placings:0 (7288)

2009: 6^{0}S,

	Starts	1st	2nd	3rd	Win & Pl
Career Total (Turf)	1	0	0	0	

Going (Turf): Sf: 0-1 GS: 0-0 Gd: 0-0 GF: 0-0 Fm: 0-0
Distance: 5f/6f: 0-1 7f-8f: 0-0 9f-13f: 0-0 14f+: 0-0
Track : LH: 0-0 RH: 0-0 Tight: 0-0 Gall: 0-0
Aids: Bl: 0-0 Vi: 0-0 Tstrap: 0-0 Ckp: 0-0
Best Rating: 29 11/09 Donc 6f soft

Best Tune

98(90) (54)53

3-y-o b f King's Best (USA)-Silver Rhapsody (USA) (Silver Hawk (USA))

J Noseda Lordship Stud

Placings:446 (3508)

2009: 10^{4}GF, 11^{4}G, 11^{6}SD,

	Starts	1st	2nd	3rd	Win & Pl
Career Total (Turf)	2	0	0	0	640
Career Total (AW)	1	0	0	0	0

Going (Turf): Sf: 0-0 GS: 0-0 Gd: 0-1 GF: 0-1 Fm: 0-0
Distance: 5f/6f: 0-0 7f-8f: 0-0 9f-13f: 0-3 14f+: 0-0
Track : LH: 0-1 RH: 0-1 Tight: 0-0 Gall: 0-0
Aids: Bl: 0-0 Vi: 0-0 Tstrap: 0-0 Ckp: 0-0
Best Rating: 54 7/09 Kemp 1m3f stand

Bestowed

96(102) (64)58

4-y-o b g Kyllachy-Granted (FR) (Cadeaux Genereux)

P D Evans (M C Chapman 21/9) Diamond Racing Ltd

Placings:004000004342413 (7856)

2009: 10^{0}GF, 9^{0}GF, 8^{4}GF, 8^{0}GF, 10^{0}G, 11^{0}G, 9^{0}GF, 9^{4}G, 9^{3}GF, 8^{4}SD, 9^{2}SD, 8^{4}SD, 9^{1}SD, 9^{3}SD,

	Starts	1st	2nd	3rd	Win & Pl
Career Total (Turf)	9	0	0	1	799
Career Total (AW)	5	1	1	1	2803

61 12/09 Wolv 1m1f103y (0-65)H STD £2047
Total win prize-money £2047

Going (Turf): Sf: 0-0 GS: 0-0 Gd: 0-3 GF: 0-6 Fm: 0-0
Distance: 5f/6f: 0-0 7f-8f: 0-1 9f-13f: 1-13 14f+: 0-0
Track : LH: 1-7 RH: 0-5 Tight: 1-10 Gall: 0-0
Aids: Bl: 0-0 Vi: 1-2 Tstrap: 0-0 Ckp: 0-0
Best Rating: 64 11/09 Wolv 1m1f103y stand

Moderate; stays 1m2f; handles Polytrack; has worn a visor.

Besty

102 71

2-y-o ch g Compton Place-Petrovna (IRE) (Petardia)

B Smart A Turton & P Langford

Placings:04301 (7115)

2009: 6^{0}S, 5^{4}GF, 6^{3}GF, 6^{0}G, 5^{1}GS,

	Starts	1st	2nd	3rd	Win & Pl
Career Total (Turf)	5	1	0	1	6192

71 10/09 Muss 5f (0-85) G-S £5180
Total win prize-money £5181

Going (Turf): Sf: 0-1 GS: 1-1 Gd: 0-1 GF: 0-2 Fm: 0-0
Distance: 5f/6f: 1-5 7f-8f: 0-0 9f-13f: 0-0 14f+: 0-0
Track : LH: 0-1 RH: 0-0 Tight: 0-0 Gall: 0-0
Aids: Bl: 0-0 Vi: 0-0 Tstrap: 0-0 Ckp: 0-0
Best Rating: 71 10/09 Muss 5f gd-sft

Fair half-brother to multiple winning sprinter Brunelleschi; effective at 5f; handles fast and easy ground.

Bet Noir (IRE)

(96) (62)64

4-y-o b m King's Best (USA)-Ivowen (USA) (Theatrical)

A W Carroll A W Carroll

Placings:0/640300-04000 (1210)

2009: 13^{0}SD, 10^{4}SD, 8^{0}SD, 8^{0}SD, 8^{0}SD,

	Starts	1st	2nd	3rd	Win & Pl
Career Total (Turf)	5	0	0	0	337
Career Total (AW)	7	0	0	1	385

Going (Turf): Sf: 0-0 GS: 0-1 Gd: 0-3 GF: 0-1 Fm: 0-0
Distance: 5f/6f: 0-0 7f-8f: 0-4 9f-13f: 0-6 14f+: 0-2
Track : LH: 0-6 RH: 0-5 Tight: 0-4 Gall: 0-3
Aids: Bl: 0-0 Vi: 0-0 Tstrap: 0-0 Ckp: 0-0
Best Rating: 64 8/08 Newb 1m2f6y gd-sft

Modest; stays 1m6f; acts on easy ground and on Polytrack.

Betony (USA)

85(85) (37)67

3-y-o b f Elusive Quality (USA)-Cala (FR) (Desert Prince (IRE))

M L W Bell Sheikh Marwan Al Maktoum

Placings:026 (5193)

2009: 7^{0}SD, 7^{2}GS, 7^{6}SD,

	Starts	1st	2nd	3rd	Win & Pl
Career Total (Turf)	1	0	1	0	848
Career Total (AW)	2	0	0	0	0

Going (Turf): Sf: 0-0 GS: 0-1 Gd: 0-0 GF: 0-0 Fm: 0-0
Distance: 5f/6f: 0-0 7f-8f: 0-3 9f-13f: 0-0 14f+: 0-0
Track : LH: 0-2 RH: 0-0 Tight: 0-2 Gall: 0-0
Aids: Bl: 0-0 Vi: 0-0 Tstrap: 0-0 Ckp: 0-0
Best Rating: 67 7/09 Yarm 7f3y gd-sft

Fair; stays 7f and acts on easy ground.

Betoula

62(78) (38)

3-y-o ch f Bertolini (USA)-Pab's Choice (Telsmoss)

Mrs A L M King C Papaioannou

Placings:0050-0 (5716)

2009: 5^{0}G,

	Starts	1st	2nd	3rd	Win & Pl
Career Total (Turf)	2	0	0	0	
Career Total (AW)	3	0	0	0	0

Going (Turf): Sf: 0-0 GS: 0-1 Gd: 0-1 GF: 0-0 Fm: 0-0
Distance: 5f/6f: 0-5 7f-8f: 0-0 9f-13f: 0-0 14f+: 0-0
Track : LH: 0-3 RH: 0-2 Tight: 0-1 Gall: 0-1
Aids: Bl: 0-0 Vi: 0-0 Tstrap: 0-0 Ckp: 0-0
Best Rating: 38 6/08 Kemp 5f stand

Betsy The Best

(69) (4)12

3-y-o ch f Best Of The Bests (IRE)-Dusty's Darling (Doyoun)

R Bastiman Scattered Friends Partnership

Placings:00-4 (0005)

2009: 8^{4}SS,

	Starts	1st	2nd	3rd	Win & Pl
Career Total (Turf)	1	0	0	0	
Career Total (AW)	2	0	0	0	0

Going (Turf): Sf: 0-1 GS: 0-0 Gd: 0-0 GF: 0-0 Fm: 0-0
Distance: 5f/6f: 0-0 7f-8f: 0-3 9f-13f: 0-0 14f+: 0-0
Track : LH: 0-2 RH: 0-0 Tight: 0-0 Gall: 0-0
Aids: Bl: 0-0 Vi: 0-0 Tstrap: 0-1 Ckp: 0-1
Best Rating: 12 10/08 Newc 7f heavy

Better Be Blue (IRE)

91(77) (47)65

2-y-o b f Big Bad Bob (IRE)-Ginger Lily (IRE) (Lucky Guest)

H J L Dunlop (Miss S Collins 16/10) Anamoine Ltd

Placings:66300340 (7501)

2009: 6^{6}S, 8^{6}Y, 8^{3}HY, 7^{0}GY, 7^{0}GF, 7^{3}G, 8^{4}SD, 7^{0}SD,

	Starts	1st	2nd	3rd	Win & Pl
Career Total (Turf)	6	0	0	2	909
Career Total (AW)	2	0	0	0	144

Going (Turf): Sf: 0-2 GS: 0-0 Gd: 0-1 GF: 0-1 Fm: 0-0
Distance: 5f/6f: 0-0 7f-8f: 0-8 9f-13f: 0-0 14f+: 0-0
Track : LH: 0-3 RH: 0-3 Tight: 0-1 Gall: 0-0
Aids: Bl: 0-0 Vi: 0-0 Tstrap: 0-0 Ckp: 0-0
Best Rating: 65 8/09 Bell 1m heavy

Better In Time (USA)

90(94) (65)60

3-y-o b f City Place (USA)-Ineda Doll (USA) (Langfuhr (CAN))

Jane Chapple-Hyam Howard Spooner

Placings:43-00 (3693)

2009: 8^{0}GF, 8^{0}G,

	Starts	1st	2nd	3rd	Win & Pl
Career Total (Turf)	2	0	0	0	
Career Total (AW)	2	0	0	1	867

Going (Turf): Sf: 0-0 GS: 0-0 Gd: 0-1 GF: 0-1 Fm: 0-0
Distance: 5f/6f: 0-0 7f-8f: 0-2 9f-13f: 0-2 14f+: 0-0
Track : LH: 0-2 RH: 0-2 Tight: 0-2 Gall: 0-2
Aids: Bl: 0-0 Vi: 0-0 Tstrap: 0-0 Ckp: 0-0
Best Rating: 65 12/08 GrLe 1m stand

Betteras Bertie

95(102) (63)72

6-y-o gr g Paris House-Suffolk Girl (Statoblest)

M Brittain Mrs V C Sugden

Placings:005000/500024244-23531010000 (6946)

2009: 8^{2}SS, 8^{3}SS, 8^{5}SD, 8^{3}SD, 8^{1}GF, 8^{0}G, 8^{1}GF, 8^{0}G, 8^{0}GF, 10^{0}GF, 8^{0}SD,

	Starts	1st	2nd	3rd	Win & Pl
Career Total (Turf)	14	2	0	0	6152
Career Total (AW)	12	0	3	2	2620

72 6/09 Pont 1m4y (0-75)H G-F £3238
69 5/09 Donc 1m (0-60)H G-F £2914
Total win prize-money £6152

Going (Turf): Sf: 0-2 GS: 0-2 Gd: 0-4 **GF: 2-6** Fm: 0-0
Distance: 5f/6f: 0-1 7f-8f: 1-14 9f-13f: 1-11 14f+: 0-0
Track : **LH: 1-20** RH: 0-2 Tight: 0-4 Gall: 0-0
Aids: Bl: 0-0 Vi: 0-1 Tstrap: 0-0 Ckp: 0-0
Best Rating: 72 6/09 Pont 1m4y gd-fm

Moderate; effective at 7f-1m; handles Fibresand and fast ground.

Bettys Touch

87 33

4-y-o b f Lujain (USA)-Fadaki Hawaki (USA) (Vice Regent (CAN))

K G Reveley T S Child

Placings:0206/000-500 (6553)

2009: 5^{5}GS, 5^{0}GF, 5^{0}GF,

	Starts	1st	2nd	3rd	Win & Pl
Career Total (Turf)	10	0	1	0	696

Going (Turf): Sf: 0-0 GS: 0-2 Gd: 0-4 GF: 0-4 Fm: 0-0
Distance: 5f/6f: 0-7 7f-8f: 0-2 9f-13f: 0-1 14f+: 0-0
Track : LH: 0-0 RH: 0-1 Tight: 0-0 Gall: 0-1
Aids: Bl: 0-0 Vi: 0-0 Tstrap: 0-0 Ckp: 0-0
Best Rating: 55 6/07 NmkJ 6f good

Betws Y Coed (IRE)

(95) (53)49

3-y-o br f Indian Haven-Tommys Queen (IRE) (Ali-Royal (IRE))

A Bailey A Bailey

Placings:06000424502-60555 (0383)

2009: 8^{6}SD, 8^{0}SD, 8^{5}SD, 8^{5}SD, 8^{5}SD,

	Starts	1st	2nd	3rd	Win & Pl
Career Total (Turf)	4	0	0	0	0
Career Total (AW)	12	0	2	0	1612

Going (Turf): Sf: 0-1 GS: 0-1 Gd: 0-2 GF: 0-0 Fm: 0-0
Distance: 5f/6f: 0-2 7f-8f: 0-7 9f-13f: 0-7 14f+: 0-0
Track : LH: 0-13 RH: 0-0 Tight: 0-7 Gall: 0-1
Aids: Bl: 0-0 Vi: 0-0 Tstrap: 0-13 Ckp: 0-13
Best Rating: 53 12/08 Wolv 1m141y stand

Moderate; stays 1m; acts on Fibresand and on Polytrack.

Bewdley

(93) (39)58

4-y-o b f Best Of The Bests (IRE)-Garota De Ipanema (FR) (Al Nasr (FR))

R E Peacock R E Peacock

Placings:506/0006500-0000 (1131)

2009: 7^{0}SD, 6^{0}SD, 9^{0}SD, 8^{0}SD,

	Starts	1st	2nd	3rd	Win & Pl
Career Total (Turf)	7	0	0	0	0
Career Total (AW)	7	0	0	0	0

Going (Turf): Sf: 0-2 GS: 0-0 Gd: 0-2 GF: 0-2 Fm: 0-1
Distance: 5f/6f: 0-1 7f-8f: 0-5 9f-13f: 0-8 14f+: 0-0
Track : LH: 0-11 RH: 0-1 Tight: 0-7 Gall: 0-0
Aids: Bl: 0-0 Vi: 0-0 Tstrap: 0-0 Ckp: 0-0
Best Rating: 58 9/07 Ches 7f2y good

Beyond Atlow

(78) (24)

4-y-o ch g And Beyond (IRE)-Argostoli (Marju (IRE))

Lucinda Featherstone J Roundtree

Placings:00 (7648)

2009: 9^{0}SD, 12^{0}SD,

	Starts	1st	2nd	3rd	Win & Pl
Career Total (Turf)	0	0	0	0	
Career Total (AW)	2	0	0	0	

Going (Turf): Sf: 0-0 GS: 0-0 Gd: 0-0 GF: 0-0 Fm: 0-0
Distance: 5f/6f: 0-0 7f-8f: 0-0 9f-13f: 0-2 14f+: 0-0
Track : LH: 0-2 RH: 0-0 Tight: 0-2 Gall: 0-0
Aids: Bl: 0-0 Vi: 0-0 Tstrap: 0-0 Ckp: 0-0
Best Rating: 24 12/09 Wolv 1m4f50y stand

Beyond Desire

104 103

2-y-o b f Invincible Spirit (IRE)-Compradore (Mujtahid (USA))

M A Jarvis Clipper Logistics

Placings:124 (6090)

2009: 6^{1}G, 6^{2}GF, 6^{4}G,

	Starts	1st	2nd	3rd	Win & Pl
Career Total (Turf)	3	1	1	0	38231

88 7/09 Gdwd 6f GD £12952
Total win prize-money £12952

Going (Turf): Sf: 0-0 GS: 0-0 **Gd: 1-2** GF: 0-1 Fm: 0-0
Distance: **5f/6f: 1-3** 7f-8f: 0-0 9f-13f: 0-0 14f+: 0-0
Track : LH: 0-0 RH: 0-0 Tight: 0-0 Gall: 0-0
Aids: Bl: 0-0 Vi: 0-0 Tstrap: 0-0 Ckp: 0-0
Best Rating: **103** 8/09 York 6f gd-fm

Smart; runner-up in the 2009 Lowther; stays 6f; acts on good ground.

Beyond The City (USA)

86(94) (54)59
2-y-o b c Elusive Quality (USA)-Whats Doin (USA) (Relaunch (USA))
R Hannon Byerley Thoroughbred Racing

Placings:000**60** **(6938)**
2009: 7^{0}G, 6^{0}GF, 8^{0}GF, 8^{6}SD, 5^{0}SD,

	Starts	1st	2nd	3rd	Win & Pl
Career Total (Turf)	3	0	0	0	
Career Total (AW)	2	0	0	0	0

Going (Turf): **Sf: 0-0 GS: 0-0 Gd: 0-1 GF: 0-2 Fm: 0-0**
Distance: 5f/6f: 0-1 7f-8f: 0-4 9f-13f: 0-0 14f+: 0-0
Track : LH: 0-1 RH: 0-3 Tight: 0-0 Gall: 0-0
Aids: Bl: 0-0 Vi: 0-0 Tstrap: 0-0 Ckp: 0-0
Best Rating: **59** 8/09 Brig 6f209y gd-fm

Beyonda Dream

73(93) (34)
3-y-o b f And Beyond (IRE)-Richenda (Mister Baileys)
Lucinda Featherstone Peaks Partnership & J Roundtree

Placings:0000 **(7751)**
2009: 10^{0}G, 13^{0}SD, 12^{0}SD, 13^{0}SD,

	Starts	1st	2nd	3rd	Win & Pl
Career Total (Turf)	1	0	0	0	
Career Total (AW)	3	0	0	0	

Going (Turf): **Sf: 0-0 GS: 0-0 Gd: 0-1 GF: 0-0 Fm: 0-0**
Distance: 5f/6f: 0-0 7f-8f: 0-0 9f-13f: 0-2 14f+: 0-2
Track : LH: 0-4 RH: 0-0 Tight: 0-3 Gall: 0-0
Aids: Bl: 0-0 Vi: 0-0 Tstrap: 0-1 Ckp: 0-1
Best Rating: **34** 11/09 Wolv 1m5f194y stand

Bianca Capello

89(95) (52)46
4-y-o b f Medicean-Totom (Mtoto)
J R Fanshawe Chris Van Hoorn

Placings:60/00-50 **(1974)**
2009: 8^{5}SD, 10^{0}F,

	Starts	1st	2nd	3rd	Win & Pl
Career Total (Turf)	4	0	0	0	0
Career Total (AW)	2	0	0	0	0

Going (Turf): **Sf: 0-1 GS: 0-0 Gd: 0-1 GF: 0-1 Fm: 0-1**
Distance: 5f/6f: 0-0 7f-8f: 0-2 9f-13f: 0-4 14f+: 0-0
Track : LH: 0-3 RH: 0-2 Tight: 0-2 Gall: 0-0
Aids: Bl: 0-0 Vi: 0-1 Tstrap: 0-0 Ckp: 0-0
Best Rating: **57** 10/07 Wwck 7f26y gd-fm

Bibiana Bay

(80) (34)
2-y-o b f Leporello (IRE)-Polisonne (Polish Precedent (USA))
B I Case SKV Racing

Placings:0 **(7799)**
2009: 5^{0}SD,

	Starts	1st	2nd	3rd	Win & Pl
Career Total (Turf)	0	0	0	0	
Career Total (AW)	1	0	0	0	

Going (Turf): **Sf: 0-0 GS: 0-0 Gd: 0-0 GF: 0-0 Fm: 0-0**
Distance: 5f/6f: 0-1 7f-8f: 0-0 9f-13f: 0-0 14f+: 0-0
Track : LH: 0-1 RH: 0-0 Tight: 0-1 Gall: 0-0
Aids: Bl: 0-0 Vi: 0-0 Tstrap: 0-0 Ckp: 0-0
Best Rating: **34** 12/09 Wolv 5f216y stand

Bibury

103(97) (78)78
3-y-o b f Royal Applause-Dahlia's Krissy (USA) (Kris S (USA))
David P Myerscough Mrs P Myerscough

Placings:5-3103303 **(7532a)**
2009: 6^{3}S, 7^{1}S, 7^{0}HY, 7^{3}SD, 8^{3}GF, 7^{0}G, 10^{3}SD,

	Starts	1st	2nd	3rd	Win & Pl
Career Total (Turf)	6	1	0	2	10388
Career Total (AW)	2	0	0	2	1427

72 4/09 Limk 7f50y SFT £8721
Total win prize-money £8721

Going (Turf): **Sf: 1-4** GS: 0-0 Gd: 0-1 GF: 0-1 Fm: 0-0
Distance: 5f/6f: 0-2 **7f-8f: 1-4** 9f-13f: 0-2 14f+: 0-0
Track : LH: 0-2 RH: 0-1 Tight: 0-0 Gall: 0-0
Aids: Bl: 0-0 Vi: 0-0 Tstrap: 0-0 Ckp: 0-0
Best Rating: **78** 11/09 Dund 1m2f150y stand

Bickersten

72(100) (73)21
3-y-o ch g Piccolo-Niseem (USA) (Hennessy (USA))
C Moore (M R Channon 16/5) J E Moore

Placings:05-116500**044** **(7650)**
2009: 7^{1}SD, 8^{1}SD, 8^{6}F, 8^{5}G, 7^{0}S, 9^{0}YS, 8^{0}SD, 8^{4}SD, 8^{4}SD,

	Starts	1st	2nd	3rd	Win & Pl
Career Total (Turf)	4	0	0	0	0
Career Total (AW)	7	2	0	0	5078

73 3/09 Ling 1m (0-75)H STD £2752
65 2/09 Ling 7f STD £2047
Total win prize-money £4799

Going (Turf): **Sf: 0-1 GS: 0-0 Gd: 0-1 GF: 0-0 Fm: 0-1**
Distance: 5f/6f: 0-0 **7f-8f: 2-9** 9f-13f: 0-2 14f+: 0-0
Track : **LH: 2-9** RH: 0-1 **Tight: 2-7** Gall: 0-0
Aids: Bl: 0-0 Vi: 0-0 Tstrap: 0-3 Ckp: 0-3
Best Rating: **73** 3/09 Ling 1m stand

Modest; effective over 1m and acts on Polytrack; has worn cheekpieces.

Bicksta

96(101) (52)54
3-y-o b f Haafhd-Premiere Dance (IRE) (Loup Solitaire (USA))
P T Midgley (E F Vaughan 11/10) R Wardlaw

Placings:0030044666 **(7780)**
2009: 7^{0}GS, 7^{0}GF, 10^{3}GF, 10^{0}GF, 10^{0}SD, 9^{4}F, 8^{4}GF, 10^{6}SS, 11^{6}SD, 11^{6}SD,

	Starts	1st	2nd	3rd	Win & Pl
Career Total (Turf)	6	0	0	1	1006
Career Total (AW)	4	0	0	0	0

Going (Turf): **Sf: 0-0 GS: 0-1 Gd: 0-0 GF: 0-4 Fm: 0-1**
Distance: 5f/6f: 0-0 7f-8f: 0-2 9f-13f: 0-8 14f+: 0-0
Track : LH: 0-7 RH: 0-1 Tight: 0-3 Gall: 0-1
Aids: Bl: 0-1 Vi: 0-3 Tstrap: 0-0 Ckp: 0-0
Best Rating: **54** 5/09 NmkR 1m2f gd-fm

Moderate; 1m; handles good to firm; has worn a visor.

Bid Art (IRE)

(95) (65)65
4-y-o b g Hawk Wing (USA)-Crystal Theatre (IRE) (King's Theatre (IRE))
Jamie Snowden Bid Art Partnership

Placings:003053/006-**000** **(0494)**
2009: 10^{0}SD, 10^{0}SD, 10^{0}SD,

	Starts	1st	2nd	3rd	Win & Pl
Career Total (Turf)	8	0	0	1	433
Career Total (AW)	4	0	0	1	302

Going (Turf): **Sf: 0-1 GS: 0-1 Gd: 0-2 GF: 0-3 Fm: 0-1**
Distance: 5f/6f: 0-3 7f-8f: 0-4 9f-13f: 0-5 14f+: 0-0
Track : LH: 0-5 RH: 0-2 Tight: 0-3 Gall: 0-1
Aids: Bl: 0-0 Vi: 0-0 Tstrap: 0-2 Ckp: 0-2
Best Rating: **65** 11/07 Kemp 1m stand

Bid For Glory

91(104) (73)98
5-y-o ch h Auction House (USA)-Woodland Steps (Bold Owl)
H J Collingridge Harraton Court One

Placings:1234/2100514/3555P0040-**060230** **(6640)**
2009: 8^{0}GF, 10^{6}GS, 8^{0}GF, 8^{2}SD, 9^{3}SD, 9^{0}SD,

	Starts	1st	2nd	3rd	Win & Pl
Career Total (Turf)	20	2	2	2	20739
Career Total (AW)	6	1	1	1	9271

95 12/07 Kemp 1m3f (0-95)H STD £6855
95 6/07 Nott 1m54y (0-95)H G-F £7124
73 7/06 NmkJ 6f G-F £3886
Total win prize-money £17866

Going (Turf): Sf: 0-0 GS: 0-5 Gd: 0-8 **GF: 2-7** Fm: 0-0
Distance: 5f/6f: 1-1 7f-8f: 0-8 **9f-13f: 2-17** 14f+: 0-0
Track : LH: 1-12 RH: 1-7 Tight: 0-6 Gall: 0-8
Aids: Bl: 0-0 Vi: 0-6 Tstrap: 0-1 Ckp: 0-1
Best Rating: **98** 4/08 Ripn 1m1f170y gd-sft

Modest; effective at 1m-1m3f; acts on fast ground and on Polytrack; has worn cheekpieces and a visor.

Bid For Gold

105(87) (36)78
5-y-o b g Auction House (USA)-Gold And Blue (IRE) (Bluebird (USA))
Jedd O'Keeffe Paul Chapman And Ba'Tat Investments

Placings:045430/313614300/0000310333100-00021145400 **(7287)**
2009: 6^{0}GF, 7^{0}SD, 5^{0}GF, 6^{2}G, 6^{1}G, 5^{1}G, 6^{4}S, 6^{5}GF, 6^{4}G, 7^{0}S, 7^{0}S,

	Starts	1st	2nd	3rd	Win & Pl
Career Total (Turf)	38	6	1	8	30621
Career Total (AW)	1	0	0	0	

78 7/09 Carl 5f193y (0-75)H GD £2729
76 6/09 Haml 6f5y (0-75)H GD £3238

72 8/08 Haml 6f5y (0-80)H G-S £7123
72 6/08 Pont 6f (0-70)H GD £3238
78 7/07 Pont 6f (0-75)H SFT £3886
56 5/07 Rdcr 6f G-F £2817
Total win prize-money £23033

Going (Turf): Sf: 1-11 GS: 1-7 **Gd: 3-10** GF: 1-10 Fm: 0-0
Distance: **5f/6f: 4-22** 7f-8f: 2-15 9f-13f: 0-2 14f+: 0-0
Track : **LH: 2-13** RH: 1-4 Tight: 0-2 Gall: 0-2
Aids: Bl: 0-1 Vi: 0-0 Tstrap: 0-1 Ckp: 0-1
Best Rating: **78** 10/09 Newc 6f good

Faur; effective over 6f; acts on any ground.

Bidable

97(105) (62)57
5-y-o b m Auction House (USA)-Dubitable (Formidable I (USA))
B Palling Flying Eight Partnership

Placings:3054/0353321400/000052006-003002210 **(7650)**
2009: 8^{0}SD, 7^{0}SD, 7^{3}G, 8^{0}G, 7^{0}G, 8^{2}SD, 8^{2}SD, 9^{1}SD, 8^{0}SD,

	Starts	1st	2nd	3rd	Win & Pl
Career Total (Turf)	22	1	2	5	8147
Career Total (AW)	10	1	2	0	3585

62 11/09 Wolv 1m1f103y (0-50)H STD £2047
66 8/07 Chep 1m14y (0-75)H G-F £3562
Total win prize-money £5609

Going (Turf): Sf: 0-4 GS: 0-4 Gd: 0-5 **GF: 1-8** Fm: 0-1
Distance: 5f/6f: 0-1 7f-8f: 0-11 **9f-13f: 2-20** 14f+: 0-0
Track : **LH: 1-20** RH: 0-2 **Tight: 1-14** Gall: 0-1
Aids: Bl: 0-0 Vi: 0-0 Tstrap: 0-0 Ckp: 0-0
Best Rating: **66** 8/07 Chep 1m14y gd-fm

Moderate; effective at around 1m; acts on most ground on turf; goes on Polytrack.

Bideeya (USA)

88(74) (36)62
2-y-o b/br f Dubawi (IRE)-Menhoubah (USA) (Dixieland Band (USA))
C E Brittain Saeed Manana

Placings:2060 **(6609)**
2009: 7^{2}GF, 7^{0}GF, 6^{6}GF, 7^{0}SD,

	Starts	1st	2nd	3rd	Win & Pl
Career Total (Turf)	3	0	1	0	1204
Career Total (AW)	1	0	0	0	

Going (Turf): **Sf: 0-0 GS: 0-0 Gd: 0-0 GF: 0-3 Fm: 0-0**
Distance: 5f/6f: 0-1 7f-8f: 0-3 9f-13f: 0-0 14f+: 0-0
Track : LH: 0-1 RH: 0-1 Tight: 0-1 Gall: 0-1
Aids: Bl: 0-0 Vi: 0-0 Tstrap: 0-1 Ckp: 0-1
Best Rating: **62** 6/09 Ches 7f2y gd-fm

Modest half-sister to a 1m2f winner; runner-up on debut over 7f on fast ground.

Bienheureux

99(103) (61)68
8-y-o b g Bien Bien (USA)-Rochea (Rock City)
Miss Gay Kelleway Mr & Mrs I Henderson

Placings:00/00002154111/342205305453243330/55101523 0550362/335630140354132255/05640464141404545620 056-3363 **(1537)**
2009: 12^{3}SS, 12^{3}SD, 14^{6}SD, 11^{3}GF,

	Starts	1st	2nd	3rd	Win & Pl
Career Total (Turf)	36	5	3	3	19584
Career Total (AW)	55	5	6	12	24311

66 5/08 NmkR 1m4f (0-70)H GD £3123
61 4/08 Brig 1m3f196y (0-60)H GD £1942
64 7/07 Brig 1m3f196y (0-65)H GD £1943
58 4/07 Brig 1m3f196y (0-60)H G-F £1943
66 8/06 Kemp 1m4f (0-65)H STD £3238
63 7/06 Sthl 1m4f (0-55)H STD £2730
69 12/04 Wolv 1m4f50y (0-62)H STD £2949
61 12/04 Wolv 1m4f50y (0-50) STD £2681
57 11/04 Ling 1m5f (0-45) STD £1617
51 7/04 Folk 1m4f F(0-55)H G-F £3080
Total win prize-money £25249

Going (Turf): Sf: 0-3 GS: 0-6 **Gd: 3-13** GF: 2-12 Fm: 0-2
Distance: 5f/6f: 0-1 7f-8f: 0-5 **9f-13f: 10-65** 14f+: 0-20
Track : **LH: 7-67** RH: 3-21 **Tight: 4-36** Gall: 1-11
Aids: Bl: 0-5 **Vi: 2-11** Tstrap: 0-2 Ckp: 0-2
Best Rating: **73** 1/05 Ling 1m5f stand

Moderate; multiple sand winner; effective at around 1m4f-2m; acts on fast ground, Polytrack and Fibresand; has worn a tongue tie and eye-shields.

Big Apple Boy (IRE)

101 94
3-y-o b c Statue Of Liberty (USA)-Go For Grace (IRE) (Shalford (IRE))
Jedd O'Keeffe Highbeck Racing

Placings:413-426410 **(3747)**
2009: 8^{4}GF, 8^{2}G, 8^{6}GF, 8^{4}GF, 6^{1}GF, 6^{0}G,

	Starts	1st	2nd	3rd	Win & Pl
Career Total (Turf)	9	2	1	1	14066

94 6/09 Pont 6f (0-85)H G-F £5180
81 9/08 Pont 6f G-F £4857
Total win prize-money £10038

Going (Turf): Sf: 0-0 GS: 0-0 Gd: 0-4 **GF: 2-5** Fm: 0-0
Distance: **5f/6f: 2-5** 7f-8f: 0-2 9f-13f: 0-2 14f+: 0-0
Track : **LH: 2-6** RH: 0-0 Tight: 0-1 Gall: 0-0
Aids: Bl: 0-0 Vi: 0-0 Tstrap: 0-0 Ckp: 0-0
Best Rating: **94** 6/09 Pont 6f gd-fm

Useful; stays 1m; acts on fast ground.

Big Audio (IRE)

101 103
2-y-o b c Oratorio (IRE)-Tarbela (IRE) (Grand Lodge (USA))
R Hannon Michael Pescod

Placings:421041 **(5214)**
2009: 6^{4}GF, 6^{2}GF, 7^{1}GF, 7^{0}GF, 7^{4}G, 8^{1}G,

	Starts	1st	2nd	3rd	Win & Pl
Career Total (Turf)	6	2	1	0	51133

101 8/09 Sals 1m GD £17031
103 6/09 Asct 7f G-F £28385
Total win prize-money £45416

Going (Turf): Sf: 0-0 GS: 0-0 **Gd: 1-2 GF: 1-4** Fm: 0-0
Distance: 5f/6f: 0-2 **7f-8f: 2-4** 9f-13f: 0-0 14f+: 0-0
Track : LH: 0-0 RH: 0-1 Tight: 0-0 Gall: 0-0
Aids: Bl: 0-0 Vi: 0-0 Tstrap: 0-0 Ckp: 0-0
Best Rating: **103** 6/09 Asct 7f gd-fm

Smart; winner of the 2009 Chesham Stakes; effective at 7f-1m; acts on fast ground.

Big Bay (USA)

103(101) (96)87
3-y-o b c Horse Chestnut (SAF)-Takipy (USA) (Persian Bold)
Jane Chapple-Hyam Jane Chapple-Hyam & Mrs B J Hirst

Placings:332011 **(7540)**
2009: 8^{3}GF, 8^{3}SD, 8^{2}G, 8^{0}GF, 8^{1}G, 8^{1}SD,

	Starts	1st	2nd	3rd	Win & Pl
Career Total (Turf)	4	1	1	1	4953
Career Total (AW)	2	1	0	1	5382

96 11/09 Kemp 1m (0-85)H STD £4727
79 10/09 Nott 1m75y GD £3238
Total win prize-money £7965

Going (Turf): Sf: 0-0 GS: 0-0 **Gd: 1-2** GF: 0-2 Fm: 0-0
Distance: 5f/6f: 0-0 7f-8f: 1-4 9f-13f: 1-2 14f+: 0-0
Track : LH: 1-1 RH: 1-2 Tight: 0-0 Gall: 0-0
Aids: Bl: 0-0 Vi: 0-0 Tstrap: 0-0 Ckp: 0-0
Best Rating: **96** 11/09 Kemp 1m stand

Useful; stays 1m; acts on fast and easy ground; goes on Polytrack.

Big Boom

103(94) (45)72
4-y-o ch g Cadeaux Genereux-Kastaway (Distant Relative)
M Quinn Andy Viner

Placings:0550-52214 **(4668)**
2009: 7^{5}SD, 6^{2}S, 6^{2}GS, 5^{1}S, 6^{4}G,

	Starts	1st	2nd	3rd	Win & Pl
Career Total (Turf)	4	1	2	0	4561
Career Total (AW)	5	0	0	0	0

72 7/09 Leic 5f218y (0-70)H SFT £2914
Total win prize-money £2914

Going (Turf): **Sf: 1-2** GS: 0-1 Gd: 0-1 GF: 0-0 Fm: 0-0
Distance: **5f/6f: 1-5** 7f-8f: 0-4 9f-13f: 0-0 14f+: 0-0
Track : LH: 0-4 RH: 0-0 Tight: 0-2 Gall: 0-1
Aids: Bl: 0-0 Vi: 0-0 Tstrap: 0-0 Ckp: 0-0
Best Rating: **72** 7/09 Leic 5f218y soft

Moderate; suited by 6f and soft ground.

Big Bound (USA)

105(106) (80)103
3-y-o b c Grand Slam (USA)-Golden Cat (USA) (Storm Cat (USA))
J H M Gosden Lady Rothschild

Placings:24-12530100 **(6327a)**
2009: 10^{1}SD, 10^{2}G, 10^{5}GF, 10^{3}GF, 10^{0}GF, 9^{1}GF, 12^{0}G, 10^{0}G,

	Starts	1st	2nd	3rd	Win & Pl
Career Total (Turf)	9	1	2	1	29098
Career Total (AW)	1	1	0	0	2730

103 7/09 Leic 1m1f218y G-F £7569
80 3/09 Ling 1m2f STD £2729
Total win prize-money £10300

Going (Turf): Sf: 0-0 GS: 0-1 Gd: 0-3 **GF: 1-5** Fm: 0-0
Distance: 5f/6f: 0-0 7f-8f: 0-0 **9f-13f: 2-10** 14f+: 0-0
Track : LH: 1-4 **RH: 1-4 Tight: 1-3** Gall: 0-1
Aids: Bl: 0-0 Vi: 0-0 Tstrap: 0-0 Ckp: 0-0
Best Rating: **103** 7/09 Gdwd 1m4f good

Smart; effective over 1m2f; acts on good/fast ground and on Polytrack.

Big Buzz (IRE)

57
2-y-o b g Redback-Aphra Benn (IRE) (In The Wings)
Mrs L Stubbs Cos We Can Partnership

Placings:0 **(4705)**
2009: 8^{0}GS,

	Starts	1st	2nd	3rd	Win & Pl
Career Total (Turf)	1	0	0	0	

Going (Turf): **Sf: 0-0 GS: 0-1 Gd: 0-0 GF: 0-0 Fm: 0-0**
Distance: 5f/6f: 0-0 7f-8f: 0-0 9f-13f: 0-1 14f+: 0-0
Track : LH: 0-1 RH: 0-0 Tight: 0-0 Gall: 0-0
Aids: Bl: 0-0 Vi: 0-0 Tstrap: 0-0 Ckp: 0-0

Big Hands Lynch (IRE)

(69) (44)
2-y-o b c Hawkeye (IRE)-Mrs Kanning (Distant View (USA))
J R Boyle Conor Murphy

Placings:000 (7663)
2009: 8⁰SD, 8⁰SD, 8⁰SD,

	Starts	1st	2nd	3rd	Win & Pl
Career Total (Turf)	0	0	0	0	
Career Total (AW)	3	0	0	0	

Going (Turf): **Sf: 0-0 GS: 0-0 Gd: 0-0 GF: 0-0 Fm: 0-0**
Distance: 5f/6f: 0-0 7f-8f: 0-3 9f-13f: 0-0 14f+: 0-0
Track : LH: 0-3 RH: 0-0 Tight: 0-3 Gall: 0-0
Aids: Bl: 0-0 Vi: 0-0 Tstrap: 0-0 Ckp: 0-0
Best Rating: **44** 12/09 Ling 1m stand

Big Nige (IRE)

90(105) (68)55
3-y-o br g Mull Of Kintyre (USA)-Queen's Quest (Rainbow Quest (USA))
J Pearce Killarney Glen

Placings:0040-03 (7882)
2009: 8⁰GF, 10³SD,

	Starts	1st	2nd	3rd	Win & Pl
Career Total (Turf)	3	0	0	0	
Career Total (AW)	3	0	0	1	620

Going (Turf): **Sf: 0-0 GS: 0-1 Gd: 0-1 GF: 0-1 Fm: 0-0**
Distance: 5f/6f: 0-0 7f-8f: 0-3 9f-13f: 0-3 14f+: 0-0
Track : LH: 0-3 RH: 0-0 Tight: 0-3 Gall: 0-0
Aids: Bl: 0-0 Vi: 0-0 Tstrap: 0-0 Ckp: 0-0
Best Rating: **68** 11/08 Wolv 1m141y stand

Modest; stays 1m; acts on Polytrack.

Big Noise

107(99) (96)99
5-y-o b h Lake Coniston (IRE)-Mitsubishi Video (IRE) (Doulab (USA))
Dr J D Scargill Theme Tune Partnership

Placings:12112/300420-15500 (6815)
2009: 7¹G, 7⁵G, 6⁵GF, 7⁰G, 7⁰G,

	Starts	1st	2nd	3rd	Win & Pl
Career Total (Turf)	14	4	1	1	28611
Career Total (AW)	2	0	2	0	3646

99	7/09	Leic	7f9y	(0-95)H	GD	£10904
89	8/07	NmkJ	7f	(0-85)H	G-F	£5181
79	6/07	NmkJ	6f	(0-80)H	SFT	£5181
71	5/07	Yarm	6f3y		GD	£1943

Total win prize-money £23211

Going (Turf): Sf: 1-2 GS: 0-1 **Gd: 2-6** GF: 1-5 Fm: 0-0
Distance: 5f/6f: 1-2 **7f-8f: 3-14** 9f-13f: 0-0 14f+: 0-0
Track : LH: 0-1 RH: 0-1 Tight: 0-0 Gall: 0-1
Aids: Bl: 0-0 Vi: 0-0 Tstrap: 0-0 Ckp: 0-0
Best Rating: **99** 7/09 Leic 7f9y good

Very useful; best at 7f; acts on most ground and on Polytrack.

Big Robert

105(107) (105)104
5-y-o b h Medicean-Top Flight Queen (Mark Of Esteem (IRE))
P D Deegan (K R Burke 28/3) Mark Gittins

Placings:2125/64031606/0605420063-350300000 (7472a)
2009: 12³G, 10⁵G, 10⁰GF, 12³SD, 11⁰SD, 10⁰SD, 12⁰SD, 10⁰SD, 10⁰SD,

	Starts	1st	2nd	3rd	Win & Pl
Career Total (Turf)	21	2	2	2	45425
Career Total (AW)	10	0	1	2	13984

102	7/07	Leic	1m1f218y	SFT	£7790
84	8/06	Sand	7f16y	GD	£4533

Total win prize-money £12324

Going (Turf): **Sf: 1-4** GS: 0-1 **Gd: 1-9** GF: 0-6 Fm: 0-0
Distance: 5f/6f: 0-0 7f-8f: 1-5 9f-13f: 1-23 14f+: 0-3
Track : LH: 0-13 **RH: 2-15** Tight: 0-3 Gall: 0-11
Aids: Bl: 0-1 Vi: 0-0 Tstrap: 0-0 Ckp: 0-0
Best Rating: **105** 9/08 GrLe 1m5f66y stand

Very useful; Listed placed; stays 1m4f; acts on good ground and softer; handles Polytrack; has worn a tongue tie.

Big Slick (IRE)

103(89) (36)62
4-y-o ch c Rossini (USA)-Why Worry Now (IRE) (College Chapel)
M Brittain Northgate Poker

Placings:00000/115306-030 (3730)
2009: 7⁰SD, 7³G, 7⁰G,

	Starts	1st	2nd	3rd	Win & Pl
Career Total (Turf)	13	2	0	2	5277
Career Total (AW)	1	0	0	0	

62	5/08	Muss	5f	(0-65)H	G-S	£2266
58	4/08	Catt	5f	(0-60)H	G-S	£2047

Total win prize-money £4314

Going (Turf): Sf: 0-3 **GS: 2-6** Gd: 0-4 GF: 0-0 Fm: 0-0
Distance: **5f/6f: 2-10** 7f-8f: 0-4 9f-13f: 0-0 14f+: 0-0
Track : LH: 0-2 RH: 0-1 Tight: 0-1 Gall: 0-1
Aids: Bl: 0-0 Vi: 0-0 Tstrap: 0-0 Ckp: 0-0
Best Rating: **62** 6/08 Newc 5f gd-sft

Moderate colt; improved since dropped to 5f; acts on easy ground.

Big Sur

(89) (60)
3-y-o ch g Selkirk (USA)-Bombazine (IRE) (Generous (IRE))
T Keddy Andrew Duffield

Placings:004 (7576)
2009: 7⁰SD, 7⁰SD, 8⁴SD,

	Starts	1st	2nd	3rd	Win & Pl
Career Total (Turf)	0	0	0	0	
Career Total (AW)	3	0	0	0	192

Going (Turf): **Sf: 0-0 GS: 0-0 Gd: 0-0 GF: 0-0 Fm: 0-0**
Distance: 5f/6f: 0-0 7f-8f: 0-3 9f-13f: 0-0 14f+: 0-0
Track : LH: 0-3 RH: 0-0 Tight: 0-3 Gall: 0-0
Aids: Bl: 0-0 Vi: 0-0 Tstrap: 0-0 Ckp: 0-0
Best Rating: **60** 11/09 Ling 1m stand

Big Talk

80 40
2-y-o b c Selkirk (USA)-Common Request (USA) (Lear Fan (USA))
S Kirk Deauville Daze Partnership

Placings:000 (7029)
2009: 8⁰GS, 9⁰GS, 8⁰S,

	Starts	1st	2nd	3rd	Win & Pl
Career Total (Turf)	3	0	0	0	

Going (Turf): **Sf: 0-1 GS: 0-2 Gd: 0-0 GF: 0-0 Fm: 0-0**
Distance: 5f/6f: 0-0 7f-8f: 0-1 9f-13f: 0-2 14f+: 0-0
Track : LH: 0-0 RH: 0-1 Tight: 0-1 Gall: 0-0
Aids: Bl: 0-0 Vi: 0-0 Tstrap: 0-0 Ckp: 0-0
Best Rating: **40** 10/09 Gdwd 1m1f gd-sft

Big Wave Bay (IRE)

86 58
2-y-o b c Alamshar (IRE)-Lady Pahia (IRE) (Pivotal)
A P Jarvis Ambrose Turnbull

Placings:640 (6046)
2009: 7⁶G, 8⁴G, 7⁰G,

	Starts	1st	2nd	3rd	Win & Pl
Career Total (Turf)	3	0	0	0	397

Going (Turf): **Sf: 0-0 GS: 0-0 Gd: 0-3 GF: 0-0 Fm: 0-0**
Distance: 5f/6f: 0-0 7f-8f: 0-3 9f-13f: 0-0 14f+: 0-0
Track : LH: 0-2 RH: 0-0 Tight: 0-1 Gall: 0-0
Aids: Bl: 0-0 Vi: 0-0 Tstrap: 0-0 Ckp: 0-0
Best Rating: **58** 8/09 Thsk 1m good

Moderate form in maidens.

Big Whitfield

91(91) (51)57
3-y-o b g Tobougg (IRE)-Natalie Jay (Ballacashtal (CAN))
M Dods Just Five Racing Partners

Placings:505 (7126)
2009: 10⁵GF, 9⁰SD, 8⁵G,

	Starts	1st	2nd	3rd	Win & Pl
Career Total (Turf)	2	0	0	0	0
Career Total (AW)	1	0	0	0	

Going (Turf): **Sf: 0-0 GS: 0-0 Gd: 0-1 GF: 0-1 Fm: 0-0**
Distance: 5f/6f: 0-0 7f-8f: 0-0 9f-13f: 0-3 14f+: 0-0
Track : LH: 0-3 RH: 0-0 Tight: 0-2 Gall: 0-0
Aids: Bl: 0-0 Vi: 0-0 Tstrap: 0-0 Ckp: 0-0
Best Rating: **57** 10/09 Nott 1m75y good

Bigalo's Star (IRE)

82(71) (40)71
3-y-o b g Xaar-Toi Toi (IRE) (In The Wings)
L A Mullaney Ian Buckley

Placings:564-000 (6840)
2009: 12⁰S, 13⁰GF, 11⁰G,

	Starts	1st	2nd	3rd	Win & Pl
Career Total (Turf)	5	0	0	0	350
Career Total (AW)	1	0	0	0	129

Going (Turf): **Sf: 0-2 GS: 0-0 Gd: 0-2 GF: 0-1 Fm: 0-0**
Distance: 5f/6f: 0-0 7f-8f: 0-3 9f-13f: 0-2 14f+: 0-1
Track : LH: 0-3 RH: 0-1 Tight: 0-2 Gall: 0-1
Aids: Bl: 0-0 Vi: 0-0 Tstrap: 0-1 Ckp: 0-1
Best Rating: 71 9/08 Donc 7f soft

Modest; stays 1m.

Bigfanofthat (IRE)

93(90) (48)64
4-y-o b g Rock Of Gibraltar (IRE)-Miss Salsa (USA) (Unbridled (USA))
M D Squance Mrs Elizabeth Macdonald

Placings:1/000-530600 (4667)
2009: 7^{5}SD, 7^{3}G, 7^{0}GF, 6^{6}S, 7^{0}SD, 8^{0}G,

	Starts	1st	2nd	3rd	Win & Pl
Career Total (Turf)	8	1	0	1	5509
Career Total (AW)	2	0	0	0	0

78 5/07 Ayr 6f G-F £5181
Total win prize-money £5182

Going (Turf): Sf: 0-3 GS: 0-1 Gd: 0-2 **GF: 1-2** Fm: 0-0
Distance: **5f/6f: 1-1** 7f-8f: 0-6 9f-13f: 0-3 14f+: 0-0
Track : LH: 0-2 RH: 0-2 Tight: 0-1 Gall: 0-0
Aids: Bl: 0-1 Vi: 0-1 Tstrap: 0-0 Ckp: 0-0
Best Rating: 78 5/07 Ayr 6f gd-fm

Modest; effective at 6f-7f; acts on a sound surface.

Bijou Dan

101 (49)71
8-y-o ch g Bijou D'Inde-Cal Norma's Lady (IRE) (Lyphard's Special (USA))
G M Moore Mrs I I Plumb

Placings:460504**2351/336**2453035500**12/6516002134110**
230**05006/56**113050050/3202115-3010515 (3728)
2009: 15^{3}GF, 16^{0}F, 15^{1}GF, 14^{0}S, 14^{5}GF, 11^{1}GF, 15^{5}G,

	Starts	1st	2nd	3rd	Win & Pl
Career Total (Turf)	40	6	3	7	22221
Career Total (AW)	31	6	4	3	27976

71 7/09 Catt 1m3f214y (0-65)H G-F £2388
71 5/09 Catt 1m7f177y (0-65)H G-F £2388
67 7/08 Ayr 1m5f13y (0-70)H G-S £3238
54 6/08 Catt 1m5f175y G-S £2047
68 5/07 Ayr 1m1f20y (0-60)H G-F £2590
65 5/07 Ayr 1m1f20y (0-60)H G-S £2590
74 7/06 Wolv 1m141y (0-80)H STD £6477
72 6/06 Wolv 1m141y (0-70)H STD £3886
66 4/06 Wolv 1m141y SF £2388
65 2/06 Sthl 7f STD £2388
68 11/05 Wolv 1m141y (0-60)H STD £2966
57 12/04 Wolv 1m141y STD £3412
Total win prize-money £36763

Going (Turf): Sf: 0-10 **GS: 3-9** Gd: 0-6 **GF: 3-14** Fm: 0-1
Distance: 5f/6f: 0-0 7f-8f: 1-14 **9f-13f: 8-48** 14f+: 3-9
Track : **LH: 12-60** RH: 0-10 **Tight: 8-43** Gall: 0-5
Aids: **Bl: 5-37** Vi: 0-2 Tstrap: 3-14 Ckp: 3-14
Best Rating: 76 9/06 Wolv 1m141y stand

Modest; effective over 7f-1m4f; acts on fast and soft ground and on sand; has worn various headgear.

Bikini Babe (IRE)

104 98
2-y-o b f Montjeu (IRE)-Zeiting (IRE) (Zieten (USA))
M Johnston A D Spence

Placings:010302 (6316a)
2009: 6^{0}GF, 7^{1}G, 7^{0}GF, 7^{3}GF, 7^{0}G, 7^{2}G,

	Starts	1st	2nd	3rd	Win & Pl
Career Total (Turf)	6	1	1	1	21763

76 6/09 Sand 7f16y GD £5180
Total win prize-money £5181

Going (Turf): Sf: 0-0 GS: 0-0 **Gd: 1-3** GF: 0-3 Fm: 0-0
Distance: 5f/6f: 0-1 **7f-8f: 1-5** 9f-13f: 0-0 14f+: 0-0
Track : LH: 0-0 **RH: 1-2** Tight: 0-0 Gall: 0-0
Aids: Bl: 0-0 Vi: 0-0 Tstrap: 0-0 Ckp: 0-0
Best Rating: 98 9/09 Curr 7f good

150,000euros purchase whose pedigree suggests speed and stamina; Listed placed; winner over 7f on good ground.

Bilash

89 68
2-y-o gr/ro c Choisir (AUS)-Goldeva (Makbul)
R Hollinshead M Pyle & Mrs T Pyle

Placings:3500 (6018)
2009: 6^{3}GF, 6^{5}GF, 6^{0}GF, 5^{0}GF,

	Starts	1st	2nd	3rd	Win & Pl
Career Total (Turf)	4	0	0	1	1156

Going (Turf): **Sf: 0-0 GS: 0-0 Gd: 0-0 GF: 0-4 Fm: 0-0**
Distance: 5f/6f: 0-3 7f-8f: 0-1 9f-13f: 0-0 14f+: 0-0
Track : LH: 0-2 RH: 0-0 Tight: 0-0 Gall: 0-0
Aids: Bl: 0-0 Vi: 0-0 Tstrap: 0-0 Ckp: 0-0
Best Rating: 68 9/09 Donc 6f gd-fm

Bilboa

87(92) (57)60
4-y-o b g Averti (IRE)-Anita Marie (IRE) (Anita's Prince)
J M Bradley Miss Diane Hill

Placings:00/023452**063445450**-000000 (5716)
2009: 5^{0}GF, 5^{0}GS, 5^{0}GF, 6^{0}G, 5^{0}G, 5^{0}G,

	Starts	1st	2nd	3rd	Win & Pl
Career Total (Turf)	15	0	2	1	2211
Career Total (AW)	8	0	0	1	289

Going (Turf): **Sf: 0-2 GS: 0-2 Gd: 0-5 GF: 0-6 Fm: 0-0**
Distance: 5f/6f: 0-19 7f-8f: 0-3 9f-13f: 0-1 14f+: 0-0
Track : LH: 0-10 RH: 0-2 Tight: 0-1 Gall: 0-7
Aids: Bl: 0-0 Vi: 0-0 Tstrap: 0-17 Ckp: 0-17
Best Rating: 60 6/08 Leic 5f218y gd-fm

Moderate; effective over 7f; acts on fast ground.

Billberry

101(105) (77)69
4-y-o gr g Diktat-Elderberry (Bin Ajwaad (IRE))
S C Williams Essex Racing Club (Billberry)

Placings:6/2011005**4**-3204032**654165** (7832)
2009: 8^{3}SD, 7^{2}SD, 6^{0}SD, 7^{4}GS, 8^{0}G, 6^{3}GF, 7^{2}F, 7^{6}SD, 7^{5}SD, 6^{4}SD, 6^{1}SD, 7^{6}SD, 6^{5}SD,

	Starts	1st	2nd	3rd	Win & Pl
Career Total (Turf)	9	0	1	1	3032
Career Total (AW)	13	3	2	1	10710

77 11/09 Ling 6f (0-70)H STD £2388
75 9/08 Ling 7f (0-55)H STD £2590
65 9/08 Kemp 7f (0-55) STD £2047
Total win prize-money £7025

Going (Turf): **Sf: 0-1 GS: 0-4 Gd: 0-2 GF: 0-1 Fm: 0-1**
Distance: 5f/6f: 1-8 **7f-8f: 2-13** 9f-13f: 0-1 14f+: 0-0
Track : **LH: 2-7** RH: 1-7 **Tight: 2-6** Gall: 0-0
Aids: Bl: 0-0 Vi: 0-0 Tstrap: 0-1 Ckp: 0-1
Best Rating: 77 11/09 Ling 6f stand

Fair; effective at 6f-1m; acts on Polytrack; has worn a tongue tie/cheekpieces.

Billich

(18) (91)84
6-y-o ch h Observatory (USA)-Pomponette (USA) (Rahy (USA))
S W Hall Claydon Hall Stud Partnership No 1

Placings:5062/231603404114/20001/0 (4857)
2009: 12^{0}SD,

	Starts	1st	2nd	3rd	Win & Pl
Career Total (Turf)	10	2	0	1	10940
Career Total (AW)	12	2	3	1	13720

84 8/07 Thsk 2m (0-85)H G-F £5181
88 11/06 Wolv 2m119y (0-75)H STD £3238
79 11/06 Wolv 2m119y (0-85)H SF £5505
81 7/06 Yarm 1m3f101y FRM £3238
Total win prize-money £17165

Going (Turf): Sf: 0-0 GS: 0-1 Gd: 0-3 **GF: 1-4 Fm: 1-2**
Distance: 5f/6f: 0-2 7f-8f: 0-2 9f-13f: 1-9 **14f+: 3-9**
Track : **LH: 4-17** RH: 0-3 **Tight: 4-17** Gall: 0-0
Aids: Bl: 0-0 Vi: 0-0 Tstrap: 0-0 Ckp: 0-0
Best Rating: 91 2/07 Ling 2m stand

Fair; stays 2m; acts on fast ground and Polytrack; can take a grip.

Billie Jean

86(94) (65)38
2-y-o b f Bertolini (USA)-Factice (USA) (Known Fact (USA))
B W Hills Phil Cunningham

Placings:0001 (7778)
2009: 5^{0}GF, 6^{0}G, 6^{0}SD, 5^{1}SD,

	Starts	1st	2nd	3rd	Win & Pl
Career Total (Turf)	2	0	0	0	
Career Total (AW)	2	1	0	0	2047

65 12/09 Sthl 5f (0-60) STD £2047
Total win prize-money £2047

Going (Turf): **Sf: 0-0 GS: 0-0 Gd: 0-1 GF: 0-1 Fm: 0-0**
Distance: **5f/6f: 1-4** 7f-8f: 0-0 9f-13f: 0-0 14f+: 0-0
Track : LH: 0-0 RH: 0-1 Tight: 0-0 Gall: 0-1
Aids: Bl: 0-0 Vi: 0-0 Tstrap: 0-0 Ckp: 0-0
Best Rating: 65 12/09 Sthl 5f stand

Modest; suited by 5f and acts on Fibresand.

Billionaire Boy (IRE)

66
2-y-o b c Acclamation-Shalwell (IRE) (Shalford (IRE))
Patrick Morris Rob Lloyd Racing Limited

Placings:5 (6381)
2009: 6^{5}GF,

	Starts	1st	2nd	3rd	Win & Pl
Career Total (Turf)	1	0	0	0	0

Going (Turf): **Sf: 0-0 GS: 0-0 Gd: 0-0 GF: 0-1 Fm: 0-0**
Distance: 5f/6f: 0-1 7f-8f: 0-0 9f-13f: 0-0 14f+: 0-0
Track : LH: 0-0 RH: 0-0 Tight: 0-0 Gall: 0-0
Aids: Bl: 0-0 Vi: 0-0 Tstrap: 0-0 Ckp: 0-0
Best Rating:

Out of an unraced half-sister to Bachir.

Billy Beetroot (USA)

99(100) (65)67

3-y-o b g Rossini (USA)-Grazia (Sharpo)

R A Harris (S C Williams 8/6) W Clifford

Placings:050-23223321140**2**000**4**6**3**000 **(7645)**

2009: 5^{2}GF, 5^{3}GF, 6^{2}G, 5^{2}G, 5^{3}GF, 5^{3}GF, 5^{2}GF, 5^{1}G, 6^{1}GF, 5^{4}GF, 6^{0}GF, **5**^{2}SD, 6^{0}GF, 6^{0}G, 5^{0}GS, 5^{4}G, **6**^{6}SD, 5^{3}G, **5**^{0}SD, **6**^{0}SD, **5**^{0}SD,

	Starts	1st	2nd	3rd	Win & Pl
Career Total (Turf)	**19**	**2**	**4**	**4**	**9884**
Career Total (AW)	**5**	**0**	**1**	**0**	**806**

59 6/09 Folk 6f G-F £2047
67 6/09 Brig 5f59y (0-70)H GD £3154
Total win prize-money £5201

Going (Turf): Sf: 0-0 GS: 0-1 **Gd: 1-7 GF: 1-11** Fm: 0-0
Distance: **5f/6f: 2-23** 7f-8f: 0-1 9f-13f: 0-0 14f+: 0-0
Track : **LH: 1-9** RH: 0-1 Tight: 0-4 Gall: 0-3
Aids: Bl: 0-6 Vi: 0-0 Tstrap: 0-3 Ckp: 0-3
Best Rating: **67** 6/09 Brig 5f59y good

Moderate; suited by 5f-6f; acts on fast ground; goes on Polytrack; has worn a tongue tie.

Billy Bowmore

89(95) (58)63

4-y-o b g Bahamian Bounty-Shaieef (IRE) (Shareef Dancer (USA))

P A Kirby Heath, O'Connell, Kirby & Fahy

Placings:0420**46**-000**66** **(3031)**

2009: 8^{0}SD, 8^{0}SD, 6^{0}GF, 7^{6}F, 6^{6}G,

	Starts	1st	2nd	3rd	Win & Pl
Career Total (Turf)	**7**	**0**	**1**	**0**	**1108**
Career Total (AW)	**4**	**0**	**0**	**0**	**0**

Going (Turf): **Sf: 0-0 GS: 0-0 Gd: 0-3 GF: 0-3 Fm: 0-1**
Distance: 5f/6f: 0-6 7f-8f: 0-5 9f-13f: 0-0 14f+: 0-0
Track : LH: 0-5 RH: 0-1 Tight: 0-3 Gall: 0-0
Aids: Bl: 0-2 Vi: 0-0 Tstrap: 0-0 Ckp: 0-0
Best Rating: **63** 7/08 Donc 6f good

Modest; effective at 6f; acts on good ground.

Billy Cadiz

73(68) (14)29

4-y-o b g Zilzal (USA)-Faraway Moon (Distant Relative)

N Tinkler Wentdale Limited

Placings:500-000 **(6847)**

2009: 6^{0}S, 6^{0}G, 7^{0}G,

	Starts	1st	2nd	3rd	Win & Pl
Career Total (Turf)	**5**	**0**	**0**	**0**	**0**
Career Total (AW)	**1**	**0**	**0**	**0**	

Going (Turf): **Sf: 0-2 GS: 0-0 Gd: 0-3 GF: 0-0 Fm: 0-0**
Distance: 5f/6f: 0-3 7f-8f: 0-2 9f-13f: 0-1 14f+: 0-0
Track : LH: 0-3 RH: 0-1 Tight: 0-3 Gall: 0-0
Aids: Bl: 0-0 Vi: 0-0 Tstrap: 0-0 Ckp: 0-0
Best Rating: **29** 7/08 Muss 7f30y good

Billy Dane (IRE)

107(93) (77)96

5-y-o b g Fayruz-Lomalou (IRE) (Lightning Dealer)

F P Murtagh James Callow

Placings:622**104**/530000/035413220360-11060022220 **(6675)**

2009: 8^{1}GF, 8^{1}GF, 8^{0}S, 8^{6}G, 7^{0}GF, 8^{0}GF, 6^{2}G, 8^{2}G, 8^{2}G, 8^{2}G, 7^{0}G,

	Starts	1st	2nd	3rd	Win & Pl
Career Total (Turf)	**32**	**3**	**8**	**4**	**67119**
Career Total (AW)	**3**	**1**	**0**	**0**	**3939**

90 5/09 Bevl 1m100y (0-85)H G-F £5180
85 4/09 Hayd 1m30y (0-85)H G-F £5504
80 6/08 Rdcr 1m (0-100)H G-F £10361
86 8/06 Wolv 7f32y STD £3238
Total win prize-money £24287

Going (Turf): Sf: 0-7 GS: 0-4 Gd: 0-9 **GF: 3-9** Fm: 0-1
Distance: 5f/6f: 0-2 7f-8f: 2-22 9f-13f: 2-11 14f+: 0-0
Track : **LH: 2-18** RH: 1-10 **Tight: 1-8** Gall: 0-7
Aids: Bl: 0-0 Vi: 0-0 Tstrap: 1-13 Ckp: 1-13
Best Rating: **96** 9/09 Ayr 1m good

Useful; stays 1m; acts on fast and soft ground; also goes on Polytrack; has worn cheekpieces.

Billy Hot Rocks (IRE)

86(96) (64)63

4-y-o b g Intikhab (USA)-Rock Abbey (IRE) (College Chapel)

Miss Gay Kelleway Hinge, Searchfield & Tamburro

Placings:0/44004**30104**-**05**00 **(1057)**

2009: 7^{0}SD, 5^{0}SD, 6^{0}SD, 7^{0}GF,

	Starts	1st	2nd	3rd	Win & Pl
Career Total (Turf)	**8**	**0**	**0**	**1**	**1046**
Career Total (AW)	**7**	**1**	**0**	**0**	**2590**

64 12/08 Kemp 6f STD £2590
Total win prize-money £2590

Going (Turf): **Sf: 0-0 GS: 0-2 Gd: 0-2 GF: 0-4 Fm: 0-0**
Distance: **5f/6f: 1-7** 7f-8f: 0-8 9f-13f: 0-0 14f+: 0-0
Track : LH: 0-5 **RH: 1-4** Tight: 0-2 Gall: 0-1
Aids: **Bl: 1-4** Vi: 0-1 Tstrap: 0-1 Ckp: 0-1
Best Rating: **64** 12/08 Ling 6f stand

Modest; effective over 6f-7f; acts on easy ground; has worn cheekpieces.

Billy Red

103(112) (82)73

5-y-o ch g Dr Fong (USA)-Liberty Bound (Primo Dominie)

J R Jenkins Mrs Irene Hampson

Placings:40**4**04**35**/65**46**410400/**0**46603**2**0**41403**-**16**00**2**2001**26****04116022** **(7656)**

2009: **6**^{1}SD, **6**^{6}SD, 6^{0}GF, **6**^{0}SD, 5^{2}GF, 5^{2}F, 5^{0}GF, 5^{0}G, 5^{1}GF, 5^{2}GF, 5^{6}GS, **5**^{0}SD, **5**^{4}SD, **5**^{1}SD, **6**^{1}SS, **5**^{6}SD, **6**^{0}SD, **6**^{2}SD, **6**^{2}SD,

	Starts	1st	2nd	3rd	Win & Pl
Career Total (Turf)	**26**	**2**	**3**	**1**	**11787**
Career Total (AW)	**23**	**4**	**3**	**2**	**17644**

80 10/09 Ling 6f (0-75)H SS £3412
75 9/09 Wolv 5f216y (0-70)H STD £2914
73 6/09 Brig 5f59y (0-65)H G-F £2590
75 1/09 GrLe 6f (0-70)H STD £3238
67 10/08 GrLe 6f (0-65)H STD £2590
66 7/07 Sand 5f6y (0-75)H GD £4533
Total win prize-money £19278

Going (Turf): Sf: 0-2 GS: 0-4 **Gd: 1-4 GF: 1-14** Fm: 0-2
Distance: **5f/6f: 6-46** 7f-8f: 0-3 9f-13f: 0-0 14f+: 0-0
Track : **LH: 5-25** RH: 0-2 Tight: 2-14 Gall: 2-6
Aids: **Bl: 6-38** Vi: 0-1 Tstrap: 0-0 Ckp: 0-0
Best Rating: **82** 12/09 Ling 6f stand

Fair; effective over 5f-6f; acts on most ground; goes on Polytrack; has worn blinkers, a visor and an eyeshield.

Billy Simmonds

37(75) (26)

4-y-o b g Man Among Men (IRE)-Lizzie Simmonds (IRE) (Common Grounds)

Miss J Feilden Mrs Jo Lambert

Placings:00 **(6022)**

2009: 7^{0}SD, 10^{0}GF,

	Starts	1st	2nd	3rd	Win & Pl
Career Total (Turf)	**1**	**0**	**0**	**0**	
Career Total (AW)	**1**	**0**	**0**	**0**	

Going (Turf): **Sf: 0-0 GS: 0-0 Gd: 0-0 GF: 0-1 Fm: 0-0**
Distance: 5f/6f: 0-0 7f-8f: 0-1 9f-13f: 0-1 14f+: 0-0
Track : LH: 0-1 RH: 0-1 Tight: 0-0 Gall: 0-0
Aids: Bl: 0-0 Vi: 0-0 Tstrap: 0-0 Ckp: 0-0
Best Rating: **26** 9/09 Kemp 7f stand

Billy Smart (IRE)

86(87) (41)58

3-y-o ch c Exceed And Excel (AUS)-Amber Tide (IRE) (Pursuit Of Love)

A J Lidderdale (D J S Ffrench Davis 16/7) Smart Racing Ltd

Placings:000-504000 **(5873)**

2009: 10^{5}GF, 8^{0}G, 7^{4}SD, 7^{0}GF, 8^{0}G, 10^{0}G,

	Starts	1st	2nd	3rd	Win & Pl
Career Total (Turf)	**7**	**0**	**0**	**0**	**0**
Career Total (AW)	**2**	**0**	**0**	**0**	**0**

Going (Turf): **Sf: 0-0 GS: 0-1 Gd: 0-4 GF: 0-2 Fm: 0-0**
Distance: 5f/6f: 0-1 7f-8f: 0-5 9f-13f: 0-3 14f+: 0-0
Track : LH: 0-8 RH: 0-0 Tight: 0-2 Gall: 0-3
Aids: Bl: 0-1 Vi: 0-0 Tstrap: 0-0 Ckp: 0-0
Best Rating: **58** 10/08 Leic 7f9y good

Billy The Gas

50

4-y-o b g Dr Fong (USA)-Hawayah (IRE) (Shareef Dancer (USA))

N Tinkler Wentdale Limited

Placings:0 **(4022)**

2009: 9^{0}GF,

	Starts	1st	2nd	3rd	Win & Pl
Career Total (Turf)	**1**	**0**	**0**	**0**	

Going (Turf): **Sf: 0-0 GS: 0-0 Gd: 0-0 GF: 0-1 Fm: 0-0**
Distance: 5f/6f: 0-0 7f-8f: 0-0 9f-13f: 0-1 14f+: 0-0
Track : LH: 0-0 RH: 0-1 Tight: 0-0 Gall: 0-0
Aids: Bl: 0-0 Vi: 0-0 Tstrap: 0-0 Ckp: 0-0

Billy's Bid

70 32

2-y-o b f Kyllachy-Bajan Blue (Lycius (USA))

I W McInnes Mrs Ann Morris

Placings:050 **(4001)**

2009: 5^{0}F, 7^{5}GF, 7^{0}GS,

	Starts	1st	2nd	3rd	Win & Pl
Career Total (Turf)	**3**	**0**	**0**	**0**	**0**

Going (Turf): **Sf: 0-0 GS: 0-1 Gd: 0-0 GF: 0-1 Fm: 0-1**
Distance: 5f/6f: 0-1 7f-8f: 0-2 9f-13f: 0-0 14f+: 0-0

Track : LH: 0-1 RH: 0-1 Tight: 0-0 Gall: 0-0
Aids: Bl: 0-0 Vi: 0-0 Tstrap: 0-0 Ckp: 0-0
Best Rating: 32 6/09 Bevl 7f100y gd-fm

Billyonair

(66) (18)

2-y-o ch g Auction House (USA)-Westmead Tango (Pursuit Of Love)

W De Best-Turner W De Best-Turner

Placings:00 (7388)

2009: 6^{0}SD, 8^{0}SD,

	Starts	1st	2nd	3rd	Win & Pl
Career Total (Turf)	0	0	0	0	
Career Total (AW)	2	0	0	0	

Going (Turf): **Sf: 0-0 GS: 0-0 Gd: 0-0 GF: 0-0 Fm: 0-0**
Distance: 5f/6f: 0-1 7f-8f: 0-1 9f-13f: 0-0 14f+: 0-0
Track : LH: 0-2 RH: 0-0 Tight: 0-2 Gall: 0-0
Aids: Bl: 0-0 Vi: 0-0 Tstrap: 0-0 Ckp: 0-0
Best Rating: 18 11/09 Ling 1m stand

Bin End

106 89

3-y-o b g King's Best (USA)-Overboard (IRE) (Rainbow Quest (USA))

M L W Bell Chris Wright & The Hon Mrs J M Corbett

Placings:3-142 (2189)

2009: 9^{1}GF, 10^{4}GF, 11^{2}GF,

	Starts	1st	2nd	3rd	Win & Pl
Career Total (Turf)	4	1	1	1	6079

80	4/09	Leic	1m1f218y		G-F	£3238

Total win prize-money £3238

Going (Turf): Sf: 0-1 GS: 0-0 Gd: 0-0 **GF: 1-3** Fm: 0-0
Distance: 5f/6f: 0-0 7f-8f: 0-0 **9f-13f: 1-4** 14f+: 0-0
Track : LH: 0-2 **RH: 1-2** Tight: 0-1 Gall: 0-1
Aids: Bl: 0-0 Vi: 0-0 Tstrap: 0-0 Ckp: 0-0
Best Rating: 89 5/09 Gdwd 1m3f gd-fm

Useful; stays 1m3f; acts on fast and soft ground.

Bin Shamardal (IRE)

84 59

2-y-o ch c Shamardal (USA)-Lonely Ahead (USA) (Rahy (USA))

B W Hills Mohamed Obaida

Placings:0 (4524)

2009: 7^{0}S,

	Starts	1st	2nd	3rd	Win & Pl
Career Total (Turf)	1	0	0	0	

Going (Turf): **Sf: 0-1 GS: 0-0 Gd: 0-0 GF: 0-0 Fm: 0-0**
Distance: 5f/6f: 0-0 7f-8f: 0-1 9f-13f: 0-0 14f+: 0-0
Track : LH: 0-0 RH: 0-1 Tight: 0-0 Gall: 0-0
Aids: Bl: 0-0 Vi: 0-0 Tstrap: 0-0 Ckp: 0-0
Best Rating: 59 8/09 Gdwd 7f soft

Binanti

85(96) (69)97

9-y-o b g Bin Ajwaad (IRE)-Princess Rosananti (IRE) (Shareef Dancer (USA))

P R Chamings Mrs J E L Wright

Placings:0641313/000420140/0660055302121/304500600 45233/0013302303300302000/6221340000/020000-600 (3469)

2009: 7^{6}GF, 7^{0}SD, 7^{0}SD,

	Starts	1st	2nd	3rd	Win & Pl
Career Total (Turf)	54	3	6	8	102633
Career Total (AW)	26	4	3	5	35371

99	6/07	Asct	7f	(0-105)H	G-S	£34276
89	3/06	Kemp	7f	(0-80)H	STD	£5505
92	12/04	Ling	1m	(0-80)	STD	£6841
89	12/04	Wolv	1m141y	(0-92)H	STD	£6671
96	8/03	Sand	7f16y	C(0-90)H	G-F	£9737
99	9/02	Gdwd	7f	C	G-F	£7830
86	9/02	Sthl	1m	F	SLW	£2982

Total win prize-money £73843

Going (Turf): Sf: 0-1 GS: 1-6 Gd: 0-17 **GF: 2-28** Fm: 0-2
Distance: 5f/6f: 0-3 **7f-8f: 6-72** 9f-13f: 1-5 14f+: 0-0
Track : LH: 3-26 RH: 3-32 **Tight: 2-20** Gall: 0-2
Aids: Bl: 0-1 **Vi: 2-21** Tstrap: 0-0 Ckp: 0-0
Best Rating: 99 8/07 Gdwd 7f good

Useful; effective over 7f-1m; suited by fast ground and Polytrack; sometimes does not find much off the bridle; has worn a visor.

Binfield (IRE)

102(103) (77)72

4-y-o b f Officer (USA)-Identify (IRE) (Persian Bold)

B G Powell N J Hitchins

Placings:02400/154-306204003060 (7423)

2009: 8^{3}SD, 8^{0}SD, 8^{6}GF, 8^{2}GF, 8^{0}GF, 9^{4}GF, 8^{0}F, 8^{0}SD, 8^{3}G, 8^{0}G, 8^{6}SD, 8^{0}SD,

	Starts	1st	2nd	3rd	Win & Pl
Career Total (Turf)	13	0	2	1	3583
Career Total (AW)	7	1	0	1	2769

77	4/08	Kemp	7f	(0-65)H	STD	£2047

Total win prize-money £2047

Going (Turf): **Sf: 0-2 GS: 0-2 Gd: 0-2 GF: 0-6 Fm: 0-1**
Distance: 5f/6f: 0-1 **7f-8f: 1-14** 9f-13f: 0-5 14f+: 0-0
Track : LH: 0-4 **RH: 1-8** Tight: 0-4 Gall: 0-1
Aids: Bl: 0-0 Vi: 0-0 Tstrap: 0-0 Ckp: 0-0
Best Rating: 77 2/09 Ling 1m stand

Modest; stays 1m; acts on fast and easy ground and on Polytrack.

Biniou (IRE)

109(108) (101)111

6-y-o b g Mozart (IRE)-Cap Coz (IRE) (Indian Ridge)

R M H Cowell Stennett, Dasmal, Rix, Barr, Mrs Penney

Placings:65313/23034410634/0000023401/030040025-1101 (4885)

2009: 5^{1}G, 5^{1}G, 6^{0}S, 5^{1}GS,

	Starts	1st	2nd	3rd	Win & Pl
Career Total (Turf)	33	6	2	6	130190
Career Total (AW)	6	0	1	1	2662

111	8/09	Nott	5f13y		G-S	£7477
111	7/09	NmkJ	5f	(0-95)H	GD	£9714
101	5/09	Thsk	5f	(0-100)H	GD	£12045
103	11/07	Fntb	6f		VS	£17568
112	8/06	Deau	5f		G-S	£17241
	8/05	Vich	5f		SFT	£6737

Total win prize-money £70783

Going (Turf): Sf: 1-6 **GS: 2-8 Gd: 2-16** GF: 0-2 Fm: 0-0
Distance: **5f/6f: 6-33** 7f-8f: 0-5 9f-13f: 0-0 14f+: 0-0
Track : LH: 0-3 **RH: 1-10** Tight: 0-0 Gall: 0-3
Aids: Bl: 0-0 Vi: 0-0 Tstrap: 0-0 Ckp: 0-0
Best Rating: 112 10/06 Lonc 5f good

Smart; ex-French; winner in Listed company; effective over 5f-6f; acts on good and easier ground and on Polytrack; has worn cheekpieces.

Binnion Bay (IRE)

97(105) (61)57

8-y-o b g Fasliyev (USA)-Literary (Woodman (USA))

J J Bridger J J Bridger

Placings:3100/0006000/5635302600000300/60020110/6 01442231410110560000050/06653443044060-61303003020000060001 (7660)

2009: 8^{6}SD, 7^{1}SD, 7^{3}SD, 7^{0}SD, 6^{3}GF, 8^{0}GF, 9^{0}GF, 10^{3}GF, 8^{0}SD, 10^{2}SD, 8^{0}GF, 8^{0}GF, 10^{0}G, 7^{0}GF, 9^{6}GF, 8^{0}SD, 10^{0}SD, 12^{0}SD, 10^{1}SD,

	Starts	1st	2nd	3rd	Win & Pl
Career Total (Turf)	34	2	0	4	10074
Career Total (AW)	59	8	5	6	23081

56	12/09	Ling	1m2f	(0-52)H	STD	£1637
59	2/09	Kemp	7f	(0-55)H	STD	£2047
75	5/07	Ling	7f	(0-75)H	G-S	£3123
82	5/07	Ling	1m	(0-75)H	STD	£3238
77	4/07	Ling	1m	(0-70)H	STD	£2914
69	3/07	Kemp	1m	(0-70)H	STD	£2914
64	2/07	Ling	7f	(0-58)H	STD	£1706
59	12/06	Ling	7f	(0-45)	STD	£1433
58	12/06	Kemp	7f	(0-45)	STD	£1365
76	5/03	Gdwd	5f	D	GD	£4771

Total win prize-money £25152

Going (Turf): Sf: 0-0 **GS: 1-3 Gd: 1-9** GF: 0-21 Fm: 0-1
Distance: 5f/6f: 1-16 **7f-8f: 8-61** 9f-13f: 1-16 14f+: 0-0
Track : **LH: 5-47** RH: 3-26 **Tight: 5-46** Gall: 0-4
Aids: **Bl: 9-53** Vi: 0-14 Tstrap: 0-5 Ckp: 0-5
Best Rating: 82 5/07 Ling 1m stand

Moderate; stays 1m2f; acts on good ground and on Polytrack; has worn blinkers and cheekpieces.

Bint Almatar (USA)

89 71

2-y-o b f Kingmambo (USA)-Firth Of Lorne (IRE) (Danehill (USA))

Saeed Bin Suroor Godolphin

Placings:10 (7187)

2009: 8^{1}GF, 8^{0}G,

	Starts	1st	2nd	3rd	Win & Pl
Career Total (Turf)	2	1	0	0	3886

71	9/09	Nott	1m75y	G-F	£3885

Total win prize-money £3886

Going (Turf): Sf: 0-0 GS: 0-0 Gd: 0-1 **GF: 1-1** Fm: 0-0
Distance: 5f/6f: 0-0 7f-8f: 0-1 **9f-13f: 1-1** 14f+: 0-0
Track : **LH: 1-1** RH: 0-0 Tight: 0-0 Gall: 0-0
Aids: Bl: 0-0 Vi: 0-0 Tstrap: 0-0 Ckp: 0-0
Best Rating: 71 9/09 Nott 1m75y gd-fm

Fair winner on debut; effective over 1m; acts on fast ground.

Bint Doyen

102 79

2-y-o br f Doyen (IRE)-Zonda (Fabulous Dancer (USA))

C E Brittain Mohammed Al Nabouda

Placings:10 (6852)

2009: 7^{1}G, 7^{0}G,

	Starts	1st	2nd	3rd	Win & Pl
Career Total (Turf)	2	1	0	0	2730

79 10/09 Folk 7f GD £2729
Total win prize-money £2730

Going (Turf): Sf: 0-0 GS: 0-0 **Gd: 1-2** GF: 0-0 Fm: 0-0
Distance: 5f/6f: 0-0 **7f-8f: 1-2** 9f-13f: 0-0 14f+: 0-0
Track : LH: 0-0 RH: 0-0 Tight: 0-0 Gall: 0-0
Aids: Bl: 0-0 Vi: 0-0 Tstrap: 0-0 Ckp: 0-0
Best Rating: 79 10/09 Folk 7f good

Useful; stays 7f and acts on good and easy ground.

Bintalaleumydarlin (IRE)

95 53
2-y-o b f Refuse To Bend (IRE)-Silly Game (IRE) (Bigstone (IRE))
M Johnston R M F Curry

Placings:04006 **(6895)**
2009: 7^{0}G, 7^{4}GS, 7^{0}G, 8^{0}G, 8^{6}GF,

	Starts	1st	2nd	3rd	Win & Pl
Career Total (Turf)	5	0	0	0	168

Going (Turf): Sf: 0-0 GS: 0-1 Gd: 0-3 GF: 0-1 Fm: 0-0
Distance: 5f/6f: 0-0 7f-8f: 0-4 9f-13f: 0-1 14f+: 0-0
Track : LH: 0-3 RH: 0-2 Tight: 0-3 Gall: 0-1
Aids: Bl: 0-0 Vi: 0-0 Tstrap: 0-0 Ckp: 0-0
Best Rating: 53 8/09 Muss 7f30y gd-sft

Bintalwaadi

79 66
2-y-o b f Barathea (IRE)-Al Durrah (USA) (Darshaan)
E A L Dunlop Hamdan Al Maktoum

Placings:2 **(4468)**
2009: 6^{2}HY,

	Starts	1st	2nd	3rd	Win & Pl
Career Total (Turf)	1	0	1	0	1156

Going (Turf): Sf: 0-1 GS: 0-0 Gd: 0-0 GF: 0-0 Fm: 0-0
Distance: 5f/6f: 0-0 7f-8f: 0-1 9f-13f: 0-0 14f+: 0-0
Track : LH: 0-0 RH: 0-0 Tight: 0-0 Gall: 0-0
Aids: Bl: 0-0 Vi: 0-0 Tstrap: 0-0 Ckp: 0-0
Best Rating: 66 7/09 Nott 6f15y heavy

Birbone (FR)

(104) (95)101
4-y-o b g Sendawar (IRE)-Labour Of Love (USA) (Silver Deputy (CAN))
Saeed Bin Suroor Godolphin

Placings:112/143330-6 **(2398)**
2009: 10^{6}SD,

	Starts	1st	2nd	3rd	Win & Pl
Career Total (Turf)	9	3	1	3	48256
Career Total (AW)	1	0	0	0	0

93 4/08 Chan 1m1f VS £12500
11/07 Pari 1m SFT £5743
10/07 Pari 1m G-S £4391
Total win prize-money £22635

Going (Turf): Sf: 1-4 GS: 1-1 Gd: 0-2 GF: 0-0 Fm: 0-0
Distance: 5f/6f: 0-0 **7f-8f: 2-3** 9f-13f: 1-7 14f+: 0-0
Track : LH: 0-2 **RH: 1-3** Tight: 0-1 Gall: 0-0
Aids: Bl: 0-0 Vi: 0-0 Tstrap: 0-1 Ckp: 0-1
Best Rating: 101 10/08 MsnL 1m1f soft

Very useful; effective at around 1m1f; acts on soft ground.

Bird On The Wire

(91) (55)
2-y-o gr f Compton Place-Pomponette (USA) (Rahy (USA))
W G M Turner Mascalls Stud

Placings:0000 **(7421)**
2009: 5^{0}SD, 6^{0}SD, 7^{0}SD, 6^{0}SD,

	Starts	1st	2nd	3rd	Win & Pl
Career Total (Turf)	0	0	0	0	
Career Total (AW)	4	0	0	0	

Going (Turf): Sf: 0-0 GS: 0-0 Gd: 0-0 GF: 0-0 Fm: 0-0
Distance: 5f/6f: 0-3 7f-8f: 0-1 9f-13f: 0-0 14f+: 0-0
Track : LH: 0-2 RH: 0-2 Tight: 0-1 Gall: 0-0
Aids: Bl: 0-0 Vi: 0-0 Tstrap: 0-1 Ckp: 0-1
Best Rating: 55 10/09 Kemp 6f stand

Birdinthehand (FR)

89(101) (67)73
3-y-o b f Nayef (USA)-Bird In The Sky (CAN) (Sky Classic (CAN))
H R A Cecil H E Sheikh Sultan Bin Khalifa Al Nahyan

Placings:322 **(3432)**
2009: 11^{3}SD, 11^{2}GF, 11^{2}GF,

	Starts	1st	2nd	3rd	Win & Pl
Career Total (Turf)	2	0	2	0	1745
Career Total (AW)	1	0	0	1	722

Going (Turf): Sf: 0-0 GS: 0-0 Gd: 0-0 GF: 0-2 Fm: 0-0
Distance: 5f/6f: 0-0 7f-8f: 0-0 9f-13f: 0-3 14f+: 0-0
Track : LH: 0-1 RH: 0-1 Tight: 0-1 Gall: 0-0
Aids: Bl: 0-0 Vi: 0-0 Tstrap: 0-0 Ckp: 0-0
Best Rating: 73 6/09 Leic 1m3f183y gd-fm

Fair; stays almost 1m4f; acts on fast ground.

Birkside

104(106) (92)94
6-y-o ch g Spinning World (USA)-Bright Hope (IRE) (Danehill (USA))
Miss L A Perratt (Ollie Pears 30/5) Ken McGarrity

Placings:05/26502/065335110051111**2121**/1410301301 0200**5004**-5010624015356 **(7118)**
2009: 12^{5}GF, 12^{0}GF, 11^{1}GF, 12^{0}GF, 11^{6}GF, 11^{2}GF, 13^{4}G, 12^{0}G, 12^{1}G, 14^{5}G, 12^{3}GF, 12^{5}SF, 12^{6}GS,

	Starts	1st	2nd	3rd	Win & Pl
Career Total (Turf)	40	8	3	5	45079
Career Total (AW)	18	7	3	0	25117

68 8/09 Muss 1m4f100y GD £2590
82 5/09 Haml 1m3f16y G-F £2729
85 7/08 York 1m4f G-F £5180
91 6/08 Ayr 1m5f13y (0-95)H G-F £11009
87 5/08 York 1m4f (0-85)H G-F £7123
96 1/08 Wolv 1m5f194y (0-85)H SS £4533
90 12/07 Wolv 1m4f50y (0-85)H STD £4857
80 12/07 Wolv 1m4f50y (0-70)H STD £3238
74 11/07 Kemp 1m2f STD £2047
71 10/07 Kemp 1m3f STD £2047
65 10/07 Rdcr 1m2f GD £3886
60 9/07 Leic 1m1f218y GD £2590
61 9/07 Ling 1m2f STD £2047
71 6/07 Ling 1m2f (0-70)H STD £2817
69 5/07 Brig 1m1f209y SFT £1943
Total win prize-money £58646

Going (Turf): Sf: 1-3 GS: 0-3 Gd: 3-19 **GF: 4-14** Fm: 0-1
Distance: 5f/6f: 0-0 7f-8f: 0-4 **9f-13f: 13-45** 14f+: 2-9
Track : **LH: 10-35** RH: 5-21 **Tight: 8-32** Gall: 2-13
Aids: Bl: 0-0 Vi: 0-0 Tstrap: 0-3 Ckp: 0-3
Best Rating: 96 1/08 Wolv 1m5f194y std-slw

Fair; effective at around 1m2f-1m6f; acts on most ground on turf but suited by fast; very effective on Polytrack; has worn a tongue tie.

Birthday Star (IRE)

(98) (48)58
7-y-o b g Desert King (IRE)-White Paper (IRE) (Marignan (USA))
Mrs L C Jewell Dr David Chapman-Jones

Placings:0/**0**43006420/**0**30610250532**5**/00040210456/00-6 **(7642)**
2009: 14^{6}SD,

	Starts	1st	2nd	3rd	Win & Pl
Career Total (Turf)	9	0	1	0	1389
Career Total (AW)	28	2	3	3	8910

63 7/07 Wolv 1m4f50y (0-60) STD £2730
66 3/06 Wolv 1m4f50y (0-60)H STD £2388
Total win prize-money £5119

Going (Turf): Sf: 0-2 GS: 0-2 Gd: 0-0 GF: 0-5 Fm: 0-0
Distance: 5f/6f: 0-1 7f-8f: 0-3 **9f-13f: 2-26** 14f+: 0-7
Track : **LH: 2-29** RH: 0-5 **Tight: 2-26** Gall: 0-1
Aids: Bl: 0-1 Vi: 0-0 Tstrap: 0-2 Ckp: 0-2
Best Rating: 67 9/06 Wolv 1m4f50y stand

Moderate; effective over 1m4f-1m6f; acts on Polytrack; has worn cheekpieces.

Bishaara (IRE)

(88) (64)
3-y-o b f Alhaarth (IRE)-Majmu (USA) (Al Nasr (FR))
J H M Gosden Hamdan Al Maktoum

Placings:4-6 **(0849)**
2009: 8^{6}SD,

	Starts	1st	2nd	3rd	Win & Pl
Career Total (Turf)	0	0	0	0	
Career Total (AW)	2	0	0	0	289

Going (Turf): Sf: 0-0 GS: 0-0 Gd: 0-0 GF: 0-0 Fm: 0-0
Distance: 5f/6f: 0-0 7f-8f: 0-2 9f-13f: 0-0 14f+: 0-0
Track : LH: 0-0 RH: 0-2 Tight: 0-0 Gall: 0-0
Aids: Bl: 0-0 Vi: 0-0 Tstrap: 0-0 Ckp: 0-0
Best Rating: 64 7/08 Kemp 7f stand

Modest; stays 7f and acts on Polytrack.

Bishop Rock (USA)

83(98) (61)60
3-y-o b c Vicar (USA)-Rhumba Rage (USA) (Nureyev (USA))
M H Tompkins Mr & Mrs G Middlebrook

Placings:06-500 **(3099)**
2009: 10^{5}SD, 9^{0}GF, 9^{0}G,

	Starts	1st	2nd	3rd	Win & Pl
Career Total (Turf)	4	0	0	0	0
Career Total (AW)	1	0	0	0	0

Going (Turf): Sf: 0-0 GS: 0-1 Gd: 0-1 GF: 0-2 Fm: 0-0
Distance: 5f/6f: 0-1 7f-8f: 0-0 9f-13f: 0-4 14f+: 0-0
Track : LH: 0-2 RH: 0-2 Tight: 0-4 Gall: 0-0

Aids: Bl: 0-0 Vi: 0-0 Tstrap: 0-0 Ckp: 0-0
Best Rating: **61** 2/09 Ling 1m2f stand

Bishopbriggs (USA)

(104) (74)**69**

4-y-o ch g Victory Gallop (CAN)-Inny River (USA) (Seattle Slew (USA))
M G Quinlan (J Ryan 27/5) Maurice Kirby

Placings:03300/**3**61056**2**4000**2**0456-000000 **(7880)**
2009: 5^{0}SD, 7^{0}SD, 6^{0}SD, 6^{0}SD, 5^{0}SD, 7^{0}SD,

	Starts	1st	2nd	3rd	Win & Pl
Career Total (Turf)	9	0	0	2	605
Career Total (AW)	18	1	2	1	4464

71 6/08 Wolv 5f216y (0-65)H STD £2388
Total win prize-money £2388

Going (Turf): **Sf: 0-1 GS: 0-1 Gd: 0-3 GF: 0-3 Fm: 0-1**
Distance: **5f/6f: 1-21** 7f-8f: 0-6 9f-13f: 0-0 14f+: 0-0
Track : **LH: 1-15** RH: 0-4 **Tight: 1-13** Gall: 0-1
Aids: Bl: 0-0 Vi: 0-0 Tstrap: 0-2 Ckp: 0-2
Best Rating: **74** 11/08 Wolv 5f216y stand

Modest; effective over 6f-1m; acts on good and faster ground and on both All-Weather surfaces.

Bitter Honey

91(89) (53)**62**

2-y-o b f Reset (AUS)-Piccolo Cativo (Komaite (USA))
Mrs G S Rees Capt James Wilson

Placings:4034005 **(7713)**
2009: 6^{4}HY, 5^{0}GF, 6^{3}S, 6^{4}GS, 5^{0}SF, 5^{0}SD, 5^{5}SD,

	Starts	1st	2nd	3rd	Win & Pl
Career Total (Turf)	4	0	0	1	1275
Career Total (AW)	3	0	0	0	0

Going (Turf): **Sf: 0-2 GS: 0-1 Gd: 0-0 GF: 0-1 Fm: 0-0**
Distance: 5f/6f: 0-7 7f-8f: 0-0 9f-13f: 0-0 14f+: 0-0
Track : LH: 0-4 RH: 0-0 Tight: 0-4 Gall: 0-0
Aids: Bl: 0-0 Vi: 0-0 Tstrap: 0-0 Ckp: 0-0
Best Rating: **62** 5/09 Hayd 6f heavy

Modest; stays 6f; acts on soft ground.

Bitter Man (IRE)

78 **71**

2-y-o b c Azamour (IRE)-Savieres (IRE) (Sadler's Wells (USA))
M R Channon Jaber Abdullah

Placings:3 **(2889)**
2009: 7^{3}G,

	Starts	1st	2nd	3rd	Win & Pl
Career Total (Turf)	1	0	0	1	770

Going (Turf): **Sf: 0-0 GS: 0-0 Gd: 0-1 GF: 0-0 Fm: 0-0**
Distance: 5f/6f: 0-0 7f-8f: 0-1 9f-13f: 0-0 14f+: 0-0
Track : LH: 0-0 RH: 0-1 Tight: 0-0 Gall: 0-0
Aids: Bl: 0-0 Vi: 0-0 Tstrap: 0-0 Ckp: 0-0
Best Rating: **71** 6/09 Sand 7f16y good

Out of a 1m3f winner; Derby entry; promise on debut over 7f on good.

Bivouac (UAE)

100(98) (60)**69**

5-y-o b g Jade Robbery (USA)-Tentpole (USA) (Rainbow Quest (USA))
G A Swinbank Mrs J M Penney

Placings:300320/432010-06504600 **(5953)**
2009: 7^{0}SD, 10^{6}GF, 10^{5}G, 8^{0}GF, 9^{4}GF, 8^{6}G, 8^{0}S, 10^{0}GF,

	Starts	1st	2nd	3rd	Win & Pl
Career Total (Turf)	15	1	2	1	5045
Career Total (AW)	5	0	0	2	929

69 6/08 Donc 1m (0-60)H GD £2810
Total win prize-money £2811

Going (Turf): Sf: 0-2 GS: 0-3 **Gd: 1-4** GF: 0-6 Fm: 0-0
Distance: 5f/6f: 0-0 **7f-8f: 1-5** 9f-13f: 0-15 14f+: 0-0
Track : **LH: 1-15** RH: 0-5 Tight: 0-7 **Gall: 1-4**
Aids: Bl: 0-0 Vi: 0-0 Tstrap: 0-0 Ckp: 0-0
Best Rating: **69** 6/08 Donc 1m good

Moderate maiden; stays 1m2f; acts on fast and soft ground.

Black Attack (IRE)

(84) (50)**74**

3-y-o br g Invincible Spirit (IRE)-Mughetta (Prince Sabo)
Paul Green Terry Cummins

Placings:20060**66-0** **(0568)**
2009: 5^{0}SD,

	Starts	1st	2nd	3rd	Win & Pl
Career Total (Turf)	5	0	1	0	1253
Career Total (AW)	3	0	0	0	0

Going (Turf): **Sf: 0-2 GS: 0-0 Gd: 0-1 GF: 0-2 Fm: 0-0**
Distance: 5f/6f: 0-4 7f-8f: 0-3 9f-13f: 0-1 14f+: 0-0
Track : LH: 0-3 RH: 0-0 Tight: 0-2 Gall: 0-0
Aids: Bl: 0-1 Vi: 0-1 Tstrap: 0-0 Ckp: 0-0
Best Rating: **74** 6/08 Ripn 5f soft

Black Baccara

92 **65**

2-y-o b f Superior Premium-Areish (IRE) (Keen)
P S McEntee Eventmaker Racehorses

Placings:1 **(1044)**
2009: 5^{1}G,

	Starts	1st	2nd	3rd	Win & Pl
Career Total (Turf)	1	1	0	0	3562

65 3/09 Folk 5f GD £3561
Total win prize-money £3562

Going (Turf): Sf: 0-0 GS: 0-0 **Gd: 1-1** GF: 0-0 Fm: 0-0
Distance: **5f/6f: 1-1** 7f-8f: 0-0 9f-13f: 0-0 14f+: 0-0
Track : LH: 0-0 RH: 0-0 Tight: 0-0 Gall: 0-0
Aids: Bl: 0-0 Vi: 0-0 Tstrap: 0-0 Ckp: 0-0
Best Rating: **65** 3/09 Folk 5f good

Cheaply-bought daughter of a 1m-1m4f winner but related to sprinters as well; narrow winner on debut over 5f on good.

Black Bear Island (IRE)

113 **113**

3-y-o b c Sadler's Wells (USA)-Kasora (IRE) (Darshaan)
Julio C Canani (A P O'Brien 8/8) R D Hubbard, R Masterson & Edward C Allred

Placings:21-3103020
2009: 10^{3}GS, 10^{1}G, 12^{0}G, 12^{3}GF, 12^{0}GS, 10^{2}G, 10^{0}F,

	Starts	1st	2nd	3rd	Win & Pl
Career Total (Turf)	9	2	2	2	179980

113 5/09 York 1m2f88y GD £85155
93 8/08 Naas 7f G-Y £9399
Total win prize-money £94555

Going (Turf): Sf: 0-0 GS: 0-2 **Gd: 1-4** GF: 0-1 Fm: 0-1
Distance: 5f/6f: 0-0 7f-8f: 1-2 9f-13f: 1-7 14f+: 0-0
Track : **LH: 2-5** RH: 0-3 Tight: 0-1 **Gall: 1-2**
Aids: Bl: 0-1 Vi: 0-0 Tstrap: 0-0 Ckp: 0-0
Best Rating: **113** 8/09 Arlt 1m2f good

Smart; Irish trained; brother to High Chaparral; landed Dante Stakes in May 2009; stays 1m2f, will get further; acts on good and easier ground.

Black Beauty

84 (59)**56**

6-y-o br g Diktat-Euridice (IRE) (Woodman (USA))
Evan Williams (M G Quinlan 7/4) R J Gambarini

Placings:0/**6**3**4**11422**4**054/000/0 **(1014)**
2009: 10^{0}G,

	Starts	1st	2nd	3rd	Win & Pl
Career Total (Turf)	15	2	2	0	12741
Career Total (AW)	2	0	0	1	433

77 5/06 Bevl 1m100y (0-70)H GD £4210
68 4/06 Folk 1m1f149y (0-70)H G-F £3238
Total win prize-money £7449

Going (Turf): Sf: 0-1 GS: 0-1 **Gd: 1-5 GF: 1-7** Fm: 0-0
Distance: 5f/6f: 0-0 7f-8f: 0-6 **9f-13f: 2-11** 14f+: 0-0
Track : LH: 0-4 **RH: 2-12 Tight: 1-6** Gall: 0-2
Aids: Bl: 0-0 Vi: 0-0 Tstrap: 0-1 Ckp: 0-1
Best Rating: **86** 6/06 Sand 1m2f7y gd-fm

Fair; stays 1m 3f; acts on most ground.

Black Cloud

71(83) (26)**45**

6-y-o gr g Cloudings (IRE)-Dutch Czarina (Prince Sabo)
G P Enright Mrs Kate Lyons & Mrs Myra Jean Fuller

Placings:0060-00 **(3774)**
2009: 16^{0}SD, 16^{0}GF,

	Starts	1st	2nd	3rd	Win & Pl
Career Total (Turf)	5	0	0	0	0
Career Total (AW)	1	0	0	0	

Going (Turf): **Sf: 0-0 GS: 0-1 Gd: 0-0 GF: 0-4 Fm: 0-0**
Distance: 5f/6f: 0-0 7f-8f: 0-0 9f-13f: 0-4 14f+: 0-2
Track : LH: 0-1 RH: 0-5 Tight: 0-4 Gall: 0-0
Aids: Bl: 0-0 Vi: 0-0 Tstrap: 0-0 Ckp: 0-0
Best Rating: **45** 6/08 Brig 1m3f196y gd-fm

Black Daddy

92(80) (40)**56**

2-y-o b g Night Shift (USA)-Sareb (FR) (Indian Ridge)
R Hannon B Bull

Placings:60003 **(6589)**
2009: 5^{6}SD, 5^{0}GF, 7^{0}G, 7^{0}GF, 6^{3}GS,

	Starts	1st	2nd	3rd	Win & Pl
Career Total (Turf)	4	0	0	1	252
Career Total (AW)	1	0	0	0	0

Going (Turf): **Sf: 0-0 GS: 0-1 Gd: 0-1 GF: 0-2 Fm: 0-0**
Distance: 5f/6f: 0-2 7f-8f: 0-3 9f-13f: 0-0 14f+: 0-0
Track : LH: 0-1 RH: 0-1 Tight: 0-1 Gall: 0-0
Aids: Bl: 0-0 Vi: 0-0 Tstrap: 0-0 Ckp: 0-0
Best Rating: **56** 8/09 Epsm 7f good

Moderate; effective over 6f; acts on easy ground.

Black Dahlia

104(106) (98)80

4-y-o br f Dansili-South Rock (Rock City)

J A Glover (A J McCabe 24/6) Paul J Dixon & Brian Morton

Placings:3460**0**/2513421542040**0**-3504346005123**0115** (7768)

2009: 8^{3}SD, 8^{5}GF, 10^{0}GF, 10^{4}G, 12^{3}GF, 8^{4}G, 9^{6}GF, 10^{0}GS, 13^{0}G, 8^{5}GF, 8^{1}GF, 8^{2}GF, 7^{3}SD, 7^{0}SD, 7^{1}SD, 7^{1}SD, 7^{5}SD,

	Starts	1st	2nd	3rd	Win & Pl
Career Total (Turf)	26	2	3	3	16200
Career Total (AW)	10	3	1	2	12774

94	11/09	Kemp	7f	(0-80)H	STD	£4727
79	11/09	Wolv	7f32y	(0-70)H	STD	£3238
75	9/09	Leic	1m60y	(0-75)H	G-F	£2914
75	6/08	Donc	1m2f60y	(0-75)H	G-F	£3238
71	4/08	GrLe	1m2f	(0-60)H	STD	£2266

Total win prize-money £16384

Going (Turf): Sf: 0-2 GS: 0-3 Gd: 0-8 **GF: 2-13** Fm: 0-0
Distance: 5f/6f: 0-1 7f-8f: 2-10 **9f-13f: 3-24** 14f+: 0-1
Track : **LH: 3-23** RH: 2-11 Tight: 1-7 **Gall: 2-9**
Aids: Bl: 0-0 Vi: 0-0 Tstrap: 0-0 Ckp: 0-0
Best Rating: **98** 12/09 Kemp 7f stand

Fair; effective over 7f-1m2f; acts on fast ground and on Polytrack.

Black Draft

71(101) (48)12

7-y-o b/br g Josr Algarhoud (IRE)-Tilia (Primo Dominie)

B Forsey Mrs Rosemary Rogers

Placings:00/**00066**/000-0000**4** (7770)

2009: 8^{0}SD, 6^{0}SD, 7^{0}SD, 7^{0}GF, 6^{4}SD,

	Starts	1st	2nd	3rd	Win & Pl
Career Total (Turf)	6	0	0	0	
Career Total (AW)	9	0	0	0	0

Going (Turf): **Sf: 0-0 GS: 0-0 Gd: 0-3 GF: 0-3 Fm: 0-0**
Distance: 5f/6f: 0-5 7f-8f: 0-6 9f-13f: 0-4 14f+: 0-0
Track : LH: 0-9 RH: 0-2 Tight: 0-8 Gall: 0-0
Aids: Bl: 0-2 Vi: 0-2 Tstrap: 0-0 Ckp: 0-0
Best Rating: **53** 5/04 Ling 5f gd-fm

Black Eagle (IRE)

103(109) (104)91

3-y-o b c Cape Cross (IRE)-Shimna (Mr Prospector (USA))

A bin Huzaim (Saeed Bin Suroor 14/11) Sheikh Hamdan Bin Mohammed Al Maktoum

Placings:51210

2009: 8^{5}GF, 10^{1}S, 9^{2}SD, 10^{1}SD, 9^{0}FT,

	Starts	1st	2nd	3rd	Win & Pl
Career Total (Turf)	2	1	0	0	3238
Career Total (AW)	3	1	1	0	13481

104	11/09	Ling	1m2f	(0-100)H	STD	£11215
91	10/09	Nott	1m2f50y		SFT	£3238

Total win prize-money £14454

Going (Turf): **Sf: 1-1** GS: 0-0 Gd: 0-0 GF: 0-1 Fm: 0-0
Distance: 5f/6f: 0-0 7f-8f: 0-0 **9f-13f: 2-5** 14f+: 0-0
Track : **LH: 2-4** RH: 0-0 **Tight: 1-2** Gall: 0-0
Aids: Bl: 0-0 Vi: 0-0 Tstrap: 0-0 Ckp: 0-0
Best Rating: **104** 11/09 Ling 1m2f stand

Very useful; stays 1m2f; acts on soft ground; goes on Polytrack.

Black Falcon (IRE)

(106) (68)62

9-y-o ch g In The Wings-Muwasim (USA) (Meadowlake (USA))

John A Harris Mrs A E Harris

Placings:31410050/**0104**/**00**000004205/**0003**/**2205**/43242 5511**50**5336202**056056**-34000 (7677)

2009: 12^{3}SS, 12^{4}SD, 12^{0}SD, 12^{0}SD, 11^{0}SD,

	Starts	1st	2nd	3rd	Win & Pl
Career Total (Turf)	31	3	2	4	28446
Career Total (AW)	29	2	5	2	16132

63	7/08	Sthl	1m4f		SS	£1978
58	6/08	Bevl	1m4f16y		G-F	£2331
92	11/04	Wolv	1m1f103y	(0-92)H	STD	£6952
95	6/03	York	1m2f88y	B(0-100)H	G-F	£15776
78	4/03	Newc	1m2f32y	D	G-F	£4085

Total win prize-money £31123

Going (Turf): Sf: 0-4 GS: 0-4 Gd: 0-12 **GF: 3-11** Fm: 0-0
Distance: 5f/6f: 0-0 7f-8f: 0-2 **9f-13f: 5-56** 14f+: 0-2
Track : **LH: 4-46** RH: 1-12 Tight: 2-20 Gall: 2-9
Aids: Bl: 0-1 Vi: 0-1 Tstrap: 0-1 Ckp: 0-1
Best Rating: **95** 6/03 York 1m2f88y gd-fm

Moderate; stays 1m4f; suited by fast and easy ground; also goes on Fibresand.

Black Jacari (IRE)

104 89

4-y-o b g Black Sam Bellamy (IRE)-Amalia (IRE) (Danehill (USA))

A King David Bellamy & Alan King

Placings:0515/31660-3 (4212)

2009: 14^{3}GF,

	Starts	1st	2nd	3rd	Win & Pl
Career Total (Turf)	10	2	0	2	9636

89	5/08	Gdwd	1m1f192y	(0-80)H	SFT	£5180
78	9/07	Chep	1m14y		G-F	£2914

Total win prize-money £8096

Going (Turf): **Sf: 1-1** GS: 0-1 Gd: 0-2 **GF: 1-6** Fm: 0-0
Distance: 5f/6f: 0-0 7f-8f: 0-1 **9f-13f: 2-8** 14f+: 0-1
Track : LH: 0-4 **RH: 1-3 Tight: 1-2** Gall: 0-3
Aids: Bl: 0-0 Vi: 0-0 Tstrap: 0-0 Ckp: 0-0
Best Rating: **89** 5/08 Gdwd 1m1f192y soft

Useful; effective at 1m2f-1m3f; acts on fast and soft ground.

Black Moma (IRE)

94(88) (36)69

5-y-o b m Averti (IRE)-Sareb (FR) (Indian Ridge)

J R Boyle Alan Moore

Placings:41212/**3304313000600**/**012226600**-00466 (5156)

2009: 6^{0}GF, 5^{0}SD, 6^{4}GF, 5^{6}G, 5^{6}GF,

	Starts	1st	2nd	3rd	Win & Pl
Career Total (Turf)	25	4	5	2	22122
Career Total (AW)	7	0	0	2	1541

66	4/08	Nott	5f13y	(0-65)H	SFT	£2047
77	6/07	Ling	5f	(0-75)H	SFT	£2817
75	8/06	Sand	5f6y		GD	£4533
60	7/06	Leic	5f2y		G-F	£3238

Total win prize-money £12637

Going (Turf): **Sf: 2-4** GS: 0-5 Gd: 1-4 GF: 1-12 Fm: 0-0
Distance: **5f/6f: 4-32** 7f-8f: 0-0 9f-13f: 0-0 14f+: 0-0
Track : LH: 0-6 RH: 0-1 Tight: 0-5 Gall: 0-3
Aids: Bl: 0-0 Vi: 0-0 Tstrap: 0-0 Ckp: 0-0
Best Rating: **79** 7/07 Sand 5f6y good

Modest; effective at 5f; acts on most types of ground, including Polytrack.

Black N Brew (USA)

101(99) (77)76

3-y-o b g Milwaukee Brew (USA)-Natural Glow (USA) (Siphon (BRZ))

J R Best Martin Long

Placings:654**2**4**2334**-**22303516** (7777)

2009: 10^{2}SD, 11^{2}SD, 10^{3}SD, 11^{0}GF, 7^{3}GS, 8^{5}SS, **10^{1}SD**, 12^{6}SD,

	Starts	1st	2nd	3rd	Win & Pl
Career Total (Turf)	6	0	1	1	1132
Career Total (AW)	11	1	3	3	9994

77	12/09	Ling	1m2f	(0-80)H	STD	£4727

Total win prize-money £4727

Going (Turf): **Sf: 0-1 GS: 0-1 Gd: 0-0 GF: 0-4 Fm: 0-0**
Distance: 5f/6f: 0-6 7f-8f: 0-5 **9f-13f: 1-6** 14f+: 0-0
Track : **LH: 1-8** RH: 0-4 **Tight: 1-8** Gall: 0-0
Aids: Bl: 0-0 Vi: 0-0 Tstrap: 0-0 Ckp: 0-0
Best Rating: **77** 12/09 Ling 1m2f stand

Fair; stays 1m2f; acts on fast ground; goes on Polytrack.

Black Nun

27(91) (61)49

3-y-o b f Fasliyev (USA)-Roxy (Rock City)

S Wynne Shropshire Wolves

Placings:3500-6006 (4065)

2009: 8^{6}SD, 12^{0}SD, 12^{0}SD, 10^{6}HY,

	Starts	1st	2nd	3rd	Win & Pl
Career Total (Turf)	3	0	0	0	0
Career Total (AW)	5	0	0	1	648

Going (Turf): **Sf: 0-2 GS: 0-0 Gd: 0-1 GF: 0-0 Fm: 0-0**
Distance: 5f/6f: 0-1 7f-8f: 0-3 9f-13f: 0-4 14f+: 0-0
Track : LH: 0-4 RH: 0-2 Tight: 0-3 Gall: 0-0
Aids: Bl: 0-1 Vi: 0-1 Tstrap: 0-0 Ckp: 0-0
Best Rating: **61** 7/08 Kemp 7f stand

Half-sister to Night Kiss, a two-time winner over 7f, including as a juvenile; promise in maiden company.

Black Or Red (IRE)

95(102) (79)71

4-y-o b g Cape Cross (IRE)-Gentle Thoughts (Darshaan)

I A Wood Graham Bradbury

Placings:003/0000052-0212406205**1** (7649)

2009: 13^{0}SD, 17^{2}GS, 16^{1}G, 16^{2}GS, **16^{4}SD**, 15^{0}S, **16^{6}SD**, 16^{2}GS, 15^{0}S, **16^{5}SD**, **16^{1}SD**,

	Starts	1st	2nd	3rd	Win & Pl
Career Total (Turf)	10	1	3	0	5475
Career Total (AW)	11	1	1	1	3813

79	12/09	Wolv	2m119y	(0-65)H	STD	£2388
71	7/09	Ffos	2m	(0-70)H	GD	£2590

Total win prize-money £4978

Going (Turf): Sf: 0-3 GS: 0-3 **Gd: 1-2** GF: 0-2 Fm: 0-0
Distance: 5f/6f: 0-0 7f-8f: 0-5 9f-13f: 0-3 **14f+: 2-13**
Track : **LH: 2-14** RH: 0-6 Tight: 1-11 Gall: 1-3

Aids: Bl: **1-11** Vi: 0-0 Tstrap: 0-0 Ckp: 0-0
Best Rating: **79** 12/09 Wolv 2m119y stand

Fair; stays 2m; acts on good and easy ground; goes on Polytrack; has worn blinkers and a tongue tie.

Black Rain

95(105) (82)79

4-y-o b g Desert Prince (IRE)-Antigua (Selkirk (USA))
M Wigham R Morecombe, SP Racing Investments SA

Placings:031/06600312-0000010 **(6900)**
2009: 10[0]S, 10[0]GF, 10[0]GS, 8[0]GF, 8[0]GF, 12[1]SF, 10[0]GF,

	Starts	1st	2nd	3rd	Win & Pl
Career Total (Turf)	15	2	0	2	8860
Career Total (AW)	3	1	1	0	4070

79 10/09 Wolv 1m4f50y (0-70)H SF £2914
78 10/08 Wind 1m3f135y (0-70)H GD £2729
75 11/07 NmkR 7f GD £4857
Total win prize-money £10502

Going (Turf): Sf: 0-3 GS: 0-3 **Gd: 2-5** GF: 0-4 Fm: 0-0
Distance: 5f/6f: 0-0 7f-8f: 1-3 **9f-13f: 2-14** 14f+: 0-1
Track : **LH: 1-7** RH: 0-6 **Tight: 2-5** Gall: 0-4
Aids: Bl: 0-0 Vi: 0-4 Tstrap: 0-0 Ckp: 0-0
Best Rating: **84** 10/07 NmkR 1m soft

Fair; stays 1m4f; acts on good and easy ground; has worn a tongue tie and a visor.

Black River Falls (USA)

94(86) (48)58

3-y-o b g Fusaichi Pegasus (USA)-La Lorgnette (CAN) (Val De L'Orne (FR))
I Semple Exchange Court Properties Ltd

Placings:4040300 **(6139)**
2009: 12[4]GF, 9[0]G, 9[4]GF, 8[0]S, 9[3]F, 12[0]SD, 11[0]G,

	Starts	1st	2nd	3rd	Win & Pl
Career Total (Turf)	6	0	0	1	890
Career Total (AW)	1	0	0	0	

Going (Turf): **Sf: 0-1 GS: 0-0 Gd: 0-2 GF: 0-2 Fm: 0-1**
Distance: 5f/6f: 0-0 7f-8f: 0-0 9f-13f: 0-7 14f+: 0-0
Track : LH: 0-3 RH: 0-4 Tight: 0-4 Gall: 0-1
Aids: Bl: 0-3 Vi: 0-0 Tstrap: 0-0 Ckp: 0-0
Best Rating: **58** 4/09 Newc 1m4f93y gd-fm

Moderate; stays 1m2f and acts on fast ground; has worn blinkers.

Black Rock Lake (IRE)

(80) (41)64

3-y-o gr f Daylami (IRE)-God Speed (IRE) (Be My Guest (USA))
T G McCourt T Cassidy

Placings:504300 **(6075)**
2009: 10[5]GF, 10[0]GY, 10[4]Y, 12[3]S, 12[0]HY, 12[0]SD,

	Starts	1st	2nd	3rd	Win & Pl
Career Total (Turf)	5	0	0	1	865
Career Total (AW)	1	0	0	0	

Going (Turf): **Sf: 0-2 GS: 0-0 Gd: 0-0 GF: 0-1 Fm: 0-0**
Distance: 5f/6f: 0-0 7f-8f: 0-0 9f-13f: 0-6 14f+: 0-0
Track : LH: 0-2 RH: 0-3 Tight: 0-1 Gall: 0-0
Aids: Bl: 0-0 Vi: 0-0 Tstrap: 0-0 Ckp: 0-0
Best Rating: **64** 8/09 Gowr 1m4f soft

Black Salix (USA)

89 50

3-y-o br f More Than Ready (USA)-Woodman's Dancer (USA) (Woodman (USA))
Mrs P Sly Michael H Sly Dr T Davies Mrs Pam Sly

Placings:400-0000 **(6390)**
2009: 6[0]GF, 8[0]GS, 8[0]GF, 8[0]GF,

	Starts	1st	2nd	3rd	Win & Pl
Career Total (Turf)	7	0	0	0	385

Going (Turf): **Sf: 0-0 GS: 0-1 Gd: 0-2 GF: 0-4 Fm: 0-0**
Distance: 5f/6f: 0-3 7f-8f: 0-1 9f-13f: 0-3 14f+: 0-0
Track : LH: 0-1 RH: 0-0 Tight: 0-0 Gall: 0-1
Aids: Bl: 0-0 Vi: 0-0 Tstrap: 0-0 Ckp: 0-0
Best Rating: **50** 5/08 Thsk 5f good

Black Sapphire

77 61

2-y-o b f Motivator-Esquiline (USA) (Gone West (USA))
Miss Amy Weaver Mrs Melba Bryce

Placings:500 **(5428)**
2009: 7[5]S, 7[0]G, 8[0]G,

	Starts	1st	2nd	3rd	Win & Pl
Career Total (Turf)	3	0	0	0	0

Going (Turf): **Sf: 0-1 GS: 0-0 Gd: 0-2 GF: 0-0 Fm: 0-0**
Distance: 5f/6f: 0-0 7f-8f: 0-3 9f-13f: 0-0 14f+: 0-0
Track : LH: 0-1 RH: 0-1 Tight: 0-1 Gall: 0-0
Aids: Bl: 0-0 Vi: 0-0 Tstrap: 0-0 Ckp: 0-0
Best Rating: **61** 7/09 NmkJ 7f soft

Black Snowflake (USA)

98 97

2-y-o b c Elusive Quality (USA)-Black Escort (USA) (Southern Halo (USA))
Saeed Bin Suroor Godolphin

Placings:2113345 **(6898)**
2009: 6[2]GF, 6[1]G, 7[1]G, 8[3]G, 8[3]S, 8[4]G, 8[5]GF,

	Starts	1st	2nd	3rd	Win & Pl
Career Total (Turf)	7	2	1	2	33441

93 7/09 Gdwd 7f H GD £12952
85 7/09 Hayd 6f GD £3238
Total win prize-money £16190

Going (Turf): Sf: 0-1 GS: 0-0 **Gd: 2-4** GF: 0-2 Fm: 0-0
Distance: 5f/6f: 1-2 7f-8f: 1-3 9f-13f: 0-2 14f+: 0-0
Track : LH: 0-2 **RH: 1-1** Tight: 0-0 Gall: 0-0
Aids: Bl: 0-0 Vi: 0-0 Tstrap: 0-0 Ckp: 0-0
Best Rating: **97** 9/09 Hayd 1m30y soft

Useful; effective over 6f; acts on fast ground.

Black Spirit (USA)

100 101

2-y-o b c Black Minnaloushe (USA)-L'Extra Honor (USA) (Hero's Honor (USA))
C G Cox A D Spence

Placings:140 **(6268)**
2009: 7[1]G, 7[4]GF, 8[0]G,

	Starts	1st	2nd	3rd	Win & Pl
Career Total (Turf)	3	1	0	0	9161

86 7/09 Asct 7f GD £6476
Total win prize-money £6476

Going (Turf): Sf: 0-0 GS: 0-0 **Gd: 1-2** GF: 0-1 Fm: 0-0
Distance: 5f/6f: 0-0 **7f-8f: 1-3** 9f-13f: 0-0 14f+: 0-0
Track : LH: 0-0 RH: 0-2 Tight: 0-0 Gall: 0-1
Aids: Bl: 0-0 Vi: 0-0 Tstrap: 0-0 Ckp: 0-0
Best Rating: **101** 8/09 Sand 7f16y gd-fm

Smart half-brother to six winners including Sun Chariot winner Majestic Roi; smart; effective over 7f; acts on good ground; has worn a tongue tie.

Black Stocking

91(97) (44)56

4-y-o br f Dansili-Mariette (Blushing Scribe (USA))
Rae Guest (M Wigham 11/5) The Hightailers

Placings:605656 **(7466)**
2009: 8[6]GF, 7[0]GF, 7[5]GS, 8[6]SD, 9[5]SD, 9[6]SD,

	Starts	1st	2nd	3rd	Win & Pl
Career Total (Turf)	3	0	0	0	0
Career Total (AW)	3	0	0	0	0

Going (Turf): **Sf: 0-0 GS: 0-1 Gd: 0-0 GF: 0-2 Fm: 0-0**
Distance: 5f/6f: 0-0 7f-8f: 0-3 9f-13f: 0-3 14f+: 0-0
Track : LH: 0-2 RH: 0-1 Tight: 0-2 Gall: 0-0
Aids: Bl: 0-0 Vi: 0-0 Tstrap: 0-0 Ckp: 0-0
Best Rating: **56** 9/09 Ling 7f gd-sft

Black Tor Figarro (IRE)

(97) (55)67

4-y-o b g Rock Of Gibraltar (IRE)-Will Be Blue (IRE) (Darshaan)
B W Duke B W Duke Racing Ms R E Tupper T H Fletcher

Placings:000/124-05 **(0668)**
2009: 12[0]SD, 16[5]SD,

	Starts	1st	2nd	3rd	Win & Pl
Career Total (Turf)	5	1	1	0	4285
Career Total (AW)	3	0	0	0	0

65 4/08 Wwck 1m2f188y (0-75)H SFT £3238
Total win prize-money £3238

Going (Turf): **Sf: 1-2** GS: 0-2 Gd: 0-0 GF: 0-1 Fm: 0-0
Distance: 5f/6f: 0-0 7f-8f: 0-2 **9f-13f: 1-5** 14f+: 0-1
Track : **LH: 1-5** RH: 0-1 Tight: 0-4 Gall: 0-0
Aids: Bl: 0-0 Vi: 0-0 Tstrap: 0-0 Ckp: 0-0
Best Rating: **67** 4/08 Wind 1m3f135y gd-fm

Modest; stays 1m3f; acts on fast and soft ground.

Blackstone Vegas

92 66

3-y-o ch g Nayef (USA)-Waqood (USA) (Riverman (USA))
J Howard Johnson Andrea & Graham Wylie

Placings:400-02 **(2627)**
2009: 12[0]GS, 11[2]GF,

	Starts	1st	2nd	3rd	Win & Pl
Career Total (Turf)	5	0	1	0	1273

Going (Turf): **Sf: 0-1 GS: 0-2 Gd: 0-0 GF: 0-2 Fm: 0-0**
Distance: 5f/6f: 0-0 7f-8f: 0-3 9f-13f: 0-2 14f+: 0-0
Track : LH: 0-1 RH: 0-4 Tight: 0-2 Gall: 0-1

Aids: Bl: 0-1 Vi: 0-0 Tstrap: 0-0 Ckp: 0-0
Best Rating: 66 7/08 York 7f heavy

Blacktoft (USA)

(107) (81)**80**
6-y-o b/br g Theatrical-Black Truffle (USA) (Mt. Livermore (USA))
Evan Williams (S C Williams 17/2) Chris Watkins & Dave Reynolds

Placings:0/3303445604132/12020520500/153344032001 410005-341113 **(0693)**
2009: 10^{3}SD, 8^{4}SD, 8^{1}SD, 10^{1}SD, 9^{1}SD, 12^{3}SD,

	Starts	1st	2nd	3rd	Win & Pl
Career Total (Turf)	20	0	3	2	8386
Career Total (AW)	29	8	2	7	28128

74 2/09 Wolv 1m1f103y STD £2914
76 2/09 Ling 1m2f STD £2047
70 2/09 Wolv 1m141y STD £2047
81 10/08 Wolv 1m1f103y STD £3238
77 9/08 Kemp 1m STD £2047
81 1/08 Kemp 1m (0-70)H STD £2590
79 1/07 Ling 1m2f (0-75)H STD £3238
72 10/06 Ling 1m2f (0-65)H STD £2914
Total win prize-money £21038

Going (Turf): Sf: 0-1 GS: 0-4 Gd: 0-6 GF: 0-8 Fm: 0-1
Distance: 5f/6f: 0-0 7f-8f: 2-12 **9f-13f: 6-37** 14f+: 0-0
Track : **LH: 6-22** RH: 2-23 **Tight: 6-21** Gall: 0-2
Aids: Bl: 0-0 Vi: 0-0 Tstrap: 0-0 Ckp: 0-0
Best Rating: 82 4/07 Wind 1m2f7y gd-fm

Fair; effective at around 1m2f-1m4f; acts well on fast ground; also goes on Polytrack; has worn an eyeshield.

Blackwater Fort (USA)

93(81) (32)**62**
3-y-o b/br g Doneraile Court (USA)-Clearwater (USA) (Seeking The Gold (USA))
J Gallagher Adweb Ltd

Placings:0322600-40400 **(4791)**
2009: 5^{4}F, 5^{0}G, 5^{4}G, 6^{0}F, 7^{0}SD,

	Starts	1st	2nd	3rd	Win & Pl
Career Total (Turf)	9	0	2	1	2422
Career Total (AW)	3	0	0	0	

Going (Turf): Sf: 0-1 GS: 0-1 Gd: 0-2 GF: 0-3 Fm: 0-2
Distance: 5f/6f: 0-10 7f-8f: 0-2 9f-13f: 0-0 14f+: 0-0
Track : LH: 0-7 RH: 0-1 Tight: 0-1 Gall: 0-2
Aids: Bl: 0-3 Vi: 0-1 Tstrap: 0-0 Ckp: 0-0
Best Rating: 62 8/08 Folk 5f gd-fm

Modest colt; effective at 5f; acts on fast and easy ground.

Blackwell Nation (IRE)

97 (68)**58**
3-y-o b f Kheleyf (USA)-No Tippling (IRE) (Unblest)
Adrian McGuinness Patrick G Carr

Placings:00050-000624 **(4137)**
2009: 6^{0}SD, 7^{0}HY, 6^{0}SD, 5^{6}GF, 6^{2}G, 5^{4}G,

	Starts	1st	2nd	3rd	Win & Pl
Career Total (Turf)	7	0	1	0	674
Career Total (AW)	4	0	0	0	

Going (Turf): Sf: 0-4 GS: 0-0 Gd: 0-2 GF: 0-1 Fm: 0-0

Distance: 5f/6f: 0-7 7f-8f: 0-4 9f-13f: 0-0 14f+: 0-0
Track : LH: 0-8 RH: 0-1 Tight: 0-0 Gall: 0-0
Aids: Bl: 0-0 Vi: 0-0 Tstrap: 0-0 Ckp: 0-0
Best Rating: 68 11/08 Dund 6f stand

Blade Of Class

(69) (6)
2-y-o b f Needwood Blade-Top Of The Class (IRE) (Rudimentary (USA))
P D Evans P D Evans

Placings:0 **(2128)**
2009: 5^{0}SD,

	Starts	1st	2nd	3rd	Win & Pl
Career Total (Turf)	0	0	0	0	
Career Total (AW)	1	0	0	0	

Going (Turf): Sf: 0-0 GS: 0-0 Gd: 0-0 GF: 0-0 Fm: 0-0
Distance: 5f/6f: 0-1 7f-8f: 0-0 9f-13f: 0-0 14f+: 0-0
Track : LH: 0-0 RH: 0-0 Tight: 0-0 Gall: 0-0
Aids: Bl: 0-0 Vi: 0-0 Tstrap: 0-0 Ckp: 0-0
Best Rating: 6 5/09 Sthl 5f stand

Blade Of Glory

75(81) (44)**35**
2-y-o ch f Needwood Blade-Jewel (IRE) (Cyrano De Bergerac)
A J McCabe Sale Of The Century

Placings:00600 **(5811)**
2009: 6^{0}G, 5^{0}SD, 7^{6}SD, 6^{0}G, 7^{0}SD,

	Starts	1st	2nd	3rd	Win & Pl
Career Total (Turf)	2	0	0	0	
Career Total (AW)	3	0	0	0	0

Going (Turf): Sf: 0-0 GS: 0-0 Gd: 0-2 GF: 0-0 Fm: 0-0
Distance: 5f/6f: 0-3 7f-8f: 0-2 9f-13f: 0-0 14f+: 0-0
Track : LH: 0-3 RH: 0-1 Tight: 0-2 Gall: 0-0
Aids: Bl: 0-0 Vi: 0-2 Tstrap: 0-1 Ckp: 0-1
Best Rating: 44 8/09 Wolv 7f32y stand

Blades Harmony

(66) (26)
2-y-o b g Needwood Blade-Yabint El Sham (Sizzling Melody)
E S McMahon R L Bedding

Placings:4 **(7836)**
2009: 7^{4}SS,

	Starts	1st	2nd	3rd	Win & Pl
Career Total (Turf)	0	0	0	0	
Career Total (AW)	1	0	0	0	0

Going (Turf): Sf: 0-0 GS: 0-0 Gd: 0-0 GF: 0-0 Fm: 0-0
Distance: 5f/6f: 0-0 7f-8f: 0-1 9f-13f: 0-0 14f+: 0-0
Track : LH: 0-1 RH: 0-0 Tight: 0-0 Gall: 0-0
Aids: Bl: 0-0 Vi: 0-0 Tstrap: 0-0 Ckp: 0-0
Best Rating: 26 12/09 Sthl 7f std-slw

£30,000 half-brother to a 5f winner, out of a multiple sprint-er scorer.

Blades Princess

98(97) (72)**91**
3-y-o ch f Needwood Blade-Breezy Palms (Tragic Role (USA))
E S McMahon R L Bedding

Placings:2110-006006 **(6669)**
2009: 5^{0}G, 5^{0}GS, 5^{6}G, 5^{0}GS, 5^{0}GF, 5^{6}SD,

	Starts	1st	2nd	3rd	Win & Pl
Career Total (Turf)	9	2	1	0	7571
Career Total (AW)	1	0	0	0	0

91 9/08 Bevl 5f SFT £3885
79 8/08 Ripn 5f G-S £2914
Total win prize-money £6800

Going (Turf): Sf: 1-1 GS: 1-4 Gd: 0-2 GF: 0-2 Fm: 0-0
Distance: **5f/6f: 2-10** 7f-8f: 0-0 9f-13f: 0-0 14f+: 0-0
Track : LH: 0-2 RH: 0-1 Tight: 0-1 Gall: 0-2
Aids: Bl: 0-1 Vi: 0-0 Tstrap: 0-1 Ckp: 0-1
Best Rating: 91 9/08 Bevl 5f soft

Useful; effective over 5f; acts on fast and easy ground.

Blaise Tower

100(105) (78)**82**
3-y-o ch g Fantastic Light (USA)-Blaise Castle (USA) (Irish River (FR))
G L Moore D J Deer

Placings:041-14030 **(4520)**
2009: 8^{1}SD, 10^{4}SD, 9^{0}G, 9^{3}G, 11^{0}G,

	Starts	1st	2nd	3rd	Win & Pl
Career Total (Turf)	3	0	0	1	963
Career Total (AW)	5	2	0	0	5301

78 1/09 Kemp 1m (0-75)H STD £2590
78 12/08 Sthl 7f STD £2047
Total win prize-money £4637

Going (Turf): Sf: 0-0 GS: 0-0 Gd: 0-3 GF: 0-0 Fm: 0-0
Distance: 5f/6f: 0-0 **7f-8f: 2-4** 9f-13f: 0-4 14f+: 0-0
Track : LH: 1-1 RH: 1-7 Tight: 0-3 Gall: 0-0
Aids: Bl: 0-0 Vi: 0-0 Tstrap: 0-0 Ckp: 0-0
Best Rating: 82 6/09 Gdwd 1m1f192y good

Fair; stays 1m2f; acts on Fibresand and Polytrack and on good ground.

Blakeneys Pet (IRE)

(68)
3-y-o b f Celtic Swing-Kathryn's Pet (Blakeney)
W G M Turner Bill Brown

Placings:0 **(7888)**
2009: 12^{0}SD,

	Starts	1st	2nd	3rd	Win & Pl
Career Total (Turf)	0	0	0	0	
Career Total (AW)	1	0	0	0	

Going (Turf): Sf: 0-0 GS: 0-0 Gd: 0-0 GF: 0-0 Fm: 0-0
Distance: 5f/6f: 0-0 7f-8f: 0-0 9f-13f: 0-1 14f+: 0-0
Track : LH: 0-1 RH: 0-0 Tight: 0-1 Gall: 0-0
Aids: Bl: 0-0 Vi: 0-0 Tstrap: 0-0 Ckp: 0-0

Blakeshall Diamond

88(94) (67)**47**
4-y-o gr f Piccolo-Hi Hoh (IRE) (Fayruz)
A J Chamberlain M A Holmes

Placings:001/26000000-0000650 **(5911)**
2009: 5^{0}SD, 5^{0}G, 5^{0}GF, 5^{0}F, 5^{6}GF, 6^{5}G, 5^{0}GF,

	Starts	1st	2nd	3rd	Win & Pl
Career Total (Turf)	9	0	0	0	0

Career Total (AW)	9	1	1	0	4159

64 11/07 Ling 5f STD £3465

Total win prize-money £3465

Going (Turf): Sf: 0-1 GS: 0-0 Gd: 0-3 GF: 0-4 Fm: 0-1
Distance: **5f/6f: 1-18** 7f-8f: 0-0 9f-13f: 0-0 14f+: 0-0
Track : **LH: 1-11** RH: 0-1 **Tight: 1-7** Gall: 0-1
Aids: Bl: 0-0 Vi: 0-0 Tstrap: 0-0 Ckp: 0-0
Best Rating: 67 1/08 Wolv 5f20y stand

Moderate; effective over 5-6f; acts on good ground and Polytrack.

Blakeshall Quest

(102) (56)**15**

9-y-o b m Piccolo-Corniche Quest (IRE) (Salt Dome (USA))
R Brotherton Bredon Hill Racing Club

Placings:600**6/21261000000/04445101000000005/0406031 30500000/02100014532030241/34600002/462433120460-0450424** **(2745)**
2009: 6^{0}SD, 5^{4}SD, 6^{5}SS, 5^{0}SD, 6^{4}SD, 6^{2}SD, 6^{4}SD,

	Starts	1st	2nd	3rd	Win & Pl
Career Total (Turf)	14	0	0	0	168
Career Total (AW)	76	9	9	7	32875

64 5/08 Sthl 6f (0-50)H STD £2729
57 12/06 Sthl 6f (0-45) STD £2047
56 4/06 Sthl 6f STD £2730
57 2/06 Sthl 6f (0-45) STD £1365
58 5/05 Sthl 6f (0-45) STD £1480
73 4/04 Wolv 6f E(0-70)H STD £3435
73 3/04 Wolv 5f E(0-75)H SS £3701
77 5/03 Sthl 6f E(0-75)H STD £3604
68 2/03 Wolv 6f D STD £3809

Total win prize-money £24904

Going (Turf): Sf: 0-3 GS: 0-3 Gd: 0-2 GF: 0-4 Fm: 0-2
Distance: **5f/6f: 9-75** 7f-8f: 0-14 9f-13f: 0-1 14f+: 0-0
Track : **LH: 9-76** RH: 0-1 **Tight: 3-28** Gall: 0-2
Aids: **Bl: 4-46** Vi: 3-28 Tstrap: 0-0 Ckp: 0-0
Best Rating: 77 5/03 Sthl 6f stand

Plating-class mare; effective over 5f-6f; acts on Polytrack but best on Fibresand.

Blakey's Boy

98 **86**

2-y-o b g Hawk Wing (USA)-Divine Grace (IRE) (Definite Article)
J L Dunlop The Blue Bar Partnership

Placings:130 **(6664)**
2009: 6^{1}S, 7^{3}GF, 8^{0}GS,

	Starts	1st	2nd	3rd	Win & Pl
Career Total (Turf)	3	1	0	1	7926

80 7/09 Sals 6f212y SFT £4695

Total win prize-money £4695

Going (Turf): Sf: 1-1 GS: 0-1 Gd: 0-0 GF: 0-1 Fm: 0-0
Distance: 5f/6f: 0-0 **7f-8f: 1-3** 9f-13f: 0-0 14f+: 0-0
Track : LH: 0-0 RH: 0-1 Tight: 0-0 Gall: 0-1
Aids: Bl: 0-0 Vi: 0-0 Tstrap: 0-0 Ckp: 0-0
Best Rating: 86 10/09 Asct 1m gd-sft

Winner on debut over 7f on soft ground; Listed placed on fast next time.

Blandford Flyer

(39) (45)**23**

6-y-o b g Soviet Star (USA)-Vento Del Oreno (FR) (Lando (GER))
M J Gingell M J Gingell

Placings:0056/000/0 **(0301)**
2009: 14^{0}SD,

	Starts	1st	2nd	3rd	Win & Pl
Career Total (Turf)	4	0	0	0	
Career Total (AW)	4	0	0	0	0

Going (Turf): Sf: 0-0 GS: 0-0 Gd: 0-1 GF: 0-3 Fm: 0-0
Distance: 5f/6f: 0-0 7f-8f: 0-5 9f-13f: 0-2 14f+: 0-1
Track : LH: 0-5 RH: 0-0 Tight: 0-3 Gall: 0-0
Aids: Bl: 0-0 Vi: 0-0 Tstrap: 0-0 Ckp: 0-0
Best Rating: 64 10/05 Ling 7f stand

Blast

92(86) (58)**59**

2-y-o ch f Avonbridge-Pain Perdu (IRE) (Waajib)
J R Gask (David P Myerscough 15/8) Fintan Shortall

Placings:00060 **(7210)**
2009: 6^{0}YS, 6^{0}G, 7^{0}SD, 5^{6}SF, 7^{0}SD,

	Starts	1st	2nd	3rd	Win & Pl
Career Total (Turf)	2	0	0	0	
Career Total (AW)	3	0	0	0	0

Going (Turf): Sf: 0-0 GS: 0-0 Gd: 0-1 GF: 0-0 Fm: 0-0
Distance: 5f/6f: 0-3 7f-8f: 0-2 9f-13f: 0-0 14f+: 0-0
Track : LH: 0-5 RH: 0-0 Tight: 0-2 Gall: 0-0
Aids: Bl: 0-2 Vi: 0-0 Tstrap: 0-0 Ckp: 0-0
Best Rating: 59 7/09 Leop 6f yld-sft

Blastie

97 **48**

4-y-o b g Josr Algarhoud (IRE)-Passerella (FR) (Brustolon)
T D Walford David Faulkner

Placings:00400 **(5953)**
2009: 8^{0}GF, 8^{0}G, 7^{4}GF, 9^{0}GF, 10^{0}GF,

	Starts	1st	2nd	3rd	Win & Pl
Career Total (Turf)	5	0	0	0	192

Going (Turf): Sf: 0-0 GS: 0-0 Gd: 0-1 GF: 0-4 Fm: 0-0
Distance: 5f/6f: 0-0 7f-8f: 0-3 9f-13f: 0-2 14f+: 0-0
Track : LH: 0-3 RH: 0-1 Tight: 0-3 Gall: 0-0
Aids: Bl: 0-0 Vi: 0-0 Tstrap: 0-0 Ckp: 0-0
Best Rating: 48 8/09 Rdcr 7f gd-fm

Blazing Buck

97(55) **74**

3-y-o ch g Fraam-Anapola (GER) (Polish Precedent (USA))
A W Carroll (H J L Dunlop 3/4) Mill House Racing Syndicate

Placings:621040-60045 **(5790)**
2009: 9^{6}SD, 10^{0}GF, 8^{0}GS, 12^{4}G, 10^{5}G,

	Starts	1st	2nd	3rd	Win & Pl
Career Total (Turf)	10	1	1	0	4205
Career Total (AW)	1	0	0	0	0

74 8/08 Wwck 7f26y SFT £2914

Total win prize-money £2914

Going (Turf): Sf: 1-2 GS: 0-3 Gd: 0-3 GF: 0-2 Fm: 0-0
Distance: 5f/6f: 0-0 **7f-8f: 1-5** 9f-13f: 0-6 14f+: 0-0
Track : **LH: 1-7** RH: 0-1 Tight: 0-2 Gall: 0-1
Aids: Bl: 0-0 Vi: 0-0 Tstrap: 0-0 Ckp: 0-0
Best Rating: 74 10/08 Bath 1m5y gd-sft

Fair; out of a half-sister nine winners in Germany; stays 7f; acts on soft ground.

Blazing Heights

101 (61)**76**

6-y-o b g Compton Place-Harrken Heights (IRE) (Belmez (USA))
J S Goldie Jim Goldie Racing Club

Placings:6162/524222640041/63025520005001**0**/0004060 354450-4005060430000000 **(7086)**
2009: 5^{4}GF, 5^{0}HY, 5^{0}G, 5^{5}GF, 5^{0}G, 5^{6}GF, 5^{0}G, 5^{4}GF, 5^{3}G, 5^{0}G, 5^{0}G, 5^{0}GS, 5^{0}GF, 5^{0}GF, 6^{0}G, 5^{0}S,

	Starts	1st	2nd	3rd	Win & Pl
Career Total (Turf)	59	3	7	3	40578
Career Total (AW)	1	0	0	0	

88 11/07 Muss 5f (0-85)H GD £5181
87 11/06 Muss 5f (0-80)H G-S £6477
69 9/05 Thsk 6f GD £4280

Total win prize-money £15939

Going (Turf): Sf: 0-13 GS: 1-9 **Gd: 2-20** GF: 0-17 Fm: 0-0
Distance: **5f/6f: 3-60** 7f-8f: 0-0 9f-13f: 0-0 14f+: 0-0
Track : LH: 0-4 RH: 0-0 Tight: 0-4 Gall: 0-0
Aids: Bl: 0-2 Vi: 0-5 Tstrap: 0-1 Ckp: 0-1
Best Rating: 89 6/07 Ayr 5f good

Moderate; seems best over 5f; acts on most ground; has worn cheekpieces.

Blessed Place

103(109) (68)**71**

9-y-o ch g Compton Place-Cathedra (So Blessed)
D J S Ffrench Davis S J Edwards

Placings:000/**32532**122350050/**00000**3354150060/**50322 21015204421021**/030241**3215333**0**430000**/**000**021060425 061**0003000**/0410**162**0002041000-0000052130 **(4907)**
2009: 6^{0}GF, 6^{0}GF, 6^{0}GF, 5^{0}G, 5^{0}SD, 5^{5}G, 5^{2}S, 5^{1}G, 5^{3}G, 5^{0}G,

	Starts	1st	2nd	3rd	Win & Pl
Career Total (Turf)	82	8	10	9	51296
Career Total (AW)	39	6	7	5	21703

62 7/09 Thsk 5f (0-75)H GD £4274
71 9/08 Sand 5f6y (0-80)H SFT £5180
68 6/08 GrLe 5f (0-65)H STD £2266
65 6/08 Wolv 5f20y (0-55)H STD £2388
71 8/07 Ches 5f16y (0-65)H G-F £2730
69 6/07 Newb 5f34y (0-70)H SFT £3562
75 7/06 Pont 5f (0-70)H G-F £4533
64 7/06 Wolv 5f216y (0-60)H STD £2730
59 10/05 Wolv 5f20y (0-45) STD £1473
67 9/05 Yarm 6f3y (0-55)H G-S £3806
59 6/05 Bath 5f161y (0-70)H GD £4856
51 5/05 Ling 6f (0-45) STD £1466
59 7/04 Wind 5f10y E(0-70)H G-S £3493
64 3/03 Ling 5f D(0-85)H STD £4693

Total win prize-money £47457

Going (Turf): Sf: 2-8 GS: 2-11 Gd: 2-21GF: 2-35 Fm: 0-7
Distance: **5f/6f: 13-115** 7f-8f: 1-5 9f-13f: 0-1 14f+: 0-0
Track : **LH: 9-57** RH: 0-5 **Tight: 6-33** Gall: 3-27
Aids: Bl: 0-1 Vi: 0-0 Tstrap: 0-6 Ckp: 0-6
Best Rating: 77 8/06 Sand 5f6y good

Moderate; effective over 5f; best suited by an easy surface on turf; goes on sand; likes to dominate; has worn a tongue tie.

Blessing Belle (IRE)

89(90) (52)**57**

3-y-o ch f Traditionally (USA)-Kind Of Loving (Diesis)
Mme G Rarick (M H Tompkins 12/5) S Collins

Placings:000-150 **(7386a)**

2009: 8^{1}G, 10^{5}SD, 8^{0}HY,

	Starts	1st	2nd	3rd	Win & Pl
Career Total (Turf)	5	1	0	0	2590
Career Total (AW)	1	0	0	0	0

57 5/09 Haml 1m65y GD £2590

Total win prize-money £2590

Going (Turf): Sf: 0-1 GS: 0-1 **Gd: 1-2** GF: 0-1 Fm: 0-0
Distance: 5f/6f: 0-0 7f-8f: 0-2 **9f-13f: 1-4** 14f+: 0-0
Track : LH: 0-2 **RH: 1-1 Tight: 1-2** Gall: 0-0
Aids: Bl: 0-0 Vi: 0-0 Tstrap: 0-0 Ckp: 0-0
Best Rating: **57** 5/09 Haml 1m65y good

Moderate; stays 1m2f; acts on Polytrack.

Blinka Me

83(86) (51)**47**
2-y-o b c Tiger Hill (IRE)-Easy To Love (USA) (Diesis)
M H Tompkins Trevor Benton

Placings:60005 **(7474)**
2009: 6^{6}G, 7^{0}G, 7^{0}G, 8^{0}GF, 10^{5}SD,

	Starts	1st	2nd	3rd	Win & Pl
Career Total (Turf)	4	0	0	0	0
Career Total (AW)	1	0	0	0	0

Going (Turf): **Sf: 0-0 GS: 0-0 Gd: 0-3 GF: 0-1 Fm: 0-0**
Distance: 5f/6f: 0-0 7f-8f: 0-3 9f-13f: 0-2 14f+: 0-0
Track : LH: 0-0 RH: 0-1 Tight: 0-0 Gall: 0-0
Aids: Bl: 0-1 Vi: 0-0 Tstrap: 0-0 Ckp: 0-0
Best Rating: **51** 11/09 Kemp 1m2f stand

Blissful Moment (USA)

95 **76**
2-y-o b/br c Dynaformer (USA)-Arabian Spell (IRE) (Desert Prince (IRE))
Sir Michael Stoute Saeed Suhail

Placings:4 **(6423)**
2009: 8^{4}GF,

	Starts	1st	2nd	3rd	Win & Pl
Career Total (Turf)	1	0	0	0	385

Going (Turf): **Sf: 0-0 GS: 0-0 Gd: 0-0 GF: 0-1 Fm: 0-0**
Distance: 5f/6f: 0-0 7f-8f: 0-1 9f-13f: 0-0 14f+: 0-0
Track : LH: 0-0 RH: 0-0 Tight: 0-0 Gall: 0-0
Aids: Bl: 0-0 Vi: 0-0 Tstrap: 0-0 Ckp: 0-0
Best Rating: **76** 10/09 NmkR 1m gd-fm

Blitzed

91 **66**
2-y-o b g Fantastic Light (USA)-Broken Peace (USA) (Devil's Bag (USA))
G L Moore Sir Eric Parker

Placings:6 **(7146)**
2009: 7^{6}G,

	Starts	1st	2nd	3rd	Win & Pl
Career Total (Turf)	1	0	0	0	0

Going (Turf): **Sf: 0-0 GS: 0-0 Gd: 0-1 GF: 0-0 Fm: 0-0**
Distance: 5f/6f: 0-0 7f-8f: 0-1 9f-13f: 0-0 14f+: 0-0
Track : LH: 0-0 RH: 0-0 Tight: 0-0 Gall: 0-0
Aids: Bl: 0-0 Vi: 0-0 Tstrap: 0-0 Ckp: 0-0
Best Rating: **66** 10/09 NmkR 7f good

Blizzard Blues (USA)

97 **98**
3-y-o ch c Mr Greeley (USA)-Blush Damask (USA) (Green Dancer (USA))
H R A Cecil Gestut Ammerland

Placings:13 **(6644)**
2009: 10^{1}G, 10^{3}G,

	Starts	1st	2nd	3rd	Win & Pl
Career Total (Turf)	2	1	0	1	11159

84 7/09 NmkJ 1m2f GD £9714

Total win prize-money £9714

Going (Turf): Sf: 0-0 GS: 0-0 **Gd: 1-2** GF: 0-0 Fm: 0-0
Distance: 5f/6f: 0-0 7f-8f: 0-0 **9f-13f: 1-2** 14f+: 0-0
Track : LH: 0-1 **RH: 1-1** Tight: 0-0 **Gall: 1-2**
Aids: **Bl: 1-1** Vi: 0-0 Tstrap: 0-0 Ckp: 0-0
Best Rating: **98** 10/09 York 1m2f88y good

Block Party

103(99) (85)**86**
3-y-o b c Dansili-Mylania (Midyan (USA))
R Charlton B E Nielsen

Placings:053-4213020 **(6773)**
2009: 8^{4}GF, 8^{2}G, 8^{1}G, 8^{3}GF, 7^{0}GF, 8^{2}SD, 8^{0}SD,

	Starts	1st	2nd	3rd	Win & Pl
Career Total (Turf)	8	1	1	2	6040
Career Total (AW)	2	0	1	0	1407

81 7/09 Wind 1m67y GD £2729

Total win prize-money £2730

Going (Turf): Sf: 0-0 GS: 0-1 **Gd: 1-4** GF: 0-3 Fm: 0-0
Distance: 5f/6f: 0-0 7f-8f: 0-8 **9f-13f: 1-2** 14f+: 0-0
Track : LH: 0-3 **RH: 1-4 Tight: 1-1** Gall: 0-1
Aids: Bl: 0-0 Vi: 0-1 Tstrap: 0-0 Ckp: 0-0
Best Rating: **86** 7/09 Hayd 1m30y good

Fair; effective over 1m; acts on good and easy ground, and Polytrack.

Blockley (USA)

93(106) (73)**70**
5-y-o b g Johannesburg (USA)-Saintly Manner (USA) (St Jovite (USA))
Ian Williams Ian Williams

Placings:50/0305204/00001-1021123600302 **(7649)**
2009: 12^{1}SD, 13^{0}SD, 13^{2}SD, 14^{1}SD, 13^{1}SD, 16^{2}G, 16^{3}SD, 10^{6}G, 10^{0}G, 11^{0}GF, 16^{3}GS, 16^{0}SD, 16^{2}SD,

	Starts	1st	2nd	3rd	Win & Pl
Career Total (Turf)	12	0	2	2	2943
Career Total (AW)	15	4	2	1	11756

62 3/09 Wolv 1m5f194y (0-75)H STD £3070
68 3/09 Sthl 1m6f (0-75)H STD £2729
64 1/09 Wolv 1m4f50y (0-55)H STD £2047
62 12/08 Kemp 1m4f (0-55)H STD £2047

Total win prize-money £9895

Going (Turf): **Sf: 0-2 GS: 0-1 Gd: 0-6 GF: 0-3 Fm: 0-0**
Distance: 5f/6f: 0-0 7f-8f: 0-1 9f-13f: 2-17 14f+: 2-9
Track : **LH: 3-21** RH: 1-5 **Tight: 2-17** Gall: 0-5
Aids: Bl: 0-1 Vi: 0-5 Tstrap: 1-3 Ckp: 1-3
Best Rating: **73** 5/09 Kemp 2m stand

Modest; stays 2m; acts on good ground; goes on sand; has worn a tongue tie/headgear.

Blow Hole (USA)

75(101) (77)**67**
4-y-o ch g Mr Greeley (USA)-Nevis (USA) (Cox's Ridge (USA))
Ray Fielder (Paul Mason 18/7) Fred Camis

Placings:404326-00 **(4083)**
2009: 10^{0}GF, 8^{0}SD,

	Starts	1st	2nd	3rd	Win & Pl
Career Total (Turf)	2	0	0	0	
Career Total (AW)	6	0	1	1	1445

Going (Turf): **Sf: 0-0 GS: 0-0 Gd: 0-0 GF: 0-2 Fm: 0-0**
Distance: 5f/6f: 0-0 7f-8f: 0-5 9f-13f: 0-3 14f+: 0-0
Track : LH: 0-3 RH: 0-4 Tight: 0-4 Gall: 0-0
Aids: Bl: 0-0 Vi: 0-0 Tstrap: 0-0 Ckp: 0-0
Best Rating: **77** 4/08 Wolv 1m141y stand

Fair half-brother to a couple of multiple sprint winners on dirt; stays 7f; acts on Polytrack.

Blow Your Mind

90 **64**
3-y-o b c Mind Games-Ashkernazy (IRE) (Salt Dome (USA))
Karen McLintock Equiname Ltd

Placings:45465-0606 **(6161)**
2009: 6^{0}GF, 5^{6}GF, 5^{0}GF, 5^{6}G,

	Starts	1st	2nd	3rd	Win & Pl
Career Total (Turf)	9	0	0	0	241

Going (Turf): **Sf: 0-1 GS: 0-0 Gd: 0-2 GF: 0-6 Fm: 0-0**
Distance: 5f/6f: 0-8 7f-8f: 0-1 9f-13f: 0-0 14f+: 0-0
Track : LH: 0-0 RH: 0-0 Tight: 0-0 Gall: 0-0
Aids: Bl: 0-1 Vi: 0-1 Tstrap: 0-0 Ckp: 0-0
Best Rating: **64** 6/08 Muss 5f gd-fm

Modest; effective over 5f; acts on fast ground; has worn a visor.

Blown It (USA)

106(103) (78)**82**
3-y-o b/br g More Than Ready (USA)-Short Shadow (USA) (Out Of Place (USA))
I Semple D G Savala

Placings:20103-43450103054 **(7478)**
2009: 6^{4}GS, 6^{3}G, 6^{4}G, 5^{5}G, 6^{0}G, 6^{1}GF, 6^{0}G, 5^{3}GF, 6^{0}G, 5^{5}SD, 6^{4}SD,

	Starts	1st	2nd	3rd	Win & Pl
Career Total (Turf)	12	1	1	2	8352
Career Total (AW)	4	1	0	1	4271

77 8/09 Ayr 6f (0-85)H G-F £4857
78 7/08 Wolv 5f216y STD £3070

Total win prize-money £7928

Going (Turf): Sf: 0-0 GS: 0-1 Gd: 0-6 **GF: 1-5** Fm: 0-0
Distance: **5f/6f: 2-15** 7f-8f: 0-1 9f-13f: 0-0 14f+: 0-0
Track : **LH: 1-3** RH: 0-1 **Tight: 1-3** Gall: 0-0
Aids: Bl: 0-1 Vi: 0-0 Tstrap: 0-2 Ckp: 0-2
Best Rating: **82** 6/08 Asct 6f gd-fm

Fair; effective over 6f; acts on fast ground and on Polytrack.

Blue Again

(80) (45)
2-y-o b f Leporello (IRE)-Forever Blue (Spectrum (IRE))
W R Swinburn Pendley Farm

Placings:0 (7537)
2009: 7^{0}SD,

	Starts	1st	2nd	3rd	Win & Pl
Career Total (Turf)	0	0	0	0	
Career Total (AW)	1	0	0	0	

Going (Turf): Sf: 0-0 GS: 0-0 Gd: 0-0 GF: 0-0 Fm: 0-0
Distance: 5f/6f: 0-0 7f-8f: 0-1 9f-13f: 0-0 14f+: 0-0
Track : LH: 0-0 RH: 0-1 Tight: 0-0 Gall: 0-0
Aids: Bl: 0-0 Vi: 0-0 Tstrap: 0-0 Ckp: 0-0
Best Rating: 45 11/09 Kemp 7f stand

Blue Angel (IRE)

103(90) (75)102
2-y-o b f Oratorio (IRE)-Blue Cloud (IRE) (Nashwan (USA))
R Hannon Oakley Street Racing

Placings:12046 (6269)
2009: 7^{1}SD, 6^{2}GS, 7^{0}G, 7^{4}G, 8^{6}G,

	Starts	1st	2nd	3rd	Win & Pl
Career Total (Turf)	4	0	1	0	8326
Career Total (AW)	1	1	0	0	3886

75 7/09 Kemp 7f STD £3885
Total win prize-money £3886

Going (Turf): Sf: 0-0 GS: 0-1 Gd: 0-3 GF: 0-0 Fm: 0-0
Distance: 5f/6f: 0-1 7f-8f: 1-4 9f-13f: 0-0 14f+: 0-0
Track : LH: 0-0 RH: 1-3 Tight: 0-0 Gall: 0-1
Aids: Bl: 0-0 Vi: 0-0 Tstrap: 0-0 Ckp: 0-0
Best Rating: 102 8/09 Gdwd 7f good

Smart; effective at 6f-7f; acts on Polytrack and good/easy ground on turf.

Blue Avon

83 57
2-y-o b f Avonbridge-Blue Nile (IRE) (Bluebird (USA))
R A Fahey H J P Farr

Placings:6020 (5938)
2009: 6^{6}G, 7^{0}G, 6^{2}GF, 7^{0}GF,

	Starts	1st	2nd	3rd	Win & Pl
Career Total (Turf)	4	0	1	0	771

Going (Turf): Sf: 0-0 GS: 0-0 Gd: 0-2 GF: 0-2 Fm: 0-0
Distance: 5f/6f: 0-2 7f-8f: 0-2 9f-13f: 0-0 14f+: 0-0
Track : LH: 0-1 RH: 0-0 Tight: 0-1 Gall: 0-0
Aids: Bl: 0-0 Vi: 0-0 Tstrap: 0-0 Ckp: 0-0
Best Rating: 57 8/09 Newc 6f gd-fm

Blue Bajan (IRE)

106 (108)113
7-y-o b g Montjeu (IRE)-Gentle Thoughts (Darshaan)
Andrew Turnell Dr John Hollowood

Placings:6001/05662136011/2315140122/2512530/244 (6854)
2009: 14^{2}GS, 12^{4}GF, 16^{4}G,

	Starts	1st	2nd	3rd	Win & Pl
Career Total (Turf)	28	6	5	3	146184
Career Total (AW)	7	2	2	0	23781

111 4/07 Epsm 1m2f18y (0-105)H G-F £24928
96 9/06 Asct 1m2f (0-90) SFT £11217
97 8/06 NmkJ 1m2f (0-90)H G-F £9067
84 10/05 Ling 1m4f (0-75)H STD £3526
77 10/05 Bath 1m3f144y (0-75)H G-F £4346
73 6/05 Leic 1m3f183y (0-65) G-F £4114
69 12/04 Wolv 1m1f103y STD £3360
Total win prize-money £60564

Going (Turf): Sf: 1-2 GS: 0-9 Gd: 1-8 GF: 4-9 Fm: 0-0
Distance: 5f/6f: 0-0 7f-8f: 0-2 9f-13f: 8-31 14f+: 0-2
Track : LH: 4-20 RH: 4-11 Tight: 5-19 Gall: 2-8
Aids: Bl: 0-1 Vi: 0-0 Tstrap: 0-0 Ckp: 0-0
Best Rating: 113 5/09 York 1m6f gd-sft

Smart and consistent; Group and Listed placed and also runner-up in 2006 Cambridgeshire; effective over 1m2f-2m; acts on most ground and Polytrack; high-class hurdler.

Blue Bond

74(82) (46)38
2-y-o ch g Monsieur Bond (IRE)-Azula (Bluebird (USA))
P T Midgley C Alton T Mather D Goult G Evans

Placings:04606060 (4858)
2009: 5^{0}GF, 5^{4}SD, 5^{6}F, 6^{0}GS, 7^{6}GF, 7^{0}S, 6^{6}SD, 7^{0}SD,

	Starts	1st	2nd	3rd	Win & Pl
Career Total (Turf)	5	0	0	0	0
Career Total (AW)	3	0	0	0	0

Going (Turf): Sf: 0-1 GS: 0-1 Gd: 0-0 GF: 0-2 Fm: 0-1
Distance: 5f/6f: 0-5 7f-8f: 0-3 9f-13f: 0-0 14f+: 0-0
Track : LH: 0-4 RH: 0-0 Tight: 0-3 Gall: 0-0
Aids: Bl: 0-1 Vi: 0-0 Tstrap: 0-1 Ckp: 0-1
Best Rating: 46 4/09 Wolv 5f20y stand

Blue Celeste

79(79) (36)13
3-y-o b f Sakhee (USA)-Ellie Ardensky (Slip Anchor)
R T Phillips R Pennant Jones

Placings:06 (7694)
2009: 10^{0}G, 10^{6}SD,

	Starts	1st	2nd	3rd	Win & Pl
Career Total (Turf)	1	0	0	0	
Career Total (AW)	1	0	0	0	0

Going (Turf): Sf: 0-0 GS: 0-0 Gd: 0-1 GF: 0-0 Fm: 0-0
Distance: 5f/6f: 0-0 7f-8f: 0-0 9f-13f: 0-2 14f+: 0-0
Track : LH: 0-2 RH: 0-0 Tight: 0-2 Gall: 0-0
Aids: Bl: 0-0 Vi: 0-0 Tstrap: 0-0 Ckp: 0-0
Best Rating: 36 12/09 Ling 1m2f stand

Blue Charm

103(108) (82)73
5-y-o b g Averti (IRE)-Exotic Forest (Dominion)
I W McInnes (S Kirk 20/1) J Morris

Placings:313/3/060304406202202113246-2332341064030 (4400)
2009: 7^{2}SS, 7^{3}SD, 7^{3}SD, 6^{2}SD, 7^{3}SD, 6^{4}GF, 8^{1}G, 8^{0}G, 8^{6}G, 7^{4}GF, 8^{0}G, 8^{3}G, 8^{0}GF,

	Starts	1st	2nd	3rd	Win & Pl
Career Total (Turf)	14	1	1	2	5381
Career Total (AW)	23	2	6	7	14911

73 4/09 Pont 1m4y (0-70)H GD £3238
75 12/08 Sthl 7f (0-62)H STD £2047
76 12/06 Kemp 6f STD £3238
Total win prize-money £8524

Going (Turf): Sf: 0-0 GS: 0-4 Gd: 1-6 GF: 0-4 Fm: 0-0
Distance: 5f/6f: 1-7 7f-8f: 1-23 9f-13f: 1-7 14f+: 0-0
Track : LH: 2-19 RH: 1-14 Tight: 0-9 Gall: 0-2
Aids: Bl: 0-0 Vi: 0-0 Tstrap: 0-0 Ckp: 0-0
Best Rating: 82 1/09 Sthl 7f std-slw

Modest; effective over 6f-1m; acts on good ground; goes on sand.

Blue Cross Boy (USA)

87(94) (54)60
4-y-o gr g Sunday Break (JPN)-Introducer (USA) (Cozzene (USA))
Adrian McGuinness Adrian McGuinness

Placings:010/00000-005203000006 (7543a)
2009: 8^{0}SD, 7^{0}GF, 6^{5}GF, 7^{2}G, 7^{0}S, 7^{3}GY, 5^{0}GF, 5^{0}GY, 5^{0}GY, 8^{0}SD, 9^{0}SD, 7^{6}SD,

	Starts	1st	2nd	3rd	Win & Pl
Career Total (Turf)	15	1	1	1	3385
Career Total (AW)	5	0	0	0	

71 8/07 Rdcr 6f GD £1808
Total win prize-money £1809

Going (Turf): Sf: 0-2 GS: 0-0 Gd: 1-4 GF: 0-5 Fm: 0-0
Distance: 5f/6f: 1-9 7f-8f: 0-10 9f-13f: 0-1 14f+: 0-0
Track : LH: 0-8 RH: 0-7 Tight: 0-1 Gall: 0-1
Aids: Bl: 0-12 Vi: 0-0 Tstrap: 0-1 Ckp: 0-1
Best Rating: 71 8/07 Rdcr 6f good

Fair; effective over 6f; acts on good ground.

Blue Dagger (IRE)

44 66
3-y-o ch g Daggers Drawn (USA)-Sports Post Lady (IRE) (M Double M (USA))
P C Haslam Blue Lion Racing VIII

Placings:400-0 (4279)
2009: 8^{0}G,

	Starts	1st	2nd	3rd	Win & Pl
Career Total (Turf)	4	0	0	0	241

Going (Turf): Sf: 0-1 GS: 0-0 Gd: 0-3 GF: 0-0 Fm: 0-0
Distance: 5f/6f: 0-2 7f-8f: 0-2 9f-13f: 0-0 14f+: 0-0
Track : LH: 0-1 RH: 0-1 Tight: 0-1 Gall: 0-1
Aids: Bl: 0-0 Vi: 0-0 Tstrap: 0-0 Ckp: 0-0
Best Rating: 66 6/08 Carl 5f soft

Blue Dynasty (USA)

95(88) (68)67
3-y-o b g Dynaformer (USA)-Saudia (USA) (Gone West (USA))
Mrs A J Perrett The Green Dot Partnership

Placings:0441-66 (3593)
2009: 11^{6}GF, 14^{6}GF,

	Starts	1st	2nd	3rd	Win & Pl
Career Total (Turf)	5	1	0	0	3623
Career Total (AW)	1	0	0	0	337

67 9/08 Bath 1m2f46y G-F £3238
Total win prize-money £3238

Going (Turf): Sf: 0-0 GS: 0-2 Gd: 0-0 GF: 1-3 Fm: 0-0
Distance: 5f/6f: 0-0 7f-8f: 0-1 9f-13f: 1-4 14f+: 0-1
Track : LH: 1-3 RH: 0-3 Tight: 1-1 Gall: 0-1
Aids: Bl: 0-1 Vi: 0-0 Tstrap: 0-0 Ckp: 0-0
Best Rating: 68 8/08 GrLe 1m stand

Modest; stays 1m2f; acts on fast ground

Blue Emirate

74 28
2-y-o b g Dubai Destination (USA)-Dorinda Gray (IRE) (Docksider (USA))

P C Haslam Blue Lion Racing VIII

Placings:300 **(5519)**
2009: 6^{3}GF, 7^{0}GF, 6^{0}G,

	Starts	1st	2nd	3rd	Win & Pl
Career Total (Turf)	3	0	0	1	385

Going (Turf): Sf: 0-0 GS: 0-0 Gd: 0-1 GF: 0-2 Fm: 0-0
Distance: 5f/6f: 0-2 7f-8f: 0-1 9f-13f: 0-0 14f+: 0-0
Track : LH: 0-1 RH: 0-0 Tight: 0-1 Gall: 0-0
Aids: Bl: 0-0 Vi: 0-0 Tstrap: 0-0 Ckp: 0-0
Best Rating: 28 6/09 Rdcr 6f gd-fm

Blue Glove (IRE)

(73) (23)
2-y-o b f Bertolini (USA)-Red Shoe (Selkirk (USA))
J A Osborne J McGarry

Placings:004 **(7874)**
2009: 8^{0}SD, 7^{0}SD, 8^{4}SD,

	Starts	1st	2nd	3rd	Win & Pl
Career Total (Turf)	0	0	0	0	
Career Total (AW)	3	0	0	0	0

Going (Turf): Sf: 0-0 GS: 0-0 Gd: 0-0 GF: 0-0 Fm: 0-0
Distance: 5f/6f: 0-0 7f-8f: 0-3 9f-13f: 0-0 14f+: 0-0
Track : LH: 0-1 RH: 0-2 Tight: 0-1 Gall: 0-0
Aids: Bl: 0-0 Vi: 0-0 Tstrap: 0-0 Ckp: 0-0
Best Rating: 23 12/09 Ling 7f stand

Blue Hills

(106) (71)**63**
8-y-o br g Vettori (IRE)-Slow Jazz (USA) (Chief's Crown (USA))
P W Hiatt Tom Pratt

Placings:052/05000**456/3303325**30106660**0001/2232415 20060/5413212010500334003103/20141323506**3400-51246040 **(1936)**
2009: 14^{5}SS, 14^{1}SD, 16^{2}SD, 14^{4}SD, 13^{6}SD, 13^{0}SD, 12^{4}SD, 13^{0}SD,

	Starts	1st	2nd	3rd	Win & Pl
Career Total (Turf)	24	0	2	2	2629
Career Total (AW)	63	10	9	12	34858

65	1/09	Sthl	1m6f	(0-65)H	STD	£1648
74	3/08	Wolv	1m5f194y	(0-70)H	STD	£1879
71	2/08	Sthl	1m6f	(0-60)H	STD	£2047
64	11/07	Wolv	1m5f194y	(0-60)H	STD	£2047
75	3/07	Sthl	1m6f	(0-65)H	STD	£2730
67	3/07	Wolv	1m5f194y	(0-70)H	STD	£2307
61	1/07	Sthl	2m	(0-70)H	STD	£2966
60	2/06	Wolv	2m119y	(0-65)H	STD	£2388
59	12/05	Wolv	1m5f194y	(0-45)	SS	£1440
61	4/05	Sthl	1m4f		STD	£3367

Total win prize-money £22824

Going (Turf): Sf: 0-0 GS: 0-9 Gd: 0-7 GF: 0-6 Fm: 0-2
Distance: 5f/6f: 0-0 7f-8f: 0-1 9f-13f: 1-23 **14f+: 9-63**
Track : **LH: 10-78** RH: 0-8 **Tight: 5-45** Gall: 0-0
Aids: **Bl: 6-38** Vi: 1-6 Tstrap: 1-9 Ckp: 1-9
Best Rating: 75 3/07 Sthl 1m6f stand

Moderate; stays 2m, but effective at shorter; acts well on sand; has worn blinkers and cheekpieces.

Blue Jack

109(105) (84)**102**
4-y-o b g Cadeaux Genereux-Fairy Flight (IRE) (Fairy King (USA))
W R Muir Martin P Graham

Placings:134/4414422046-320615101100 **(6091)**
2009: 5^{3}GF, 5^{2}GF, 6^{0}GF, 6^{6}GF, 5^{1}GF, 5^{5}GF, 5^{1}G, 5^{0}G, 5^{1}GS, 5^{1}GF, 5^{0}GS, 6^{0}G,

	Starts	1st	2nd	3rd	Win & Pl
Career Total (Turf)	22	6	3	1	49671
Career Total (AW)	3	0	0	1	1444

102	8/09	Sand	5f6y	(0-100)H	G-F	£12462
99	7/09	Gdwd	5f	(0-90)H	G-S	£12952
95	7/09	Wind	5f10y	(0-85)H	GD	£5180
91	6/09	Sand	5f6y	(0-85)H	G-F	£5180
82	5/08	Bevl	5f	(0-85)H	GD	£4209
71	10/07	Nott	5f13y		G-S	£3238

Total win prize-money £43224

Going (Turf): Sf: 0-0 **GS: 2-5 Gd: 2-7 GF: 2-9** Fm: 0-1
Distance: **5f/6f: 6-25** 7f-8f: 0-0 9f-13f: 0-0 14f+: 0-0
Track : LH: 0-5 RH: 0-0 Tight: 0-2 **Gall: 1-5**
Aids: **Bl: 4-8** Vi: 0-0 Tstrap: 0-0 Ckp: 0-0
Best Rating: 102 8/09 Sand 5f6y gd-fm

Very useful; effective over 5f-6f; acts on good and easier ground; goes on Polytrack; has worn blinkers.

Blue Jet (USA)

100(95) (59)**61**
5-y-o b g Black Minnaloushe (USA)-Clickety Click (USA) (Sovereign Dancer (USA))
M E Sowersby (R M Whitaker 6/10) The Southwold Set

Placings:00/0010530/025300651245-063200036 **(6559)**
2009: 16^{0}F, 11^{6}GF, 14^{3}GF, 14^{2}GF, 14^{0}SD, 13^{0}S, 14^{0}GF, 13^{3}GF, 15^{6}G,

	Starts	1st	2nd	3rd	Win & Pl
Career Total (Turf)	27	2	2	4	12469
Career Total (AW)	3	0	1	0	771

61	9/08	Hayd	1m6f	G-F	£6476
59	7/07	Catt	1m5f175y	G-F	£3238

Total win prize-money £9715

Going (Turf): Sf: 0-5 GS: 0-4 Gd: 0-6 **GF: 2-11** Fm: 0-1
Distance: 5f/6f: 0-0 7f-8f: 0-2 9f-13f: 0-4 **14f+: 2-24**
Track : **LH: 2-27** RH: 0-3 **Tight: 1-18** Gall: 0-7
Aids: Bl: 0-0 Vi: 0-1 Tstrap: 0-2 Ckp: 0-2
Best Rating: 62 10/07 Newc 2m19y good

Moderate; stays 2m; acts on fast ground.

Blue Lyric

89(100) (79)**59**
2-y-o b f Refuse To Bend (IRE)-Powder Blue (Daylami (IRE))
L M Cumani Fittocks Stud & Andrew Bengough

Placings:63611 **(7611)**
2009: 6^{6}GF, 5^{3}SD, 8^{6}GF, 7^{1}SD, 7^{1}SD,

	Starts	1st	2nd	3rd	Win & Pl
Career Total (Turf)	2	0	0	0	0
Career Total (AW)	3	2	0	1	6121

79	12/09	Kemp	7f	(0-85)	STD	£3885
78	11/09	Kemp	7f	(0-65)	STD	£1706

Total win prize-money £5592

Going (Turf): **Sf: 0-0 GS: 0-0 Gd: 0-0 GF: 0-2 Fm: 0-0**
Distance: 5f/6f: 0-1 **7f-8f: 2-4** 9f-13f: 0-0 14f+: 0-0
Track : LH: 0-1 **RH: 2-2** Tight: 0-1 Gall: 0-0
Aids: Bl: 0-0 Vi: 0-0 Tstrap: 0-0 Ckp: 0-0
Best Rating: 79 12/09 Kemp 7f stand

Fair; stays 7f; acts on Polytrack.

Blue Maiden

105 **104**
2-y-o b f Medicean-Bluebelle (Generous (IRE))
P J McBride Peter Charter

Placings:2125 **(6447)**
2009: 6^{2}GF, 6^{1}G, 7^{2}G, 7^{5}GF,

	Starts	1st	2nd	3rd	Win & Pl
Career Total (Turf)	4	1	2	0	18180

80	7/09	NmkJ	6f	GD	£4533

Total win prize-money £4533

Going (Turf): Sf: 0-0 GS: 0-0 **Gd: 1-2** GF: 0-2 Fm: 0-0
Distance: **5f/6f: 1-1** 7f-8f: 0-3 9f-13f: 0-0 14f+: 0-0
Track : LH: 0-0 RH: 0-0 Tight: 0-0 Gall: 0-0
Aids: Bl: 0-0 Vi: 0-0 Tstrap: 0-0 Ckp: 0-0
Best Rating: 104 8/09 NmkJ 7f good

Very useful; Group 3 placed; stays 7f; acts on good and fast ground.

Blue Monday

96(108) (104)**119**
8-y-o b g Darshaan-Lunda (IRE) (Soviet Star (USA))
R Charlton R A Pegum

Placings:011/31421/21143314/500400/2012-44 **(5059a)**
2009: 10^{4}GS, 10^{4}G,

	Starts	1st	2nd	3rd	Win & Pl
Career Total (Turf)	27	8	4	3	503120
Career Total (AW)	1	0	0	0	

119	9/08	Newb	1m3f5y		GD	£36900
119	9/06	Newb	1m3f5y		GD	£28390
108	6/06	Lonc	1m2f		G-S	£27586
116	5/06	Gdwd	1m1f192y		SFT	£17034
113	10/05	NmkR	1m1f	H	SFT	£75400
105	5/05	Rdcr	1m2f	(0-105)H	G-F	£32500
96	11/03	Donc	1m	C	GD	£4932
88	10/03	York	7f205y	D	G-F	£5762

Total win prize-money £228505

Going (Turf): Sf: 2-5 GS: 1-5 **Gd: 3-10** GF: 2-6 Fm: 0-1
Distance: 5f/6f: 0-0 7f-8f: 2-5 **9f-13f: 6-22** 14f+: 0-1
Track : **LH: 4-13** RH: 2-9 Tight: 2-4 **Gall: 3-11**
Aids: Bl: 0-0 Vi: 0-0 Tstrap: 0-0 Ckp: 0-0
Best Rating: 119 9/08 Newb 1m3f5y good

Smart; winner of the 2005 Cambridgeshire; Group 3 winner and third in the Eclipse Stakes and Juddmonte International in 2006; raced in Australia in 2007; stays 1m4f and acts on any ground; has a decent turn of foot.

Blue Neptune

80(99) (64)**34**
2-y-o ch c Compton Place-Centre Court (Second Set (IRE))
W R Muir Martin P Graham

Placings:060100336 **(7871)**
2009: 5^{0}G, 5^{6}GF, 5^{0}SD, 5^{1}SD, 5^{0}SD, 5^{0}SD, 5^{3}SD, 5^{3}SD, 5^{6}SD,

	Starts	1st	2nd	3rd	Win & Pl
Career Total (Turf)	2	0	0	0	0
Career Total (AW)	7	1	0	2	2735

64	10/09	Kemp	5f	6(0-60)	STD	£2047

Total win prize-money £2047

Going (Turf): **Sf: 0-0 GS: 0-0 Gd: 0-1 GF: 0-1 Fm: 0-0**
Distance: **5f/6f: 1-9** 7f-8f: 0-0 9f-13f: 0-0 14f+: 0-0
Track : LH: 0-4 **RH: 1-4** Tight: 0-4 Gall: 0-1
Aids: Bl: 0-0 Vi: 0-0 Tstrap: 0-0 Ckp: 0-0
Best Rating: 64 10/09 Kemp 5f stand

Modest; suited by 5f; acts on Polytrack.

Blue Noodles

104(103) (72)72

3-y-o b g Reset (AUS)-Gleam Of Light (IRE) (Danehill (USA))

P D Evans (Ollie Pears 9/8) Diamond Racing Ltd

Placings:460-03351523623112 **(6790)**

2009: 6^{0}SD, 5^{3}GF, 7^{3}GF, 6^{5}GF, 6^{1}GS, 5^{5}G, 5^{2}GF, 6^{3}G, 5^{6}G, 7^{2}S, 7^{3}HY, 7^{1}GS, 7^{1}SD, 6^{2}G,

	Starts	1st	2nd	3rd	Win & Pl
Career Total (Turf)	15	2	3	4	8292
Career Total (AW)	2	1	0	0	2730

72	9/09	Wolv	7f32y	(0-65)H	STD	£2729
72	9/09	Chep	7f16y		G-S	£1942
66	5/09	Newc	6f		G-S	£2072

Total win prize-money £6745

Going (Turf): Sf: 0-2 **GS: 2-4** Gd: 0-5 GF: 0-4 Fm: 0-0
Distance: 5f/6f: 1-9 **7f-8f: 2-8** 9f-13f: 0-0 14f+: 0-0
Track : **LH: 1-9** RH: 0-1 **Tight: 1-7** Gall: 0-0
Aids: Bl: 0-0 Vi: 0-0 Tstrap: 0-0 Ckp: 0-0
Best Rating: **72** 10/09 Brig 6f209y good

Modest; suited by 6f-7f; acts on most ground and on Polytrack.

Blue Nymph

99(99) (93)82

3-y-o ch f Selkirk (USA)-Blue Icon (Peintre Celebre (USA))

R M Beckett J H Richmond-Watson

Placings:5-22211 **(6875)**

2009: 11^{2}SD, 12^{2}SD, 11^{2}G, 12^{1}SD, 14^{1}SD,

	Starts	1st	2nd	3rd	Win & Pl
Career Total (Turf)	2	0	1	0	771
Career Total (AW)	4	2	2	0	10022

93	10/09	Sthl	1m6f	(0-85)H	STD	£5504
78	9/09	Kemp	1m4f		STD	£2590

Total win prize-money £8095

Going (Turf): **Sf: 0-0 GS: 0-1 Gd: 0-1 GF: 0-0 Fm: 0-0**
Distance: 5f/6f: 0-0 7f-8f: 0-0 9f-13f: 1-5 14f+: 1-1
Track : LH: 1-4 RH: 1-2 Tight: 0-1 Gall: 0-0
Aids: Bl: 0-0 Vi: 0-0 Tstrap: 0-0 Ckp: 0-0
Best Rating: **93** 10/09 Sthl 1m6f stand

Useful; stays 1m4f; acts on Fibresand and Polytrack.

Blue Rum (IRE)

88(73) (30)52

2-y-o b g Pyrus (USA)-Secret Combe (IRE) (Mujadil (USA))

P C Haslam Blue Lion Racing VIII & Miss K Theobald

Placings:34560 **(7421)**

2009: 5^{3}F, 5^{4}GF, 6^{5}GS, 6^{6}GS, 6^{0}SD,

	Starts	1st	2nd	3rd	Win & Pl
Career Total (Turf)	4	0	0	1	636
Career Total (AW)	1	0	0	0	

Going (Turf): **Sf: 0-0 GS: 0-2 Gd: 0-0 GF: 0-1 Fm: 0-1**
Distance: 5f/6f: 0-4 7f-8f: 0-1 9f-13f: 0-0 14f+: 0-0
Track : LH: 0-1 RH: 0-0 Tight: 0-0 Gall: 0-0
Aids: Bl: 0-0 Vi: 0-0 Tstrap: 0-2 Ckp: 0-2
Best Rating: **52** 4/09 Rdcr 5f gd-fm

Blue Sky Basin

104(106) (105)108

4-y-o b g Desert Prince (IRE)-Kimba (USA) (Kris S (USA))

Saeed Bin Suroor (M bin Shafya 13/3) Godolphin

Placings:4103/0111-00310 **(1861)**

2009: 7^{0}G, 7^{0}FT, 6^{3}GF, 7^{1}SD, 7^{0}GF,

	Starts	1st	2nd	3rd	Win & Pl
Career Total (Turf)	9	2	0	2	37003
Career Total (AW)	4	3	0	0	18682

105	3/09	Jebl	7f	(85-100)H	STD	£11363
108	7/08	Gdwd	7f	(0-105)H	G-F	£24924
96	7/08	Kemp	7f	(0-85)H	STD	£4727
87	6/08	Newb	7f	(0-75)H	GD	£2590
76	8/07	Kemp	7f		STD	£2590

Total win prize-money £46196

Going (Turf): Sf: 0-1 GS: 0-0 **Gd: 1-3 GF: 1-5** Fm: 0-0
Distance: 5f/6f: 0-0 **7f-8f: 5-13** 9f-13f: 0-0 14f+: 0-0
Track : LH: 0-4 **RH: 3-5** Tight: 0-0 Gall: 0-3
Aids: Bl: 0-0 Vi: 0-0 Tstrap: 0-0 Ckp: 0-0
Best Rating: **108** 7/08 Gdwd 7f gd-fm

Smart; stays 7f; acts on good and fast ground; also goes on Polytrack.

Blue Sky Thinking (IRE)

(98) (72)89

10-y-o b g Danehill Dancer (IRE)-Lauretta Blue (IRE) (Bluebird (USA))

K R Burke Mrs Elaine M Burke

Placings:3121/016334/**1560346200/03/6211116/14-00** **(0105)**

2009: 8^{0}SS, 9^{0}SD,

	Starts	1st	2nd	3rd	Win & Pl
Career Total (Turf)	18	4	2	5	37799
Career Total (AW)	15	5	1	0	29905

72	3/08	Wolv	1m141y		STD	£1483
71	5/07	Newc	1m3y		G-S	£1943
72	4/07	Wolv	1m141y		SF	£2730
79	3/07	Wolv	1m141y		STD	£3238
76	3/07	Wolv	1m1f103y		SF	£3071
104	1/04	Ling	1m2f	C(0-100)H	STD	£14993
94	8/03	Thsk	1m	C(0-90)	G-F	£8449
94	8/02	Sals	1m	C(0-90)	G-F	£7497
86	7/02	Asct	1m	D	GD	£6857

Total win prize-money £50263

Going (Turf): Sf: 0-1 GS: 1-4 Gd: 1-6 **GF: 2-7** Fm: 0-0
Distance: 5f/6f: 0-0 7f-8f: 3-13 **9f-13f: 6-20** 14f+: 0-0
Track : **LH: 6-25** RH: 0-3 **Tight: 6-16** Gall: 0-5
Aids: Bl: 0-0 Vi: 0-0 Tstrap: 0-0 Ckp: 0-0
Best Rating: **105** 2/04 Ling 1m2f stand

Fair gelding; formerly useful and has had his problems; stays 1m2f, but effective at shorter; suited by a sound surface.

Blue Sparkle (IRE)

89 67

2-y-o b f Acclamation-Westlife (IRE) (Mind Games)

Mrs A J Perrett The Green Dot Partnership

Placings:303 **(5604)**

2009: 6^{3}GF, 6^{0}GF, 6^{3}S,

	Starts	1st	2nd	3rd	Win & Pl
Career Total (Turf)	3	0	0	2	1493

Going (Turf): **Sf: 0-1 GS: 0-0 Gd: 0-0 GF: 0-2 Fm: 0-0**
Distance: 5f/6f: 0-2 7f-8f: 0-1 9f-13f: 0-0 14f+: 0-0
Track : LH: 0-0 RH: 0-0 Tight: 0-0 Gall: 0-1
Aids: Bl: 0-0 Vi: 0-0 Tstrap: 0-0 Ckp: 0-0
Best Rating: **67** 9/09 Sals 6f212y soft

Useful; suited by 7f and soft ground.

Blue Spartan (IRE)

86 82

4-y-o gr g Spartacus (IRE)-Bridelina (FR) (Linamix (FR))

C J Mann (B J Meehan 14/5) W A Harrison-Allan

Placings:0016-0 **(1603)**

2009: 8^{0}GF,

	Starts	1st	2nd	3rd	Win & Pl
Career Total (Turf)	5	1	0	0	2461

82	5/08	Chep	1m14y	SFT	£2460

Total win prize-money £2461

Going (Turf): **Sf: 1-1** GS: 0-1 Gd: 0-2 GF: 0-1 Fm: 0-0
Distance: 5f/6f: 0-0 7f-8f: 0-2 **9f-13f: 1-3** 14f+: 0-0
Track : LH: 0-0 RH: 0-2 Tight: 0-1 Gall: 0-0
Aids: Bl: 0-0 Vi: 0-0 Tstrap: 0-0 Ckp: 0-0
Best Rating: **82** 5/08 Chep 1m14y soft

Useful; stays 1m; acts on soft ground.

Blue Spinnaker (IRE)

97 91

10-y-o b g Bluebird (USA)-Suedoise (Kris)

M W Easterby G Sparkes G Hart S Curtis & T Dewhirst

Placings:0/23132414004/014104634/0200006300/0310000000/00042030000005/12100051402200-006000600 **(6900)**

2009: 10^{0}GS, 8^{0}GF, 9^{6}GF, 8^{0}GS, 8^{0}G, 8^{0}GF, 8^{6}GS, 8^{0}S, 10^{0}GF,

	Starts	1st	2nd	3rd	Win & Pl
Career Total (Turf)	78	8	7	6	153422

89	7/08	York	1m	(0-90)H	HVY	£10361
89	4/08	Thsk	1m	(0-70)H	G-S	£3885
88	4/08	Donc	1m2f60y	(0-70)H	G-S	£3123
108	5/06	York	1m2f88y	(0-100)H	G-S	£16516
111	5/04	Rdcr	1m2f	B(0-105)H	G-F	£32500
106	5/04	Thsk	1m	C(0-95)H	GD	£12818
94	8/03	Hayd	1m30y	C(0-90)H	G-F	£9872
76	6/03	Donc	5f	D	GD	£5449

Total win prize-money £94527

Going (Turf): Sf: 1-17 **GS: 3-17** Gd: 2-17 GF: 2-25 Fm: 0-2
Distance: 5f/6f: 1-3 7f-8f: 3-24 **9f-13f: 4-51** 14f+: 0-0
Track : **LH: 7-53** RH: 0-10 Tight: 3-11 Gall: 3-31
Aids: Bl: 0-2 Vi: 0-0 Tstrap: 0-1 Ckp: 0-1
Best Rating: **112** 10/04 NmkR 1m1f good

Useful; stays 1m2f; acts on most types of ground; has worn blinkers and cheekpieces.

Blue Tango (IRE)

97(101) (73)71

3-y-o ch c Noverre (USA)-It Takes Two (IRE) (Alzao (USA))

Mrs A J Perrett The Green Dot Partnership

Placings:04120-4000301060 **(6910)**

2009: 10^{4}SD, 10^{0}SD, 11^{0}GF, 14^{0}G, 14^{3}SD, 14^{0}G, 12^{1}SD, 12^{0}SD, 12^{6}SD, 10^{0}G,

	Starts	1st	2nd	3rd	Win & Pl
Career Total (Turf)	7	1	0	0	2589
Career Total (AW)	8	1	1	1	5645

66	9/09	Wolv	1m4f50y	(0-75)H	STD	£3561
71	10/08	Bath	1m5y		G-S	£2396

Total win prize-money £5958

Going (Turf): Sf: 0-1 **GS: 1-1** Gd: 0-4 GF: 0-1 Fm: 0-0
Distance: 5f/6f: 0-0 7f-8f: 0-4 **9f-13f: 2-8** 14f+: 0-3
Track : **LH: 2-8** RH: 0-4 **Tight: 2-8** Gall: 0-0
Aids: **Bl: 1-5** Vi: 0-0 Tstrap: 0-0 Ckp: 0-0
Best Rating: **73** 11/08 Ling 1m stand

Modest; stays 1m6f; acts on easy ground and on Polytrack and Fibresand.

Blue Tomato

105(107) (88)**93**

8-y-o b g Orpen (USA)-Ocean Grove (IRE) (Fairy King (USA))

Miss L A Perratt (D Nicholls 17/7) Ken McGarrity

Placings:4111503/0/646200033033000/30002111230503 50/00630/10450510050314-22221313052311021400 **(6051)**

2009: 5^{2}SD, 5^{2}SD, 6^{2}SD, 5^{2}SD, 5^{1}SD, 5^{3}SD, 5^{1}SD, 5^{3}SD, 5^{0}GF, 6^{5}GF, 6^{2}F, 7^{3}SD, 5^{1}GF, 5^{1}G, 6^{0}GF, 5^{2}G, 5^{1}G, 5^{4}G, 5^{0}GF, 5^{0}G,

	Starts	1st	2nd	3rd	Win & Pl
Career Total (Turf)	**62**	**11**	**5**	**9**	**99768**
Career Total (AW)	**16**	**3**	**4**	**4**	**11704**

82	7/09	Haml	5f4y		GD	£2266
84	6/09	Muss	5f	(0-105)H	GD	£7771
71	5/09	Muss	5f		G-F	£2590
75	3/09	Wolv	5f216y		STD	£1942
85	3/09	Wolv	5f216y		STD	£2047
88	10/08	Wolv	5f20y		STD	£2047
93	6/08	Haml	6f5y	(0-90)H	G-F	£10361
91	3/08	Muss	5f	(0-85)H	GD	£6477
96	7/06	Hayd	6f	(0-80)H	G-F	£6477
88	6/06	Newc	6f	(0-75)H	G-F	£4857
81	6/06	Gdwd	6f	(0-70)H	GD	£3562
105	8/03	York	6f3y	C H	G-F	£11407
94	8/03	Gdwd	6f	C H	GD	£10790
73	7/03	York	6f3y	E	G-F	£9308

Total win prize-money £81907

Going (Turf): Sf: 0-3 GS: 0-1 Gd: 5-21 **GF: 6-33** Fm: 0-4
Distance: **5f/6f: 11-60** 7f-8f: 3-17 9f-13f: 0-1 14f+: 0-0
Track : **LH: 3-17** RH: 0-5 **Tight: 3-12** Gall: 0-6
Aids: Bl: 0-0 Vi: 0-0 Tstrap: 2-12 Ckp: 2-12
Best Rating: **105** 8/03 York 6f3y gd-fm

Fair; Listed placed at two; stays 6f; acts on fast ground and on Polytrack; has worn cheekpieces.

Blue Turk

104(97) (64)**59**

4-y-o b g Where Or When (IRE)-Pearly River (Elegant Air)

J R Boyle (G M Lyons 21/6) Byerley Thoroughbred Racing

Placings:6660-60201400 **(7225)**

2009: 7^{6}GF, 7^{0}SD, 7^{2}GS, 8^{0}G, 10^{1}SD, 8^{4}SD, 12^{0}SD, 10^{0}SD,

	Starts	1st	2nd	3rd	Win & Pl
Career Total (Turf)	5	0	1	0	605
Career Total (AW)	7	1	0	0	**2047**

64	9/09	Kemp	1m2f	(0-65)H	STD	£2047

Total win prize-money £2047

Going (Turf): **Sf: 0-0 GS: 0-1 Gd: 0-2 GF: 0-1 Fm: 0-1**
Distance: 5f/6f: 0-0 7f-8f: 0-7 **9f-13f: 1-5** 14f+: 0-0
Track : LH: 0-6 **RH: 1-4** Tight: 0-0 Gall: 0-0
Aids: Bl: 0-0 Vi: 0-0 Tstrap: 0-0 Ckp: 0-0
Best Rating: **65** 3/08 Dund 7f stand

Modest; stays 1m2f; acts on Polytrack.

Blue Warrior (IRE)

15

4-y-o b g Touch Of The Blues (FR)-Warrior Wings (Indian Ridge)

J R Best Paul And Donna Rooks

Placings:0 **(3161)**

2009: 6^{0}GF,

	Starts	1st	2nd	3rd	Win & Pl
Career Total (Turf)	1	0	0	0	

Going (Turf): **Sf: 0-0 GS: 0-0 Gd: 0-0 GF: 0-1 Fm: 0-0**
Distance: 5f/6f: 0-1 7f-8f: 0-0 9f-13f: 0-0 14f+: 0-0
Track : LH: 0-0 RH: 0-0 Tight: 0-0 Gall: 0-0
Aids: Bl: 0-0 Vi: 0-0 Tstrap: 0-0 Ckp: 0-0

Blue Zephyr

(85) (61)

2-y-o br c Pastoral Pursuits-Pippa's Dancer (IRE) (Desert Style (IRE))

W R Muir M Graham, T Langley & G Cox

Placings:5 **(1119)**

2009: 5^{5}SD,

	Starts	1st	2nd	3rd	Win & Pl
Career Total (Turf)	0	0	0	0	
Career Total (AW)	1	0	0	0	0

Going (Turf): **Sf: 0-0 GS: 0-0 Gd: 0-0 GF: 0-0 Fm: 0-0**
Distance: 5f/6f: 0-1 7f-8f: 0-0 9f-13f: 0-0 14f+: 0-0
Track : LH: 0-1 RH: 0-0 Tight: 0-1 Gall: 0-0
Aids: Bl: 0-0 Vi: 0-0 Tstrap: 0-0 Ckp: 0-0
Best Rating: **61** 4/09 Ling 5f stand

Bluebaru

72(62) **28**

3-y-o b g Bahamian Bounty-Gina Of Hithermoor (Reprimand)

L R James Brian Womersley

Placings:000-0 **(1335)**

2009: 6^{0}GF,

	Starts	1st	2nd	3rd	Win & Pl
Career Total (Turf)	3	0	0	0	
Career Total (AW)	1	0	0	0	

Going (Turf): **Sf: 0-1 GS: 0-0 Gd: 0-1 GF: 0-1 Fm: 0-0**
Distance: 5f/6f: 0-3 7f-8f: 0-0 9f-13f: 0-1 14f+: 0-0
Track : LH: 0-3 RH: 0-0 Tight: 0-0 Gall: 0-0
Aids: Bl: 0-0 Vi: 0-1 Tstrap: 0-0 Ckp: 0-0
Best Rating: **28** 7/08 Pont 6f good

Bluebell Ridge (IRE)

(103) (70)**44**

4-y-o b f Distant Music (USA)-Miss Indigo (Indian Ridge)

D W P Arbuthnot The Bluebell Ridge Partnership

Placings:56/000041144-01 **(0299)**

2009: 12^{0}SD, 12^{1}SD,

	Starts	1st	2nd	3rd	Win & Pl
Career Total (Turf)	3	0	0	0	
Career Total (AW)	10	3	0	0	**7026**

69	1/09	Wolv	1m4f50y	(0-75)H	STD	£2729
66	10/08	Kemp	1m4f	(0-65)H	STD	£1706
60	10/08	Kemp	1m4f		STD	£2590

Total win prize-money £7026

Going (Turf): **Sf: 0-0 GS: 0-0 Gd: 0-2 GF: 0-1 Fm: 0-0**
Distance: 5f/6f: 0-0 7f-8f: 0-4 **9f-13f: 3-8** 14f+: 0-1
Track : LH: 1-4 **RH: 2-8 Tight: 1-5** Gall: 0-0
Aids: Bl: 0-1 Vi: 0-0 Tstrap: 0-0 Ckp: 0-0
Best Rating: **70** 11/08 Wolv 1m5f194y stand

Modest; stays 1m4f; acts on Polytrack.

Bluebird Chariot

86(87) (40)**40**

6-y-o b g Bluebird (USA)-Boadicea's Chariot (Commanche Run)

J M Bradley J M Bradley

Placings:0300-5006 **(7520)**

2009: 6^{5}F, 7^{0}GS, 5^{0}G, 7^{6}SD,

	Starts	1st	2nd	3rd	Win & Pl
Career Total (Turf)	7	0	0	1	353
Career Total (AW)	1	0	0	0	0

Going (Turf): **Sf: 0-1 GS: 0-1 Gd: 0-2 GF: 0-1 Fm: 0-2**
Distance: 5f/6f: 0-2 7f-8f: 0-5 9f-13f: 0-1 14f+: 0-0
Track : LH: 0-4 RH: 0-0 Tight: 0-2 Gall: 0-1
Aids: Bl: 0-0 Vi: 0-0 Tstrap: 0-0 Ckp: 0-0
Best Rating: **40** 11/09 Ling 7f stand

Very moderate; effective at 7f; acts on fast ground.

Bluebok

97(106) (75)**67**

8-y-o ch g Indian Ridge-Blue Sirocco (Bluebird (USA))

J M Bradley E A Hayward

Placings:5/230/4024113202600/04204154215455415/452 0002063404/006003006013244-063354212350356013562505044 **(7657)**

2009: 5^{0}SD, 5^{6}SD, 5^{3}SD, 5^{3}SD, 5^{5}SD, 5^{4}SD, 5^{2}SD, 5^{1}SD, 5^{2}SD, 5^{3}GF, 5^{5}F, 5^{0}G, 5^{3}SD, 5^{5}F, 5^{6}GF, 5^{0}GF, 5^{1}SD, 5^{3}SD, 5^{5}G, 5^{6}G, 5^{2}G, 5^{5}G, 5^{0}SD,

	Starts	1st	2nd	3rd	Win & Pl
Career Total (Turf)	**62**	**6**	**9**	**4**	**59619**
Career Total (AW)	**28**	**2**	**3**	**6**	**9256**

69	7/09	Ling	5f	(0-65)H	STD	£2047
73	4/09	Wolv	5f20y	(0-60)H	STD	£2047
67	10/08	Gdwd	5f	(0-70)H	G-F	£3561
88	9/06	Yarm	5f43y	(0-85)H	G-F	£6232
90	7/06	Yarm	5f43y	(0-85)H	FRM	£6232
91	6/06	Muss	5f	H	G-F	£9715
85	7/05	Hayd	5f	(0-70)H	G-F	£3653
74	6/05	Bath	5f161y	(0-70)H	FRM	£4515

Total win prize-money £38005

Going (Turf): Sf: 0-3 GS: 0-4 Gd: 0-18 **GF: 4-32** Fm: 2-5
Distance: **5f/6f: 8-87** 7f-8f: 0-3 9f-13f: 0-0 14f+: 0-0
Track : **LH: 3-35** RH: 0-7 **Tight: 2-23** Gall: 1-6
Aids: **Bl: 3-39** Vi: 0-0 Tstrap: 0-0 Ckp: 0-0
Best Rating: **91** 6/06 Muss 5f gd-fm

Moderate; best over 5f; acts on fast ground; goes on Polytrack; has worn a tongue tie and blinkers.

Bluecrop Boy

(99) (57)**44**

5-y-o b g Zaha (CAN)-Pearl Dawn (IRE) (Jareer (USA))

D J S Ffrench Davis Mrs J E Taylor

Placings:6060003/2-6 **(5885)**

2009: 16^{6}SD,

	Starts	1st	2nd	3rd	Win & Pl
Career Total (Turf)	3	0	0	1	302
Career Total (AW)	6	0	1	0	605

Going (Turf): **Sf: 0-1 GS: 0-1 Gd: 0-1 GF: 0-0 Fm: 0-0**
Distance: 5f/6f: 0-0 7f-8f: 0-0 9f-13f: 0-7 14f+: 0-2
Track : LH: 0-8 RH: 0-1 Tight: 0-7 Gall: 0-0

Aids: Bl: 0-1 Vi: 0-1 Tstrap: 0-1 Ckp: 0-1
Best Rating: **57** 11/08 Sthl 1m4f stand

Moderate; stays 1m4f; acts on easy ground and Fibresand; has worn a visor and cheekpieces.

Bluegrass Lion (USA)

91(74) **50**

3-y-o b/br g Volponi (USA)-Exactly Dixie (USA) (Dixie Brass (USA))
Paul Green Bluegrass Racing Ltd

Placings:50 **(7504)**
2009: 11^{5}GF, 12^{0}SD,

	Starts	1st	2nd	3rd	Win & Pl
Career Total (Turf)	1	0	0	0	0
Career Total (AW)	1	0	0	0	

Going (Turf): **Sf: 0-0 GS: 0-0 Gd: 0-0 GF: 0-1 Fm: 0-0**
Distance: 5f/6f: 0-0 7f-8f: 0-0 9f-13f: 0-2 14f+: 0-0
Track : LH: 0-1 RH: 0-1 Tight: 0-0 Gall: 0-0
Aids: Bl: 0-0 Vi: 0-0 Tstrap: 0-0 Ckp: 0-0
Best Rating: **50** 9/09 Leic 1m3f183y gd-fm

Bluejain

(104) (87)**73**

4-y-o b g Lujain (USA)-Belle Of The Blues (IRE) (Blues Traveller (IRE))
Miss Gay Kelleway Countrywide Classics Limited

Placings:00/0116552312-P **(0199)**
2009: 8^{P}SD,

	Starts	1st	2nd	3rd	Win & Pl
Career Total (Turf)	6	1	0	0	2218
Career Total (AW)	7	2	2	1	8790

84	12/08	GrLe	1m2f	(0-75)H	STD	£2914
79	7/08	Kemp	1m	(0-65)H	STD	£2047
64	7/08	Catt	7f		G-F	£2217

Total win prize-money £7179

Going (Turf): Sf: 0-1 GS: 0-1 Gd: 0-0 **GF: 1-4** Fm: 0-0
Distance: 5f/6f: 0-1 **7f-8f: 2-7** 9f-13f: 1-5 14f+: 0-0
Track : **LH: 2-6** RH: 1-4 Tight: 1-2 Gall: 1-4
Aids: Bl: 0-0 Vi: 0-0 Tstrap: 0-0 Ckp: 0-0
Best Rating: **87** 12/08 GrLe 1m stand

Fair; effective at around 1m-1m2f; acted on fast ground and Polytrack (DEAD).

Blues Jazz

(89) (49)

3-y-o b g Josr Algarhoud (IRE)-Belle Of The Blues (IRE) (Blues Traveller (IRE))
Miss Gay Kelleway Countrywide Classics Ltd & Gay Kelleway

Placings:0 **(6223)**
2009: 8^{0}SD,

	Starts	1st	2nd	3rd	Win & Pl
Career Total (Turf)	0	0	0	0	
Career Total (AW)	1	0	0	0	

Going (Turf): **Sf: 0-0 GS: 0-0 Gd: 0-0 GF: 0-0 Fm: 0-0**
Distance: 5f/6f: 0-0 7f-8f: 0-1 9f-13f: 0-0 14f+: 0-0
Track : LH: 0-0 RH: 0-1 Tight: 0-0 Gall: 0-0
Aids: Bl: 0-0 Vi: 0-0 Tstrap: 0-0 Ckp: 0-0
Best Rating: **49** 9/09 Kemp 1m stand

Blues Minor (IRE)

73(97) (72)**68**

4-y-o b g Acclamation-Narbayda (IRE) (Kahyasi)
M Mullineaux Bluestone Partnership

Placings:42501/000320016-0000 **(5683)**
2009: 7^{0}SD, 7^{0}SF, 10^{0}GS, 8^{0}SD,

	Starts	1st	2nd	3rd	Win & Pl
Career Total (Turf)	12	1	1	1	4779
Career Total (AW)	6	1	1	0	2973

72	11/08	Wolv	1m141y	(0-67)H⁻	STD	£2388
79	10/07	Gdwd	7f		SFT	£3238

Total win prize-money £5627

Going (Turf): **Sf: 1-2** GS: 0-5 Gd: 0-1 GF: 0-3 Fm: 0-1
Distance: 5f/6f: 0-3 7f-8f: 1-10 9f-13f: 1-5 14f+: 0-0
Track : LH: 1-7 RH: 1-3 **Tight: 1-6** Gall: 0-0
Aids: **Bl: 1-5** Vi: 0-0 Tstrap: 0-0 Ckp: 0-0
Best Rating: **79** 10/07 Gdwd 7f soft

Modest; effective over 7f-1m; acts on easy ground; goes on Polytrack.

Bluie

100 **79**

2-y-o b g Ishiguru (USA)-Flying Highest (Spectrum (IRE))
D Nicholls The Three K's

Placings:04311144 **(6048)**
2009: 5^{0}GF, 6^{4}GS, 6^{3}GS, 6^{1}G, 6^{1}S, 6^{1}GS, 6^{4}GS, 6^{4}G,

	Starts	1st	2nd	3rd	Win & Pl
Career Total (Turf)	8	3	0	1	25759

79	8/09	Haml	6f5y		G-S	£4209
78	8/09	Gdwd	6f	H	SFT	£12952
68	7/09	Hayd	6f		GD	£5504

Total win prize-money £22666

Going (Turf): **Sf: 1-1 GS: 1-4 Gd: 1-2** GF: 0-1 Fm: 0-0
Distance: **5f/6f: 2-7** 7f-8f: 1-1 9f-13f: 0-0 14f+: 0-0
Track : LH: 0-0 RH: 0-0 Tight: 0-0 Gall: 0-0
Aids: Bl: 0-0 Vi: 0-0 Tstrap: 0-0 Ckp: 0-0
Best Rating: **79** 9/09 Ayr 6f good

Fair; effective over 6f; acts on easy ground.

Blushing (IRE)

87(57) **61**

2-y-o b f Fasliyev (USA)-Danseuse Du Bois (USA) (Woodman (USA))
B J Meehan B J Meehan

Placings:540 **(5368)**
2009: 5^{5}F, 6^{4}GF, 6^{0}SD,

	Starts	1st	2nd	3rd	Win & Pl
Career Total (Turf)	2	0	0	0	385
Career Total (AW)	1	0	0	0	

Going (Turf): **Sf: 0-0 GS: 0-0 Gd: 0-0 GF: 0-1 Fm: 0-1**
Distance: 5f/6f: 0-2 7f-8f: 0-1 9f-13f: 0-0 14f+: 0-0
Track : LH: 0-2 RH: 0-0 Tight: 0-1 Gall: 0-1
Aids: Bl: 0-0 Vi: 0-0 Tstrap: 0-0 Ckp: 0-0
Best Rating: **61** 7/09 Newb 6f8y gd-fm

Modest half-sister to Saucy Brown; stays 6f; acts on fast ground.

Blushing Bertie

(74) (39)

3-y-o b g Bertolini (USA)-Blushing Sunrise (USA) (Cox's Ridge (USA))
J W Unett James Unett

Placings:00-0 **(3228)**
2009: 8^{0}SD,

	Starts	1st	2nd	3rd	Win & Pl
Career Total (Turf)	1	0	0	0	
Career Total (AW)	2	0	0	0	

Going (Turf): **Sf: 0-0 GS: 0-0 Gd: 0-0 GF: 0-1 Fm: 0-0**
Distance: 5f/6f: 0-1 7f-8f: 0-1 9f-13f: 0-1 14f+: 0-0
Track : LH: 0-2 RH: 0-0 Tight: 0-2 Gall: 0-0
Aids: Bl: 0-0 Vi: 0-0 Tstrap: 0-0 Ckp: 0-0
Best Rating: **39** 6/09 Wolv 1m141y stand

Blushing Dreamer (IRE)

(76) (23)

3-y-o ch f Frenchmans Bay (FR)-Second Dream (IRE) (Second Set (IRE))
Miss N A Lloyd-Beavis S Lloyd-Beavis

Placings:0000-0 **(7615)**
2009: 8^{0}SD,

	Starts	1st	2nd	3rd	Win & Pl
Career Total (Turf)	1	0	0	0	
Career Total (AW)	4	0	0	0	

Going (Turf): **Sf: 0-1 GS: 0-0 Gd: 0-0 GF: 0-0 Fm: 0-0**
Distance: 5f/6f: 0-0 7f-8f: 0-3 9f-13f: 0-2 14f+: 0-0
Track : LH: 0-4 RH: 0-1 Tight: 0-3 Gall: 0-1
Aids: Bl: 0-1 Vi: 0-1 Tstrap: 0-0 Ckp: 0-0
Best Rating: **23** 11/08 Wolv 7f32y stand

Blushing Heart

(91) (50)**61**

5-y-o b m Observatory (USA)-Navarazi (Arazi (USA))
G M Moore Mrs D N B Pearson

Placings:66/6/506-50 **(0368)**
2009: 12^{5}SD, 12^{0}SD,

	Starts	1st	2nd	3rd	Win & Pl
Career Total (Turf)	6	0	0	0	140
Career Total (AW)	2	0	0	0	0

Going (Turf): **Sf: 0-3 GS: 0-2 Gd: 0-1 GF: 0-0 Fm: 0-0**
Distance: 5f/6f: 0-1 7f-8f: 0-2 9f-13f: 0-4 14f+: 0-1
Track : LH: 0-5 RH: 0-0 Tight: 0-0 Gall: 0-0
Aids: Bl: 0-0 Vi: 0-0 Tstrap: 0-0 Ckp: 0-0
Best Rating: **76** 10/06 MsnL 1m good

Modest; stays 1m4f.

Blushing Hilary (IRE)

(96) (58)**65**

6-y-o ch m City On A Hill (USA)-Trinida (Jaazeiro (USA))
Mrs S J Humphrey Yen Hall Farm Racing

Placings:6434504200/33445354/54300/352500-0 **(0248)**
2009: 12^{0}SD,

	Starts	1st	2nd	3rd	Win & Pl
Career Total (Turf)	21	0	2	4	6650
Career Total (AW)	9	0	0	2	1240

Going (Turf): **Sf: 0-1 GS: 0-2 Gd: 0-10 GF: 0-7 Fm: 0-1**
Distance: 5f/6f: 0-1 7f-8f: 0-6 9f-13f: 0-14 14f+: 0-9
Track : LH: 0-15 RH: 0-11 Tight: 0-18 Gall: 0-1

Aids: Bl: 0-3 Vi: 0-6 Tstrap: 0-10 Ckp: 0-10
Best Rating: 75 9/06 Bevl 1m4f16y gd-fm

Moderate sort; stays 1m4f; acts on easy ground; still a maiden; has worn headgear.

Blushing Maid

93(94) (63)67

3-y-o br f Namid-Music Maid (IRE) (Inzar (USA))
H S Howe Roly Roper

Placings:04010-466660600 (6362)
2009: 5^{4}F, 5^{6}F, 6^{0}SD, 5^{6}GF, 5^{6}GF, 6^{0}SD, 6^{6}GF, 6^{0}SD, 6^{0}GF,

	Starts	1st	2nd	3rd	Win & Pl
Career Total (Turf)	11	1	0	0	4065
Career Total (AW)	3	0	0	0	0

65	6/08	Bath	5f161y		FRM	£3367

Total win prize-money £3368

Going (Turf): Sf: 0-0 GS: 0-0 Gd: 0-4 GF: 0-4 **Fm: 1-3**
Distance: **5f/6f: 1-14** 7f-8f: 0-0 9f-13f: 0-0 14f+: 0-0
Track : **LH: 1-8** RH: 0-1 Tight: 0-2 **Gall: 1-6**
Aids: Bl: 0-0 Vi: 0-0 Tstrap: 0-0 Ckp: 0-0
Best Rating: 67 5/08 Sals 5f good

Fair; effective at around 5f; acts on firm ground and Polytrack.

Blushing Soul (USA)

(69) (70)

3-y-o ch g Perfect Soul (IRE)-Kalimenta (USA) (Rahy (USA))
L A Dace (Miss P Robson 8/12) Let's Have Fun Syndicate

Placings:330-00 (7888)
2009: 10^{0}SD, 12^{0}SD,

	Starts	1st	2nd	3rd	Win & Pl
Career Total (Turf)	0	0	0	0	
Career Total (AW)	5	0	0	2	1436

Going (Turf): Sf: 0-0 GS: 0-0 Gd: 0-0 GF: 0-0 Fm: 0-0
Distance: 5f/6f: 0-0 7f-8f: 0-3 9f-13f: 0-2 14f+: 0-0
Track : LH: 0-5 RH: 0-0 Tight: 0-1 Gall: 0-0
Aids: Bl: 0-2 Vi: 0-0 Tstrap: 0-2 Ckp: 0-2
Best Rating: 70 10/08 Dund 1m stand

Blythe Knight (IRE)

104(98) (99)117

9-y-o ch g Selkirk (USA)-Blushing Barada (USA) (Blushing Groom (FR))
J J Quinn Maxilead Limited

Placings:02/15150430/4146300065/2264340040300/1034 0430/203110430/24531310205-206500 (4404)
2009: 8^{2}SD, 8^{0}GF, 8^{6}GF, 8^{5}G, 8^{0}G, 9^{0}G,

	Starts	1st	2nd	3rd	Win & Pl
Career Total (Turf)	64	8	4	10	323226
Career Total (AW)	3	0	3	0	27561

114	7/08	Ches	7f2y		GD	£24978
116	6/08	Epsm	1m114y		GD	£28385
115	6/07	Epsm	1m114y		GD	£42585
107	5/07	York	1m	(0-110)H	G-S	£20744
106	3/06	Rdcr	1m	H	SFT	£62320
108	4/04	Epsm	1m2f18yB(0-105)H		SFT	£17400
103	6/03	Pont	1m2f6yC(0-90)		G-F	£10398
84	3/03	Donc	1m2f60y	D	GD	£5434

Total win prize-money £212246

Going (Turf): Sf: 2-13 GS: 1-9 **Gd: 4-20** GF: 1-20 Fm: 0-2
Distance: 5f/6f: 0-0 7f-8f: 3-26 **9f-13f: 5-41** 14f+: 0-0
Track : **LH: 7-32** RH: 0-14 **Tight: 4-12** Gall: 2-23
Aids: Bl: 0-1 Vi: 0-1 Tstrap: 0-6 Ckp: 0-6
Best Rating: 117 3/08 Donc 1m gd-sft

Smart; winner of Group 3 Diomed Stakes in 2007 and 2008; effective from 7f-1m4f; handles fast ground, but may be better on softer; also acts on Polytrack; smart hurdler.

Bo McGinty (IRE)

104(109) (80)89

8-y-o ch g Fayruz-Georges Park Lady (IRE) (Tirol)
R A Fahey Paddy McGinty & Bo Turnbull

Placings:301/012004515/060004003502010000/06000054 02143060046/0024430443025012334 0/2122530016066100002 0-643543224460453500555 (7870)
2009: 5^{6}SS, 5^{4}SD, 6^{3}SD, 5^{5}SD, 5^{4}SD, 5^{3}SD, 5^{2}SD, 5^{2}SD, 5^{4}GF, 5^{4}GF, 5^{6}GF, 6^{0}GS, 5^{4}GF, 5^{5}GF, 5^{3}GF, 5^{5}GF, 5^{0}SD, 5^{0}SD, 5^{5}SD, 5^{5}SD, 6^{5}SS,

	Starts	1st	2nd	3rd	Win & Pl
Career Total (Turf)	84	7	7	8	98945
Career Total (AW)	25	2	5	3	18582

89	6/08	Ches	5f16y	(0-90)H	GD	£8831
87	4/08	Sthl	5f	(0-80)H	STD	£4533
84	2/08	Sthl	5f	(0-75)H	STD	£2593
87	9/07	Hayd	5f	(0-80)H	G-F	£6477
89	6/06	Bevl	5f	(0-95)H	G-F	£8096
93	9/05	Carl	5f193y	(0-85)H	G-F	£6922
89	9/04	Sand	5f6y	(0-85)H	GD	£8303
84	5/04	Haml	6f5y	C(0-95)H	G-S	£9326
78	8/03	Carl	5f	E	G-F	£3718

Total win prize-money £58801

Going (Turf): Sf: 0-11 GS: 1-11 Gd: 2-22 **GF: 4-38** Fm: 0-2
Distance: **5f/6f: 8-102** 7f-8f: 1-7 9f-13f: 0-0 14f+: 0-0
Track : LH: 1-26 **RH: 2-6** Tight: 1-18 Gall: 1-3
Aids: **Bl: 6-59** Vi: 0-17 Tstrap: 0-3 Ckp: 0-3
Best Rating: 93 9/05 Carl 5f193y gd-fm

Modest; effective over 5f-6f; acts on most ground and on Fibresand; has worn blinkers and a visor.

Bob Goes Electric (IRE)

79 39

2-y-o br c Camacho-Gracious Gretclo (Common Grounds)
J R Best John Mayne

Placings:0 (1669)
2009: 5^{0}G,

	Starts	1st	2nd	3rd	Win & Pl
Career Total (Turf)	1	0	0	0	

Going (Turf): Sf: 0-0 GS: 0-0 Gd: 0-1 GF: 0-0 Fm: 0-0
Distance: 5f/6f: 0-1 7f-8f: 0-0 9f-13f: 0-0 14f+: 0-0
Track : LH: 0-0 RH: 0-0 Tight: 0-0 Gall: 0-0
Aids: Bl: 0-0 Vi: 0-0 Tstrap: 0-0 Ckp: 0-0
Best Rating: 39 5/09 Gdwd 5f good

A £19,000 half-brother to Grafton, Malahide Express, Granston and Our Kes.

Bob Stock (IRE)

97(102) (66)67

3-y-o b g Dubai Destination (USA)-Red Rita (IRE) (Kefaah (USA))
W J Musson B N Fulton

Placings:0000-200003 (7650)
2009: 8^{2}GF, 8^{0}GF, 7^{0}GF, 8^{0}S, 7^{0}SD, 8^{3}SD,

	Starts	1st	2nd	3rd	Win & Pl
Career Total (Turf)	8	0	1	0	605
Career Total (AW)	2	0	0	1	353

Going (Turf): Sf: 0-1 GS: 0-1 Gd: 0-0 GF: 0-6 Fm: 0-0
Distance: 5f/6f: 0-2 7f-8f: 0-5 9f-13f: 0-3 14f+: 0-0
Track : LH: 0-4 RH: 0-1 Tight: 0-1 Gall: 0-1
Aids: Bl: 0-0 Vi: 0-0 Tstrap: 0-0 Ckp: 0-0
Best Rating: 67 5/09 Wwck 1m22y gd-fm

Moderate; effective over 1m; acts on Polytrack.

Bob's Your Uncle

104(101) (61)61

6-y-o br g Zilzal (USA)-Bob's Princess (Bob's Return (IRE))
J G Portman A S B Portman

Placings:5046040/40141140200/03212355602/3025002 0-03060 (5246)
2009: 11^{0}GF, 16^{3}G, 16^{0}SD, 16^{6}GF, 13^{0}F,

	Starts	1st	2nd	3rd	Win & Pl
Career Total (Turf)	30	3	4	2	13936
Career Total (AW)	13	1	2	2	3946

65	6/07	Ling	1m4f	(0-55)H	STD	£2047
68	6/06	Wind	1m3f135y	(0-70)H	G-S	£3238
64	6/06	Ling	1m3f106y	(0-60)H	FRM	£2730
60	4/06	Wind	1m2f7y		GD	£3238

Total win prize-money £11256

Going (Turf): Sf: 0-2 **GS: 1-3 Gd: 1-11** GF: 0-11 **Fm: 1-3**
Distance: 5f/6f: 0-0 7f-8f: 0-5 **9f-13f: 4-25** 14f+: 0-13
Track : **LH: 2-24** RH: 1-13 **Tight: 4-27** Gall: 0-0
Aids: Bl: 0-0 Vi: 0-0 Tstrap: 0-0 Ckp: 0-0
Best Rating: 71 8/06 Wind 1m3f135y good

Moderate; effective at around 1m4f; acts on easy ground; also goes on Polytrack.

Bobal Girl

(96) (53)44

4-y-o ch f Tobougg (IRE)-Al Guswa (Shernazar)
M D Squance Dr David Marlin

Placings:002/053000550-0 (0043)
2009: 8^{0}SD,

	Starts	1st	2nd	3rd	Win & Pl
Career Total (Turf)	5	0	0	0	0
Career Total (AW)	8	0	1	1	1141

Going (Turf): Sf: 0-0 GS: 0-0 Gd: 0-2 GF: 0-3 Fm: 0-0
Distance: 5f/6f: 0-1 7f-8f: 0-4 9f-13f: 0-7 14f+: 0-1
Track : LH: 0-8 RH: 0-4 Tight: 0-5 Gall: 0-2
Aids: Bl: 0-1 Vi: 0-0 Tstrap: 0-0 Ckp: 0-0
Best Rating: 53 6/08 Ling 1m4f stand

Bobbie Soxer (IRE)

103(98) (77)83

3-y-o br f Pivotal-Fantasy Girl (IRE) (Marju (IRE))
J L Dunlop Windflower Overseas Holdings Inc

Placings:041064-221400240 (6723)
2009: 7^{2}SD, 6^{2}GF, 5^{1}GF, 6^{4}GF, 6^{0}GF, 6^{0}GF, 6^{2}GF, 5^{4}F, 6^{0}SD,

	Starts	1st	2nd	3rd	Win & Pl
Career Total (Turf)	12	2	2	0	14233
Career Total (AW)	3	0	1	0	1792

83	5/09	Leic	5f218y	(0-80)H	G-F	£4857
72	7/08	Folk	7f		G-F	£4209

Total win prize-money £9066

Going (Turf): Sf: 0-0 GS: 0-0 Gd: 0-0 **GF: 2-11** Fm: 0-1
Distance: 5f/6f: 1-10 7f-8f: 1-5 9f-13f: 0-0 14f+: 0-0
Track : LH: 0-3 RH: 0-2 Tight: 0-1 Gall: 0-2
Aids: Bl: 0-0 Vi: 0-0 Tstrap: 0-0 Ckp: 0-0
Best Rating: **83** 8/09 Nott 6f15y gd-fm

Fair; suited by 6f-7f and fast ground.

Bobble Rock (IRE)

78(81) (27)53
3-y-o ch c Rock Of Gibraltar (IRE)-Torosay Spring (First Trump)
J R Best David Thorpe & Partners

Placings:360000 (6371)
2009: 7^{3}GF, 7^{6}GS, 6^{0}G, 8^{0}GF, 7^{0}SD, 11^{0}SD,

	Starts	1st	2nd	3rd	Win & Pl
Career Total (Turf)	4	0	0	1	403
Career Total (AW)	2	0	0	0	

Going (Turf): **Sf: 0-0 GS: 0-1 Gd: 0-1 GF: 0-2 Fm: 0-0**
Distance: 5f/6f: 0-1 7f-8f: 0-3 9f-13f: 0-2 14f+: 0-0
Track : LH: 0-0 RH: 0-2 Tight: 0-0 Gall: 0-0
Aids: Bl: 0-1 Vi: 0-0 Tstrap: 0-0 Ckp: 0-0
Best Rating: **53** 7/09 Yarm 7f3y gd-sft

Bobby Charles

81 (87)63
8-y-o ch g Polish Precedent (USA)-Dina Line (USA) (Diesis)
Dr J D Scargill Silent Partners

Placings:043/1621121/3300543/505/0-0 (4054)
2009: 10^{0}S,

	Starts	1st	2nd	3rd	Win & Pl
Career Total (Turf)	11	3	1	0	16629
Career Total (AW)	11	1	1	4	9321

86	10/05	Yarm	1m2f21y	(0-80)H	HVY	£6890
76	4/05	Thsk	1m4f	(0-70)	SFT	£4007
72	4/05	Folk	1m1f149y	(0-65)	SFT	£3386
66	1/05	Ling	1m2f		STD	£3445

Total win prize-money £17729

Going (Turf): **Sf: 3-7** GS: 0-2 Gd: 0-1 GF: 0-1 Fm: 0-0
Distance: 5f/6f: 0-0 7f-8f: 0-1 **9f-13f: 4-21** 14f+: 0-0
Track : **LH: 3-15** RH: 1-7 **Tight: 4-12** Gall: 0-2
Aids: Bl: 0-0 Vi: 0-0 Tstrap: 0-0 Ckp: 0-0
Best Rating: **87** 2/06 Ling 1m2f stand

Fair; stays 1m 4f; suited by soft ground but acts on Polytrack.

Bobby McGee

82 43
2-y-o b f Captain Rio-Al Kahina (Mark Of Esteem (IRE))
Jedd O'Keeffe The Hut Partnership

Placings:6 (6408)
2009: 6^{6}GF,

	Starts	1st	2nd	3rd	Win & Pl
Career Total (Turf)	1	0	0	0	0

Going (Turf): **Sf: 0-0 GS: 0-0 Gd: 0-0 GF: 0-1 Fm: 0-0**
Distance: 5f/6f: 0-1 7f-8f: 0-0 9f-13f: 0-0 14f+: 0-0
Track : LH: 0-0 RH: 0-0 Tight: 0-0 Gall: 0-0
Aids: Bl: 0-0 Vi: 0-0 Tstrap: 0-0 Ckp: 0-0
Best Rating: **43** 10/09 Ayr 6f gd-fm

Bobby's Doll

80(90) (57)48
2-y-o ch f Needwood Blade-Nine To Five (Imp Society (USA))
T T Clement Ms Sarah Jensen

Placings:60445 (7584)
2009: 6^{6}GF, 5^{0}SF, 6^{4}SD, 6^{4}SD, 7^{5}SF,

	Starts	1st	2nd	3rd	Win & Pl
Career Total (Turf)	1	0	0	0	0
Career Total (AW)	4	0	0	0	192

Going (Turf): **Sf: 0-0 GS: 0-0 Gd: 0-0 GF: 0-1 Fm: 0-0**
Distance: 5f/6f: 0-4 7f-8f: 0-1 9f-13f: 0-0 14f+: 0-0
Track : LH: 0-2 RH: 0-2 Tight: 0-2 Gall: 0-0
Aids: Bl: 0-0 Vi: 0-0 Tstrap: 0-0 Ckp: 0-0
Best Rating: **57** 10/09 Kemp 6f stand

Moderate; stays 7f; acts on Polytrack.

Bobeachway (IRE)

82 51
3-y-o b g Chevalier (IRE)-Miss Barcelona (IRE) (Mac's Imp (USA))
M Dods N A Riddell

Placings:005 (2105)
2009: 8^{0}GF, 8^{0}GF, 9^{5}GS,

	Starts	1st	2nd	3rd	Win & Pl
Career Total (Turf)	3	0	0	0	0

Going (Turf): **Sf: 0-0 GS: 0-1 Gd: 0-0 GF: 0-2 Fm: 0-0**
Distance: 5f/6f: 0-0 7f-8f: 0-1 9f-13f: 0-2 14f+: 0-0
Track : LH: 0-2 RH: 0-1 Tight: 0-2 Gall: 0-0
Aids: Bl: 0-0 Vi: 0-0 Tstrap: 0-0 Ckp: 0-0
Best Rating: **51** 5/09 Ripn 1m1f gd-sft

Bobering

(99) (43)43
9-y-o b g Bob's Return (IRE)-Ring The Rafters (Batshoof)
B P J Baugh J H Chrimes And Mr & Mrs G W Hannam

Placings:0/0000/0052053643/15/61400024630/450453000 0-006006 (7719)
2009: 10^{0}SD, 9^{0}SD, 9^{6}SD, 9^{0}SD, 9^{0}SD, 9^{6}SD,

	Starts	1st	2nd	3rd	Win & Pl
Career Total (Turf)	5	0	0	0	
Career Total (AW)	39	2	2	4	5757

61	1/07	Wolv	1m1f103y	(0-50)H	SS	£2388
49	12/06	Wolv	1m141y	(0-45)	STD	£1365

Total win prize-money £3754

Going (Turf): **Sf: 0-0 GS: 0-0 Gd: 0-3 GF: 0-2 Fm: 0-0**
Distance: 5f/6f: 0-0 7f-8f: 0-3 **9f-13f: 2-41** 14f+: 0-0
Track : **LH: 2-42** RH: 0-2 **Tight: 2-33** Gall: 0-1
Aids: Bl: 0-0 Vi: 0-0 Tstrap: 0-0 Ckp: 0-0
Best Rating: **61** 1/07 Wolv 1m1f103y std-slw

Plating-class gelding; acts on Polytrack; has shown that he stays 1m4f, but is best over shorter.

Bobs Dreamflight

95(97) (81)72
3-y-o b g Royal Applause-Millybaa (USA) (Anabaa (USA))
D K Ivory Rahul Bajaj & Dean Ivory

Placings:3521-2000200 (7516)
2009: 5^{2}SD, 5^{0}GF, 6^{0}GF, 7^{0}GF, 6^{2}G, 6^{0}SD, 7^{0}SD,

	Starts	1st	2nd	3rd	Win & Pl
Career Total (Turf)	5	0	1	1	1541
Career Total (AW)	6	1	2	0	5042

77	12/08	Ling	6f	STD	£2729

Total win prize-money £2730

Going (Turf): **Sf: 0-1 GS: 0-0 Gd: 0-1 GF: 0-3 Fm: 0-0**
Distance: **5f/6f: 1-9** 7f-8f: 0-2 9f-13f: 0-0 14f+: 0-0
Track : **LH: 1-3** RH: 0-3 **Tight: 1-2** Gall: 0-2
Aids: Bl: 0-0 Vi: 0-0 Tstrap: 0-0 Ckp: 0-0
Best Rating: **81** 1/09 Wolv 5f216y stand

Fair; stays 6f and acts on Polytrack and good ground on turf.

Bobski (IRE)

100(105) (91)82
7-y-o b g Victory Note (USA)-Vivid Impression (Cure The Blues (USA))
M Keller (Miss Gay Kelleway 26/4) Stall Barton Mills

Placings:1110560/633005061/1600004623/0652323600-643320230 (1539)
2009: 7^{6}SD, 8^{4}SD, 8^{3}SD, 8^{3}SD, 8^{2}SD, 8^{0}SD, 8^{2}GF, 7^{3}GF, 8^{0}G,

	Starts	1st	2nd	3rd	Win & Pl
Career Total (Turf)	23	1	2	5	13745
Career Total (AW)	22	4	3	3	23234

93	1/07	Ling	1m	(0-85)H	STD	£4857
91	11/06	Ling	7f	(0-85)H	STD	£5505
82	5/05	Donc	7f	(0-85)H	G-F	£7111
78	4/05	Ling	7f	(0-70)H	STD	£3446
72	2/05	Ling	6f		STD	£4065

Total win prize-money £24987

Going (Turf): Sf: 0-0 GS: 0-0 Gd: 0-8 **GF: 1-13** Fm: 0-2
Distance: 5f/6f: 1-4 **7f-8f: 4-34** 9f-13f: 0-7 14f+: 0-0
Track : **LH: 4-28** RH: 0-7 **Tight: 4-22** Gall: 0-1
Aids: Bl: 0-1 Vi: 0-0 Tstrap: 0-14 Ckp: 0-14
Best Rating: **93** 1/07 Ling 1m stand

Modest; effective at around 7f-1m; acts on a sound surface; also goes on Polytrack; has worn cheekpieces.

Body Gold (ARG)

71 19
6-y-o b g Body Glove (ARG)-Aurifera (ARG) (Climber (USA))
P J Makin Alexander Harper

Placings:541140/3024/000 (7373)
2009: 12^{0}GF, 10^{0}S, 12^{0}SD,

	Starts	1st	2nd	3rd	Win & Pl
Career Total (Turf)	3	0	0	0	0
Career Total (AW)	10	2	1	1	22623

10/06	Plmo	1m3f	FST	£9638

Total win prize-money £13299

Going (Turf): **Sf: 0-1 GS: 0-0 Gd: 0-1 GF: 0-1 Fm: 0-1**
Distance: 5f/6f: 0-0 7f-8f: 0-2 **9f-13f: 2-11** 14f+: 0-0
Track : LH: 0-2 RH: 0-1 Tight: 0-1 Gall: 0-1
Aids: Bl: 0-0 Vi: 0-0 Tstrap: 0-0 Ckp: 0-0
Best Rating: **19** 9/09 Asct 1m4f gd-fm

Boffin

94(92) (50)60
4-y-o b g Kalanisi (IRE)-Phi Beta Kappa (USA) (Diesis)
Eve Johnson Houghton Mrs R F Johnson Houghton

Placings:046400000 (7814)

2009: 10^{0}GF, 12^{4}SD, 12^{6}GF, 11^{4}GF, 11^{0}G, 10^{0}G, 10^{0}SD, 8^{0}SD, 8^{0}SD,

	Starts	1st	2nd	3rd	Win & Pl
Career Total (Turf)	5	0	0	0	192
Career Total (AW)	4	0	0	0	0

Going (Turf): **Sf: 0-0 GS: 0-0 Gd: 0-2 GF: 0-3 Fm: 0-0**
Distance: 5f/6f: 0-0 7f-8f: 0-0 9f-13f: 0-9 14f+: 0-0
Track : LH: 0-8 RH: 0-1 Tight: 0-6 Gall: 0-2
Aids: Bl: 0-0 Vi: 0-0 Tstrap: 0-3 Ckp: 0-3
Best Rating: **60** 5/09 Wind 1m2f7y gd-fm

Boga (IRE)

100(74) (48)**64**

2-y-o b f Invincible Spirit (IRE)-Miznapp (Pennekamp (USA))
R J Hodges (M R Channon 25/5) Miss R Dobson

Placings:413450**0** (5310)
2009: **5**^{4}SD, 5^{1}GF, 6^{3}GS, 5^{4}GF, 5^{5}F, 6^{0}GF, **5**^{0}SD,

	Starts	1st	2nd	3rd	Win & Pl
Career Total (Turf)	5	1	0	1	3050
Career Total (AW)	2	0	0	0	289

61 5/09 Bath 5f11y G-F £1942
Total win prize-money £1943

Going (Turf): Sf: 0-0 GS: 0-1 Gd: 0-0 **GF: 1-3** Fm: 0-1
Distance: **5f/6f: 1-6** 7f-8f: 0-1 9f-13f: 0-0 14f+: 0-0
Track : **LH: 1-3** RH: 0-1 Tight: 0-1 **Gall: 1-2**
Aids: Bl: 0-0 Vi: 0-0 Tstrap: 0-0 Ckp: 0-0
Best Rating: **64** 5/09 Newc 6f gd-sft

Modest; effective over 5-6f; acts on fast and easy ground.

Bogside Theatre (IRE)

93(83) (32)**99**

5-y-o b m Fruits Of Love (USA)-Royal Jubilee (IRE) (King's Theatre (IRE))
G M Moore B Lappin

Placings:161402/52332020-000**4** (7091)
2009: 16^{0}GF, 12^{0}G, 13^{0}G, **14**^{4}SD,

	Starts	1st	2nd	3rd	Win & Pl
Career Total (Turf)	17	2	4	2	50691
Career Total (AW)	1	0	0	0	722

89 7/07 Haml 1m5f9y (0-85)H G-S £7772
73 6/07 Newc 1m2f32y GD £3303
Total win prize-money £11075

Going (Turf): Sf: 0-4 **GS: 1-3 Gd: 1-7** GF: 0-2 Fm: 0-1
Distance: 5f/6f: 0-0 7f-8f: 0-0 9f-13f: 1-4 14f+: 1-14
Track : LH: 1-11 RH: 1-7 Tight: 1-4 Gall: 1-7
Aids: Bl: 0-0 Vi: 0-0 Tstrap: 0-0 Ckp: 0-0
Best Rating: **99** 8/08 Asct 2m gd-sft

Very useful; stays 2m; acts on good and softer ground; likes to race prominently.

Bogula (IRE)

93 **61**

3-y-o b f Tagula (IRE)-Bobbydazzle (Rock Hopper)
Mrs A Duffield Mrs Ann Starkie & Partner

Placings:440400 (6766)
2009: 10^{4}GF, 9^{4}GF, 10^{0}GF, 10^{4}GF, 9^{0}GF, 12^{0}GS,

	Starts	1st	2nd	3rd	Win & Pl
Career Total (Turf)	6	0	0	0	673

Going (Turf): **Sf: 0-0 GS: 0-1 Gd: 0-0 GF: 0-5 Fm: 0-0**
Distance: 5f/6f: 0-0 7f-8f: 0-0 9f-13f: 0-6 14f+: 0-0
Track : LH: 0-4 RH: 0-2 Tight: 0-3 Gall: 0-1
Aids: Bl: 0-0 Vi: 0-0 Tstrap: 0-0 Ckp: 0-0
Best Rating: **61** 6/09 Ripn 1m1f170y gd-fm

Boho Chic

99(96) (59)**69**

3-y-o b f Kyllachy-Summer Lightning (IRE) (Tamure (IRE))
George Baker P K Gardner

Placings:430-**00**161**02** (6914)
2009: 7^{0}SD, **6**^{0}SD, 5^{1}G, 5^{6}F, 5^{1}GF, **5**^{0}SD, **6**^{2}SD,

	Starts	1st	2nd	3rd	Win & Pl
Career Total (Turf)	6	2	0	1	4927
Career Total (AW)	4	0	1	0	605

69 9/09 Brig 5f213y (0-58)H G-F £2137
59 9/09 Bath 5f161y GD £1942
Total win prize-money £4080

Going (Turf): Sf: 0-1 GS: 0-1 **Gd: 1-1 GF: 1-2** Fm: 0-1
Distance: **5f/6f: 2-9** 7f-8f: 0-1 9f-13f: 0-0 14f+: 0-0
Track : **LH: 2-7** RH: 0-1 Tight: 0-3 **Gall: 1-2**
Aids: Bl: 0-0 Vi: 0-0 Tstrap: 2-4 Ckp: 2-4
Best Rating: **69** 9/09 Brig 5f213y gd-fm

Modest; effective over 5f-6f; acts on good ground and on Polytrack.

Bohobe (IRE)

100(93) (63)**65**

4-y-o b f Noverre (USA)-Green Life (Green Desert (USA))
Rae Guest Tremousser Partnership

Placings:461300/60**5**54000-2**0**10100 (5504)
2009: 6^{2}G, **6**^{0}SD, 6^{1}GF, 6^{0}GF, 6^{1}G, 6^{0}S, 5^{0}G,

	Starts	1st	2nd	3rd	Win & Pl
Career Total (Turf)	18	3	1	1	9090
Career Total (AW)	3	0	0	0	241

63 6/09 Sals 6f (0-75)H G-F £3238
70 7/07 Catt 5f G-S £3562
Total win prize-money £6800

Going (Turf): Sf: 0-3 **GS: 1-1 Gd: 1-6 GF: 1-7** Fm: 0-1
Distance: **5f/6f: 2-11** 7f-8f: 1-10 9f-13f: 0-0 14f+: 0-0
Track : LH: 0-4 RH: 0-0 Tight: 0-2 Gall: 0-0
Aids: Bl: 0-1 Vi: 0-0 Tstrap: 0-0 Ckp: 0-0
Best Rating: **70** 8/07 Rdcr 6f firm

Moderate; effective over 6f; acts on fast and soft ground.

Bois Joli (IRE)

(104) (81)**78**

4-y-o b f Orpen (USA)-Claba Di San Jore (IRE) (Barathea (IRE))
M Botti Effevi Snc Di Villa Felice & C

Placings:21/25543601-3 (0456)
2009: 11^{3}SD,

	Starts	1st	2nd	3rd	Win & Pl
Career Total (Turf)	6	1	2	0	15450
Career Total (AW)	5	1	0	2	4573

81 10/08 Wolv 1m4f50y (0-75)H STD £3885
11/07 Siro 1m1f SFT £8446
Total win prize-money £12332

Going (Turf): **Sf: 1-2** GS: 0-1 Gd: 0-3 GF: 0-0 Fm: 0-0
Distance: 5f/6f: 0-0 7f-8f: 0-3 **9f-13f: 2-8** 14f+: 0-0
Track : **LH: 1-2** RH: 0-6 **Tight: 1-2** Gall: 0-1
Aids: Bl: 0-0 Vi: 0-0 Tstrap: 0-0 Ckp: 0-0
Best Rating: **81** 10/08 Wolv 1m4f50y stand

Fair; ex-Italian; effective up to 1m4f; acts on good and soft ground; also goes on Polytrack.

Bojangles Andrews

81 **51**

2-y-o b c Avonbridge-Polished Up (Polish Precedent (USA))
B G Powell Jay Three Racing

Placings:04000 (7056)
2009: 7^{0}G, 6^{4}GF, 6^{0}G, 6^{0}GS, 7^{0}GF,

	Starts	1st	2nd	3rd	Win & Pl
Career Total (Turf)	5	0	0	0	385

Going (Turf): **Sf: 0-0 GS: 0-1 Gd: 0-2 GF: 0-2 Fm: 0-0**
Distance: 5f/6f: 0-2 7f-8f: 0-3 9f-13f: 0-0 14f+: 0-0
Track : LH: 0-0 RH: 0-0 Tight: 0-0 Gall: 0-1
Aids: Bl: 0-0 Vi: 0-1 Tstrap: 0-0 Ckp: 0-0
Best Rating: **51** 8/09 Wind 6f gd-fm

Bolanderi (USA)

100(80) (51)**80**

4-y-o ch g Seeking The Gold (USA)-Lilium (Nashwan (USA))
Andrew Turnell Maori Partnership

Placings:33334512 (5869)
2009: **10**^{3}SD, 8^{3}G, 9^{3}F, 10^{3}GF, 11^{4}GF, 11^{5}F, 9^{1}GF, 8^{2}G,

	Starts	1st	2nd	3rd	Win & Pl
Career Total (Turf)	7	1	1	3	5981
Career Total (AW)	1	0	0	1	482

78 9/09 Leic 1m1f218y (0-70)H G-F £3238
Total win prize-money £3238

Going (Turf): Sf: 0-0 GS: 0-0 Gd: 0-2 **GF: 1-3** Fm: 0-2
Distance: 5f/6f: 0-0 7f-8f: 0-1 **9f-13f: 1-7** 14f+: 0-0
Track : LH: 0-4 **RH: 1-3** Tight: 0-3 Gall: 0-1
Aids: Bl: 0-1 Vi: 0-0 Tstrap: 0-0 Ckp: 0-0
Best Rating: **80** 9/09 Ffos 1m good

Fair; stays 1m2f; acts on fast ground.

Bolckow

(97) (59)**59**

6-y-o b g Marju (IRE)-Stamatina (Warning)
J T Stimpson J T Stimpson

Placings:6/40530565465**103**/**152204030**/**0021003445-0** (5377)
2009: 11^{0}SD,

	Starts	1st	2nd	3rd	Win & Pl
Career Total (Turf)	16	1	0	0	2576
Career Total (AW)	19	2	3	4	8063

59 6/08 Haml 1m4f17y (0-60)H G-F £2047
68 1/07 Sthl 1m4f (0-55)H STD £2730
58 11/06 Sthl 1m3f STD £1706
Total win prize-money £6483

Going (Turf): Sf: 0-3 GS: 0-0 Gd: 0-3 **GF: 1-8** Fm: 0-2
Distance: 5f/6f: 0-0 7f-8f: 0-3 **9f-13f: 3-30** 14f+: 0-2
Track : **LH: 2-29** RH: 1-6 **Tight: 1-10** Gall: 0-0
Aids: Bl: 0-0 Vi: 0-0 Tstrap: 0-0 Ckp: 0-0
Best Rating: **68** 3/07 Sthl 1m4f stand

Moderate; stays 1m4f; acts on fast ground; also goes on Fibresand and Polytrack.

Bold Account (IRE)

75(92) (66)**66**

3-y-o b/br g Bold Fact (USA)-Generate (Generous (IRE))

Garry Moss Brooklands Racing

Placings:05021155432-040503000 **(4621)**

2009: 6^0SD, 6^4SD, 5^0SD, 6^5SD, 5^0GF, 5^3SD, 6^0G, 6^0SD, 5^0G,

	Starts	1st	2nd	3rd	Win & Pl
Career Total (Turf)	11	2	1	0	6588
Career Total (AW)	9	0	1	2	1209

66	8/08	Ayr	6f	(0-65)	SFT	£2914
66	8/08	Ripn	6f		G-S	£2729

Total win prize-money £5644

Going (Turf): **Sf: 1-3 GS: 1-2** Gd: 0-3 GF: 0-3 Fm: 0-0
Distance: **5f/6f: 2-17** 7f-8f: 0-3 9f-13f: 0-0 14f+: 0-0
Track : LH: 0-9 RH: 0-1 Tight: 0-2 Gall: 0-1
Aids: Bl: 0-0 Vi: 0-0 Tstrap: 0-8 Ckp: 0-8
Best Rating: **66** 10/08 GrLe 6f stand

Modest; effective over 6f; acts on easy ground; goes on Fibresand.

Bold Adventure

99(106) (72)**69**

5-y-o ch g Arkadian Hero (USA)-Impatiente (USA) (Vaguely Noble)

W J Musson W J Musson

Placings:000/00403**1110/020563000-12126640500** **(7785)**

2009: 16^1SD, 16^2SD, 16^1SD, 13^2SD, 16^6SD, 13^6SD, 14^4GS, 13^0SD, 16^5SD, 16^0SD, 13^0SD,

	Starts	1st	2nd	3rd	Win & Pl
Career Total (Turf)	12	0	0	1	802
Career Total (AW)	20	5	3	1	17273

72	3/09	Wolv	2m119y	(0-75)H	STD	£3070
67	2/09	Wolv	2m119y	(0-55)H	STD	£2388
73	10/07	Wolv	1m5f194y	(0-70)H	STD	£3238
69	9/07	Wolv	1m5f194y	(0-75)H	STD	£3071
61	9/07	Kemp	2m	(0-65)H	STD	£2047

Total win prize-money £13817

Going (Turf): **Sf: 0-2 GS: 0-2 Gd: 0-4 GF: 0-4 Fm: 0-0**
Distance: 5f/6f: 0-2 7f-8f: 0-1 9f-13f: 0-9 **14f+: 5-20**
Track : **LH: 4-23** RH: 1-5 **Tight: 4-21** Gall: 0-2
Aids: Bl: 0-0 Vi: 0-0 Tstrap: 0-0 Ckp: 0-0
Best Rating: **75** 5/08 GrLe 1m6f stand

Modest; effective over 1m6f-2m; acts well on Polytrack; handles easy ground on turf.

Bold Alaska (IRE)

(87) (67)**85**

6-y-o b g Cape Cross (IRE)-Dramatic Entry (IRE) (Persian Bold)

Peter Grayson R Teatum And S Kamis

Placings:16/00 (7253)

2009: 8^0SD, 6^0SD,

	Starts	1st	2nd	3rd	Win & Pl
Career Total (Turf)	2	1	0	0	4858
Career Total (AW)	2	0	0	0	

85	5/06	NmkR	1m	GD	£4857

Total win prize-money £4858

Going (Turf): Sf: 0-1 GS: 0-0 **Gd: 1-1** GF: 0-0 Fm: 0-0
Distance: 5f/6f: 0-1 **7f-8f: 1-3** 9f-13f: 0-0 14f+: 0-0
Track : LH: 0-1 RH: 0-1 Tight: 0-1 Gall: 0-0
Aids: Bl: 0-0 Vi: 0-0 Tstrap: 0-0 Ckp: 0-0
Best Rating: **85** 5/06 NmkR 1m good

Bold Argument (IRE)

105(95) (56)**74**

6-y-o ch g Shinko Forest (IRE)-Ivory Bride (Domynsky)

Mrs P N Dutfield Simon Dutfield

Placings:00/**542**016000/**04400045**/151062501-003100000 **(5608)**

2009: 7^0SD, 6^0GS, 6^3GF, 6^1GF, 5^0GF, 5^0G, 6^0G, 5^0GF, 5^0S,

	Starts	1st	2nd	3rd	Win & Pl
Career Total (Turf)	29	5	1	1	17566
Career Total (AW)	8	0	1	0	964

74	6/09	Wind	6f	(0-80)H	G-F	£4857
74	9/08	Sals	5f	(0-70)H	GD	£3238
73	6/08	Nott	6f15y	(0-65)H	G-F	£2047
64	5/08	Nott	6f15y	(0-60)H	GD	£2047
78	7/06	Wind	6f	(0-70)H	G-F	£3238

Total win prize-money £15428

Going (Turf): Sf: 0-4 GS: 0-3 Gd: 2-6 **GF: 3-16** Fm: 0-0
Distance: **5f/6f: 3-26** 7f-8f: 2-11 9f-13f: 0-0 14f+: 0-0
Track : LH: 0-6 RH: 0-6 Tight: 0-2 **Gall: 2-10**
Aids: Bl: 0-1 Vi: 0-0 Tstrap: 0-0 Ckp: 0-0
Best Rating: **78** 7/06 Wind 6f gd-fm

Modest sprinter; acts on fast ground; has worn a tongue strap.

Bold Bomber

93(92) (51)**51**

3-y-o b c Kyllachy-Latina (IRE) (King's Theatre (IRE))

Paul Green Paul Green (Oaklea)

Placings:004-0000040060 **(7615)**

2009: 5^0GF, 8^0GF, 8^0F, 5^0GF, 6^0G, 5^4G, 5^0GS, 9^0GF, 7^6SD, 8^0SD,

	Starts	1st	2nd	3rd	Win & Pl
Career Total (Turf)	10	0	0	0	0
Career Total (AW)	3	0	0	0	0

Going (Turf): **Sf: 0-1 GS: 0-2 Gd: 0-2 GF: 0-4 Fm: 0-1**
Distance: 5f/6f: 0-7 7f-8f: 0-4 9f-13f: 0-2 14f+: 0-0
Track : LH: 0-3 RH: 0-4 Tight: 0-2 Gall: 0-0
Aids: Bl: 0-1 Vi: 0-0 Tstrap: 0-0 Ckp: 0-0
Best Rating: **51** 11/09 Sthl 7f stand

Bold Cross (IRE)

104(104) (75)**87**

6-y-o b g Cape Cross (IRE)-Machikane Akaiito (IRE) (Persian Bold)

E G Bevan E G Bevan

Placings:00642224/05050/**5045000121633**/013160562145 60-16621314042050 **(5887)**

2009: 7^1GF, 8^6SD, 8^6HY, 8^2GF, 8^1GF, 7^3GS, 8^1GF, 7^4G, 8^0G, 7^4GF, 10^2GF, 7^0G, 10^5G, 8^0SD,

	Starts	1st	2nd	3rd	Win & Pl
Career Total (Turf)	44	6	7	2	36922
Career Total (AW)	10	2	0	2	9128

85	6/09	Donc	1m	(0-80)H	G-F	£4857
76	6/09	Hayd	1m30y	(0-80)H	G-F	£5180
76	5/09	Chep	7f16y	(0-70)H	G-F	£2914
73	8/08	Wolv	1m141y	(0-80)H	STD	£6476
66	6/08	Leic	7f9y	(0-75)H	G-F	£4857
71	5/08	Bath	1m5y	(0-70)H	G-F	£2590
68	9/07	Wwck	7f26y	(0-60)H	G-F	£3238
58	9/07	Wolv	7f32y	(0-55)	STD	£2047

Total win prize-money £32162

Going (Turf): Sf: 0-9 GS: 0-1 Gd: 0-16 **GF: 6-18** Fm: 0-0
Distance: 5f/6f: 0-2 **7f-8f: 5-24** 9f-13f: 3-28 14f+: 0-0
Track : **LH: 6-27** RH: 0-11 **Tight: 3-15** Gall: 1-2
Aids: Bl: 0-0 Vi: 0-0 Tstrap: 0-0 Ckp: 0-0
Best Rating: **87** 8/09 Bath 1m2f46y gd-fm

Fair; effective at around 7f-1m; acts on a fast surface and on Polytrack.

Bold Diktator

91(60) (83)**68**

7-y-o b g Diktat-Madam Bold (Never So Bold)

R M Whitaker R M Whitaker

Placings:066/50533041105420/0011605600**1/1106106006** **4/300** **(6861)**

2009: 8^3GF, 8^0GF, 8^0SD,

	Starts	1st	2nd	3rd	Win & Pl
Career Total (Turf)	29	5	1	3	26676
Career Total (AW)	13	3	0	0	8577

85	4/07	Sand	1m14y	(0-80)H	GD	£6477
83	2/07	Wolv	1m141y	(0-75)H	STD	£3071
77	1/07	Ling	1m	(0-75)H	STD	£2914
74	12/06	Wolv	1m141y	(0-65)H	STD	£2590
80	6/06	Ling	7f140y	(0-75)H	G-F	£3238
78	6/06	Bath	1m5y	(0-70)H	FRM	£4533
74	8/05	Ling	7f	(0-70)H	G-F	£3814
72	8/05	Bath	1m5y	(0-70)H	FRM	£4613

Total win prize-money £31254

Going (Turf): Sf: 0-0 GS: 0-3 Gd: 1-5 **GF: 2-16 Fm: 2-5**
Distance: 5f/6f: 0-0 7f-8f: 3-18 **9f-13f: 5-24** 14f+: 0-0
Track : **LH: 5-25** RH: 1-6 **Tight: 5-22** Gall: 0-1
Aids: **Bl: 3-11** Vi: 0-0 Tstrap: 0-0 Ckp: 0-0
Best Rating: **85** 4/07 Sand 1m14y good

Moderate handicapper; effective at around 1m; acts on fast ground and on Polytrack; has worn blinkers; likes to race prominently.

Bold Diva

(103) (65)**50**

4-y-o ch m Bold Edge-Trina's Pet (Efisio)

A W Carroll Mrs P Izamis

Placings:000400000/**002433550**0456**05120-550243434623** **(2134)**

2009: 6^5SS, 6^5SD, 7^0SD, 7^2SD, 7^4SD, 6^3SD, 8^4SD, 8^3SD, 7^4SD, 7^6SD, 7^2SD, 6^3SD,

	Starts	1st	2nd	3rd	Win & Pl
Career Total (Turf)	14	0	0	0	481
Career Total (AW)	25	1	4	5	5669

63	11/08	Kemp	6f	(0-55)H	STD	£1706

Total win prize-money £1706

Going (Turf): **Sf: 0-2 GS: 0-3 Gd: 0-0 GF: 0-6 Fm: 0-3**
Distance: **5f/6f: 1-19** 7f-8f: 0-16 9f-13f: 0-4 14f+: 0-0
Track : LH: 0-21 **RH: 1-9** Tight: 0-10 Gall: 0-4
Aids: Bl: 0-2 **Vi: 1-28** Tstrap: 0-0 Ckp: 0-0
Best Rating: **65** 12/08 Sthl 7f stand

Moderate; suited by 6f-7f; acts on Fibresand and Polytrack; has worn a visor.

Bold Hawk

75(90) (44)**50**

3-y-o b g Mujahid (USA)-Girl Next Door (Local Suitor (USA))

Mrs C A Dunnett Stranger Than Fiction Syndicate

Placings:500-0000 **(3743)**

2009: 6^0GF, 6^0G, 6^0G, 6^0SD,

	Starts	1st	2nd	3rd	Win & Pl
Career Total (Turf)	6	0	0	0	0
Career Total (AW)	1	0	0	0	

Going (Turf): **Sf: 0-0 GS: 0-0 Gd: 0-3 GF: 0-3 Fm: 0-0**
Distance: 5f/6f: 0-3 7f-8f: 0-4 9f-13f: 0-0 14f+: 0-0
Track : LH: 0-1 RH: 0-0 Tight: 0-1 Gall: 0-0
Aids: Bl: 0-2 Vi: 0-0 Tstrap: 0-1 Ckp: 0-1
Best Rating: **50** 5/08 NmkR 5f gd-fm

Bold Haze

69 **14**
7-y-o ch g Bold Edge-Melody Park (Music Boy)
Miss S E Hall Miss S E Hall

Placings:304/102023400/00402020/5160000/00-0 **(1924)**
2009: 6^{0}F,

	Starts	1st	2nd	3rd	Win & Pl
Career Total (Turf)	**29**	**2**	**4**	**2**	**13656**
Career Total (AW)	**1**	**0**	**0**	**0**	

69 6/07 Carl 5f193y (0-60)H G-S £2047
69 4/05 Ripn 6f (0-75)H SFT £3409
Total win prize-money £5458

Going (Turf): **Sf: 1-9 GS: 1-3** Gd: 0-6 GF: 0-9 Fm: 0-2
Distance: **5f/6f: 2-22** 7f-8f: 0-7 9f-13f: 0-1 14f+: 0-0
Track : LH: 0-3 **RH: 1-3** Tight: 0-3 Gall: 0-0
Aids: Bl: 0-0 **Vi: 1-14** Tstrap: 0-0 Ckp: 0-0
Best Rating: **75** 7/05 Donc 6f gd-fm

Bold Indian (IRE)

102(94) (71)**66**
5-y-o b g Indian Danehill (IRE)-Desert Gift (Green Desert (USA))
M E Sowersby (I Semple 30/8) Racing Ladies 1

Placings:00**323**/3500100105**350**/25542300-**50**563523223 **(6488)**
2009: 8^{5}SD, 9^{0}SD, 8^{5}GF, 8^{6}GF, 8^{3}GF, 9^{5}G, 8^{2}GS, 7^{3}GF, 10^{2}GF, 10^{2}GF, 10^{3}GF,

	Starts	1st	2nd	3rd	Win & Pl
Career Total (Turf)	**28**	**2**	**5**	**5**	**11458**
Career Total (AW)	**9**	**0**	**1**	**3**	**2606**

57 8/07 Haml 1m65y G-F £2388
59 6/07 Catt 7f G-F £2730
Total win prize-money £5119

Going (Turf): Sf: 0-3 GS: 0-4 Gd: 0-4 **GF: 2-15** Fm: 0-1
Distance: 5f/6f: 0-2 7f-8f: 1-14 9f-13f: 1-21 14f+: 0-0
Track : LH: 1-18 RH: 1-16 **Tight: 2-28** Gall: 0-0
Aids: Bl: 0-0 Vi: 0-0 Tstrap: 0-3 Ckp: 0-3
Best Rating: **73** 4/07 Muss 1m1f gd-fm

Modest; effective over 7f-1m1f; acts on a sound surface and on Polytrack.

Bold Marc (IRE)

104(96) (76)**86**
7-y-o b g Bold Fact (USA)-Zara's Birthday (IRE) (Waajib)
A P Jarvis (K R Burke 25/7) Market Avenue Racing Club Ltd

Placings:4121064**635**/22400220**540**/630430040641**2225**/4510010000/**00**1002500061**22**00-0244331004**06** **(7220)**
2009: 7^{0}F, 7^{2}GF, 8^{4}HY, 7^{4}GF, 8^{3}SD, 7^{3}GF, 7^{1}GF, 7^{0}GF, 7^{0}G, 7^{4}SD, 7^{0}SD, 7^{6}S,

	Starts	1st	2nd	3rd	Win & Pl
Career Total (Turf)	**64**	**8**	**11**	**3**	**89545**
Career Total (AW)	**11**	**0**	**1**	**2**	**3694**

86 7/09 Catt 7f (0-80)H G-F £5180
86 10/08 Catt 7f (0-75)H G-S £2590
84 4/08 Hayd 1m30y (0-85)H G-S £4857
90 6/07 Carl 7f200y (0-80)H G-S £19431
86 5/07 Hayd 1m30y (0-80)H G-F £6477
86 10/06 Catt 7f (0-75)H SFT £3238
83 5/04 Rdcr 5f E G-F £3503
79 4/04 Muss 5f F G-F £3347
Total win prize-money £48627

Going (Turf): Sf: 1-12 GS: 3-15 Gd: 0-11 **GF: 4-23** Fm: 0-3
Distance: 5f/6f: 2-30 **7f-8f: 4-32** 9f-13f: 2-13 14f+: 0-0
Track : **LH: 5-37** RH: 1-11 **Tight: 3-23** Gall: 0-5
Aids: Bl: 0-0 Vi: 0-2 Tstrap: 1-5 Ckp: 1-5
Best Rating: **90** 6/07 Carl 7f200y gd-sft

Fair; effective over 7f-1m; acts on most ground on turf; goes on Fibresand; has worn a visor and cheekpieces; likes to race prominently.

Bold Minstrel (IRE)

(68) (45)**84**
7-y-o br g Bold Fact (USA)-Ponda Rosa (IRE) (Case Law)
M Quinn The Boys From The Shed Partnership

Placings:0321242556**2**/001/50016**303**/**00**021060**000**/6046 00-0 **(0474)**
2009: 5^{0}SD,

	Starts	1st	2nd	3rd	Win & Pl
Career Total (Turf)	**33**	**4**	**4**	**2**	**23631**
Career Total (AW)	**7**	**0**	**1**	**1**	**2115**

84 5/07 Yarm 5f43y (0-75)H GD £2914
84 8/06 Wind 5f10y (0-75)H GD £3238
82 5/05 Rdcr 5f (0-85)H FRM £6973
65 7/04 Ches 5f16y E GD £3376
Total win prize-money £16504

Going (Turf): Sf: 0-2 GS: 0-5 **Gd: 3-8** GF: 0-16 Fm: 1-2
Distance: **5f/6f: 4-40** 7f-8f: 0-0 9f-13f: 0-0 14f+: 0-0
Track : **LH: 1-15** RH: 0-0 Tight: 1-10 Gall: 1-5
Aids: Bl: 0-0 Vi: 0-1 Tstrap: 0-0 Ckp: 0-0
Best Rating: **84** 5/07 Yarm 5f43y good

Moderate sprinter; effective over 5f; acts on good and fast ground.

Bold Ring

98(101) (64)**62**
3-y-o ch f Bold Edge-Floppie Disk (Magic Ring (IRE))
E J Creighton Daniel Creighton

Placings:06**510**-2000601460136**42043445** **(7158)**
2009: 7^{2}SD, 7^{0}SD, 5^{0}GF, 7^{0}GF, 5^{6}GF, 6^{0}GF, 6^{1}F, 6^{4}GF, 6^{6}GF, 6^{0}G, 6^{1}GF, 6^{3}F, 6^{6}GF, 5^{4}SD, 6^{2}SD, 6^{0}SD, 5^{4}SD, 6^{3}GF, 5^{4}SD, 6^{4}SD, 7^{5}SD,

	Starts	1st	2nd	3rd	Win & Pl
Career Total (Turf)	**14**	**2**	**0**	**2**	**4875**
Career Total (AW)	**12**	**1**	**2**	**0**	**3515**

62 7/09 Nott 6f15y (0-65)H G-F £1942
61 5/09 Wwck 6f (0-65)H FRM £2047
57 10/08 Kemp 6f (0-60) STD £1706
Total win prize-money £5696

Going (Turf): Sf: 0-0 GS: 0-1 Gd: 0-1 **GF: 1-10 Fm: 1-2**
Distance: **5f/6f: 2-17** 7f-8f: 1-9 9f-13f: 0-0 14f+: 0-0
Track : LH: 1-14 RH: 1-2 Tight: 0-10 Gall: 0-2
Aids: Bl: 0-0 Vi: 0-0 Tstrap: 0-0 Ckp: 0-0
Best Rating: **64** 9/09 Ling 6f stand

Modest; effective at 6f; acts on fast ground and on Polytrack.

Bold Rose

102(101) (62)**67**
3-y-o ch f Bold Edge-Bowden Rose (Dashing Blade)
M D I Usher Ushers Court

Placings:03040**224**-**5010**100600001 **(7880)**
2009: 6^{5}SD, 6^{0}SD, 5^{1}SD, 5^{0}SD, 6^{1}GF, 6^{0}GF, 6^{0}G, 6^{6}G, 5^{0}G, 6^{0}S, 6^{0}S, 5^{0}SD, 7^{1}SD,

	Starts	1st	2nd	3rd	Win & Pl
Career Total (Turf)	**11**	**1**	**1**	**0**	**3230**
Career Total (AW)	**10**	**2**	**1**	**1**	**4893**

12/09 Ling 7f (0-52)H STD £1637
67 5/09 Chep 6f16y (0-65)H G-F £2266
60 2/09 Sthl 5f (0-65)H STD £2047
Total win prize-money £5952

Going (Turf): Sf: 0-3 GS: 0-1 Gd: 0-4 **GF: 1-2** Fm: 0-1
Distance: 5f/6f: 1-16 **7f-8f: 2-5** 9f-13f: 0-0 14f+: 0-0
Track : **LH: 1-5** RH: 0-1 **Tight: 1-3** Gall: 0-3
Aids: Bl: 0-0 Vi: 0-0 Tstrap: 3-9 Ckp: 3-9
Best Rating: **67** 5/09 Chep 6f16y gd-fm

Moderate; effective over 5f-6f; acts on fast and soft ground; goes on both AW surfaces; has worn cheekpieces.

Bold Tie

93 **75**
3-y-o ch g Bold Edge-Level Pegging (IRE) (Common Grounds)
R Hannon Lady Whent

Placings:01-5 **(2562)**
2009: 5^{5}GF,

	Starts	1st	2nd	3rd	Win & Pl
Career Total (Turf)	**3**	**1**	**0**	**0**	**3562**

75 10/08 Wind 6f GD £3561
Total win prize-money £3562

Going (Turf): Sf: 0-0 GS: 0-0 **Gd: 1-1** GF: 0-2 Fm: 0-0
Distance: **5f/6f: 1-3** 7f-8f: 0-0 9f-13f: 0-0 14f+: 0-0
Track : LH: 0-0 RH: 0-0 Tight: 0-0 **Gall: 1-2**
Aids: Bl: 0-0 Vi: 0-0 Tstrap: 0-0 Ckp: 0-0
Best Rating: **75** 10/08 Wind 6f good

Boldinor

99(98) (57)**67**
6-y-o b g Inchinor-Rambold (Rambo Dancer (CAN))
M R Bosley Ron Collins

Placings:1505**0**2000**000**/01601066**050**-00053433260 **(6335)**
2009: 5^{0}GS, 6^{0}GF, 6^{0}GF, 5^{5}GF, 6^{3}F, 5^{4}GS, 6^{3}GF, 6^{3}G, 5^{2}F, 6^{6}GF, 5^{0}GF,

	Starts	1st	2nd	3rd	Win & Pl
Career Total (Turf)	**24**	**2**	**2**	**3**	**8649**
Career Total (AW)	**10**	**1**	**0**	**0**	**3239**

67 7/08 Leic 5f218y (0-70)H GD £3885
62 6/08 Leic 5f218y GD £1942
67 2/06 Wolv 5f216y STD £3238
Total win prize-money £9068

Going (Turf): Sf: 0-1 GS: 0-4 **Gd: 2-5** GF: 0-11 Fm: 0-3
Distance: **5f/6f: 3-21** 7f-8f: 0-12 9f-13f: 0-1 14f+: 0-0
Track : **LH: 1-14** RH: 0-5 **Tight: 1-7** Gall: 0-3
Aids: Bl: 0-0 Vi: 0-0 Tstrap: 0-0 Ckp: 0-0
Best Rating: **69** 7/06 Bath 5f161y good

Moderate; stays 6f; acts on good/fast ground and Polytrack; looks slightly quirky.

Bollin Andrew

81 46

2-y-o b c Bollin Eric-Bollin Roberta (Bob's Return (IRE))

T D Easterby Sir Neil Westbrook

Placings:000 **(5951)**

2009: 7^{0}GF, 7^{0}S, 9^{0}GF,

	Starts	1st	2nd	3rd	Win & Pl
Career Total (Turf)	3	0	0	0	

Going (Turf): **Sf: 0-1 GS: 0-0 Gd: 0-0 GF: 0-2 Fm: 0-0**
Distance: 5f/6f: 0-0 7f-8f: 0-2 9f-13f: 0-1 14f+: 0-0
Track : LH: 0-2 RH: 0-0 Tight: 0-2 Gall: 0-0
Aids: Bl: 0-0 Vi: 0-0 Tstrap: 0-0 Ckp: 0-0
Best Rating: **46** 9/09 Rdcr 1m1f gd-fm

Bollin Dolly

103 74

6-y-o ch m Bien Bien (USA)-Bollin Roberta (Bob's Return (IRE))

T D Easterby Sir Neil Westbrook

Placings:0/56233536/0540/1214 **(7247)**

2009: 10^{1}GF, 10^{2}GF, 10^{1}GF, 10^{4}S,

	Starts	1st	2nd	3rd	Win & Pl
Career Total (Turf)	17	2	2	3	10602

74 10/09 Pont 1m2f6y (0-75)H G-F £3238
70 8/09 Rdcr 1m2f (0-75)H G-F £2590
Total win prize-money £5828

Going (Turf): Sf: 0-1 GS: 0-2 Gd: 0-4 **GF: 2-9** Fm: 0-1
Distance: 5f/6f: 0-0 7f-8f: 0-1 **9f-13f: 2-16** 14f+: 0-0
Track : **LH: 2-10** RH: 0-6 **Tight: 1-8** Gall: 0-0
Aids: Bl: 0-0 Vi: 0-0 Tstrap: 0-0 Ckp: 0-0
Best Rating: **74** 10/09 Pont 1m2f6y gd-fm

Modest; stays 1m4f; acts on fast and easy ground.

Bollin Felix

108 98

5-y-o br g Generous (IRE)-Bollin Magdalene (Teenoso (USA))

T D Easterby Sir Neil Westbrook

Placings:6660/413113036/4323131203-5524 **(2895)**

2009: 16^{5}GF, 12^{5}GS, 16^{2}G, 16^{4}GS,

	Starts	1st	2nd	3rd	Win & Pl
Career Total (Turf)	27	5	3	7	50976

97 9/08 Thsk 2m (0-85)H SFT £5569
92 7/08 Hayd 1m6f (0-85)H HVY £5504
83 7/07 Ripn 1m4f10y (0-75)H HVY £5181
81 7/07 Pont 1m4f8y (0-65)H SFT £3238
63 5/07 Nott 1m6f15y (0-75)H GD £3886
Total win prize-money £23381

Going (Turf): **Sf: 4-7** GS: 0-6 Gd: 1-9 GF: 0-5 Fm: 0-0
Distance: 5f/6f: 0-0 7f-8f: 0-3 9f-13f: 2-7 **14f+: 3-17**
Track : **LH: 4-18** RH: 1-7 **Tight: 2-6** Gall: 0-10
Aids: **Bl: 5-20** Vi: 0-2 Tstrap: 0-0 Ckp: 0-0
Best Rating: **98** 9/08 Donc 1m6f132y soft

Useful; stays 2m and very much suited by soft ground; usually wears blinkers/visor.

Bollin Franny

92(106) (58)44

5-y-o br g Bertolini (USA)-Bollin Ann (Anshan)

J E Long P Saxon

Placings:5215665/0260506/**0006330022-5036050060** **(6038)**

2009: 5^{5}SD, 5^{0}SD, 6^{3}SD, 6^{6}SD, 5^{0}F, 6^{5}SD, 6^{0}SD, 6^{0}G, 6^{6}GF, 6^{0}GF,

	Starts	1st	2nd	3rd	Win & Pl
Career Total (Turf)	21	1	2	0	5717
Career Total (AW)	13	0	2	3	1998

68 6/06 Ripn 5f G-F £3886
Total win prize-money £3886

Going (Turf): Sf: 0-1 GS: 0-2 Gd: 0-5 **GF: 1-10** Fm: 0-3
Distance: **5f/6f: 1-32** 7f-8f: 0-2 9f-13f: 0-0 14f+: 0-0
Track : LH: 0-17 RH: 0-3 Tight: 0-11 Gall: 0-2
Aids: Bl: 0-1 Vi: 0-0 Tstrap: 0-1 Ckp: 0-1
Best Rating: **70** 5/06 Thsk 5f firm

Moderate; stays 6f; acts on fast ground and on Polytrack; has worn headgear.

Bollin Freddie

94(93) (51)59

5-y-o ch g Golden Snake (USA)-Bollin Roberta (Bob's Return (IRE))

A J Lockwood Highgreen Partnership

Placings:040/0066/063063154-01 **(2803)**

2009: 12^{0}GS, 9^{1}F,

	Starts	1st	2nd	3rd	Win & Pl
Career Total (Turf)	17	2	0	2	7765
Career Total (AW)	1	0	0	0	0

59 6/09 Bevl 1m1f207y (0-70)H FRM £4209
52 9/08 Bevl 1m1f207y (0-55)H HVY £2637
Total win prize-money £6846

Going (Turf): **Sf: 1-4** GS: 0-3 Gd: 0-3 GF: 0-5 **Fm: 1-2**
Distance: 5f/6f: 0-1 7f-8f: 0-2 **9f-13f: 2-14** 14f+: 0-1
Track : LH: 0-8 **RH: 2-9** Tight: 0-9 Gall: 0-2
Aids: Bl: 0-0 Vi: 0-0 Tstrap: 0-0 Ckp: 0-0
Best Rating: **59** 6/09 Bevl 1m1f207y firm

Moderate; stays 1m4f and acts on most ground.

Bollin Greta

98 76

4-y-o b/br f Mtoto-Bollin Zola (Alzao (USA))

T D Easterby Sir Neil Westbrook

Placings:0/253411-44531 **(3563)**

2009: 12^{4}F, 14^{4}G, 14^{5}GS, 12^{3}GS, 12^{1}G,

	Starts	1st	2nd	3rd	Win & Pl
Career Total (Turf)	12	3	1	2	12679

76 7/09 Donc 1m4f (0-70)H GD £3238
74 10/08 Rdcr 1m6f19y (0-75)H GD £3238
67 10/08 Pont 1m4f8y (0-70)H GD £3885
Total win prize-money £10362

Going (Turf): Sf: 0-2 GS: 0-2 **Gd: 3-5** GF: 0-2 Fm: 0-1
Distance: 5f/6f: 0-0 7f-8f: 0-2 **9f-13f: 2-7** 14f+: 1-3
Track : **LH: 3-6** RH: 0-5 Tight: 1-6 Gall: 1-1
Aids: Bl: 0-0 Vi: 0-0 Tstrap: 0-0 Ckp: 0-0
Best Rating: **76** 7/09 Donc 1m4f good

Modest; stays 1m6f; acts on easy ground.

Bollin Jasmine

46

2-y-o b f Silver Patriarch (IRE)-Bollin Zola (Alzao (USA))

T D Easterby Sir Neil Westbrook

Placings:0 **(6214)**

2009: 7^{0}GF,

	Starts	1st	2nd	3rd	Win & Pl
Career Total (Turf)	1	0	0	0	

Going (Turf): **Sf: 0-0 GS: 0-0 Gd: 0-0 GF: 0-1 Fm: 0-0**
Distance: 5f/6f: 0-0 7f-8f: 0-1 9f-13f: 0-0 14f+: 0-0
Track : LH: 0-0 RH: 0-0 Tight: 0-0 Gall: 0-0
Aids: Bl: 0-0 Vi: 0-0 Tstrap: 0-0 Ckp: 0-0

Bollin Judith

103(83) (53)77

3-y-o b f Bollin Eric-Bollin Nellie (Rock Hopper)

T D Easterby Sir Neil Westbrook

Placings:006-431336212 **(7170)**

2009: 12^{4}GF, 12^{3}GF, 14^{1}GF, 14^{3}G, 12^{3}G, 16^{6}GF, 14^{2}GF, 14^{1}GF, 15^{2}S,

	Starts	1st	2nd	3rd	Win & Pl
Career Total (Turf)	11	2	2	3	9275
Career Total (AW)	1	0	0	0	0

73 10/09 Rdcr 1m6f19y (0-75)H G-F £2590
60 5/09 Rdcr 1m6f19y (0-65)H G-F £2047
Total win prize-money £4637

Going (Turf): Sf: 0-2 GS: 0-0 Gd: 0-3 **GF: 2-6** Fm: 0-0
Distance: 5f/6f: 0-0 7f-8f: 0-1 9f-13f: 0-5 **14f+: 2-6**
Track : **LH: 2-9** RH: 0-2 **Tight: 2-7** Gall: 0-0
Aids: Bl: 0-0 Vi: 0-0 Tstrap: 0-0 Ckp: 0-0
Best Rating: **77** 10/09 Ayr 1m7f soft

Modest; effective over 1m6f; acts on fast ground.

Bollin Julie

89 47

2-y-o b f Bollin Eric-Bollin Nellie (Rock Hopper)

T D Easterby Sir Neil Westbrook

Placings:00 **(7243)**

2009: 8^{0}GS, 8^{0}S,

	Starts	1st	2nd	3rd	Win & Pl
Career Total (Turf)	2	0	0	0	

Going (Turf): **Sf: 0-1 GS: 0-1 Gd: 0-0 GF: 0-0 Fm: 0-0**
Distance: 5f/6f: 0-0 7f-8f: 0-1 9f-13f: 0-1 14f+: 0-0
Track : LH: 0-2 RH: 0-0 Tight: 0-0 Gall: 0-1
Aids: Bl: 0-0 Vi: 0-0 Tstrap: 0-0 Ckp: 0-0
Best Rating: **47** 11/09 Nott 1m75y soft

Bollin Rachel

66 18

2-y-o gr f Silver Patriarch (IRE)-Bollin Ann (Anshan)

T D Easterby Sir Neil Westbrook

Placings:0 **(3170)**

2009: 7^{0}GF,

	Starts	1st	2nd	3rd	Win & Pl
Career Total (Turf)	1	0	0	0	

Going (Turf): **Sf: 0-0 GS: 0-0 Gd: 0-0 GF: 0-1 Fm: 0-0**
Distance: 5f/6f: 0-0 7f-8f: 0-1 9f-13f: 0-0 14f+: 0-0
Track : LH: 0-0 RH: 0-0 Tight: 0-0 Gall: 0-0
Aids: Bl: 0-0 Vi: 0-0 Tstrap: 0-0 Ckp: 0-0
Best Rating: **18** 6/09 Rdcr 7f gd-fm

Bollywood (IRE)

(98) (47)51

6-y-o ch g Indian Rocket-La Fille De Cirque (Cadeaux Genereux)

J J Bridger J J Bridger

Placings:006/**21066000000046400264000/04065450052 00004/0400406B400-0** **(7888)**

2009: 12^{0}SD,

	Starts	1st	2nd	3rd	Win & Pl
Career Total (Turf)	27	0	1	0	2079
Career Total (AW)	28	1	2	0	3742

71 1/06 Ling 7f STD £2388

Total win prize-money £2389

Going (Turf): Sf: 0-5 GS: 0-6 Gd: 0-4 GF: 0-12 Fm: 0-0
Distance: 5f/6f: 0-11 **7f-8f: 1-30** 9f-13f: 0-14 14f+: 0-0
Track : **LH: 1-22** RH: 0-18 **Tight: 1-18** Gall: 0-3
Aids: Bl: 0-2 Vi: 0-0 Tstrap: 0-5 Ckp: 0-5
Best Rating: 71 1/06 Ling 7f stand

Moderate performer; stays 1m1f; acts on Polytrack.

Bollywood Style

(101) (62)
4-y-o b m Josr Algarhoud (IRE)-Dane Dancing (IRE) (Danehill (USA))
J R Best Miss Sara Furnival

Placings:224304/4201260 **(7716)**
2009: 8^{4}SD, 7^{2}SD, 8^{0}SD, 7^{1}SD, 7^{2}SD, 6^{6}SD, 7^{0}SD,

	Starts	1st	2nd	3rd	Win & Pl
Career Total (Turf)	0	0	0	0	
Career Total (AW)	13	1	4	1	4647

62 2/09 Ling 7f (0-60)H STD £2047

Total win prize-money £2047

Going (Turf): Sf: 0-0 GS: 0-0 Gd: 0-0 GF: 0-0 Fm: 0-0
Distance: 5f/6f: 0-3 **7f-8f: 1-8** 9f-13f: 0-2 14f+: 0-0
Track : **LH: 1-10** RH: 0-3 **Tight: 1-10** Gall: 0-0
Aids: Bl: 0-0 Vi: 0-0 Tstrap: 0-0 Ckp: 0-0
Best Rating: 62 11/09 Ling 7f stand

Moderate; effective at 7f; acts on Polytrack.

Bolodenka (IRE)

103(100) (86)**101**
7-y-o b g Soviet Star (USA)-My-Lorraine (IRE) (Mac's Imp (USA))
R A Fahey Aidan J Ryan

Placings:023/105166/2011240/34500500104/400163-0000200540 **(7848)**
2009: 8^{0}SD, 8^{0}GF, 8^{0}G, 7^{0}GF, 9^{2}GS, 8^{0}G, 8^{0}S, 7^{5}SD, 8^{4}SD, 9^{0}SD,

	Starts	1st	2nd	3rd	Win & Pl
Career Total (Turf)	37	6	3	2	136699
Career Total (AW)	6	0	1	1	3381

101 9/08 Ayr 1m (0-100)H HVY £26170
98 8/07 Ripn 1m (0-100)H G-F £12464
98 8/06 Gway 7f H GD £44896
94 8/06 Gway 1m100y (60-90)H G-F £8101
87 7/05 NmkJ 1m (0-80)H GD £6333
84 5/05 NmkR 1m (0-75)H GD £4362

Total win prize-money £102328

Going (Turf): Sf: 1-6 GS: 0-9 **Gd: 3-9** GF: 2-10 Fm: 0-0
Distance: 5f/6f: 0-3 **7f-8f: 5-23** 9f-13f: 1-17 14f+: 0-0
Track : LH: 1-18 **RH: 3-9 Tight: 1-11** Gall: 0-8
Aids: Bl: 0-0 Vi: 0-0 Tstrap: 0-0 Ckp: 0-0
Best Rating: 105 9/06 York 1m2f88y good

Useful; effective over 1m-1m2f; seems to handle any ground and Polytrack; usually held up.

Bolshoi King (IRE)

75 **34**
3-y-o b g Fasliyev (USA)-Nawaji (USA) (Trempolino (USA))
B J Meehan Favourites Racing XXII

Placings:060 **(3459)**
2009: 8^{0}G, 6^{6}GF, 6^{0}GF,

	Starts	1st	2nd	3rd	Win & Pl
Career Total (Turf)	3	0	0	0	0

Going (Turf): Sf: 0-0 GS: 0-0 Gd: 0-1 GF: 0-2 Fm: 0-0
Distance: 5f/6f: 0-2 7f-8f: 0-0 9f-13f: 0-1 14f+: 0-0
Track : LH: 0-1 RH: 0-0 Tight: 0-0 Gall: 0-1
Aids: Bl: 0-0 Vi: 0-0 Tstrap: 0-1 Ckp: 0-1
Best Rating: 34 6/09 Nott 1m75y good

Bolton Hall (IRE)

95(97) (47)**50**
7-y-o b g Imperial Ballet (IRE)-Muneera (USA) (Green Dancer (USA))
W K Goldsworthy David Hughes Mike Evans and Partners

Placings:1656500/05314526404230/000000321455/6000 3231230030/0000-6604040 **(5873)**
2009: 13^{6}SD, 16^{6}SD, 12^{0}GF, 17^{4}G, 16^{0}G, 11^{4}GF, 10^{0}G,

	Starts	1st	2nd	3rd	Win & Pl
Career Total (Turf)	52	4	5	5	42442
Career Total (AW)	6	0	0	2	857

69 8/07 Bevl 1m100y (0-65)H GD £3123
70 8/06 Haml 1m1f36y (0-80)H G-F £6477
80 5/05 Leic 7f9y (0-80)H G-F £7334
80 6/04 Bevl 5f B G F £11669

Total win prize-money £28605

Going (Turf): Sf: 0-4 GS: 0-3 Gd: 1-21 **GF: 3-23** Fm: 0-1
Distance: 5f/6f: 1-5 7f-8f: 1-25 **9f-13f: 2-24** 14f+: 0-4
Track : LH: 0-26 **RH: 2-23 Tight: 1-18** Gall: 0-2
Aids: Bl: 0-0 Vi: 0-0 Tstrap: 0-11 Ckp: 0-11
Best Rating: 80 6/05 Nott 1m54y gd-fm

Modest handicapper; was effective at around 1m.

Bom Boms (IRE)

(74) (20)
2-y-o b c Fayruz-Mechilie (Belmez (USA))
Tom Dascombe Manor House Stables LLP

Placings:00 **(6638)**
2009: 5^{0}SD, 7^{0}SD,

	Starts	1st	2nd	3rd	Win & Pl
Career Total (Turf)	0	0	0	0	
Career Total (AW)	2	0	0	0	

Going (Turf): Sf: 0-0 GS: 0-0 Gd: 0-0 GF: 0-0 Fm: 0-0
Distance: 5f/6f: 0-1 7f-8f: 0-1 9f-13f: 0-0 14f+: 0-0
Track : LH: 0-2 RH: 0-0 Tight: 0-2 Gall: 0-0
Aids: Bl: 0-0 Vi: 0-0 Tstrap: 0-0 Ckp: 0-0
Best Rating: 20 9/09 Wolv 5f20y stand

Bombadero (IRE)

90 **67**
2-y-o b c Sadler's Wells (USA)-Fantasy Girl (IRE) (Marju (IRE))
J L Dunlop Windflower Overseas Holdings Inc

Placings:04 **(7034)**
2009: 8^{0}G, 8^{4}S,

	Starts	1st	2nd	3rd	Win & Pl
Career Total (Turf)	2	0	0	0	361

Going (Turf): Sf: 0-1 GS: 0-0 Gd: 0-1 GF: 0-0 Fm: 0-0
Distance: 5f/6f: 0-0 7f-8f: 0-2 9f-13f: 0-0 14f+: 0-0
Track : LH: 0-0 RH: 0-0 Tight: 0-0 Gall: 0-0
Aids: Bl: 0-0 Vi: 0-0 Tstrap: 0-0 Ckp: 0-0
Best Rating: 67 10/09 Newb 1m soft

Bombardier Wells

(105) (74)**69**
4-y-o b g Red Ransom (USA)-Bow River Gold (Rainbow Quest (USA))
R H York (C J Down 18/5) Arun Green

Placings:50/1060600560-1 **(0500)**
2009: 10^{1}SD,

	Starts	1st	2nd	3rd	Win & Pl
Career Total (Turf)	5	0	0	0	0
Career Total (AW)	8	2	0	0	4310

63 2/09 Ling 1m2f STD £1978
74 4/08 Ling 7f STD £2331

Total win prize-money £4310

Going (Turf): Sf: 0-0 GS: 0-1 Gd: 0-1 GF: 0-3 Fm: 0-0
Distance: 5f/6f: 0-2 7f-8f: 1-8 9f-13f: 1-3 14f+: 0-0
Track : **LH: 2-7** RH: 0-2 **Tight: 2-6** Gall: 0-0
Aids: Bl: 0-2 Vi: 0-0 Tstrap: 0-1 Ckp: 0-1
Best Rating: 74 4/08 Ling 7f stand

Modest; stays 1m2f; acts on Polytrack.

Bombay Mist

39(72) (11)
2-y-o b f Rambling Bear-Paris Mist (Paris House)
R C Guest Malcolm Penney

Placings:00 **(7331)**
2009: 5^{0}GF, 5^{0}SD,

	Starts	1st	2nd	3rd	Win & Pl
Career Total (Turf)	1	0	0	0	
Career Total (AW)	1	0	0	0	

Going (Turf): Sf: 0-0 GS: 0-0 Gd: 0-0 GF: 0-1 Fm: 0-0
Distance: 5f/6f: 0-2 7f-8f: 0-0 9f-13f: 0-0 14f+: 0-0
Track : LH: 0-0 RH: 0-0 Tight: 0-0 Gall: 0-0
Aids: Bl: 0-0 Vi: 0-0 Tstrap: 0-0 Ckp: 0-0
Best Rating: 11 11/09 Sthl 5f stand

Bomber Brown (IRE)

106(102) (78)**79**
3-y-o b g Pyrus (USA)-Secret Of Gold (IRE) (Peintre Celebre (USA))
P W Chapple-Hyam Baggies Racing

Placings:034213540 **(6680)**
2009: 8^{0}SD, 10^{3}SD, 8^{4}GF, 10^{2}GF, 9^{1}GS, 10^{3}GS, 10^{5}SD, 11^{4}GF, 10^{0}G,

	Starts	1st	2nd	3rd	Win & Pl
Career Total (Turf)	6	1	1	1	4865
Career Total (AW)	3	0	0	1	403

75 7/09 Yarm 1m1f G-S £2590

Total win prize-money £2590

Going (Turf): Sf: 0-0 **GS: 1-2** Gd: 0-1 GF: 0-3 Fm: 0-0
Distance: 5f/6f: 0-0 7f-8f: 0-1 **9f-13f: 1-8** 14f+: 0-0
Track : **LH: 1-5** RH: 0-4 **Tight: 1-5** Gall: 0-1
Aids: Bl: 0-0 Vi: 0-0 Tstrap: 0-0 Ckp: 0-0
Best Rating: 79 7/09 Yarm 1m2f21y gd-fm

Fair; acts on Polytrack and most ground; stays 1m2f.

Bomber Command (USA)

90(111) (99)82

6-y-o b g Stravinsky (USA)-Parish Manor (USA) (Waquoit (USA))

J W Hills Gary & Linnet Woodward (2)

Placings:0321/3500**641213**/**225**001**265600**/00630**4**10136-500006021060 **(7375)**

2009: 8^{5}SD, 7^{0}SD, 8^{0}GF, 7^{0}GF, 8^{0}G, 8^{6}SD, 7^{0}G, 8^{2}SD, 8^{1}SD, 8^{0}SD, 8^{6}SF, 8^{0}SD,

	Starts	1st	2nd	3rd	Win & Pl
Career Total (Turf)	16	1	1	1	10835
Career Total (AW)	33	6	5	4	56155

90	9/09	Kemp	1m	(0-85)H	STD	£4984
99	7/08	GrLe	1m	(0-90)H	STD	£7477
92	6/08	Kemp	7f	(0-85)H	STD	£4209
82	7/07	Asct	7f	(0-85)H	G-F	£6477
97	12/06	Kemp	7f	(0-85)H	STD	£5505
91	11/06	Kemp	7f	(0-85)H	STD	£5505
78	11/05	Wolv	7f32y		STD	£3500

Total win prize-money £37659

Going (Turf): Sf: 0-2 GS: 0-1 Gd: 0-7 **GF: 1-5** Fm: 0-1
Distance: 5f/6f: 0-2 **7f-8f: 7-40** 9f-13f: 0-7 14f+: 0-0
Track : LH: 2-17 **RH: 4-18** Tight: 1-16 Gall: 1-2
Aids: Bl: 0-3 **Vi: 4-19** Tstrap: 0-2 Ckp: 0-2
Best Rating: 101 3/07 Ling 1m stand

Useful; effective over 7f-1m; acts on fast ground and on Polytrack; has worn blinkers, cheekpieces and a visor.

Bombie Boy

56

4-y-o b g Tobougg (IRE)-Waraqa (USA) (Red Ransom (USA))

F P Murtagh (K W Hogg 17/6) Anthony White

Placings:6 **(3022)**

2009: 9^{6}G,

	Starts	1st	2nd	3rd	Win & Pl
Career Total (Turf)	1	0	0	0	0

Going (Turf): Sf: 0-0 GS: 0-0 Gd: 0-1 GF: 0-0 Fm: 0-0
Distance: 5f/6f: 0-0 7f-8f: 0-0 9f-13f: 0-1 14f+: 0-0
Track : LH: 0-0 RH: 0-1 Tight: 0-1 Gall: 0-0
Aids: Bl: 0-0 Vi: 0-0 Tstrap: 0-0 Ckp: 0-0

Bombina

100 78

3-y-o b f Lomitas-Firebelly (Nicolotte)

P W Chapple-Hyam C G P Wyatt

Placings:10-12435 **(4720)**

2009: 8^{1}GF, 10^{2}G, 8^{4}S, 7^{3}S, 8^{5}G,

	Starts	1st	2nd	3rd	Win & Pl
Career Total (Turf)	7	2	1	1	9133

77	5/09	NmkR	1m	(0-75)H	G-F	£3885
71	10/08	Yarm	1m3y		GD	£3532

Total win prize-money £7418

Going (Turf): Sf: 0-2 GS: 0-1 **Gd: 1-3 GF: 1-1** Fm: 0-0
Distance: 5f/6f: 0-0 7f-8f: 1-4 9f-13f: 1-3 14f+: 0-0
Track : LH: 0-1 RH: 0-0 Tight: 0-0 Gall: 0-0
Aids: Bl: 0-0 Vi: 0-0 Tstrap: 0-0 Ckp: 0-0
Best Rating: 78 6/09 Nott 1m2f50y good

Fair; stays 1m; effective on good/fast ground.

Bon Spiel

101(109) (105)92

5-y-o b h Singspiel (IRE)-L'Affaire Monique (Machiavellian (USA))

L M Cumani Aston House Stud

Placings:56204064/0110305122**23**-500050 **(6795)**

2009: 12^{5}GF, 10^{0}GF, 10^{0}SD, 10^{0}G, 9^{5}GF, 10^{0}S,

	Starts	1st	2nd	3rd	Win & Pl
Career Total (Turf)	22	3	3	1	29485
Career Total (AW)	4	0	1	1	7667

7/08	Siro	1m110y	H	GD	£4688
3/08	Capa	1m3f		GD	£5514
1/08	Pisa	1m1f110y		HVY	£3860

Total win prize-money £14063

Going (Turf): Sf: 1-9 GS: 0-1 **Gd: 2-8** GF: 0-3 Fm: 0-0
Distance: 5f/6f: 0-0 7f-8f: 0-1 **9f-13f: 3-25** 14f+: 0-0
Track : LH: 0-6 **RH: 1-4** Tight: 0-2 Gall: 0-3
Aids: Bl: 0-0 Vi: 0-0 Tstrap: 0-0 Ckp: 0-0
Best Rating: 105 12/08 Ling 1m2f stand

Smart; ex-Italian; stays 1m2f; acts on good and soft ground; goes on Polytrack.

Bona Fortuna

(87) (51)

2-y-o ch g Mark Of Esteem (IRE)-Time Honoured (Sadler's Wells (USA))

Sir Mark Prescott Galaxy Sports Management Ltd

Placings:000 **(7266)**

2009: 7^{0}SD, 7^{0}SD, 8^{0}SD,

	Starts	1st	2nd	3rd	Win & Pl
Career Total (Turf)	0	0	0	0	
Career Total (AW)	3	0	0	0	

Going (Turf): Sf: 0-0 GS: 0-0 Gd: 0-0 GF: 0-0 Fm: 0-0
Distance: 5f/6f: 0-0 7f-8f: 0-3 9f-13f: 0-0 14f+: 0-0
Track : LH: 0-3 RH: 0-0 Tight: 0-2 Gall: 0-0
Aids: Bl: 0-0 Vi: 0-0 Tstrap: 0-0 Ckp: 0-0
Best Rating: 51 9/09 Wolv 7f32y stand

Bonamassa

(77) (31)

2-y-o b c Sulamani (IRE)-Anastasia Venture (Lion Cavern (USA))

M J Attwater Canisbay Bloodstock

Placings:00 **(7763)**

2009: 8^{0}SD, 8^{0}SD,

	Starts	1st	2nd	3rd	Win & Pl
Career Total (Turf)	0	0	0	0	
Career Total (AW)	2	0	0	0	

Going (Turf): Sf: 0-0 GS: 0-0 Gd: 0-0 GF: 0-0 Fm: 0-0
Distance: 5f/6f: 0-0 7f-8f: 0-2 9f-13f: 0-0 14f+: 0-0
Track : LH: 0-1 RH: 0-1 Tight: 0-1 Gall: 0-0
Aids: Bl: 0-0 Vi: 0-0 Tstrap: 0-0 Ckp: 0-0
Best Rating: 31 11/09 Ling 1m stand

Bonasera (IRE)

77(48) 32

2-y-o b f Kheleyf (USA)-Jumlah (Unfuwain (USA))

A Berry Jim & Helen Bowers

Placings:566000 **(7088)**

2009: 5^{5}GF, 5^{6}GF, 7^{6}S, 6^{0}GS, 6^{0}GF, 6^{0}SD,

	Starts	1st	2nd	3rd	Win & Pl
Career Total (Turf)	5	0	0	0	0
Career Total (AW)	1	0	0	0	

Going (Turf): Sf: 0-1 GS: 0-1 Gd: 0-0 GF: 0-3 Fm: 0-0
Distance: 5f/6f: 0-5 7f-8f: 0-1 9f-13f: 0-0 14f+: 0-0
Track : LH: 0-2 RH: 0-0 Tight: 0-0 Gall: 0-0
Aids: Bl: 0-0 Vi: 0-0 Tstrap: 0-0 Ckp: 0-0
Best Rating: 32 9/09 Newc 6f gd-sft

Bond Casino

(94) (63)54

5-y-o b m Kyllachy-Songsheet (Dominion)

G R Oldroyd R C Bond

Placings:50/0300042**213430**/00402**0650036-00** **(0790)**

2009: 14^{0}SS, 12^{0}SD,

	Starts	1st	2nd	3rd	Win & Pl
Career Total (Turf)	16	0	2	1	2457
Career Total (AW)	13	1	1	3	3992

63	9/07	Wolv	1m4f50y	(0-60)H	STD	£2047

Total win prize-money £2048

Going (Turf): Sf: 0-2 GS: 0-1 Gd: 0-5 GF: 0-8 Fm: 0-0
Distance: 5f/6f: 0-6 7f-8f: 0-1 **9f-13f: 1-13** 14f+: 0-9
Track : LH: 1-20 RH: 0-3 **Tight: 1-14** Gall: 0-3
Aids: Bl: 0-0 Vi: 0-4 Tstrap: 0-3 Ckp: 0-3
Best Rating: 63 11/07 Wolv 1m5f194y stand

Moderate; effective over 1m4f; acts on fast ground and Polytrack.

Bond City (IRE)

105(106) (94)102

7-y-o b g Trans Island-Where's Charlotte (Sure Blade (USA))

G R Oldroyd R C Bond

Placings:013352501**21**/3060410**4**046300/200501042/2230 0333004200/53000046010001500-0550206030000000 **(7083)**

2009: 6^{0}S, 6^{5}GF, 6^{5}GF, 7^{0}G, 7^{2}SF, 6^{0}G, 6^{6}G, 6^{0}G, 5^{3}SD, 7^{0}S, 7^{0}SD, 6^{0}G, 7^{0}G, 6^{0}SD, 7^{0}S,

	Starts	1st	2nd	3rd	Win & Pl
Career Total (Turf)	72	5	7	9	132360
Career Total (AW)	8	2	1	1	12445

96	9/08	Hayd	6f	(0-90)	HVY	£10361
94	8/08	Ripn	6f	(0-95)H	GD	£9346
108	8/06	Epsm	5f	(0-105)H	G-S	£18696
102	6/05	NmkJ	5f	(0-100)H	G-F	£11952
94	10/04	Ling	5f		STD	£4872
87	10/04	Wolv	5f20y		STD	£4212
80	6/04	Carl	5f	E	GD	£5772

Total win prize-money £65214

Going (Turf): Sf: 1-10 GS: 1-9 **Gd: 2-28** GF: 1-23 Fm: 0-2
Distance: 5f/6f: 7-71 7f-8f: 0-9 9f-13f: 0-0 14f+: 0-0
Track : LH: 2-16 RH: 1-1 **Tight: 2-10** Gall: 1-3
Aids: Bl: 0-2 Vi: 0-0 Tstrap: 0-6 Ckp: 0-6
Best Rating: 111 10/06 NmkR 5f gd-sft

Useful; Group and Listed placed; effective at 5f-6f; acts on most types of ground and on Polytrack; has worn cheek-pieces and blinkers; likes to race prominently.

Bond Cruz

(95) (26)22

6-y-o b g King's Best (USA)-Arabis (Arazi (USA))

T Keddy A C Maylam

Placings:065/0000P/0/50-0 **(7549)**

2009: 12^{0}SD,

	Starts	1st	2nd	3rd	Win & Pl
Career Total (Turf)	7	0	0	0	0
Career Total (AW)	5	0	0	0	0

Going (Turf): Sf: 0-2 GS: 0-0 Gd: 0-1 GF: 0-3 Fm: 0-1
Distance: 5f/6f: 0-0 7f-8f: 0-6 9f-13f: 0-6 14f+: 0-0
Track : LH: 0-8 RH: 0-3 Tight: 0-6 Gall: 0-0
Aids: Bl: 0-2 Vi: 0-2 Tstrap: 0-1 Ckp: 0-1
Best Rating: 52 12/05 Sthl 1m stand

Bond Fastrac

103(88) (53)93
2-y-o b c Monsieur Bond (IRE)-Kanisfluh (Pivotal)
G R Oldroyd R C Bond

Placings:5125 (5763)
2009: 5^{5}SD, 6^{1}GF, 6^{2}GF, 6^{5}GF,

	Starts	1st	2nd	3rd	Win & Pl
Career Total (Turf)	3	1	1	0	8978
Career Total (AW)	1	0	0	0	0

80 7/09 Rdcr 6f G-F £3753
Total win prize-money £3753

Going (Turf): Sf: 0-0 GS: 0-0 Gd: 0-0 **GF: 1-3** Fm: 0-0
Distance: **5f/6f: 1-4** 7f-8f: 0-0 9f-13f: 0-0 14f+: 0-0
Track : LH: 0-1 RH: 0-0 Tight: 0-1 Gall: 0-0
Aids: Bl: 0-0 Vi: 0-0 Tstrap: 0-0 Ckp: 0-0
Best Rating: 93 8/09 York 6f gd-fm

Useful; effective over 6f; acts on fast ground.

Bond Together

88(84) (50)48
2-y-o ch g Monsieur Bond (IRE)-My Bonus (Cyrano De Bergerac)
P D Evans Jim Ennis

Placings:02305 (4153)
2009: 5^{0}GF, 5^{2}SD, 5^{3}SD, 6^{0}GS, 6^{5}G,

	Starts	1st	2nd	3rd	Win & Pl
Career Total (Turf)	3	0	0	0	0
Career Total (AW)	2	0	1	1	1310

Going (Turf): Sf: 0-0 GS: 0-1 Gd: 0-1 GF: 0-1 Fm: 0-0
Distance: 5f/6f: 0-4 7f-8f: 0-1 9f-13f: 0-0 14f+: 0-0
Track : LH: 0-2 RH: 0-0 Tight: 0-2 Gall: 0-0
Aids: Bl: 0-1 Vi: 0-1 Tstrap: 0-0 Ckp: 0-0
Best Rating: 50 5/09 Wolv 5f20y stand

Moderate; effective over 5f; acts on Polytrack.

Bondage (IRE)

86(92) (62)57
2-y-o b g Whipper (USA)-Shamah (Unfuwain (USA))
J R Fanshawe Mrs Andrew Crawshaw & Chris Van Hoorn

Placings:566 (7763)
2009: 7^{5}G, 7^{6}SD, 8^{6}SD,

	Starts	1st	2nd	3rd	Win & Pl
Career Total (Turf)	1	0	0	0	148
Career Total (AW)	2	0	0	0	0

Going (Turf): Sf: 0-0 GS: 0-0 Gd: 0-1 GF: 0-0 Fm: 0-0
Distance: 5f/6f: 0-0 7f-8f: 0-3 9f-13f: 0-0 14f+: 0-0
Track : LH: 0-0 RH: 0-2 Tight: 0-0 Gall: 0-0
Aids: Bl: 0-0 Vi: 0-0 Tstrap: 0-0 Ckp: 0-0
Best Rating: 62 12/09 Kemp 1m stand

Modest; stays 7f but should stay further; acts on Polytrack; should improve.

Bonded (IRE)

82(91) (70)51
2-y-o b c Oasis Dream-Lovealoch (IRE) (Lomond (USA))
B J Meehan Coleman Bloodstock Limited

Placings:033 (7764)
2009: 8^{0}S, 8^{3}SD, 8^{3}SD,

	Starts	1st	2nd	3rd	Win & Pl
Career Total (Turf)	1	0	0	0	
Career Total (AW)	2	0	0	2	1059

Going (Turf): Sf: 0-1 GS: 0-0 Gd: 0-0 GF: 0-0 Fm: 0-0
Distance: 5f/6f: 0-0 7f-8f: 0-2 9f-13f: 0-1 14f+: 0-0
Track : LH: 0-1 RH: 0-1 Tight: 0-1 Gall: 0-0
Aids: Bl: 0-0 Vi: 0-0 Tstrap: 0-0 Ckp: 0-0
Best Rating: 70 12/09 Kemp 1m stand

Fair; stays 1m; acts on Polytrack.

Bonfire Knight

102(88) (71)80
2-y-o b c Red Ransom (USA)-Attune (Singspiel (IRE))
J J Quinn Ross Harmon

Placings:23102 (5515)
2009: 7^{2}SD, 6^{3}S, 7^{1}G, 6^{0}GF, 8^{2}GF,

	Starts	1st	2nd	3rd	Win & Pl
Career Total (Turf)	4	1	1	1	14278
Career Total (AW)	1	0	1	0	1156

67 8/09 Catt 7f GD £3238
Total win prize-money £3238

Going (Turf): Sf: 0-1 GS: 0-0 **Gd: 1-1** GF: 0-2 Fm: 0-0
Distance: 5f/6f: 0-2 **7f-8f: 1-2** 9f-13f: 0-1 14f+: 0-0
Track : **LH: 1-3** RH: 0-0 **Tight: 1-2** Gall: 0-0
Aids: Bl: 0-0 Vi: 0-0 Tstrap: 0-0 Ckp: 0-0
Best Rating: 80 8/09 Newc 1m3y gd-fm

Fair; stays 1m; acts on good and fats ground; goes on Polytrack; has worn a tongue tie.

Bonheurs Art (IRE)

99 76
2-y-o b f Acclamation-Anneliina (Cadeaux Genereux)
B W Hills Matthew Green

Placings:4252 (6905)
2009: 6^{4}G, 6^{2}GF, 6^{5}G, 6^{2}G,

	Starts	1st	2nd	3rd	Win & Pl
Career Total (Turf)	4	0	2	0	3209

Going (Turf): Sf: 0-0 GS: 0-0 Gd: 0-3 GF: 0-1 Fm: 0-0
Distance: 5f/6f: 0-4 7f-8f: 0-0 9f-13f: 0-0 14f+: 0-0
Track : LH: 0-0 RH: 0-0 Tight: 0-0 Gall: 0-2
Aids: Bl: 0-0 Vi: 0-0 Tstrap: 0-0 Ckp: 0-0
Best Rating: 76 8/09 Wind 6f gd-fm

Fair; suited by 6f and acts on fast ground.

Bonne

95(92) (52)68
4-y-o b f Namid-Jouet (Reprimand)
Miss J R Tooth Raymond Tooth

Placings:0402134-00000 (4536)
2009: 7^{0}SD, 6^{0}G, 6^{0}G, 6^{0}G, 6^{0}S,

	Starts	1st	2nd	3rd	Win & Pl
Career Total (Turf)	8	1	1	1	4895
Career Total (AW)	4	0	0	0	173

68 7/08 Nott 6f15y (0-70)H GD £3238
Total win prize-money £3238

Going (Turf): Sf: 0-2 GS: 0-2 **Gd: 1-4** GF: 0-0 Fm: 0-0
Distance: 5f/6f: 0-7 **7f-8f: 1-5** 9f-13f: 0-0 14f+: 0-0
Track : LH: 0-3 RH: 0-1 Tight: 0-3 Gall: 0-1
Aids: Bl: 0-3 Vi: 0-0 Tstrap: 0-0 Ckp: 0-0
Best Rating: 68 7/08 Nott 6f15y good

Bonnet O'Bonnie

79(96) (55)10
5-y-o br m Makbul-Parkside Prospect (Piccolo)
J Mackie J M Graham

Placings:0/44645000/30-200 (3972)
2009: 6^{2}SD, 6^{0}SD, 5^{0}GS,

	Starts	1st	2nd	3rd	Win & Pl
Career Total (Turf)	3	0	0	0	0
Career Total (AW)	11	0	1	1	1344

Going (Turf): Sf: 0-0 GS: 0-2 Gd: 0-1 GF: 0-0 Fm: 0-0
Distance: 5f/6f: 0-9 7f-8f: 0-4 9f-13f: 0-1 14f+: 0-0
Track : LH: 0-11 RH: 0-1 Tight: 0-8 Gall: 0-0
Aids: Bl: 0-0 Vi: 0-0 Tstrap: 0-0 Ckp: 0-0
Best Rating: 55 3/09 Sthl 6f stand

Moderate; effective at around 7f; acts on Polytrack.

Bonnie Bea

65(87) (49)5
3-y-o b f Royal Applause-Boojum (Mujtahid (USA))
B I Case Itchen Valley Stud

Placings:0-40 (6741)
2009: 8^{4}SD, 8^{0}GS,

	Starts	1st	2nd	3rd	Win & Pl
Career Total (Turf)	1	0	0	0	
Career Total (AW)	2	0	0	0	0

Going (Turf): Sf: 0-0 GS: 0-1 Gd: 0-0 GF: 0-0 Fm: 0-0
Distance: 5f/6f: 0-0 7f-8f: 0-1 9f-13f: 0-2 14f+: 0-0
Track : LH: 0-2 RH: 0-1 Tight: 0-3 Gall: 0-0
Aids: Bl: 0-0 Vi: 0-0 Tstrap: 0-0 Ckp: 0-0
Best Rating: 49 9/09 Wolv 1m141y stand

Bonnie Brae

96(91) (61)67
2-y-o b f Mujahid (USA)-Skara Brae (Inchinor)
G G Margarson Mrs T A Foreman

Placings:02 (6962)
2009: 8^{0}SD, 6^{2}G,

	Starts	1st	2nd	3rd	Win & Pl
Career Total (Turf)	1	0	1	0	1132
Career Total (AW)	1	0	0	0	

Going (Turf): Sf: 0-0 GS: 0-0 Gd: 0-1 GF: 0-0 Fm: 0-0
Distance: 5f/6f: 0-0 7f-8f: 0-2 9f-13f: 0-0 14f+: 0-0
Track : LH: 0-1 RH: 0-1 Tight: 0-0 Gall: 0-0
Aids: Bl: 0-0 Vi: 0-0 Tstrap: 0-0 Ckp: 0-0
Best Rating: 67 10/09 Brig 6f209y good

Modest; effective over 7f; acts on good ground.

Bonnie Charlie

110(100) (76)**109**

3-y-o ch c Intikhab (USA)-Scottish Exile (IRE) (Ashkalani (IRE))

R Hannon Thurloe Thoroughbreds XXII

Placings:122132-5604442 **(6815)**

2009: 8^{5}SD, 7^{6}S, 6^{0}GF, 7^{4}GF, 6^{4}G, 6^{4}GS, 7^{2}G,

	Starts	1st	2nd	3rd	Win & Pl
Career Total (Turf)	12	2	4	1	119249
Career Total (AW)	1	0	0	0	0

96	9/08	Donc	6f		SFT	£10904
88	4/08	Wind	5f10y		G-S	£2729

Total win prize-money £13634

Going (Turf): **Sf: 1-3 GS: 1-3** Gd: 0-4 GF: 0-2 Fm: 0-0
Distance: **5f/6f: 2-8** 7f-8f: 0-5 9f-13f: 0-0 14f+: 0-0
Track : LH: 0-0 RH: 0-1 Tight: 0-0 **Gall: 1-1**
Aids: Bl: 0-0 Vi: 0-0 Tstrap: 0-0 Ckp: 0-0
Best Rating: **109** 10/09 Asct 6f gd-sft

Smart; placed at Group 3 level; stays 7f; acts on good and softer ground.

Bonnie Prince Blue

103(110) (80)**83**

6-y-o ch g Tipsy Creek (USA)-Heart So Blue (Dilum (USA))

D Nicholls Middleham Park Racing XVII

Placings:114/45042400/610030463643002/16010006000-240031543 **(7337)**

2009: 6^{2}GS, 5^{4}G, 6^{0}G, 6^{0}G, 5^{3}G, 5^{1}GS, 5^{5}S, 5^{4}SD, 6^{3}SD,

	Starts	1st	2nd	3rd	Win & Pl
Career Total (Turf)	33	4	2	2	35363
Career Total (AW)	13	2	1	3	13259

83	8/09	Catt	5f212y	(0-75)H	G-S	£2914
91	4/08	Folk	6f	(0-85)H	G-S	£4209
90	1/08	Sthl	6f	(0-85)H	STD	£4210
88	5/07	Kemp	7f	(0-80)H	STD	£5181
87	8/05	Wind	6f		GD	£4901
83	7/05	Newb	6f8y		G-S	£5622

Total win prize-money £27039

Going (Turf): Sf: 0-9 **GS: 3-7** Gd: 1-11 GF: 0-6 Fm: 0-0
Distance: **5f/6f: 4-20** 7f-8f: 2-21 9f-13f: 0-5 14f+: 0-0
Track : **LH: 2-18** RH: 1-8 Tight: 1-10 Gall: 1-2
Aids: **Bl: 3-18** Vi: 0-0 Tstrap: 0-0 Ckp: 0-0
Best Rating: **93** 8/06 Pont 1m4y good

Fair; effective over 6f-7f; acts on good and softer ground; also goes on sand; has worn blinkers.

Bonus (IRE)

(111) (115)**96**

9-y-o b g Cadeaux Genereux-Khamseh (Thatching)

G A Butler The Bonus Partnership

Placings:025/321112515/600056/3060411/152/3020006141/13234004302-23346 **(0781)**

2009: 7^{2}SD, 6^{3}SD, 8^{3}SD, 8^{4}SD, 7^{6}SD,

	Starts	1st	2nd	3rd	Win & Pl
Career Total (Turf)	30	5	4	2	112411
Career Total (AW)	24	5	4	6	109327

106	1/08	Ling	6f		STD	£6543
96	12/07	Kemp	7f		STD	£14762
110	10/07	Kemp	6f	(0-100)H	STD	£24928
104	1/06	Ling	7f	(0-100)H	STD	£12954
103	12/05	Wolv	5f216y	(0-100)H	STD	£11571
93	8/05	Wind	6f		GD	£4966
110	8/03	Curr	6f		GD	£29545
110	5/03	Ling	6f	B(0-105)H	GD	£34800
111	5/03	Sals	6f	B(0-100)H	G-S	£12249
91	4/03	NmkR	6f	D	G-F	£5447

Total win prize-money £157769

Going (Turf): Sf: 0-0 GS: 1-6 **Gd: 3-12** GF: 1-11 Fm: 0-1
Distance: **5f/6f: 8-36** 7f-8f: 2-18 9f-13f: 0-0 14f+: 0-0
Track : **LH: 3-16** RH: 2-9 **Tight: 3-13** Gall: 1-10
Aids: Bl: 0-6 **Vi: 1-2** Tstrap: 0-2 Ckp: 0-2
Best Rating: **115** 1/08 Kemp 6f stand

Smart on the All-Weather/useful on turf; Listed winner; effective over 5f-7f; acts on most ground and Polytrack; has worn blinkers, cheekpieces, tongue tie and a visor; usually held up.

Bonzo

(94) (54)**21**

4-y-o b g Where Or When (IRE)-Making Memories (IRE) (Alzao (USA))

P Howling M A Shipman

Placings:0606050-0 **(0169)**

2009: 13^{0}SD,

	Starts	1st	2nd	3rd	Win & Pl
Career Total (Turf)	1	0	0	0	0
Career Total (AW)	7	0	0	0	0

Going (Turf): **Sf: 0-0 GS: 0-0 Gd: 0-0 GF: 0-1 Fm: 0-0**
Distance: 5f/6f: 0-0 7f-8f: 0-0 9f-13f: 0-4 14f+: 0-4
Track : LH: 0-6 RH: 0-2 Tight: 0-2 Gall: 0-4
Aids: Bl: 0-1 Vi: 0-0 Tstrap: 0-0 Ckp: 0-0
Best Rating: **54** 9/08 GrLe 1m6f stand

Boo

93(99) (77)**61**

7-y-o b g Namaqualand (USA)-Violet (IRE) (Mukaddamah (USA))

J W Unett M E Hughes

Placings:4640/361411323011/25466000350005/0000600500/20006-5604 **(7127)**

2009: 12^{5}SD, 8^{6}G, 9^{0}SD, 10^{4}G,

	Starts	1st	2nd	3rd	Win & Pl
Career Total (Turf)	29	2	1	4	30349
Career Total (AW)	20	3	2	0	29508

98	12/05	Wolv	1m1f103y	(0-100)H	STD	£11446
87	12/05	Wolv	1m1f103y	(0-85)H	STD	£5733
83	7/05	Carl	1m1f61y	(0-70)H	G-F	£3604
70	7/05	Ayr	1m	(0-75)H	G-F	£4098
69	6/05	Wolv	1m141y	(0-75)H	STD	£3583

Total win prize-money £28467

Going (Turf): Sf: 0-3 GS: 0-4 Gd: 0-11 **GF: 2-10** Fm: 0-1
Distance: 5f/6f: 0-2 7f-8f: 1-3 **9f-13f: 4-44** 14f+: 0-0
Track : **LH: 4-36** RH: 1-6 **Tight: 3-22** Gall: 0-8
Aids: Bl: 0-1 **Vi: 2-20** Tstrap: 0-1 Ckp: 0-1
Best Rating: **103** 3/07 Ling 1m2f stand

Useful; stays 1m2f; suited by fast ground and on Polytrack.

Boogie Dancer

(94) (62)**68**

5-y-o b m Tobougg (IRE)-Bolero (Rainbow Quest (USA))

H S Howe Mrs V W Jones

Placings:000303/3400/4-0 **(0115)**

2009: 8^{0}SD,

	Starts	1st	2nd	3rd	Win & Pl
Career Total (Turf)	7	0	0	2	1637
Career Total (AW)	5	0	0	1	674

Going (Turf): **Sf: 0-0 GS: 0-2 Gd: 0-2 GF: 0-3 Fm: 0-0**
Distance: 5f/6f: 0-0 7f-8f: 0-7 9f-13f: 0-5 14f+: 0-0
Track : LH: 0-3 RH: 0-5 Tight: 0-4 Gall: 0-0
Aids: Bl: 0-0 Vi: 0-1 Tstrap: 0-0 Ckp: 0-0
Best Rating: **68** 5/07 Sand 1m1f gd-sft

Modest; effective at around 1m1f; acts on good ground; also goes on Polytrack.

Boogie Diva

96 **78**

2-y-o b f Tobougg (IRE)-Distant Diva (Distant Relative)

M Botti Norcroft Park Stud

Placings:3203 **(6567)**

2009: 7^{3}GF, 7^{2}GF, 7^{0}GF, 7^{3}GF,

	Starts	1st	2nd	3rd	Win & Pl
Career Total (Turf)	4	0	1	2	2793

Going (Turf): **Sf: 0-0 GS: 0-0 Gd: 0-0 GF: 0-4 Fm: 0-0**
Distance: 5f/6f: 0-0 7f-8f: 0-4 9f-13f: 0-0 14f+: 0-0
Track : LH: 0-0 RH: 0-0 Tight: 0-0 Gall: 0-0
Aids: Bl: 0-0 Vi: 0-0 Tstrap: 0-0 Ckp: 0-0
Best Rating: **78** 8/09 NmkJ 7f gd-fm

Fair; stays 1m; acts on fast ground.

Boogie Waltzer

94(93) (53)**52**

2-y-o b f Tobougg (IRE)-Upping The Tempo (Dunbeath (USA))

S C Williams Michael Edwards and John Parsons

Placings:0654263 **(7748)**

2009: 6^{0}G, 7^{6}F, 5^{5}S, 6^{4}SD, 5^{2}S, 5^{6}SD, 5^{3}SD,

	Starts	1st	2nd	3rd	Win & Pl
Career Total (Turf)	4	0	1	0	964
Career Total (AW)	3	0	0	1	602

Going (Turf): **Sf: 0-2 GS: 0-0 Gd: 0-1 GF: 0-0 Fm: 0-1**
Distance: 5f/6f: 0-6 7f-8f: 0-1 9f-13f: 0-0 14f+: 0-0
Track : LH: 0-3 RH: 0-1 Tight: 0-3 Gall: 0-0
Aids: Bl: 0-0 Vi: 0-0 Tstrap: 0-0 Ckp: 0-0
Best Rating: **53** 12/09 Wolv 5f20y stand

Moderate; effective over 5f-6f; acts on soft ground; goes on Polytrack.

Book Of Truth (USA)

87(71) (31)**57**

2-y-o b/br c Truluck (USA)-Elise's Notebook (USA) (Notebook (USA))

D M Simcock Sultan Ali

Placings:0000 **(5868)**

2009: 7^{0}GF, 7^{0}S, 7^{0}SD, 8^{0}G,

	Starts	1st	2nd	3rd	Win & Pl
Career Total (Turf)	3	0	0	0	
Career Total (AW)	1	0	0	0	

Going (Turf): **Sf: 0-1 GS: 0-0 Gd: 0-1 GF: 0-1 Fm: 0-0**
Distance: 5f/6f: 0-0 7f-8f: 0-4 9f-13f: 0-0 14f+: 0-0
Track : LH: 0-1 RH: 0-2 Tight: 0-0 Gall: 0-1
Aids: Bl: 0-0 Vi: 0-0 Tstrap: 0-0 Ckp: 0-0
Best Rating: **57** 7/09 Sand 7f16y gd-fm

Bookiebasher Babe (IRE)

99(104) (74)**72**

4-y-o b f Orpen (USA)-Jay Gee (IRE) (Second Set (IRE))

M Quinn J Henry, J Blake & A Newby

Placings:0602/15132040002041-6406411052050**0** **(6703)**

2009: 8^{6}SD, 8^{4}SD, 8^{0}SD, 8^{6}SD, 8^{4}SD, 8^{1}SD, 8^{1}SD, 9^{0}GF, 9^{5}GF, 8^{2}S, 8^{0}GS, 10^{5}GS, 9^{0}SD, 8^{0}SS,

	Starts	1st	2nd	3rd	Win & Pl
Career Total (Turf)	10	0	1	1	1541
Career Total (AW)	22	5	3	0	20327

74	5/09	Sthl	1m	(0-80)H	STD	£6476
70	4/09	Sthl	1m	(0-80)H	STD	£5180
71	12/08	Sthl	1m		STD	£2047
68	3/08	Wolv	1m141y	(0-65)H	STD	£2047
67	1/08	Sthl	1m	(0-70)H	STD	£2525

Total win prize-money £18277

Going (Turf): Sf: 0-2 GS: 0-5 Gd: 0-0 GF: 0-3 Fm: 0-0
Distance: 5f/6f: 0-2 **7f-8f: 4-15** 9f-13f: 1-15 14f+: 0-0
Track : **LH: 5-22** RH: 0-4 **Tight: 1-12** Gall: 0-2
Aids: Bl: 0-0 Vi: 0-2 Tstrap: 0-0 Ckp: 0-0
Best Rating: 74 5/09 Sthl 1m stand

Fair; stays 1m and acts on sand; likes to race prominently.

Bookiesindex Boy

93(106) (79)**65**

5-y-o b/br g Piccolo-United Passion (Emarati (USA))

J R Jenkins Robin Stevens

Placings:6053002512/322002002405/14600032054016-50600032200 **(7682)**

2009: 5^{5}SD, 5^{0}SD, 5^{6}SD, 5^{0}GS, 5^{0}GF, 5^{0}GF, 5^{3}GS, 5^{2}SD, 5^{2}SD, 5^{0}SD, 5^{0}SD,

	Starts	1st	2nd	3rd	Win & Pl
Career Total (Turf)	22	0	3	3	5035
Career Total (AW)	25	3	6	1	17450

79	12/08	Kemp	5f	(0-75)H	STD	£2590
79	3/08	Wolv	5f20y	(0-85)H	STD	£4857
73	10/06	Wolv	5f20y		SF	£3238

Total win prize-money £10687

Going (Turf): Sf: 0-3 GS: 0-5 Gd: 0-4 GF: 0-10 Fm: 0-0
Distance: **5f/6f: 3-47** 7f-8f: 0-9 9f-13f: 0-0 14f+: 0-0
Track : **LH: 2-18** RH: 1-4 **Tight: 2-15** Gall: 0-3
Aids: Bl: 1-14 **Vi: 2-18** Tstrap: 0-0 Ckp: 0-0
Best Rating: 79 12/08 Kemp 5f stand

Fair; suited by 5f; acts on easy ground; goes on Polytrack; has worn blinkers and a visor.

Bookiesindex Girl (IRE)

83(95) (52)**45**

2-y-o b f Rakti-Distant Valley (Distant Relative)

J R Jenkins Bookmakers Index Ltd

Placings:0060046231 **(7887)**

2009: 5^{0}GF, 6^{0}G, 5^{6}SD, 6^{0}SD, 6^{0}GF, 6^{4}SD, 6^{6}SD, 7^{2}SD, 8^{3}SD, 7^{1}SD,

	Starts	1st	2nd	3rd	Win & Pl
Career Total (Turf)	3	0	0	0	
Career Total (AW)	7	1	1	1	2531

	12/09	Ling	7f	(0-60)	STD	£1637

Total win prize-money £1638

Going (Turf): Sf: 0-0 GS: 0-0 Gd: 0-1 GF: 0-2 Fm: 0-0
Distance: 5f/6f: 0-6 **7f-8f: 1-4** 9f-13f: 0-0 14f+: 0-0
Track : **LH: 1-5** RH: 0-1 **Tight: 1-1** Gall: 0-0
Aids: Bl: 0-0 Vi: 0-0 Tstrap: 0-0 Ckp: 0-0
Best Rating: 52 11/09 Sthl 7f stand

Moderate; effective over 7f; acts on Fibresand.

Bootleg

70 **14**

3-y-o b g Bahamian Bounty-Asbo (Abou Zouz (USA))

D Nicholls The Untouchable Partnership

Placings:6-0 **(1831)**

2009: 6^{0}GS,

	Starts	1st	2nd	3rd	Win & Pl
Career Total (Turf)	2	0	0	0	0

Going (Turf): Sf: 0-1 GS: 0-1 Gd: 0-0 GF: 0-0 Fm: 0-0
Distance: 5f/6f: 0-0 7f-8f: 0-2 9f-13f: 0-0 14f+: 0-0
Track : LH: 0-1 RH: 0-0 Tight: 0-0 Gall: 0-0
Aids: Bl: 0-0 Vi: 0-0 Tstrap: 0-0 Ckp: 0-0
Best Rating: 14 5/09 Haml 6f5y gd-sft

Boquito (IRE)

92(98) (77)**62**

2-y-o b c Rahy (USA)-Fantasia Girl (IRE) (Caerleon (USA))

Miss Amy Weaver Mrs Melba Bryce

Placings:0401135 **(7003)**

2009: 6^{0}G, 5^{4}S, 6^{0}G, 8^{1}SD, 8^{1}SD, 8^{3}SD, 8^{5}SD,

	Starts	1st	2nd	3rd	Win & Pl
Career Total (Turf)	3	0	0	0	361
Career Total (AW)	4	2	0	1	4672

77	9/09	Kemp	1m	(0-75)	STD	£2047
69	9/09	Kemp	1m	(0-65)	STD	£2047

Total win prize-money £4094

Going (Turf): Sf: 0-1 GS: 0-0 Gd: 0-2 GF: 0-0 Fm: 0-0
Distance: 5f/6f: 0-2 **7f-8f: 2-4** 9f-13f: 0-1 14f+: 0-0
Track : LH: 0-1 **RH: 2-3** Tight: 0-1 Gall: 0-0
Aids: Bl: 0-0 Vi: 0-0 Tstrap: 0-0 Ckp: 0-0
Best Rating: 77 9/09 Kemp 1m stand

Fair; stays 1m; best effort on Polytrack.

Borasco (USA)

96(102) (83)**91**

4-y-o ch m Stormy Atlantic (USA)-Seek (USA) (Devil's Bag (USA))

T D Barron Mrs Christine Barron

Placings:361033/0115-55000255 **(7813)**

2009: 6^{5}SD, 7^{5}GS, 7^{0}GF, 7^{0}SD, 7^{0}S, 7^{2}SD, 6^{5}SD, 7^{5}SD,

	Starts	1st	2nd	3rd	Win & Pl
Career Total (Turf)	12	3	0	2	12993
Career Total (AW)	6	0	1	1	1279

91	8/08	Rdcr	7f	(0-80)H	GD	£4857
80	6/08	Newc	7f	(0-75)H	G-S	£4533
74	6/07	Rdcr	7f		SFT	£2169

Total win prize-money £11560

Going (Turf): Sf: 1-2 GS: 1-3 Gd: 1-2 GF: 0-5 Fm: 0-0
Distance: 5f/6f: 0-7 **7f-8f: 3-11** 9f-13f: 0-0 14f+: 0-0
Track : LH: 0-7 RH: 0-0 Tight: 0-5 Gall: 0-0
Aids: Bl: 0-0 Vi: 0-0 Tstrap: 0-0 Ckp: 0-0
Best Rating: 91 8/08 Rdcr 7f good

Modest; effective over 7f; acts on good and softer ground; goes on Polytrack.

Border Artist

(98) (59)**54**

10-y-o ch g Selkirk (USA)-Aunt Tate (Tate Gallery (USA))

J Pearce Jeff Pearce

Placings:665100/60060040530000/442101604031160000/0010043455/62555/0030050230422222311062604040/452066030601600000/6665004406-S **(1958)**

2009: 6^{S}F,

	Starts	1st	2nd	3rd	Win & Pl
Career Total (Turf)	79	9	8	5	55248
Career Total (AW)	31	0	2	2	1713

65	9/07	Yarm	7f3y	(0-60)H	GD	£2914
70	8/06	Yarm	7f3y	(0-70)H	GD	£3562
63	7/06	Yarm	7f3y	(0-70)H	FRM	£3627
68	5/04	Muss	7f30y	E(0-70)H	G-F	£4260
73	7/03	Bevl	7f100y	D(0-80)H	G-F	£8443
67	7/03	Epsm	6f	D(0-80)H	G-F	£5811
66	5/03	Muss	7f30y	D(0-85)H	G-F	£6838
64	5/03	Muss	7f30y	F(0-65)H	G-S	£3393
69	7/01	Wind	6f	D	G-F	£3893

Total win prize-money £42745

Going (Turf): Sf: 0-6 GS: 1-7 Gd: 2-14 **GF: 5-42** Fm: 1-10
Distance: 5f/6f: 2-22 **7f-8f: 7-79** 9f-13f: 0-9 14f+: 0-0
Track : LH: 1-52 **RH: 4-21 Tight: 4-37** Gall: 1-6
Aids: Bl: 0-4 Vi: 0-4 Tstrap: 0-5 Ckp: 0-5
Best Rating: 73 7/03 Bevl 7f100y gd-fm

Moderate handicapper; effective at around 7f; acts on a sound surface; likes Yarmouth and Musselburgh.

Border Owl (IRE)

101(103) (85)**81**

4-y-o b g Selkirk (USA)-Nightbird (IRE) (Night Shift (USA))

P Salmon (N J Gifford 27/2) Viscount Environmental

Placings:052/034331534-053050505 **(7711)**

2009: 12^{0}GF, 8^{5}HY, 8^{3}F, 8^{0}GS, 7^{5}GF, 8^{0}GF, 8^{5}GF, 8^{0}SD, 8^{5}SD,

	Starts	1st	2nd	3rd	Win & Pl
Career Total (Turf)	16	1	0	4	5896
Career Total (AW)	5	0	1	1	2037

74	7/08	Wind	1m67y	G-F	£2729

Total win prize-money £2730

Going (Turf): Sf: 0-3 GS: 0-4 Gd: 0-2 **GF: 1-6** Fm: 0-1
Distance: 5f/6f: 0-0 7f-8f: 0-11 **9f-13f: 1-10** 14f+: 0-0
Track : LH: 0-11 **RH: 1-8 Tight: 1-7** Gall: 0-3
Aids: Bl: 0-0 Vi: 0-1 Tstrap: 0-0 Ckp: 0-0
Best Rating: 85 10/08 Kemp 1m stand

Fair; stays 1m1f; acts on good ground; also goes on Polytrack and handles Fibresand.

Border Patrol

105 **115**

3-y-o b c Selkirk (USA)-Ffestiniog (IRE) (Efisio)

R Charlton Elite Racing Club

Placings:3-111102 **(7208a)**

2009: 8^{1}S, 6^{1}G, 8^{1}G, 8^{1}S, 7^{0}GS, 8^{2}VS,

	Starts	1st	2nd	3rd	Win & Pl
Career Total (Turf)	7	4	1	1	105752

115	9/09	Curr	1m	SFT	£39126
110	5/09	Sand	1m14y	GD	£22708
111	5/09	Newb	6f8y	GD	£22708
95	4/09	Newb	1m	SFT	£4857

Total win prize-money £89399

Going (Turf): Sf: 2-2 GS: 0-2 **Gd: 2-2** GF: 0-0 Fm: 0-0
Distance: 5f/6f: 0-0 **7f-8f: 3-6** 9f-13f: 1-1 14f+: 0-0
Track : LH: 0-1 **RH: 2-3** Tight: 0-0 **Gall: 1-1**
Aids: Bl: 0-0 Vi: 0-0 Tstrap: 0-0 Ckp: 0-0

Best Rating: **115** 11/09 StCl 1m v soft

Smart; dual Listed winner; effective over 1m; acts on good and easier ground.

Border Tale

95(94) (44)59

9-y-o b g Selkirk (USA)-Likely Story (IRE) (Night Shift (USA))

James Moffatt DJM - Arnold Headdock

Placings:00430340/223142361254/**010**/03400/**030006**/30/0-0022230 **(5734)**

2009: 12^{0}SD, 13^{0}SF, 16^{2}GS, 13^{2}GF, 13^{2}GF, 11^{3}S, 16^{0}GS,

	Starts	1st	2nd	3rd	Win & Pl
Career Total (Turf)	34	2	7	6	32736
Career Total (AW)	10	1	0	2	3953

86 2/04 Wolv 1m4f F(0-85)H SS £2877
84 6/03 Ches 1m4f66yD(0-85)H GD £7065
78 5/03 Wind 1m3f135yE(0-70)H GD £3760
Total win prize-money £13703

Going (Turf): Sf: 0-6 GS: 0-5 **Gd: 2-8** GF: 0-14 Fm: 0-1
Distance: 5f/6f: 0-2 7f-8f: 0-5 **9f-13f: 3-27** 14f+: 0-10
Track : **LH: 2-29** RH: 0-7 **Tight: 3-24** Gall: 0-6
Aids: Bl: 0-0 Vi: 0-5 Tstrap: 0-5 Ckp: 0-5
Best Rating: **86** 2/04 Wolv 1m4f std-slw

Modest handicapper on turf and sand; also winning hurdler; stays 2m and handles soft ground, but better on faster.

Borderlescott

117 (105)121

7-y-o b g Compton Place-Jeewan (Touching Wood (USA))

R Bastiman James Edgar & William Donaldson

Placings:6031/51511231/1421262/2200220422/12223131-32514160 **(7745a)**

2009: 5^{3}GF, 5^{2}HY, 5^{5}GF, 5^{1}GF, 5^{4}G, 5^{1}GF, 5^{6}G, 6^{0}G,

	Starts	1st	2nd	3rd	Win & Pl
Career Total (Turf)	43	11	13	5	592487
Career Total (AW)	2	1	1	0	29529

121 8/09 York 5f G-F £136248
109 7/09 Ches 5f16y G-F £22708
105 10/08 Dund 5f STD £23933
121 8/08 NmkJ 5f GD £93670
113 5/08 Muss 5f G-S £12462
114 8/06 Gdwd 6f H G-F £62320
109 5/06 York 6f (0-100)H SFT £12954
105 10/05 York 6f (0-100)H SFT £19500
93 8/05 Ripn 6f (0-80)H G-F £6856
84 8/05 Rdcr 6f (0-85)H G-F £5930
81 6/05 Hayd 6f (0-80)H G-F £7396
74 7/04 Haml 6f5y D G-F £5187
Total win prize-money £409167

Going (Turf): Sf: 2-4 GS: 1-8 Gd: 1-10 **GF: 7-21** Fm: 0-0
Distance: **5f/6f: 11-43** 7f-8f: 1-2 9f-13f: 0-0 14f+: 0-0
Track : **LH: 2-4** RH: 0-2 **Tight: 1-3** Gall: 0-2
Aids: Bl: 0-0 Vi: 0-0 Tstrap: 0-0 Ckp: 0-0
Best Rating: **121** 8/09 York 5f gd-fm

Group class; winner of the 2006 Stewards' Cup; won the Group 1 Nunthorpe Stakes in both 2008 and 2009; effective at 5f-6f; acts on most ground; likes to race prominently; tough and durable and a credit to his connections.

Born A Dancer (IRE)

86 54

2-y-o b f Danehill Dancer (IRE)-Born Beautiful (USA) (Silver Deputy (CAN))

J W Hills Gordian Troeller

Placings:00 **(6241)**

2009: 6^{0}GF, 6^{0}G,

	Starts	1st	2nd	3rd	Win & Pl
Career Total (Turf)	2	0	0	0	

Going (Turf): **Sf: 0-0 GS: 0-0 Gd: 0-1 GF: 0-1 Fm: 0-0**
Distance: 5f/6f: 0-0 7f-8f: 0-2 9f-13f: 0-0 14f+: 0-0
Track : LH: 0-0 RH: 0-0 Tight: 0-0 Gall: 0-0
Aids: Bl: 0-0 Vi: 0-0 Tstrap: 0-0 Ckp: 0-0
Best Rating: **54** 8/09 Newb 6f8y gd-fm

Born Romantic

88(78) (22)44

3-y-o b f High Chaparral (IRE)-Maid For Romance (Pursuit Of Love)

H J L Dunlop Normandie Stud Ltd

Placings:00 **(3025)**

2009: 10^{0}S, 10^{0}SD,

	Starts	1st	2nd	3rd	Win & Pl
Career Total (Turf)	1	0	0	0	
Career Total (AW)	1	0	0	0	

Going (Turf): **Sf: 0-1 GS: 0-0 Gd: 0-0 GF: 0-0 Fm: 0-0**
Distance: 5f/6f: 0-0 7f-8f: 0-0 9f-13f: 0-2 14f+: 0-0
Track : LH: 0-1 RH: 0-1 Tight: 0-0 Gall: 0-1
Aids: Bl: 0-0 Vi: 0-0 Tstrap: 0-0 Ckp: 0-0
Best Rating: **44** 5/09 Newb 1m2f6y soft

Born To Be King (USA)

98 103

3-y-o b c Storm Cat (USA)-Quarter Moon (IRE) (Sadler's Wells (USA))

A P O'Brien Mrs J Magnier & Mrs R Henry

Placings:021-3060 **(2992)**

2009: 8^{3}GF, 8^{0}G, 10^{6}G, 8^{0}GF,

	Starts	1st	2nd	3rd	Win & Pl
Career Total (Turf)	7	1	1	1	16629

87 8/08 Gowr 7f G-Y £8637
Total win prize-money £8638

Going (Turf): **Sf: 0-0 GS: 0-0 Gd: 0-2 GF: 0-3 Fm: 0-0**
Distance: 5f/6f: 0-2 **7f-8f: 1-4** 9f-13f: 0-1 14f+: 0-0
Track : LH: 0-2 **RH: 1-3** Tight: 0-0 Gall: 0-1
Aids: Bl: 0-1 Vi: 0-0 Tstrap: 0-0 Ckp: 0-0
Best Rating: **103** 3/09 Leop 1m gd-fm

Useful; effective over 7f; acts on fast and easy ground.

Born To Perform

91 55

4-y-o b g Theatrical-My Hansel (USA) (Hansel (USA))

G A Swinbank J N Swinbank

Placings:0550 **(5289)**

2009: 12^{0}GF, 9^{5}GF, 9^{5}G, 8^{0}GS,

	Starts	1st	2nd	3rd	Win & Pl
Career Total (Turf)	4	0	0	0	0

Going (Turf): **Sf: 0-0 GS: 0-1 Gd: 0-1 GF: 0-2 Fm: 0-0**
Distance: 5f/6f: 0-0 7f-8f: 0-1 9f-13f: 0-3 14f+: 0-0
Track : LH: 0-1 RH: 0-3 Tight: 0-2 Gall: 0-1
Aids: Bl: 0-0 Vi: 0-0 Tstrap: 0-0 Ckp: 0-0
Best Rating: **55** 7/09 Carl 1m1f61y good

Born Tobouggie (GER)

107(111) (106)103

4-y-o b f Tobougg (IRE)-Braissim (Dancing Brave (USA))

H R A Cecil The Sticky Wicket Syndicate

Placings:12613015-13 **(1667)**

2009: 8^{1}SD, 8^{3}G,

	Starts	1st	2nd	3rd	Win & Pl
Career Total (Turf)	7	3	1	1	22480
Career Total (AW)	3	1	0	1	24904

106 4/09 Kemp 1m STD £22708
103 10/08 Leic 1m60y GD £7569
95 8/08 Wind 1m67y (0-85)H G-S £5698
75 4/08 Nott 1m54y SFT £2104
Total win prize-money £38082

Going (Turf): **Sf: 1-2 GS: 1-1 Gd: 1-3** GF: 0-0 Fm: 0-1
Distance: 5f/6f: 0-0 7f-8f: 1-5 **9f-13f: 3-5** 14f+: 0-0
Track : LH: 1-5 **RH: 3-4 Tight: 1-3** Gall: 0-1
Aids: Bl: 0-0 Vi: 0-0 Tstrap: 0-0 Ckp: 0-0
Best Rating: **106** 4/09 Kemp 1m stand

Smart; Listed winner; effective at around 1m; acts on good and soft ground; goes on Polytrack.

Born West (USA)

(103) (62)71

5-y-o b g Gone West (USA)-Admirer (USA) (Private Terms (USA))

M C Banks (N B King 6/4) M C Banks

Placings:030/34243/0-0300 **(1154)**

2009: 13^{0}SD, 16^{3}SD, 16^{0}SD, 16^{0}SD,

	Starts	1st	2nd	3rd	Win & Pl
Career Total (Turf)	4	0	1	1	1283
Career Total (AW)	9	0	0	3	1235

Going (Turf): **Sf: 0-0 GS: 0-1 Gd: 0-1 GF: 0-2 Fm: 0-0**
Distance: 5f/6f: 0-0 7f-8f: 0-1 9f-13f: 0-4 14f+: 0-8
Track : LH: 0-12 RH: 0-1 Tight: 0-12 Gall: 0-0
Aids: Bl: 0-2 Vi: 0-0 Tstrap: 0-0 Ckp: 0-0
Best Rating: **71** 9/07 Catt 1m7f177y good

Modest gelding; placed in low grade handicaps at up to 2m; acts on a sound surface and Polytrack.

Borodinsky

86 (42)52

8-y-o b g Magic Ring (IRE)-Valldemosa (Music Boy)

R E Barr Mrs R E Barr

Placings:000/50402402/00351362/0006400**40**/**06**053366341200/00500-606 **(3539)**

2009: 8^{6}GF, 7^{0}GF, 7^{6}F,

	Starts	1st	2nd	3rd	Win & Pl
Career Total (Turf)	47	2	4	5	13193
Career Total (AW)	4	0	0	0	0

57 8/07 Catt 7f (0-65)H FRM £2730
58 8/05 Catt 7f (0-55)H G-F £3109
Total win prize-money £5839

Going (Turf): Sf: 0-2 GS: 0-5 Gd: 0-12 **GF: 1-20 Fm: 1-8**
Distance: 5f/6f: 0-12 **7f-8f: 2-35** 9f-13f: 0-4 14f+: 0-0
Track : **LH: 2-19** RH: 0-8 **Tight: 2-18** Gall: 0-0
Aids: Bl: 0-0 Vi: 0-2 Tstrap: 0-2 Ckp: 0-2
Best Rating: **69** 8/07 Rdcr 1m gd-fm

Moderate; effective up to 1m; acts on good and fast ground; has worn a visor and cheekpieces.

Borouj (IRE)

(81) (61)**61**
7-y-o ch g Unfuwain (USA)-Amanah (USA) (Mr Prospector (USA))
Joss Saville Lowbeck Racing Syndicate

Placings:023261/000/40000-00 **(0603)**
2009: 8^{0}SD, 12^{0}SD,

	Starts	1st	2nd	3rd	Win & Pl
Career Total (Turf)	13	1	2	1	7409
Career Total (AW)	3	0	0	0	

73 9/05 Haml 1m1f36y SFT £3497
Total win prize-money £3497

Going (Turf): **Sf: 1-1** GS: 0-1 Gd: 0-4 GF: 0-2 Fm: 0-1
Distance: 5f/6f: 0-0 7f-8f: 0-5 **9f-13f: 1-10** 14f+: 0-1
Track : LH: 0-6 **RH: 1-8 Tight: 1-3** Gall: 0-1
Aids: Bl: 0-0 **Vi: 1-2** Tstrap: 0-1 Ckp: 0-1
Best Rating: 81 7/05 Newb 1m1f gd-sft

Borromeo (USA)

95 **64**
3-y-o ch g Mr Greeley (USA)-Luxury On The Lake (USA) (Salt Lake (USA))
M Johnston Sheikh Hamdan Bin Mohammed Al Maktoum

Placings:0632 **(3260)**
2009: 8^{0}GS, 10^{6}GF, 11^{3}GF, 11^{2}F,

	Starts	1st	2nd	3rd	Win & Pl
Career Total (Turf)	4	0	1	1	1291

Going (Turf): Sf: 0-0 GS: 0-1 Gd: 0-0 GF: 0-2 Fm: 0-1
Distance: 5f/6f: 0-0 7f-8f: 0-0 9f-13f: 0-4 14f+: 0-0
Track : LH: 0-2 RH: 0-2 Tight: 0-1 Gall: 0-0
Aids: Bl: 0-0 Vi: 0-0 Tstrap: 0-0 Ckp: 0-0
Best Rating: 64 6/09 Bath 1m3f144y firm

Modest; stays 1m3f plus; acts on fast ground.

Bosamcliff (IRE)

102(108) (73)**69**
4-y-o b f Daylami (IRE)-L'Animee (Green Tune (USA))
P D Evans (B G Powell 28/4) W Clifford

Placings:06/6021046-5640233115 **(7641)**
2009: 6^{5}GF, 8^{6}GF, 8^{4}G, 10^{0}GF, 8^{2}G, 7^{3}G, 10^{3}G, 9^{1}S, 12^{1}SD, 11^{5}SD,

	Starts	1st	2nd	3rd	Win & Pl
Career Total (Turf)	13	2	2	2	7253
Career Total (AW)	6	1	0	0	2730

73 11/09 Sthl 1m4f (0-70)H STD £2729
69 10/09 Ayr 1m1f20y (0-60)H SFT £2266
69 8/08 Ayr 1m2f (0-65)H SFT £2590
Total win prize-money £7587

Going (Turf): Sf: 2-4 GS: 0-0 Gd: 0-6 GF: 0-3 Fm: 0-0
Distance: 5f/6f: 0-1 7f-8f: 0-2 **9f-13f: 3-16** 14f+: 0-0
Track : **LH: 3-13** RH: 0-3 Tight: 0-7 Gall: 0-0
Aids: Bl: 0-0 Vi: 0-0 Tstrap: 0-0 Ckp: 0-0
Best Rating: 73 11/09 Sthl 1m4f stand

Modest; effective over 1m2f-1m4f; acts on easy ground and Fibresand.

Boscage (USA)

74(108) (97)**74**
4-y-o b g Forestry (USA)-Prospinsky (USA) (Mr Prospector (USA))
M Johnston Sheikh Hamdan Bin Mohammed Al Maktoum

Placings:1140 **(1352)**
2009: 8^{1}SD, 8^{1}SD, 8^{4}GF, 8^{0}S,

	Starts	1st	2nd	3rd	Win & Pl
Career Total (Turf)	2	0	0	0	625
Career Total (AW)	2	2	0	0	7318

97 3/09 Sthl 1m (0-85)H STD £4727
86 3/09 Ling 1m STD £2590
Total win prize-money £7317

Going (Turf): Sf: 0-1 GS: 0-0 Gd: 0-0 GF: 0-1 Fm: 0-0
Distance: 5f/6f: 0-0 **7f-8f: 2-3** 9f-13f: 0-1 14f+: 0-0
Track : **LH: 2-3** RH: 0-0 **Tight: 1-2** Gall: 0-0
Aids: Bl: 0-0 Vi: 0-0 Tstrap: 0-0 Ckp: 0-0
Best Rating: 97 3/09 Sthl 1m stand

Very useful; stays 1m, should get further; acts on sand.

Boss Hog

95(110) (73)**55**
4-y-o b g Key Of Luck (USA)-Dania (GER) (Night Shift (USA))
P T Midgley (R Curtis 18/3) D I Perry

Placings:430000222-21530050505050056420 **(7051)**
2009: 7^{2}SD, 7^{1}SD, 8^{5}SD, 7^{3}SD, 7^{0}SD, 8^{0}GF, 7^{5}SD, 7^{0}SD, 7^{5}F, 7^{0}G, 7^{5}G, 7^{0}G, 7^{0}G, 5^{5}GS, 7^{6}GF, 8^{4}GF, 8^{2}SD, 7^{0}SD,

	Starts	1st	2nd	3rd	Win & Pl
Career Total (Turf)	12	0	0	0	0
Career Total (AW)	15	1	5	2	6421

72 2/09 Sthl 7f STD £2729
Total win prize-money £2730

Going (Turf): Sf: 0-1 GS: 0-2 Gd: 0-5 GF: 0-3 Fm: 0-1
Distance: 5f/6f: 0-2 **7f-8f: 1-22** 9f-13f: 0-3 14f+: 0-0
Track : **LH: 1-15** RH: 0-8 Tight: 0-4 Gall: 0-0
Aids: Bl: 0-1 Vi: 0-0 Tstrap: 0-2 Ckp: 0-2
Best Rating: 73 1/09 Wolv 7f32y stand

Modest; effective at around 1m; acts on Fibresand; has worn cheekpieces.

Boss's Destination

87 **65**
2-y-o b g Dubai Destination (USA)-Blushing Sunrise (USA) (Cox's Ridge (USA))
G A Swinbank G H Bell

Placings:55 **(4847)**
2009: 5^{5}G, 7^{5}G,

	Starts	1st	2nd	3rd	Win & Pl
Career Total (Turf)	2	0	0	0	0

Going (Turf): Sf: 0-0 GS: 0-0 Gd: 0-2 GF: 0-0 Fm: 0-0
Distance: 5f/6f: 0-1 7f-8f: 0-1 9f-13f: 0-0 14f+: 0-0
Track : LH: 0-1 RH: 0-1 Tight: 0-1 Gall: 0-1
Aids: Bl: 0-0 Vi: 0-0 Tstrap: 0-0 Ckp: 0-0
Best Rating: 65 8/09 Thsk 7f good

Bossy Kitty

106 **77**
2-y-o ch f Avonbridge-Between The Sticks (Pharly (FR))
N Tinkler Leeds Plywood And Doors Ltd

Placings:05003425013110 **(7290)**
2009: 5^{0}GF, 5^{5}GF, 5^{0}GS, 5^{0}GF, 5^{3}G, 5^{4}GF, 5^{2}G, 5^{5}GF, 6^{0}GF, 5^{1}GS, 5^{3}S, 5^{1}GF, 6^{1}G, 6^{0}S,

	Starts	1st	2nd	3rd	Win & Pl
Career Total (Turf)	14	3	1	2	9115

68 10/09 Ayr 5f (0-75) G-F £2914
66 9/09 Ripn 5f G-S £2914
Total win prize-money £5828

Going (Turf): Sf: 0-2 **GS: 1-2 Gd: 1-3 GF: 1-7** Fm: 0-0
Distance: **5f/6f: 3-14** 7f-8f: 0-0 9f-13f: 0-0 14f+: 0-0
Track : LH: 0-1 RH: 0-0 Tight: 0-1 Gall: 0-0
Aids: Bl: 0-0 Vi: 0-0 Tstrap: 0-0 Ckp: 0-0
Best Rating: 77 10/09 York 6f good

Fair; effective over 5f-6f; acts on fast and easy ground.

Boston Blue

(91) (66)
2-y-o b g Halling (USA)-City Of Gold (IRE) (Sadler's Wells (USA))
W J Knight Mr & Mrs I H Bendelow

Placings:45 **(7388)**
2009: 8^{4}SD, 8^{5}SD,

	Starts	1st	2nd	3rd	Win & Pl
Career Total (Turf)	0	0	0	0	
Career Total (AW)	2	0	0	0	0

Going (Turf): Sf: 0-0 GS: 0-0 Gd: 0-0 GF: 0-0 Fm: 0-0
Distance: 5f/6f: 0-0 7f-8f: 0-2 9f-13f: 0-0 14f+: 0-0
Track : LH: 0-2 RH: 0-0 Tight: 0-2 Gall: 0-0
Aids: Bl: 0-0 Vi: 0-0 Tstrap: 0-0 Ckp: 0-0
Best Rating: 66 10/09 Ling 1m stand

Bosun Breese

(96) (61)**89**
4-y-o b g Bahamian Bounty-Nellie Melba (Hurricane Sky (AUS))
T D Barron Estio Capital Racing

Placings:3413002/0620064102-0 **(7414)**
2009: 5^{0}SD,

	Starts	1st	2nd	3rd	Win & Pl
Career Total (Turf)	16	2	3	2	23256
Career Total (AW)	2	0	0	0	0

86 7/08 Sand 5f6y (0-80)H G-F £5504
75 6/07 Sand 5f6y G-S £3886
Total win prize-money £9391

Going (Turf): Sf: 0-0 **GS: 1-3** Gd: 0-3 **GF: 1-10** Fm: 0-0
Distance: **5f/6f: 2-18** 7f-8f: 0-0 9f-13f: 0-0 14f+: 0-0
Track : LH: 0-3 RH: 0-1 Tight: 0-1 Gall: 0-2
Aids: Bl: 0-0 Vi: 0-0 Tstrap: 0-0 Ckp: 0-0
Best Rating: 89 5/08 Wind 5f10y gd-fm

Useful; effective over 5f-6f; handles most ground; has worn a tongue-tie.

Botanist

89 **82**
2-y-o b c Selkirk (USA)-Red Camellia (Polar Falcon (USA))
Sir Michael Stoute Cheveley Park Stud

Placings:021 **(6759)**
2009: 7^{0}GF, 8^{2}GS, 8^{1}G,

	Starts	1st	2nd	3rd	Win & Pl
Career Total (Turf)	3	1	1	0	6722

82 10/09 Leic 1m60y GD £5180
Total win prize-money £5181

Going (Turf): Sf: 0-0 GS: 0-1 **Gd: 1-1** GF: 0-1 Fm: 0-0
Distance: 5f/6f: 0-0 7f-8f: 0-1 **9f-13f: 1-2** 14f+: 0-0
Track : LH: 0-0 **RH: 1-2** Tight: 0-0 Gall: 0-0

Aids: Bl: 0-0 Vi: 0-0 Tstrap: 0-0 Ckp: 0-0
Best Rating: 82 10/09 Leic 1m60y good

Useful; stays 1m; acts on god and easy ground.

Both Ends Burning (IRE)

83 31
2-y-o ch f Choisir (AUS)-Giadamar (IRE) (Be My Guest (USA))
J S Wainwright Charles Wentworth

Placings:00 (4817)
2009: 6[0]GF, 7[0]GF,

	Starts	1st	2nd	3rd	Win & Pl
Career Total (Turf)	2	0	0	0	

Going (Turf): Sf: 0-0 GS: 0-0 Gd: 0-0 GF: 0-2 Fm: 0-0
Distance: 5f/6f: 0-1 7f-8f: 0-1 9f-13f: 0-0 14f+: 0-0
Track : LH: 0-0 RH: 0-0 Tight: 0-0 Gall: 0-0
Aids: Bl: 0-0 Vi: 0-0 Tstrap: 0-0 Ckp: 0-0
Best Rating: 31 7/09 Rdcr 6f gd-fm

Botham (USA)

102(99) (58)71
5-y-o b/br g Cryptoclearance (USA)-Oval (USA) (Kris S (USA))
J S Goldie Caledonia Racing

Placings:006/005504025/6013350054354-01206101260010 (7172)
2009: 5[0]GF, 8[1]GF, 6[2]GF, 8[0]G, 7[6]G, 6[1]G, 6[0]GF, 6[1]GS, 5[2]GS, 6[6]GF, 9[0]G, 8[0]GF, 7[1]G, 7[0]S,

	Starts	1st	2nd	3rd	Win & Pl
Career Total (Turf)	30	5	2	3	15696
Career Total (AW)	9	0	1	0	877

71	10/09	Ayr	7f50y	(0-70)H	GD	£2914
69	8/09	Haml	6f5y	(0-65)H	G-S	£2266
66	7/09	Haml	6f5y	(0-60)H	GD	£2266
55	5/09	Haml	1m65y	(0-55)H	G-F	£2307
61	6/08	Haml	6f5y	(0-60)H	G-F	£2966

Total win prize-money £12723

Going (Turf): Sf: 0-5 GS: 1-3 Gd: 2-9 GF: 2-13 Fm: 0-0
Distance: 5f/6f: 0-10 7f-8f: 4-18 9f-13f: 1-9 14f+: 0-2
Track : LH: 1-17 RH: 1-7 Tight: 1-10 Gall: 0-0
Aids: Bl: 0-5 Vi: 0-0 Tstrap: 0-0 Ckp: 0-0
Best Rating: 71 10/09 Ayr 7f50y good

Modest; stays 1m6f, but has the speed for 5f; acts on most ground and on sand.

Bothwell Castle (IRE)

87(83) (41)57
2-y-o b g Captain Rio-Majesty's Nurse (Indian King (USA))
P C Haslam Blue Lion Racing VIII & M T Buckley

Placings:03400 (6639)
2009: 6[0]GS, 6[3]G, 6[4]GF, 6[0]GS, 8[0]SD,

	Starts	1st	2nd	3rd	Win & Pl
Career Total (Turf)	4	0	0	1	620
Career Total (AW)	1	0	0	0	

Going (Turf): Sf: 0-0 GS: 0-2 Gd: 0-1 GF: 0-1 Fm: 0-0
Distance: 5f/6f: 0-3 7f-8f: 0-1 9f-13f: 0-1 14f+: 0-0
Track : LH: 0-1 RH: 0-0 Tight: 0-1 Gall: 0-0
Aids: Bl: 0-0 Vi: 0-0 Tstrap: 0-1 Ckp: 0-1
Best Rating: 57 6/09 Rdcr 6f good

Moderate; stays 6f; acts on a sound surface.

Bothy

108 91
3-y-o ch g Pivotal-Villa Carlotta (Rainbow Quest (USA))
B Ellison (R M Beckett 15/10) Dan Gilbert

Placings:2-164 (6795)
2009: 8[1]G, 11[6]GF, 10[4]S,

	Starts	1st	2nd	3rd	Win & Pl
Career Total (Turf)	4	1	1	0	6748

88	4/09	Epsm	1m114y	GD	£4533

Total win prize-money £4533

Going (Turf): Sf: 0-1 GS: 0-1 Gd: 1-1 GF: 0-1 Fm: 0-0
Distance: 5f/6f: 0-0 7f-8f: 0-1 9f-13f: 1-3 14f+: 0-0
Track : LH: 1-2 RH: 0-1 Tight: 1-2 Gall: 0-0
Aids: Bl: 0-0 Vi: 0-0 Tstrap: 0-0 Ckp: 0-0
Best Rating: 91 10/09 Nott 1m2f50y soft

Very useful; stays 1m2f, should get further; acts on soft ground.

Botley Bell

87(79) (52)59
2-y-o b f Imperial Dancer-Curbridge Bell (Fraam)
M R Channon Capital

Placings:00600 (4384)
2009: 5[0]GF, 7[0]SD, 6[6]GF, 6[0]G, 6[0]G,

	Starts	1st	2nd	3rd	Win & Pl
Career Total (Turf)	4	0	0	0	0
Career Total (AW)	1	0	0	0	

Going (Turf): Sf: 0-0 GS: 0-0 Gd: 0-2 GF: 0-2 Fm: 0-0
Distance: 5f/6f: 0-1 7f-8f: 0-4 9f-13f: 0-0 14f+: 0-0
Track : LH: 0-0 RH: 0-1 Tight: 0-0 Gall: 0-0
Aids: Bl: 0-0 Vi: 0-1 Tstrap: 0-0 Ckp: 0-0
Best Rating: 59 7/09 Nott 6f15y gd-fm

Bouggie Daize

93 70
3-y-o b f Tobougg (IRE)-Milly's Lass (Mind Games)
C G Cox Ken Lock Racing

Placings:52405-00 (4326)
2009: 8[0]GF, 6[0]GF,

	Starts	1st	2nd	3rd	Win & Pl
Career Total (Turf)	7	0	1	0	8233

Going (Turf): Sf: 0-1 GS: 0-1 Gd: 0-2 GF: 0-3 Fm: 0-0
Distance: 5f/6f: 0-1 7f-8f: 0-6 9f-13f: 0-0 14f+: 0-0
Track : LH: 0-0 RH: 0-1 Tight: 0-0 Gall: 0-0
Aids: Bl: 0-0 Vi: 0-0 Tstrap: 0-0 Ckp: 0-0
Best Rating: 70 9/08 Asct 6f110y good

Fair; effective over 6f; acts on fast ground.

Bould Mover

108(84) (51)105
2-y-o b c Kyllachy-Maugwenna (Danehill (USA))
R Curtis H Downs & D Looney

Placings:43115024 (6660)
2009: 5[4]SD, 5[3]G, 5[1]GF, 5[1]GF, 5[5]G, 6[0]G, 5[2]GF, 5[4]GS,

	Starts	1st	2nd	3rd	Win & Pl
Career Total (Turf)	7	2	1	1	30224
Career Total (AW)	1	0	0	0	385

91	7/09	Bevl	5f	G-F	£5180
74	6/09	Muss	5f	G-F	£2729

Total win prize-money £7911

Going (Turf): Sf: 0-0 GS: 0-1 Gd: 0-3 GF: 2-3 Fm: 0-0
Distance: 5f/6f: 2-8 7f-8f: 0-0 9f-13f: 0-0 14f+: 0-0
Track : LH: 0-0 RH: 0-1 Tight: 0-0 Gall: 0-0
Aids: Bl: 0-0 Vi: 0-0 Tstrap: 0-0 Ckp: 0-0
Best Rating: 105 9/09 Donc 5f gd-fm

Very useful; Group 2 placed; effective over 5f; acts on fast ground; handles Polytrack.

Boule Masquee

(95) (69)83
5-y-o ch m Compton Place-Burqa (Nashwan (USA))
David P Myerscough D Farrington

Placings:0/241/00150000-035 (6120)
2009: 5[0]S, 7[3]SD, 5[5]SD,

	Starts	1st	2nd	3rd	Win & Pl
Career Total (Turf)	11	2	1	0	13146
Career Total (AW)	4	0	0	1	517

83	7/08	Fair	6f	(50-80)H	GD	£6351
78	6/07	Naas	6f	(47-70)H	G-Y	£4668

Total win prize-money £11020

Going (Turf): Sf: 0-2 GS: 0-1 Gd: 1-3 GF: 0-2 Fm: 0-0
Distance: 5f/6f: 2-8 7f-8f: 0-7 9f-13f: 0-0 14f+: 0-0
Track : LH: 1-9 RH: 1-4 Tight: 0-2 Gall: 0-0
Aids: Bl: 0-1 Vi: 0-0 Tstrap: 0-1 Ckp: 0-1
Best Rating: 83 7/08 Fair 6f good

Fair; effective over 6f-7f; acts on good ground.

Bound By Honour (SAF)

109(108) (101)101
6-y-o b g Rambo Dancer (CAN)-Child Of Grace (SAF) (Only A Pound)
G L Moore (H J Brown 26/2) Blue Diamond Racing

Placings:21230220/001151204/2311453-40050400216 (7789)
2009: 8[4]G, 10[0]G, 12[0]G, 10[5]GF, 10[0]GF, 9[4]GF, 10[0]GF, 10[0]GF, 10[2]SD, 10[1]SD, 9[6]SD,

	Starts	1st	2nd	3rd	Win & Pl
Career Total (Turf)	32	6	6	3	74723
Career Total (AW)	3	1	1	0	14785

101	11/09	Ling	1m2f	(0-100)H	STD	£11215
	4/08	Turf	1m2f		GD	£13786
	3/08	Turf	1m4f55y	H	GD	£6204
	9/07	Vaal	1m2f		GD	£3849
	7/07	Vaal	1m4f	H	GD	£3623
	6/07	Vaal	1m2f		GD	£3396
	4/06	Vaal	7f		GD	£3331

Total win prize-money £45409

Going (Turf): Sf: 0-2 GS: 0-0 Gd: 6-25 GF: 0-5 Fm: 0-0
Distance: 5f/6f: 0-0 7f-8f: 1-9 9f-13f: 6-25 14f+: 0-1
Track : LH: 1-10 RH: 0-1 Tight: 1-5 Gall: 0-6
Aids: Bl: 1-11 Vi: 0-0 Tstrap: 0-0 Ckp: 0-0
Best Rating: 101 11/09 Ling 1m2f stand

Very useful; ex-South African; effective at 1m2f-1m4f; acts on fast ground and on Polytrack; has worn blinkers and a tongue tie.

Bound For Stardom

65 2

2-y-o b f Royal Applause-Liberty Bound (Primo Dominie)
W S Kittow Boswell,Maitland-Jones,Williams & Urquhart

Placings:0 (5379)
2009: 5^0G,

	Starts	1st	2nd	3rd	Win & Pl
Career Total (Turf)	1	0	0	0	

Going (Turf): Sf: 0-0 GS: 0-0 Gd: 0-1 GF: 0-0 Fm: 0-0
Distance: 5f/6f: 0-1 7f-8f: 0-0 9f-13f: 0-0 14f+: 0-0
Track : LH: 0-1 RH: 0-0 Tight: 0-0 Gall: 0-1
Aids: Bl: 0-0 Vi: 0-0 Tstrap: 0-0 Ckp: 0-0
Best Rating: 2 8/09 Bath 5f161y good

Boundless Applause

96(95) (45)54

3-y-o b f Royal Applause-Liberty Bound (Primo Dominie)
I A Wood M I Forbes

Placings:00-030431050 (7774)
2009: 5^0F, 6^3G, 6^0G, 6^4GF, 5^3G, 6^1GF, 5^0SD, 6^5SD, 6^0SD,

	Starts	1st	2nd	3rd	Win & Pl
Career Total (Turf)	8	1	0	2	2682
Career Total (AW)	3	0	0	0	0

54	9/09	Yarm	6f3y	(0-60)H	G-F	£2007

Total win prize-money £2008

Going (Turf): Sf: 0-0 GS: 0-0 Gd: 0-3 **GF: 1-4** Fm: 0-1
Distance: 5f/6f: 0-9 **7f-8f: 1-2** 9f-13f: 0-0 14f+: 0-0
Track : LH: 0-5 RH: 0-0 Tight: 0-3 Gall: 0-2
Aids: Bl: 0-0 Vi: 0-0 Tstrap: 0-1 Ckp: 0-1
Best Rating: 54 9/09 Yarm 6f3y gd-fm

Moderate sprinter; acts on fast ground.

Boundless Prospect (USA)

102(112) (74)71

10-y-o b g Boundary (USA)-Cape (USA) (Mr Prospector (USA))
P D Evans Diamond Racing Ltd

Placings:0/01012035/005500/**00**0023160**00**/**556**0133226 143**200**/6554150000**146**/**44**603**0**3415134**0445**/**563**015141 440**213**-**312120321** (7779)
2009: 8^3SS, 12^1SD, 11^2SD, 11^1SD, 10^2GS, 12^0S, 12^3SD, 11^2SD, 12^1SD,

	Starts	1st	2nd	3rd	Win & Pl
Career Total (Turf)	59	10	5	7	74119
Career Total (AW)	38	6	4	5	19168

72	12/09	Sthl	1m4f	(0-70)H	STD	£2729
62	3/09	Sthl	1m3f		STD	£2047
52	1/09	Wolv	1m4f50y		STD	£2047
74	12/08	Sthl	1m	(0-65)H	STD	£2047
67	6/08	Leic	1m1f218y		GD	£2331
67	4/08	Donc	1m		G-S	£2729
67	3/08	Sthl	1m		STD	£1774
81	10/07	Yarm	1m3y		SFT	£2072
81	9/07	Rdcr	1m		G-S	£4728
77	11/06	Sthl	1m	(0-70)H	STD	£3238
89	6/06	Yarm	1m3y	(0-80)H	GD	£6232
86	9/05	Yarm	1m3y	(0-85)H	G-F	£7864
81	7/05	NmkJ	1m	(0-75)H	G-F	£4206
82	7/04	Newb	7f	D(0-80)H	GD	£6032
90	6/02	Leic	7f9y	D(0-80)H	GD	£7800
79	4/02	Nott	6f15y	D	GD	£3883

Total win prize-money £61766

Going (Turf): Sf: 1-6 GS: 2-9 **Gd: 5-21** GF: 2-20 Fm: 0-3
Distance: 5f/6f: 0-2 **7f-8f: 9-61** 9f-13f: 7-34 14f+: 0-0
Track : **LH: 6-44** RH: 1-23 **Tight: 1-22** Gall: 0-6
Aids: Bl: 0-1 Vi: 0-1 Tstrap: 0-2 Ckp: 0-2
Best Rating: 95 8/02 NmkJ 7f gd-fm

Modest; stays 1m4f, acts on most ground and on sand; usually held up.

Bountiful Bay

68(107) (63)51

4-y-o b f Bahamian Bounty-My Preference (Reference Point)
Matthew Salaman (M Salaman 27/7) J H Widdows

Placings:0000**5**220-020050 (7835)
2009: 6^0GF, 6^2SD, 5^0SD, 5^0SD, 6^5SD, 6^0SD,

	Starts	1st	2nd	3rd	Win & Pl
Career Total (Turf)	5	0	0	0	
Career Total (AW)	9	0	3	0	1612

Going (Turf): Sf: 0-1 GS: 0-1 Gd: 0-1 GF: 0-2 Fm: 0-0
Distance: 5f/6f: 0-11 7f-8f: 0-1 9f-13f: 0-2 14f+: 0-0
Track : LH: 0-6 RH: 0-6 Tight: 0-5 Gall: 0-2
Aids: Bl: 0-0 Vi: 0-0 Tstrap: 0-0 Ckp: 0-0
Best Rating: 63 11/08 Kemp 5f stand

Moderate; effective at 5f; acts on Polytrack; has worn a tongue tie.

Bounty Box

109 100

3-y-o b f Bahamian Bounty-Bible Box (IRE) (Bin Ajwaad (IRE))
C F Wall John E Sims

Placings:341-31126 (6814)
2009: 5^3G, 6^1G, 6^1GF, 6^2GF, 6^6G,

	Starts	1st	2nd	3rd	Win & Pl
Career Total (Turf)	8	3	1	2	42855

95	8/09	NmkJ	6f	(0-105)H	G-F	£24924
89	7/09	NmkJ	6f	(0-95)H	GD	£9346
82	10/08	Leic	5f218y		G-S	£2590

Total win prize-money £36861

Going (Turf): Sf: 0-0 **GS: 1-1 Gd: 1-4 GF: 1-3** Fm: 0-0
Distance: **5f/6f: 3-7** 7f-8f: 0-1 9f-13f: 0-0 14f+: 0-0
Track : LH: 0-0 RH: 0-0 Tight: 0-0 Gall: 0-1
Aids: Bl: 0-0 Vi: 0-0 Tstrap: 0-0 Ckp: 0-0
Best Rating: 100 10/09 NmkR 6f gd-fm

Useful; effective over 6f; acts on fast and easy ground.

Bounty Reef

91(76) (33)56

3-y-o b f Bahamian Bounty-Shaieef (IRE) (Shareef Dancer (USA))
P D Evans Mrs I M Folkes

Placings:50002140-00560040 (6369)
2009: 9^0GF, 8^0GF, 7^5GF, 10^6GF, 10^0G, 7^0GF, 7^4GS, 10^0GF,

	Starts	1st	2nd	3rd	Win & Pl
Career Total (Turf)	14	1	1	0	3503
Career Total (AW)	2	0	0	0	

56	9/08	Rdcr	1m	(0-65)	G-S	£2266

Total win prize-money £2267

Going (Turf): Sf: 0-3 **GS: 1-2** Gd: 0-1 GF: 0-8 Fm: 0-0
Distance: 5f/6f: 0-2 **7f-8f: 1-9** 9f-13f: 0-5 14f+: 0-0
Track : LH: 0-6 RH: 0-3 Tight: 0-3 Gall: 0-1
Aids: Bl: 0-0 Vi: 0-2 Tstrap: 0-0 Ckp: 0-0
Best Rating: 56 9/08 Rdcr 1m gd-sft

Moderate; stays 1m and acts on easy ground; has worn a visor.

Bourbon Highball (IRE)

(85) (25)61

4-y-o b g Catcher In The Rye (IRE)-Be Exciting (IRE) (Be My Guest (USA))
P C Haslam Middleham Park Racing XXXIV

Placings:05300/360-0 (0107)
2009: 12^0SD,

	Starts	1st	2nd	3rd	Win & Pl
Career Total (Turf)	7	0	0	2	1262
Career Total (AW)	2	0	0	0	

Going (Turf): Sf: 0-2 GS: 0-2 Gd: 0-2 GF: 0-1 Fm: 0-0
Distance: 5f/6f: 0-3 7f-8f: 0-3 9f-13f: 0-3 14f+: 0-0
Track : LH: 0-4 RH: 0-2 Tight: 0-3 Gall: 0-0
Aids: Bl: 0-0 Vi: 0-0 Tstrap: 0-1 Ckp: 0-1
Best Rating: 61 5/08 Haml 1m65y gd-sft

Bourn Fair

(90) (53)31

3-y-o ch f Systematic-Astelia (Sabrehill (USA))
P J McBride The Bourn Partnership

Placings:000-30000 (7802)
2009: 9^3SF, 9^0SD, 12^0SD, 12^0SD, 8^0SD,

	Starts	1st	2nd	3rd	Win & Pl
Career Total (Turf)	1	0	0	0	
Career Total (AW)	7	0	0	1	302

Going (Turf): Sf: 0-0 GS: 0-0 Gd: 0-1 GF: 0-0 Fm: 0-0
Distance: 5f/6f: 0-0 7f-8f: 0-2 9f-13f: 0-6 14f+: 0-0
Track : LH: 0-7 RH: 0-0 Tight: 0-4 Gall: 0-2
Aids: Bl: 0-0 Vi: 0-0 Tstrap: 0-0 Ckp: 0-0
Best Rating: 53 11/08 GrLe 1m stand

Modest; stays 1m1f; handles Polytrack.

Bourne

102(105) (78)72

3-y-o gr g Linamix (FR)-L'Affaire Monique (Machiavellian (USA))
L M Cumani Aston House Stud

Placings:4044 (6613)
2009: 8^4GF, 10^0GF, 10^4G, 12^4SD,

	Starts	1st	2nd	3rd	Win & Pl
Career Total (Turf)	3	0	0	0	601
Career Total (AW)	1	0	0	0	351

Going (Turf): Sf: 0-0 GS: 0-0 Gd: 0-1 GF: 0-2 Fm: 0-0
Distance: 5f/6f: 0-0 7f-8f: 0-1 9f-13f: 0-3 14f+: 0-0
Track : LH: 0-1 RH: 0-2 Tight: 0-0 Gall: 0-0
Aids: Bl: 0-0 Vi: 0-0 Tstrap: 0-0 Ckp: 0-0
Best Rating: 78 10/09 Kemp 1m4f stand

Fair; stays 1m4f; acts on Polytrack.

Bourse (IRE)

99(103) (68)71

4-y-o b g Dubai Destination (USA)-Quarter Note (USA) (Danehill (USA))

A G Foster A G Foster

Placings:00/6401300336461-**0465500045506** **(5947)**

2009: 9^{0}SD, 8^{4}SD, 8^{6}GF, 8^{5}F, 9^{5}G, 10^{0}GS, 8^{0}GF, 9^{0}G, 8^{4}GS, 9^{5}G, 10^{5}GF, 12^{0}S, 12^{6}G,

	Starts	1st	2nd	3rd	Win & Pl
Career Total (Turf)	**26**	**2**	**0**	**3**	**9281**
Career Total (AW)	**2**	**0**	**0**	**0**	**0**

71	11/08	Muss	1m1f	(0-80)H	SFT	£5180
65	5/08	Muss	1m	(0-60)H	G-F	£2266

Total win prize-money £7448

Going (Turf): **Sf: 1-6** GS: 0-3 Gd: 0-8 **GF: 1-7** Fm: 0-2
Distance: 5f/6f: 0-2 7f-8f: 1-10 9f-13f: 1-16 14f+: 0-0
Track : LH: 0-9 **RH: 2-16 Tight: 2-18** Gall: 0-3
Aids: Bl: 0-3 Vi: 0-0 Tstrap: 0-4 Ckp: 0-4
Best Rating: **71** 11/08 Muss 1m1f soft

Modest; stays 1m1f and acts on most ground; has worn blinkers.

Bouvardia

105 101

3-y-o b f Oasis Dream-Arabesque (Zafonic (USA))

H R A Cecil K Abdulla

Placings:2210-2112 **(5069)**

2009: 5^{2}G, 6^{1}F, 6^{1}GF, 6^{2}GF,

	Starts	1st	2nd	3rd	Win & Pl
Career Total (Turf)	**8**	**3**	**4**	**0**	**55916**

101	5/09	NmkR	6f	(0-105)H	G-F	£24924
97	5/09	Nott	6f15y	(0-95)H	FRM	£9714
80	9/08	Yarm	6f3y		GD	£5046

Total win prize-money £39684

Going (Turf): Sf: 0-2 GS: 0-0 **Gd: 1-3 GF: 1-2 Fm: 1-1**
Distance: 5f/6f: 1-4 **7f-8f: 2-4** 9f-13f: 0-0 14f+: 0-0
Track : LH: 0-2 RH: 0-0 Tight: 0-0 Gall: 0-0
Aids: Bl: 0-0 Vi: 0-0 Tstrap: 0-0 Ckp: 0-0
Best Rating: **101** 5/09 NmkR 6f gd-fm

Very useful; effective over 5f-7f; acts on any ground.

Bow Beaver (USA)

93 79

2-y-o b c Vindication (USA)-Miss Carolina (USA) (Unbridled (USA))

J Howard Johnson W M G Black & J Howard Johnson

Placings:120 **(6134)**

2009: 5^{1}GF, 7^{2}GF, 6^{0}G,

	Starts	1st	2nd	3rd	Win & Pl
Career Total (Turf)	**3**	**1**	**1**	**0**	**4587**

79	6/09	Carl	5f	G-F	£3238

Total win prize-money £3238

Going (Turf): Sf: 0-0 GS: 0-0 Gd: 0-1 **GF: 1-2** Fm: 0-0
Distance: **5f/6f: 1-1** 7f-8f: 0-2 9f-13f: 0-0 14f+: 0-0
Track : LH: 0-0 **RH: 1-1** Tight: 0-0 **Gall: 1-1**
Aids: Bl: 0-0 Vi: 0-0 Tstrap: 0-0 Ckp: 0-0
Best Rating: **79** 8/09 Newc 7f gd-fm

Fair juvenile; probably stays 7f.

Bow To No One (IRE)

101(103) (89)69

3-y-o b f Refuse To Bend (IRE)-Deadly Buzz (IRE) (Darshaan)

A P Jarvis Geoffrey Bishop

Placings:543044111 **(7178)**

2009: 10^{5}GF, 8^{4}SD, 9^{3}GF, 10^{0}G, 8^{4}GF, 11^{4}G, 12^{1}GF, 12^{1}SD, 16^{1}SD,

	Starts	1st	2nd	3rd	Win & Pl
Career Total (Turf)	**6**	**1**	**0**	**1**	**4829**
Career Total (AW)	**3**	**2**	**0**	**0**	**7679**

89	10/09	Kemp	2m	(0-85)H	STD	£4727
82	10/09	Kemp	1m4f	(0-75)H	STD	£2590
69	10/09	Pont	1m4f8y	(0-70)H	G-F	£3885

Total win prize-money £11203

Going (Turf): Sf: 0-0 GS: 0-0 Gd: 0-2 **GF: 1-4** Fm: 0-0
Distance: 5f/6f: 0-0 7f-8f: 0-1 **9f-13f: 2-7** 14f+: 1-1
Track : LH: 1-3 **RH: 2-5** Tight: 0-1 Gall: 0-2
Aids: Bl: 0-0 Vi: 0-0 Tstrap: 0-0 Ckp: 0-0
Best Rating: **89** 10/09 Kemp 2m stand

Fair; stays 1m4f; acts on fast ground; goes on Polytrack.

Bowder Stone (IRE)

99 86

4-y-o b g Rock Of Gibraltar (IRE)-Ghita (IRE) (Zilzal (USA))

E J Alston Mr & Mrs G Middlebrook

Placings:0/32353213036-00 **(1826)**

2009: 10^{0}G, 12^{0}GF,

	Starts	1st	2nd	3rd	Win & Pl
Career Total (Turf)	**14**	**1**	**2**	**5**	**12929**

86	8/08	Ches	1m2f75y	(0-75)H	GD	£4435

Total win prize-money £4436

Going (Turf): Sf: 0-2 GS: 0-4 **Gd: 1-5** GF: 0-3 Fm: 0-0
Distance: 5f/6f: 0-1 7f-8f: 0-3 **9f-13f: 1-10** 14f+: 0-0
Track : **LH: 1-8** RH: 0-3 **Tight: 1-6** Gall: 0-3
Aids: Bl: 0-0 Vi: 0-0 Tstrap: 0-0 Ckp: 0-0
Best Rating: **86** 8/08 Ches 1m2f75y good

Fair; effective over 1m-1m2f; acts on good and soft ground.

Bowdler's Magic

89(97) (73)44

2-y-o b c Hernando (FR)-Slew The Moon (ARG) (Kitwood (USA))

M Johnston Paul Dean

Placings:021 **(7491)**

2009: 8^{0}GS, 9^{2}SD, 8^{1}SD,

	Starts	1st	2nd	3rd	Win & Pl
Career Total (Turf)	**1**	**0**	**0**	**0**	
Career Total (AW)	**2**	**1**	**1**	**0**	**4394**

73	11/09	Wolv	1m141y	STD	£3238

Total win prize-money £3238

Going (Turf): **Sf: 0-0 GS: 0-1 Gd: 0-0 GF: 0-0 Fm: 0-0**
Distance: 5f/6f: 0-0 7f-8f: 0-1 **9f-13f: 1-2** 14f+: 0-0
Track : **LH: 1-2** RH: 0-1 **Tight: 1-3** Gall: 0-0
Aids: Bl: 0-0 Vi: 0-0 Tstrap: 0-0 Ckp: 0-0
Best Rating: **73** 11/09 Wolv 1m141y stand

Fair; stays 1m1f; acts on Polytrack; type to improve further.

Bowmaker

(101) (79)

2-y-o b g Dubawi (IRE)-Viola Da Braccio (IRE) (Vettori (IRE))

M Johnston Sheikh Hamdan Bin Mohammed Al Maktoum

Placings:1 **(7087)**

2009: 6^{1}SD,

	Starts	1st	2nd	3rd	Win & Pl
Career Total (Turf)	**0**	**0**	**0**	**0**	
Career Total (AW)	**1**	**1**	**0**	**0**	**3412**

79	10/09	Sthl	6f	STD	£3412

Total win prize-money £3412

Going (Turf): **Sf: 0-0 GS: 0-0 Gd: 0-0 GF: 0-0 Fm: 0-0**
Distance: **5f/6f: 1-1** 7f-8f: 0-0 9f-13f: 0-0 14f+: 0-0
Track : **LH: 1-1** RH: 0-0 Tight: 0-0 Gall: 0-0
Aids: Bl: 0-0 Vi: 0-0 Tstrap: 0-0 Ckp: 0-0
Best Rating: **79** 10/09 Sthl 6f stand

Easy winner on debut; effective over 6f; acts on Fibresand.

Bowsers Beau

87(99) (65)52

3-y-o br g Sakhee (USA)-Shawahid (USA) (A.P. Indy (USA))

M P Tregoning Mrs Simon Aldridge

Placings:442 **(6941)**

2009: 9^{4}G, 8^{4}SD, 12^{2}SD,

	Starts	1st	2nd	3rd	Win & Pl
Career Total (Turf)	**1**	**0**	**0**	**0**	**289**
Career Total (AW)	**2**	**0**	**1**	**0**	**771**

Going (Turf): **Sf: 0-0 GS: 0-0 Gd: 0-1 GF: 0-0 Fm: 0-0**
Distance: 5f/6f: 0-0 7f-8f: 0-1 9f-13f: 0-2 14f+: 0-0
Track : LH: 0-0 RH: 0-3 Tight: 0-1 Gall: 0-0
Aids: Bl: 0-0 Vi: 0-0 Tstrap: 0-0 Ckp: 0-0
Best Rating: **65** 10/09 Kemp 1m4f stand

Promise in maidens on Polytrack and good ground; stays at least 1m.

Box Office

88 86

3-y-o b c Storming Home-Dream Ticket (USA) (Danzig (USA))

M Johnston Sheikh Hamdan Bin Mohammed Al Maktoum

Placings:231-6 **(1559)**

2009: 8^{6}GF,

	Starts	1st	2nd	3rd	Win & Pl
Career Total (Turf)	**4**	**1**	**1**	**1**	**6447**

86	10/08	Leic	7f9y	GD	£4857

Total win prize-money £4857

Going (Turf): Sf: 0-2 GS: 0-0 **Gd: 1-1** GF: 0-1 Fm: 0-0
Distance: 5f/6f: 0-1 **7f-8f: 1-2** 9f-13f: 0-1 14f+: 0-0
Track : LH: 0-0 RH: 0-0 Tight: 0-0 Gall: 0-0
Aids: Bl: 0-0 Vi: 0-0 Tstrap: 0-0 Ckp: 0-0
Best Rating: **86** 10/08 Leic 7f9y good

Useful; effective over 7f; acts on good and soft ground.

Boy Blue

106(81) (51)87

4-y-o b c Observatory (USA)-Rowan Flower (IRE) (Ashkalani (IRE))

P Salmon Wandahome

Placings:521/046100-5340340000 **(7287)**

2009: 8^{5}GF, 8^{3}GF, 8^{4}GS, 7^{0}GF, 7^{3}S, 8^{4}GS, 8^{0}S, 8^{0}SD, 7^{0}S, 7^{0}S,

	Starts	1st	2nd	3rd	Win & Pl
Career Total (Turf)	18	2	1	2	15184
Career Total (AW)	1	0	0	0	

86 7/08 Ayr 1m (0-85)H GD £4857
85 9/07 Ayr 7f50y SFT £5181
Total win prize-money £10039

Going (Turf): **Sf: 1-7** GS: 0-4 **Gd: 1-2** GF: 0-5 Fm: 0-0
Distance: 5f/6f: 0-0 **7f-8f: 2-16** 9f-13f: 0-3 14f+: 0-0
Track : **LH: 2-14** RH: 0-0 Tight: 0-4 Gall: 0-2
Aids: Bl: 0-0 Vi: 0-0 Tstrap: 0-0 Ckp: 0-0
Best Rating: 87 6/09 Newc 7f soft

Useful; stays 1m; acts on most ground.

Boy Dancer (IRE)

91(99) (46)65
6-y-o ch g Danehill Dancer (IRE)-Mary Gabry (IRE) (Kris)
J J Quinn A Turton & S Brown

Placings:000/0535102050/**5036**50020/**06**001463130-00000002 **(7499)**
2009: 9^{0}GF, 7^{0}F, 9^{0}G, 8^{0}GF, 12^{0}S, 9^{0}GF, 11^{0}G, 8^{2}SD,

	Starts	1st	2nd	3rd	Win & Pl
Career Total (Turf)	34	3	2	3	10581
Career Total (AW)	7	0	1	1	844

65 7/08 Rdcr 1m2f (0-70)H G-F £2590
60 6/08 Carl 7f200y (0-65)H GD £2047
66 6/06 Carl 5f193y (0-60)H G-F £2730
Total win prize-money £7367

Going (Turf): Sf: 0-4 GS: 0-6 Gd: 1-8 **GF: 2-15** Fm: 0-1
Distance: 5f/6f: 1-7 7f-8f: 1-21 9f-13f: 1-13 14f+: 0-0
Track : LH: 1-22 **RH: 2-14 Tight: 1-11** Gall: 0-1
Aids: Bl: 0-0 Vi: 0-0 Tstrap: 0-4 Ckp: 0-4
Best Rating: 67 8/06 Carl 5f193y good

Moderate; type that needs things to drop right; stays 1m2f; acts on fast ground; has worn cheekpieces.

Boy Racer (IRE)

52(98) (67)67
4-y-o br g Singspiel (IRE)-Gombay Girl (USA) (Woodman (USA))
C J Teague Tony Duffy & Michael Marsh

Placings:3500-00 **(7118)**
2009: 7^{0}GF, 12^{0}GS,

	Starts	1st	2nd	3rd	Win & Pl
Career Total (Turf)	5	0	0	0	0
Career Total (AW)	1	0	0	1	385

Going (Turf): **Sf: 0-0 GS: 0-1 Gd: 0-2 GF: 0-2 Fm: 0-0**
Distance: 5f/6f: 0-0 7f-8f: 0-1 9f-13f: 0-5 14f+: 0-0
Track : LH: 0-4 RH: 0-1 Tight: 0-4 Gall: 0-0
Aids: Bl: 0-0 Vi: 0-0 Tstrap: 0-0 Ckp: 0-0
Best Rating: 67 4/08 Yarm 1m3f101y gd-fm

Boy The Bell

(92) (68)
2-y-o b g Choisir (AUS)-Bella Beguine (Komaite (USA))
J A Osborne D J P Turner

Placings:032 **(7708)**
2009: 7^{0}SD, 5^{3}SD, 6^{2}SD,

	Starts	1st	2nd	3rd	Win & Pl
Career Total (Turf)	0	0	0	0	
Career Total (AW)	3	0	1	1	1008

Going (Turf): **Sf: 0-0 GS: 0-0 Gd: 0-0 GF: 0-0 Fm: 0-0**
Distance: 5f/6f: 0-2 7f-8f: 0-1 9f-13f: 0-0 14f+: 0-0
Track : LH: 0-3 RH: 0-0 Tight: 0-2 Gall: 0-0
Aids: Bl: 0-0 Vi: 0-0 Tstrap: 0-0 Ckp: 0-0
Best Rating: 68 12/09 Sthl 6f stand

Modest; stays 6f; acts on Polytrack and Fibresand.

Boycott (IRE)

85(90) (62)61
2-y-o b g Refuse To Bend (IRE)-Withorwithoutyou (IRE) (Danehill (USA))
J H M Gosden H R H Princess Haya Of Jordan

Placings:000043 **(6609)**
2009: 7^{0}GF, 7^{0}G, 7^{0}GF, 7^{0}GS, 8^{4}SD, 7^{3}SD,

	Starts	1st	2nd	3rd	Win & Pl
Career Total (Turf)	4	0	0	0	
Career Total (AW)	2	0	0	1	302

Going (Turf): **Sf: 0-0 GS: 0-1 Gd: 0-1 GF: 0-2 Fm: 0-0**
Distance: 5f/6f: 0-0 7f-8f: 0-6 9f-13f: 0-0 14f+: 0-0
Track : LH: 0-2 RH: 0-2 Tight: 0-2 Gall: 0-0
Aids: Bl: 0-4 Vi: 0-0 Tstrap: 0-0 Ckp: 0-0
Best Rating: 62 9/09 Kemp 1m stand

Modest; stays 1m; acts on Polytrack; has worn blinkers.

Boz

103(110) (99)97
5-y-o gr h Grand Lodge (USA)-Dali's Grey (Linamix (FR))
M Gasparini (L M Cumani 19/8) Francesca Turri

Placings:000003**11111**/**3**100**1**0**50**1-340040
2009: 12^{3}GF, 14^{4}GF, 12^{0}GF, 12^{0}GF, 14^{4}G, 14^{0}G,

	Starts	1st	2nd	3rd	Win & Pl
Career Total (Turf)	14	1	0	3	15780
Career Total (AW)	13	7	0	1	28109

99 10/08 Kemp 1m4f (0-90)H STD £7477
90 7/08 Donc 1m4f (0-80)H GD £5180
90 5/08 GrLe 1m6f (0-80)H STD £4533
85 11/07 Wolv 1m5f194y (0-85)H STD £4549
84 10/07 Wolv 1m4f50y (0-75)H STD £3238
79 10/07 Wolv 1m4f50y (0-70)H STD £2968
70 9/07 Wolv 1m4f50y (0-60)H STD £2388
67 9/07 Kemp 1m2f (0-50)H STD £2047
Total win prize-money £32385

Going (Turf): Sf: 0-0 GS: 0-1 **Gd: 1-7** GF: 0-6 Fm: 0-0
Distance: 5f/6f: 0-0 7f-8f: 0-2 **9f-13f: 6-18** 14f+: 2-7
Track : **LH: 6-16** RH: 2-10 **Tight: 4-8** Gall: 2-10
Aids: Bl: 0-4 **Vi: 1-3** Tstrap: 0-0 Ckp: 0-0
Best Rating: 99 10/08 Kemp 1m4f stand

Useful; effective from 1m4f-1m6f; acts on good ground and on Polytrack; has worn a visor/blinkers.

Brad's Luck (IRE)

99(95) (55)62
3-y-o ch g Lucky Story (USA)-Seymour (IRE) (Eagle Eyed (USA))
M Blanshard C McKenna

Placings:006-440000**0002** **(6859)**
2009: 10^{4}HY, 10^{4}GF, 9^{0}GF, 10^{0}GS, 11^{0}GS, 12^{0}SD, 9^{0}SF, 16^{0}SS, 16^{2}SD,

	Starts	1st	2nd	3rd	Win & Pl
Career Total (Turf)	8	0	0	0	553
Career Total (AW)	4	0	1	0	705

Going (Turf): **Sf: 0-1 GS: 0-3 Gd: 0-1 GF: 0-3 Fm: 0-0**
Distance: 5f/6f: 0-0 7f-8f: 0-2 9f-13f: 0-8 14f+: 0-2
Track : LH: 0-9 RH: 0-1 Tight: 0-7 Gall: 0-1
Aids: Bl: 0-0 Vi: 0-0 Tstrap: 0-0 Ckp: 0-0
Best Rating: 62 6/09 Ches 1m2f75y gd-fm

Modest sort; stays 2m; acts on sand and fast turf.

Braddock (IRE)

102(100) (73)70
6-y-o b g Pivotal-Sedna (FR) (Bering)
S Donohoe Mrs Samantha Donohoe

Placings:11/**1650**/0000015-6300000**3**26 **(7053)**
2009: 6^{6}YS, 7^{3}Y, 7^{0}HY, 6^{0}HY, 7^{0}Y, 7^{0}SH, 7^{0}S, 6^{3}S, 6^{2}SD, 6^{6}SD,

	Starts	1st	2nd	3rd	Win & Pl
Career Total (Turf)	19	4	0	2	17939
Career Total (AW)	5	0	1	0	771

68 10/08 Tipp 7f100y (45-60)H HVY £4318
85 5/07 Newc 7f (0-75)H G-S £3886
73 4/06 Nott 1m54y (0-65)H SFT £2730
60 3/06 Sthl 7f HVY £3886
Total win prize-money £14821

Going (Turf): **Sf: 3-11** GS: 1-2 Gd: 0-1 GF: 0-0 Fm: 0-0
Distance: 5f/6f: 0-7 **7f-8f: 3-15** 9f-13f: 1-2 14f+: 0-0
Track : **LH: 3-9** RH: 0-6 **Tight: 1-3** Gall: 0-0
Aids: Bl: 0-1 Vi: 0-0 Tstrap: 1-8 Ckp: 1-8
Best Rating: 85 5/07 Newc 7f gd-sft

Modest; effective over 6f-1m; acts on Polytrack and on heavy ground; has worn cheekpieces, blinkers and a tongue-tie.

Bradford (IRE)

96(77) (47)73
2-y-o b c Pyrus (USA)-Lypharden (IRE) (Lyphard's Special (USA))
K R Burke M Nelmes-Crocker

Placings:4246 **(4152)**
2009: 6^{4}G, 6^{2}G, 7^{4}SD, 7^{6}G,

	Starts	1st	2nd	3rd	Win & Pl
Career Total (Turf)	3	0	1	0	1336
Career Total (AW)	1	0	0	0	289

Going (Turf): **Sf: 0-0 GS: 0-0 Gd: 0-3 GF: 0-0 Fm: 0-0**
Distance: 5f/6f. 0-2 7f-8f: 0-2 9f-13f: 0-0 14f+: 0-0
Track : LH: 0-1 RH: 0-0 Tight: 0-1 Gall: 0-0
Aids: Bl: 0-0 Vi: 0-1 Tstrap: 0-0 Ckp: 0-0
Best Rating: 73 6/09 Newc 6f good

Fair; stays 6f; ,acts on good ground.

Brads House (IRE)

76 37
7-y-o b g Rossini (USA)-Gold Stamp (Golden Act (USA))
J G M O'Shea K W Bell & Son Ltd

Placings:0/415316443/00 **(6021)**
2009: 12^{0}GF, 17^{0}GF,

	Starts	1st	2nd	3rd	Win & Pl
Career Total (Turf)	12	2	0	2	16882

90 6/05 Gdwd 1m4f (0-85)H GD £6909
78 4/05 Haml 1m3f16y G-S £3367
Total win prize-money £10277

Going (Turf): Sf: 0-1 **GS: 1-5 Gd: 1-3** GF: 0-2 Fm: 0-1
Distance: 5f/6f: 0-0 7f-8f: 0-1 **9f-13f: 2-8** 14f+: 0-3
Track : LH: 0-8 **RH: 2-4 Tight: 2-4** Gall: 0-3

Aids: Bl: 0-0 Vi: 0-0 Tstrap: 0-0 Ckp: 0-0
Best Rating: **92** 9/05 Hayd 1m6f gd-sft

Useful performer; a winner in 2005 at Hamilton and Goodwood; stays 14 furlongs but shapes as though he will get further; acts on most ground.

Brae Hill (IRE)

108(96) (74)**97**
3-y-o b g Fath (USA)-Auriga (Belmez (USA))
M L W Bell Thurloe Partners

Placings:2103230-01002 (6278)
2009: 6^{0}GF, 7^{1}GF, 7^{0}GS, 7^{0}SD, 7^{2}GF,

	Starts	1st	2nd	3rd	Win & Pl
Career Total (Turf)	11	2	3	2	47812
Career Total (AW)	1	0	0	0	

97 6/09 Ches 7f2y (0-90)H G-F £8831
87 5/08 Leic 5f2y G-F £2590
Total win prize-money £11421

Going (Turf): Sf: 0-1 GS: 0-2 Gd: 0-1 **GF: 2-7** Fm: 0-0
Distance: 5f/6f: 1-7 7f-8f: 1-5 9f-13f: 0-0 14f+: 0-0
Track : **LH: 1-3** RH: 0-1 **Tight: 1-3** Gall: 0-1
Aids: Bl: 0-0 Vi: 0-0 Tstrap: 0-0 Ckp: 0-0
Best Rating: **97** 9/09 Ches 7f2y gd-fm

Very useful; effective at 6f-7f; acts on fast ground but handles soft.

Braggadocio

(15)
2-y-o br g Fraam-Brangane (IRE) (Anita's Prince)
P Winkworth P Winkworth

Placings:0 (3744)
2009: 6^{0}SD,

	Starts	1st	2nd	3rd	Win & Pl
Career Total (Turf)	0	0	0	0	
Career Total (AW)	1	0	0	0	

Going (Turf): Sf: 0-0 GS: 0-0 Gd: 0-0 GF: 0-0 Fm: 0-0
Distance: 5f/6f: 0-1 7f-8f: 0-0 9f-13f: 0-0 14f+: 0-0
Track : LH: 0-1 RH: 0-0 Tight: 0-1 Gall: 0-0
Aids: Bl: 0-0 Vi: 0-0 Tstrap: 0-0 Ckp: 0-0

Brahms And Mist (FR)

(85) (8)
9-y-o b g River Mist (USA)-Strabit (Stradavinsky)
D J S Ffrench Davis Mrs Meregan Norwood

Placings:0-0 (7367)
2009: 12^{0}SD,

	Starts	1st	2nd	3rd	Win & Pl
Career Total (Turf)	0	0	0	0	
Career Total (AW)	2	0	0	0	

Going (Turf): Sf: 0-0 GS: 0-0 Gd: 0-0 GF: 0-0 Fm: 0-0
Distance: 5f/6f: 0-0 7f-8f: 0-0 9f-13f: 0-2 14f+: 0-0
Track : LH: 0-2 RH: 0-0 Tight: 0-2 Gall: 0-0
Aids: Bl: 0-0 Vi: 0-0 Tstrap: 0-0 Ckp: 0-0
Best Rating: **8** 11/08 Ling 1m4f stand

Braille

93 **71**
4-y-o b g Bahamian Bounty-Branston Gem (So Factual (USA))
T D Walford N Maher A Quirke C Backhouse

Placings:00401-0000 (4620)
2009: 5^{0}GF, 5^{0}G, 5^{0}GF, 5^{0}G,

	Starts	1st	2nd	3rd	Win & Pl
Career Total (Turf)	9	1	0	0	3155

71 7/08 Rdcr 5f (0-70)H GD £2914
Total win prize-money £2914

Going (Turf): Sf: 0-0 GS: 0-0 **Gd: 1-5** GF: 0-4 Fm: 0-0
Distance: **5f/6f: 1-9** 7f-8f: 0-0 9f-13f: 0-0 14f+: 0-0
Track : LH: 0-2 RH: 0-0 Tight: 0-1 Gall: 0-0
Aids: Bl: 0-0 Vi: 0-0 Tstrap: 0-0 Ckp: 0-0
Best Rating: **71** 7/08 Rdcr 5f good

Modest sprinter; blind in one eye; best over 5f; acts on good ground.

Bramalea

103(105) (73)**72**
4-y-o b f Whitmore's Conn (USA)-Aster (IRE) (Danehill (USA))
B W Duke P J Cave

Placings:00553106U100-330232420403314 (6498)
2009: 9^{3}SD, 10^{3}GF, 10^{0}SD, 10^{2}F, 10^{3}G, 11^{2}GS, 10^{4}F, 11^{2}S, 10^{0}G, 11^{4}GS, 10^{0}SD, 12^{3}GS, 11^{3}GS, 12^{1}SD, 12^{4}SF,

	Starts	1st	2nd	3rd	Win & Pl
Career Total (Turf)	14	0	3	5	5095
Career Total (AW)	13	3	0	1	7100

69 9/09 Wolv 1m4f50y (0-60)H STD £2388
73 10/08 Wolv 1m141y (0-65)H STD £2047
62 8/08 GrLe 1m (0-65)H STD £1942
Total win prize-money £6378

Going (Turf): Sf: 0-1 GS: 0-6 Gd: 0-2 GF: 0-3 Fm: 0-2
Distance: 5f/6f: 0-0 7f-8f: 1-3 **9f-13f: 2-24** 14f+: 0-0
Track : **LH: 3-24** RH: 0-3 **Tight: 2-19** Gall: 1-4
Aids: Bl: 0-0 Vi: 0-0 Tstrap: 0-1 Ckp: 0-1
Best Rating: **73** 10/08 Wolv 1m141y stand

Modest; stays 1m2f; acts on good and easy ground and on Polytrack; likes to race prominently.

Brambleberry

81(95) (86)**62**
2-y-o b f Cape Cross (IRE)-Miss Satamixa (FR) (Linamix (FR))
Tom Dascombe Grant Thornton Racing Club

Placings:105155 (6179)
2009: 5^{1}SD, 5^{0}G, 6^{5}G, 5^{1}SD, 5^{5}SD, 5^{5}GF,

	Starts	1st	2nd	3rd	Win & Pl
Career Total (Turf)	3	0	0	0	0
Career Total (AW)	3	2	0	0	7447

86 8/09 Ling 5f STD £3885
79 6/09 Ling 5f STD £3561
Total win prize-money £7448

Going (Turf): Sf: 0-0 GS: 0-0 Gd: 0-2 GF: 0-1 Fm: 0-0
Distance: **5f/6f: 2-5** 7f-8f: 0-1 9f-13f: 0-0 14f+: 0-0
Track : **LH: 2-4** RH: 0-0 **Tight: 2-4** Gall: 0-0
Aids: Bl: 0-0 Vi: 0-0 Tstrap: 0-0 Ckp: 0-0
Best Rating: **86** 8/09 Ling 5f stand

Useful; effective over 5f; acts on Polytrack.

Bramshaw (USA)

(91) (72)
2-y-o gr/ro c Langfuhr (CAN)-Milagra (USA) (Maria's Mon (USA))
Mrs A J Perrett Paul & Clare Cuttill, Brenda Karn-Smith

Placings:1 (7537)
2009: 7^{1}SD,

	Starts	1st	2nd	3rd	Win & Pl
Career Total (Turf)	0	0	0	0	
Career Total (AW)	1	1	0	0	3238

72 11/09 Kemp 7f STD £3238
Total win prize-money £3238

Going (Turf): Sf: 0-0 GS: 0-0 Gd: 0-0 GF: 0-0 Fm: 0-0
Distance: 5f/6f: 0-0 **7f-8f: 1-1** 9f-13f: 0-0 14f+: 0-0
Track : LH: 0-0 **RH: 1-1** Tight: 0-0 Gall: 0-0
Aids: Bl: 0-0 Vi: 0-0 Tstrap: 0-0 Ckp: 0-0
Best Rating: **72** 11/09 Kemp 7f stand

Created good impression on debut; stays 7f but should be suited by 1m; acts on Polytrack; potentially useful.

Bramshill Lady (IRE)

85 **66**
2-y-o gr/ro f Verglas (IRE)-Jinx Johnson (IRE) (Desert King (IRE))
Pat Eddery Devenish, Eddery, Hancock and Mathews

Placings:4500 (7055)
2009: 5^{4}G, 5^{5}GF, 7^{0}GF, 7^{0}GF,

	Starts	1st	2nd	3rd	Win & Pl
Career Total (Turf)	4	0	0	0	289

Going (Turf): Sf: 0-0 GS: 0-0 Gd: 0-1 GF: 0-3 Fm: 0-0
Distance: 5f/6f: 0-2 7f-8f: 0-2 9f-13f: 0-0 14f+: 0-0
Track : LH: 0-0 RH: 0-0 Tight: 0-0 Gall: 0-2
Aids: Bl: 0-0 Vi: 0-0 Tstrap: 0-0 Ckp: 0-0
Best Rating: **66** 6/09 Wind 5f10y gd-fm

Brananx (USA)

86 **48**
2-y-o b c Red Ransom (USA)-Shady Reflection (USA) (Sultry Song (USA))
K A Ryan J Hanson

Placings:0 (6990)
2009: 7^{0}G,

	Starts	1st	2nd	3rd	Win & Pl
Career Total (Turf)	1	0	0	0	

Going (Turf): Sf: 0-0 GS: 0-0 Gd: 0-1 GF: 0-0 Fm: 0-0
Distance: 5f/6f: 0-0 7f-8f: 0-1 9f-13f: 0-0 14f+: 0-0
Track : LH: 0-0 RH: 0-0 Tight: 0-0 Gall: 0-0
Aids: Bl: 0-0 Vi: 0-0 Tstrap: 0-0 Ckp: 0-0
Best Rating: **48** 10/09 Donc 7f good

Branderburgo (IRE)

93 **89**
2-y-o b c High Chaparral (IRE)-Farhad (Red Ransom (USA))
L Riccardi (M Botti 7/11) Tenuta Dorna Di Montaltuzzo SRL

Placings:6353034
2009: 6^{6}GF, 7^{3}G, 7^{5}G, 8^{3}GF, 8^{0}GF, 9^{3}S, 8^{4}G,

	Starts	1st	2nd	3rd	Win & Pl
Career Total (Turf)	7	0	0	3	11410

Going (Turf): Sf: 0-1 GS: 0-0 Gd: 0-3 GF: 0-3 Fm: 0-0
Distance: 5f/6f: 0-1 7f-8f: 0-3 9f-13f: 0-3 14f+: 0-0

Track : LH: 0-1 RH: 0-2 Tight: 0-1 Gall: 0-0
Aids: Bl: 0-0 Vi: 0-0 Tstrap: 0-2 Ckp: 0-2
Best Rating: 89 12/09 Sira 1m good

Fair; stays 7f and acts on good ground.

Brandy Butter

88(91) (54)**54**
3-y-o ch g Domedriver (IRE)-Brand (Shareef Dancer (USA))
D E Pipe (A M Balding 21/10) M C Pipe

Placings:06054 (6935)
2009: 10^{0}SD, 10^{6}SD, 12^{0}SD, 12^{5}SD, 17^{4}G,

	Starts	1st	2nd	3rd	Win & Pl
Career Total (Turf)	1	0	0	0	192
Career Total (AW)	4	0	0	0	0

Going (Turf): Sf: 0-0 GS: 0-0 Gd: 0-1 GF: 0-0 Fm: 0-0
Distance: 5f/6f: 0-0 7f-8f: 0-0 9f-13f: 0-4 14f+: 0-1
Track : LH: 0-4 RH: 0-1 Tight: 0-4 Gall: 0-0
Aids: Bl: 0-0 Vi: 0-3 Tstrap: 0-0 Ckp: 0-0
Best Rating: 54 10/09 Bath 2m1f34y good

Brandywell Boy (IRE)

103(105) (79)**74**
6-y-o b g Danetime (IRE)-Alexander Eliott (IRE) (Night Shift (USA))
D J S Ffrench Davis P B Gallagher

Placings:42431022/000036620640256/000003002003202 1226/503024463225140444-0313000042013640452215246010 (7832)
2009: 6^{0}SD, 6^{3}SD, 5^{1}SD, 5^{3}SD, 6^{0}SD, 5^{0}G, 6^{0}SD, 5^{0}F, 5^{4}G, 5^{2}GF, 5^{0}G, 5^{1}GF, 5^{3}G, 5^{6}GF, 5^{4}G, 5^{0}GF, 5^{4}G, 5^{5}GF, 5^{2}S, 5^{2}GF, 5^{1}G, 5^{5}GF, 5^{2}SD, 5^{4}SD,

	Starts	1st	2nd	3rd	Win & Pl
Career Total (Turf)	49	3	10	6	44351
Career Total (AW)	38	4	7	3	22328

79	11/09	Ling	6f	(0-85)H	STD	£4727
70	9/09	Gdwd	5f	(0-70)H	GD	£3238
67	6/09	Newb	5f34y	(0-70)H	G-F	£3238
77	2/09	Ling	5f		STD	£2047
77	11/08	Kemp	6f		STD	£2047
75	11/07	Kemp	6f	(0-65)H	STD	£2047
78	7/05	Thsk	5f		GD	£6825

Total win prize-money £24170

Going (Turf): Sf: 0-3 GS: 0-0 **Gd: 2-16** GF: 1-27 Fm: 0-3
Distance: 5f/6f: 7-84 7f-8f: 0-3 9f-13f: 0-0 14f+: 0-0
Track : LH: 2-30 RH: 2-15 **Tight: 2-21** Gall: 0-12
Aids: Bl: 0-3 Vi: 0-1 Tstrap: 0-2 Ckp: 0-2
Best Rating: 89 11/05 Ling 6f stand

Fair; effective over 5f-6f; acts on good and faster ground and on Polytrack; has worn headgear.

Brannagh (USA)

89(99) (76)**74**
2-y-o ch c Hennessy (USA)-Green Room (USA) (Theatrical)
J Noseda Ms Gillian Khosla And Caroline Green

Placings:33 (7130)
2009: 6^{3}GF, 7^{3}SD,

	Starts	1st	2nd	3rd	Win & Pl
Career Total (Turf)	1	0	0	1	770
Career Total (AW)	1	0	0	1	655

Going (Turf): Sf: 0-0 GS: 0-0 Gd: 0-0 GF: 0-1 Fm: 0-0
Distance: 5f/6f: 0-1 7f-8f: 0-1 9f-13f: 0-0 14f+: 0-0
Track : LH: 0-1 RH: 0-0 Tight: 0-1 Gall: 0-0
Aids: Bl: 0-0 Vi: 0-0 Tstrap: 0-0 Ckp: 0-0
Best Rating: 76 10/09 Ling 7f stand

Fair; effective over 7f; acts on Polytrack.

Brasingaman Eric

85(82) (51)**43**
2-y-o b c Bollin Eric-Serene Pearl (IRE) (Night Shift (USA))
Mrs G S Rees R Morgan

Placings:446 (3716)
2009: 5^{4}G, 6^{4}G, 7^{6}SD,

	Starts	1st	2nd	3rd	Win & Pl
Career Total (Turf)	2	0	0	0	481
Career Total (AW)	1	0	0	0	0

Going (Turf): Sf: 0-0 GS: 0-0 Gd: 0-2 GF: 0-0 Fm: 0-0
Distance: 5f/6f: 0-2 7f-8f: 0-1 9f-13f: 0-0 14f+: 0-0
Track : LH: 0-1 RH: 0-0 Tight: 0-1 Gall: 0-0
Aids: Bl: 0-0 Vi: 0-0 Tstrap: 0-0 Ckp: 0-0
Best Rating: 51 7/09 Wolv 7f32y stand

Brasingaman Hifive

100(102) (74)**84**
4-y-o b f High Estate-Our Miss Florence (Carlitin)
Mrs G S Rees R Morgan

Placings:16/6051200-0353060 (7125)
2009: 8^{0}GF, 8^{3}HY, 8^{5}G, 7^{3}G, 8^{0}GF, 8^{6}SD, 8^{0}G,

	Starts	1st	2nd	3rd	Win & Pl
Career Total (Turf)	15	2	1	2	12255
Career Total (AW)	1	0	0	0	0

79	8/08	Hayd	1m30y	(0-80)H	G-S	£5504
76	9/07	Hayd	7f30y		G-F	£2590

Total win prize-money £8096

Going (Turf): Sf: 0-1 **GS: 1-2** Gd: 0-6 **GF: 1-6** Fm: 0-0
Distance: 5f/6f: 0-0 7f-8f: 1-8 9f-13f: 1-8 14f+: 0-0
Track : **LH: 2-12** RH: 0-0 Tight: 0-3 Gall: 0-0
Aids: Bl: 0-0 Vi: 0-0 Tstrap: 0-0 Ckp: 0-0
Best Rating: 84 9/08 Rdcr 1m gd-sft

Fair; stays 1m; acts on fast and easy ground.

Brassini

102(93) (68)**96**
4-y-o gr g Bertolini (USA)-Silver Spell (Aragon)
B R Millman The Links Partnership

Placings:433116300/5410332130420-003510 (3335)
2009: 7^{0}SD, 6^{0}G, 7^{3}GF, 7^{5}G, 7^{1}G, 7^{0}GF,

	Starts	1st	2nd	3rd	Win & Pl
Career Total (Turf)	26	5	2	7	46422
Career Total (AW)	2	0	0	0	0

91	6/09	Sand	7f16y	(0-100)H	GD	£11215
93	7/08	Sand	7f16y	(0-90)H	G-F	£7771
87	5/08	Ling	6f	(0-80)H	G-F	£6231
76	7/07	Chep	5f16y		SFT	£4533
76	6/07	Ches	5f16y		GD	£5181

Total win prize-money £34934

Going (Turf): Sf: 1-2 GS: 0-3 **Gd: 2-7 GF: 2-13** Fm: 0-1
Distance: 5f/6f: 3-15 7f-8f: 2-12 9f-13f: 0-1 14f+: 0-0
Track : LH: 1-3 **RH: 2-8 Tight: 1-3** Gall: 0-1
Aids: Bl: 0-0 Vi: 0-0 Tstrap: 0-0 Ckp: 0-0
Best Rating: 96 10/08 Gdwd 6f gd-sft

Useful; effective at 6f-7f and acted on most ground; (DEAD).

Bravalto

(92) (52)**59**
3-y-o b c Falbrav (IRE)-Bunty Boo (Noalto)
B Smart Pinnacle Falbrav Partnership

Placings:06-6 (7730)
2009: 7^{6}SD,

	Starts	1st	2nd	3rd	Win & Pl
Career Total (Turf)	2	0	0	0	0
Career Total (AW)	1	0	0	0	0

Going (Turf): Sf: 0-1 GS: 0-1 Gd: 0-0 GF: 0-0 Fm: 0-0
Distance: 5f/6f: 0-2 7f-8f: 0-1 9f-13f: 0-0 14f+: 0-0
Track : LH: 0-1 RH: 0-0 Tight: 0-1 Gall: 0-0
Aids: Bl: 0-0 Vi: 0-0 Tstrap: 0-0 Ckp: 0-0
Best Rating: 59 11/08 Donc 6f soft

Some ability over 6f on soft ground.

Brave Ambition (IRE)

66(73) (30)**22**
2-y-o b g Spartacus (IRE)-I Want You Now (IRE) (Nicolotte)
R C Guest (Garry Moss 28/7) Brooklands Racing

Placings:0000 (7419)
2009: 5^{0}SD, 6^{0}GF, 7^{0}GF, 7^{0}SD,

	Starts	1st	2nd	3rd	Win & Pl
Career Total (Turf)	2	0	0	0	
Career Total (AW)	2	0	0	0	

Going (Turf): Sf: 0-0 GS: 0-0 Gd: 0-0 GF: 0-2 Fm: 0-0
Distance: 5f/6f: 0-2 7f-8f: 0-2 9f-13f: 0-0 14f+: 0-0
Track : LH: 0-1 RH: 0-1 Tight: 0-0 Gall: 0-0
Aids: Bl: 0-0 Vi: 0-0 Tstrap: 0-0 Ckp: 0-0
Best Rating: 30 6/09 Sthl 5f stand

Brave Beat

80(83) (38)**43**
3-y-o b g Beat Hollow-Be Brave (FR) (Green Forest (USA))
H J L Dunlop Lord Maclaurin

Placings:0000 (3593)
2009: 12^{0}SD, 12^{0}G, 10^{0}G, 14^{0}GF,

	Starts	1st	2nd	3rd	Win & Pl
Career Total (Turf)	3	0	0	0	
Career Total (AW)	1	0	0	0	

Going (Turf): Sf: 0-0 GS: 0-0 Gd: 0-2 GF: 0-1 Fm: 0-0
Distance: 5f/6f: 0-0 7f-8f: 0-0 9f-13f: 0-3 14f+: 0-1
Track : LH: 0-2 RH: 0-2 Tight: 0-0 Gall: 0-0
Aids: Bl: 0-1 Vi: 0-0 Tstrap: 0-0 Ckp: 0-0
Best Rating: 43 5/09 Chep 1m4f23y good

Brave Bugsy (IRE)

103(96) (60)**66**
6-y-o b g Mujadil (USA)-Advancing (IRE) (Ela-Mana-Mou)
A M Balding West Mercia Fork Trucks Ltd

Placings:443016440-5261 (3997)
2009: 17^{5}GS, 17^{2}F, 16^{6}SD, 17^{1}G,

	Starts	1st	2nd	3rd	Win & Pl
Career Total (Turf)	8	2	1	0	5694
Career Total (AW)	5	0	0	1	536

61	7/09	Bath	2m1f34y	(0-65)H	GD	£2914
66	5/08	Bath	2m1f34y	(0-65)H	G-F	£1846

Total win prize-money £4760

Going (Turf): Sf: 0-1 GS: 0-1 **Gd: 1-4 GF: 1-1** Fm: 0-1
Distance: 5f/6f: 0-0 7f-8f: 0-0 9f-13f: 0-3 **14f+: 2-10**
Track : **LH: 2-11** RH: 0-2 **Tight: 2-10** Gall: 0-0
Aids: Bl: 0-0 **Vi: 1-3** Tstrap: 0-0 Ckp: 0-0
Best Rating: 66 5/08 Bath 2m1f34y gd-fm

Moderate; stays 2m1f; acts on fast ground; has worn a visor.

Brave Dealer

94 **63**

3-y-o ch g Falbrav (IRE)-Sharp Terms (Kris)
R Charlton Thurloe Thoroughbreds XXII

Placings:060 (3703)
2009: 10^{0}S, 10^{6}G, 10^{0}GS,

	Starts	1st	2nd	3rd	Win & Pl
Career Total (Turf)	3	0	0	0	0

Going (Turf): Sf: 0-1 GS: 0-1 Gd: 0-1 GF: 0-0 Fm: 0-0
Distance: 5f/6f: 0-0 7f-8f: 0-0 9f-13f: 0-3 14f+: 0-0
Track : LH: 0-2 RH: 0-1 Tight: 0-0 Gall: 0-1
Aids: Bl: 0-0 Vi: 0-0 Tstrap: 0-0 Ckp: 0-0
Best Rating: 63 6/09 Sand 1m2f7y good

Brave Decision

(94) (70)

2-y-o gr g With Approval (CAN)-Brave Vanessa (USA) (Private Account (USA))
A J McCabe Khalifa Dasmal

Placings:3 (7859)
2009: 7^{3}SD,

	Starts	1st	2nd	3rd	Win & Pl
Career Total (Turf)	0	0	0	0	
Career Total (AW)	1	0	0	1	482

Going (Turf): Sf: 0-0 GS: 0-0 Gd: 0-0 GF: 0-0 Fm: 0-0
Distance: 5f/6f: 0-0 7f-8f: 0-1 9f-13f: 0-0 14f+: 0-0
Track : LH: 0-1 RH: 0-0 Tight: 0-1 Gall: 0-0
Aids: Bl: 0-0 Vi: 0-0 Tstrap: 0-0 Ckp: 0-0
Best Rating: 70 12/09 Wolv 7f32y stand

Modest; stays 7f; acts on Polytrack.

Brave Enough (USA)

(92) (65)

2-y-o b c Yes It's True (USA)-Courageous (USA) (Kingmambo (USA))
M A Magnusson Eastwind Racing Ltd and Martha Trussell

Placings:05 (7859)
2009: 7^{0}SD, 7^{5}SD,

	Starts	1st	2nd	3rd	Win & Pl
Career Total (Turf)	0	0	0	0	
Career Total (AW)	2	0	0	0	0

Going (Turf): Sf: 0-0 GS: 0-0 Gd: 0-0 GF: 0-0 Fm: 0-0
Distance: 5f/6f: 0-0 7f-8f: 0-2 9f-13f: 0-0 14f+: 0-0
Track : LH: 0-2 RH: 0-0 Tight: 0-2 Gall: 0-0
Aids: Bl: 0-0 Vi: 0-0 Tstrap: 0-0 Ckp: 0-0
Best Rating: 65 12/09 Wolv 7f32y stand

Modest; stays 7f; acts on Polytrack.

Brave Ghurka

89(89) (59)**67**

2-y-o b g Bahamian Bounty-Wondrous Maid (GER) (Mondrian I (GER))
S Kirk Ivory, Lee & Pearson

Placings:06550 (7824)
2009: 6^{0}S, 6^{6}GS, 7^{5}SD, 7^{5}SD, 7^{0}SD,

	Starts	1st	2nd	3rd	Win & Pl
Career Total (Turf)	2	0	0	0	0
Career Total (AW)	3	0	0	0	0

Going (Turf): Sf: 0-1 GS: 0-1 Gd: 0-0 GF: 0-0 Fm: 0-0
Distance: 5f/6f: 0-1 7f-8f: 0-4 9f-13f: 0-0 14f+: 0-0
Track : LH: 0-2 RH: 0-1 Tight: 0-2 Gall: 0-1
Aids: Bl: 0-0 Vi: 0-0 Tstrap: 0-0 Ckp: 0-0
Best Rating: 67 10/09 Wind 6f gd-sft

Brave Knave (IRE)

56 **43**

4-y-o b c Averti (IRE)-Recall (IRE) (Revoque (IRE))
B De Haan Mrs D Vaughan

Placings:006-6 (3432)
2009: 11^{6}GF,

	Starts	1st	2nd	3rd	Win & Pl
Career Total (Turf)	4	0	0	0	0

Going (Turf): Sf: 0-1 GS: 0-1 Gd: 0-1 GF: 0-1 Fm: 0-0
Distance: 5f/6f: 0-0 7f-8f: 0-0 9f-13f: 0-4 14f+: 0-0
Track : LH: 0-1 RH: 0-2 Tight: 0-2 Gall: 0-0
Aids: Bl: 0-0 Vi: 0-0 Tstrap: 0-0 Ckp: 0-0
Best Rating: 43 7/08 Leic 1m1f218y good

Brave Mave

102(106) (83)**74**

4-y-o gr m Daylami (IRE)-Baalbek (Barathea (IRE))
Jane Chapple-Hyam (W Jarvis 29/9) J W Munroe Construction Ltd

Placings:051/60020003210-05050 (7505)
2009: 12^{0}SD, 12^{5}GF, 11^{0}GF, 13^{5}SD, 12^{0}SD,

	Starts	1st	2nd	3rd	Win & Pl
Career Total (Turf)	11	1	1	1	5703
Career Total (AW)	8	1	1	0	3789

83	11/08	Sthl	1m4f	(0-70)H	STD	£2729
71	10/07	Leic	7f9y		SFT	£4210

Total win prize-money £6940

Going (Turf): Sf: 1-4 GS: 0-2 Gd: 0-0 GF: 0-5 Fm: 0-0
Distance: 5f/6f: 0-1 7f-8f: 1-2 9f-13f: 1-16 14f+: 0-0
Track : **LH: 1-9** RH: 0-6 Tight: 0-5 Gall: 0-2
Aids: Bl: 0-3 Vi: 0-0 Tstrap: 0-0 Ckp: 0-0
Best Rating: 83 11/08 Sthl 1m4f stand

Modest; stays 1m4f; acts on soft ground; goes on Fibresand.

Brave Optimist (IRE)

(71) (23)**36**

4-y-o b f Diktat-Maine Lobster (USA) (Woodman (USA))
Paul Green J H Davey

Placings:00-6 (0556)
2009: 8^{6}SD,

	Starts	1st	2nd	3rd	Win & Pl
Career Total (Turf)	1	0	0	0	
Career Total (AW)	2	0	0	0	0

Going (Turf): Sf: 0-0 GS: 0-1 Gd: 0-0 GF: 0-0 Fm: 0-0
Distance: 5f/6f: 0-0 7f-8f: 0-1 9f-13f: 0-2 14f+: 0-0
Track : LH: 0-3 RH: 0-0 Tight: 0-3 Gall: 0-0
Aids: Bl: 0-0 Vi: 0-0 Tstrap: 0-0 Ckp: 0-0
Best Rating: 36 9/08 Catt 7f gd-sft

Brave Prospector

111 **110**

4-y-o b c Oasis Dream-Simply Times (USA) (Dodge (USA))
P W Chapple-Hyam Saleh Al Homaizi & Imad Al Sagar

Placings:244/0041000-000103 (6661)
2009: 6^{0}GF, 6^{0}S, 5^{0}GF, 6^{1}GF, 6^{0}G, 6^{3}GS,

	Starts	1st	2nd	3rd	Win & Pl
Career Total (Turf)	16	2	1	1	89887

107	9/09	Donc	6f110y	(0-105)H	G-F	£12952
108	6/08	York	6f	(0-105)H	GD	£64760

Total win prize-money £77712

Going (Turf): Sf: 0-5 GS: 0-2 **Gd: 1-5 GF: 1-3** Fm: 0-1
Distance: 5f/6f: 1-11 7f-8f: 1-5 9f-13f: 0-0 14f+: 0-0
Track : LH: 0-1 RH: 0-0 Tight: 0-1 Gall: 0-1
Aids: Bl: 0-0 Vi: 0-0 Tstrap: 0-0 Ckp: 0-0
Best Rating: 110 10/09 Asct 6f gd-sft

Smart; effective at 6f-7f; acts on most ground on turf; has worn a tongue tie.

Braveheart Move (IRE)

103(95) (78)**98**

3-y-o b g Cape Cross (IRE)-Token Gesture (IRE) (Alzao (USA))
Sir Mark Prescott Moyglare Stud Farm Ltd

Placings:01-10101 (6138)
2009: 12^{1}GF, 12^{0}G, 12^{1}GF, 14^{0}GF, 13^{1}G,

	Starts	1st	2nd	3rd	Win & Pl
Career Total (Turf)	6	3	0	0	29977
Career Total (AW)	1	1	0	0	3071

98	9/09	Haml	1m5f9y	(0-95)H	GD	£10592
94	8/09	Pont	1m4f8y	(0-90)H	G-F	£9346
90	5/09	Ches	1m4f66y	(0-95)H	G-F	£10037
78	9/08	Wolv	7f32y		SF	£3070

Total win prize-money £33049

Going (Turf): Sf: 0-0 GS: 0-0 Gd: 1-3 **GF: 2-3** Fm: 0-0
Distance: 5f/6f: 0-0 7f-8f: 1-2 **9f-13f: 2-3** 14f+: 1-2
Track : **LH: 3-4** RH: 1-2 **Tight: 3-4** Gall: 0-1
Aids: Bl: 0-0 Vi: 0-0 Tstrap: 0-0 Ckp: 0-0
Best Rating: 98 9/09 Haml 1m5f9y good

Useful; stays 1m4f; acts on fast ground; goes on Polytrack.

Bravely (IRE)

102 81

5-y-o b g Rock Of Gibraltar (IRE)-Raghida (IRE) (Nordico (USA))

T D Easterby Habton Farms

Placings:05000/3001003-34220601040020 (7123)

2009: 7^{3}GF, 7^{4}F, 7^{2}GS, 7^{2}GF, 6^{0}G, 7^{6}GF, 7^{0}G, 5^{1}GS, 5^{0}G, 6^{4}GF, 5^{0}GF, 5^{0}GF, 5^{2}GF, 5^{0}G,

	Starts	1st	2nd	3rd	Win & Pl
Career Total (Turf)	26	2	3	3	17965

81 7/09 Newc 5f (0-85)H G-S £5046

78 6/08 Fair 7f G-Y £6605

Total win prize-money £11651

Going (Turf): Sf: 0-4 **GS: 1-3** Gd: 0-7 GF: 0-8 Fm: 0-1

Distance: 5f/6f: 1-12 7f-8f: 1-13 9f-13f: 0-1 14f+: 0-0

Track : LH: 0-8 **RH: 1-3** Tight: 0-3 Gall: 0-2

Aids: Bl: 0-0 Vi: 0-0 Tstrap: 0-0 Ckp: 0-0

Best Rating: 89 9/07 Curr 6f yield

Fair; ex-Irish; stays 7f and acts on most ground.

Bravely Fought (IRE)

105(92) (98)96

4-y-o b g Indian Ridge-Amazing Tale (Shareef Dancer (USA))

Sabrina J Harty Dolittle Syndicate

Placings:0/10250-0110650003 (7567a)

2009: 7^{0}GF, 10^{1}G, 10^{1}G, 9^{0}G, 10^{6}SD, 9^{5}GY, 8^{0}S, 8^{0}G, 10^{0}SD, 12^{3}SD,

	Starts	1st	2nd	3rd	Win & Pl
Career Total (Turf)	10	2	0	0	22646
Career Total (AW)	6	1	1	1	11902

95 7/09 Fair 1m2f (60-100)H GD £13588

90 6/09 Leop 1m2f (60-90)H GD £9056

82 2/08 Dund 1m STD £6351

Total win prize-money £28997

Going (Turf): Sf: 0-3 GS: 0-0 **Gd: 2-4** GF: 0-2 Fm: 0-0

Distance: 5f/6f: 0-0 7f-8f: 1-7 **9f-13f: 2-9** 14f+: 0-0

Track : LH: 1-7 RH: 1-6 Tight: 0-1 Gall: 0-1

Aids: **Bl: 1-4** Vi: 0-0 Tstrap: 0-0 Ckp: 0-0

Best Rating: 98 11/09 Dund 1m4f stand

Very useful; Irish trained; effective over 1m2f; acts on good ground.

Bravo Belle (IRE)

71

2-y-o b f Bertolini (USA)-Dazilyn Lady (USA) (Zilzal (USA))

T H Caldwell Thorn Cross

Placings:5 (7217)

2009: 5^{5}S,

	Starts	1st	2nd	3rd	Win & Pl
Career Total (Turf)	1	0	0	0	0

Going (Turf): Sf: 0-1 GS: 0-0 Gd: 0-0 GF: 0-0 Fm: 0-0

Distance: 5f/6f: 0-1 7f-8f: 0-0 9f-13f: 0-0 14f+: 0-0

Track : LH: 0-1 RH: 0-0 Tight: 0-1 Gall: 0-0

Aids: Bl: 0-0 Vi: 0-0 Tstrap: 0-0 Ckp: 0-0

Bravo Blue (IRE)

65 6

2-y-o b f Mark Of Esteem (IRE)-Fantazia (Zafonic (USA))

T H Caldwell Thorn Cross

Placings:060 (6991)

2009: 6^{0}GF, 7^{6}G, 7^{0}G,

	Starts	1st	2nd	3rd	Win & Pl
Career Total (Turf)	3	0	0	0	0

Going (Turf): Sf: 0-0 GS: 0-0 Gd: 0-2 GF: 0-1 Fm: 0-0

Distance: 5f/6f: 0-1 7f-8f: 0-2 9f-13f: 0-0 14f+: 0-0

Track : LH: 0-0 RH: 0-0 Tight: 0-0 Gall: 0-0

Aids: Bl: 0-0 Vi: 0-0 Tstrap: 0-0 Ckp: 0-0

Best Rating: 6 10/09 Donc 7f good

Bravo Bravo

26

2-y-o b g Sadler's Wells (USA)-Top Table (Shirley Heights)

Eve Johnson Houghton Derek And Jean Clee

Placings:0 (5831)

2009: 8^{0}GF,

	Starts	1st	2nd	3rd	Win & Pl
Career Total (Turf)	1	0	0	0	

Going (Turf): Sf: 0-0 GS: 0-0 Gd: 0-0 GF: 0-1 Fm: 0-0

Distance: 5f/6f: 0-0 7f-8f: 0-0 9f-13f: 0-1 14f+: 0-0

Track : LH: 0-0 RH: 0-1 Tight: 0-0 Gall: 0-0

Aids: Bl: 0-0 Vi: 0-0 Tstrap: 0-0 Ckp: 0-0

Bravo Echo

102(103) (91)94

3-y-o b c Oasis Dream-Bold Empress (USA) (Diesis)

M J Attwater (J H M Gosden 11/9) Canisbay Bloodstock

Placings:010-035135 (7827)

2009: 7^{0}GS, 7^{3}GF, 7^{5}GF, 8^{1}G, 8^{3}GF, 8^{5}SD,

	Starts	1st	2nd	3rd	Win & Pl
Career Total (Turf)	8	2	0	2	19245
Career Total (AW)	1	0	0	0	415

89 7/09 NmkJ 1m (0-100)H GD £12462

89 10/08 Leic 7f9y GD £4857

Total win prize-money £17319

Going (Turf): Sf: 0-1 GS: 0-1 **Gd: 2-2** GF: 0-4 Fm: 0-0

Distance: 5f/6f: 0-0 **7f-8f: 2-8** 9f-13f: 0-1 14f+: 0-0

Track : LH: 0-0 RH: 0-3 Tight: 0-0 Gall: 0-0

Aids: Bl: 0-0 Vi: 0-0 Tstrap: 0-0 Ckp: 0-0

Best Rating: 94 9/09 Sand 1m14y gd-fm

Useful; effective at 7f-1m; acts on good and fast ground.

Brazilian Brush (IRE)

82(109) (68)74

4-y-o ch g Captain Rio-Ejder (IRE) (Indian Ridge)

J M Bradley J M Bradley

Placings:344/0130000041-0006006006 (7680)

2009: 5^{0}SD, 6^{0}SD, 5^{0}SD, 5^{6}SD, 5^{0}G, 5^{0}GF, 6^{6}G, 5^{0}G, 6^{0}SD, 6^{6}SD,

	Starts	1st	2nd	3rd	Win & Pl
Career Total (Turf)	11	1	0	2	4490
Career Total (AW)	12	1	0	0	2735

68 10/08 GrLe 6f STD £2590

74 5/08 Gdwd 5f (0-70)H SFT £3238

Total win prize-money £5828

Going (Turf): Sf: 1-1 GS: 0-2 Gd: 0-5 GF: 0-3 Fm: 0-0

Distance: **5f/6f: 2-20** 7f-8f: 0-3 9f-13f: 0-0 14f+: 0-0

Track : **LH: 1-12** RH: 0-2 Tight: 0-6 **Gall: 1-6**

Aids: Bl: 0-0 Vi: 0-0 Tstrap: 0-1 Ckp: 0-1

Best Rating: 74 5/08 Gdwd 5f soft

Modest; stays 6f and acts on Polytrack; has worn a tongue tie.

Breach Of Peace (USA)

96(84) (54)67

3-y-o b f Royal Academy (USA)-Hasardeuse (USA) (Distant View (USA))

R Charlton K Abdulla

Placings:0-0665 (2567)

2009: 7^{0}SD, 8^{6}GF, 8^{6}GF, 9^{5}GF,

	Starts	1st	2nd	3rd	Win & Pl
Career Total (Turf)	4	0	0	0	0
Career Total (AW)	1	0	0	0	

Going (Turf): Sf: 0-0 GS: 0-0 Gd: 0-1 GF: 0-3 Fm: 0-0

Distance: 5f/6f: 0-0 7f-8f: 0-3 9f-13f: 0-2 14f+: 0-0

Track : LH: 0-0 RH: 0-3 Tight: 0-2 Gall: 0-0

Aids: Bl: 0-0 Vi: 0-0 Tstrap: 0-0 Ckp: 0-0

Best Rating: 67 5/09 NmkR 1m gd-fm

Breadstick

95(92) (67)71

3-y-o br f Diktat-Poilane (Kris)

H Morrison Penelope Bossom & Bloomsbury Stud

Placings:035-20646 (5628)

2009: 9^{2}G, 9^{0}GF, 8^{6}G, 8^{4}SD, 7^{6}GS,

	Starts	1st	2nd	3rd	Win & Pl
Career Total (Turf)	5	0	1	0	964
Career Total (AW)	3	0	0	1	770

Going (Turf): Sf: 0-0 GS: 0-1 Gd: 0-3 GF: 0-1 Fm: 0-0

Distance: 5f/6f: 0-0 7f-8f: 0-5 9f-13f: 0-3 14f+: 0-0

Track : LH: 0-3 RH: 0-2 Tight: 0-3 Gall: 0-2

Aids: Bl: 0-1 Vi: 0-0 Tstrap: 0-0 Ckp: 0-0

Best Rating: 71 5/09 Gdwd 1m1f192y good

Modest; stays 1m2f and acts on Polytrack and fast ground.

Breakevie (IRE)

89 50

3-y-o b f Mull Of Kintyre (USA)-Skehana (IRE) (Mukaddamah (USA))

R A Fahey Jonathan Gill

Placings:30-40 (2154)

2009: 6^{4}G, 7^{0}GF,

	Starts	1st	2nd	3rd	Win & Pl
Career Total (Turf)	4	0	0	1	578

Going (Turf): Sf: 0-1 GS: 0-0 Gd: 0-2 GF: 0-1 Fm: 0-0

Distance: 5f/6f: 0-3 7f-8f: 0-1 9f-13f: 0-0 14f+: 0-0

Track : LH: 0-0 RH: 0-1 Tight: 0-1 Gall: 0-0

Aids: Bl: 0-0 Vi: 0-0 Tstrap: 0-0 Ckp: 0-0

Best Rating: 50 10/08 Catt 5f good

Moderate; suited by 5f and good ground.

Breakheart (IRE)

99 74

2-y-o b g Sakhee (USA)-Exorcet (FR) (Selkirk (USA))

A M Balding J C Smith

Placings:02 (6930)
2009: 7^{0}G, 8^{2}G,

	Starts	1st	2nd	3rd	Win & Pl
Career Total (Turf)	2	0	1	0	674

Going (Turf): Sf: 0-0 GS: 0-0 Gd: 0-2 GF: 0-0 Fm: 0-0
Distance: 5f/6f: 0-0 7f-8f: 0-1 9f-13f: 0-1 14f+: 0-0
Track : LH: 0-1 RH: 0-0 Tight: 0-1 Gall: 0-0
Aids: Bl: 0-0 Vi: 0-0 Tstrap: 0-0 Ckp: 0-0
Best Rating: 74 10/09 Bath 1m5y good

Modest; effective over 1m; acts on good ground.

Breathless Kiss (USA)

100 71
2-y-o b f Roman Ruler (USA)-Crusading Miss Cox (USA) (Crusader Sword (USA))
K A Ryan Mrs Angie Bailey

Placings:16 (5521)
2009: 5^{1}S, 6^{6}G,

	Starts	1st	2nd	3rd	Win & Pl
Career Total (Turf)	2	1	0	0	4291

71 7/09 Donc 5f SFT £3885
Total win prize-money £3886

Going (Turf): Sf: 1-1 GS: 0-0 Gd: 0-1 GF: 0-0 Fm: 0-0
Distance: 5f/6f: 1-2 7f-8f: 0-0 9f-13f: 0-0 14f+: 0-0
Track : LH: 0-0 RH: 0-0 Tight: 0-0 Gall: 0-0
Aids: Bl: 0-0 Vi: 0-0 Tstrap: 0-0 Ckp: 0-0
Best Rating: 71 7/09 Donc 5f soft

Useful; efective over 5f; acts in soft ground.

Breeze Of The Air

87 55
2-y-o ch c Compton Place-Dixieanna (Night Shift (USA))
M R Channon Jaber Abdullah

Placings:665 (4194)
2009: 5^{6}F, 6^{6}G, 7^{5}GS,

	Starts	1st	2nd	3rd	Win & Pl
Career Total (Turf)	3	0	0	0	0

Going (Turf): Sf: 0-0 GS: 0-1 Gd: 0-1 GF: 0-0 Fm: 0-1
Distance: 5f/6f: 0-2 7f-8f: 0-1 9f-13f: 0-0 14f+: 0-0
Track : LH: 0-1 RH: 0-0 Tight: 0-0 Gall: 0-2
Aids: Bl: 0-0 Vi: 0-0 Tstrap: 0-0 Ckp: 0-0
Best Rating: 55 7/09 Leic 7f9y gd-sft

Brenda Duke

85(75) (17)43
2-y-o ch f Bachelor Duke (USA)-Fiina (Most Welcome)
J G Portman J G B Portman

Placings:00 (7120)
2009: 7^{0}SD, 8^{0}GF,

	Starts	1st	2nd	3rd	Win & Pl
Career Total (Turf)	1	0	0	0	
Career Total (AW)	1	0	0	0	

Going (Turf): Sf: 0-0 GS: 0-0 Gd: 0-0 GF: 0-1 Fm: 0-0
Distance: 5f/6f: 0-0 7f-8f: 0-1 9f-13f: 0-1 14f+: 0-0
Track : LH: 0-1 RH: 0-1 Tight: 0-0 Gall: 0-0
Aids: Bl: 0-0 Vi: 0-0 Tstrap: 0-0 Ckp: 0-0
Best Rating: 43 10/09 Nott 1m75y gd-fm

Brenin Taran

104(100) (87)93
3-y-o gr g Lujain (USA)-Silver Chime (Robellino (USA))
D M Simcock Mrs Ann Simcock

Placings:4215-106440220 (6240)
2009: 5^{1}F, 5^{0}GF, 5^{6}G, 5^{4}GF, 5^{4}GF, 6^{0}GF, 5^{2}SD, 5^{2}F, 6^{0}G,

	Starts	1st	2nd	3rd	Win & Pl
Career Total (Turf)	11	2	2	0	17216
Career Total (AW)	2	0	1	0	1407

90 4/09 Thsk 5f (0-90)H FRM £8159
81 5/08 Yarm 5f43y G-F £3218
Total win prize-money £11379

Going (Turf): Sf: 0-0 GS: 0-0 Gd: 0-4 GF: 1-5 Fm: 1-2
Distance: 5f/6f: 2-13 7f-8f: 0-0 9f-13f: 0-0 14f+: 0-0
Track : LH: 0-3 RH: 0-2 Tight: 0-1 Gall: 0-1
Aids: Bl: 0-0 Vi: 0-0 Tstrap: 0-3 Ckp: 0-3
Best Rating: 93 9/09 Bath 5f161y firm

Useful; effective at 5f; acts on a sound surface; has worn cheekpieces.

Brer Rabbit

89(99) (69)56
3-y-o b f Invincible Spirit (IRE)-Red Rabbit (Suave Dancer (USA))
Seamus Fahey (B W Hills 15/10) Michael Allen

Placings:0003-210060060 (7782)
2009: 8^{2}SD, 8^{1}SD, 10^{0}SD, 9^{0}SD, 9^{6}SD, 8^{0}G, 9^{0}SD, 8^{6}SF, 8^{0}SD,

	Starts	1st	2nd	3rd	Win & Pl
Career Total (Turf)	4	0	0	0	
Career Total (AW)	9	1	1	1	3070

69 3/09 Wolv 1m141y (0-65)H STD £2047
Total win prize-money £2047

Going (Turf): Sf: 0-0 GS: 0-1 Gd: 0-2 GF: 0-1 Fm: 0-0
Distance: 5f/6f: 0-3 7f-8f: 0-3 9f-13f: 1-7 14f+: 0-0
Track : LH: 1-7 RH: 0-3 Tight: 1-7 Gall: 0-2
Aids: Bl: 0-0 Vi: 0-0 Tstrap: 0-0 Ckp: 0-0
Best Rating: 69 3/09 Wolv 1m141y stand

Moderate; stays 1m and acts on Polytrack.

Brett Vale (IRE)

110(102) (91)91
3-y-o br g Sinndar (IRE)-Pinta (IRE) (Ahonoora)
P R Hedger (Sir Mark Prescott 19/9) P C F Racing Ltd

Placings:055011215610213 (7811)
2009: 5^{0}SD, 6^{5}SD, 6^{5}SD, 7^{0}SD, 10^{1}SD, 9^{1}G, 11^{2}S, 10^{1}G, 10^{5}G, 10^{6}SD, 12^{1}GF, 9^{0}SD, 12^{2}SD, 16^{1}SD, 12^{3}SD,

	Starts	1st	2nd	3rd	Win & Pl
Career Total (Turf)	5	3	1	0	14473
Career Total (AW)	10	2	1	1	8884

91 12/09 Kemp 2m (0-85)H STD £4727
80 9/09 NmkR 1m4f G-F £6476
91 8/09 Sand 1m2f7y (0-80)H GD £4857
78 6/09 Brig 1m1f209y (0-65)H GD £2523
76 6/09 Ling 1m2f (0-60)H STD £2047
Total win prize-money £20630

Going (Turf): Sf: 0-1 GS: 0-0 Gd: 2-3 GF: 1-1 Fm: 0-0
Distance: 5f/6f: 0-3 7f-8f: 0-1 9f-13f: 4-10 14f+: 1-1
Track : LH: 2-10 RH: 3-5 Tight: 1-8 Gall: 1-1
Aids: Bl: 0-0 Vi: 0-0 Tstrap: 0-0 Ckp: 0-0
Best Rating: 91 12/09 Kemp 2m stand

Useful; stays 2m; acts on Polytrack.

Briannsta (IRE)

95(102) (58)59
7-y-o b g Bluebird (USA)-Nacote (IRE) (Mtoto)
J E Long P Saxon

Placings:6521001/20131000040204000/0000113/4002050 06/000063000-640352406130000 (7774)
2009: 7^{6}SD, 7^{4}SD, 6^{0}SD, 6^{3}SD, 5^{5}GS, 6^{2}GF, 7^{4}GF, 6^{0}GF, 5^{6}GF, 5^{1}SD, 7^{3}SD, 5^{0}SD, 6^{0}SD, 6^{0}SD, 6^{0}SD,

	Starts	1st	2nd	3rd	Win & Pl
Career Total (Turf)	41	3	5	2	37778
Career Total (AW)	24	4	0	3	16484

57 10/09 Wolv 5f216y (0-52)H STD £2388
85 11/06 Wolv 5f216y (0-75)H STD £3562
82 10/06 Wolv 5f216y (0-75)H STD £3238
91 5/05 Haml 6f5y (0-85)H GD £9614
92 5/05 Ches 6f18y (0-90)H G-S £10496
78 11/04 Ling 7f STD £5476
77 8/04 Wwck 7f26y E G-S £4004
Total win prize-money £38780

Going (Turf): Sf: 0-4 GS: 2-9 Gd: 1-11 GF: 0-17 Fm: 0-0
Distance: 5f/6f: 3-42 7f-8f: 4-21 9f-13f: 0-2 14f+: 0-0
Track : LH: 6-25 RH: 0-10 Tight: 5-20 Gall: 0-3
Aids: Bl: 1-11 Vi: 0-1 Tstrap: 0-0 Ckp: 0-0
Best Rating: 94 9/05 Gdwd 6f gd-fm

Moderate; effective over 5f-7f; acts on most ground on turf; goes on Polytrack; has worn blinkers.

Briary Mac

93 68
2-y-o b f Royal Applause-Red May (IRE) (Persian Bold)
N Bycroft J A Swinburne

Placings:254 (7217)
2009: 6^{2}GF, 5^{5}S, 5^{4}S,

	Starts	1st	2nd	3rd	Win & Pl
Career Total (Turf)	3	0	1	0	1156

Going (Turf): Sf: 0-2 GS: 0-0 Gd: 0-0 GF: 0-1 Fm: 0-0
Distance: 5f/6f: 0-3 7f-8f: 0-0 9f-13f: 0-0 14f+: 0-0
Track : LH: 0-2 RH: 0-0 Tight: 0-2 Gall: 0-0
Aids: Bl: 0-0 Vi: 0-0 Tstrap: 0-0 Ckp: 0-0
Best Rating: 68 10/09 Rdcr 6f gd-fm

Brick Red

101(94) (78)84
2-y-o ch g Dubawi (IRE)-Duchcov (Caerleon (USA))
A M Balding Brick Racing

Placings:0162 (6693)
2009: 7^{0}GF, 6^{1}SD, 7^{6}GF, 7^{2}GS,

	Starts	1st	2nd	3rd	Win & Pl
Career Total (Turf)	3	0	1	0	1638
Career Total (AW)	1	1	0	0	

Going (Turf): Sf: 0-0 GS: 0-1 Gd: 0-0 GF: 0-2 Fm: 0-0
Distance: 5f/6f: 1-1 7f-8f: 0-3 9f-13f: 0-0 14f+: 0-0
Track : LH: 0-0 RH: 1-2 Tight: 0-0 Gall: 0-0
Aids: Bl: 0-0 Vi: 0-0 Tstrap: 0-0 Ckp: 0-0
Best Rating: 84 10/09 Gdwd 7f gd-sft

Bricks And Porter (IRE)

103(89) (65)67
9-y-o b g College Chapel-Camassina (IRE) (Taufan (USA))

T G McCourt Mrs Una Lynch

Placings:00001400/32304160/42206/2400032150/042546650400/000/**5**0310500**60**-030000050**000** (7343a)

2009: 7^{0}SH, 10^{3}HY, 10^{0}HY, 10^{0}GF, 10^{0}GF, 10^{0}G, 8^{0}S, 10^{5}GY, 9^{0}G, **12**^{0}SD, **12**^{0}SD, **12**^{0}SD,

	Starts	1st	2nd	3rd	Win & Pl
Career Total (Turf)	62	4	6	5	65825
Career Total (AW)	6	0	0	0	

66	5/08	Curr	1m2f	(60-90)H	FRM	£9573
92	10/05	Curr	1m	(60-100)H	GD	£13851
80	9/03	Gway	1m100y	(50-80)H	G-Y	£6944
76	9/02	Gway	7f	(0-85)H	HVY	£7975

Total win prize-money £38345

Going (Turf): **Sf: 1-14** GS: 0-0 **Gd: 1-13** GF: 0-12 **Fm: 1-2**
Distance: 5f/6f: 0-12 7f-8f: 2-30 9f-13f: 2-26 14f+: 0-0
Track : LH: 0-23 **RH: 2-27** Tight: 0-2 **Gall: 1-10**
Aids: **Bl: 3-37** Vi: 0-1 Tstrap: 0-4 Ckp: 0-4
Best Rating: **94** 4/06 Navn 1m gd-fm

Brideview

64 (58)**15**

3-y-o ch f Kyllachy-Dolce Piccata (Piccolo)
Edgar Byrne (P J Prendergast 24/4) Mrs M Murphy

Placings:360-000 (3176)

2009: 6^{0}SD, 5^{0}F, 5^{0}GF,

	Starts	1st	2nd	3rd	Win & Pl
Career Total (Turf)	3	0	0	0	
Career Total (AW)	3	0	0	1	653

Going (Turf): **Sf: 0-0 GS: 0-0 Gd: 0-0 GF: 0-1 Fm: 0-2**
Distance: 5f/6f: 0-6 7f-8f: 0-0 9f-13f: 0-0 14f+: 0-0
Track : LH: 0-5 RH: 0-0 Tight: 0-0 Gall: 0-1
Aids: Bl: 0-0 Vi: 0-0 Tstrap: 0-1 Ckp: 0-1
Best Rating: **58** 4/08 Dund 5f stand

Bridge Note (USA)

80(87) (44)**28**

3-y-o b f Stravinsky (USA)-Myrtle (Batshoof)
J Noseda Budget Stable

Placings:00 (1840)

2009: 6^{0}SD, 6^{0}GF,

	Starts	1st	2nd	3rd	Win & Pl
Career Total (Turf)	1	0	0	0	
Career Total (AW)	1	0	0	0	

Going (Turf): **Sf: 0-0 GS: 0-0 Gd: 0-0 GF: 0-1 Fm: 0-0**
Distance: 5f/6f: 0-1 7f-8f: 0-1 9f-13f: 0-0 14f+: 0-0
Track : LH: 0-1 RH: 0-0 Tight: 0-0 Gall: 0-0
Aids: Bl: 0-0 Vi: 0-0 Tstrap: 0-0 Ckp: 0-0
Best Rating: **44** 4/09 Sthl 6f stand

Bridge Of Fermoy (IRE)

(101) (76)**60**

4-y-o b g Danetime (IRE)-Banco Solo (Distant Relative)
D C O'Brien (Miss Gay Kelleway 23/2) C Attrell

Placings:6020**414/131141221**0**060-50650060** (6917)

2009: 7^{5}SD, **8**^{0}SD, 7^{6}SD, 8^{5}SD, **8**^{0}SD, **10**^{0}SD, **10**^{6}SD, **12**^{0}SD,

	Starts	1st	2nd	3rd	Win & Pl
Career Total (Turf)	5	0	1	0	1156
Career Total (AW)	23	6	2	1	14684

75	4/08	Wolv	7f32y		STD	£2047
74	3/08	Ling	1m2f		STD	£2047
74	3/08	Wolv	1m141y		STD	£2590
71	2/08	Kemp	1m		STD	£2047
71	1/08	Kemp	1m		STD	£2047
63	9/07	Kemp	1m	(0-65)	STD	£2047

Total win prize-money £12830

Going (Turf): **Sf: 0-2 GS: 0-0 Gd: 0-0 GF: 0-3 Fm: 0-0**
Distance: 5f/6f: 0-1 **7f-8f: 4-19** 9f-13f: 2-8 14f+: 0-0
Track : LH: 3-16 RH: 3-8 **Tight: 3-16** Gall: 0-0
Aids: **Bl: 3-12** Vi: 2-5 Tstrap: 0-3 Ckp: 0-3
Best Rating: **76** 12/08 Ling 1m stand

Fair; best at around 1m-1m2f; acts on Polytrack.

Bridge Of Gold (USA)

98(100) (78)**100**

3-y-o b c Giant's Causeway (USA)-Lady Doc (USA) (Doc's Leader (USA))
M A Magnusson Eastwind Racing Ltd and Martha Trussell

Placings:144 (3298)

2009: 8^{1}S, 8^{4}G, 8^{4}SD,

	Starts	1st	2nd	3rd	Win & Pl
Career Total (Turf)	2	1	0	0	7005
Career Total (AW)	1	0	0	0	577

90	4/09	Newb	1m	SFT	£4857

Total win prize-money £4857

Going (Turf): **Sf: 1-1** GS: 0-0 Gd: 0-1 GF: 0-0 Fm: 0-0
Distance: 5f/6f: 0-0 **7f-8f: 1-2** 9f-13f: 0-1 14f+: 0-0
Track : LH: 0-0 RH: 0-2 Tight: 0-0 Gall: 0-0
Aids: Bl: 0-0 Vi: 0-0 Tstrap: 0-0 Ckp: 0-0
Best Rating: **100** 5/09 Sand 1m14y good

Smart; stays 1m; acts on soft ground.

Bridge Valley

100 **78**

2-y-o ch g Avonbridge-Go Between (Daggers Drawn (USA))
R Hannon D J Deer

Placings:45321300 (7290)

2009: 6^{4}GS, 6^{5}GF, 7^{3}GF, 6^{2}S, 5^{1}G, 6^{3}GF, 7^{0}GS, 6^{0}S,

	Starts	1st	2nd	3rd	Win & Pl
Career Total (Turf)	8	1	1	2	4956

78	8/09	Sand	5f6y	GD	£3238

Total win prize-money £3238

Going (Turf): Sf: 0-2 GS: 0-2 **Gd: 1-1** GF: 0-3 Fm: 0-0
Distance: **5f/6f: 1-5** 7f-8f: 0-3 9f-13f: 0-0 14f+: 0-0
Track : LH: 0-2 RH: 0-0 Tight: 0-0 Gall: 0-4
Aids: Bl: 0-0 Vi: 0-0 Tstrap: 0-0 Ckp: 0-0
Best Rating: **78** 8/09 Sand 5f6y good

Fair; effective at 5-7f; effective on fast and soft ground.

Bridgewater Boys

107(109) (76)**72**

8-y-o b g Atraf-Dunloe (IRE) (Shaadi (USA))
T J Pitt (P D Evans 11/3) Two Up Two Down

Placings:405423025621**5/413112150**0**6304/00**206003602**0623/041310031**403**002/3300416424**22412**212/11143161**5121-**234612130**22**0**200600** (6097)

2009: **13**^{2}SD, **13**^{3}SD, **16**^{4}SD, **13**^{6}SD, **12**^{1}SD, **12**^{2}SD, **11**^{1}SD, 12^{3}SD, 12^{0}G, 12^{2}GF, 12^{2}F, **12**^{0}SD, 13^{2}G, 18^{0}G, 12^{0}GF, 13^{6}GF, 11^{0}SD, 13^{0}GF,

	Starts	1st	2nd	3rd	Win & Pl
Career Total (Turf)	44	6	10	3	44317
Career Total (AW)	61	14	10	10	45297

69	3/09	Sthl	1m3f		STD	£2047
71	2/09	Ling	1m4f		STD	£2047
69	12/08	Ling	1m2f		STD	£1978
67	12/08	Wolv	1m4f50y		STD	£2047
74	10/08	Ling	1m2f	(0-75)H	STD	£2729
62	6/08	Ling	1m4f		STD	£1774
72	3/08	Ling	1m4f	(0-70)H	STD	£2331
71	1/08	Kemp	1m2f	(0-65)H	STD	£2047
71	1/08	Ling	1m2f		STD	£1774
71	10/07	Brig	1m1f209y	(0-60)H	GD	£2047
57	8/07	Wind	1m3f135y		SFT	£3886
63	3/07	Sthl	1m3f		STD	£2184
70	5/06	Bevl	1m100y	(0-70)H	G-S	£4533
69	2/06	Wolv	1m141y	(0-70)H	STD	£3886
63	2/06	Wolv	1m141y	(0-58)H	STD	£2388
83	6/04	Ripn	6f	C(0-95)H	G-F	£8607
76	5/04	Hayd	6f	D(0-85)H	G-F	£6077
73	5/04	Sals	6f	E(0-75)H	GD	£3757
73	1/04	Wolv	7f	E(0-70)H	SS	£3255
64	11/03	Wolv	6f	F	STD	£2289

Total win prize-money £61692

Going (Turf): Sf: 1-5 GS: 1-6 **Gd: 2-13 GF: 2-16** Fm: 0-4
Distance: 5f/6f: 4-21 7f-8f: 1-18 **9f-13f: 15-59** 14f+: 0-7
Track : **LH: 14-72** RH: 2-14 **Tight: 12-52** Gall: 0-6
Aids: **Bl: 15-84** Vi: 0-2 Tstrap: 3-10 Ckp: 3-10
Best Rating: **83** 6/04 Ripn 6f gd-fm

Fair; effective at around 1m2f-1m4f; acts on most ground and on sand; has worn headgear.

Brief Candle

102(92) (77)**83**

3-y-o br f Diktat-Bright Hope (IRE) (Danehill (USA))
W R Swinburn Pendley Farm

Placings:3010-5050 (6243)

2009: 8^{5}GF, 9^{0}G, 8^{5}GF, 8^{0}G,

	Starts	1st	2nd	3rd	Win & Pl
Career Total (Turf)	7	1	0	0	4857
Career Total (AW)	1	0	0	1	722

82	8/08	Sand	7f16y	GD	£4857

Total win prize-money £4857

Going (Turf): Sf: 0-0 GS: 0-0 **Gd: 1-4** GF: 0-3 Fm: 0-0
Distance: 5f/6f: 0-0 **7f-8f: 1-6** 9f-13f: 0-2 14f+: 0-0
Track : LH: 0-0 **RH: 1-6** Tight: 0-1 Gall: 0-1
Aids: Bl: 0-0 Vi: 0-0 Tstrap: 0-0 Ckp: 0-0
Best Rating: **83** 8/09 Wind 1m67y gd-fm

Useful; suited by 7f and fast ground; has worn a tongue tie.

Brief Encounter (IRE)

107(103) (105)**103**

3-y-o br g Pyrus (USA)-Just One Look (Barathea (IRE))
A M Balding Thurloe Thoroughbreds XXII

Placings:3**2**1-6101**62**50 (6480)

2009: 7^{6}GS, 7^{1}GF, 8^{0}GF, 8^{1}GF, 8^{6}S, **8**^{2}SD, 8^{5}GF, 9^{0}GF,

	Starts	1st	2nd	3rd	Win & Pl
Career Total (Turf)	9	3	0	1	45909
Career Total (AW)	2	0	2	0	4117

100	7/09	NmkJ	1m	(0-100)H	G-F	£24924
94	5/09	York	7f	(0-100)H	G-F	£16190
81	9/08	Bath	5f161y		G-F	£3238

Total win prize-money £44352

Going (Turf): Sf: 0-1 GS: 0-1 Gd: 0-0 **GF: 3-7** Fm: 0-0

Distance: 5f/6f: 1-3 **7f-8f: 2-7** 9f-13f: 0-1 14f+: 0-0
Track : **LH: 2-3** RH: 0-2 Tight: 0-0 **Gall: 2-3**
Aids: Bl: 0-0 Vi: 0-0 Tstrap: 0-0 Ckp: 0-0
Best Rating: 105 8/09 Kemp 1m stand

Very useful; effective over 7f-1m; acts on fast ground; goes on Polytrack.

Brief Look

103(110) (94)**90**
3-y-o b f Sadler's Wells (USA)-Half Glance (Danehill (USA))
H R A Cecil K Abdulla

Placings:221130 **(6734)**
2009: 10^{2}GF, **11^{2}SD**, 12^{1}SD, **12^{1}SD**, 12^{3}GF, 14^{0}S,

	Starts	1st	2nd	3rd	Win & Pl
Career Total (Turf)	3	0	1	1	2504
Career Total (AW)	3	2	1	0	9671

86	9/09	Ling	1m4f	(0-85)H	STD	£5828
94	8/09	Kemp	1m4f		STD	£2590

Total win prize-money £8418

Going (Turf): Sf: 0-1 GS: 0-0 Gd: 0-0 GF: 0-2 Fm: 0-0
Distance: 5f/6f: 0-0 7f-8f: 0-0 **9f-13f: 2-5** 14f+: 0-1
Track : LH: 1-3 RH: 1-3 **Tight: 1-2** Gall: 0-2
Aids: Bl: 0-0 Vi: 0-0 Tstrap: 0-0 Ckp: 0-0
Best Rating: 94 8/09 Kemp 1m4f stand

Fair; effective over 1m2f-1m3f; acts on fast ground; goes on Fibresand.

Brierty (IRE)

100(104) (82)**83**
3-y-o b f Statue Of Liberty (USA)-Bridelina (FR) (Linamix (FR))
D Carroll G P Clarke

Placings:01012-02641550500 **(7801)**
2009: 7^{0}GS, 7^{2}F, 8^{6}GF, 6^{4}G, 5^{1}G, 6^{5}GF, 6^{5}GF, 6^{0}G, **6^{5}SD**, 6^{0}SD, 7^{0}SD,

	Starts	1st	2nd	3rd	Win & Pl
Career Total (Turf)	12	2	2	0	16207
Career Total (AW)	4	1	0	0	4080

83	7/09	York	5f89y	(0-80)H	GD	£5180
81	9/08	GrLe	6f	(0-70)	STD	£4079
68	5/08	Wwck	5f110y		G-F	£3070

Total win prize-money £12332

Going (Turf): Sf: 0-1 GS: 0-1 **Gd: 1-4 GF: 1-5** Fm: 0-1
Distance: 5f/6f: 3-9 7f-8f: 0-7 9f-13f: 0-0 14f+: 0-0
Track : LH: 2-5 RH: 0-2 Tight: 0-3 **Gall: 1-1**
Aids: Bl: 0-0 Vi: 0-1 Tstrap: 0-0 Ckp: 0-0
Best Rating: 83 7/09 York 5f89y good

Useful; effective over 5-7f; acts on good to firm and Polytrack.

Briery Blaze

(90) (54)**58**
6-y-o b m Dansili-Sabonis (USA) (The Minstrel (CAN))
T Wall C G Johnson

Placings:6460/0030/006002504041640/0006-050 **(0567)**
2009: 5^{0}SD, 5^{5}SD, 12^{0}SD,

	Starts	1st	2nd	3rd	Win & Pl
Career Total (Turf)	16	0	1	1	1636
Career Total (AW)	14	1	0	0	2116

54	10/07	Wolv	5f216y	(0-50)H	STD	£2115

Total win prize-money £2116

Going (Turf): Sf: 0-1 GS: 0-4 Gd: 0-3 GF: 0-7 Fm: 0-1
Distance: 5f/6f: 1-11 7f-8f: 0-13 9f-13f: 0-6 14f+: 0-0
Track : LH: 1-18 RH: 0-6 **Tight: 1-17** Gall: 0-0
Aids: Bl: 1-7 Vi: 0-0 Tstrap: 0-3 Ckp: 0-3
Best Rating: 64 6/05 Donc 6f gd-fm

Plating-class filly; stays mile but won only race at 6f; acts on a sound surface; has worn blinkers.

Briery Lane (IRE)

79(95) (54)**56**
8-y-o ch g Tagula (IRE)-Branston Berry (IRE) (Mukaddamah (USA))
J M Bradley J M Bradley

Placings:06300043046/25014032004/440201200430/0460 04-060006 **(3673)**
2009: 5^{0}SD, 5^{6}SD, 5^{0}SD, 5^{0}SD, 6^{0}GF, 5^{6}F,

	Starts	1st	2nd	3rd	Win & Pl
Career Total (Turf)	37	2	4	4	10822
Career Total (AW)	9	0	0	0	0

64	8/07	Bath	5f11y	(0-60)H	G-S	£2266
69	5/06	Rdcr	6f	(0-60)H	G-F	£2307

Total win prize-money £4575

Going (Turf): Sf: 0-6 **GS: 1-4** Gd: 0-7 **GF: 1-17** Fm: 0-3
Distance: 5f/6f: 2-39 7f-8f: 0-7 9f-13f: 0-0 14f+: 0-0
Track : LH: 1-17 RH: 0-1 Tight: 0-9 **Gall: 1-3**
Aids: Bl: 0-0 Vi: 0-0 Tstrap: 1-14 Ckp: 1-14
Best Rating: 69 8/06 Rdcr 6f good

Moderate sprinter; won 5f Class 6 handicap at Bath August 2007; stays 6f; acts on good to firm and good to soft as well as Polytrack.

Brigadoon

90(96) (72)**63**
2-y-o b c Compton Place-Briggsmaid (Elegant Air)
W Jarvis William Jarvis

Placings:023 **(7637)**
2009: 7^{0}G, 7^{2}SD, 5^{3}SD,

	Starts	1st	2nd	3rd	Win & Pl
Career Total (Turf)	1	0	0	0	0
Career Total (AW)	2	0	1	1	1236

Going (Turf): Sf: 0-0 GS: 0-0 Gd: 0-1 GF: 0-0 Fm: 0-0
Distance: 5f/6f: 0-1 7f-8f: 0-2 9f-13f: 0-0 14f+: 0-0
Track : LH: 0-1 RH: 0-0 Tight: 0-0 Gall: 0-0
Aids: Bl: 0-0 Vi: 0-0 Tstrap: 0-0 Ckp: 0-0
Best Rating: 72 11/09 Sthl 7f stand

Fair; stays 7f and acts on Fibresand.

Bright Falcon

89(91) (57)**73**
4-y-o ch g Hawk Wing (USA)-Cream Tease (Pursuit Of Love)
J Balding (S Parr 23/6) Willie McKay

Placings:1/5000000-0000000100 **(6005)**
2009: 7^{0}SD, 16^{0}F, 21^{0}F, 7^{0}GF, 8^{0}G, 8^{0}GF, 8^{0}GF, 6^{1}G, 6^{0}GF, 7^{0}GF,

	Starts	1st	2nd	3rd	Win & Pl
Career Total (Turf)	15	2	0	0	9962
Career Total (AW)	3	0	0	0	

55	6/09	Ripn	6f		GD	£2590
74	10/07	York	1m		G-S	£7124

Total win prize-money £9715

Going (Turf): Sf: 0-2 **GS: 1-4 Gd: 1-2** GF: 0-5 Fm: 0-2
Distance: 5f/6f: 1-3 7f-8f: 1-7 9f-13f: 0-5 14f+: 0-3
Track : LH: 1-8 RH: 0-4 Tight: 0-5 **Gall: 1-2**
Aids: Bl: 1-5 Vi: 0-1 Tstrap: 0-1 Ckp: 0-1
Best Rating: 74 10/07 York 1m gd-sft

Useful; stays 1m and acts on easy ground; has worn blinkers and a tongue tie.

Bright Sparky (GER)

106(104) (56)**54**
6-y-o ch g Dashing Blade-Braissim (Dancing Brave (USA))
M W Easterby Rupert Armitage & Graham Sparkes

Placings:3600/00/426-1003002 **(7751)**
2009: 11^{1}SD, 12^{0}SD, 9^{0}GF, 14^{3}GF, 16^{0}GS, 15^{0}G, 13^{2}SD,

	Starts	1st	2nd	3rd	Win & Pl
Career Total (Turf)	10	0	0	2	824
Career Total (AW)	6	1	2	0	2857

56	2/09	Sthl	1m3f	(0-52)H	STD	£1648

Total win prize-money £1648

Going (Turf): Sf: 0-1 GS: 0-1 Gd: 0-4 GF: 0-4 Fm: 0-0
Distance: 5f/6f: 0-3 7f-8f: 0-2 **9f-13f: 1-5** 14f+: 0-6
Track : LH: 1-8 RH: 0-4 Tight: 0-6 Gall: 0-0
Aids: Bl: 1-4 Vi: 0-3 Tstrap: 0-0 Ckp: 0-0
Best Rating: 56 12/09 Wolv 1m5f194y stand

Moderate; stays 1m6f; acts on Fibresand and Polytrack; has worn blinkers.

Bright Wire (IRE)

84(89) (45)**44**
3-y-o b g Elusive City (USA)-Alinga (IRE) (King's Theatre (IRE))
M Madgwick Recycled Products Limited

Placings:00-40060000 **(7888)**
2009: 7^{4}SD, 8^{0}GF, **10^{0}SD**, 11^{6}GF, 12^{0}SD, 11^{0}G, 16^{0}G, 12^{0}SD,

	Starts	1st	2nd	3rd	Win & Pl
Career Total (Turf)	6	0	0	0	0
Career Total (AW)	4	0	0	0	0

Going (Turf): Sf: 0-1 GS: 0-0 Gd: 0-3 GF: 0-2 Fm: 0-0
Distance: 5f/6f: 0-1 7f-8f: 0-2 9f-13f: 0-6 14f+: 0-1
Track : LH: 0-7 RH: 0-2 Tight: 0-7 Gall: 0-0
Aids: Bl: 0-0 Vi: 0-1 Tstrap: 0-0 Ckp: 0-0
Best Rating: 45 4/09 Ling 7f stand

Brilliana

104(100) (75)**89**
3-y-o b f Danehill Dancer (IRE)-Streak Of Silver (USA) (Dynaformer (USA))
D R Lanigan Ms Nicola Mahoney

Placings:6-32512 **(5771)**
2009: 10^{3}GF, 10^{2}GF, **10^{5}SD**, 11^{1}GF, 12^{2}GF,

	Starts	1st	2nd	3rd	Win & Pl
Career Total (Turf)	5	1	2	1	6188
Career Total (AW)	1	0	0	0	0

82	8/09	Bath	1m3f144y		G-F	£2719

Total win prize-money £2720

Going (Turf): Sf: 0-1 GS: 0-0 Gd: 0-0 **GF: 1-4** Fm: 0-0
Distance: 5f/6f: 0-0 7f-8f: 0-1 **9f-13f: 1-5** 14f+: 0-0
Track : LH: 1-5 RH: 0-0 **Tight: 1-3** Gall: 0-1
Aids: Bl: 0-0 Vi: 0-0 Tstrap: 0-0 Ckp: 0-0
Best Rating: 89 9/09 Epsm 1m4f10y gd-fm

Fair; stays 1m4f; acts on fast ground and Fibresand.

Bring It On Home

(97) (57)**69**
5-y-o b g Beat Hollow-Dernier Cri (Slip Anchor)

Mrs S Leech (G L Moore 24/3) C J Leech

Placings:00/60006/33-2 (0603)
2009: 12²SD,

	Starts	1st	2nd	3rd	Win & Pl
Career Total (Turf)	6	0	0	0	0
Career Total (AW)	4	0	1	2	1292

Going (Turf): Sf: 0-0 GS: 0-0 Gd: 0-3 GF: 0-2 Fm: 0-1
Distance: 5f/6f: 0-0 7f-8f: 0-2 9f-13f: 0-6 14f+: 0-2
Track : LH: 0-3 RH: 0-6 Tight: 0-3 Gall: 0-1
Aids: Bl: 0-2 Vi: 0-0 Tstrap: 0-0 Ckp: 0-0
Best Rating: 69 7/07 Sand 1m2f7y good

Modest; stays 1m4f and acts on sand; has worn blinkers.

Bring Sweets (IRE)

83 **44**
2-y-o b g Firebreak-Missperon (IRE) (Orpen (USA))
B Ellison Koo's Racing Club

Placings:0660 (7055)
2009: 5⁰GF, 5⁶GF, 5⁶GF, 7⁰GF,

	Starts	1st	2nd	3rd	Win & Pl
Career Total (Turf)	4	0	0	0	0

Going (Turf): Sf: 0-0 GS: 0-0 Gd: 0-0 GF: 0-4 Fm: 0-0
Distance: 5f/6f: 0-3 7f-8f: 0-1 9f-13f: 0-0 14f+: 0-0
Track : LH: 0-0 RH: 0-1 Tight: 0-0 Gall: 0-1
Aids: Bl: 0-0 Vi: 0-0 Tstrap: 0-0 Ckp: 0-0
Best Rating: 44 5/09 Ripn 5f gd-fm

Brink

95(89) (47)**64**
2-y-o b f Powerscourt-Fonage (Zafonic (USA))
T J Pitt Ferrybank Properties Limited

Placings:532 (7114)
2009: 8⁵SD, 7³G, 7²GS,

	Starts	1st	2nd	3rd	Win & Pl
Career Total (Turf)	2	0	1	1	1559
Career Total (AW)	1	0	0	0	0

Going (Turf): Sf: 0-0 GS: 0-1 Gd: 0-1 GF: 0-0 Fm: 0-0
Distance: 5f/6f: 0-0 7f-8f: 0-2 9f-13f: 0-1 14f+: 0-0
Track : LH: 0-2 RH: 0-1 Tight: 0-3 Gall: 0-0
Aids: Bl: 0-0 Vi: 0-0 Tstrap: 0-0 Ckp: 0-0
Best Rating: 64 10/09 Catt 7f good

Brinscall

94(87) (51)**70**
2-y-o b f Lucky Story (USA)-Happy Lady (FR) (Cadeaux Genereux)
R A Fahey (T D Easterby 13/8) David W Armstrong

Placings:53604245 (7618)
2009: 5⁵F, 6³S, 6⁶GS, 7⁰G, 6⁴GS, 6²GF, 7⁴G, 5⁵SD,

	Starts	1st	2nd	3rd	Win & Pl
Career Total (Turf)	7	0	1	1	1864
Career Total (AW)	1	0	0	0	0

Going (Turf): Sf: 0-1 GS: 0-2 Gd: 0-2 GF: 0-1 Fm: 0-1
Distance: 5f/6f: 0-6 7f-8f: 0-2 9f-13f: 0-0 14f+: 0-0
Track : LH: 0-3 RH: 0-1 Tight: 0-2 Gall: 0-0
Aids: Bl: 0-0 Vi: 0-0 Tstrap: 0-0 Ckp: 0-0

Best Rating: 70 9/09 Newc 6f gd-fm

Fair; stays 6f and acts on fast ground.

Brisbane (IRE)

85 **71**
2-y-o b g Kheleyf (USA)-Waroonga (IRE) (Brief Truce (USA))
J H M Gosden H R H Princess Haya Of Jordan

Placings:420 (2940)
2009: 6⁴G, 6²G, 6⁰GF,

	Starts	1st	2nd	3rd	Win & Pl
Career Total (Turf)	3	0	1	0	1569

Going (Turf): Sf: 0-0 GS: 0-0 Gd: 0-2 GF: 0-1 Fm: 0-0
Distance: 5f/6f: 0-1 7f 8f: 0-2 9f-13f: 0-0 14f+: 0-0
Track : LH: 0-0 RH: 0-0 Tight: 0-0 Gall: 0-0
Aids: Bl: 0-0 Vi: 0-0 Tstrap: 0-0 Ckp: 0-0
Best Rating: 71 5/09 Yarm 6f3y good

Fair; effective over 6f; acts on fast ground.

Bristol Delauriere (FR)

(74) (19)
5-y-o b g Epistolaire (IRE)-Shenedova (FR) (Hellios (USA))
Miss N A Lloyd-Beavis Miss Wendy Gill

Placings:0 (6225)
2009: 12⁰SD,

	Starts	1st	2nd	3rd	Win & Pl
Career Total (Turf)	0	0	0	0	
Career Total (AW)	1	0	0	0	

Going (Turf): Sf: 0-0 GS: 0-0 Gd: 0-0 GF: 0-0 Fm: 0-0
Distance: 5f/6f: 0-0 7f-8f: 0-0 9f-13f: 0-1 14f+: 0-0
Track : LH: 0-0 RH: 0-1 Tight: 0-0 Gall: 0-0
Aids: Bl: 0-0 Vi: 0-0 Tstrap: 0-0 Ckp: 0-0
Best Rating: 19 9/09 Kemp 1m4f stand

Broad Calrn

102(105) (91)**94**
3-y-o b g Green Desert (USA)-Celtic Cross (Selkirk (USA))
R Charlton The Queen

Placings:2-31013104 (6702)
2009: 7³GS, 8¹GS, 7⁰G, 7¹GF, 7³G, 7¹G, 7⁰GF, 7⁴SS,

	Starts	1st	2nd	3rd	Win & Pl
Career Total (Turf)	8	3	1	2	19654
Career Total (AW)	1	0	0	0	0

92	8/09	Wwck	7f26y	(0-85)H	GD	£4984
86	7/09	Sand	7f16y	(0-90)H	G F	£7771
80	5/09	Hayd	1m30y		G-S	£3238

Total win prize-money £15994

Going (Turf): Sf: 0-0 **GS: 1-2 Gd: 1-4 GF: 1-2** Fm: 0-0
Distance: 5f/6f: 0-0 **7f-8f: 2-8** 9f-13f: 1-1 14f+: 0-0
Track : **LH: 2-3** RH: 1-3 Tight: 0-1 Gall: 0-0
Aids: Bl: 0-0 Vi: 0-0 Tstrap: 0-0 Ckp: 0-0
Best Rating: 94 8/09 Sand 7f16y good

Useful; effective over 7f-1m; acts on fast and easy ground.

Broad Town Girl

53(90) (36)
6-y-o b m Woodborough (USA)-Fortunes Course (IRE) (Crash Course)

W S Coltherd J W Purves

Placings:005000/500-0 (3023)
2009: 12⁰G,

	Starts	1st	2nd	3rd	Win & Pl
Career Total (Turf)	1	0	0	0	
Career Total (AW)	9	0	0	0	0

Going (Turf): Sf: 0-0 GS: 0-0 Gd: 0-1 GF: 0-0 Fm: 0-0
Distance: 5f/6f: 0-0 7f-8f: 0-5 9f-13f: 0-5 14f+: 0-0
Track : LH: 0-7 RH: 0-3 Tight: 0-8 Gall: 0-0
Aids: Bl: 0-0 Vi: 0-1 Tstrap: 0-0 Ckp: 0-0
Best Rating: 36 1/08 Wolv 7f32y stand

Brockfield

97 **62**
3-y-o ch c Falbrav (IRE)-Irish Light (USA) (Irish River (FR))
M Brittain Mel Brittain

Placings:4055 (4660)
2009: 8⁴GF, 8⁰G, 8⁵G, 8⁵G,

	Starts	1st	2nd	3rd	Win & Pl
Career Total (Turf)	4	0	0	0	241

Going (Turf): Sf: 0-0 GS: 0-0 Gd: 0-3 GF: 0-1 Fm: 0-0
Distance: 5f/6f: 0-0 7f-8f: 0-3 9f-13f: 0-1 14f+: 0-0
Track : LH: 0-2 RH: 0-2 Tight: 0-2 Gall: 0-1
Aids: Bl: 0-0 Vi: 0-0 Tstrap: 0-0 Ckp: 0-0
Best Rating: 62 6/09 Ripn 1m gd-fm

Modest; stays 1m; handles a sound surface.

Broctune Papa Gio

70 **23**
2-y-o b g Tobougg (IRE)-Fairlie (Halling (USA))
K G Reveley D Playforth

Placings:0 (6821)
2009: 8⁰GF,

	Starts	1st	2nd	3rd	Win & Pl
Career Total (Turf)	1	0	0	0	

Going (Turf): Sf: 0-0 GS: 0-0 Gd: 0-0 GF: 0-1 Fm: 0-0
Distance: 5f/6f: 0-0 7f-8f: 0-1 9f-13f: 0-0 14f+: 0-0
Track : LH: 0-0 RH: 0-0 Tight: 0-0 Gall: 0-0
Aids: Bl: 0-0 Vi: 0-0 Tstrap: 0-0 Ckp: 0-0
Best Rating: 23 10/09 Rdcr 1m gd-fm

Brody's Boy

67
2-y-o ch c Tumbleweed Ridge-Raffelina (USA) (Carson City (USA))
G L Moore Geoff Buck

Placings:0 (7145)
2009: 6⁰G,

	Starts	1st	2nd	3rd	Win & Pl
Career Total (Turf)	1	0	0	0	

Going (Turf): Sf: 0-0 GS: 0-0 Gd: 0-1 GF: 0-0 Fm: 0-0
Distance: 5f/6f: 0-1 7f-8f: 0-0 9f-13f: 0-0 14f+: 0-0
Track : LH: 0-0 RH: 0-0 Tight: 0-0 Gall: 0-0
Aids: Bl: 0-0 Vi: 0-0 Tstrap: 0-0 Ckp: 0-0

Bromhead (USA)

93(103) (73)**60**

3-y-o ch g Johannesburg (USA)-Caramel Queen (NZ) (Turbulent Dancer (USA))

Mrs C A Dunnett (B J Meehan 12/5) Messrs Linder,Machin,Power & C Dunnett

Placings:51444005000030 **(7094)**

2009: 7^5SD, 10^1SD, 10^4SD, 8^4SD, 8^4SD, 6^0F, 8^0SD, 9^5S, 10^0G, 8^0GF, 7^0GF, 9^0SF, 11^0G, 11^3GF, 10^0G,

	Starts	1st	2nd	3rd	Win & Pl
Career Total (Turf)	8	0	0	1	289
Career Total (AW)	7	1	0	0	2730

70 1/09 Ling 1m2f STD £2729

Total win prize-money £2730

Going (Turf): **Sf: 0-1 GS: 0-0 Gd: 0-3 GF: 0-3 Fm: 0-1**
Distance: 5f/6f: 0-0 7f-8f: 0-5 **9f-13f: 1-10** 14f+: 0-0
Track : **LH: 1-10** RH: 0-3 **Tight: 1-9** Gall: 0-0
Aids: Bl: 0-0 Vi: 0-0 Tstrap: 0-0 Ckp: 0-0
Best Rating: 73 2/09 Ling 1m2f stand

Modest; effective over 1m2f; acts on Polytrack; has worn a tongue tie and eyeshield.

Bronte's Hope

88(91) (58)**56**

5-y-o ch m Gorse-General Jane (Be My Chief (USA))

M P Tregoning M P N Tregoning

Placings:5/14/0000-3 **(1421)**

2009: 6^3G,

	Starts	1st	2nd	3rd	Win & Pl
Career Total (Turf)	1	0	0	1	302
Career Total (AW)	7	1	0	0	2915

71 1/07 Ling 6f STD £2914

Total win prize-money £2915

Going (Turf): **Sf: 0-0 GS: 0-0 Gd: 0-1 GF: 0-0 Fm: 0-0**
Distance: **5f/6f: 1-6** 7f-8f: 0-2 9f-13f: 0-0 14f+: 0-0
Track : **LH: 1-4** RH: 0-3 **Tight: 1-4** Gall: 0-0
Aids: Bl: 0-0 Vi: 0-0 Tstrap: 0-1 Ckp: 0-1
Best Rating: 71 1/07 Ling 6f stand

Bronze Beau

98(88) (54)**69**

2-y-o ch g Compton Place-Bella Cantata (Singspiel (IRE))

Mrs L Stubbs D Arundale

Placings:54205232436 **(7213)**

2009: 5^5SD, 5^4GF, 5^2GS, 5^0GS, 5^5GF, 5^2G, 5^3GS, 5^2GF, 5^4GF, 5^3G, 5^6SD,

	Starts	1st	2nd	3rd	Win & Pl
Career Total (Turf)	9	0	3	2	4005
Career Total (AW)	2	0	0	0	0

Going (Turf): **Sf: 0-0 GS: 0-3 Gd: 0-2 GF: 0-4 Fm: 0-0**
Distance: 5f/6f: 0-11 7f-8f: 0-0 9f-13f: 0-0 14f+: 0-0
Track : LH: 0-1 RH: 0-1 Tight: 0-1 Gall: 0-1
Aids: Bl: 0-0 Vi: 0-0 Tstrap: 0-0 Ckp: 0-0
Best Rating: 69 8/09 Thsk 5f good

Modest; effective over 5f; acts on fast ground.

Bronze Cannon (USA)

116(110) (112)**122**

4-y-o b/br c Lemon Drop Kid (USA)-Victoria Cross (IRE) (Mark Of Esteem (IRE))

J H M Gosden Ramzan Kadyrov

Placings:011/11035-331140 **(6324a)**

2009: 10^3SD, 10^3SD, 12^1GF, 12^1GF, 12^4SD, 12^0G,

	Starts	1st	2nd	3rd	Win & Pl
Career Total (Turf)	7	4	0	1	152764
Career Total (AW)	7	2	0	2	23182

122 6/09 Asct 1m4f G-F £70962
119 5/09 NmkR 1m4f G-F £56770
112 5/08 NmkR 1m2f (0-100)H GD £11656
104 4/08 NmkR 1m2f (0-95)H GD £9066
88 10/07 Kemp 1m (0-85) STD £2817
77 9/07 Kemp 1m STD £4210

Total win prize-money £155483

Going (Turf): Sf: 0-0 GS: 0-1 **Gd: 2-3 GF: 2-2** Fm: 0-1
Distance: 5f/6f: 0-0 7f-8f: 2-3 **9f-13f: 4-11** 14f+: 0-0
Track : LH: 0-2 **RH: 4-8** Tight: 0-2 **Gall: 2-3**
Aids: Bl: 0-0 Vi: 0-0 Tstrap: 0-0 Ckp: 0-0
Best Rating: 122 6/09 Asct 1m4f gd-fm

Group-class; winner of the 2009 Jockey Club Stakes and Hardwicke Stakes; stays 1m4f; acts on good/fast ground and on Polytrack.

Bronze Prince

(98) (81)

2-y-o b c Oasis Dream-Sweet Pea (Persian Bold)

Saeed Bin Suroor Godolphin

Placings:1 **(7376)**

2009: 7^1SD,

	Starts	1st	2nd	3rd	Win & Pl
Career Total (Turf)	0	0	0	0	
Career Total (AW)	1	1	0	0	3238

81 11/09 Wolv 7f32y STD £3238

Total win prize-money £3238

Going (Turf): **Sf: 0-0 GS: 0-0 Gd: 0-0 GF: 0-0 Fm: 0-0**
Distance: 5f/6f: 0-0 **7f-8f: 1-1** 9f-13f: 0-0 14f+: 0-0
Track : **LH: 1-1** RH: 0-0 **Tight: 1-1** Gall: 0-0
Aids: Bl: 0-0 Vi: 0-0 Tstrap: 0-0 Ckp: 0-0
Best Rating: 81 11/09 Wolv 7f32y stand

Useful; stays 7f; acts on Polytrack.

Brooklands Bay (IRE)

(92) (68)

2-y-o b g Pyrus (USA)-Brooklands Time (IRE) (Danetime (IRE))

J R Weymes High Moor Racing 1

Placings:1 **(6858)**

2009: 8^1SD,

	Starts	1st	2nd	3rd	Win & Pl
Career Total (Turf)	0	0	0	0	
Career Total (AW)	1	1	0	0	2388

68 10/09 Wolv 1m141y STD £2388

Total win prize-money £2388

Going (Turf): **Sf: 0-0 GS: 0-0 Gd: 0-0 GF: 0-0 Fm: 0-0**
Distance: 5f/6f: 0-0 7f-8f: 0-0 **9f-13f: 1-1** 14f+: 0-0
Track : **LH: 1-1** RH: 0-0 **Tight: 1-1** Gall: 0-0
Aids: Bl: 0-0 Vi: 0-0 Tstrap: 0-0 Ckp: 0-0
Best Rating: 68 10/09 Wolv 1m141y stand

Modest; stays 1m; acts on Polytrack.

Brooklyn Spirit

99 **73**

3-y-o ch g Cadeaux Genereux-Serengeti Bride (USA) (Lion Cavern (USA))

C G Cox Gwyn Powell and Peter Ridgers

Placings:0-100 **(6420)**

2009: 10^1G, 12^0GF, 11^0GF,

	Starts	1st	2nd	3rd	Win & Pl
Career Total (Turf)	4	1	0	0	3238

73 6/09 Sand 1m2f7y GD £3238

Total win prize-money £3238

Going (Turf): Sf: 0-1 GS: 0-0 **Gd: 1-1** GF: 0-2 Fm: 0-0
Distance: 5f/6f: 0-0 7f-8f: 0-1 **9f-13f: 1-3** 14f+: 0-0
Track : LH: 0-0 **RH: 1-3** Tight: 0-2 Gall: 0-0
Aids: Bl: 0-0 Vi: 0-0 Tstrap: 0-0 Ckp: 0-0
Best Rating: 73 6/09 Sand 1m2f7y good

Fair; stays 1m2f; acts on fast ground.

Brooksby

103(101) (73)**68**

3-y-o b f Diktat-Lovely Lyca (Night Shift (USA))

L A Dace (R Hannon 15/8) Winterfields Farm Ltd

Placings:0336631-60563242450300 **(7392)**

2009: 8^6SD, 9^0GF, 7^5SD, 8^6GS, 7^3G, 8^2GF, 7^4SD, 8^2SD, 8^4G, 8^5SD, 9^0GF, 7^3SS, 8^0SD, 10^0SD,

	Starts	1st	2nd	3rd	Win & Pl
Career Total (Turf)	11	0	1	3	2712
Career Total (AW)	10	1	1	2	4025

73 11/08 Kemp 1m (0-70) STD £2590

Total win prize-money £2590

Going (Turf): **Sf: 0-1 GS: 0-2 Gd: 0-4 GF: 0-4 Fm: 0-0**
Distance: 5f/6f: 0-2 **7f-8f: 1-14** 9f-13f: 0-5 14f+: 0-0
Track : LH: 0-6 **RH: 1-9** Tight: 0-8 Gall: 0-1
Aids: **Bl: 1-13** Vi: 0-2 Tstrap: 0-0 Ckp: 0-0
Best Rating: 73 11/08 Kemp 1m stand

Modest; effective at around 1m; acts on soft ground; goes on Polytrack; has worn blinkers.

Broomfield Buddy

59

3-y-o b f Reel Buddy (USA)-Tancred Arms (Clantime)

D W Barker G E Fawcett

Placings:00-0 **(1451)**

2009: 7^0GF,

	Starts	1st	2nd	3rd	Win & Pl
Career Total (Turf)	3	0	0	0	

Going (Turf): **Sf: 0-0 GS: 0-1 Gd: 0-1 GF: 0-1 Fm: 0-0**
Distance: 5f/6f: 0-2 7f-8f: 0-1 9f-13f: 0-0 14f+: 0-0
Track : LH: 0-2 RH: 0-0 Tight: 0-2 Gall: 0-0
Aids: Bl: 0-0 Vi: 0-0 Tstrap: 0-0 Ckp: 0-0

Broomielaw

109(111) (95)**105**

5-y-o ch g Rock Of Gibraltar (IRE)-Peony (Lion Cavern (USA))

E A L Dunlop Lady Ferguson

Placings:2/41/1006 **(7465)**

2009: 10^1G, 10^0GF, 12^0S, 12^6SD,

	Starts	1st	2nd	3rd	Win & Pl
Career Total (Turf)	6	2	1	0	17663
Career Total (AW)	1	0	0	0	234

105 8/09 NmkJ 1m2f (0-90)H GD £9066
97 8/07 Donc 1m2f60y G-F £6477

Total win prize-money £15543

Going (Turf): Sf: 0-1 GS: 0-0 **Gd: 1-1 GF: 1-4** Fm: 0-0
Distance: 5f/6f: 0-0 7f-8f: 0-1 **9f-13f: 2-6** 14f+: 0-0
Track : LH: 1-4 RH: 1-1 Tight: 0-1 **Gall: 2-4**
Aids: Bl: 0-0 Vi: 0-0 Tstrap: 0-0 Ckp: 0-0
Best Rating: 105 8/09 NmkJ 1m2f good

Very useful; effective over 1m2f; acts on good/fast ground; was off the track for two years from August 2007.

Brootommitty (IRE)

76 **36**
2-y-o b f Azamour (IRE)-Polyandry (IRE) (Pennekamp (USA))
I Semple Kevin Thomson Steven Whittaker Scott Brown

Placings:4 **(5330)**
2009: 7^{4}S,

	Starts	1st	2nd	3rd	Win & Pl
Career Total (Turf)	1	0	0	0	394

Going (Turf): Sf: 0-1 GS: 0-0 Gd: 0-0 GF: 0-0 Fm: 0-0
Distance: 5f/6f: 0-0 7f-8f: 0-1 9f-13f: 0-0 14f+: 0-0
Track : LH: 0-1 RH: 0-0 Tight: 0-0 Gall: 0-0
Aids: Bl: 0-0 Vi: 0-0 Tstrap: 0-0 Ckp: 0-0
Best Rating: 36 8/09 Ayr 7f50y soft

Brother Barry (USA)

97(96) (64)**65**
4-y-o b/br g Forestry (USA)-Saratoga Sugar (USA) (Gone West (USA))
G A Swinbank S Rudolf

Placings:6/000000-430 **(2316)**
2009: 8^{4}SD, 7^{3}GF, 5^{0}GF,

	Starts	1st	2nd	3rd	Win & Pl
Career Total (Turf)	9	0	0	1	443
Career Total (AW)	1	0	0	0	0

Going (Turf): Sf: 0-1 GS: 0-1 Gd: 0-3 GF: 0-4 Fm: 0-0
Distance: 5f/6f: 0-4 7f-8f: 0-5 9f-13f: 0-1 14f+: 0-0
Track : LH: 0-2 RH: 0-1 Tight: 0-1 Gall: 0-1
Aids: Bl: 0-0 Vi: 0-0 Tstrap: 0-0 Ckp: 0-0
Best Rating: 65 4/08 NmkR 7f good

Brother Cha (IRE)

99 **82**
3-y-o ch c Indian Ridge-Sun On The Sea (IRE) (Bering)
M G Quinlan Exors of The Late Cathal M Ryan

Placings:01 **(5181)**
2009: 7^{0}GF, 7^{1}G,

	Starts	1st	2nd	3rd	Win & Pl
Career Total (Turf)	2	1	0	0	2752

82 8/09 Chep 7f16y GD £2752
Total win prize-money £2752

Going (Turf): Sf: 0-0 GS: 0-0 **Gd: 1-1** GF: 0-1 Fm: 0-0
Distance: 5f/6f: 0-0 **7f-8f: 1-2** 9f-13f: 0-0 14f+: 0-0
Track : LH: 0-0 RH: 0-0 Tight: 0-0 Gall: 0-0
Aids: Bl: 0-0 Vi: 0-0 Tstrap: 0-0 Ckp: 0-0
Best Rating: 82 8/09 Chep 7f16y good

Broughton Beck (IRE)

(97) (58)
3-y-o ch g Distant Music (USA)-Mauras Pride (IRE) (Cadeaux Genereux)
R F Fisher Des Johnston

Placings:60-64 **(0659)**
2009: 10^{6}SD, 9^{4}SD,

	Starts	1st	2nd	3rd	Win & Pl
Career Total (Turf)	0	0	0	0	
Career Total (AW)	4	0	0	0	0

Going (Turf): Sf: 0-0 GS: 0-0 Gd: 0-0 GF: 0-0 Fm: 0-0
Distance: 5f/6f: 0-0 7f-8f: 0-1 9f-13f: 0-3 14f+: 0-0
Track : LH: 0-4 RH: 0-0 Tight: 0-3 Gall: 0-0
Aids: Bl: 0-0 Vi: 0-0 Tstrap: 0-0 Ckp: 0-0
Best Rating: 58 2/09 Wolv 1m1f103y stand

Broughtons Day

72 **50**
2-y-o b g Mujahid (USA)-Rainy Day Song (Persian Bold)
W J Musson Broughton Thermal Insulation

Placings:6 **(5029)**
2009: 6^{6}GF,

	Starts	1st	2nd	3rd	Win & Pl
Career Total (Turf)	1	0	0	0	0

Going (Turf): Sf: 0-0 GS: 0-0 Gd: 0-0 GF: 0-1 Fm: 0-0
Distance: 5f/6f: 0-1 7f-8f: 0-0 9f-13f: 0-0 14f+: 0-0
Track : LH: 0-0 RH: 0-0 Tight: 0-0 Gall: 0-0
Aids: Bl: 0-0 Vi: 0-0 Tstrap: 0-0 Ckp: 0-0
Best Rating: 50 8/09 NmkJ 6f gd-fm

Broughtons Flight (IRE)

(107) (67)**67**
4-y-o ch f Hawk Wing (USA)-Aldburgh (Bluebird (USA))
W J Musson Broughton Bloodstock

Placings:0052/0020004-230 **(0320)**
2009: 10^{2}SD, 10^{3}SD, 10^{0}SD,

	Starts	1st	2nd	3rd	Win & Pl
Career Total (Turf)	7	0	1	0	964
Career Total (AW)	7	0	2	1	1636

Going (Turf): Sf: 0-3 GS: 0-0 Gd: 0-2 GF: 0-2 Fm: 0-0
Distance: 5f/6f: 0-0 7f-8f: 0-6 9f-13f: 0-8 14f+: 0-0
Track : LH: 0-7 RH: 0-4 Tight: 0-5 Gall: 0-2
Aids: Bl: 0-0 Vi: 0-0 Tstrap: 0-0 Ckp: 0-0
Best Rating: 67 7/08 Bevl 1m1f207y gd-fm

Moderate; stays 1m2f and acts on Polytrack.

Broughtons Paradis (IRE)

101(97) (61)**68**
3-y-o b f Royal Applause-Amankila (IRE) (Revoque (IRE))
W J Musson Broughton Thermal Insulation

Placings:000-232163265 **(7831)**
2009: 10^{2}SD, 8^{3}GF, 12^{2}G, 11^{1}G, 12^{6}SD, 11^{3}GS, 10^{2}G, 12^{6}SD, 12^{5}SD,

	Starts	1st	2nd	3rd	Win & Pl
Career Total (Turf)	7	1	2	2	4689
Career Total (AW)	5	0	1	0	605

68 8/09 Yarm 1m3f101y (0-65)H GD £2072
Total win prize-money £2072

Going (Turf): Sf: 0-0 GS: 0-1 **Gd: 1-4** GF: 0-2 Fm: 0-0
Distance: 5f/6f: 0-2 7f-8f: 0-2 **9f-13f: 1-8** 14f+: 0-0
Track : **LH: 1-4** RH: 0-4 **Tight: 1-5** Gall: 0-2
Aids: Bl: 0-0 Vi: 0-0 Tstrap: 0-0 Ckp: 0-0
Best Rating: 68 8/09 Yarm 1m3f101y good

Moderate; stays 1m4f; acts on good ground.

Broughtons Point

91(85) (43)**41**
3-y-o b f Falbrav (IRE)-Glowing Reference (Reference Point)
W J Musson Broughton Thermal Insulation

Placings:6000 **(7660)**
2009: 10^{6}GF, 8^{0}SD, 9^{0}SD, 10^{0}SD,

	Starts	1st	2nd	3rd	Win & Pl
Career Total (Turf)	1	0	0	0	0
Career Total (AW)	3	0	0	0	

Going (Turf): Sf: 0-0 GS: 0-0 Gd: 0-0 GF: 0-1 Fm: 0-0
Distance: 5f/6f: 0-0 7f-8f: 0-0 9f-13f: 0-4 14f+: 0-0
Track : LH: 0-4 RH: 0-0 Tight: 0-4 Gall: 0-0
Aids: Bl: 0-0 Vi: 0-0 Tstrap: 0-0 Ckp: 0-0
Best Rating: 43 9/09 Wolv 1m141y stand

Broughtons Silk

101(95) (51)**60**
4-y-o b f Medicean-Soviet Cry (Soviet Star (USA))
W J Musson Broughton Thermal Insulation

Placings:5-000016560 **(6945)**
2009: 8^{0}G, 7^{0}SD, 8^{0}SF, 8^{0}GS, 8^{1}G, 8^{6}G, 10^{5}GF, 8^{6}SD, 8^{0}SD,

	Starts	1st	2nd	3rd	Win & Pl
Career Total (Turf)	5	1	0	0	1943
Career Total (AW)	5	0	0	0	0

60 8/09 Yarm 1m3y (0-65)H GD £1942
Total win prize-money £1943

Going (Turf): Sf: 0-0 GS: 0-1 **Gd: 1-3** GF: 0-1 Fm: 0-0
Distance: 5f/6f: 0-0 7f-8f: 0-2 **9f-13f: 1-8** 14f+: 0-0
Track : LH: 0-6 RH: 0-1 Tight: 0-5 Gall: 0-0
Aids: Bl: 0-0 Vi: 0-0 Tstrap: 0-0 Ckp: 0-0
Best Rating: 60 8/09 Yarm 1m3y good

Moderate; effective over 1m; acts on good ground.

Brouhaha

109(105) (90)**85**
5-y-o b g Bahhare (USA)-Top Of The Morning (Keen)
Tom Dascombe Grant Thornton Racing Club

Placings:005/000502/02332240-111010106240220P20 **(7789)**
2009: 9^{1}SD, 8^{1}SD, 9^{1}SD, 9^{0}SD, 10^{1}SD, 11^{0}SD, 8^{1}SD, 8^{0}GF, 10^{6}SD, 8^{2}SD, 10^{4}G, 8^{0}HY, 9^{2}G, 10^{2}GF, 9^{0}SD, 8^{6}SF, 9^{2}SF, 9^{0}SD,

	Starts	1st	2nd	3rd	Win & Pl
Career Total (Turf)	19	0	4	2	5434
Career Total (AW)	16	5	4	0	20517

90 4/09 Wolv 1m141y (0-80)H STD £5180
86 3/09 Kemp 1m2f (0-75)H STD £2590
79 2/09 Wolv 1m1f103y (0-75)H STD £2729
73 2/09 Wolv 1m141y (0-75)H STD £2729
68 1/09 Wolv 1m1f103y STD £2729
Total win prize-money £15961

Going (Turf): Sf: 0-2 GS: 0-4 Gd: 0-8 GF: 0-5 Fm: 0-0

Distance: 5f/6f: 0-1 7f-8f: 0-12 **9f-13f: 5-22** 14f+: 0-0
Track : **LH: 4-16** RH: 1-9 **Tight: 4-12** Gall: 0-1
Aids: Bl: 0-0 Vi: 0-0 Tstrap: 0-1 Ckp: 0-1
Best Rating: 90 11/09 Wolv 1m1f103y std-fst

Useful; effective over 1m-1m2f; acts on Polytrack.

Brown Lentic (IRE)

(98) (51)**41**
3-y-o b c Invincible Spirit (IRE)-Indienne (IRE) (Indian Ridge)
Miss J Feilden Miss J Feilden

Placings:000**06**-15500 **(1529)**
2009: 5^{1}SD, 5^{5}SD, 5^{5}SD, 5^{0}SD, 5^{0}SD,

	Starts	1st	2nd	3rd	Win & Pl
Career Total (Turf)	3	0	0	0	
Career Total (AW)	7	1	0	0	2047

51 1/09 Ling 5f (0-60)H STD £2047
Total win prize-money £2047

Going (Turf): **Sf: 0-1 GS: 0-1 Gd: 0-0 GF: 0-1 Fm: 0-0**
Distance: **5f/6f: 1-10** 7f-8f: 0-0 9f-13f: 0-0 14f+: 0-0
Track : **LH: 1-6** RH: 0-1 **Tight: 1-5** Gall: 0-2
Aids: Bl: 0-0 Vi: 0-0 Tstrap: 0-0 Ckp: 0-0
Best Rating: 51 1/09 Ling 5f stand

Moderate; effective over 5f; acts on Polytrack.

Brunelleschi

105(103) (81)**86**
6-y-o ch g Bertolini (USA)-Petrovna (IRE) (Petardia)
P L Gilligan Dr Susan Barnes

Placings:4142**503**/546056**000**/2111066020/0100000000-11102015000 **(7189)**
2009: 6^{1}SD, 6^{1}SD, 6^{1}GF, 6^{0}GF, 6^{2}GF, 6^{0}SD, 6^{1}G, 6^{5}GF, 5^{0}GS, 7^{0}SD, 7^{0}G,

	Starts	1st	2nd	3rd	Win & Pl
Career Total (Turf)	37	7	4	0	33817
Career Total (AW)	10	2	0	1	6214

86 8/09 NmkJ 6f (0-85)H GD £5180
81 4/09 Wind 6f (0-75)H G-F £2729
81 3/09 Kemp 6f (0-75)H STD £2590
73 3/09 Ling 6f (0-70)H STD £2590
82 6/08 NmkJ 6f (0-80)H G-F £6476
84 5/07 Yarm 6f3y (0-75)H GD £2839
82 5/07 NmkR 6f (0-75)H GD £3886
79 5/07 Nott 6f15y (0-60)H GD £2457
78 7/05 Wind 5f10y G-F £4173
Total win prize-money £32922

Going (Turf): Sf: 0-2 GS: 0-9 **Gd: 4-10** GF: 3-15 Fm: 0-1
Distance: **5f/6f: 7-40** 7f-8f: 2-7 9f-13f: 0-0 14f+: 0-0
Track : LH: 1-7 RH: 1-4 Tight: 1-6 **Gall: 2-4**
Aids: **Bl: 8-30** Vi: 0-4 Tstrap: 0-0 Ckp: 0-0
Best Rating: 86 8/09 NmkJ 6f good

Fair; suited by 6f; acts on good ground and on Polytrack; often wears blinkers; can start slowly.

Brunette (IRE)

88(88) (75)**60**
2-y-o br f Camacho-Hidden Agenda (FR) (Machiavellian (USA))
R Hannon Mrs J Wood

Placings:0224000 **(6391)**
2009: 6^{0}GF, 7^{2}SD, 7^{2}SD, 8^{4}GS, 8^{0}G, 9^{0}GF, 10^{0}GF,

	Starts	1st	2nd	3rd	Win & Pl
Career Total (Turf)	5	0	0	0	241
Career Total (AW)	2	0	2	0	2312

Going (Turf): **Sf: 0-0 GS: 0-1 Gd: 0-1 GF: 0-3 Fm: 0-0**
Distance: 5f/6f: 0-1 7f-8f: 0-3 9f-13f: 0-3 14f+: 0-0
Track : LH: 0-2 RH: 0-2 Tight: 0-0 Gall: 0-0
Aids: Bl: 0-0 Vi: 0-0 Tstrap: 0-0 Ckp: 0-0
Best Rating: 75 6/09 Kemp 7f stand

Brunston

108 **92**
3-y-o gr g High Chaparral (IRE)-Molly Mello (GER) (Big Shuffle (USA))
R Charlton Seasons Holidays

Placings:00-215104 **(3618)**
2009: 7^{2}G, 9^{1}GF, 11^{5}GS, 11^{1}GF, 12^{0}GF, 11^{4}GF,

	Starts	1st	2nd	3rd	Win & Pl
Career Total (Turf)	8	2	1	0	13740

90 5/09 Gdwd 1m3f (0-85)H G-F £6476
81 5/09 Sals 1m1f198y (0-85)H G-F £4857
Total win prize-money £11333

Going (Turf): Sf: 0-0 GS: 0-3 Gd: 0-1 **GF: 2-4** Fm: 0-0
Distance: 5f/6f: 0-0 7f-8f: 0-3 **9f-13f: 2-5** 14f+: 0-0
Track : LH: 0-3 **RH: 2-3 Tight: 2-2** Gall: 0-2
Aids: Bl: 0-0 Vi: 0-0 Tstrap: 0-0 Ckp: 0-0
Best Rating: 92 7/09 Hayd 1m3f200y gd-fm

Useful; stays 1m4f; acts on good and faster ground.

Brushing

101 **71**
3-y-o ch f Medicean-Seasonal Blossom (IRE) (Fairy King (USA))
M H Tompkins Dullingham Park

Placings:0-16 **(6015)**
2009: 6^{1}G, 7^{6}G,

	Starts	1st	2nd	3rd	Win & Pl
Career Total (Turf)	3	1	0	0	2720

71 8/09 Yarm 6f3y GD £2719
Total win prize-money £2720

Going (Turf): Sf: 0-0 GS: 0-0 **Gd: 1-3** GF: 0-0 Fm: 0-0
Distance: 5f/6f: 0-0 **7f-8f: 1-3** 9f-13f: 0-0 14f+: 0-0
Track : LH: 0-1 RH: 0-0 Tight: 0-0 Gall: 0-0
Aids: Bl: 0-0 Vi: 0-0 Tstrap: 0-0 Ckp: 0-0
Best Rating: 71 8/09 Yarm 6f3y good

Fair; effective over 6f; acts on good ground.

Brut

99(81) (58)**76**
7-y-o b g Mind Games-Champenoise (Forzando)
D W Barker D W Barker

Placings:0620**556**/**366**2233004515030222/300150035000 053/**240**5061021153004101/**00**301005006-0056035 **(3020)**
2009: 5^{0}GF, 5^{0}GF, 5^{5}GF, 5^{6}F, 5^{0}GF, 5^{3}GF, 5^{5}G,

	Starts	1st	2nd	3rd	Win & Pl
Career Total (Turf)	70	8	7	9	38942
Career Total (AW)	8	0	1	1	1224

76 5/08 Catt 5f (0-70)H GD £2729
70 11/07 Catt 5f G-F £2730
75 9/07 Haml 5f4y (0-70)H G-S £3238
74 6/07 Haml 6f5y (0-75)H GD £3886
70 6/07 Haml 6f5y (0-60)H GD £2637
67 5/07 Haml 5f4y (0-60)H G-F £2388
74 6/06 Catt 5f (0-70)H G-F £3886
65 7/05 Thsk 6f (0-70)H GD £4264
Total win prize-money £25762

Going (Turf): Sf: 0-5 GS: 1-10 **Gd: 4-26** GF: 3-24 Fm: 0-5
Distance: **5f/6f: 6-70** 7f-8f: 2-8 9f-13f: 0-0 14f+: 0-0
Track : LH: 0-15 RH: 0-0 Tight: 0-8 Gall: 0-0
Aids: Bl: 0-0 Vi: 0-1 Tstrap: 6-36 Ckp: 6-36
Best Rating: 76 5/08 Catt 5f good

Moderate handicapper; effective from 5f-6f; acts on any ground; goes well at Hamilton.

Bruton Street (USA)

105 **89**
3-y-o b/br g Dynaformer (USA)-Fit For A Queen (USA) (Fit To Fight (USA))
J H M Gosden H R H Princess Haya Of Jordan

Placings:0-3435321 **(7221)**
2009: 10^{3}G, 10^{4}GS, 10^{3}G, 12^{5}G, 10^{3}GS, 10^{2}GS, 11^{1}S,

	Starts	1st	2nd	3rd	Win & Pl
Career Total (Turf)	8	1	1	3	6015

89 11/09 Catt 1m3f214y SFT £2914
Total win prize-money £2914

Going (Turf): **Sf: 1-1** GS: 0-3 Gd: 0-4 GF: 0-0 Fm: 0-0
Distance: 5f/6f: 0-0 7f-8f: 0-0 **9f-13f: 1-8** 14f+: 0-0
Track : **LH: 1-4** RH: 0-4 **Tight: 1-3** Gall: 0-2
Aids: Bl: 0-0 Vi: 0-0 Tstrap: 0-0 Ckp: 0-0
Best Rating: 89 11/09 Catt 1m3f214y soft

Useful; stays 1m4f; acts on good and soft ground.

Brynfa Boy

96(98) (71)**62**
3-y-o b g Namid-Funny Girl (IRE) (Darshaan)
P W D'Arcy The Golf Oil Partnership

Placings:0-0005251 **(7714)**
2009: 6^{0}G, 6^{0}GF, 5^{0}G, 6^{5}G, 5^{2}GF, 5^{5}GF, 5^{1}SD,

	Starts	1st	2nd	3rd	Win & Pl
Career Total (Turf)	6	0	1	0	1156
Career Total (AW)	2	1	0	0	2730

71 12/09 Wolv 5f20y STD £2729
Total win prize-money £2730

Going (Turf): **Sf: 0-0 GS: 0-0** Gd: 0-3 **GF: 0-3 Fm: 0-0**
Distance: **5f/6f: 1-6** 7f-8f: 0-2 9f-13f: 0-0 14f+: 0-0
Track : **LH: 1-2** RH: 0-0 **Tight: 1-1** Gall: 0-2
Aids: Bl: 0-0 Vi: 0-0 Tstrap: 0-0 Ckp: 0-0
Best Rating: 71 12/09 Wolv 5f20y stand

Modest; effective over 5f; acts on fast ground on Polytrack.

Buachaill Dona (IRE)

108(104) (101)**110**
6-y-o b g Namid-Serious Contender (IRE) (Tenby)
D Nicholls Mike Browne

Placings:2/11216/4603100/**0**3550100-00160202006 **(6180)**
2009: 6^{0}G, 6^{0}G, 6^{1}SD, 6^{6}G, 5^{0}GF, 5^{2}G, 6^{0}S, 5^{2}G, 5^{0}GF, 5^{0}GF, 5^{6}GF,

	Starts	1st	2nd	3rd	Win & Pl
Career Total (Turf)	30	5	4	2	80513
Career Total (AW)	2	1	0	0	6476

101 4/09 Kemp 6f STD £6476
110 6/08 Newc 5f (0-105)H G-S £18693
107 9/07 Muss 5f (0-95)H G-F £7772
103 8/06 York 5f (0-100)H G-S £16192
87 7/06 Catt 5f (0-85)H FRM £7772
65 4/06 Thsk 6f G-S £3562
Total win prize-money £60468

Going (Turf): Sf: 0-2 **GS: 3-6** Gd: 0-11 GF: 1-10 Fm: 1-1
Distance: **5f/6f: 6-30** 7f-8f: 0-2 9f-13f: 0-0 14f+: 0-0
Track : LH: 0-6 **RH: 1-1** Tight: 0-1 Gall: 0-5
Aids: Bl: 0-0 Vi: 0-0 Tstrap: 0-0 Ckp: 0-0
Best Rating: 110 6/08 Newc 5f gd-sft

Smart; effective over 5f-6f; acts on most ground; goes on Polytrack.

Buail Isteach (IRE)

91(91) (44)**47**
4-y-o b f Acclamation-Its All Eurs (IRE) (Barathea (IRE))
E J Creighton Four Provinces Partnership

Placings:0-0605000 (3946)
2009: 7^{0}SD, 7^{6}SD, 7^{0}SD, 7^{5}GF, 7^{0}GF, 5^{0}F, 7^{0}GF,

	Starts	1st	2nd	3rd	Win & Pl
Career Total (Turf)	4	0	0	0	0
Career Total (AW)	4	0	0	0	0

Going (Turf): **Sf: 0-0 GS: 0-0 Gd: 0-0 GF: 0-3 Fm: 0-1**
Distance: 5f/6f: 0-1 7f-8f: 0-7 9f-13f: 0-0 14f+: 0-0
Track : LH: 0-6 RH: 0-0 Tight: 0-3 Gall: 0-1
Aids: Bl: 0-3 Vi: 0-0 Tstrap: 0-0 Ckp: 0-0
Best Rating: 47 5/09 Yarm 7f3y gd-fm

Bubbelas

92 **73**
2-y-o b f Pastoral Pursuits-Arctic High (Polar Falcon (USA))
J J Quinn C D Carr

Placings:015604 (6169)
2009: 5^{0}G, 6^{1}G, 6^{5}GS, 7^{6}GS, 5^{0}GF, 5^{4}GF,

	Starts	1st	2nd	3rd	Win & Pl
Career Total (Turf)	6	1	0	0	3479

73 6/09 Pont 6f GD £3238
Total win prize-money £3238

Going (Turf): Sf: 0-0 GS: 0-2 **Gd: 1-2** GF: 0-2 Fm: 0-0
Distance: **5f/6f: 1-5** 7f-8f: 0-1 9f-13f: 0-0 14f+: 0-0
Track : **LH: 1-4** RH: 0-0 Tight: 0-2 Gall: 0-0
Aids: Bl: 0-0 Vi: 0-0 Tstrap: 0-0 Ckp: 0-0
Best Rating: 73 6/09 Pont 6f good

Bubber (IRE)

86(88) (52)**42**
2-y-o b f Westerner-Bubble N Squeak (IRE) (Catrail (USA))
R A Fahey R F White

Placings:640 (7799)
2009: 5^{6}S, **7^{4}**SD, **5^{0}**SD,

	Starts	1st	2nd	3rd	Win & Pl
Career Total (Turf)	1	0	0	0	0
Career Total (AW)	2	0	0	0	192

Going (Turf): **Sf: 0-1 GS: 0-0 Gd: 0-0 GF: 0-0 Fm: 0-0**
Distance: 5f/6f: 0-2 7f-8f: 0-1 9f-13f: 0-0 14f+: 0-0
Track : LH: 0-3 RH: 0-0 Tight: 0-2 Gall: 0-0
Aids: Bl: 0-0 Vi: 0-0 Tstrap: 0-0 Ckp: 0-0
Best Rating: 52 12/09 Wolv 5f216y stand

Moderate; stays 6f but will be suited by further; acts on Polytrack; one to keep an eye on.

Bubbly Bellini (IRE)

89(102) (76)**73**
2-y-o b g Mull Of Kintyre (USA)-Gwapa (IRE) (Imperial Frontier (USA))
George Baker (A Bailey 14/12) Mrs C E S Baker

Placings:6455**621212** (7868)
2009: 6^{6}GF, 5^{4}G, 7^{5}GF, 6^{5}G, 7^{6}SF, **6^{2}**SD, **5^{1}**SD, **5^{2}**SD, **5^{1}**SS, 7^{2}SS,

	Starts	1st	2nd	3rd	Win & Pl
Career Total (Turf)	4	0	0	0	385
Career Total (AW)	6	2	3	0	7094

76 12/09 Sthl 5f SS £2047
69 12/09 Wolv 5f216y STD £2729
Total win prize-money £4777

Going (Turf): **Sf: 0-0 GS: 0-0 Gd: 0-2 GF: 0-2 Fm: 0-0**
Distance: **5f/6f: 2-7** 7f-8f: 0-3 9f-13f: 0-0 14f+: 0-0
Track : **LH: 1-5** RH: 0-0 **Tight: 1-4** Gall: 0-0
Aids: Bl: 0-0 Vi: 0-0 Tstrap: 1-3 Ckp: 1-3
Best Rating: 76 12/09 Sthl 5f std-slw

Fair; effective over 5f-7f; acts on fast ground; goes on Polytrack and Fibresand; has worn cheekpieces.

Bubbly Braveheart (IRE)

94(97) (65)**67**
2-y-o b g Cape Cross (IRE)-Infinity (FR) (Bering)
A Bailey The Champagne Club

Placings:05606204216 (7731)
2009: **6^{0}**SD, 7^{5}G, 7^{6}G, 7^{0}GS, 8^{6}G, **8^{2}**SD, 8^{0}S, **8^{4}**SD, **8^{2}**SD, **8^{1}**SD, 9^{6}SD,

	Starts	1st	2nd	3rd	Win & Pl
Career Total (Turf)	5	0	0	0	0
Career Total (AW)	6	1	2	0	3720

64 12/09 Wolv 1m141y STD £2047
Total win prize-money £2047

Going (Turf): **Sf: 0-1 GS: 0-1 Gd: 0-3 GF: 0-0 Fm: 0-0**
Distance: 5f/6f: 0-1 7f-8f: 0-5 **9f-13f: 1-5** 14f+: 0-0
Track : **LH: 1-7** RH: 0-2 **Tight: 1-6** Gall: 0-0
Aids: Bl: 0-4 Vi: 0-0 Tstrap: 1-2 Ckp: 1-2
Best Rating: 67 6/09 Sand 7f16y good

Modest; stays 1m; acts on good ground; goes on Polytrack; has worn blinkers and cheekpieces.

Bubses Boy

99(96) (60)**61**
3-y-o ch g Needwood Blade-Welcome Home (Most Welcome)
P Howling (M L W Bell 5/8) Paul Terry

Placings:004-3**04**041506400 (7392)
2009: 9^{3}GS, **11^{0}**SD, **10^{4}**SD, 10^{0}GF, 10^{4}G, 10^{1}G, 16^{5}GF, **11^{0}**SD, **12^{6}**SD, 12^{4}GF, **12^{0}**SD, **10^{0}**SD,

	Starts	1st	2nd	3rd	Win & Pl
Career Total (Turf)	9	1	0	1	3314
Career Total (AW)	6	0	0	0	0

61 8/09 Yarm 1m2f21y GD £2201
Total win prize-money £2202

Going (Turf): Sf: 0-2 GS: 0-2 **Gd: 1-2** GF: 0-3 Fm: 0-0
Distance: 5f/6f: 0-1 7f-8f: 0-2 **9f-13f: 1-11** 14f+: 0-1
Track : **LH: 1-7** RH: 0-5 **Tight: 1-6** Gall: 0-0
Aids: Bl: 0-0 Vi: 0-0 Tstrap: 0-0 Ckp: 0-0
Best Rating: 61 8/09 Yarm 1m2f21y good

Moderate; stays 1m2f; seems best on good ground.

Buccellati

112 **118**
5-y-o ch h Soviet Star (USA)-Susi Wong (IRE) (Selkirk (USA))
A M Balding Mr & Mrs P McMahon & Mr & Mrs R Gorell

Placings:012/454056111/04514116-310430 **(7744a)**
2009: 10^{3}G, 13^{1}GF, 12^{0}G, 12^{4}G, 12^{3}F, 12^{0}G,

	Starts	1st	2nd	3rd	Win & Pl
Career Total (Turf)	26	8	1	2	391457

116 5/09 Ches 1m5f89y G-F £42577
117 10/08 Newb 1m4f5y SFT £36900
113 10/08 NmkR 1m4f G-F £24978
110 7/08 Asct 1m2f (0-105)H G-F £11215
105 10/07 Asct 1m4f (0-105)H G-S £46740
100 9/07 Ches 1m2f75y (0-100)H GD £21188
97 9/07 Donc 1m2f60y (0-85) G-F £11217
75 8/06 Wwck 7f26y GD £2590
Total win prize-money £197412

Going (Turf): Sf: 1-3 GS: 1-3 Gd: 2-11 **GF: 4-7** Fm: 0-2
Distance: 5f/6f: 0-1 7f-8f: 1-3 **9f-13f: 6-21** 14f+: 1-1
Track : **LH: 5-10** RH: 3-13 Tight: 2-5 **Gall: 5-9**
Aids: Bl: 0-1 **Vi: 7-16** Tstrap: 0-0 Ckp: 0-0
Best Rating: 118 4/09 Sand 1m2f7y good

Group class; effective over 1m2f-1m4f; acts on most ground; usually visored; usually held up.

Buck Cannon (IRE)

(93) (52)
4-y-o b g High Chaparral (IRE)-Folgore (USA) (Irish River (FR))
P M Phelan Ermyn Lodge Stud

Placings:00060-0 **(0061)**
2009: **8^{0}**SD,

	Starts	1st	2nd	3rd	Win & Pl
Career Total (Turf)	1	0	0	0	
Career Total (AW)	5	0	0	0	0

Going (Turf): **Sf: 0-0 GS: 0-1 Gd: 0-0 GF: 0-0 Fm: 0-0**
Distance: 5f/6f: 0-0 7f-8f: 0-4 9f-13f: 0-2 14f+: 0-0
Track : LH: 0-2 RH: 0-4 Tight: 0-3 Gall: 0-0
Aids: Bl: 0-0 Vi: 0-0 Tstrap: 0-0 Ckp: 0-0
Best Rating: 52 3/08 Ling 1m stand

Bucked Off (SAF)

106(89) (97)**94**
5-y-o b g Casey Tibbs (IRE)-See Me Fly (SAF) (Caesour (USA))
T P Tate (H J Brown 13/3) Mrs Fitri Hay

Placings:4/1356242033402/300-64530440 (6665)
2009: 8^{6}FT, 10^{4}G, 10^{5}GF, **9^{3}**SD, 12^{0}GF, 10^{4}GS, 8^{4}GF, 10^{0}GS,

	Starts	1st	2nd	3rd	Win & Pl
Career Total (Turf)	23	1	3	4	20460
Career Total (AW)	2	0	0	1	3403

1/07 Keni 5f GD £2119
Total win prize-money £2120

Going (Turf): Sf: 0-5 GS: 0-2 **Gd: 1-13** GF: 0-3 Fm: 0-0
Distance: **5f/6f: 1-5** 7f-8f: 0-9 9f-13f: 0-10 14f+: 0-0
Track : LH: 0-5 RH: 0-1 Tight: 0-0 Gall: 0-5
Aids: Bl: 0-0 Vi: 0-0 Tstrap: 0-0 Ckp: 0-0
Best Rating: 97 3/09 Jebl 1m1f stand

Very useful; formerly trained in South Africa and Dubai; stays 1m2f; acts on most types of ground.

Buckie Boy (IRE)

101(105) (86)**78**

3-y-o b g Bahri (USA)-Woodren (USA) (Woodman (USA))
J S Goldie (H R A Cecil 11/10) North South Partnership

Placings:424352130 **(7117)**
2009: 10^4GF, 10^2GF, 10^4GF, 10^3GF, 10^5SD, 12^2SD, 12^1SD, 13^3SS, 16^0GS,

	Starts	1st	2nd	3rd	Win & Pl
Career Total (Turf)	5	0	1	1	1740
Career Total (AW)	4	1	1	1	3676

86 9/09 Kemp 1m4f STD £2590
Total win prize-money £2590

Going (Turf): Sf: 0-0 GS: 0-1 Gd: 0-0 GF: 0-4 Fm: 0-0
Distance: 5f/6f: 0-0 7f-8f: 0-0 **9f-13f: 1-8** 14f+: 0-1
Track : LH: 0-4 **RH: 1-5** Tight: 0-6 Gall: 0-0
Aids: Bl: 0-4 Vi: 0-1 Tstrap: 0-0 Ckp: 0-0
Best Rating: 86 9/09 Kemp 1m4f stand

Useful; effective at 1m2f-1m5f; goes on fast ground; acts on Polytrack; has worn blinkers/visor.

Buckle Up

88(92) (44)**42**

3-y-o ch g Primo Valentino (IRE)-Ambitious (Ardkinglass)
D K Ivory Marcoe Electrical And Dean Ivory

Placings:000-50060640 **(4425)**
2009: 6^5SD, 7^0SD, 5^0GS, 7^6SD, 9^0G, 8^6GF, 8^4GS, 7^0S,

	Starts	1st	2nd	3rd	Win & Pl
Career Total (Turf)	7	0	0	0	144
Career Total (AW)	4	0	0	0	0

Going (Turf): Sf: 0-1 GS: 0-2 Gd: 0-2 GF: 0-2 Fm: 0-0
Distance: 5f/6f: 0-5 7f-8f: 0-3 9f-13f: 0-3 14f+: 0-0
Track : LH: 0-5 RH: 0-3 Tight: 0-2 Gall: 0-3
Aids: Bl: 0-0 Vi: 0-0 Tstrap: 0-3 Ckp: 0-3
Best Rating: 44 2/09 Kemp 6f stand

Buddhist Monk

106(101) (79)**94**

4-y-o b g Dr Fong (USA)-Circle Of Light (Anshan)
Ian Williams Dr Marwan Koukash

Placings:25222120-633350001121 **(6248)**
2009: 10^6G, 10^3G, 12^3GF, 14^3GF, 14^5GF, 16^0S, 12^0GS, 16^0GF, 9^1F, 9^1GF, 9^2GF, 10^1GF,

	Starts	1st	2nd	3rd	Win & Pl
Career Total (Turf)	17	3	5	3	28110
Career Total (AW)	3	1	1	0	2818

77 9/09 Hayd 1m2f95y G-F £6476
82 9/09 Leic 1m1f218y G-F £2590
79 9/09 Brig 1m1f209y FRM £1942
78 9/08 Kemp 1m4f STD £2047
Total win prize-money £13056

Going (Turf): Sf: 0-1 GS: 0-3 Gd: 0-3 **GF: 2-9** Fm: 1-1
Distance: 5f/6f: 0-0 7f-8f: 0-2 **9f-13f: 4-13** 14f+: 0-5
Track : LH: 2-11 RH: 2-8 Tight: 0-5 Gall: 0-8
Aids: Bl: 0-0 Vi: 1-1 Tstrap: 1-3 Ckp: 1-3
Best Rating: 94 5/09 York 1m6f gd-fm

Useful; effective at around 1m2f-1m6f; acts on quick ground; goes on Polytrack; has looked quirky; has worn a tongue tie.

Buddy Holly

100(104) (87)**84**

4-y-o b g Reel Buddy (USA)-Night Symphonie (Cloudings (IRE))
Pat Eddery Hayman, Pearson, Phillips & McGuinness

Placings:00/0112103445-3431406020 **(6724)**
2009: 11^3SD, 12^4G, 10^3G, 10^1SD, 10^4GS, 10^0GF, 9^6S, 8^0SD, 12^2G, 12^0SD,

	Starts	1st	2nd	3rd	Win & Pl
Career Total (Turf)	17	3	2	2	15462
Career Total (AW)	5	1	0	1	5594

87 6/09 Kemp 1m2f (0-80)H STD £4727
84 6/08 Sand 1m2f7y (0-75)H GD £4533
73 4/08 Bath 1m2f46y (0-70)H SFT £2914
68 4/08 Nott 1m54y (0-65)H SFT £2047
Total win prize-money £14221

Going (Turf): Sf: 2-5 GS: 0-3 Gd: 1-6 GF: 0-3 Fm: 0-0
Distance: 5f/6f: 0-1 7f-8f: 0-3 **9f-13f: 4-18** 14f+: 0-0
Track : LH: 2-8 RH: 2-12 **Tight: 1-8** Gall: 0-3
Aids: Bl: 0-0 **Vi: 1-5** Tstrap: 0-0 Ckp: 0-0
Best Rating: 87 6/09 Kemp 1m2f stand

Useful; stays 1m2f; acts on good and soft ground; goes on Polytrack.

Buddy Marvellous (IRE)

(90) (34)**55**

3-y-o ch g Redback-La Paola (IRE) (Common Grounds)
R A Harris Drag Star On Swan

Placings:65503000-00 **(0308)**
2009: 7^0SD, 6^0SD,

	Starts	1st	2nd	3rd	Win & Pl
Career Total (Turf)	6	0	0	1	404
Career Total (AW)	4	0	0	0	

Going (Turf): Sf: 0-0 GS: 0-2 Gd: 0-3 GF: 0-1 Fm: 0-0
Distance: 5f/6f: 0-7 7f-8f: 0-3 9f-13f: 0-0 14f+: 0-0
Track : LH: 0-5 RH: 0-2 Tight: 0-2 Gall: 0-2
Aids: Bl: 0-1 Vi: 0-0 Tstrap: 0-1 Ckp: 0-1
Best Rating: 55 4/08 Wind 5f10y good

Plating-class; suited by 5f and good ground.

Buds Dilemma

(94) (45)**50**

5-y-o b m Anabaa (USA)-Lady Thynn (FR) (Crystal Glitters (USA))
D A Rees (S Gollings 25/4) Monty Belton

Placings:0/0500060/40-40 **(0802)**
2009: 7^4SD, 8^0SD,

	Starts	1st	2nd	3rd	Win & Pl
Career Total (Turf)	9	0	0	0	192
Career Total (AW)	3	0	0	0	0

Going (Turf): Sf: 0-1 GS: 0-1 Gd: 0-5 GF: 0-2 Fm: 0-0
Distance: 5f/6f: 0-1 7f-8f: 0-6 9f-13f: 0-5 14f+: 0-0
Track : LH: 0-5 RH: 0-6 Tight: 0-6 Gall: 0-0
Aids: Bl: 0-2 Vi: 0-0 Tstrap: 0-0 Ckp: 0-0
Best Rating: 50 9/07 Ches 1m2f75y good

Budva

(89) (62)

2-y-o b c Kylian (USA)-Danlu (USA) (Danzig (USA))
H Morrison H Morrison

Placings:030 **(7638)**
2009: 8^0SD, 8^3SD, 8^0SD,

	Starts	1st	2nd	3rd	Win & Pl
Career Total (Turf)	0	0	0	0	
Career Total (AW)	3	0	0	1	385

Going (Turf): Sf: 0-0 GS: 0-0 Gd: 0-0 GF: 0-0 Fm: 0-0
Distance: 5f/6f: 0-0 7f-8f: 0-3 9f-13f: 0-0 14f+: 0-0
Track : LH: 0-3 RH: 0-0 Tight: 0-0 Gall: 0-0
Aids: Bl: 0-0 Vi: 0-0 Tstrap: 0-0 Ckp: 0-0
Best Rating: 62 11/09 Sthl 1m stand

Buffett

91(95) (66)**66**

2-y-o b c Bertolini (USA)-Batik (IRE) (Peintre Celebre (USA))
L M Cumani Aston House Stud

Placings:6554 **(6211)**
2009: 6^6GF, 7^5G, 6^5G, 8^4SD,

	Starts	1st	2nd	3rd	Win & Pl
Career Total (Turf)	3	0	0	0	0
Career Total (AW)	1	0	0	0	0

Going (Turf): Sf: 0-0 GS: 0-0 Gd: 0-2 GF: 0-1 Fm: 0-0
Distance: 5f/6f: 0-1 7f-8f: 0-3 9f-13f: 0-0 14f+: 0-0
Track : LH: 0-1 RH: 0-1 Tight: 0-1 Gall: 0-0
Aids: Bl: 0-0 Vi: 0-0 Tstrap: 0-0 Ckp: 0-0
Best Rating: 66 9/09 Kemp 1m stand

Bugaku

97(110) (96)**91**

4-y-o b g Montjeu (IRE)-Bryony Brind (IRE) (Kris)
Sir Michael Stoute Mrs Denis Haynes

Placings:0/1306400 **(6681)**
2009: 10^1GF, 10^3SD, 10^0GS, 10^6G, 11^4SD, 14^0GF, 12^0G,

	Starts	1st	2nd	3rd	Win & Pl
Career Total (Turf)	6	1	0	0	3886
Career Total (AW)	2	0	0	1	1652

86 5/09 Sand 1m2f7y G-F £3885
Total win prize-money £3886

Going (Turf): Sf: 0-1 GS: 0-1 Gd: 0-2 **GF: 1-2** Fm: 0-0
Distance: 5f/6f: 0-0 7f-8f: 0-1 **9f-13f: 1-6** 14f+: 0-1
Track : LH: 0-3 **RH: 1-4** Tight: 0-0 Gall: 0-4
Aids: Bl: 0-0 Vi: 0-0 Tstrap: 0-0 Ckp: 0-0
Best Rating: 96 6/09 Kemp 1m2f stand

Useful; stays 1m3f; acts on fast ground and Polytrack.

Bugsy's Boy

92(99) (73)**77**

5-y-o b g Double Trigger (IRE)-Bugsy's Sister (Aragon)
George Baker Seaton Partnership

Placings:06040210/0112004-2 **(6622)**
2009: 16^2G,

	Starts	1st	2nd	3rd	Win & Pl
Career Total (Turf)	6	1	2	0	5069
Career Total (AW)	10	2	1	0	4700

77 3/08 Pont 2m1f216y (0-75)H G-S £3238
73 2/08 Wolv 2m119y (0-65)H STD £2047
69 12/07 Wolv 2m119y (0-65)H STD £2047
Total win prize-money £7335

Going (Turf): Sf: 0-0 **GS: 1-3** Gd: 0-2 GF: 0-1 Fm: 0-0
Distance: 5f/6f: 0-0 7f-8f: 0-2 9f-13f: 0-3 **14f+: 3-11**
Track : **LH: 3-11** RH: 0-5 **Tight: 2-6** Gall: 0-1
Aids: Bl: 0-0 Vi: 0-0 Tstrap: 2-4 Ckp: 2-4
Best Rating: 77 10/09 Newb 2m good

Modest; stays 2m2f; acts on easy ground; goes on Polytrack; has worn cheekpieces.

Bulberry Hill

(96) (46)45

8-y-o b g Makbul-Hurtleberry (IRE) (Tirol)
R W Price Dhafi Al Marri

Placings:0550035/6015502301/2233601051 4/2200004/40 0-06 **(1439)**
2009: 14^{0}SD, 16^{6}SD,

	Starts	1st	2nd	3rd	Win & Pl
Career Total (Turf)	7	0	0	0	0
Career Total (AW)	33	4	5	4	10602

57 12/06 Sthl 2m (0-45) STD £2047
53 10/06 Sthl 2m (0-45) STD £2013
53 12/05 Sthl 1m4f (0-40) STD £1440
48 5/05 Sthl 1m4f (0-45) STD £1477
Total win prize-money £6978

Going (Turf): **Sf: 0-0 GS: 0-1 Gd: 0-2 GF: 0-3 Fm: 0-1**
Distance: 5f/6f: 0-0 7f-8f: 0-3 9f-13f: 2-20 14f+: 2-17
Track : **LH: 4-35** RH: 0-3 Tight: 0-12 Gall: 0-1
Aids: Bl: 0-0 Vi: 0-0 Tstrap: 0-0 Ckp: 0-0
Best Rating: **67** 2/07 Sthl 2m slow

Moderate; stays 2m; acts on both All-Weather surfaces; has worn tongue tie.

Bulella

(93) (61)48

3-y-o b f Makbul-Bella Tutrice (IRE) (Woodborough (USA))
Garry Moss Brooklands Racing

Placings:00062302-3 **(0041)**
2009: 6^{3}SS,

	Starts	1st	2nd	3rd	Win & Pl
Career Total (Turf)	3	0	0	0	
Career Total (AW)	6	0	2	2	1814

Going (Turf): **Sf: 0-0 GS: 0-2 Gd: 0-0 GF: 0-1 Fm: 0-0**
Distance: 5f/6f: 0-8 7f-8f: 0-1 9f-13f: 0-0 14f+: 0-0
Track : LH: 0-7 RH: 0-0 Tight: 0-1 Gall: 0-1
Aids: Bl: 0-0 Vi: 0-0 Tstrap: 0-0 Ckp: 0-0
Best Rating: **61** 1/09 Sthl 6f std-slw

Moderate; suited by 6f and Fibresand.

Bull Market (IRE)

81(101) (76)84

6-y-o b g Danehill (USA)-Paper Moon (IRE) (Lake Coniston (IRE))
M S Tuck (Ian Williams 18/3) Luckley Arms Partnership

Placings:221/30605/1001314060-300002 **(7490)**
2009: 8^{3}SD, 9^{0}SD, 12^{0}GS, 13^{0}SD, 8^{0}SS, 12^{2}SD,

	Starts	1st	2nd	3rd	Win & Pl
Career Total (Turf)	14	2	0	2	12999
Career Total (AW)	10	2	3	1	10269

84 6/08 Hayd 1m2f120y (0-85)H G-F £5504
79 5/08 Hayd 1m3f200y (0-75)H G-F £5310
76 4/08 Kemp 1m4f STD £2047
76 12/05 Sthl 1m STD £4061
Total win prize-money £16923

Going (Turf): Sf: 0-0 GS: 0-3 Gd: 0-5 **GF: 2-6** Fm: 0-0
Distance: 5f/6f: 0-0 7f-8f: 1-3 **9f-13f: 3-19** 14f+: 0-2
Track : **LH: 3-19** RH: 1-5 Tight: 0-13 Gall: 0-4
Aids: Bl: 0-0 Vi: 0-0 Tstrap: 0-0 Ckp: 0-0
Best Rating: **84** 6/08 Hayd 1m2f120y gd-fm

Modest; stays 1m4f; acts on most ground; also goes on Polytrack and Fibresand.

Bullet Duck (IRE)

79 27

2-y-o br/gr f Redback-Helibel (IRE) (Pivotal)
Tom Dascombe Manor House Stables LLP

Placings:00 **(6591)**
2009: 6^{0}GF, 6^{0}GS,

	Starts	1st	2nd	3rd	Win & Pl
Career Total (Turf)	2	0	0	0	

Going (Turf): **Sf: 0-0 GS: 0-1 Gd: 0-0 GF: 0-1 Fm: 0-0**
Distance: 5f/6f: 0-1 7f-8f: 0-1 9f-13f: 0-0 14f+: 0-0
Track : LH: 0-0 RH: 0-0 Tight: 0-0 Gall: 0-0
Aids: Bl: 0-0 Vi: 0-0 Tstrap: 0-0 Ckp: 0-0
Best Rating: **27** 10/09 Nott 6f15y gd-sft

Bullet Man (USA)

107(107) (87)94

4-y-o br g Mr Greeley (USA)-Silk Tapestry (USA) (Tank's Prospect (USA))
L M Cumani Kevin Bailey & Ms Nicola Mahoney

Placings:23/41-661200 **(5437)**
2009: 10^{6}G, 10^{6}GS, 10^{1}GF, 10^{2}GF, 12^{0}GF, 10^{0}GF,

	Starts	1st	2nd	3rd	Win & Pl
Career Total (Turf)	7	1	2	0	9433
Career Total (AW)	3	1	0	1	5358

89 5/09 NmkR 1m2f (0-85)H G-F £5828
87 12/08 Ling 1m2f (0-80)H STD £4727
Total win prize-money £10555

Going (Turf): Sf: 0-0 GS: 0-1 Gd: 0-1 **GF: 1-5** Fm: 0-0
Distance: 5f/6f: 0-0 7f-8f: 0-3 **9f-13f: 2-7** 14f+: 0-0
Track : **LH: 1-6** RH: 0-2 **Tight: 1-3** Gall: 0-3
Aids: Bl: 0-0 Vi: 0-0 Tstrap: 0-0 Ckp: 0-0
Best Rating: **94** 6/09 Pont 1m2f6y gd-fm

Useful; effective over 1m2f; acts on Polytrack and fast ground.

Bullet Train

94 77

2-y-o b c Sadler's Wells (USA)-Kind (IRE) (Danehill (USA))
H R A Cecil K Abdulla

Placings:1 **(7099)**
2009: 8^{1}G,

	Starts	1st	2nd	3rd	Win & Pl
Career Total (Turf)	1	1	0	0	3469

77 10/09 Yarm 1m3y GD £3469
Total win prize-money £3469

Going (Turf): Sf: 0-0 GS: 0-0 **Gd: 1-1** GF: 0-0 Fm: 0-0
Distance: 5f/6f: 0-0 7f-8f: 0-0 **9f-13f: 1-1** 14f+: 0-0
Track : LH: 0-0 RH: 0-0 Tight: 0-0 Gall: 0-0
Aids: Bl: 0-0 Vi: 0-0 Tstrap: 0-0 Ckp: 0-0
Best Rating: **77** 10/09 Yarm 1m3y good

Fair; stays 1m; acts on good ground.

Bulwark (IRE)

100(91) (74)108

7-y-o b g Montjeu (IRE)-Bulaxie (Bustino)
Ian Williams JSM Fabrications Ltd

Placings:045/3212133121/561030442/03300505/14050-6605000 **(7402)**
2009: 16^{6}G, 21^{6}GF, 14^{0}GF, 16^{5}GS, 18^{0}G, 16^{0}G, 16^{0}SD,

	Starts	1st	2nd	3rd	Win & Pl
Career Total (Turf)	40	6	4	5	176610
Career Total (AW)	2	0	0	1	4665

108 5/08 Ches 2m2f147y H GD £74772
101 6/06 Hayd 2m45y (0-100)H G-F £17449
97 9/05 Nott 2m9y (0-85)H GD £5947
87 9/05 NmkJ 1m6f175y (0-80)H G-F £5973
79 6/05 Yarm 1m6f17y (0-75)H FRM £4208
76 5/05 Wwck 1m4f134y (0-70)H GD £3746
Total win prize-money £112099

Going (Turf): Sf: 0-3 GS: 0-5 **Gd: 3-13** GF: 2-18 Fm: 1-1
Distance: 5f/6f: 0-0 7f-8f: 0-2 9f-13f: 1-7 **14f+: 5-33**
Track : **LH: 5-18** RH: 1-22 **Tight: 2-9** Gall: 1-19
Aids: **Bl: 5-23** Vi: 1-8 Tstrap: 0-0 Ckp: 0-0
Best Rating: **111** 5/07 Sand 2m78y gd-sft

Useful; Group placed and winner of the 2008 Chester Cup; stays 2m2f; acts on most ground; has worn blinkers, an eyeshield and a visor; usually held up.

Bumble Rose (IRE)

87 41

6-y-o b m Kornado-Bukowina (GER) (Windwurf (GER))
A G Foster (Miss Lucinda V Russell 3/3) S A Rose

Placings:06050 **(3023)**
2009: 12^{0}GF, 10^{6}GS, 9^{0}G, 9^{5}F, 12^{0}G,

	Starts	1st	2nd	3rd	Win & Pl
Career Total (Turf)	5	0	0	0	0

Going (Turf): **Sf: 0-0 GS: 0-1 Gd: 0-2 GF: 0-1 Fm: 0-1**
Distance: 5f/6f: 0-0 7f-8f: 0-0 9f-13f: 0-5 14f+: 0-0
Track : LH: 0-2 RH: 0-3 Tight: 0-3 Gall: 0-1
Aids: Bl: 0-0 Vi: 0-0 Tstrap: 0-3 Ckp: 0-3
Best Rating: **41** 6/09 Ayr 1m1f20y firm

Bun Oir (USA)

89 61

2-y-o b/br c Seeking The Gold (USA)-Fraulein (Acatenango (GER))
R Hannon Peter O'Callaghan

Placings:0000 **(6735)**
2009: 7^{0}G, 7^{0}G, 7^{0}G, 8^{0}GS,

	Starts	1st	2nd	3rd	Win & Pl
Career Total (Turf)	4	0	0	0	

Going (Turf): **Sf: 0-0 GS: 0-1 Gd: 0-3 GF: 0-0 Fm: 0-0**
Distance: 5f/6f: 0-0 7f-8f: 0-3 9f-13f: 0-1 14f+: 0-0
Track : LH: 0-1 RH: 0-1 Tight: 0-1 Gall: 0-1
Aids: Bl: 0-0 Vi: 0-0 Tstrap: 0-0 Ckp: 0-0
Best Rating: **61** 8/09 NmkJ 7f good

Bun Penny

72 36

3-y-o ch f Bertolini (USA)-Mint Royale (IRE) (Cadeaux Genereux)
G M Moore Evelyn Duchess Of Sutherland

Placings:600-00 **(2970)**
2009: 7^{0}GF, 5^{0}GF,

	Starts	1st	2nd	3rd	Win & Pl
Career Total (Turf)	5	0	0	0	0

Going (Turf): **Sf: 0-0 GS: 0-1 Gd: 0-2 GF: 0-2 Fm: 0-0**
Distance: 5f/6f: 0-4 7f-8f: 0-1 9f-13f: 0-0 14f+: 0-0
Track : LH: 0-1 RH: 0-2 Tight: 0-1 Gall: 0-0

Aids: Bl: 0-0 Vi: 0-0 Tstrap: 0-0 Ckp: 0-0
Best Rating: 36 7/08 Ayr 6f good

Bundle Up

83(96) (57)53
6-y-o b m Diktat-Bundle (Cadeaux Genereux)
J L Flint (P D Evans 4/5) J L Flint

Placings:040/500214P-0560 (6859)
2009: 11⁰SD, 12⁵GF, 11⁶GF, 16⁰SD,

	Starts	1st	2nd	3rd	Win & Pl
Career Total (Turf)	6	1	1	0	2547
Career Total (AW)	8	0	0	0	433

53 8/08 Brig 1m3f196y (0-55)H G-F £1942
Total win prize-money £1943

Going (Turf): Sf: 0-0 GS: 0-1 Gd: 0-1 GF: 1-4 Fm: 0-0
Distance: 5f/6f: 0-0 7f-8f: 0-1 9f-13f: 1-10 14f+: 0-3
Track : LH: 1-8 RH: 0-4 Tight: 0-7 Gall: 0-1
Aids: Bl: 0-0 Vi: 0-0 Tstrap: 0-0 Ckp: 0-0
Best Rating: 58 6/07 Gdwd 1m good

Moderate; stays 1m3f; handles quick ground; has worn a tongue tie.

Bungie

(88) (48)35
5-y-o gr g Forzando-Sweet Whisper (Petong)
Jennie Candlish Ms Jennie Candlish

Placings:5004614/40000/0300-0 (0133)
2009: 7⁰SD,

	Starts	1st	2nd	3rd	Win & Pl
Career Total (Turf)	8	0	0	1	591
Career Total (AW)	9	1	0	0	3283

64 12/06 Wolv 5f20y STD £2730
Total win prize-money £2730

Going (Turf): Sf: 0-3 GS: 0-1 Gd: 0-1 GF: 0-3 Fm: 0-0
Distance: 5f/6f: 1-13 7f-8f: 0-4 9f-13f: 0-0 14f+: 0-0
Track : LH: 1-8 RH: 0-0 Tight: 1-8 Gall: 0-0
Aids: Bl: 0-3 Vi: 0-1 Tstrap: 0-0 Ckp: 0-0
Best Rating: 64 12/06 Wolv 5f20y stand

Bureaucrat

104 96
7-y-o b g Machiavellian (USA)-Lajna (Be My Guest (USA))
M F Harris (P J Hobbs 8/11) Mrs Susan Granger

Placings:46/41100/100-000 (4988)
2009: 12⁰G, 14⁰G, 13⁰GF,

	Starts	1st	2nd	3rd	Win & Pl
Career Total (Turf)	12	3	0	0	23976
Career Total (AW)	1	0	0	0	

96 6/08 Epsm 1m4f10y (0-100)H GD £15577
98 7/05 Nott 1m1f213y (0-70) GD £3445
86 6/05 Sals 1m1f198y (0-70) G-F £4241
Total win prize-money £23264

Going (Turf): Sf: 0-2 GS: 0-2 Gd: 2-4 GF: 1-4 Fm: 0-0
Distance: 5f/6f: 0-0 7f-8f: 0-2 9f-13f: 3-8 14f+: 0-3
Track : LH: 2-6 RH: 1-4 Tight: 2-7 Gall: 0-3
Aids: Bl: 0-0 Vi: 0-0 Tstrap: 0-1 Ckp: 0-1
Best Rating: 98 7/05 Nott 1m1f213y good

Very useful; stays 1m4f; acts on good and faster ground; multiple winner over hurdles/fences.

Burgau Royal

95 74
2-y-o b c Noverre (USA)-Regal Ransom (IRE) (Anabaa (USA))
M R Channon Nick Quesnel

Placings:422 (5445)
2009: 6⁴G, 6²GF, 6²GF,

	Starts	1st	2nd	3rd	Win & Pl
Career Total (Turf)	3	0	2	0	2227

Going (Turf): Sf: 0-0 GS: 0-0 Gd: 0-1 GF: 0-2 Fm: 0-0
Distance: 5f/6f: 0-3 7f-8f: 0-0 9f-13f: 0-0 14f+: 0-0
Track : LH: 0-0 RH: 0-0 Tight: 0-0 Gall: 0-2
Aids: Bl: 0-0 Vi: 0-0 Tstrap: 0-0 Ckp: 0-0
Best Rating: 74 8/09 Wind 6f gd-fm

Fair; suited by 6f and acts on fast ground.

Burgundy Ice (USA)

104(107) (96)87
3-y-o gr/ro f Storm Cat (USA)-Cara Rafaela (USA) (Quiet American (USA))
Saeed Bin Suroor Godolphin

Placings:10-20312 (6946)
2009: 8²GF, 8⁰GF, 8³GF, 8¹SD, 8²SD,

	Starts	1st	2nd	3rd	Win & Pl
Career Total (Turf)	5	1	1	1	7888
Career Total (AW)	2	1	1	0	6462

95 10/09 Kemp 1m (0-85)H STD £4727
77 10/08 Leic 7f9y SFT £4857
Total win prize-money £9584

Going (Turf): Sf: 1-1 GS: 0-1 Gd: 0-0 GF: 0-3 Fm: 0-0
Distance: 5f/6f: 0-0 7f-8f: 2-6 9f-13f: 0-1 14f+: 0-0
Track : LH: 0-2 RH: 1-3 Tight: 0-1 Gall: 0-1
Aids: Bl: 0-0 Vi: 0-0 Tstrap: 0-0 Ckp: 0-0
Best Rating: 96 10/09 Sthl 1m stand

Useful; stays 7f and acts on soft ground.

Burj Nahar

103 87
2-y-o b c Shamardal (USA)-Melikah (IRE) (Lammtarra (USA))
Saeed Bin Suroor Godolphin

Placings:1 (7243)
2009: 8¹S,

	Starts	1st	2nd	3rd	Win & Pl
Career Total (Turf)	1	1	0	0	4209

87 11/09 Nott 1m75y SFT £4209
Total win prize-money £4209

Going (Turf): Sf: 1-1 GS: 0-0 Gd: 0-0 GF: 0-0 Fm: 0-0
Distance: 5f/6f: 0-0 7f-8f: 0-0 9f-13f: 1-1 14f+: 0-0
Track : LH: 1-1 RH: 0-0 Tight: 0-0 Gall: 0-0
Aids: Bl: 0-0 Vi: 0-0 Tstrap: 0-0 Ckp: 0-0
Best Rating: 87 11/09 Nott 1m75y soft

Impressive winner on debut; effective over 1m; acts on soft ground.

Burma Rock (IRE)

100(102) (87)79
3-y-o b g Danehill Dancer (IRE)-Burmese Princess (USA) (King Of Kings (IRE))
L M Cumani Drones Racing

Placings:022-345421 (7048)
2009: 6³GF, 8⁴GF, 7⁵G, 8⁴GF, 9²SD, 10¹SD,

	Starts	1st	2nd	3rd	Win & Pl
Career Total (Turf)	7	0	2	1	3606
Career Total (AW)	2	1	1	0	3396

87 10/09 Kemp 1m2f (0-75)H STD £2590
Total win prize-money £2590

Going (Turf): Sf: 0-1 GS: 0-0 Gd: 0-3 GF: 0-3 Fm: 0-0
Distance: 5f/6f: 0-0 7f-8f: 0-6 9f-13f: 1-3 14f+: 0-0
Track : LH: 0-3 RH: 1-1 Tight: 0-1 Gall: 0-0
Aids: Bl: 0-0 Vi: 0-0 Tstrap: 0-0 Ckp: 0-0
Best Rating: 87 10/09 Kemp 1m2f stand

Fair; stays 1m2f; acts on good ground; goes on Polytrack.

Burnbank (IRE)

(72)75
6-y-o ch g Danehill Dancer (IRE)-Roseau (Nashwan (USA))
J M Jefferson The Hacking Partnership

Placings:60/225/6-P (0559)
2009: 12ᴾSD,

	Starts	1st	2nd	3rd	Win & Pl
Career Total (Turf)	4	0	1	0	3289
Career Total (AW)	3	0	1	0	964

Going (Turf): Sf: 0-0 GS: 0-0 Gd: 0-1 GF: 0-3 Fm: 0-0
Distance: 5f/6f: 0-0 7f-8f: 0-2 9f-13f: 0-5 14f+: 0-0
Track : LH: 0-6 RH: 0-1 Tight: 0-5 Gall: 0-0
Aids: Bl: 0-0 Vi: 0-0 Tstrap: 0-0 Ckp: 0-0
Best Rating: 75 4/06 Epsm 1m114y good

Burnbrake

77(101) (71)73
4-y-o b g Mujahid (USA)-Duena (Grand Lodge (USA))
L Montague Hall B H Page

Placings:045/01400045-650450 (7236)
2009: 8⁶SD, 10⁵SD, 10⁰GS, 8⁴SD, 8⁵SD, 8⁰SD,

	Starts	1st	2nd	3rd	Win & Pl
Career Total (Turf)	7	1	0	0	4463
Career Total (AW)	10	0	0	0	0

73 5/08 NmkR 7f (0-70)H GD £3885
Total win prize-money £3886

Going (Turf): Sf: 0-1 GS: 0-1 Gd: 1-5 GF: 0-0 Fm: 0-0
Distance: 5f/6f: 0-0 7f-8f: 1-15 9f-13f: 0-2 14f+: 0-0
Track : LH: 0-6 RH: 0-6 Tight: 0-4 Gall: 0-2
Aids: Bl: 0-0 Vi: 0-2 Tstrap: 0-0 Ckp: 0-0
Best Rating: 73 5/08 NmkR 7f good

Modest; effective over 7f; acts on good ground.

Burnett (IRE)

91 85
2-y-o b c Dynaformer (USA)-Secret Garden (IRE) (Danehill (USA))
Saeed Bin Suroor Godolphin

Placings:10 (7030)
2009: 8¹GS, 7⁰S,

	Starts	1st	2nd	3rd	Win & Pl
Career Total (Turf)	2	1	0	0	3886

85 10/09 Newc 1m G-S £3885
Total win prize-money £3886

Going (Turf): Sf: 0-1 GS: 1-1 Gd: 0-0 GF: 0-0 Fm: 0-0
Distance: 5f/6f: 0-0 7f-8f: 1-2 9f-13f: 0-0 14f+: 0-0

Track : LH: 1-1 RH: 0-0 Tight: 0-0 Gall: 1-1
Aids: Bl: 0-0 Vi: 0-0 Tstrap: 0-0 Ckp: 0-0
Best Rating: 85 10/09 Newc 1m gd-sft

Useful; 460,000gns purchase; stays 1m and acts on easy ground.

Burning Incense (IRE)

96(96) (82)**91**

6-y-o b g Namid-Night Scent (IRE) (Scenic)
M Dods Andrew Tinkler

Placings:05/6223123102/06050054/40630600-0060 **(6765)**
2009: 5^{0}GS, 7^{0}GS, 7^{6}SF, 6^{0}G,

	Starts	1st	2nd	3rd	Win & Pl
Career Total (Turf)	29	2	4	3	46756
Career Total (AW)	3	0	0	0	0

100 8/06 NmkJ 6f (0-105)H GD £18696
93 6/06 Wind 6f (0-85)H G-S £6477
Total win prize-money £25173

Going (Turf): Sf: 0-8 GS: 1-8 Gd: 1-7 GF: 0-6 Fm: 0-0
Distance: 5f/6f: 2-25 7f-8f: 0-7 9f-13f: 0-0 14f+: 0-0
Track : LH: 0-5 RH: 0-1 Tight: 0-3 Gall: 1-5
Aids: Bl: 1-7 Vi: 0-0 Tstrap: 0-4 Ckp: 0-4
Best Rating: 105 9/06 Asct 6f gd-sft

Fair; effective over 6f; acts on fast ground, but probably best with some ease; has worn blinkers and cheekpieces.

Burning Thread (IRE)

(79) (38)

2-y-o b g Captain Rio-Desert Rose (Green Desert (USA))
T J Etherington Tim Etherington

Placings:0 **(7618)**
2009: 5^{0}SD,

	Starts	1st	2nd	3rd	Win & Pl
Career Total (Turf)	0	0	0	0	
Career Total (AW)	1	0	0	0	

Going (Turf): Sf: 0-0 GS: 0-0 Gd: 0-0 GF: 0-0 Fm: 0-0
Distance: 5f/6f: 0-1 7f-8f: 0-0 9f-13f: 0-0 14f+: 0-0
Track : LH: 0-1 RH: 0-0 Tight: 0-1 Gall: 0-0
Aids: Bl: 0-0 Vi: 0-0 Tstrap: 0-0 Ckp: 0-0
Best Rating: 38 12/09 Wolv 5f216y stand

Burns Night

105(96) (77)**83**

3-y-o ch c Selkirk (USA)-Night Frolic (Night Shift (USA))
M Johnston Sheikh Hamdan Bin Mohammed Al Maktoum

Placings:613240050 **(6907)**
2009: 7^{6}GF, 8^{1}GF, 8^{3}GF, 8^{2}GF, 8^{4}G, 7^{0}GF, 10^{0}G, 9^{5}SD, 10^{0}G,

	Starts	1st	2nd	3rd	Win & Pl
Career Total (Turf)	8	1	1	1	5446
Career Total (AW)	1	0	0	0	0

77 6/09 Bevl 1m100y G-F £2590
Total win prize-money £2590

Going (Turf): Sf: 0-0 GS: 0-0 Gd: 0-3 GF: 1-5 Fm: 0-0
Distance: 5f/6f: 0-0 7f-8f: 0-3 9f-13f: 1-6 14f+: 0-0
Track : LH: 0-3 RH: 1-4 Tight: 0-3 Gall: 0-0
Aids: Bl: 0-1 Vi: 0-0 Tstrap: 0-0 Ckp: 0-0
Best Rating: 83 7/09 Newb 1m gd-fm

Useful; effective at around 1m1f and acts on fast ground and Polytrack; has worn blinkers.

Burnt Cream

87 **62**

2-y-o b f Exceed And Excel (AUS)-Basbousate Nadia (Wolfhound (USA))
B Smart Mrs Patricia Brown

Placings:44 **(6179)**
2009: 5^{4}G, 5^{4}GF,

	Starts	1st	2nd	3rd	Win & Pl
Career Total (Turf)	2	0	0	0	702

Going (Turf): Sf: 0-0 GS: 0-0 Gd: 0-1 GF: 0-1 Fm: 0-0
Distance: 5f/6f: 0-2 7f-8f: 0-0 9f-13f: 0-0 14f+: 0-0
Track : LH: 0-0 RH: 0-0 Tight: 0-0 Gall: 0-0
Aids: Bl: 0-0 Vi: 0-0 Tstrap: 0-0 Ckp: 0-0
Best Rating: 62 9/09 Bevl 5f gd-fm

Burnwynd Boy

106 **106**

4-y-o b g Tobougg (IRE)-Cadeau Speciale (Cadeaux Genereux)
D Nicholls Robert Reid

Placings:110030/2030030-0000030 **(6135)**
2009: 6^{0}GF, 7^{0}GF, 6^{0}GS, 6^{0}G, 6^{0}G, 6^{3}G, 6^{0}G,

	Starts	1st	2nd	3rd	Win & Pl
Career Total (Turf)	20	2	1	4	22787

86 5/07 Pont 6f GD £9348
80 5/07 Newc 6f G-S £3886
Total win prize-money £13234

Going (Turf): Sf: 0-3 GS: 1-3 Gd: 1-8 GF: 0-6 Fm: 0-0
Distance: 5f/6f: 2-11 7f-8f: 0-8 9f-13f: 0-1 14f+: 0-0
Track : LH: 1-3 RH: 0-0 Tight: 0-1 Gall: 0-0
Aids: Bl: 0-1 Vi: 0-1 Tstrap: 0-1 Ckp: 0-1
Best Rating: 106 6/08 Newc 6f soft

Fair; Group placed; suited by 6f; acts on most ground; has worn a visor/cheekpieces.

Burtondale Boy (IRE)

80(70) **39**

2-y-o b g Shinko Forest (IRE)-Irish Moss (USA) (Irish River (FR))
P T Midgley A Taylor Snr, A Taylor Jnr, M Wainman

Placings:000000 **(6555)**
2009: 5^{0}GF, 5^{0}F, 6^{0}GF, 5^{0}GF, 5^{0}SD, 5^{0}G,

	Starts	1st	2nd	3rd	Win & Pl
Career Total (Turf)	5	0	0	0	
Career Total (AW)	1	0	0	0	

Going (Turf): Sf: 0-0 GS: 0-0 Gd: 0-1 GF: 0-3 Fm: 0-1
Distance: 5f/6f: 0-6 7f-8f: 0-0 9f-13f: 0-0 14f+: 0-0
Track : LH: 0-0 RH: 0-0 Tight: 0-0 Gall: 0-0
Aids: Bl: 0-0 Vi: 0-0 Tstrap: 0-1 Ckp: 0-1
Best Rating: 39 3/09 Donc 5f gd-fm

Bury St Edmunds

72(70) (19)**52**

2-y-o ch c Zafeen (FR)-Naivety (Machiavellian (USA))
A G Newcombe J R Salter

Placings:054000 **(7731)**
2009: 6^{0}S, 5^{5}G, 8^{4}GF, 7^{0}GF, 8^{0}SD, 9^{0}SD,

	Starts	1st	2nd	3rd	Win & Pl
Career Total (Turf)	4	0	0	0	0
Career Total (AW)	2	0	0	0	

Going (Turf): Sf: 0-1 GS: 0-0 Gd: 0-1 GF: 0-2 Fm: 0-0
Distance: 5f/6f: 0-1 7f-8f: 0-3 9f-13f: 0-2 14f+: 0-0
Track : LH: 0-3 RH: 0-1 Tight: 0-2 Gall: 0-1
Aids: Bl: 0-0 Vi: 0-0 Tstrap: 0-0 Ckp: 0-0
Best Rating: 52 8/09 Wind 1m67y gd-fm

Bury Treasure (IRE)

(97) (69)**59**

4-y-o ch g Choisir (AUS)-Future Treasure (Habitat)
Miss Gay Kelleway M M Foulger

Placings:040/312600506-00 **(0362)**
2009: 10^{0}SD, 8^{0}SD,

	Starts	1st	2nd	3rd	Win & Pl
Career Total (Turf)	7	0	0	0	265
Career Total (AW)	7	1	1	1	3120

62 1/08 Wolv 1m141y (0-65)H STD £2047
Total win prize-money £2048

Going (Turf): Sf: 0-1 GS: 0-2 Gd: 0-2 GF: 0-2 Fm: 0-0
Distance: 5f/6f: 0-2 7f-8f: 0-6 9f-13f: 1-6 14f+: 0-0
Track : LH: 1-10 RH: 0-1 Tight: 1-4 Gall: 0-4
Aids: Bl: 0-0 Vi: 0-0 Tstrap: 0-1 Ckp: 0-1
Best Rating: 69 2/08 Wolv 1m141y stand

Modest; effective at around 1m; acts Polytrack.

Burza

107(95) (63)**76**

3-y-o ch f Bold Edge-Welcome Star (IRE) (Most Welcome)
J Mackie Norman A Blyth

Placings:150315030 **(5940)**
2009: 8^{1}SD, 8^{5}SD, 7^{0}GF, 8^{3}GF, 10^{1}GF, 10^{5}S, 10^{0}G, 9^{3}GF, 8^{0}GF,

	Starts	1st	2nd	3rd	Win & Pl
Career Total (Turf)	7	1	0	2	6914
Career Total (AW)	2	1	0	0	3211

73 6/09 Newb 1m2f6y (0-85)H G-F £5180
63 2/09 Wolv 1m141y STD £3070
Total win prize-money £8252

Going (Turf): Sf: 0-1 GS: 0-0 Gd: 0-1 GF: 1-5 Fm: 0-0
Distance: 5f/6f: 0-0 7f-8f: 0-1 9f-13f: 2-8 14f+: 0-0
Track : LH: 2-6 RH: 0-2 Tight: 1-3 Gall: 1-2
Aids: Bl: 0-0 Vi: 0-0 Tstrap: 0-0 Ckp: 0-0
Best Rating: 76 8/09 Gdwd 1m1f gd-fm

Fair; stays 1m; acts on Polytrack.

Buscador (USA)

(106) (69)**50**

10-y-o ch g Crafty Prospector (USA)-Fairway Flag (USA) (Fairway Phantom (USA))
W M Brisbourne David Robson

Placings:0660/0303611061/00000010/0612216260/03030315400133/0304032620004/121343124510-20540355 **(1533)**
2009: 9^{2}SD, 9^{0}SD, 9^{5}SD, 13^{4}SD, 13^{0}SD, 12^{3}SD, 9^{5}SD, 12^{5}SD,

	Starts	1st	2nd	3rd	Win & Pl
Career Total (Turf)	18	0	0	2	1472
Career Total (AW)	61	12	8	10	40457

67 3/08 Wolv 1m4f50y (0-60)H STD £2047
69 2/08 Wolv 1m4f50y STD £2590
64 1/08 Wolv 1m4f50y (0-50)H STD £1774
62 1/08 Wolv 1m1f103y (0-52)H STD £2047
66 11/06 Wolv 1m1f103y (0-60)H STD £2730
67 3/06 Wolv 1m1f103y (0-60)H STD £2047

68 3/05 Wolv 1m1f103y STD £2933
66 2/05 Wolv 1m1f103y STD £2639
76 12/04 Wolv 1m1f103y (0-77)H STD £3373
76 12/03 Wolv 1m1f79yE(0-70)H SLW £2135
74 7/03 Wolv 1m1f79yE(0-75)H FST £3633
65 7/03 Wolv 1m1f79y G STD £2982
Total win prize-money £30937

Going (Turf): Sf: 0-2 GS: 0-1 Gd: 0-8 GF: 0-5 Fm: 0-2
Distance: 5f/6f: 0-1 7f-8f: 0-4 9f-13f: 12-72 14f+: 0-2
Track : LH: 12-74 RH: 0-0 Tight: 12-65 Gall: 0-1
Aids: Bl: 0-0 Vi: 0-0 Tstrap: 0-0 Ckp: 0-0
Best Rating: 76 12/04 Wolv 1m1f103y stand

Moderate; stays 1m4f; acts on Polytrack.

Bush Master

96(102) (70)67
2-y-o b g Hunting Lion (IRE)-Patandon Girl (IRE) (Night Shift (USA))
J R Boyle (R Hannon 14/10) The Vine Associates

Placings:0023264200406 (7655)
2009: 5^0GF, 6^0G, 7^2SD, 6^3GF, 5^2GF, 6^6F, 6^4GF, 5^2SS, 5^0G, 6^0SD, 5^4SD, 7^0SD, 6^6SD,

	Starts	1st	2nd	3rd	Win & Pl
Career Total (Turf)	7	0	1	1	2287
Career Total (AW)	6	0	2	0	1776

Going (Turf): Sf: 0-0 GS: 0-0 Gd: 0-2 GF: 0-4 Fm: 0-1
Distance: 5f/6f: 0-10 7f-8f: 0-3 9f-13f: 0-0 14f+: 0-0
Track : LH: 0-5 RH: 0-2 Tight: 0-4 Gall: 0-3
Aids: Bl: 0-0 Vi: 0-0 Tstrap: 0-0 Ckp: 0-0
Best Rating: 70 10/09 Kemp 6f stand

Modest; stays 7f and acts on Polytrack.

Bush Tucker (IRE)

98(90) (73)85
2-y-o b c Choisir (AUS)-Queen's Victory (Mujadil (USA))
P Winkworth Mrs Tessa Winkworth

Placings:2213 (5769)
2009: 5^2G, 5^2SD, 5^1GF, 6^3GF,

	Starts	1st	2nd	3rd	Win & Pl
Career Total (Turf)	3	1	1	1	4110
Career Total (AW)	1	0	1	0	992

77 8/09 Bath 5f11y G-F £1942
Total win prize-money £1943

Going (Turf): Sf: 0-0 GS: 0-0 Gd: 0-1 GF: 1-2 Fm: 0-0
Distance: 5f/6f: 1-4 7f-8f: 0-0 9f-13f: 0-0 14f+: 0-0
Track : LH: 1-3 RH: 0-0 Tight: 0-2 Gall: 1-2
Aids: Bl: 0-0 Vi: 0-0 Tstrap: 0-0 Ckp: 0-0
Best Rating: 85 9/09 Epsm 6f gd-fm

Useful; suited by 5-6f and fast ground.

Bushman

108(104) (82)111
5-y-o gr g Maria's Mon (USA)-Housa Dancer (FR) (Fabulous Dancer (USA))
D M Simcock Khalifa Dasmal

Placings:31120-06051203 (7186)
2009: 10^0G, 10^6GF, 8^0G, 8^5GS, 8^1G, 8^2S, 9^0G, 8^3G,

	Starts	1st	2nd	3rd	Win & Pl
Career Total (Turf)	12	3	2	1	46940
Career Total (AW)	1	0	0	1	363

109 8/09 NmkJ 1m GD £12462
110 5/08 Sand 1m14y (0-95)H SFT £9346
95 4/08 Wind 1m2f7y GD £2729
Total win prize-money £24539

Going (Turf): Sf: 1-3 GS: 0-1 Gd: 2-6 GF: 0-2 Fm: 0-0
Distance: 5f/6f: 0-0 7f-8f: 1-4 9f-13f: 2-9 14f+: 0-0
Track : LH: 0-4 RH: 2-5 Tight: 1-3 Gall: 0-0
Aids: Bl: 0-0 Vi: 0-0 Tstrap: 0-0 Ckp: 0-0
Best Rating: 111 10/09 NmkR 1m good

Smart; effective over 1m-1m2f; acts on most ground; goes on Polytrack.

Bushranger (IRE)

108 (102)119
3-y-o b c Danetime (IRE)-Danz Danz (Efisio)
David Wachman D Smith, Mrs J Magnier, M Tabor

Placings:1213110-400 (5657)
2009: 6^4HY, 6^0GF, 6^0GS,

	Starts	1st	2nd	3rd	Win & Pl
Career Total (Turf)	9	4	1	1	339737
Career Total (AW)	1	0	0	0	

119 10/08 NmkR 6f G-F £111893
116 8/08 Deau 6f G-S £147051
112 7/08 Curr 6f63y G-Y £35900
90 6/08 Tipp 5f GD £9573
Total win prize-money £304420

Going (Turf): Sf: 0-1 GS: 1-2 Gd: 1-1 GF: 1-4 Fm: 0-0
Distance: 5f/6f: 3-8 7f-8f: 1-1 9f-13f: 0-1 14f+: 0-0
Track : LH: 1-2 RH: 1-1 Tight: 0-0 Gall: 0-0
Aids: Bl: 0-0 Vi: 0-1 Tstrap: 0-0 Ckp: 0-0
Best Rating: 119 10/08 NmkR 6f gd-fm

High class; Irish trained; winner of the Prix Morny and Middle Park Stakes in 2008; suited by 6f; acts on easy and fast ground; has worn a visor.

Bushveld (IRE)

(108) (85)26
3-y-o b c Cape Cross (IRE)-Gold Sunrise (USA) (Forty Niner (USA))
M Johnston Sheikh Hamdan Bin Mohammed Al Maktoum

Placings:041-22 (0312)
2009: 10^2SD, 8^2SD,

	Starts	1st	2nd	3rd	Win & Pl
Career Total (Turf)	2	0	0	0	289
Career Total (AW)	3	1	2	0	5728

79 11/08 Wolv 1m141y STD £2914
Total win prize-money £2914

Going (Turf): Sf: 0-2 GS: 0-0 Gd: 0-0 GF: 0-0 Fm: 0-0
Distance: 5f/6f: 0-0 7f-8f: 0-3 9f-13f: 1-2 14f+: 0-0
Track : LH: 1-2 RH: 0-2 Tight: 1-1 Gall: 0-0
Aids: Bl: 0-0 Vi: 0-0 Tstrap: 0-0 Ckp: 0-0
Best Rating: 85 1/09 Kemp 1m2f stand

Fair; stays 1m2f; acts on Polytrack; should improve further.

Bushy Dell (IRE)

100(107) (76)91
4-y-o br f King Charlemagne (USA)-Nisibis (In The Wings)
Miss J Feilden R J Creese

Placings:51/2006151624-05505105 (7867)
2009: 13^0SD, 12^5G, 12^5SD, 12^0G, 11^5GF, 13^1SD, 13^0SD, 14^5SS,

	Starts	1st	2nd	3rd	Win & Pl
Career Total (Turf)	4	0	0	0	1076
Career Total (AW)	16	4	2	0	16086

75 9/09 Wolv 1m5f194y (0-80)H STD £5046
75 9/08 Wolv 1m4f50y (0-75)H STD £3238
73 8/08 Kemp 1m3f (0-75)H STD £2590
65 10/07 Wolv 1m141y STD £2047
Total win prize-money £12922

Going (Turf): Sf: 0-0 GS: 0-0 Gd: 0-2 GF: 0-2 Fm: 0-0
Distance: 5f/6f: 0-0 7f-8f: 0-2 9f-13f: 3-13 14f+: 1-5
Track : LH: 3-10 RH: 1-8 Tight: 3-7 Gall: 0-3
Aids: Bl: 0-0 Vi: 0-0 Tstrap: 0-0 Ckp: 0-0
Best Rating: 91 8/09 Wind 1m3f135y gd-fm

Modest; effective up to 1m6f; acts on Polytrack.

Business As Usual

90(97) (87)80
2-y-o b c Invincible Spirit (IRE)-Lesgor (USA) (Irish River (FR))
M A Jarvis P Makin

Placings:12 (6779)
2009: 7^1GF, 8^2SS,

	Starts	1st	2nd	3rd	Win & Pl
Career Total (Turf)	1	1	0	0	5046
Career Total (AW)	1	0	1	0	1542

80 9/09 Yarm 7f3y G-F £5046
Total win prize-money £5046

Going (Turf): Sf: 0-0 GS: 0-0 Gd: 0-0 GF: 1-1 Fm: 0-0
Distance: 5f/6f: 0-0 7f-8f: 1-2 9f-13f: 0-0 14f+: 0-0
Track : LH: 0-1 RH: 0-0 Tight: 0-1 Gall: 0-0
Aids: Bl: 0-0 Vi: 0-0 Tstrap: 0-0 Ckp: 0-0
Best Rating: 87 10/09 Ling 1m std-slw

Useful; suited by 7f and fast ground.

Business Class (BRZ)

97(103) (73)64
4-y-o b g Thignon Lafre (BRZ)-Dioner (BRZ) (Rotioner (BRZ))
D Nicholls Michael Reay

Placings:3-330003154 (7423)
2009: 8^3SD, 7^3GF, 7^0GS, 7^0G, 8^0GF, 7^3GF, 8^1SD, 9^5GS, 8^4SD,

	Starts	1st	2nd	3rd	Win & Pl
Career Total (Turf)	7	0	0	3	1300
Career Total (AW)	3	1	0	1	2774

73 9/09 Sthl 1m (0-60)H STD £2388
Total win prize-money £2388

Going (Turf): Sf: 0-0 GS: 0-3 Gd: 0-1 GF: 0-3 Fm: 0-0
Distance: 5f/6f: 0-0 7f-8f: 1-9 9f-13f: 0-1 14f+: 0-0
Track : LH: 1-6 RH: 0-2 Tight: 0-4 Gall: 0-0
Aids: Bl: 0-0 Vi: 0-0 Tstrap: 0-0 Ckp: 0-0
Best Rating: 73 9/09 Sthl 1m stand

Modest; stays 1m; acts on fast ground and on Fibresand.

Businessman

97 83
2-y-o b c Acclamation-Venus Rising (Observatory (USA))
M Johnston Sheikh Hamdan Bin Mohammed Al Maktoum

Placings:1P (5521)
2009: 6^1GF, 6^PG,

	Starts	1st	2nd	3rd	Win & Pl
Career Total (Turf)	2	1	0	0	16190

83 8/09 York 6f G-F £16190
Total win prize-money £16190

Going (Turf): Sf: 0-0 GS: 0-0 Gd: 0-1 GF: 1-1 Fm: 0-0
Distance: 5f/6f: 1-2 7f-8f: 0-0 9f-13f: 0-0 14f+: 0-0

Track : LH: 0-0 RH: 0-0 Tight: 0-0 Gall: 0-0
Aids: Bl: 0-0 Vi: 0-0 Tstrap: 0-0 Ckp: 0-0
Best Rating: 83 8/09 York 6f gd-fm

Useful debut winner; effective over 6f; acts on fast ground.

Bussell Along (IRE)

94(84) (47)52
3-y-o b f Mujadil (USA)-Waaedah (USA) (Halling (USA))
M L W Bell Robert Frosell

Placings:5560-0343 (4177)
2009: 7^{0}GF, 7^{3}GF, 9^{4}G, 10^{3}GS,

	Starts	1st	2nd	3rd	Win & Pl
Career Total (Turf)	7	0	0	2	674
Career Total (AW)	1	0	0	0	0

Going (Turf): Sf: 0-2 GS: 0-1 Gd: 0-1 GF: 0-3 Fm: 0-0
Distance: 5f/6f: 0-3 7f-8f: 0-3 9f-13f: 0-2 14f+: 0-0
Track : LH: 0-2 RH: 0-1 Tight: 0-3 Gall: 0-0
Aids: Bl: 0-0 Vi: 0-0 Tstrap: 0-0 Ckp: 0-0
Best Rating: 52 9/08 Leic 7f9y soft

Moderate; stays 1m2f; acts on a sound surface.

Bustan (IRE)

96(101) (73)86
10-y-o b g Darshaan-Dazzlingly Radiant (Try My Best (USA))
G C Bravery Mrs J Morley

Placings:11543/442/32046/002060406004/12030002000/51231000-3000000 (5367)
2009: 8^{3}G, 8^{0}GF, 10^{0}GF, 8^{0}GF, 8^{0}G, 8^{0}G, 9^{0}F,

	Starts	1st	2nd	3rd	Win & Pl
Career Total (Turf)	46	5	6	4	88171
Career Total (AW)	5	0	0	1	8700

86 7/08 Bevl 1m100y (0-85)H G-F £4727
83 4/08 Sand 1m14y (0-80)H GD £7123
98 4/07 Thsk 7f (0-90)H FRM £7772
105 6/02 NmkR 1m2f A G-F £14094
80 5/02 Kemp 1m D GD £4407
Total win prize-money £38124

Going (Turf): Sf: 0-2 GS: 0-7 Gd: 2-16 GF: 2-19 Fm: 1-2
Distance: 5f/6f: 0-0 7f-8f: 2-19 9f-13f: 3-32 14f+: 0-0
Track : LH: 1-17 RH: 3-20 Tight: 1-14 Gall: 1-11
Aids: Bl: 0-1 Vi: 0-0 Tstrap: 0-2 Ckp: 0-2
Best Rating: 116 8/02 York 1m3f195y good

Useful; effective over 7f-1m2f; acts on most ground.

Bustard Bay (IRE)

90 56
2-y-o b g Footstepsinthesand-Toy Show (IRE) (Danehill (USA))
J G Given J David Abell

Placings:50500 (6590)
2009: 5^{5}G, 7^{0}GS, 7^{5}G, 7^{0}GF, 6^{0}GS,

	Starts	1st	2nd	3rd	Win & Pl
Career Total (Turf)	5	0	0	0	0

Going (Turf): Sf: 0-0 GS: 0-2 Gd: 0-2 GF: 0-1 Fm: 0-0
Distance: 5f/6f: 0-1 7f-8f: 0-4 9f-13f: 0-0 14f+: 0-0
Track : LH: 0-1 RH: 0-0 Tight: 0-1 Gall: 0-0
Aids: Bl: 0-0 Vi: 0-0 Tstrap: 0-0 Ckp: 0-0
Best Rating: 56 7/09 Leic 7f9y gd-sft

Buster Hyvonen (IRE)

(109) (101)89
7-y-o b g Dansili-Serotina (IRE) (Mtoto)
J R Fanshawe Simon Gibson

Placings:2/2104/642102/3/12231-00 (1007)
2009: 11^{0}SD, 16^{0}SD,

	Starts	1st	2nd	3rd	Win & Pl
Career Total (Turf)	9	1	2	2	8996
Career Total (AW)	10	3	4	0	19270

101 6/08 Kemp 1m4f (0-85)H STD £4209
88 2/08 Wolv 1m5f194y (0-85)H STD £4210
78 8/06 Gdwd 1m3f (0-75)H G-F £4857
71 7/05 Ling 1m STD £2590
Total win prize-money £15867

Going (Turf): Sf: 0-0 GS: 0-2 Gd: 0-1 GF: 1-6 Fm: 0-0
Distance: 5f/6f: 0-0 7f-8f: 1-3 9f-13f: 2-10 14f+: 1-6
Track : LH: 2-6 RH: 2-11 Tight: 3-6 Gall: 0-3
Aids: Bl: 0-0 Vi: 0-0 Tstrap: 0-0 Ckp: 0-0
Best Rating: 101 6/08 Kemp 1m4f stand

Useful; stays 2m; acts on fast ground; also goes on Polytrack.

Butch And Sundance

96 88
2-y-o b g Captain Rio-Be My Wish (Be My Chief (USA))
B J Meehan Abbott Racing Limited

Placings:0162030 (6993)
2009: 6^{0}GF, 6^{1}G, 7^{6}G, 6^{2}GF, 6^{0}GF, 8^{3}G, 8^{0}GS,

	Starts	1st	2nd	3rd	Win & Pl
Career Total (Turf)	7	1	1	1	5808

77 7/09 Yarm 6f3y GD £2978
Total win prize-money £2979

Going (Turf): Sf: 0-0 GS: 0-1 Gd: 1-3 GF: 0-3 Fm: 0-0
Distance: 5f/6f: 0-2 7f-8f: 1-5 9f-13f: 0-0 14f+: 0-0
Track : LH: 0-2 RH: 0-0 Tight: 0-0 Gall: 0-2
Aids: Bl: 0-2 Vi: 0-0 Tstrap: 0-0 Ckp: 0-0
Best Rating: 88 9/09 Ayr 1m good

Useful; suited by 6f and good or faster ground.

Bute Street

78(96) (53)34
4-y-o b g Superior Premium-Hard To Follow (Dilum (USA))
R J Hodges J W Mursell

Placings:00/00310 (7154)
2009: 11^{0}GF, 9^{0}SD, 13^{3}SD, 16^{1}SD, 16^{0}SD,

	Starts	1st	2nd	3rd	Win & Pl
Career Total (Turf)	3	0	0	0	
Career Total (AW)	4	1	0	1	2691

53 10/09 Wolv 2m119y (0-65)H STD £2388
Total win prize-money £2388

Going (Turf): Sf: 0-0 GS: 0-1 Gd: 0-0 GF: 0-2 Fm: 0-0
Distance: 5f/6f: 0-1 7f-8f: 0-1 9f-13f: 0-2 14f+: 1-3
Track : LH: 1-6 RH: 0-0 Tight: 1-5 Gall: 0-1
Aids: Bl: 0-0 Vi: 0-0 Tstrap: 0-0 Ckp: 0-0
Best Rating: 53 10/09 Wolv 2m119y stand

Butstillitmoves (IRE)

(90) (55)
3-y-o b f Galileo (IRE)-Deuxieme (IRE) (Second Empire (IRE))
J H M Gosden Ms Rachel D S Hood

Placings:6 (0876)
2009: 10^{6}SD,

	Starts	1st	2nd	3rd	Win & Pl
Career Total (Turf)	0	0	0	0	
Career Total (AW)	1	0	0	0	0

Going (Turf): Sf: 0-0 GS: 0-0 Gd: 0-0 GF: 0-0 Fm: 0-0
Distance: 5f/6f: 0-0 7f-8f: 0-0 9f-13f: 0-1 14f+: 0-0
Track : LH: 0-0 RH: 0-1 Tight: 0-0 Gall: 0-0
Aids: Bl: 0-0 Vi: 0-0 Tstrap: 0-0 Ckp: 0-0
Best Rating: 55 3/09 Kemp 1m2f stand

Buxton

104(109) (79)86
5-y-o b g Auction House (USA)-Dam Certain (IRE) (Damister (USA))
R Ingram Peter J Burton

Placings:0/21034364300040/611020604550100003-20000643050 (6614)
2009: 6^{2}GF, 6^{0}GS, 7^{0}GF, 6^{0}GF, 7^{0}G, 7^{6}G, 6^{4}GF, 6^{3}SD, 7^{0}SD, 7^{5}SD, 8^{0}SD,

	Starts	1st	2nd	3rd	Win & Pl
Career Total (Turf)	17	1	2	0	6260
Career Total (AW)	28	3	1	5	17920

83 9/08 Brig 6f209y (0-75)H GD £2838
89 2/08 Ling 6f (0-85)H STD £4100
85 2/08 Ling 6f (0-75)H STD £2590
71 5/07 Wolv 7f32y STD £3071
Total win prize-money £12602

Going (Turf): Sf: 0-0 GS: 0-1 Gd: 1-8 GF: 0-7 Fm: 0-1
Distance: 5f/6f: 2-16 7f-8f: 2-28 9f-13f: 0-1 14f+: 0-0
Track : LH: 4-23 RH: 0-13 Tight: 3-20 Gall: 0-3
Aids: Bl: 0-1 Vi: 0-0 Tstrap: 0-0 Ckp: 0-0
Best Rating: 93 3/08 Wolv 7f32y stand

Fair; effective over 6f-7f; acts on good ground and on Polytrack; has worn a tongue tie.

Buy On The Red

97(105) (78)78
8-y-o b g Komaite (USA)-Red Rosein (Red Sunset)
D Nicholls R Haim

Placings:424/221102001240/000560060/0054304405304321/2401522003640/615055303566-02301U606012 (7808)
2009: 7^{0}F, 7^{2}GF, 6^{3}G, 5^{0}GF, 5^{1}GF, 5^{U}G, 5^{6}G, 5^{0}G, 5^{6}GS, 5^{0}GS, 5^{1}SD, 5^{2}SD,

	Starts	1st	2nd	3rd	Win & Pl
Career Total (Turf)	45	5	6	2	48192
Career Total (AW)	32	3	5	5	27722

70 12/09 Ling 5f STD £1978
78 6/09 Leic 5f2y (0-70)H G-F £2498
78 5/08 Bath 5f161y (0-70)H G-F £2590
74 8/07 Wind 6f (0-70)H G-F £3238
87 12/06 Wolv 7f32y (0-85)H STD £5505
94 11/04 Ling 7f (0-92)H STD £6792
87 5/04 NmkR 6f C(0-100)H G-F £26000
79 5/04 Brig 5f213y D G-F £3464
Total win prize-money £52069

Going (Turf): Sf: 0-1 GS: 0-2 Gd: 0-15 **GF: 5-24** Fm: 0-3
Distance: **5f/6f: 6-55** 7f-8f: 2-22 9f-13f: 0-0 14f+: 0-0
Track : **LH: 5-44** RH: 0-4 **Tight: 3-34** Gall: 2-5
Aids: Bl: 1-16 Vi: 0-2 Tstrap: 2-24 Ckp: 2-24
Best Rating: **102** 12/04 Ling 6f stand

Modest; effective over 5f-7f; acts on fast ground; also goes on Polytrack; has worn blinkers.

Buzz Bird

84 **51**
2-y-o b f Danbird (AUS)-Ashtaroute (USA) (Holy Bull (USA))
T D Barron Twinacre Nurseries Ltd

Placings:0000 **(6215)**
2009: 7^{0}G, 7^{0}GF, 6^{0}GF, 8^{0}GF,

	Starts	1st	2nd	3rd	Win & Pl
Career Total (Turf)	4	0	0	0	

Going (Turf): **Sf: 0-0 GS: 0-0 Gd: 0-1 GF: 0-3 Fm: 0-0**
Distance: 5f/6f: 0-1 7f-8f: 0-3 9f-13f: 0-0 14f+: 0-0
Track : LH: 0-1 RH: 0-0 Tight: 0-1 Gall: 0-0
Aids: Bl: 0-0 Vi: 0-0 Tstrap: 0-0 Ckp: 0-0
Best Rating: **51** 8/09 Rdcr 7f gd-fm

Buzzword

109 **115**
2-y-o b c Pivotal-Bustling (Danehill (USA))
Saeed Bin Suroor Godolphin

Placings:21221355 **(7304a)**
2009: 6^{2}GF, 6^{1}G, 6^{2}G, 7^{2}GF, 7^{1}GS, 7^{3}G, 7^{5}G, 8^{5}F,

	Starts	1st	2nd	3rd	Win & Pl
Career Total (Turf)	8	2	3	1	138456

114 9/09 Lonc 7f G-S £38835
89 7/09 Wind 6f GD £2729
Total win prize-money £41565

Going (Turf): Sf: 0-0 **GS: 1-1 Gd: 1-4** GF: 0-2 Fm: 0-1
Distance: 5f/6f: 1-3 7f-8f: 1-5 9f-13f: 0-0 14f+: 0-0
Track : LH: 0-1 **RH: 1-3** Tight: 0-0 **Gall: 1-2**
Aids: Bl: 0-0 Vi: 0-0 Tstrap: 0-0 Ckp: 0-0
Best Rating: **115** 10/09 Lonc 7f good

Group class; winner at Group 3 level and runner-up in the Group 2 Richmond Stakes; decent efforts in Group 1 races since; effective at up to 1m; acts on fast and easy ground.

By Command

100(99) (62)**96**
4-y-o b g Red Ransom (USA)-Rafha (Kris)
J W Hills Gary And Linnet Woodward

Placings:45/153000-05463400**3044** **(6940)**
2009: 10^{0}GF, 10^{5}G, 10^{4}G, 10^{6}G, 12^{3}S, 10^{4}GF, 8^{0}G, 8^{0}G, 10^{3}GS, 9^{0}SD, 9^{4}GF, 10^{4}SD,

	Starts	1st	2nd	3rd	Win & Pl
Career Total (Turf)	18	1	0	3	8080
Career Total (AW)	2	0	0	0	0

93 4/08 Wind 1m2f7y G-S £2729
Total win prize-money £2730

Going (Turf): Sf: 0-3 **GS: 1-3** Gd: 0-7 GF: 0-5 Fm: 0-0
Distance: 5f/6f: 0-0 7f-8f: 0-2 **9f-13f: 1-18** 14f+: 0-0
Track : LH: 0-6 **RH: 1-13 Tight: 1-8** Gall: 0-2
Aids: Bl: 0-2 Vi: 0-0 Tstrap: 0-2 Ckp: 0-2
Best Rating: **96** 5/08 Ling 1m3f106y gd-fm

Fair; stays 1m2f and acts on easy ground.

By Request

94 **60**
3-y-o b f Giant's Causeway (USA)-Approach (Darshaan)
Sir Mark Prescott Denford Stud

Placings:06 **(5718)**
2009: 8^{0}G, 11^{6}G,

	Starts	1st	2nd	3rd	Win & Pl
Career Total (Turf)	2	0	0	0	0

Going (Turf): **Sf: 0-0 GS: 0-0 Gd: 0-2 GF: 0-0 Fm: 0-0**
Distance: 5f/6f: 0-0 7f-8f: 0-1 9f-13f: 0-1 14f+: 0-0
Track : LH: 0-1 RH: 0-1 Tight: 0-2 Gall: 0-0
Aids: Bl: 0-0 Vi: 0-0 Tstrap: 0-0 Ckp: 0-0
Best Rating: **60** 9/09 Bath 1m3f144y good

By The Sea (IRE)

90(54) (48)**49**
4-y-o b f Monashee Mountain (USA)-Sesame Heights (IRE) (High Estate)
M P Sunderland Horsin Around Syndicate

Placings:00-060260 **(7143)**
2009: 8^{0}YS, 10^{6}GF, 9^{0}GF, 9^{2}HY, 8^{6}SD, 9^{0}SD,

	Starts	1st	2nd	3rd	Win & Pl
Career Total (Turf)	4	0	1	0	1250
Career Total (AW)	4	0	0	0	

Going (Turf): **Sf: 0-1 GS: 0-0 Gd: 0-0 GF: 0-2 Fm: 0-0**
Distance: 5f/6f: 0-0 7f-8f: 0-2 9f-13f: 0-6 14f+: 0-0
Track : LH: 0-6 RH: 0-1 Tight: 0-1 Gall: 0-0
Aids: Bl: 0-2 Vi: 0-0 Tstrap: 0-0 Ckp: 0-0
Best Rating: **49** 9/09 Tipp 1m1f heavy

Moderate; effective at 1m1f; handles heavy.

By The Wind (IRE)

(82) (21)
3-y-o b g Iron Mask (USA)-Macha Rua (IRE) (Eagle Eyed (USA))
T J Etherington Tim Etherington

Placings:000 **(4860)**
2009: 5^{0}SD, 5^{0}SD, 5^{0}SD,

	Starts	1st	2nd	3rd	Win & Pl
Career Total (Turf)	0	0	0	0	
Career Total (AW)	3	0	0	0	

Going (Turf): **Sf: 0-0 GS: 0-0 Gd: 0-0 GF: 0-0 Fm: 0-0**
Distance: 5f/6f: 0-3 7f-8f: 0-0 9f-13f: 0-0 14f+: 0-0
Track : LH: 0-2 RH: 0-0 Tight: 0-2 Gall: 0-0
Aids: Bl: 0-0 Vi: 0-0 Tstrap: 0-0 Ckp: 0-0
Best Rating: **21** 3/09 Ling 5f stand

Byron Bay

89(97) (64)**73**
7-y-o b g My Best Valentine-Candarela (Damister (USA))
R Johnson James S Kennerley And Miss Jenny Hall

Placings:005030**0**/0102502421/**5**112602455**056**/**5**24**0**/050 600000-000100234500 **(7349)**
2009: 12^{0}SD, 16^{0}GS, 12^{0}GS, 8^{1}SD, 8^{0}GS, 8^{0}GS, 8^{2}SD, 8^{3}GS, 8^{4}GF, 8^{5}SD, 10^{0}GF, 7^{0}SD,

	Starts	1st	2nd	3rd	Win & Pl
Career Total (Turf)	39	1	5	2	21139
Career Total (AW)	16	4	2	0	19988

62 6/09 Sthl 1m (0-60)H STD £2047
91 3/06 Wolv 7f32y (0-85)H STD £5505
85 2/06 Sthl 1m (0-75)H STD £3238
83 12/05 Sthl 1m (0-70)H STD £5796
74 5/05 Haml 1m1f36y G-S £3510
Total win prize-money £20098

Going (Turf): Sf: 0-8 **GS: 1-14** Gd: 0-5 GF: 0-10 Fm: 0-2
Distance: 5f/6f: 0-2 **7f-8f: 4-32** 9f-13f: 1-20 14f+: 0-1
Track : **LH: 4-37** RH: 1-7 **Tight: 2-18** Gall: 0-5
Aids: Bl: 0-0 Vi: 0-1 Tstrap: 0-8 Ckp: 0-8
Best Rating: **91** 2/07 Sthl 1m stand

Moderate; stays 1m2f but effective at shorter; acts on soft ground and Fibresand; suited by forcing tactics; has been tried in cheekpieces.

C'Mon You Irons (IRE)

103(104) (73)**85**
4-y-o b g Orpen (USA)-Laissez Faire (IRE) (Tagula (IRE))
M R Hoad double-r-racing.com

Placings:410/30600**436401**-**2444**02111005 **(6564)**
2009: 7^{2}SD, 7^{4}SD, 6^{4}SD, 7^{4}SD, 6^{0}GF, 6^{2}GF, 6^{1}GF, 6^{1}GF, 6^{1}S, 6^{0}G, 6^{0}G, 6^{5}GS,

	Starts	1st	2nd	3rd	Win & Pl
Career Total (Turf)	16	4	1	1	15288
Career Total (AW)	10	1	1	1	3446

85 7/09 Pont 6f (0-75)H SFT £3238
82 7/09 Wind 6f (0-75)H G-F £2729
76 6/09 Wind 6f (0-70)H G-F £2729
70 12/08 Ling 6f STD £1978
77 9/07 Haml 6f5y G-S £3886
Total win prize-money £14563

Going (Turf): Sf: 1-3 GS: 1-2 Gd: 0-6 **GF: 2-4** Fm: 0-1
Distance: **5f/6f: 4-21** 7f-8f: 1-5 9f-13f: 0-0 14f+: 0-0
Track : **LH: 2-9** RH: 0-4 Tight: 1-6 **Gall: 2-4**
Aids: Bl: 0-3 Vi: 0-0 Tstrap: 0-0 Ckp: 0-0
Best Rating: **85** 7/09 Pont 6f soft

Fair; stays 7f but effective at 6f; acts on most ground and on Polytrack.

Cabal

(96) (72)
2-y-o b f Kyllachy-Secret Flame (Machiavellian (USA))
Sir Michael Stoute Cheveley Park Stud

Placings:2 **(7376)**
2009: 7^{2}SD,

	Starts	1st	2nd	3rd	Win & Pl
Career Total (Turf)	0	0	0	0	
Career Total (AW)	1	0	1	0	964

Going (Turf): **Sf: 0-0 GS: 0-0 Gd: 0-0 GF: 0-0 Fm: 0-0**
Distance: 5f/6f: 0-0 7f-8f: 0-1 9f-13f: 0-0 14f+: 0-0
Track : LH: 0-1 RH: 0-0 Tight: 0-1 Gall: 0-0
Aids: Bl: 0-0 Vi: 0-0 Tstrap: 0-0 Ckp: 0-0
Best Rating: **72** 11/09 Wolv 7f32y stand

Cabernet Sauvignon

97(97) (75)**75**
3-y-o br g Dansili-Halcyon Daze (Halling (USA))
Gordon Elliott (J W Hills 5/7) In Vino Veritas Partnership

Placings:632-0625**3**600 **(7729)**

2009: 7^{0}GF, 8^{6}F, 8^{2}GF, 8^{5}GF, 7^{3}F, 7^{6}SD, 8^{0}G, 7^{0}SD,

	Starts	1st	2nd	3rd	Win & Pl
Career Total (Turf)	7	0	1	1	1492
Career Total (AW)	4	0	1	1	1576

Going (Turf): **Sf: 0-0 GS: 0-0 Gd: 0-2 GF: 0-3 Fm: 0-2**
Distance: 5f/6f: 0-1 7f-8f: 0-8 9f-13f: 0-2 14f+: 0-0
Track : LH: 0-8 RH: 0-3 Tight: 0-3 Gall: 0-1
Aids: Bl: 0-1 Vi: 0-0 Tstrap: 0-0 Ckp: 0-0
Best Rating: **75** 12/08 Ling 7f stand

Fair; effective over 1m; acts on fast ground; goes on Polytrack.

Cabopino (IRE)

(96) (53)**37**
4-y-o ch f Captain Rio-Fey Rouge (IRE) (Fayruz)
K R Burke Clipper Logistics

Placings:043-05 **(0367)**
2009: 6^{0}SD, 5^{5}SD,

	Starts	1st	2nd	3rd	Win & Pl
Career Total (Turf)	1	0	0	0	
Career Total (AW)	4	0	0	1	482

Going (Turf): **Sf: 0-0 GS: 0-0 Gd: 0-1 GF: 0-0 Fm: 0-0**
Distance: 5f/6f: 0-4 7f-8f: 0-1 9f-13f: 0-0 14f+: 0-0
Track : LH: 0-2 RH: 0-1 Tight: 0-1 Gall: 0-0
Aids: Bl: 0-0 Vi: 0-0 Tstrap: 0-0 Ckp: 0-0
Best Rating: **53** 12/08 Kemp 7f stand

Cactus Curtsey

89(92) (48)**53**
3-y-o b f Royal Applause-Prairie Flower (IRE) (Zieten (USA))
J R Fanshawe J H Richmond-Watson

Placings:30500 **(5403)**
2009: 7^{3}G, 8^{0}S, 8^{5}GF, 5^{0}SD, 7^{0}G,

	Starts	1st	2nd	3rd	Win & Pl
Career Total (Turf)	4	0	0	1	722
Career Total (AW)	1	0	0	0	

Going (Turf): **Sf: 0-1 GS: 0-0 Gd: 0-2 GF: 0-1 Fm: 0-0**
Distance: 5f/6f: 0-1 7f-8f: 0-4 9f-13f: 0-0 14f+: 0-0
Track : LH: 0-1 RH: 0-0 Tight: 0-1 Gall: 0-0
Aids: Bl: 0-0 Vi: 0-0 Tstrap: 0-0 Ckp: 0-0
Best Rating: **53** 7/09 Donc 7f good

Cactus King

91(100) (81)**87**
6-y-o b g Green Desert (USA)-Apache Star (Arazi (USA))
P M Phelan Tony Smith

Placings:031/5363000/10060/133000-50360 **(2708)**
2009: 7^{5}SD, 8^{0}SD, 9^{3}G, 10^{6}SD, 12^{0}SD,

	Starts	1st	2nd	3rd	Win & Pl
Career Total (Turf)	14	0	0	5	6372
Career Total (AW)	12	3	0	1	11500

81	3/08	Kemp	1m		STD	£2047
87	4/07	Ling	1m2f	(0-85)H	STD	£4857
82	11/05	Ling	1m		STD	£3899

Total win prize-money £10805

Going (Turf): **Sf: 0-1 GS: 0-4 Gd: 0-3 GF: 0-6 Fm: 0-0**
Distance: 5f/6f: 0-0 **7f-8f: 2-10** 9f-13f: 1-16 14f+: 0-0
Track : **LH: 2-12** RH: 1-10 **Tight: 2-14** Gall: 0-0
Aids: Bl: 0-2 Vi: 0-0 Tstrap: 0-2 Ckp: 0-2

Best Rating: **94** 6/06 Wind 1m67y gd-fm

Useful; stays 1m2f; acts on fast ground and Polytrack.

Cadeaux Fax

100(100) (72)**66**
4-y-o ch g Largesse-Facsimile (Superlative)
B R Millman Mrs Mette Campbell-Andenaes

Placings:000-5042013215 **(6909)**
2009: 8^{5}GF, 8^{0}GF, 7^{4}HY, 8^{2}G, 8^{0}G, 7^{1}G, 7^{3}GS, 6^{2}GF, 8^{1}SD, 8^{5}G,

	Starts	1st	2nd	3rd	Win & Pl
Career Total (Turf)	11	1	2	1	4232
Career Total (AW)	2	1	0	0	2047

72	10/09	Kemp	1m	(0-60)H	STD	£2047
63	8/09	Chep	7f16y	(0-65)H	GD	£2266

Total win prize-money £4314

Going (Turf): Sf: 0-2 GS: 0-1 **Gd: 1-5** GF: 0-3 Fm: 0-0
Distance: 5f/6f: 0-0 **7f-8f: 2-6** 9f-13f: 0-7 14f+: 0-0
Track : LH: 0-3 **RH: 1-3** Tight: 0-1 Gall: 0-0
Aids: Bl: 0-0 Vi: 0-0 Tstrap: 0-0 Ckp: 0-0
Best Rating: **72** 10/09 Kemp 1m stand

Modest; effective at 7f; acts on most ground.

Cadley Road (IRE)

102 **95**
2-y-o b c Elusive City (USA)-Rouge Noir (USA) (Saint Ballado (CAN))
R Hannon J R May

Placings:31266 **(7030)**
2009: 7^{3}GF, 7^{1}GF, 7^{2}G, 8^{6}G, 7^{6}S,

	Starts	1st	2nd	3rd	Win & Pl
Career Total (Turf)	5	1	1	1	26044

89	7/09	Sand	7f16y	G-F	£5180

Total win prize-money £5181

Going (Turf): Sf: 0-1 GS: 0-0 Gd: 0-2 **GF: 1-2** Fm: 0-0
Distance: 5f/6f: 0-0 **7f-8f: 1-5** 9f-13f: 0-0 14f+: 0-0
Track : LH: 0-1 **RH: 1-3** Tight: 0-1 Gall: 0-1
Aids: Bl: 0-0 Vi: 0-0 Tstrap: 0-0 Ckp: 0-0
Best Rating: **95** 10/09 Newb 7f soft

Useful; Listed placed; stays 7f and acts on fast ground.

Cadre (IRE)

107(93) (87)**104**
4-y-o b g King's Best (USA)-Desert Frolic (IRE) (Persian Bold)
J H M Gosden H R H Princess Haya Of Jordan

Placings:0/1-0160430 **(6270)**
2009: 7^{0}SD, 8^{1}GF, 8^{6}G, 8^{0}GF, 8^{4}G, 8^{3}GS, 7^{0}G,

	Starts	1st	2nd	3rd	Win & Pl
Career Total (Turf)	7	1	0	1	12895
Career Total (AW)	2	1	0	0	2590

103	5/09	Yarm	1m3y	(0-95)H	G-F	£7477
87	9/08	Kemp	7f		STD	£2590

Total win prize-money £10067

Going (Turf): Sf: 0-0 GS: 0-1 Gd: 0-4 **GF: 1-2** Fm: 0-0
Distance: 5f/6f: 0-0 7f-8f: 1-6 9f-13f: 1-3 14f+: 0-0
Track : LH: 0-1 **RH: 1-3** Tight: 0-1 Gall: 0-0
Aids: Bl: 0-0 Vi: 0-0 Tstrap: 0-0 Ckp: 0-0
Best Rating: **104** 9/09 Sand 1m14y gd-sft

Very useful; effective over 7f-1m; acts on fast ground and on Polytrack.

Caerlaverock (IRE)

104 **85**
4-y-o br g Statue Of Liberty (USA)-Daziyra (IRE) (Doyoun)
G A Swinbank Mr & Mrs Duncan Davidson

Placings:51330 **(2895)**
2009: 12^{5}GF, 11^{1}G, 12^{3}G, 12^{3}GS, 16^{0}GS,

	Starts	1st	2nd	3rd	Win & Pl
Career Total (Turf)	5	1	0	2	4270

80	5/09	Haml	1m3f16y	GD	£2729

Total win prize-money £2730

Going (Turf): Sf: 0-0 GS: 0-2 **Gd: 1-2** GF: 0-1 Fm: 0-0
Distance: 5f/6f: 0-0 7f-8f: 0-0 **9f-13f: 1-4** 14f+: 0-1
Track : LH: 0-4 **RH: 1-1 Tight: 1-1** Gall: 0-3
Aids: Bl: 0-2 Vi: 0-0 Tstrap: 0-0 Ckp: 0-0
Best Rating: **85** 6/09 Donc 1m4f gd-sft

Useful; stays 1m4f and acts on good ground; as worn blinkers; bumper winner.

Caerus (USA)

96(98) (71)**64**
3-y-o b c Greatness (USA)-Bellewood (USA) (Alydar (USA))
W J Knight Ellis Glasscock Tracey

Placings:330-06603 **(3672)**
2009: 8^{0}SD, 6^{6}G, 7^{6}GF, 8^{0}GF, 6^{3}F,

	Starts	1st	2nd	3rd	Win & Pl
Career Total (Turf)	4	0	0	1	347
Career Total (AW)	4	0	0	2	1031

Going (Turf): **Sf: 0-0 GS: 0-0 Gd: 0-1 GF: 0-2 Fm: 0-1**
Distance: 5f/6f: 0-2 7f-8f: 0-6 9f-13f: 0-0 14f+: 0-0
Track : LH: 0-3 RH: 0-2 Tight: 0-2 Gall: 0-0
Aids: Bl: 0-0 Vi: 0-2 Tstrap: 0-0 Ckp: 0-0
Best Rating: **71** 9/08 Wolv 7f32y std-fst

Modest; effective over 7f; acts on Polytrack.

Cafe Fiore (IRE)

(89) (50)**42**
3-y-o b f Clodovil (IRE)-Carpet Lover (IRE) (Fayruz)
T J Pitt T J Pitt

Placings:005003-0 **(0091)**
2009: 5^{0}SD,

	Starts	1st	2nd	3rd	Win & Pl
Career Total (Turf)	2	0	0	0	
Career Total (AW)	5	0	0	1	482

Going (Turf): **Sf: 0-0 GS: 0-1 Gd: 0-0 GF: 0-1 Fm: 0-0**
Distance: 5f/6f: 0-7 7f-8f: 0-0 9f-13f: 0-0 14f+: 0-0
Track : LH: 0-6 RH: 0-0 Tight: 0-4 Gall: 0-0
Aids: Bl: 0-2 Vi: 0-1 Tstrap: 0-0 Ckp: 0-0
Best Rating: **50** 10/08 Wolv 5f216y stand

Cafe Greco

94(90) (70)**73**
2-y-o b g Red Ransom (USA)-Mocca (IRE) (Sri Pekan (USA))
P J Makin Countess Of Lonsdale

Placings:240504 **(6735)**
2009: 6^{2}G, 6^{4}S, 8^{0}SD, 7^{5}SD, 8^{0}SD, 8^{4}GS,

	Starts	1st	2nd	3rd	Win & Pl
Career Total (Turf)	3	0	1	0	1746

Career Total (AW)	3	0	0	0	188

Going (Turf): **Sf: 0-1 GS: 0-1 Gd: 0-1 GF: 0-0 Fm: 0-0**
Distance: 5f/6f: 0-0 7f-8f: 0-5 9f-13f: 0-1 14f+: 0-0
Track : LH: 0-2 RH: 0-2 Tight: 0-3 Gall: 0-0
Aids: Bl: 0-0 Vi: 0-1 Tstrap: 0-0 Ckp: 0-0
Best Rating: **73** 6/09 Sals 6f212y good

Fair; stays 7f; acts on Polytrack.

Cake (IRE)

103(105) (90)**98**
4-y-o b f Acclamation-Carpet Lady (IRE) (Night Shift (USA))
R Hannon Des Anderson

Placings:1135501203/00256352-01205000 **(5871)**
2009: 5^{0}GS, 5^{1}G, 5^{2}GF, 5^{0}GF, 6^{5}GS, 5^{0}G, 5^{0}GF, 5^{0}G,

	Starts	1st	2nd	3rd	Win & Pl
Career Total (Turf)	24	3	3	3	52060
Career Total (AW)	2	1	1	0	8510

98	5/09	Gdwd	5f	(0-90)H	GD	£7771
99	8/07	Newb	5f34y		GD	£12207
79	5/07	Sals	5f		G-F	£6477
66	4/07	Ling	5f		STD	£2914

Total win prize-money £29371

Going (Turf): Sf: 0-2 GS: 0-4 **Gd: 2-10** GF: 1-8 Fm: 0-0
Distance: **5f/6f: 4-24** 7f-8f: 0-2 9f-13f: 0-0 14f+: 0-0
Track : **LH: 1-2** RH: 0-1 **Tight: 1-2** Gall: 0-1
Aids: Bl: 0-0 Vi: 0-0 Tstrap: 0-0 Ckp: 0-0
Best Rating: **102** 10/07 Asct 5f gd-sft

Very useful; winner in Listed company and Group placed at two; suited by 5f; acts on most ground and on Polytrack; likes to race prominently.

Cake Stand

82(90) (52)**55**
3-y-o b g Haafhd-Galette (Caerleon (USA))
J A R Toller P C J Dalby & R Schuster

Placings:0-05050P **(6771)**
2009: 7^{0}G, 8^{5}GF, 8^{0}S, 7^{5}SD, 7^{0}GF, 8^{P}SD,

	Starts	1st	2nd	3rd	Win & Pl
Career Total (Turf)	5	0	0	0	0
Career Total (AW)	2	0	0	0	0

Going (Turf): **Sf: 0-1 GS: 0-0 Gd: 0-1 GF: 0-3 Fm: 0-0**
Distance: 5f/6f: 0-0 7f-8f: 0-6 9f-13f: 0-1 14f+: 0-0
Track : LH: 0-1 RH: 0-1 Tight: 0-1 Gall: 0-0
Aids: Bl: 0-0 Vi: 0-3 Tstrap: 0-0 Ckp: 0-0
Best Rating: **55** 5/09 NmkR 1m gd-fm

Calabaza

78(90) (44)**62**
7-y-o ch g Zaha (CAN)-Mo Stopher (Sharpo)
M J Attwater Canisbay Bloodstock

Placings:03300510/034000/605000201010**0**/0002**6**00-00 **(3917)**
2009: 6^{0}G, 5^{0}G,

	Starts	1st	2nd	3rd	Win & Pl
Career Total (Turf)	32	3	2	3	16192
Career Total (AW)	4	0	0	0	0

69	10/07	Brig	5f59y	(0-70)H	G-S	£3238
68	10/07	Wwck	6f	(0-65)H	G-F	£2047
71	8/05	Gdwd	6f		GD	£6711

Total win prize-money £11998

Going (Turf): Sf: 0-1 **GS: 1-5 Gd: 1-19 GF: 1-7** Fm: 0-0
Distance: **5f/6f: 3-29** 7f-8f: 0-7 9f-13f: 0-0 14f+: 0-0

Track : **LH: 2-8** RH: 0-2 Tight: 0-2 Gall: 0-4
Aids: Bl: 1-10 Vi: 0-0 Tstrap: 2-12 Ckp: 2-12
Best Rating: **73** 8/06 NmkJ 6f gd-fm

Modest; effective at around six furlongs; acts on good ground; has worn blinkers and cheekpieces.

Calahonda

96(103) (87)**86**
3-y-o ch f Haafhd-Californie (IRE) (Rainbow Quest (USA))
P W D'Arcy Gongolphin & Racing

Placings:261410241-0560041 **(5329)**
2009: 7^{0}S, 6^{5}GF, 6^{6}SD, 6^{0}SD, 7^{0}G, 7^{4}SD, 8^{1}SD,

	Starts	1st	2nd	3rd	Win & Pl
Career Total (Turf)	9	2	1	0	10002
Career Total (AW)	7	2	1	0	13124

81	8/09	Sthl	1m	(0-70)H	STD	£5051
87	11/08	GrLe	6f		STD	£6854
82	9/08	Yarm	7f3y	(0-85)	GD	£4037
70	8/08	Yarm	7f3y		GD	£2331

Total win prize-money £18273

Going (Turf): Sf: 0-1 GS: 0-2 **Gd: 2-4** GF: 0-2 Fm: 0-0
Distance: 5f/6f: **1-7 7f-8f: 3-9** 9f-13f: 0-0 14f+: 0-0
Track : **LH: 2-3** RH: 0-5 Tight: 0-1 **Gall: 1-1**
Aids: Bl: 0-0 Vi: 0-0 Tstrap: 0-1 Ckp: 0-1
Best Rating: **87** 11/08 GrLe 6f stand

Fair; stays 1m; acts on good and softer ground and on sand; has worn cheekpieces and an eyeshield.

Calaloo (IRE)

102(94) (81)**82**
3-y-o b g Dansili-Maraami (Selkirk (USA))
C R Egerton Brimacombe, McNally, Rickman & Sangster

Placings:431-0**3345**25**0**0 **(6936)**
2009: 8^{0}GF, 11^{3}G, 12^{3}SD, 12^{4}SD, 10^{5}G, 10^{2}GF, 10^{5}GF, 12^{0}SD, 11^{0}G,

	Starts	1st	2nd	3rd	Win & Pl
Career Total (Turf)	9	1	1	2	5286
Career Total (AW)	3	0	0	1	1088

78	10/08	Bath	1m5y		G-S	£2396

Total win prize-money £2396

Going (Turf): Sf: 0-1 **GS: 1-1** Gd: 0-3 GF: 0-3 Fm: 0-1
Distance: 5f/6f: 0-1 7f-8f: 0-1 **9f-13f: 1-10** 14f+: 0-0
Track : **LH: 1-5** RH: 0-4 **Tight: 1-5** Gall: 0-1
Aids: Bl: 0-5 Vi: 0-0 Tstrap: 0-0 Ckp: 0-0
Best Rating: **82** 5/09 Wind 1m3f135y good

Fair; stays 1m4f; acts on good and easy ground and Polytrack; has worn blinkers.

Calatrava Cape (IRE)

101 **73**
2-y-o b/br f Cape Cross (IRE)-Pershaan (IRE) (Darshaan)
J L Dunlop Windflower Overseas Holdings Inc

Placings:50062 **(6232)**
2009: 7^{5}GF, 7^{0}GS, 7^{0}GF, 8^{6}GF, 8^{2}GF,

	Starts	1st	2nd	3rd	Win & Pl
Career Total (Turf)	5	0	1	0	1349

Going (Turf): **Sf: 0-0 GS: 0-1 Gd: 0-0 GF: 0-4 Fm: 0-0**
Distance: 5f/6f: 0-0 7f-8f: 0-4 9f-13f: 0-1 14f+: 0-0
Track : LH: 0-1 RH: 0-2 Tight: 0-0 Gall: 0-0
Aids: Bl: 0-0 Vi: 0-0 Tstrap: 0-0 Ckp: 0-0
Best Rating: **73** 9/09 Pont 1m4y gd-fm

Modest; stays 1m; acts on fast ground.

Calculating (IRE)

100(108) (78)**84**
5-y-o b g Machiavellian (USA)-Zaheemah (USA) (El Prado (IRE))
M D I Usher Brian Rogan

Placings:0/55002505**222**/**5123211300660000602**3-**64405421U33042301341310** **(7867)**
2009: 16^{6}SD, 16^{4}SD, 14^{4}SD, 16^{0}SD, 16^{5}SD, 13^{4}SD, 14^{2}SD, 14^{1}SD, 15^{U}G, 13^{3}SD, 16^{3}G, 16^{0}G, 16^{4}SD, 16^{2}SD, 16^{3}SD, 16^{0}GS, 12^{1}G, 14^{3}G, 16^{4}SD, 13^{1}SD, 16^{3}SD, 16^{1}SD, 14^{0}SS,

	Starts	1st	2nd	3rd	Win & Pl
Career Total (Turf)	21	1	1	2	5421
Career Total (AW)	34	6	8	6	41035

74	12/09	Sthl	2m	(0-75)H	STD	£2729
70	11/09	Wolv	1m5f194y	(0-85)H	STD	£5046
55	7/09	Epsm	1m4f10y	(0-70)H	GD	£3238
68	3/09	Sthl	1m6f	(0-75)H	STD	£2590
91	3/08	Kemp	2m	(0-105)H	STD	£9971
88	3/08	Wolv	2m119y	(0-85)H	STD	£4210
76	1/08	Sthl	1m3f		STD	£2457

Total win prize-money £30242

Going (Turf): Sf: 0-0 GS: 0-7 **Gd: 1-10** GF: 0-4 Fm: 0-0
Distance: 5f/6f: 0-0 7f-8f: 0-4 9f-13f: 2-15 **14f+: 5-36**
Track : **LH: 6-33** RH: 1-18 **Tight: 3-18** Gall: 0-4
Aids: Bl: 0-0 Vi: 0-0 Tstrap: 0-1 Ckp: 0-1
Best Rating: **93** 4/08 GrLe 2m stand

Modest; effective from 1m3f-2m; acts on Polytrack and Fibresand.

Calculus Affair (IRE)

(89) (58)
2-y-o b c Trans Island-Where's Charlotte (Sure Blade (USA))
J Noseda Mrs Susan Roy

Placings:45 **(7886)**
2009: 7^{4}SD, 7^{5}SD,

	Starts	1st	2nd	3rd	Win & Pl
Career Total (Turf)	0	0	0	0	
Career Total (AW)	2	0	0	0	265

Going (Turf): **Sf: 0-0 GS: 0-0 Gd: 0-0 GF: 0-0 Fm: 0-0**
Distance: 5f/6f: 0-0 7f-8f: 0-2 9f-13f: 0-0 14f+: 0-0
Track : LH: 0-2 RH: 0-0 Tight: 0-2 Gall: 0-0
Aids: Bl: 0-0 Vi: 0-0 Tstrap: 0-0 Ckp: 0-0
Best Rating: **58** 12/09 Ling 7f stand

Caldercruix (USA)

95 **67**
2-y-o ch c Rahy (USA)-Al Theraab (USA) (Roberto (USA))
T P Tate Mrs Fitri Hay

Placings:003 **(6990)**
2009: 7^{0}GF, 7^{0}G, 7^{3}G,

	Starts	1st	2nd	3rd	Win & Pl
Career Total (Turf)	3	0	0	1	674

Going (Turf): **Sf: 0-0 GS: 0-0 Gd: 0-2 GF: 0-1 Fm: 0-0**
Distance: 5f/6f: 0-0 7f-8f: 0-3 9f-13f: 0-0 14f+: 0-0
Track : LH: 0-1 RH: 0-0 Tight: 0-0 Gall: 0-1
Aids: Bl: 0-0 Vi: 0-0 Tstrap: 0-0 Ckp: 0-0

Best Rating: 67 10/09 Donc 7f good

Caldermud (IRE)

90(85) (52)67

2-y-o ch c Chineur (FR)-Dalal (Cadeaux Genereux)
J R Best Tony Perkins & James D Cameron

Placings:50 (5778)
2009: 6^{5}G, 6^{0}SD,

	Starts	1st	2nd	3rd	Win & Pl
Career Total (Turf)	1	0	0	0	0
Career Total (AW)	1	0	0	0	

Going (Turf): Sf: 0-0 GS: 0-0 Gd: 0-1 GF: 0-0 Fm: 0-0
Distance: 5f/6f: 0-2 7f-8f: 0-0 9f-13f: 0-0 14f+: 0-0
Track : LH: 0-0 RH: 0-1 Tight: 0-0 Gall: 0-1
Aids: Bl: 0-0 Vi: 0-0 Tstrap: 0-0 Ckp: 0-0
Best Rating: 67 8/09 Wind 6f good

Calders

61

2-y-o b f Monsieur Bond (IRE)-Delicious (Dominion)
A Berry Andrew Calderbank

Placings:000 (4800)
2009: 5^{0}GF, 5^{0}S, 6^{0}GF,

	Starts	1st	2nd	3rd	Win & Pl
Career Total (Turf)	3	0	0	0	

Going (Turf): Sf: 0-1 GS: 0-0 Gd: 0-0 GF: 0-2 Fm: 0-0
Distance: 5f/6f: 0-3 7f-8f: 0-0 9f-13f: 0-0 14f+: 0-0
Track : LH: 0-1 RH: 0-0 Tight: 0-1 Gall: 0-0
Aids: Bl: 0-0 Vi: 0-0 Tstrap: 0-0 Ckp: 0-0

Caledonia Princess

90(109) (74)74

3-y-o b f Kyllachy-Granuaile O'Malley (IRE) (Mark Of Esteem (IRE))
R Curtis Isla & Colin Cage

Placings:60214-0060055100 (7634)
2009: 8^{0}GF, 7^{0}GS, 6^{0}SD, 7^{0}SD, 6^{0}GS, 6^{5}SD, 6^{5}SD, 5^{1}SD, 5^{0}SD, 5^{0}SD,

	Starts	1st	2nd	3rd	Win & Pl
Career Total (Turf)	8	1	1	0	4777
Career Total (AW)	7	1	0	0	3238

74 11/09 Wolv 5f20y (0-70)H STD £3238
74 9/08 Leic 5f218y (0-85) GD £3885
Total win prize-money £7124

Going (Turf): Sf: 0-1 GS: 0-3 **Gd: 1-1** GF: 0-3 Fm: 0-0
Distance: **5f/6f: 2-13** 7f-8f: 0-2 9f-13f: 0-0 14f+: 0-0
Track : **LH: 1-6** RH: 0-3 **Tight: 1-3** Gall: 0-2
Aids: **Bl: 1-3** Vi: 0-0 Tstrap: 0-0 Ckp: 0-0
Best Rating: 74 11/09 Wolv 5f20y stand

Modest; effective over 6f; acts on good ground/Polytrack; has worn blinkers.

California Bright (IRE)

88 56

3-y-o ch f Rock Of Gibraltar (IRE)-Woodyousmileforme (USA) (Woodman (USA))
J G Given Brighton Farm Ltd

Placings:03 (2659)
2009: 10^{0}G, 11^{3}G,

	Starts	1st	2nd	3rd	Win & Pl
Career Total (Turf)	2	0	0	1	482

Going (Turf): Sf: 0-0 GS: 0-0 Gd: 0-2 GF: 0-0 Fm: 0-0
Distance: 5f/6f: 0-0 7f-8f: 0-0 9f-13f: 0-2 14f+: 0-0
Track : LH: 0-2 RH: 0-0 Tight: 0-1 Gall: 0-0
Aids: Bl: 0-0 Vi: 0-0 Tstrap: 0-0 Ckp: 0-0
Best Rating: 56 6/09 Catt 1m3f214y good

Call For Liberty (IRE)

95(86) (75)60

4-y-o b c Statue Of Liberty (USA)-Give A Whistle (IRE) (Mujadil (USA))
B Smart Prime Equestrian

Placings:0225/1040-05 (2269)
2009: 7^{0}SD, 7^{5}G,

	Starts	1st	2nd	3rd	Win & Pl
Career Total (Turf)	6	0	2	0	2187
Career Total (AW)	4	1	0	0	4605

75 1/08 Jebl 6f FST £4062
Total win prize-money £4063

Going (Turf): Sf: 0-0 GS: 0-1 Gd: 0-2 GF: 0-3 Fm: 0-0
Distance: **5f/6f: 1-6** 7f-8f: 0-4 9f-13f: 0-0 14f+: 0-0
Track : LH: 0-3 RH: 0-1 Tight: 0-3 Gall: 0-1
Aids: Bl: 0-2 Vi: 0-0 Tstrap: 0-0 Ckp: 0-0
Best Rating: 79 8/07 Hayd 6f gd-fm

Modest form in maidens at 6f on fast ground.

Call It On (IRE)

107 91

3-y-o ch g Raise A Grand (IRE)-Birthday Present (Cadeaux Genereux)
M H Tompkins GPD Ltd

Placings:041-03532630 (6996)
2009: 10^{0}GF, 8^{3}G, 10^{5}G, 10^{3}G, 10^{2}G, 10^{6}GF, 10^{3}GS, 10^{0}GS,

	Starts	1st	2nd	3rd	Win & Pl
Career Total (Turf)	11	1	1	3	9473

86 10/08 Wind 1m67y G-S £5018
Total win prize-money £5019

Going (Turf): Sf: 0-0 **GS: 1-3** Gd: 0-4 GF: 0-4 Fm: 0-0
Distance: 5f/6f: 0-0 7f-8f: 0-2 **9f-13f: 1-9** 14f+: 0-0
Track : LH: 0-4 **RH: 1-4 Tight: 1-3** Gall: 0-3
Aids: Bl: 0-0 Vi: 0-0 Tstrap: 0-0 Ckp: 0-0
Best Rating: 91 10/09 Wind 1m2f7y gd-sft

Useful; stays 1m2f; acts on easy and good ground.

Call Me Al (IRE)

76(85) (73)60

4-y-o b g Alhaarth (IRE)-Takarna (IRE) (Mark Of Esteem (IRE))
J J Lambe J J Lambe

Placings:50/0000046-00 (2441)
2009: 16^{0}SD, 8^{0}GF,

	Starts	1st	2nd	3rd	Win & Pl
Career Total (Turf)	5	0	0	0	
Career Total (AW)	6	0	0	0	256

Going (Turf): Sf: 0-0 GS: 0-0 Gd: 0-0 GF: 0-2 Fm: 0-1
Distance: 5f/6f: 0-1 7f-8f: 0-4 9f-13f: 0-5 14f+: 0-1
Track : LH: 0-5 RH: 0-2 Tight: 0-2 Gall: 0-0
Aids: Bl: 0-0 Vi: 0-0 Tstrap: 0-0 Ckp: 0-0
Best Rating: 73 11/07 Dund 1m stand

Call Me Courageous (IRE)

94(80) (15)54

3-y-o ch g Captain Rio-Golden Concorde (Super Concorde (USA))
R A Harris (A B Haynes 5/8) Ridge House Stables Ltd

Placings:5600450-00042000 (5628)
2009: 8^{0}GF, 8^{0}F, 5^{0}F, 5^{4}F, 6^{2}G, 5^{0}GF, 6^{0}SD, 7^{0}GS,

	Starts	1st	2nd	3rd	Win & Pl
Career Total (Turf)	13	0	1	0	867
Career Total (AW)	2	0	0	0	

Going (Turf): Sf: 0-3 GS: 0-2 Gd: 0-2 GF: 0-3 Fm: 0-3
Distance: 5f/6f: 0-9 7f-8f: 0-4 9f-13f: 0-2 14f+: 0-0
Track : LH: 0-8 RH: 0-1 Tight: 0-1 Gall: 0-1
Aids: Bl: 0-0 Vi: 0-1 Tstrap: 0-2 Ckp: 0-2
Best Rating: 61 4/08 Nott 5f13y soft

Call Me Rosy (IRE)

90(64) (60)46

5-y-o ch m Shinko Forest (IRE)-Fanciful (IRE) (Mujtahid (USA))
B Smart Mrs Patricia Brown

Placings:02400/3040/00-500 (3484)
2009: 7^{5}GF, 6^{0}GF, 6^{0}GF,

	Starts	1st	2nd	3rd	Win & Pl
Career Total (Turf)	5	0	0	0	0
Career Total (AW)	9	0	1	1	1758

Going (Turf): Sf: 0-0 GS: 0-0 Gd: 0-0 GF: 0-5 Fm: 0-0
Distance: 5f/6f: 0-9 7f-8f: 0-5 9f-13f: 0-0 14f+: 0-0
Track : LH: 0-8 RH: 0-2 Tight: 0-7 Gall: 0-0
Aids: Bl: 0-0 Vi: 0-0 Tstrap: 0-0 Ckp: 0-0
Best Rating: 65 10/06 Wolv 5f216y std-fst

Call Of Duty (IRE)

100 (75)62

4-y-o br g Storming Home-Blushing Barada (USA) (Blushing Groom (FR))
Mrs Dianne Sayer T W Rebanks

Placings:12/0006042400 (6184)
2009: 10^{0}GS, 6^{0}GF, 8^{0}GS, 7^{6}G, 9^{0}GF, 13^{4}G, 12^{2}GS, 11^{4}GF, 15^{0}S, 9^{0}GF,

	Starts	1st	2nd	3rd	Win & Pl
Career Total (Turf)	10	0	1	0	1375
Career Total (AW)	2	1	1	0	3099

73 12/07 Ling 1m STD £1943
Total win prize-money £1943

Going (Turf): Sf: 0-1 GS: 0-3 Gd: 0-2 GF: 0-4 Fm: 0-0
Distance: 5f/6f: 0-0 **7f-8f: 1-5** 9f-13f: 0-6 14f+: 0-1
Track : **LH: 1-5** RH: 0-7 **Tight: 1-7** Gall: 0-1
Aids: Bl: 0-0 Vi: 0-0 Tstrap: 0-0 Ckp: 0-0
Best Rating: 75 12/07 Ling 1m stand

Modest; stays 1m2f; acts on fast ground and on Polytrack.

Call Of Ktulu (IRE)

76 32

4-y-o b g Noverre (USA)-Yankee Dancer (Groom Dancer (USA))
J S Wainwright Charles Wentworth

Placings:00/00-000 **(3558)**
2009: 8^{0}GF, 8^{0}GF, 7^{0}GF,

	Starts	1st	2nd	3rd	Win & Pl
Career Total (Turf)	7	0	0	0	

Going (Turf): Sf: 0-0 GS: 0-0 Gd: 0-2 GF: 0-5 Fm: 0-0
Distance: 5f/6f: 0-0 7f-8f: 0-5 9f-13f: 0-2 14f+: 0-0
Track : LH: 0-4 RH: 0-2 Tight: 0-4 Gall: 0-1
Aids: Bl: 0-1 Vi: 0-1 Tstrap: 0-2 Ckp: 0-2
Best Rating: 32 5/09 Thsk 1m gd-fm

Call Of The Kings

80(75) (32)55

2-y-o b g Acclamation-Surrey Down (USA) (Forest Wildcat (USA))
R A Teal J Morton

Placings:40 **(6629)**
2009: 6^{4}GF, 7^{0}SS,

	Starts	1st	2nd	3rd	Win & Pl
Career Total (Turf)	1	0	0	0	289
Career Total (AW)	1	0	0	0	

Going (Turf): Sf: 0-0 GS: 0-0 Gd: 0-0 GF: 0-1 Fm: 0-0
Distance: 5f/6f: 0-1 7f-8f: 0-1 9f-13f: 0-0 14f+: 0-0
Track : LH: 0-1 RH: 0-0 Tight: 0-1 Gall: 0-0
Aids: Bl: 0-1 Vi: 0-0 Tstrap: 0-0 Ckp: 0-0
Best Rating: 55 6/09 Gdwd 6f gd-fm

Call To Arms (IRE)

91 78

2-y-o br g Shamardal (USA)-Requesting (Rainbow Quest (USA))
M Johnston Sheikh Hamdan Bin Mohammed Al Maktoum

Placings:232 **(5958)**
2009: 6^{2}G, 6^{3}GF, 6^{2}GF,

	Starts	1st	2nd	3rd	Win & Pl
Career Total (Turf)	3	0	2	1	3006

Going (Turf): Sf: 0-0 GS: 0-0 Gd: 0-1 GF: 0-2 Fm: 0-0
Distance: 5f/6f: 0-3 7f-8f: 0-0 9f-13f: 0-0 14f+: 0-0
Track : LH: 0-0 RH: 0-0 Tight: 0-0 Gall: 0-0
Aids: Bl: 0-0 Vi: 0-0 Tstrap: 0-0 Ckp: 0-0
Best Rating: 78 6/09 Thsk 6f good

Useful; stays 6f and acts on good/fast ground.

Call To Reason (IRE)

90 78

2-y-o ch f Pivotal-Venturi (Danehill Dancer (IRE))
J Noseda The Socrates Partnership

Placings:2 **(7182)**
2009: 7^{2}G,

	Starts	1st	2nd	3rd	Win & Pl
Career Total (Turf)	1	0	1	0	1445

Going (Turf): Sf: 0-0 GS: 0-0 Gd: 0-1 GF: 0-0 Fm: 0-0
Distance: 5f/6f: 0-0 7f-8f: 0-1 9f-13f: 0-0 14f+: 0-0
Track : LH: 0-0 RH: 0-0 Tight: 0-0 Gall: 0-0
Aids: Bl: 0-0 Vi: 0-0 Tstrap: 0-0 Ckp: 0-0
Best Rating: 78 10/09 NmkR 7f good

Calle Vistamar

2-y-o ch f Stage Pass-Champagne Bubbleigh Vii (Damsire Unregistered)
S Wynne Kevin Holmes

Placings:0P **(6122)**
2009: 5^{0}SD, 7^{P}SD,

	Starts	1st	2nd	3rd	Win & Pl
Career Total (Turf)	0	0	0	0	
Career Total (AW)	2	0	0	0	

Going (Turf): Sf: 0-0 GS: 0-0 Gd: 0-0 GF: 0-0 Fm: 0-0
Distance: 5f/6f: 0-1 7f-8f: 0-1 9f-13f: 0-0 14f+: 0-0
Track : LH: 0-2 RH: 0-0 Tight: 0-2 Gall: 0-0
Aids: Bl: 0-0 Vi: 0-0 Tstrap: 0-0 Ckp: 0-0

Calley Ho

70(95) (70)66

3-y-o b g Kyllachy-Lucayan Belle (Cadeaux Genereux)
Mrs L Stubbs Mrs L Stubbs

Placings:4150643000-00 **(3862)**
2009: 6^{0}G, 8^{0}GF,

	Starts	1st	2nd	3rd	Win & Pl
Career Total (Turf)	7	1	0	0	2855
Career Total (AW)	5	0	0	1	602

62 6/08 Haml 6f5y G-F £2590
Total win prize-money £2590

Going (Turf): Sf: 0-0 GS: 0-0 Gd: 0-4 **GF: 1-3** Fm: 0-0
Distance: 5f/6f: 0-5 **7f-8f: 1-6** 9f-13f: 0-1 14f+: 0-0
Track : LH: 0-5 RH: 0-2 Tight: 0-0 Gall: 0-3
Aids: Bl: 0-0 Vi: 0-0 Tstrap: 0-0 Ckp: 0-0
Best Rating: 70 9/08 Kemp 6f stand

Modest; should stay 7f; acts on fast ground.

Calligrapher (USA)

94(88) (67)85

3-y-o ch g Rahy (USA)-Calista (Caerleon (USA))
M A Jarvis Sheikh Ahmed Al Maktoum

Placings:514-06 **(2821)**
2009: 6^{0}GF, 6^{6}GF,

	Starts	1st	2nd	3rd	Win & Pl
Career Total (Turf)	4	1	0	0	4857
Career Total (AW)	1	0	0	0	330

85 9/08 Pont 6f G-F £4857
Total win prize-money £4857

Going (Turf): Sf: 0-0 GS: 0-0 Gd: 0-1 **GF: 1-3** Fm: 0-0
Distance: **5f/6f: 1-4** 7f-8f: 0-1 9f-13f: 0-0 14f+: 0-0
Track : **LH: 1-2** RH: 0-0 Tight: 0-1 Gall: 0-0
Aids: Bl: 0-0 Vi: 0-0 Tstrap: 0-0 Ckp: 0-0
Best Rating: 85 9/08 Pont 6f gd-fm

Very useful; suited by 6f and fast ground.

Calling Birds (IRE)

91(91) (49)39

3-y-o b f Royal Applause-Jezyah (USA) (Chief's Crown (USA))
Karen George (J A Osborne 21/4) Mrs Isabel Fraser

Placings:6-050060 **(4084)**
2009: 8^{0}SD, 10^{5}SD, 10^{0}G, 9^{0}GF, 9^{6}GF, 10^{0}SD,

	Starts	1st	2nd	3rd	Win & Pl
Career Total (Turf)	3	0	0	0	0
Career Total (AW)	4	0	0	0	0

Going (Turf): Sf: 0-0 GS: 0-0 Gd: 0-1 GF: 0-2 Fm: 0-0
Distance: 5f/6f: 0-0 7f-8f: 0-1 9f-13f: 0-6 14f+: 0-0
Track : LH: 0-6 RH: 0-1 Tight: 0-5 Gall: 0-0
Aids: Bl: 0-1 Vi: 0-2 Tstrap: 0-2 Ckp: 0-2
Best Rating: 49 3/09 Ling 1m2f stand

Calling Victory (FR)

91(96) (66)49

3-y-o b f Vettori (IRE)-Calling Card (Bering)
M Botti Mrs R J Jacobs

Placings:22600 **(2709)**
2009: 8^{2}SD, 8^{2}SD, 10^{6}G, 10^{0}G, 10^{0}SD,

	Starts	1st	2nd	3rd	Win & Pl
Career Total (Turf)	2	0	0	0	0
Career Total (AW)	3	0	2	0	1461

Going (Turf): Sf: 0-0 GS: 0-0 Gd: 0-2 GF: 0-0 Fm: 0-0
Distance: 5f/6f: 0-0 7f-8f: 0-0 9f-13f: 0-5 14f+: 0-0
Track : LH: 0-5 RH: 0-0 Tight: 0-4 Gall: 0-0
Aids: Bl: 0-1 Vi: 0-0 Tstrap: 0-0 Ckp: 0-0
Best Rating: 66 2/09 Wolv 1m141y stand

Moderate; stays 1m; acts on Polytrack.

Callis Wood

78 35

3-y-o br f Shinko Forest (IRE)-Meltonby (Sayf El Arab (USA))
Ollie Pears N Hetherton

Placings:00 **(2105)**
2009: 7^{0}GF, 9^{0}GS,

	Starts	1st	2nd	3rd	Win & Pl
Career Total (Turf)	2	0	0	0	

Going (Turf): Sf: 0-0 GS: 0-1 Gd: 0-0 GF: 0-1 Fm: 0-0
Distance: 5f/6f: 0-0 7f-8f: 0-1 9f-13f: 0-1 14f+: 0-0
Track : LH: 0-0 RH: 0-1 Tight: 0-1 Gall: 0-0
Aids: Bl: 0-0 Vi: 0-0 Tstrap: 0-0 Ckp: 0-0
Best Rating: 35 4/09 Rdcr 7f gd-fm

Callisto Moon

107(100) (69)88

5-y-o b g Mujahid (USA)-Nursling (IRE) (Kahyasi)
R Curtis B Bedford & Mrs Gill White

Placings:426603252/5016/422024-45115110 **(7117)**

2009: 16^{4}SD, 14^{5}SD, 14^{1}G, 14^{1}GF, 16^{5}GF, 14^{1}GF, 17^{1}F, 16^{0}GS,

	Starts	1st	2nd	3rd	Win & Pl
Career Total (Turf)	16	5	3	0	40388
Career Total (AW)	11	0	3	1	3056

88	9/09	Bath	2m1f34y	(0-100)H	FRM	£17446
87	7/09	Sand	1m6f	(0-85)H	G-F	£4857
83	6/09	Muss	1m6f	(0-75)H	G-F	£3238
78	6/09	Sand	1m6f	(0-85)H	GD	£5828
69	4/07	Wwck	1m2f188y	(0-75)H	G-F	£3238

Total win prize-money £34609

Going (Turf): Sf: 0-0 GS: 0-2 Gd: 1-5 **GF: 3-8** Fm: 1-1
Distance: 5f/6f: 0-2 7f-8f: 0-3 9f-13f: 1-9 **14f+: 4-13**
Track : LH: 2-13 **RH: 3-12 Tight: 2-10** Gall: 0-2
Aids: Bl: 0-2 Vi: 0-0 Tstrap: 3-7 Ckp: 3-7
Best Rating: 88 9/09 Bath 2m1f34y firm

Useful; stays 2m1f; acts on fast ground and on Polytrack; has worn cheekpieces.

Calm And Serene (USA)

87 **47**

2-y-o b f Quiet American (USA)-Charm Away (USA) (Silver Charm (USA))
Rae Guest Mrs Melba Bryce

Placings:00 **(6786)**
2009: 8^{0}GS, 7^{0}G,

	Starts	1st	2nd	3rd	Win & Pl
Career Total (Turf)	2	0	0	0	

Going (Turf): Sf: 0-0 GS: 0-1 Gd: 0-1 GF: 0-0 Fm: 0-0
Distance: 5f/6f: 0-0 7f-8f: 0-1 9f-13f: 0-1 14f+: 0-0
Track : LH: 0-2 RH: 0-0 Tight: 0-0 Gall: 0-0
Aids: Bl: 0-0 Vi: 0-0 Tstrap: 0-0 Ckp: 0-0
Best Rating: 47 10/09 Brig 7f214y good

Calm Storm (IRE)

79(89) (63)**33**

2-y-o b c Whipper (USA)-Dark Hyacinth (IRE) (Darshaan)
J Noseda Saeed Suhail

Placings:06600 **(6735)**
2009: 7^{0}G, 6^{6}SD, 6^{6}SD, 8^{0}SD, 8^{0}GS,

	Starts	1st	2nd	3rd	Win & Pl
Career Total (Turf)	2	0	0	0	
Career Total (AW)	3	0	0	0	0

Going (Turf): Sf: 0-0 GS: 0-1 Gd: 0-1 GF: 0-0 Fm: 0-0
Distance: 5f/6f: 0-2 7f-8f: 0-2 9f-13f: 0-1 14f+: 0-0
Track : LH: 0-1 RH: 0-3 Tight: 0-2 Gall: 0-0
Aids: Bl: 0-0 Vi: 0-1 Tstrap: 0-0 Ckp: 0-0
Best Rating: 63 9/09 Kemp 6f stand

Modest; should be suited by 7f; acts on Polytrack.

Calmdownmate (IRE)

98(104) (80)**85**

4-y-o b g Danehill Dancer (IRE)-Lady Digby (IRE) (Petorius)
Mrs R A Carr Ruth Carr Racing

Placings:62150/00000303215-12010100350 **(7758)**
2009: 5^{1}SD, 5^{2}SD, 5^{0}SD, 6^{1}SD, 6^{0}GF, 5^{1}SD, 5^{0}G, 6^{0}GF, 6^{3}SD, 6^{5}SD, 5^{0}SD,

	Starts	1st	2nd	3rd	Win & Pl
Career Total (Turf)	14	1	1	1	6619
Career Total (AW)	13	4	2	2	12703

80	5/09	Sthl	5f	(0-75)H	STD	£3756
75	2/09	Sthl	6f	(0-70)H	STD	£2590
75	1/09	Sthl	5f		STD	£2047
70	12/08	Sthl	5f		STD	£2047
89	8/07	Ripn	6f		G-F	£4210

Total win prize-money £14650

Going (Turf): Sf: 0-1 GS: 0-2 Gd: 0-6 **GF: 1-5** Fm: 0-0
Distance: **5f/6f: 5-24** 7f-8f: 0-3 9f-13f: 0-0 14f+: 0-0
Track : **LH: 1-8** RH: 0 0 Tight: 0-1 Gall: 0-2
Aids: Bl: 0-3 Vi: 0-1 Tstrap: 0-0 Ckp: 0-0
Best Rating: 89 8/07 York 7f good

Modest; effective over 5f-7f; acts on good and fast ground; goes on Fibresand; has worn blinkers.

Caltire (GER)

(95) (66)**65**

4-y-o b g Pentire-Caluna (SWI) (Lagunas)
M G Quinlan N J Jones

Placings:6011522/06601066-**660** **(0872)**
2009: 12^{6}SD, 12^{6}SD, 10^{0}SD,

	Starts	1st	2nd	3rd	Win & Pl
Career Total (Turf)	9	1	0	0	2526
Career Total (AW)	9	2	2	0	5576

65	5/08	Brig	1m1f209y	(0-65)H	G-S	£2525
57	11/07	Ling	1m		STD	£2047
48	10/07	Ling	1m		STD	£2047

Total win prize-money £6622

Going (Turf): Sf: 0-1 **GS: 1-6** Gd: 0-1 GF: 0-1 Fm: 0-0
Distance: 5f/6f: 0-0 **7f-8f: 2-3** 9f-13f: 1-15 14f+: 0-0
Track : **LH: 3-13** RH: 0-4 **Tight: 2-12** Gall: 0-0
Aids: **Bl: 3-12** Vi: 0-0 Tstrap: 0-0 Ckp: 0-0
Best Rating: 66 1/08 Wolv 1m1f103y stand

Modest; stays 1m2f; acts on easy ground; also goes on Polytrack; often wears blinkers.

Calypso Bay (IRE)

97(92) (56)**85**

3-y-o b c Galileo (IRE)-Poule De Luxe (IRE) (Cadeaux Genereux)
J Noseda D Smith, Mrs J Magnier, M Tabor

Placings:306 **(2488)**
2009: 10^{3}GF, 10^{0}GF, 10^{6}SD,

	Starts	1st	2nd	3rd	Win & Pl
Career Total (Turf)	2	0	0	1	770
Career Total (AW)	1	0	0	0	0

Going (Turf): Sf: 0-0 GS: 0-0 Gd: 0-0 GF: 0-2 Fm: 0-0
Distance: 5f/6f: 0-0 7f-8f: 0-0 9f-13f: 0-3 14f+: 0-0
Track : LH: 0-2 RH: 0-0 Tight: 0-2 Gall: 0-0
Aids: Bl: 0-0 Vi: 0-0 Tstrap: 0-0 Ckp: 0-0
Best Rating: 85 4/09 NmkR 1m2f gd-fm

Calypso Girl (IRE)

95(87) (65)**76**

3-y-o gr f Verglas (IRE)-Clochette (IRE) (Namaqualand (USA))
P D Evans Mrs I M Folkes

Placings:0135600006-050500000 **(5716)**
2009: 7^{0}GF, 5^{5}GF, 6^{0}G, 6^{5}GF, 6^{0}F, 5^{0}G, 6^{0}S, 6^{0}G, 5^{0}G,

	Starts	1st	2nd	3rd	Win & Pl
Career Total (Turf)	16	1	0	1	7374
Career Total (AW)	3	0	0	0	0

74	4/08	Nott	5f13y		SFT	£3626

Total win prize-money £3627

Going (Turf): **Sf: 1-4** GS: 0-1 Gd: 0-7 GF: 0-3 Fm: 0-1
Distance: **5f/6f: 1-17** 7f-8f: 0-2 9f-13f: 0-0 14f+: 0-0
Track : LH: 0-3 RH: 0-1 Tight: 0-1 Gall: 0-4
Aids: Bl: 0-0 Vi: 0-1 Tstrap: 0-0 Ckp: 0-0
Best Rating: 76 9/08 Sals 6f good

Fair; best at 5f; handles good and soft ground.

Calypso Prince

(83) (42)**54**

3-y-o ch g Lucky Story (USA)-Eleonora D'Arborea (Prince Sabo)
M D I Usher M D I Usher

Placings:003000000-000 **(0506)**
2009: 7^{0}SD, 5^{0}SD, 10^{0}SD,

	Starts	1st	2nd	3rd	Win & Pl
Career Total (Turf)	4	0	0	1	424
Career Total (AW)	8	0	0	0	

Going (Turf): Sf: 0-1 GS: 0-0 Gd: 0-1 GF: 0-1 Fm: 0-1
Distance: 5f/6f: 0-5 7f-8f: 0-6 9f-13f: 0-1 14f+: 0-0
Track : LH: 0-8 RH: 0-2 Tight: 0-5 Gall: 0-2
Aids: Bl: 0-0 Vi: 0-5 Tstrap: 0-2 Ckp: 0-2
Best Rating: 54 6/08 Brig 5f213y firm

Calypso Star (IRE)

87(95) (68)**47**

2-y-o ch c Exceed And Excel (AUS)-Reematna (Sabrehill (USA))
R Hannon A C Pickford & N A Woodcock

Placings:60022 **(7335)**
2009: 6^{6}G, 7^{0}SS, 8^{0}G, 8^{2}SD, 8^{2}SD,

	Starts	1st	2nd	3rd	Win & Pl
Career Total (Turf)	2	0	0	0	0
Career Total (AW)	3	0	2	0	1384

Going (Turf): Sf: 0-0 GS: 0-0 Gd: 0-2 GF: 0-0 Fm: 0-0
Distance: 5f/6f: 0-0 7f-8f: 0-4 9f-13f: 0-1 14f+: 0-0
Track : LH: 0-3 RH: 0-1 Tight: 0-2 Gall: 0-0
Aids: Bl: 0-0 Vi: 0-0 Tstrap: 0-0 Ckp: 0-0
Best Rating: 68 11/09 Sthl 1m stand

Modest; stays 1m; acts on Polytrack and Fibresand; sure to win a race.

Calzaghe (IRE)

99(111) (72)**75**

5-y-o ch g Galileo (IRE)-Novelette (Darshaan)
Jim Best (F Sheridan 23/3) Chipstead Racehorse Owners Club

Placings:004/226351/3010602520-53404015 **(1537)**
2009: 12^{5}SD, 12^{3}SD, 12^{4}SD, 12^{0}SD, 12^{4}SD, 12^{0}GF, 13^{1}SD, 11^{5}GF,

	Starts	1st	2nd	3rd	Win & Pl
Career Total (Turf)	16	1	2	2	5895
Career Total (AW)	11	2	2	1	7467

70	4/09	Ling	1m5f	(0-65)H	STD	£1878
75	4/08	Sthl	1m4f	(0-70)H	G-F	£2456
75	9/07	Wolv	1m4f50y	(0-65)H	STD	£3071

Total win prize-money £7406

Going (Turf): Sf: 0-0 GS: 0-1 Gd: 0-6 **GF: 1-9** Fm: 0-0
Distance: 5f/6f: 0-0 7f-8f: 0-1 **9f-13f: 3-23** 14f+: 0-3
Track: **LH: 3-19** RH: 0-6 **Tight: 3-14** Gall: 0-6
Aids: Bl: 0-0 **Vi: 2-20** Tstrap: 0-0 Ckp: 0-0
Best Rating: **75** 4/09 Brig 1m3f196y gd-fm

Fair; stays 1m4f; acts on fast ground and Polytrack; has worn a visor.

Camacho Flyer (IRE)

93(74) (27)**69**
2-y-o b g Camacho-Despondent (IRE) (Broken Hearted)
P T Midgley Peedeetee Syndicate

Placings:0000451060 **(6841)**
2009: 5^{0}GF, 5^{0}GF, 5^{0}G, 6^{0}GF, 5^{4}GF, **5^{5}SD**, 5^{1}GS, 5^{0}G, 5^{6}GF, 5^{0}G,

	Starts	1st	2nd	3rd	Win & Pl
Career Total (Turf)	9	1	0	0	2677
Career Total (AW)	1	0	0	0	0

69 8/09 Catt 5f G-S £2388
Total win prize-money £2388

Going (Turf): Sf: 0-0 **GS: 1-1** Gd: 0-3 GF: 0-5 Fm: 0-0
Distance: **5f/6f: 1-10** 7f-8f: 0-0 9f-13f: 0-0 14f+: 0-0
Track: LH: 0-0 RH: 0-0 Tight: 0-0 Gall: 0-0
Aids: Bl: 0-0 **Vi: 1-3** Tstrap: 0-2 Ckp: 0-2
Best Rating: **69** 8/09 Catt 5f gd-sft

Camacho half-brother to a couple of winning sprinters; winner over 5f on easy ground; has worn a visor.

Cambuslang (IRE)

87 **59**
2-y-o b c Chevalier (IRE)-Zafine (Zafonic (USA))
I Semple Exchange Court Properties Ltd

Placings:533000 **(6134)**
2009: 5^{5}G, 5^{3}GF, 7^{3}G, 6^{0}GS, 6^{0}GS, 6^{0}G,

	Starts	1st	2nd	3rd	Win & Pl
Career Total (Turf)	6	0	0	2	1011

Going (Turf): **Sf: 0-0 GS: 0-2 Gd: 0-3 GF: 0-1 Fm: 0-0**
Distance: 5f/6f: 0-3 7f-8f: 0-3 9f-13f: 0-0 14f+: 0-0
Track: LH: 0-1 RH: 0-0 Tight: 0-0 Gall: 0-0
Aids: Bl: 0-0 Vi: 0-0 Tstrap: 0-1 Ckp: 0-1
Best Rating: **59** 7/09 Ayr 7f50y good

Moderate; suited by 5f and fast ground.

Came Back (IRE)

(108) (99)**63**
6-y-o ch g Bertolini (USA)-Distant Decree (USA) (Distant View (USA))
Miss A Stokell Ms Caron Stokell

Placings:0/341001035/241002115500202/3111101024411-645500 **(1565)**
2009: 6^{6}SS, 6^{4}SD, 6^{5}SD, 5^{5}SD, 5^{0}SF, 5^{0}SD,

	Starts	1st	2nd	3rd	Win & Pl
Career Total (Turf)	2	0	0	0	
Career Total (AW)	42	12	5	3	43550

69 12/08 Sthl 6f STD £1978
86 12/08 Sthl 6f STD £1978
99 5/08 GrLe 6f (0-90)H STD £6938
98 3/08 Sthl 6f (0-85)H STD £4533
88 3/08 Ling 6f (0-80)H STD £4100
87 2/08 Sthl 6f SS £1774
75 2/08 Sthl 6f STD £1774
82 4/07 Wolv 5f216y (0-70)H STD £3071
81 3/07 Wolv 5f216y (0-70)H STD £3071
72 2/07 Sthl 6f (0-60)H STD £1706
68 10/06 Ling 6f STD £3238
57 2/06 Ling 6f STD £3886
Total win prize-money £38055

Going (Turf): **Sf: 0-1 GS: 0-0 Gd: 0-0 GF: 0-0 Fm: 0-1**
Distance: **5f/6f: 12-44** 7f-8f: 0-0 9f-13f: 0-0 14f+: 0-0
Track: **LH: 12-37** RH: 0-3 **Tight: 5-22** Gall: 1-3
Aids: Bl: 0-0 Vi: 0-0 Tstrap: 0-0 Ckp: 0-0
Best Rating: **99** 5/08 GrLe 6f stand

Very useful; effective over 6f; acts on both Polytrack and Fibresand.

Camelot Queen

81(82) (37)**27**
4-y-o gr f Baryshnikov (AUS)-Guarded Expression (Siberian Express (USA))
W S Kittow D & J Racing

Placings:0600 **(1703)**
2009: 8^{0}SD, 7^{6}SD, 8^{0}SD, 6^{0}GF,

	Starts	1st	2nd	3rd	Win & Pl
Career Total (Turf)	1	0	0	0	
Career Total (AW)	3	0	0	0	0

Going (Turf): **Sf: 0-0 GS: 0-0 Gd: 0-0 GF: 0-1 Fm: 0-0**
Distance: 5f/6f: 0-1 7f-8f: 0-3 9f-13f: 0-0 14f+: 0-0
Track: LH: 0-1 RH: 0-2 Tight: 0-1 Gall: 0-0
Aids: Bl: 0-0 Vi: 0-0 Tstrap: 0-0 Ckp: 0-0
Best Rating: **37** 2/09 Wolv 7f32y stand

Camera Shy (IRE)

102(100) (57)**59**
5-y-o ch g Pivotal-Shy Danceuse (FR) (Groom Dancer (USA))
K A Morgan Michael Ogburn

Placings:000100P-311 **(3308)**
2009: 10^{3}G, 10^{1}G, 11^{1}GF,

	Starts	1st	2nd	3rd	Win & Pl
Career Total (Turf)	5	2	0	1	6784
Career Total (AW)	5	1	0	0	2047

59 6/09 Leic 1m3f183y (0-75)H G-F £3885
57 6/09 Yarm 1m2f21y (0-60)H GD £2590
57 6/08 Ling 1m4f (0-55)H STD £2047
Total win prize-money £8523

Going (Turf): Sf: 0-0 GS: 0-0 **Gd: 1-3 GF: 1-2** Fm: 0-0
Distance: 5f/6f: 0-0 7f-8f: 0-2 **9f-13f: 3-8** 14f+: 0-0
Track: **LH: 2-8** RH: 1-2 **Tight: 2-7** Gall: 0-0
Aids: Bl: 0-0 Vi: 0-0 Tstrap: 0-1 Ckp: 0-1
Best Rating: **59** 6/09 Leic 1m3f183y gd-fm

Moderate; stays 1m4f and acts on Polytrack and good/fast ground; has worn cheekpieces.

Camerooney

88(99) (53)**49**
6-y-o b g Sugarfoot-Enkindle (Relkino)
B Ellison Mrs Jean Stapleton

Placings:0400/060-43060 **(7855)**
2009: 7^{4}GF, 8^{3}SD, 9^{0}SD, 7^{6}SD, 8^{0}SS,

	Starts	1st	2nd	3rd	Win & Pl
Career Total (Turf)	6	0	0	0	0
Career Total (AW)	6	0	0	1	302

Going (Turf): **Sf: 0-0 GS: 0-1 Gd: 0-3 GF: 0-1 Fm: 0-1**
Distance: 5f/6f: 0-0 7f-8f: 0-3 9f-13f: 0-9 14f+: 0-0
Track: LH: 0-10 RH: 0-1 Tight: 0-6 Gall: 0-1
Aids: Bl: 0-0 Vi: 0-0 Tstrap: 0-0 Ckp: 0-0
Best Rating: **53** 11/09 Wolv 1m141y stand

Moderate; effective over 1m; acts on Polytrack; has worn an eyeshield.

Camilla Knight (IRE)

68(83) (34)**29**
3-y-o ch f Night Shift (USA)-Koukla Mou (Keen)
W R Swinburn The Pendley Partners

Placings:00 **(5747)**
2009: 7^{0}SD, 7^{0}GF,

	Starts	1st	2nd	3rd	Win & Pl
Career Total (Turf)	1	0	0	0	
Career Total (AW)	1	0	0	0	

Going (Turf): **Sf: 0-0 GS: 0-0 Gd: 0-0 GF: 0-1 Fm: 0-0**
Distance: 5f/6f: 0-0 7f-8f: 0-2 9f-13f: 0-0 14f+: 0-0
Track: LH: 0-0 RH: 0-1 Tight: 0-0 Gall: 0-0
Aids: Bl: 0-0 Vi: 0-0 Tstrap: 0-0 Ckp: 0-0
Best Rating: **34** 8/09 Kemp 7f stand

Camomile

82(70) **26**
3-y-o b f Xaar-Pretty Davis (USA) (Trempolino (USA))
Miss Tracy Waggott (K A Ryan 16/10) Miss Mandy Hetherington

Placings:5600 **(7796)**
2009: 7^{5}GS, 6^{6}S, 6^{0}GF, 7^{0}SS,

	Starts	1st	2nd	3rd	Win & Pl
Career Total (Turf)	3	0	0	0	0
Career Total (AW)	1	0	0	0	

Going (Turf): **Sf: 0-1 GS: 0-1 Gd: 0-0 GF: 0-1 Fm: 0-0**
Distance: 5f/6f: 0-1 7f-8f: 0-3 9f-13f: 0-0 14f+: 0-0
Track: LH: 0-2 RH: 0-0 Tight: 0-1 Gall: 0-0
Aids: Bl: 0-0 Vi: 0-0 Tstrap: 0-0 Ckp: 0-0
Best Rating: **26** 7/09 Catt 7f gd-sft

Campaigner

89(86) (38)**52**
2-y-o b c Dansili-Rosapenna (IRE) (Spectrum (IRE))
J W Hills Tom and Kate Ellis

Placings:0006000 **(6586)**
2009: 6^{0}G, 6^{0}GF, 7^{0}G, 5^{6}SD, 6^{0}SD, 7^{0}GF, 7^{0}SD,

	Starts	1st	2nd	3rd	Win & Pl
Career Total (Turf)	4	0	0	0	
Career Total (AW)	3	0	0	0	0

Going (Turf): **Sf: 0-0 GS: 0-0 Gd: 0-2 GF: 0-2 Fm: 0-0**
Distance: 5f/6f: 0-4 7f-8f: 0-3 9f-13f: 0-0 14f+: 0-0
Track: LH: 0-1 RH: 0-4 Tight: 0-1 Gall: 0-0
Aids: Bl: 0-0 Vi: 0-0 Tstrap: 0-0 Ckp: 0-0
Best Rating: **52** 9/09 Gdwd 7f gd-fm

Campanologist (USA)

115 (102)**119**
4-y-o b c Kingmambo (USA)-Ring Of Music (Sadler's Wells (USA))
Saeed Bin Suroor Godolphin

Placings:1410/113142-02021320 (6850)
2009: 10^{0}G, 12^{2}GF, 12^{0}G, 10^{2}G, 10^{1}GF, 11^{3}GF, 12^{2}GF, 10^{0}G,

	Starts	1st	2nd	3rd	Win & Pl
Career Total (Turf)	17	5	4	2	327524
Career Total (AW)	1	1	0	0	16193

113 8/09 Wind 1m2f7y G-F £39739
111 6/08 Asct 1m4f FRM £134317
109 4/08 NmkR 1m1f GD £17031
102 3/08 Kemp 1m1f STD £16192
90 9/07 Hayd 1m30y G-F £12954
82 8/07 Sand 7f16y GD £4533
Total win prize-money £224769

Going (Turf): Sf: 0-1 GS: 0-0 **Gd: 2-7 GF: 2-8** Fm: 1-1
Distance: 5f/6f: 0-0 7f-8f: 1-3 **9f-13f: 5-15** 14f+: 0-0
Track : LH: 1-6 **RH: 4-10** Tight: 1-2 Gall: 1-8
Aids: Bl: 0-0 Vi: 0-0 Tstrap: 0-0 Ckp: 0-0
Best Rating: **119** 7/08 Sand 1m2f7y gd-fm

Group class; winner of the 2008 King Edward VII Stakes at Royal Ascot; effective over 1m1f-1m4f; acts on good and fast ground and Polytrack.

Campbells Lad

90 (60)**33**
8-y-o b g Mind Games-T O O Mamma'S (IRE) (Classic Secret (USA))
A Berry PCB Racing

Placings:0540/54005302432/0604040400/065466402/50 1435/0 (2264)
2009: 11^{0}G,

	Starts	1st	2nd	3rd	Win & Pl
Career Total (Turf)	30	1	2	2	5736
Career Total (AW)	12	0	1	1	1017

62 7/07 Catt 1m3f214y GD £2730
Total win prize-money £2730

Going (Turf): Sf: 0-2 GS: 0-6 **Gd: 1-9** GF: 0-11 Fm: 0-2
Distance: 5f/6f: 0-4 7f-8f: 0-11 **9f-13f: 1-26** 14f+: 0-1
Track : **LH: 1-26** RH: 0-12 **Tight: 1-21** Gall: 0-0
Aids: Bl: 0-2 Vi: 0-0 Tstrap: 0-2 Ckp: 0-2
Best Rating: **62** 8/07 Catt 1m3f214y firm

Campli (IRE)

105(103) (76)**76**
7-y-o b g Zafonic (USA)-Sept A Neuf (Be My Guest (USA))
B Ellison Racing Management & Training Ltd

Placings:2305303/00600-25201364 (3264)
2009: 9^{2}SD, 8^{5}SD, 7^{2}GF, 7^{0}GF, 7^{1}SD, 7^{3}GF, 7^{6}GF, 7^{4}G,

	Starts	1st	2nd	3rd	Win & Pl
Career Total (Turf)	16	0	2	4	4748
Career Total (AW)	4	1	1	0	4656

76 4/09 Wolv 7f32y (0-75)H STD £3885
Total win prize-money £3886

Going (Turf): **Sf: 0-0 GS: 0-0 Gd: 0-6 GF: 0-9 Fm: 0-1**
Distance: 5f/6f: 0-0 **7f-8f: 1-6** 9f-13f: 0-10 14f+: 0-4
Track : **LH: 1-13** RH: 0-6 **Tight: 1-12** Gall: 0-4
Aids: Bl: 0-0 Vi: 0-0 Tstrap: 0-0 Ckp: 0-0
Best Rating: **76** 4/09 Wolv 7f32y stand

Modest; bumper winner; effective at around 7f-1m4f; acts on fast ground.

Camps Bay (USA)

107 **106**
5-y-o b g Cozzene (USA)-Seewillo (USA) (Pleasant Colony (USA))
Mrs A J Perrett Mr & Mrs R Scott

Placings:053/131205/20300-4000440 (7018)
2009: 12^{4}GF, 14^{0}G, 14^{0}GF, 12^{0}GF, 12^{4}GF, 12^{4}G, 12^{0}GS,

	Starts	1st	2nd	3rd	Win & Pl
Career Total (Turf)	21	2	2	3	44074

86 7/07 Wind 1m3f135y (0-85)H G-F £5047
80 5/07 Sals 1m1f198y (0-80)H G-F £5181
Total win prize-money £10229

Going (Turf): Sf: 0-1 GS: 0-3 Gd: 0-6 **GF: 2-11** Fm: 0-0
Distance: 5f/6f: 0-0 7f-8f: 0-2 **9f-13f: 2-14** 14f+: 0-5
Track : LH: 0-8 **RH: 1-11 Tight: 2-6** Gall: 0-11
Aids: Bl: 0-1 Vi: 0-0 Tstrap: 0-2 Ckp: 0-2
Best Rating: **106** 7/08 Hayd 1m3f200y soft

Very useful; stays 1m4f; acts on fast and soft ground.

Can Can Star

105(108) (89)**86**
6-y-o br h Lend A Hand-Carrie Can Can (Green Tune (USA))
A W Carroll K F Coleman

Placings:30356340/212214024022/0006311-431143544406153423330342 (7734)
2009: 11^{4}SD, 12^{3}SD, 10^{1}SD, 10^{1}SD, 10^{4}SD, 8^{3}SD, 10^{5}G, 8^{4}SD, 10^{4}GF, 9^{4}G, 10^{0}GF, 10^{6}SD, 10^{1}GF, 9^{5}S, 8^{3}GF, 10^{4}GF, 8^{2}GF, 12^{3}SD, 10^{3}GF, 10^{0}G, 10^{3}SD, 10^{4}SD, 8^{2}SD,

	Starts	1st	2nd	3rd	Win & Pl
Career Total (Turf)	28	2	5	5	18321
Career Total (AW)	22	5	3	5	20037

83 7/09 Nott 1m2f50y (0-75)H G-F £2590
84 2/09 Ling 1m2f (0-75)H STD £2900
79 1/09 Ling 1m2f (0-70)H STD £2900
72 12/08 Ling 1m2f (0-60)H STD £1706
68 11/08 Ling 1m2f (0-65)H STD £2047
76 4/07 Leic 1m1f218y (0-70)H G-F £3238
65 1/07 Wolv 1m1f103y STD £2047
Total win prize-money £17430

Going (Turf): Sf: 0-4 GS: 0-3 Gd: 0-6 **GF: 2-12** Fm: 0-3
Distance: 5f/6f: 0-0 7f-8f: 0-5 **9f-13f: 7-45** 14f+: 0-0
Track : **LH: 6-30** RH: 1-20 **Tight: 5-26** Gall: 0-4
Aids: Bl: 0-1 Vi: 0-0 Tstrap: 0-0 Ckp: 0-0
Best Rating: **89** 11/09 Ling 1m2f stand

Useful; stays 1m2f; acts on most ground on turf; goes on Polytrack.

Canadian Danehill (IRE)

107(109) (87)**99**
7-y-o b g Indian Danehill (IRE)-San Jovita (CAN) (St Jovite (USA))
R M H Cowell T W Morley

Placings:0003/32615433121004005000/34110220205320050036/2111314026535303131 6/000102550000000154-30236312611000066 (7866)
2009: 5^{3}SS, 5^{0}SD, 5^{2}SD, 5^{3}SD, 5^{6}SD, 5^{3}SD, 5^{1}GF, 5^{2}GF, 5^{6}GF, 5^{1}G, 5^{1}G, 5^{0}G, 5^{0}GF, 5^{0}GS, 5^{0}SD, 5^{0}SD, 5^{8}SS,

	Starts	1st	2nd	3rd	Win & Pl
Career Total (Turf)	53	7	6	6	59242
Career Total (AW)	46	9	5	9	48180

99 7/09 NmkJ 5f (0-95)H GD £9714
95 7/09 Sand 5f6y (0-95)H GD £7771
90 5/09 NmkR 5f (0-80)H G-F £5180
86 12/08 Wolv 5f20y (0-75)H STD £3885
99 3/08 Sthl 5f (0-100)H STD £10687
90 9/07 Yarm 5f43y (0-85)H GD £6232
92 8/07 Sand 5f6y (0-75)H G-F £4533
93 3/07 Sthl 5f (0-75)H STD £3071
84 2/07 Wolv 5f20y (0-65)H STD £2730
83 2/07 Sthl 5f (0-58)H STD £1876
78 1/07 Wolv 5f20y (0-62)H SS £2730
73 2/06 Wolv 5f20y (0-65)H STD £2388
68 1/06 Wolv 7f32y (0-58)H STD £2047
67 5/05 NmkR 6f (0-70)H G-F £3490
65 5/05 Brig 5f59y (0-70)H FRM £5720
60 2/05 Sthl 5f STD £3406
Total win prize-money £75467

Going (Turf): Sf: 0-6 GS: 0-8 **Gd: 3-14 GF: 3-22** Fm: 1-3
Distance: **5f/6f: 15-90** 7f-8f: 1-8 9f-13f: 0-1 14f+: 0-0
Track : **LH: 6-41** RH: 0-1 **Tight: 5-25** Gall: 0-7
Aids: Bl: 0-0 Vi: 0-0 Tstrap: 15-71 Ckp: 15-71
Best Rating: **99** 7/09 NmkJ 5f good

Useful; effective over 5f-7f; acts on most ground and on sand; wears cheekpieces.

Canary Girl

86(86) (19)**35**
6-y-o br m Primo Valentino (IRE)-Cumbrian Concerto (Petong)
G Prodromou Mrs B Hodgkinson

Placings:0000/00050004/05000/000-600 (7062)
2009: 6^{6}F, 8^{0}G, 7^{0}GF,

	Starts	1st	2nd	3rd	Win & Pl
Career Total (Turf)	18	0	0	0	0
Career Total (AW)	5	0	0	0	0

Going (Turf): **Sf: 0-2 GS: 0-0 Gd: 0-3 GF: 0-11 Fm: 0-2**
Distance: 5f/6f: 0-5 7f-8f: 0-12 9f-13f: 0-6 14f+: 0-0
Track : LH: 0-7 RH: 0-3 Tight: 0-4 Gall: 0-2
Aids: Bl: 0-0 Vi: 0-5 Tstrap: 0-1 Ckp: 0-1
Best Rating: **41** 7/06 Thsk 1m firm

Candilejas

90(94) (63)**44**
3-y-o br f Diktat-Nacho Venture (FR) (Rainbow Quest (USA))
R J Smith Pedro Rosas

Placings:0530-0000 (7433)
2009: 8^{0}G, 12^{0}SD, 10^{0}SD, 8^{0}SD,

	Starts	1st	2nd	3rd	Win & Pl
Career Total (Turf)	1	0	0	0	
Career Total (AW)	7	0	0	1	404

Going (Turf): **Sf: 0-0 GS: 0-0 Gd: 0-1 GF: 0-0 Fm: 0-0**
Distance: 5f/6f: 0-0 7f-8f: 0-3 9f-13f: 0-5 14f+: 0-0
Track : LH: 0-5 RH: 0-3 Tight: 0-6 Gall: 0-0
Aids: Bl: 0-0 Vi: 0-0 Tstrap: 0-1 Ckp: 0-1
Best Rating: **63** 10/08 Wolv 7f32y stand

Moderate; stays 1m; acts on Polytrack; should win a race.

Candle

104(100) (89)**96**
6-y-o br m Dansili-Celia Brady (Last Tycoon)
T R George Thoroughbred Ladies

Placings:2102020/3331/0426004-000 (4840)
2009: 16^{0}SD, 14^{0}G, 12^{0}SD,

	Starts	1st	2nd	3rd	Win & Pl
Career Total (Turf)	17	1	4	3	22748
Career Total (AW)	4	1	0	0	3239

91 10/07 Gdwd 1m4f (0-95)H SFT £7772
81 6/06 Kemp 1m2f STD £3238
Total win prize-money £11011

Going (Turf): **Sf: 1-4** GS: 0-6 Gd: 0-3 GF: 0-2 Fm: 0-2
Distance: 5f/6f: 0-0 7f-8f: 0-0 **9f-13f: 2-16** 14f+: 0-5
Track : LH: 0-6 **RH: 2-15 Tight: 1-8** Gall: 0-8
Aids: Bl: 0-0 Vi: 0-0 Tstrap: 0-0 Ckp: 0-0
Best Rating: **96** 7/08 NmkJ 1m4f soft

Useful; effective over 1m4f-1m6f; acts on good and soft ground and on Polytrack.

Candleshoe (IRE)

90 **69**
2-y-o b f Danehill Dancer (IRE)-Keepers Dawn (IRE) (Alzao (USA))
R Hannon Mrs J Wood

Placings:405 **(5096)**
2009: 6^{4}GF, 7^{0}GS, 6^{5}GF,

	Starts	1st	2nd	3rd	Win & Pl
Career Total (Turf)	3	0	0	0	414

Going (Turf): **Sf: 0-0 GS: 0-1 Gd: 0-0 GF: 0-2 Fm: 0-0**
Distance: 5f/6f: 0-2 7f-8f: 0-1 9f-13f: 0-0 14f+: 0-0
Track : LH: 0-0 RH: 0-1 Tight: 0-0 Gall: 0-2
Aids: Bl: 0-0 Vi: 0-0 Tstrap: 0-0 Ckp: 0-0
Best Rating: **69** 7/09 Wind 6f gd-fm

Modest form in maidens at 6-7f; handles fast ground.

Candy Anchor (FR)

(97) (48)**47**
10-y-o b m Slip Anchor-Kandavu (Safawan)
R E Peacock R E Peacock

Placings:5000/0243400/00306/200/5/000/V6/6205600-F **(2337)**
2009: 11^{F}GF,

	Starts	1st	2nd	3rd	Win & Pl
Career Total (Turf)	15	0	1	2	2164
Career Total (AW)	18	0	2	0	800

Going (Turf): **Sf: 0-1 GS: 0-1 Gd: 0-5 GF: 0-6 Fm: 0-2**
Distance: 5f/6f: 0-0 7f-8f: 0-6 9f-13f: 0-26 14f+: 0-1
Track : LH: 0-24 RH: 0-7 Tight: 0-22 Gall: 0-0
Aids: Bl: 0-10 Vi: 0-0 Tstrap: 0-0 Ckp: 0-0
Best Rating: **48** 1/08 Wolv 1m4f50y stand

Candy Ride (IRE)

98 **80**
3-y-o ch f Pivotal-Mia Mambo (USA) (Affirmed (USA))
E A L Dunlop Rick Barnes

Placings:521210 **(7291)**
2009: 7^{5}GS, 8^{2}G, 8^{1}G, 8^{2}GF, 9^{1}G, 10^{0}S,

	Starts	1st	2nd	3rd	Win & Pl
Career Total (Turf)	6	2	2	0	7541
80 7/09 Sand	1m1f	(0-75)H		GD	£3238
74 6/09 Nott	1m75y			GD	£2590

Total win prize-money £5828

Going (Turf): Sf: 0-1 GS: 0-1 **Gd: 2-3** GF: 0-1 Fm: 0-0
Distance: 5f/6f: 0-0 7f-8f: 0-1 **9f-13f: 2-5** 14f+: 0-0
Track : LH: 1-2 RH: 1-3 Tight: 0-2 Gall: 0-1
Aids: Bl: 0-0 Vi: 0-0 Tstrap: 0-0 Ckp: 0-0
Best Rating: **80** 7/09 Sand 1m1f good

Fair; stays 1m1f; acts on good and fast ground.

Candy Rose

95(97) (58)**63**
4-y-o b f Tobougg (IRE)-Cottage Maid (Inchinor)
M P Tregoning Miss S Sharp

Placings:66520-06406 **(6940)**
2009: 8^{0}SD, 9^{6}GF, 7^{4}F, 7^{0}SD, 10^{6}SD,

	Starts	1st	2nd	3rd	Win & Pl
Career Total (Turf)	4	0	1	0	1204
Career Total (AW)	6	0	0	0	0

Going (Turf): **Sf: 0-0 GS: 0-1 Gd: 0-0 GF: 0-2 Fm: 0-1**
Distance: 5f/6f: 0-0 7f-8f: 0-5 9f-13f: 0-5 14f+: 0-0
Track : LH: 0-4 RH: 0-5 Tight: 0-3 Gall: 0-1
Aids: Bl: 0-0 Vi: 0-0 Tstrap: 0-1 Ckp: 0-1
Best Rating: **63** 10/08 Gdwd 1m gd-fm

Candyfloss Girl

94(93) (65)**64**
2-y-o b f Intikhab (USA)-Annatalia (Pivotal)
H J L Dunlop Stephen J Buckmaster

Placings:006315300 **(7033)**
2009: 6^{0}GF, 6^{0}GF, 5^{6}G, 6^{3}SD, 5^{1}SD, 6^{5}SD, 6^{3}SD, 7^{0}GF, 7^{0}S,

	Starts	1st	2nd	3rd	Win & Pl
Career Total (Turf)	5	0	0	0	0
Career Total (AW)	4	1	0	2	3010
62 8/09 Kemp	5f	(0-65)		STD	£2047

Total win prize-money £2047

Going (Turf): **Sf: 0-1 GS: 0-0 Gd: 0-1 GF: 0-3 Fm: 0-0**
Distance: **5f/6f: 1-5** 7f-8f: 0-4 9f-13f: 0-0 14f+: 0-0
Track : LH: 0-1 **RH: 1-4** Tight: 0-0 Gall: 0-1
Aids: Bl: 0-0 Vi: 0-0 Tstrap: 0-0 Ckp: 0-0
Best Rating: **65** 9/09 Kemp 6f stand

Modest; stays 6f; acts on Polytrack; tail-flasher.

Cane Cat (IRE)

95(94) (54)**61**
2-y-o b/br f One Cool Cat (USA)-Seven Wonders (USA) (Rahy (USA))
A W Carroll John W Egan

Placings:564065436020 **(7749)**
2009: 5^{5}GF, 5^{6}GF, 5^{4}GF, 5^{0}GF, 7^{6}SD, 6^{5}GF, 5^{4}SD, 6^{3}GS, 6^{6}G, 5^{0}S, 5^{2}SD, 5^{0}SD,

	Starts	1st	2nd	3rd	Win & Pl
Career Total (Turf)	8	0	0	1	454
Career Total (AW)	4	0	1	0	705

Going (Turf): **Sf: 0-1 GS: 0-1 Gd: 0-1 GF: 0-5 Fm: 0-0**
Distance: 5f/6f: 0-10 7f-8f: 0-2 9f-13f: 0-0 14f+: 0-0
Track : LH: 0-5 RH: 0-1 Tight: 0-3 Gall: 0-2
Aids: Bl: 0-0 Vi: 0-0 Tstrap: 0-0 Ckp: 0-0
Best Rating: **61** 5/09 Chep 5f16y gd-fm

Moderate; effective over 6f; acts on easy ground and Polytrack.

Canford Cliffs (IRE)

113 **118**
2-y-o b c Tagula (IRE)-Mrs Marsh (Marju (IRE))
R Hannon The Heffer Syndicate

Placings:113 **(5299a)**
2009: 6^{1}G, 6^{1}GF, 6^{3}G,

	Starts	1st	2nd	3rd	Win & Pl
Career Total (Turf)	3	2	0	1	100467
118 6/09 Asct	6f			G-F	£56770
97 5/09 Newb	6f8y			GD	£4857

Total win prize-money £61627

Going (Turf): Sf: 0-0 GS: 0-0 **Gd: 1-2 GF: 1-1** Fm: 0-0
Distance: 5f/6f: 1-2 7f-8f: 1-1 9f-13f: 0-0 14f+: 0-0
Track : LH: 0-0 RH: 0-1 Tight: 0-0 Gall: 0-0
Aids: Bl: 0-0 Vi: 0-0 Tstrap: 0-0 Ckp: 0-0
Best Rating: **118** 6/09 Asct 6f gd-fm

High-class juvenile; free-going type; won the 2009 Coventry Stakes; effective over 6f; acts on fast and easy ground.

Canmoss (USA)

97(102) (70)**70**
3-y-o ch c Maria's Mon (USA)-Dance For Free (CAN) (Fly So Free (USA))
A Bonin (E J O'Neill 11/7) C Martin

Placings:00001-25621000
2009: 12^{2}G, 12^{5}GF, 14^{6}F, 12^{2}FT, 12^{1}SD, 12^{0}G, 15^{0}VS, 12^{0}VS,

	Starts	1st	2nd	3rd	Win & Pl
Career Total (Turf)	8	0	1	0	964
Career Total (AW)	5	2	1	0	14823
70 8/09 Deau	1m4f			STD	£8738
64 12/08 GrLe	1m2f	(0-75)		STD	£2590

Total win prize-money £11328

Going (Turf): **Sf: 0-2 GS: 0-0 Gd: 0-2 GF: 0-1 Fm: 0-1**
Distance: 5f/6f: 0-0 7f-8f: 0-2 **9f-13f: 2-9** 14f+: 0-2
Track : **LH: 1-9** RH: 0-1 Tight: 0-1 **Gall: 1-2**
Aids: Bl: 0-1 Vi: 0-0 Tstrap: 0-1 Ckp: 0-1
Best Rating: **70** 8/09 Deau 1m4f stand

Modest; stays 1m4f; acts on good ground; goes on Polytrack.

Cannonball (USA)

109 (81)**121**
4-y-o b/br g Catienus (USA)-No Deadline (USA) (Skywalker (USA))
Wesley A Ward Kenneth L & Sarah K Ramsey

Placings:641133/360103-42262130 **(7745a)**
2009: 5^{4}F, 5^{2}G, 5^{2}G, 5^{6}GF, 6^{2}GF, 5^{1}F, 6^{3}F, 6^{0}G,

	Starts	1st	2nd	3rd	Win & Pl
Career Total (Turf)	17	4	3	5	369818
Career Total (AW)	3	0	0	0	5590
121 9/09 Sara	5f110y			FRM	£31125
5/08 Belm	6f			GD	£23291
10/07 Belm	1m			YLD	£24244
80 9/07 Belm	6f			FRM	£14082

Total win prize-money £92743

Going (Turf): Sf: 0-0 GS: 0-0 Gd: 1-4 GF: 0-2 **Fm: 2-8**
Distance: **5f/6f: 3-11** 7f-8f: 1-4 9f-13f: 0-5 14f+: 0-0
Track : LH: 0-3 RH: 0-0 Tight: 0-0 Gall: 0-0
Aids: Bl: 0-1 Vi: 0-0 Tstrap: 0-0 Ckp: 0-0
Best Rating: **121** 9/09 Sara 5f110y firm

Smart sprinter; US trained; acts on good ground; stays 1m, but efective at 5f; has worn blinkers/tongue tie.

Canongate

82 (84)**92**
5-y-o gr g Highest Honor (FR)-Tremiere (FR) (Anabaa (USA))
Miss E C Lavelle Lady Bland

Placings:00/541100/0266-00 **(4957)**
2009: 10^{0}G, 9^{0}G,

	Starts	1st	2nd	3rd	Win & Pl
Career Total (Turf)	12	1	1	0	28988
Career Total (AW)	2	1	0	0	8446

89 5/07 Lonc 1m H HVY £18419
84 3/07 Deau 6f110y H STD £8446
Total win prize-money £26865

Going (Turf): Sf: 1-3 GS: 0-2 Gd: 0-3 GF: 0-1 Fm: 0-0
Distance: 5f/6f: 0-0 7f-8f: 2-11 9f-13f: 0-3 14f+: 0-0
Track : LH: 0-2 RH: 0-3 Tight: 0-0 Gall: 0-1
Aids: Bl: 0-0 Vi: 0-0 Tstrap: 0-0 Ckp: 0 0
Best Rating: 92 5/08 StCl 1m v soft

Useful; formerly French trained; stays a mile; goes well in testing ground.

Cansili Star

97 81
2-y-o b g Dansili-Canis Star (Wolfhound (USA))
M A Jarvis A D Spence

Placings:24524 (6561)
2009: 6^{2}GF, 7^{4}GS, 6^{5}GF, 7^{2}GF, 7^{4}G,

	Starts	1st	2nd	3rd	Win & Pl
Career Total (Turf)	5	0	2	0	2819

Going (Turf): Sf: 0-0 GS: 0-1 Gd: 0-1 GF: 0-3 Fm: 0-0
Distance: 5f/6f: 0-1 7f-8f: 0-4 9f-13f: 0-0 14f+: 0-0
Track : LH: 0-1 RH: 0-1 Tight: 0-0 Gall: 0-0
Aids: Bl: 0-0 Vi: 0-0 Tstrap: 0-0 Ckp: 0-0
Best Rating: 81 9/09 Gdwd 7f gd-fm

Useful; stays 7f and best on fast ground.

Cantabilly (IRE)

(101) (67)69
6-y-o b g Distant Music (USA)-Cantaloupe (Priolo (USA))
R J Hodges Mrs S G Clapp

Placings:560/330206214501154/240/500-0645 (0835)
2009: 10^{0}SD, 10^{6}SD, 13^{4}SF, 16^{5}SD,

	Starts	1st	2nd	3rd	Win & Pl
Career Total (Turf)	19	1	3	1	12204
Career Total (AW)	9	2	0	1	7680

85 10/06 Ling 1m2f (0-70)H STD £3238
75 10/06 Wolv 1m1f103y (0-70)H SF £3238
72 7/06 Epsm 1m2f18y (0-80)H G-F £7772
Total win prize-money £14250

Going (Turf): Sf: 0-3 GS: 0-4 Gd: 0-7 GF: 1-2 Fm: 0-3
Distance: 5f/6f: 0-0 7f-8f: 0-3 9f-13f: 3-19 14f+: 0-6
Track : LH: 3-17 RH: 0-7 Tight: 3-16 Gall: 0-1
Aids: Bl: 0-0 Vi: 0-0 Tstrap: 0-0 Ckp: 0-0
Best Rating: 88 4/07 Kemp 2m stand

Modest; stays 1m2f; acts on fast and soft ground; also goes on Polytrack.

Canton Road

93(96) (59)64
3-y-o b g Galileo (IRE)-Welsh Diva (Selkirk (USA))
P F I Cole D S Lee & W Fyfe

Placings:0-26030 (5679)
2009: 11^{2}GF, 12^{6}SD, 11^{0}GF, 11^{3}SD, 12^{0}SD,

	Starts	1st	2nd	3rd	Win & Pl
Career Total (Turf)	3	0	1	0	964
Career Total (AW)	3	0	0	1	453

Going (Turf): Sf: 0-0 GS: 0-1 Gd: 0-0 GF: 0-2 Fm: 0-0
Distance: 5f/6f: 0-0 7f-8f: 0-1 9f-13f: 0-5 14f+: 0-0
Track : LH: 0-4 RH: 0-1 Tight: 0-2 Gall: 0-1
Aids: Bl: 0-2 Vi: 0-0 Tstrap: 0-0 Ckp: 0-0
Best Rating: 64 6/09 Leic 1m3f183y gd-fm

Modest; stays 1m3f and acts on fast ground; has worn blinkers and a tongue tie.

Canucatcher (IRE)

(86) (37)32
3-y-o b f Catcher In The Rye (IRE)-Never Zal (Zilzal (USA))
T D Walford David Jones

Placings:060-4 (0883)
2009: 11^{4}SD,

	Starts	1st	2nd	3rd	Win & Pl
Career Total (Turf)	3	0	0	0	0
Career Total (AW)	1	0	0	0	0

Going (Turf): Sf: 0-3 GS: 0-0 Gd: 0-0 GF: 0-0 Fm: 0-0
Distance: 5f/6f: 0-0 7f-8f: 0-2 9f-13f: 0-2 14f+: 0-0
Track : LH: 0-2 RH: 0-0 Tight: 0-0 Gall: 0-0
Aids: Bl: 0-0 Vi: 0-0 Tstrap: 0-0 Ckp: 0-0
Best Rating: 37 3/09 Sthl 1m3f stand

Canwinn (IRE)

104(95) (77)102
3-y-o b c Refuse To Bend (IRE)-Born To Glamour (Ajdal (USA))
M R Channon Sheikh Ahmed Al Maktoum

Placings:3333123O-66004302 (5670)
2009: 8^{6}SD, 10^{6}G, 8^{0}HY, 8^{0}GF, 8^{4}GF, 8^{3}GF, 8^{0}GF, 8^{2}S,

	Starts	1st	2nd	3rd	Win & Pl
Career Total (Turf)	15	1	2	6	38551
Career Total (AW)	1	0	0	0	540

83 8/08 Nott 1m75y SFT £3885
Total win prize-money £3886

Going (Turf): Sf: 1-3 GS: 0-2 Gd: 0-5 GF: 0-5 Fm: 0-0
Distance: 5f/6f: 0-1 7f-8f: 0-10 9f-13f: 1-5 14f+: 0-0
Track : LH: 1-6 RH: 0-3 Tight: 0-3 Gall: 0-0
Aids: Bl: 0-0 Vi: 0-4 Tstrap: 0-0 Ckp: 0-0
Best Rating: 102 9/08 Lonc 1m good

Useful; Group placed at two; stays 1m and acts on most ground; has worn a visor.

Canyon Ranch

103 71
3-y-o b c Danehill Dancer (IRE)-Model Queen (USA) (Kingmambo (USA))
L M Cumani Lady C Warren & The Hon Mrs H Herbert

Placings:402 (3690)
2009: 8^{4}GF, 8^{0}G, 8^{2}G,

	Starts	1st	2nd	3rd	Win & Pl
Career Total (Turf)	3	0	1	0	1348

Going (Turf): Sf: 0-0 GS: 0-0 Gd: 0-2 GF: 0-1 Fm: 0-0
Distance: 5f/6f: 0-0 7f-8f: 0-3 9f-13f: 0-0 14f+: 0-0
Track : LH: 0-1 RH: 0-1 Tight: 0-1 Gall: 0-1
Aids: Bl: 0-0 Vi: 0-0 Tstrap: 0-0 Ckp: 0-0
Best Rating: 71 7/09 Ripn 1m good

Fair; stays 1m; acts on good ground.

Caoba

99 68
5-y-o b m Hernando (FR)-Seeker (Rainbow Quest (USA))
V R A Dartnall Exe Valley Racing

Placings:0/032/10 (2429)
2009: 16^{1}G, 16^{0}G,

	Starts	1st	2nd	3rd	Win & Pl
Career Total (Turf)	6	1	1	1	6915

68 5/09 Nott 2m9y (0-70)H GD £2590
Total win prize-money £2590

Going (Turf): Sf: 0-1 GS: 0-1 Gd: 1-4 GF: 0-0 Fm: 0-0
Distance: 5f/6f: 0-0 7f-8f: 0-1 9f-13f: 0-3 14f+: 1-2
Track : LH: 1-3 RH: 0-1 Tight: 0-1 Gall: 0-0
Aids: Bl: 0-0 Vi: 0-0 Tstrap: 0-1 Ckp: 0-1
Best Rating: 68 5/09 Nott 2m9y good

Modest; winning hurdler; stays very well; acts on most ground.

Caol Ila (IRE)

83(90) (55)52
2-y-o b f Invincible Spirit (IRE)-Pink Cashmere (IRE) (Polar Falcon (USA))
J G Given Danethorpe Racing Partnership

Placings:506634 (7778)
2009: 5^{5}SD, 6^{0}GF, 5^{6}SD, 5^{6}SD, 5^{3}SD, 5^{4}SD,

	Starts	1st	2nd	3rd	Win & Pl
Career Total (Turf)	1	0	0	0	
Career Total (AW)	5	0	0	1	403

Going (Turf): Sf: 0-0 GS: 0-0 Gd: 0-0 GF: 0-1 Fm: 0-0
Distance: 5f/6f: 0-6 7f-8f: 0-0 9f-13f: 0-0 14f+: 0-0
Track : LH: 0-3 RH: 0-1 Tight: 0-3 Gall: 0-0
Aids: Bl: 0-0 Vi: 0-0 Tstrap: 0-0 Ckp: 0-0
Best Rating: 55 11/09 Wolv 5f20y stand

Moderate sprinter; handles Polytrack.

Cap St Jean (IRE)

(104) (73)66
5-y-o b g Cape Cross (IRE)-Karminiya (IRE) (Primo Dominie)
R Hollinshead R Hollinshead

Placings:440020533233/2061456350030-22412610 (2576)
2009: 7^{2}SS, 7^{2}SD, 7^{4}SS, 7^{1}SD, 7^{2}SD, 7^{6}SD, 7^{1}SD, 7^{0}SD,

	Starts	1st	2nd	3rd	Win & Pl
Career Total (Turf)	12	1	1	3	4107
Career Total (AW)	21	2	5	3	8575

73 4/09 Sthl 7f STD £2047
68 2/09 Wolv 7f32y (0-60)H STD £2388
66 5/08 Leic 7f9y G-F £1748
Total win prize-money £6184

Going (Turf): Sf: 0-0 GS: 0-2 Gd: 0-5 GF: 1-4 Fm: 0-1
Distance: 5f/6f: 0-4 7f-8f: 3-20 9f-13f: 0-9 14f+: 0-0
Track : LH: 2-26 RH: 0-4 Tight: 1-12 Gall: 0-0
Aids: Bl: 0-0 Vi: 0-0 Tstrap: 3-19 Ckp: 3-19
Best Rating: 73 4/09 Sthl 7f stand

Moderate; effective at around 1m-1m1f; acts on a sound surface and on sand.

Capable Guest (IRE)

104(110) (91)94

7-y-o b/br g Cape Cross (IRE)-Alexander Confranc (IRE) (Magical Wonder (USA))

M R Channon M Channon

Placings:33321434/2006000200000/1300043660/5001006000335/102203010000036026300-40064505063103325 (7357)

2009: 9^{4}SD, 8^{0}G, 8^{0}G, 10^{6}GF, 12^{4}G, 10^{5}GS, 11^{0}F, 13^{5}GF, 15^{0}GF, 12^{6}SD, 12^{3}G, 12^{1}GF, 12^{0}SD, 12^{3}S, 12^{3}GS, 13^{2}SD, 13^{5}SD,

	Starts	1st	2nd	3rd	Win & Pl
Career Total (Turf)	71	4	6	14	130607
Career Total (AW)	11	2	1	0	20475

72	9/09	Newc	1m4f93y	(0-75)H	G-F	£3139
99	5/08	Rdcr	1m2f	(0-105)H	G-F	£32380
97	1/08	Kemp	1m	(0-95)H	STD	£6543
97	4/07	Sand	1m14y	(0-100)H	GD	£12464
97	2/06	Ling	1m	(0-95)H	STD	£11217
86	8/04	Leic	7f9y	D	G-F	£5798

Total win prize-money £71543

Going (Turf): Sf: 0-13 GS: 0-9 Gd: 1-20 **GF: 3-27** Fm: 0-2
Distance: 5f/6f: 0-2 7f-8f: 3-38 9f-13f: 3-38 14f+: 0-4
Track: **LH: 3-36** RH: 2-22 **Tight: 2-21** Gall: 1-17
Aids: Bl: 0-1 **Vi: 2-27** Tstrap: 0-0 Ckp: 0-0
Best Rating: **106** 9/04 Lonc 1m gd-sft

Modest; effective over 1m-1m4f; acts on most ground and on Polytrack; has worn a visor; usually held up.

Capacity (IRE)

89 75

2-y-o b c Cape Cross (IRE)-Carry On Katie (USA) (Fasliyev (USA))

M Johnston Sheikh Hamdan Bin Mohammed Al Maktoum

Placings:4522 (4558)

2009: 5^{4}GF, 6^{5}G, 6^{2}S, 6^{2}G,

	Starts	1st	2nd	3rd	Win & Pl
Career Total (Turf)	4	0	2	0	2986

Going (Turf): **Sf: 0-1 GS: 0-0 Gd: 0-2 GF: 0-1 Fm: 0-0**
Distance: 5f/6f: 0-3 7f-8f: 0-1 9f-13f: 0-0 14f+: 0-0
Track: LH: 0-1 RH: 0-0 Tight: 0-1 Gall: 0-0
Aids: Bl: 0-0 Vi: 0-0 Tstrap: 0-0 Ckp: 0-0
Best Rating: **75** 8/09 Ches 6f18y good

Fair; effective over 6f; acts on good and soft ground.

Capania (IRE)

(98) (61)57

5-y-o br m Cape Cross (IRE)-Gentle Papoose (Commanche Run)

E G Bevan J Swinnerton & Miss S Howell

Placings:0/3643/05304400-0 (0473)

2009: 7^{0}SD,

	Starts	1st	2nd	3rd	Win & Pl
Career Total (Turf)	2	0	0	1	385
Career Total (AW)	12	0	0	2	655

Going (Turf): **Sf: 0-0 GS: 0-0 Gd: 0-0 GF: 0-2 Fm: 0-0**
Distance: 5f/6f: 0-1 7f-8f: 0-6 9f-13f: 0-7 14f+: 0-0
Track: LH: 0-11 RH: 0-2 Tight: 0-8 Gall: 0-1
Aids: Bl: 0-0 Vi: 0-1 Tstrap: 0-2 Ckp: 0-2
Best Rating: **61** 10/07 Kemp 1m stand

Cape Amber (IRE)

102 111

4-y-o b f Cape Cross (IRE)-Maramba (Rainbow Quest (USA))

R M Beckett Five Horses Ltd

Placings:1/260361-5 (4903)

2009: 9^{5}GF,

	Starts	1st	2nd	3rd	Win & Pl
Career Total (Turf)	8	2	1	1	53785

111	9/08	Yarm	1m2f21y	GD	£22432
84	8/07	NmkJ	7f	FRM	£4533

Total win prize-money £26966

Going (Turf): Sf: 0-0 GS: 0-1 **Gd: 1-3** GF: 0-3 **Fm: 1-1**
Distance: 5f/6f: 0-0 7f-8f: 1-1 9f-13f: 1-7 14f+: 0-0
Track: **LH: 1-3** RH: 0-4 **Tight: 1-4** Gall: 0-3
Aids: Bl: 0-0 Vi: 0-0 Tstrap: 0-0 Ckp: 0-0
Best Rating: **111** 9/08 Yarm 1m2f21y good

Smart; Group and Listed placed; stays 1m2f and acts on fast ground.

Cape Cobra

88(97) (60)60

5-y-o ch g Inchinor-Cape Merino (Clantime)

H Morrison Mrs Marguerite Walker

Placings:4231/666-24000 (7503)

2009: 8^{2}G, 7^{4}SD, 7^{0}SF, 6^{0}SD, 5^{0}SD,

	Starts	1st	2nd	3rd	Win & Pl
Career Total (Turf)	6	1	2	0	5423
Career Total (AW)	6	0	0	1	302

69	10/07	Rdcr	6f	GD	£2817

Total win prize-money £2817

Going (Turf): Sf: 0-0 GS: 0-2 **Gd: 1-3** GF: 0-1 Fm: 0-0
Distance: **5f/6f: 1-4** 7f-8f: 0-8 9f-13f: 0-0 14f+: 0-0
Track: LH: 0-3 RH: 0-2 Tight: 0-2 Gall: 0-0
Aids: **Bl: 1-5** Vi: 0-0 Tstrap: 0-0 Ckp: 0-0
Best Rating: **69** 10/07 Rdcr 6f good

Modest; stays 7f; acts on fast ground and on Polytrack.

Cape Colony

105(107) (86)84

4-y-o gr c Cape Town (IRE)-Lucky Princess (Bijou D'Inde)

R Hannon P D Merritt

Placings:0/601104120012-0065104 (3273)

2009: 11^{0}SD, 12^{0}SF, 12^{6}SD, 12^{5}SD, 12^{1}GS, 14^{0}G, 12^{4}SD,

	Starts	1st	2nd	3rd	Win & Pl
Career Total (Turf)	9	3	1	0	12646
Career Total (AW)	11	2	1	0	8770

84	6/09	Donc	1m4f	(0-85)H	G-S	£5180
83	12/08	Kemp	1m4f	(0-80)H	STD	£5180
80	6/08	Pont	1m4f8y	(0-70)H	GD	£3238
71	4/08	Wind	1m3f135y	(0-75)H	GD	£3070
71	4/08	Kemp	1m4f	(0-60)H	STD	£2047

Total win prize-money £18718

Going (Turf): Sf: 0-0 GS: 1-3 **Gd: 2-3** GF: 0-3 Fm: 0-0
Distance: 5f/6f: 0-0 7f-8f: 0-2 **9f-13f: 5-16** 14f+: 0-2
Track: LH: 2-8 RH: 2-11 Tight: 1-5 Gall: 1-3
Aids: Bl: 0-0 Vi: 0-0 Tstrap: 0-0 Ckp: 0-0
Best Rating: **86** 12/08 Kemp 1m4f stand

Fair; stays 1m4f, handles good ground and Polytrack.

Cape D'Or (IRE)

93 74

2-y-o b c Cape Cross (IRE)-Sombreffe (Polish Precedent (USA))

R Hannon Patrick J Fahey

Placings:53 (3376)

2009: 6^{5}GF, 7^{3}GF,

	Starts	1st	2nd	3rd	Win & Pl
Career Total (Turf)	2	0	0	1	482

Going (Turf): **Sf: 0-0 GS: 0-0 Gd: 0-0 GF: 0-2 Fm: 0-0**
Distance: 5f/6f: 0-1 7f-8f: 0-1 9f-13f: 0-0 14f+: 0-0
Track: LH: 0-0 RH: 0-0 Tight: 0-0 Gall: 0-0
Aids: Bl: 0-0 Vi: 0-0 Tstrap: 0-0 Ckp: 0-0
Best Rating: **74** 6/09 NmkJ 6f gd-fm

100,000gns half-brother to, among others, high-class 1m-1m2f performer Ransom O'War; promise on debut over 6f on fast ground.

Cape Dancer (IRE)

91(95) (45)46

5-y-o b m Cape Cross (IRE)-Yankee Dancer (Groom Dancer (USA))

J S Wainwright Charles Wentworth

Placings:34506/606P0000/06444255000-6 (2723)

2009: 10^{6}G,

	Starts	1st	2nd	3rd	Win & Pl
Career Total (Turf)	19	0	1	1	1834
Career Total (AW)	6	0	0	0	96

Going (Turf): **Sf: 0-5 GS: 0-3 Gd: 0-6 GF: 0-5 Fm: 0-0**
Distance: 5f/6f: 0-3 7f-8f: 0-10 9f-13f: 0-12 14f+: 0-0
Track: LH: 0-12 RH: 0-9 Tight: 0-8 Gall: 0-2
Aids: Bl: 0-0 Vi: 0-0 Tstrap: 0-8 Ckp: 0-8
Best Rating: **63** 8/06 Thsk 7f gd-sft

Cape Express (IRE)

104(111) (102)94

4-y-o b g Cape Cross (IRE)-Lilissa (IRE) (Doyoun)

M A Jarvis A D Spence

Placings:51-1364 (5004)

2009: 12^{1}SD, 11^{3}SD, 12^{6}G, 10^{4}G,

	Starts	1st	2nd	3rd	Win & Pl
Career Total (Turf)	2	0	0	0	1501
Career Total (AW)	4	2	0	1	11319

101	1/09	Wolv	1m4f50y	(0-85)H	STD	£4857
80	12/08	Wolv	1m4f50y		STD	£2729

Total win prize-money £7587

Going (Turf): **Sf: 0-0 GS: 0-0 Gd: 0-2 GF: 0-0 Fm: 0-0**
Distance: 5f/6f: 0-0 7f-8f: 0-0 **9f-13f: 2-6** 14f+: 0-0
Track: **LH: 2-3** RH: 0-3 **Tight: 2-4** Gall: 0-1
Aids: Bl: 0-0 Vi: 0-0 Tstrap: 0-0 Ckp: 0-0
Best Rating: **102** 3/09 Kemp 1m3f stand

Very useful; stays 1m4f; acts on Polytrack.

Cape Greko

87(99) (61)58

7-y-o ro g Loup Sauvage (USA)-Onefortheditch (USA) (With Approval (CAN))

B G Powell Holistic Racing Ltd

Placings:21/535/000250/506053/0-000640 (7608)

2009: 16^{0}S, 9^{0}G, 12^{0}SD, 16^{6}SD, 12^{4}SD, 16^{0}SD,

	Starts	1st	2nd	3rd	Win & Pl
Career Total (Turf)	14	1	1	2	11857
Career Total (AW)	10	0	1	0	2624

98 7/04 Asct 7f D GD £5564

Total win prize-money £5564

Going (Turf): Sf: 0-3 GS: 0-2 **Gd: 1-7** GF: 0-2 Fm: 0-0
Distance: 5f/6f: 0-0 **7f-8f: 1-9** 9f-13f: 0-12 14f+: 0-3
Track : LH: 0-6 RH: 0-14 Tight: 0-8 Gall: 0-2
Aids: Bl: 0-0 Vi: 0-9 Tstrap: 0-0 Ckp: 0-0
Best Rating: **98** 7/04 Asct 7f good

Modest; probably stays 2m; acts on most types of ground; has worn a visor.

Cape Hawk (IRE)

108(108) (104)**97**

5-y-o b g Cape Cross (IRE)-Hawksbill Special (IRE) (Taufan (USA))

R Hannon Thurloe Thoroughbreds XVII

Placings:6/221414/1541402030-00346042051 (6695)

2009: 8^{0}SD, 8^{0}G, 8^{3}GF, 8^{4}G, 8^{6}GF, 8^{0}G, 9^{4}3, 8^{2}GF, 7^{0}GF, 8^{5}GF, 8^{1}GS,

	Starts	1st	2nd	3rd	Win & Pl
Career Total (Turf)	20	2	2	1	28783
Career Total (AW)	8	3	2	1	29312

91 10/09 Gdwd 1m (0-85)H G-S £5180
97 7/08 Asct 1m (0-95)H G-S £9066
102 4/08 Kemp 1m (0-85)H STD £4209
89 8/07 Kemp 1m (0-85)H STD £4728
86 6/07 Kemp 1m (0-80)H STD £4728

Total win prize-money £27912

Going (Turf): Sf: 0-4 **GS: 2-4** Gd: 0-5 GF: 0-7 Fm: 0-0
Distance: 5f/6f: 0-0 **7f-8f: 5-22** 9f-13f: 0-6 14f+: 0-0
Track : LH: 0-1 **RH: 5-23** Tight: 0-3 **Gall: 1-4**
Aids: Bl: 0-0 Vi: 0-1 Tstrap: 0-0 Ckp: 0-0
Best Rating: **104** 10/08 Kemp 1m stand

Useful; best at 1m; suited by easy ground and Polytrack; likes to race prominently.

Cape Kimberley

82(97) (74)**47**

2-y-o b g Arakan (USA)-Etoile Volant (USA) (Silver Hawk (USA))

J G Given J David Abell

Placings:4506215 (7453)

2009: 6^{4}SD, 6^{5}SD, 6^{0}GS, 5^{6}SD, 6^{2}SD, 6^{1}SD, 6^{5}SD,

	Starts	1st	2nd	3rd	Win & Pl
Career Total (Turf)	1	0	0	0	
Career Total (AW)	6	1	1	0	3764

74 11/09 Sthl 6f (0-70) STD £2729

Total win prize-money £2730

Going (Turf): Sf: 0-0 GS: 0-1 Gd: 0-0 GF: 0-0 Fm: 0-0
Distance: **5f/6f: 1-7** 7f-8f: 0-0 9f-13f: 0-0 14f+: 0-0
Track : **LH: 1-4** RH: 0-1 Tight: 0-0 Gall: 0-0
Aids: Bl: 0-0 Vi: 0-0 Tstrap: 0-0 Ckp: 0-0
Best Rating: **74** 11/09 Kemp 6f stand

Fair; stays 6f; acts on Fibresand.

Cape Marien (IRE)

90(100) (84)**68**

3-y-o b f Cape Cross (IRE)-Marienbad (FR) (Darshaan)

D R Lanigan Saif Ali

Placings:0102113 (7005)

2009: 10^{0}G, 11^{1}GF, 11^{0}GS, 12^{2}SD, 13^{1}SD, 12^{1}SD, 16^{3}SD,

	Starts	1st	2nd	3rd	Win & Pl
Career Total (Turf)	3	1	0	0	2730
Career Total (AW)	4	2	1	1	6137

84 10/09 Kemp 1m4f (0-65)H STD £2047
72 10/09 Wolv 1m5f194y (0-65)H STD £2729
68 6/09 Wind 1m3f135y G-F £2729

Total win prize-money £7507

Going (Turf): Sf: 0-0 GS: 0-1 Gd: 0-1 **GF: 1-1** Fm: 0-0
Distance: 5f/6f: 0-0 7f-8f: 0-0 **9f-13f: 2-5** 14f+: 1-2
Track : LH: 1-3 RH: 1-3 **Tight: 2-4** Gall: 0-0
Aids: Bl: 0-0 Vi: 0-0 Tstrap: 0-0 Ckp: 0-0
Best Rating: **84** 10/09 Kemp 1m4f stand

Fair filly; half-sister to Arc winner Marienbard; stays 1m6f; acts on fast ground and on Polytrack; progressive.

Cape Melody

99(87) (39)**79**

3-y-o b f Piccolo-Cape Charlotte (Mon Tresor)

H Morrison Morrison, Eavis, Usher

Placings:0224162540 (6964)

2009: 7^{0}SD, 6^{2}GF, 6^{2}GF, 6^{4}GF, 6^{1}GF, 7^{6}GF, 6^{2}G, 5^{5}GF, 6^{4}GS, 5^{0}G,

	Starts	1st	2nd	3rd	Win & Pl
Career Total (Turf)	9	1	3	0	6477
Career Total (AW)	1	0	0	0	

77 6/09 Chep 6f16y (0-70)H G-F £2719

Total win prize-money £2720

Going (Turf): Sf: 0-0 GS: 0-1 Gd: 0-2 **GF: 1-6** Fm: 0-0
Distance: 5f/6f: 0-7 **7f-8f: 1-3** 9f-13f: 0-0 14f+: 0-0
Track : LH: 0-2 RH: 0-1 Tight: 0-0 Gall: 0-0
Aids: Bl: 0-0 Vi: 0-0 Tstrap: 0-0 Ckp: 0-0
Best Rating: **79** 7/09 Ffos 6f good

Cape Of Luck (IRE)

99(100) (76)**81**

6-y-o b g Cape Cross (IRE)-Fledgling (Efisio)

P M Phelan Celtic Contractors Limited

Placings:1252100/601000/2606060500/0306400-430040 (2244)

2009: 12^{4}SD, 10^{3}SD, 12^{0}SD, 10^{0}GF, 12^{4}GF, 10^{0}GF,

	Starts	1st	2nd	3rd	Win & Pl
Career Total (Turf)	21	2	3	1	20571
Career Total (AW)	16	1	0	1	6144

89 6/06 NmkJ 7f (0-85)H G-F £6477
86 10/05 Ling 6f STD £4842
73 6/05 Sand 5f6y G-F £4134

Total win prize-money £15454

Going (Turf): Sf: 0-0 GS: 0-3 Gd: 0-6 **GF: 2-11** Fm: 0-1
Distance: **5f/6f: 2-7** 7f-8f: 1-18 9f-13f: 0-12 14f+: 0-0
Track : **LH: 1-9** RH: 0-16 **Tight: 1-11** Gall: 0-2
Aids: Bl: 0-2 Vi: 0-0 Tstrap: 0-5 Ckp: 0-5
Best Rating: **96** 6/07 Folk 7f good

Moderate; effective at around 7f-1m2f; acts on fast ground; goes on Polytrack; has won cheekpieces and a tongue tie.

Cape Of Storms

(107) (68)**60**

6-y-o b g Cape Cross (IRE)-Lloc (Absalom)

R Brotherton Arthur Clayton

Placings:30000365000/5052060052/22123252300000-64451355100 (7795)

2009: 6^{6}SS, 6^{4}SD, 6^{4}SD, 6^{5}SD, 6^{1}SS, 7^{3}SD, 6^{5}SD, 7^{5}SD, 6^{1}SD, 6^{0}SD, 6^{0}SS,

	Starts	1st	2nd	3rd	Win & Pl
Career Total (Turf)	12	0	0	1	482
Career Total (AW)	34	3	7	4	12934

68 3/09 Sthl 6f (0-65)H STD £2047
60 2/09 Sthl 6f (0-55)H SS £2047
67 2/08 Sthl 6f SS £2457

Total win prize-money £6551

Going (Turf): Sf: 0-2 GS: 0-1 Gd: 0-2 GF: 0-6 Fm: 0-1
Distance: **5f/6f: 3-24** 7f-8f: 0-13 9f-13f: 0-9 14f+: 0-0
Track : **LH: 3-39** RH: 0-4 Tight: 0-18 Gall: 0-0
Aids: **Bl: 1-8** Vi: 0-1 Tstrap: 0-2 Ckp: 0-2
Best Rating: **70** 4/08 Wolv 7f32y stand

Modest; effective at around 6f; acts on sand; sometimes wears blinkers.

Cape Quarter (USA)

(98) (78)

3-y-o b g Elusive Quality (USA)-June Moon (IRE) (Sadler's Wells (USA))

W J Haggas Bernard Kantor

Placings:5-1 (7353)

2009: 7^{1}SD,

	Starts	1st	2nd	3rd	Win & Pl
Career Total (Turf)	0	0	0	0	
Career Total (AW)	2	1	0	0	5118

65 11/09 Sthl 7f STD £5118

Total win prize-money £5118

Going (Turf): Sf: 0-0 GS: 0-0 Gd: 0-0 GF: 0-0 Fm: 0-0
Distance: 5f/6f: 0-0 **7f-8f: 1-2** 9f-13f: 0-0 14f+: 0-0
Track : **LH: 1-2** RH: 0-0 Tight: 0-1 Gall: 0-0
Aids: Bl: 0-0 Vi: 0-0 Tstrap: 0-0 Ckp: 0-0
Best Rating: **78** 10/08 Ling 7f stand

Fair; stays 7f and acts on Fibresand.

Cape Roberto (IRE)

79(93) (56)**56**

4-y-o b g Cape Cross (IRE)-Kalwada (USA) (Roberto (USA))

John Berry Michael Ogburn

Placings:04050000-0 (7094)

2009: 10^{0}G,

	Starts	1st	2nd	3rd	Win & Pl
Career Total (Turf)	4	0	0	0	0
Career Total (AW)	5	0	0	0	0

Going (Turf): Sf: 0-0 GS: 0-1 Gd: 0-1 GF: 0-2 Fm: 0-0
Distance: 5f/6f: 0-1 7f-8f: 0-6 9f-13f: 0-2 14f+: 0-0
Track : LH: 0-4 RH: 0-2 Tight: 0-2 Gall: 0-2
Aids: Bl: 0-0 Vi: 0-0 Tstrap: 0-0 Ckp: 0-0
Best Rating: **56** 8/08 GrLe 1m stand

Cape Rock

104(99) (76)**87**

4-y-o b g Cape Cross (IRE)-Wildwood Flower (Distant Relative)

W J Knight Mrs B Sumner

Placings:005/62522523-1233 **(5182)**
2009: 7^{1}GF, 6^{2}G, 7^{3}G, 7^{3}G,

	Starts	1st	2nd	3rd	Win & Pl
Career Total (Turf)	13	1	5	2	11077
Career Total (AW)	2	0	0	1	403

80 6/09 Chep 7f16y (0-70)H G-F £3238
Total win prize-money £3238

Going (Turf): Sf: 0-1 GS: 0-3 Gd: 0-6 **GF: 1-3** Fm: 0-0
Distance: 5f/6f: 0-3 **7f-8f: 1-12** 9f-13f: 0-0 14f+: 0-0
Track : LH: 0-2 RH: 0-0 Tight: 0-2 Gall: 0-1
Aids: Bl: 0-0 Vi: 0-0 Tstrap: 0-1 Ckp: 0-1
Best Rating: **87** 7/09 NmkJ 7f good

Fair; suited by 6f-7f; acts on good and soft ground.

Cape Royal

104(100) (73)**84**
9-y-o b g Prince Sabo-Indigo (Primo Dominie)
J M Bradley E A Hayward

Placings:6/210220/06106020320/41305000000001265222 40/05020050436050421026036 0/62100504502005200/004 6600065104504030351 0-0632303220512200000544005 **(7808)**
2009: 5^{0}GF, 5^{6}GF, 5^{3}GF, 5^{2}GF, 5^{3}GF, 5^{0}G, 5^{3}G, 5^{2}S, 5^{2}HY, 6^{0}GF, 5^{5}GF, 5^{1}GF, 5^{2}GF, 5^{2}GF, 5^{0}SD, 5^{0}GF, 5^{0}SD, 5^{0}G, 5^{5}SD, 5^{4}SD, 5^{4}SD, 5^{0}SD, 5^{0}SD, 5^{5}SD,

	Starts	1st	2nd	3rd	Win & Pl
Career Total (Turf)	114	9	20	8	151949
Career Total (AW)	14	0	0	1	1385

78 8/09 Wind 5f10y (0-70)H G-F £2729
81 10/08 Nott 5f13y (0-75)H HVY £3238
84 7/08 Nott 5f13y (0-75)H G-F £3238
99 4/07 Epsm 5f (0-95)H G-F £8101
101 9/06 Hayd 5f (0-100)H HVY £18696
99 8/05 Sand 5f6y (0-100)H SFT £11050
100 4/05 Donc 5f (0-100)H GD £12209
93 4/04 Epsm 5f C(0-95)H SFT £9117
73 6/03 Nott 5f13y E G-F £3721
Total win prize-money £72103

Going (Turf): **Sf: 4-21** GS: 0-17Gd: 1-30**GF: 4-46** Fm: 0-0
Distance: **5f/6f: 9-128** 7f-8f: 0-0 9f-13f: 0-0 14f+: 0-0
Track : LH: 0-25 RH: 0-2 Tight: 0-17 **Gall: 1-7**
Aids: **Bl: 4-74** Vi: 0-0 Tstrap: 0-0 Ckp: 0-0
Best Rating: **104** 9/05 Hayd 5f gd-sft

Fair; best at 5f; acts on most ground; usually wears blinkers and a tongue tie; likes to race prominently.

Cape Tribulation

92 **91**
5-y-o b g Hernando (FR)-Gay Fantastic (Ela-Mana-Mou)
J M Jefferson J David Abell

Placings:015-00 **(7018)**
2009: 16^{0}G, 12^{0}GS,

	Starts	1st	2nd	3rd	Win & Pl
Career Total (Turf)	5	1	0	0	2914

83 10/08 Nott 1m2f50y SFT £2914
Total win prize-money £2914

Going (Turf): **Sf: 1-1** GS: 0-2 Gd: 0-2 GF: 0-0 Fm: 0-0
Distance: 5f/6f: 0-0 7f-8f: 0-0 **9f-13f: 1-3** 14f+: 0-2
Track : **LH: 1-5** RH: 0-0 Tight: 0-0 Gall: 0-2
Aids: Bl: 0-0 Vi: 0-0 Tstrap: 0-0 Ckp: 0-0
Best Rating: **91** 10/08 Donc 1m6f132y good

Useful; effective over 1m2f; acts on soft ground.

Cape Vale (IRE)

109 **93**
4-y-o b g Cape Cross (IRE)-Wolf Cleugh (IRE) (Last Tycoon)
D Nicholls Lady O'Reilly

Placings:11/42500-04052121020 **(7015)**
2009: 5^{0}GF, 6^{4}G, 6^{0}G, 5^{5}G, 5^{2}GF, 6^{1}G, 6^{2}G, 6^{1}GF, 6^{0}G, 5^{2}G, 5^{0}GS,

	Starts	1st	2nd	3rd	Win & Pl
Career Total (Turf)	18	4	4	0	28433

93 9/09 Hayd 6f (0-85)H G-F £5504
89 7/09 Ffos 6f (0-80)H GD £4857
83 9/07 Ayr 6f (0-85) SFT £6477
78 8/07 Thsk 6f G-F £4533
Total win prize-money £21373

Going (Turf): Sf: 1-1 GS: 0-2 Gd: 1-9 **GF: 2-6** Fm: 0-0
Distance: **5f/6f: 4-17** 7f-8f: 0-1 9f-13f: 0-0 14f+: 0-0
Track : LH: 0-3 RH: 0-0 Tight: 0-2 Gall: 0-0
Aids: Bl: 0-0 Vi: 0-0 Tstrap: 0-0 Ckp: 0-0
Best Rating: **93** 10/09 Catt 5f good

Useful; effective over 5f-7f; acts on most ground on turf.

Capeability (IRE)

107(102) (77)**91**
3-y-o b g Cape Cross (IRE)-Mennetou (IRE) (Entrepreneur)
M R Channon The Totally Incapables

Placings:06-226600025 **(7620)**
2009: 8^{2}SD, 8^{2}SD, 10^{6}GF, 10^{6}GF, 8^{0}GF, 10^{0}GS, 10^{0}S, 10^{2}SD, 9^{5}SD,

	Starts	1st	2nd	3rd	Win & Pl
Career Total (Turf)	7	0	0	0	3920
Career Total (AW)	4	0	3	0	2571

Going (Turf): **Sf: 0-1 GS: 0-1 Gd: 0-0 GF: 0-5 Fm: 0-0**
Distance: 5f/6f: 0-1 7f-8f: 0-2 9f-13f: 0-8 14f+: 0-0
Track : LH: 0-7 RH: 0-2 Tight: 0-3 Gall: 0-1
Aids: Bl: 0-0 Vi: 0-0 Tstrap: 0-0 Ckp: 0-0
Best Rating: **91** 4/09 NmkR 1m2f gd-fm

Useful; effective over 1m; acts on Polytrack.

Capefly

(106) (71)**71**
4-y-o b f Cape Cross (IRE)-Patacake Patacake (USA) (Bahri (USA))
P W Chapple-Hyam Miss Alfiya Shaykhutdinova

Placings:0332/0-30 **(0281)**
2009: 6^{3}SD, 6^{0}SD,

	Starts	1st	2nd	3rd	Win & Pl
Career Total (Turf)	4	0	1	2	1975
Career Total (AW)	3	0	0	1	482

Going (Turf): **Sf: 0-1 GS: 0-0 Gd: 0-2 GF: 0-0 Fm: 0-1**
Distance: 5f/6f: 0-6 7f-8f: 0-1 9f-13f: 0-0 14f+: 0-0
Track : LH: 0-5 RH: 0-0 Tight: 0-2 Gall: 0-3
Aids: Bl: 0-0 Vi: 0-0 Tstrap: 0-0 Ckp: 0-0
Best Rating: **71** 1/09 GrLe 6f stand

Modest; best at about 6f; acts on good or faster ground; has worn a tongue tie.

Capercaillie (USA)

103 **90**
2-y-o ch f Elusive Quality (USA)-Silent Eskimo (USA) (Eskimo (USA))
M Johnston Sheikh Hamdan Bin Mohammed Al Maktoum

Placings:11440 **(6677)**
2009: 5^{1}GF, 5^{1}G, 5^{4}GF, 6^{4}G, 6^{0}G,

	Starts	1st	2nd	3rd	Win & Pl
Career Total (Turf)	5	2	0	0	28592

90 6/09 Muss 5f GD £15577
84 5/09 Muss 5f G-F £3885
Total win prize-money £19464

Going (Turf): Sf: 0-0 GS: 0-0 **Gd: 1-3 GF: 1-2** Fm: 0-0
Distance: **5f/6f: 2-5** 7f-8f: 0-0 9f-13f: 0-0 14f+: 0-0
Track : LH: 0-0 RH: 0-0 Tight: 0-0 Gall: 0-0
Aids: Bl: 0-0 Vi: 0-0 Tstrap: 0-0 Ckp: 0-0
Best Rating: **90** 7/09 NmkJ 6f good

Very useful, effective at 5f; acts on good and faster ground.

Capistrano

(102) (54)**54**
6-y-o b g Efisio-Washita (Valiyar)
Paul Mason Mick White & Paul Mason

Placings:003/6150/606000/54062600-40 **(1439)**
2009: 11^{4}SD, 16^{0}SD,

	Starts	1st	2nd	3rd	Win & Pl
Career Total (Turf)	14	1	0	0	3886
Career Total (AW)	9	0	1	1	1414

76 5/06 Ripn 1m1f170y (0-70)H GD £3886
Total win prize-money £3886

Going (Turf): Sf: 0-2 GS: 0-5 **Gd: 1-2** GF: 0-5 Fm: 0-0
Distance: 5f/6f: 0-2 7f-8f: 0-4 **9f-13f: 1-14** 14f+: 0-3
Track : LH: 0-12 **RH: 1-8 Tight: 1-9** Gall: 0-1
Aids: Bl: 0-3 Vi: 0-0 Tstrap: 0-2 Ckp: 0-2
Best Rating: **76** 5/06 Ripn 1m1f170y good

Moderate; stays 1m5f; acts on good ground; also goes on Polytrack.

Capital Attraction (USA)

77 **68**
2-y-o ch c Speightstown (USA)-Cecilia's Crown (USA) (Chief's Crown (USA))
H R A Cecil H E Sheikh Sultan Bin Khalifa Al Nahyan

Placings:4 **(6759)**
2009: 8^{4}G,

	Starts	1st	2nd	3rd	Win & Pl
Career Total (Turf)	1	0	0	0	385

Going (Turf): **Sf: 0-0 GS: 0-0 Gd: 0-1 GF: 0-0 Fm: 0-0**
Distance: 5f/6f: 0-0 7f-8f: 0-0 9f-13f: 0-1 14f+: 0-0
Track : LH: 0-0 RH: 0-1 Tight: 0-0 Gall: 0-0
Aids: Bl: 0-0 Vi: 0-0 Tstrap: 0-0 Ckp: 0-0
Best Rating: **68** 10/09 Leic 1m60y good

Capitalise (IRE)

(102) (63)**65**
6-y-o b g City On A Hill (USA)-Prime Interest (IRE) (Kings Lake (USA))
Miss Gay Kelleway David Jenkins

Placings:000/05066500242/02343323/243112410-00054 **(0835)**
2009: 13^{0}SD, 16^{0}SD, 13^{0}SD, 13^{5}SF, 16^{4}SD,

	Starts	1st	2nd	3rd	Win & Pl
Career Total (Turf)	14	1	1	0	4035
Career Total (AW)	22	2	5	5	9887

65	5/08	Yarm	2m	(0-70)H	G-F	£2590
62	3/08	Ling	1m5f	(0-75)H	STD	£2590
55	2/08	Ling	1m5f	(0-60)H	STD	£1876

Total win prize-money £7058

Going (Turf): Sf: 0-1 GS: 0-1 Gd: 0-4 **GF: 1-4** Fm: 0-4
Distance: 5f/6f: 0-0 7f-8f: 0-4 **9f-13f: 2-11** 14f+: 1-21
Track : **LH: 3-30** RH: 0-5 **Tight: 3-26** Gall: 0-2
Aids: Bl: 0-1 Vi: 0-1 Tstrap: 0-1 Ckp: 0-1
Best Rating: 65 5/08 Yarm 2m gd-fm

Moderate; effective at around 1m5f-2m; acts on Polytrack; has worn visor.

Capitelli (IRE)

103(95) (70)81
3-y-o b f Cape Cross (IRE)-Dear Girl (IRE) (Fairy King (USA))
R Hannon The Royal Ascot Racing Club

Placings:26656-5035 **(7238)**
2009: 9^{5}F, 9^{0}GF, 10^{3}G, 12^{5}SD,

	Starts	1st	2nd	3rd	Win & Pl
Career Total (Turf)	6	0	1	1	2041
Career Total (AW)	3	0	0	0	74

Going (Turf): Sf: 0-0 GS: 0-1 Gd: 0-3 GF: 0-1 Fm: 0-1
Distance: 5f/6f: 0-0 7f-8f: 0-4 9f-13f: 0-5 14f+: 0-0
Track : LH: 0-3 RH: 0-4 Tight: 0-4 Gall: 0-1
Aids: Bl: 0-0 Vi: 0-0 Tstrap: 0-0 Ckp: 0-0
Best Rating: 81 9/08 Newb 7f good

Fair; stays 1m2f; acts on good ground.

Capo Regime

101(100) (76)68
3-y-o ch g Captain Rio-Ashtree Belle (Up And At 'Em)
P Howling (D Nicholls 1/7) Paul Terry

Placings:530-0103055030630 **(7762)**
2009: 5^{0}GF, 6^{1}SD, 5^{0}SD, 7^{3}GF, 7^{0}S, 8^{5}GS, 8^{5}G, 8^{0}G, 7^{3}SS, 7^{0}G, 8^{6}SD, 6^{3}SD, 7^{0}SD,

	Starts	1st	2nd	3rd	Win & Pl
Career Total (Turf)	10	0	0	2	924
Career Total (AW)	6	1	0	2	2652

76	5/09	Sthl	6f		STD	£2047

Total win prize-money £2047

Going (Turf): Sf: 0-2 GS: 0-1 Gd: 0-4 GF: 0-3 Fm: 0-0
Distance: **5f/6f: 1-7** 7f-8f: 0-8 9f-13f: 0-1 14f+: 0-0
Track : **LH: 1-6** RH: 0-2 Tight: 0-2 Gall: 0-0
Aids: Bl: 0-0 **Vi: 1-6** Tstrap: 0-0 Ckp: 0-0
Best Rating: 76 5/09 Sthl 6f stand

Modest; best at 5f but stays further.

Capone (IRE)

104(109) (95)79
4-y-o b g Daggers Drawn (USA)-Order Of The Day (USA) (Dayjur (USA))
R Curtis (Garry Moss 8/8) Brooklands Racing

Placings:643/61623540-061130652316 **(7862)**
2009: 7^{0}G, 7^{6}G, 6^{1}G, 6^{1}G, 6^{3}GF, 5^{0}VS, 7^{6}S, 6^{5}SD, 6^{2}SD, 6^{3}SD, 6^{1}SD, 5^{6}SD,

	Starts	1st	2nd	3rd	Win & Pl
Career Total (Turf)	17	3	1	2	11769
Career Total (AW)	6	1	1	2	7940

95	12/09	Kemp	6f	(0-85)H	STD	£5180
79	8/09	Yarm	6f3y	(0-70)H	GD	£2978
72	7/09	Donc	6f	(0-70)H	GD	£3412
74	5/08	Thsk	6f	(0-75)H	GD	£3885

Total win prize-money £15458

Going (Turf): Sf: 0-4 GS: 0-1 **Gd: 3-8** GF: 0-3 Fm: 0-0
Distance: **5f/6f: 3-17** 7f-8f: 1-6 9f-13f: 0-0 14f+: 0-0
Track : LH: 0-8 **RH: 1-2** Tight: 0-6 Gall: 0-0
Aids: Bl: 0-1 Vi: 0-0 Tstrap: 0-0 Ckp: 0-0
Best Rating: 95 12/09 Kemp 6f stand

Useful; effective over 6f; acts on most ground; goes on Polytrack.

Cappagh Strand (USA)

95(94) (67)61
3-y-o b f Grand Slam (USA)-Quiet Eclipse (USA) (Quiet American (USA))
David P Myerscough Glenview House Stud

Placings:0033550 **(7525a)**
2009: 7^{0}SD, 8^{0}GY, 7^{3}GF, 8^{3}SD, 8^{5}SD, 6^{5}SD, 5^{0}SD,

	Starts	1st	2nd	3rd	Win & Pl
Career Total (Turf)	2	0	0	1	403
Career Total (AW)	5	0	0	1	403

Going (Turf): Sf: 0-0 GS: 0-0 Gd: 0-0 GF: 0-1 Fm: 0-0
Distance: 5f/6f: 0-2 7f-8f: 0-4 9f-13f: 0-1 14f+: 0-0
Track : LH: 0-6 RH: 0-0 Tight: 0-1 Gall: 0-0
Aids: Bl: 0-0 Vi: 0-0 Tstrap: 0-0 Ckp: 0-0
Best Rating: 67 9/09 Wolv 1m141y stand

Modest; stays 7f and acts on fast ground.

Capped For Victory (USA)

(94) (48)54
8-y-o b g Red Ransom (USA)-Nazoo (IRE) (Nijinsky (CAN))
W Storey (G A Swinbank 21/1) W Storey

Placings:232/200/00/00/0300-60 **(1131)**
2009: 8^{6}SS, 8^{0}SD,

	Starts	1st	2nd	3rd	Win & Pl
Career Total (Turf)	13	0	3	2	8458
Career Total (AW)	3	0	0	0	0

Going (Turf): Sf: 0-1 GS: 0-2 Gd: 0-4 GF: 0-6 Fm: 0-0
Distance: 5f/6f: 0-1 7f-8f: 0-8 9f-13f: 0-7 14f+: 0-0
Track : LH: 0-8 RH: 0-3 Tight: 0-5 Gall: 0-1
Aids: Bl: 0-1 Vi: 0-0 Tstrap: 0-0 Ckp: 0-0
Best Rating: 98 8/03 York 6f217y gd-fm

Capricorn Run (USA)

105(112) (106)106
6-y-o b/br g Elusive Quality (USA)-Cercida (USA) (Copelan (USA))
A J McCabe Khalifa Dasmal & Placida Racing

Placings:610/0/0054010102110 10/1230046000600000-36413100036200040 **(7768)**
2009: 8^{3}SD, 8^{6}SD, 7^{4}SD, 7^{1}SD, 7^{3}SD, 7^{1}SD, 8^{0}SD, 7^{0}SD, 6^{0}GF, 7^{3}GF, 6^{6}GF, 7^{2}SD, 7^{0}GF, 6^{0}G, 7^{0}G, 6^{4}SD, 7^{0}SD,

	Starts	1st	2nd	3rd	Win & Pl
Career Total (Turf)	22	2	0	1	12614
Career Total (AW)	30	7	3	3	75758

101	2/09	Ling	7f	(0-100)H	STD	£11656
97	2/09	Kemp	7f	(0-100)H	STD	£11215
111	1/08	Ling	1m		STD	£6624
111	11/07	Ling	7f	(0-100)H	STD	£9971
105	11/07	Ling	7f	(0-95)H	STD	£6855
103	10/07	Ling	7f	(0-95)H	STD	£7166
96	9/07	NmkR	6f	(0-85)H	FRM	£5181
87	9/07	Ling	6f	(0-80)H	STD	£5181
82	9/05	Newb	7f		G-F	£5577

Total win prize-money £69431

Going (Turf): Sf: 0-0 GS: 0-2 Gd: 0-8 **GF: 1-11 Fm: 1-1**
Distance: 5f/6f: 2-15 **7f-8f: 7-32** 9f-13f: 0-5 14f+: 0-0
Track : **LH: 6-27** RH: 1-6 **Tight: 6-23** Gall: 0-2
Aids: Bl: 0-4 **Vi: 7-32** Tstrap: 1-7 Ckp: 1-7
Best Rating: 111 1/08 Wolv 1m141y stand

Very useful; stays 1m; acts on fast ground and on Polytrack; has worn various headgear; can break very slowly.

Capricornus (USA)

(96) (72)
2-y-o ch c Rahy (USA)-Silent Partner (USA) (Capote (USA))
M Johnston Sheikh Hamdan Bin Mohammed Al Maktoum

Placings:41 **(7859)**
2009: 8^{4}SD, 7^{1}SD,

	Starts	1st	2nd	3rd	Win & Pl
Career Total (Turf)	0	0	0	0	
Career Total (AW)	2	1	0	0	3527

72	12/09	Wolv	7f32y		STD	£3238

Total win prize-money £3238

Going (Turf): Sf: 0-0 GS: 0-0 Gd: 0-0 GF: 0-0 Fm: 0-0
Distance: 5f/6f: 0-0 **7f-8f: 1-2** 9f-13f: 0-0 14f+: 0-0
Track : **LH: 1-1** RH: 0-1 **Tight: 1-1** Gall: 0-0
Aids: Bl: 0-0 Vi: 0-0 Tstrap: 0-0 Ckp: 0-0
Best Rating: 72 12/09 Wolv 7f32y stand

Fair; effective over 7f; acts on Polytrack; should improve further.

Caprio (IRE)

105(111) (87)86
4-y-o ch g Captain Rio-Disarm (IRE) (Bahamian Bounty)
J R Boyle (Tom Dascombe 21/4) M Khan X2

Placings:056112/42235632054-2122325130522201 **(7558)**
2009: 7^{2}SD, 6^{1}SD, 7^{2}SF, 7^{2}SD, 7^{3}SD, 7^{2}SD, 7^{5}SD, 6^{1}GF, 6^{3}GF, 6^{0}SD, 6^{5}G, 7^{2}G, 7^{2}G, 6^{2}F, 7^{0}SD, 7^{1}SD,

	Starts	1st	2nd	3rd	Win & Pl
Career Total (Turf)	12	1	4	2	9935
Career Total (AW)	21	4	7	2	24915

87	11/09	Wolv	7f32y	(0-90)H	STD	£7569
86	5/09	Gdwd	6f	(0-80)H	G-F	£5180
79	2/09	Kemp	6f	(0-85)H	STD	£4857
68	11/07	Kemp	6f	(0-65)	STD	£2047
71	11/07	Wolv	5f216y	(0-60)	STD	£2047

Total win prize-money £21704

Going (Turf): Sf: 0-1 GS: 0-1 Gd: 0-5 **GF: 1-3** Fm: 0-2
Distance: **5f/6f: 4-15** 7f-8f: 1-18 9f-13f: 0-0 14f+: 0-0
Track : LH: 2-19 RH: 2-7 **Tight: 2-12** Gall: 0-2
Aids: Bl: 0-1 Vi: 0-0 Tstrap: 0-1 Ckp: 0-1
Best Rating: 87 11/09 Wolv 7f32y stand

Useful; effective over 6f-7f; acts on fast and easy ground; also goes on Fibresand and Polytrack.

Captain Blake (IRE)

79(68) (20)38
2-y-o b/br g Captain Rio-Green Flower (USA) (Fappiano (USA))

P D Evans (A B Haynes 15/4) Bathwick Gold Partnership

Placings:000060 (6215)
2009: 5[0]SD, 5[0]GF, 6[0]G, 8[0]GS, 8[6]G, 8[0]GF,

	Starts	1st	2nd	3rd	Win & Pl
Career Total (Turf)	5	0	0	0	0
Career Total (AW)	1	0	0	0	

Going (Turf): Sf: 0-0 GS: 0-1 Gd: 0-2 GF: 0-2 Fm: 0-0
Distance: 5f/6f: 0-2 7f-8f: 0-3 9f-13f: 0-1 14f+: 0-0
Track : LH: 0-2 RH: 0-0 Tight: 0-1 Gall: 0-1
Aids: Bl: 0-0 Vi: 0-0 Tstrap: 0-0 Ckp: 0-0
Best Rating: 38 9/09 Ffos 1m good

Captain Bluebird (IRE)

91(73) (37)61

2-y-o ch c Captain Rio-Dolly Blue (IRE) (Pennekamp (USA))
D Donovan Philip Mclaughlin

Placings:504 (4564)
2009: 6[5]SD, 6[0]G, 6[4]G,

	Starts	1st	2nd	3rd	Win & Pl
Career Total (Turf)	2	0	0	0	361
Career Total (AW)	1	0	0	0	0

Going (Turf): Sf: 0-0 GS: 0-0 Gd: 0-2 GF: 0-0 Fm: 0-0
Distance: 5f/6f: 0-2 7f-8f: 0-1 9f-13f: 0-0 14f+: 0-0
Track : LH: 0-1 RH: 0-0 Tight: 0-1 Gall: 0-0
Aids: Bl: 0-0 Vi: 0-0 Tstrap: 0-0 Ckp: 0-0
Best Rating: 61 8/09 Newb 6f8y good

Modest; best effort over 6f on fast ground.

Captain Bradz (USA)

(81) (31)

3-y-o ch c Diesis-Garden Rose (IRE) (Caerleon (USA))
P T Midgley Darren & Annaley Yates

Placings:00-260 (0273)
2009: 8[2]SS, 7[6]SD, 5[0]SD,

	Starts	1st	2nd	3rd	Win & Pl
Career Total (Turf)	2	0	0	0	
Career Total (AW)	3	0	1	0	605

Going (Turf): Sf: 0-0 GS: 0-0 Gd: 0-0 GF: 0-2 Fm: 0-0
Distance: 5f/6f: 0-3 7f-8f: 0-2 9f-13f: 0-0 14f+: 0-0
Track : LH: 0-3 RH: 0-1 Tight: 0-1 Gall: 0-0
Aids: Bl: 0-0 Vi: 0-0 Tstrap: 0-0 Ckp: 0-0
Best Rating: 31 1/09 Sthl 1m std-slw

Very moderate; stays 1m and acts on Fibresand.

Captain Brilliance (USA)

109 108

4-y-o ch c Officer (USA)-Bloomin Genius (USA) (Beau Genius (CAN))
J Noseda Bluehills Racing Limited

Placings:21/120063 (7019)
2009: 7[1]GF, 7[2]GF, 7[0]G, 8[0]GF, 8[6]GF, 7[3]GS,

	Starts	1st	2nd	3rd	Win & Pl
Career Total (Turf)	8	2	2	1	40485

105 6/09 NmkJ 7f (0-95)H G-F £9714
83 8/07 NmkJ 6f G-F £6477
Total win prize-money £16191

Going (Turf): Sf: 0-0 GS: 0-1 Gd: 0-1 GF: 2-6 Fm: 0-0
Distance: 5f/6f: 1-2 7f-8f: 1-6 9f-13f: 0-0 14f+: 0-0
Track : LH: 0-1 RH: 0-0 Tight: 0-0 Gall: 0-1
Aids: Bl: 0-0 Vi: 0-1 Tstrap: 0-0 Ckp: 0-0
Best Rating: 108 10/09 Donc 7f gd-sft

Smart; effective over 6f-7f; acts on fast ground; has worn a visor.

Captain Carey

102(96) (79)91

3-y-o b g Fraam-Brigadiers Bird (IRE) (Mujadil (USA))
M S Saunders M S Saunders

Placings:0630-01162515 (5245)
2009: 5[0]SD, 5[1]SD, 5[1]GF, 5[6]G, 5[2]G, 5[5]GS, 5[1]G, 5[5]F,

	Starts	1st	2nd	3rd	Win & Pl
Career Total (Turf)	7	2	1	0	9506
Career Total (AW)	5	1	0	1	3183

91 6/09 Wind 5f10y (0-85)H GD £5180
74 4/09 Bath 5f11y (0-70)H G-F £2590
79 3/09 Sthl 5f (0-70)H STD £2729
Total win prize-money £10501

Going (Turf): Sf: 0-0 GS: 0-1 Gd: 1-3 GF: 1-2 Fm: 0-1
Distance: 5f/6f: 3-10 7f-8f: 0-2 9f-13f: 0-0 14f+: 0-0
Track : LH: 1-6 RH: 0-1 Tight: 0-3 Gall: 2-5
Aids: Bl: 0-0 Vi: 0-0 Tstrap: 0-0 Ckp: 0-0
Best Rating: 91 6/09 Wind 5f10y good

Fair; effective over 5f-6f; acts on fast ground and on Fibresand.

Captain Cash

85 37

2-y-o ch g Kyllachy-Fission (Efisio)
T D Easterby Habton Farms

Placings:000 (5407)
2009: 5[0]GF, 6[0]GF, 8[0]G,

	Starts	1st	2nd	3rd	Win & Pl
Career Total (Turf)	3	0	0	0	

Going (Turf): Sf: 0-0 GS: 0-0 Gd: 0-1 GF: 0-2 Fm: 0-0
Distance: 5f/6f: 0-2 7f-8f: 0-1 9f-13f: 0-0 14f+: 0-0
Track : LH: 0-1 RH: 0-0 Tight: 0-1 Gall: 0-0
Aids: Bl: 0-0 Vi: 0-0 Tstrap: 0-0 Ckp: 0-0
Best Rating: 37 6/09 Ripn 5f gd-fm

Captain Cavendish (IRE)

67(94) (59)

3-y-o b g Captain Rio-Fahan (IRE) (Sri Pekan (USA))
A Bailey The Glenbuccaneers

Placings:010203-600000 (5403)
2009: 7[6]SD, 7[0]SD, 7[0]SD, 7[0]G, 9[0]SD, 7[0]G,

	Starts	1st	2nd	3rd	Win & Pl
Career Total (Turf)	2	0	0	0	
Career Total (AW)	10	1	1	1	3256

54 10/08 Wolv 7f32y SF £2047
Total win prize-money £2047

Going (Turf): Sf: 0-0 GS: 0-0 Gd: 0-2 GF: 0-0 Fm: 0-0
Distance: 5f/6f: 0-0 7f-8f: 1-9 9f-13f: 0-3 14f+: 0-0
Track : LH: 1-10 RH: 0-0 Tight: 1-7 Gall: 0-1
Aids: Bl: 1-6 Vi: 0-3 Tstrap: 0-2 Ckp: 0-2
Best Rating: 59 12/08 Wolv 7f32y stand

Modest; effective over 1m; acts on Polytrack.

Captain Clint (IRE)

82(78) (14)47

2-y-o b g Captain Rio-Lake Poopo (IRE) (Persian Heights)
M H Tompkins Raceworld

Placings:0000 (7335)
2009: 6[0]GF, 7[0]G, 7[0]G, 8[0]SD,

	Starts	1st	2nd	3rd	Win & Pl
Career Total (Turf)	3	0	0	0	
Career Total (AW)	1	0	0	0	

Going (Turf): Sf: 0-0 GS: 0-0 Gd: 0-2 GF: 0-1 Fm: 0-0
Distance: 5f/6f: 0-0 7f-8f: 0-4 9f-13f: 0-0 14f+: 0-0
Track : LH: 0-1 RH: 0-0 Tight: 0-0 Gall: 0-0
Aids: Bl: 0-0 Vi: 0-0 Tstrap: 0-0 Ckp: 0-0
Best Rating: 47 8/09 Yarm 6f3y gd-fm

Captain Cool (IRE)

97(93) (43)50

2-y-o ch g Captain Rio-Aiaie (Zafonic (USA))
R Hannon Mrs John Lee

Placings:500650432 (7887)
2009: 5[5]GF, 5[0]GF, 6[0]GF, 7[6]G, 8[5]GF, 8[0]G, 6[4]G, 7[3]SD, 7[2]SD,

	Starts	1st	2nd	3rd	Win & Pl
Career Total (Turf)	7	0	0	0	283
Career Total (AW)	2	0	1	1	736

Going (Turf): Sf: 0-0 GS: 0-0 Gd: 0-3 GF: 0-4 Fm: 0-0
Distance: 5f/6f: 0-3 7f-8f: 0-4 9f-13f: 0-2 14f+: 0-0
Track : LH: 0-3 RH: 0-3 Tight: 0-3 Gall: 0-1
Aids: Bl: 0-0 Vi: 0-0 Tstrap: 0-0 Ckp: 0-0
Best Rating: 50 8/09 Bevl 7f100y good

Moderate; stays 7f; acts on Polytrack.

Captain Dancer (IRE)

99(68) (5)77

3-y-o ch g Danehill Dancer (IRE)-Rain Flower (IRE) (Indian Ridge)
B W Hills R J Arculli

Placings:01-056 (6997)
2009: 7[0]SD, 6[5]S, 7[6]G,

	Starts	1st	2nd	3rd	Win & Pl
Career Total (Turf)	4	1	0	0	4857
Career Total (AW)	1	0	0	0	

76 10/08 NmkR 7f G-S £4857
Total win prize-money £4857

Going (Turf): Sf: 0-1 GS: 1-1 Gd: 0-1 GF: 0-1 Fm: 0-0
Distance: 5f/6f: 0-0 7f-8f: 1-5 9f-13f: 0-0 14f+: 0-0
Track : LH: 0-1 RH: 0-0 Tight: 0-0 Gall: 0-0
Aids: Bl: 0-0 Vi: 0-0 Tstrap: 0-0 Ckp: 0-0
Best Rating: 77 10/09 Sals 6f212y soft

175,000euros son of an unraced half-sister to Dr Devious and Archway; effective over 7f; acts on fast and easy ground.

Captain Dunne (IRE)

108(106) (101)105
4-y-o b g Captain Rio-Queen Bodicea (IRE) (Revoque (IRE))
T D Easterby Middleham Park Racing Xv

Placings:0143/0033021001330-02200656310 **(6678)**
2009: 6^{0}GF, 5^{2}G, 5^{2}GF, 5^{0}G, 5^{0}G, 5^{6}G, 5^{5}GF, 5^{6}GS, 5^{3}GF, 5^{1}GF, 6^{0}G,

	Starts	1st	2nd	3rd	Win & Pl
Career Total (Turf)	27	3	3	6	54324
Career Total (AW)	1	1	0	0	9066

105 9/09 Bevl 5f G-F £7477
101 9/08 Sthl 5f (0-90)H STD £9066
89 8/08 Thsk 5f (0-85)H SFT £5569
72 5/07 Hayd 5f G-F £2817
Total win prize-money £24929

Going (Turf): Sf: 1-5 GS: 0-5 Gd: 0-9 **GF: 2-8** Fm: 0-0
Distance: **5f/6f: 4-28** 7f-8f: 0-0 9f-13f: 0-0 14f+: 0-0
Track : LH: 0-1 RH: 0-0 Tight: 0-0 Gall: 0-0
Aids: Bl: 0-0 Vi: 0-0 Tstrap: 0-0 Ckp: 0-0
Best Rating: **105** 9/09 Bevl 5f gd-fm

Very useful; effective at 5f; acts on most ground and on Fibresand; suited by forcing tactics.

Captain Ellis (USA)

102(78) (33)85
3-y-o b g Five Star Day (USA)-Adventure (USA) (Unbridled's Song (USA))
A P Jarvis (K R Burke 11/7) Mogeely Stud & Mrs Maura Gittins

Placings:2220-3100 **(5375)**
2009: 8^{3}G, 8^{1}F, 7^{0}GF, 8^{0}SD,

	Starts	1st	2nd	3rd	Win & Pl
Career Total (Turf)	7	1	3	1	7535
Career Total (AW)	1	0	0	0	

81 7/09 Hayd 1m30y FRM £3238
Total win prize-money £3238

Going (Turf): Sf: 0-1 GS: 0-0 Gd: 0-3 GF: 0-2 **Fm: 1-1**
Distance: 5f/6f: 0-3 7f-8f: 0-3 **9f-13f: 1-2** 14f+: 0-0
Track : **LH: 1-3** RH: 0-0 Tight: 0-0 Gall: 0-0
Aids: Bl: 0-0 Vi: 0-0 Tstrap: 0-1 Ckp: 0-1
Best Rating: **85** 7/08 Hayd 6f good

Useful; stays 1m; acts on any ground.

Captain Flack

96(97) (61)54
3-y-o ch g Lucky Story (USA)-Au Contraire (Groom Dancer (USA))
J A R Toller M A Whelton

Placings:00-01034 **(5483)**
2009: 10^{0}SD, 12^{1}SD, 14^{0}GF, 12^{3}SD, 14^{4}GF,

	Starts	1st	2nd	3rd	Win & Pl
Career Total (Turf)	4	0	0	0	173
Career Total (AW)	3	1	0	1	2350

58 6/09 Ling 1m4f STD £2047
Total win prize-money £2047

Going (Turf): **Sf: 0-0 GS: 0-0 Gd: 0-1 GF: 0-3 Fm: 0-0**
Distance: 5f/6f: 0-0 7f-8f: 0-2 **9f-13f: 1-3** 14f+: 0-2
Track : **LH: 1-5** RH: 0-0 **Tight: 1-4** Gall: 0-0
Aids: **Bl: 1-4** Vi: 0-0 Tstrap: 0-0 Ckp: 0-0
Best Rating: **61** 8/09 Wolv 1m4f50y stand

Moderate; stays 1m4f; acts on Polytrack; has worn blinkers.

Captain Flasheart (IRE)

103(101) (73)81
3-y-o ch g Captain Rio-Catfoot Lane (Batshoof)
S C Williams Paul W Stevens

Placings:5-550311 **(5998)**
2009: 5^{5}SD, 5^{5}SD, 7^{0}S, 8^{3}S, 8^{1}SD, 7^{1}GF,

	Starts	1st	2nd	3rd	Win & Pl
Career Total (Turf)	3	1	0	1	2489
Career Total (AW)	4	1	0	0	2590

81 9/09 Yarm 7f3y (0-60)H G-F £2007
73 9/09 Kemp 1m (0-70)H STD £2590
Total win prize-money £4598

Going (Turf): Sf: 0-2 GS: 0-0 Gd: 0-0 **GF: 1-1** Fm: 0-0
Distance: 5f/6f: 0-3 **7f-8f: 2-4** 9f-13f: 0-0 14f+: 0-0
Track : LH: 0-0 **RH: 1-5** Tight: 0-1 Gall: 0-0
Aids: Bl: 0-0 Vi: 0-0 Tstrap: 0-0 Ckp: 0-0
Best Rating: **81** 9/09 Yarm 7f3y gd-fm

Fair; stays 1m; acts on fast ground and on Polytrack.

Captain Gerrard (IRE)

108 113
4-y-o b c Oasis Dream-Delphinus (Soviet Star (USA))
B Smart R C Bond

Placings:6231131411/1400-0004002060006 **(7015)**
2009: 6^{0}GF, 5^{0}HY, 5^{0}G, 5^{4}GF, 5^{0}GY, 5^{0}G, 5^{2}GF, 5^{0}GF, 5^{6}GF, 5^{0}GF, 5^{0}GF, 6^{0}G, 5^{6}GS,

	Starts	1st	2nd	3rd	Win & Pl
Career Total (Turf)	27	6	2	2	145408

113 5/08 NmkR 5f G-F £28385
110 10/07 Asct 5f G-S £22712
110 9/07 Ayr 5f SFT £17034
105 8/07 York 5f GD £17781
97 7/07 Ches 5f16y HVY £9148
99 6/07 Ches 5f16y SFT £4728
Total win prize-money £99788

Going (Turf): **Sf: 3-5** GS: 1-4 Gd: 1-6 GF: 1-11 Fm: 0-0
Distance: **5f/6f: 6-27** 7f-8f: 0-0 9f-13f: 0-0 14f+: 0-0
Track : **LH: 2-3** RH: 0-0 **Tight: 2-3** Gall: 0-0
Aids: Bl: 0-2 Vi: 0-0 Tstrap: 0-0 Ckp: 0-0
Best Rating: **113** 5/08 NmkR 5f gd-fm

Very useful; winner of the Group 3 Cornwallis Stakes as a juvenile and Group 3 Palace House Stakes on three-year-old return; best at 5f; acts on fast ground, but revels in the mud; likes to race prominently; has worn blinkers.

Captain Hook

(91) (34)65
5-y-o b g Rock Of Gibraltar (IRE)-Biloxi (Caerleon (USA))
Daniel Mark Loughnane Michael V Kirby

Placings:3030/002040406-0000 **(4554a)**
2009: 13^{0}SD, 14^{0}G, 12^{0}Y, 16^{0}YS,

	Starts	1st	2nd	3rd	Win & Pl
Career Total (Turf)	15	0	1	2	3511
Career Total (AW)	2	0	0	0	

Going (Turf): **Sf: 0-4 GS: 0-0 Gd: 0-4 GF: 0-0 Fm: 0-0**
Distance: 5f/6f: 0-0 7f-8f: 0-1 9f-13f: 0-6 14f+: 0-10
Track : LH: 0-4 RH: 0-12 Tight: 0-1 Gall: 0-0
Aids: Bl: 0-3 Vi: 0-0 Tstrap: 0-9 Ckp: 0-9

Best Rating: **72** 7/07 Leop 1m soft

Captain Imperial (IRE)

96(95) (68)73
3-y-o b g Captain Rio-Imperialist (IRE) (Imperial Frontier (USA))
R Bastiman (T P Tate 17/10) Chris Myers & Partners 3

Placings:03102-0PP035000 **(7594)**
2009: 10^{0}G, 12^{P}G, 12^{P}G, 12^{0}S, 8^{3}G, 7^{5}S, 8^{0}SD, 12^{0}SD, 13^{0}SD,

	Starts	1st	2nd	3rd	Win & Pl
Career Total (Turf)	10	1	0	2	5391
Career Total (AW)	4	0	1	0	1156

73 8/08 Thsk 7f SFT £4274
Total win prize-money £4274

Going (Turf): **Sf: 1-4** GS: 0-1 Gd: 0-4 GF: 0-1 Fm: 0-0
Distance: 5f/6f: 0-1 **7f-8f: 1-6** 9f-13f: 0-6 14f+: 0-1
Track : **LH: 1-12** RH: 0-1 **Tight: 1-8** Gall: 0-2
Aids: Bl: 0-0 Vi: 0-0 Tstrap: 0-0 Ckp: 0-0
Best Rating: **73** 8/08 Thsk 7f soft

Fair; effective at 7f-1m; acts on soft ground; goes on Fibresand.

Captain Jacksparra (IRE)

104(103) (88)91
5-y-o b g Danehill (USA)-Push A Venture (Shirley Heights)
K A Ryan J Duddy,B McDonald,A Heeney,M McMenamin

Placings:436/2112220051/00250400-02000231005 **(5779)**
2009: 7^{0}GF, 7^{2}GF, 7^{0}SD, 7^{0}G, 7^{0}SD, 9^{2}GF, 8^{3}GF, 8^{1}SD, 7^{0}G, 7^{0}SD, 8^{5}SD,

	Starts	1st	2nd	3rd	Win & Pl
Career Total (Turf)	21	1	5	2	15202
Career Total (AW)	11	3	2	0	13395

82 7/09 Ling 1m STD £2047
91 9/07 Ling 7f (0-85)H G-F £5181
82 3/07 Ling 7f (0-85)H STD £5505
53 3/07 Sthl 6f STD £2968
Total win prize-money £15703

Going (Turf): Sf: 0-1 GS: 0-2 Gd: 0-5 **GF: 1-12** Fm: 0-1
Distance: 5f/6f: 1-4 **7f-8f: 3-26** 9f-13f: 0-2 14f+: 0-0
Track : **LH: 3-20** RH: 0-4 **Tight: 2-13** Gall: 0-2
Aids: Bl: 0-0 Vi: 0-0 Tstrap: 0-4 Ckp: 0-4
Best Rating: **91** 5/08 Catt 7f gd-fm

Fair; effective at 7f-1m; acts on fast ground; goes on sand; likes to race prominently; has worn cheekpieces.

Captain Kallis (IRE)

101(100) (64)64
3-y-o ch g Captain Rio-Alicedale (USA) (Trempolino (USA))
D J S Ffrench Davis Hargood Limited

Placings:640402136-32550300 **(5632)**
2009: 6^{3}SD, 6^{2}GF, 6^{5}F, 5^{5}G, 6^{0}SD, 5^{3}S, 6^{0}G, 6^{0}GS,

	Starts	1st	2nd	3rd	Win & Pl
Career Total (Turf)	10	0	1	1	1555
Career Total (AW)	8	1	1	2	5733

63 11/08 Sthl 6f STD £3753
Total win prize-money £3753

Going (Turf): **Sf: 0-1 GS: 0-2 Gd: 0-2 GF: 0-4 Fm: 0-1**

Distance: **5f/6f: 1-13** 7f-8f: 0-5 9f-13f: 0-0 14f+: 0-0
Track : **LH: 1-12** RH: 0-0 Tight: 0-1 Gall: 0-2
Aids: Bl: 0-0 Vi: 0-1 Tstrap: 0-0 Ckp: 0-0
Best Rating: 64 5/09 Chep 6f16y gd-fm

Modest; effective over 6f; acts on most ground; goes on Fibresand; has worn a tongue tie.

Captain Macarry (IRE)

106(108) (96)**96**
4-y-o ch g Captain Rio-Grannys Reluctance (IRE) (Anita's Prince)
B Smart Anthony D Gee

Placings:6100/00**12-441**60130**5121**0**1** (6944)
2009: 7^{4}SS, 7^{4}SD, **7^{1}SD**, 7^{6}GF, 7^{0}GF, **7^{1}GF**, 8^{3}GF, 7^{0}S, 8^{5}GF, **6^{1}G**, 7^{2}GF, **7^{1}SD**, 7^{0}G, **7^{1}SD**,

	Starts	1st	2nd	3rd	Win & Pl
Career Total (Turf)	15	3	1	1	16218
Career Total (AW)	7	4	1	0	16419

96	10/09	Kemp	7f	(0-85)H	STD	£4727
90	9/09	Wolv	7f32y	(0-80)H	STD	£5046
96	8/09	Carl	6f192y	(0-85)H	GD	£4727
89	5/09	Bevl	7f100y	(0-75)H	G-F	£2752
80	2/09	Wolv	7f32y	(0-75)H	STD	£3070
80	12/08	Sthl	7f	(0-65)H	STD	£2047
73	9/07	York	6f		G-F	£6541

Total win prize-money £28912

Going (Turf): Sf: 0-2 GS: 0-0 Gd: 1-5 **GF: 2-8** Fm: 0-0
Distance: 5f/6f: 1-5 **7f-8f: 6-15** 9f-13f: 0-2 14f+: 0-0
Track : LH: 3-7 RH: 3-6 **Tight: 2-3** Gall: 0-0
Aids: Bl: 0-0 **Vi: 6-16** Tstrap: 0-0 Ckp: 0-0
Best Rating: 96 10/09 Kemp 7f stand

Useful; effective at 7f-1m; acts on fast ground; goes on sand; often visored.

Captain Mainwaring

95(98) (61)**66**
4-y-o b g Auction House (USA)-Shalyah (IRE) (Shalford (IRE))
N P Littmoden John B Waterfall

Placings:004/64**1**2005-300050 (4156)
2009: 13^{3}SD, 13^{0}SD, 12^{0}SD, 12^{0}GF, 10^{5}G, 11^{0}G,

	Starts	1st	2nd	3rd	Win & Pl
Career Total (Turf)	11	1	1	0	2936
Career Total (AW)	5	0	0	1	302

65	5/08	Chep	1m4f23y	(0-60)H	SFT	£2331

Total win prize-money £2331

Going (Turf): **Sf: 1-3** GS: 0-1 Gd: 0-3 GF: 0-4 Fm: 0-0
Distance: 5f/6f: 0-0 7f-8f: 0-1 **9f-13f: 1-13** 14f+: 0-2
Track : **LH: 1-12** RH: 0-2 Tight: 0-7 Gall: 0-2
Aids: Bl: 0-4 Vi: 0-0 Tstrap: 0-2 Ckp: 0-2
Best Rating: 66 6/08 Ling 1m3f106y good

Moderate; stays 1m5f; acts on soft ground and Polytrack.

Captain Oats (IRE)

97 (54)**54**
6-y-o b g Bahhare (USA)-Adarika (Kings Lake (USA))
Mrs P Ford K R Ford

Placings:50300/0046/03/604642 (5720)
2009: 10^{6}GF, 12^{0}GS, 10^{4}G, 11^{6}GF, 8^{4}G, 13^{2}G,

	Starts	1st	2nd	3rd	Win & Pl
Career Total (Turf)	13	0	1	2	2851
Career Total (AW)	4	0	0	0	192

Going (Turf): **Sf: 0-1 GS: 0-2 Gd: 0-4 GF: 0-4 Fm: 0-1**
Distance: 5f/6f: 0-0 7f-8f: 0-4 9f-13f: 0-12 14f+: 0-1
Track : LH: 0-11 RH: 0-4 Tight: 0-5 Gall: 0-1
Aids: Bl: 0-0 Vi: 0-0 Tstrap: 0-2 Ckp: 0-2
Best Rating: 71 8/05 Tral 1m good

Very moderate; stays 1m2f; acts on fast and easy ground; has worn cheekpieces.

Captain Peachey

85 **36**
3-y-o b c Pursuit Of Love-Dekelsmary (Komaite (USA))
B R Millman The Peachey Syndicate

Placings:000600 (4690)
2009: 7^{0}GF, 6^{0}GF, 7^{0}GS, 5^{6}GF, 5^{0}GF, 5^{0}G,

	Starts	1st	2nd	3rd	Win & Pl
Career Total (Turf)	6	0	0	0	0

Going (Turf): **Sf: 0-0 GS: 0-1 Gd: 0-1 GF: 0-4 Fm: 0-0**
Distance: 5f/6f: 0-4 7f-8f: 0-2 9f-13f: 0-0 14f+: 0-0
Track : LH: 0-2 RH: 0-0 Tight: 0-0 Gall: 0-1
Aids: Bl: 0-1 Vi: 0-0 Tstrap: 0-0 Ckp: 0-0
Best Rating: 36 6/09 Nott 5f13y gd-fm

Captain Ramius (IRE)

96(99) (100)**87**
3-y-o b c Kheleyf (USA)-Princess Mood (GER) (Muhtarram (USA))
S A Callaghan Mrs Clodagh McStay

Placings:111-06 (2278)
2009: 8^{0}SD, 7^{6}GF,

	Starts	1st	2nd	3rd	Win & Pl
Career Total (Turf)	1	0	0	0	540
Career Total (AW)	4	3	0	0	44247

100	10/08	Dund	7f	STD	£33507
84	9/08	Kemp	7f	STD	£6854
78	8/08	Kemp	7f	STD	£3885

Total win prize-money £44247

Going (Turf): **Sf: 0-0 GS: 0-0 Gd: 0-0 GF: 0-1 Fm: 0-0**
Distance: 5f/6f: 0-0 **7f-8f: 3-5** 9f-13f: 0-0 14f+: 0-0
Track : LH: 1-1 **RH: 2-3** Tight: 0-0 Gall: 0-0
Aids: Bl: 0-0 Vi: 0-0 Tstrap: 0-0 Ckp: 0-0
Best Rating: 100 10/08 Dund 7f stand

Useful half-brother to very smart multiple 6f-7f winner Kingsgate Prince, and 1m winner Smuggler's Bay; winner of first three starts over 7f, including in Listed company, on Polytrack.

Captain Royale (IRE)

102(95) (61)**60**
4-y-o ch g Captain Rio-Paix Royale (Royal Academy (USA))
Miss Tracy Waggott H Conlon

Placings:61600/0004205-000054621650 (7241)
2009: 8^{0}GF, 7^{0}SD, 7^{0}GS, 6^{0}SD, 6^{5}G, 6^{4}GF, 6^{6}GF, 5^{2}S, **5^{1}G**, 5^{6}GF, 6^{5}G, 5^{0}S,

	Starts	1st	2nd	3rd	Win & Pl
Career Total (Turf)	16	2	1	0	9148
Career Total (AW)	8	0	1	0	605

60	9/09	Haml	5f4y	(0-65)H	GD	£1942
86	6/07	Ripn	6f		SFT	£3562

Total win prize-money £5505

Going (Turf): **Sf: 1-5** GS: 0-1 **Gd: 1-5** GF: 0-4 Fm: 0-0
Distance: **5f/6f: 2-13** 7f-8f: 0-10 9f-13f: 0-1 14f+: 0-0
Track : LH: 0-8 RH: 0-3 Tight: 0-1 Gall: 0-1
Aids: Bl: 0-0 Vi: 0-2 Tstrap: 1-10 Ckp: 1-10
Best Rating: 86 8/07 Curr 6f sft-hvy

Modest; suited by 6f; acts on soft ground and on sand; has worn cheekpieces.

Captain Sachin (IRE)

2-y-o b g Captain Rio-Belalzao (IRE) (Alzao (USA))
T J Etherington Exors Of The Late C Hoggard

Placings:P (1661)
2009: 5^{P}G,

	Starts	1st	2nd	3rd	Win & Pl
Career Total (Turf)	1	0	0	0	

Going (Turf): **Sf: 0-0 GS: 0-0 Gd: 0-1 GF: 0-0 Fm: 0-0**
Distance: 5f/6f: 0-1 7f-8f: 0-0 9f-13f: 0-0 14f+: 0-0
Track : LH: 0-0 RH: 0-0 Tight: 0-0 Gall: 0-0
Aids: Bl: 0-0 Vi: 0-0 Tstrap: 0-0 Ckp: 0-0

Captain Scooby

106 **75**
3-y-o b g Captain Rio-Scooby Dooby Do (Atraf)
R M Whitaker Paul Davies (H'gte)

Placings:332140-3343451600 (6798)
2009: 6^{3}GF, 6^{3}GF, 6^{4}HY, 6^{3}GS, 6^{4}GF, 6^{5}G, **5^{1}GS**, 6^{6}S, 5^{0}GF, 6^{0}S,

	Starts	1st	2nd	3rd	Win & Pl
Career Total (Turf)	16	2	1	5	17557

75	8/09	Carl	5f	(0-80)H	G-S	£6476
74	8/08	Bevl	5f	(0-85)	SFT	£5180

Total win prize-money £11657

Going (Turf): **Sf: 1-7 GS: 1-2** Gd: 0-1 GF: 0-6 Fm: 0-0
Distance: **5f/6f: 2-14** 7f-8f: 0-2 9f-13f: 0-0 14f+: 0-0
Track : LH: 0-2 **RH: 1-1** Tight: 0-1 **Gall: 1-1**
Aids: Bl: 0-0 Vi: 0-1 Tstrap: 0-1 Ckp: 0-1
Best Rating: 75 8/09 Carl 5f gd-sft

Fair; effective over 5f; acts on soft ground.

Captain Sirus (FR)

68(89) (44)
6-y-o b g Fly To The Stars-Zudika (IRE) (Ezzoud (IRE))
P Butler P Butler

Placings:000/0/**06000**-0 (1876)
2009: 7^{0}GF,

	Starts	1st	2nd	3rd	Win & Pl
Career Total (Turf)	5	0	0	0	
Career Total (AW)	5	0	0	0	0

Going (Turf): **Sf: 0-0 GS: 0-0 Gd: 0-0 GF: 0-5 Fm: 0-0**
Distance: 5f/6f: 0-1 7f-8f: 0-7 9f-13f: 0-2 14f+: 0-0
Track : LH: 0-4 RH: 0-4 Tight: 0-2 Gall: 0-0
Aids: Bl: 0-0 Vi: 0-0 Tstrap: 0-1 Ckp: 0-1
Best Rating: 44 9/08 Kemp 1m stand

Captain Teddo

75(67) (5)**14**

3-y-o ch c Auction House (USA)-Charlottevalentina (IRE) (Perugino (USA))

R Ingram Stuart Higgins

Placings:000 **(5900)**

2009: 6^{0}G, 7^{0}SD, 5^{0}F,

	Starts	1st	2nd	3rd	Win & Pl
Career Total (Turf)	2	0	0	0	
Career Total (AW)	1	0	0	0	

Going (Turf): Sf: 0-0 GS: 0-0 Gd: 0-1 GF: 0-0 Fm: 0-1
Distance: 5f/6f: 0-2 7f-8f: 0-1 9f-13f: 0-0 14f+: 0-0
Track : LH: 0-1 RH: 0-1 Tight: 0-0 Gall: 0-1
Aids: Bl: 0-0 Vi: 0-0 Tstrap: 0-0 Ckp: 0-0
Best Rating: **14** 8/09 Ling 6f good

Captain Walcot

(96) (59)**55**

3-y-o b g Fantastic Light (USA)-Princess Minnie (Mistertopogigo (IRE))

R Hannon The Early Bath Partnership

Placings:00000435-56 **(0287)**

2009: 10^{b}SD, 8^{6}SD,

	Starts	1st	2nd	3rd	Win & Pl
Career Total (Turf)	4	0	0	0	
Career Total (AW)	6	0	0	1	241

Going (Turf): Sf: 0-0 GS: 0-0 Gd: 0-1 GF: 0-3 Fm: 0-0
Distance: 5f/6f: 0-0 7f-8f: 0-7 9f-13f: 0-3 14f+: 0-0
Track : LH: 0-4 RH: 0-3 Tight: 0-3 Gall: 0-1
Aids: Bl: 0-5 Vi: 0-0 Tstrap: 0-1 Ckp: 0-1
Best Rating: **59** 11/08 Kemp 1m stand

Modest; stays 7f; has worn blinkers and cheekpieces.

Captain's Paradise (IRE)

84(83) (35)**42**

2-y-o b f Rock Of Gibraltar (IRE)-Minnie Habit (Habitat)

Sir Mark Prescott Denford Stud

Placings:00 **(4278)**

2009: 5^{0}SD, 7^{0}G,

	Starts	1st	2nd	3rd	Win & Pl
Career Total (Turf)	1	0	0	0	
Career Total (AW)	1	0	0	0	

Going (Turf): Sf: 0-0 GS: 0-0 Gd: 0-1 GF: 0-0 Fm: 0-0
Distance: 5f/6f: 0-1 7f-8f: 0-1 9f-13f: 0-0 14f+: 0-0
Track : LH: 0-2 RH: 0-0 Tight: 0-2 Gall: 0-0
Aids: Bl: 0-0 Vi: 0-0 Tstrap: 0-0 Ckp: 0-0
Best Rating: **42** 7/09 Thsk 7f good

Captainrisk (IRE)

107(97) (76)**76**

3-y-o b g Captain Rio-Helderberg (USA) (Diesis)

Mrs C A Dunnett (M Botti 20/6) P Fisher

Placings:220-2313525 **(4914)**

2009: 8^{2}SD, 8^{3}SD, 7^{1}SD, 7^{3}SD, 7^{5}GF, 8^{2}G, 7^{5}G,

	Starts	1st	2nd	3rd	Win & Pl
Career Total (Turf)	4	0	2	0	2293
Career Total (AW)	6	1	2	2	5469

73 2/09 Wolv 7f32y (0-75)H STD £2914
Total win prize-money £2914

Going (Turf): Sf: 0-0 GS: 0-0 Gd: 0-2 GF: 0-2 Fm: 0-0
Distance: 5f/6f: 0-0 **7f-8f: 1-6** 9f-13f: 0-4 14f+: 0-0
Track : **LH: 1-7** RH: 0-1 **Tight: 1-4** Gall: 0-0
Aids: Bl: 0-1 **Vi: 1-3** Tstrap: 0-1 Ckp: 0-1
Best Rating: **76** 6/09 Hayd 1m30y good

Fair; stays 1m; acts on Polytrack; has worn blinkers/visor.

Capucci

106(104) (88)**87**

4-y-o b g King's Best (USA)-Design Perfection (USA) (Diesis)

J J Quinn Ross Harmon

Placings:0551503-65362650415 **(6846)**

2009: 8^{6}GF, 8^{5}GF, 8^{3}GF, 8^{6}GF, 7^{2}SD, 6^{6}G, 9^{5}S, 8^{0}GF, 7^{4}GF, 7^{1}SF, 7^{5}G,

	Starts	1st	2nd	3rd	Win & Pl
Career Total (Turf)	16	1	0	2	5098
Career Total (AW)	2	1	1	0	4645

88 10/09 Wolv 7f32y SF £3238
87 6/08 Newb 1m (0-75)H GD £2590
Total win prize-money £5828

Going (Turf): Sf: 0-1 GS: 0-2 **Gd: 1-6** GF: 0-7 Fm: 0-0
Distance: 5f/6f: 0-1 **7f-8f: 2-11** 9f-13f: 0-6 14f+: 0-0
Track : **LH: 1-8** RH: 0-4 **Tight: 1-4** Gall: 0-0
Aids: Bl: 0-0 Vi: 0-0 Tstrap: 1-2 Ckp: 1-2
Best Rating: **88** 10/09 Wolv 7f32y std-fst

Useful; stays 7f-1m; acts on fast ground and on Polytrack; has worn a tongue-tie.

Cara's Request (AUS)

103(95) (55)**82**

4-y-o gr g Urgent Request (IRE)-Carahill (AUS) (Danehill (USA))

D Nicholls (L M Cumani 18/6) Stewart Aitken

Placings:521-055030 **(7172)**

2009: 8^{0}S, 8^{5}GF, 6^{5}GF, 7^{0}G, 7^{3}S, 7^{0}S,

	Starts	1st	2nd	3rd	Win & Pl
Career Total (Turf)	8	1	1	1	5673
Career Total (AW)	1	0	0	0	0

82 10/08 Nott 1m75y HVY £3238
Total win prize-money £3238

Going (Turf): **Sf: 1-5** GS: 0-0 Gd: 0-1 GF: 0-2 Fm: 0-0
Distance: 5f/6f: 0-1 7f-8f: 0-4 **9f-13f: 1-4** 14f+: 0-0
Track : **LH: 1-7** RH: 0-1 Tight: 0-1 Gall: 0-2
Aids: Bl: 0-0 Vi: 0-0 Tstrap: 0-0 Ckp: 0-0
Best Rating: **82** 10/08 Nott 1m75y heavy

Fair; effective over 7f-1m; acts on soft ground.

Caracal

82 **61**

2-y-o b c Dubai Destination (USA)-Desert Lynx (IRE) (Green Desert (USA))

M Johnston Sheikh Hamdan Bin Mohammed Al Maktoum

Placings:04 **(4307)**

2009: 7^{0}GF, 7^{4}GS,

	Starts	1st	2nd	3rd	Win & Pl
Career Total (Turf)	2	0	0	0	313

Going (Turf): Sf: 0-0 GS: 0-1 Gd: 0-0 GF: 0-1 Fm: 0-0
Distance: 5f/6f: 0-0 7f-8f: 0-2 9f-13f: 0-0 14f+: 0-0
Track : LH: 0-1 RH: 0-0 Tight: 0-0 Gall: 0-0
Aids: Bl: 0-0 Vi: 0-0 Tstrap: 0-0 Ckp: 0-0
Best Rating: **61** 7/09 Newc 7f gd-sft

Caracciola (GER)

110 **109**

12-y-o b g Lando (GER)-Capitolina (FR) (Empery (USA))

B W Hills (N J Henderson 20/6) P J D Pottinger

Placings:6/11111404/0/3212/6541-114 **(4457)**

2009: 14^{1}GF, 21^{1}GF, 16^{4}G,

	Starts	1st	2nd	3rd	Win & Pl
Career Total (Turf)	21	9	2	1	229512

99 6/09 Asct 2m5f159y G-F £31155
104 5/09 York 1m6f G-F £22708
109 10/08 NmkR 2m2f H GD £99696
95 9/07 Bath 2m1f34y (0-100)H FRM £10094
7/01 Duss 1m3f H GD £4886
6/01 Colo 1m3f H GD £5212
5/01 Badn 1m4f H GD £3909
5/01 Colo 1m3f H SFT £1954
4/01 Gels 1m1f HVY £1140
Total win prize-money £180754

Going (Turf): Sf: 2-3 GS: 0-4 **Gd: 4-7** GF: 2-5 Fm: 1-1
Distance: 5f/6f: 0-0 7f-8f: 0-1 **9f-13f: 5-8** 14f+: 4-12
Track : LH: 3-4 **RH: 4-12** Tight: 1-3 **Gall: 3-9**
Aids: Bl: 0-0 Vi: 0-0 Tstrap: 0-0 Ckp: 0-0
Best Rating: **109** 10/08 NmkR 2m2f good

Smart; winner of the 2008 Cesarewitch and 2009 Queen Alexandra; effective from 1m6f-2m5f and acts on most types of ground; useful hurdler/chaser.

Caramelita

97(93) (67)**71**

2-y-o b f Deportivo-Apple Of My Eye (Fraam)

J R Jenkins La Senoritas

Placings:552433 **(7674)**

2009: 6^{5}G, 6^{5}GF, 6^{2}GS, 5^{4}GF, 6^{3}SD, 5^{3}SD,

	Starts	1st	2nd	3rd	Win & Pl
Career Total (Turf)	4	0	1	0	1186
Career Total (AW)	2	0	0	2	933

Going (Turf): Sf: 0-0 GS: 0-1 Gd: 0-1 GF: 0-2 Fm: 0-0
Distance: 5f/6f: 0-5 7f-8f: 0-1 9f-13f: 0-0 14f+: 0-0
Track : LH: 0-0 RH: 0-1 Tight: 0-0 Gall: 0-1
Aids: Bl: 0-0 Vi: 0-0 Tstrap: 0-0 Ckp: 0-0
Best Rating: **71** 10/09 Folk 6f gd-sft

Modest; suited by 5f-6f and easy ground; acts on Fibresand too.

Caranbola

99 **91**

3-y-o br f Lucky Story (USA)-Ladywell Blaise (IRE) (Turtle Island (IRE))

M Brittain Mel Brittain

Placings:21222513650-6600003520 **(6159)**

2009: 5^{6}F, 6^{6}GS, 6^{0}GF, 6^{0}G, 6^{0}G, 6^{0}GS, 6^{3}GF, 6^{5}G, 5^{2}GF, 5^{0}G,

	Starts	1st	2nd	3rd	Win & Pl
Career Total (Turf)	21	2	5	2	30860

89 8/08 Hayd 6f SFT £6476
70 4/08 Ripn 5f GD £2914
Total win prize-money £9390

Going (Turf): **Sf: 1-2** GS: 0-5 **Gd: 1-8** GF: 0-5 Fm: 0-1
Distance: **5f/6f: 2-21** 7f-8f: 0-0 9f-13f: 0-0 14f+: 0-0

Track : LH: 0-0 RH: 0-0 Tight: 0-0 Gall: 0-0
Aids: Bl: 0-0 Vi: 0-0 Tstrap: 0-0 Ckp: 0-0
Best Rating: 91 8/08 Ripn 5f gd-sft

Very useful; effective over 5f-6f; acts on most ground; tough.

Caravan Of Dreams (IRE)

(98) (69)63
3-y-o b f Anabaa (USA)-Smart 'n Noble (USA) (Smarten (USA))
M A Jarvis P D Savill

Placings:60530-5 (0317)
2009: 7^{5}SD,

	Starts	1st	2nd	3rd	Win & Pl
Career Total (Turf)	2	0	0	0	0
Career Total (AW)	4	0	0	1	605

Going (Turf): Sf: 0-0 GS: 0-0 Gd: 0-0 GF: 0-2 Fm: 0-0
Distance: 5f/6f: 0-0 7f-8f: 0-5 9f-13f: 0-1 14f+: 0-0
Track : LH: 0-3 RH: 0-2 Tight: 0-2 Gall: 0-1
Aids: Bl: 0-0 Vi: 0-0 Tstrap: 0-0 Ckp: 0-0
Best Rating: 69 12/08 Kemp 1m stand

Modest; half-sister to the high-class 1m4f/2m performer Royal And Regal; stays 1m2f; acts on Polytrack.

Carbon Hoofprint

108(99) (80)86
3-y-o b g Green Tune (USA)-Salome's Attack (Anabaa (USA))
P J Makin The Billinomas

Placings:32362212654 (7350)
2009: 8^{3}SD, 8^{2}SD, 7^{3}G, 10^{6}GF, 8^{2}GF, 8^{2}GF, 8^{1}GS, 8^{2}F, 8^{6}GF, 7^{5}SD, 7^{4}SD,

	Starts	1st	2nd	3rd	Win & Pl
Career Total (Turf)	7	1	3	1	6728
Career Total (AW)	4	0	1	1	1209

85	8/09	Bath	1m5y	(0-75)H	G-S	£2719

Total win prize-money £2720

Going (Turf): Sf: 0-0 GS: 1-1 Gd: 0-1 GF: 0-4 Fm: 0-1
Distance: 5f/6f: 0-0 7f-8f: 0-8 9f-13f: 1-3 14f+: 0-0
Track : LH: 1-6 RH: 0-3 Tight: 1-5 Gall: 0-0
Aids: Bl: 0-0 Vi: 0-0 Tstrap: 0-0 Ckp: 0-0
Best Rating: 86 8/09 Bath 1m5y firm

Useful; stays 1m; acts on fast and easy ground; goes on Polytrack.

Carbon Print (USA)

90 61
4-y-o ch g Johannesburg (USA)-Caithness (USA) (Roberto (USA))
P R Webber The Dream On Partnership

Placings:0-00450 (5484)
2009: 10^{0}GF, 9^{0}G, 10^{4}S, 10^{5}GS, 10^{0}GF,

	Starts	1st	2nd	3rd	Win & Pl
Career Total (Turf)	6	0	0	0	289

Going (Turf): Sf: 0-1 GS: 0-2 Gd: 0-1 GF: 0-2 Fm: 0-0
Distance: 5f/6f: 0-0 7f-8f: 0-1 9f-13f: 0-5 14f+: 0-0
Track : LH: 0-2 RH: 0-3 Tight: 0-4 Gall: 0-1
Aids: Bl: 0-0 Vi: 0-0 Tstrap: 0-0 Ckp: 0-0
Best Rating: 61 7/09 NmkJ 1m2f soft

Carcinetto (IRE)

108(107) (94)102
7-y-o b m Danetime (IRE)-Dolphin Stamp (IRE) (Dolphin Street (FR))
P D Evans Mrs Sally Edwards

Placings:0000160/05050012220314623/03410413623303115132/064601024004310503605055013230024160046100346402500 (7768)
2009: 5^{5}SD, 5^{5}SD, 6^{0}SD, 5^{1}GF, 7^{3}GF, 7^{2}F, 7^{3}GF, 5^{0}G, 5^{0}GF, 6^{2}F, 6^{4}GS, 7^{1}GF, 6^{6}GF, 6^{0}GF, 7^{0}GF, 6^{4}G, 6^{6}GF, 7^{1}GF, 7^{0}GF, 7^{0}GF, 7^{3}GF, 6^{4}GF, 7^{6}GF, 8^{4}SD, 8^{0}SD,

	Starts	1st	2nd	3rd	Win & Pl
Career Total (Turf)	46	5	7	5	89475
Career Total (AW)	49	8	3	8	40199

102	8/09	Ches	7f122y	H	G-F	£24924
101	6/09	Leic	7f9y		G-F	£12462
92	4/09	Bath	5f161y	(0-85)H	G-F	£5180
91	7/08	NmkJ	6f	(0-95)H	G-F	£9346
86	5/08	Kemp	6f	(0-85)H	STD	£4209
85	11/07	Wolv	5f216y	(0-80)H	STD	£4728
81	10/07	Wolv	5f216y	(0-75)H	STD	£3238
76	9/07	Wolv	5f216y	(0-75)H	STD	£3071
73	4/07	Wolv	7f32y	(0-60)H	SF	£2388
66	2/07	Wolv	7f32y	(0-58)H	STD	£1706
63	11/06	Ling	6f		STD	£2590
53	7/06	Bath	5f11y		FRM	£2331
55	9/05	Wolv	5f216y	(0-45)	STD	£1487

Total win prize-money £77667

Going (Turf): Sf: 0-1 GS: 0-3 Gd: 0-15 GF: 4-23 Fm: 1-4
Distance: 5f/6f: 9-50 7f-8f: 4-43 9f-13f: 0-2 14f+: 0-0
Track : LH: 10-57 RH: 1-11 Tight: 8-46 Gall: 2-9
Aids: Bl: 0-0 Vi: 1-5 Tstrap: 1-5 Ckp: 1-5
Best Rating: 102 8/09 Ches 7f122y gd-fm

Very useful; Listed placed; effective from 5f-7f; acts on fast ground and on Polytrack; likes to race prominently.

Cardenio (USA)

85(86) (31)48
3-y-o b/br f Proud Citizen (USA)-Divine Diva (USA) (Theatrical)
J R Gask For Sale

Placings:00000 (6771)
2009: 6^{0}GF, 6^{0}GF, 6^{0}GF, 7^{0}SD, 8^{0}SD,

	Starts	1st	2nd	3rd	Win & Pl
Career Total (Turf)	3	0	0	0	
Career Total (AW)	2	0	0	0	

Going (Turf): Sf: 0-0 GS: 0-0 Gd: 0-0 GF: 0-3 Fm: 0-0
Distance: 5f/6f: 0-2 7f-8f: 0-3 9f-13f: 0-0 14f+: 0-0
Track : LH: 0-1 RH: 0-1 Tight: 0-1 Gall: 0-0
Aids: Bl: 0-0 Vi: 0-0 Tstrap: 0-0 Ckp: 0-0
Best Rating: 48 7/09 Newb 6f8y gd-fm

Cardinal

100(98) (57)62
4-y-o ch c Pivotal-Fictitious (Machiavellian (USA))
R A Harris Mrs Ruth M Serrell

Placings:00524500 (7370)
2009: 8^{0}SD, 6^{0}GF, 6^{5}GF, 6^{2}S, 7^{4}GS, 6^{5}GS, 7^{0}G, 5^{0}SD,

	Starts	1st	2nd	3rd	Win & Pl
Career Total (Turf)	6	0	1	0	1156
Career Total (AW)	2	0	0	0	

Going (Turf): Sf: 0-1 GS: 0-2 Gd: 0-1 GF: 0-2 Fm: 0-0
Distance: 5f/6f: 0-4 7f-8f: 0-4 9f-13f: 0-0 14f+: 0-0

Track : LH: 0-2 RH: 0-0 Tight: 0-2 Gall: 0-0
Aids: Bl: 0-0 Vi: 0-0 Tstrap: 0-0 Ckp: 0-0
Best Rating: 62 7/09 Ripn 6f soft

Cardinal James (IRE)

(90) (51)
5-y-o br g Bishop Of Cashel-Dilwara (IRE) (Lashkari)
Miss Tor Sturgis James Roberts

Placings:5 (0670)
2009: 11^{5}SD,

	Starts	1st	2nd	3rd	Win & Pl
Career Total (Turf)	0	0	0	0	
Career Total (AW)	1	0	0	0	0

Going (Turf): Sf: 0-0 GS: 0-0 Gd: 0-0 GF: 0-0 Fm: 0-0
Distance: 5f/6f: 0-0 7f-8f: 0-0 9f-13f: 0-1 14f+: 0-0
Track : LH: 0-0 RH: 0-1 Tight: 0-0 Gall: 0-0
Aids: Bl: 0-0 Vi: 0-0 Tstrap: 0-0 Ckp: 0-0
Best Rating: 51 2/09 Kemp 1m3f stand

Cardossi

83 40
2-y-o ch f Dr Fong (USA)-English Harbour (Sabrehill (USA))
M L W Bell W J Gredley

Placings:0 (6921)
2009: 8^{0}GF,

	Starts	1st	2nd	3rd	Win & Pl
Career Total (Turf)	1	0	0	0	

Going (Turf): Sf: 0-0 GS: 0-0 Gd: 0-0 GF: 0-1 Fm: 0-0
Distance: 5f/6f: 0-0 7f-8f: 0-0 9f-13f: 0-1 14f+: 0-0
Track : LH: 0-0 RH: 0-0 Tight: 0-0 Gall: 0-0
Aids: Bl: 0-0 Vi: 0-0 Tstrap: 0-0 Ckp: 0-0
Best Rating: 40 10/09 Yarm 1m3y gd-fm

Cariad Coch

77(80) (37)33
2-y-o b f Reset (AUS)-Silly Mid-On (Midyan (USA))
Mrs L Stubbs Mrs L J Williams

Placings:50000 (6343)
2009: 5^{5}GF, 5^{0}SD, 6^{0}HY, 5^{0}SF, 5^{0}SD,

	Starts	1st	2nd	3rd	Win & Pl
Career Total (Turf)	2	0	0	0	0
Career Total (AW)	3	0	0	0	

Going (Turf): Sf: 0-1 GS: 0-0 Gd: 0-0 GF: 0-1 Fm: 0-0
Distance: 5f/6f: 0-5 7f-8f: 0-0 9f-13f: 0-0 14f+: 0-0
Track : LH: 0-2 RH: 0-0 Tight: 0-2 Gall: 0-0
Aids: Bl: 0-0 Vi: 0-0 Tstrap: 0-0 Ckp: 0-0
Best Rating: 37 8/09 Wolv 5f20y std-fst

Caribbean Coral

99(99) (73)87
10-y-o ch g Brief Truce (USA)-Caribbean Star (Soviet Star (USA))
A B Haynes T Hosier

Placings:01540/2024306/016000012/02110030440/00000000/06033142066100/01330300000/2045610500-34002243311202436 (6341)

2009: 5^{3}SD, 5^{4}SD, 5^{0}SD, 6^{0}G, 5^{2}GF, 6^{2}G, 5^{4}GF, 6^{3}GF, 6^{3}GF, 5^{1}F, 5^{1}GF, 6^{2}GF, 5^{0}F, 5^{2}F, 5^{4}F, 5^{3}G, 5^{6}GF,

	Starts	1st	2nd	3rd	Win & Pl
Career Total (Turf)	88	11	10	10	159001
Career Total (AW)	4	0	0	1	385

68	6/09	Brig	5f213y		G-F	£1942
70	6/09	Bath	5f161y		FRM	£1942
78	6/08	Ripn	6f		SFT	£2914
96	5/07	Ches	5f16y	(0-100)H	GD	£13248
95	9/06	Ches	5f16y	(0-85)H	G-F	£5829
91	7/06	Wwck	5f110y	(0-85)H	G-F	£5297
106	6/04	Newc	5f	B(0-105)H	SFT	£17400
100	6/04	Epsm	5f	B(0-105)H	G-F	£43500
95	10/03	Newc	5f	D(0-85)H	GD	£3080
92	6/03	Sand	5f6y	D(0-85)H	G-F	£5752
79	7/01	Brig	5f213y E		FRM	£2919

Total win prize-money £103827

Going (Turf): Sf: 2-9 GS: 0-10Gd: 2-24 **GF: 5-36** Fm: 2-9
Distance: **5f/6f: 11-89** 7f-8f: 0-3 9f-13f: 0-0 14f+: 0-0
Track : **LH: 6-23** RH: 0-1 **Tight: 2-9** Gall: 1-8
Aids: Bl: 0-0 Vi: 1-5 Tstrap: 1-7 Ckp: 1-7
Best Rating: **106** 6/04 Newc 5f soft

Modest; effective over 5f-6f; acts on most types of ground; usually held up; has worn cheekpieces and visor.

Caribou Island

87 **62**

2-y-o b c Dansili-Lake Nipigon (Selkirk (USA))
Saeed Bin Suroor Godolphin

Placings:5 **(4638)**
2009: 6^{5}GF,

	Starts	1st	2nd	3rd	Win & Pl
Career Total (Turf)	1	0	0	0	150

Going (Turf): **Sf: 0-0 GS: 0-0 Gd: 0-0 GF: 0-1 Fm: 0-0**
Distance: 5f/6f: 0-0 7f-8f: 0-1 9f-13f: 0-0 14f+: 0-0
Track : LH: 0-1 RH: 0-0 Tight: 0-0 Gall: 0-0
Aids: Bl: 0-0 Vi: 0-0 Tstrap: 0-0 Ckp: 0-0
Best Rating: **62** 8/09 Brig 6f209y gd-fm

Carioca (IRE)

91 **71**

2-y-o br f Rakti-Cidaris (IRE) (Persian Bold)
M Botti The Great Partnership

Placings:46 **(4792)**
2009: 7^{4}GS, 7^{6}G,

	Starts	1st	2nd	3rd	Win & Pl
Career Total (Turf)	2	0	0	0	0

Going (Turf): **Sf: 0-0 GS: 0-1 Gd: 0-1 GF: 0-0 Fm: 0-0**
Distance: 5f/6f: 0-0 7f-8f: 0-2 9f-13f: 0-0 14f+: 0-0
Track : LH: 0-0 RH: 0-0 Tight: 0-0 Gall: 0-0
Aids: Bl: 0-0 Vi: 0-0 Tstrap: 0-0 Ckp: 0-0
Best Rating: **71** 7/09 Donc 7f gd-sft

Carlcol Girl

82(64) (9)**45**

2-y-o b f Where Or When (IRE)-Capstick (JPN) (Machiavellian (USA))
Mrs C A Dunnett M M Foulger

Placings:000500 **(7097)**
2009: 7^{0}G, 7^{0}G, 7^{0}SD, 8^{5}GF, 8^{0}GS, 7^{0}G,

	Starts	1st	2nd	3rd	Win & Pl
Career Total (Turf)	5	0	0	0	188
Career Total (AW)	1	0	0	0	

Going (Turf): **Sf: 0-0 GS: 0-1 Gd: 0-3 GF: 0-1 Fm: 0-0**
Distance: 5f/6f: 0-0 7f-8f: 0-4 9f-13f: 0-2 14f+: 0-0
Track : LH: 0-1 RH: 0-1 Tight: 0-2 Gall: 0-0
Aids: Bl: 0-0 Vi: 0-3 Tstrap: 0-1 Ckp: 0-1
Best Rating: **45** 9/09 Yarm 1m3y gd-fm

Carlesimo (IRE)

61(76) (30)**83**

11-y-o b/br g Erins Isle-Diamond Display (IRE) (Shardari)
Noel Meade Hollyville Syndicate

Placings:006/6612225/64/04200/1/11/150/511-00 **(7578)**
2009: 12^{0}S, 13^{0}SF,

	Starts	1st	2nd	3rd	Win & Pl
Career Total (Turf)	27	7	4	0	50355
Career Total (AW)	1	0	0	0	

64	7/08	Wxfd	1m5f		G-F	£4318
57	7/08	Wxfd	1m5f		GD	£4318
86	6/06	Lcop	2m	(60-90)H	GD	£7148
81	7/05	Gway	2m	(50-80)H	G-F	£7596
74	6/05	Bell	1m6f	(50-80)H	GD	£6615
74	6/04	Gowr	1m4f	(60-90)H	G-F	£7299
74	5/01	Gowr	1m1f100y	(0-85)H	GD	£5008

Total win prize-money £42305

Going (Turf): Sf: 0-4 GS: 0-0 **Gd: 4-6** GF: 3-9 Fm: 0-1
Distance: 5f/6f: 0-1 7f-8f: 0-3 **9f-13f: 4-14** 14f+: 3-9
Track : LH: 2-10 **RH: 4-8** Tight: 0-1 Gall: 0-0
Aids: Bl: 0-1 Vi: 0-0 Tstrap: 0-0 Ckp: 0-0
Best Rating: **88** 6/06 Gowr 2m gd-fm

Carleton

101(101) (80)**96**

4-y-o b g Hunting Lion (IRE)-Canadian Capers (Ballacashtal (CAN))
W J Musson The Square Table

Placings:1016005040360/0020000030-506443 **(3928)**
2009: 6^{5}GS, 6^{0}GS, 6^{6}GF, 6^{4}GF, 7^{4}SD, 7^{3}SF,

	Starts	1st	2nd	3rd	Win & Pl
Career Total (Turf)	27	2	1	2	23618
Career Total (AW)	2	0	0	1	1465

92	6/07	Bath	5f11y	G-S	£4533
78	5/07	Wind	5f10y	G-S	£4533

Total win prize-money £9068

Going (Turf): Sf: 0-2 **GS: 2-10** Gd: 0-6 GF: 0-8 Fm: 0-1
Distance: **5f/6f: 2-21** 7f-8f: 0-8 9f-13f: 0-0 14f+: 0-0
Track : **LH: 1-4** RH: 0-1 Tight: 0-3 **Gall: 2-5**
Aids: Bl: 0-0 Vi: 0-0 Tstrap: 0-0 Ckp: 0-0
Best Rating: **97** 9/07 Ayr 5f soft

Useful; Listed placed at two; effective over 5f-7f; acts on most ground, but probably best on an easy surface.

Carlitos Spirit (IRE)

103(105) (81)**87**

5-y-o ch g Redback-Negria (IRE) (Al Hareb (USA))
B R Millman Karmaa Racing Limited

Placings:456054/025204415/55211201060-50053105650 **(6212)**
2009: 7^{5}SD, 7^{0}GF, 8^{0}G, 7^{5}GF, 7^{3}GF, 7^{1}GF, 8^{0}GS, 7^{5}GF, 8^{6}SD, 8^{5}SD, 7^{0}SD,

	Starts	1st	2nd	3rd	Win & Pl
Career Total (Turf)	25	4	3	1	19574
Career Total (AW)	12	1	1	0	3939

84	6/09	Ling	7f140y	(0-75)H	G-F	£3070
87	8/08	NmkJ	1m	(0-80)H	G-F	£6476
82	5/08	Ling	7f	(0-75)H	G-F	£3123
78	4/08	Nott	1m54y	(0-65)H	SFT	£1942
69	12/07	Kemp	1m	(0-58)H	STD	£2047

Total win prize-money £16661

Going (Turf): Sf: 1-4 GS: 0-5 Gd: 0-5 **GF: 3-9** Fm: 0-2
Distance: 5f/6f: 0-4 **7f-8f: 4-26** 9f-13f: 1-7 14f+: 0-0
Track : LH: 1-6 RH: 1-16 Tight: 0-4 Gall: 0-2
Aids: Bl: 0-1 Vi: 0-0 Tstrap: 0-0 Ckp: 0-0
Best Rating: **87** 8/08 NmkJ 1m gd-fm

Useful; effective over 7f-1m; acts on good/fast ground and Polytrack.

Carlton Mac

93(98) (44)**58**

4-y-o ch g Timeless Times (USA)-Julie's Gift (Presidium)
N Bycroft S D Rose

Placings:00060000/000003630-01006 **(6177)**
2009: 12^{0}GS, 15^{1}G, 12^{0}G, 15^{0}S, 12^{6}GF,

	Starts	1st	2nd	3rd	Win & Pl
Career Total (Turf)	22	1	0	2	2769
Career Total (AW)	1	0	0	0	

46	8/09	Catt	1m7f177y	GD	£2047

Total win prize-money £2047

Going (Turf): Sf: 0-3 GS: 0-4 **Gd: 1-8** GF: 0-6 Fm: 0-1
Distance: 5f/6f: 0-5 7f-8f: 0-7 9f-13f: 0-8 **14f+: 1-3**
Track : **LH: 1-9** RH: 0-5 **Tight: 1-10** Gall: 0-1
Aids: Bl: 0-5 Vi: 0-1 Tstrap: 1-5 Ckp: 1-5
Best Rating: **58** 11/08 Catt 1m3f214y heavy

Carlton Scroop (FR)

(105) (67)**64**

6-y-o ch g Priolo (USA)-Elms Schooldays (Emarati (USA))
J Jay David Fremel

Placings:000/1324/162640440/4054-1322U1 **(0871)**
2009: 11^{1}SD, 16^{3}SD, 12^{2}SD, 16^{2}SD, 12^{U}SD, 12^{1}SD,

	Starts	1st	2nd	3rd	Win & Pl
Career Total (Turf)	6	0	0	1	908
Career Total (AW)	20	4	4	1	12051

67	3/09	Ling	1m4f	(0-60)H	STD	£2047
55	1/09	Kemp	1m3f	(0-52)H	STD	£1706
69	3/07	Wolv	1m4f50y	(0-60)H	SF	£2730
51	4/06	Kemp	1m2f	(0-45)	STD	£2388

Total win prize-money £8872

Going (Turf): **Sf: 0-1 GS: 0-1 Gd: 0-3 GF: 0-1 Fm: 0-0**
Distance: 5f/6f: 0-0 7f-8f: 0-2 **9f-13f: 4-17** 14f+: 0-7
Track : LH: 2-18 RH: 2-8 **Tight: 2-17** Gall: 0-1
Aids: **Bl: 4-21** Vi: 0-0 Tstrap: 0-0 Ckp: 0-0
Best Rating: **69** 3/07 Wolv 1m4f50y std-fst

Moderate; effective at around 1m4f and stays 2m; acts on Polytrack; has worn blinkers.

Carmela Maria

99(103) (68)**64**

4-y-o b f Medicean-Carmela Owen (Owington)
M E Sowersby (S C Williams 5/9) Mrs Janet Cooper & M E Sowersby

Placings:0/0062341-00235556226 **(6097)**
2009: 10^{0}G, 10^{0}SD, 12^{2}GF, 10^{3}GS, 10^{5}GF, 11^{5}F, 11^{5}S, 9^{6}GF, 10^{2}GF, 12^{2}SD, 13^{6}GF,

	Starts	1st	2nd	3rd	Win & Pl
Career Total (Turf)	15	0	3	1	2546
Career Total (AW)	4	1	1	1	4134

68 9/08 GrLe 1m2f (0-60)H STD £3043
Total win prize-money £3044

Going (Turf): **Sf: 0-2 GS: 0-3 Gd: 0-2 GF: 0-7 Fm: 0-1**
Distance: 5f/6f: 0-0 7f-8f: 0-4 **9f-13f: 1-14** 14f+: 0-1
Track : **LH: 1-10** RH: 0-5 Tight: 0-10 **Gall: 1-2**
Aids: Bl: 0-0 Vi: 0-0 Tstrap: 0-3 Ckp: 0-3
Best Rating: **68** 9/08 GrLe 1m2f stand

Moderate; stays 1m4f; acts on fast ground and Polytrack; has worn cheekpieces.

Carmenero (GER)

100(101) (78)80

6-y-o b g Barathea (IRE)-Claire Fraser (USA) (Gone West (USA))
C R Dore (W R Muir 7/8) Andrew Page

Placings:40244051245/20520605602**6**/300**16**00**3**44**0**6**352**/2406**504235254-644510046500** (7735)
2009: 7⁶SD, 6⁴G, 7⁴SD, 7⁵G, 5¹GS, 7⁰SD, 7⁰GF, 7⁴SD, 6⁶SS, 6⁵GS, 7⁰SD, 5⁰SD,

	Starts	1st	2nd	3rd	Win & Pl
Career Total (Turf)	32	2	4	1	14102
Career Total (AW)	31	1	5	3	11563

56 8/09 Brig 5f213y G-S £1942
81 6/07 Ling 1m (0-75)H STD £2914
74 8/05 Bath 5f11y FRM £2884
Total win prize-money £7742

Going (Turf): Sf: 0-1 **GS: 1-3** Gd: 0-11 GF: 0-13 **Fm: 1-4**
Distance: **5f/6f: 2-16** 7f-8f: 1-43 9f-13f: 0-4 14f+: 0-0
Track : **LH: 3-38** RH: 0-13 Tight: 1-27 Gall: 1-5
Aids: Bl: 0-0 Vi: 0-0 Tstrap: 1-2 Ckp: 1-2
Best Rating: **83** 6/06 NmkJ 7f gd-fm

Fair; effective over 7f-1m; acts on good and faster ground; goes on Polytrack.

Carnaby Street (IRE)

105 102

2-y-o b c Le Vie Dei Colori-Prodigal Daughter (Alhaarth (IRE))
R Hannon Noodles Racing

Placings:0202011 (7030)
2009: 6⁰GF, 6²G, 6⁰GF, 6²GF, 6⁰GF, 6¹GS, 7¹S,

	Starts	1st	2nd	3rd	Win & Pl
Career Total (Turf)	7	2	2	0	101337

102 10/09 Newb 7f SFT £28385
88 10/09 Gdwd 6f G-S £3238
Total win prize-money £31623

Going (Turf): **Sf: 1-1 GS: 1-1** Gd: 0-1 GF: 0-4 Fm: 0-0
Distance: 5f/6f: 1-4 7f-8f: 1-3 9f-13f: 0-0 14f+: 0-0
Track : LH: 0-0 RH: 0-0 Tight: 0-0 Gall: 0-1
Aids: Bl: 0-0 Vi: 0-0 Tstrap: 0-0 Ckp: 0-0
Best Rating: **102** 10/09 Newb 7f soft

Useful; suited by 6f; acts on quick ground.

Carnacki (USA)

(71) (24)

2-y-o b c Ghostzapper (USA)-Guana (FR) (Sillery (USA))
J Noseda Ballygallon Stud Limited

Placings:0 (5807)
2009: 7⁰SD,

	Starts	1st	2nd	3rd	Win & Pl
Career Total (Turf)	0	0	0	0	
Career Total (AW)	1	0	0	0	

Going (Turf): **Sf: 0-0 GS: 0-0 Gd: 0-0 GF: 0-0 Fm: 0-0**
Distance: 5f/6f: 0-0 7f-8f: 0-1 9f-13f: 0-0 14f+: 0-0
Track : LH: 0-0 RH: 0-1 Tight: 0-0 Gall: 0-0
Aids: Bl: 0-0 Vi: 0-0 Tstrap: 0-0 Ckp: 0-0
Best Rating: **24** 9/09 Kemp 7f stand

Carnaval Court (IRE)

92(98) (57)60

2-y-o b f Saffron Walden (FR)-Bellagio Princess (Kris)
A M Balding G W Chong

Placings:040002 (6721)
2009: 6⁰G, 6⁴G, 8⁰G, 8⁰SD, 7⁰GF, 8²SD,

	Starts	1st	2nd	3rd	Win & Pl
Career Total (Turf)	4	0	0	0	202
Career Total (AW)	2	0	1	0	771

Going (Turf): **Sf: 0-0 GS: 0-0 Gd: 0-3 GF: 0-1 Fm: 0-0**
Distance: 5f/6f: 0-1 7f-8f: 0-4 9f-13f: 0-1 14f+: 0-0
Track : LH: 0-1 RH: 0-2 Tight: 0-0 Gall: 0-0
Aids: Bl: 0-1 Vi: 0-1 Tstrap: 0-0 Ckp: 0-0
Best Rating: **60** 8/09 Chep 6f16y good

Modest; effective over 1m; acts on Polytrack.

Carnival Dream

97(97) (58)56

4-y-o b f Carnival Dancer-Reach The Wind (USA) (Relaunch (USA))
H A McWilliams J D Riches

Placings:5442355**0**55/400-**00**0403042260**01**0 (7579)
2009: 7⁰SD, 8⁰SF, 7⁰F, 7⁴GF, 9⁰GF, 8³GF, 8⁰G, 8⁴GF, 7²GF, 6²HY, 7⁶GF, 7⁰GF, 8⁰SD, 5¹SD, 7⁰SF,

	Starts	1st	2nd	3rd	Win & Pl
Career Total (Turf)	20	0	3	2	3216
Career Total (AW)	8	1	0	0	2047

58 11/09 Wolv 5f216y (0-52)H STD £2047
Total win prize-money £2047

Going (Turf): **Sf: 0-2 GS: 0-2 Gd: 0-4 GF: 0-10 Fm: 0-2**
Distance: **5f/6f: 1-9** 7f-8f: 0-16 9f-13f: 0-3 14f+: 0-0
Track : **LH: 1-13** RH: 0-4 **Tight: 1-12** Gall: 0-0
Aids: Bl: 0-6 Vi: 0-0 Tstrap: 0-6 Ckp: 0-6
Best Rating: **65** 8/07 Rdcr 7f firm

Moderate; effective over 6f-7f; acts on most ground and on Polytrack; has worn blinkers.

Carnival Fair

80(54) 45

4-y-o b f Carnival Dancer-Testament (Darshaan)
S Wynne (R A Fahey 30/5) Carnival Racing Limited

Placings:050000 (7318)
2009: 8⁰GF, 12⁵GF, 12⁰GF, 8⁰GF, 11⁰G, 12⁰SD,

	Starts	1st	2nd	3rd	Win & Pl
Career Total (Turf)	5	0	0	0	0
Career Total (AW)	1	0	0	0	

Going (Turf): **Sf: 0-0 GS: 0-0 Gd: 0-1 GF: 0-4 Fm: 0-0**
Distance: 5f/6f: 0-0 7f-8f: 0-1 9f-13f: 0-5 14f+: 0-0
Track : LH: 0-2 RH: 0-2 Tight: 0-2 Gall: 0-1
Aids: Bl: 0-0 Vi: 0-1 Tstrap: 0-0 Ckp: 0-0
Best Rating: **45** 4/09 Muss 1m4f100y gd-fm

Carnival Time (IRE)

74 28

2-y-o ch g Captain Rio-Latest (IRE) (Bob Back (USA))
C G Cox The Revellers

Placings:00 (4933)
2009: 6⁰GF, 6⁰G,

	Starts	1st	2nd	3rd	Win & Pl
Career Total (Turf)	2	0	0	0	

Going (Turf): **Sf: 0-0 GS: 0-0 Gd: 0-1 GF: 0-1 Fm: 0-0**
Distance: 5f/6f: 0-1 7f-8f: 0-1 9f-13f: 0-0 14f+: 0-0
Track : LH: 0-0 RH: 0-0 Tight: 0-0 Gall: 0-1
Aids: Bl: 0-1 Vi: 0-0 Tstrap: 0-0 Ckp: 0-0
Best Rating: **28** 7/09 Wind 6f gd-fm

Carnivore

97(105) (81)84

7-y-o ch g Zafonic (USA)-Ermine (IRE) (Cadeaux Genereux)
T D Barron The Meat Eaters

Placings:2/0025/1312261/6010**365**/306**01**-**016**200**165** (7833)
2009: 7⁰SD, 8¹SD, 7⁶SD, 7²GS, 7⁰GF, 7⁰G, 7¹GF, 7⁶SD, 7⁵SD,

	Starts	1st	2nd	3rd	Win & Pl
Career Total (Turf)	22	5	5	2	32090
Career Total (AW)	11	2	0	1	6939

83 9/09 Rdcr 7f (0-70)H G-F £2590
78 2/09 Wolv 1m141y STD £2978
81 12/08 Wolv 7f32y (0-75)H STD £3238
85 6/07 Muss 7f30y (0-85)H G-S £5505
81 9/06 Newb 7f (0-85)H GD £6477
74 8/06 Newc 7f (0-75)H G-F £5181
68 6/06 Muss 7f30y (0-55)H FRM £2730
Total win prize-money £28701

Going (Turf): Sf: 0-1 GS: 1-4 Gd: 1-6 **GF: 2-7** Fm: 1-4
Distance: 5f/6f: 0-5 **7f-8f: 6-27** 9f-13f: 1-1 14f+: 0-0
Track : LH: 2-10 RH: 2-10 **Tight: 4-11** Gall: 0-1
Aids: Bl: 0-0 Vi: 0-0 Tstrap: 0-0 Ckp: 0-0
Best Rating: **86** 10/07 Ling 7f stand

Fair; effective over 7f-1m; acts on fast ground; goes on Polytrack; has worn tongue tie.

Carole Os (IRE)

(79) (27)39

4-y-o b f Catcher In The Rye (IRE)-Kuda Chantik (IRE) (Lashkari)
S W Hall J Howard, J Goddard, Mrs M Silcock

Placings:00/00-0 (0725)
2009: 8⁰SD,

	Starts	1st	2nd	3rd	Win & Pl
Career Total (Turf)	3	0	0	0	
Career Total (AW)	2	0	0	0	

Going (Turf): **Sf: 0-1 GS: 0-0 Gd: 0-0 GF: 0-1 Fm: 0-1**
Distance: 5f/6f: 0-2 7f-8f: 0-2 9f-13f: 0-1 14f+: 0-0
Track : LH: 0-5 RH: 0-0 Tight: 0-3 Gall: 0-0
Aids: Bl: 0-0 Vi: 0-0 Tstrap: 0-0 Ckp: 0-0
Best Rating: **64** 9/07 Wwck 6f gd-fm

Carpe Diem

99(90) (48)**59**

4-y-o b g Stravinsky (USA)-Spare That Tree (AUS) (Woodman (USA))

R A Fahey Mrs V Fahey

Placings:66005-40230**6**0400 **(5982)**

2009: 8^{4}GF, 8^{0}GF, 7^{2}F, 7^{3}GF, 8^{0}GF, 8^{6}SD, 7^{0}G, 8^{4}G, 9^{0}G, 8^{0}GF,

	Starts	1st	2nd	3rd	Win & Pl
Career Total (Turf)	14	0	1	1	1907
Career Total (AW)	1	0	0	0	0

Going (Turf): **Sf: 0-1 GS: 0-0 Gd: 0-4 GF: 0-8 Fm: 0-1**
Distance: 5f/6f: 0-1 7f-8f: 0-10 9f-13f: 0-4 14f+: 0-0
Track : LH: 0-4 RH: 0-9 Tight: 0-4 Gall: 0-0
Aids: Bl: 0-0 Vi: 0-5 Tstrap: 0-1 Ckp: 0-1
Best Rating: **59** 6/09 Carl 7f200y gd-fm

Moderate; stays 1m2f; has worn a visor.

Carr Hall (IRE)

(98) (55)**58**

6-y-o b g Rossini (USA)-Pidgeon Bay (IRE) (Perugino (USA))

B G Powell (Mrs J L Le Brocq 28/11) Mrs J L Le Brocq

Placings:5020030/5504346/4031123/6564561**50445** **(7888)**

2009: 10^{6}G, 12^{5}G, 12^{6}F, 14^{4}GF, 12^{5}GS, 12^{6}GS, 12^{1}GF, 8^{5}F, 13^{0}SF, **12**^{4}SD, 13^{4}SD, **12**^{5}SD,

	Starts	1st	2nd	3rd	Win & Pl
Career Total (Turf)	28	3	2	3	8643
Career Total (AW)	5	0	0	1	353

8/09	LesL	1m4f	H	G-F	£1460
7/07	LesL	1m4f		GD	£2200
7/07	LesL	1m110y	H	GD	£1460

Total win prize-money £5120

Going (Turf): Sf: 0-2 GS: 0-4 **Gd: 2-13** GF: 1-7 Fm: 0-2
Distance: 5f/6f: 0-1 7f-8f: 0-8 **9f-13f: 3-21** 14f+: 0-3
Track : **LH: 3-21** RH: 0-5 Tight: 0-7 Gall: 0-0
Aids: Bl: 0-1 Vi: 0-0 Tstrap: 0-1 Ckp: 0-1
Best Rating: **63** 9/07 Wolv 1m4f50y stand

Moderate; stays 1m4f; acts on good ground and on Polytrack.

Carragold

95(96) (56)**58**

3-y-o b c Diktat-Shadow Roll (IRE) (Mark Of Esteem (IRE))

M Brittain Mel Brittain

Placings:4635**250** **(7732)**

2009: 6^{4}GF, 6^{6}GS, 7^{3}GF, 8^{5}GF, 8^{2}GF, 9^{5}SD, 12^{0}SD,

	Starts	1st	2nd	3rd	Win & Pl
Career Total (Turf)	5	0	1	1	1132
Career Total (AW)	2	0	0	0	0

Going (Turf): **Sf: 0-0 GS: 0-1 Gd: 0-0 GF: 0-4 Fm: 0-0**
Distance: 5f/6f: 0-2 7f-8f: 0-1 9f-13f: 0-4 14f+: 0-0
Track : LH: 0-2 RH: 0-2 Tight: 0-2 Gall: 0-0
Aids: Bl: 0-0 Vi: 0-0 Tstrap: 0-0 Ckp: 0-0
Best Rating: **58** 9/09 Bevl 1m100y gd-fm

Modest; stays at least a mile.

Carrazara (IRE)

79(79) (40)**29**

3-y-o b f Namid-Carrozzina (Vettori (IRE))

Edgar Byrne Mayne-Hamilton

Placings:60000 **(3174)**

2009: 10^{6}SD, 10^{0}GS, 8^{0}GF, 5^{0}G, 7^{0}GF,

	Starts	1st	2nd	3rd	Win & Pl
Career Total (Turf)	4	0	0	0	
Career Total (AW)	1	0	0	0	0

Going (Turf): **Sf: 0-0 GS: 0-1 Gd: 0-1 GF: 0-2 Fm: 0-0**
Distance: 5f/6f: 0-1 7f-8f: 0-1 9f-13f: 0-3 14f+: 0-0
Track : LH: 0-3 RH: 0-0 Tight: 0-1 Gall: 0-1
Aids: Bl: 0-1 Vi: 0-0 Tstrap: 0-0 Ckp: 0-0
Best Rating: **40** 2/09 Ling 1m2f stand

Carries Lass

85 **42**

2-y-o br f Auction House (USA)-Carranita (IRE) (Anita's Prince)

J A Osborne D J P Turner

Placings:0660 **(3626)**

2009: 5^{0}GF, 5^{6}F, 6^{6}GF, 5^{0}G,

	Starts	1st	2nd	3rd	Win & Pl
Career Total (Turf)	4	0	0	0	0

Going (Turf): **Sf: 0-0 GS: 0-0 Gd: 0-1 GF: 0-2 Fm: 0-1**
Distance: 5f/6f: 0-4 7f-8f: 0-0 9f-13f: 0-0 14f+: 0-0
Track : LH: 0-1 RH: 0-0 Tight: 0-0 Gall: 0-2
Aids: Bl: 0-2 Vi: 0-0 Tstrap: 0-0 Ckp: 0-0
Best Rating: **42** 6/09 Wind 6f gd-fm

Carry On Cleo

(92) (60)**56**

4-y-o ch f First Trump-Classy Cleo (IRE) (Mujadil (USA))

A Berry Alan Berry

Placings:3000**0633601310/04450**3160140044050-**0006** **(0581)**

2009: 9^{0}SD, 9^{0}SD, 9^{0}SD, 9^{6}SD,

	Starts	1st	2nd	3rd	Win & Pl
Career Total (Turf)	14	1	0	2	3964
Career Total (AW)	22	3	0	3	8169

56	7/08	Ripn	1m1f170y	HVY	£2729
56	4/08	Wolv	1m141y	STD	£2047
60	12/07	Wolv	1m141y	STD	£2388
53	12/07	Wolv	1m141y	STD	£2730

Total win prize-money £9896

Going (Turf): **Sf: 1-4** GS: 0-4 Gd: 0-3 GF: 0-3 Fm: 0-0
Distance: 5f/6f: 0-5 7f-8f: 0-6 **9f-13f: 4-25** 14f+: 0-0
Track : **LH: 3-24** RH: 1-9 **Tight: 4-25** Gall: 0-1
Aids: Bl: 2-10 Vi: 2-16 Tstrap: 0-0 Ckp: 0-0
Best Rating: **60** 12/07 Wolv 1m141y stand

Moderate; effective at around 1m-1m2f; acts on easy ground; also goes on Polytrack; has worn a visor and blinkers.

Carsington

81 **40**

5-y-o ch m And Beyond (IRE)-Nutmeg Point (Nashwan (USA))

Lucinda Featherstone J Roundtree

Placings:0 **(2447)**

2009: 10^{0}GS,

	Starts	1st	2nd	3rd	Win & Pl
Career Total (Turf)	1	0	0	0	

Going (Turf): **Sf: 0-0 GS: 0-1 Gd: 0-0 GF: 0-0 Fm: 0-0**
Distance: 5f/6f: 0-0 7f-8f: 0-0 9f-13f: 0-1 14f+: 0-0
Track : LH: 0-1 RH: 0-0 Tight: 0-0 Gall: 0-0
Aids: Bl: 0-0 Vi: 0-0 Tstrap: 0-0 Ckp: 0-0
Best Rating: **40** 5/09 Hayd 1m2f95y gd-sft

Carson's Spirit (USA)

71 (73)**71**

5-y-o ch g Carson City (USA)-Pascarina (FR) (Exit To Nowhere (USA))

J R Gask (W S Kittow 17/1) K B Hodges

Placings:1006/540/5-0 **(3577)**

2009: 6^{0}GF,

	Starts	1st	2nd	3rd	Win & Pl
Career Total (Turf)	7	1	0	0	3923
Career Total (AW)	2	0	0	0	0

78	4/06	Bath	5f11y	G-S	£3562

Total win prize-money £3562

Going (Turf): Sf: 0-1 **GS: 1-2** Gd: 0-0 GF: 0-4 Fm: 0-0
Distance: **5f/6f: 1-2** 7f-8f: 0-4 9f-13f: 0-3 14f+: 0-0
Track : **LH: 1-3** RH: 0-1 Tight: 0-1 **Gall: 1-1**
Aids: Bl: 0-1 Vi: 0-0 Tstrap: 0-0 Ckp: 0-0
Best Rating: **81** 6/06 Asct 6f gd-fm

Carte D'Oro (IRE)

91 **59**

3-y-o b f Medaglia D'Oro (USA)-Prospectress (USA) (Mining (USA))

R M Beckett Five Horses Ltd

Placings:0-05504 **(5568)**

2009: 10^{0}GF, 10^{5}GF, 9^{5}GF, 9^{0}GF, 9^{4}F,

	Starts	1st	2nd	3rd	Win & Pl
Career Total (Turf)	6	0	0	0	144

Going (Turf): **Sf: 0-0 GS: 0-0 Gd: 0-1 GF: 0-4 Fm: 0-1**
Distance: 5f/6f: 0-0 7f-8f: 0-1 9f-13f: 0-5 14f+: 0-0
Track : LH: 0-3 RH: 0-2 Tight: 0-3 Gall: 0-1
Aids: Bl: 0-0 Vi: 0-0 Tstrap: 0-0 Ckp: 0-0
Best Rating: **59** 6/09 Newb 1m2f6y gd-fm

Carte Diamond (USA)

104(113) (103)**108**

8-y-o ch g Theatrical-Liteup My Life (USA) (Green Dancer (USA))

B Ellison Ashley Carr

Placings:11231/20/330R00200-630003 **(7091)**

2009: 12^{6}G, **16**^{3}SD, 18^{0}GF, 16^{0}S, 12^{0}G, **14**^{3}SD,

	Starts	1st	2nd	3rd	Win & Pl
Career Total (Turf)	20	3	3	3	120935
Career Total (AW)	2	0	0	2	2564

108	11/04	Donc	1m4f	(0-110)H	SFT	£35425
99	7/04	York	1m3f198y	B(0-100)H	G-S	£12910
91	6/04	Rdcr	1m3f	D	GD	£3513

Total win prize-money £51849

Going (Turf): **Sf: 1-6 GS: 1-3 Gd: 1-9** GF: 0-2 Fm: 0-0
Distance: 5f/6f: 0-0 7f-8f: 0-0 **9f-13f: 3-12** 14f+: 0-10
Track : **LH: 3-18** RH: 0-4 Tight: 1-6 **Gall: 2-12**
Aids: Bl: 0-1 Vi: 0-0 Tstrap: 0-0 Ckp: 0-0
Best Rating: **116** 8/05 York 1m5f197y good

Very useful; missed whole of 2006 and 2007 seasons due

to injury; stays 2m and acts on most ground; has worn a tongue tie; winning hurdler.

Carter

98(98) (62)63

3-y-o b g Reset (AUS)-Cameo Role (GER) (Acatenango (GER))

W M Brisbourne W M Clare

Placings:645-04105662 **(7049)**

2009: 8^{0}GF, 8^{4}G, 10^{1}GF, 10^{0}G, 10^{5}S, 11^{6}G, 10^{6}SD, 12^{2}SD,

	Starts	1st	2nd	3rd	Win & Pl
Career Total (Turf)	7	1	0	0	4216
Career Total (AW)	4	0	1	0	605

63 6/09 Ches 1m2f75y (0-70)H G-F £4047

Total win prize-money £4047

Going (Turf): Sf: 0-1 GS: 0-0 Gd: 0-3 **GF: 1-2** Fm: 0-1
Distance: 5f/6f: 0-0 7f-8f: 0-2 **9f-13f: 1-9** 14f+: 0-0
Track : **LH: 1-7** RH: 0-4 **Tight: 1-7** Gall: 0-0
Aids: Bl: 0-0 Vi: 0-0 Tstrap: 0-0 Ckp: 0-0
Best Rating: 63 6/09 Ches 1m2f75y gd-fm

Modest; stays 1m4f; acts on fast ground; goes on Polytrack.

Cartoon

86 79

3-y-o br f Danehill Dancer (IRE)-Elfin Laughter (Alzao (USA))

M A Jarvis Highclere Thoroughbred Racing-SunChariot

Placings:0-1 **(1406)**

2009: 8^{1}GF,

	Starts	1st	2nd	3rd	Win & Pl
Career Total (Turf)	2	1	0	0	2730

79 4/09 Wind 1m67y G-F £2729

Total win prize-money £2730

Going (Turf): Sf: 0-0 GS: 0-1 Gd: 0-0 **GF: 1-1** Fm: 0-0
Distance: 5f/6f: 0-0 7f-8f: 0-1 **9f-13f: 1-1** 14f+: 0-0
Track : LH: 0-0 **RH: 1-1 Tight: 1-1** Gall: 0-0
Aids: Bl: 0-0 Vi: 0-0 Tstrap: 0-0 Ckp: 0-0
Best Rating: 79 4/09 Wind 1m67y gd-fm

Useful; effective at 1m; acts on fast ground.

Cartoonist (IRE)

(73) (18)55

6-y-o ch g Fruits Of Love (USA)-Verusa (IRE) (Petorius)

M Mullineaux Miss E Cross

Placings:000/3000/0 **(0213)**

2009: 12^{0}SD,

	Starts	1st	2nd	3rd	Win & Pl
Career Total (Turf)	5	0	0	1	482
Career Total (AW)	3	0	0	0	

Going (Turf): Sf: 0-1 GS: 0-2 Gd: 0-2 GF: 0-0 Fm: 0-0
Distance: 5f/6f: 0-0 7f-8f: 0-0 9f-13f: 0-8 14f+: 0-0
Track : LH: 0-6 RH: 0-2 Tight: 0-4 Gall: 0-0
Aids: Bl: 0-0 Vi: 0-0 Tstrap: 0-1 Ckp: 0-1
Best Rating: 57 10/05 Bath 1m5y gd-sft

Carved Emerald

(94) (86)84

4-y-o b f Pivotal-Emerald Peace (IRE) (Green Desert (USA))

D R C Elsworth (R Gibson 13/4) Mike Watson

Placings:5210-056050 **(7026)**

2009: 7^{0}SD, 7^{5}SD, 8^{6}G, 7^{0}SD, 6^{5}SD, 6^{0}SD,

	Starts	1st	2nd	3rd	Win & Pl
Career Total (Turf)	3	0	0	0	0
Career Total (AW)	7	1	1	0	13897

84 8/08 Deau 6f110y STD £10662

Total win prize-money £10662

Going (Turf): Sf: 0-2 GS: 0-0 Gd: 0-1 GF: 0-0 Fm: 0-0
Distance: 5f/6f: 0-2 **7f-8f: 1-8** 9f-13f: 0-0 14f+: 0-0
Track : LH: 0-1 RH: 0-3 Tight: 0-0 Gall: 0-0
Aids: **Bl: 1-5** Vi: 0-0 Tstrap: 0-1 Ckp: 0-1
Best Rating: 86 3/09 Capa 7f stand

Casablanca Minx (IRE)

100(100) (61)56

6-y-o br m Desert Story (IRE)-Conspire (IRE) (Turtle Island (IRE))

A G Juckes (Miss Gay Kelleway 13/8) Whispering Winds

Placings:446361103040513OO/3111105005/00205504003 24106123403324403323б/544234045216306000225303OO 40-601000424556050 **(7750)**

2009: 8^{6}SD, 10^{0}SD, 12^{1}SD, 12^{0}SD, 12^{0}GF, 11^{0}GF, 9^{4}GF, 10^{2}G, 11^{4}G, 11^{5}GS, 12^{5}G, 9^{6}SD, 9^{0}SD, 12^{5}SD, 13^{0}SD,

	Starts	1st	2nd	3rd	Win & Pl
Career Total (Turf)	28	2	3	4	10395
Career Total (AW)	74	9	7	11	36601

58	2/09	Wolv	1m4f50y (0-52)H	STD	£1648
62	3/08	Wolv	1m1f103y (0-60)H	STD	£2047
66	8/07	Wolv	7f32y (0-60)H	STD	£2914
58	7/07	Wolv	1m141y (0-65)H	STD	£2388
78	2/06	Wolv	1m141y (0-85)H	STD	£5505
59	2/06	Ling	1m	STD	£3886
73	1/06	Wolv	1m141y	STD	£2730
64	1/06	Ling	1m (0-65)H	STD	£2388
60	11/05	Ling	7f	STD	£3575
59	6/05	Brig	5f213y	FRM	£2912
60	6/05	Folk	5f	G-F	£2912

Total win prize-money £32909

Going (Turf): Sf: 0-1 GS: 0-3 Gd: 0-8 **GF: 1-14 Fm: 1-2**
Distance: 5f/6f: 2-12 7f-8f: 4-17 **9f-13f: 5-72** 14f+: 0-1
Track : **LH: 10-84** RH: 0-7 **Tight: 9-76** Gall: 0-2
Aids: Bl: 0-24 **Vi: 4-48** Tstrap: 0-0 Ckp: 0-0
Best Rating: 78 2/06 Wolv 1m141y stand

Moderate; stays 1m4f; acts on fast ground; also goes on Polytrack; has worn blinkers and a visor.

Casanova Kid

87(81) (38)41

2-y-o b c Pastoral Pursuits-Dust (Green Desert (USA))

E J Creighton Mrs Mary Tobin

Placings:60600 **(7477)**

2009: 5^{6}G, 6^{0}SD, 6^{6}GF, 5^{0}G, 6^{0}SD,

	Starts	1st	2nd	3rd	Win & Pl
Career Total (Turf)	3	0	0	0	0
Career Total (AW)	2	0	0	0	

Going (Turf): Sf: 0-0 GS: 0-0 Gd: 0-2 GF: 0-1 Fm: 0-0
Distance: 5f/6f: 0-5 7f-8f: 0-0 9f-13f: 0-0 14f+: 0-0
Track : LH: 0-1 RH: 0-1 Tight: 0-1 Gall: 0-1
Aids: Bl: 0-0 Vi: 0-0 Tstrap: 0-0 Ckp: 0-0
Best Rating: 41 10/09 Wind 5f10y good

Cascata (IRE)

102(94) (73)88

3-y-o b f Montjeu (IRE)-Leaping Water (Sure Blade (USA))

L M Cumani S Stuckey

Placings:1-4624 **(6113)**

2009: 9^{4}SD, 9^{6}GF, 9^{2}GF, 12^{4}GF,

	Starts	1st	2nd	3rd	Win & Pl
Career Total (Turf)	3	0	1	0	2561
Career Total (AW)	2	1	0	0	4142

71 11/08 GrLe 1m STD £3925

Total win prize-money £3926

Going (Turf): Sf: 0-0 GS: 0-0 Gd: 0-0 GF: 0-3 Fm: 0-0
Distance: 5f/6f: 0-0 **7f-8f: 1-1** 9f-13f: 0-4 14f+: 0-0
Track : **LH: 1-2** RH: 0-3 Tight: 0-3 **Gall: 1-2**
Aids: Bl: 0-0 Vi: 0-0 Tstrap: 0-0 Ckp: 0-0
Best Rating: 88 8/09 Ripn 1m1f170y gd-fm

Fair; stays 1m1f and should stay further; acts on Polytrack; should improve.

Casewick Star

55

2-y-o ch f Reset (AUS)-Be My Tinker (Be My Chief (USA))

P W D'Arcy J Cleeve

Placings:0 **(4383)**

2009: 5^{0}G,

	Starts	1st	2nd	3rd	Win & Pl
Career Total (Turf)	1	0	0	0	

Going (Turf): Sf: 0-0 GS: 0-0 Gd: 0-1 GF: 0-0 Fm: 0-0
Distance: 5f/6f: 0-1 7f-8f: 0-0 9f-13f: 0-0 14f+: 0-0
Track : LH: 0-0 RH: 0-0 Tight: 0-0 Gall: 0-0
Aids: Bl: 0-0 Vi: 0-0 Tstrap: 0-0 Ckp: 0-0

Casey's Rebel (IRE)

78 32

2-y-o b f Antonius Pius (USA)-Agent Scully (IRE) (Simply Great (FR))

M G Quinlan John W Casey

Placings:400 **(5543)**

2009: 6^{4}HY, 7^{0}GS, 7^{0}GF,

	Starts	1st	2nd	3rd	Win & Pl
Career Total (Turf)	3	0	0	0	289

Going (Turf): Sf: 0-1 GS: 0-1 Gd: 0-0 GF: 0-1 Fm: 0-0
Distance: 5f/6f: 0-0 7f-8f: 0-3 9f-13f: 0-0 14f+: 0-0
Track : LH: 0-0 RH: 0-0 Tight: 0-0 Gall: 0-0
Aids: Bl: 0-0 Vi: 0-0 Tstrap: 0-0 Ckp: 0-0
Best Rating: 32 8/09 NmkJ 7f gd-sft

Cash In The Attic

91(96) (52)58

3-y-o b f Auction House (USA)-Aziz Presenting (IRE) (Charnwood Forest (IRE))

M R Channon M Channon

Placings:03350000-26044650 **(4425)**

2009: 8^{2}SD, 8^{6}SD, 8^{0}SD, 8^{4}SD, 7^{4}GF, 7^{6}F, 8^{5}F, 7^{0}S,

	Starts	1st	2nd	3rd	Win & Pl
Career Total (Turf)	9	0	0	2	934
Career Total (AW)	7	0	1	0	605

Going (Turf): Sf: 0-4 GS: 0-0 Gd: 0-0 GF: 0-3 Fm: 0-2

Distance: 5f/6f: 0-7 7f-8f: 0-8 9f-13f: 0-1 14f+: 0-0
Track : LH: 0-8 RH: 0-3 Tight: 0-5 Gall: 0-0
Aids: Bl: 0-0 Vi: 0-0 Tstrap: 0-0 Ckp: 0-0
Best Rating: 58 8/08 Sand 5f6y soft

Moderate; stays 1m; acts on fast and soft ground; goes on Polytrack.

Cash On (IRE)

81(103) (71)**28**
7-y-o ch g Spectrum (IRE)-Lady Lucre (IRE) (Last Tycoon)
Karen George Mrs Clare E Smith

Placings:00/664100/6/0/6300-5400 (2182)
2009: 12^{5}SD, 13^{4}SD, 16^{0}SD, 11^{0}G,

	Starts	1st	2nd	3rd	Win & Pl
Career Total (Turf)	6	0	0	0	333
Career Total (AW)	12	1	0	1	3422

70 9/05 Ling 1m4f STD £2940
Total win prize-money £2940

Going (Turf): **Sf: 0-1 GS: 0-1 Gd: 0-2 GF: 0-2 Fm: 0-0**
Distance: 5f/6f: 0-0 7f-8f: 0-2 **9f-13f: 1-13** 14f+: 0-3
Track : **LH: 1-14** RH: 0-3 **Tight: 1-13** Gall: 0-1
Aids: Bl: 0-0 Vi: 0-2 Tstrap: 0-8 Ckp: 0-8
Best Rating: 74 7/05 NmkJ 1m4f gd-fm

Modest; suffers from foot problems; stays 1m5f; acts on Polytrack.

Cash Queen Anna (IRE)

99 **79**
2-y-o b f Dr Fong (USA)-Cashel Queen (USA) (Kingmambo (USA))
B W Hills South Bank Thoroughbred Racing

Placings:32212 (6481)
2009: 6^{3}S, 7^{2}GF, 7^{2}G, 7^{1}GF, 7^{2}GF,

	Starts	1st	2nd	3rd	Win & Pl
Career Total (Turf)	5	1	3	1	13144

71 9/09 Rdcr 7f G-F £3885
Total win prize-money £3886

Going (Turf): Sf: 0-1 GS: 0-0 Gd: 0-1 **GF: 1-3** Fm: 0-0
Distance: 5f/6f: 0-0 **7f-8f: 1-5** 9f-13f: 0-0 14f+: 0-0
Track : LH: 0-1 RH: 0-0 Tight: 0-1 Gall: 0-0
Aids: Bl: 0-0 Vi: 0-0 Tstrap: 0-0 Ckp: 0-0
Best Rating: 79 10/09 NmkR 7f gd-fm

Fair filly; effective at 7f; goes well on fast ground.

Cashelgar (IRE)

109 **119**
3-y-o b c Anabaa (USA)-Tropical Barth (IRE) (Peintre Celebre (USA))
A De Royer-Dupre Sir Robert Ogden

Placings:22-124 (4367a)
2009: 10^{1}GS, 10^{2}GF, 10^{4}GS,

	Starts	1st	2nd	3rd	Win & Pl
Career Total (Turf)	5	1	3	0	59449

97 5/09 StCl 1m2f110y G-S £16505
Total win prize-money £16505

Going (Turf): Sf: 0-0 **GS: 1-3** Gd: 0-0 GF: 0-1 Fm: 0-0
Distance: 5f/6f: 0-0 7f-8f: 0-2 **9f-13f: 1-3** 14f+: 0-0
Track : **LH: 1-1** RH: 0-2 Tight: 0-0 Gall: 0-1
Aids: Bl: 0-0 Vi: 0-0 Tstrap: 0-0 Ckp: 0-0
Best Rating: 119 6/09 Asct 1m2f gd-fm

Group-class; stays 1m2f; acts on fast and easy ground.

Cashleen (USA)

92(76) (31)**67**
3-y-o ch f Lemon Drop Kid (USA)-Radu Cool (USA) (Carnivalay (USA))
K A Ryan L Rutherford Mrs R G Hillen Mrs J Ryan

Placings:10-000056 (4940)
2009: 9^{0}SD, 6^{0}GF, 8^{0}GF, 7^{0}GF, 6^{5}GF, 7^{6}GF,

	Starts	1st	2nd	3rd	Win & Pl
Career Total (Turf)	7	1	0	0	2914
Career Total (AW)	1	0	0	0	

67 9/08 Hayd 6f G-F £2914
Total win prize-money £2914

Going (Turf): Sf: 0-1 GS: 0-0 Gd: 0-0 **GF: 1-6** Fm: 0-0
Distance: **5f/6f: 1-2** 7f-8f: 0-4 9f-13f: 0-2 14f+: 0-0
Track : LH: 0-2 RH: 0-0 Tight: 0-1 Gall: 0-0
Aids: Bl: 0-1 Vi: 0-0 Tstrap: 0-2 Ckp: 0-2
Best Rating: 67 9/08 Hayd 6f gd-fm

Casilda (IRE)

108(105) (96)**101**
4-y-o b f Cape Cross (IRE)-Koniya (IRE) (Doyoun)
A M Balding Jon Haseler

Placings:511422-3206 (6093)
2009: 10^{3}SD, 9^{2}GF, 10^{0}GF, 10^{6}G,

	Starts	1st	2nd	3rd	Win & Pl
Career Total (Turf)	9	2	3	0	36293
Career Total (AW)	1	0	0	1	1156

83 6/08 Sals 1m1f198y (0-85)H G-F £6476
76 5/08 Gdwd 1m1f G-F £3238
Total win prize-money £9714

Going (Turf): Sf: 0-1 GS: 0-1 Gd: 0-2 **GF: 2-5** Fm: 0-0
Distance: 5f/6f: 0-0 7f-8f: 0-0 **9f-13f: 2-10** 14f+: 0-0
Track : LH: 0-3 **RH: 2-6 Tight: 2-6** Gall: 0-1
Aids: Bl: 0-0 Vi: 0-0 Tstrap: 0-0 Ckp: 0-0
Best Rating: 101 5/09 NmkR 1m1f gd-fm

Very useful; stays 1m4f but possibly best at 1m2f; acts on fast and soft ground and Polytrack.

Casino Night

104(88) (52)**80**
4-y-o ch f Night Shift (USA)-Come Fly With Me (Bluebird (USA))
F P Murtagh (R Johnson 25/6) Barry Robson

Placings:435610650/015334045201154510-502000403423144060 (6648)
2009: 11^{5}SD, 8^{0}SD, 8^{2}GF, 7^{0}GF, 8^{0}GF, 9^{0}G, 8^{4}G, 6^{0}GF, 9^{3}GF, 8^{4}GF, 9^{2}G, 11^{3}G, 9^{1}S, 9^{4}S, 9^{4}S, 8^{0}G, 12^{6}GF, 10^{0}G,

	Starts	1st	2nd	3rd	Win & Pl
Career Total (Turf)	40	6	3	4	29588
Career Total (AW)	5	0	0	1	578

80 8/09 Haml 1m1f36y (0-75)H SFT £3238
74 10/08 NmkR 1m (0-75)H G-S £6476
71 9/08 Haml 1m65y (0-60)H SFT £2266
64 8/08 Haml 1m65y (0-70)H SFT £3885
65 5/08 Bevl 7f100y (0-60)H GD £1683
62 8/07 Newc 7f GD £2266
Total win prize-money £19818

Going (Turf): **Sf: 3-7** GS: 1-2 Gd: 2-17 GF: 0-12 Fm: 0-2
Distance: 5f/6f: 0-0 7f-8f: 3-22 9f-13f: 3-23 14f+: 0-0
Track : LH: 0-15 **RH: 4-21 Tight: 3-21** Gall: 0-2
Aids: Bl: 0-0 Vi: 0-0 Tstrap: 0-2 Ckp: 0-2
Best Rating: 80 8/09 Ayr 1m1f20y soft

Fair; stays 1m2f; acts on good and softer ground and on Polytrack; likes to race prominently.

Cassidy K

86 **55**
2-y-o ch f Zafeen (FR)-Alizar (IRE) (Rahy (USA))
D W Thompson (J Howard Johnson 6/10) J Hamilton

Placings:3253300 (7218)
2009: 5^{3}GF, 6^{2}GS, 6^{5}GF, 6^{3}GF, 7^{3}GF, 7^{0}G, 7^{0}S,

	Starts	1st	2nd	3rd	Win & Pl
Career Total (Turf)	7	0	1	3	2620

Going (Turf): **Sf: 0-1 GS: 0-1 Gd: 0-1 GF: 0-4 Fm: 0-0**
Distance: 5f/6f: 0-4 7f-8f: 0-3 9f-13f: 0-0 14f+: 0-0
Track : LH: 0-2 RH: 0-1 Tight: 0-2 Gall: 0-0
Aids: Bl: 0-0 Vi: 0-0 Tstrap: 0-0 Ckp: 0-0
Best Rating: 55 5/09 Newc 6f gd-fm

Cassique Lady (IRE)

110 (85)**103**
4-y-o b f Langfuhr (CAN)-Palacoona (FR) (Last Tycoon)
Mrs L Wadham Mr And Mrs A E Pakenham

Placings:110-03120 (5796)
2009: 8^{0}G, 11^{3}G, 10^{1}GS, 14^{2}G, 14^{0}G,

	Starts	1st	2nd	3rd	Win & Pl
Career Total (Turf)	7	3	1	1	58969
Career Total (AW)	1	0	0	0	

102 6/09 Wwck 1m2f188y G-S £22708
89 7/08 Klny 1m3f GD £8129
79 6/08 Navn 1m2f FRM £6605
Total win prize-money £37442

Going (Turf): Sf: 0-0 **GS: 1-1 Gd: 1-5** GF: 0-0 **Fm: 1-1**
Distance: 5f/6f: 0-0 7f-8f: 0-1 **9f-13f: 3-5** 14f+: 0-2
Track : **LH: 3-6** RH: 0-2 Tight: 0-1 Gall: 0-1
Aids: Bl: 0-0 Vi: 0-0 Tstrap: 0-0 Ckp: 0-0
Best Rating: 103 5/09 Hayd 1m3f200y good

Listed class; effective over 1m2f-1m6f; acts on easy and fast ground.

Cast Of Stars (IRE)

93(97) (70)**68**
2-y-o b g Nayef (USA)-Scarpe Rosse (IRE) (Sadler's Wells (USA))
R M Beckett D P Barrie & M J Rees

Placings:052 (7683)
2009: 8^{0}G, 9^{5}GS, 10^{2}SD,

	Starts	1st	2nd	3rd	Win & Pl
Career Total (Turf)	2	0	0	0	0
Career Total (AW)	1	0	1	0	771

Going (Turf): **Sf: 0-0 GS: 0-1 Gd: 0-1 GF: 0-0 Fm: 0-0**
Distance: 5f/6f: 0-0 7f-8f: 0-0 9f-13f: 0-3 14f+: 0-0
Track : LH: 0-0 RH: 0-2 Tight: 0-1 Gall: 0-0
Aids: Bl: 0-0 Vi: 0-0 Tstrap: 0-0 Ckp: 0-0
Best Rating: 70 12/09 Kemp 1m2f stand

Fair; stays 1m2f; acts on Polytrack.

Castaneous (IRE)

96(103) (66)**51**
5-y-o b g Lahib (USA)-Witchy Native (IRE) (Be My Native (USA))
P J Rothwell Celtic Dragon Syndicate

Placings:03-10000 (3287a)
2009: 12^{1}SD, 12^{0}SD, 10^{0}GY, 12^{0}Y, 10^{0}GF,

	Starts	1st	2nd	3rd	Win & Pl
Career Total (Turf)	3	0	0	0	
Career Total (AW)	4	1	0	1	3133

66 1/09 Wolv 1m4f50y STD £2729
Total win prize-money £2730

Going (Turf): **Sf: 0-0 GS: 0-0 Gd: 0-0 GF: 0-1 Fm: 0-0**
Distance: 5f/6f: 0-0 7f-8f: 0-0 **9f-13f: 1-7** 14f+: 0-0
Track : **LH: 1-6** RH: 0-1 **Tight: 1-2** Gall: 0-0
Aids: **Bl: 1-3** Vi: 0-0 Tstrap: 0-1 Ckp: 0-1
Best Rating: **66** 1/09 Wolv 1m4f50y stand

Modest; stays 1m4f; acts on Polytrack.

Castano

98(101) (69)**74**
5-y-o br g Makbul-Royal Orchid (IRE) (Shalford (IRE))
B R Millman H G Gooding & Mrs A A Gooding

Placings:3220/52510004/0266134204046-33604041550 (7348)
2009: 6^{3}G, 6^{3}GF, 6^{6}GF, 6^{0}GF, 7^{4}SD, 5^{0}S, 6^{4}G, 5^{1}SD, 6^{5}GS, 7^{5}GF, 7^{0}SD,

	Starts	1st	2nd	3rd	Win & Pl
Career Total (Turf)	29	2	5	4	13313
Career Total (AW)	7	1	0	0	2730

61 9/09 Wolv 5f216y (0-55)H STD £2729
71 8/08 Sals 6f212y (0-70)H SFT £3238
74 6/07 Folk 5f SFT £2914
Total win prize-money £8883

Going (Turf): **Sf: 2-8** GS: 0-6 Gd: 0-5 GF: 0-8 Fm: 0-2
Distance: **5f/6f: 2-17** 7f-8f: 1-17 9f-13f: 0-2 14f+: 0-0
Track : **LH: 1-5** RH: 0-4 **Tight: 1-3** Gall: 0-2
Aids: Bl: 0-0 Vi: 0-1 Tstrap: 1-14 Ckp: 1-14
Best Rating: **74** 9/08 Leic 7f9y heavy

Moderate; effective over 5f-7f; acts on varying ground; has worn cheekpieces.

Castellina

96(97) (55)**96**
5-y-o ch m Medicean-Protectorate (Hector Protector (USA))
E J Creighton (P J Hobbs 5/5) Mrs Mary Tobin

Placings:4/31232115/1521-2000 (6668)
2009: 10^{2}GF, 10^{0}SD, 14^{0}GF, 9^{0}SD,

	Starts	1st	2nd	3rd	Win & Pl
Career Total (Turf)	14	4	4	2	47547
Career Total (AW)	3	1	0	0	7432

83 8/08 Deau 1m2f SFT £8088
82 4/08 StCl 1m2f110y HVY £9559
10/07 Bord 1m GD £8783
105 8/07 Deau 1m1f110y STD £7432
Total win prize-money £37917

Going (Turf): **Sf: 2-3** GS: 0-0 Gd: 1-3 GF: 0-2 Fm: 0-0
Distance: 5f/6f: 0-0 7f-8f: 1-4 **9f-13f: 4-12** 14f+: 0-1
Track : LH: 1-5 RH: 1-2 Tight: 0-3 Gall: 0-0
Aids: Bl: 0-0 Vi: 0-0 Tstrap: 0-0 Ckp: 0-0
Best Rating: **105** 8/07 Deau 1m1f110y stand

Fair; multiple winner in France; effective at around 1m2f; acts on fast and soft ground.

Caster Sugar (USA)

109(90) (56)**84**
3-y-o b f Cozzene (USA)-OnlyRoyale(IRE)(Caerleon (USA))
R Hannon Mrs James Wigan

Placings:452200-3045116211 (6420)
2009: 6^{3}G, 7^{0}GF, 7^{4}SD, 8^{5}G, 8^{1}GF, 8^{1}G, 9^{6}G, 10^{2}GF, 9^{1}F, 11^{1}GF,

	Starts	1st	2nd	3rd	Win & Pl
Career Total (Turf)	14	4	3	1	22022
Career Total (AW)	2	0	0	0	192

84 10/09 Gdwd 1m3f (0-80)H G-F £6476
79 9/09 Brig 1m1f209y (0-70)H FRM £3154
70 7/09 Epsm 1m114y (0-75)H GD £3238
69 7/09 Sals 1m (0-70)H G-F £4695
Total win prize-money £17563

Going (Turf): Sf: 0-0 GS: 0-1 Gd: 1-5 **GF: 2-7** Fm: 1-1
Distance: 5f/6f: 0-0 7f-8f: 1-7 **9f-13f: 3-9** 14f+: 0-0
Track : **LH: 2-3** RH: 1-6 **Tight: 2-4** Gall: 0-0
Aids: Bl: 0-0 Vi: 0-0 Tstrap: 0-0 Ckp: 0-0
Best Rating: **84** 10/09 Gdwd 1m3f gd-fm

Modest; stays 1m and acts on fast ground.

Casting Couch (IRE)

95(67) (48)**68**
3-y-o b f Royal Applause-Mcqueenie (IRE) (Danehill (USA))
B W Hills C Wright & The Hon Mrs J M Corbett

Placings:45-4030 (5789)
2009: 7^{4}GF, 6^{0}GF, 7^{3}G, 7^{0}G,

	Starts	1st	2nd	3rd	Win & Pl
Career Total (Turf)	5	0	0	1	1063
Career Total (AW)	1	0	0	0	0

Going (Turf): **Sf: 0-0 GS: 0-0 Gd: 0-3 GF: 0-2 Fm: 0-0**
Distance: 5f/6f: 0-1 7f-8f: 0-5 9f-13f: 0-0 14f+: 0-0
Track : LH: 0-1 RH: 0-1 Tight: 0-0 Gall: 0-1
Aids: Bl: 0-0 Vi: 0-0 Tstrap: 0-0 Ckp: 0-0
Best Rating: **68** 8/09 Chep 7f16y good

First foal of a sister to a Group 3 winner and half-sister to Champion Hurdle winner Alderbrook; some ability in maiden company.

Castle Myth (USA)

91(104) (67)**54**
3-y-o b/br g Johannesburg (USA)-Castlemania (CAN) (Bold Ruckus (USA))
B Ellison Locketts Legends

Placings:400-0030000241530 (7857)
2009: 7^{0}GF, 11^{0}SD, 9^{3}SD, 8^{0}G, 10^{0}G, 10^{0}S, 8^{0}GS, 9^{2}SD, 9^{4}SD, 8^{1}SD, 8^{5}SD, 8^{3}SD, 9^{0}SD,

	Starts	1st	2nd	3rd	Win & Pl
Career Total (Turf)	8	0	0	0	444
Career Total (AW)	8	1	1	2	3440

67 11/09 Wolv 1m141y (0-65)H STD £2047
Total win prize-money £2047

Going (Turf): **Sf: 0-2 GS: 0-2 Gd: 0-2 GF: 0-2 Fm: 0-0**
Distance: 5f/6f: 0-2 7f-8f: 0-5 **9f-13f: 1-9** 14f+: 0-0
Track : **LH: 1-12** RH: 0-1 **Tight: 1-9** Gall: 0-1
Aids: **Bl: 1-7** Vi: 0-0 Tstrap: 0-0 Ckp: 0-0
Best Rating: **67** 11/09 Wolv 1m141y stand

Modest; effective over 1m-1m2f; handles Polytrack; has worn a tongue tie and blinkers.

Castlebury (IRE)

102 **71**
4-y-o b g Spartacus (IRE)-La Vie En Rouge (IRE) (College Chapel)
G A Swinbank Mrs V McGee & A Butler

Placings:0/0432535-45040145 (4821)
2009: 8^{4}G, 9^{5}GS, 8^{0}G, 7^{4}G, 6^{0}GS, 10^{1}G, 8^{4}GS, 8^{5}GF,

	Starts	1st	2nd	3rd	Win & Pl
Career Total (Turf)	16	1	1	2	6257

67 7/09 Pont 1m2f6y (0-70)H GD £3885
Total win prize-money £3886

Going (Turf): Sf: 0-1 GS: 0-5 **Gd: 1-5** GF: 0-4 Fm: 0-1
Distance: 5f/6f: 0-3 7f-8f: 0-4 **9f-13f: 1-9** 14f+: 0-0
Track : **LH: 1-6** RH: 0-4 Tight: 0-3 Gall: 0-0
Aids: Bl: 0-1 Vi: 0-0 Tstrap: 0-0 Ckp: 0-0
Best Rating: **71** 5/08 Newc 1m3y gd-fm

Modest; stays 1m2f; acts on good to firm and good to soft.

Castlecarra (IRE)

91(93) (33)**46**
4-y-o b g Mull Of Kintyre (USA)-Sketch Pad (Warning)
J Hetherton Mrs Elizabeth Bell

Placings:360000 (7681)
2009: 5^{3}GF, 6^{6}GF, 5^{0}GS, 5^{0}S, 9^{0}SD, 6^{0}SD,

	Starts	1st	2nd	3rd	Win & Pl
Career Total (Turf)	4	0	0	1	409
Career Total (AW)	2	0	0	0	

Going (Turf): **Sf: 0-1 GS: 0-1 Gd: 0-0 GF: 0-2 Fm: 0-0**
Distance: 5f/6f: 0-5 7f-8f: 0-0 9f-13f: 0-1 14f+: 0-0
Track : LH: 0-2 RH: 0-0 Tight: 0-1 Gall: 0-0
Aids: Bl: 0-1 Vi: 0-0 Tstrap: 0-0 Ckp: 0-0
Best Rating: **46** 8/09 Bevl 5f gd-fm

Castlefish (IRE)

78 **33**
5-y-o b g Carrowkeel (IRE)-Haven Island (IRE) (Revoque (IRE))
D Burchell S Hyde

Placings:00/00 (5632)
2009: 8^{0}F, 6^{0}GS,

	Starts	1st	2nd	3rd	Win & Pl
Career Total (Turf)	4	0	0	0	

Going (Turf): **Sf: 0-2 GS: 0-1 Gd: 0-0 GF: 0-0 Fm: 0-1**
Distance: 5f/6f: 0-1 7f-8f: 0-2 9f-13f: 0-1 14f+: 0-0
Track : LH: 0-1 RH: 0-1 Tight: 0-1 Gall: 0-0
Aids: Bl: 0-0 Vi: 0-0 Tstrap: 0-0 Ckp: 0-0
Best Rating: **33** 8/09 Bath 1m5y firm

Castles In The Air

107(106) (95)**97**
4-y-o b g Oasis Dream-Dance Parade (USA) (Gone West (USA))
R A Fahey Jim McGrath

Placings:5042/010300-0162010220 (6270)
2009: 6^{0}GF, 6^{1}GS, 6^{6}G, 7^{2}G, 8^{0}G, 7^{1}G, 7^{0}G, 7^{2}SD, 6^{2}GF, 7^{0}G,

	Starts	1st	2nd	3rd	Win & Pl
Career Total (Turf)	18	3	2	1	21895
Career Total (AW)	2	0	2	0	3781

97 7/09 Asct 7f (0-90)H GD £7495
88 5/09 Haml 6f5y (0-75)H G-S £3412
77 5/08 Hayd 6f (0-80)H G-F £4533
Total win prize-money £15440

Going (Turf): Sf: 0-1 **GS: 1-2 Gd: 1-10 GF: 1-4** Fm: 0-1
Distance: 5f/6f: 1-9 **7f-8f: 2-11** 9f-13f: 0-0 14f+: 0-0
Track : LH: 0-4 RH: 0-0 Tight: 0-2 Gall: 0-0
Aids: Bl: 0-0 Vi: 0-1 Tstrap: 0-0 Ckp: 0-0
Best Rating: 97 9/09 Asct 7f good

Very useful; effective over 6-7f; acts on fast ground; has worn a visor.

Casual Conquest (IRE)

115 **123**
4-y-o b g Hernando (FR)-Lady Luck (IRE) (Kris)
D K Weld Moyglare Stud Farm

Placings:1/132-21310 **(5688a)**
2009: 12^{2}GF, 10^{1}HY, 10^{3}YS, 10^{1}SH, 10^{0}GY,

	Starts	1st	2nd	3rd	Win & Pl
Career Total (Turf)	**9**	**4**	**2**	**2**	**695787**
121 8/09 Curr 1m2f				SH	£68106
123 5/09 Curr 1m2f110y				HVY	£168203
119 5/08 Leop 1m2f				GD	£59742
88 9/07 Leop 7f				G-F	£8797

Total win prize-money £304851

Going (Turf): Sf: 1-1 GS: 0-0 **Gd: 1-2 GF: 1-2** Fm: 0-0
Distance: 5f/6f: 0-0 7f-8f: 1-1 **9f-13f: 3-8** 14f+: 0-0
Track : LH: 2-5 RH: 2-4 Tight: 0-1 Gall: 0-1
Aids: Bl: 0-1 Vi: 0-0 Tstrap: 0-0 Ckp: 0-0
Best Rating: 123 5/09 Curr 1m2f110y heavy

Group class; Irish trained; third in the Derby and second in the Irish Derby in 2008 won the Tattersalls Gold Cup in 2009; effective at 1m2f-1m4f; acts on fast and heavy ground; has worn a tongue tie and blinkers.

Casual Garcia

101(96) (56)**80**
4-y-o gr g Hernando (FR)-Frosty Welcome (USA) (With Approval (CAN))
N J Gifford (Sir Mark Prescott 13/9) Ne'Er Do Wells Ii

Placings:00000/01611-060406 **(5917)**
2009: 16^{0}GF, 16^{6}GF, 21^{0}G, 17^{4}GF, 15^{0}GS, 16^{6}GF,

	Starts	1st	2nd	3rd	Win & Pl
Career Total (Turf)	**13**	**2**	**0**	**0**	**4926**
Career Total (AW)	**3**	**1**	**0**	**0**	**1774**
80 8/08 Folk 1m7f92y (0-70)H				G-F	£2590
70 7/08 Nott 2m9y (0-60)H				G-F	£2047
56 6/08 Ling 1m4f				STD	£1774

Total win prize-money £6411

Going (Turf): Sf: 0-1 GS: 0-1 Gd: 0-1 **GF: 2-8** Fm: 0-2
Distance: 5f/6f: 0-1 7f-8f: 0-2 9f-13f: 1-4 **14f+: 2-9**
Track : **LH: 2-9** RH: 1-6 **Tight: 2-7** Gall: 0-1
Aids: **Bl: 3-10** Vi: 0-0 Tstrap: 0-0 Ckp: 0-0
Best Rating: 80 8/08 Folk 1m7f92y gd-fm

Modest; stays 2m; acts on Polytrack and fast turf; has worn blinkers.

Cat Hunter

82(95) (65)**64**
2-y-o b f One Cool Cat (USA)-Eoz (IRE) (Sadler's Wells (USA))
Mrs A J Perrett David Cohen

Placings:5310 **(7187)**
2009: 6^{5}SD, 7^{3}GF, 7^{1}SD, 8^{0}G,

	Starts	1st	2nd	3rd	Win & Pl
Career Total (Turf)	**2**	**0**	**0**	**1**	**482**
Career Total (AW)	**2**	**1**	**0**	**0**	**2388**
65 10/09 Ling 7f				STD	£2388

Total win prize-money £2388

Going (Turf): Sf: 0-0 GS: 0-0 Gd: 0-1 GF: 0-1 Fm: 0-0
Distance: 5f/6f: 0-1 **7f-8f: 1-3** 9f-13f: 0-0 14f+: 0-0
Track : **LH: 1-3** RH: 0-0 **Tight: 1-2** Gall: 0-0
Aids: Bl: 0-0 Vi: 0-0 Tstrap: 0-0 Ckp: 0-0
Best Rating: 65 10/09 Ling 7f stand

Fair; stays 7f and acts on Polytrack.

Cat Junior (USA)

110(107) (89)**117**
4-y-o b/br c Storm Cat (USA)-Luna Wells (IRE) (Sadler's Wells (USA))
B J Meehan Roldvale Limited

Placings:1/644022-03324 **(6503a)**
2009: 8^{0}FT, 6^{3}SD, 7^{3}GF, 7^{2}GF, 7^{4}GS,

	Starts	1st	2nd	3rd	Win & Pl
Career Total (Turf)	**10**	**1**	**3**	**1**	**115099**
Career Total (AW)	**2**	**0**	**0**	**1**	**1926**
91 8/07 Newb 6f8y				G-F	£5829

Total win prize-money £5829

Going (Turf): Sf: 0-0 GS: 0-1 Gd: 0-3 **GF: 1-6** Fm: 0-0
Distance: 5f/6f: 0-1 **7f-8f: 1-9** 9f-13f: 0-2 14f+: 0-0
Track : LH: 0-3 RH: 0-5 Tight: 0-1 Gall: 0-4
Aids: Bl: 0-0 Vi: 0-0 Tstrap: 0-0 Ckp: 0-0
Best Rating: 117 7/08 Chan 1m good

Listed class; Group 2 placed; effective at 1m; acts on good and faster ground; has worn tongue tie.

Cat Six (USA)

86(87) (26)**21**
5-y-o b m Tale Of The Cat (USA)-Hurricane Warning (USA) (Thunder Gulch (USA))
Samantha Pearce (T Wall 11/8) D B Roberts

Placings:0/055035000006/00 **(4373)**
2009: 12^{0}GF, 12^{0}SD,

	Starts	1st	2nd	3rd	Win & Pl
Career Total (Turf)	**10**	**0**	**0**	**0**	**0**
Career Total (AW)	**5**	**0**	**0**	**1**	**353**

Going (Turf): Sf: 0-0 GS: 0-1 Gd: 0-4 GF: 0-4 Fm: 0-1
Distance: 5f/6f: 0-0 7f-8f: 0-2 9f-13f: 0-13 14f+: 0-0
Track : LH: 0-12 RH: 0-1 Tight: 0-6 Gall: 0-0
Aids: Bl: 0-1 Vi: 0-0 Tstrap: 0-1 Ckp: 0-1
Best Rating: 64 8/07 Hayd 1m30y gd-fm

Catai

(82) (34)
5-y-o b h Mark Of Esteem (IRE)-China (Royal Academy (USA))
P Monteith Dennis J Coppola

Placings:0/S36001230/63115341-0 **(0566)**
2009: 12^{0}SD,

	Starts	1st	2nd	3rd	Win & Pl
Career Total (Turf)	**17**	**4**	**1**	**4**	**16258**
Career Total (AW)	**2**	**0**	**0**	**0**	**0**
8/08 Gros 1m4f H				GD	£3676
6/08 Siro 1m2f				GD	£2574
5/08 Livo 1m1f165y				GD	£1471
10/07 Gros 1m165y H				GD	£2703

Total win prize-money £10424

Going (Turf): Sf: 0-2 GS: 0-0 **Gd: 4-15** GF: 0-0 Fm: 0-0
Distance: 5f/6f: 0-0 7f-8f: 0-5 **9f-13f: 4-14** 14f+: 0-0
Track : LH: 0-1 RH: 0-0 Tight: 0-1 Gall: 0-0
Aids: Bl: 0-0 Vi: 0-0 Tstrap: 0-0 Ckp: 0-0
Best Rating: 34 2/09 Wolv 1m4f50y stand

Catalan Bay (AUS)

103(107) (82)**81**
5-y-o b m Rock Of Gibraltar (IRE)-Kim Angel (AUS) (Serheed (USA))
J R Gask Horses First Racing Limited

Placings:41105100/64640-2420546 **(6020)**
2009: 6^{2}SD, 7^{4}SF, 6^{2}G, 6^{0}GS, 7^{5}G, 7^{4}G, 6^{6}GF,

	Starts	1st	2nd	3rd	Win & Pl
Career Total (Turf)	**18**	**3**	**1**	**0**	**33441**
Career Total (AW)	**2**	**0**	**1**	**0**	**1217**
9/07 Moon 1m H				GD	£9677
8/07 Sann 6f H				SFT	£6290
4/07 Sann 6f110y H				GD	£6290

Total win prize-money £22257

Going (Turf): Sf: 1-1 GS: 0-3 **Gd: 2-13** GF: 0-1 Fm: 0-0
Distance: 5f/6f: 1-7 **7f-8f: 2-11** 9f-13f: 0-2 14f+: 0-0
Track : LH: 0-3 RH: 0-0 Tight: 0-2 Gall: 0-0
Aids: Bl: 0-1 Vi: 0-1 Tstrap: 0-0 Ckp: 0-0
Best Rating: 97 2/08 Moon 7f110y good

Fair; effective over 6f-1m; acts on Polytrack; has worn a visor.

Catalina Sunrise (USA)

(75) (56)
3-y-o ch f Malibu Moon (USA)-Jealous Forum (USA) (Open Forum (USA))
J E Pease (L M Cumani 25/6) Christopher Wright

Placings:00
2009: 8^{0}SD, 9^{0}SD,

	Starts	1st	2nd	3rd	Win & Pl
Career Total (Turf)	**0**	**0**	**0**	**0**	
Career Total (AW)	**2**	**0**	**0**	**0**	

Going (Turf): Sf: 0-0 GS: 0-0 Gd: 0-0 GF: 0-0 Fm: 0-0
Distance: 5f/6f: 0-0 7f-8f: 0-1 9f-13f: 0-1 14f+: 0-0
Track : LH: 0-0 RH: 0-1 Tight: 0-0 Gall: 0-0
Aids: Bl: 0-0 Vi: 0-0 Tstrap: 0-0 Ckp: 0-0
Best Rating: 56 8/09 Deau 1m1f110y stand

Catawollow

80(48) **44**
2-y-o b f Beat Hollow-Catalonia (IRE) (Catrail (USA))
R C Guest Bamboozelem

Placings:000 **(7638)**
2009: 5^{0}GF, 8^{0}S, 8^{0}SD,

	Starts	1st	2nd	3rd	Win & Pl
Career Total (Turf)	**2**	**0**	**0**	**0**	
Career Total (AW)	**1**	**0**	**0**	**0**	

Going (Turf): Sf: 0-1 GS: 0-0 Gd: 0-0 GF: 0-1 Fm: 0-0
Distance: 5f/6f: 0-1 7f-8f: 0-1 9f-13f: 0-1 14f+: 0-0
Track : LH: 0-2 RH: 0-0 Tight: 0-0 Gall: 0-0
Aids: Bl: 0-0 Vi: 0-0 Tstrap: 0-0 Ckp: 0-0
Best Rating: 44 11/09 Nott 1m75y soft

Catbells (IRE)

91 75

2-y-o ch f Rakti-Moonbi Ridge (IRE) (Definite Article)

A Bailey C M & Mrs S A Martin

Placings:25060 (6481)

2009: 6^{2}GF, 6^{5}GF, 6^{0}GS, 6^{0}G, 7^{0}GF,

	Starts	1st	2nd	3rd	Win & Pl
Career Total (Turf)	5	0	1	0	3342

Going (Turf): Sf: 0-0 GS: 0-1 Gd: 0-1 GF: 0-3 Fm: 0-0
Distance: 5f/6f: 0-3 7f-8f: 0-2 9f-13f: 0-0 14f+: 0-0
Track : LH: 0-1 RH: 0-0 Tight: 0-1 Gall: 0-0
Aids: Bl: 0-0 Vi: 0-0 Tstrap: 0-0 Ckp: 0-0
Best Rating: 75 9/09 Ayr 6f good

Half-brother to the useful 2yo 6f winner Exhibition; effective over 6f; acts on fast ground.

Catch Key (IRE)

89 51

3-y-o b f Key Of Luck (USA)-Catch Me (Rudimentary (USA))

T D Easterby Ryedale Partners No 4

Placings:6404 (3610)

2009: 7^{6}GF, 7^{4}GF, 7^{0}GF, 9^{4}GF,

	Starts	1st	2nd	3rd	Win & Pl
Career Total (Turf)	4	0	0	0	433

Going (Turf): Sf: 0-0 GS: 0-0 Gd: 0-0 GF: 0-4 Fm: 0-0
Distance: 5f/6f: 0-0 7f-8f: 0-3 9f-13f: 0-1 14f+: 0-0
Track : LH: 0-1 RH: 0-3 Tight: 0-1 Gall: 0-0
Aids: Bl: 0-0 Vi: 0-0 Tstrap: 0-0 Ckp: 0-0
Best Rating: 51 5/09 Bevl 7f100y gd-fm

Catch Roy (IRE)

80 60

3-y-o b g Catcher In The Rye (IRE)-Top Of Jumbo (IRE) (Fayruz)

Daniel Mark Loughnane (Timothy Doyle 3/8) Raymond Yeung

Placings:00-004000 (5184)

2009: 8^{0}G, 10^{0}GF, 6^{4}S, 7^{0}GF, 6^{0}S, 5^{0}G,

	Starts	1st	2nd	3rd	Win & Pl
Career Total (Turf)	8	0	0	0	279

Going (Turf): Sf: 0-2 GS: 0-0 Gd: 0-2 GF: 0-4 Fm: 0-0
Distance: 5f/6f: 0-4 7f-8f: 0-2 9f-13f: 0-2 14f+: 0-0
Track : LH: 0-3 RH: 0-2 Tight: 0-0 Gall: 0-0
Aids: Bl: 0-0 Vi: 0-0 Tstrap: 0-0 Ckp: 0-0
Best Rating: 60 6/08 Limk 7f50y gd-fm

Catchanova (IRE)

85(89) (65)58

2-y-o b c Catcher In The Rye (IRE)-Head For The Stars (IRE) (Head For Heights)

Eve Johnson Houghton Andrew Wyer Darrell Blake Hugh Arthur

Placings:00630 (7235)

2009: 6^{0}GF, 5^{0}G, 6^{6}G, 7^{3}SD, 8^{0}SD,

	Starts	1st	2nd	3rd	Win & Pl
Career Total (Turf)	3	0	0	0	0
Career Total (AW)	2	0	0	1	302

Going (Turf): Sf: 0-0 GS: 0-0 Gd: 0-2 GF: 0-1 Fm: 0-0
Distance: 5f/6f: 0-3 7f-8f: 0-2 9f-13f: 0-0 14f+: 0-0
Track : LH: 0-1 RH: 0-2 Tight: 0-0 Gall: 0-2
Aids: Bl: 0-0 Vi: 0-0 Tstrap: 0-0 Ckp: 0-0
Best Rating: 65 9/09 Kemp 7f stand

Catcher Of Dreams (IRE)

12 (62)45

3-y-o b c Catcher In The Rye (IRE)-No Islands (Lomond (USA))

A G Foster A G Foster

Placings:000-0 (7173)

2009: 9^{0}S,

	Starts	1st	2nd	3rd	Win & Pl
Career Total (Turf)	2	0	0	0	
Career Total (AW)	2	0	0	0	

Going (Turf): Sf: 0-2 GS: 0-0 Gd: 0-0 GF: 0-0 Fm: 0-0
Distance: 5f/6f: 0-1 7f-8f: 0-2 9f-13f: 0-1 14f+: 0-0
Track : LH: 0-3 RH: 0-1 Tight: 0-0 Gall: 0-1
Aids: Bl: 0-0 Vi: 0-0 Tstrap: 0-0 Ckp: 0-0
Best Rating: 62 9/08 Dund 7f stand

Catchmeifyoucan (FR)

74(94) (61)60

3-y-o b g Marju (IRE)-Catch Us (FR) (Selkirk (USA))

Andrew Turnell (C G Cox 19/10) Miss S Douglas-Pennant

Placings:0060 (6910)

2009: 10^{0}GF, 10^{0}G, 10^{6}SD, 10^{0}G,

	Starts	1st	2nd	3rd	Win & Pl
Career Total (Turf)	3	0	0	0	
Career Total (AW)	1	0	0	0	0

Going (Turf): Sf: 0-0 GS: 0-0 Gd: 0-2 GF: 0-1 Fm: 0-0
Distance: 5f/6f: 0-0 7f-8f: 0-0 9f-13f: 0-4 14f+: 0-0
Track : LH: 0-0 RH: 0-4 Tight: 0-2 Gall: 0-1
Aids: Bl: 0-1 Vi: 0-0 Tstrap: 0-0 Ckp: 0-0
Best Rating: 61 9/09 Kemp 1m2f stand

Catchpenny

90(89) (53)47

3-y-o b f Piccolo-Noble Penny (Pennekamp (USA))

K A Ryan Guy Reed

Placings:335020 (7579)

2009: 6^{3}HY, 5^{3}GS, 5^{5}SD, 7^{0}SD, 6^{2}SD, 7^{0}SF,

	Starts	1st	2nd	3rd	Win & Pl
Career Total (Turf)	2	0	0	2	857
Career Total (AW)	4	0	1	0	907

Going (Turf): Sf: 0-1 GS: 0-1 Gd: 0-0 GF: 0-0 Fm: 0-0
Distance: 5f/6f: 0-3 7f-8f: 0-3 9f-13f: 0-0 14f+: 0-0
Track : LH: 0-4 RH: 0-0 Tight: 0-2 Gall: 0-0
Aids: Bl: 0-0 Vi: 0-0 Tstrap: 0-2 Ckp: 0-2
Best Rating: 53 11/09 Sthl 6f stand

Moderate; effective over 6f; acts on Fibresand.

Cate Washington

82(89) (33)25

6-y-o b m Superior Premium-Willisa (Polar Falcon (USA))

Mrs L Williamson G D Kendrick

Placings:000/000600/0/00000 (2517)

2009: 5^{0}SD, 5^{0}SD, 7^{0}SD, 10^{0}GF, 11^{0}F,

	Starts	1st	2nd	3rd	Win & Pl
Career Total (Turf)	9	0	0	0	0
Career Total (AW)	6	0	0	0	

Going (Turf): Sf: 0-2 GS: 0-1 Gd: 0-2 GF: 0-3 Fm: 0-1
Distance: 5f/6f: 0-7 7f-8f: 0-6 9f-13f: 0-2 14f+: 0-0
Track : LH: 0-9 RH: 0-1 Tight: 0-6 Gall: 0-1
Aids: Bl: 0-0 Vi: 0-0 Tstrap: 0-0 Ckp: 0-0
Best Rating: 48 10/05 Newc 7f soft

Categorical

98 (69)70

6-y-o b g Diktat-Zibet (Kris)

Miss Lucinda V Russell (K G Reveley 6/5) Rug, Grub & Pub Partnership

Placings:0413/0630005/446/360-0 (1242)

2009: 16^{0}F,

	Starts	1st	2nd	3rd	Win & Pl
Career Total (Turf)	17	0	0	3	2520
Career Total (AW)	1	1	0	0	3783

78 7/05 Sthl 5f STD £3783

Total win prize-money £3783

Going (Turf): Sf: 0-5 GS: 0-0 Gd: 0-3 GF: 0-7 Fm: 0-2
Distance: 5f/6f: 1-4 7f-8f: 0-4 9f-13f: 0-3 14f+: 0-7
Track : LH: 0-7 RH: 0-3 Tight: 0-9 Gall: 0-0
Aids: Bl: 0-0 Vi: 0-0 Tstrap: 0-0 Ckp: 0-0
Best Rating: 82 9/05 Donc 7f heavy

Modest; stays 2m; acts on good ground.

Catherine (IRE)

(84) (49)55

3-y-o ch f Modigliani (USA)-Jillians Pride (IRE) (Persian Mews)

Mark L Fagan C J Kiernan

Placings:000-400000 (7371)

2009: 8^{4}Y, 7^{0}HY, 7^{0}GY, 6^{0}GY, 7^{0}SD, 5^{0}SD,

	Starts	1st	2nd	3rd	Win & Pl
Career Total (Turf)	6	0	0	0	279
Career Total (AW)	3	0	0	0	

Going (Turf): Sf: 0-1 GS: 0-0 Gd: 0-0 GF: 0-0 Fm: 0-0
Distance: 5f/6f: 0-1 7f-8f: 0-8 9f-13f: 0-0 14f+: 0-0
Track : LH: 0-4 RH: 0-5 Tight: 0-1 Gall: 0-0
Aids: Bl: 0-0 Vi: 0-0 Tstrap: 0-0 Ckp: 0-0
Best Rating: 55 7/09 Gowr 1m yield

Catherines Call (IRE)

(81) (50)

2-y-o b f Captain Rio-It's Academic (Royal Academy (USA))

D Donovan Philip Mclaughlin

Placings:6 (5638)

2009: 6^{6}SD,

	Starts	1st	2nd	3rd	Win & Pl
Career Total (Turf)	0	0	0	0	

Career Total (AW)	1	0	0	0	0

Going (Turf): Sf: 0-0 GS: 0-0 Gd: 0-0 GF: 0-0 Fm: 0-0
Distance: 5f/6f: 0-1 7f-8f: 0-0 9f-13f: 0-0 14f+: 0-0
Track: LH: 0-0 RH: 0-1 Tight: 0-0 Gall: 0-0
Aids: Bl: 0-0 Vi: 0-0 Tstrap: 0-0 Ckp: 0-0
Best Rating: 50 9/09 Kemp 6f stand

Cativo

82(92) (49)36
3-y-o b f Deportivo-Catriona (Bustino)
B R Millman Ashley House Racing

Placings:0-005500 (7829)
2009: 8^{0}GF, 7^{0}G, 6^{5}SD, 8^{5}SD, 7^{0}SD, 7^{0}SD,

	Starts	1st	2nd	3rd	Win & Pl
Career Total (Turf)	3	0	0	0	
Career Total (AW)	4	0	0	0	0

Going (Turf): Sf: 0-0 GS: 0-0 Gd: 0-2 GF: 0-1 Fm: 0-0
Distance: 5f/6f: 0-1 7f-8f: 0-5 9f-13f: 0-1 14f+: 0-0
Track: LH: 0-3 RH: 0-3 Tight: 0-1 Gall: 0-0
Aids: Bl: 0-0 Vi: 0-0 Tstrap: 0-0 Ckp: 0-0
Best Rating: 49 12/09 Kemp 7f stand

Cativo Cavallino

99(102) (78)81
6-y-o ch g Bertolini (USA)-Sea Isle (Selkirk (USA))
J E Long P Saxon

Placings:6532/0000000000/111415014/55420643360600-5433263135 (7432)
2009: 7^{5}SD, 6^{4}SD, 7^{3}SD, 6^{3}GS, 6^{2}G, 7^{6}SD, 7^{3}GF, 6^{1}SD, 7^{3}SD, 7^{5}SD,

	Starts	1st	2nd	3rd	Win & Pl
Career Total (Turf)	17	1	2	3	5940
Career Total (AW)	30	5	1	4	14845

71	9/09	Kemp	6f	(0-65)H	STD	£2047
84	10/07	Kemp	6f	(0-75)H	STD	£2817
76	8/07	Ling	6f	(0-70)H	GD	£2817
69	4/07	Ling	7f	(0-65)H	STD	£2388
61	3/07	Ling	6f	(0-52)H	STD	£1706
55	2/07	Ling	7f	(0-60)H	STD	£1706

Total win prize-money £13482

Going (Turf): Sf: 0-3 GS: 0-4 **Gd: 1-3** GF: 0-7 Fm: 0-0
Distance: **5f/6f: 4-24** 7f-8f: 2-19 9f-13f: 0-3 14f+: 0-1
Track: **LH: 3-20** RH: 2-13 **Tight: 3-19** Gall: 0-4
Aids: Bl: 0-0 Vi: 0-0 Tstrap: 0-1 Ckp: 0-1
Best Rating: 84 10/07 Kemp 6f stand

Modest; effective at around 6f-7f; acts on good ground and Polytrack; goes well for Natalia Gemelova.

Catskill

96(84) (25)58
7-y-o ch g Inchinor-Manhattan Sunset (USA) (El Gran Senor (USA))
Adrian McGuinness K G C Syndicate

Placings:65626/0130600/0/30400 (7649)
2009: 13^{3}G, 14^{0}Y, 12^{4}HY, 14^{0}YS, 16^{0}SD,

	Starts	1st	2nd	3rd	Win & Pl
Career Total (Turf)	15	1	1	2	5788
Career Total (AW)	3	0	0	0	

77	5/06	Yarm	1m2f21y	(0-65)H	GD	£3108

Total win prize-money £3109

Going (Turf): Sf: 0-1 GS: 0-2 **Gd: 1-8** GF: 0-1 Fm: 0-0
Distance: 5f/6f: 0-0 7f-8f: 0-2 **9f-13f: 1-12** 14f+: 0-4
Track: **LH: 1-8** RH: 0-8 **Tight: 1-8** Gall: 0-1
Aids: Bl: 0-5 Vi: 0-0 Tstrap: 0-1 Ckp: 0-1
Best Rating: 77 5/06 Yarm 1m2f21y good

Caucus

96 70
2-y-o b c Cape Cross (IRE)-Maid To Perfection (Sadler's Wells (USA))
J L Dunlop Normandie Stud Ltd

Placings:004 (5542)
2009: 6^{0}S, 7^{0}GF, 7^{4}GF,

	Starts	1st	2nd	3rd	Win & Pl
Career Total (Turf)	3	0	0	0	361

Going (Turf): Sf: 0-1 GS: 0-0 Gd: 0-0 GF: 0-2 Fm: 0-0
Distance: 5f/6f: 0-0 7f-8f: 0-3 9f-13f: 0-0 14f+: 0-0
Track: LH: 0-0 RH: 0-0 Tight: 0-0 Gall: 0-0
Aids: Bl: 0-0 Vi: 0-0 Tstrap: 0-0 Ckp: 0-0
Best Rating: 70 9/09 Leic 7f9y gd-fm

Caught In Paradise (IRE)

(73) 59
4-y-o b g Catcher In The Rye (IRE)-Paradis (Bijou D'Inde)
D W Thompson D Morland

Placings:52151000/0000024500-0 (0061)
2009: 8^{0}SD,

	Starts	1st	2nd	3rd	Win & Pl
Career Total (Turf)	18	2	2	0	6171
Career Total (AW)	1	0	0	0	

59	7/07	Yarm	5f43y	G-F	£1943
59	6/07	Hayd	5f	G-F	£2817

Total win prize-money £4760

Going (Turf): Sf: 0-1 GS: 0-2 Gd: 0-5 **GF: 2-9** Fm: 0-1
Distance: **5f/6f: 2-9** 7f-8f: 0-7 9f-13f: 0-3 14f+: 0-0
Track: LH: 0-6 RH: 0-4 Tight: 0-5 Gall: 0-2
Aids: Bl: 0-2 Vi: 0-0 Tstrap: 0-2 Ckp: 0-2
Best Rating: 59 7/07 Yarm 5f43y gd-fm

Plating-class; effective over sprint distances; acts on fast ground; has worn cheekpieces/tongue tie.

Caught On Camera

100(88) (59)58
3-y-o b f Red Ransom (USA)-Colorsnap (Shirley Heights)
M L W Bell Helena Springfield Ltd

Placings:000-0403 (4944)
2009: 10^{0}SD, 9^{4}GF, 12^{0}G, 10^{3}GF,

	Starts	1st	2nd	3rd	Win & Pl
Career Total (Turf)	4	0	0	1	308
Career Total (AW)	3	0	0	0	

Going (Turf): Sf: 0-0 GS: 0-1 Gd: 0-1 GF: 0-2 Fm: 0-0
Distance: 5f/6f: 0-1 7f-8f: 0-2 9f-13f: 0-4 14f+: 0-0
Track: LH: 0-4 RH: 0-2 Tight: 0-2 Gall: 0-4
Aids: Bl: 0-0 Vi: 0-0 Tstrap: 0-0 Ckp: 0-0
Best Rating: 59 9/08 Kemp 7f stand

Moderate; effective at 1m2f.

Cause For Applause (IRE)

84(96) (56)42
3-y-o b f Royal Applause-Polyandry (IRE) (Pennekamp (USA))
R Craggs (B Smart 26/3) Gerry Slater & Allen Evans

Placings:006-10440500 (7726)
2009: 8^{1}SS, 8^{0}SD, 8^{4}SD, 8^{4}SD, 8^{0}GF, 8^{5}SD, 9^{0}SD, 7^{0}SD,

	Starts	1st	2nd	3rd	Win & Pl
Career Total (Turf)	3	0	0	0	
Career Total (AW)	8	1	0	0	2047

56	1/09	Sthl	1m	SS	£2047

Total win prize-money £2047

Going (Turf): Sf: 0-0 GS: 0-1 Gd: 0-1 GF: 0-1 Fm: 0-0
Distance: 5f/6f: 0-1 **7f-8f: 1-8** 9f-13f: 0-2 14f+: 0-0
Track: **LH: 1-10** RH: 0-0 Tight: 0-4 Gall: 0-1
Aids: Bl: 0-0 **Vi: 1-5** Tstrap: 0-0 Ckp: 0-0
Best Rating: 56 1/09 Sthl 1m std-slw

Very moderate; stays 1m and acts on Fibresand; has worn a visor.

Causeway Coast (USA)

76 36
2-y-o b/br f Giant's Causeway (USA)-Manda Island (USA) (Dynaformer (USA))
P W Chapple-Hyam Plantation Stud

Placings:0 (6992)
2009: 8^{0}GS,

	Starts	1st	2nd	3rd	Win & Pl
Career Total (Turf)	1	0	0	0	

Going (Turf): Sf: 0-0 GS: 0-1 Gd: 0-0 GF: 0-0 Fm: 0-0
Distance: 5f/6f: 0-0 7f-8f: 0-1 9f-13f: 0-0 14f+: 0-0
Track: LH: 0-1 RH: 0-0 Tight: 0-0 Gall: 0-1
Aids: Bl: 0-0 Vi: 0-0 Tstrap: 0-0 Ckp: 0-0
Best Rating: 36 10/09 Donc 1m gd-sft

Causeway King (USA)

72(102) (62)68
3-y-o ch g Giant's Causeway (USA)-A P Petal (USA) (A.P. Indy (USA))
A King R S Brookhouse

Placings:005-050 (5286)
2009: 8^{0}SD, 11^{5}SD, 12^{0}GF,

	Starts	1st	2nd	3rd	Win & Pl
Career Total (Turf)	3	0	0	0	
Career Total (AW)	3	0	0	0	0

Going (Turf): Sf: 0-0 GS: 0-0 Gd: 0-2 GF: 0-1 Fm: 0-0
Distance: 5f/6f: 0-0 7f-8f: 0-4 9f-13f: 0-2 14f+: 0-0
Track: LH: 0-1 RH: 0-4 Tight: 0-1 Gall: 0-1
Aids: Bl: 0-0 Vi: 0-0 Tstrap: 0-0 Ckp: 0-0
Best Rating: 68 8/08 Sand 7f16y good

Modest maiden form to date.

Caustic Wit (IRE)

101(95) (68)67
11-y-o b g Cadeaux Genereux-Baldemosa (FR) (Lead On Time (USA))

M S Saunders Mrs Sandra Jones

Placings:501216/0000/0003030/1011112200466/0000044 20040/000000201100201302341650652646001221434330 0520/00610200546000600-651504000 **(5065)**

2009: 6^{6}G, 5^{5}GF, 6^{1}GF, 6^{5}GF, 6^{0}GF, 5^{4}F, 6^{0}G, 5^{0}S, 5^{0}GF,

	Starts	1st	2nd	3rd	Win & Pl
Career Total (Turf)	84	13	9	4	95189
Career Total (AW)	31	2	3	3	9359

63	5/09	Chep	6f16y	(0-65)H	G-F	£2266
63	5/08	Brig	5f213y	(0-70)H	G-F	£2396
72	7/07	Folk	5f	(0-70)H	G-F	£3238
69	6/07	Ling	5f	(0-75)H	GD	£2817
67	8/06	Wolv	5f216y	(0-60)H	STD	£2730
81	7/06	Epsm	6f	(0-80)H	GD	£5505
76	6/06	Wind	6f	(0-80)H	G-F	£6477
74	6/06	Bath	5f161y	(0-70)H	FRM	£3886
91	6/04	Wind	6f	D(0-80)H	G-F	£5720
81	6/04	Sals	6f	C(0-90)H	G-F	£8792
73	5/04	Leic	5f218y	E(0-75)H	G-F	£5629
71	5/04	Folk	6f	E(0-70)H	SFT	£3523
67	1/04	Wolv	6f	F(0-60)H	STD	£2975
98	9/00	NmkR	6f	C(0-95)	GD	£8866
89	7/00	Donc	6f	D	GD	£3753

Total win prize-money £68577

Going (Turf): Sf: 1-10 GS: 0-13Gd: 4-18**GF: 7-37** Fm: 1-6
Distance: **5f/6f: 14-101** 7f-8f: 1-149f-13f: 0-0 14f+: 0-0
Track : **LH: 5-44** RH: 0-7 Tight: 3-21 Gall: 3-31
Aids: Bl: 0-0 Vi: 0-0 Tstrap: 8-52 Ckp: 8-52
Best Rating: **98** 9/00 NmkR 6f good

Modest sprinter; effective over 5f-6f; acts on Polytrack; has worn cheekpieces.

Cavalry Guard (USA)

102(103) (58)**57**

5-y-o ch g Officer (USA)-Leeward City (USA) (Carson City (USA))
T D McCarthy Inside Track Racing Club

Placings:2240/5260/300600000012-4643305200002023 **(7880)**

2009: 7^{4}SD, 8^{6}SD, 7^{4}SD, 7^{3}SD, 8^{3}SD, 7^{0}SD, 8^{5}SD, 8^{2}F, 7^{0}GF, 7^{0}G, 8^{0}GF, 8^{0}SD, 7^{2}SD, 8^{0}SD, 7^{2}SD, 7^{3}SD,

	Starts	1st	2nd	3rd	Win & Pl
Career Total (Turf)	14	0	4	0	4046
Career Total (AW)	23	1	3	4	5455

54	12/08	Ling	7f	(0-55)H	STD	£2047

Total win prize-money £2047

Going (Turf): **Sf: 0-1 GS: 0-3 Gd: 0-3 GF: 0-5 Fm: 0-2**
Distance: 5f/6f: 0-2 **7f-8f: 1-28** 9f-13f: 0-7 14f+: 0-0
Track : **LH: 1-19** RH: 0-9 **Tight: 1-17** Gall: 0-1
Aids: **Bl: 1-16** Vi: 0-2 Tstrap: 0-4 Ckp: 0-4
Best Rating: **78** 7/06 NmkJ 6f gd-fm

Moderate; effective at around 7f; acts on good ground; goes on Polytrack; has worn blinkers.

Cave Of The Giant (IRE)

85 **49**

7-y-o b g Giant's Causeway (USA)-Maroussie (FR) (Saumarez)
T D McCarthy A D Spence

Placings:50/30/5 **(3423)**

2009: 14^{5}G,

	Starts	1st	2nd	3rd	Win & Pl
Career Total (Turf)	5	0	0	1	1784

Going (Turf): **Sf: 0-0 GS: 0-1 Gd: 0-3 GF: 0-1 Fm: 0-0**
Distance: 5f/6f: 0-0 7f-8f: 0-0 9f-13f: 0-2 14f+: 0-3
Track : LH: 0-0 RH: 0-5 Tight: 0-3 Gall: 0-0
Aids: Bl: 0-1 Vi: 0-0 Tstrap: 0-0 Ckp: 0-0
Best Rating: **71** 9/06 Sals 1m6f15y gd-sft

Cavendish

(96) (69)**77**

5-y-o b g Pursuit Of Love-Bathwick Babe (IRE) (Sri Pekan (USA))
J M P Eustace The Cavendish Partnership

Placings:00006/3405143656/001162330-0 **(6258)**

2009: 13^{0}SD,

	Starts	1st	2nd	3rd	Win & Pl
Career Total (Turf)	12	3	1	2	9548
Career Total (AW)	13	0	0	2	741

71	5/08	Catt	1m7f177y	(0-65)H	GD	£2047
68	4/08	Yarm	1m6f17y	(0-55)H	GD	£2266
65	6/07	Wwck	1m2f188y	(0-60)H	G-S	£2730

Total win prize-money £7044

Going (Turf): Sf: 0-0 GS: 1-5 **Gd: 2-5** GF: 0-2 Fm: 0-0
Distance: 5f/6f: 0-3 7f-8f: 0-2 9f-13f: 1-12 **14f+: 2-8**
Track : **LH: 3-17** RH: 0-6 **Tight: 2-16** Gall: 0-2
Aids: **Bl: 3-18** Vi: 0-1 Tstrap: 0-0 Ckp: 0-0
Best Rating: **77** 7/08 Newb 2m good

Fair; effective over 2m; acts on easy ground; also goes on Polytrack; usually blinkered.

Cavendish Road (IRE)

101(100) (74)**72**

3-y-o b g Bachelor Duke (USA)-Gronchi Rosa (IRE) (Nashwan (USA))
W R Muir C L A Edginton

Placings:5201000503-104131033 **(7065)**

2009: 7^{1}GF, 8^{0}GF, 6^{4}GF, 6^{1}F, 7^{3}F, 7^{1}F, 8^{0}G, 7^{3}GF, 8^{3}SD,

	Starts	1st	2nd	3rd	Win & Pl
Career Total (Turf)	14	4	1	2	12701
Career Total (AW)	5	0	0	2	746

71	8/09	Brig	7f214y	(0-65)H	FRM	£2590
64	6/09	Brig	6f209y	(0-70)H	FRM	£3154
62	4/09	Folk	7f	(0-60)H	G-F	£2047
70	8/08	Brig	6f209y		GD	£2964

Total win prize-money £10756

Going (Turf): Sf: 0-0 GS: 0-0 Gd: 1-5 GF: 1-6 **Fm: 2-3**
Distance: 5f/6f: 0-5 **7f-8f: 4-12** 9f-13f: 0-2 14f+: 0-0
Track : **LH: 3-13** RH: 0-1 Tight: 0-4 Gall: 0-2
Aids: Bl: 0-4 Vi: 0-0 Tstrap: 0-0 Ckp: 0-0
Best Rating: **74** 10/09 Ling 1m stand

Modest; effective at 7f on fast ground.

Caviar

92(86) (58)**69**

2-y-o gr f Thunder Gulch (USA)-Cozzene'Saffair (USA) (Black Tie Affair)
R Hannon Highclere Thoroughbred Racing (Donoghue)

Placings:306 **(3733)**

2009: 6^{3}GS, 6^{0}GF, 6^{6}SD,

	Starts	1st	2nd	3rd	Win & Pl
Career Total (Turf)	2	0	0	1	722
Career Total (AW)	1	0	0	0	0

Going (Turf): **Sf: 0-0 GS: 0-1 Gd: 0-0 GF: 0-1 Fm: 0-0**
Distance: 5f/6f: 0-3 7f-8f: 0-0 9f-13f: 0-0 14f+: 0-0
Track : LH: 0-1 RH: 0-1 Tight: 0-0 Gall: 0-0
Aids: Bl: 0-0 Vi: 0-0 Tstrap: 0-0 Ckp: 0-0
Best Rating: **69** 6/09 Donc 6f gd-sft

Fair; stays 6f and acts on good ground.

Cavitie

88(94) (55)**55**

3-y-o b g Teofilio (IRE)-Kirriemuir (Lochnager)
Andrew Reid (E J Creighton 22/4) A S Reid

Placings:000-602260 **(6777)**

2009: 6^{6}SD, 6^{0}GF, 5^{2}G, 5^{2}SD, 6^{6}G, 6^{0}SD,

	Starts	1st	2nd	3rd	Win & Pl
Career Total (Turf)	4	0	1	0	705
Career Total (AW)	5	0	1	0	605

Going (Turf): **Sf: 0-1 GS: 0-0 Gd: 0-2 GF: 0-1 Fm: 0-0**
Distance: 5f/6f: 0-6 7f-8f: 0-3 9f-13f: 0-0 14f+: 0-0
Track : LH: 0-2 RH: 0-2 Tight: 0-1 Gall: 0-1
Aids: Bl: 0-0 Vi: 0-0 Tstrap: 0-0 Ckp: 0-0
Best Rating: **55** 6/09 Sthl 5f stand

Moderate; effective over 5f; acts on good ground and on Fibresand.

Cawdor (IRE)

103 **83**

3-y-o b g Kyllachy-Dim Ots (Alhijaz)
H Candy Thurloe Thoroughbreds XIV

Placings:342-232001 **(6798)**

2009: 5^{2}GF, 6^{3}GF, 5^{2}G, 7^{0}GF, 6^{0}G, 6^{1}S,

	Starts	1st	2nd	3rd	Win & Pl
Career Total (Turf)	9	1	3	2	7383

83	10/09	Nott	6f15y	(0-75)H	SFT	£2590

Total win prize-money £2590

Going (Turf): **Sf: 1-3** GS: 0-0 Gd: 0-2 GF: 0-4 Fm: 0-0
Distance: 5f/6f: 0-7 **7f-8f: 1-2** 9f-13f: 0-0 14f+: 0-0
Track : LH: 0-2 RH: 0-0 Tight: 0-1 Gall: 0-4
Aids: Bl: 0-1 Vi: 0-0 Tstrap: 0-0 Ckp: 0-0
Best Rating: **83** 10/09 Nott 6f15y soft

Fair; suited by 5f; acts on soft and fast ground.

Cayman Fox

103(104) (77)**64**

4-y-o ch f Cayman Kai (IRE)-Kalarram (Muhtarram (USA))
James Moffatt R R Whitton

Placings:4266350/002240-0512352042246 **(7634)**

2009: 5^{0}GF, 5^{5}GF, 5^{1}G, 5^{2}GF, 5^{3}S, 5^{5}GF, 5^{2}SD, 5^{0}GS, 5^{4}SD, 5^{2}SD, 5^{2}SD, 5^{4}SD, 5^{6}SD,

	Starts	1st	2nd	3rd	Win & Pl
Career Total (Turf)	16	1	2	2	5918
Career Total (AW)	10	0	5	0	5329

64	6/09	Haml	5f4y	GD	£2266

Total win prize-money £2267

Going (Turf): Sf: 0-4 GS: 0-1 **Gd: 1-6** GF: 0-5 Fm: 0-0
Distance: **5f/6f: 1-26** 7f-8f: 0-0 9f-13f: 0-0 14f+: 0-0
Track : LH: 0-12 RH: 0-0 Tight: 0-11 Gall: 0-0
Aids: Bl: 0-0 Vi: 0-0 Tstrap: 0-0 Ckp: 0-0
Best Rating: **77** 11/08 Wolv 5f20y stand

Modest; effective over 5f; acts on most ground; has worn an eyeshield.

Cayman Sky

100(98) (65)69

3-y-o b g Fantastic Light (USA)-Comme Ca (Cyrano De Bergerac)

R Hannon I A N Wight

Placings:004-643642003034 (7049)

2009: 10^{6}SD, 10^{4}GF, 11^{3}GS, 11^{6}GF, 11^{4}G, 14^{2}G, 11^{0}GF, 11^{0}GS, 12^{3}SD, 11^{0}GS, 12^{3}SD, 12^{4}SD,

	Starts	1st	2nd	3rd	Win & Pl
Career Total (Turf)	9	0	1	1	1800
Career Total (AW)	6	0	0	2	688

Going (Turf): **Sf: 0-0 GS: 0-3 Gd: 0-3 GF: 0-3 Fm: 0-0**
Distance: 5f/6f: 0-0 7f-8f: 0-3 9f-13f: 0-11 14f+: 0-1
Track : LH: 0-5 RH: 0-5 Tight: 0-10 Gall: 0-1
Aids: Bl: 0-14 Vi: 0-0 Tstrap: 0-0 Ckp: 0-0
Best Rating: **69** 4/09 Wind 1m3f135y gd-sft

Modest; stays 1m2f; acts on fast ground; has worn blinkers.

Cayo Costa (IRE)

53

2-y-o ch f Kheleyf (USA)-Tropical Paradise (USA) (Manila (USA))

A J McCabe Sale Of The Century

Placings:0 (7120)

2009: 8^{0}GF,

	Starts	1st	2nd	3rd	Win & Pl
Career Total (Turf)	1	0	0	0	

Going (Turf): **Sf: 0-0 GS: 0-0 Gd: 0-0 GF: 0-1 Fm: 0-0**
Distance: 5f/6f: 0-0 7f-8f: 0-0 9f-13f: 0-1 14f+: 0-0
Track : LH: 0-1 RH: 0-0 Tight: 0-0 Gall: 0-0
Aids: Bl: 0-0 Vi: 0-0 Tstrap: 0-0 Ckp: 0-0
Best Rating:

Cecil's Gift

80(74) (23)40

2-y-o b f Act One-Poyle Jenny (Piccolo)

W G M Turner Mrs Tracy Turner

Placings:050 (3709)

2009: 6^{0}GF, 5^{5}G, 5^{0}SD,

	Starts	1st	2nd	3rd	Win & Pl
Career Total (Turf)	2	0	0	0	0
Career Total (AW)	1	0	0	0	

Going (Turf): **Sf: 0-0 GS: 0-0 Gd: 0-1 GF: 0-1 Fm: 0-0**
Distance: 5f/6f: 0-3 7f-8f: 0-0 9f-13f: 0-0 14f+: 0-0
Track : LH: 0-0 RH: 0-0 Tight: 0-0 Gall: 0-1
Aids: Bl: 0-0 Vi: 0-0 Tstrap: 0-0 Ckp: 0-0
Best Rating: **40** 6/09 Chep 5f16y good

Cecily

94(108) (85)79

3-y-o b f Oasis Dream-Odette (Pursuit Of Love)

Sir Mark Prescott C G Rowles Nicholson

Placings:01-3546324144340 (7613)

2009: 5^{3}SD, 5^{5}SD, 5^{4}SD, 5^{6}SD, 5^{3}SD, 6^{2}SD, 5^{4}G, 5^{1}SD, 5^{4}SD, 5^{4}GF, 6^{3}SD, 5^{4}SD, 6^{0}SD,

	Starts	1st	2nd	3rd	Win & Pl
Career Total (Turf)	4	1	0	0	4613
Career Total (AW)	11	1	1	3	9896
83 4/09 Wolv 5f216y (0-80)H				STD	£5180
79 6/08 Wwck 5f				G-F	£3626

Total win prize-money £8808

Going (Turf): Sf: 0-0 GS: 0-0 Gd: 0-1 **GF: 1-3** Fm: 0-0
Distance: **5f/6f: 2-15** 7f-8f: 0-0 9f-13f: 0-0 14f+: 0-0
Track : **LH: 2-6** RH: 0-6 **Tight: 1-4** Gall: 0-0
Aids: Bl: 0-3 Vi: 0-0 Tstrap: 0-0 Ckp: 0-0
Best Rating: **85** 11/09 Kemp 5f stand

Fair; stays 6f; acts on fast ground and Polytrack; has worn blinkers.

Cecily Parsley

95(73) (6)49

3-y-o b f Fantastic Light (USA)-Salim Toto (Mtoto)

H Morrison L A Garfield

Placings:5060 (6445)

2009: 12^{5}GF, 11^{0}G, 11^{6}GF, 12^{0}SS,

	Starts	1st	2nd	3rd	Win & Pl
Career Total (Turf)	3	0	0	0	0
Career Total (AW)	1	0	0	0	

Going (Turf): **Sf: 0-0 GS: 0-0 Gd: 0-1 GF: 0-2 Fm: 0-0**
Distance: 5f/6f: 0-0 7f-8f: 0-0 9f-13f: 0-4 14f+: 0-0
Track : LH: 0-4 RH: 0-0 Tight: 0-3 Gall: 0-1
Aids: Bl: 0-0 Vi: 0-0 Tstrap: 0-0 Ckp: 0-0
Best Rating: **49** 7/09 Bath 1m3f144y good

Cecina Marina

97(88) (20)52

6-y-o b m Sugarfoot-Chasetown Cailin (Suave Dancer (USA))

Mrs K Walton B D Howell and G D Brumby

Placings:00503640/4540200-030020035 (7080)

2009: 11^{0}SD, 13^{3}GF, 14^{0}GF, 13^{0}GF, 11^{2}S, 9^{0}GF, 10^{0}GF, 11^{3}G, 11^{5}S,

	Starts	1st	2nd	3rd	Win & Pl
Career Total (Turf)	22	0	2	3	2858
Career Total (AW)	2	0	0	0	

Going (Turf): **Sf: 0-4 GS: 0-3 Gd: 0-6 GF: 0-9 Fm: 0-0**
Distance: 5f/6f: 0-0 7f-8f: 0-2 9f-13f: 0-17 14f+: 0-5
Track : LH: 0-13 RH: 0-9 Tight: 0-15 Gall: 0-0
Aids: Bl: 0-0 Vi: 0-0 Tstrap: 0-1 Ckp: 0-1
Best Rating: **52** 10/09 Catt 1m3f214y good

Moderate; stays 1m4f; acts on easy ground.

Ceedwell

103 90

2-y-o ch f Exceed And Excel (AUS)-Muja Farewell (Mujtahid (USA))

E Libaud (B Smart 8/7) Prime Equestrian

Placings:11365 (5739a)

2009: 5^{1}GF, 5^{1}GF, 5^{3}GF, 6^{6}G, 8^{5}GS,

	Starts	1st	2nd	3rd	Win & Pl
Career Total (Turf)	5	2	0	1	21423
90 6/09 Catt 5f				G-F	£4094
74 5/09 Carl 5f				G-F	£3885

Total win prize-money £7980

Going (Turf): Sf: 0-0 GS: 0-1 Gd: 0-1 **GF: 2-3** Fm: 0-0
Distance: **5f/6f: 2-4** 7f-8f: 0-0 9f-13f: 0-1 14f+: 0-0
Track : LH: 0-0 **RH: 1-1** Tight: 0-0 **Gall: 1-1**
Aids: Bl: 0-0 Vi: 0-0 Tstrap: 0-0 Ckp: 0-0
Best Rating: **90** 6/09 Asct 5f gd-fm

Very useful; effective over 5f and acts on fast ground.

Ceilidh House

95 80

2-y-o ch f Selkirk (USA)-Villa Carlotta (Rainbow Quest (USA))

R M Beckett J H Richmond-Watson

Placings:1 (6593)

2009: 8^{1}GS,

	Starts	1st	2nd	3rd	Win & Pl
Career Total (Turf)	1	1	0	0	2914
80 10/09 Nott 1m75y				G-S	£2914

Total win prize-money £2914

Going (Turf): Sf: 0-0 **GS: 1-1** Gd: 0-0 GF: 0-0 Fm: 0-0
Distance: 5f/6f: 0-0 7f-8f: 0-0 **9f-13f: 1-1** 14f+: 0-0
Track : **LH: 1-1** RH: 0-0 Tight: 0-0 Gall: 0-0
Aids: Bl: 0-0 Vi: 0-0 Tstrap: 0-0 Ckp: 0-0
Best Rating: **80** 10/09 Nott 1m75y gd-sft

Impressive winner on debut; effective over 1m; acts on easy ground.

Celebrian

68(85) (56)8

2-y-o b f Fasliyev (USA)-Triplemoon (USA) (Trempolino (USA))

W R Swinburn David Taylor & Don Clark

Placings:000 (7451)

2009: 6^{0}S, 7^{0}SD, 8^{0}SD,

	Starts	1st	2nd	3rd	Win & Pl
Career Total (Turf)	1	0	0	0	
Career Total (AW)	2	0	0	0	

Going (Turf): **Sf: 0-1 GS: 0-0 Gd: 0-0 GF: 0-0 Fm: 0-0**
Distance: 5f/6f: 0-0 7f-8f: 0-3 9f-13f: 0-0 14f+: 0-0
Track : LH: 0-1 RH: 0-1 Tight: 0-1 Gall: 0-0
Aids: Bl: 0-0 Vi: 0-0 Tstrap: 0-0 Ckp: 0-0
Best Rating: **56** 11/09 Kemp 1m stand

Celendine

83 58

2-y-o b f Oratorio (IRE)-Affaire D'Amour (Hernando (FR))

G A Swinbank R H Hall

Placings:0 (6154)

2009: 6^{0}G,

	Starts	1st	2nd	3rd	Win & Pl
Career Total (Turf)	1	0	0	0	

Going (Turf): **Sf: 0-0 GS: 0-0 Gd: 0-1 GF: 0-0 Fm: 0-0**
Distance: 5f/6f: 0-0 7f-8f: 0-1 9f-13f: 0-0 14f+: 0-0
Track : LH: 0-0 RH: 0-0 Tight: 0-0 Gall: 0-0
Aids: Bl: 0-0 Vi: 0-0 Tstrap: 0-0 Ckp: 0-0
Best Rating: **58** 9/09 Haml 6f5y good

Celestial Dream (IRE)

98(98) (69)65

3-y-o b f Oasis Dream-Lochangel (Night Shift (USA))

A M Balding J C Smith

Placings:43-213 (2654)

2009: 5^{2}F, 5^{1}SD, 5^{3}F,

	Starts	1st	2nd	3rd	Win & Pl
Career Total (Turf)	3	0	1	1	1802
Career Total (AW)	2	1	0	1	3600

69 5/09 Ling 5f (0-75)H STD £3070

Total win prize-money £3071

Going (Turf): **Sf: 0-0 GS: 0-1 Gd: 0-0 GF: 0-0 Fm: 0-2**
Distance: **5f/6f: 1-5** 7f-8f: 0-0 9f-13f: 0-0 14f+: 0-0
Track : **LH: 1-5** RH: 0-0 **Tight: 1-1** Gall: 0-3
Aids: Bl: 0-0 Vi: 0-0 Tstrap: 0-0 Ckp: 0-0
Best Rating: **69** 5/09 Ling 5f stand

Modest; stays 6f and acts on fast ground and Polytrack.

Celestial Girl

(89) (53)
2-y-o b f Dubai Destination (USA)-Brightest Star (Unfuwain (USA))
H Morrison Helena Springfield Ltd

Placings:0 (7859)
2009: 7^{0}SD,

	Starts	1st	2nd	3rd	Win & Pl
Career Total (Turf)	0	0	0	0	
Career Total (AW)	1	0	0	0	

Going (Turf): **Sf: 0-0 GS: 0-0 Gd: 0-0 GF: 0-0 Fm: 0-0**
Distance: 5f/6f: 0-0 7f-8f: 0-1 9f-13f: 0-0 14f+: 0-0
Track : LH: 0-1 RH: 0-0 Tight: 0-1 Gall: 0-0
Aids: Bl: 0-0 Vi: 0-0 Tstrap: 0-0 Ckp: 0-0
Best Rating: **53** 12/09 Wolv 7f32y stand

Celestial Tryst

95 74
2-y-o b f Tobougg (IRE)-Celestial Welcome (Most Welcome)
G M Moore Celestial Tryst Partnership

Placings:0160 (6693)
2009: 5^{0}G, 7^{1}G, 8^{6}G, 7^{0}GS,

	Starts	1st	2nd	3rd	Win & Pl
Career Total (Turf)	4	1	0	0	3886

72 7/09 Donc 7f GD £3885

Total win prize-money £3886

Going (Turf): Sf: 0-0 GS: 0-1 **Gd: 1-3** GF: 0-0 Fm: 0-0
Distance: 5f/6f: 0-1 **7f-8f: 1-3** 9f-13f: 0-0 14f+: 0-0
Track : LH: 0-0 RH: 0-3 Tight: 0-0 Gall: 0-1
Aids: Bl: 0-0 Vi: 0-0 Tstrap: 0-0 Ckp: 0-0
Best Rating: **74** 8/09 Deau 1m good

Fair; stays 7f; acts on good ground; may improve further.

Cellarmaster (IRE)

(89) (43)
8-y-o ch g Alhaarth (IRE)-Cheeky Weeky (Cadeaux Genereux)
Mark Gillard Ascot Park Polo Club

Placings:352/31430/000/0-0 (0190)
2009: 16^{0}SD,

	Starts	1st	2nd	3rd	Win & Pl
Career Total (Turf)	10	1	0	3	7231
Career Total (AW)	3	0	1	0	858

82 7/04 Nott 1m1f213yE(0-75)H GD £4192

Total win prize-money £4193

Going (Turf): Sf: 0-2 GS: 0-2 **Gd: 1-4** GF: 0-2 Fm: 0-0
Distance: 5f/6f: 0-0 7f-8f: 0-1 **9f-13f: 1-10** 14f+: 0-2
Track : **LH: 1-6** RH: 0-5 Tight: 0-4 Gall: 0-3
Aids: Bl: 0-0 Vi: 0-0 Tstrap: 0-0 Ckp: 0-0
Best Rating: **84** 8/04 NmkJ 1m2f gd-sft

Celtic Carisma

99 51
7-y-o b m Celtic Swing-Kathryn's Pet (Blakeney)
K G Reveley Bill Brown

Placings:00/00100114/01005000/60264 (5734)
2009: 16^{6}GS, 14^{0}GF, 16^{2}G, 17^{6}GF, 16^{4}GS,

	Starts	1st	2nd	3rd	Win & Pl
Career Total (Turf)	23	4	1	0	11191

63 4/06 Sthl 2m (0-65)H GD £2730
55 9/05 Newc 2m19y (0-65)H G-F £2865
58 8/05 Rdcr 1m6f19y (0-55)H GD £2943
47 5/05 Carl 1m3f206y (0-40) G-F £1512

Total win prize-money £10050

Going (Turf): Sf: 0-5 GS: 0-4 **Gd: 2-4 GF: 2-9** Fm: 0-1
Distance: 5f/6f: 0-1 7f-8f: 0-1 9f-13f: 1-6 **14f+: 3-15**
Track : **LH: 3-17** RH: 1-3 **Tight: 2-8** Gall: 1-7
Aids: Bl: 0-0 Vi: 0-0 Tstrap: 0-0 Ckp: 0-0
Best Rating: **63** 4/06 Sthl 2m good

Modest; suited by 2m; acts on fast ground.

Celtic Change (IRE)

105(97) (73)87
5-y-o br g Celtic Swing-Changi (IRE) (Lear Fan (USA))
M Dods P Taylor

Placings:44/5622120/30355405-2006116200 (6485)
2009: 8^{2}GF, 9^{0}G, 8^{0}GS, 7^{6}G, 8^{1}G, 8^{1}GF, 8^{6}GF, 8^{2}GF, 8^{0}G, 8^{0}GF,

	Starts	1st	2nd	3rd	Win & Pl
Career Total (Turf)	26	3	5	2	24253
Career Total (AW)	1	0	0	0	0

87 7/09 Bevl 1m100y (0-85)H G-F £5180
87 7/09 Hayd 1m30y (0-75)H GD £4857
78 7/07 Rdcr 1m (0-75)H G-S £3886

Total win prize-money £13924

Going (Turf): Sf: 0-2 **GS: 1-6 Gd: 1-11 GF: 1-7** Fm: 0-0
Distance: 5f/6f: 0-0 7f-8f: 1-15 **9f-13f: 2-12** 14f+: 0-0
Track : LH: 1-11 RH: 1-5 Tight: 0-5 Gall: 0-6
Aids: **Bl: 2-6** Vi: 0-3 Tstrap: 0-3 Ckp: 0-3
Best Rating: **87** 7/09 Bevl 1m100y gd-fm

Useful; effective over 1m-1m2f; acts on good and easier ground; has worn various headgear.

Celtic Charlie (FR)

(88) (34)19
4-y-o ch c Until Sundown (USA)-India Regalona (USA) (Dehere (USA))
P M Phelan Celtic Contractors Limited

Placings:266/050-0 (6770)
2009: 12^{0}SD,

	Starts	1st	2nd	3rd	Win & Pl
Career Total (Turf)	2	0	0	0	0
Career Total (AW)	5	0	1	0	771

Going (Turf): **Sf: 0-1 GS: 0-0 Gd: 0-0 GF: 0-1 Fm: 0-0**
Distance: 5f/6f: 0-1 7f-8f: 0-5 9f-13f: 0-1 14f+: 0-0
Track : LH: 0-3 RH: 0-3 Tight: 0-3 Gall: 0-0
Aids: Bl: 0-0 Vi: 0-0 Tstrap: 0-0 Ckp: 0-0
Best Rating: **64** 12/07 Ling 1m stand

Celtic Commitment

(98) (67)67
3-y-o gr c Mull Of Kintyre (USA)-Grey Again (Unfuwain (USA))
R Hannon J M Connolly

Placings:00246240-5 (0231)
2009: 8^{5}SD,

	Starts	1st	2nd	3rd	Win & Pl
Career Total (Turf)	3	0	0	0	260
Career Total (AW)	6	0	2	0	2938

Going (Turf): **Sf: 0-1 GS: 0-0 Gd: 0-1 GF: 0-1 Fm: 0-0**
Distance: 5f/6f: 0-2 7f-8f: 0-5 9f-13f: 0-2 14f+: 0-0
Track : LH: 0-3 RH: 0-4 Tight: 0-0 Gall: 0-3
Aids: Bl: 0-0 Vi: 0-0 Tstrap: 0-0 Ckp: 0-0
Best Rating: **67** 11/08 GrLe 1m stand

Modest; effective over 1m; acts on Polytrack.

Celtic Gold (USA)

102(104) (71)73
5-y-o b g Elusive Quality (USA)-Fortune (IRE) (Night Shift (USA))
Andrew Turnell L G Kimber

Placings:63-16562 (1514)
2009: 12^{1}SD, 10^{6}SD, 12^{5}SD, 12^{6}SD, 9^{2}GF,

	Starts	1st	2nd	3rd	Win & Pl
Career Total (Turf)	1	0	1	0	964
Career Total (AW)	6	1	0	1	3211

64 1/09 Ling 1m4f STD £2729

Total win prize-money £2730

Going (Turf): **Sf: 0-0 GS: 0-0 Gd: 0-0 GF: 0-1 Fm: 0-0**
Distance: 5f/6f: 0-0 7f-8f: 0-1 **9f-13f: 1-6** 14f+: 0-0
Track : **LH: 1-4** RH: 0-3 **Tight: 1-3** Gall: 0-1
Aids: Bl: 0-0 Vi: 0-0 Tstrap: 0-0 Ckp: 0-0
Best Rating: **73** 4/09 Leic 1m1f218y gd-fm

Fair sort; stays 1m4f; handles Polytrack.

Celtic Lass

82(87) (44)39
3-y-o b f Celtic Swing-Nsx (Roi Danzig (USA))
M A Jarvis H R H Sultan Ahmad Shah

Placings:60 (4145)
2009: 10^{6}SD, 10^{0}GF,

	Starts	1st	2nd	3rd	Win & Pl
Career Total (Turf)	1	0	0	0	
Career Total (AW)	1	0	0	0	0

Going (Turf): **Sf: 0-0 GS: 0-0 Gd: 0-0 GF: 0-1 Fm: 0-0**
Distance: 5f/6f: 0-0 7f-8f: 0-0 9f-13f: 0-2 14f+: 0-0
Track : LH: 0-0 RH: 0-2 Tight: 0-1 Gall: 0-0
Aids: Bl: 0-0 Vi: 0-0 Tstrap: 0-0 Ckp: 0-0
Best Rating: **44** 6/09 Kemp 1m2f stand

Celtic Lynn (IRE)

100 83
4-y-o br f Celtic Swing-Sheryl Lynn (Miller's Mate)
M Dods P Taylor

Placings:314020-155360 (5697)
2009: 7^{1}GS, 7^{5}GF, 8^{5}GS, 7^{3}G, 8^{6}GS, 7^{0}GS,

	Starts	1st	2nd	3rd	Win & Pl
Career Total (Turf)	12	2	1	2	9844

83 5/09 Newc 7f (0-75)H G-S £2866
78 5/08 Donc 6f GD £3238
Total win prize-money £6104

Going (Turf): Sf: 0-2 **GS: 1-6 Gd: 1-3** GF: 0-1 Fm: 0-0
Distance: 5f/6f: 1-2 7f-8f: 1-8 9f-13f: 0-2 14f+: 0-0
Track : LH: 0-2 RH: 0-2 Tight: 0-1 Gall: 0-1
Aids: Bl: 0-0 Vi: 0-0 Tstrap: 0-0 Ckp: 0-0
Best Rating: 83 5/09 Newc 7f gd-sft

Fair; effective at 6f-7f; acts on good and easy ground.

Celtic Ransom

83(80) (36)58
2-y-o b c Red Ransom (USA)-Welsh Valley (USA) (Irish River (FR))
J W Hills Mrs Kingham,K Mercer,G Charles,R Benton

Placings:000 (7050)
2009: 7^{0}GF, 6^{0}G, 7^{0}SD,

	Starts	1st	2nd	3rd	Win & Pl
Career Total (Turf)	2	0	0	0	
Career Total (AW)	1	0	0	0	

Going (Turf): **Sf: 0-0 GS: 0-0 Gd: 0-1 GF: 0-1 Fm: 0-0**
Distance: 5f/6f: 0-0 7f-8f: 0-3 9f-13f: 0-0 14f+: 0-0
Track : LH: 0-0 RH: 0-1 Tight: 0-0 Gall: 0-0
Aids: Bl: 0-0 Vi: 0-0 Tstrap: 0-0 Ckp: 0-0
Best Rating: 58 9/09 Newb 7f gd-fm

Celtic Rebel (IRE)

81(99) (58)46
3-y-o b g Bahri (USA)-Farjah (IRE) (Charnwood Forest (IRE))
S A Callaghan Phil Cunningham

Placings:6002630-4U0 (1455)
2009: 6^{4}SD, 5^{U}SD, 5^{0}GF,

	Starts	1st	2nd	3rd	Win & Pl
Career Total (Turf)	3	0	0	0	0
Career Total (AW)	7	0	1	1	990

Going (Turf): **Sf: 0-0 GS: 0-2 Gd: 0-0 GF: 0-1 Fm: 0-0**
Distance: 5f/6f: 0-9 7f-8f: 0-1 9f-13f: 0-0 14f+: 0-0
Track : LH: 0-4 RH: 0-2 Tight: 0-2 Gall: 0-2
Aids: Bl: 0-0 Vi: 0-0 Tstrap: 0-1 Ckp: 0-1
Best Rating: 58 2/09 Kemp 6f stand

Moderate; effective over 5f; acts on Polytrack.

Celtic Sovereign (IRE)

(100) (68)
3-y-o b g Celtic Swing-Penny Ha'Penny (Bishop Of Cashel)
M G Quinlan Burns Farm Racing

Placings:1 (7829)
2009: 7^{1}SD,

	Starts	1st	2nd	3rd	Win & Pl
Career Total (Turf)	0	0	0	0	
Career Total (AW)	1	1	0	0	2047

68 12/09 Kemp 7f STD £2047
Total win prize money £2047

Going (Turf): **Sf: 0-0 GS: 0-0 Gd: 0-0 GF: 0-0 Fm: 0-0**
Distance: 5f/6f: 0-0 **7f-8f: 1-1** 9f-13f: 0-0 14f+: 0-0
Track : LH: 0-0 **RH: 1-1** Tight: 0-0 Gall: 0-0
Aids: Bl: 0-0 Vi: 0-0 Tstrap: 0-0 Ckp: 0-0
Best Rating: 68 12/09 Kemp 7f stand

Winner on debut; effective over 7f; acts on Polytrack.

Celtic Spirit (IRE)

96(115) (100)78
6-y-o ch g Pivotal-Cavernista (Lion Cavern (USA))
G L Moore Miss S Bowles

Placings:612133/41/410002-50 (1458)
2009: 12^{5}SD, 12^{0}G,

	Starts	1st	2nd	3rd	Win & Pl
Career Total (Turf)	9	3	0	2	16961
Career Total (AW)	7	1	2	0	16649

100 4/08 Kemp 1m4f (0-105)H STD £9969
96 6/07 Sals 1m1f198y (0-95)H G-S £7124
89 8/06 Sand 1m2f7y (0-80)H GD £5505
74 5/06 Chep 1m14y HVY £3368
Total win prize-money £25968

Going (Turf): **Sf: 1-3 GS: 1-2 Gd: 1-4** GF: 0-0 Fm: 0-0
Distance: 5f/6f: 0-0 7f-8f: 0-0 **9f-13f: 4-15** 14f+: 0-1
Track : LH: 0-7 **RH: 3-8 Tight: 1-6** Gall: 0-3
Aids: Bl: 0-1 Vi: 0-0 Tstrap: 0-1 Ckp: 0-1
Best Rating: 100 4/08 Kemp 1m4f stand

Very useful; stays 1m5f; acts on good and softer ground and on Polytrack; likes to race prominently; has worn blinkers.

Celtic Step

104(104) (67)84
5-y-o br g Selkirk (USA)-Inchiri (Sadler's Wells (USA))
P D Niven Mrs Muriel Ward

Placings:01315/0000/302202-030054332 (7723)
2009: 8^{0}GS, 8^{3}S, 7^{0}GF, 8^{0}GS, 8^{5}SD, 7^{4}S, 8^{3}SD, 8^{3}SD, 8^{2}SD,

	Starts	1st	2nd	3rd	Win & Pl
Career Total (Turf)	15	2	3	2	16962
Career Total (AW)	9	0	1	3	1751

80 10/06 Catt 7f (0-85) SFT £6477
81 9/06 Leic 7f9y G-F £4533
Total win prize-money £11011

Going (Turf): **Sf: 1-6** GS: 0-3 Gd: 0-2 **GF: 1-4** Fm: 0-0
Distance: 5f/6f: 0-0 **7f-8f: 2-19** 9f-13f: 0-5 14f+: 0-0
Track : **LH: 1-19** RH: 0-3 **Tight: 1-11** Gall: 0-3
Aids: **Bl: 1-6** Vi: 0-0 Tstrap: 0-1 Ckp: 0-1
Best Rating: 86 10/06 Newb 1m heavy

Modest; stays 1m; handles good and softer ground and Polytrack; has worn blinkers.

Celtic Sultan (IRE)

109 108
5-y-o b g Celtic Swing-Farjah (IRE) (Charnwood Forest (IRE))
T P Tate Mrs Sylvia Clegg and Louise Worthington

Placings:21300/4344314/15000000-0012020000004300 (7294)
2009: 6^{0}GF, 7^{0}GF, 7^{1}G, 7^{2}GF, 7^{0}GF, 7^{2}G, 7^{0}GF, 7^{0}G, 7^{0}GF, 6^{0}GF, 7^{4}GF, 7^{3}GF, 7^{0}G, 7^{0}S,

	Starts	1st	2nd	3rd	Win & Pl
Career Total (Turf)	34	4	3	4	62243

96 5/09 Catt 7f (0-90)H GD £7771
108 5/08 Ches 7f122y (0-100)H GD £13246
105 10/07 NmkR 7f (0-100)H G-F £12464
90 7/06 Hayd 6f G-F £3886
Total win prize-money £37368

Going (Turf): Sf: 0-3 GS: 0-0 **Gd: 2-13 GF: 2-17** Fm: 0-1
Distance: 5f/6f: 1-9 **7f-8f: 3-24** 9f-13f: 0-1 14f+: 0-0
Track : **LH: 2-11** RH: 0-2 **Tight: 2-8** Gall: 0-3
Aids: Bl: 0-0 Vi: 0-0 Tstrap: 0-0 Ckp: 0-0
Best Rating: 108 5/08 Ches 7f122y good

Useful; effective over 6f-7f; acts on good and faster ground.

Celticello (IRE)

(96) (74)83
7-y-o b/br g Celtic Swing-Viola Royale (IRE) (Royal Academy (USA))
Paul Murphy (Jamie Snowden 6/6) Ms A Hughes

Placings:64116/00/4/164430230030-0 (0584)
2009: 12^{0}SD,

	Starts	1st	2nd	3rd	Win & Pl
Career Total (Turf)	17	3	1	2	15869
Career Total (AW)	4	0	0	1	963

79 5/08 Chep 1m2f36y (0-75)H SFT £3561
92 6/05 Newc 1m (0-80)H GD £6223
80 5/05 Ripn 1m SFT £3477
Total win prize-money £13263

Going (Turf): **Sf: 2-3** GS: 0-6 Gd: 1-5 GF: 0-3 Fm: 0-0
Distance: 5f/6f: 0-0 **7f-8f: 2-5** 9f-13f: 1-15 14f+: 0-1
Track : **LH: 2-13** RH: 1-5 Tight: 1-4 Gall: 1-4
Aids: Bl: 0-0 Vi: 0-0 Tstrap: 0-2 Ckp: 0-2
Best Rating: 92 6/05 Newc 1m good

Fair; stays 1m3f; acts on good and soft ground.

Centenary (IRE)

93 (48)49
5-y-o b g Traditionally (USA)-Catherinofaragon (USA) (Chief's Crown (USA))
M W Easterby S Hudson S Blankley

Placings:532363410/000002005/0046-00 (3171)
2009: 16^{0}G, 14^{0}GF,

	Starts	1st	2nd	3rd	Win & Pl
Career Total (Turf)	20	1	2	3	8681
Career Total (AW)	4	0	0	0	0

69 9/06 Newc 1m GD £3886
Total win prize-money £3886

Going (Turf): Sf: 0-1 GS: 0-2 **Gd: 1-5** GF: 0-11 Fm: 0-1
Distance: 5f/6f: 0-1 **7f-8f: 1-8** 9f-13f: 0-10 14f+: 0-5
Track : **LH: 1-14** RH: 0-6 Tight: 0-10 **Gall: 1-2**
Aids: Bl: 0-1 Vi: 0-1 Tstrap: 0-6 Ckp: 0-6
Best Rating: 71 8/06 Newc 7f gd-fm

Modest gelding; suited by a mile; acts on fast and easy ground.

Centenerola (USA)

(83) (38)85
4-y-o b f Century City (IRE)-Lady Angharad (IRE) (Tenby)
D Shaw Simon Mapletoft Racing & R G Botham

Placings:05/3100000-0 (0039)
2009: 8^{0}SS,

	Starts	1st	2nd	3rd	Win & Pl
Career Total (Turf)	7	1	0	1	5135
Career Total (AW)	3	0	0	0	

85 4/08 Donc 7f G-S £4533
Total win prize-money £4533

Going (Turf): Sf: 0-2 **GS: 1-3** Gd: 0-2 GF: 0-0 Fm: 0-0
Distance: 5f/6f: 0-1 **7f-8f: 1-9** 9f-13f: 0-0 14f+: 0-0
Track : LH: 0-2 RH: 0-2 Tight: 0-1 Gall: 0-0
Aids: Bl: 0-1 Vi: 0-1 Tstrap: 0-0 Ckp: 0-0
Best Rating: 85 4/08 Donc 7f gd-sft

Useful; effective at 7f; goes well on soft ground.

Centennial (IRE)

106 **114**

4-y-o gr c Dalakhani (IRE)-Lurina (IRE) (Lure (USA))
J H M Gosden Michael O'Flynn

Placings:3112/1400133-26000 (5932a)
2009: 12^{2}S, 14^{6}GS, 20^{0}GF, 16^{0}G, 15^{0}G,

	Starts	1st	2nd	3rd	Win & Pl
Career Total (Turf)	**16**	**4**	**2**	**3**	**156805**
114 8/08 Gdwd 1m4f				G-S	£56770
107 4/08 Sand 1m2f7y				GD	£26681
99 9/07 Newb 1m				G-F	£11217
83 8/07 NmkJ 1m				G-F	£4533

Total win prize-money £99204

Going (Turf): Sf: 0-2 GS: 1-3 Gd: 1-5 **GF: 2-5** Fm: 0-0
Distance: 5f/6f: 0-0 7f-8f: 2-4 9f-13f: 2-7 14f+: 0-5
Track : LH: 0-4 **RH: 2-9 Tight: 1-2** Gall: 0-4
Aids: **Bl: 1-7** Vi: 0-1 Tstrap: 0-0 Ckp: 0-0
Best Rating: 114 9/08 Lonc 1m4f gd-sft

Group class; winner of the Group 3 Sandown Classic Trial and Great Voltigeur Stakes in 2008; effective at around 1m2f-1m4f but appears to stay further; acts on most ground; has worn blinkers.

Centigrade (IRE)

98 **89**

2-y-o gr g Verglas (IRE)-American Queen (FR) (Fairy King (USA))
W J Haggas Highclere Thoroughbred Racing (Verglas)

Placings:411 (6088)
2009: 6^{4}G, 7^{1}G, 8^{1}G,

	Starts	1st	2nd	3rd	Win & Pl
Career Total (Turf)	**3**	**2**	**0**	**0**	**16409**
89 9/09 Ayr 1m H				GD	£12462
78 8/09 Wwck 7f26y				GD	£3561

Total win prize-money £16024

Going (Turf): Sf: 0-0 GS: 0-0 **Gd: 2-3** GF: 0-0 Fm: 0-0
Distance: 5f/6f: 0-1 **7f-8f: 2-2** 9f-13f: 0-0 14f+: 0-0
Track : **LH: 2-2** RH: 0-0 Tight: 0-0 Gall: 0-0
Aids: Bl: 0-0 Vi: 0-0 Tstrap: 0-0 Ckp: 0-0
Best Rating: 89 9/09 Ayr 1m good

Useful; stays 1m; acts on good ground.

Centime

88 **51**

2-y-o b f Royal Applause-Argent Du Bois (USA) (Silver Hawk (USA))
B J Meehan Car Colston Hall Stud

Placings:00 (6992)
2009: 6^{0}S, 8^{0}GS,

	Starts	1st	2nd	3rd	Win & Pl
Career Total (Turf)	**2**	**0**	**0**	**0**	

Going (Turf): **Sf: 0-1 GS: 0-1 Gd: 0-0 GF: 0-0 Fm: 0-0**
Distance: 5f/6f: 0-0 7f-8f: 0-2 9f-13f: 0-0 14f+: 0-0
Track : LH: 0-1 RH: 0-0 Tight: 0-0 Gall: 0-1
Aids: Bl: 0-0 Vi: 0-0 Tstrap: 0-0 Ckp: 0-0
Best Rating: 51 10/09 Sals 6f212y soft

Centurio

96 **78**

2-y-o b c Pivotal-Grain Of Gold (Mr Prospector (USA))
R Charlton B E Nielsen

Placings:32 (6617)
2009: 8^{3}GS, 8^{2}G,

	Starts	1st	2nd	3rd	Win & Pl
Career Total (Turf)	**2**	**0**	**1**	**1**	**2216**

Going (Turf): **Sf: 0-0 GS: 0-1 Gd: 0-1 GF: 0-0 Fm: 0-0**
Distance: 5f/6f: 0-0 7f-8f: 0-1 9f-13f: 0-1 14f+: 0-0
Track : LH: 0-0 RH: 0-1 Tight: 0-0 Gall: 0-0
Aids: Bl: 0-0 Vi: 0-0 Tstrap: 0-0 Ckp: 0-0
Best Rating: 78 10/09 Newb 1m good

Cereal Killer (IRE)

90 **71**

2-y-o br c Xaar-Snap Crackle Pop (IRE) (Statoblest)
R Hannon The Major Shear

Placings:004 (6696)
2009: 5^{0}GF, 7^{0}GF, 6^{4}GS,

	Starts	1st	2nd	3rd	Win & Pl
Career Total (Turf)	**3**	**0**	**0**	**0**	**241**

Going (Turf): **Sf: 0-0 GS: 0-1 Gd: 0-0 GF: 0-2 Fm: 0-0**
Distance: 5f/6f: 0-2 7f-8f: 0-1 9f-13f: 0-0 14f+: 0-0
Track : LH: 0-0 RH: 0-0 Tight: 0-0 Gall: 0-0
Aids: Bl: 0-0 Vi: 0-0 Tstrap: 0-0 Ckp: 0-0
Best Rating: 71 10/09 Gdwd 6f gd-sft

Ceremonial Jade (UAE)

59(112) (112)**62**

6-y-o b g Jade Robbery (USA)-Talah (Danehill (USA))
M Botti Giuliano Manfredini

Placings:12011/2042002331/242101163-510303 (7768)
2009: 6^{5}SD, 7^{1}SD, 7^{0}GF, 7^{3}SD, 6^{0}SD, 7^{3}SD,

	Starts	1st	2nd	3rd	Win & Pl
Career Total (Turf)	**10**	**1**	**2**	**1**	**14513**
Career Total (AW)	**20**	**7**	**4**	**4**	**123549**
109 3/09 Wolv 7f32y				STD	£22708
112 9/08 GrLe 6f				STD	£24924
110 7/08 GrLe 6f				STD	£7788
113 5/08 Ling 7f (0-105)H				STD	£12462
105 11/07 Ling 6f (0-100)H				STD	£9971
101 10/06 Ling 7f (0-90)H				STD	£10594
96 9/06 Kemp 7f (0-85)H				STD	£6477
77 6/06 Bevl 1m100y				G-F	£5181

Total win prize-money £100107

Going (Turf): Sf: 0-1 GS: 0-1 Gd: 0-2 **GF: 1-5** Fm: 0-1
Distance: 5f/6f: 3-9 **7f-8f: 4-20** 9f-13f: 1-1 14f+: 0-0
Track : **LH: 6-15** RH: 2-7 **Tight: 4-13** Gall: 2-3
Aids: Bl: 0-0 Vi: 0-0 Tstrap: 1-4 Ckp: 1-4
Best Rating: 113 5/08 Ling 7f stand

Smart on sand/very useful on turf; Listed winner; effective over 6f-1m; acts on fast ground; suited to Polytrack; has worn cheekpieces and a tongue tie.

Cerito

46(107) (88)**91**

3-y-o ch g Bahamian Bounty-Pascali (Compton Place)
J R Boyle Inside Track Racing Club

Placings:1663010-0460 (7511)
2009: 6^{0}GS, 5^{4}SD, 6^{6}SD, 5^{0}SD,

	Starts	1st	2nd	3rd	Win & Pl
Career Total (Turf)	**8**	**2**	**0**	**1**	**13215**
Career Total (AW)	**3**	**0**	**0**	**0**	**673**
91 9/08 Muss 5f (0-90)				SFT	£7477
86 5/08 Bath 5f11y				G-F	£3626

Total win prize-money £11104

Going (Turf): **Sf: 1-2** GS: 0-1 Gd: 0-2 **GF: 1-3** Fm: 0-0
Distance: **5f/6f: 2-10** 7f-8f: 0-1 9f-13f: 0-0 14f+: 0-0
Track : **LH: 1-3** RH: 0-1 Tight: 0-2 **Gall: 1-1**
Aids: Bl: 0-0 Vi: 0-0 Tstrap: 0-0 Ckp: 0-0
Best Rating: 91 9/08 Muss 5f soft

Very useful; effective over 5f; acts on fast and soft ground.

Certain Justice (USA)

(97) (72)**76**

11-y-o gr g Lit De Justice (USA)-Pure Misk (Rainbow Quest (USA))
Stef Liddiard Mrs Stef Liddiard

Placings:11/32250/5402062152/0506040/065050/1032514 06020/01323/5254020002/0300-0 (0094)
2009: 7^{0}SD,

	Starts	1st	2nd	3rd	Win & Pl
Career Total (Turf)	**42**	**4**	**9**	**4**	**67659**
Career Total (AW)	**20**	**2**	**2**	**1**	**9245**
76 7/06 Leic 7f9y (0-70)				GD	£5047
80 7/05 Sthl 6f (0-75)H				STD	£3869
74 2/05 Sthl 7f (0-70)H				STD	£3439
95 8/02 NmkJ 7f B(0-105)H				SFT	£19500
106 5/00 Wind 5f10y B				G-F	£7308
85 4/00 NmkR 5f D				SFT	£4914

Total win prize-money £44077

Going (Turf): **Sf: 2-8** GS: 0-8 Gd: 1-15 GF: 1-10 Fm: 0-1
Distance: 5f/6f: 3-14 7f-8f: 3-41 9f-13f: 0-7 14f+: 0-0
Track : **LH: 2-27** RH: 0-5 Tight: 0-11 **Gall: 1-4**
Aids: **Bl: 1-3** Vi: 0-0 Tstrap: 0-1 Ckp: 0-1
Best Rating: 106 5/00 Wind 5f10y gd-fm

Fair; effective at up to 1m; best with give on turf but acts on both All-Weather surfaces; has worn an eyeshield.

Certifiable

(97) (54)**37**

8-y-o b g Deploy-Gentle Irony (Mazilier (USA))
Miss Z C Davison Mrs S E Colville

Placings:411505002410/00050000/16400-0 (0211)
2009: 8^{0}SD,

	Starts	1st	2nd	3rd	Win & Pl
Career Total (Turf)	**3**	**0**	**0**	**0**	**676**
Career Total (AW)	**23**	**4**	**1**	**0**	**13749**
53 1/08 Kemp 1m (0-50)H				STD	£2047
72 12/04 Wolv 7f32y				STD	£2968
76 3/04 Ling 1m E(0-70)				STD	£3464
71 2/04 Ling 1m D				STD	£4212

Total win prize-money £12693

Going (Turf): **Sf: 0-0 GS: 0-2 Gd: 0-0 GF: 0-0 Fm: 0-1**
Distance: 5f/6f: 0-0 **7f-8f: 4-18** 9f-13f: 0-8 14f+: 0-0
Track : **LH: 3-17** RH: 1-9 **Tight: 3-15** Gall: 0-2
Aids: Bl: 0-0 Vi: 0-1 Tstrap: 0-2 Ckp: 0-2
Best Rating: 77 12/04 Ling 1m stand

Moderate; suited by 1m; acts on Polytrack.

Cesare

112(105) (99)**123**

8-y-o b g Machiavellian (USA)-Tromond (Lomond (USA))

J R Fanshawe Cheveley Park Stud

Placings:210/1113/01015/151240/1443-25354 **(6030)**

2009: 8^{2}GF, 8^{5}GF, 8^{3}G, 8^{5}G, 8^{4}SD,

	Starts	1st	2nd	3rd	Win & Pl
Career Total (Turf)	24	8	3	3	339926
Career Total (AW)	3	1	0	0	10740

123	4/08	Asct	1m		SFT	£17031
121	7/07	Asct	1m		GD	£48263
121	5/07	Asct	1m		G-F	£17034
111	8/06	Wwck	7f26y		GD	£6477
108	6/06	Asct	1m	H	G-F	£62320
106	7/05	Ling	1m	(0-90)	STD	£10173
96	5/05	Ripn	1m	(0-90)H	SFT	£9525
80	4/05	Leic	7f9y	(0-85)H	SFT	£6869
69	4/04	Bevl	1m100y	D	G-S	£4186

Total win prize-money £181878

Going (Turf): **Sf: 3-6** GS: 1-4 Gd: 2-8 GF: 2-6 Fm: 0-0
Distance: 5f/6f: 0-0 **7f-8f: 8-23** 9f-13f: 1-4 14f+: 0-0
Track : LH: 2-6 **RH: 3-9 Tight: 2-4** Gall: 1-5
Aids: Bl: 0-0 Vi: 0-0 Tstrap: 0-0 Ckp: 0-0
Best Rating: **123** 4/08 Asct 1m soft

Group class; winner of the 2006 Royal Hunt Cup; Group 2 winner in 2007; stays 1m; acts on most ground; also goes on Polytrack; likes Ascot.

Chabal (IRE)

103 **116**

2-y-o b c Galileo (IRE)-Vagary (IRE) (Zafonic (USA))

J S Bolger Lady O'Reilly/ Mrs J S Bolger

Placings:120 **(6849)**

2009: 7^{1}GY, 7^{2}SH, 7^{0}G,

	Starts	1st	2nd	3rd	Win & Pl
Career Total (Turf)	3	1	1	0	57954

86	9/09	Leop	7f	G-Y	£11740

Total win prize-money £11740

Going (Turf): **Sf: 0-0 GS: 0-0 Gd: 0-1 GF: 0-0 Fm: 0-0**
Distance: 5f/6f: 0-0 **7f-8f: 1-3** 9f-13f: 0-0 14f+: 0-0
Track : **LH: 1-1** RH: 0-0 Tight: 0-0 Gall: 0-0
Aids: Bl: 0-0 Vi: 0-0 Tstrap: 0-0 Ckp: 0-0
Best Rating: **116** 9/09 Curr 7f sft-hvy

Smart juvenile; runner-up in the Group 1 National Stakes; stays at least 7f; goes well with cut in the ground; has joined Godolphin.

Chachamaidee (IRE)

99 **93**

2-y-o b f Footstepsinthesand-Canterbury Lace (USA) (Danehill (USA))

H R A Cecil R A H Evans

Placings:1365 **(5199)**

2009: 6^{1}GF, 6^{3}GF, 7^{6}G, 6^{5}GF,

	Starts	1st	2nd	3rd	Win & Pl
Career Total (Turf)	4	1	0	1	14466

79	6/09	Ling	6f	G-F	£3561

Total win prize-money £3562

Going (Turf): Sf: 0-0 GS: 0-0 Gd: 0-1 **GF: 1-3** Fm: 0-0
Distance: **5f/6f: 1-3** 7f-8f: 0-1 9f-13f: 0-0 14f+: 0-0
Track : LH: 0-0 RH: 0-0 Tight: 0-0 Gall: 0-0
Aids: Bl: 0-0 Vi: 0-0 Tstrap: 0-0 Ckp: 0-0
Best Rating: **93** 6/09 Asct 6f gd-fm

Very useful; Group 3 placed; effective over 6f; acts on fast ground.

Chadwell Spring (IRE)

103(93) (68)**74**

3-y-o b f Statue Of Liberty (USA)-Cresalin (Coquelin (USA))

Miss J Feilden R J Creese

Placings:0026-30036160140 **(6474)**

2009: 8^{3}SD, 8^{0}SD, 8^{0}G, 7^{3}G, 7^{6}GF, 9^{1}GF, 8^{6}G, 10^{0}SD, 8^{1}GF, 8^{4}GF, 8^{0}GF,

	Starts	1st	2nd	3rd	Win & Pl
Career Total (Turf)	11	2	0	1	7892
Career Total (AW)	4	0	1	1	2505

74	9/09	Epsm	1m114y	(0-80)H	G-F	£5180
67	7/09	Ling	1m1f	(0-60)H	G-F	£2047

Total win prize-money £7228

Going (Turf): Sf: 0-1 GS: 0-1 Gd: 0-4 **GF: 2-5** Fm: 0-0
Distance: 5f/6f: 0-0 7f-8f: 0-5 **9f-13f: 2-10** 14f+: 0-0
Track : **LH: 2-8** RH: 0-0 **Tight: 2-6** Gall: 0-1
Aids: Bl: 0-0 Vi: 0-0 Tstrap: 0-2 Ckp: 0-2
Best Rating: **74** 9/09 Epsm 1m114y gd-fm

Modest; stays 1m1f; acts on fast ground and on Polytrack.

Chain Of Events

88 **73**

2-y-o ch g Nayef (USA)-Ermine (IRE) (Cadeaux Genereux)

B W Hills Sir A Ferguson,Cavendish InvLtd,J Hanson

Placings:30 **(5793)**

2009: 7^{3}S, 8^{0}GF,

	Starts	1st	2nd	3rd	Win & Pl
Career Total (Turf)	2	0	0	1	963

Going (Turf): **Sf: 0-1 GS: 0-0 Gd: 0-0 GF: 0-1 Fm: 0-0**
Distance: 5f/6f: 0-0 7f-8f: 0-2 9f-13f: 0-0 14f+: 0-0
Track : LH: 0-0 RH: 0-0 Tight: 0-0 Gall: 0-0
Aids: Bl: 0-0 Vi: 0-0 Tstrap: 0-0 Ckp: 0-0
Best Rating: **73** 7/09 Newb 7f soft

Chain Of Office

87 **72**

2-y-o ch f Mark Of Esteem (IRE)-Lady Mayor (Kris)

W J Haggas J M Greetham

Placings:610 **(6923)**

2009: 7^{6}GF, 8^{1}GF, 8^{0}GF,

	Starts	1st	2nd	3rd	Win & Pl
Career Total (Turf)	3	1	0	0	5181

72	9/09	Ffos	1m	G-F	£5180

Total win prize-money £5181

Going (Turf): Sf: 0-0 GS: 0-0 Gd: 0-0 **GF: 1-3** Fm: 0-0
Distance: 5f/6f: 0-0 **7f-8f: 1-2** 9f-13f: 0-1 14f+: 0-0
Track : **LH: 1-1** RH: 0-0 Tight: 0-0 **Gall: 1-1**
Aids: Bl: 0-0 Vi: 0-0 Tstrap: 0-0 Ckp: 0-0
Best Rating: **72** 9/09 Ffos 1m gd-fm

Fair; effective over 1m; acts on fast ground.

Chairman Pat (USA)

92(87) (65)**70**

2-y-o ch c Proud Citizen (USA)-Sejm's Lunar Star (USA) (Sejm (USA))

Tom Dascombe De La Warr Racing (P Wiener Memorial)

Placings:0525060 **(6793)**

2009: 6^{0}GF, 7^{5}SD, 7^{2}G, 6^{5}F, 8^{0}G, 7^{6}GF, 8^{0}S,

	Starts	1st	2nd	3rd	Win & Pl
Career Total (Turf)	6	0	1	0	1177
Career Total (AW)	1	0	0	0	0

Going (Turf): **Sf: 0-1 GS: 0-0 Gd: 0-2 GF: 0-2 Fm: 0-1**
Distance: 5f/6f: 0-1 7f-8f: 0-5 9f-13f: 0-1 14f+: 0-0
Track : LH: 0-2 RH: 0-2 Tight: 0-0 Gall: 0-0
Aids: Bl: 0-0 Vi: 0-0 Tstrap: 0-0 Ckp: 0-0
Best Rating: **70** 8/09 Brig 6f209y firm

Chalentina

(97) (52)**59**

6-y-o b m Primo Valentino (IRE)-Chantilly Myth (Sri Pekan (USA))

J E Long T H Bambridge

Placings:403/52521200**4**/**04**0303340**5**0**3**/000000-34500 **(0853)**

2009: 7^{3}SD, 6^{4}SD, 7^{5}SD, 7^{0}SD, 6^{0}SD,

	Starts	1st	2nd	3rd	Win & Pl
Career Total (Turf)	17	1	3	3	9180
Career Total (AW)	18	0	0	3	1231

70	7/06	Yarm	7f3y	FRM	£3238

Total win prize-money £3239

Going (Turf): Sf: 0-0 GS: 0-2 Gd: 0-3 GF: 0-10 **Fm: 1-2**
Distance: 5f/6f: 0-3 **7f-8f: 1-25** 9f-13f: 0-7 14f+: 0-0
Track : LH: 0-20 RH: 0-6 Tight: 0-15 Gall: 0-0
Aids: Bl: 0-1 Vi: 0-0 Tstrap: 0-0 Ckp: 0-0
Best Rating: **78** 9/06 Catt 7f gd-sft

Plater; formerly fair; probably best over 7f; acts on fast ground and Polytrack.

Chalice Welcome

99(106) (75)**74**

6-y-o b g Most Welcome-Blue Peru (IRE) (Perugino (USA))

N B King The Dyball Partnership

Placings:0000/**2**0**3**06**4**/5440/01-1**2**6**2**1000161 **(7695)**

2009: 10^{1}SD, 9^{2}SD, 10^{6}SD, 10^{2}SD, 9^{1}F, 10^{0}GF, 11^{0}G, 10^{0}F, 11^{1}GF, 10^{6}GF, 12^{1}SD,

	Starts	1st	2nd	3rd	Win & Pl
Career Total (Turf)	11	2	0	0	5569
Career Total (AW)	16	3	3	1	8051

75	12/09	Ling	1m4f	(0-70)H	STD	£2729
74	9/09	Yarm	1m3f101y	(0-70)H	G-F	£3238
66	5/09	Brig	1m1f209y	(0-60)H	FRM	£2331
59	1/09	Ling	1m2f	(0-55)H	STD	£1706
54	12/08	GrLe	1m2f	(0-45)	STD	£1706

Total win prize-money £11711

Going (Turf): Sf: 0-0 GS: 0-0 Gd: 0-3 **GF: 1-5 Fm: 1-3**
Distance: 5f/6f: 0-3 7f-8f: 0-6 **9f-13f: 5-18** 14f+: 0-0
Track : **LH: 5-17** RH: 0-5 **Tight: 3-15** Gall: 1-1
Aids: Bl: 0-1 Vi: 0-1 Tstrap: 0-0 Ckp: 0-0
Best Rating: **75** 12/09 Ling 1m4f stand

Fair; stays 1m4f; acts on fast ground; goes on Polytrack; has worn a visor and blinkers.

Chalk Hill Blue

82(94) (54)**62**

3-y-o b f Reset (AUS)-Golubitsa (IRE) (Bluebird (USA))

Eve Johnson Houghton Fyfield Racing

Placings:026-06000 (4224)
2009: 10^{0}GF, 10^{6}SD, 8^{0}G, 11^{0}G, 10^{0}G,

	Starts	1st	2nd	3rd	Win & Pl
Career Total (Turf)	6	0	1	0	867
Career Total (AW)	2	0	0	0	0

Going (Turf): Sf: 0-1 GS: 0-0 Gd: 0-3 GF: 0-2 Fm: 0-0
Distance: 5f/6f: 0-0 7f-8f: 0-3 9f-13f: 0-5 14f+: 0-0
Track : LH: 0-4 RH: 0-1 Tight: 0-3 Gall: 0-0
Aids: Bl: 0-1 Vi: 0-0 Tstrap: 0-0 Ckp: 0-0
Best Rating: 62 8/08 Wwck 7f26y soft

Promising efforts in maidens over 7f on fast and soft ground.

Challenging (UAE)

91 53
3-y-o b f Halling (USA)-Small Change (IRE) (Danzig (USA))
M W Easterby Stephen J Curtis

Placings:062-00 (3610)
2009: 8^{0}GF, 9^{0}GF,

	Starts	1st	2nd	3rd	Win & Pl
Career Total (Turf)	5	0	1	0	1156

Going (Turf): Sf: 0-1 GS: 0-1 Gd: 0-0 GF: 0-3 Fm: 0-0
Distance: 5f/6f: 0-0 7f-8f: 0-2 9f-13f: 0-3 14f+: 0-0
Track : LH: 0-2 RH: 0-3 Tight: 0-2 Gall: 0-0
Aids: Bl: 0-0 Vi: 0-0 Tstrap: 0-0 Ckp: 0-0
Best Rating: 53 11/08 Muss 7f30y soft

Moderate; stays 7f and acts on soft ground.

Champagne All Day

75 8
3-y-o ch g Timeless Times (USA)-Miss Ceylon (Brief Truce (USA))
S P Griffiths T Grant & J Horsfall

Placings:0 (6823)
2009: 6^{0}GF,

	Starts	1st	2nd	3rd	Win & Pl
Career Total (Turf)	1	0	0	0	

Going (Turf): Sf: 0-0 GS: 0-0 Gd: 0-0 GF: 0-1 Fm: 0-0
Distance: 5f/6f: 0-1 7f-8f: 0-0 9f-13f: 0-0 14f+: 0-0
Track : LH: 0-0 RH: 0-0 Tight: 0-0 Gall: 0-0
Aids: Bl: 0-0 Vi: 0-0 Tstrap: 0-0 Ckp: 0-0
Best Rating: 8 10/09 Rdcr 6f gd-fm

Champagne Cocktail (IRE)

(94) (51)
8-y-o b g Dushyantor (USA)-Kunuz (Ela-Mana-Mou)
R J Price McGahon & Price

Placings:032/30 (3029)
2009: 12^{3}SD, 16^{0}SD,

	Starts	1st	2nd	3rd	Win & Pl
Career Total (Turf)	3	0	1	1	1545
Career Total (AW)	2	0	0	1	353

Going (Turf): Sf: 0-0 GS: 0-0 Gd: 0-2 GF: 0-1 Fm: 0-0
Distance: 5f/6f: 0-0 7f-8f: 0-0 9f-13f: 0-3 14f+: 0-2
Track : LH: 0-1 RH: 0-4 Tight: 0-0 Gall: 0-0
Aids: Bl: 0-1 Vi: 0-0 Tstrap: 0-0 Ckp: 0-0
Best Rating: 68 8/05 Tram 2m good

Modest; stays 2m; acts on good ground and on Fibresand.

Champagne Fizz (IRE)

91(96) (60)67
3-y-o gr f King Charlemagne (USA)-Silver Moon (Environment Friend)
Miss Jo Crowley Mrs Liz Nelson

Placings:3306-606301 (7765)
2009: 7^{6}GF, 7^{0}G, 9^{6}GF, 12^{3}SS, 12^{0}SD, 11^{1}SD,

	Starts	1st	2nd	3rd	Win & Pl
Career Total (Turf)	6	0	0	2	1204
Career Total (AW)	4	1	0	1	2299

59 12/09 Kemp 1m3f STD £2047
Total win prize-money £2047

Going (Turf): Sf: 0-0 GS: 0-1 Gd: 0-2 GF: 0-3 Fm: 0-0
Distance: 5f/6f: 0-2 7f-8f: 0-4 9f-13f: 1-4 14f+: 0-0
Track : LH: 0-3 RH: 1-2 Tight: 0-4 Gall: 0-0
Aids: Bl: 0-0 Vi: 0-0 Tstrap: 0-0 Ckp: 0-0
Best Rating: 67 8/08 Newb 7f gd-sft

Fair; effective over 7f; acts on fast and easy ground.

Champagne Future

105 86
3-y-o b f Compton Place-Jade Pet (Petong)
W R Swinburn The Enthusiasts

Placings:0-312 (2058)
2009: 6^{3}GF, 5^{1}GF, 5^{2}GS,

	Starts	1st	2nd	3rd	Win & Pl
Career Total (Turf)	4	1	1	1	4951

82 4/09 Bath 5f161y G-F £2590
Total win prize-money £2590

Going (Turf): Sf: 0-0 GS: 0-1 Gd: 0-0 GF: 1-3 Fm: 0-0
Distance: 5f/6f: 1-4 7f-8f: 0-0 9f-13f: 0-0 14f+: 0-0
Track : LH: 1-2 RH: 0-0 Tight: 0-0 Gall: 1-1
Aids: Bl: 0-0 Vi: 0-0 Tstrap: 0-0 Ckp: 0-0
Best Rating: 86 5/09 York 5f gd-sft

Fair; stays 6f; acts on fast ground; progressive.

Champagne Shadow (IRE)

(104) (67)71
8-y-o b g Kahyasi-Moet (IRE) (Mac's Imp (USA))
J Pearce Miss Audrey Lanham

Placings:04/040202320030/R1/3441354121302333/05011 1145264/13130506600-43 (3382)
2009: 14^{4}SD, 12^{3}SD,

	Starts	1st	2nd	3rd	Win & Pl
Career Total (Turf)	9	1	0	0	4189
Career Total (AW)	48	9	6	11	38262

65 2/08 Ling 1m5f STD £1774
59 1/08 Wolv 1m5f194y STD £1774
77 7/07 Ling 2m (0-70)H STD £2817
68 7/07 Wolv 1m4f50y STD £2184
64 6/07 Wolv 1m4f50y SF £2590
56 6/07 Ling 1m4f STD £2968
71 8/06 Catt 1m3f214y (0-75)H SFT £3747
66 6/06 Ling 1m4f STD £2388
67 3/06 Ling 1m4f STD £3238
76 6/05 Ling 1m4f STD £3474
Total win prize-money £26961

Going (Turf): Sf: 1-2 GS: 0-0 Gd: 0-4 GF: 0-2 Fm: 0-1
Distance: 5f/6f: 0-0 7f-8f: 0-3 9f-13f: 8-30 14f+: 2-24
Track : LH: 10-48 RH: 0-6 Tight: 10-46 Gall: 0-2
Aids: Bl: 3-22 Vi: 0-0 Tstrap: 5-21 Ckp: 5-21
Best Rating: 86 2/06 Ling 2m stand

Modest; completed four-timer on Polytrack in the summer of 2007; stays 2m but effective over shorter; acts on soft ground; also goes well on Polytrack; has worn cheekpieces.

Champagne Style (USA)

103(97) (82)100
2-y-o ch c Lion Heart (USA)-Statute (USA) (Verzy (CAN))
B J Meehan Roldvale Limited

Placings:221 (6811)
2009: 7^{2}G, 7^{2}SD, 8^{1}G,

	Starts	1st	2nd	3rd	Win & Pl
Career Total (Turf)	2	1	1	0	10310
Career Total (AW)	1	0	1	0	964

100 10/09 NmkR 1m GD £9346
Total win prize-money £9347

Going (Turf): Sf: 0-0 GS: 0-0 Gd: 1-2 GF: 0-0 Fm: 0-0
Distance: 5f/6f: 0-0 7f-8f: 1-3 9f-13f: 0-0 14f+: 0-0
Track : LH: 0-1 RH: 0-1 Tight: 0-1 Gall: 0-0
Aids: Bl: 0-0 Vi: 0-0 Tstrap: 0-0 Ckp: 0-0
Best Rating: 100 10/09 NmkR 1m good

Useful; stays 1m; acts on good ground.

Champagnelifestyle

88 85
2-y-o b f Montjeu (IRE)-White Rose (GER) (Platini (GER))
B W Hills Betfair Club ROA

Placings:10 (6852)
2009: 7^{1}S, 7^{0}G,

	Starts	1st	2nd	3rd	Win & Pl
Career Total (Turf)	2	1	0	0	5181

85 7/09 NmkJ 7f SFT £5180
Total win prize-money £5181

Going (Turf): Sf: 1-1 GS: 0-0 Gd: 0-1 GF: 0-0 Fm: 0-0
Distance: 5f/6f: 0-0 7f-8f: 1-2 9f-13f: 0-0 14f+: 0-0
Track : LH: 0-0 RH: 0-0 Tight: 0-0 Gall: 0-0
Aids: Bl: 0-0 Vi: 0-0 Tstrap: 0-0 Ckp: 0-0
Best Rating: 85 7/09 NmkJ 7f soft

Useful; 140,000gns foal but unsold as a yearling; daughter of Montjeu and half-sister to a 1m2f winner in France; made a winning debut over 7f on soft ground.

Champain Sands (IRE)

103(88) (61)71
10-y-o b g Green Desert (USA)-Grecian Bride (IRE) (Groom Dancer (USA))
E J Alston Geoff & Astrid Long

Placings:0/01/30200062/34250006/153624020045/02054 411440/64305031464023/0230053005-02421000000 (5418)
2009: 8^{0}F, 8^{2}F, 8^{4}GF, 7^{2}GF, 8^{1}F, 7^{0}GF, 7^{0}G, 7^{0}GF, 8^{0}G, 8^{0}F, 7^{0}GF,

	Starts	1st	2nd	3rd	Win & Pl
Career Total (Turf)	69	4	10	6	32556
Career Total (AW)	9	2	0	2	5605

65 6/09 Thsk 1m (0-75)H FRM £4274
69 8/07 Thsk 1m (0-75)H G-F £3238
72 8/06 Thsk 1m (0-70)H G-F £3238
66 7/06 Carl 6f192y (0-70)H FRM £3238
56 3/05 Wolv 1m1f103y (0-45) STD £1470
54 12/02 Wolv 1m1f79y D STD £3362
Total win prize-money £18824

Going (Turf): Sf: 0-4 GS: 0-6 Gd: 0-13 **GF: 2-38 Fm: 2-8**
Distance: 5f/6f: 0-0 **7f-8f: 4-37** 9f-13f: 2-41 14f+: 0-0
Track : **LH: 5-46** RH: 1-28 **Tight: 5-36** Gall: 0-2
Aids: Bl: 0-1 Vi: 0-1 Tstrap: 0-0 Ckp: 0-0
Best Rating: 74 9/07 Muss 7f30y good

Modest; effective over 7f-1m2f; acts on fast ground; also goes on Polytrack.

Champion Girl (IRE)

93(86) (40)65
3-y-o b f Captain Rio-Sea Of Serenity (USA) (Conquistador Cielo (USA))
D Haydn Jones Joseph E Keeling

Placings:0020-00400 (5628)
2009: 6⁰G, 8⁰SD, 7⁴S, 8⁰SF, 7⁰GS,

	Starts	1st	2nd	3rd	Win & Pl
Career Total (Turf)	5	0	1	0	1011
Career Total (AW)	4	0	0	0	

Going (Turf): Sf: 0-2 GS: 0-2 Gd: 0-1 GF: 0-0 Fm: 0-0
Distance: 5f/6f: 0-1 7f-8f: 0-5 9f-13f: 0-3 14f+: 0-0
Track : LH: 0-3 RH: 0-1 Tight: 0-3 Gall: 0-1
Aids: Bl: 0-1 Vi: 0-0 Tstrap: 0-0 Ckp: 0-0
Best Rating: 65 10/08 Folk 7f soft

Chandika

100(101) (65)65
3-y-o b f Exceed And Excel (AUS)-Jitterbug (IRE) (Marju (IRE))
C G Cox B D H & R J H Preston

Placings:06532661 (7224)
2009: 6⁰GF, 6⁶GF, 6⁵GF, 5³G, 5²GF, 5⁶GS, 5⁶GF, 5¹SD,

	Starts	1st	2nd	3rd	Win & Pl
Career Total (Turf)	7	0	1	1	1367
Career Total (AW)	1	1	0	0	2267

65 11/09 Kemp 5f (0-70)H STD £2266
Total win prize-money £2267

Going (Turf): Sf: 0-0 GS: 0-1 Gd: 0-1 GF: 0-5 Fm: 0-0
Distance: 5f/6f: 1-7 7f-8f: 0-1 9f-13f: 0-0 14f+: 0-0
Track : LH: 0-1 **RH: 1-1** Tight: 0-0 Gall: 0-2
Aids: Bl: 0-0 Vi: 0-0 Tstrap: 1-1 Ckp: 1-1
Best Rating: 65 11/09 Kemp 5f stand

Modest; suited by 5f; acts on fast ground and on Polytrack; has worn cheekpieces.

Chandrayaan

92(92) (66)62
2-y-o ch g Bertolini (USA)-Muffled (USA) (Mizaaya)
E A L Dunlop Mohammed Jaber

Placings:0050410 (6609)
2009: 7⁰G, 7⁰S, 7⁵SD, 7⁰S, 6⁴GS, 5¹SD, 7⁰SD,

	Starts	1st	2nd	3rd	Win & Pl
Career Total (Turf)	4	0	0	0	241
Career Total (AW)	3	1	0	0	2388

66 9/09 Wolv 5f216y (0-65)H STD £2388
Total win prize-money £2388

Going (Turf): Sf: 0-2 GS: 0-1 Gd: 0-1 GF: 0-0 Fm: 0-0
Distance: 5f/6f: 1-2 7f-8f: 0-5 9f-13f: 0-0 14f+: 0-0
Track : LH: 1-3 RH: 0-1 **Tight: 1-3** Gall: 0-0
Aids: Bl: 0-0 **Vi: 1-3** Tstrap: 0-0 Ckp: 0-0
Best Rating: 66 9/09 Wolv 5f216y stand

Modest; stays 6f; acts on Polytrack and easy ground; has worn a visor.

Changing Skies (IRE)

90 111
4-y-o b f Sadler's Wells (USA)-Magnificent Style (USA) (Silver Hawk (USA))
B J Meehan Sangster Family

Placings:3/2361253-4 (2013)
2009: 10⁴G,

	Starts	1st	2nd	3rd	Win & Pl
Career Total (Turf)	9	1	2	3	36290

94 7/08 Leic 1m1f218y GD £3238
Total win prize-money £3238

Going (Turf): Sf: 0-2 GS: 0-3 **Gd: 1-3** GF: 0-1 Fm: 0-0
Distance: 5f/6f: 0-0 7f-8f: 0-1 **9f-13f: 1-8** 14f+: 0-0
Track : LH: 0-3 **RH: 1-5** Tight: 0-1 Gall: 0-3
Aids: Bl: 0-0 Vi: 0-0 Tstrap: 0-0 Ckp: 0-0
Best Rating: 111 8/08 Deau 1m2f soft

Smart; best at around 1m2f; acts on fast and easy ground.

Changing The Guard

110(104) (84)91
3-y-o b g King's Best (USA)-Our Queen Of Kings (Arazi (USA))
R A Fahey I L Davies

Placings:1221325150 (4455)
2009: 5¹SD, 5²SD, 7²SD, 7¹SD, 8³SD, 7²GF, 7⁵HY, 10¹G, 10⁵G, 9⁰G,

	Starts	1st	2nd	3rd	Win & Pl
Career Total (Turf)	5	1	1	0	18385
Career Total (AW)	5	2	2	1	11650

91 6/09 York 1m2f88y (0-100)H GD £14247
82 3/09 Wolv 7f32y (0-85)H STD £4857
69 1/09 GrLe 5f STD £2590
Total win prize-money £21694

Going (Turf): Sf: 0-1 GS: 0-0 **Gd: 1-3** GF: 0-1 Fm: 0-0
Distance: 5f/6f: 1-2 7f-8f: 1-5 9f-13f: 1-3 14f+: 0-0
Track : LH: 3-6 RH: 0-4 Tight: 1-4 **Gall: 2-3**
Aids: Bl: 0-0 **Vi: 1-3** Tstrap: 0-0 Ckp: 0-0
Best Rating: 91 7/09 NmkJ 1m2f good

Useful; stays 1m2f; acts on good and faster ground and on Polytrack; has worn a visor.

Changingoftheguard (IRE)

106 117
3-y-o b c Montjeu (IRE)-Miletrian (IRE) (Marju (IRE))
David Hayes (A P O'Brien 12/9) R P & Mrs C C Legh et al

Placings:5-231126 (5861)
2009: 10²GF, 10³HY, 10¹GF, 12¹GF, 14²GF, 14⁶GF,

	Starts	1st	2nd	3rd	Win & Pl
Career Total (Turf)	7	2	2	1	97855

104 6/09 DRoy 1m4f190y H G-F £40844
93 6/09 Navn 1m2f G-F £7379
Total win prize-money £48225

Going (Turf): Sf: 0-1 GS: 0-0 Gd: 0-0 **GF: 2-5** Fm: 0-0
Distance: 5f/6f: 0-0 7f-8f: 0-1 **9f-13f: 2-4** 14f+: 0-2
Track : LH: 1-5 RH: 1-2 Tight: 0-1 Gall: 0-2
Aids: Bl: 0-0 Vi: 0-0 Tstrap: 0-0 Ckp: 0-0
Best Rating: 117 8/09 York 1m6f gd-fm

Smart; Irish trained; unlucky second in the Ebor; stays 1m6f; acts on any gound; progressive.

Channel Crossing

89 (42)73
7-y-o b g Deploy-Wave Dancer (Dance In Time (CAN))
S Wynne Miss Gillian Milner

Placings:400/00002300/02012330-043000 (6969)
2009: 9⁰GF, 9⁴GF, 11³GF, 11⁰GF, 11⁰GS, 11⁰G,

	Starts	1st	2nd	3rd	Win & Pl
Career Total (Turf)	21	1	3	3	9666
Career Total (AW)	4	0	0	1	297

72 7/08 Leic 1m3f183y (0-80)H G-F £4857
Total win prize-money £4857

Going (Turf): Sf: 0-4 GS: 0-5 Gd: 0-4 **GF: 1-8** Fm: 0-0
Distance: 5f/6f: 0-0 7f-8f: 0-0 **9f-13f: 1-22** 14f+: 0-3
Track : LH: 0-10 **RH: 1-14** Tight: 0-10 Gall: 0-2
Aids: Bl: 0-0 Vi: 0-0 Tstrap: 0-4 Ckp: 0-4
Best Rating: 73 9/08 Haml 1m3f16y gd-sft

Modest; stays 1m4f; acts on any ground.

Chanrossa (IRE)

90(106) (69)62
3-y-o b f Galileo (IRE)-Palacoona (FR) (Last Tycoon)
E A L Dunlop St Albans Bloodstock LLP

Placings:0-56055**0202202** (7882)
2009: 10⁵GF, 10⁶GF, 11⁰GF, 12⁵G, 11⁵SD, 12⁰SD, 10²SS, 10⁰SD, 10²SD, 10²SD, 12⁰SD, 10²SD,

	Starts	1st	2nd	3rd	Win & Pl
Career Total (Turf)	5	0	0	0	0
Career Total (AW)	8	0	4	0	2499

Going (Turf): Sf: 0-0 GS: 0-1 Gd: 0-1 GF: 0-3 Fm: 0-0
Distance: 5f/6f: 0-0 7f-8f: 0-0 9f-13f: 0-13 14f+: 0-0
Track : LH: 0-7 RH: 0-5 Tight: 0-6 Gall: 0-2
Aids: Bl: 0-0 Vi: 0-0 Tstrap: 0-3 Ckp: 0-3
Best Rating: 69 11/09 Ling 1m2f stand

Modest; effective over 1m2f, acts on Polytrack; has worn cheekpieces.

Chantilly Creme (USA)

103 100
2-y-o b f Johannesburg (USA)-Creme De La Creme (FR) (Vettori (IRE))
R Gibson L B Robbins

Placings:152100 (6269)
2009: 5¹G, 5⁵GF, 5²G, 6¹S, 7⁰G, 8⁰G,

	Starts	1st	2nd	3rd	Win & Pl
Career Total (Turf)	6	2	1	0	61159

98 8/09 Buch 6f SFT £26699
82 5/09 Lonc 5f GD £16505

Total win prize-money £43204

Going (Turf): **Sf: 1-1** GS: 0-0 **Gd: 1-4** GF: 0-1 Fm: 0-0
Distance: **5f/6f: 2-4** 7f-8f: 0-2 9f-13f: 0-0 14f+: 0-0
Track : LH: 0-0 RH: 0-2 Tight: 0-0 Gall: 0-1
Aids: Bl: 0-0 Vi: 0-0 Tstrap: 0-0 Ckp: 0-0
Best Rating: **100** 9/09 Asct 1m good

Useful; French trained; suited by 5-6f and acts on good and soft ground.

Chantilly Dancer (IRE)

96(86) (47)58
3-y-o b f Danehill Dancer (IRE)-Antiguan Jane (Shirley Heights)
M Quinn John Quorn

Placings:0U46400-5660454165 **(6001)**
2009: 8⁵SD, 8⁶SD, 8⁶SD, 10⁰SD, 8⁴G, 8⁵GF, 10⁴GF, 9¹G, 10⁶G, 10⁵GF,

	Starts	1st	2nd	3rd	Win & Pl
Career Total (Turf)	9	1	0	0	2414
Career Total (AW)	8	0	0	0	0

51 6/09 Yarm 1m1f GD £1942
Total win prize-money £1943

Going (Turf): Sf: 0-1 GS: 0-0 **Gd: 1-5** GF: 0-3 Fm: 0-0
Distance: 5f/6f: 0-3 7f-8f: 0-7 **9f-13f: 1-7** 14f+: 0-0
Track : **LH: 1-13** RH: 0-1 **Tight: 1-8** Gall: 0-2
Aids: Bl: 0-0 Vi: 0-1 Tstrap: 0-0 Ckp: 0-0
Best Rating: **58** 8/08 Yarm 7f3y good

Moderate; effective at 7f-1m; acts on good ground.

Chantilly Jewel (USA)

98(98) (56)60
4-y-o b f Century City (IRE)-Betty's Star (USA) (Pentelicus (USA))
R M H Cowell Bottisham Heath Stud

Placings:004555204016400 **(7710)**
2009: 6⁰SD, 7⁰SD, 6⁴SD, 5⁵SD, 6⁵SD, 6⁶GF, 5²GF, 5⁰G, 5⁴S, 5⁰GS, 5¹SD, 5⁶SD, 5⁴SD, 5⁰SD, 5⁰SD,

	Starts	1st	2nd	3rd	Win & Pl
Career Total (Turf)	5	0	1	0	973
Career Total (AW)	10	1	0	0	2730

56 9/09 Ling 5f STD £2729
Total win prize-money £2730

Going (Turf): **Sf: 0-1 GS: 0-1 Gd: 0-1 GF: 0-2 Fm: 0-0**
Distance: **5f/6f: 1-13** 7f-8f: 0-2 9f-13f: 0-0 14f+: 0-0
Track : **LH: 1-8** RH: 0-1 **Tight: 1-5** Gall: 0-0
Aids: **Bl: 1-4** Vi: 0-5 Tstrap: 0-3 Ckp: 0-3
Best Rating: **60** 6/09 Rdcr 5f gd-fm

Modest sprinter.

Chantilly Passion (FR)

22
8-y-o b g Double Trigger (IRE)-Chantilly Fashion (FR) (Northern Fashion (USA))
B Storey F S Storey

Placings:0 **(3314)**
2009: 10⁰GF,

	Starts	1st	2nd	3rd	Win & Pl
Career Total (Turf)	1	0	0	0	

Going (Turf): **Sf: 0-0 GS: 0-0 Gd: 0-0 GF: 0-1 Fm: 0-0**
Distance: 5f/6f: 0-0 7f-8f: 0-0 9f-13f: 0-1 14f+: 0-0
Track : LH: 0-1 RH: 0-0 Tight: 0-0 Gall: 0-1
Aids: Bl: 0-0 Vi: 0-0 Tstrap: 0-0 Ckp: 0-0

Chantilly Pearl (USA)

98(101) (68)69
3-y-o b/br f Smart Strike (CAN)-Cataballerina (USA) (Tabasco Cat (USA))
J G Given Mrs B E Wilkinson

Placings:1-04625420 **(7512)**
2009: 8⁰GF, 6⁴GF, 10⁶F, 8²GF, 8⁵GF, 8⁴SD, 9²SD, 10⁰SD,

	Starts	1st	2nd	3rd	Win & Pl
Career Total (Turf)	5	0	1	0	1602
Career Total (AW)	4	1	1	0	6433

68 12/08 GrLe 6f STD £5180
Total win prize-money £5181

Going (Turf): **Sf: 0-0 GS: 0-0 Gd: 0-0 GF: 0-4 Fm: 0-1**
Distance: **5f/6f: 1-1** 7f-8f: 0-3 9f-13f: 0-5 14f+: 0-0
Track : **LH: 1-4** RH: 0-3 Tight: 0-4 **Gall: 1-1**
Aids: Bl: 0-0 Vi: 0-0 Tstrap: 0-0 Ckp: 0-0
Best Rating: **69** 8/09 Newc 1m3y gd-fm

Modest; stays 1m1f; acts on Polytrack.

Chantilly Tiffany

107(104) (98)108
5-y-o ch m Pivotal-Gaily Royal (IRE) (Royal Academy (USA))
E A L Dunlop Ballygallon Stud Limited

Placings:141066004/25402121-0040346 **(7044a)**
2009: 7⁰GF, 8⁰HY, 8⁴GF, 7⁰G, 8³SD, 7⁴GF, 7⁶S,

	Starts	1st	2nd	3rd	Win & Pl
Career Total (Turf)	22	4	2	0	77950
Career Total (AW)	2	0	1	1	6883

108 10/08 Badn 7f SFT £22059
103 8/08 Duss 7f GD £13235
91 5/07 NmkR 1m G-F £6477
75 4/07 NmkR 1m G-F £6477
Total win prize-money £48248

Going (Turf): Sf: 1-4 GS: 0-3 Gd: 1-4 **GF: 2-11** Fm: 0-0
Distance: 5f/6f: 0-0 **7f-8f: 4-20** 9f-13f: 0-4 14f+: 0-0
Track : LH: 1-3 RH: 1-10 Tight: 0-0 Gall: 0-1
Aids: Bl: 0-2 Vi: 0-0 Tstrap: 0-0 Ckp: 0-0
Best Rating: **108** 10/08 Badn 7f soft

Smart; Group 3 winner in Germany; effective over 7f-1m; acts on most ground; also goes on Polytrack; has worn blinkers.

Chaperno (USA)

99(103) (95)97
2-y-o b/br c More Than Ready (USA)-Timeless Forest (USA) (Forestry (USA))
Saeed Bin Suroor Godolphin

Placings:22103621 **(7063)**
2009: 6²GF, 6²S, 6¹GF, 7⁰G, 6³G, 6⁶SD, 6²GF, 6¹SD,

	Starts	1st	2nd	3rd	Win & Pl
Career Total (Turf)	6	1	3	1	13136
Career Total (AW)	2	1	0	0	4561

92 10/09 Ling 6f STD £3885
88 7/09 York 6f G-F £6670
Total win prize-money £10556

Going (Turf): Sf: 0-1 GS: 0-0 Gd: 0-2 **GF: 1-3** Fm: 0-0

Distance: **5f/6f: 2-7** 7f-8f: 0-1 9f-13f: 0-0 14f+: 0-0
Track : **LH: 1-1** RH: 0-2 **Tight: 1-1** Gall: 0-1
Aids: Bl: 0-0 Vi: 0-1 Tstrap: 0-0 Ckp: 0-0
Best Rating: **97** 7/09 Gdwd 7f good

Very useful; effective over 6f; acts on most ground; has worn a visor.

Chapter (IRE)

81(90) (46)52
7-y-o ch g Sinndar (IRE)-Web Of Intrigue (Machiavellian (USA))
S E H Sherwood (Mrs A L M King 5/5) The Hon Mrs S Sherwood

Placings:22035/0013U5U0/30063060/400600020/150606 R-00 **(1770)**
2009: 12⁰SD, 10⁰GF,

	Starts	1st	2nd	3rd	Win & Pl
Career Total (Turf)	35	2	3	4	12453
Career Total (AW)	4	0	0	0	0

52 5/08 Brig 1m1f209y (0-60)HG-F £2137
73 5/05 Wind 1m67y (0-70)H G-F £3585
Total win prize-money £5722

Going (Turf): Sf: 0-0 GS: 0-3 Gd: 0-7 **GF: 2-22** Fm: 0-3
Distance: 5f/6f: 0-0 7f-8f: 0-5 **9f-13f: 2-33** 14f+: 0-1
Track : LH: 1-19 RH: 1-14 **Tight: 1-12** Gall: 0-2
Aids: Bl: 0-6 Vi: 0-1 Tstrap: 1-13 Ckp: 1-13
Best Rating: **75** 6/05 NmkJ 1m gd-fm

Moderate handicapper; stays a mile; acts on good to firm.

Chapter And Verse (IRE)

102(108) (88)85
3-y-o gr g One Cool Cat (USA)-Beautiful Hill (IRE) (Danehill (USA))
Mike Murphy (B W Hills 14/10) D J Ellis

Placings:026-1461004322 **(7560)**
2009: 10¹GF, 10⁴GF, 10⁶G, 8¹GF, 8⁰GF, 8⁰GF, 8⁴SD, 10³SD, 8²SD, 8²SD,

	Starts	1st	2nd	3rd	Win & Pl
Career Total (Turf)	9	2	1	0	14311
Career Total (AW)	4	0	2	1	5820

85 8/09 Ripn 1m (0-90)H G-F £7569
76 4/09 Pont 1m2f6y G-F £5180
Total win prize-money £12751

Going (Turf): Sf: 0-0 GS: 0-0 Gd: 0-3 **GF: 2-6** Fm: 0-0
Distance: 5f/6f: 0-0 7f-8f: 1-7 9f-13f: 1-6 14f+: 0-0
Track : LH: 1-3 RH: 1-7 **Tight: 1-3** Gall: 0-1
Aids: Bl: 0-0 Vi: 0-0 Tstrap: 0-0 Ckp: 0-0
Best Rating: **88** 11/09 Wolv 1m141y stand

Useful; stays 1m2f; acts on fast ground and on Polytrack.

Chardonnay

88(93) (74)63
2-y-o br f Piccolo-Icy (Mind Games)
G A Swinbank Guy Reed

Placings:31 **(6638)**
2009: 6³GF, 7¹SD,

	Starts	1st	2nd	3rd	Win & Pl
Career Total (Turf)	1	0	0	1	530
Career Total (AW)	1	1	0	0	2047

74 10/09 Wolv 7f32y STD £2047
Total win prize-money £2047

Going (Turf): **Sf: 0-0 GS: 0-0 Gd: 0-0 GF: 0-1 Fm: 0-0**

Distance: 5f/6f: 0-1 **7f-8f: 1-1** 9f-13f: 0-0 14f+: 0-0
Track : **LH: 1-1** RH: 0-0 **Tight: 1-1** Gall: 0-0
Aids: Bl: 0-0 Vi: 0-0 Tstrap: 0-0 Ckp: 0-0
Best Rating: **74** 10/09 Wolv 7f32y stand

Fair; stays 7f and acts on Polytrack.

Chardonnay Star (IRE)

66(66) (7)8

2-y-o b f Bertolini (USA)-Coup De Coeur (IRE) (Kahyasi)
C J Teague Roland Bowman

Placings:000 (7420)
2009: 5^{0}G, 6^{0}HY, 7^{0}SD,

	Starts	1st	2nd	3rd	Win & Pl
Career Total (Turf)	2	0	0	0	
Career Total (AW)	1	0	0	0	

Going (Turf): **Sf: 0-1 GS: 0-0 Gd: 0-1 GF: 0-0 Fm: 0-0**
Distance: 5f/6f: 0-2 7f-8f: 0-1 9f-13f: 0-0 14f+: 0-0
Track : LH: 0-1 RH: 0-0 Tight: 0-0 Gall: 0-0
Aids: Bl: 0-0 Vi: 0-0 Tstrap: 0-0 Ckp: 0-0
Best Rating: **8** 5/09 Thsk 5f good

Charger

100 76

3-y-o b g Rock Of Gibraltar (IRE)-Ruthless Rose (USA) (Conquistador Cielo (USA))
Paul Stafford (J Noseda 15/10) Any News Syndicate

Placings:40401 (6789)
2009: 10^{4}GF, 10^{0}G, 9^{4}GF, 10^{0}GS, 11^{1}G,

	Starts	1st	2nd	3rd	Win & Pl
Career Total (Turf)	5	1	0	0	4032

76	10/09	Brig	1m3f196y	GD	£3406

Total win prize-money £3406

Going (Turf): Sf: 0-0 GS: 0-1 **Gd: 1-2** GF: 0-2 Fm: 0-0
Distance: 5f/6f: 0-0 7f-8f: 0-0 **9f-13f: 1-5** 14f+: 0-0
Track : **LH: 1-2** RH: 0-3 Tight: 0-1 Gall: 0-2
Aids: Bl: 0-0 Vi: 0-0 Tstrap: 0-0 Ckp: 0-0
Best Rating: **76** 10/09 Brig 1m3f196y good

Fair; stays 1m4f and acts on good ground.

Charging Indian (IRE)

95(99) (78)74

3-y-o b g Chevalier (IRE)-Kathy Tolfa (IRE) (Sri Pekan (USA))
P T Midgley (D R Lanigan 15/7) David Mann

Placings:1-0000051454 (7794)
2009: 7^{0}SD, 8^{0}G, 6^{0}G, 7^{0}G, 8^{0}SD, 12^{5}GS, 11^{1}SD, 12^{4}SD, 12^{5}SD, 11^{4}SS,

	Starts	1st	2nd	3rd	Win & Pl
Career Total (Turf)	5	1	0	0	4209
Career Total (AW)	6	1	0	0	3562

71	10/09	Sthl	1m3f	(0-75)H	STD	£3561
74	6/08	Ripn	5f		SFT	£4209

Total win prize-money £7771

Going (Turf): **Sf: 1-1** GS: 0-1 Gd: 0-3 GF: 0-0 Fm: 0-0
Distance: 5f/6f: 1-2 7f-8f: 0-3 9f-13f: 1-6 14f+: 0-0
Track : **LH: 1-8** RH: 0-2 Tight: 0-0 Gall: 0-1
Aids: Bl: 0-0 Vi: 0-0 Tstrap: 1-4 Ckp: 1-4
Best Rating: **78** 4/09 Kemp 7f stand

Modest; stays 1m3f; handles Fibresand; has worn cheek-pieces.

Charismatic Lady

92 65

3-y-o ch f Bertolini (USA)-Norcroft Lady (Mujtahid (USA))
Jane Chapple-Hyam (M Botti 5/8) Norcroft Park Stud

Placings:0-65305000 (6924)
2009: 8^{0}F, 10^{5}GF, 10^{3}F, 12^{0}S, 10^{5}G, 6^{0}GF, 8^{0}GF, 8^{0}GF,

	Starts	1st	2nd	3rd	Win & Pl
Career Total (Turf)	9	0	0	1	482

Going (Turf): **Sf: 0-1 GS: 0-0 Gd: 0-1 GF: 0-5 Fm: 0-2**
Distance: 5f/6f: 0-0 7f-8f: 0-2 9f-13f: 0-7 14f+: 0-0
Track : LH: 0-7 RH: 0-0 Tight: 0-3 Gall: 0-0
Aids: Bl: 0-1 Vi: 0-0 Tstrap: 0-0 Ckp: 0-0
Best Rating: **65** 7/09 Rdcr 1m2f firm

Charity Belle (USA)

107 106

3-y-o b f Empire Maker (USA)-Sweet Charity (USA) (A.P. Indy (USA))
J H M Gosden H R H Princess Haya Of Jordan

Placings:142150 (6853)
2009: 10^{1}GF, 10^{4}GF, 10^{2}G, 10^{1}G, 12^{5}GS, 12^{0}G,

	Starts	1st	2nd	3rd	Win & Pl
Career Total (Turf)	6	2	1	0	50950

106	8/09	Deau	1m2f	GD	£38835
83	5/09	Newc	1m2f32y	G-F	£3238

Total win prize-money £42073

Going (Turf): Sf: 0-0 GS: 0-1 **Gd: 1-3 GF: 1-2** Fm: 0-0
Distance: 5f/6f: 0-0 7f-8f: 0-0 **9f-13f: 2-6** 14f+: 0-0
Track : LH: 1-3 RH: 1-3 Tight: 0-0 **Gall: 1-4**
Aids: Bl: 0-0 Vi: 0-0 Tstrap: 0-0 Ckp: 0-0
Best Rating: **106** 10/09 Lonc 1m4f110y gd-sft

Group-class; best at around 1m2f; acts on fast ground.

Charity Fair

96 49

2-y-o ch f Bahamian Bounty-Be Most Welcome (Most Welcome)
A Berry Jim Kennan & Alan Berry

Placings:6050060300044 (7168)
2009: 5^{6}GS, 5^{0}GF, 5^{5}GF, 6^{0}G, 6^{0}GS, 6^{6}GF, 7^{0}GF, 6^{3}S, 7^{0}GF, 8^{0}GF, 6^{0}G, 7^{4}GS, 7^{4}S,

	Starts	1st	2nd	3rd	Win & Pl
Career Total (Turf)	13	0	0	1	1011

Going (Turf): **Sf: 0-2 GS: 0-3 Gd: 0-2 GF: 0-6 Fm: 0-0**
Distance: 5f/6f: 0-8 7f-8f: 0-5 9f-13f: 0-0 14f+: 0-0
Track : LH: 0-3 RH: 0-2 Tight: 0-3 Gall: 0-1
Aids: Bl: 0-0 Vi: 0-0 Tstrap: 0-1 Ckp: 0-1
Best Rating: **49** 8/09 Ayr 6f soft

Very moderate; stays 6f and acts on soft ground.

Charles Bear

(90) (57)

2-y-o br f Needwood Blade-Zamyatina (IRE) (Danehill Dancer (IRE))
E S McMahon B Dunn

Placings:04 (7799)
2009: 7^{0}SD, 5^{4}SD,

	Starts	1st	2nd	3rd	Win & Pl
Career Total (Turf)	0	0	0	0	
Career Total (AW)	2	0	0	0	0

Going (Turf): **Sf: 0-0 GS: 0-0 Gd: 0-0 GF: 0-0 Fm: 0-0**
Distance: 5f/6f: 0-1 7f-8f: 0-1 9f-13f: 0-0 14f+: 0-0
Track : LH: 0-2 RH: 0-0 Tight: 0-2 Gall: 0-0
Aids: Bl: 0-0 Vi: 0-0 Tstrap: 0-0 Ckp: 0-0
Best Rating: **57** 12/09 Wolv 5f216y stand

Moderate; stays 6f; acts on Polytrack.

Charles Darwin (IRE)

99(106) (68)86

6-y-o ch g Tagula (IRE)-Seymour (IRE) (Eagle Eyed (USA))
M Blanshard The Breeze-In Partnership

Placings:062261013245/4003302152334/5004000/01500 0022040-460063000150 (7330)
2009: 6^{4}SD, 6^{6}SD, 5^{0}GF, 6^{0}HY, 6^{6}GF, 7^{3}GF, 8^{0}GF, 7^{0}GS, 6^{0}GF, 5^{1}SD, 5^{5}SD, 6^{0}SD,

	Starts	1st	2nd	3rd	Win & Pl
Career Total (Turf)	48	4	7	6	52814
Career Total (AW)	8	1	0	0	4079

68	9/09	Wolv	5f216y	(0-70)H	STD	£3238
86	5/08	Donc	6f	(0-80)H	G-F	£4857
95	7/06	Asct	6f	(0-100)H	G-F	£16192
82	8/05	Nott	6f15y		GD	£3571
74	7/05	Donc	5f		G-F	£4108

Total win prize-money £31968

Going (Turf): Sf: 0-9 GS: 0-11 Gd: 1-5 **GF: 3-22** Fm: 0-1
Distance: **5f/6f: 4-51** 7f-8f: 1-4 9f-13f: 0-1 14f+: 0-0
Track : **LH: 1-8** RH: 0-4 **Tight: 1-5** Gall: 0-1
Aids: **Bl: 1-3** Vi: 0-0 Tstrap: 0-2 Ckp: 0-2
Best Rating: **95** 9/06 Asct 6f gd-sft

Modest; suited by 6f; acts on fast ground and Polytrack; likes to race prominently; has worn headgear.

Charles Parnell (IRE)

91(109) (89)81

6-y-o b g Elnadim (USA)-Titania (Fairy King (USA))
S P Griffiths (M Dods 10/10) J N Griffiths

Placings:335/3100024264/050000454110444133/4440640 2555502211-200503526556 (7729)
2009: 6^{2}SS, 5^{0}G, 6^{0}GS, 6^{5}SD, 6^{0}SD, 5^{3}GS, 6^{5}G, 7^{2}SD, 5^{6}SD, 5^{5}SD, 5^{5}SD, 7^{6}SD,

	Starts	1st	2nd	3rd	Win & Pl
Career Total (Turf)	46	4	4	6	24690
Career Total (AW)	13	2	3	0	11066

88	12/08	Sthl	6f	(0-80)H	STD	£4857
86	12/08	Sthl	6f	(0-75)H	STD	£2729
78	9/07	Ayr	5f	(0-70)H	G-S	£5181
78	7/07	Catt	5f212y	(0-60)H	G-S	£2590
72	7/07	Ayr	6f	(0-65)H	GD	£2730
67	6/06	Rdcr	6f		FRM	£3238

Total win prize-money £21329

Going (Turf): Sf: 0-9 **GS: 2-9** Gd: 1-14 GF: 0-12 Fm: 1-2
Distance: **5f/6f: 6-50** 7f-8f: 0-9 9f-13f: 0-0 14f+: 0-0
Track : **LH: 3-24** RH: 0-3 **Tight: 1-12** Gall: 0-0
Aids: Bl: 0-4 Vi: 0-2 Tstrap: 0-2 Ckp: 0-2
Best Rating: **89** 1/09 Sthl 6f std-slw

Fair; effective over 6-7f; acts on most ground on turf; goes on Fibresand; handles Polytrack; has worn blinkers; usually held up.

Charleston

(90) (49)

8-y-o ch g Pursuit Of Love-Discomatic (USA) (Roberto (USA))

R Rowe Richard Rowe

Placings:2224000/6/0/006 (0750)

2009: 14^{0}SD, 13^{0}SD, 12^{6}SD,

	Starts	1st	2nd	3rd	Win & Pl
Career Total (Turf)	4	0	3	0	3921
Career Total (AW)	8	0	0	0	276

Going (Turf): Sf: 0-1 GS: 0-0 Gd: 0-1 GF: 0-2 Fm: 0-0
Distance: 5f/6f: 0-0 7f-8f: 0-1 9f-13f: 0-9 14f+: 0-2
Track : LH: 0-10 RH: 0-1 Tight: 0-9 Gall: 0-2
Aids: Bl: 0-1 Vi: 0-0 Tstrap: 0-0 Ckp: 0-0
Best Rating: 73 6/04 Chep 1m2f36y good

Charlevoix (IRE)

103(95) (74)78

4-y-o b f King Charlemagne (USA)-Cayman Sound (Turtle Island (IRE))

C F Wall M Sinclair

Placings:060/11440-5140 (3076)

2009: 8^{5}G, 8^{1}GF, 8^{4}GF, 8^{0}G,

	Starts	1st	2nd	3rd	Win & Pl
Career Total (Turf)	10	3	0	0	7839
Career Total (AW)	2	0	0	0	192

76	4/09	Yarm	1m3y	(0-75)H	G-F	£2590
78	7/08	Yarm	1m1f	(0-70)H	G-F	£2719
69	5/08	Rdcr	1m	(0-60)H	G-F	£2047

Total win prize-money £7357

Going (Turf): Sf: 0-3 GS: 0-1 Gd: 0-2 GF: 3-4 Fm: 0-0
Distance: 5f/6f: 0-2 7f-8f: 1-3 9f-13f: 2-7 14f+: 0-0
Track : LH: 1-3 RH: 0-3 Tight: 1-2 Gall: 0-2
Aids: Bl: 0-0 Vi: 0-0 Tstrap: 0-0 Ckp: 0-0
Best Rating: 78 7/08 Yarm 1m1f gd-fm

Fair; stays 1m1f and acts on fast ground.

Charlie Allnut

88(101) (50)58

4-y-o b g Desert Style (IRE)-Queen Of Africa (USA) (Peintre Celebre (USA))

S Wynne David Manning Associates

Placings:60554205-003300 (7459)

2009: 7^{0}SD, 5^{0}SD, 7^{3}SD, 6^{3}SD, 7^{0}GF, 7^{0}SD,

	Starts	1st	2nd	3rd	Win & Pl
Career Total (Turf)	7	0	1	0	578
Career Total (AW)	7	0	0	2	605

Going (Turf): Sf: 0-0 GS: 0-0 Gd: 0-4 GF: 0-3 Fm: 0-0
Distance: 5f/6f: 0-5 7f-8f: 0-8 9f-13f: 0-1 14f+: 0-0
Track : LH: 0-9 RH: 0-1 Tight: 0-6 Gall: 0-0
Aids: Bl: 0-8 Vi: 0-1 Tstrap: 0-1 Ckp: 0-1
Best Rating: 58 9/08 Leic 7f9y good

Moderate; effective at around 7f; acts on good ground; goes on Fibresand.

Charlie Be (IRE)

90(66) (47)44

4-y-o ch g King Charlemagne (USA)-Miriana (IRE) (Bluebird (USA))

Mrs P N Dutfield Mrs Nerys Dutfield

Placings:60000/000550-00 (5120)

2009: 10^{0}G, 6^{0}F,

	Starts	1st	2nd	3rd	Win & Pl
Career Total (Turf)	10	0	0	0	0
Career Total (AW)	3	0	0	0	0

Going (Turf): Sf: 0-1 GS: 0-1 Gd: 0-4 GF: 0-1 Fm: 0-3
Distance: 5f/6f: 0-3 7f-8f: 0-2 9f-13f: 0-8 14f+: 0-0
Track : LH: 0-9 RH: 0-1 Tight: 0-7 Gall: 0-0
Aids: Bl: 0-0 Vi: 0-0 Tstrap: 0-0 Ckp: 0-0
Best Rating: 57 5/07 Sals 5f gd-sft

Charlie Bear

81(99) (51)46

8-y-o ch h Bahamian Bounty-Abi (Chief's Crown (USA))

Miss Z C Davison Charlie's Starrs

Placings:500/0203/00605/3550155431460/45200000/0020 0640000-004060 (1200)

2009: 16^{0}SS, 12^{0}SD, 11^{4}SD, 11^{0}SD, 11^{6}SD, 12^{0}GF,

	Starts	1st	2nd	3rd	Win & Pl
Career Total (Turf)	30	2	2	1	9739
Career Total (AW)	20	0	1	2	1625

66	7/06	Sals	1m	(0-75)H	G-F	£3747
64	4/06	Yarm	7f3y	(0-65)H	G-F	£2914

Total win prize-money £6663

Going (Turf): Sf: 0-2 GS: 0-7 Gd: 0-6 GF: 2-14 Fm: 0-1
Distance: 5f/6f: 0-6 7f-8f: 2-27 9f-13f: 0-16 14f+: 0-1
Track : LH: 0-16 RH: 0-14 Tight: 0-13 Gall: 0-1
Aids: Bl: 0-3 Vi: 0-0 Tstrap: 0-6 Ckp: 0-6
Best Rating: 73 10/04 Wolv 7f32y stand

Moderate; effective at around 7f-1m; acts on fast ground; also goes on Polytrack.

Charlie Cool

109(100) (82)101

6-y-o ch h Rainbow Quest (USA)-Tigwa (Cadeaux Genereux)

Mrs R A Carr (J H M Gosden 27/6) Middleham Park Racing Xxiv

Placings:210/31203/31430413064/0001460020006 (7583)

2009: 8^{0}FT, 8^{0}GS, 10^{0}G, 10^{1}GF, 10^{4}G, 8^{6}G, 10^{0}G, 8^{0}GF, 10^{2}GS, 10^{0}G, 10^{0}S, 9^{0}SD, 9^{6}SF,

	Starts	1st	2nd	3rd	Win & Pl
Career Total (Turf)	27	5	3	3	164841
Career Total (AW)	5	0	0	2	7108

99	2/09	Ndas	1m2f	(95-110)H	G-F	£50000
111	6/07	Nott	1m54y		GD	£11217
111	2/07	Ndas	1m2f	(90-105)H	GD	£33673
103	8/06	Hayd	1m30y	(0-95)H	G-F	£11334
83	8/05	York	7f		G-F	£7936

Total win prize-money £114163

Going (Turf): Sf: 0-1 GS: 0-4 Gd: 2-16 GF: 3-6 Fm: 0-0
Distance: 5f/6f: 0-0 7f-8f: 1-8 9f-13f: 4-24 14f+: 0-0
Track : LH: 5-19 RH: 0-7 Tight: 0-4 Gall: 3-14
Aids: Bl: 0-1 Vi: 1-6 Tstrap: 0-4 Ckp: 0-4
Best Rating: 111 6/07 Nott 1m54y good

Very useful; stays 1m2f but effective at 1m; acts on fast and easy ground and sand; usually held up; has worn a visor and blinkers.

Charlie Delta

95(102) (65)78

6-y-o b g Pennekamp (USA)-Papita (IRE) (Law Society (USA))

R A Harris Robert & Nina Bailey

Placings:6014450130450030/01463020434400045321/500 0012211000600/41215030-0060042001035614 (7879)

2009: 7^{0}GF, 5^{0}GF, 5^{6}GF, 6^{0}GF, 5^{0}G, 7^{4}G, 7^{2}GS, 8^{0}F, 7^{0}GF, 6^{1}SD, 7^{0}SD, 7^{3}SD, 7^{5}SD, 7^{6}SD, 5^{1}SD, 6^{4}SD,

	Starts	1st	2nd	3rd	Win & Pl
Career Total (Turf)	43	8	3	2	36890
Career Total (AW)	32	3	3	5	11593

65	12/09	Wolv	5f216y	(0-63)H	STD	£1706
61	10/09	Kemp	6f	(0-52)H	STD	£2047
78	6/08	NmkJ	7f	(0-70)H	FRM	£3885
72	5/08	Sals	6f	(0-65)H	G-F	£2810
73	6/07	Sals	6f212y		G-F	£3238
69	5/07	Yarm	6f3y		GD	£1943
66	4/07	Yarm	6f3y		G-F	£1943
77	1/07	Sthl	6f		STD	£2184
83	6/06	Nott	6f15y	(0-75)H	G-F	£3886
81	9/05	Ayr	6f	(0-85)	GD	£7020
70	6/05	Brig	5f213y		FRM	£2877

Total win prize-money £33542

Going (Turf): Sf: 0-4 GS: 0-4 Gd: 2-11 GF: 4-19 Fm: 2-5
Distance: 5f/6f: 6-48 7f-8f: 5-26 9f-13f: 0-1 14f+: 0-0
Track : LH: 3-34 RH: 1-3 Tight: 1-24 Gall: 0-2
Aids: Bl: 7-29 Vi: 0-4 Tstrap: 1-9 Ckp: 1-9
Best Rating: 86 10/06 Ayr 6f heavy

Moderate; effective at around 6f-7f; has yet to win on ground worse than good but handles Fibresand and Polytrack; has worn headgear.

Charlie Farnsbarns (IRE)

109 116

5-y-o b g Cape Cross (IRE)-Lafleur (IRE) (Grand Lodge (USA))

B J Meehan The English Girls

Placings:215012/2/15021-05435614 (6812)

2009: 8^{0}G, 10^{5}G, 12^{4}GF, 9^{3}GF, 8^{5}GF, 8^{6}S, 9^{1}GF, 9^{4}G,

	Starts	1st	2nd	3rd	Win & Pl
Career Total (Turf)	20	5	4	1	130375

104	9/09	Newb	1m1f	G-F	£7477
116	10/08	NmkR	1m1f	GD	£36900
100	5/08	York	1m208y	G-F	£10361
105	10/06	Asct	7f	G-S	£9348
86	6/06	NmkJ	6f	G-F	£4533

Total win prize-money £68622

Going (Turf): Sf: 0-3 GS: 1-2 Gd: 1-5 GF: 3-9 Fm: 0-0
Distance: 5f/6f: 1-1 7f-8f: 1-5 9f-13f: 3-14 14f+: 0-0
Track : LH: 2-5 RH: 0-6 Tight: 0-3 Gall: 2-4
Aids: Bl: 0-1 Vi: 0-0 Tstrap: 0-0 Ckp: 0-0
Best Rating: 116 10/08 NmkR 1m1f good

Smart; Group 3 winner; effective over 7f-1m2f; acts on most ground; has worn blinkers.

Charlie Green (IRE)

(83) (33)35

4-y-o b g Traditionally (USA)-Saninka (IRE) (Doyoun)

Paul Green Paddy Mason

Placings:000/0000-0 (7790)

2009: 12^{0}SD,

	Starts	1st	2nd	3rd	Win & Pl
Career Total (Turf)	4	0	0	0	
Career Total (AW)	4	0	0	0	

Going (Turf): Sf: 0-0 GS: 0-0 Gd: 0-1 GF: 0-3 Fm: 0-0
Distance: 5f/6f: 0-3 7f-8f: 0-1 9f-13f: 0-4 14f+: 0-0

Track : LH: 0-6 RH: 0-1 Tight: 0-4 Gall: 0-1
Aids: Bl: 0-0 Vi: 0-2 Tstrap: 0-0 Ckp: 0-0
Best Rating: 35 7/07 Carl 5f gd-fm

Charlie Oxo

(56) 27
4-y-o br g Puissance-Aegean Mist (Prince Sabo)
B P J Baugh G B Hignett

Placings:000/0 (7464)
2009: 7[0]SD,

	Starts	1st	2nd	3rd	Win & Pl
Career Total (Turf)	3	0	0	0	
Career Total (AW)	1	0	0	0	

Going (Turf): **Sf: 0-1 GS: 0-1 Gd: 0-0 GF: 0-1 Fm: 0-0**
Distance: 5f/6f: 0-3 7f-8f: 0-1 9f-13f: 0-0 14f+: 0-0
Track : LH: 0-1 RH: 0-0 Tight: 0-1 Gall: 0-0
Aids: Bl: 0-0 Vi: 0-0 Tstrap: 0-0 Ckp: 0-0
Best Rating: 27 10/07 Nott 5f13y gd-sft

Charlie Smirke (USA)

93(96) (68)62
3-y-o b g Gulch (USA)-Two Altazano (USA) (Manzotti (USA))
G L Moore R E Anderson

Placings:02336-6060322 (7826)
2009: 10[6]SD, 8[0]GF, 9[6]GS, 9[0]G, 7[3]SD, 8[2]SD, 8[2]SD,

	Starts	1st	2nd	3rd	Win & Pl
Career Total (Turf)	4	0	0	0	0
Career Total (AW)	8	0	3	3	4046

Going (Turf): **Sf: 0-0 GS: 0-1 Gd: 0-2 GF: 0-1 Fm: 0-0**
Distance: 5f/6f: 0-0 7f-8f: 0-8 9f-13f: 0-4 14f+: 0-0
Track : LH: 0-6 RH: 0-6 Tight: 0-4 Gall: 0-1
Aids: Bl: 0-2 Vi: 0-0 Tstrap: 0-0 Ckp: 0-0
Best Rating: 68 9/08 Ling 7f stand

Modest; effective at 7f-1m; acts on Polytrack.

Charlie Tipple

108 90
5-y-o b g Diktat-Swing Of The Tide (Sri Pekan (USA))
T D Easterby Norman Jackson

Placings:6103/0041425452/345550301651-250200035 (7060)
2009: 8[2]F, 8[5]GF, 8[0]GS, 8[2]G, 8[0]GF, 8[0]GF, 9[0]S, 8[3]GF, 8[5]GF,

	Starts	1st	2nd	3rd	Win & Pl
Career Total (Turf)	35	4	4	4	48137
87	10/08 Rdcr	1m	H	GD	£18693
85	8/08 Rdcr	1m	(0-90)H	GD	£7771
78	7/07 Nott	6f15y	(0-70)H	HVY	£2914
68	6/06 Newc	6f		G-F	£4533

Total win prize-money £33913

Going (Turf): Sf: 1-7 GS: 0-3 **Gd: 2-9** GF: 1-14 Fm: 0-2
Distance: 5f/6f: 1-6 **7f-8f: 3-19** 9f-13f: 0-10 14f+: 0-0
Track : LH: 0-9 RH: 0-10 Tight: 0-7 Gall: 0-2
Aids: Bl: 1-1 Vi: 0-0 Tstrap: 1-18 Ckp: 1-18
Best Rating: 90 6/09 Hayd 1m30y good

Useful; stays 1m and acts on any ground; has worn cheekpieces and blinkers.

Charlie Tokyo (IRE)

105(109) (99)91
6-y-o b g Trans Island-Ellistown Lady (IRE) (Red Sunset)
R A Fahey Stanley Yu

Placings:1423602/606242120/01241604/004400600-0530314002 (6986)
2009: 12[0]GS, 10[5]GF, 10[3]GF, 12[0]G, 10[3]GS, 9[1]HY, 10[4]GS, 10[0]GS, 10[0]G, 10[2]G,

	Starts	1st	2nd	3rd	Win & Pl
Career Total (Turf)	39	5	7	3	149501
Career Total (AW)	4	0	0	0	1635
88	8/09 Leic	1m1f218y	(0-85)H	HVY	£4857
104	7/07 York	1m208y	H	HVY	£93480
91	4/07 Pont	1m2f6y	(0-100)H	GD	£11217
89	10/06 Wind	1m2f7y	(0-85)H	SFT	£6477
69	6/05 Wind	6f		G-F	£4316

Total win prize-money £120348

Going (Turf): **Sf: 3-8** GS: 0-11 Gd: 1-11 GF: 1-9 Fm: 0-0
Distance: 5f/6f: 1-2 7f-8f: 0-4 **9f-13f: 4-37** 14f+: 0-0
Track : LH: 2-26 RH: 2-13 Tight: 1-14 **Gall: 2-12**
Aids: **Bl: 3-13** Vi: 1-17 Tstrap: 0-0 Ckp: 0-0
Best Rating: 106 7/07 York 1m2f88y heavy

Useful; winner of the 2007 John Smith's Cup at York; stays 1m2f; acts on most ground and on Polytrack; wears blinkers or a visor.

Charlietoo

93(91) (53)67
3-y-o b g King Charlemagne (USA)-Ticcatoo (IRE) (Dolphin Street (FR))
E G Bevan (R Hollinshead 2/4) E G Bevan

Placings:200000 (5610)
2009: 5[2]GF, 7[0]SD, 7[0]SD, 7[0]GF, 6[0]G, 5[0]SD,

	Starts	1st	2nd	3rd	Win & Pl
Career Total (Turf)	3	0	1	0	578
Career Total (AW)	3	0	0	0	

Going (Turf): **Sf: 0-0 GS: 0-0 Gd: 0-1 GF: 0-2 Fm: 0-0**
Distance: 5f/6f: 0-2 7f-8f: 0-4 9f-13f: 0-0 14f+: 0-0
Track : LH: 0-3 RH: 0-0 Tight: 0-3 Gall: 0-0
Aids: Bl: 0-0 Vi: 0-0 Tstrap: 0-0 Ckp: 0-0
Best Rating: 67 4/09 Leic 5f218y gd-fm

Modest; effective over 6f; acts on fast ground.

Charlotte Grey

(103) (64)64
5-y-o gr m Wizard King-Great Intent (Aragon)
P J McBride N Davies

Placings:32344005211 2/442001640263640 0050/2103040 664260355-1120 (0607)
2009: 6[1]SS, 7[1]SD, 6[2]SD, 7[0]SD,

	Starts	1st	2nd	3rd	Win & Pl
Career Total (Turf)	10	0	0	1	2051
Career Total (AW)	41	6	8	4	22290
63	1/09 Sthl	7f	(0-52)H	STD	£2047
60	1/09 Sthl	6f	(0-52)H	SS	£2047
55	1/08 Wolv	5f216y	(0-45)	STD	£1365
67	4/07 Wolv	5f20y	(0-65)H	STD	£2388
62	12/06 Wolv	5f216y	(0-65)	STD	£2730
64	12/06 Wolv	5f216y		STD	£1365

Total win prize-money £11943

Going (Turf): **Sf: 0-1 GS: 0-0 Gd: 0-4 GF: 0-5 Fm: 0-0**
Distance: **5f/6f: 5-41** 7f-8f: 1-9 9f-13f: 0-1 14f+: 0-0

Track : **LH: 6-32** RH: 0-4 **Tight: 4-24** Gall: 0-1
Aids: Bl: 0-0 Vi: 0-0 Tstrap: 0-0 Ckp: 0-0
Best Rating: 67 7/07 Wolv 5f20y stand

Moderate; effective over 5f-6f; acts on sand; suited by forcing tactics.

Charlotte Point (USA)

106(101) (88)89
3-y-o b f Distorted Humor (USA)-Skygusty (USA) (Skywalker (USA))
P F I Cole C Wright & The Hon Mrs J M Corbett

Placings:6321-21123000 (6907)
2009: 8[2]SD, 8[1]GF, 8[1]GF, 8[2]G, 8[3]SD, 8[0]GF, 8[0]SD, 10[0]G,

	Starts	1st	2nd	3rd	Win & Pl
Career Total (Turf)	6	2	1	0	7879
Career Total (AW)	6	1	2	2	8259
84	5/09 Gdwd	1m	(0-85)H	G-F	£5180
73	10/08 GrLe	1m		STD	£3885

Total win prize-money £9067

Going (Turf): Sf: 0-1 GS: 0-0 Gd: 0-2 **GF: 2-3** Fm: 0-0
Distance: 5f/6f: 0-0 **7f-8f: 2-9** 9f-13f: 1-3 14f+: 0-0
Track : **LH: 2-6** RH: 1-5 Tight: 0-2 **Gall: 1-3**
Aids: Bl: 0-0 Vi: 0-0 Tstrap: 0-0 Ckp: 0-0
Best Rating: 89 6/09 NmkJ 1m good

Fair; stays 1m; acts on fast ground; handles Polytrack.

Charlottesometimes (USA)

81(84) (48)48
2-y-o b/br f Dehere (USA)-Alexander Charlote (IRE) (Titus Livius (FR))
D M Simcock Mrs Ann Simcock

Placings:646 (4379)
2009: 7[6]SD, 5[4]GF, 5[6]G,

	Starts	1st	2nd	3rd	Win & Pl
Career Total (Turf)	2	0	0	0	208
Career Total (AW)	1	0	0	0	0

Going (Turf): **Sf: 0-0 GS: 0-0 Gd: 0-1 GF: 0-1 Fm: 0-0**
Distance: 5f/6f: 0-2 7f-8f: 0-1 9f-13f: 0-0 14f+: 0-0
Track : LH: 0-2 RH: 0-0 Tight: 0-1 Gall: 0-1
Aids: Bl: 0-0 Vi: 0-0 Tstrap: 0-0 Ckp: 0-0
Best Rating: 48 7/09 Brig 5f213y gd-fm

Charm School

113(112) (99)111
4-y-o b g Dubai Destination (USA)-Eve (Rainbow Quest (USA))
J H M Gosden H R H Princess Haya Of Jordan

Placings:12033-00451501 (7293)
2009: 8[0]GF, 8[0]S, 7[4]GF, 10[5]G, 11[1]SD, 10[5]GF, 9[0]GF, 12[1]S,

	Starts	1st	2nd	3rd	Win & Pl
Career Total (Turf)	11	2	1	2	71990
Career Total (AW)	2	1	0	0	7353
111	11/09 Donc	1m4f	H	SFT	£59194
99	9/09 Kemp	1m3f	(0-95)H	STD	£7352
86	3/08 Donc	7f		SFT	£4048

Total win prize-money £70596

Going (Turf): **Sf: 2-4** GS: 0-2 Gd: 0-1 GF: 0-4 Fm: 0-0
Distance: 5f/6f: 0-0 7f-8f: 1-6 **9f-13f: 2-7** 14f+: 0-0
Track : LH: 1-4 RH: 1-3 Tight: 0-2 **Gall: 1-2**
Aids: Bl: 0-1 Vi: 0-0 Tstrap: 0-0 Ckp: 0-0

Best Rating: **111** 11/09 Donc 1m4f soft

Very useful; effective at 1m2f-1m4f; won the November Handicap in 2009; acts on fast and soft ground; goes on Polytrack; has worn an eyeshield and blinkers.

Charmaxjoanne

77(31) 49

2-y-o ch f Lucky Story (USA)-Dance Of The Swans (IRE) (Try My Best (USA))

P C Haslam M C Mason

Placings:040 (7616)

2009: 5^{0}G, 7^{4}GF, 8^{0}SD,

	Starts	1st	2nd	3rd	Win & Pl
Career Total (Turf)	2	0	0	0	164
Career Total (AW)	1	0	0	0	

Going (Turf): **Sf: 0-0 GS: 0-0 Gd: 0-1 GF: 0-1 Fm: 0-0**
Distance: 5f/6f: 0-1 7f-8f: 0-1 9f-13f: 0-1 14f+: 0-0
Track : LH: 0-1 RH: 0-0 Tight: 0-1 Gall: 0-0
Aids: Bl: 0-0 Vi: 0-0 Tstrap: 0-0 Ckp: 0-0
Best Rating: **49** 8/09 Newc 7f gd-fm

Moderate; stays 7f; acts on a sound surface.

Charmel's Lad

(99) (62)64

4-y-o ch g Compton Place-Fittonia (FR) (Ashkalani (IRE))

W R Swinburn Alan Le Herissier

Placings:506/55004030-0455 (0934)

2009: 7^{0}SD, 6^{4}SD, 6^{5}SD, 7^{5}SD,

	Starts	1st	2nd	3rd	Win & Pl
Career Total (Turf)	5	0	0	0	0
Career Total (AW)	10	0	0	1	444

Going (Turf): **Sf: 0-0 GS: 0-2 Gd: 0-0 GF: 0-3 Fm: 0-0**
Distance: 5f/6f: 0-7 7f-8f: 0-7 9f-13f: 0-1 14f+: 0-0
Track : LH: 0-8 RH: 0-4 Tight: 0-4 Gall: 0-2
Aids: Bl: 0-0 Vi: 0-2 Tstrap: 0-1 Ckp: 0-1
Best Rating: **64** 10/07 Leic 7f9y gd-sft

Moderate; stays 7f; acts on Polytrack; has worn a tongue tie.

Charminamix (IRE)

104 (93)91

6-y-o gr g Linamix (FR)-Cheeky Charm (USA) (Nureyev (USA))

A J Martin D N O'Connor

Placings:0410/4/22-0500620 (7567a)

2009: 10^{0}GF, 10^{5}SD, 12^{0}GF, 9^{0}G, 10^{6}GF, 10^{2}SD, 12^{0}SD,

	Starts	1st	2nd	3rd	Win & Pl
Career Total (Turf)	10	1	1	0	19023
Career Total (AW)	4	0	2	0	10537

87 5/06 Lonc 1m110y G-S £6552
Total win prize-money £6552

Going (Turf): Sf: 0-1 **GS: 1-1** Gd: 0-3 GF: 0-4 Fm: 0-1
Distance: 5f/6f: 0-0 7f-8f: 0-2 **9f-13f: 1-12** 14f+: 0-0
Track : LH: 0-8 RH: 0-3 Tight: 0-1 Gall: 0-1
Aids: Bl: 0-0 Vi: 0-0 Tstrap: 0-0 Ckp: 0-0
Best Rating: **93** 8/08 Dund 1m2f150y stand

Useful; effective over 1m2f; acts on easy ground and on Polytrack.

Charming Escort

(98) (62)45

5-y-o ch g Rossini (USA)-Iktizawa (Entrepreneur)

T T Clement P Charalambous

Placings:5/5011354-60 (0118)

2009: 8^{6}SD, 7^{0}SD,

	Starts	1st	2nd	3rd	Win & Pl
Career Total (Turf)	1	0	0	0	466
Career Total (AW)	9	2	0	1	5029

61 10/08 Kemp 7f (0-55) STD £2047
55 10/08 Kemp 1m (0-55) STD £2047
Total win prize-money £4094

Going (Turf): **Sf: 0-0 GS: 0-0 Gd: 0-1 GF: 0-0 Fm: 0-0**
Distance: 5f/6f: 0-0 **7f-8f: 2-10** 9f-13f: 0-0 14f+: 0-0
Track : LH: 0-3 **RH: 2-6** Tight: 0-3 Gall: 0-0
Aids: Bl: 0-0 Vi: 0-1 Tstrap: 0-0 Ckp: 0-0
Best Rating: **67** 9/06 Kemp 1m stand

Moderate; effective over 7f-1m; acts on Polytrack; has worn a visor.

Charpoy Cobra

91(92) (61)64

2-y-o b f Mark Of Esteem (IRE)-Duena (Grand Lodge (USA))

J A R Toller The Cobra Partnership

Placings:0630 (6923)

2009: 7^{0}G, 8^{6}SD, 8^{3}SS, 8^{0}GF,

	Starts	1st	2nd	3rd	Win & Pl
Career Total (Turf)	2	0	0	0	
Career Total (AW)	2	0	0	1	403

Going (Turf): **Sf: 0-0 GS: 0-0 Gd: 0-1 GF: 0-1 Fm: 0-0**
Distance: 5f/6f: 0-0 7f-8f: 0-3 9f-13f: 0-1 14f+: 0-0
Track : LH: 0-1 RH: 0-1 Tight: 0-1 Gall: 0-0
Aids: Bl: 0-0 Vi: 0-0 Tstrap: 0-0 Ckp: 0-0
Best Rating: **64** 8/09 NmkJ 7f good

Chartist

101(96) (76)93

4-y-o ch g Choisir (AUS)-Sareb (FR) (Indian Ridge)

B P J Baugh (D Nicholls 18/6) Martin Hignett

Placings:01/502200005-5400000 (6596)

2009: 7^{5}GF, 7^{4}GF, 6^{0}G, 5^{0}GF, 5^{0}GS, 5^{0}GS, 6^{0}GS,

	Starts	1st	2nd	3rd	Win & Pl
Career Total (Turf)	16	1	2	0	10612
Career Total (AW)	2	0	0	0	373

84 10/07 Nott 5f13y G-F £2914
Total win prize-money £2915

Going (Turf): Sf: 0-3 GS: 0-4 Gd: 0-3 **GF: 1-6** Fm: 0-0
Distance: **5f/6f: 1-15** 7f-8f: 0-3 9f-13f: 0-0 14f+: 0-0
Track : LH: 0-2 RH: 0-2 Tight: 0-3 Gall: 0-0
Aids: Bl: 0-0 Vi: 0-1 Tstrap: 0-0 Ckp: 0-0
Best Rating: **93** 5/08 Ches 5f16y good

Useful; effective over 5f and acts on most ground.

Chasca (IRE)

98(101) (69)72

3-y-o b f Namid-Daganya (IRE) (Danehill Dancer (IRE))

Mrs A J Perrett Lady Clague

Placings:1410650 (6739)

2009: 6^{1}SD, 6^{4}SD, 6^{1}GF, 5^{0}GF, 6^{6}G, 5^{5}SD, 6^{0}GS,

	Starts	1st	2nd	3rd	Win & Pl
Career Total (Turf)	4	1	0	0	3071
Career Total (AW)	3	1	0	0	2218

72 4/09 Folk 6f (0-70)H G-F £3070
66 3/09 Ling 6f STD £2217
Total win prize-money £5289

Going (Turf): Sf: 0-0 GS: 0-1 Gd: 0-1 **GF: 1-2** Fm: 0-0
Distance: **5f/6f: 2-7** 7f-8f: 0-0 9f-13f: 0-0 14f+: 0-0
Track : **LH: 1-4** RH: 0-0 **Tight: 1-3** Gall: 0-1
Aids: Bl: 0-0 Vi: 0-0 Tstrap: 0-0 Ckp: 0-0
Best Rating: **72** 4/09 Folk 6f gd-fm

Modest; suited by 6f and Polytrack; also acts on fast ground.

Chase End

(90) (45)

3-y-o ch f Arkadian Hero (USA)-Sestina (FR) (Bering)

J M P Eustace Malvern Hills Racing

Placings:60 (0236)

2009: 6^{6}SD, 5^{0}SD,

	Starts	1st	2nd	3rd	Win & Pl
Career Total (Turf)	0	0	0	0	
Career Total (AW)	2	0	0	0	0

Going (Turf): **Sf: 0-0 GS: 0-0 Gd: 0-0 GF: 0-0 Fm: 0-0**
Distance: 5f/6f: 0-2 7f-8f: 0-0 9f-13f: 0-0 14f+: 0-0
Track : LH: 0-2 RH: 0-0 Tight: 0-1 Gall: 0-1
Aids: Bl: 0-0 Vi: 0-0 Tstrap: 0-0 Ckp: 0-0
Best Rating: **45** 1/09 GrLe 6f stand

Chasing Amy

71(94) (61)57

3-y-o b f Namid-Inspiring (IRE) (Anabaa (USA))

M G Quinlan Burns Farm Racing

Placings:3520-000060 (6344)

2009: 6^{0}GF, 6^{0}G, 8^{0}SD, 7^{0}SD, 7^{6}SD, 5^{0}SD,

	Starts	1st	2nd	3rd	Win & Pl
Career Total (Turf)	4	0	0	1	578
Career Total (AW)	6	0	1	0	504

Going (Turf): **Sf: 0-0 GS: 0-1 Gd: 0-1 GF: 0-2 Fm: 0-0**
Distance: 5f/6f: 0-3 7f-8f: 0-6 9f-13f: 0-1 14f+: 0-0
Track : LH: 0-5 RH: 0-1 Tight: 0-4 Gall: 0-1
Aids: Bl: 0-2 Vi: 0-0 Tstrap: 0-0 Ckp: 0-0
Best Rating: **61** 8/08 Ling 6f stand

Modest; effective over 6f; acts on Polytrack.

Chasing Stars

112 99

4-y-o ch f Observatory (USA)-Post Modern (USA) (Nureyev (USA))

Mme C Head-Maarek K Abdulla

Placings:1/3110431-040

2009: 7^{0}GF, 7^{4}G, 8^{0}VS,

	Starts	1st	2nd	3rd	Win & Pl
Career Total (Turf)	11	4	0	2	72105

99 11/08 StCl 1m HVY £20221
87 6/08 MsnL 1m GD £12500
97 5/08 Lonc 7f GD £10662
79 11/07 StCl 7f HVY £7095
Total win prize-money £50478

Going (Turf): **Sf: 2-3** GS: 0-0 **Gd: 2-5** GF: 0-1 Fm: 0-0
Distance: 5f/6f: 0-0 **7f-8f: 4-11** 9f-13f: 0-0 14f+: 0-0
Track : **LH: 2-4** RH: 1-3 Tight: 0-0 Gall: 0-0
Aids: Bl: 0-0 Vi: 0-0 Tstrap: 0-0 Ckp: 0-0

Best Rating: 99 11/08 StCl 1m heavy

Very useful French-trained filly; effective at 7f and a mile; handles plenty of ease in the ground.

Chat De La Burg (USA)

91(96) (76)**76**

2-y-o ch c Johannesburg (USA)-Catsuit (USA) (Sir Cat (USA))

J R Best Kent Bloodstock

Placings:21 (6971)

2009: 6^{2}GF, 5^{1}SD,

	Starts	1st	2nd	3rd	Win & Pl
Career Total (Turf)	1	0	1	0	1542
Career Total (AW)	1	1	0	0	2590

76 10/09 Kemp 5f STD £2590

Total win prize-money £2590

Going (Turf): Sf: 0-0 GS: 0-0 Gd: 0-0 GF: 0-1 Fm: 0-0
Distance: 5f/6f: 1-2 7f-8f: 0-0 9f-13f: 0-0 14f+: 0-0
Track : LH: 0-0 RH: 1-1 Tight: 0-0 Gall: 0-0
Aids: Bl: 0-0 Vi: 0-0 Tstrap: 0-0 Ckp: 0-0
Best Rating: 76 10/09 Kemp 5f stand

Useful; effective over 5f-6f; acts on Polytrack.

Chat De Soie (IRE)

92(82) (39)**61**

2-y-o b f Barathea (IRE)-Margay (IRE) (Marju (IRE))

J S Moore Mrs Sandy Briddon

Placings:05404 (6200)

2009: 7^{0}G, 7^{5}GF, 7^{4}GF, 8^{0}SD, 9^{4}G,

	Starts	1st	2nd	3rd	Win & Pl
Career Total (Turf)	4	0	0	0	722
Career Total (AW)	1	0	0	0	

Going (Turf): Sf: 0-0 GS: 0-0 Gd: 0-2 GF: 0-2 Fm: 0-0
Distance: 5f/6f: 0-0 7f-8f: 0-4 9f-13f: 0-1 14f+: 0-0
Track : LH: 0-0 RH: 0-3 Tight: 0-1 Gall: 0-0
Aids: Bl: 0-0 Vi: 0-0 Tstrap: 0-0 Ckp: 0-0
Best Rating: 61 9/09 Gdwd 1m1f good

Chatanoogachoo choo

102(100) (65)**69**

4-y-o ch f Piccolo-Taza (Persian Bold)

M Hill Martin Hill

Placings:4030-0264034444 (7790)

2009: 10^{0}GF, 8^{2}GF, 7^{6}S, 8^{4}G, 8^{0}GF, 9^{3}GF, 12^{4}SD, 8^{4}SD, 9^{4}SD, 12^{4}SD,

	Starts	1st	2nd	3rd	Win & Pl
Career Total (Turf)	10	0	1	2	2691
Career Total (AW)	4	0	0	0	856

Going (Turf): Sf: 0-2 GS: 0-0 Gd: 0-1 GF: 0-7 Fm: 0-0
Distance: 5f/6f: 0-0 7f-8f: 0-3 9f-13f: 0-11 14f+: 0-0
Track : LH: 0-7 RH: 0-4 Tight: 0-9 Gall: 0-1
Aids: Bl: 0-0 Vi: 0-0 Tstrap: 0-0 Ckp: 0-0
Best Rating: 69 7/09 Bath 1m5y good

Modest; stays 1m2f; acts on fast ground and on Polytrack.

Chateau Zara

(80) (48)

2-y-o b f Zaha (CAN)-Glensara (Petoski)

C G Cox Basingstoke Commercials

Placings:0 (7024)

2009: 7^{0}SD,

	Starts	1st	2nd	3rd	Win & Pl
Career Total (Turf)	0	0	0	0	
Career Total (AW)	1	0	0	0	

Going (Turf): Sf: 0-0 GS: 0-0 Gd: 0-0 GF: 0-0 Fm: 0-0
Distance: 5f/6f: 0-0 7f-8f: 0-1 9f-13f: 0-0 14f+: 0-0
Track : LH: 0-0 RH: 0-1 Tight: 0-0 Gall: 0-0
Aids: Bl: 0-0 Vi: 0-0 Tstrap: 0-0 Ckp: 0-0
Best Rating: 48 10/09 Kemp 7f stand

Chateauneuf (IRE)

95(95) (54)**56**

3-y-o b f Marju (IRE)-Night Eyes (IRE) (Night Shift (USA))

W M Brisbourne (B W Hills 26/10) D Slingsby

Placings:06-665550 (7374)

2009: 8^{6}G, 8^{6}G, 8^{5}HY, 10^{5}SD, 12^{5}SD, 9^{0}SD,

	Starts	1st	2nd	3rd	Win & Pl
Career Total (Turf)	5	0	0	0	0
Career Total (AW)	3	0	0	0	0

Going (Turf): Sf: 0-1 GS: 0-0 Gd: 0-4 GF: 0-0 Fm: 0-0
Distance: 5f/6f: 0-0 7f-8f: 0-3 9f-13f: 0-5 14f+: 0-0
Track : LH: 0-3 RH: 0-4 Tight: 0-2 Gall: 0-0
Aids: Bl: 0-0 Vi: 0-0 Tstrap: 0-2 Ckp: 0-2
Best Rating: 56 6/09 Gdwd 1m good

Chatterszaha

73(94) (64)**54**

3-y-o ch f Zaha (CAN)-Chatter's Princess (Cadeaux Genereux)

C Drew C Drew

Placings:45400-0000 (7100)

2009: 6^{0}SD, 5^{0}SD, 7^{0}SD, 5^{0}G,

	Starts	1st	2nd	3rd	Win & Pl
Career Total (Turf)	2	0	0	0	337
Career Total (AW)	7	0	0	0	361

Going (Turf): Sf: 0-0 GS: 0-0 Gd: 0-1 GF: 0-1 Fm: 0-0
Distance: 5f/6f: 0-8 7f-8f: 0-1 9f-13f: 0-0 14f+: 0-0
Track : LH: 0-6 RH: 0-1 Tight: 0-2 Gall: 0-3
Aids: Bl: 0-0 Vi: 0-1 Tstrap: 0-0 Ckp: 0-0
Best Rating: 64 9/08 GrLe 6f stand

Chaussini

101 **76**

2-y-o b f Dubawi (IRE)-Miss Chaussini (IRE) (Rossini (USA))

J A R Toller M E Wates

Placings:0320 (7147)

2009: 6^{0}GF, 6^{3}GF, 6^{2}G, 6^{0}G,

	Starts	1st	2nd	3rd	Win & Pl
Career Total (Turf)	4	0	1	1	2490

Going (Turf): Sf: 0-0 GS: 0-0 Gd: 0-2 GF: 0-2 Fm: 0-0
Distance: 5f/6f: 0-2 7f-8f: 0-2 9f-13f: 0-0 14f+: 0-0
Track : LH: 0-0 RH: 0-0 Tight: 0-0 Gall: 0-0
Aids: Bl: 0-0 Vi: 0-0 Tstrap: 0-0 Ckp: 0-0
Best Rating: 76 10/09 NmkR 6f good

Fair; effective over 6f; acts on good ground.

Cheam Forever (USA)

107(100) (69)**80**

3-y-o b g Exchange Rate (USA)-Many Charms (USA) (St Jovite (USA))

R Charlton H R H Sultan Ahmad Shah

Placings:300-300113314 (6545)

2009: 7^{3}SD, 6^{0}F, 7^{0}SD, 8^{1}GS, 7^{1}GF, 8^{3}F, 8^{3}GF, 8^{1}GF, 8^{4}GF,

	Starts	1st	2nd	3rd	Win & Pl
Career Total (Turf)	8	3	0	2	11194
Career Total (AW)	4	0	0	2	1006

80 9/09 Wwck 1m22y (0-75)H G-F £2914
75 8/09 Brig 7f214y (0-70)H G-F £3280
67 7/09 Pont 1m4y (0-70)H G-S £3238

Total win prize-money £9432

Going (Turf): Sf: 0-0 GS: 1-2 Gd: 0-0 GF: 2-4 Fm: 0-2
Distance: 5f/6f: 0-2 7f-8f: 1-5 9f-13f: 2-5 14f+: 0-0
Track : LH: 3-9 RH: 0-1 Tight: 0-4 Gall: 0-0
Aids: Bl: 0-0 Vi: 1-1 Tstrap: 0-0 Ckp: 0-0
Best Rating: 80 9/09 Wwck 1m22y gd-fm

Modest; effective over 7f-1m; acts on Polytrack and fast ground.

Cheap Street

94(99) (59)**73**

5-y-o ch g Compton Place-Anneliina (Cadeaux Genereux)

J G Portman A S B Portman

Placings:03241101/0500060/305043600-00265 (5634)

2009: 7^{0}SD, 6^{0}G, 6^{2}GF, 7^{6}G, 7^{5}GS,

	Starts	1st	2nd	3rd	Win & Pl
Career Total (Turf)	25	3	2	3	37849
Career Total (AW)	4	0	0	0	0

90 10/06 NmkR 6f (0-95) G-S £5181
84 8/06 NmkJ 6f SFT £24625
73 8/06 Wind 6f G-F £3886

Total win prize-money £33693

Going (Turf): Sf: 1-3 GS: 1-8 Gd: 0-6 GF: 1-8 Fm: 0-0
Distance: 5f/6f: 3-18 7f-8f: 0-10 9f-13f: 0-1 14f+: 0-0
Track : LH: 0-4 RH: 0-4 Tight: 0-2 Gall: 1-8
Aids: Bl: 0-3 Vi: 0-0 Tstrap: 0-0 Ckp: 0-0
Best Rating: 90 10/06 NmkR 6f gd-sft

Modest; stays 6f; acts on fast and easy ground.

Cheap Thrills

101(100) (75)**77**

3-y-o ch f Bertolini (USA)-Licence To Thrill (Wolfhound (USA))

J A Osborne Mr And Mrs Christopher Wright

Placings:03-1321305003614 (7870)

2009: 6^{1}SD, 6^{3}SD, 7^{2}F, 7^{1}GF, 7^{3}G, 7^{0}GF, 7^{5}SD, 7^{0}SD, 5^{0}SD, 6^{3}SD, 6^{6}SD, 6^{1}SD, 6^{4}SS,

	Starts	1st	2nd	3rd	Win & Pl
Career Total (Turf)	4	1	1	1	5282
Career Total (AW)	11	2	0	3	5757

69 12/09 Sthl 6f (0-70) STD £2047
77 5/09 NmkR 7f (0-70)H G-F £3885
66 1/09 Ling 6f STD £2217

Total win prize-money £8151

Going (Turf): Sf: 0-0 GS: 0-0 Gd: 0-1 **GF: 1-2** Fm: 0-1
Distance: **5f/6f: 2-9** 7f-8f: 1-6 9f-13f: 0-0 14f+: 0-0
Track : **LH: 2-10** RH: 0-3 **Tight: 1-7** Gall: 0-0
Aids: Bl: 0-0 Vi: 0-0 Tstrap: 0-0 Ckp: 0-0
Best Rating: **77** 5/09 NmkR 7f gd-fm

Modest; effective at 6f-7f; acts on Polytrack and fast ground.

Check The Anchor (IRE)

79 **43**
2-y-o ch g Observatory (USA)-Fleet River (USA) (Riverman (USA))
N Tinkler P D Savill

Placings:000 **(6214)**
2009: 6^{0}GF, 9^{0}GF, 7^{0}GF,

	Starts	1st	2nd	3rd	Win & Pl
Career Total (Turf)	3	0	0	0	

Going (Turf): **Sf: 0-0 GS: 0-0 Gd: 0-0 GF: 0-3 Fm: 0-0**
Distance: 5f/6f: 0-1 7f-8f: 0-1 9f-13f: 0-1 14f+: 0-0
Track : LH: 0-1 RH: 0-0 Tight: 0-1 Gall: 0-0
Aids: Bl: 0-0 Vi: 0-0 Tstrap: 0-0 Ckp: 0-0
Best Rating: **43** 9/09 Rdcr 1m1f gd-fm

Check Up (IRE)

(90) (40)**62**
8-y-o b g Frimaire-Melons Lady (IRE) (The Noble Player (USA))
J L Flint Andrew Leyshon

Placings:3/21200060-0 **(0444)**
2009: 12^{0}SD,

	Starts	1st	2nd	3rd	Win & Pl
Career Total (Turf)	6	1	2	1	3615
Career Total (AW)	4	0	0	0	

61 7/08 Wind 1m3f135y G-F £2047
Total win prize-money £2047

Going (Turf): Sf: 0-1 GS: 0-1 Gd: 0-2 **GF: 1-2** Fm: 0-0
Distance: 5f/6f: 0-0 7f-8f: 0-0 **9f-13f: 1-8** 14f+: 0-2
Track : LH: 0-6 RH: 0-2 **Tight: 1-5** Gall: 0-1
Aids: Bl: 0-0 Vi: 0-0 Tstrap: 0-2 Ckp: 0-2
Best Rating: **62** 8/08 Chep 1m4f23y soft

Checklow (USA)

110(107) (94)**98**
4-y-o b g Street Cry (IRE)-Comstock Queen (USA) (Silver Hawk (USA))
J Noseda Mrs Susan Roy

Placings:3140-252000 **(6665)**
2009: 8^{2}SD, 8^{5}SD, 10^{2}GF, 10^{0}GF, 8^{0}G, 10^{0}GS,

	Starts	1st	2nd	3rd	Win & Pl
Career Total (Turf)	7	1	1	1	8288
Career Total (AW)	3	0	1	0	3705

77 4/08 Wind 1m2f7y G-F £2729
Total win prize-money £2730

Going (Turf): Sf: 0-0 GS: 0-1 Gd: 0-3 **GF: 1-3** Fm: 0-0
Distance: 5f/6f: 0-0 7f-8f: 0-2 **9f-13f: 1-8** 14f+: 0-0
Track : LH: 0-4 **RH: 1-5 Tight: 1-2** Gall: 0-4
Aids: Bl: 0-0 Vi: 0-1 Tstrap: 0-1 Ckp: 0-1
Best Rating: **98** 5/09 York 1m2f88y gd-fm

Very useful; suited by 1m2f; acts on fast ground and on Polytrack; has worn a visor and cheekpieces.

Cheeky Crumpet

71 **10**
3-y-o b f Mind Games-Woore Lass (IRE) (Persian Bold)
A Berry Mrs Margaret Forsyth

Placings:00 **(1335)**
2009: 6^{0}GF, 6^{0}GF,

	Starts	1st	2nd	3rd	Win & Pl
Career Total (Turf)	2	0	0	0	

Going (Turf): **Sf: 0-0 GS: 0-0 Gd: 0-0 GF: 0-2 Fm: 0-0**
Distance: 5f/6f: 0-2 7f-8f: 0-0 9f-13f: 0-0 14f+: 0-0
Track : LH: 0-1 RH: 0-0 Tight: 0-0 Gall: 0-0
Aids: Bl: 0-0 Vi: 0-0 Tstrap: 0-0 Ckp: 0-0
Best Rating: **10** 4/09 Pont 6f gd-fm

Cheerfully

79 **54**
2-y-o br f Sadler's Wells (USA)-Light Of Morn (Daylami (IRE))
J H M Gosden George Strawbridge

Placings:0 **(7182)**
2009: 7^{0}G,

	Starts	1st	2nd	3rd	Win & Pl
Career Total (Turf)	1	0	0	0	

Going (Turf): **Sf: 0-0 GS: 0-0 Gd: 0-1 GF: 0-0 Fm: 0-0**
Distance: 5f/6f: 0-0 7f-8f: 0-1 9f-13f: 0-0 14f+: 0-0
Track : LH: 0-0 RH: 0-0 Tight: 0-0 Gall: 0-0
Aids: Bl: 0-0 Vi: 0-0 Tstrap: 0-0 Ckp: 0-0
Best Rating: **54** 10/09 NmkR 7f good

Cheers Big Ears (IRE)

86(95) (56)**54**
3-y-o br c Kheleyf (USA)-Grey Galava (Generous (IRE))
J R Best Michael Hanratty

Placings:6403 **(7069)**
2009: 7^{6}SD, 7^{4}GF, 6^{0}GF, 6^{3}SD,

	Starts	1st	2nd	3rd	Win & Pl
Career Total (Turf)	2	0	0	0	192
Career Total (AW)	2	0	0	1	252

Going (Turf): **Sf: 0-0 GS: 0-0 Gd: 0-0 GF: 0-2 Fm: 0-0**
Distance: 5f/6f: 0-2 7f-8f: 0-2 9f-13f: 0-0 14f+: 0-0
Track : LH: 0-2 RH: 0-0 Tight: 0-2 Gall: 0-0
Aids: Bl: 0-0 Vi: 0-0 Tstrap: 0-0 Ckp: 0-0
Best Rating: **56** 10/09 Ling 6f stand

Cheers For Thea (IRE)

96(103) (76)**62**
4-y-o gr f Distant Music (USA)-Popiplu (USA) (Cozzene (USA))
T D Easterby Ron George

Placings:605012-02353443101 **(6349)**
2009: 9^{0}GF, 9^{2}GF, 10^{3}F, 10^{5}G, 9^{3}F, 12^{4}S, 11^{4}G, 9^{3}SD, 8^{1}SD, 8^{0}GF, 8^{1}SD,

	Starts	1st	2nd	3rd	Win & Pl
Career Total (Turf)	14	1	2	2	6596
Career Total (AW)	3	2	0	1	5130

76 9/09 Wolv 1m141y (0-65)H STD £2388
70 9/09 Wolv 1m141y (0-60)H STD £2388
60 7/08 Pont 1m2f6y (0-70)H GD £3885
Total win prize-money £8662

Going (Turf): Sf: 0-2 GS: 0-1 **Gd: 1-5** GF: 0-4 Fm: 0-2
Distance: 5f/6f: 0-0 7f-8f: 0-2 **9f-13f: 3-15** 14f+: 0-0
Track : **LH: 3-11** RH: 0-6 **Tight: 2-6** Gall: 0-1
Aids: **Bl: 2-4** Vi: 0-0 Tstrap: 0-0 Ckp: 0-0
Best Rating: **76** 9/09 Wolv 1m141y stand

Moderate; stays 1m2f but effective at 1m; acts on Polytrack and a sound surface on turf; has worn blinkers and a tongue-tie.

Cheery Cat (USA)

97(97) (56)**68**
5-y-o b/br g Catienus (USA)-Olinka (USA) (Wolfhound (USA))
J Balding (D W Barker 6/7) The Cataractonium Racing Syndicate

Placings:03000/60213441306/0100045565F-040005451030 **(7703)**
2009: 6^{0}SD, 7^{4}F, 7^{0}GF, 7^{0}GF, 8^{0}GS, 7^{5}GS, 6^{4}GF, 7^{5}GF, 6^{1}SD, 7^{0}SD, 5^{3}SD, 6^{0}SD,

	Starts	1st	2nd	3rd	Win & Pl
Career Total (Turf)	32	3	1	3	13405
Career Total (AW)	7	1	0	1	2008

56 10/09 Ling 6f (0-55)H STD £1706
68 5/08 Haml 6f5y (0-75)H G-F £3412
66 8/07 Rdcr 7f (0-65)H GD £2817
63 6/07 Pont 6f (0-75)H G-S £3886
Total win prize-money £11821

Going (Turf): Sf: 0-3 **GS: 1-6 Gd: 1-7 GF: 1-13** Fm: 0-3
Distance: 5f/6f: 2-11 7f-8f: 2-27 9f-13f: 0-1 14f+: 0-0
Track : **LH: 2-18** RH: 0-8 **Tight: 1-16** Gall: 0-0
Aids: Bl: 0-0 Vi: 0-1 Tstrap: 4-29 Ckp: 4-29
Best Rating: **68** 5/08 Haml 6f5y gd-fm

Moderate; stays 7f but fully effective over shorter; acts on fast and easy ground; has worn cheekpieces.

Cheetah

96 **78**
2-y-o b f Tiger Hill (IRE)-Kassiyra (IRE) (Kendor (FR))
L M Cumani Fittocks Stud

Placings:23 **(6992)**
2009: 8^{2}GF, 8^{3}GS,

	Starts	1st	2nd	3rd	Win & Pl
Career Total (Turf)	2	0	1	1	2312

Going (Turf): **Sf: 0-0 GS: 0-1 Gd: 0-0 GF: 0-1 Fm: 0-0**
Distance: 5f/6f: 0-0 7f-8f: 0-2 9f-13f: 0-0 14f+: 0-0
Track : LH: 0-2 RH: 0-0 Tight: 0-0 Gall: 0-2
Aids: Bl: 0-0 Vi: 0-0 Tstrap: 0-0 Ckp: 0-0
Best Rating: **78** 10/09 Donc 1m gd-sft

Runner-up on debut; effective over 1m; acts on fast ground.

Cheetah Beetah

77(79) (6)**25**
3-y-o ch f Compton Place-Scylla (Rock City)
H S Howe (M Halford 24/6) Roly Roper

Placings:060006 **(5500)**
2009: 6^{0}G, 6^{6}S, 6^{0}GF, 8^{0}GS, 6^{0}SD, 5^{6}G,

	Starts	1st	2nd	3rd	Win & Pl
Career Total (Turf)	5	0	0	0	0
Career Total (AW)	1	0	0	0	

Going (Turf): **Sf: 0-1 GS: 0-1 Gd: 0-2 GF: 0-1 Fm: 0-0**
Distance: 5f/6f: 0-5 7f-8f: 0-0 9f-13f: 0-1 14f+: 0-0
Track : LH: 0-2 RH: 0-2 Tight: 0-1 Gall: 0-0
Aids: Bl: 0-0 Vi: 0-0 Tstrap: 0-0 Ckp: 0-0
Best Rating: **25** 8/09 Chep 5f16y good

Chef De Camp (FR)

(77) (21)
6-y-o gr g Smadoun (FR)-Jolie Cheftaine (FR) (Chef De Clan (FR))
M R Hoad R P C Hoad

Placings:5/0-6 **(0119)**
2009: 10^{6}SD,

	Starts	1st	2nd	3rd	Win & Pl
Career Total (Turf)	2	0	0	0	304
Career Total (AW)	1	0	0	0	0

Going (Turf): **Sf: 0-1 GS: 0-1 Gd: 0-0 GF: 0-0 Fm: 0-0**
Distance: 5f/6f: 0-0 7f-8f: 0-0 9f-13f: 0-2 14f+: 0-1
Track : LH: 0-1 RH: 0-0 Tight: 0-1 Gall: 0-0
Aids: Bl: 0-0 Vi: 0-0 Tstrap: 0-0 Ckp: 0-0
Best Rating: **21** 1/09 Ling 1m2f stand

Chelsea Morning (USA)

89 **72**
2-y-o ch f Giant's Causeway (USA)-Binya (GER) (Royal Solo (IRE))
B W Hills Mr & Mrs Christopher Wright

Placings:3 **(3810)**
2009: 7^{3}GF,

	Starts	1st	2nd	3rd	Win & Pl
Career Total (Turf)	1	0	0	1	770

Going (Turf): **Sf: 0-0 GS: 0-0 Gd: 0-0 GF: 0-1 Fm: 0-0**
Distance: 5f/6f: 0-0 7f-8f: 0-1 9f-13f: 0-0 14f+: 0-0
Track : LH: 0-0 RH: 0-0 Tight: 0-0 Gall: 0-0
Aids: Bl: 0-0 Vi: 0-0 Tstrap: 0-0 Ckp: 0-0
Best Rating: **72** 7/09 Newb 7f gd-fm

Fair; stays 7f and acts on fast ground.

Chenin (IRE)

66(87) (41)
3-y-o b f Statue Of Liberty (USA)-Baltic Beach (IRE) (Polish Precedent (USA))
Peter Grayson Haldane Racing & D L Rhodes

Placings:0000065 **(5645)**
2009: 6^{0}SD, 5^{0}SD, 5^{0}GF, 5^{0}SD, 5^{0}SD, 5^{6}SD, 5^{5}SD,

	Starts	1st	2nd	3rd	Win & Pl
Career Total (Turf)	1	0	0	0	
Career Total (AW)	6	0	0	0	0

Going (Turf): **Sf: 0-0 GS: 0-0 Gd: 0-0 GF: 0-1 Fm: 0-0**
Distance: 5f/6f: 0-7 7f-8f: 0-0 9f-13f: 0-0 14f+: 0-0
Track : LH: 0-4 RH: 0-1 Tight: 0-4 Gall: 0-0
Aids: Bl: 0-1 Vi: 0-0 Tstrap: 0-0 Ckp: 0-0
Best Rating: **41** 4/09 Kemp 5f stand

Cherish The Moment (IRE)

101 **75**
3-y-o b c Galileo (IRE)-Belleclaire (IRE) (Bigstone (IRE))
B W Hills J Hanson & Cavendish Investing Ltd

Placings:6-300234 **(6698)**
2009: 9^{3}GF, 10^{0}G, 12^{0}G, 10^{2}GF, 11^{3}GF, 12^{4}GS,

	Starts	1st	2nd	3rd	Win & Pl
Career Total (Turf)	7	0	1	2	1931

Going (Turf): **Sf: 0-0 GS: 0-2 Gd: 0-2 GF: 0-3 Fm: 0-0**
Distance: 5f/6f: 0-0 7f-8f: 0-1 9f-13f: 0-6 14f+: 0-0
Track : LH: 0-2 RH: 0-4 Tight: 0-4 Gall: 0-0
Aids: Bl: 0-0 Vi: 0-0 Tstrap: 0-1 Ckp: 0-1
Best Rating: **75** 8/09 Wind 1m2f7y gd-fm

Fair; effective over 1m2f; acts on fast ground.

Cherri Fosfate

100(106) (74)**74**
5-y-o b g Mujahid (USA)-Compradore (Mujtahid (USA))
D Carroll (Paul W Flynn 14/5) Stoppers

Placings:21005**522/13042201300**6000**5**00**6**14/1**0**1244300 **01**-50 **(2998)**
2009: 8^{5}F, 7^{0}GF,

	Starts	1st	2nd	3rd	Win & Pl
Career Total (Turf)	21	3	2	1	10589
Career Total (AW)	21	4	4	2	16179

74 12/08 Wolv 1m1f103y (0-65)H STD £2729
71 5/08 Ripn 1m1f170y GD £2590
55 4/08 Ripn 1m1f170y GD £2590
58 9/07 Rdcr 1m2f G-S £2047
77 3/07 Wolv 1m141y (0-75)H STD £3886
63 1/07 Wolv 5f216y STD £2730
67 5/06 Kemp 6f STD £1706
Total win prize-money £18280

Going (Turf): Sf: 0-6 GS: 1-4 **Gd: 2-3** GF: 0-6 Fm: 0-1
Distance: 5f/6f: 2-12 7f-8f: 0-13 **9f-13f: 5-17** 14f+: 0-0
Track : **LH: 4-29** RH: 3-9 **Tight: 6-24** Gall: 0-0
Aids: **Bl: 2-15** Vi: 1-9 Tstrap: 0-2 Ckp: 0-2
Best Rating: **79** 4/07 Wolv 7f32y stand

Modest; stays 1m2f but effective over shorter; acts on easy ground; also goes on Polytrack.

Cherries On Top (IRE)

(89) (42)**36**
4-y-o ch g Elnadim (USA)-Easy Going (Hamas (IRE))
D Nicholls Cherries Racing

Placings:06005-R **(1769)**
2009: 7^{R}GF,

	Starts	1st	2nd	3rd	Win & Pl
Career Total (Turf)	4	0	0	0	0
Career Total (AW)	2	0	0	0	0

Going (Turf): **Sf: 0-0 GS: 0-0 Gd: 0-0 GF: 0-4 Fm: 0-0**
Distance: 5f/6f: 0-4 7f-8f: 0-2 9f-13f: 0-0 14f+: 0-0
Track : LH: 0-5 RH: 0-0 Tight: 0-3 Gall: 0-1
Aids: Bl: 0-0 Vi: 0-0 Tstrap: 0-0 Ckp: 0-0
Best Rating: **42** 9/08 Ling 5f stand

Cherry Bee

99 **72**
2-y-o gr f Acclamation-Norfolk Lavender (CAN) (Ascot Knight (CAN))
M Johnston Favourites Racing IV

Placings:24231 **(5320)**
2009: 5^{2}GF, 5^{4}GS, 6^{2}G, 6^{3}GS, 8^{1}GF,

	Starts	1st	2nd	3rd	Win & Pl
Career Total (Turf)	5	1	2	1	7339

72 8/09 Wind 1m67y (0-85) G-F £3885
Total win prize-money £3886

Going (Turf): Sf: 0-0 GS: 0-2 Gd: 0-1 **GF: 1-2** Fm: 0-0
Distance: 5f/6f: 0-3 7f-8f: 0-1 **9f-13f: 1-1** 14f+: 0-0
Track : LH: 0-0 **RH: 1-1 Tight: 1-1** Gall: 0-0
Aids: Bl: 0-0 Vi: 0-0 Tstrap: 0-0 Ckp: 0-0
Best Rating: **72** 8/09 Wind 1m67y gd-fm

Modest; stays 1m; acts on fast ground.

Cherry Belle (IRE)

92(84) (46)**58**
3-y-o b f Red Ransom (USA)-Pondicherry (USA) (Sir Wimborne (USA))
P D Evans P D Evans

Placings:6510**3**02635265-0006 **(6172)**
2009: 8^{0}GF, 10^{0}GF, 10^{0}GF, 9^{6}GF,

	Starts	1st	2nd	3rd	Win & Pl
Career Total (Turf)	15	1	2	2	4302
Career Total (AW)	2	0	0	0	0

54 6/08 Rdcr 7f G-F £1683
Total win prize-money £1684

Going (Turf): Sf: 0-2 GS: 0-2 Gd: 0-2 **GF: 1-9** Fm: 0-0
Distance: 5f/6f: 0-1 **7f-8f: 1-9** 9f-13f: 0-7 14f+: 0-0
Track : LH: 0-7 RH: 0-4 Tight: 0-6 Gall: 0-0
Aids: Bl: 0-0 **Vi: 1-13** Tstrap: 0-0 Ckp: 0-0
Best Rating: **58** 9/08 Wind 1m67y gd-fm

Moderate sort; stays 1m; acts on fast ground; has worn a visor.

Cherry Plum

(87) (46)
3-y-o ch f Medicean-Putuna (Generous (IRE))
A M Balding J C, J R And S R Hitchins

Placings:04 **(0695)**
2009: 8^{0}SD, 8^{4}SD,

	Starts	1st	2nd	3rd	Win & Pl
Career Total (Turf)	0	0	0	0	
Career Total (AW)	2	0	0	0	192

Going (Turf): **Sf: 0-0 GS: 0-0 Gd: 0-0 GF: 0-0 Fm: 0-0**
Distance: 5f/6f: 0-0 7f-8f: 0-1 9f-13f: 0-1 14f+: 0-0
Track : LH: 0-1 RH: 0-1 Tight: 0-1 Gall: 0-0
Aids: Bl: 0-0 Vi: 0-0 Tstrap: 0-0 Ckp: 0-0
Best Rating: **46** 2/09 Wolv 1m141y stand

Chesapeake Bay

61 (68)**69**
4-y-o b g High Chaparral (IRE)-Coyote (Indian Ridge)
J J Lambe B G Dallat

Placings:34054/06 **(2440)**
2009: 12^{0}SW, 9^{6}GF,

	Starts	1st	2nd	3rd	Win & Pl
Career Total (Turf)	5	0	0	1	1633
Career Total (AW)	2	0	0	0	

Going (Turf): Sf: 0-1 GS: 0-0 Gd: 0-0 GF: 0-2 Fm: 0-1
Distance: 5f/6f: 0-0 7f-8f: 0-5 9f-13f: 0-2 14f+: 0-0
Track : LH: 0-3 RH: 0-2 Tight: 0-1 Gall: 0-0
Aids: Bl: 0-1 Vi: 0-0 Tstrap: 0-0 Ckp: 0-0
Best Rating: 69 10/07 Navn 1m firm

Cheshire Lady (IRE)

80 43
2-y-o b f Marju (IRE)-Kiris World (Distant Relative)
W M Brisbourne Four Cheshire Gents

Placings:60 (3633)
2009: 5^{6}GF, 5^{0}G,

	Starts	1st	2nd	3rd	Win & Pl
Career Total (Turf)	2	0	0	0	0

Going (Turf): Sf: 0-0 GS: 0-0 Gd: 0-1 GF: 0-1 Fm: 0-0
Distance: 5f/6f: 0-2 7f-8f: 0-0 9f-13f: 0-0 14f+: 0-0
Track : LH: 0-1 RH: 0-0 Tight: 0-1 Gall: 0-0
Aids: Bl: 0-0 Vi: 0-0 Tstrap: 0-0 Ckp: 0-0
Best Rating: 43 6/09 Ches 5f16y gd-fm

Cheshire Prince

109 97
5-y-o br g Desert Prince (IRE)-Bundle Up (USA) (Miner's Mark (USA))
N B King (W M Brisbourne 5/10) Across The Pond Partnership

Placings:0140655420/50325311/630622113B600-1002206006 (6546)
2009: 10^{1}GF, 10^{0}GF, 12^{0}G, 10^{2}GS, 10^{2}G, 10^{0}G, 13^{6}GF, 10^{0}GF, 11^{0}GF, 10^{6}GF,

	Starts	1st	2nd	3rd	Win & Pl
Career Total (Turf)	41	6	6	4	53082

94	5/09	Ches	1m2f75y	(0-100)H	G-F	£14193
93	8/08	Ches	1m4f66y	(0-85)H	GD	£5828
81	7/08	Ches	1m2f75y	(0-80)H	GD	£5828
73	8/07	Ches	1m2f75y	(0-75)H	G-F	£3400
68	8/07	Newc	1m2f32y	(0-65)H	G-F	£2137
66	5/06	Yarm	6f3y		GD	£2266

Total win prize-money £33653

Going (Turf): Sf: 0-4 GS: 0-4 Gd: 3-12 GF: 3-21 Fm: 0-0
Distance: 5f/6f: 0-2 7f-8f: 1-8 9f-13f: 5-29 14f+: 0-2
Track : LH: 5-32 RH: 0-5 Tight: 4-19 Gall: 1-8
Aids: Bl: 0-0 Vi: 0-0 Tstrap: 0-0 Ckp: 0-0
Best Rating: 97 7/09 NmkJ 1m2f good

Very useful; stays 1m4f, but effective at 1m2f; acts on most ground; goes well at Chester.

Cheshire Rose

96(100) (67)69
4-y-o ch f Bertolini (USA)-Merch Rhyd-Y-Grug (Sabrehill (USA))
A M Hales (T D Barron 15/5) Gary P Martin

Placings:10000/2504162060-562063350050 (7397)
2009: 5^{5}SD, 5^{6}SD, 5^{2}SD, 5^{0}GF, 5^{6}GS, 6^{3}S, 5^{3}GS, 5^{5}SD, 5^{0}G, 5^{0}SD, 5^{5}SD, 5^{0}SD,

	Starts	1st	2nd	3rd	Win & Pl
Career Total (Turf)	19	2	2	2	8710
Career Total (AW)	8	0	1	0	1156

69	8/08	Ayr	5f	(0-65)H	G-S	£2590
69	7/07	Ripn	5f		HVY	£3238

Total win prize-money £5829

Going (Turf): Sf: 1-9 GS: 1-5 Gd: 0-3 GF: 0-2 Fm: 0-0
Distance: 5f/6f: 2-26 7f-8f: 0-1 9f-13f: 0-0 14f+: 0-0
Track : LH: 0-5 RH: 0-1 Tight: 0-5 Gall: 0-0
Aids: Bl: 0-1 Vi: 0-0 Tstrap: 0-6 Ckp: 0-6
Best Rating: 69 8/08 Ayr 5f gd-sft

Modest; suited by 5f; acts on soft ground.

Cheveton

109(108) (106)103
5-y-o ch g Most Welcome-Attribute (Warning)
R J Price Mrs K Oseman

Placings:02443211111520-152303050120 (7015)
2009: 5^{1}SD, 5^{5}GS, 5^{2}G, 5^{3}G, 5^{0}G, 5^{3}GF, 6^{0}G, 5^{5}G, 6^{0}GF, 5^{1}GS, 6^{2}G, 5^{0}GS,

	Starts	1st	2nd	3rd	Win & Pl
Career Total (Turf)	20	5	4	3	72248
Career Total (AW)	6	2	1	0	19511

101	9/09	Hayd	5f	(0-100)H	G-S	£18693
106	3/09	Sthl	5f	(0-100)H	STD	£11215
96	8/08	GrLe	5f	(0-90)H	STD	£7569
96	8/08	Newb	5f34y	(0-85)H	GD	£4857
89	7/08	Asct	5f	(0-85)H	G-S	£6476
89	7/08	Hayd	5f	(0-75)H	SFT	£4857
80	6/08	Sand	5f6y	(0-80)H	GD	£5180

Total win prize-money £58850

Going (Turf): Sf: 1-3 GS: 2-5 Gd: 2-10 GF: 0-2 Fm: 0-0
Distance: 5f/6f: 7-24 7f-8f: 0-1 9f-13f: 0-1 14f+: 0-0
Track : LH: 1-7 RH: 0-0 Tight: 0-3 Gall: 1-3
Aids: Bl: 0-0 Vi: 0-0 Tstrap: 0-0 Ckp: 0-0
Best Rating: 106 3/09 Sthl 5f stand

Very useful; effective over 5f-6f; acts on good and softer ground and on Polytrack.

Cheveyo (IRE)

(89) (73)68
3-y-o br g Celtic Swing-La Catalane (IRE) (Marju (IRE))
Patrick Morris (G M Lyons 25/11) D & D Coatings Ltd

Placings:354240200 (7829)
2009: 7^{3}GF, 8^{5}G, 8^{4}GY, 6^{2}SD, 6^{4}SD, 8^{0}S, 6^{2}SD, 8^{0}SD, 7^{0}SD,

	Starts	1st	2nd	3rd	Win & Pl
Career Total (Turf)	4	0	0	1	1142
Career Total (AW)	5	0	2	0	3466

Going (Turf): Sf: 0-1 GS: 0-0 Gd: 0-1 GF: 0-1 Fm: 0-0
Distance: 5f/6f: 0-3 7f-8f: 0-5 9f-13f: 0-1 14f+: 0-0
Track : LH: 0-6 RH: 0-3 Tight: 0-0 Gall: 0-0
Aids: Bl: 0-0 Vi: 0-0 Tstrap: 0-0 Ckp: 0-0
Best Rating: 73 10/09 Dund 6f stand

Cheviot (USA)

104(94) (75)90
3-y-o b g Rahy (USA)-Camlet (Green Desert (USA))
M A Jarvis Sheikh Ahmed Al Maktoum

Placings:0144-232 (3375)
2009: 6^{2}GF, 6^{3}GF, 7^{2}GF,

	Starts	1st	2nd	3rd	Win & Pl
Career Total (Turf)	6	0	2	1	7273
Career Total (AW)	1	1	0	0	3886

75	9/08	Kemp	6f	STD	£3885

Total win prize-money £3886

Going (Turf): Sf: 0-0 GS: 0-1 Gd: 0-1 GF: 0-4 Fm: 0-0
Distance: 5f/6f: 1-5 7f-8f: 0-2 9f-13f: 0-0 14f+: 0-0
Track : LH: 0-1 RH: 1-1 Tight: 0-1 Gall: 0-1
Aids: Bl: 0-0 Vi: 0-0 Tstrap: 0-2 Ckp: 0-2
Best Rating: 90 4/09 Ripn 6f gd-fm

Useful; stays 7f; acts on fast ground and on Polytrack; has worn cheekpieces.

Cheyenne Chant

(82) (46)
2-y-o ch f Singspiel (IRE)-Apache Song (USA) (Dynaformer (USA))
Sir Mark Prescott Lord Derby

Placings:500 (7491)
2009: 7^{5}SD, 7^{0}SD, 8^{0}SD,

	Starts	1st	2nd	3rd	Win & Pl
Career Total (Turf)	0	0	0	0	
Career Total (AW)	3	0	0	0	0

Going (Turf): Sf: 0-0 GS: 0-0 Gd: 0-0 GF: 0-0 Fm: 0-0
Distance: 5f/6f: 0-0 7f-8f: 0-2 9f-13f: 0-1 14f+: 0-0
Track : LH: 0-3 RH: 0-0 Tight: 0-2 Gall: 0-0
Aids: Bl: 0-0 Vi: 0-0 Tstrap: 0-0 Ckp: 0-0
Best Rating: 46 11/09 Wolv 1m141y stand

Cheyenne Red (IRE)

101(90) (57)71
3-y-o br g Namid-Red Leggings (Shareef Dancer (USA))
M Dods The Westerners

Placings:44423213412 (6798)
2009: 6^{4}SD, 6^{4}GS, 6^{4}G, 5^{2}GF, 6^{3}GF, 5^{2}G, 6^{1}S, 5^{3}GF, 6^{4}S, 6^{1}G, 6^{2}S,

	Starts	1st	2nd	3rd	Win & Pl
Career Total (Turf)	10	2	3	2	9769
Career Total (AW)	1	0	0	0	0

71	9/09	Haml	6f5y	(0-70)H	GD	£3238
67	8/09	Haml	6f5y		SFT	£2590

Total win prize-money £5828

Going (Turf): Sf: 1-3 GS: 0-1 Gd: 1-3 GF: 0-3 Fm: 0-0
Distance: 5f/6f: 0-7 7f-8f: 2-4 9f-13f: 0-0 14f+: 0-0
Track : LH: 0-2 RH: 0-1 Tight: 0-0 Gall: 0-1
Aids: Bl: 0-0 Vi: 0-0 Tstrap: 0-0 Ckp: 0-0
Best Rating: 71 9/09 Haml 6f5y good

Modest; effective at 6f; acts on good ground.

Chia (IRE)

(103) (60)66
6-y-o ch m Ashkalani (IRE)-Motley (Rainbow Quest (USA))
D Haydn Jones Mrs E M Haydn Jones

Placings:66020063/054005302232/21623424632262/153005-0000 (7856)
2009: 9^{0}SD, 9^{0}SD, 9^{0}SD, 9^{0}SD,

	Starts	1st	2nd	3rd	Win & Pl
Career Total (Turf)	14	0	2	2	2624
Career Total (AW)	30	2	8	4	15796

71	1/08	Wolv	1m1f103y	(0-75)H	STD	£2457
71	1/07	Wolv	1m1f103y	(0-70)H	SS	£3238

Total win prize-money £5696

Going (Turf): Sf: 0-1 GS: 0-1 Gd: 0-2 GF: 0-8 Fm: 0-2
Distance: 5f/6f: 0-2 7f-8f: 0-12 9f-13f: 2-30 14f+: 0-0
Track : LH: 2-31 RH: 0-8 Tight: 2-30 Gall: 0-2

Aids: Bl: 0-0 Vi: 0-1 Tstrap: 1-14 Ckp: 1-14
Best Rating: 72 1/08 Wolv 1m1f103y stand

Modest but consistent mare; effective at around 1m1f-1m4f; acts on Polytrack but handles fast turf.

Chiberta King

112 97
3-y-o b g King's Best (USA)-Glam Rock (Nashwan (USA))
A M Balding The Pink Hat Racing Partnership

Placings:006-1120220 (6302)
2009: 11¹GF, 12¹GF, 12²GF, 12⁰G, 12²GS, 14²G, 12⁰GF,

	Starts	1st	2nd	3rd	Win & Pl
Career Total (Turf)	10	2	3	0	32814

89 5/09 NmkR 1m4f (0-95)H G-F £9714
77 4/09 Wind 1m3f135y (0-75)H G-F £3070
Total win prize-money £12785

Going (Turf): Sf: 0-0 GS: 0-1 Gd: 0-4 **GF: 2-5** Fm: 0-0
Distance: 5f/6f: 0-0 7f-8f: 0-3 **9f-13f: 2-6** 14f+: 0-1
Track: LH: 0-1 **RH: 1-6** Tight: 1-2 Gall: 1-5
Aids: Bl: 0-0 Vi: 0-0 Tstrap: 0-0 Ckp: 0-0
Best Rating: 97 9/09 Ffos 1m6f good

Useful; stays 1m6f; acts on fast ground.

Chic Shanique (USA)

92(99) (57)59
3-y-o b/br f Dynaformer (USA)-Toll Order (USA) (Loup Sauvage (USA))
Tom Dascombe Mrs A G Kavanagh & Partners

Placings:65-00250 (4156)
2009: 8⁰S, 10⁰SD, 12²F, 12⁵SD, 11⁰G,

	Starts	1st	2nd	3rd	Win & Pl
Career Total (Turf)	3	0	1	0	723
Career Total (AW)	4	0	0	0	0

Going (Turf): **Sf: 0-1 GS: 0-0 Gd: 0-1 GF: 0-0 Fm: 0-1**
Distance: 5f/6f: 0-0 7f-8f: 0-3 9f-13f: 0-4 14f+: 0-0
Track: LH: 0-5 RH: 0-1 Tight: 0-6 Gall: 0-0
Aids: Bl: 0-0 Vi: 0-0 Tstrap: 0-0 Ckp: 0-0
Best Rating: 59 6/09 Bevl 1m4f16y firm

Moderate sort; stays 1m4f; handles quick ground.

Chicago Cop (IRE)

(69) (15)83
3-y-o b g Fasliyev (USA)-Sassari (IRE) (Darshaan)
D Nicholls The Untouchable Partnership

Placings:16-0 (1214)
2009: 7⁰SD,

	Starts	1st	2nd	3rd	Win & Pl
Career Total (Turf)	2	1	0	0	6152
Career Total (AW)	1	0	0	0	

83 5/08 York 6f GD £6152
Total win prize-money £6152

Going (Turf): Sf: 0-0 GS: 0-0 **Gd: 1-1** GF: 0-1 Fm: 0-0
Distance: **5f/6f: 1-2** 7f-8f: 0-1 9f-13f: 0-0 14f+: 0-0
Track: LH: 0-0 RH: 0-1 Tight: 0-0 Gall: 0-0
Aids: Bl: 0-0 Vi: 0-0 Tstrap: 0-0 Ckp: 0-0
Best Rating: 83 5/08 York 6f good

Chicamia

85(88) (41)27
5-y-o b m Kyllachy-Inflation (Primo Dominie)
M Mullineaux Abbey Racing

Placings:00/00630/00000 (7753)
2009: 8⁰G, 10⁰GF, 9⁰SD, 16⁰SD, 8⁰SD,

	Starts	1st	2nd	3rd	Win & Pl
Career Total (Turf)	9	0	0	1	454
Career Total (AW)	3	0	0	0	

Going (Turf): **Sf: 0-1 GS: 0-1 Gd: 0-4 GF: 0-3 Fm: 0-0**
Distance: 5f/6f: 0-3 7f-8f: 0-2 9f-13f: 0-6 14f+: 0-1
Track: LH: 0-9 RH: 0-1 Tight: 0-7 Gall: 0-0
Aids: Bl: 0-1 Vi: 0-0 Tstrap: 0-1 Ckp: 0-1
Best Rating: 43 8/07 Ches 7f122y gd-fm

Chicane

(79) (51)
2-y-o b f Motivator-Wosaita (Generous (IRE))
W J Haggas St Albans Bloodstock LLP

Placings:4 (7396)
2009: 7⁴SD,

	Starts	1st	2nd	3rd	Win & Pl
Career Total (Turf)	0	0	0	0	
Career Total (AW)	1	0	0	0	289

Going (Turf): **Sf: 0-0 GS: 0-0 Gd: 0-0 GF: 0-0 Fm: 0-0**
Distance: 5f/6f: 0-0 7f-8f: 0-1 9f-13f: 0-0 14f+: 0-0
Track: LH: 0-1 RH: 0-0 Tight: 0-1 Gall: 0-0
Aids: Bl: 0-0 Vi: 0-0 Tstrap: 0-0 Ckp: 0-0
Best Rating: 51 11/09 Wolv 7f32y stand

Modest; should stay 1m; acts on Polytrack; sure to improve.

Chicha Morada (USA)

(85) (57)
2-y-o b f Tale Of The Cat (USA)-Unbridled Charmer (USA) (Unbridled (USA))
D M Simcock El Catorce

Placings:6 (3979)
2009: 7⁶SD,

	Starts	1st	2nd	3rd	Win & Pl
Career Total (Turf)	0	0	0	0	
Career Total (AW)	1	0	0	0	0

Going (Turf): **Sf: 0-0 GS: 0-0 Gd: 0-0 GF: 0-0 Fm: 0-0**
Distance: 5f/6f: 0-0 7f-8f: 0-1 9f-13f: 0-0 14f+: 0-0
Track: LH: 0-0 RH: 0-1 Tight: 0-0 Gall: 0-0
Aids: Bl: 0-0 Vi: 0-0 Tstrap: 0-0 Ckp: 0-0
Best Rating: 57 7/09 Kemp 7f stand

Chichen Daawe

96(86) (32)55
3-y-o b f Daawe (USA)-Chichen Itza (Shareef Dancer (USA))
B Ellison Mrs Andrea M Mallinson

Placings:5553021540 (7214)
2009: 8⁵GF, 6⁵GS, 7⁵GS, 8³GF, 8⁰GF, 10²GF, 10¹G, 9⁵GF, 10⁴GF, 13⁰SD,

	Starts	1st	2nd	3rd	Win & Pl
Career Total (Turf)	9	1	1	1	3249
Career Total (AW)	1	0	0	0	

55 9/09 Ffos 1m2f (0-55)H GD £2266
Total win prize-money £2267

Going (Turf): Sf: 0-0 GS: 0-2 **Gd: 1-1** GF: 0-6 Fm: 0-0
Distance: 5f/6f: 0-1 7f-8f: 0-2 **9f-13f: 1-6** 14f+: 0-1
Track: **LH: 1-4** RH: 0-3 Tight: 0-2 **Gall: 1-2**
Aids: Bl: 0-0 Vi: 0-0 Tstrap: 0-0 Ckp: 0-0
Best Rating: 55 9/09 Ffos 1m2f good

Moderate; stays 1m2f; acts on good and faster ground.

Chichi (IRE)

(86) (35)
2-y-o b f Tomba-Chiffon (Polish Precedent (USA))
R Hannon Mrs P Good

Placings:00 (7885)
2009: 7⁰SD, 7⁰SD,

	Starts	1st	2nd	3rd	Win & Pl
Career Total (Turf)	0	0	0	0	
Career Total (AW)	2	0	0	0	

Going (Turf): **Sf: 0-0 GS: 0-0 Gd: 0-0 GF: 0-0 Fm: 0-0**
Distance: 5f/6f: 0-0 7f-8f: 0-2 9f-13f: 0-0 14f+: 0-0
Track: LH: 0-2 RH: 0-0 Tight: 0-2 Gall: 0-0
Aids: Bl: 0-0 Vi: 0-0 Tstrap: 0-0 Ckp: 0-0
Best Rating: 35 12/09 Ling 7f stand

Chichina (USA)

74(81) (39)46
2-y-o b f Afleet Alex (USA)-St Aye (USA) (Nureyev (USA))
M Johnston Mrs Christine E Budden

Placings:000 (6858)
2009: 6⁰GS, 7⁰GF, 8⁰SD,

	Starts	1st	2nd	3rd	Win & Pl
Career Total (Turf)	2	0	0	0	
Career Total (AW)	1	0	0	0	

Going (Turf): **Sf: 0-0 GS: 0-1 Gd: 0-0 GF: 0-1 Fm: 0-0**
Distance: 5f/6f: 0-1 7f-8f: 0-1 9f-13f: 0-1 14f+: 0-0
Track: LH: 0-2 RH: 0-0 Tight: 0-1 Gall: 0-0
Aids: Bl: 0-0 Vi: 0-0 Tstrap: 0-0 Ckp: 0-0
Best Rating: 46 10/09 Wwck 7f26y gd-fm

Chicita Banana

91(87) (65)69
2-y-o b f Danehill Dancer (IRE)-Night Frolic (Night Shift (USA))
George Baker Findlay & Bloom

Placings:01200330 (6227)
2009: 5⁰GF, 5¹GF, 5²GF, 5⁰GS, 6⁰GF, 7³SD, 5³G, 6⁰SD,

	Starts	1st	2nd	3rd	Win & Pl
Career Total (Turf)	6	1	1	1	5652
Career Total (AW)	2	0	0	1	385

68 4/09 Bath 5f11y G-F £3561
Total win prize-money £3562

Going (Turf): Sf: 0-0 GS: 0-1 Gd: 0-1 **GF: 1-4** Fm: 0-0
Distance: **5f/6f: 1-7** 7f-8f: 0-1 9f-13f: 0-0 14f+: 0-0
Track: **LH: 1-2** RH: 0-2 Tight: 0-0 **Gall: 1-1**
Aids: Bl: 0-0 Vi: 0-0 Tstrap: 0-0 Ckp: 0-0
Best Rating: 69 4/09 Thsk 5f gd-fm

Fair filly; effective from 5-7f; acts on good ground and Polytrack.

Chicora (USA)

96(94) (66)66

3-y-o b f Congaree (USA)-Old Money (AUS) (Old Spice (AUS))

J H M Gosden H R H Princess Haya Of Jordan

Placings:536302 **(5222)**

2009: 7^5GF, 8^3SD, 9^6G, 10^3GF, 10^0GF, 8^2G,

	Starts	1st	2nd	3rd	Win & Pl
Career Total (Turf)	5	0	1	1	1367
Career Total (AW)	1	0	0	1	385

Going (Turf): **Sf: 0-0 GS: 0-0 Gd: 0-2 GF: 0-3 Fm: 0-0**
Distance: 5f/6f: 0-0 7f-8f: 0-2 9f-13f: 0-4 14f+: 0-0
Track : LH: 0-3 RH: 0-2 Tight: 0-3 Gall: 0-1
Aids: Bl: 0-0 Vi: 0-0 Tstrap: 0-0 Ckp: 0-0
Best Rating: **66** 8/09 Sand 1m14y good

Fair; stays 1m; acts on fast ground and on Polytrack.

Chief Editor

111 (99)118

5-y-o b g Tomba-Princess Zara (Reprimand)

M A Jarvis Mrs P Good

Placings:1312/41/2126013-1F **(1676)**

2009: 5^1GS, 5^FGF,

	Starts	1st	2nd	3rd	Win & Pl
Career Total (Turf)	13	4	3	2	57557
Career Total (AW)	2	2	0	0	11701

118	4/09	Newb	5f34y	(0-110)H	G-S	£11215
112	9/08	Hayd	6f	(0-100)H	G-F	£12952
103	4/08	Nott	5f13y	(0-95)H	G-S	£6542
99	11/07	Wolv	5f20y	(0-95)H	STD	£8970
87	5/06	York	5f		G-S	£8420
76	4/06	Sthl	5f		STD	£2730

Total win prize-money £50832

Going (Turf): Sf: 0-7 **GS: 3-3** Gd: 0-1 GF: 1-2 Fm: 0-0
Distance: **5f/6f: 6-15** 7f-8f: 0-0 9f-13f: 0-0 14f+: 0-0
Track : **LH: 1-1** RH: 0-0 **Tight: 1-1** Gall: 0-0
Aids: Bl: 0-0 Vi: 0-0 Tstrap: 0-0 Ckp: 0-0
Best Rating: **118** 4/09 Newb 5f34y gd-sft

Smart; Listed placed; effective over 5-6f; acts on any ground and on sand; often held up.

Chief Exec

93(106) (81)54

7-y-o br g Zafonic (USA)-Shot At Love (IRE) (Last Tycoon)

J R Gask Stuart Dobb & Miss Kate Dobb

Placings:0212/4005405440/133005200P05003/404222020335/01442006-001264023544 **(7801)**

2009: 7^0G, 7^0SD, 7^1SD, 7^2SD, 7^6G, 7^4SD, 8^0SD, 7^2SD, 7^3SD, 7^5SD, 7^4SD, 7^4SD,

	Starts	1st	2nd	3rd	Win & Pl
Career Total (Turf)	14	0	2	0	2061
Career Total (AW)	47	4	8	6	32638

79	7/09	Wolv	7f32y	(0-65)H	STD	£2388
82	2/08	Wolv	7f32y	(0-70)H	STD	£2331
88	1/06	Ling	7f	(0-80)H	STD	£5505
81	11/04	Ling	7f		STD	£4550

Total win prize-money £14775

Going (Turf): **Sf: 0-1 GS: 0-2 Gd: 0-5 GF: 0-6 Fm: 0-0**
Distance: 5f/6f: 0-8 **7f-8f: 4-51** 9f-13f: 0-2 14f+: 0-0
Track : **LH: 4-41** RH: 0-8 **Tight: 4-40** Gall: 0-1
Aids: **Bl: 2-15** Vi: 0-3 Tstrap: 0-2 Ckp: 0-2
Best Rating: **88** 1/06 Ling 7f stand

Fair; effective at around 7f; acts on good ground; also goes on Polytrack; has worn blinkers and a visor.

Chief Of Ten

67(63) (14)20

2-y-o ch c Doyen (IRE)-Fudge (Polar Falcon (USA))

D R Lanigan Saif Ali & Saeed H Altayer

Placings:00 **(7388)**

2009: 8^0S, 8^0SD,

	Starts	1st	2nd	3rd	Win & Pl
Career Total (Turf)	1	0	0	0	
Career Total (AW)	1	0	0	0	

Going (Turf): **Sf: 0-1 GS: 0-0 Gd: 0-0 GF: 0-0 Fm: 0-0**
Distance: 5f/6f: 0-0 7f-8f: 0-1 9f-13f: 0-1 14f+: 0-0
Track : LH: 0-2 RH: 0-0 Tight: 0-1 Gall: 0-0
Aids: Bl: 0-0 Vi: 0-0 Tstrap: 0-0 Ckp: 0-0
Best Rating: **20** 11/09 Nott 1m75y soft

Chief Red Cloud (USA)

95(100) (72)65

3-y-o b/br g Cherokee Run (USA)-Pertuisane (Zamindar (USA))

A P Jarvis (K R Burke 15/7) Market Avenue Racing Club Ltd

Placings:00-4144350 **(6437)**

2009: 7^4F, 8^1SD, 8^4SD, 8^4G, 5^3SD, 7^5SD, 7^0SD,

	Starts	1st	2nd	3rd	Win & Pl
Career Total (Turf)	4	0	0	0	625
Career Total (AW)	5	1	0	1	2538

67	6/09	Kemp	1m	(0-60)H	STD	£1942

Total win prize-money £1943

Going (Turf): **Sf: 0-1 GS: 0-0 Gd: 0-2 GF: 0-0 Fm: 0-1**
Distance: 5f/6f: 0-2 **7f-8f: 1-6** 9f-13f: 0-1 14f+: 0-0
Track : LH: 0-4 **RH: 1-3** Tight: 0-3 Gall: 0-0
Aids: Bl: 0-0 Vi: 0-0 Tstrap: 0-0 Ckp: 0-0
Best Rating: **72** 9/09 Wolv 7f32y stand

Modest; stays 1m and acts on Polytrack.

Chief Wild Cat (IRE)

56(82) (42)68

3-y-o b g One Cool Cat (USA)-Soft (USA) (Lear Fan (USA))

C Moore D J Dolan

Placings:4500-000 **(1757a)**

2009: 5^0SD, 5^0SD, 7^0HY,

	Starts	1st	2nd	3rd	Win & Pl
Career Total (Turf)	5	0	0	0	543
Career Total (AW)	2	0	0	0	

Going (Turf): **Sf: 0-2 GS: 0-0 Gd: 0-0 GF: 0-0 Fm: 0-0**
Distance: 5f/6f: 0-5 7f-8f: 0-2 9f-13f: 0-0 14f+: 0-0
Track : LH: 0-5 RH: 0-1 Tight: 0-1 Gall: 0-0
Aids: Bl: 0-0 Vi: 0-0 Tstrap: 0-0 Ckp: 0-0
Best Rating: **68** 4/08 Leop 6f gd-yld

Chief Wren (USA)

(82) (51)

2-y-o b f Elusive Quality (USA)-Sea Gift (USA) (A.P. Indy (USA))

E F Vaughan Ali Saeed

Placings:6 **(7624)**

2009: 8^6SD,

	Starts	1st	2nd	3rd	Win & Pl
Career Total (Turf)	0	0	0	0	
Career Total (AW)	1	0	0	0	0

Going (Turf): **Sf: 0-0 GS: 0-0 Gd: 0-0 GF: 0-0 Fm: 0-0**
Distance: 5f/6f: 0-0 7f-8f: 0-1 9f-13f: 0-0 14f+: 0-0
Track : LH: 0-1 RH: 0-0 Tight: 0-1 Gall: 0-0
Aids: Bl: 0-0 Vi: 0-0 Tstrap: 0-0 Ckp: 0-0
Best Rating: **51** 12/09 Ling 1m stand

Chifah

86(79) (35)45

2-y-o b f Choisir (AUS)-Danifah (IRE) (Perugino (USA))

P D Evans E A R Morgans

Placings:066 **(2319)**

2009: 5^0GF, 5^6SD, 6^6G,

	Starts	1st	2nd	3rd	Win & Pl
Career Total (Turf)	2	0	0	0	0
Career Total (AW)	1	0	0	0	0

Going (Turf): **Sf: 0-0 GS: 0-0 Gd: 0-1 GF: 0-1 Fm: 0-0**
Distance: 5f/6f: 0-2 7f-8f: 0-1 9f-13f: 0-0 14f+: 0-0
Track : LH: 0-0 RH: 0-0 Tight: 0-0 Gall: 0-0
Aids: Bl: 0-0 Vi: 0-0 Tstrap: 0-0 Ckp: 0-0
Best Rating: **45** 5/09 Chep 6f16y good

Chiff Chaff

92(109) (57)62

5-y-o b m Mtoto-Hen Harrier (Polar Falcon (USA))

C R Dore J A Higson & Castles UK

Placings:000/3255200/06520300331651200-3000 **(4388)**

2009: 13^3SD, 15^0GF, 16^0SD, 16^0G,

	Starts	1st	2nd	3rd	Win & Pl
Career Total (Turf)	14	2	2	1	6533
Career Total (AW)	17	0	2	4	2557

60	8/08	Ripn	2m	(0-65)H	G-S	£2590
53	7/08	Yarm	2m	(0-65)H	G-F	£2072

Total win prize-money £4662

Going (Turf): Sf: 0-4 **GS: 1-3** Gd: 0-1 **GF: 1-6** Fm: 0-0
Distance: 5f/6f: 0-0 7f-8f: 0-3 9f-13f: 0-10 **14f+: 2-18**
Track : LH: 1-24 RH: 1-6 **Tight: 2-23** Gall: 0-0
Aids: Bl: 0-0 Vi: 0-0 Tstrap: 0-0 Ckp: 0-0
Best Rating: **68** 4/07 Wolv 1m4f50y stand

Moderate; stays 2m; acts on soft ground; also goes on Polytrack.

Child Of Our Time (IRE)

93 61

2-y-o b f Oratorio (IRE)-Shariyfa (FR) (Zayyani)

P W Chapple-Hyam Hintlesham Racing

Placings:00 **(6921)**

2009: 7^0GF, 8^0GF,

	Starts	1st	2nd	3rd	Win & Pl
Career Total (Turf)	2	0	0	0	

Going (Turf): **Sf: 0-0 GS: 0-0 Gd: 0-0 GF: 0-2 Fm: 0-0**
Distance: 5f/6f: 0-0 7f-8f: 0-1 9f-13f: 0-1 14f+: 0-0
Track : LH: 0-0 RH: 0-0 Tight: 0-0 Gall: 0-0
Aids: Bl: 0-0 Vi: 0-0 Tstrap: 0-0 Ckp: 0-0
Best Rating: **61** 10/09 Yarm 1m3y gd-fm

Chilean Fizz

82 47

2-y-o b f Domedriver (IRE)-Alter Ego (Alzao (USA))
Mrs A Duffield I Farrington

Placings:0540 (5337)
2009: 6[0]GF, 5[5]G, 5[4]G, 5[0]GS,

	Starts	1st	2nd	3rd	Win & Pl
Career Total (Turf)	4	0	0	0	289

Going (Turf): Sf: 0-0 GS: 0-1 Gd: 0-2 GF: 0-1 Fm: 0-0
Distance: 5f/6f: 0-4 7f-8f: 0-0 9f-13f: 0-0 14f+: 0-0
Track : LH: 0-1 RH: 0-0 Tight: 0-0 Gall: 0-0
Aids: Bl: 0-0 Vi: 0-0 Tstrap: 0-0 Ckp: 0-0
Best Rating: 47 7/09 Muss 5f good

Chill Out Charley

59

2-y-o b g Cyrano De Bergerac-We're Joken (Statoblest)
J J Bridger Mrs D E Johnston

Placings:00 (3403)
2009: 5[0]G, 6[0]GF,

	Starts	1st	2nd	3rd	Win & Pl
Career Total (Turf)	2	0	0	0	

Going (Turf): Sf: 0-0 GS: 0-0 Gd: 0-1 GF: 0-1 Fm: 0-0
Distance: 5f/6f: 0-2 7f-8f: 0-0 9f-13f: 0-0 14f+: 0-0
Track : LH: 0-1 RH: 0-0 Tight: 0-0 Gall: 0-1
Aids: Bl: 0-0 Vi: 0-0 Tstrap: 0-0 Ckp: 0-0
Best Rating:

Chilly Filly (IRE)

83(87) (69)73

3-y-o b f Montjeu (IRE)-Chill Seeking (USA) (Theatrical)
M Johnston J Barson

Placings:43230-21 (1349)
2009: 12[2]SD, 12[1]GF,

	Starts	1st	2nd	3rd	Win & Pl
Career Total (Turf)	6	1	1	2	7173
Career Total (AW)	1	0	1	0	806

70 4/09 Donc 1m4f G-F £4857
Total win prize-money £4857

Going (Turf): Sf: 0-3 GS: 0-1 Gd: 0-0 **GF: 1-2** Fm: 0-0
Distance: 5f/6f: 0-0 7f-8f: 0-2 **9f-13f: 1-5** 14f+: 0-0
Track : **LH: 1-5** RH: 0-2 Tight: 0-2 **Gall: 1-1**
Aids: Bl: 0-0 Vi: 0-0 Tstrap: 0-0 Ckp: 0-0
Best Rating: 73 8/08 Bevl 7f100y soft

Modest; stays 7f and acts on soft ground.

Chimbonda

87(93) (63)67

3-y-o ch c Dr Fong (USA)-Ambonnay (Ashkalani (IRE))
S Parr Willie McKay

Placings:544003054350-0204506050 (3020)
2009: 5[0]SD, 5[2]SD, 5[0]SD, 5[4]SD, 5[5]SD, 5[0]GF, 5[6]GF, 8[0]G, 5[5]GF, 5[0]G,

	Starts	1st	2nd	3rd	Win & Pl
Career Total (Turf)	10	0	0	1	1521
Career Total (AW)	12	0	1	1	1147

Going (Turf): Sf: 0-3 GS: 0-0 Gd: 0-2 GF: 0-5 Fm: 0-0
Distance: 5f/6f: 0-20 7f-8f: 0-1 9f-13f: 0-1 14f+: 0-0
Track : LH: 0-10 RH: 0-1 Tight: 0-8 Gall: 0-0
Aids: Bl: 0-3 Vi: 0-4 Tstrap: 0-1 Ckp: 0-1
Best Rating: 67 8/08 Thsk 5f soft

Fair; best around 5-6f; acts on good to firm; has worn blinkers and cheekpieces.

Chin Wag (IRE)

97 (76)69

5-y-o b g Iron Mask (USA)-Sweet Chat (IRE) (Common Grounds)
J S Goldie Miss L Mcfadzean & E Nisbet

Placings:13105/0064510/50031024525000-305060 (5513)
2009: 8[3]G, 9[0]G, 6[5]G, 6[0]GS, 6[6]GF, 8[0]GF,

	Starts	1st	2nd	3rd	Win & Pl
Career Total (Turf)	30	3	2	3	20588
Career Total (AW)	2	1	0	0	2257

64 6/08 Ayr 1m (0-55)H G-F £3070
72 10/07 Kemp 7f STD £2047
86 7/06 NmkJ 6f G-S £7124
81 6/06 Leic 5f218y G-F £3886
Total win prize-money £16130

Going (Turf): Sf: 0-3 GS: 1-9 Gd: 0-10 **GF: 2-8** Fm: 0-0
Distance: 5f/6f: 2-8 7f-8f: 2-14 9f-13f: 0-10 14f+: 0-0
Track : LH: 1-14 RH: 1-8 Tight: 0-11 Gall: 0-0
Aids: Bl: 0-1 Vi: 0-2 Tstrap: 2-13 Ckp: 2-13
Best Rating: 86 7/06 NmkJ 6f gd-sft

Modest; effective at 7f; acts on fast and easy ground and Polytrack.

China Bay

70(79) (43)7

2-y-o b f Reset (AUS)-Kathryn Janeway (IRE) (In The Wings)
P M Phelan (Tom Dascombe 15/6) The Constructive Partnership

Placings:6506 (7106)
2009: 5[6]SD, 5[5]SD, 6[0]GF, 8[6]SD,

	Starts	1st	2nd	3rd	Win & Pl
Career Total (Turf)	1	0	0	0	
Career Total (AW)	3	0	0	0	0

Going (Turf): Sf: 0-0 GS: 0-0 Gd: 0-0 GF: 0-1 Fm: 0-0
Distance: 5f/6f: 0-3 7f-8f: 0-1 9f-13f: 0-0 14f+: 0-0
Track : LH: 0-1 RH: 0-1 Tight: 0-1 Gall: 0-1
Aids: Bl: 0-0 Vi: 0-0 Tstrap: 0-0 Ckp: 0-0
Best Rating: 43 6/09 Sthl 5f stand

China Lily (USA)

89(80) (45)53

2-y-o b/br f Street Cry (IRE)-Lil Lisa Can (USA) (Lil's Lad (USA))
Saeed Bin Suroor Godolphin

Placings:60 (6436)
2009: 7[6]GF, 7[0]SD,

	Starts	1st	2nd	3rd	Win & Pl
Career Total (Turf)	1	0	0	0	0
Career Total (AW)	1	0	0	0	

Going (Turf): Sf: 0-0 GS: 0-0 Gd: 0-0 GF: 0-1 Fm: 0-0
Distance: 5f/6f: 0-0 7f-8f: 0-2 9f-13f: 0-0 14f+: 0-0
Track : LH: 0-1 RH: 0-1 Tight: 0-1 Gall: 0-0
Aids: Bl: 0-0 Vi: 0-0 Tstrap: 0-0 Ckp: 0-0
Best Rating: 53 9/09 Bevl 7f100y gd-fm

Chincoteague (IRE)

100 66

3-y-o b f Daylami (IRE)-Blue Water (USA) (Bering)
B J Meehan Mrs R Philipps

Placings:32 (6332)
2009: 11[3]G, 10[2]F,

	Starts	1st	2nd	3rd	Win & Pl
Career Total (Turf)	2	0	1	1	1561

Going (Turf): Sf: 0-0 GS: 0-0 Gd: 0-1 GF: 0-0 Fm: 0-1
Distance: 5f/6f: 0-0 7f-8f: 0-0 9f-13f: 0-2 14f+: 0-0
Track : LH: 0-2 RH: 0-0 Tight: 0-2 Gall: 0-0
Aids: Bl: 0-0 Vi: 0-0 Tstrap: 0-0 Ckp: 0-0
Best Rating: 66 9/09 Bath 1m2f46y firm

Modest; stays 1m3f; acts on fast ground.

Chinese Democracy (USA)

83(88) (45)49

2-y-o b f Proud Citizen (USA)-Double's Lass (USA) (Mr. Leader (USA))
P F I Cole Mr & Mrs C Wright & P F I Cole

Placings:6045 (6938)
2009: 5[6]GF, 6[0]GF, 5[4]F, 5[5]SD,

	Starts	1st	2nd	3rd	Win & Pl
Career Total (Turf)	3	0	0	0	385
Career Total (AW)	1	0	0	0	0

Going (Turf): Sf: 0-0 GS: 0-0 Gd: 0-0 GF: 0-2 Fm: 0-1
Distance: 5f/6f: 0-4 7f-8f: 0-0 9f-13f: 0-0 14f+: 0-0
Track : LH: 0-2 RH: 0-1 Tight: 0-0 Gall: 0-1
Aids: Bl: 0-0 Vi: 0-0 Tstrap: 0-0 Ckp: 0-0
Best Rating: 49 6/09 Bath 5f11y firm

Chinese Profit

88(84) (40)56

4-y-o b g Acclamation-Tancholo (So Factual (USA))
G C Bravery J P Carrington

Placings:00/00-200000 (7723)
2009: 7[2]GF, 8[0]GF, 8[0]SD, 10[0]SD, 7[0]GF, 8[0]SD,

	Starts	1st	2nd	3rd	Win & Pl
Career Total (Turf)	7	0	1	0	771
Career Total (AW)	3	0	0	0	

Going (Turf): Sf: 0-0 GS: 0-2 Gd: 0-2 GF: 0-3 Fm: 0-0
Distance: 5f/6f: 0-1 7f-8f: 0-7 9f-13f: 0-2 14f+: 0-0
Track : LH: 0-2 RH: 0-1 Tight: 0-1 Gall: 0-0
Aids: Bl: 0-0 Vi: 0-0 Tstrap: 0-1 Ckp: 0-1
Best Rating: 58 11/07 NmkR 7f good

Chink Of Light

82 52

2-y-o ch c Dr Fong (USA)-Isle Of Flame (Shirley Heights)
A M Balding David Brownlow

Placings:0 (7244)
2009: 8[0]S,

	Starts	1st	2nd	3rd	Win & Pl
Career Total (Turf)	1	0	0	0	

Going (Turf): **Sf: 0-1 GS: 0-0 Gd: 0-0 GF: 0-0 Fm: 0-0**
Distance: 5f/6f: 0-0 7f-8f: 0-0 9f-13f: 0-1 14f+: 0-0
Track : LH: 0-1 RH: 0-0 Tight: 0-0 Gall: 0-0
Aids: Bl: 0-0 Vi: 0-0 Tstrap: 0-0 Ckp: 0-0
Best Rating: **52** 11/09 Nott 1m75y soft

Chinoise (IRE)

88(57) **48**
2-y-o b f Chineur (FR)-Grey Pursuit (IRE) (Pursuit Of Love)
P M Phelan Mrs Norah M Kennedy

Placings:50 (3979)
2009: 6^5GF, 7^0SD,

	Starts	1st	2nd	3rd	Win & Pl
Career Total (Turf)	1	0	0	0	0
Career Total (AW)	1	0	0	0	

Going (Turf): **Sf: 0-0 GS: 0-0 Gd: 0-0 GF: 0-1 Fm: 0-0**
Distance: 5f/6f: 0-1 7f-8f: 0-1 9f-13f: 0-0 14f+: 0-0
Track : LH: 0-0 RH: 0-1 Tight: 0-0 Gall: 0-1
Aids: Bl: 0-0 Vi: 0-0 Tstrap: 0-0 Ckp: 0-0
Best Rating: **48** 6/09 Wind 6f gd-fm

Chintz (IRE)

102 **107**
3-y-o b f Danehill Dancer (IRE)-Gold Dodger (USA) (Slew O'Gold (USA))
David Wachman Mrs John Magnier

Placings:1221-0506400 (6884a)
2009: 7^0GF, 8^5HY, 8^0GF, 9^6S, 9^4HY, 8^0S, 8^0GY,

	Starts	1st	2nd	3rd	Win & Pl
Career Total (Turf)	11	2	2	0	75860
107 9/08 Curr 7f			YLD	£38294	
90 6/08 Leop 7f			G-F	£9573	

Total win prize-money £47868

Going (Turf): Sf: 0-4 GS: 0-0 Gd: 0-1 **GF: 1-3** Fm: 0-0
Distance: 5f/6f: 0-1 **7f-8f: 2-8** 9f-13f: 0-2 14f+: 0-0
Track : **LH: 1-4** RH: 0-5 Tight: 0-0 Gall: 0-3
Aids: Bl: 0-0 Vi: 0-0 Tstrap: 0-3 Ckp: 0-3
Best Rating: **107** 9/08 Curr 7f yield

Smart; winner in Group 3 company; effective over 7f; acts on fast and easy ground.

Chip N Pin

85 **46**
5-y-o b m Erhaab (USA)-Vallauris (Faustus (USA))
T D Easterby Mrs M H Easterby

Placings:5/0420400323/60-0 (3499)
2009: 11^0GF,

	Starts	1st	2nd	3rd	Win & Pl
Career Total (Turf)	14	0	2	2	2820

Going (Turf): **Sf: 0-1 GS: 0-2 Gd: 0-3 GF: 0-7 Fm: 0-1**
Distance: 5f/6f: 0-0 7f-8f: 0-4 9f-13f: 0-9 14f+: 0-1
Track : LH: 0-7 RH: 0-7 Tight: 0-10 Gall: 0-1
Aids: Bl: 0-1 Vi: 0-0 Tstrap: 0-0 Ckp: 0-0
Best Rating: **57** 5/07 Bevl 1m1f207y gd-fm

Poor maiden; seems best at 10 furlongs; acts on fast ground.

Chipolini (IRE)

87(70) **59**
3-y-o b g Bertolini (USA)-Chimere (FR) (Soviet Lad (USA))
D Carroll G P Clarke

Placings:00306-00050 (3562)
2009: 5^0F, 9^0GF, 7^0SD, 6^5G, 5^0GF,

	Starts	1st	2nd	3rd	Win & Pl
Career Total (Turf)	9	0	0	1	289
Career Total (AW)	1	0	0	0	

Going (Turf): **Sf: 0-1 GS: 0-0 Gd: 0-3 GF: 0-4 Fm: 0-1**
Distance: 5f/6f: 0-8 7f-8f: 0-2 9f-13f: 0-0 14f+: 0-0
Track : LH: 0-2 RH: 0-3 Tight: 0-1 Gall: 0-2
Aids: Bl: 0-1 Vi: 0-1 Tstrap: 0-0 Ckp: 0-0
Best Rating: **59** 6/08 Bevl 5f gd-fm

Chips O'Toole (IRE)

102(94) (83)**88**
2-y-o b c Fasliyev (USA)-Miss Megs (IRE) (Croco Rouge (IRE))
B J Meehan Abbott Racing Limited

Placings:32301264 (7150)
2009: 5^3G, 6^2G, 5^3G, 5^0G, 6^1GF, 5^2G, 6^6SD, 6^4G,

	Starts	1st	2nd	3rd	Win & Pl
Career Total (Turf)	7	1	2	2	7861
Career Total (AW)	1	0	0	0	0
82 10/09 Gdwd 6f	(0-80)H			G-F	£3885

Total win prize-money £3886

Going (Turf): Sf: 0-0 GS: 0-0 Gd: 0-6 **GF: 1-1** Fm: 0-0
Distance: **5f/6f: 1-7** 7f-8f: 0-1 9f-13f: 0-0 14f+: 0-0
Track : LH: 0-2 RH: 0-1 Tight: 0-0 Gall: 0-1
Aids: Bl: 0-0 Vi: 0-0 Tstrap: 0-0 Ckp: 0-0
Best Rating: **88** 10/09 Catt 5f good

Fair; suited by 5-6f and good ground.

Chjimes (IRE)

100(117) (92)**79**
5-y-o b g Fath (USA)-Radiance (IRE) (Thatching)
C R Dore Sean J Murphy

Placings:123005040/464222223/533660431431006005l-1311460603636065 (7872)
2009: 5^1SD, 6^3SD, 5^1SD, 5^1SD, 5^4SD, 5^6SD, 5^0S, 6^6G, 5^0G, 5^3SD, 5^6SD, 5^3SD, 5^6SS, 5^0SD, 5^6SD, 5^5SD,

	Starts	1st	2nd	3rd	Win & Pl
Career Total (Turf)	21	1	6	2	22534
Career Total (AW)	33	6	0	7	31577
92 3/09 Ling 5f	(0-85)H			STD	£4857
88 2/09 Ling 5f	(0-85)H			STD	£4857
83 1/09 Ling 5f	(0-85)H			STD	£4857
80 11/08 Ling 6f	(0-70)H			STD	£2729
81 7/08 Ling 6f	(0-70)H			STD	£2590
78 6/08 Ling 7f	(0-80)H			STD	£5180
70 4/06 Nott 5f13y				SFT	£3886

Total win prize-money £28958

Going (Turf): **Sf: 1-8** GS: 0-1 Gd: 0-7 GF: 0-4 Fm: 0-0
Distance: **5f/6f: 6-37** 7f-8f: 1-16 9f-13f: 0-1 14f+: 0-0
Track : **LH: 6-31** RH: 0-6 **Tight: 6-25** Gall: 0-1
Aids: Bl: 0-0 Vi: 0-1 Tstrap: 0-0 Ckp: 0-0
Best Rating: **94** 5/06 Curr 5f gd-yld

Useful; placed in Listed company at two; stays 7f; acts on most ground and on Polytrack; can look quirky.

Choc'A'Moca (IRE)

73 **35**
2-y-o b g Camacho-Dear Catch (IRE) (Bluebird (USA))
I W McInnes John Milburn - Andrew Stephenson

Placings:000 (7079)
2009: 5^0GF, 7^0S, 5^0S,

	Starts	1st	2nd	3rd	Win & Pl
Career Total (Turf)	3	0	0	0	

Going (Turf): **Sf: 0-2 GS: 0-0 Gd: 0-0 GF: 0-1 Fm: 0-0**
Distance: 5f/6f: 0-2 7f-8f: 0-1 9f-13f: 0-0 14f+: 0-0
Track : LH: 0-2 RH: 0-0 Tight: 0-2 Gall: 0-0
Aids: Bl: 0-1 Vi: 0-0 Tstrap: 0-0 Ckp: 0-0
Best Rating: **35** 4/09 Bevl 5f gd-fm

Chock A Block (IRE)

110 **110**
3-y-o gr c Dalakhani (IRE)-Choc Ice (IRE) (Kahyasi)
Saeed Bin Suroor Godolphin

Placings:1-5310 (7031)
2009: 11^5G, 10^3G, 12^1GF, 12^0S,

	Starts	1st	2nd	3rd	Win & Pl
Career Total (Turf)	5	2	0	1	38617
110 10/09 NmkR 1m4f			G-F	£22708	
91 10/08 Lonc 1m1f			G-S	£12500	

Total win prize-money £35208

Going (Turf): Sf: 0-1 **GS: 1-1** Gd: 0-2 **GF: 1-1** Fm: 0-0
Distance: 5f/6f: 0-0 7f-8f: 0-0 **9f-13f: 2-5** 14f+: 0-0
Track : LH: 0-2 **RH: 2-3** Tight: 0-1 **Gall: 1-3**
Aids: Bl: 0-0 Vi: 0-0 Tstrap: 0-0 Ckp: 0-0
Best Rating: **110** 10/09 NmkR 1m4f gd-fm

Smart; ex-French; stays 1m4f and acts on most ground.

Chocolate Caramel (USA)

(104) (74)**89**
7-y-o b g Storm Creek (USA)-Sandhill (BRZ) (Baynoun)
R A Fahey Jonathan Gill

Placings:521/5142526/510/646324445/1010612-40 (7867)
2009: 12^4SD, 14^0SS,

	Starts	1st	2nd	3rd	Win & Pl
Career Total (Turf)	20	3	4	0	38728
Career Total (AW)	11	3	1	1	20093
89 7/08 Bevl 2m35y	(0-85)H			GD	£12952
78 5/08 York 1m4f				GD	£7123
91 4/08 GrLe 1m6f	(0-85)H			STD	£4533
92 6/06 Ling 1m4f	(0-85)H			STD	£5505
90 5/05 Leic 1m1f218y	(0-85)H			SFT	£7147
81 11/04 Ling 1m2f				STD	£6922

Total win prize-money £44184

Going (Turf): Sf: 1-4 GS: 0-5 **Gd: 2-5** GF: 0-6 Fm: 0-0
Distance: 5f/6f: 0-0 7f-8f: 0-1 **9f-13f: 4-20** 14f+: 2-10
Track : **LH: 4-19** RH: 2-12 **Tight: 3-15** Gall: 2-11
Aids: Bl: 0-1 Vi: 0-0 Tstrap: 0-0 Ckp: 0-0
Best Rating: **92** 6/06 Ling 1m4f stand

Fair; stays 2m; acts on good and soft ground; also goes on Polytrack; has worn blinkers.

Chocolate Cookie (IRE)

96(100) (66)**72**
2-y-o b f Desert Style (IRE)-Back At De Front (IRE) (Cape Cross (IRE))
J R Boyle (R Hannon 3/10) Mrs Pippa Boyle

Placings:303443221 (7435)
2009: 6^{3}G, 5^{0}GS, 5^{3}G, 7^{4}GF, 5^{4}G, 7^{3}SD, 5^{2}SF, 6^{2}SD, 7^{1}SD,

	Starts	1st	2nd	3rd	Win & Pl
Career Total (Turf)	5	0	0	2	4788
Career Total (AW)	4	1	2	1	3591

66 11/09 Ling 7f STD £1978
Total win prize-money £1979

Going (Turf): Sf: 0-0 GS: 0-1 Gd: 0-3 GF: 0-1 Fm: 0-0
Distance: 5f/6f: 0-6 7f-8f: 1-3 9f-13f: 0-0 14f+: 0-0
Track : LH: 1-3 RH: 0-2 Tight: 1-2 Gall: 0-2
Aids: Bl: 0-0 Vi: 0-0 Tstrap: 0-0 Ckp: 0-0
Best Rating: 72 7/09 Newb 5f34y gd-sft

Modest; stays 7f; acts on Polytrack.

Chocolicious (IRE)

101(92) (65)71
3-y-o b/br f Captain Rio-Queenfisher (Scottish Reel)
B Smart Mrs Trisha Laughton

Placings:6054-413131 (2355)
2009: 7^{4}SD, 5^{1}GF, 7^{3}SD, 6^{1}GF, 6^{3}GS, 5^{1}GF,

	Starts	1st	2nd	3rd	Win & Pl
Career Total (Turf)	7	3	0	1	7084
Career Total (AW)	3	0	0	1	302

71 5/09 Leic 5f218y G-F £2590
68 4/09 Rdcr 6f G-F £2047
63 4/09 Leic 5f218y G-F £1942
Total win prize-money £6580

Going (Turf): Sf: 0-0 GS: 0-3 Gd: 0-0 GF: 3-4 Fm: 0-0
Distance: 5f/6f: 3-7 7f-8f: 0-3 9f-13f: 0-0 14f+: 0-0
Track : LH: 0-4 RH: 0-0 Tight: 0-1 Gall: 0-0
Aids: Bl: 0-0 Vi: 3-5 Tstrap: 0-0 Ckp: 0-0
Best Rating: 71 5/09 Leic 5f218y gd-fm

Modest; effective over 6f; acts on fast and easy ground.

Choctaw Nation

93 66
5-y-o b g Sadler's Wells (USA)-Space Quest (Rainbow Quest (USA))
J J Lambe Mrs Rita Lee

Placings:0453 (4600)
2009: 14^{0}G, 12^{4}G, 12^{5}GF, 12^{3}G,

	Starts	1st	2nd	3rd	Win & Pl
Career Total (Turf)	4	0	0	1	851

Going (Turf): Sf: 0-0 GS: 0-0 Gd: 0-3 GF: 0-1 Fm: 0-0
Distance: 5f/6f: 0-0 7f-8f: 0-0 9f-13f: 0-3 14f+: 0-1
Track : LH: 0-3 RH: 0-1 Tight: 0-1 Gall: 0-0
Aids: Bl: 0-0 Vi: 0-0 Tstrap: 0-0 Ckp: 0-0
Best Rating: 66 8/09 Ripn 1m4f10y good

Modest; stays 1m4f; acts on a sound surface.

Choice

94 67
2-y-o b f Azamour (IRE)-Poise (IRE) (Rainbow Quest (USA))
Sir Michael Stoute Cheveley Park Stud

Placings:6 (6921)
2009: 8^{6}GF,

	Starts	1st	2nd	3rd	Win & Pl
Career Total (Turf)	1	0	0	0	0

Going (Turf): Sf: 0-0 GS: 0-0 Gd: 0-0 GF: 0-1 Fm: 0-0
Distance: 5f/6f: 0-0 7f-8f: 0-0 9f-13f: 0-1 14f+: 0-0
Track : LH: 0-0 RH: 0-0 Tight: 0-0 Gall: 0-0
Aids: Bl: 0-0 Vi: 0-0 Tstrap: 0-0 Ckp: 0-0
Best Rating: 67 10/09 Yarm 1m3y gd-fm

Choir Solo

82 38
2-y-o b f Medicean-Choirgirl (Unfuwain (USA))
J H M Gosden Cheveley Park Stud

Placings:0 (6921)
2009: 8^{0}GF,

	Starts	1st	2nd	3rd	Win & Pl
Career Total (Turf)	1	0	0	0	

Going (Turf): Sf: 0-0 GS: 0-0 Gd: 0-0 GF: 0-1 Fm: 0-0
Distance: 5f/6f: 0-0 7f-8f: 0-0 9f-13f: 0-1 14f+: 0-0
Track : LH: 0-0 RH: 0-0 Tight: 0-0 Gall: 0-0
Aids: Bl: 0-1 Vi: 0-0 Tstrap: 0-0 Ckp: 0-0
Best Rating: 38 10/09 Yarm 1m3y gd-fm

Choiseau (IRE)

104(104) (80)91
4-y-o b g Choisir (AUS)-Little Linnet (Be My Guest (USA))
Pat Eddery Pat Eddery Racing (Danehill Dancer)

Placings:02/21-42 (4501)
2009: 6^{4}SD, 7^{2}G,

	Starts	1st	2nd	3rd	Win & Pl
Career Total (Turf)	5	1	3	0	5866
Career Total (AW)	1	0	0	0	385

84 6/08 Yarm 6f3y G-F £2590
Total win prize-money £2590

Going (Turf): Sf: 0-0 GS: 0-0 Gd: 0-3 GF: 1-2 Fm: 0-0
Distance: 5f/6f: 0 2 7f-8f: 1-4 9f-13f: 0-0 14f+: 0-0
Track : LH: 0-1 RH: 0-0 Tight: 0-0 Gall: 0-0
Aids: Bl: 0-0 Vi: 0-0 Tstrap: 0-0 Ckp: 0-0
Best Rating: 91 7/09 NmkJ 7f good

Useful; stays 6f, should get further; acts on a sound surface; handles Fibresand.

Choisharp (IRE)

100(92) (62)74
3-y-o b c Choisir (AUS)-Ballea Queen (IRE) (College Chapel)
M Botti Giuliano Manfredini

Placings:44-6423231 (5480)
2009: 6^{6}SD, 5^{4}GF, 5^{2}GF, 6^{3}G, 5^{2}F, 6^{3}G, 5^{1}GF,

	Starts	1st	2nd	3rd	Win & Pl
Career Total (Turf)	6	1	2	2	5832
Career Total (AW)	3	0	0	0	265

74 8/09 Yarm 5f43y (0-70)H G-F £3154
Total win prize-money £3154

Going (Turf): Sf: 0-0 GS: 0-0 Gd: 0-2 GF: 1-3 Fm: 0-1
Distance: 5f/6f: 1-7 7f-8f: 0-2 9f-13f: 0-0 14f+: 0-0
Track : LH: 0-3 RH: 0-1 Tight: 0-1 Gall: 0-0
Aids: Bl: 1-2 Vi: 0-0 Tstrap: 0-0 Ckp: 0-0
Best Rating: 74 8/09 Yarm 5f43y gd-fm

Modest; seems suited by 5f; acts on fast ground; has tried blinkers.

Chookie Avon

84(91) (61)62
2-y-o ch g Avonbridge-Lady Of Windsor (IRE) (Woods Of Windsor (USA))
I Semple Raeburn Brick Limited

Placings:0663 (7493)
2009: 6^{0}GS, 6^{6}G, 7^{6}SD, 8^{3}SD,

	Starts	1st	2nd	3rd	Win & Pl
Career Total (Turf)	2	0	0	0	0
Career Total (AW)	2	0	0	1	403

Going (Turf): Sf: 0-0 GS: 0-1 Gd: 0-1 GF: 0-0 Fm: 0-0
Distance: 5f/6f: 0-1 7f-8f: 0-2 9f-13f: 0-1 14f+: 0-0
Track : LH: 0-2 RH: 0-0 Tight: 0-2 Gall: 0-0
Aids: Bl: 0-0 Vi: 0-0 Tstrap: 0-0 Ckp: 0-0
Best Rating: 62 9/09 Haml 6f5y good

Modest; stays 7f; acts on Polytrack.

Chookie Hamilton

109(109) (85)79
5-y-o ch g Compton Place-Lady Of Windsor (IRE) (Woods Of Windsor (USA))
I Semple Raeburn Brick Limited

Placings:043043112/1100606054/15242136-240111250063115 (7573)
2009: 12^{2}SS, 13^{4}SD, 12^{0}GF, 13^{1}G, 11^{1}GF, 13^{1}G, 13^{2}G, 13^{5}G, 10^{0}S, 13^{0}SD, 13^{6}G, 13^{3}SD, 12^{1}SD, 12^{1}SD, 13^{5}SD,

	Starts	1st	2nd	3rd	Win & Pl
Career Total (Turf)	27	5	3	3	28960
Career Total (AW)	15	6	2	1	29687

85 11/09 Wolv 1m4f50y (0-85)H STD £5046
85 11/09 Wolv 1m4f50y (0-70)H STD £3885
77 6/09 Ayr 1m5f13y (0-75)H GD £3412
71 5/09 Carl 1m3f107y (0-80)H G-F £5180
65 5/09 Haml 1m5f9y (0-80)H GD £6476
67 9/08 Muss 1m4f (0-65)H SFT £2590
64 6/08 Muss 1m4f (0-70)H G-F £3885
84 1/07 Wolv 1m141y (0-85)H STD £4857
76 1/07 Wolv 1m1f103y (0-85)H STD £5505
66 12/06 Sthl 1m (0-85) STD £4857
66 11/06 Wolv 1m141y STD £2730
Total win prize-money £48428

Going (Turf): Sf: 1-6 GS: 0-4 Gd: 2-10 GF: 2-6 Fm: 0-1
Distance: 5f/6f: 0-0 7f-8f: 1-5 9f-13f: 8-28 14f+: 2-9
Track : LH: 7-27 RH: 4-15 Tight: 8-28 Gall: 0-1
Aids: Bl: 0-1 Vi: 0-1 Tstrap: 0-2 Ckp: 0-2
Best Rating: 85 11/09 Wolv 1m4f50y stand

Fair; effective at around 1m4f-1m6f; acts on fast and soft ground; goes on sand.

Chookie Heiton (IRE)

95(96) (65)68
11-y-o br g Fumo Di Londra (IRE)-Royal Wolff (Prince Tenderfoot (USA))
I Semple Raeburn Brick Limited

Placings:2/6314162/021310/00010/450010/002031000/4060/6000/500400-50600 (2964)
2009: 6^{5}SD, 5^{0}SD, 5^{6}G, 6^{0}GF, 5^{0}GF,

	Starts	1st	2nd	3rd	Win & Pl
Career Total (Turf)	48	7	4	3	107179
Career Total (AW)	5	0	0	0	0

112 8/05 Bevl 5f GD £17400
109 8/04 Bevl 5f A G-S £17400

105	7/02	Newb	6f8y	B(0-105)H	G-F	£11205
102	5/02	York	6f	B(0-105)H	G-F	£15877
84	8/01	Newc	6f	D(0-80)	GD	£4104
77	5/01	Rdcr	6f	E	FRM	£2891

Total win prize-money £68879

Going (Turf): Sf: 0-2 GS: 1-8 **Gd: 3-11** GF: 2-25 Fm: 1-2
Distance: **5f/6f: 6-41** 7f-8f: 1-12 9f-13f: 0-0 14f+: 0-0
Track : LH: 0-6 RH: 0-1 Tight: 0-4 Gall: 0-2
Aids: Bl: 0-0 Vi: 0-0 Tstrap: 0-1 Ckp: 0-1
Best Rating: **113** 8/03 Donc 6f good

Modest; suited by 5f-6f; acts on a sound surface; regressing; has worn cheekpieces.

Choosy Floosy

88(80) (29)47
3-y-o b f Lend A Hand-In The Stocks (Reprimand)
Pat Eddery Paul Dean

Placings:50000 (7666)
2009: 8^{5}G, 8^{0}SD, 8^{0}GF, 11^{0}G, 10^{0}SD,

	Starts	1st	2nd	3rd	Win & Pl
Career Total (Turf)	3	0	0	0	0
Career Total (AW)	2	0	0	0	

Going (Turf): **Sf: 0-0 GS: 0-0 Gd: 0-2 GF: 0-1 Fm: 0-0**
Distance: 5f/6f: 0-0 7f-8f: 0-0 9f-13f: 0-5 14f+: 0-0
Track : LH: 0-4 RH: 0-1 Tight: 0-2 Gall: 0-0
Aids: Bl: 0-0 Vi: 0-0 Tstrap: 0-0 Ckp: 0-0
Best Rating: **47** 9/09 Nott 1m75y gd-fm

Choral Festival

96(98) (75)74
3-y-o b f Pivotal-Choirgirl (Unfuwain (USA))
J J Bridger (Sir Mark Prescott 6/8) Mrs Liz Gardner

Placings:022-100 (7831)
2009: 12^{1}SD, 11^{0}GS, 12^{0}SD,

	Starts	1st	2nd	3rd	Win & Pl
Career Total (Turf)	2	0	1	0	1493
Career Total (AW)	4	1	1	0	5042

73	7/09	Sthl	1m4f	STD	£3885

Total win prize-money £3886

Going (Turf): **Sf: 0-1 GS: 0-1 Gd: 0-0 GF: 0-0 Fm: 0-0**
Distance: 5f/6f: 0-0 7f-8f: 0-3 **9f-13f: 1-3** 14f+: 0-0
Track : **LH: 1-3** RH: 0-3 Tight: 0-0 Gall: 0-0
Aids: Bl: 0-0 Vi: 0-0 Tstrap: 0-0 Ckp: 0-0
Best Rating: **75** 9/08 Sthl 1m stand

Fair; stays 1m4f; acts on soft ground and on Fibresand.

Choral Service

95 71
3-y-o ch g Pivotal-Choir Mistress (Chief Singer)
W J Haggas Cheveley Park Stud

Placings:0-043 (3321)
2009: 8^{0}G, 8^{4}G, 10^{3}GF,

	Starts	1st	2nd	3rd	Win & Pl
Career Total (Turf)	4	0	0	1	621

Going (Turf): **Sf: 0-1 GS: 0-0 Gd: 0-2 GF: 0-1 Fm: 0-0**
Distance: 5f/6f: 0-0 7f-8f: 0-0 9f-13f: 0-4 14f+: 0-0
Track : LH: 0-2 RH: 0-0 Tight: 0-0 Gall: 0-0
Aids: Bl: 0-0 Vi: 0-0 Tstrap: 0-0 Ckp: 0-0
Best Rating: **71** 6/09 Wwck 1m2f188y gd-fm

Choree (IRE)

83 34
3-y-o ch f Choisir (AUS)-Reem Al Fala (Green Desert (USA))
T D Easterby R Sidebottom

Placings:640 (3003)
2009: 6^{6}GF, 5^{4}G, 5^{0}GF,

	Starts	1st	2nd	3rd	Win & Pl
Career Total (Turf)	3	0	0	0	0

Going (Turf): **Sf: 0-0 GS: 0-0 Gd: 0-1 GF: 0-2 Fm: 0-0**
Distance: 5f/6f: 0-3 7f-8f: 0-0 9f-13f: 0-0 14f+: 0-0
Track : LH: 0-1 RH: 0-0 Tight: 0-1 Gall: 0-0
Aids: Bl: 0-0 Vi: 0-0 Tstrap: 0-0 Ckp: 0-0
Best Rating: **34** 5/09 Catt 5f212y good

Choreography

101(82) (48)86
6-y-o ch g Medicean-Stark Ballet (USA) (Nureyev (USA))
Jim Best Bill Wallace

Placings:6/35045114/00000326306422/0131010-00006065100 (6562)
2009: 6^{0}G, 5^{0}GF, 7^{0}GF, 7^{0}G, 6^{6}F, 5^{0}GS, 6^{6}F, 6^{5}GF, 6^{1}F, 7^{0}GF, 7^{0}GS,

	Starts	1st	2nd	3rd	Win & Pl
Career Total (Turf)	39	6	3	4	35890
Career Total (AW)	2	0	0	0	

77	9/09	Brig	6f209y	(0-75)H	FRM	£3280
86	8/08	Brig	7f214y	(0-80)H	G-F	£15480
81	6/08	Brig	6f209y	(0-75)H	FRM	£2849
79	6/08	Brig	6f209y	(0-65)H	FRM	£2525
79	8/06	Haml	6f5y	(0-65)H	GD	£2730
69	8/06	Muss	7f30y	(0-65)H	G-F	£3412

Total win prize-money £30278

Going (Turf): Sf: 0-2 GS: 0-6 Gd: 1-5 GF: 2-18 **Fm: 3-8**
Distance: 5f/6f: 0-14 **7f-8f: 6-26** 9f-13f: 0-1 14f+: 0-0
Track : **LH: 4-14** RH: 1-10 **Tight: 1-10** Gall: 0-1
Aids: Bl: 1-3 Vi: 0-2 Tstrap: 3-11 Ckp: 3-11
Best Rating: **86** 8/08 Brig 7f214y gd-fm

Fair; effective over 6f-7f and best on fast ground; has worn cheekpieces.

Chorus Boy

86(80) (47)40
2-y-o ch c Kyllachy-Dame Jude (Dilum (USA))
G G Margarson Stableside Racing

Placings:00656 (7501)
2009: 6^{0}GF, 6^{0}G, 7^{6}G, 8^{5}SD, 7^{6}SD,

	Starts	1st	2nd	3rd	Win & Pl
Career Total (Turf)	3	0	0	0	0
Career Total (AW)	2	0	0	0	0

Going (Turf): **Sf: 0-0 GS: 0-0 Gd: 0-2 GF: 0-1 Fm: 0-0**
Distance: 5f/6f: 0-2 7f-8f: 0-3 9f-13f: 0-0 14f+: 0-0
Track : LH: 0-2 RH: 0-0 Tight: 0-1 Gall: 0-1
Aids: Bl: 0-3 Vi: 0-0 Tstrap: 0-0 Ckp: 0-0
Best Rating: **47** 11/09 Ling 1m stand

Chosen Forever

85(102) (69)66
4-y-o b g Choisir (AUS)-Forever Bond (Danetime (IRE))
G R Oldroyd R C Bond

Placings:10260-0006311 (7857)
2009: 5^{0}GF, 8^{0}SD, 6^{0}GF, 7^{6}SF, 8^{3}SD, 9^{1}SD, 9^{1}SD,

	Starts	1st	2nd	3rd	Win & Pl
Career Total (Turf)	5	1	0	0	3753
Career Total (AW)	7	2	1	1	4761

	12/09	Wolv	1m1f103y	(0-60)H	STD	£1706
65	12/09	Wolv	1m1f103y	(0-55)H	STD	£2047
63	7/08	Donc	6f		GD	£3753

Total win prize-money £7506

Going (Turf): Sf: 0-0 GS: 0-0 **Gd: 1-3** GF: 0-2 Fm: 0-0
Distance: 5f/6f: 1-3 7f-8f: 0-6 **9f-13f: 2-3** 14f+: 0-0
Track : **LH: 2-7** RH: 0-1 **Tight: 2-6** Gall: 0-0
Aids: Bl: 0-0 Vi: 0-0 Tstrap: 0-1 Ckp: 0-1
Best Rating: **69** 10/08 Wolv 7f32y stand

Modest; stays 1m2f; acts on good ground and on Polytrack.

Chosen One (IRE)

102(103) (66)68
4-y-o ch g Choisir (AUS)-Copious (IRE) (Generous (IRE))
B Smart Ceffyl Racing

Placings:5110-000034203 (7738)
2009: 6^{0}GS, 6^{0}G, 6^{0}G, 5^{0}G, 5^{3}GS, 5^{4}S, 5^{2}S, 5^{0}SD, 6^{3}SD,

	Starts	1st	2nd	3rd	Win & Pl
Career Total (Turf)	11	2	1	1	7832
Career Total (AW)	2	0	0	1	337

68	9/08	Haml	6f5y	(0-70)H	SFT	£3885
66	8/08	Catt	5f212y		GD	£2590

Total win prize-money £6476

Going (Turf): **Sf: 1-3** GS: 0-3 **Gd: 1-5** GF: 0-0 Fm: 0-0
Distance: 5f/6f: 1-10 7f-8f: 1-3 9f-13f: 0-0 14f+: 0-0
Track : **LH: 1-3** RH: 0-1 **Tight: 1-3** Gall: 0-0
Aids: Bl: 0-0 Vi: 0-0 Tstrap: 0-0 Ckp: 0-0
Best Rating: **68** 9/08 Haml 6f5y soft

Modest; effective over 6f; acts on good and softer ground.

Chosen Son (IRE)

(101) (69)
3-y-o b/br g Kheleyf (USA)-Choice Pickings (IRE) (Among Men (USA))
P J O'Gorman N S Yong

Placings:6033-000403003 (7510)
2009: 5^{0}SD, 6^{0}SD, 5^{0}SD, 7^{4}SD, 7^{0}SD, 5^{3}SD, 5^{0}SD, 5^{0}SD, 5^{3}SD,

	Starts	1st	2nd	3rd	Win & Pl
Career Total (Turf)	0	0	0	0	
Career Total (AW)	13	0	0	4	1769

Going (Turf): **Sf: 0-0 GS: 0-0 Gd: 0-0 GF: 0-0 Fm: 0-0**
Distance: 5f/6f: 0-11 7f-8f: 0-2 9f-13f: 0-0 14f+: 0-0
Track : LH: 0-4 RH: 0-8 Tight: 0-2 Gall: 0-2
Aids: Bl: 0-0 Vi: 0-0 Tstrap: 0-0 Ckp: 0-0
Best Rating: **69** 11/08 Kemp 5f stand

Fair; suited by 5f and Polytrack; has worn a tongue tie.

Chris's Jem

96(93) (60)58
3-y-o b f Makbul-Royal Orchid (IRE) (Shalford (IRE))
J R Jenkins A C Murphy

Placings:02150650 (6377)
2009: 6^{0}SD, 6^{2}G, 5^{1}GF, 5^{5}GF, 5^{0}S, 5^{6}SD, 5^{5}F, 6^{0}SD,

	Starts	1st	2nd	3rd	Win & Pl
Career Total (Turf)	5	1	1	0	3536
Career Total (AW)	3	0	0	0	0

58	4/09	Folk	5f	G-F	£2729

Total win prize-money £2730

Going (Turf): Sf: 0-1 GS: 0-0 Gd: 0-1 **GF: 1-2** Fm: 0-1
Distance: **5f/6f: 1-8** 7f-8f: 0-0 9f-13f: 0-0 14f+: 0-0
Track : LH: 0-1 RH: 0-2 Tight: 0-1 Gall: 0-0
Aids: Bl: 0-0 Vi: 0-0 Tstrap: 0-0 Ckp: 0-0
Best Rating: **60** 8/09 Kemp 5f stand

Modest filly; stays 6f; effective on good and fast ground.

Christina Rossetti

88(81) (66)**64**
3-y-o b f Falbrav (IRE)-First Exhibit (Machiavellian (USA))
J H M Gosden Ms Rachel D S Hood

Placings:30 **(1302)**
2009: 8^{3}SD, 7^{0}GF,

	Starts	1st	2nd	3rd	Win & Pl
Career Total (Turf)	1	0	0	0	
Career Total (AW)	1	0	0	1	385

Going (Turf): **Sf: 0-0 GS: 0-0 Gd: 0-0 GF: 0-1 Fm: 0-0**
Distance: 5f/6f: 0-0 7f-8f: 0-2 9f-13f: 0-0 14f+: 0-0
Track : LH: 0-0 RH: 0-1 Tight: 0-0 Gall: 0-0
Aids: Bl: 0-0 Vi: 0-0 Tstrap: 0-0 Ckp: 0-0
Best Rating: **66** 3/09 Kemp 1m stand

Christmas Carnival

82(93) (79)**71**
2-y-o ch c Cadeaux Genereux-Ellebanna (Tina's Pet)
B J Meehan Jaber Abdullah

Placings:53 **(6672)**
2009: 7^{5}GF, 8^{3}SD,

	Starts	1st	2nd	3rd	Win & Pl
Career Total (Turf)	1	0	0	0	0
Career Total (AW)	1	0	0	1	403

Going (Turf): **Sf: 0-0 GS: 0-0 Gd: 0-0 GF: 0-1 Fm: 0-0**
Distance: 5f/6f: 0-0 7f-8f: 0-1 9f-13f: 0-1 14f+: 0-0
Track : LH: 0-1 RH: 0-0 Tight: 0-1 Gall: 0-0
Aids: Bl: 0-0 Vi: 0-0 Tstrap: 0-0 Ckp: 0-0
Best Rating: **79** 10/09 Wolv 1m141y stand

Christmas Coming

(89) (70)
2-y-o b c Cape Cross (IRE)-Aunty Rose (IRE) (Caerleon (USA))
D R C Elsworth Gordon Li

Placings:402 **(7773)**
2009: 7^{4}SD, 8^{0}SD, 7^{2}SD,

	Starts	1st	2nd	3rd	Win & Pl
Career Total (Turf)	0	0	0	0	
Career Total (AW)	3	0	1	0	1252

Going (Turf): **Sf: 0-0 GS: 0-0 Gd: 0-0 GF: 0-0 Fm: 0-0**
Distance: 5f/6f: 0-0 7f-8f: 0-3 9f-13f: 0-0 14f+: 0-0
Track : LH: 0-1 RH: 0-2 Tight: 0-1 Gall: 0-0
Aids: Bl: 0-0 Vi: 0-0 Tstrap: 0-0 Ckp: 0-0
Best Rating: **70** 9/09 Kemp 7f stand

Christmascamet wice

16(92) (60)
3-y-o b f Monsieur Bond (IRE)-My Poppet (Midyan (USA))
J A Osborne J A Osborne

Placings:3600 **(1982)**
2009: 6^{3}SD, 6^{6}SD, 5^{0}SD, 5^{0}F,

	Starts	1st	2nd	3rd	Win & Pl
Career Total (Turf)	1	0	0	0	
Career Total (AW)	3	0	0	1	385

Going (Turf): **Sf: 0-0 GS: 0-0 Gd: 0-0 GF: 0-0 Fm: 0-1**
Distance: 5f/6f: 0-4 7f-8f: 0-0 9f-13f: 0-0 14f+: 0-0
Track : LH: 0-4 RH: 0-0 Tight: 0-3 Gall: 0-1
Aids: Bl: 0-0 Vi: 0-0 Tstrap: 0-0 Ckp: 0-0
Best Rating: **60** 3/09 Ling 6f stand

Christopher Wren (USA)

94(86) (59)**73**
2-y-o ch c D'Wildcat (USA)-Ashley's Coy (USA) (Country Pine (USA))
J R Best Kingsgate Racing

Placings:3031 **(6736)**
2009: 7^{3}SD, 8^{0}SD, 7^{3}GF, 8^{1}GS,

	Starts	1st	2nd	3rd	Win & Pl
Career Total (Turf)	2	1	0	1	2870
Career Total (AW)	2	0	0	1	353

73 10/09 Wind 1m67y (0-75) G-S £2388
Total win prize-money £2388

Going (Turf): Sf: 0-0 **GS: 1-1** Gd: 0-0 GF: 0-1 Fm: 0-0
Distance: 5f/6f: 0-0 7f-8f: 0-3 **9f-13f: 1-1** 14f+: 0-0
Track : LH: 0-1 **RH: 1-3 Tight: 1-2** Gall: 0-0
Aids: Bl: 0-0 Vi: 0-0 Tstrap: 0-0 Ckp: 0-0
Best Rating: **73** 10/09 Wind 1m67y gd-sft

Modest; stays 7f and acts on Polytrack.

Christophers Quest

84(94) (69)**67**
4-y-o b g Forzando-Kaprisky (IRE) (Red Sunset)
Miss N A Lloyd-Beavis Miss V Dunn H Davies

Placings:230360-00 **(6908)**
2009: 8^{0}GF, 8^{0}G,

	Starts	1st	2nd	3rd	Win & Pl
Career Total (Turf)	6	0	0	1	578
Career Total (AW)	2	0	1	1	1040

Going (Turf): **Sf: 0-0 GS: 0-2 Gd: 0-2 GF: 0-2 Fm: 0-0**
Distance: 5f/6f: 0-0 7f-8f: 0-6 9f-13f: 0-2 14f+: 0-0
Track : LH: 0-3 RH: 0-1 Tight: 0-4 Gall: 0-0
Aids: Bl: 0-0 Vi: 0-0 Tstrap: 0-0 Ckp: 0-0
Best Rating: **69** 4/08 Ling 7f stand

Modest half-brother to two middle-distance winners on the Flat and a winner over hurdles; stays 7f.

Chushka

96 **60**
2-y-o ch f Pivotal-Ravine (Indian Ridge)
B Smart Crossfields Racing

Placings:44 **(5949)**
2009: 6^{4}GF, 6^{4}GF,

	Starts	1st	2nd	3rd	Win & Pl
Career Total (Turf)	2	0	0	0	265

Going (Turf): **Sf: 0-0 GS: 0-0 Gd: 0-0 GF: 0-2 Fm: 0-0**
Distance: 5f/6f: 0-2 7f-8f: 0-0 9f-13f: 0-0 14f+: 0-0
Track : LH: 0-0 RH: 0-0 Tight: 0-0 Gall: 0-0
Aids: Bl: 0-0 Vi: 0-0 Tstrap: 0-0 Ckp: 0-0
Best Rating: **60** 7/09 Rdcr 6f gd-fm

Has shown signs of ability over 6f.

Cian Rooney (IRE)

90 **74**
2-y-o b g Camacho-Exponent (USA) (Exbourne (USA))
Mrs A Duffield Findlay & Bloom

Placings:0410 **(4803)**
2009: 5^{0}GF, 5^{4}GF, 5^{1}G, 6^{0}GF,

	Starts	1st	2nd	3rd	Win & Pl
Career Total (Turf)	4	1	0	0	4774

74 7/09 Pont 5f GD £4533
Total win prize-money £4533

Going (Turf): Sf: 0-0 GS: 0-0 **Gd: 1-1** GF: 0-3 Fm: 0-0
Distance: **5f/6f: 1-4** 7f-8f: 0-0 9f-13f: 0-0 14f+: 0-0
Track : **LH: 1-1** RH: 0-1 Tight: 0-0 Gall: 0-1
Aids: Bl: 0-0 Vi: 0-0 Tstrap: 0-0 Ckp: 0-0
Best Rating: **74** 7/09 Pont 5f good

Fair; effective over 5f; acts on fast ground.

Ciara Eile (IRE)

97 (17)**54**
9-y-o b m Victory Note (USA)-Graceful Resign (Most Welcome)
D Carroll John Joseph Fitzpatrick

Placings:005/0400/0000/0660/03160/5504/0-40 **(2344)**
2009: 12^{4}GS, 14^{0}GF,

	Starts	1st	2nd	3rd	Win & Pl
Career Total (Turf)	26	1	0	1	5595
Career Total (AW)	1	0	0	0	

53 7/06 Naas 1m (40-60)H G-F £4288
Total win prize-money £4289

Going (Turf): Sf: 0-4 GS: 0-1 Gd: 0-4 **GF: 1-6** Fm: 0-5
Distance: 5f/6f: 0-3 **7f-8f: 1-9** 9f-13f: 0-14 14f+: 0-1
Track : **LH: 1-11** RH: 0-8 Tight: 0-1 Gall: 0-1
Aids: Bl: 0-2 Vi: 0-0 Tstrap: 0-0 Ckp: 0-0
Best Rating: **69** 10/02 Curr 6f yield

Cigalas

101 **80**
4-y-o ch g Selkirk (USA)-Langoustine (AUS) (Danehill (USA))
Mrs J C McGregor William Allan

Placings:04/510-00045000 **(6157)**
2009: 8^{0}GF, 7^{0}GF, 9^{0}G, 8^{4}G, 8^{5}G, 8^{0}G, 7^{0}GF, 9^{0}G,

	Starts	1st	2nd	3rd	Win & Pl
Career Total (Turf)	13	1	0	0	3994

80 8/08 Wwck 7f26y SFT £3238
Total win prize-money £3238

Going (Turf): **Sf: 1-1** GS: 0-0 Gd: 0-7 GF: 0-5 Fm: 0-0
Distance: 5f/6f: 0-1 **7f-8f: 1-10** 9f-13f: 0-2 14f+: 0-0
Track : **LH: 1-5** RH: 0-4 Tight: 0-4 Gall: 0-0

Aids: Bl: 0-0 Vi: 0-0 Tstrap: 0-0 Ckp: 0-0
Best Rating: 83 9/07 Donc 7f gd-fm

Fair; effective at 7f; acts on a any ground.

Cilium (IRE)

103 (80)89

3-y-o b f War Chant (USA)-Venturi (Danehill Dancer (IRE))
Andrew Oliver A Hanahoe

Placings:23015000 (6884a)
2009: 8^{2}GY, 8^{3}S, 7^{0}GY, 8^{1}GY, 9^{5}HY, 7^{0}GF, 10^{0}SD, 8^{0}GY,

	Starts	1st	2nd	3rd	Win & Pl
Career Total (Turf)	7	1	1	1	11592
Career Total (AW)	1	0	0	0	

79 8/09 Leop 1m G-Y £8385
Total win prize-money £8386

Going (Turf): Sf: 0-2 GS: 0-0 Gd: 0-0 GF: 0-1 Fm: 0-0
Distance: 5f/6f: 0-0 7f-8f: 1-6 9f-13f: 0-2 14f+: 0-0
Track : LH: 1-5 RH: 0-2 Tight: 0-0 Gall: 0-1
Aids: Bl: 0-0 Vi: 0-0 Tstrap: 0-0 Ckp: 0-0
Best Rating: 89 8/09 Curr 1m1f heavy

Cill Rialaig

112(102) (82)96

4-y-o gr f Environment Friend-Pang Valley Girl (Rock Hopper)
H Morrison Pangfield Partners

Placings:4331216160 (7291)
2009: 11^{4}GF, 12^{3}SD, 12^{3}GF, 9^{1}GF, 9^{2}GF, 10^{1}G, 10^{6}GF, 10^{1}GS, 10^{6}S, 10^{0}S,

	Starts	1st	2nd	3rd	Win & Pl
Career Total (Turf)	9	3	1	1	29816
Career Total (AW)	1	0	0	1	385

96 10/09 Asct 1m2f (0-105)H G-S £11215
91 8/09 Epsm 1m2f18y (0-90)H GD £7771
82 6/09 Sals 1m1f198y (0-85)H G-F £6799
Total win prize-money £25787

Going (Turf): Sf: 0-2 GS: 1-1 Gd: 1-1 GF: 1-5 Fm: 0-0
Distance: 5f/6f: 0-0 7f-8f: 0-0 9f-13f: 3-10 14f+: 0-0
Track : LH: 1-4 RH: 2-6 Tight: 2-4 Gall: 1-4
Aids: Bl: 0-0 Vi: 0-0 Tstrap: 0-0 Ckp: 0-0
Best Rating: 96 10/09 Asct 1m2f gd-sft

Very useful; bumper winner; effective over 1m2f-1m4f; acts on fast and easy ground.

Cils Blancs (IRE)

101(90) (49)63

3-y-o b f Barathea (IRE)-Immortelle (Arazi (USA))
B Smart Mrs Julie Martin

Placings:60135 (7349)
2009: 8^{6}GF, 8^{0}GS, 7^{1}GS, 7^{3}G, 7^{5}SD,

	Starts	1st	2nd	3rd	Win & Pl
Career Total (Turf)	4	1	0	1	5955
Career Total (AW)	1	0	0	0	0

63 8/09 Thsk 7f G-S £5569
Total win prize-money £5569

Going (Turf): Sf: 0-0 GS: 1-2 Gd: 0-1 GF: 0-1 Fm: 0-0
Distance: 5f/6f: 0-0 7f-8f: 1-3 9f-13f: 0-2 14f+: 0-0
Track : LH: 1-4 RH: 0-1 Tight: 1-2 Gall: 0-0
Aids: Bl: 0-0 Vi: 0-0 Tstrap: 0-0 Ckp: 0-0
Best Rating: 63 8/09 Thsk 7f gd-sft

Cima De Triomphe (IRE)

114 119

4-y-o gr c Galileo (IRE)-Sopran Londa (IRE) (Danehill (USA))
L M Cumani Teruya Yoshida

Placings:13/43110100-614400 (7196a)
2009: 10^{6}G, 10^{1}G, 10^{4}G, 10^{4}G, 12^{0}GS, 10^{0}G,

	Starts	1st	2nd	3rd	Win & Pl
Career Total (Turf)	16	5	0	2	473094

115 5/09 Sand 1m2f7y GD £36900
110 9/08 Siro 1m2f G-S £6250
108 5/08 Capa 1m3f G-F £334559
93 4/08 Siro 1m2f SFT £20588
10/07 Siro 1m110y GD £6757
Total win prize-money £405055

Going (Turf): Sf: 1-2 GS: 1-4 Gd: 2-9 GF: 1-1 Fm: 0-0
Distance: 5f/6f: 0-0 7f-8f: 0-0 9f-13f: 5-16 14f+: 0-0
Track : LH: 0-2 RH: 3-10 Tight: 0-0 Gall: 0-0
Aids: Bl: 0-2 Vi: 0-0 Tstrap: 0-0 Ckp: 0-0
Best Rating: 119 10/08 Lonc 1m4f gd-sft

Group-class; ex-Italian; winner of the 2008 Italian Derby and 2009 Brigadier Gerard Stakes on British debut; probably best over 1m2f; acts on good and softer ground; has worn a tongue tie.

Cindy Incidentally

85(97) (47)43

3-y-o ch f Shinko Forest (IRE)-Bayrami (Emarati (USA))
Miss Gay Kelleway Tim Urry

Placings:556-64000326P0 (6255)
2009: 5^{6}SD, 5^{4}SD, 5^{0}SD, 5^{0}G, 5^{0}GF, 5^{3}GF, 7^{2}GS, 5^{6}GF, 7^{P}S, 7^{0}SD,

	Starts	1st	2nd	3rd	Win & Pl
Career Total (Turf)	7	0	1	1	1058
Career Total (AW)	6	0	0	0	0

Going (Turf): Sf: 0-2 GS: 0-1 Gd: 0-1 GF: 0-3 Fm: 0-0
Distance: 5f/6f: 0-10 7f-8f: 0-3 9f-13f: 0-0 14f+: 0-0
Track : LH: 0-10 RH: 0-0 Tight: 0-9 Gall: 0-0
Aids: Bl: 0-5 Vi: 0-0 Tstrap: 0-1 Ckp: 0-1
Best Rating: 47 2/09 Wolv 5f20y stand

Cinematic (IRE)

64(103) (77)82

6-y-o b g Bahhare (USA)-Eastern Star (IRE) (Sri Pekan (USA))
J R Boyle Inside Track Racing Club

Placings:0310/0504/00301224560241/5-2005 (1604)
2009: 10^{2}SD, 10^{0}SD, 10^{0}GF, 10^{5}SD,

	Starts	1st	2nd	3rd	Win & Pl
Career Total (Turf)	11	1	1	1	6601
Career Total (AW)	16	2	3	1	10108

77 11/07 Wolv 1m1f103y (0-75)H STD £2710
74 3/07 Ling 1m2f (0-70)H STD £3071
73 9/05 Ayr 6f GD £3419
Total win prize-money £9201

Going (Turf): Sf: 0-1 GS: 0-2 Gd: 1-4 GF: 0-4 Fm: 0-0
Distance: 5f/6f: 1-5 7f-8f: 0-7 9f-13f: 2-15 14f+: 0-0
Track : LH: 2-14 RH: 0-7 Tight: 2-12 Gall: 0-1
Aids: Bl: 0-0 Vi: 0-0 Tstrap: 0-0 Ckp: 0-0
Best Rating: 82 5/07 Hayd 1m2f120y gd-fm

Modest handicapper; effective at 1m2f; acts on good ground and on Polytrack.

Cipher

101 84

3-y-o b g Reset (AUS)-Subtle Charm (Machiavellian (USA))
M Johnston Sheikh Hamdan Bin Mohammed Al Maktoum

Placings:013 (3394)
2009: 6^{0}GF, 8^{1}G, 8^{3}S,

	Starts	1st	2nd	3rd	Win & Pl
Career Total (Turf)	3	1	0	1	2794

84 6/09 Rdcr 1m GD £2047
Total win prize-money £2047

Going (Turf): Sf: 0-1 GS: 0-0 Gd: 1-1 GF: 0-1 Fm: 0-0
Distance: 5f/6f: 0-1 7f-8f: 1-2 9f-13f: 0-0 14f+: 0-0
Track : LH: 0-1 RH: 0-0 Tight: 0-0 Gall: 0-1
Aids: Bl: 0-0 Vi: 0-0 Tstrap: 0-0 Ckp: 0-0
Best Rating: 84 6/09 Rdcr 1m good

Useful; much better effort to win Redcar maiden on second start; stays 1m and should stay 1m2f; acts on good ground; sure to improve and win more races.

Circle Dance (IRE)

100(99) (71)74

4-y-o b/br g Namid-Rivana (Green Desert (USA))
Miss M E Rowland (D Shaw 14/8) S Mapletoft & M E Rowland

Placings:00/033040004-23365100500330400 (7678)
2009: 5^{2}SD, 5^{3}SD, 5^{3}SD, 5^{6}SD, 5^{5}SD, 5^{1}SF, 5^{0}GF, 5^{0}SD, 5^{5}GF, 5^{0}GF, 6^{0}SD, 6^{3}GS, 6^{3}G, 6^{0}GS, 6^{4}GF, 5^{0}G, 7^{0}SD,

	Starts	1st	2nd	3rd	Win & Pl
Career Total (Turf)	18	0	0	4	2471
Career Total (AW)	10	1	1	2	4556

71 3/09 Wolv 5f20y SF £2729
Total win prize-money £2730

Going (Turf): Sf: 0-4 GS: 0-2 Gd: 0-3 GF: 0-5 Fm: 0-1
Distance: 5f/6f: 1-24 7f-8f: 0-4 9f-13f: 0-0 14f+: 0-0
Track : LH: 1-10 RH: 0-2 Tight: 1-3 Gall: 0-1
Aids: Bl: 0-0 Vi: 1-17 Tstrap: 0-1 Ckp: 0-1
Best Rating: 74 6/08 Cork 6f gd-fm

Modest sprinter; ex-Irish; acts on Polytrack; has worn a visor.

Circuit Dancer (IRE)

95 (73)76

9-y-o b g Mujadil (USA)-Trysinger (IRE) (Try My Best (USA))
D Nicholls David Fish

Placings:003521/665020122316/340105040040/350000060400/0110230242601/0000041040/60005023240-05065 (3484)
2009: 5^{0}GF, 5^{5}GF, 5^{0}GF, 6^{6}G, 6^{5}GF,

	Starts	1st	2nd	3rd	Win & Pl
Career Total (Turf)	78	7	9	6	85352
Career Total (AW)	3	1	0	0	3239

80 9/07 Ches 5f16y (0-85)H G-F £5829
88 9/06 Ches 5f16y (0-85)H G-F £7772
73 5/06 Kemp 6f (0-65)H STD £3238
76 4/06 Catt 5f212y (0-65)H FRM £2730
99 6/04 York 6f3y B(0-100)H G-F £12423
94 8/03 Ches 6f18y C(0-95)H G-F £13942
88 7/03 Hayd 6f D(0-85)H G-F £5050
84 9/02 Muss 5f D G-F £4927

Total win prize-money £55915

Going (Turf): Sf: 0-7 GS: 0-8 Gd: 0-23 **GF: 6-37** Fm: 1-3
Distance: **5f/6f: 6-66** 7f-8f: 2-15 9f-13f: 0-0 14f+: 0-0
Track : **LH: 4-17** RH: 1-3 **Tight: 4-13** Gall: 0-2
Aids: Bl: 0-0 Vi: 0-0 Tstrap: 0-3 Ckp: 0-3
Best Rating: 99 6/04 York 6f3y gd-fm

Modest; effective over 5f-6f; suited by fast ground; has worn cheekpieces.

Circumvent

101(96) (95)106

2-y-o ch g Tobougg (IRE)-Seren Devious (Dr Devious (IRE))
P F I Cole The Fairy Story Partnership

Placings:12112 **(6889a)**
2009: 6[1]SD, 7[2]SD, 7[1]GF, 8[1]VS, 9[2]GS,

	Starts	1st	2nd	3rd	Win & Pl
Career Total (Turf)	3	2	1	0	59550
Career Total (AW)	2	1	1	0	6562
104 10/09 StCl	1m		VS		£38835
95 9/09 Leic	7f9y		G-F		£5180
78 8/09 Sthl	6f		STD		£4640

Total win prize-money £48656

Going (Turf): Sf: 0-0 GS: 0-1 Gd: 0-0 **GF: 1-1** Fm: 0-0
Distance: 5f/6f: 1-1 **7f-8f: 2-3** 9f-13f: 0-1 14f+: 0-0
Track : **LH: 2-2** RH: 0-2 Tight: 0-0 Gall: 0-0
Aids: Bl: 0-0 Vi: 0-0 Tstrap: 0-0 Ckp: 0-0
Best Rating: 106 10/09 Lonc 1m1f gd-sft

Very useful; suited by 6f-7f; acts on fast ground; goes on Fibresand and Polytrack.

Circus Clown (IRE)

87 60

4-y-o b g Vettori (IRE)-Comic (IRE) (Be My Chief (USA))
P Monteith David McKenzie

Placings:65405-6 **(6156)**
2009: 11[6]G,

	Starts	1st	2nd	3rd	Win & Pl
Career Total (Turf)	6	0	0	0	241

Going (Turf): **Sf: 0-2 GS: 0-1 Gd: 0-3 GF: 0-0 Fm: 0-0**
Distance: 5f/6f: 0-0 7f-8f: 0-0 9f-13f: 0-4 14f+: 0-2
Track : LH: 0-3 RH: 0-3 Tight: 0-3 Gall: 0-2
Aids: Bl: 0-0 Vi: 0-1 Tstrap: 0-0 Ckp: 0-0
Best Rating: 60 7/08 Haml 1m3f16y good

Circus Girl (IRE)

(82) (55)

2-y-o ch f Bertolini (USA)-Blew Her Top (USA) (Blushing John (USA))
R M Beckett J C Smith

Placings:5 (7325)
2009: 7[5]SD,

	Starts	1st	2nd	3rd	Win & Pl
Career Total (Turf)	0	0	0	0	
Career Total (AW)	1	0	0	0	0

Going (Turf): **Sf: 0-0 GS: 0-0 Gd: 0-0 GF: 0-0 Fm: 0-0**
Distance: 5f/6f: 0-0 7f-8f: 0-1 9f-13f: 0-0 14f+: 0-0
Track : LH: 0-0 RH: 0-1 Tight: 0-0 Gall: 0-0
Aids: Bl: 0-0 Vi: 0-0 Tstrap: 0-0 Ckp: 0-0
Best Rating: 55 11/09 Kemp 7f stand

Citizenship

103(90) (73)81

3-y-o b g Beat Hollow-Three More (USA) (Sanglamore (USA))
Ian Williams Dr Marwan Koukash

Placings:060-615514422620 **(7263a)**
2009: 7[6]SD, 9[1]SD, 9[5]GF, 12[5]GF, 11[1]G, 12[4]G, 14[4]S, 11[2]G, 11[2]GS, 10[6]G, 12[2]HY, 12[0]HY,

	Starts	1st	2nd	3rd	Win & Pl
Career Total (Turf)	13	1	3	0	12864
Career Total (AW)	2	1	0	0	2730
78 5/09 Leic	1m3f183y (0-70)H			GD	£2590
73 2/09 Wolv	1m1f103y (0-75)H			STD	£2729

Total win prize-money £5320

Going (Turf): Sf: 0-4 GS: 0-1 **Gd: 1-6** GF: 0-2 Fm: 0-0
Distance: 5f/6f: 0-0 7f-8f: 0-4 **9f-13f: 2-10** 14f+: 0-1
Track : LH: 1-8 RH: 1-5 **Tight: 1-6** Gall: 0-1
Aids: Bl: 0-1 Vi: 0-0 Tstrap: 0-0 Ckp: 0-0
Best Rating: 81 8/09 Gdwd 1m3f good

Fair; stays 1m4f; acts well on soft ground; has worn blinkers and a tongue tie.

Citrus Star (USA)

103 102

2-y-o b g Broken Vow (USA)-Twist A Lime (USA) (Copelan (USA))
C F Wall Induna Racing Partners Two

Placings:2113 **(7016)**
2009: 6[2]GF, 5[1]GF, 5[1]G, 6[3]GS,

	Starts	1st	2nd	3rd	Win & Pl
Career Total (Turf)	4	2	1	1	12339
102 10/09 Wind	5f10y (0-95)			GD	£5180
84 9/09 Pont	5f			G-F	£3238

Total win prize-money £8419

Going (Turf): Sf: 0-0 GS: 0-1 **Gd: 1-1 GF: 1-2** Fm: 0-0
Distance: **5f/6f: 2-3** 7f-8f: 0-1 9f-13f: 0-0 14f+: 0-0
Track : **LH: 1-1** RH: 0-0 Tight: 0-0 **Gall: 1-1**
Aids: Bl: 0-0 Vi: 0-0 Tstrap: 0-0 Ckp: 0-0
Best Rating: 102 10/09 Wind 5f10y good

Very useful; Listed placed; effective over 5f; acts on good and faster ground.

City Dancer (IRE)

107 (89)99

3-y-o b f Elusive City (USA)-Calypso Dancer (FR) (Celtic Swing)
A Berry J N S Quigley

Placings:021-3345623006 **(6135)**
2009: 5[3]G, 5[3]GF, 5[4]G, 5[5]G, 5[6]G, 5[2]GF, 6[3]G, 6[0]GF, 5[0]GF, 6[6]G,

	Starts	1st	2nd	3rd	Win & Pl
Career Total (Turf)	12	0	2	3	33545
Career Total (AW)	1	1	0	0	9574
89 10/08 Dund	5f		STD		£9573

Total win prize-money £9574

Going (Turf): **Sf: 0-1 GS: 0-0 Gd: 0-6 GF: 0-4 Fm: 0-0**
Distance: **5f/6f: 1-11** 7f-8f: 0-2 9f-13f: 0-0 14f+: 0-0
Track : **LH: 1-4** RH: 0-0 Tight: 0-2 Gall: 0-0
Aids: Bl: 0-0 Vi: 0-0 Tstrap: 0-0 Ckp: 0-0
Best Rating: 99 5/09 Ches 5f16y gd-fm

Very useful: ex-Irish; Listed placed; best at 5f but stays 6f; acts on most ground and on Polytrack.

City For Conquest (IRE)

93(95) (57)56

6-y-o b m City On A Hill (USA)-Northern Life (IRE) (Distinctly North (USA))
John A Harris M F Schofield

Placings:6013140244/1005544053140532000/6220000200 45/00032413436335100-64565600 **(4225)**
2009: 6[8]SD, 5[4]GF, 6[5]SD, 7[6]GF, 5[5]GF, 7[6]GF, 5[0]GF, 6[0]G,

	Starts	1st	2nd	3rd	Win & Pl
Career Total (Turf)	35	2	2	5	16166
Career Total (AW)	30	4	4	3	14728
57 11/08 Sthl	6f	(0-50)H		STD	£1706
54 7/08 Ling	5f	(0-65)H		STD	£2047
74 9/06 Wolv	5f20y	(0-70)H		STD	£3238
72 3/06 Wolv	5f20y			STD	£2730
74 7/05 Donc	5f			G-F	£4810
74 5/05 Catt	5f			FRM	£2989

Total win prize-money £17521

Going (Turf): Sf: 0-3 GS: 0-3 Gd: 0-7 **GF: 1-20 Fm: 1-2**
Distance: **5f/6f: 6-61** 7f-8f: 0-4 9f-13f: 0-0 14f+: 0-0
Track : **LH: 4-30** RH: 0-2 **Tight: 3-22** Gall: 0-1
Aids: Bl: 0-25 **Vi: 4-17** Tstrap: 0-1 Ckp: 0-1
Best Rating: 80 10/05 Muss 5f good

Moderate; stays 6f; acts on fast ground and on Polytrack.

City Gossip (IRE)

88(91) (64)51

2-y-o b f Shinko Forest (IRE)-Lady At War (Warning)
M G Quinlan Mrs J Quinlan

Placings:50442 **(7781)**
2009: 5[5]SD, 5[0]SF, 8[4]GF, 7[4]SD, 7[2]SD,

	Starts	1st	2nd	3rd	Win & Pl
Career Total (Turf)	1	0	0	0	0
Career Total (AW)	4	0	1	0	605

Going (Turf): **Sf: 0-0 GS: 0-0 Gd: 0-0 GF: 0-1 Fm: 0-0**
Distance: 5f/6f: 0-2 7f-8f: 0-2 9f-13f: 0-1 14f+: 0-0
Track : LH: 0-5 RH: 0-0 Tight: 0-2 Gall: 0-0
Aids: Bl: 0-0 Vi: 0-0 Tstrap: 0-0 Ckp: 0-0
Best Rating: 64 9/09 Wolv 5f216y stand

Modest; effective over 7f; acts on Polytrack.

City Hustler (USA)

(99) (63)43

4-y-o b g Century City (IRE)-French Buster (USA) (Housebuster (USA))
Adrian McGuinness (Sean Thornton 23/6) Gringos Syndicate

Placings:042524/0065 **(7667)**
2009: 11[0]Y, 13[0]SD, 12[6]SD, 9[5]SD,

	Starts	1st	2nd	3rd	Win & Pl
Career Total (Turf)	4	0	0	0	192
Career Total (AW)	6	0	2	0	1808

Going (Turf): **Sf: 0-0 GS: 0-1 Gd: 0-0 GF: 0-2 Fm: 0-0**
Distance: 5f/6f: 0-0 7f-8f: 0-5 9f-13f: 0-4 14f+: 0-1
Track : LH: 0-6 RH: 0-1 Tight: 0-6 Gall: 0-0
Aids: Bl: 0-0 Vi: 0-0 Tstrap: 0-0 Ckp: 0-0
Best Rating: 72 10/07 Ling 7f stand

City Leader (IRE)

116 **118**

4-y-o gr c Fasliyev (USA)-Kanmary (FR) (Kenmare (FR))
B J Meehan Roldvale Ltd, Sangster Family & A K Collins

Placings:1212/6162340-4054 **(7313a)**
2009: 11^{4}GF, 9^{0}GS, 10^{5}G, 10^{4}HY,

	Starts	1st	2nd	3rd	Win & Pl
Career Total (Turf)	15	3	3	1	266095

109	5/08	Gdwd	1m3f	GD	£17031
108	9/07	Asct	1m	SFT	£70975
85	7/07	Asct	7f	G-S	£6800

Total win prize-money £94807

Going (Turf): **Sf: 1-2 GS: 1-3 Gd: 1-7** GF: 0-2 Fm: 0-1
Distance: 5f/6f: 0-0 **7f-8f: 2-5** 9f-13f: 1-10 14f+: 0-0
Track : LH: 0-1 **RH: 2-8** Tight: 1-1 Gall: 1-3
Aids: Bl: 0-2 Vi: 0-0 Tstrap: 0-0 Ckp: 0-0
Best Rating: **118** 10/09 NmkR 1m2f good

Group class; winner of the Group 2 Royal Lodge Stakes and runner-up in the Group 1 Racing Post Trophy in 2007; stays 1m 3f; acts on most ground.

City Line (IRE)

55 **60**

2-y-o b c Antonius Pius (USA)-Indian Myth (USA) (Lear Fan (USA))
John Joseph Murphy Mrs John J Murphy

Placings:3060 **(5543)**
2009: 7^{3}HY, 8^{0}YS, 8^{6}YS, 7^{0}GF,

	Starts	1st	2nd	3rd	Win & Pl
Career Total (Turf)	4	0	0	1	1034

Going (Turf): **Sf: 0-1 GS: 0-0 Gd: 0-0 GF: 0-1 Fm: 0-0**
Distance: 5f/6f: 0-0 7f-8f: 0-2 9f-13f: 0-2 14f+: 0-0
Track : LH: 0-2 RH: 0-1 Tight: 0-0 Gall: 0-0
Aids: Bl: 0-0 Vi: 0-0 Tstrap: 0-0 Ckp: 0-0
Best Rating: **60** 5/09 Tipp 7f100y heavy

City Of Rome (IRE)

82 **52**

2-y-o b c Elusive City (USA)-Marain (IRE) (Marju (IRE))
R Hannon Cunningham Family

Placings:0500 **(5715)**
2009: 7^{0}G, 6^{5}S, 6^{0}GF, 8^{0}G,

	Starts	1st	2nd	3rd	Win & Pl
Career Total (Turf)	4	0	0	0	0

Going (Turf): **Sf: 0-1 GS: 0-0 Gd: 0-2 GF: 0-1 Fm: 0-0**
Distance: 5f/6f: 0-0 7f-8f: 0-3 9f-13f: 0-1 14f+: 0-0
Track : LH: 0-1 RH: 0-1 Tight: 0-1 Gall: 0-0
Aids: Bl: 0-0 Vi: 0-0 Tstrap: 0-0 Ckp: 0-0
Best Rating: **52** 7/09 Sand 7f16y good

City Of The Kings (IRE)

106(100) (83)**101**

4-y-o b g Cape Cross (IRE)-Prima Volta (Primo Dominie)
G A Harker John J Maguire

Placings:0411/0516400-21100000 **(7060)**
2009: 8^{2}GF, 9^{1}GS, 8^{1}GF, 8^{0}GS, 8^{0}G, 8^{0}GF, 7^{0}G, 8^{0}GF,

	Starts	1st	2nd	3rd	Win & Pl
Career Total (Turf)	17	4	1	0	39705
Career Total (AW)	2	1	0	0	3239

101	7/09	York	1m	(0-100)H	G-F	£11656
96	6/09	Ripn	1m1f	(0-90)H	G-S	£8723
92	6/08	NmkJ	1m		G-F	£4533
83	9/07	Ches	7f2y	(0-95)	G-F	£9463
77	8/07	Kemp	1m		STD	£3238

Total win prize-money £37616

Going (Turf): Sf: 0-0 GS: 1-4 Gd: 0-4 **GF: 3-9** Fm: 0-0
Distance: 5f/6f: 0-1 **7f-8f: 4-11** 9f-13f: 1-7 14f+: 0-0
Track : LH: 2-5 RH: 2-9 **Tight: 2-4** Gall: 1-4
Aids: Bl: 0-0 Vi: 0-0 Tstrap: 0-0 Ckp: 0-0
Best Rating: **101** 7/09 York 1m gd-fm

Very useful; stays 1m1f; acts on fast and easy ground; goes on Polytrack.

City Stable (IRE)

78(101) (86)**77**

4-y-o b g Machiavellian (USA)-Rainbow City (IRE) (Rainbow Quest (USA))
M Wigham G Swan

Placings:223/02**10**-0366**00** **(4235)**
2009: 13^{0}SD, 12^{3}SD, 12^{6}SD, 12^{6}SD, 12^{0}GF, 12^{0}GF,

	Starts	1st	2nd	3rd	Win & Pl
Career Total (Turf)	7	0	3	1	3536
Career Total (AW)	6	1	0	1	5483

86	8/08	GrLe	1m6f	(0-80)H	STD	£5180

Total win prize-money £5181

Going (Turf): **Sf: 0-0 GS: 0-2 Gd: 0-3 GF: 0-2 Fm: 0-0**
Distance: 5f/6f: 0-0 7f-8f: 0-2 9f-13f: 0-8 **14f+: 1-3**
Track : **LH: 1-9** RH: 0-3 Tight: 0-6 **Gall: 1-3**
Aids: Bl: 0-0 Vi: 0-0 Tstrap: 0-0 Ckp: 0-0
Best Rating: **86** 8/08 GrLe 1m6f stand

Fair; stays 1m6f; acts on good and softer ground; goes on Polytrack.

City Style (USA)

107 **108**

3-y-o ch g City Zip (USA)-Brattothecore (CAN) (Katahaula County (CAN))
Saeed Bin Suroor Godolphin

Placings:1214-1134 **(7186)**
2009: 6^{1}G, 7^{1}G, 7^{3}G, 8^{4}G,

	Starts	1st	2nd	3rd	Win & Pl
Career Total (Turf)	6	3	0	1	163975
Career Total (AW)	2	1	1	0	5548

104	3/09	Ndas	7f110y	GD	£62500
108	2/09	Ndas	6f110y	GD	£20833
95	9/08	Loud	1m110y	FRM	£45226
	7/08	Lstp	5f110y	FST	£3135

Total win prize-money £131695

Going (Turf): Sf: 0-0 GS: 0-0 **Gd: 2-4** GF: 0-0 Fm: 1-2
Distance: 5f/6f: 1-2 **7f-8f: 2-5** 9f-13f: 1-1 14f+: 0-0
Track : **LH: 2-4** RH: 0-0 Tight: 0-0 **Gall: 2-2**
Aids: Bl: 0-0 Vi: 0-0 Tstrap: 0-0 Ckp: 0-0
Best Rating: **108** 2/09 Ndas 6f110y good

Smart; effective over 6f-1m; acts on good ground.

City Vaults Girl (IRE)

94 **69**

2-y-o b f Oratorio (IRE)-Uriah (GER) (Acatenango (GER))
R A Fahey City Vaults Racing

Placings:33543 **(6923)**
2009: 6^{3}GF, 6^{3}G, 7^{5}G, 8^{4}GF, 8^{3}GF,

	Starts	1st	2nd	3rd	Win & Pl
Career Total (Turf)	5	0	0	3	1964

Going (Turf): **Sf: 0-0 GS: 0-0 Gd: 0-2 GF: 0-3 Fm: 0-0**
Distance: 5f/6f: 0-2 7f-8f: 0-2 9f-13f: 0-1 14f+: 0-0
Track : LH: 0-2 RH: 0-0 Tight: 0-0 Gall: 0-1
Aids: Bl: 0-0 Vi: 0-0 Tstrap: 0-0 Ckp: 0-0
Best Rating: **69** 10/09 Yarm 1m3y gd-fm

Modest; stays 7f; acts on fast ground.

City Well

(73)

6-y-o b g Sadler's Wells (USA)-City Dance (USA) (Seattle Slew (USA))
Mrs L J Young Mrs Laura J Young

Placings:31/0-00 **(6432)**
2009: 13^{0}SD, 16^{0}SD,

	Starts	1st	2nd	3rd	Win & Pl
Career Total (Turf)	1	0	0	0	
Career Total (AW)	4	1	0	1	3492

73	3/06	Wolv	1m4f50y	STD	£2914

Total win prize-money £2915

Going (Turf): **Sf: 0-0 GS: 0-0 Gd: 0-0 GF: 0-1 Fm: 0-0**
Distance: 5f/6f: 0-0 7f-8f: 0-0 **9f-13f: 1-2** 14f+: 0-3
Track : **LH: 1-4** RH: 0-1 **Tight: 1-4** Gall: 0-1
Aids: Bl: 0-1 Vi: 0-0 Tstrap: 0-0 Ckp: 0-0
Best Rating: **73** 3/06 Wolv 1m4f50y stand

Cityscape

106 **112**

3-y-o ch c Selkirk (USA)-Tantina (USA) (Distant View (USA))
R Charlton K Abdulla

Placings:212-20 **(1675)**
2009: 7^{2}S, 8^{0}GF,

	Starts	1st	2nd	3rd	Win & Pl
Career Total (Turf)	5	1	3	0	49049

104	9/08	Sals	1m	GD	£4695

Total win prize-money £4695

Going (Turf): Sf: 0-1 GS: 0-0 **Gd: 1-3** GF: 0-1 Fm: 0-0
Distance: 5f/6f: 0-0 **7f-8f: 1-5** 9f-13f: 0-0 14f+: 0-0
Track : LH: 0-0 RH: 0-1 Tight: 0-0 Gall: 0-1
Aids: Bl: 0-0 Vi: 0-0 Tstrap: 0-0 Ckp: 0-0
Best Rating: **112** 9/08 Asct 1m good

Group class; runner-up in the 2008 Royal Lodge and 2009 Greenham; stays 1m; acts on good and softer ground.

Claddagh

82(96) (62)**49**

2-y-o b g Dubai Destination (USA)-Ring Of Love (Magic Ring (IRE))
M Johnston Sheikh Hamdan Bin Mohammed Al Maktoum

Placings:634 **(7865)**
2009: 9^{6}GF, 8^{3}SD, 8^{4}SS,

	Starts	1st	2nd	3rd	Win & Pl
Career Total (Turf)	1	0	0	0	0
Career Total (AW)	2	0	0	1	770

Going (Turf): **Sf: 0-0 GS: 0-0 Gd: 0-0 GF: 0-1 Fm: 0-0**
Distance: 5f/6f: 0-0 7f-8f: 0-2 9f-13f: 0-1 14f+: 0-0

Track : LH: 0-3 RH: 0-0 Tight: 0-1 Gall: 0-0
Aids: Bl: 0-0 Vi: 0-0 Tstrap: 0-0 Ckp: 0-0
Best Rating: 62 12/09 Sthl 1m stand

Modest; half-brother to a smart filly Bahia Breeze.

Claimant (IRE)

82 **46**

2-y-o b g Acclamation-Between The Winds (USA) (Diesis)
Miss J R Tooth Raymond Tooth

Placings:00 (4286)
2009: 7^{0}S, 7^{0}G,

	Starts	1st	2nd	3rd	Win & Pl
Career Total (Turf)	2	0	0	0	

Going (Turf): Sf: 0-1 GS: 0-0 Gd: 0-1 GF: 0-0 Fm: 0-0
Distance: 5f/6f: 0-0 7f-8f: 0-2 9f-13f: 0-0 14f+: 0-0
Track : LH: 0-1 RH: 0-0 Tight: 0-0 Gall: 0-1
Aids: Bl: 0-0 Vi: 0-0 Tstrap: 0-0 Ckp: 0-0
Best Rating: 46 7/09 Newb 7f soft

Clairvoyance (IRE)

(91) (74)

2-y-o b f Shamardal (USA)-Crystal View (IRE) (Imperial Ballet (IRE))
J H M Gosden H R H Princess Haya Of Jordan

Placings:2 (7450)
2009: 8^{2}SD,

	Starts	1st	2nd	3rd	Win & Pl
Career Total (Turf)	0	0	0	0	
Career Total (AW)	1	0	1	0	964

Going (Turf): Sf: 0-0 GS: 0-0 Gd: 0-0 GF: 0-0 Fm: 0-0
Distance: 5f/6f: 0-0 7f-8f: 0-1 9f-13f: 0-0 14f+: 0-0
Track : LH: 0-0 RH: 0-1 Tight: 0-0 Gall: 0-0
Aids: Bl: 0-0 Vi: 0-0 Tstrap: 0-0 Ckp: 0-0
Best Rating: 74 11/09 Kemp 1m stand

Useful; stays 1m and acts on Polytrack.

Clan Piper

78 **45**

2-y-o b c Exceed And Excel (AUS)-Song Of Skye (Warning)
J H M Gosden H R H Princess Haya Of Jordan

Placings:040 (5006)
2009: 5^{0}GS, 6^{4}GF, 6^{0}G,

	Starts	1st	2nd	3rd	Win & Pl
Career Total (Turf)	3	0	0	0	283

Going (Turf): Sf: 0-0 GS: 0-1 Gd: 0-1 GF: 0-1 Fm: 0-0
Distance: 5f/6f: 0-1 7f-8f: 0-2 9f-13f: 0-0 14f+: 0-0
Track : LH: 0-0 RH: 0-0 Tight: 0-0 Gall: 0-0
Aids: Bl: 0-0 Vi: 0-0 Tstrap: 0-0 Ckp: 0-0
Best Rating: 45 5/09 Yarm 6f3y gd-fm

100,000gns half-brother to two winners at up to 1m; disappointing favourite on debut on easy ground.

Clanachy

90 **37**

3-y-o b f Kyllachy-Antonia's Dream (Clantime)
A G Foster D W Shaw

Placings:00004 (6308)
2009: 9^{0}G, 8^{0}G, 7^{0}GF, 5^{0}G, 5^{4}GF,

	Starts	1st	2nd	3rd	Win & Pl
Career Total (Turf)	5	0	0	0	192

Going (Turf): Sf: 0-0 GS: 0-0 Gd: 0-3 GF: 0-2 Fm: 0-0
Distance: 5f/6f: 0-2 7f-8f: 0-2 9f-13f: 0-1 14f+: 0-0
Track : LH: 0-1 RH: 0-1 Tight: 0-2 Gall: 0-0
Aids: Bl: 0-0 Vi: 0-0 Tstrap: 0-0 Ckp: 0-0
Best Rating: 37 9/09 Muss 5f good

Clare Glen (IRE)

95(69) (65)**65**

3-y-o b f Sakhee (USA)-Desert Grouse (USA) (Gulch (USA))
Lee Smyth Leslie Laverty

Placings:0304404040 (7301a)
2009: 8^{0}G, 8^{3}GF, 10^{0}G, 8^{4}G, 8^{4}SD, 8^{0}SD, 10^{4}SD, 10^{0}S, 10^{4}SD, 12^{0}SD,

	Starts	1st	2nd	3rd	Win & Pl
Career Total (Turf)	5	0	0	1	1009
Career Total (AW)	5	0	0	0	1254

Going (Turf): Sf: 0-1 GS: 0-0 Gd: 0-3 GF: 0-1 Fm: 0-0
Distance: 5f/6f: 0-0 7f-8f: 0-4 9f-13f: 0-6 14f+: 0-0
Track : LH: 0-8 RH: 0-2 Tight: 0-2 Gall: 0-1
Aids: Bl: 0-0 Vi: 0-0 Tstrap: 0-5 Ckp: 0-5
Best Rating: 65 10/09 Dund 1m2f150y stand

Clarietta

99 **98**

2-y-o b/br f Shamardal (USA)-Claxon (Caerleon (USA))
J L Dunlop Bluehills Racing Limited

Placings:01153 (7187)
2009: 7^{0}GF, 7^{1}GS, 7^{1}GS, 8^{5}GF, 8^{3}G,

	Starts	1st	2nd	3rd	Win & Pl
Career Total (Turf)	5	2	0	1	16023
86	8/09	NmkJ	7f	G-S	£5180
78	7/09	Donc	7f	G-S	£5459

Total win prize-money £10640

Going (Turf): Sf: 0-0 **GS: 2-2** Gd: 0-1 GF: 0-2 Fm: 0-0
Distance: 5f/6f: 0-0 **7f-8f: 2-5** 9f-13f: 0-0 14f+: 0-0
Track : LH: 0-0 RH: 0-0 Tight: 0-0 Gall: 0-0
Aids: Bl: 0-0 Vi: 0-0 Tstrap: 0-0 Ckp: 0-0
Best Rating: 98 9/09 Donc 1m gd-fm

Very useful; stays 7f; handles fast and easy ground.

Clarity Of Passion

(84) (33)

4-y-o br f Zamindar (USA)-Millazure (USA) (Dayjur (USA))
James Halpin Hugh J O'Brien

Placings:000 (7753)
2009: 10^{0}SD, 10^{0}SD, 8^{0}SD,

	Starts	1st	2nd	3rd	Win & Pl
Career Total (Turf)	0	0	0	0	
Career Total (AW)	3	0	0	0	

Going (Turf): Sf: 0-0 GS: 0-0 Gd: 0-0 GF: 0-0 Fm: 0-0
Distance: 5f/6f: 0-0 7f-8f: 0-0 9f-13f: 0-3 14f+: 0-0
Track : LH: 0-3 RH: 0-0 Tight: 0-1 Gall: 0-0
Aids: Bl: 0-0 Vi: 0-0 Tstrap: 0-0 Ckp: 0-0
Best Rating: 33 11/09 Dund 1m2f150y stand

Clash City Rocker

76 **25**

3-y-o bl g Needwood Blade-Wandering Stranger (Petong)
G A Swinbank P C Thompson

Placings:0 (4276)
2009: 7^{0}G,

	Starts	1st	2nd	3rd	Win & Pl
Career Total (Turf)	1	0	0	0	

Going (Turf): Sf: 0-0 GS: 0-0 Gd: 0-1 GF: 0-0 Fm: 0-0
Distance: 5f/6f: 0-0 7f-8f: 0-1 9f-13f: 0-0 14f+: 0-0
Track : LH: 0-1 RH: 0-0 Tight: 0-1 Gall: 0-0
Aids: Bl: 0-0 Vi: 0-0 Tstrap: 0-0 Ckp: 0-0
Best Rating: 25 7/09 Thsk 7f good

Clashnacree (IRE)

103 **84**

2-y-o b/br c Footstepsinthesand-Miss Moore (IRE) (Tagula (IRE))
T Stack Dublin Blue Syndicate

Placings:2202 (4723a)
2009: 6^{2}HY, 6^{2}G, 5^{0}GF, 6^{2}G,

	Starts	1st	2nd	3rd	Win & Pl
Career Total (Turf)	4	0	3	0	8284

Going (Turf): Sf: 0-1 GS: 0-0 Gd: 0-2 GF: 0-1 Fm: 0-0
Distance: 5f/6f: 0-4 7f-8f: 0-0 9f-13f: 0-0 14f+: 0-0
Track : LH: 0-2 RH: 0-0 Tight: 0-0 Gall: 0-0
Aids: Bl: 0-0 Vi: 0-0 Tstrap: 0-0 Ckp: 0-0
Best Rating: 84 8/09 Leop 6f good

Class Attraction (IRE)

109 (83)**98**

5-y-o b m Act One-She's All Class (USA) (Rahy (USA))
J E Hammond P D Savill

Placings:23221/210-214450 (5472)
2009: 9^{2}GS, 9^{1}G, 10^{4}GS, 8^{4}VS, 8^{5}G, 9^{0}GF,

	Starts	1st	2nd	3rd	Win & Pl
Career Total (Turf)	11	2	4	0	61964
Career Total (AW)	3	1	1	1	10709
87	6/09	Lonc	1m1f165y	GD	£16019
98	10/08	Chan	1m1f	G-S	£12132
	12/07	Deau	1m1f110y	STD	£5743

Total win prize-money £33894

Going (Turf): Sf: 0-2 **GS: 1-4 Gd: 1-2** GF: 0-1 Fm: 0-0
Distance: 5f/6f: 0-0 7f-8f: 0-4 **9f-13f: 3-10** 14f+: 0-0
Track : LH: 0-2 **RH: 2-6** Tight: 0-1 Gall: 0-0
Aids: Bl: 0-0 Vi: 0-0 Tstrap: 0-0 Ckp: 0-0
Best Rating: 98 5/09 Chan 1m1f110y gd-sft

Class Is Class (IRE)

113 **103**

3-y-o b g Montjeu (IRE)-Hector's Girl (Hector Protector (USA))

Sir Michael Stoute R Ahamad & P Scott

Placings:02-13240 **(6662)**
2009: 8^{1}G, 10^{3}G, 12^{2}GF, 10^{4}GF, 12^{0}GS,

	Starts	1st	2nd	3rd	Win & Pl
Career Total (Turf)	7	1	2	1	21404

87 5/09 Yarm 1m3y GD £2525
Total win prize-money £2526

Going (Turf): Sf: 0-1 GS: 0-1 **Gd: 1-3** GF: 0-2 Fm: 0-0
Distance: 5f/6f: 0-0 7f-8f: 0-0 **9f-13f: 1-7** 14f+: 0-0
Track : LH: 0-3 RH: 0-3 Tight: 0-0 Gall: 0-4
Aids: Bl: 0-0 Vi: 0-0 Tstrap: 0-0 Ckp: 0-0
Best Rating: 103 9/09 Newb 1m2f6y gd-fm

Very useful; stays 1m4f; acts on most ground on turf.

Classic Blue (IRE)

94(103) (60)43
5-y-o b m Tagula (IRE)-Palace Blue (IRE) (Dara Monarch)
Ian Williams Boston R S Ian Bennett

Placings:000/0000/2215021250-0500 **(7855)**
2009: 8^{0}G, 10^{5}G, 9^{0}GF, 8^{0}SS,

	Starts	1st	2nd	3rd	Win & Pl
Career Total (Turf)	7	0	0	0	0
Career Total (AW)	14	2	4	0	6756

59 10/08 Kemp 1m1f (0-50)H STD £2047
60 2/08 Kemp 1m2f (0-55)H STD £2047
Total win prize-money £4095

Going (Turf): **Sf: 0-0 GS: 0-1 Gd: 0-2 GF: 0-4 Fm: 0-0**
Distance: 5f/6f: 0-1 7f-8f: 0-3 **9f-13f: 2-17** 14f+: 0-0
Track : LH: 0-14 **RH: 2-5** Tight: 0-7 Gall: 0-2
Aids: Bl: 0-0 Vi: 0-0 Tstrap: 0-0 Ckp: 0-0
Best Rating: 60 10/08 GrLe 1m2f stand

Moderate; stays 1m2f; acts on Polytrack.

Classic Colori (IRE)

99 89
2-y-o b c Le Vie Dei Colori-Beryl (Bering)
Tom Dascombe The Classic Strollers Partnership

Placings:10 **(7030)**
2009: 6^{1}GF, 7^{0}S,

	Starts	1st	2nd	3rd	Win & Pl
Career Total (Turf)	2	1	0	0	3886

88 7/09 Wind 6f G-F £3885
Total win prize-money £3886

Going (Turf): Sf: 0-1 GS: 0-0 Gd: 0-0 **GF: 1-1** Fm: 0-0
Distance: **5f/6f: 1-1** 7f-8f: 0-1 9f-13f: 0-0 14f+: 0-0
Track : LH: 0-0 RH: 0-0 Tight: 0-0 **Gall: 1-1**
Aids: Bl: 0-0 Vi: 0-0 Tstrap: 0-0 Ckp: 0-0
Best Rating: 89 10/09 Newb 7f soft

Useful; suited by 6f and acts on fast ground.

Classic Contours (USA)

99 77
3-y-o b g Najran (USA)-What's Up Kittycat (USA) (Tabasco Cat (USA))
J J Quinn Elsa Crankshaw Gordon Allan

Placings:0026-0511234344 **(5952)**
2009: 7^{0}GF, 9^{5}GF, 12^{1}GS, 12^{1}GF, 12^{2}GF, 12^{3}GF, 12^{4}GF, 14^{3}GF, 14^{4}GS, 14^{4}GF,

	Starts	1st	2nd	3rd	Win & Pl
Career Total (Turf)	14	2	2	2	9957

71 5/09 Bevl 1m4f16 (0-60)H G-F £2590
64 5/09 Haml 1m4f17 (0-70)H G-S £3238
Total win prize-money £5828

Going (Turf): Sf: 0-0 **GS: 1-3** Gd: 0-1 **GF: 1-10** Fm: 0-0
Distance: 5f/6f: 0-1 7f-8f: 0-4 **9f-13f: 2-6** 14f+: 0-3
Track : LH: 0-5 **RH: 2-7 Tight: 2-8** Gall: 0-1
Aids: Bl: 0-0 Vi: 0-0 Tstrap: 0-0 Ckp: 0-0
Best Rating: 77 7/09 Nott 1m6f15y gd-fm

Modest; stays 1m4f; acts on fast and easy ground.

Classic Dancer

49(78) (9)
4-y-o b f Groom Dancer (USA)-Versatility (Teenoso (USA))
Andrew Turnell (Jane Chapple-Hyam 30/8) Cromhall Stud

Placings:00-0 **(4617)**
2009: 15^{0}G,

	Starts	1st	2nd	3rd	Win & Pl
Career Total (Turf)	1	0	0	0	
Career Total (AW)	2	0	0	0	

Going (Turf): **Sf: 0-0 GS: 0-0 Gd: 0-1 GF: 0-0 Fm: 0-0**
Distance: 5f/6f: 0-0 7f-8f: 0-0 9f-13f: 0-1 14f+: 0-2
Track : LH: 0-3 RH: 0-0 Tight: 0-2 Gall: 0-1
Aids: Bl: 0-0 Vi: 0-0 Tstrap: 0-0 Ckp: 0-0
Best Rating: 9 12/08 GrLe 1m5f66y stand

Classic Descent

100(98) (85)90
4-y-o b g Auction House (USA)-Polish Descent (IRE) (Danehill (USA))
P J Makin Joseph Joyce

Placings:432/10-0600 **(6944)**
2009: 7^{0}GF, 7^{6}SD, 7^{0}G, 7^{0}SD,

	Starts	1st	2nd	3rd	Win & Pl
Career Total (Turf)	6	1	1	0	6818
Career Total (AW)	3	0	0	1	337

90 5/08 NmkR 7f GD £5180
Total win prize-money £5181

Going (Turf): Sf: 0-0 GS: 0-1 **Gd: 1-3** GF: 0-2 Fm: 0-0
Distance: 5f/6f: 0-2 **7f-8f: 1-7** 9f-13f: 0-0 14f+: 0-0
Track : LH: 0-1 RH: 0-2 Tight: 0-1 Gall: 0-0
Aids: Bl: 0-0 Vi: 0-0 Tstrap: 0-0 Ckp: 0-0
Best Rating: 90 6/08 Donc 1m gd-sft

Very useful; stays 7f; acts on good ground and on Polytrack.

Classic Legend

105(110) (93)90
4-y-o b f Galileo (IRE)-Lady Lahar (Fraam)
B J Meehan Mrs Moira McNamara

Placings:11/3604-00516 **(4166)**
2009: 8^{0}GF, 8^{0}G, 8^{5}GF, 10^{1}G, 10^{6}G,

	Starts	1st	2nd	3rd	Win & Pl
Career Total (Turf)	10	3	0	1	26105
Career Total (AW)	1	0	0	0	2148

90 7/09 Hayd 1m2f95y (0-85)H GD £5504
93 11/07 NmkR 1m GD £12491
82 10/07 Nott 1m54y G-F £3238
Total win prize-money £21236

Going (Turf): Sf: 0-0 GS: 0-0 **Gd: 2-7** GF: 1-3 Fm: 0-0
Distance: 5f/6f: 0-0 7f-8f: 1-5 **9f-13f: 2-6** 14f+: 0-0
Track : **LH: 2-5** RH: 0-3 Tight: 0-2 Gall: 0-2
Aids: Bl: 0-0 Vi: 0-0 Tstrap: 0-0 Ckp: 0-0
Best Rating: 93 11/08 Kemp 1m stand

Useful; former Listed winner; effective over 1m-1m2f; acts on good/fast ground.

Classic Port (FR)

92(102) (103)100
5-y-o gr h Slickly (FR)-Portella (GER) (Protektor (GER))
J R Best Ashards Partnership

Placings:1/31/4060-6 **(3282)**
2009: 8^{6}GF,

	Starts	1st	2nd	3rd	Win & Pl
Career Total (Turf)	7	2	0	1	17644
Career Total (AW)	1	0	0	0	2335

96 4/07 MsnL 1m GD £11486
10/06 Mans 7f110y SFT £2758
Total win prize-money £14245

Going (Turf): **Sf: 1-2** GS: 0-1 **Gd: 1-2** GF: 0-2 Fm: 0-0
Distance: 5f/6f: 0-0 **7f-8f: 2-6** 9f-13f: 0-2 14f+: 0-0
Track : LH: 0-2 RH: 0-2 Tight: 0-2 Gall: 0-0
Aids: Bl: 0-0 Vi: 0-0 Tstrap: 0-0 Ckp: 0-0
Best Rating: 103 3/08 Wolv 1m141y stand

Classic Punch (IRE)

106 111
6-y-o b g Mozart (IRE)-Rum Cay (USA) (Our Native (USA))
D R C Elsworth The Classic Bunch

Placings:03/100200/115200/0040204-020130234 **(6452)**
2009: 13^{0}GF, 12^{2}G, 12^{0}GF, 12^{1}GF, 12^{3}G, 12^{0}G, 10^{2}G, 11^{3}GF, 12^{4}GF,

	Starts	1st	2nd	3rd	Win & Pl
Career Total (Turf)	30	4	5	3	95368

107 4/09 Ripn 1m4f10y G-F £7477
114 7/07 NmkJ 1m4f G-F £9971
111 6/07 NmkJ 1m4f SFT £15330
89 6/06 Wind 1m2f7y G-F £3886
Total win prize-money £36665

Going (Turf): Sf: 1-2 GS: 0-5 Gd: 0-12 **GF: 3-10** Fm: 0-1
Distance: 5f/6f: 0-0 7f-8f: 0-2 **9f-13f: 4-23** 14f+: 0-5
Track : LH: 0-6 **RH: 4-19** Tight: 2-6 Gall: 2-18
Aids: Bl: 0-0 Vi: 0-0 Tstrap: 0-0 Ckp: 0-0
Best Rating: 114 8/07 Wind 1m3f135y good

Smart; Listed winner; best at around 1m4f; acts on most ground; suited by forcing tactics.

Classic Vintage (USA)

111 103
3-y-o b c El Prado (IRE)-Cellars Shiraz (USA) (Kissin Kris (USA))
Mrs A J Perrett R & P Scott A & J Powell Gallagher Stud

Placings:011-60131640 **(6662)**
2009: 10^{6}G, 11^{0}HY, 12^{1}GF, 12^{3}GF, 12^{1}G, 14^{6}GF, 14^{4}G, 12^{0}GS,

	Starts	1st	2nd	3rd	Win & Pl
Career Total (Turf)	11	4	0	1	57533

103 7/09 Gdwd 1m4f (0-105)H GD £37386
95 6/09 Sals 1m4f (0-95)H G-F £7477
86 10/08 Bath 1m5y G-S £3756
83 9/08 Sand 1m14y SFT £5180
Total win prize-money £53800

Going (Turf): Sf: 1-2 GS: 1-2 Gd: 1-4 GF: 1-3 Fm: 0-0
Distance: 5f/6f: 0-0 7f-8f: 0-1 9f-13f: 4-8 14f+: 0-2
Track : LH: 1-3 RH: 3-8 Tight: 3-4 Gall: 0-3
Aids: Bl: 0-0 Vi: 0-0 Tstrap: 0-0 Ckp: 0-0
Best Rating: 103 7/09 Gdwd 1m4f good

Very useful; stays 1m4f; acts on fast and soft ground.

Classical Piece (USA)

89(88) (69)53
2-y-o b g Brahms (USA)-Nueva (USA) (Jade Hunter (USA))
Mrs D J Sanderson R J Budge

Placings:040 (7289)
2009: 7⁰SD, 7⁴SD, 6⁰S,

	Starts	1st	2nd	3rd	Win & Pl
Career Total (Turf)	1	0	0	0	
Career Total (AW)	2	0	0	0	0

Going (Turf): Sf: 0-1 GS: 0-0 Gd: 0-0 GF: 0-0 Fm: 0-0
Distance: 5f/6f: 0-1 7f-8f: 0-2 9f-13f: 0-0 14f+: 0-0
Track : LH: 0-1 RH: 0-1 Tight: 0-1 Gall: 0-0
Aids: Bl: 0-0 Vi: 0-0 Tstrap: 0-0 Ckp: 0-0
Best Rating: 69 10/09 Ling 7f stand

Classical Rhythm (IRE)

100(95) (60)68
4-y-o ch g Traditionally (USA)-Golden Angel (USA) (Slew O'Gold (USA))
J R Boyle Inside Track Racing Club

Placings:060060/10304006040-64600004230 (5444)
2009: 10⁶GF, 11⁴G, 10⁶G, 12⁰SD, 11⁰G, 12⁰G, 10⁰G, 10⁴G, 11²GF, 12³GF, 11⁰GF,

	Starts	1st	2nd	3rd	Win & Pl
Career Total (Turf)	20	1	1	2	4576
Career Total (AW)	8	0	0	0	0

66 4/08 Folk 1m1f149y (0-75)H G-S £2331
Total win prize-money £2331

Going (Turf): Sf: 0-0 GS: 1-3 Gd: 0-8 GF: 0-9 Fm: 0-0
Distance: 5f/6f: 0-2 7f-8f: 0-5 9f-13f: 1-21 14f+: 0-0
Track : LH: 0-13 RH: 1-9 Tight: 1-12 Gall: 0-2
Aids: Bl: 0-2 Vi: 0-0 Tstrap: 0-0 Ckp: 0 0
Best Rating: 68 7/08 Nott 1m2f50y gd-sft

Modest sort; effective at around 1m2f; handles easy ground; has worn blinkers.

Classically (IRE)

94(101) (73)84
3-y-o b g Indian Haven-Specifically (USA) (Sky Classic (CAN))
R Charlton P Gleeson

Placings:2-3000314 (6977)
2009: 10³G, 10⁰GF, 10⁰G, 10⁰S, 8³SD, 8¹SD, 8⁴SD,

	Starts	1st	2nd	3rd	Win & Pl
Career Total (Turf)	5	0	1	1	2312
Career Total (AW)	3	1	0	1	2542

73 10/09 Kemp 1m STD £2047
Total win prize-money £2047

Going (Turf): Sf: 0-2 GS: 0-0 Gd: 0-2 GF: 0-1 Fm: 0-0
Distance: 5f/6f: 0-0 7f-8f: 1-3 9f-13f: 0-5 14f+: 0-0
Track : LH: 0-2 RH: 1-4 Tight: 0-1 Gall: 0-2
Aids: Bl: 0-0 Vi: 0-0 Tstrap: 0-0 Ckp: 0-0

Best Rating: 84 3/09 Donc 1m2f60y good

Fair; stays 1m2f; acts on soft ground and Polytrack.

Classlin

83 49
2-y-o b f Bertolini (USA)-Class Wan (Safawan)
J S Goldie Frank & Annette Brady

Placings:0500 (6409)
2009: 6⁰GF, 5⁵GS, 6⁰G, 5⁰GF,

	Starts	1st	2nd	3rd	Win & Pl
Career Total (Turf)	4	0	0	0	0

Going (Turf): Sf: 0-0 GS: 0-1 Gd: 0-1 GF: 0-2 Fm: 0-0
Distance: 5f/6f: 0-4 7f-8f: 0-0 9f-13f: 0-0 14f+: 0-0
Track : LH: 0-0 RH: 0-0 Tight: 0-0 Gall: 0-0
Aids: Bl: 0-0 Vi: 0-0 Tstrap: 0-0 Ckp: 0-0
Best Rating: 49 9/09 Ayr 6f good

Moderate form to date.

Clayton Flick (IRE)

77(89) (52)45
2-y-o b c Kheleyf (USA)-Mambodorga (USA) (Kingmambo (USA))
A B Haynes Ms J Loylert

Placings:000062 (7756)
2009: 8⁰SD, 7⁰F, 6⁰G, 5⁰SD, 8⁶SD, 7²SD,

	Starts	1st	2nd	3rd	Win & Pl
Career Total (Turf)	2	0	0	0	
Career Total (AW)	4	0	1	0	605

Going (Turf): Sf: 0-0 GS: 0-0 Gd: 0-1 GF: 0-0 Fm: 0-1
Distance: 5f/6f: 0-1 7f-8f: 0-4 9f-13f: 0-1 14f+: 0-0
Track : LH: 0-3 RH: 0-1 Tight: 0-2 Gall: 0-0
Aids: Bl: 0-0 Vi: 0-1 Tstrap: 0-0 Ckp: 0-0
Best Rating: 52 12/09 Sthl 7f stand

Moderate; stays 7f; acts on Fibresand; has worn a visor.

Clear Hand

93(79) (52)50
3-y-o b g Lend A Hand-Miss Maisey (IRE) (Entrepreneur)
B R Millman Clear Racing & P Tosh

Placings:000-00604300 (6170)
2009: 10⁰SD, 7⁰GF, 6⁶S, 6⁰GF, 5⁴GF, 6³G, 6⁰GS, 7⁰GF,

	Starts	1st	2nd	3rd	Win & Pl
Career Total (Turf)	9	0	0	1	529
Career Total (AW)	2	0	0	0	

Going (Turf): Sf: 0-1 GS: 0-1 Gd: 0-2 GF: 0-5 Fm: 0-0
Distance: 5f/6f: 0-2 7f-8f: 0-8 9f-13f: 0-1 14f+: 0-0
Track : LH: 0-4 RH: 0-0 Tight: 0-2 Gall: 0-0
Aids: Bl: 0-6 Vi: 0-0 Tstrap: 0-0 Ckp: 0-0
Best Rating: 52 9/08 Ling 7f stand

Moderate; stays 6f; acts on most ground; has worn blinkers.

Clear Ice (IRE)

87(94) (74)56
2-y-o gr g Verglas (IRE)-Mynu Girl (IRE) (Charnwood Forest (IRE))
D Nicholls J P Honeyman

Placings:5540002212510 (7805)
2009: 6⁵G, 5⁵GF, 6⁴G, 5⁰GF, 6⁰GF, 5⁰GF, 5²SD, 6²SD, 5¹SD, 6²SD, 7⁵SD, 6¹SD, 6⁰SD,

	Starts	1st	2nd	3rd	Win & Pl
Career Total (Turf)	6	0	0	0	409
Career Total (AW)	7	2	3	0	7396

74 12/09 Sthl 6f (0-75) STD £2729
67 11/09 Sthl 5f STD £2047
Total win prize-money £4777

Going (Turf): Sf: 0-0 GS: 0-0 Gd: 0-2 GF: 0-4 Fm: 0-0
Distance: 5f/6f: 2-12 7f-8f: 0-1 9f-13f: 0-0 14f+: 0-0
Track : LH: 1-6 RH: 0-1 Tight: 0-2 Gall: 0-0
Aids: Bl: 0-0 Vi: 0-0 Tstrap: 0-0 Ckp: 0-0
Best Rating: 74 12/09 Sthl 6f stand

Modest; suited by 5f-6f; acts on Fibresand.

Clear Reef

105(104) (88)88
5-y-o b h Hernando (FR)-Trinity Reef (Bustino)
Jane Chapple-Hyam Mrs Jane Chapple-Hyam

Placings:04611/525000156351-6254531002505131 (7867)
2009: 12⁰SD, 14²SD, 12⁵SD, 12⁴SD, 12⁵SD, 12³SD, 14¹S, 16⁰G, 12⁰GF, 14²G, 12⁵G, 16⁰G, 14⁵S, 16¹SD, 16³SD, 14¹SS,

	Starts	1st	2nd	3rd	Win & Pl
Career Total (Turf)	14	2	1	0	11979
Career Total (AW)	19	5	2	3	26727

12/09 Sthl 1m6f (0-85)H SS £4984
87 11/09 Wolv 2m119y (0-85)H STD £5046
88 5/09 Hayd 1m6f (0-80)H SFT £5504
87 12/08 Wolv 1m4f50y (0-85)H STD £6308
82 8/08 Thsk 2m (0-75)H GD £4274
77 1/08 Sthl 1m6f (0-75)H STD £2461
78 12/07 Sthl 1m3f (0-70)H SS £2968
Total win prize-money £31548

Going (Turf): Sf: 1-3 GS: 0-1 Gd: 1-8 GF: 0-2 Fm: 0-0
Distance: 5f/6f: 0-0 7f-8f: 0-0 9f-13f: 2-13 14f+: 5-20
Track : LH: 7-19 RH: 0-14 Tight: 3-7 Gall: 0-10
Aids: Bl: 0-0 Vi: 0-0 Tstrap: 3-12 Ckp: 3-12
Best Rating: 91 2/08 Sthl 1m6f std-slw

Useful; stays 2m; acts on good ground; goes on sand; has worn cheekpieces.

Clear Sailing

94(108) (80)82
6-y-o b g Selkirk (USA)-Welsh Autumn (Tenby)
Ollie Pears We-Know Partnership

Placings:31/500/10451-2122460321 (7631)
2009: 8²SS, 10¹SD, 8²SD, 8²SD, 8⁴SD, 9⁶SD, 10⁰GS, 8³SD, 8²SD, 8¹SD,

	Starts	1st	2nd	3rd	Win & Pl
Career Total (Turf)	8	2	0	1	5987
Career Total (AW)	12	3	4	1	10578

74 12/09 Wolv 1m141y (0-70) STD £3238
75 1/09 GrLe 1m2f STD £2590
80 12/08 Sthl 1m STD £1978
82 8/08 Nott 1m2f50y (0-75)H SFT £2914
83 10/06 Nott 1m1f213y SFT £2590
Total win prize-money £13312

Going (Turf): Sf: 2-4 GS: 0-2 Gd: 0-1 GF: 0-1 Fm: 0-0
Distance: 5f/6f: 0-0 7f-8f: 1-5 9f-13f: 4-14 14f+: 0-1
Track : LH: 5-16 RH: 0-4 Tight: 1-8 Gall: 1-2
Aids: Bl: 0-0 Vi: 0-0 Tstrap: 3-13 Ckp: 3-13
Best Rating: 83 10/06 Nott 1m1f213y soft

Modest; effective over 1m-1m2f; acts on soft ground and on sand; has worn cheekpieces.

Clearing House

(91) (55)
4-y-o ch g Zamindar (USA)-Easy Option (IRE) (Prince Sabo)
R W Price Kevin Chapman

Placings:066-000 **(6587)**
2009: 12^{0}SD, 7^{0}SD, 7^{0}SD,

	Starts	1st	2nd	3rd	Win & Pl
Career Total (Turf)	0	0	0	0	
Career Total (AW)	6	0	0	0	0

Going (Turf): **Sf: 0-0 GS: 0-0 Gd: 0-0 GF: 0-0 Fm: 0-0**
Distance: 5f/6f: 0-0 7f-8f: 0-5 9f-13f: 0-1 14f+: 0-0
Track : LH: 0-4 RH: 0-2 Tight: 0-2 Gall: 0-1
Aids: Bl: 0-0 Vi: 0-0 Tstrap: 0-0 Ckp: 0-0
Best Rating: **57** 4/08 GrLe 1m stand

Cleaver

106(104) (82)86
8-y-o ch g Kris-Much Too Risky (Bustino)
Lady Herries Lady Herries and Friends

Placings:0/50/01/000446111/4433220/5313020-32360 **(6995)**
2009: 16^{3}S, 16^{2}G, 16^{3}GS, 16^{6}GS, 14^{0}GS,

	Starts	1st	2nd	3rd	Win & Pl
Career Total (Turf)	28	5	4	3	28058
Career Total (AW)	5	0	0	3	3023

85	5/08	Newb	1m5f61y	(0-75)H	SFT	£2590
81	11/06	Nott	1m1f213y	(0-75)H	SFT	£3886
75	10/06	Newc	1m4f93y	(0-70)H	SFT	£3238
73	9/06	Haml	1m3f16y	(0-65)H	G-S	£3238
72	10/05	Newc	1m2f32y	(0-60)H	SFT	£3462

Total win prize-money £16416

Going (Turf): **Sf: 4-12** GS: 1-7 Gd: 0-7 GF: 0-2 Fm: 0-0
Distance: 5f/6f: 0-0 7f-8f: 0-1 **9f-13f: 4-23** 14f+: 1-9
Track : **LH: 4-20** RH: 1-12 Tight: 1-9 **Gall: 3-11**
Aids: Bl: 0-0 Vi: 0-0 Tstrap: 0-0 Ckp: 0-0
Best Rating: **86** 6/09 York 2m88y gd-sft

Fair; effective over 1m2f-1m6f; suited by soft ground.

Cleisthenes (USA)

106 87
3-y-o b g Pleasantly Perfect (USA)-Do The Mambo (USA) (Kingmambo (USA))
W J Haggas Findlay & Bloom

Placings:1 **(1956)**
2009: 5^{1}F,

	Starts	1st	2nd	3rd	Win & Pl
Career Total (Turf)	1	1	0	0	3785

87	5/09	Brig	5f213y	FRM	£3784

Total win prize-money £3785

Going (Turf): Sf: 0-0 GS: 0-0 Gd: 0-0 GF: 0-0 **Fm: 1-1**
Distance: **5f/6f: 1-1** 7f-8f: 0-0 9f-13f: 0-0 14f+: 0-0
Track : **LH: 1-1** RH: 0-0 Tight: 0-0 Gall: 0-0
Aids: Bl: 0-0 Vi: 0-0 Tstrap: 0-0 Ckp: 0-0
Best Rating: **87** 5/09 Brig 5f213y firm

Fair; suited by 6f and fast ground.

Clerical (USA)

90(97) (59)47
3-y-o b g Yes It's True (USA)-Clerical Etoile (ARG) (The Watcher (USA))
R M H Cowell J Sargeant

Placings:000030343-30554250 **(7614)**
2009: 5^{3}SD, 6^{0}G, 5^{5}SD, 5^{5}GF, 6^{4}SD, 7^{2}SD, 8^{5}SD, 7^{0}SD,

	Starts	1st	2nd	3rd	Win & Pl
Career Total (Turf)	7	0	0	0	118
Career Total (AW)	10	0	1	4	2550

Going (Turf): **Sf: 0-0 GS: 0-1 Gd: 0-2 GF: 0-4 Fm: 0-0**
Distance: 5f/6f: 0-11 7f-8f: 0-6 9f-13f: 0-0 14f+: 0-0
Track : LH: 0-5 RH: 0-5 Tight: 0-2 Gall: 0-3
Aids: Bl: 0-0 Vi: 0-1 Tstrap: 0-9 Ckp: 0-9
Best Rating: **59** 12/08 GrLe 6f stand

Moderate; stays 6f and acts on Polytrack.

Clerk's Choice (IRE)

112(93) (74)90
3-y-o b g Bachelor Duke (USA)-Credit Crunch (IRE) (Caerleon (USA))
W Jarvis M C Banks

Placings:050223-3310243 **(6571)**
2009: 7^{3}GS, 9^{3}GF, 9^{1}G, 10^{0}G, 10^{2}GF, 10^{4}GF, 11^{3}GF,

	Starts	1st	2nd	3rd	Win & Pl
Career Total (Turf)	10	1	2	3	14870
Career Total (AW)	3	0	1	1	1108

89	6/09	Sand	1m1f	(0-90)H	GD	£7771

Total win prize-money £7771

Going (Turf): Sf: 0-0 GS: 0-2 **Gd: 1-2** GF: 0-6 Fm: 0-0
Distance: 5f/6f: 0-1 7f-8f: 0-6 **9f-13f: 1-6** 14f+: 0-0
Track : LH: 0-5 **RH: 1-4** Tight: 0-4 Gall: 0-1
Aids: Bl: 0-0 Vi: 0-0 Tstrap: 0-0 Ckp: 0-0
Best Rating: **90** 9/09 Yarm 1m2f21y gd-fm

Useful; stays 1m2f; acts on most ground and on sand.

Cleveland

(101) (71)57
7-y-o b g Pennekamp (USA)-Clerio (Soviet Star (USA))
R Hollinshead Mrs Susy Haslehurst

Placings:006000/0001130/02526324550/031532360330-62 **(0619)**
2009: 6^{6}SD, 6^{2}SD,

	Starts	1st	2nd	3rd	Win & Pl
Career Total (Turf)	15	0	0	2	578
Career Total (AW)	23	3	5	5	11056

71	1/08	Sthl	5f	(0-60)H	STD	£2457
72	11/06	Sthl	7f	(0-45)	STD	£1365
57	11/06	Sthl	7f		STD	£2388

Total win prize-money £6211

Going (Turf): **Sf: 0-2 GS: 0-3 Gd: 0-7 GF: 0-3 Fm: 0-0**
Distance: 5f/6f: 1-20 **7f-8f: 2-16** 9f-13f: 0-2 14f+: 0-0
Track : **LH: 2-28** RH: 0-1 Tight: 0-4 Gall: 0-0
Aids: Bl: 0-0 Vi: 0-0 Tstrap: 0-0 Ckp: 0-0
Best Rating: **73** 5/07 Sthl 7f stand

Modest; suited by 5f-7f and acts on Fibresand.

Clever Molly (IRE)

97(87) (46)57
2-y-o b f Mull Of Kintyre (USA)-Mother Molly (USA) (Irish River (FR))
E J Alston J Stephenson

Placings:05264300 **(6355)**
2009: 5^{0}G, 5^{5}G, 5^{2}GF, 5^{6}G, 5^{4}G, 5^{3}GF, 6^{0}GS, 5^{0}SD,

	Starts	1st	2nd	3rd	Win & Pl
Career Total (Turf)	7	0	1	1	1426
Career Total (AW)	1	0	0	0	

Going (Turf): **Sf: 0-0 GS: 0-1 Gd: 0-4 GF: 0-2 Fm: 0-0**
Distance: 5f/6f: 0-8 7f-8f: 0-0 9f-13f: 0-0 14f+: 0-0
Track : LH: 0-0 RH: 0-2 Tight: 0-0 Gall: 0-0
Aids: Bl: 0-0 Vi: 0-0 Tstrap: 0-0 Ckp: 0-0
Best Rating: **57** 9/09 Rdcr 5f gd-fm

Modest; suited by 5f and fast ground.

Clever Omneya (USA)

87(89) (42)36
3-y-o ch f Toccet (USA)-Clever Empress (Crafty Prospector (USA))
J R Jenkins Sheik Ahmad Yousuf Al Sabah

Placings:0005 **(7686)**
2009: 5^{0}S, 5^{0}SD, 6^{0}SD, 6^{5}SD,

	Starts	1st	2nd	3rd	Win & Pl
Career Total (Turf)	1	0	0	0	
Career Total (AW)	3	0	0	0	0

Going (Turf): **Sf: 0-1 GS: 0-0 Gd: 0-0 GF: 0-0 Fm: 0-0**
Distance: 5f/6f: 0-4 7f-8f: 0-0 9f-13f: 0-0 14f+: 0-0
Track : LH: 0-1 RH: 0-2 Tight: 0-1 Gall: 0-0
Aids: Bl: 0-0 Vi: 0-0 Tstrap: 0-0 Ckp: 0-0
Best Rating: **42** 12/09 Kemp 6f stand

Clientele (USA)

101(104) (87)88
3-y-o b/br g Mr Greeley (USA)-Pracer (USA) (Lyphard (USA))
M Johnston Sheikh Hamdan Bin Mohammed Al Maktoum

Placings:410240P **(6830)**
2009: 11^{4}GF, 8^{1}G, 8^{0}GF, 7^{2}G, 8^{4}SD, 7^{0}G, 8^{P}SF,

	Starts	1st	2nd	3rd	Win & Pl
Career Total (Turf)	5	1	1	0	4923
Career Total (AW)	2	0	0	0	378

82	7/09	Pont	1m4y	GD	£3238

Total win prize-money £3238

Going (Turf): Sf: 0-0 GS: 0-0 **Gd: 1-3** GF: 0-2 Fm: 0-0
Distance: 5f/6f: 0-0 7f-8f: 0-2 **9f-13f: 1-5** 14f+: 0-0
Track : **LH: 1-5** RH: 0-2 Tight: 0-4 Gall: 0-0
Aids: Bl: 0-0 Vi: 0-0 Tstrap: 0-0 Ckp: 0-0
Best Rating: **88** 8/09 Wwck 7f26y good

Useful; effective over 7f-1m; acts on good ground.

Clifton Bridge

(97) (79)
2-y-o b g Avonbridge-Ambitious (Ardkinglass)
R M Beckett Landmark Racing Limited

Placings:51 **(7843)**
2009: 6^{5}SD, 5^{1}SD,

	Starts	1st	2nd	3rd	Win & Pl
Career Total (Turf)	0	0	0	0	
Career Total (AW)	2	1	0	0	3886

79	12/09	Wolv	5f20y	STD	£3885

Total win prize-money £3886

Going (Turf): **Sf: 0-0 GS: 0-0 Gd: 0-0 GF: 0-0 Fm: 0-0**
Distance: **5f/6f: 1-2** 7f-8f: 0-0 9f-13f: 0-0 14f+: 0-0

Track : LH: 1-1 RH: 0-1 Tight: 1-1 Gall: 0-0
Aids: Bl: 0-0 Vi: 0-0 Tstrap: 0-0 Ckp: 0-0
Best Rating: 79 12/09 Wolv 5f20y stand

Fair; suited by 5f and Polytrack.

Clifton Dancer

101 **98**

4-y-o b f Fraam-Crofters Ceilidh (Scottish Reel)
Tom Dascombe Clifton Partners

Placings:035100/51160-3000 **(4423)**
2009: 7^3GS, 8^0G, 7^0GF, 7^0G,

	Starts	1st	2nd	3rd	Win & Pl
Career Total (Turf)	15	3	0	2	34923

98	6/08	Wwck	7f26y		G-F	£14760
92	5/08	Newb	7f	(0-85)H	GD	£6476
79	9/07	Ling	7f	(0-75)	G-F	£3238

Total win prize-money £24475

Going (Turf): Sf: 0-2 GS: 0-2 Gd: 1-6 **GF: 2-5** Fm: 0-0
Distance: 5f/6f: 0-2 **7f-8f: 3-13** 9f-13f: 0-0 14f+: 0-0
Track : **LH: 1-3** RH: 0-2 Tight: 0-0 Gall: 0-2
Aids: Bl: 0-0 Vi: 0-0 Tstrap: 0-0 Ckp: 0-0
Best Rating: 98 6/08 Wwck 7f26y gd-fm

Very useful; Listed winner; best at 7f; acts on good and faster ground; likes to race prominently.

Clifton Encore (USA)

73 **4**

2-y-o b f War Chant (USA)-Theatrical Pause (USA) (Theatrical)
Tom Dascombe Clifton Partners

Placings:0 **(6932)**
2009: 5^0G,

	Starts	1st	2nd	3rd	Win & Pl
Career Total (Turf)	1	0	0	0	

Going (Turf): **Sf: 0-0 GS: 0-0 Gd: 0-1 GF: 0-0 Fm: 0-0**
Distance: 5f/6f: 0-1 7f-8f: 0-0 9f-13f: 0-0 14f+: 0-0
Track : LH: 0-1 RH: 0-0 Tight: 0-0 Gall: 0-1
Aids: Bl: 0-0 Vi: 0-0 Tstrap: 0-0 Ckp: 0-0
Best Rating: 4 10/09 Bath 5f11y good

Clifton Kid (IRE)

(44)

2-y-o b g Danbird (AUS)-Flossytoo (Royal Applause)
R C Guest Brooklands Racing

Placings:6 **(7836)**
2009: 7^6SS,

	Starts	1st	2nd	3rd	Win & Pl
Career Total (Turf)	0	0	0	0	
Career Total (AW)	1	0	0	0	0

Going (Turf): **Sf: 0-0 GS: 0-0 Gd: 0-0 GF: 0-0 Fm: 0-0**
Distance: 5f/6f: 0-0 7f-8f: 0-1 9f-13f: 0-0 14f+: 0-0
Track : LH: 0-1 RH: 0-0 Tight: 0-0 Gall: 0-0
Aids: Bl: 0-0 Vi: 0-0 Tstrap: 0-0 Ckp: 0-0

Climate (IRE)

(107) (63)**36**

10-y-o ch g Catrail (USA)-Burishki (Chilibang)
P D Evans J E Abbey

Placings:23000421/23403122/0034400050S30/54021630002/6/0431103/3111033004056542/266511620211060400 1053-0560010 **(7857)**
2009: 9^0SD, 8^5SD, 8^6SD, 8^0SD, 9^0SD, 8^1SD, 9^0SD,

	Starts	1st	2nd	3rd	Win & Pl
Career Total (Turf)	34	1	3	7	17369
Career Total (AW)	59	13	8	5	45753

61	12/09	Wolv	1m141y	(0-55)H	STD	£2047
61	12/08	Wolv	1m1f103y	(0-55)H	STD	£2047
68	4/08	Wolv	1m141y		STD	£2729
56	4/08	Wolv	1m1f103y		STD	£2456
64	2/08	Wolv	1m141y	(0-58)H	STD	£1774
60	2/08	Ling	1m2f	(0-55)H	STD	£1876
64	2/07	Wolv	1m141y		STD	£2388
68	1/07	Wolv	1m141y		SS	£2388
74	1/07	Wolv	1m1f103y		STD	£2388
71	10/06	Wolv	1m1f103y		STD	£3238
73	10/06	Wolv	7f32y	(0-68)H	STD	£3238
79	5/04	Ling	1m	E(0-70)H	STD	£3513
86	6/02	Ches	7f122y	D(0-80)	G-F	£4075
67	1/02	Ling	1m	D	STD	£2810

Total win prize-money £36978

Going (Turf): Sf: 0-4 GS: 0-4 Gd: 0-5 **GF: 1-20** Fm: 0-1
Distance: 5f/6f: 0-4 7f-8f: 4-40 **9f-13f: 10-49** 14f+: 0-0
Track : **LH: 14-56** RH: 0-20 **Tight: 14-58** Gall: 0-4
Aids: Bl: 1-11 Vi: 4-17 Tstrap: 4-17 Ckp: 4-17
Best Rating: 93 6/03 Gdwd 1m gd-fm

Moderate; effective over 1m-1m2f; acts on fast ground; goes on Polytrack; has worn blinkers/visor/cheekpieces.

Clincher

89(85) (26)**39**

3-y-o b f Royal Applause-Clincher Club (Polish Patriot (USA))
J A Osborne Mr & Mrs G Middlebrook & D Redvers

Placings:500 **(7411)**
2009: 6^5G, 5^0SD, 5^0SD,

	Starts	1st	2nd	3rd	Win & Pl
Career Total (Turf)	1	0	0	0	0
Career Total (AW)	2	0	0	0	

Going (Turf): **Sf: 0-0 GS: 0-0 Gd: 0-1 GF: 0-0 Fm: 0-0**
Distance: 5f/6f: 0-3 7f-8f: 0-0 9f-13f: 0-0 14f+: 0-0
Track : LH: 0-2 RH: 0-0 Tight: 0-2 Gall: 0-1
Aids: Bl: 0-0 Vi: 0-0 Tstrap: 0-0 Ckp: 0-0
Best Rating: 39 10/09 Wind 6f good

Clinging Vine (USA)

(89) (61)

3-y-o b/br f Fusaichi Pegasus (USA)-Nemea (USA) (The Minstrel (CAN))
R Hannon T Hyde & Mrs P Shanahan

Placings:60-0 **(0201)**
2009: 8^0SD,

	Starts	1st	2nd	3rd	Win & Pl
Career Total (Turf)	0	0	0	0	
Career Total (AW)	3	0	0	0	0

Going (Turf): **Sf: 0-0 GS: 0-0 Gd: 0-0 GF: 0-0 Fm: 0-0**
Distance: 5f/6f: 0-0 7f-8f: 0-3 9f-13f: 0-0 14f+: 0-0
Track : LH: 0-2 RH: 0-1 Tight: 0-1 Gall: 0-1
Aids: Bl: 0-0 Vi: 0-0 Tstrap: 0-0 Ckp: 0-0
Best Rating: 61 9/08 Kemp 7f stand

Half-sister to Lovers Knot and Foodbroker Founder.

Clipperdown (IRE)

98(102) (69)**66**

8-y-o b g Green Desert (USA)-Maroussie (FR) (Saumarez)
E J Creighton Travel Spot LLP

Placings:3016/14160210/6656244123/5/0560-02323000250 **(6668)**
2009: 9^0GF, 10^2SD, 12^3SD, 10^2SD, 11^3GF, 9^0F, 10^0GS, 9^0GF, 9^2F, 10^5SD, 9^0SD,

	Starts	1st	2nd	3rd	Win & Pl
Career Total (Turf)	30	4	4	3	67040
Career Total (AW)	8	1	2	1	15579

	10/06	SnAt	1m		FRM	£17791
93	9/05	Ling	1m2f	(0-95)H	STD	£11402
84	7/05	Ripn	1m1f170y	(0-80)H	G-F	£6500
86	6/05	Ripn	1m	(0-80)H	G-F	£6958
75	8/04	Pont	1m4y	D	G-F	£5395

Total win prize-money £48047

Going (Turf): Sf: 0-0 GS: 0-2 Gd: 0-6 **GF: 3-11** Fm: 1-11
Distance: 5f/6f: 0-0 7f-8f: 2-9 **9f-13f: 3-29** 14f+: 0-0
Track : **LH: 3-21** RH: 2-6 **Tight: 3-15** Gall: 0-5
Aids: Bl: 0-1 Vi: 0-0 Tstrap: 0-2 Ckp: 0-2
Best Rating: 110 1/07 SnAt 1m2f firm

Moderate; formerly smart; spent 2006 and early 2007 in the US; suited by 1m2f; acts on fast ground; goes on Polytrack; has worn a tongue tie.

Clippity Clop (IRE)

93(100) (70)**58**

3-y-o b g Clodovil (IRE)-Son Chou (Cyrano De Bergerac)
J A Osborne J A Osborne

Placings:1004600 **(6807)**
2009: 8^1SD, 10^0GF, 14^0GF, 10^4GF, 8^6G, 9^0SD, 12^0SD,

	Starts	1st	2nd	3rd	Win & Pl
Career Total (Turf)	4	0	0	0	0
Career Total (AW)	3	1	0	0	2590

70	3/09	Sthl	1m	STD	£2590

Total win prize-money £2590

Going (Turf): **Sf: 0-0 GS: 0-0 Gd: 0-1 GF: 0-3 Fm: 0-0**
Distance: 5f/6f: 0-0 **7f-8f: 1-1** 9f-13f: 0-5 14f+: 0-1
Track : **LH: 1-6** RH: 0-0 Tight: 0-4 Gall: 0-0
Aids: Bl: 0-0 Vi: 0-0 Tstrap: 0-0 Ckp: 0-0
Best Rating: 70 3/09 Sthl 1m stand

Modest; made winning debut in 1m Fibresand maiden; failed to build on it.

Clockmaker (IRE)

93 **86**

3-y-o b c Danetime (IRE)-Lady Ingabelle (IRE) (Catrail (USA))
J H M Gosden H R H Princess Haya Of Jordan

Placings:2 **(1355)**
2009: 8^2S,

	Starts	1st	2nd	3rd	Win & Pl
Career Total (Turf)	1	0	1	0	1445

Going (Turf): **Sf: 0-1 GS: 0-0 Gd: 0-0 GF: 0-0 Fm: 0-0**
Distance: 5f/6f: 0-0 7f-8f: 0-1 9f-13f: 0-0 14f+: 0-0
Track : LH: 0-0 RH: 0-0 Tight: 0-0 Gall: 0-0
Aids: Bl: 0-0 Vi: 0-0 Tstrap: 0-0 Ckp: 0-0
Best Rating: 86 4/09 Newb 1m soft

Clopf (IRE)

107 (74)**83**

8-y-o b g Dr Massini (IRE)-Chroma (IRE) (Supreme Leader)

Andrew Heffernan (E J O'Grady 14/4) Bernard Anthony Heffernan

Placings:10/0-105040 **(7261a)**

2009: 16^{1}G, 20^{0}GF, **17^{5}SD**, 14^{0}S, 16^{4}G, 16^{0}HY,

	Starts	1st	2nd	3rd	Win & Pl
Career Total (Turf)	8	2	0	0	18634
Career Total (AW)	1	0	0	0	

82 5/09 Leop 2m (60-90)H GD £9056
75 4/07 Tipp 1m6f G-F £7470
Total win prize-money £16527

Going (Turf): Sf: 0-4 GS: 0-0 **Gd: 1-2 GF: 1-2** Fm: 0-0
Distance: 5f/6f: 0-0 7f-8f: 0-0 9f-13f: 0-0 **14f+: 2-9**
Track : **LH: 2-5** RH: 0-4 Tight: 0-0 Gall: 0-1
Aids: Bl: 0-1 Vi: 0-0 Tstrap: 0-0 Ckp: 0-0
Best Rating: 83 9/09 Curr 2m good

Useful; smart hurdler; winning chaser; effective over 2m; goes on any ground.

Close Alliance (USA)

101(99) (94)**97**

3-y-o b c Gone West (USA)-Shoogle (USA) (A.P. Indy (USA))

J H M Gosden K Abdulla

Placings:1-064 **(1678)**

2009: 9^{0}SD, 8^{6}GF, 10^{4}GF,

	Starts	1st	2nd	3rd	Win & Pl
Career Total (Turf)	2	0	0	0	3563
Career Total (AW)	2	1	0	0	4533

85 10/08 GrLe 1m STD £4533
Total win prize-money £4533

Going (Turf): Sf: 0-0 GS: 0-0 Gd: 0-0 GF: 0-2 Fm: 0-0
Distance: 5f/6f: 0-0 **7f-8f: 1-2** 9f-13f: 0-2 14f+: 0-0
Track : **LH: 1-1** RH: 0-1 Tight: 0-0 **Gall: 1-1**
Aids: Bl: 0-0 Vi: 0-0 Tstrap: 0-0 Ckp: 0-0
Best Rating: 97 5/09 NmkR 1m2f gd-fm

Fair; stays 1m; acts on Polytrack; likely to improve.

Cloud's End

82(100) (73)**68**

2-y-o b f Dubawi (IRE)-Kangra Valley (Indian Ridge)

W J Haggas Manor Farm Stud & Miss S Hoare

Placings:31 **(6722)**

2009: 6^{3}GF, **6^{1}SD**,

	Starts	1st	2nd	3rd	Win & Pl
Career Total (Turf)	1	0	0	1	578
Career Total (AW)	1	1	0	0	4533

73 10/09 Kemp 6f STD £4533
Total win prize-money £4533

Going (Turf): Sf: 0-0 GS: 0-0 Gd: 0-0 GF: 0-1 Fm: 0-0
Distance: **5f/6f: 1-1** 7f-8f: 0-1 9f-13f: 0-0 14f+: 0-0
Track : LH: 0-0 **RH: 1-1** Tight: 0-0 Gall: 0-0
Aids: Bl: 0-0 Vi: 0-0 Tstrap: 0-0 Ckp: 0-0
Best Rating: 73 10/09 Kemp 6f stand

Fair; effective over 6f; acts on Polytrack.

Cloudesley (IRE)

105(99) (71)**74**

3-y-o b g Trans Island-Decatur (Deploy)

A M Balding Kingsclere Racing CLub

Placings:55-62236266 **(6761)**

2009: 7^{6}SD, 8^{2}GF, 8^{2}GS, 9^{3}G, 9^{6}GF, 8^{2}SD, 10^{6}G, 9^{6}G,

	Starts	1st	2nd	3rd	Win & Pl
Career Total (Turf)	6	0	2	1	3006
Career Total (AW)	4	0	1	0	605

Going (Turf): Sf: 0-0 GS: 0-1 Gd: 0-3 GF: 0-2 Fm: 0-0
Distance: 5f/6f: 0-1 7f-8f: 0-4 9f-13f: 0-5 14f+: 0-0
Track : LH: 0-3 RH: 0-5 Tight: 0-5 Gall: 0-0
Aids: Bl: 0-0 Vi: 0-1 Tstrap: 0-1 Ckp: 0-1
Best Rating: 74 6/09 Sand 1m1f good

Fair; stays 1m1f; acts on fast and soft ground.

Cloudy City (USA)

92 **70**

2-y-o b/br g Giant's Causeway (USA)-Mambo Slew (USA) (Kingmambo (USA))

M Johnston A D Spence

Placings:643 **(5428)**

2009: 7^{6}G, 8^{4}G, 8^{3}G,

	Starts	1st	2nd	3rd	Win & Pl
Career Total (Turf)	3	0	0	1	866

Going (Turf): Sf: 0-0 GS: 0-0 Gd: 0-3 GF: 0-0 Fm: 0-0
Distance: 5f/6f: 0-0 7f-8f: 0-2 9f-13f: 0-1 14f+: 0-0
Track : LH: 0-0 RH: 0-3 Tight: 0-0 Gall: 0-0
Aids: Bl: 0-0 Vi: 0-0 Tstrap: 0-0 Ckp: 0-0
Best Rating: 70 8/09 Gdwd 1m good

Modest; stays 1m; acts on good ground.

Cloudy Start

106(114) (108)**108**

3-y-o b c Oasis Dream-Set Fair (USA) (Alleged (USA))

H R A Cecil K Abdulla

Placings:0321-0311204 **(5855)**

2009: 7^{0}GS, 7^{3}GF, 7^{1}G, 8^{1}SD, 8^{2}G, 8^{0}G, 7^{4}GF,

	Starts	1st	2nd	3rd	Win & Pl
Career Total (Turf)	10	2	2	2	26774
Career Total (AW)	1	1	0	0	7771

108 6/09 Kemp 1m STD £7771
96 6/09 Epsm 7f (0-100)H GD £12462
91 10/08 Rdcr 7f GD £5536
Total win prize-money £25770

Going (Turf): Sf: 0-1 GS: 0-1 **Gd: 2-5** GF: 0-3 Fm: 0-0
Distance: 5f/6f: 0-0 **7f-8f: 3-10** 9f-13f: 0-1 14f+: 0-0
Track : LH: 1-2 RH: 1-3 **Tight: 1-2** Gall: 0-0
Aids: Bl: 0-0 Vi: 0-0 Tstrap: 0-0 Ckp: 0-0
Best Rating: 108 7/09 NmkJ 1m good

Smart; stays 1m; acts on good and faster ground and on Polytrack.

Clovis

101(101) (73)**71**

4-y-o b g Kingmambo (USA)-Darling Flame (USA) (Capote (USA))

Andrew Turnell (N P Mulholland 28/8) The Chosen Few

Placings:564625/430430000-15560026016 **(6210)**

2009: 10^{1}SD, 10^{5}SD, 10^{5}SD, 11^{6}G, 12^{0}SD, 10^{0}GF, 10^{2}F, 10^{6}GF, 10^{0}G, 11^{1}G, 12^{6}SD,

	Starts	1st	2nd	3rd	Win & Pl
Career Total (Turf)	16	1	1	2	4080
Career Total (AW)	10	1	1	0	4471

61 8/09 Bath 1m3f144y GD £1942
65 2/09 Kemp 1m2f STD £3238
Total win prize-money £5181

Going (Turf): Sf: 0-1 GS: 0-4 **Gd: 1-7** GF: 0-3 Fm: 0-1
Distance: 5f/6f: 0-0 7f-8f: 0-1 **9f-13f: 2-24** 14f+: 0-1
Track : LH: 1-15 RH: 1-11 **Tight: 1-16** Gall: 0-1
Aids: Bl: 1-12 Vi: 0-0 Tstrap: 1-5 Ckp: 1-5
Best Rating: 78 11/07 Nott 1m54y gd-fm

Modest; stays 1m4f; acts on a sound surface and Fibresand; has worn blinkers and cheekpieces.

Clowance House

110 **94**

3-y-o ch g Galileo (IRE)-Corsican Sunset (USA) (Thunder Gulch (USA))

R Charlton Seasons Holidays

Placings:43-313036 **(5870)**

2009: 11^{3}GS, 12^{1}GF, 12^{3}GF, 16^{0}GF, 14^{3}GF, 14^{6}G,

	Starts	1st	2nd	3rd	Win & Pl
Career Total (Turf)	8	1	0	4	8692

78 5/09 Sals 1m4f G-F £3885
Total win prize-money £3886

Going (Turf): Sf: 0-1 GS: 0-1 Gd: 0-2 **GF: 1-4** Fm: 0-0
Distance: 5f/6f: 0-0 7f-8f: 0-2 **9f-13f: 1-3** 14f+: 0-3
Track : LH: 0-2 **RH: 1-4 Tight: 1-1** Gall: 0-4
Aids: Bl: 0-0 Vi: 0-0 Tstrap: 0-0 Ckp: 0-0
Best Rating: 94 6/09 Asct 2m gd-fm

Very useful; stays 1m6f; acts on any ground.

Club Tahiti

103 **90**

3-y-o b f Hernando (FR)-Freni (GER) (Sternkoenig (IRE))

R Charlton Seasons Holidays

Placings:10-043 **(4422)**

2009: 10^{0}GF, 8^{4}GS, 9^{3}G,

	Starts	1st	2nd	3rd	Win & Pl
Career Total (Turf)	5	1	0	1	8305

87 10/08 Newb 6f110y G-S £5504
Total win prize-money £5505

Going (Turf): Sf: 0-1 **GS: 1-2** Gd: 0-1 GF: 0-1 Fm: 0-0
Distance: 5f/6f: 0-0 **7f-8f: 1-3** 9f-13f: 0-2 14f+: 0-0
Track : LH: 0-1 RH: 0-1 Tight: 0-1 Gall: 0-1
Aids: Bl: 0-0 Vi: 0-0 Tstrap: 0-0 Ckp: 0-0
Best Rating: 90 7/09 Gdwd 1m1f good

Useful; stays 1m; acts on soft ground.

Clueless

(91) (33)**90**

7-y-o b g Royal Applause-Pure (Slip Anchor)

G A Charlton Northumbria Leisure Ltd

Placings:43/4221512/2400600/5000060-6 **(0923)**

2009: 12^{6}SD,

	Starts	1st	2nd	3rd	Win & Pl
Career Total (Turf)	23	2	4	1	29386
Career Total (AW)	1	0	0	0	0

95 9/05 Yarm 1m2f21y (0-90)H G-F £12298
86 7/05 NmkJ 1m4f G-F £4842
Total win prize-money £17141

Going (Turf): Sf: 0-3 GS: 0-3 Gd: 0-7 **GF: 2-10** Fm: 0-0
Distance: 5f/6f: 0-0 7f-8f: 0-1 **9f-13f: 2-18** 14f+: 0-5
Track : LH: 1-14 RH: 1-6 Tight: 1-6 Gall: 1-6
Aids: Bl: 0-5 Vi: 0-0 Tstrap: 0-1 Ckp: 0-1

Best Rating: 95 10/05 NmkR 1m2f soft

Useful; stays 1m5f; acts on fast and soft ground; has worn blinkers.

Clumber Place

101(95) (64)69

3-y-o ch f Compton Place-Inquirendo (USA) (Roberto (USA))

R C Guest The Clumber Park Syndicate

Placings:1-060601 (5941)

2009: 8^{0}SD, 7^{6}GF, 8^{0}F, 10^{6}G, 8^{0}S, 7^{1}G,

	Starts	1st	2nd	3rd	Win & Pl
Career Total (Turf)	6	2	0	0	5505
Career Total (AW)	1	0	0	0	

59	9/09	Muss	7f30y	(0-65)H	GD	£2266
69	4/08	Pont	5f		G-S	£3238

Total win prize-money £5505

Going (Turf): Sf: 0-1 **GS: 1-1 Gd: 1-2** GF: 0-1 Fm: 0-1
Distance: 5f/6f: 1-1 7f-8f: 1-4 9f-13f: 0-2 14f+: 0-0
Track : LH: 1-3 RH: 1-4 **Tight: 1-2** Gall: 0-0
Aids: Bl: 0-0 Vi: 0-0 Tstrap: 0-0 Ckp: 0-0
Best Rating: 69 4/08 Pont 5f gd-sft

Moderate; stays 7f and acts on good and easier ground.

Clumber Pursuits

65 4

2-y-o ch f Pastoral Pursuits-Inquirendo (USA) (Roberto (USA))

S A Harris S & D Bloodstock

Placings:00 (5439)

2009: 6^{0}GF, 6^{0}GF,

	Starts	1st	2nd	3rd	Win & Pl
Career Total (Turf)	2	0	0	0	

Going (Turf): **Sf: 0-0 GS: 0-0 Gd: 0-0 GF: 0-2 Fm: 0-0**
Distance: 5f/6f: 0-1 7f-8f: 0-1 9f-13f: 0-0 14f+: 0-0
Track : LH: 0-0 RH: 0-0 Tight: 0-0 Gall: 0-0
Aids: Bl: 0-0 Vi: 0-0 Tstrap: 0-0 Ckp: 0-0
Best Rating: 4 8/09 Yarm 6f3y gd-fm

Well beaten in 6f maidens.

Cluny

95(83) (35)62

3-y-o b f Celtic Swing-Muschana (Deploy)

J R Fanshawe Nigel & Carolyn Elwes

Placings:0-34400 (7049)

2009: 9^{3}GF, 10^{4}GF, 12^{4}GF, 11^{0}GS, 12^{0}SD,

	Starts	1st	2nd	3rd	Win & Pl
Career Total (Turf)	4	0	0	1	836
Career Total (AW)	2	0	0	0	

Going (Turf): **Sf: 0-0 GS: 0-1 Gd: 0-0 GF: 0-3 Fm: 0-0**
Distance: 5f/6f: 0-0 7f-8f: 0-1 9f-13f: 0-5 14f+: 0-0
Track : LH: 0-2 RH: 0-3 Tight: 0-5 Gall: 0-0
Aids: Bl: 0-0 Vi: 0-0 Tstrap: 0-0 Ckp: 0-0
Best Rating: 62 4/09 Folk 1m1f149y gd-fm

Cnoc Moy (IRE)

(100) (80)86

5-y-o b g Mull Of Kintyre (USA)-Ewar Sunrise (Shavian)

O Sherwood Mrs C Hardman

Placings:0/062101120/5 (0459)

2009: 16^{5}SD,

	Starts	1st	2nd	3rd	Win & Pl
Career Total (Turf)	4	2	1	0	11643
Career Total (AW)	7	1	1	0	2792

83	7/07	Sand	1m14y	(0-80)H	GD	£6477
77	7/07	Wind	1m67y	(0-70)H	G-S	£3238
74	4/07	Ling	1m	(0-60)H	STD	£2388

Total win prize-money £12105

Going (Turf): Sf: 0-0 **GS: 1-1 Gd: 1-2** GF: 0-1 Fm: 0-0
Distance: 5f/6f: 0-0 7f-8f: 1-4 **9f-13f: 2-6** 14f+: 0-1
Track : LH: 1-5 **RH: 2-5 Tight: 2-7** Gall: 0-0
Aids: Bl: 0-0 Vi: 0-0 Tstrap: 0-0 Ckp: 0-0
Best Rating: 86 8/07 Wind 1m67y gd-fm

Fair; effective over 1m; acts on good ground; also goes on Polytrack.

Co Dependent (USA)

(98) (68)39

3-y-o ch c Cozzene (USA)-Glowing Breeze (USA) (Southern Halo (USA))

J A Osborne Mountgrange Stud

Placings:006-032 (0716)

2009: 9^{0}SD, 8^{3}SD, 8^{2}SD,

	Starts	1st	2nd	3rd	Win & Pl
Career Total (Turf)	1	0	0	0	
Career Total (AW)	5	0	1	1	1292

Going (Turf): **Sf: 0-0 GS: 0-0 Gd: 0-0 GF: 0-1 Fm: 0-0**
Distance: 5f/6f: 0-1 7f-8f: 0-3 9f-13f: 0-2 14f+: 0-0
Track : LH: 0-2 RH: 0-3 Tight: 0-2 Gall: 0-0
Aids: Bl: 0-0 Vi: 0-0 Tstrap: 0-0 Ckp: 0-0
Best Rating: 68 2/09 Wolv 1m141y stand

Moderate; stays 1m; acts on Polytrack.

Cobo Bay

108 (83)103

4-y-o b g Primo Valentino (IRE)-Fisher Island (IRE) (Sri Pekan (USA))

K A Ryan The C H F Partnership

Placings:4341101/1300635-000421300 (7294)

2009: 8^{0}GF, 8^{0}S, 10^{0}G, 9^{4}GS, 8^{2}G, 8^{1}HY, 7^{3}GS, 8^{0}G, 7^{0}S,

	Starts	1st	2nd	3rd	Win & Pl
Career Total (Turf)	21	4	1	3	41832
Career Total (AW)	2	1	0	1	3561

99	7/09	Nott	1m75y	(0-85)H	HVY	£6231
104	4/08	Ripn	1m	(0-95)H	G-S	£8756
92	9/07	Ayr	1m	(0-95)	G-S	£12464
85	8/07	NmkJ	1m		SFT	£5181
83	8/07	Wolv	7f32y		STD	£3238

Total win prize-money £35872

Going (Turf): **Sf: 2-7 GS: 2-6** Gd: 0-6 GF: 0-2 Fm: 0-0
Distance: 5f/6f: 0-2 **7f-8f: 4-15** 9f-13f: 1-6 14f+: 0-0
Track : **LH: 3-8** RH: 1-5 **Tight: 2-7** Gall: 0-0
Aids: **Bl: 1-4** Vi: 0-1 Tstrap: 0-7 Ckp: 0-7
Best Rating: 104 4/08 Ripn 1m gd-sft

Very useful; effective at 7f-1m; acts on soft ground; also goes on Polytrack; has worn cheekpieces, a visor and blinkers.

Cobos

90(90) (64)53

3-y-o b f Royal Applause-Darya (USA) (Gulch (USA))

A M Hales (Ms E L McWilliam 15/7) Andrew L Cohen

Placings:055-0060 (3980)

2009: 8^{0}G, 10^{0}GF, 9^{6}F, 8^{0}SD,

	Starts	1st	2nd	3rd	Win & Pl
Career Total (Turf)	4	0	0	0	0
Career Total (AW)	3	0	0	0	0

Going (Turf): **Sf: 0-0 GS: 0-0 Gd: 0-2 GF: 0-1 Fm: 0-1**
Distance: 5f/6f: 0-0 7f-8f: 0-5 9f-13f: 0-2 14f+: 0-0
Track : LH: 0-4 RH: 0-2 Tight: 0-3 Gall: 0-1
Aids: Bl: 0-0 Vi: 0-0 Tstrap: 0-1 Ckp: 0-1
Best Rating: 64 10/08 GrLe 1m stand

Cockney Class (USA)

94 75

2-y-o gr/ro c Speightstown (USA)-Snappy Little Cat (USA) (Tactical Cat (USA))

B J Meehan Roldvale Limited

Placings:33 (4499)

2009: 7^{3}G, 7^{3}G,

	Starts	1st	2nd	3rd	Win & Pl
Career Total (Turf)	2	0	0	2	1926

Going (Turf): **Sf: 0-0 GS: 0-0 Gd: 0-2 GF: 0-0 Fm: 0-0**
Distance: 5f/6f: 0-0 7f-8f: 0-2 9f-13f: 0-0 14f+: 0-0
Track : LH: 0-0 RH: 0-0 Tight: 0-0 Gall: 0-0
Aids: Bl: 0-0 Vi: 0-0 Tstrap: 0-0 Ckp: 0-0
Best Rating: 75 7/09 NmkJ 7f good

Fair; stays 7f; acts on good ground.

Cockney Colonel (USA)

71 18

2-y-o b/br g Dixie Union (USA)-Kristina's Wish (USA) (Smart Strike (CAN))

E J Creighton The Ultimate Racing Fraternity

Placings:00 (4153)

2009: 5^{0}G, 6^{0}G,

	Starts	1st	2nd	3rd	Win & Pl
Career Total (Turf)	2	0	0	0	

Going (Turf): **Sf: 0-0 GS: 0-0 Gd: 0-2 GF: 0-0 Fm: 0-0**
Distance: 5f/6f: 0-1 7f-8f: 0-1 9f-13f: 0-0 14f+: 0-0
Track : LH: 0-0 RH: 0-0 Tight: 0-0 Gall: 0-1
Aids: Bl: 0-0 Vi: 0-0 Tstrap: 0-0 Ckp: 0-0
Best Rating: 18 7/09 Wind 5f10y good

Cocktail Party (IRE)

90(97) (55)62

3-y-o b f Acclamation-Irish Moss (USA) (Irish River (FR))

J W Hills Tony Waspe Partnership

Placings:40052164-0002040**543** (7703)

2009: 6^{0}GF, 6^{0}G, 8^{0}GS, 5^{0}GS, 5^{2}G, 5^{0}GS, 5^{4}GF, 6^{0}G, 5^{5}SD, 5^{4}SD, 6^{3}SD,

	Starts	1st	2nd	3rd	Win & Pl
Career Total (Turf)	15	1	2	0	4704
Career Total (AW)	4	0	0	1	302

62	10/08	Nott	5f13y	(0-65)	SFT	£2729

Total win prize-money £2730

Going (Turf):	**Sf: 1-3** GS: 0-4 Gd: 0-3 GF: 0-5 Fm: 0-0
Distance:	**5f/6f: 1-17** 7f-8f: 0-1 9f-13f: 0-1 14f+: 0-0
Track :	LH: 0-2 RH: 0-4 Tight: 0-1 Gall: 0-5
Aids:	Bl: 0-0 Vi: 0-0 Tstrap: 0-0 Ckp: 0-0
Best Rating:	**62** 10/08 Nott 5f13y soft

Moderate; effective over 5f-6f; acts on fast and soft ground; goes on Polytrack; has worn a tongue tie.

Coco L'Escargot

(87) (41)**56**
5-y-o b m Slip Anchor-Dafne (Nashwan (USA))
J R Jenkins Nick Hodge

Placings:505603356-6 **(0058)**
2009: 11^{6}SD,

	Starts	1st	2nd	3rd	Win & Pl
Career Total (Turf)	4	0	0	2	931
Career Total (AW)	6	0	0	0	0

Going (Turf):	**Sf: 0-1 GS: 0-1 Gd: 0-0 GF: 0-2 Fm: 0-0**
Distance:	5f/6f: 0-0 7f-8f: 0-1 9f-13f: 0-8 14f+: 0-1
Track :	LH: 0-5 RH: 0-5 Tight: 0-1 Gall: 0-2
Aids:	Bl: 0-0 Vi: 0-6 Tstrap: 0-0 Ckp: 0-0
Best Rating:	**56** 10/08 Catt 1m3f214y gd-sft

Moderate; stays 1m4f; acts on soft ground and Polytrack; has worn a visor.

Coconut Moon

99(99) (77)**72**
7-y-o b m Bahamian Bounty-Lunar Ridge (Indian Ridge)
A Berry The Coconutters

Placings:6/0013/001325200100/000223265021020/4000 51660000-00000U0404000 **(7219)**
2009: 5^{0}GF, 5^{0}GF, 5^{0}SD, 5^{0}GF, 5^{0}GF, 5^{U}G, 5^{0}GF, 6^{4}G, 6^{0}GS, 6^{4}GF, 5^{0}G, 6^{0}GF, 5^{0}S,

	Starts	1st	2nd	3rd	Win & Pl
Career Total (Turf)	47	2	7	2	27113
Career Total (AW)	11	3	0	1	9922
77 7/08 Ling 5f	(0-65)H			STD	£2590
85 9/07 Ches 5f16y	(0-85)H			G-F	£5829
83 8/06 Ches 5f16y	(0-85)H			GD	£5829
62 6/06 Wolv 5f20y	(0-70)H			SS	£3238
70 11/05 Wolv 5f20y				STD	£3481

Total win prize-money £20968

Going (Turf):	Sf: 0-4 GS: 0-6 **Gd: 1-12 GF: 1-24** Fm: 0-1
Distance:	**5f/6f: 5-57** 7f-8f: 0-1 9f-13f: 0-0 14f+: 0-0
Track :	**LH: 5-26** RH: 0-2 **Tight: 5-22** Gall: 0-4
Aids:	Bl: 0-3 Vi: 0-0 Tstrap: 0-0 Ckp: 0-0
Best Rating:	**86** 9/07 Ches 5f16y gd-fm

Moderate formerly fair; suited by 5f; acts on fast ground and on Polytrack; suited by a turning left-handed track; likes to race prominently.

Coconut Shy

(98) (72)**89**
3-y-o b f Bahamian Bounty-Lets Be Fair (Efisio)
G Prodromou F Butler

Placings:265110600-43 **(4372)**
2009: 6^{4}SD, 6^{3}SD,

	Starts	1st	2nd	3rd	Win & Pl
Career Total (Turf)	8	2	1	0	6891
Career Total (AW)	3	0	0	1	471
75 8/08 Wwck 5f110y	(0-75)			SFT	£3238
74 8/08 Yarm 6f3y				G-S	£2072

Total win prize-money £5310

Going (Turf):	**Sf: 1-3 GS: 1-4** Gd: 0-1 GF: 0-0 Fm: 0-0
Distance:	5f/6f: 1-8 7f-8f: 1-3 9f-13f: 0-0 14f+: 0-0
Track :	**LH: 1-4** RH: 0-0 Tight: 0-1 Gall: 0-0
Aids:	Bl: 0-0 Vi: 0-0 Tstrap: 0-0 Ckp: 0-0
Best Rating:	**89** 9/08 Donc 5f soft

Useful; stays 6f; acts on easy ground; has worn a tongue tie.

Coda Agency

(105) (71)**55**
6-y-o b g Agnes World (USA)-The Frog Lady (IRE) (Al Hareb (USA))
D W P Arbuthnot Banfield, Thompson

Placings:006/365355063232/054600/13151615-0100 **(5642)**
2009: 16^{0}SD, 16^{1}SD, 16^{0}SD, 16^{0}SD,

	Starts	1st	2nd	3rd	Win & Pl
Career Total (Turf)	13	0	1	0	1002
Career Total (AW)	20	5	1	5	13632
71 6/09 Kemp 2m	(0-65)H			STD	£2047
71 10/08 Ling 2m	(0-65)H			STD	£2047
65 5/08 Kemp 2m	(0-75)H			STD	£2590
64 3/08 Kemp 2m	(0-70)H			STD	£2590
61 2/08 Sthl 1m4f	(0-55)H			SS	£1774

Total win prize-money £11050

Going (Turf):	**Sf: 0-1 GS: 0-2 Gd: 0-4 GF: 0-6 Fm: 0-0**
Distance:	5f/6f: 0-0 7f-8f: 0-2 9f-13f: 1-12 **14f+: 4-19**
Track :	LH: 2-19 **RH: 3-13 Tight: 1-14** Gall: 0-1
Aids:	Bl: 0-0 Vi: 0-0 Tstrap: 0-0 Ckp: 0-0
Best Rating:	**71** 6/09 Kemp 2m stand

Modest; winning hurdler; stays 2m1f; acts on easy ground; goes on sand.

Coeur Brule (FR)

80(88) (47)**41**
3-y-o b g Polish Summer-Sally's Cry (FR) (Freedom Cry)
Miss S L Davison (Edgar Byrne 26/11) David Turner

Placings:00-00 **(5990)**
2009: 9^{0}G, 16^{0}SD,

	Starts	1st	2nd	3rd	Win & Pl
Career Total (Turf)	1	0	0	0	
Career Total (AW)	3	0	0	0	

Going (Turf):	**Sf: 0-0 GS: 0-0 Gd: 0-1 GF: 0-0 Fm: 0-0**
Distance:	5f/6f: 0-1 7f-8f: 0-1 9f-13f: 0-1 14f+: 0-1
Track :	LH: 0-2 RH: 0-2 Tight: 0-3 Gall: 0-0
Aids:	Bl: 0-0 Vi: 0-0 Tstrap: 0-0 Ckp: 0-0
Best Rating:	**47** 11/08 Wolv 7f32y stand

Coeur Courageux (FR)

84(99) (76)**39**
7-y-o b g Xaar-Linoise (FR) (Caerwent)
M D Squance M D Squance

Placings:0/210300/U000/600640160040/0060-000 **(1258)**
2009: 7^{0}SD, 8^{0}SD, 7^{0}G,

	Starts	1st	2nd	3rd	Win & Pl
Career Total (Turf)	17	0	0	1	4001
Career Total (AW)	13	2	1	0	9772
86 8/07 Wolv 7f32y	(0-75)H			STD	£3071
85 3/05 Ling 7f				STD	£5213

Total win prize-money £8284

Going (Turf):	**Sf: 0-2 GS: 0-2 Gd: 0-4 GF: 0-8 Fm: 0-1**
Distance:	5f/6f: 0-5 **7f-8f: 2-20** 9f-13f: 0-5 14f+: 0-0
Track :	**LH: 2-16** RH: 0-7 **Tight: 2-12** Gall: 0-1
Aids:	Bl: 0-0 Vi: 0-0 Tstrap: 0-1 Ckp: 0-1
Best Rating:	**103** 5/05 Gdwd 1m good

Useful; effective over 6f-1m; acts on a sound surface and on Polytrack.

Coeur De Lionne (IRE)

101(105) (93)**84**
5-y-o b g Invincible Spirit (IRE)-Lionne (Darshaan)
E A L Dunlop The Lamprell Partnership

Placings:622/1432011/000003-60100326 **(7720)**
2009: 9^{6}GS, 10^{0}GS, 12^{1}G, 12^{0}S, 12^{0}GF, 10^{3}SD, 13^{2}SD, 12^{6}SD,

	Starts	1st	2nd	3rd	Win & Pl
Career Total (Turf)	15	1	2	1	12244
Career Total (AW)	9	3	2	2	22662
84 8/09 NmkJ 1m4f	(0-85)H			GD	£5180
106 9/07 Kemp 1m4f	(0-95)H			STD	£6855
99 9/07 Kemp 1m3f	(0-90)H			STD	£6855
73 4/07 Kemp 1m3f				STD	£2047

Total win prize-money £20939

Going (Turf):	Sf: 0-1 GS: 0-4 **Gd: 1-7** GF: 0-3 Fm: 0-0
Distance:	5f/6f: 0-0 7f-8f: 0-3 **9f-13f: 4-20** 14f+: 0-1
Track :	LH: 0-10 **RH: 4-12** Tight: 0-5 **Gall: 1-10**
Aids:	Bl: 0-0 Vi: 0-0 Tstrap: 0-1 Ckp: 0-1
Best Rating:	**106** 9/07 Kemp 1m4f stand

Useful; stays 1m4f; goes very well on Polytrack and good ground on turf.

Cognac Boy (USA)

98(103) (63)**57**
3-y-o b/br g Hennessy (USA)-City Sleeper (USA) (Carson City (USA))
A B Haynes (R Hannon 14/1) Abacus Employment Services Ltd

Placings:0462-514540002430 **(5502)**
2009: 8^{5}SD, 7^{1}SD, 7^{4}SD, 8^{5}SD, 7^{4}SD, 6^{0}F, 7^{0}SD, 5^{0}SD, 7^{2}F, 7^{4}GF, 7^{3}GF, 7^{0}G,

	Starts	1st	2nd	3rd	Win & Pl
Career Total (Turf)	6	0	1	1	1073
Career Total (AW)	10	1	1	0	3157
63 1/09 Ling 7f				STD	£2047

Total win prize-money £2047

Going (Turf):	**Sf: 0-0 GS: 0-0 Gd: 0-1 GF: 0-3 Fm: 0-2**
Distance:	5f/6f: 0-2 **7f-8f: 1-14** 9f-13f: 0-0 14f+: 0-0
Track :	**LH: 1-11** RH: 0-2 **Tight: 1-8** Gall: 0-0
Aids:	**Bl: 1-5** Vi: 0-4 Tstrap: 0-1 Ckp: 0-1
Best Rating:	**63** 1/09 Ling 7f stand

Modest; stays 1m; effective on Polytrack; has worn blinkers.

Coiled Spring

97 **82**
3-y-o b g Observatory (USA)-Balmy (Zafonic (USA))
Mrs A J Perrett K Abdulla

Placings:364-34 **(2090)**
2009: 10^{3}G, 12^{4}G,

	Starts	1st	2nd	3rd	Win & Pl
Career Total (Turf)	5	0	0	2	1930

Going (Turf):	**Sf: 0-0 GS: 0-1 Gd: 0-3 GF: 0-1 Fm: 0-0**

Distance: 5f/6f: 0-0 7f-8f: 0-2 9f-13f: 0-3 14f+: 0-0
Track : LH: 0-2 RH: 0-1 Tight: 0-3 Gall: 0-0
Aids: Bl: 0-0 Vi: 0-0 Tstrap: 0-0 Ckp: 0-0
Best Rating: 82 9/08 NmkR 1m gd-fm

Useful; stays 1m2f; acts on good/fast ground.

Coill Glas (IRE)

(95) (57)
4-y-o b g Green Desert (USA)-Forest Express (AUS) (Kaaptive Edition (NZ))
W J Haggas Brian Wallace

Placings:0-3 (0080)
2009: 8³SD,

	Starts	1st	2nd	3rd	Win & Pl
Career Total (Turf)	0	0	0	0	
Career Total (AW)	2	0	0	1	403

Going (Turf): Sf: 0-0 GS: 0-0 Gd: 0-0 GF: 0-0 Fm: 0-0
Distance: 5f/6f: 0-0 7f-8f: 0-1 9f-13f: 0-1 14f+: 0-0
Track : LH: 0-2 RH: 0-0 Tight: 0-2 Gall: 0-0
Aids: Bl: 0-0 Vi: 0-0 Tstrap: 0-0 Ckp: 0-0
Best Rating: 57 12/08 Wolv 7f32y stand

Coin From Heaven (IRE)

99 86
2-y-o b f Invincible Spirit (IRE)-Capital Gain (FR) (Bluebird (USA))
R A Fahey G Morrin

Placings:310 (7147)
2009: 6³GF, 6¹GF, 6⁰G,

	Starts	1st	2nd	3rd	Win & Pl
Career Total (Turf)	3	1	0	1	4367
81	10/09 Rdcr	6f		G-F	£3885

Total win prize-money £3886

Going (Turf): Sf: 0-0 GS: 0-0 Gd: 0-1 **GF: 1-2** Fm: 0-0
Distance: **5f/6f: 1-3** 7f-8f: 0-0 9f-13f: 0-0 14f+: 0-0
Track : LH: 0-0 RH: 0-0 Tight: 0-0 Gall: 0-0
Aids: Bl: 0-0 Vi: 0-0 Tstrap: 0-0 Ckp: 0-0
Best Rating: 86 10/09 NmkR 6f good

Fair filly; effective at 6f; acts on fast ground.

Coin Of The Realm (IRE)

105(104) (78)93
4-y-o b g Galileo (IRE)-Common Knowledge (Rainbow Quest (USA))
G L Moore B Siddle & B D Haynes

Placings:2432140-4100 (6662)
2009: 12⁴G, 12¹G, 12⁰GF, 12⁰GS,

	Starts	1st	2nd	3rd	Win & Pl
Career Total (Turf)	9	1	2	1	16519
Career Total (AW)	2	1	0	0	2590
93	6/09 Epsm	1m4f10y (0-100)H		GD	£12462
78	7/08 Ling	1m4f		STD	£2590

Total win prize-money £15052

Going (Turf): Sf: 0-3 GS: 0-1 **Gd: 1-4** GF: 0-1 Fm: 0-0
Distance: 5f/6f: 0-0 7f-8f: 0-0 **9f-13f: 2-11** 14f+: 0-0
Track : **LH: 2-7** RH: 0-3 **Tight: 2-5** Gall: 0-2
Aids: Bl: 0-0 Vi: 0-0 Tstrap: 0-0 Ckp: 0-0
Best Rating: 93 6/09 Epsm 1m4f10y good

Useful; effective at around 1m4f; acts on most ground and on Polytrack.

Cojo (IRE)

92(91) (47)76
2-y-o b f Rock Of Gibraltar (IRE)-Love Excelling (FR) (Polish Precedent (USA))
B J Meehan Exors of the Late F C T Wilson

Placings:625 (7140)
2009: 6⁶GF, 6²S, 8⁵SD,

	Starts	1st	2nd	3rd	Win & Pl
Career Total (Turf)	2	0	1	0	867
Career Total (AW)	1	0	0	0	0

Going (Turf): Sf: 0-1 GS: 0-0 Gd: 0-0 GF: 0-1 Fm: 0-0
Distance: 5f/6f: 0-0 7f-8f: 0-2 9f-13f: 0-1 14f+: 0-0
Track : LH: 0-1 RH: 0-0 Tight: 0-1 Gall: 0-0
Aids: Bl: 0-0 Vi: 0-0 Tstrap: 0-0 Ckp: 0-0
Best Rating: 76 10/09 Sals 6f212y soft

Fair; stays 7f; acts on soft ground.

Colangnik (USA)

88(100) (72)52
3-y-o b f Sky Classic (CAN)-Rainbow Strike (USA) (Smart Strike (CAN))
J R Best Folan Lees Halligan

Placings:0333-00**6**00**6**00 (7392)
2009: 10⁰G, 9⁰GF, 10⁶SD, 12⁰SD, 10⁰SS, 8⁶SD, 10⁰SD, 10⁰SD,

	Starts	1st	2nd	3rd	Win & Pl
Career Total (Turf)	3	0	0	0	
Career Total (AW)	9	0	0	3	1430

Going (Turf): Sf: 0-0 GS: 0-1 Gd: 0-1 GF: 0-1 Fm: 0-0
Distance: 5f/6f: 0-1 7f-8f: 0-4 9f-13f: 0-7 14f+: 0-0
Track : LH: 0-7 RH: 0-4 Tight: 0-7 Gall: 0-1
Aids: Bl: 0-0 Vi: 0-2 Tstrap: 0-0 Ckp: 0-0
Best Rating: 72 11/08 Kemp 1m stand

Fair; stays 1m and acts on Polytrack.

Cold Mountain (IRE)

93 51
7-y-o b g Inchinor-Streak Of Silver (USA) (Dynaformer (USA))
J W Mullins Woodford Valley Racing

Placings:0/0005000/0-3 (4935)
2009: 18³G,

	Starts	1st	2nd	3rd	Win & Pl
Career Total (Turf)	10	0	0	1	337

Going (Turf): Sf: 0-1 GS: 0-1 Gd: 0-3 GF: 0-5 Fm: 0-0
Distance: 5f/6f: 0-0 7f-8f: 0-3 9f-13f: 0-4 14f+: 0-3
Track : LH: 0-2 RH: 0-6 Tight: 0-1 Gall: 0-0
Aids: Bl: 0-1 Vi: 0-0 Tstrap: 0-4 Ckp: 0-4
Best Rating: 57 5/05 Gowr 1m gd-fm

Cold Quest (USA)

91 (86)97
5-y-o b g Seeking The Gold (USA)-Polaire (IRE) (Polish Patriot (USA))
Miss L A Perratt Ken McGarrity

Placings:13/30/20-000660 (6984)
2009: 10⁰G, 10⁰GF, 9⁰GS, 9⁶G, 9⁶GF, 7⁰G,

	Starts	1st	2nd	3rd	Win & Pl
Career Total (Turf)	11	1	1	1	11409
Career Total (AW)	1	0	0	1	1059
81	8/06 Leic	7f9y		G-S	£7790

Total win prize-money £7790

Going (Turf): Sf: 0-1 **GS: 1-2** Gd: 0-6 GF: 0-2 Fm: 0-0
Distance: 5f/6f: 0-0 **7f-8f: 1-3** 9f-13f: 0-9 14f+: 0-0
Track : LH: 0-5 RH: 0-6 Tight: 0-5 Gall: 0-3
Aids: Bl: 0-0 Vi: 0-0 Tstrap: 0-2 Ckp: 0-2
Best Rating: 98 7/07 NmkJ 1m2f good

Very useful; stays 1m2f; acts on good and easy ground; also goes on Polytrack; has worn cheekpieces.

Cold Turkey

(111) (93)98
9-y-o b/br g Polar Falcon (USA)-South Rock (Rock City)
G L Moore A Grinter

Placings:04540/**65**0142200**11112**/**113241**2400**205**/**13124**
102003**1**/**4511**0400**2**/0**64**/**3**0**1**0-00**6**60**3** (1435)
2009: 10⁰SD, 12⁰SD, 10⁶SD, 10⁶SD, 12⁰SD, 16³SD,

	Starts	1st	2nd	3rd	Win & Pl
Career Total (Turf)	25	4	3	0	45938
Career Total (AW)	41	11	6	5	114865
93	2/08 Ling	1m4f	(0-85)H	STD	£4100
97	4/06 Kemp	2m	(0-105)H	STD	£11217
99	3/06 Ling	1m5f	(0-100)H	STD	£12464
98	12/05 Wolv	1m4f50y	(0-100)H	STD	£11458
98	3/05 Kemp	2m	(0-105)H	G-S	£11988
93	2/05 Ling	1m4f	(0-100)H	STD	£14807
95	1/05 Ling	1m4f	(0-85)H	STD	£6741
91	4/04 Epsm	1m4f10y	C(0-95)H	SFT	£15892
97	1/04 Ling	1m4f	C(0-95)H	STD	£10637
87	1/04 Ling	1m4f	C(0-90)H	STD	£7293
83	11/03 Ling	1m4f	F(0-80)H	STD	£3234
83	11/03 Ling	1m5f	F(0-75)H	STD	£2257
74	10/03 Ling	1m4f	E(0-70)H	STD	£2261
78	10/03 Gdwd	1m3f	E	G-F	£2982
71	7/03 Leic	1m1f218y	E	GD	£3454

Total win prize-money £120792

Going (Turf): Sf: 1-4 GS: 1-6 Gd: 1-4 GF: 1-10 Fm: 0-1
Distance: 5f/6f: 0-1 7f-8f: 0-5 **9f-13f: 13-47** 14f+: 2-13
Track : **LH: 11-46** RH: 4-14 **Tight: 12-45** Gall: 0-6
Aids: Bl: 0-0 Vi: 0-0 Tstrap: 0-0 Ckp: 0-0
Best Rating: 99 11/06 Ling 1m4f stand

Useful on turf and Polytrack; winner of the 2005 and 2006 Queen's Prize; effective from 1m4f to 2m; acts on any ground; likes to be held up.

Coleorton Choice

101(92) (74)87
3-y-o ch c Choisir (AUS)-Tayovullin (IRE) (Shalford (IRE))
K A Ryan Coleorton Moor Racing

Placings:530311-2451060 (7227)
2009: 5²F, 6⁴GF, 6⁵G, 6¹G, 6⁰G, 6⁶SD, 6⁰SD,

	Starts	1st	2nd	3rd	Win & Pl
Career Total (Turf)	11	3	1	2	24916
Career Total (AW)	2	0	0	0	176
87	5/09 Ayr	6f	(0-85)H	GD	£5828
84	9/08 Ayr	6f	(0-95)	HVY	£9066
78	8/08 Ripn	6f		G-S	£4533

Total win prize-money £19427

Going (Turf): Sf: 1-2 GS: 1-1 Gd: 1-4 GF: 0-2 Fm: 0-2
Distance: **5f/6f: 3-13** 7f-8f: 0-0 9f-13f: 0-0 14f+: 0-0
Track : LH: 0-2 RH: 0-1 Tight: 0-0 Gall: 0-0
Aids: Bl: 0-0 Vi: 0-0 Tstrap: 0-0 Ckp: 0-0
Best Rating: 87 5/09 Ayr 6f good

Useful; effective over 5f-6f; acts on any ground.

Coleorton Dancer

94(103) (81)74

7-y-o ch g Danehill Dancer (IRE)-Tayovullin (IRE) (Shalford (IRE))

K A Ryan A C Henson

Placings:04440111100/15240500/2400040/000055203/3640456443304300-00 **(2852)**

2009: 5^{0}GF, 6^{0}G,

	Starts	1st	2nd	3rd	Win & Pl
Career Total (Turf)	42	5	2	2	66070
Career Total (AW)	12	0	1	3	2456

99	4/05	Ripn	6f	(0-95)H	SFT	£8940
89	8/04	NmkJ	6f	B	G-S	£14040
82	8/04	Ches	5f16y	D	GD	£6873
87	8/04	Nott	5f13y	E	GD	£3916
80	8/04	Thsk	5f	E	G-S	£4192

Total win prize-money £37963

Going (Turf): Sf: 1-7 **GS: 2-11 Gd: 2-15** GF: 0-9 Fm: 0-0
Distance: **5f/6f: 5-42** 7f-8f: 0-11 9f-13f: 0-1 14f+: 0-0
Track : **LH: 1-19** RH: 0-2 **Tight: 1-12** Gall: 0-0
Aids: Bl: 0-5 Vi: 0-0 Tstrap: 0-8 Ckp: 0-8
Best Rating: **105** 5/05 NmkR 6f gd-sft

Very useful at his best; now modest; effective over 5f-6f; acts on good and softer ground and Fibresand; has worn blinkers and cheekpieces.

Colepeper

104 90

2-y-o b c Cape Cross (IRE)-Autumn Wealth (IRE) (Cadeaux Genereux)

M Johnston Sheikh Hamdan Bin Mohammed Al Maktoum

Placings:2015 **(6643)**

2009: 6^{2}S, 7^{0}S, 5^{1}GF, 6^{5}G,

	Starts	1st	2nd	3rd	Win & Pl
Career Total (Turf)	4	1	1	0	5042

87	9/09	Catt	5f212y	G-F	£3885

Total win prize-money £3886

Going (Turf): Sf: 0-2 GS: 0-0 Gd: 0-1 **GF: 1-1** Fm: 0-0
Distance: **5f/6f: 1-2** 7f-8f: 0-2 9f-13f: 0-0 14f+: 0-0
Track : **LH: 1-2** RH: 0-0 **Tight: 1-2** Gall: 0-0
Aids: Bl: 0-0 Vi: 0-0 Tstrap: 0-0 Ckp: 0-0
Best Rating: **90** 10/09 York 6f good

Useful; stays 6f; acts on most ground.

Colin Staite

(26) 21

3-y-o b g Superior Premium-Downclose Duchess (King's Signet (USA))

R Brotherton Arthur Clayton

Placings:0050-0 **(0092)**

2009: 7^{0}SD,

	Starts	1st	2nd	3rd	Win & Pl
Career Total (Turf)	3	0	0	0	0
Career Total (AW)	2	0	0	0	

Going (Turf): **Sf: 0-1 GS: 0-0 Gd: 0-0 GF: 0-1 Fm: 0-1**
Distance: 5f/6f: 0-3 7f-8f: 0-2 9f-13f: 0-0 14f+: 0-0
Track : LH: 0-3 RH: 0-0 Tight: 0-1 Gall: 0-1
Aids: Bl: 0-1 Vi: 0-0 Tstrap: 0-0 Ckp: 0-0
Best Rating: **21** 7/08 Chep 5f16y soft

Collateral Damage (IRE)

109(102) (92)102

6-y-o b g Orpen (USA)-Jay Gee (IRE) (Second Set (IRE))

T D Easterby Middleham Park Racing Xxv

Placings:342315/021536232/00505330600/150454654-420005341111311 **(7294)**

2009: 8^{4}GF, 8^{2}G, 8^{0}GF, 8^{0}GS, 7^{0}GF, 8^{5}GF, 8^{3}G, 8^{4}GF, 8^{1}S, 8^{1}GF, 8^{1}G, 8^{1}GF, 8^{3}SD, 8^{1}S, 7^{1}S,

	Starts	1st	2nd	3rd	Win & Pl
Career Total (Turf)	47	9	5	6	133484
Career Total (AW)	3	0	0	2	2410

102	11/09	Donc	7f	(0-105)H	SFT	£25904
99	10/09	Ayr	1m	(0-90)H	SFT	£9714
92	10/09	Rdcr	1m	H	G-F	£18693
89	9/09	Ayr	1m	(0-85)H	GD	£6152
84	9/09	Rdcr	1m	(0-85)H	G-F	£5180
86	8/09	Ayr	1m	(0-80)H	SFT	£5828
89	3/08	Pont	1m4y	(0-95)H	G-S	£7478
93	5/06	York	7f	(0-95)H	SFT	£9715
79	10/05	Newc	7f		SFT	£3857

Total win prize-money £92524

Going (Turf): **Sf: 5-12** GS: 1-8 Gd: 1-14 GF: 2-13 Fm: 0-0
Distance: 5f/6f: 0-2 **7f-8f: 8-25** 9f-13f: 1-23 14f+: 0-0
Track : **LH: 6-26** RH: 0-12 Tight: 0-14 **Gall: 1-7**
Aids: Bl: 0-2 Vi: 0-0 Tstrap: 0-0 Ckp: 0-0
Best Rating: **102** 11/09 Donc 7f soft

Useful; effective at around 7f-1m2f; acts on fast and soft ground; has worn blinkers and a tongue tie.

College Land Boy

79 47

5-y-o b g Cois Na Tine (IRE)-Welcome Lu (Most Welcome)

A Kirtley A Kirtley

Placings:6/0000/066006000-0 **(6184)**

2009: 9^{0}GF,

	Starts	1st	2nd	3rd	Win & Pl
Career Total (Turf)	15	0	0	0	0

Going (Turf): **Sf: 0-1 GS: 0-4 Gd: 0-3 GF: 0-7 Fm: 0-0**
Distance: 5f/6f: 0-4 7f-8f: 0-5 9f-13f: 0-5 14f+: 0-1
Track : LH: 0-7 RH: 0-3 Tight: 0-6 Gall: 0-1
Aids: Bl: 0-0 Vi: 0-1 Tstrap: 0-0 Ckp: 0-0
Best Rating: **61** 8/06 Hayd 6f gd-fm

Collingwood (IRE)

96(102) (71)65

7-y-o br g Machiavellian (USA)-Almaaseh (IRE) (Dancing Brave (USA))

T M Walsh Mrs Helen Walsh

Placings:31/001033/2250554-3053160 **(6129a)**

2009: 5^{3}SD, 12^{0}SW, 8^{5}SD, 5^{3}SD, 7^{1}GF, 6^{6}SD, 7^{0}G,

	Starts	1st	2nd	3rd	Win & Pl
Career Total (Turf)	8	1	0	2	6841
Career Total (AW)	14	2	2	3	14402

65	6/09	Leop	7f	(50-70)H	G-F	£5702
61	9/07	Layt	7f		STD	£4902
63	9/06	Layt	7f		STD	£5003

Total win prize-money £15608

Going (Turf): Sf: 0-0 GS: 0-0 Gd: 0-3 **GF: 1-3** Fm: 0-1
Distance: 5f/6f: 0-8 **7f-8f: 3-10** 9f-13f: 0-3 14f+: 0-1
Track : **LH: 3-18** RH: 0-0 Tight: 0-1 Gall: 0-0
Aids: Bl: 0-10 Vi: 0-0 Tstrap: 0-0 Ckp: 0-0
Best Rating: **71** 5/09 Dund 5f stand

Modest sort; effective at 7f but won a bumper in early career; has worn a tongue tie.

Colombard (IRE)

93(99) (65)57

4-y-o b g Almutawakel-Searching Star (Rainbow Quest (USA))

Patrick Morris W J Crosbie

Placings:01/4400000-0045064366252444430 **(7889)**

2009: 7^{0}F, 6^{0}SD, 6^{4}F, 6^{5}GF, 7^{0}SD, 7^{6}GF, 7^{4}G, 6^{3}SD, 6^{6}GF, 7^{6}SD, 6^{2}SD, 5^{5}SD, 5^{2}SD, 5^{4}SD, 6^{4}SD, 5^{4}SD, 6^{4}SD, 5^{3}SD, 5^{0}SD,

	Starts	1st	2nd	3rd	Win & Pl
Career Total (Turf)	10	0	0	0	781
Career Total (AW)	18	1	2	2	7966

78	10/07	Dund	6f	STD	£5836

Total win prize-money £5836

Going (Turf): **Sf: 0-0 GS: 0-0 Gd: 0-1 GF: 0-5 Fm: 0-2**
Distance: **5f/6f: 1-16** 7f-8f: 0-12 9f-13f: 0-0 14f+: 0-0
Track : LH: 0-18 RH: 0-2 Tight: 0-11 Gall: 0-0
Aids: Bl: 0-7 Vi: 0-6 Tstrap: 0-0 Ckp: 0-0
Best Rating: **78** 10/07 Dund 6f stand

Moderate; stays 6f; acts on fast ground; goes on Polytrack; has worn a visor and blinkers.

Colonel Carter (IRE)

97 80

2-y-o br c Danehill Dancer (IRE)-Pina Colada (Sabrehill (USA))

B J Meehan Mrs B V Sangster

Placings:34 **(6592)**

2009: 7^{3}GF, 8^{4}GS,

	Starts	1st	2nd	3rd	Win & Pl
Career Total (Turf)	2	0	0	1	987

Going (Turf): **Sf: 0-0 GS: 0-1 Gd: 0-0 GF: 0-1 Fm: 0-0**
Distance: 5f/6f: 0-0 7f-8f: 0-1 9f-13f: 0-1 14f+: 0-0
Track : LH: 0-1 RH: 0-0 Tight: 0-0 Gall: 0-0
Aids: Bl: 0-0 Vi: 0-0 Tstrap: 0-0 Ckp: 0-0
Best Rating: **80** 9/09 Newb 7f gd-fm

Useful prospect; effective over 7f; acts on fast ground.

Colonel Flay

104(100) (71)79

5-y-o ch g Danehill Dancer (IRE)-Bobbie Dee (Blakeney)

Mrs P N Dutfield John Boswell

Placings:200/360055/1625316-1523355 **(7066)**

2009: 14^{1}F, 14^{5}G, 14^{2}G, 14^{3}GF, 14^{3}G, 12^{5}GF, 12^{5}SD,

	Starts	1st	2nd	3rd	Win & Pl
Career Total (Turf)	20	3	3	4	17597
Career Total (AW)	3	0	0	0	0

78	5/09	Nott	1m6f15y	(0-85)H	FRM	£6476
75	8/08	Sals	1m6f21y	(0-70)H	G-F	£3238
73	5/08	Sthl	1m4f	(0-65)H	GD	£1910

Total win prize-money £11625

Going (Turf): Sf: 0-2 GS: 0-2 **Gd: 1-7 GF: 1-8 Fm: 1-1**
Distance: 5f/6f: 0-1 7f-8f: 0-2 9f-13f: 1-10 **14f+: 2-10**
Track : **LH: 2-7** RH: 1-14 **Tight: 2-13** Gall: 0-2
Aids: Bl: 0-0 Vi: 0-0 Tstrap: 0-0 Ckp: 0-0
Best Rating: **79** 6/09 Sals 1m6f21y good

Fair; suited by 1m4f-1m6f; acts on a sound surface; also goes on Fibresand.

Colonel Henry

(86) (50)

2-y-o br g Imperial Dancer-Spark Of Life (Rainbows For Life (CAN))

S Dow R Gurney

Placings:0 **(7763)**

2009: 8^{0}SD,

	Starts	1st	2nd	3rd	Win & Pl
Career Total (Turf)	0	0	0	0	
Career Total (AW)	1	0	0	0	

Going (Turf): **Sf: 0-0 GS: 0-0 Gd: 0-0 GF: 0-0 Fm: 0-0**
Distance: 5f/6f: 0-0 7f-8f: 0-1 9f-13f: 0-0 14f+: 0-0
Track : LH: 0-0 RH: 0-1 Tight: 0-0 Gall: 0-0
Aids: Bl: 0-0 Vi: 0-0 Tstrap: 0-0 Ckp: 0-0
Best Rating: **50** 12/09 Kemp 1m stand

Colonel Mak

99 91

2-y-o br g Makbul-Colonel's Daughter (Colonel Collins (USA))

D H Brown Norton Common Farm Racing

Placings:0312134365 **(7016)**

2009: 6^{0}GF, 6^{3}GF, 6^{1}GF, 6^{2}GS, 6^{1}G, 6^{3}GS, 6^{4}GF, 6^{3}GF, 6^{6}GF, 6^{5}GS,

	Starts	1st	2nd	3rd	Win & Pl
Career Total (Turf)	**10**	**2**	**1**	**3**	**14291**

91 7/09 Haml 6f5y GD £5180
76 6/09 Haml 6f5y G-F £2266
Total win prize-money £7448

Going (Turf): Sf: 0-0 GS: 0-3 **Gd: 1-1 GF: 1-6** Fm: 0-0
Distance: 5f/6f: 0-7 **7f-8f: 2-3** 9f-13f: 0-0 14f+: 0-0
Track : LH: 0-1 RH: 0-0 Tight: 0-0 Gall: 0-0
Aids: Bl: 0-0 Vi: 0-0 Tstrap: 0-0 Ckp: 0-0
Best Rating: **91** 10/09 Donc 6f gd-sft

Very useful; stays 6f; acts on good and faster ground.

Colonel Munro (IRE)

(71) (29)

2-y-o b c Azamour (IRE)-Zooming (IRE) (Indian Ridge)

D Nicholls Mrs C C Regalado-Gonzalez

Placings:0 **(6431)**

2009: 8^{0}SD,

	Starts	1st	2nd	3rd	Win & Pl
Career Total (Turf)	0	0	0	0	
Career Total (AW)	1	0	0	0	

Going (Turf): **Sf: 0-0 GS: 0-0 Gd: 0-0 GF: 0-0 Fm: 0-0**
Distance: 5f/6f: 0-0 7f-8f: 0-0 9f-13f: 0-1 14f+: 0-0
Track : LH: 0-1 RH: 0-0 Tight: 0-1 Gall: 0-0
Aids: Bl: 0-0 Vi: 0-0 Tstrap: 0-0 Ckp: 0-0
Best Rating: **29** 10/09 Wolv 1m141y stand

Colonel Sherman (USA)

85(110) (74)54

4-y-o b/br h Mr Greeley (USA)-Spankin 'n Fannin (USA) (Lear Fan (USA))

P A Kirby (L A Dace 15/4) Ms Toni Nash

Placings:003422-1233000060 **(7840)**

2009: 10^{1}SD, 10^{2}SD, 12^{3}SD, 8^{3}SD, 8^{0}G, 10^{0}GS, 8^{0}SD, 12^{0}SD, 9^{6}SD, 12^{0}SS,

	Starts	1st	2nd	3rd	Win & Pl
Career Total (Turf)	5	0	0	1	289
Career Total (AW)	11	1	3	2	4800

71 1/09 Ling 1m2f (0-55)H STD £2047
Total win prize-money £2047

Going (Turf): **Sf: 0-0 GS: 0-2 Gd: 0-2 GF: 0-1 Fm: 0-0**
Distance: 5f/6f: 0-1 7f-8f: 0-1 **9f-13f: 1-14** 14f+: 0-0
Track : **LH: 1-9** RH: 0-6 **Tight: 1-8** Gall: 0-1
Aids: Bl: 0-0 Vi: 0-0 Tstrap: 0-0 Ckp: 0-0
Best Rating: **74** 2/09 Kemp 1m4f stand

Moderate; effective over 1m4f; acts on good ground and on Polytrack.

Colorus (IRE)

103(105) (84)77

6-y-o b g Night Shift (USA)-Duck Over (Warning)

W J H Ratcliffe J Sheard & W J S Ratcliffe

Placings:14300/00060060/010100600350/53030252503 04042-003462102510001060102320 **(7866)**

2009: 5^{0}SD, 5^{0}SD, 5^{3}SD, 5^{4}SD, 5^{6}SD, 5^{2}SD, 5^{1}SD, 5^{0}GF, 5^{2}SD, 5^{5}SD, 5^{1}G, 5^{0}G, 5^{0}GF, 5^{0}GF, 5^{1}GF, 5^{0}G, 5^{6}GF, 5^{0}G, 5^{1}SD, 5^{0}SD, 5^{2}SD, 5^{3}SD, 5^{2}SD,

	Starts	1st	2nd	3rd	Win & Pl
Career Total (Turf)	**47**	**4**	**2**	**5**	**22929**
Career Total (AW)	**19**	**3**	**5**	**2**	**17605**

77 10/09 Sthl 5f (0-70)H STD £3412
77 9/09 Yarm 5f43y (0-85)H G-F £5046
73 7/09 Wind 5f10y (0-75)H GD £2729
74 3/09 Sthl 5f (0-70)H STD £3412
85 5/07 Thsk 5f (0-85)H GD £5181
76 4/07 Ripn 5f (0-75)H G-F £3238
77 7/05 Sthl 5f STD £3770
Total win prize-money £26791

Going (Turf): Sf: 0-5 GS: 0-6 **Gd: 2-17 GF: 2-17** Fm: 0 2
Distance: **5f/6f: 7-63** 7f-8f: 0-3 9f-13f: 0-0 14f+: 0-0
Track : LH: 0-9 RH: 0-2 Tight: 0-5 **Gall: 1-3**
Aids: Bl: 0-2 Vi: 0-1 Tstrap: 4-27 Ckp: 4-27
Best Rating: **92** 8/05 York 5f good

Fair; effective over 5f; acts on fast ground and on sand; has worn blinkers, cheekpieces and a visor.

Colour Of Money

(100) (65)46

4-y-o br g Kyllachy-Euridice (IRE) (Woodman (USA))

S A Callaghan Michael Tabor

Placings:000-1540 **(2686)**

2009: 7^{1}SD, 7^{5}SD, 8^{4}SD, 7^{0}SD,

	Starts	1st	2nd	3rd	Win & Pl
Career Total (Turf)	3	0	0	0	
Career Total (AW)	4	1	0	0	2047

63 3/09 Ling 7f (0-55)H STD £2047
Total win prize-money £2047

Going (Turf): **Sf: 0-0 GS: 0-2 Gd: 0-0 GF: 0-1 Fm: 0-0**
Distance: 5f/6f: 0-2 **7f-8f: 1-5** 9f-13f: 0-0 14f+: 0-0
Track : **LH: 1-4** RH: 0-0 **Tight: 1-4** Gall: 0-0
Aids: Bl: 0-0 Vi: 0-0 Tstrap: 0-1 Ckp: 0-1
Best Rating: **65** 5/09 Ling 1m stand

Modest half-brother to seven winners, including Hazyview, stays 1m; acts on Polytrack.

Colour Trooper (IRE)

100(99) (67)75

4-y-o ch g Traditionally (USA)-Viola Royale (IRE) (Royal Academy (USA))

D E Pipe (P Winkworth 10/7) W Clifford

Placings:0/05100-5500 **(3811)**

2009: 11^{5}G, 10^{5}G, 11^{0}GF, 10^{0}GF,

	Starts	1st	2nd	3rd	Win & Pl
Career Total (Turf)	7	0	0	0	0
Career Total (AW)	3	1	0	0	2047

67 9/08 Ling 1m STD £2047
Total win prize-money £2047

Going (Turf): **Sf: 0-0 GS: 0-0 Gd: 0-3 GF: 0-4 Fm: 0-0**
Distance: 5f/6f: 0-0 **7f-8f: 1-4** 9f-13f: 0-6 14f+: 0-0
Track : **LH: 1-6** RH: 0-3 **Tight: 1-7** Gall: 0-1
Aids: Bl: 0-2 Vi: 0-0 Tstrap: 0-1 Ckp: 0-1
Best Rating: **75** 8/08 Sals 1m1f198y gd-fm

Fair; effective over 1m-1m2f; acts on Polytrack; has worn blinkers.

Colourful Move

96(103) (67)63

4-y-o b c Rainbow Quest (USA)-Flit (USA) (Lyphard (USA))

P G Murphy Mrs Dianne Murphy

Placings:6023-431402004335 **(7750)**

2009: 12^{4}SS, 16^{3}SD, 16^{1}SD, 14^{4}GF, 16^{0}G, 16^{2}SD, 16^{0}G, 16^{0}SD, 16^{4}SD, 16^{3}SD, 14^{3}SD, 13^{5}SD,

	Starts	1st	2nd	3rd	Win & Pl
Career Total (Turf)	5	0	0	0	241
Career Total (AW)	11	1	2	4	4602

65 4/09 Kemp 2m (0-65)H STD £1942
Total win prize-money £1943

Going (Turf): **Sf: 0-1 GS: 0-0 Gd: 0-2 GF: 0-2 Fm: 0-0**
Distance: 5f/6f: 0-0 7f-8f: 0-0 9f-13f: 0-5 **14f+: 1-11**
Track : LH: 0-11 **RH: 1-5** Tight: 0-6 Gall: 0-1
Aids: Bl: 0-0 Vi: 0-0 Tstrap: 0-0 Ckp: 0-0
Best Rating: **67** 11/08 Sthl 1m4f stand

Moderate; effective over 1m4f; acts on Fibresand and Polytrack.

Coloursoftheglen (IRE)

98(91) (75)83

2-y-o ch c Le Vie Dei Colori-Gertie Laurie (Lomond (USA))

Eddie Truman (Tom Dascombe 31/7) Michael D Lewis

Placings:221250

2009: 6^{2}S, 7^{2}GF, 7^{1}SD, 7^{2}GS, 7^{5}G, 8^{0}F,

	Starts	1st	2nd	3rd	Win & Pl
Career Total (Turf)	5	0	3	0	3215
Career Total (AW)	1	1	0	0	3886

75 6/09 Wolv 7f32y STD £3885
Total win prize-money £3886

Going (Turf): **Sf: 0-1 GS: 0-1 Gd: 0-1 GF: 0-1 Fm: 0-1**
Distance: 5f/6f: 0-1 **7f-8f: 1-5** 9f-13f: 0-0 14f+: 0-0
Track : **LH: 1-2** RH: 0-1 **Tight: 1-1** Gall: 0-0
Aids: Bl: 0-0 Vi: 0-0 Tstrap: 0-0 Ckp: 0-0
Best Rating: **83** 11/09 Holl 1m firm

Fair; stays 7f; acts on most ground and on Polytrack.

Comadoir (IRE)

97(100) (81)77

3-y-o ch c Medecis-Hymn Of The Dawn (USA) (Phone Trick (USA))

Miss Jo Crowley Mrs Liz Nelson

Placings:2222525323-13406510606 **(7656)**

2009: 5^{1}SD, 5^{3}SD, 6^{4}SD, 6^{0}SD, 7^{6}SD, 7^{5}GF, 6^{1}SD, 6^{0}SD, 6^{6}SD, 6^{0}SD, 6^{6}SD,

	Starts	1st	2nd	3rd	Win & Pl
Career Total (Turf)	7	0	5	0	10563
Career Total (AW)	14	2	1	3	8613

81 7/09 Ling 6f (0-75)H STD £2729
79 1/09 Ling 5f STD £2729
Total win prize-money £5460

Going (Turf): **Sf: 0-3 GS: 0-0 Gd: 0-0 GF: 0-3 Fm: 0-1**
Distance: **5f/6f: 2-17** 7f-8f: 0-4 9f-13f: 0-0 14f+: 0-0
Track : **LH: 2-13** RH: 0-6 **Tight: 2-8** Gall: 0-1
Aids: Bl: 0-2 Vi: 0-0 Tstrap: 0-0 Ckp: 0-0
Best Rating: **81** 7/09 Ling 6f stand

Fair; stays 6f; acts on most ground and on Polytrack.

Come And Go (UAE)

100 81

3-y-o b g Halling (USA)-Woven Silk (USA) (Danzig (USA))

G A Swinbank B Valentine

Placings:03140-05562020 **(5340)**

2009: 7^{0}GF, 10^{5}GF, 8^{5}S, 8^{6}GF, 6^{2}G, 6^{0}S, 6^{2}GF, 7^{0}GS,

	Starts	1st	2nd	3rd	Win & Pl
Career Total (Turf)	13	1	2	1	10359

78 8/08 Hayd 6f G-S £3885
Total win prize-money £3886

Going (Turf): Sf: 0-4 **GS: 1-3** Gd: 0-1 GF: 0-5 Fm: 0-0
Distance: **5f/6f: 1-7** 7f-8f: 0-5 9f-13f: 0-1 14f+: 0-0
Track : LH: 0-5 RH: 0-1 Tight: 0-3 Gall: 0-1
Aids: Bl: 0-0 Vi: 0-0 Tstrap: 0-0 Ckp: 0-0
Best Rating: **81** 8/08 Ripn 6f gd-sft

Useful; effective at 6-7f and acts on most ground.

Come April

89 (79)67

5-y-o b m Singspiel (IRE)-So Admirable (Suave Dancer (USA))

P R Webber Denford Stud

Placings:1/00 **(6900)**

2009: 12^{0}G, 10^{0}GF,

	Starts	1st	2nd	3rd	Win & Pl
Career Total (Turf)	2	0	0	0	
Career Total (AW)	1	1	0	0	2915

79 6/07 Ling 1m2f STD £2914
Total win prize-money £2915

Going (Turf): **Sf: 0-0 GS: 0-0 Gd: 0-1 GF: 0-1 Fm: 0-0**
Distance: 5f/6f: 0-0 7f-8f: 0-0 **9f-13f: 1-3** 14f+: 0-0
Track : **LH: 1-2** RH: 0-1 **Tight: 1-2** Gall: 0-0
Aids: Bl: 0-0 Vi: 0-0 Tstrap: 0-0 Ckp: 0-0
Best Rating: **79** 6/07 Ling 1m2f stand

Come On Buckers (IRE)

89(100) (62)62

3-y-o ch g Fath (USA)-Deerussa (IRE) (Jareer (USA))

E J Creighton The Vixens

Placings:4413220002-0532066024150620 **(7224)**

2009: 5^{0}SD, 6^{5}F, 5^{3}SD, 5^{2}F, 6^{0}GF, 6^{6}SD, 7^{6}S, 8^{0}G, 7^{2}SD, 7^{4}SD, 6^{1}SD, 5^{5}SD, 5^{0}SD, 5^{6}SD, 5^{2}SD, 5^{0}SD,

	Starts	1st	2nd	3rd	Win & Pl
Career Total (Turf)	12	1	3	1	4355
Career Total (AW)	14	1	3	1	4365

62 9/09 Kemp 6f (0-60)H STD £2047
59 5/08 Chep 6f16y SFT £1910
Total win prize-money £3958

Going (Turf): **Sf: 1-5** GS: 0-0 Gd: 0-1 GF: 0-4 Fm: 0-2
Distance: 5f/6f: 1-15 7f-8f: 1-9 9f-13f: 0-2 14f+: 0-0
Track : LH: 0-12 **RH: 1-4** Tight: 0-9 Gall: 0-1
Aids: **Bl: 1-7** Vi: 0-3 Tstrap: 0-1 Ckp: 0-1
Best Rating: **62** 10/09 Wolv 5f216y stand

Modest; effective over 5f-6f; acts on fast ground and on Polytrack; has worn blinkers.

Come On Safari (IRE)

93(93) (71)80

2-y-o b g Antonius Pius (USA)-Calypso Dancer (FR) (Celtic Swing)

P Winkworth Rupert Williams

Placings:0415 **(7434)**

2009: 6^{0}GF, 5^{4}G, 7^{1}GF, 8^{5}SD,

	Starts	1st	2nd	3rd	Win & Pl
Career Total (Turf)	3	1	0	0	2884
Career Total (AW)	1	0	0	0	0

80 8/09 Folk 7f G-F £2729
Total win prize-money £2730

Going (Turf): Sf: 0-0 GS: 0-0 Gd: 0-1 **GF: 1-2** Fm: 0-0
Distance: 5f/6f: 0-2 **7f-8f: 1-2** 9f-13f: 0-0 14f+: 0-0
Track : LH: 0-2 RH: 0-0 Tight: 0-1 Gall: 0-2
Aids: Bl: 0-0 Vi: 0-0 Tstrap: 0-0 Ckp: 0-0
Best Rating: **80** 8/09 Folk 7f gd-fm

Useful; effective over 7f; acts on fast ground.

Come On Toby

(81) (21)30

3-y-o b g Piccolo-Fleeting Moon (Fleetwood (IRE))

Miss Amy Weaver Philip Mclaughlin

Placings:000-0 **(0839)**

2009: 8^{0}SD,

	Starts	1st	2nd	3rd	Win & Pl
Career Total (Turf)	3	0	0	0	
Career Total (AW)	1	0	0	0	

Going (Turf): **Sf: 0-0 GS: 0-0 Gd: 0-1 GF: 0-2 Fm: 0-0**
Distance: 5f/6f: 0-1 7f-8f: 0-3 9f-13f: 0-0 14f+: 0-0
Track : LH: 0-1 RH: 0-0 Tight: 0-1 Gall: 0-1
Aids: Bl: 0-0 Vi: 0-0 Tstrap: 0-0 Ckp: 0-0
Best Rating: **30** 10/08 NmkR 7f gd-fm

Comedy Act

82(83) (41)50

2-y-o b g Motivator-Comic (IRE) (Be My Chief (USA))

Sir Mark Prescott Neil Greig - Osborne House

Placings:500 **(4790)**

2009: 7^{5}GF, 7^{0}GF, 8^{0}SD,

	Starts	1st	2nd	3rd	Win & Pl
Career Total (Turf)	2	0	0	0	0
Career Total (AW)	1	0	0	0	

Going (Turf): **Sf: 0-0 GS: 0-0 Gd: 0-0 GF: 0-2 Fm: 0-0**
Distance: 5f/6f: 0-0 7f-8f: 0-3 9f-13f: 0-0 14f+: 0-0
Track : LH: 0-2 RH: 0-0 Tight: 0-2 Gall: 0-0
Aids: Bl: 0-0 Vi: 0-0 Tstrap: 0-0 Ckp: 0-0
Best Rating: **50** 6/09 Leic 7f9y gd-fm

Comedy Hall (USA)

101(91) (78)93

2-y-o b c Valid Expectations (USA)-Comedy At The Met (USA) (Metfield (USA))

M Johnston Sheikh Hamdan Bin Mohammed Al Maktoum

Placings:52101 **(6541)**

2009: 6^{5}G, 6^{2}SD, 5^{1}S, 6^{0}G, 6^{1}GF,

	Starts	1st	2nd	3rd	Win & Pl
Career Total (Turf)	4	2	0	0	11507
Career Total (AW)	1	0	1	0	1370

93 10/09 Wwck 6f (0-95) G-F £8095
83 9/09 Catt 5f SFT £3412
Total win prize-money £11507

Going (Turf): **Sf: 1-1** GS: 0-0 Gd: 0-2 **GF: 1-1** Fm: 0-0
Distance: **5f/6f: 2-5** 7f-8f: 0-0 9f-13f: 0-0 14f+: 0-0
Track : **LH: 1-2** RH: 0-0 Tight: 0-0 Gall: 0-0
Aids: Bl: 0-0 Vi: 0-0 Tstrap: 0-0 Ckp: 0-0
Best Rating: **93** 10/09 Wwck 6f gd-fm

Useful; effective at 5-6f and acts on Fibresand and soft ground.

Comeintothespace (IRE)

90(103) (57)43

7-y-o b g Tagula (IRE)-Playa Del Sol (IRE) (Alzao (USA))

R A Farrant Rodney Farrant

Placings:00006**062**/**112046**20000442040**000**/**040**0003500 6/**132310061140**/0-405006000 **(3269)**

2009: 12^{4}SD, 9^{0}SD, 12^{5}SD, 11^{0}SD, 13^{0}SD, 10^{6}GF, 11^{0}GF, 10^{0}GS, 8^{0}SD,

	Starts	1st	2nd	3rd	Win & Pl
Career Total (Turf)	31	0	2	1	5459
Career Total (AW)	30	6	3	2	17590

57 4/07 Ling 1m4f STD £2184
57 4/07 Kemp 1m4f (0-50)H STD £2047
56 3/07 Ling 1m2f (0-52)H STD £2047
54 1/07 Kemp 1m (0-45) STD £1365
67 2/05 Wolv 1m141y (0-70)H STD £3373
63 1/05 Wolv 1m141y STD £2583
Total win prize-money £13602

Going (Turf): **Sf: 0-1 GS: 0-2 Gd: 0-8 GF: 0-14 Fm: 0-2**
Distance: 5f/6f: 0-0 7f-8f: 1-18 **9f-13f: 5-41** 14f+: 0-2
Track : **LH: 4-46** RH: 2-12 **Tight: 4-27** Gall: 0-2
Aids: Bl: 0-2 Vi: 0-0 Tstrap: 0-3 Ckp: 0-3
Best Rating: **73** 4/05 Ling 1m2f stand

Moderate; ex-Irish; effective over 1m4f; acts well on Polytrack.

Coming Back

94(99) (77)87

3-y-o ch f Fantastic Light (USA)-Return (USA) (Sadler's Wells (USA))

J H M Gosden K Abdulla

Placings:6-125 **(3251)**

2009: 10^{1}SD, 9^{2}F, 10^{5}GF,

	Starts	1st	2nd	3rd	Win & Pl
Career Total (Turf)	3	0	1	0	2216
Career Total (AW)	1	1	0	0	2590

77 3/09 Kemp 1m2f STD £2590
Total win prize-money £2590

Going (Turf): Sf: 0-0 GS: 0-1 Gd: 0-0 GF: 0-1 Fm: 0-1
Distance: 5f/6f: 0-0 7f-8f: 0-1 9f-13f: 1-3 14f+: 0-0
Track : LH: 0-1 RH: 1-2 Tight: 0-1 Gall: 0-1
Aids: Bl: 0-0 Vi: 0-0 Tstrap: 0-0 Ckp: 0-0
Best Rating: 87 5/09 Sals 1m1f198y firm

Useful; stays 1m2f; handles Polytrack.

Commanche Raider (IRE)

98 73
2-y-o b g Tale Of The Cat (USA)-Alsharq (IRE) (Machiavellian (USA))
M Dods Doug Graham

Placings:41 (6556)
2009: 5^{4}GF, 5^{1}G,

	Starts	1st	2nd	3rd	Win & Pl
Career Total (Turf)	2	1	0	0	4498

73 10/09 Catt 5f GD £4209
Total win prize-money £4209

Going (Turf): Sf: 0-0 GS: 0-0 Gd: 1-1 GF: 0-1 Fm: 0-0
Distance: 5f/6f: 1-2 7f-8f: 0-0 9f-13f: 0-0 14f+: 0-0
Track : LH: 0-0 RH: 0-0 Tight: 0-0 Gall: 0-0
Aids: Bl: 0-0 Vi: 0-0 Tstrap: 0-0 Ckp: 0-0
Best Rating: 73 10/09 Catt 5f good

Fair sprinter; acts on good ground.

Command Marshal (FR)

(89) (59)79
6-y-o b g Commands (AUS)-Marsakara (IRE) (Turtle Island (IRE))
M J Scudamore Eddie Moss

Placings:0/3521046/3/320620P0-66 (7873)
2009: 16^{6}SD, 16^{6}SD,

	Starts	1st	2nd	3rd	Win & Pl
Career Total (Turf)	16	1	3	3	14568
Career Total (AW)	3	0	0	0	0

10/06 Nant 1m4f H G-S £4827
Total win prize-money £4828

Going (Turf): Sf: 0-6 GS: 1-4 Gd: 0-2 GF: 0-2 Fm: 0-1
Distance: 5f/6f: 0-0 7f-8f: 0-2 9f-13f: 1-9 14f+: 0-8
Track : LH: 0-11 RH: 0-2 Tight: 0-5 Gall: 0-2
Aids: Bl: 0-0 Vi: 0-0 Tstrap: 0-0 Ckp: 0-0
Best Rating: 79 7/08 Ches 1m7f195y good

Commander Wish

100(104) (52)80
6-y-o ch g Arkadian Hero (USA)-Flighty Dancer (Pivotal)
Lucinda Featherstone J Roundtree

Placings:030000/00U/0001160/424023113000-300000060006660 (7651)
2009: 5^{3}G, 6^{0}GF, 5^{0}GF, 5^{0}G, 5^{0}G, 5^{0}GF, 5^{0}GF, 5^{6}GF, 5^{0}GF, 5^{0}SD, 6^{0}GF, 5^{6}S, 5^{6}S, 5^{6}SD, 5^{0}SD,

	Starts	1st	2nd	3rd	Win & Pl
Career Total (Turf)	26	2	1	4	9576
Career Total (AW)	17	2	1	0	4358

74 8/08 Pont 5f (0-75)H GD £3885
71 7/08 Bevl 5f (0-65)H GD £2266
67 11/07 Wolv 5f20y (0-60)H STD £2047
63 10/07 Wolv 5f20y (0-45) STD £1706
Total win prize-money £9907

Going (Turf): Sf: 0-4 GS: 0-1 Gd: 2-10 GF: 0-10 Fm: 0-1
Distance: 5f/6f: 4-33 7f-8f: 0-7 9f-13f: 0-1 14f+: 0-2
Track : LH: 3-17 RH: 0-6 Tight: 2-15 Gall: 0-0
Aids: Bl: 0-0 Vi: 0-0 Tstrap: 4-28 Ckp: 4-28
Best Rating: 80 8/09 Bevl 5f gd-fm

Modest; effective over 5f-6f; acts on good ground; also goes on Polytrack; often wears cheekpieces.

Commandingpresence (USA)

93(96) (69)55
3-y-o b/br f Thunder Gulch (USA)-Sehra (USA) (Silver Hawk (USA))
J J Bridger (Ms J S Doyle 22/5) W Wood

Placings:2-030000600634056360 (7771)
2009: 8^{0}SD, 7^{3}SD, 8^{0}SD, 8^{0}SD, 7^{0}SD, 7^{0}GF, 7^{6}SD, 10^{0}GF, 9^{0}GF, 7^{6}SD, 7^{3}GS, 5^{4}SD, 7^{0}SD, 7^{5}SD, 8^{6}SD, 6^{3}SD, 6^{6}SD, 6^{0}SD,

	Starts	1st	2nd	3rd	Win & Pl
Career Total (Turf)	4	0	0	1	403
Career Total (AW)	15	0	1	2	1512

Going (Turf): Sf: 0-0 GS: 0-1 Gd: 0-0 GF: 0-3 Fm: 0-0
Distance: 5f/6f: 0-4 7f-8f: 0-13 9f-13f: 0-2 14f+: 0-0
Track : LH: 0-12 RH: 0-6 Tight: 0-11 Gall: 0-0
Aids: Bl: 0-2 Vi: 0-1 Tstrap: 0-1 Ckp: 0-1
Best Rating: 69 12/08 Wolv 7f32y stand

Very moderate; stays 7f; acts on easy ground and on Polytrack.

Commando Scott (IRE)

102(99) (72)73
8-y-o b g Danetime (IRE)-Faye (Monsanto (FR))
I W McInnes Mrs Ann Morris

Placings:4340/10022261 1500/0030006360/04223101000 36330/000006105012 3020/000025540 (5673)
2009: 7^{0}G, 6^{0}S, 7^{0}S, 7^{0}GF, 7^{2}SD, 6^{5}S, 8^{5}G, 7^{4}SD, 8^{0}S,

	Starts	1st	2nd	3rd	Win & Pl
Career Total (Turf)	62	7	7	8	102180
Career Total (AW)	5	0	1	0	994

98 9/07 Ayr 7f50y (0-90)H G-S £11217
98 5/07 NmkR 6f (0-100)H G-S £11658
99 5/06 Ayr 6f (0-90)H SFT £11658
93 5/06 Ayr 7f50y (0-90)H GD £11658
93 7/04 Donc 6f D(0-85)H SFT £5671
93 7/04 Hayd 6f D(0-85)H SFT £5165
69 4/04 Thsk 6f E G-S £3682
Total win prize-money £60713

Going (Turf): Sf: 3-20 GS: 3-12 Gd: 1-17 GF: 0-11 Fm: 0-2
Distance: 5f/6f: 5-33 7f-8f: 2-32 9f-13f: 0-2 14f+: 0-0
Track : LH: 2-21 RH: 0-6 Tight: 0-15 Gall: 0-0
Aids: Bl: 0-1 Vi: 0-0 Tstrap: 0-0 Ckp: 0-0
Best Rating: 99 10/07 Donc 6f good

Fair on turf; modest on all-weather; effective over 6f-7f; acts on most ground, but well suited by cut.

Commissionaire

96 80
2-y-o b c Medicean-Appointed One (USA) (Danzig (USA))
J H M Gosden Cheveley Park Stud

Placings:1 (7095)
2009: 8^{1}G,

	Starts	1st	2nd	3rd	Win & Pl
Career Total (Turf)	1	1	0	0	3469

80 10/09 Yarm 1m3y GD £3469
Total win prize-money £3469

Going (Turf): Sf: 0-0 GS: 0-0 Gd: 1-1 GF: 0-0 Fm: 0-0
Distance: 5f/6f: 0-0 7f-8f: 0-0 9f-13f: 1-1 14f+: 0-0
Track : LH: 0-0 RH: 0-0 Tight: 0-0 Gall: 0-0
Aids: Bl: 0-0 Vi: 0-0 Tstrap: 0-0 Ckp: 0-0
Best Rating: 80 10/09 Yarm 1m3y good

Useful winner on debut over 1m on good.

Common Diva

105(107) (77)77
3-y-o ch f Auction House (USA)-Vida (IRE) (Wolfhound (USA))
A J McCabe Alotincommon Partnership

Placings:031540000 4-31410136265530 (6667)
2009: 8^{3}SD, 8^{1}SD, 8^{4}SD, 8^{1}SD, 8^{0}SD, 8^{1}SD, 7^{3}SD, 9^{6}SD, 8^{2}GF, 8^{6}GS, 8^{5}G, 8^{5}GF, 8^{3}SD, 7^{0}SD,

	Starts	1st	2nd	3rd	Win & Pl
Career Total (Turf)	9	1	1	1	6330
Career Total (AW)	15	3	0	3	9872

71 3/09 Wolv 1m141y STD £2729
71 2/09 Wolv 1m141y (0-70)H STD £2729
70 1/09 Wolv 1m141y (0-70)H STD £2729
73 6/08 Pont 6f GD £3238
Total win prize-money £11428

Going (Turf): Sf: 0-0 GS: 0-1 Gd: 1-3 GF: 0-5 Fm: 0-0
Distance: 5f/6f: 1-6 7f-8f: 0-7 9f-13f: 3-11 14f+: 0-0
Track : LH: 4-17 RH: 0-2 Tight: 3-13 Gall: 0-1
Aids: Bl: 0-0 Vi: 0-0 Tstrap: 0-0 Ckp: 0-0
Best Rating: 77 5/09 Pont 1m4y good

Fair; effective over 1m; acts on good ground; goes on Polytrack.

Competitor

(108) (67)39
8-y-o b g Danzero (AUS)-Ceanothus (IRE) (Bluebird (USA))
J Akehurst John Akehurst

Placings:10/2005060506/000001/2506131300003/010103 0000/01216000000606-655 (0588)
2009: 10^{6}SD, 12^{5}SD, 10^{5}SD,

	Starts	1st	2nd	3rd	Win & Pl
Career Total (Turf)	15	1	0	0	3500
Career Total (AW)	43	7	3	4	18560

67 3/08 Ling 1m2f STD £1774
59 2/08 Ling 1m4f STD £1774
67 3/07 Ling 1m2f (0-60)H STD £1706
54 1/07 Ling 1m2f STD £2184
63 4/06 Ling 1m2f STD £2388
62 3/06 Ling 1m4f STD £2388
63 12/05 Ling 1m2f STD £2518
62 10/03 Rdcr 1m E FRM £3500
Total win prize-money £18236

Going (Turf): Sf: 0-1 GS: 0-3 Gd: 0-4 GF: 0-5 Fm: 1-2
Distance: 5f/6f: 0-0 7f-8f: 1-3 9f-13f: 7-55 14f+: 0-0
Track : LH: 7-46 RH: 0-11 Tight: 7-47 Gall: 0-2
Aids: Bl: 2-8 Vi: 5-33 Tstrap: 0-3 Ckp: 0-3
Best Rating: 71 1/04 Ling 1m2f stand

Modest; effective over 1m2f-1m4f; acts on Polytrack.

Complete Frontline (GER)

84(97) (60)57

4-y-o ch g Tertullian (USA)-Carola Rouge (Arazi (USA))

K R Burke Frontline Bathrooms

Placings:052/300450334200-00 **(2155)**

2009: 8^{0}F, 9^{0}GF,

	Starts	1st	2nd	3rd	Win & Pl
Career Total (Turf)	12	0	1	2	3333
Career Total (AW)	5	0	1	1	1117

Going (Turf): Sf: 0-2 GS: 0-1 Gd: 0-3 GF: 0-4 Fm: 0-2
Distance: 5f/6f: 0-7 7f-8f: 0-7 9f-13f: 0-3 14f+: 0-0
Track : LH: 0-5 RH: 0-5 Tight: 0-6 Gall: 0-1
Aids: Bl: 0-0 Vi: 0-1 Tstrap: 0-2 Ckp: 0-2
Best Rating: 61 7/07 York 6f heavy

Moderate; effective at around 1m; acts on soft ground; also goes on Polytrack.

Comprimario (IRE)

66 9

3-y-o b g Montjeu (IRE)-Soubrette (USA) (Opening Verse (USA))

N A Twiston-Davies (J L Dunlop 3/5) Mrs M E Slade

Placings:6 **(1708)**

2009: 12^{6}GF,

	Starts	1st	2nd	3rd	Win & Pl
Career Total (Turf)	1	0	0	0	0

Going (Turf): Sf: 0-0 GS: 0-0 Gd: 0-0 GF: 0-1 Fm: 0-0
Distance: 5f/6f: 0-0 7f-8f: 0-0 9f-13f: 0-1 14f+: 0-0
Track : LH: 0-0 RH: 0-1 Tight: 0-1 Gall: 0-0
Aids: Bl: 0-0 Vi: 0-0 Tstrap: 0-0 Ckp: 0-0
Best Rating: 9 5/09 Sals 1m4f gd-fm

Compton Blue

103(89) (52)78

3-y-o b c Compton Place-Blue Goddess (IRE) (Blues Traveller (IRE))

R Hannon Godfrey Wilson

Placings:505-046100021 **(6908)**

2009: 6^{0}GF, 6^{4}G, 6^{6}SD, 8^{1}G, 8^{0}SD, 7^{0}G, 8^{0}G, 8^{2}G, 8^{1}G,

	Starts	1st	2nd	3rd	Win & Pl
Career Total (Turf)	10	2	1	0	6432
Career Total (AW)	2	0	0	0	0
78	10/09 Wind	1m67y	(0-70)H	GD	£2388
70	8/09 Sand	1m14y	(0-75)H	GD	£3238

Total win prize-money £5626

Going (Turf): Sf: 0-0 GS: 0-2 Gd: 2-6 GF: 0-2 Fm: 0-0
Distance: 5f/6f: 0-2 7f-8f: 0-7 9f-13f: 2-3 14f+: 0-0
Track : LH: 0-0 RH: 2-6 Tight: 1-2 Gall: 0-1
Aids: Bl: 1-1 Vi: 0-0 Tstrap: 0-0 Ckp: 0-0
Best Rating: 78 10/09 Wind 1m67y good

Modest; effective over 7f-1m; acts on good and easy ground.

Compton Charlie

74(93) (52)64

5-y-o b g Compton Place-Tell Tale Fox (Tel Quel (FR))

J G Portman A S B Portman

Placings:053/0002/15242504-000 **(3503)**

2009: 12^{0}GF, 11^{0}GF, 12^{0}GF,

	Starts	1st	2nd	3rd	Win & Pl
Career Total (Turf)	14	1	3	0	4867
Career Total (AW)	4	0	0	1	482
57	4/08 Folk	1m4f	(0-60)H	G-S	£2047

Total win prize-money £2047

Going (Turf): Sf: 0-1 GS: 1-5 Gd: 0-2 GF: 0-6 Fm: 0-0
Distance: 5f/6f: 0-2 7f-8f: 0-2 9f-13f: 1-13 14f+: 0-1
Track : LH: 0-6 RH: 1-8 Tight: 1-11 Gall: 0-3
Aids: Bl: 0-0 Vi: 0-0 Tstrap: 0-1 Ckp: 0-1
Best Rating: 64 7/08 Sals 1m4f gd-fm

Moderate; stays 1m4f; acts on soft ground; also goes on Fibresand.

Compton Classic

97(102) (74)67

7-y-o b g Compton Place-Ayr Classic (Local Suitor (USA))

J R Boyle (Tom Dascombe 22/1) John Hopkins (t/a South Hatch Racing)

Placings:0660/042000045000060/012620601406513220/0 2051120031461031001345/102400022-02032202140203060 **(7224)**

2009: 6^{0}SD, 6^{2}SD, 5^{0}SD, 6^{3}SD, 6^{2}SD, 5^{2}SD, 6^{0}SD, 6^{2}SD, 6^{1}SD, 6^{4}SD, 6^{0}SD, 5^{2}G, 5^{0}GS, 5^{3}S, 6^{0}SD, 5^{6}S, 5^{0}SD,

	Starts	1st	2nd	3rd	Win & Pl
Career Total (Turf)	56	7	7	4	32221
Career Total (AW)	30	4	8	2	13852
74	4/09 Kemp	6f	(0-65)H	STD	£2047
72	1/08 Wolv	5f20y		STD	£2047
77	11/07 Kemp	6f		STD	£2047
64	10/07 Muss	5f		GD	£2590
82	8/07 Ayr	6f	(0-75)H	G-S	£3886
78	7/07 Ayr	5f	(0-65)H	GD	£2590
71	6/07 Muss	5f	(0-65)H	GD	£3238
59	6/07 Carl	5f	(0-70)H	G-S	£3238
59	9/06 Ayr	5f	(0-58)H	SFT	£2866
58	7/06 Ayr	5f	(0-55)H	GD	£2966
52	4/06 Wolv	5f20y	(0-45)	STD	£1365

Total win prize-money £28888

Going (Turf): Sf: 1-12 GS: 2-14 Gd: 4-16 GF: 0-13 Fm: 0-1
Distance: 5f/6f: 11-84 7f-8f: 0-2 9f-13f: 0-0 14f+: 0-0
Track : LH: 2-18 RH: 3-17 Tight: 2-14 Gall: 1-7
Aids: Bl: 0-1 Vi: 2-11 Tstrap: 7-51 Ckp: 7-51
Best Rating: 82 8/07 Ayr 6f gd-sft

Modest; effective over 5f-6f; acts on most ground and on Polytrack; has worn cheekpieces, a visor and a tongue tie.

Compton Falcon

(103) (64)73

5-y-o ch g Peintre Celebre (USA)-Lesgor (USA) (Irish River (FR))

H Candy (G A Butler 2/1) Erik Penser

Placings:303660/2466345334-30 **(5577)**

2009: 12^{3}SD, 11^{0}SD,

	Starts	1st	2nd	3rd	Win & Pl
Career Total (Turf)	8	0	0	3	1165
Career Total (AW)	10	0	1	3	2358

Going (Turf): Sf: 0-0 GS: 0-3 Gd: 0-2 GF: 0-2 Fm: 0-1
Distance: 5f/6f: 0-0 7f-8f: 0-0 9f-13f: 0-13 14f+: 0-5
Track : LH: 0-14 RH: 0-4 Tight: 0-9 Gall: 0-3
Aids: Bl: 0-1 Vi: 0-1 Tstrap: 0-0 Ckp: 0-0
Best Rating: 73 7/07 Bath 1m2f46y gd-sft

Moderate; stays 1m4f; acts on good ground and on Polytrack; has worn tongue tie, but has looked reluctant.

Compton Ford

98(96) (57)68

3-y-o ch g Compton Place-Coffee Time (IRE) (Efisio)

M Dods Septimus Racing Group

Placings:0654160-312546045 **(4596)**

2009: 5^{3}GF, 5^{1}GF, 5^{2}GF, 5^{5}G, 5^{4}GF, 5^{6}GF, 5^{0}GS, 5^{4}SF, 5^{5}G,

	Starts	1st	2nd	3rd	Win & Pl
Career Total (Turf)	14	2	1	1	5316
Career Total (AW)	2	0	0	0	0
65	4/09 Catt	5f	(0-60)H	G-F	£2183
61	8/08 Muss	5f		GD	£1942

Total win prize-money £4127

Going (Turf): Sf: 0-1 GS: 0-2 Gd: 1-3 GF: 1-8 Fm: 0-0
Distance: 5f/6f: 2-16 7f-8f: 0-0 9f-13f: 0-0 14f+: 0-0
Track : LH: 0-1 RH: 0-0 Tight: 0-1 Gall: 0-0
Aids: Bl: 0-1 Vi: 0-1 Tstrap: 0-1 Ckp: 0-1
Best Rating: 68 5/09 Muss 5f gd-fm

Modest; best at 5f and acts on good ground.

Compton Lad

36 (11)37

6-y-o b g Compton Place-Kintara (Cyrano De Bergerac)

D A Nolan Miss M McFadyen-Murray

Placings:54033630400660/050030000/00000000/000-0 **(2157)**

2009: 5^{0}GF,

	Starts	1st	2nd	3rd	Win & Pl
Career Total (Turf)	32	0	0	3	1936
Career Total (AW)	4	0	0	1	364

Going (Turf): Sf: 0-3 GS: 0-7 Gd: 0-6 GF: 0-16 Fm: 0-0
Distance: 5f/6f: 0-34 7f-8f: 0-2 9f-13f: 0-0 14f+: 0-0
Track : LH: 0-3 RH: 0-0 Tight: 0-3 Gall: 0-0
Aids: Bl: 0-1 Vi: 0-0 Tstrap: 0-9 Ckp: 0-9
Best Rating: 50 8/06 Ayr 5f gd-fm

Compton Park

(71) (42)

2-y-o ch c Compton Place-Corps De Ballet (IRE) (Fasliyev (USA))

W J Knight Mrs P G M Jamison

Placings:0 **(7538)**

2009: 7^{0}SD,

	Starts	1st	2nd	3rd	Win & Pl
Career Total (Turf)	0	0	0	0	
Career Total (AW)	1	0	0	0	

Going (Turf): Sf: 0-0 GS: 0-0 Gd: 0-0 GF: 0-0 Fm: 0-0
Distance: 5f/6f: 0-0 7f-8f: 0-1 9f-13f: 0-0 14f+: 0-0
Track : LH: 0-0 RH: 0-1 Tight: 0-0 Gall: 0-0
Aids: Bl: 0-0 Vi: 0-0 Tstrap: 0-0 Ckp: 0-0
Best Rating: 42 11/09 Kemp 7f stand

Compton Rose

97 69

4-y-o ch f Compton Place-Benjarong (Sharpo)

H Candy Mrs J E L Wright

Placings:5/343500-00000 **(5792)**

2009: 5^{0}GF, 5^{0}GF, 6^{0}GF, 6^{0}G, 5^{0}G,

	Starts	1st	2nd	3rd	Win & Pl
Career Total (Turf)	12	0	0	2	1155

Going (Turf): Sf: 0-1 GS: 0-1 Gd: 0-4 GF: 0-6 Fm: 0-0
Distance: 5f/6f: 0-11 7f-8f: 0-1 9f-13f: 0-0 14f+: 0-0
Track : LH: 0-1 RH: 0-0 Tight: 0-0 Gall: 0-3
Aids: Bl: 0-0 Vi: 0-0 Tstrap: 0-0 Ckp: 0-0
Best Rating: 69 9/08 Gdwd 5f gd-fm

Compton Way

85 **40**
2-y-o b c Compton Place-Never Away (Royal Applause)
B W Hills Mrs Barbara James

Placings:00 **(7289)**
2009: 6^{0}G, 6^{0}S,

	Starts	1st	2nd	3rd	Win & Pl
Career Total (Turf)	2	0	0	0	

Going (Turf): Sf: 0-1 GS: 0-0 Gd: 0-1 GF: 0-0 Fm: 0-0
Distance: 5f/6f: 0-2 7f-8f: 0-0 9f-13f: 0-0 14f+: 0-0
Track : LH: 0-0 RH: 0-0 Tight: 0-0 Gall: 0-0
Aids: Bl: 0-0 Vi: 0-0 Tstrap: 0-0 Ckp: 0-0
Best Rating: 40 10/09 NmkR 6f good

Out of a half-sister to three winners including the high-class Never A Doubt; unplaced in 6f maidens.

Compton's Eleven

102(106) (88)**90**
8-y-o gr g Compton Place-Princess Tara (Prince Sabo)
M R Channon PCM Racing

Placings:5110033/000052122220/100203002050255622 6/12440002022503/605000243015530 0/504201600002000300-5220050046525020605 3 **(6985)**
2009: 7^{5}SD, 7^{2}SD, 6^{2}SD, 7^{0}F, 7^{0}GF, 7^{5}GF, 7^{0}GF, 7^{0}GF, 7^{4}GF, 7^{6}GS, 7^{5}G, 7^{2}G, 7^{5}G, 7^{0}GF, 7^{2}GF, 7^{0}G, 7^{6}G, 7^{0}GF, 7^{5}GF, 7^{3}G,

	Starts	1st	2nd	3rd	Win & Pl
Career Total (Turf)	99	7	19	7	228689
Career Total (AW)	7	0	2	1	3971

90	6/08	Donc	7f	(0-90)H	G-S	£9714
89	8/07	NmkJ	6f	(0-85)H	GD	£12464
103	1/06	Ndas	6f110y	(95-110)H	G-F	£45348
102	1/05	Ndas	6f	(90-105)H	G-F	£37239
93	7/04	Haml	6f5y	D(0-75)	GD	£6162
94	9/03	Gdwd	6f	D(0-85)H	G-F	£2975
85	8/03	Yarm	5f43y	D	G-F	£4953

Total win prize-money £118857

Going (Turf): Sf: 0-10 GS: 1-18 Gd: 2-26 **GF: 4-44** Fm: 0-1
Distance: 5f/6f: 4-30 7f-8f: 3-75 9f-13f: 0-1 14f+: 0-0
Track : LH: 2-28 RH: 0-15 Tight: 0-13 **Gall: 2-11**
Aids: Bl: 0-0 Vi: 0-0 Tstrap: 0-0 Ckp: 0-0
Best Rating: 106 8/06 Gdwd 7f good

Fair; effective at 6f-7f; acts on most ground and on Polytrack.

Comptonspirit

99(97) (66)**73**
5-y-o ch m Compton Place-Croeso Cynnes (Most Welcome)
B P J Baugh G B Hignett

Placings:U/034643462146/5442226156064-0204563403524 **(6379)**
2009: 5^{0}SD, 5^{2}F, 5^{0}GF, 5^{4}F, 5^{6}HY, 5^{0}GF, 5^{3}GF, 5^{4}G, 5^{0}G, 5^{3}GF, 5^{5}GF, 6^{2}GF, 5^{4}GF,

	Starts	1st	2nd	3rd	Win & Pl
Career Total (Turf)	29	2	6	3	14575
Career Total (AW)	10	0	0	1	961

73	7/08	Pont	5f	(0-70)H	G-F	£3885
72	8/07	Ayr	5f	(0-65)H	G-F	£2730

Total win prize-money £6616

Going (Turf): Sf: 0-3 GS: 0-3 Gd: 0-6 **GF: 2-15** Fm: 0-2
Distance: 5f/6f: 2-36 7f-8f: 0-3 9f-13f: 0-0 14f+: 0-0
Track : LH: 1-18 RH: 0-0 Tight: 0-11 Gall: 0-1
Aids: Bl: 0-0 Vi: 0-0 Tstrap: 1-7 Ckp: 1-7
Best Rating: 73 4/09 Rdcr 5f firm

Modest; effective over 5-6f; acts on most ground.

Comrade Cotton

100(102) (65)**62**
5-y-o b g Royal Applause-Cutpurse Moll (Green Desert (USA))
J Ryan John Ryan Racing Partnership

Placings:06/21020454004/004350201024 2-04040332100 (2824)
2009: 7^{0}SD, 7^{4}SD, 7^{0}SD, 8^{4}SD, 6^{0}G, 8^{3}F, 9^{3}F, 10^{2}GF, 11^{1}GF, 10^{0}GF, 8^{0}SD,

	Starts	1st	2nd	3rd	Win & Pl
Career Total (Turf)	14	1	3	2	6390
Career Total (AW)	23	2	3	1	7528

54	5/09	Leic	1m3f183y	(0-60)H	G-F	£2590
60	11/08	Ling	7f	(0-58)H	STD	£1706
66	1/07	Ling	6f	(0-70)H	STD	£2914

Total win prize-money £7211

Going (Turf): Sf: 0-2 GS: 0-3 Gd: 0-3 **GF: 1-3** Fm: 0-3
Distance: 5f/6f: 1-11 7f-8f: 1-19 9f-13f: 1-7 14f+: 0-0
Track : LH: 2-26 RH: 1-5 **Tight: 2-16** Gall: 0-2
Aids: Bl: 0-1 Vi: 0-5 Tstrap: 1-12 Ckp: 1-12
Best Rating: 66 6/07 NmkJ 6f soft

Moderate; effective up to 1m4f; acts on good/fast ground; goes on Polytrack; has worn cheekpieces.

Comradeship (IRE)

98(99) (76)**80**
2-y-o ch c Dubawi (IRE)-Friendlier (Zafonic (USA))
J H M Gosden H R H Princess Haya Of Jordan

Placings:0265621 **(7335)**
2009: 8^{0}G, 8^{2}G, 8^{6}GF, 8^{5}GS, 8^{6}G, 8^{2}SD, 8^{1}SD,

	Starts	1st	2nd	3rd	Win & Pl
Career Total (Turf)	5	0	1	0	1156
Career Total (AW)	2	1	1	0	3597

75	11/09	Sthl	1m	(0-70)	STD	£2729

Total win prize-money £2730

Going (Turf): Sf: 0-0 GS: 0-1 Gd: 0-3 GF: 0-1 Fm: 0-0
Distance: 5f/6f: 0-0 **7f-8f: 1-4** 9f-13f: 0-3 14f+: 0-0
Track : LH: 1-4 RH: 0-0 Tight: 0-0 Gall: 0-1
Aids: Bl: 1-2 Vi: 0-0 Tstrap: 0-0 Ckp: 0-0
Best Rating: 80 8/09 Chep 1m14y good

Fair; stays 1m; acts on Fibresand; has worn blinkers.

Con Artist (IRE)

(92) (80)
2-y-o b c Invincible Spirit (IRE)-Hoodwink (IRE) (Selkirk (USA))
Saeed Bin Suroor Godolphin

Placings:31 **(7390)**
2009: 8^{3}SD, 8^{1}SD,

	Starts	1st	2nd	3rd	Win & Pl
Career Total (Turf)	0	0	0	0	
Career Total (AW)	2	1	0	1	3845

80	11/09	Ling	1m	STD	£3412

Total win prize-money £3412

Going (Turf): Sf: 0-0 GS: 0-0 Gd: 0-0 GF: 0-0 Fm: 0-0
Distance: 5f/6f: 0-0 **7f-8f: 1-2** 9f-13f: 0-0 14f+: 0-0
Track : LH: 1-2 RH: 0-0 **Tight: 1-1** Gall: 0-0
Aids: Bl: 0-0 Vi: 0-0 Tstrap: 0-0 Ckp: 0-0
Best Rating: 80 11/09 Ling 1m stand

Fair; effective over 1m; acts on Polytrack.

Conclave (IRE)

(93) (30)**61**
5-y-o b m Key Of Luck (USA)-Dathuil (IRE) (Royal Academy (USA))
W P Mullins (Adrian Sexton 20/2) S Buggy

Placings:00/020204/460-00 **(7547a)**
2009: 16^{0}SD, 10^{0}SD,

	Starts	1st	2nd	3rd	Win & Pl
Career Total (Turf)	7	0	2	0	1849
Career Total (AW)	6	0	0	0	183

Going (Turf): Sf: 0-1 GS: 0-0 Gd: 0-0 GF: 0-2 Fm: 0-0
Distance: 5f/6f: 0-2 7f-8f: 0-3 9f-13f: 0-6 14f+: 0-2
Track : LH: 0-7 RH: 0-4 Tight: 0-1 Gall: 0-0
Aids: Bl: 0-2 Vi: 0-0 Tstrap: 0-2 Ckp: 0-2
Best Rating: 61 3/08 Cork 1m2f50y sft-hvy

Conclusive

81(90) (56)**50**
3-y-o b g Selkirk (USA)-Never A Doubt (Night Shift (USA))
R M Beckett Thurloe Thoroughbreds XXIII

Placings:0-0005 **(3302)**
2009: 7^{0}SD, 7^{0}GF, 6^{0}GF, 8^{5}SD,

	Starts	1st	2nd	3rd	Win & Pl
Career Total (Turf)	3	0	0	0	
Career Total (AW)	2	0	0	0	0

Going (Turf): Sf: 0-0 GS: 0-1 Gd: 0-0 GF: 0-2 Fm: 0-0
Distance: 5f/6f: 0-0 7f-8f: 0-5 9f-13f: 0-0 14f+: 0-0
Track : LH: 0-0 RH: 0-2 Tight: 0-0 Gall: 0-0
Aids: Bl: 0-0 Vi: 0-0 Tstrap: 0-1 Ckp: 0-1
Best Rating: 56 4/09 Kemp 7f stand

Concorde Kiss (USA)

(85) (55)
2-y-o b f Harlan's Holiday (USA)-Saraa Ree (USA) (Caro)
S Kirk Mr & Mrs Christopher Wright

Placings:050 **(7865)**
2009: 8^{0}SD, 8^{5}SD, 8^{0}SS,

	Starts	1st	2nd	3rd	Win & Pl
Career Total (Turf)	0	0	0	0	
Career Total (AW)	3	0	0	0	0

Going (Turf): Sf: 0-0 GS: 0-0 Gd: 0-0 GF: 0-0 Fm: 0-0
Distance: 5f/6f: 0-0 7f-8f: 0-2 9f-13f: 0-1 14f+: 0-0
Track : LH: 0-3 RH: 0-0 Tight: 0-2 Gall: 0-0
Aids: Bl: 0-0 Vi: 0-0 Tstrap: 0-0 Ckp: 0-0
Best Rating: 55 12/09 Wolv 1m141y stand

Half-sister to a number of winners including Grade 1 winner Sarafan; moderate form so far.

Conduit (IRE)

118 (79)127

4-y-o ch c Dalakhani (IRE)-Well Head (IRE) (Sadler's Wells (USA))

Sir Michael Stoute Ballymacoll Stud

Placings:031/312111-231414 (7593a)

2009: 10^{2}G, 10^{3}G, 12^{1}G, 12^{4}G, 12^{1}F, 12^{4}F,

	Starts	1st	2nd	3rd	Win & Pl
Career Total (Turf)	13	6	2	2	3547479
Career Total (AW)	2	1	0	1	4368

123 11/09 SnAt 1m4f FRM £1125000
127 7/09 Asct 1m4f GD £567700
127 10/08 SnAt 1m4f FRM £866985
124 9/08 Donc 1m6f132y SFT £283850
114 7/08 Gdwd 1m4f GD £39739
104 6/08 Epsm 1m2f18y (0-105)H GD £31155
79 9/07 Wolv 1m141y STD £3886

Total win prize-money £2918315

Going (Turf): Sf: 1-1 GS: 0-1 **Gd: 3-6** GF: 0-1 Fm: 2-4
Distance: 5f/6f: 0-0 7f-8f: 0-2 **9f-13f: 6-12** 14f+: 1-1
Track : **LH: 5-6** RH: 2-8 **Tight: 3-3** Gall: 2-3
Aids: Bl: 0-0 Vi: 0-0 Tstrap: 0-0 Ckp: 0-0
Best Rating: **127** 7/09 Asct 1m4f good

Top class; winner of Gordon Stakes, St Leger and Breeders' Cup Turf in 2008; landed the 2009 King George before finishing fourth in the Arc and winning the Breeders' Cup Turf for the second time; best over 1m4f; acts on a sound surface but handles cut and acts on sand; usually held up and appreciates a decent pace.

Confessional

102(99) (75)80

2-y-o b g Dubawi (IRE)-Golden Nun (Bishop Of Cashel)

T D Easterby T G & Mrs M E Holdcroft

Placings:0032021 (7217)

2009: 6^{0}GS, 5^{0}GF, 5^{3}GS, 5^{2}GF, 6^{0}GF, 5^{2}SD, 5^{1}S,

	Starts	1st	2nd	3rd	Win & Pl
Career Total (Turf)	6	1	1	1	4524
Career Total (AW)	1	0	1	0	964

80 11/09 Catt 5f212y SFT £2388

Total win prize-money £2388

Going (Turf): **Sf: 1-1** GS: 0-2 Gd: 0-0 GF: 0-3 Fm: 0-0
Distance: **5f/6f: 1-7** 7f-8f: 0-0 9f-13f: 0-0 14f+: 0-0
Track : **LH: 1-2** RH: 0-0 **Tight: 1-2** Gall: 0-0
Aids: Bl: 0-1 Vi: 0-0 Tstrap: 0-0 Ckp: 0-0
Best Rating: **80** 11/09 Catt 5f212y soft

Useful; stays 6f; acts on most ground on turf; goes on Polytrack.

Confide In Me

96(99) (63)66

5-y-o b g Medicean-Confidante (USA) (Dayjur (USA))

G A Butler A D Spence & Mr And Mrs P Hargreaves

Placings:0/0030-2124506551045 (7586)

2009: 8^{2}GF, 9^{1}GF, 10^{2}G, 9^{4}G, 8^{5}SD, 10^{0}G, 8^{6}SD, 8^{5}SF, 7^{5}GF, 8^{1}SD, 8^{0}SD, 8^{4}SD, 8^{5}SD,

	Starts	1st	2nd	3rd	Win & Pl
Career Total (Turf)	8	1	2	0	4460
Career Total (AW)	10	1	0	1	2792

61 10/09 Wolv 1m141y (0-55)H STD £2388
66 6/09 Folk 1m1f149y (0-70)H G-F £3070

Total win prize-money £5459

Going (Turf): Sf: 0-0 GS: 0-0 Gd: 0-4 **GF: 1-4** Fm: 0-0
Distance: 5f/6f: 0-0 7f-8f: 0-6 **9f-13f: 2-12** 14f+: 0-0
Track : LH: 1-10 RH: 1-6 **Tight: 2-8** Gall: 0-0
Aids: Bl: 0-2 Vi: 0-0 Tstrap: 1-4 Ckp: 1-4
Best Rating: **66** 6/09 Folk 1m1f149y gd-fm

Moderate; stays 1m and acts on Polytrack; has worn cheek-pieces and a tongue-tie.

Confidentiality (IRE)

93(106) (91)81

5-y-o b m Desert Style (IRE)-Confidential (Generous (IRE))

M Wigham (Edward Lynam 25/11) J M Cullinan

Placings:0504**111111/4324**00460-**15064**600**512** (7848)

2009: **10**^{1}SD, **8**^{5}SD, **12**^{0}SD, 10^{6}GF, **10**^{4}SD, 10^{6}G, 10^{0}GY, **10**^{0}SD, 8^{5}SD, **10**^{1}SD, **9**^{2}SD,

	Starts	1st	2nd	3rd	Win & Pl
Career Total (Turf)	12	0	0	0	703
Career Total (AW)	18	8	2	1	28397

87 12/09 Ling 1m2f (0-85)H STD £4727
91 1/09 Ling 1m2f (0-85)H STD £4857
87 12/07 Wolv 1m141y (0-70)H STD £2817
83 12/07 Wolv 1m1f103y (0-70)H STD £2968
88 12/07 Wolv 1m141y (0-64)H STD £2047
74 11/07 Wolv 1m1f103y (0-55)H STD £2047
65 11/07 Kemp 1m (0-65)H STD £2047
57 11/07 Ling 1m (0-55)H STD £2047

Total win prize-money £23562

Going (Turf): **Sf: 0-3 GS: 0-0 Gd: 0-2 GF: 0-3 Fm: 0-1**
Distance: 5f/6f: 0-0 7f-8f: 2-10 **9f-13f: 6-20** 14f+: 0-0
Track : **LH: 7-20** RH: 1-9 **Tight: 7-13** Gall: 0-3
Aids: Bl: 0-0 Vi: 0-0 Tstrap: 0-0 Ckp: 0-0
Best Rating: **91** 12/09 Wolv 1m1f103y stand

Useful; has had spells in Ireland; stays 1m1f; acts very well on Polytrack.

Confront

115(105) (95)119

4-y-o b g Nayef (USA)-Contiguous (USA) (Danzig (USA))

Sir Michael Stoute K Abdulla

Placings:21/**54**-124221116 (7746a)

2009: 9^{1}GF, 8^{2}G, 10^{4}G, 8^{2}GF, 8^{2}GF, 7^{1}GF, 8^{1}S, 8^{1}GF, 8^{6}G,

	Starts	1st	2nd	3rd	Win & Pl
Career Total (Turf)	12	5	4	0	181610
Career Total (AW)	1	0	0	0	577

117 10/09 NmkR 1m G-F £36900
116 9/09 Hayd 1m30y SFT £22708
114 5/09 NmkR 1m1f H G-F £31155
112 10/07 Asct 7f G-S £7478

Total win prize-money £98242

Going (Turf): Sf: 1-2 GS: 1-1 Gd: 0-3 **GF: 3-6** Fm: 0-0
Distance: 5f/6f: 0-0 **7f-8f: 3-9** 9f-13f: 2-4 14f+: 0-0
Track : **LH: 2-4** RH: 0-3 Tight: 0-1 **Gall: 1-3**
Aids: Bl: 0-0 Vi: 0-0 Tstrap: 0-0 Ckp: 0-0
Best Rating: **119** 7/09 Asct 1m gd-fm

Group class; Group 3winner; effective over 7f-1m1f; acts on fast and easy ground; has worn earplugs.

Confuchias (IRE)

107(108) (109)107

5-y-o b h Cape Cross (IRE)-Schust Madame (IRE) (Second Set (IRE))

Pat Eddery (K R Burke 26/2) Pattern Racing UK Ltd

Placings:311/250150/6460053**105**-06560004**342** (7795)

2009: 6^{0}G, 6^{6}GF, 6^{5}GF, 6^{6}GF, 6^{0}GF, 6^{0}G, 6^{0}G, 7^{4}S, 7^{3}SD, **6**^{4}SD, 6^{2}SS,

	Starts	1st	2nd	3rd	Win & Pl
Career Total (Turf)	24	3	1	2	104371
Career Total (AW)	6	1	1	1	11108

109 11/08 Kemp 7f STD £7477
114 6/07 Newc 6f HVY £28390
103 10/06 Leop 7f SFT £31427
91 10/06 Naas 6f Y-S £8577

Total win prize-money £75873

Going (Turf): **Sf: 2-5** GS: 0-4 Gd: 0-6 GF: 0-5 Fm: 0-0
Distance: 5f/6f: 2-16 7f-8f: 2-14 9f-13f: 0-0 14f+: 0-0
Track : **LH: 2-9** RH: 1-5 Tight: 0-0 Gall: 0-6
Aids: Bl: 0-0 Vi: 0-0 Tstrap: 0-2 Ckp: 0-2
Best Rating: **114** 6/07 Newc 6f heavy

Very useful; winner in Group 3 company; effective over 6f-7f; goes well with cut in the ground; acts on Fibresand; has worn cheekpieces.

Confucius Fortune (IRE)

86(93) (80)48

2-y-o gr g Verglas (IRE)-Duck Over (Warning)

J R Boyle Albert Kwok

Placings:01 (6372)

2009: 6^{0}G, 7^{1}SD,

	Starts	1st	2nd	3rd	Win & Pl
Career Total (Turf)	1	0	0	0	
Career Total (AW)	1	1	0	0	2590

80 9/09 Kemp 7f STD £2590

Total win prize-money £2590

Going (Turf): **Sf: 0-0 GS: 0-0 Gd: 0-1 GF: 0-0 Fm: 0-0**
Distance: 5f/6f: 0-1 **7f-8f: 1-1** 9f-13f: 0-0 14f+: 0-0
Track : LH: 0-0 **RH: 1-1** Tight: 0-0 Gall: 0-1
Aids: Bl: 0-0 Vi: 0-0 Tstrap: 0-0 Ckp: 0-0
Best Rating: **80** 9/09 Kemp 7f stand

Useful; effective at 7f; acts well on Polytrack.

Coniston Wood

81(83) (46)45

3-y-o b f Needwood Blade-Litewska (IRE) (Mujadil (USA))

M W Easterby T Bannister, M Hall & G Fawcett

Placings:600-50 (1247)

2009: 8^{5}SD, 5^{0}F,

	Starts	1st	2nd	3rd	Win & Pl
Career Total (Turf)	2	0	0	0	
Career Total (AW)	3	0	0	0	0

Going (Turf): **Sf: 0-0 GS: 0-0 Gd: 0-1 GF: 0-0 Fm: 0-1**
Distance: 5f/6f: 0-3 7f-8f: 0-2 9f-13f: 0-0 14f+: 0-0
Track : LH: 0-2 RH: 0-0 Tight: 0-0 Gall: 0-0
Aids: Bl: 0-1 Vi: 0-0 Tstrap: 0-0 Ckp: 0-0
Best Rating: **46** 7/08 Sthl 5f stand

Conjecture

93 (46)68

7-y-o b g Danzig (USA)-Golden Opinion (USA) (Slew O'Gold (USA))

R Bastiman The McMaster Springford Partnership

Placings:5101234/503524066026**6**/0**0**52342320/00416010-25604600 (5443)

2009: 5^{2}GF, 6^{5}G, 6^{6}GF, 5^{0}G, 5^{4}G, 5^{6}S, 6^{0}GF, 6^{0}GF,

	Starts	1st	2nd	3rd	Win & Pl
Career Total (Turf)	41	3	7	4	20158
Career Total (AW)	5	1	0	0	4147

68	9/08	Brig	5f213y	(0-58)H	G-F	£2331
62	7/08	Ayr	5f	(0-65)H	GD	£2637
71	4/05	Muss	5f	(0-70)H	GD	£4057
66	2/05	Ling	5f		STD	£4147

Total win prize-money £13173

Going (Turf): Sf: 0-4 GS: 0-3 **Gd: 2-13** GF: 1-19 Fm: 0-2
Distance: **5f/6f: 4-44** 7f-8f: 0-2 9f-13f: 0-0 14f+: 0-0
Track : **LH: 2-11** RH: 0-1 **Tight: 1-9** Gall: 0-0
Aids: Bl: 0-1 Vi: 0-1 Tstrap: 0-0 Ckp: 0-0
Best Rating: 81 7/05 Hayd 5f gd-fm

Modest; effective at around 6f; acts on fast ground; goes on Polytrack.

Conniption (IRE)

100 **94**

2-y-o b f Danehill Dancer (IRE)-Showbiz (IRE) (Sadler's Wells (USA))
B J Meehan Exors of the Late F C T Wilson

Placings:1554 **(7147)**
2009: 6^{1}S, 6^{5}S, 6^{5}G, 6^{4}G,

	Starts	1st	2nd	3rd	Win & Pl
Career Total (Turf)	**4**	**1**	**0**	**0**	**10925**

88	7/09	Newb	6f8y	SFT	£6476

Total win prize-money £6476

Going (Turf): **Sf: 1-2** GS: 0-0 Gd: 0-2 GF: 0-0 Fm: 0-0
Distance: 5f/6f: 0-3 **7f-8f: 1-1** 9f-13f: 0-0 14f+: 0-0
Track : LH: 0-0 RH: 0-0 Tight: 0-0 Gall: 0-0
Aids: Bl: 0-0 Vi: 0-0 Tstrap: 0-0 Ckp: 0-0
Best Rating: 94 10/09 NmkR 6f good

Very useful; winner on debut; effective over 6f; acts on soft ground.

Connor's Choice

97(101) (70)**69**

4-y-o b g Bertolini (USA)-Susan's Dowry (Efisio)
Andrew Turnell Andrew Turnell

Placings:00232/20460000016-012012 **(7480)**
2009: 6^{0}GF, 6^{1}GF, 6^{2}GS, 6^{0}SD, 7^{1}SF, 7^{2}SD,

	Starts	1st	2nd	3rd	Win & Pl
Career Total (Turf)	**11**	**1**	**3**	**1**	**5265**
Career Total (AW)	**11**	**2**	**2**	**0**	**6027**

68	10/09	Wolv	7f32y	(0-60)H	SF	£2388
60	8/09	Ling	6f		G-F	£2047
67	10/08	Ling	6f		STD	£1978

Total win prize-money £6414

Going (Turf): Sf: 0-1 GS: 0-1 Gd: 0-3 **GF: 1-6** Fm: 0-0
Distance: **5f/6f: 2-9** 7f-8f: 1-13 9f-13f: 0-0 14f+: 0-0
Track : **LH: 2-10** RH: 0-5 **Tight: 2-6** Gall: 0-2
Aids: Bl: 0-2 Vi: 0-0 Tstrap: 0-0 Ckp: 0-0
Best Rating: 78 5/08 Ling 7f stand

Modest; stays 7f; acts on fast ground and on Polytrack; has worn blinkers.

Conny Nobel (IRE)

(88) (51)**56**

5-y-o gr g Marju (IRE)-Beauharnaise (FR) (Linamix (FR))
C Roberts Irish Legend Racing Team

Placings:052/0005560250325/3 **(0566)**
2009: 12^{3}SD,

	Starts	1st	2nd	3rd	Win & Pl
Career Total (Turf)	**5**	**0**	**1**	**1**	**983**
Career Total (AW)	**12**	**0**	**2**	**1**	**2308**

Going (Turf): **Sf: 0-1 GS: 0-0 Gd: 0-1 GF: 0-2 Fm: 0-1**
Distance: 5f/6f: 0-0 7f-8f: 0-5 9f-13f: 0-9 14f+: 0-3
Track : LH: 0-11 RH: 0-6 Tight: 0-9 Gall: 0-0
Aids: Bl: 0-0 Vi: 0-1 Tstrap: 0-5 Ckp: 0-5
Best Rating: 65 12/06 Wolv 7f32y stand

Moderate gelding; stays well; acts on good and soft ground and Polytrack.

Cono Zur (FR)

93 **79**

2-y-o b c Anabaa (USA)-Alaskan Idol (USA) (Carson City (USA))
M Johnston T T Bloodstocks

Placings:10 **(7218)**
2009: 7^{1}GF, 7^{0}S,

	Starts	1st	2nd	3rd	Win & Pl
Career Total (Turf)	**2**	**1**	**0**	**0**	**6231**

79	8/09	Newc	7f	G-F	£6231

Total win prize-money £6231

Going (Turf): Sf: 0-1 GS: 0-0 Gd: 0-0 **GF: 1-1** Fm: 0-0
Distance: 5f/6f: 0-0 **7f-8f: 1-2** 9f-13f: 0-0 14f+: 0-0
Track : LH: 0-1 RH: 0-0 Tight: 0-1 Gall: 0-0
Aids: Bl: 0-0 Vi: 0-0 Tstrap: 0-0 Ckp: 0-0
Best Rating: 79 8/09 Newc 7f gd-fm

Winner on debut; effective over 7f; acts on fast ground.

Conquisto

107(90) (60)**96**

4-y-o ch g Hernando (FR)-Seal Indigo (IRE) (Glenstal (USA))
S Gollings (C G Cox 19/9) P J Martin

Placings:060/2102604-5150400 **(7573)**
2009: 12^{5}G, 12^{1}G, 12^{5}GS, 14^{0}S, 13^{4}G, 12^{0}S, 13^{0}SD,

	Starts	1st	2nd	3rd	Win & Pl
Career Total (Turf)	**16**	**2**	**2**	**0**	**14535**
Career Total (AW)	**1**	**0**	**0**	**0**	

93	7/09	Donc	1m4f	(0-85)H	GD	£4857
89	4/08	Hayd	1m2f120y	(0-75)H	G-S	£2590

Total win prize-money £7447

Going (Turf): Sf: 0-5 **GS: 1-6 Gd: 1-5** GF: 0-0 Fm: 0-0
Distance: 5f/6f: 0-1 7f-8f: 0-2 **9f-13f: 2-12** 14f+: 0-2
Track : **LH: 2-9** RH: 0-5 Tight: 0-1 **Gall: 1-3**
Aids: Bl: 0-0 Vi: 0-0 Tstrap: 0-0 Ckp: 0-0
Best Rating: 96 8/09 Asct 1m4f gd-sft

Useful; stays 1m4f; handles good and easy ground.

Conry (IRE)

106(101) (80)**89**

3-y-o ch g Captain Rio-Altizaf (Zafonic (USA))
Patrick Morris (Ms Caroline Hutchinson 19/7) Mrs S J Kelly

Placings:20003000-40416144012 **(7220)**
2009: 7^{4}Y, 6^{0}HY, 6^{4}GF, 7^{1}G, 6^{6}S, 7^{1}GS, 7^{4}GF, 7^{4}SD, 8^{0}SD, 7^{1}S, 7^{2}S,

	Starts	1st	2nd	3rd	Win & Pl
Career Total (Turf)	**15**	**3**	**2**	**1**	**22468**
Career Total (AW)	**4**	**0**	**0**	**0**	**351**

86	10/09	Catt	7f	(0-85)H	SFT	£5180
84	8/09	Catt	7f	(0-80)H	G-S	£5180
75	6/09	Tipp	7f100y	(47-70)H	GD	£5702

Total win prize-money £16064

Going (Turf): **Sf: 1-7 GS: 1-1 Gd: 1-2** GF: 0-2 Fm: 0-0
Distance: 5f/6f: 0-9 **7f-8f: 3-10** 9f-13f: 0-0 14f+: 0-0
Track : **LH: 3-10** RH: 0-3 **Tight: 2-4** Gall: 0-0
Aids: Bl: 0-0 Vi: 0-0 Tstrap: 0-1 Ckp: 0-1
Best Rating: 89 11/09 Catt 7f soft

Useful; stays 7f; acts on good and softer ground; handles Polytrack.

Consequence

91(61) **42**

3-y-o gr g Paris House-Scrutinize (IRE) (Selkirk (USA))
A Dickman Keith Fitzsimons-Blanche M Bennett

Placings:40-06 **(4805)**
2009: 7^{0}G, 7^{6}GF,

	Starts	1st	2nd	3rd	Win & Pl
Career Total (Turf)	**2**	**0**	**0**	**0**	**0**
Career Total (AW)	**2**	**0**	**0**	**0**	**0**

Going (Turf): **Sf: 0-0 GS: 0-0 Gd: 0-1 GF: 0-1 Fm: 0-0**
Distance: 5f/6f: 0-1 7f-8f: 0-3 9f-13f: 0-0 14f+: 0-0
Track : LH: 0-3 RH: 0-0 Tight: 0-1 Gall: 0-0
Aids: Bl: 0-0 Vi: 0-0 Tstrap: 0-0 Ckp: 0-0
Best Rating: 42 8/09 Rdcr 7f gd-fm

Consequential

83(96) (71)**64**

2-y-o b f Pivotal-Thirteen Tricks (USA) (Grand Slam (USA))
D M Simcock The Consequential Partnership

Placings:62 **(7717)**
2009: 7^{6}G, 8^{2}SD,

	Starts	1st	2nd	3rd	Win & Pl
Career Total (Turf)	**1**	**0**	**0**	**0**	**0**
Career Total (AW)	**1**	**0**	**1**	**0**	**2454**

Going (Turf): **Sf: 0-0 GS: 0-0 Gd: 0-1 GF: 0-0 Fm: 0-0**
Distance: 5f/6f: 0-0 7f-8f: 0-1 9f-13f: 0-1 14f+: 0-0
Track : LH: 0-1 RH: 0-0 Tight: 0-1 Gall: 0-0
Aids: Bl: 0-0 Vi: 0-0 Tstrap: 0-0 Ckp: 0-0
Best Rating: 71 12/09 Wolv 1m141y stand

Fair; stays 1m; acts on Polytrack.

Consider Yourself (USA)

86 **64**

2-y-o gr/ro f Afleet Alex (USA)-Champagne Royale (USA) (French Deputy (USA))
M L W Bell C Wright & The Hon Mrs J M Corbett

Placings:00 **(6062)**
2009: 7^{0}G, 8^{0}GF,

	Starts	1st	2nd	3rd	Win & Pl
Career Total (Turf)	**2**	**0**	**0**	**0**	

Going (Turf): **Sf: 0-0 GS: 0-0 Gd: 0-1 GF: 0-1 Fm: 0-0**
Distance: 5f/6f: 0-0 7f-8f: 0-2 9f-13f: 0-0 14f+: 0-0
Track : LH: 0-0 RH: 0-0 Tight: 0-0 Gall: 0-0
Aids: Bl: 0-0 Vi: 0-0 Tstrap: 0-0 Ckp: 0-0
Best Rating: 64 9/09 NmkR 1m gd-fm

Constant Cheers (IRE)

101(100) (78)**86**

6-y-o b g Royal Applause-Juno Marlowe (IRE) (Danehill (USA))

W R Swinburn Mr & Mrs W R Swinburn

Placings:000/04050/33144/51156-451545 **(5875)**
2009: 9^{4}GF, **10^{5}SD**, 10^{1}G, 10^{5}GF, 10^{4}GF, 9^{5}GF,

	Starts	1st	2nd	3rd	Win & Pl
Career Total (Turf)	**16**	**4**	**0**	**1**	**14551**
Career Total (AW)	**8**	**0**	**0**	**1**	**593**

81	7/09	Epsm	1m2f18y (0-75)H	GD	£3238
86	7/08	Newb	1m3f5y (0-70)H	G-F	£2590
78	6/08	Wwck	1m2f188y (0-65)H	G-F	£2388
67	8/07	Wind	1m3f135y (0-70)H	G-F	£3238

Total win prize-money £11455

Going (Turf): Sf: 0-1 GS: 0-2 Gd: 1-2 **GF: 3-10** Fm: 0-1
Distance: 5f/6f: 0-0 7f-8f: 0-3 **9f-13f: 4-21** 14f+: 0-0
Track : **LH: 3-13** RH: 0-7 **Tight: 2-12** Gall: 1-1
Aids: Bl: 0-0 Vi: 0-2 Tstrap: 1-6 Ckp: 1-6
Best Rating: **86** 7/08 Newb 1m3f5y gd-fm

Fair; gets 1m2f; acts on fast ground and Polytrack; has worn cheekpieces.

Constant Contact

102 **89**
2-y-o b c Passing Glance-Floriana (Selkirk (USA))
A M Balding Kingsclere Racing CLub

Placings:0512 **(6471)**
2009: 7^{0}GF, 6^{5}F, 7^{1}G, 7^{2}GF,

	Starts	1st	2nd	3rd	Win & Pl
Career Total (Turf)	**4**	**1**	**1**	**0**	**7630**

88	8/09	Epsm	7f	GD	£5180

Total win prize-money £5181

Going (Turf): Sf: 0-0 GS: 0-0 **Gd: 1-1** GF: 0-2 Fm: 0-1
Distance: 5f/6f: 0-0 **7f-8f: 1-4** 9f-13f: 0-0 14f+: 0-0
Track : **LH: 1-4** RH: 0-0 **Tight: 1-2** Gall: 0-0
Aids: Bl: 0-0 Vi: 0-0 Tstrap: 0-0 Ckp: 0-0
Best Rating: **89** 10/09 Epsm 7f gd-fm

Useful; stays 7f; acts on fast ground.

Consult

(77) (33)
2-y-o ch g Dr Fong (USA)-Merle (Selkirk (USA))
Sir Mark Prescott W E Sturt - Osborne House III

Placings:600 **(7326)**
2009: 7^{6}SD, 8^{0}SD, 7^{0}SD,

	Starts	1st	2nd	3rd	Win & Pl
Career Total (Turf)	**0**	**0**	**0**	**0**	
Career Total (AW)	**3**	**0**	**0**	**0**	**0**

Going (Turf): **Sf: 0-0 GS: 0-0 Gd: 0-0 GF: 0-0 Fm: 0-0**
Distance: 5f/6f: 0-0 7f-8f: 0-3 9f-13f: 0-0 14f+: 0-0
Track : LH: 0-2 RH: 0-1 Tight: 0-1 Gall: 0-0
Aids: Bl: 0-0 Vi: 0-0 Tstrap: 0-0 Ckp: 0-0
Best Rating: **33** 10/09 Sthl 7f stand

Contemplate

90 (83) (28) **59**
3-y-o ch f Compton Place-Billie Blue (Ballad Rock)
Dr J D Scargill R A Dalton & Silent Partners

Placings:0-60020 **(6925)**
2009: 7^{6}SD, 8^{0}G, 7^{0}GF, 7^{2}GF, 7^{0}GF,

	Starts	1st	2nd	3rd	Win & Pl
Career Total (Turf)	**5**	**0**	**1**	**0**	**771**
Career Total (AW)	**1**	**0**	**0**	**0**	**0**

Going (Turf): **Sf: 0-1 GS: 0-0 Gd: 0-1 GF: 0-3 Fm: 0-0**
Distance: 5f/6f: 0-1 7f-8f: 0-4 9f-13f: 0-1 14f+: 0-0
Track : LH: 0-1 RH: 0-0 Tight: 0-0 Gall: 0-0
Aids: Bl: 0-2 Vi: 0-0 Tstrap: 0-0 Ckp: 0-0
Best Rating: **59** 10/09 Leic 7f9y gd-fm

Plating-class; stays 7f; acts on fast ground; has worn blinkers.

Contest (IRE)

109 (111) (115) **111**
5-y-o b h Danehill Dancer (IRE)-Mala Mala (IRE) (Brief Truce (USA))
C Theodorakis (D M Simcock 10/1) Mrs T Nanos & C Theodorakis

Placings:41130/100000-10654210300200 **(6579a)**
2009: 6^{1}SD, 6^{0}G, 6^{6}GF, 6^{5}G, 6^{4}GF, 5^{2}VS, 6^{1}G, 5^{0}G, 5^{3}G, 6^{0}G, 5^{0}G, 6^{2}G, 7^{0}GS, 5^{0}VS,

	Starts	1st	2nd	3rd	Win & Pl
Career Total (Turf)	**23**	**4**	**2**	**2**	**114131**
Career Total (AW)	**2**	**1**	**0**	**0**	**7771**

111	4/09	Chan	6f		GD	£25243
115	1/09	Ling	6f		STD	£7771
108	5/08	Cork	6f		YLD	£23933
104	5/07	Naas	6f	(60-100)H	GD	£11436
74	4/07	Navn	5f		FRM	£6069

Total win prize-money £74454

Going (Turf): Sf: 0-0 GS: 0-2 **Gd: 2-11** GF: 0-4 Fm: 1-1
Distance: **5f/6f: 5-22** 7f-8f: 0-3 9f-13f: 0-0 14f+: 0-0
Track : **LH: 3-9** RH: 0-4 **Tight: 1-1** Gall: 0-4
Aids: **Bl: 1-11** Vi: 0-0 Tstrap: 0-2 Ckp: 0-2
Best Rating: **115** 1/09 Ling 6f stand

Smart; effective at up to 6f; acts on good or faster ground.

Contract Caterer (IRE)

99 **86**
2-y-o b c Azamour (IRE)-Nawaji (USA) (Trempolino (USA))
Pat Eddery ABM Catering Limited

Placings:42141 **(5742)**
2009: 6^{4}S, 7^{2}GF, 7^{1}GF, 7^{4}G, 8^{1}GF,

	Starts	1st	2nd	3rd	Win & Pl
Career Total (Turf)	**5**	**2**	**1**	**0**	**9651**

86	9/09	Gdwd	1m (0-85)H	G-F	£3885
77	7/09	Catt	7f	G-F	£3238

Total win prize-money £7124

Going (Turf): Sf: 0-1 GS: 0-0 Gd: 0-1 **GF: 2-3** Fm: 0-0
Distance: 5f/6f: 0-1 **7f-8f: 2-4** 9f-13f: 0-0 14f+: 0-0
Track : LH: 1-1 RH: 1-2 **Tight: 1-1** Gall: 0-0
Aids: Bl: 0-0 Vi: 0-0 Tstrap: 0-0 Ckp: 0-0
Best Rating: **86** 9/09 Gdwd 1m gd-fm

Useful; effective at 1m; handles fast and soft ground.

Contrada

(95) (59) **70**
4-y-o b g Medicean-Trounce (Barathea (IRE))
J A B Old W E Sturt

Placings:0/6000130-0 **(1073)**
2009: 12^{0}SD,

	Starts	1st	2nd	3rd	Win & Pl
Career Total (Turf)	**7**	**1**	**0**	**0**	**2331**
Career Total (AW)	**2**	**0**	**0**	**1**	**289**

70	9/08	Brig	1m1f209y (0-65)H	G-F	£2331

Total win prize-money £2331

Going (Turf): Sf: 0-1 GS: 0-3 Gd: 0-1 **GF: 1-2** Fm: 0-0
Distance: 5f/6f: 0-0 7f-8f: 0-3 **9f-13f: 1-6** 14f+: 0-0
Track : **LH: 1-5** RH: 0-0 Tight: 0-4 Gall: 0-1
Aids: Bl: 0-1 Vi: 0-0 Tstrap: 0-0 Ckp: 0-0
Best Rating: **70** 9/08 Brig 1m1f209y gd-fm

Modest; stays 1m2f; acts on fast ground.

Contrary (IRE)

(84) (53)
2-y-o ch f Mark Of Esteem (IRE)-Crystal Gaze (IRE) (Rainbow Quest (USA))
E J O'Neill (E A L Dunlop 21/9) Ballygallon Stud Limited

Placings:01 **(7166a)**
2009: 7^{0}SD, 7^{1}VS,

	Starts	1st	2nd	3rd	Win & Pl
Career Total (Turf)	**1**	**1**	**0**	**0**	**6311**
Career Total (AW)	**1**	**0**	**0**	**0**	

10/09 Moul	7f	VS	£6311

Total win prize-money £6311

Going (Turf): **Sf: 0-0 GS: 0-0 Gd: 0-0 GF: 0-0 Fm: 0-0**
Distance: 5f/6f: 0-0 **7f-8f: 1-2** 9f-13f: 0-0 14f+: 0-0
Track : LH: 0-0 RH: 0-1 Tight: 0-0 Gall: 0-0
Aids: Bl: 0-0 Vi: 0-0 Tstrap: 0-0 Ckp: 0-0
Best Rating: **53** 9/09 Kemp 7f stand

Contredanse (IRE)

93 (90) (72) **71**
2-y-o br f Danehill Dancer (IRE)-Ahdaab (USA) (Rahy (USA))
B J Meehan Exors of the Late F C T Wilson

Placings:003 **(7450)**
2009: 7^{0}GF, 7^{0}GF, 8^{3}SD,

	Starts	1st	2nd	3rd	Win & Pl
Career Total (Turf)	**2**	**0**	**0**	**0**	**7840**
Career Total (AW)	**1**	**0**	**0**	**1**	**482**

Going (Turf): **Sf: 0-0 GS: 0-0 Gd: 0-0 GF: 0-2 Fm: 0-0**
Distance: 5f/6f: 0-0 7f-8f: 0-3 9f-13f: 0-0 14f+: 0-0
Track : LH: 0-0 RH: 0-1 Tight: 0-0 Gall: 0-0
Aids: Bl: 0-0 Vi: 0-0 Tstrap: 0-0 Ckp: 0-0
Best Rating: **72** 11/09 Kemp 1m stand

Useful; stays 1m and acts on Polytrack.

Convallaria (FR)

(102) (67) **40**
6-y-o b m Cape Cross (IRE)-Scarlet Davis (FR) (Ti King (FR))
C F Wall Mrs Claude Lilley

Placings:00/6200053/2020001001-204500 **(3983)**
2009: 7^{2}SD, 8^{0}SD, 7^{4}SD, 7^{5}SD, 7^{0}SD, 7^{0}SD,

	Starts	1st	2nd	3rd	Win & Pl
Career Total (Turf)	**6**	**0**	**1**	**0**	**636**
Career Total (AW)	**19**	**2**	**3**	**1**	**6011**

64	11/08	Kemp	7f	(0-55)H	STD	£1706
62	8/08	Ling	7f	(0-65)H	STD	£2047

Total win prize-money £3753

Going (Turf): **Sf: 0-1 GS: 0-2 Gd: 0-2 GF: 0-1 Fm: 0-0**
Distance: 5f/6f: 0-0 **7f-8f: 2-19** 9f-13f: 0-6 14f+: 0-0
Track : LH: 1-12 RH: 1-8 **Tight: 1-11** Gall: 0-0
Aids: **Bl: 2-9** Vi: 0-0 Tstrap: 0-0 Ckp: 0-0
Best Rating: **67** 2/09 Kemp 7f stand

Modest; stays 1m; acts on Polytrack and on good ground on turf; has worn blinkers.

Converti

97(79) (57)**56**

5-y-o b g Averti (IRE)-Conquestadora (Hernando (FR))

Mrs H J Manners (H J Manners 6/9) Exors Of The Late H J Manners

Placings:000/**0**2**05**1**0**/**05043540-50** **(4092)**

2009: 14^{5}GF, 16^{0}GS,

	Starts	1st	2nd	3rd	Win & Pl
Career Total (Turf)	**13**	**1**	**0**	**1**	**3541**
Career Total (AW)	**6**	**0**	**1**	**0**	**605**
53 7/07 Wind 1m3f135y				G-F	£3238

Total win prize-money £3239

Going (Turf): Sf: 0-0 GS: 0-3 Gd: 0-2 **GF: 1-8** Fm: 0-0
Distance: 5f/6f: 0-1 7f-8f: 0-2 **9f-13f: 1-14** 14f+: 0-2
Track : LH: 0-9 RH: 0-3 **Tight: 1-12** Gall: 0-1
Aids: Bl: 0-2 Vi: 0-0 Tstrap: 0-0 Ckp: 0-0
Best Rating: 57 6/07 Ling 1m4f stand

Convince (USA)

104(103) (63)**67**

8-y-o ch g Mt. Livermore (USA)-Conical (Zafonic (USA))

J L Flint (K M Prendergast 17/9) M Matthews (Mid-Glamorgan)

Placings:32104/00056500/61450650/503030560026/6351 0000660/00006-31314152052605**1** **(7726)**

2009: 7^{3}SD, 6^{1}SD, 7^{3}SD, 6^{1}SD, 6^{4}SD, 6^{1}GS, 7^{5}GF, 7^{2}G, 6^{0}G, 7^{5}GF, 6^{2}GS, 5^{6}SD, 7^{0}SD, 7^{1}SD,

	Starts	1st	2nd	3rd	Win & Pl
Career Total (Turf)	**51**	**4**	**4**	**4**	**21114**
Career Total (AW)	**13**	**3**	**0**	**2**	**3916**
58 5/09 Brig 6f209y (0-65)H				G-S	£2590
57 3/09 Sthl 6f (0-50)H				STD	£2047
52 1/09 Kemp 6f (0-45)				STD	£1364
61 5/07 Leic 7f9y				G-F	£2590
81 5/05 Hayd 5f (0-75)H				GD	£3569
91 8/03 Wind 6f D				G-F	£4407

Total win prize-money £16570

Going (Turf): Sf: 0-1 GS: 1-9 Gd: 1-14 **GF: 2-25** Fm: 0-2
Distance: **5f/6f: 4-30** 7f-8f: 3-27 9f-13f: 0-7 14f+: 0-0
Track : **LH: 3-24** RH: 1-9 Tight: 0-4 **Gall: 1-9**
Aids: Bl: 0-3 Vi: 0-2 Tstrap: 2-16 Ckp: 2-16
Best Rating: 91 8/03 Wind 6f gd-fm

Moderate; effective at around 5f-1m; acts on easy ground; acts on Fibresand and Polytrack; has worn cheekpieces.

Convitezza

80 **29**

3-y-o b f Domedriver (IRE)-Condoleezza (USA) (Cozzene (USA))

M E Sowersby I L Westwood

Placings:605600 **(6997)**

2009: 8^{6}GF, 8^{0}G, 10^{5}GF, 8^{6}GF, 7^{0}GF, 7^{0}G,

	Starts	1st	2nd	3rd	Win & Pl
Career Total (Turf)	**6**	**0**	**0**	**0**	**0**

Going (Turf): Sf: 0-0 GS: 0-0 Gd: 0-2 GF: 0-4 Fm: 0-0
Distance: 5f/6f: 0-0 7f-8f: 0-3 9f-13f: 0-3 14f+: 0-0
Track : LH: 0-3 RH: 0-1 Tight: 0-1 Gall: 0-0
Aids: Bl: 0-0 Vi: 0-0 Tstrap: 0-0 Ckp: 0-0
Best Rating: 29 8/09 Pont 1m4y gd-fm

Convivial Spirit

(98) (72)**64**

5-y-o b g Lake Coniston (IRE)-Ruby Princess (IRE) (Mac's Imp (USA))

E F Vaughan A M Pickering

Placings:632004/**2131**5004506535**3**/**42506034646-0** **(0357)**

2009: 8^{0}SD,

	Starts	1st	2nd	3rd	Win & Pl
Career Total (Turf)	**13**	**0**	**1**	**1**	**1638**
Career Total (AW)	**20**	**2**	**2**	**4**	**9315**
72 3/07 Ling 7f (0-70)H				STD	£2914
69 2/07 Wolv 5f216y (0-65)H				SS	£2730

Total win prize-money £5645

Going (Turf): Sf: 0-1 GS: 0-1 Gd: 0-5 GF: 0-6 Fm: 0-0
Distance: 5f/6f: 1-12 7f-8f: 1-17 9f-13f: 0-4 14f+: 0-0
Track : **LH: 2-21** RH: 0-4 **Tight: 2-17** Gall: 0-1
Aids: Bl: 0-0 Vi: 0-1 Tstrap: 0-1 Ckp: 0-1
Best Rating: 72 2/08 Kemp 1m stand

Modest; stays 1m; acts on easy ground and Polytrack.

Cook's Endeavour (USA)

104(94) (66)**81**

3-y-o b g Gone West (USA)-Weekend In London (USA) (Belong To Me (USA))

K A Ryan Graham Frankland

Placings:03130-0033000206 **(7350)**

2009: 8^{0}GF, 7^{0}GS, 7^{3}GF, 6^{3}GS, 7^{0}GF, 7^{0}GS, 7^{0}SD, 8^{2}GF, 7^{0}GF, 7^{6}SD,

	Starts	1st	2nd	3rd	Win & Pl
Career Total (Turf)	**13**	**1**	**1**	**4**	**9707**
Career Total (AW)	**2**	**0**	**0**	**0**	**0**
81 7/08 Leic 5f218y				G-F	£5180

Total win prize-money £5181

Going (Turf): Sf: 0-1 GS: 0-3 Gd: 0-2 **GF: 1-7** Fm: 0-0
Distance: **5f/6f: 1-3** 7f-8f: 0-11 9f-13f: 0-1 14f+: 0-0
Track : LH: 0-3 RH: 0-1 Tight: 0-3 Gall: 0-0
Aids: Bl: 0-0 Vi: 0-0 Tstrap: 0-2 Ckp: 0-2
Best Rating: 81 9/08 Donc 7f soft

Fair; stays 1m and acts on most ground.

Cookie Galore

94(90) (48)**53**

2-y-o ch f Monsieur Bond (IRE)-Ginger Cookie (Bold Edge)

J A Glover Dixon, Denniff, Youdan

Placings:60403 **(6938)**

2009: 5^{6}GF, 5^{0}GF, 6^{4}SD, 6^{0}S, 5^{3}SD,

	Starts	1st	2nd	3rd	Win & Pl
Career Total (Turf)	**3**	**0**	**0**	**0**	**0**
Career Total (AW)	**2**	**0**	**0**	**1**	**302**

Going (Turf): Sf: 0-1 GS: 0-0 Gd: 0-0 GF: 0-2 Fm: 0-0
Distance: 5f/6f: 0-4 7f-8f: 0-1 9f-13f: 0-0 14f+: 0-0
Track : LH: 0-1 RH: 0-1 Tight: 0-0 Gall: 0-0
Aids: Bl: 0-0 Vi: 0-0 Tstrap: 0-0 Ckp: 0-0
Best Rating: 53 9/09 Rdcr 5f gd-fm

Cool Art (IRE)

91(96) (80)**71**

3-y-o b g One Cool Cat (USA)-Fee Faw Fum (IRE) (Great Commotion (USA))

J S Wainwright (Peter Grayson 2/10) Mrs Z Wentworth

Placings:51010613-00406600400 **(6989)**

2009: 7^{0}SD, 7^{0}SD, 7^{4}SD, 6^{0}GF, 6^{6}G, 5^{6}GF, 6^{0}SD, 6^{0}SD, 7^{4}SS, 6^{0}GF, 6^{0}G,

	Starts	1st	2nd	3rd	Win & Pl
Career Total (Turf)	**9**	**1**	**0**	**0**	**3785**
Career Total (AW)	**10**	**2**	**0**	**1**	**5865**
77 11/08 Ling 7f				STD	£2047
77 9/08 Ling 6f (0-75)				STD	£3238
66 5/08 Yarm 6f3y				G-F	£3784

Total win prize-money £9070

Going (Turf): Sf: 0-0 GS: 0-0 Gd: 0-3 **GF: 1-6** Fm: 0-0
Distance: 5f/6f: 1-9 **7f-8f: 2-10** 9f-13f: 0-0 14f+: 0-0
Track : **LH: 2-9** RH: 0-1 **Tight: 2-7** Gall: 0-2
Aids: **Bl: 1-9** Vi: 0-0 Tstrap: 0-0 Ckp: 0-0
Best Rating: 80 11/08 Ling 7f stand

Fair; stays 7f; acts on fast ground and on Polytrack; has worn blinkers.

Cool Baranca (GER)

105 **82**

3-y-o b f Beat Hollow-Cool Storm (IRE) (Rainbow Quest (USA))

P Monteith (P Schiergen 25/7) Dennis J Coppola

Placings:024312 **(7169)**

2009: 8^{0}G, 7^{2}G, 8^{4}GS, 9^{3}G, 9^{1}G, 8^{2}S,

	Starts	1st	2nd	3rd	Win & Pl
Career Total (Turf)	**6**	**1**	**2**	**1**	**7593**
74 10/09 Ayr 1m1f20y (0-70)				GD	£3238

Total win prize-money £3238

Going (Turf): Sf: 0-1 GS: 0-1 **Gd: 1-4** GF: 0-0 Fm: 0-0
Distance: 5f/6f: 0-0 7f-8f: 0-4 **9f-13f: 1-2** 14f+: 0-0
Track : **LH: 1-3** RH: 0-1 Tight: 0-1 Gall: 0-1
Aids: Bl: 0-0 Vi: 0-0 Tstrap: 0-0 Ckp: 0-0
Best Rating: 82 10/09 Ayr 1m soft

Modest; stays 1m1f and acts on good ground.

Cool Ebony

100(95) (67)**83**

6-y-o br g Erhaab (USA)-Monawara (IRE) (Namaqualand (USA))

P J Makin Wedgewood Estates

Placings:005/5035411200/56044631250/163300-0561 **(4824)**

2009: 8^{0}SD, 8^{5}G, 8^{6}GF, 8^{1}G,

	Starts	1st	2nd	3rd	Win & Pl
Career Total (Turf)	**33**	**5**	**2**	**4**	**24912**
Career Total (AW)	**1**	**0**	**0**	**0**	
77 8/09 Wind 1m67y (0-70)H				GD	£2729
83 5/08 Bath 1m5y (0-75)H				G-F	£3885
78 9/07 Muss 1m (0-75)H				G-F	£3886
82 8/06 Bath 1m5y (0-75)H				FRM	£4210
76 7/06 Hayd 1m30y (0-70)H				G-F	£5505

Total win prize-money £20217

Going (Turf): Sf: 0-1 GS: 0-4 Gd: 1-12 **GF: 3-15** Fm: 1-1
Distance: 5f/6f: 0-0 7f-8f: 1-14 **9f-13f: 4-19** 14f+: 0-1
Track : **LH: 3-21** RH: 2-9 **Tight: 4-19** Gall: 0-2
Aids: Bl: 0-0 Vi: 0-0 Tstrap: 0-1 Ckp: 0-1
Best Rating: 83 5/08 Bath 1m5y gd-fm

Fair; effective over 1m; acts on fast ground.

Cool Fashion (IRE)

89(93) (46)43

4-y-o b f Orpen (USA)-Fun Fashion (IRE) (Polish Patriot (USA))

Ollie Pears 21st Century Racing

Placings:00/50000006-00 (2529)

2009: 5^0F, 5^0GF,

	Starts	1st	2nd	3rd	Win & Pl
Career Total (Turf)	7	0	0	0	
Career Total (AW)	5	0	0	0	0

Going (Turf): Sf: 0-0 GS: 0-0 Gd: 0-4 GF: 0-2 Fm: 0-1
Distance: 5f/6f: 0-10 7f-8f: 0-2 9f-13f: 0-0 14f+: 0-0
Track : LH: 0-5 RH: 0-2 Tight: 0-4 Gall: 0-1
Aids: Bl: 0-7 Vi: 0-3 Tstrap: 0-0 Ckp: 0-0
Best Rating: 46 2/08 Wolv 5f20y stand

Cool Hand Jake

87(104) (87)65

3-y-o b g Storming Home-Monawara (IRE) (Namaqualand (USA))

P J Makin Wedgewood Estates

Placings:04-1611030 (6209)

2009: 8^1SD, 8^6GF, 8^1SD, 8^1SD, 8^0SD, 8^3SD, 10^0SD,

	Starts	1st	2nd	3rd	Win & Pl
Career Total (Turf)	2	0	0	0	0
Career Total (AW)	7	3	0	1	12171

85	6/09	Kemp	1m	(0-80)H	STD	£4727
78	6/09	Wolv	1m141y	(0-70)H	STD	£3885
69	1/09	Kemp	1m		STD	£2590

Total win prize-money £11203

Going (Turf): Sf: 0-0 GS: 0-1 Gd: 0-0 GF: 0-1 Fm: 0-0
Distance: 5f/6f: 0-0 **7f-8f: 2-5** 9f-13f: 1-4 14f+: 0-0
Track : LH: 1-3 **RH: 2-6 Tight: 1-2** Gall: 0-0
Aids: Bl: 0-0 Vi: 0-0 Tstrap: 0-0 Ckp: 0-0
Best Rating: 87 9/09 Kemp 1m stand

Useful; stays 1m; acts on Polytrack; has worn a tongue-tie.

Cool Judgement (IRE)

107 101

4-y-o b g Peintre Celebre (USA)-Sadinga (IRE) (Sadler's Wells (USA))

M A Jarvis H R H Sultan Ahmad Shah

Placings:301/123306-2 (1709)

2009: 14^2GF,

	Starts	1st	2nd	3rd	Win & Pl
Career Total (Turf)	10	2	2	3	21413

91	5/08	Gdwd	1m3f	(0-80)H	G-S	£4533
78	10/07	Gdwd	1m1f		SFT	£4533

Total win prize-money £9067

Going (Turf): Sf: 1-4 GS: 1-2 Gd: 0-1 GF: 0-3 Fm: 0-0
Distance: 5f/6f: 0-0 7f-8f: 0-2 **9f-13f: 2-5** 14f+: 0-3
Track : LH: 0-2 **RH: 2-7 Tight: 2-4** Gall: 0-3
Aids: Bl: 0-0 Vi: 0-0 Tstrap: 0-0 Ckp: 0-0
Best Rating: 101 5/09 Sals 1m6f21y gd-fm

Very useful; Listed placed; stays 1m5f and acts on soft ground.

Cool Kitten (IRE)

83 50

2-y-o b f One Cool Cat (USA)-Zoom Lens (IRE) (Caerleon (USA))

W J Knight G Roddick

Placings:006 (6786)

2009: 6^0GF, 7^0GF, 7^6G,

	Starts	1st	2nd	3rd	Win & Pl
Career Total (Turf)	3	0	0	0	0

Going (Turf): Sf: 0-0 GS: 0-0 Gd: 0-1 GF: 0-2 Fm: 0-0
Distance: 5f/6f: 0-1 7f-8f: 0-2 9f-13f: 0-0 14f+: 0-0
Track : LH: 0-1 RH: 0-0 Tight: 0-0 Gall: 0-0
Aids: Bl: 0-0 Vi: 0-0 Tstrap: 0-0 Ckp: 0-0
Best Rating: 50 5/09 Ling 6f gd-fm

Cool Libby (IRE)

96(76) (30)50

3-y-o br f One Cool Cat (USA)-Cosabawn (IRE) (Barathea (IRE))

A B Haynes T Hosier

Placings:00-0600 (5540a)

2009: 8^0GS, 8^6F, 10^0GS, 8^0F,

	Starts	1st	2nd	3rd	Win & Pl
Career Total (Turf)	5	0	0	0	0
Career Total (AW)	1	0	0	0	

Going (Turf): Sf: 0-0 GS: 0-3 Gd: 0-0 GF: 0-0 Fm: 0-2
Distance: 5f/6f: 0-0 7f-8f: 0-1 9f-13f: 0-5 14f+: 0-0
Track : LH: 0-4 RH: 0-1 Tight: 0-3 Gall: 0-0
Aids: Bl: 0-0 Vi: 0-0 Tstrap: 0-0 Ckp: 0-0
Best Rating: 50 10/08 Bath 1m5y gd-sft

Cool Madam

81(78) (29)13

3-y-o b f Ishiguru (USA)-Face The Judge (USA) (Benny The Dip (USA))

D Flood D A Drake

Placings:0-0500 (1578)

2009: 6^0SD, 5^5SD, 6^0SD, 10^0G,

	Starts	1st	2nd	3rd	Win & Pl
Career Total (Turf)	1	0	0	0	
Career Total (AW)	4	0	0	0	0

Going (Turf): Sf: 0-0 GS: 0-0 Gd: 0-1 GF: 0-0 Fm: 0-0
Distance: 5f/6f: 0-3 7f-8f: 0-1 9f-13f: 0-1 14f+: 0-0
Track : LH: 0-5 RH: 0-0 Tight: 0-3 Gall: 0-1
Aids: Bl: 0-0 Vi: 0-0 Tstrap: 0-1 Ckp: 0-1
Best Rating: 29 2/09 Wolv 5f20y stand

Cool Sands (IRE)

81(106) (78)56

7-y-o b g Trans Island-Shalerina (USA) (Shalford (IRE))

J G Given Peter Swann

Placings:006/6412043500001043O5/516004000000125/30 3133155110600004O4/25440564040001004141240-050000052332 (7835)

2009: 6^0SS, 7^5SD, 5^0GF, 6^0SD, 6^0SD, 6^0SD, 6^0SD, 5^5SD, 6^2SD, 5^3SD, 6^3SD, 6^2SD,

	Starts	1st	2nd	3rd	Win & Pl
Career Total (Turf)	20	0	0	1	992
Career Total (AW)	71	11	6	7	40748

75	11/08	Sthl	6f	(0-75)H	STD	£4094
73	10/08	Kemp	6f	(0-65)H	STD	£1706
71	7/08	Sthl	6f	(0-75)H	STD	£2729
77	5/07	Sthl	6f	(0-80)H	STD	£5181
75	3/07	Kemp	6f	(0-75)H	STD	£2914
73	2/07	Kemp	6f	(0-65)H	STD	£2047
71	2/07	Sthl	6f	(0-70)H	STD	£3241
64	12/06	Sthl	7f	(0-53)H	STD	£2047
68	3/06	Ling	7f	(0-70)H	STD	£2914
63	11/05	Sthl	6f	(0-55)H	STD	£2893
56	2/05	Ling	6f	(0-55)H	STD	£2877

Total win prize-money £32651

Going (Turf): Sf: 0-5 GS: 0-6 Gd: 0-5 GF: 0-4 Fm: 0-0
Distance: 5f/6f: 9-53 7f-8f: 2-35 9f-13f: 0-3 14f+: 0-0
Track : LH: 8-64 RH: 3-16 **Tight: 2-34** Gall: 0-2
Aids: Bl: 0-0 **Vi: 9-71** Tstrap: 0-0 Ckp: 0-0
Best Rating: 78 11/08 Sthl 6f stand

Moderate; best over 6f; acts on most ground on turf; also goes on sand; has worn a visor.

Cool Sonata (IRE)

(89) (36)42

3-y-o b f One Cool Cat (USA)-Sonatina (Distant Relative)

M Brittain Mel Brittain

Placings:20600030-0 (0228)

2009: 8^0SD,

	Starts	1st	2nd	3rd	Win & Pl
Career Total (Turf)	6	0	1	0	605
Career Total (AW)	3	0	0	1	388

Going (Turf): Sf: 0-0 GS: 0-1 Gd: 0-2 GF: 0-3 Fm: 0-0
Distance: 5f/6f: 0-5 7f-8f: 0-3 9f-13f: 0-1 14f+: 0-0
Track : LH: 0-3 RH: 0-1 Tight: 0-1 Gall: 0-1
Aids: Bl: 0-0 Vi: 0-0 Tstrap: 0-0 Ckp: 0-0
Best Rating: 42 5/08 Catt 5f good

Moderate; effective over 7f; acts on Fibresand.

Cool Strike (UAE)

112(94) (67)93

3-y-o b g Halling (USA)-Velour (Mtoto)

A M Balding Mrs P Hastings

Placings:520-021315 (4408)

2009: 10^0GF, 11^2G, 11^1F, 12^3GF, 12^1GF, 14^5G,

	Starts	1st	2nd	3rd	Win & Pl
Career Total (Turf)	7	2	1	1	14682
Career Total (AW)	2	0	1	0	806

93	7/09	NmkJ	1m4f	(0-90)H	G-F	£9714
82	6/09	Bath	1m3f144y	(0-70)H	FRM	£2719

Total win prize-money £12434

Going (Turf): Sf: 0-1 GS: 0-0 Gd: 0-2 **GF: 1-3 Fm: 1-1**
Distance: 5f/6f: 0-0 7f-8f: 0-2 **9f-13f: 2-6** 14f+: 0-1
Track : LH: 1-3 RH: 1-5 Tight: 1-6 Gall: 1-1
Aids: Bl: 0-0 **Vi: 2-5** Tstrap: 0-0 Ckp: 0-0
Best Rating: 93 7/09 Gdwd 1m6f good

Useful; stays 1m4f; handles quick ground; has worn a visor.

Cool Valentine

99(95) (78)82

2-y-o b c One Cool Cat (USA)-Miss Mirasol (Sheikh Albadou)

A M Balding Mick and Janice Mariscotti

Placings:246144 (6373)

2009: 6^{2}SD, 6^{4}G, 5^{6}G, 7^{1}GF, 8^{4}GF, 8^{4}SD,

	Starts	1st	2nd	3rd	Win & Pl
Career Total (Turf)	4	1	0	0	5710
Career Total (AW)	2	0	1	0	1195

79 8/09 Sand 7f16y (0-85) G-F £5180
Total win prize-money £5181

Going (Turf): Sf: 0-0 GS: 0-0 Gd: 0-2 **GF: 1-2** Fm: 0-0
Distance: 5f/6f: 0-3 **7f-8f: 1-3** 9f-13f: 0-0 14f+: 0-0
Track : LH: 0-3 **RH: 1-3** Tight: 0-2 Gall: 0-1
Aids: Bl: 0-0 Vi: 0-0 Tstrap: 0-0 Ckp: 0-0
Best Rating: **82** 9/09 Gdwd 1m gd-fm

Fair; half-brother to the dual 1m2f winner Dark Prospect; stays 7f; acts on Polytrack and quick ground.

Coole Dodger (IRE)

102(94) (52)**75**
4-y-o ch g Where Or When (IRE)-Shining High (Shirley Heights)
B Ellison Koo's Racing Club

Placings:04403/24054410001520-00606330 (6358)
2009: 9^{0}GS, 7^{0}GF, 7^{6}GF, 7^{0}SD, 9^{6}GF, 8^{3}HY, 8^{3}G, 8^{0}SD,

	Starts	1st	2nd	3rd	Win & Pl
Career Total (Turf)	14	2	1	2	7393
Career Total (AW)	13	0	1	1	1140

75 6/08 Wind 1m67y (0-70)H G-F £2729
72 4/08 Leic 1m60y (0-70)H G-S £2590
Total win prize-money £5320

Going (Turf): Sf: 0-4 **GS: 1-3** Gd: 0-2 **GF: 1-5** Fm: 0-0
Distance: 5f/6f: 0-4 7f-8f: 0-11 **9f-13f: 2-12** 14f+: 0-0
Track : LH: 0-4 **RH: 2-21 Tight: 1-7** Gall: 0-0
Aids: Bl: 0-0 Vi: 0-0 Tstrap: 0-0 Ckp: 0-0
Best Rating: **75** 6/08 Wind 1m67y gd-fm

Fair; effective at around 1m; acts on fast and easy ground; also goes on Polytrack.

Coolella (IRE)

88(78) (44)**53**
2-y-o gr f Verglas (IRE)-Tianella (GER) (Acatenango (GER))
J R Weymes High Moor Racing 3

Placings:03606 (6125)
2009: 6^{0}S, 5^{3}G, 6^{6}SD, 6^{0}S, 8^{6}SD,

	Starts	1st	2nd	3rd	Win & Pl
Career Total (Turf)	3	0	0	1	385
Career Total (AW)	2	0	0	0	0

Going (Turf): Sf: 0-2 GS: 0-0 Gd: 0-1 GF: 0-0 Fm: 0-0
Distance: 5f/6f: 0-4 7f-8f: 0-0 9f-13f: 0-1 14f+: 0-0
Track : LH: 0-3 RH: 0-1 Tight: 0-1 Gall: 0-0
Aids: Bl: 0-0 Vi: 0-0 Tstrap: 0-0 Ckp: 0-0
Best Rating: **53** 8/09 Carl 5f193y good

Coolminx (IRE)

101 91
2-y-o b f One Cool Cat (USA)-Greta D'Argent (IRE) (Great Commotion (USA))
R A Fahey Mrs H Steel

Placings:112 (6677)
2009: 5^{1}GS, 5^{1}GF, 6^{2}G,

	Starts	1st	2nd	3rd	Win & Pl
Career Total (Turf)	3	2	1	0	17408

83 9/09 Bevl 5f G-F £3885
81 9/09 York 5f89y G-S £6799
Total win prize-money £10686

Going (Turf): Sf: 0-0 **GS: 1-1** Gd: 0-1 **GF: 1-1** Fm: 0-0
Distance: **5f/6f: 2-3** 7f-8f: 0-0 9f-13f: 0-0 14f+: 0-0
Track : LH: 0-0 RH: 0-0 Tight: 0-0 Gall: 0-0
Aids: Bl: 0-0 Vi: 0-0 Tstrap: 0-0 Ckp: 0-0
Best Rating: **91** 10/09 York 6f good

Very useful; effective over 5f-6f; acts on fast and easy ground.

Coolnaharan (IRE)

100(96) (66)**58**
9-y-o b g Blues Traveller (IRE)-Alma Assembly (General Assembly (USA))
Lee Smyth (John C McConnell 6/8) Pircan Partnership

Placings:0000/010/06/0**6**/02**600161** (7718)
2009: 15^{0}S, 10^{2}G, **12**^{6}SD, **10**^{0}SD, 9^{0}S, **9**^{1}SD, **9**^{6}SD, **9**^{1}SD,

	Starts	1st	2nd	3rd	Win & Pl
Career Total (Turf)	13	1	1	0	5483
Career Total (AW)	6	2	0	0	3753

66 12/09 Wolv 1m1f103y (0-60)H STD £2047
60 11/09 Wolv 1m1f103y (0-55) STD £1706
48 7/04 Bell 1m (33-60)H GD £4866
Total win prize-money £8619

Going (Turf): Sf: 0-2 GS: 0-0 **Gd: 1-4** GF: 0-2 Fm: 0-2
Distance: 5f/6f: 0-0 7f-8f: 1-4 **9f-13f: 2-14** 14f+: 0-1
Track : **LH: 3-11** RH: 0-2 **Tight: 2-4** Gall: 0-0
Aids: Bl: 0-0 Vi: 0-0 Tstrap: 2-3 Ckp: 2-3
Best Rating: **66** 12/09 Wolv 1m1f103y stand

Modest; stays 1m2f; handles Polytrack; has worn cheek-pieces.

Coolree Star (IRE)

100(100) (80)**73**
2-y-o ch g Kheleyf (USA)-Amount (Salse (USA))
J A Glover (W R Muir 20/7) Sexy Six Partnership

Placings:0150201020 (7625)
2009: 5^{0}G, 6^{1}G, 6^{5}S, 6^{0}SD, 6^{2}GF, 6^{0}G, 6^{1}G, 6^{0}S, 6^{2}SD, 6^{0}SD,

	Starts	1st	2nd	3rd	Win & Pl
Career Total (Turf)	7	2	1	0	5776
Career Total (AW)	3	0	1	0	771

73 10/09 Wind 6f (0-75) GD £2388
67 7/09 Yarm 6f3y GD £1942
Total win prize-money £4331

Going (Turf): Sf: 0-2 GS: 0-0 **Gd: 2-4** GF: 0-1 Fm: 0-0
Distance: 5f/6f: 1-9 7f-8f: 1-1 9f-13f: 0-0 14f+: 0-0
Track : LH: 0-1 RH: 0-2 Tight: 0-1 **Gall: 1-2**
Aids: Bl: 0-0 Vi: 0-0 Tstrap: 0-0 Ckp: 0-0
Best Rating: **80** 11/09 Kemp 6f stand

Fair; effective over 6f; acts on fast ground and on Polytrack.

Cooper Island Kid (USA)

86(90) (48)**61**
3-y-o b/br g Arch (USA)-Raven Quiver (USA) (Old Trieste (USA))
P W D'Arcy Mrs Jan Harris

Placings:000-0000 (4470)
2009: 11^{0}GF, 8^{0}SD, 11^{0}GS, 16^{0}HY,

	Starts	1st	2nd	3rd	Win & Pl
Career Total (Turf)	4	0	0	0	
Career Total (AW)	3	0	0	0	

Going (Turf): Sf: 0-1 GS: 0-2 Gd: 0-0 GF: 0-1 Fm: 0-0
Distance: 5f/6f: 0-1 7f-8f: 0-3 9f-13f: 0-2 14f+: 0-1
Track : LH: 0-5 RH: 0-0 Tight: 0-2 Gall: 0-2
Aids: Bl: 0-0 Vi: 0-0 Tstrap: 0-0 Ckp: 0-0
Best Rating: **61** 10/08 NmkR 7f gd-sft

Cooperman

88 **40**
3-y-o b g Sulamani (IRE)-Minibule (FR) (Funambule (USA))
P T Midgley Camela Racing Limited

Placings:04000 (3976)
2009: 10^{0}G, 10^{4}GF, 10^{0}G, 12^{0}GF, 11^{0}GS,

	Starts	1st	2nd	3rd	Win & Pl
Career Total (Turf)	5	0	0	0	204

Going (Turf): Sf: 0-0 GS: 0-1 Gd: 0-2 GF: 0-2 Fm: 0-0
Distance: 5f/6f: 0-0 7f-8f: 0-0 9f-13f: 0-5 14f+: 0-0
Track : LH: 0-5 RH: 0-0 Tight: 0-1 Gall: 0-3
Aids: Bl: 0-0 Vi: 0-0 Tstrap: 0-0 Ckp: 0-0
Best Rating: **40** 6/09 Donc 1m4f gd-fm

Coordinated Cut (IRE)

94 **93**
2-y-o b c Montjeu (IRE)-Apache Star (Arazi (USA))
P W Chapple-Hyam Lawrie Inman

Placings:10 (7017)
2009: 8^{1}GF, 8^{0}GS,

	Starts	1st	2nd	3rd	Win & Pl
Career Total (Turf)	2	1	0	0	6800

85 9/09 Donc 1m G-F £6799
Total win prize-money £6800

Going (Turf): Sf: 0-0 GS: 0-1 Gd: 0-0 **GF: 1-1** Fm: 0-0
Distance: 5f/6f: 0-0 **7f-8f: 1-2** 9f-13f: 0-0 14f+: 0-0
Track : LH: 0-0 RH: 0-0 Tight: 0-0 Gall: 0-0
Aids: Bl: 0-0 Vi: 0-0 Tstrap: 0-0 Ckp: 0-0
Best Rating: **93** 10/09 Donc 1m gd-sft

Useful; middle-distance prospect; made winning debut over 1m on fast ground.

Copper Dock (IRE)

102 (100)**86**
5-y-o b g Docksider (USA)-Sundown (Polish Precedent (USA))
T G McCourt Barry Doyle

Placings:000000/010505630/01260136230-36000054003121 (7566a)
2009: **5**^{3}SD, **6**^{6}SD, 5^{0}GF, 5^{0}GF, 5^{0}S, 5^{0}G, **6**^{5}SD, **5**^{4}SD, 5^{0}GF, 7^{0}SD, 7^{3}SD, **6**^{1}SD, **6**^{2}SD, **6**^{1}SD,

	Starts	1st	2nd	3rd	Win & Pl
Career Total (Turf)	24	1	1	2	8825
Career Total (AW)	16	4	2	3	49277

100 11/09 Dund 6f H STD £13904
93 10/09 Dund 6f (60-100)H STD £13588
83 7/08 Dund 5f (50-80)H STD £6605
66 5/08 Dund 5f (50-70)H STD £5334
62 4/07 Tipp 5f (42-70)H G-F £5135
Total win prize-money £44570

Going (Turf): Sf: 0-3 GS: 0-0 Gd: 0-5 **GF: 1-8** Fm: 0-2
Distance: **5f/6f: 5-36** 7f-8f: 0-4 9f-13f: 0-0 14f+: 0-0
Track : **LH: 5-29** RH: 0-0 Tight: 0-0 Gall: 0-0
Aids: Bl: 0-2 Vi: 0-0 Tstrap: 0-1 Ckp: 0-1
Best Rating: 100 11/09 Dund 6f stand

Useful; effective over sprint trips on a sound surface and on Polytrack; has worn headgear/tongue tie.

Copper King

(104) (60)**44**
5-y-o ch g Ishiguru (USA)-Dorissio (IRE) (Efisio)
Miss Tor Sturgis Paul Reason

Placings:036060152104/3240263041600/42500050010-005041050 (7438)
2009: 7^{0}SD, 8^{0}SD, 8^{5}SD, 7^{0}SD, 7^{4}SD, 8^{1}SD, 8^{0}SD, 8^{5}SD, 8^{0}SD,

	Starts	1st	2nd	3rd	Win & Pl
Career Total (Turf)	15	2	1	2	8942
Career Total (AW)	31	3	3	1	8902

55 6/09 Ling 1m (0-60)H STD £2047
60 11/08 Kemp 1m (0-50)H STD £2047
59 7/07 Carl 6f192y G-F £2047
68 10/06 Wwck 7f26y SFT £2388
Total win prize-money £8531

Going (Turf): **Sf: 1-2** GS: 0-1 Gd: 0-5 **GF: 1-6** Fm: 0-1
Distance: 5f/6f: 0-6 **7f-8f: 5-32** 9f-13f: 0-8 14f+: 0-0
Track : **LH: 3-30** RH: 2-12 **Tight: 2-21** Gall: 0-1
Aids: Bl: 0-0 **Vi: 1-3** Tstrap: 0-1 Ckp: 0-1
Best Rating: 82 1/07 Ling 7f stand

Moderate; stays 1m; acts on easy ground and on Polytrack.

Copper Penny

82 **52**
2-y-o b f Dansili-Makara (Lion Cavern (USA))
D R Lanigan Saif Ali & Saeed H Altayer

Placings:0 (4792)
2009: 7^{0}G,

	Starts	1st	2nd	3rd	Win & Pl
Career Total (Turf)	1	0	0	0	

Going (Turf): **Sf: 0-0 GS: 0-0 Gd: 0-1 GF: 0-0 Fm: 0-0**
Distance: 5f/6f: 0-0 7f-8f: 0-1 9f-13f: 0-0 14f+: 0-0
Track : LH: 0-0 RH: 0-0 Tight: 0-0 Gall: 0-0
Aids: Bl: 0-0 Vi: 0-0 Tstrap: 0-0 Ckp: 0-0
Best Rating: 52 8/09 NmkJ 7f good

Copper Sovereign

76(73) (18)**18**
7-y-o ch g Compton Place-Lady Kitty (Petong)
Jamie Poulton Exceat Partnership

Placings:000 (6703)
2009: 6^{0}G, 7^{0}GF, 8^{0}SS,

	Starts	1st	2nd	3rd	Win & Pl
Career Total (Turf)	2	0	0	0	
Career Total (AW)	1	0	0	0	

Going (Turf): **Sf: 0-0 GS: 0-0 Gd: 0-1 GF: 0-1 Fm: 0-0**
Distance: 5f/6f: 0-1 7f-8f: 0-2 9f-13f: 0-0 14f+: 0-0
Track : LH: 0-1 RH: 0-0 Tight: 0-1 Gall: 0-0
Aids: Bl: 0-0 Vi: 0-0 Tstrap: 0-0 Ckp: 0-0
Best Rating: 18 10/09 Ling 1m std-slw

Copperbeech (IRE)

107(110) (101)**105**
3-y-o b f Red Ransom (USA)-Aynthia (USA) (Zafonic (USA))
Saeed Bin Suroor Godolphin

Placings:113-63023 (7291)
2009: 9^{6}GF, 10^{3}SD, 10^{0}G, 11^{2}GF, 10^{3}S,

	Starts	1st	2nd	3rd	Win & Pl
Career Total (Turf)	7	2	1	2	52547
Career Total (AW)	1	0	0	1	1101

97 9/08 Lonc 1m G-S £12500
90 8/08 Deau 1m SFT £8088
Total win prize-money £20588

Going (Turf): **Sf: 1-2 GS: 1-2** Gd: 0-1 GF: 0-2 Fm: 0-0
Distance: 5f/6f: 0-0 **7f-8f: 2-3** 9f-13f: 0-5 14f+: 0-0
Track : LH: 0-1 **RH: 1-4** Tight: 0-1 Gall: 0-1
Aids: Bl: 0-0 Vi: 0-0 Tstrap: 0-0 Ckp: 0-0
Best Rating: 105 10/08 Lonc 1m gd-sft

Smart; third in the Prix Marcel Boussac as a juvenile; probably stays 1m4f; acts on fast and soft ground and Polytrack.

Copperwood

91(104) (67)**56**
4-y-o ch g Bahamian Bounty-Sophielu (Rudimentary (USA))
M Blanshard Mrs Rosemary K Wilkerson

Placings:245/6606050005-36306261 (7591)
2009: 8^{3}SD, 7^{6}SD, 8^{3}SD, 8^{0}SD, 7^{6}GF, 7^{2}SD, 7^{6}SD, 7^{1}SD,

	Starts	1st	2nd	3rd	Win & Pl
Career Total (Turf)	8	0	1	0	1252
Career Total (AW)	13	1	1	2	2714

67 11/09 Kemp 7f (0-60)H STD £1619
Total win prize-money £1619

Going (Turf): **Sf: 0-1 GS: 0-3 Gd: 0-1 GF: 0-3 Fm: 0-0**
Distance: 5f/6f: 0-2 **7f-8f: 1-17** 9f-13f: 0-2 14f+: 0-0
Track : LH: 0-8 **RH: 1-7** Tight: 0-7 Gall: 0-0
Aids: Bl: 0-1 Vi: 0-0 Tstrap: 0-0 Ckp: 0-0
Best Rating: 74 9/07 Hayd 7f30y gd-fm

Moderate; effective over 7f-1m; acts on good ground; goes on Polytrack.

Coral Point (IRE)

92(77) (36)**53**
3-y-o ch g Hawkeye (IRE)-Green Crystal (Green Dancer (USA))
S Curran John Duddy

Placings:00000-5 (2772)
2009: 11^{5}G,

	Starts	1st	2nd	3rd	Win & Pl
Career Total (Turf)	2	0	0	0	0
Career Total (AW)	4	0	0	0	

Going (Turf): **Sf: 0-0 GS: 0-1 Gd: 0-1 GF: 0-0 Fm: 0-0**
Distance: 5f/6f: 0-0 7f-8f: 0-3 9f-13f: 0-3 14f+: 0-0
Track : LH: 0-4 RH: 0-0 Tight: 0-5 Gall: 0-0
Aids: Bl: 0-0 Vi: 0-0 Tstrap: 0-0 Ckp: 0-0
Best Rating: 53 6/09 Wind 1m3f135y good

Coral Shores

101(109) (62)**69**
4-y-o b f Carnival Dancer-Leading Role (Cadeaux Genereux)
P W Hiatt P W Hiatt & Charlotte Bird

Placings:30065060/662221260402153535350-6045554133140503 (7641)
2009: 8^{6}SD, 10^{0}SD, 11^{4}SD, 10^{5}SD, 11^{5}SD, 13^{5}SD, 11^{4}GF, 10^{1}F, 11^{3}GF, 11^{3}F, 10^{1}GS, 11^{4}GF, 11^{0}GF, 9^{5}G, 9^{0}SD, 11^{3}SD,

	Starts	1st	2nd	3rd	Win & Pl
Career Total (Turf)	21	3	1	6	10659
Career Total (AW)	24	1	4	1	4497

69 6/09 Wwck 1m2f188y (0-65)H G-S £2047
67 5/09 Wwck 1m2f188y (0-55)H FRM £2047
68 6/08 Pont 1m2f6y (0-70)H GD £3123
51 2/08 Ling 1m2f STD £1774
Total win prize-money £8992

Going (Turf): Sf: 0-2 **GS: 1-5 Gd: 1-2** GF: 0-9 **Fm: 1-3**
Distance: 5f/6f: 0-1 7f-8f: 0-9 **9f-13f: 4-35** 14f+: 0-0
Track : **LH: 4-34** RH: 0-9 **Tight: 1-14** Gall: 0-1
Aids: Bl: 0-0 **Vi: 4-34** Tstrap: 0-0 Ckp: 0-0
Best Rating: 69 6/09 Wwck 1m2f188y gd-sft

Modest; effective at around 1m2f-1m4f; acts on good ground and on sand; often visored.

Coralamber (IRE)

77(76) (32)**35**
2-y-o gr f Monsieur Bond (IRE)-Silver Sun (Green Desert (USA))
Garry Moss Brooklands Racing

Placings:0605 (3495)
2009: 5^{0}GF, 6^{6}F, 5^{0}SD, 5^{5}GF,

	Starts	1st	2nd	3rd	Win & Pl
Career Total (Turf)	3	0	0	0	0
Career Total (AW)	1	0	0	0	

Going (Turf): **Sf: 0-0 GS: 0-0 Gd: 0-0 GF: 0-2 Fm: 0-1**
Distance: 5f/6f: 0-4 7f-8f: 0-0 9f-13f: 0-0 14f+: 0-0
Track : LH: 0-0 RH: 0-0 Tight: 0-0 Gall: 0-0
Aids: Bl: 0-0 Vi: 0-0 Tstrap: 0-0 Ckp: 0-0
Best Rating: 35 5/09 Sals 5f gd-fm

Cordell (IRE)

100(105) (98)**70**
4-y-o b g Fasliyev (USA)-Urgele (FR) (Zafonic (USA))
R Ingram (R Hannon 7/8) M&R Refurbishments Ltd

Placings:4403016/31-500006100000 (6924)
2009: 8^{5}SD, 8^{0}S, 8^{0}GF, 7^{0}G, 10^{0}G, 8^{6}G, 7^{1}GS, 8^{0}GF, 7^{0}GF, 8^{0}SS, 7^{0}SS, 8^{0}GF,

	Starts	1st	2nd	3rd	Win & Pl
Career Total (Turf)	15	1	0	1	3643
Career Total (AW)	6	2	0	1	10828

70 8/09 Brig 7f214y G-S £2072
98 3/08 Kemp 1m (0-85)H STD £4210
78 9/07 Kemp 1m STD £4210
Total win prize-money £10492

Going (Turf): Sf: 0-2 **GS: 1-2** Gd: 0-6 GF: 0-5 Fm: 0-0
Distance: 5f/6f: 0-4 **7f-8f: 3-12** 9f-13f: 0-5 14f+: 0-0
Track : LH: 1-5 **RH: 2-7** Tight: 0-4 Gall: 0-1
Aids: Bl: 0-0 Vi: 0-0 Tstrap: 0-0 Ckp: 0-0
Best Rating: 98 4/09 Kemp 1m stand

Very useful; stays 1m; acts on good ground and on Polytrack; likes to race prominently.

Cordiality

82(82) (53)**56**
2-y-o b g Kingsalsa (USA)-Peace (Sadler's Wells (USA))
P G Murphy (J R Fanshawe 7/10) The Golden Anorak Partnership

Placings:000 **(7638)**
2009: 8^{0}SD, 8^{0}GS, 8^{0}SD,

	Starts	1st	2nd	3rd	Win & Pl
Career Total (Turf)	1	0	0	0	
Career Total (AW)	2	0	0	0	

Going (Turf): Sf: 0-0 GS: 0-1 Gd: 0-0 GF: 0-0 Fm: 0-0
Distance: 5f/6f: 0-0 7f-8f: 0-2 9f-13f: 0-1 14f+: 0-0
Track : LH: 0-2 RH: 0-1 Tight: 0-0 Gall: 0-0
Aids: Bl: 0-0 Vi: 0-0 Tstrap: 0-0 Ckp: 0-0
Best Rating: 56 10/09 Nott 1m75y gd-sft

Cordoba

(100) (76)
3-y-o b f Oasis Dream-Spanish Sun (USA) (El Prado (IRE))
Sir Michael Stoute K Abdulla

Placings:1 **(3508)**
2009: 11^{1}SD,

	Starts	1st	2nd	3rd	Win & Pl
Career Total (Turf)	0	0	0	0	
Career Total (AW)	1	1	0	0	2590

76 7/09 Kemp 1m3f STD £2590
Total win prize-money £2590

Going (Turf): Sf: 0-0 GS: 0-0 Gd: 0-0 GF: 0-0 Fm: 0-0
Distance: 5f/6f: 0-0 7f-8f: 0-0 9f-13f: 1-1 14f+: 0-0
Track : LH: 0-0 RH: 1-1 Tight: 0-0 Gall: 0-0
Aids: Bl: 0-0 Vi: 0-0 Tstrap: 0-0 Ckp: 0-0
Best Rating: 76 7/09 Kemp 1m3f stand

Fair; stays 1m3f; acts on Polytrack.

Core Element (IRE)

89 (53)67
2-y-o b f Consolidator (USA)-Millstream (USA) (Dayjur (USA))
J G Coogan (Adrian Sexton 22/7) S Buggy

Placings:300000 **(5920a)**
2009: 6^{3}G, 6^{0}GF, 6^{0}GY, 5^{0}S, 6^{0}SD, 6^{0}S,

	Starts	1st	2nd	3rd	Win & Pl
Career Total (Turf)	5	0	0	1	1206
Career Total (AW)	1	0	0	0	

Going (Turf): Sf: 0-2 GS: 0-0 Gd: 0-1 GF: 0-1 Fm: 0-0
Distance: 5f/6f: 0-6 7f-8f: 0-0 9f-13f: 0-0 14f+: 0-0
Track : LH: 0-3 RH: 0-0 Tight: 0-0 Gall: 0-0
Aids: Bl: 0-1 Vi: 0-0 Tstrap: 0-0 Ckp: 0-0
Best Rating: 67 6/09 Curr 6f good

Modest; effective over 6f; acts on good ground.

Corking (IRE)

97(84) (46)59
4-y-o b f Montjeu (IRE)-Scanno's Choice (IRE) (Pennine Walk)
J L Flint T A Jones

Placings:00/502023-0010 **(2519)**
2009: 14^{0}SS, 13^{0}SD, 17^{1}GS, 17^{0}F,

	Starts	1st	2nd	3rd	Win & Pl
Career Total (Turf)	8	1	2	1	3896
Career Total (AW)	4	0	0	0	

59 5/09 Bath 2m1f34y (0-65)H G-S £2109
Total win prize-money £2110

Going (Turf): Sf: 0-1 GS: 1-3 Gd: 0-3 GF: 0-0 Fm: 0-1
Distance: 5f/6f: 0-0 7f-8f: 0-2 9f-13f: 0-5 14f+: 1-5
Track : LH: 1-9 RH: 0-2 Tight: 1-7 Gall: 0-0
Aids: Bl: 0-1 Vi: 0-0 Tstrap: 0-0 Ckp: 0-0
Best Rating: 59 5/09 Bath 2m1f34y gd-sft

Moderate; stays 2m1f; acts on easy ground.

Corlough Mountain

91(101) (55)66
5-y-o ch g Inchinor-Two Step (Mujtahid (USA))
P Butler Miss M Bryant

Placings:225/2350531/600403263000040050-1616000000 **(7608)**
2009: 12^{1}SD, 12^{6}SD, 12^{1}SD, 13^{6}SD, 11^{0}GF, 6^{0}GF, 9^{0}F, 10^{0}GF, 12^{0}SD, 16^{0}SD,

	Starts	1st	2nd	3rd	Win & Pl
Career Total (Turf)	17	0	2	3	2781
Career Total (AW)	21	3	2	1	9348

55 2/09 Wolv 1m4f50y (0-52)H STD £1648
54 1/09 Kemp 1m4f (0-60)H STD £1977
74 12/07 Ling 7f (0-70)H STD £2817
Total win prize-money £6443

Going (Turf): Sf: 0-3 GS: 0-3 Gd: 0-2 GF: 0-7 Fm: 0-2
Distance: 5f/6f: 0-6 7f-8f: 1-18 9f-13f: 2-11 14f+: 0-3
Track : LH: 2-23 RH: 1-6 Tight: 2-18 Gall: 0-0
Aids: Bl: 0-0 Vi: 0-0 Tstrap: 0-9 Ckp: 0-9
Best Rating: 74 12/07 Ling 7f stand

Moderate; stays 2m; acts on fast ground; also goes on Polytrack; has worn cheekpieces/tongue tie.

Cornish Baroness

58
2-y-o b f Reset (AUS)-Milady Lillie (IRE) (Distinctly North (USA))
R Hannon Paul Blows & David Owen

Placings:0 **(5547)**
2009: 8^{0}GF,

	Starts	1st	2nd	3rd	Win & Pl
Career Total (Turf)	1	0	0	0	

Going (Turf): Sf: 0-0 GS: 0-0 Gd: 0-0 GF: 0-1 Fm: 0-0
Distance: 5f/6f: 0-0 7f-8f: 0-0 9f-13f: 0-1 14f+: 0-0
Track : LH: 0-0 RH: 0-1 Tight: 0-0 Gall: 0-0
Aids: Bl: 0-0 Vi: 0-0 Tstrap: 0-0 Ckp: 0-0

Cornish Beau (IRE)

94(95) (66)68
2-y-o ch c Pearl Of Love (IRE)-Marimar (IRE) (Grand Lodge (USA))
M H Tompkins M Winter

Placings:5362 **(7267)**
2009: 7^{5}G, 7^{3}GF, 8^{6}GS, 8^{2}SD,

	Starts	1st	2nd	3rd	Win & Pl
Career Total (Turf)	3	0	0	1	403
Career Total (AW)	1	0	1	0	1831

Going (Turf): Sf: 0-0 GS: 0-1 Gd: 0-1 GF: 0-1 Fm: 0-0
Distance: 5f/6f: 0-0 7f-8f: 0-3 9f-13f: 0-1 14f+: 0-0
Track : LH: 0-1 RH: 0-0 Tight: 0-0 Gall: 0-0
Aids: Bl: 0-0 Vi: 0-0 Tstrap: 0-0 Ckp: 0-0
Best Rating: 68 8/09 Folk 7f gd-fm

Modest; stays 1m; acts on fast ground and on Fibresand.

Cornish Castle (USA)

101 76
3-y-o ch g Mizzen Mast (USA)-Rouwaki (USA) (Miswaki (USA))
Joss Saville (T D Walford 14/10) Lowbeck Racing Syndicate

Placings:00-011404 **(3489)**
2009: 10^{0}G, 8^{1}GF, 8^{1}GF, 8^{4}GF, 9^{0}GF, 8^{4}G,

	Starts	1st	2nd	3rd	Win & Pl
Career Total (Turf)	8	2	0	0	5244

76 4/09 Nott 1m75y (0-65)H G-F £2047
76 4/09 Nott 1m75y (0-70)H G-F £2590
Total win prize-money £4637

Going (Turf): Sf: 0-0 GS: 0-0 Gd: 0-3 GF: 2-5 Fm: 0-0
Distance: 5f/6f: 0-0 7f-8f: 0-4 9f-13f: 2-4 14f+: 0-0
Track : LH: 2-4 RH: 0-1 Tight: 0-2 Gall: 0-1
Aids: Bl: 0-1 Vi: 0-0 Tstrap: 0-0 Ckp: 0-0
Best Rating: 76 4/09 Nott 1m75y gd-fm

Modest; effective at around 1m; acts on fast ground.

Cornus

107(110) (80)83
7-y-o ch g Inchinor-Demerger (USA) (Distant View (USA))
J A Glover (A J McCabe 6/6) Paul J Dixon

Placings:11220/6630545353105303/6050000064400/61050532630300015004110420/533040200353066052360005265-011530603104060056060 **(7795)**
2009: 7^{0}SD, 7^{1}SD, 6^{1}SD, 7^{5}SD, 7^{3}SF, 5^{0}SD, 8^{6}SD, 7^{0}GF, 7^{3}GF, 6^{1}F, 7^{0}GF, 6^{4}GF, 6^{0}G, 7^{6}S, 7^{0}G, 7^{0}SD, 7^{5}GS, 6^{6}GF, 7^{0}G, 7^{6}SD, 6^{0}SS,

	Starts	1st	2nd	3rd	Win & Pl
Career Total (Turf)	69	7	6	10	61509
Career Total (AW)	39	3	1	5	15451

82 4/09 Thsk 6f (0-75)H FRM £4274
77 2/09 Ling 6f (0-75)H STD £2729
78 1/09 Wolv 7f32y (0-75)H STD £2729
87 10/07 Nott 6f15y (0-70)H SFT £3238
81 10/07 Nott 6f15y (0-70)H G-S £2914
76 9/07 Thsk 6f (0-75)H G-F £3886
79 2/07 Wolv 5f216y (0-75)H STD £3238
81 9/05 Bevl 5f GD £8607
89 4/04 NmkR 5f C G-S £7186
80 4/04 Wind 5f10y E G-S £3454
Total win prize-money £42261

Going (Turf): Sf: 1-14 GS: 3-15 Gd: 1-15 GF: 1-23 Fm: 1-2
Distance: 5f/6f: 7-66 7f-8f: 3-41 9f-13f: 0-1 14f+: 0-0
Track : LH: 3-44 RH: 0-2 Tight: 3-36 Gall: 1-6
Aids: Bl: 7-69 Vi: 0-0 Tstrap: 0-2 Ckp: 0-2
Best Rating: 103 5/05 Newb 6f8y gd-fm

Fair; stays 7f; acts on good and softer ground; goes on sand; often wears an eyeshield and blinkers.

Coronado's Gold (USA)

94 (40)63
8-y-o ch g Coronado's Quest (USA)-Debit My Account (USA) (Classic Account (USA))
B Ellison S Hawe

Placings:4432100/0050/**05**/10640/2662506020-0003 **(2263)**
2009: 15[0]GF, 12[0]GF, 15[0]GF, 9[3]G,

	Starts	1st	2nd	3rd	Win & Pl
Career Total (Turf)	29	2	4	2	20177
Career Total (AW)	3	0	0	0	0

60 6/07 Hayd 1m2f120y (0-65)H G-F £2867
8/04 Elsp 1m110y FRM £8246
Total win prize-money £11114

Going (Turf): Sf: 0-0 GS: 0-5 Gd: 0-8 **GF: 1-10 Fm: 1-6**
Distance: 5f/6f: 0-0 7f-8f: 0-8 **9f-13f: 2-15** 14f+: 0-9
Track : **LH: 1-18** RH: 0-7 Tight: 0-17 Gall: 0-3
Aids: Bl: 0-0 Vi: 0-0 Tstrap: 0-2 Ckp: 0-2
Best Rating: **63** 5/08 Catt 1m7f177y good

Moderate; stays 2m and acts on fast ground.

Coronaria

33
2-y-o b f Starcraft (NZ)-Anthos (GER) (Big Shuffle (USA))
W J Haggas Cheveley Park Stud

Placings:0 **(4331)**
2009: 6[0]G,

	Starts	1st	2nd	3rd	Win & Pl
Career Total (Turf)	1	0	0	0	

Going (Turf): **Sf: 0-0 GS: 0-0 Gd: 0-1 GF: 0-0 Fm: 0-0**
Distance: 5f/6f: 0-1 7f-8f: 0-0 9f-13f: 0-0 14f+: 0-0
Track : LH: 0-0 RH: 0-0 Tight: 0-0 Gall: 0-0
Aids: Bl: 0-0 Vi: 0-0 Tstrap: 0-0 Ckp: 0-0

Corporal Maddox

102 **104**
2-y-o b c Royal Applause-Noble View (USA) (Distant View (USA))
H R A Cecil (A P Jarvis 19/8) Mogeely Stud & Mrs Maura Gittins

Placings:41133616 **(7016)**
2009: 5[4]GF, 5[1]GF, 6[1]G, 5[3]G, 7[3]G, 6[6]GF, 7[1]GS, 6[6]GS,

	Starts	1st	2nd	3rd	Win & Pl
Career Total (Turf)	8	3	0	2	49967

104 10/09 Asct 7f G-S £8411
96 6/09 Epsm 6f GD £17031
74 5/09 Haml 5f4y G-F £3885
Total win prize-money £29329

Going (Turf): Sf: 0-0 **GS: 1-2 Gd: 1-3 GF: 1-3** Fm: 0-0
Distance: **5f/6f: 2-6** 7f-8f: 1-2 9f-13f: 0-0 14f+: 0-0
Track : **LH: 1-1** RH: 0-1 **Tight: 1-1** Gall: 0-0
Aids: Bl: 0-0 Vi: 0-0 Tstrap: 0-0 Ckp: 0-0
Best Rating: **104** 10/09 Asct 7f gd-sft

Smart; won the Listed Woodcote Stakes at Epsom; stays 7f; acts on fast and easy ground.

Corr Point (IRE)

(79) (49)
2-y-o b c Azamour (IRE)-Naazeq (Nashwan (USA))
J A Osborne J Duddy & R A Pegum

Placings:000 **(7538)**
2009: 7[0]SD, 7[0]SD, 7[0]SD,

	Starts	1st	2nd	3rd	Win & Pl
Career Total (Turf)	0	0	0	0	
Career Total (AW)	3	0	0	0	

Going (Turf): **Sf: 0-0 GS: 0-0 Gd: 0-0 GF: 0-0 Fm: 0-0**
Distance: 5f/6f: 0-0 7f-8f: 0-3 9f-13f: 0-0 14f+: 0-0
Track : LH: 0-1 RH: 0-2 Tight: 0-1 Gall: 0-0
Aids: Bl: 0-0 Vi: 0-0 Tstrap: 0-0 Ckp: 0-0
Best Rating: **49** 11/09 Kemp 7f stand

Corrib (IRE)

99(101) (60)**53**
6-y-o b m Lahib (USA)-Montana Miss (IRE) (Earl Of Barking (IRE))
B Palling Bryn Palling

Placings:1150**50**/00**210060**/0003501320**0**/**0063**3400-6404433055 **(7803)**
2009: 12[6]SD, 11[4]SD, 11[0]F, 10[4]F, 12[4]GF, 9[3]GF, 10[3]G, 11[0]G, 9[5]SD, 9[5]SD,

	Starts	1st	2nd	3rd	Win & Pl
Career Total (Turf)	25	3	1	5	12747
Career Total (AW)	18	1	1	1	5395

68 8/07 Newb 1m1f (0-70)H GD £3238
75 7/06 Wolv 7f32y (0-75)H STD £3886
76 6/05 Chep 6f16y G-F £3454
70 5/05 Bath 5f11y GD £2583
Total win prize-money £13163

Going (Turf): Sf: 0-3 GS: 0-4 **Gd: 2-8** GF: 1-8 Fm: 0-2
Distance: 5f/6f: 1-4 **7f-8f: 2-12** 9f-13f: 1-26 14f+: 0-1
Track : **LH: 3-32** RH: 0-1 Tight: 1-22 **Gall: 2-4**
Aids: Bl: 0-0 Vi: 0-0 Tstrap: 0-0 Ckp: 0-0
Best Rating: **78** 6/05 NmkJ 6f good

Moderate; stays 1m4f; acts on a sound surface and Polytrack.

Corriolanus (GER)

99(103) (67)**73**
9-y-o b g Zamindar (USA)-Caesarea (GER) (Generous (IRE))
A M Balding Kingsclere Racing CLub

Placings:33/1263/**3000606100021**/2125630/5402/5000600/3-30641 **(2040)**
2009: 10[3]SD, 10[0]SD, 12[6]SD, 10[4]G, 12[1]GS,

	Starts	1st	2nd	3rd	Win & Pl
Career Total (Turf)	34	4	4	4	153073
Career Total (AW)	9	1	1	3	22533

73 5/09 Newb 1m4f5y (0-75)H G-S £2590
108 2/05 Ndas 1m4f H G-F £59244
108 11/04 Ling 1m2f (0-107)H STD £11971
102 8/04 NmkJ 1m2f C G-F £8398
3/03 Frnk 1m2f GD £1948
Total win prize-money £84152

Going (Turf): Sf: 0-4 GS: 1-3 Gd: 1-12 **GF: 2-12** Fm: 0-3
Distance: 5f/6f: 0-0 7f-8f: 0-3 **9f-13f: 5-40** 14f+: 0-0
Track : **LH: 4-30** RH: 1-11 Tight: 1-12 **Gall: 3-21**
Aids: Bl: 0-2 Vi: 0-0 Tstrap: 1-4 Ckp: 1-4
Best Rating: **114** 2/05 Ndas 1m4f gd-fm

Fair; effective from 1m2f-1m4f; acts on fast ground; also goes on Polytrack.

Corrybrough

106(106) (86)**114**
4-y-o ch c Kyllachy-Calamanco (Clantime)
H Candy Thurloe Thoroughbreds XXI

Placings:21/111254-50 **(5657)**
2009: 6[5]SD, 6[0]GS,

	Starts	1st	2nd	3rd	Win & Pl
Career Total (Turf)	9	4	2	0	59496
Career Total (AW)	1	0	0	0	0

114 6/08 Sand 5f6y GD £14760
111 5/08 Bevl 5f G-F £6542
102 4/08 Sand 5f6y (0-100)H G-S £9969
92 10/07 Wind 6f SFT £2817
Total win prize-money £34090

Going (Turf): **Sf: 1-4 GS: 1-2 Gd: 1-2 GF: 1-1** Fm: 0-0
Distance: **5f/6f: 4-9** 7f-8f: 0-1 9f-13f: 0-0 14f+: 0-0
Track : LH: 0-1 RH: 0-1 Tight: 0-1 **Gall: 1-1**
Aids: Bl: 0-0 Vi: 0-0 Tstrap: 0-0 Ckp: 0-0
Best Rating: **114** 9/08 Donc 6f soft

Group class; effective at 5f-6f; acts on most ground.

Corsica (IRE)

97 **79**
2-y-o b c Cape Cross (IRE)-Cedar Sea (IRE) (Persian Bold)
M Johnston Sheikh Hamdan Bin Mohammed Al Maktoum

Placings:2551 **(6982)**
2009: 8[2]GF, 8[5]G, 8[5]GF, 8[1]G,

	Starts	1st	2nd	3rd	Win & Pl
Career Total (Turf)	4	1	1	0	6144

74 10/09 Ayr 1m GD £5180
Total win prize-money £5181

Going (Turf): Sf: 0-0 GS: 0-0 **Gd: 1-2** GF: 0-2 Fm: 0-0
Distance: 5f/6f: 0-0 **7f-8f: 1-2** 9f-13f: 0-2 14f+: 0-0
Track : **LH: 1-2** RH: 0-2 Tight: 0-1 Gall: 0-0
Aids: Bl: 0-0 Vi: 0-0 Tstrap: 0-0 Ckp: 0-0
Best Rating: **79** 8/09 Sand 1m14y gd-fm

Fair; stays 1m and acts on good ground.

Corton Charlemagne (IRE)

101(94) (63)**77**
3-y-o b f King Charlemagne (USA)-Teller (ARG) (Southern Halo (USA))
Rae Guest Cheval Ct, Alexander, Bottriell & Guest

Placings:2304-025113155 **(6387)**
2009: 7[0]SD, 6[2]F, 6[5]G, 5[1]G, 5[1]GF, 5[3]GF, 5[1]F, 5[5]GF, 5[5]GF,

	Starts	1st	2nd	3rd	Win & Pl
Career Total (Turf)	8	3	1	1	11228
Career Total (AW)	5	0	1	1	1975

77 9/09 Folk 5f (0-75)H FRM £3885
77 8/09 Newc 5f (0-70)H G-F £3238
72 8/09 Wind 5f10y (0-75)H GD £2729
Total win prize-money £9854

Going (Turf): Sf: 0-0 GS: 0-0 **Gd: 1-2 GF: 1-4 Fm: 1-2**
Distance: **5f/6f: 3-12** 7f-8f: 0-1 9f-13f: 0-0 14f+: 0-0
Track : LH: 0-6 RH: 0-1 Tight: 0-3 **Gall: 1-3**
Aids: Bl: 0-0 Vi: 0-0 Tstrap: 0-0 Ckp: 0-0
Best Rating: **77** 9/09 Folk 5f firm

Modest; effective over 5-6f; acts on Polytrack.

Corum (IRE)

93(86) (89)**73**
6-y-o b g Galileo (IRE)-Vallee Des Reves (USA) (Kingmambo (USA))
D E Pipe (Mrs K Waldron 15/7) Kilcash Bloodstock Limited

Placings:0/16200/03106/**6**0604-0 **(3788)**
2009: 14[0]GF,

	Starts	1st	2nd	3rd	Win & Pl
Career Total (Turf)	14	1	1	1	7393
Career Total (AW)	3	1	0	0	6017

89	6/07	Wolv	1m5f194y (0-85)H	STD	£5829
82	6/06	Sand	1m2f7y	G-F	£4533

Total win prize-money £10363

Going (Turf): Sf: 0-2 GS: 0-1 Gd: 0-3 **GF: 1-7** Fm: 0-1
Distance: 5f/6f: 0-0 7f-8f: 0-1 9f-13f: 1-6 14f+: 1-10
Track : LH: 1-10 RH: 1-6 **Tight: 1-5** Gall: 0-3
Aids: Bl: 0-0 Vi: 0-0 Tstrap: 1-9 Ckp: 1-9
Best Rating: 92 8/06 NmkJ 1m4f good

Modest; stays 2m; acts on good or faster ground; also goes on Polytrack; has worn cheekpieces.

Cosimo

102(89) (69)**72**

3-y-o ch g Medicean-Flight Soundly (IRE) (Caerleon (USA))
Sir Michael Stoute Sir Evelyn De Rothschild

Placings:02-5425 **(3636)**
2009: 9^{5}GF, 11^{4}G, 9^{2}GF, 10^{5}G,

	Starts	1st	2nd	3rd	Win & Pl
Career Total (Turf)	5	0	1	0	1806
Career Total (AW)	1	0	1	0	964

Going (Turf): Sf: 0-1 GS: 0-0 Gd: 0-2 GF: 0-2 Fm: 0-0
Distance: 5f/6f: 0-0 7f-8f: 0-2 9f-13f: 0-4 14f+: 0-0
Track : LH: 0-2 RH: 0-2 Tight: 0-1 Gall: 0-1
Aids: Bl: 0-0 Vi: 0-2 Tstrap: 0-0 Ckp: 0-0
Best Rating: 72 7/09 Nott 1m2f50y good

Fair; effective over 1m2f; acts on Polytrack and good ground; has worn a visor.

Cosimo de Medici

(98) (58)

2-y-o b g Medicean-Wish (Danehill (USA))
H Morrison Bevan, Doyle & Lawrence

Placings:650 **(7736)**
2009: 5^{6}SD, 6^{5}SD, 6^{0}SD,

	Starts	1st	2nd	3rd	Win & Pl
Career Total (Turf)	0	0	0	0	
Career Total (AW)	3	0	0	0	0

Going (Turf): Sf: 0-0 GS: 0-0 Gd: 0-0 GF: 0-0 Fm: 0-0
Distance: 5f/6f: 0-3 7f-8f: 0-0 9f-13f: 0-0 14f+: 0-0
Track : LH: 0-2 RH: 0-1 Tight: 0-2 Gall: 0-0
Aids: Bl: 0-0 Vi: 0-0 Tstrap: 0-0 Ckp: 0-0
Best Rating: 58 11/09 Ling 5f stand

Cosmea

102 (51)**86**

4-y-o b f Compton Place-St James's Antigua (IRE) (Law Society (USA))
A King Barbury Castle Stud

Placings:60400/0211240-14034 **(6060)**
2009: 10^{1}GF, 10^{4}GF, 9^{0}GF, 12^{3}GF, 12^{4}GF,

	Starts	1st	2nd	3rd	Win & Pl
Career Total (Turf)	16	3	2	1	14808
Career Total (AW)	1	0	0	0	

82	7/08	Newb	1m2f6y (0-80)H	GD	£4857
73	6/08	Wind	1m3f135y (0-70)H	G-F	£2729

Total win prize-money £7587

Going (Turf): Sf: 0-2 GS: 0-0 Gd: 1-2 **GF: 2-12** Fm: 0-0
Distance: 5f/6f: 0-2 7f-8f: 0-4 **9f-13f: 3-11** 14f+: 0-0
Track : LH: 1-6 RH: 1-8 Tight: 1-9 Gall: 1-3
Aids: Bl: 0-0 Vi: 0-0 Tstrap: 0-0 Ckp: 0-0
Best Rating: 86 9/09 Gdwd 1m4f gd-fm

Useful; stays 1m4f, but effective at shorter; acts on a sound surface.

Cosmic

77 **44**

3-y-o b g Nayef (USA)-Urania (Most Welcome)
T D Easterby Jim McGrath

Placings:00 **(1522)**
2009: 9^{0}F, 9^{0}GF,

	Starts	1st	2nd	3rd	Win & Pl
Career Total (Turf)	2	0	0	0	

Going (Turf): Sf: 0-0 GS: 0-0 Gd: 0-0 GF: 0-1 Fm: 0-1
Distance: 5f/6f: 0-0 7f-8f: 0-0 9f-13f: 0-2 14f+: 0-0
Track : LH: 0-1 RH: 0-1 Tight: 0-2 Gall: 0-0
Aids: Bl: 0-0 Vi: 0-0 Tstrap: 0-0 Ckp: 0-0
Best Rating: 44 4/09 Rdcr 1m1f firm

Cosmic Destiny (IRE)

100(104) (78)**76**

7-y-o b m Soviet Star (USA)-Cruelle (USA) (Irish River (FR))
E F Vaughan A M Pickering

Placings:0/**24**06330630310/**0**505363401055**0650/0036**40 4**5**313**22**11324/**2**00323433000**41-000**5533540400000 **(7657)**
2009: **5**^{0}SD, **5**^{0}SD, **6**^{0}SD, 5^{5}GF, 5^{5}G, 5^{3}GF, 5^{3}GF, 5^{5}GF, 5^{4}GF, 5^{0}F, 5^{4}GF, 5^{0}GF, 5^{0}GF, 5^{0}G, **6**^{0}SD, **5**^{0}SD,

	Starts	1st	2nd	3rd	Win & Pl
Career Total (Turf)	55	4	2	14	21767
Career Total (AW)	24	2	4	2	9263

78	12/08	Wolv	5f20y	(0-65)H	STD	£2388
73	8/07	Brig	5f59y	(0-65)H	G-S	£2137
65	8/07	Bath	5f11y	(0-75)H	FRM	£3238
61	6/07	Brig	5f59y	(0-60)H	FRM	£2072
67	7/06	Ling	5f	(0-55)H	STD	£2388
65	9/05	Gdwd	5f	(0-70)H	G-F	£3411

Total win prize-money £15638

Going (Turf): Sf: 0-1 GS: 1-9 Gd: 0-12 GF: 1-24 **Fm: 2-9**
Distance: 5f/6f: 6-79 7f-8f: 0-0 9f-13f: 0-0 14f+: 0-0
Track : LH: 5-52 RH: 0-1 **Tight: 2-24** Gall: 1-6
Aids: Bl: 0-0 Vi: 0-0 Tstrap: 0-0 Ckp: 0-0
Best Rating: 78 12/08 Wolv 5f20y stand

Modest; seems best over 5f; acts on most ground and on Polytrack; usually held up.

Cosmic Orbit

83 **56**

2-y-o b c Royal Applause-Susquehanna Days (USA) (Chief's Crown (USA))
K R Burke Findlay & Bloom

Placings:55 **(4308)**
2009: 7^{5}GF, 7^{5}GS,

	Starts	1st	2nd	3rd	Win & Pl
Career Total (Turf)	2	0	0	0	0

Going (Turf): Sf: 0-0 GS: 0-1 Gd: 0-0 GF: 0-1 Fm: 0-0
Distance: 5f/6f: 0-0 7f-8f: 0-2 9f-13f: 0-0 14f+: 0-0
Track : LH: 0-0 RH: 0-0 Tight: 0-0 Gall: 0-0
Aids: Bl: 0-0 Vi: 0-0 Tstrap: 0-0 Ckp: 0-0
Best Rating: 56 7/09 Newc 7f gd-sft

Cosmic Sun

108 **102**

3-y-o b g Helissio (FR)-Cosmic Case (Casteddu)
R A Fahey The Cosmic Cases

Placings:02222024-00131443 **(5823)**
2009: 10^{0}GF, 12^{0}G, 12^{1}GF, 11^{3}GF, 12^{1}G, 12^{4}G, 14^{4}GF, 14^{3}GF,

	Starts	1st	2nd	3rd	Win & Pl
Career Total (Turf)	16	2	5	2	67715

94	7/09	York	1m4f	(0-100)H	GD	£11527
89	6/09	Asct	1m4f	(0-105)H	G-F	£31155

Total win prize-money £42682

Going (Turf): Sf: 0-2 GS: 0-2 **Gd: 1-3 GF: 1-9** Fm: 0-0
Distance: 5f/6f: 0-2 7f-8f: 0-6 **9f-13f: 2-6** 14f+: 0-2
Track : LH: 1-8 RH: 1-5 Tight: 0-4 **Gall: 2-6**
Aids: Bl: 0-0 Vi: 0-0 Tstrap: 0-0 Ckp: 0-0
Best Rating: 102 8/09 York 1m6f gd-fm

Very useful; winner of the King George V Handicap in 2009; stays 1m6f; acts on any ground.

Cosmopolitan

103 **96**

4-y-o ch f Cadeaux Genereux-Parisian Elegance (Zilzal (USA))
J H M Gosden H R H Princess Haya Of Jordan

Placings:03-110100 **(6267)**
2009: 8^{1}GF, 8^{1}GF, 8^{0}G, 8^{1}GS, 7^{0}G, 8^{0}G,

	Starts	1st	2nd	3rd	Win & Pl
Career Total (Turf)	8	3	0	1	24172

96	7/09	Newb	1m	(0-100)H	G-S	£12462
91	6/09	NmkJ	1m	(0-85)H	G-F	£6476
84	6/09	Gdwd	1m		G-F	£3885

Total win prize-money £22824

Going (Turf): Sf: 0-2 GS: 1-1 Gd: 0-3 **GF: 2-2** Fm: 0-0
Distance: 5f/6f: 0-0 **7f-8f: 3-8** 9f-13f: 0-0 14f+: 0-0
Track : LH: 0-0 **RH: 1-4** Tight: 0-0 Gall: 0-1
Aids: Bl: 0-0 Vi: 0-0 Tstrap: 0-0 Ckp: 0-0
Best Rating: 96 7/09 Newb 1m gd-sft

Very useful; stays 1m and acts on fast and soft ground.

Cossack Prince

103(103) (78)**73**

4-y-o b g Dubai Destination (USA)-Danemere (IRE) (Danehill (USA))
Mrs L J Mongan Mrs P J Sheen

Placings:041/0004205**321-010124000** **(7823)**
2009: 12^{0}SD, 12^{1}SD, 12^{0}SD, 12^{1}GF, 12^{2}GF, 9^{4}G, 12^{0}GF, 11^{0}GS, 10^{0}SD,

	Starts	1st	2nd	3rd	Win & Pl
Career Total (Turf)	15	1	2	1	6970
Career Total (AW)	7	3	1	0	7397

73	5/09	Gdwd	1m4f	(0-75)H	G-F	£3238
78	2/09	Kemp	1m4f		STD	£2047
73	10/08	Kemp	1m4f	(0-65)H	STD	£1706
78	11/07	Wolv	1m141y		STD	£2968

Total win prize-money £9960

Going (Turf): Sf: 0-0 GS: 0-3 Gd: 0-4 **GF: 1-8** Fm: 0-0
Distance: 5f/6f: 0-0 7f-8f: 0-1 **9f-13f: 4-17** 14f+: 0-4
Track : LH: 1-13 **RH: 3-8 Tight: 2-11** Gall: 0-2
Aids: Bl: 0-0 Vi: 0-0 Tstrap: 0-2 Ckp: 0-2
Best Rating: 78 2/09 Kemp 1m4f stand

Fair; effective at around 1m4f-1m7f; acts on good and fast ground; goes on Polytrack; has been tried in cheekpieces.

Cote D'Argent

99 **68**

6-y-o b g Lujain (USA)-In The Groove (Night Shift (USA))
C J Down (L Lungo 19/6) Culm Valley Racing

Placings:3531/0/00-3042 **(3095)**
2009: 12^{3}GS, 12^{0}GS, 16^{4}G, 13^{2}G,

	Starts	1st	2nd	3rd	Win & Pl
Career Total (Turf)	**11**	**1**	**1**	**3**	**7180**

84 11/05 Muss 7f30y SFT £4197
Total win prize-money £4197

Going (Turf): **Sf: 1-1** GS: 0-4 Gd: 0-3 GF: 0-3 Fm: 0-0
Distance: 5f/6f: 0-0 **7f-8f: 1-5** 9f-13f: 0-4 14f+: 0-2
Track : LH: 0-8 **RH: 1-1 Tight: 1-1** Gall: 0-3
Aids: Bl: 0-0 Vi: 0-0 Tstrap: 0-0 Ckp: 0-0
Best Rating: **84** 11/05 Muss 7f30y soft

Modest; stays 1m5f; acts on good and soft ground.

Cotillion

104 **81**

3-y-o b g Sadler's Wells (USA)-Riberac (Efisio)
W J Haggas Mr & Mrs G Middlebrook

Placings:262524 **(7221)**
2009: 10^{2}S, 10^{6}GF, 12^{2}G, 12^{5}G, 10^{2}GS, 11^{4}S,

	Starts	1st	2nd	3rd	Win & Pl
Career Total (Turf)	6	0	3	0	4456

Going (Turf): **Sf: 0-2 GS: 0-1 Gd: 0-2 GF: 0-1 Fm: 0-0**
Distance: 5f/6f: 0-0 7f-8f: 0-0 9f-13f: 0-6 14f+: 0-0
Track : LH: 0-3 RH: 0-3 Tight: 0-2 Gall: 0-3
Aids: Bl: 0-0 Vi: 0-0 Tstrap: 0-0 Ckp: 0-0
Best Rating: **81** 10/09 Nott 1m2f50y gd-sft

Useful; stays 1m2f; acts on soft ground.

Cotswold Village (AUS)

(86) (32)

3-y-o b f Hawk Wing (USA)-Scenic Bold Dancer (AUS) (Scenic)
M R Bosley Colin Rogers

Placings:0 **(7439)**
2009: 10^{0}SD,

	Starts	1st	2nd	3rd	Win & Pl
Career Total (Turf)	0	0	0	0	
Career Total (AW)	1	0	0	0	

Going (Turf): **Sf: 0-0 GS: 0-0 Gd: 0-0 GF: 0-0 Fm: 0-0**
Distance: 5f/6f: 0-0 7f-8f: 0-0 9f-13f: 0-1 14f+: 0-0
Track : LH: 0-1 RH: 0-0 Tight: 0-1 Gall: 0-0
Aids: Bl: 0-0 Vi: 0-0 Tstrap: 0-0 Ckp: 0-0
Best Rating: **32** 11/09 Ling 1m2f stand

Cotswolds

104 **82**

4-y-o br g Green Desert (USA)-Valley Of Gold (FR) (Shirley Heights)
M Johnston Sheikh Hamdan Bin Mohammed Al Maktoum

Placings:0-10531 **(3560)**
2009: 7^{1}GF, 7^{0}G, 8^{5}GF, 8^{3}GF, 8^{1}GF,

	Starts	1st	2nd	3rd	Win & Pl
Career Total (Turf)	**6**	**2**	**0**	**1**	**9039**

82 7/09 Bevl 1m100y (0-85)H G-F £5180
80 5/09 Catt 7f G-F £2914
Total win prize-money £8095

Going (Turf): Sf: 0-1 GS: 0-0 Gd: 0-1 **GF: 2-4** Fm: 0-0
Distance: 5f/6f: 0-0 7f-8f: 1-3 9f-13f: 1-3 14f+: 0-0
Track : LH: 1-1 RH: 1-4 **Tight: 1-1** Gall: 0-0
Aids: Bl: 0-0 Vi: 0-0 Tstrap: 0-0 Ckp: 0-0
Best Rating: **82** 7/09 Bevl 1m100y gd-fm

Fair; stays 1m and acts on fast ground.

Cottam Breeze

31 (19)**29**

4-y-o b f Diktat-Flower Breeze (USA) (Rahy (USA))
J S Wainwright Peter Easterby

Placings:00000/0 **(2805)**
2009: 7^{0}F,

	Starts	1st	2nd	3rd	Win & Pl
Career Total (Turf)	5	0	0	0	
Career Total (AW)	1	0	0	0	

Going (Turf): **Sf: 0-0 GS: 0-2 Gd: 0-0 GF: 0-2 Fm: 0-1**
Distance: 5f/6f: 0-1 7f-8f: 0-4 9f-13f: 0-1 14f+: 0-0
Track : LH: 0-2 RH: 0-3 Tight: 0-1 Gall: 0-0
Aids: Bl: 0-0 Vi: 0-0 Tstrap: 0-1 Ckp: 0-1
Best Rating: **29** 7/07 Rdcr 7f gd-sft

Cotton Top (IRE)

90(85) (59)**68**

2-y-o b f Fath (USA)-Common Cause (Polish Patriot (USA))
M R Channon Mrs T Burns

Placings:3000 **(7616)**
2009: 7^{3}GF, 7^{0}SD, 7^{0}G, 8^{0}SD,

	Starts	1st	2nd	3rd	Win & Pl
Career Total (Turf)	2	0	0	1	605
Career Total (AW)	2	0	0	0	

Going (Turf): **Sf: 0-0 GS: 0-0 Gd: 0-1 GF: 0-1 Fm: 0-0**
Distance: 5f/6f: 0-0 7f-8f: 0-3 9f-13f: 0-1 14f+: 0-0
Track : LH: 0-4 RH: 0-0 Tight: 0-3 Gall: 0-0
Aids: Bl: 0-0 Vi: 0-0 Tstrap: 0-0 Ckp: 0-0
Best Rating: **68** 9/09 Wwck 7f26y gd-fm

Modest; stays 7f; acts on fast ground.

Cottonfields (USA)

88(90) (52)**57**

3-y-o gr/ro g Maria's Mon (USA)-Known Romance (USA) (Known Fact (USA))
Mrs H S Main Wetumpka Racing

Placings:005 **(4979)**
2009: 7^{0}GS, 10^{0}GF, 10^{5}SD,

	Starts	1st	2nd	3rd	Win & Pl
Career Total (Turf)	2	0	0	0	
Career Total (AW)	1	0	0	0	0

Going (Turf): **Sf: 0-0 GS: 0-1 Gd: 0-0 GF: 0-1 Fm: 0-0**
Distance: 5f/6f: 0-0 7f-8f: 0-1 9f-13f: 0-2 14f+: 0-0
Track : LH: 0-0 RH: 0-2 Tight: 0-1 Gall: 0-0
Aids: Bl: 0-0 Vi: 0-0 Tstrap: 0-0 Ckp: 0-0
Best Rating: **57** 5/09 Newb 7f gd-sft

Coughlans Locke (IRE)

104(99) (54)**62**

6-y-o b g All My Dreams (IRE)-Inniu (IRE) (Tirol)
Kieran P Cotter R J Cotter

Placings:0040000-0414400 **(7798)**
2009: 9^{0}G, 11^{4}YS, 9^{1}Y, 10^{4}YS, 9^{4}G, 8^{0}Y, 9^{0}SS,

	Starts	1st	2nd	3rd	Win & Pl
Career Total (Turf)	**11**	**1**	**0**	**0**	**6433**
Career Total (AW)	**3**	**0**	**0**	**0**	

62 7/09 Baln 1m1f (47-65)H YLD £5031
Total win prize-money £5032

Going (Turf): **Sf: 0-2 GS: 0-0 Gd: 0-3 GF: 0-0 Fm: 0-0**
Distance: 5f/6f: 0-0 7f-8f: 0-4 **9f-13f: 1-10** 14f+: 0-0
Track : LH: 0-6 **RH: 1-8** Tight: 0-2 Gall: 0-1
Aids: **Bl: 1-5** Vi: 0-0 Tstrap: 0-0 Ckp: 0-0
Best Rating: **62** 7/09 Baln 1m1f yield

Could It Be Magic

95(91) (69)**72**

2-y-o b c Dubai Destination (USA)-Lomapamar (Nashwan (USA))
W G M Turner Mascalls Stud

Placings:63525530 **(7654)**
2009: 5^{6}GF, 6^{3}G, 7^{5}GF, 6^{2}G, 6^{5}SD, 6^{5}S, 7^{3}SD, 7^{0}SD,

	Starts	1st	2nd	3rd	Win & Pl
Career Total (Turf)	5	0	1	1	1532
Career Total (AW)	3	0	0	1	385

Going (Turf): **Sf: 0-1 GS: 0-0 Gd: 0-2 GF: 0-2 Fm: 0-0**
Distance: 5f/6f: 0-4 7f-8f: 0-4 9f-13f: 0-0 14f+: 0-0
Track : LH: 0-3 RH: 0-1 Tight: 0-3 Gall: 0-0
Aids: Bl: 0-0 Vi: 0-0 Tstrap: 0-5 Ckp: 0-5
Best Rating: **72** 8/09 Chep 6f16y good

Fair; best at around 6f on a sound surface; has worn cheek-pieces.

Councellor (FR)

101(113) (97)**79**

7-y-o b g Gilded Time (USA)-Sudden Storm Bird (USA) (Storm Bird (CAN))
Stef Liddiard ownaracehorse.co.uk

Placings:3442/043322141032/3301464/003312014400400 2314114365/005405313444031-125400620 **(2883)**
2009: 8^{1}SS, 7^{2}SD, 8^{5}SD, 7^{4}SD, 7^{0}SD, 8^{0}GF, 7^{6}GF, 7^{2}G, 7^{0}G,

	Starts	1st	2nd	3rd	Win & Pl
Career Total (Turf)	**28**	**3**	**4**	**5**	**27432**
Career Total (AW)	**44**	**8**	**4**	**8**	**67052**

97 1/09 Sthl 1m (0-100)H SS £11656
90 12/08 Wolv 7f32y (0-95)H STD £7569
79 5/08 Gdwd 7f (0-80)H G-F £4533
94 11/07 Wolv 7f32y (0-85)H STD £4857
85 11/07 Ling 1m (0-85)H STD £4728
83 10/07 Wolv 7f32y STD £2047
91 3/07 Kemp 1m (0-85)H STD £4728
86 2/07 Sthl 1m (0-75)H STD £3238
84 3/06 Wolv 5f216y (0-80)H STD £5505
80 9/05 Epsm 7f (0-75)H GD £4190
70 8/05 Epsm 7f GD £3376
Total win prize-money £56434

Going (Turf): Sf: 0-1 GS: 0-1 **Gd: 2-13** GF: 1-12 Fm: 0-1
Distance: 5f/6f: 1-8 **7f-8f: 10-56** 9f-13f: 0-8 14f+: 0-0
Track : **LH: 9-42** RH: 2-19 **Tight: 7-30** Gall: 0-2

Aids: Bl: 0-0 Vi: 0-1 Tstrap: 0-0 Ckp: 0-0
Best Rating: 97 2/09 Kemp 1m stand

Very useful; effective at around 7f-1m; acts on most ground on turf and on sand; wears a tongue tie; likes to race prominently; can pull hard.

Count Bertoni (IRE)

97(90) (60)**74**

2-y-o b c Bertolini (USA)-Queen Sceptre (IRE) (Fairy King (USA))
S Gollings (T P Tate 5/7) P J Martin

Placings:2654342 (7218)
2009: 6^{2}GS, 6^{6}GF, 7^{5}G, 7^{4}G, 7^{3}G, 7^{4}SD, 7^{2}S,

	Starts	1st	2nd	3rd	Win & Pl
Career Total (Turf)	6	0	2	1	3472
Career Total (AW)	1	0	0	0	409

Going (Turf): **Sf: 0-1 GS: 0-1 Gd: 0-3 GF: 0-1 Fm: 0-0**
Distance: 5f/6f: 0-2 7f-8f: 0-5 9f-13f: 0-0 14f+: 0-0
Track : LH: 0-5 RH: 0-0 Tight: 0-1 Gall: 0-1
Aids: Bl: 0-1 Vi: 0-0 Tstrap: 0-0 Ckp: 0-0
Best Rating: 74 5/09 Newc 6f gd-sft

Fair; stays 7f; acts on fast and soft ground.

Count Ceprano (IRE)

100(112) (88)**89**

5-y-o b g Desert Prince (IRE)-Camerlata (Common Grounds)
C R Dore Chris Marsh

Placings:412/435000/**335132221**0625024514**00000-422646600**0053006000 (5998)
2009: 5^{4}SD, 6^{2}SD, 5^{2}SD, 6^{6}SD, 7^{4}SD, 7^{6}SD, 6^{6}SD, 7^{0}GF, 6^{0}GF, 7^{0}SD, 7^{5}GF, 8^{3}G, 8^{0}GF, 7^{0}GS, 8^{6}GS, 8^{0}HY, 8^{0}SD, 7^{0}GF,

	Starts	1st	2nd	3rd	Win & Pl
Career Total (Turf)	21	1	1	1	17564
Career Total (AW)	30	3	7	4	25246

89	8/08	Gdwd	1m1f	(0-90)H	G-F	£12952
86	4/08	Wolv	7f32y	(0-85)H	STD	£4209
75	2/08	Ling	7f	(0-75)H	STD	£2590
76	9/06	Ling	6f		STD	£3886

Total win prize-money £23638

Going (Turf): Sf: 0-2 GS: 0-2 Gd: 0-6 **GF: 1-10** Fm: 0-1
Distance: 5f/6f: 1-11 **7f-8f: 2-31** 9f-13f: 1-9 14f+: 0-0
Track : **LH: 3-26** RH: 1-17 **Tight: 4-22** Gall: 0-3
Aids: Bl: 0-0 Vi: 0-0 Tstrap: 0-2 Ckp: 0-2
Best Rating: 89 8/08 Gdwd 1m1f gd-fm

Fair; stays 1m1f; acts on fast ground and on Polytrack.

Count Cougar (USA)

(92) (41)**19**

9-y-o b g Sir Cat (USA)-Gold Script (USA) (Seeking The Gold (USA))
S P Griffiths Mrs C Grant

Placings:44200/43U060**010**/30060000**05**/45441311430000500/0025104100004064/11211260010/600000-00 (7503)
2009: 5^{0}SD, 6^{0}SD,

	Starts	1st	2nd	3rd	Win & Pl
Career Total (Turf)	21	0	1	3	2957
Career Total (AW)	54	11	3	1	33619

80	12/07	Sthl	5f	(0-85)H	SS	£4728
81	4/07	Sthl	5f	(0-70)H	STD	£3238
78	3/07	Sthl	6f	(0-75)H	STD	£3071
74	1/07	Sthl	6f	(0-65)H	STD	£2388
69	1/07	Sthl	6f	(0-55)H	STD	£1706
72	5/06	Sthl	6f	(0-70)H	STD	£3238
68	4/06	Sthl	5f	(0-60)H	STD	£2730
72	6/05	Wolv	5f216y	(0-55)H	STD	£2639
63	6/05	Wolv	5f216y	(0-55)H	STD	£3018
57	4/05	Sthl	6f	(0-45)	STD	£1473
73	10/03	Sthl	5f	F(0-60)H	STD	£2042

Total win prize-money £30276

Going (Turf): **Sf: 0-2 GS: 0-1 Gd: 0-2 GF: 0-14 Fm: 0-2**
Distance: **5f/6f: 11-68** 7f-8f: 0-7 9f-13f: 0-0 14f+: 0-0
Track : **LH: 7-38** RH: 0-5 **Tight: 2-16** Gall: 0-3
Aids: Bl: 0-1 Vi: 0-0 Tstrap: 0-2 Ckp: 0-2
Best Rating: 82 5/07 Sthl 5f stand

Fair sprinter; effective over5f-6f; acts on Polytrack, but very effective on Fibresand; likes to race prominently.

Count Lucien

92 **70**

3-y-o b c Danehill Dancer (IRE)-Paquita (IRE) (Sadler's Wells (USA))
J H M Gosden Nigel & Carolyn Elwes

Placings:405 (4246)
2009: 10^{4}GF, 10^{0}G, 8^{5}GF,

	Starts	1st	2nd	3rd	Win & Pl
Career Total (Turf)	3	0	0	0	289

Going (Turf): **Sf: 0-0 GS: 0-0 Gd: 0-1 GF: 0-2 Fm: 0-0**
Distance: 5f/6f: 0-0 7f-8f: 0-0 9f-13f: 0-3 14f+: 0-0
Track : LH: 0-0 RH: 0-3 Tight: 0-0 Gall: 0-0
Aids: Bl: 0-0 Vi: 0-0 Tstrap: 0-0 Ckp: 0-0
Best Rating: 70 5/09 Sand 1m2f7y gd-fm

Modest; stays 1m2f; acts on fast ground.

Count Of Anjou (USA)

88(90) (71)**65**

2-y-o b/br c Lion Heart (USA)-Woodmaven (USA) (Woodman (USA))
R Hannon J A Lazzari

Placings:502 (7537)
2009: 6^{5}G, 8^{0}S, 7^{2}SD,

	Starts	1st	2nd	3rd	Win & Pl
Career Total (Turf)	2	0	0	0	0
Career Total (AW)	1	0	1	0	964

Going (Turf): **Sf: 0-1 GS: 0-0 Gd: 0-1 GF: 0-0 Fm: 0-0**
Distance: 5f/6f: 0-0 7f-8f: 0-3 9f-13f: 0-0 14f+: 0-0
Track : LH: 0-0 RH: 0-1 Tight: 0-0 Gall: 0-0
Aids: Bl: 0-0 Vi: 0-0 Tstrap: 0-0 Ckp: 0-0
Best Rating: 71 11/09 Kemp 7f stand

Fair; stays 7f; acts on Polytrack.

Count Of Tuscany (USA)

100(103) (78)**77**

3-y-o b c Arch (USA)-Corsini (Machiavellian (USA))
Mrs A J Perrett K Abdulla

Placings:3-231 (6941)
2009: 12^{2}G, 9^{3}GF, 12^{1}SD,

	Starts	1st	2nd	3rd	Win & Pl
Career Total (Turf)	3	0	1	2	2745
Career Total (AW)	1	1	0	0	2590

78	10/09	Kemp	1m4f	STD	£2590

Total win prize-money £2590

Going (Turf): **Sf: 0-0 GS: 0-1 Gd: 0-1 GF: 0-1 Fm: 0-0**
Distance: 5f/6f: 0-0 7f-8f: 0-1 **9f-13f: 1-3** 14f+: 0-0
Track : LH: 0-0 **RH: 1-3** Tight: 0-1 Gall: 0-1
Aids: Bl: 0-0 Vi: 0-0 Tstrap: 0-0 Ckp: 0-0
Best Rating: 78 10/09 Kemp 1m4f stand

Fair; seems to stay 1m4f; acts on easy ground.

Count On Guest

94 **63**

3-y-o ch g Fantastic Light (USA)-Countess Guest (IRE) (Spectrum (IRE))
G G Margarson John Guest

Placings:04-500002000 (5972)
2009: 10^{5}G, 11^{0}GS, 10^{0}GF, 8^{0}GF, 12^{0}GF, 8^{2}G, 7^{0}F, 7^{0}G, 7^{0}GF,

	Starts	1st	2nd	3rd	Win & Pl
Career Total (Turf)	11	0	1	0	737

Going (Turf): **Sf: 0-0 GS: 0-1 Gd: 0-3 GF: 0-6 Fm: 0-1**
Distance: 5f/6f: 0-0 7f-8f: 0-5 9f-13f: 0-6 14f+: 0-0
Track : LH: 0-3 RH: 0-2 Tight: 0-5 Gall: 0-0
Aids: Bl: 0-1 Vi: 0-0 Tstrap: 0-0 Ckp: 0-0
Best Rating: 63 7/08 Yarm 7f3y gd-fm

Count Paris (USA)

(95) (74)**75**

3-y-o ch c Pivotal-Dearly (Rahy (USA))
M Johnston Sheikh Hamdan Bin Mohammed Al Maktoum

Placings:60311340-**04** (1434)
2009: 6^{0}SD, 7^{4}SD,

	Starts	1st	2nd	3rd	Win & Pl
Career Total (Turf)	8	2	0	2	12768
Career Total (AW)	2	0	0	0	351

73	9/08	Haml	6f5y	(0-85)	SFT	£7123
69	9/08	Ling	7f	(0-75)	SFT	£3238

Total win prize-money £10362

Going (Turf): **Sf: 2-4** GS: 0-1 Gd: 0-3 GF: 0-0 Fm: 0-0
Distance: 5f/6f: 0-5 **7f-8f: 2-5** 9f-13f: 0-0 14f+: 0-0
Track : LH: 0-1 RH: 0-2 Tight: 0-0 Gall: 0-0
Aids: Bl: 0-0 Vi: 0-0 Tstrap: 0-0 Ckp: 0-0
Best Rating: 75 10/08 Donc 7f good

Fair; effective at 6f-7f; acts on good and softer ground.

Count Trevisio (IRE)

98(100) (85)**71**

6-y-o b g Danehill (USA)-Stylish (Anshan)
J R Gask Horses First Racing Limited

Placings:10/1320/12003/**0-603645**0 (2495)
2009: 7^{6}SD, 8^{0}SD, 9^{3}SD, 12^{6}SF, 9^{4}SD, 8^{5}SD, 8^{0}GF,

	Starts	1st	2nd	3rd	Win & Pl
Career Total (Turf)	12	3	2	2	36416
Career Total (AW)	7	0	0	1	1318

95	1/07	Ndas	1m194y	(85-94)H	GD	£6675
99	6/06	Sand	1m1f	(0-90)H	G-F	£8096
77	9/05	Wwck	7f26y		GD	£3315

Total win prize-money £18087

Going (Turf): Sf: 0-1 GS: 0-1 **Gd: 2-4** GF: 1-6 Fm: 0-0
Distance: 5f/6f: 0-0 7f-8f: 1-9 **9f-13f: 2-10** 14f+: 0-0
Track: LH: 1-9 RH: 1-4 Tight: 0-6 Gall: 0-2
Aids: Bl: 0-0 Vi: 0-0 Tstrap: 0-2 Ckp: 0-2
Best Rating: **108** 2/07 Ndas 1m2f good

Very useful; stays 1m2f; acts on good and faster ground; effective from the front.

Countdown

98(102) (89)88
7-y-o ch g Pivotal-Quiz Time (Efisio)
R A Fahey (M D Squance 19/6) David W Armstrong

Placings:3211205/0033/2502005203413/356541166000/0 03003520510-05000 (5697)
2009: 6[0]GF, 7[5]GF, 7[0]SD, 7[0]GF, 7[0]GS,

	Starts	1st	2nd	3rd	Win & Pl
Career Total (Turf)	43	5	4	6	54112
Career Total (AW)	10	1	2	2	9809

89	10/08	Kemp	7f	(0-80)H	STD	£5180
92	7/07	York	7f	(0-100)H	HVY	£12464
89	7/07	Catt	7f	(0-90)H	G-S	£7124
85	10/06	Catt	7f	(0-85)H	SFT	£6477
89	8/04	Sand	5f6y	D	SFT	£6841
78	8/04	Hayd	5f	D	GD	£4901

Total win prize-money £42989

Going (Turf): **Sf: 3-10** GS: 1-10 Gd: 1-7 GF: 0-15 Fm: 0-1
Distance: 5f/6f: 2-22 **7f-8f: 4-31** 9f-13f: 0-0 14f+: 0-0
Track: **LH: 3-21** RH: 1-5 **Tight: 2-17** Gall: 1-5
Aids: Bl: 0-10 Vi: 0-4 Tstrap: 0-0 Ckp: 0-0
Best Rating: **92** 7/07 York 7f heavy

Useful; effective at up to 7f; acts on easy ground; also goes on Polytrack; has worn blinkers and a visor.

Countenance

96(91) (68)65
3-y-o ch g Medicean-Glamorous (Sanglamore (USA))
W J Haggas Highclere Thoroughbred Racing (Ormonde)

Placings:03400 (6784)
2009: 9[0]GF, 9[3]GS, 8[4]SD, 10[0]GS, 10[0]SS,

	Starts	1st	2nd	3rd	Win & Pl
Career Total (Turf)	3	0	0	1	530
Career Total (AW)	2	0	0	0	0

Going (Turf): Sf: 0-0 GS: 0-2 Gd: 0-0 GF: 0-1 Fm: 0-0
Distance: 5f/6f: 0-0 7f-8f: 0-1 9f-13f: 0-4 14f+: 0-0
Track: LH: 0-3 RH: 0-2 Tight: 0-3 Gall: 0-1
Aids: Bl: 0-0 Vi: 0-0 Tstrap: 0-0 Ckp: 0-0
Best Rating: **68** 6/09 Ling 1m stand

Countenance Divine

83 63
2-y-o ch f Pivotal-Sundari (IRE) (Danehill (USA))
B W Hills Lady Bamford

Placings:0 (7182)
2009: 7[0]G,

	Starts	1st	2nd	3rd	Win & Pl
Career Total (Turf)	1	0	0	0	

Going (Turf): Sf: 0-0 GS: 0-0 Gd: 0-1 GF: 0-0 Fm: 0-0
Distance: 5f/6f: 0-0 7f-8f: 0-1 9f-13f: 0-0 14f+: 0-0
Track: LH: 0-0 RH: 0-0 Tight: 0-0 Gall: 0-0
Aids: Bl: 0-0 Vi: 0-0 Tstrap: 0-0 Ckp: 0-0
Best Rating: **63** 10/09 NmkR 7f good

Countess Comet (IRE)

86 57
2-y-o b f Medicean-Countess Sybil (IRE) (Dr Devious (IRE))
R M Beckett Lady Cobham & Giles Irwin

Placings:4 (6792)
2009: 8[4]S,

	Starts	1st	2nd	3rd	Win & Pl
Career Total (Turf)	1	0	0	0	0

Going (Turf): Sf: 0-1 GS: 0-0 Gd: 0-0 GF: 0-0 Fm: 0-0
Distance: 5f/6f: 0-0 7f-8f: 0-0 9f-13f: 0-1 14f+: 0-0
Track: LH: 0-1 RH: 0-0 Tight: 0-0 Gall: 0-0
Aids: Bl: 0-0 Vi: 0-0 Tstrap: 0-0 Ckp: 0-0
Best Rating: **57** 10/09 Nott 1m75y soft

Countess Zara (IRE)

98(87) (52)70
3-y-o b f Xaar-Lochridge (Indian Ridge)
A M Balding J C Smith

Placings:00350-0554 (3281)
2009: 7[0]SD, 8[5]G, 6[5]GF, 6[4]GF,

	Starts	1st	2nd	3rd	Win & Pl
Career Total (Turf)	6	0	0	1	939
Career Total (AW)	3	0	0	0	

Going (Turf): Sf: 0-0 GS: 0-2 Gd: 0-2 GF: 0-2 Fm: 0-0
Distance: 5f/6f: 0-2 7f-8f: 0-7 9f-13f: 0-0 14f+: 0-0
Track: LH: 0-1 RH: 0-4 Tight: 0-2 Gall: 0-0
Aids: Bl: 0-1 Vi: 0-2 Tstrap: 0-0 Ckp: 0-0
Best Rating: **70** 10/08 Muss 7f30y gd-sft

Fair; grand-daughter of Lochsong; effective over 7f.

Country Princess (FR)

84 57
2-y-o b f Country Reel (USA)-Millefiori (USA) (Machiavellian (USA))
R M Beckett R Roberts

Placings:040 (2047)
2009: 5[0]GF, 5[4]GF, 6[0]GF,

	Starts	1st	2nd	3rd	Win & Pl
Career Total (Turf)	3	0	0	0	265

Going (Turf): Sf: 0-0 GS: 0-0 Gd: 0-0 GF: 0-3 Fm: 0-0
Distance: 5f/6f: 0-3 7f-8f: 0-0 9f-13f: 0-0 14f+: 0-0
Track: LH: 0-1 RH: 0-0 Tight: 0-0 Gall: 0-2
Aids: Bl: 0-0 Vi: 0-0 Tstrap: 0-0 Ckp: 0-0
Best Rating: **57** 5/09 Wind 5f10y gd-fm

Country Road (IRE)

103(89) (68)74
3-y-o b c Montjeu (IRE)-Souffle (Zafonic (USA))
P W Chapple-Hyam M Tabor, Mrs J Magnier & D Smith

Placings:0365 (6974)
2009: 10[0]S, 10[3]G, 10[6]S, 11[5]SD,

	Starts	1st	2nd	3rd	Win & Pl
Career Total (Turf)	3	0	0	1	433
Career Total (AW)	1	0	0	0	0

Going (Turf): Sf: 0-2 GS: 0-0 Gd: 0-1 GF: 0-0 Fm: 0-0
Distance: 5f/6f: 0-0 7f-8f: 0-0 9f-13f: 0-4 14f+: 0-0
Track: LH: 0-3 RH: 0-1 Tight: 0-0 Gall: 0-1
Aids: Bl: 0-0 Vi: 0-0 Tstrap: 0-0 Ckp: 0-0
Best Rating: **74** 8/09 Wwck 1m2f188y good

Moderate; stays 1m2f; acts on good and soft ground.

Countrycraft

78 32
2-y-o b g Pastoral Pursuits-Turn Back (Pivotal)
Miss S E Hall C Platts

Placings:0 (3606)
2009: 5[0]GF,

	Starts	1st	2nd	3rd	Win & Pl
Career Total (Turf)	1	0	0	0	

Going (Turf): Sf: 0-0 GS: 0-0 Gd: 0-0 GF: 0-1 Fm: 0-0
Distance: 5f/6f: 0-1 7f-8f: 0-0 9f-13f: 0-0 14f+: 0-0
Track: LH: 0-0 RH: 0-0 Tight: 0-0 Gall: 0-0
Aids: Bl: 0-0 Vi: 0-0 Tstrap: 0-0 Ckp: 0-0
Best Rating: **32** 7/09 Bevl 5f gd-fm

Countrymans Dream

87 39
2-y-o b g Mark Of Esteem (IRE)-Lateralle (IRE) (Unfuwain (USA))
J R Weymes Jackson,Heaton,Clarke,Pratt & Web Racing

Placings:05000 (6215)
2009: 5[0]GF, 5[5]GF, 5[0]GF, 7[0]G, 8[0]GF,

	Starts	1st	2nd	3rd	Win & Pl
Career Total (Turf)	5	0	0	0	0

Going (Turf): Sf: 0-0 GS: 0-0 Gd: 0-1 GF: 0-4 Fm: 0-0
Distance: 5f/6f: 0-3 7f-8f: 0-2 9f-13f: 0-0 14f+: 0-0
Track: LH: 0-0 RH: 0-3 Tight: 0-0 Gall: 0-1
Aids: Bl: 0-0 Vi: 0-0 Tstrap: 0-0 Ckp: 0-0
Best Rating: **39** 6/09 Carl 5f gd-fm

Countrystyle Lass (IRE)

88(89) (43)43
3-y-o b f Kheleyf (USA)-Davis Rock (Rock City)
P Winkworth Countrystyle Recycling Ltd

Placings:04000 (6339)
2009: 8[0]G, 8[4]G, 8[0]GF, 7[0]SD, 6[0]GF,

	Starts	1st	2nd	3rd	Win & Pl
Career Total (Turf)	4	0	0	0	0
Career Total (AW)	1	0	0	0	

Going (Turf): Sf: 0-0 GS: 0-0 Gd: 0-2 GF: 0-2 Fm: 0-0
Distance: 5f/6f: 0-0 7f-8f: 0-2 9f-13f: 0-3 14f+: 0-0
Track: LH: 0-2 RH: 0-3 Tight: 0-4 Gall: 0-0
Aids: Bl: 0-0 Vi: 0-0 Tstrap: 0-0 Ckp: 0-0
Best Rating: **43** 9/09 Ling 7f stand

Countrywide City (IRE)

73(87) (64)75

3-y-o b g Elusive City (USA)-Handy Station (IRE) (Desert Style (IRE))

Jane Southcombe K A Parr

Placings:4212305-000 **(3428)**

2009: 6^{0}GF, 5^{0}F, 5^{0}GF,

	Starts	1st	2nd	3rd	Win & Pl
Career Total (Turf)	9	1	2	1	6671
Career Total (AW)	1	0	0	0	165
69 6/08 Wwck 5f			FRM	£2914	

Total win prize-money £2914

Going (Turf): Sf: 0-0 GS: 0-1 Gd: 0-2 GF: 0-4 **Fm: 1-2**
Distance: **5f/6f: 1-10** 7f-8f: 0-0 9f-13f: 0-0 14f+: 0-0
Track : **LH: 1-6** RH: 0-0 Tight: 0-3 Gall: 0-2
Aids: Bl: 0-0 Vi: 0-0 Tstrap: 0-0 Ckp: 0-0
Best Rating: **75** 7/08 Ches 5f16y gd-sft

Fair; effective at 5f-6f; acts on good and faster ground.

Countrywide Comet (IRE)

(92) (47)60

4-y-o b g Desert Style (IRE)-Darzao (IRE) (Alzao (USA))

P Howling Mrs J P Howling

Placings:545430110055/564-000400 **(0802)**

2009: 7^{0}SD, 8^{0}SD, 8^{0}SD, 9^{4}SD, 8^{0}SD, 8^{0}SD,

	Starts	1st	2nd	3rd	Win & Pl
Career Total (Turf)	5	1	0	1	2769
Career Total (AW)	16	1	0	0	3239
62 10/07 Ling 6f			STD	£3238	
60 10/07 Rdcr 7f			GD	£2047	

Total win prize-money £5287

Going (Turf): Sf: 0-0 GS: 0-0 **Gd: 1-2** GF: 0-3 Fm: 0-0
Distance: 5f/6f: 1-9 7f-8f: 1-9 9f-13f: 0-3 14f+: 0-0
Track : **LH: 1-13** RH: 0-4 **Tight: 1-8** Gall: 0-0
Aids: **Bl: 2-8** Vi: 0-0 Tstrap: 0-1 Ckp: 0-1
Best Rating: **62** 10/07 Ling 6f stand

Modest; effective over 6f-7f; acts on a sound surface.

Countrywide Ice (IRE)

88(68) 50

2-y-o gr g Verglas (IRE)-Samaritan Woman (IRE) (Priolo (USA))

K A Ryan Countrywide Racing

Placings:00004050 **(5519)**

2009: 5^{0}GF, 5^{0}SD, 5^{0}GF, 5^{0}SD, 5^{4}S, 6^{0}GF, 6^{5}HY, 6^{0}G,

	Starts	1st	2nd	3rd	Win & Pl
Career Total (Turf)	6	0	0	0	241
Career Total (AW)	2	0	0	0	

Going (Turf): **Sf: 0-2 GS: 0-0 Gd: 0-1 GF: 0-3 Fm: 0-0**
Distance: 5f/6f: 0-7 7f-8f: 0-1 9f-13f: 0-0 14f+: 0-0
Track : LH: 0-0 RH: 0-0 Tight: 0-0 Gall: 0-0
Aids: Bl: 0-4 Vi: 0-0 Tstrap: 0-1 Ckp: 0-1
Best Rating: **50** 7/09 Hayd 5f soft

Countrywide Jaime (IRE)

(79) (33)

3-y-o b f Danetime (IRE)-Naraina (IRE) (Desert Story (IRE))

M Wigham (S A Callaghan 31/1) Countrywide Steel & Tubes Ltd

Placings:0-560 **(7652)**

2009: 5^{5}SD, 5^{6}SD, 8^{0}SD,

	Starts	1st	2nd	3rd	Win & Pl
Career Total (Turf)	0	0	0	0	
Career Total (AW)	4	0	0	0	0

Going (Turf): **Sf: 0-0 GS: 0-0 Gd: 0-0 GF: 0-0 Fm: 0-0**
Distance: 5f/6f: 0-3 7f-8f: 0-1 9f-13f: 0-0 14f+: 0-0
Track : LH: 0-4 RH: 0-0 Tight: 0-3 Gall: 0-1
Aids: Bl: 0-0 Vi: 0-0 Tstrap: 0-0 Ckp: 0-0
Best Rating: **33** 1/09 GrLe 5f stand

Countrywide Sun

78 17

7-y-o b g Benny The Dip (USA)-Sundae Girl (USA) (Green Dancer (USA))

A C Whillans Chas N Whillans

Placings:0002400/0/0 **(2159)**

2009: 14^{0}GF,

	Starts	1st	2nd	3rd	Win & Pl
Career Total (Turf)	8	0	1	0	1130
Career Total (AW)	1	0	0	0	297

Going (Turf): **Sf: 0-0 GS: 0-2 Gd: 0-3 GF: 0-3 Fm: 0-0**
Distance: 5f/6f: 0-1 7f-8f: 0-5 9f-13f: 0-2 14f+: 0-1
Track : LH: 0-3 RH: 0-1 Tight: 0-2 Gall: 0-1
Aids: Bl: 0-1 Vi: 0-0 Tstrap: 0-5 Ckp: 0-5
Best Rating: **56** 8/04 Sthl 7f stand

Coup De Torchon (FR)

76(83) (26)56

4-y-o b f Namid-Tashtiyana (IRE) (Doyoun)

J A Osborne Cavendish Star Racing

Placings:04030-0 **(4305)**

2009: 7^{0}G,

	Starts	1st	2nd	3rd	Win & Pl
Career Total (Turf)	3	0	0	1	688
Career Total (AW)	3	0	0	0	

Going (Turf): **Sf: 0-0 GS: 0-0 Gd: 0-2 GF: 0-0 Fm: 0-1**
Distance: 5f/6f: 0-0 7f-8f: 0-5 9f-13f: 0-1 14f+: 0-0
Track : LH: 0-4 RH: 0-1 Tight: 0-1 Gall: 0-0
Aids: Bl: 0-0 Vi: 0-0 Tstrap: 0-0 Ckp: 0-0
Best Rating: **56** 6/08 Wwck 7f26y firm

Moderate; probably stays 7f; acts on fast ground.

Courageous (IRE)

101 99

3-y-o ch c Refuse To Bend (IRE)-Bella Bella (IRE) (Sri Pekan (USA))

B Smart H E Sheikh Rashid Bin Mohammed

Placings:1525-03000 **(7019)**

2009: 7^{0}GF, 7^{3}GF, 7^{0}GF, 8^{0}G, 7^{0}GS,

	Starts	1st	2nd	3rd	Win & Pl
Career Total (Turf)	9	1	1	1	17124
76 7/08 Rdcr 7f			GD	£3399	

Total win prize-money £3400

Going (Turf): Sf: 0-1 GS: 0-2 **Gd: 1-3** GF: 0-3 Fm: 0-0
Distance: 5f/6f: 0-0 **7f-8f: 1-8** 9f-13f: 0-1 14f+: 0-0
Track : LH: 0-2 RH: 0-0 Tight: 0-0 Gall: 0-1
Aids: Bl: 0-0 Vi: 0-0 Tstrap: 0-0 Ckp: 0-0
Best Rating: **99** 10/08 Donc 1m good

Veru useful; best at around 7f; acts on fast and soft ground.

Course De Diamante (IRE)

98 68

3-y-o b f Galileo (IRE)-Desert Bluebell (Kalaglow)

D R Lanigan Diamond Racing Ltd

Placings:0645 **(3462)**

2009: 8^{0}F, 9^{6}GF, 10^{4}GF, 11^{5}GF,

	Starts	1st	2nd	3rd	Win & Pl
Career Total (Turf)	4	0	0	0	289

Going (Turf): **Sf: 0-0 GS: 0-0 Gd: 0-0 GF: 0-3 Fm: 0-1**
Distance: 5f/6f: 0-0 7f-8f: 0-0 9f-13f: 0-4 14f+: 0-0
Track : LH: 0-2 RH: 0-1 Tight: 0-2 Gall: 0-1
Aids: Bl: 0-0 Vi: 0-0 Tstrap: 0-0 Ckp: 0-0
Best Rating: **68** 6/09 Newb 1m2f6y gd-fm

Court Drinking (USA)

(81) (42)

2-y-o ch c Alke (USA)-Royal Forum (USA) (Open Forum (USA))

J R Best Illegal Racing Partnership

Placings:6 **(7618)**

2009: 5^{6}SD,

	Starts	1st	2nd	3rd	Win & Pl
Career Total (Turf)	0	0	0	0	
Career Total (AW)	1	0	0	0	0

Going (Turf): **Sf: 0-0 GS: 0-0 Gd: 0-0 GF: 0-0 Fm: 0-0**
Distance: 5f/6f: 0-1 7f-8f: 0-0 9f-13f: 0-0 14f+: 0-0
Track : LH: 0-1 RH: 0-0 Tight: 0-1 Gall: 0-0
Aids: Bl: 0-0 Vi: 0-0 Tstrap: 0-0 Ckp: 0-0
Best Rating: **42** 12/09 Wolv 5f216y stand

Green on debut over 6f on Polytrack.

Court Gown (IRE)

94 77

2-y-o b f Zafeen (FR)-Silk Law (IRE) (Barathea (IRE))

E S McMahon J C Fretwell

Placings:21 **(5440)**

2009: 7^{2}G, 7^{1}GF,

	Starts	1st	2nd	3rd	Win & Pl
Career Total (Turf)	2	1	1	0	4394
77 8/09 Rdcr 7f			G-F	£3238	

Total win prize-money £3238

Going (Turf): Sf: 0-0 GS: 0-0 Gd: 0-1 **GF: 1-1** Fm: 0-0
Distance: 5f/6f: 0-0 **7f-8f: 1-2** 9f-13f: 0-0 14f+: 0-0
Track : LH: 0-0 RH: 0-0 Tight: 0-0 Gall: 0-0

Aids: Bl: 0-0 Vi: 0-0 Tstrap: 0-0 Ckp: 0-0
Best Rating: 77 8/09 Rdcr 7f gd-fm

Fair; stays 7f and should stay 1m; acts on good ground.

Court Masterpiece

107 (100)108
9-y-o b h Polish Precedent (USA)-Easy Option (IRE) (Prince Sabo)
J J Quinn Maxilead Limited

Placings:61/42301/35421436/4212213315/6321300/05/350034 (6312)
2009: 7[3]GF, 7[5]G, 8[0]G, 7[0]GF, 10[3]GS, 9[4]GF,

	Starts	1st	2nd	3rd	Win & Pl
Career Total (Turf)	37	7	5	9	702136
Career Total (AW)	3	0	1	0	37934

124 8/06 Gdwd 1m G-F £180134
117 10/05 Lonc 7f SFT £81050
117 7/05 Gdwd 7f G-S £72500
119 6/05 Gdwd 1m G-S £17400
115 7/04 Asct 7f B H G-F £87000
106 8/03 Gdwd 1m A GD £20300
88 8/02 York 6f D GD £18294
Total win prize-money £476679

Going (Turf): Sf: 1-3 **GS: 2-6 Gd: 2-11 GF: 2-15** Fm: 0-2
Distance: 5f/6f: 1-1 **7f-8f: 6-37** 9f-13f: 0-2 14f+: 0-0
Track: LH: 0-9 **RH: 5-13** Tight: 0-3 Gall: 0-7
Aids: Bl: 0-0 Vi: 0-0 Tstrap: 0-0 Ckp: 0-0
Best Rating: 124 8/06 Gdwd 1m gd-fm

Group-class before going to stud; returned to the track in 2009; won the Group 1 Prix de la Foret in 2005 and Group 1 Sussex Stakes in 2006; effective at 7f-1m; acts on most ground.

Court Princess

84(101) (68)35
6-y-o b m Mtoto-Fairfields Cone (Celtic Cone)
George Baker (C E Longsdon 1/1) Derek & Cheryl Holder

Placings:050410 (7873)
2009: 11[0]G, 12[5]SD, 11[0]SD, 16[4]SD, 16[1]SD, 16[0]SD,

	Starts	1st	2nd	3rd	Win & Pl
Career Total (Turf)	1	0	0	0	
Career Total (AW)	5	1	0	0	1912

68 12/09 Ling 2m (0-60)H STD £1911
Total win prize-money £1912

Going (Turf): **Sf: 0-0 GS: 0-0 Gd: 0-1 GF: 0-0 Fm: 0-0**
Distance: 5f/6f: 0-0 7f-8f: 0-0 9f-13f: 0-3 **14f+: 1-3**
Track: **LH: 1-2** RH: 0-4 **Tight: 1-2** Gall: 0-0
Aids: Bl: 0-0 Vi: 0-0 Tstrap: 0-0 Ckp: 0-0
Best Rating: 68 12/09 Ling 2m stand

Modest; stays 2m; acts on Polytrack.

Court Wing (IRE)

69(56) 21
3-y-o b f Hawk Wing (USA)-Nicely (IRE) (Bustino)
George Baker Derek & Cheryl Holder

Placings:000 (2192)
2009: 7[0]SD, 8[0]F, 9[0]GF,

	Starts	1st	2nd	3rd	Win & Pl
Career Total (Turf)	2	0	0	0	
Career Total (AW)	1	0	0	0	

Going (Turf): **Sf: 0-0 GS: 0-0 Gd: 0-0 GF: 0-1 Fm: 0-1**
Distance: 5f/6f: 0-0 7f-8f: 0-1 9f-13f: 0-2 14f+: 0-0
Track: LH: 0-1 RH: 0-2 Tight: 0-1 Gall: 0-0
Aids: Bl: 0-0 Vi: 0-0 Tstrap: 0-0 Ckp: 0-0
Best Rating: 21 5/09 Nott 1m75y firm

Cousin Charlie

(92) (66)31
3-y-o b g Choisir (AUS)-Michelle Ma Belle (IRE) (Shareef Dancer (USA))
S Kirk Mrs Michelle Cousins

Placings:003-0 (0160)
2009: 7[0]SD,

	Starts	1st	2nd	3rd	Win & Pl
Career Total (Turf)	1	0	0	0	
Career Total (AW)	3	0	0	1	530

Going (Turf): **Sf: 0-0 GS: 0-1 Gd: 0-0 GF: 0-0 Fm: 0-0**
Distance: 5f/6f: 0-0 7f-8f: 0-4 9f-13f: 0-0 14f+: 0-0
Track: LH: 0-2 RH: 0-1 Tight: 0-2 Gall: 0-0
Aids: Bl: 0-0 Vi: 0-0 Tstrap: 0-0 Ckp: 0-0
Best Rating: 66 12/08 Wolv 7f32y stand

Moderate; stays 7f and acts on Polytrack.

Cover Drive (USA)

(96) (74)61
6-y-o br g Giant's Causeway (USA)-Woodland Orchid (IRE) (Woodman (USA))
Miss E J Baker (Christian Wroe 22/1) Mrs M J Arnold

Placings:0541/**3442/5300/50000650-06** (0244)
2009: 12[0]SD, 10[6]SD,

	Starts	1st	2nd	3rd	Win & Pl
Career Total (Turf)	5	0	0	0	531
Career Total (AW)	17	1	1	2	9274

78 12/05 Ndas 7f FST £2765
Total win prize-money £2766

Going (Turf): **Sf: 0-0 GS: 0-1 Gd: 0-2 GF: 0-2 Fm: 0-0**
Distance: 5f/6f: 0-1 **7f-8f: 1-6** 9f-13f: 0-15 14f+: 0-0
Track: LH: 0-2 RH: 0-5 Tight: 0-2 Gall: 0-0
Aids: Bl: 0-8 Vi: 0-1 Tstrap: 0-0 Ckp: 0-0
Best Rating: 81 1/07 Jebl 1m1f fast

Moderate; stays 1m4f.

Covert Ambition

104(105) (111)110
4-y-o ch c Singspiel (IRE)-Super Tassa (IRE) (Lahib (USA))
Saeed Bin Suroor Godolphin

Placings:1-1226 (5609)
2009: 10[1]SD, 10[2]G, 10[2]GS, 14[6]S,

	Starts	1st	2nd	3rd	Win & Pl
Career Total (Turf)	4	1	2	0	20688
Career Total (AW)	1	1	0	0	7353

111 6/09 Kemp 1m2f (0-95)H STD £7352
98 10/08 Nott 1m2f50y G-S £3238
Total win prize-money £10591

Going (Turf): Sf: 0-1 **GS: 1-2** Gd: 0-1 GF: 0-0 Fm: 0-0
Distance: 5f/6f: 0-0 7f-8f: 0-0 **9f-13f: 2-4** 14f+: 0-1
Track: LH: 1-2 RH: 1-3 Tight: 0-1 Gall: 0-1
Aids: Bl: 0-0 Vi: 0-0 Tstrap: 0-0 Ckp: 0-0
Best Rating: 111 6/09 Kemp 1m2f stand

Smart; Listed placed; stays 1m2f; acts on good and easy ground and on Polytrack.

Covert Mission

91(97) (66)61
6-y-o b m Overbury (IRE)-Peg's Permission (Ra Nova)
P D Evans Lost Souls Racing

Placings:56000**300**/0120-54 (7085)
2009: 12[5]SF, 11[4]S,

	Starts	1st	2nd	3rd	Win & Pl
Career Total (Turf)	7	1	0	0	2047
Career Total (AW)	7	0	1	1	1008

61 10/08 Catt 1m3f214y (0-60)H G-S £2047
Total win prize-money £2047

Going (Turf): Sf: 0-2 **GS: 1-1** Gd: 0-0 GF: 0-3 Fm: 0-1
Distance: 5f/6f: 0-0 7f-8f: 0-0 **9f-13f: 1-11** 14f+: 0-3
Track: **LH: 1-12** RH: 0-2 **Tight: 1-10** Gall: 0-1
Aids: Bl: 0-0 Vi: 0-0 Tstrap: 0-0 Ckp: 0-0
Best Rating: 66 11/08 Wolv 1m5f194y stand

Modest; stays 1m5f; acts on easy ground; goes on Polytrack.

Coyote Creek

98 91
5-y-o b g Zilzal (USA)-High Barn (Shirley Heights)
E F Vaughan Gibson, Goddard, Hamer & Hawkes

Placings:643/332032/4310460-020 (2898)
2009: 10[0]G, 12[2]GS, 12[0]GS,

	Starts	1st	2nd	3rd	Win & Pl
Career Total (Turf)	19	1	3	5	11488

91 5/08 Donc 1m4f (0-85)H GD £4857
Total win prize-money £4857

Going (Turf): Sf: 0-2 GS: 0-2 **Gd: 1-7** GF: 0-7 Fm: 0-1
Distance: 5f/6f: 0-0 7f-8f: 0-2 **9f-13f: 1-15** 14f+: 0-2
Track: **LH: 1-11** RH: 0-5 Tight: 0-7 **Gall: 1-9**
Aids: Bl: 0-1 **Vi: 1-5** Tstrap: 0-1 Ckp: 0-1
Best Rating: 91 6/08 Wind 1m3f135y gd-fm

Useful; stays 1m4f and acts on good and faster ground; has worn blinkers and a visor.

Cozy Tiger (USA)

(85) (76)70
4-y-o gr g Hold That Tiger (USA)-Cozelia (USA) (Cozzene (USA))
W J Musson McHugh & Partners

Placings:32/0604-6 (0310)
2009: 11[6]SD,

	Starts	1st	2nd	3rd	Win & Pl
Career Total (Turf)	3	0	0	0	0
Career Total (AW)	4	0	1	1	1229

Going (Turf): **Sf: 0-1 GS: 0-1 Gd: 0-1 GF: 0-0 Fm: 0-0**
Distance: 5f/6f: 0-0 7f-8f: 0-3 9f-13f: 0-4 14f+: 0-0
Track: LH: 0-2 RH: 0-4 Tight: 0-3 Gall: 0-1
Aids: Bl: 0-0 Vi: 0-0 Tstrap: 0-0 Ckp: 0-0
Best Rating: 76 11/07 Wolv 1m141y stand

Crackdown (IRE)

108 107
3-y-o b c Refuse To Bend (IRE)-Whitefoot (Be My Chief (USA))
M Johnston Sheikh Hamdan Bin Mohammed Al Maktoum

Placings:32361-102200 (4486)
2009: 8[1]GF, 8[0]GF, 8[2]G, 8[2]GF, 7[0]G, 8[0]G,

	Starts	1st	2nd	3rd	Win & Pl
Career Total (Turf)	11	2	3	2	42862

101	4/09	Ripn	1m	(0-95)H	G-F	£8723
84	9/08	Leic	7f9y		GD	£5180

Total win prize-money £13904

Going (Turf): Sf: 0-2 GS: 0-0 **Gd: 1-4 GF: 1-5** Fm: 0-0
Distance: 5f/6f: 0-1 **7f-8f: 2-8** 9f-13f: 0-2 14f+: 0-0
Track : LH: 0-1 **RH: 1-3 Tight: 1-1** Gall: 0-0
Aids: Bl: 0-0 Vi: 0-0 Tstrap: 0-0 Ckp: 0-0
Best Rating: 107 7/09 Sand 1m14y good

Very useful; stays 1m; seems to handle most ground; suited by forcing tactics.

Crackentorp

106(107) (91)99
4-y-o b g Generous (IRE)-Raspberry Sauce (Niniski (USA))
R M Beckett R A Pegum

Placings:311-202 (6546)
2009: 12^2G, 12^0GF, 10^2GF,

	Starts	1st	2nd	3rd	Win & Pl
Career Total (Turf)	4	0	2	1	6359
Career Total (AW)	2	2	0	0	9744

91	9/08	Ling	1m2f	(0-90)H	STD	£7477
87	8/08	Ling	1m2f		STD	£2266

Total win prize-money £9744

Going (Turf): **Sf: 0-0 GS: 0-0 Gd: 0-1 GF: 0-3 Fm: 0-0**
Distance: 5f/6f: 0-0 7f-8f: 0-0 **9f-13f: 2-6** 14f+: 0-0
Track : **LH: 2-3** RH: 0-3 **Tight: 2-3** Gall: 0-1
Aids: Bl: 0-0 Vi: 0-0 Tstrap: 0-0 Ckp: 0-0
Best Rating: 99 10/09 Wwck 1m2f188y gd-fm

Useful; stays 1m2f and acts on Polytrack.

Cracking Lass (IRE)

100 77
2-y-o b f Whipper (USA)-Lady From Limerick (IRE) (Rainbows For Life (CAN))
R A Fahey Mel Roberts and Ms Nicola Meese

Placings:00150 (6477)
2009: 6^0S, 6^0GF, 7^1S, 6^5GF, 7^0GF,

	Starts	1st	2nd	3rd	Win & Pl
Career Total (Turf)	5	1	0	0	19333

68	9/09	Thsk	7f	SFT	£5342

Total win prize-money £5343

Going (Turf): **Sf: 1-2** GS: 0-0 Gd: 0-0 GF: 0-3 Fm: 0-0
Distance: 5f/6f: 0-3 **7f-8f: 1-2** 9f-13f: 0-0 14f+: 0-0
Track : **LH: 1-1** RH: 0-0 **Tight: 1-1** Gall: 0-0
Aids: Bl: 0-0 Vi: 0-0 Tstrap: 0-0 Ckp: 0-0
Best Rating: 77 10/09 NmkR 7f gd-fm

Fair half-sister to Tagula Sunrise, Lord Links and Pacific Pride; winner on third start over 7f on soft.

Crag Path

84(99) (59)50
3-y-o b f Celtic Swing-Juvenilia (IRE) (Masterclass (USA))
D R C Elsworth G B Partnership

Placings:4300 (1531)
2009: 8^4SD, 10^3SD, 9^0GF, 8^0SD,

	Starts	1st	2nd	3rd	Win & Pl
Career Total (Turf)	1	0	0	0	
Career Total (AW)	3	0	0	1	403

Going (Turf): **Sf: 0-0 GS: 0-0 Gd: 0-0 GF: 0-1 Fm: 0-0**
Distance: 5f/6f: 0-0 7f-8f: 0-1 9f-13f: 0-3 14f+: 0-0
Track : LH: 0-3 RH: 0-1 Tight: 0-4 Gall: 0-0
Aids: Bl: 0-0 Vi: 0-0 Tstrap: 0-0 Ckp: 0-0
Best Rating: 59 4/09 Wolv 1m141y stand

Moderate; stays 1m2f; acts on Polytrack.

Cragganmore Creek

85(97) (53)46
6-y-o b g Tipsy Creek (USA)-Polish Abbey (Polish Precedent (USA))
D Morris Stag & Huntsman

Placings:1/50000600**3144**/340303002525**0**/13160002-2524060**6**000 (7608)
2009: 11^2SD, 12^5SD, 12^2SD, 11^4SD, 12^0SD, 10^6GF, 11^0G, 11^6GF, 11^0SD, 16^0SS, 16^0SD,

	Starts	1st	2nd	3rd	Win & Pl
Career Total (Turf)	10	0	0	0	0
Career Total (AW)	35	4	5	5	10713

59	2/08	Sthl	1m3f	(0-52)H	STD	£1714
55	1/08	Sthl	2m	(0-60)H	STD	£1351
63	11/06	Sthl	1m4f	(0-45)	STD	£1706
53	12/05	Wolv	1m141y		STD	£1405

Total win prize-money £6178

Going (Turf): **Sf: 0-1 GS: 0-1 Gd: 0-1 GF: 0-6 Fm: 0-1**
Distance: 5f/6f: 0-0 7f-8f: 0-0 **9f-13f: 3-33** 14f+: 1-12
Track : **LH: 4-39** RH: 0-4 **Tight: 1-19** Gall: 0-0
Aids: Bl: 1-7 Vi: 1-20 Tstrap: 0-2 Ckp: 0-2
Best Rating: 63 11/06 Sthl 1m4f stand

Moderate; stays 2m and acts on sand; has worn a visor.

Craicattack (IRE)

98(93) (67)76
2-y-o ch g Arakan (USA)-Jack-N-Jilly (IRE) (Anita's Prince)
J S Moore W Adams & J S Moore

Placings:021630305 (7846)
2009: 6^0GF, 6^2GF, 5^1GF, 5^6GF, 5^3GF, 6^0S, 6^3GF, 6^0GF, 7^5SD,

	Starts	1st	2nd	3rd	Win & Pl
Career Total (Turf)	8	1	1	2	7461
Career Total (AW)	1	0	0	0	212

73	6/09	Brig	5f213y	G-F	£3532

Total win prize-money £3532

Going (Turf): Sf: 0-1 GS: 0-0 Gd: 0-0 **GF: 1-7** Fm: 0-0
Distance: **5f/6f: 1-7** 7f-8f: 0-2 9f-13f: 0-0 14f+: 0-0
Track : **LH: 1-4** RH: 0-1 Tight: 0-1 Gall: 0-0
Aids: Bl: 0-0 Vi: 0-0 Tstrap: 0-0 Ckp: 0-0
Best Rating: 76 9/09 Newb 6f8y gd-fm

Fair; effective over 6f; acts on fast ground.

Craighall

89 62
2-y-o b f Dubawi (IRE)-Craigmill (Slip Anchor)
D M Simcock Major M G Wyatt

Placings:0 (6992)
2009: 8^0GS,

	Starts	1st	2nd	3rd	Win & Pl
Career Total (Turf)	1	0	0	0	

Going (Turf): **Sf: 0-0 GS: 0-1 Gd: 0-0 GF: 0-0 Fm: 0-0**
Distance: 5f/6f: 0-0 7f-8f: 0-1 9f-13f: 0-0 14f+: 0-0
Track : LH: 0-1 RH: 0-0 Tight: 0-0 Gall: 0-1
Aids: Bl: 0-0 Vi: 0-0 Tstrap: 0-0 Ckp: 0-0
Best Rating: 62 10/09 Donc 1m gd-sft

Cranworth Blaze

93(94) (49)46
5-y-o b m Diktat-Julietta Mia (USA) (Woodman (USA))
A G Newcombe (T J Etherington 28/8) Mike Clark

Placings:000/40045/0046**5200**-00000 (6966)
2009: 5^0F, 5^0GF, 7^0G, 6^0G, 9^0G,

	Starts	1st	2nd	3rd	Win & Pl
Career Total (Turf)	16	0	0	0	563
Career Total (AW)	5	0	1	0	771

Going (Turf): **Sf: 0-0 GS: 0-0 Gd: 0-8 GF: 0-6 Fm: 0-2**
Distance: 5f/6f: 0-12 7f-8f: 0-5 9f-13f: 0-4 14f+: 0-0
Track : LH: 0-8 RH: 0-3 Tight: 0-6 Gall: 0-3
Aids: Bl: 0-5 Vi: 0-0 Tstrap: 0-0 Ckp: 0-0
Best Rating: 49 9/08 GrLe 5f stand

Poor maiden; effective at 5f but stays further; acts on fast ground/Polytrack.

Crazy Bold (GER)

95(87) (34)44
6-y-o ch g Erminius (GER)-Crazy Love (GER) (Presto)
A W Carroll (D G Bridgwater 13/4) Mrs Susan Keable

Placings:00010400/00422556005/215531-55 (4880)
2009: 11^5SD, 10^5GS,

	Starts	1st	2nd	3rd	Win & Pl
Career Total (Turf)	22	2	3	0	7653
Career Total (AW)	6	1	0	1	1618

3/08	Colo	1m	H	HVY	£2205
1/08	Dort	1m110y	H	STD	£1176
7/06	Hamb	1m2f	H	GD	£2758

Total win prize-money £6141

Going (Turf): **Sf: 1-7** GS: 0-1 **Gd: 1-12** GF: 0-0 Fm: 0-0
Distance: 5f/6f: 0-1 7f-8f: 1-7 **9f-13f: 2-20** 14f+: 0-0
Track : LH: 0-2 RH: 0-0 Tight: 0-0 Gall: 0-0
Aids: Bl: 0-0 Vi: 0-0 Tstrap: 0-0 Ckp: 0-0
Best Rating: 44 8/09 Nott 1m2f50y gd-sft

Crazy Chris

102(104) (83)70
4-y-o b m Ishiguru (USA)-Ellopassoff (Librate)
B Palling (Tom Dascombe 21/10) E R Griffiths

Placings:2451 (7512)
2009: 8^2SD, 10^4GF, 10^5G, 10^1SD,

	Starts	1st	2nd	3rd	Win & Pl
Career Total (Turf)	2	0	0	0	433
Career Total (AW)	2	1	1	0	3396

83	11/09	Kemp	1m2f	(0-70)H	STD	£2590

Total win prize-money £2590

Going (Turf): **Sf: 0-0 GS: 0-0 Gd: 0-1 GF: 0-1 Fm: 0-0**
Distance: 5f/6f: 0-0 7f-8f: 0-1 **9f-13f: 1-3** 14f+: 0-0
Track : LH: 0-3 **RH: 1-1** Tight: 0-3 Gall: 0-0
Aids: Bl: 0-0 Vi: 0-0 Tstrap: 0-0 Ckp: 0-0
Best Rating: 83 11/09 Kemp 1m2f stand

Modest; stays 1m2f and acts on Polytrack; bumper winner.

Crazy Colours

(101) (63)
3-y-o ch g Dalakhani (IRE)-Eternity Ring (Alzao (USA))
Jane Chapple-Hyam Howard Spooner

Placings:00-46 (0295)
2009: 8^4SD, 9^6SD,

	Starts	1st	2nd	3rd	Win & Pl
Career Total (Turf)	0	0	0	0	

	Starts	1st	2nd	3rd	Win & Pl
Career Total (AW)	4	0	0	0	192

Going (Turf): Sf: 0-0 GS: 0-0 Gd: 0-0 GF: 0-0 Fm: 0-0
Distance: 5f/6f: 0-0 7f-8f: 0-3 9f-13f: 0-1 14f+: 0-0
Track : LH: 0-3 RH: 0-1 Tight: 0-2 Gall: 0-1
Aids: Bl: 0-2 Vi: 0-0 Tstrap: 0-1 Ckp: 0-1
Best Rating: 63 1/09 Kemp 1m stand

Creative (IRE)

99(91) (57)63
4-y-o b g Acclamation-Pride Of Pendle (Grey Desire)
M H Tompkins Miss Clare Hollest

Placings:426033/000000-52206424 (3109)
2009: 6^{5}G, 6^{2}SD, 5^{2}G, 6^{0}SD, 6^{6}GF, 6^{4}GF, 5^{2}G, 5^{4}GF,

	Starts	1st	2nd	3rd	Win & Pl
Career Total (Turf)	18	0	3	2	3117
Career Total (AW)	2	0	1	0	605

Going (Turf): Sf: 0-1 GS: 0-4 Gd: 0-6 GF: 0-7 Fm: 0-0
Distance: 5f/6f: 0-8 7f-8f: 0-9 9f-13f: 0-3 14f+: 0-0
Track : LH: 0-4 RH: 0-2 Tight: 0-3 Gall: 0-0
Aids: Bl: 0-2 Vi: 0-3 Tstrap: 0-0 Ckp: 0-0
Best Rating: 68 6/07 Haml 6f5y gd-fm

Modest; stays 7f; acts on most types of ground.

Credential

102(100) (58)58
7-y-o b g Dansili-Sabria (USA) (Miswaki (USA))
John A Harris Mrs A E Harris

Placings:5403/0020041/250002300/140300-042106 (4880)
2009: 10^{0}G, 10^{4}G, 11^{2}GF, 11^{1}SD, 12^{0}GF, 10^{6}GS,

	Starts	1st	2nd	3rd	Win & Pl
Career Total (Turf)	25	1	3	3	6127
Career Total (AW)	8	2	1	0	4994

58 7/09 Sthl 1m3f (0-65)H STD £1942
58 7/08 Yarm 1m3f101y (0-65)H G-F £1942
66 1/07 Sthl 1m3f STD £2184
Total win prize-money £6070

Going (Turf): Sf: 0-6 GS: 0-4 Gd: 0-6 **GF: 1-9** Fm: 0-0
Distance: 5f/6f: 0-0 7f-8f: 0-3 **9f-13f: 3-30** 14f+: 0-0
Track : **LH: 3-25** RH: 0-6 **Tight: 1-11** Gall: 0-2
Aids: Bl: 0-0 Vi: 0-0 Tstrap: 0-3 Ckp: 0-3
Best Rating: 76 9/05 Donc 1m gd-sft

Moderate; stays 1m4f; acts on Fibresand and easy ground.

Credit Swap

105(100) (84)98
4-y-o b g Diktat-Locharia (Wolfhound (USA))
M Wigham Your Golf Travel Ltd

Placings:4/210352-050420511123 (6307)
2009: 5^{0}SD, 6^{5}SD, 6^{0}GF, 6^{4}GF, 7^{2}GF, 7^{0}SD, 7^{5}GF, 8^{1}GF, 8^{1}G, 8^{1}G, 8^{2}GF, 8^{3}GF,

	Starts	1st	2nd	3rd	Win & Pl
Career Total (Turf)	15	4	3	2	27145
Career Total (AW)	4	0	1	0	1542

96 7/09 NmkJ 1m (0-80)H GD £5180
98 7/09 Asct 1m (0-85)H GD £6476
87 7/09 Newb 1m (0-80)H G-F £5828
71 6/08 Ling 6f G-F £2331
Total win prize-money £19816

Going (Turf): Sf: 0-3 GS: 0-0 **Gd: 2-2 GF: 2-10** Fm: 0-0
Distance: 5f/6f: 1-6 **7f-8f: 3-13** 9f-13f: 0-0 14f+: 0-0
Track : LH: 0-2 RH: 0-2 Tight: 0-2 Gall: 0-0
Aids: Bl: 0-0 Vi: 0-0 Tstrap: 0-0 Ckp: 0-0
Best Rating: 98 7/09 Asct 1m good

Fair; effective over 6f-1m and acts on fast ground.

Creese

95 80
2-y-o b f Halling (USA)-Why Dubai (USA) (Kris S (USA))
H R A Cecil Malih L Al Basti

Placings:1 (5284)
2009: 7^{1}GF,

	Starts	1st	2nd	3rd	Win & Pl
Career Total (Turf)	1	1	0	0	4371

80 8/09 Folk 7f G-F £4371
Total win prize-money £4371

Going (Turf): Sf: 0-0 GS: 0-0 Gd: 0-0 **GF: 1-1** Fm: 0-0
Distance: 5f/6f: 0-0 **7f-8f: 1-1** 9f-13f: 0-0 14f+: 0-0
Track : LH: 0-0 RH: 0-0 Tight: 0-0 Gall: 0-0
Aids: Bl: 0-0 Vi: 0-0 Tstrap: 0-0 Ckp: 0-0
Best Rating: 80 8/09 Folk 7f gd-fm

Winner on debut; effective over 7f; acts on fast ground.

Creevy (IRE)

90(91) (54)56
2-y-o b f Trans Island-Kilbride Lass (IRE) (Lahib (USA))
S Kirk Creevies Cronies Partnership

Placings:0500206646 (7788)
2009: 7^{0}GF, 7^{5}SD, 8^{0}G, 7^{0}GF, 7^{2}GF, 8^{0}GF, 8^{6}SD, 7^{6}SD, 10^{4}SD, 8^{6}SD,

	Starts	1st	2nd	3rd	Win & Pl
Career Total (Turf)	5	0	1	0	771
Career Total (AW)	5	0	0	0	192

Going (Turf): Sf: 0-0 GS: 0-0 Gd: 0-1 GF: 0-4 Fm: 0-0
Distance: 5f/6f: 0-0 7f-8f: 0-6 9f-13f: 0-4 14f+: 0-0
Track : LH: 0-4 RH: 0-2 Tight: 0-2 Gall: 0-0
Aids: Bl: 0-0 Vi: 0-0 Tstrap: 0-0 Ckp: 0-0
Best Rating: 56 9/09 Wwck 7f26y gd-fm

Modest; stays 7f; acts on Polytrack.

Creshendo

90(89) (55)71
3-y-o b g Kyllachy-Dry Wit (IRE) (Desert Prince (IRE))
R M Beckett Mrs David Aykroyd

Placings:1-0050 (2349)
2009: 6^{0}SD, 7^{0}SD, 5^{5}F, 5^{0}GF,

	Starts	1st	2nd	3rd	Win & Pl
Career Total (Turf)	3	1	0	0	3238
Career Total (AW)	2	0	0	0	

71 5/08 Gdwd 6f SFT £3238
Total win prize-money £3238

Going (Turf): **Sf: 1-1** GS: 0-0 Gd: 0-0 GF: 0-1 Fm: 0-1
Distance: **5f/6f: 1-4** 7f-8f: 0-1 9f-13f: 0-0 14f+: 0-0
Track : LH: 0-2 RH: 0-1 Tight: 0-1 Gall: 0-1
Aids: Bl: 0-1 Vi: 0-1 Tstrap: 0-1 Ckp: 0-1
Best Rating: 71 5/08 Gdwd 6f soft

Cridda Boy

80 28
3-y-o ch g Mark Of Esteem (IRE)-Second Affair (IRE) (Pursuit Of Love)
A G Newcombe D G Staddon

Placings:000 (2795)
2009: 8^{0}GF, 10^{0}S, 6^{0}GF,

	Starts	1st	2nd	3rd	Win & Pl
Career Total (Turf)	3	0	0	0	

Going (Turf): Sf: 0-1 GS: 0-0 Gd: 0-0 GF: 0-2 Fm: 0-0
Distance: 5f/6f: 0-0 7f-8f: 0-1 9f-13f: 0-2 14f+: 0-0
Track : LH: 0-2 RH: 0-0 Tight: 0-0 Gall: 0-1
Aids: Bl: 0-0 Vi: 0-0 Tstrap: 0-0 Ckp: 0-0
Best Rating: 28 5/09 Newb 1m2f6y soft

Crime Scene (IRE)

107 (93)118
6-y-o b g Royal Applause-Crime (USA) (Gulch (USA))
Saeed Bin Suroor (M bin Shafya 5/3) Godolphin

Placings:1/13200020103/41141/604-510261062 (7215a)
2009: 10^{5}FT, 12^{1}GS, 12^{0}GF, 12^{2}G, 12^{6}GF, 10^{1}GS, 12^{0}G, 12^{6}G, 16^{2}GS,

	Starts	1st	2nd	3rd	Win & Pl
Career Total (Turf)	28	8	4	2	657657
Career Total (AW)	1	0	0	0	1705

112 7/09 Newb 1m2f6y G-S £22708
112 1/09 Ndas 1m4f (95-110)H G-S £50000
115 10/07 Newb 1m4f5y SFT £26686
107 3/07 Ndas 1m4f (100-112)H GD £53571
92 2/07 Ndas 1m4f (90-105)H GD £33673
103 9/06 Sthl 1m4f (0-95)H G-F £9715
91 5/06 Muss 1m (0-85)H G-F £7772
75 6/05 Newc 6f GD £6864
Total win prize-money £210991

Going (Turf): Sf: 1-3 GS: 2-5 **Gd: 3-12** GF: 2-8 Fm: 0-0
Distance: 5f/6f: 1-1 7f-8f: 1-2 **9f-13f: 6-25** 14f+: 0-1
Track : **LH: 6-15** RH: 1-10 Tight: 2-6 **Gall: 5-16**
Aids: Bl: 0-1 Vi: 0-0 Tstrap: 0-0 Ckp: 0-0
Best Rating: 118 11/09 Flem 2m gd-sft

Smart; stays 1m4f but effective at 1m2f; handles most ground.

Crime Writer (USA)

100 80
3-y-o b g Elusive Quality (USA)-Larrocha (IRE) (Sadler's Wells (USA))
M Johnston Sheikh Hamdan Bin Mohammed Al Maktoum

Placings:3210360 (4597)
2009: 6^{3}GF, 7^{2}F, 7^{1}G, 7^{0}G, 7^{3}G, 7^{6}GF, 9^{0}G,

	Starts	1st	2nd	3rd	Win & Pl
Career Total (Turf)	7	1	1	2	5926

76 6/09 Ayr 7f50y GD £3885
Total win prize-money £3886

Going (Turf): Sf: 0-0 GS: 0-0 **Gd: 1-4** GF: 0-2 Fm: 0-1
Distance: 5f/6f: 0-0 **7f-8f: 1-6** 9f-13f: 0-1 14f+: 0-0
Track : **LH: 1-2** RH: 0-3 Tight: 0-2 Gall: 0-0
Aids: Bl: 0-0 Vi: 0-0 Tstrap: 0-0 Ckp: 0-0
Best Rating: 80 7/09 Epsm 7f good

Fair; effective at 7f, should stay further; acts on good/fast ground.

Crimea (IRE)

106(98) (67)90
3-y-o b g Kheleyf (USA)-Russian Countess (USA) (Nureyev (USA))

M Johnston Sheikh Hamdan Bin Mohammed Al Maktoum

Placings:1610 **(7202)**
2009: 5^{1}GF, 5^{6}G, 5^{1}GF, 5^{0}SD,

	Starts	1st	2nd	3rd	Win & Pl
Career Total (Turf)	**3**	**2**	**0**	**0**	**9066**
Career Total (AW)	**1**	**0**	**0**	**0**	

90	7/09	Haml	5f4y	(0-80)H	G-F	£6476
81	6/09	Thsk	5f		G-F	£2590

Total win prize-money £9066

Going (Turf): Sf: 0-0 GS: 0-0 Gd: 0-1 **GF: 2-2** Fm: 0-0
Distance: **5f/6f: 2-4** 7f-8f: 0-0 9f-13f: 0-0 14f+: 0-0
Track : LH: 0-1 RH: 0-0 Tight: 0-1 Gall: 0-0
Aids: Bl: 0-0 Vi: 0-0 Tstrap: 0-0 Ckp: 0-0
Best Rating: **90** 7/09 Haml 5f4y gd-fm

Fair; suited by 5f; acts on fast ground.

Crimson Fern (IRE)

108(106) (96)**102**
5-y-o ch m Titus Livius (FR)-Crimada (IRE) (Mukaddamah (USA))
M S Saunders M S Saunders

Placings:0310/421140012131105230-5026P **(2704)**
2009: 5^{5}SD, 5^{0}GS, 5^{2}G, 5^{6}GF, 5^{P}GF,

	Starts	1st	2nd	3rd	Win & Pl
Career Total (Turf)	**17**	**4**	**3**	**2**	**50494**
Career Total (AW)	**10**	**3**	**1**	**1**	**8182**

101	7/08	Asct	5f	(0-105)H	G-S	£11215
95	7/08	Sand	5f6y	(0-95)H	G-F	£9066
88	6/08	Sand	5f6y	(0-85)H	SFT	£5180
84	5/08	Gdwd	5f	(0-70)H	G-F	£3238
69	1/08	Wolv	5f216y	(0-60)H	STD	£2047
66	1/08	Ling	6f	(0-65)H	STD	£1813
56	10/07	Wolv	7f32y		STD	£2388

Total win prize-money £34951

Going (Turf): Sf: 1-2 GS: 1-2 Gd: 0-5 **GF: 2-8** Fm: 0-0
Distance: **5f/6f: 6-26** 7f-8f: 1-1 9f-13f: 0-0 14f+: 0-0
Track : **LH: 3-10** RH: 0-2 **Tight: 3-8** Gall: 0-3
Aids: Bl: 0-0 Vi: 0-0 Tstrap: 0-0 Ckp: 0-0
Best Rating: **102** 8/08 Sand 5f6y good

Very useful; best at 5f but stays 7f; acts on most ground; also acts on Polytrack.

Crimson Flame (IRE)

(92) (48)**73**
6-y-o b g Celtic Swing-Wish List (IRE) (Mujadil (USA))
M S Tuck G S Tuck

Placings:544346434/446500656262040000/06/0-4 **(7858)**
2009: 8^{4}SD,

	Starts	1st	2nd	3rd	Win & Pl
Career Total (Turf)	**24**	**0**	**2**	**2**	**8006**
Career Total (AW)	**7**	**0**	**0**	**0**	**289**

Going (Turf): **Sf: 0-1 GS: 0-0 Gd: 0-8 GF: 0-12 Fm: 0-3**
Distance: 5f/6f: 0-0 7f-8f: 0-10 9f-13f: 0-20 14f+: 0-1
Track : LH: 0-14 RH: 0-9 Tight: 0-14 Gall: 0-0
Aids: Bl: 0-0 Vi: 0-5 Tstrap: 0-0 Ckp: 0-0
Best Rating: **77** 9/05 Donc 1m gd-fm

Crimson Mist

87(83) (23)**39**
3-y-o b g Red Ransom (USA)-Lavinia Fontana (IRE) (Sharpo)
J J Quinn Elsa Crankshaw & G Allan

Placings:060 **(4277)**
2009: 6^{0}GS, 6^{6}SD, 7^{0}G,

	Starts	1st	2nd	3rd	Win & Pl
Career Total (Turf)	**2**	**0**	**0**	**0**	
Career Total (AW)	**1**	**0**	**0**	**0**	**0**

Going (Turf): **Sf: 0-0 GS: 0-1 Gd: 0-1 GF: 0-0 Fm: 0-0**
Distance: 5f/6f: 0-2 7f-8f: 0-1 9f-13f: 0-0 14f+: 0-0
Track : LH: 0-2 RH: 0-0 Tight: 0-1 Gall: 0-0
Aids: Bl: 0-0 Vi: 0-0 Tstrap: 0-0 Ckp: 0-0
Best Rating: **39** 6/09 Ripn 6f gd-sft

Crimson Mitre

99(101) (79)**68**
4-y-o b h Bishop Of Cashel-Pink Champagne (Cosmonaut)
J Jay Burns, Clarke & Fremel

Placings:0040/4100-40021045 **(7779)**
2009: 12^{4}SD, 12^{0}GS, 12^{0}SD, 14^{2}SD, 12^{1}SD, 12^{0}SD, 11^{4}GF, 12^{5}SD,

	Starts	1st	2nd	3rd	Win & Pl
Career Total (Turf)	**8**	**1**	**0**	**0**	**2416**
Career Total (AW)	**8**	**1**	**1**	**0**	**2652**

79	7/09	Sthl	1m4f	(0-65)H	STD	£2047
68	4/08	Sthl	1m3f		G-F	£1774

Total win prize-money £3821

Going (Turf): Sf: 0-0 GS: 0-4 Gd: 0-1 **GF: 1-2** Fm: 0-0
Distance: 5f/6f: 0-0 7f-8f: 0-2 **9f-13f: 2-11** 14f+: 0-3
Track : **LH: 2-12** RH: 0-2 **Tight: 1-3** Gall: 0-2
Aids: Bl: 0-0 Vi: 0-0 Tstrap: 0-0 Ckp: 0-0
Best Rating: **79** 7/09 Sthl 1m4f stand

Modest; stays 1m6f; acts on Fibresand.

Crimson Ribbon (USA)

104(109) (90)**85**
3-y-o b f Lemon Drop Kid (USA)-Victoria Cross (IRE) (Mark Of Esteem (IRE))
J H M Gosden A E Oppenheimer

Placings:310560 **(7366)**
2009: 9^{3}SD, 12^{1}GF, 10^{0}GF, 10^{5}G, 13^{6}SD, 10^{0}SD,

	Starts	1st	2nd	3rd	Win & Pl
Career Total (Turf)	**3**	**1**	**0**	**0**	**5181**
Career Total (AW)	**3**	**0**	**0**	**1**	**943**

73	5/09	NmkR	1m4f	G-F	£5180

Total win prize-money £5181

Going (Turf): Sf: 0-0 GS: 0-0 Gd: 0-1 **GF: 1-2** Fm: 0-0
Distance: 5f/6f: 0-0 7f-8f: 0-0 **9f-13f: 1-6** 14f+: 0-0
Track : LH: 0-5 **RH: 1-1** Tight: 0-4 **Gall: 1-2**
Aids: Bl: 0-0 Vi: 0-0 Tstrap: 0-0 Ckp: 0-0
Best Rating: **90** 10/09 Ling 1m5f stand

Fair filly; stays 1m5f; acts on fast ground.

Cripsey Brook

101 **68**
11-y-o ch g Lycius (USA)-Duwon (IRE) (Polish Precedent (USA))
K G Reveley Reveley Farms

Placings:450/504100/000430162/121116511330/6600256 0005/0322634010/05204202240/11044650635/500-06543400060 **(6768)**
2009: 10^{0}F, 12^{6}GS, 14^{5}GF, 14^{4}GF, 14^{3}GF, 14^{4}F, 12^{0}G, 14^{0}GF, 12^{0}G, 14^{6}GF, 12^{0}GS,

	Starts	1st	2nd	3rd	Win & Pl
Career Total (Turf)	**87**	**11**	**9**	**7**	**96993**

80	4/07	Nott	1m1f213y	(0-75)H	G-F	£3238
81	4/07	Pont	1m4f8y	(0-75)H	GD	£3886
84	10/05	Rdcr	1m2f	(0-75)H	G-F	£3845
93	8/03	Ripn	1m2f	C(0-90)H	G-F	£8566
89	8/03	Hayd	1m2f120y	D(0-80)H	G-F	£5638
87	7/03	Hayd	1m2f120y	C(0-90)H	G-F	£10043
81	6/03	Newc	1m2f32y	D(0-75)	G-F	£5759
81	6/03	Nott	1m1f213y	D(0-80)H	FRM	£6058
57	5/03	Newc	1m2f32y	E(0-65)	G-F	£3877
63	9/02	Rdcr	1m2f	G(0-60)H	FRM	£2499
73	6/01	Brig	6f209y	E(0-70)H	G-F	£2975

Total win prize-money £56388

Going (Turf): Sf: 0-4 GS: 0-10 Gd: 1-30 **GF: 8-31** Fm: 2-12
Distance: 5f/6f: 0-2 7f-8f 1-10 **9f-13f: 10-61** 14f+: 0-14
Track : **LH: 10-68** RH: 1-11 **Tight: 3-29** Gall: 2-27
Aids: Bl: 0-1 Vi: 0-0 Tstrap: 0-0 Ckp: 0-0
Best Rating: **95** 9/03 Donc 1m2f60y good

Fair; stays 1m4f, but effective over shorter; suited by fast ground; usually wears a tongue tie.

Criterion

96(100) (78)**81**
4-y-o b g Dr Fong (USA)-Film Script (Unfuwain (USA))
Ian Williams Mrs Ruth M Serrell

Placings:04/21240-600004 **(7854)**
2009: 16^{6}SD, 16^{0}S, 18^{0}G, 16^{0}GF, 10^{0}SD, 8^{4}SS,

	Starts	1st	2nd	3rd	Win & Pl
Career Total (Turf)	**10**	**1**	**2**	**0**	**6979**
Career Total (AW)	**3**	**0**	**0**	**0**	**0**

71	5/08	Thsk	1m4f	GD	£3885

Total win prize-money £3886

Going (Turf): Sf: 0-2 GS: 0-1 **Gd: 1-4** GF: 0-3 Fm: 0-0
Distance: 5f/6f: 0-0 7f-8f: 0-2 **9f-13f: 1-5** 14f+: 0-6
Track : **LH: 1-7** RH: 0-5 **Tight: 1-5** Gall: 0-1
Aids: Bl: 0-0 Vi: 0-2 Tstrap: 0-2 Ckp: 0-2
Best Rating: **81** 6/08 Ches 1m4f66y good

Fair; effective from 1m4f-1m6f; acts on good and easier ground; has worn a visor and cheekpieces.

Critical Moment (USA)

102 **96**
2-y-o b c Aptitude (USA)-Rouwaki (USA) (Miswaki (USA))
B W Hills K Abdulla

Placings:315 **(7030)**
2009: 7^{3}G, 7^{1}GF, 7^{5}S,

	Starts	1st	2nd	3rd	Win & Pl
Career Total (Turf)	**3**	**1**	**0**	**1**	**7248**

84	9/09	Newb	7f	G-F	£5180

Total win prize-money £5181

Going (Turf): Sf: 0-1 GS: 0-0 Gd: 0-1 **GF: 1-1** Fm: 0-0
Distance: 5f/6f: 0-0 **7f-8f: 1-3** 9f-13f: 0-0 14f+: 0-0
Track : LH: 0-0 RH: 0-0 Tight: 0-0 Gall: 0-0
Aids: Bl: 0-0 Vi: 0-0 Tstrap: 0-0 Ckp: 0-0
Best Rating: **96** 10/09 Newb 7f soft

Useful; stays 7f; acts on fast ground.

Critical Path (IRE)

101(101) (72)79

3-y-o b f Noverre (USA)-Elemental (Rudimentary (USA))

A M Balding Trebles Holford Thoroughbreds

Placings:431645 **(7366)**

2009: 8^{4}SD, 8^{3}G, 10^{1}GF, 10^{6}GS, 10^{4}GS, 10^{5}SD,

	Starts	1st	2nd	3rd	Win & Pl
Career Total (Turf)	4	1	0	1	4080
Career Total (AW)	2	0	0	0	192

79 7/09 Epsm 1m2f18y G-F £3238

Total win prize-money £3238

Going (Turf): Sf: 0-0 GS: 0-2 Gd: 0-1 **GF: 1-1** Fm: 0-0
Distance: 5f/6f: 0-0 7f-8f: 0-2 **9f-13f: 1-4** 14f+: 0-0
Track : **LH: 1-2** RH: 0-4 **Tight: 1-3** Gall: 0-0
Aids: Bl: 0-0 Vi: 0-0 Tstrap: 0-0 Ckp: 0-0
Best Rating: **79** 7/09 Epsm 1m2f18y gd-fm

Fair filly; stays 1m2f; acts on good ground, but likes it softer.

Criticize (USA)

87(92) (57)71

3-y-o b g Mizzen Mast (USA)-Euphonize (USA) (Seattle Slew (USA))

R Charlton K Abdulla

Placings:244 **(5751)**

2009: 7^{2}GS, 7^{4}G, 8^{4}SD,

	Starts	1st	2nd	3rd	Win & Pl
Career Total (Turf)	2	0	1	0	2071
Career Total (AW)	1	0	0	0	0

Going (Turf): **Sf: 0-0 GS: 0-1 Gd: 0-1 GF: 0-0 Fm: 0-0**
Distance: 5f/6f: 0-0 7f-8f: 0-3 9f-13f: 0-0 14f+: 0-0
Track : LH: 0-1 RH: 0-0 Tight: 0-1 Gall: 0-0
Aids: Bl: 0-0 Vi: 0-0 Tstrap: 0-0 Ckp: 0-0
Best Rating: **71** 5/09 Newb 7f gd-sft

Modest half-brother to a sprint winner on the dirt in the US; stays7f; acts on easy ground.

Crocodile Bay (IRE)

93(105) (81)93

6-y-o b g Spectrum (IRE)-Shenkara (IRE) (Night Shift (USA))

John A Harris Stan Wright

Placings:5112030633/000/0022050054212236120600240 03230010-22504060040 **(4887)**

2009: 6^{2}SS, 7^{2}SD, 6^{5}SD, 8^{0}SD, 6^{4}G, 7^{0}SD, 7^{6}GF, 8^{0}GF, 7^{0}GF, 7^{4}SD, 7^{0}G,

	Starts	1st	2nd	3rd	Win & Pl
Career Total (Turf)	38	4	7	4	40746
Career Total (AW)	19	1	4	2	6709

69 12/08 Sthl 7f STD £1978
93 5/08 Bevl 1m100y (0-90)H G-F £6799
81 10/07 Newc 1m3y (0-70)H GD £3562
85 5/05 Donc 5f GD £4134
80 4/05 Wind 5f10y GD £4316

Total win prize-money £20791

Going (Turf): Sf: 0-6 GS: 0-3 **Gd: 3-13** GF: 1-16 Fm: 0-0
Distance: 5f/6f: 2-9 7f-8f: 1-34 9f-13f: 2-14 14f+: 0-0
Track : LH: 1-25 RH: 1-15 Tight: 0-14 **Gall: 1-2**
Aids: **Bl: 1-9** Vi: 0-0 Tstrap: 0-0 Ckp: 0-0
Best Rating: **93** 5/08 Newc 7f gd-fm

Modest; effective over 7f-1m; acts well on a sound surface and on sand.

Crocus Rose

103(100) (79)82

3-y-o b f Royal Applause-Crodelle (IRE) (Formidable (USA))

H J L Dunlop When Harry Met Rosie Partnership

Placings:0-6532131 **(6995)**

2009: 10^{6}GF, 11^{5}SD, 12^{3}G, 14^{2}HY, 14^{1}G, 16^{3}SD, 14^{1}GS,

	Starts	1st	2nd	3rd	Win & Pl
Career Total (Turf)	6	2	1	1	11159
Career Total (AW)	2	0	0	1	703

82 10/09 Donc 1m6f132y (0-85)H G-S £6476
74 8/09 Sals 1m6f21y (0-70)H GD £3238

Total win prize-money £9714

Going (Turf): Sf: 0-2 **GS: 1-1 Gd: 1-2** GF: 0-1 Fm: 0-0
Distance: 5f/6f: 0-0 7f-8f: 0-0 9f-13f: 0-4 **14f+: 2-4**
Track : LH: 1-5 RH: 1-3 Tight: 1-1 Gall: 1-3
Aids: Bl: 0-0 Vi: 0-0 Tstrap: 0-0 Ckp: 0-0
Best Rating: **82** 10/09 Donc 1m6f132y gd-sft

Fair; stays 1m6f; acts on good and on heavy ground; should improve.

Croeso Cusan

96 67

4-y-o b f Diktat-Croeso Croeso (Most Welcome)

J L Spearing Oxstalls Farm Stud

Placings:6/04064312-0604025 **(7248)**

2009: 8^{0}GF, 8^{6}GS, 10^{0}G, 8^{4}GS, 7^{0}G, 9^{2}S, 10^{5}HY,

	Starts	1st	2nd	3rd	Win & Pl
Career Total (Turf)	16	1	2	1	4273

63 9/08 Brig 7f214y (0-65)H SFT £2072

Total win prize-money £2072

Going (Turf): **Sf: 1-4** GS: 0-3 Gd: 0-6 GF: 0-3 Fm: 0-0
Distance: 5f/6f: 0-3 **7f-8f: 1-5** 9f-13f: 0-8 14f+: 0-0
Track : **LH: 1-9** RH: 0-1 Tight: 0-1 Gall: 0-2
Aids: Bl: 0-0 Vi: 0-0 Tstrap: 0-0 Ckp: 0-0
Best Rating: **67** 10/08 Brig 7f214y good

Moderate; dam was a prolific winning sprinter; effective over 1m; acts on easy ground.

Croeso Ynol

94 41

3-y-o ch f Medicean-Croeso Croeso (Most Welcome)

J L Spearing Oxstalls Farm Stud

Placings:00466 **(6005)**

2009: 6^{0}GF, 6^{0}G, 7^{4}G, 6^{6}G, 7^{6}GF,

	Starts	1st	2nd	3rd	Win & Pl
Career Total (Turf)	5	0	0	0	204

Going (Turf): **Sf: 0-0 GS: 0-0 Gd: 0-3 GF: 0-2 Fm: 0-0**
Distance: 5f/6f: 0-2 7f-8f: 0-3 9f-13f: 0-0 14f+: 0-0
Track : LH: 0-0 RH: 0-0 Tight: 0-0 Gall: 0-1
Aids: Bl: 0-0 Vi: 0-0 Tstrap: 0-0 Ckp: 0-0
Best Rating: **41** 8/09 Chep 6f16y good

Croft Bridge

91(74) (26)48

2-y-o ch g Avonbridge-Aahgowangowan (IRE) (Tagula (IRE))

M Dods Les Waugh

Placings:0500 **(6494)**

2009: 5^{0}G, 5^{5}S, 6^{0}G, 5^{0}SF,

	Starts	1st	2nd	3rd	Win & Pl
Career Total (Turf)	3	0	0	0	0
Career Total (AW)	1	0	0	0	

Going (Turf): **Sf: 0-1 GS: 0-0 Gd: 0-2 GF: 0-0 Fm: 0-0**
Distance: 5f/6f: 0-4 7f-8f: 0-0 9f-13f: 0-0 14f+: 0-0
Track : LH: 0-1 RH: 0-0 Tight: 0-1 Gall: 0-0
Aids: Bl: 0-0 Vi: 0-0 Tstrap: 0-0 Ckp: 0-0
Best Rating: **48** 8/09 Muss 5f soft

Croisultan (IRE)

110 (83)100

3-y-o ch c Refuse To Bend (IRE)-Zoudie (Ezzoud (IRE))

Liam McAteer Brunabonne Syndicate

Placings:00441213-6210304440 **(6320a)**

2009: 6^{6}SH, 5^{2}S, 5^{1}HY, 7^{0}G, 5^{3}G, 5^{0}HY, 6^{4}S, 5^{4}S, 6^{4}SH, 7^{0}G,

	Starts	1st	2nd	3rd	Win & Pl
Career Total (Turf)	17	3	1	2	46608
Career Total (AW)	1	0	1	0	5618

100 5/09 Navn 5f182y HVY £12589
89 10/08 Navn 5f H SH £7621
86 8/08 Bell 5f (50-80) G-Y £6859

Total win prize-money £27070

Going (Turf): **Sf: 1-6** GS: 0-0 Gd: 0-5 GF: 0-2 Fm: 0-0
Distance: **5f/6f: 3-13** 7f-8f: 0-5 9f-13f: 0-0 14f+: 0-0
Track : **LH: 3-11** RH: 0-3 Tight: 0-1 Gall: 0-0
Aids: Bl: 0-1 Vi: 0-0 Tstrap: 0-0 Ckp: 0-0
Best Rating: **100** 8/09 Curr 6f sft-hvy

Croix Rouge (USA)

(100) (65)70

7-y-o b g Chester House (USA)-Rougeur (USA) (Blushing Groom (FR))

R J Smith Mrs Jayne Smith

Placings:30016/2143/3511/5004111450/51-606 **(7766)**

2009: 12^{6}SD, 16^{0}SD, 11^{6}SD,

	Starts	1st	2nd	3rd	Win & Pl
Career Total (Turf)	6	1	0	1	3687
Career Total (AW)	22	7	1	2	39810

3/08 Mija 1m5f STD £4411
7/07 Mija 1m2f110y H STD £3378
6/07 Mija 1m2f110y STD £4054
6/07 Mija 1m2f110y STD £2702
8/06 Mija 1m3f STD £2413
8/06 Mija 1m5f STD £2413
5/05 Mija 1m2f110y STD £5106
11/04 Mija 1m55y STD £2112

Total win prize-money £26594

Going (Turf): **Sf: 0-1 GS: 0-0 Gd: 0-2 GF: 0-2 Fm: 0-0**
Distance: 5f/6f: 0-0 7f-8f: 0-2 **9f-13f: 8-22** 14f+: 0-4
Track : LH: 0-3 RH: 0-4 Tight: 0-2 Gall: 0-0
Aids: Bl: 0-1 Vi: 0-0 Tstrap: 0-0 Ckp: 0-0
Best Rating: **70** 9/04 Wwck 7f26y gd-fm

Croon

94(73) (13)47

7-y-o b g Sinndar (IRE)-Shy Minstrel (USA) (The Minstrel (CAN))

Andrew Turnell Ferrybank Properties Limited

Placings:651/5/3144156/444/00 (6584)
2009: 11^{0}GF, 12^{0}SD,

	Starts	1st	2nd	3rd	Win & Pl
Career Total (Turf)	**6**	**1**	**0**	**1**	**9626**
Career Total (AW)	**10**	**2**	**0**	**0**	**11403**

83 7/06 Epsm 1m4f10y (0-75)H G-F £5505
82 5/06 Ling 1m4f (0-85)H STD £6477
68 12/04 Wolv 7f32y STD £3386
Total win prize-money £15369

Going (Turf): Sf: 0-0 GS: 0-1 Gd: 0-2 **GF: 1-2** Fm: 0-1
Distance: 5f/6f: 0-0 7f-8f: 1-3 **9f-13f: 2-9** 14f+: 0-4
Track : **LH: 3-11** RH: 0-4 **Tight: 3-13** Gall: 0-1
Aids: Bl: 0-0 Vi: 0-0 Tstrap: 0-1 Ckp: 0-1
Best Rating: **85** 7/06 Asct 1m4f good

Fair handicapper; stays 1m4f; acts on fast ground and Polytrack.

Crosby Jemma

(64) **48**
5-y-o ch m Lomitas-Gino's Spirits (Perugino (USA))
M E Sowersby R D Seldon

Placings:006/2055260/0650-0 (0221)
2009: 8^{0}SD,

	Starts	1st	2nd	3rd	Win & Pl
Career Total (Turf)	**14**	**0**	**2**	**0**	**1927**
Career Total (AW)	**1**	**0**	**0**	**0**	

Going (Turf): **Sf: 0-0 GS: 0-0 Gd: 0-3 GF: 0-8 Fm: 0-3**
Distance: 5f/6f: 0-2 7f-8f: 0-5 9f-13f: 0-8 14f+: 0-0
Track : LH: 0-10 RH: 0-4 Tight: 0-9 Gall: 0-1
Aids: Bl: 0-0 Vi: 0-0 Tstrap: 0-0 Ckp: 0-0
Best Rating: **48** 8/07 Muss 1m gd-fm

Moderate; stays 1m; acts on fast ground.

Cross Key (IRE)

85 **56**
2-y-o b f Trans Island-Cayman Sunrise (IRE) (Peintre Celebre (USA))
R A Fahey Ballinlough Castle Racing

Placings:445 (5146)
2009: 5^{4}S, 6^{4}G, 5^{5}GS,

	Starts	1st	2nd	3rd	Win & Pl
Career Total (Turf)	**3**	**0**	**0**	**0**	**697**

Going (Turf): **Sf: 0-1 GS: 0-1 Gd: 0-1 GF: 0-0 Fm: 0-0**
Distance: 5f/6f: 0-3 7f-8f: 0-0 9f-13f: 0-0 14f+: 0-0
Track : LH: 0-0 RH: 0-1 Tight: 0-0 Gall: 0-1
Aids: Bl: 0-0 Vi: 0-0 Tstrap: 0-0 Ckp: 0-0
Best Rating: **56** 7/09 Ripn 5f soft

Cross Of Lorraine (IRE)

96 (72)**69**
6-y-o b g Pivotal-My-Lorraine (IRE) (Mac's Imp (USA))
J Wade John Wade

Placings:342212/433020425/3000-00060004 (5465)
2009: 5^{0}G, 6^{0}G, 8^{0}GS, 7^{6}GF, 8^{0}GF, 7^{0}G, 7^{0}S, 7^{4}GF,

	Starts	1st	2nd	3rd	Win & Pl
Career Total (Turf)	**21**	**0**	**2**	**3**	**4835**
Career Total (AW)	**6**	**1**	**3**	**1**	**6390**

69 12/06 Wolv 5f216y STD £3238
Total win prize-money £3239

Going (Turf): **Sf: 0-4 GS: 0-5 Gd: 0-5 GF: 0-7 Fm: 0-0**
Distance: **5f/6f: 1-13** 7f-8f: 0-12 9f-13f: 0-2 14f+: 0-0
Track : **LH: 1-6** RH: 0-7 **Tight: 1-6** Gall: 0-0
Aids: **Bl: 1-27** Vi: 0-0 Tstrap: 0-0 Ckp: 0-0
Best Rating: **72** 7/07 Ayr 6f gd-sft

Modest; effective over 5f-7f; acts well on Polytrack.

Cross Reef

89(94) (64)**46**
4-y-o b f Cape Cross (IRE)-Mureefa (USA) (Bahri (USA))
R A Harris Peter A Price

Placings:006000000 (5965)
2009: 7^{0}SD, 10^{0}GF, 9^{6}SD, 8^{0}GF, 11^{0}F, 8^{0}SD, 8^{0}SD, 7^{0}S, 7^{0}GS,

	Starts	1st	2nd	3rd	Win & Pl
Career Total (Turf)	**5**	**0**	**0**	**0**	
Career Total (AW)	**4**	**0**	**0**	**0**	**0**

Going (Turf): **Sf: 0-1 GS: 0-1 Gd: 0-0 GF: 0-2 Fm: 0-1**
Distance: 5f/6f: 0-0 7f-8f: 0-4 9f-13f: 0-5 14f+: 0-0
Track : LH: 0-5 RH: 0-1 Tight: 0-5 Gall: 0-0
Aids: Bl: 0-0 Vi: 0-1 Tstrap: 0-2 Ckp: 0-2
Best Rating: **64** 3/09 Ling 7f stand

Cross Section (USA)

89(99) (71)**57**
3-y-o b/br f Cape Cross (IRE)-Demure (Machiavellian (USA))
E F Vaughan Ali Saeed

Placings:2-56424 (7826)
2009: 7^{5}GF, 6^{6}G, 7^{4}SD, 8^{2}SD, 8^{4}SD,

	Starts	1st	2nd	3rd	Win & Pl
Career Total (Turf)	**2**	**0**	**0**	**0**	**0**
Career Total (AW)	**4**	**0**	**2**	**0**	**2155**

Going (Turf): **Sf: 0-0 GS: 0-0 Gd: 0-1 GF: 0-1 Fm: 0-0**
Distance: 5f/6f: 0-1 7f-8f: 0-4 9f-13f: 0-1 14f+: 0-0
Track : LH: 0-3 RH: 0-2 Tight: 0-2 Gall: 0-0
Aids: Bl: 0-0 Vi: 0-0 Tstrap: 0-1 Ckp: 0-1
Best Rating: **71** 10/08 Ling 7f stand

Modest; best suited by 7f and Polytrack.

Cross The Boss (IRE)

57 **4**
2-y-o b g Cape Cross (IRE)-Lady Salsa (IRE) (Gone West (USA))
P C Haslam Widdop Wanderers

Placings:0 (6991)
2009: 7^{0}G,

	Starts	1st	2nd	3rd	Win & Pl
Career Total (Turf)	**1**	**0**	**0**	**0**	

Going (Turf): **Sf: 0-0 GS: 0-0 Gd: 0-1 GF: 0-0 Fm: 0-0**
Distance: 5f/6f: 0-0 7f-8f: 0-1 9f-13f: 0-0 14f+: 0-0
Track : LH: 0-0 RH: 0-0 Tight: 0-0 Gall: 0-0
Aids: Bl: 0-0 Vi: 0-0 Tstrap: 0-0 Ckp: 0-0
Best Rating: **4** 10/09 Donc 7f good

Cross The Line (IRE)

(102) (88)**71**
7-y-o b g Cape Cross (IRE)-Baalbek (Barathea (IRE))
A P Jarvis Geoffrey Bishop

Placings:4/00122/232451202102/6252440060/56006500-23 (1067)
2009: 8^{2}SD, 8^{3}SD,

	Starts	1st	2nd	3rd	Win & Pl
Career Total (Turf)	**19**	**1**	**3**	**0**	**12810**
Career Total (AW)	**19**	**2**	**7**	**2**	**26032**

91 9/06 Kemp 1m (0-85)H STD £5505
80 7/06 Kemp 1m (0-80)H STD £5505
74 8/05 York 1m (0-75)H G-F £5792
Total win prize-money £16802

Going (Turf): Sf: 0-1 GS: 0-3 Gd: 0-7 **GF: 1-8** Fm: 0-0
Distance: 5f/6f: 0-1 **7f-8f: 3-31** 9f-13f: 0-6 14f+: 0-0
Track : LH: 1-11 **RH: 2-16** Tight: 0-6 **Gall: 1-4**
Aids: Bl: 0-0 Vi: 0-1 Tstrap: 0-0 Ckp: 0-0
Best Rating: **95** 10/06 Ling 1m stand

Modest; suited by around 1m; acts on fast ground and Polytrack.

Crossbow Creek

101(109) (89)**88**
11-y-o b g Lugana Beach-Roxy River (Ardross)
M G Rimell Mark Rimell

Placings:610/512050/5603103006-600515 (6734)
2009: 16^{6}SD, 12^{0}SD, 11^{0}GF, 11^{5}GF, 12^{1}G, 14^{5}S,

	Starts	1st	2nd	3rd	Win & Pl
Career Total (Turf)	**14**	**2**	**1**	**2**	**15571**
Career Total (AW)	**11**	**2**	**0**	**0**	**8196**

81 9/09 Asct 1m4f (0-80)H GD £6002
88 5/08 York 1m4f (0-80)H GD £6246
88 7/07 Kemp 1m2f (0-80)H STD £4728
83 8/06 Ling 1m4f STD £3238
Total win prize-money £20215

Going (Turf): Sf: 0-1 GS: 0-2 **Gd: 2-4** GF: 0-7 Fm: 0-0
Distance: 5f/6f: 0-0 7f-8f: 0-9 **9f-13f: 4-21** 14f+: 0-4
Track : LH: 2-7 RH: 2-17 Tight: 1-9 **Gall: 2-8**
Aids: Bl: 0-0 Vi: 0-0 Tstrap: 0-0 Ckp: 0-0
Best Rating: **90** 9/07 Kemp 1m3f stand

Fair; stays 1m4f; acts on fast ground; goes on Polytrack.

Crowded House

109(98) (94)**120**
3-y-o ch c Rainbow Quest (USA)-Wiener Wald (USA) (Woodman (USA))
B J Meehan J P Reddam, Mrs Carmen Burrell, J Harvey

Placings:0121-06 (2705)
2009: 10^{0}G, 12^{6}G,

	Starts	1st	2nd	3rd	Win & Pl
Career Total (Turf)	**5**	**1**	**1**	**0**	**361098**
Career Total (AW)	**1**	**1**	**0**	**0**	**5181**

120 10/08 Donc 1m GD £122623
94 9/08 Kemp 1m STD £5180
Total win prize-money £127804

Going (Turf): Sf: 0-0 GS: 0-0 **Gd: 1-4** GF: 0-1 Fm: 0-0
Distance: 5f/6f: 0-0 **7f-8f: 2-4** 9f-13f: 0-2 14f+: 0-0
Track : LH: 0-2 **RH: 1-1** Tight: 0-1 Gall: 0-1
Aids: Bl: 0-0 Vi: 0-0 Tstrap: 0-0 Ckp: 0-0
Best Rating: **120** 10/08 Donc 1m good

Group class; 75,000gns half-brother to several winners

including Heron Bay; winner of the Racing Post Trophy in 2008; effective at stays 1m, stays further; acts on Polytrack and good and fast turf.

Crown (IRE)

97 88

2-y-o b f Royal Applause-Bolivia (USA) (Distant View (USA))
R Hannon Mrs J Wood

Placings:501105540 **(6447)**
2009: 5⁵GF, 5⁰GF, 5¹GF, 5¹GF, 5⁰GF, 6⁵G, 7⁵GF, 6⁴GF, 7⁰GF,

	Starts	1st	2nd	3rd	Win & Pl
Career Total (Turf)	9	2	0	0	11490

86 5/09 Wind 5f10y G-F £4857
82 5/09 Wind 5f10y G-F £2729
Total win prize-money £7587

Going (Turf): Sf: 0-0 GS: 0-0 Gd: 0-1 **GF: 2-8** Fm: 0-0
Distance: **5f/6f: 2-6** 7f-8f: 0-3 9f-13f: 0-0 14f+: 0-0
Track : LH: 0-2 RH: 0-1 Tight: 0-1 **Gall: 2-3**
Aids: Bl: 0-0 Vi: 0-0 Tstrap: 0-0 Ckp: 0-0
Best Rating: **88** 7/09 NmkJ 6f good

Useful; effective over 5f-7f; acts on fast ground.

Crown Affair (IRE)

74(88) (58)37

3-y-o b f Royal Applause-Alyousufeya (IRE) (Kingmambo (USA))
J W Hills Mr And Mrs Thomas Ellis

Placings:0P-**44000** **(5016)**
2009: 7⁴SD, 8⁴SD, 8⁰SD, 9⁰GF, 8⁰SD,

	Starts	1st	2nd	3rd	Win & Pl
Career Total (Turf)	3	0	0	0	
Career Total (AW)	4	0	0	0	192

Going (Turf): **Sf: 0-0 GS: 0-0 Gd: 0-1 GF: 0-2 Fm: 0-0**
Distance: 5f/6f: 0-0 7f-8f: 0-6 9f-13f: 0-1 14f+: 0-0
Track : LH: 0-5 RH: 0-0 Tight: 0-5 Gall: 0-0
Aids: Bl: 0-0 Vi: 0-0 Tstrap: 0-0 Ckp: 0-0
Best Rating: **58** 2/09 Ling 1m stand

Crown Choice

98(103) (97)78

4-y-o b g King's Best (USA)-Belle Allemande (CAN) (Royal Academy (USA))
W R Swinburn P W Harris

Placings:30-11000 **(7185)**
2009: 7¹SD, 7¹SD, 7⁰GF, 7⁰SS, 8⁰G,

	Starts	1st	2nd	3rd	Win & Pl
Career Total (Turf)	4	0	0	1	891
Career Total (AW)	3	2	0	0	7843

97 4/09 Kemp 7f (0-85)H STD £4604
85 4/09 Kemp 7f STD £3238
Total win prize-money £7843

Going (Turf): **Sf: 0-0 GS: 0-0 Gd: 0-2 GF: 0-2 Fm: 0-0**
Distance: 5f/6f: 0-0 **7f-8f: 2-7** 9f-13f: 0-0 14f+: 0-0
Track : LH: 0-1 **RH: 2-4** Tight: 0-1 Gall: 0-0
Aids: Bl: 0-0 Vi: 0-0 Tstrap: 0-0 Ckp: 0-0
Best Rating: **97** 4/09 Kemp 7f stand

Useful; stays 1m but effective at 7f; acts on good ground; goes on Polytrack.

Croy (IRE)

(45)

4-y-o b f Elnadim (USA)-Flower Fairy (FR) (Fairy King (USA))
S Parr Willie McKay

Placings:05 **(0488)**
2009: 6⁰SD, 8⁵SS,

	Starts	1st	2nd	3rd	Win & Pl
Career Total (Turf)	0	0	0	0	
Career Total (AW)	2	0	0	0	0

Going (Turf): **Sf: 0-0 GS: 0-0 Gd: 0-0 GF: 0-0 Fm: 0-0**
Distance: 5f/6f: 0-1 7f-8f: 0-1 9f-13f: 0-0 14f+: 0-0
Track : LH: 0-2 RH: 0-0 Tight: 0-0 Gall: 0-0
Aids: Bl: 0-0 Vi: 0-0 Tstrap: 0-0 Ckp: 0-0

Cruciform (IRE)

59 31

3-y-o b/br g Cape Cross (IRE)-Tshusick (Dancing Brave (USA))
D Nicholls Lady O'Reilly

Placings:0-0 **(5394)**
2009: 7⁰GF,

	Starts	1st	2nd	3rd	Win & Pl
Career Total (Turf)	2	0	0	0	

Going (Turf): **Sf: 0-0 GS: 0-0 Gd: 0-1 GF: 0-1 Fm: 0-0**
Distance: 5f/6f: 0-0 7f-8f: 0-2 9f-13f: 0-0 14f+: 0-0
Track : LH: 0-0 RH: 0-0 Tight: 0-0 Gall: 0-0
Aids: Bl: 0-0 Vi: 0-0 Tstrap: 0-0 Ckp: 0-0
Best Rating: **31** 7/08 Curr 7f good

Cruikadyke

104(95) (72)93

3-y-o b c Kyllachy-Shoshone (Be My Chief (USA))
P F I Cole Mrs Fitri Hay

Placings:105-60036100 **(5999)**
2009: 8⁶G, 8⁰HY, 8⁰G, 9³GF, 10⁶G, 8¹GF, 8⁰SD, 8⁰GF,

	Starts	1st	2nd	3rd	Win & Pl
Career Total (Turf)	10	2	0	1	11389
Career Total (AW)	1	0	0	0	

83 7/09 Sals 1m G-F £3238
82 7/08 York 6f G-F £6670
Total win prize-money £9908

Going (Turf): Sf: 0-1 GS: 0-0 Gd: 0-4 **GF: 2-4** Fm: 0-0
Distance: 5f/6f: 1-1 7f-8f: 1-4 9f-13f: 0-6 14f+: 0-0
Track : LH: 0-3 RH: 0-3 Tight: 0-1 Gall: 0-0
Aids: Bl: 0-0 Vi: 0-0 Tstrap: 0-0 Ckp: 0-0
Best Rating: **93** 9/08 Curr 7f yield

Useful; probably stays 1m2f; acts on fast ground.

Cruise Control

78(84) (47)20

3-y-o b g Piccolo-Urban Dancer (IRE) (Generous (IRE))
R J Price Cruise Control Partnership

Placings:0-600000 **(6255)**
2009: 5⁶SD, 8⁰G, 7⁰S, 6⁰G, 8⁰SD, 7⁰SD,

	Starts	1st	2nd	3rd	Win & Pl
Career Total (Turf)	3	0	0	0	
Career Total (AW)	4	0	0	0	0

Going (Turf): **Sf: 0-1 GS: 0-0 Gd: 0-2 GF: 0-0 Fm: 0-0**
Distance: 5f/6f: 0-1 7f-8f: 0-4 9f-13f: 0-2 14f+: 0-0
Track : LH: 0-5 RH: 0-0 Tight: 0-4 Gall: 0-0
Aids: Bl: 0-0 Vi: 0-0 Tstrap: 0-0 Ckp: 0-0
Best Rating: **47** 1/09 Wolv 5f216y stand

Cruise Director

(96) (62)89

9-y-o b g Zilzal (USA)-Briggsmaid (Elegant Air)
Ian Williams Ian Williams

Placings:005/51322103/0301002455/**4254**0210/64000/405 /042006640-**034** **(0743)**
2009: 13⁰SD, 12³SD, 14⁴SD,

	Starts	1st	2nd	3rd	Win & Pl
Career Total (Turf)	31	3	4	0	34298
Career Total (AW)	18	1	2	4	12876

93 5/05 York 1m4f (0-95)H SFT £10255
88 4/04 Wind 1m3f135yD(0-85)H G-S £5622
83 4/03 Wind 1m3f135yD(0-85)H GD £5638
69 2/03 Ling 1m E(0-70)H STD £3269
Total win prize-money £24787

Going (Turf): **Sf: 1-8 GS: 1-7 Gd: 1-13** GF: 0-3 Fm: 0-0
Distance: 5f/6f: 0-1 7f-8f: 1-5 **9f-13f: 3-39** 14f+: 0-4
Track : **LH: 2-40** RH: 0-7 **Tight: 3-24** Gall: 1-16
Aids: Bl: 0-0 Vi: 0-0 Tstrap: 0-0 Ckp: 0-0
Best Rating: **93** 5/05 York 1m4f soft

Fair; stays 1m4f; seems best with cut in the ground.

Crunched

95(97) (73)73

2-y-o b c Dubai Destination (USA)-Amica (Averti (IRE))
M L W Bell R P B Michaelson

Placings:5431 **(7193)**
2009: 7⁵HY, 8⁴G, 7³GF, 8¹SD,

	Starts	1st	2nd	3rd	Win & Pl
Career Total (Turf)	3	0	0	1	674
Career Total (AW)	1	1	0	0	3238

73 10/09 Wolv 1m141y STD £3238
Total win prize-money £3238

Going (Turf): **Sf: 0-1 GS: 0-0 Gd: 0-1 GF: 0-1 Fm: 0-0**
Distance: 5f/6f: 0-0 7f-8f: 0-3 **9f-13f: 1-1** 14f+: 0-0
Track : **LH: 1-1** RH: 0-2 **Tight: 1-1** Gall: 0-0
Aids: Bl: 0-0 Vi: 0-0 Tstrap: 0-0 Ckp: 0-0
Best Rating: **73** 10/09 Wolv 1m141y stand

Modest; stays 1m; acts on good ground and Polytrack.

Crush (IRE)

(74) (25)

3-y-o b c Kheleyf (USA)-Premier Amour (Salmon Leap (USA))
D M Simcock Khalifa Dasmal

Placings:6 **(1108)**
2009: 7⁶SD,

	Starts	1st	2nd	3rd	Win & Pl
Career Total (Turf)	0	0	0	0	
Career Total (AW)	1	0	0	0	0

Going (Turf): **Sf: 0-0 GS: 0-0 Gd: 0-0 GF: 0-0 Fm: 0-0**
Distance: 5f/6f: 0-0 7f-8f: 0-1 9f-13f: 0-0 14f+: 0-0
Track : LH: 0-1 RH: 0-0 Tight: 0-1 Gall: 0-0
Aids: Bl: 0-0 Vi: 0-0 Tstrap: 0-0 Ckp: 0-0
Best Rating: **25** 4/09 Wolv 7f32y stand

Crushing (IRE)

95(93) (52)67

2-y-o b g Kheleyf (USA)-Filmgame (IRE) (Be My Guest (USA))

A J McCabe (T D Barron 25/9) David W Armstrong

Placings:426050005 (7788)

2009: 5^4GF, 6^2GS, 5^6GF, 6^0GF, 7^5GF, 7^0SD, 5^0SD, 5^0SD, 8^5SD,

	Starts	1st	2nd	3rd	Win & Pl
Career Total (Turf)	5	0	1	0	1565
Career Total (AW)	4	0	0	0	0

Going (Turf): Sf: 0-0 GS: 0-1 Gd: 0-0 GF: 0-4 Fm: 0-0
Distance: 5f/6f: 0-6 7f-8f: 0-2 9f-13f: 0-1 14f+: 0-0
Track : LH: 0-4 RH: 0-0 Tight: 0-4 Gall: 0-0
Aids: Bl: 0-0 Vi: 0-0 Tstrap: 0-2 Ckp: 0-2
Best Rating: 67 6/09 Ripn 6f gd-sft

Modest; stays 6f; acts on easy ground; has worn cheek-pieces.

Crux

98 (40)58

7-y-o b g Pivotal-Penny Dip (Cadeaux Genereux)

R E Barr Mrs R E Barr

Placings:0/06000**005**/0/06060/0-06633P (3490)

2009: 7^0F, 7^6GF, 8^6GF, 9^3G, 8^3GS, 8^PG,

	Starts	1st	2nd	3rd	Win & Pl
Career Total (Turf)	17	0	0	2	867
Career Total (AW)	5	0	0	0	0

Going (Turf): Sf: 0-1 GS: 0-2 Gd: 0-7 GF: 0-6 Fm: 0-1
Distance: 5f/6f: 0-6 7f-8f: 0-12 9f-13f: 0-4 14f+: 0-0
Track : LH: 0-9 RH: 0-4 Tight: 0-9 Gall: 0-0
Aids: Bl: 0-0 Vi: 0-0 Tstrap: 0-0 Ckp: 0-0
Best Rating: 58 6/09 Muss 1m1f good

Moderate perfomer; stays a mile; acts on Polytrack and easy ground on turf.

Cry Alot Boy

98(102) (81)79

6-y-o ch g Spinning World (USA)-Intellectuelle (Caerleon (USA))

K A Morgan K A Morgan

Placings:626261260 (7775)

2009: 8^6SD, 10^2S, 8^6G, 10^2GF, 10^6GF, 9^1S, **10^2SD**, 10^6SD, 10^0SD,

	Starts	1st	2nd	3rd	Win & Pl
Career Total (Turf)	5	1	2	0	6658
Career Total (AW)	4	0	1	0	806
79 7/09 Leic	1m1f218y (0-80)H			SFT	£4731

Total win prize-money £4731

Going (Turf): Sf: 1-2 GS: 0-0 Gd: 0-1 GF: 0-2 Fm: 0-0
Distance: 5f/6f: 0-0 7f-8f: 0-1 **9f-13f: 1-8** 14f+: 0-0
Track : LH: 0-7 **RH: 1-1** Tight: 0-4 Gall: 0-0
Aids: Bl: 0-0 Vi: 0-0 Tstrap: 0-0 Ckp: 0-0
Best Rating: 81 11/09 Ling 1m2f stand

Fair; bumper winner; stays 1m2f; acts on any ground.

Cry For The Moon (USA)

98 84

3-y-o b g Street Cry (IRE)-Kafaf (USA) (Zilzal (USA))

J H Culloty (Mrs A J Perrett 29/9) Four Long Lives Syndicate

Placings:003-1334065 (6368)

2009: 12^1G, 14^3GF, 14^3GF, 14^4GF, 12^0G, 12^6GF, 14^5GF,

	Starts	1st	2nd	3rd	Win & Pl
Career Total (Turf)	10	1	0	3	5939
79 4/09 Pont	1m4f8y (0-75)H			GD	£3238

Total win prize-money £3238

Going (Turf): Sf: 0-0 GS: 0-0 **Gd: 1-5** GF: 0-5 Fm: 0-0
Distance: 5f/6f: 0-0 7f-8f: 0-2 **9f-13f: 1-4** 14f+: 0-4
Track : **LH: 1-2** RH: 0-6 Tight: 0-3 Gall: 0-0
Aids: Bl: 0-0 Vi: 0-0 Tstrap: 0-0 Ckp: 0-0
Best Rating: 84 6/09 Sals 1m6f21y gd-fm

Fair; stays 1m4f; acts on good ground.

Cry Of Freedom (USA)

73(95) (77)99

3-y-o b c Street Cry (IRE)-Tustarta (USA) (Trempolino (USA))

M Johnston Sheikh Hamdan Bin Mohammed Al Maktoum

Placings:11000-50 (1291)

2009: 8^5SD, 10^0GF,

	Starts	1st	2nd	3rd	Win & Pl
Career Total (Turf)	6	2	0	0	22212
Career Total (AW)	1	0	0	0	1076
99 8/08 Newb 7f				G-S	£17031
81 7/08 Sand 7f16y				G-F	£5180

Total win prize-money £22212

Going (Turf): Sf: 0-1 **GS: 1-1** Gd: 0-1 **GF: 1-3** Fm: 0-0
Distance: 5f/6f: 0-0 **7f-8f: 2-6** 9f-13f: 0-1 14f+: 0-0
Track : LH: 0-1 **RH: 1-2** Tight: 0-1 Gall: 0-0
Aids: Bl: 0-1 Vi: 0-0 Tstrap: 0-0 Ckp: 0-0
Best Rating: 99 8/08 Newb 7f gd-sft

Very useful; winner in Listed company; stays at least 7f; handles quick and easy ground; has worn blinkers.

Cry Of Truth (IRE)

99 50

3-y-o b f Danetime (IRE)-Clandolly (IRE) (Burslem)

D W Barker Raymond Gomersall

Placings:6040 (2593)

2009: 7^6GF, 7^0GF, 6^4GF, 6^0F,

	Starts	1st	2nd	3rd	Win & Pl
Career Total (Turf)	4	0	0	0	241

Going (Turf): Sf: 0-0 GS: 0-0 Gd: 0-0 GF: 0-3 Fm: 0-1
Distance: 5f/6f: 0-2 7f-8f: 0-2 9f-13f: 0-0 14f+: 0-0
Track : LH: 0-2 RH: 0-0 Tight: 0-2 Gall: 0-0
Aids: Bl: 0-0 Vi: 0-0 Tstrap: 0-0 Ckp: 0-0
Best Rating: 50 5/09 Ripn 6f gd-fm

Cry Presto (USA)

(93) (46)44

5-y-o b g Street Cry (IRE)-Sabaah Elfull (Kris)

S T Nolan J P Prunty

Placings:00345**026**/**01**005**000**/0-05**50** (7547a)

2009: 7^0Y, 14^5YS, **16^5SD**, 10^0SD,

	Starts	1st	2nd	3rd	Win & Pl
Career Total (Turf)	13	0	0	1	1659
Career Total (AW)	8	1	1	0	4360
66 3/07 Ling	1m4f			STD	£2914

Total win prize-money £2915

Going (Turf): Sf: 0-1 GS: 0-3 Gd: 0-4 GF: 0-3 Fm: 0-0
Distance: 5f/6f: 0-0 7f-8f: 0-9 **9f-13f: 1-8** 14f+: 0-4
Track : **LH: 1-7** RH: 0-6 **Tight: 1-5** Gall: 0-1
Aids: Bl: 0-7 Vi: 0-0 Tstrap: 0-2 Ckp: 0-2
Best Rating: 87 8/06 Newb 7f good

Fair; stays 1m4f; acts on Polytrack.

Crystal B Good (USA)

97(92) (41)58

3-y-o b/br f Successful Appeal (USA)-Unbridled Run (USA) (Unbridled (USA))

J R Best Martin Long

Placings:60404200 (7890)

2009: 6^0SD, 6^0SD, 7^4GF, 8^0G, 6^4GF, 5^2G, 6^0SD, 6^0SD,

	Starts	1st	2nd	3rd	Win & Pl
Career Total (Turf)	4	0	1	0	1156
Career Total (AW)	4	0	0	0	0

Going (Turf): Sf: 0-0 GS: 0-0 Gd: 0-2 GF: 0-2 Fm: 0-0
Distance: 5f/6f: 0-6 7f-8f: 0-2 9f 13f: 0-0 14f+: 0-0
Track : LH: 0-4 RH: 0-1 Tight: 0-4 Gall: 0-0
Aids: Bl: 0-0 Vi: 0-0 Tstrap: 0-0 Ckp: 0-0
Best Rating: 58 7/09 Leic 5f218y good

Modest sprinter; best on good/fast ground.

Crystal Bridge

65(77) (28)23

2-y-o b f Avonbridge-Heaven-Liegh-Grey (Grey Desire)

Mrs L Williamson Anthony Thomas Sykes

Placings:06000 (7816)

2009: 5^0G, 5^6GF, 5^0GF, 8^0SD, 8^0SD,

	Starts	1st	2nd	3rd	Win & Pl
Career Total (Turf)	3	0	0	0	0
Career Total (AW)	2	0	0	0	

Going (Turf): Sf: 0-0 GS: 0-0 Gd: 0-1 GF: 0-2 Fm: 0-0
Distance: 5f/6f: 0-3 7f-8f: 0-0 9f-13f: 0-2 14f+: 0-0
Track : LH: 0-3 RH: 0-0 Tight: 0-3 Gall: 0-0
Aids: Bl: 0-0 Vi: 0-0 Tstrap: 0-1 Ckp: 0-1
Best Rating: 28 10/09 Wolv 1m141y stand

Crystal Capella

110 (75)116

4-y-o b f Cape Cross (IRE)-Crystal Star (Mark Of Esteem (IRE))

Sir Michael Stoute Sir Evelyn De Rothschild

Placings:2/211111-152 (6853)

2009: 10^1G, 10^5G, 12^2G,

	Starts	1st	2nd	3rd	Win & Pl
Career Total (Turf)	9	6	2	0	190148
Career Total (AW)	1	0	1	0	935
116 5/09 York	1m2f88y			GD	£36900
110 10/08 NmkR	1m4f			GD	£60829
104 9/08 Asct	1m4f			GD	£24978
102 8/08 Gdwd	1m1f192y (0-110)H			SFT	£24978
98 7/08 York	1m2f88y (0-90)H			G-F	£9714
79 5/08 Newc	1m2f32y			G-F	£3561

Total win prize-money £160964

Going (Turf): Sf: 1-1 GS: 0-0 **Gd: 3-6** GF: 2-2 Fm: 0-0
Distance: 5f/6f: 0-0 7f-8f: 0-1 **9f-13f: 6-9** 14f+: 0-0
Track : LH: 3-5 RH: 3-5 Tight: 1-2 **Gall: 5-6**

Aids: Bl: 0-0 Vi: 0-0 Tstrap: 0-0 Ckp: 0-0
Best Rating: **116** 5/09 York 1m2f88y good

Group class; winner of the Group 2 Pride Stakes in 2008; stays 1m4f; acts on fast and soft ground; also goes on Polytrack.

Crystal Crown (IRE)

71(94) (60)**9**
5-y-o b g Grand Lodge (USA)-Top Crystal (IRE) (Sadler's Wells (USA))
B G Powell Michael Poland

Placings:60/03-0 **(2243)**
2009: 8^{0}GF,

	Starts	1st	2nd	3rd	Win & Pl
Career Total (Turf)	4	0	0	0	
Career Total (AW)	1	0	0	1	403

Going (Turf): **Sf: 0-0 GS: 0-0 Gd: 0-1 GF: 0-2 Fm: 0-0**
Distance: 5f/6f: 0-0 7f-8f: 0-2 9f-13f: 0-3 14f+: 0-0
Track : LH: 0-4 RH: 0-0 Tight: 0-0 Gall: 0-0
Aids: Bl: 0-0 Vi: 0-0 Tstrap: 0-0 Ckp: 0-0
Best Rating: **73** 4/07 Leop 1m2f good

Fair; best at about 1m; handles Fibresand; has worn a tongue tie.

Crystal Feather

98(106) (59)**66**
3-y-o ch f Monsieur Bond (IRE)-Prince's Feather (IRE) (Cadeaux Genereux)
E F Vaughan Featherbed Ladies

Placings:5-3361613 **(5524)**
2009: 7^{3}SD, 7^{3}SD, 10^{6}SD, 8^{1}SD, 10^{6}GF, 9^{1}G, 9^{3}G,

	Starts	1st	2nd	3rd	Win & Pl
Career Total (Turf)	3	1	0	1	2506
Career Total (AW)	5	1	0	2	2652
66 8/09 Yarm 1m1f (0-65)H				GD	£2072
59 5/09 Wolv 1m141y (0-55)				STD	£2047

Total win prize-money £4119

Going (Turf): Sf: 0-0 GS: 0-0 **Gd: 1-2** GF: 0-1 Fm: 0-0
Distance: 5f/6f: 0-1 7f-8f: 0-2 **9f-13f: 2-5** 14f+: 0-0
Track : **LH: 2-7** RH: 0-1 **Tight: 2-6** Gall: 0-0
Aids: Bl: 0-0 Vi: 0-0 Tstrap: 0-0 Ckp: 0-0
Best Rating: **66** 8/09 Yarm 1m1f good

Moderate; stays 1m2f; acts on Polytrack.

Crystal Gale (IRE)

93 **71**
2-y-o gr f Verglas (IRE)-Mango Groove (IRE) (Unfuwain (USA))
W J Knight O J Williams

Placings:30335 **(5627)**
2009: 6^{3}GF, 6^{0}GF, 7^{3}GS, 8^{3}G, 8^{5}GS,

	Starts	1st	2nd	3rd	Win & Pl
Career Total (Turf)	5	0	0	3	1980

Going (Turf): **Sf: 0-0 GS: 0-2 Gd: 0-1 GF: 0-2 Fm: 0-0**
Distance: 5f/6f: 0-2 7f-8f: 0-2 9f-13f: 0-1 14f+: 0-0
Track : LH: 0-0 RH: 0-0 Tight: 0-0 Gall: 0-0
Aids: Bl: 0-0 Vi: 0-0 Tstrap: 0-0 Ckp: 0-0
Best Rating: **71** 7/09 Donc 7f gd-sft

Fair: stays 1m; acts on most ground.

Crystal Glass

61(71) (24)
2-y-o b g Exceed And Excel (AUS)-Cumbrian Crystal (Mind Games)
T D Easterby Habton Farms

Placings:006 **(7420)**
2009: 7^{0}G, 6^{0}S, 7^{6}SD,

	Starts	1st	2nd	3rd	Win & Pl
Career Total (Turf)	2	0	0	0	
Career Total (AW)	1	0	0	0	0

Going (Turf): **Sf: 0-1 GS: 0-0 Gd: 0-1 GF: 0-0 Fm: 0-0**
Distance: 5f/6f: 0-1 7f-8f: 0-2 9f-13f: 0-0 14f+: 0-0
Track : LH: 0-1 RH: 0-0 Tight: 0-0 Gall: 0-0
Aids: Bl: 0-0 Vi: 0-0 Tstrap: 0-0 Ckp: 0-0
Best Rating: **24** 11/09 Sthl 7f stand

Crystal Moments

101(103) (91)**93**
3-y-o b f Haafhd-Celestial Choir (Celestial Storm (USA))
E A L Dunlop Mohammed Jaber

Placings:14110-200254410 **(7292)**
2009: 6^{2}SD, 6^{0}GF, 5^{0}GF, 6^{2}G, 6^{5}GF, 6^{4}G, 6^{4}SS, 7^{1}S, 6^{0}S,

	Starts	1st	2nd	3rd	Win & Pl
Career Total (Turf)	10	2	1	0	17529
Career Total (AW)	4	2	1	0	11357
93 10/09 Newb 7f (0-95)H				SFT	£9066
87 8/08 Wolv 5f216y (0-85)				STD	£4533
84 7/08 Kemp 6f				STD	£3885
78 5/08 Sand 5f6y				G-F	£4533

Total win prize-money £22018

Going (Turf): **Sf: 1-2** GS: 0-0 Gd: 0-4 **GF: 1-4** Fm: 0-0
Distance: **5f/6f: 3-11** 7f-8f: 1-3 9f-13f: 0-0 14f+: 0-0
Track : LH: 1-3 RH: 1-1 **Tight: 1-3** Gall: 0-0
Aids: Bl: 0-0 Vi: 0-0 Tstrap: 0-0 Ckp: 0-0
Best Rating: **93** 10/09 Newb 7f soft

Useful; effective at 5f-7f; acts on good/fast ground and on Polytrack.

Crystal Prince

81(98) (68)**76**
5-y-o b g Marju (IRE)-Crystal Ring (IRE) (Kris)
C E Longsdon Bulls & Bears

Placings:00/243/4045-0 **(2983)**
2009: 11^{0}GF,

	Starts	1st	2nd	3rd	Win & Pl
Career Total (Turf)	9	0	1	1	2045
Career Total (AW)	1	0	0	0	0

Going (Turf): **Sf: 0-2 GS: 0-0 Gd: 0-1 GF: 0-6 Fm: 0-0**
Distance: 5f/6f: 0-0 7f-8f: 0-1 9f-13f: 0-9 14f+: 0-0
Track : LH: 0-7 RH: 0-2 Tight: 0-2 Gall: 0-2
Aids: Bl: 0-2 Vi: 0-0 Tstrap: 0-1 Ckp: 0-1
Best Rating: **77** 4/07 Nott 1m1f213y gd-fm

Fair; effective over 1m4f; acts on fast ground; has worn cheekpieces, blinkers and a tongue tie.

Crystallize

96(97) (65)**69**
3-y-o b g Bertolini (USA)-Adamas (IRE) (Fairy King (USA))
A B Haynes Mrs A De Weck & P De Weck

Placings:0035-065114400464 **(7715)**
2009: 8^{0}SD, 7^{6}GF, 7^{5}GF, 7^{1}SD, 7^{1}G, 7^{4}G, 6^{4}GF, 6^{0}G, 7^{0}SD, 7^{4}SD, 7^{6}SD, 7^{4}SD,

	Starts	1st	2nd	3rd	Win & Pl
Career Total (Turf)	9	1	0	1	2722
Career Total (AW)	7	1	0	0	2388
69 5/09 Yarm 7f3y (0-60)H				GD	£2072
62 5/09 Wolv 7f32y (0-60)H				STD	£2388

Total win prize-money £4460

Going (Turf): Sf: 0-1 GS: 0-0 **Gd: 1-3** GF: 0-5 Fm: 0-0
Distance: 5f/6f: 0-0 **7f-8f: 2-15** 9f-13f: 0-1 14f+: 0-0
Track : **LH: 1-9** RH: 0-2 **Tight: 1-5** Gall: 0-0
Aids: Bl: 0-0 Vi: 0-0 Tstrap: 0-0 Ckp: 0-0
Best Rating: **69** 5/09 Yarm 7f3y good

Modest; effective over 7f; acts on good and soft ground; handles Polytrack.

Crystany (IRE)

101(101) (94)**98**
4-y-o b f Green Desert (USA)-Crystal Music (USA) (Nureyev (USA))
E A L Dunlop Ballygallon Stud Limited

Placings:4512/4234664-056 **(2886)**
2009: 6^{0}HY, 6^{5}F, 6^{6}G,

	Starts	1st	2nd	3rd	Win & Pl
Career Total (Turf)	13	1	2	1	27248
Career Total (AW)	1	0	0	0	211
81 9/07 Ripn 6f				G-F	£3886

Total win prize-money £3886

Going (Turf): Sf: 0-1 GS: 0-2 Gd: 0-7 **GF: 1-2** Fm: 0-1
Distance: **5f/6f: 1-9** 7f-8f: 0-5 9f-13f: 0-0 14f+: 0-0
Track : LH: 0-1 RH: 0-2 Tight: 0-1 Gall: 0-0
Aids: Bl: 0-1 Vi: 0-0 Tstrap: 0-0 Ckp: 0-0
Best Rating: **98** 5/08 Nott 6f15y good

Very useful; Listed placed; effective over 6f; acts on fast ground; handles Polytrack.

Cuccinello (IRE)

66 **10**
6-y-o b m Makbul-Costa Verde (King Of Spain)
K W Hogg (I McMath 24/3) K W Hogg

Placings:000/00/0 **(2718)**
2009: 9^{0}G,

	Starts	1st	2nd	3rd	Win & Pl
Career Total (Turf)	6	0	0	0	

Going (Turf): **Sf: 0-0 GS: 0-2 Gd: 0-3 GF: 0-1 Fm: 0-0**
Distance: 5f/6f: 0-2 7f-8f: 0-3 9f-13f: 0-1 14f+: 0-0
Track : LH: 0-0 RH: 0-3 Tight: 0-1 Gall: 0-0
Aids: Bl: 0-0 Vi: 0-0 Tstrap: 0-0 Ckp: 0-0
Best Rating: **10** 5/06 Carl 5f193y gd-sft

Cuckoo Rock (IRE)

75 **32**
2-y-o b g Refuse To Bend (IRE)-Ringmoor Down (Pivotal)
J G Portman Prof C D Green

Placings:00 **(5787)**
2009: 7^{0}GF, 8^{0}G,

	Starts	1st	2nd	3rd	Win & Pl
Career Total (Turf)	2	0	0	0	

Going (Turf): **Sf: 0-0 GS: 0-0 Gd: 0-1 GF: 0-1 Fm: 0-0**
Distance: 5f/6f: 0-0 7f-8f: 0-1 9f-13f: 0-1 14f+: 0-0

Track : LH: 0-0 RH: 0-1 Tight: 0-0 Gall: 0-0

Aids: Bl: 0-0 Vi: 0-0 Tstrap: 0-0 Ckp: 0-0

Best Rating: 32 7/09 Sand 7f16y gd-fm

Cuis Ghaire (IRE)

113 **112**

3-y-o b f Galileo (IRE)-Scribonia (IRE) (Danehill (USA))

J S Bolger Mrs J S Bolger & D H W Dobson

Placings:11120-200 **(6848)**

2009: 8^{2}GF, 8^{0}HY, 7^{0}G,

	Starts	1st	2nd	3rd	Win & Pl
Career Total (Turf)	8	3	2	0	190123

101	6/08	Asct	6f	1	FRM	£39739
105	6/08	Naas	6f		G-F	£47867
89	5/08	Naas	6f		GD	£6605

Total win prize-money £94212

Going (Turf): Sf: 0-2 GS: 0-0 **Gd: 1-2 GF: 1-3 Fm: 1-1**

Distance: **5f/6f: 3-3** 7f-8f: 0-5 9f-13f: 0-0 14f+: 0-0

Track : **LH: 2-4** RH: 0-1 Tight: 0-0 Gall: 0-1

Aids: Bl: 0-0 Vi: 0-0 Tstrap: 0-0 Ckp: 0-0

Best Rating: **112** 5/09 NmkR 1m gd fm

Group class; runner-up in the 1000 Guineas; effective over 6f-1m; acts on good and fast ground.

Cullybackey (IRE)

94(91) (41)**52**

4-y-o ch f Golan (IRE)-Leitrim Lodge (IRE) (Classic Music (USA))

J R Boyle (G A Swinbank 17/6) Hubert Brown Kerr

Placings:0360-060**506** **(7533)**

2009: 8^{0}GF, 9^{6}G, 12^{0}G, 6^{5}SD, 7^{0}SD, 6^{6}SD,

	Starts	1st	2nd	3rd	Win & Pl
Career Total (Turf)	7	0	0	1	385
Career Total (AW)	3	0	0	0	0

Going (Turf): **Sf: 0-0 GS: 0-2 Gd: 0-3 GF: 0-2 Fm: 0-0**

Distance: 5f/6f: 0-3 7f-8f: 0-3 9f-13f: 0-4 14f+: 0-0

Track : LH: 0-4 RH: 0-4 Tight: 0-4 Gall: 0-0

Aids: Bl: 0-1 Vi: 0-0 Tstrap: 0-0 Ckp: 0-0

Best Rating: **52** 9/08 Rdcr 6f gd-sft

Cultivar

94 **71**

2-y-o b c Xaar-New Orchid (USA) (Quest For Fame)

B W Hills K Abdulla

Placings:36 **(5542)**

2009: 7^{3}GF, 7^{6}GF,

	Starts	1st	2nd	3rd	Win & Pl
Career Total (Turf)	2	0	0	1	722

Going (Turf): **Sf: 0-0 GS: 0-0 Gd: 0-0 GF: 0-2 Fm: 0-0**

Distance: 5f/6f: 0-0 7f-8f: 0-2 9f-13f: 0-0 14f+: 0-0

Track : LH: 0-0 RH: 0-0 Tight: 0-0 Gall: 0-0

Aids: Bl: 0-0 Vi: 0-0 Tstrap: 0-0 Ckp: 0-0

Best Rating: **71** 8/09 Newb 7f gd-fm

Cultured Pride (IRE)

97 **77**

2-y-o ch f King's Best (USA)-Cultured Pearl (IRE) (Lammtarra (USA))

R Hannon D G Churston & R E Greatorex

Placings:015530 **(6241)**

2009: 6^{0}GF, 6^{1}G, 6^{5}GF, 7^{5}GS, 8^{3}GF, 6^{0}G,

	Starts	1st	2nd	3rd	Win & Pl
Career Total (Turf)	6	1	0	1	5759

70	6/09	Gdwd	6f	GD	£5180

Total win prize-money £5181

Going (Turf): Sf: 0-0 GS: 0-1 **Gd: 1-2** GF: 0-3 Fm: 0-0

Distance: **5f/6f: 1-2** 7f-8f: 0-4 9f-13f: 0-0 14f+: 0-0

Track : LH: 0-0 RH: 0-1 Tight: 0-0 Gall: 0-0

Aids: Bl: 0-0 Vi: 0-0 Tstrap: 0-0 Ckp: 0-0

Best Rating: **77** 9/09 Gdwd 1m gd-fm

Fair; probably stays 1m.

Cumana Bay

108(100) (82)**89**

3-y-o b f Dansili-Mayaro Bay (Robellino (USA))

R Hannon J R Shannon

Placings:61**45**-**2**212165205 **(7133)**

2009: 7^{2}SD, 8^{2}GF, 7^{1}GF, 8^{2}GF, 8^{1}G, 7^{8}G, 6^{5}GF, 8^{2}GF, 7^{0}GF, 7^{5}SD,

	Starts	1st	2nd	3rd	Win & Pl
Career Total (Turf)	10	3	3	0	21930
Career Total (AW)	4	0	1	0	998

89	6/09	NmkJ	1m	(0-90)H	GD	£9066
82	5/09	Newb	7f	(0-75)H	G-F	£2590
67	9/08	Sand	5f6y		SFT	£5180

Total win prize-money £16837

Going (Turf): **Sf: 1-1** GS: 0-0 **Gd: 1-3 GF: 1-6** Fm: 0-0

Distance: 5f/6f: 1-2 **7f-8f: 2-10** 9f-13f: 0-2 14f+: 0-0

Track : LH: 0-3 RH: 0-4 Tight: 0-5 Gall: 0-0

Aids: Bl: 0-0 Vi: 0-0 Tstrap: 0-0 Ckp: 0-0

Best Rating: **89** 6/09 NmkJ 1m good

Useful; effective over 7f-1m; acts on most ground on turf; goes on Polytrack.

Cumbrian Gold (USA)

(76) (41)

3-y-o ch g Gilded Time (USA)-Brackenber (USA) (Lycius (USA))

B Smart Pinnacle Gilded Time Partnership

Placings:006-0 **(0383)**

2009: 8^{0}SD,

	Starts	1st	2nd	3rd	Win & Pl
Career Total (Turf)	0	0	0	0	
Career Total (AW)	4	0	0	0	0

Going (Turf): **Sf: 0-0 GS: 0-0 Gd: 0-0 GF: 0-0 Fm: 0-0**

Distance: 5f/6f: 0-0 7f-8f: 0-2 9f-13f: 0-2 14f+: 0-0

Track : LH: 0-4 RH: 0-0 Tight: 0-2 Gall: 0-0

Aids: Bl: 0-0 Vi: 0-1 Tstrap: 0-0 Ckp: 0-0

Best Rating: **41** 11/08 Wolv 1m141y stand

Cumbrian Knight (IRE)

(92) (67)**53**

11-y-o b g Presenting-Crashrun (Crash Course)

J M Jefferson J M Jefferson

Placings:0/04040**510**/**10004052**/**14032**/**13010-00** **(0301)**

2009: 16^{0}SS, 14^{0}SD,

	Starts	1st	2nd	3rd	Win & Pl
Career Total (Turf)	11	0	0	0	542
Career Total (AW)	18	5	2	2	12162

67	11/08	Sthl	1m6f	(0-65)H	STD	£1977
61	1/08	Sthl	2m	(0-60)H	STD	£1351
61	1/07	Wolv	2m119y	(0-60)H	STD	£2307
67	1/06	Wolv	2m119y	(0-60)H	STD	£1977
71	11/05	Wolv	1m5f194y	(0-65)H	STD	£2787

Total win prize-money £10404

Going (Turf): **Sf: 0-1 GS: 0-0 Gd: 0-2 GF: 0-8 Fm: 0-0**

Distance: 5f/6f: 0-0 7f-8f: 0-0 9f-13f: 0-10 **14f+: 5-19**

Track : **LH: 5-25** RH: 0-4 **Tight: 3-20** Gall: 0-0

Aids: Bl: 0-0 Vi: 0-0 Tstrap: 0-0 Ckp: 0-0

Best Rating: **71** 11/05 Wolv 1m5f194y stand

Modest; winning hurdler; effective over 1m6f-2m; acts on Fibresand and Polytrack.

Cumulus Nimbus

93 **85**

2-y-o ch c Muhtathir-Supreme Talent (Desert King (IRE))

R Hannon Mrs John Lee

Placings:12033 **(6756)**

2009: 7^{1}G, 7^{2}GS, 7^{0}GF, 7^{3}GS, 7^{3}G,

	Starts	1st	2nd	3rd	Win & Pl
Career Total (Turf)	5	1	1	2	12229

82	7/09	Ling	7f	GD	£3561

Total win prize-money £3562

Going (Turf): Sf: 0-0 GS: 0-2 **Gd: 1-2** GF: 0-1 Fm: 0-0

Distance: 5f/6f: 0-0 **7f-8f: 1-5** 9f-13f: 0-0 14f+: 0-0

Track : LH: 0-0 RH: 0-3 Tight: 0-0 Gall: 0-0

Aids: Bl: 0-0 Vi: 0-0 Tstrap: 0-0 Ckp: 0-0

Best Rating: **85** 9/09 Sand 7f16y gd-sft

Useful; effective over 7f; acts on good ground.

Cunning Plan (IRE)

89 **50**

2-y-o ch c Bachelor Duke (USA)-Madamaa (IRE) (Alzao (USA))

P W Chapple-Hyam A B S Webb & Partner

Placings:06 **(6922)**

2009: 7^{0}GF, 6^{6}GF,

	Starts	1st	2nd	3rd	Win & Pl
Career Total (Turf)	2	0	0	0	0

Going (Turf): **Sf: 0-0 GS: 0-0 Gd: 0-0 GF: 0-2 Fm: 0-0**

Distance: 5f/6f: 0-0 7f-8f: 0-2 9f-13f: 0-0 14f+: 0-0

Track : LH: 0-0 RH: 0-1 Tight: 0-0 Gall: 0-0

Aids: Bl: 0-0 Vi: 0-0 Tstrap: 0-0 Ckp: 0-0

Best Rating: **50** 10/09 Yarm 6f3y gd-fm

Cupid's Glory

87(105) (88)**83**

7-y-o b g Pursuit Of Love-Doctor's Glory (USA) (Elmaamul (USA))

G L Moore K Johnson, K Jessup

Placings:6111314/0122/3/00060454/62502120206-500 **(7539)**

2009: 9^{5}G, 9^{0}SD, 12^{0}SD,

	Starts	1st	2nd	3rd	Win & Pl
Career Total (Turf)	15	3	4	1	74220
Career Total (AW)	19	3	2	1	24291

83	9/08	GrLe	1m2f	(0-75)H	STD	£3561

109	8/05	Ches	7f122y		G-F	£8978
108	10/04	Newb	7f		SFT	£23200
107	8/04	Ling	7f	E	STD	£3601
97	8/04	Ches	6f18y	C	SFT	£9353
80	8/04	Ling	6f	F	STD	£3555

Total win prize-money £52251

Going (Turf): **Sf: 2-2** GS: 0-3 Gd: 0-5 GF: 1-3 Fm: 0-0
Distance: 5f/6f: 1-2 **7f-8f: 4-15** 9f-13f: 1-17 14f+: 0-0
Track : **LH: 5-20** RH: 0-11 **Tight: 4-18** Gall: 1-4
Aids: Bl: 0-1 Vi: 0-0 Tstrap: 0-6 Ckp: 0-6
Best Rating: **115** 8/05 Deau 1m gd-sft

Useful; formerly smart; winner of the Group 3 Horris Hill Stakes at two; stays 1m2f; acts on good and softer and on Polytrack; has worn blinkers and cheekpieces.

Curacao

103(108) (78)**83**

3-y-o br g Sakhee (USA)-Bourbonella (Rainbow Quest (USA))
Mrs A J Perrett Mrs S Conway, Coombelands Racing Stables

Placings:666-23511343 (6388)
2009: 11^{2}SD, **12^{3}**SD, 11^{5}GF, 12^{1}S, 14^{1}GF, 14^{3}G, **16^{4}**SD, 16^{3}GF,

	Starts	1st	2nd	3rd	Win & Pl
Career Total (Turf)	6	2	0	2	8161
Career Total (AW)	5	0	1	1	2022

83	7/09	Sals	1m6f21y	(0-75)H	G-F	£3238
75	7/09	Sals	1m4f	(0-75)H	SFT	£3238

Total win prize-money £6476

Going (Turf): **Sf: 1-1** GS: 0-0 Gd: 0-1 **GF: 1-4** Fm: 0-0
Distance: 5f/6f: 0-0 7f-8f: 0-3 9f-13f: 1-4 14f+: 1-4
Track : LH: 0-5 **RH: 2-6 Tight: 2-6** Gall: 0-0
Aids: Bl: 0-0 Vi: 0-0 Tstrap: 0-0 Ckp: 0-0
Best Rating: **83** 7/09 Sals 1m6f21y gd-fm

Moderate; stays 1m4f; acts on Polytrack.

Curlew (IRE)

76 **30**

3-y-o b g Cape Cross (IRE)-Billbill (USA) (Storm Cat (USA))
M Johnston Sheikh Hamdan Bin Mohammed Al Maktoum

Placings:0 (3485)
2009: 8^{0}GF,

	Starts	1st	2nd	3rd	Win & Pl
Career Total (Turf)	1	0	0	0	

Going (Turf): **Sf: 0-0 GS: 0-0 Gd: 0-0 GF: 0-1 Fm: 0-0**
Distance: 5f/6f: 0-0 7f-8f: 0-0 9f-13f: 0-1 14f+: 0-0
Track : LH: 0-0 RH: 0-1 Tight: 0-1 Gall: 0-0
Aids: Bl: 0-0 Vi: 0-0 Tstrap: 0-0 Ckp: 0-0
Best Rating: **30** 6/09 Haml 1m65y gd-fm

Curtain Call (FR)

114 **115**

4-y-o b c Sadler's Wells (USA)-Apsara (FR) (Darshaan)
L M Cumani Mrs P K Cooper and Partners

Placings:62215/1050-16442**P** (5662)
2009: 10^{1}HY, 9^{6}S, 12^{4}S, 10^{4}G, 10^{2}SH, **12^{P}**SD,

	Starts	1st	2nd	3rd	Win & Pl
Career Total (Turf)	14	3	3	0	217084
Career Total (AW)	1	0	0	0	

115	5/09	Curr	1m2f	HVY	£53640
113	4/08	Nott	1m2f50y	G-S	£12462
112	9/07	Curr	1m	YLD	£54898

Total win prize-money £121002

Going (Turf): **Sf: 1-6 GS: 1-1** Gd: 0-4 GF: 0-0 Fm: 0-0
Distance: 5f/6f: 0-0 7f-8f: 1-5 **9f-13f: 2-10** 14f+: 0-0
Track : LH: 1-5 **RH: 2-7** Tight: 0-1 **Gall: 1-2**
Aids: Bl: 0-0 Vi: 0-0 Tstrap: 0-0 Ckp: 0-0
Best Rating: **115** 8/09 Curr 1m2f sft-hvy

Group class; ex-Irish; winner of the Group 2 Beresford Stakes in 2007; stays 1m2f and acts on soft ground.

Curtains

100 **89**

2-y-o b f Dubawi (IRE)-Voile (IRE) (Barathea (IRE))
S Dow The Pull Yourself Together Partnership

Placings:332054 (3396)
2009: 5^{3}GF, 5^{3}GF, 6^{2}GF, 5^{0}G, 6^{5}GF, 6^{4}G,

	Starts	1st	2nd	3rd	Win & Pl
Career Total (Turf)	6	0	1	2	5321

Going (Turf): **Sf: 0-0 GS: 0-0 Gd: 0-2 GF: 0-4 Fm: 0-0**
Distance: 5f/6f: 0-6 7f-8f: 0-0 9f-13f: 0-0 14f+: 0-0
Track : LH: 0-3 RH: 0-0 Tight: 0-0 Gall: 0-1
Aids: Bl: 0-0 Vi: 0-0 Tstrap: 0-0 Ckp: 0-0
Best Rating: **89** 6/09 NmkJ 6f good

Useful; effective at 5f-6f; acts on fast ground.

Custody (IRE)

102(97) (85)**73**

3-y-o b g Fusaichi Pegasus (USA)-Shahtoush (IRE) (Alzao (USA))
Sir Michael Stoute Highclere Thoroughbred Racing (Eclipse)

Placings:62222-5630 (6595)
2009: 10^{5}G, 9^{6}GF, **12^{3}**SD, 10^{0}GS,

	Starts	1st	2nd	3rd	Win & Pl
Career Total (Turf)	6	0	2	0	2650
Career Total (AW)	3	0	2	1	3237

Going (Turf): **Sf: 0-1 GS: 0-1 Gd: 0-2 GF: 0-2 Fm: 0-0**
Distance: 5f/6f: 0-1 7f-8f: 0-3 9f-13f: 0-5 14f+: 0-0
Track : LH: 0-4 RH: 0-3 Tight: 0-2 Gall: 0-0
Aids: Bl: 0-1 Vi: 0-2 Tstrap: 0-1 Ckp: 0-1
Best Rating: **85** 10/08 Ling 7f stand

Fair; stays 1m; acts on fast ground and on Polytrack; has worn blinkers and a visor.

Cut And Thrust (IRE)

95(100) (78)**62**

3-y-o b g Haafhd-Ego (Green Desert (USA))
M Wellings (M A Jarvis 6/10) Nicholls Family

Placings:660351-162000 (7830)
2009: 7^{1}SD, 8^{6}SD, 8^{2}SD, 8^{0}SD, 7^{0}GS, 7^{0}SD,

	Starts	1st	2nd	3rd	Win & Pl
Career Total (Turf)	2	0	0	0	
Career Total (AW)	10	2	1	1	5455

78	1/09	Kemp	7f	(0-75)H	STD	£2590
78	12/08	Ling	7f	(0-60)	STD	£1706

Total win prize-money £4296

Going (Turf): **Sf: 0-0 GS: 0-2 Gd: 0-0 GF: 0-0 Fm: 0-0**
Distance: 5f/6f: 0-1 **7f-8f: 2-10** 9f-13f: 0-1 14f+: 0-0
Track : LH: 1-3 RH: 1-8 **Tight: 1-2** Gall: 0-0
Aids: Bl: 0-0 Vi: 0-0 Tstrap: 2-7 Ckp: 2-7
Best Rating: **78** 1/09 Kemp 7f stand

Modest; effective over 7f; acts on Fibresand and on Polytrack; has worn cheekpieces.

Cut The Cackle (IRE)

99(103) (81)**84**

3-y-o b f Danetime (IRE)-Alexander Anapolis (IRE) (Spectrum (IRE))
P Winkworth P Winkworth

Placings:101-62604255 (7253)
2009: 5^{6}GF, **6^{2}**SD, 6^{6}G, 6^{0}GF, 5^{4}GF, 6^{2}GF, **6^{5}**SD, **6^{5}**SD,

	Starts	1st	2nd	3rd	Win & Pl
Career Total (Turf)	8	2	1	0	11950
Career Total (AW)	3	0	1	0	1445

84	10/08	Wind	5f10y	(0-95)	G-S	£5180
80	8/08	Sand	5f6y		GD	£3885

Total win prize-money £9067

Going (Turf): Sf: 0-0 **GS: 1-1 Gd: 1-3** GF: 0-4 Fm: 0-0
Distance: **5f/6f: 2-11** 7f-8f: 0-0 9f-13f: 0-0 14f+: 0-0
Track : LH: 0-2 RH: 0-1 Tight: 0-2 **Gall: 1-2**
Aids: Bl: 0-0 Vi: 0-0 Tstrap: 0-0 Ckp: 0-0
Best Rating: **84** 10/08 Wind 5f10y gd-sft

Fair; effective at 5f; acts on fast and soft ground.

Cute Ass (IRE)

106 **94**

4-y-o b f Fath (USA)-John's Ballad (IRE) (Ballad Rock)
K R Burke Bigwigs Bloodstock II

Placings:3241232/200050-2 (2591)
2009: 5^{2}GF,

	Starts	1st	2nd	3rd	Win & Pl
Career Total (Turf)	14	1	5	2	32814

72	8/07	Muss	5f	GD	£3886

Total win prize-money £3886

Going (Turf): Sf: 0-3 GS: 0-2 **Gd: 1-3** GF: 0-6 Fm: 0-0
Distance: **5f/6f: 1-14** 7f-8f: 0-0 9f-13f: 0-0 14f+: 0-0
Track : LH: 0-1 RH: 0-1 Tight: 0-0 Gall: 0-1
Aids: Bl: 0-0 Vi: 0-1 Tstrap: 0-0 Ckp: 0-0
Best Rating: **102** 10/07 Asct 5f gd-sft

Very useful; placed in Listed and Group company; effective over 5-6f and acts on most ground; has worn a visor; likes to race prominently.

Cuthbert (IRE)

91(101) (63)**66**

2-y-o ch c Bertolini (USA)-Tequise (IRE) (Victory Note (USA))
W Jarvis The Square Mile Syndicate

Placings:324063**051** (7885)
2009: 5^{3}GF, 6^{2}G, 7^{4}G, 6^{0}GS, 7^{6}GS, 6^{3}GF, **7^{0}**SD, **7^{5}**SD, **7^{1}**SD,

	Starts	1st	2nd	3rd	Win & Pl
Career Total (Turf)	6	0	1	2	2172
Career Total (AW)	3	1	0	0	1638

12/09	Ling	7f	STD	£1637

Total win prize-money £1638

Going (Turf): **Sf: 0-0 GS: 0-2 Gd: 0-2 GF: 0-2 Fm: 0-0**
Distance: 5f/6f: 0-2 **7f-8f: 1-7** 9f-13f: 0-0 14f+: 0-0
Track : **LH: 1-7** RH: 0-0 **Tight: 1-5** Gall: 0-0
Aids: Bl: 0-2 Vi: 0-0 Tstrap: 0-0 Ckp: 0-0
Best Rating: **66** 7/09 Ling 7f good

Modest; stays 7f; acts on good ground.

Cuts Both Ways (USA)

87(73) (31)53

2-y-o b g Johannesburg (USA)-Wise Investor (USA) (Belong To Me (USA))

P F I Cole A D Spence

Placings:4003 **(7056)**

2009: 6^{4}GF, 7^{0}SD, 8^{0}G, 7^{3}GF,

	Starts	1st	2nd	3rd	Win & Pl
Career Total (Turf)	3	0	0	1	614
Career Total (AW)	1	0	0	0	

Going (Turf): Sf: 0-0 GS: 0-0 Gd: 0-1 GF: 0-2 Fm: 0-0
Distance: 5f/6f: 0-1 7f-8f: 0-2 9f-13f: 0-1 14f+: 0-0
Track : LH: 0-1 RH: 0-0 Tight: 0-1 Gall: 0-0
Aids: Bl: 0-1 Vi: 0-0 Tstrap: 0-0 Ckp: 0-0
Best Rating: 53 8/09 Folk 6f gd-fm

Cwm Rhondda (USA)

109(76) (16)79

4-y-o b f Gulch (USA)-Frayne (USA) (Red Ransom (USA))

P W Chapple-Hyam Hinllesham Thoroughbreds

Placings:000025-05114150 **(6003)**

2009: 8^{0}SD, 8^{5}F, 10^{1}GF, 10^{1}G, 12^{4}GF, 10^{1}GF, 9^{5}GF, 10^{0}GF,

	Starts	1st	2nd	3rd	Win & Pl
Career Total (Turf)	13	3	1	0	8005
Career Total (AW)	1	0	0	0	

79 7/09 Yarm 1m2f21y (0-70)H G-F £2719
74 5/09 Yarm 1m2f21y (0-55)H GD £2072
71 5/09 Yarm 1m2f21y (0-60)H G-F £2072
Total win prize-money £6864

Going (Turf): Sf: 0-2 GS: 0-1 Gd: 1-2 GF: 2-7 Fm: 0-1
Distance: 5f/6f: 0-0 7f-8f: 0-2 9f-13f: 3-11 14f+: 0-1
Track : LH: 3-10 RH: 0-3 Tight: 3-6 Gall: 0-2
Aids: Bl: 0-0 Vi: 0-0 Tstrap: 0-0 Ckp: 0-0
Best Rating: 79 7/09 Yarm 1m2f21y gd-fm

Fair; seems best over 1m2f; acts on fast and soft ground; goes well at Yarmouth.

Cwmni

98(95) (50)53

3-y-o b f Auction House (USA)-Sontime (Son Pardo)

B Palling Flying Eight Partnership

Placings:6052-640400100 **(5633)**

2009: 7^{6}SD, 7^{4}SD, 10^{0}SD, 6^{4}F, 7^{0}GF, 6^{0}G, 5^{1}G, 6^{0}G, 6^{0}GS,

	Starts	1st	2nd	3rd	Win & Pl
Career Total (Turf)	7	1	0	0	3479
Career Total (AW)	6	0	1	0	806

53 7/09 Bath 5f161y GD £3238
Total win prize-money £3238

Going (Turf): Sf: 0-0 GS: 0-2 Gd: 1-3 GF: 0-1 Fm: 0-1
Distance: 5f/6f: 1-3 7f-8f: 0-9 9f-13f: 0-1 14f+: 0-0
Track : LH: 1-8 RH: 0-0 Tight: 0-5 Gall: 1-2
Aids: Bl: 0-0 Vi: 0-0 Tstrap: 0-0 Ckp: 0-0
Best Rating: 53 7/09 Bath 5f161y good

Moderate; stays 7f; acts on Polytrack and good ground on turf.

Cyan Eyed

91(92) (65)54

2-y-o b f Orpen (USA)-Morale (Bluebird (USA))

Tom Dascombe Timeform Betfair Racing Club Partnership

Placings:002 **(6970)**

2009: 6^{0}S, 6^{0}G, 5^{2}SD,

	Starts	1st	2nd	3rd	Win & Pl
Career Total (Turf)	2	0	0	0	
Career Total (AW)	1	0	1	0	605

Going (Turf): Sf: 0-1 GS: 0-0 Gd: 0-1 GF: 0-0 Fm: 0-0
Distance: 5f/6f: 0-1 7f-8f: 0-2 9f-13f: 0-0 14f+: 0-0
Track : LH: 0-0 RH: 0-1 Tight: 0-0 Gall: 0-0
Aids: Bl: 0-0 Vi: 0-0 Tstrap: 0-0 Ckp: 0-0
Best Rating: 65 10/09 Kemp 5f stand

Modest; effective over 5f; acts on Polytrack.

Cyber Space

87(88) (52)32

5-y-o b g Medicean-Coyaima (GER) (Night Shift (USA))

B J McMath Cyber Space Partnership

Placings:0004 **(4538)**

2009: 8^{0}SD, 7^{0}SD, 10^{0}GF, 10^{4}SD,

	Starts	1st	2nd	3rd	Win & Pl
Career Total (Turf)	1	0	0	0	
Career Total (AW)	3	0	0	0	0

Going (Turf): Sf: 0-0 GS: 0-0 Gd: 0-0 GF: 0-1 Fm: 0-0
Distance: 5f/6f: 0-0 7f-8f: 0-2 9f-13f: 0-2 14f+: 0-0
Track : LH: 0-4 RH: 0-0 Tight: 0-4 Gall: 0-0
Aids: Bl: 0-0 Vi: 0-0 Tstrap: 0-0 Ckp: 0-0
Best Rating: 52 8/09 Ling 1m2f stand

Cyborg

104(97) (84)84

5-y-o ch g Halling (USA)-Ciboure (Norwick (USA))

C Byrnes (D R C Elsworth 12/10) Patrick Wilmott

Placings:6630-453315354 **(6724)**

2009: 11^{4}GS, 12^{5}GF, 12^{3}GF, 12^{3}GF, 13^{1}GF, 16^{5}GS, 12^{3}G, 14^{5}G, 12^{4}SD,

	Starts	1st	2nd	3rd	Win & Pl
Career Total (Turf)	11	1	0	4	6443
Career Total (AW)	2	0	0	0	351

84 7/09 Newb 1m5f61y (0-75)H G-F £3238
Total win prize-money £3238

Going (Turf): Sf: 0-0 GS: 0-3 Gd: 0-2 GF: 1-6 Fm: 0-0
Distance: 5f/6f: 0-0 7f-8f: 0-0 9f-13f: 0-9 14f+: 1-4
Track : LH: 1-7 RH: 0-5 Tight: 0-4 Gall: 1-5
Aids: Bl: 0-0 Vi: 0-0 Tstrap: 0-0 Ckp: 0-0
Best Rating: 84 10/09 Kemp 1m4f stand

Useful; stays 1m5f and acts on fast ground.

Cyflymder (IRE)

103(97) (83)99

3-y-o b g Mujadil (USA)-Nashwan Star (IRE) (Nashwan (USA))

R Hannon Amblestock Partnership

Placings:04100-1041112432U0 **(7294)**

2009: 7^{1}SD, 7^{0}SD, 6^{4}GF, 7^{1}GF, 7^{1}GF, 7^{1}G, 8^{2}GS, 7^{4}GF, 7^{3}G, 7^{2}GF, 7^{U}GS, 7^{0}S,

	Starts	1st	2nd	3rd	Win & Pl
Career Total (Turf)	15	4	2	1	29673
Career Total (AW)	2	1	0	0	4857

95 7/09 Sand 7f16y (0-95)H GD £7477
93 6/09 NmkJ 7f (0-85)H G-F £6476
85 6/09 Sand 7f16y (0-85)H G-F £5180
83 3/09 Ling 7f (0-85)H STD £4857
77 8/08 Ches 6f18y SFT £3238
Total win prize-money £27229

Going (Turf): Sf: 1-2 GS: 0-2 Gd: 1-5 GF: 2-6 Fm: 0-0
Distance: 5f/6f: 0-3 7f-8f: 5-13 9f-13f: 0-1 14f+: 0-0
Track : LH: 2-8 RH: 2-3 Tight: 2-4 Gall: 0-0
Aids: Bl: 0-0 Vi: 0-0 Tstrap: 0-0 Ckp: 0-0
Best Rating: 99 9/09 Ches 7f122y gd-fm

Very useful; effective over 6f-7f; acts on fast and soft ground and Polytrack.

Cyfrwys (IRE)

81(96) (52)52

8-y-o b m Foxhound (USA)-Divine Elegance (IRE) (College Chapel)

B Palling Bryn Palling

Placings:42524/022606106/534102450020/50006/266046 6/0403030-60000 **(2352)**

2009: 8^{6}SD, 7^{0}SD, 7^{0}SD, 7^{0}GF, 8^{0}GF,

	Starts	1st	2nd	3rd	Win & Pl
Career Total (Turf)	34	2	6	3	12798
Career Total (AW)	16	0	1	0	1500

69 6/05 Chep 6f16y (0-65)H GD £3557
Total win prize-money £3557

Going (Turf): Sf: 0-1 GS: 0-2 Gd: 2-14 GF: 0-16 Fm: 0-1
Distance: 5f/6f: 1-24 7f-8f: 1-25 9f-13f: 0-1 14f+: 0-0
Track : LH: 1-26 RH: 0-3 Tight: 1-15 Gall: 0-6
Aids: Bl: 0-0 Vi: 0-2 Tstrap: 0-18 Ckp: 0-18
Best Rating: 78 10/03 Wind 6f gd-fm

Moderate mare; stays 7f; acts on fast ground.

Cygnet

104 90

3-y-o b c Dansili-Ballet Princess (Muhtarram (USA))

L M Cumani Lady Milford Haven & The Hon Mrs Steel

Placings:01-2 **(6002)**

2009: 10^{2}GF,

	Starts	1st	2nd	3rd	Win & Pl
Career Total (Turf)	3	1	1	0	5651

80 10/08 Nott 1m75y G-S £3412
Total win prize-money £3412

Going (Turf): Sf: 0-0 GS: 1-1 Gd: 0-1 GF: 0-1 Fm: 0-0
Distance: 5f/6f: 0-0 7f-8f: 0-1 9f-13f: 1-2 14f+: 0-0
Track : LH: 1-2 RH: 0-1 Tight: 0-1 Gall: 0-0
Aids: Bl: 0-0 Vi: 0-0 Tstrap: 0-0 Ckp: 0-0
Best Rating: 90 9/09 Yarm 1m2f21y gd-fm

Useful; stays 1m2f and acts on most ground.

Cygnet Committee (IRE)

90 55

2-y-o gr f Kheleyf (USA)-Forest Light (IRE) (Rainbow Quest (USA))

J S Wainwright Charles Wentworth

Placings:00054340060 **(7098)**

2009: 5^{0}G, 7^{0}GF, 6^{0}GF, 5^{5}G, 6^{4}GF, 7^{3}GF, 6^{4}G, 5^{0}GF, 6^{0}GS, 7^{6}GF, 7^{0}G,

	Starts	1st	2nd	3rd	Win & Pl
Career Total (Turf)	11	0	0	1	327

Going (Turf): Sf: 0-0 GS: 0-1 Gd: 0-4 GF: 0-6 Fm: 0-0

Distance: 5f/6f: 0-5 7f-8f: 0-6 9f-13f: 0-0 14f+: 0-0
Track : LH: 0-0 RH: 0-0 Tight: 0-0 Gall: 0-0
Aids: Bl: 0-7 Vi: 0-0 Tstrap: 0-1 Ckp: 0-1
Best Rating: **55** 8/09 Newc 7f gd-fm

Moderate; stays 7f; acts on fast ground; has worn blinkers and cheekpieces.

Cyril The Squirrel

(100) (51)
5-y-o b g Cyrano De Bergerac-All Done (Northern State (USA))
Karen George R E Baskerville

Placings:406/4230-0 (1728)
2009: 10^{0}SD,

	Starts	1st	2nd	3rd	Win & Pl
Career Total (Turf)	0	0	0	0	
Career Total (AW)	8	0	1	1	971

Going (Turf): **Sf: 0-0 GS: 0-0 Gd: 0-0 GF: 0-0 Fm: 0-0**
Distance: 5f/6f: 0-0 7f-8f: 0-1 9f-13f: 0-7 14f+: 0-0
Track : LH: 0-5 RH: 0-3 Tight: 0-5 Gall: 0-0
Aids: Bl: 0-1 Vi: 0-0 Tstrap: 0-2 Ckp: 0-2
Best Rating: **51** 2/08 Ling 1m4f stand

D'Artagnans Dream

98(97) (65)**67**
3-y-o b g Cyrano De Bergerac-Kairine (IRE) (Kahyasi)
G D Blake Adrian Smith

Placings:0006-00066240 (7049)
2009: 9^{0}GF, 8^{0}G, 8^{0}GS, 8^{6}GS, 8^{6}SD, 12^{2}SS, 12^{4}SD, 12^{0}SD,

	Starts	1st	2nd	3rd	Win & Pl
Career Total (Turf)	6	0	0	0	0
Career Total (AW)	6	0	1	0	504

Going (Turf): **Sf: 0-1 GS: 0-3 Gd: 0-1 GF: 0-1 Fm: 0-0**
Distance: 5f/6f: 0-0 7f-8f: 0-4 9f-13f: 0-8 14f+: 0-0
Track : LH: 0-6 RH: 0-3 Tight: 0-6 Gall: 0-0
Aids: Bl: 0-4 Vi: 0-0 Tstrap: 0-2 Ckp: 0-2
Best Rating: **67** 8/08 Newb 7f gd-sft

Moderate; stays 1m4f; acts on Polytrack; has worn blinkers.

D'Urberville

84(89) (56)**55**
2-y-o b g Auction House (USA)-Laser Crystal (IRE) (King's Theatre (IRE))
J R Jenkins (R Ingram 9/6) Mrs Wendy Jenkins

Placings:0050046 (7884)
2009: 5^{0}GF, 6^{0}GF, 7^{5}F, 8^{0}GF, 7^{0}SD, 7^{4}SD, 7^{6}SD,

	Starts	1st	2nd	3rd	Win & Pl
Career Total (Turf)	4	0	0	0	0
Career Total (AW)	3	0	0	0	140

Going (Turf): **Sf: 0-0 GS: 0-0 Gd: 0-0 GF: 0-3 Fm: 0-1**
Distance: 5f/6f: 0-2 7f-8f: 0-5 9f-13f: 0-0 14f+: 0-0
Track : LH: 0-3 RH: 0-1 Tight: 0-2 Gall: 0-0
Aids: Bl: 0-0 Vi: 0-0 Tstrap: 0-0 Ckp: 0-0
Best Rating: **56** 11/09 Ling 7f stand

Da Bomber (IRE)

73(94) (53)**58**
4-y-o b g Tagula (IRE)-Talahari (IRE) (Roi Danzig (USA))
J W Unett Philip Bourchier

Placings:5-00000 (7754)
2009: 8^{0}HY, 8^{0}GS, 7^{0}GF, 9^{0}SD, 8^{0}SD,

	Starts	1st	2nd	3rd	Win & Pl
Career Total (Turf)	4	0	0	0	0
Career Total (AW)	2	0	0	0	

Going (Turf): **Sf: 0-1 GS: 0-1 Gd: 0-0 GF: 0-2 Fm: 0-0**
Distance: 5f/6f: 0-0 7f-8f: 0-2 9f-13f: 0-4 14f+: 0-0
Track : LH: 0-4 RH: 0-1 Tight: 0-2 Gall: 0-0
Aids: Bl: 0-0 Vi: 0-0 Tstrap: 0-0 Ckp: 0-0
Best Rating: **58** 5/08 Leic 7f9y gd-fm

Daaweitza

108(99) (77)**94**
6-y-o ch g Daawe (USA)-Chichen Itza (Shareef Dancer (USA))
B Ellison Mrs Andrea M Mallinson

Placings:6006200**404/15**0622312106/003151360**4**0/06014 1100600430-000630224050150204**533** (7724)
2009: 10^{0}G, 8^{0}GF, 7^{0}GF, 8^{6}G, 7^{3}G, 7^{0}GF, 8^{2}GF, 7^{2}G, 7^{4}G, 6^{0}G, 6^{5}G, 7^{0}G, 10^{1}GF, 8^{5}GF, **9**^{0}SD, 8^{2}GF, 10^{0}S, 8^{4}GF, **12**^{5}SD, **16**^{3}SD, 12^{3}SD,

	Starts	1st	2nd	3rd	Win & Pl
Career Total (Turf)	58	7	7	5	73716
Career Total (AW)	11	2	0	2	7989

83	8/09	Rdcr	1m2f	(0-75)H	G-F	£3123
94	6/08	Ches	7f2y	(0-95)H	G-F	£8200
86	5/08	Catt	7f	(0-90)H	G-F	£7771
87	5/08	Catt	7f	(0-80)H	GD	£4209
87	5/07	Hayd	1m30y	(0-90)H	G-F	£9715
83	5/07	Muss	7f30y	(0-90)H	G-F	£8413
79	8/06	Rdcr	1m	(0-85)H	G-F	£6477
82	7/06	Wolv	1m141y	(0-75)H	STD	£3238
75	1/06	Sthl	1m		STD	£3238

Total win prize-money £54387

Going (Turf): Sf: 0-8 GS: 0-7 Gd: 1-18 **GF: 6-24** Fm: 0-1
Distance: 5f/6f: 0-8 **7f-8f: 6-37** 9f-13f: 3-23 14f+: 0-1
Track : **LH: 7-31** RH: 1-11 **Tight: 6-20** Gall: 0-3
Aids: **Bl: 1-11** Vi: 0-1 Tstrap: 0-3 Ckp: 0-3
Best Rating: **94** 6/08 Ches 7f2y gd-fm

Fair; effective over 7f-1m; acts on most ground on turf; goes on sand; has been tried in most headgear.

Dabbers Ridge (IRE)

102(101) (83)**93**
7-y-o b h Indian Ridge-Much Commended (Most Welcome)
I W McInnes M Shirley

Placings:0/22132442/31130153/03000160/10600000-0040013160**640**050 (7719)
2009: 7^{0}SD, 8^{0}GF, 7^{4}G, 7^{0}GS, **7**^{0}SD, 7^{1}GF, **7**^{3}SD, 7^{1}F, 9^{6}G, 8^{0}GF, 8^{6}SS, 7^{4}SS, 7^{0}S, **7**^{0}SD, **7**^{5}SD, **9**^{0}SD,

	Starts	1st	2nd	3rd	Win & Pl
Career Total (Turf)	41	8	4	5	177619
Career Total (AW)	8	0	0	1	302

71	7/09	Rdcr	7f		FRM	£2914
81	6/09	Rdcr	7f		G-F	£2590
106	4/08	Wwck	7f26y		SFT	£6799
109	9/07	Hayd	6f	(0-100)H	SFT	£12954
109	7/06	Asct	7f	H	G-F	£93480
108	5/06	Ches	7f122y	(0-100)H	G-S	£14826
99	4/06	Thsk	7f	(0-90)H	GD	£11658
83	5/05	York	7f		SFT	£7189

Total win prize-money £152412

Going (Turf): **Sf: 3-9** GS: 1-7 Gd: 1-14 GF: 2-9 Fm: 1-2
Distance: 5f/6f: 1-4 **7f-8f: 7-43** 9f-13f: 0-2 14f+: 0-0
Track : **LH: 4-20** RH: 0-4 **Tight: 2-12** Gall: 1-5
Aids: Bl: 0-2 Vi: 0-0 Tstrap: 0-1 Ckp: 0-1
Best Rating: **109** 9/07 Hayd 6f soft

Very useful; seems best over 6f-7f; acts on fast ground but better on a soft surface; has worn cheekpieces.

Daddy Cool

(91) (37)**82**
5-y-o b g Kyllachy-Addicted To Love (Touching Wood (USA))
W G M Turner Mascalls Stud

Placings:63/124116000/0000000-0 (0096)
2009: 5^{0}SD,

	Starts	1st	2nd	3rd	Win & Pl
Career Total (Turf)	7	1	0	0	7772
Career Total (AW)	12	2	1	1	7274

82	4/07	Thsk	5f	(0-90)H	FRM	£7772
75	3/07	Kemp	5f	(0-70)H	STD	£2914
66	1/07	Kemp	5f		STD	£2914

Total win prize-money £13602

Going (Turf): Sf: 0-0 GS: 0-1 Gd: 0-1 GF: 0-4 **Fm: 1-1**
Distance: **5f/6f: 3-18** 7f-8f: 0-1 9f-13f: 0-0 14f+: 0-0
Track : LH: 0-9 **RH: 2-4** Tight: 0-8 Gall: 0-1
Aids: Bl: 0-2 Vi: 0-1 Tstrap: 0-1 Ckp: 0-1
Best Rating: **82** 4/07 Thsk 5f firm

Daddy's Gift (IRE)

102(113) (91)**84**
3-y-o b f Trans Island-Lady Corduff (IRE) (Titus Livius (FR))
R Hannon Charlee & Hollie Allan

Placings:33**1**0**3**631300-**21**003505600**31** (7613)
2009: **6**^{2}SD, **6**^{1}SD, 7^{0}GS, 6^{0}GF, 6^{3}GF, 6^{5}G, 6^{0}GF, 7^{5}GF, 7^{6}GF, 6^{0}SD, **6**^{0}SD, 8^{3}SD, **6**^{1}SD,

	Starts	1st	2nd	3rd	Win & Pl
Career Total (Turf)	16	1	0	5	6793
Career Total (AW)	8	3	1	2	20897

91	12/09	Kemp	6f	(0-85)H	STD	£4727
90	3/09	Kemp	6f	(0-105)H	STD	£11215
81	9/08	Folk	6f		SFT	£3885
76	6/08	Ling	6f		STD	£2266

Total win prize-money £22096

Going (Turf): **Sf: 1-3** GS: 0-2 Gd: 0-2 GF: 0-9 Fm: 0-0
Distance: **5f/6f: 4-15** 7f-8f: 0-9 9f-13f: 0-0 14f+: 0-0
Track : LH: 1-4 **RH: 2-7 Tight: 1-4** Gall: 0-2
Aids: Bl: 0-0 Vi: 0-1 Tstrap: 0-0 Ckp: 0-0
Best Rating: **91** 12/09 Kemp 6f stand

Useful; effective over 6f-7f; acts on most ground; goes on Polytrack; has worn a visor.

Dado Mush

91(104) (50)**42**
6-y-o b g Almushtarak (IRE)-Princess Of Spain (King Of Spain)
T T Clement John W Barnard

Placings:00/**6**41460**000**/003**0111/131206**0**06-0**00**030** (7784)
2009: **8**^{0}SD, 8^{0}G, **9**^{0}SD, **8**^{0}SD, **12**^{3}SD, **8**^{0}SD,

	Starts	1st	2nd	3rd	Win & Pl
Career Total (Turf)	12	1	0	1	4935
Career Total (AW)	21	5	1	2	15890

79 5/08 Sthl 1m (0-85)H STD £5504
79 1/08 Sthl 1m (0-70)H STD £2593
74 12/07 Sthl 1m (0-57)H STD £2047
71 12/07 Sthl 1m (0-65)H SS £2047
65 12/07 Sthl 1m (0-62)H STD £2047
59 7/06 Ripn 1m GD £4533
Total win prize-money £18777

Going (Turf): Sf: 0-2 GS: 0-1 **Gd: 1-5** GF: 0-3 Fm: 0-1
Distance: 5f/6f: 0-1 **7f-8f: 6-23** 9f-13f: 0-9 14f+: 0-0
Track : **LH: 5-22** RH: 1-6 **Tight: 1-5** Gall: 0-2
Aids: Bl: 0-0 Vi: 0-1 Tstrap: 5-19 Ckp: 5-19
Best Rating: **79** 5/08 Sthl 1m stand

Fair; suited by 1m but stays further; acts on easy ground and on Fibresand; wears cheekpieces.

Dafeef

100 **87**
2-y-o b c Medicean-Almahab (USA) (Danzig (USA))
Saeed Bin Suroor Godolphin

Placings:21 (5431)
2009: 6^{2}GF, 6^{1}G,

	Starts	1st	2nd	3rd	Win & Pl
Career Total (Turf)	2	1	1	0	6578

87 8/09 NmkJ 6f GD £5180
Total win prize-money £5181

Going (Turf): Sf: 0-0 GS: 0-0 **Gd: 1-1** GF: 0-1 Fm: 0-0
Distance: **5f/6f: 1-2** 7f-8f: 0-0 9f-13f: 0-0 14f+: 0-0
Track : LH: 0-0 RH: 0-0 Tight: 0-0 Gall: 0-0
Aids: Bl: 0-0 Vi: 0-0 Tstrap: 0-0 Ckp: 0-0
Best Rating: **87** 8/09 NmkJ 6f good

Useful; suited by 6f and fast ground.

Daft Lad

80(58) **54**
2-y-o b/br c Danbird (AUS)-Stolen Melody (Robellino (USA))
L A Mullaney Bavill & White

Placings:000000 (5519)
2009: 5^{0}GF, 5^{0}GS, 5^{0}SD, 5^{0}GF, 5^{0}G, 6^{0}G,

	Starts	1st	2nd	3rd	Win & Pl
Career Total (Turf)	5	0	0	0	
Career Total (AW)	1	0	0	0	

Going (Turf): **Sf: 0-0 GS: 0-1 Gd: 0-2 GF: 0-2 Fm: 0-0**
Distance: 5f/6f: 0-6 7f-8f: 0-0 9f-13f: 0-0 14f+: 0-0
Track : LH: 0-0 RH: 0-0 Tight: 0-0 Gall: 0-0
Aids: Bl: 0-0 Vi: 0-3 Tstrap: 0-0 Ckp: 0-0
Best Rating: **54** 8/09 Bevl 5f good

Daggerman

(99) (55)**36**
4-y-o ch g Daggers Drawn (USA)-Another Mans Cause (FR) (Highest Honor (FR))
R Curtis John Wardle

Placings:00/30-000 (0674)
2009: 12^{0}SD, 12^{0}SD, 8^{0}SD,

	Starts	1st	2nd	3rd	Win & Pl
Career Total (Turf)	1	0	0	0	
Career Total (AW)	6	0	0	1	403

Going (Turf): **Sf: 0-0 GS: 0-0 Gd: 0-0 GF: 0-1 Fm: 0-0**
Distance: 5f/6f: 0-1 7f-8f: 0-4 9f-13f: 0-2 14f+: 0-0
Track : LH: 0-5 RH: 0-2 Tight: 0-1 Gall: 0-0
Aids: Bl: 0-0 Vi: 0-0 Tstrap: 0-0 Ckp: 0-0
Best Rating: **55** 11/08 Sthl 7f stand

Modest; stays 7f and acts on Fibresand.

Dahaam

90(97) (79)**76**
2-y-o b c Red Ransom (USA)-Almansoora (USA) (Bahri (USA))
Saeed Bin Suroor Godolphin

Placings:221 (6772)
2009: 7^{2}G, 8^{2}SD, 8^{1}SD,

	Starts	1st	2nd	3rd	Win & Pl
Career Total (Turf)	1	0	1	0	1060
Career Total (AW)	2	1	1	0	5475

79 10/09 Kemp 1m STD £3885
Total win prize-money £3886

Going (Turf): **Sf: 0-0 GS: 0-0 Gd: 0-1 GF: 0-0 Fm: 0-0**
Distance: 5f/6f: 0-0 **7f-8f: 1-3** 9f-13f: 0-0 14f+: 0-0
Track : LH: 0-1 **RH: 1-2** Tight: 0-0 Gall: 0-0
Aids: Bl: 0-0 Vi: 0-0 Tstrap: 0-0 Ckp: 0-0
Best Rating: **79** 10/09 Kemp 1m stand

Promising debut over 7f on good ground.

Dahakaa

90(98) (79)**78**
2-y-o ch c Bertolini (USA)-Dorrati (USA) (Dubai Millennium)
M A Jarvis Sheikh Ahmed Al Maktoum

Placings:31 (4856)
2009: 5^{3}GF, 5^{1}SD,

	Starts	1st	2nd	3rd	Win & Pl
Career Total (Turf)	1	0	0	1	770
Career Total (AW)	1	1	0	0	4209

79 8/09 Wolv 5f216y STD £4209
Total win prize-money £4209

Going (Turf): **Sf: 0-0 GS: 0-0 Gd: 0-0 GF: 0-1 Fm: 0-0**
Distance: **5f/6f: 1-2** 7f-8f: 0-0 9f-13f: 0-0 14f+: 0-0
Track : **LH: 1-1** RH: 0-0 **Tight: 1-1** Gall: 0-0
Aids: Bl: 0-0 Vi: 0-0 Tstrap: 0-0 Ckp: 0-0
Best Rating: **79** 8/09 Wolv 5f216y stand

Fair; stays 6f and acts on Polytrack.

Dahama

63(84) (40)**64**
3-y-o b f Green Desert (USA)-Darling Flame (USA) (Capote (USA))
C E Brittain Saeed Manana

Placings:050-40 (3010)
2009: 7^{4}SD, 6^{0}G,

	Starts	1st	2nd	3rd	Win & Pl
Career Total (Turf)	4	0	0	0	0
Career Total (AW)	1	0	0	0	0

Going (Turf): **Sf: 0-0 GS: 0-0 Gd: 0-4 GF: 0-0 Fm: 0-0**
Distance: 5f/6f: 0-1 7f-8f: 0-4 9f-13f: 0-0 14f+: 0-0
Track : LH: 0-2 RH: 0-0 Tight: 0-0 Gall: 0-0
Aids: Bl: 0-0 Vi: 0-0 Tstrap: 0-0 Ckp: 0-0
Best Rating: **64** 9/08 Wwck 7f26y good

Dahes (IRE)

82 **58**
2-y-o b c Azamour (IRE)-Delphie Queen (IRE) (Desert Sun)
A Al Raihe (B Smart 12/8) Ali Rashid Al Raihe

Placings:503
2009: 6^{5}GF, 7^{0}G, 6^{3}FT,

	Starts	1st	2nd	3rd	Win & Pl
Career Total (Turf)	2	0	0	0	0
Career Total (AW)	1	0	0	1	1250

Going (Turf): **Sf: 0-0 GS: 0-0 Gd: 0-1 GF: 0-1 Fm: 0-0**
Distance: 5f/6f: 0-1 7f-8f: 0-2 9f-13f: 0-0 14f+: 0-0
Track : LH: 0-0 RH: 0-1 Tight: 0-0 Gall: 0-0
Aids: Bl: 0-0 Vi: 0-0 Tstrap: 0-0 Ckp: 0-0
Best Rating: **58** 6/09 Haml 6f5y gd-fm

Daily Double

99(99) (63)**60**
3-y-o gr g Needwood Blade-Coffee To Go (Environment Friend)
H J Manners (D K Ivory 24/6) Exors Of The Late H J Manners

Placings:0554000-551360002 (3257)
2009: 7^{5}SD, 7^{5}SD, 8^{1}SD, 10^{3}G, 8^{6}SD, 8^{0}G, 10^{0}GF, 10^{0}SD, 8^{2}F,

	Starts	1st	2nd	3rd	Win & Pl
Career Total (Turf)	7	0	1	1	981
Career Total (AW)	9	1	0	0	2240

63 3/09 Ling 1m STD £2047
Total win prize-money £2047

Going (Turf): **Sf: 0-1 GS: 0-1 Gd: 0-2 GF: 0-2 Fm: 0-1**
Distance: 5f/6f: 0-4 **7f-8f: 1-7** 9f-13f: 0-5 14f+: 0-0
Track : **LH: 1-7** RH: 0-7 **Tight: 1-8** Gall: 0-2
Aids: Bl: 0-1 Vi: 0-0 Tstrap: 0-0 Ckp: 0-0
Best Rating: **63** 3/09 Ling 1m stand

Modest; stays 1m and acts on Polytrack.

Daily Planet (IRE)

(85) (35)**40**
3-y-o ch g Titus Livius (FR)-Flattering News (USA) (Pleasant Colony (USA))
B W Duke Brendan W Duke Racing

Placings:000000500-P (4240)
2009: 7^{P}F,

	Starts	1st	2nd	3rd	Win & Pl
Career Total (Turf)	7	0	0	0	
Career Total (AW)	3	0	0	0	0

Going (Turf): **Sf: 0-2 GS: 0-0 Gd: 0-2 GF: 0-2 Fm: 0-1**
Distance: 5f/6f: 0-0 7f-8f: 0-7 9f-13f: 0-3 14f+: 0-0
Track : LH: 0-4 RH: 0-3 Tight: 0-2 Gall: 0-0
Aids: Bl: 0-0 Vi: 0-1 Tstrap: 0-3 Ckp: 0-3
Best Rating: **40** 7/08 Sand 7f16y gd-fm

Daisy Brown

89 **52**
2-y-o b f Exceed And Excel (AUS)-Hazy Heights (Shirley Heights)
N Tinkler Mrs Beverley Brown

Placings:5024660 (6589)

2009: 5^{5}G, 6^{0}G, 5^{2}G, 5^{4}GF, 5^{6}G, 5^{6}GF, 6^{0}GS,

	Starts	1st	2nd	3rd	Win & Pl
Career Total (Turf)	7	0	1	0	1022

Going (Turf): Sf: 0-0 GS: 0-1 Gd: 0-4 GF: 0-2 Fm: 0-0
Distance: 5f/6f: 0-6 7f-8f: 0-1 9f-13f: 0-0 14f+: 0-0
Track : LH: 0-0 RH: 0-0 Tight: 0-0 Gall: 0-0
Aids: Bl: 0-0 Vi: 0-0 Tstrap: 0-0 Ckp: 0-0
Best Rating: 52 8/09 Bevl 5f good

Daisy Moses (IRE)

88(94) (51)74
3-y-o br f Mull Of Kintyre (USA)-Starring (FR) (Ashkalani (IRE))
D Nicholls Mrs Trisha Laughton

Placings:10-0006 (3953)
2009: 5^{0}GF, 7^{0}S, 5^{0}SD, 6^{6}SD,

	Starts	1st	2nd	3rd	Win & Pl
Career Total (Turf)	4	1	0	0	3238
Career Total (AW)	2	0	0	0	0

74 5/08 Donc 5f GD £3238
Total win prize-money £3238

Going (Turf): Sf: 0-1 GS: 0-0 Gd: 1-1 GF: 0-1 Fm: 0-1
Distance: 5f/6f: 1-5 7f-8f: 0-1 9f-13f: 0-0 14f+: 0-0
Track : LH: 0-3 RH: 0-0 Tight: 0-1 Gall: 0-0
Aids: Bl: 0-0 Vi: 0-0 Tstrap: 0-0 Ckp: 0-0
Best Rating: 74 5/08 Donc 5f good

Useful prospect; debut winner at Doncaster over 5f on good ground.

Daisys Fantasy

4-y-o br f Diktat-Double Fantasy (Mind Games)
S Parr Willie McKay

Placings:6 (0488)
2009: 8^{6}SS,

	Starts	1st	2nd	3rd	Win & Pl
Career Total (Turf)	0	0	0	0	
Career Total (AW)	1	0	0	0	0

Going (Turf): Sf: 0-0 GS: 0-0 Gd: 0-0 GF: 0-0 Fm: 0-0
Distance: 5f/6f: 0-0 7f-8f: 0-1 9f-13f: 0-0 14f+: 0-0
Track : LH: 0-1 RH: 0-0 Tight: 0-0 Gall: 0-0
Aids: Bl: 0-0 Vi: 0-0 Tstrap: 0-0 Ckp: 0-0

Dajen

88(96) (66)40
3-y-o b c Kyllachy-Eau Rouge (Grand Lodge (USA))
D M Simcock Tick Tock Partnership

Placings:0064 (7479)
2009: 6^{0}S, 6^{0}G, 7^{6}SD, 7^{4}SD,

	Starts	1st	2nd	3rd	Win & Pl
Career Total (Turf)	2	0	0	0	
Career Total (AW)	2	0	0	0	0

Going (Turf): Sf: 0-1 GS: 0-0 Gd: 0-1 GF: 0-0 Fm: 0-0
Distance: 5f/6f: 0-1 7f-8f: 0-3 9f-13f: 0-0 14f+: 0-0
Track : LH: 0-1 RH: 0-1 Tight: 0-1 Gall: 0-1
Aids: Bl: 0-0 Vi: 0-0 Tstrap: 0-0 Ckp: 0-0
Best Rating: 66 11/09 Kemp 7f stand

Modest; effective over 7f; acts on Polytrack.

Dakiyah (IRE)

102(109) (93)89
5-y-o b m Observatory (USA)-Darariyna (IRE) (Shirley Heights)
Mrs L J Mongan Mrs P J Sheen

Placings:44221236/0022421-401365 (7589)
2009: 11^{4}GF, 9^{0}GF, 12^{1}SD, 12^{3}G, 14^{6}GF, 12^{5}SD,

	Starts	1st	2nd	3rd	Win & Pl
Career Total (Turf)	14	2	4	2	28090
Career Total (AW)	7	1	2	0	10029

86 6/09 Kemp 1m4f (0-85)H STD £4727
85 6/08 Gdwd 1m1f192y (0-80)H GD £4533
9/07 Nanc 1m1f165y G-S £6418
Total win prize-money £15679

Going (Turf): Sf: 0-1 GS: 1-2 Gd: 1-7 GF: 0-3 Fm: 0-0
Distance: 5f/6f: 0-0 7f-8f: 0-2 9f-13f: 3-18 14f+: 0-1
Track : LH: 0-2 RH: 2-11 Tight: 1-5 Gall: 0-1
Aids: Bl: 0-0 Vi: 0-0 Tstrap: 2-8 Ckp: 2-8
Best Rating: 93 11/09 Kemp 1m4f stand

Fair; ex-French; effective at around 1m4f; acts on Polytrack; has worn cheekpieces.

Dakota Hills

(94) (69)71
3-y-o ch g Danehill Dancer (IRE)-Karla June (Unfuwain (USA))
J R Best D Cunningham, A O'Brien & T Caston

Placings:24202-00 (7518)
2009: 7^{0}SD, 6^{0}SD,

	Starts	1st	2nd	3rd	Win & Pl
Career Total (Turf)	2	0	0	0	0
Career Total (AW)	5	0	3	0	3758

Going (Turf): Sf: 0-0 GS: 0-0 Gd: 0-1 GF: 0-0 Fm: 0-1
Distance: 5f/6f: 0-5 7f-8f: 0-2 9f-13f: 0-0 14f+: 0-0
Track : LH: 0-5 RH: 0-1 Tight: 0-2 Gall: 0-2
Aids: Bl: 0-0 Vi: 0-0 Tstrap: 0-0 Ckp: 0-0
Best Rating: 71 7/08 Ling 5f firm

Fair; suited by 5f-6f; acts on Polytrack.

Dalarossie

99(93) (61)67
4-y-o b g Kyllachy-Damalis (IRE) (Mukaddamah (USA))
E J Alston Liam & Tony Ferguson

Placings:643556/0300416500-00635062024 (6380)
2009: 5^{0}GF, 5^{0}F, 5^{6}GF, 6^{3}GS, 6^{5}G, 6^{0}GF, 5^{6}GF, 5^{2}G, 5^{0}GS, 5^{2}G, 5^{4}GF,

	Starts	1st	2nd	3rd	Win & Pl
Career Total (Turf)	24	1	2	2	5958
Career Total (AW)	3	0	0	1	302

67 8/08 Ripn 5f (0-65)H GD £2590
Total win prize-money £2590

Going (Turf): Sf: 0-4 GS: 0-3 Gd: 1-7 GF: 0-9 Fm: 0-1
Distance: 5f/6f: 1-26 7f-8f: 0-1 9f-13f: 0-0 14f+: 0-0
Track : LH: 0-7 RH: 0-1 Tight: 0-5 Gall: 0-1
Aids: Bl: 0-1 Vi: 0-0 Tstrap: 0-0 Ckp: 0-0
Best Rating: 67 8/08 Ripn 5f good

Modest sprinter; seems best at 5f; acts on good ground; also goes on Polytrack.

Dalepak Flyer (IRE)

85(94) (58)57
3-y-o ch c Noverre (USA)-Hartstown House (IRE) (Primo Dominie)
Paul Mason Mick White

Placings:5400-54000 (3464)
2009: 5^{5}SD, 7^{4}SF, 7^{0}GF, 6^{0}SD, 5^{0}SD,

	Starts	1st	2nd	3rd	Win & Pl
Career Total (Turf)	4	0	0	0	250
Career Total (AW)	5	0	0	0	0

Going (Turf): Sf: 0-1 GS: 0-0 Gd: 0-0 GF: 0-2 Fm: 0-1
Distance: 5f/6f: 0-7 7f-8f: 0-2 9f-13f: 0-0 14f+: 0-0
Track : LH: 0-6 RH: 0-1 Tight: 0-3 Gall: 0-2
Aids: Bl: 0-1 Vi: 0-0 Tstrap: 0-1 Ckp: 0-1
Best Rating: 58 3/09 Wolv 7f32y std-fst

Moderate; stays 7f; acts on Polytrack.

Dalesway

92 66
3-y-o b g Muhtarram (USA)-Si Si Si (Lomitas)
R A Fahey The G-Guck Group

Placings:60-36 (5072)
2009: 8^{3}G, 8^{6}GF,

	Starts	1st	2nd	3rd	Win & Pl
Career Total (Turf)	4	0	0	1	838

Going (Turf): Sf: 0-1 GS: 0-0 Gd: 0-1 GF: 0-2 Fm: 0-0
Distance: 5f/6f: 0-0 7f-8f: 0-1 9f-13f: 0-3 14f+: 0-0
Track : LH: 0-4 RH: 0-0 Tight: 0-1 Gall: 0-0
Aids: Bl: 0-0 Vi: 0-0 Tstrap: 0-0 Ckp: 0-0
Best Rating: 66 7/09 Thsk 1m good

Modest; effective at 1m; acts on good ground.

Dallool

(101) (62)39
8-y-o b g Unfuwain (USA)-Sardonic (Kris)
P M Phelan Celtic Contractors Limited

Placings:5144100/0005/06/00-3 (0668)
2009: 16^{3}SD,

	Starts	1st	2nd	3rd	Win & Pl
Career Total (Turf)	8	2	0	0	12717
Career Total (AW)	8	0	0	1	428

92 8/04 Hayd 1m3f200yD(0-80)H GD £5746
78 4/04 Hayd 1m3f200y D SFT £5395
Total win prize-money £11141

Going (Turf): Sf: 1-2 GS: 0-2 Gd: 1-2 GF: 0-1 Fm: 0-0
Distance: 5f/6f: 0-0 7f-8f: 0-2 9f-13f: 2-13 14f+: 0-1
Track : LH: 2-7 RH: 0-3 Tight: 0-1 Gall: 0-4
Aids: Bl: 0-0 Vi: 0-1 Tstrap: 0-0 Ckp: 0-0
Best Rating: 92 8/04 Hayd 1m3f200y good

Dalmunzie (IRE)

75 16
3-y-o ch f Choisir (AUS)-Berenice (ITY) (Marouble)
J J Quinn Geoffrey Van Cutsem

Placings:00 (2789)
2009: 5^{0}G, 8^{0}G,

	Starts	1st	2nd	3rd	Win & Pl
Career Total (Turf)	2	0	0	0	

Going (Turf): Sf: 0-0 GS: 0-0 Gd: 0-2 GF: 0-0 Fm: 0-0
Distance: 5f/6f: 0-1 7f-8f: 0-1 9f-13f: 0-0 14f+: 0-0
Track : LH: 0-1 RH: 0-0 Tight: 0-1 Gall: 0-0
Aids: Bl: 0-0 Vi: 0-0 Tstrap: 0-0 Ckp: 0-0
Best Rating: 16 5/09 Catt 5f212y good

Dalradian (IRE)

101(98) (92)78
3-y-o b g Dansili-Aethra (USA) (Trempolino (USA))
W J Knight Canisbay Bloodstock

Placings:0640-1026103 (3988)
2009: 8^{1}SD, 7^{0}GS, 8^{2}GF, 8^{6}GF, 8^{1}SD, 8^{0}G, 8^{3}SD,

	Starts	1st	2nd	3rd	Win & Pl
Career Total (Turf)	7	0	1	0	1445
Career Total (AW)	4	2	0	1	10099

88 5/09 Ling 1m (0-85)H STD £5828
75 3/09 Ling 1m STD £2729
Total win prize-money £8558

Going (Turf): Sf: 0-0 GS: 0-2 Gd: 0-2 GF: 0-3 Fm: 0-0
Distance: 5f/6f: 0-1 7f-8f: 2-8 9f-13f: 0-2 14f+: 0-0
Track : LH: 2-4 RH: 0-2 Tight: 2-4 Gall: 0-0
Aids: Bl: 0-0 Vi: 0-0 Tstrap: 0-0 Ckp: 0-0
Best Rating: 92 7/09 Ling 1m stand

Fair; stays 1m; acts on fast ground; goes on Polytrack.

Dalrymple (IRE)

93(94) (55)55
3-y-o ch g Daylami (IRE)-Dallaah (Green Desert (USA))
M Madgwick (Ian Williams 7/6) Collingwood Investment Properties Ltd

Placings:601050600600 (7549)
2009: 8^{6}SD, 12^{0}SD, 10^{1}G, 11^{0}GF, 10^{5}GF, 9^{0}GF, 6^{6}G, 12^{0}SD, 9^{0}GF, 9^{6}GS, 11^{0}G, 12^{0}SD,

	Starts	1st	2nd	3rd	Win & Pl
Career Total (Turf)	8	1	0	0	2730
Career Total (AW)	4	0	0	0	0

55 4/09 Wind 1m2f7y GD £2729
Total win prize-money £2730

Going (Turf): Sf: 0-0 GS: 0-1 Gd: 1-3 GF: 0-4 Fm: 0-0
Distance: 5f/6f: 0-0 7f-8f: 0-1 9f-13f: 1-11 14f+: 0-0
Track : LH: 0-8 RH: 1-3 Tight: 1-8 Gall: 0-0
Aids: Bl: 0-0 Vi: 0-1 Tstrap: 0-0 Ckp: 0-0
Best Rating: 55 4/09 Wind 1m2f7y good

Modest; stays 1m2f; acts on a sound surface.

Daltaban (FR)

81(87) (32)85
5-y-o ch g Rainbow Quest (USA)-Daltaiyma (IRE) (Doyoun)
P Salmon Ann And Eric Lumley

Placings:641/000-0006 (7712)
2009: 18^{0}G, 15^{0}S, 8^{0}SD, 12^{6}SD,

	Starts	1st	2nd	3rd	Win & Pl
Career Total (Turf)	7	1	0	0	8514
Career Total (AW)	3	0	0	0	0

84 6/07 Chan 1m2f110y SFT £7095
Total win prize-money £7095

Going (Turf): Sf: 1-4 GS: 0-1 Gd: 0-1 GF: 0-1 Fm: 0-0
Distance: 5f/6f: 0-0 7f-8f: 0-1 9f-13f: 1-6 14f+: 0-3
Track : LH: 0-4 RH: 1-4 Tight: 0-2 Gall: 0-2
Aids: Bl: 1-3 Vi: 0-1 Tstrap: 0-0 Ckp: 0-0
Best Rating: 85 5/08 Gdwd 1m4f soft

Fair; better known as a hurdler; effective at around 1m4f; acts on soft ground; has worn blinkers.

Damaniyat Girl (USA)

108(99) (79)106
3-y-o ch f Elusive Quality (USA)-Dabaweyaa (Shareef Dancer (USA))
W J Haggas Mohamed Obaida

Placings:21-25024201 (6814)
2009: 7^{2}GF, 7^{5}GF, 8^{0}GF, 7^{2}GF, 8^{4}GF, 8^{2}G, 8^{0}G, 6^{1}G,

	Starts	1st	2nd	3rd	Win & Pl
Career Total (Turf)	9	1	4	0	119512
Career Total (AW)	1	1	0	0	3562

103 10/09 NmkR 6f GD £22708
79 10/08 Kemp 6f STD £3561
Total win prize-money £26270

Going (Turf): Sf: 0-0 GS: 0-0 Gd: 1-3 GF: 0-6 Fm: 0-0
Distance: 5f/6f: 2-3 7f-8f: 0-6 9f-13f: 0-1 14f+: 0-0
Track : LH: 0-2 RH: 1-3 Tight: 0-1 Gall: 0-1
Aids: Bl: 1-5 Vi: 0-0 Tstrap: 0-0 Ckp: 0-0
Best Rating: 106 9/09 Veli 1m good

Smart; placed in Group 3 company; Listed winner; effective over 6f-1m; acts on fast ground; goes on Polytrack; has worn blinkers.

Damascus Gold

78 54
5-y-o b h Thowra (FR)-Damasquiner (Casteddu)
Miss Z C Davison Miss P I Westbrook

Placings:0/540-00 (6692)
2009: 11^{0}GF, 16^{0}GS,

	Starts	1st	2nd	3rd	Win & Pl
Career Total (Turf)	6	0	0	0	192

Going (Turf): Sf: 0-1 GS: 0-3 Gd: 0-1 GF: 0-1 Fm: 0-0
Distance: 5f/6f: 0-0 7f-8f: 0-0 9f-13f: 0-5 14f+: 0-1
Track : LH: 0-1 RH: 0-5 Tight: 0-4 Gall: 0-1
Aids: Bl: 0-3 Vi: 0-0 Tstrap: 0-2 Ckp: 0-2
Best Rating: 61 4/08 Folk 1m4f gd-sft

Dame Anouska (IRE)

90 (60)78
3-y-o b f Exceed And Excel (AUS)-True Joy (IRE) (Zilzal (USA))
E J O'Neill Frank Cosgrove

Placings:24525201 (7386a)
2009: 7^{2}GF, 8^{4}S, 8^{5}VS, 9^{2}S, 9^{5}G, 7^{2}F, 9^{0}SD, 8^{1}HY,

	Starts	1st	2nd	3rd	Win & Pl
Career Total (Turf)	7	1	3	0	19895
Career Total (AW)	1	0	0	0	

67 11/09 MsnL 1m HVY £10194
Total win prize-money £10194

Going (Turf): Sf: 1-3 GS: 0-0 Gd: 0-1 GF: 0-1 Fm: 0-1
Distance: 5f/6f: 0-0 7f-8f: 1-5 9f-13f: 0-3 14f+: 0-0
Track : LH: 0-2 RH: 0-0 Tight: 0-1 Gall: 0-0
Aids: Bl: 0-0 Vi: 0-0 Tstrap: 1-1 Ckp: 1-1
Best Rating: 78 10/09 Mans 7f firm

Modest; effective at 7f, appears to stays further; acts on fast ground and handles soft.

Dame Shanakill (USA)

(83) (36)
2-y-o ch f Mr Greeley (USA)-Innovate (USA) (Relaunch (USA))
H R A Cecil Mogeely Stud & Mrs Maura Gittins

Placings:0 (7050)
2009: 7^{0}SD,

	Starts	1st	2nd	3rd	Win & Pl
Career Total (Turf)	0	0	0	0	
Career Total (AW)	1	0	0	0	

Going (Turf): Sf: 0-0 GS: 0-0 Gd: 0-0 GF: 0-0 Fm: 0-0
Distance: 5f/6f: 0-0 7f-8f: 0-1 9f-13f: 0-0 14f+: 0-0
Track : LH: 0-0 RH: 0-1 Tight: 0-0 Gall: 0-0
Aids: Bl: 0-0 Vi: 0-0 Tstrap: 0-0 Ckp: 0-0
Best Rating: 36 10/09 Kemp 7f stand

Dametime (IRE)

100(103) (78)78
3-y-o b f Danetime (IRE)-Fee Eria (FR) (Always Fair (USA))
Daniel Mark Loughnane Brian Forkan

Placings:506305-6061102600400 (6833a)
2009: 6^{6}SD, 7^{0}HY, 6^{6}SD, 6^{1}G, 6^{1}SD, 6^{0}G, 6^{2}G, 6^{6}S, 6^{0}YS, 6^{0}S, 6^{4}SD, 5^{0}SD, 5^{0}SD,

	Starts	1st	2nd	3rd	Win & Pl
Career Total (Turf)	13	1	1	1	6372
Career Total (AW)	6	1	0	0	3589

77 6/09 Ling 6f (0-75)H STD £3238
73 5/09 Chep 6f16y (0-70)H GD £2914
Total win prize-money £6152

Going (Turf): Sf: 0-6 GS: 0-0 Gd: 1-3 GF: 0-1 Fm: 0-0
Distance: 5f/6f: 1-16 7f-8f: 1-3 9f-13f: 0-0 14f+: 0-0
Track : LH: 1-10 RH: 0-1 Tight: 1-2 Gall: 0-0
Aids: Bl: 0-0 Vi: 0-0 Tstrap: 0-0 Ckp: 0-0
Best Rating: 78 9/09 Kemp 6f stand

Fair; suited by 6f; acts on good and soft ground and Polytrack; has worn a tongue tie.

Damien (IRE)

102(102) (98)108
3-y-o gr c Namid-Miss Shaan (FR) (Darshaan)
B W Hills The Hon Mrs J M Corbett & C Wright

Placings:14240-4630 (3747)
2009: 7^{4}SD, 6^{6}GF, 6^{3}G, 6^{0}G,

	Starts	1st	2nd	3rd	Win & Pl
Career Total (Turf)	8	1	1	1	88502
Career Total (AW)	1	0	0	0	3222

79 7/08 Wind 6f G-F £4209
Total win prize-money £4209

Going (Turf): Sf: 0-1 GS: 0-1 Gd: 0-4 GF: 1-2 Fm: 0-0
Distance: 5f/6f: 1-6 7f-8f: 0-3 9f-13f: 0-0 14f+: 0-0
Track : LH: 0-1 RH: 0-0 Tight: 0-1 Gall: 1-1
Aids: Bl: 0-0 Vi: 0-0 Tstrap: 0-0 Ckp: 0-0
Best Rating: 108 9/08 Newb 6f8y good

Smart half-brother to a winning sprinter and winning miler in France: successful on debut over 6f on fast ground and good efforts in defeat in sales races afterwards; acts on fast and soft ground.

Damietta (USA)

94(91) (79)75

2-y-o b f More Than Ready (USA)-Dixie Eyes Blazing (USA) (Gone West (USA))

Saeed Bin Suroor Godolphin

Placings:3100 **(5797)**

2009: 6^{3}G, 7^{1}SD, 7^{0}GF, 6^{0}GF,

	Starts	1st	2nd	3rd	Win & Pl
Career Total (Turf)	3	0	0	1	1926
Career Total (AW)	1	1	0	0	3886

79 8/09 Kemp 7f STD £3885

Total win prize-money £3886

Going (Turf): **Sf: 0-0 GS: 0-0 Gd: 0-1 GF: 0-2 Fm: 0-0**
Distance: 5f/6f: 0-1 **7f-8f: 1-3** 9f-13f: 0-0 14f+: 0-0
Track : LH: 0-0 **RH: 1-1** Tight: 0-0 Gall: 0-0
Aids: Bl: 0-0 Vi: 0-0 Tstrap: 0-0 Ckp: 0-0
Best Rating: **79** 8/09 Kemp 7f stand

Useful; stays 7f and acts on Polytrack.

Damika (IRE)

104(102) (97)111

6-y-o ch g Namid-Emly Express (IRE) (High Estate)

R M Whitaker G B Bedford

Placings:2212/115220310/03200100610/4220316254640-00006043 **(6278)**

2009: 5^{0}G, 7^{0}GF, 7^{0}S, 6^{0}G, 6^{6}GF, 6^{0}GS, 7^{4}G, 7^{3}GF,

	Starts	1st	2nd	3rd	Win & Pl
Career Total (Turf)	40	6	6	4	103957
Career Total (AW)	5	1	3	0	8979

110 7/08 Hayd 6f SFT £15577
99 10/07 NmkR 7f (0-100)H SFT £12464
96 9/07 Ripn 6f (0-90)H G-F £11217
94 8/06 Rdcr 6f (0-85)H GD £6477
81 5/06 Ling 7f (0-70)H GD £3886
75 5/06 Newc 6f (0-70)H G-F £4210
8/05 Mija 5f110y STD £4255

Total win prize-money £58088

Going (Turf): **Sf: 2-9** GS: 0-6 **Gd: 2-12 GF: 2-13** Fm: 0-0
Distance: **5f/6f: 5-29** 7f-8f: 2-15 9f-13f: 0-1 14f+: 0-0
Track : LH: 0-8 RH: 0-2 Tight: 0-2 Gall: 0-2
Aids: Bl: 0-0 Vi: 0-0 Tstrap: 0-1 Ckp: 0-1
Best Rating: **111** 7/08 NmkJ 7f good

Very useful; Listed placed; effective over 6f-7f; acts on most ground, but probably best on soft.

Damini (USA)

94(82) (57)75

3-y-o b f Seeking The Gold (USA)-Dalisay (IRE) (Sadler's Wells (USA))

Sir Michael Stoute Philip Newton

Placings:0250-0 **(2607)**

2009: 8^{0}GF,

	Starts	1st	2nd	3rd	Win & Pl
Career Total (Turf)	4	0	1	0	1558
Career Total (AW)	1	0	0	0	

Going (Turf): **Sf: 0-1 GS: 0-0 Gd: 0-1 GF: 0-2 Fm: 0-0**
Distance: 5f/6f: 0-0 7f-8f: 0-3 9f-13f: 0-2 14f+: 0-0
Track : LH: 0-2 RH: 0-1 Tight: 0-0 Gall: 0-0
Aids: Bl: 0-0 Vi: 0-0 Tstrap: 0-0 Ckp: 0-0
Best Rating: **75** 8/08 Folk 7f gd-fm

Fair; stays 7f; acts on fast ground.

Dan Buoy (FR)

(75) (17)78

6-y-o b g Slip Anchor-Bramosia (Forzando)

R C Guest Bamboozelem

Placings:6/4252/04220/0 **(7598)**

2009: 16^{0}SD,

	Starts	1st	2nd	3rd	Win & Pl
Career Total (Turf)	8	0	4	0	4412
Career Total (AW)	3	0	0	0	241

Going (Turf): **Sf: 0-3 GS: 0-2 Gd: 0-2 GF: 0-1 Fm: 0-0**
Distance: 5f/6f: 0-0 7f-8f: 0-1 9f-13f: 0-8 14f+: 0-2
Track : LH: 0-7 RH: 0-4 Tight: 0-6 Gall: 0-1
Aids: Bl: 0-0 Vi: 0-0 Tstrap: 0-1 Ckp: 0-1
Best Rating: **78** 7/07 Wwck 1m4f134y soft

Dan Tucker

(98) (67)74

5-y-o b g Dansili-Shapely (USA) (Alleged (USA))

Jim Best Alan Clarke

Placings:006/11303360562/062354315544024-4 **(0877)**

2009: 12^{4}SD,

	Starts	1st	2nd	3rd	Win & Pl
Career Total (Turf)	23	2	3	3	9227
Career Total (AW)	7	1	0	2	2983

72 7/08 Catt 1m3f214y (0-65)H G-F £2217
72 4/07 Sthl 1m3f (0-60)H GD £2388
75 3/07 Kemp 1m2f (0-60)H STD £1365

Total win prize-money £5972

Going (Turf): Sf: 0-1 GS: 0-7 **Gd: 1-8 GF: 1-7** Fm: 0-0
Distance: 5f/6f: 0-1 7f-8f: 0-2 **9f-13f: 3-25** 14f+: 0-2
Track : **LH: 2-17** RH: 1-9 **Tight: 2-13** Gall: 0-4
Aids: Bl: 0-2 Vi: 0-0 Tstrap: 0-0 Ckp: 0-0
Best Rating: **75** 6/07 Kemp 1m4f stand

Modest; stays 1m4f; acts on soft ground; also goes on Polytrack.

Dance And Dance (IRE)

101(106) (91)84

3-y-o b c Royal Applause-Caldy Dancer (IRE) (Soviet Star (USA))

E F Vaughan Mohammed Rashid

Placings:6-322162051203 **(7523)**

2009: 6^{3}SD, 6^{2}SD, 7^{2}SD, 7^{1}SD, 7^{6}SD, 7^{2}GF, 7^{0}GF, 7^{5}GF, 7^{1}SD, 7^{2}SD, 7^{0}SD, 8^{3}SD,

	Starts	1st	2nd	3rd	Win & Pl
Career Total (Turf)	3	0	1	0	1542
Career Total (AW)	10	2	3	2	11564

91 10/09 Kemp 7f (0-80)H STD £4727
78 2/09 Ling 7f STD £2729

Total win prize-money £7457

Going (Turf): **Sf: 0-0 GS: 0-0 Gd: 0-0 GF: 0-3 Fm: 0-0**
Distance: 5f/6f: 0-3 **7f-8f: 2-10** 9f-13f: 0-0 14f+: 0-0
Track : LH: 1-8 RH: 1-3 **Tight: 1-5** Gall: 0-1
Aids: Bl: 0-0 Vi: 0-0 Tstrap: 0-0 Ckp: 0-0
Best Rating: **91** 10/09 Kemp 7f stand

Useful; effective over 6f-1m; acts on Polytrack.

Dance Card

104 77

4-y-o b f Cape Cross (IRE)-Dance On (Caerleon (USA))

A G Foster S C B Limited

Placings:0-4100 **(6764)**

2009: 8^{4}G, 7^{1}GF, 7^{0}G, 6^{0}G,

	Starts	1st	2nd	3rd	Win & Pl
Career Total (Turf)	5	1	0	0	4126

77 8/09 Newc 7f G-F £3885

Total win prize-money £3886

Going (Turf): Sf: 0-0 GS: 0-0 Gd: 0-4 **GF: 1-1** Fm: 0-0
Distance: 5f/6f: 0-2 **7f-8f: 1-2** 9f-13f: 0-1 14f+: 0-0
Track : LH: 0-2 RH: 0-0 Tight: 0-0 Gall: 0-0
Aids: Bl: 0-0 Vi: 0-0 Tstrap: 0-0 Ckp: 0-0
Best Rating: **77** 8/09 Newc 7f gd-fm

Fair; stays 7f; acts on fast ground; has worn a tongue tie.

Dance Club (IRE)

100(97) (63)70

3-y-o b f Fasliyev (USA)-Two Clubs (First Trump)

W Jarvis Dr John Fike

Placings:6066-02140 **(6070)**

2009: 8^{0}GS, 6^{2}G, 7^{1}GF, 7^{4}GF, 7^{0}SD,

	Starts	1st	2nd	3rd	Win & Pl
Career Total (Turf)	7	1	1	0	3835
Career Total (AW)	2	0	0	0	

70 8/09 Yarm 7f3y (0-70)H G-F £2849

Total win prize-money £2849

Going (Turf): Sf: 0-2 GS: 0-1 Gd: 0-1 **GF: 1-3** Fm: 0-0
Distance: 5f/6f: 0-2 **7f-8f: 1-6** 9f-13f: 0-1 14f+: 0-0
Track : LH: 0-2 RH: 0-0 Tight: 0-2 Gall: 0-0
Aids: Bl: 0-0 Vi: 0-0 Tstrap: 0-0 Ckp: 0-0
Best Rating: **70** 8/09 Yarm 7f3y gd-fm

Modest; likes 7f on quick ground.

Dance East

86 45

2-y-o b f Shamardal (USA)-Russian Dance (USA) (Nureyev (USA))

J Noseda Cheveley Park Stud

Placings:0 **(5317)**

2009: 6^{0}GF,

	Starts	1st	2nd	3rd	Win & Pl
Career Total (Turf)	1	0	0	0	

Going (Turf): **Sf: 0-0 GS: 0-0 Gd: 0-0 GF: 0-1 Fm: 0-0**
Distance: 5f/6f: 0-1 7f-8f: 0-0 9f-13f: 0-0 14f+: 0-0
Track : LH: 0-0 RH: 0-0 Tight: 0-0 Gall: 0-1
Aids: Bl: 0-0 Vi: 0-0 Tstrap: 0-0 Ckp: 0-0
Best Rating: **45** 8/09 Wind 6f gd-fm

Dance For Julie (IRE)

99 76

2-y-o b f Redback-Dancing Steps (Zafonic (USA))

P C Haslam Mark James

Placings:32216 **(6134)**

2009: 6^{3}GF, 6^{2}GF, 5^{2}GF, 6^{1}S, 6^{6}G,

	Starts	1st	2nd	3rd	Win & Pl
Career Total (Turf)	5	1	2	1	6846

76 9/09 Thsk 6f SFT £4274

Total win prize-money £4274

Going (Turf): **Sf: 1-1** GS: 0-0 Gd: 0-1 GF: 0-3 Fm: 0-0
Distance: **5f/6f: 1-4** 7f-8f: 0-1 9f-13f: 0-0 14f+: 0-0

Track : LH: 0-1 RH: 0-0 Tight: 0-0 Gall: 0-0
Aids: Bl: 0-0 Vi: 0-0 Tstrap: 0-0 Ckp: 0-0
Best Rating: 76 9/09 Thsk 6f soft

Fair; suited by 6f; handles soft and fast ground.

Dance Gdansk (IRE)

(91) (55)
3-y-o b c Fasliyev (USA)-Tordasia (IRE) (Dr Devious (IRE))
M Blanshard Ms Francesca Baring

Placings:00050 **(7649)**
2009: 12^{0}SD, 12^{0}SD, 12^{0}SD, 16^{5}SD, 16^{0}SD,

	Starts	1st	2nd	3rd	Win & Pl
Career Total (Turf)	0	0	0	0	
Career Total (AW)	5	0	0	0	0

Going (Turf): Sf: 0-0 GS: 0-0 Gd: 0-0 GF: 0-0 Fm: 0-0
Distance: 5f/6f: 0-0 7f-8f: 0-0 9f-13f: 0-3 14f+: 0-2
Track : LH: 0-3 RH: 0-2 Tight: 0-3 Gall: 0-0
Aids: Bl: 0-0 Vi: 0-0 Tstrap: 0-0 Ckp: 0-0
Best Rating: 55 11/09 Ling 1m4f stand

Dance Sauvage

87 50
6-y-o ch g Groom Dancer (USA)-Peace Dance (Bikala)
B Storey Mr & Mrs T I Gourley

Placings:000/020622046/5F0350-0004 **(5161)**
2009: 14^{0}GF, 16^{0}G, 17^{0}G, 11^{4}S,

	Starts	1st	2nd	3rd	Win & Pl
Career Total (Turf)	22	0	3	1	2944

Going (Turf): Sf: 0-3 GS: 0-1 Gd: 0-9 GF: 0-9 Fm: 0-0
Distance: 5f/6f: 0-1 7f-8f: 0-2 9f-13f: 0-6 14f+: 0-13
Track : LH: 0-11 RH: 0-9 Tight: 0-13 Gall: 0-4
Aids: Bl: 0-0 Vi: 0-0 Tstrap: 0-0 Ckp: 0-0
Best Rating: 58 10/07 Rdcr 1m6f19y good

Moderate; stays 1m5f; acts on fast ground.

Dance Society

78 49
3-y-o b g Mull Of Kintyre (USA)-Gracious Imp (USA) (Imp Society (USA))
T D Easterby S A Heley

Placings:000-50 **(2719)**
2009: 6^{5}GF, 7^{0}G,

	Starts	1st	2nd	3rd	Win & Pl
Career Total (Turf)	5	0	0	0	0

Going (Turf): Sf: 0-3 GS: 0-0 Gd: 0-1 GF: 0-1 Fm: 0-0
Distance: 5f/6f: 0-1 7f-8f: 0-3 9f-13f: 0-1 14f+: 0-0
Track : LH: 0-0 RH: 0-4 Tight: 0-1 Gall: 0-0
Aids: Bl: 0-2 Vi: 0-0 Tstrap: 0-0 Ckp: 0-0
Best Rating: 49 9/08 Bevl 7f100y soft

Dance The Star (USA)

100(113) (95)92
4-y-o b/br c Dynaformer (USA)-Dance The Slew (USA) (Slew City Slew (USA))
D M Simcock Sultan Ali

Placings:3011013-60424023 **(7720)**
2009: 10^{6}SD, 12^{0}GF, 12^{4}SD, 11^{2}SD, 12^{4}GF, 12^{0}G, 12^{2}SD, 12^{3}SD,

	Starts	1st	2nd	3rd	Win & Pl
Career Total (Turf)	5	1	0	0	3296
Career Total (AW)	10	2	2	3	17018

92 10/08 Kemp 1m4f (0-85)H STD £6476
88 7/08 Ling 1m4f (0-75)H STD £2590
76 6/08 Wind 1m3f135y G-F £2729
Total win prize-money £11796

Going (Turf): Sf: 0-0 GS: 0-0 Gd: 0-2 **GF: 1-3** Fm: 0-0
Distance: 5f/6f: 0-0 7f-8f: 0-0 **9f-13f: 3-14** 14f+: 0-1
Track : LH: 1-5 RH: 1-9 **Tight: 2-5** Gall: 0-3
Aids: Bl: 0-0 Vi: 0-0 Tstrap: 0-0 Ckp: 0-0
Best Rating: 95 11/09 Wolv 1m4f50y stand

Useful; stays 1m4f; acts on fast ground and on Polytrack.

Dance With Chance (IRE)

72(82) (51)39
2-y-o b f Kalanisi (IRE)-Persian Lass (IRE) (Grand Lodge (USA))
W R Swinburn Dr Jamal Ahmadzadeh

Placings:00 **(7183)**
2009: 7^{0}SD, 7^{0}G,

	Starts	1st	2nd	3rd	Win & Pl
Career Total (Turf)	1	0	0	0	
Career Total (AW)	1	0	0	0	

Going (Turf): Sf: 0-0 GS: 0-0 Gd: 0-1 GF: 0-0 Fm: 0-0
Distance: 5f/6f: 0-0 7f-8f: 0-2 9f-13f: 0-0 14f+: 0-0
Track : LH: 0-1 RH: 0-0 Tight: 0-1 Gall: 0-0
Aids: Bl: 0-0 Vi: 0-0 Tstrap: 0-0 Ckp: 0-0
Best Rating: 51 9/09 Ling 7f stand

Dancealot Lady (USA)

89(68) (23)50
2-y-o b f Theatrical-Guadaira (IRE) (Grand Lodge (USA))
P Winkworth Stuart Matheson

Placings:0060 **(5715)**
2009: 6^{0}S, 6^{0}SD, 7^{6}GF, 8^{0}G,

	Starts	1st	2nd	3rd	Win & Pl
Career Total (Turf)	3	0	0	0	0
Career Total (AW)	1	0	0	0	

Going (Turf): Sf: 0-1 GS: 0-0 Gd: 0-1 GF: 0-1 Fm: 0-0
Distance: 5f/6f: 0-1 7f-8f: 0-2 9f-13f: 0-1 14f+: 0-0
Track : LH: 0-2 RH: 0-0 Tight: 0-2 Gall: 0-0
Aids: Bl: 0-0 Vi: 0-0 Tstrap: 0-0 Ckp: 0-0
Best Rating: 50 8/09 Folk 7f gd-fm

Danceintothelight

87 72
2-y-o gr g Dansili-Kali (Linamix (FR))
K A Ryan Mrs T P Hyde

Placings:5642 **(6982)**
2009: 8^{5}F, 8^{6}G, 8^{4}GS, 8^{2}G,

	Starts	1st	2nd	3rd	Win & Pl
Career Total (Turf)	4	0	1	0	1830

Going (Turf): Sf: 0-0 GS: 0-1 Gd: 0-2 GF: 0-0 Fm: 0-1

Distance: 5f/6f: 0-0 7f-8f: 0-2 9f-13f: 0-2 14f+: 0-0
Track : LH: 0-2 RH: 0-2 Tight: 0-1 Gall: 0-1
Aids: Bl: 0-0 Vi: 0-0 Tstrap: 0-0 Ckp: 0-0
Best Rating: 72 10/09 Ayr 1m good

Fair; stays 1m and acts on good ground.

Dancelectic (IRE)

80(69) (17)15
3-y-o b c Barathea (IRE)-Sheer Spirit (IRE) (Caerleon (USA))
D R Lanigan Paul Dean

Placings:000-0 **(1578)**
2009: 10^{0}G,

	Starts	1st	2nd	3rd	Win & Pl
Career Total (Turf)	1	0	0	0	
Career Total (AW)	3	0	0	0	

Going (Turf): Sf: 0-0 GS: 0-0 Gd: 0-1 GF: 0-0 Fm: 0-0
Distance: 5f/6f: 0-0 7f-8f: 0-2 9f-13f: 0-2 14f+: 0-0
Track : LH: 0-3 RH: 0-1 Tight: 0-2 Gall: 0-1
Aids: Bl: 0-0 Vi: 0-0 Tstrap: 0-0 Ckp: 0-0
Best Rating: 17 11/08 GrLe 1m stand

Dancer In Demand (IRE)

(97) (75)75
4-y-o ch g Danehill Dancer (IRE)-Sought Out (IRE) (Rainbow Quest (USA))
Sir Michael Stoute Ballymacoll Stud

Placings:30-2 **(1286)**
2009: 12^{2}SD,

	Starts	1st	2nd	3rd	Win & Pl
Career Total (Turf)	2	0	0	1	794
Career Total (AW)	1	0	1	0	771

Going (Turf): Sf: 0-0 GS: 0-0 Gd: 0-1 GF: 0-1 Fm: 0-0
Distance: 5f/6f: 0-0 7f-8f: 0-0 9f-13f: 0-3 14f+: 0-0
Track : LH: 0-2 RH: 0-1 Tight: 0-0 Gall: 0-2
Aids: Bl: 0-0 Vi: 0-0 Tstrap: 0-0 Ckp: 0-0
Best Rating: 75 4/09 Kemp 1m4f stand

Fair; stays 1m4f and should stay further; acts on Polytrack.

Dancer's Legacy

101(98) (67)80
4-y-o ch g Nayef (USA)-Blond Moment (USA) (Affirmed (USA))
J R Boyle (E A L Dunlop 30/4) Miltil Consortium

Placings:00130/5150000-000604534 **(6565)**
2009: 8^{0}GF, 10^{0}G, 10^{0}GF, 8^{6}G, 8^{0}GF, 7^{4}F, 7^{5}F, 10^{3}SD, 9^{4}GS,

	Starts	1st	2nd	3rd	Win & Pl
Career Total (Turf)	17	2	0	1	7603
Career Total (AW)	4	0	0	1	289

80 5/08 Nott 1m75y (0-75)H GD £3238
68 8/07 Wwck 7f26y G-F £3238
Total win prize-money £6477

Going (Turf): Sf: 0-0 GS: 0-3 **Gd: 1-5 GF: 1-7** Fm: 0-2
Distance: 5f/6f: 0-0 7f-8f: 1-9 9f-13f: 1-12 14f+: 0-0
Track : **LH: 2-7** RH: 0-9 Tight: 0-7 Gall: 0-1
Aids: Bl: 0-0 Vi: 0-1 Tstrap: 0-1 Ckp: 0-1
Best Rating: 80 5/08 Nott 1m75y good

Fair; stays 1m; effective on fast ground; has worn tongue tie and cheekpieces.

Dancing Again

72(76) (5)12

3-y-o ch f Reel Buddy (USA)-Batchworth Breeze (Beveled (USA))

E A Wheeler Tony Arnold & Nick Hill

Placings:0000 (7254)

2009: 8^{0}GF, 6^{0}G, 5^{0}SD, 5^{0}SD,

	Starts	1st	2nd	3rd	Win & Pl
Career Total (Turf)	2	0	0	0	
Career Total (AW)	2	0	0	0	

Going (Turf): Sf: 0-0 GS: 0-0 Gd: 0-1 GF: 0-1 Fm: 0-0
Distance: 5f/6f: 0-3 7f-8f: 0-0 9f-13f: 0-1 14f+: 0-0
Track : LH: 0-2 RH: 0-1 Tight: 0-3 Gall: 0-1
Aids: Bl: 0-0 Vi: 0-0 Tstrap: 0-0 Ckp: 0-0
Best Rating: 12 5/09 Wind 1m67y gd-fm

Dancing David (IRE)

96 109

2-y-o b c Danehill Dancer (IRE)-Seek Easy (USA) (Seeking The Gold (USA))

B J Meehan Catesby W Clay

Placings:214 (7017)

2009: 8^{2}GS, 8^{1}G, 8^{4}GS,

	Starts	1st	2nd	3rd	Win & Pl
Career Total (Turf)	3	1	1	0	16994

85 10/09 Newb 1m GD £4857

Total win prize-money £4857

Going (Turf): Sf: 0-0 GS: 0-2 Gd: 1-1 GF: 0-0 Fm: 0-0
Distance: 5f/6f: 0-0 7f-8f: 1-3 9f-13f: 0-0 14f+: 0-0
Track : LH: 0-0 RH: 0-0 Tight: 0-0 Gall: 0-0
Aids: Bl: 0-0 Vi: 0-0 Tstrap: 0-0 Ckp: 0-0
Best Rating: 109 10/09 Donc 1m gd-sft

Very useful; stays 1m; acts on good and softer ground.

Dancing Deano (IRE)

(104) (75)62

7-y-o b g Second Empire (IRE)-Ultimate Beat (USA) (Go And Go)

R Hollinshead Ron Wood

Placings:0605/01325023540/126003000/0500116/341043 6020341-522460 (0934)

2009: 7^{5}SD, 8^{2}SD, 8^{2}SD, 8^{4}SD, 7^{6}SD, 7^{0}SD,

	Starts	1st	2nd	3rd	Win & Pl
Career Total (Turf)	25	2	3	3	10978
Career Total (AW)	25	4	3	3	10711

68 12/08 Wolv 7f32y STD £2388
75 6/08 Sthl 7f STD £1774
67 12/07 Sthl 7f STD £2047
52 11/07 Wolv 7f32y (0-45) STD £1619
59 5/06 Carl 5f193y G-S £2590
63 5/05 Chep 6f16y (0-60)H G-S £2667

Total win prize-money £13087

Going (Turf): Sf: 0-2 GS: 2-5 Gd: 0-10 GF: 0-7 Fm: 0-1
Distance: 5f/6f: 1-14 7f-8f: 5-30 9f-13f: 0-6 14f+: 0-0
Track : LH: 4-33 RH: 1-4 Tight: 2-21 Gall: 0-0
Aids: Bl: 0-0 Vi: 4-25 Tstrap: 0-0 Ckp: 0-0
Best Rating: 75 6/08 Sthl 7f stand

Modest; effective over 7f; acts on most ground and on sand.

Dancing Duo

89(102) (62)56

5-y-o b m Groom Dancer (USA)-Affaire Royale (IRE) (Royal Academy (USA))

D Shaw Mrs Lyndsey Shaw

Placings:0061/002000300/0033400502003-620020 (1634)

2009: 8^{6}SS, 8^{2}SD, 7^{0}SD, 8^{0}SD, 8^{2}SF, 7^{0}GF,

	Starts	1st	2nd	3rd	Win & Pl
Career Total (Turf)	6	0	1	0	0
Career Total (AW)	26	1	3	4	5724

60 10/06 Wolv 7f32y SF £2388

Total win prize-money £2389

Going (Turf): Sf: 0-1 GS: 0-1 Gd: 0-0 GF: 0-4 Fm: 0-0
Distance: 5f/6f: 0-4 7f-8f: 1-25 9f-13f: 0-3 14f+: 0-0
Track : LH: 1-19 RH: 0-7 Tight: 1-14 Gall: 0-2
Aids: Bl: 0-0 Vi: 0-27 Tstrap: 0-0 Ckp: 0-0
Best Rating: 62 10/07 Kemp 7f stand

Moderate; stays 1m; effective on both sand surfaces.

Dancing Freddy (IRE)

100(98) (77)85

2-y-o b c Chineur (FR)-Majesty's Dancer (IRE) (Danehill Dancer (IRE))

J G Given Danethorpe Racing Partnership

Placings:221306050320 (7290)

2009: 5^{2}SD, 5^{2}GF, 5^{1}GF, 5^{3}G, 5^{0}GF, 6^{6}F, 5^{0}G, 5^{5}SD, 6^{0}GF, 5^{3}SF, 5^{2}GS, 6^{0}S,

	Starts	1st	2nd	3rd	Win & Pl
Career Total (Turf)	9	1	2	1	8405
Career Total (AW)	3	0	1	1	1633

75 5/09 Nott 5f13y G-F £3885

Total win prize-money £3886

Going (Turf): Sf: 0-1 GS: 0-1 Gd: 0-2 GF: 1-4 Fm: 0-1
Distance: 5f/6f: 1-12 7f-8f: 0-0 9f-13f: 0-0 14f+: 0-0
Track : LH: 0-3 RH: 0-0 Tight: 0-3 Gall: 0-0
Aids: Bl: 0-0 Vi: 0-0 Tstrap: 0-0 Ckp: 0-0
Best Rating: 85 6/09 Muss 5f good

Useful; suited by 5f; goes on fast ground and on Polytrack.

Dancing Ghost (IRE)

75(84) (16)18

3-y-o gr f Verglas (IRE)-Ghost Dance (IRE) (Lure (USA))

Jane Chapple-Hyam Mrs Jane Chapple-Hyam

Placings:00 (7332)

2009: 7^{0}G, 12^{0}SD,

	Starts	1st	2nd	3rd	Win & Pl
Career Total (Turf)	1	0	0	0	
Career Total (AW)	1	0	0	0	

Going (Turf): Sf: 0-0 GS: 0-0 Gd: 0-1 GF: 0-0 Fm: 0-0
Distance: 5f/6f: 0-0 7f-8f: 0-1 9f-13f: 0-1 14f+: 0-0
Track : LH: 0-1 RH: 0-0 Tight: 0-0 Gall: 0-0
Aids: Bl: 0-0 Vi: 0-0 Tstrap: 0-0 Ckp: 0-0
Best Rating: 18 7/09 NmkJ 7f good

Dancing Jest (IRE)

105 (19)69

5-y-o b m Averti (IRE)-Mezzanine (Sadler's Wells (USA))

Rae Guest Mrs J E Lury and O T Lury

Placings:50/021606/5423-02212500 (6174)

2009: 8^{0}GF, 10^{2}GF, 10^{2}GF, 9^{1}GF, 8^{2}GF, 9^{5}GF, 8^{0}GF, 8^{0}GF,

	Starts	1st	2nd	3rd	Win & Pl
Career Total (Turf)	19	2	5	1	11206
Career Total (AW)	1	0	0	0	

69 6/09 Leic 1m1f218y (0-75)H G-F £3885
65 8/07 Yarm 1m3y (0-75)H G-F £2914

Total win prize-money £6801

Going (Turf): Sf: 0-1 GS: 0-2 Gd: 0-0 GF: 2-14 Fm: 0-2
Distance: 5f/6f: 0-1 7f-8f: 0-6 9f-13f: 2-13 14f+: 0-0
Track : LH: 0-11 RH: 1-5 Tight: 0-10 Gall: 0-0
Aids: Bl: 0-0 Vi: 0-0 Tstrap: 0-0 Ckp: 0-0
Best Rating: 69 6/09 Wind 1m67y gd-fm

Modest; effective at around 1m1f; acts on fast ground.

Dancing Lyra

96(101) (70)67

8-y-o b g Alzao (USA)-Badaayer (USA) (Silver Hawk (USA))

R A Fahey Aidan J Ryan Racing

Placings:0300/611240605/060340640003/115500/2660/50-026251544 (3974)

2009: 10^{0}SD, 11^{2}SD, 12^{6}SD, 11^{2}SD, 9^{5}GF, 12^{1}SD, 12^{5}GS, 14^{4}SD, 11^{4}GS,

	Starts	1st	2nd	3rd	Win & Pl
Career Total (Turf)	36	3	2	2	50847
Career Total (AW)	10	2	2	1	9982

67 6/09 Sthl 1m4f (0-60)H STD £2388
88 3/06 Muss 1m (0-85)H HVY £6477
86 3/06 Sthl 7f (0-85)H HVY £6477
95 5/04 Sals 1m1f198yC(0-100)H SFT £9187
75 2/04 Ling 1m2f D STD £5174

Total win prize-money £29703

Going (Turf): Sf: 3-4 GS: 0-7 Gd: 0-11 GF: 0-14 Fm: 0-0
Distance: 5f/6f: 0-1 7f-8f: 2-6 9f-13f: 3-35 14f+: 0-4
Track : LH: 3-26 RH: 2-13 Tight: 4-21 Gall: 0-10
Aids: Bl: 0-0 Vi: 0-0 Tstrap: 0-0 Ckp: 0-0
Best Rating: 95 5/04 Sals 1m1f198y soft

Modest; effective at up to 1m4f, acts on most types of ground and on Fibresand, but revels in the mud.

Dancing Maite

105(102) (78)89

4-y-o ch g Ballet Master (USA)-Ace Maite (Komaite (USA))

S R Bowring Stuart Burgan

Placings:044/3022030432116-431201041400560 (7617)

2009: 7^{4}SD, 7^{3}SD, 5^{1}SD, 5^{2}GF, 8^{0}GF, 6^{1}GF, 7^{0}G, 7^{4}S, 6^{1}G, 6^{4}G, 6^{0}GF, 6^{0}GF, 6^{5}GF, 6^{6}SD, 7^{0}SD,

	Starts	1st	2nd	3rd	Win & Pl
Career Total (Turf)	19	3	2	2	18636
Career Total (AW)	12	2	2	2	8351

89 6/09 York 6f (0-80)H GD £7123
83 5/09 NmkR 6f (0-75)H G-F £3885
78 4/09 Wolv 5f216y (0-70)H STD £3238
76 10/08 Leic 7f9y G-S £2590
68 10/08 Sthl 7f STD £2866

Total win prize-money £19704

Going (Turf): Sf: 0-2 GS: 1-1 Gd: 1-8 GF: 1-8 Fm: 0-0
Distance: 5f/6f: 3-15 7f-8f: 2-15 9f-13f: 0-1 14f+: 0-0
Track : LH: 2-17 RH: 0-2 Tight: 1-10 Gall: 0-0
Aids: Bl: 0-0 Vi: 0-0 Tstrap: 0-0 Ckp: 0-0
Best Rating: 89 6/09 York 6f good

Fair; effective over 6f-1m; acts on most ground on turf; goes on Fibresand and Polytrack.

Dancing Poppy

85(92) (56)60

2-y-o b f Kyllachy-Broughtons Motto (Mtoto)

M R Channon The Ranway Partnership

Placings:53006 (6722)

2009: 6^{5}G, 7^{3}GF, 7^{0}SD, 7^{0}GF, 6^{6}SD,

	Starts	1st	2nd	3rd	Win & Pl
Career Total (Turf)	3	0	0	1	337
Career Total (AW)	2	0	0	0	0

Going (Turf): Sf: 0-0 GS: 0-0 Gd: 0-1 GF: 0-2 Fm: 0-0
Distance: 5f/6f: 0-2 7f-8f: 0-3 9f-13f: 0-0 14f+: 0-0
Track : LH: 0-2 RH: 0-2 Tight: 0-2 Gall: 0-0
Aids: Bl: 0-0 Vi: 0-0 Tstrap: 0-0 Ckp: 0-0
Best Rating: 60 6/09 Pont 6f good

Dancing Queen (IRE)

89 72

2-y-o ch f Danehill Dancer (IRE)-Elauyun (IRE) (Muhtarram (USA))

M A Magnusson Eastwind Racing Ltd and Martha Trussell

Placings:652 (6284)

2009: 7^{6}G, 8^{5}GF, 8^{2}GF,

	Starts	1st	2nd	3rd	Win & Pl
Career Total (Turf)	3	0	1	0	1156

Going (Turf): Sf: 0-0 GS: 0-0 Gd: 0-1 GF: 0-2 Fm: 0-0
Distance: 5f/6f: 0-0 7f-8f: 0-2 9f-13f: 0-1 14f+: 0-0
Track : LH: 0-1 RH: 0-1 Tight: 0-0 Gall: 0-0
Aids: Bl: 0-0 Vi: 0-0 Tstrap: 0-0 Ckp: 0-0
Best Rating: 72 9/09 Hayd 1m30y gd-fm

Fair; stays 1m; acts on fast ground.

Dancing Red Devil (IRE)

94 77

2-y-o b f Desert Style (IRE)-Mannsara (IRE) (Royal Academy (USA))

Paul Green Daniel Britton & Chris Clarke

Placings:15550 (5274a)

2009: 5^{1}GF, 5^{5}GF, 5^{5}HY, 6^{5}GF, 6^{0}S,

	Starts	1st	2nd	3rd	Win & Pl
Career Total (Turf)	5	1	0	0	6273

77	6/09	Ches	5f16y		G-F	£5180

Total win prize-money £5181

Going (Turf): Sf: 0-2 GS: 0-0 Gd: 0-0 **GF: 1-3** Fm: 0-0
Distance: **5f/6f: 1-5** 7f-8f: 0-0 9f-13f: 0-0 14f+: 0-0
Track : **LH: 1-2** RH: 0-1 **Tight: 1-2** Gall: 0-0
Aids: Bl: 0-1 Vi: 0-0 Tstrap: 0-0 Ckp: 0-0
Best Rating: 77 6/09 Ches 5f16y gd-fm

Made winning debut over 5f on fast ground.

Dancing Rhythm

97(91) (60)63

4-y-o b g Piccolo-Will You Dance (Shareef Dancer (USA))

M S Saunders Chris Scott

Placings:000-00050 (1970)

2009: 8^{0}SD, 8^{0}GF, 7^{0}GF, 6^{5}GF, 5^{0}F,

	Starts	1st	2nd	3rd	Win & Pl
Career Total (Turf)	6	0	0	0	0
Career Total (AW)	2	0	0	0	

Going (Turf): Sf: 0-0 GS: 0-1 Gd: 0-0 GF: 0-4 Fm: 0-1
Distance: 5f/6f: 0-2 7f-8f: 0-4 9f-13f: 0-2 14f+: 0-0
Track : LH: 0-5 RH: 0-1 Tight: 0-4 Gall: 0-0
Aids: Bl: 0-0 Vi: 0-0 Tstrap: 0-0 Ckp: 0-0
Best Rating: 63 5/09 Sals 6f gd-fm

Dancing Storm

101 (56)71

6-y-o b m Trans Island-Stormswell (Persian Bold)

W S Kittow The Quintet Partnership

Placings:4660/6014500/610544/21435663-06504060 (6968)

2009: 8^{0}GF, 8^{6}GF, 8^{5}GF, 10^{0}GF, 8^{4}GF, 8^{0}GF, 8^{6}G, 7^{0}G,

	Starts	1st	2nd	3rd	Win & Pl
Career Total (Turf)	28	3	1	2	13035
Career Total (AW)	5	0	0	0	0

71	5/08	Chep	1m14y	(0-70)H	SFT	£3238
61	7/07	Brig	7f214y	(0-60)H	GD	£2072
61	7/06	Chep	1m14y	(0-70)H	G-F	£5181

Total win prize-money £10493

Going (Turf): Sf: 1-3 GS: 0-4 **Gd: 1-8 GF: 1-13** Fm: 0-0
Distance: 5f/6f: 0-4 7f-8f: 1-8 **9f-13f: 2-21** 14f+: 0-0
Track : **LH: 1-13** RH: 0-4 Tight: 0-12 Gall: 0-1
Aids: Bl: 0-0 Vi: 0-0 Tstrap: 0-1 Ckp: 0-1
Best Rating: 71 5/08 Chep 1m14y soft

Moderate; dual winner of 1m Class 5 handicaps at Chepstow; stays 1m; acts on most ground; also goes on Polytrack.

Dancing Wave

100(98) (59)65

3-y-o b f Baryshnikov (AUS)-Wavet (Pursuit Of Love)

M C Chapman Roy Gowans

Placings:542000046-122260336041200020 (7838)

2009: 6^{1}SS, 7^{2}SD, 7^{2}SD, 7^{2}SD, 5^{6}SD, 7^{0}GF, 6^{3}SD, 7^{3}GF, 10^{6}GF, 7^{0}G, 5^{4}GF, 5^{1}GF, 5^{2}GF, 5^{0}G, 6^{0}SD, 5^{0}GF, 6^{2}GF, 6^{0}SD, 5^{0}SS,

	Starts	1st	2nd	3rd	Win & Pl
Career Total (Turf)	17	1	3	1	5554
Career Total (AW)	11	1	3	1	4365

61	6/09	Rdcr	5f	(0-60)H	G-F	£2047
55	1/09	Sthl	6f		SS	£2047

Total win prize-money £4094

Going (Turf): Sf: 0-3 GS: 0-1 Gd: 0-4 **GF: 1-9** Fm: 0-0
Distance: **5f/6f: 2-19** 7f-8f: 0-8 9f-13f: 0-1 14f+: 0-0
Track : **LH: 1-11** RH: 0-2 Tight: 0-1 Gall: 0-4
Aids: Bl: 0-0 Vi: 0-0 Tstrap: 0-0 Ckp: 0-0
Best Rating: 65 10/09 Yarm 6f3y gd-fm

Moderate; stays 7f; acts on soft ground and on Fibresand; likes to race prominently.

Dancing Welcome

94(101) (65)57

3-y-o b f Kyllachy-Highland Gait (Most Welcome)

J M Bradley J M Bradley

Placings:60-300460235224402121300 (7860)

2009: 5^{3}SD, 5^{0}SD, 5^{0}SD, 5^{4}G, 6^{6}GF, 5^{0}F, 5^{2}SD, 5^{3}SF, 6^{5}G, 5^{2}GF, 6^{2}G, 6^{4}GF, 7^{4}GS, 7^{0}GF, 6^{2}SD, 7^{1}SD, 6^{2}SD, 7^{1}SD, 7^{3}SD, 7^{0}SD, 7^{0}SD,

	Starts	1st	2nd	3rd	Win & Pl
Career Total (Turf)	11	0	2	0	1628
Career Total (AW)	12	2	3	3	6165

65	11/09	Ling	7f	(0-58)H	STD	£1637
57	11/09	Kemp	7f	(0-55)H	STD	£1706

Total win prize-money £3344

Going (Turf): Sf: 0-0 GS: 0-2 Gd: 0-3 GF: 0-5 Fm: 0-1
Distance: 5f/6f: 0-13 **7f-8f: 2-10** 9f-13f: 0-0 14f+: 0-0
Track : LH: 1-12 RH: 1-4 **Tight: 1-7** Gall: 0-1
Aids: **Bl: 2-18** Vi: 0-0 Tstrap: 0-0 Ckp: 0-0
Best Rating: 65 11/09 Ling 7f stand

Moderate; stays 7f; acts on fast and easy ground; goes on Polytrack; has worn blinkers.

Dancing Wizard

(86) (53)

5-y-o ch g Dancing Spree (USA)-Magic Legs (Reprimand)

Norma Twomey R J Turton

Placings:2/54-0 (0969)

2009: 9^{0}SD,

	Starts	1st	2nd	3rd	Win & Pl
Career Total (Turf)	0	0	0	0	
Career Total (AW)	4	0	1	0	1050

Going (Turf): Sf: 0-0 GS: 0-0 Gd: 0-0 GF: 0-0 Fm: 0-0
Distance: 5f/6f: 0-0 7f-8f: 0-3 9f-13f: 0-1 14f+: 0-0
Track : LH: 0-3 RH: 0-1 Tight: 0-3 Gall: 0-0
Aids: Bl: 0-0 Vi: 0-0 Tstrap: 0-0 Ckp: 0-0
Best Rating: 53 2/08 Wolv 7f32y stand

Dancourt (IRE)

108(96) (75)98

3-y-o b g Cadeaux Genereux-Stage Struck (IRE) (Sadler's Wells (USA))

Sir Michael Stoute Ballymacoll Stud

Placings:034-22114 (4781)

2009: 8^{2}SD, 9^{2}G, 8^{1}G, 10^{1}GF, 10^{4}G,

	Starts	1st	2nd	3rd	Win & Pl
Career Total (Turf)	5	2	1	0	22833
Career Total (AW)	3	0	1	1	2408

97	7/09	Sand	1m2f7y	(0-90)H	G-F	£7771
87	7/09	NmkJ	1m	(0-90)H	GD	£9714

Total win prize-money £17485

Going (Turf): Sf: 0-0 GS: 0-0 **Gd: 1-4 GF: 1-1** Fm: 0-0
Distance: 5f/6f: 0-1 7f-8f: 1-4 9f-13f: 1-3 14f+: 0-0
Track : LH: 0-4 **RH: 1-2** Tight: 0-2 Gall: 0-1
Aids: Bl: 0-0 Vi: 0-0 Tstrap: 0-0 Ckp: 0-0
Best Rating: 98 8/09 Hayd 1m2f95y good

Very useful; stays 1m2f; acts on fast ground; goes on Polytrack.

Dandarrell

93(86) (58)62

2-y-o b g Makbul-Dress Design (IRE) (Brief Truce (USA))

Miss J A Camacho Miss Julie Camacho

Placings:52 (7420)

2009: 6^{5}S, 7^{2}SD,

	Starts	1st	2nd	3rd	Win & Pl
Career Total (Turf)	1	0	0	0	0
Career Total (AW)	1	0	1	0	771

Going (Turf): Sf: 0-1 GS: 0-0 Gd: 0-0 GF: 0-0 Fm: 0-0
Distance: 5f/6f: 0-1 7f-8f: 0-1 9f-13f: 0-0 14f+: 0-0

Track : LH: 0-1 RH: 0-0 Tight: 0-0 Gall: 0-0
Aids: Bl: 0-0 Vi: 0-0 Tstrap: 0-0 Ckp: 0-0
Best Rating: 62 11/09 Donc 6f soft

Moderate; effective over 6f; acts on soft ground.

Danderek

(93) (57)
3-y-o ch g Fantastic Light (USA)-Maureena (IRE) (Grand Lodge (USA))
R A Fahey Derek Rowlands & Daniel Keenan

Placings:4 **(7765)**
2009: 11^{4}SD,

	Starts	1st	2nd	3rd	Win & Pl
Career Total (Turf)	0	0	0	0	
Career Total (AW)	1	0	0	0	0

Going (Turf): Sf: 0-0 GS: 0-0 Gd: 0-0 GF: 0-0 Fm: 0-0
Distance: 5f/6f: 0-0 7f-8f: 0-0 9f-13f: 0-1 14f+: 0-0
Track : LH: 0-0 RH: 0-1 Tight: 0-0 Gall: 0-0
Aids: Bl: 0-0 Vi: 0-0 Tstrap: 0-0 Ckp: 0-0
Best Rating: 57 12/09 Kemp 1m3f stand

Dandino

94 76
2-y-o br c Dansili-Generous Diana (Generous (IRE))
J G Given Elite Racing Club

Placings:02 **(7121)**
2009: 8^{0}GS, 8^{2}GF,

	Starts	1st	2nd	3rd	Win & Pl
Career Total (Turf)	2	0	1	0	1156

Going (Turf): Sf: 0-0 GS: 0-1 Gd: 0-0 GF: 0-1 Fm: 0-0
Distance: 5f/6f: 0-0 7f-8f: 0-1 9f-13f: 0-1 14f+: 0-0
Track : LH: 0-2 RH: 0-0 Tight: 0-0 Gall: 0-1
Aids: Bl: 0-0 Vi: 0-0 Tstrap: 0-0 Ckp: 0-0
Best Rating: 76 10/09 Nott 1m75y gd-fm

Fair; effective over 1m; acts on good ground.

Dandy Man (IRE)

110 118
6-y-o b h Mozart (IRE)-Lady Alexander (IRE) (Night Shift (USA))
Saeed Bin Suroor Godolphin

Placings:0115/214103/1225320/04300-00050144 **(6427)**
2009: 5^{0}GF, 5^{0}G, 5^{0}GF, 5^{5}G, 5^{0}GF, 5^{1}GF, 5^{4}GF, 5^{4}GF,

	Starts	1st	2nd	3rd	Win & Pl
Career Total (Turf)	30	6	4	3	277776

107	9/09	Leic	5f2y	G-F	£7477
122	4/07	Naas	5f	GD	£21993
117	7/06	Curr	5f	G-F	£44896
114	5/06	NmkR	5f	G-F	£28390
102	8/05	Tipp	5f	YLD	£27702
80	8/05	Naas	6f	GD	£10157

Total win prize-money £140616

Going (Turf): Sf: 0-1 GS: 0-2 Gd: 2-9 **GF: 3-14** Fm: 0-0
Distance: 5f/6f: 6-30 7f-8f: 0-0 9f-13f: 0-0 14f+: 0-0
Track : LH: 3-6 RH: 0-0 Tight: 0-0 Gall: 0-0
Aids: Bl: 0-1 Vi: 0-0 Tstrap: 0-0 Ckp: 0-0
Best Rating: 122 6/07 Asct 5f gd-fm

Smart; formerly Irish trained; winner in Group 3 company and placed at a higher level; effective at 6f, but best over 5f; best on a sound surface; has worn a tongue tie and blinkers; likes to race prominently.

Dane Cottage

73 4
2-y-o ch f Beat Hollow-Lady Soleas (Be My Guest (USA))
Miss Gay Kelleway Holistic Racing Ltd

Placings:0 **(6903)**
2009: 5^{0}G,

	Starts	1st	2nd	3rd	Win & Pl
Career Total (Turf)	1	0	0	0	

Going (Turf): Sf: 0-0 GS: 0-0 Gd: 0-1 GF: 0-0 Fm: 0-0
Distance: 5f/6f: 0-1 7f-8f: 0-0 9f-13f: 0-0 14f+: 0-0
Track : LH: 0-0 RH: 0-0 Tight: 0-0 Gall: 0-1
Aids: Bl: 0-0 Vi: 0-0 Tstrap: 0-0 Ckp: 0-0
Best Rating: 4 10/09 Wind 5f10y good

Danehill Destiny

107 107
3-y-o b f Danehill Dancer (IRE)-Comeraincomeshine (IRE) (Night Shift (USA))
W J Haggas Cheveley Park Stud

Placings:1104430-3166 **(5921a)**
2009: 7^{3}S, 6^{1}G, 6^{6}G, 6^{6}S,

	Starts	1st	2nd	3rd	Win & Pl
Career Total (Turf)	11	3	0	2	54002

107	5/09	Hayd	6f	GD	£22708
95	6/08	Wind	5f10y	G-S	£3626
83	4/08	NmkR	5f	GD	£4533

Total win prize-money £30868

Going (Turf): Sf: 0-4 GS: 1-1 **Gd: 2-3** GF: 0-3 Fm: 0-0
Distance: 5f/6f: 3-10 7f-8f: 0-1 9f-13f: 0-0 14f+: 0-0
Track : LH: 0-0 RH: 0-0 Tight: 0-0 **Gall: 1-1**
Aids: Bl: 0-1 Vi: 0-0 Tstrap: 0-0 Ckp: 0-0
Best Rating: 107 5/09 Hayd 6f good

Smart; effective over 5f-6f; acts best on good or softer ground; has worn blinkers and a tongue tie.

Danehill Intellect (IRE)

94(83) (60)69
2-y-o ch f Danehill Dancer (IRE)-Intellectuelle (Caerleon (USA))
G A Butler Woodcote Stud Ltd

Placings:64 **(5547)**
2009: 7^{6}SD, 8^{4}GF,

	Starts	1st	2nd	3rd	Win & Pl
Career Total (Turf)	1	0	0	0	361
Career Total (AW)	1	0	0	0	0

Going (Turf): Sf: 0-0 GS: 0-0 Gd: 0-0 GF: 0-1 Fm: 0-0
Distance: 5f/6f: 0-0 7f-8f: 0-1 9f-13f: 0-1 14f+: 0-0
Track : LH: 0-0 RH: 0-2 Tight: 0-0 Gall: 0-0
Aids: Bl: 0-0 Vi: 0-0 Tstrap: 0-0 Ckp: 0-0
Best Rating: 69 9/09 Leic 1m60y gd-fm

Danehill's Pearl (IRE)

100 103
3-y-o b f Danehill Dancer (IRE)-Mother Of Pearl (IRE) (Sadler's Wells (USA))
Tom Dascombe Paul Murphy

Placings:1561 **(4334a)**
2009: 7^{1}GS, 10^{5}G, 10^{6}GF, 10^{1}S,

	Starts	1st	2nd	3rd	Win & Pl
Career Total (Turf)	4	2	0	0	33496

103	7/09	Vich	1m2f	SFT	£26699
76	4/09	Newb	7f	G-S	£5180

Total win prize-money £31880

Going (Turf): Sf: 1-1 GS: 1-1 Gd: 0-1 GF: 0-1 Fm: 0-0
Distance: 5f/6f: 0-0 7f-8f: 1-1 9f-13f: 1-3 14f+: 0-0
Track : LH: 0-2 **RH: 1-1** Tight: 0-0 Gall: 0-2
Aids: Bl: 0-0 Vi: 0-0 Tstrap: 0-0 Ckp: 0-0
Best Rating: 103 7/09 Vich 1m2f soft

165,000gns foal and a half-sister to winners at 1m plus from the family of Turtle Island; winner on debut over 7f on easy ground and Listed winner over 1m2f on soft in France.

Danehillsundance (IRE)

103(101) (91)94
5-y-o b g Danehill Dancer (IRE)-Rosie's Guest (IRE) (Be My Guest (USA))
D H Brown (S Parr 6/3) J P Hardiman

Placings:4322**341**/211010400/**6**200045000-**6**00031050 **(6900)**
2009: 5^{6}SD, 7^{0}G, 8^{0}GF, 7^{0}GF, 10^{3}G, 8^{1}GF, 8^{0}GF, 8^{5}GF, 10^{0}GF,

	Starts	1st	2nd	3rd	Win & Pl
Career Total (Turf)	28	4	4	2	40829
Career Total (AW)	7	1	0	1	4893

80	7/09	Bevl	1m100y	(0-80)H	G-F	£4727
99	9/07	Donc	7f	(0-100)H	G-F	£12464
90	7/07	Sand	7f16y	(0-95)H	GD	£8724
87	6/07	Nott	1m54y	(0-85)H	G-F	£4857
71	12/06	Ling	7f		STD	£3562

Total win prize-money £34336

Going (Turf): Sf: 0-2 GS: 0-4 Gd: 1-12 **GF: 3-10** Fm: 0-0
Distance: 5f/6f: 0-6 **7f-8f: 3-16** 9f-13f: 2-13 14f+: 0-0
Track : LH: 2-17 RH: 2-7 **Tight: 1-8** Gall: 0-1
Aids: Bl: 0-0 Vi: 0-0 Tstrap: 0-0 Ckp: 0-0
Best Rating: 99 10/07 Pont 1m4y good

Fair; effective over 7f-1m2f; acts on most ground; has worn a tongue tie.

Danetime Lily (IRE)

101 (67)80
5-y-o b m Danetime (IRE)-Millie's Lily (IRE) (Distinctly North (USA))
Ms Joanna Morgan Derek Healy

Placings:0000112/2101000-015504 **(4831a)**
2009: 5^{0}GF, 5^{1}GF, 5^{5}S, 5^{5}G, 5^{0}HY, 5^{4}S,

	Starts	1st	2nd	3rd	Win & Pl
Career Total (Turf)	18	5	2	0	36818
Career Total (AW)	2	0	0	0	

77	6/09	DRoy	5f	(50-80)H	G-F	£7044
77	6/08	Navn	5f	H	FRM	£11966
74	6/08	Tipp	5f	(50-80)H	GD	£6351
61	10/07	Navn	5f	(42-60)H	G-F	£4435
51	8/07	DRoy	5f	(42-60)H	GD	£3968

Total win prize-money £33766

Going (Turf): Sf: 0-4 GS: 0-0 **Gd: 2-5 GF: 2-4** Fm: 1-3
Distance: 5f/6f: 5-17 7f-8f: 0-2 9f-13f: 0-1 14f+: 0-0
Track : LH: 3-8 RH: 2-5 Tight: 0-0 Gall: 0-0
Aids: Bl: 0-0 Vi: 0-0 Tstrap: 0-4 Ckp: 0-4
Best Rating: 80 7/09 NmkJ 5f good

Danetime Panther (IRE)

100(99) (79)78

5-y-o b g Danetime (IRE)-Annotate (Groom Dancer (USA))

Ian Williams Jenny & Mark Pitman Racing Club

Placings:0/010/535402430-0035 **(2798)**

2009: 8^{0}G, 10^{0}S, 9^{3}G, 12^{5}GF,

	Starts	1st	2nd	3rd	Win & Pl
Career Total (Turf)	13	0	0	3	3095
Career Total (AW)	4	1	1	0	4937

76 4/07 Sthl 1m STD £3071

Total win prize-money £3071

Going (Turf): **Sf: 0-2 GS: 0-2 Gd: 0-3 GF: 0-6 Fm: 0-0**
Distance: 5f/6f: 0-1 **7f-8f: 1-5** 9f-13f: 0-11 14f+: 0-0
Track : **LH: 1-3** RH: 0-11 Tight: 0-5 Gall: 0-2
Aids: Bl: 0-1 Vi: 0-0 Tstrap: 0-2 Ckp: 0-2
Best Rating: 79 9/08 Kemp 1m stand

Fair; stays 1m2f; acts on Fibresand and fast turf.

Danger Mulally

90(100) (73)68

2-y-o b g Governor Brown (USA)-Glittering Image (IRE) (Sadler's Wells (USA))

A M Balding John Dwyer

Placings:0510001 **(7685)**

2009: 6^{0}GF, 7^{5}GF, 7^{1}GF, 7^{0}G, 8^{0}SD, 8^{0}SD, 8^{1}SD,

	Starts	1st	2nd	3rd	Win & Pl
Career Total (Turf)	4	1	0	0	3400
Career Total (AW)	3	1	0	0	3886

73 12/09 Kemp 1m (0-85) STD £3885
68 7/09 Wwck 7f26y G-F £3399

Total win prize-money £7286

Going (Turf): Sf: 0-0 GS: 0-0 Gd: 0-1 **GF: 1-3** Fm: 0-0
Distance: 5f/6f: 0-1 **7f-8f: 2-6** 9f-13f: 0-0 14f+: 0-0
Track : LH: 1-3 RH: 1-1 Tight: 0-2 Gall: 0-0
Aids: Bl: 0-0 Vi: 0-0 Tstrap: 0-0 Ckp: 0-0
Best Rating: 73 12/09 Kemp 1m stand

Fair; effective over 7f-1m; acts on fast ground and Polytrack; has worn cheekpieces/tongue tie.

Dangerous Midge (USA)

107 91

3-y-o b c Lion Heart (USA)-Adored Slew (USA) (Seattle Slew (USA))

B J Meehan Iraj Parvizi

Placings:0131 **(5828)**

2009: 10^{0}G, 9^{1}G, 10^{3}G, 10^{1}GF,

	Starts	1st	2nd	3rd	Win & Pl
Career Total (Turf)	4	2	0	1	14195

91 9/09 Donc 1m2f60y (0-85) G-F £9346
82 6/09 Sals 1m1f198y GD £3885

Total win prize-money £13233

Going (Turf): Sf: 0-0 GS: 0-0 **Gd: 1-3 GF: 1-1** Fm: 0-0
Distance: 5f/6f: 0-0 7f-8f: 0-0 **9f-13f: 2-4** 14f+: 0-0
Track : LH: 1-2 RH: 1-2 Tight: 1-2 Gall: 1-1
Aids: Bl: 0-0 Vi: 0-0 Tstrap: 0-0 Ckp: 0-0
Best Rating: 91 9/09 Donc 1m2f60y gd-fm

Useful; effective over 1m2f; acts on good and faster ground.

Dani's Girl (IRE)

99(92) (76)93

6-y-o b/br m Second Empire (IRE)-Quench The Lamp (IRE) (Glow (USA))

P M Phelan (P A Fahy 31/7) Clive Craig

Placings:0012160/5052040030**0**/30200**0**-0035001 **(7873)**

2009: 8^{0}G, 10^{0}GF, 10^{0}G, 11^{3}Y, 12^{5}G, 12^{0}GF, 10^{0}GF, 16^{1}SD,

	Starts	1st	2nd	3rd	Win & Pl
Career Total (Turf)	29	2	3	3	32535
Career Total (AW)	3	1	0	0	2590

12/09 Kemp 2m (0-75)H STD £2590
83 8/06 Gway 7f (60-90)H G-F £13468
74 6/06 Fair 7f FRM £5718

Total win prize-money £21778

Going (Turf): Sf: 0-3 GS: 0-0 Gd: 0-6 **GF: 1-7 Fm: 1-3**
Distance: 5f/6f: 0-0 **7f-8f: 2-16** 9f-13f: 0-15 14f+: 1-1
Track : LH: 0-10 **RH: 3-17** Tight: 0-3 Gall: 0-4
Aids: Bl: 0-1 Vi: 0-0 Tstrap: 0-0 Ckp: 0-0
Best Rating: 100 6/07 Naas 7f gd-yld

Fair; effective over 2m; acts on Polytrack.

Daniel Thomas (IRE)

95(106) (79)75

7-y-o b g Dansili-Last Look (Rainbow Quest (USA))

Mrs A L M King George Martin

Placings:22321/3/**06**/**6**5050000/**26**114006420-0000243051 **(7858)**

2009: 8^{0}GF, 8^{0}GF, 8^{0}SS, 10^{0}SD, 8^{2}SD, 8^{4}SD, 8^{3}SD, 8^{0}SD, 9^{5}SD, 8^{1}SD,

	Starts	1st	2nd	3rd	Win & Pl
Career Total (Turf)	18	1	3	2	9504
Career Total (AW)	19	3	3	1	12483

12/09 Wolv 1m141y STD £2047
75 5/08 Rdcr 1m1f (0-70)H G-F £2331
73 5/08 Ling 1m (0-70)H STD £2590
88 10/04 Ling 7f STD £5148

Total win prize-money £12116

Going (Turf): Sf: 0-2 GS: 0-2 Gd: 0-4 **GF: 1-10** Fm: 0-0
Distance: 5f/6f: 0-2 7f-8f: 2-21 9f-13f: 2-14 14f+: 0-0
Track : **LH: 4-16** RH: 0-14 **Tight: 4-16** Gall: 0-0
Aids: Bl: 0-0 **Vi: 1-2** Tstrap: 0-4 Ckp: 0-4
Best Rating: 89 12/06 Ling 1m stand

Modest; stays 1m1f; acts on most ground and on Polytrack; has worn cheekpieces/visor.

Daniella De Bruijn (IRE)

97(96) (72)74

2-y-o b f Orpen (USA)-Ardent Lady (Alhaarth (IRE))

A B Haynes Ms J Loylert

Placings:4412451430 **(7139)**

2009: 5^{4}GF, 5^{4}GF, 6^{1}S, 6^{2}GF, 6^{4}G, 5^{5}GF, 8^{1}SD, 7^{4}SD, 8^{3}SD, 9^{0}SD,

	Starts	1st	2nd	3rd	Win & Pl
Career Total (Turf)	6	1	1	0	5571
Career Total (AW)	4	1	0	1	2774

72 10/09 Wolv 1m141y STD £2388
74 5/09 Hayd 6f SFT £2914

Total win prize-money £5302

Going (Turf): **Sf: 1-1** GS: 0-0 Gd: 0-1 GF: 0-4 Fm: 0-0
Distance: 5f/6f: 1-5 7f-8f: 0-3 9f-13f: 1-2 14f+: 0-0
Track : **LH: 1-3** RH: 0-2 **Tight: 1-2** Gall: 0-1
Aids: Bl: 0-0 Vi: 0-0 Tstrap: 0-0 Ckp: 0-0
Best Rating: 74 6/09 Chep 6f16y gd-fm

Fair filly; stays 1m and acts on most ground and Polytrack.

Danies Boy (IRE)

99(97) (69)70

3-y-o b c Elusive City (USA)-Daniela Samuel (USA) (No Robbery)

R Hannon Simon Leech

Placings:4331 **(2009)**

2009: 7^{4}SD, 7^{3}SD, 7^{3}GF, 6^{1}F,

	Starts	1st	2nd	3rd	Win & Pl
Career Total (Turf)	2	1	0	1	3692
Career Total (AW)	2	0	0	1	596

66 5/09 Sals 6f212y FRM £3238

Total win prize-money £3238

Going (Turf): Sf: 0-0 GS: 0-0 Gd: 0-0 GF: 0-1 **Fm: 1-1**
Distance: 5f/6f: 0-0 **7f-8f: 1-4** 9f-13f: 0-0 14f+: 0-0
Track : LH: 0-2 RH: 0-1 Tight: 0-1 Gall: 0-0
Aids: Bl: 0-0 Vi: 0-0 Tstrap: 0-0 Ckp: 0-0
Best Rating: 70 4/09 Wwck 7f26y gd-fm

Fair; effective on Polytrack and fast turf; stays 7f.

Danish Art (IRE)

94(100) (76)77

4-y-o b g Danehill Dancer (IRE)-Lady Ounavarra (IRE) (Simply Great (FR))

M W Easterby E A Brook

Placings:36/310053-0600065 **(5982)**

2009: 7^{0}SD, 6^{6}SD, 7^{0}SD, 7^{0}SD, 7^{0}GF, 7^{6}SD, 8^{5}GF,

	Starts	1st	2nd	3rd	Win & Pl
Career Total (Turf)	7	1	0	2	6144
Career Total (AW)	8	0	0	1	403

77 6/08 NmkJ 6f (0-80)H FRM £5180

Total win prize-money £5181

Going (Turf): Sf: 0-1 GS: 0-0 Gd: 0-0 GF: 0-5 **Fm: 1-1**
Distance: **5f/6f: 1-4** 7f-8f: 0-10 9f-13f: 0-1 14f+: 0-0
Track : LH: 0-6 RH: 0-3 Tight: 0-3 Gall: 0-0
Aids: Bl: 0-0 Vi: 0-0 Tstrap: 0-0 Ckp: 0-0
Best Rating: 77 6/08 NmkJ 6f firm

Moderate; effective over 6f-7f; acts on fast ground; goes on Polytrack.

Dannios

78(93) (63)57

3-y-o b c Tobougg (IRE)-Fleuve D'Or (IRE) (Last Tycoon)

L M Cumani P Booth & D Boorer

Placings:330-000 **(4734)**

2009: 8^{0}G, 8^{0}GF, 9^{0}GS,

	Starts	1st	2nd	3rd	Win & Pl
Career Total (Turf)	4	0	0	1	385
Career Total (AW)	2	0	0	1	252

Going (Turf): **Sf: 0-0 GS: 0-1 Gd: 0-1 GF: 0-2 Fm: 0-0**
Distance: 5f/6f: 0-3 7f-8f: 0-0 9f-13f: 0-3 14f+: 0-0
Track : LH: 0-4 RH: 0-0 Tight: 0-1 Gall: 0-1
Aids: Bl: 0-1 Vi: 0-0 Tstrap: 0-0 Ckp: 0-0
Best Rating: 63 8/08 Ling 6f stand

Modest so far; effective over 6f; acts on Polytrack.

Danny's Choice

97 87

2-y-o ch f Compton Place-Pie High (Salse (USA))

R M Beckett G B Partnership

Placings:21610 **(6241)**

2009: 5^{2}GF, 5^{1}G, 5^{6}G, 6^{1}F, 6^{0}G,

	Starts	1st	2nd	3rd	Win & Pl
Career Total (Turf)	**5**	**2**	**1**	**0**	**7421**

73 9/09 Folk 6f FRM £3885
70 7/09 Nott 5f13y GD £2729
Total win prize-money £6616

Going (Turf): Sf: 0-0 GS: 0-0 **Gd: 1-3** GF: 0-1 **Fm: 1-1**
Distance: **5f/6f: 2-4** 7f-8f: 0-1 9f-13f: 0-0 14f+: 0-0
Track : LH: 0-0 RH: 0-1 Tight: 0-0 Gall: 0-0
Aids: Bl: 0-0 Vi: 0-0 Tstrap: 0-0 Ckp: 0-0
Best Rating: **87** 8/09 Deau 5f good

Fair; effective at 5f on good ground.

Dansant

113(113) (117)113

5-y-o b h Dansili-La Balagna (Kris)

G A Butler Mrs Barbara M Keller

Placings:1230251511/10044611-26135 **(5023)**

2009: 10^{2}SD, 10^{6}FT, 10^{1}SD, 12^{3}GF, 13^{5}GF,

	Starts	1st	2nd	3rd	Win & Pl
Career Total (Turf)	**13**	**2**	**2**	**2**	**67649**
Career Total (AW)	**10**	**6**	**1**	**0**	**120053**

117 3/09 Kemp 1m2f STD £22708
116 12/08 Ling 1m2f STD £22708
108 11/08 Kemp 1m4f STD £22708
103 2/08 Ling 1m2f STD £14762
116 12/07 Kemp 1m4f STD £14762
108 11/07 Kemp 1m4f STD £14762
102 9/07 Donc 1m6f132y (0-110)H G-F £32385
86 4/07 Wind 1m2f7y G-F £3238
Total win prize-money £148037

Going (Turf): Sf: 0-2 GS: 0-0 Gd: 0-4 **GF: 2-7** Fm: 0-0
Distance: 5f/6f: 0-0 7f-8f: 0-0 **9f-13f: 7-18** 14f+: 1-5
Track : LH: 3-9 **RH: 5-14 Tight: 3-6** Gall: 1-7
Aids: Bl: 0-0 Vi: 0-0 Tstrap: 0-0 Ckp: 0-0
Best Rating: **117** 3/09 Kemp 1m2f stand

Smart; multiple Listed winner and Group placed; stays 1m6f, but effective over shorter; acts on most ground, but very effective on Polytrack.

Danse On Wood

91(102) (70)60

3-y-o b c Dansili-Woodwin (IRE) (Woodman (USA))

J Noseda Mr And Mrs J D Cotton

Placings:00200 **(6975)**

2009: 10^{0}GF, 12^{0}GF, 12^{2}SD, 16^{0}SD, 12^{0}SD,

	Starts	1st	2nd	3rd	Win & Pl
Career Total (Turf)	**2**	**0**	**0**	**0**	
Career Total (AW)	**3**	**0**	**1**	**0**	**806**

Going (Turf): **Sf: 0-0 GS: 0-0 Gd: 0-0 GF: 0-2 Fm: 0-0**
Distance: 5f/6f: 0-0 7f-8f: 0-0 9f-13f: 0-4 14f+: 0-1
Track : LH: 0-2 RH: 0-2 Tight: 0-1 Gall: 0-1
Aids: Bl: 0-0 Vi: 0-0 Tstrap: 0-0 Ckp: 0-0
Best Rating: **70** 7/09 Ling 1m4f stand

Fair; stays 1m4f and acts on Polytrack.

Dansili Dancer

109(107) (105)105

7-y-o b g Dansili-Magic Slipper (Habitat)

C G Cox The Loyal Troupers

Placings:21552/0010114/6050153/066535-3416004 **(6302)**

2009: 12^{3}SD, 12^{4}GF, 12^{1}GF, 12^{6}GF, 11^{0}GF, 14^{0}GF, 12^{4}GF,

	Starts	1st	2nd	3rd	Win & Pl
Career Total (Turf)	**29**	**6**	**2**	**1**	**175733**
Career Total (AW)	**3**	**0**	**0**	**2**	**5816**

105 5/09 Donc 1m4f (0-100)H G-F £16190
106 8/07 Hayd 1m3f200y H G-F £52972
104 8/06 Hayd 1m2f120y (0-105)H G-F £49856
101 7/06 Sand 1m2f7y (0-100)H G-F £11217
98 6/06 Gdwd 1m (0-100)H G-F £13087
91 6/05 Gdwd 1m GD £3610
Total win prize-money £146934

Going (Turf): Sf: 0-2 GS: 0-2 Gd: 1-7 **GF: 5-18** Fm: 0-0
Distance: 5f/6f: 0-0 7f-8f: 2-7 **9f-13f: 4-20** 14f+: 0-5
Track : LH: 3-12 RH: 3-14 Tight: 0-7 **Gall: 1-10**
Aids: Bl: 0-0 Vi: 0-0 Tstrap: 0-1 Ckp: 0-1
Best Rating: **108** 9/07 Hayd 1m6f gd-fm

Smart; effective from 1m2f-1m6f; acts on good and faster ground and Polytrack; has worn cheekpieces.

Dansilver

(104) (67)67

5-y-o b g Dansili-Silver Gyre (IRE) (Silver Hawk (USA))

A W Carroll John W Egan

Placings:5052062000/25/16050-231 **(0252)**

2009: 12^{2}SD, 12^{3}SD, 16^{1}SD,

	Starts	1st	2nd	3rd	Win & Pl
Career Total (Turf)	**15**	**1**	**2**	**0**	**3547**
Career Total (AW)	**5**	**1**	**2**	**1**	**3308**

67 1/09 Wolv 2m119y (0-65)H STD £1706
67 4/08 Sthl 2m (0-65)H G-F £1774
Total win prize-money £3480

Going (Turf): Sf: 0-5 GS: 0-0 Gd: 0-3 **GF: 1-5** Fm: 0-2
Distance: 5f/6f: 0-1 7f-8f: 0-7 9f-13f: 0-5 **14f+: 2-7**
Track : **LH: 2-12** RH: 0-3 **Tight: 2-8** Gall: 0-0
Aids: Bl: 0-0 Vi: 0-0 Tstrap: 0-1 Ckp: 0-1
Best Rating: **67** 1/09 Wolv 2m119y stand

Moderate; stays 2m; acts on most ground on turf; goes on Polytrack; winning hurdler.

Dansimar

84 (72)61

5-y-o gr m Daylami (IRE)-Hylandra (USA) (Bering)

Miss Venetia Williams Let's Live Racing

Placings:305/63063232303423/53 **(2127)**

2009: 14^{5}G, 17^{3}GS,

	Starts	1st	2nd	3rd	Win & Pl
Career Total (Turf)	**13**	**0**	**1**	**6**	**3617**
Career Total (AW)	**6**	**0**	**2**	**2**	**2182**

Going (Turf): **Sf: 0-0 GS: 0-1 Gd: 0-7 GF: 0-4 Fm: 0-1**
Distance: 5f/6f: 0-0 7f-8f: 0-1 9f-13f: 0-9 14f+: 0-9
Track : LH: 0-9 RH: 0-8 Tight: 0-10 Gall: 0-2
Aids: Bl: 0-0 Vi: 0-0 Tstrap: 0-0 Ckp: 0-0
Best Rating: **72** 7/07 Kemp 1m4f stand

Modest; stays 2m2f; acts on a sound surface and Polytrack.

Dantari (IRE)

98(104) (68)65

4-y-o b c Alhaarth (IRE)-Daniysha (IRE) (Doyoun)

Evan Williams Ian Brice

Placings:405-636 **(4168)**

2009: 13^{6}SD, 14^{3}GF, 16^{6}G,

	Starts	1st	2nd	3rd	Win & Pl
Career Total (Turf)	**3**	**0**	**0**	**1**	**578**
Career Total (AW)	**3**	**0**	**0**	**0**	**377**

Going (Turf): **Sf: 0-0 GS: 0-0 Gd: 0-1 GF: 0-1 Fm: 0-0**
Distance: 5f/6f: 0-0 7f-8f: 0-1 9f-13f: 0-3 14f+: 0-2
Track : LH: 0-6 RH: 0-0 Tight: 0-1 Gall: 0-1
Aids: Bl: 0-1 Vi: 0-0 Tstrap: 0-0 Ckp: 0-0
Best Rating: **68** 9/08 Dund 1m stand

Dante Deo (USA)

94(93) (55)59

3-y-o b f Proud Citizen (USA)-Best Feature (USA) (El Gran Senor (USA))

T D Barron Patrick Toes & R G Toes

Placings:42-6005160 **(2236)**

2009: 9^{6}SD, 7^{0}SD, 8^{0}GF, 7^{5}GF, 7^{1}GF, 8^{6}F, 8^{0}GS,

	Starts	1st	2nd	3rd	Win & Pl
Career Total (Turf)	**5**	**1**	**0**	**0**	**1910**
Career Total (AW)	**4**	**0**	**1**	**0**	**869**

59 5/09 Bevl 7f100y (0-60)H G-F £1910
Total win prize-money £1910

Going (Turf): Sf: 0-0 GS: 0-1 Gd: 0-0 **GF: 1-3** Fm: 0-1
Distance: 5f/6f: 0-0 **7f-8f: 1-6** 9f-13f: 0-3 14f+: 0-0
Track : LH: 0-4 **RH: 1-2** Tight: 0-1 Gall: 0-1
Aids: Bl: 0-0 Vi: 0-0 Tstrap: 0-0 Ckp: 0-0
Best Rating: **59** 5/09 Bevl 7f100y gd-fm

Modest; effective over 7f; acts on Fibresand.

Danube (IRE)

90 62

2-y-o b f Montjeu (IRE)-Darabela (IRE) (Desert King (IRE))

H R A Cecil Gestut Ammerland

Placings:5 **(5547)**

2009: 8^{5}GF,

	Starts	1st	2nd	3rd	Win & Pl
Career Total (Turf)	**1**	**0**	**0**	**0**	**0**

Going (Turf): **Sf: 0-0 GS: 0-0 Gd: 0-0 GF: 0-1 Fm: 0-0**
Distance: 5f/6f: 0-0 7f-8f: 0-0 9f-13f: 0-1 14f+: 0-0
Track : LH: 0-0 RH: 0-1 Tight: 0-0 Gall: 0-0
Aids: Bl: 0-0 Vi: 0-0 Tstrap: 0-0 Ckp: 0-0
Best Rating: **62** 9/09 Leic 1m60y gd-fm

Danum Dancer

96(99) (68)62

5-y-o ch g Allied Forces (USA)-Branston Dancer (Rudimentary (USA))

N Bycroft G Hart, B Abbott, R McGrane, K Senior

Placings:6452001016/050605000/0-03504100 **(7870)**

2009: 6^{0}G, 6^{3}S, 5^{5}SD, 5^{0}SD, 6^{4}SD, 6^{1}SD, 7^{0}SD, 6^{0}SS,

	Starts	1st	2nd	3rd	Win & Pl
Career Total (Turf)	**22**	**2**	**1**	**1**	**126849**
Career Total (AW)	**6**	**1**	**0**	**0**	**1706**

68 12/09 Sthl 6f (0-60)H STD £1706
91 9/06 Rdcr 6f GD £113560

87 8/06 Bevl 5f G-S £9715
Total win prize-money £124982

Going (Turf): Sf: 0-3 **GS: 1-5 Gd: 1-7** GF: 0-6 Fm: 0-1
Distance: **5f/6f: 3-25** 7f-8f: 0-3 9f-13f: 0-0 14f+: 0-0
Track : **LH: 1-4** RH: 0-0 Tight: 0-0 Gall: 0-0
Aids: **Bl: 3-15** Vi: 0-0 Tstrap: 0-0 Ckp: 0-0
Best Rating: 94 9/06 York 5f good

Moderate; former Listed winner; effective over 5f-6f; acts on fast and easy ground; usually wears blinkers.

Danvilla

(62)
2-y-o b f Dansili-Newtown Villa (Spectrum (IRE))
P R Webber Shully Liebermann

Placings:0 **(6628)**
2009: 8^{0}SS,

	Starts	1st	2nd	3rd	Win & Pl
Career Total (Turf)	0	0	0	0	
Career Total (AW)	1	0	0	0	

Going (Turf): **Sf: 0-0 GS: 0-0 Gd: 0-0 GF: 0-0 Fm: 0-0**
Distance: 5f/6f: 0-0 7f-8f: 0-1 9f-13f: 0-0 14f+: 0-0
Track : LH: 0-1 RH: 0-0 Tight: 0-1 Gall: 0-0
Aids: Bl: 0-0 Vi: 0-0 Tstrap: 0-0 Ckp: 0-0

Danzadil (IRE)

96(96) (56)**60**
3-y-o b f Mujadil (USA)-Changari (USA) (Gulch (USA))
R A Teal The Rat Racers

Placings:503P40-0003004 **(7069)**
2009: 6^{0}G, 6^{0}SD, 5^{0}G, 7^{3}G, 7^{0}SD, 7^{0}GF, 6^{4}SD,

	Starts	1st	2nd	3rd	Win & Pl
Career Total (Turf)	8	0	0	2	1107
Career Total (AW)	5	0	0	0	0

Going (Turf): **Sf: 0-0 GS: 0-1 Gd: 0-4 GF: 0-3 Fm: 0-0**
Distance: 5f/6f: 0-8 7f-8f: 0-5 9f-13f: 0-0 14f+: 0-0
Track : LH: 0-6 RH: 0-2 Tight: 0-5 Gall: 0-3
Aids: Bl: 0-0 Vi: 0-0 Tstrap: 0-0 Ckp: 0-0
Best Rating: 60 6/08 Sals 5f gd-fm

Modest; effective over 6f; acts on easy ground.

Danzatrice

107 **76**
7-y-o b m Tamure (IRE)-Miss Petronella (Petoski)
C W Thornton 980 Racing

Placings:055/00/0305114144/02255416654602/22122453431650-2016063254200 **(7170)**
2009: 16^{2}GF, 14^{0}GF, 16^{1}GF, 16^{6}GS, 16^{0}GF, 16^{8}GF, 16^{3}GS, 16^{2}G, 16^{5}G, 16^{4}GS, 17^{2}G, 18^{0}G, 15^{0}S,

	Starts	1st	2nd	3rd	Win & Pl
Career Total (Turf)	56	7	10	4	43851

76	5/09	Ripn	2m	(0-70)H	G-F	£3238
71	8/08	Muss	1m6f	(0-75)H	GD	£3885
70	5/08	Ripn	2m	(0-70)H	GD	£3238
68	8/07	Muss	1m5f	(0-65)H	G-F	£2498
59	8/06	Muss	1m6f	(0-65)H	GD	£3238
58	8/06	Ayr	1m7f	(0-60)H	G-F	£3238
55	8/06	Muss	1m5f	(0-60)H	GD	£3296

Total win prize-money £22635

Going (Turf): Sf: 0-8 GS: 0-10 **Gd: 4-21**GF: 3-16 Fm: 0-1
Distance: 5f/6f: 0-2 7f-8f: 0-1 9f-13f: 2-9 **14f+: 5-44**
Track : LH: 1-24 **RH: 6-29 Tight: 6-31** Gall: 0-13
Aids: Bl: 0-0 Vi: 0-0 Tstrap: 0-0 Ckp: 0-0
Best Rating: 76 5/09 Ripn 2m gd-fm

Fair; stays 2m but effective at shorter; acts on fast and easy ground; often goes well at Musselburgh.

Danzig Fox

98(98) (57)**64**
4-y-o b g Foxhound (USA)-Via Dolorosa (Chaddleworth (IRE))
M Mullineaux Southley Racing Partnership

Placings:160/004300000-050000 **(7085)**
2009: 5^{0}SD, 7^{5}GF, 8^{0}S, 6^{0}GS, 7^{0}SD, 11^{0}S,

	Starts	1st	2nd	3rd	Win & Pl
Career Total (Turf)	13	1	0	1	4766
Career Total (AW)	5	0	0	0	

65 7/07 Ayr 6f GD £3238
Total win prize-money £3239

Going (Turf): Sf: 0-4 GS: 0-3 **Gd: 1-3** GF: 0-3 Fm: 0-0
Distance: **5f/6f: 1-7** 7f-8f: 0-10 9f-13f: 0-1 14f+: 0-0
Track : LH: 0-14 RH: 0-0 Tight: 0-12 Gall: 0-0
Aids: Bl: 0-2 Vi: 0-0 Tstrap: 0-1 Ckp: 0-1
Best Rating: 65 7/07 Ayr 6f good

Modest; suited by 6f and good ground; has worn cheek-pieces.

Danzili Bay

87(95) (67)**71**
7-y-o b h Dansili-Lady Bankes (IRE) (Alzao (USA))
A W Carroll Winding Wheel Partnership

Placings:4410/21414/0/0416304-0 **(1890)**
2009: 6^{0}GF,

	Starts	1st	2nd	3rd	Win & Pl
Career Total (Turf)	17	4	1	1	28459
Career Total (AW)	1	0	0	0	313

71	6/08	Sals	6f	(0-75)H	G-F	£3238
95	7/05	Hayd	6f	(0-90)H	G-F	£10029
86	5/05	Leic	5f218y	(0-80)	G-F	£6890
78	9/04	Rdcr	5f		G-F	£2975

Total win prize-money £23133

Going (Turf): Sf: 0-1 GS: 0-3 Gd: 0-1 **GF: 4-11** Fm: 0-1
Distance: **5f/6f: 4-17** 7f-8f: 0-1 9f-13f: 0-0 14f+: 0-0
Track : LH: 0-4 RH: 0-0 Tight: 0-0 Gall: 0-5
Aids: Bl: 0-0 Vi: 0-0 Tstrap: 0-0 Ckp: 0-0
Best Rating: 95 7/05 Hayd 6f gd-fm

Modest; effective over 5f-6f; handles most ground, but best on fast; likes to race prominently.

Danzoe (IRE)

97 **77**
2-y-o b g Kheleyf (USA)-Fiaba (Precocious)
D Donovan Philip Mclaughlin

Placings:226140050 **(6693)**
2009: 5^{2}GF, 5^{2}GF, 6^{6}G, 6^{1}GS, 5^{4}GF, 5^{0}G, 5^{0}GF, 7^{5}GF, 7^{0}GS,

	Starts	1st	2nd	3rd	Win & Pl
Career Total (Turf)	9	1	2	0	6787

77 6/09 Ripn 6f G-S £4209
Total win prize-money £4209

Going (Turf): Sf: 0-0 **GS: 1-2** Gd: 0-2 GF: 0-5 Fm: 0-0
Distance: **5f/6f: 1-7** 7f-8f: 0-2 9f-13f: 0-0 14f+: 0-0
Track : LH: 0-1 RH: 0-1 Tight: 0-0 Gall: 0-0
Aids: Bl: 0-0 Vi: 0-0 Tstrap: 0-0 Ckp: 0-0
Best Rating: 77 7/09 Leic 5f218y gd-fm

Fair; effective over 6f; acts on fast and easy ground.

Daphne Du Maurier (IRE)

76 **35**
2-y-o b f Arakan (USA)-Butter Knife (IRE) (Sure Blade (USA))
I Semple Allan McWilliam/Christopher McWilliam

Placings:0500 **(5942)**
2009: 6^{0}GF, 6^{5}GF, 5^{0}GS, 7^{0}G,

	Starts	1st	2nd	3rd	Win & Pl
Career Total (Turf)	4	0	0	0	0

Going (Turf): **Sf: 0-0 GS: 0-1 Gd: 0-1 GF: 0-2 Fm: 0-0**
Distance: 5f/6f: 0-3 7f-8f: 0-1 9f-13f: 0-0 14f+: 0-0
Track : LH: 0-0 RH: 0-1 Tight: 0-1 Gall: 0-0
Aids: Bl: 0-0 Vi: 0-0 Tstrap: 0-0 Ckp: 0-0
Best Rating: 35 8/09 Ayr 6f gd-fm

Dar Es Salaam

102 **84**
5-y-o ch g King's Best (USA)-Place De L'Opera (Sadler's Wells (USA))
James Moffatt (J S Goldie 1/8) John Macgregor

Placings:521500/303352164-603060 **(6995)**
2009: 12^{6}G, 10^{0}S, 12^{3}G, 10^{0}GS, 10^{6}G, 14^{0}GS,

	Starts	1st	2nd	3rd	Win & Pl
Career Total (Turf)	20	2	2	4	14593
Career Total (AW)	1	0	0	0	

83	9/08	Newb	1m2f6y	(0-85)H	GD	£5180
84	7/07	Pont	1m2f6y		GD	£3886

Total win prize-money £9067

Going (Turf): Sf: 0-4 GS: 0-3 **Gd: 2-10** GF: 0-3 Fm: 0-0
Distance: 5f/6f: 0-0 7f-8f: 0-0 **9f-13f: 2-19** 14f+: 0-2
Track : **LH: 2-14** RH: 0-7 Tight: 0-3 **Gall: 1-12**
Aids: Bl: 0-0 Vi: 0-0 Tstrap: 0-0 Ckp: 0-0
Best Rating: 84 9/08 Sand 1m2f7y soft

Fair; effective at around 1m2f-1m4f; acts on good and soft ground.

Dar Re Mi

116 **119**
4-y-o b f Singspiel (IRE)-Darara (Top Ville)
J H M Gosden Watership Down Stud

Placings:2/13311223-211553 **(7310a)**
2009: 10^{2}G, 10^{1}Y, 12^{1}GF, 12^{5}G, 12^{5}G, 12^{3}F,

	Starts	1st	2nd	3rd	Win & Pl
Career Total (Turf)	15	5	4	4	820178

119	8/09	York	1m4f	G-F	£175987
110	6/09	Curr	1m2f	YLD	£131067
109	8/08	Deau	1m4f110y	G-S	£29412
106	7/08	NmkJ	1m4f	G-F	£24978
93	4/08	Sand	1m2f7y	G-S	£5180

Total win prize-money £366627

Going (Turf): Sf: 0-0 **GS: 2-4** Gd: 0-6 **GF: 2-3** Fm: 0-1
Distance: 5f/6f: 0-0 7f-8f: 0-1 **9f-13f: 5-14** 14f+: 0-0
Track : LH: 1-5 **RH: 4-9** Tight: 0-0 **Gall: 2-5**
Aids: Bl: 0-0 Vi: 0-0 Tstrap: 0-0 Ckp: 0-0
Best Rating: 119 10/09 Lonc 1m4f good

High class; winner of Group 1 Pretty Polly Stakes and the Group 1 Yorkshire Oaks in 2009; finished first but disqualified from the Prix Vermeille; fifth in the Arc and third in the Breeders' Cup Turf; effective at up to 1m4f; acts on fast and easy ground.

Daraahem (IRE)

99 **106**

4-y-o ch g Act One-Shamah (Unfuwain (USA))
B W Hills Hamdan Al Maktoum

Placings:0/210310-1 **(1790)**
2009: 18^{1}GF,

	Starts	1st	2nd	3rd	Win & Pl
Career Total (Turf)	8	3	1	1	97003

106 5/09 Ches 2m2f147y H G-F £74772
103 8/08 Hayd 1m6f (0-95)H SFT £9714
95 5/08 Ches 1m2f75y GD £7123
Total win prize-money £91610

Going (Turf): **Sf: 1-1** GS: 0-0 **Gd: 1-5 GF: 1-2** Fm: 0-0
Distance: 5f/6f: 0-0 7f-8f: 0-1 9f-13f: 1-4 **14f+: 2-3**
Track : **LH: 3-4** RH: 0-2 **Tight: 2-2** Gall: 0-2
Aids: Bl: 0-0 Vi: 0-0 Tstrap: 0-0 Ckp: 0-0
Best Rating: **106** 5/09 Ches 2m2f147y gd-fm

Smart; won the Chester Cup in 2009; stays 2m2f; acts on fast and easy ground.

Daraiym (IRE)

106(101) (57)**65**

4-y-o b g Peintre Celebre (USA)-Dararita (IRE) (Halo (USA))
Paul Green Paul Boyers

Placings:400000**304**-5**1**16 **(1399)**
2009: 16^{5}SD, 15^{1}GF, 17^{1}GF, 21^{6}F,

	Starts	1st	2nd	3rd	Win & Pl
Career Total (Turf)	8	2	0	0	5819
Career Total (AW)	5	0	0	1	589

59 4/09 Pont 2m1f216y (0-75)H G-F £3238
54 4/09 Catt 1m7f177y (0-65)H G-F £2388
Total win prize-money £5626

Going (Turf): Sf: 0-0 GS: 0-1 Gd: 0-2 **GF: 2-4** Fm: 0-1
Distance: 5f/6f: 0-0 7f-8f: 0-0 9f-13f: 0-5 **14f+: 2-8**
Track : **LH: 2-13** RH: 0-0 **Tight: 1-7** Gall: 0-0
Aids: Bl: 0-0 Vi: 0-0 Tstrap: 0-0 Ckp: 0-0
Best Rating: **65** 4/08 Hayd 1m3f200y gd-sft

Moderate; stays 2m and acts on fast ground.

Darcey

105(94) (75)**77**

3-y-o ch f Noverre (USA)-Firozi (Forzando)
Miss Amy Weaver (R A Fahey 16/9) Michael Bringloe

Placings:515-5302**11316**300 **(7149)**
2009: 7^{5}GF, 6^{3}GF, 7^{0}S, 6^{2}GF, 7^{1}GF, 6^{1}GF, 7^{3}S, 8^{1}GF, 8^{6}SD, 8^{3}GF, 7^{0}SD, 8^{0}G,

	Starts	1st	2nd	3rd	Win & Pl
Career Total (Turf)	13	4	1	3	13805
Career Total (AW)	2	0	0	0	0

77 9/09 Yarm 1m3y G-F £3238
73 8/09 Ripn 6f G-F £2590
65 8/09 Newc 7f G-F £1942
77 9/08 Catt 5f212y G-S £3561
Total win prize-money £11333

Going (Turf): Sf: 0-3 GS: 1-1 Gd: 0-2 **GF: 3-7** Fm: 0-0
Distance: **5f/6f: 2-5** 7f-8f: 1-8 9f-13f: 1-2 14f+: 0-0
Track : **LH: 1-5** RH: 0-3 **Tight: 1-2** Gall: 0-1
Aids: Bl: 0-0 Vi: 0-0 Tstrap: 0-0 Ckp: 0-0
Best Rating: **77** 10/09 Wwck 1m22y gd-fm

Fair; stays 1m and acts on most ground.

Darcy's Pride (IRE)

100(92) (43)**69**

5-y-o b/br m Danetime (IRE)-Cox's Ridge (IRE) (Indian Ridge)
P T Midgley (D W Barker 3/7) T Shepherd & A Turton

Placings:0064/1440116265200/065026002000-0104003002104030 **(7280)**
2009: 5^{0}GF, 5^{1}F, 5^{0}GF, 5^{4}GF, 5^{0}GF, 5^{0}GF, 5^{3}GF, 5^{0}G, 5^{0}G, 5^{2}GF, 5^{1}GF, 6^{0}GF, 5^{4}GF, 5^{0}GF, 5^{3}GF, 5^{0}SD,

	Starts	1st	2nd	3rd	Win & Pl
Career Total (Turf)	45	5	5	2	20023
Career Total (AW)	1	0	0	0	

61 8/09 Newc 5f (0-55)H G-F £2331
64 4/09 Rdcr 5f (0-70)H FRM £2590
74 6/07 Carl 5f (0-60)H GD £2047
66 6/07 Newc 5f (0-75)H GD £3562
61 4/07 Catt 5f (0-65)H G-F £2730
Total win prize-money £13261

Going (Turf): Sf: 0-2 GS: 0-6 **Gd: 2-10 GF: 2-25** Fm: 1-2
Distance: **5f/6f: 5-46** 7f-8f: 0-0 9f-13f: 0-0 14f+: 0-0
Track : LH: 0-7 **RH: 1-5** Tight: 0-4 **Gall: 1-5**
Aids: Bl: 0-0 Vi: 0-0 Tstrap: 0-0 Ckp: 0-0
Best Rating: **76** 8/07 Haml 5f4y gd-fm

Modest sprinter; suited by 5f; acts on fast ground; has worn a tongue tie.

Daredevil Dan

95 **65**

3-y-o b g Golden Snake (USA)-Tiempo (King Of Spain)
M H Tompkins Dullingham Park

Placings:0-3303 **(6789)**
2009: 10^{3}G, 10^{3}GF, 13^{0}G, 11^{3}G,

	Starts	1st	2nd	3rd	Win & Pl
Career Total (Turf)	5	0	0	3	1280

Going (Turf): **Sf: 0-0 GS: 0-0 Gd: 0-3 GF: 0-2 Fm: 0-0**
Distance: 5f/6f: 0-0 7f-8f: 0-1 9f-13f: 0-4 14f+: 0-0
Track : LH: 0-3 RH: 0-1 Tight: 0-2 Gall: 0-1
Aids: Bl: 0-0 Vi: 0-0 Tstrap: 0-0 Ckp: 0-0
Best Rating: **65** 5/09 Yarm 1m2f21y gd-fm

Dareh (IRE)

85(96) (66)**62**

3-y-o b f Invincible Spirit (IRE)-Delage (Bellypha)
M Johnston Sheikh Hamdan Bin Mohammed Al Maktoum

Placings:333-20 **(1736)**
2009: 6^{2}SD, 6^{0}GS,

	Starts	1st	2nd	3rd	Win & Pl
Career Total (Turf)	2	0	0	1	433
Career Total (AW)	3	0	1	2	1953

Going (Turf): **Sf: 0-1 GS: 0-1 Gd: 0-0 GF: 0-0 Fm: 0-0**
Distance: 5f/6f: 0-4 7f-8f: 0-1 9f-13f: 0-0 14f+: 0-0
Track : LH: 0-3 RH: 0-0 Tight: 0-2 Gall: 0-1
Aids: Bl: 0-0 Vi: 0-0 Tstrap: 0-0 Ckp: 0-0
Best Rating: **66** 10/08 GrLe 6f stand

Fair; stays 7f and acts on Polytrack.

Darfour

96 **68**

5-y-o b g Inchinor-Gai Bulga (Kris)
M Hill (J S Goldie 17/10) Martin Hill

Placings:60100/153000/5443656-245066 **(5941)**
2009: 9^{2}F, 8^{4}G, 10^{5}GF, 8^{0}GF, 8^{6}GS, 7^{6}G,

	Starts	1st	2nd	3rd	Win & Pl
Career Total (Turf)	24	2	1	2	11511

77 5/07 Newc 7f (0-75)H GD £3562
74 7/06 Ling 7f G-F £3886
Total win prize-money £7448

Going (Turf): Sf: 0-5 GS: 0-2 **Gd: 1-6 GF: 1-10** Fm: 0-1
Distance: 5f/6f: 0-2 **7f-8f: 2-13** 9f-13f: 0-9 14f+: 0-0
Track : LH: 0-9 RH: 0-4 Tight: 0-4 Gall: 0-2
Aids: Bl: 0-0 Vi: 0-2 Tstrap: 0-2 Ckp: 0-2
Best Rating: **77** 5/07 Newc 7f good

Modest; effective over 7f-1m; acts on fast and soft ground.

Daring Dream (GER)

104(101) (65)**70**

4-y-o ch c Big Shuffle (USA)-Daring Action (Arazi (USA))
J S Goldie (A P Jarvis 5/7) Ambrose Turnbull

Placings:6434320/040060**025**-**450321406** **(6984)**
2009: 8^{4}SD, 7^{5}SD, 8^{0}SD, 8^{3}GF, 7^{2}F, 7^{1}S, 6^{4}GF, 6^{0}G, 7^{6}G,

	Starts	1st	2nd	3rd	Win & Pl
Career Total (Turf)	19	1	2	3	10027
Career Total (AW)	6	0	1	0	648

70 8/09 Ayr 7f50y (0-65)H SFT £2388
Total win prize-money £2388

Going (Turf): **Sf: 1-5** GS: 0-4 Gd: 0-3 GF: 0-6 Fm: 0-1
Distance: 5f/6f: 0-7 **7f-8f: 1-14** 9f-13f: 0-4 14f+: 0-0
Track : **LH: 1-8** RH: 0-7 Tight: 0-1 Gall: 0-1
Aids: Bl: 0-0 Vi: 0-6 Tstrap: 0-0 Ckp: 0-0
Best Rating: **74** 9/07 Ayr 1m gd-sft

Modest; effective over 6f-1m; acts on most ground.

Daring Racer (GER)

102(100) (70)**64**

6-y-o ch g Big Shuffle (USA)-Daring Action (Arazi (USA))
Tim Vaughan (Mrs L J Mongan 20/8) The Spoofing Ten Partnership

Placings:54/54321/000**2240**/356**200620**-43565 **(5186)**
2009: 9^{4}GF, 9^{3}GF, 8^{5}GF, 9^{6}GF, 10^{5}GF,

	Starts	1st	2nd	3rd	Win & Pl
Career Total (Turf)	21	1	3	3	16394
Career Total (AW)	7	0	2	0	1189

72 9/06 Badn 1m1f GD £2897
Total win prize-money £2897

Going (Turf): Sf: 0-4 GS: 0-1 **Gd: 1-7** GF: 0-9 Fm: 0-0
Distance: 5f/6f: 0-0 7f-8f: 0-2 **9f-13f: 1-19** 14f+: 0-7
Track : **LH: 1-13** RH: 0-10 Tight: 0-10 Gall: 0-2
Aids: Bl: 0-0 Vi: 0-0 Tstrap: 0-8 Ckp: 0-8
Best Rating: **72** 9/06 Badn 1m1f good

Moderate; stays 2m; acts on Polytrack and fast turf.

Dark Camellia

92(97) (66)**50**

4-y-o b f Olden Times-Miss Mirror (Magic Mirror)
H J L Dunlop Barry Marsden

Placings:00/2033532-550**0506100** **(7591)**
2009: 6^{5}SD, 7^{5}GF, 7^{0}GF, 6^{0}SD, 7^{5}SD, 7^{0}SD, 8^{6}SD, 8^{1}SD, 8^{0}SD, 7^{0}SD,

	Starts	1st	2nd	3rd	Win & Pl
Career Total (Turf)	5	0	0	0	0

	Starts	1st	2nd	3rd	Win & Pl
Career Total (AW)	14	1	2	3	4233

64 11/09 Kemp 1m STD £2047

Total win prize-money £2047

Going (Turf): **Sf: 0-1 GS: 0-0 Gd: 0-0 GF: 0-4 Fm: 0-0**
Distance: 5f/6f: 0-3 **7f-8f: 1-14** 9f-13f: 0-2 14f+: 0-0
Track : LH: 0-7 **RH: 1-9** Tight: 0-7 Gall: 0-0
Aids: Bl: 0-1 Vi: 0-0 Tstrap: 0-0 Ckp: 0-0
Best Rating: **66** 11/08 Kemp 7f stand

Moderate; stays 1m and acts on Polytrack; has worn a tongue-tie.

Dark Desert

(84) (41)**43**

3-y-o b c Best Of The Bests (IRE)-Dune Safari (IRE) (Key Of Luck (USA))
A G Newcombe A G Newcombe

Placings:00004-5 **(0196)**
2009: 8^{5}SD,

	Starts	1st	2nd	3rd	Win & Pl
Career Total (Turf)	3	0	0	0	
Career Total (AW)	3	0	0	0	0

Going (Turf): **Sf: 0-0 GS: 0-1 Gd: 0-1 GF: 0-1 Fm: 0-0**
Distance: 5f/6f: 0-4 7f-8f: 0-1 9f-13f: 0-1 14f+: 0-0
Track : LH: 0-4 RH: 0-0 Tight: 0-1 Gall: 0-1
Aids: Bl: 0-0 Vi: 0-0 Tstrap: 0-0 Ckp: 0-0
Best Rating: **43** 7/08 Sals 6f gd-fm

Dark Echoes

90(84) (48)**59**

3-y-o bl g Diktat-Calamanco (Clantime)
Jedd O'Keeffe Ken And Delia Shaw-KGS Consulting LLP

Placings:400-5055054 **(6880)**
2009: 8^{5}GS, 8^{0}G, 8^{5}GS, 11^{5}S, 10^{0}GS, 8^{5}HY, 7^{4}SD,

	Starts	1st	2nd	3rd	Win & Pl
Career Total (Turf)	9	0	0	0	1371
Career Total (AW)	1	0	0	0	0

Going (Turf): **Sf: 0-2 GS: 0-5 Gd: 0-1 GF: 0-1 Fm: 0-0**
Distance: 5f/6f: 0-3 7f-8f: 0-2 9f-13f: 0-5 14f+: 0-0
Track : LH: 0-6 RH: 0-1 Tight: 0-3 Gall: 0-1
Aids: Bl: 0-1 Vi: 0-0 Tstrap: 0-0 Ckp: 0-0
Best Rating: **59** 8/08 Hayd 6f gd-sft

Plating-class half-brother to Corrybrough; not built on promising debut.

Dark Energy

(97) (63)**76**

5-y-o br g Observatory (USA)-Waterfowl Creek (IRE) (Be My Guest (USA))
M J Scudamore (R A Harris 10/8) The Yes No Wait Sorries

Placings:3/0040201/504-40650 **(7695)**
2009: 12^{4}G, 16^{0}SD, 13^{6}SD, 13^{5}SD, 12^{0}SD,

	Starts	1st	2nd	3rd	Win & Pl
Career Total (Turf)	12	1	1	1	6487
Career Total (AW)	4	0	0	0	0

77 10/07 Newc 1m2f32y (0-70)H G-S £3886

Total win prize-money £3886

Going (Turf): Sf: 0-2 **GS: 1-5** Gd: 0-4 GF: 0-1 Fm: 0-0
Distance: 5f/6f: 0-0 7f-8f: 0-3 **9f-13f: 1-7** 14f+: 0-6
Track : **LH: 1-13** RH: 0-3 Tight: 0-8 **Gall: 1-2**
Aids: Bl: 0-0 Vi: 0-0 Tstrap: 0-0 Ckp: 0-0

Best Rating: **77** 10/07 Newc 1m2f32y gd-sft

Modest; stays 1m 2f; acts on soft ground.

Dark Eyes (IRE)

97(94) (74)**81**

2-y-o b f Camacho-Sherkova (USA) (State Dinner (USA))
D J Coakley Barliffey Racing

Placings:13530 **(7187)**
2009: 5^{1}G, 6^{3}GF, 7^{5}SD, 7^{3}GF, 8^{0}G,

	Starts	1st	2nd	3rd	Win & Pl
Career Total (Turf)	4	1	0	2	5834
Career Total (AW)	1	0	0	0	0

78 7/09 Bath 5f161y GD £2072

Total win prize-money £2072

Going (Turf): Sf: 0-0 GS: 0-0 **Gd: 1-2** GF: 0-2 Fm: 0-0
Distance: **5f/6f: 1-2** 7f-8f: 0-3 9f-13f: 0-0 14f+: 0-0
Track : **LH: 1-2** RH: 0-0 Tight: 0-1 **Gall: 1-1**
Aids: Bl: 0-0 Vi: 0-0 Tstrap: 0-0 Ckp: 0-0
Best Rating: **81** 10/09 NmkR 7f gd-fm

Fair; stays 7f; handles good and fast ground.

Dark Lane

102 **86**

3-y-o b g Namid-Corps De Ballet (IRE) (Fasliyev (USA))
R A Fahey (T D Barron 8/7) David W Armstrong

Placings:3512-10205030 **(6050)**
2009: 6^{1}G, 6^{0}GF, 5^{2}GS, 6^{0}G, 5^{5}G, 6^{0}G, 6^{3}GF, 6^{0}G,

	Starts	1st	2nd	3rd	Win & Pl
Career Total (Turf)	12	2	2	2	32469

85 5/09 Hayd 6f (0-85)H GD £5504
71 8/08 NmkJ 6f G-F £21665

Total win prize-money £27171

Going (Turf): Sf: 0-1 GS: 0-1 **Gd: 1-6 GF: 1-4** Fm: 0-0
Distance: **5f/6f: 2-12** 7f-8f: 0-0 9f-13f: 0-0 14f+: 0-0
Track : LH: 0-0 RH: 0-0 Tight: 0-0 Gall: 0-0
Aids: Bl: 0-0 Vi: 0-0 Tstrap: 0-1 Ckp: 0-1
Best Rating: **86** 9/09 Hayd 6f gd-fm

Useful; 46,000gns first foal of a sprint winner; effective at 5f-6f; acts on good ground

Dark Mischief

107(103) (91)**102**

3-y-o b g Namid-Syrian Queen (Slip Anchor)
H Candy First Of Many Partnership

Placings:15-1505031 **(5959)**
2009: 6^{1}GF, 6^{5}GF, 6^{0}G, 6^{5}GF, 7^{0}GS, 6^{3}SD, 6^{1}GF,

	Starts	1st	2nd	3rd	Win & Pl
Career Total (Turf)	8	3	0	0	27082
Career Total (AW)	1	0	0	1	1156

102 9/09 Hayd 6f (0-90) G-F £10361
95 4/09 NmkR 6f (0-100)H G-F £12952
82 6/08 Wind 6f G-F £3302

Total win prize-money £26617

Going (Turf): Sf: 0-0 GS: 0-1 Gd: 0-2 **GF: 3-5** Fm: 0-0
Distance: **5f/6f: 3-8** 7f-8f: 0-1 9f-13f: 0-0 14f+: 0-0
Track : LH: 0-1 RH: 0-1 Tight: 0-1 **Gall: 1-1**
Aids: Bl: 0-0 Vi: 0-0 Tstrap: 0-0 Ckp: 0-0
Best Rating: **102** 9/09 Hayd 6f gd-fm

Very useful; effective over 6f and acts on fast ground.

Dark Moment

99 **76**

3-y-o gr g Spartacus (IRE)-Dim Ofan (Petong)
A Dickman Construction Crew Racing Partnership

Placings:00060-1R411106 **(6847)**
2009: 7^{1}GF, 7^{R}G, 8^{4}GF, 7^{1}G, 6^{1}GF, 6^{1}S, 7^{0}GF, 7^{6}G,

	Starts	1st	2nd	3rd	Win & Pl
Career Total (Turf)	13	4	0	0	9616

76 8/09 Haml 6f5y (0-65)H SFT £2388
71 8/09 Newc 6f (0-60)H G-F £2201
65 8/09 Muss 7f30y (0-65)H GD £2590
58 6/09 Muss 7f30y (0-55)H G-F £2266

Total win prize-money £9447

Going (Turf): Sf: 1-2 GS: 0-2 Gd: 1-4 **GF: 2-4** Fm: 0-1
Distance: 5f/6f: 1-2 **7f-8f: 3-10** 9f-13f: 0-1 14f+: 0-0
Track : LH: 0-3 **RH: 2-4 Tight: 2-7** Gall: 0-0
Aids: Bl: 0-0 Vi: 0-0 Tstrap: 3-5 Ckp: 3-5
Best Rating: **76** 8/09 Haml 6f5y soft

Modest; effective at 6-7f; acts on fast ground; can refuse to race; has worn cheekpieces.

Dark Oasis

96(99) (61)**61**

3-y-o b g Dubai Destination (USA)-Silent Waters (Polish Precedent (USA))
M C Chapman (K A Ryan 8/5) F Michael

Placings:00025-200223003605 **(5376)**
2009: 8^{2}SD, 9^{0}SF, 9^{0}GF, 8^{2}G, 9^{2}GF, 11^{3}GF, 12^{0}G, 10^{0}S, 16^{3}G, 16^{6}HY, 14^{0}G, 16^{5}SD,

	Starts	1st	2nd	3rd	Win & Pl
Career Total (Turf)	12	0	2	2	2330
Career Total (AW)	5	0	2	0	1914

Going (Turf): **Sf: 0-2 GS: 0-0 Gd: 0-5 GF: 0-5 Fm: 0-0**
Distance: 5f/6f: 0-1 7f-8f: 0-4 9f-13f: 0-8 14f+: 0-4
Track : LH: 0-7 RH: 0-7 Tight: 0-8 Gall: 0-1
Aids: Bl: 0-5 Vi: 0-0 Tstrap: 0-2 Ckp: 0-2
Best Rating: **61** 5/09 Ripn 1m1f170y gd-fm

Modest; effective over 7f-1m2f; goes on fast; acts on Fibresand and Polytrack.

Dark Planet

92(79) (53)**56**

6-y-o ch g Singspiel (IRE)-Warning Shadows (IRE) (Cadeaux Genereux)
D W Thompson A J Duffield

Placings:0004/2164404/00400005/226-00000 **(1765)**
2009: 8^{0}SS, 12^{0}SD, 12^{0}GF, 10^{0}GF, 11^{0}GF,

	Starts	1st	2nd	3rd	Win & Pl
Career Total (Turf)	14	1	2	0	6225
Career Total (AW)	13	0	1	0	1451

65 4/06 Bevl 1m1f207y (0-75)H G-F £4210

Total win prize-money £4210

Going (Turf): Sf: 0-4 GS: 0-1 Gd: 0-3 **GF: 1-6** Fm: 0-0
Distance: 5f/6f: 0-0 7f-8f: 0-3 **9f-13f: 1-22** 14f+: 0-2
Track : LH: 0-19 **RH: 1-6** Tight: 0-13 Gall: 0-2
Aids: Bl: 0-0 Vi: 0-10 Tstrap: 0-5 Ckp: 0-5
Best Rating: **66** 3/07 Kemp 1m4f stand

Moderate; suited by 1m2f; acts on fast ground.

Dark Prospect

104(106) (88)**91**

4-y-o b g Nayef (USA)-Miss Mirasol (Sheikh Albadou)

M A Jarvis Michael Hill

Placings:60/53321222-01520430 **(6907)**

2009: 10^{0}G, 9^{1}G, **10^{5}SD**, 10^{2}GS, 9^{0}G, 10^{4}GF, 10^{3}GS, 10^{0}G,

	Starts	1st	2nd	3rd	Win & Pl
Career Total (Turf)	15	1	4	3	13655
Career Total (AW)	3	1	1	0	4311

91 5/09 Leic 1m1f218y (0-80)H GD £4857
79 9/08 Kemp 1m2f (0-75)H STD £2590
Total win prize-money £7447

Going (Turf): Sf: 0-2 GS: 0-4 **Gd: 1-6** GF: 0-2 Fm: 0-1
Distance: 5f/6f: 0-0 7f-8f: 0-0 **9f-13f: 2-18** 14f+: 0-0
Track : LH: 0-10 **RH: 2-6** Tight: 0-6 Gall: 0-2
Aids: Bl: 0-2 Vi: 0-0 Tstrap: 0-3 Ckp: 0-3
Best Rating: 91 10/09 Nott 1m2f50y gd-sft

Useful; effective over 1m-1m2f; acts on fast ground; also goes on Polytrack; has worn cheekpieces and blinkers.

Dark Quest

103 **71**

3-y-o b f Rainbow Quest (USA)-Pure Grain (Polish Precedent (USA))
J L Dunlop R Barnett

Placings:04523 **(4743)**

2009: 10^{0}GS, 12^{4}GF, 12^{5}GF, 10^{2}GS, 14^{3}GS,

	Starts	1st	2nd	3rd	Win & Pl
Career Total (Turf)	5	0	1	1	1926

Going (Turf): Sf: 0-0 GS: 0-3 Gd: 0-0 GF: 0-2 Fm: 0-0
Distance: 5f/6f: 0-0 7f-8f: 0-0 9f-13f: 0-4 14f+: 0-1
Track : LH: 0-4 RH: 0-1 Tight: 0-1 Gall: 0-2
Aids: Bl: 0-0 Vi: 0-0 Tstrap: 0-0 Ckp: 0-0
Best Rating: 71 5/09 NmkR 1m4f gd-fm

Dark Ranger

97(98) (64)**64**

3-y-o b/br g Where Or When (IRE)-Dark Raider (IRE) (Definite Article)
T J Pitt Recycled Products Limited

Placings:00000-31331230054 **(7742)**

2009: 8^{3}SD, 8^{1}SD, 8^{3}SD, 10^{3}GS, **10^{1}SD**, 10^{2}GF, 9^{3}GF, 8^{0}G, 8^{0}SD, 10^{5}SD, 8^{4}SD,

	Starts	1st	2nd	3rd	Win & Pl
Career Total (Turf)	6	0	1	2	2036
Career Total (AW)	10	2	0	2	4824

57 5/09 Ling 1m2f (0-55) STD £1942
57 3/09 Ling 1m (0-60)H STD £2047
Total win prize-money £3990

Going (Turf): Sf: 0-1 GS: 0-1 Gd: 0-2 GF: 0-2 Fm: 0-0
Distance: 5f/6f: 0-2 7f-8f: 1-8 9f-13f: 1-6 14f+: 0-0
Track : **LH: 2-10** RH: 0-4 **Tight: 2-7** Gall: 0-1
Aids: Bl: 0-0 Vi: 0-0 Tstrap: 0-0 Ckp: 0-0
Best Rating: 64 12/09 Kemp 1m stand

Moderate; effective over 1m but stays 1m2f; acts on Polytrack and fast ground.

Dark Tara

(108) (70)**75**

4-y-o br f Diktat-Karisal (IRE) (Persian Bold)
John Joseph Hanlon (R A Fahey 27/1) Miss Rachel O'Neill

Placings:4160006/0-0150 **(7163a)**

2009: 5^{0}SD, 7^{1}SD, 6^{5}SD, 8^{0}SD,

	Starts	1st	2nd	3rd	Win & Pl
Career Total (Turf)	8	1	0	0	7138
Career Total (AW)	4	1	0	0	3071

70 1/09 Wolv 7f32y (0-70)H STD £3070
71 7/07 York 6f HVY £6800
Total win prize-money £9872

Going (Turf): Sf: 1-4 GS: 0-1 Gd: 0-2 GF: 0-1 Fm: 0-0
Distance: 5f/6f: 1-10 7f-8f: 1-2 9f-13f: 0-0 14f+: 0-0
Track : **LH: 1-6** RH: 0-0 **Tight: 1-2** Gall: 0-0
Aids: Bl: 0-2 Vi: 0-0 Tstrap: 0-2 Ckp: 0-2
Best Rating: 75 8/07 Gdwd 6f gd-fm

Fair suited by 6f; acts on most ground; has worn a tongie tie and cheekpieces.

Dark Velvet (IRE)

83(87) (18)**63**

3-y-o b f Statue Of Liberty (USA)-Lovingit (IRE) (Fasliyev (USA))
E J Alston The Five Go Racing Partnership

Placings:006-0005000 **(7787)**

2009: 7^{0}F, 7^{0}GF, 6^{0}S, 8^{5}GS, 5^{0}S, 7^{0}SD, 7^{0}SD,

	Starts	1st	2nd	3rd	Win & Pl
Career Total (Turf)	8	0	0	0	0
Career Total (AW)	2	0	0	0	

Going (Turf): Sf: 0-2 GS: 0-1 Gd: 0-2 GF: 0-2 Fm: 0-1
Distance: 5f/6f: 0-4 7f-8f: 0-5 9f-13f: 0-1 14f+: 0-0
Track : LH: 0-5 RH: 0-1 Tight: 0-4 Gall: 0-0
Aids: Bl: 0-1 Vi: 0-0 Tstrap: 0-1 Ckp: 0-1
Best Rating: 63 7/08 Ripn 5f good

Darley Star

(99) (57)**62**

4-y-o gr f King's Best (USA)-Amellnaa (IRE) (Sadler's Wells (USA))
R A Harris Peter A Price

Placings:660/0500002100-600 **(0918)**

2009: 10^{6}SD, 11^{0}SD, 11^{0}SD,

	Starts	1st	2nd	3rd	Win & Pl
Career Total (Turf)	6	0	0	0	0
Career Total (AW)	10	1	1	0	2521

57 10/08 GrLe 1m2f (0-55)H STD £1942
Total win prize-money £1943

Going (Turf): Sf: 0-0 GS: 0-1 Gd: 0-1 GF: 0-4 Fm: 0-0
Distance: 5f/6f: 0-0 7f-8f: 0-7 **9f-13f: 1-9** 14f+: 0-0
Track : **LH: 1-9** RH: 0-4 Tight: 0-4 **Gall: 1-2**
Aids: Bl: 0-0 Vi: 0-0 Tstrap: 0-2 Ckp: 0-2
Best Rating: 62 8/07 Donc 7f gd-fm

Modest; stays 1m2f; acts on Polytrack.

Darley Sun (IRE)

112(95) (61)**111**

3-y-o b c Tiger Hill (IRE)-Sagamartha (Rainbow Quest (USA))
D M Simcock Abdullah Saeed Belhab

Placings:040-61412121 **(6851)**

2009: 11^{6}SD, 14^{1}F, 14^{4}GF, 14^{1}GF, 14^{2}GF, 16^{1}G, 18^{2}GF, 18^{1}G,

	Starts	1st	2nd	3rd	Win & Pl
Career Total (Turf)	10	4	2	0	144295
Career Total (AW)	1	0	0	0	0

111 10/09 NmkR 2m2f H GD £99696
102 7/09 Asct 2m (0-100)H GD £12952
83 6/09 Hayd 1m6f (0-75)H G-F £3238
77 5/09 Nott 1m6f15y (0-75)H FRM £4857
Total win prize-money £120743

Going (Turf): Sf: 0-1 GS: 0-1 **Gd: 2-2** GF: 1-5 Fm: 1-1
Distance: 5f/6f: 0-0 7f-8f: 0-1 9f-13f: 0-3 **14f+: 4-7**
Track : LH: 2-4 RH: 2-5 Tight: 0-2 **Gall: 2-3**
Aids: Bl: 0-0 Vi: 0-0 Tstrap: 0-0 Ckp: 0-0
Best Rating: 111 10/09 NmkR 2m2f good

Smart; Group placed; winner of the 2009 Cesarewitch; stays 2m2f and acts on fast ground.

Darling Buds

(90) (56)

2-y-o b f Reel Buddy (USA)-Its Another Gift (Primo Dominie)
K A Ryan Margaret's Partnership

Placings:065 **(7799)**

2009: 5^{0}SD, 6^{6}SD, 5^{5}SD,

	Starts	1st	2nd	3rd	Win & Pl
Career Total (Turf)	0	0	0	0	
Career Total (AW)	3	0	0	0	0

Going (Turf): Sf: 0-0 GS: 0-0 Gd: 0-0 GF: 0-0 Fm: 0-0
Distance: 5f/6f: 0-3 7f-8f: 0-0 9f-13f: 0-0 14f+: 0-0
Track : LH: 0-3 RH: 0-0 Tight: 0-2 Gall: 0-0
Aids: Bl: 0-0 Vi: 0-0 Tstrap: 0-0 Ckp: 0-0
Best Rating: 56 12/09 Wolv 5f216y stand

Moderate; stays 6f; acts on Polytrack.

Darshonin

89 **61**

2-y-o ch g Pivotal-Incheni (IRE) (Nashwan (USA))
J Noseda Nurlan Bizakov

Placings:00 **(6478)**

2009: 6^{0}GF, 7^{0}GF,

	Starts	1st	2nd	3rd	Win & Pl
Career Total (Turf)	2	0	0	0	

Going (Turf): Sf: 0-0 GS: 0-0 Gd: 0-0 GF: 0-2 Fm: 0-0
Distance: 5f/6f: 0-0 7f-8f: 0-2 9f-13f: 0-0 14f+: 0-0
Track : LH: 0-0 RH: 0-0 Tight: 0-0 Gall: 0-0
Aids: Bl: 0-0 Vi: 0-0 Tstrap: 0-0 Ckp: 0-0
Best Rating: 61 9/09 Newb 6f8y gd-fm

200,000gns purchase by Pivotal; promise in maiden company.

Dart

93(101) (73)**49**

5-y-o br m Diktat-Eilean Shona (Suave Dancer (USA))
Mrs S Lamyman (J R Fanshawe 8/6) Mrs S Lamyman

Placings:302321/4164-25054021 **(7842)**

2009: 14^{2}SS, 14^{5}SD, 14^{0}S, 17^{5}G, 14^{4}SD, 14^{0}SD, 14^{2}SD, 14^{1}SS,

	Starts	1st	2nd	3rd	Win & Pl
Career Total (Turf)	3	0	1	0	867
Career Total (AW)	15	3	3	2	9695

68 12/09 Sthl 1m6f (0-65)H SS £2047
73 11/08 Sthl 2m (0-75)H STD £2729
78 12/07 Sthl 1m3f STD £2047
Total win prize-money £6825

Going (Turf): Sf: 0-1 GS: 0-1 Gd: 0-1 GF: 0-0 Fm: 0-0
Distance: 5f/6f: 0-0 7f-8f: 0-0 9f-13f: 1-6 **14f+: 2-12**
Track : **LH: 3-15** RH: 0-3 Tight: 0-2 Gall: 0-1
Aids: Bl: 0-0 Vi: 0-0 Tstrap: 0-0 Ckp: 0-0
Best Rating: 78 12/07 Sthl 1m3f stand

Modest; stays 2m; acts on easy ground and on Fibresand.

Darwin's Dragon

90(93) (66)66

3-y-o ch g Royal Dragon (USA)-Darwinia (GER) (Acatenango (GER))

P F I Cole Mrs E A Bass

Placings:05033-00000 (3302)

2009: 8^{0}GF, 8^{0}GF, 7^{0}SD, 7^{0}GF, 8^{0}SD,

	Starts	1st	2nd	3rd	Win & Pl
Career Total (Turf)	4	0	0	0	
Career Total (AW)	6	0	0	2	605

Going (Turf): Sf: 0-0 GS: 0-0 Gd: 0-0 GF: 0-4 Fm: 0-0
Distance: 5f/6f: 0-0 7f-8f: 0-9 9f-13f: 0-1 14f+: 0-0
Track : LH: 0-5 RH: 0-2 Tight: 0-4 Gall: 0-0
Aids: Bl: 0-1 Vi: 0-0 Tstrap: 0-0 Ckp: 0-0
Best Rating: 66 12/08 Ling 1m stand

Fair; stays 1m and acts on sand.

Daryainur (IRE)

63(81) (40)33

2-y-o br f Auction House (USA)-Maylan (IRE) (Lashkari)

W De Best-Turner W De Best-Turner

Placings:000 (7064)

2009: 7^{0}GF, 8^{0}G, 8^{0}SD,

	Starts	1st	2nd	3rd	Win & Pl
Career Total (Turf)	2	0	0	0	
Career Total (AW)	1	0	0	0	

Going (Turf): Sf: 0-0 GS: 0-0 Gd: 0-1 GF: 0-1 Fm: 0-0
Distance: 5f/6f: 0-0 7f-8f: 0-2 9f-13f: 0-1 14f+: 0-0
Track : LH: 0-1 RH: 0-1 Tight: 0-1 Gall: 0-0
Aids: Bl: 0-0 Vi: 0-0 Tstrap: 0-0 Ckp: 0-0
Best Rating: 40 10/09 Ling 1m stand

Daryal (IRE)

80 33

8-y-o b g Night Shift (USA)-Darata (IRE) (Vayrann)

G L Moore Let's Live Racing

Placings:63233/134/0 (3697)

2009: 11^{0}G,

	Starts	1st	2nd	3rd	Win & Pl
Career Total (Turf)	8	1	1	3	10357
Career Total (AW)	1	0	0	1	2430

81 8/07 Ches 1m4f66y (0-75)H G-F £3435
Total win prize-money £3435

Going (Turf): Sf: 0-2 GS: 0-2 Gd: 0-2 GF: 1-2 Fm: 0-0
Distance: 5f/6f: 0-0 7f-8f: 0-0 9f-13f: 1-8 14f+: 0-1
Track : LH: 1-3 RH: 0-0 Tight: 1-2 Gall: 0-1
Aids: Bl: 0-1 Vi: 0-0 Tstrap: 0-0 Ckp: 0-0
Best Rating: 84 9/07 Hayd 1m6f soft

Fair; ex-French; winning hurdler; stays 1m6f; acts on fast and soft ground; has worn blinkers.

Dash Back (USA)

104(104) (83)80

4-y-o b f Sahm (USA)-Nadwah (USA) (Shadeed (USA))

Adrian McGuinness Edward Battersby

Placings:2/50500-02201005000002414 (7673)

2009: 7^{0}GF, 7^{2}Y, 7^{2}SD, 7^{0}GF, 7^{1}G, 7^{0}S, 7^{0}Y, 6^{5}G, 7^{0}Y, 8^{0}G, 7^{0}SD, 8^{0}GF, 8^{0}G, 5^{2}SD, 5^{4}SD, 7^{1}SD, 5^{4}SD,

	Starts	1st	2nd	3rd	Win & Pl
Career Total (Turf)	14	1	2	0	11990
Career Total (AW)	9	1	2	0	5933

83 12/09 Wolv 7f32y (0-70)H STD £3238
78 6/09 Cork 7f (50-80)H GD £7044
Total win prize-money £10282

Going (Turf): Sf: 0-1 GS: 0-0 Gd: 1-6 GF: 0-3 Fm: 0-0
Distance: 5f/6f: 0-9 7f-8f: 2-13 9f-13f: 0-1 14f+: 0-0
Track : LH: 1-15 RH: 1-5 Tight: 1-4 Gall: 0-0
Aids: Bl: 0-0 Vi: 0-0 Tstrap: 0-0 Ckp: 0-0
Best Rating: 83 12/09 Wolv 7f32y stand

Fair; stays 7f; acts on Polytrack.

Dasheena

(104) (77)61

6-y-o b m Magic Ring (IRE)-Sweet And Lucky (Lucky Wednesday)

A J McCabe Paul J Dixon

Placings:000100/234004036/60202050305104303112/33 332005064000-060 (0242)

2009: 5^{0}SD, 7^{6}SD, 7^{0}SD,

	Starts	1st	2nd	3rd	Win & Pl
Career Total (Turf)	15	2	0	0	7191
Career Total (AW)	37	2	5	9	11862

77 12/07 Sthl 7f (0-60)H STD £2047
64 12/07 Wolv 7f32y (0-62)H STD £1706
61 9/07 Catt 7f (0-60)H GD £2730
54 9/05 Carl 5f193y (0-75) FRM £3698
Total win prize-money £10183

Going (Turf): Sf: 0-3 GS: 0-0 Gd: 1-3 GF: 0-8 Fm: 1-1
Distance: 5f/6f: 1-27 7f-8f: 3-25 9f-13f: 0-0 14f+: 0-0
Track : LH: 3-38 RH: 1-1 Tight: 2-28 Gall: 0-0
Aids: Bl: 3-31 Vi: 0-1 Tstrap: 0-3 Ckp: 0-3
Best Rating: 77 12/07 Sthl 7f stand

Moderate; suited by 6f-7f; handles fast ground; also goes on both Fibresand and Polytrack.

Dasher Reilly (USA)

(88) (50)5

8-y-o b g Ghazi (USA)-Kutira (USA) (Dixieland Band (USA))

A Sadik A Sadik

Placings:0/00-00 (0249)

2009: 16^{0}SD, 16^{0}SD,

	Starts	1st	2nd	3rd	Win & Pl
Career Total (Turf)	1	0	0	0	
Career Total (AW)	4	0	0	0	

Going (Turf): Sf: 0-0 GS: 0-0 Gd: 0-0 GF: 0-0 Fm: 0-0
Distance: 5f/6f: 0-0 7f-8f: 0-0 9f-13f: 0-3 14f+: 0-2
Track : LH: 0-4 RH: 0-0 Tight: 0-3 Gall: 0-0
Aids: Bl: 0-2 Vi: 0-0 Tstrap: 0-0 Ckp: 0-0
Best Rating: 50 12/08 Wolv 1m4f50y stand

Dashing Daniel

82(91) (47)38

4-y-o gr g Zamindar (USA)-Etienne Lady (IRE) (Imperial Frontier (USA))

N J Vaughan Owen Promotions Limited

Placings:60-000 (3331)

2009: 8^{0}GF, 6^{0}GF, 7^{0}GF,

	Starts	1st	2nd	3rd	Win & Pl
Career Total (Turf)	3	0	0	0	
Career Total (AW)	2	0	0	0	0

Going (Turf): Sf: 0-0 GS: 0-0 Gd: 0-0 GF: 0-3 Fm: 0-0
Distance: 5f/6f: 0-1 7f-8f: 0-3 9f-13f: 0-1 14f+: 0-0
Track : LH: 0-3 RH: 0-0 Tight: 0-3 Gall: 0-0
Aids: Bl: 0-0 Vi: 0-0 Tstrap: 0-1 Ckp: 0-1
Best Rating: 47 9/08 Wolv 7f32y std-fst

Dashing Doc (IRE)

97(74) (43)77

2-y-o ch g Dr Fong (USA)-Dashiba (Dashing Blade)

D R C Elsworth J C Smith

Placings:0344314 (5970)

2009: 6^{0}SD, 7^{3}GF, 7^{4}GF, 7^{4}GS, 7^{3}GS, 8^{1}G, 8^{4}GF,

	Starts	1st	2nd	3rd	Win & Pl
Career Total (Turf)	6	1	0	2	7822
Career Total (AW)	1	0	0	0	

77 8/09 NmkJ 1m GD £5180
Total win prize-money £5181

Going (Turf): Sf: 0-0 GS: 0-2 Gd: 1-1 GF: 0-3 Fm: 0-0
Distance: 5f/6f: 0-1 7f-8f: 1-5 9f-13f: 0-1 14f+: 0-0
Track : LH: 0-2 RH: 0-0 Tight: 0-2 Gall: 0-0
Aids: Bl: 0-0 Vi: 0-0 Tstrap: 0-0 Ckp: 0-0
Best Rating: 77 8/09 NmkJ 1m good

Modest; stays 7f and acts on fast ground.

Database (IRE)

97 77

2-y-o ch c Singspiel (IRE)-Memory Green (USA) (Green Forest (USA))

Saeed Bin Suroor Godolphin

Placings:31 (6931)

2009: 8^{3}G, 8^{1}G,

	Starts	1st	2nd	3rd	Win & Pl
Career Total (Turf)	2	1	0	1	2989

77 10/09 Bath 1m5y GD £2266
Total win prize-money £2267

Going (Turf): Sf: 0-0 GS: 0-0 Gd: 1-2 GF: 0-0 Fm: 0-0
Distance: 5f/6f: 0-0 7f-8f: 0-1 9f-13f: 1-1 14f+: 0-0
Track : LH: 1-1 RH: 0-0 Tight: 1-1 Gall: 0-0
Aids: Bl: 0-0 Vi: 0-0 Tstrap: 0-0 Ckp: 0-0
Best Rating: 77 10/09 Bath 1m5y good

Fair; effective over 1m; acts on good ground.

Dauntsey Park (IRE)

75(85) (55)49

2-y-o ch c Refuse To Bend (IRE)-Shauna's Honey (IRE) (Danehill (USA))

Miss Tor Sturgis Miss Ann Sturgis

Placings:0006 (7389)

2009: 6^{0}G, 7^{0}G, 8^{0}SD, 7^{6}SD,

	Starts	1st	2nd	3rd	Win & Pl
Career Total (Turf)	2	0	0	0	
Career Total (AW)	2	0	0	0	35

Going (Turf): Sf: 0-0 GS: 0-0 Gd: 0-2 GF: 0-0 Fm: 0-0
Distance: 5f/6f: 0-1 7f-8f: 0-3 9f-13f: 0-0 14f+: 0-0
Track : LH: 0-1 RH: 0-1 Tight: 0-1 Gall: 0-1
Aids: Bl: 0-0 Vi: 0-0 Tstrap: 0-0 Ckp: 0-0
Best Rating: 55 11/09 Ling 7f stand

Davana

89(97) (49)**42**

3-y-o b f Primo Valentino (IRE)-Bombay Sapphire (Be My Chief (USA))

W J H Ratcliffe T B Tarn

Placings:000-06356335 (7814)

2009: 6^{0}GF, 8^{6}GF, 8^{3}GS, 9^{5}SD, 12^{6}SD, 8^{3}SF, 8^{3}SD, 8^{5}SD,

	Starts	1st	2nd	3rd	Win & Pl
Career Total (Turf)	6	0	0	1	289
Career Total (AW)	5	0	0	2	655

Going (Turf): **Sf: 0-0 GS: 0-1 Gd: 0-1 GF: 0-4 Fm: 0-0**
Distance: 5f/6f: 0-2 7f-8f: 0-3 9f-13f: 0-6 14f+: 0-0
Track : LH: 0-5 RH: 0-3 Tight: 0-5 Gall: 0-0
Aids: Bl: 0-0 Vi: 0-0 Tstrap: 0-0 Ckp: 0-0
Best Rating: **49** 12/09 Wolv 1m141y stand

Plating-class; stays 1m; acts on Polytrack.

Davaye

74 (41)**67**

5-y-o b m Bold Edge-Last Impression (Imp Society (USA))

K R Burke The Baltika Partnership

Placings:345314/04504006/0 (2032)

2009: 5^{0}G,

	Starts	1st	2nd	3rd	Win & Pl
Career Total (Turf)	14	1	0	2	7492
Career Total (AW)	1	0	0	0	0

66 8/06 Muss 5f G-F £5181
Total win prize-money £5182

Going (Turf): Sf: 0-2 GS: 0-2 Gd: 0-4 **GF: 1-6** Fm: 0-0
Distance: **5f/6f: 1-11** 7f-8f: 0-4 9f-13f: 0-0 14f+: 0-0
Track : LH: 0-1 RH: 0-3 Tight: 0-2 Gall: 0-1
Aids: Bl: 0-0 Vi: 0-0 Tstrap: 0-0 Ckp: 0-0
Best Rating: **67** 8/06 Hayd 5f gd-fm

Dave Diamond

3-y-o b g Deportivo-Blossoming (Vague Shot)

P D Evans W Clifford

Placings:0 (3862)

2009: 8^{0}GF,

	Starts	1st	2nd	3rd	Win & Pl
Career Total (Turf)	1	0	0	0	

Going (Turf): **Sf: 0-0 GS: 0-0 Gd: 0-0 GF: 0-1 Fm: 0-0**
Distance: 5f/6f: 0-0 7f-8f: 0-0 9f-13f: 0-1 14f+: 0-0
Track : LH: 0-1 RH: 0-0 Tight: 0-0 Gall: 0-0
Aids: Bl: 0-0 Vi: 0-0 Tstrap: 0-0 Ckp: 0-0

Davenport (IRE)

(103) (76)**85**

7-y-o b g Bold Fact (USA)-Semence D'Or (FR) (Kaldoun (FR))

B R Millman M A Swift and A J Chapman

Placings:02/441100430140/04421030005424/1560055/04 150520432-305 (0384)

2009: 8^{3}SS, 9^{0}SD, 11^{5}SD,

	Starts	1st	2nd	3rd	Win & Pl
Career Total (Turf)	28	5	1	1	24543
Career Total (AW)	21	1	4	3	12599

79 5/08 Gdwd 1m1f (0-70)H G-F £3115
83 1/07 Sthl 1m (0-75)H SLW £2914
86 5/06 Sand 1m14y (0-80)H G-S £6477
89 10/05 NmkR 1m (0-75)H SFT £3402
78 4/05 Wind 1m67y (0-70)H G-S £3575
74 4/05 Nott 1m54y (0-70)H SFT £3754
Total win prize-money £23240

Going (Turf): **Sf: 2-6 GS: 2-4** Gd: 0-10 GF: 1-8 Fm: 0-0
Distance: 5f/6f: 0-0 7f-8f: 2-16 **9f-13f: 4-33** 14f+: 0-0
Track : LH: 2-34 **RH: 3-11 Tight: 2-20** Gall: 0-2
Aids: Bl: 0-0 Vi: 0-0 Tstrap: 1-19 Ckp: 1-19
Best Rating: **89** 10/05 NmkR 1m soft

Fair; effective at around 1m1f-1m4f; acts on most ground; goes on sand; has worn cheekpieces.]

Davids City (IRE)

(92) (53)

5-y-o b g Laveron-Irelands Own (IRE) (Commanche Run)

G A Harker David Adair

Placings:500 (7670)

2009: 13^{5}SD, 13^{0}SF, 12^{0}SD,

	Starts	1st	2nd	3rd	Win & Pl
Career Total (Turf)	0	0	0	0	
Career Total (AW)	3	0	0	0	0

Going (Turf): **Sf: 0-0 GS: 0-0 Gd: 0-0 GF: 0-0 Fm: 0-0**
Distance: 5f/6f: 0-0 7f-8f: 0-0 9f-13f: 0-1 14f+: 0-2
Track : LH: 0-3 RH: 0-0 Tight: 0-3 Gall: 0-0
Aids: Bl: 0-0 Vi: 0-0 Tstrap: 0-0 Ckp: 0-0
Best Rating: **53** 10/09 Wolv 1m5f194y stand

Davids Mark

90(111) (63)**55**

9-y-o b g Polar Prince (IRE)-Star Of Flanders (Puissance)

J R Jenkins Mrs Wendy Jenkins

Placings:00161033555003503 0/03444120032043 6/06006/ 2030406046105234 1/00530244/41436045-512004066040 (7835)

2009: 6^{5}SD, 6^{1}SD, 6^{2}SD, 6^{0}SD, 6^{0}SD, 6^{4}G, 6^{0}F, 5^{6}F, 6^{6}SD, 5^{0}SD, 6^{4}SD, 6^{0}SD,

	Starts	1st	2nd	3rd	Win & Pl
Career Total (Turf)	28	3	2	4	13575
Career Total (AW)	55	4	4	7	12815

59 1/09 Ling 6f (0-52)H STD £2047
55 1/08 Kemp 6f (0-50)H STD £2047
58 12/06 Kemp 5f (0-45) STD £1365
53 7/06 Yarm 5f43y (0-60)H FRM £2388
58 8/04 Wind 5f10y E(0-70)H G-F £3493
65 3/03 Folk 6f E(0-70)H GD £3594
66 2/03 Ling 6f G STD £3003
Total win prize-money £17941

Going (Turf): Sf: 0-1 GS: 0-1 **Gd: 1-4 GF: 1-16 Fm: 1-6**
Distance: **5f/6f: 7-77** 7f-8f: 0-6 9f-13f: 0-0 14f+: 0-0
Track : LH: 2-43 RH: 2-19 **Tight: 2-31** Gall: 1-6
Aids: Bl: 0-0 Vi: 0-6 Tstrap: 0-2 Ckp: 0-2
Best Rating: **68** 4/03 Wwck 5f gd-fm

Moderate sprinter; acts on Polytrack.

Davids Matador

96(94) (57)**71**

3-y-o b g Dansili-Mousseline (USA) (Barathea (IRE))

Eve Johnson Houghton David Herbert

Placings:054-606665505 (7002)

2009: 8^{6}GF, 9^{0}G, 7^{6}GF, 8^{6}GS, 7^{6}GF, 7^{5}SD, 6^{5}SD, 6^{0}GF, 5^{5}SD,

	Starts	1st	2nd	3rd	Win & Pl
Career Total (Turf)	9	0	0	0	325
Career Total (AW)	3	0	0	0	0

Going (Turf): **Sf: 0-0 GS: 0-2 Gd: 0-3 GF: 0-4 Fm: 0-0**
Distance: 5f/6f: 0-3 7f-8f: 0-6 9f-13f: 0-3 14f+: 0-0
Track : LH: 0-4 RH: 0-3 Tight: 0-4 Gall: 0-0
Aids: Bl: 0-1 Vi: 0-0 Tstrap: 0-2 Ckp: 0-2
Best Rating: **71** 10/08 Sals 1m good

Dawn Storm (IRE)

(99) (56)

4-y-o ch g City On A Hill (USA)-Flames (Blushing Flame (USA))

J L Spearing Miss P Cooper

Placings:0/0533 (7842)

2009: 9^{0}SD, 12^{5}SD, 16^{3}SD, 14^{3}SS,

	Starts	1st	2nd	3rd	Win & Pl
Career Total (Turf)	0	0	0	0	
Career Total (AW)	5	0	0	2	655

Going (Turf): **Sf: 0-0 GS: 0-0 Gd: 0-0 GF: 0-0 Fm: 0-0**
Distance: 5f/6f: 0-1 7f-8f: 0-0 9f-13f: 0-2 14f+: 0-2
Track : LH: 0-5 RH: 0-0 Tight: 0-4 Gall: 0-0
Aids: Bl: 0-1 Vi: 0-0 Tstrap: 0-1 Ckp: 0-1
Best Rating: **56** 12/09 Sthl 1m6f std-slw

Moderate; stays 2m; acts on Polytrack.

Dawn Wind

76(93) (50)**45**

4-y-o b f Vettori (IRE)-Topper (IRE) (Priolo (USA))

I A Wood Paddy Barrett

Placings:0003/00000000U40060-633000 (4389)

2009: 12^{6}SD, 11^{3}SD, 12^{3}SF, 12^{0}SD, 17^{0}G, 8^{0}G,

	Starts	1st	2nd	3rd	Win & Pl
Career Total (Turf)	12	0	0	0	155
Career Total (AW)	12	0	0	3	907

Going (Turf): **Sf: 0-3 GS: 0-2 Gd: 0-3 GF: 0-4 Fm: 0-0**
Distance: 5f/6f: 0-0 7f-8f: 0-6 9f-13f: 0-17 14f+: 0-1
Track : LH: 0-12 RH: 0-7 Tight: 0-11 Gall: 0-2
Aids: Bl: 0-6 Vi: 0-5 Tstrap: 0-5 Ckp: 0-5
Best Rating: **58** 9/07 Kemp 1m stand

Moderate; effective over 1m3f; acts on Polytrack; has worn headgear and a tongue-tie.

Dawnbreak (USA)

95(94) (77)**86**

2-y-o ch f Distorted Humor (USA)-Dawn Princess (USA) (Polish Numbers (USA))

Saeed Bin Suroor Godolphin

Placings:162 (6756)

2009: 7^{1}SD, 7^{6}GF, 7^{2}G,

	Starts	1st	2nd	3rd	Win & Pl
Career Total (Turf)	2	0	1	0	2287
Career Total (AW)	1	1	0	0	3886

77 9/09 Ling 7f STD £3885
Total win prize-money £3886

Going (Turf): **Sf: 0-0 GS: 0-0 Gd: 0-1 GF: 0-1 Fm: 0-0**
Distance: 5f/6f: 0-0 **7f-8f: 1-3** 9f-13f: 0-0 14f+: 0-0
Track : **LH: 1-1** RH: 0-0 **Tight: 1-1** Gall: 0-0
Aids: Bl: 0-0 Vi: 0-0 Tstrap: 0-0 Ckp: 0-0
Best Rating: **86** 10/09 Leic 7f9y good

Useful; stays 7f; acts on Polytrack and good ground.

Dawson Creek (IRE)

90(107) (71)47

5-y-o ch g Titus Livius (FR)-Particular Friend (Cadeaux Genereux)

B Gubby Brian Gubby

Placings:000/040012041/222241306200-000600 (7693)

2009: 7^{0}SD, 7^{0}SD, 7^{0}GF, 10^{6}SD, 7^{0}SD, 8^{0}SD,

	Starts	1st	2nd	3rd	Win & Pl
Career Total (Turf)	4	0	0	0	
Career Total (AW)	26	3	6	1	10655

71 8/08 Ling 7f (0-70)H STD £2590
62 12/07 Ling 7f (0-52)H STD £1943
52 10/07 Ling 1m2f (0-45) STD £2047
Total win prize-money £6581

Going (Turf): Sf: 0-1 GS: 0-0 Gd: 0-0 GF: 0-3 Fm: 0-0
Distance: 5f/6f: 0-1 7f-8f: 2-20 9f-13f: 1-9 14f+: 0-0
Track : LH: 3-21 RH: 0-8 Tight: 3-21 Gall: 0-1
Aids: Bl: 0-1 Vi: 0-0 Tstrap: 0-3 Ckp: 0-3
Best Rating: 71 8/08 Ling 7f stand

Modest; effective over 7f-1m2f; acts on Polytrack.

Day Care

(96) (58)46

8-y-o gr g Daylami (IRE)-Ancara (Dancing Brave (USA))

R McGlinchey P Joseph O'Brien

Placings:2/5/0/000/30050-232 (7214)

2009: 12^{2}SD, 10^{3}SD, 13^{2}SD,

	Starts	1st	2nd	3rd	Win & Pl
Career Total (Turf)	11	0	1	1	2470
Career Total (AW)	3	0	2	1	2360

Going (Turf): Sf: 0-1 GS: 0-0 Gd: 0-3 GF: 0-2 Fm: 0-0
Distance: 5f/6f: 0-0 7f-8f: 0-0 9f-13f: 0-8 14f+: 0-6
Track : LH: 0-4 RH: 0-10 Tight: 0-2 Gall: 0-0
Aids: Bl: 0-2 Vi: 0-0 Tstrap: 0-1 Ckp: 0-1
Best Rating: 68 9/04 Gdwd 1m1f192y good

Moderate; effective over 1m5f; acts on Polytrack.

Day In Dubai

91(76) (18)53

3-y-o b f Dubai Destination (USA)-Pazzazz (IRE) (Green Desert (USA))

J J Bridger Allsorts

Placings:060-60000005 (7198)

2009: 6^{6}GF, 6^{0}F, 5^{0}G, 7^{0}G, 6^{0}GF, 7^{0}GS, 6^{0}G, 10^{5}SD,

	Starts	1st	2nd	3rd	Win & Pl
Career Total (Turf)	9	0	0	0	0
Career Total (AW)	2	0	0	0	0

Going (Turf): Sf: 0-0 GS: 0-2 Gd: 0-4 GF: 0-2 Fm: 0-1
Distance: 5f/6f: 0-6 7f-8f: 0-4 9f-13f: 0-1 14f+: 0-0
Track : LH: 0-1 RH: 0-1 Tight: 0-1 Gall: 0-1
Aids: Bl: 0-0 Vi: 0-0 Tstrap: 0-0 Ckp: 0-0
Best Rating: 53 9/08 Newb 6f8y good

Day Of The Eagle (IRE)

99 82

3-y-o b g Danehill Dancer (IRE)-Puck's Castle (Shirley Heights)

L M Cumani Chris Wright & Andy MacDonald

Placings:03531 (7149)

2009: 8^{0}G, 9^{3}G, 9^{5}GF, 8^{3}G, 8^{1}G,

	Starts	1st	2nd	3rd	Win & Pl
Career Total (Turf)	5	1	0	2	7439

82 10/09 NmkR 1m (0-75)H GD £6476
Total win prize-money £6476

Going (Turf): Sf: 0-0 GS: 0-0 Gd: 1-4 GF: 0-1 Fm: 0-0
Distance: 5f/6f: 0-0 7f-8f: 1-2 9f-13f: 0-3 14f+: 0-0
Track : LH: 0-2 RH: 0-2 Tight: 0-3 Gall: 0-1
Aids: Bl: 0-0 Vi: 0-0 Tstrap: 0-0 Ckp: 0-0
Best Rating: 82 10/09 NmkR 1m good

Fair; stays 1m2f; acts on good ground.

Dayanara (USA)

91(87) (49)53

3-y-o b/br f Action This Day (USA)-Dana Did It (USA) (Wagon Limit (USA))

Mrs S Leech (C G Cox 20/10) C J Leech

Placings:00066 (6917)

2009: 8^{0}G, 8^{0}SD, 11^{0}G, 12^{6}SS, 12^{6}SD,

	Starts	1st	2nd	3rd	Win & Pl
Career Total (Turf)	2	0	0	0	
Career Total (AW)	3	0	0	0	0

Going (Turf): Sf: 0-0 GS: 0-0 Gd: 0-2 GF: 0-0 Fm: 0-0
Distance: 5f/6f: 0-0 7f-8f: 0-1 9f-13f: 0-4 14f+: 0-0
Track : LH: 0-3 RH: 0-2 Tight: 0-4 Gall: 0-0
Aids: Bl: 0-1 Vi: 0-0 Tstrap: 0-0 Ckp: 0-0
Best Rating: 53 9/09 Bath 1m3f144y good

Dayia (IRE)

109(111) (92)93

5-y-o br m Act One-Masharik (IRE) (Caerleon (USA))

J Pearce Lady Green

Placings:43441-325142 (7117)

2009: 15^{3}G, 16^{2}SD, 16^{5}G, 13^{1}SD, 18^{4}G, 16^{2}GS,

	Starts	1st	2nd	3rd	Win & Pl
Career Total (Turf)	5	0	1	1	12364
Career Total (AW)	6	2	1	1	9729

92 10/09 Wolv 1m5f194y (0-80)H STD £5046
83 12/08 GrLe 1m6f (0-75)H STD £3238
Total win prize-money £8284

Going (Turf): Sf: 0-0 GS: 0-1 Gd: 0-3 GF: 0-1 Fm: 0-0
Distance: 5f/6f: 0-0 7f-8f: 0-0 9f-13f: 0-1 14f+: 2-10
Track : LH: 2-6 RH: 0-5 Tight: 1-6 Gall: 1-3
Aids: Bl: 0-0 Vi: 0-0 Tstrap: 0-0 Ckp: 0-0
Best Rating: 93 10/09 Muss 2m gd-sft

Useful; stays 2m2f; acts on good and easier ground and on Polytrack.

Days Of Pleasure (IRE)

(95) (67)

4-y-o b g Fraam-Altizaf (Zafonic (USA))

C Gordon E J Farrant

Placings:5523130-0 (0202)

2009: 12^{0}SD,

	Starts	1st	2nd	3rd	Win & Pl
Career Total (Turf)	0	0	0	0	
Career Total (AW)	8	1	1	2	3185

64 3/08 Sthl 7f STD £1774
Total win prize-money £1775

Going (Turf): Sf: 0-0 GS: 0-0 Gd: 0-0 GF: 0-0 Fm: 0-0
Distance: 5f/6f: 0-0 7f-8f: 1-6 9f-13f: 0-2 14f+: 0-0
Track : LH: 1-7 RH: 0-1 Tight: 0-4 Gall: 0-0
Aids: Bl: 0-0 Vi: 0-0 Tstrap: 0-0 Ckp: 0-0
Best Rating: 67 2/08 Wolv 7f32y stand

Modest; stays 1m2f; acts on sand.

Days Of Thunder (IRE)

72(79) (26)21

4-y-o b g Choisir (AUS)-Grazina (Mark Of Esteem (IRE))

B R Summers K W Bradley

Placings:000/00000 (7817)

2009: 8^{0}GF, 6^{0}SD, 7^{0}HY, 9^{0}GF, 9^{0}SD,

	Starts	1st	2nd	3rd	Win & Pl
Career Total (Turf)	6	0	0	0	
Career Total (AW)	2	0	0	0	

Going (Turf): Sf: 0-1 GS: 0-1 Gd: 0-2 GF: 0-2 Fm: 0-0
Distance: 5f/6f: 0-3 7f-8f: 0-2 9f-13f: 0-3 14f+: 0-0
Track : LH: 0-4 RH: 0-1 Tight: 0-1 Gall: 0-0
Aids: Bl: 0-0 Vi: 0-0 Tstrap: 0-0 Ckp: 0-0
Best Rating: 26 12/09 Wolv 1m1f103y stand

Dazakhee

84(88) (46)47

2-y-o ch f Sakhee (USA)-Ziya (IRE) (Lion Cavern (USA))

P T Midgley Darren & Annaley Yates

Placings:40005 (7335)

2009: 6^{4}F, 7^{0}G, 6^{0}GF, 6^{0}GS, 8^{5}SD,

	Starts	1st	2nd	3rd	Win & Pl
Career Total (Turf)	4	0	0	0	481
Career Total (AW)	1	0	0	0	0

Going (Turf): Sf: 0-0 GS: 0-1 Gd: 0-1 GF: 0-1 Fm: 0-1
Distance: 5f/6f: 0-3 7f-8f: 0-2 9f-13f: 0-0 14f+: 0-0
Track : LH: 0-2 RH: 0-0 Tight: 0-1 Gall: 0-0
Aids: Bl: 0-0 Vi: 0-0 Tstrap: 0-1 Ckp: 0-1
Best Rating: 47 9/09 Newc 6f gd-sft

Moderate; stays 1m; acts on Fibresand.

Dazed And Amazed

104(103) (87)88

5-y-o b g Averti (IRE)-Amazed (Clantime)

R Hannon Mrs R Ablett

Placings:315145006/354100050006/0440000013-140400540 (6631)

2009: 5^{1}GF, 6^{4}G, 5^{0}G, 5^{4}F, 5^{0}GF, 5^{0}GS, 5^{5}G, 5^{4}GF, 6^{0}SS,

	Starts	1st	2nd	3rd	Win & Pl
Career Total (Turf)	35	4	0	1	38997
Career Total (AW)	5	1	0	2	17026

88 4/09 Bath 5f161y (0-85)H G-F £4727
86 9/08 Bath 5f11y G-F £2266
102 6/07 Kemp 5f STD £14762
95 6/06 Newb 6f8y GD £13343
81 5/06 NmkR 5f G-S £4533
Total win prize-money £39634

Going (Turf): Sf: 0-2 GS: 1-7 Gd: 1-10 GF: 2-15 Fm: 0-1
Distance: 5f/6f: 4-35 7f-8f: 1-5 9f-13f: 0-0 14f+: 0-0
Track : LH: 2-6 RH: 1-4 Tight: 0-1 Gall: 2-4
Aids: Bl: 0-2 Vi: 0-0 Tstrap: 0-0 Ckp: 0-0

Best Rating: 102 6/07 Kemp 5f stand

Useful; winner in Listed company; effective at 5f-6f; handles most ground and Polytrack; has worn blinkers and a tongue tie.

Dazeen

94 72

2-y-o b g Zafeen (FR)-Bond Finesse (IRE) (Danehill Dancer (IRE))

P T Midgley Darren & Annaley Yates

Placings:02524 (5392)

2009: 6^{0}G, 5^{2}GF, 6^{5}GF, 5^{2}GS, 6^{4}GF,

	Starts	1st	2nd	3rd	Win & Pl
Career Total (Turf)	5	0	2	0	2236

Going (Turf): Sf: 0-0 GS: 0-1 Gd: 0-1 GF: 0-3 Fm: 0-0
Distance: 5f/6f: 0-5 7f-8f: 0-0 9f-13f: 0-0 14f+: 0-0
Track : LH: 0-0 RH: 0-1 Tight: 0-0 Gall: 0-1
Aids: Bl: 0-0 Vi: 0-0 Tstrap: 0-0 Ckp: 0-0
Best Rating: 72 8/09 Newc 6f gd-fm

Modest; effective over 5f; acts on fast ground.

Dazinski

111 91

3-y-o ch g Sulamani (IRE)-Shuheb (Nashwan (USA))

M H Tompkins Mrs Beryl Lockey

Placings:0165-53231310 (7151)

2009: 12^{5}GF, 12^{3}GS, 14^{2}S, 14^{3}GF, 15^{1}GF, 16^{3}GF, 16^{1}GF, 16^{0}G,

	Starts	1st	2nd	3rd	Win & Pl
Career Total (Turf)	12	3	1	3	17473

91 9/09 Nott 2m9y (0-85)H G-F £6476
86 8/09 Ches 1m7f195y (0-85)H G-F £5504
68 7/08 Yarm 7f3y G-F £2201
Total win prize-money £14183

Going (Turf): Sf: 0-1 GS: 0-1 Gd: 0-1 **GF: 3-8** Fm: 0-1
Distance: 5f/6f: 0-0 7f-8f: 1-3 9f-13f: 0-3 **14f+: 2-6**
Track : **LH: 2-4** RH: 0-4 **Tight: 1-5** Gall: 0-2
Aids: Bl: 0-0 Vi: 0-0 Tstrap: 0-0 Ckp: 0-0
Best Rating: 91 9/09 Nott 2m9y gd-fm

Useful; stays 2m; acts on fast ground.

Dazzling Bay

99(108) (85)80

9-y-o b g Mind Games-Adorable Cherub (USA) (Halo (USA))

T D Easterby Ghmw Racing

Placings:2153640053/021110206/6035200300/006000/160000/0032100-062300 (5516)

2009: 6^{0}GF, 6^{6}GF, 6^{2}GF, 6^{3}GF, 6^{0}G, 6^{0}GF,

	Starts	1st	2nd	3rd	Win & Pl
Career Total (Turf)	49	5	5	5	134403
Career Total (AW)	5	1	1	1	6819

85 11/08 Kemp 6f (0-80)H STD £5180
97 5/06 Ripn 6f (0-90)H GD £9348
110 6/03 Ripn 6f C(0-95)H G-F £9064
104 6/03 York 6f3y B(0-105)H G-F £57525
91 5/03 NmkR 6f C(0-100)H G-F £26000
77 5/02 Haml 5f4y D SFT £4290
Total win prize-money £111409

Going (Turf): Sf: 1-9 GS: 0-4 Gd: 1-11 **GF: 3-21** Fm: 0-4
Distance: **5f/6f: 5-46** 7f-8f: 1-8 9f-13f: 0-0 14f+: 0-0
Track : LH: 0-5 **RH: 1-1** Tight: 0-3 Gall: 0-2
Aids: **Bl: 1-20** Vi: 0-0 Tstrap: 0-0 Ckp: 0-0
Best Rating: 110 6/03 Ripn 6f gd-fm

Fair; seems best at 6f; likes fast ground; goes on Polytrack; has worn blinkers and an eyeshield.

Dazzling Begum

101(108) (60)55

4-y-o br f Okawango (USA)-Dream On Me (Prince Sabo)

J Pearce Macniler Racing Partnership

Placings:4144032-40226300603314503160015 (7842)

2009: 12^{4}SD, 12^{0}SD, 12^{2}SD, 12^{2}SD, 12^{6}SD, 12^{3}SD, 13^{0}SD, 12^{0}SD, 11^{6}GF, 11^{0}G, 14^{3}GF, 12^{3}GF, 14^{1}SD, 16^{4}G, 12^{5}G, 13^{0}S, 16^{3}SD, 15^{1}GF, 13^{6}SD, 16^{0}SD, 14^{0}SD, 12^{1}SD,

	Starts	1st	2nd	3rd	Win & Pl
Career Total (Turf)	11	2	0	2	5028
Career Total (AW)	19	2	3	3	6983

56 12/09 Wolv 1m4f50y (0-60)H STD £2047
54 9/09 Folk 1m7f92y (0-60)H G-F £2047
60 7/09 Sthl 1m6f (0-65)H STD £2047
51 10/08 Leic 1m1f218y SFT £1942
Total win prize-money £8084

Going (Turf): **Sf: 1-3** GS: 0-0 Gd: 0-4 **GF: 1-4** Fm: 0-0
Distance: 5f/6f: 0-0 7f-8f: 0-1 9f-13f: 2-18 14f+: 2-11
Track : LH: 2-24 RH: 2-5 **Tight: 2-14** Gall: 0-1
Aids: Bl: 0-1 Vi: 0-5 Tstrap: 2-10 Ckp: 2-10
Best Rating: 60 7/09 Sthl 1m6f stand

Moderate; stays 2m; acts on good and easy ground; goes on Fibresand; has worn a visor and cheekpieces.

Dazzling Colours

89(87) (38)41

4-y-o b c Oasis Dream-Dazzle (Gone West (USA))

T T Clement John W Barnard

Placings:6/00000 (4158)

2009: 7^{0}SD, 8^{0}G, 7^{0}SD, 5^{0}F, 10^{0}G,

	Starts	1st	2nd	3rd	Win & Pl
Career Total (Turf)	4	0	0	0	0
Career Total (AW)	2	0	0	0	

Going (Turf): **Sf: 0-0 GS: 0-0 Gd: 0-2 GF: 0-1 Fm: 0-1**
Distance: 5f/6f: 0-2 7f-8f: 0-2 9f-13f: 0-2 14f+: 0-0
Track : LH: 0-4 RH: 0-1 Tight: 0-3 Gall: 0-0
Aids: Bl: 0-0 Vi: 0-2 Tstrap: 0-0 Ckp: 0-0
Best Rating: 63 9/07 Hayd 6f gd-fm

Dazzling Light (UAE)

106(102) (69)82

4-y-o b/br f Halling (USA)-Crown Of Light (Mtoto)

J S Goldie M Mackay, S Bruce, J S Goldie

Placings:3234-3232154003245 (7117)

2009: 9^{3}GF, 12^{2}GF, 11^{3}G, 12^{2}GF, 14^{1}GF, 11^{5}GF, 12^{4}GF, 12^{0}GF, 16^{0}GS, 13^{3}G, 13^{2}GF, 13^{4}GF, 16^{5}GS,

	Starts	1st	2nd	3rd	Win & Pl
Career Total (Turf)	16	1	4	4	17170
Career Total (AW)	1	0	0	1	385

82 5/09 Muss 1m6f (0-85)H G-F £6231
Total win prize-money £6231

Going (Turf): Sf: 0-0 GS: 0-3 Gd: 0-3 **GF: 1-10** Fm: 0-0
Distance: 5f/6f: 0-0 7f-8f: 0-0 9f-13f: 0-11 **14f+: 1-6**
Track : LH: 0-10 **RH: 1-7 Tight: 1-8** Gall: 0-6
Aids: Bl: 0-0 Vi: 0-0 Tstrap: 0-0 Ckp: 0-0
Best Rating: 82 9/09 Ches 1m5f89y gd-fm

Fair; effective at 1m2f-1m6f; acts on fast ground; goes on Polytrack.

De Soto

80 70

8-y-o b g Hernando (FR)-Vanessa Bell (IRE) (Lahib (USA))

P R Webber P A Deal & M J Silver

Placings:44 (4743)

2009: 12^{4}GF, 14^{4}GS,

	Starts	1st	2nd	3rd	Win & Pl
Career Total (Turf)	2	0	0	0	409

Going (Turf): **Sf: 0-0 GS: 0-1 Gd: 0-0 GF: 0-1 Fm: 0-0**
Distance: 5f/6f: 0-0 7f-8f: 0-0 9f-13f: 0-1 14f+: 0-1
Track : LH: 0-2 RH: 0-0 Tight: 0-1 Gall: 0-0
Aids: Bl: 0-0 Vi: 0-0 Tstrap: 0-0 Ckp: 0-0
Best Rating: 70 7/09 Wwck 1m4f134y gd-fm

Deacon Blues

99 79

2-y-o b c Compton Place-Persario (Bishop Of Cashel)

J R Fanshawe Jan & Peter Hopper & Michelle Morris

Placings:51 (7058)

2009: 6^{5}GS, 5^{1}GF,

	Starts	1st	2nd	3rd	Win & Pl
Career Total (Turf)	2	1	0	0	5181

79 10/09 Leic 5f218y G-F £5180
Total win prize-money £5181

Going (Turf): Sf: 0-0 GS: 0-1 Gd: 0-0 **GF: 1-1** Fm: 0-0
Distance: **5f/6f: 1-1** 7f-8f: 0-1 9f-13f: 0-0 14f+: 0-0
Track : LH: 0-0 RH: 0-0 Tight: 0-0 Gall: 0-0
Aids: Bl: 0-0 Vi: 0-0 Tstrap: 0-0 Ckp: 0-0
Best Rating: 79 10/09 Leic 5f218y gd-fm

Fair; stays 6f; acts on fast ground.

Dead Cat Bounce (IRE)

86(95) (60)54

3-y-o b c Mujadil (USA)-Where's Charlotte (Sure Blade (USA))

J Pearce Jeff Pearce

Placings:4-0602004 (2169)

2009: 8^{0}SD, 8^{6}SD, 9^{0}SF, 10^{2}SD, 8^{0}G, 9^{0}GF, 8^{4}GF,

	Starts	1st	2nd	3rd	Win & Pl
Career Total (Turf)	3	0	0	0	144
Career Total (AW)	5	0	1	0	605

Going (Turf): **Sf: 0-0 GS: 0-0 Gd: 0-1 GF: 0-2 Fm: 0-0**
Distance: 5f/6f: 0-0 7f-8f: 0-3 9f-13f: 0-5 14f+: 0-0
Track : LH: 0-5 RH: 0-1 Tight: 0-6 Gall: 0-0
Aids: Bl: 0-3 Vi: 0-0 Tstrap: 0-1 Ckp: 0-1
Best Rating: 60 3/09 Ling 1m2f stand

Modest; stays 1m2f and acts on Polytrack; has worn blinkers and a tongue tie.

Dead Womans Pass (IRE)

90 39

2-y-o b f High Chaparral (IRE)-Pedicure (Atticus (USA))

N Wilson G J Paver

Placings:00005 (7114)

2009: 6^{0}GF, 7^{0}G, 5^{0}GS, 7^{0}GF, 7^{5}GS,

	Starts	1st	2nd	3rd	Win & Pl
Career Total (Turf)	5	0	0	0	0

Going (Turf): Sf: 0-0 GS: 0-2 Gd: 0-1 GF: 0-2 Fm: 0-0
Distance: 5f/6f: 0-2 7f-8f: 0-3 9f-13f: 0-0 14f+: 0-0
Track : LH: 0-2 RH: 0-1 Tight: 0-1 Gall: 0-1
Aids: Bl: 0-0 Vi: 0-0 Tstrap: 0-0 Ckp: 0-0
Best Rating: 39 10/09 Muss 7f30y gd-sft

Deadline (UAE)

(91) (49)**74**

5-y-o ch g Machiavellian (USA)-Time Changes (USA) (Danzig (USA))
Mrs A M Thorpe (P T Midgley 9/5) Hanford's Chemist Ltd

Placings:6520/3332060143560/0000-56 **(0857)**
2009: 8^{5}SD, 11^{6}SD,

	Starts	1st	2nd	3rd	Win & Pl
Career Total (Turf)	18	1	2	2	8005
Career Total (AW)	5	0	0	2	1031

68 8/07 Newc 1m1f9y (0-70) G-F £3469
Total win prize-money £3470

Going (Turf): Sf: 0-1 GS: 0-2 Gd: 0-4 **GF: 1-11** Fm: 0-0
Distance: 5f/6f: 0-3 7f-8f: 0-9 **9f-13f: 1-11** 14f+: 0-0
Track : **LH: 1-16** RH: 0-3 Tight: 0-9 **Gall: 1-3**
Aids: Bl: 0-0 Vi: 0-0 Tstrap: 0-2 Ckp: 0-2
Best Rating: 76 9/06 Pont 6f gd-fm

Deadly Encounter (IRE)

107 **86**

3-y-o br g Lend A Hand-Cautious Joe (First Trump)
R A Fahey J J Staunton

Placings:15500-51644 **(4459)**
2009: 7^{5}S, 7^{1}GF, 7^{6}GF, 7^{4}G, 7^{4}GS,

	Starts	1st	2nd	3rd	Win & Pl
Career Total (Turf)	10	2	0	0	11702

80 6/09 Hayd 7f30y (0-85)H G-F £6476
86 5/08 Bevl 5f GD £2331
Total win prize-money £8807

Going (Turf): Sf: 0-2 GS: 0-2 **Gd: 1-2 GF: 1-4** Fm: 0-0
Distance: 5f/6f: 1-5 7f-8f: 1-5 9f-13f: 0-0 14f+: 0-0
Track : **LH: 1-3** RH: 0-2 Tight: 0-1 Gall: 0-0
Aids: Bl: 0-0 Vi: 0-0 Tstrap: 0-0 Ckp: 0-0
Best Rating: 86 5/08 Bevl 5f good

Fair; effective at 7f; acts on fast ground.

Deadly Secret (USA)

104 **96**

3-y-o b g Johannesburg (USA)-Lypink (USA) (Lyphard (USA))
R A Fahey J J Staunton

Placings:15200-002050 **(5070)**
2009: 7^{0}GF, 8^{0}HY, 8^{2}S, 8^{0}GF, 8^{5}GS, 8^{0}GF,

	Starts	1st	2nd	3rd	Win & Pl
Career Total (Turf)	11	1	2	0	20960

85 6/08 Haml 6f5y G-F £4533
Total win prize-money £4533

Going (Turf): Sf: 0-3 GS: 0-2 Gd: 0-2 **GF: 1-4** Fm: 0-0
Distance: 5f/6f: 0-2 **7f-8f: 1-6** 9f-13f: 0-3 14f+: 0-0
Track : LH: 0-4 RH: 0-0 Tight: 0-0 Gall: 0-1
Aids: Bl: 0-0 Vi: 0-0 Tstrap: 0-0 Ckp: 0-0
Best Rating: 96 8/08 Ripn 6f gd-sft

Useful; stays 1m and acts on most ground.

Deal (IRE)

94 **86**

2-y-o b f Invincible Spirit (IRE)-Desert Order (IRE) (Desert King (IRE))
R Hannon Mrs Madeleine Mangan

Placings:3315300 **(4989)**
2009: 5^{3}GF, 5^{3}GF, 5^{1}GS, 5^{5}G, 6^{3}S, 6^{0}G, 5^{0}GF,

	Starts	1st	2nd	3rd	Win & Pl
Career Total (Turf)	7	1	0	3	8905

81 6/09 Wwck 5f G-S £3885
Total win prize-money £3886

Going (Turf): Sf: 0-1 **GS: 1-1** Gd: 0-2 GF: 0-3 Fm: 0-0
Distance: **5f/6f: 1-6** 7f-8f: 0-1 9f-13f: 0-0 14f+: 0-0
Track : **LH: 1-2** RH: 0-0 Tight: 0-0 Gall: 0-1
Aids: Bl: 0-0 Vi: 0-0 Tstrap: 0-0 Ckp: 0-0
Best Rating: 86 7/09 Newb 6f8y soft

Useful; effective over 5-6f and acts on most ground.

Dealmaker Frank (USA)

(89) (53)**69**

4-y-o b g Diesis-Armourette (USA) (Rahy (USA))
Daniel Mark Loughnane Leo Cox

Placings:54260600/00603343206-000 **(6224)**
2009: 9^{0}G, 11^{0}GY, 8^{0}SD,

	Starts	1st	2nd	3rd	Win & Pl
Career Total (Turf)	20	0	2	3	6127
Career Total (AW)	2	0	0	0	

Going (Turf): **Sf: 0-1 GS: 0-0 Gd: 0-7 GF: 0-1 Fm: 0-0**
Distance: 5f/6f: 0-1 7f-8f: 0-8 9f-13f: 0-13 14f+: 0-0
Track : LH: 0-7 RH: 0-12 Tight: 0-0 Gall: 0-0
Aids: Bl: 0-0 Vi: 0-0 Tstrap: 0-1 Ckp: 0-1
Best Rating: 72 6/07 Leop 7f good

Dean Iarracht (IRE)

101(98) (60)**68**

3-y-o b g Danetime (IRE)-Sirdhana (Selkirk (USA))
Miss Tracy Waggott (M Dods 18/9) Michael Howarth

Placings:22305-363404300543 **(7632)**
2009: 7^{3}GF, 7^{6}SD, 7^{3}GF, 8^{4}GF, 7^{0}GF, 8^{4}S, 9^{3}G, 10^{0}S, 8^{0}S, 8^{5}G, 8^{4}S, 9^{3}SD,

	Starts	1st	2nd	3rd	Win & Pl
Career Total (Turf)	15	0	2	4	4381
Career Total (AW)	2	0	0	1	308

Going (Turf): **Sf: 0-5 GS: 0-1 Gd: 0-4 GF: 0-5 Fm: 0-0**
Distance: 5f/6f: 0-4 7f-8f: 0-8 9f-13f: 0-5 14f+: 0-0
Track : LH: 0-8 RH: 0-2 Tight: 0-4 Gall: 0-0
Aids: Bl: 0-1 Vi: 0-1 Tstrap: 0-2 Ckp: 0-2
Best Rating: 68 7/09 Hayd 1m30y soft

Moderate; stays 6f and acts on fast ground; has worn blinkers and a tongue tie.

Dear Maurice

103(104) (83)**91**

5-y-o b g Indian Ridge-Shamaiel (IRE) (Lycius (USA))
E A L Dunlop Abdul Rahman Al Khalifa

Placings:4/0611600-4304426330 **(6973)**
2009: 9^{4}G, 9^{3}GS, 8^{0}HY, 8^{4}G, 10^{4}G, 8^{2}GF, 8^{6}GF, 8^{3}GF, 9^{3}SD, 10^{0}SD,

	Starts	1st	2nd	3rd	Win & Pl
Career Total (Turf)	15	2	1	2	10382
Career Total (AW)	3	0	0	1	755

91 6/08 Wind 1m67y (0-75)H G-F £3070
88 6/08 Wind 1m67y (0-75)H G-F £3070
Total win prize-money £6142

Going (Turf): Sf: 0-4 GS: 0-1 Gd: 0-3 **GF: 2-7** Fm: 0-0
Distance: 5f/6f: 0-0 7f-8f: 0-2 **9f-13f: 2-16** 14f+: 0-0
Track : LH: 0-5 **RH: 2-11 Tight: 2-10** Gall: 0-1
Aids: Bl: 0-1 Vi: 0-2 Tstrap: 0-1 Ckp: 0-1
Best Rating: 91 6/08 Wind 1m67y gd-fm

Fair; stays 1m; acts on fast ground; has worn blinkers.

Dear Mr Fantasy (IRE)

81(88) (61)**47**

2-y-o b c Kingsalsa (USA)-Heart Ofthe Matter (Rainbow Quest (USA))
J W Hills Christopher Wright & Mrs J A Wright

Placings:5001000 **(6639)**
2009: 6^{5}SD, 6^{0}GF, 7^{0}G, 7^{1}SD, 7^{0}SD, 8^{0}SD, 8^{0}SD,

	Starts	1st	2nd	3rd	Win & Pl
Career Total (Turf)	2	0	0	0	
Career Total (AW)	5	1	0	0	3238

61 8/09 Wolv 7f32y STD £3238
Total win prize-money £3238

Going (Turf): **Sf: 0-0 GS: 0-0 Gd: 0-1 GF: 0-1 Fm: 0-0**
Distance: 5f/6f: 0-2 **7f-8f: 1-4** 9f-13f: 0-1 14f+: 0-0
Track : **LH: 1-4** RH: 0-1 **Tight: 1-4** Gall: 0-0
Aids: Bl: 0-0 Vi: 0-0 Tstrap: 0-0 Ckp: 0-0
Best Rating: 61 8/09 Wolv 7f32y stand

Moderate 3,000gns colt out of a half-sister to three winners including the useful Silver Pivotal; stays 7f; acts on Polytrack.

Deauville Flyer

100 **86**

3-y-o b g Dubai Destination (USA)-Reaf (In The Wings)
T D Easterby Mr And Mrs J D Cotton

Placings:603134123 **(6995)**
2009: 7^{6}GF, 8^{0}GF, 12^{3}GF, 12^{1}GF, 12^{3}GS, 14^{4}G, 14^{1}HY, 16^{2}GS, 14^{3}GS,

	Starts	1st	2nd	3rd	Win & Pl
Career Total (Turf)	9	2	1	3	12060

82 7/09 Hayd 1m6f (0-70)H HVY £3238
72 6/09 Donc 1m4f (0-70)H G-F £4209
Total win prize-money £7447

Going (Turf): **Sf: 1-1** GS: 0-3 Gd: 0-1 **GF: 1-4** Fm: 0-0
Distance: 5f/6f: 0-0 7f-0f: 0-2 9f-13f: 1-3 14f+: 1-4
Track : **LH: 2-6** RH: 0-2 Tight: 0-2 **Gall: 1-5**
Aids: Bl: 0-0 Vi: 0-0 Tstrap: 0-0 Ckp: 0-0
Best Rating: 86 10/09 Donc 1m6f132y gd-sft

Fair; stays 2m; acts on fast and on heavy ground; type to win more races.

Deauville Post (FR)

104 **86**

2-y-o b c American Post-Loyola (FR) (Sicyos (USA))
R Hannon Jaber Abdullah

Placings:0423 **(5399)**

2009: 7^{0}G, 7^{4}G, 7^{2}G, 8^{3}G,

	Starts	1st	2nd	3rd	Win & Pl
Career Total (Turf)	4	0	1	1	2697

Going (Turf): Sf: 0-0 GS: 0-0 Gd: 0-4 GF: 0-0 Fm: 0-0

Distance: 5f/6f: 0-0 7f-8f: 0-4 9f-13f: 0-0 14f+: 0-0

Track : LH: 0-1 RH: 0-2 Tight: 0-1 Gall: 0-0

Aids: Bl: 0-0 Vi: 0-0 Tstrap: 0-0 Ckp: 0-0

Best Rating: 86 8/09 NmkJ 1m good

Useful; stays 1m.

Debdene Bank (IRE)

97(99) (67)**69**

6-y-o b m Pivotal-Nedaarah (Reference Point)

Mrs Mary Hambro Mrs Richard Hambro

Placings:4/056-56002023236 **(7594)**

2009: 8^{5}SD, 9^{6}SD, 8^{0}SD, 10^{0}GF, 11^{2}G, 12^{0}SD, 10^{2}G, 8^{3}SF, 13^{2}SD, 12^{3}SD, 13^{6}SD,

	Starts	1st	2nd	3rd	Win & Pl
Career Total (Turf)	6	0	2	0	1740
Career Total (AW)	9	0	1	2	1363

Going (Turf): Sf: 0-1 GS: 0-0 Gd: 0-2 GF: 0-3 Fm: 0-0

Distance: 5f/6f: 0-1 7f-8f: 0-3 9f-13f: 0-9 14f+: 0-2

Track : LH: 0-10 RH: 0-3 Tight: 0-8 Gall: 0-1

Aids: Bl: 0-0 Vi: 0-0 Tstrap: 0-0 Ckp: 0-0

Best Rating: 69 5/08 Wind 1m67y gd-fm

Modest; stays 1m43f; acts on good ground; goes on Polytrack.

Debord (FR)

72(90) (45)**67**

6-y-o ch g Sendawar (IRE)-Partie De Dames (USA) (Bering)

Jamie Poulton Les Best

Placings:00410000/02000/0-06 **(4703)**

2009: 16^{0}SD, 15^{6}GF,

	Starts	1st	2nd	3rd	Win & Pl
Career Total (Turf)	13	1	1	0	7873
Career Total (AW)	4	0	0	0	

67 6/06 Sand 1m14y (0-80)H GD £6477

Total win prize-money £6477

Going (Turf): Sf: 0-2 GS: 0-3 **Gd: 1-5** GF: 0-3 Fm: 0-0

Distance: 5f/6f: 0-0 7f-8f: 0-5 **9f-13f: 1-5** 14f+: 0-7

Track : LH: 0-7 **RH: 1-9** Tight: 0-8 Gall: 0-0

Aids: Bl: 0-1 Vi: 0-0 Tstrap: 0-0 Ckp: 0-0

Best Rating: 67 6/06 Sand 1m14y good

Debussy (IRE)

111(95) (90)**115**

3-y-o b c Diesis-Opera Comique (FR) (Singspiel (IRE))

J H M Gosden H R H Princess Haya Of Jordan

Placings:4-1130016 **(5084a)**

2009: 10^{1}SD, 10^{1}G, 12^{3}GF, 12^{0}G, 12^{0}GF, 10^{1}GS, 10^{6}G,

	Starts	1st	2nd	3rd	Win & Pl
Career Total (Turf)	6	2	0	1	241360
Career Total (AW)	2	1	0	0	4857

115 7/09 MsnL 1m2f G-S £221359

108 4/09 Epsm 1m2f18y GD £12462

90 3/09 Ling 1m2f STD £4857

Total win prize-money £238678

Going (Turf): Sf: 0-0 **GS: 1-1 Gd: 1-3** GF: 0-2 Fm: 0-0

Distance: 5f/6f: 0-0 7f-8f: 0-1 **9f-13f: 3-7** 14f+: 0-0

Track : **LH: 2-5** RH: 0-2 **Tight: 2-5** Gall: 0-1

Aids: Bl: 0-0 Vi: 0-0 Tstrap: 0-1 Ckp: 0-1

Best Rating: 115 8/09 Deau 1m2f good

Smart; effective over 1m2f; acts on good ground and Polytrack.

Decameron (USA)

102(101) (87)**96**

4-y-o b g Theatrical-Morning Pride (IRE) (Machiavellian (USA))

R A Harris (Sir Michael Stoute 30/5) Paul Moulton

Placings:32120566-5005400 **(7845)**

2009: 8^{5}G, 7^{0}GF, 8^{0}SD, 9^{5}G, 8^{4}SD, 8^{0}SD, 7^{0}SD,

	Starts	1st	2nd	3rd	Win & Pl
Career Total (Turf)	9	1	2	1	12439
Career Total (AW)	6	0	0	0	485

89 6/08 York 1m GD £6540

Total win prize-money £6541

Going (Turf): Sf: 0-1 GS: 0-0 **Gd: 1-4** GF: 0-4 Fm: 0-0

Distance: 5f/6f: 0-0 **7f-8f: 1-9** 9f-13f: 0-6 14f+: 0-0

Track : **LH: 1-8** RH: 0-3 Tight: 0-4 **Gall: 1-2**

Aids: Bl: 0-0 Vi: 0-1 Tstrap: 0-1 Ckp: 0-1

Best Rating: 96 7/08 NmkJ 1m gd-fm

Useful; effective at around 1m; acts on good and fast ground and Polytrack.

December

85(99) (61)**63**

3-y-o b g Oasis Dream-Winter Solstice (Unfuwain (USA))

Mrs C A Dunnett (Sir Michael Stoute 19/6) P D West

Placings:0-00356 **(7831)**

2009: 8^{0}S, 10^{0}GF, 10^{3}SD, 12^{5}SD, 12^{6}SD,

	Starts	1st	2nd	3rd	Win & Pl
Career Total (Turf)	3	0	0	0	
Career Total (AW)	3	0	0	1	403

Going (Turf): Sf: 0-1 GS: 0-0 Gd: 0-1 GF: 0-1 Fm: 0-0

Distance: 5f/6f: 0-0 7f-8f: 0-2 9f-13f: 0-4 14f+: 0-0

Track : LH: 0-2 RH: 0-3 Tight: 0-2 Gall: 0-1

Aids: Bl: 0-0 Vi: 0-0 Tstrap: 0-0 Ckp: 0-0

Best Rating: 63 6/09 NmkJ 1m2f gd-fm

December Draw (IRE)

99(103) (86)**87**

3-y-o br g Medecis-New York (IRE) (Danzero (AUS))

W J Knight Brook House

Placings:31-35306 **(7684)**

2009: 8^{3}GF, 9^{5}G, 8^{3}GF, 8^{0}SD, 10^{6}SD,

	Starts	1st	2nd	3rd	Win & Pl
Career Total (Turf)	3	0	0	2	2149
Career Total (AW)	4	1	0	1	2700

75 12/08 Ling 1m STD £2047

Total win prize-money £2047

Going (Turf): Sf: 0-0 GS: 0-0 Gd: 0-1 GF: 0-2 Fm: 0-0

Distance: 5f/6f: 0-0 **7f-8f: 1-3** 9f-13f: 0-4 14f+: 0-0

Track : **LH: 1-3** RH: 0-4 **Tight: 1-5** Gall: 0-1

Aids: Bl: 0-0 Vi: 0-0 Tstrap: 0-1 Ckp: 0-1

Best Rating: 87 5/09 Wind 1m67y gd-fm

Useful; effective over 1m and acts on Polytrack.

Decency (IRE)

88(82) (46)**43**

2-y-o b f Celtic Swing-Siem Reap (USA) (El Gran Senor (USA))

E A L Dunlop Highclere Thoroughbred Racing (St Simon)

Placings:000 **(7317)**

2009: 6^{0}SD, 6^{0}G, 5^{0}SD,

	Starts	1st	2nd	3rd	Win & Pl
Career Total (Turf)	1	0	0	0	
Career Total (AW)	2	0	0	0	

Going (Turf): Sf: 0-0 GS: 0-0 Gd: 0-1 GF: 0-0 Fm: 0-0

Distance: 5f/6f: 0-3 7f-8f: 0-0 9f-13f: 0-0 14f+: 0-0

Track : LH: 0-2 RH: 0-0 Tight: 0-2 Gall: 0-0

Aids: Bl: 0-0 Vi: 0-0 Tstrap: 0-0 Ckp: 0-0

Best Rating: 46 11/09 Wolv 5f216y stand

Dechiper (IRE)

103 (35)**75**

7-y-o b/br g Almutawakel-Safiya (USA) (Riverman (USA))

R Johnson L Armstrong

Placings:000/0442/04004151236/031054320660-551021206040404 **(6899)**

2009: 12^{5}GF, 10^{5}GF, 12^{1}GS, 16^{0}GS, 11^{2}GF, 10^{1}G, 10^{2}S, 11^{0}G, 10^{6}G, 8^{0}GF, 8^{4}GF, 12^{0}GS, 12^{4}GF, 16^{0}GS, 17^{4}GF,

	Starts	1st	2nd	3rd	Win & Pl
Career Total (Turf)	42	5	5	3	24651
Career Total (AW)	3	0	0	0	

72 6/09 Newc 1m2f32y (0-75)H GD £3238

70 5/09 Newc 1m4f93y (0-70)H G-S £2978

71 5/08 Newc 1m2f32y (0-65)H G-F £2752

65 8/07 Newc 1m2f32y (0-75)H GD £3469

63 7/07 Newc 1m2f32y (0-60)H GD £2266

Total win prize-money £14706

Going (Turf): Sf: 0-5 GS: 1-10 **Gd: 3-12** GF: 1-12 Fm: 0-0

Distance: 5f/6f: 0-1 7f-8f: 0-8 **9f-13f: 5-31** 14f+: 0-5

Track : **LH: 5-32** RH: 0-6 Tight: 0-4 **Gall: 5-24**

Aids: Bl: 0-0 Vi: 0-0 Tstrap: 0-2 Ckp: 0-2

Best Rating: 75 6/09 Newc 1m2f32y soft

Modest; effective at 1m2f-2m; likes fast ground; goes well at Newcastle; has worn cheekpieces.

Decider (USA)

88(104) (69)**50**

6-y-o ch g High Yield (USA)-Nikita Moon (USA) (Secret Hello (USA))

R A Harris Robert Bailey

Placings:5000045211/000006600/2115500000-0363634240020450313410224 **(7807)**

2009: 5^{0}SD, 5^{3}SD, 5^{6}SD, 5^{3}SD, 5^{6}SD, 5^{3}SD, 5^{4}SD, 5^{2}SD, 5^{4}SD, 5^{0}SD, 5^{0}SD, 5^{2}SD, 5^{0}SD, 6^{4}SD, 5^{5}SD, 5^{0}GS, 5^{3}GF, 5^{1}SD, 5^{3}SD, 5^{4}SD, 5^{1}SD, 6^{0}SD,

	Starts	1st	2nd	3rd	Win & Pl
Career Total (Turf)	18	0	0	1	626
Career Total (AW)	36	6	6	4	19992

68 11/09 Wolv 5f20y STD £2047

61 9/09 Wolv 5f20y (0-55)H STD £2388

77 3/08 Sthl 5f (0-60)H STD £1911

64 2/08 Wolv 5f216y (0-55)H STD £1774

63 12/06 Kemp 5f (0-58)H STD £3412

62 11/06 Sthl 5f STD £3238

Total win prize-money £14773

Going (Turf): Sf: 0-1 GS: 0-4 Gd: 0-3 GF: 0-10 Fm: 0-0

Distance: **5f/6f: 6-51** 7f-8f: 0-3 9f-13f: 0-0 14f+: 0-0

Track : **LH: 3-28** RH: 1-6 **Tight: 3-22** Gall: 0-4

Aids: Bl: 0-5 Vi: 0-0 Tstrap: 2-13 Ckp: 2-13
Best Rating: 77 3/08 Sthl 5f stand

Modest; effective over 5f-6f; acts on sand; has worn cheek-pieces.

Decimus Meridius (IRE)

86 62

2-y-o ch c Danehill Dancer (IRE)-Simaat (USA) (Mr Prospector (USA))
J Howard Johnson Transcend Bloodstock LLP

Placings:300 **(6136)**
2009: 7³G, 8⁰G, 8⁰G,

	Starts	1st	2nd	3rd	Win & Pl
Career Total (Turf)	3	0	0	1	482

Going (Turf): Sf: 0-0 GS: 0-0 Gd: 0-3 GF: 0-0 Fm: 0-0
Distance: 5f/6f: 0-0 7f-8f: 0-2 9f-13f: 0-1 14f+: 0-0
Track: LH: 0-2 RH: 0-1 Tight: 0-3 Gall: 0-0
Aids: Bl: 0-0 Vi: 0-0 Tstrap: 0-0 Ckp: 0-0
Best Rating: 62 8/09 Catt 7f good

Decision

108 88

3-y-o b g Royal Applause-Corinium (IRE) (Turtle Island (IRE))
C G Cox A D Spence

Placings:0353-22423001 **(6907)**
2009: 10²GF, 10²S, 10⁴GS, 10²GF, 12³G, 10⁰GF, 10⁰GF, 10¹G,

	Starts	1st	2nd	3rd	Win & Pl
Career Total (Turf)	12	1	3	3	17007

85 10/09 Wind 1m2f7y (0-85)H GD £4857
Total win prize-money £4857

Going (Turf): Sf: 0-2 GS: 0-2 **Gd: 1-4** GF: 0-4 Fm: 0-0
Distance: 5f/6f: 0-0 7f-8f: 0-2 **9f-13f: 1-10** 14f+: 0-0
Track: LH: 0-5 **RH: 1-5 Tight: 1-2** Gall: 0-3
Aids: Bl: 0-0 Vi: 0-0 Tstrap: 0-1 Ckp: 0-1
Best Rating: 88 5/09 Newb 1m2f6y soft

Useful; stays 1m2f; acts on fast ground.

Deckchair

93(98) (60)54

3-y-o b f Monsieur Bond (IRE)-Silver Sun (Green Desert (USA))
S Curran (H J Collingridge 7/8) Dave Clayton

Placings:0006123-3544015004505 **(7535)**
2009: 5³SD, 6⁵SD, 5⁴SD, 6⁴SD, 7⁰SD, 5¹SD, 5⁵GF, 5⁰SD, 6⁰G, 7⁴GF, 7⁵GF, 7⁰SS, 6⁵SD,

	Starts	1st	2nd	3rd	Win & Pl
Career Total (Turf)	5	0	0	0	0
Career Total (AW)	15	2	1	2	6732

60 3/09 Wolv 5f216y STD £2047
55 11/08 Wolv 5f216y STD £3238
Total win prize-money £5285

Going (Turf): Sf: 0-0 GS: 0-0 Gd: 0-2 GF: 0-3 Fm: 0-0
Distance: **5f/6f: 2-10** 7f-8f: 0-10 9f-13f: 0-0 14f+: 0-0
Track: **LH: 2-11** RH: 0-4 **Tight: 2-9** Gall: 0-2
Aids: Bl: 0-0 **Vi: 2-18** Tstrap: 0-0 Ckp: 0-0
Best Rating: 60 3/09 Wolv 5f216y stand

Moderate; effective over 6f and acts on Polytrack; has worn a visor.

Decorative (IRE)

97 87

2-y-o b f Danehill Dancer (IRE)-Source Of Life (IRE) (Fasliyev (USA))
M A Jarvis Highclere Thoroughbred Racing Royal Pal

Placings:1 **(5478)**
2009: 6¹GF,

	Starts	1st	2nd	3rd	Win & Pl
Career Total (Turf)	1	1	0	0	4289

87 8/09 Yarm 6f3y G-F £4289
Total win prize-money £4289

Going (Turf): Sf: 0-0 GS: 0-0 Gd: 0-0 **GF: 1-1** Fm: 0-0
Distance: 5f/6f: 0-0 **7f-8f: 1-1** 9f-13f: 0-0 14f+: 0-0
Track: LH: 0-0 RH: 0-0 Tight: 0-0 Gall: 0-0
Aids: Bl: 0-0 Vi: 0-0 Tstrap: 0-0 Ckp: 0-0
Best Rating: 87 8/09 Yarm 6f3y gd-fm

Useful; stays 6f; acts on fast ground.

Decorum (USA)

96(100) (79)80

3-y-o b c Dynaformer (USA)-Shy Greeting (ARG) (Shy Tom (USA))
J H M Gosden George Strawbridge & Arthur Hancock

Placings:064-33252 **(6789)**
2009: 10³GF, 11³GS, 12²SD, 13⁵G, 11²G,

	Starts	1st	2nd	3rd	Win & Pl
Career Total (Turf)	5	0	1	2	2199
Career Total (AW)	3	0	1	0	1869

Going (Turf): Sf: 0-0 GS: 0-2 Gd: 0-2 GF: 0-1 Fm: 0-0
Distance: 5f/6f: 0-0 7f-8f: 0-2 9f-13f: 0-6 14f+: 0-0
Track: LH: 0-6 RH: 0-1 Tight: 0-1 Gall: 0-5
Aids: Bl: 0-1 Vi: 0-0 Tstrap: 0-0 Ckp: 0-0
Best Rating: 80 5/09 Newb 1m3f5y gd-sft

Fair; stays 1m2f; acts on fast ground and on Polytrack; has worn a tongue tie.

Decree Absolute (USA)

90 74

2-y-o b/br g Orientate (USA)-Midriff (USA) (Naevus (USA))
Miss J R Tooth J R May

Placings:1200 **(6367)**
2009: 6¹GF, 6²GF, 7⁰G, 7⁰GF,

	Starts	1st	2nd	3rd	Win & Pl
Career Total (Turf)	4	1	1	0	5227

69 6/09 Sals 6f G-F £2914
Total win prize-money £2914

Going (Turf): Sf: 0-0 GS: 0-0 Gd: 0-1 **GF: 1-3** Fm: 0-0
Distance: **5f/6f: 1-2** 7f-8f: 0-2 9f-13f: 0-0 14f+: 0-0
Track: LH: 0-2 RH: 0-0 Tight: 0-0 Gall: 0-0
Aids: Bl: 0-0 Vi: 0-0 Tstrap: 0-0 Ckp: 0-0
Best Rating: 74 6/09 Pont 6f gd-fm

Winner on debut; effective over 6f; acts on fast ground.

Dedante

(95) (63)63

3-y-o br f One Cool Cat (USA)-Cloridja (Indian Ridge)
D K Ivory Three Cool Cats

Placings:52324025-660R **(4155)**
2009: 5⁶SD, 5⁶SD, 5⁰SD, 6ᴿG,

	Starts	1st	2nd	3rd	Win & Pl
Career Total (Turf)	3	0	1	0	1811
Career Total (AW)	9	0	2	1	1953

Going (Turf): Sf: 0-0 GS: 0-0 Gd: 0-1 GF: 0-1 Fm: 0-1
Distance: 5f/6f: 0-11 7f-8f: 0-1 9f-13f: 0-0 14f+: 0-0
Track: LH: 0-8 RH: 0-0 Tight: 0-8 Gall: 0-0
Aids: Bl: 0-5 Vi: 0-0 Tstrap: 0-0 Ckp: 0-0
Best Rating: 63 6/08 Ches 5f16y gd-fm

Moderate; effective over 5f; acts on fast ground and on sand; has worn blinkers.

Dee Cee Elle

87(96) (53)50

5-y-o b m Groom Dancer (USA)-Missouri (Charnwood Forest (IRE))
D Burchell C Friel

Placings:605501/2114140066/0-053 **(4862)**
2009: 16⁰SD, 11⁵F, 16³SD,

	Starts	1st	2nd	3rd	Win & Pl
Career Total (Turf)	14	2	1	0	7203
Career Total (AW)	6	2	0	1	6676

73 5/07 Bevl 1m4f16y (0-70)H GD £3562
76 4/07 Sthl 1m3f (0-65)H STD £3071
63 4/07 Sthl 1m3f (0-60)H GD £2388
57 11/06 Wolv 1m1f103y (0-65) STD £2900
Total win prize-money £11923

Going (Turf): Sf: 0-2 GS: 0-1 **Gd: 2-3** GF: 0-6 Fm: 0-2
Distance: 5f/6f: 0-2 7f-8f: 0-1 **9f-13f: 4-14** 14f+: 0-3
Track: **LH: 3-10** RH: 1-7 **Tight: 3-12** Gall: 0-0
Aids: Bl: 0-0 Vi: 0-0 Tstrap: 0-3 Ckp: 0-3
Best Rating: 76 4/07 Sthl 1m3f stand

Modest filly; probably stays 1m6f; acts on fast ground and Polytrack.

Deely Plaza

90(92) (70)70

2-y-o b g Compton Place-Anchorage (IRE) (Slip Anchor)
R Hannon Mrs J Wood

Placings:04454 **(6895)**
2009: 6⁰GF, 6⁴SD, 7⁴GF, 8⁵GS, 8⁴GF,

	Starts	1st	2nd	3rd	Win & Pl
Career Total (Turf)	4	0	0	0	649
Career Total (AW)	1	0	0	0	265

Going (Turf): Sf: 0-0 GS: 0-1 Gd: 0-0 GF: 0-3 Fm: 0-0
Distance: 5f/6f: 0-2 7f-8f: 0-1 9f-13f: 0-2 14f+: 0-0
Track: LH: 0-2 RH: 0-2 Tight: 0-2 Gall: 0-1
Aids: Bl: 0-0 Vi: 0-0 Tstrap: 0-0 Ckp: 0-0
Best Rating: 70 9/09 Ches 7f2y gd-fm

Fair; effective over 6f but should be better suited by 7f; best effort on Polytrack; should win a race.

Deep Winter

99(91) (64)91

4-y-o ch f Pivotal-Russian Snows (IRE) (Sadler's Wells (USA))
R A Fahey G Morrin

Placings:4001110143-23000 **(4328)**
2009: 8²GF, 8³G, 9⁰GF, 10⁰GF, 10⁰G,

	Starts	1st	2nd	3rd	Win & Pl
Career Total (Turf)	14	3	1	2	20036
Career Total (AW)	1	1	0	0	1943

87 8/08 Ayr 1m2f (0-85)H SFT £7352

82 7/08 Carl 1m1f61y (0-70)H FRM £2590
72 7/08 Haml 1m65y (0-70)H GD £3238
64 6/08 GrLe 1m (0-60)H STD £1942
Total win prize-money £15124

Going (Turf): **Sf: 1-1** GS: 0-1 **Gd: 1-4** GF: 0-7 **Fm: 1-1**
Distance: 5f/6f: 0-3 7f-8f: 1-3 **9f-13f: 3-9** 14f+: 0-0
Track : LH: 2-8 RH: 2-3 Tight: 1-4 Gall: 1-3
Aids: Bl: 0-0 Vi: 0-0 Tstrap: 0-0 Ckp: 0-0
Best Rating: **91** 4/09 Hanv 1m good

Useful; stays 1m2f; acts on most ground and on Polytrack; likes to race prominently.

Defector (IRE)

98(104) (77)**73**
3-y-o b g Fasliyev (USA)-Rich Dancer (Halling (USA))
W R Muir David Knox & Partners

Placings:4325-503**20401523305 31** (7876)
2009: 6^{5}GF, 7^{0}G, 6^{3}GF, **6**^{2}SD, 6^{0}G, **6**^{4}SD, **6**^{0}SD, 7^{1}SD, 7^{5}SD, 7^{2}SD, 7^{3}SD, 7^{3}SD, 7^{0}SD, 7^{5}SD, 7^{3}SD, 7^{1}SD,

	Starts	1st	2nd	3rd	Win & Pl
Career Total (Turf)	7	0	1	1	9589
Career Total (AW)	13	2	2	4	8781

12/09 Kemp 7f (0-70)H STD £2590
76 9/09 Kemp 7f (0-75)H STD £2590
Total win prize-money £5180

Going (Turf): **Sf: 0-0 GS: 0-0 Gd: 0-3 GF: 0-4 Fm: 0-0**
Distance: 5f/6f: 0-8 **7f-8f: 2-12** 9f-13f: 0-0 14f+: 0-0
Track : LH: 0-7 **RH: 2-7** Tight: 0-4 Gall: 0-1
Aids: Bl: 0-3 Vi: 0-0 Tstrap: 0-1 Ckp: 0-1
Best Rating: **77** 10/09 Kemp 7f stand

Fair; effective over 6f-7f; handles fast ground; goes on Fibresand and Polytrack; not straightforward.

Defi (IRE)

91(91) (75)**55**
7-y-o b g Rainbow Quest (USA)-Danse Classique (IRE) (Night Shift (USA))
D A Nolan Miss M McFadyen-Murray

Placings:4431100/206553603**00/304**304051100**0040/6502** 000**124/3**600000-600000 (5364)
2009: 9^{6}GF, 9^{0}G, 7^{0}GF, 7^{0}GF, 8^{0}G, 8^{0}S,

	Starts	1st	2nd	3rd	Win & Pl
Career Total (Turf)	44	5	2	4	40903
Career Total (AW)	13	0	1	2	2070

70 11/07 Muss 1m GD £2590
76 8/06 Haml 1m65y G-F £2730
76 7/06 Haml 1m65y (0-65)H G-F £3238
80 8/04 Tipp 7f100y G-F £11002
86 7/04 Gway 7f G-F £10315
Total win prize-money £29878

Going (Turf): Sf: 0-4 GS: 0-2 Gd: 1-11 **GF: 4-23** Fm: 0-2
Distance: 5f/6f: 0-3 **7f-8f: 3-20** 9f-13f: 2-34 14f+: 0-0
Track : LH: 0-23 **RH: 4-27 Tight: 3-38** Gall: 0-1
Aids: **Bl: 3-35** Vi: 0-0 Tstrap: 0-8 Ckp: 0-8
Best Rating: **89** 4/05 NmkR 1m gd-fm

Modest; stays 1m; acts on fast ground; not very consistent.

Definightly

97 **94**
3-y-o b/br g Diktat-Perfect Night (Danzig Connection (USA))
R Charlton S Emmet And Miss R Emmet

Placings:521210-060 (2934)
2009: 6^{0}GF, 7^{6}HY, 6^{0}G,

	Starts	1st	2nd	3rd	Win & Pl
Career Total (Turf)	9	2	2	0	18095

94 10/08 Donc 7f GD £9714
91 9/08 Ling 6f SFT £2914
Total win prize-money £12628

Going (Turf): **Sf: 1-3** GS: 0-1 **Gd: 1-4** GF: 0-1 Fm: 0-0
Distance: 5f/6f: 1-4 7f-8f: 1-5 9f-13f: 0-0 14f+: 0-0
Track : LH: 0-1 RH: 0-0 Tight: 0-0 Gall: 0-0
Aids: Bl: 0-0 Vi: 0-0 Tstrap: 0-0 Ckp: 0-0
Best Rating: **94** 10/08 Donc 7f good

Useful; stays 7f; handles good, but acts well on soft ground.

Deirdre

79(87) (71)**78**
2-y-o b f Dubawi (IRE)-Dolores (Danehill (USA))
J H M Gosden Normandie Stud Ltd

Placings:51 (6762)
2009: 7^{5}SD, 8^{1}GS,

	Starts	1st	2nd	3rd	Win & Pl
Career Total (Turf)	1	1	0	0	3886
Career Total (AW)	1	0	0	0	0

78 10/09 Newc 1m G-S £3885
Total win prize-money £3886

Going (Turf): Sf: 0-0 **GS: 1-1** Gd: 0-0 GF: 0-0 Fm: 0-0
Distance: 5f/6f: 0-0 **7f-8f: 1-2** 9f-13f: 0-0 14f+: 0-0
Track : **LH: 1-1** RH: 0-1 Tight: 0-0 **Gall: 1-1**
Aids: Bl: 0-0 Vi: 0-0 Tstrap: 0-0 Ckp: 0-0
Best Rating: **78** 10/09 Newc 1m gd-sft

Fair; stays 1m; acts on easy ground.

Delegator

114 **123**
3-y-o b c Dansili-Indian Love Bird (Efisio)
Saeed Bin Suroor (B J Meehan 16/6) Godolphin

Placings:215-1202035 (7308a)
2009: 8^{1}GF, 8^{2}GF, 8^{0}HY, 8^{2}GF, 8^{0}G, 8^{3}GF, 8^{5}F,

	Starts	1st	2nd	3rd	Win & Pl
Career Total (Turf)	10	2	3	1	265916

118 4/09 NmkR 1m G-F £36900
91 8/08 NmkJ 7f GD £5180
Total win prize-money £42082

Going (Turf): Sf: 0-1 GS: 0-1 **Gd: 1-3 GF: 1-4** Fm: 0-1
Distance: 5f/6f: 0-0 **7f-8f: 2-10** 9f-13f: 0-0 14f+: 0-0
Track : LH: 0-1 RH: 0-4 Tight: 0-0 Gall: 0-3
Aids: Bl: 0-0 Vi: 0-0 Tstrap: 0-0 Ckp: 0-0
Best Rating: **123** 6/09 Asct 1m gd-fm

Group class; impressive winner of the Craven Stakes in 2009 before finishing runner-up in the 2000 Guineas; also second in the St James's Palace Stakes; left Brian Meehan prior to winning the Celebration Mile at Goodwood (subsequently disqualified); effective at 1m; acts on fast and easy ground.

Deloria

93(92) (72)**74**
2-y-o ch f Mark Of Esteem (IRE)-Denica (IRE) (Night Shift (USA))
Eve Johnson Houghton Skeltools Ltd

Placings:215060 (6906)
2009: 6^{2}GF, 6^{1}GF, **6**^{5}SD, 7^{0}GF, 6^{6}GF, 6^{0}G,

	Starts	1st	2nd	3rd	Win & Pl
Career Total (Turf)	5	1	1	0	5603
Career Total (AW)	1	0	0	0	0

72 7/09 Sals 6f G-F £3885
Total win prize-money £3886

Going (Turf): Sf: 0-0 GS: 0-0 Gd: 0-1 **GF: 1-4** Fm: 0-0
Distance: **5f/6f: 1-3** 7f-8f: 0-3 9f-13f: 0-0 14f+: 0-0
Track : LH: 0-0 RH: 0-1 Tight: 0-0 Gall: 0-1
Aids: Bl: 0-1 Vi: 0-0 Tstrap: 0-0 Ckp: 0-0
Best Rating: **74** 7/09 Newb 6f8y gd-fm

Fair filly; effective over 6f on fast ground.

Delta Sky (IRE)

87(81) (52)**62**
2-y-o ch f Refuse To Bend (IRE)-Delta Blues (IRE) (Digamist (USA))
Miss Amy Weaver Bringloe, White, Lennox

Placings:0050 (7884)
2009: 6^{0}GF, 7^{0}G, **6**^{5}SD, 7^{0}SD,

	Starts	1st	2nd	3rd	Win & Pl
Career Total (Turf)	2	0	0	0	
Career Total (AW)	2	0	0	0	0

Going (Turf): **Sf: 0-0 GS: 0-0 Gd: 0-1 GF: 0-1 Fm: 0-0**
Distance: 5f/6f: 0-1 7f-8f: 0-3 9f-13f: 0-0 14f+: 0-0
Track : LH: 0-2 RH: 0-0 Tight: 0-2 Gall: 0-0
Aids: Bl: 0-0 Vi: 0-0 Tstrap: 0-0 Ckp: 0-0
Best Rating: **62** 7/09 Sals 6f212y gd-fm

Demeanour (USA)

98(103) (75)**74**
3-y-o ch f Giant's Causeway (USA)-Akuna Bay (USA) (Mr Prospector (USA))
E A L Dunlop Highclere Thoroughbred Racing (Eclipse)

Placings:430-**23434233** (6975)
2009: **10**^{2}SD, 10^{3}GF, 10^{4}G, **12**^{3}SD, **11**^{4}SD, **9**^{2}SD, **9**^{3}SD, **12**^{3}SD,

	Starts	1st	2nd	3rd	Win & Pl
Career Total (Turf)	5	0	0	2	1609
Career Total (AW)	6	0	2	3	3158

Going (Turf): **Sf: 0-0 GS: 0-1 Gd: 0-2 GF: 0-2 Fm: 0-0**
Distance: 5f/6f: 0-0 7f-8f: 0-3 9f-13f: 0-8 14f+: 0-0
Track : LH: 0-5 RH: 0-3 Tight: 0-5 Gall: 0-0
Aids: Bl: 0-0 Vi: 0-1 Tstrap: 0-2 Ckp: 0-2
Best Rating: **75** 10/09 Kemp 1m4f stand

Fair; stays 1m2f; acts on good ground; goes on Polytrack.

Democrate

96 (86)**113**
4-y-o gr/ro c Dalakhani (IRE)-Aiglonne (USA) (Silver Hawk (USA))
Saeed Bin Suroor Godolphin

Placings:22/210-00 (5004)
2009: 10^{0}G, 10^{0}G,

	Starts	1st	2nd	3rd	Win & Pl
Career Total (Turf)	6	1	2	0	62323
Career Total (AW)	1	0	1	0	3784

113 5/08 Lonc 1m3f G-S £54485
Total win prize-money £54485

Going (Turf): Sf: 0-2 **GS: 1-1** Gd: 0-2 GF: 0-0 Fm: 0-0
Distance: 5f/6f: 0-0 7f-8f: 0-1 **9f-13f: 1-6** 14f+: 0-0
Track : LH: 0-1 **RH: 1-5** Tight: 0-0 Gall: 0-1
Aids: Bl: 0-0 Vi: 0-0 Tstrap: 0-0 Ckp: 0-0
Best Rating: **113** 5/08 Lonc 1m3f gd-sft

Demolition

110(100) (72)**96**

5-y-o ch g Starborough-Movie Star (IRE) (Barathea (IRE))

N Wilson M Wormald

Placings:0/0221656/54221060-315051234124 **(6644)**

2009: 10^{3}GF, 12^{1}GF, 9^{5}GF, 12^{0}GF, 12^{5}G, 12^{1}G, 9^{2}G, 9^{3}G, 12^{4}S, 10^{1}GS, 13^{2}G, 10^{4}G,

	Starts	1st	2nd	3rd	Win & Pl
Career Total (Turf)	25	5	6	2	46013
Career Total (AW)	3	0	0	0	

96	9/09	Ayr	1m2f	(0-100)H	G-S	£12952
84	7/09	York	1m4f		GD	£5180
89	4/09	Bevl	1m4f16y	(0-85)H	G-F	£4727
84	8/08	Ripn	1m1f170y	(0-85)H	GD	£4731
78	8/07	Sals	1m1f198y		G-F	£4857

Total win prize-money £32449

Going (Turf): Sf: 0-2 GS: 1-3 **Gd: 2-12 GF: 2-8** Fm: 0-0
Distance: 5f/6f: 0-0 7f-8f: 0-2 **9f-13f: 5-25** 14f+: 0-1
Track : LH: 2-15 **RH: 3-12 Tight: 3-11** Gall: 1-7
Aids: Bl: 0-0 Vi: 0-0 Tstrap: 3-11 Ckp: 3-11
Best Rating: **96** 9/09 Ayr 1m2f gd-sft

Useful; effective over 1m2f-1m4f; acts on good ground; has worn cheekpieces.

Demonstrative (USA)

91(86) (51)**71**

2-y-o b g Elusive Quality (USA)-Loving Pride (USA) (Quiet American (USA))

M Johnston Sheikh Hamdan Bin Mohammed Al Maktoum

Placings:032346 **(7168)**

2009: 6^{0}GF, 6^{3}G, 7^{2}GF, 7^{3}GF, 7^{4}SD, 7^{6}S,

	Starts	1st	2nd	3rd	Win & Pl
Career Total (Turf)	5	0	1	2	4220
Career Total (AW)	1	0	0	0	289

Going (Turf): **Sf: 0-1 GS: 0-0 Gd: 0-1 GF: 0-3 Fm: 0-0**
Distance: 5f/6f: 0-1 7f-8f: 0-5 9f-13f: 0-0 14f+: 0-0
Track : LH: 0-5 RH: 0-0 Tight: 0-2 Gall: 0-0
Aids: Bl: 0-0 Vi: 0-0 Tstrap: 0-0 Ckp: 0-0
Best Rating: **71** 9/09 Ches 7f2y gd-fm

Fair; stays 7f; acts on good and fast ground.

Den Maschine

97(91) (55)**57**

4-y-o b g Sakhee (USA)-Flamingo Flower (USA) (Diesis)

B N Pollock (Ollie Pears 15/7) Paul Morgan

Placings:50424200 **(5679)**

2009: 9^{5}SD, 9^{0}F, 9^{4}GF, 12^{2}GF, 12^{4}SD, 11^{2}GS, 10^{0}GF, 12^{0}SD,

	Starts	1st	2nd	3rd	Win & Pl
Career Total (Turf)	5	0	2	0	1668
Career Total (AW)	3	0	0	0	144

Going (Turf): **Sf: 0-0 GS: 0-1 Gd: 0-0 GF: 0-3 Fm: 0-1**
Distance: 5f/6f: 0-0 7f-8f: 0-0 9f-13f: 0-8 14f+: 0-0
Track : LH: 0-5 RH: 0-3 Tight: 0-6 Gall: 0-1
Aids: Bl: 0-0 Vi: 0-0 Tstrap: 0-1 Ckp: 0-1
Best Rating: **57** 6/09 Ripn 1m4f10y gd-fm

Modest; stays 1m4f.

Den's Boy

46(81) (35)**2**

4-y-o b g Josr Algarhoud (IRE)-Den's-Joy (Archway (IRE))

S Curran Patsys Crew

Placings:0/000-60 **(3207)**

2009: 7^{6}G, 8^{0}G,

	Starts	1st	2nd	3rd	Win & Pl
Career Total (Turf)	3	0	0	0	0
Career Total (AW)	3	0	0	0	

Going (Turf): **Sf: 0-0 GS: 0-0 Gd: 0-3 GF: 0-0 Fm: 0-0**
Distance: 5f/6f: 0-1 7f-8f: 0-3 9f-13f: 0-2 14f+: 0-0
Track : LH: 0-4 RH: 0-0 Tight: 0-3 Gall: 0-1
Aids: Bl: 0-0 Vi: 0-0 Tstrap: 0-0 Ckp: 0-0
Best Rating: **35** 1/08 Ling 1m stand

Den's Gift (IRE)

103(107) (90)**89**

5-y-o gr/ro g City On A Hill (USA)-Romanylei (IRE) (Blues Traveller (IRE))

C G Cox Mrs Olive Shaw

Placings:304/**11/33**4332202**06-1**032455**22** **(7883)**

2009: 8^{1}SD, 8^{0}G, 7^{3}G, 7^{2}GS, 7^{4}GF, 8^{5}G, 7^{5}GF, 8^{2}SD, 8^{2}SD,

	Starts	1st	2nd	3rd	Win & Pl
Career Total (Turf)	17	0	4	4	13606
Career Total (AW)	8	3	2	2	15337

87	1/09	Ling	1m	(0-85)H	STD	£4857
87	12/07	Kemp	1m	(0-75)H	STD	£2590
79	11/07	Ling	7f		STD	£2968

Total win prize-money £10417

Going (Turf): **Sf: 0-3 GS: 0-3 Gd: 0-5 GF: 0-6 Fm: 0-0**
Distance: 5f/6f: 0-3 **7f-8f: 3-19** 9f-13f: 0-3 14f+: 0-0
Track : **LH: 2-10** RH: 1-8 **Tight: 2-9** Gall: 0-1
Aids: **Bl: 1-17** Vi: 0-0 Tstrap: 0-0 Ckp: 0-0
Best Rating: **90** 12/09 Ling 1m stand

Useful; effective at 1m; acts on fast and easy ground; also goes on Polytrack; has worn blinkers.

Dencolstina

61(70) (9)

2-y-o b f Lujain (USA)-Buthaina (IRE) (Bahhare (USA))

T H Caldwell (Joss Saville 13/8) Colin Mather & Stephen Tomkinson

Placings:005 **(4939)**

2009: 5^{0}F, 5^{0}SD, 7^{5}GF,

	Starts	1st	2nd	3rd	Win & Pl
Career Total (Turf)	2	0	0	0	0
Career Total (AW)	1	0	0	0	

Going (Turf): **Sf: 0-0 GS: 0-0 Gd: 0-0 GF: 0-1 Fm: 0-1**
Distance: 5f/6f: 0-2 7f-8f: 0-1 9f-13f: 0-0 14f+: 0-0
Track : LH: 0-1 RH: 0-0 Tight: 0-1 Gall: 0-0
Aids: Bl: 0-0 Vi: 0-0 Tstrap: 0-0 Ckp: 0-0
Best Rating: **9** 8/09 Wolv 5f216y stand

Denices Desert

92(82) (26)**45**

3-y-o b f Green Desert (USA)-Denice (Night Shift (USA))

M Botti Mrs R J Jacobs

Placings:0400 **(7438)**

2009: 8^{0}SD, 10^{4}F, 10^{0}G, 8^{0}SD,

	Starts	1st	2nd	3rd	Win & Pl
Career Total (Turf)	2	0	0	0	289
Career Total (AW)	2	0	0	0	

Going (Turf): **Sf: 0-0 GS: 0-0 Gd: 0-1 GF: 0-0 Fm: 0-1**
Distance: 5f/6f: 0-0 7f-8f: 0-1 9f-13f: 0-3 14f+: 0-0
Track : LH: 0-4 RH: 0-0 Tight: 0-4 Gall: 0-0
Aids: Bl: 0-1 Vi: 0-0 Tstrap: 0-0 Ckp: 0-0
Best Rating: **45** 9/09 Bath 1m2f46y firm

Denton (NZ)

101(101) (73)**74**

6-y-o b g Montjeu (IRE)-Melora (NZ) (Sir Tristram)

J R Gask Horses First Racing Limited

Placings:56/5/2020-**011**1**0** **(6936)**

2009: 8^{0}SD, 10^{1}SD, 10^{1}GS, 9^{1}SD, 11^{0}G,

	Starts	1st	2nd	3rd	Win & Pl
Career Total (Turf)	9	1	2	0	4057
Career Total (AW)	3	2	0	0	5626

73	10/09	Wolv	1m1f103y	(0-75)H	STD	£3238
74	8/09	Nott	1m2f50y	(0-65)H	G-S	£1942
64	8/09	Ling	1m2f	(0-55)H	STD	£2388

Total win prize-money £7569

Going (Turf): Sf: 0-1 **GS: 1-2** Gd: 0-6 GF: 0-0 Fm: 0-0
Distance: 5f/6f: 0-0 7f-8f: 0-5 **9f-13f: 3-7** 14f+: 0-0
Track : **LH: 3-5** RH: 0-0 **Tight: 2-3** Gall: 0-0
Aids: Bl: 0-0 Vi: 0-0 Tstrap: 0-0 Ckp: 0-0
Best Rating: **74** 8/09 Nott 1m2f50y gd-sft

Denton Diva

96(102) (66)**63**

3-y-o b f Tobougg (IRE)-Seeking Utopia (Wolfhound (USA))

M Dods Denton Hall Racing Ltd

Placings:33401-420436 **(5326)**

2009: 6^{4}SD, 6^{2}SD, 7^{0}GF, 6^{4}SD, 6^{3}GS, 6^{6}SD,

	Starts	1st	2nd	3rd	Win & Pl
Career Total (Turf)	5	0	0	3	1453
Career Total (AW)	6	1	1	0	4067

66	11/08	Sthl	6f	STD	£3070

Total win prize-money £3071

Going (Turf): **Sf: 0-2 GS: 0-1 Gd: 0-1 GF: 0-1 Fm: 0-0**
Distance: **5f/6f: 1-6** 7f-8f: 0-5 9f-13f: 0-0 14f+: 0-0
Track : **LH: 1-7** RH: 0-2 Tight: 0-4 Gall: 0-0
Aids: Bl: 0-0 Vi: 0-2 Tstrap: 0-1 Ckp: 0-1
Best Rating: **66** 11/08 Sthl 6f stand

Modest form over 7f but effective at 6f; handles soft ground and Fibresand.

Denton Ryal

80(82) (41)**58**

2-y-o b f Trade Fair-My Valentina (Royal Academy (USA))

S W James Clive Dennett

Placings:00 **(6920)**

2009: 7^{0}SD, 8^{0}GF,

	Starts	1st	2nd	3rd	Win & Pl
Career Total (Turf)	1	0	0	0	
Career Total (AW)	1	0	0	0	

Going (Turf): **Sf: 0-0 GS: 0-0 Gd: 0-0 GF: 0-1 Fm: 0-0**
Distance: 5f/6f: 0-0 7f-8f: 0-1 9f-13f: 0-1 14f+: 0-0
Track : LH: 0-1 RH: 0-0 Tight: 0-1 Gall: 0-0
Aids: Bl: 0-0 Vi: 0-0 Tstrap: 0-0 Ckp: 0-0
Best Rating: **58** 10/09 Yarm 1m3y gd-fm

Deo Valente (IRE)

86(97) (67)76

4-y-o b g Dubai Destination (USA)-Pack Ice (USA) (Wekiva Springs (USA))

J M Bradley Roger Miles, Val Smith, Tony Stamp

Placings:03/3002-00003000 **(7703)**

2009: 8^0GF, 7^0GF, 8^0SD, 7^0G, 5^0SD, 5^3SD, 5^0S, 5^0SD, 6^0SD,

	Starts	1st	2nd	3rd	Win & Pl
Career Total (Turf)	9	0	1	2	2331
Career Total (AW)	6	0	0	1	302

Going (Turf): **Sf: 0-1 GS: 0-2 Gd: 0-3 GF: 0-3 Fm: 0-0**
Distance: 5f/6f: 0-5 7f-8f: 0-8 9f-13f: 0-2 14f+: 0-0
Track : LH: 0-3 RH: 0-4 Tight: 0-3 Gall: 0-0
Aids: Bl: 0-4 Vi: 0-0 Tstrap: 0-1 Ckp: 0-1
Best Rating: **84** 10/07 NmkR 7f good

Fair; effective over 1m; acts on fast and easy ground.

Deora De

63 16

2-y-o b f Night Shift (USA)-Photo Flash (IRE) (Bahamian Bounty)

E A L Dunlop St Albans Bloodstock LLP

Placings:0 **(6730)**

2009: 6^0S,

	Starts	1st	2nd	3rd	Win & Pl
Career Total (Turf)	1	0	0	0	

Going (Turf): **Sf: 0-1 GS: 0-0 Gd: 0-0 GF: 0-0 Fm: 0-0**
Distance: 5f/6f: 0-0 7f-8f: 0-1 9f-13f: 0-0 14f+: 0-0
Track : LH: 0-0 RH: 0-0 Tight: 0-0 Gall: 0-0
Aids: Bl: 0-0 Vi: 0-0 Tstrap: 0-0 Ckp: 0-0
Best Rating: **16** 10/09 Sals 6f212y soft

Deportista

73(95) (49)14

3-y-o ch f Deportivo-Wadenhoe (IRE) (Persian Bold)

J A Pickering J A Pickering

Placings:000040 **(7818)**

2009: 5^0SD, 7^0GF, 9^0SD, 8^0SD, 8^4SD, 9^0SD,

	Starts	1st	2nd	3rd	Win & Pl
Career Total (Turf)	1	0	0	0	
Career Total (AW)	5	0	0	0	0

Going (Turf): **Sf: 0-0 GS: 0-0 Gd: 0-0 GF: 0-1 Fm: 0-0**
Distance: 5f/6f: 0-1 7f-8f: 0-2 9f-13f: 0-3 14f+: 0-0
Track : LH: 0-4 RH: 0-1 Tight: 0-4 Gall: 0-0
Aids: Bl: 0-0 Vi: 0-0 Tstrap: 0-0 Ckp: 0-0
Best Rating: **49** 12/09 Wolv 1m141y stand

Deportment

103 88

3-y-o b f Barathea (IRE)-Tina Heights (Shirley Heights)

J R Fanshawe Chippenham Lodge Stud

Placings:3521 **(7101)**

2009: 10^3S, 10^5GF, 10^2GF, 10^1G,

	Starts	1st	2nd	3rd	Win & Pl
Career Total (Turf)	4	1	1	1	6689

88 10/09 Yarm 1m2f21y (0-80)H GD £5051

Total win prize-money £5051

Going (Turf): Sf: 0-1 GS: 0-0 **Gd: 1-1** GF: 0-2 Fm: 0-0
Distance: 5f/6f: 0-0 7f-8f: 0-0 **9f-13f: 1-4** 14f+: 0-0
Track : **LH: 1-4** RH: 0-0 **Tight: 1-2** Gall: 0-2
Aids: Bl: 0-0 Vi: 0-0 Tstrap: 0-0 Ckp: 0-0
Best Rating: **88** 10/09 Yarm 1m2f21y good

Fair; stays 1m2f; acts on most ground.

Deposer (IRE)

110(102) (99)112

3-y-o b g Kheleyf (USA)-Bezant (IRE) (Zamindar (USA))

J R Best Kent Bloodstock

Placings:216640-02432 **(3011)**

2009: 9^0SD, 8^2SD, 10^4GF, 8^3G, 7^2GF,

	Starts	1st	2nd	3rd	Win & Pl
Career Total (Turf)	6	0	2	1	29827
Career Total (AW)	5	1	1	0	24234

96 7/08 Ling 6f STD £2388

Total win prize-money £2388

Going (Turf): **Sf: 0-0 GS: 0-1 Gd: 0-2 GF: 0-3 Fm: 0-0**
Distance: **5f/6f: 1-3** 7f-8f: 0-4 9f-13f: 0-4 14f+: 0-0
Track : **LH: 1-5** RH: 0-2 **Tight: 1-4** Gall: 0-0
Aids: Bl: 0-0 Vi: 0-0 Tstrap: 0-0 Ckp: 0-0
Best Rating: **112** 6/09 Asct 7f gd-fm

Smart; stays 1m2f, also effective at shorter; acts on fast ground; also goes on Polytrack.

Der Rosenkavalier (IRE)

80(78) (36)34

3-y-o gr g Captain Rio-Brooks Masquerade (Absalom)

C Grant (A M Balding 30/5) Gareth Cheshire

Placings:0-60 **(2496)**

2009: 5^6G, 6^0GF,

	Starts	1st	2nd	3rd	Win & Pl
Career Total (Turf)	2	0	0	0	0
Career Total (AW)	1	0	0	0	

Going (Turf): **Sf: 0-0 GS: 0-0 Gd: 0-1 GF: 0-1 Fm: 0-0**
Distance: 5f/6f: 0-2 7f-8f: 0-1 9f-13f: 0-0 14f+: 0-0
Track : LH: 0-1 RH: 0-0 Tight: 0-1 Gall: 0-0
Aids: Bl: 0-0 Vi: 0-0 Tstrap: 0-0 Ckp: 0-0
Best Rating: **36** 6/08 Wolv 5f216y stand

Deraaya (IRE)

(99) (76)82

4-y-o b f Mujahid (USA)-Hawafiz (Nashwan (USA))

K A Morgan P Doughty

Placings:063-530 **(3272)**

2009: 7^5SD, 6^3SD, 6^0SD,

	Starts	1st	2nd	3rd	Win & Pl
Career Total (Turf)	3	0	0	1	2426
Career Total (AW)	3	0	0	1	385

Going (Turf): **Sf: 0-2 GS: 0-1 Gd: 0-0 GF: 0-0 Fm: 0-0**
Distance: 5f/6f: 0-2 7f-8f: 0-4 9f-13f: 0-0 14f+: 0-0
Track : LH: 0-4 RH: 0-1 Tight: 0-2 Gall: 0-0
Aids: Bl: 0-0 Vi: 0-0 Tstrap: 0-0 Ckp: 0-0
Best Rating: **82** 5/08 StCl 7f soft

Derbaas (USA)

104 106

3-y-o b c Seeking The Gold (USA)-Sultana (USA) (Storm Cat (USA))

E A L Dunlop Hamdan Al Maktoum

Placings:4133-53430 **(6732)**

2009: 9^5GF, 8^3HY, 8^4G, 8^3S, 8^0S,

	Starts	1st	2nd	3rd	Win & Pl
Career Total (Turf)	9	1	0	4	31847

88 7/08 Asct 7f G-F £7771

Total win prize-money £7771

Going (Turf): Sf: 0-4 GS: 0-0 Gd: 0-1 **GF: 1-4** Fm: 0-0
Distance: 5f/6f: 0-0 **7f-8f: 1-6** 9f-13f: 0-3 14f+: 0-0
Track : LH: 0-2 RH: 0-0 Tight: 0-0 Gall: 0-0
Aids: Bl: 0-0 Vi: 0-0 Tstrap: 0-0 Ckp: 0-0
Best Rating: **106** 5/09 Hayd 1m30y heavy

Smart; Group and Listed placed; effective over 7f-1m; acts on most ground; likes to race prominently.

Derby Desire (IRE)

(67) (33)22

5-y-o b m Swallow Flight (IRE)-Jaldi (IRE) (Nordico (USA))

D G Duggan Damien G Duggan

Placings:00/000-0 **(7369)**

2009: 9^0SD,

	Starts	1st	2nd	3rd	Win & Pl
Career Total (Turf)	2	0	0	0	
Career Total (AW)	4	0	0	0	

Going (Turf): **Sf: 0-0 GS: 0-0 Gd: 0-0 GF: 0-1 Fm: 0-1**
Distance: 5f/6f: 0-0 7f-8f: 0-3 9f-13f: 0-3 14f+: 0-0
Track : LH: 0-2 RH: 0-2 Tight: 0-1 Gall: 0-0
Aids: Bl: 0-1 Vi: 0-0 Tstrap: 0-0 Ckp: 0-0
Best Rating: **33** 4/08 Dund 1m stand

Derringbay (IRE)

85(84) (63)27

3-y-o b g Mull Of Kintyre (USA)-Rustle In The Wind (Barathea (IRE))

Mme G Rarick (M H Tompkins 21/6) Mme G Rarick

Placings:00-30000002 **(6980a)**

2009: 9^3SD, 10^0SD, 8^0GF, 10^0GF, 8^0GF, 6^0GF, 9^0G, 9^2SD,

	Starts	1st	2nd	3rd	Win & Pl
Career Total (Turf)	6	0	0	0	
Career Total (AW)	4	0	1	1	2619

Going (Turf): **Sf: 0-1 GS: 0-0 Gd: 0-1 GF: 0-4 Fm: 0-0**
Distance: 5f/6f: 0-1 7f-8f: 0-2 9f-13f: 0-7 14f+: 0-0
Track : LH: 0-5 RH: 0-2 Tight: 0-3 Gall: 0-1
Aids: Bl: 0-2 Vi: 0-0 Tstrap: 0-0 Ckp: 0-0
Best Rating: **63** 1/09 GrLe 1m1f46y stand

Derval (IRE)

73 37

2-y-o b f One Cool Cat (USA)-Sagrada (GER) (Primo Dominie)

K A Ryan Mrs E O'Leary

Placings:000 **(5553)**

2009: 5^0S, 5^0G, 5^0GS,

	Starts	1st	2nd	3rd	Win & Pl
Career Total (Turf)	3	0	0	0	

Going (Turf): **Sf: 0-1 GS: 0-1 Gd: 0-1 GF: 0-0 Fm: 0-0**
Distance: 5f/6f: 0-3 7f-8f: 0-0 9f-13f: 0-0 14f+: 0-0
Track : LH: 0-0 RH: 0-0 Tight: 0-0 Gall: 0-0
Aids: Bl: 0-0 Vi: 0-0 Tstrap: 0-0 Ckp: 0-0
Best Rating: **37** 7/09 Leic 5f218y soft

Descargo

(81) (11)**23**
5-y-o ch m Delta Dancer-Secret Miss (Beveled (USA))
C R Dore D A Drake

Placings:0/200/0 (7815)
2009: 5^0SD,

	Starts	1st	2nd	3rd	Win & Pl
Career Total (Turf)	1	0	0	0	
Career Total (AW)	4	0	1	0	877

Going (Turf): **Sf: 0-0 GS: 0-0 Gd: 0-0 GF: 0-1 Fm: 0-0**
Distance: 5f/6f: 0-5 7f-8f: 0-0 9f-13f: 0-0 14f+: 0-0
Track : LH: 0-3 RH: 0-1 Tight: 0-3 Gall: 0-0
Aids: Bl: 0-0 Vi: 0-0 Tstrap: 0-0 Ckp: 0-0
Best Rating: **54** 1/07 Wolv 5f20y stand

Desdamona (IRE)

74 **27**
3-y-o b f Desert Style (IRE)-Tattymulmona Queen (USA) (Royal Academy (USA))
A Berry Alan Berry

Placings:05-00000 (4397)
2009: 8^0G, 9^0GF, 9^0GF, 9^0G, 12^0GF,

	Starts	1st	2nd	3rd	Win & Pl
Career Total (Turf)	7	0	0	0	0

Going (Turf): **Sf: 0-1 GS: 0-0 Gd: 0-3 GF: 0-3 Fm: 0-0**
Distance: 5f/6f: 0-1 7f-8f: 0-1 9f-13f: 0-5 14f+: 0-0
Track : LH: 0-1 RH: 0-5 Tight: 0-4 Gall: 0-0
Aids: Bl: 0-0 Vi: 0-0 Tstrap: 0-0 Ckp: 0-0
Best Rating: **27** 5/09 Haml 1m65y good

Desert Aisling (IRE)

80(88) (43)**51**
2-y-o gr f Verglas (IRE)-Desert Sprite (IRE) (Tagula (IRE))
Edgar Byrne Mayne-Hamilton

Placings:00060 (7335)
2009: 5^0GF, 7^0G, 8^0G, 9^6SD, 8^0SD,

	Starts	1st	2nd	3rd	Win & Pl
Career Total (Turf)	3	0	0	0	
Career Total (AW)	2	0	0	0	0

Going (Turf): **Sf: 0-0 GS: 0-0 Gd: 0-2 GF: 0-1 Fm: 0-0**
Distance: 5f/6f: 0-1 7f-8f: 0-3 9f-13f: 0-1 14f+: 0-0
Track : LH: 0-3 RH: 0-1 Tight: 0-1 Gall: 0-0
Aids: Bl: 0-0 Vi: 0-0 Tstrap: 0-0 Ckp: 0-0
Best Rating: **51** 6/09 Sand 7f16y good

Desert Auction (IRE)

102(87) (69)**87**
2-y-o b c Desert Style (IRE)-Double Gamble (Ela-Mana-Mou)
R Hannon A J Ilsley, K T Ivory & G Battocchi

Placings:3311004016565 (7013)
2009: 5^3SD, 5^3SD, 5^1GF, 5^1GF, 6^0G, 5^0GF, 6^4GF, 5^0GS, 7^1G, 8^6G, 7^5GF, 7^6GF, 7^5GS,

	Starts	1st	2nd	3rd	Win & Pl
Career Total (Turf)	11	3	0	0	16353
Career Total (AW)	2	0	0	2	1174

87	8/09	Newb	7f	GD	£3885
84	5/09	Gdwd	5f	G-F	£8723
80	4/09	Folk	5f	G-F	£2729

Total win prize-money £15339

Going (Turf): Sf: 0-0 GS: 0-2 Gd: 1-3 **GF: 2-6** Fm: 0-0
Distance: **5f/6f: 2-8** 7f-8f: 1-5 9f-13f: 0-0 14f+: 0-0
Track : LH: 0-2 RH: 0-1 Tight: 0-2 Gall: 0-0
Aids: Bl: 0-0 Vi: 0-0 Tstrap: 0-0 Ckp: 0-0
Best Rating: **87** 10/09 Donc 7f gd-sft

Useful; stays 7f; acts on good/fast ground; goes on Polytrack.

Desert Ben (IRE)

93 (62)**68**
6-y-o b g Desert Prince (IRE)-Benefits Galore (IRE) (Brief Truce (USA))
Peter Casey (C Grant 19/8) Mrs Peter Casey

Placings:0040003/0001**343**/5123035205-0300005**3**41 (7525a)
2009: 7^0G, 5^3G, 7^0G, 5^0S, 8^0GF, 6^0GF, 5^5S, 5^3GY, 8^4SD, 5^1SD,

	Starts	1st	2nd	3rd	Win & Pl
Career Total (Turf)	29	2	2	5	13052
Career Total (AW)	5	1	0	2	6122

62	11/09	Dund	5f	(47-65)H	STD	£4696
59	4/08	Navn	5f182y	(45-60)H	G-Y	£4318
56	10/07	Cork	5f	(42-60)H	GD	£3968

Total win prize-money £12984

Going (Turf): Sf: 0-5 GS: 0-0 **Gd: 1-7** GF: 0-5 Fm: 0-5
Distance: **5f/6f: 3-20** 7f-8f: 0-12 9f-13f: 0-2 14f+: 0-0
Track : **LH: 2-18** RH: 0-4 Tight: 0-4 Gall: 0-0
Aids: **Bl: 2-16** Vi: 0-1 Tstrap: 0-2 Ckp: 0-2
Best Rating: **68** 7/08 Tipp 5f good

Desert Bump

(99) (70)
3-y-o b f Medicean-Greenfly (Green Desert (USA))
E F Vaughan Mrs Emma Kennedy

Placings:42-12 (0441)
2009: 7^1SD, 8^2SD,

	Starts	1st	2nd	3rd	Win & Pl
Career Total (Turf)	0	0	0	0	
Career Total (AW)	4	1	2	0	4294

68	1/09	Wolv	7f32y	STD	£2590

Total win prize-money £2590

Going (Turf): **Sf: 0-0 GS: 0-0 Gd: 0-0 GF: 0-0 Fm: 0-0**
Distance: 5f/6f: 0-2 **7f-8f: 1-2** 9f-13f: 0-0 14f+: 0-0
Track : **LH: 1-4** RH: 0-0 **Tight: 1-3** Gall: 0-1
Aids: Bl: 0-0 Vi: 0-0 Tstrap: 0-0 Ckp: 0-0
Best Rating: **70** 2/09 Ling 1m stand

Fair; effective over 7f, acts on Polytrack.

Desert Creek (IRE)

106 **98**
3-y-o ch c Refuse To Bend (IRE)-Flagship (Rainbow Quest (USA))
Sir Michael Stoute Saeed Suhail

Placings:21-1105 (4296)
2009: 8^1GF, 8^1HY, 8^0GF, 8^5G,

	Starts	1st	2nd	3rd	Win & Pl
Career Total (Turf)	6	3	1	0	67141

98	5/09	Hayd	1m30y	H	HVY	£52963
93	5/09	Wind	1m67y	(0-90)H	G-F	£8095
82	10/08	Yarm	7f3y		SFT	£3974

Total win prize-money £65033

Going (Turf): **Sf: 2-2** GS: 0-0 Gd: 0-2 GF: 1-2 Fm: 0-0
Distance: 5f/6f: 0-1 7f-8f: 1-3 **9f-13f: 2-2** 14f+: 0-0
Track : LH: 1-1 RH: 1-1 **Tight: 1-1** Gall: 0-1
Aids: Bl: 0-0 Vi: 0-0 Tstrap: 0-0 Ckp: 0-0
Best Rating: **98** 5/09 Hayd 1m30y heavy

Very useful; stays 1m; acts on fast and heavy ground.

Desert Destiny

103 (86)**71**
9-y-o b g Desert Prince (IRE)-High Savannah (Rousillon (USA))
C Grant Chris Grant

Placings:010/15054/02521/0010006/204/350-0401255 (3679)
2009: 8^0G, 10^4GS, 9^0GF, 13^1GF, 14^2GF, 14^5F, 14^5G,

	Starts	1st	2nd	3rd	Win & Pl
Career Total (Turf)	32	4	4	1	118928
Career Total (AW)	1	0	0	0	584

63	6/09	Catt	1m5f175y		G-F	£2047
108	3/05	Ndas	1m	(100-112)H	G-F	£59244
109	4/03	NmkR	7f	C	G-F	£8450
88	7/02	NmkJ	7f	D	G-F	£4849

Total win prize-money £74592

Going (Turf): Sf: 0-3 GS: 0-4 Gd: 0-8 **GF: 4-16** Fm: 0-1
Distance: 5f/6f: 0-0 **7f-8f: 3-18** 9f-13f: 0-11 14f+: 1-4
Track : **LH: 2-15** RH: 0-8 Tight: 1-11 Gall: 1-8
Aids: Bl: 0-0 **Vi: 1-12** Tstrap: 0-3 Ckp: 0-3
Best Rating: **112** 6/04 NmkJ 7f gd-fm

Modest; formerly smart when placed at Group level; stays 1m6f and acts on most ground.

Desert Dreamer (IRE)

107(106) (85)**88**
8-y-o b g Green Desert (USA)-Follow That Dream (Darshaan)
P D Evans (Tom Dascombe 18/3) R Piff

Placings:415420/5060000/**2**0**5**46340**0**01**4**00132/**4**000**2**02**0**21**0**0314050**500/6**040**2**5041**126**0**060551**/**0362121104**3652**322-1331**132201254120064**6001600002263** (7891)
2009: 7^1SD, 7^3SD, 7^3SD, 7^1SD, 7^1SD, 6^3GF, 6^2GF, 6^2GF, 7^0GF, 7^1GF, 7^2G, 7^5G, 7^4GS, 7^1GF, 7^2GF, 7^0GF, 7^0G, 7^6GF, 7^4G, 7^6GF, 7^0SD, 7^0SD, 7^1GF, 7^6SS, 7^0SD,

	Starts	1st	2nd	3rd	Win & Pl
Career Total (Turf)	66	8	9	5	75116
Career Total (AW)	53	9	10	5	40187

88	9/09	Ches	7f2y	(0-95)H	G-F	£11009
85	6/09	Ches	7f2y	(0-85)H	G-F	£5180
79	5/09	Wwck	7f26y	(0-85)H	G-F	£5180
77	3/09	Ling	7f		STD	£2047
75	3/09	Ling	7f		STD	£2047
80	1/09	Kemp	7f		STD	£2590
80	4/08	Kemp	7f		STD	£2047
87	3/08	Ling	7f		STD	£1774
83	3/08	Ling	7f	(0-75)H	STD	£2914
76	12/07	Ling	7f		STD	£1943
83	7/07	Kemp	7f		STD	£2914
79	7/07	Brig	6f209y	(0-80)H	G-F	£4605

76	8/06	Wind	6f		GD	£4533
88	7/06	Brig	6f209y	(0-80)H	FRM	£6232
88	9/05	Ling	7f	(0-80)H	STD	£6883
85	8/05	NmkJ	6f	(0-85)H	SFT	£6032
91	7/03	Newb	7f	D	GD	£7702

Total win prize-money £75641

Going (Turf): Sf: 1-3 GS: 0-10 Gd: 2-22 **GF: 4-30** Fm: 1-1
Distance: 5f/6f: 2-28 **7f-8f: 15-86** 9f-13f: 0-5 14f+: 0-0
Track : **LH: 11-64** RH: 3-26 **Tight: 8-53** Gall: 1-7
Aids: Bl: 0-1 Vi: 0-0 Tstrap: 0-1 Ckp: 0-1
Best Rating: **96** 8/03 Ripn 6f good

Fair; stays 1m, but effective over shorter; acts on most ground on turf; goes on Polytrack; has worn a tongue tie, blinkers and cheekpieces.

Desert Dust

(97) (49)**48**
6-y-o b g Vettori (IRE)-Dust (Green Desert (USA))
H J Collingridge J W J McCullough

Placings:600/430000200524153**5**/4300/55-5006 **(7839)**
2009: 6^{5}SD, 6^{0}SD, 5^{0}SD, 5^{6}SS,

	Starts	1st	2nd	3rd	Win & Pl
Career Total (Turf)	**7**	**0**	**1**	**0**	**964**
Career Total (AW)	**22**	**1**	**1**	**3**	**3342**

58 11/06 Wolv 5f20y (0-45) STD £1365
Total win prize-money £1365

Going (Turf): **Sf: 0-0 GS: 0-2 Gd: 0-2 GF: 0-2 Fm: 0-1**
Distance: **5f/6f: 1-27** 7f-8f: 0-2 9f-13f: 0-0 14f+: 0-0
Track : **LH: 1-15** RH: 0-2 **Tight: 1-12** Gall: 0-1
Aids: Bl: 0-2 **Vi: 1-8** Tstrap: 0-6 Ckp: 0-6
Best Rating: **58** 11/06 Kemp 5f stand

Very moderate; most effective at 5f; acts on Polytrack and soft ground; has worn various headgear.

Desert Fairy

93(93) (50)**46**
3-y-o b f Tobougg (IRE)-Regal Fairy (IRE) (Desert King (IRE))
J W Unett A H Bennett

Placings:000-0566354 **(7802)**
2009: 10^{0}GF, 9^{5}GF, 12^{6}SD, 9^{6}SD, 12^{3}SD, 12^{5}SD, 8^{4}SD,

	Starts	1st	2nd	3rd	Win & Pl
Career Total (Turf)	**3**	**0**	**0**	**0**	**0**
Career Total (AW)	**7**	**0**	**0**	**1**	**353**

Going (Turf): **Sf: 0-0 GS: 0-1 Gd: 0-0 GF: 0-2 Fm: 0-0**
Distance: 5f/6f: 0-0 7f-8f: 0-2 9f-13f: 0-8 14f+: 0-0
Track : LH: 0-7 RH: 0-3 Tight: 0-4 Gall: 0-2
Aids: Bl: 0-0 Vi: 0-0 Tstrap: 0-0 Ckp: 0-0
Best Rating: **50** 12/09 Wolv 1m4f50y stand

Moderate; stays 1m4f and acts on Polytrack.

Desert Falls

98(103) (86)**84**
3-y-o b g Pyrus (USA)-Sally Traffic (River Falls)
R M Whitaker J Barry Pemberton

Placings:53343**114**-4043503200 **(7356)**
2009: 5^{4}F, 6^{0}GF, 6^{4}GF, 6^{3}GF, 6^{5}G, 6^{0}S, 6^{3}GF, 7^{2}GF, 7^{0}GF, 7^{0}SD,

	Starts	1st	2nd	3rd	Win & Pl
Career Total (Turf)	**14**	**0**	**1**	**5**	**7021**
Career Total (AW)	**4**	**2**	**0**	**0**	**11945**

86	9/08	GrLe	6f	STD	£6476
82	9/08	GrLe	6f	STD	£5180

Total win prize-money £11657

Going (Turf): **Sf: 0-2 GS: 0-1 Gd: 0-2 GF: 0-8 Fm: 0-1**
Distance: **5f/6f: 2-14** 7f-8f: 0-4 9f-13f: 0-0 14f+: 0-0
Track : **LH: 2-6** RH: 0-2 Tight: 0-3 **Gall: 2-2**
Aids: Bl: 0-0 Vi: 0-0 Tstrap: 0-0 Ckp: 0-0
Best Rating: **86** 9/08 GrLe 6f stand

Useful on AW; fair on turf; stays 6f; best on Polytrack.

Desert Fever

94 **72**
3-y-o b g Dubai Destination (USA)-Gaijin (Caerleon (USA))
N A Twiston-Davies (B W Hills 16/7) H R Mould

Placings:0-6006 **(4004)**
2009: 7^{6}GF, 10^{0}GF, 10^{0}G, 10^{6}GS,

	Starts	1st	2nd	3rd	Win & Pl
Career Total (Turf)	**5**	**0**	**0**	**0**	**0**

Going (Turf): **Sf: 0-0 GS: 0-1 Gd: 0-2 GF: 0-2 Fm: 0-0**
Distance: 5f/6f: 0-1 7f-8f: 0-1 9f-13f: 0-3 14f+: 0-0
Track : LH: 0-2 RH: 0-2 Tight: 0-0 Gall: 0-3
Aids: Bl: 0-0 Vi: 0-0 Tstrap: 0-0 Ckp: 0-0
Best Rating: **72** 7/09 NmkJ 1m2f good

Desert Forest (IRE)

98 **70**
2-y-o b g Desert Style (IRE)-Minehostess (IRE) (Shernazar)
J Howard Johnson Transcend Bloodstock LLP

Placings:022240 **(6821)**
2009: 6^{0}GF, 6^{2}G, 7^{2}GF, 7^{2}GS, 7^{4}GF, 8^{0}GF,

	Starts	1st	2nd	3rd	Win & Pl
Career Total (Turf)	**6**	**0**	**3**	**0**	**2815**

Going (Turf): **Sf: 0-0 GS: 0-1 Gd: 0-1 GF: 0-4 Fm: 0-0**
Distance: 5f/6f: 0-2 7f-8f: 0-4 9f-13f: 0-0 14f+: 0-0
Track : LH: 0-2 RH: 0-0 Tight: 0-2 Gall: 0-0
Aids: Bl: 0-0 Vi: 0-0 Tstrap: 0-1 Ckp: 0-1
Best Rating: **70** 7/09 Catt 7f gd-sft

Fair; stays 6f and should stay 7f; should improve.

Desert Hawk

97(102) (58)**60**
8-y-o b g Cape Cross (IRE)-Milling (IRE) (In The Wings)
W M Brisbourne J Jones Racing Ltd

Placings:00540062020/053503600/6213433/31000300551
334303145**0532**/004030615240606**3**-
054021650340005**00000** **(7670)**
2009: 12^{0}SD, 12^{5}SD, 12^{4}SD, 10^{0}SD, 12^{2}SD, 9^{1}SD, 9^{6}SD, 9^{5}SD, 9^{0}SD, 12^{3}SD, 11^{4}GF, 10^{0}G, 10^{0}G, 11^{0}GS, 10^{5}G, 12^{0}GF, 9^{0}SD, 12^{0}SD, 13^{0}SD, 12^{0}SD, 12^{0}SD,

	Starts	1st	2nd	3rd	Win & Pl
Career Total (Turf)	**49**	**2**	**3**	**7**	**11143**
Career Total (AW)	**39**	**4**	**3**	**8**	**13281**

55	2/09	Wolv	1m1f103y	(0-50)H	STD	£2047
58	8/08	Wolv	1m1f103y	(0-60)H	STD	£2388
57	8/07	Yarm	1m2f21y	(0-65)H	GD	£2137
61	6/07	Yarm	1m2f21y	(0-60)H	G-S	£1943
62	1/07	Wolv	1m1f103y	(0-52)H	STD	£2149
56	2/06	Wolv	1m1f103y	(0-55)H	SF	£2047

Total win prize-money £12713

Going (Turf): Sf: 0-6 **GS: 1-6 Gd: 1-17** GF: 0-20 Fm: 0-0
Distance: 5f/6f: 0-0 7f-8f: 0-6 **9f-13f: 6-80** 14f+: 0-2
Track : **LH: 6-68** RH: 0-14 **Tight: 6-59** Gall: 0-8
Aids: **Bl: 3-28** Vi: 0-2 Tstrap: 0-0 Ckp: 0-0
Best Rating: **71** 9/04 Bath 1m5y good

Moderate; seems best at around 1m2f, but stays further; acts on fast ground; also goes on Polytrack; has worn blinkers.

Desert Hunter (IRE)

97(98) (54)**57**
6-y-o b g Desert Story (IRE)-She-Wolff (IRE) (Pips Pride)
Micky Hammond The Rectangle Partnership

Placings:0660/053100/34400004/3200200000-0010250 **(5289)**
2009: 7^{0}F, 8^{0}GF, 7^{1}GF, 7^{0}F, 8^{2}GF, 8^{5}S, 8^{0}GS,

	Starts	1st	2nd	3rd	Win & Pl
Career Total (Turf)	**28**	**2**	**2**	**2**	**8474**
Career Total (AW)	**7**	**0**	**1**	**1**	**806**

57	6/09	Carl	7f200y	(0-65)H	G-F	£2047
53	7/06	Catt	5f212y	(0-70)H	G-F	£3886

Total win prize-money £5933

Going (Turf): Sf: 0-2 GS: 0-3 Gd: 0-5 **GF: 2-14** Fm: 0-4
Distance: 5f/6f: 1-18 7f-8f: 1-14 9f-13f: 0-3 14f+: 0-0
Track : LH: 1-11 RH: 1-13 **Tight: 1-9** Gall: 0-2
Aids: Bl: 0-0 Vi: 0-0 Tstrap: 0-0 Ckp: 0-0
Best Rating: **57** 6/09 Pont 1m4y gd-fm

Moderate; suited by 6f-7f; acts on fast ground; also goes on Polytrack.

Desert Icon (IRE)

105(97) (69)**86**
3-y-o b g Desert Style (IRE)-Gilded Vanity (IRE) (Indian Ridge)
W J Knight B & Mrs D Willis, B & Mrs M Pullin

Placings:41P-0620600 **(6240)**
2009: 6^{0}SD, 6^{6}GF, 6^{2}G, 6^{0}S, 6^{6}GF, 6^{0}SD, 6^{0}G,

	Starts	1st	2nd	3rd	Win & Pl
Career Total (Turf)	**8**	**1**	**1**	**0**	**23398**
Career Total (AW)	**2**	**0**	**0**	**0**	

78 7/08 Wind 6f SFT £3885
Total win prize-money £3886

Going (Turf): **Sf: 1-2** GS: 0-0 Gd: 0-2 GF: 0-4 Fm: 0-0
Distance: **5f/6f: 1-10** 7f-8f: 0-0 9f-13f: 0-0 14f+: 0-0
Track : LH: 0-1 RH: 0-1 Tight: 0-1 **Gall: 1-2**
Aids: Bl: 0-0 Vi: 0-0 Tstrap: 0-0 Ckp: 0-0
Best Rating: **86** 7/09 NmkJ 6f good

Useful; effective over 6f; acts on soft and fast ground.

Desert Kiss

103(102) (80)**88**
4-y-o b f Cape Cross (IRE)-Kiss And Don'Tell (USA) (Rahy (USA))
W R Swinburn The Capers

Placings:032-4011240 **(5833)**
2009: 8^{4}G, 8^{0}GF, 8^{1}SD, 8^{1}GF, 8^{2}G, 8^{4}GF, 8^{0}GF,

	Starts	1st	2nd	3rd	Win & Pl
Career Total (Turf)	**9**	**1**	**2**	**1**	**11494**
Career Total (AW)	**1**	**1**	**0**	**0**	**2590**

82	7/09	Asct	1m	(0-90)H	G-F	£7771
80	6/09	Kemp	1m	(0-70)H	STD	£2590

Total win prize-money £10361

Going (Turf): Sf: 0-0 GS: 0-0 Gd: 0-3 **GF: 1-6** Fm: 0-0
Distance: 5f/6f: 0-0 **7f-8f: 2-3** 9f-13f: 0-7 14f+: 0-0
Track : LH: 0-1 **RH: 1-5** Tight: 0-4 Gall: 0-0

Aids: Bl: 0-0 Vi: 0-0 Tstrap: 0-0 Ckp: 0-0
Best Rating: 88 9/09 Sand 1m14y gd-fm

Fair; effective over 1m; acts on fast ground.

Desert Lark

(93) (48)**44**
4-y-o b g Sakhee (USA)-Oyster Catcher (IRE) (Bluebird (USA))
K A Ryan David Gibbons & Tracey Gaunt

Placings:60/0-0240 (0647)
2009: 8^{0}SD, 12^{2}SD, 9^{4}SD, 10^{0}SD,

	Starts	1st	2nd	3rd	Win & Pl
Career Total (Turf)	3	0	0	0	0
Career Total (AW)	4	0	1	0	403

Going (Turf): Sf: 0-0 GS: 0-1 Gd: 0-1 GF: 0-1 Fm: 0-0
Distance: 5f/6f: 0-1 7f-8f: 0-3 9f-13f: 0-3 14f+: 0-0
Track : LH: 0-4 RH: 0-2 Tight: 0-4 Gall: 0-0
Aids: Bl: 0-0 Vi: 0-0 Tstrap: 0-0 Ckp: 0-0
Best Rating: 48 2/09 Kemp 1m4f stand

Moderate sort; stays 1m4f; handles Polytrack.

Desert Leader (IRE)

94(101) (53)**39**
8-y-o b g Green Desert (USA)-Za Aamah (USA) (Mr Prospector (USA))
W M Brisbourne R Rickett

Placings:002000/04062031126/302650/104400040/500-004000 (6342)
2009: 12^{0}SD, 12^{0}SD, 12^{4}SD, 12^{0}GF, 12^{0}SD, 12^{0}SD,

	Starts	1st	2nd	3rd	Win & Pl
Career Total (Turf)	11	0	0	0	288
Career Total (AW)	30	3	4	2	16670

78	1/07	Wolv	1m4f50y	(0-75)H	STD	£3238
84	12/05	Wolv	1m1f103y	(0-70)H	STD	£3396
77	11/05	Wolv	1m1f103y	(0-70)H	STD	£3524

Total win prize-money £10160

Going (Turf): Sf: 0-1 GS: 0-3 Gd: 0-2 GF: 0-4 Fm: 0-1
Distance: 5f/6f: 0-1 7f-8f: 0-5 9f-13f: 3-35 14f+: 0-0
Track : LH: 3-38 RH: 0-1 Tight: 3-29 Gall: 0-2
Aids: Bl: 0-0 Vi: 0-0 Tstrap: 0-0 Ckp: 0-0
Best Rating: 85 12/05 Wolv 1m1f103y stand

Modest gelding; effective at between 9f and 1m4f; acts on Polytrack.

Desert Liaison

83 **62**
2-y-o b f Dansili-Toffee Nosed (Selkirk (USA))
J Noseda Saeed Suhail

Placings:0 (4797)
2009: 7^{0}G,

	Starts	1st	2nd	3rd	Win & Pl
Career Total (Turf)	1	0	0	0	

Going (Turf): Sf: 0-0 GS: 0-0 Gd: 0-1 GF: 0-0 Fm: 0-0
Distance: 5f/6f: 0-0 7f-8f: 0-1 9f-13f: 0-0 14f+: 0-0
Track : LH: 0-0 RH: 0-0 Tight: 0-0 Gall: 0-0
Aids: Bl: 0-0 Vi: 0-0 Tstrap: 0-0 Ckp: 0-0
Best Rating: 62 8/09 NmkJ 7f good

Desert Light (IRE)

(107) (63)**43**
8-y-o b g Desert Sun-Nacote (IRE) (Mtoto)
D Shaw ownaracehorse.co.uk (Shaw)

Placings:00000060/13002252300/00402426506/3150014130000056444/64603331440105554/046400641000000-006052 (0508)
2009: 6^{0}SD, 6^{0}SD, 6^{6}SD, 5^{0}SD, 5^{5}SD, 5^{2}SD,

	Starts	1st	2nd	3rd	Win & Pl
Career Total (Turf)	9	0	1	0	1128
Career Total (AW)	80	7	5	7	22798

60	3/08	Kemp	6f	(0-55)H	STD	£2047
66	4/07	Wolv	5f216y	(0-60)H	STD	£2307
57	3/07	Wolv	5f216y		STD	£2047
66	4/06	Ling	6f	(0-60)H	STD	£2730
59	3/06	Wolv	5f216y	(0-45)	STD	£1876
54	2/06	Wolv	5f216y	(0-52)H	STD	£2388
62	1/04	Ling	6f	F(0-60)	STD	£2884

Total win prize-money £16284

Going (Turf): Sf: 0-2 GS: 0-2 Gd: 0-2 GF: 0-3 Fm: 0-0
Distance: 5f/6f: 7-85 7f-8f: 0-3 9f-13f: 0-1 14f+: 0-0
Track : LH: 6-58 RH: 1-18 Tight: 6-48 Gall: 0-2
Aids: Bl: 0-0 Vi: 7-79 Tstrap: 0-0 Ckp: 0-0
Best Rating: 69 5/06 Kemp 6f stand

Moderate sprinter; stays 6f; acts on Polytrack; often wears a visor; looks a tricky ride.

Desert Lord

87 (101)**111**
9-y-o b g Green Desert (USA)-Red Carnival (USA) (Mr Prospector (USA))
K A Ryan Bull & Bell Partnership

Placings:32210/610136/000000600551060060/31051222510/36025330/2303000-00 (2704)
2009: 5^{0}G, 5^{0}GF,

	Starts	1st	2nd	3rd	Win & Pl
Career Total (Turf)	50	6	7	5	315627
Career Total (AW)	8	1	0	3	17318

119	10/06	Lonc	5f		GD	£98517
105	6/06	Epsm	5f	H	G-F	£46740
98	4/06	Muss	5f	(0-85)H	GD	£6477
96	7/05	Pont	5f	(0-90)H	G-F	£9340
96	12/04	Ling	6f	(0-107)H	STD	£12006
91	8/04	NmkJ	7f	B(0-105)H	G-F	£19500
78	9/02	Chep	6f16y	D	G-F	£3556

Total win prize-money £196136

Going (Turf): Sf: 0-4 GS: 0-4 Gd: 2-12 GF: 4-28 Fm: 0-0
Distance: 5f/6f: 5-45 7f-8f: 2-13 9f-13f: 0-0 14f+: 0-0
Track : LH: 2-18 RH: 0-1 Tight: 1-9 Gall: 0-5
Aids: Bl: 3-29 Vi: 0-0 Tstrap: 1-6 Ckp: 1-6
Best Rating: 119 10/06 Lonc 5f good

Group class; winner of the Group 1 Prix de L'Abbaye in 2006; effective at up to 7f, but best over sprint distances; acts on most ground and on Polytrack; often wears blinkers, but has worn cheekpieces; likes to race prominently.

Desert Lover (IRE)

92(96) (51)**50**
7-y-o b g Desert Prince (IRE)-Crystal Flute (Lycius (USA))
A M Hales (R J Price 12/7) Gary P Martin

Placings:6/500050521036/61113510426000/050421340000654354/4025025-0003600 (4640)
2009: 7^{0}SD, 8^{0}SD, 8^{0}SD, 9^{3}SD, 8^{6}GF, 7^{0}GF, 11^{0}GF,

	Starts	1st	2nd	3rd	Win & Pl
Career Total (Turf)	11	0	0	0	289
Career Total (AW)	48	6	5	5	16970

61	3/07	Sthl	7f	(0-52)H	STD	£1706
68	3/06	Wolv	7f32y	(0-70)H	STD	£3886
64	2/06	Wolv	7f32y	(0-52)H	STD	£2047
64	2/06	Sthl	1m	(0-52)H	STD	£2388
58	1/06	Sthl	7f	(0-45)	STD	£1365
54	11/05	Sthl	7f	(0-45)	SS	£1457

Total win prize-money £12851

Going (Turf): Sf: 0-1 GS: 0-2 Gd: 0-1 GF: 0-7 Fm: 0-0
Distance: 5f/6f: 0-8 7f-8f: 6-38 9f-13f: 0-13 14f+: 0-0
Track : LH: 6-51 RH: 0-3 Tight: 2-32 Gall: 0-0
Aids: Bl: 0-0 Vi: 0-6 Tstrap: 1-9 Ckp: 1-9
Best Rating: 68 5/06 Kemp 6f stand

Moderate; effective over 7f-1m; acts well on Fibresand/Polytrack.

Desert Mile (IRE)

102(93) (80)**76**
6-y-o b m Desert Style (IRE)-Maiskaya (IRE) (Mark Of Esteem (IRE))
Ollie Pears (Edward Lynam 26/10) Ollie Pears

Placings:0000/26/03110212/010053605-06060000 (7762)
2009: 8^{0}G, 8^{6}GF, 10^{0}GY, 8^{6}G, 9^{0}Y, 8^{0}SD, 7^{0}SD, 7^{0}SD,

	Starts	1st	2nd	3rd	Win & Pl
Career Total (Turf)	21	4	2	1	36939
Career Total (AW)	10	0	1	1	1632

76	6/08	Curr	1m	(60-90)H	FRM	£12924
73	9/07	List	1m	(60-90)H	G-F	£10996
61	7/07	Klny	1m100y		G-Y	£4435
69	7/07	Bell	1m	(42-60)H	Y-S	£4435

Total win prize-money £32791

Going (Turf): Sf: 0-2 GS: 0-0 Gd: 0-6 GF: 1-4 Fm: 1-1
Distance: 5f/6f: 0-1 7f-8f: 3-20 9f-13f: 1-10 14f+: 0-0
Track : LH: 3-23 RH: 1-4 Tight: 0-1 Gall: 1-1
Aids: Bl: 0-0 Vi: 0-0 Tstrap: 0-1 Ckp: 0-1
Best Rating: 80 10/08 Dund 1m stand

Desert Opal

(109) (79)**80**
9-y-o ch g Cadeaux Genereux-Nullarbor (Green Desert (USA))
C R Dore Mrs Louise Marsh

Placings:5/0142110/005060/00040006501100６/45016025020020340020131 1/04614134100155552/36456640665015100-6044 (0481)
2009: 5^{6}SD, 5^{0}SD, 5^{4}SD, 5^{4}SD,

	Starts	1st	2nd	3rd	Win & Pl
Career Total (Turf)	38	6	3	2	45810
Career Total (AW)	52	9	3	2	30596

76	11/08	Kemp	5f	(0-65)H	STD	£2047
73	9/08	GrLe	5f	(0-60)H	STD	£2590
79	10/07	Wolv	5f20y		STD	£2047
80	7/07	Sand	5f6y	(0-75)H	G-S	£4533
77	5/07	Bevl	5f	(0-70)H	GD	£3562
76	4/07	Nott	5f13y	(0-70)H	G-F	£3238
80	12/06	Wolv	5f20y	(0-75)H	STD	£5181
71	12/06	Wolv	5f20y	(0-65)H	STD	£2730
71	11/06	Wolv	5f20y	(0-60)H	SF	£2730
67	3/06	Wolv	5f20y	(0-65)H	STD	£2730
72	9/05	Wolv	5f216y	(0-70)H	STD	£3455
73	9/05	Wolv	5f216y	(0-60)H	STD	£3056
101	9/03	Hayd	1m30y	C(0-95)H	SFT	£12463
95	7/03	Newb	1m	D(0-85)H	GD	£6448
76	5/03	Sals	6f	D	G-S	£5629

Total win prize-money £62443

Going (Turf): Sf: 1-10 **GS: 2-7 Gd: 2-12** GF: 1-9 Fm: 0-0
Distance: **5f/6f: 13-66** 7f-8f: 1-18 9f-13f: 1-6 14f+: 0-0
Track : **LH: 9-51** RH: 1-11 **Tight: 7-43** Gall: 1-7
Aids: Bl: 3-28 Vi: 0-1 Tstrap: 6-16 Ckp: 6-16
Best Rating: **101** 9/03 Hayd 1m30y soft

Modest; suited by 5f; acts on most ground and on sand; likes to come late; usually wears cheekpieces but has sported blinkers.

Desert Phantom (USA)

89 98

3-y-o b c Arch (USA)-Junkinthetrunk (USA) (Top Account (USA))
D M Simcock Ahmad Al Shaikh

Placings:1115-0 (7292)
2009: 6^0S,

	Starts	1st	2nd	3rd	Win & Pl
Career Total (Turf)	5	3	0	0	35400

95 8/08 Ripn 6f G-S £17031
95 8/08 Wind 6f G-S £7771
87 7/08 Hayd 6f HVY £3238
Total win prize-money £28040

Going (Turf): Sf: 1-2 **GS: 2-3** Gd: 0-0 GF: 0-0 Fm: 0-0
Distance: **5f/6f: 3-4** 7f-8f: 0-1 9f-13f: 0-0 14f+: 0-0
Track : LH: 0-0 RH: 0-1 Tight: 0-0 **Gall: 1-1**
Aids: Bl: 0-0 Vi: 0-0 Tstrap: 0-0 Ckp: 0-0
Best Rating: **98** 10/08 Lonc 7f gd-sft

Very useful; effective over 6-7f; acts with give in the ground.

Desert Poppy (IRE)

94(103) (76)73

2-y-o b f Oasis Dream-Flanders (IRE) (Common Grounds)
W R Swinburn Oasis Dreamers

Placings:62122 (7372)
2009: 6^6SD, 5^2F, 5^1SD, 5^2SD, 5^2SD,

	Starts	1st	2nd	3rd	Win & Pl
Career Total (Turf)	1	0	1	0	809
Career Total (AW)	4	1	2	0	5064

73 10/09 Kemp 5f STD £2590
Total win prize-money £2590

Going (Turf): **Sf: 0-0 GS: 0-0 Gd: 0-0 GF: 0-0 Fm: 0-1**
Distance: **5f/6f: 1-5** 7f-8f: 0-0 9f-13f: 0-0 14f+: 0-0
Track : LH: 0-3 **RH: 1-2** Tight: 0-2 Gall: 0-1
Aids: Bl: 0-0 Vi: 0-0 Tstrap: 0-0 Ckp: 0-0
Best Rating: **76** 11/09 Wolv 5f20y stand

Fair; stays 6f; acts on Polytrack; may do better.

Desert Pride

101(98) (65)70

4-y-o b g Desert Style (IRE)-Dalu (IRE) (Dancing Brave (USA))
W S Kittow M E Harris

Placings:25/22000-340354650 (7241)
2009: 6^3SD, 7^4GF, 5^0SD, 6^3GF, 6^5GF, 5^4GF, 6^6SD, 5^5G, 5^0S,

	Starts	1st	2nd	3rd	Win & Pl
Career Total (Turf)	9	0	1	1	1603
Career Total (AW)	7	0	2	1	1612

Going (Turf): **Sf: 0-2 GS: 0-0 Gd: 0-1 GF: 0-6 Fm: 0-0**
Distance: 5f/6f: 0-13 7f-8f: 0-3 9f-13f: 0-0 14f+: 0-0
Track : LH: 0-6 RH: 0-2 Tight: 0-5 Gall: 0-1
Aids: Bl: 0-0 Vi: 0-6 Tstrap: 0-0 Ckp: 0-0
Best Rating: **70** 6/08 Ling 6f gd-fm

Modest; effective at 6f; acts on fast ground; has worn a visor.

Desert Rat (IRE)

(97) (43)67

5-y-o b g Desert Sun-Virtue Rewarded (IRE) (Darshaan)
Tim Vaughan The Rat Pack

Placings:066050/0560224213400/00000-4 (0647)
2009: 10^4SD,

	Starts	1st	2nd	3rd	Win & Pl
Career Total (Turf)	24	1	3	1	8657
Career Total (AW)	2	0	0	0	120

66 7/07 Baln 1m1f (47-60)H G-Y £4202
Total win prize-money £4202

Going (Turf): **Sf: 0-4 GS: 0-1 Gd: 0-3 GF: 0-8 Fm: 0-0**
Distance: 5f/6f: 0-2 7f-8f: 0-14 **9f-13f: 1-10** 14f+: 0-0
Track : LH: 0-13 **RH: 1-6** Tight: 0-5 Gall: 0-0
Aids: Bl: 0-2 Vi: 0-2 Tstrap: 1-9 Ckp: 1-9
Best Rating: **67** 8/07 Gway 1m100y good

Plating-class; stays 1m2f; acts on Polytrack; has worn cheekpieces.

Desert Recluse (IRE)

(86) (41)

2-y-o ch c Redback-Desert Design (Desert King (IRE))
Pat Eddery Pat Eddery Racing (Storm Bird)

Placings:000 (7885)
2009: 7^0SD, 7^0SD, 7^0SD,

	Starts	1st	2nd	3rd	Win & Pl
Career Total (Turf)	0	0	0	0	
Career Total (AW)	3	0	0	0	

Going (Turf): **Sf: 0-0 GS: 0-0 Gd: 0-0 GF: 0-0 Fm: 0-0**
Distance: 5f/6f: 0-0 7f-8f: 0-3 9f-13f: 0-0 14f+: 0-0
Track : LH: 0-2 RH: 0-1 Tight: 0-2 Gall: 0-0
Aids: Bl: 0-0 Vi: 0-0 Tstrap: 0-0 Ckp: 0-0
Best Rating: **41** 10/09 Kemp 7f stand

Desert Sage

100 73

2-y-o ch f Selkirk (USA)-Prairie Flower (IRE) (Zieten (USA))
R M Beckett J H Richmond-Watson

Placings:2 (6592)
2009: 8^2GS,

	Starts	1st	2nd	3rd	Win & Pl
Career Total (Turf)	1	0	1	0	867

Going (Turf): **Sf: 0-0 GS: 0-1 Gd: 0-0 GF: 0-0 Fm: 0-0**
Distance: 5f/6f: 0-0 7f-8f: 0-0 9f-13f: 0-1 14f+: 0-0
Track : LH: 0-1 RH: 0-0 Tight: 0-0 Gall: 0-0
Aids: Bl: 0-0 Vi: 0-0 Tstrap: 0-0 Ckp: 0-0
Best Rating: **73** 10/09 Nott 1m75y gd-sft

Runner-up on debut; effective over 1m; acts on easy ground.

Desert Sea (IRE)

111(101) (103)103

6-y-o b g Desert Sun-Sea Of Time (USA) (Gilded Time (USA))
D W P Arbuthnot Bonusprint

Placings:000/001211/042010/10626-14100 (5823)
2009: 16^1SD, 18^4GF, 16^1G, 14^0GF, 14^0GF,

	Starts	1st	2nd	3rd	Win & Pl
Career Total (Turf)	18	3	1	0	69010
Career Total (AW)	7	4	2	0	27012

103 7/09 Sand 2m78y GD £22708
103 3/09 Kemp 2m (0-105)H STD £11215
97 6/08 Sand 1m6f (0-85)H GD £5180
89 8/07 Donc 2m2f (0-105)H G-F £31160
90 9/06 Kemp 2m (0-80)H STD £5505
85 7/06 Ling 2m (0-70)H STD £3238
72 6/06 Wolv 1m4f50y (0-65)H STD £2730
Total win prize-money £81739

Going (Turf): Sf: 0-5 GS: 0-3 **Gd: 2-4** GF: 1-6 Fm: 0-0
Distance: 5f/6f: 0-0 7f-8f: 0-2 9f-13f: 1-5 **14f+: 6-18**
Track : LH: 3-12 **RH: 4-11 Tight: 2-5** Gall: 1-10
Aids: Bl: 0-0 Vi: 0-0 Tstrap: 0-0 Ckp: 0-0
Best Rating: **103** 7/09 Sand 2m78y good

Very useful; Listed winner; stays 2m2f; acts on fast ground and on Polytrack; usually held up.

Desert Streak (FR)

69(99) (74)49

3-y-o b c Green Desert (USA)-Niner's Home (USA) (Forty Niner (USA))
R Simpson (C G Cox 16/9) H E Sheikh Sultan Bin Khalifa Al Nahyan

Placings:00-0124064
2009: 10^0GF, 7^1SD, 7^2SD, 6^4SD, 7^0SD, 7^6GF, 6^4FT,

	Starts	1st	2nd	3rd	Win & Pl
Career Total (Turf)	3	0	0	0	
Career Total (AW)	6	1	1	0	3955

64 8/09 Ling 7f (0-60)H STD £2047
Total win prize-money £2047

Going (Turf): **Sf: 0-0 GS: 0-0 Gd: 0-1 GF: 0-2 Fm: 0-0**
Distance: 5f/6f: 0-3 **7f-8f: 1-5** 9f-13f: 0-1 14f+: 0-0
Track : **LH: 1-4** RH: 0-2 **Tight: 1-4** Gall: 0-0
Aids: Bl: 0-0 Vi: 0-0 Tstrap: 0-2 Ckp: 0-2
Best Rating: **74** 8/09 Wolv 7f32y stand

Modest; effective over 6f-7f; acts on Polytrack; has worn cheekpieces.

Desert Strike

98(99) (79)77

3-y-o b g Bertolini (USA)-Mary Jane (Tina's Pet)
P F I Cole P F I Cole Ltd

Placings:053214-15325050 (7329)
2009: 5^1SD, 5^5SD, 5^3G, 5^2GF, 5^5GF, 5^0GF, 6^5G, 6^0SD,

	Starts	1st	2nd	3rd	Win & Pl
Career Total (Turf)	6	0	1	2	2467
Career Total (AW)	8	2	1	0	3786

74 12/08 GrLe 5f STD £2590
Total win prize-money £2590

Going (Turf): **Sf: 0-0 GS: 0-0 Gd: 0-2 GF: 0-4 Fm: 0-0**
Distance: **5f/6f: 2-14** 7f-8f: 0-0 9f-13f: 0-0 14f+: 0-0
Track : **LH: 2-6** RH: 0-2 Tight: 0-2 **Gall: 2-6**
Aids: Bl: 0-0 Vi: 0-0 Tstrap: 0-1 Ckp: 0-1
Best Rating: **79** 1/09 GrLe 5f stand

Fair; suited by 5f; acts on fast ground; goes on Fibresand and Polytrack.

Desert Vision

100(107) (87)65

5-y-o b g Alhaarth (IRE)-Fragrant Oasis (USA) (Rahy (USA))

M W Easterby A Black,R Edmonds,J Holdroyd,J Quickfall

Placings:562-0000011212 (7851)

2009: 11^{0}SD, 8^{0}S, 12^{0}SF, 10^{0}GS, 10^{0}HY, 12^{1}SD, 9^{1}SD, 9^{2}SD, 9^{1}SS, 11^{2}SS,

	Starts	1st	2nd	3rd	Win & Pl
Career Total (Turf)	3	0	0	0	
Career Total (AW)	10	3	3	0	9673

82 12/09 Wolv 1m1f103y (0-65)H SS £2047
75 12/09 Wolv 1m1f103y (0-75)H STD £2810
71 11/09 Wolv 1m4f50y (0-65)H STD £2047
Total win prize-money £6905

Going (Turf): Sf: 0-2 GS: 0-1 Gd: 0-0 GF: 0-0 Fm: 0-0
Distance: 5f/6f: 0-0 7f-8f: 0-1 9f-13f: 3-12 14f+: 0-0
Track: LH: 3-13 RH: 0-0 Tight: 3-9 Gall: 0-1
Aids: Bl: 1-1 Vi: 2-4 Tstrap: 0-0 Ckp: 0-0
Best Rating: 87 12/09 Sthl 1m3f std-slw

Fair; effective over 1m1f-1m4f; acts on Polytrack and Fibresand; has worn a tongue tie/blinkers/visor.

Desire To Excel (IRE)

102(91) (63)81

3-y-o b g Desert Style (IRE)-Sanpala (Sanglamore (USA))

P F I Cole H R H Sultan Ahmad Shah

Placings:3540-10111 (4453)

2009: 7^{1}GF, 7^{0}SD, 7^{1}GF, 8^{1}GF, 8^{1}G,

	Starts	1st	2nd	3rd	Win & Pl
Career Total (Turf)	8	4	0	1	19770
Career Total (AW)	1	0	0	0	

81 7/09 Epsm 1m114y (0-80)H GD £5180
79 7/09 Bevl 1m100y (0-80)H G-F £5180
77 6/09 Leic 7f9y (0-80)H G-F £5180
72 4/09 Muss 7f30y G-F £2590
Total win prize-money £18133

Going (Turf): Sf: 0-0 GS: 0-0 Gd: 1-2 GF: 3-6 Fm: 0-0
Distance: 5f/6f: 0-3 7f-8f: 2-4 9f-13f: 2-2 14f+: 0-0
Track: LH: 1-2 RH: 2-2 Tight: 2-2 Gall: 0-0
Aids: Bl: 0-1 Vi: 0-0 Tstrap: 0-0 Ckp: 0-0
Best Rating: 81 7/09 Epsm 1m114y good

Fair; effective at 7f but stays 1m plus; acts on fast ground.

Desperate Dan

105(106) (83)83

8-y-o b g Danzero (AUS)-Alzianah (Alzao (USA))

A B Haynes Joe McCarthy

Placings:102/643002046/331600030306/3300620401552 1300/3134432324311601230-30115112224012001350014442 (7535)

2009: 5^{3}SD, 5^{0}SD, 5^{1}SD, 5^{1}SD, 5^{5}SD, 5^{1}SD, 5^{1}SD, 5^{2}SD, 5^{2}SD, 5^{2}SD, 5^{4}GF, 6^{0}G, 5^{1}F, 5^{2}F, 5^{0}F, 5^{0}G, 5^{1}G, 5^{3}GS, 5^{5}G, 6^{0}G, 5^{0}F, 5^{1}F, 5^{4}SD, 5^{4}SD,

	Starts	1st	2nd	3rd	Win & Pl
Career Total (Turf)	49	5	7	9	33958
Career Total (AW)	37	10	5	7	42970

75 9/09 Bath 5f11y FRM £2072
83 7/09 Bath 5f11y (0-75)H GD £4209
77 5/09 Bath 5f161y (0-85)H FRM £4857
83 4/09 Wolv 5f20y STD £2729
77 3/09 Wolv 5f20y STD £2047
81 3/09 Wolv 5f20y STD £2729
74 2/09 Wolv 5f20y STD £2047
69 9/08 GrLe 5f STD £2590
77 8/08 Bath 5f161y (0-75)H G-S £2914
66 7/08 Bath 5f11y FRM £2266
78 4/08 Wolv 5f20y STD £2388
83 11/07 Ling 5f (0-75)H STD £3238
73 8/07 Wolv 5f20y STD £2914
94 1/06 Sthl 5f (0-85)H STD £6477
86 8/03 Ling 6f E STD £3779
Total win prize-money £47262

Going (Turf): Sf: 0-3 GS: 1-6 Gd: 1-15 GF: 0-17 Fm: 3-8
Distance: 5f/6f: 15-84 7f-8f: 0-2 9f-13f: 0-0 14f+: 0-0
Track: LH: 14-47 RH: 0-1 Tight: 8-26 Gall: 6-16
Aids: Bl: 5-43 Vi: 7-23 Tstrap: 0-2 Ckp: 0-2
Best Rating: 96 7/05 Newb 6f8y gd-fm

Fair; suited by 5f; acts on fast ground; goes well on sand; has worn blinkers, a visor and cheekpieces.

Destination Alm

93 77

2-y-o b c Dubai Destination (USA)-Tessa Reef (IRE) (Mark Of Esteem (IRE))

Saeed Bin Suroor Godolphin

Placings:41 (5000)

2009: 7^{4}S, 7^{1}G,

	Starts	1st	2nd	3rd	Win & Pl
Career Total (Turf)	2	1	0	0	4848

77 8/09 NmkJ 7f GD £3885
Total win prize-money £3886

Going (Turf): Sf: 0-1 GS: 0-0 Gd: 1-1 GF: 0-0 Fm: 0-0
Distance: 5f/6f: 0-0 7f-8f: 1-2 9f-13f: 0-0 14f+: 0-0
Track: LH: 0-0 RH: 0-1 Tight: 0-0 Gall: 0-0
Aids: Bl: 0-0 Vi: 0-0 Tstrap: 0-0 Ckp: 0-0
Best Rating: 77 8/09 NmkJ 7f good

Destinationunknown (USA)

71(94) (55)

3-y-o b f Arch (USA)-Private Funds (USA) (Private Terms (USA))

A J McCabe (W J Haggas 14/3) Findlay & Bloom

Placings:5560 (1926)

2009: 7^{5}SD, 8^{5}SD, 8^{6}SD, 8^{0}F,

	Starts	1st	2nd	3rd	Win & Pl
Career Total (Turf)	1	0	0	0	
Career Total (AW)	3	0	0	0	0

Going (Turf): Sf: 0-0 GS: 0-0 Gd: 0-0 GF: 0-0 Fm: 0-1
Distance: 5f/6f: 0-0 7f-8f: 0-4 9f-13f: 0-0 14f+: 0-0
Track: LH: 0-2 RH: 0-1 Tight: 0-1 Gall: 0-0
Aids: Bl: 0-1 Vi: 0-0 Tstrap: 0-1 Ckp: 0-1
Best Rating: 55 2/09 Sthl 1m stand

Destiny Blue (IRE)

(86) (65)

2-y-o b c Danehill Dancer (IRE)-Arpege (IRE) (Sadler's Wells (USA))

J A Osborne Mr & Mrs I H Bendelow

Placings:4 (7388)

2009: 8^{4}SD,

	Starts	1st	2nd	3rd	Win & Pl
Career Total (Turf)	0	0	0	0	
Career Total (AW)	1	0	0	0	0

Going (Turf): Sf: 0-0 GS: 0-0 Gd: 0-0 GF: 0-0 Fm: 0-0
Distance: 5f/6f: 0-0 7f-8f: 0-1 9f-13f: 0-0 14f+: 0-0
Track: LH: 0-1 RH: 0-0 Tight: 0-1 Gall: 0-0
Aids: Bl: 0-0 Vi: 0-0 Tstrap: 0-0 Ckp: 0-0
Best Rating: 65 11/09 Ling 1m stand

Destiny Rules

55

2-y-o br f Endoli (USA)-Up The Order (Forzando)

John Berry Hyseven Bloodstock

Placings:0 (6542)

2009: 6^{0}GF,

	Starts	1st	2nd	3rd	Win & Pl
Career Total (Turf)	1	0	0	0	

Going (Turf): Sf: 0-0 GS: 0-0 Gd: 0-0 GF: 0-1 Fm: 0-0
Distance: 5f/6f: 0-1 7f-8f: 0-0 9f-13f: 0-0 14f+: 0-0
Track: LH: 0-1 RH: 0-0 Tight: 0-0 Gall: 0-0
Aids: Bl: 0-0 Vi: 0-0 Tstrap: 0-0 Ckp: 0-0

Destiny's Dancer

82 44

2-y-o b f Dubai Destination (USA)-Cybinka (Selkirk (USA))

P C Haslam Mark James

Placings:565 (5253)

2009: 5^{5}S, 6^{6}GF, 6^{5}GF,

	Starts	1st	2nd	3rd	Win & Pl
Career Total (Turf)	3	0	0	0	0

Going (Turf): Sf: 0-1 GS: 0-0 Gd: 0-0 GF: 0-2 Fm: 0-0
Distance: 5f/6f: 0-3 7f-8f: 0-0 9f-13f: 0-0 14f+: 0-0
Track: LH: 0-1 RH: 0-0 Tight: 0-1 Gall: 0-0
Aids: Bl: 0-0 Vi: 0-0 Tstrap: 0-0 Ckp: 0-0
Best Rating: 44 8/09 Ripn 6f gd-fm

Destinys Dream (IRE)

105 77

4-y-o b f Mull Of Kintyre (USA)-Dream Of Jenny (Caerleon (USA))

Miss Tracy Waggott H Conlon

Placings:406025136/6455-441460631050 (6490)

2009: 12^{4}GF, 9^{4}GF, 12^{1}F, 10^{4}G, 10^{6}GS, 7^{0}G, 10^{6}S, 12^{3}GF, 12^{1}G, 11^{0}S, 13^{5}GF, 10^{0}GF,

	Starts	1st	2nd	3rd	Win & Pl
Career Total (Turf)	25	3	1	2	16083

77 8/09 Ches 1m4f66y (0-85)H GD £5828
74 4/09 Thsk 1m4f (0-75)H FRM £4274
71 9/07 Bevl 7f100y (0-65) G-F £3238
Total win prizo-money £13341

Going (Turf): Sf: 0-4 GS: 0-1 Gd: 1-8 GF: 1-10 Fm: 1-2
Distance: 5f/6f: 0-4 7f-8f: 1-5 9f-13f: 2-15 14f+: 0-1
Track: LH: 2-13 RH: 1-7 Tight: 2-6 Gall: 0-4
Aids: Bl: 0-0 Vi: 0-0 Tstrap: 0-0 Ckp: 0-0
Best Rating: 77 8/09 Ches 1m4f66y good

Fair; stays 1m4f; acts on good and faster ground.

Deuce

101(102) (70)69

3-y-o ch f Where Or When (IRE)-Justbetweenfriends (USA) (Diesis)

Eve Johnson Houghton Henry Marsh

Placings:04-02002212350 (7005)
2009: 10^{0}GF, 11^{2}GF, 14^{0}G, 12^{0}GF, 12^{2}SD, 12^{2}SD, 16^{1}GF, 16^{2}GF, 13^{3}SD, 16^{5}SD, 16^{0}SD,

	Starts	1st	2nd	3rd	Win & Pl
Career Total (Turf)	7	1	2	0	3642
Career Total (AW)	6	0	2	1	2556

64 8/09 Nott 2m9y (0-65)H G-F £2266
Total win prize-money £2267

Going (Turf): Sf: 0-0 GS: 0-1 Gd: 0-1 **GF: 1-5** Fm: 0-0
Distance: 5f/6f: 0-0 7f-8f: 0-1 9f-13f: 0-6 **14f+: 1-6**
Track : **LH: 1-9** RH: 0-3 Tight: 0-9 Gall: 0-0
Aids: **Bl: 1-10** Vi: 0-0 Tstrap: 0-0 Ckp: 0-0
Best Rating: 70 10/09 Wolv 2m119y stand

Modest; stays 1m4f and acts on Polytrack; has worn blinkers.

Deutschland (USA)

105 (91) **105**
6-y-o b g Red Ransom (USA)-Rhine Valley (USA) (Danzig (USA))
W P Mullins Allan McLuckie

Placings:454/3231/1105 (5824)
2009: 13^{1}GF, 17^{1}SD, 14^{0}GF, 18^{5}GF,

	Starts	1st	2nd	3rd	Win & Pl
Career Total (Turf)	8	2	0	1	16386
Career Total (AW)	3	1	1	1	13331

91 7/09 Dund 2m1f H STD £11404
82 6/09 Navn 1m5f (50-85)H G-F £7044
83 5/06 Ayr 1m2f (0-70) SFT £5505
Total win prize-money £23954

Going (Turf): **Sf: 1-2** GS: 0-0 Gd: 0-1 **GF: 1-5** Fm: 0-0
Distance: 5f/6f: 0-1 7f-8f: 0-2 **9f-13f: 2-5** 14f+: 1-3
Track : **LH: 3-9** RH: 0-0 Tight: 0-2 Gall: 0-3
Aids: Bl: 0-0 Vi: 0-0 Tstrap: 1-2 Ckp: 1-2
Best Rating: 105 8/09 York 1m6f gd-fm

Very useful; stays 2m1f; acts on good and softer ground and on Polytrack; has worn cheekpieces; winning hurdler/chase .

Devassa

98 (84) (43) **60**
2-y-o b f Reel Buddy (USA)-Signs And Wonders (Danehill (USA))
C G Cox J D R Cruden

Placings:632400 (6970)
2009: 5^{6}GF, 5^{3}G, 5^{2}G, 5^{4}GF, 5^{0}SF, 5^{0}SD,

	Starts	1st	2nd	3rd	Win & Pl
Career Total (Turf)	4	0	1	1	1146
Career Total (AW)	2	0	0	0	

Going (Turf): **Sf: 0-0 GS: 0-0 Gd: 0-2 GF: 0-2 Fm: 0-0**
Distance: 5f/6f: 0-6 7f-8f: 0-0 9f-13f: 0-0 14f+: 0-0
Track : LH: 0-4 RH: 0-1 Tight: 0-1 Gall: 0-3
Aids: Bl: 0-0 Vi: 0-0 Tstrap: 0-0 Ckp: 0-0
Best Rating: 60 9/09 Bath 5f11y good

Modest; effective over 5f; acts on good ground.

Develop U

80 (86) (39) **37**
2-y-o b g Mutazayid (IRE)-Verdura (Green Desert (USA))
W G M Turner Developing Performance Partnership Ltd

Placings:005 (7616)
2009: 8^{0}GF, 10^{0}SD, 8^{5}SD,

	Starts	1st	2nd	3rd	Win & Pl
Career Total (Turf)	1	0	0	0	
Career Total (AW)	2	0	0	0	0

Going (Turf): **Sf: 0-0 GS: 0-0 Gd: 0-0 GF: 0-1 Fm: 0-0**
Distance: 5f/6f: 0-0 7f-8f: 0-0 9f-13f: 0-3 14f+: 0-0
Track : LH: 0-2 RH: 0-1 Tight: 0-1 Gall: 0-0
Aids: Bl: 0-0 Vi: 0-0 Tstrap: 0-0 Ckp: 0-0
Best Rating: 39 12/09 Wolv 1m141y stand

Dever Dream

93 **68**
2-y-o b f Medicean-Sharplaw Venture (Polar Falcon (USA))
W J Haggas Exors of the Late F C T Wilson

Placings:5 (6061)
2009: 6^{5}GF,

	Starts	1st	2nd	3rd	Win & Pl
Career Total (Turf)	1	0	0	0	0

Going (Turf): **Sf: 0-0 GS: 0-0 Gd: 0-0 GF: 0-1 Fm: 0-0**
Distance: 5f/6f: 0-1 7f-8f: 0-0 9f-13f: 0-0 14f+: 0-0
Track : LH: 0-0 RH: 0-0 Tight: 0-0 Gall: 0-0
Aids: Bl: 0-0 Vi: 0-0 Tstrap: 0-0 Ckp: 0-0
Best Rating: 68 9/09 NmkR 6f gd-fm

Deviant Ways

(51)
3-y-o b f Celtic Swing-Khwezi (Bering)
S Kirk Sylvester Kirk

Placings:0 (1585)
2009: 8^{0}SD,

	Starts	1st	2nd	3rd	Win & Pl
Career Total (Turf)	0	0	0	0	
Career Total (AW)	1	0	0	0	

Going (Turf): **Sf: 0-0 GS: 0-0 Gd: 0-0 GF: 0-0 Fm: 0-0**
Distance: 5f/6f: 0-0 7f-8f: 0-1 9f-13f: 0-0 14f+: 0-0
Track : LH: 0-1 RH: 0-0 Tight: 0-1 Gall: 0-0
Aids: Bl: 0-0 Vi: 0-0 Tstrap: 0-0 Ckp: 0-0

Devil To Pay

102 **81**
3-y-o b g Red Ransom (USA)-My Way (IRE) (Marju (IRE))
A King (J L Dunlop 23/10) Horace 5

Placings:600-012200 (6995)
2009: 10^{0}GF, 9^{1}G, 12^{2}GF, 14^{2}GF, 14^{0}G, 14^{0}GS,

	Starts	1st	2nd	3rd	Win & Pl
Career Total (Turf)	9	1	2	0	5165

71 5/09 Gdwd 1m1f192y (0-70)H GD £3238
Total win prize-money £3238

Going (Turf): Sf: 0-0 GS: 0-2 **Gd: 1-4** GF: 0-3 Fm: 0-0
Distance: 5f/6f: 0-0 7f-8f: 0-3 **9f-13f: 1-3** 14f+: 0-3
Track : LH: 0-3 **RH: 1-3 Tight: 1-3** Gall: 0-2
Aids: Bl: 0-0 Vi: 0-0 Tstrap: 0-0 Ckp: 0-0
Best Rating: 81 7/09 Sals 1m6f21y gd-fm

Fair; stays 1m4f; acts on fast ground.

Devil You Know (IRE)

100 (103) (83) **86**
3-y-o b g Elusive City (USA)-Certainly Brave (Indian Ridge)
D R C Elsworth Raymond Tooth

Placings:414124004 (5974)
2009: 5^{4}GS, 6^{1}GF, 5^{4}G, 6^{1}SD, 6^{2}GF, 6^{4}G, 5^{0}G, 6^{0}G, 5^{4}GF,

	Starts	1st	2nd	3rd	Win & Pl
Career Total (Turf)	8	1	1	0	5531
Career Total (AW)	1	1	0	0	4727

83 6/09 Kemp 6f (0-80)H STD £4727
78 5/09 Nott 6f15y G-F £2590
Total win prize-money £7317

Going (Turf): Sf: 0-0 GS: 0-1 Gd: 0-4 **GF: 1-3** Fm: 0-0
Distance: 5f/6f: 1-8 7f-8f: 1-1 9f-13f: 0-0 14f+: 0-0
Track : LH: 0-0 **RH: 1-1** Tight: 0-0 Gall: 0-1
Aids: Bl: 0-0 Vi: 0-0 Tstrap: 0-0 Ckp: 0-0
Best Rating: 86 6/09 Wind 6f gd-fm

Useful; stays 6f; acts on fast ground and Polytrack.

Devinius (IRE)

97 (79) (17) **66**
4-y-o ch f Choisir (AUS)-Vampress (IRE) (Marju (IRE))
G A Swinbank The Jags Syndicate

Placings:3305516-403006 (6998)
2009: 7^{4}G, 7^{0}G, 10^{3}GS, 8^{0}G, 7^{0}G, 9^{6}SD,

	Starts	1st	2nd	3rd	Win & Pl
Career Total (Turf)	12	1	0	3	6441
Career Total (AW)	1	0	0	0	0

66 8/08 Thsk 1m (0-75)H SFT £4274
Total win prize-money £4274

Going (Turf): **Sf: 1-2** GS: 0-2 Gd: 0-7 GF: 0-1 Fm: 0-0
Distance: 5f/6f: 0-1 **7f-8f: 1-8** 9f-13f: 0-4 14f+: 0-0
Track : **LH: 1-6** RH: 0-3 **Tight: 1-7** Gall: 0-1
Aids: Bl: 0-0 Vi: 0-0 Tstrap: 0-0 Ckp: 0-0
Best Rating: 66 8/08 Thsk 1m soft

Modest; stays 1m; acts on soft ground.

Devolution (IRE)

(71) (51)
11-y-o b g Distinctly North (USA)-Election Special (Chief Singer)
Miss C Dyson Miss C Dyson

Placings:523R0011/5025140/001/0/0 (1568)
2009: 11^{0}SD,

	Starts	1st	2nd	3rd	Win & Pl
Career Total (Turf)	11	2	2	0	17022
Career Total (AW)	9	2	0	1	7247

82 7/03 Leic 1m1f218yD(0-80)H GD £5681
82 10/02 Yarm 1m2f21yD(0-85)H SFT £8998
87 12/01 Ling 1m E(0-75)H STD £2793
83 11/01 Ling 1m E(0-75)H STD £3391
Total win prize-money £20865

Going (Turf): **Sf: 1-1** GS: 0-2 **Gd: 1-3** GF: 0-5 Fm: 0-0
Distance: 5f/6f: 0-2 7f-8f: 2-7 9f-13f: 2-11 14f+: 0-0
Track : **LH: 3-13** RH: 1-2 **Tight: 3-8** Gall: 0-1
Aids: Bl: 0-0 Vi: 0-0 Tstrap: 0-0 Ckp: 0-0
Best Rating: 87 12/01 Ling 1m stand

Useful handicapper on turf and Polytrack; suited by a mile to ten furlongs and acts on good or softer ground on turf.

Devon Diva

76(85) (49)4

3-y-o b f Systematic-General Jane (Be My Chief (USA))

J F Panvert (C J Down 13/8) Miss Jennifer Dorey

Placings:5-00 **(6934)**

2009: 8⁰SD, 10⁰G,

	Starts	1st	2nd	3rd	Win & Pl
Career Total (Turf)	1	0	0	0	
Career Total (AW)	2	0	0	0	0

Going (Turf): Sf: 0-0 GS: 0-0 Gd: 0-1 GF: 0-0 Fm: 0-0
Distance: 5f/6f: 0-1 7f-8f: 0-0 9f-13f: 0-2 14f+: 0-0
Track : LH: 0-3 RH: 0-0 Tight: 0-3 Gall: 0-0
Aids: Bl: 0-0 Vi: 0-0 Tstrap: 0-0 Ckp: 0-0
Best Rating: 49 11/08 Wolv 5f216y stand

Devotee (USA)

90(103) (103)59

3-y-o ch f Elusive Quality (USA)-Danuta (USA) (Sunday Silence (USA))

Saeed Bin Suroor Godolphin

Placings:13-0100 **(1698)**

2009: 8⁰FT, 9¹FT, 8⁰GF, 10⁰FT,

	Starts	1st	2nd	3rd	Win & Pl
Career Total (Turf)	1	0	0	0	
Career Total (AW)	5	2	0	1	149375
103 2/09 Ndas 1m1f				FST	£104166
8/08 Sara 6f110y				FST	£18693

Total win prize-money £122860

Going (Turf): Sf: 0-0 GS: 0-0 Gd: 0-0 GF: 0-1 Fm: 0-0
Distance: 5f/6f: 0-0 7f-8f: 1-3 9f-13f: 1-3 14f+: 0-0
Track : **LH: 1-3** RH: 0-0 Tight: 0-0 **Gall: 1-2**
Aids: Bl: 0-0 Vi: 0-0 Tstrap: 0-0 Ckp: 0-0
Best Rating: 103 2/09 Ndas 1m1f fast

Listed class; winner of the UAE Oaks; stays 1m1f; acts on dirt.

Devotion To Duty (IRE)

97 83

3-y-o b c Montjeu (IRE)-Charmante (USA) (Alydar (USA))

B W Hills J Hanson & Cavendish Investing Ltd

Placings:0-40160 **(6681)**

2009: 10⁴GF, 10⁰GF, 10¹GS, 12⁶S, 12⁰G,

	Starts	1st	2nd	3rd	Win & Pl
Career Total (Turf)	6	1	0	0	3623
83 5/09 Hayd 1m2f95y				G-S	£3238

Total win prize-money £3238

Going (Turf): Sf: 0-1 **GS: 1-1** Gd: 0-1 GF: 0-3 Fm: 0-0
Distance: 5f/6f: 0-0 7f-8f: 0-1 **9f-13f: 1-5** 14f+: 0-0
Track : **LH: 1-4** RH: 0-0 Tight: 0-1 Gall: 0-2
Aids: Bl: 0-0 Vi: 0-0 Tstrap: 0-0 Ckp: 0-0
Best Rating: 83 5/09 Hayd 1m2f95y gd-sft

Useful; stays 1m2f; acts on fast and easy ground.

Deyas Dream

98(93) (66)75

3-y-o b f Clodovil (IRE)-Dream On Deya (IRE) (Dolphin Street (FR))

A M Balding Miss A V Hill

Placings:453046-0606 **(2949)**

2009: 7⁰SD, 8⁶G, 7⁰F, 6⁶GF,

	Starts	1st	2nd	3rd	Win & Pl
Career Total (Turf)	7	0	0	0	577
Career Total (AW)	3	0	0	1	578

Going (Turf): Sf: 0-2 GS: 0-0 Gd: 0-2 GF: 0-2 Fm: 0-1
Distance: 5f/6f: 0-3 7f-8f: 0-6 9f-13f: 0-1 14f+: 0-0
Track : LH: 0-4 RH: 0-1 Tight: 0-3 Gall: 0-0
Aids: Bl: 0-0 Vi: 0-0 Tstrap: 0-0 Ckp: 0-0
Best Rating: 75 5/08 Newb 6f8y soft

Fair; effective over 6f; acts on good ground.

Dhaawiah (USA)

(104) (89)

3-y-o b f Elusive Quality (USA)-Huja (IRE) (Alzao (USA))

Saeed Bin Suroor Godolphin

Placings:210 **(5665)**

2009: 8²SD, 7¹SD, 7⁰SD,

	Starts	1st	2nd	3rd	Win & Pl
Career Total (Turf)	0	0	0	0	
Career Total (AW)	3	1	1	0	4333
89 8/09 Ling 7f				STD	£3561

Total win prize-money £3562

Going (Turf): Sf: 0-0 GS: 0-0 Gd: 0-0 GF: 0-0 Fm: 0-0
Distance: 5f/6f: 0-0 **7f-8f: 1-3** 9f-13f: 0-0 14f+: 0-0
Track : **LH: 1-1** RH: 0-2 **Tight: 1-1** Gall: 0-0
Aids: Bl: 0-0 Vi: 0-0 Tstrap: 0-0 Ckp: 0-0
Best Rating: 89 8/09 Ling 7f stand

Useful; stays 7f and acts on Polytrack.

Dhan Dhana (IRE)

76(84) (50)48

2-y-o b f Dubawi (IRE)-Kylemore (IRE) (Sadler's Wells (USA))

W J Haggas Mohammed Jaber

Placings:000 **(7183)**

2009: 7⁰SD, 7⁰SD, 7⁰G,

	Starts	1st	2nd	3rd	Win & Pl
Career Total (Turf)	1	0	0	0	
Career Total (AW)	2	0	0	0	

Going (Turf): Sf: 0-0 GS: 0-0 Gd: 0-1 GF: 0-0 Fm: 0-0
Distance: 5f/6f: 0-0 7f-8f: 0-3 9f-13f: 0-0 14f+: 0-0
Track : LH: 0-1 RH: 0-1 Tight: 0-1 Gall: 0-0
Aids: Bl: 0-0 Vi: 0-0 Tstrap: 0-0 Ckp: 0-0
Best Rating: 50 9/09 Ling 7f stand

Dhania (IRE)

103(92) (70)73

3-y-o b g Gulch (USA)-Novograd (USA) (Gentlemen (ARG))

R A Teal M Vickers

Placings:4-4400233302 **(6788)**

2009: 8⁴SD, 8⁴G, 10⁰GF, 8⁰G, 11²G, 10³G, 11³GF, 12³GF, 12⁰SS, 11²G,

	Starts	1st	2nd	3rd	Win & Pl
Career Total (Turf)	8	0	2	3	2757
Career Total (AW)	3	0	0	0	265

Going (Turf): Sf: 0-0 GS: 0-0 Gd: 0-5 GF: 0-3 Fm: 0-0
Distance: 5f/6f: 0-0 7f-8f: 0-1 9f-13f: 0-10 14f+: 0-0
Track : LH: 0-5 RH: 0-3 Tight: 0-8 Gall: 0-0
Aids: Bl: 0-6 Vi: 0-1 Tstrap: 0-0 Ckp: 0-0
Best Rating: 73 4/09 Epsm 1m114y good

Modest; stays 1m4f and acts on good ground; has worn blinkers.

Dhaular Dhar (IRE)

105 (93)106

7-y-o b h Indian Ridge-Pescara (IRE) (Common Grounds)

J S Goldie Middleham Park Racing XLV

Placings:210/0000645205 1/6052105043021610/2001400 6404000500/05012020004040-3000600040 **(7294)**

2009: 7³GF, 7⁰GF, 7⁰GF, 7⁰G, 7⁶G, 7⁰GF, 7⁰G, 7⁰GF, 7⁴G, 7⁰S,

	Starts	1st	2nd	3rd	Win & Pl
Career Total (Turf)	69	7	7	2	157936
Career Total (AW)	2	0	0	0	0
101 5/08 Donc 7f	(0-100)H			GD	£15577
105 5/07 Ches 7f122y	(0-100)H			GD	£13248
100 10/06 Catt 5f	(0-100)H			SFT	£14573
96 10/06 Catt 5f212y	(0-85)H			GD	£5505
90 6/06 Ches 7f2y	(0-95)H			GD	£10094
83 10/05 Gdwd 1m	(0-80)H			GD	£6870
89 9/04 Ches 7f2y				GD	£5085

Total win prize-money £70956

Going (Turf): Sf: 1-9 GS: 0-10 **Gd: 6-26** GF: 0-23 Fm: 0-1
Distance: 5f/6f: 2-19 **7f-8f: 5-46** 9f-13f: 0-6 14f+: 0-0
Track : **LH: 4-24** RH: 1-6 **Tight: 4-23** Gall: 0-2
Aids: Bl: 0-0 Vi: 0-0 Tstrap: 0-0 Ckp: 0-0
Best Rating: 106 5/09 Asct 7f gd-fm

Very useful; stays 7f, but effective at shorter; acts on most ground on turf.

Dherghaam (IRE)

102 79

2-y-o b c Exceed And Excel (AUS)-Alnasreya (IRE) (Machiavellian (USA))

E A L Dunlop Hamdan Al Maktoum

Placings:302 **(6922)**

2009: 6³GF, 6⁰GF, 6²GF,

	Starts	1st	2nd	3rd	Win & Pl
Career Total (Turf)	3	0	1	1	3540

Going (Turf): Sf: 0-0 GS: 0-0 Gd: 0-0 GF: 0-3 Fm: 0-0
Distance: 5f/6f: 0-2 7f-8f: 0-1 9f-13f: 0-0 14f+: 0-0
Track : LH: 0-0 RH: 0-0 Tight: 0-0 Gall: 0-0
Aids: Bl: 0-0 Vi: 0-0 Tstrap: 0-0 Ckp: 0-0
Best Rating: 79 10/09 Yarm 6f3y gd-fm

Fair; stays 6f; acts on quick ground.

Dhhamaan (IRE)

93(99) (61)70

4-y-o b g Dilshaan-Safe Care (IRE) (Caerleon (USA))

Mrs R A Carr S B Clark

Placings:320002132/341111465000000-000403000000 **(7754)**

2009: 7⁰SD, 7⁰SD, 7⁰SD, 5⁴SD, 5⁰SD, 8³SF, 7⁰SD, 5⁰SD, 7⁰SD, 6⁰GF, 7⁰SD, 8⁰SD,

	Starts	1st	2nd	3rd	Win & Pl
Career Total (Turf)	11	0	0	1	578
Career Total (AW)	25	5	3	3	16122
79 4/08 Kemp 7f				STD	£2047
79 3/08 Wolv 7f32y				STD	£2730
77 3/08 Kemp 7f				STD	£2047

78 2/08 Ling 7f STD £1774
70 11/07 Ling 7f STD £2047
Total win prize-money £10648

Going (Turf): Sf: 0-2 GS: 0-1 Gd: 0-4 GF: 0-4 Fm: 0-0
Distance: 5f/6f: 0-9 **7f-8f: 5-23** 9f-13f: 0-4 14f+: 0-0
Track : **LH: 3-27** RH: 2-4 **Tight: 3-26** Gall: 0-0
Aids: **Bl: 3-23** Vi: 2-6 Tstrap: 0-0 Ckp: 0-0
Best Rating: 79 4/08 Kemp 7f stand

Fair; effective at up to 1m; acts on fast ground and Polytrack; has worn blinkers and a visor.

Dhushan

98 **88**
3-y-o b g Rainbow Quest (USA)-Abyaan (IRE) (Ela-Mana-Mou)
M A Jarvis Sheikh Ahmed Al Maktoum

Placings:41000 **(5419)**
2009: 11^{4}GS, 12^{1}G, 16^{0}GF, 13^{0}G, 9^{0}GF,

	Starts	1st	2nd	3rd	Win & Pl
Career Total (Turf)	5	1	0	0	3105

88 5/09 Chep 1m4f23y GD £2719
Total win prize-money £2720

Going (Turf): Sf: 0-0 GS: 0-1 **Gd: 1-2** GF: 0-2 Fm: 0-0
Distance: 5f/6f: 0-0 7f-8f: 0-0 **9f-13f: 1-4** 14f+: 0-1
Track : **LH: 1-2** RH: 0-3 Tight: 0-0 Gall: 0-3
Aids: Bl: 0-1 Vi: 0-0 Tstrap: 0-0 Ckp: 0-0
Best Rating: 88 5/09 Chep 1m4f23y good

Useful; stays 1m4f and acts on good ground; has worn blinkers.

Di Stefano

103 **98**
2-y-o b g Bahamian Bounty-Marisa (GER) (Desert Sun)
M R Channon Jon and Julia Aisbitt

Placings:441320305 **(6398)**
2009: 5^{4}GS, 5^{4}G, 5^{1}GF, 5^{3}GF, 5^{2}G, 6^{0}GF, 6^{3}G, 6^{0}GF, 6^{5}GF,

	Starts	1st	2nd	3rd	Win & Pl
Career Total (Turf)	9	1	1	2	20221

79 6/09 Ripn 5f G-F £4209
Total win prize-money £4209

Going (Turf): Sf: 0-0 GS: 0-1 Gd: 0-3 **GF: 1-5** Fm: 0-0
Distance: **5f/6f: 1-8** 7f-8f: 0-1 9f-13f: 0-0 14f+: 0-0
Track : LH: 0-0 RH: 0-0 Tight: 0-0 Gall: 0-0
Aids: Bl: 0-0 Vi: 0-2 Tstrap: 0-0 Ckp: 0-0
Best Rating: 98 6/09 Asct 5f gd-fm

Very useful; Listed placed; effective over 5-6f; acts on good and fast ground; has worn a visor.

Diabolical (USA)

103(112) (119)**119**
6-y-o ch h Artax (USA)-Bonnie Byerly (USA) (Dayjur (USA))
Saeed Bin Suroor Godolphin

Placings:12232/4210111012/3211/410065022-3336 **(3140)**
2009: 6^{3}FT, 6^{3}FT, 6^{3}G, 6^{6}GF,

	Starts	1st	2nd	3rd	Win & Pl
Career Total (Turf)	13	2	3	1	259959
Career Total (AW)	19	7	5	4	564859

119 3/08 Ndas 6f FST £60301
114 7/07 Sara 6f H FST £76530
111 5/07 Piml 6f H FST £61224
10/06 Phil 6f H FST £34883
8/06 Dela 1m110y FRM £26162
7/06 Dela 1m110y SLP £20302
6/06 Monm 1m FRM £13953
4/06 Dela 1m FST £13255
98 7/05 Belm 5f110y FST £13437
Total win prize-money £320053

Going (Turf): Sf: 0-3 GS: 0-0 Gd: 0-3 GF: 0-2 **Fm: 2-5**
Distance: **5f/6f: 5-18** 7f-8f: 2-8 9f-13f: 2-6 14f+: 0-0
Track : **LH: 1-8** RH: 0-1 Tight: 0-0 **Gall: 1-5**
Aids: Bl: 0-0 Vi: 0-0 Tstrap: 0-0 Ckp: 0-0
Best Rating: 119 10/08 SnAt 6f110y firm

Group class; multiple Graded winner in the US and Group winner in Dubai; effective at around 6f; acts on fast ground and also goes on dirt.

Dialect

89(97) (74)**74**
3-y-o b f Diktat-Welsh Autumn (Tenby)
Mrs A J Perrett K Abdulla

Placings:031-00 **(6621)**
2009: 8^{0}GF, 8^{0}G,

	Starts	1st	2nd	3rd	Win & Pl
Career Total (Turf)	3	0	0	1	722
Career Total (AW)	2	1	0	0	3562

74 11/08 Kemp 7f STD £3561
Total win prize-money £3562

Going (Turf): Sf: 0-0 GS: 0-1 Gd: 0-1 GF: 0-1 Fm: 0-0
Distance: 5f/6f: 0-0 **7f-8f: 1-3** 9f-13f: 0-2 14f+: 0-0
Track : LH: 0-1 **RH: 1-3** Tight: 0-1 Gall: 0-1
Aids: Bl: 0-0 Vi: 0-0 Tstrap: 0-0 Ckp: 0-0
Best Rating: 74 11/08 Kemp 7f stand

Fair maiden form; effective over 7f; acts on easy ground.

Dialogue

100(104) (89)**84**
3-y-o b c Singspiel (IRE)-Zonda (Fabulous Dancer (USA))
G A Harker (M Johnston 25/7) A Findlay

Placings:541011-00560 **(6490)**
2009: 10^{0}S, 10^{0}G, 10^{5}GF, 12^{6}G, 10^{0}GF,

	Starts	1st	2nd	3rd	Win & Pl
Career Total (Turf)	8	0	0	0	385
Career Total (AW)	3	3	0	0	15273

89 12/08 Wolv 1m141y STD £6854
89 11/08 Wolv 1m141y (0-85) STD £5180
80 9/08 Ling 7f STD £3238
Total win prize-money £15273

Going (Turf): Sf: 0-1 GS: 0-0 Gd: 0-4 GF: 0-3 Fm: 0-0
Distance: 5f/6f: 0-0 7f-8f: 1-4 **9f-13f: 2-7** 14f+: 0-0
Track : **LH: 3-7** RH: 0-3 **Tight: 3-6** Gall: 0-3
Aids: Bl: 0-0 Vi: 0-0 Tstrap: 0-0 Ckp: 0-0
Best Rating: 89 12/08 Wolv 1m141y stand

Useful; stays 1m and acts on Polytrack.

Diam Queen (GER)

93(98) (85)**69**
2-y-o b f Lando (GER)-Dance Solo (Sadler's Wells (USA))
L M Cumani Jaber Abdullah

Placings:121 **(7434)**
2009: 7^{1}F, 8^{2}SD, 8^{1}SD,

	Starts	1st	2nd	3rd	Win & Pl
Career Total (Turf)	1	1	0	0	3238
Career Total (AW)	2	1	1	0	5235

85 11/09 Ling 1m (0-85)H STD £3885
69 9/09 Folk 7f FRM £3238
Total win prize-money £7124

Going (Turf): Sf: 0-0 GS: 0-0 Gd: 0-0 GF: 0-0 **Fm: 1-1**
Distance: 5f/6f: 0-0 **7f-8f: 2-2** 9f-13f: 0-1 14f+: 0-0
Track : **LH: 1-2** RH: 0-0 **Tight: 1-2** Gall: 0-0
Aids: Bl: 0-0 Vi: 0-0 Tstrap: 0-0 Ckp: 0-0
Best Rating: 85 11/09 Ling 1m stand

Useful; effective over 1m; acts quick ground; goes on Polytrack.

Diamond Affair (IRE)

86(87) (62)**56**
2-y-o b f Namid-Subtle Affair (IRE) (Barathea (IRE))
M G Quinlan L Cashman & M C Fahy

Placings:632400000 **(6554)**
2009: 5^{6}GF, 5^{3}GF, 5^{2}SD, 5^{4}G, 5^{0}G, 5^{0}G, 5^{0}SD, 5^{0}GF, 5^{0}GF,

	Starts	1st	2nd	3rd	Win & Pl
Career Total (Turf)	7	0	0	1	722
Career Total (AW)	2	0	1	0	806

Going (Turf): Sf: 0-0 GS: 0-0 Gd: 0-3 GF: 0-4 Fm: 0-0
Distance: 5f/6f: 0-9 7f-8f: 0-0 9f-13f: 0-0 14f+: 0-0
Track : LH: 0-0 RH: 0-0 Tight: 0-0 Gall: 0-0
Aids: Bl: 0-0 Vi: 0-0 Tstrap: 0-0 Ckp: 0-0
Best Rating: 62 6/09 Sthl 5f stand

Modest; suited by 5f and acts on fast ground.

Diamond Blade

102(100) (71)**59**
3-y-o ch g Needwood Blade-Branston Gem (So Factual (USA))
T D Easterby D A West

Placings:0-233204564111 **(7681)**
2009: 6^{2}SD, 6^{3}GF, 5^{3}G, 6^{2}GF, 6^{0}GF, 5^{4}S, 5^{5}GF, 5^{6}GS, 6^{4}GF, 6^{1}GF, 6^{1}SD, 6^{1}SD,

	Starts	1st	2nd	3rd	Win & Pl
Career Total (Turf)	10	1	1	2	3744
Career Total (AW)	3	2	1	0	4621

71 12/09 Sthl 6f (0-60)H STD £1706
65 11/09 Sthl 6f (0-60)H STD £1706
59 9/09 Rdcr 6f (0-65)H G-F £1706
Total win prize-money £5118

Going (Turf): Sf: 0-1 GS: 0-2 Gd: 0-1 **GF: 1-6** Fm: 0-0
Distance: **5f/6f: 3-13** 7f-8f: 0-0 9f-13f: 0-0 14f+: 0-0
Track : **LH: 2-3** RH: 0-1 Tight: 0-0 Gall: 0-0
Aids: Bl: 0-0 Vi: 0-0 Tstrap: 3-4 Ckp: 3-4
Best Rating: 71 12/09 Sthl 6f stand

Moderate; effective over 6f; acts on fast ground; goes on Fibresand; has worn cheekpieces.

Diamond Daisy (IRE)

101(93) (62)**76**
3-y-o b f Elnadim (USA)-Charlotte's Dancer (Kris)
Mrs A Duffield John and Elaine Culf and John Gatenby

Placings:360-22344113626 **(6365)**
2009: 7^{2}GF, 8^{2}SD, 8^{3}G, 7^{4}GF, 6^{4}G, 7^{1}GF, 8^{1}G, 8^{3}GF, 8^{6}S, 8^{2}GF, 8^{6}GF,

	Starts	1st	2nd	3rd	Win & Pl
Career Total (Turf)	13	2	2	3	10215
Career Total (AW)	1	0	1	0	1156

72 8/09 Thsk 1m (0-75)H GD £4274

67 7/09 Bevl 7f100y (0-65)H G-F £2428
Total win prize-money £6702

Going (Turf): Sf: 0-1 GS: 0-1 **Gd: 1-5 GF: 1-6** Fm: 0-0
Distance: 5f/6f: 0-3 **7f-8f: 2-7** 9f-13f: 0-4 14f+: 0-0
Track : LH: 1-8 RH: 1-3 **Tight: 1-5** Gall: 0-0
Aids: Bl: 0-0 Vi: 0-0 Tstrap: 0-0 Ckp: 0-0
Best Rating: 76 9/09 Pont 1m4y gd-fm

Modest; effective over 1m; acts on fast and easy ground; handles Polytrack.

Diamond Dee

89(89) (46)48
3-y-o ch f Deploy-Diamond Swan (Colonel Collins (USA))
M D I Usher M D I Usher

Placings:60 (2395)
2009: 7⁶GF, 10⁰SD,

	Starts	1st	2nd	3rd	Win & Pl
Career Total (Turf)	1	0	0	0	0
Career Total (AW)	1	0	0	0	

Going (Turf): Sf: 0-0 GS: 0-0 Gd: 0-0 GF: 0-1 Fm: 0-0
Distance: 5f/6f: 0-0 7f-8f: 0-1 9f-13f: 0-1 14f+: 0-0
Track : LH: 0-1 RH: 0-0 Tight: 0-1 Gall: 0-0
Aids: Bl: 0-0 Vi: 0-0 Tstrap: 0-0 Ckp: 0-0
Best Rating: 48 5/09 Ling 7f gd-fm

Diamond Duchess (IRE)

94(95) (73)72
2-y-o ch f Dubawi (IRE)-Tarakana (USA) (Shahrastani (USA))
D R Lanigan Saif Ali

Placings:4315330 (6391)
2009: 6⁴GF, 7³G, 8¹GS, 8⁵G, 8³G, 8³SD, 10⁰GF,

	Starts	1st	2nd	3rd	Win & Pl
Career Total (Turf)	6	1	0	2	4509
Career Total (AW)	1	0	0	1	302

72 8/09 Hayd 1m30y G-S £3238
Total win prize-money £3238

Going (Turf): Sf: 0-0 **GS: 1-1** Gd: 0-3 GF: 0-2 Fm: 0-0
Distance: 5f/6f: 0-0 7f-8f: 0-4 **9f-13f: 1-3** 14f+: 0-0
Track : **LH: 1-3** RH: 0-1 Tight: 0-1 Gall: 0-0
Aids: Bl: 0-0 Vi: 0-0 Tstrap: 0-0 Ckp: 0-0
Best Rating: 73 9/09 Kemp 1m stand

Fair; stays 1m; acts on fast and easy ground.

Diamond Fire (IRE)

95(97) (59)56
5-y-o b g King Charlemagne (USA)-Diamond Sun (Primo Dominie)
Adrian McGuinness Adrian McGuinness

Placings:304/33123/00060460140-520403054012 (7542a)
2009: 8⁵G, 7²GF, 8⁰G, 5⁴Y, 8⁰HY, 6³SD, 7⁰GY, 7⁵GF, 5⁴GY, 5⁰GY, 5¹SD, 7²SD,

	Starts	1st	2nd	3rd	Win & Pl
Career Total (Turf)	23	1	2	4	9871
Career Total (AW)	8	2	1	1	9011

57 11/09 Wolv 5f216y (0-52)H STD £2047
52 9/08 Dund 1m (45-60)H STD £5080
7/07 Aabe 6f GD £1418
Total win prize-money £8547

Going (Turf): Sf: 0-5 GS: 0-0 **Gd: 1-7** GF: 0-4 Fm: 0-0
Distance: **5f/6f: 2-10** 7f-8f: 1-19 9f-13f: 0-2 14f+: 0-0
Track : **LH: 2-17** RH: 0-6 **Tight: 1-1** Gall: 0-1
Aids: **Bl: 2-11** Vi: 0-0 Tstrap: 0-0 Ckp: 0-0
Best Rating: 59 11/09 Dund 7f stand

Moderate; effective between 6f and 1m; acts on sand; has worn headgear.

Diamond Jo (IRE)

66(52) 32
3-y-o b f Johannesburg (USA)-Still As Sweet (IRE) (Fairy King (USA))
Patrick Morris Rob Lloyd Racing Limited

Placings:00-00 (4347)
2009: 7⁰GF, 9⁰G,

	Starts	1st	2nd	3rd	Win & Pl
Career Total (Turf)	3	0	0	0	
Career Total (AW)	1	0	0	0	

Going (Turf): Sf: 0-1 GS: 0-0 Gd: 0-1 GF: 0-1 Fm: 0-0
Distance: 5f/6f: 0-0 7f-8f: 0-2 9f-13f: 0-2 14f+: 0-0
Track : LH: 0-2 RH: 0-1 Tight: 0-2 Gall: 0-0
Aids: Bl: 0-0 Vi: 0-0 Tstrap: 0-0 Ckp: 0-0
Best Rating: 32 10/08 Newc 7f heavy

Diamond Johnny G (USA)

84(86) (70)77
2-y-o b c Omega Code (USA)-My Dancin Girl (USA) (Sun War Dancer (USA))
J R Best John Griffin Owen Mullen

Placings:260 (3779)
2009: 6²SD, 5⁶GF, 6⁰G,

	Starts	1st	2nd	3rd	Win & Pl
Career Total (Turf)	2	0	0	0	1215
Career Total (AW)	1	0	1	0	705

Going (Turf): Sf: 0-0 GS: 0-0 Gd: 0-1 GF: 0-1 Fm: 0-0
Distance: 5f/6f: 0-3 7f-8f: 0-0 9f-13f: 0-0 14f+: 0-0
Track : LH: 0-1 RH: 0-0 Tight: 0-1 Gall: 0-0
Aids: Bl: 0-0 Vi: 0-0 Tstrap: 0-0 Ckp: 0-0
Best Rating: 77 6/09 Asct 5f gd-fm

Promising debut in 6f Polytrack maiden; sixth in Norfolk Stakes next time.

Diamond Lass (IRE)

99(97) (48)68
4-y-o b f Rock Of Gibraltar (IRE)-Keralba (USA) (Sheikh Albadou)
R A Fahey Mel Roberts and Ms Nicola Meese

Placings:456/300520005 (7403)
2009: 7³F, 8⁰SD, 9⁰G, 9⁵GF, 9²G, 10⁰GF, 8⁰GF, 10⁰GF, 8⁵SD,

	Starts	1st	2nd	3rd	Win & Pl
Career Total (Turf)	10	0	1	1	1599
Career Total (AW)	2	0	0	0	0

Going (Turf): Sf: 0-0 GS: 0-1 Gd: 0-2 GF: 0-6 Fm: 0-1
Distance: 5f/6f: 0-2 7f-8f: 0-3 9f-13f: 0-7 14f+: 0-0
Track : LH: 0-8 RH: 0-2 Tight: 0-4 Gall: 0-1
Aids: Bl: 0-0 Vi: 0-0 Tstrap: 0-0 Ckp: 0-0
Best Rating: 68 4/09 Thsk 7f firm

Modest; effective at up to9f; acts on good ground.

Diamond Laura

97(106) (78)85
2-y-o gr f Lucky Story (USA)-Erracht (Emarati (USA))
Mrs R A Carr (P D Evans 20/7) Middleham Park Racing XXXII

Placings:221401112320 (6292)
2009: 5²GF, 5²G, 5¹SD, 5⁴GS, 5⁰GF, 5¹SD, 5¹G, 6¹G, 6²GS, 6³GF, 5²SD, 6⁰SD,

	Starts	1st	2nd	3rd	Win & Pl
Career Total (Turf)	8	2	3	1	14343
Career Total (AW)	4	2	1	0	8095

82 8/09 Ches 6f18y GD £5180
71 7/09 Bevl 5f GD £2729
76 7/09 Wolv 5f216y STD £2729
78 5/09 Wolv 5f20y STD £4209
Total win prize-money £14850

Going (Turf): Sf: 0-0 GS: 0-2 **Gd: 2-3** GF: 0-3 Fm: 0-0
Distance: **5f/6f: 3-9** 7f-8f: 1-3 9f-13f: 0-0 14f+: 0-0
Track : **LH: 3-5** RH: 0-1 **Tight: 3-5** Gall: 0-1
Aids: Bl: 0-0 Vi: 0-0 Tstrap: 0-0 Ckp: 0-0
Best Rating: 85 8/09 Haml 6f5y gd-sft

Useful; effective over 5f-6f; acts on good ground and on Polytrack.

Diamond Paula (IRE)

75(78) (26)26
3-y-o b f Spartacus (IRE)-Balgren (IRE) (Ballad Rock)
P D Evans Diamond Racing Ltd

Placings:60 (5228)
2009: 7⁶G, 8⁰SF,

	Starts	1st	2nd	3rd	Win & Pl
Career Total (Turf)	1	0	0	0	0
Career Total (AW)	1	0	0	0	

Going (Turf): Sf: 0-0 GS: 0-0 Gd: 0-1 GF: 0-0 Fm: 0-0
Distance: 5f/6f: 0-0 7f-8f: 0-1 9f-13f: 0-1 14f+: 0-0
Track : LH: 0-1 RH: 0-0 Tight: 0-1 Gall: 0-0
Aids: Bl: 0-0 Vi: 0-0 Tstrap: 0-0 Ckp: 0-0
Best Rating: 26 8/09 Wolv 1m141y std-fst

Diamond Surprise

(96) (70)59
3-y-o b f Mark Of Esteem (IRE)-Lucky Dip (Tirol)
R J Smith (R Curtis 26/2) Miss Jackie Penny

Placings:5053-221300 (7229)
2009: 6²SD, 6²SD, 6¹SD, 8³SD, 6⁰SD, 8⁰SD,

	Starts	1st	2nd	3rd	Win & Pl
Career Total (Turf)	3	0	0	0	0
Career Total (AW)	7	1	2	2	4448

70 2/09 Sthl 6f (0-65)H STD £2047
Total win prize-money £2047

Going (Turf): Sf: 0-2 GS: 0-0 Gd: 0-0 GF: 0-1 Fm: 0-0
Distance: **5f/6f: 1-6** 7f-8f: 0-4 9f-13f: 0-0 14f+: 0-0
Track : **LH: 1-7** RH: 0-2 Tight: 0-2 Gall: 0-0
Aids: Bl: 0-0 Vi: 0-0 Tstrap: 0-0 Ckp: 0-0
Best Rating: 70 2/09 Sthl 6f stand

Modest; stays 6f and probably gets 7f; acts on Fibresand.

Diamond Twister (USA)

102(104) (78)72

3-y-o b c Omega Code (USA)-King's Pact (USA) (Slewacide (USA))

J R Best John Best

Placings:66236-3412646550200**24602005** (7524)

2009: 6^{3}SD, 8^{4}SD, 10^{1}SD, 10^{2}SD, 9^{6}GF, 12^{4}SD, 12^{6}SD, 10^{5}GF, 9^{5}G, 12^{0}GF, 7^{2}GF, 8^{0}G, 10^{0}GS, 7^{2}SD, 8^{4}SD, 7^{6}F, 9^{0}SD, 8^{2}SD, 10^{0}SD, 8^{0}SD, 10^{5}SD,

	Starts	1st	2nd	3rd	Win & Pl
Career Total (Turf)	10	0	1	0	907
Career Total (AW)	16	1	4	2	10855

71 2/09 Ling 1m2f STD £2729

Total win prize-money £2730

Going (Turf): Sf: 0-0 GS: 0-1 Gd: 0-2 GF: 0-6 Fm: 0-1
Distance: 5f/6f: 0-5 7f-8f: 0-8 9f-13f: 1-13 14f+: 0-0
Track : LH: 1-10 RH: 0-11 Tight: 1-11 Gall: 0-4
Aids: Bl: 0-0 Vi: 0-0 Tstrap: 0-0 Ckp: 0-0
Best Rating: 78 4/09 Kemp 1m4f stand

Modest; stays 1m2f; acts on fast groundsd; goes on Polytrack; has worn a tongue tie.

Diana's Choice (SAF)

112(106) (98)108

5-y-o b m Windrush (USA)-Fly To The Stars (SAF) (Desert Team (USA))

M F De Kock Sheikh Mohammed Bin Khalifa Al Maktoum

Placings:1/142114/6351-3114400 (4297)

2009: 6^{3}FT, 6^{1}GF, 6^{1}GF, 6^{4}FT, 6^{4}GF, 6^{0}G, 7^{0}G,

	Starts	1st	2nd	3rd	Win & Pl
Career Total (Turf)	16	7	1	1	125922
Career Total (AW)	2	0	0	1	20833

108 2/09 Ndas 6f110y (95-110)H G-F £50000
103 2/09 Ndas 6f (95-110)H G-F £50000
5/08 Keni 6f GD £5055
5/07 Keni 6f GD £4528
5/07 Keni 6f SFT £4528
1/07 Keni 5f GD £4528
12/06 Keni 4f GD £2987

Total win prize-money £121629

Going (Turf): Sf: 1-2 GS: 0-0 Gd: 4-11 GF: 2-3 Fm: 0-0
Distance: 5f/6f: 5-13 7f-8f: 1-4 9f-13f: 0-0 14f+: 0-0
Track : LH: 2-4 RH: 0-0 Tight: 0-0 Gall: 2-4
Aids: Bl: 0-0 Vi: 0-0 Tstrap: 0-0 Ckp: 0-0
Best Rating: 108 2/09 Ndas 6f110y gd-fm

Smart; successful in South Africa and Dubai; suited by 6f and fast ground.

Diane's Choice

94(100) (59)78

6-y-o ch m Komaite (USA)-Ramajana (USA) (Shadeed (USA))

Miss Gay Kelleway The Dark Side, Gay Kelleway

Placings:6330/**26151123**/0300025100**450**/**600**0001002103400-5060**330210003444405** (7880)

2009: 5^{5}GS, 5^{0}GF, 5^{6}GF, 5^{0}GF, 5^{3}SD, 5^{3}SD, 5^{0}GF, 5^{2}G, 5^{1}S, 5^{0}G, 5^{0}SD, 5^{0}SD, 6^{3}GF, 5^{4}GF, 5^{4}G, 7^{4}SD, 8^{4}SD, 6^{0}SD, 7^{5}SD,

	Starts	1st	2nd	3rd	Win & Pl
Career Total (Turf)	40	5	4	5	31873
Career Total (AW)	20	2	1	3	17325

63 8/09 Bath 5f11y (0-75)H SFT £3238
74 7/08 Brig 5f59y (0-70)H FRM £2775
92 8/07 Kemp 6f (0-105)H STD £9971
88 8/06 Leic 5f2y (0-90)H GD £11217
78 8/06 Ling 5f (0-75)H G-S £3238
69 2/06 Ling 5f STD £3886

Total win prize-money £34328

Going (Turf): Sf: 1-6 GS: 2-7 Gd: 1-11 GF: 0-15 Fm: 1-1
Distance: 5f/6f: 7-55 7f-8f: 0-5 9f-13f: 0-0 14f+: 0-0
Track : LH: 3-27 RH: 1-4 Tight: 1-13 Gall: 1-9
Aids: Bl: 0-3 Vi: 0-2 Tstrap: 0-2 Ckp: 0-2
Best Rating: 92 8/07 Kemp 6f stand

Moderate; effective at 5f-7f; acts on fast and easy ground; goes on Polytrack; has worn blinkers and an eyeshield.

Diapason (IRE)

103(103) (62)72

3-y-o b f Mull Of Kintyre (USA)-Suaad (IRE) (Fools Holme (USA))

Tom Dascombe John Brown

Placings:54-310000**61** (7861)

2009: 7^{3}GF, 7^{1}G, 8^{0}G, 7^{0}G, 8^{0}GF, 8^{0}GF, 7^{6}SD, 7^{1}SD,

	Starts	1st	2nd	3rd	Win & Pl
Career Total (Turf)	8	1	0	1	4129
Career Total (AW)	2	1	0	0	1706

12/09 Wolv 7f32y (0-65)H STD £1706
72 7/09 Leic 7f9y (0-70) GD £3238

Total win prize-money £4944

Going (Turf): Sf: 0-0 GS: 0-1 Gd: 1-4 GF: 0-3 Fm: 0-0
Distance: 5f/6f: 0-2 7f-8f: 2-6 9f-13f: 0-2 14f+: 0-0
Track : LH: 1-3 RH: 0-3 Tight: 1-3 Gall: 0-1
Aids: Bl: 0-0 Vi: 0-0 Tstrap: 0-0 Ckp: 0-0
Best Rating: 72 7/09 Leic 7f9y good

Fair; stays 7f; acts on good/fast ground and on Polytrack.

Dice (IRE)

101(96) (79)80

3-y-o b c Kalanisi (IRE)-Rain Dancer (IRE) (Sadler's Wells (USA))

L M Cumani DIC Racing Syndicate

Placings:03-20612622 (6543)

2009: 7^{2}G, 10^{0}GS, 9^{6}GF, 11^{1}F, 14^{2}G, 12^{6}GS, 13^{2}SD, 14^{2}GF,

	Starts	1st	2nd	3rd	Win & Pl
Career Total (Turf)	9	1	3	1	6796
Career Total (AW)	1	0	1	0	867

72 7/09 Brig 1m3f196y (0-75)H FRM £3406

Total win prize-money £3406

Going (Turf): Sf: 0-1 GS: 0-3 Gd: 0-2 GF: 0-2 Fm: 1-1
Distance: 5f/6f: 0-1 7f-8f: 0-2 9f-13f: 1-4 14f+: 0-3
Track : LH: 1-5 RH: 0-2 Tight: 0-4 Gall: 0-0
Aids: Bl: 0-0 Vi: 0-0 Tstrap: 0-0 Ckp: 0-0
Best Rating: 80 10/09 Wwck 1m6f213y gd-fm

Modest; stays 1m4f; acts on fast and soft ground.

Dicey Affair

93(96) (65)58

3-y-o b f Medicean-Lucky Dice (Perugino (USA))

G L Moore Heart Of The South Racing

Placings:0004-00400066064 (7877)

2009: 7^{0}SD, 6^{0}SD, 7^{4}GF, 7^{0}F, 7^{0}GS, 7^{0}GF, 7^{6}SS, 7^{6}G, 7^{0}G, 6^{6}SD, 7^{4}SD,

	Starts	1st	2nd	3rd	Win & Pl
Career Total (Turf)	8	0	0	0	241
Career Total (AW)	7	0	0	0	0

Going (Turf): Sf: 0-0 GS: 0-2 Gd: 0-2 GF: 0-3 Fm: 0-1
Distance: 5f/6f: 0-2 7f-8f: 0-13 9f-13f: 0-0 14f+: 0-0
Track : LH: 0-7 RH: 0-2 Tight: 0-5 Gall: 0-0
Aids: Bl: 0-0 Vi: 0-0 Tstrap: 0-1 Ckp: 0-1
Best Rating: 65 10/08 Ling 7f stand

Dichoh

101(108) (86)67

6-y-o b g Diktat-Hoh Dancer (Indian Ridge)

M Madgwick (Rae Guest 4/5) Derek J Willis

Placings:0121/65110260263/5230445-12110020052114364 (7664)

2009: 8^{1}SD, 8^{2}SD, 8^{1}SD, 8^{1}SD, 8^{0}SD, 7^{0}SD, 8^{2}GF, 11^{0}SD, 8^{0}G, 7^{5}GS, 8^{2}SD, 8^{1}GF, 7^{1}SS, 7^{4}G, 8^{3}SD, 8^{6}SD, 8^{4}SD,

	Starts	1st	2nd	3rd	Win & Pl
Career Total (Turf)	7	1	1	0	3529
Career Total (AW)	32	8	6	3	36435

82 10/09 Ling 7f (0-70) SS £1706
64 9/09 Sals 1m (0-65)H G-F £2719
79 3/09 Ling 1m STD £2047
78 3/09 Wolv 1m141y STD £1978
86 1/09 Wolv 1m141y STD £2729
94 3/07 Sthl 1m (0-85)H STD £4857
87 2/07 Sthl 1m (0-85)H STD £4857
81 12/06 Kemp 7f (0-70)H STD £4857
70 11/06 Wolv 7f32y SF £2590

Total win prize-money £28347

Going (Turf): Sf: 0-1 GS: 0-2 Gd: 0-2 GF: 1-2 Fm: 0-0
Distance: 5f/6f: 0-0 7f-8f: 7-30 9f-13f: 2-9 14f+: 0-0
Track : LH: 7-27 RH: 1-9 Tight: 5-20 Gall: 0-0
Aids: Bl: 0-2 Vi: 2-14 Tstrap: 3-6 Ckp: 3-6
Best Rating: 94 4/07 Sthl 1m stand

Modest; stays 1m and acts on sand; has worn various headgear.

Dick Turpin (IRE)

107 112

2-y-o b c Arakan (USA)-Merrily (Sharrood (USA))

R Hannon John Manley

Placings:111156 (6849)

2009: 6^{1}GS, 6^{1}G, 6^{1}G, 6^{1}S, 7^{5}G, 7^{6}G,

	Starts	1st	2nd	3rd	Win & Pl
Career Total (Turf)	6	4	0	0	208752

109 8/09 Fair 6f SFT £142718
108 7/09 Gdwd 6f GD £45416
99 7/09 Sals 6f GD £3885
86 6/09 Wind 6f G-S £2729

Total win prize-money £194750

Going (Turf): Sf: 1-1 GS: 1-1 Gd: 2-4 GF: 0-0 Fm: 0-0
Distance: 5f/6f: 4-4 7f-8f: 0-2 9f-13f: 0-0 14f+: 0-0
Track : LH: 0-0 RH: 1-2 Tight: 0-0 Gall: 1-1
Aids: Bl: 0-0 Vi: 0-0 Tstrap: 0-0 Ckp: 0-0
Best Rating: 112 10/09 Lonc 7f good

Smart; winner of the Group 2 Richmond at Goodwood and a valuable sales race at Fairyhouse; effective at 6f and acts on good and easy ground.

Dickie Deano

(84) (22)

5-y-o b g Sooty Tern-Chez Bonito (IRE) (Persian Bold)

J M Bradley Mrs J K Bradley

Placings:0/0050/0-0 (0647)

2009: 10^{0}SD,

	Starts	1st	2nd	3rd	Win & Pl
Career Total (Turf)	1	0	0	0	
Career Total (AW)	6	0	0	0	0

Going (Turf): Sf: 0-0 GS: 0-1 Gd: 0-0 GF: 0-0 Fm: 0-0
Distance: 5f/6f: 0-0 7f-8f: 0-1 9f-13f: 0-6 14f+: 0-0
Track : LH: 0-5 RH: 0-1 Tight: 0-6 Gall: 0-0
Aids: Bl: 0-0 Vi: 0-0 Tstrap: 0-0 Ckp: 0-0
Best Rating: 39 2/07 Wolv 1m1f103y std-slw

Dickie Le Davoir

106(104) (64)**87**
5-y-o b g Kyllachy-Downeaster Alexa (USA) (Red Ryder (USA))
R C Guest (John A Harris 24/9) Stan Wright

Placings:5140204P3/241000003614/1422122236660612 1014000500600-05004354521003005460 **(7681)**
2009: 5^{0}SD, 6^{5}SD, 6^{0}GF, 5^{0}GF, 5^{4}SD, 6^{3}G, 6^{5}G, 5^{4}GF, 7^{5}SD, 5^{2}GF, 6^{1}GS, 5^{0}GF, 6^{0}S, 5^{3}SD, 7^{0}GS, 5^{0}GF, 6^{5}SD, 5^{4}SD, 5^{6}SD, 6^{0}SD,

	Starts	1st	2nd	3rd	Win & Pl
Career Total (Turf)	42	6	4	2	50149
Career Total (AW)	28	3	5	3	11446

82	7/09	Pont	6f	(0-90)H	G-S	£9346
87	7/08	Pont	6f	(0-90)H	GD	£9346
81	6/08	Leic	5f218y	(0-75)H	G-F	£3238
63	6/08	Haml	6f5y		G-F	£2047
79	2/08	Kemp	7f		STD	£2047
78	1/08	Sthl	6f		STD	£1911
72	12/07	Wolv	7f32y		STD	£2388
93	5/07	Nott	6f15y	(0-95)H	G-S	£11658
75	5/06	Hayd	5f		HVY	£3238

Total win prize-money £45225

Going (Turf): Sf: 1-11 **GS: 2-8** Gd: 1-10 **GF: 2-13** Fm: 0-0
Distance: **5f/6f: 5-51** 7f-8f: 4-19 9f-13f: 0-0 14f+: 0-0
Track : **LH: 4-34** RH: 1-3 **Tight: 1-12** Gall: 0-1
Aids: **Bl: 1-7** Vi: 0-5 Tstrap: 0-2 Ckp: 0-2
Best Rating: 93 5/07 Nott 6f15y gd-sft

Moderate; effective over 6f-7f; acts on most ground and on sand; has been visored; usually held up.

Dictation

(85) (36)**44**
7-y-o b/br m Diktat-Monaiya (Shareef Dancer (USA))
Mrs Valerie Keatley A Kennedy

Placings:5230100/0000050/604552/05000-0 **(0275)**
2009: 9^{0}SD,

	Starts	1st	2nd	3rd	Win & Pl
Career Total (Turf)	19	1	1	1	7361
Career Total (AW)	7	0	1	0	605

72	7/05	Baln	1m1f	(50-70)H	G-F	£5145

Total win prize-money £5146

Going (Turf): Sf: 0-1 GS: 0-0 Gd: 0-4 **GF: 1-8** Fm: 0-0
Distance: 5f/6f: 0-0 7f-8f: 0-5 **9f-13f: 1-21** 14f+: 0-0
Track : LH: 0-13 **RH: 1-12** Tight: 0-3 Gall: 0-0
Aids: **Bl: 1-21** Vi: 0-0 Tstrap: 0-1 Ckp: 0-1
Best Rating: 72 7/05 Baln 1m1f gd-fm

Diddums

100(95) (84)**77**
3-y-o b g Royal Applause-Sahara Shade (USA) (Shadeed (USA))
P S McEntee (J W Hills 24/10) Aspen Bloodstock Ltd

Placings:21402-400053150660000 **(7890)**
2009: 5^{4}GF, 6^{0}SD, 7^{0}G, 7^{0}SF, 6^{5}GF, 6^{3}GF, 6^{1}GF, 6^{5}GF, 6^{0}G, 6^{6}SD, 6^{0}SD, 6^{0}SD, 7^{0}SD, 6^{0}SD, 6^{0}SD,

	Starts	1st	2nd	3rd	Win & Pl
Career Total (Turf)	10	2	0	1	10044

	Starts	1st	2nd	3rd	Win & Pl
Career Total (AW)	10	0	2	0	2448

71	8/09	Gdwd	6f	(0-70)H	G-F	£3238
76	8/08	Donc	6f		GD	£5180

Total win prize-money £8419

Going (Turf): Sf: 0-0 GS: 0-0 **Gd: 1-3 GF: 1-7** Fm: 0-0
Distance: **5f/6f: 2-16** 7f-8f: 0-4 9f-13f: 0-0 14f+: 0-0
Track : LH: 0-7 RH: 0-4 Tight: 0-7 Gall: 0-0
Aids: Bl: 0-2 Vi: 0-0 Tstrap: 0-0 Ckp: 0-0
Best Rating: 84 10/08 Wolv 5f216y stand

Modest; effective over 6f; acts on good ground; also goes on Polytrack; has worn blinkers.

Die Haard

(88) (59)
3-y-o ch g Haafhd-Decision Maid (USA) (Diesis)
J R Gask For Sale

Placings:000-0 **(6442)**
2009: 7^{0}SS,

	Starts	1st	2nd	3rd	Win & Pl
Career Total (Turf)	0	0	0	0	
Career Total (AW)	4	0	0	0	

Going (Turf): Sf: 0-0 GS: 0-0 Gd: 0-0 GF: 0-0 Fm: 0-0
Distance: 5f/6f: 0-1 7f-8f: 0-3 9f-13f: 0-0 14f+: 0-0
Track : LH: 0-4 RH: 0-0 Tight: 0-3 Gall: 0-1
Aids: Bl: 0-0 Vi: 0-0 Tstrap: 0-0 Ckp: 0-0
Best Rating: 59 11/08 GrLe 6f stand

Diego Rivera

94(99) (69)**72**
4-y-o b g Orpen (USA)-Manuka Too (IRE) (First Trump)
P J Makin Mrs P J Makin and Mrs R B Denny

Placings:0022520-6401000360 **(6904)**
2009: 8^{6}SD, 8^{4}SD, 8^{0}SD, 7^{1}SD, 8^{0}SD, 7^{0}G, 7^{0}SD, 7^{3}SD, 7^{6}SD, 6^{0}G,

	Starts	1st	2nd	3rd	Win & Pl
Career Total (Turf)	7	0	2	0	2698
Career Total (AW)	10	1	1	1	3888

69	4/09	Wolv	7f32y	(0-65)H	STD	£2729

Total win prize-money £2730

Going (Turf): Sf: 0-2 GS: 0-1 Gd: 0-3 GF: 0-1 Fm: 0-0
Distance: 5f/6f: 0-4 **7f-8f: 1-13** 9f-13f: 0-0 14f+: 0-0
Track : **LH: 1-8** RH: 0-3 **Tight: 1-7** Gall: 0-1
Aids: Bl: 0-0 Vi: 0-1 Tstrap: 0-0 Ckp: 0-0
Best Rating: 72 7/08 Newb 6f8y soft

Modest; effective over 6f; acts on soft ground; also goes on Polytrack.

Dies Solis

84 **56**
2-y-o ch c Exceed And Excel (AUS)-Rose Of America (Brief Truce (USA))
I Semple A Gauley

Placings:556 **(7167)**
2009: 7^{5}G, 6^{5}GF, 7^{6}S,

	Starts	1st	2nd	3rd	Win & Pl
Career Total (Turf)	3	0	0	0	0

Going (Turf): Sf: 0-1 GS: 0-0 Gd: 0-1 GF: 0-1 Fm: 0-0
Distance: 5f/6f: 0-1 7f-8f: 0-2 9f-13f: 0-0 14f+: 0-0
Track : LH: 0-2 RH: 0-0 Tight: 0-0 Gall: 0-0
Aids: Bl: 0-0 Vi: 0-0 Tstrap: 0-0 Ckp: 0-0
Best Rating: 56 9/09 Ayr 7f50y good

Modest form in maidens at 6-7f.

Dig Deep (IRE)

105(102) (79)**86**
7-y-o b g Entrepreneur-Diamond Quest (Rainbow Quest (USA))
J J Quinn Roberts Green Whittall-Williams Savidge

Placings:41140/0010/2201000130004001/6056000002-00440010052 **(7506)**
2009: 5^{0}GF, 5^{0}G, 5^{4}G, 5^{4}GF, 6^{0}GF, 7^{0}G, 7^{1}G, 7^{0}GF, 7^{0}SD, 5^{5}SD, 6^{2}SD,

	Starts	1st	2nd	3rd	Win & Pl
Career Total (Turf)	34	4	1	1	33728
Career Total (AW)	12	3	3	0	17244

77	8/09	Chep	7f16y	(0-85)H	GD	£5180
91	10/07	Pont	5f	(0-85)H	GD	£5181
96	7/07	Asct	5f	(0-85)H	G-F	£6477
104	4/07	Wolv	5f20y	(0-85)H	STD	£4857
91	12/06	Wolv	7f32y	(0-85)H	STD	£5297
81	9/05	Newb	7f	(0-80)H	G-F	£6962
61	6/05	Wolv	7f32y		STD	£2576

Total win prize-money £36534

Going (Turf): Sf: 0-1 GS: 0-8 **Gd: 2-10 GF: 2-14** Fm: 0-1
Distance: 5f/6f: 3-32 **7f-8f: 4-14** 9f-13f: 0-0 14f+: 0-0
Track : **LH: 4-20** RH: 0-5 **Tight: 3-14** Gall: 0-2
Aids: Bl: 0-0 Vi: 0-0 Tstrap: 0-0 Ckp: 0-0
Best Rating: 104 4/07 Wolv 5f20y stand

Fair; effective from 5f-6f; acts on fast ground and on sand.

Digger Derek (IRE)

98(96) (62)**73**
3-y-o b g Key Of Luck (USA)-Carson Dancer (USA) (Carson City (USA))
R A Fahey Dr W D Ashworth

Placings:35420411-450360440 **(6703)**
2009: 8^{4}SD, 9^{5}GF, 12^{0}GF, 10^{3}GF, 9^{6}G, 9^{0}G, 10^{4}S, 8^{4}G, 8^{0}SS,

	Starts	1st	2nd	3rd	Win & Pl
Career Total (Turf)	14	2	1	2	9983
Career Total (AW)	3	0	0	0	361

73	10/08	Nott	1m75y	(0-70)	G-S	£3238
71	10/08	Catt	7f	(0-85)	GD	£3885

Total win prize-money £7124

Going (Turf): Sf: 0-2 **GS: 1-2 Gd: 1-4** GF: 0-6 Fm: 0-0
Distance: 5f/6f: 0-1 7f-8f: 1-9 9f-13f: 1-7 14f+: 0-0
Track : **LH: 2-11** RH: 0-4 **Tight: 1-7** Gall: 0-0
Aids: Bl: 0-0 Vi: 0-0 Tstrap: 0-0 Ckp: 0-0
Best Rating: 73 10/08 Nott 1m75y gd-sft

Modest; stays 7f and acts on good and softer ground.

Diggeratt (USA)

99(99) (71)**77**
3-y-o gr/ro f Maria's Mon (USA)-Miss Exhilaration (USA) (Gulch (USA))
R A Fahey J A Rattigan

Placings:5120-05266113530 **(6370)**
2009: 7^{0}S, 6^{5}GF, 7^{2}G, 8^{6}GF, 7^{6}G, 7^{1}G, 8^{1}CF, 8^{3}SD, 7^{5}GF, 8^{3}SD, 8^{0}SD,

	Starts	1st	2nd	3rd	Win & Pl
Career Total (Turf)	12	3	2	0	11229
Career Total (AW)	3	0	0	2	605

72	8/09	Rdcr	1m	G-F	£2047
70	8/09	Carl	7f200y	GD	£2047
70	7/08	Pont	6f	GD	£1533

Total win prize-money £8627

Going (Turf): Sf: 0-1 GS: 0-1 **Gd: 2-5** GF: 1-4 Fm: 0-1

Distance:	5f/6f: 1-3 **7f-8f: 2-12** 9f-13f: 0-0 14f+: 0-0
Track :	LH: 1-3 RH: 1-5 Tight: 0-1 Gall: 0-0
Aids:	Bl: 0-0 Vi: 0-0 Tstrap: 0-2 Ckp: 0-2
Best Rating:	**77** 6/09 Donc 7f good

Fair; effective over 6f-1m; acts on good and fast ground.

Digit

87(73) (23)**62**

3-y-o ch f Reel Buddy (USA)-Compact Disc (IRE) (Royal Academy (USA))

B Smart B Smart

Placings:0245532210-0300 **(5621)**

2009: 6^{0}F, 6^{3}GF, 8^{0}GS, 7^{0}S,

	Starts	1st	2nd	3rd	Win & Pl
Career Total (Turf)	**13**	**1**	**3**	**2**	**5467**
Career Total (AW)	**1**	**0**	**0**	**0**	
62	10/08	Rdcr	7f	GD	£2388

Total win prize-money £2388

Going (Turf):	Sf: 0-2 GS: 0-4 **Gd: 1-3** GF: 0-3 Fm: 0-1
Distance:	5f/6f: 0-5 **7f-8f: 1-8** 9f-13f: 0-1 14f+: 0-0
Track :	LH: 0-5 RH: 0-2 Tight: 0-5 Gall: 0-0
Aids:	Bl: 0-0 Vi: 0-0 Tstrap: 0-0 Ckp: 0-0
Best Rating:	**62** 10/08 Rdcr 7f good

Modest; effective at around 6f-7f; acts on fast and soft ground.

Digital

100(104) (80)**85**

12-y-o ch g Safawan-Heavenly Goddess (Soviet Star (USA))

M R Channon W G R Wightman

Placings:423021/2020031000/0001633030445/051260202 04216002/**0**3403600522200022050 64/0400004256102120 5006/3500105003**620**/06443660424204502612 3130/**2**1033 4303020662-54540003600 **(5073)**

2009: 5^{5}G, 6^{4}GF, 6^{5}G, 5^{4}GF, 5^{0}GF, 5^{0}G, 6^{0}GF, 5^{3}GF, 5^{6}S, 5^{0}GF, 5^{0}GF,

	Starts	1st	2nd	3rd	Win & Pl
Career Total (Turf)	**146**	**11**	**24**	**17**	**150648**
Career Total (AW)	**5**	**0**	**1**	**0**	**771**

84	4/08	Bath	5f11y	(0-75)H	GD	£2590
79	9/07	Rdcr	5f	(0-70)H	G-S	£2817
68	9/07	Bath	5f161y	(0-75)H	FRM	£2979
81	5/06	Bath	5f161y	(0-70)H	SFT	£3562
80	8/05	Wind	6f	(0-70)	G-F	£4108
74	7/05	Carl	6f192y	(0-70)H	G-F	£3511
101	9/03	Gdwd	7f	B(0-105)H	G-F	£10776
91	5/03	Ling	7f140y	D(0-80)	GD	£5703
92	5/02	Newb	7f	D(0-85)H	G-S	£5642
94	7/01	York	6f214y	C(0-90)H	GD	£9880
91	10/00	Nott	1m54y	E(0-75)H	SFT	£3172

Total win prize-money £54741

Going (Turf):	Sf: 2-27GS: 2-18**Gd: 3-43 GF: 3-54** Fm: 1-3
Distance:	5f/6f: 5-49 7f-8f: 5-92 9f-13f: 1-9 14f+: 0-0
Track :	**LH: 5-41** RH: 2-24 Tight: 0-16 **Gall: 5-23**
Aids:	Bl: 0-0 **Vi: 2-21** Tstrap: 0-0 Ckp: 0-0
Best Rating:	**101** 10/03 Donc 7f gd-fm

Fair; stays 1m, but effective at much shorter; acts on most types of ground; has worn a visor.

Dijeerr (USA)

103(110) (110)**113**

5-y-o b h Danzig (USA)-Sharp Minister (CAN) (Deputy Minister (CAN))

Saeed Bin Suroor (M bin Shafya 28/3) Godolphin

Placings:2121/022/2221204-001051 **(5855)**

2009: 7^{0}GS, 8^{0}G, 8^{1}FT, 8^{0}FT, 8^{5}GF, 7^{1}GF,

	Starts	1st	2nd	3rd	Win & Pl
Career Total (Turf)	**18**	**4**	**8**	**0**	**130165**
Career Total (AW)	**2**	**1**	**0**	**0**	**45833**

106	9/09	Ches	7f122y	G-F	£9066
110	2/09	Ndas	1m	FST	£45833
113	8/08	NmkJ	1m	GD	£12462
106	10/06	Newb	7f	HVY	£22712
88	9/06	Leic	7f9y	G-F	£4533

Total win prize-money £94607

Going (Turf):	Sf: 1-3 GS: 0-2 Gd: 1-8 **GF: 2-5** Fm: 0-0
Distance:	5f/6f: 0-1 **7f-8f: 5-16** 9f-13f: 0-3 14f+: 0-0
Track :	**LH: 2-9** RH: 0-2 Tight: 1-3 Gall: 1-7
Aids:	Bl: 0-0 **Vi: 3-13** Tstrap: 0-0 Ckp: 0-0
Best Rating:	**113** 8/08 NmkJ 1m good

Smart; effective up to 1m; handles most ground; has worn a tongue tie and a visor.

Diktalina

96(97) (64)**56**

3-y-o b f Diktat-Oiselina (FR) (Linamix (FR))

Mrs A M Thorpe (W R Muir 20/10) The Cartmel Syndicate

Placings:060-0021450200 **(6917)**

2009: 11^{0}GS, 12^{0}GF, 12^{2}SD, 11^{1}G, 12^{4}SD, 11^{5}G, 13^{0}G, 13^{2}GF, 16^{0}GF, 12^{0}SD,

	Starts	1st	2nd	3rd	Win & Pl
Career Total (Turf)	**8**	**1**	**1**	**0**	**2652**
Career Total (AW)	**5**	**0**	**1**	**0**	**605**
56	7/09	Wind	1m3f135y	GD	£2047

Total win prize-money £2047

Going (Turf):	Sf: 0-0 GS: 0-1 **Gd: 1-4** GF: 0-3 Fm: 0-0
Distance:	5f/6f: 0-0 7f-8f: 0-3 **9f-13f: 1-7** 14f+: 0-3
Track :	LH: 0-9 RH: 0-1 **Tight: 1-11** Gall: 0-1
Aids:	Bl: 0-0 Vi: 0-0 Tstrap: 0-0 Ckp: 0-0
Best Rating:	**64** 10/08 Ling 1m stand

Moderate; stays 1m4f; acts on good ground and on Polytrack.

Diktaram

82(90) (45)**46**

3-y-o b g Diktat-Aries (GER) (Big Shuffle (USA))

J R Weymes High Moor Racing 5

Placings:0-56000 **(3954)**

2009: 11^{5}SD, 12^{6}GF, 12^{0}GS, 12^{0}SD, 14^{0}SD,

	Starts	1st	2nd	3rd	Win & Pl
Career Total (Turf)	**2**	**0**	**0**	**0**	**0**
Career Total (AW)	**4**	**0**	**0**	**0**	**0**

Going (Turf):	**Sf: 0-0 GS: 0-1 Gd: 0-0 GF: 0-1 Fm: 0-0**
Distance:	5f/6f: 0-0 7f-8f: 0-0 9f-13f: 0-5 14f+: 0-1
Track :	LH: 0-4 RH: 0-2 Tight: 0-4 Gall: 0-0
Aids:	Bl: 0-0 Vi: 0-1 Tstrap: 0-1 Ckp: 0-1
Best Rating:	**46** 4/09 Muss 1m4f100y gd-fm

Diktat Queen

98 **75**

3-y-o b f Diktat-Sakura Queen (IRE) (Woodman (USA))

Rae Guest Barry Stewart

Placings:6100 **(6937)**

2009: 7^{6}GF, 7^{1}G, 8^{0}G, 8^{0}G,

	Starts	1st	2nd	3rd	Win & Pl
Career Total (Turf)	**4**	**1**	**0**	**0**	**2590**
75	9/09	Chep	7f16y	GD	£2590

Total win prize-money £2590

Going (Turf):	Sf: 0-0 GS: 0-0 **Gd: 1-3** GF: 0-1 Fm: 0-0
Distance:	5f/6f: 0-0 **7f-8f: 1-2** 9f-13f: 0-2 14f+: 0-0
Track :	LH: 0-2 RH: 0-0 Tight: 0-1 Gall: 0-1
Aids:	Bl: 0-0 Vi: 0-0 Tstrap: 0-0 Ckp: 0-0
Best Rating:	**75** 9/09 Chep 7f16y good

Diktatorship (IRE)

(107) (54)**50**

6-y-o b g Diktat-Polka Dancer (Dancing Brave (USA))

Jennie Candlish The J C R Partnership

Placings:50044/000032500**U0**/351600242120**2400630**/46-23356 **(7750)**

2009: 13^{2}SD, 12^{3}SD, 12^{3}SD, 16^{5}SD, 13^{6}SD,

	Starts	1st	2nd	3rd	Win & Pl
Career Total (Turf)	**15**	**0**	**1**	**1**	**1588**
Career Total (AW)	**27**	**2**	**5**	**4**	**7961**

60	5/07	Sthl	1m3f	(0-45)	STD	£1876
59	1/07	Wolv	1m4f50y	(0-45)	STD	£1911

Total win prize-money £3788

Going (Turf):	**Sf: 0-1 GS: 0-2 Gd: 0-3 GF: 0-9 Fm: 0-0**
Distance:	5f/6f: 0-4 7f-8f: 0-4 **9f-13f: 2-23** 14f+: 0-11
Track :	**LH: 2-33** RH: 0-4 **Tight: 1-26** Gall: 0-1
Aids:	Bl: 0-2 Vi: 0-3 Tstrap: 1-7 Ckp: 1-7
Best Rating:	**73** 6/05 Donc 6f gd-fm

Moderate; stays at least 1m4f; acts on sand.

Dillenda

78 **56**

3-y-o b/br f Lend A Hand-Samadilla (IRE) (Mujadil (USA))

T D Easterby W T Whittle

Placings:062-00 **(2786)**

2009: 7^{0}GF, 7^{0}GF,

	Starts	1st	2nd	3rd	Win & Pl
Career Total (Turf)	**5**	**0**	**1**	**0**	**605**

Going (Turf):	**Sf: 0-1 GS: 0-1 Gd: 0-0 GF: 0-3 Fm: 0-0**
Distance:	5f/6f: 0-1 7f-8f: 0-4 9f-13f: 0-0 14f+: 0-0
Track :	LH: 0-1 RH: 0-2 Tight: 0-1 Gall: 0-0
Aids:	Bl: 0-0 Vi: 0-0 Tstrap: 0-0 Ckp: 0-0
Best Rating:	**56** 9/08 Hayd 6f gd-fm

Moderate; effective over 7f; acts on easy ground.

Dilli Dancer

92(93) (54)**64**

4-y-o b f Dansili-Cup Of Kindness (USA) (Secretariat (USA))

G D Blake Adrian Smith

Placings:5460405 **(6777)**

2009: 6^{5}GF, 6^{4}GF, 5^{6}S, 7^{0}G, 7^{4}SD, 5^{0}SD, 6^{5}SD,

	Starts	1st	2nd	3rd	Win & Pl
Career Total (Turf)	**4**	**0**	**0**	**0**	**241**
Career Total (AW)	**3**	**0**	**0**	**0**	**0**

Going (Turf):	**Sf: 0-1 GS: 0-0 Gd: 0-1 GF: 0-2 Fm: 0-0**
Distance:	5f/6f: 0-5 7f-8f: 0-2 9f-13f: 0-0 14f+: 0-0
Track :	LH: 0-1 RH: 0-3 Tight: 0-1 Gall: 0-0
Aids:	Bl: 0-0 Vi: 0-0 Tstrap: 0-0 Ckp: 0-0
Best Rating:	**64** 5/09 Sals 6f gd-fm

Dimaire

97(94) (64)**64**

2-y-o b f Kheleyf (USA)-Dim Ots (Alhijaz)

D Haydn Jones G J Hicks

Placings:00622432 (7748)

2009: 6^{0}SD, 7^{0}SD, 5^{6}G, 5^{2}G, 5^{2}SD, 5^{4}G, 5^{3}SD, 5^{2}SD,

	Starts	1st	2nd	3rd	Win & Pl
Career Total (Turf)	3	0	1	0	1421
Career Total (AW)	5	0	2	1	2177

Going (Turf): Sf: 0-0 GS: 0-0 Gd: 0-3 GF: 0-0 Fm: 0-0
Distance: 5f/6f: 0-7 7f-8f: 0-1 9f-13f: 0-0 14f+: 0-0
Track : LH: 0-4 RH: 0-1 Tight: 0-2 Gall: 0-2
Aids: Bl: 0-0 Vi: 0-0 Tstrap: 0-0 Ckp: 0-0
Best Rating: 64 9/09 Sthl 5f stand

Modest; suited by 5f; acts on good ground; goes on Fibresand and Polytrack.

Diman Waters (IRE)

91 **65**

2-y-o br g Namid-Phantom Waters (Pharly (FR))

E J Alston Con Harrington

Placings:5406 (7242)

2009: 6^{5}S, 6^{4}GF, 6^{0}S, 5^{6}S,

	Starts	1st	2nd	3rd	Win & Pl
Career Total (Turf)	4	0	0	0	361

Going (Turf): Sf: 0-3 GS: 0-0 Gd: 0-0 GF: 0-1 Fm: 0-0
Distance: 5f/6f: 0-3 7f-8f: 0-1 9f-13f: 0-0 14f+: 0-0
Track : LH: 0-0 RH: 0-0 Tight: 0-0 Gall: 0-0
Aids: Bl: 0-0 Vi: 0-0 Tstrap: 0-0 Ckp: 0-0
Best Rating: 65 6/09 Donc 6f gd-fm

Modest; stays 6f; acts on fast ground.

Dimashq

98(93) (33)**61**

7-y-o b m Mtoto-Agwaas (IRE) (Rainbow Quest (USA))

P T Midgley A Bell

Placings:00620034100/0021000/56/33156-0656151053200 (7336)

2009: 12^{0}G, 16^{6}GF, 14^{5}GF, 13^{6}GF, 12^{1}GS, 11^{5}GF, 11^{1}GS, 12^{0}G, 13^{5}G, 12^{3}G, 13^{2}G, 11^{0}S, 14^{0}SD,

	Starts	1st	2nd	3rd	Win & Pl
Career Total (Turf)	33	5	3	4	16584
Career Total (AW)	5	0	0	0	0

54	7/09	Catt	1m3f214y		G-S	£2388
54	6/09	Ripn	1m4f10y	(0-65)H	G-S	£2810
61	7/08	Muss	1m5f	(0-65)H	G-F	£2498
48	8/06	Bevl	2m35y	(0-60)H	GD	£3238
52	10/05	Wwck	1m4f134y		GD	£1298

Total win prize-money £12235

Going (Turf): Sf: 0-2 GS: 2-3 Gd: 2-14 GF: 1-13 Fm: 0-1
Distance: 5f/6f: 0-0 7f-8f: 0-1 9f-13f: 4-21 14f+: 1-16
Track : LH: 2-22 RH: 3-15 Tight: 4-27 Gall: 0-2
Aids: Bl: 0-0 Vi: 0-0 Tstrap: 0-0 Ckp: 0-0
Best Rating: 61 7/08 Muss 1m5f gd-fm

Moderate; stays 2m but effective at 1m4f; acts on fast and easy ground.

Diminuto

(104) (80)**78**

5-y-o b m Iron Mask (USA)-Thicket (Wolfhound (USA))

M D I Usher R H Brookes

Placings:33255530631044331114/2204224331543110503020/263055450660156502000-000600 (0946)

2009: 5^{0}SD, 7^{0}SD, 5^{0}SD, 5^{6}SD, 6^{0}SD, 6^{0}SD,

	Starts	1st	2nd	3rd	Win & Pl
Career Total (Turf)	24	3	2	5	15252
Career Total (AW)	44	4	6	6	21706

69	7/08	Wolv	5f216y	(0-60)H	STD	£2388
78	7/07	Catt	5f	(0-85)H	GD	£5181
72	7/07	Bath	5f161y	(0-75)H	G-S	£2979
67	5/07	Sthl	5f	(0-70)H	STD	£3562
63	12/06	Sthl	5f	(0-75)	STD	£3238
54	12/06	Sthl	5f	(0-75)	STD	£3238
55	8/06	Bath	5f11y		FRM	£2266

Total win prize-money £22856

Going (Turf): Sf: 0-2 GS: 1-5 Gd: 1-6 GF: 0-8 Fm: 1-3
Distance: 5f/6f: 7-65 7f-8f: 0-3 9f-13f: 0-0 14f+: 0-0
Track : LH: 3-34 RH: 0-8 Tight: 1-16 Gall: 2-11
Aids: Bl: 0-0 Vi: 0-0 Tstrap: 0-0 Ckp: 0-0
Best Rating: 80 1/08 Sthl 5f stand

Modest; suited by 5f-6f; acts on fast ground; also goes on Fibresand and Polytrack.

Dingaan (IRE)

103(107) (93)**88**

6-y-o b g Tagula (IRE)-Boughtbyphone (Warning)

A M Balding Lady C S Cadbury

Placings:033/110165050/010006004444/40222334200-003421460 (6429)

2009: 7^{0}GF, 7^{0}G, 7^{3}G, 7^{4}GF, 8^{2}G, 8^{1}GF, 8^{4}F, 8^{6}GF, 8^{0}GF,

	Starts	1st	2nd	3rd	Win & Pl
Career Total (Turf)	32	2	4	5	42402
Career Total (AW)	12	3	1	0	43312

86	7/09	Bath	1m5y	(0-80)H	G-F	£6308
93	6/07	Gdwd	6f	(0-100)H	GD	£16514
94	5/06	Kemp	7f	(0-105)H	STD	£28044
89	1/06	Ling	6f	(0-85)H	STD	£6477
84	1/06	Ling	6f		STD	£3238

Total win prize-money £60583

Going (Turf): Sf: 0-0 GS: 0-8 Gd: 1-10 GF: 1-12 Fm: 0-2
Distance: 5f/6f: 3-16 7f-8f: 1-26 9f-13f: 1-2 14f+: 0-0
Track : LH: 3-13 RH: 1-10 Tight: 3-12 Gall: 0-2
Aids: Bl: 0-1 Vi: 0-4 Tstrap: 0-5 Ckp: 0-5
Best Rating: 94 5/06 Kemp 7f stand

Useful; effective over 6f-7f; acts on fast ground; also goes on Polytrack; has worn blinkers, cheekpieces and a visor.

Dinkie Short

89(85) (56)**62**

2-y-o b g Reset (AUS)-Spring Sunrise (Robellino (USA))

W R Muir Mrs D Vaughan

Placings:06600 (6586)

2009: 7^{0}G, 8^{6}G, 7^{6}GF, 8^{0}SD, 7^{0}SD,

	Starts	1st	2nd	3rd	Win & Pl
Career Total (Turf)	3	0	0	0	0
Career Total (AW)	2	0	0	0	

Going (Turf): Sf: 0-0 GS: 0-0 Gd: 0-2 GF: 0-1 Fm: 0-0
Distance: 5f/6f: 0-0 7f-8f: 0-4 9f-13f: 0-1 14f+: 0-0
Track : LH: 0-2 RH: 0-3 Tight: 0-2 Gall: 0-0
Aids: Bl: 0-1 Vi: 0-0 Tstrap: 0-0 Ckp: 0-0
Best Rating: 62 8/09 Gdwd 1m good

Dinky Deb

30(60) (16)

2-y-o ch f Captain Rio-Debinnair (FR) (Wolfhound (USA))

D K Ivory D R Tucker

Placings:060 (2457)

2009: 5^{0}SD, 5^{6}SD, 5^{0}GF,

	Starts	1st	2nd	3rd	Win & Pl
Career Total (Turf)	1	0	0	0	
Career Total (AW)	2	0	0	0	0

Going (Turf): Sf: 0-0 GS: 0-0 Gd: 0-0 GF: 0-1 Fm: 0-0
Distance: 5f/6f: 0-3 7f-8f: 0-0 9f-13f: 0-0 14f+: 0-0
Track : LH: 0-2 RH: 0-0 Tight: 0-2 Gall: 0-0
Aids: Bl: 0-0 Vi: 0-0 Tstrap: 0-0 Ckp: 0-0
Best Rating: 16 5/09 Ling 5f stand

Dinkys Diamond (IRE)

82 **54**

2-y-o b g Modigliani (USA)-Along Came Molly (Dr Fong (USA))

B Ellison Dorothy & William Gibson

Placings:0650 (6046)

2009: 6^{0}S, 7^{6}GS, 6^{5}G, 7^{0}G,

	Starts	1st	2nd	3rd	Win & Pl
Career Total (Turf)	4	0	0	0	0

Going (Turf): Sf: 0-1 GS: 0-1 Gd: 0-2 GF: 0-0 Fm: 0-0
Distance: 5f/6f: 0-2 7f-8f: 0-2 9f-13f: 0-0 14f+: 0-0
Track : LH: 0-1 RH: 0-0 Tight: 0-0 Gall: 0-0
Aids: Bl: 0-0 Vi: 0-0 Tstrap: 0-0 Ckp: 0-0
Best Rating: 54 8/09 Ripn 6f good

Dinner Date

99(106) (76)**64**

7-y-o ch g Groom Dancer (USA)-Misleading Lady (Warning)

T Keddy Mrs H Keddy

Placings:0/05605001066/2130000500/3456120/0151030615-40000003321310 (7684)

2009: 8^{4}SD, 8^{0}SD, 8^{0}SD, 10^{0}G, 10^{0}GF, 8^{0}G, 10^{0}GF, 10^{3}GF, 10^{3}GF, 10^{2}SD, 8^{1}SD, 8^{3}SD, 8^{1}SD, 10^{0}SD,

	Starts	1st	2nd	3rd	Win & Pl
Career Total (Turf)	19	1	1	3	5353
Career Total (AW)	34	7	2	3	19055

76	11/09	Kemp	1m	(0-75)H	STD	£2590
74	10/09	Kemp	1m	(0-65)H	STD	£1706
72	11/08	Kemp	1m	(0-70)H	STD	£2266
71	4/08	Kemp	1m	(0-65)H	STD	£2047
68	3/08	Kemp	1m	(0-65)H	STD	£2047
62	11/07	Kemp	1m2f	(0-52)H	STD	£2047
68	5/06	Kemp	1m2f	(0-65)H	STD	£3238
52	8/05	Yarm	1m2f21y		G-F	£2912

Total win prize-money £18857

Going (Turf): Sf: 0-2 GS: 0-1 Gd: 0-3 GF: 1-13 Fm: 0-0
Distance: 5f/6f: 0-0 7f-8f: 5-13 9f-13f: 3-40 14f+: 0-0
Track : LH: 1-24 RH: 7-27 Tight: 1-19 Gall: 0-5
Aids: Bl: 0-0 Vi: 0-0 Tstrap: 0-0 Ckp: 0-0
Best Rating: 76 11/09 Kemp 1m stand

Modest; effective from 1m-1m2f; acts on fast ground and on Polytrack.

Dirar (IRE)

101(116) (96)**95**

4-y-o b g King's Best (USA)-Dibiya (IRE) (Caerleon (USA))

Gordon Elliott Michael White

Placings:31/25625310-2051 **(7720)**

2009: 14^{2}G, 18^{0}G, 10^{5}SD, 12^{1}SD,

	Starts	1st	2nd	3rd	Win & Pl
Career Total (Turf)	8	1	1	2	12080
Career Total (AW)	6	2	2	0	23442

96 12/09 Wolv 1m4f50y (0-100)H STD £11215

95 8/08 Dpat 1m4f110y G-Y £7621

82 11/07 Dund 1m STD £5836

Total win prize-money £24673

Going (Turf): Sf: 0-0 GS: 0-0 Gd: 0-4 GF: 0-1 Fm: 0-0

Distance: 5f/6f: 0-0 7f-8f: 1-3 9f-13f: 2-9 14f+: 0-2

Track : LH: 1-8 RH: 1-4 Tight: 1-1 Gall: 0-1

Aids: Bl: 0-0 Vi: 0-0 Tstrap: 0-0 Ckp: 0-0

Best Rating: 96 12/09 Wolv 1m4f50y stand

Very useful; stays 1m6f; handles good going and Polytrack.

Direct Debit (IRE)

101(101) (84)**66**

6-y-o b g Dansili-Dimple (Fairy King (USA))

M Wellings Nicholls Family

Placings:5/12320/0003213/00416-05003040 **(3689)**

2009: 8^{0}SD, 7^{5}SD, 10^{0}SD, 10^{0}GF, 8^{3}G, 7^{0}GF, 8^{4}GF, 8^{0}G,

	Starts	1st	2nd	3rd	Win & Pl
Career Total (Turf)	16	1	2	4	14785
Career Total (AW)	10	2	1	0	7362

81 11/08 Wolv 1m141y STD £1978

85 7/07 Asct 1m G-F £6477

76 1/06 Ling 1m STD £3071

Total win prize-money £11527

Going (Turf): Sf: 0-0 GS: 0-1 Gd: 0-5 GF: 1-10 Fm: 0-0

Distance: 5f/6f: 0-0 7f-8f: 2-16 9f-13f: 1-10 14f+: 0-0

Track : LH: 2-12 RH: 0-5 Tight: 2-12 Gall: 0-0

Aids: Bl: 0-0 Vi: 0-0 Tstrap: 0-1 Ckp: 0-1

Best Rating: 92 4/06 Sand 1m14y good

Fair; effective from 7f-1m2f; acts on decent ground on turf, also acts on Polytrack.

Directa's Digger (IRE)

90(51) **76**

5-y-o b h Daggers Drawn (USA)-Chita Rivera (Chief Singer)

M J Scudamore M Scudamore

Placings:633/2354/02121105-0 **(2445)**

2009: 14^{0}GS,

	Starts	1st	2nd	3rd	Win & Pl
Career Total (Turf)	15	3	3	3	15336
Career Total (AW)	1	0	0	0	0

63 6/08 Muss 2m2f37y (0-70)H G-F £4209

76 6/08 Carl 1m6f32y (0-70)H G-F £2590

71 5/08 Hayd 1m6f (0-70)H GD £2590

Total win prize-money £9389

Going (Turf): Sf: 0-5 GS: 0-2 Gd: 1-3 GF: 2-5 Fm: 0-0

Distance: 5f/6f: 0-0 7f-8f: 0-3 9f-13f: 0-3 14f+: 3-10

Track : LH: 1-8 RH: 2-3 Tight: 1-4 Gall: 0-2

Aids: Bl: 0-0 Vi: 3-8 Tstrap: 0-1 Ckp: 0-1

Best Rating: 76 6/08 Carl 1m6f32y gd-fm

Fair; stays 2m2f; acts on good ground; has worn a visor and cheekpieces.

Director's Chair

98(100) (66)**72**

4-y-o b g Catcher In The Rye (IRE)-Capegulch (USA) (Gulch (USA))

Miss J Feilden Ocean Trailers Ltd

Placings:5322001500-0104006 **(7440)**

2009: 10^{0}SD, 10^{1}G, 10^{0}GF, 10^{4}GF, 10^{0}S, 8^{0}G, 12^{6}SD,

	Starts	1st	2nd	3rd	Win & Pl
Career Total (Turf)	8	2	2	0	5785
Career Total (AW)	9	0	0	1	363

72 3/09 Donc 1m2f60y (0-70)H GD £2498

70 7/08 Yarm 1m2f21y (0-65)H G-F £1942

Total win prize-money £4441

Going (Turf): Sf: 0-1 GS: 0-0 Gd: 1-2 GF: 1-5 Fm: 0-0

Distance: 5f/6f: 0-0 7f-8f: 0-2 9f-13f: 2-15 14f+: 0-0

Track : LH: 2-11 RH: 0-6 Tight: 1-6 Gall: 1-5

Aids: Bl: 0-4 Vi: 0-0 Tstrap: 0-2 Ckp: 0-2

Best Rating: 72 3/09 Donc 1m2f60y good

Modest; effective over 1m2f; acts on fast ground.

Directorship

98 **83**

3-y-o br c Diktat-Away To Me (Exit To Nowhere (USA))

P R Chamings Mrs Lyon, Mrs Hayton & Exors Mrs Jenkins

Placings:04-01660 **(6740)**

2009: 10^{0}S, 8^{1}GF, 8^{6}GF, 10^{6}GF, 10^{0}GS,

	Starts	1st	2nd	3rd	Win & Pl
Career Total (Turf)	7	1	0	0	3647

83 7/09 Sand 1m14y G-F £3238

Total win prize-money £3238

Going (Turf): Sf: 0-2 GS: 0-2 Gd: 0-0 GF: 1-3 Fm: 0-0

Distance: 5f/6f: 0-0 7f-8f: 0-2 9f-13f: 1-5 14f+: 0-0

Track : LH: 0-1 RH: 1-4 Tight: 0-1 Gall: 0-1

Aids: Bl: 0-0 Vi: 0-0 Tstrap: 0-0 Ckp: 0-0

Best Rating: 83 7/09 Sand 1m14y gd-fm

Useful; stays 1m; acts on fast ground; handles cut.

Diriculous

97(110) (107)**94**

5-y-o b g Diktat-Sheila's Secret (IRE) (Bluebird (USA))

T G Mills Sherwoods Transport Ltd

Placings:41/151213150131322-306030500 **(6949)**

2009: 6^{3}SD, 6^{0}S, 6^{6}SD, 6^{0}GF, 6^{3}G, 6^{0}G, 6^{5}SD, 6^{0}SS, 6^{0}SD,

	Starts	1st	2nd	3rd	Win & Pl
Career Total (Turf)	7	0	0	3	3274
Career Total (AW)	19	7	3	2	36348

103 8/08 GrLe 6f (0-95)H STD £7477

93 7/08 GrLe 6f (0-85)H STD £5180

85 5/08 Sthl 6f (0-80)H STD £4533

83 4/08 Sthl 6f (0-75)H STD £3561

78 2/08 Kemp 6f (0-75)H STD £2590

73 1/08 Sthl 6f (0-60)H STD £1911

66 11/07 Kemp 6f STD £2047

Total win prize-money £27303

Going (Turf): Sf: 0-2 GS: 0-1 Gd: 0-2 GF: 0-2 Fm: 0-0

Distance: 5f/6f: 7-26 7f-8f: 0-0 9f-13f: 0-0 14f+: 0-0

Track : LH: 5-13 RH: 2-6 Tight: 0-4 Gall: 2-6

Aids: Bl: 0-4 Vi: 0-0 Tstrap: 0-1 Ckp: 0-1

Best Rating: 107 12/08 GrLe 6f stand

Smart; effective over 6f; acts on most ground on turf; goes on sand.

Discanti (IRE)

105(92) (58)**84**

4-y-o ch g Distant Music (USA)-Gertie Laurie (Lomond (USA))

T D Easterby The Lapin Blanc Racing Partnership

Placings:06306/41313-3603645100 **(6647)**

2009: 5^{3}GF, 5^{6}SD, 5^{0}G, 5^{3}GF, 5^{6}GF, 5^{4}GF, 5^{5}G, 5^{1}G, 5^{0}GF, 5^{0}G,

	Starts	1st	2nd	3rd	Win & Pl
Career Total (Turf)	18	3	0	5	18256
Career Total (AW)	2	0	0	0	0

84 8/09 Bevl 5f (0-85)H GD £5180

81 6/08 Ayr 5f (0-85)H G-F £6476

75 5/08 Muss 5f (0-65)H G-F £2266

Total win prize-money £13924

Going (Turf): Sf: 0-2 GS: 0-0 Gd: 1-7 GF: 2-9 Fm: 0-0

Distance: 5f/6f: 3-20 7f-8f: 0-0 9f-13f: 0-0 14f+: 0-0

Track : LH: 0-1 RH: 0-0 Tight: 0-0 Gall: 0-0

Aids: Bl: 0-0 Vi: 0-0 Tstrap: 0-0 Ckp: 0-0

Best Rating: 84 8/09 Bevl 5f good

Fair; effective over 5f-6f; acts on most ground.

Dishdasha (IRE)

(112) (81)

7-y-o b g Desert Prince (IRE)-Counterplot (IRE) (Last Tycoon)

Mrs A M Thorpe Tristar

Placings:0030005/6062301060000/003056/25/1214 **(0848)**

2009: 13^{1}SD, 12^{2}SD, 12^{1}SD, 12^{4}SD,

	Starts	1st	2nd	3rd	Win & Pl
Career Total (Turf)	9	0	0	1	418
Career Total (AW)	23	3	3	2	8503

81 2/09 Kemp 1m4f (0-70)H STD £2590

62 1/09 GrLe 1m5f66y (0-65)H STD £1942

52 3/05 Ling 6f (0-45) STD £1435

Total win prize-money £5968

Going (Turf): Sf: 0-0 GS: 0-1 Gd: 0-1 GF: 0-5 Fm: 0-2

Distance: 5f/6f: 1-12 7f-8f: 0-7 9f-13f: 1-12 14f+: 1-1

Track : LH: 2-20 RH: 1-5 Tight: 1-13 Gall: 1-1

Aids: Bl: 0-0 Vi: 0-0 Tstrap: 0-0 Ckp: 0-0

Best Rating: 81 2/09 Kemp 1m4f stand

Modest; stays 1m4f; acts on Polytrack; has worn a tongue tie.

Dispol Antonio (IRE)

90 **54**

2-y-o b g Antonius Pius (USA)-Brief Fairy (IRE) (Brief Truce (USA))

P T Midgley W B Imison

Placings:000556 **(4503)**

2009: 6^{0}GS, 6^{0}GF, 7^{0}GF, 7^{5}GF, 7^{5}S, 7^{6}G,

	Starts	1st	2nd	3rd	Win & Pl
Career Total (Turf)	6	0	0	0	0

Going (Turf): Sf: 0-1 GS: 0-1 Gd: 0-1 GF: 0-3 Fm: 0-0

Distance: 5f/6f: 0-2 7f-8f: 0-4 9f-13f: 0-0 14f+: 0-0

Track : LH: 0-3 RH: 0-1 Tight: 0-3 Gall: 0-0

Aids: Bl: 0-0 Vi: 0-4 Tstrap: 0-0 Ckp: 0-0

Best Rating: 54 7/09 Catt 7f soft

Dispol Diva

102(97) (64)**67**

3-y-o b f Deportivo-Kingston Rose (GER) (Robellino (USA))

P T Midgley W B Imison

Placings:610364333-**461**215360235 **(4506)**
2009: 8^{4}SD, **8**^{6}SD, **11**^{1}SD, 11^{2}GF, 12^{1}GF, 12^{5}G, 12^{3}GS, 12^{6}GF, 12^{0}GF, 9^{2}GF, 11^{3}GS, 12^{5}G,

	Starts	1st	2nd	3rd	Win & Pl
Career Total (Turf)	18	2	2	6	9278
Career Total (AW)	3	1	0	0	2047
66 4/09 Bevl	1m4f16y (0-70)H			G-F	£2590
64 3/09 Sthl	1m3f			STD	£2047
54 4/08 Bevl	5f			G-S	£2428

Total win prize-money £7065

Going (Turf): Sf: 0-3 **GS: 1-5** Gd: 0-3 **GF: 1-7** Fm: 0-0
Distance: 5f/6f: 1-3 7f-8f: 0-7 **9f-13f: 2-11** 14f+: 0-0
Track : LH: 1-9 RH: 1-7 **Tight: 1-6** Gall: 0-1
Aids: Bl: 0-0 **Vi: 2-16** Tstrap: 0-0 Ckp: 0-0
Best Rating: **67** 5/09 Haml 1m4f17y gd-sft

Moderate; stays 1m3f; acts on easy ground and on Fibresand; has worn a visor.

Dispol Fay (IRE)

80(81) (32)**32**
2-y-o b f Fayruz-Hever Rosina (Efisio)
P T Midgley W B Imison

Placings:00**00** **(7637)**
2009: 5^{0}G, 5^{0}S, **5**^{0}SD, **5**^{0}SD,

	Starts	1st	2nd	3rd	Win & Pl
Career Total (Turf)	2	0	0	0	
Career Total (AW)	2	0	0	0	

Going (Turf): **Sf: 0-1 GS: 0-0 Gd: 0-1 GF: 0-0 Fm: 0-0**
Distance: 5f/6f: 0-4 7f-8f: 0-0 9f-13f: 0-0 14f+: 0-0
Track : LH: 0-1 RH: 0-0 Tight: 0-1 Gall: 0-0
Aids: Bl: 0-0 Vi: 0-0 Tstrap: 0-0 Ckp: 0-0
Best Rating: **32** 11/09 Sthl 5f stand

Dispol Grand (IRE)

99(97) (72)**72**
3-y-o b g Raise A Grand (IRE)-Hever Rosina (Efisio)
P T Midgley W B Imison

Placings:000414234-**32**62431214540406 **(5517)**
2009: 5^{3}SD, **5**^{2}SD, 5^{6}GF, 5^{2}GF, 5^{4}GF, 5^{3}GF, 5^{1}G, 5^{2}GF, 5^{1}G, 5^{4}GS, 5^{6}G, 5^{4}GF, 5^{0}G, 5^{4}GF, 6^{0}G, 5^{8}GF,

	Starts	1st	2nd	3rd	Win & Pl
Career Total (Turf)	22	3	2	2	14369
Career Total (AW)	3	0	2	1	2340
72 6/09 Newc	5f	(0-75)H		GD	£3238
69 5/09 Ayr	5f	(0-70)H		GD	£2914
65 8/08 Muss	5f			SFT	£3885

Total win prize-money £10038

Going (Turf): Sf: 1-5 GS: 0-2 **Gd: 2-6** GF: 0-9 Fm: 0-0
Distance: **5f/6f: 3-25** 7f-8f: 0-0 9f-13f: 0-0 14f+: 0-0
Track : LH: 0-1 RH: 0-1 Tight: 0-0 Gall: 0-1
Aids: Bl: 0-0 Vi: 0-0 Tstrap: 0-0 Ckp: 0-0
Best Rating: **72** 6/09 Newc 5f good

Modest; effective at sprint trips; handles easy and fast ground; goes on Fibresand.

Dispol Kabira

92 **56**
2-y-o b f Kheleyf (USA)-Ablr (Soviet Star (USA))
D W Thompson (P T Midgley 22/7) J Greenbank

Placings:0616640600000 **(7056)**
2009: 5^{0}GF, 5^{6}GF, 5^{1}GS, 6^{6}GS, 6^{6}GF, 6^{4}F, 7^{0}S, 6^{6}HY, 5^{0}GF, 5^{0}GF, 6^{0}GS, 7^{0}GF, 7^{0}GF,

	Starts	1st	2nd	3rd	Win & Pl
Career Total (Turf)	13	1	0	0	2590
56 5/09 Haml	5f4y		G-S	£2590	

Total win prize-money £2590

Going (Turf): Sf: 0-2 **GS: 1-3** Gd: 0-0 GF: 0-7 Fm: 0-1
Distance: **5f/6f: 1-8** 7f-8f: 0-5 9f-13f: 0-0 14f+: 0-0
Track : LH: 0-1 RH: 0-0 Tight: 0-1 Gall: 0-0
Aids: Bl: 0-0 Vi: 0-0 Tstrap: 0-0 Ckp: 0-0
Best Rating: **56** 5/09 Haml 5f4y gd-sft

Dispol Keasha

96 **77**
2-y-o ch f Kheleyf (USA)-Easy Mover (IRE) (Bluebird (USA))
T D Barron W B Imison

Placings:2164 **(2714)**
2009: 5^{2}GF, 5^{1}G, 5^{6}GS, 5^{4}G,

	Starts	1st	2nd	3rd	Win & Pl
Career Total (Turf)	4	1	1	0	8152
77 5/09 Muss	5f		GD	£5828	

Total win prize-money £5828

Going (Turf): Sf: 0-0 GS: 0-1 **Gd: 1-2** GF: 0-1 Fm: 0-0
Distance: **5f/6f: 1-4** 7f-8f: 0-0 9f-13f: 0-0 14f+: 0-0
Track : LH: 0-0 RH: 0-0 Tight: 0-0 Gall: 0-0
Aids: Bl: 0-0 Vi: 0-0 Tstrap: 0-0 Ckp: 0-0
Best Rating: **77** 5/09 Muss 5f good

Fair, speedy filly; effective at 5f on fast ground.

Dispol Kylie (IRE)

99(81) (46)**84**
3-y-o b f Kheleyf (USA)-Professional Mom (USA) (Spinning World (USA))
P T Midgley W B Imison

Placings:11061300-**0**043440535 **(5626)**
2009: **5**^{0}SD, 5^{0}F, 5^{4}GF, 5^{3}G, 5^{4}GF, 5^{4}GS, 5^{0}GS, 5^{5}S, 5^{3}GF, 5^{5}S,

	Starts	1st	2nd	3rd	Win & Pl
Career Total (Turf)	17	3	0	3	19857
Career Total (AW)	1	0	0	0	
84 8/08 Thsk	5f		GD	£8159	
84 5/08 Thsk	5f		GD	£5180	
66 4/08 Donc	5f		SFT	£3885	

Total win prize-money £17227

Going (Turf): Sf: 1-5 GS: 0-3 **Gd: 2-3** GF: 0-5 Fm: 0-1
Distance: **5f/6f: 3-18** 7f-8f: 0-0 9f-13f: 0-0 14f+: 0-0
Track : LH: 0-0 RH: 0-0 Tight: 0-0 Gall: 0-0
Aids: Bl: 0-0 Vi: 0-0 Tstrap: 0-1 Ckp: 0-1
Best Rating: **84** 8/08 Thsk 5f good

Modest, effective over 5f; acts on good and soft ground.

Distant Dreamer (USA)

77(81) (9)**12**
3-y-o ch f Rahy (USA)-Khazayin (USA) (Bahri (USA))
Rae Guest Mrs Paula Smith

Placings:0500 **(7726)**
2009: 6^{0}S, 8^{5}GF, 7^{0}GS, **7**^{0}SD,

	Starts	1st	2nd	3rd	Win & Pl
Career Total (Turf)	3	0	0	0	108
Career Total (AW)	1	0	0	0	

Going (Turf): **Sf: 0-1 GS: 0-1 Gd: 0-0 GF: 0-1 Fm: 0-0**
Distance: 5f/6f: 0-1 7f-8f: 0-3 9f-13f: 0-0 14f+: 0-0
Track : LH: 0-1 RH: 0-0 Tight: 0-0 Gall: 0-0
Aids: Bl: 0-0 Vi: 0-0 Tstrap: 0-0 Ckp: 0-0
Best Rating: **12** 9/09 Ling 7f gd-sft

Distant Memories (IRE)

109 **108**
3-y-o b g Falbrav (IRE)-Amathia (IRE) (Darshaan)
T P Tate Mrs Fitri Hay

Placings:61-20112 **(7077a)**
2009: 11^{2}HY, 10^{0}G, 9^{1}S, 9^{1}GS, 10^{2}Y,

	Starts	1st	2nd	3rd	Win & Pl
Career Total (Turf)	7	3	2	0	31161
108 9/09 Ripn	1m1f170y (0-90)H			G-S	£8723
96 7/09 Ripn	1m1f170y (0-85)H			SFT	£6938
84 11/08 Ayr	7f50y			HVY	£3885

Total win prize-money £19548

Going (Turf): **Sf: 2-3** GS: 1-1 Gd: 0-2 GF: 0-0 Fm: 0-0
Distance: 5f/6f: 0-0 7f-8f: 1-2 **9f-13f: 2-5** 14f+: 0-0
Track : LH: 1-4 **RH: 2-2 Tight: 2-2** Gall: 0-1
Aids: Bl: 0-0 Vi: 0-0 Tstrap: 0-0 Ckp: 0-0
Best Rating: **108** 9/09 Ripn 1m1f170y gd-sft

Very useful; stays 1m4f but effective at shorter; acts on soft ground; likes to race prominently.

Distant Pleasure

96 **65**
5-y-o b m Diktat-Our Pleasure (IRE) (Lake Coniston (IRE))
M Dods Pontefract Racecourse Racing Syndicate

Placings:601400/60001322-60060 **(6984)**
2009: 8^{6}G, 8^{0}G, 8^{0}S, 7^{6}S, 7^{0}G,

	Starts	1st	2nd	3rd	Win & Pl
Career Total (Turf)	19	2	2	1	6731
65 8/08 Carl	6f192y (0-60)H			GD	£2047
56 6/07 Rdcr	1m			G-F	£2047

Total win prize-money £4095

Going (Turf): Sf: 0-6 GS: 0-2 **Gd: 1-6 GF: 1-4** Fm: 0-1
Distance: 5f/6f: 0-0 **7f-8f: 2-11** 9f-13f: 0-8 14f+: 0-0
Track : LH: 0-14 **RH: 1-3** Tight: 0-2 Gall: 0-0
Aids: Bl: 0-0 Vi: 0-0 Tstrap: 0-2 Ckp: 0-2
Best Rating: **65** 8/08 Carl 6f192y good

Moderate; effective over 7f-1m; acts on any ground on turf.

Distant Sun (USA)

101(108) (89)**80**
5-y-o b g Distant View (USA)-The Great Flora (USA) (Unaccounted For (USA))
Miss L A Perratt Ken McGarrity

Placings:3/**32**04**0**1552413430/**1132**00004-00004103 **(7119)**
2009: 6^{0}G, 8^{0}GF, 5^{0}GS, 5^{0}G, 5^{4}G, 5^{1}GF, 6^{0}GF, 5^{3}GS,

	Starts	1st	2nd	3rd	Win & Pl
Career Total (Turf)	25	3	1	3	11932
Career Total (AW)	8	2	2	3	11148
74 9/09 Muss	5f	(0-65)H		G-F	£2590
89 2/08 Wolv	5f20y	(0-80)H		STD	£4533
82 1/08 Wolv	5f216y	(0-75)H		STD	£2331
76 8/07 Haml	6f5y	(0-65)H		G-S	£2388
60 5/07 Ayr	6f	(0-70)		G-F	£2914

Total win prize-money £14760

Going (Turf): Sf: 0-1 GS: 1-3 Gd: 0-12 **GF: 2-9** Fm: 0-0
Distance: **5f/6f: 4-18** 7f-8f: 1-14 9f-13f: 0-1 14f+: 0-0
Track : **LH: 2-14** RH: 0-4 **Tight: 2-15** Gall: 0-0
Aids: Bl: 0-0 Vi: 0-0 Tstrap: 0-2 Ckp: 0-2
Best Rating: **89** 3/08 Wolv 5f216y stand

Modest; effective from 5f-7f; acts on most ground and on Polytrack.

Distant Vision (IRE)

98(91) (40)**54**
6-y-o br m Distant Music (USA)-Najeyba (Indian Ridge)
H A McWilliams Ian Swarbrick & J D Riches

Placings:66/360005/00005/356030-00243004205 **(6856)**
2009: 5^0SD, 6^0G, 5^2F, 5^4GF, 5^3GF, 5^0GF, 5^0GF, 5^4GF, 5^2G, 6^0GF, 5^5SD,

	Starts	1st	2nd	3rd	Win & Pl
Career Total (Turf)	23	0	2	4	3499
Career Total (AW)	7	0	0	0	0

Going (Turf): **Sf: 0-1 GS: 0-2 Gd: 0-6 GF: 0-12 Fm: 0-2**
Distance: 5f/6f: 0-17 7f-8f: 0-10 9f-13f: 0-3 14f+: 0-0
Track : LH: 0-10 RH: 0-5 Tight: 0-5 Gall: 0-1
Aids: Bl: 0-7 Vi: 0-1 Tstrap: 0-3 Ckp: 0-3
Best Rating: **54** 7/09 Hayd 5f good

Plating class; probably best over sprint distances; best on fast ground; has worn cheekpieces and blinkers.

Distinctive

103 **101**
2-y-o b f Tobougg (IRE)-Blue Azure (USA) (American Chance (USA))
B Smart Mr & Mrs G Middlebrook

Placings:3110 **(6852)**
2009: 6^3G, 6^1GF, 6^1G, 7^0G,

	Starts	1st	2nd	3rd	Win & Pl
Career Total (Turf)	4	2	0	1	43969
101 9/09 Ayr 6f			GD		£39739
78 8/09 Rdcr 6f			G-F		£3238

Total win prize-money £42977

Going (Turf): Sf: 0-0 GS: 0-0 **Gd: 1-3 GF: 1-1** Fm: 0-0
Distance: **5f/6f: 2-3** 7f-8f: 0-1 9f-13f: 0-0 14f+: 0-0
Track : LH: 0-0 RH: 0-0 Tight: 0-0 Gall: 0-0
Aids: Bl: 0-0 Vi: 0-0 Tstrap: 0-0 Ckp: 0-0
Best Rating: **101** 9/09 Ayr 6f good

Very useful; effective over 6f; acts on fast ground.

Distinctive Image (USA)

104(110) (101)**84**
4-y-o b c Mineshaft (USA)-Dock Leaf (USA) (Woodman (USA))
R Hollinshead Stevenson Leadbeater & Hollinshead

Placings:0/214-12204421 **(4840)**
2009: 12^1SF, 12^2SD, 12^2SD, 12^0GF, 12^4SD, 11^4GS, 12^2G, 12^1SD,

	Starts	1st	2nd	3rd	Win & Pl
Career Total (Turf)	4	0	2	0	3059
Career Total (AW)	8	3	2	0	33097
101 8/09 Sthl 1m4f (0-90)H				STD	£10037
88 3/09 Wolv 1m4f50y (0-90)H				SF	£9462
86 9/08 GrLe 1m2f				STD	£6476

Total win prize-money £25976

Going (Turf): **Sf: 0-1 GS: 0-1 Gd: 0-1 GF: 0-1 Fm: 0-0**
Distance: 5f/6f: 0-0 7f-8f: 0-1 **9f-13f: 3-11** 14f+: 0-0
Track : **LH: 3-9** RH: 0-3 Tight: 1-6 Gall: 1-3
Aids: Bl: 0-0 Vi: 0-0 Tstrap: 0-0 Ckp: 0-0
Best Rating: **101** 8/09 Sthl 1m4f stand

Veyr useful; stays 1m4f; acts on good and turf but better on artifical surfaces.

Distinctly Game

(109) (90)**86**
7-y-o b g Mind Games-Distinctly Blu (IRE) (Distinctly North (USA))
K A Ryan Mr & Mrs Julian And Rosie Richer

Placings:2221422/4600000/000/41303000000501/143356 6304-54142430 **(1313)**
2009: 5^5SD, 6^4SD, 6^1SD, 6^4SD, 6^2SD, 5^4SD, 6^3SD, 5^0SD,

	Starts	1st	2nd	3rd	Win & Pl
Career Total (Turf)	25	1	4	0	83033
Career Total (AW)	24	4	2	6	29004
84 1/09 Ling 6f (0-75)H				STD	£2900
90 1/08 Kemp 6f (0-80)H				STD	£4210
84 11/07 Ling 6f (0-85)H				STD	£4404
94 1/07 Kemp 6f (0-85)H				STD	£4728
80 6/04 York 5f3y E				G-F	£5070

Total win prize-money £21312

Going (Turf): Sf: 0-1 GS: 0-3 Gd: 0-9 **GF: 1-12** Fm: 0-0
Distance: **5f/6f: 5-49** 7f-8f: 0-0 9f-13f: 0-0 14f+: 0-0
Track : LH: 2-19 RH: 2-5 **Tight: 2-14** Gall: 0-3
Aids: Bl: 0-1 Vi: 0-0 Tstrap: 0-1 Ckp: 0-1
Best Rating: **103** 6/05 Chan 5f good

Fair; effective over 5f-6f; acts on good or faster ground and on Polytrack; has worn cheekpieces.

Ditzy Diva

61(48) **24**
3-y-o b f Imperial Dancer-Runs In The Family (Distant Relative)
B G Powell K Rhatigan

Placings:00-0 **(5531)**
2009: 10^0G,

	Starts	1st	2nd	3rd	Win & Pl
Career Total (Turf)	2	0	0	0	
Career Total (AW)	1	0	0	0	

Going (Turf): **Sf: 0-1 GS: 0-0 Gd: 0-1 GF: 0-0 Fm: 0-0**
Distance: 5f/6f: 0-0 7f-8f: 0-1 9f-13f: 0-2 14f+: 0-0
Track : LH: 0-2 RH: 0-1 Tight: 0-0 Gall: 0-0
Aids: Bl: 0-0 Vi: 0-0 Tstrap: 0-0 Ckp: 0-0
Best Rating: **24** 10/08 Nott 1m75y soft

Divertimenti (IRE)

79(110) (74)**55**
5-y-o b g Green Desert (USA)-Ballet Shoes (IRE) (Ela-Mana-Mou)
S R Bowring (C R Dore 22/10) K Nicholls

Placings:33300/5156133414245/254021060500644-401640064003 **(7839)**
2009: 7^4SD, 8^0SD, 7^1SD, 7^6SD, 7^4SD, 7^0GF, 7^0SD, 7^6SD, 10^4SD, 8^0SD, 12^0SD, 5^3SS,

	Starts	1st	2nd	3rd	Win & Pl
Career Total (Turf)	8	1	0	3	5610
Career Total (AW)	37	4	3	3	15962
74 1/09 Ling 7f (0-65)H				STD	£2047
83 3/08 Wolv 7f32y (0-75)H				STD	£2730
83 8/07 Ling 7f (0-70)H				STD	£2817
71 4/07 Leic 5f218y				G-F	£2266
75 2/07 Ling 6f				STD	£3071

Total win prize-money £12932

Going (Turf): Sf: 0-1 GS: 0-0 Gd: 0-4 **GF: 1-2** Fm: 0-1
Distance: 5f/6f: 2-12 **7f-8f: 3-30** 9f-13f: 0-3 14f+: 0-0
Track : **LH: 4-30** RH: 0-9 **Tight: 4-24** Gall: 0-0
Aids: Bl: 1-7 Vi: 0-0 Tstrap: 2-14 Ckp: 2-14
Best Rating: **83** 3/08 Wolv 7f32y stand

Moderate; effective over 7f-1m; acts on fast ground; goes on sand.

Divinatore

98(97) (68)**65**
3-y-o b g Sakhee (USA)-Divina Mia (Dowsing (USA))
D Haydn Jones The Preseli Partnership

Placings:6-42200455 **(7699)**
2009: 8^4SD, 9^2SD, 8^2GF, 11^0GS, 10^0G, 11^4G, 8^5SD, 10^5SD,

	Starts	1st	2nd	3rd	Win & Pl
Career Total (Turf)	4	0	1	0	1156
Career Total (AW)	5	0	1	0	806

Going (Turf): **Sf: 0-0 GS: 0-1 Gd: 0-2 GF: 0-1 Fm: 0-0**
Distance: 5f/6f: 0-0 7f-8f: 0-3 9f-13f: 0-6 14f+: 0-0
Track : LH: 0-4 RH: 0-4 Tight: 0-4 Gall: 0-1
Aids: Bl: 0-0 Vi: 0-0 Tstrap: 0-1 Ckp: 0-1
Best Rating: **68** 2/09 Wolv 1m1f103y stand

Modest; effective at around 1m1f; acts on Polytrack.

Divine Design (IRE)

88 (18)**48**
5-y-o b m Barathea (IRE)-Tortue (IRE) (Turtle Island (IRE))
Seamus G O'Donnell See How She is Today Syndicate

Placings:050/050000-000 **(4344)**
2009: 7^0GF, 6^0GY, 7^0G,

	Starts	1st	2nd	3rd	Win & Pl
Career Total (Turf)	11	0	0	0	
Career Total (AW)	1	0	0	0	

Going (Turf): **Sf: 0-2 GS: 0-0 Gd: 0-1 GF: 0-2 Fm: 0-2**
Distance: 5f/6f: 0-3 7f-8f: 0-8 9f-13f: 0-1 14f+: 0-0
Track : LH: 0-4 RH: 0-4 Tight: 0-0 Gall: 0-1
Aids: Bl: 0-1 Vi: 0-0 Tstrap: 0-1 Ckp: 0-1
Best Rating: **78** 10/06 Curr 1m heavy

Divine Force

95(102) (68)**56**
3-y-o b g Bertolini (USA)-Malcesine (IRE) (Auction Ring (USA))
M Wigham (J A Osborne 10/3) R J Lorenz

Placings:5253600521 **(7602)**
2009: 7^5SD, 7^2SD, 7^5SD, 6^3SD, 6^6SD, 6^0GF, 6^0SD, 6^5GF, 7^2SD, 6^1SD,

	Starts	1st	2nd	3rd	Win & Pl
Career Total (Turf)	2	0	0	0	0
Career Total (AW)	8	1	2	1	3230
68 12/09 Ling 6f (0-60)H				STD	£1637

Total win prize-money £1638

Going (Turf): **Sf: 0-0 GS: 0-0 Gd: 0-0 GF: 0-2 Fm: 0-0**
Distance: **5f/6f: 1-4** 7f-8f: 0-6 9f-13f: 0-0 14f+: 0-0

Track : LH: 1-7 RH: 0-1 Tight: 1-6 Gall: 0-0
Aids: Bl: 0-0 Vi: 0-0 Tstrap: 0-0 Ckp: 0-0
Best Rating: 68 12/09 Ling 6f stand

Modest; effective over 6f-7f; acts on Polytrack.

Divine Spirit

101(92) (63)**84**
8-y-o b g Foxhound (USA)-Vocation (IRE) (Royal Academy (USA))
M Dods The Newcastle Racing Club

Placings:454304442161/00036103603/000005022306344 05304/041430020060605/0636203223211041 1/00006510 00-020560000000 (7081)
2009: 5^{0}GF, 5^{2}G, 5^{0}HY, 5^{5}G, 5^{6}GF, 5^{0}S, 5^{0}G, 5^{0}G, 5^{0}GS, 5^{0}SD, 5^{0}SD, 5^{0}S,

	Starts	1st	2nd	3rd	Win & Pl
Career Total (Turf)	93	9	9	10	77260
Career Total (AW)	4	0	0	1	829

84	8/08	Bevl	5f	(0-85)H	G-S	£5180
89	9/07	Ayr	5f	(0-85)H	SFT	£6477
67	9/07	Muss	5f	(0-80)H	G-S	£5505
81	8/07	Nott	5f13y	(0-75)H	GD	£3238
73	7/07	Bevl	5f	(0-75)H	GD	£3238
76	6/06	Catt	5f212y	(0-80)H	G-F	£7772
88	6/04	Ayr	5f	D(0-85)H	GD	£6799
83	9/03	Muss	5f	C(0-95)	G-F	£8141
78	8/03	Catt	5f	F	FRM	£3255

Total win prize-money £49608

Going (Turf): Sf: 1-10 GS: 2-14 Gd: 3-27 GF: 2-36 Fm: 1-6
Distance: 5f/6f: 9-96 7f-8f: 0-1 9f-13f: 0-0 14f+: 0-0
Track : LH: 1-20 RH: 0-7 Tight: 1-10 Gall: 0-7
Aids: Bl: 0-7 Vi: 0-0 Tstrap: 2-17 Ckp: 2-17
Best Rating: 89 9/07 Ayr 5f soft

Fair sprinter; suited by 5f; acts on fast and easy ground; has worn cheekpieces and blinkers.

Divine White

94(93) (62)**45**
6-y-o ch m College Chapel-Snowy Mantle (Siberian Express (USA))
G P Enright Homebred Racing

Placings:00264/00534026/3050000/0-3020000400 (7869)
2009: 6^{3}SS, 6^{0}SD, 6^{2}SD, 6^{0}SD, 6^{0}GF, 7^{0}GS, 6^{0}GF, 6^{4}GF, 6^{0}G, 6^{0}SS,

	Starts	1st	2nd	3rd	Win & Pl
Career Total (Turf)	19	0	1	1	2085
Career Total (AW)	12	0	2	2	2513

Going (Turf): Sf: 0-2 GS: 0-2 Gd: 0-2 GF: 0-13 Fm: 0-0
Distance: 5f/6f: 0-12 7f-8f: 0-15 9f-13f: 0-4 14f+: 0-0
Track : LH: 0-15 RH: 0-3 Tight: 0-7 Gall: 0-4
Aids: Bl: 0-1 Vi: 0-2 Tstrap: 0-3 Ckp: 0-3
Best Rating: 62 3/09 Sthl 6f stand

Moderate; effective over 6f; acts on Polytrack and on Fibresand.

Dixey

101(103) (93)**96**
4-y-o br f Diktat-Hoh Dancer (Indian Ridge)
M A Jarvis T G Warner

Placings:152/01-5040240520 (7294)
2009: 8^{6}SD, 7^{0}SD, 7^{4}G, 7^{0}SF, 7^{2}G, 8^{4}SD, 7^{0}G, 8^{5}G, 7^{2}S, 7^{0}S,

	Starts	1st	2nd	3rd	Win & Pl
Career Total (Turf)	9	1	2	0	19269
Career Total (AW)	6	1	1	0	6159

92	6/08	Leic	7f9y	GD	£12462
88	6/07	Kemp	7f	STD	£3562

Total win prize-money £16024

Going (Turf): Sf: 0-2 GS: 0-0 Gd: 1-6 GF: 0-1 Fm: 0-0
Distance: 5f/6f: 0-0 7f-8f: 2-14 9f-13f: 0-1 14f+: 0-0
Track : LH: 0-5 RH: 1-5 Tight: 0-4 Gall: 0-0
Aids: Bl: 0-0 Vi: 0-0 Tstrap: 0-2 Ckp: 0-2
Best Rating: 96 10/09 Newb 7f soft

Very useful; stays 7f; acts on good ground; goes on Polytrack.

Dixi Heights

86(72) (18)**59**
2-y-o b f Golan (IRE)-Ninfa Of Cisterna (Polish Patriot (USA))
J R Boyle The Dixi Racing Partnership

Placings:66300 (6589)
2009: 5^{6}SD, 6^{6}GF, 5^{3}S, 5^{0}G, 6^{0}GS,

	Starts	1st	2nd	3rd	Win & Pl
Career Total (Turf)	4	0	0	1	530
Career Total (AW)	1	0	0	0	0

Going (Turf): Sf: 0-1 GS: 0-1 Gd: 0-1 GF: 0-1 Fm: 0-0
Distance: 5f/6f: 0-4 7f-8f: 0-1 9f-13f: 0-0 14f+: 0-0
Track : LH: 0-1 RH: 0-1 Tight: 0-0 Gall: 0-1
Aids: Bl: 0-0 Vi: 0-0 Tstrap: 0-0 Ckp: 0-0
Best Rating: 59 7/09 Leic 5f218y soft

Dixie Bright (USA)

87(98) (74)**61**
2-y-o b/br g Dixie Union (USA)-Tell Me Now (USA) (A.P. Indy (USA))
J G Given Brighton Farm Ltd

Placings:01500002 (7056)
2009: 5^{0}G, 5^{1}SD, 6^{5}GS, 7^{0}SD, 7^{0}SD, 6^{0}SD, 8^{0}SD, 7^{2}GF,

	Starts	1st	2nd	3rd	Win & Pl
Career Total (Turf)	3	0	1	0	674
Career Total (AW)	5	1	0	0	3886

74	6/09	Wolv	5f216y	STD	£3885

Total win prize-money £3886

Going (Turf): Sf: 0-0 GS: 0-1 Gd: 0-1 GF: 0-1 Fm: 0-0
Distance: 5f/6f: 1-4 7f-8f: 0-3 9f-13f: 0-1 14f+: 0-0
Track : LH: 1-5 RH: 0-1 Tight: 1-4 Gall: 0-0
Aids: Bl: 0-1 Vi: 0-1 Tstrap: 0-0 Ckp: 0-0
Best Rating: 74 6/09 Wolv 5f216y stand

Fair; stays 6f; acts on Polytrack.

Dizziness (USA)

82 **65**
2-y-o b f Stormy Atlantic (USA)-Danzante (USA) (Danzig (USA))
R Charlton K Abdulla

Placings:6 (3356)
2009: 6^{6}GS,

	Starts	1st	2nd	3rd	Win & Pl
Career Total (Turf)	1	0	0	0	0

Going (Turf): Sf: 0-0 GS: 0-1 Gd: 0-0 GF: 0-0 Fm: 0-0
Distance: 5f/6f: 0-1 7f-8f: 0-0 9f-13f: 0-0 14f+: 0-0
Track : LH: 0-0 RH: 0-0 Tight: 0-0 Gall: 0-0
Aids: Bl: 0-0 Vi: 0-0 Tstrap: 0-0 Ckp: 0-0
Best Rating: 65 6/09 NmkJ 6f gd-sft

Half-sister to seven winners, including the Group 1 scorer Monzante; promise on debut over 6f on easy ground.

Djalalabad (FR)

98(101) (64)**53**
5-y-o b m King's Best (USA)-Daraydala (IRE) (Royal Academy (USA))
Mrs C A Dunnett Far Afield

Placings:340066200/000400060300501 0-10560040506340306 (7787)
2009: 7^{1}SD, 8^{0}GF, 7^{5}SD, 6^{6}GF, 7^{0}F, 6^{0}GF, 7^{4}SD, 8^{0}SD, 8^{5}SD, 7^{0}GF, 7^{6}SD, 8^{3}SD, 8^{4}SD, 7^{0}SD, 8^{3}SD, 8^{0}SD, 7^{6}SD,

	Starts	1st	2nd	3rd	Win & Pl
Career Total (Turf)	25	0	1	1	1781
Career Total (AW)	17	2	0	3	4974

64	3/09	Wolv	7f32y	(0-55)H	STD	£2047
59	9/08	Kemp	7f	(0-50)H	STD	£2047

Total win prize-money £4094

Going (Turf): Sf: 0-1 GS: 0-6 Gd: 0-5 GF: 0-12 Fm: 0-1
Distance: 5f/6f: 0-1 7f-8f: 2-27 9f-13f: 0-14 14f+: 0-0
Track : LH: 1-22 RH: 1-9 Tight: 1-11 Gall: 0-2
Aids: Bl: 0-0 Vi: 0-2 Tstrap: 2-19 Ckp: 2-19
Best Rating: 64 3/09 Wolv 7f32y stand

Moderate; effective over 7f-1m; acts on good ground; goes on Polytrack; has worn tonguestrap/cheekpieces.

Django Reinhardt

53(88) (59)
3-y-o b g Tobougg (IRE)-Alexander Ballet (Mind Games)
J R Gask For Sale

Placings:0-000 (5809)
2009: 6^{0}SD, 5^{0}S, 6^{0}SD,

	Starts	1st	2nd	3rd	Win & Pl
Career Total (Turf)	1	0	0	0	
Career Total (AW)	3	0	0	0	

Going (Turf): Sf: 0-1 GS: 0-0 Gd: 0-0 GF: 0-0 Fm: 0-0
Distance: 5f/6f: 0-4 7f-8f: 0-0 9f-13f: 0-0 14f+: 0-0
Track : LH: 0-1 RH: 0-2 Tight: 0-1 Gall: 0-0
Aids: Bl: 0-0 Vi: 0-0 Tstrap: 0-0 Ckp: 0-0
Best Rating: 59 10/08 Kemp 6f stand

Do Be Brave (IRE)

71(91) (58)
3-y-o ch g Kheleyf (USA)-Fear Not (IRE) (Alzao (USA))
Paul Mason Seven Plus Seven

Placings:30 0000 (3985)
2009: 7^{0}SD, 7^{0}SD, 8^{0}SD, 10^{0}GF,

	Starts	1st	2nd	3rd	Win & Pl
Career Total (Turf)	2	0	0	0	
Career Total (AW)	4	0	0	1	385

Going (Turf): Sf: 0-1 GS: 0-0 Gd: 0-0 GF: 0-1 Fm: 0-0
Distance: 5f/6f: 0-0 7f-8f: 0-5 9f-13f: 0-1 14f+: 0-0
Track : LH: 0-2 RH: 0-3 Tight: 0-1 Gall: 0-0
Aids: Bl: 0-0 Vi: 0-0 Tstrap: 0-0 Ckp: 0-0
Best Rating: 58 8/08 Kemp 7f stand

Do More Business (IRE)

92(91) (65)69

2-y-o b g Dubai Destination (USA)-Tokyo Song (USA) (Stravinsky (USA))

P M Phelan Timesquare Ltd

Placings:100546 **(5967)**

2009: 5^{1}GF, 7^{0}GF, 7^{0}G, 5^{5}SD, 6^{4}SD, 6^{6}GS,

	Starts	1st	2nd	3rd	Win & Pl
Career Total (Turf)	4	1	0	0	6476
Career Total (AW)	2	0	0	0	168

69 5/09 Gdwd 5f G-F £6476

Total win prize-money £6476

Going (Turf): Sf: 0-0 GS: 0-1 Gd: 0-1 **GF: 1-2** Fm: 0-0
Distance: **5f/6f: 1-4** 7f-8f: 0-2 9f-13f: 0-0 14f+: 0-0
Track : LH: 0-2 RH: 0-1 Tight: 0-2 Gall: 0-0
Aids: Bl: 0-0 Vi: 0-0 Tstrap: 0-0 Ckp: 0-0
Best Rating: **69** 5/09 Gdwd 5f gd-fm

Modest; stays 6f; acts on fast ground and on Polytrack.

Do The Deal (IRE)

87 (63)71

3-y-o ch f Halling (USA)-Cairns (UAE) (Cadeaux Genereux)

D M Leigh (J J Quinn 21/6) Dominic Fagan

Placings:33-4500350 **(7563a)**

2009: 7^{4}GF, 9^{5}GF, 8^{0}GF, 6^{0}SD, 10^{3}SD, 10^{5}SD, 8^{0}SD,

	Starts	1st	2nd	3rd	Win & Pl
Career Total (Turf)	5	0	0	2	1169
Career Total (AW)	4	0	0	1	483

Going (Turf): **Sf: 0-0 GS: 0-1 Gd: 0-0 GF: 0-4 Fm: 0-0**
Distance: 5f/6f: 0-1 7f-8f: 0-4 9f-13f: 0-4 14f+: 0-0
Track : LH: 0-7 RH: 0-1 Tight: 0-2 Gall: 0-0
Aids: Bl: 0-3 Vi: 0-0 Tstrap: 0-1 Ckp: 0-1
Best Rating: **71** 9/08 Ches 7f2y gd-fm

Modest; effective over 7f; acts on fast and easy ground.

Do The Strand (IRE)

99 87

3-y-o b c Galileo (IRE)-Aiming Upwards (Blushing Flame (USA))

B W Hills Suzanne & Nigel Williams

Placings:041 **(4519)**

2009: 8^{0}S, 10^{4}G, 10^{1}S,

	Starts	1st	2nd	3rd	Win & Pl
Career Total (Turf)	3	1	0	0	3960

87 8/09 Donc 1m2f60y SFT £3238

Total win prize-money £3238

Going (Turf): **Sf: 1-2** GS: 0-0 Gd: 0-1 GF: 0-0 Fm: 0-0
Distance: 5f/6f: 0-0 7f-8f: 0-1 **9f-13f: 1-2** 14f+: 0-0
Track : **LH: 1-1** RH: 0-1 Tight: 0-0 **Gall: 1-2**
Aids: Bl: 0-0 Vi: 0-0 Tstrap: 0-0 Ckp: 0-0
Best Rating: **87** 8/09 Donc 1m2f60y soft

Useful; stays 1m2f; acts in soft ground.

Dobravany (IRE)

91(96) (52)60

5-y-o b g Danehill Dancer (IRE)-Eadaoin (USA) (King Of Kings (IRE))

K A Morgan (Adrian McGuinness 22/1) John Sheridan

Placings:0001660200/0560000605-005235 **(3552)**

2009: 8^{0}SD, 9^{0}SD, 8^{5}SD, 8^{2}SD, 9^{3}SD, 11^{5}GF,

	Starts	1st	2nd	3rd	Win & Pl
Career Total (Turf)	18	1	1	0	7336
Career Total (AW)	8	0	1	1	692

76 6/07 Navn 1m2f (50-80)H Y-S £6303

Total win prize-money £6303

Going (Turf): **Sf: 0-5 GS: 0-0 Gd: 0-3 GF: 0-4 Fm: 0-0**
Distance: 5f/6f: 0-1 7f-8f: 0-5 **9f-13f: 1-20** 14f+: 0-0
Track : **LH: 1-9** RH: 0-12 Tight: 0-5 Gall: 0-0
Aids: Bl: 0-5 Vi: 0-3 Tstrap: 0-2 Ckp: 0-2
Best Rating: **76** 6/07 Navn 1m2f yld-sft

Doc Jones (IRE)

101(99) (74)78

3-y-o ch g Docksider (USA)-Quick Return (Polish Precedent (USA))

P D Evans Barry McCabe

Placings:2-5421045250355 **(5901)**

2009: 7^{5}SD, 6^{4}GF, 7^{2}F, 7^{1}F, 6^{0}SD, 7^{4}GF, 6^{5}GF, 6^{2}GS, 7^{5}GF, 5^{0}G, 7^{3}SD, 5^{5}G, 5^{5}F,

	Starts	1st	2nd	3rd	Win & Pl
Career Total (Turf)	11	1	3	0	8250
Career Total (AW)	3	0	0	1	626

72 6/09 Thsk 7f FRM £4274

Total win prize-money £4274

Going (Turf): Sf: 0-0 GS: 0-2 Gd: 0-2 GF: 0-4 **Fm: 1-3**
Distance: 5f/6f: 0-7 **7f-8f: 1-7** 9f-13f: 0-0 14f+: 0-0
Track : **LH: 1-7** RH: 0-1 **Tight: 1-4** Gall: 0-4
Aids: Bl: 0-0 Vi: 0-0 Tstrap: 0-1 Ckp: 0-1
Best Rating: **78** 7/09 Hayd 6f gd-sft

Modest; stays 7f; acts on most ground on turf and Polytrack.

Docofthebay (IRE)

109(108) (103)112

5-y-o ch g Docksider (USA)-Baize (Efisio)

J A Osborne Paul J Dixon

Placings:21/22132112326/4420520-3000033500 **(6480)**

2009: 8^{3}SD, 10^{0}G, 10^{0}GF, 10^{0}SD, 8^{0}GF, 8^{3}GF, 8^{3}G, 8^{5}GS, 8^{0}GF, 9^{0}GF,

	Starts	1st	2nd	3rd	Win & Pl
Career Total (Turf)	26	3	7	4	140178
Career Total (AW)	4	1	1	1	6089

99 8/07 Gdwd 7f (0-100)H GD £24928
91 7/07 Asct 7f (0-90)H G-F £9715
86 5/07 Thsk 1m (0-85)H GD £5181
72 11/06 Sthl 1m STD £1911

Total win prize-money £41737

Going (Turf): Sf: 0-1 GS: 0-3 **Gd: 2-6** GF: 1-15 Fm: 0-1
Distance: 5f/6f: 0-0 **7f-8f: 4-16** 9f-13f: 0-14 14f+: 0-0
Track : **LH: 2-14** RH: 1-6 **Tight: 1-6** Gall: 0-7
Aids: Bl: 0-4 Vi: 0-0 Tstrap: 0-4 Ckp: 0-4
Best Rating: **112** 6/08 Asct 1m gd-fm

Very useful; runner-up in the 2007 Cambridgeshire and the 2008 Royal Hunt Cup; effective at around 1m, but does stay further; acts on fast ground and on Polytrack and Fibresand; has worn blinkers and cheekpieces; usually held up and can start slowly.

Doctor Crane (USA)

101(91) (83)98

3-y-o b g Doneraile Court (USA)-Sharons Song (USA) (Badger Land (USA))

J H M Gosden Ms Rachel D S Hood

Placings:11506-41 **(2296)**

2009: 10^{4}G, 10^{1}GF,

	Starts	1st	2nd	3rd	Win & Pl
Career Total (Turf)	6	3	0	0	25035
Career Total (AW)	1	0	0	0	468

98 5/09 NmkR 1m2f (0-100)H G-F £12952
92 7/08 Newb 7f GD £7477
82 6/08 Donc 7f G-F £3238

Total win prize-money £23667

Going (Turf): Sf: 0-0 GS: 0-0 Gd: 1-2 **GF: 2-4** Fm: 0-0
Distance: 5f/6f: 0-0 **7f-8f: 2-5** 9f-13f: 1-2 14f+: 0-0
Track : LH: 0-1 RH: 0-1 Tight: 0-0 Gall: 0-1
Aids: Bl: 0-0 Vi: 0-0 Tstrap: 0-0 Ckp: 0-0
Best Rating: **98** 5/09 NmkR 1m2f gd-fm

Very useful; stays 1m2f and acts on fast ground; likes to race prominently.

Doctor Delta

66(95) (48)46

4-y-o b c Dr Fong (USA)-Delta Tempo (IRE) (Bluebird (USA))

M Brittain Mel Brittain

Placings:04000-40400 **(2609)**

2009: 8^{4}SD, 8^{0}SD, 9^{4}SD, 12^{0}SD, 12^{0}GF,

	Starts	1st	2nd	3rd	Win & Pl
Career Total (Turf)	5	0	0	0	216
Career Total (AW)	5	0	0	0	0

Going (Turf): **Sf: 0-1 GS: 0-1 Gd: 0-1 GF: 0-2 Fm: 0-0**
Distance: 5f/6f: 0-0 7f-8f: 0-2 9f-13f: 0-8 14f+: 0-0
Track : LH: 0-5 RH: 0-5 Tight: 0-7 Gall: 0-0
Aids: Bl: 0-0 Vi: 0-1 Tstrap: 0-0 Ckp: 0-0
Best Rating: **48** 1/09 Wolv 1m1f103y stand

Doctor Fremantle

109 120

4-y-o b c Sadler's Wells (USA)-Summer Breeze (Rainbow Quest (USA))

Sir Michael Stoute K Abdulla

Placings:221/21440-10110 **(6850)**

2009: 10^{1}GF, 12^{0}GF, 12^{1}G, 11^{1}GF, 10^{0}G,

	Starts	1st	2nd	3rd	Win & Pl
Career Total (Turf)	13	5	3	0	277593

120 9/09 Newb 1m3f5y G-F £36900
116 7/09 NmkJ 1m4f GD £56770
110 5/09 Ches 1m2f75y G-F £36900
115 5/08 Ches 1m4f66y G-F £36900
89 10/07 Nott 1m54y G-F £3562

Total win prize-money £171035

Going (Turf): Sf: 0-1 GS: 0-1 Gd: 1-5 **GF: 4-5** Fm: 0-1
Distance: 5f/6f: 0-0 7f-8f: 0-2 **9f-13f: 5-10** 14f+: 0-1
Track : **LH: 4-6** RH: 1-3 Tight: 2-3 Gall: 2-4
Aids: Bl: 0-0 Vi: 0-0 Tstrap: 0-0 Ckp: 0-0
Best Rating: **120** 9/09 Newb 1m3f5y gd-fm

Group class; winner of the Group 3 Chester Vase and fourth in the Derby in 2008; winner of the Group 3 Huxley Stakes in 2009 and the Group 2 Princess Of Wales's

Stakes; effective from 1m2f-1m4f; acts on good and faster ground.

Doctor Hilary

(101) (83)**62**

7-y-o b g Mujahid (USA)-Agony Aunt (Formidable (USA))

A B Haynes double-r-racing.com

Placings:412325/**0215**/**2115**/365030/**040400-00** **(7673)**

2009: 6^{0}SD, 5^{0}SD,

	Starts	1st	2nd	3rd	Win & Pl
Career Total (Turf)	**7**	**1**	**2**	**1**	**10077**
Career Total (AW)	**21**	**3**	**2**	**2**	**34930**

99	12/06	Ndas	5f110y		STD	£9523
96	11/06	Ndas	6f	(80-105)H	FST	£7619
99	11/05	Ndas	5f110y	(75-100)H	FST	£5531
70	5/04	Ayr	6f	E	G-F	£3666

Total win prize-money £26341

Going (Turf): Sf: 0-0 GS: 0-1 Gd: 0-1 **GF: 1-5** Fm: 0-0
Distance: **5f/6f: 4-26** 7f-8f: 0-1 9f-13f: 0-1 14f+: 0-0
Track : LH: 0-11 RH: 0-1 Tight: 0-3 Gall: 0-8
Aids: Bl: 0-2 **Vi: 3-21** Tstrap: 0-0 Ckp: 0-0
Best Rating: **109** 1/07 Ndas 6f fast

Very useful; effective over 5f-6f; has had a spell in Dubai; acts on fast ground; also goes on dirt; often visored/tongue tied.

Doctor Of Music (IRE)

82 **43**

3-y-o ch g Dr Fong (USA)-Sublime Beauty (USA) (Caerleon (USA))

B Smart Dr Philip Brown

Placings:0600 **(6184)**

2009: 7^{0}G, 8^{6}G, 8^{0}G, 9^{0}GF,

	Starts	1st	2nd	3rd	Win & Pl
Career Total (Turf)	**4**	**0**	**0**	**0**	**0**

Going (Turf): **Sf: 0-0 GS: 0-0 Gd: 0-3 GF: 0-1 Fm: 0-0**
Distance: 5f/6f: 0-0 7f-8f: 0-2 9f-13f: 0-2 14f+: 0-0
Track : LH: 0-3 RH: 0-1 Tight: 0-2 Gall: 0-0
Aids: Bl: 0-0 Vi: 0-0 Tstrap: 0-0 Ckp: 0-0
Best Rating: **43** 7/09 Thsk 1m good

Doctor Parkes

109 **89**

3-y-o b g Diktat-Lucky Parkes (Full Extent (USA))

E J Alston Joseph Heler

Placings:3241-10410 **(6283)**

2009: 5^{1}GF, 5^{0}GS, 5^{4}GF, 5^{1}G, 5^{0}GF,

	Starts	1st	2nd	3rd	Win & Pl
Career Total (Turf)	**9**	**3**	**1**	**1**	**25107**

89	8/09	Ripn	5f	(0-85)H	GD	£4857
86	5/09	Ches	5f16y	(0-100)H	G-F	£14193
71	8/08	Catt	5f		GD	£2388

Total win prize-money £21438

Going (Turf): Sf: 0-0 GS: 0-3 **Gd: 2-2** GF: 1-4 Fm: 0-0
Distance: **5f/6f: 3-8** 7f-8f: 0-1 9f-13f: 0-0 14f+: 0-0
Track : **LH: 1-1** RH: 0-0 **Tight: 1-1** Gall: 0-0
Aids: Bl: 0-0 Vi: 0-0 Tstrap: 0-0 Ckp: 0-0
Best Rating: **89** 8/09 Ripn 5f good

Useful; effective at 5f-6f; acts on fast and easy ground.

Doctor Zhivago

(97) (76)

2-y-o b c Shamardal (USA)-Balalaika (Sadler's Wells (USA))

M Johnston Sheikh Hamdan Bin Mohammed Al Maktoum

Placings:1 **(7638)**

2009: 8^{1}SD,

	Starts	1st	2nd	3rd	Win & Pl
Career Total (Turf)	**0**	**0**	**0**	**0**	
Career Total (AW)	**1**	**1**	**0**	**0**	**4094**

76	12/09	Sthl	1m		STD	£4094

Total win prize-money £4094

Going (Turf): **Sf: 0-0 GS: 0-0 Gd: 0-0 GF: 0-0 Fm: 0-0**
Distance: 5f/6f: 0-0 **7f-8f: 1-1** 9f-13f: 0-0 14f+: 0-0
Track : **LH: 1-1** RH: 0-0 Tight: 0-0 Gall: 0-0
Aids: Bl: 0-0 Vi: 0-0 Tstrap: 0-0 Ckp: 0-0
Best Rating: **76** 12/09 Sthl 1m stand

Useful; stays 1m and acts on Fibresand.

Dodaa (USA)

(106) (61)**61**

6-y-o b g Dayjur (USA)-Ra'A (USA) (Diesis)

N Wilson Hurn Racing Club

Placings:00001/33100000055/11361121310-05065300 **(7839)**

2009: 5^{0}SS, 5^{5}SD, 5^{0}SD, 5^{6}SD, 5^{5}SD, 5^{3}SD, 5^{0}SD, 5^{0}SS,

	Starts	1st	2nd	3rd	Win & Pl
Career Total (Turf)	**4**	**0**	**0**	**0**	
Career Total (AW)	**32**	**8**	**1**	**5**	**15913**

73	5/08	Wolv	5f20y		STD	£2047
81	3/08	Ling	5f	(0-65)H	STD	£2047
60	3/08	Ling	5f	(0-55)H	STD	£2252
58	2/08	Wolv	5f20y	(0-50)H	STD	£1684
56	1/08	Kemp	5f	(0-45)	STD	£1365
55	1/08	Wolv	5f20y	(0-45)	SS	£1365
56	2/07	Sthl	5f	(0-45)	STD	£1365
45	12/06	Sthl	6f	(0-45)	STD	£1876

Total win prize-money £14003

Going (Turf): **Sf: 0-0 GS: 0-3 Gd: 0-0 GF: 0-1 Fm: 0-0**
Distance: **5f/6f: 8-32** 7f-8f: 0-2 9f-13f: 0-2 14f+: 0-0
Track : **LH: 6-25** RH: 1-2 **Tight: 5-18** Gall: 0-0
Aids: Bl: 0-3 Vi: 0-0 Tstrap: 0-0 Ckp: 0-0
Best Rating: **81** 3/08 Ling 5f stand

Modest; effective over 5f; acts on sand; likes to dominate.

Doggerbank (IRE)

102 **89**

3-y-o b f Oasis Dream-Discreet Brief (IRE) (Darshaan)

H R A Cecil G Schoeningh

Placings:2121 **(4948)**

2009: 10^{2}GF, 12^{1}GF, 13^{2}G, 12^{1}GF,

	Starts	1st	2nd	3rd	Win & Pl
Career Total (Turf)	**4**	**2**	**2**	**0**	**12162**

89	8/09	Sals	1m4f	(0-80)H	G-F	£6799
73	7/09	Wwck	1m4f134y		G-F	£2914

Total win prize-money £9714

Going (Turf): Sf: 0-0 GS: 0-0 Gd: 0-1 **GF: 2-3** Fm: 0-0
Distance: 5f/6f: 0-0 7f-8f: 0-0 **9f-13f: 2-4** 14f+: 0-0
Track : LH: 1-2 RH: 1-2 **Tight: 1-2** Gall: 0-1
Aids: Bl: 0-0 Vi: 0-0 Tstrap: 0-0 Ckp: 0-0
Best Rating: **89** 8/09 Sals 1m4f gd-fm

Useful; stays 1m4f; acts on fast ground.

Dohasa (IRE)

111(109) (113)**110**

4-y-o b g Bold Fact (USA)-Zara's Birthday (IRE) (Waajib)

G M Lyons Sean Jones

Placings:54561216/61641U-33320201121 **(7768)**

2009: 6^{3}GF, 6^{3}GF, 6^{3}GF, 7^{2}Y, 6^{0}GF, 7^{2}G, 7^{0}G, 7^{1}SD, 7^{1}G, 7^{2}GF, 7^{1}SD,

	Starts	1st	2nd	3rd	Win & Pl
Career Total (Turf)	**21**	**4**	**3**	**3**	**113742**
Career Total (AW)	**4**	**3**	**1**	**0**	**62944**

109	12/09	Kemp	7f		STD	£22708
96	9/09	Curr	7f		GD	£15168
86	9/09	Dund	7f		STD	£11069
113	8/08	Dund	6f	H	STD	£26327
101	5/08	Leop	6f		G-F	£11966
98	10/07	Navn	5f	H	G-F	£5836
92	9/07	Tipp	5f		FRM	£5836

Total win prize-money £98912

Going (Turf): Sf: 0-1 GS: 0-1 Gd: 1-7 **GF: 2-8** Fm: 1-1
Distance: **5f/6f: 4-16** 7f-8f: 3-9 9f-13f: 0-0 14f+: 0-0
Track : **LH: 5-14** RH: 1-1 Tight: 0-0 Gall: 0-3
Aids: Bl: 0-1 Vi: 0-0 Tstrap: 0-0 Ckp: 0-0
Best Rating: **113** 8/08 Dund 6f stand

Smart; Irish trained; Group placed; stays 7f; best on fast ground and also goes on Polytrack; has worn blinkers.

Dollar Express (USA)

(96) (62)

3-y-o ch g Broken Vow (USA)-Feminine (USA) (Tale Of The Cat (USA))

E W Tuer (J Noseda 27/3) E Tuer

Placings:66444 **(0978)**

2009: 7^{6}SD, 7^{6}SD, 8^{4}SD, 12^{4}SD, 12^{4}SD,

	Starts	1st	2nd	3rd	Win & Pl
Career Total (Turf)	**0**	**0**	**0**	**0**	
Career Total (AW)	**5**	**0**	**0**	**0**	**192**

Going (Turf): **Sf: 0-0 GS: 0-0 Gd: 0-0 GF: 0-0 Fm: 0-0**
Distance: 5f/6f: 0-0 7f-8f: 0-2 9f-13f: 0-3 14f+: 0-0
Track : LH: 0-4 RH: 0-1 Tight: 0-3 Gall: 0-0
Aids: Bl: 0-0 Vi: 0-0 Tstrap: 0-0 Ckp: 0-0
Best Rating: **62** 3/09 Kemp 1m4f stand

Dolly No Hair

87(82) (43)**65**

4-y-o ch g Reel Buddy (USA)-Champagne Grandy (Vaigly Great)

N Wilson (D W Barker 19/6) Colin Marginson & Tony Dolphin

Placings:002/03200000-**6000060** **(7270)**

2009: 9^{6}F, 8^{0}GF, 8^{0}GF, 8^{0}G, 7^{0}GF, 7^{6}SD, 6^{0}SD,

	Starts	1st	2nd	3rd	Win & Pl
Career Total (Turf)	**16**	**0**	**2**	**1**	**1888**
Career Total (AW)	**2**	**0**	**0**	**0**	**0**

Going (Turf): **Sf: 0-2 GS: 0-2 Gd: 0-5 GF: 0-6 Fm: 0-1**
Distance: 5f/6f: 0-7 7f-8f: 0-9 9f-13f: 0-2 14f+: 0-0
Track : LH: 0-6 RH: 0-1 Tight: 0-1 Gall: 0-0
Aids: Bl: 0-1 Vi: 0-0 Tstrap: 0-1 Ckp: 0-1
Best Rating: **67** 10/07 Newc 7f good

Modest; effective at 7f; acts on most ground.

Dolly Penrose

106 **87**

4-y-o b f Hernando (FR)-Mistinguett (IRE) (Doyoun)
C J Down (M R Channon 4/11) Geoffrey Rowe

Placings:432421025-3502241066620 **(7148)**
2009: 16^{3}GF, 16^{5}GF, 16^{0}G, 14^{2}G, 13^{2}GF, 15^{4}GF, 14^{1}S, 14^{0}G, 16^{6}GS, 16^{6}G, 14^{6}GF, 17^{2}GF, 12^{0}G,

	Starts	1st	2nd	3rd	Win & Pl
Career Total (Turf)	22	2	6	2	34388

87	7/09	Hayd	1m6f	(0-85)H	SFT	£5504
83	7/08	York	1m6f	(0-95)H	HVY	£9714

Total win prize-money £15219

Going (Turf): **Sf: 2-2** GS: 0-3 Gd: 0-9 GF: 0-8 Fm: 0-0
Distance: 5f/6f: 0-0 7f-8f: 0-0 9f-13f: 0-5 **14f+: 2-17**
Track : **LH: 2-12** RH: 0-10 Tight: 0-8 **Gall: 1-7**
Aids: Bl: 0-0 Vi: 0-3 Tstrap: 0-0 Ckp: 0-0
Best Rating: **87** 10/09 Pont 2m1f216y gd-fm

Useful; stays 2m2f; acts on most ground; has worn a visor.

Dolly Will Do

80(57) **47**

2-y-o b f Bahamian Bounty-Desert Flower (Green Desert (USA))
N P Mulholland Larkinglass II

Placings:050000 **(5498)**
2009: 5^{0}GF, 5^{5}GF, 5^{0}GF, 6^{0}SD, 5^{0}G, 8^{0}G,

	Starts	1st	2nd	3rd	Win & Pl
Career Total (Turf)	5	0	0	0	0
Career Total (AW)	1	0	0	0	

Going (Turf): **Sf: 0-0 GS: 0-0 Gd: 0-2 GF: 0-3 Fm: 0-0**
Distance: 5f/6f: 0-5 7f-8f: 0-0 9f-13f: 0-1 14f+: 0-0
Track : LH: 0-4 RH: 0-0 Tight: 0-1 Gall: 0-3
Aids: Bl: 0-0 Vi: 0-0 Tstrap: 0-0 Ckp: 0-0
Best Rating: **47** 5/09 Bath 5f11y gd-fm

Dolores Ortiz (IRE)

86 **56**

3-y-o b f High Chaparral (IRE)-Ma N'leme Biche (USA) (Key To The Kingdom (USA))
S C Williams Mrs Jane Bailey

Placings:00000 **(4719)**
2009: 8^{0}GF, 8^{0}G, 10^{0}GF, 10^{0}G, 8^{0}G,

	Starts	1st	2nd	3rd	Win & Pl
Career Total (Turf)	5	0	0	0	

Going (Turf): **Sf: 0-0 GS: 0-0 Gd: 0-3 GF: 0-2 Fm: 0-0**
Distance: 5f/6f: 0-0 7f-8f: 0-1 9f-13f: 0-4 14f+: 0-0
Track : LH: 0-1 RH: 0-2 Tight: 0-2 Gall: 0-0
Aids: Bl: 0-0 Vi: 0-1 Tstrap: 0-0 Ckp: 0-0
Best Rating: **56** 5/09 Wind 1m67y good

Dolphin Rock

98(94) (67)**68**

2-y-o b g Mark Of Esteem (IRE)-Lark In The Park (IRE) (Grand Lodge (USA))
Mrs G S Rees Mia Racing

Placings:035424632 **(6901)**
2009: 6^{0}G, 5^{3}SD, 6^{5}G, 7^{4}SD, 7^{2}SD, 7^{4}GF, 8^{6}SD, 8^{3}S, 8^{2}GF,

	Starts	1st	2nd	3rd	Win & Pl
Career Total (Turf)	5	0	1	1	1926
Career Total (AW)	4	0	1	1	1927

Going (Turf): **Sf: 0-1 GS: 0-0 Gd: 0-2 GF: 0-2 Fm: 0-0**
Distance: 5f/6f: 0-3 7f-8f: 0-3 9f-13f: 0-3 14f+: 0-0
Track : LH: 0-7 RH: 0-0 Tight: 0-4 Gall: 0-0
Aids: Bl: 0-0 Vi: 0-0 Tstrap: 0-0 Ckp: 0-0
Best Rating: **68** 10/09 Pont 1m4y gd-fm

Fair; stays 7f and acts on Polytrack.

Dom Polski

(98) (66)

3-y-o b g Polish Precedent (USA)-Camerlata (Common Grounds)
W R Swinburn Davis, Larking, Coomes-Waugh & Nash

Placings:44503 **(6608)**
2009: 7^{4}SD, 7^{4}SD, 7^{5}SD, 8^{0}SD, 8^{3}SD,

	Starts	1st	2nd	3rd	Win & Pl
Career Total (Turf)	0	0	0	0	
Career Total (AW)	5	0	0	1	302

Going (Turf): **Sf: 0-0 GS: 0-0 Gd: 0-0 GF: 0-0 Fm: 0-0**
Distance: 5f/6f: 0-0 7f-8f: 0-4 9f-13f: 0-1 14f+: 0-0
Track : LH: 0-2 RH: 0-3 Tight: 0-2 Gall: 0-0
Aids: Bl: 0-0 Vi: 0-0 Tstrap: 0-0 Ckp: 0-0
Best Rating: **66** 10/09 Kemp 1m stand

Moderate; stays 1m; acts on Polytrack; has worn a tongue tie.

Domada

38(33)

4-y-o ch f Domedriver (IRE)-Estimada (Mark Of Esteem (IRE))
W J H Ratcliffe The Wensley Partnership

Placings:00 **(2229)**
2009: 7^{0}SD, 8^{0}HY,

	Starts	1st	2nd	3rd	Win & Pl
Career Total (Turf)	1	0	0	0	
Career Total (AW)	1	0	0	0	

Going (Turf): **Sf: 0-1 GS: 0-0 Gd: 0-0 GF: 0-0 Fm: 0-0**
Distance: 5f/6f: 0-0 7f-8f: 0-1 9f-13f: 0-1 14f+: 0-0
Track : LH: 0-2 RH: 0-0 Tight: 0-0 Gall: 0-0
Aids: Bl: 0-0 Vi: 0-0 Tstrap: 0-0 Ckp: 0-0

Dome Rocket

102(99) (79)**83**

3-y-o b g Domedriver (IRE)-Sea Ridge (Slip Anchor)
W J Knight Bluehills Racing Limited

Placings:222-54121000 **(6594)**
2009: 11^{5}SD, 9^{4}G, 9^{1}SD, 10^{2}GF, 10^{1}G, 9^{0}G, 10^{0}SD, 10^{0}GS,

	Starts	1st	2nd	3rd	Win & Pl
Career Total (Turf)	7	1	3	0	9179
Career Total (AW)	4	1	1	0	3886

83	7/09	Epsm	1m2f18y	(0-80)H	GD	£5180
70	6/09	Wolv	1m1f103y		STD	£2729

Total win prize-money £7911

Going (Turf): Sf: 0-1 GS: 0-2 **Gd: 1-3** GF: 0-1 Fm: 0-0
Distance: 5f/6f: 0-0 7f-8f: 0-0 **9f-13f: 2-11** 14f+: 0-0
Track : **LH: 2-6** RH: 0-5 **Tight: 2-6** Gall: 0-0
Aids: Bl: 0-0 Vi: 0-0 Tstrap: 1-4 Ckp: 1-4
Best Rating: **83** 7/09 Epsm 1m2f18y good

Useful; effective over 1m2f; acts on good and easy ground, and on Polytrack; has worn cheekpieces.

Domesday (UAE)

94(51) (51)**43**

8-y-o b g Cape Cross (IRE)-Deceive (Machiavellian (USA))
T T Clement R L Gray

Placings:005/00003240/000-400 **(6392)**
2009: 10^{4}G, 8^{0}G, 10^{0}GF,

	Starts	1st	2nd	3rd	Win & Pl
Career Total (Turf)	13	0	1	1	1011
Career Total (AW)	4	0	0	0	0

Going (Turf): **Sf: 0-2 GS: 0-3 Gd: 0-5 GF: 0-3 Fm: 0-0**
Distance: 5f/6f: 0-0 7f-8f: 0-5 9f-13f: 0-11 14f+: 0-1
Track : LH: 0-10 RH: 0-5 Tight: 0-10 Gall: 0-1
Aids: Bl: 0-0 Vi: 0-2 Tstrap: 0-1 Ckp: 0-1
Best Rating: **53** 9/07 Thsk 1m gd-fm

Moderate; best at 1m; acts on good ground.

Domination

94(82) (37)**70**

2-y-o b g Motivator-Soliza (IRE) (Intikhab (USA))
H Morrison Michael Kerr-Dineen & Bob Tullett

Placings:406 **(7266)**
2009: 9^{4}GS, 8^{0}S, 8^{6}SD,

	Starts	1st	2nd	3rd	Win & Pl
Career Total (Turf)	2	0	0	0	385
Career Total (AW)	1	0	0	0	0

Going (Turf): **Sf: 0-1 GS: 0-1 Gd: 0-0 GF: 0-0 Fm: 0-0**
Distance: 5f/6f: 0-0 7f-8f: 0-2 9f-13f: 0-1 14f+: 0-0
Track : LH: 0-1 RH: 0-1 Tight: 0-1 Gall: 0-0
Aids: Bl: 0-0 Vi: 0-0 Tstrap: 0-0 Ckp: 0-0
Best Rating: **70** 10/09 Gdwd 1m1f gd-sft

Don Pele (IRE)

102(107) (78)**77**

7-y-o b g Monashee Mountain (USA)-Big Fandango (Bigstone (IRE))
R A Harris (J Pearce 18/5) Robert Bailey

Placings:02110/5400060/5100002612/06323002136/0064020230506220-12634411325530004405630 4 **(7890)**
2009: 6^{1}SS, 5^{2}SD, 6^{6}SD, 6^{3}SD, 6^{4}SD, 5^{4}SD, 5^{1}SD, 5^{1}SD, 6^{3}SD, 6^{2}SD, 6^{5}SD, 6^{5}G, 6^{3}GF, 5^{0}GF, 6^{0}GF, 6^{0}SD, 6^{4}G, 5^{4}S, 5^{0}GF, 6^{5}SD, 5^{6}SD, 5^{3}SD, 5^{0}SS,

	Starts	1st	2nd	3rd	Win & Pl
Career Total (Turf)	48	4	5	5	49530
Career Total (AW)	25	4	6	3	17449

74	3/09	Wolv	5f216y		STD	£1978
78	2/09	Ling	5f	(0-70)H	STD	£2900
78	1/09	Sthl	6f		SS	£2047
87	9/07	Gdwd	6f	(0-80)H	G-S	£4857
87	12/06	Wolv	5f216y		STD	£2730
96	6/06	York	6f	(0-100)H	G-F	£12954
103	7/04	Newb	6f8y	A	GD	£14500
83	6/04	Wind	6f	E	G-F	£3630

Total win prize-money £45598

Going (Turf): Sf: 0-7 GS: 1-8 Gd: 1-10 **GF: 2-23** Fm: 0-0
Distance: **5f/6f: 7-65** 7f-8f: 1-8 9f-13f: 0-0 14f+: 0-0
Track : **LH: 4-24** RH: 0-4 **Tight: 3-14** Gall: 1-11
Aids: Bl: 0-11 Vi: 0-0 Tstrap: 4-36 Ckp: 4-36
Best Rating: **103** 7/04 Newb 6f8y good

Moderate; effective at 5f-6f; acts on most ground and on sand; often wears cheekpieces.

Don Picolo

(95) (59)39

4-y-o b g Bertolini (USA)-Baby Come Back (IRE) (Fayruz)

R Curtis Pedro Rosas

Placings:0600/53310440-0 (0489)

2009: 7^{0}SS,

	Starts	1st	2nd	3rd	Win & Pl
Career Total (Turf)	3	0	0	0	0
Career Total (AW)	10	1	0	2	2435

59	2/08	Sthl	7f	(0-60)H	STD	£1911

Total win prize-money £1911

Going (Turf):	Sf: 0-1 GS: 0-0 Gd: 0-1 GF: 0-1 Fm: 0-0
Distance:	5f/6f: 0-2 7f-8f: 1-10 9f-13f: 0-1 14f+: 0-0
Track :	LH: 1-10 RH: 0-1 Tight: 0-3 Gall: 0-0
Aids:	Bl: 1-7 Vi: 0-0 Tstrap: 0-0 Ckp: 0-0
Best Rating:	59 2/08 Sthl 7f stand

Moderate handicapper; stays 7f; acts on Fibresand; has worn blinkers and an eyeshield.

Don Pietro

105(106) (77)74

6-y-o b g Bertolini (USA)-Silver Spell (Aragon)

R Curtis Mrs Joanna Hughes

Placings:210232225/0302503/01150324010-4362452141 (5243)

2009: 10^{4}SD, 8^{3}SD, 7^{6}SS, 8^{2}SD, 10^{4}SD, 9^{5}SD, 8^{2}GF, 10^{1}G, 10^{4}G, 8^{1}F,

	Starts	1st	2nd	3rd	Win & Pl
Career Total (Turf)	19	4	5	2	22090
Career Total (AW)	18	2	4	3	10753

74	8/09	Bath	1m5y	(0-80)H	FRM	£4727
61	7/09	Bath	1m2f46y		GD	£1942
76	11/08	GrLe	1m2f	(0-70)H	STD	£2590
	5/08	Lanc	1m	H	G-F	£1860
74	4/08	Wolv	1m141y	(0-70)H	STD	£2729
73	5/06	Leic	1m60y		G-S	£4533

Total win prize-money £18384

Going (Turf):	Sf: 0-3 GS: 1-2 Gd: 1-6 GF: 1-6 Fm: 1-2
Distance:	5f/6f: 0-0 7f-8f: 1-10 9f-13f: 5-27 14f+: 0-0
Track :	LH: 4-23 RH: 1-8 Tight: 3-17 Gall: 1-3
Aids:	Bl: 0-2 Vi: 0-1 Tstrap: 1-7 Ckp: 1-7
Best Rating:	85 10/06 Bath 1m5y good

Modest; effective over 1m-1m2f; acts on most ground on turf; goes on Polytrack; has worn cheekpieces.

Don Stefano

(51)

2-y-o b g Deportivo-Molly Music (Music Boy)

W G M Turner Darren Coombes

Placings:0 (5371)

2009: 8^{0}SD,

	Starts	1st	2nd	3rd	Win & Pl
Career Total (Turf)	0	0	0	0	
Career Total (AW)	1	0	0	0	

Going (Turf):	Sf: 0-0 GS: 0-0 Gd: 0-0 GF: 0-0 Fm: 0-0
Distance:	5f/6f: 0-0 7f-8f: 0-1 9f-13f: 0-0 14f+: 0-0
Track :	LH: 0-1 RH: 0-0 Tight: 0-0 Gall: 0-0
Aids:	Bl: 0-0 Vi: 0-0 Tstrap: 0-0 Ckp: 0-0

Don't Panic (IRE)

110

5-y-o ch g Fath (USA)-Torrmana (IRE) (Ela-Mana-Mou)

R J Hodges (P W Chapple-Hyam 29/4) A B S Webb

Placings:4410/0063151/12240R-RR (1600)

2009: 8^{R}GF, 8^{R}GF,

	Starts	1st	2nd	3rd	Win & Pl
Career Total (Turf)	19	4	2	1	71414

114	3/08	Donc	1m	H	G-S	£24928
100	10/07	Gdwd	1m	(0-85)H	SFT	£7124
90	9/07	Gdwd	1m	(0-80)H	G-F	£5181
87	9/06	Wwck	7f26y		G-S	£2590

Total win prize-money £39826

Going (Turf):	Sf: 1-4 GS: 2-4 Gd: 0-3 GF: 1-8 Fm: 0-0
Distance:	5f/6f: 0-1 7f-8f: 4-15 9f-13f: 0-3 14f+: 0-0
Track :	LH: 1-4 RH: 2-4 Tight: 0-2 Gall: 0-1
Aids:	Bl: 0-1 Vi: 0-0 Tstrap: 0-0 Ckp: 0-0
Best Rating:	114 3/08 Donc 1m gd-sft

Smart; winner of the 2008 Spring Mile at Doncaster; stays 1m; acts well in soft ground.

Don't Stop Me Now (IRE)

103(104) (71)70

4-y-o b f Catcher In The Rye (IRE)-Persian Flower (Persian Heights)

John Joseph Hanlon (J Howard Johnson 3/4) Glafy Syndicate

Placings:00021-1006003 (6785)

2009: 16^{1}GF, 10^{0}GF, 10^{0}G, 14^{6}GF, 15^{0}GF, 16^{0}GY, 16^{3}SS,

	Starts	1st	2nd	3rd	Win & Pl
Career Total (Turf)	7	1	0	0	3886
Career Total (AW)	5	1	1	1	4828

70	4/09	Muss	2m	(0-70)H	G-F	£3885
71	7/08	GrLe	1m6f		STD	£3561

Total win prize-money £7448

Going (Turf):	Sf: 0-0 GS: 0-0 Gd: 0-1 GF: 1-5 Fm: 0-0
Distance:	5f/6f: 0-0 7f-8f: 0-0 9f-13f: 0-6 14f+: 2-6
Track :	LH: 1-7 RH: 1-5 Tight: 1-5 Gall: 1-2
Aids:	Bl: 0-0 Vi: 0-0 Tstrap: 0-2 Ckp: 0-2
Best Rating:	71 7/08 GrLe 1m6f stand

Modest; winning hurdler; stays 2m; acts on Polytrack and fast turf.

Don't Tell Mary (IRE)

93 99

2-y-o b f Starcraft (NZ)-Only In Dreams (Polar Falcon (USA))

Tom Dascombe K P Trowbridge

Placings:11006 (7033)

2009: 5^{1}F, 5^{1}GF, 5^{0}GF, 5^{0}GS, 7^{6}S,

	Starts	1st	2nd	3rd	Win & Pl
Career Total (Turf)	5	2	0	0	21322

99	5/09	Bevl	5f	G-F	£17031
85	5/09	Bath	5f11y	FRM	£3885

Total win prize-money £20917

Going (Turf):	Sf: 0-1 GS: 0-1 Gd: 0-0 GF: 1-2 Fm: 1-1
Distance:	5f/6f: 2-4 7f-8f: 0-1 9f-13f: 0-0 14f+: 0-0
Track :	LH: 1-1 RH: 0-0 Tight: 0-0 Gall: 1-1
Aids:	Bl: 0-0 Vi: 0-0 Tstrap: 0-0 Ckp: 0-0
Best Rating:	99 5/09 Bevl 5f gd-fm

Smart; winner in Listed company; suited by 5f and fast ground.

Dona Alba (IRE)

106 98

4-y-o b f Peintre Celebre (USA)-Fantastic Fantasy (IRE) (Lahib (USA))

J L Dunlop Windflower Overseas Holdings Inc

Placings:412/0150-34005 (5137)

2009: 10^{3}G, 10^{4}GF, 12^{0}G, 9^{0}G, 10^{5}GF,

	Starts	1st	2nd	3rd	Win & Pl
Career Total (Turf)	12	2	1	1	17365

94	6/08	Leic	1m1f218y	(0-85)H	GD	£4209
83	9/07	Folk	7f		G-F	£3465

Total win prize-money £7674

Going (Turf):	Sf: 0-0 GS: 0-2 Gd: 1-5 GF: 1-5 Fm: 0-0
Distance:	5f/6f: 0-0 7f-8f: 1-2 9f-13f: 1-10 14f+: 0-0
Track :	LH: 0-3 RH: 1-7 Tight: 0-4 Gall: 0-2
Aids:	Bl: 0-0 Vi: 0-0 Tstrap: 0-0 Ckp: 0-0
Best Rating:	98 4/09 Epsm 1m2f18y good

Very useful; stays 1m2f; acts on good and faster ground.

Donair

76 43

2-y-o ch c Nayef (USA)-Darwinia (GER) (Acatenango (GER))

P F I Cole Mrs E A Bass

Placings:00 (7121)

2009: 7^{0}G, 8^{0}GF,

	Starts	1st	2nd	3rd	Win & Pl
Career Total (Turf)	2	0	0	0	

Going (Turf):	Sf: 0-0 GS: 0-0 Gd: 0-1 GF: 0-1 Fm: 0-0
Distance:	5f/6f: 0-0 7f-8f: 0-1 9f-13f: 0-1 14f+: 0-0
Track :	LH: 0-1 RH: 0-0 Tight: 0-0 Gall: 0-0
Aids:	Bl: 0-0 Vi: 0-0 Tstrap: 0-0 Ckp: 0-0
Best Rating:	43 10/09 Leic 7f9y good

Donard Lodge (IRE)

(91) (53)40

4-y-o b f Elnadim (USA)-Knockatotaun (Spectrum (IRE))

Patrick Martin (J Balding 9/2) George Doyle

Placings:000/6120000540-60560 (7542a)

2009: 5^{6}SD, 7^{0}SD, 6^{5}G, 6^{6}SD, 7^{0}SD,

	Starts	1st	2nd	3rd	Win & Pl
Career Total (Turf)	4	0	0	0	
Career Total (AW)	14	1	1	0	5940

58	3/08	Dund	6f	(45-65)H	STD	£4572

Total win prize-money £4573

Going (Turf):	Sf: 0-0 GS: 0-0 Gd: 0-1 GF: 0-2 Fm: 0-1
Distance:	5f/6f: 1-10 7f-8f: 0-8 9f-13f: 0-0 14f+: 0-0
Track :	LH: 1-14 RH: 0-1 Tight: 0-2 Gall: 0-1
Aids:	Bl: 0-0 Vi: 0-0 Tstrap: 0-1 Ckp: 0-1
Best Rating:	60 4/08 Dund 6f stand

Moderate; effective at 6f; handles good ground; has worn a tongue tie.

Donativum

109 114

3-y-o gr/ro g Cadeaux Genereux-Miss Universe (IRE) (Warning)

Saeed Bin Suroor Godolphin

Placings:420111-4515543 (6848)

2009: 7^{4}GF, 7^{5}GF, 8^{1}GS, 8^{5}S, 8^{5}G, 8^{4}GF, 7^{3}G,

	Starts	1st	2nd	3rd	Win & Pl
Career Total (Turf)	13	4	1	1	904928

103 7/09 Deau 1m G-S £26699
113 10/08 SnAt 1m FRM £306633
105 10/08 NmkR 7f G-F £541700
88 8/08 Yarm 6f3y G-S £3784
Total win prize-money £878817

Going (Turf): Sf: 0-1 **GS: 2-2** Gd: 0-4 GF: 1-5 Fm: 1-1
Distance: 5f/6f: 0-2 **7f-8f: 4-11** 9f-13f: 0-0 14f+: 0-0
Track : LH: 1-1 RH: 1-3 Tight: 0-0 Gall: 0-0
Aids: Bl: 0-1 Vi: 0-0 Tstrap: 0-0 Ckp: 0-0
Best Rating: **114** 10/09 NmkR 7f good

Smart; winner of the Tattersalls Timeform Million and the Breeders' Cup Juvenile Turf in 2008; stays 1m; acts on good and easy ground, and on Pro-Ride.

Doncaster Rover (USA)

109(95) (84)**109**
3-y-o b g War Chant (USA)-Rebridled Dreams (USA) (Unbridled's Song (USA))
D H Brown (S Parr 21/3) P Holling I Raeburn S Halsall S Bolland

Placings:2165-021310 (5079a)
2009: 7^{0}SD, 6^{2}G, 6^{1}GF, 6^{3}S, 6^{1}G, 6^{0}SH,

	Starts	1st	2nd	3rd	Win & Pl
Career Total (Turf)	9	3	2	1	73891
Career Total (AW)	1	0	0	0	

108 8/09 Ches 6f18y GD £22708
107 7/09 Hayd 6f G-F £15577
95 5/08 Ches 5f16y GD £13085
Total win prize-money £51371

Going (Turf): Sf: 0-2 GS: 0-2 **Gd: 2-3** GF: 1-1 Fm: 0-0
Distance: **5f/6f: 2-7** 7f-8f: 1-3 9f-13f: 0-0 14f+: 0-0
Track : **LH: 2-3** RH: 0-0 **Tight: 2-3** Gall: 0-0
Aids: Bl: 0-0 Vi: 0-0 Tstrap: 0-0 Ckp: 0-0
Best Rating: **109** 7/09 Newb 6f8y soft

Smart; Listed winner; Group 3 placed; stays 6f; acts on good and softer ground.

Doncosaque (IRE)

102(107) (87)**83**
3-y-o b c Xaar-Darabela (IRE) (Desert King (IRE))
P Howling Glenn Birch

Placings:462501151-3341363056 (3220)
2009: 10^{3}SD, 10^{3}SD, 8^{4}SD, 10^{1}SD, 8^{3}SD, 10^{6}GF, 9^{3}GF, 10^{0}GF, 9^{5}GF, 8^{6}GF,

	Starts	1st	2nd	3rd	Win & Pl
Career Total (Turf)	8	0	0	1	891
Career Total (AW)	11	4	1	3	18571

87 2/09 Ling 1m2f (0-85)H STD £4857
85 12/08 Wolv 1m141y (0-85) STD £5046
75 11/08 Wolv 1m141y STD £2388
80 11/08 GrLe 1m STD £2590
Total win prize-money £14881

Going (Turf): **Sf: 0-1 GS: 0-0 Gd: 0-1 GF: 0-6 Fm: 0-0**
Distance: 5f/6f: 0-0 7f-8f: 1-5 **9f-13f: 3-14** 14f+: 0-0
Track : **LH: 4-10** RH: 0-6 **Tight: 3-9** Gall: 1-2
Aids: Bl: 0-0 Vi: 0-0 Tstrap: 0-0 Ckp: 0-0
Best Rating: **87** 2/09 Ling 1m2f stand

Useful; effective over 1m-1m2f; acts on Polytrack and fast ground.

Dongola (IRE)

62 **13**
2-y-o b f Xaar-Laura Margaret (Persian Bold)
P Winkworth P Winkworth

Placings:0 (1569)
2009: 5^{0}G,

	Starts	1st	2nd	3rd	Win & Pl
Career Total (Turf)	1	0	0	0	

Going (Turf): **Sf: 0-0 GS: 0-0 Gd: 0-1 GF: 0-0 Fm: 0-0**
Distance: 5f/6f: 0-1 7f-8f: 0-0 9f-13f: 0-0 14f+: 0-0
Track : LH: 0-0 RH: 0-0 Tight: 0-0 Gall: 0-1
Aids: Bl: 0-0 Vi: 0-0 Tstrap: 0-0 Ckp: 0-0
Best Rating: **13** 4/09 Wind 5f10y good

Donna Elvira

84(69) (15)**72**
2-y-o b f Doyen (IRE)-Impatiente (USA) (Vaguely Noble)
R Hannon Geoff Howard-Spink

Placings:20 (7106)
2009: 8^{2}S, 8^{0}SD,

	Starts	1st	2nd	3rd	Win & Pl
Career Total (Turf)	1	0	1	0	867
Career Total (AW)	1	0	0	0	

Going (Turf): **Sf: 0-1 GS: 0-0 Gd: 0-0 GF: 0-0 Fm: 0-0**
Distance: 5f/6f: 0-0 7f-8f: 0-2 9f-13f: 0-0 14f+: 0-0
Track : LH: 0-0 RH: 0-1 Tight: 0-0 Gall: 0-0
Aids: Bl: 0-0 Vi: 0-0 Tstrap: 0-0 Ckp: 0-0
Best Rating: **72** 10/09 Sals 1m soft

Fair; stays 1m; acts on soft.

Donny Bowl

82 **26**
4-y-o b c Presidium-Perpetuo (Mtoto)
I W McInnes Keith Brown Properties (hull) Ltd

Placings:60 (6755)
2009: 6^{6}GF, 7^{0}G,

	Starts	1st	2nd	3rd	Win & Pl
Career Total (Turf)	2	0	0	0	0

Going (Turf): **Sf: 0-0 GS: 0-0 Gd: 0-1 GF: 0-1 Fm: 0-0**
Distance: 5f/6f: 0-0 7f-8f: 0-2 9f-13f: 0-0 14f+: 0-0
Track : LH: 0-0 RH: 0-0 Tight: 0-0 Gall: 0-0
Aids: Bl: 0-0 Vi: 0-0 Tstrap: 0-0 Ckp: 0-0
Best Rating: **26** 9/09 Yarm 6f3y gd-fm

Dontbugthebunny (USA)

79(89) (50)**50**
2-y-o ch f Theatrical-Stravinia (USA) (Stravinsky (USA))
George Baker Jerry Jamgotchian

Placings:425053 (7419)
2009: 6^{4}G, 8^{2}GF, 7^{5}SD, 9^{0}SD, 8^{5}SD, 7^{3}SD,

	Starts	1st	2nd	3rd	Win & Pl
Career Total (Turf)	2	0	1	0	821
Career Total (AW)	4	0	0	1	302

Going (Turf): **Sf: 0-0 GS: 0-0 Gd: 0-1 GF: 0-1 Fm: 0-0**
Distance: 5f/6f: 0-1 7f-8f: 0-3 9f-13f: 0-2 14f+: 0-0
Track : LH: 0-4 RH: 0-1 Tight: 0-3 Gall: 0-0
Aids: Bl: 0-0 Vi: 0-0 Tstrap: 0-0 Ckp: 0-0
Best Rating: **50** 11/09 Sthl 7f stand

Moderate; effective over 7f-1m; acts on Fibresand.

Dontpaytheferry man (USA)

95(100) (59)**57**
4-y-o ch g Wiseman's Ferry (USA)-Expletive Deleted (USA) (Dr Blum (USA))
B Ellison (R A Fahey 24/9) Koo's Racing Club

Placings:65/002643-23333306 (6770)
2009: 11^{2}SD, 12^{3}SD, 11^{3}SD, 10^{3}G, 11^{3}GS, 12^{3}S, 13^{0}SD, 12^{6}SD,

	Starts	1st	2nd	3rd	Win & Pl
Career Total (Turf)	6	0	0	3	1300
Career Total (AW)	10	0	2	3	2098

Going (Turf): **Sf: 0-3 GS: 0-1 Gd: 0-2 GF: 0-0 Fm: 0-0**
Distance: 5f/6f: 0-1 7f-8f: 0-2 9f-13f: 0-11 14f+: 0-2
Track : LH: 0-7 RH: 0-8 Tight: 0-5 Gall: 0-1
Aids: Bl: 0-0 Vi: 0-0 Tstrap: 0-1 Ckp: 0-1
Best Rating: **59** 11/08 Kemp 1m4f stand

Moderate; stays 1m4f and acts on Polytrack; has worn a tongue tie; winning hurdler.

Dontriskit

(70) (15)
3-y-o ch f Bertolini (USA)-Risky Valentine (Risk Me (FR))
J L Spearing J Spearing

Placings:0 (0154)
2009: 7^{0}SD,

	Starts	1st	2nd	3rd	Win & Pl
Career Total (Turf)	0	0	0	0	
Career Total (AW)	1	0	0	0	

Going (Turf): **Sf: 0-0 GS: 0-0 Gd: 0-0 GF: 0-0 Fm: 0-0**
Distance: 5f/6f: 0-0 7f-8f: 0-1 9f-13f: 0-0 14f+: 0-0
Track : LH: 0-0 RH: 0-1 Tight: 0-0 Gall: 0-0
Aids: Bl: 0-0 Vi: 0-0 Tstrap: 0-0 Ckp: 0-0
Best Rating: **15** 1/09 Kemp 7f stand

Dontuwishitwere so

94(100) (69)**43**
3-y-o b g Kyllachy-Prospering (Prince Sabo)
P W D'Arcy The Redesdalers

Placings:2100005554 (7869)
2009: 6^{2}SD, 6^{1}SD, 6^{0}SD, 7^{0}SD, 6^{0}G, 8^{0}GS, 6^{5}SD, 6^{5}SD, 7^{5}SD, 6^{4}SS,

	Starts	1st	2nd	3rd	Win & Pl
Career Total (Turf)	2	0	0	0	
Career Total (AW)	8	1	1	0	3541

63 3/09 Sthl 6f STD £2590
Total win prize-money £2590

Going (Turf): **Sf: 0-0 GS: 0-1 Gd: 0-1 GF: 0-0 Fm: 0-0**
Distance: **5f/6f: 1-7** 7f-8f: 0-3 9f-13f: 0-0 14f+: 0-0
Track : **LH: 1-6** RH: 0-2 Tight: 0-1 Gall: 0-1
Aids: Bl: 0-0 Vi: 0-1 Tstrap: 0-0 Ckp: 0-0
Best Rating: **69** 3/09 Sthl 6f stand

Moderate; suited by 6f and acts on Fibresand.

Doon Haymer (IRE)

103 **85**

4-y-o b g Barathea (IRE)-Mutige (Warning)

I Semple Gordon McDowall

Placings:33201/0600345200-31406 **(5361)**

2009: 9^{3}GF, 9^{1}G, 9^{4}S, 9^{0}S, 9^{6}S,

	Starts	1st	2nd	3rd	Win & Pl
Career Total (Turf)	20	2	2	4	12666
79 7/09 Haml	1m1f36y (0-70)H		GD	£3238	
79 11/07 Ayr	7f50y		HVY	£3562	

Total win prize-money £6800

Going (Turf): **Sf: 1-9** GS: 0-3 **Gd: 1-5** GF: 0-3 Fm: 0-0
Distance: 5f/6f: 0-0 7f-8f: 1-7 9f-13f: 1-13 14f+: 0-0
Track : LH: 1-8 RH: 1-9 **Tight: 1-9** Gall: 0-3
Aids: Bl: 0-0 **Vi: 1-7** Tstrap: 0-1 Ckp: 0-1
Best Rating: **85** 5/08 Haml 1m3f16y gd-fm

Fair; stays 1m1f and acts on most ground; has worn a visor.

Doonigan (IRE)

12(79) (17)**51**

5-y-o b g Val Royal (FR)-Music In My Life (IRE) (Law Society (USA))

G Brown T Bramble

Placings:064/00502/0-00 **(2127)**

2009: 11^{0}SD, 17^{0}GS,

	Starts	1st	2nd	3rd	Win & Pl
Career Total (Turf)	6	0	1	0	838
Career Total (AW)	5	0	0	0	241

Going (Turf): **Sf: 0-0 GS: 0-4 Gd: 0-2 GF: 0-0 Fm: 0-0**
Distance: 5f/6f: 0-2 7f-8f: 0-3 9f-13f: 0-4 14f+: 0-2
Track : LH: 0-5 RH: 0-4 Tight: 0-4 Gall: 0-1
Aids: Bl: 0-1 Vi: 0-1 Tstrap: 0-1 Ckp: 0-1
Best Rating: **53** 10/06 NmkR 6f gd-sft

Moderate; stays 1m2f; acts on good ground.

Doorock (IRE)

90(87) (52)**60**

5-y-o b g Redback-Prime Time Girl (Primo Dominie)

S T Nolan J P Prunty

Placings:00/00060105 0/**5440631426**-335015000 **(7444a)**

2009: 7^{3}GY, 5^{3}GF, 5^{5}G, 6^{0}S, 7^{1}S, 7^{5}S, 7^{0}S, 5^{0}SD, 8^{0}SD,

	Starts	1st	2nd	3rd	Win & Pl
Career Total (Turf)	25	3	1	3	17848
Career Total (AW)	5	0	0	0	271
57 8/09 Tipp	7f100y	(47-65)H	SFT	£5366	
54 8/08 Bell	5f	(45-60)H	G-Y	£4826	
53 8/07 Bell	5f	(42-60)H	FRM	£4435	

Total win prize-money £14629

Going (Turf): **Sf: 1-8** GS: 0-0 Gd: 0-4 GF: 0-2 **Fm: 1-4**
Distance: **5f/6f: 2-23** 7f-8f: 1-7 9f-13f: 0-0 14f+: 0-0
Track : **LH: 3-23** RH: 0-4 Tight: 0-1 Gall: 0-0
Aids: Bl: 0-0 Vi: 0-0 Tstrap: 3-20 Ckp: 3-20
Best Rating: **60** 8/09 DRoy 7f soft

Dorback

97 **87**

2-y-o ch c Kyllachy-Pink Supreme (Night Shift (USA))

H Candy Thurloe Thoroughbreds XXIV

Placings:16205 **(7150)**

2009: 6^{1}GF, 6^{6}GS, 5^{2}GF, 6^{0}G, 6^{5}G,

	Starts	1st	2nd	3rd	Win & Pl
Career Total (Turf)	5	1	1	0	3824
87 6/09 Wind	6f		G-F	£2388	

Total win prize-money £2388

Going (Turf): Sf: 0-0 GS: 0-1 Gd: 0-2 **GF: 1-2** Fm: 0-0
Distance: **5f/6f: 1-4** 7f-8f: 0-1 9f-13f: 0-0 14f+: 0-0
Track : LH: 0-0 RH: 0-0 Tight: 0-0 **Gall: 1-1**
Aids: Bl: 0-0 Vi: 0-0 Tstrap: 0-0 Ckp: 0-0
Best Rating: **87** 9/09 Bevl 5f gd-fm

Useful; effective at 5-6f; acts on fast ground.

Doric Echo

100(80) (32)**78**

3-y-o b g Bertolini (USA)-Latour (Sri Pekan (USA))

B Smart Doric Dream Partnership

Placings:453315-50054300 **(6824)**

2009: 7^{5}GF, 7^{0}G, 7^{0}GF, 7^{5}G, 8^{4}S, 8^{3}G, 7^{0}SD, 7^{0}GF,

	Starts	1st	2nd	3rd	Win & Pl
Career Total (Turf)	13	1	0	3	6265
Career Total (AW)	1	0	0	0	
78 10/08 Ayr	6f	(0-75)	HVY	£2914	

Total win prize-money £2914

Going (Turf): **Sf: 1-4** GS: 0-0 Gd: 0-4 GF: 0-5 Fm: 0-0
Distance: **5f/6f: 1-5** 7f-8f: 0-9 9f-13f: 0-0 14f+: 0-0
Track : LH: 0-7 RH: 0-1 Tight: 0-1 Gall: 0-1
Aids: Bl: 0-0 Vi: 0-0 Tstrap: 0-1 Ckp: 0-1
Best Rating: **78** 10/08 Ayr 6f heavy

Fair; effective over 6f; acts on fast and testing ground.

Doric Lady

106(110) (86)**85**

4-y-o b f Kyllachy-Tanasie (Cadeaux Genereux)

J A R Toller Buckingham Thoroughbreds I

Placings:632/4050131-414100001 **(7395)**

2009: 6^{4}GS, 5^{1}GF, 6^{4}G, 5^{1}G, 6^{0}G, 5^{0}GF, 5^{0}GF, 5^{0}G, 6^{1}SD,

	Starts	1st	2nd	3rd	Win & Pl
Career Total (Turf)	17	4	1	1	19559
Career Total (AW)	2	1	0	1	5566
86 11/09 Ling	6f	(0-85)H	STD	£5180	
85 7/09 Donc	5f	(0-80)H	GD	£4857	
85 5/09 Leic	5f218y	(0-80)H	G-F	£6231	
83 10/08 Yarm	6f3y	(0-75)H	SFT	£2849	
70 9/08 Yarm	6f3y		GD	£2901	

Total win prize-money £22020

Going (Turf): Sf: 1-2 GS: 0-2 **Gd: 2-5** GF: 1-7 Fm: 0-1
Distance: **5f/6f: 3-16** 7f-8f: 2-3 9f-13f: 0-0 14f+: 0-0
Track : **LH: 1-4** RH: 0-0 **Tight: 1-2** Gall: 0-1
Aids: Bl: 0-0 Vi: 0-0 Tstrap: 0-0 Ckp: 0-0
Best Rating: **86** 11/09 Ling 6f stand

Useful; effective over 5f-6f; acts on good ground; goes on Polytrack.

Dormer Fleet

90(69) (28)**78**

2-y-o b c Kyllachy-Petong's Pet (Petong)

J H M Gosden C J Murfitt

Placings:0100 **(7290)**

2009: 7^{0}SD, 6^{1}S, 7^{0}G, 6^{0}S,

	Starts	1st	2nd	3rd	Win & Pl
Career Total (Turf)	3	1	0	0	2388
Career Total (AW)	1	0	0	0	
78 10/09 Nott	6f15y		SFT	£2388	

Total win prize-money £2388

Going (Turf): **Sf: 1-2** GS: 0-0 Gd: 0-1 GF: 0-0 Fm: 0-0
Distance: 5f/6f: 0-1 **7f-8f: 1-3** 9f-13f: 0-0 14f+: 0-0
Track : LH: 0-0 RH: 0-1 Tight: 0-0 Gall: 0-0
Aids: Bl: 0-0 Vi: 0-0 Tstrap: 0-0 Ckp: 0-0
Best Rating: **78** 10/09 Nott 6f15y soft

Fair; stays 6f and acts on easy ground.

Dorn Dancer (IRE)

103(87) (54)**80**

7-y-o b m Danehill Dancer (IRE)-Appledorn (Doulab (USA))

W M Brisbourne (D W Barker 3/6) The Ebor Partnership

Placings:01500600/050005540000/1246403350302466/4341004051560043/33133256163260-**0000006000**0 **(6846)**

2009: 6^{0}SD, 7^{0}GF, 6^{0}GF, 6^{0}GS, 5^{0}GF, 8^{0}GF, 6^{6}G, 7^{0}G, 7^{0}SF, 7^{0}SD, 7^{0}G,

	Starts	1st	2nd	3rd	Win & Pl
Career Total (Turf)	74	6	4	10	39016
Career Total (AW)	3	0	0	0	
79 6/08 Hayd	6f	(0-75)H	GD	£2590	
71 4/08 Nott	5f13y	(0-70)H	SFT	£2590	
66 7/07 Ayr	6f	(0-85)H	GD	£6232	
67 5/07 Ayr	6f	(0-75)H	G-S	£4533	
66 3/06 Muss	5f	(0-70)H	HVY	£3886	
73 6/04 Ches	5f16y D		G-F	£5343	

Total win prize-money £25175

Going (Turf): **Sf: 2-15** GS: 1-16 **Gd: 2-27** GF: 1-15 Fm: 0-1
Distance: **5f/6f: 6-53** 7f-8f: 0-24 9f-13f: 0-0 14f+: 0-0
Track : **LH: 1-21** RH: 0-4 **Tight: 1-15** Gall: 0-1
Aids: Bl: 0-3 Vi: 0-0 Tstrap: 0-1 Ckp: 0-1
Best Rating: **80** 7/08 Ayr 6f good

Fair; effective at 5f-6f and acts on most ground, but probably best with some ease; has been tried in blinkers.

Dot's Delight

92(101) (51)**49**

5-y-o b m Golden Snake (USA)-Hotel California (IRE) (Last Tycoon)

M G Rimell Mrs S E Lindley

Placings:003022**440/0313434-01044** **(5246)**

2009: 10^{0}SD, 13^{1}SF, 11^{0}SD, 11^{4}GS, 13^{4}F,

	Starts	1st	2nd	3rd	Win & Pl
Career Total (Turf)	8	0	2	1	1808
Career Total (AW)	13	2	0	3	5211
51 7/09 Wolv	1m5f194y (0-65)H		SF	£2388	
47 2/08 Sthl	1m4f		STD	£1911	

Total win prize-money £4299

Going (Turf): **Sf: 0-0 GS: 0-2 Gd: 0-2 GF: 0-3 Fm: 0-1**
Distance: 5f/6f: 0-0 7f-8f: 0-0 9f-13f: 1-17 14f+: 1-4
Track : **LH: 2-17** RH: 0-4 **Tight: 1-12** Gall: 0-1
Aids: Bl: 0-3 Vi: 0-0 Tstrap: 0-2 Ckp: 0-2
Best Rating: **58** 11/07 Wolv 1m1f103y stand

Moderate; suited by around 1m4f-1m5f; acts on soft ground; goes on Fibresand and Polytrack; has been tried in blinkers, cheekpieces and a tongue tie.

Double Act

(100) (82)**59**

3-y-o br g Where Or When (IRE)-Secret Flame (Machiavellian (USA))

Evan Williams (J Noseda 21/1) R E R Williams

Placings:00162-113 (0547)

2009: 8^{1}SD, 8^{1}SD, 8^{3}SD,

	Starts	1st	2nd	3rd	Win & Pl
Career Total (Turf)	2	0	0	0	
Career Total (AW)	6	3	1	1	8627

76	1/09	Kemp	1m	STD	£2047
78	1/09	Wolv	1m141y	STD	£2047
80	11/08	Wolv	7f32y	STD	£2729

Total win prize-money £6824

Going (Turf): **Sf: 0-0 GS: 0-0 Gd: 0-2 GF: 0-0 Fm: 0-0**
Distance: 5f/6f: 0-1 **7f-8f: 2-5** 9f-13f: 1-2 14f+: 0-0
Track : **LH: 2-4** RH: 1-2 **Tight: 2-4** Gall: 0-1
Aids: Bl: 0-0 Vi: 0-0 Tstrap: 0-0 Ckp: 0-0
Best Rating: 82 12/08 Wolv 1m141y stand

Useful but races in claimers; stays 1m; acts on Polytrack; has worn a tongue tie.

Double Banded (IRE)

104 (73)**94**

5-y-o b g Mark Of Esteem (IRE)-Bronzewing (Beldale Flutter (USA))

K A Ryan (Ian Williams 20/6) Dr Marwan Koukash

Placings:000/006113112/1400063-006624 (6115)

2009: 18^{0}GF, 16^{0}G, 14^{6}G, 13^{6}GF, 15^{2}GF, 18^{4}GF,

	Starts	1st	2nd	3rd	Win & Pl
Career Total (Turf)	23	5	2	1	42741
Career Total (AW)	2	0	0	1	454

97	4/08	Nott	1m6f15y	(0-95)H	G-S	£9346
92	11/07	NmkR	2m	(0-90)H	GD	£7772
80	10/07	Rdcr	1m6f19y	(0-75)H	GD	£2817
73	9/07	Rdcr	1m6f19y	(0-70)H	FRM	£2817
61	8/07	Newc	1m4f93y	(0-65)H	GD	£3238

Total win prize-money £25992

Going (Turf): Sf: 0-1 GS: 1-4 **Gd: 3-10** GF: 0-7 Fm: 1-1
Distance: 5f/6f: 0-0 7f-8f: 0-3 9f-13f: 1-4 **14f+: 4-18**
Track : **LH: 4-14** RH: 1-9 Tight: 2-12 Gall: 2-5
Aids: Bl: 0-0 Vi: 0-0 Tstrap: 0-2 Ckp: 0-2
Best Rating: 97 4/08 Nott 1m6f15y gd-sft

Useful; stays 2m; acts on most ground on turf; goes on Polytrack; has worn cheekpieces.

Double Bill (USA)

(104) (79)**74**

5-y-o b/br g Mr Greeley (USA)-Salty Perfume (USA) (Salt Lake (USA))

P F I Cole P F I Cole Ltd

Placings:0/14000/632000-3 (7861)

2009: 7^{3}SD,

	Starts	1st	2nd	3rd	Win & Pl
Career Total (Turf)	6	1	0	0	3886
Career Total (AW)	7	0	1	2	2289

74	5/07	Leic	5f218y	G-F	£3886

Total win prize-money £3886

Going (Turf): Sf: 0-0 GS: 0-3 Gd: 0-1 **GF: 1-2** Fm: 0-0
Distance: **5f/6f: 1-10** 7f-8f: 0-3 9f-13f: 0-0 14f+: 0-0
Track : LH: 0-2 RH: 0-3 Tight: 0-2 Gall: 0-1
Aids: Bl: 0-2 Vi: 0-0 Tstrap: 0-1 Ckp: 0-1
Best Rating: 79 6/07 Kemp 6f stand

Modest; stays 7f; acts on fast ground, on Polytrack and Fibresand.

Double Carpet (IRE)

74(104) (71)**58**

6-y-o b g Lahib (USA)-Cupid Miss (Anita's Prince)

G Woodward Mr & Mrs Bloom

Placings:050/002020/030100/055003011-00060 (4225)

2009: 5^{0}SD, 5^{0}SD, 6^{0}G, 5^{6}SD, 6^{0}G,

	Starts	1st	2nd	3rd	Win & Pl
Career Total (Turf)	16	1	1	1	4684
Career Total (AW)	13	2	1	1	5337

71	12/08	Wolv	5f216y	(0-60)H	SF	£2047
55	12/08	GrLe	6f	(0-50)H	STD	£2266
65	10/07	Ayr	6f	(0-70)H	G-S	£3238

Total win prize-money £7553

Going (Turf): Sf: 0-3 **GS: 1-4** Gd: 0-7 GF: 0-2 Fm: 0-0
Distance: **5f/6f: 3-19** 7f-8f: 0-10 9f-13f: 0-0 14f+: 0-0
Track : **LH: 2-13** RH: 0-2 Tight: 1-6 Gall: 1-2
Aids: Bl: 0-0 Vi: 0-0 Tstrap: 0-0 Ckp: 0-0
Best Rating: 71 12/08 Wolv 5f216y std-fst

Modest; seems suited by 6f; acts on easy ground; goes on Fibresand.

Double Exposure

87(77) (20)**45**

5-y-o b g Double Trigger (IRE)-Last Night's Fun (IRE) (Law Society (USA))

Jamie Poulton Oceana racing

Placings:00/03 (6417)

2009: 11^{0}SD, 14^{3}GF,

	Starts	1st	2nd	3rd	Win & Pl
Career Total (Turf)	2	0	0	1	482
Career Total (AW)	2	0	0	0	

Going (Turf): **Sf: 0-1 GS: 0-0 Gd: 0-0 GF: 0-1 Fm: 0-0**
Distance: 5f/6f: 0-0 7f-8f: 0-1 9f-13f: 0-2 14f+: 0-1
Track : LH: 0-2 RH: 0-2 Tight: 0-3 Gall: 0-0
Aids: Bl: 0-0 Vi: 0-0 Tstrap: 0-0 Ckp: 0-0
Best Rating: 49 12/06 Ling 1m stand

Double Fortune

(82) (47)

2-y-o b f Singspiel (IRE)-Four-Legged Friend (Aragon)

Jamie Poulton R W Huggins

Placings:0 (7764)

2009: 8^{0}SD,

	Starts	1st	2nd	3rd	Win & Pl
Career Total (Turf)	0	0	0	0	
Career Total (AW)	1	0	0	0	

Going (Turf): **Sf: 0-0 GS: 0-0 Gd: 0-0 GF: 0-0 Fm: 0-0**
Distance: 5f/6f: 0-0 7f-8f: 0-1 9f-13f: 0-0 14f+: 0-0
Track : LH: 0-0 RH: 0-1 Tight: 0-0 Gall: 0-0
Aids: Bl: 0-0 Vi: 0-0 Tstrap: 0-0 Ckp: 0-0
Best Rating: 47 12/09 Kemp 1m stand

Double Moon

88 **46**

3-y-o b g Makbul-Emoona (FR) (Linamix (FR))

George Baker Mrs P Scott-Dunn

Placings:0406 (4669)

2009: 9^{0}G, 7^{4}GF, 7^{0}GF, 10^{6}G,

	Starts	1st	2nd	3rd	Win & Pl
Career Total (Turf)	4	0	0	0	216

Going (Turf): **Sf: 0-0 GS: 0-0 Gd: 0-2 GF: 0-2 Fm: 0-0**
Distance: 5f/6f: 0-0 7f-8f: 0-2 9f-13f: 0-2 14f+: 0-0
Track : LH: 0-3 RH: 0-1 Tight: 0-2 Gall: 0-0
Aids: Bl: 0-0 Vi: 0-0 Tstrap: 0-0 Ckp: 0-0
Best Rating: 46 7/09 Wwck 7f26y gd-fm

Double Rollover

66(83) (43)

2-y-o b c Fantastic Light (USA)-Princess Miletrian (IRE) (Danehill (USA))

W R Muir Linkslade Lottery

Placings:000500 (6034)

2009: 7^{0}GS, 7^{0}S, 7^{0}GF, 7^{5}SD, 7^{0}SD, 8^{0}GF,

	Starts	1st	2nd	3rd	Win & Pl
Career Total (Turf)	4	0	0	0	
Career Total (AW)	2	0	0	0	0

Going (Turf): **Sf: 0-1 GS: 0-1 Gd: 0-0 GF: 0-2 Fm: 0-0**
Distance: 5f/6f: 0-0 7f-8f: 0-5 9f-13f: 0-1 14f+: 0-0
Track : LH: 0-2 RH: 0-1 Tight: 0-2 Gall: 0-0
Aids: Bl: 0-2 Vi: 0-1 Tstrap: 0-2 Ckp: 0-2
Best Rating: 43 8/09 Wolv 7f32y stand

Double Spectre (IRE)

100(98) (65)**74**

7-y-o b g Spectrum (IRE)-Phantom Ring (Magic Ring (IRE))

Jean-Rene Auvray The Dragon Partnership

Placings:45320/350302013/01040556/002130000-3600300 (7112)

2009: 14^{3}SD, 11^{6}GF, 11^{0}F, 12^{0}GF, 16^{3}G, 15^{0}GF, 12^{0}SD,

	Starts	1st	2nd	3rd	Win & Pl
Career Total (Turf)	33	3	3	6	15296
Career Total (AW)	5	0	0	1	385

71	6/08	Sals	1m4f	(0-70)H	G-F	£3238
72	4/07	Bath	1m2f46y	(0-65)H	FRM	£2266
71	9/06	Sand	1m14y	(0-65)H	G-F	£3238

Total win prize-money £8744

Going (Turf): Sf: 0-1 GS: 0-2 Gd: 0-14 **GF: 2-13** Fm: 1-3
Distance: 5f/6f: 0-0 7f-8f: 0-1 **9f-13f: 3-33** 14f+: 0-4
Track : LH: 1-18 **RH: 2-18 Tight: 2-19** Gall: 0-7
Aids: Bl: 0-1 Vi: 0-0 Tstrap: 0-0 Ckp: 0-0
Best Rating: 74 6/08 Newb 1m3f5y gd-fm

Modest; effective over 1m2f-1m4f; acts on a sound surface.

Double Valentine

79(102) (62)**45**

6-y-o ch m Primo Valentino (IRE)-Charlottevalentina (IRE) (Perugino (USA))

R Ingram Ellangowan Racing Partners

Placings:00000/0626020/030006U0166625400/31321556 50501460-3005600005 (7520)

2009: 7^{3}SD, 8^{0}SD, 8^{0}SD, 9^{5}SD, 10^{6}SD, 8^{0}SD, 8^{0}GF, 8^{0}SD, 7^{0}SD, 7^{5}SD,

	Starts	1st	2nd	3rd	Win & Pl
Career Total (Turf)	14	0	1	1	1215

Career Total (AW)	41	4	3	3	10291	
62	12/08 Kemp	1m	(0-50)H	STD	£2047	
61	2/08 Ling	7f	(0-60)H	STD	£1876	
56	1/08 Kemp	6f	(0-45)	STD	£1365	
51	8/07 Ling	6f	(0-45)	STD	£2047	

Total win prize-money £7337

Going (Turf): Sf: 0-0 **GS: 0-1 Gd: 0-2 GF: 0-10 Fm: 0-1**
Distance: 5f/6f: 2-20 7f-8f: 2-32 9f-13f: 0-3 14f+: 0-0
Track : LH: 2-23 RH: 2-20 **Tight: 2-20** Gall: 0-3
Aids: Bl: 0-2 Vi: 0-0 Tstrap: 0-0 Ckp: 0-0
Best Rating: **62** 3/09 Kemp 7f stand

Moderate; seems best suited to 6f-7f; acts on good ground; also goes on Polytrack; has worn blinkers; tricky ride.

Double Whammy

98 **63**

3-y-o b g Systematic-Honor Rouge (IRE) (Highest Honor (FR))
Jamie Poulton R W Huggins

Placings:055 **(5578)**
2009: 10^{0}GF, 11^{5}G, 11^{5}GF,

	Starts	1st	2nd	3rd	Win & Pl
Career Total (Turf)	3	0	0	0	0

Going (Turf): **Sf: 0-0 GS: 0-0 Gd: 0-1 GF: 0-2 Fm: 0-0**
Distance: 5f/6f: 0-0 7f-8f: 0-0 9f-13f: 0-3 14f+: 0-0
Track : LH: 0-2 RH: 0-1 Tight: 0-2 Gall: 0-0
Aids: Bl: 0-0 Vi: 0-0 Tstrap: 0-0 Ckp: 0-0
Best Rating: **63** 7/09 Bath 1m3f144y good

Doubly Guest

102 **76**

5-y-o b m Barathea Guest-Countess Guest (IRE) (Spectrum (IRE))
Tim Vaughan (B W Hills 25/7) M Khan X2

Placings:03031/000420051/326 **(5857)**
2009: 16^{3}GF, 16^{2}G, 15^{6}GF,

	Starts	1st	2nd	3rd	Win & Pl	
Career Total (Turf)	17	2	2	3	10790	
73	10/07 Bath	2m1f34y	(0-75)H	GD	£3238	
74	10/06 Pont	1m4y	(0-75)	G-S	£3886	

Total win prize-money £7125

Going (Turf): Sf: 0-4 **GS: 1-5 Gd: 1-3** GF: 0-5 Fm: 0-0
Distance: 5f/6f: 0-1 7f-8f: 0-2 9f-13f: 1-10 14f+: 1-4
Track : **LH: 2-8** RH: 0-5 **Tight: 1-9** Gall: 0-1
Aids: Bl: 0-0 Vi: 0-0 Tstrap: 1-2 Ckp: 1-2
Best Rating: **76** 7/09 Ling 2m good

Modest; stays 2m; acts on soft ground; has worn cheek-pieces.

Doubnov (FR)

81(102) (70)**42**

6-y-o gr g Linamix (FR)-Karmitycia (FR) (Last Tycoon)
Ian Williams Dr Marwan Koukash

Placings:153116/10112/232-00010 **(7811)**
2009: 12^{0}GS, 10^{0}SD, 10^{0}GS, 12^{1}SD, 12^{0}SD,

	Starts	1st	2nd	3rd	Win & Pl
Career Total (Turf)	15	5	3	2	96222
Career Total (AW)	4	2	0	0	9220
70	11/09 Ling	1m4f	STD	£1978	
102	7/07 Diep	1m3f	SFT	£18918	
104	5/07 Pari	1m3f	SFT	£8108	
	2/07 Toul	1m2f	HVY	£7432	
	10/06 Mars	1m2f	GD	£7586	
94	8/06 Deau	1m1f110y	STD	£7241	
	3/06 Fntb	1m1f	HVY	£6551	

Total win prize-money £57817

Going (Turf): **Sf: 4-6** GS: 0-2 Gd: 1-6 GF: 0-0 Fm: 0-0
Distance: 5f/6f: 0-0 7f-8f: 0-0 **9f-13f: 7-19** 14f+: 0-0
Track : **LH: 1-6** RH: 0-5 **Tight: 1-2** Gall: 0-5
Aids: Bl: 0-0 Vi: 0-0 Tstrap: 1-2 Ckp: 1-2
Best Rating: **104** 5/07 Pari 1m3f soft

Very useful; ex-French; stays 1m4f; acts on good ground.

Doubtful Sound (USA)

(113) (102)**69**

5-y-o b g Diesis-Roam Free (USA) (Unbridled (USA))
R Hollinshead Phil Pye

Placings:2/21066/514612405120422152211 5-143606 **(7414)**
2009: 6^{1}SD, 5^{4}SD, 5^{3}SD, 5^{6}SD, 5^{0}SD, 5^{6}SD,

	Starts	1st	2nd	3rd	Win & Pl
Career Total (Turf)	7	1	1	0	2454
Career Total (AW)	27	7	7	1	40011
101	1/09 Ling	6f	(0-100)H	STD	£11656
96	12/08 Wolv	5f20y	(0-85)H	STD	£5180
88	11/08 Wolv	5f216y	(0-75)H	STD	£3238
78	10/08 Wolv	5f216y	STD	£2388	
68	5/08 Yarm	6f3y	G-F	£1683	
78	3/08 Wolv	5f20y	STD	£2730	
79	1/08 Wolv	5f20y	STD	£2457	
76	3/07 Wolv	5f216y	SF	£3412	

Total win prize-money £32748

Going (Turf): Sf: 0-0 GS: 0-1 Gd: 0-2 **GF: 1-4** Fm: 0-0
Distance: **5f/6f: 7-31** 7f-8f: 1-3 9f-13f: 0-0 14f+: 0-0
Track : **LH: 7-24** RH: 0-0 **Tight: 7-17** Gall: 0-5
Aids: Bl: 1-4 Vi: 0-0 Tstrap: 4-14 Ckp: 4-14
Best Rating: **102** 2/09 Wolv 5f20y stand

Useful; effective over 5f-7f; acts on fast ground and on sand; has worn cheekpieces.

Douchkette (FR)

81 **42**

3-y-o b f Califet (FR)-Douchka (FR) (Fijar Tango (FR))
John Berry (F Belmont 9/5) Just The Two Of Us

Placings:00 **(4057)**
2009: 8^{0}G, 8^{0}S,

	Starts	1st	2nd	3rd	Win & Pl
Career Total (Turf)	2	0	0	0	

Going (Turf): **Sf: 0-1 GS: 0-0 Gd: 0-1 GF: 0-0 Fm: 0-0**
Distance: 5f/6f: 0-0 7f-8f: 0-1 9f-13f: 0-1 14f+: 0-0
Track : LH: 0-0 RH: 0-1 Tight: 0-1 Gall: 0-0
Aids: Bl: 0-0 Vi: 0-0 Tstrap: 0-0 Ckp: 0-0
Best Rating: **42** 7/09 Wind 1m67y good

Dove (IRE)

96(101) (70)**75**

4-y-o b f Sadler's Wells (USA)-Golden Digger (USA) (Mr Prospector (USA))
J H M Gosden H R H Princess Haya Of Jordan

Placings:02/10 **(7131)**
2009: 10^{1}GS, 13^{0}SD,

	Starts	1st	2nd	3rd	Win & Pl	
Career Total (Turf)	2	1	1	0	4560	
Career Total (AW)	2	0	0	0		
75	7/09 Pont	1m2f6y		G-S	£3885	

Total win prize-money £3886

Going (Turf): Sf: 0-1 **GS: 1-1** Gd: 0-0 GF: 0-0 Fm: 0-0
Distance: 5f/6f: 0-0 7f-8f: 0-1 **9f-13f: 1-3** 14f+: 0-0
Track : **LH: 1-3** RH: 0-0 Tight: 0-2 Gall: 0-0
Aids: Bl: 0-0 Vi: 0-0 Tstrap: 0-0 Ckp: 0-0
Best Rating: **87** 10/07 Yarm 1m3y soft

Fair half-sister to Naheef; stays 1m; acts on soft ground.

Dove Cottage (IRE)

103 (65)**83**

7-y-o b g Great Commotion (USA)-Pooka (Dominion)
W S Kittow Reg Gifford

Placings:6531254/0000130/241104/043054/210400-5404210 **(6936)**
2009: 9^{5}G, 10^{4}G, 10^{0}GF, 10^{4}G, 12^{2}GF, 12^{1}GS, 11^{0}G,

	Starts	1st	2nd	3rd	Win & Pl	
Career Total (Turf)	38	6	4	3	33390	
Career Total (AW)	1	0	0	0	241	
79	10/09 Folk	1m4f	(0-70)H	G-S	£2729	
83	5/08 Gdwd	1m3f	(0-70)H	G-F	£3238	
73	6/06 Chep	1m2f36y	(0-70)H	G-F	£3886	
70	6/06 Chep	1m2f36y	(0-65)H	G-F	£2914	
64	8/05 Gdwd	1m1f192y	(0-70)H	GD	£4478	
60	8/04 Chep	6f16y	E	G-F	£4173	

Total win prize-money £21421

Going (Turf): Sf: 0-8 GS: 1-6 Gd: 1-11 **GF: 4-11** Fm: 0-2
Distance: 5f/6f: 0-3 7f-8f: 1-5 **9f-13f: 5-31** 14f+: 0-0
Track : LH: 2-23 **RH: 3-10 Tight: 3-13** Gall: 0-3
Aids: Bl: 0-0 Vi: 0-0 Tstrap: 0-1 Ckp: 0-1
Best Rating: **83** 5/08 Gdwd 1m3f gd-fm

Modest; stays 1m4f and acts on most ground; suited by forcing tactics.

Dove Mews

95(93) (57)**81**

3-y-o b f Namid-Flying Fulmar (Bahamian Bounty)
M L W Bell Sir Thomas Pilkington

Placings:13402-006420 **(5989)**
2009: 6^{0}GF, 6^{0}GF, 6^{6}GS, 7^{4}G, 7^{2}G, 6^{0}SD,

	Starts	1st	2nd	3rd	Win & Pl
Career Total (Turf)	10	1	2	1	10575
Career Total (AW)	1	0	0	0	
72	6/08 NmkJ	6f	G-F	£5180	

Total win prize-money £5181

Going (Turf): Sf: 0-2 GS: 0-2 Gd: 0-2 **GF: 1-4** Fm: 0-0
Distance: **5f/6f: 1-7** 7f-8f: 0-4 9f-13f: 0-0 14f+: 0-0
Track : LH: 0-2 RH: 0-1 Tight: 0-1 Gall: 0-0
Aids: Bl: 0-0 Vi: 0-0 Tstrap: 0-0 Ckp: 0-0
Best Rating: **81** 10/08 Wwck 6f soft

Fair; suited by 7f; acts on fast and easy ground.

Dovedon Angel

51(94) (56)**37**

3-y-o b f Winged Love (IRE)-Alexander Star (IRE) (Inzar (USA))
Miss Gay Kelleway Whatley, Baber & Clark

Placings:0-50432 **(7765)**
2009: 10^{5}SD, 11^{0}S, 12^{4}SD, 10^{3}SD, 11^{2}SD,

	Starts	1st	2nd	3rd	Win & Pl
Career Total (Turf)	2	0	0	0	
Career Total (AW)	4	0	1	1	846

Going (Turf): Sf: 0-1 GS: 0-1 Gd: 0-0 GF: 0-0 Fm: 0-0
Distance: 5f/6f: 0-0 7f-8f: 0-1 9f-13f: 0-5 14f+: 0-0
Track : LH: 0-4 RH: 0-1 Tight: 0-4 Gall: 0-0
Aids: Bl: 0-0 Vi: 0-0 Tstrap: 0-0 Ckp: 0-0
Best Rating: 56 12/09 Kemp 1m3f stand

Moderate; suited by 1m2f and Polytrack.

Dovedon Diva

88 52

2-y-o b f Generous (IRE)-Alexander Star (IRE) (Inzar (USA))
T Keddy The Diva Partnership

Placings:P00 (7288)
2009: 8^{P}S, 7^{0}G, 6^{0}S,

	Starts	1st	2nd	3rd	Win & Pl
Career Total (Turf)	3	0	0	0	

Going (Turf): Sf: 0-2 GS: 0-0 Gd: 0-1 GF: 0-0 Fm: 0-0
Distance: 5f/6f: 0-1 7f-8f: 0-1 9f-13f: 0-1 14f+: 0-0
Track : LH: 0-1 RH: 0-0 Tight: 0-0 Gall: 0-0
Aids: Bl: 0-0 Vi: 0-0 Tstrap: 0-0 Ckp: 0-0
Best Rating: 52 11/09 Donc 6f soft

Dovedon Earl

(93) (56)

3-y-o b g Millkom-Syrian Flutist (Shaamit (IRE))
T Keddy Michael C Whatley

Placings:04 (7590)
2009: 10^{0}SD, 12^{4}SD,

	Starts	1st	2nd	3rd	Win & Pl
Career Total (Turf)	0	0	0	0	
Career Total (AW)	2	0	0	0	192

Going (Turf): Sf: 0-0 GS: 0-0 Gd: 0-0 GF: 0-0 Fm: 0-0
Distance: 5f/6f: 0-0 7f-8f: 0-0 9f-13f: 0-2 14f+: 0-0
Track : LH: 0-0 RH: 0-2 Tight: 0-0 Gall: 0-0
Aids: Bl: 0-0 Vi: 0-0 Tstrap: 0-0 Ckp: 0-0
Best Rating: 56 11/09 Kemp 1m4f stand

Dovedon Hero

78(93) (66)40

9-y-o ch g Millkom-Hot Topic (IRE) (Desse Zenny (USA))
P J McBride P J McBride

Placings:21403301 6/00204602034242012/364606160030 503/51655325202605 0/46224/3-00 (2129)
2009: 10^{0}G, 12^{0}SD,

	Starts	1st	2nd	3rd	Win & Pl
Career Total (Turf)	32	3	5	4	38819
Career Total (AW)	32	2	6	4	18761

76 2/06 Ling 1m5f (0-75)H STD £3238
84 5/05 NmkR 2m (0-95)H G-F £13452
77 12/04 Ling 1m5f (0-77)H STD £3446
87 10/03 Leic 1m3f183yC(0-90)H G-F £6593
72 7/03 Bath 1m2f46y D FRM £3692
Total win prize-money £30423

Going (Turf): Sf: 0-0 GS: 0-1 Gd: 0-9 GF: 2-20 Fm: 1-2
Distance: 5f/6f: 0-0 7f-8f: 0-0 9f-13f: 4-46 14f+: 1-18
Track : LH: 3-41 RH: 2-23 Tight: 3-29 Gall: 1-19
Aids: Bl: 4-49 Vi: 0-0 Tstrap: 0-2 Ckp: 0-2
Best Rating: 87 10/03 Leic 1m3f183y gd-fm

Modest handicapper; does not always give the impression that he is giving his all in a finish; effective between one and a half to two miles; suited by fast ground and Polytrack.

Dower Glen

87 67

2-y-o b f Camacho-Aimee's Delight (Robellino (USA))
I Semple Gordon McDowall

Placings:520353460 (5976)
2009: 5^{5}GF, 5^{2}GS, 5^{0}GF, 5^{3}GF, 5^{5}GF, 5^{3}G, 5^{4}GF, 5^{6}S, 5^{0}GF,

	Starts	1st	2nd	3rd	Win & Pl
Career Total (Turf)	9	0	1	2	1752

Going (Turf): Sf: 0-1 GS: 0-1 Gd: 0-1 GF: 0-6 Fm: 0-0
Distance: 5f/6f: 0-9 7f-8f: 0-0 9f-13f: 0-0 14f+: 0-0
Track : LH: 0-0 RH: 0-0 Tight: 0-0 Gall: 0-0
Aids: Bl: 0-2 Vi: 0-0 Tstrap: 0-0 Ckp: 0-0
Best Rating: 67 5/09 Bevl 5f gd-fm

Moderate; effective over 5f; acts on fast and on easy ground.

Dowlleh

65(85) (71)36

5-y-o b g Noverre (USA)-Al Persian (IRE) (Persian Bold)
G Brown Mrs K W Sneath

Placings:222522145/60546P500/00-0 (5729)
2009: 6^{0}GS,

	Starts	1st	2nd	3rd	Win & Pl
Career Total (Turf)	16	1	4	0	11049
Career Total (AW)	5	0	1	0	1349

74 8/06 Brig 6f209y G-F £4210
Total win prize-money £4210

Going (Turf): Sf: 0-1 GS: 0-3 Gd: 0-4 GF: 1-7 Fm: 0-1
Distance: 5f/6f: 0-12 7f-8f: 1-8 9f-13f: 0-1 14f+: 0-0
Track : LH: 1-9 RH: 0-2 Tight: 0-5 Gall: 0-2
Aids: Bl: 0-0 Vi: 0-0 Tstrap: 0-2 Ckp: 0-2
Best Rating: 82 9/06 Ayr 6f gd-sft

Fair; suited by 6f-7f; acts on fast ground and Polytrack.

Downhill Skier (IRE)

97(106) (69)70

5-y-o ch g Danehill Dancer (IRE)-Duchy Of Cornwall (USA) (The Minstrel (CAN))
W M Brisbourne Miss P D Insull

Placings:02300/0000-1164224304101600445 (7480)
2009: 7^{1}SD, 7^{1}SD, 7^{6}SD, 7^{4}SD, 7^{2}SD, 7^{2}SD, 7^{4}SD, 8^{3}SD, 8^{0}SD, 8^{4}SD, 7^{1}SD, 7^{0}SD, 6^{1}G, 6^{6}GF, 7^{0}S, 6^{0}GS, 6^{4}SD, 7^{4}SD, 7^{5}SD,

	Starts	1st	2nd	3rd	Win & Pl
Career Total (Turf)	12	1	1	1	7400
Career Total (AW)	16	3	2	1	9627

70 7/09 Thsk 6f (0-70)H GD £4338
67 4/09 Wolv 7f32y (0-75)H STD £3238
68 1/09 Wolv 7f32y (0-60)H STD £2047
66 1/09 Kemp 7f (0-60)H STD £2047
Total win prize-money £11671

Going (Turf): Sf: 0-2 GS: 0-1 Gd: 1-1 GF: 0-2 Fm: 0-0
Distance: 5f/6f: 1-4 7f-8f: 3-21 9f-13f: 0-3 14f+: 0-0
Track : LH: 2-15 RH: 1-7 Tight: 2-9 Gall: 0-0
Aids: Bl: 0-5 Vi: 0-0 Tstrap: 0-0 Ckp: 0-0
Best Rating: 70 7/09 Thsk 6f good

Modest; effective at 6-7f; handles Polytrack and easy ground.

Downhiller (IRE)

109(109) (99)105

4-y-o ch g Alhaarth (IRE)-Ski For Gold (Shirley Heights)
J L Dunlop Windflower Overseas Holdings Inc

Placings:0222/13416432-010 (1790)
2009: 16^{0}SD, 16^{1}GF, 18^{0}GF,

	Starts	1st	2nd	3rd	Win & Pl
Career Total (Turf)	12	3	4	1	32425
Career Total (AW)	3	0	0	1	2240

105 4/09 Ripn 2m (0-100)H G-F £15577
92 7/08 Newb 1m4f5y (0-85)H G-F £5180
87 4/08 Leic 1m1f218y SFT £2590
Total win prize-money £23349

Going (Turf): Sf: 1-1 GS: 0-1 Gd: 0-4 GF: 2-6 Fm: 0-0
Distance: 5f/6f: 0-0 7f-8f: 0-2 9f-13f: 2-7 14f+: 1-6
Track : LH: 1-5 RH: 2-9 Tight: 1-3 Gall: 1-3
Aids: Bl: 0-0 Vi: 0-0 Tstrap: 0-0 Ckp: 0-0
Best Rating: 105 4/09 Ripn 2m gd-fm

Very useful; stays 2m; acts on most ground and on Polytrack.

Downing Street (IRE)

98 82

8-y-o b g Sadler's Wells (USA)-Photographie (USA) (Trempolino (USA))
Jennie Candlish Alan Baxter

Placings:540/104/400-40 (5235)
2009: 14^{4}F, 16^{0}GF,

	Starts	1st	2nd	3rd	Win & Pl
Career Total (Turf)	11	1	0	0	5336

83 8/07 Thsk 2m (0-75)H G-F £3886
Total win prize-money £3886

Going (Turf): Sf: 0-0 GS: 0-1 Gd: 0-4 GF: 1-5 Fm: 0-1
Distance: 5f/6f: 0-0 7f-8f: 0-1 9f-13f: 0-2 14f+: 1-8
Track : LH: 1-7 RH: 0-4 Tight: 1-2 Gall: 0-5
Aids: Bl: 1-3 Vi: 0-4 Tstrap: 0-1 Ckp: 0-1
Best Rating: 83 8/07 Thsk 2m gd-fm

Downstream

(86) (52)40

3-y-o b f Marju (IRE)-Sister Moonshine (FR) (Piccolo)
D M Simcock Major M G Wyatt

Placings:600-0 (0135)
2009: 5^{0}SD,

	Starts	1st	2nd	3rd	Win & Pl
Career Total (Turf)	1	0	0	0	0
Career Total (AW)	3	0	0	0	

Going (Turf): Sf: 0-0 GS: 0-1 Gd: 0-0 GF: 0-0 Fm: 0-0
Distance: 5f/6f: 0-3 7f-8f: 0-1 9f-13f: 0-0 14f+: 0-0
Track : LH: 0-3 RH: 0-0 Tight: 0-2 Gall: 0-1
Aids: Bl: 0-1 Vi: 0-0 Tstrap: 0-0 Ckp: 0-0
Best Rating: 52 10/08 Ling 7f stand

Downtoobusiness

75(82) (50)43

2-y-o b g Desert Sun-Mariette (Blushing Scribe (USA))
Karen George Adrian Parr & Karen George

Placings:000 (5312)
2009: 7^{0}GF, 7^{0}SD, 8^{0}SD,

	Starts	1st	2nd	3rd	Win & Pl
Career Total (Turf)	1	0	0	0	
Career Total (AW)	2	0	0	0	

Going (Turf): Sf: 0-0 GS: 0-0 Gd: 0-0 GF: 0-1 Fm: 0-0
Distance: 5f/6f: 0-0 7f-8f: 0-3 9f-13f: 0-0 14f+: 0-0
Track : LH: 0-2 RH: 0-1 Tight: 0-1 Gall: 0-0
Aids: Bl: 0-0 Vi: 0-0 Tstrap: 0-0 Ckp: 0-0
Best Rating: 50 7/09 Ling 7f stand

Doyenne Dream

82 43

2-y-o b f Doyen (IRE)-Cribella (USA) (Robellino (USA))
J M P Eustace Hockham Lodge Stud

Placings:0 (7095)
2009: 8^{0}G,

	Starts	1st	2nd	3rd	Win & Pl
Career Total (Turf)	1	0	0	0	

Going (Turf): Sf: 0-0 GS: 0-0 Gd: 0-1 GF: 0-0 Fm: 0-0
Distance: 5f/6f: 0-0 7f-8f: 0-0 9f-13f: 0-1 14f+: 0-0
Track : LH: 0-0 RH: 0-0 Tight: 0-0 Gall: 0-0
Aids: Bl: 0-0 Vi: 0-0 Tstrap: 0-0 Ckp: 0-0
Best Rating: 43 10/09 Yarm 1m3y good

Dr Brass

74(101) (73)81

4-y-o b g Dr Fong (USA)-Tropical Heights (FR) (Shirley Heights)
B N Pollock R Catton

Placings:0043160-000 (1571)
2009: 10^{0}SD, 12^{0}SD, 11^{0}GS,

	Starts	1st	2nd	3rd	Win & Pl
Career Total (Turf)	6	1	0	1	5339
Career Total (AW)	4	0	0	0	168

81 8/08 Bath 1m2f46y (0-80)H G-S £4857
Total win prize-money £4857

Going (Turf): Sf: 0-2 GS: 1-2 Gd: 0-2 GF: 0-0 Fm: 0-0
Distance: 5f/6f: 0-0 7f-8f: 0-1 9f-13f: 1-9 14f+: 0-0
Track : LH: 1-7 RH: 0-2 Tight: 1-7 Gall: 0-2
Aids: Bl: 1-4 Vi: 0-0 Tstrap: 0-1 Ckp: 0-1
Best Rating: 81 8/08 Bath 1m2f46y gd-sft

Dr Finley (IRE)

93 71

2-y-o ch g Dr Fong (USA)-Farrfesheena (USA) (Rahy (USA))
M L W Bell Sheikh Marwan Al Maktoum

Placings:4243 (6786)
2009: 7^{4}S, 7^{2}S, 6^{4}F, 7^{3}G,

	Starts	1st	2nd	3rd	Win & Pl
Career Total (Turf)	4	0	1	1	1690

Going (Turf): Sf: 0-2 GS: 0-0 Gd: 0-1 GF: 0-0 Fm: 0-1
Distance: 5f/6f: 0-0 7f-8f: 0-4 9f-13f: 0-0 14f+: 0-0
Track : LH: 0-2 RH: 0-0 Tight: 0-0 Gall: 0-0
Aids: Bl: 0-0 Vi: 0-0 Tstrap: 0-0 Ckp: 0-0
Best Rating: 71 10/09 Brig 7f214y good

Fair; stays 1m and acts on good ground.

Dr Jameson (IRE)

101(99) (66)77

3-y-o b g Orpen (USA)-Touraneena (Robellino (USA))
R A Fahey Black Velvet Racing

Placings:23324-31505603 (7782)
2009: 8^{3}GF, 7^{1}GF, 8^{5}GF, 10^{0}GF, 8^{5}GF, 9^{6}SD, 8^{0}SD, 8^{3}SD,

	Starts	1st	2nd	3rd	Win & Pl
Career Total (Turf)	10	1	2	3	6584
Career Total (AW)	3	0	0	1	302

76 5/09 Bevl 7f100y G-F £2590
Total win prize-money £2590

Going (Turf): Sf: 0-2 GS: 0-1 Gd: 0-1 GF: 1-6 Fm: 0-0
Distance: 5f/6f: 0-2 7f-8f: 1-5 9f-13f: 0-6 14f+: 0-0
Track : LH: 0-7 RH: 1-2 Tight: 0-3 Gall: 0-1
Aids: Bl: 0-1 Vi: 0-1 Tstrap: 0-0 Ckp: 0-0
Best Rating: 77 10/08 Donc 1m good

Modest; effective over 7f; acts on most ground.

Dr Light (IRE)

(99) (52)56

5-y-o b g Medicean-Allumette (Rainbow Quest (USA))
M A Peill Miss Anna Bramall

Placings:06/000/04000-50 (0567)
2009: 11^{5}SD, 12^{0}SD,

	Starts	1st	2nd	3rd	Win & Pl
Career Total (Turf)	6	0	0	0	0
Career Total (AW)	6	0	0	0	0

Going (Turf): Sf: 0-0 GS: 0-0 Gd: 0-2 GF: 0-4 Fm: 0-0
Distance: 5f/6f: 0-0 7f-8f: 0-1 9f-13f: 0-11 14f+: 0-0
Track : LH: 0-9 RH: 0-3 Tight: 0-8 Gall: 0-0
Aids: Bl: 0-0 Vi: 0-0 Tstrap: 0-0 Ckp: 0-0
Best Rating: 56 6/08 Nott 1m2f50y gd-fm

Dr Livingstone (IRE)

108(109) (90)95

4-y-o b g Dr Fong (USA)-Radhwa (FR) (Shining Steel)
C R Egerton Longmoor Holdings Ltd

Placings:034/410103-2652 (7035)
2009: 10^{2}G, 10^{6}G, 11^{5}SD, 10^{2}S,

	Starts	1st	2nd	3rd	Win & Pl
Career Total (Turf)	11	2	2	2	17807
Career Total (AW)	2	0	0	0	275

92 9/08 Sand 1m2f7y (0-85)H SFT £6476
81 5/08 Sals 1m1f198y (0-80)H GD £4533
Total win prize-money £11009

Going (Turf): Sf: 1-4 GS: 0-0 Gd: 1-6 GF: 0-1 Fm: 0-0
Distance: 5f/6f: 0-0 7f-8f: 0-3 9f-13f: 2-10 14f+: 0-0
Track : LH: 0-5 RH: 2-8 Tight: 1-4 Gall: 0-1
Aids: Bl: 0-0 Vi: 0-0 Tstrap: 0-0 Ckp: 0-0
Best Rating: 95 10/09 Newb 1m2f6y soft

Useful; stays 1m2f and acts on most ground.

Dr Mathias

85(84) (62)70

2-y-o b g Dubai Destination (USA)-Herminoe (Rainbow Quest (USA))
P D Evans (W R Muir 12/9) Shropshire Wolves

Placings:0100 (7003)
2009: 8^{0}G, 8^{1}G, 8^{0}SD, 8^{0}SD,

	Starts	1st	2nd	3rd	Win & Pl
Career Total (Turf)	2	1	0	0	3238
Career Total (AW)	2	0	0	0	

70 9/09 Ffos 1m GD £3238
Total win prize-money £3238

Going (Turf): Sf: 0-0 GS: 0-0 Gd: 1-2 GF: 0-0 Fm: 0-0
Distance: 5f/6f: 0-0 7f-8f: 1-2 9f-13f: 0-2 14f+: 0-0
Track : LH: 1-3 RH: 0-1 Tight: 0-2 Gall: 1-1
Aids: Bl: 0-0 Vi: 0-0 Tstrap: 0-0 Ckp: 0-0
Best Rating: 70 9/09 Ffos 1m good

Fair; stays 1m and acts on good ground.

Dr McFab

96(89) (36)52

5-y-o ch g Dr Fong (USA)-Barbera (Barathea (IRE))
Miss Tor Sturgis Chris Grant & Michael H Burke

Placings:02/53224/0000-0300 (5367)
2009: 13^{0}SF, 10^{3}F, 11^{0}GF, 9^{0}F,

	Starts	1st	2nd	3rd	Win & Pl
Career Total (Turf)	8	0	0	1	543
Career Total (AW)	7	0	3	1	3633

Going (Turf): Sf: 0-1 GS: 0-1 Gd: 0-1 GF: 0-3 Fm: 0-2
Distance: 5f/6f: 0-0 7f-8f: 0-4 9f-13f: 0-10 14f+: 0-1
Track : LH: 0-13 RH: 0-2 Tight: 0-9 Gall: 0-3
Aids: Bl: 0-0 Vi: 0-1 Tstrap: 0-2 Ckp: 0-2
Best Rating: 72 4/07 Wolv 1m1f103y stand

Moderate; stays 1m4f; acts on fast ground; has worn cheekpieces/visor.

Dr Wintringham (IRE)

101(102) (70)66

3-y-o b f Monsieur Bond (IRE)-Shirley Collins (Robellino (USA))
Karen George (J S Moore 26/6) Mrs Isabel Fraser

Placings:430-033533214402 (7591)
2009: 6^{0}G, 5^{3}GF, 5^{3}F, 6^{5}GS, 6^{3}GF, 6^{3}G, 6^{2}S, 8^{1}G, 8^{4}GF, 8^{4}F, 8^{0}GF, 7^{2}SD,

	Starts	1st	2nd	3rd	Win & Pl
Career Total (Turf)	12	1	1	4	4323
Career Total (AW)	3	0	1	1	1468

66 8/09 Chep 1m14y (0-55)H GD £2266
Total win prize-money £2267

Going (Turf): Sf: 0-1 GS: 0-1 Gd: 1-4 GF: 0-4 Fm: 0-2
Distance: 5f/6f: 0-10 7f-8f: 0-2 9f-13f: 1-3 14f+: 0-0
Track : LH: 0-3 RH: 0-3 Tight: 0-3 Gall: 0-2
Aids: Bl: 0-0 Vi: 0-0 Tstrap: 0-0 Ckp: 0-0
Best Rating: 70 11/09 Kemp 7f stand

Modest; stays 1m; acts on fast ground and on Polytrack.

Draco Boy

76(69) (20)46

2-y-o gr g Silver Patriarch (IRE)-Miss Tchente (FR) (Tehente (FR))
Andrew Turnell Mayden Stud

Placings:000 (6629)
2009: 6^{0}GF, 7^{0}G, 7^{0}SS,

	Starts	1st	2nd	3rd	Win & Pl
Career Total (Turf)	2	0	0	0	
Career Total (AW)	1	0	0	0	

Going (Turf): Sf: 0-0 GS: 0-0 Gd: 0-1 GF: 0-1 Fm: 0-0
Distance: 5f/6f: 0-1 7f-8f: 0-2 9f-13f: 0-0 14f+: 0-0
Track : LH: 0-2 RH: 0-0 Tight: 0-1 Gall: 0-0
Aids: Bl: 0-0 Vi: 0-0 Tstrap: 0-0 Ckp: 0-0

Best Rating: 46 8/09 Wwck 7f26y good

Dragon Flame (IRE)

98(89) (41)77

6-y-o b g Tagula (IRE)-Noble Rocket (Reprimand)

M Quinn A Newby

Placings:444500/2400/13015-016300 (5480)

2009: 5^{0}SD, 5^{1}GF, 5^{6}G, 5^{3}G, 5^{0}HY, 5^{0}GF,

	Starts	1st	2nd	3rd	Win & Pl
Career Total (Turf)	19	3	1	2	11132
Career Total (AW)	2	0	0	0	

77 5/09 Yarm 5f43y (0-75)H G-F £2719
72 10/08 Nott 5f13y (0-65)H G-S £2047
66 4/08 Yarm 5f43y GD £2590
Total win prize-money £7357

Going (Turf): Sf: 0-7 **GS: 1-3 Gd: 1-6 GF: 1-3** Fm: 0-0
Distance: **5f/6f: 3-15** 7f-8f: 0-6 9f-13f: 0-0 14f+: 0-0
Track : LH: 0-3 RH: 0-0 Tight: 0-1 Gall: 0-2
Aids: Bl: 0-0 **Vi: 1-7** Tstrap: 0-0 Ckp: 0-0
Best Rating: 77 5/09 Yarm 5f43y gd-fm

Modest; effective at around 5f; acts on good and soft ground; sometimes visored.

Dragon Slayer (IRE)

102(103) (68)79

7-y-o ch g Night Shift (USA)-Arandora Star (USA) (Sagace (FR))

John A Harris Mrs A E Harris

Placings:3642/432103110022/62340231313050/13500400 426/0501F53140400-00535662120451 (7127)

2009: 10^{0}G, 10^{0}G, 10^{5}F, 11^{3}G, 10^{5}GF, 10^{6}GF, 10^{6}G, 9^{2}S, 10^{1}G, 10^{2}G, 10^{0}GF, 9^{4}GF, 10^{5}GF, 10^{1}G,

	Starts	1st	2nd	3rd	Win & Pl
Career Total (Turf)	42	8	2	5	41732
Career Total (AW)	26	2	7	5	18787

74 10/09 Nott 1m2f50y (0-65)H GD £1977
68 7/09 Yarm 1m2f21y (0-60)H GD £1942
79 8/08 Sand 1m2f7y (0-75)H GD £6246
77 7/08 Nott 1m2f50y (0-75)H G-S £2914
86 1/07 Wolv 1m1f103y (0-75)H STD £3238
85 6/06 NmkJ 1m2f (0-85)H G-F £5297
78 3/06 Yarm 1m2f21y (0-80)H FRM £7790
76 8/05 Hayd 1m30y (0-70)H G-F £3661
73 8/05 Epsm 1m114y (0-70)H GD £4544
65 3/05 Sthl 6f STD £3334
Total win prize-money £40948

Going (Turf): Sf: 0-4 GS: 1-2 **Gd: 4-15** GF: 2-16 Fm: 1-3
Distance: 5f/6f: 1-8 7f-8f: 0-3 **9f-13f: 9-57** 14f+: 0-0
Track : **LH: 8-54** RH: 2-13 **Tight: 4-35** Gall: 1-8
Aids: Bl: 0-0 Vi: 0-0 Tstrap: 1-4 Ckp: 1-4
Best Rating: 86 1/07 Wolv 1m1f103y std-slw

Modest; stays 1m4f, but effective at shorter; acts on good and faster ground; goes on sand.

Dragonessa (IRE)

95(83) (42)57

2-y-o b f Red Ransom (USA)-Principessa (Machiavellian (USA))

B Palling Derek And Jean Clee

Placings:0001020 (7242)

2009: 5^{0}GF, 5^{0}SD, 7^{0}SD, 6^{1}GS, 5^{0}SD, 6^{2}GS, 5^{0}S,

	Starts	1st	2nd	3rd	Win & Pl
Career Total (Turf)	4	1	1	0	3742
Career Total (AW)	3	0	0	0	

57 9/09 Ling 6f (0-70) G-S £3238
Total win prize-money £3238

Going (Turf): Sf: 0-1 **GS: 1-2** Gd: 0-0 GF: 0-1 Fm: 0-0
Distance: **5f/6f: 1-5** 7f-8f: 0-2 9f-13f: 0-0 14f+: 0-0
Track : LH: 0-2 RH: 0-1 Tight: 0-2 Gall: 0-0
Aids: Bl: 0-0 Vi: 0-0 Tstrap: 0-0 Ckp: 0-0
Best Rating: 57 10/09 Nott 6f15y gd-sft

Modest; stays 6f; acts on easy ground.

Dramatic Jewel (USA)

77(96) (65)26

3-y-o b g Diesis-Seeking The Jewel (USA) (Seeking The Gold (USA))

J W Hills Ted Voute

Placings:06043 (6497)

2009: 8^{0}G, 10^{6}SD, 12^{0}SD, 10^{4}SD, 9^{3}SF,

	Starts	1st	2nd	3rd	Win & Pl
Career Total (Turf)	1	0	0	0	
Career Total (AW)	4	0	0	1	545

Going (Turf): **Sf: 0-0 GS: 0-0 Gd: 0-1 GF: 0-0 Fm: 0-0**
Distance: 5f/6f: 0-0 7f-8f: 0-0 9f-13f: 0-5 14f+: 0-0
Track : LH: 0-3 RH: 0-1 Tight: 0-3 Gall: 0-0
Aids: Bl: 0-0 Vi: 0-0 Tstrap: 0-0 Ckp: 0-0
Best Rating: 65 9/09 Kemp 1m2f stand

Dramatic Solo

103(107) (74)73

4-y-o ch f Nayef (USA)-Just Dreams (Salse (USA))

A P Jarvis (K R Burke 25/7) Malih L Al Basti

Placings:40/6452310555-164343413351333 (6822)

2009: 16^{1}SD, 13^{6}SD, 16^{4}SD, 13^{3}SD, 17^{4}GF, 16^{3}GF, 12^{4}GF, 13^{1}GF, 14^{3}G, 14^{3}F, 14^{5}GF, 14^{1}G, 12^{3}GF, 14^{3}G, 14^{3}GF,

	Starts	1st	2nd	3rd	Win & Pl
Career Total (Turf)	18	3	1	7	16678
Career Total (AW)	9	1	0	1	2593

70 8/09 Muss 1m6f (0-65)H GD £2590
70 5/09 Muss 1m5f (0-65)H G-F £2590
74 1/09 Ling 2m (0-65)H STD £2047
73 7/08 Thsk 1m4f (0-80)H G-F £5569
Total win prize-money £12796

Going (Turf): Sf: 0-0 GS: 0-1 Gd: 1-3 **GF: 2-13** Fm: 0-1
Distance: 5f/6f: 0-0 7f-8f: 0-1 9f-13f: 2-12 14f+: 2-14
Track : LH: 2-17 RH: 2-9 **Tight: 4-19** Gall: 0-5
Aids: **Bl: 4-20** Vi: 0-1 Tstrap: 0-0 Ckp: 0-0
Best Rating: 74 1/09 Ling 2m stand

Fair; stays 2m; acts on quick ground and on Polytrack; has worn blinkers and a visor.

Drawn Gold

102(101) (68)72

5-y-o b g Daggers Drawn (USA)-Gold Belt (IRE) (Bellypha)

R Hollinshead Tim Leadbeater

Placings:4/441/3203456-024014230063 (7594)

2009: 9^{0}SD, 12^{2}SD, 11^{4}GF, 14^{0}GS, 12^{1}GS, 12^{4}GF, 11^{2}G, 12^{3}GF, 12^{0}G, 16^{0}G, 13^{6}SD, 13^{3}SD,

	Starts	1st	2nd	3rd	Win & Pl
Career Total (Turf)	18	2	2	3	11240
Career Total (AW)	5	0	1	1	1010

66 6/09 Wwck 1m4f134y (0-60)H G-S £1977
71 11/07 NmkR 1m (0-75)H GD £3238
Total win prize-money £5217

Going (Turf): Sf: 0-2 **GS: 1-3 Gd: 1-6** GF: 0-7 Fm: 0-0
Distance: 5f/6f: 0-1 7f-8f: 1-1 9f-13f: 1-17 14f+: 0-4
Track : **LH: 1-18** RH: 0-3 Tight: 0-10 Gall: 0-1
Aids: Bl: 0-0 Vi: 0-0 Tstrap: 0-0 Ckp: 0-0
Best Rating: 72 6/08 Ches 1m2f75y gd-fm

Moderate; stays 1m6f; acts on fast and soft ground; goes on Polytrack.

Drawnfromthepast (IRE)

104(104) (91)95

4-y-o ch g Tagula (IRE)-Ball Cat (FR) (Cricket Ball (USA))

J A Osborne H R H Prince of Saxe-Weimar

Placings:61150/4060004444 (7395)

2009: 6^{4}SD, 6^{0}GS, 6^{6}G, 7^{0}GF, 6^{0}GF, 6^{0}GF, 6^{4}SD, 6^{4}SD, 5^{4}SD, 6^{4}SD,

	Starts	1st	2nd	3rd	Win & Pl
Career Total (Turf)	10	2	0	0	36172
Career Total (AW)	5	0	0	0	1946

98 6/07 Asct 5f G-F £31229
86 6/07 Brig 5f213y G-F £2849
Total win prize-money £34079

Going (Turf): Sf: 0-0 GS: 0-2 Gd: 0-2 **GF: 2-6** Fm: 0-0
Distance: **5f/6f: 2-12** 7f-8f: 0-3 9f-13f: 0-0 14f+: 0-0
Track : **LH: 1-3** RH: 0-3 Tight: 0-2 Gall: 0-0
Aids: Bl: 0-0 Vi: 0-0 Tstrap: 0-0 Ckp: 0-0
Best Rating: 98 6/07 Asct 5f gd-fm

Useful; landed Windsor Castle Stakes at Royal Ascot in 2007; effective over 5f-6f; acts on fast ground; has worn a tongue tie.

Dream Catch Me (IRE)

64(86) (48)

3-y-o b f Xaar-Dancerette (Groom Dancer (USA))

J R Boyle Mrs Pippa Boyle

Placings:4360 (1618)

2009: 6^{4}SD, 6^{3}SD, 5^{6}SD, 6^{0}GF,

	Starts	1st	2nd	3rd	Win & Pl
Career Total (Turf)	1	0	0	0	
Career Total (AW)	3	0	0	1	454

Going (Turf): **Sf: 0-0 GS: 0-0 Gd: 0-0 GF: 0-1 Fm: 0-0**
Distance: 5f/6f: 0-4 7f-8f: 0-0 9f-13f: 0-0 14f+: 0-0
Track : LH: 0-3 RH: 0-0 Tight: 0-3 Gall: 0-0
Aids: Bl: 0-0 Vi: 0-0 Tstrap: 0-0 Ckp: 0-0
Best Rating: 48 2/09 Ling 6f stand

Moderate form in 6f Polytrack maidens.

Dream Date (IRE)

(99) (80)44

3-y-o b f Oasis Dream-Femme Fatale (Fairy King (USA))

J L Eyre (W J Haggas 23/1) Rachael Teasdale Racing

Placings:0430022-113 (0276)

2009: 7^{1}SD, 7^{1}SD, 6^{3}SD,

	Starts	1st	2nd	3rd	Win & Pl
Career Total (Turf)	2	0	0	0	
Career Total (AW)	8	2	2	2	13072

80 1/09 Wolv 7f32y (0-85)H STD £5180

76 1/09 Ling 7f (0-85)H STD £4857
Total win prize-money £10038

Going (Turf): **Sf: 0-0 GS: 0-1 Gd: 0-0 GF: 0-1 Fm: 0-0**
Distance: 5f/6f: 0-3 **7f-8f: 2-7** 9f-13f: 0-0 14f+: 0-0
Track : **LH: 2-6** RH: 0-1 **Tight: 2-5** Gall: 0-2
Aids: Bl: 0-0 Vi: 0-0 Tstrap: 0-0 Ckp: 0-0
Best Rating: **80** 1/09 Wolv 7f32y stand

Fair; stays 7f and acts on Polytrack.

Dream Desert (IRE)

104(107) (93)93
4-y-o ch c Elnadim (USA)-Bravo Dancer (Acatenango (GER))
M R Channon Ahmed Jaber

Placings:1134-36000 (3443a)
2009: 11^{3}SD, 12^{6}G, 10^{0}GF, 10^{0}G, 12^{0}S,

	Starts	1st	2nd	3rd	Win & Pl
Career Total (Turf)	6	0	0	1	4326
Career Total (AW)	3	2	0	1	11136

85 3/08 Wolv 1m1f103y (0-95)H STD £7124
77 2/08 Wolv 1m141y STD £2331
Total win prize-money £9457

Going (Turf): **Sf: 0-1 GS: 0-0 Gd: 0-3 GF: 0-2 Fm: 0-0**
Distance: 5f/6f: 0-0 7f-8f: 0-0 **9f-13f: 2-9** 14f+: 0-0
Track : **LH: 2-6** RH: 0-2 **Tight: 2-5** Gall: 0-1
Aids: Bl: 0-0 Vi: 0-0 Tstrap: 0-0 Ckp: 0-0
Best Rating: **93** 3/09 Kemp 1m3f stand

Useful; stays 1m4f; acts on Polytrack and on fast ground on turf.

Dream Eater (IRE)

115 (79)116
4-y-o gr c Night Shift (USA)-Kapria (FR) (Simon Du Desert (FR))
A M Balding J C Smith

Placings:32463316/53-2205444120 (6304)
2009: 7^{2}GF, 8^{2}G, 8^{0}S, 8^{5}GF, 7^{4}G, 8^{4}GF, 7^{4}G, 7^{1}GF, 8^{2}GF, 6^{0}GF,

	Starts	1st	2nd	3rd	Win & Pl
Career Total (Turf)	19	2	3	4	435752
Career Total (AW)	1	0	1	0	1542

97 9/07 Donc 6f110y G-F £191533
Total win prize-money £191533

Going (Turf): Sf: 0-1 GS: 0-0 Gd: 0-7 **GF: 2-11** Fm: 0-0
Distance: 5f/6f: 0-7 **7f-8f: 2-12** 9f-13f: 0-1 14f+: 0-0
Track : **LH: 1-2** RH: 0-5 Tight: 0-0 **Gall: 1-2**
Aids: Bl: 0-0 Vi: 0-0 Tstrap: 0-0 Ckp: 0-0
Best Rating: **116** 9/09 Veli 1m gd-fm

Smart; Listed winner; Group placed; effective over 6f-1m; acts on good and faster ground and on Polytrack; has worn a tongue tie.

Dream Express (IRE)

102(101) (73)78
4-y-o b g Fasliyev (USA)-Lothlorien (USA) (Woodman (USA))
P Howling (M Dods 8/8) Paul Terry

Placings:642300/41313300-003000114354066050O (7716)
2009: 7^{0}SD, 7^{0}F, 7^{3}GS, 7^{0}GS, 7^{0}GF, 7^{0}G, 7^{1}GF, 6^{1}G, 7^{4}GS, 6^{3}GF, 7^{5}SD, 5^{4}SD, 5^{0}SD, 6^{6}GF, 6^{6}GS, 7^{0}SD, 6^{5}SD, 8^{0}SD, 7^{0}SD,

	Starts	1st	2nd	3rd	Win & Pl
Career Total (Turf)	24	3	1	6	11899
Career Total (AW)	9	1	0	0	2645

68 7/09 Ayr 6f GD £2047
70 7/09 Bevl 7f100y G-F £2266
75 7/08 Catt 7f (0-75)H GD £2590
76 5/08 Wolv 7f32y (0-70) STD £2456
Total win prize-money £9361

Going (Turf): Sf: 0-1 GS: 0-9 **Gd: 2-7** GF: 1-6 Fm: 0-1
Distance: 5f/6f: 1-10 **7f-8f: 3-22** 9f-13f: 0-1 14f+: 0-0
Track : **LH: 2-14** RH: 1-6 **Tight: 2-15** Gall: 0-1
Aids: Bl: 0-2 Vi: 0-2 Tstrap: 0-1 Ckp: 0-1
Best Rating: **78** 8/08 Carl 6f192y good

Modest; stays 7f and acts on most ground; has worn a visor.

Dream Huntress

98(103) (67)64
3-y-o ch f Dubai Destination (USA)-Dream Lady (Benny The Dip (USA))
J W Hills (B J Meehan 17/1) Longview Stud & Bloodstock Ltd

Placings:060041-002503 (7693)
2009: 10^{0}SD, 8^{0}SD, 7^{2}G, 7^{5}G, 8^{0}SD, 8^{3}SD,

	Starts	1st	2nd	3rd	Win & Pl
Career Total (Turf)	5	0	1	0	771
Career Total (AW)	7	1	0	1	3022

60 12/08 Wolv 1m141y (0-65) STD £2729
Total win prize-money £2730

Going (Turf): **Sf: 0-0 GS: 0-0 Gd: 0-3 GF: 0-2 Fm: 0-0**
Distance: 5f/6f: 0-0 7f-8f: 0-7 **9f-13f: 1-5** 14f+: 0-0
Track : **LH: 1-8** RH: 0-1 **Tight: 1-6** Gall: 0-0
Aids: Bl: 0-0 Vi: 0-0 Tstrap: 0-0 Ckp: 0-0
Best Rating: **67** 12/09 Ling 1m stand

Modest; stays 1m; acts on good ground; goes on Polytrack.

Dream In Blue

91(102) (66)49
4-y-o b g Oasis Dream-Blue Birds Fly (Rainbow Quest (USA))
J A Glover (J A Osborne 4/8) Paul J Dixon & Brian Morton

Placings:22206004613 (7851)
2009: 11^{2}SD, 13^{2}SD, 12^{2}SD, 17^{0}GF, 17^{6}G, 15^{0}G, 11^{0}G, 12^{4}SD, 12^{6}SD, 11^{1}SD, 11^{3}SS,

	Starts	1st	2nd	3rd	Win & Pl
Career Total (Turf)	4	0	0	0	0
Career Total (AW)	7	1	3	1	4833

66 12/09 Sthl 1m3f STD £2047
Total win prize-money £2047

Going (Turf): **Sf: 0-0 GS: 0-0 Gd: 0-3 GF: 0-1 Fm: 0-0**
Distance: 5f/6f: 0-0 7f-8f: 0-0 **9f-13f: 1-8** 14f+: 0-3
Track : **LH: 1-10** RH: 0-1 Tight: 0-6 Gall: 0-0
Aids: Bl: 0-1 Vi: 0-0 Tstrap: 1-5 Ckp: 1-5
Best Rating: **66** 12/09 Sthl 1m3f stand

Modest; stays 1m5f; acts on both AW surfaces; has worn cheekpieces.

Dream In Waiting

89(103) (80)84
3-y-o b f Oasis Dream-Lady In Waiting (Kylian (USA))
B J Meehan Pegasus Racing Ltd

Placings:543140-03 (7141)
2009: 10^{0}G, 8^{3}SD,

	Starts	1st	2nd	3rd	Win & Pl
Career Total (Turf)	7	1	0	1	28566
Career Total (AW)	1	0	0	1	755

83 9/08 Donc 6f110y H SFT £25904
Total win prize-money £25904

Going (Turf): **Sf: 1-2** GS: 0-1 Gd: 0-2 GF: 0-2 Fm: 0-0
Distance: 5f/6f: 0-1 **7f-8f: 1-5** 9f-13f: 0-2 14f+: 0-0
Track : LH: 0-3 RH: 0-0 Tight: 0-2 Gall: 0-1
Aids: Bl: 0-0 Vi: 0-0 Tstrap: 0-0 Ckp: 0-0
Best Rating: **84** 11/08 NmkR 1m gd-sft

Useful; out of Sun Chariot Stakes winner Lady In Waiting; won over extended 6f; acts on soft ground.

Dream Lodge (IRE)

112(110) (103)111
5-y-o ch g Grand Lodge (USA)-Secret Dream (IRE) (Zafonic (USA))
R A Fahey (J G Given 14/5) The G-Guck Group

Placings:3416/3225531212/0240030012060-030010144254 (6485)
2009: 8^{0}GF, 8^{3}GF, 9^{0}GF, 8^{0}G, 8^{1}G, 10^{0}GF, 8^{1}GS, 8^{4}G, 10^{4}GF, 8^{2}GF, 10^{5}G, 8^{4}GF,

	Starts	1st	2nd	3rd	Win & Pl
Career Total (Turf)	27	4	3	3	79953
Career Total (AW)	12	2	4	2	21226

106 7/09 Donc 1m G-S £7771
107 6/09 Rdcr 1m (0-95)H GD £7477
103 7/08 Donc 1m G-F £7771
97 10/07 Pont 1m4y (0-95)H GD £9348
84 8/07 Wolv 1m141y (0-80)H STD £4857
84 10/06 Wolv 7f32y STD £4731
Total win prize-money £41957

Going (Turf): Sf: 0-1 GS: 1-3 **Gd: 2-10** GF: 1-13 Fm: 0-0
Distance: 5f/6f: 0-0 **7f-8f: 4-17** 9f-13f: 2-22 14f+: 0-0
Track : **LH: 3-27** RH: 0-3 **Tight: 2-12** Gall: 0-7
Aids: Bl: 0-0 **Vi: 1-7** Tstrap: 0-0 Ckp: 0-0
Best Rating: **111** 10/09 Rdcr 1m gd-fm

Smart; stays 1m2f but effective at 1m; acts on a sound surface and on Polytrack; has worn a visor.

Dream Mountain

(91) (41)62
6-y-o b g Mozart (IRE)-Statua (IRE) (Statoblest)
Ms J S Doyle Ms J S Doyle

Placings:321005/000264/100066/000 (1069)
2009: 14^{0}SD, 12^{0}SD, 16^{0}SD,

	Starts	1st	2nd	3rd	Win & Pl
Career Total (Turf)	8	1	2	1	5294
Career Total (AW)	13	1	0	0	1947

59 1/07 Kemp 2m (0-65)H STD £1706
60 9/05 Newc 7f G-F £2737
Total win prize-money £4443

Going (Turf): Sf: 0-1 GS: 0-2 Gd: 0-1 **GF: 1-4** Fm: 0-0
Distance: 5f/6f: 0-2 7f-8f: 1-5 9f-13f: 0-8 14f+: 1-6
Track : LH: 0-11 **RH: 1-8** Tight: 0-6 Gall: 0-1
Aids: Bl: 0-0 Vi: 0-1 Tstrap: 0-1 Ckp: 0-1
Best Rating: **64** 9/05 Catt 5f212y gd-fm

Fair sort; stays seven furlongs; acts on fast ground.

Dream Number (IRE)

92(89) (63)71

2-y-o ch f Fath (USA)-Very Nice (Daylami (IRE))

W R Muir Linkslade Lottery

Placings:533510 (7320)

2009: 5^{5}G, 5^{3}G, 5^{3}F, 6^{5}SD, 7^{1}GF, 7^{0}SD,

	Starts	1st	2nd	3rd	Win & Pl
Career Total (Turf)	4	1	0	2	3249
Career Total (AW)	2	0	0	0	0

71 10/09 Leic 7f9y (0-65) G-F £2266

Total win prize-money £2267

Going (Turf): Sf: 0-0 GS: 0-0 Gd: 0-2 GF: 1-1 Fm: 0-1
Distance: 5f/6f: 0-4 7f-8f: 1-2 9f-13f: 0-0 14f+: 0-0
Track : LH: 0-3 RH: 0-1 Tight: 0-1 Gall: 0-2
Aids: Bl: 0-0 Vi: 0-0 Tstrap: 0-0 Ckp: 0-0
Best Rating: 71 10/09 Leic 7f9y gd-fm

Moderate; suited by 5f and good ground.

Dream Of Fortune (IRE)

91(108) (86)78

5-y-o b g Danehill Dancer (IRE)-Tootling (IRE) (Pennine Walk)

M G Quinlan Norman Jones Snr

Placings:5041/061400201-33124600403331 (7823)

2009: 9^{3}SD, 10^{3}SD, 9^{1}SD, 9^{2}SD, 10^{4}SD, 10^{6}G, 12^{0}G, 9^{0}SD, 8^{4}SS, 10^{0}SD, 12^{3}SD, 10^{3}SD, 10^{3}SD, 10^{1}SD,

	Starts	1st	2nd	3rd	Win & Pl
Career Total (Turf)	6	0	0	0	289
Career Total (AW)	21	5	2	5	23444

79 12/09 Kemp 1m2f (0-75)H STD £2590
83 2/09 Wolv 1m1f103y (0-85)H STD £4857
86 12/08 GrLe 1m2f (0-80)H STD £5504
76 4/08 GrLe 1m2f (0-70)H STD £2590
72 10/07 Ling 1m2f (0-70)H STD £2817

Total win prize-money £18359

Going (Turf): Sf: 0-0 GS: 0-0 Gd: 0-4 GF: 0-2 Fm: 0-0
Distance: 5f/6f: 0-0 7f-8f: 0-6 9f-13f: 5-21 14f+: 0-0
Track : LH: 4-18 RH: 1-7 Tight: 2-14 Gall: 2-6
Aids: Bl: 0-2 Vi: 0-0 Tstrap: 0-0 Ckp: 0-0
Best Rating: 86 3/09 Wolv 1m1f103y stand

Fair; stays 1m2f; acts on Polytrack; has worn a tongue tie.

Dream Of Gerontius (IRE)

83(69) (46)29

2-y-o b f Oratorio (IRE)-Shades Of Rosegold (IRE) (Bluebird (USA))

R Hannon Mrs J Wood

Placings:0300 (5543)

2009: 5^{0}G, 5^{3}SD, 6^{0}GF, 7^{0}GF,

	Starts	1st	2nd	3rd	Win & Pl
Career Total (Turf)	3	0	0	0	
Career Total (AW)	1	0	0	1	746

Going (Turf): Sf: 0-0 GS: 0-0 Gd: 0-1 GF: 0-2 Fm: 0-0
Distance: 5f/6f: 0-2 7f-8f: 0-2 9f-13f: 0-0 14f+: 0-0
Track : LH: 0-1 RH: 0-1 Tight: 0-0 Gall: 0-1
Aids: Bl: 0-1 Vi: 0-0 Tstrap: 0-0 Ckp: 0-0
Best Rating: 46 5/09 Kemp 5f stand

Dream Of Olwyn (IRE)

103(92) (65)75

4-y-o b f Nayef (USA)-Jam (IRE) (Arazi (USA))

J G Given Alex Owen

Placings:0025305216-120 (7248)

2009: 10^{1}F, 10^{2}GS, 10^{0}HY,

	Starts	1st	2nd	3rd	Win & Pl
Career Total (Turf)	11	2	3	0	9520
Career Total (AW)	2	0	0	1	289

75 5/09 Nott 1m2f50y (0-75)H FRM £3885
69 10/08 Nott 1m2f50y (0-65)H HVY £2307

Total win prize-money £6194

Going (Turf): Sf: 1-4 GS: 0-2 Gd: 0-3 GF: 0-1 Fm: 1-1
Distance: 5f/6f: 0-0 7f-8f: 0-3 9f-13f: 2-10 14f+: 0-0
Track : LH: 2-13 RH: 0-0 Tight: 0-1 Gall: 0-2
Aids: Bl: 0-0 Vi: 0-0 Tstrap: 0-0 Ckp: 0-0
Best Rating: 75 5/09 Hayd 1m2f95y gd-sft

Modest; stays 1m2f; acts on fast ground and on Polytrack.

Dream On Connie

96(97) (60)66

3-y-o b g Cape Cross (IRE)-Fantasize (Groom Dancer (USA))

W J Knight Mrs G Cotton

Placings:0500650300 (7022)

2009: 8^{0}GF, 10^{5}SD, 10^{0}GF, 8^{0}G, 8^{6}G, 9^{5}GF, 9^{0}GF, 10^{3}GF, 9^{0}GF, 10^{0}SD,

	Starts	1st	2nd	3rd	Win & Pl
Career Total (Turf)	8	0	0	1	289
Career Total (AW)	2	0	0	0	0

Going (Turf): Sf: 0-0 GS: 0-0 Gd: 0-2 GF: 0-6 Fm: 0-0
Distance: 5f/6f: 0-0 7f-8f: 0-1 9f-13f: 0-9 14f+: 0-0
Track : LH: 0-3 RH: 0-7 Tight: 0-5 Gall: 0-1
Aids: Bl: 0-0 Vi: 0-1 Tstrap: 0-1 Ckp: 0-1
Best Rating: 66 8/09 Sals 1m1f198y gd-fm

Modest; stays 1m2f and acts on fast ground.

Dream Rainbow

61(96) (66)72

4-y-o b g Oasis Dream-Bint Zamayem (IRE) (Rainbow Quest (USA))

Joss Saville Ownaracehorse.co.uk (Lowbeck)

Placings:522/60-000 (4977)

2009: 6^{0}GS, 7^{0}SD, 7^{0}GF,

	Starts	1st	2nd	3rd	Win & Pl
Career Total (Turf)	5	0	2	0	1088
Career Total (AW)	3	0	0	0	0

Going (Turf): Sf: 0-0 GS: 0-1 Gd: 0-1 GF: 0-2 Fm: 0-1
Distance: 5f/6f: 0-4 7f-8f: 0-4 9f-13f: 0-0 14f+: 0-0
Track : LH: 0-5 RH: 0-1 Tight: 0-3 Gall: 0-0
Aids: Bl: 0-0 Vi: 0-1 Tstrap: 0-0 Ckp: 0-0
Best Rating: 72 6/07 DRoy 5f firm

Dream Spinner

90(93) (66)70

2-y-o b g Royal Applause-Dream Quest (Rainbow Quest (USA))

J L Dunlop Bluehills Racing Limited

Placings:454063 (6533)

2009: 7^{4}G, 7^{5}GF, 6^{4}F, 8^{0}G, 8^{6}SD, 10^{3}GF,

	Starts	1st	2nd	3rd	Win & Pl
Career Total (Turf)	5	0	0	1	1391
Career Total (AW)	1	0	0	0	0

Going (Turf): Sf: 0-0 GS: 0-0 Gd: 0-2 GF: 0-2 Fm: 0-1
Distance: 5f/6f: 0-0 7f-8f: 0-5 9f-13f: 0-1 14f+: 0-0
Track : LH: 0-3 RH: 0-2 Tight: 0-0 Gall: 0-0
Aids: Bl: 0-0 Vi: 0-0 Tstrap: 0-0 Ckp: 0-0
Best Rating: 70 10/09 Pont 1m2f6y gd-fm

Fair; seems to stay 1m2f; acts on a sound surface.

Dream Street Rose (USA)

(26)

4-y-o b/br f Yankee Victor (USA)-Dixie Fine (USA) (L'Emigrant (USA))

K R Burke Mrs Elaine M Burke

Placings:0 (1530)

2009: 8^{0}SD,

	Starts	1st	2nd	3rd	Win & Pl
Career Total (Turf)	0	0	0	0	
Career Total (AW)	1	0	0	0	

Going (Turf): Sf: 0-0 GS: 0-0 Gd: 0-0 GF: 0-0 Fm: 0-0
Distance: 5f/6f: 0-0 7f-8f: 0-0 9f-13f: 0-1 14f+: 0-0
Track : LH: 0-1 RH: 0-0 Tight: 0-1 Gall: 0-0
Aids: Bl: 0-0 Vi: 0-0 Tstrap: 0-0 Ckp: 0-0

Dream Theme

101(97) (61)91

6-y-o b g Distant Music (USA)-Xaymara (USA) (Sanglamore (USA))

D Nicholls The Untouchable Partnership

Placings:03/161130/30/50000500-0320 (1921)

2009: 7^{0}GF, 7^{3}SD, 6^{2}G, 5^{0}F,

	Starts	1st	2nd	3rd	Win & Pl
Career Total (Turf)	20	2	1	3	40515
Career Total (AW)	2	1	0	1	5808

103 8/06 Leic 7f9y (0-100)H GD £12464
95 8/06 Gdwd 7f (0-100)H G-F £24928
80 4/06 Kemp 7f STD £5505

Total win prize-money £42897

Going (Turf): Sf: 0-3 GS: 0-2 Gd: 1-5 GF: 1-9 Fm: 0-1
Distance: 5f/6f: 0-8 7f-8f: 3-13 9f-13f: 0-1 14f+: 0-0
Track : LH: 0-5 RH: 2-2 Tight: 0-2 Gall: 0-0
Aids: Bl: 0-0 Vi: 0-1 Tstrap: 0-0 Ckp: 0-0
Best Rating: 103 8/06 Leic 7f9y good

Useful; stays 7f; acts on a sound surface and on Polytrack; usually held up.

Dream Win

88 75

3-y-o b g Oasis Dream-Wince (Selkirk (USA))

Sir Michael Stoute K Abdulla

Placings:5-5 (1255)

2009: 8^{5}G,

	Starts	1st	2nd	3rd	Win & Pl
Career Total (Turf)	2	0	0	0	129

Going (Turf): Sf: 0-0 GS: 0-0 Gd: 0-2 GF: 0-0 Fm: 0-0

Distance: 5f/6f: 0-0 7f-8f: 0-1 9f-13f: 0-1 14f+: 0-0
Track : LH: 0-0 RH: 0-0 Tight: 0-0 Gall: 0-0
Aids: Bl: 0-0 Vi: 0-0 Tstrap: 0-0 Ckp: 0-0
Best Rating: 75 10/08 Donc 7f good

Dreamcoat

94 **73**
3-y-o ch c Pivotal-Follow A Dream (USA) (Gone West (USA))
J H M Gosden Cheveley Park Stud

Placings:0-430 **(2857)**
2009: 8^{4}S, 7^{3}GS, 8^{0}G,

	Starts	1st	2nd	3rd	Win & Pl
Career Total (Turf)	4	0	0	1	1276

Going (Turf): Sf: 0-1 GS: 0-1 Gd: 0-2 GF: 0-0 Fm: 0-0
Distance: 5f/6f: 0-0 7f-8f: 0-3 9f-13f: 0-1 14f+: 0-0
Track : LH: 0-1 RH: 0-0 Tight: 0-0 Gall: 0-0
Aids: Bl: 0-0 Vi: 0-0 Tstrap: 0-0 Ckp: 0-0
Best Rating: 73 4/09 Newb 1m soft

Fair half-brother to Pipedreamer; stays 1m; acts on good.

Dreamonandon (IRE)

91 **61**
3-y-o b g Val Royal (FR)-Boley Lass (IRE) (Archway (IRE))
G A Swinbank R Haggas

Placings:666-600 **(3018)**
2009: 9^{6}GF, 8^{0}G, 8^{0}G,

	Starts	1st	2nd	3rd	Win & Pl
Career Total (Turf)	6	0	0	0	0

Going (Turf): Sf: 0-2 GS: 0-1 Gd: 0-2 GF: 0-1 Fm: 0-0
Distance: 5f/6f: 0-2 7f-8f: 0-2 9f-13f: 0-2 14f+: 0-0
Track : LH: 0-3 RH: 0-2 Tight: 0-4 Gall: 0-0
Aids: Bl: 0-0 Vi: 0-0 Tstrap: 0-0 Ckp: 0-0
Best Rating: 61 4/09 Bevl 1m1f207y gd-fm

Dreams Jewel

82(110) (62)**56**
9-y-o b g Dreams End-Jewel Of The Nile (Glenstal (USA))
C Roberts Allan Ashcroft

Placings:60/020404/14124000-3000 **(7594)**
2009: 16^{3}SD, 14^{0}SD, 16^{0}G, 13^{0}SD,

	Starts	1st	2nd	3rd	Win & Pl
Career Total (Turf)	10	0	1	0	1397
Career Total (AW)	10	2	1	1	5259

67 3/08 Wolv 1m5f194y (0-70)H STD £1879
62 2/08 Sthl 1m6f (0-65)H SS £1911
Total win prize-money £3790

Going (Turf): Sf: 0-0 GS: 0-4 Gd: 0-2 GF: 0-4 Fm: 0-0
Distance: 5f/6f: 0-0 7f-8f: 0-0 9f-13f: 0-7 **14f+: 2-13**
Track : LH: 2-18 RH: 0-2 **Tight: 1-9** Gall: 0-1
Aids: Bl: 0-0 Vi: 0-0 Tstrap: 0-0 Ckp: 0-0
Best Rating: 67 3/08 Sthl 2m stand

Modest; stays 2m; acts on easy ground and Fibresand; winning hurdler.

Dreamspeed (IRE)

100 **97**
2-y-o b c Barathea (IRE)-Kapria (FR) (Simon Du Desert (FR))
A M Balding J C Smith

Placings:1055 **(6268)**
2009: 7^{1}G, 7^{0}G, 8^{5}G, 8^{5}G,

	Starts	1st	2nd	3rd	Win & Pl
Career Total (Turf)	4	1	0	0	11367

79 7/09 Sand 7f16y GD £6476
Total win prize-money £6476

Going (Turf): Sf: 0-0 GS: 0-0 **Gd: 1-4** GF: 0-0 Fm: 0-0
Distance: 5f/6f: 0-0 **7f-8f: 1-4** 9f-13f: 0-0 14f+: 0-0
Track : LH: 0-0 **RH: 1-3** Tight: 0-0 Gall: 0-1
Aids: Bl: 0-0 Vi: 0-0 Tstrap: 0-0 Ckp: 0-0
Best Rating: 97 7/09 Gdwd 7f good

Very useful; probably stays 7f; acts on good ground.

Dreamwalk (IRE)

107 **85**
3-y-o b g Bahri (USA)-Celtic Silhouette (FR) (Celtic Swing)
R Curtis (R M Beckett 2/10) R P Behan

Placings:2360-21044201 **(6454)**
2009: 10^{2}G, 10^{1}GF, 10^{0}G, 9^{4}GF, 10^{4}G, 11^{2}F, 9^{0}GF, 10^{1}GF,

	Starts	1st	2nd	3rd	Win & Pl
Career Total (Turf)	12	2	3	1	7705

82 10/09 NmkR 1m2f (0-85)H G-F £0
74 5/09 Yarm 1m2f21y G-F £2590
Total win prize-money £2590

Going (Turf): Sf: 0-0 GS: 0-1 Gd: 0-4 **GF: 2-6** Fm: 0-1
Distance: 5f/6f: 0-0 7f-8f: 0-3 **9f-13f: 2-9** 14f+: 0-0
Track : LH: 1-5 RH: 0-3 **Tight: 1-6** Gall: 0-0
Aids: Bl: 0-0 **Vi: 1-4** Tstrap: 0-0 Ckp: 0-0
Best Rating: 85 7/09 Bath 1m2f46y good

Fair; stays 1m2f; acts on good ground; has worn a visor.

Dreamy Eyed (IRE)

65(92) (54)**10**
2-y-o b f Shamardal (USA)-Misty Eyed (IRE) (Paris House)
Mrs P N Dutfield Mrs Jan Fuller

Placings:0000 **(6938)**
2009: 6^{0}G, 6^{0}S, 5^{0}SD, 5^{0}SD,

	Starts	1st	2nd	3rd	Win & Pl
Career Total (Turf)	2	0	0	0	
Career Total (AW)	2	0	0	0	

Going (Turf): Sf: 0-1 GS: 0-0 Gd: 0-1 GF: 0-0 Fm: 0-0
Distance: 5f/6f: 0-3 7f-8f: 0-1 9f-13f: 0-0 14f+: 0-0
Track : LH: 0-0 RH: 0-2 Tight: 0-0 Gall: 0-0
Aids: Bl: 0-0 Vi: 0-0 Tstrap: 0-0 Ckp: 0-0
Best Rating: 54 10/09 Kemp 5f stand

Dressed To Dance (IRE)

101(101) (78)**93**
5-y-o b m Namid-Costume Drama (USA) (Alleged (USA))
R A Harris (P D Evans 6/5) Ridge House Stables Ltd

Placings:00422/11546216060/000113511102000034-4365143420200 **(6739)**
2009: 7^{4}SD, 6^{3}SD, 5^{6}SD, 7^{5}SD, 5^{1}GF, 6^{4}GF, 6^{3}G, 6^{4}GF, 5^{2}G, 6^{0}F, 6^{2}G, 5^{0}GF, 6^{0}GS,

	Starts	1st	2nd	3rd	Win & Pl
Career Total (Turf)	35	7	4	3	28862
Career Total (AW)	12	2	2	1	8284

54 5/09 Bath 5f161y G-F £2183
93 6/08 Wind 6f (0-70)H G-F £2729
83 6/08 Bath 5f161y (0-75)H FRM £2914
78 6/08 Wind 6f (0-80)H G-F £5051
63 5/08 Wind 6f G-F £2593
71 5/08 Rdcr 6f G-F £2047
71 7/07 Folk 7f (0-65)H G-S £2388
68 2/07 Wolv 7f32y STD £3238
63 1/07 Wolv 7f32y STD £2388
Total win prize-money £25536

Going (Turf): Sf: 0-3 GS: 1-9 Gd: 0-8 **GF: 5-13** Fm: 1-2
Distance: 5f/6f: 6-26 7f-8f: 3-20 9f-13f: 0-1 14f+: 0-0
Track : LH: 4-18 RH: 0-2 Tight: 2-8 **Gall: 5-15**
Aids: Bl: 3-10 **Vi: 6-26** Tstrap: 0-0 Ckp: 0-0
Best Rating: 93 7/08 Pont 6f gd-fm

Fair; effective over 5f-7f; acts on most ground on turf; goes on Polytrack; has worn blinkers and a visor.

Drews Lane

72 **45**
2-y-o b f Forzando-Emerald Dream (IRE) (Vision (USA))
W G M Turner Mrs Tracy Turner

Placings:6060 **(5543)**
2009: 7^{6}G, 7^{0}G, 8^{6}GF, 7^{0}GF,

	Starts	1st	2nd	3rd	Win & Pl
Career Total (Turf)	4	0	0	0	0

Going (Turf): Sf: 0-0 GS: 0-0 Gd: 0-2 GF: 0-2 Fm: 0-0
Distance: 5f/6f: 0-0 7f-8f: 0-3 9f-13f: 0-1 14f+: 0-0
Track : LH: 0-1 RH: 0-1 Tight: 0-2 Gall: 0-0
Aids: Bl: 0-0 Vi: 0-0 Tstrap: 0-2 Ckp: 0-2
Best Rating: 45 8/09 Wind 1m67y gd-fm

Drift And Dream

93 **71**
2-y-o b f Exceed And Excel (AUS)-Sea Drift (FR) (Warning)
C F Wall Lady Juliet Tadgell

Placings:1522 **(5992)**
2009: 5^{1}G, 6^{5}G, 5^{2}GF, 5^{2}S,

	Starts	1st	2nd	3rd	Win & Pl
Career Total (Turf)	4	1	2	0	4647

65 6/09 Yarm 5f43y GD £2719
Total win prize-money £2720

Going (Turf): Sf: 0-1 GS: 0-0 **Gd: 1-2** GF: 0-1 Fm: 0-0
Distance: 5f/6f: 1-4 7f-8f: 0-0 9f-13f: 0-0 14f+: 0-0
Track : LH: 0-0 RH: 0-0 Tight: 0-0 Gall: 0-0
Aids: Bl: 0-0 Vi: 0-0 Tstrap: 0-0 Ckp: 0-0
Best Rating: 71 9/09 Sand 5f6y soft

Fair; effective at 5f; acts on most ground.

Drifting Gold

101(106) (77)**81**
5-y-o ch m Bold Edge-Driftholme (Safawan)
C G Cox Martin C Oliver

Placings:2522035/42122150106/61666006-31554401225000 **(6801)**
2009: 5^{3}SD, 5^{1}SD, 5^{5}SD, 5^{5}SD, 5^{4}SD, 5^{4}SD, 5^{0}G, 5^{1}GF, 5^{2}GF, 5^{2}GF, 6^{5}SD, 5^{0}GF, 5^{0}GF, 5^{0}SD,

	Starts	1st	2nd	3rd	Win & Pl
Career Total (Turf)	16	3	2	1	12680
Career Total (AW)	24	3	6	1	17996

78 4/09 Brig 5f59y (0-70)H G-F £3280
77 1/09 Kemp 5f (0-70)H STD £5051
81 1/08 Wolv 5f20y (0-75)H STD £2590
74 8/07 Wind 5f10y (0-70)H G-F £3238
71 6/07 Gdwd 5f (0-70)H GD £3562
77 2/07 Wolv 5f20y STD £2817
Total win prize-money £20540

Going (Turf): Sf: 0-0 GS: 0-0 Gd: 1-5 **GF: 2-11** Fm: 0-0
Distance: **5f/6f: 6-38** 7f-8f: 0-2 9f-13f: 0-0 14f+: 0-0
Track : **LH: 3-26** RH: 1-3 **Tight: 2-22** Gall: 1-5
Aids: **Bl: 5-24** Vi: 1-7 Tstrap: 0-1 Ckp: 0-1
Best Rating: **81** 5/09 Leic 5f2y gd-fm

Fair sprinter; suited by 5f; acts on a sound surface; goes on Polytrack; has worn blinkers and a visor.

Drill Sergeant

111 111
4-y-o br g Rock Of Gibraltar (IRE)-Dolydille (IRE) (Dolphin Street (FR))
M Johnston J Barson

Placings:320/1254503210333-000203332156324025 **(7031)**
2009: 10⁰G, 13⁰GF, 16⁰GF, 12²G, 10⁰G, 12³GF, 12³G, 12³GF, 12²G, 12¹GF, 11⁵GF, 14⁶GF, 14³G, 16²GF, 18⁴GF, 12⁰GF, 12²GF, 12⁵S,

	Starts	1st	2nd	3rd	Win & Pl
Career Total (Turf)	34	3	7	9	184510

110 6/09 Asct 1m4f (0-105)H G-F £31155
106 8/08 Bevl 1m1f207y (0-105)H SFT £25904
96 4/08 Newc 1m2f32y G-S £2914
Total win prize-money £59973

Going (Turf): **Sf: 1-4 GS: 1-4** Gd: 0-10 **GF: 1-14** Fm: 0-1
Distance: 5f/6f: 0-1 7f-8f: 0-2 **9f-13f: 3-25** 14f+: 0-6
Track : LH: 1-14 **RH: 2-13** Tight: 0-5 **Gall: 2-16**
Aids: Bl: 0-0 Vi: 0-0 Tstrap: 0-0 Ckp: 0-0
Best Rating: **111** 7/09 Gdwd 1m6f good

Smart; winner of the 2009 Duke Of Edinburgh Handicap and Group placed; effective at 1m4f but stays 2m; acts on any ground; likes to race prominently.

Drinking Buddy

91 54
2-y-o ch g Reel Buddy (USA)-Tancred Arms (Clantime)
D W Thompson (K A Ryan 14/8) Opus Industrial Services Partnership

Placings:553426000 **(7055)**
2009: 6⁵S, 7⁵G, 6³GF, 7⁴GF, 6²G, 5⁶GF, 6⁰GS, 8⁰GF, 7⁰GF,

	Starts	1st	2nd	3rd	Win & Pl
Career Total (Turf)	9	0	1	1	1108

Going (Turf): **Sf: 0-1 GS: 0-1 Gd: 0-2 GF: 0-5 Fm: 0-0**
Distance: 5f/6f: 0-4 7f-8f: 0-4 9f-13f: 0-1 14f+: 0-0
Track : LH: 0-4 RH: 0-0 Tight: 0-3 Gall: 0-0
Aids: Bl: 0-0 Vi: 0-0 Tstrap: 0-0 Ckp: 0-0
Best Rating: **54** 8/09 Catt 7f gd-fm

Driven (IRE)

102(104) (80)79
4-y-o b g Domedriver (IRE)-Wonderful World (GER) (Dashing Blade)
Mrs A J Perrett A D Spence

Placings:404/056-125303000 **(6790)**
2009: 7¹GF, 8²SD, 8⁵GF, 7³GF, 8⁰GF, 6³F, 7⁰SD, 7⁰GF, 6⁰G,

	Starts	1st	2nd	3rd	Win & Pl
Career Total (Turf)	13	1	0	2	6884
Career Total (AW)	2	0	1	0	907

79 4/09 Brig 7f214y (0-70)H G-F £3280
Total win prize-money £3280

Going (Turf): Sf: 0-0 GS: 0-1 Gd: 0-4 **GF: 1-7** Fm: 0-1
Distance: 5f/6f: 0-0 **7f-8f: 1-12** 9f-13f: 0-3 14f+: 0-0
Track : **LH: 1-8** RH: 0-3 Tight: 0-4 Gall: 0-0
Aids: Bl: 0-0 Vi: 0-0 Tstrap: 0-0 Ckp: 0-0
Best Rating: **80** 5/09 Ling 1m stand

Fair half-brother to Ayr Gold Cup winner Advanced; stays 1m; handles fast and easy ground and Polytrack.

Drizzi (IRE)

(87) (30)72
8-y-o b g Night Shift (USA)-Woopi Gold (IRE) (Last Tycoon)
Jim Best Eagle Bloodstock & Racing

Placings:5131/43523132401000/3403612/04240105202/1104222212100323/2-0 **(7842)**
2009: 14⁰SS,

	Starts	1st	2nd	3rd	Win & Pl
Career Total (Turf)	47	10	10	6	87655
Career Total (AW)	7	0	3	2	2558

72 9/07 Muss 1m4f GD £2590
8/07 Gros 1m165y H SFT £8614
4/07 Pisa 1m2f GD £1520
3/07 Pisa 1m2f GD £1520
10/06 Pisa 1m2f GD £1551
5/05 Siro 1m4f GD £7092
10/04 Siro 1m5f GD £5986
5/04 Siro 1m3f GD £8803
12/03 Agno 1m2f GD £5519
11/03 Capa 1m1f HVY £6494
Total win prize-money £49692

Going (Turf): Sf: 2-9 GS: 0-2 **Gd: 8-34** GF: 0-2 Fm: 0-0
Distance: 5f/6f: 0-0 7f-8f: 0-3 **9f-13f: 10-47** 14f+: 0-4
Track : LH: 0-6 **RH: 1-3 Tight: 1-5** Gall: 0-0
Aids: Bl: 0-0 Vi: 0-0 Tstrap: 1-6 Ckp: 1-6
Best Rating: **72** 9/07 Muss 1m4f good

Modest; multiple winner in Italy; effective at around 1m-1m5f; acts on Fibresand and Polytrack.

Drogba (ARG)

(101) (69)
4-y-o b c Lucky Roberto (USA)-Gattara (ARG) (Potrillazo (ARG))
M Botti El Catorce

Placings:1211-6 **(7810)**
2009: 8⁶SD,

	Starts	1st	2nd	3rd	Win & Pl
Career Total (Turf)	0	0	0	0	
Career Total (AW)	5	3	1	0	6441

6/08 Mrco 7f STD £2516
5/08 Mrco 6f110y STD £2052
2/08 Mrco 5f STD £1221
Total win prize-money £5789

Going (Turf): **Sf: 0-0 GS: 0-0 Gd: 0-0 GF: 0-0 Fm: 0-0**
Distance: 5f/6f: 1-2 **7f-8f: 2-3** 9f-13f: 0-0 14f+: 0-0
Track : LH: 0-1 RH: 0-0 Tight: 0-1 Gall: 0-0
Aids: Bl: 0-0 Vi: 0-1 Tstrap: 0-0 Ckp: 0-0
Best Rating: **69** 12/09 Ling 1m stand

Drombeg Pride (IRE)

(97) (31)43
5-y-o b g High Account (USA)-Proserpina (Most Welcome)
G P Enright Blue & Silver Partnership

Placings:0/000/000-0 **(0190)**
2009: 16⁰SD,

	Starts	1st	2nd	3rd	Win & Pl
Career Total (Turf)	7	0	0	0	
Career Total (AW)	1	0	0	0	

Going (Turf): **Sf: 0-1 GS: 0-1 Gd: 0-0 GF: 0-1 Fm: 0-1**
Distance: 5f/6f: 0-0 7f-8f: 0-2 9f-13f: 0-4 14f+: 0-2
Track : LH: 0-6 RH: 0-2 Tight: 0-2 Gall: 0-0
Aids: Bl: 0-0 Vi: 0-0 Tstrap: 0-0 Ckp: 0-0
Best Rating: **43** 7/07 Naas 1m2f soft

Dromore (IRE)

95(81) (58)75
2-y-o ch g Traditionally (USA)-Try To Catch Me (USA) (Shareef Dancer (USA))
A M Balding I G Burbidge

Placings:0100 **(6993)**
2009: 7⁰SD, 6¹GF, 8⁰GF, 8⁰GS,

	Starts	1st	2nd	3rd	Win & Pl
Career Total (Turf)	3	1	0	0	2914
Career Total (AW)	1	0	0	0	

75 8/09 Sals 6f212y G-F £2914
Total win prize-money £2914

Going (Turf): Sf: 0-0 GS: 0-1 Gd: 0-0 **GF: 1-2** Fm: 0-0
Distance: 5f/6f: 0-0 **7f-8f: 1-4** 9f-13f: 0-0 14f+: 0-0
Track : LH: 0-2 RH: 0-0 Tight: 0-1 Gall: 0-1
Aids: Bl: 0-0 Vi: 0-0 Tstrap: 0-0 Ckp: 0-0
Best Rating: **75** 8/09 Sals 6f212y gd-fm

Fair half-brother to Storming Home; efffective at 7f; acts on fast ground.

Drop The Hammer

99(81) (22)63
3-y-o b f Lucky Story (USA)-Paperweight (In The Wings)
T P Tate A Crowther

Placings:20-603153000 **(6822)**
2009: 10⁶GS, 12⁰GF, 12³GF, 14¹G, 14⁵SD, 16³GF, 16⁰GS, 16⁰GF, 14⁰GF,

	Starts	1st	2nd	3rd	Win & Pl
Career Total (Turf)	10	1	1	2	4982
Career Total (AW)	1	0	0	0	0

60 7/09 Hayd 1m6f (0-70)H GD £3238
Total win prize-money £3238

Going (Turf): Sf: 0-2 GS: 0-2 **Gd: 1-1** GF: 0-5 Fm: 0-0
Distance: 5f/6f: 0-0 7f-8f: 0-1 9f-13f: 0-4 **14f+: 1-6**
Track : **LH: 1-8** RH: 0-2 Tight: 0-3 Gall: 0-3
Aids: Bl: 0-0 Vi: 0-0 Tstrap: 0-0 Ckp: 0-0
Best Rating: **63** 10/08 Newc 7f heavy

Moderate; stays 1m6f; acts on fast ground.

Drubinca

80 43
2-y-o b g Dubai Destination (USA)-Racina (Bluebird (USA))
S C Williams Mad Man Plus One

Placings:005 (6364)
2009: 6^{0}G, 7^{0}GF, 7^{5}GF,

	Starts	1st	2nd	3rd	Win & Pl
Career Total (Turf)	3	0	0	0	0

Going (Turf): Sf: 0-0 GS: 0-0 Gd: 0-1 GF: 0-2 Fm: 0-0
Distance: 5f/6f: 0-1 7f-8f: 0-2 9f-13f: 0-0 14f+: 0-0
Track : LH: 0-1 RH: 0-0 Tight: 0-0 Gall: 0-1
Aids: Bl: 0-0 Vi: 0-0 Tstrap: 0-0 Ckp: 0-0
Best Rating: 43 9/09 Wwck 7f26y gd-fm

Drum Dragon

101(100) (78)74
3-y-o b f Beat Hollow-Qilin (IRE) (Second Set (IRE))
M H Tompkins David P Noblett

Placings:04-0216346146 (7539)
2009: 6^{0}GF, 8^{2}SD, 8^{1}GF, 8^{6}G, 10^{3}HY, 10^{4}GS, 12^{6}GF, 11^{1}G, 12^{4}SD, 12^{6}SD,

	Starts	1st	2nd	3rd	Win & Pl
Career Total (Turf)	9	2	0	1	6372
Career Total (AW)	3	0	1	0	1349

72 10/09 Catt 1m3f214y GD £2729
70 6/09 Haml 1m65y G-F £2590
Total win prize-money £5320

Going (Turf): Sf: 0-1 GS: 0-2 Gd: 1-3 GF: 1-3 Fm: 0-0
Distance: 5f/6f: 0-2 7f-8f: 0-1 9f-13f: 2-9 14f+: 0-0
Track : LH: 1-7 RH: 1-4 Tight: 2-4 Gall: 0-0
Aids: Bl: 0-0 Vi: 0-0 Tstrap: 0-0 Ckp: 0-0
Best Rating: 78 6/09 Wolv 1m141y stand

Fair; effective over 1m4f; acts on good ground and on Polytrack.

Drum Major (IRE)

100(99) (74)73
4-y-o b g Sadler's Wells (USA)-Phantom Gold (Machiavellian (USA))
G L Moore Miss Sarah Anne Phillips

Placings:0405002104-4025050 (5217)
2009: 12^{4}SD, 13^{0}SD, 13^{2}GF, 11^{5}GF, 16^{0}SD, 11^{5}GS, 14^{0}G,

	Starts	1st	2nd	3rd	Win & Pl
Career Total (Turf)	10	0	2	0	1734
Career Total (AW)	7	1	0	0	3472

58 10/08 GrLe 1m5f66y STD £2914
Total win prize-money £2914

Going (Turf): Sf: 0-1 GS: 0-2 Gd: 0-2 GF: 0-5 Fm: 0-0
Distance: 5f/6f: 0-0 7f-8f: 0-0 9f-13f: 0-12 14f+: 1-5
Track : LH: 1-9 RH: 0-7 Tight: 0-9 Gall: 1-4
Aids: Bl: 0-1 Vi: 0-0 Tstrap: 0-0 Ckp: 0-0
Best Rating: 74 1/09 Ling 1m4f stand

Modest; stays 1m5f; handles fast and soft ground; also goes on Polytrack.

Drumadoon Bay (IRE)

93 56
5-y-o b g Marju (IRE)-Mythical Creek (USA) (Pleasant Tap (USA))
G A Swinbank R H Hall

Placings:000204-04P6 (3683)
2009: 7^{0}GF, 8^{4}GF, 10^{P}G, 7^{6}GS,

	Starts	1st	2nd	3rd	Win & Pl
Career Total (Turf)	10	0	1	0	1293

Going (Turf): Sf: 0-1 GS: 0-2 Gd: 0-3 GF: 0-3 Fm: 0-1
Distance: 5f/6f: 0-1 7f-8f: 0-4 9f-13f: 0-4 14f+: 0-1
Track : LH: 0-4 RH: 0-5 Tight: 0-3 Gall: 0-1
Aids: Bl: 0-0 Vi: 0-0 Tstrap: 0-0 Ckp: 0-0
Best Rating: 56 7/08 Klny 1m100y good

Drumbeat (IRE)

108 108
3-y-o b c Montjeu (IRE)-Maskaya (IRE) (Machiavellian (USA))
A P O'Brien Derrick Smith

Placings:32215542-2360022 (4216a)
2009: 9^{2}GF, 10^{3}GF, 8^{6}HY, 10^{0}G, 12^{0}GY, 9^{2}Y, 8^{2}S,

	Starts	1st	2nd	3rd	Win & Pl
Career Total (Turf)	15	1	6	2	137005

89 8/08 Gowr 7f HVY £8637
Total win prize-money £8638

Going (Turf): Sf: 1-7 GS: 0-0 Gd: 0-2 GF: 0-2 Fm: 0-0
Distance: 5f/6f: 0-0 7f-8f: 1-9 9f-13f: 0-6 14f+: 0-0
Track : LH: 0-3 RH: 1-7 Tight: 0-1 Gall: 0-1
Aids: Bl: 0-0 Vi: 0-0 Tstrap: 0-0 Ckp: 0-0
Best Rating: 108 11/08 StCl 1m2f heavy

Smart; stays 7f; handles good and softer ground.

Drumfire (IRE)

111 115
5-y-o b h Danehill Dancer (IRE)-Witch Of Fife (USA) (Lear Fan (USA))
M Johnston Kennet Valley Thoroughbreds Iv

Placings:12130/2F/332163604-3420140 (5447)
2009: 10^{3}GF, 10^{4}G, 12^{2}GF, 12^{0}G, 9^{1}G, 12^{4}G, 10^{0}GF,

	Starts	1st	2nd	3rd	Win & Pl
Career Total (Turf)	23	4	4	5	207668

115 7/09 Gdwd 1m1f192y H GD £31155
114 8/08 NmkJ 1m2f GD £12462
99 8/06 Sand 7f16y GD £22712
86 6/06 Bevl 7f100y G-F £5505
Total win prize-money £71834

Going (Turf): Sf: 0-3 GS: 0-1 Gd: 3-11 GF: 1-7 Fm: 0-0
Distance: 5f/6f: 0-0 7f-8f: 2-9 9f-13f: 2-14 14f+: 0-0
Track : LH: 0-2 RH: 4-12 Tight: 1-6 Gall: 1-2
Aids: Bl: 0-0 Vi: 0-0 Tstrap: 0-0 Ckp: 0-0
Best Rating: 115 7/09 Gdwd 1m1f192y good

Smart; Group and Listed placed; stays 1m4f; acts on most ground.

Drumhallagh (IRE)

73(98) (53)10
4-y-o b g Barathea (IRE)-Nashua Song (IRE) (Kahyasi)
Tom Dascombe R George & J Brown

Placings:000/0-00 (1254)
2009: 13^{0}SF, 10^{0}GF,

	Starts	1st	2nd	3rd	Win & Pl
Career Total (Turf)	4	0	0	0	
Career Total (AW)	2	0	0	0	

Going (Turf): Sf: 0-0 GS: 0-1 Gd: 0-0 GF: 0-3 Fm: 0-0
Distance: 5f/6f: 0-1 7f-8f: 0-2 9f-13f: 0-2 14f+: 0-1
Track : LH: 0-4 RH: 0-0 Tight: 0-2 Gall: 0-1
Aids: Bl: 0-1 Vi: 0-0 Tstrap: 0-0 Ckp: 0-0
Best Rating: 60 8/07 Bath 5f161y gd-fm

Drumpellier (IRE)

92(86) (50)61
2-y-o ch f Rakti-Early Memory (USA) (Devil's Bag (USA))
P T Midgley R Wardlaw & Peter Mee

Placings:46654104 (4975)
2009: 5^{4}GF, 5^{6}F, 5^{6}GF, 6^{5}GS, 5^{4}SD, 6^{1}S, 6^{0}GS, 5^{4}GF,

	Starts	1st	2nd	3rd	Win & Pl
Career Total (Turf)	7	1	0	0	709
Career Total (AW)	1	0	0	0	0

Going (Turf): Sf: 1-1 GS: 0-2 Gd: 0-0 GF: 0-3 Fm: 0-1
Distance: 5f/6f: 1-7 7f-8f: 0-1 9f-13f: 0-0 14f+: 0-0
Track : LH: 0-2 RH: 0-1 Tight: 0-1 Gall: 0-1
Aids: Bl: 0-0 Vi: 0-0 Tstrap: 0-0 Ckp: 0-0
Best Rating: 61 8/09 Catt 5f212y gd-fm

Modest; stays 6f; acts on most ground.

Drunken Sailor (IRE)

114 (77)104
4-y-o b g Tendulkar (USA)-Ronni Pancake (Mujadil (USA))
Paul W Flynn J J Keogh

Placings:000/2341121024-50221162 (6106)
2009: 10^{5}GF, 10^{0}GF, 12^{2}GF, 12^{2}GY, 12^{1}SH, 12^{1}G, 14^{6}S, 10^{2}GF,

	Starts	1st	2nd	3rd	Win & Pl
Career Total (Turf)	19	5	5	1	118695
Career Total (AW)	2	0	1	0	1635

92 8/09 Gowr 1m4f (60-90)H GD £9727
85 7/09 Gway 1m4f H SH £41082
79 8/08 Baln 1m1f (50-80)H Y-S £6605
76 6/08 DRoy 1m2f100y (45-60)H G-Y £4318
62 6/08 Fair 7f (45-65)H GD £4572
Total win prize-money £66308

Going (Turf): Sf: 0-3 GS: 0-0 Gd: 2-3 GF: 0-5 Fm: 0-1
Distance: 5f/6f: 0-0 7f-8f: 1-7 9f-13f: 4-13 14f+: 0-1
Track : LH: 0-6 RH: 5-13 Tight: 0-0 Gall: 0-2
Aids: Bl: 2-9 Vi: 0-0 Tstrap: 1-4 Ckp: 1-4
Best Rating: 104 9/09 Newb 1m2f6y gd-fm

Very useful; effective at around 1m2f-1m4f; acts on most types of ground on turf; has worn blinkers/tongue tie.

Drussell (IRE)

87(101) (69)63
3-y-o b g Orpen (USA)-Cahermee Queen (USA) (King Of Kings (IRE))
S Donohoe Mrs Samantha Donohoe

Placings:10000 (7048)
2009: 12^{1}SF, 15^{0}GF, 14^{0}GF, 10^{0}SD, 10^{0}SD,

	Starts	1st	2nd	3rd	Win & Pl
Career Total (Turf)	2	0	0	0	
Career Total (AW)	3	1	0	0	2047

68 3/09 Wolv 1m4f50y SF £2047
Total win prize-money £2047

Going (Turf): Sf: 0-0 GS: 0-0 Gd: 0-0 GF: 0-2 Fm: 0-0
Distance: 5f/6f: 0-0 7f-8f: 0-0 9f-13f: 1-3 14f+: 0-2
Track : LH: 1-2 RH: 0-3 Tight: 1-3 Gall: 0-0
Aids: Bl: 0-0 Vi: 0-0 Tstrap: 0-0 Ckp: 0-0
Best Rating: 69 10/09 Kemp 1m2f stand

Dry Speedfit (IRE)

85(97) (72)57

4-y-o b g Desert Style (IRE)-Annmary Girl (Zafonic (USA))

Micky Hammond Oakwood Racing Partnership

Placings:1050/**5**0000**5**000**R**-0 (3862)

2009: 8^{0}GF,

	Starts	1st	2nd	3rd	Win & Pl
Career Total (Turf)	10	1	0	0	3356
Career Total (AW)	5	0	0	0	0

84	6/07	Wind	6f		SFT	£3238

Total win prize-money £3239

Going (Turf): **Sf: 1-2** GS: 0-3 Gd: 0-2 GF: 0-3 Fm: 0-0
Distance: **5f/6f: 1-4** 7f-8f: 0-7 9f-13f: 0-4 14f+: 0-0
Track : LH: 0-4 RH: 0-3 Tight: 0-1 **Gall: 1-2**
Aids: Bl: 0-2 Vi: 0-1 Tstrap: 0-0 Ckp: 0-0
Best Rating: **93** 7/07 NmkJ 7f gd-fm

Modest; regressive in 2008, seems best at 1m; acts on soft ground; has worn blinkers.

Dualagi

99(99) (67)71

5-y-o b m Royal Applause-Lady Melbourne (IRE) (Indian Ridge)

M R Bosley Inca Financial Services

Placings:0/143532416050/45146002550250-0021034653340 (6933)

2009: 6^{0}SD, 6^{0}GF, 5^{2}F, 6^{1}GF, 6^{0}GF, 6^{3}SD, 6^{4}SD, 6^{6}GS, 5^{5}S, 6^{3}GF, 6^{3}GF, 6^{4}GF, 5^{0}G,

	Starts	1st	2nd	3rd	Win & Pl
Career Total (Turf)	32	3	3	4	15630
Career Total (AW)	8	1	1	1	4121

64	5/09	Sals	6f	(0-65)H	G-F	£3043
71	5/08	Bath	5f161y	(0-70)H	G-F	£2590
71	8/07	Sand	5f6y	(0-75)H	G-S	£4533
60	3/07	Ling	5f		STD	£2914

Total win prize-money £13083

Going (Turf): Sf: 0-5 GS: 1-8 Gd: 0-3 **GF: 2-13** Fm: 0-3
Distance: **5f/6f: 4-35** 7f-8f: 0-5 9f-13f: 0-0 14f+: 0-0
Track : **LH: 2-10** RH: 0-5 Tight: 1-2 Gall: 1-7
Aids: Bl: 0-0 Vi: 0-0 Tstrap: 0-1 Ckp: 0-1
Best Rating: **71** 5/08 Bath 5f161y gd-fm

Modest; stays 6f; acts on soft ground and on Polytrack.

Duar Mapel (USA)

94(100) (73)65

3-y-o b g Lemon Drop Kid (USA)-Pitchacurve (USA) (Defrere (USA))

N Bertran De Balanda (Paul Mason 13/6) Prime Equestrian SARL

Placings:003-30060 (2909)

2009: 8^{3}SD, 8^{0}GS, 10^{0}GF, 11^{6}F, 10^{0}HO,

	Starts	1st	2nd	3rd	Win & Pl
Career Total (Turf)	5	0	0	0	0
Career Total (AW)	3	0	0	2	981

Going (Turf): **Sf: 0-0 GS: 0-2 Gd: 0-0 GF: 0-1 Fm: 0-1**
Distance: 5f/6f: 0-0 7f-8f: 0-3 9f-13f: 0-5 14f+: 0-0
Track : LH: 0-3 RH: 0-3 Tight: 0-4 Gall: 0-0
Aids: Bl: 0-5 Vi: 0-1 Tstrap: 0-0 Ckp: 0-0
Best Rating: **73** 10/08 Kemp 1m stand

Modest; effective over 1m; acts on Polytrack.

Dubai Bounty

(95) (66)

2-y-o ch f Dubai Destination (USA)-Mary Read (Bahamian Bounty)

G A Butler The Distaff 2 Partnership

Placings:1 (7844)

2009: 8^{1}SD,

	Starts	1st	2nd	3rd	Win & Pl
Career Total (Turf)	0	0	0	0	
Career Total (AW)	1	1	0	0	3886

66	12/09	Wolv	1m141y	STD	£3885

Total win prize-money £3886

Going (Turf): **Sf: 0-0 GS: 0-0 Gd: 0-0 GF: 0-0 Fm: 0-0**
Distance: 5f/6f: 0-0 7f-8f: 0-0 **9f-13f: 1-1** 14f+: 0-0
Track : **LH: 1-1** RH: 0-0 **Tight: 1-1** Gall: 0-0
Aids: Bl: 0-0 Vi: 0-0 Tstrap: 0-0 Ckp: 0-0
Best Rating: **66** 12/09 Wolv 1m141y stand

Fair; stays 1m and acts on Polytrack.

Dubai Creek (IRE)

88(96) (62)50

3-y-o b g Cape Cross (IRE)-Humilis (IRE) (Sadler's Wells (USA))

D McCain Jnr (M Johnston 10/10) Timeform Betfair Racing Club Ltd

Placings:55 (6673)

2009: 10^{5}GF, 9^{5}SD,

	Starts	1st	2nd	3rd	Win & Pl
Career Total (Turf)	1	0	0	0	0
Career Total (AW)	1	0	0	0	0

Going (Turf): **Sf: 0-0 GS: 0-0 Gd: 0-0 GF: 0-1 Fm: 0-0**
Distance: 5f/6f: 0-0 7f-8f: 0-0 9f-13f: 0-2 14f+: 0-0
Track : LH: 0-2 RH: 0-0 Tight: 0-2 Gall: 0-0
Aids: Bl: 0-0 Vi: 0-0 Tstrap: 0-0 Ckp: 0-0
Best Rating: **62** 10/09 Wolv 1m1f103y stand

Dubai Crest

103(96) (69)91

3-y-o b g Dubai Destination (USA)-On The Brink (Mind Games)

Mrs A J Perrett A D Spence

Placings:00461232-12000164650 (6907)

2009: 9^{1}GF, 10^{2}GF, 10^{0}G, 12^{0}GF, 11^{0}G, 10^{1}G, 9^{6}GF, 10^{4}F, 10^{6}G, 10^{5}GF, 10^{0}G,

	Starts	1st	2nd	3rd	Win & Pl
Career Total (Turf)	18	2	3	1	17412
Career Total (AW)	1	1	0	0	2047

90	8/09	Wind	1m2f7y	(0-85)H	GD	£5180
86	4/09	Bevl	1m1f207y	(0-80)H	G-F	£4727
69	9/08	Kemp	1m	(0-65)	STD	£2047

Total win prize-money £11955

Going (Turf): Sf: 0-1 GS: 0-2 **Gd: 1-7 GF: 1-7** Fm: 0-1
Distance: 5f/6f: 0-0 7f-8f: 1-5 **9f-13f: 2-14** 14f+: 0-0
Track : LH: 0-5 **RH: 3-12 Tight: 1-6** Gall: 0-2
Aids: Bl: 0-1 Vi: 0-0 Tstrap: 0-0 Ckp: 0-0
Best Rating: **91** 5/09 NmkR 1m2f gd-fm

Useful; stays 1m2f; acts on most ground and on Polytrack; has worn binkers.

Dubai Diva

90(101) (70)47

3-y-o b f Dubai Destination (USA)-Marine City (JPN) (Carnegie (IRE))

C F Wall Peter Botham

Placings:000-40140 (7760)

2009: 11^{4}SD, 11^{0}S, 16^{1}SD, 16^{4}SD, 16^{0}SD,

	Starts	1st	2nd	3rd	Win & Pl
Career Total (Turf)	2	0	0	0	
Career Total (AW)	6	1	0	0	2831

70	11/09	Ling	2m	(0-70)H	STD	£2590

Total win prize-money £2590

Going (Turf): **Sf: 0-1 GS: 0-1 Gd: 0-0 GF: 0-0 Fm: 0-0**
Distance: 5f/6f: 0-0 7f-8f: 0-1 9f-13f: 0-4 **14f+: 1-3**
Track : **LH: 1-7** RH: 0-0 **Tight: 1-4** Gall: 0-1
Aids: Bl: 0-0 Vi: 0-0 Tstrap: 0-0 Ckp: 0-0
Best Rating: **70** 11/09 Ling 2m stand

Modest; effective over 2m; acts on Polytrack.

Dubai Dynamo

90(110) (97)99

4-y-o b g Kyllachy-Miss Mercy (IRE) (Law Society (USA))

P F I Cole Mrs Fitri Hay

Placings:5021035116/50040600-100P0 (6732)

2009: 8^{1}SD, 8^{0}SD, 8^{0}GF, 8^{P}G, 8^{0}S,

	Starts	1st	2nd	3rd	Win & Pl
Career Total (Turf)	18	3	0	1	143638
Career Total (AW)	5	1	1	0	7997

97	4/09	Kemp	1m	(0-95)H	STD	£7352
95	10/07	Rdcr	6f		GD	£125285
86	9/07	Donc	7f	(0-95)	G-F	£9715
75	6/07	Gdwd	6f		GD	£2752

Total win prize-money £145107

Going (Turf): Sf: 0-3 GS: 0-3 **Gd: 2-5** GF: 1-7 Fm: 0-0
Distance: 5f/6f: 2-7 7f-8f: 2-16 9f-13f: 0-0 14f+: 0-0
Track : LH: 0-5 **RH: 1-5** Tight: 0-0 Gall: 0-3
Aids: Bl: 0-1 Vi: 0-0 Tstrap: 0-0 Ckp: 0-0
Best Rating: **99** 6/08 Asct 1m gd-fm

Useful; effective over 6f-1m; acts on most types of ground on turf; goes on Fibresand; has worn blinkers.

Dubai Echo (USA)

105 85

3-y-o b/br g Mr Greeley (USA)-Entendu (USA) (Diesis)

Sir Michael Stoute Saeed Suhail

Placings:04-2414 (3526)

2009: 10^{2}GF, 9^{4}G, 9^{1}GF, 10^{4}GF,

	Starts	1st	2nd	3rd	Win & Pl
Career Total (Turf)	6	1	1	0	4862

81	6/09	Ripn	1m1f170y	G-F	£3238

Total win prize-money £3238

Going (Turf): Sf: 0-1 GS: 0-0 Gd: 0-1 **GF: 1-4** Fm: 0-0
Distance: 5f/6f: 0-0 7f-8f: 0-1 **9f-13f: 1-5** 14f+: 0-0
Track : LH: 0-2 **RH: 1-3 Tight: 1-4** Gall: 0-0
Aids: Bl: 0-0 Vi: 0-0 Tstrap: 0-0 Ckp: 0-0
Best Rating: **85** 4/09 Wind 1m2f7y gd-fm

Useful; effective at about a mile; handles quick ground.

Dubai Gem

92 66

3-y-o b f Fantastic Light (USA)-Reflectance (Sadler's Wells (USA))

Jamie Poulton Ormonde Racing

Placings:655 (2679)

2009: 8^{6}GF, 9^{5}GF, 8^{5}GF,

	Starts	1st	2nd	3rd	Win & Pl
Career Total (Turf)	3	0	0	0	0

Going (Turf): Sf: 0-0 GS: 0-0 Gd: 0-0 GF: 0-3 Fm: 0-0
Distance: 5f/6f: 0-0 7f-8f: 0-2 9f-13f: 0-1 14f+: 0-0
Track : LH: 0-0 RH: 0-3 Tight: 0-1 Gall: 0-0
Aids: Bl: 0-0 Vi: 0-0 Tstrap: 0-0 Ckp: 0-0
Best Rating: 66 5/09 Gdwd 1m1f192y gd-fm

Dubai Hills

93 81

3-y-o b g Dubai Destination (USA)-Hill Welcome (Most Welcome)

B Smart H E Sheikh Rashid Bin Mohammed

Placings:0210-400 (5523)

2009: 6^{4}GF, 6^{0}G, 6^{0}G,

	Starts	1st	2nd	3rd	Win & Pl
Career Total (Turf)	7	1	1	0	6019
81 9/08 Hayd 6f			HVY	£3885	

Total win prize-money £3886

Going (Turf): Sf: 1-2 GS: 0-0 Gd: 0-3 GF: 0-2 Fm: 0-0
Distance: 5f/6f: 1-5 7f-8f: 0-2 9f-13f: 0-0 14f+: 0-0
Track : LH: 0-0 RH: 0-0 Tight: 0-0 Gall: 0-0
Aids: Bl: 0-0 Vi: 0-0 Tstrap: 0-0 Ckp: 0-0
Best Rating: 81 9/08 Hayd 6f heavy

Useful; stays 6f; acts on soft ground.

Dubai Legend

96(90) (62)78

3-y-o ch f Cadeaux Genereux-Royal Future (IRE) (Royal Academy (USA))

D M Simcock Ahmad Al Shaikh

Placings:0250-10500 (6798)

2009: 6^{1}GF, 6^{0}G, 6^{5}G, 6^{0}GF, 6^{0}S,

	Starts	1st	2nd	3rd	Win & Pl
Career Total (Turf)	7	1	1	0	13383
Career Total (AW)	2	0	0	0	0
73 5/09 Sals 6f			G-F	£3885	

Total win prize-money £3886

Going (Turf): Sf: 0-1 GS: 0-1 Gd: 0-2 GF: 1-3 Fm: 0-0
Distance: 5f/6f: 1-5 7f-8f: 0-4 9f-13f: 0-0 14f+: 0-0
Track : LH: 0-0 RH: 0-2 Tight: 0-0 Gall: 0-1
Aids: Bl: 0-0 Vi: 0-0 Tstrap: 0-0 Ckp: 0-0
Best Rating: 78 10/08 NmkR 7f gd-fm

Promising sort; effective at 6f; acts with give in the ground; handles Polytrack.

Dubai Media (CAN)

89(91) (68)66

2-y-o b f Songandaprayer (USA)-Forty Gran (USA) (El Gran Senor (USA))

D M Simcock Ahmad Al Shaikh

Placings:04 (7135)

2009: 7^{0}G, 7^{4}SD,

	Starts	1st	2nd	3rd	Win & Pl
Career Total (Turf)	1	0	0	0	
Career Total (AW)	1	0	0	0	327

Going (Turf): Sf: 0-0 GS: 0-0 Gd: 0-1 GF: 0-0 Fm: 0-0
Distance: 5f/6f: 0-0 7f-8f: 0-2 9f-13f: 0-0 14f+: 0-0
Track : LH: 0-1 RH: 0-0 Tight: 0-1 Gall: 0-0
Aids: Bl: 0-0 Vi: 0-0 Tstrap: 0-0 Ckp: 0-0
Best Rating: 68 10/09 Ling 7f stand

Dubai Meydan (IRE)

(104) (90)85

4-y-o b g High Chaparral (IRE)-Miss Golden Sands (Kris)

Miss Gay Kelleway M K Armitt & N Spence

Placings:30/412655P-0U31 (7111)

2009: 8^{0}SD, 7^{U}SD, 7^{3}SD, 7^{1}SD,

	Starts	1st	2nd	3rd	Win & Pl
Career Total (Turf)	7	1	1	1	6776
Career Total (AW)	6	1	0	1	5745
90 10/09 Kemp 7f	(0-80)H		STD	£4727	
80 5/08 Catt 7f			GD	£2590	

Total win prize-money £7317

Going (Turf): Sf: 0-1 GS: 0-2 Gd: 1-2 GF: 0-2 Fm: 0-0
Distance: 5f/6f: 0-0 7f-8f: 2-12 9f-13f: 0-1 14f+: 0-0
Track : LH: 1-6 RH: 1-4 Tight: 1-3 Gall: 0-1
Aids: Bl: 0-1 Vi: 0-0 Tstrap: 0-0 Ckp: 0-0
Best Rating: 90 10/09 Kemp 7f stand

Useful maiden; effective at 7f; acts on good ground.

Dubai Miracle (USA)

92(93) (79)98

2-y-o ch c Consolidator (USA)-East Cape (USA) (Mr Prospector (USA))

D M Simcock Ahmad Al Shaikh

Placings:43120 (6268)

2009: 6^{4}SD, 7^{3}SD, 7^{1}SD, 8^{2}G, 8^{0}G,

	Starts	1st	2nd	3rd	Win & Pl
Career Total (Turf)	2	0	1	0	6456
Career Total (AW)	3	1	0	1	2966
79 7/09 Ling 7f			STD	£2388	

Total win prize-money £2388

Going (Turf): Sf: 0-0 GS: 0-0 Gd: 0-2 GF: 0-0 Fm: 0-0
Distance: 5f/6f: 0-1 7f-8f: 1-4 9f-13f: 0-0 14f+: 0-0
Track : LH: 1-2 RH: 0-2 Tight: 1-2 Gall: 0-1
Aids: Bl: 0-0 Vi: 0-0 Tstrap: 0-0 Ckp: 0-0
Best Rating: 98 8/09 Sals 1m good

Fair; stays 1m and acts on Polytrack and good ground.

Dubai Petal (IRE)

(96) (64)77

4-y-o b f Dubai Destination (USA)-Out Of Egypt (USA) (Red Ransom (USA))

J S Moore S A Belton

Placings:0404/52145523200-0 (0103)

2009: 12^{0}SD,

	Starts	1st	2nd	3rd	Win & Pl
Career Total (Turf)	14	1	3	1	8711
Career Total (AW)	2	0	0	0	
74 4/08 Wind 1m3f135y	(0-75)H		G-F	£2729	

Total win prize-money £2730

Going (Turf): Sf: 0-2 GS: 0-8 Gd: 0-1 GF: 1-3 Fm: 0-0
Distance: 5f/6f: 0-2 7f-8f: 0-3 9f-13f: 1-8 14f+: 0-3
Track : LH: 0-9 RH: 0-2 Tight: 1-7 Gall: 0-2
Aids: Bl: 0-0 Vi: 0-0 Tstrap: 0-0 Ckp: 0-0
Best Rating: 77 5/08 Gdwd 1m1f192y soft

Fair; stays an extended 1m3f; acts on fast and easy ground.

Dubai Phantom (USA)

71(89) (66)30

2-y-o b g Arch (USA)-Sharp Apple (USA) (Diesis)

D M Simcock Ahmad Al Shaikh

Placings:053 (6858)

2009: 8^{0}G, 8^{5}SD, 8^{3}SD,

	Starts	1st	2nd	3rd	Win & Pl
Career Total (Turf)	1	0	0	0	
Career Total (AW)	2	0	0	1	353

Going (Turf): Sf: 0-0 GS: 0-0 Gd: 0-1 GF: 0-0 Fm: 0-0
Distance: 5f/6f: 0-0 7f-8f: 0-1 9f-13f: 0-2 14f+: 0-0
Track : LH: 0-1 RH: 0-1 Tight: 0-1 Gall: 0-0
Aids: Bl: 0-2 Vi: 0-0 Tstrap: 0-0 Ckp: 0-0
Best Rating: 66 10/09 Wolv 1m141y stand

Dubai Set

103 89

2-y-o ch c Reset (AUS)-Bint Makbul (Makbul)

R Hannon Malih L Al Basti

Placings:4322131 (7290)

2009: 6^{4}GF, 6^{3}GF, 6^{2}GF, 5^{2}G, 6^{1}GF, 6^{3}GS, 6^{1}S,

	Starts	1st	2nd	3rd	Win & Pl
Career Total (Turf)	7	2	2	2	14496
89 11/09 Donc 6f	(0-85)		SFT	£6476	
78 8/09 Ling 6f			G-F	£3561	

Total win prize-money £10038

Going (Turf): Sf: 1-1 GS: 0-1 Gd: 0-1 GF: 1-4 Fm: 0-0
Distance: 5f/6f: 2-7 7f-8f: 0-0 9f-13f: 0-0 14f+: 0-0
Track : LH: 0-1 RH: 0-0 Tight: 0-0 Gall: 0-4
Aids: Bl: 0-0 Vi: 0-0 Tstrap: 0-0 Ckp: 0-0
Best Rating: 89 11/09 Donc 6f soft

Useful; stays 6f and acts on soft and fast ground.

Dubai Storming

(98) (81)

3-y-o b g Storming Home-Tropical Breeze (IRE) (Kris)

E A L Dunlop Salem Suhail

Placings:0-511450 (5667)

2009: 10^{5}SD, 11^{1}SD, 12^{1}SD, 10^{4}SD, 12^{5}SD, 11^{0}SD,

	Starts	1st	2nd	3rd	Win & Pl
Career Total (Turf)	0	0	0	0	
Career Total (AW)	7	2	0	0	5258
77 3/09 Wolv 1m4f50y	(0-75)H		STD	£2729	
69 2/09 Kemp 1m3f			STD	£2047	

Total win prize-money £4777

Going (Turf): Sf: 0-0 GS: 0-0 Gd: 0-0 GF: 0-0 Fm: 0-0
Distance: 5f/6f: 0-0 7f-8f: 0-1 9f-13f: 2-6 14f+: 0-0
Track : LH: 1-3 RH: 1-4 Tight: 1-3 Gall: 0-0
Aids: Bl: 0-1 Vi: 0-0 Tstrap: 0-0 Ckp: 0-0
Best Rating: 81 3/09 Ling 1m2f stand

Modest; effective over 1m4f; acts on Polytrack; has worn blinkers.

Dubai To Barnsley

102(101) (56)**61**

4-y-o b g Superior Premium-Oakwell Ace (Clantime)

D A Nolan (Garry Moss 29/1) J Hampson

Placings:003060100**5220-00424450**0 **(7460)**

2009: 6^{0}SD, 6^{0}SD, 5^{4}GF, 5^{2}GF, 5^{4}GF, 5^{4}G, 5^{5}G, 7^{0}SD, 5^{0}SD,

	Starts	1st	2nd	3rd	Win & Pl
Career Total (Turf)	14	1	1	1	4141
Career Total (AW)	8	0	2	0	1279

51 8/08 Bevl 5f (0-60)H SFT £2900

Total win prize-money £2900

Going (Turf): **Sf: 1-3** GS: 0-0 Gd: 0-6 GF: 0-5 Fm: 0-0
Distance: **5f/6f: 1-20** 7f-8f: 0-2 9f-13f: 0-0 14f+: 0-0
Track : LH: 0-7 RH: 0-0 Tight: 0-3 Gall: 0-3
Aids: Bl: 0-0 Vi: 0-0 Tstrap: 0-1 Ckp: 0-1
Best Rating: **61** 6/09 Muss 5f gd-fm

Moderate; effective at 5f-6f; acts on fast and soft ground; goes on Polytrack.

Dubai Tsunami

(67) (15)**28**

3-y-o gr f Fantastic Light (USA)-Citrine Spirit (IRE) (Soviet Star (USA))

E A L Dunlop Salem Suhail

Placings:05-0 **(3228)**

2009: 8^{0}SD,

	Starts	1st	2nd	3rd	Win & Pl
Career Total (Turf)	2	0	0	0	0
Career Total (AW)	1	0	0	0	

Going (Turf): **Sf: 0-0 GS: 0-2 Gd: 0-0 GF: 0-0 Fm: 0-0**
Distance: 5f/6f: 0-2 7f-8f: 0-0 9f-13f: 0-1 14f+: 0-0
Track : LH: 0-2 RH: 0-0 Tight: 0-1 Gall: 0-0
Aids: Bl: 0-0 Vi: 0-0 Tstrap: 0-0 Ckp: 0-0
Best Rating: **28** 5/08 NmkR 6f gd-sft

Dam is well related and won over 1m at three.

Dubai's Touch

101(113) (109)**109**

5-y-o b h Dr Fong (USA)-Noble Peregrine (Lomond (USA))

M Johnston Salem Suhail

Placings:64113310/1010024/**24**000433460-400100 **(4768)**

2009: 8^{4}GF, 8^{0}G, 8^{0}GF, 8^{1}G, 8^{0}G, 8^{0}GS,

	Starts	1st	2nd	3rd	Win & Pl
Career Total (Turf)	28	5	1	4	110150
Career Total (AW)	4	1	1	0	26196

103 7/09 Asct 1m (0-95)H GD £7771
112 8/07 Gdwd 1m G-F £17034
109 3/07 Kemp 1m STD £14762
99 8/06 Newb 7f GD £13343
87 7/06 Pont 6f G-F £7478
80 6/06 Ripn 6f G-F £4533

Total win prize-money £64923

Going (Turf): Sf: 0-3 GS: 0-4 Gd: 2-9 **GF: 3-12** Fm: 0-0
Distance: 5f/6f: 2-6 **7f-8f: 4-17** 9f-13f: 0-9 14f+: 0-0
Track : LH: 1-8 **RH: 3-12** Tight: 0-2 **Gall: 1-5**
Aids: **Bl: 1-3** Vi: 0-0 Tstrap: 0-0 Ckp: 0-0
Best Rating: **112** 8/07 Gdwd 1m gd-fm

Very useful; winner in Listed company; effective at around 1m-1m2f; acts on good and faster ground and on Polytrack; has worn blinkers.

Dubara Reef (IRE)

58(74) (24)

2-y-o ch g Dubawi (IRE)-Mamara Reef (Salse (USA))

Paul Green The Four Aces

Placings:000 **(7463)**

2009: 7^{0}S, 8^{0}GF, 7^{0}SD,

	Starts	1st	2nd	3rd	Win & Pl
Career Total (Turf)	2	0	0	0	
Career Total (AW)	1	0	0	0	

Going (Turf): **Sf: 0-1 GS: 0-0 Gd: 0-0 GF: 0-1 Fm: 0-0**
Distance: 5f/6f: 0-0 7f-8f: 0-2 9f-13f: 0-1 14f+: 0-0
Track : LH: 0-3 RH: 0-0 Tight: 0-2 Gall: 0-0
Aids: Bl: 0-0 Vi: 0-0 Tstrap: 0-0 Ckp: 0-0
Best Rating: **24** 11/09 Wolv 7f32y stand

Dubawi Heights

103 **96**

2-y-o b f Dubawi (IRE)-Rosie's Posy (IRE) (Suave Dancer (USA))

S A Callaghan F W Golding, E Kirtland & N A Callaghan

Placings:053226 **(6852)**

2009: 6^{0}GF, 6^{5}GS, 6^{3}GF, 6^{2}G, 7^{2}GF, 7^{6}G,

	Starts	1st	2nd	3rd	Win & Pl
Career Total (Turf)	6	0	2	1	238380

Going (Turf): **Sf: 0-0 GS: 0-1 Gd: 0-2 GF: 0-3 Fm: 0-0**
Distance: 5f/6f: 0-3 7f-8f: 0-3 9f-13f: 0-0 14f+: 0-0
Track : LH: 0-0 RH: 0-0 Tight: 0-0 Gall: 0-0
Aids: Bl: 0-0 Vi: 0-0 Tstrap: 0-0 Ckp: 0-0
Best Rating: **96** 8/09 York 6f gd-fm

Smart; Group 2 placed; effective over 6-7f; acts on fast ground.

Dubawi King

79 **42**

2-y-o b g Dubawi (IRE)-Laughing Girl (USA) (Woodman (USA))

N Tinkler D Bloy & P Beecroft

Placings:00 **(7121)**

2009: 8^{0}GS, 8^{0}GF,

	Starts	1st	2nd	3rd	Win & Pl
Career Total (Turf)	2	0	0	0	

Going (Turf): **Sf: 0-0 GS: 0-1 Gd: 0-0 GF: 0-1 Fm: 0-0**
Distance: 5f/6f: 0-0 7f-8f: 0-0 9f-13f: 0-2 14f+: 0-0
Track : LH: 0-2 RH: 0-0 Tight: 0-0 Gall: 0-0
Aids: Bl: 0-0 Vi: 0-0 Tstrap: 0-0 Ckp: 0-0
Best Rating: **42** 10/09 Nott 1m75y gd-fm

Dubawi Phantom

99 **104**

2-y-o ch c Dubawi (IRE)-Anna Amalia (IRE) (In The Wings)

D M Simcock Sultan Ali

Placings:5621360 **(7030)**

2009: 5^{5}GF, 7^{6}G, 7^{2}G, 7^{1}G, 7^{3}GF, 8^{6}GS, 7^{0}S,

	Starts	1st	2nd	3rd	Win & Pl
Career Total (Turf)	7	1	1	1	12923

83 7/09 Epsm 7f GD £5180

Total win prize-money £5180

Going (Turf): Sf: 0-1 GS: 0-1 **Gd: 1-3** GF: 0-2 Fm: 0-0
Distance: 5f/6f: 0-1 **7f-8f: 1-6** 9f-13f: 0-0 14f+: 0-0
Track : **LH: 1-2** RH: 0-3 **Tight: 1-1** Gall: 0-1
Aids: Bl: 0-2 Vi: 0-0 Tstrap: 0-0 Ckp: 0-0
Best Rating: **104** 8/09 Sand 7f16y gd-fm

Smart; Group placed; effective over 7f; acts on good ground; has worn blinkers.

Dubburg (USA)

100(102) (62)**69**

4-y-o ch g Johannesburg (USA)-Plaisir Des Yeux (FR) (Funambule (USA))

W J Musson K A Cosby

Placings:515050-0650630 **(7248)**

2009: 8^{0}SD, 9^{6}GF, 9^{5}GF, 10^{0}GS, 9^{6}SD, 12^{3}SF, 10^{0}HY,

	Starts	1st	2nd	3rd	Win & Pl
Career Total (Turf)	8	1	0	0	7621
Career Total (AW)	5	0	0	1	433

69 4/08 Limk 6f160y SH £7621

Total win prize-money £7621

Going (Turf): **Sf: 0-1 GS: 0-1 Gd: 0-0 GF: 0-4 Fm: 0-0**
Distance: 5f/6f: 0-1 **7f-8f: 1-5** 9f-13f: 0-7 14f+: 0-0
Track : LH: 0-6 RH: 0-5 Tight: 0-3 Gall: 0-1
Aids: Bl: 0-1 Vi: 0-0 Tstrap: 0-0 Ckp: 0-0
Best Rating: **69** 5/08 Leop 7f gd-fm

Modest; stays 1m2f; acts on fast ground.

Ducal Daisey

91 **29**

3-y-o b f Shahrastani (USA)-Jimgareen (IRE) (Lahib (USA))

A B Haynes Abacus Employment Services Ltd

Placings:0 **(5381)**

2009: 11^{0}G,

	Starts	1st	2nd	3rd	Win & Pl
Career Total (Turf)	1	0	0	0	

Going (Turf): **Sf: 0-0 GS: 0-0 Gd: 0-1 GF: 0-0 Fm: 0-0**
Distance: 5f/6f: 0-0 7f-8f: 0-0 9f-13f: 0-1 14f+: 0-0
Track : LH: 0-1 RH: 0-0 Tight: 0-1 Gall: 0-0
Aids: Bl: 0-0 Vi: 0-0 Tstrap: 0-0 Ckp: 0-0
Best Rating: **29** 8/09 Bath 1m3f144y good

Ducal Destiny

70 **45**

2-y-o b c Reset (AUS)-Lucky Thing (Green Desert (USA))

J R Weymes Thoroughbred Partners

Placings:55 **(2784)**

2009: 5^{5}GF, 6^{5}GF,

	Starts	1st	2nd	3rd	Win & Pl
Career Total (Turf)	2	0	0	0	0

Going (Turf): **Sf: 0-0 GS: 0-0 Gd: 0-0 GF: 0-2 Fm: 0-0**
Distance: 5f/6f: 0-2 7f-8f: 0-0 9f-13f: 0-0 14f+: 0-0
Track : LH: 0-0 RH: 0-0 Tight: 0-0 Gall: 0-0
Aids: Bl: 0-0 Vi: 0-0 Tstrap: 0-0 Ckp: 0-0
Best Rating: **45** 5/09 Muss 5f gd-fm

Ducal Regancy Duke

85(65) **56**

5-y-o gr g Bertolini (USA)-Fun Run (USA) (Skip Away (USA))

C J Teague A Skelton

Placings:0300500-0604000 (5147)
2009: 7⁰GF, 14⁰GF, 14⁰GF, 9⁴G, 9⁰G, 9⁰G, 5⁰GS,

	Starts	1st	2nd	3rd	Win & Pl
Career Total (Turf)	13	0	0	1	495
Career Total (AW)	1	0	0	0	

Going (Turf): Sf: 0-1 GS: 0-2 Gd: 0-4 GF: 0-6 Fm: 0-0
Distance: 5f/6f: 0-2 7f-8f: 0-3 9f-13f: 0-6 14f+: 0-3
Track : LH: 0-6 RH: 0-6 Tight: 0-9 Gall: 0-0
Aids: Bl: 0-1 Vi: 0-2 Tstrap: 0-4 Ckp: 0-4
Best Rating: 56 6/08 Rdcr 1m gd-fm

Ducal Regancy Red

(98) (57)44
5-y-o ch m Bertolini (USA)-One For Jeannie (Clantime)
C J Teague Regancy Bloodstock

Placings:00060/3213060430000-06 (0919)
2009: 5⁰SD, 5⁰SD,

	Starts	1st	2nd	3rd	Win & Pl
Career Total (Turf)	8	0	0	1	337
Career Total (AW)	12	1	1	2	2646

51 2/08 Kemp 5f (0-45) STD £1295
Total win prize-money £1295

Going (Turf): Sf: 0-1 GS: 0-2 Gd: 0-2 GF: 0-3 Fm: 0-0
Distance: 5f/6f: 1-19 7f-8f: 0-1 9f-13f: 0-4 14f+: 0-0
Track : LH: 0-7 RH: 1-1 Tight: 0-5 Gall: 0-0
Aids: Bl: 0-0 Vi: 0-0 Tstrap: 0-0 Ckp: 0-0
Best Rating: 57 2/08 Sthl 5f std-slw

Plating-class sprinter; acts on both All-Weather surfaces.

Duchess Dora (IRE)

100 90
2-y-o b f Tagula (IRE)-Teodora (IRE) (Fairy King (USA))
J J Quinn The Clay Family

Placings:3121156 (6677)
2009: 5³F, 5¹GF, 5²GF, 5¹GF, 5¹GF, 5⁵G, 6⁶G,

	Starts	1st	2nd	3rd	Win & Pl
Career Total (Turf)	7	3	1	1	17341

90 8/09 Bevl 5f (0-85) G-F £6476
84 8/09 Sand 5f6y G-F £3885
76 5/09 Catt 5f G-F £2183
Total win prize-money £12546

Going (Turf): Sf: 0-0 GS: 0-0 Gd: 0-2 GF: 3-4 Fm: 0-1
Distance: 5f/6f: 3-7 7f-8f: 0-0 9f-13f: 0-0 14f+: 0-0
Track : LH: 0-1 RH: 0-0 Tight: 0-0 Gall: 0-0
Aids: Bl: 0-0 Vi: 0-0 Tstrap: 0-0 Ckp: 0-0
Best Rating: 90 8/09 Bevl 5f gd-fm

Very useful; effective over 5f and acts on fast ground.

Duchess Of Alba

67(58) 2
4-y-o b f Compton Place-Marie La Rose (FR) (Night Shift (USA))
G C Bravery M Klaton & Mrs F E Bravery

Placings:000 (6166)
2009: 8⁰G, 8⁰GF, 12⁰SD,

	Starts	1st	2nd	3rd	Win & Pl
Career Total (Turf)	2	0	0	0	
Career Total (AW)	1	0	0	0	

Going (Turf): Sf: 0-0 GS: 0-0 Gd: 0-1 GF: 0-1 Fm: 0-0
Distance: 5f/6f: 0-0 7f-8f: 0-1 9f-13f: 0-2 14f+: 0-0
Track : LH: 0-0 RH: 0-2 Tight: 0-0 Gall: 0-0
Aids: Bl: 0-0 Vi: 0-0 Tstrap: 0-0 Ckp: 0-0
Best Rating: 2 8/09 Sand 1m14y good

Duchess Of Doom (IRE)

81(91) (19)47
3-y-o b f Exceed And Excel (AUS)-Tallahassee Spirit (THA) (Presidential (USA))
C Gordon (S A Callaghan 18/5) N A Dunger

Placings:000-000 (6001)
2009: 7⁰GF, 8⁰SD, 10⁰GF,

	Starts	1st	2nd	3rd	Win & Pl
Career Total (Turf)	4	0	0	0	
Career Total (AW)	2	0	0	0	

Going (Turf): Sf: 0-1 GS: 0-0 Gd: 0-0 GF: 0-3 Fm: 0-0
Distance: 5f/6f: 0-2 7f-8f: 0-2 9f-13f: 0-2 14f+: 0-0
Track : LH: 0-3 RH: 0-0 Tight: 0-3 Gall: 0-1
Aids: Bl: 0-0 Vi: 0-0 Tstrap: 0-0 Ckp: 0-0
Best Rating: 47 6/08 Wind 6f gd-fm

Duchess Ravel (IRE)

83 59
2-y-o br f Bachelor Duke (USA)-Bolero Again (IRE) (Sadler's Wells (USA))
R Hannon Ballylinch Stud

Placings:3 (3458)
2009: 5³GF,

	Starts	1st	2nd	3rd	Win & Pl
Career Total (Turf)	1	0	0	1	403

Going (Turf): Sf: 0-0 GS: 0-0 Gd: 0-0 GF: 0-1 Fm: 0-0
Distance: 5f/6f: 0-1 7f-8f: 0-0 9f-13f: 0-0 14f+: 0-0
Track : LH: 0-0 RH: 0-0 Tight: 0-0 Gall: 0-1
Aids: Bl: 0-0 Vi: 0-0 Tstrap: 0-0 Ckp: 0-0
Best Rating: 59 6/09 Wind 5f10y gd-fm

Dudley

80 44
2-y-o ch g Compton Place-Just A Glimmer (Bishop Of Cashel)
J G Portman Berkeley Racing

Placings:000 (4478)
2009: 6⁰GF, 6⁰GF, 5⁰G,

	Starts	1st	2nd	3rd	Win & Pl
Career Total (Turf)	3	0	0	0	

Going (Turf): Sf: 0-0 GS: 0-0 Gd: 0-1 GF: 0-2 Fm: 0-0
Distance: 5f/6f: 0-3 7f-8f: 0-0 9f-13f: 0-0 14f+: 0-0
Track : LH: 0-1 RH: 0-0 Tight: 0-0 Gall: 0-2
Aids: Bl: 0-0 Vi: 0-0 Tstrap: 0-0 Ckp: 0-0
Best Rating: 44 6/09 Sals 6f gd-fm

Dudley Docker (IRE)

93(107) (80)75
7-y-o b g Victory Note (USA)-Nordic Abu (IRE) (Nordico (USA))
D C O'Brien (P R Webber 24/10) Joshua Pearce

Placings:0022/P0521050405/00226400004124664/12642 1101320/0362235101060-640064545 (7668)
2009: 7⁶SD, 7⁴SD, 7⁰SD, 8⁰SD, 9⁶GF, 8⁴GF, 8⁵GF, 8⁴G, 9⁵SD,

	Starts	1st	2nd	3rd	Win & Pl
Career Total (Turf)	25	4	1	1	15911
Career Total (AW)	41	4	10	2	26027

75 4/08 Sthl 7f (0-80)H G-F £4209
84 3/08 Ling 1m (0-85)H STD £6232
70 8/07 Hayd 1m30y (0-70)H G-F £2817
70 4/07 Sthl 7f (0-70)H GD £3071
69 2/07 Wolv 1m141y STD £2388
78 1/07 Sthl 1m (0-70)H STD £3071
69 11/06 Wolv 7f32y (0-58)H SF £2730
69 6/05 NmkJ 1m (0-70)H G-F £3573
Total win prize-money £28093

Going (Turf): Sf: 0-1 GS: 0-1 Gd: 1-7 GF: 3-15 Fm: 0-1
Distance: 5f/6f: 0-3 7f-8f: 6-50 9f-13f: 2-13 14f+: 0-0
Track : LH: 7-50 RH: 0-10 Tight: 5-29 Gall: 0-1
Aids: Bl: 3-15 Vi: 1-3 Tstrap: 0-2 Ckp: 0-2
Best Rating: 84 3/08 Ling 1m stand

Modest; effective at around 1m; acts on fast ground; also goes on Fibresand and Polytrack; has worn blinkers and cheekpieces.

Duellist

(82) (60)
2-y-o b c Dubawi (IRE)-Satin Flower (USA) (Shadeed (USA))
M Johnston Sheikh Hamdan Bin Mohammed Al Maktoum

Placings:4 (7864)
2009: 6⁴SS,

	Starts	1st	2nd	3rd	Win & Pl
Career Total (Turf)	0	0	0	0	
Career Total (AW)	1	0	0	0	192

Going (Turf): Sf: 0-0 GS: 0-0 Gd: 0-0 GF: 0-0 Fm: 0-0
Distance: 5f/6f: 0-1 7f-8f: 0-0 9f-13f: 0-0 14f+: 0-0
Track : LH: 0-1 RH: 0-0 Tight: 0-0 Gall: 0-0
Aids: Bl: 0-0 Vi: 0-0 Tstrap: 0-0 Ckp: 0-0
Best Rating: 60 12/09 Sthl 6f std-slw

Duff (IRE)

108(115) (116)117
6-y-o b g Spinning World (USA)-Shining Prospect (Lycius (USA))
Edward Lynam Kilboy Estate

Placings:61244/303/243120/10611-20100110 (7746a)
2009: 6²SD, 6⁰GF, 7¹G, 6⁰GF, 5⁰G, 7¹GF, 7¹GF, 8⁰G,

	Starts	1st	2nd	3rd	Win & Pl
Career Total (Turf)	24	6	3	3	283172
Career Total (AW)	3	2	1	0	54024

117 10/09 Tipp 7f100y G-F £45436
117 9/09 Donc 7f G-F £90832
110 6/09 Leop 7f GD £41019
116 12/08 Kemp 7f STD £22708
116 11/08 Ling 6f STD £22708
109 8/08 Cork 1m G-Y £23933
110 8/07 York 7f GD £20744
81 5/05 Gowr 7f G-F £8331
Total win prize-money £275714

Going (Turf): Sf: 0-2 GS: 0-1 Gd: 2-12 **GF: 3-8** Fm: 0-0
Distance: 5f/6f: 1-7 **7f-8f: 7-20** 9f-13f: 0-0 14f+: 0-0
Track : **LH: 4-7** RH: 3-10 Tight: 1-2 Gall: 1-3
Aids: Bl: 0-0 Vi: 0-0 Tstrap: 0-0 Ckp: 0-0
Best Rating: **117** 10/09 Tipp 7f100y gd-fm

Smart; Irish-trained; winner in Group 2 and 3 company and multiple Listed winner; effective at 6f-1m; acts on most ground and on Polytrack; likes to race prominently.

Dugatti

66
3-y-o b c Bertolini (USA)-Go Polar (Polar Falcon (USA))
Mike Murphy The Chalfont Partnership

Placings:00 **(1592)**
2009: 7^{0}GF, 5^{0}GS,

	Starts	1st	2nd	3rd	Win & Pl
Career Total (Turf)	2	0	0	0	

Going (Turf): **Sf: 0-0 GS: 0-1 Gd: 0-0 GF: 0-1 Fm: 0-0**
Distance: 5f/6f: 0-1 7f-8f: 0-1 9f-13f: 0-0 14f+: 0-0
Track : LH: 0-1 RH: 0-0 Tight: 0-0 Gall: 0-0
Aids: Bl: 0-0 Vi: 0-0 Tstrap: 0-0 Ckp: 0-0

Duke Of Bothwell (USA)

83(69) (1)**44**
3-y-o ch g Hennessy (USA)-Crooked Wood (USA) (Woodman (USA))
R A Fahey James Gaffney

Placings:0500 **(6414)**
2009: 5^{0}SD, 6^{5}S, 7^{0}GF, 7^{0}GF,

	Starts	1st	2nd	3rd	Win & Pl
Career Total (Turf)	3	0	0	0	0
Career Total (AW)	1	0	0	0	

Going (Turf): **Sf: 0-1 GS: 0-0 Gd: 0-0 GF: 0-2 Fm: 0-0**
Distance: 5f/6f: 0-1 7f-8f: 0-3 9f-13f: 0-0 14f+: 0-0
Track : LH: 0-2 RH: 0-0 Tight: 0-1 Gall: 0-0
Aids: Bl: 0-0 Vi: 0-0 Tstrap: 0-0 Ckp: 0-0
Best Rating: **44** 8/09 Haml 6f5y soft

Duke Of Burgundy (FR)

103 **74**
6-y-o b g Danehill (USA)-Valley Of Gold (FR) (Shirley Heights)
Jennie Candlish Alan Baxter

Placings:6226 **(6595)**
2009: 12^{6}G, 10^{2}G, 8^{2}GS, 10^{6}GS,

	Starts	1st	2nd	3rd	Win & Pl
Career Total (Turf)	4	0	2	0	2000

Going (Turf): **Sf: 0-0 GS: 0-2 Gd: 0-2 GF: 0-0 Fm: 0-0**
Distance: 5f/6f: 0-0 7f-8f: 0-1 9f-13f: 0-3 14f+: 0-0
Track : LH: 0-3 RH: 0-1 Tight: 0-1 Gall: 0-1
Aids: Bl: 0-0 Vi: 0-0 Tstrap: 0-0 Ckp: 0-0
Best Rating: **74** 8/09 Wwck 1m2f188y good

Fair; dual bumper winner; stays 1m2f plus; acts on a sound surface.

Duke Of Milan (IRE)

99(103) (71)**61**
6-y-o ch g Desert Prince (IRE)-Abyat (USA) (Shadeed (USA))
Tom Dascombe (G C Bravery 4/2) G D Newton

Placings:45/36360**1003060/5**0**5**0466**50035/041**33055**420-2220634225** **(4479)**
2009: 6^{2}SD, 7^{2}SD, 7^{2}SD, 7^{0}SD, 8^{6}GF, 6^{3}G, 6^{4}GF, 7^{2}SD, 6^{2}GF, 5^{5}G,

	Starts	1st	2nd	3rd	Win & Pl
Career Total (Turf)	20	0	1	4	3222
Career Total (AW)	27	2	5	3	9456

60 4/08 Kemp 6f (0-58)H STD £2047
74 9/06 Ling 6f (0-70)H STD £3238
Total win prize-money £5286

Going (Turf): **Sf: 0-1 GS: 0-0 Gd: 0-6 GF: 0-12 Fm: 0-0**
Distance: **5f/6f: 2-30** 7f-8f: 0-13 9f-13f: 0-4 14f+: 0-0
Track : LH: 1-17 RH: 1-20 **Tight: 1-13** Gall: 0-4
Aids: Bl: 0-1 Vi: 0-4 Tstrap: 0-1 Ckp: 0-1
Best Rating: **76** 6/05 Curr 7f gd-fm

Modest; effective at 6f-7f; acts on good ground; also goes on Polytrack; has worn a visor.

Duke Of Normandy (IRE)

93(99) (68)**52**
3-y-o gr g Refuse To Bend (IRE)-Marie De Bayeux (FR) (Turgeon (USA))
B P J Baugh (M Johnston 23/3) Stuart M Mercer

Placings:00-**464232**004000**060** **(7369)**
2009: 7^{4}SD, 7^{6}SD, 9^{4}SD, 9^{2}SF, 8^{3}SD, 9^{2}SD, 9^{0}GF, 8^{0}G, 10^{4}GF, 10^{0}S, 10^{0}G, 10^{0}G, 8^{0}SD, 9^{6}SD, 9^{0}SD,

	Starts	1st	2nd	3rd	Win & Pl
Career Total (Turf)	7	0	0	0	301
Career Total (AW)	10	0	2	1	1911

Going (Turf): **Sf: 0-1 GS: 0-0 Gd: 0-4 GF: 0-2 Fm: 0-0**
Distance: 5f/6f: 0-0 7f-8f: 0-5 9f-13f: 0-12 14f+: 0-0
Track : LH: 0-13 RH: 0-2 Tight: 0-12 Gall: 0-0
Aids: Bl: 0-0 Vi: 0-0 Tstrap: 0-1 Ckp: 0-1
Best Rating: **68** 3/09 Wolv 1m1f103y stand

Modest; stays 1m1f; handles Polytack and fast turf.

Duke Of Rainford

89(95) (53)**51**
2-y-o gr g Bahamian Bounty-Night Haven (Night Shift (USA))
M Herrington (D Nicholls 14/9) P Ringer

Placings:0031063000 **(7778)**
2009: 5^{0}GF, 5^{0}GF, 5^{3}SD, 5^{1}S, 5^{0}GS, 5^{6}GF, 5^{3}SD, 5^{0}GF, 5^{0}SD, 5^{0}SD,

	Starts	1st	2nd	3rd	Win & Pl
Career Total (Turf)	6	1	0	0	0
Career Total (AW)	4	0	0	2	688

Going (Turf): **Sf: 1-1** GS: 0-1 Gd: 0-0 GF: 0-4 Fm: 0-0
Distance: **5f/6f: 1-10** 7f-8f: 0-0 9f-13f: 0-0 14f+: 0-0
Track : LH: 0-1 RH: 0-2 Tight: 0-1 Gall: 0-0
Aids: **Bl: 1-2** Vi: 0-0 Tstrap: 0-0 Ckp: 0-0
Best Rating: **53** 9/09 Kemp 5f stand

Moderate; effective over 5f; acts on soft ground.

Duke Of Urbino

71(92) (50)**20**
3-y-o ch g Medicean-Nefeli (First Trump)
K A Ryan Mr & Mrs Duncan Davidson

Placings:4500 **(5362)**
2009: 7^{4}SD, 6^{5}SD, 8^{0}G, 6^{0}S,

	Starts	1st	2nd	3rd	Win & Pl
Career Total (Turf)	2	0	0	0	
Career Total (AW)	2	0	0	0	0

Going (Turf): **Sf: 0-1 GS: 0-0 Gd: 0-1 GF: 0-0 Fm: 0-0**
Distance: 5f/6f: 0-2 7f-8f: 0-1 9f-13f: 0-1 14f+: 0-0
Track : LH: 0-3 RH: 0-0 Tight: 0-0 Gall: 0-0
Aids: Bl: 0-0 Vi: 0-0 Tstrap: 0-1 Ckp: 0-1
Best Rating: **50** 2/09 Sthl 7f stand

Dukes Art

98(104) (85)**83**
3-y-o b c Bachelor Duke (USA)-Creme Caramel (USA) (Septieme Ciel (USA))
J A R Toller Matthew Green

Placings:3-44**01120** **(7027)**
2009: 8^{4}G, 8^{4}GF, 8^{0}SD, 7^{1}G, 7^{1}G, 7^{2}SD, 7^{0}SD,

	Starts	1st	2nd	3rd	Win & Pl
Career Total (Turf)	4	2	0	0	9929
Career Total (AW)	4	0	1	1	1760

80 7/09 Yarm 7f3y (0-80)H GD £4667
83 7/09 Donc 7f GD £4857
Total win prize-money £9525

Going (Turf): Sf: 0-0 GS: 0-0 **Gd: 2-3** GF: 0-1 Fm: 0-0
Distance: 5f/6f: 0-0 **7f-8f: 2-6** 9f-13f: 0-2 14f+: 0-0
Track : LH: 0-2 RH: 0-2 Tight: 0-2 Gall: 0-0
Aids: Bl: 0-0 Vi: 0-0 Tstrap: 0-0 Ckp: 0-0
Best Rating: **85** 8/09 Kemp 7f stand

Useful; stays 1m, but suited by 7f; acts on fast ground; goes on Polytrack.

Dulce Domum

94(85) (46)**44**
3-y-o b f Dansili-Enclave (USA) (Woodman (USA))
A B Haynes The Villains

Placings:00-53005**6**56 **(4142)**
2009: 8^{5}SD, 9^{3}SD, 10^{0}GF, 12^{0}SD, 12^{5}F, 12^{6}SD, 9^{5}F, 16^{6}G,

	Starts	1st	2nd	3rd	Win & Pl
Career Total (Turf)	4	0	0	0	0
Career Total (AW)	6	0	0	1	353

Going (Turf): **Sf: 0-0 GS: 0-0 Gd: 0-1 GF: 0-1 Fm: 0-2**
Distance: 5f/6f: 0-0 7f-8f: 0-3 9f-13f: 0-6 14f+: 0-1
Track : LH: 0-7 RH: 0-3 Tight: 0-7 Gall: 0-0
Aids: Bl: 0-0 Vi: 0-1 Tstrap: 0-0 Ckp: 0-0
Best Rating: **46** 11/08 Ling 1m stand

Modest; stays 1m1f; acts on Polytrack.

Dulcie

102(106) (78)**83**
3-y-o b f Hernando (FR)-Dulcinea (Selkirk (USA))
M H Tompkins Trevor Benton

Placings:01-033210 **(7151)**
2009: 9^{0}GF, 14^{3}S, 16^{3}G, 16^{2}SD, 16^{1}GS, 16^{0}G,

	Starts	1st	2nd	3rd	Win & Pl
Career Total (Turf)	7	2	0	2	13176

Career Total (AW)	1	0	1	0	1927

83 9/09 York 2m88y (0-80)H G-S £5828
75 10/08 Gdwd 1m1f G-S £5180
Total win prize-money £11009

Going (Turf): Sf: 0-1 **GS: 2-2** Gd: 0-2 GF: 0-2 Fm: 0-0
Distance: 5f/6f: 0-0 7f-8f: 0-1 9f-13f: 1-2 14f+: 1-5
Track : LH: 1-3 RH: 1-4 Tight: 1-2 Gall: 1-3
Aids: Bl: 0-0 Vi: 0-0 Tstrap: 0-0 Ckp: 0-0
Best Rating: 83 9/09 York 2m88y gd-sft

Fair; stays 2m; acts on easy ground; goes on Fibresand.

Dunaskin (IRE)

103(106) (98)**101**
9-y-o b g Bahhare (USA)-Mirwara (IRE) (Darshaan)
B Ellison Koo's Racing Club

Placings:56602236/61210105053/005631110/3006/**2030** 0200/**6061302200**/20205**624-40560**66226 **(7867)**
2009: 14^{4}GF, 18^{0}GF, 12^{5}G, 12^{6}GF, 12^{0}G, 12^{6}SD, 13^{6}SD, 14^{2}SD, 11^{2}SD, 14^{6}SS,

	Starts	1st	2nd	3rd	Win & Pl
Career Total (Turf)	58	7	8	6	152288
Career Total (AW)	11	0	4	0	10234

100 6/07 Pont 1m2f6y (0-90)H G-S £9348
104 8/04 York 1m2f88yB(0-105)H SFT £13305
93 8/04 Hayd 1m2f120yB(0-105)H GD £43500
86 7/04 Newc 1m2f32y D(0-80) GD £5746
92 5/03 Ripn 1m C(0-90)H G-S £9251
83 4/03 Bevl 1m1f207yD(0-80)H G-F £5525
77 4/03 Ripn 1m2f E(0-70)H G-F £4182
Total win prize-money £90858

Going (Turf): Sf: 1-10 **GS: 2-9 Gd: 2-16 GF: 2-20** Fm: 0-3
Distance: 5f/6f: 0-5 7f-8f: 1-6 **9f-13f: 6-52** 14f+: 0-6
Track : **LH: 4-44** RH: 3-17 Tight: 2-14 Gall: 2-26
Aids: Bl: 0-0 Vi: 0-1 Tstrap: 1-1 Ckp: 1-1
Best Rating: 110 9/07 Ayr 1m2f gd-sft

Fair; Listed placed; stays 1m6f; acts on most ground; has worn headgear; very effective under forcing tactics.

Duncan

111 **120**
4-y-o b c Dalakhani (IRE)-Dolores (Danehill (USA))
J H M Gosden Normandie Stud Ltd

Placings:22160-11403 **(4780)**
2009: 10^{1}G, 12^{1}GF, 12^{4}G, 12^{0}G, 10^{3}G,

	Starts	1st	2nd	3rd	Win & Pl
Career Total (Turf)	10	3	2	1	80726

116 5/09 Asct 1m4f G-F £22708
113 4/09 Epsm 1m2f18y (0-105)H GD £31155
97 9/08 Pont 1m2f6y G-S £3885
Total win prize-money £57749

Going (Turf): Sf: 0-0 **GS: 1-3 Gd: 1-4 GF: 1-3** Fm: 0-0
Distance: 5f/6f: 0-0 7f-8f: 0-1 **9f-13f: 3-9** 14f+: 0-0
Track : **LH: 2-4** RH: 1-4 Tight: 1-3 Gall: 1-3
Aids: Bl: 0-0 Vi: 0-0 Tstrap: 0-0 Ckp: 0-0
Best Rating: 120 6/09 Epsm 1m4f10y good

Group class; effective over 1m2f-1m4f; acts on fast and easy ground.

Dundry

(100) (81)**86**
8-y-o b g Bin Ajwaad (IRE)-China's Pearl (Shirley Heights)
G L Moore Ms J Lambert

Placings:0/332210/502100206/3006/1133405/**00-24** **(0485)**
2009: 12^{2}SD, 13^{4}SD,

	Starts	1st	2nd	3rd	Win & Pl
Career Total (Turf)	24	1	4	5	24874
Career Total (AW)	7	3	1	0	13367

86 2/07 Ling 1m4f (0-85)H STD £4857
80 1/07 Sthl 1m4f (0-85)H STD £4857
85 5/05 York 1m5f197y (0-85)H SFT £11202
82 9/04 Ling 1m4f STD £2891
Total win prize-money £23809

Going (Turf): **Sf: 1-4** GS: 0-9 Gd: 0-4 GF: 0-7 Fm: 0-0
Distance: 5f/6f: 0-0 7f-8f: 0-1 **9f-13f: 3-15** 14f+: 1-15
Track : **LH: 4-22** RH: 0-7 **Tight: 2-13** Gall: 1-6
Aids: Bl: 0-0 Vi: 0-0 Tstrap: 4-25 Ckp: 4-25
Best Rating: 88 4/07 Newb 2m gd-fm

Fair; effective from 1m4f-2m; acts on most ground, including Fibresand and Polytrack; usually wears cheekpieces.

Duneen Dream (USA)

(101) (52)**54**
4-y-o ch g Hennessy (USA)-T N T Red (USA) (Explosive Red (CAN))
Mrs N S Evans John Berry (Gwent)

Placings:00401/3600036-**00054** **(7751)**
2009: 9^{0}SD, 9^{0}SD, 12^{0}SF, 12^{5}SD, 13^{4}SD,

	Starts	1st	2nd	3rd	Win & Pl
Career Total (Turf)	5	0	0	1	302
Career Total (AW)	12	1	0	1	2502

57 1/08 Wolv 1m1f103y (0-65)H STD £2047
Total win prize-money £2048

Going (Turf): **Sf: 0-2 GS: 0-1 Gd: 0-0 GF: 0-1 Fm: 0-1**
Distance: 5f/6f: 0-1 7f-8f: 0-4 **9f-13f: 1-11** 14f+: 0-1
Track : **LH: 1-13** RH: 0-2 **Tight: 1-9** Gall: 0-2
Aids: Bl: 0-0 Vi: 0-0 Tstrap: 0-0 Ckp: 0-0
Best Rating: 60 1/08 Wolv 1m1f103y stand

Modest gelding; won extended 9f Class 6 handicap at Wolverhampton January 2008; stays 9f; acts on firm ground and Polytrack.

Dunelight (IRE)

(108) (108)**113**
6-y-o ch h Desert Sun-Badee'A (IRE) (Marju (IRE))
C G Cox Mr And Mrs P Hargreaves

Placings:231/31021230/03153420/2013-**62** **(7768)**
2009: 8^{6}SD, 7^{2}SD,

	Starts	1st	2nd	3rd	Win & Pl
Career Total (Turf)	23	5	5	6	194584
Career Total (AW)	2	0	1	0	9148

109 6/08 Wind 1m67y G-F £14760
113 6/07 Gdwd 1m G-F £17034
111 7/06 Asct 1m H GD £46740
98 5/06 NmkR 1m (0-100)H G-F £16192
83 9/05 NmkR 1m GD £4192
Total win prize-money £98920

Going (Turf): Sf: 0-0 GS: 0-1 Gd: 2-9 **GF: 3-13** Fm: 0-0
Distance: 5f/6f: 0-0 **7f-8f: 4-19** 9f-13f: 1-6 14f+: 0-0
Track : LH: 0-1 **RH: 2-13 Tight: 1-3** Gall: 0-2
Aids: Bl: 0-2 **Vi: 3-17** Tstrap: 0-0 Ckp: 0-0
Best Rating: 113 5/08 Wind 1m67y gd-fm

Smart; winner in Listed company; effective at around 7f-1m; acts on good and faster ground; wears blinkers or a visor; suited by forcing tactics.

Dunes Queen (USA)

94(99) (81)**82**
3-y-o b f Elusive Quality (USA)-Queen's Logic (IRE) (Grand Lodge (USA))
M R Channon Jaber Abdullah

Placings:3-1554 **(2373)**
2009: 6^{1}SD, 7^{5}GF, 6^{5}GS, 5^{4}GF,

	Starts	1st	2nd	3rd	Win & Pl
Career Total (Turf)	4	0	0	1	3444
Career Total (AW)	1	1	0	0	4727

81 3/09 Kemp 6f STD £4727
Total win prize-money £4727

Going (Turf): **Sf: 0-0 GS: 0-2 Gd: 0-0 GF: 0-2 Fm: 0-0**
Distance: **5f/6f: 1-2** 7f-8f: 0-3 9f-13f: 0-0 14f+: 0-0
Track : LH: 0-0 **RH: 1-1** Tight: 0-0 Gall: 0-0
Aids: Bl: 0-0 Vi: 0-0 Tstrap: 0-0 Ckp: 0-0
Best Rating: 82 4/09 NmkR 7f gd-fm

Useful; effective over 6f; acts on Polytrack.

Dunfishin (IRE)

(53)
2-y-o ch c Chineur (FR)-Sisal (IRE) (Danehill (USA))
M S Tuck M Bell

Placings:0 **(7859)**
2009: 7^{0}SD,

	Starts	1st	2nd	3rd	Win & Pl
Career Total (Turf)	0	0	0	0	
Career Total (AW)	1	0	0	0	

Going (Turf): **Sf: 0-0 GS: 0-0 Gd: 0-0 GF: 0-0 Fm: 0-0**
Distance: 5f/6f: 0-0 7f-8f: 0-1 9f-13f: 0-0 14f+: 0-0
Track : LH: 0-1 RH: 0-0 Tight: 0-1 Gall: 0-0
Aids: Bl: 0-0 Vi: 0-0 Tstrap: 0-0 Ckp: 0-0

Dungannon

86 **60**
2-y-o b g Monsieur Bond (IRE)-May Light (Midyan (USA))
A M Balding I G Burbidge

Placings:5 **(3218)**
2009: 6^{5}GF,

	Starts	1st	2nd	3rd	Win & Pl
Career Total (Turf)	1	0	0	0	0

Going (Turf): **Sf: 0-0 GS: 0-0 Gd: 0-0 GF: 0-1 Fm: 0-0**
Distance: 5f/6f: 0-1 7f-8f: 0-0 9f-13f: 0-0 14f+: 0-0
Track : LH: 0-0 RH: 0-0 Tight: 0-0 Gall: 0-1
Aids: Bl: 0-0 Vi: 0-0 Tstrap: 0-0 Ckp: 0-0
Best Rating: 60 6/09 Wind 6f gd-fm

Dunn'o (IRE)

108 **102**
4-y-o b g Cape Cross (IRE)-Indian Express (Indian Ridge)
C G Cox Dennis Shaw

Placings:342/102251462-016106030 **(6249)**
2009: 8^{0}GF, 8^{1}G, 7^{6}GF, 8^{1}G, 8^{0}GF, 8^{6}GS, 7^{0}GF, 7^{3}GF, 8^{0}GF,

	Starts	1st	2nd	3rd	Win & Pl
Career Total (Turf)	21	4	4	2	43534

102 5/09 Sand 1m14y (0-95)H GD £9346
96 4/09 Sand 1m14y (0-100)H GD £11215
88 8/08 Sand 7f16y (0-90)H G-S £7771

83 4/08 Bath 5f11y GD £3238
Total win prize-money £31572

Going (Turf): Sf: 0-2 GS: 1-2 **Gd: 3-6** GF: 0-11 Fm: 0-0
Distance: 5f/6f: 1-7 7f-8f: 1-10 **9f-13f: 2-4** 14f+: 0-0
Track : LH: 1-6 **RH: 3-5** Tight: 0-2 **Gall: 1-5**
Aids: Bl: 0-0 Vi: 0-0 Tstrap: 0-0 Ckp: 0-0
Best Rating: **102** 5/09 Sand 1m14y good

Very useful; stays 1m; acts on most ground.

Dunwhinny

(80) (44)
2-y-o b g Tobougg (IRE)-Possibility (Robellino (USA))
P W D'Arcy Gongolphin & Racing

Placings:000 (3957)
2009: 6^{0}SD, 7^{0}SD, 7^{0}S,

	Starts	1st	2nd	3rd	Win & Pl
Career Total (Turf)	1	0	0	0	
Career Total (AW)	2	0	0	0	

Going (Turf): **Sf: 0-1 GS: 0-0 Gd: 0-0 GF: 0-0 Fm: 0-0**
Distance: 5f/6f: 0-1 7f-8f: 0-2 9f-13f: 0-0 14f+: 0-0
Track : LH: 0-1 RH: 0-1 Tight: 0-1 Gall: 0-0
Aids: Bl: 0-0 Vi: 0-0 Tstrap: 0-0 Ckp: 0-0
Best Rating: **44** 7/09 Wolv 7f32y stand

Duplicity

95(89) (68)95
2-y-o b c Cadeaux Genereux-Artful (IRE) (Green Desert (USA))
R Hannon The Early Bath P'ship & Bloomsbury Stud

Placings:4215 (6752a)
2009: 7^{4}SD, 7^{2}GF, 6^{1}S, 6^{5}VS,

	Starts	1st	2nd	3rd	Win & Pl
Career Total (Turf)	3	1	1	0	21926
Career Total (AW)	1	0	0	0	289

95 7/09 Newb 6f8y SFT £17031
Total win prize-money £17031

Going (Turf): **Sf: 1-1** GS: 0-0 Gd: 0-0 GF: 0-1 Fm: 0-0
Distance: 5f/6f: 0-1 **7f-8f: 1-3** 9f-13f: 0-0 14f+: 0-0
Track : LH: 0-1 RH: 0-1 Tight: 0-0 Gall: 0-0
Aids: Bl: 0-0 Vi: 0-0 Tstrap: 0-0 Ckp: 0-0
Best Rating: **95** 7/09 Newb 6f8y soft

Very useful; Listed winner; effective over 6f-7f; acts on most ground.

Durgan

91(92) (64)69
3-y-o b c Dansili-Peryllys (Warning)
Mrs L C Jewell E A Condon

Placings:06-406 (7833)
2009: 7^{4}GS, 7^{0}GF, 7^{6}SD,

	Starts	1st	2nd	3rd	Win & Pl
Career Total (Turf)	4	0	0	0	457
Career Total (AW)	1	0	0	0	0

Going (Turf): **Sf: 0-0 GS: 0-1 Gd: 0-2 GF: 0-1 Fm: 0-0**
Distance: 5f/6f: 0-0 7f-8f: 0-5 9f-13f: 0-0 14f+: 0-0
Track : LH: 0-0 RH: 0-3 Tight: 0-0 Gall: 0-0
Aids: Bl: 0-0 Vi: 0-0 Tstrap: 0-0 Ckp: 0-0
Best Rating: **69** 9/08 Newb 7f good

Fair; effective over 7f; acts on easy ground.

Durham Express (IRE)

99 72
2-y-o b g Acclamation-Edwina (IRE) (Caerleon (USA))
M Dods M J Sedgewick

Placings:314 (6841)
2009: 5^{3}G, 5^{1}GF, 5^{4}G,

	Starts	1st	2nd	3rd	Win & Pl
Career Total (Turf)	3	1	0	1	2995

72 9/09 Rdcr 5f G-F £2047
Total win prize-money £2047

Going (Turf): Sf: 0-0 GS: 0-0 Gd: 0-2 **GF: 1-1** Fm: 0-0
Distance: **5f/6f: 1-3** 7f-8f: 0-0 9f-13f: 0-0 14f+: 0-0
Track : LH: 0-0 RH: 0-0 Tight: 0-0 Gall: 0-0
Aids: Bl: 0-0 Vi: 0-0 Tstrap: 0-0 Ckp: 0-0
Best Rating: **72** 9/09 Rdcr 5f gd-fm

Fair; effective over 5f; acts on fast ground.

Durham Reflection (IRE)

102 75
2-y-o b g Pastoral Pursuits-Opari (IRE) (Night Shift (USA))
J Howard Johnson Transcend Bloodstock LLP

Placings:5652351 (5942)
2009: 6^{5}GS, 6^{6}GF, 7^{5}GS, 6^{2}GF, 6^{3}S, 7^{5}GF, 7^{1}G,

	Starts	1st	2nd	3rd	Win & Pl
Career Total (Turf)	7	1	1	1	3677

75 9/09 Muss 7f30y GD £1942
Total win prize-money £1943

Going (Turf): Sf: 0-1 GS: 0-2 **Gd: 1-1** GF: 0-3 Fm: 0-0
Distance: 5f/6f: 0-2 **7f-8f: 1-5** 9f-13f: 0-0 14f+: 0-0
Track : LH: 0-1 **RH: 1-1 Tight: 1-2** Gall: 0-0
Aids: Bl: 0-0 Vi: 0-0 Tstrap: 0-1 Ckp: 0-1
Best Rating: **75** 9/09 Muss 7f30y good

Fair; stays 7f and acts on good ground.

Durham Town (IRE)

89(73) (34)62
2-y-o b g Arakan (USA)-Southern Spectrum (IRE) (Spectrum (IRE))
D K Ivory K T Ivory

Placings:04066 (4915)
2009: 5^{0}G, 5^{4}GF, 7^{0}SD, 6^{6}G, 7^{6}G,

	Starts	1st	2nd	3rd	Win & Pl
Career Total (Turf)	4	0	0	0	0
Career Total (AW)	1	0	0	0	

Going (Turf): **Sf: 0-0 GS: 0-0 Gd: 0-3 GF: 0-1 Fm: 0-0**
Distance: 5f/6f: 0-3 7f-8f: 0-2 9f-13f: 0-0 14f+: 0-0
Track : LH: 0-0 RH: 0-1 Tight: 0-0 Gall: 0-3
Aids: Bl: 0-0 Vi: 0-0 Tstrap: 0-0 Ckp: 0-0
Best Rating: **62** 4/09 Wind 5f10y gd-fm

During The War (USA)

78(78) (39)65
2-y-o b g Lion Heart (USA)-Carson's Star (USA) (Carson City (USA))
C A Dwyer (L M Cumani 5/10) Mrs Shelley Dwyer

Placings:005 (7552)
2009: 7^{0}SD, 7^{0}GF, 7^{5}SD,

	Starts	1st	2nd	3rd	Win & Pl
Career Total (Turf)	1	0	0	0	
Career Total (AW)	2	0	0	0	0

Going (Turf): **Sf: 0-0 GS: 0-0 Gd: 0-0 GF: 0-1 Fm: 0-0**
Distance: 5f/6f: 0-0 7f-8f: 0-3 9f-13f: 0-0 14f+: 0-0
Track : LH: 0-2 RH: 0-1 Tight: 0-1 Gall: 0-0
Aids: Bl: 0-0 Vi: 0-0 Tstrap: 0-0 Ckp: 0-0
Best Rating: **65** 10/09 Wwck 7f26y gd-fm

Dushstorm (IRE)

(107) (75)52
8-y-o b g Dushyantor (USA)-Between The Winds (USA) (Diesis)
R J Price R J Price

Placings:61/4664165000/**403**4510610/1200421/61105**100**/ 1613112000006000**5200-0** (0078)
2009: 8^{0}SD,

	Starts	1st	2nd	3rd	Win & Pl
Career Total (Turf)	36	9	2	0	42194
Career Total (AW)	22	4	2	2	10465

71	4/08	Kemp	1m2f		STD	£2266
75	4/08	Kemp	1m		STD	£2266
72	2/08	Ling	1m		STD	£1774
62	1/08	Ling	1m		STD	£1774
	7/07	Siro	1m1f	H	GD	£3378
	4/07	Pisa	1m2f	H	HVY	£4054
	2/07	Pisa	1m2f	H	HVY	£2703
	12/06	Pisa	7f110y	H	VS	£4138
	3/06	Siro	1m1f	H	GD	£2759
	11/05	Siro	1m	H	VS	£2837
	4/05	Siro	1m1f	H	HVY	£4255
	8/04	Var	1m3f165y	H	GD	£7042
	12/03	Pisa	1m2f		GD	£4870

Total win prize-money £44120

Going (Turf): Sf: 3-13 GS: 0-1 **Gd: 4-19** GF: 0-0 Fm: 0-0
Distance: 5f/6f: 0-0 7f-8f: 5-17 **9f-13f: 8-41** 14f+: 0-0
Track : LH: 2-17 **RH: 6-12 Tight: 2-14** Gall: 0-2
Aids: Bl: 0-0 Vi: 0-0 Tstrap: 3-8 Ckp: 3-8
Best Rating: **75** 4/08 Kemp 1m stand

Modest; multiple winner in Italy; effective at around 1m-1m3f; acts on good and softer ground and on Polytrack.

Dusk

90(103) (71)71
4-y-o b g Fantastic Light (USA)-Dark Veil (USA) (Gulch (USA))
Evan Williams (Mrs S J Humphrey 16/8) R E R Williams

Placings:5005/6363**362354-35**00 (4158)
2009: 12^{3}SD, 12^{5}SD, 10^{0}GS, 10^{0}G,

	Starts	1st	2nd	3rd	Win & Pl
Career Total (Turf)	11	0	0	3	1131
Career Total (AW)	7	0	1	2	1945

Going (Turf): **Sf: 0-2 GS: 0-1 Gd: 0-2 GF: 0-6 Fm: 0-0**
Distance: 5f/6f: 0-0 7f-8f: 0-3 9f-13f: 0-14 14f+: 0-1
Track : LH: 0-9 RH: 0-6 Tight: 0-7 Gall: 0-1
Aids: Bl: 0-11 Vi: 0-0 Tstrap: 0-0 Ckp: 0-0
Best Rating: **71** 10/08 Kemp 1m4f stand

Modest; effective at around 1m2f; acts on fast ground and on Polytrack.

Duster

93(89) (73)62

2-y-o b g Pastoral Pursuits-Spring Clean (FR) (Danehill (USA))

H Morrison M T Bevan

Placings:2250 (6905)

2009: 7^{2}SD, 6^{2}SD, 7^{5}SD, 6^{0}G,

	Starts	1st	2nd	3rd	Win & Pl
Career Total (Turf)	1	0	0	0	
Career Total (AW)	3	0	2	0	1861

Going (Turf): Sf: 0-0 GS: 0-0 Gd: 0-1 GF: 0-0 Fm: 0-0
Distance: 5f/6f: 0-2 7f-8f: 0-2 9f-13f: 0-0 14f+: 0-0
Track : LH: 0-3 RH: 0-0 Tight: 0-2 Gall: 0-1
Aids: Bl: 0-0 Vi: 0-0 Tstrap: 0-0 Ckp: 0-0
Best Rating: 73 7/09 Ling 7f stand

Modest; effective over 6f-7f; acts on Fibresand and Polytrack.

Dustry (IRE)

96(98) (69)73

3-y-o b c Chevalier (IRE)-Church Mice (IRE) (Petardia)

R Hannon D J Walker

Placings:010-005000 (5628)

2009: 8^{0}SD, 8^{0}SD, 8^{5}GF, 10^{0}GS, 8^{0}GS, 7^{0}GS,

	Starts	1st	2nd	3rd	Win & Pl
Career Total (Turf)	7	1	0	0	3238
Career Total (AW)	2	0	0	0	
73 9/08 Leic	5f218y		SFT	£3238	

Total win prize-money £3238

Going (Turf): Sf: 1-1 GS: 0-5 Gd: 0-0 GF: 0-1 Fm: 0-0
Distance: 5f/6f: 1-1 7f-8f: 0-5 9f-13f: 0-3 14f+: 0-0
Track : LH: 0-2 RH: 0-3 Tight: 0-2 Gall: 0-0
Aids: Bl: 0-2 Vi: 0-0 Tstrap: 0-0 Ckp: 0-0
Best Rating: 73 9/08 Leic 5f218y soft

Fair; effective over 6f; acts on soft ground.

Dusty Spirit

103(94) (60)76

2-y-o b c Invincible Spirit (IRE)-Dusty Dazzler (IRE) (Titus Livius (FR))

W G M Turner T.O.C.S. Ltd

Placings:604032410 (7290)

2009: 5^{6}SD, 5^{0}G, 5^{4}G, 5^{0}SD, 5^{3}GF, 5^{2}GF, 5^{4}SS, 5^{1}G, 6^{0}S,

	Starts	1st	2nd	3rd	Win & Pl
Career Total (Turf)	6	1	1	1	5294
Career Total (AW)	3	0	0	0	241
76 10/09 Bath	5f11y		GD	£3561	

Total win prize-money £3562

Going (Turf): Sf: 0-1 GS: 0-0 Gd: 1-3 GF: 0-2 Fm: 0-0
Distance: 5f/6f: 1-9 7f-8f: 0-0 9f-13f: 0-0 14f+: 0-0
Track : LH: 1-4 RH: 0-0 Tight: 0-3 Gall: 1-1
Aids: Bl: 0-0 Vi: 0-0 Tstrap: 0-0 Ckp: 0-0
Best Rating: 76 10/09 Bath 5f11y good

Fair; effective over 5f; acts on good ground.

Dutiful

86(95) (61)59

2-y-o ch c Dubawi (IRE)-Pelagia (IRE) (Lycius (USA))

M R Channon Wood Street Syndicate II

Placings:0600310 (7654)

2009: 7^{0}GF, 8^{6}GS, 6^{0}GF, 7^{0}SD, 7^{3}SD, 7^{1}SF, 7^{0}SD,

	Starts	1st	2nd	3rd	Win & Pl
Career Total (Turf)	3	0	0	0	0
Career Total (AW)	4	1	0	1	2668
61 11/09 Wolv	7f32y	(0-60)	SF	£2388	

Total win prize-money £2388

Going (Turf): Sf: 0-0 GS: 0-1 Gd: 0-0 GF: 0-2 Fm: 0-0
Distance: 5f/6f: 0-0 7f-8f: 1-7 9f-13f: 0-0 14f+: 0-0
Track : LH: 1-3 RH: 0-1 Tight: 1-3 Gall: 0-0
Aids: Bl: 0-0 Vi: 0-0 Tstrap: 0-0 Ckp: 0-0
Best Rating: 61 11/09 Wolv 7f32y std-fst

Moderate; effective over 7f; acts on Polytrack.

Duty And Destiny (IRE)

92(104) (77)73

2-y-o b f Montjeu (IRE)-Swilly (USA) (Irish River (FR))

B J Meehan Sangster Family & M Green

Placings:4422 (7359)

2009: 7^{4}S, 7^{4}G, 10^{2}F, 8^{2}SD,

	Starts	1st	2nd	3rd	Win & Pl
Career Total (Turf)	3	0	1	0	1516
Career Total (AW)	1	0	1	0	964

Going (Turf): Sf: 0-1 GS: 0-0 Gd: 0-1 GF: 0-0 Fm: 0-1
Distance: 5f/6f: 0-0 7f-8f: 0-2 9f-13f: 0-2 14f+: 0-0
Track : LH: 0-2 RH: 0-0 Tight: 0-2 Gall: 0-0
Aids: Bl: 0-0 Vi: 0-0 Tstrap: 0-0 Ckp: 0-0
Best Rating: 77 11/09 Wolv 1m141y stand

Fair; effective over 1m2f; acts on fast ground.

Duty Free (IRE)

96(99) (71)87

5-y-o b g Rock Of Gibraltar (IRE)-Photographie (USA) (Trempolino (USA))

C R Egerton Lady Laidlaw Of Rothiemay

Placings:54/54211252/0000-00 (1581)

2009: 12^{0}SD, 11^{0}G,

	Starts	1st	2nd	3rd	Win & Pl
Career Total (Turf)	11	1	3	0	11265
Career Total (AW)	5	1	0	0	2048
80 8/07 Sand	1m6f	(0-80)H	GD	£6477	
78 7/07 Kemp	1m4f	(0-65)H	STD	£2047	

Total win prize-money £8525

Going (Turf): Sf: 0-0 GS: 0-2 Gd: 1-7 GF: 0-2 Fm: 0-0
Distance: 5f/6f: 0-0 7f-8f: 0-1 9f-13f: 1-9 14f+: 1-6
Track : LH: 0-8 RH: 2-8 Tight: 0-8 Gall: 0-4
Aids: Bl: 0-0 Vi: 0-0 Tstrap: 0-1 Ckp: 0-1
Best Rating: 91 10/07 NmkR 1m6f good

Useful; stays 1m6f; acts on good and fast ground; also goes on Polytrack.

Dvinsky (USA)

102(110) (92)74

8-y-o b g Stravinsky (USA)-Festive Season (USA) (Lypheor)

P Howling Richard Berenson

Placings:02042523104243000245362006/400421260350 4300340234/10003341200235052345001 6/064314213242 461655031330321- 2154005222565000260420520160 54663 (7875)

2009: 5^{7}SD, 6^{1}SD, 6^{5}SD, 7^{4}SD, 5^{0}SD, 6^{0}SD, 5^{5}SD, 7^{2}SD, 6^{2}SD, 6^{2}GF, 6^{5}SD, 7^{6}SD, 6^{5}GF, 6^{0}SD, 6^{0}GF, 7^{0}SD, 6^{2}GF, 6^{6}SD, 6^{0}GF, 6^{4}SD, 6^{2}GF, 6^{0}SD, 7^{5}SD,

	Starts	1st	2nd	3rd	Win & Pl
Career Total (Turf)	48	3	9	4	26119
Career Total (AW)	93	10	14	15	64576
82 10/09 Kemp	7f	(0-75)H	STD	£2266	
92 1/09 GrLe	6f	(0-85)H	STD	£5051	
85 12/08 Wolv	5f216y	(0-85)H	STD	£5046	
86 10/08 Kemp	6f	(0-85)H	STD	£5180	
88 7/08 Kemp	6f	(0-85)H	STD	£4727	
80 4/08 Ling	7f	(0-70)H	STD	£2331	
78 2/08 Kemp	6f	(0-70)H	STD	£2590	
75 12/07 Kemp	6f	(0-70)H	STD	£2817	
78 4/07 Kemp	6f	(0-75)H	STD	£3886	
77 6/06 Pont	6f	(0-70)H	G-F	£3886	
73 5/05 Chep	7f16y	(0-70)H	G-S	£3746	
88 9/03 Gdwd	6f	D	G-F	£2975	

Total win prize-money £44505

Going (Turf): Sf: 0-3 GS: 1-5 Gd: 0-7 GF: 2-30 Fm: 0-3
Distance: 5f/6f: 10-86 7f-8f: 3-48 9f-13f: 0-7 14f+: 0-0
Track : LH: 5-73 RH: 6-40 Tight: 3-52 Gall: 1-13
Aids: Bl: 7-59 Vi: 1-9 Tstrap: 0-1 Ckp: 0-1
Best Rating: 92 3/09 Kemp 7f stand

Fair; effective over 6f-7f; acts on most ground on turf; also goes on Polytrack; has worn blinkers; likes to race prominently; goes well at Kempton.

Dylanesque

102 79

2-y-o b f Royal Applause-Ventura Highway (Machiavellian (USA))

M A Jarvis Helena Springfield Ltd

Placings:0160 (7013)

2009: 6^{0}GF, 6^{1}GF, 7^{6}GF, 7^{0}GS,

	Starts	1st	2nd	3rd	Win & Pl
Career Total (Turf)	4	1	0	0	5046
77 9/09 Yarm	6f3y		G-F	£5046	

Total win prize-money £5046

Going (Turf): Sf: 0-0 GS: 0-1 Gd: 0-0 GF: 1-3 Fm: 0-0
Distance: 5f/6f: 0-0 7f-8f: 1-4 9f-13f: 0-0 14f+: 0-0
Track : LH: 0-1 RH: 0-0 Tight: 0-1 Gall: 0-0
Aids: Bl: 0-0 Vi: 0-0 Tstrap: 0-0 Ckp: 0-0
Best Rating: 79 10/09 Epsm 7f gd-fm

Fair half-sister to Alessandro Volta; promise on debut over 6f on fast ground.

Dyna Waltz

104(96) (82)103

2-y-o b f Dynaformer (USA)-Valentine Waltz (IRE) (Be My Guest (USA))

J H M Gosden George Strawbridge

Placings:3215 (6269)

2009: 7^{3}S, 7^{2}G, 8^{1}SD, 8^{5}G,

	Starts	1st	2nd	3rd	Win & Pl
Career Total (Turf)	3	0	1	1	8176
Career Total (AW)	1	1	0	0	4533
82 8/09 Kemp	1m		STD	£4533	

Total win prize-money £4533

Going (Turf): Sf: 0-1 GS: 0-0 Gd: 0-2 GF: 0-0 Fm: 0-0
Distance: 5f/6f: 0-0 7f-8f: 1-4 9f-13f: 0-0 14f+: 0-0
Track : LH: 0-0 RH: 1-2 Tight: 0-0 Gall: 0-1
Aids: Bl: 0-0 Vi: 0-0 Tstrap: 0-0 Ckp: 0-0
Best Rating: 103 9/09 Asct 1m good

Smart filly; stays 1m; acts on good ground and Polytrack.

Dynamic Drive (IRE)

(89) (63)
2-y-o b c Motivator-Biriyani (IRE) (Danehill (USA))
W R Swinburn P W Harris

Placings:6 (6772)
2009: 8^{6}SD,

	Starts	1st	2nd	3rd	Win & Pl
Career Total (Turf)	0	0	0	0	
Career Total (AW)	1	0	0	0	0

Going (Turf): Sf: 0-0 GS: 0-0 Gd: 0-0 GF: 0-0 Fm: 0-0
Distance: 5f/6f: 0-0 7f-8f: 0-1 9f-13f: 0-0 14f+: 0-0
Track : LH: 0-0 RH: 0-1 Tight: 0-0 Gall: 0-0
Aids: Bl: 0-0 Vi: 0-0 Tstrap: 0-0 Ckp: 0-0
Best Rating: **63** 10/09 Kemp 1m stand

Dynamic Idol (USA)

(88) (57)
2-y-o b/br c Dynaformer (USA)-El Nafis (USA) (Kingmambo (USA))
M A Magnusson Eastwind Racing Ltd and Martha Trussell

Placings:4 (7638)
2009: 8^{4}SD,

	Starts	1st	2nd	3rd	Win & Pl
Career Total (Turf)	0	0	0	0	
Career Total (AW)	1	0	0	0	0

Going (Turf): Sf: 0-0 GS: 0-0 Gd: 0-0 GF: 0-0 Fm: 0-0
Distance: 5f/6f: 0-0 7f-8f: 0-1 9f-13f: 0-0 14f+: 0-0
Track : LH: 0-1 RH: 0-0 Tight: 0-0 Gall: 0-0
Aids: Bl: 0-0 Vi: 0-0 Tstrap: 0-0 Ckp: 0-0
Best Rating: **57** 12/09 Sthl 1m stand

$250,000 half-brother to the high-class Nasheej; well beaten on debut over 1m on Fibresand.

Dynamo Dave (USA)

95(101) (54)**53**
4-y-o b g Distorted Humor (USA)-Nothing Special (CAN) (Tejabo (CAN))
M D I Usher R H Brookes

Placings:60/6U050000-3604000005661040000103 (7877)
2009: 8^{3}SD, 8^{6}SD, 8^{0}SD, 8^{4}SD, 7^{0}SD, 10^{0}SD, 10^{0}G, 9^{F}, 11^{0}G, 10^{0}GF, 9^{5}G, 10^{6}F, 7^{6}F, 6^{1}F, 6^{0}S, 6^{4}SD, 6^{0}GF, 6^{0}GF, 6^{0}GF, 5^{0}GF, 7^{1}SD, 7^{0}SD, 7^{3}SD,

	Starts	1st	2nd	3rd	Win & Pl
Career Total (Turf)	15	1	0	0	2047
Career Total (AW)	18	1	0	2	2252

54	11/09	Ling	7f	(0-58)H	STD	£1637
53	7/09	Folk	6f		FRM	£2047

Total win prize-money £3685

Going (Turf): Sf: 0-1 GS: 0-0 Gd: 0-3 GF: 0-7 **Fm: 1-4**
Distance: 5f/6f: 1-7 7f-8f: 1-16 9f-13f: 0-10 14f+: 0-0
Track : **LH: 1-23** RH: 0-3 **Tight: 1-18** Gall: 0-2
Aids: **Bl: 2-10** Vi: 0-2 Tstrap: 0-1 Ckp: 0-1
Best Rating: **60** 11/07 Ling 1m stand

Moderate; effective over 6f-1m; acts on fast ground; goes on Polytrack; has worn blinkers.

Dynasty

100 (84)**83**
2-y-o b c Danehill Dancer (IRE)-Dash To The Top (Montjeu (IRE))
A P O'Brien Mrs John Magnier

Placings:2301 (7159a)
2009: 6^{2}S, 7^{3}GY, 7^{0}GF, 6^{1}SD,

	Starts	1st	2nd	3rd	Win & Pl
Career Total (Turf)	3	0	1	1	13117
Career Total (AW)	1	1	0	0	9057

84	10/09	Dund	6f	STD	£9056

Total win prize-money £9057

Going (Turf): **Sf: 0-1 GS: 0-0 Gd: 0-0 GF: 0-1 Fm: 0-0**
Distance: **5f/6f: 1-2** 7f-8f: 0-2 9f-13f: 0-0 14f+: 0-0
Track : **LH: 1-2** RH: 0-1 Tight: 0-0 Gall: 0-0
Aids: Bl: 0-0 Vi: 0-0 Tstrap: 0-0 Ckp: 0-0
Best Rating: **84** 10/09 Dund 6f stand

Useful; out of a high-class winner at 1m-1m4f; effective over 6f-7f; acts with give in the ground; has displayed an awkward head carriage.

Dzesmin (POL)

103(95) (64)**89**
7-y-o b g Professional (IRE)-Dzakarta (POL) (Aprizzo (IRE))
R A Fahey JAS Partnership

Placings:12121/121113/43016/004304302510/5005155-5665 (3313)
2009: 11^{5}SD, 12^{6}GF, 14^{6}GF, 16^{5}GF,

	Starts	1st	2nd	3rd	Win & Pl
Career Total (Turf)	35	10	4	4	59138
Career Total (AW)	4	0	0	0	361

89	8/08	Ches	1m4f66y	(0-85)H	SFT	£5504
86	9/07	Catt	1m3f214y	(0-90)H	GD	£7124
83	9/06	Catt	1m3f214y	(0-90)H	G-F	£9715
	9/05	Sluz	1m6f		G-F	£3548
	8/05	Sluz	1m2f		G-F	£2087
	7/05	Sluz	1m4f		G-F	£8348
	5/05	Sluz	1m		G-F	£2435
	10/04	Sluz	1m		SFT	£3507
	9/04	Sluz	6f110y		GD	£1791
	6/04	Sluz	6f		GD	£955

Total win prize-money £45017

Going (Turf): Sf: 2-6 GS: 0-1 Gd: 3-11 **GF: 5-17** Fm: 0-0
Distance: 5f/6f: 1-1 7f-8f: 3-5 **9f-13f: 5-25** 14f+: 1-8
Track : **LH: 3-22** RH: 0-6 **Tight: 3-12** Gall: 0-12
Aids: Bl: 0-0 Vi: 0-0 Tstrap: 2-17 Ckp: 2-17
Best Rating: **89** 8/08 Ches 1m4f66y soft

Fair; ex-Polish; effective at around 1m4f; acts on most ground; sometimes wears cheekpieces; winning hurdler.

Eager To Bow (IRE)

79 **50**
3-y-o b g Acclamation-Tullawadgeen (IRE) (Sinndar (IRE))
P R Chamings Mrs J E L Wright

Placings:600-06 (3672)
2009: 8^{0}GF, 6^{6}F,

	Starts	1st	2nd	3rd	Win & Pl
Career Total (Turf)	5	0	0	0	0

Going (Turf): **Sf: 0-2 GS: 0-0 Gd: 0-0 GF: 0-2 Fm: 0-1**
Distance: 5f/6f: 0-1 7f-8f: 0-3 9f-13f: 0-1 14f+: 0-0
Track : LH: 0-2 RH: 0-0 Tight: 0-0 Gall: 0-0
Aids: Bl: 0-1 Vi: 0-0 Tstrap: 0-0 Ckp: 0-0
Best Rating: **50** 10/08 Folk 7f soft

Eagle Nebula

96(102) (67)**62**
5-y-o ch g Observatory (USA)-Tarocchi (USA) (Affirmed (USA))
B R Johnson Tann Racing

Placings:64025634-000401225 (7695)
2009: 7^{0}SD, 7^{0}SD, 7^{0}SD, 10^{4}G, 11^{0}SD, 9^{1}SD, 10^{2}SD, 16^{2}SD, 12^{5}SD,

	Starts	1st	2nd	3rd	Win & Pl
Career Total (Turf)	2	0	0	1	876
Career Total (AW)	15	1	3	0	4342

61	9/09	Wolv	1m1f103y	(0-52)H	STD	£2388

Total win prize-money £2388

Going (Turf): **Sf: 0-0 GS: 0-1 Gd: 0-1 GF: 0-0 Fm: 0-0**
Distance: 5f/6f: 0-1 7f-8f: 0-7 **9f-13f: 1-8** 14f+: 0-1
Track : **LH: 1-7** RH: 0-10 **Tight: 1-6** Gall: 0-1
Aids: Bl: 0-0 Vi: 0-1 Tstrap: 0-0 Ckp: 0-0
Best Rating: **67** 6/08 Kemp 1m stand

Moderate; effective at 1m2f-2m; acts on easy ground and on Polytrack.

Earlsmedic

107(108) (97)**90**
4-y-o ch g Dr Fong (USA)-Area Girl (Jareer (USA))
S C Williams Mad Man Plus One

Placings:6/0552511100-510040043115 (7862)
2009: 6^{5}GF, 6^{1}GF, 6^{0}G, 6^{0}GF, 5^{4}GF, 6^{0}G, 6^{0}GF, 6^{4}GF, 6^{3}SD, 6^{1}SD, 6^{1}SD, 5^{5}SD,

	Starts	1st	2nd	3rd	Win & Pl
Career Total (Turf)	18	4	1	0	23176
Career Total (AW)	5	2	0	1	13202

97	11/09	Kemp	6f	(0-80)H	STD	£4727
90	11/09	Kemp	6f	(0-95)H	STD	£7352
90	5/09	Yarm	6f3y	(0-80)H	G-F	£5180
88	8/08	NmkJ	6f	(0-85)H	GD	£6476
88	8/08	NmkJ	6f	(0-85)H	GD	£6476
81	8/08	Haml	6f5y		GD	£3238

Total win prize-money £33451

Going (Turf): Sf: 0-3 GS: 0-3 **Gd: 3-5** GF: 1-7 Fm: 0-0
Distance: **5f/6f: 4-13** 7f-8f: 2-8 9f-13f: 0-2 14f+: 0-0
Track : LH: 0-6 **RH: 2-4** Tight: 0-3 Gall: 0-0
Aids: Bl: 0-0 **Vi: 4-11** Tstrap: 0-0 Ckp: 0-0
Best Rating: **97** 11/09 Kemp 6f stand

Useful; stays 7f but very effective at shorter; handles Polytrack and a sound surface on turf; has worn a visor and eyeshield.

Early Dart

2-y-o b f Auction House (USA)-Cozette (IRE) (Danehill Dancer (IRE))
A Berry Mr and Mrs Calderbank

Placings:P (7717)
2009: 8^{P}SD,

	Starts	1st	2nd	3rd	Win & Pl
Career Total (Turf)	0	0	0	0	
Career Total (AW)	1	0	0	0	

Going (Turf): **Sf: 0-0 GS: 0-0 Gd: 0-0 GF: 0-0 Fm: 0-0**
Distance: 5f/6f: 0-0 7f-8f: 0-0 9f-13f: 0-1 14f+: 0-0
Track : LH: 0-1 RH: 0-0 Tight: 0-1 Gall: 0-0
Aids: Bl: 0-0 Vi: 0-0 Tstrap: 0-0 Ckp: 0-0

Early Girl

(71) (27)
4-y-o b f Compton Place-Reciprocal (IRE) (Night Shift (USA))
P D Evans J Wotherspoon

Placings:04 **(0488)**
2009: 11[0]SD, 8[4]SS,

	Starts	1st	2nd	3rd	Win & Pl
Career Total (Turf)	0	0	0	0	
Career Total (AW)	2	0	0	0	0

Going (Turf): **Sf: 0-0 GS: 0-0 Gd: 0-0 GF: 0-0 Fm: 0-0**
Distance: 5f/6f: 0-0 7f-8f: 0-1 9f-13f: 0-1 14f+: 0-0
Track : LH: 0-1 RH: 0-1 Tight: 0-0 Gall: 0-0
Aids: Bl: 0-0 Vi: 0-0 Tstrap: 0-0 Ckp: 0-0
Best Rating: 27 1/09 Kemp 1m3f stand

Early Morning Rain (IRE)

84 44
3-y-o b f Rock Of Gibraltar (IRE)-Honorine (IRE) (Mark Of Esteem (IRE))
Rae Guest Ashley House Stud

Placings:00 **(4786)**
2009: 6[0]GF, 6[0]G,

	Starts	1st	2nd	3rd	Win & Pl
Career Total (Turf)	2	0	0	0	

Going (Turf): **Sf: 0-0 GS: 0-0 Gd: 0-1 GF: 0-1 Fm: 0-0**
Distance: 5f/6f: 0-1 7f-8f: 0-1 9f-13f: 0-0 14f+: 0-0
Track : LH: 0-0 RH: 0-0 Tight: 0-0 Gall: 0-0
Aids: Bl: 0-0 Vi: 0-0 Tstrap: 0-0 Ckp: 0-0
Best Rating: 44 6/09 Sals 6f212y gd-fm

Earmark

(103) (58)43
6-y-o b g Halling (USA)-Earlene (IRE) (In The Wings)
Seamus Fahey (James McAuley 17/6) J J Dunne

Placings:0500/40002 **(6860)**
2009: 8[4]SD, 8[0]Y, 10[0]HY, 7[0]S, 9[2]SD,

	Starts	1st	2nd	3rd	Win & Pl
Career Total (Turf)	6	0	0	0	
Career Total (AW)	3	0	1	0	1024

Going (Turf): **Sf: 0-3 GS: 0-0 Gd: 0-2 GF: 0-0 Fm: 0-0**
Distance: 5f/6f: 0-0 7f-8f: 0-6 9f-13f: 0-2 14f+: 0-1
Track : LH: 0-5 RH: 0-3 Tight: 0-1 Gall: 0-1
Aids: Bl: 0-0 Vi: 0-0 Tstrap: 0-4 Ckp: 0-4
Best Rating: 65 10/07 Gowr 7f good

East Of The Sun (IRE)

92 55
3-y-o ch g Dr Fong (USA)-Arabis (Arazi (USA))
G Verheye (T P Tate 1/9) G Verheye

Placings:50000
2009: 10[5]S, 12[0]GF, 12[0]G, 16[0]GS, 7[0]HY,

	Starts	1st	2nd	3rd	Win & Pl
Career Total (Turf)	5	0	0	0	0

Going (Turf): **Sf: 0-2 GS: 0-1 Gd: 0-1 GF: 0-1 Fm: 0-0**
Distance: 5f/6f: 0-0 7f-8f: 0-1 9f-13f: 0-3 14f+: 0-1
Track : LH: 0-2 RH: 0-2 Tight: 0-2 Gall: 0-1
Aids: Bl: 0-1 Vi: 0-0 Tstrap: 0-0 Ckp: 0-0
Best Rating: 55 5/09 Hayd 1m2f95y soft

Easterly Breeze (IRE)

(101) (72)77
5-y-o b g Green Desert (USA)-Chiang Mai (IRE) (Sadler's Wells (USA))
Mrs L J Young (M S Tuck 5/9) Total Plumbing Supporters Club

Placings:255234/04200-004643 **(7578)**
2009: 8[0]SD, 12[0]SD, 12[4]SD, 9[6]SD, 12[4]SD, 13[3]SF,

	Starts	1st	2nd	3rd	Win & Pl
Career Total (Turf)	8	0	1	1	2132
Career Total (AW)	9	0	2	1	2081

Going (Turf): **Sf: 0-0 GS: 0-1 Gd: 0-1 GF: 0-4 Fm: 0-0**
Distance: 5f/6f: 0-0 7f-8f: 0-3 9f-13f: 0-13 14f+: 0-1
Track : LH: 0-13 RH: 0-4 Tight: 0-8 Gall: 0-1
Aids: Bl: 0-5 Vi: 0-0 Tstrap: 0-1 Ckp: 0-1
Best Rating: 77 5/07 Newb 1m2f6y gd-sft

Modest; suited by 1m2f; acts on fast and easy ground; handles Polytrack; has worn blinkers, a tongue tie and cheekpieces.

Eastern Anthem (IRE)

109 120
5-y-o b h Singspiel (IRE)-Kazzia (GER) (Zinaad)
Saeed Bin Suroor (M bin Shafya 28/3) Godolphin

Placings:1/32/2316-11165322 **(6324a)**
2009: 10[1]G, 12[1]G, 12[1]G, 12[6]G, 20[5]GF, 12[3]G, 12[2]S, 12[2]G,

	Starts	1st	2nd	3rd	Win & Pl
Career Total (Turf)	15	5	4	3	2344415

120	3/09	Ndas	1m4f		GD	£2083333
118	2/09	Ndas	1m4f	(95-112)H	GD	£62500
112	2/09	Ndas	1m2f	(95-110)H	GD	£50000
89	7/08	NmkJ	1m4f		G-F	£9969
84	10/06	Nott	1m54y		SFT	£2590

Total win prize-money £2208394

Going (Turf): Sf: 1-3 GS: 0-1 **Gd: 3-8** GF: 1-3 Fm: 0-0
Distance: 5f/6f: 0-0 7f-8f: 0-0 **9f-13f: 5-12** 14f+: 0-3
Track : **LH: 4-8** RH: 1-6 Tight: 0-3 **Gall: 4-7**
Aids: Bl: 0-0 Vi: 0-0 Tstrap: 0-0 Ckp: 0-0
Best Rating: 120 3/09 Ndas 1m4f good

Smart; Listed placed in Britain; won the Group 1 Dubai Sheema Classic in 2009; stays 1m4f; acts on any ground; has worn a tongue tie.

Eastern Aria (UAE)

109(101) (87)105
3-y-o br f Halling (USA)-Badraan (USA) (Danzig (USA))
M Johnston Sheikh Hamdan Bin Mohammed Al Maktoum

Placings:2131021210141214 **(6872a)**
2009: 8[2]SD, 8[1]SD, 8[3]SD, 10[1]SD, 10[0]S, 10[2]SD, 9[1]G, 10[2]GF, 10[1]GF, 10[0]G, 11[1]G, 10[4]GF, 9[1]GF, 10[2]G, 12[1]GS, 10[4]F,

	Starts	1st	2nd	3rd	Win & Pl
Career Total (Turf)	11	5	2	0	120339
Career Total (AW)	5	2	2	1	8563

102	9/09	StCl	1m4f		G-S	£26699
105	8/09	Bevl	1m1f207y	(0-105)H	G-F	£25904
101	8/09	Gdwd	1m3f	(0-90)H	GD	£12462
93	7/09	Epsm	1m2f18y	(0-85)H	G-F	£4857
86	6/09	Gdwd	1m1f192y	(0-80)H	GD	£6476
83	3/09	Ling	1m2f	(0-75)H	STD	£2729
75	2/09	Sthl	1m		STD	£2590

Total win prize-money £81718

Going (Turf): Sf: 0-1 GS: 1-1 **Gd: 2-4 GF: 2-4** Fm: 0-1
Distance: 5f/6f: 0-0 7f-8f: 1-2 **9f-13f: 6-14** 14f+: 0-0
Track : **LH: 4-11** RH: 3-5 **Tight: 4-8** Gall: 0-3
Aids: Bl: 0-0 Vi: 0-0 Tstrap: 0-0 Ckp: 0-0
Best Rating: 105 8/09 Bevl 1m1f207y gd-fm

Smart; effective at 1m2f-1m3f; acts on good/fast ground; goes on sand.

Eastern Empire

106(91) (73)92
3-y-o b g Dubai Destination (USA)-Possessive Artiste (Shareef Dancer (USA))
J W Hills Wai Kuen Chan

Placings:00-3110643 **(5419)**
2009: 7[3]SD, 8[1]GF, 8[1]GF, 8[0]GF, 8[6]G, 8[4]GF, 9[3]GF,

	Starts	1st	2nd	3rd	Win & Pl
Career Total (Turf)	7	2	0	1	12648
Career Total (AW)	2	0	0	1	482

91	5/09	Gdwd	1m	(0-85)H	G-F	£4857
87	5/09	Gdwd	1m		G-F	£3238

Total win prize-money £8095

Going (Turf): Sf: 0-0 GS: 0-0 Gd: 0-2 **GF: 2-5** Fm: 0-0
Distance: 5f/6f: 0-0 **7f-8f: 2-7** 9f-13f: 0-2 14f+: 0-0
Track : LH: 0-2 **RH: 2-5** Tight: 0-1 Gall: 0-0
Aids: Bl: 0-0 Vi: 0-0 Tstrap: 0-0 Ckp: 0-0
Best Rating: 92 8/09 Bevl 1m1f207y gd-fm

Useful; stays 1m; acts on fast ground and on Polytrack; likes to race prominently.

Eastern Gift

103(102) (79)84
4-y-o ch g Cadeaux Genereux-Dahshah (Mujtahid (USA))
Miss Gay Kelleway KingsClubSyndicate

Placings:452212044/0000400421 3-50000022230060 0625 **(7860)**
2009: 8[5]SD, 8[0]GF, 7[0]GF, 7[0]GF, 10[0]GF, 8[0]S, 9[2]F, 9[2]GF, 8[2]GF, 8[3]G, 8[0]SD, 8[0]SF, 7[6]SD, 7[0]SD, 8[0]SD, 7[6]SD, 9[2]SD, 7[5]SD,

	Starts	1st	2nd	3rd	Win & Pl
Career Total (Turf)	21	1	6	1	29097
Career Total (AW)	17	1	2	1	5112

77	11/08	Kemp	1m	(0-70)H	STD £2590
85	9/07	Ches	7f2y	G-F	£6800

Total win prize-money £9391

Going (Turf): Sf: 0-3 GS: 0-1 Gd: 0-6 **GF: 1-10** Fm: 0-1
Distance: 5f/6f: 0-3 **7f-8f: 2-27** 9f-13f: 0-8 14f+: 0-0
Track : LH: 1-18 RH: 1-10 **Tight: 1-13** Gall: 0-2
Aids: Bl: 0-0 Vi: 0-1 Tstrap: 0-3 Ckp: 0-3
Best Rating: 95 9/07 Gdwd 1m gd-fm

Modest; effective over 6f-1m; acts on most ground; likes to race prominently; can take a hold; has worn a visor.

Eastern Hills

100(90) (69)80
4-y-o b g Dubai Destination (USA)-Rainbow Mountain (Rainbow Quest (USA))
J S Wainwright Charles Wentworth

Placings:40201-003300602445 **(7247)**
2009: 8^{0}GS, 7^{0}GF, 6^{3}G, 5^{3}G, 7^{0}G, 7^{0}G, 6^{6}G, 7^{0}G, 6^{2}GS, 7^{4}G, 7^{4}G, 10^{5}S,

	Starts	1st	2nd	3rd	Win & Pl
Career Total (Turf)	15	1	2	2	8541
Career Total (AW)	2	0	0	0	0

80 6/08 Sand 7f16y (0-85)H G-S £5180
Total win prize-money £5181

Going (Turf): Sf: 0-1 **GS: 1-4** Gd: 0-8 GF: 0-2 Fm: 0-0
Distance: 5f/6f: 0-3 **7f-8f: 1-12** 9f-13f: 0-2 14f+: 0-0
Track : LH: 0-8 **RH: 1-3** Tight: 0-3 Gall: 0-2
Aids: Bl: 0-0 Vi: 0-3 Tstrap: 0-0 Ckp: 0-0
Best Rating: 80 6/08 Sand 7f16y gd-sft

Modest; suited by 6f-7f; acts on good and easy ground; has worn a visor.

Eastern Warrior

107(92) (62)**79**
3-y-o ch g Barathea (IRE)-Shakalaka Baby (Nashwan (USA))
J W Hills Wai Kuen Chan & Mark Wilson Leung

Placings:040-22215653 **(6937)**
2009: 8^{2}GF, 7^{2}S, 8^{2}G, 8^{1}G, 8^{5}GF, 8^{6}G, 8^{5}GF, 8^{3}G,

	Starts	1st	2nd	3rd	Win & Pl
Career Total (Turf)	9	1	3	1	6995
Career Total (AW)	2	0	0	0	265

79 7/09 Ripn 1m GD £3238
Total win prize-money £3238

Going (Turf): Sf: 0-1 GS: 0-1 **Gd: 1-4** GF: 0-3 Fm: 0-0
Distance: 5f/6f: 0-0 **7f-8f: 1-4** 9f-13f: 0-7 14f+: 0-0
Track : LH: 0-7 **RH: 1-3 Tight: 1-3** Gall: 0-1
Aids: Bl: 0-0 Vi: 0-0 Tstrap: 0-0 Ckp: 0-0
Best Rating: 79 7/09 Ripn 1m good

Fair; effective at around 7f-1m; acts on most types of ground.

Eastfields Lad

(83) (33)**29**
7-y-o b g Overbury (IRE)-Honey Day (Lucky Wednesday)
S R Bowring S R Bowring

Placings:06000/0/00 **(0619)**
2009: 7^{0}SD, 6^{0}SD,

	Starts	1st	2nd	3rd	Win & Pl
Career Total (Turf)	3	0	0	0	0
Career Total (AW)	5	0	0	0	

Going (Turf): Sf: 0-0 GS: 0-0 Gd: 0-1 GF: 0-2 Fm: 0-0
Distance: 5f/6f: 0-2 7f-8f: 0-4 9f-13f: 0-2 14f+: 0-0
Track : LH: 0-5 RH: 0-2 Tight: 0-0 Gall: 0-0
Aids: Bl: 0-3 Vi: 0-0 Tstrap: 0-0 Ckp: 0-0
Best Rating: 33 2/09 Sthl 7f stand

Eastwell Smiles

99(104) (63)**60**
5-y-o gr g Erhaab (USA)-Miss University (USA) (Beau Genius (CAN))
R T Phillips Eastwell Manor Racing Ltd

Placings:630/5050 **(2760)**
2009: 13^{5}SD, 16^{0}SD, 15^{5}G, 16^{0}GF,

	Starts	1st	2nd	3rd	Win & Pl
Career Total (Turf)	2	0	0	0	0
Career Total (AW)	5	0	0	1	419

Going (Turf): Sf: 0-0 GS: 0-0 Gd: 0-1 GF: 0-1 Fm: 0-0
Distance: 5f/6f: 0-0 7f-8f: 0-0 9f-13f: 0-4 14f+: 0-3
Track : LH: 0-4 RH: 0-3 Tight: 0-6 Gall: 0-0
Aids: Bl: 0-0 Vi: 0-0 Tstrap: 0-1 Ckp: 0-1
Best Rating: 69 6/07 Ling 1m2f stand

Modest; stays 1m5f; acts on Polytrack.

Easy Target (FR)

85(101) (90)**102**
4-y-o ch c Danehill Dancer (IRE)-Aiming (Highest Honor (FR))
G L Moore (X Nakkachdji 15/7) The Pink Punters

Placings:11054/313562-00015016 **(4983)**
2009: 6^{0}G, 8^{0}FT, 6^{0}FT, 9^{1}GS, 9^{5}GS, 7^{0}S, 8^{1}G, 8^{6}SD,

	Starts	1st	2nd	3rd	Win & Pl
Career Total (Turf)	16	5	1	2	57425
Career Total (AW)	3	0	0	0	138

72 7/09 MsnL 1m GD £7282
5/09 Stma 1m1f G-S £6311
102 7/08 Newb 7f GD £7477
93 7/07 Pont 6f SFT £6477
77 6/07 Nott 6f15y G-F £3562
Total win prize-money £31109

Going (Turf): Sf: 1-3 GS: 1-2 **Gd: 2-8** GF: 1-3 Fm: 0-0
Distance: 5f/6f: 1-4 **7f-8f: 3-11** 9f-13f: 1-4 14f+: 0-0
Track : **LH: 1-7** RH: 0-2 Tight: 0-0 Gall: 0-4
Aids: Bl: 0-1 Vi: 0-0 Tstrap: 0-0 Ckp: 0-0
Best Rating: 102 9/08 Newb 7f good

Very useful; effective at around 6f-1m; acts on most ground; has worn blinkers.

Easy Terms

83 **54**
2-y-o b f Trade Fair-Effie (Royal Academy (USA))
B R Millman T E Pocock

Placings:0 **(2175)**
2009: 6^{0}G,

	Starts	1st	2nd	3rd	Win & Pl
Career Total (Turf)	1	0	0	0	

Going (Turf): Sf: 0-0 GS: 0-0 Gd: 0-1 GF: 0-0 Fm: 0-0
Distance: 5f/6f: 0-1 7f-8f: 0-0 9f-13f: 0-0 14f+: 0-0
Track : LH: 0-0 RH: 0-0 Tight: 0-0 Gall: 0-0
Aids: Bl: 0-0 Vi: 0-0 Tstrap: 0-0 Ckp: 0-0
Best Rating: 54 5/09 Gdwd 6f good

Easy Wonder (GER)

79(103) (51)**60**
4-y-o b m Royal Dragon (USA)-Emy Coasting (USA) (El Gran Senor (USA))
I A Wood Paddy Barrett

Placings:6344301/**46003005444535460-0064403006004** **(7880)**
2009: 5^{0}SD, 7^{0}SD, 5^{6}SD, 6^{4}SD, 6^{4}SD, 5^{0}GF, 6^{3}SD, 5^{0}F, 5^{0}GF, 5^{6}SD, 6^{0}SD, 8^{0}SD, 7^{4}SD,

	Starts	1st	2nd	3rd	Win & Pl
Career Total (Turf)	19	0	0	3	15213
Career Total (AW)	18	1	0	2	2710

66 11/07 Wolv 5f216y STD £1892
Total win prize-money £1893

Going (Turf): Sf: 0-4 GS: 0-2 Gd: 0-4 GF: 0-7 Fm: 0-2
Distance: **5f/6f: 1-24** 7f-8f: 0-12 9f-13f: 0-1 14f+: 0-0
Track : **LH: 1-27** RH: 0-4 **Tight: 1-11** Gall: 0-4
Aids: Bl: 0-11 Vi: 0-0 Tstrap: 0-6 Ckp: 0-6
Best Rating: 71 9/07 Dort 6f heavy

Moderate; effective over 6f; acts on a sound surface; goes on Polytrack; has worn blinkers.

Eau Good

(56) (86)**89**
5-y-o ch g Cadeaux Genereux-Girl's Best Friend (Nicolotte)
G J Smith P Voce

Placings:233132/5220**1030500/56-0** **(0009)**
2009: 7^{0}SS,

	Starts	1st	2nd	3rd	Win & Pl
Career Total (Turf)	12	1	1	3	10184
Career Total (AW)	8	1	3	1	8730

89 4/07 Wind 1m67y (0-85)H G-F £6477
85 12/06 Wolv 5f216y STD £3238
Total win prize-money £9716

Going (Turf): Sf: 0-4 GS: 0-1 Gd: 0-5 **GF: 1-2** Fm: 0-0
Distance: 5f/6f: 1-6 7f-8f: 0-7 9f-13f: 1-7 14f+: 0-0
Track : LH: 1-7 RH: 1-7 **Tight: 2-5** Gall: 0-3
Aids: Bl: 0-1 Vi: 0-0 Tstrap: 0-0 Ckp: 0-0
Best Rating: 89 4/07 Wind 1m67y gd-fm

Useful; effective at around 1m; acts on easy ground and on sand.

Ebert

(102) (75)**95**
6-y-o b g Polish Precedent (USA)-Fanfare (Deploy)
R A Fahey G H Leatham & M A Leatham

Placings:032/451423/24634/66-3334 **(0423)**
2009: 13^{3}SD, 12^{3}SD, 12^{3}SD, 12^{4}SD,

	Starts	1st	2nd	3rd	Win & Pl
Career Total (Turf)	14	1	2	2	16308
Career Total (AW)	6	0	1	4	2058

79 7/06 Sals 1m (0-85)H G-F £7124
Total win prize-money £7125

Going (Turf): Sf: 0-1 GS: 0-1 Gd: 0-7 **GF: 1-4** Fm: 0-1
Distance: 5f/6f: 0-0 **7f-8f: 1-9** 9f-13f: 0-10 14f+: 0-1
Track : LH: 0-10 RH: 0-6 Tight: 0-7 Gall: 0-1
Aids: Bl: 0-1 Vi: 0-0 Tstrap: 0-1 Ckp: 0-1
Best Rating: 95 6/07 Gdwd 1m gd-fm

Useful; stays 1m; acts on fast ground and on Polytrack.

Ebiayn (FR)

98(97) (82)**79**
3-y-o b g Monsun (GER)-Drei (USA) (Lyphard (USA))
A King (M A Jarvis 3/10) Winter Madness

Placings:3-3344 **(6475)**
2009: 8^{3}S, 8^{3}SD, 12^{4}G, 10^{4}GF,

	Starts	1st	2nd	3rd	Win & Pl
Career Total (Turf)	4	0	0	2	1900
Career Total (AW)	1	0	0	1	403

Going (Turf): Sf: 0-1 GS: 0-1 Gd: 0-1 GF: 0-1 Fm: 0-0
Distance: 5f/6f: 0-0 7f-8f: 0-2 9f-13f: 0-3 14f+: 0-0
Track : LH: 0-3 RH: 0-1 Tight: 0-2 Gall: 0-1
Aids: Bl: 0-0 Vi: 0-0 Tstrap: 0-0 Ckp: 0-0
Best Rating: 82 6/09 Ling 1m stand

Useful; stays 1m2f; acts on fast ground.

Ebony Boom (IRE)

91(99) (74)**74**

2-y-o b c Boreal (GER)-Elegant As Well (IRE) (Sadler's Wells (USA))

H R A Cecil Gestut Ammerland

Placings:0423 (7199)

2009: 7^{0}HY, 7^{4}SD, 8^{2}GF, 8^{3}SD,

	Starts	1st	2nd	3rd	Win & Pl
Career Total (Turf)	2	0	1	0	1542
Career Total (AW)	2	0	0	1	543

Going (Turf): **Sf: 0-1 GS: 0-0 Gd: 0-0 GF: 0-1 Fm: 0-0**
Distance: 5f/6f: 0-0 7f-8f: 0-3 9f-13f: 0-1 14f+: 0-0
Track : LH: 0-3 RH: 0-0 Tight: 0-3 Gall: 0-0
Aids: Bl: 0-0 Vi: 0-0 Tstrap: 0-0 Ckp: 0-0
Best Rating: **74** 11/09 Ling 1m stand

Fair; stays 1m; acts on fast ground; goes on Polytrack.

Ebony Eyes

100(101) (85)**66**

3-y-o br f King's Best (USA)-Qui Liz (USA) (Benny The Dip (USA))

W J Knight D G Hardisty Bloodstock

Placings:635**6131** (7476)

2009: 9^{6}G, 9^{3}GF, 10^{5}GF, 10^{6}SD, 11^{1}SD, 12^{3}SD, 12^{1}SD,

	Starts	1st	2nd	3rd	Win & Pl
Career Total (Turf)	3	0	0	1	403
Career Total (AW)	4	2	0	1	5023

85 11/09 Kemp 1m4f (0-75)H STD £2590
68 9/09 Kemp 1m3f (0-65)H STD £2047
Total win prize-money £4637

Going (Turf): **Sf: 0-0 GS: 0-0 Gd: 0-1 GF: 0-2 Fm: 0-0**
Distance: 5f/6f: 0-0 7f-8f: 0-0 **9f-13f: 2-7** 14f+: 0-0
Track : LH: 0-3 **RH: 2-4** Tight: 0-4 Gall: 0-0
Aids: Bl: 0-0 Vi: 0-0 Tstrap: 0-0 Ckp: 0-0
Best Rating: **85** 11/09 Kemp 1m4f stand

Fair; stays 1m4f and acts on most ground, including Polytrack.

Eborbrav

85 **47**

3-y-o b g Falbrav (IRE)-Eboracum (IRE) (Alzao (USA))

T D Easterby A Arton

Placings:0-50 (2090)

2009: 10^{5}GS, 12^{0}G,

	Starts	1st	2nd	3rd	Win & Pl
Career Total (Turf)	3	0	0	0	0

Going (Turf): **Sf: 0-0 GS: 0-1 Gd: 0-1 GF: 0-1 Fm: 0-0**
Distance: 5f/6f: 0-0 7f-8f: 0-1 9f-13f: 0-2 14f+: 0-0
Track : LH: 0-2 RH: 0-0 Tight: 0-1 Gall: 0-1
Aids: Bl: 0-0 Vi: 0-0 Tstrap: 0-0 Ckp: 0-0
Best Rating: **47** 5/09 Newc 1m2f32y gd-sft

Ebraam (USA)

103(113) (105)**98**

6-y-o b g Red Ransom (USA)-Futuh (USA) (Diesis)

S Curran (Mike Murphy 1/12) L M Power

Placings:0/0210/**006641233201 1261/2136334300234405 42-0531035000340031222** (7862)

2009: 6^{0}SD, 5^{5}SD, 5^{3}SD, 5^{1}SD, 7^{0}SD, 5^{3}SD, 5^{5}G, 6^{0}GF, 6^{0}GF, 5^{0}G, 5^{3}G, 5^{4}G, 5^{0}G, 5^{0}G, 6^{3}SD, 5^{1}SD, 6^{2}SD, 5^{2}SD, 5^{2}SD,

	Starts	1st	2nd	3rd	Win & Pl
Career Total (Turf)	19	1	1	4	10299
Career Total (AW)	39	7	9	7	81599

103 11/09 Wolv 5f216y STD £2388
103 2/09 Wolv 5f216y (0-95)H STD £9462
102 2/08 Ling 5f (0-100)H STD £9971
98 12/07 Ling 6f (0-100)H STD £9971
86 11/07 Ling 6f (0-85)H STD £4857
87 10/07 Wolv 5f20y (0-70)H STD £3071
68 7/07 Wolv 5f216y (0-60)H STD £2388
72 9/06 Catt 7f G-F £2590
Total win prize-money £44701

Going (Turf): Sf: 0-1 GS: 0-3 Gd: 0-11 **GF: 1-4** Fm: 0-0
Distance: **5f/6f: 7-45** 7f-8f: 1-13 9f-13f: 0-0 14f+: 0-0
Track : **LH: 8-36** RH: 0-5 **Tight: 8-31** Gall: 0-2
Aids: Bl: 0-0 Vi: 0-0 Tstrap: 0-0 Ckp: 0-0
Best Rating: **105** 11/09 Ling 6f stand

Very useful; effective over 5f-7f; acts on fast ground; goes on sand; has worn a tongue-tie.

Echo Dancer

100(103) (74)**62**

3-y-o br g Danehill Dancer (IRE)-Entail (USA) (Riverman (USA))

T Wall (S A Callaghan 24/7) The Wenlock Edge Optimists

Placings:5-1**0062000** (7615)

2009: 8^{1}SD, 8^{0}GF, 8^{0}SD, 10^{6}SD, 8^{2}SD, 8^{0}GS, 11^{0}SD, 8^{0}SD,

	Starts	1st	2nd	3rd	Win & Pl
Career Total (Turf)	2	0	0	0	
Career Total (AW)	7	1	1	0	3751

67 1/09 Sthl 1m STD £2729
Total win prize-money £2730

Going (Turf): **Sf: 0-0 GS: 0-1 Gd: 0-0 GF: 0-1 Fm: 0-0**
Distance: 5f/6f: 0-0 **7f-8f: 1-5** 9f-13f: 0-4 14f+: 0-0
Track : **LH: 1-6** RH: 0-1 Tight: 0-3 Gall: 0-0
Aids: Bl: 0-0 Vi: 0-0 Tstrap: 0-0 Ckp: 0-0
Best Rating: **74** 7/09 Sthl 1m stand

Modest; stays 1m; acts on Fibresand.

Echo Forest

78(75) (41)**42**

3-y-o b g Mark Of Esteem (IRE)-Engulfed (USA) (Gulch (USA))

J R Best Tim Hedin

Placings:050-00 (3919)

2009: 9^{0}GF, 11^{0}G,

	Starts	1st	2nd	3rd	Win & Pl
Career Total (Turf)	3	0	0	0	0
Career Total (AW)	2	0	0	0	

Going (Turf): **Sf: 0-0 GS: 0-0 Gd: 0-1 GF: 0-2 Fm: 0-0**
Distance: 5f/6f: 0-0 7f-8f: 0-3 9f-13f: 0-2 14f+: 0-0
Track : LH: 0-4 RH: 0-0 Tight: 0-4 Gall: 0-0
Aids: Bl: 0-0 Vi: 0-0 Tstrap: 0-0 Ckp: 0-0
Best Rating: **42** 9/08 Brig 6f209y gd-fm

Eclipsed (USA)

68 **20**

2-y-o ch c Proud Citizen (USA)-Kamareyah (IRE) (Hamas (IRE))

J R Best Kent Bloodstock

Placings:00 (6737)

2009: 7^{0}G, 6^{0}GS,

	Starts	1st	2nd	3rd	Win & Pl
Career Total (Turf)	2	0	0	0	

Going (Turf): **Sf: 0-0 GS: 0-1 Gd: 0-1 GF: 0-0 Fm: 0-0**
Distance: 5f/6f: 0-1 7f-8f: 0-1 9f-13f: 0-0 14f+: 0-0
Track : LH: 0-0 RH: 0-0 Tight: 0-0 Gall: 0-1
Aids: Bl: 0-0 Vi: 0-0 Tstrap: 0-0 Ckp: 0-0
Best Rating: **20** 10/09 Wind 6f gd-sft

Ecole D'Art (USA)

108 (59)**76**

8-y-o b g Theatrical-Colour Chart (USA) (Mr Prospector (USA))

J J Lambe Mighty Macs Syndicate

Placings:113030/2333/000-501 (6053)

2009: 8^{5}GF, 10^{0}GF, 17^{1}G,

	Starts	1st	2nd	3rd	Win & Pl
Career Total (Turf)	15	3	1	5	51429
Career Total (AW)	1	0	0	0	

76 9/09 Ayr 2m1f105y (0-80)H GD £6476
96 6/04 Lonc 1m2f GD £15845
5/04 StCl 1m2f110y SFT £6338
Total win prize-money £28659

Going (Turf): Sf: 1-3 GS: 0-1 **Gd: 2-7** GF: 0-2 Fm: 0-0
Distance: 5f/6f: 0-0 7f-8f: 0-1 **9f-13f: 2-14** 14f+: 1-1
Track : **LH: 2-6** RH: 1-8 Tight: 0-0 Gall: 0-0
Aids: Bl: 0-0 Vi: 0-0 Tstrap: 0-0 Ckp: 0-0
Best Rating: **103** 7/05 Chan 1m2f good

Fair; stays 2m1f; acts on good ground.

Ed's A Red

71 **29**

2-y-o b f Auction House (USA)-Gracious Imp (USA) (Imp Society (USA))

A Berry Sporting Kings

Placings:460 (5958)

2009: 6^{4}GF, 6^{6}GF, 6^{0}GF,

	Starts	1st	2nd	3rd	Win & Pl
Career Total (Turf)	3	0	0	0	481

Going (Turf): **Sf: 0-0 GS: 0-0 Gd: 0-0 GF: 0-3 Fm: 0-0**
Distance: 5f/6f: 0-2 7f-8f: 0-1 9f-13f: 0-0 14f+: 0-0
Track : LH: 0-1 RH: 0-0 Tight: 0-1 Gall: 0-0
Aids: Bl: 0-0 Vi: 0-0 Tstrap: 0-0 Ckp: 0-0
Best Rating: **29** 8/09 Hayd 6f gd-fm

Ed's Pride (IRE)

(98) (51)**35**

3-y-o b c Catcher In The Rye (IRE)-Queenliness (Exit To Nowhere (USA))

K A Ryan E Duffy

Placings:0065-4455 (0793)

2009: 8^{4}SD, 9^{4}SD, 8^{5}SD, 7^{5}SD,

	Starts	1st	2nd	3rd	Win & Pl
Career Total (Turf)	3	0	0	0	0
Career Total (AW)	5	0	0	0	0

Going (Turf): **Sf: 0-0 GS: 0-0 Gd: 0-0 GF: 0-3 Fm: 0-0**
Distance: 5f/6f: 0-2 7f-8f: 0-4 9f-13f: 0-2 14f+: 0-0
Track : LH: 0-5 RH: 0-0 Tight: 0-2 Gall: 0-0

Aids: Bl: 0-5 Vi: 0-0 Tstrap: 0-1 Ckp: 0-1
Best Rating: 51 3/09 Sthl 7f stand

Very moderate; stays 1m; acts on Polytrack; has worn blinkers.

Edas

102(104) (74)**75**
7-y-o b g Celtic Swing-Eden (IRE) (Polish Precedent (USA))
T A K Cuthbert (R A Harris 7/6) Mrs Joyce Cuthbert

Placings:4614000/0666**525**/3363/002204-**1323243346201** **(7113)**
2009: 11^{1}SD, 11^{3}SD, 11^{2}SD, 12^{3}GF, 11^{2}G, 12^{4}GF, 12^{3}SD, 13^{3}GF, 11^{4}G, 13^{6}HY, 10^{2}GF, 12^{0}GS, 9^{1}GS,

	Starts	1st	2nd	3rd	Win & Pl
Career Total (Turf)	31	2	4	5	13141
Career Total (AW)	6	1	2	2	5647

75	10/09	Muss	1m1f	(0-65)H	G-S	£2498
73	1/09	Sthl	1m3f	(0-70)H	STD	£3070
79	6/05	Folk	1m1f149y		G-F	£3532

Total win prize-money £9102

Going (Turf): Sf: 0-6 **GS: 1-5** Gd: 0-8 **GF: 1-9** Fm: 0-3
Distance: 5f/6f: 0-0 7f-8f: 0-0 **9f-13f: 3-35** 14f+: 0-2
Track : LH: 1-18 **RH: 2-19 Tight: 2-23** Gall: 0-4
Aids: Bl: 0-0 Vi: 0-1 Tstrap: 0-2 Ckp: 0-2
Best Rating: 84 7/05 Folk 1m1f149y firm

Modest; stays 1m4f; acts on most types of turf, Fibresand and Polytrack; has worn a visor.

Eddie Boy

93(89) (59)**68**
3-y-o b g Tobougg (IRE)-Maristax (Reprimand)
M L W Bell C A Gershinson

Placings:036-30004 **(5127)**
2009: 11^{3}SD, 8^{0}GF, 9^{0}G, 10^{0}GS, 9^{4}GF,

	Starts	1st	2nd	3rd	Win & Pl
Career Total (Turf)	6	0	0	1	642
Career Total (AW)	2	0	0	1	302

Going (Turf): **Sf: 0-1 GS: 0-2 Gd: 0-1 GF: 0-2 Fm: 0-0**
Distance: 5f/6f: 0-0 7f-8f: 0-3 9f-13f: 0-5 14f+: 0-0
Track : LH: 0-3 RH: 0-4 Tight: 0-2 Gall: 0-1
Aids: Bl: 0-0 Vi: 0-1 Tstrap: 0-0 Ckp: 0-0
Best Rating: 68 9/08 Bevl 7f100y soft

Ede's

(65) (32)
9-y-o ch g Bijou D'Inde-Ballagarrow Girl (North Stoke)
P M Phelan Ede's (uk) Ltd

Placings:560/65/0/0 **(7328)**
2009: 16^{0}SD,

	Starts	1st	2nd	3rd	Win & Pl
Career Total (Turf)	5	0	0	0	0
Career Total (AW)	2	0	0	0	

Going (Turf): **Sf: 0-1 GS: 0-0 Gd: 0-2 GF: 0-2 Fm: 0-0**
Distance: 5f/6f: 0-1 7f-8f: 0-2 9f-13f: 0-3 14f+: 0-1
Track : LH: 0-2 RH: 0-2 Tight: 0-2 Gall: 0-0
Aids: Bl: 0-0 Vi: 0-0 Tstrap: 0-0 Ckp: 0-0
Best Rating: 52 3/02 Kemp 5f good

–

Ede's Dot Com (IRE)

104(100) (64)**66**
5-y-o b g Trans Island-Kilkee Bay (IRE) (Case Law)
P M Phelan Ede's (uk) Ltd

Placings:01340/65004020/26-3300021 **(7105)**
2009: 8^{3}SD, 8^{3}SD, 6^{0}SD, 8^{0}SD, 12^{0}SD, 7^{2}G, 7^{1}SD,

	Starts	1st	2nd	3rd	Win & Pl
Career Total (Turf)	7	0	2	0	2407
Career Total (AW)	15	2	1	3	6973

64	10/09	Kemp	7f	(0-55)	STD	£2047
74	7/06	Ling	6f		STD	£2590

Total win prize-money £4638

Going (Turf): **Sf: 0-0 GS: 0-3 Gd: 0-2 GF: 0-2 Fm: 0-0**
Distance: 5f/6f: 1-9 7f-8f: 1-11 9f-13f: 0-2 14f+: 0-0
Track : LH: 1-11 RH: 1-6 **Tight: 1-9** Gall: 0-1
Aids: Bl: 0-0 Vi: 0-0 Tstrap: 0-0 Ckp: 0-0
Best Rating: 79 9/06 NmkR 6f gd-fm

Modest; effective over 6f; acts on Polytrack.

Eden Park

82(85) (56)**31**
3-y-o ch f Tobougg (IRE)-Aegean Flame (Anshan)
M Dods J M & Mrs E E Ranson

Placings:340-00 **(2132)**
2009: 5^{0}GF, 6^{0}SD,

	Starts	1st	2nd	3rd	Win & Pl
Career Total (Turf)	3	0	0	1	347
Career Total (AW)	2	0	0	0	0

Going (Turf): **Sf: 0-0 GS: 0-0 Gd: 0-1 GF: 0-2 Fm: 0-0**
Distance: 5f/6f: 0-5 7f-8f: 0-0 9f-13f: 0-0 14f+: 0-0
Track : LH: 0-1 RH: 0-0 Tight: 0-0 Gall: 0-0
Aids: Bl: 0-0 Vi: 0-0 Tstrap: 0-0 Ckp: 0-0
Best Rating: 56 6/08 Sthl 5f stand

Edge Closer

110(112) (111)**117**
5-y-o b h Bold Edge-Blue Goddess (IRE) (Blues Traveller (IRE))
R Hannon Godfrey Wilson

Placings:1/21110/**12**6105010-0036 **(4087)**
2009: 6^{0}GF, 6^{0}GF, 6^{3}GF, 6^{6}S,

	Starts	1st	2nd	3rd	Win & Pl
Career Total (Turf)	16	5	1	1	67414
Career Total (AW)	3	2	1	0	17131

117	8/08	NmkJ	6f		G-F	£24978
117	6/08	Sals	6f		GD	£17031
111	3/08	Kemp	6f		STD	£6543
106	8/07	Kemp	6f	(0-95)H	STD	£6855
96	7/07	Asct	6f	(0-85)H	GD	£6477
85	7/07	Asct	6f	(0-80)H	G-F	£6477
70	11/06	Wind	6f		G-S	£3238

Total win prize-money £71602

Going (Turf): Sf: 0-2 GS: 1-2 **Gd: 2-6 GF: 2-6** Fm: 0-0
Distance: **5f/6f: 7-16** 7f-8f: 0-3 9f-13f: 0-0 14f+: 0-0
Track : LH: 0-1 **RH: 2-2** Tight: 0-1 **Gall: 1-4**
Aids: Bl: 0-0 Vi: 0-0 Tstrap: 0-0 Ckp: 0-0
Best Rating: 117 8/08 NmkJ 6f gd-fm

Smart; winner in Listed company; effective at around 6f; acts on any ground and on Polytrack; has worn a tongue tie; likes to race prominently.

Edge End

(92) (61)**61**
5-y-o ch g Bold Edge-Rag Time Belle (Raga Navarro (ITY))
P D Evans Mrs I M Folkes

Placings:6/5500/0000300-600 **(7460)**
2009: 6^{6}SD, 5^{0}SD, 5^{0}SD,

	Starts	1st	2nd	3rd	Win & Pl
Career Total (Turf)	9	0	0	0	0
Career Total (AW)	6	0	0	1	353

Going (Turf): **Sf: 0-0 GS: 0-2 Gd: 0-2 GF: 0-3 Fm: 0-2**
Distance: 5f/6f: 0-12 7f-8f: 0-3 9f-13f: 0-0 14f+: 0-0
Track : LH: 0-8 RH: 0-1 Tight: 0-5 Gall: 0-2
Aids: Bl: 0-1 Vi: 0-2 Tstrap: 0-3 Ckp: 0-3
Best Rating: 61 7/08 Ling 6f stand

Edgefour (IRE)

(92) (50)**53**
5-y-o b m King's Best (USA)-Highshaan (Pistolet Bleu (IRE))
B I Case D Allen

Placings:00/000/04-6 **(6225)**
2009: 12^{6}SD,

	Starts	1st	2nd	3rd	Win & Pl
Career Total (Turf)	4	0	0	0	
Career Total (AW)	4	0	0	0	0

Going (Turf): **Sf: 0-0 GS: 0-2 Gd: 0-1 GF: 0-1 Fm: 0-0**
Distance: 5f/6f: 0-0 7f-8f: 0-4 9f-13f: 0-4 14f+: 0-0
Track : LH: 0-4 RH: 0-3 Tight: 0-3 Gall: 0-1
Aids: Bl: 0-0 Vi: 0-0 Tstrap: 0-0 Ckp: 0-0
Best Rating: 53 7/07 Wind 1m67y gd-sft

Edgewater (IRE)

95(98) (83)**78**
2-y-o b g Bahamian Bounty-Esteemed Lady (IRE) (Mark Of Esteem (IRE))
J Akehurst (B J Meehan 24/10) One More Bid Partnership

Placings:04324141 **(7878)**
2009: 6^{0}G, 6^{4}GF, 7^{3}SD, 7^{2}SD, 8^{4}G, 6^{1}GF, 7^{4}SD, 6^{1}SD,

	Starts	1st	2nd	3rd	Win & Pl
Career Total (Turf)	4	1	0	0	3719
Career Total (AW)	4	1	1	1	5365

83	12/09	Ling	6f	(0-85)	STD	£3885
78	10/09	Pont	6f	(0-85)	G-F	£3238

Total win prize-money £7124

Going (Turf): Sf: 0-0 GS: 0-0 Gd: 0-2 **GF: 1-2** Fm: 0-0
Distance: **5f/6f: 2-4** 7f-8f: 0-3 9f-13f: 0-1 14f+: 0-0
Track : **LH: 2-3** RH: 0-2 **Tight: 1-2** Gall: 0-1
Aids: Bl: 0-0 Vi: 0-0 Tstrap: 0-0 Ckp: 0-0
Best Rating: 83 12/09 Ling 6f stand

Useful; effective over 6f-7f; acts on Polytrack.

Edgeworth (IRE)

103(97) (66)**79**
3-y-o b g Pyrus (USA)-Credibility (Komaite (USA))
B G Powell K Rhatigan

Placings:3050-4243011561006 **(7189)**
2009: 7^{4}SD, 7^{2}SD, 7^{4}G, 8^{3}GF, 8^{0}GF, 8^{1}GF, 8^{1}GF, 8^{5}G, 8^{6}GS, 8^{1}GF, 8^{0}G, 8^{0}SD, 7^{6}G,

	Starts	1st	2nd	3rd	Win & Pl
Career Total (Turf)	13	3	0	2	11622

Career Total (AW) 4 0 1 0 605
79 9/09 Leic 1m60y (0-75)H G-F £3885
71 6/09 NmkJ 1m (0-75)H G-F £3885
68 6/09 Wind 1m67y (0-70)H G-F £2729
Total win prize-money £10502

Going (Turf): Sf: 0-0 GS: 0-3 Gd: 0-5 **GF: 3-5** Fm: 0-0
Distance: 5f/6f: 0-2 7f-8f: 1-10 **9f-13f: 2-5** 14f+: 0-0
Track : LH: 0-7 **RH: 2-6 Tight: 1-5** Gall: 0-2
Aids: Bl: 0-0 Vi: 0-0 Tstrap: 0-0 Ckp: 0-0
Best Rating: 79 9/09 Leic 1m60y gd-fm

Fair; effective over 1m; acts on fast ground.

Edinburgh Knight (IRE)

63 29

2-y-o b c Selkirk (USA)-Pippas Song (Reference Point)
P W D'Arcy Knights Racing

Placings:0 (5029)
2009: 6⁰GF,

	Starts	1st	2nd	3rd	Win & Pl
Career Total (Turf)	1	0	0	0	

Going (Turf): Sf: 0-0 GS: 0-0 Gd: 0-0 GF: 0-1 Fm: 0-0
Distance: 5f/6f: 0-1 7f-8f: 0-0 9f-13f: 0-0 14f+: 0-0
Track : LH: 0-0 RH: 0-0 Tight: 0-0 Gall: 0-0
Aids: Bl: 0-0 Vi: 0-0 Tstrap: 0-0 Ckp: 0-0
Best Rating: 29 8/09 NmkJ 6f gd-fm

Edith's Boy (IRE)

100(106) (75)70

3-y-o ch g Trans Island-My Ramona (Alhijaz)
S Dow A Lindsay

Placings:4602-343243521210 (7808)
2009: 5³SD, 5⁴SD, 6³SD, 6²SD, 6⁴SD, 5³G, 5⁵GS, 5²GF, 5¹SD, 5²G, 5¹SD, 5⁰SD,

	Starts	1st	2nd	3rd	Win & Pl
Career Total (Turf)	4	0	2	1	2427
Career Total (AW)	12	2	2	2	7711

75 11/09 Ling 5f (0-70)H STD £2729
62 9/09 Kemp 5f STD £2047
Total win prize-money £4777

Going (Turf): Sf: 0-0 GS: 0-1 Gd: 0-2 GF: 0-1 Fm: 0-0
Distance: **5f/6f: 2-16** 7f-8f: 0-0 9f-13f: 0-0 14f+: 0-0
Track : LH: 1-12 RH: 1-2 **Tight: 1-9** Gall: 0-2
Aids: Bl: 0-0 Vi: 0-0 Tstrap: 0-0 Ckp: 0-0
Best Rating: 75 11/09 Ling 5f stand

Modest; effective at around 6f; acts on fast ground and on Polytrack.

Edward Lear

60(70) (32)1

2-y-o b c Refuse To Bend (IRE)-Darrery (Darshaan)
E F Vaughan Ali Saeed

Placings:00 (6842)
2009: 8⁰SD, 7⁰G,

	Starts	1st	2nd	3rd	Win & Pl
Career Total (Turf)	1	0	0	0	
Career Total (AW)	1	0	0	0	

Going (Turf): Sf: 0-0 GS: 0-0 Gd: 0-1 GF: 0-0 Fm: 0-0
Distance: 5f/6f: 0-0 7f-8f: 0-2 9f-13f: 0-0 14f+: 0-0
Track : LH: 0-2 RH: 0-0 Tight: 0-2 Gall: 0-0
Aids: Bl: 0-0 Vi: 0-0 Tstrap: 0-0 Ckp: 0-0
Best Rating: 32 9/09 Ling 1m stand

Edward Longshanks (USA)

80 49

2-y-o b c More Than Ready (USA)-Amour Mio (USA) (Private Terms (USA))
T P Tate Mrs Fitri Hay

Placings:000 (6763)
2009: 7⁰GF, 9⁰GF, 8⁰GS,

	Starts	1st	2nd	3rd	Win & Pl
Career Total (Turf)	3	0	0	0	

Going (Turf): Sf: 0-0 GS: 0-1 Gd: 0-0 GF: 0-2 Fm: 0-0
Distance: 5f/6f: 0-0 7f-8f: 0-2 9f-13f: 0-1 14f+: 0-0
Track : LH: 0-2 RH: 0-0 Tight: 0-1 Gall: 0-1
Aids: Bl: 0-0 Vi: 0-0 Tstrap: 0-0 Ckp: 0-0
Best Rating: 49 10/09 Newc 1m gd sft

Edward Whymper

93(97) (69)64

2-y-o ch g Bahamian Bounty-Sosumi (Be My Chief (USA))
M H Tompkins P A Sakal

Placings:000023522 (7604)
2009: 6⁰GF, 6⁰GF, 6⁰G, 7⁰SD, 7²GF, 8³GS, 7⁵SD, 7²SD, 8²SD,

	Starts	1st	2nd	3rd	Win & Pl
Career Total (Turf)	5	0	1	1	1124
Career Total (AW)	4	0	2	0	1310

Going (Turf): Sf: 0-0 GS: 0-1 Gd: 0-1 GF: 0-3 Fm: 0-0
Distance: 5f/6f: 0-1 7f-8f: 0-7 9f-13f: 0-1 14f+: 0-0
Track : LH: 0-2 RH: 0-3 Tight: 0-3 Gall: 0-0
Aids: Bl: 0-0 Vi: 0-0 Tstrap: 0-0 Ckp: 0-0
Best Rating: 69 12/09 Ling 1m stand

Modest; effective over 7f; acts on fast gound; goes on Polytrack.

Eeny Mac (IRE)

78 39

2-y-o ch g Redback-Sally Green (IRE) (Common Grounds)
N Bycroft N Bycroft

Placings:000 (4888)
2009: 5⁰G, 7⁰GS, 7⁰G,

	Starts	1st	2nd	3rd	Win & Pl
Career Total (Turf)	3	0	0	0	

Going (Turf): Sf: 0-0 GS: 0-1 Gd: 0-2 GF: 0-0 Fm: 0-0
Distance: 5f/6f: 0-1 7f-8f: 0-2 9f-13f: 0-0 14f+: 0-0
Track : LH: 0-0 RH: 0-1 Tight: 0-0 Gall: 0-0
Aids: Bl: 0-0 Vi: 0-0 Tstrap: 0-0 Ckp: 0-0
Best Rating: 39 8/09 Bevl 7f100y good

Effervesce (IRE)

(77) (47)

2-y-o ch f Galileo (IRE)-Royal Fizz (IRE) (Royal Academy (USA))
Sir Michael Stoute Cheveley Park Stud

Placings:5 (7396)
2009: 7⁵SD,

	Starts	1st	2nd	3rd	Win & Pl
Career Total (Turf)	0	0	0	0	
Career Total (AW)	1	0	0	0	0

Going (Turf): Sf: 0-0 GS: 0-0 Gd: 0-0 GF: 0-0 Fm: 0-0
Distance: 5f/6f: 0-0 7f-8f: 0-1 9f-13f: 0-0 14f+: 0-0
Track : LH: 0-1 RH: 0-0 Tight: 0-1 Gall: 0-0
Aids: Bl: 0-0 Vi: 0-0 Tstrap: 0-0 Ckp: 0-0
Best Rating: 47 11/09 Wolv 7f32y stand

Modest on evidence so far; should stay 1m; acts on Polytrack; sure to improve.

Efficiency

94(97) (81)73

3-y-o b f Efisio-Trounce (Barathea (IRE))
M Blanshard The First Timers

Placings:0521-0600000 (7586)
2009: 7⁰SD, 7⁶GS, 8⁰SD, 8⁰S, 10⁰G, 9⁰SD, 8⁰SD,

	Starts	1st	2nd	3rd	Win & Pl
Career Total (Turf)	4	0	0	0	0
Career Total (AW)	7	1	1	0	5235

81 12/08 Kemp 7f (0-85) STD £3885
Total win prize-money £3886

Going (Turf): Sf: 0-2 GS: 0-1 Gd: 0-1 GF: 0-0 Fm: 0-0
Distance: 5f/6f: 0-0 **7f-8f: 1-9** 9f-13f: 0-2 14f+: 0-0
Track : LH: 0-3 **RH: 1-6** Tight: 0-1 Gall: 0-1
Aids: Bl: 0-0 Vi: 0-0 Tstrap: 0-0 Ckp: 0-0
Best Rating: 81 12/08 Kemp 7f stand

Fair; stays 1m and acts on Polytrack.

Effigy

106(99) (80)86

5-y-o b g Efisio-Hymne D'Amour (USA) (Dixieland Band (USA))
H Candy The Earl Cadogan

Placings:04/0036053/26460321134-0232333226 (6695)
2009: 8⁰GF, 8²GF, 8³GF, 8²GF, 8³GF, 8³G, 9³S, 8²GF, 8²GF, 8⁶GS,

	Starts	1st	2nd	3rd	Win & Pl
Career Total (Turf)	27	2	6	7	22679
Career Total (AW)	3	0	0	1	944

80 9/08 Pont 1m4y (0-70)H G-S £3238
76 9/08 Sals 1m (0-70)H GD £3238
Total win prize-money £6476

Going (Turf): Sf: 0-5 **GS: 1-6 Gd: 1-7** GF: 0-9 Fm: 0-0
Distance: 5f/6f: 0-2 7f-8f: 1-13 9f-13f: 1-15 14f+: 0-0
Track : **LH: 1-10** RH: 0-12 Tight: 0-9 Gall: 0-4
Aids: Bl: 0-0 Vi: 0-0 Tstrap: 0-0 Ckp: 0-0
Best Rating: 86 5/09 Newb 1m gd-fm

Fair; effective over 1m; acts on good and easy ground; goes on Polytrack.

Effort

73(98) (86)97

3-y-o ch g Dr Fong (USA)-Party Doll (Be My Guest (USA))
A bin Huzaim (M Johnston 24/4) Sheikh Hamdan Bin Mohammed Al Maktoum

Placings:124003303-606600
2009: 6⁶SD, 8⁰G, 7⁶FT, 6⁶FT, 5⁰FT, 5⁰FT,

	Starts	1st	2nd	3rd	Win & Pl
Career Total (Turf)	9	1	1	2	10099

	Starts	1st	2nd	3rd	Win & Pl
Career Total (AW)	6	0	0	1	788

89	5/08	Carl	5f		G-F	£3626

Total win prize-money £3627

Going (Turf): Sf: 0-1 GS: 0-2 Gd: 0-2 **GF: 1-4** Fm: 0-0
Distance: **5f/6f: 1-12** 7f-8f: 0-2 9f-13f: 0-1 14f+: 0-0
Track : LH: 0-2 **RH: 1-3** Tight: 0-2 **Gall: 1-1**
Aids: Bl: 0-0 Vi: 0-0 Tstrap: 0-0 Ckp: 0-0
Best Rating: **97** 6/08 Asct 5f gd-fm

Very useful; effective over 5f-6f; acts on most ground.

Efidium

97 (54)**69**

11-y-o b g Presidium-Efipetite (Efisio)
N Bycroft N Bycroft

Placings:5000010/6000002000005100/002025360050/0110 14026514600046/20423153541200/000302446035010000/ 3553660403320/00056156205043350/3020210220-0053025350030400 **(7062)**

2009: 7^0F, 7^0GF, 9^5GF, 8^3G, 8^0GF, 7^2F, 7^5GF, 6^3G, 8^5GF, 8^0G, 7^0GF, 9^3GF, 10^0GF, 10^4GF, 12^0GS, 7^0GF,

	Starts	1st	2nd	3rd	Win & Pl
Career Total (Turf)	132	10	15	15	79932
Career Total (AW)	8	1	0	0	2170

69	7/08	Rdcr	1m	(0-75)H	GD	£2914
70	6/07	Rdcr	1m	(0-75)H	G-S	£2817
71	9/05	Thsk	1m	(0-70)H	GD	£4327
76	7/04	Thsk	1m	C(0-95)H	FRM	£9587
73	5/04	York	6f217y	D(0-80)H	G-F	£5882
76	7/03	Carl	6f192y	E(0-70)H	FRM	£4160
70	5/03	Donc	7f	E(0-70)H	GD	£4426
69	5/03	Rdcr	7f	F	G-F	£3542
65	4/03	Ripn	1m	E(0-70)H	G-F	£3946
57	8/01	Rdcr	6f	F(0-60)	G-F	£2590
60	12/00	Sthl	5f	F	STD	£2170

Total win prize-money £46365

Going (Turf): Sf: 0-13GS: 1-10Gd: 3-26**GF: 4-57**Fm: 2-26
Distance: 5f/6f: 2-25 **7f-8f: 9-105** 9f-13f: 0-1014f+: 0-0
Track : **LH: 3-48** RH: 2-28 **Tight: 3-31** Gall: 1-10
Aids: **Bl: 1-22** Vi: 0-0 Tstrap: 0-0 Ckp: 0-0
Best Rating: **79** 8/04 Rdcr 1m gd-fm

Modest; stays 1m, but effective at shorter; acts on most types of ground.

Efisio Princess

103(107) (73)**72**

6-y-o br m Efisio-Hardiprincess (Keen)
J E Long Miss M B Fernandes

Placings:031/012/0033130-14040140 **(7738)**

2009: 6^1SD, 7^4SD, 6^0S, 6^4G, 5^0G, 6^1GS, 6^4SD, 6^0SD,

	Starts	1st	2nd	3rd	Win & Pl
Career Total (Turf)	14	3	1	3	9858
Career Total (AW)	7	2	0	1	5862

72	10/09	Wind	6f	(0-70)H	G-S	£2388
70	1/09	Sthl	6f	(0-70)H	STD	£2729
73	11/08	Sthl	6f	(0-70)H	STD	£2729
66	10/07	Wind	6f	(0-70)H	SFT	£2817
55	10/06	Wwck	6f21y		SFT	£2590

Total win prize-money £13256

Going (Turf): **Sf: 2-4** GS: 1-4 Gd: 0-6 GF: 0-0 Fm: 0-0
Distance: **5f/6f: 4-14** 7f-8f: 1-7 9f-13f: 0-0 14f+: 0-0
Track : **LH: 3-7** RH: 0-2 Tight: 0-0 **Gall: 2-4**
Aids: Bl: 0-0 Vi: 0-0 Tstrap: 0-0 Ckp: 0-0
Best Rating: **73** 11/08 Sthl 6f stand

Modest; effective over 6f; goes well on soft ground; acts on Fibresand.

Efistorm

105(99) (83)**93**

8-y-o b g Efisio-Abundance (Cadeaux Genereux)
C R Dore Sean J Murphy

Placings:211/14000/003/0203145605301/0616166531402 01250/003146004006606-4012561330500 **(6279)**

2009: 5^4SD, 5^0SD, 5^1G, 5^2G, 5^5GF, 5^6S, 5^1G, 5^3G, 5^3GF, 5^0GF, 5^5GF, 5^0GF, 6^0GF,

	Starts	1st	2nd	3rd	Win & Pl
Career Total (Turf)	42	9	4	4	83311
Career Total (AW)	28	3	1	3	18698

88	7/09	Muss	5f	(0-80)H	GD	£6476
85	4/09	Wind	5f10y	(0-80)H	GD	£4857
93	7/08	Pont	5f	(0-90)H	GD	£9346
94	8/07	NmkJ	5f	(0-85)H	SFT	£5181
91	6/07	Sand	5f6y	(0-80)H	G-S	£5181
80	4/07	Wind	5f10y	(0-80)H	G-F	£5181
69	1/07	Wolv	5f20y		SS	£3238
86	12/06	Wolv	5f20y	(0-80)H	STD	£6477
87	3/06	Sthl	5f	(0-70)H	STD	£3238
	3/04	Siro	6f		HLD	£10563
	10/03	Siro	5f		HVY	£9740
	9/03	Siro	5f		G-S	£6494

Total win prize-money £75978

Going (Turf): Sf: 2-10 GS: 2-9 **Gd: 3-8** GF: 1-13 Fm: 0-0
Distance: **5f/6f: 12-69** 7f-8f: 0-1 9f-13f: 0-0 14f+: 0-0
Track : LH: 3-17 RH: 3-8 Tight: 2-12 Gall: 2-5
Aids: Bl: 0-0 Vi: 0-0 Tstrap: 0-2 Ckp: 0-2
Best Rating: **95** 9/07 Hayd 5f soft

Useful; seems best suited by 5f; acts well on easy ground; also goes on sand.

Eforetta (GER)

103(105) (67)**65**

7-y-o ch m Dr Fong (USA)-Erminora (GER) (Highest Honor (FR))
A W Carroll John W Egan

Placings:000/0120000/0023031123/34351600/04543114 **(2429)**

2009: 16^0SS, 12^4SD, 12^5SD, 14^4SD, 16^3SD, 16^1SD, 16^1SD, 16^4G,

	Starts	1st	2nd	3rd	Win & Pl
Career Total (Turf)	9	0	0	2	1797
Career Total (AW)	27	6	3	4	18879

67	5/09	Kemp	2m	(0-75)H	STD	£2590
63	4/09	Sthl	2m	(0-65)H	STD	£2047
71	5/07	Sthl	1m6f	(0-70)H	STD	£3886
68	5/06	Sthl	1m6f	(0-75)H	STD	£3238
63	5/06	Sthl	1m6f	(0-45)	STD	£1876
54	5/05	Sthl	7f	(0-45)	STD	£1484

Total win prize-money £15123

Going (Turf): **Sf: 0-2 GS: 0-3 Gd: 0-2 GF: 0-2 Fm: 0-0**
Distance: 5f/6f: 0-3 7f-8f: 1-5 9f-13f: 0-11 **14f+: 5-17**
Track : **LH: 5-31** RH: 1-3 Tight: 0-6 Gall: 0-2
Aids: Bl: 0-1 Vi: 0-0 Tstrap: 0-1 Ckp: 0-1
Best Rating: **71** 5/07 Sthl 1m6f stand

Moderate; stays 2m; acts on sand; has worn blinkers and cheekpieces.

Egyptian Lord

(102) (43)**57**

6-y-o ch g Bold Edge-Calypso Lady (IRE) (Priolo (USA))
Peter Grayson Haldane Racing & D L Rhodes

Placings:0003035612/10030630000040/53141121050450 006006/00250400-0U00 **(7838)**

2009: 5^0SD, 5^UG, 5^0SD, 5^0SS,

	Starts	1st	2nd	3rd	Win & Pl
Career Total (Turf)	15	0	0	3	1799
Career Total (AW)	41	6	3	2	23416

83	3/07	Sthl	5f	(0-85)H	STD	£5181
79	3/07	Sthl	5f	(0-70)H	STD	£3071
73	2/07	Sthl	5f	(0-65)H	STD	£2388
74	2/07	Sthl	5f	(0-58)H	STD	£1876
72	1/06	Ling	5f	(0-70)H	STD	£3238
66	12/05	Sthl	5f	(0-75)	STD	£4010

Total win prize-money £19769

Going (Turf): **Sf: 0-1 GS: 0-0 Gd: 0-7 GF: 0-7 Fm: 0-0**
Distance: **5f/6f: 6-55** 7f-8f: 0-1 9f-13f: 0-0 14f+: 0-0
Track : **LH: 1-25** RH: 0-2 **Tight: 1-24** Gall: 0-0
Aids: **Bl: 6-38** Vi: 0-1 Tstrap: 0-0 Ckp: 0-0
Best Rating: **83** 3/07 Sthl 5f stand

Moderate; effective at around 5f; goes very well on Fibresand acts on Polytrack.

Egyptology (IRE)

85(85) (63)**58**

2-y-o ch g Shamardal (USA)-Golden Digger (USA) (Mr Prospector (USA))
M Johnston Sheikh Hamdan Bin Mohammed Al Maktoum

Placings:065 **(7430)**

2009: 8^0G, 7^6SD, 7^5SD,

	Starts	1st	2nd	3rd	Win & Pl
Career Total (Turf)	1	0	0	0	
Career Total (AW)	2	0	0	0	0

Going (Turf): **Sf: 0-0 GS: 0-0 Gd: 0-1 GF: 0-0 Fm: 0-0**
Distance: 5f/6f: 0-0 7f-8f: 0-2 9f-13f: 0-1 14f+: 0-0
Track : LH: 0-1 RH: 0-1 Tight: 0-1 Gall: 0-0
Aids: Bl: 0-0 Vi: 0-0 Tstrap: 0-0 Ckp: 0-0
Best Rating: **63** 11/09 Kemp 7f stand

Ei Tanniola (IRE)

10(48)

4-y-o b f Dr Massini (IRE)-Academic Accuracy (Environment Friend)
G J Smith (M J Gingell 1/1) Jestadreeme

Placings:00 **(2149)**

2009: 7^0SD, 8^0G,

	Starts	1st	2nd	3rd	Win & Pl
Career Total (Turf)	1	0	0	0	
Career Total (AW)	1	0	0	0	

Going (Turf): **Sf: 0-0 GS: 0-0 Gd: 0-1 GF: 0-0 Fm: 0-0**
Distance: 5f/6f: 0-0 7f-8f: 0-1 9f-13f: 0-1 14f+: 0-0
Track : LH: 0-1 RH: 0-1 Tight: 0-0 Gall: 0-0
Aids: Bl: 0-0 Vi: 0-0 Tstrap: 0-2 Ckp: 0-2

Eight Hours

95(87) (60)**64**

2-y-o b g Bahamian Bounty-Alchimie (IRE) (Sri Pekan (USA))
R A Fahey Aidan J Ryan

Placings:010210 **(6048)**

2009: 5^0GF, 5^1SD, 6^0GF, 6^2S, 6^1G, 6^0G,

	Starts	1st	2nd	3rd	Win & Pl
Career Total (Turf)	5	1	1	0	5400
Career Total (AW)	1	1	0	0	3071

64	9/09	Ripn	6f	GD	£4533
60	4/09	Wolv	5f20y	STD	£3070

Total win prize-money £7604

Going (Turf): Sf: 0-1 GS: 0-0 **Gd: 1-2** GF: 0-2 Fm: 0-0
Distance: **5f/6f: 2-6** 7f-8f: 0-0 9f-13f: 0-0 14f+: 0-0
Track : **LH: 1-1** RH: 0-0 **Tight: 1-1** Gall: 0-0
Aids: Bl: 0-1 Vi: 0-0 Tstrap: 0-0 Ckp: 0-0
Best Rating: **64** 9/09 Ripn 6f good

Modest; effective over 5f-6f; acts on soft ground and on Polytrack.

Eightdaysaweek

93(102) (65)**51**

3-y-o b f Montjeu (IRE)-Figlette (Darshaan)
A J McCabe (S Kirk 25/8) T R Pearson

Placings:00-6**1**20**4**0**10454053** **(7794)**
2009: 10[6]GF, **11**[1]SD, **11**[2]SD, 11[0]G, **14**[4]SD, 10[0]G, **11**[1]SD, **16**[0]SD, 13[4]SD, **9**[5]SD, **11**[4]SD, 7[0]SD, **11**[5]SD, **11**[3]SS,

	Starts	1st	2nd	3rd	Win & Pl
Career Total (Turf)	5	0	0	0	0
Career Total (AW)	11	2	1	1	7052

65	8/09	Sthl	1m3f		STD	£3043
58	4/09	Sthl	1m3f	(0-60)H	STD	£2047

Total win prize-money £5091

Going (Turf): **Sf: 0-0 GS: 0-1 Gd: 0-2 GF: 0-2 Fm: 0-0**
Distance: 5f/6f: 0-0 7f-8f: 0-3 **9f-13f: 2-10** 14f+: 0-3
Track : **LH: 2-12** RH: 0-2 Tight: 0-6 Gall: 0-0
Aids: Bl: 0-0 Vi: 0-0 Tstrap: 0-4 Ckp: 0-4
Best Rating: **65** 8/09 Sthl 1m3f stand

Moderate; effective at around 1m3f; acts on Fibresand.

Eighteenfifty

58(104) (77)

5-y-o ch g Hernando (FR)-Colleville (Pharly (FR))
B W Hills (N J Henderson 10/7) Richard Morecombe

Placings:1302 **(5094)**
2009: **12**[1]SD, **13**[3]SD, 10[0]G, **16**[2]SD,

	Starts	1st	2nd	3rd	Win & Pl
Career Total (Turf)	1	0	0	0	
Career Total (AW)	3	1	1	1	4859

72	2/09	Wolv	1m4f50y	STD	£2729

Total win prize-money £2730

Going (Turf): **Sf: 0-0 GS: 0-0 Gd: 0-1 GF: 0-0 Fm: 0-0**
Distance: 5f/6f: 0-0 7f-8f: 0-0 **9f-13f: 1-1** 14f+: 0-3
Track : **LH: 1-2** RH: 0-2 **Tight: 1-2** Gall: 0-1
Aids: Bl: 0-0 Vi: 0-0 Tstrap: 0-0 Ckp: 0-0
Best Rating: **77** 8/09 Kemp 2m stand

Fair; bumper winner; effective over 1m4f; acts on Polytrack.

Eijaaz (IRE)

102 **69**

8-y-o b g Green Desert (USA)-Kismah (Machiavellian (USA))
G A Harker A S Ward

Placings:0040**0/01304**4603134040/**0466**020660/2422000355/3114400231-06206300 **(7222)**
2009: 12[0]GS, 9[0]GF, 10[2]GF, 10[0]G, 13[6]G, 10[3]GF, 10[0]GF, 13[0]S,

	Starts	1st	2nd	3rd	Win & Pl
Career Total (Turf)	47	4	6	6	18838
Career Total (AW)	11	1	0	1	3994

69	11/08	Catt	1m5f175y	(0-75)H	HVY	£2590
62	6/08	Nott	1m2f50y	(0-60)H	G-F	£2047
56	5/08	Catt	1m3f214y		G-F	£2047
60	5/05	Leic	1m1f218y		GD	£2982
65	1/05	Ling	1m2f	(0-55)H	STD	£2958

Total win prize-money £12624

Going (Turf): Sf: 1-5 GS: 0-5 Gd: 1-11 **GF: 2-24** Fm: 0-2
Distance: 5f/6f: 0-0 7f-8f: 0-4 **9f-13f: 4-50** 14f+: 1-4
Track : **LH: 4-47** RH: 1-10 **Tight: 3-35** Gall: 0-7
Aids: Bl: 0-0 Vi: 0-1 Tstrap: 0-3 Ckp: 0-3
Best Rating: **69** 6/09 Rdcr 1m2f gd-fm

Modest; suited by 1m2f-1m4f; acts on fast ground.

Eimear's Pride (IRE)

65 **32**

9-y-o b g Sri Pekan (USA)-Elinor Dashwood (IRE) (Fools Holme (USA))
Daniel Mark Loughnane DNA Syndicate

Placings:00000/055/340/0/0 **(3444)**
2009: 16[0]GF,

	Starts	1st	2nd	3rd	Win & Pl
Career Total (Turf)	13	0	0	1	1055

Going (Turf): **Sf: 0-0 GS: 0-0 Gd: 0-3 GF: 0-6 Fm: 0-0**
Distance: 5f/6f: 0-0 7f-8f: 0-4 9f-13f: 0-4 14f+: 0-5
Track : LH: 0-2 RH: 0-4 Tight: 0-1 Gall: 0-0
Aids: Bl: 0-1 Vi: 0-0 Tstrap: 0-0 Ckp: 0-0
Best Rating: **65** 5/04 Wxfd 2m gd-fm

Eisteddfod

106(107) (107)**111**

8-y-o ch g Cadeaux Genereux-Ffestiniog (IRE) (Efisio)
P F I Cole Elite Racing Club

Placings:1331111/34511210/3650020305/**13**010410/305006-1**2**02**44** **(7837)**
2009: **6**[1]SD, **6**[2]SD, 6[0]GF, 6[2]S, **6**[4]SD, 7[4]SS,

	Starts	1st	2nd	3rd	Win & Pl
Career Total (Turf)	38	10	3	6	191856
Career Total (AW)	7	2	1	1	17944

107	3/09	Kemp	6f		STD	£7477
111	9/07	Sand	7f16y		GD	£14762
105	5/07	Leic	7f9y		SFT	£6232
96	3/07	Kemp	6f		STD	£6855
116	8/05	Deau	6f		G-S	£26596
116	6/05	Wind	6f	(0-105)H	GD	£29000
112	5/05	Gdwd	6f	(0-100)H	GD	£15335
110	9/04	Hayd	6f	(0-100)H	SFT	£20553
98	9/04	Ayr	6f	H	SFT	£18049
93	8/04	Sals	6f212y	D(0-80)	G-S	£8209
87	7/04	Wind	6f	D(0-80)	G-F	£6870
75	5/04	Folk	5f	D	SFT	£3740

Total win prize-money £163683

Going (Turf): **Sf: 4-8** GS: 2-13 Gd: 3-11 GF: 1-5 Fm: 0-0
Distance: **5f/6f: 9-28** 7f-8f: 3-17 9f-13f: 0-0 14f+: 0-0
Track : LH: 0-6 **RH: 4-10** Tight: 0-5 **Gall: 2-5**
Aids: Bl: 0-4 Vi: 0-0 Tstrap: 0-1 Ckp: 0-1
Best Rating: **116** 8/05 Deau 6f gd-sft

Smart; winner in Group 3 company abroad; effective at up to 7f; seems best on soft ground, but has won on faster and on Polytrack; has worn blinkers, cheekpieces and a tongue tie.

Ejaab

95(93) (79)**76**

2-y-o b/br g Kyllachy-Whittle Woods Girl (Emarati (USA))
W J Haggas Hamdan Al Maktoum

Placings:4130 **(5692)**
2009: 5[4]GF, 5[1]S, **6**[3]SD, 7[0]GS,

	Starts	1st	2nd	3rd	Win & Pl
Career Total (Turf)	3	1	0	0	4413
Career Total (AW)	1	0	0	1	578

76	7/09	Catt	5f212y	SFT	£3691

Total win prize-money £3691

Going (Turf): **Sf: 1-1** GS: 0-1 Gd: 0-0 GF: 0-1 Fm: 0-0
Distance: **5f/6f: 1-3** 7f-8f: 0-1 9f-13f: 0-0 14f+: 0-0
Track : **LH: 1-2** RH: 0-1 **Tight: 1-1** Gall: 0-1
Aids: Bl: 0-0 Vi: 0-0 Tstrap: 0-0 Ckp: 0-0
Best Rating: **79** 8/09 Kemp 6f stand

Fair; suited by 6f and soft ground.

Ejeed (USA)

92(98) (69)**50**

4-y-o b g Rahy (USA)-Lahan (Unfuwain (USA))
Miss Z C Davison Mrs J Irvine

Placings:0/0**5**0-00**06046** (7826)
2009: 7[0]GF, 6[0]GF, **6**[0]SD, 7[6]SD, **8**[0]SD, **8**[4]SD, **8**[6]SD,

	Starts	1st	2nd	3rd	Win & Pl
Career Total (Turf)	5	0	0	0	
Career Total (AW)	6	0	0	0	0

Going (Turf): **Sf: 0-0 GS: 0-1 Gd: 0-0 GF: 0-4 Fm: 0-0**
Distance: 5f/6f: 0-2 7f-8f: 0-6 9f-13f: 0-3 14f+: 0-0
Track : LH: 0-2 RH: 0-6 Tight: 0-0 Gall: 0-0
Aids: Bl: 0-0 Vi: 0-0 Tstrap: 0-4 Ckp: 0-4
Best Rating: **69** 11/09 Kemp 1m stand

Moderate; stays 7f; acts on Polytrack; has worn cheek-pieces.

Ektimaal

97(108) (86)**78**

6-y-o ch g Bahamian Bounty-Secret Circle (Magic Ring (IRF))
E A L Dunlop The Serendipity Partnership

Placings:06432/**1111**05000**2/35**-6**0461505** (7832)
2009: 8[6]GF, **7**[0]SD, **8**[4]SD, **7**[6]SD, **6**[1]SD, **6**[5]SD, **7**[0]SD, **6**[5]SD,

	Starts	1st	2nd	3rd	Win & Pl
Career Total (Turf)	10	0	1	1	1758
Career Total (AW)	15	5	1	1	25438

86	11/09	Ling	6f	(0-80)H	STD	£4857
98	3/07	Wolv	7f32y	(0-85)H	STD	£5505
90	1/07	Wolv	7f32y	(0-75)H	SS	£3071
87	1/07	Kemp	7f	(0-80)H	STD	£4728
79	1/07	Kemp	7f		STD	£2047

Total win prize-money £20209

Going (Turf): **Sf: 0-1 GS: 0-1 Gd: 0-4 GF: 0-4 Fm: 0-0**
Distance: 5f/6f: 1-3 **7f-8f: 4-17** 9f-13f: 0-5 14f+: 0-0
Track : **LH: 3-13** RH: 2-9 **Tight: 3-11** Gall: 0-0
Aids: Bl: 0-0 Vi: 0-0 Tstrap: 0-0 Ckp: 0-0
Best Rating: **98** 3/07 Wolv 7f32y stand

Useful; best at 6f-7f; acts on soft ground and Polytrack; has worn a tongue tie.

El Ameen

102(86) (49)**79**

3-y-o b c Haafhd-Gracious (Grand Lodge (USA))
M Johnston Hamdan Al Maktoum

Placings:33220 (6780)
2009: 7[3]G, 8[3]GF, 7[2]GF, 7[2]GF, 8[0]SS,

	Starts	1st	2nd	3rd	Win & Pl
Career Total (Turf)	4	0	2	2	3468
Career Total (AW)	1	0	0	0	

Going (Turf): **Sf: 0-0 GS: 0-0 Gd: 0-1 GF: 0-3 Fm: 0-0**
Distance: 5f/6f: 0-0 7f-8f: 0-4 9f-13f: 0-1 14f+: 0-0
Track : LH: 0-2 RH: 0-0 Tight: 0-1 Gall: 0-0
Aids: Bl: 0-1 Vi: 0-0 Tstrap: 0-0 Ckp: 0-0
Best Rating: 79 7/09 NmkJ 7f good

Fair; stays 1m; acts on fast ground.

El Bravo

101(106) (80)82
3-y-o ch g Falbrav (IRE)-Alessandra (Generous (IRE))
G L Moore D J Deer

Placings:04231265 **(2208)**
2009: 7^{0}SD, 10^{4}SD, 12^{2}SD, 12^{3}SD, 12^{1}SD, 11^{2}GF, 11^{6}GS, 14^{5}GF,

	Starts	1st	2nd	3rd	Win & Pl
Career Total (Turf)	3	0	1	0	907
Career Total (AW)	5	1	1	1	3939

80 4/09 Wolv 1m4f50y STD £2729
Total win prize-money £2730

Going (Turf): **Sf: 0-0 GS: 0-1 Gd: 0-0 GF: 0-2 Fm: 0-0**
Distance: 5f/6f: 0-0 7f-8f: 0-1 **9f-13f: 1-6** 14f+: 0-1
Track : **LH: 1-6** RH: 0-1 **Tight: 1-6** Gall: 0-1
Aids: Bl: 0-0 Vi: 0-0 Tstrap: 0-0 Ckp: 0-0
Best Rating: 82 4/09 Wind 1m3f135y gd-fm

Fair; stays 1m4f; acts on Polytrack.

El Dececy (USA)

105(107) (85)93
5-y-o b g Seeking The Gold (USA)-Ashraakat (USA) (Danzig (USA))
J Balding (S Parr 4/7) Willie McKay

Placings:030/3133600006/3323111000**6500-652**30316100010**1005** **(4040)**
2009: 6^{6}SD, 6^{5}SD, 5^{2}SD, 8^{3}SD, 7^{0}GF, 8^{3}GF, 7^{1}F, 7^{6}GF, 5^{1}GF, 10^{0}G, 10^{0}GF, 5^{0}G, 7^{1}GF, 8^{0}GF, 7^{1}GF, 7^{0}GF, 5^{0}G, 9^{5}G,

	Starts	1st	2nd	3rd	Win & Pl
Career Total (Turf)	38	8	1	8	30156
Career Total (AW)	7	0	1	1	1769

66 6/09 Chep 7f16y G-F £1942
75 5/09 Rdcr 7f G-F £2047
70 4/09 Brig 5f213y G-F £1942
68 4/09 Rdcr 7f FRM £1942
92 7/08 Haml 1m65y (0-75)H G-S £3885
93 7/08 Nott 1m75y (0-70)H G-F £3238
81 6/08 Wwck 1m22y (0-70)H G-F £3123
81 5/07 Pont 1m2f6y G-F £4533
Total win prize-money £22657

Going (Turf): Sf: 0-1 GS: 1-4 Gd: 0-11 **GF: 6-21** Fm: 1-1
Distance: 5f/6f: 1-8 7f-8f: 3-14 **9f-13f: 4-22** 14f+: 0-1
Track : **LH: 4-20** RH: 1-12 **Tight: 1-13** Gall: 0-6
Aids: Bl: 0-4 Vi: 0-1 Tstrap: 3-6 Ckp: 3-6
Best Rating: 93 7/08 Nott 1m75y gd-fm

Fair; amazingly he is effective over 5f-2m; acts on fast ground and on Polytrack; has worn various headgear.

El Diego (IRE)

(105) (87)70
5-y-o b g Sadler's Wells (USA)-Goncharova (USA) (Gone West (USA))
J R Gask Horses First Racing Limited

Placings:6/54/65-11260 **(6634)**
2009: 12^{1}SS, 12^{1}SD, 14^{2}SD, 12^{6}SD, 12^{0}SS,

	Starts	1st	2nd	3rd	Win & Pl
Career Total (Turf)	2	0	0	0	
Career Total (AW)	8	2	1	0	7441

79 1/09 Wolv 1m4f50y (0-75)H STD £2729
71 1/09 Sthl 1m4f SS £2729
Total win prize-money £5460

Going (Turf): **Sf: 0-0 GS: 0-0 Gd: 0-0 GF: 0-1 Fm: 0-0**
Distance: 5f/6f: 0-0 7f-8f: 0-1 **9f-13f: 2-7** 14f+: 0-2
Track : **LH: 2-7** RH: 0-1 **Tight: 1-3** Gall: 0-0
Aids: Bl: 0-0 Vi: 0-0 Tstrap: 0-0 Ckp: 0-0
Best Rating: 87 1/09 Sthl 1m6f stand

Fair; stays 1m4f; acts on Fibresand and Polytrack.

El Libertador (USA)

102(98) (73)73
3-y-o b/br g Giant's Causeway (USA)-Istikbal (USA) (Kingmambo (USA))
E A Wheeler J L Day

Placings:0-4430404235 **(7456)**
2009: 8^{4}GF, 8^{4}SD, 8^{3}GF, 9^{0}GF, 8^{4}GF, 7^{0}GF, 8^{4}G, 8^{2}G, 8^{3}SD, 8^{5}SD,

	Starts	1st	2nd	3rd	Win & Pl
Career Total (Turf)	8	0	1	1	2931
Career Total (AW)	3	0	0	1	545

Going (Turf): **Sf: 0-0 GS: 0-0 Gd: 0-2 GF: 0-5 Fm: 0-0**
Distance: 5f/6f: 0-0 7f-8f: 0-5 9f-13f: 0-6 14f+: 0-0
Track : LH: 0-2 RH: 0-7 Tight: 0-4 Gall: 0-0
Aids: Bl: 0-0 Vi: 0-0 Tstrap: 0-0 Ckp: 0-0
Best Rating: 73 11/09 Ling 1m stand

Fair; stays 1m; acts on fast ground and Polytrack.

El Loco Uno (USA)

96(99) (86)76
3-y-o ch c Fusaichi Pegasus (USA)-La Vida Loca (IRE) (Caerleon (USA))
H R A Cecil H E Sheikh Sultan Bin Khalifa Al Nahyan

Placings:25100 **(4814)**
2009: 8^{2}GF, 8^{5}SD, 8^{1}SD, 8^{0}GF, 7^{0}HY,

	Starts	1st	2nd	3rd	Win & Pl
Career Total (Turf)	3	0	1	0	964
Career Total (AW)	2	1	0	0	2730

86 6/09 Ling 1m STD £2729
Total win prize-money £2730

Going (Turf): **Sf: 0-1 GS: 0-0 Gd: 0-0 GF: 0-2 Fm: 0-0**
Distance: 5f/6f: 0-0 **7f-8f: 1-4** 9f-13f: 0-1 14f+: 0-0
Track : **LH: 1-1** RH: 0-3 **Tight: 1-3** Gall: 0-0
Aids: Bl: 0-0 Vi: 0-0 Tstrap: 0-0 Ckp: 0-0
Best Rating: 86 6/09 Ling 1m stand

Fair; stays 1m; acts on Polytrack.

El Potro

101(97) (49)62
7-y-o b g Forzando-Gaelic Air (Ballad Rock)
J R Holt Mrs Lisa Else

Placings:0004/436411/0240000060020202/042502232210615/2050540000-5000050 **(7869)**
2009: 6^{5}GF, 5^{0}GS, 6^{0}G, 5^{0}S, 7^{0}SD, 5^{5}SD, 6^{0}SS,

	Starts	1st	2nd	3rd	Win & Pl
Career Total (Turf)	24	2	3	0	8671
Career Total (AW)	34	2	7	2	11634

66 10/07 Nott 5f13y (0-65)H SFT £2047
65 7/07 Pont 5f (0-70)H G-S £3886
68 12/05 Wolv 5f20y (0-60)H STD £2515
67 11/05 Sthl 5f STD £3348
Total win prize-money £11799

Going (Turf): **Sf: 1-10 GS: 1-4** Gd: 0-5 GF: 0-5 Fm: 0-0
Distance: **5f/6f: 4-55** 7f-8f: 0-3 9f-13f: 0-0 14f+: 0-0
Track : **LH: 2-26** RH: 0-3 **Tight: 1-18** Gall: 0-3
Aids: Bl: 0-1 Vi: 0-0 Tstrap: 0-0 Ckp: 0-0
Best Rating: 73 4/08 Nott 5f13y soft

Moderate; effective at 5f-6f; acts on easy ground; also goes on Fibresand and Polytrack.

El Presidente (IRE)

92 (88)86
4-y-o gr g Daylami (IRE)-Todi (IRE) (Spinning World (USA))
N B King (M Halford 22/3) Across The Pond Partnership

Placings:234100206-500 **(6002)**
2009: 10^{5}SW, 8^{0}S, 10^{0}GF,

	Starts	1st	2nd	3rd	Win & Pl
Career Total (Turf)	9	1	1	1	8928
Career Total (AW)	3	0	1	0	3090

86 8/08 Bell 1m G-Y £6605
Total win prize-money £6605

Going (Turf): **Sf: 0-4 GS: 0-0 Gd: 0-2 GF: 0-1 Fm: 0-0**
Distance: 5f/6f: 0-0 **7f-8f: 1-7** 9f-13f: 0-5 14f+: 0-0
Track : **LH: 1-7** RH: 0-5 Tight: 0-1 Gall: 0-2
Aids: Bl: 0-1 Vi: 0-0 Tstrap: 1-7 Ckp: 1-7
Best Rating: 88 10/08 Dund 1m stand

Ela Gorrie Mou

98 73
3-y-o b f Mujahid (USA)-Real Flame (Cyrano De Bergerac)
T T Clement P Charalambous

Placings:00-04511 **(5869)**
2009: 8^{0}F, 9^{4}GS, 8^{5}HY, 8^{1}GF, 8^{1}G,

	Starts	1st	2nd	3rd	Win & Pl
Career Total (Turf)	7	2	0	0	7381

73 9/09 Ffos 1m (0-70)H GD £4857
69 8/09 Yarm 1m3y (0-60)H G-F £2331
Total win prize-money £7188

Going (Turf): Sf: 0-1 GS: 0-1 **Gd: 1-1 GF: 1-3** Fm: 0-1
Distance: 5f/6f: 0-0 7f-8f: 1-3 9f-13f: 1-4 14f+: 0-0
Track : **LH: 1-4** RH: 0-0 Tight: 0-1 **Gall: 1-1**
Aids: Bl: 0-0 Vi: 0-0 Tstrap: 0-0 Ckp: 0-0
Best Rating: 73 9/09 Ffos 1m good

Modest; stays 1m and acts on good or faster ground.

Elaala (USA)

83(95) (57)51
7-y-o ch m Aljabr (USA)-Nufuth (USA) (Nureyev (USA))
B D Leavy Moorland Racing

Placings:660054/14/0/10-5 **(2163)**
2009: 16^{5}G,

	Starts	1st	2nd	3rd	Win & Pl
Career Total (Turf)	6	0	0	0	232
Career Total (AW)	6	2	0	0	3412

57 11/08 Sthl 1m6f (0-60)H STD £2047
54 3/06 Sthl 1m6f (0-45) STD £1365
Total win prize-money £3412

Going (Turf): **Sf: 0-1 GS: 0-1 Gd: 0-4 GF: 0-0 Fm: 0-0**
Distance: 5f/6f: 0-0 7f-8f: 0-0 9f-13f: 0-5 **14f+: 2-7**
Track : **LH: 2-11** RH: 0-1 Tight: 0-4 Gall: 0-0
Aids: Bl: 0-0 Vi: 0-0 Tstrap: 0-0 Ckp: 0-0
Best Rating: 58 4/05 Pont 1m2f6y good

Moderate; stays 1m6f and acts on Fibresand; winning hurdler.

Elation (IRE)

(95) (70)

2-y-o b f Cape Cross (IRE)-Attraction (Efisio)

M Johnston Duke Of Roxburghe

Placings:41 **(7772)**

2009: 6^{4}SD, 7^{1}SD,

	Starts	1st	2nd	3rd	Win & Pl
Career Total (Turf)	**0**	**0**	**0**	**0**	
Career Total (AW)	**2**	**1**	**0**	**0**	**3826**

70 12/09 Ling 7f STD £3561

Total win prize-money £3562

Going (Turf): **Sf: 0-0 GS: 0-0 Gd: 0-0 GF: 0-0 Fm: 0-0**
Distance: 5f/6f: 0-1 **7f-8f: 1-1** 9f-13f: 0-0 14f+: 0-0
Track : **LH: 1-1** RH: 0-1 **Tight: 1-1** Gall: 0-0
Aids: Bl: 0-0 Vi: 0-0 Tstrap: 0-0 Ckp: 0-0
Best Rating: **70** 12/09 Ling 7f stand

Out of the top-class filly Attraction; useful prospect; effective at 7f; acts on Polytrack.

Eldalil

(83) (63)

2-y-o br f Singspiel (IRE)-White House (Pursuit Of Love)

Sir Michael Stoute Hamdan Al Maktoum

Placings:6 **(5639)**

2009: 7^{6}SD,

	Starts	1st	2nd	3rd	Win & Pl
Career Total (Turf)	**0**	**0**	**0**	**0**	
Career Total (AW)	**1**	**0**	**0**	**0**	**140**

Going (Turf): **Sf: 0-0 GS: 0-0 Gd: 0-0 GF: 0-0 Fm: 0-0**
Distance: 5f/6f: 0-0 7f-8f: 0-1 9f-13f: 0-0 14f+: 0-0
Track : LH: 0-0 RH: 0-1 Tight: 0-0 Gall: 0-0
Aids: Bl: 0-0 Vi: 0-0 Tstrap: 0-0 Ckp: 0-0
Best Rating: **63** 9/09 Kemp 7f stand

Eleanor Eloise (USA)

96(101) (58)49

5-y-o b m Minardi (USA)-Javana (USA) (Sandpit (BRZ))

J R Gask Horses First Racing Limited

Placings:65/205450623-04040 **(5019)**

2009: 7^{0}SD, 5^{4}SD, 5^{0}F, 6^{4}GS, 7^{0}GF,

	Starts	1st	2nd	3rd	Win & Pl
Career Total (Turf)	**4**	**0**	**0**	**0**	**217**
Career Total (AW)	**12**	**0**	**2**	**1**	**1635**

Going (Turf): **Sf: 0-0 GS: 0-2 Gd: 0-0 GF: 0-1 Fm: 0-1**
Distance: 5f/6f: 0-9 7f-8f: 0-7 9f-13f: 0-0 14f+: 0-0
Track : LH: 0-11 RH: 0-4 Tight: 0-6 Gall: 0-3
Aids: Bl: 0-3 Vi: 0-0 Tstrap: 0-3 Ckp: 0-3
Best Rating: **58** 12/08 Kemp 7f stand

Moderate; suited by 6f; acts on Polytrack; has worn cheekpieces.

Eleanora Duse (IRE)

81(95) (78)38

2-y-o b f Azamour (IRE)-Drama Class (IRE) (Caerleon (USA))

Sir Michael Stoute Ballymacoll Stud

Placings:601 **(7451)**

2009: 7^{6}SD, 7^{0}GF, 8^{1}SD,

	Starts	1st	2nd	3rd	Win & Pl
Career Total (Turf)	**1**	**0**	**0**	**0**	
Career Total (AW)	**2**	**1**	**0**	**0**	**3238**

78 11/09 Kemp 1m STD £3238

Total win prize-money £3238

Going (Turf): **Sf: 0-0 GS: 0-0 Gd: 0-0 GF: 0-1 Fm: 0-0**
Distance: 5f/6f: 0-0 **7f-8f: 1-3** 9f-13f: 0-0 14f+: 0-0
Track : LH: 0-0 **RH: 1-2** Tight: 0-0 Gall: 0-0
Aids: Bl: 0-0 Vi: 0-0 Tstrap: 0-0 Ckp: 0-0
Best Rating: **78** 11/09 Kemp 1m stand

Useful; stays 1m and acts on Polytrack.

Electioneer (USA)

97 79

2-y-o b g Elusive Quality (USA)-Secret Charm (IRE) (Green Desert (USA))

M Johnston Sheikh Hamdan Bin Mohammed Al Maktoum

Placings:410 **(5033)**

2009: 5^{4}F, 5^{1}GF, 5^{0}GF,

	Starts	1st	2nd	3rd	Win & Pl
Career Total (Turf)	**3**	**1**	**0**	**0**	**4312**

79 7/09 Bevl 5f G-F £4047

Total win prize-money £4047

Going (Turf): Sf: 0-0 GS: 0-0 Gd: 0-0 **GF: 1-2** Fm: 0-1
Distance: **5f/6f: 1-3** 7f-8f: 0-0 9f-13f: 0-0 14f+: 0-0
Track : LH: 0-1 RH: 0-0 Tight: 0-0 Gall: 0-1
Aids: Bl: 0-0 Vi: 0-0 Tstrap: 0-0 Ckp: 0-0
Best Rating: **79** 7/09 Bevl 5f gd-fm

Fair; seffective at 5f; acts on fast ground.

Electric City (IRE)

85(86) (63)73

2-y-o b f Elusive City (USA)-Accell (IRE) (Magical Wonder (USA))

M G Quinlan Eddie Tynan

Placings:0346 **(5841)**

2009: 7^{0}SD, 6^{3}G, 6^{4}S, 7^{6}SD,

	Starts	1st	2nd	3rd	Win & Pl
Career Total (Turf)	**2**	**0**	**0**	**1**	**987**
Career Total (AW)	**2**	**0**	**0**	**0**	**0**

Going (Turf): **Sf: 0-1 GS: 0-0 Gd: 0-1 GF: 0-0 Fm: 0-0**
Distance: 5f/6f: 0-2 7f-8f: 0-2 9f-13f: 0-0 14f+: 0-0
Track : LH: 0-2 RH: 0-0 Tight: 0-2 Gall: 0-0
Aids: Bl: 0-0 Vi: 0-0 Tstrap: 0-0 Ckp: 0-0
Best Rating: **73** 7/09 NmkJ 6f good

Electric Feel

100 100

2-y-o b f Firebreak-Night Gypsy (Mind Games)

M Botti Joseph Barton

Placings:16321 **(7033)**

2009: 6^{1}GF, 6^{6}GF, 6^{3}G, 7^{2}GF, 7^{1}S,

	Starts	1st	2nd	3rd	Win & Pl
Career Total (Turf)	**5**	**2**	**1**	**1**	**36203**

100 10/09 Newb 7f SFT £17031
77 5/09 NmkR 6f G-F £5180

Total win prize-money £22212

Going (Turf): **Sf: 1-1** GS: 0-0 Gd: 0-1 **GF: 1-3** Fm: 0-0
Distance: 5f/6f: 1-3 7f-8f: 1-2 9f-13f: 0-0 14f+: 0-0
Track : LH: 0-1 RH: 0-0 Tight: 0-0 Gall: 0-0
Aids: Bl: 0-0 Vi: 0-0 Tstrap: 0-0 Ckp: 0-0
Best Rating: **100** 10/09 Newb 7f soft

Very useful; Listed placed; effective over 6-7f; acts on fast ground.

Electric Warrior (IRE)

(106) (92)92

6-y-o b g Bold Fact (USA)-Dungeon Princess (IRE) (Danehill (USA))

C R Dore (K R Burke 22/2) Liam Breslin

Placings:0/0601113654/2500212254/1321544000431314-2115000060 **(7858)**

2009: 7^{2}SD, 8^{1}SD, 8^{1}SD, 7^{5}SD, 7^{0}SD, 8^{0}SD, 8^{0}SD, 7^{0}SD, 7^{0}SD, 7^{6}SD, 8^{0}SD,

	Starts	1st	2nd	3rd	Win & Pl
Career Total (Turf)	**15**	**3**	**1**	**1**	**19448**
Career Total (AW)	**33**	**7**	**5**	**3**	**41766**

78 2/09 Ling 1m STD £1878
75 2/09 Ling 1m STD £2047
80 12/08 Ling 7f STD £1978
73 11/08 GrLe 1m STD £2590
94 3/08 Dund 1m H STD £12445
92 1/08 Kemp 1m STD £2047
91 7/07 Kemp 1m (0-80)H STD £4728
85 6/06 Newc 7f (0-75)H G-F £4857
77 6/06 Pont 6f (0-75)H G-F £4533
72 6/06 Hayd 1m30y (0-75)H G-F £3238

Total win prize-money £40347

Going (Turf): Sf: 0-1 GS: 0-5 Gd: 0-2 **GF: 3-7** Fm: 0-0
Distance: 5f/6f: 1-2 **7f-8f: 8-36** 9f-13f: 1-10 14f+: 0-0
Track : **LH: 6-28** RH: 2-15 **Tight: 3-13** Gall: 1-1
Aids: Bl: 0-0 Vi: 0-0 Tstrap: 0-0 Ckp: 0-0
Best Rating: **94** 3/08 Dund 1m stand

Fair; stays 1m, acts on fast ground and on Polytrack.

Electrolyser (IRE)

105(103) (90)102

4-y-o gr c Daylami (IRE)-Iviza (IRE) (Sadler's Wells (USA))

C G Cox Mr And Mrs P Hargreaves

Placings:21210-4510 **(6851)**

2009: 12^{4}GS, 16^{5}S, 16^{1}GF, 18^{0}G,

	Starts	1st	2nd	3rd	Win & Pl
Career Total (Turf)	**7**	**2**	**1**	**0**	**43822**
Career Total (AW)	**2**	**1**	**1**	**0**	**3025**

102 9/09 Asct 2m G-F £22708
99 10/08 Leic 1m3f183y (0-100)H SFT £11215
82 2/08 Ling 1m2f STD £2331

Total win prize-money £36256

Going (Turf): **Sf: 1-3** GS: 0-1 Gd: 0-1 **GF: 1-2** Fm: 0-0
Distance: 5f/6f: 0-0 7f-8f: 0-0 **9f-13f: 2-6** 14f+: 1-3
Track : LH: 1-5 **RH: 2-3** Tight: 1-2 Gall: 1-5
Aids: Bl: 0-0 Vi: 0-0 Tstrap: 0-0 Ckp: 0-0
Best Rating: **102** 9/09 Asct 2m gd-fm

Very useful; stays 2m; acts on fast and easy ground, and on Polytrack.

Elegant Dancer (IRE)

79 **47**

2-y-o ch f Choisir (AUS)-Sofistication (IRE) (Dayjur (USA))
Paul Green Derek A Howard

Placings:403 **(2161)**
2009: 5^{4}F, 5^{0}GF, 5^{3}GF,

	Starts	1st	2nd	3rd	Win & Pl
Career Total (Turf)	3	0	0	1	818

Going (Turf): **Sf: 0-0 GS: 0-0 Gd: 0-0 GF: 0-2 Fm: 0-1**
Distance: 5f/6f: 0-3 7f-8f: 0-0 9f-13f: 0-0 14f+: 0-0
Track : LH: 0-1 RH: 0-0 Tight: 0-0 Gall: 0-0
Aids: Bl: 0-0 Vi: 0-0 Tstrap: 0-0 Ckp: 0-0
Best Rating: **47** 5/09 Nott 5f13y gd-fm

Elements (IRE)

93(88) (46)**49**

3-y-o b f Rock Of Gibraltar (IRE)-Ghita (IRE) (Zilzal (USA))
E J Alston Mr & Mrs G Middlebrook

Placings:0-660000 **(6987)**
2009: 8^{6}HY, 7^{6}G, 8^{0}HY, 7^{0}S, 8^{0}SD, 9^{0}G,

	Starts	1st	2nd	3rd	Win & Pl
Career Total (Turf)	5	0	0	0	0
Career Total (AW)	2	0	0	0	

Going (Turf): **Sf: 0-3 GS: 0-0 Gd: 0-2 GF: 0-0 Fm: 0-0**
Distance: 5f/6f: 0-0 7f-8f: 0-3 9f-13f: 0-4 14f+: 0-0
Track : LH: 0-6 RH: 0-1 Tight: 0-5 Gall: 0-0
Aids: Bl: 0-0 Vi: 0-0 Tstrap: 0-0 Ckp: 0-0
Best Rating: **49** 9/09 Catt 7f soft

Elevate Bambina

(61) (1)**37**

3-y-o b f Spartacus (IRE)-Miri (IRE) (Sillery (USA))
A Berry Elevate Equestrian Ltd

Placings:000-6 **(0530)**
2009: 7^{6}SD,

	Starts	1st	2nd	3rd	Win & Pl
Career Total (Turf)	2	0	0	0	
Career Total (AW)	2	0	0	0	0

Going (Turf): **Sf: 0-2 GS: 0-0 Gd: 0-0 GF: 0-0 Fm: 0-0**
Distance: 5f/6f: 0-0 7f-8f: 0-4 9f-13f: 0-0 14f+: 0-0
Track : LH: 0-2 RH: 0-1 Tight: 0-1 Gall: 0-0
Aids: Bl: 0-0 Vi: 0-0 Tstrap: 0-0 Ckp: 0-0
Best Rating: **37** 9/08 Bevl 7f100y soft

Elevate Bobbob

(82) (29)

3-y-o b g Observatory (USA)-Grandma Lily (IRE) (Bigstone (IRE))
A Berry PCB Racing

Placings:00000 **(7796)**
2009: 8^{0}SD, 8^{0}SD, 7^{0}SD, 12^{0}SD, 7^{0}SS,

	Starts	1st	2nd	3rd	Win & Pl
Career Total (Turf)	0	0	0	0	
Career Total (AW)	5	0	0	0	

Going (Turf): **Sf: 0-0 GS: 0-0 Gd: 0-0 GF: 0-0 Fm: 0-0**
Distance: 5f/6f: 0-0 7f-8f: 0-3 9f-13f: 0-2 14f+: 0-0
Track : LH: 0-5 RH: 0-0 Tight: 0-2 Gall: 0-0
Aids: Bl: 0-0 Vi: 0-1 Tstrap: 0-0 Ckp: 0-0
Best Rating: **29** 12/09 Sthl 7f std-slw

Elhamri

99(106) (95)**94**

5-y-o b/br g Noverre (USA)-Seamstress (IRE) (Barathea (IRE))
S Kirk Liam Breslin

Placings:1611455/6050006/60104000100-0400000 **(4907)**
2009: 5^{0}GS, 5^{4}G, 5^{0}GF, 5^{0}GF, 5^{0}SD, 5^{0}G, 5^{0}G,

	Starts	1st	2nd	3rd	Win & Pl
Career Total (Turf)	29	4	0	0	134987
Career Total (AW)	4	1	0	0	8332

95	9/08	GrLe	5f	(0-95)H	STD	£7771
94	5/08	Gdwd	5f	(0-100)H	G-F	£10361
106	7/06	Newb	5f34y		GD	£76725
103	6/06	Asct	5f		G-F	£31229
82	4/06	Wind	5f10y		GD	£3886

Total win prize-money £129973

Going (Turf): Sf: 0-1 GS: 0-8 **Gd: 2-11 GF: 2-9** Fm: 0-0
Distance: **5f/6f: 5-32** 7f-8f: 0-1 9f-13f: 0-0 14f+: 0-0
Track : **LH: 1-6** RH: 0-1 Tight: 0-3 **Gall: 2-4**
Aids: Bl: 0-0 Vi: 0-0 Tstrap: 0-0 Ckp: 0-0
Best Rating: **106** 7/06 Newb 5f34y good

Useful; winner of the Windsor Castle Stakes and Weatherbys Super Sprint as a juvenile; suited by 5f; acts on a sound surface and on Polytrack.

Elie Shore

82(85) (54)**47**

2-y-o b f Tobougg (IRE)-Mitsuki (Puissance)
P C Haslam Middleham Park Racing Xvi

Placings:50000 **(7616)**
2009: 7^{5}GF, 8^{0}G, 8^{0}SD, 8^{0}GF, 8^{0}SD,

	Starts	1st	2nd	3rd	Win & Pl
Career Total (Turf)	3	0	0	0	0
Career Total (AW)	2	0	0	0	

Going (Turf): **Sf: 0-0 GS: 0-0 Gd: 0-1 GF: 0-2 Fm: 0-0**
Distance: 5f/6f: 0-0 7f-8f: 0-1 9f-13f: 0-4 14f+: 0-0
Track : LH: 0-3 RH: 0-1 Tight: 0-3 Gall: 0-0
Aids: Bl: 0-0 Vi: 0-3 Tstrap: 0-0 Ckp: 0-0
Best Rating: **54** 10/09 Wolv 1m141y stand

Elijah Pepper (USA)

109(104) (66)**74**

4-y-o ch g Crafty Prospector (USA)-Dovie Dee (USA) (Housebuster (USA))
T D Barron Wensleydale Bacon Limited

Placings:352015/531-165530005 **(7735)**
2009: 6^{1}GF, 6^{6}GF, 6^{5}GF, 6^{5}F, 6^{3}GF, 7^{0}G, 6^{0}GF, 6^{0}GF, 5^{5}SD,

	Starts	1st	2nd	3rd	Win & Pl
Career Total (Turf)	16	2	1	3	9699
Career Total (AW)	2	1	0	0	2218

74	5/09	Thsk	6f	(0-75)H	G-F	£4274
67	8/08	Pont	6f	(0-75)H	GD	£3885
76	10/07	Wolv	5f216y		STD	£2218

Total win prize-money £10378

Going (Turf): Sf: 0-0 GS: 0-2 **Gd: 1-3 GF: 1-10** Fm: 0-1
Distance: **5f/6f: 3-17** 7f-8f: 0-1 9f-13f: 0-0 14f+: 0-0
Track : **LH: 2-5** RH: 0-1 **Tight: 1-4** Gall: 0-1
Aids: Bl: 0-1 Vi: 0-0 Tstrap: 0-0 Ckp: 0-0
Best Rating: **76** 10/07 Wolv 5f216y stand

Fair; effective over 6f; acts on good and easy ground; also goes on Polytrack.

Elisiario (IRE)

79(107) (81)**38**

4-y-o b g Clodovil (IRE)-Kahla (Green Desert (USA))
J R Boyle John Hopkins, J-P Lim & keith Marsden

Placings:052-211260 **(4060)**
2009: 7^{2}SD, 7^{1}SD, 7^{1}SD, 8^{2}SD, 7^{6}SD, 8^{0}S,

	Starts	1st	2nd	3rd	Win & Pl
Career Total (Turf)	2	0	0	0	
Career Total (AW)	7	2	3	0	11738

80	4/09	Sthl	7f	(0-80)H	STD	£4857
74	3/09	Sthl	7f		STD	£3412

Total win prize-money £8269

Going (Turf): **Sf: 0-2 GS: 0-0 Gd: 0-0 GF: 0-0 Fm: 0-0**
Distance: 5f/6f: 0-0 **7f-8f: 2-9** 9f-13f: 0-0 14f+: 0-0
Track : **LH: 2-4** RH: 0-3 Tight: 0-1 Gall: 0-1
Aids: Bl: 0-0 Vi: 0-0 Tstrap: 0-0 Ckp: 0-0
Best Rating: **81** 5/09 Ling 1m stand

Fair; effective at up to a mile; handles Polytrack and Fibresand.

Elite Land

105(101) (69)**72**

6-y-o b g Namaqualand (USA)-Petite Elite (Anfield)
B Ellison Dan Gilbert

Placings:05000000/2045544200/0/51024162126332-45431 **(6102)**
2009: 12^{4}G, 13^{5}G, 12^{4}GF, 12^{3}GS, 13^{1}GF,

	Starts	1st	2nd	3rd	Win & Pl
Career Total (Turf)	36	4	5	2	14904
Career Total (AW)	2	0	1	1	907

71	9/09	Catt	1m5f175y (0-65)H	G-F	£2047
66	8/08	Catt	1m3f214y (0-75)H	G-S	£2498
58	7/08	Catt	1m3f214y	G-F	£2217
52	6/08	Ripn	1m4f10y (0-60)H	SFT	£2590

Total win prize-money £9353

Going (Turf): Sf: 1-2 GS: 1-5 Gd: 0-10 **GF: 2-17** Fm: 0-2
Distance: 5f/6f: 0-3 7f-8f: 0-6 **9f-13f: 3-24** 14f+: 1-5
Track : **LH: 3-18** RH: 1-15 **Tight: 4-21** Gall: 0-4
Aids: Bl: 0-5 Vi: 0-0 Tstrap: 0-1 Ckp: 0-1
Best Rating: **72** 9/08 Haml 1m5f9y gd-sft

Modest; stays 1m5f; acts on fast and soft ground; goes on Fibresand; has worn cheekpieces.

Eliza Doolittle

96(97) (64)**59**

3-y-o b f Royal Applause-Green Supreme (Primo Dominie)
J R Fanshawe Mrs C C Regalado-Gonzalez

Placings:64641 **(7051)**
2009: 6^{6}S, 6^{4}G, 5^{6}SD, 6^{4}GF, 7^{1}SD,

	Starts	1st	2nd	3rd	Win & Pl
Career Total (Turf)	3	0	0	0	375
Career Total (AW)	2	1	0	0	1706

64	10/09	Kemp	7f	(0-60)H	STD	£1706

Total win prize-money £1706

Going (Turf): **Sf: 0-1 GS: 0-0 Gd: 0-1 GF: 0-1 Fm: 0-0**
Distance: 5f/6f: 0-1 **7f-8f: 1-4** 9f-13f: 0-0 14f+: 0-0
Track : LH: 0-1 **RH: 1-1** Tight: 0-1 Gall: 0-0

Aids: Bl: 0-0 Vi: 0-0 Tstrap: 0-0 Ckp: 0-0
Best Rating: **64** 10/09 Kemp 7f stand

Moderate; stays 7f; acts on Polytrack.

Elizabelle (IRE)

88(80) (55)65
2-y-o b f Westerner-Jus'Chillin' (IRE) (Elbio)
R Hannon The Southside Partnership

Placings:0300 **(5589)**
2009: 6^{0}GF, 7^{3}GS, 7^{0}SD, 7^{0}GS,

	Starts	1st	2nd	3rd	Win & Pl
Career Total (Turf)	3	0	0	1	433
Career Total (AW)	1	0	0	0	

Going (Turf): **Sf: 0-0 GS: 0-2 Gd: 0-0 GF: 0-1 Fm: 0-0**
Distance: 5f/6f: 0-0 7f-8f: 0-4 9f-13f: 0-0 14f+: 0-0
Track : LH: 0-1 RH: 0-1 Tight: 0-1 Gall: 0-0
Aids: Bl: 0-0 Vi: 0-0 Tstrap: 0-0 Ckp: 0-0
Best Rating: **65** 7/09 Leic 7f9y gd-sft

Elizabeth's Quest

(86) (22)60
4-y-o b f Piccolo-Reina (Homeboy)
Miss N A Lloyd-Beavis Miss N A Lloyd-Beavis

Placings:5040/006000-00 **(7250)**
2009: 7^{0}SD, 10^{0}SD,

	Starts	1st	2nd	3rd	Win & Pl
Career Total (Turf)	6	0	0	0	337
Career Total (AW)	6	0	0	0	0

Going (Turf): **Sf: 0-1 GS: 0-0 Gd: 0-1 GF: 0-4 Fm: 0-0**
Distance: 5f/6f: 0-4 7f-8f: 0-5 9f-13f: 0-3 14f+: 0-0
Track : LH: 0-7 RH: 0-3 Tight: 0-5 Gall: 0-1
Aids: Bl: 0-0 Vi: 0-0 Tstrap: 0-2 Ckp: 0-2
Best Rating: **60** 8/07 Wind 6f good

Elk Trail (IRE)

91(100) (71)81
4-y-o ch g Captain Rio-Panpipes (USA) (Woodman (USA))
M Mullineaux (Mrs P Sly 9/12) Bluestone Partnership

Placings:6426/2363550002-4436 **(7247)**
2009: 8^{4}SS, 8^{4}SD, 12^{3}SD, 10^{6}S,

	Starts	1st	2nd	3rd	Win & Pl
Career Total (Turf)	13	0	2	2	3768
Career Total (AW)	5	0	1	1	1058

Going (Turf): **Sf: 0-2 GS: 0-0 Gd: 0-4 GF: 0-6 Fm: 0-1**
Distance: 5f/6f: 0-0 7f-8f: 0-7 9f-13f: 0-11 14f+: 0-0
Track : LH: 0-12 RH: 0-4 Tight: 0-6 Gall: 0-1
Aids: Bl: 0-1 Vi: 0-0 Tstrap: 0-0 Ckp: 0-0
Best Rating: **81** 7/08 Ripn 1m1f170y good

Modest; suited by 1m1f; acts on fast ground.

Elkhart Lake (IRE)

(96) (45)49
4-y-o b g Fath (USA)-Danny's Joy (IRE) (Maelstrom Lake)
Adrian McGuinness John G Daly

Placings:000005045-4000 **(6597a)**
2009: 7^{4}SD, 7^{0}SD, 6^{0}GY, 5^{0}GY,

	Starts	1st	2nd	3rd	Win & Pl
Career Total (Turf)	7	0	0	0	
Career Total (AW)	6	0	0	0	168

Going (Turf): **Sf: 0-1 GS: 0-0 Gd: 0-0 GF: 0-1 Fm: 0-2**
Distance: 5f/6f: 0-7 7f-8f: 0-5 9f-13f: 0-1 14f+: 0-0
Track : LH: 0-7 RH: 0-3 Tight: 0-3 Gall: 0-1
Aids: Bl: 0-2 Vi: 0-0 Tstrap: 0-0 Ckp: 0-0
Best Rating: **49** 5/08 Limk 7f50y firm

Plater; effective over 6f-7f; acts on Polytrack; has worn blinkers and a tongue tie.

Elkhorn

103(102) (67)68
7-y-o b g Indian Ridge-Rimba (USA) (Dayjur (USA))
Miss J A Camacho Lee Bolingbroke Racing 2

Placings:05400/00006430611110/0216204300/005050603-30003452024633 **(6926)**
2009: 5^{3}SD, 5^{0}SD, 6^{0}G, 5^{0}SD, 6^{3}GF, 6^{4}GF, 6^{5}G, 6^{2}GF, 6^{0}GF, 6^{2}GF, 6^{4}GS, 6^{6}GF, 6^{3}GF, 6^{3}GF,

	Starts	1st	2nd	3rd	Win & Pl
Career Total (Turf)	45	5	4	5	27929
Career Total (AW)	7	0	0	2	706

85	6/07	Haml	5f4y	(0-80)H	G-S	£6477
80	9/06	Rdcr	5f	(0-70)H	GD	£5181
66	9/06	Rdcr	6f	(0-65)H	FRM	£2388
72	9/06	Rdcr	6f	(0-70)H	G-F	£3238
62	8/06	Rdcr	6f	(0-65)H	GD	£2730

Total win prize-money £20017

Going (Turf): Sf: 0-4 GS: 1-8 **Gd: 2-19** GF: 1-13 Fm: 1-1
Distance: **5f/6f: 5-37** 7f-8f: 0-14 9f-13f: 0-1 14f+: 0-0
Track : LH: 0-11 RH: 0-2 Tight: 0-7 Gall: 0-4
Aids: **Bl: 5-29** Vi: 0-10 Tstrap: 0-5 Ckp: 0-5
Best Rating: **89** 7/07 Newc 5f good

Modest; effective at 5f-6f; acts on good and easier ground; goes on Polytrack; often wears blinkers; can miss the break.

Ella

106(95) (73)96
5-y-o b m Pivotal-Flossy (Efisio)
G A Swinbank Guy Reed

Placings:035311-0433 **(7293)**
2009: 12^{0}SD, 9^{4}GS, 10^{3}S, 12^{3}S,

	Starts	1st	2nd	3rd	Win & Pl
Career Total (Turf)	7	2	0	3	32061
Career Total (AW)	3	0	0	1	363

95	7/08	York	1m4f	(0-100)H	HVY	£11656
85	4/08	Pont	1m2f6y	(0-90)H	HVY	£9346

Total win prize-money £21004

Going (Turf): **Sf: 2-5** GS: 0-1 Gd: 0-1 GF: 0-0 Fm: 0-0
Distance: 5f/6f: 0-0 7f-8f: 0-1 **9f-13f: 2-9** 14f+: 0-0
Track : **LH: 2-7** RH: 0-3 Tight: 0-3 **Gall: 1-2**
Aids: Bl: 0-0 Vi: 0-0 Tstrap: 0-0 Ckp: 0-0
Best Rating: **96** 11/09 Donc 1m4f soft

Very useful; stays 1m4f, but effective over shorter; acts well on soft ground.

Ella Grace (USA)

94 65
2-y-o b/br f Broken Vow (USA)-Shy Swan (USA) (Nureyev (USA))
R A Fahey Matt Morgan & Lauren Stapley

Placings:40024 **(6391)**
2009: 5^{4}GF, 6^{0}S, 6^{0}GF, 8^{2}GF, 10^{4}GF,

	Starts	1st	2nd	3rd	Win & Pl
Career Total (Turf)	5	0	1	0	1059

Going (Turf): **Sf: 0-1 GS: 0-0 Gd: 0-0 GF: 0-4 Fm: 0-0**
Distance: 5f/6f: 0-3 7f-8f: 0-1 9f-13f: 0-1 14f+: 0-0
Track : LH: 0-1 RH: 0-0 Tight: 0-0 Gall: 0-0
Aids: Bl: 0-0 Vi: 0-0 Tstrap: 0-0 Ckp: 0-0
Best Rating: **65** 9/09 Rdcr 1m gd-fm

Ella Woodcock (IRE)

102(104) (71)86
5-y-o b g Daggers Drawn (USA)-Hollow Haze (USA) (Woodman (USA))
E J Alston (C Grant 27/4) Derrick Mossop

Placings:000/2332111122/0000604242000-300063056215 **(7798)**
2009: 12^{3}GF, 8^{0}S, 8^{0}GF, 9^{0}G, 13^{6}GF, 8^{3}GF, 9^{0}SD, 8^{5}SD, 8^{6}SD, 8^{2}SD, 9^{1}SD, 9^{5}SS,

	Starts	1st	2nd	3rd	Win & Pl
Career Total (Turf)	29	4	5	2	28222
Career Total (AW)	9	1	2	2	6262

71	12/09	Wolv	1m1f103y	(0-75)H	STD	£3885
75	9/07	Haml	1m1f36y		GD	£5181
83	9/07	Yarm	1m3y		GD	£4731
77	9/07	Ripn	1m	(0-70)H	G-F	£3886
74	8/07	Folk	7f	(0-75)H	G-S	£3238

Total win prize-money £20925

Going (Turf): Sf: 0-3 GS: 1-4 **Gd: 2-10** GF: 1-11 Fm: 0-1
Distance: 5f/6f: 0-3 7f-8f: 2-9 **9f-13f: 3-25** 14f+: 0-1
Track : LH: 1-26 **RH: 2-7 Tight: 3-16** Gall: 0-6
Aids: Bl: 0-6 Vi: 0-0 Tstrap: 0-7 Ckp: 0-7
Best Rating: **92** 10/07 Donc 1m2f60y good

Modest; stays 1m2f; acts on most ground; goes on Polytrack; has worn blinkers and cheekpieces.

Ellbeedee (IRE)

86 56
2-y-o b f Dalakhani (IRE)-Tochar Ban (USA) (Assert)
M A Jarvis Stephen Dartnell

Placings:0 **(6992)**
2009: 8^{0}GS,

	Starts	1st	2nd	3rd	Win & Pl
Career Total (Turf)	1	0	0	0	

Going (Turf): **Sf: 0-0 GS: 0-1 Gd: 0-0 GF: 0-0 Fm: 0-0**
Distance: 5f/6f: 0-0 7f-8f: 0-1 9f-13f: 0-0 14f+: 0-0
Track : LH: 0-1 RH: 0-0 Tight: 0-0 Gall: 0-1
Aids: Bl: 0-0 Vi: 0-0 Tstrap: 0-0 Ckp: 0-0
Best Rating: **56** 10/09 Donc 1m gd-sft

Ellemujie

107(103) (91)96
4-y-o b g Mujahid (USA)-Jennelle (Nomination)
D K Ivory Mrs J A Cornwell & John G Smith

Placings:01032635034/03323232654-451000045006 **(6973)**
2009: 8^{4}G, 8^{5}GF, 8^{1}GF, 8^{0}GF, 8^{0}G, 8^{0}G, 8^{0}GF, 10^{4}GF, 8^{5}GF, 8^{0}GF, 9^{0}GF, 10^{0}SD,

	Starts	1st	2nd	3rd	Win & Pl
Career Total (Turf)	28	1	4	5	33468

	Starts	1st	2nd	3rd	Win & Pl
Career Total (AW)	6	1	0	2	4898

96 6/09 Sand 1m14y (0-90)H G-F £7771
77 6/07 Kemp 6f STD £2914
Total win prize-money £10686

Going (Turf): Sf: 0-1 GS: 0-2 Gd: 0-8 **GF: 1-17** Fm: 0-0
Distance: 5f/6f: 1-5 7f-8f: 0-17 9f-13f: 1-12 14f+: 0-0
Track : LH: 0-4 **RH: 2-13** Tight: 0-5 Gall: 0-3
Aids: Bl: 0-0 Vi: 0-0 Tstrap: 0-0 Ckp: 0-0
Best Rating: **96** 6/09 Sand 1m14y gd-fm

Useful; effective from 1m-1m2f; acts on good and faster ground and on Polytrack.

Ellen Vannin (IRE)

92(88) (54)**55**
2-y-o ch f Tagula (IRE)-Felin Special (Lyphard's Special (USA))
Eve Johnson Houghton Mrs J E O'Halloran

Placings:6000 **(6905)**
2009: 6^{6}GF, 7^{0}G, 7^{0}SD, 6^{0}G,

	Starts	1st	2nd	3rd	Win & Pl
Career Total (Turf)	3	0	0	0	0
Career Total (AW)	1	0	0	0	

Going (Turf): **Sf: 0-0 GS: 0-0 Gd: 0-2 GF: 0-1 Fm: 0-0**
Distance: 5f/6f: 0-2 7f-8f: 0-2 9f-13f: 0-0 14f+: 0-0
Track : LH: 0-2 RH: 0-0 Tight: 0-1 Gall: 0-1
Aids: Bl: 0-0 Vi: 0-0 Tstrap: 0-0 Ckp: 0-0
Best Rating: **55** 8/09 Wwck 7f26y good

Ellies Image

82(69) (24)**47**
2-y-o b f Lucky Story (USA)-Crown City (USA) (Coronado's Quest (USA))
B P J Baugh F Gillespie

Placings:0000 **(5839)**
2009: 5^{0}GF, 7^{0}SD, 7^{0}GF, 8^{0}SD,

	Starts	1st	2nd	3rd	Win & Pl
Career Total (Turf)	2	0	0	0	
Career Total (AW)	2	0	0	0	

Going (Turf): **Sf: 0-0 GS: 0-0 Gd: 0-0 GF: 0-2 Fm: 0-0**
Distance: 5f/6f: 0-1 7f-8f: 0-2 9f-13f: 0-1 14f+: 0-0
Track : LH: 0-2 RH: 0-0 Tight: 0-2 Gall: 0-0
Aids: Bl: 0-0 Vi: 0-0 Tstrap: 0-0 Ckp: 0-0
Best Rating: **47** 8/09 Rdcr 7f gd-fm

Ellies Inspiration

59
4-y-o b f Puissance-Star View Lady (Precocious)
M Mullineaux Michael Mullineaux

Placings:000 **(2446)**
2009: 6^{0}F, 8^{0}HY, 8^{0}GS,

	Starts	1st	2nd	3rd	Win & Pl
Career Total (Turf)	3	0	0	0	

Going (Turf): **Sf: 0-1 GS: 0-1 Gd: 0-0 GF: 0-0 Fm: 0-1**
Distance: 5f/6f: 0-1 7f-8f: 0-0 9f-13f: 0-2 14f+: 0-0
Track : LH: 0-3 RH: 0-0 Tight: 0-0 Gall: 0-0
Aids: Bl: 0-0 Vi: 0-0 Tstrap: 0-0 Ckp: 0-0

Elliptical (USA)

104(98) (84)**93**
3-y-o b g Arch (USA)-Citidance Missy (USA) (Citidancer (USA))
G A Butler Keen As Mustard

Placings:53-101360 **(6795)**
2009: 9^{1}G, 10^{0}G, 8^{1}S, 7^{3}GF, 8^{6}SD, 10^{0}S,

	Starts	1st	2nd	3rd	Win & Pl
Career Total (Turf)	5	2	0	1	9443
Career Total (AW)	3	0	0	1	571

93 7/09 Sals 1m (0-85)H SFT £4857
82 5/09 Gdwd 1m1f192y GD £3238
Total win prize-money £8095

Going (Turf): **Sf: 1-2** GS: 0-0 **Gd: 1-2** GF: 0-1 Fm: 0-0
Distance: 5f/6f: 0-0 7f-8f: 1-4 9f-13f: 1-4 14f+: 0-0
Track : LH: 0-4 **RH: 1-2 Tight: 1-3** Gall: 0-1
Aids: Bl: 0-0 Vi: 0-0 Tstrap: 0-1 Ckp: 0-1
Best Rating: **93** 7/09 Sals 1m soft

Useful; stays 1m2f; acts on good and softer ground and on Polytrack.

Elliwan

88(103) (65)**77**
4-y-o b g Nayef (USA)-Ashbilya (USA) (Nureyev (USA))
M W Easterby Two Old Pals

Placings:03/20**600006-6134**00 **(7499)**
2009: **10**^{6}SD, **12**^{1}SD, **11**^{3}SD, **11**^{4}SD, 12^{0}GS, **8**^{0}SD,

	Starts	1st	2nd	3rd	Win & Pl
Career Total (Turf)	5	0	1	1	1223
Career Total (AW)	11	1	0	1	2336

65 3/09 Sthl 1m4f (0-55)H STD £2047
Total win prize-money £2047

Going (Turf): **Sf: 0-1 GS: 0-1 Gd: 0-1 GF: 0-2 Fm: 0-0**
Distance: 5f/6f: 0-0 7f-8f: 0-4 **9f-13f: 1-12** 14f+: 0-0
Track : **LH: 1-15** RH: 0-1 Tight: 0-7 Gall: 0-1
Aids: **Bl: 1-6** Vi: 0-0 Tstrap: 0-0 Ckp: 0-0
Best Rating: **77** 6/08 Rdcr 1m2f gd-fm

Moderate; stays 1m4f; acts on fast ground and on Fibresand; has worn blinkers.

Ellmau

106(111) (89)**91**
4-y-o ch g Dr Fong (USA)-Triple Sharp (Selkirk (USA))
E S McMahon (A J McCabe 26/6) Premspace Ltd

Placings:1350/**64405510-0**04414 **(7018)**
2009: **10**^{0}SD, 10^{0}G, 10^{4}GF, 10^{4}GF, 10^{1}GS, 12^{4}GS,

	Starts	1st	2nd	3rd	Win & Pl
Career Total (Turf)	12	1	0	1	20330
Career Total (AW)	6	2	0	0	8012

90 10/09 Nott 1m2f50y (0-85)H G-S £6476
89 10/08 Sthl 1m3f (0-85)H STD £5828
76 5/07 Sthl 6f STD £2184
Total win prize-money £14488

Going (Turf): Sf: 0-2 **GS: 1-2** Gd: 0-2 GF: 0-6 Fm: 0-0
Distance: 5f/6f: 1-1 7f-8f: 0-3 **9f-13f: 2-14** 14f+: 0-0
Track : **LH: 3-11** RH: 0-5 Tight: 0-4 Gall: 0-4
Aids: Bl: 0-0 Vi: 0-0 Tstrap: 0-0 Ckp: 0-0
Best Rating: **100** 7/07 NmkJ 7f gd-fm

Very useful; Group placed at two; stays 1m4f; acts on fast and soft ground; goes on Fibresand.

Ellmollell

85(84) (48)**42**
2-y-o b f Piccolo-Runs In The Family (Distant Relative)
S Kirk The Sweet Peas

Placings:00050000 **(7706)**
2009: 5^{0}G, 5^{0}GF, 6^{0}SD, 5^{5}G, 6^{0}G, 7^{0}SD, 8^{0}SD, 8^{0}SD,

	Starts	1st	2nd	3rd	Win & Pl
Career Total (Turf)	4	0	0	0	0
Career Total (AW)	4	0	0	0	

Going (Turf): **Sf: 0-0 GS: 0-0 Gd: 0-3 GF: 0-1 Fm: 0-0**
Distance: 5f/6f: 0-4 7f-8f: 0-3 9f-13f: 0-1 14f+: 0-0
Track : LH: 0-3 RH: 0-1 Tight: 0-2 Gall: 0-2
Aids: Bl: 0-0 Vi: 0-0 Tstrap: 0-0 Ckp: 0-0
Best Rating: **48** 7/09 Kemp 6f stand

Has shown signs of minor ability.

Elmfield Giant (USA)

95(88) (68)**78**
2-y-o ch g Giant's Causeway (USA)-Princess Atoosa (USA) (Gone West (USA))
R A Fahey Mike Browne

Placings:0624 **(5371)**
2009: 6^{0}S, 7^{6}GF, 7^{2}GF, 8^{4}SD,

	Starts	1st	2nd	3rd	Win & Pl
Career Total (Turf)	3	0	1	0	964
Career Total (AW)	1	0	0	0	313

Going (Turf): **Sf: 0-1 GS: 0-0 Gd: 0-0 GF: 0-2 Fm: 0-0**
Distance: 5f/6f: 0-1 7f-8f: 0-3 9f-13f: 0-0 14f+: 0-0
Track : LH: 0-1 RH: 0-1 Tight: 0-0 Gall: 0-0
Aids: Bl: 0-0 Vi: 0-0 Tstrap: 0-0 Ckp: 0-0
Best Rating: **78** 8/09 Newc 7f gd-fm

Elms School Story

90 **37**
3-y-o b f Lucky Story (USA)-Elms Schoolgirl (Emarati (USA))
Miss Venetia Williams Elms School Racing

Placings:0 **(5531)**
2009: 10^{0}G,

	Starts	1st	2nd	3rd	Win & Pl
Career Total (Turf)	1	0	0	0	

Going (Turf): **Sf: 0-0 GS: 0-0 Gd: 0-1 GF: 0-0 Fm: 0-0**
Distance: 5f/6f: 0-0 7f-8f: 0-0 9f-13f: 0-1 14f+: 0-0
Track : LH: 0-1 RH: 0-0 Tight: 0-0 Gall: 0-0
Aids: Bl: 0-0 Vi: 0-0 Tstrap: 0-0 Ckp: 0-0
Best Rating: **37** 8/09 Wwck 1m2f188y good

Elna Bright

107(110) (99)**93**
4-y-o b g Elnadim (USA)-Acicula (IRE) (Night Shift (USA))
B R Johnson (P D Evans 29/7) Peter Crate

Placings:3211602/**2**05-**3**1605142**2**03210**410** **(7827)**
2009: **8**^{3}SD, 8^{1}GF, 8^{6}G, 7^{0}GF, 8^{5}GF, 6^{1}GF, 7^{4}GF, 6^{2}GF, **8**^{2}SD, 7^{0}G, 8^{3}G, 7^{2}GF, 8^{1}GF, 10^{0}GF, **10**^{4}SD, **7**^{1}SD, **8**^{0}SD,

	Starts	1st	2nd	3rd	Win & Pl
Career Total (Turf)	21	5	4	2	43507

	Starts	1st	2nd	3rd	Win & Pl
Career Total (AW)	6	1	2	1	16117

99	11/09	Ling	7f	(0-100)H	STD	£11527
93	9/09	Asct	1m	(0-100)H	G-F	£12462
82	6/09	Sals	6f212y		G-F	£3238
93	4/09	Bath	1m5y		G-F	£8418
86	7/07	NmkJ	7f		G-F	£6477
70	6/07	Brig	5f213y		FRM	£2914

Total win prize-money £45038

Going (Turf): Sf: 0-1 GS: 0-0 Gd: 0-7 **GF: 4-12** Fm: 1-1
Distance: 5f/6f: 1-4 **7f-8f: 4-17** 9f-13f: 1-6 14f+: 0-0
Track : **LH: 3-12** RH: 0-6 **Tight: 2-7** Gall: 0-2
Aids: Bl: 0-0 Vi: 0-0 Tstrap: 0-0 Ckp: 0-0
Best Rating: **99** 11/09 Ling 7f stand

Useful; effective over 6f-1m; acts on fast ground; goes on Polytrack.

Elnawin

100(106) (108)**104**
3-y-o b c Elnadim (USA)-Acicula (IRE) (Night Shift (USA))
R Hannon Noodles Racing

Placings:4111-255 **(2035)**
2009: 7^{2}SD, 6^{5}GF, 6^{5}G,

	Starts	1st	2nd	3rd	Win & Pl
Career Total (Turf)	5	2	0	0	167043
Career Total (AW)	2	1	1	0	41297

108	9/08	Kemp	6f	STD	£28385
104	8/08	NmkJ	6f	GD	£160620
85	7/08	Sals	6f	G-F	£3885

Total win prize-money £192892

Going (Turf): Sf: 0-0 GS: 0-0 **Gd: 1-2 GF: 1-3** Fm: 0-0
Distance: **5f/6f: 3-5** 7f-8f: 0-2 9f-13f: 0-0 14f+: 0-0
Track : LH: 0-1 **RH: 1-1** Tight: 0-1 Gall: 0-0
Aids: Bl: 0-0 Vi: 0-0 Tstrap: 0-0 Ckp: 0-0
Best Rating: **108** 9/08 Kemp 6f stand

Smart; winner in Group 3 company; effective over 6f; acts on a sound surface; goes on Polytrack.

Eloise

91(97) (56)**39**
3-y-o ch f Hernando (FR)-Eternelle (Green Desert (USA))
Sir Mark Prescott Miss K Rausing

Placings:50016 **(5812)**
2009: 12^{5}SD, 11^{0}SD, 12^{0}G, 11^{1}SD, 16^{6}SD,

	Starts	1st	2nd	3rd	Win & Pl
Career Total (Turf)	1	0	0	0	
Career Total (AW)	4	1	0	0	2072

56	8/09	Sthl	1m3f	(0-50)H	STD	£2072

Total win prize-money £2072

Going (Turf): **Sf: 0-0 GS: 0-0 Gd: 0-1 GF: 0-0 Fm: 0-0**
Distance: 5f/6f: 0-0 7f-8f: 0-0 **9f-13f: 1-4** 14f+: 0-1
Track : **LH: 1-4** RH: 0-1 Tight: 0-1 Gall: 0-0
Aids: **Bl: 1-2** Vi: 0-0 Tstrap: 0-0 Ckp: 0-0
Best Rating: **56** 8/09 Sthl 1m3f stand

Moderate; stays 1m3f and acts on Fibresand; has worn blinkers.

Elsie Jo (IRE)

(98) (56)**42**
3-y-o b f Catcher In The Rye (IRE)-Joy St Clair (IRE) (Try My Best (USA))
M Wigham E J Evans

Placings:060-230 **(0831)**
2009: 7^{2}SD, 7^{3}SD, 5^{0}SD,

	Starts	1st	2nd	3rd	Win & Pl
Career Total (Turf)	2	0	0	0	
Career Total (AW)	4	0	1	1	907

Going (Turf): **Sf: 0-0 GS: 0-0 Gd: 0-1 GF: 0-1 Fm: 0-0**
Distance: 5f/6f: 0-4 7f-8f: 0-2 9f-13f: 0-0 14f+: 0-0
Track : LH: 0-4 RH: 0-0 Tight: 0-3 Gall: 0-1
Aids: Bl: 0-0 Vi: 0-0 Tstrap: 0-0 Ckp: 0-0
Best Rating: **56** 2/09 Ling 7f stand

Moderate; effective over 7f; acts on Polytrack.

Elsie's Orphan

(94) (59)
2-y-o br f Pastoral Pursuits-Elsie Plunkett (Mind Games)
P R Chamings Mrs J E L Wright

Placings:06 **(6582)**
2009: 6^{0}SD, 5^{6}SD,

	Starts	1st	2nd	3rd	Win & Pl
Career Total (Turf)	0	0	0	0	
Career Total (AW)	2	0	0	0	0

Going (Turf): **Sf: 0-0 GS: 0-0 Gd: 0-0 GF: 0-0 Fm: 0-0**
Distance: 5f/6f: 0-2 7f-8f: 0-0 9f-13f: 0-0 14f+: 0-0
Track : LH: 0-0 RH: 0-2 Tight: 0-0 Gall: 0-0
Aids: Bl: 0-0 Vi: 0-0 Tstrap: 0-0 Ckp: 0-0
Best Rating: **59** 10/09 Kemp 5f stand

Elspeth's Boy (USA)

(107) (80)
2-y-o b/br c Tiznow (USA)-Miss Waki Club (USA) (Miswaki (USA))
J R Best D Gorton

Placings:1 **(7209)**
2009: 7^{1}SD,

	Starts	1st	2nd	3rd	Win & Pl
Career Total (Turf)	0	0	0	0	
Career Total (AW)	1	1	0	0	3238

80	11/09	Wolv	7f32y	STD	£3238

Total win prize-money £3238

Going (Turf): **Sf: 0-0 GS: 0-0 Gd: 0-0 GF: 0-0 Fm: 0-0**
Distance: 5f/6f: 0-0 **7f-8f: 1-1** 9f-13f: 0-0 14f+: 0-0
Track : **LH: 1-1** RH: 0-0 **Tight: 1-1** Gall: 0-0
Aids: Bl: 0-0 Vi: 0-0 Tstrap: 0-0 Ckp: 0-0
Best Rating: **80** 11/09 Wolv 7f32y stand

Winner on debut; effective over 7f; acts on Polytrack.

Eltheeb

96 **66**
2-y-o gr c Red Ransom (USA)-Snowdrops (Gulch (USA))
J L Dunlop Hamdan Al Maktoum

Placings:0003 **(6965)**
2009: 7^{0}G, 7^{0}GS, 8^{0}GS, 7^{3}G,

	Starts	1st	2nd	3rd	Win & Pl
Career Total (Turf)	4	0	0	1	816

Going (Turf): **Sf: 0-0 GS: 0-2 Gd: 0-2 GF: 0-0 Fm: 0-0**
Distance: 5f/6f: 0-0 7f-8f: 0-3 9f-13f: 0-1 14f+: 0-0
Track : LH: 0-2 RH: 0-0 Tight: 0-0 Gall: 0-0
Aids: Bl: 0-0 Vi: 0-0 Tstrap: 0-0 Ckp: 0-0
Best Rating: **66** 10/09 Brig 7f214y good

Elusive Award (USA)

79 (99)**81**
2-y-o b c Elusive Quality (USA)-Victoria Cross (IRE) (Mark Of Esteem (IRE))
Andrew Oliver Peter Thomas

Placings:110 **(7017)**
2009: 7^{1}G, 7^{1}SD, 8^{0}GS,

	Starts	1st	2nd	3rd	Win & Pl
Career Total (Turf)	2	1	0	0	11740
Career Total (AW)	1	1	0	0	11405

99	9/09	Dund	7f	STD	£11404
81	8/09	Leop	7f	GD	£11740

Total win prize-money £23145

Going (Turf): Sf: 0-0 GS: 0-1 **Gd: 1-1** GF: 0-0 Fm: 0-0
Distance: 5f/6f: 0-0 **7f-8f: 2-3** 9f-13f: 0-0 14f+: 0-0
Track : **LH: 2-2** RH: 0-0 Tight: 0-0 Gall: 0-0
Aids: Bl: 0-0 Vi: 0-0 Tstrap: 0-0 Ckp: 0-0
Best Rating: **99** 9/09 Dund 7f stand

Very useful; stays 7f; acts on good ground and on Polytrack.

Elusive Dreams (USA)

(103) (67)**70**
5-y-o ch g Elusive Quality (USA)-Bally Five (USA) (Miswaki (USA))
P Howling The Circle Bloodstock I Limited

Placings:50100/500620224063-0020 **(0946)**
2009: 6^{0}SD, 6^{0}SD, 6^{2}SD, 6^{0}SD,

	Starts	1st	2nd	3rd	Win & Pl
Career Total (Turf)	4	1	1	0	5532
Career Total (AW)	17	0	3	1	2217

65	8/07	Sals	6f212y	G-S	£4857

Total win prize-money £4858

Going (Turf): Sf: 0-0 **GS: 1-2** Gd: 0-0 GF: 0-2 Fm: 0-0
Distance: 5f/6f: 0-9 **7f-8f: 1-12** 9f-13f: 0-0 14f+: 0-0
Track : LH: 0-13 RH: 0-4 Tight: 0-11 Gall: 0-1
Aids: Bl: 0-0 Vi: 0-9 Tstrap: 0-0 Ckp: 0-0
Best Rating: **71** 9/07 Ling 1m stand

Moderate; effective over 6f-7f; acts on Polytrack.

Elusive Fame (USA)

91(105) (81)**68**
3-y-o b g Elusive Quality (USA)-Advancing Star (USA) (Soviet Star (USA))
M Johnston Mark Johnston Racing Ltd

Placings:1-005001616000010363 **(7854)**
2009: 6^{0}GF, 7^{0}GS, 6^{5}GF, 7^{0}GF, 6^{0}GF, 6^{1}SD, 6^{6}SD, 7^{1}SD, 7^{6}SD, 8^{0}SD, 7^{0}SD, 8^{0}SD, 8^{0}SF, 7^{0}SD, 8^{1}SD, 8^{0}SD, 8^{3}SD, 8^{6}SD, 8^{3}SS,

	Starts	1st	2nd	3rd	Win & Pl
Career Total (Turf)	5	0	0	0	0
Career Total (AW)	15	4	0	2	15541

79	11/09	Sthl	1m	(0-70)H	STD	£2729
78	8/09	Sthl	7f	(0-80)H	STD	£5180
76	7/09	Sthl	6f	(0-70)H	STD	£2729
81	11/08	Wolv	7f32y		STD	£4094

Total win prize-money £14735

Going (Turf): **Sf: 0-0 GS: 0-1 Gd: 0-0 GF: 0-4 Fm: 0-0**
Distance: 5f/6f: 1-4 **7f-8f: 3-15** 9f-13f: 0-1 14f+: 0-0
Track : **LH: 4-13** RH: 0-3 **Tight: 1-5** Gall: 0-0
Aids: **Bl: 2-12** Vi: 0-1 Tstrap: 0-0 Ckp: 0-0

Best Rating: **81** 11/08 Wolv 7f32y stand

Fair; effective over 6f-1m; acts on Fibresand and Polytrack; has worn blinkers.

Elusive Glen (IRE)

(89) (49)

3-y-o b c Elusive City (USA)-Glenarff (USA) (Irish River (FR))

M Johnston Douglas Livingston

Placings:5P (1474)

2009: 8^{5}SD, 8^{P}GF,

	Starts	1st	2nd	3rd	Win & Pl
Career Total (Turf)	1	0	0	0	
Career Total (AW)	1	0	0	0	0

Going (Turf): **Sf: 0-0 GS: 0-0 Gd: 0-0 GF: 0-1 Fm: 0-0**
Distance: 5f/6f: 0-0 7f-8f: 0-1 9f-13f: 0-1 14f+: 0-0
Track : LH: 0-1 RH: 0-1 Tight: 0-0 Gall: 0-0
Aids: Bl: 0-0 Vi: 0-0 Tstrap: 0-0 Ckp: 0-0
Best Rating: **49** 3/09 Sthl 1m stand

Elusive Hawk (IRE)

96(109) (83)73

5-y-o b g Noverre (USA)-Two Clubs (First Trump)

B J Curley (A P Stringer 13/1) Curley Leisure

Placings:5/01100065-22631050 (7758)

2009: 6^{2}SD, 7^{2}G, 7^{6}GF, 6^{3}SD, 6^{1}SD, 5^{0}G, 6^{5}SD, 5^{0}SD,

	Starts	1st	2nd	3rd	Win & Pl
Career Total (Turf)	6	0	1	0	655
Career Total (AW)	11	3	1	1	9090
83 7/09 Sthl 6f	(0-75)H			STD	£2729
80 7/08 Sthl 6f	(0-70)H			STD	£2729
71 2/08 Sthl 6f				STD	£2457

Total win prize-money £7917

Going (Turf): **Sf: 0-3 GS: 0-0 Gd: 0-2 GF: 0-1 Fm: 0-0**
Distance: **5f/6f: 3-12** 7f-8f: 0-5 9f-13f: 0-0 14f+: 0-0
Track : **LH: 3-12** RH: 0-0 Tight: 0-2 Gall: 0-1
Aids: Bl: 0-0 Vi: 0-0 Tstrap: 0-0 Ckp: 0-0
Best Rating: **83** 7/09 Sthl 6f stand

Fair; suited by 6f-7f; acts on good ground and on Fibresand.

Elusive Muse

89 56

3-y-o ch g Exit To Nowhere (USA)-Dance A Dream (Sadler's Wells (USA))

M Dods Mould Pritchard & Woodhouse

Placings:5640 (5442)

2009: 8^{5}GF, 8^{6}G, 11^{4}GF, 14^{0}GF,

	Starts	1st	2nd	3rd	Win & Pl
Career Total (Turf)	4	0	0	0	241

Going (Turf): **Sf: 0-0 GS: 0-0 Gd: 0-1 GF: 0-3 Fm: 0-0**
Distance: 5f/6f: 0-0 7f-8f: 0-1 9f-13f: 0-2 14f+: 0-1
Track : LH: 0-3 RH: 0-1 Tight: 0-3 Gall: 0-0
Aids: Bl: 0-0 Vi: 0-0 Tstrap: 0-0 Ckp: 0-0
Best Rating: **56** 4/09 Ripn 1m gd-fm

Elusive Pimpernel (USA)

111 115

2-y-o b/br c Elusive Quality (USA)-Cara Fantasy (IRE) (Sadler's Wells (USA))

J L Dunlop Windflower Overseas Holdings Inc

Placings:112 (7017)

2009: 7^{1}G, 7^{1}GF, 8^{2}GS,

	Starts	1st	2nd	3rd	Win & Pl
Career Total (Turf)	3	2	1	0	82384
109 8/09 York 7f			G-F		£29630
89 7/09 NmkJ 7f			GD		£9714

Total win prize-money £39344

Going (Turf): Sf: 0-0 GS: 0-1 **Gd: 1-1 GF: 1-1** Fm: 0-0
Distance: 5f/6f: 0-0 **7f-8f: 2-3** 9f-13f: 0-0 14f+: 0-0
Track : **LH: 1-1** RH: 0-0 Tight: 0-0 **Gall: 1-1**
Aids: Bl: 0-0 Vi: 0-0 Tstrap: 0-0 Ckp: 0-0
Best Rating: **115** 10/09 Donc 1m gd-sft

Group class; winner of the Group 3 Acomb Stakes and runner-up in the Group 1 Racing Post Trophy at two; stays 1m and acts on most ground.

Elusive Ronnie (IRE)

84(100) (65)57

3-y-o b g One Cool Cat (USA)-Elusive Kitty (USA) (Elusive Quality (USA))

R A Teal R J Ryan

Placings:002045505512-50353400012200 (7890)

2009: 6^{5}SD, 6^{0}SD, 5^{3}SD, 6^{5}SD, 7^{3}SD, 7^{4}G, 5^{0}F, 5^{0}GF, 7^{0}SD, 5^{1}SD, 6^{2}SD, 6^{2}SD, 6^{0}SD, 6^{0}SD,

	Starts	1st	2nd	3rd	Win & Pl
Career Total (Turf)	9	0	1	0	742
Career Total (AW)	17	2	3	2	6303
56 11/09 Kemp 5f	(0-50)H			STD	£2047
59 12/08 Ling 6f				STD	£1978

Total win prize-money £4026

Going (Turf): **Sf: 0-1 GS: 0-1 Gd: 0-1 GF: 0-5 Fm: 0-1**
Distance: **5f/6f: 2-21** 7f-8f: 0-5 9f-13f: 0-0 14f+: 0-0
Track : LH: 1-15 RH: 1-4 **Tight: 1-12** Gall: 0-1
Aids: Bl: 1-6 Vi: 0-0 Tstrap: 1-15 Ckp: 1-15
Best Rating: **65** 11/09 Ling 6f stand

Moderate; stays 6f; acts on most ground and on Polytrack; has worn cheekpieces and blinkers.

Elusive Style (IRE)

83 38

3-y-o b f Elusive City (USA)-Brooklands Lodge (USA) (Grand Lodge (USA))

S P Griffiths Ms Elizabeth Grant

Placings:003000 (7219)

2009: 7^{0}GF, 8^{0}G, 7^{3}GS, 8^{0}HY, 10^{0}GF, 5^{0}S,

	Starts	1st	2nd	3rd	Win & Pl
Career Total (Turf)	6	0	0	1	353

Going (Turf): **Sf: 0-2 GS: 0-1 Gd: 0-1 GF: 0-2 Fm: 0-0**
Distance: 5f/6f: 0-1 7f-8f: 0-3 9f-13f: 0-2 14f+: 0-0
Track : LH: 0-3 RH: 0-1 Tight: 0-4 Gall: 0-0
Aids: Bl: 0-0 Vi: 0-0 Tstrap: 0-0 Ckp: 0-0
Best Rating: **38** 7/09 Catt 7f gd-sft

Elusive Sue (USA)

100 76

2-y-o b/br f Elusive Quality (USA)-Show Me The Stage (USA) (Slew The Surgeon (USA))

R A Fahey P D Smith Holdings Ltd

Placings:02201 (5958)

2009: 5^{0}GS, 5^{2}GF, 6^{2}GF, 6^{0}GF, 6^{1}GF,

	Starts	1st	2nd	3rd	Win & Pl
Career Total (Turf)	5	1	2	0	6150
76 9/09 Hayd 6f			G-F		£3885

Total win prize-money £3886

Going (Turf): Sf: 0-0 GS: 0-1 Gd: 0-0 **GF: 1-4** Fm: 0-0
Distance: **5f/6f: 1-5** 7f-8f: 0-0 9f-13f: 0-0 14f+: 0-0
Track : LH: 0-0 RH: 0-0 Tight: 0-0 Gall: 0-0
Aids: Bl: 0-0 Vi: 0-0 Tstrap: 0-0 Ckp: 0-0
Best Rating: **76** 9/09 Hayd 6f gd-fm

Fair; effective over 6f; acts on fast ground.

Elusive Trader (USA)

96(94) (79)72

2-y-o b/br c Elusive Quality (USA)-Kumari Continent (USA) (Kris S (USA))

R Hannon Trevor C Stewart

Placings:231 (5977)

2009: 5^{2}SD, 6^{3}SD, 5^{1}GF,

	Starts	1st	2nd	3rd	Win & Pl
Career Total (Turf)	1	1	0	0	3238
Career Total (AW)	2	0	1	1	1734
72 9/09 Bevl 5f			G-F		£3238

Total win prize-money £3238

Going (Turf): Sf: 0-0 GS: 0-0 Gd: 0-0 **GF: 1-1** Fm: 0-0
Distance: **5f/6f: 1-3** 7f-8f: 0-0 9f-13f: 0-0 14f+: 0-0
Track : LH: 0-1 RH: 0-1 Tight: 0-1 Gall: 0-0
Aids: Bl: 0-0 Vi: 0-0 Tstrap: 0-0 Ckp: 0-0
Best Rating: **79** 8/09 Ling 5f stand

Fair; effective over 5f; acts on Polytrack.

Elusive Warrior (USA)

93(108) (79)46

6-y-o b g Elusive Quality (USA)-Love To Fight (CAN) (Fit To Fight (USA))

A J McCabe Mrs M J McCabe

Placings:43305/5043061500002**0110**/004**0422**05/3206101 02642123060135524-344040622 (7762)

2009: 7^{3}SS, 7^{4}SD, 7^{4}SD, 7^{0}SD, 6^{4}SD, 7^{0}GF, 7^{6}SD, 7^{2}SD, 7^{2}SD,

	Starts	1st	2nd	3rd	Win & Pl
Career Total (Turf)	22	1	0	3	5958
Career Total (AW)	42	6	10	4	24556
79 10/08 Sthl 7f	(0-75)H			STD	£3412
74 6/08 Sthl 7f	(0-60)H			STD	£1774
67 4/08 Sthl 7f	(0-70)H			STD	£3399
65 3/08 Sthl 7f	(0-60)H			STD	£1943
68 12/06 Sthl 7f	(0-53)H			STD	£2047
69 12/06 Sthl 7f	(0-60)H			STD	£3071
64 6/06 Brig 6f209y	(0-70)H			FRM	£3238

Total win prize-money £18887

Going (Turf): Sf: 0-1 GS: 0-0 Gd: 0-7 GF: 0-8 **Fm: 1-6**
Distance: 5f/6f: 0-15 **7f-8f: 7-47** 9f-13f: 0-2 14f+: 0-0
Track : **LH: 7-49** RH: 0-2 Tight: 0-12 Gall: 0-2
Aids: Bl: 0-2 Vi: 0-0 Tstrap: 7-47 Ckp: 7-47

Best Rating: 79 10/08 Sthl 7f stand

Modest; effective at around 7f; acts on Fibresand and Polytrack; has worn cheekpieces; likes to race prominently.

Elusive Wave (IRE)

112 **118**

3-y-o b f Elusive City (USA)-Multicolour Wave (IRE) (Rainbow Quest (USA))
J-C Rouget Martin S Schwartz

Placings:1112-1142R **(5710a)**
2009: 7^{1}GS, 8^{1}G, 8^{4}GF, 8^{2}S, 8^{R}GS,

	Starts	1st	2nd	3rd	Win & Pl
Career Total (Turf)	9	5	2	0	434477

117 5/09 Lonc 1m GD £221903
114 4/09 MsnL 7f G-S £38835
102 8/08 Deau 7f GD £29412
100 7/08 Lonc 7f GD £20221
81 5/08 Gdwd 6f GD £3561
Total win prize-money £313933

Going (Turf): Sf: 0-1 GS: 1-3 **Gd: 4-4** GF: 0-1 Fm: 0-0
Distance: 5f/6f: 1-1 **7f-8f: 4-8** 9f-13f: 0-0 14f+: 0-0
Track : LH: 0-0 **RH: 2-4** Tight: 0-0 Gall: 0-1
Aids: Bl: 0-0 Vi: 0-0 Tstrap: 0-0 Ckp: 0-0
Best Rating: 118 8/09 Deau 1m soft

High-class; winner of the 2009 Poule d'Essai des Pouliches; stays 1m and acts on good ground.

Elvira Madigan

(99) (73)

2-y-o b f Sakhee (USA)-Santa Isobel (Nashwan (USA))
A M Balding J C & S R Hitchins

Placings:433 **(7763)**
2009: 8^{4}SD, 8^{3}SD, 8^{3}SD,

	Starts	1st	2nd	3rd	Win & Pl
Career Total (Turf)	0	0	0	0	
Career Total (AW)	3	0	0	2	1171

Going (Turf): Sf: 0-0 GS: 0-0 Gd: 0-0 GF: 0-0 Fm: 0-0
Distance: 5f/6f: 0-0 7f-8f: 0-3 9f-13f: 0-0 14f+: 0-0
Track : LH: 0-1 RH: 0-2 Tight: 0-1 Gall: 0-0
Aids: Bl: 0-0 Vi: 0-0 Tstrap: 0-0 Ckp: 0-0
Best Rating: 73 12/09 Kemp 1m stand

Email Exit (IRE)

91 **56**

2-y-o ch c Titus Livius (FR)-Christoph's Girl (Efisio)
C F Wall Des Thurlby

Placings:00004 **(6589)**
2009: 5^{0}G, 6^{0}G, 6^{0}G, 5^{0}GF, 6^{4}GS,

	Starts	1st	2nd	3rd	Win & Pl
Career Total (Turf)	5	0	0	0	0

Going (Turf): Sf: 0-0 GS: 0-1 Gd: 0-3 GF: 0-1 Fm: 0-0
Distance: 5f/6f: 0-3 7f-8f: 0-2 9f-13f: 0-0 14f+: 0-0
Track : LH: 0-1 RH: 0-0 Tight: 0-0 Gall: 0-1
Aids: Bl: 0-0 Vi: 0-0 Tstrap: 0-0 Ckp: 0-0
Best Rating: 56 9/09 Rdcr 5f gd-fm

Embra (IRE)

90(99) (64)**68**

4-y-o b g Monashee Mountain (USA)-Ivory Turner (Efisio)
T J Etherington The Carpe Diem Partnership

Placings:0/03531-00030302 **(7503)**
2009: 5^{0}GF, 5^{0}GF, 5^{0}GF, 6^{3}SD, 6^{0}G, 5^{3}SD, 6^{0}SD, 5^{2}SD,

	Starts	1st	2nd	3rd	Win & Pl
Career Total (Turf)	8	1	0	2	3359
Career Total (AW)	6	0	1	2	1244

68 7/08 Ayr 5f (0-65)H GD £2492
Total win prize-money £2492

Going (Turf): Sf: 0-0 GS: 0-1 **Gd: 1-3** GF: 0-4 Fm: 0-0
Distance: 5f/6f: 1-13 7f-8f: 0-1 9f-13f: 0-0 14f+: 0-0
Track : LH: 0-3 RH: 0-3 Tight: 0-2 Gall: 0-1
Aids: Bl: 0-0 Vi: 0-0 Tstrap: 0-0 Ckp: 0-0
Best Rating: 68 7/08 Ayr 5f good

Moderate brother to Fullandby; stays 6f; acts on fast ground, Polytrack and Fibresand.

Embsay Crag

113 **85**

3-y-o b g Elmaamul (USA)-Wigman Lady (IRE) (Tenby)
Mrs K Walton Keep The Faith Partnership

Placings:55501-46515241430 **(6996)**
2009: 7^{4}GF, 8^{6}GF, 8^{5}GF, 10^{1}GF, 12^{5}GF, 10^{2}S, 11^{4}GS, 10^{1}GF, 11^{4}GF, 10^{3}G, 10^{0}GS,

	Starts	1st	2nd	3rd	Win & Pl
Career Total (Turf)	16	3	1	1	18736

83 8/09 Ches 1m2f75y (0-90)H G-F £8831
73 6/09 Ches 1m2f75y (0-70)H G-F £4209
65 10/08 Leic 7f9y (0-65) G-S £2590
Total win prize-money £15630

Going (Turf): Sf: 0-2 GS: 1-4 Gd: 0-2 **GF: 2-8** Fm: 0-0
Distance: 5f/6f: 0-3 7f-8f: 1-3 **9f-13f: 2-10** 14f+: 0-0
Track : LH: 2-10 RH: 0-2 **Tight: 2-4** Gall: 0-2
Aids: Bl: 0-0 Vi: 0-0 Tstrap: 0-0 Ckp: 0-0
Best Rating: 85 10/09 York 1m2f88y good

Fair; stays 1m2f; acts on easy ground.

Emeebee

95(102) (80)**79**

3-y-o b g Medicean-Broughtons Motto (Mtoto)
W J Musson Broughton Thermal Insulation

Placings:41-033 **(7356)**
2009: 8^{0}SD, 7^{3}G, 7^{3}SD,

	Starts	1st	2nd	3rd	Win & Pl
Career Total (Turf)	2	0	0	1	987
Career Total (AW)	3	1	0	1	3500

73 12/08 Wolv 7f32y STD £2729
Total win prize-money £2730

Going (Turf): Sf: 0-1 GS: 0-0 Gd: 0-1 GF: 0-0 Fm: 0-0
Distance: 5f/6f: 0-0 **7f-8f: 1-5** 9f-13f: 0-0 14f+: 0-0
Track : LH: 1-3 RH: 0-1 **Tight: 1-2** Gall: 0-0
Aids: Bl: 0-0 Vi: 0-0 Tstrap: 0-0 Ckp: 0-0
Best Rating: 80 11/09 Wolv 7f32y stand

Landed a gamble on second start; effective at 7f; handles Polytrack.

Emerald Commander (IRE)

110 **109**

2-y-o b c Pivotal-Brigitta (IRE) (Sadler's Wells (USA))
Saeed Bin Suroor (R Hannon 5/9) Godolphin

Placings:41212 **(7207a)**
2009: 7^{4}G, 7^{1}S, 7^{2}GF, 8^{1}S, 8^{2}VS,

	Starts	1st	2nd	3rd	Win & Pl
Career Total (Turf)	5	2	2	0	93757

109 9/09 Hayd 1m30y SFT £19869
88 7/09 Newb 7f SFT £6476
Total win prize-money £26346

Going (Turf): Sf: 2-2 GS: 0-0 Gd: 0-1 GF: 0-1 Fm: 0-0
Distance: 5f/6f: 0-0 7f-8f: 1-4 9f-13f: 1-1 14f+: 0-0
Track : **LH: 1-3** RH: 0-0 Tight: 0-0 Gall: 0-1
Aids: Bl: 0-0 Vi: 0-0 Tstrap: 0-0 Ckp: 0-0
Best Rating: 109 11/09 StCl 1m v soft

Useful; effective over 7f; acts on soft and quick ground.

Emerald Girl (IRE)

102 **73**

2-y-o b f Chineur (FR)-Faypool (IRE) (Fayruz)
R A Fahey M Wynne

Placings:3213514 **(6643)**
2009: 5^{3}GF, 5^{2}G, 5^{1}GF, 5^{3}G, 5^{5}GF, 6^{1}G, 6^{4}G,

	Starts	1st	2nd	3rd	Win & Pl
Career Total (Turf)	7	2	1	2	12587

73 9/09 Haml 6f5y (0-85)H GD £6476
69 7/09 Bevl 5f G-F £3238
Total win prize-money £9714

Going (Turf): Sf: 0-0 GS: 0-0 **Gd: 1-4 GF: 1-3** Fm: 0-0
Distance: 5f/6f: 1-6 7f-8f: 1-1 9f-13f: 0-0 14f+: 0-0
Track : LH: 0-1 RH: 0-2 Tight: 0-1 Gall: 0-1
Aids: Bl: 0-0 Vi: 0-0 Tstrap: 0-0 Ckp: 0-0
Best Rating: 73 9/09 Haml 6f5y good

Modest; effective over 5f-6f; acts on fast ground.

Emerald Glade (IRE)

90 **54**

2-y-o b f Azamour (IRE)-Woodland Glade (Mark Of Esteem (IRE))
T D Easterby D A West

Placings:6005 **(5980)**
2009: 6^{6}G, 7^{0}G, 6^{0}GF, 7^{5}GF,

	Starts	1st	2nd	3rd	Win & Pl
Career Total (Turf)	4	0	0	0	0

Going (Turf): Sf: 0-0 GS: 0-0 Gd: 0-2 GF: 0-2 Fm: 0-0
Distance: 5f/6f: 0-2 7f-8f: 0-2 9f-13f: 0-0 14f+: 0-0
Track : LH: 0-1 RH: 0-1 Tight: 0-1 Gall: 0-0
Aids: Bl: 0-0 Vi: 0-0 Tstrap: 0-0 Ckp: 0-0
Best Rating: 54 9/09 Bevl 7f100y gd-fm

Emerald Hawk (IRE)

88 **36**

3-y-o b/br c Hawk Wing (USA)-Fabulous Pet (Somethingfabulous (USA))
D H Brown (S Parr 7/4) Bezwell Fixings Limited

Placings:00005 **(6899)**
2009: 10^{0}GF, 7^{0}G, 7^{0}GF, 11^{0}GS, 17^{5}GF,

	Starts	1st	2nd	3rd	Win & Pl
Career Total (Turf)	5	0	0	0	0

Going (Turf): Sf: 0-0 GS: 0-1 Gd: 0-1 GF: 0-3 Fm: 0-0

Distance: 5f/6f: 0-0 7f-8f: 0-2 9f-13f: 0-2 14f+: 0-1
Track : LH: 0-2 RH: 0-1 Tight: 0-1 Gall: 0-0
Aids: Bl: 0-1 Vi: 0-2 Tstrap: 0-0 Ckp: 0-0
Best Rating: **36** 8/09 Bevl 7f100y gd-fm

Emerald Rock (CAN)

84(108) (63)**50**

4-y-o b g Johannesburg (USA)-Classic Jones (CAN) (Regal Classic (CAN))
Tom Dascombe (N J Vaughan 16/2) The Whack Pack

Placings:6/**46405** **(6818)**
2009: 9^{4}SD, 8^{6}SD, 9^{4}SD, 12^{0}SD, 10^{5}GF,

	Starts	1st	2nd	3rd	Win & Pl
Career Total (Turf)	2	0	0	0	0
Career Total (AW)	4	0	0	0	0

Going (Turf): **Sf: 0-0 GS: 0-0 Gd: 0-0 GF: 0-2 Fm: 0-0**
Distance: 5f/6f: 0-0 7f-8f: 0-1 9f-13f: 0-5 14f+: 0-0
Track : LH: 0-5 RH: 0-1 Tight: 0-4 Gall: 0-0
Aids: Bl: 0-0 Vi: 0-0 Tstrap: 0-2 Ckp: 0-2
Best Rating: **63** 2/09 Wolv 1m1f103y stand

Modest; effective over 1m1f; acts on Polytrack.

Emerald Wilderness (IRE)

93(112) (106)**97**

5-y-o b g Green Desert (USA)-Simla Bibi (Indian Ridge)
A King Terry Warner & David Sewell

Placings:4236/**322221421102303**/150-**21601** **(4315)**
2009: 12^{2}SD, 11^{1}SD, 9^{6}GF, 10^{0}G, 10^{1}G,

	Starts	1st	2nd	3rd	Win & Pl
Career Total (Turf)	20	3	5	3	37350
Career Total (AW)	7	3	3	1	23881

97	7/09	NmkJ	1m2f	(0-95)H	GD	£8723
106	2/09	Kemp	1m3f	(0-100)H	STD	£11215
102	4/08	GrLe	1m	(0-95)H	STD	£6623
95	7/07	Folk	1m1f149y	(0-85)H	G-F	£4857
91	7/07	Wind	1m2f7y	(0-85)H	G-S	£6477

Total win prize-money £37897

Going (Turf): Sf: 0-0 **GS: 1-5 Gd: 1-5 GF: 1-9** Fm: 0-1
Distance: 5f/6f: 0-0 7f-8f: 1-7 **9f-13f: 5-20** 14f+: 0-0
Track : LH: 2-10 **RH: 4-13 Tight: 3-15** Gall: 2-3
Aids: **Bl: 1-2** Vi: 0-0 Tstrap: 0-0 Ckp: 0-0
Best Rating: **106** 2/09 Kemp 1m3f stand

Very useful; effective from 1m-1m4f; acts on most ground and on Polytrack; has worn blinkers.

Emeralda

83 **42**

3-y-o b f Desert Prince (IRE)-Edouna (FR) (Doyoun)
Pat Eddery Baron F C Oppenheim

Placings:60 **(1579)**
2009: 10^{6}GF, 10^{0}G,

	Starts	1st	2nd	3rd	Win & Pl
Career Total (Turf)	2	0	0	0	0

Going (Turf): **Sf: 0-0 GS: 0-0 Gd: 0-1 GF: 0-1 Fm: 0-0**
Distance: 5f/6f: 0-0 7f-8f: 0-0 9f-13f: 0-2 14f+: 0-0
Track : LH: 0-2 RH: 0-0 Tight: 0-1 Gall: 0-0
Aids: Bl: 0-0 Vi: 0-0 Tstrap: 0-0 Ckp: 0-0
Best Rating: **42** 4/09 Bath 1m2f46y good

Emeralds Spirit (IRE)

91 **57**

2-y-o b f Rock Of Gibraltar (IRE)-Spiritual Air (Royal Applause)
J R Weymes T A Scothern

Placings:60665 **(6232)**
2009: 5^{6}G, 6^{0}G, 7^{6}G, 5^{6}G, 8^{5}GF,

	Starts	1st	2nd	3rd	Win & Pl
Career Total (Turf)	5	0	0	0	0

Going (Turf): **Sf: 0-0 GS: 0-0 Gd: 0-4 GF: 0-1 Fm: 0-0**
Distance: 5f/6f: 0-3 7f-8f: 0-1 9f-13f: 0-1 14f+: 0-0
Track : LH: 0-2 RH: 0-0 Tight: 0-1 Gall: 0-0
Aids: Bl: 0-0 Vi: 0-0 Tstrap: 0-0 Ckp: 0-0
Best Rating: **57** 5/09 Donc 5f good

Emily Harley (IRE)

84 (37)**50**

3-y-o b f Sulamani (IRE)-Princess Bankes (Vettori (IRE))
W G M Turner (E Danel 14/9) T Lightbowne

Placings:5-00003065 **(6935)**
2009: 7^{0}SD, 7^{0}G, 9^{0}G, 11^{0}G, 14^{3}G, 12^{0}SD, 15^{6}GS, 17^{5}G,

	Starts	1st	2nd	3rd	Win & Pl
Career Total (Turf)	7	0	0	1	3136
Career Total (AW)	2	0	0	0	

Going (Turf): **Sf: 0-1 GS: 0-1 Gd: 0-5 GF: 0-0 Fm: 0-0**
Distance: 5f/6f: 0-0 7f-8f: 0-3 9f-13f: 0-3 14f+: 0-3
Track : LH: 0-2 RH: 0-1 Tight: 0-1 Gall: 0-0
Aids: Bl: 0-0 Vi: 0-0 Tstrap: 0-0 Ckp: 0-0
Best Rating: **50** 9/09 StCl 1m7f gd-sft

Emirates Champion

98(92) (75)**104**

3-y-o b c Haafhd-Janaat (Kris)
Saeed Bin Suroor Godolphin

Placings:1-51 **(6986)**
2009: 11^{5}GF, 10^{1}G,

	Starts	1st	2nd	3rd	Win & Pl
Career Total (Turf)	2	1	0	0	4857
Career Total (AW)	1	1	0	0	3238

104	10/09	Ayr	1m2f	(0-85)H	GD	£4857
75	11/08	GrLe	1m		STD	£3238

Total win prize-money £8095

Going (Turf): Sf: 0-0 GS: 0-0 **Gd: 1-1** GF: 0-1 Fm: 0-0
Distance: 5f/6f: 0-0 7f-8f: 1-1 9f-13f: 1-2 14f+: 0-0
Track : **LH: 2-2** RH: 0-1 Tight: 0-1 **Gall: 1-1**
Aids: Bl: 0-0 Vi: 0-0 Tstrap: 0-0 Ckp: 0-0
Best Rating: **104** 10/09 Ayr 1m2f good

Very useful; stays 1m2f; acts on good ground and on Polytrack; has worn a tongue-tie.

Emirates Dream (USA)

104 **105**

2-y-o b c Kingmambo (USA)-My Boston Gal (USA) (Boston Harbor (USA))
Saeed Bin Suroor Godolphin

Placings:1433 **(6811)**
2009: 7^{1}G, 7^{4}GS, 8^{3}G, 8^{3}G,

	Starts	1st	2nd	3rd	Win & Pl
Career Total (Turf)	4	1	0	2	28458

81	7/09	York	7f	GD	£7641

Total win prize-money £7642

Going (Turf): Sf: 0-0 GS: 0-1 **Gd: 1-3** GF: 0-0 Fm: 0-0
Distance: 5f/6f: 0-0 **7f-8f: 1-4** 9f-13f: 0-0 14f+: 0-0
Track : **LH: 1-1** RH: 0-1 Tight: 0-0 **Gall: 1-1**
Aids: Bl: 0-0 Vi: 0-0 Tstrap: 0-0 Ckp: 0-0
Best Rating: **105** 9/09 Lonc 1m good

Very useful; stays 7f; acts on good ground.

Emirates Hills

98 **73**

2-y-o b f Dubawi (IRE)-Starstone (Diktat)
E F Vaughan Ali Saeed

Placings:50100 **(6169)**
2009: 6^{5}G, 7^{0}G, 6^{1}GF, 6^{0}GF, 5^{0}GF,

	Starts	1st	2nd	3rd	Win & Pl
Career Total (Turf)	5	1	0	0	3886

72	8/09	Wind	6f	G-F	£3885

Total win prize-money £3886

Going (Turf): Sf: 0-0 GS: 0-0 Gd: 0-2 **GF: 1-3** Fm: 0-0
Distance: **5f/6f: 1-3** 7f-8f: 0-2 9f-13f: 0-0 14f+: 0-0
Track : LH: 0-0 RH: 0-0 Tight: 0-0 **Gall: 1-1**
Aids: Bl: 0-0 Vi: 0-1 Tstrap: 0-0 Ckp: 0-0
Best Rating: **73** 9/09 Donc 6f110y gd-fm

Fair; stays 6f plus; acts on fast ground.

Emirates Roadshow (USA)

103 **92**

3-y-o ch g Distorted Humor (USA)-Just A Bird (USA) (Storm Bird (CAN))
Saeed Bin Suroor Godolphin

Placings:6221-230020 **(5475)**
2009: 8^{2}GF, 8^{3}S, 8^{0}GF, 10^{0}G, 8^{2}GF, 9^{0}GF,

	Starts	1st	2nd	3rd	Win & Pl
Career Total (Turf)	10	1	4	1	14491

87	10/08	NmkR	7f	G-S	£4857

Total win prize-money £4857

Going (Turf): Sf: 0-1 **GS: 1-1** Gd: 0-3 GF: 0-5 Fm: 0-0
Distance: 5f/6f: 0-0 **7f-8f: 1-6** 9f-13f: 0-4 14f+: 0-0
Track : LH: 0-1 RH: 0-3 Tight: 0-3 Gall: 0-1
Aids: Bl: 0-0 Vi: 0-0 Tstrap: 0-0 Ckp: 0-0
Best Rating: **92** 5/09 Wind 1m67y gd-fm

Useful; stays 1m and acts on most ground; suited by forcing tactics.

Emirates Sports

104(101) (91)**88**

3-y-o b c King's Best (USA)-Time Saved (Green Desert (USA))
Saeed Bin Suroor Godolphin

Placings:41-153 **(4801)**
2009: 8^{1}SD, 7^{5}GF, 8^{3}GF,

	Starts	1st	2nd	3rd	Win & Pl
Career Total (Turf)	3	0	0	1	1540
Career Total (AW)	2	2	0	0	7965

91	7/09	Kemp	1m	(0-85)H	STD	£4727

80 11/08 GrLe 6f STD £3238
Total win prize-money £7965

Going (Turf): **Sf: 0-0 GS: 0-1 Gd: 0-0 GF: 0-2 Fm: 0-0**
Distance: 5f/6f: 1-2 7f-8f: 1-3 9f-13f: 0-0 14f+: 0-0
Track : LH: 1-1 RH: 1-2 Tight: 0-0 **Gall: 1-1**
Aids: Bl: 0-0 Vi: 0-0 Tstrap: 0-0 Ckp: 0-0
Best Rating: **91** 7/09 Kemp 1m stand

Useful; effective over 6f-1m; acts on Polytrack.

Emirates World (IRE)

(96) (73)**71**
3-y-o b g Exceed And Excel (AUS)-Enrich (USA) (Dynaformer (USA))
A E Jessop (M Johnston 22/3) Mrs Gloria Jessop

Placings:540-155 **(0924)**
2009: 7^{1}SD, 7^{5}SD, 7^{5}SD,

	Starts	1st	2nd	3rd	Win & Pl
Career Total (Turf)	2	0	0	0	192
Career Total (AW)	4	1	0	0	2730

73 1/09 Ling 7f STD £2729
Total win prize-money £2730

Going (Turf): **Sf: 0-1 GS: 0-0 Gd: 0-1 GF: 0-0 Fm: 0-0**
Distance: 5f/6f: 0-1 **7f-8f: 1-5** 9f-13f: 0-0 14f+: 0-0
Track : **LH: 1-3** RH: 0-1 **Tight: 1-1** Gall: 0-1
Aids: Bl: 0-0 Vi: 0-1 Tstrap: 0-0 Ckp: 0-0
Best Rating: **73** 1/09 Ling 7f stand

Fair; effective over 7f; acts on Polytrack.

Emiratesdotcom

90 **40**
3-y-o b g Pivotal-Teggiano (IRE) (Mujtahid (USA))
M Johnston Sheikh Hamdan Bin Mohammed Al Maktoum

Placings:0000 **(6188)**
2009: 9^{0}GF, 8^{0}G, 8^{0}G, 15^{0}GF,

	Starts	1st	2nd	3rd	Win & Pl
Career Total (Turf)	4	0	0	0	

Going (Turf): **Sf: 0-0 GS: 0-0 Gd: 0-2 GF: 0-2 Fm: 0-0**
Distance: 5f/6f: 0-0 7f-8f: 0-2 9f-13f: 0-1 14f+: 0-1
Track : LH: 0-2 RH: 0-2 Tight: 0-4 Gall: 0-0
Aids: Bl: 0-0 Vi: 0-0 Tstrap: 0-0 Ckp: 0-0
Best Rating: **40** 7/09 Thsk 1m good

Emma Dora (IRE)

90(89) (54)**71**
2-y-o b f Medaglia D'Oro (USA)-My Girl Lisa (USA) (With Approval (CAN))
D R C Elsworth G B Partnership

Placings:051600566 **(7359)**
2009: 6^{0}GF, 6^{5}G, 6^{1}GS, 6^{6}G, 8^{0}G, 8^{0}SD, 8^{5}GS, 7^{6}G, 8^{6}SD,

	Starts	1st	2nd	3rd	Win & Pl
Career Total (Turf)	7	1	0	0	5181
Career Total (AW)	2	0	0	0	0

71 6/09 NmkJ 6f G-S £5180
Total win prize-money £5181

Going (Turf): Sf: 0-0 **GS: 1-2** Gd: 0-4 GF: 0-1 Fm: 0-0
Distance: **5f/6f: 1-2** 7f-8f: 0-5 9f-13f: 0-2 14f+: 0-0
Track : LH: 0-1 RH: 0-2 Tight: 0-2 Gall: 0-0
Aids: Bl: 0-0 Vi: 0-0 Tstrap: 0-0 Ckp: 0-0
Best Rating: **71** 6/09 NmkJ 6f gd-sft

Fair; effective over 6f; acts on easy ground.

Emma Jean Lass (IRE)

92(93) (68)**59**
2-y-o b f Choisir (AUS)-Enlisted (IRE) (Sadler's Wells (USA))
P D Evans (J S Moore 6/10) Roger Ambrose & William Reilly

Placings:26420030 **(7849)**
2009: 5^{2}SD, 5^{6}GF, 5^{4}G, 5^{2}G, 6^{0}GF, 6^{0}GS, 5^{3}SD, 6^{0}SS,

	Starts	1st	2nd	3rd	Win & Pl
Career Total (Turf)	5	0	1	0	1517
Career Total (AW)	3	0	1	1	1209

Going (Turf): **Sf: 0-0 GS: 0-1 Gd: 0-2 GF: 0-2 Fm: 0-0**
Distance: 5f/6f: 0-8 7f-8f: 0-0 9f-13f: 0-0 14f+: 0-0
Track : LH: 0-5 RH: 0-0 Tight: 0-2 Gall: 0-3
Aids: Bl: 0-0 Vi: 0-0 Tstrap: 0-0 Ckp: 0-0
Best Rating: **68** 3/09 Ling 5f stand

Modest; effective over 5f; acts on Polytrack.

Emmrooz

107 **107**
4-y-o b c Red Ransom (USA)-Nasmatt (Danehill (USA))
Saeed Bin Suroor Godolphin

Placings:2103/22 **(2606)**
2009: 8^{2}GF, 8^{2}GF,

	Starts	1st	2nd	3rd	Win & Pl
Career Total (Turf)	6	1	3	1	36291

90 9/07 Gdwd 1m G-F £5505
Total win prize-money £5505

Going (Turf): Sf: 0-2 GS: 0-0 Gd: 0-1 **GF: 1-3** Fm: 0-0
Distance: 5f/6f: 0-0 **7f-8f: 1-4** 9f-13f: 0-2 14f+: 0-0
Track : LH: 0-2 **RH: 1-3** Tight: 0-0 Gall: 0-2
Aids: Bl: 0-0 Vi: 0-0 Tstrap: 0-0 Ckp: 0-0
Best Rating: **107** 2/09 Ndas 1m194y gd-fm

Smart; stays 1m; handles soft but acts best on fast ground.

Emotive

83 (59)**32**
6-y-o b g Pursuit Of Love-Ruby Julie (Clantime)
F P Murtagh Hurst Farm Racing

Placings:0050/20600110620003000300/5 **(5307)**
2009: 13^{5}HY,

	Starts	1st	2nd	3rd	Win & Pl
Career Total (Turf)	19	2	1	2	9009
Career Total (AW)	6	0	1	0	964

66 6/06 Wwck 1m22y (0-60)H G-F £2730
63 5/06 Leic 1m60y G-S £3886
Total win prize-money £6616

Going (Turf): Sf: 0-1 **GS: 1-4** Gd: 0-7 **GF: 1-4** Fm: 0-3
Distance: 5f/6f: 0-1 7f-8f: 0-8 **9f-13f: 2-12** 14f+: 0-4
Track : LH: 1-11 RH: 1-9 Tight: 0-10 Gall: 0-0
Aids: Bl: 0-5 Vi: 0-0 Tstrap: 0-3 Ckp: 0-3
Best Rating: **66** 8/06 Leic 1m60y good

Modest; seems best over 1m; acts on most ground.

Emperor Claudius (USA)

101 **103**
2-y-o b c Giant's Causeway (USA)-Virginia Waters (USA) (Kingmambo (USA))
A P O'Brien M Tabor, D Smith & Mrs John Magnier

Placings:31266 **(5859)**
2009: 6^{3}G, 6^{1}GF, 7^{2}GF, 7^{6}GF, 7^{6}GF,

	Starts	1st	2nd	3rd	Win & Pl
Career Total (Turf)	5	1	1	1	23488

92 6/09 Fair 6f G-F £9056
Total win prize-money £9057

Going (Turf): Sf: 0-0 GS: 0-0 Gd: 0-1 **GF: 1-4** Fm: 0-0
Distance: **5f/6f: 1-2** 7f-8f: 0-3 9f-13f: 0-0 14f+: 0-0
Track : LH: 0-1 **RH: 1-1** Tight: 0-0 Gall: 0-0
Aids: Bl: 0-0 Vi: 0-0 Tstrap: 0-0 Ckp: 0-0
Best Rating: **103** 6/09 Asct 7f gd-fm

Very useful; Listed placed; stays 7f; acts on fast ground.

Emperor Court (IRE)

104(108) (89)**89**
5-y-o ch h Singspiel (IRE)-Tarquina (USA) (Niniski (USA))
P J Makin Four Seasons Racing Ltd

Placings:034432/212165302-005143535 **(6830)**
2009: 9^{0}SD, 10^{0}SD, 10^{5}SD, 10^{1}GF, 9^{4}GF, 10^{3}GF, 10^{5}GF, 8^{3}SD, 8^{5}SF,

	Starts	1st	2nd	3rd	Win & Pl
Career Total (Turf)	10	2	0	3	13237
Career Total (AW)	14	1	4	2	8002

89 6/09 Hayd 1m2f95y (0-85)H G-F £5504
85 4/08 Wind 1m2f7y (0-80)H G-F £5180
76 2/08 Ling 1m2f (0-75)H STD £2590
Total win prize-money £13277

Going (Turf): Sf: 0-0 GS: 0-0 Gd: 0-2 **GF: 2-8** Fm: 0-0
Distance: 5f/6f: 0-0 7f-8f: 0-5 **9f-13f: 3-19** 14f+: 0-0
Track : **LH: 2-13** RH: 1-10 **Tight: 2-15** Gall: 0-1
Aids: Bl: 0-0 Vi: 0-0 Tstrap: 0-0 Ckp: 0-0
Best Rating: **89** 10/09 Wolv 1m141y std-fst

Useful; effective at around 1m2f; acts on fast ground; also goes on Polytrack.

Emperor's Well

97(99) (53)**64**
10-y-o ch g First Trump-Catherines Well (Junius (USA))
M W Easterby A Chandler & L Westwood

Placings:5535000/0500/000204146/0311200/0030001452 00/00000202060/033211206000/030615320330-0000024553 **(7142)**
2009: 8^{0}GF, 8^{0}G, 8^{0}GF, 8^{0}G, 8^{0}GF, 7^{2}G, 8^{4}G, 9^{5}GF, 8^{5}SD, 9^{3}SD,

	Starts	1st	2nd	3rd	Win & Pl
Career Total (Turf)	76	7	8	9	36198
Career Total (AW)	8	0	1	1	1158

61 7/08 Thsk 1m (0-55)H G-F £3139
74 7/07 Bevl 7f100y (0-65)H GD £3238
68 7/07 Ripn 1m (0-70)H HVY £3886
68 8/05 Bevl 1m100y (0-55)H G-F £3454
69 9/04 Bevl 1m1f207y (0-55)H G-F £3680
66 9/04 Bevl 1m100y (0-55)H G-F £3684
63 9/03 Pont 1m4y F(0-60)H G-F £3234
Total win prize-money £24319

Going (Turf): Sf: 1-10 GS: 0-8 Gd: 1-16 **GF: 5-36** Fm: 0-6
Distance: 5f/6f: 0-13 7f-8f: 3-23 **9f-13f: 4-48** 14f+: 0-0
Track : LH: 2-37 **RH: 5-32 Tight: 2-22** Gall: 0-4
Aids: **Bl: 5-50** Vi: 0-1 Tstrap: 0-0 Ckp: 0-0
Best Rating: **74** 7/07 Bevl 7f100y good

Moderate; stays 1m2f; acts on fast and easy ground; blinkers.

Empire Seeker (USA)

91(93) (53)60

4-y-o br g Seeking The Gold (USA)-Lady From Shanghai (USA) (Storm Cat (USA))

Mrs H S Main Wetumpka Racing

Placings:0/0005-**0006** **(4538)**

2009: 10[0]SD, 11[0]SD, 8[0]G, 10[6]SD,

	Starts	1st	2nd	3rd	Win & Pl
Career Total (Turf)	6	0	0	0	0
Career Total (AW)	3	0	0	0	0

Going (Turf): **Sf: 0-2 GS: 0-0 Gd: 0-2 GF: 0-2 Fm: 0-0**
Distance: 5f/6f: 0-0 7f-8f: 0-2 9f-13f: 0-7 14f+: 0-0
Track : LH: 0-3 RH: 0-3 Tight: 0-4 Gall: 0-0
Aids: Bl: 0-0 Vi: 0-0 Tstrap: 0-1 Ckp: 0-1
Best Rating: **62** 10/07 Newb 1m soft

Empowered (IRE)

109(105) (88)94

4-y-o b c Fasliyev (USA)-Funsie (FR) (Saumarez)

W J Haggas Cheveley Park Stud

Placings:41-211 **(1826)**

2009: 9[2]SD, 10[1]G, 12[1]GF,

	Starts	1st	2nd	3rd	Win & Pl
Career Total (Turf)	3	2	0	0	5049
Career Total (AW)	2	1	1	0	5427

94 5/09 Donc 1m2f60y (0-85)H GD £4857
85 10/08 Kemp 1m2f STD £3885
Total win prize-money £8743

Going (Turf): Sf: 0-1 GS: 0-0 **Gd: 1-1 GF: 1-1** Fm: 0-0
Distance: 5f/6f: 0-0 7f-8f: 0-0 **9f-13f: 3-5** 14f+: 0-0
Track : **LH: 2-3** RH: 1-2 Tight: 1-2 Gall: 1-1
Aids: Bl: 0-0 Vi: 0-0 Tstrap: 0-0 Ckp: 0-0
Best Rating: **94** 5/09 Donc 1m2f60y good

Useful; effective over 1m2f; acts on Polytrack.

Empress Leizu (IRE)

85(85) (52)44

2-y-o b f Chineur (FR)-Silk Point (IRE) (Barathea (IRE))

E A L Dunlop Mrs Janice Quy

Placings:0001 **(7669)**

2009: 8[0]GF, 8[0]SD, 8[0]SD, 8[1]SD,

	Starts	1st	2nd	3rd	Win & Pl
Career Total (Turf)	1	0	0	0	
Career Total (AW)	3	1	0	0	2730

52 12/09 Wolv 1m141y STD £2729
Total win prize-money £2730

Going (Turf): **Sf: 0-0 GS: 0-0 Gd: 0-0 GF: 0-1 Fm: 0-0**
Distance: 5f/6f: 0-0 7f-8f: 0-2 **9f-13f: 1-2** 14f+: 0-0
Track : **LH: 1-2** RH: 0-1 **Tight: 1-2** Gall: 0-0
Aids: Bl: 0-0 Vi: 0-0 Tstrap: 0-0 Ckp: 0-0
Best Rating: **52** 12/09 Wolv 1m141y stand

Moderate filly; stays 1m well; acts on Polytrack.

Empressofboogie

89(83) (47)53

2-y-o b f Tobougg (IRE)-Akhira (Emperor Jones (USA))

M Dods Mrs C E Dods

Placings:4450 **(6431)**

2009: 6[4]GF, 6[4]S, 7[5]G, 8[0]SD,

	Starts	1st	2nd	3rd	Win & Pl
Career Total (Turf)	3	0	0	0	510
Career Total (AW)	1	0	0	0	

Going (Turf): **Sf: 0-1 GS: 0-0 Gd: 0-1 GF: 0-1 Fm: 0-0**
Distance: 5f/6f: 0-2 7f-8f: 0-1 9f-13f: 0-1 14f+: 0-0
Track : LH: 0-1 RH: 0-1 Tight: 0-2 Gall: 0-0
Aids: Bl: 0-0 Vi: 0-0 Tstrap: 0-0 Ckp: 0-0
Best Rating: **53** 8/09 Newc 6f gd-fm

Moderate half-sister to the very useful sprinter Empress Jain and another winner; improved on debut over 6f on soft.

En Fuego

95 77

2-y-o b c Firebreak-Yanomami (USA) (Slew O'Gold (USA))

P W Chapple-Hyam Michael Daffey & Robert Markwick

Placings:03 **(7096)**

2009: 6[0]G, 7[3]G,

	Starts	1st	2nd	3rd	Win & Pl
Career Total (Turf)	2	0	0	1	595

Going (Turf): **Sf: 0-0 GS: 0-0 Gd: 0-2 GF: 0-0 Fm: 0-0**
Distance: 5f/6f: 0-1 7f-8f: 0-1 9f-13f: 0-0 14f+: 0-0
Track : LH: 0-0 RH: 0-0 Tight: 0-0 Gall: 0-0
Aids: Bl: 0-0 Vi: 0-0 Tstrap: 0-0 Ckp: 0-0
Best Rating: **77** 10/09 Yarm 7f3y good

Enact

106 100

3-y-o b f Kyllachy-Constitute (USA) (Gone West (USA))

Sir Michael Stoute Cheveley Park Stud

Placings:10-200051223 **(6814)**

2009: 6[2]GF, 7[0]GF, 7[0]HY, 6[0]G, 7[5]GS, 6[1]GF, 6[2]S, 6[2]G, 6[3]G,

	Starts	1st	2nd	3rd	Win & Pl
Career Total (Turf)	11	2	3	1	31052

97 8/09 Nott 6f15y (0-90)H G-F £9066
74 9/08 Wind 6f G-F £3561
Total win prize-money £12628

Going (Turf): Sf: 0-3 GS: 0-1 Gd: 0-3 **GF: 2-4** Fm: 0-0
Distance: 5f/6f: 1-5 7f-8f: 1-6 9f-13f: 0-0 14f+: 0-0
Track : LH: 0-2 RH: 0-1 Tight: 0-0 **Gall: 1-2**
Aids: Bl: 0-0 Vi: 0-0 Tstrap: 0-0 Ckp: 0-0
Best Rating: **100** 9/09 Asct 6f good

Very useful; effective at 6f-7f; acts on fast and easy ground.

Encircled

95(106) (95)92

5-y-o b m In The Wings-Ring Of Esteem (Mark Of Esteem (IRE))

J R Jenkins Fhad Al Harthi

Placings:05031/0130/03020304-**623050** **(6724)**

2009: 12[6]SD, 12[2]SD, 10[3]GF, 10[0]SD, 11[5]GF, 12[0]SD,

	Starts	1st	2nd	3rd	Win & Pl
Career Total (Turf)	15	1	1	4	14189
Career Total (AW)	8	1	1	1	7486

81 6/07 Wind 1m2f7y (0-80)H GD £6477
66 12/06 Wolv 1m1f103y STD £3412
Total win prize-money £9890

Going (Turf): Sf: 0-2 GS: 0-5 **Gd: 1-5** GF: 0-3 Fm: 0-0
Distance: 5f/6f: 0-0 7f-8f: 0-2 **9f-13f: 2-21** 14f+: 0-0
Track : LH: 1-12 RH: 1-9 **Tight: 2-7** Gall: 0-8
Aids: Bl: 0-0 Vi: 0-0 Tstrap: 0-0 Ckp: 0-0
Best Rating: **95** 11/08 Kemp 1m4f stand

Fair; stays 1m4f; acts on good ground and Polytrack.

Encore Belle

94(81) (26)59

4-y-o b f Beat Hollow-Rada's Daughter (Robellino (USA))

Mouse Hamilton-Fairley Rectory Racing

Placings:04045-6360606 **(4220)**

2009: 10[6]SD, 10[3]GF, 9[6]GF, 10[0]GF, 11[6]F, 9[0]GF, 10[6]G,

	Starts	1st	2nd	3rd	Win & Pl
Career Total (Turf)	11	0	0	1	767
Career Total (AW)	1	0	0	0	0

Going (Turf): **Sf: 0-1 GS: 0-1 Gd: 0-2 GF: 0-6 Fm: 0-1**
Distance: 5f/6f: 0-0 7f-8f: 0-2 9f-13f: 0-10 14f+: 0-0
Track : LH: 0-8 RH: 0-2 Tight: 0-6 Gall: 0-0
Aids: Bl: 0-0 Vi: 0-1 Tstrap: 0-0 Ckp: 0-0
Best Rating: **59** 4/09 Wwck 1m2f188y gd-fm

Moderate; stays 1m2f; acts on fast and easy ground.

Endeavoured (IRE)

32(77) (46)26

3-y-o b g Peintre Celebre (USA)-Addaya (IRE) (Persian Bold)

D Carroll Diamond Racing Ltd

Placings:00-0 **(6788)**

2009: 11[0]G,

	Starts	1st	2nd	3rd	Win & Pl
Career Total (Turf)	2	0	0	0	
Career Total (AW)	1	0	0	0	

Going (Turf): **Sf: 0-1 GS: 0-0 Gd: 0-1 GF: 0-0 Fm: 0-0**
Distance: 5f/6f: 0-0 7f-8f: 0-1 9f-13f: 0-2 14f+: 0-0
Track : LH: 0-2 RH: 0-1 Tight: 0-0 Gall: 0-0
Aids: Bl: 0-1 Vi: 0-0 Tstrap: 0-0 Ckp: 0-0
Best Rating: **46** 11/08 Kemp 7f stand

Enderby Spirit (GR)

106 108

3-y-o gr c Invincible Spirit (IRE)-Arctic Ice (IRE) (Zafonic (USA))

B Smart Philip & Patricia Brown

Placings:2212-42613000 **(6661)**

2009: 5[4]GF, 6[2]GF, 6[6]G, 6[1]GF, 6[3]G, 6[0]S, 6[0]GF, 6[0]GS,

	Starts	1st	2nd	3rd	Win & Pl
Career Total (Turf)	12	2	4	1	47544

105 7/09 Hayd 6f (0-100)H G-F £12952
87 10/08 Nott 5f13y G-S £3885
Total win prize-money £16838

Going (Turf): Sf: 0-1 **GS: 1-3** Gd: 0-4 **GF: 1-4** Fm: 0-0
Distance: **5f/6f: 2-11** 7f-8f: 0-1 9f-13f: 0-0 14f+: 0-0
Track : LH: 0-1 RH: 0-0 Tight: 0-1 Gall: 0-0
Aids: Bl: 0-0 Vi: 0-0 Tstrap: 0-0 Ckp: 0-0
Best Rating: **108** 7/09 NmkJ 6f good

Smart; Listed placed; effective over 5f-6f; acts on most ground.

England (IRE)

78 55

2-y-o b c Bertolini (USA)-Radha (Bishop Of Cashel)
N P Littmoden Franconson Partners 2

Placings:556 **(3403)**
2009: 6^5G, 5^5G, 6^6GF,

	Starts	1st	2nd	3rd	Win & Pl
Career Total (Turf)	3	0	0	0	150

Going (Turf): **Sf: 0-0 GS: 0-0 Gd: 0-2 GF: 0-1 Fm: 0-0**
Distance: 5f/6f: 0-2 7f-8f: 0-1 9f-13f: 0-0 14f+: 0-0
Track : LH: 0-0 RH: 0-0 Tight: 0-0 Gall: 0-1
Aids: Bl: 0-0 Vi: 0-0 Tstrap: 0-0 Ckp: 0-0
Best Rating: **55** 6/09 Sand 5f6y good

Moderate form in maidens so far.

English Archer

90 11

6-y-o b g Rock City-Fire Sprite (Mummy's Game)
A Kirtley M F Hyman

Placings:46/5000005/6601620000/00000 **(6183)**
2009: 14^0GF, 12^0S, 16^0GS, 16^0GS, 9^0GF,

	Starts	1st	2nd	3rd	Win & Pl
Career Total (Turf)	24	1	1	0	3336

54 7/07 Haml 1m3f16y (0-65)H G-S £2388
Total win prize-money £2389

Going (Turf): Sf: 0-3 **GS: 1-6** Gd: 0-5 GF: 0-10 Fm: 0-0
Distance: 5f/6f: 0-2 7f-8f: 0-5 **9f-13f: 1-14** 14f+: 0-3
Track : LH: 0-11 **RH: 1-11 Tight: 1-13** Gall: 0-2
Aids: Bl: 0-0 Vi: 0-0 Tstrap: 0-2 Ckp: 0-2
Best Rating: **54** 8/07 Folk 1m4f gd-sft

English City (IRE)

101 (45)56

6-y-o ch h City On A Hill (USA)-Toledana (IRE) (Sure Blade (USA))
Mrs L B Normile Peter Carnaby

Placings:00400/01244334/0/50-35 **(5359)**
2009: 14^3G, 13^5S,

	Starts	1st	2nd	3rd	Win & Pl
Career Total (Turf)	16	1	1	3	5671
Career Total (AW)	2	0	0	0	0

59 5/06 Rdcr 1m2f GD £2388
Total win prize-money £2389

Going (Turf): Sf: 0-3 GS: 0-2 **Gd: 1-4** GF: 0-6 Fm: 0-1
Distance: 5f/6f: 0-2 7f-8f: 0-4 **9f-13f: 1-9** 14f+: 0-3
Track : **LH: 1-8** RH: 0-7 **Tight: 1-7** Gall: 0-2
Aids: Bl: 0-0 Vi: 0-0 Tstrap: 0-1 Ckp: 0-1
Best Rating: **61** 7/06 Carl 1m1f61y firm

Moderate; suited by 1m2f; acts on easy and fast ground.

Engulf (IRE)

74 56

2-y-o b c Danehill Dancer (IRE)-All Embracing (IRE) (Night Shift (USA))
W J Haggas Findlay & Bloom

Placings:5 **(5029)**
2009: 6^5GF,

	Starts	1st	2nd	3rd	Win & Pl
Career Total (Turf)	1	0	0	0	0

Going (Turf): **Sf: 0-0 GS: 0-0 Gd: 0-0 GF: 0-1 Fm: 0-0**
Distance: 5f/6f: 0-1 7f-8f: 0-0 9f-13f: 0-0 14f+: 0-0
Track : LH: 0-0 RH: 0-0 Tight: 0-0 Gall: 0-0
Aids: Bl: 0-0 Vi: 0-0 Tstrap: 0-0 Ckp: 0-0
Best Rating: **56** 8/09 NmkJ 6f gd-fm

Enhancing

82(100) (54)67

3-y-o b f Hawk Wing (USA)-Enhance (Entrepreneur)
J A Glover (A J McCabe 19/6)
Dixon,Cartwright,Adams,Morton,Nbria Ieis

Placings:63-0360004 **(6804)**
2009: 10^0G, 7^3SD, 8^6GS, 7^0GF, 7^0SD, 7^0G, 9^4SD,

	Starts	1st	2nd	3rd	Win & Pl
Career Total (Turf)	6	0	0	1	530
Career Total (AW)	3	0	0	1	482

Going (Turf): **Sf: 0-0 GS: 0-2 Gd: 0-3 GF: 0-1 Fm: 0-0**
Distance: 5f/6f: 0-0 7f-8f: 0-6 9f-13f: 0-3 14f+: 0-0
Track : LH: 0-4 RH: 0-0 Tight: 0-3 Gall: 0-1
Aids: Bl: 0-0 Vi: 0-2 Tstrap: 0-1 Ckp: 0-1
Best Rating: **67** 8/08 Rdcr 7f gd-sft

Fair; effective over 7f; acts on easy ground.

Enjoy The Moment

89 105

6-y-o b g Generous (IRE)-Denial (Sadler's Wells (USA))
J A Osborne Mrs Judy Wilson & Martin Landau

Placings:06/51265/0301040/6040-60 **(6851)**
2009: 17^6F, 18^0G,

	Starts	1st	2nd	3rd	Win & Pl
Career Total (Turf)	20	2	1	1	65812

106 6/07 Asct 2m5f159y SFT £34276
85 6/06 Brig 1m3f196y FRM £3886
Total win prize-money £38162

Going (Turf): **Sf: 1-3** GS: 0-3 Gd: 0-3 GF: 0-9 **Fm: 1-2**
Distance: 5f/6f: 0-0 7f-8f: 0-0 9f-13f: 1-7 14f+: 1-13
Track : LH: 1-7 RH: 1-13 Tight: 0-6 **Gall: 1-10**
Aids: Bl: 0-0 Vi: 0-0 Tstrap: 0-0 Ckp: 0-0
Best Rating: **106** 6/07 Asct 2m5f159y soft

Very useful; winner of the 2007 Queen Alexandra Stakes; stays extreme distances, but effective at shorter; acts on most ground; usually held up.

Enjoyment

91 63

2-y-o b f Dansili-Have Fun (Indian Ridge)
M L W Bell The Rare Quality Partnership

Placings:40 **(4666)**
2009: 7^4G, 7^0G,

	Starts	1st	2nd	3rd	Win & Pl
Career Total (Turf)	2	0	0	0	289

Going (Turf): **Sf: 0-0 GS: 0-0 Gd: 0-2 GF: 0-0 Fm: 0-0**
Distance: 5f/6f: 0-0 7f-8f: 0-2 9f-13f: 0-0 14f+: 0-0
Track : LH: 0-0 RH: 0-0 Tight: 0-0 Gall: 0-0
Aids: Bl: 0-0 Vi: 0-0 Tstrap: 0-0 Ckp: 0-0
Best Rating: **63** 7/09 Donc 7f good

Promise on debut; stays 7f; acts on good ground; sure to improve and win a race.

Enlightenment (IRE)

(89) (64)48

9-y-o b g Presenting-Shaiybaniyda (He Loves Me)
Evan Williams T Hywel Jones

Placings:10 **(4169)**
2009: 13^1SD, 12^0G,

	Starts	1st	2nd	3rd	Win & Pl
Career Total (Turf)	1	0	0	0	
Career Total (AW)	1	1	0	0	2730

64 2/09 Ling 1m5f STD £2729
Total win prize-money £2730

Going (Turf): **Sf: 0-0 GS: 0-0 Gd: 0-1 GF: 0-0 Fm: 0-0**
Distance: 5f/6f: 0-0 7f-8f: 0-0 **9f-13f: 1-2** 14f+: 0-0
Track : **LH: 1-2** RH: 0-0 **Tight: 1-1** Gall: 0-1
Aids: Bl: 0-0 Vi: 0-0 Tstrap: 0-0 Ckp: 0-0
Best Rating: **64** 2/09 Ling 1m5f stand

Maiden winner; stays 1m5f; handles Polytrack.

Enlist

(104) (69)

5-y-o b g Beat Hollow-Dawna (Polish Precedent (USA))
A J Lidderdale Miss Lauren Meek

Placings:05/36 **(1133)**
2009: 9^3SD, 9^6SD,

	Starts	1st	2nd	3rd	Win & Pl
Career Total (Turf)	2	0	0	0	946
Career Total (AW)	2	0	0	1	433

Going (Turf): **Sf: 0-0 GS: 0-2 Gd: 0-0 GF: 0-0 Fm: 0-0**
Distance: 5f/6f: 0-0 7f-8f: 0-0 9f-13f: 0-3 14f+: 0-1
Track : LH: 0-2 RH: 0-0 Tight: 0-2 Gall: 0-0
Aids: Bl: 0-0 Vi: 0-0 Tstrap: 0-0 Ckp: 0-0
Best Rating: **69** 4/09 Wolv 1m1f103y stand

Enroller (IRE)

111 112

4-y-o b c Marju (IRE)-Walk On Quest (FR) (Rainbow Quest (USA))
W R Muir D G Clarke & C L A Edginton

Placings:054/12156454-1465560 **(7031)**
2009: 12^1S, 12^4GF, 12^6G, 16^5G, 16^5GF, 12^6G, 12^0S,

	Starts	1st	2nd	3rd	Win & Pl
Career Total (Turf)	18	3	1	0	92701

112 4/09 Newb 1m4f5y SFT £36900
96 5/08 NmkR 1m4f (0-95)H G-S £9066
80 4/08 Leic 1m3f183y SFT £2590
Total win prize-money £48557

Going (Turf): **Sf: 2-7** GS: 1-3 Gd: 0-4 GF: 0-3 Fm: 0-1
Distance: 5f/6f: 0-0 7f-8f: 0-2 **9f-13f: 3-10** 14f+: 0-6
Track : LH: 1-5 **RH: 2-11** Tight: 0-1 **Gall: 2-9**
Aids: Bl: 0-0 Vi: 0-0 Tstrap: 0-0 Ckp: 0-0
Best Rating: **112** 4/09 Newb 1m4f5y soft

Group class; stays at least 1m6f but effective at 1m4f; acts in soft ground.

Ensign's Trick

66 (26)63

5-y-o b m Cayman Kai (IRE)-River Ensign (River God (USA))
W M Brisbourne Mrs Mary Brisbourne

Placings:0303104400/0310206500/403020002000-0 **(6924)**
2009: 8^{0}GF,

	Starts	1st	2nd	3rd	Win & Pl
Career Total (Turf)	32	2	3	4	11246
Career Total (AW)	2	0	0	0	

68 5/07 Chep 6f16y (0-65)H G-F £2266
68 7/06 Ripn 6f G-F £2590
Total win prize-money £4858

Going (Turf): Sf: 0-1 GS: 0-9 Gd: 0-8 **GF: 2-14** Fm: 0-0
Distance: 5f/6f: 1-14 7f-8f: 1-19 9f-13f: 0-1 14f+: 0-0
Track : LH: 0-13 RH: 0-2 Tight: 0-9 Gall: 0-2
Aids: Bl: 0-0 Vi: 0-0 Tstrap: 0-0 Ckp: 0-0
Best Rating: 70 8/06 Ches 6f18y good

Moderate; suited by 6f-7f; acts on fast ground.

Ensnare

99(104) (82)**71**
4-y-o b g Pivotal-Entrap (USA) (Phone Trick (USA))
Ian Williams (A M Hales 16/2) C Owen

Placings:0461100126 **(7633)**
2009: 8^{0}SD, 10^{4}SD, 9^{6}SD, 8^{1}SD, 9^{1}G, 10^{0}GF, 8^{0}GF, 8^{1}SD, 8^{2}SD, 8^{6}SD,

	Starts	1st	2nd	3rd	Win & Pl
Career Total (Turf)	3	1	0	0	2267
Career Total (AW)	7	2	1	0	5723

82 11/09 Kemp 1m (0-65)H STD £2047
71 7/09 Ayr 1m1f20y (0-65)H GD £2266
68 6/09 Wolv 1m141y (0-60)H STD £2729
Total win prize-money £7044

Going (Turf): Sf: 0-0 GS: 0-0 **Gd: 1-1** GF: 0-2 Fm: 0-0
Distance: 5f/6f: 0-0 7f-8f: 1-3 **9f-13f: 2-7** 14f+: 0-0
Track : **LH: 2-6** RH: 1-4 **Tight: 1-6** Gall: 0-0
Aids: Bl: 0-0 Vi: 0-0 Tstrap: 0-0 Ckp: 0-0
Best Rating: 82 11/09 Kemp 1m stand

Fair; stays 1m and acts on Polytrack.

Enthusius

96(95) (58)**45**
6-y-o b g Generous (IRE)-Edouna (FR) (Doyoun)
G L Moore Fontwell Park Partnership

Placings:00/0/1403/5000 **(6692)**
2009: 14^{5}SD, 11^{0}GF, 16^{0}GF, 16^{0}GS,

	Starts	1st	2nd	3rd	Win & Pl
Career Total (Turf)	7	0	0	0	
Career Total (AW)	4	1	0	1	2679

60 2/07 Ling 1m4f (0-50)H STD £2388
Total win prize-money £2389

Going (Turf): **Sf: 0-1 GS: 0-1 Gd: 0-1 GF: 0-4 Fm: 0-0**
Distance: 5f/6f: 0-0 7f-8f: 0-0 **9f-13f: 1-7** 14f+: 0-4
Track : **LH: 1-7** RH: 0-3 **Tight: 1-8** Gall: 0-1
Aids: Bl: 0-2 Vi: 0-0 Tstrap: 0-0 Ckp: 0-0
Best Rating: 60 2/07 Ling 1m4f stand

Moderate; stays 2m; acts best on Polytrack.

Enticement

109 **102**
3-y-o b f Montjeu (IRE)-Ecoutila (USA) (Rahy (USA))
Sir Michael Stoute The Queen

Placings:11-3010 **(7128a)**
2009: 10^{3}GF, 12^{0}S, 10^{1}G, 10^{0}VS,

	Starts	1st	2nd	3rd	Win & Pl
Career Total (Turf)	6	3	0	1	50301

100 10/09 NmkR 1m2f GD £22708
99 11/08 NmkR 1m G-S £17031
75 10/08 Nott 1m75y G-S £3561
Total win prize-money £43301

Going (Turf): Sf: 0-1 **GS: 2-2** Gd: 1-1 GF: 0-1 Fm: 0-0
Distance: 5f/6f: 0-0 7f-8f: 1-1 **9f-13f: 2-5** 14f+: 0-0
Track : **LH: 1-4** RH: 0-0 Tight: 0-0 Gall: 0-1
Aids: Bl: 0-0 Vi: 0-0 Tstrap: 0-0 Ckp: 0-0
Best Rating: 102 5/09 York 1m2f88y gd-fm

Smart; winner in Listed company; stays 1m2f; acts on good and soft ground.

Entreat

106(101) (76)**84**
3-y-o ch f Pivotal-River Saint (USA) (Irish River (FR))
Sir Michael Stoute Cheveley Park Stud

Placings:6-3353130 **(6250)**
2009: 10^{3}G, 9^{3}F, 11^{5}G, **10^{3}SD**, 9^{1}GF, 10^{3}GS, 8^{0}GF,

	Starts	1st	2nd	3rd	Win & Pl
Career Total (Turf)	7	1	0	3	4927
Career Total (AW)	1	0	0	1	403

84 8/09 Folk 1m1f149y G-F £2729
Total win prize-money £2730

Going (Turf): Sf: 0-0 GS: 0-2 Gd: 0-2 **GF: 1-2** Fm: 0-1
Distance: 5f/6f: 0-0 7f-8f: 0-1 **9f-13f: 1-7** 14f+: 0-0
Track : LH: 0-3 **RH: 1-4 Tight: 1-3** Gall: 0-0
Aids: Bl: 0-0 **Vi: 1-3** Tstrap: 0-0 Ckp: 0-0
Best Rating: 84 9/09 Sand 1m2f7y gd-sft

Useful stays 1m2f; acts on fast and easy ground.

Eolith

97(93) (83)**83**
2-y-o ch f Pastoral Pursuits-Evening Guest (FR) (Be My Guest (USA))
W J Knight Mrs Alison Ruggles

Placings:11 **(5639)**
2009: 7^{1}G, 7^{1}SD,

	Starts	1st	2nd	3rd	Win & Pl
Career Total (Turf)	1	1	0	0	4857
Career Total (AW)	1	1	0	0	7477

83 9/09 Kemp 7f STD £7477
83 8/09 NmkJ 7f GD £4857
Total win prize-money £12334

Going (Turf): Sf: 0-0 GS: 0-0 **Gd: 1-1** GF: 0-0 Fm: 0-0
Distance: 5f/6f: 0-0 **7f-8f: 2-2** 9f-13f: 0-0 14f+: 0-0
Track : LH: 0-0 **RH: 1-1** Tight: 0-0 Gall: 0-0
Aids: Bl: 0-0 Vi: 0-0 Tstrap: 0-0 Ckp: 0-0
Best Rating: 83 9/09 Kemp 7f stand

Useful; effective over 7f; acts on good ground and on Polytrack.

Epic (IRE)

97(89) (76)**76**
2-y-o b g Celtic Swing-Needwood Epic (Midyan (USA))
M Johnston Racegoers Club Owners Group

Placings:651303 **(7804)**
2009: 7^{6}GF, 7^{5}SD, 7^{1}GF, 8^{3}SD, 8^{0}SD, 8^{3}SD,

	Starts	1st	2nd	3rd	Win & Pl
Career Total (Turf)	2	1	0	0	2914
Career Total (AW)	4	0	0	2	1429

76 9/09 Bevl 7f100y G-F £2914
Total win prize-money £2914

Going (Turf): Sf: 0-0 GS: 0-0 Gd: 0-0 **GF: 1-2** Fm: 0-0
Distance: 5f/6f: 0-0 **7f-8f: 1-3** 9f-13f: 0-3 14f+: 0-0
Track : LH: 0-4 **RH: 1-2** Tight: 0-4 Gall: 0-0
Aids: Bl: 0-0 Vi: 0-0 Tstrap: 0-0 Ckp: 0-0
Best Rating: 76 10/09 Wolv 1m141y stand

Fair sort; effective at 7f; acts on fast ground and on Polytrack.

Epic Odyssey

78(107) (87)**85**
4-y-o ch g Dubai Destination (USA)-Royal Gift (Cadeaux Genereux)
Lee Smyth (J R Gask 26/3) Mark Devlin

Placings:605/422143400624-2130 **(2389)**
2009: 6^{2}SD, 6^{1}SD, 5^{3}SD, 6^{0}G,

	Starts	1st	2nd	3rd	Win & Pl
Career Total (Turf)	9	1	2	0	16729
Career Total (AW)	10	1	2	2	9421

76 2/09 Kemp 6f STD £1942
83 6/08 Curr 6f FRM £8129
Total win prize-money £10072

Going (Turf): Sf: 0-2 GS: 0-0 Gd: 0-3 GF: 0-1 **Fm: 1-1**
Distance: **5f/6f: 2-17** 7f-8f: 0-2 9f-13f: 0-0 14f+: 0-0
Track : LH: 0-12 **RH: 1-1** Tight: 0-2 Gall: 0-3
Aids: Bl: 0-0 Vi: 0-0 Tstrap: 0-2 Ckp: 0-2
Best Rating: 87 12/08 GrLe 6f stand

Epidaurian King (IRE)

92(104) (68)**64**
6-y-o b g King's Best (USA)-Thurayya (Nashwan (USA))
D Shaw Market Avenue Racing Club Ltd

Placings:6/003000041/11002450430105б-5625006 **(2264)**
2009: 11^{5}SD, 9^{6}SD, 12^{2}SD, 12^{5}SD, 9^{0}GF, 7^{0}GF, 11^{6}G,

	Starts	1st	2nd	3rd	Win & Pl
Career Total (Turf)	5	0	0	1	262
Career Total (AW)	27	4	2	1	8901

68 10/08 Kemp 1m (0-60)H STD £2047
68 1/08 Kemp 7f (0-50)H STD £2047
58 1/08 Wolv 7f32y (0-45) STD £1365
59 12/07 Ling 7f (0-52)H STD £1943
Total win prize-money £7403

Going (Turf): **Sf: 0-0 GS: 0-0 Gd: 0-3 GF: 0-2 Fm: 0-0**
Distance: 5f/6f: 0-8 **7f-8f: 4-17** 9f-13f: 0-7 14f+: 0-0
Track : LH: 2-19 RH: 2-13 **Tight: 2-15** Gall: 0-0
Aids: Bl: 0-0 **Vi: 4-16** Tstrap: 0-0 Ckp: 0-0
Best Rating: 68 10/08 Kemp 1m stand

Modest; stays 1m4f; acts on Polytrack; has worn a visor.

Epsom Salts

105(102) (77)**84**
4-y-o b g Josr Algarhoud (IRE)-Captive Heart (Conquistador Cielo (USA))
P M Phelan The Epsom Racegoers

Placings:000/0052111222-004015413130 **(6473)**
2009: 15^{0}G, 16^{0}G, 16^{4}GF, 11^{0}GF, 12^{1}GF, 13^{5}GF, 11^{4}F, 12^{1}GF, 12^{3}G, 12^{1}GF, 18^{3}GF, 12^{0}GF,

	Starts	1st	2nd	3rd	Win & Pl
Career Total (Turf)	16	3	0	2	20457
Career Total (AW)	9	3	4	0	11049

84 9/09 Epsm 1m4f10y (0-80)H G-F £6476
76 8/09 Epsm 1m4f10y (0-80)H G-F £4996
72 7/09 Epsm 1m4f10y (0-75)H G-F £3238
69 11/08 Ling 1m4f (0-70)H STD £2637
66 11/08 Ling 1m5f (0-75)H STD £2729

63	10/08	Kemp	1m4f	(0-60)H	STD	£2047

Total win prize-money £22125

Going (Turf): Sf: 0-1 GS: 0-1 Gd: 0-4 **GF: 3-9** Fm: 0-1
Distance: 5f/6f: 0-2 7f-8f: 0-1 **9f-13f: 6-16** 14f+: 0-6
Track : **LH: 5-17** RH: 1-7 **Tight: 5-18** Gall: 0-3
Aids: Bl: 0-0 Vi: 0-0 Tstrap: 0-0 Ckp: 0-0
Best Rating: **84** 9/09 Epsm 1m4f10y gd-fm

Fair; stays 2m but effective at shorter; acts on fast ground; goes on Polytrack; goes well at Epsom.

Equiano (FR)

110 **119**

4-y-o b c Acclamation-Entente Cordiale (IRE) (Ela-Mana-Mou)
B W Hills J Acheson

Placings:210133/212140-200000050 **(6522a)**
2009: 6^{2}GF, 6^{0}CF, 5^{0}G, 5^{0}GF, 6^{0}GF, 5^{0}G, 5^{0}GF, 6^{5}GS, 5^{0}G,

	Starts	1st	2nd	3rd	Win & Pl
Career Total (Turf)	**21**	**4**	**4**	**2**	**233754**

119	6/08	Asct	5f	G-F	£141925
111	5/08	Chan	5f110y	GD	£12500
	9/07	Madr	7f	GD	£4054
	8/07	Sans	6f110y	GD	£4054

Total win prize-money £162533

Going (Turf): Sf: 0-4 GS: 0-2 **Gd: 3-9** GF: 1-6 Fm: 0-0
Distance: 5f/6f: 2-16 7f-8f: 2-4 9f-13f: 0-0 14f+: 0-0
Track : LH: 0-0 RH: 0-0 Tight: 0-0 Gall: 0-0
Aids: Bl: 0-2 Vi: 0-0 Tstrap: 0-0 Ckp: 0-0
Best Rating: **119** 6/08 Asct 5f gd-fm

Smart; formerly Spanish-trained; winner of the 2008 King's Stand Stakes; effective from 5f-7f; acts on most ground; has worn blinkers.

Equinine (IRE)

102(96) (74)**76**

3-y-o ch f Namid-Goldilocks (IRE) (Caerleon (USA))
Peter Grayson (B W Hills 26/9) Jasper Partnership

Placings:0426-303**2**1200 **(7358)**
2009: 7^{3}GF, 7^{0}G, 7^{3}GS, 7^{2}SD, 6^{1}GF, 6^{2}GF, 7^{0}SD, 5^{0}SD,

	Starts	1st	2nd	3rd	Win & Pl
Career Total (Turf)	**9**	**1**	**2**	**2**	**6741**
Career Total (AW)	**3**	**0**	**1**	**0**	**605**

73	9/09	Rdcr	6f	G-F	£2590

Total win prize-money £2590

Going (Turf): Sf: 0-1 GS: 0-2 Gd: 0-1 **GF: 1-5** Fm: 0-0
Distance: **5f/6f: 1-7** 7f-8f: 0-5 9f-13f: 0-0 14f+: 0-0
Track : LH: 0-2 RH: 0-2 Tight: 0-2 Gall: 0-1
Aids: Bl: 0-0 Vi: 0-0 Tstrap: 0-0 Ckp: 0-0
Best Rating: **76** 9/09 Gdwd 6f gd-fm

Modest; stays 7f; acts on fast and soft ground; goes on Polytrack.

Equinity

96(94) (56)**52**

3-y-o b f Ishiguru (USA)-Notable Lady (IRE) (Victory Note (USA))
J Pearce Killarney Glen

Placings:04005-6040100502 **(7879)**
2009: 5^{6}SD, 6^{0}SD, 5^{4}F, 5^{0}G, 6^{1}GF, 6^{0}GF, 6^{0}SD, 6^{5}SD, 6^{0}SD, 6^{2}SD,

	Starts	1st	2nd	3rd	Win & Pl
Career Total (Turf)	**6**	**1**	**0**	**0**	**2240**
Career Total (AW)	**9**	**0**	**1**	**0**	**849**

52	8/09	Folk	6f	(0-65)H	G-F	£2047

Total win prize-money £2047

Going (Turf): Sf: 0-0 GS: 0-1 Gd: 0-2 **GF: 1-2** Fm: 0-1
Distance: **5f/6f: 1-12** 7f-8f: 0-3 9f-13f: 0-0 14f+: 0-0
Track : LH: 0-7 RH: 0-3 Tight: 0-4 Gall: 0-1
Aids: Bl: 0-0 Vi: 0-0 Tstrap: 0-0 Ckp: 0-0
Best Rating: **56** 10/08 Kemp 6f stand

Moderate; effective over 6f; acts on Polytrack.

Equipe De Nuit

102(94) (70)**83**

3-y-o ch c Sulamani (IRE)-Denica (IRE) (Night Shift (USA))
S C Williams Hamill, Ostlere & George

Placings:22-**6**00632344**5**100 **(6755)**
2009: 7^{6}SD, 10^{0}GF, 10^{0}G, 10^{6}G, 9^{3}GF, 10^{2}GF, 9^{3}GF, 10^{4}GF, 8^{4}SD, 8^{5}GF, 7^{1}GF, 6^{0}GF, 7^{0}G,

	Starts	1st	2nd	3rd	Win & Pl
Career Total (Turf)	**12**	**1**	**2**	**2**	**5112**
Career Total (AW)	**3**	**0**	**1**	**0**	**915**

73	9/09	Leic	7f9y	G-F	£1942

Total win prize-money £1943

Going (Turf): Sf: 0-0 GS: 0-0 Gd: 0-4 **GF: 1-8** Fm: 0-0
Distance: 5f/6f: 0-1 **7f-8f: 1-6** 9f-13f: 0-8 14f+: 0-0
Track : LH: 0-7 RH: 0-4 Tight: 0-5 Gall: 0-1
Aids: Bl: 0-0 Vi: 0-0 Tstrap: 0-0 Ckp: 0-0
Best Rating: **83** 8/08 NmkJ 7f good

Fair; stays 7f; acts on fast and easy ground; goes on Polytrack.

Equuleus Pictor

105(105) (93)**94**

5-y-o br g Piccolo-Vax Rapide (Sharpo)
J L Spearing Masonaires

Placings:63**5**/0100044/0651462231133O-0411560034023 **(7866)**
2009: 5^{0}GF, 5^{4}G, 5^{1}HY, 5^{1}GS, 5^{5}G, 5^{6}G, 5^{0}GS, 5^{0}GS, 5^{3}C, 5^{4}G, 5^{0}GS, 5^{2}SD, 5^{3}SS,

	Starts	1st	2nd	3rd	Win & Pl
Career Total (Turf)	**34**	**6**	**2**	**5**	**36532**
Career Total (AW)	**3**	**0**	**1**	**1**	**3432**

93	6/09	York	5f	(0-90)H	G-S	£7641
93	5/09	Hayd	5f	(0-85)H	HVY	£6476
86	8/08	Wind	5f10y	(0-85)H	G-S	£5375
82	8/08	Nott	5f13y	(0-70)H	SFT	£3238
75	5/08	Yarm	5f43y	(0-75)H	G-S	£2590
71	7/07	Ayr	6f	(0-70)H	G-S	£3886

Total win prize-money £29207

Going (Turf): Sf: 2-4 **GS: 4-12** Gd: 0-14 GF: 0-4 Fm: 0-0
Distance: **5f/6f: 6-33** 7f-8f: 0-4 9f-13f: 0-0 14f+: 0-0
Track : LH: 0-3 RH: 0-0 Tight: 0-1 **Gall: 1-8**
Aids: Bl: 0-0 Vi: 0-0 Tstrap: 0-0 Ckp: 0-0
Best Rating: **94** 10/09 York 5f good

Useful; effective over 5f-6f; acts on most ground on turf; goes on Polytrack.

Erebus (IRE)

85(92) (64)**58**

2-y-o b c Fasliyev (USA)-Velvet Slipper (Muhtafal (USA))
S Kirk The Classics Partnership

Placings:006 **(7859)**
2009: 6^{0}GS, 7^{0}SD, 7^{6}SD,

	Starts	1st	2nd	3rd	Win & Pl
Career Total (Turf)	**1**	**0**	**0**	**0**	
Career Total (AW)	**2**	**0**	**0**	**0**	**0**

Going (Turf): **Sf: 0-0 GS: 0-1 Gd: 0-0 GF: 0-0 Fm: 0-0**
Distance: 5f/6f: 0-1 7f-8f: 0-2 9f-13f: 0-0 14f+: 0-0
Track : LH: 0-1 RH: 0-1 Tight: 0-1 Gall: 0-1
Aids: Bl: 0-0 Vi: 0-0 Tstrap: 0-0 Ckp: 0-0
Best Rating: **64** 12/09 Wolv 7f32y stand

Ereeford

(71)

3-y-o b g Ishiguru (USA)-Miss Twiddles (IRE) (Desert King (IRE))
M W Easterby Clark Industrial Services Partnership

Placings:60 **(1476)**
2009: 5^{6}SD, 7^{0}SD,

	Starts	1st	2nd	3rd	Win & Pl
Career Total (Turf)	**0**	**0**	**0**	**0**	
Career Total (AW)	**2**	**0**	**0**	**0**	**0**

Going (Turf): **Sf: 0-0 GS: 0-0 Gd: 0-0 GF: 0-0 Fm: 0-0**
Distance: 5f/6f: 0-1 7f-8f: 0-1 9f-13f: 0-0 14f+: 0-0
Track : LH: 0-1 RH: 0-0 Tight: 0-0 Gall: 0-0
Aids: Bl: 0-0 Vi: 0-0 Tstrap: 0-0 Ckp: 0-0

Erfaan (USA)

86 **65**

2-y-o b/br c Forest Camp (USA)-Look For Good (USA) (Unbridled's Song (USA))
B W Hills Hamdan Al Maktoum

Placings:00 **(3750)**
2009: 6^{0}GF, 7^{0}G,

	Starts	1st	2nd	3rd	Win & Pl
Career Total (Turf)	**2**	**0**	**0**	**0**	

Going (Turf): **Sf: 0-0 GS: 0-0 Gd: 0-1 GF: 0-1 Fm: 0-0**
Distance: 5f/6f: 0-0 7f-8f: 0-2 9f-13f: 0-0 14f+: 0-0
Track : LH: 0-0 RH: 0-0 Tight: 0-0 Gall: 0-0
Aids: Bl: 0-0 Vi: 0-0 Tstrap: 0-0 Ckp: 0-0
Best Rating: **65** 7/09 NmkJ 7f good

Ergo (FR)

101(104) (71)**76**

5-y-o b h Grand Lodge (USA)-Erhawah (Mark Of Esteem (IRE))
James Moffatt Mrs Eileen M Milligan

Placings:0/0036411320/5000-112154004 **(5886)**
2009: 8^{1}SD, 8^{1}SD, 7^{2}GF, 8^{1}G, 8^{5}G, 10^{4}G, 8^{0}S, 8^{0}GF, 8^{4}SD,

	Starts	1st	2nd	3rd	Win & Pl
Career Total (Turf)	**20**	**3**	**2**	**2**	**20263**
Career Total (AW)	**4**	**2**	**0**	**0**	**4407**

76	5/09	Haml	1m65y	(0-70)H	GD	£3238
71	3/09	Wolv	1m141y	(0-60)H	STD	£2047
59	2/09	Wolv	1m141y	(0-60)H	STD	£2047
	5/07	Saln	1m4f		SFT	£6081
	5/07	Orai	1m3f		GD	£2702

Total win prize-money £16116

Going (Turf): Sf: 1-6 GS: 0-2 **Gd: 2-8** GF: 0-2 Fm: 0-0
Distance: 5f/6f: 0-0 7f-8f: 0-3 **9f-13f: 5-19** 14f+: 0-2
Track : **LH: 2-12** RH: 1-2 **Tight: 3-7** Gall: 0-4
Aids: **Bl: 4-13** Vi: 1-6 Tstrap: 0-1 Ckp: 0-1
Best Rating: **76** 5/09 Haml 1m65y good

Modest; stays 1m4f, but fully effective at around 1m; acts on fast ground and on Polytrack; usually wears headgear.

Erinjay (IRE)

(96) (75)

3-y-o b g Bachelor Duke (USA)-Quinella (Generous (IRE))

M Wigham Seyhan Osman & Robert Kibble

Placings:01 **(7826)**

2009: 5^{0}SD, 8^{1}SD,

	Starts	1st	2nd	3rd	Win & Pl
Career Total (Turf)	0	0	0	0	
Career Total (AW)	2	1	0	0	2590

75 12/09 Kemp 1m STD £2590

Total win prize-money £2590

Going (Turf): **Sf: 0-0 GS: 0-0 Gd: 0-0 GF: 0-0 Fm: 0-0**
Distance: 5f/6f: 0-1 **7f-8f: 1-1** 9f-13f: 0-0 14f+: 0-0
Track : LH: 0-1 **RH: 1-1** Tight: 0-1 Gall: 0-0
Aids: Bl: 0-0 Vi: 0-0 Tstrap: 0-0 Ckp: 0-0
Best Rating: **75** 12/09 Kemp 1m stand

Modest; stays 1m; acts on Polytrack.

Ermine And Velvet

103(84) (39)88

3-y-o ch f Nayef (USA)-Ermine (IRE) (Cadeaux Genereux)

C E Brittain Saeed Manana

Placings:40220020 **(6267)**

2009: 7^{4}GS, 8^{0}SD, 7^{2}GS, 7^{2}G, 7^{0}GF, 8^{0}GF, 6^{2}GF, 8^{0}G,

	Starts	1st	2nd	3rd	Win & Pl
Career Total (Turf)	7	0	3	0	11980
Career Total (AW)	1	0	0	0	

Going (Turf): **Sf: 0-0 GS: 0-2 Gd: 0-2 GF: 0-3 Fm: 0-0**
Distance: 5f/6f: 0-0 7f-8f: 0-8 9f-13f: 0-0 14f+: 0-0
Track : LH: 0-2 RH: 0-2 Tight: 0-1 Gall: 0-1
Aids: Bl: 0-0 Vi: 0-0 Tstrap: 0-0 Ckp: 0-0
Best Rating: **88** 6/09 Epsm 7f good

Useful; effective over 7f; acts on good and easy ground.

Ermine Grey

104(102) (63)66

8-y-o gr g Wolfhound (USA)-Impulsive Decision (IRE) (Nomination)

S Gollings L M Baker

Placings:0651016/00344030/62040043/0566245255050/0 4231030606/2422524512414-555034 **(6668)**

2009: 8^{5}SD, 10^{5}SD, 8^{5}G, 8^{0}SD, 8^{3}GS, 9^{4}SD,

	Starts	1st	2nd	3rd	Win & Pl
Career Total (Turf)	38	3	4	5	18941
Career Total (AW)	28	2	5	1	10861

66	7/08	Chep	1m14y	(0-75)H	G-F	£3885
63	5/08	Chep	1m14y	(0-65)H	GD	£2104
62	7/07	Hayd	1m30y	(0-65)H	HVY	£3238
82	11/03	Wolv	7f	E(0-75)	STD	£2086
73	9/03	Sthl	1m	D	SLW	£2912

Total win prize-money £14228

Going (Turf): **Sf: 1-9** GS: 0-6 **Gd: 1-12 GF: 1-10** Fm: 0-1
Distance: 5f/6f: 0-3 7f-8f: 2-17 **9f-13f: 3-46** 14f+: 0-0
Track : **LH: 3-42** RH: 0-11 **Tight: 1-24** Gall: 0-3
Aids: Bl: 0-6 **Vi: 2-16** Tstrap: 0-2 Ckp: 0-2
Best Rating: **84** 2/05 Wolv 1m141y stand

Moderate; made successful return to turf when landing 1m Class 6 handicap at Chepstow May 2006; came from a long way back when landing similar event at the same venue in July; effective over 1m-1m2f; acts on most ground; also goes on Polytrack.

Ermine Sea

107 (77)93

6-y-o b g Rainbow Quest (USA)-Bint Pasha (USA) (Affirmed (USA))

Miss H C Knight Lady Bamford & Alice Bamford

Placings:0/22231505/3065 **(5346)**

2009: 16^{3}GF, 20^{0}GF, 16^{6}G, 14^{5}G,

	Starts	1st	2nd	3rd	Win & Pl
Career Total (Turf)	12	1	2	2	18240
Career Total (AW)	1	0	1	0	1638

86 7/06 Newb 1m4f5y GD £5181

Total win prize-money £5182

Going (Turf): Sf: 0-1 GS: 0-2 **Gd: 1-4** GF: 0-5 Fm: 0-0
Distance: 5f/6f: 0-0 7f-8f: 0-1 **9f-13f: 1-4** 14f+: 0-8
Track : **LH: 1-4** RH: 0-8 Tight: 0-2 **Gall: 1-5**
Aids: Bl: 0-1 Vi: 0-0 Tstrap: 0-1 Ckp: 0-1
Best Rating: **100** 6/06 Asct 2m gd-fm

Very useful; Group placed; stays 2m, but effective over shorter; acts on fast ground and Polytrack; likes to race prominently.

Ermyn Express

(93) (63)

2-y-o b f Selkirk (USA)-Aymara (Darshaan)

P M Phelan Ermyn Lodge Stud

Placings:0034 **(7825)**

2009: 7^{0}SD, 8^{0}SD, 6^{3}SD, 8^{4}SD,

	Starts	1st	2nd	3rd	Win & Pl
Career Total (Turf)	0	0	0	0	
Career Total (AW)	4	0	0	1	403

Going (Turf): **Sf: 0-0 GS: 0-0 Gd: 0-0 GF: 0-0 Fm: 0-0**
Distance: 5f/6f: 0-1 7f-8f: 0-3 9f-13f: 0-0 14f+: 0-0
Track : LH: 0-2 RH: 0-2 Tight: 0-2 Gall: 0-0
Aids: Bl: 0-0 Vi: 0-0 Tstrap: 0-0 Ckp: 0-0
Best Rating: **63** 12/09 Ling 6f stand

Modest; effective over 6f; acts on Polytrack.

Ermyn Lodge

105(102) (81)81

3-y-o br g Singspiel (IRE)-Rosewood Belle (USA) (Woodman (USA))

P M Phelan Ermyn Lodge Stud & Heatherwold Stud

Placings:000-12532122 **(6388)**

2009: 12^{1}SD, 11^{2}GS, 14^{5}F, 16^{3}SD, 14^{2}G, 14^{1}G, 16^{2}SD, 16^{2}GF,

	Starts	1st	2nd	3rd	Win & Pl
Career Total (Turf)	7	1	3	0	9035
Career Total (AW)	4	1	1	1	4321

69	8/09	Sand	1m6f	(0-80)H	GD	£4857
62	3/09	Kemp	1m4f	(0-60)H	STD	£2047

Total win prize-money £6904

Going (Turf): Sf: 0-0 GS: 0-2 **Gd: 1-2** GF: 0-2 Fm: 0-1
Distance: 5f/6f: 0-0 7f-8f: 0-0 9f-13f: 1-5 14f+: 1-6
Track : LH: 0-3 **RH: 2-7** Tight: 0-3 Gall: 0-1
Aids: Bl: 0-0 **Vi: 1-4** Tstrap: 0-0 Ckp: 0-0
Best Rating: **81** 9/09 Nott 2m9y gd-fm

Fair; stays 2m; acts on fast ground; goes on Polytrack.

Ermyntrude

72(87) (56)41

2-y-o b/br f Rock Of Gibraltar (IRE)-Ruthie (Pursuit Of Love)

P M Phelan Timesquare Ltd

Placings:5040 **(7654)**

2009: 8^{5}SS, 8^{0}S, 8^{4}SD, 7^{0}SD,

	Starts	1st	2nd	3rd	Win & Pl
Career Total (Turf)	1	0	0	0	
Career Total (AW)	3	0	0	0	289

Going (Turf): **Sf: 0-1 GS: 0-0 Gd: 0-0 GF: 0-0 Fm: 0-0**
Distance: 5f/6f: 0-0 7f-8f: 0-4 9f-13f: 0-0 14f+: 0-0
Track : LH: 0-2 RH: 0-1 Tight: 0-2 Gall: 0-0
Aids: Bl: 0-0 Vi: 0-0 Tstrap: 0-0 Ckp: 0-0
Best Rating: **56** 10/09 Ling 1m std-slw

Ernies Keep

87(49) 46

3-y-o ch g Young Ern-Croeso Cynnes (Most Welcome)

W Storey Thistle And Rose Racing

Placings:004000-0050000 **(5733)**

2009: 9^{0}GF, 9^{0}GF, 11^{5}GF, 12^{0}F, 15^{0}G, 14^{0}GF, 12^{0}GS,

	Starts	1st	2nd	3rd	Win & Pl
Career Total (Turf)	13	0	0	0	0
Career Total (AW)	1	0	0	0	

Going (Turf): **Sf: 0-0 GS: 0-2 Gd: 0-4 GF: 0-5 Fm: 0-2**
Distance: 5f/6f: 0-5 7f-8f: 0-2 9f-13f: 0-5 14f+: 0-2
Track : LH: 0-5 RH: 0-4 Tight: 0-7 Gall: 0-1
Aids: Bl: 0-0 Vi: 0-0 Tstrap: 0-1 Ckp: 0-1
Best Rating: **46** 10/08 Catt 7f gd-sft

Erra Go On

(91) (60)57

8-y-o ch g Atraf-Pastelle (Tate Gallery (USA))

G T Lynch Mrs Mary T Kelly

Placings:500/041201205646/066004411000/6004000400/ 00-006000 **(7383a)**

2009: 7^{0}SD, 8^{0}SD, 9^{6}GF, 11^{0}YS, 16^{0}YS, 10^{0}SD,

	Starts	1st	2nd	3rd	Win & Pl
Career Total (Turf)	38	4	2	0	28871
Career Total (AW)	7	0	0	0	0

83	8/06	Tral	1m	(60-90)H	YLD	£7624
78	8/06	Tipp	7f100y	(50-70)H	GD	£4765
79	7/04	DRoy	7f	(50-80)H	FRM	£6082
78	6/04	Naas	6f	(37-70)H	G-F	£4866

Total win prize-money £23340

Going (Turf): Sf: 0-2 GS: 0-0 **Gd: 1-9 GF: 1-17 Fm: 1-2**
Distance: 5f/6f: 1-9 **7f-8f: 3-29** 9f-13f: 0-5 14f+: 0-2
Track : **LH: 2-18** RH: 1-16 Tight: 0-4 Gall: 0-1
Aids: Bl: 0-1 Vi: 0-0 Tstrap: 0-0 Ckp: 0-0
Best Rating: **85** 7/04 Curr 7f good

Four times a winner at up to a mile in Ireland; acts on firm and good to soft.

Errigal Lad

107(92) (61)88

4-y-o ch g Bertolini (USA)-La Belle Vie (Indian King (USA))

J Balding (K A Ryan 31/7) R L Crowe

Placings:210/003431-25026560 **(5516)**

2009: 6^{2}GF, 7^{5}S, 7^{0}G, 6^{2}GF, 6^{6}GS, 6^{5}G, 6^{6}G, 6^{0}GF,

	Starts	1st	2nd	3rd	Win & Pl
Career Total (Turf)	16	2	3	2	14396
Career Total (AW)	1	0	0	0	

86	9/08	Leic	5f218y	(0-85)H	SFT	£4857
76	9/07	Hayd	6f		G-F	£2590

Total win prize-money £7448

Going (Turf): **Sf: 1-3** GS: 0-4 Gd: 0-5 **GF: 1-4** Fm: 0-0
Distance: **5f/6f: 2-11** 7f-8f: 0-6 9f-13f: 0-0 14f+: 0-0
Track : LH: 0-2 RH: 0-2 Tight: 0-0 Gall: 0-0
Aids: Bl: 0-2 Vi: 0-0 Tstrap: 0-4 Ckp: 0-4
Best Rating: **88** 6/09 Donc 6f gd-fm

Useful; effective over 6f; acts on most ground; has worn blinkers and cheekpieces.

Errol Flynn (IRE)

92(82) (30)51
3-y-o b/br g Danehill Dancer (IRE)-Warusha (GER) (Shareef Dancer (USA))
B G Powell (R A Harris 28/8) W Clifford

Placings:00000 **(6705)**
2009: 8^{0}GF, 8^{0}G, 10^{0}GF, 11^{0}G, 10^{0}SS,

	Starts	1st	2nd	3rd	Win & Pl
Career Total (Turf)	4	0	0	0	
Career Total (AW)	1	0	0	0	

Going (Turf): **Sf: 0-0 GS: 0-0 Gd: 0-2 GF: 0-2 Fm: 0-0**
Distance: 5f/6f: 0-0 7f-8f: 0-1 9f-13f: 0-4 14f+: 0-0
Track : LH: 0-2 RH: 0-1 Tight: 0-3 Gall: 0-0
Aids: Bl: 0-1 Vi: 0-0 Tstrap: 0-2 Ckp: 0-2
Best Rating: **51** 8/09 Wind 1m2f7y gd-fm

Ertiyaad

(79) (48)
2-y-o b f Sakhee (USA)-Asawer (IRE) (Darshaan)
Sir Michael Stoute Hamdan Al Maktoum

Placings:0 **(7325)**
2009: 7^{0}SD,

	Starts	1st	2nd	3rd	Win & Pl
Career Total (Turf)	0	0	0	0	
Career Total (AW)	1	0	0	0	

Going (Turf): **Sf: 0-0 GS: 0-0 Gd: 0-0 GF: 0-0 Fm: 0-0**
Distance: 5f/6f: 0-0 7f-8f: 0-1 9f-13f: 0-0 14f+: 0-0
Track : LH: 0-0 RH: 0-1 Tight: 0-0 Gall: 0-0
Aids: Bl: 0-0 Vi: 0-0 Tstrap: 0-0 Ckp: 0-0
Best Rating: **48** 11/09 Kemp 7f stand

Esaar (USA)

98 85
2-y-o b c Mr Greeley (USA)-Al Desima (Emperor Jones (USA))
B W Hills Hamdan Al Maktoum

Placings:32 **(6451)**
2009: 7^{3}GF, 7^{2}GF,

	Starts	1st	2nd	3rd	Win & Pl
Career Total (Turf)	2	0	1	1	2649

Going (Turf): **Sf: 0-0 GS: 0-0 Gd: 0-0 GF: 0-2 Fm: 0-0**
Distance: 5f/6f: 0-0 7f-8f: 0-2 9f-13f: 0-0 14f+: 0-0
Track : LH: 0-0 RH: 0-0 Tight: 0-0 Gall: 0-0
Aids: Bl: 0-0 Vi: 0-0 Tstrap: 0-0 Ckp: 0-0
Best Rating: **85** 10/09 NmkR 7f gd-fm

Useful; stays 7f; acts on fast ground.

Escape Artist

78 43
2-y-o gr g Act One-Free At Last (Shirley Heights)
T D Easterby Habtons Baggie Rams

Placings:006 **(4888)**
2009: 7^{0}G, 7^{0}GF, 7^{6}G,

	Starts	1st	2nd	3rd	Win & Pl
Career Total (Turf)	3	0	0	0	0

Going (Turf): **Sf: 0-0 GS: 0-0 Gd: 0-2 GF: 0-1 Fm: 0-0**
Distance: 5f/6f: 0-0 7f-8f: 0-3 9f-13f: 0-0 14f+: 0-0
Track : LH: 0-1 RH: 0-2 Tight: 0-0 Gall: 0-1
Aids: Bl: 0-0 Vi: 0-0 Tstrap: 0-0 Ckp: 0-0
Best Rating: **43** 7/09 Bevl 7f100y gd-fm

Escape Wall

(70) (12)
8-y-o ch g Kirkwall-Island Escape (IRE) (Turtle Island (IRE))
R J Hodges Michael Potter

Placings:0 **(6703)**
2009: 8^{0}SS,

	Starts	1st	2nd	3rd	Win & Pl
Career Total (Turf)	0	0	0	0	
Career Total (AW)	1	0	0	0	

Going (Turf): **Sf: 0-0 GS: 0-0 Gd: 0-0 GF: 0-0 Fm: 0-0**
Distance: 5f/6f: 0-0 7f-8f: 0-1 9f-13f: 0-0 14f+: 0-0
Track : LH: 0-1 RH: 0-0 Tight: 0-1 Gall: 0-0
Aids: Bl: 0-0 Vi: 0-0 Tstrap: 0-0 Ckp: 0-0
Best Rating: **12** 10/09 Ling 1m std-slw

Eseej (USA)

101(111) (82)78
4-y-o ch g Aljabr (USA)-Jinaan (USA) (Mr Prospector (USA))
P W Hiatt P W Hiatt

Placings:06/0505001-642110020610404 **(7851)**
2009: 12^{6}SD, 11^{4}SD, 12^{2}SD, 12^{1}SD, 12^{1}SD, 12^{0}SD, 12^{0}G, 11^{2}GF, 12^{0}GF, 10^{6}SD, 11^{1}SD, 16^{0}G, 13^{4}SD, 12^{0}SD, 11^{4}SS,

	Starts	1st	2nd	3rd	Win & Pl
Career Total (Turf)	8	0	1	0	806
Career Total (AW)	16	4	1	0	13477

82	10/09	Sthl	1m3f	(0-85)H	STD	£5504
81	3/09	Sthl	1m4f	(0-65)H	STD	£2047
73	2/09	Wolv	1m4f50y	(0-75)H	STD	£2729
66	12/08	Kemp	1m3f		STD	£2047

Total win prize-money £12329

Going (Turf): **Sf: 0-0 GS: 0-1 Gd: 0-4 GF: 0-3 Fm: 0-0**
Distance: 5f/6f: 0-3 7f-8f: 0-0 **9f-13f: 4-19** 14f+: 0-2
Track : **LH: 3-11** RH: 1-9 **Tight: 1-6** Gall: 0-2
Aids: Bl: 0-0 Vi: 0-0 Tstrap: 0-0 Ckp: 0-0
Best Rating: **82** 10/09 Sthl 1m3f stand

Fair; stays 1m4f; acts on Fibresand and Polytrack.

Esoterica (IRE)

108 97
6-y-o b g Bluebird (USA)-Mysterious Plans (IRE) (Last Tycoon)
J S Goldie Mrs S E Bruce

Placings:3/3036441232306/000440215411405442/00232 321142004-60511500056401 **(6815)**
2009: 7^{6}GF, 7^{0}G, 8^{5}GS, 8^{1}G, 7^{1}GF, 7^{5}GF, 8^{0}GF, 7^{0}G, 7^{0}GF, 7^{5}GF, 7^{6}S, 6^{4}G, 7^{0}GF, 7^{1}G,

	Starts	1st	2nd	3rd	Win & Pl
Career Total (Turf)	60	9	8	7	67216

97	10/09	NmkR	7f	(0-105)H	GD	£11215
96	6/09	Ayr	7f50y	(0-85)H	G-F	£4727
81	5/09	Ayr	1m	(0-75)H	GD	£3885
86	7/08	York	7f	(0-80)H	G-F	£6476
79	7/08	Ayr	1m	(0-85)H	G-S	£6476
68	9/07	Thsk	1m	(0-75)H	G-F	£3886
75	9/07	Rdcr	7f	(0-70)H	G-F	£2817
65	8/07	Thsk	7f	(0-70)H	G-F	£3886
68	6/06	Muss	1m	(0-65)H	FRM	£3412

Total win prize-money £46783

Going (Turf): Sf: 0-6 GS: 1-8 Gd: 2-15 **GF: 5-28** Fm: 1-3
Distance: 5f/6f: 0-5 **7f-8f: 9-49** 9f-13f: 0-6 14f+: 0-0
Track : **LH: 6-34** RH: 1-15 **Tight: 3-27** Gall: 1-3
Aids: **Bl: 5-30** Vi: 4-13 Tstrap: 0-3 Ckp: 0-3
Best Rating: **97** 10/09 NmkR 7f good

Useful; effective at 7f-1m; acts on most ground; has worn blinkers/visor.

Especially Special (IRE)

97(99) (75)72
3-y-o b f Exceed And Excel (AUS)-Super Trouper (FR) (Nashwan (USA))
Peter Grayson (S Kirk 24/10) Jasper Partnership

Placings:010-60404040 **(7808)**
2009: 5^{6}GF, 6^{0}SD, 7^{4}SD, 7^{0}SS, 5^{4}SD, 5^{0}SD, 5^{4}SD, 5^{0}SD,

	Starts	1st	2nd	3rd	Win & Pl
Career Total (Turf)	3	0	0	0	0
Career Total (AW)	8	1	0	0	5397

75	9/08	GrLe	5f	STD £5180

Total win prize-money £5181

Going (Turf): **Sf: 0-0 GS: 0-1 Gd: 0-0 GF: 0-2 Fm: 0-0**
Distance: **5f/6f: 1-9** 7f-8f: 0-2 9f-13f: 0-0 14f+: 0-0
Track : **LH: 1-7** RH: 0-1 Tight: 0-6 **Gall: 1-2**
Aids: Bl: 0-0 Vi: 0-0 Tstrap: 0-0 Ckp: 0-0
Best Rating: **75** 9/08 GrLe 5f stand

Modest; suited by 5f and acts on Polytrack.

Espero (IRE)

97(104) (86)82
3-y-o b g Celtic Swing-Zota (IRE) (Barathea (IRE))
R A Farrant M Sawers

Placings:00-263211 **(7141)**
2009: 8^{2}G, 9^{6}GS, 7^{3}SD, 7^{2}SD, 8^{1}SD, 8^{1}SD,

	Starts	1st	2nd	3rd	Win & Pl
Career Total (Turf)	4	0	1	0	964
Career Total (AW)	4	2	1	1	8990

86	10/09	Wolv	1m141y	(0-85)H	STD	£5046
72	9/09	Wolv	1m141y		STD	£2388

Total win prize-money £7434

Going (Turf): **Sf: 0-2 GS: 0-1 Gd: 0-1 GF: 0-0 Fm: 0-0**
Distance: 5f/6f: 0-0 7f-8f: 0-4 **9f-13f: 2-4** 14f+: 0-0
Track : **LH: 2-5** RH: 0-2 **Tight: 2-4** Gall: 0-1
Aids: Bl: 0-0 Vi: 0-0 Tstrap: 0-0 Ckp: 0-0
Best Rating: **86** 10/09 Wolv 1m141y stand

Fair; stays 1m but effective at 7f; acts on Polytrack and good ground on turf.

Espiritu (FR)

105 107
3-y-o b g Dansili-Red Bravo (USA) (Red Ransom (USA))
J Noseda Sir Robert Ogden

Placings:34-521403002 **(6665)**

2009: 7^{5}GF, 8^{2}G, 7^{1}F, 8^{4}GF, 7^{0}GF, 8^{3}G, 8^{0}GF, 8^{0}GF, 10^{2}GS,

	Starts	1st	2nd	3rd	Win & Pl
Career Total (Turf)	11	1	2	2	17120

89 6/09 Bevl 7f100y FRM £2914
Total win prize-money £2914

Going (Turf): Sf: 0-1 GS: 0-1 Gd: 0-3 GF: 0-5 **Fm: 1-1**
Distance: 5f/6f: 0-0 **7f-8f: 1-9** 9f-13f: 0-2 14f+: 0-0
Track : LH: 0-0 **RH: 1-2** Tight: 0-0 Gall: 0-1
Aids: Bl: 0-0 **Vi: 1-6** Tstrap: 0-1 Ckp: 0-1
Best Rating: **107** 10/09 Asct 1m2f gd-sft

Very useful; effective over 1m-1m2f; acts on good/fast ground; has worn a visor.

Espresso Steps (USA)

(80) (25)
3-y-o b/br f Medaglia D'Oro (USA)-Walk On Gold (USA) (Seeking The Gold (USA))
P Howling The Circle Bloodstock I Limited

Placings:060 (7730)
2009: 5^{0}SD, 8^{6}SD, 7^{0}SD,

	Starts	1st	2nd	3rd	Win & Pl
Career Total (Turf)	0	0	0	0	
Career Total (AW)	3	0	0	0	0

Going (Turf): **Sf: 0-0 GS: 0-0 Gd: 0-0 GF: 0-0 Fm: 0-0**
Distance: 5f/6f: 0-1 7f-8f: 0-2 9f-13f: 0-0 14f+: 0-0
Track : LH: 0-3 RH: 0-0 Tight: 0-3 Gall: 0-0
Aids: Bl: 0-0 Vi: 0-0 Tstrap: 0-0 Ckp: 0-0
Best Rating: **25** 11/09 Wolv 5f216y stand

Esprit De Midas

105(102) (83)93
3-y-o b g Namid-Spritzeria (Bigstone (IRE))
K A Ryan Joseph Ogden, J Hanson, John Ogden

Placings:050-111616 (7639)
2009: 7^{1}SD, 7^{1}SD, 7^{1}SD, 6^{6}SD, 5^{1}G, 6^{6}SD,

	Starts	1st	2nd	3rd	Win & Pl
Career Total (Turf)	4	1	0	0	4857
Career Total (AW)	5	3	0	0	6824

93 5/09 Leic 5f218y (0-80)H GD £4857
81 2/09 Sthl 7f (0-60)H STD £2047
83 2/09 Sthl 7f (0-70)H STD £2729
76 2/09 Sthl 7f (0-60)H STD £2047
Total win prize-money £11681

Going (Turf): Sf: 0-0 GS: 0-2 **Gd: 1-1** GF: 0-1 Fm: 0-0
Distance: 5f/6f: 1-6 **7f-8f: 3-3** 9f-13f: 0-0 14f+: 0-0
Track : **LH: 3-6** RH: 0-0 Tight: 0-0 Gall: 0-1
Aids: Bl: 0-0 Vi: 0-0 Tstrap: 0-0 Ckp: 0-0
Best Rating: **93** 5/09 Leic 5f218y good

Useful; stays 7f and acts on Fibresand.

Espy

101(108) (73)82
4-y-o b g Piccolo-Running Glimpse (IRE) (Runnett)
I W McInnes (S Kirk 24/10) Keith Brown Properties (hull) Ltd

Placings:532114-000623042034062 (7673)
2009: 5^{0}GF, 6^{0}SD, 6^{0}GF, 5^{6}GF, 5^{2}F, 5^{3}F, 5^{0}G, 5^{4}S, 5^{2}GF, 5^{0}GF, 5^{3}SD, 5^{4}SD, 6^{0}GS, 6^{6}SD, 5^{2}SD,

	Starts	1st	2nd	3rd	Win & Pl
Career Total (Turf)	13	1	3	1	7532
Career Total (AW)	8	1	1	2	6234

82 5/08 NmkR 5f (0-75)H G-F £3885
86 5/08 Kemp 5f (0-85)H STD £4209
Total win prize-money £8095

Going (Turf): Sf: 0-1 GS: 0-2 Gd: 0-2 **GF: 1-6** Fm: 0-2
Distance: **5f/6f: 2-21** 7f-8f: 0-0 9f-13f: 0-0 14f+: 0-0
Track : LH: 0-8 **RH: 1-5** Tight: 0-3 Gall: 0-6
Aids: Bl: 0-0 Vi: 0-0 Tstrap: 0-0 Ckp: 0-0
Best Rating: **86** 5/08 Kemp 5f stand

Modest; effective over 5f-6f; acts on most ground and on Polytrack.

Essexbridge

98(93) (72)77
2-y-o b c Avonbridge-Aonach Mor (Anabaa (USA))
R Hannon Morecombe Elsom Notley Burnham

Placings:421 (6962)
2009: 7^{4}GF, 7^{2}SS, 6^{1}G,

	Starts	1st	2nd	3rd	Win & Pl
Career Total (Turf)	2	1	0	0	4169
Career Total (AW)	1	0	1	0	1060

77 10/09 Brig 6f209y GD £3784
Total win prize-money £3784

Going (Turf): Sf: 0-0 GS: 0-0 **Gd: 1-1** GF: 0-1 Fm: 0-0
Distance: 5f/6f: 0-0 **7f-8f: 1-3** 9f-13f: 0-0 14f+: 0-0
Track : **LH: 1-2** RH: 0-0 Tight: 0-1 Gall: 0-0
Aids: Bl: 0-0 Vi: 0-0 Tstrap: 0-0 Ckp: 0-0
Best Rating: **77** 10/09 Brig 6f209y good

Fair; stays 7f; acts on a sound surface and Polytrack.

Estate

(94) (74)80
7-y-o b g Montjeu (IRE)-Fig Tree Drive (USA) (Miswaki (USA))
D E Pipe R S Brookhouse

Placings:44/3630/0110142/46320-0 (7701)
2009: 16^{0}SD,

	Starts	1st	2nd	3rd	Win & Pl
Career Total (Turf)	14	2	1	2	13757
Career Total (AW)	5	1	1	1	3309

80 11/07 Muss 2m (0-80)H GD £6477
75 10/07 Wolv 2m119y (0-65)H STD £2047
69 10/07 Gdwd 2m (0-70)H SFT £3238
Total win prize-money £11764

Going (Turf): **Sf: 1-4** GS: 0-1 **Gd: 1-4** GF: 0-4 Fm: 0-0
Distance: 5f/6f: 0-0 7f-8f: 0-2 9f-13f: 0-5 **14f+: 3-12**
Track : LH: 1-8 **RH: 2-9 Tight: 3-7** Gall: 0-2
Aids: Bl: 0-2 Vi: 0-0 Tstrap: 0-0 Ckp: 0-0
Best Rating: **82** 11/07 Wolv 2m119y stand

Fair; effective at around 2m; handles most types of ground; winning hurdler.

Esteem Dancer

(83) (49)
3-y-o ch g Mark Of Esteem (IRE)-Lake Diva (Docksider (USA))
J G Given P B Doyle

Placings:0-400 (0808)
2009: 7^{4}SD, 7^{0}SD, 8^{0}SD,

	Starts	1st	2nd	3rd	Win & Pl
Career Total (Turf)	0	0	0	0	
Career Total (AW)	4	0	0	0	192

Going (Turf): **Sf: 0-0 GS: 0-0 Gd: 0-0 GF: 0-0 Fm: 0-0**
Distance: 5f/6f: 0-0 7f-8f: 0-4 9f-13f: 0-0 14f+: 0-0
Track : LH: 0-3 RH: 0-1 Tight: 0-2 Gall: 0-0
Aids: Bl: 0-0 Vi: 0-0 Tstrap: 0-0 Ckp: 0-0
Best Rating: **49** 12/08 Wolv 7f32y stand

Esteem Lord

90(101) (69)69
3-y-o ch g Mark Of Esteem (IRE)-Milady Lillie (IRE) (Distinctly North (USA))
Jamie Poulton Paul Blows, Bill Brown, Ian Brown

Placings:0-022000 (3274)
2009: 8^{0}SD, 8^{2}SD, 8^{2}SD, 7^{0}GF, 8^{0}GF, 8^{0}SD,

	Starts	1st	2nd	3rd	Win & Pl
Career Total (Turf)	2	0	0	0	
Career Total (AW)	5	0	2	0	1734

Going (Turf): **Sf: 0-0 GS: 0-0 Gd: 0-0 GF: 0-2 Fm: 0-0**
Distance: 5f/6f: 0-0 7f-8f: 0-7 9f-13f: 0-0 14f+: 0-0
Track : LH: 0-2 RH: 0-3 Tight: 0-2 Gall: 0-0
Aids: Bl: 0-0 Vi: 0-0 Tstrap: 0-0 Ckp: 0-0
Best Rating: **69** 4/09 NmkR 7f gd-fm

Esteem Machine (USA)

99(109) (83)91
5-y-o b g Mark Of Esteem (IRE)-Theme (IRE) (Sadler's Wells (USA))
R A Teal M Vickers

Placings:342522121230/02100-05040210004456 (7603)
2009: 7^{0}SD, 7^{5}SD, 6^{0}GS, 5^{4}GF, 5^{0}GF, 5^{2}GF, 6^{1}G, 6^{0}GF, 6^{0}G, 6^{0}GF, 6^{4}SD, 6^{4}G, 7^{5}SD, 8^{6}SD,

	Starts	1st	2nd	3rd	Win & Pl
Career Total (Turf)	20	3	5	1	28754
Career Total (AW)	11	1	2	1	11500

90 7/09 NmkJ 6f (0-90)H GD £9066
99 4/08 GrLe 6f (0-90)H STD £6938
93 8/07 NmkJ 6f (0-85)H SFT £5181
79 7/07 Ling 7f GD £2730
Total win prize-money £23917

Going (Turf): Sf: 1-3 GS: 0-2 **Gd: 2-7** GF: 0-8 Fm: 0-0
Distance: **5f/6f: 3-17** 7f-8f: 1-14 9f-13f: 0-0 14f+: 0-0
Track : **LH: 1-6** RH: 0-6 Tight: 0-5 **Gall: 1-3**
Aids: Bl: 0-0 Vi: 0-2 Tstrap: 0-0 Ckp: 0-0
Best Rating: **99** 4/08 GrLe 6f stand

Useful; suited by 5f-7f; acts on most ground and on Polytrack; has worn a visor; suited by forcing tactics.

Estejo (GER)

108 111
5-y-o b h Johan Cruyff-Este (GER) (The Noble Player (USA))
R Rohne Giovanni Martone

Placings:11210/24461510-60100 (7313a)
2009: 10^{6}GF, 10^{0}GF, 10^{1}G, 9^{0}GS, 10^{0}HY,

	Starts	1st	2nd	3rd	Win & Pl
Career Total (Turf)	18	6	2	0	158528

9/09 Siro 1m2f GD £16990
111 11/08 Capa 1m2f HVY £79412
8/08 Siro 1m2f GD £6250
6/07 Siro 1m2f GD £27364
4/07 Siro 1m4f GD £8445
3/07 Siro 1m2f GD £6756
Total win prize-money £145220

Going (Turf): Sf: 1-4 GS: 0-1 **Gd: 5-10** GF: 0-3 Fm: 0-0
Distance: 5f/6f: 0-0 7f-8f: 0-0 **9f-13f: 6-18** 14f+: 0-0
Track : LH: 0-0 **RH: 2-10** Tight: 0-0 Gall: 0-1
Aids: Bl: 0-0 Vi: 0-0 Tstrap: 0-0 Ckp: 0-0
Best Rating: 111 11/08 Capa 1m2f heavy

Smart; German trained; effective from 1m2f-1m4f; acts on most types of ground.

Estonia

78 **36**

2-y-o b f Exceed And Excel (AUS)-Global Trend (Bluebird (USA))
J H M Gosden K Abdulla

Placings:0 **(5026)**
2009: 6[0]GF,

	Starts	1st	2nd	3rd	Win & Pl
Career Total (Turf)	1	0	0	0	

Going (Turf): **Sf: 0-0 GS: 0-0 Gd: 0-0 GF: 0-1 Fm: 0-0**
Distance: 5f/6f: 0-0 7f-8f: 0-1 9f-13f: 0-0 14f+: 0-0
Track : LH: 0-0 RH: 0-0 Tight: 0-0 Gall: 0-0
Aids: Bl: 0-0 Vi: 0-0 Tstrap: 0-0 Ckp: 0-0
Best Rating: 36 8/09 Newb 6f8y gd-fm

Showed abiltiy on debut over 6f on fast ground.

Esuvia (IRE)

97(95) (71)**66**

2-y-o b f Whipper (USA)-Aoife (IRE) (Thatching)
B Smart Ceffyl Racing

Placings:321 **(7708)**
2009: 6[3]S, 5[2]SD, 6[1]SD,

	Starts	1st	2nd	3rd	Win & Pl
Career Total (Turf)	1	0	0	1	915
Career Total (AW)	2	1	1	0	2853

71 12/09 Sthl 6f STD £2047
Total win prize-money £2047

Going (Turf): **Sf: 0-1 GS: 0-0 Gd: 0-0 GF: 0-0 Fm: 0-0**
Distance: **5f/6f: 1-3** 7f-8f: 0-0 9f-13f: 0-0 14f+: 0-0
Track : **LH: 1-2** RH: 0-0 Tight: 0-1 Gall: 0-0
Aids: Bl: 0-0 Vi: 0-0 Tstrap: 0-0 Ckp: 0-0
Best Rating: 71 12/09 Sthl 6f stand

Fair half-sister to smart sprinter Resplendent Glory; stays 6f; acts on soft ground; handles Polytrack; goes well on Fibresand.

Etain (IRE)

(101) (71)**74**

5-y-o b m Alhaarth (IRE)-Brogan's Well (IRE) (Caerleon (USA))
Mrs Lawney Hill C J Collins

Placings:30416/00235**0**-0 **(7225)**
2009: 10[0]SD,

	Starts	1st	2nd	3rd	Win & Pl
Career Total (Turf)	8	1	0	1	4153
Career Total (AW)	4	0	1	1	1301

74 6/07 Wind 1m2f7y (0-70)H SFT £3238
Total win prize-money £3239

Going (Turf): **Sf: 1-1** GS: 0-1 Gd: 0-4 GF: 0-2 Fm: 0-0
Distance: 5f/6f: 0-0 7f-8f: 0-2 **9f-13f: 1-9** 14f+: 0-1
Track : LH: 0-6 **RH: 1-6 Tight: 1-4** Gall: 0-4
Aids: Bl: 0-0 Vi: 0-0 Tstrap: 0-1 Ckp: 0-1
Best Rating: 74 6/07 Wind 1m2f7y soft

Modest; stays 1m2f; acts on soft ground.

Eternal Instinct

94 **79**

2-y-o b f Exceed And Excel (AUS)-Glenhurich (IRE) (Sri Pekan (USA))
J S Goldie J S Goldie, F Connor, G Brown

Placings:10001030004 **(7115)**
2009: 5[1]GF, 5[0]GS, 5[0]G, 6[0]GF, 5[1]GS, 5[0]GS, 5[3]GS, 6[0]GF, 6[0]GF, 6[0]G, 5[4]GS,

	Starts	1st	2nd	3rd	Win & Pl
Career Total (Turf)	11	2	0	1	19833

79 7/09 Muss 5f G-S £5180
73 4/09 Hayd 5f G-F £3885
Total win prize-money £9067

Going (Turf): Sf: 0-0 **GS: 1-5** Gd: 0-2 **GF: 1-4** Fm: 0-0
Distance: **5f/6f: 2-10** 7f-8f: 0-1 9f-13f: 0-0 14f+: 0-0
Track : LH: 0-0 RH: 0-0 Tight: 0-0 Gall: 0-0
Aids: Bl: 0-0 Vi: 0-0 Tstrap: 0-0 Ckp: 0-0
Best Rating: 79 7/09 Muss 5f gd-sft

Fair; from a prolific family from 5f to 1m4f; effective at 5f; acts on fast and easy ground.

Eternal Optimist (IRE)

(96) (58)**56**

4-y-o b f Bahri (USA)-Shore Lark (USA) (Storm Bird (CAN))
Paul Green J H Davey

Placings:000036**0563**/650**2604**-0 **(0655)**
2009: 5[0]SD,

	Starts	1st	2nd	3rd	Win & Pl
Career Total (Turf)	9	0	0	1	530
Career Total (AW)	9	0	1	1	1058

Going (Turf): **Sf: 0-1 GS: 0-2 Gd: 0-3 GF: 0-3 Fm: 0-0**
Distance: 5f/6f: 0-5 7f-8f: 0-6 9f-13f: 0-7 14f+: 0-0
Track : LH: 0-13 RH: 0-1 Tight: 0-12 Gall: 0-0
Aids: Bl: 0-0 Vi: 0-1 Tstrap: 0-1 Ckp: 0-1
Best Rating: 58 11/08 Wolv 1m141y stand

Moderate; effective over 1m; acts on Polytrack.

Ethics Girl (IRE)

110(104) (81)**82**

3-y-o b f Hernando (FR)-Palinisa (FR) (Night Shift (USA))
John Berry The 1997 Partnership

Placings:00-620151042**333** **(7583)**
2009: 7[6]G, 9[2]GF, 10[0]G, 8[1]GF, 10[5]G, 9[1]G, 9[0]GF, 9[4]GF, 12[2]GF, 12[3]SD, 13[3]SD, 9[3]SF,

	Starts	1st	2nd	3rd	Win & Pl
Career Total (Turf)	11	2	2	0	11515
Career Total (AW)	3	0	0	3	2281

81 8/09 Sand 1m1f (0-85)H GD £4857
75 7/09 Chep 1m14y (0-70)H G-F £3238
Total win prize-money £8095

Going (Turf): Sf: 0-1 GS: 0-1 **Gd: 1-4 GF: 1-5** Fm: 0-0
Distance: 5f/6f: 0-1 7f-8f: 0-2 **9f-13f: 2-11** 14f+: 0-0
Track : LH: 0-6 **RH: 1-5** Tight: 0-7 Gall: 0-0
Aids: Bl: 0-0 Vi: 0-0 Tstrap: 0-0 Ckp: 0-0
Best Rating: 82 10/09 Epsm 1m4f10y gd-fm

Fair; stays 1m4f; acts on good and faster ground; handles Polytrack.

Etoile D'Or (IRE)

(68) **61**

5-y-o ch m Soviet Star (USA)-Christeningpresent (IRE) (Cadeaux Genereux)
Tim Vaughan (M J Gingell 31/3) Treoes Racing Club

Placings:053/0060621/0-**0** **(0493)**
2009: 12[0]SD,

	Starts	1st	2nd	3rd	Win & Pl
Career Total (Turf)	11	1	1	1	3029
Career Total (AW)	1	0	0	0	

61 10/07 Yarm 1m3f101y SFT £1943
Total win prize-money £1943

Going (Turf): **Sf: 1-2** GS: 0-2 Gd: 0-5 GF: 0-1 Fm: 0-1
Distance: 5f/6f: 0-2 7f-8f: 0-2 **9f-13f: 1-8** 14f+: 0-0
Track : **LH: 1-6** RH: 0-2 **Tight: 1-3** Gall: 0-2
Aids: Bl: 0-0 Vi: 0-0 Tstrap: 0-0 Ckp: 0-0
Best Rating: 63 10/06 Newc 7f soft

Modest; stays 1m3f; acts on easy ground.

Eton Fable (IRE)

103(109) (78)**84**

4-y-o b g Val Royal (FR)-Lina Story (Linamix (FR))
W J H Ratcliffe The Gathering

Placings:50405/030132400-**2315300012** **(5067)**
2009: 10[2]SD, 12[3]SD, 12[1]GF, 10[5]G, 14[3]G, 14[0]GF, 17[0]G, 12[0]G, 11[1]F, 12[2]GF,

	Starts	1st	2nd	3rd	Win & Pl
Career Total (Turf)	22	3	2	3	25879
Career Total (AW)	2	0	1	1	1985

79 8/09 Brig 1m3f196y (0-80)H FRM £12384
81 4/09 Pont 1m4f8y (0-75)H G-F £3238
72 7/08 Pont 1m4y G-F £3885
Total win prize-money £19508

Going (Turf): Sf: 0-3 GS: 0-2 Gd: 0-9 **GF: 2-7** Fm: 1-1
Distance: 5f/6f: 0-1 7f-8f: 0-3 **9f-13f: 3-17** 14f+: 0-3
Track : **LH: 3-19** RH: 0-4 Tight: 0-7 Gall: 0-6
Aids: Bl: 0-0 Vi: 0-1 Tstrap: 2-10 Ckp: 2-10
Best Rating: 84 8/09 Pont 1m4f8y gd-fm

Fair; effective at 1m2f-1m6f; acts on soft ground and Polytrack; has worn cheekpieces.

Eton Rifles (IRE)

108 **96**

4-y-o b g Pivotal-Maritsa (IRE) (Danehill (USA))
J Howard Johnson Transcend Bloodstock LLP

Placings:521-313231 **(6135)**
2009: 7[3]GS, 6[1]HY, 6[3]GS, 7[2]GS, 6[3]GS, 6[1]G,

	Starts	1st	2nd	3rd	Win & Pl
Career Total (Turf)	9	3	2	3	29538

96 9/09 Haml 6f5y GD £12462
96 5/09 Hayd 6f (0-80)H HVY £6476
86 9/08 Catt 7f G-S £2590
Total win prize-money £21528

Going (Turf): **Sf: 1-1 GS: 1-6 Gd: 1-2** GF: 0-0 Fm: 0-0
Distance: 5f/6f: 1-3 **7f-8f: 2-6** 9f-13f: 0-0 14f+: 0-0
Track : **LH: 1-3** RH: 0-0 **Tight: 1-1** Gall: 0-1
Aids: Bl: 0-0 Vi: 0-0 Tstrap: 0-0 Ckp: 0-0
Best Rating: 96 9/09 Haml 6f5y good

Useful; effective over 6f-7f; acts on soft ground.

Etruscan (IRE)

92(82) (35)79

4-y-o b g Selkirk (USA)-Maddelina (IRE) (Sadler's Wells (USA))

C Gordon Edgeley, Larking, Nash & Nuttall

Placings:20/245 **(7780)**

2009: 8^{2}GS, 12^{4}S, 11^{5}SD,

	Starts	1st	2nd	3rd	Win & Pl
Career Total (Turf)	4	0	2	0	1819
Career Total (AW)	1	0	0	0	0

Going (Turf): **Sf: 0-1 GS: 0-2 Gd: 0-0 GF: 0-1 Fm: 0-0**
Distance: 5f/6f: 0-0 7f-8f: 0-0 9f-13f: 0-5 14f+: 0-0
Track : LH: 0-4 RH: 0-1 Tight: 0-1 Gall: 0-1
Aids: Bl: 0-0 Vi: 0-0 Tstrap: 0-0 Ckp: 0-0
Best Rating: **79** 10/09 Newb 1m4f5y soft

Fair; stays 1m and acts on easy ground.

Ettrick Mill

72(91) (71)23

3-y-o ch g Selkirk (USA)-Milly-M (Cadeaux Genereux)

M Johnston Mark Johnston Racing Ltd

Placings:0554 **(6158)**

2009: 8^{0}SD, 8^{5}SD, 10^{5}GF, 9^{4}G,

	Starts	1st	2nd	3rd	Win & Pl
Career Total (Turf)	2	0	0	0	192
Career Total (AW)	2	0	0	0	0

Going (Turf): **Sf: 0-0 GS: 0-0 Gd: 0-1 GF: 0-1 Fm: 0-0**
Distance: 5f/6f: 0-0 7f-8f: 0-2 9f-13f: 0-2 14f+: 0-0
Track : LH: 0-3 RH: 0-1 Tight: 0-3 Gall: 0-0
Aids: Bl: 0-0 Vi: 0-0 Tstrap: 0-0 Ckp: 0-0
Best Rating: **71** 2/09 Ling 1m stand

Fair; stays 1m; acts on Polytrack.

Eureka Moment

(102) (68)70

4-y-o b f Alhaarth (IRE)-Burn Baby Burn (IRE) (King's Theatre (IRE))

E A L Dunlop St Albans Bloodstock LLP

Placings:4650302**202315-424** **(0393)**

2009: 13^{4}SD, 12^{2}SD, 13^{4}SD,

	Starts	1st	2nd	3rd	Win & Pl
Career Total (Turf)	6	0	0	1	482
Career Total (AW)	10	1	4	1	6500

65 12/08 Sthl 1m4f STD £2729

Total win prize-money £2730

Going (Turf): **Sf: 0-0 GS: 0-0 Gd: 0-1 GF: 0-5 Fm: 0-0**
Distance: 5f/6f: 0-0 7f-8f: 0-0 **9f-13f: 1-13** 14f+: 0-3
Track : **LH: 1-10** RH: 0-6 Tight: 0-6 Gall: 0-4
Aids: Bl: 0-1 Vi: 0-0 Tstrap: 0-0 Ckp: 0-0
Best Rating: **70** 4/08 Wind 1m2f7y good

Modest; stays 1m6f; acts on good ground; goes on Polytrack; has worn blinkers.

Euroceleb (IRE)

(106) (73)57

4-y-o ch f Peintre Celebre (USA)-Eurobird (Ela-Mana-Mou)

H Morrison Stonethorn Stud Farms Limited

Placings:0454-30 **(0219)**

2009: 12^{3}SS, 13^{0}SD,

	Starts	1st	2nd	3rd	Win & Pl
Career Total (Turf)	2	0	0	0	192
Career Total (AW)	4	0	0	1	644

Going (Turf): **Sf: 0-1 GS: 0-1 Gd: 0-0 GF: 0-0 Fm: 0-0**
Distance: 5f/6f: 0-0 7f-8f: 0-0 9f-13f: 0-4 14f+: 0-2
Track : LH: 0-5 RH: 0-1 Tight: 0-4 Gall: 0-1
Aids: Bl: 0-0 Vi: 0-0 Tstrap: 0-1 Ckp: 0-1
Best Rating: **73** 11/08 Ling 1m4f stand

Modest; stays 1m4f and acts on sand.

European Dream (IRE)

99 90

6-y-o br g Kalanisi (IRE)-Tereed Elhawa (Cadeaux Genereux)

R C Guest You Trotters

Placings:00154/214335300/10611010/000-006 **(7245)**

2009: 8^{0}S, 8^{0}S, 8^{6}S,

	Starts	1st	2nd	3rd	Win & Pl
Career Total (Turf)	28	6	1	3	63148

108	7/07	York	1m208y	(0-100)H	SFT	£11658
102	6/07	Rdcr	1m	(0-100)H	SFT	£11658
97	5/07	Ripn	1m	(0-100)H	GD	£10094
95	3/07	Newc	1m3y	H	G-S	£15580
82	5/06	Newc	1m3y	(0-70)H	G-F	£5181
63	8/05	Newc	7f		SFT	£2373

Total win prize-money £56547

Going (Turf): **Sf: 3-11** GS: 1-3 Gd: 1-5 GF: 1-9 Fm: 0-0
Distance: 5f/6f: 0-0 7f-8f: 3-14 9f-13f: 3-14 14f+: 0-0
Track : LH: 1-13 RH: 1-2 Tight: 1-4 Gall: 1-6
Aids: Bl: 0-0 Vi: 0-0 Tstrap: 3-11 Ckp: 3-11
Best Rating: **108** 7/07 York 1m208y soft

Very useful; stays 1m1f; acts on most ground, but seems best on soft; has worn cheekpieces; usually held up.

Eurotanz (IRE)

96(89) (64)64

3-y-o b f Danehill Dancer (IRE)-Eurostorm (USA) (Storm Bird (CAN))

H Morrison Stonethorn Stud Farms Limited

Placings:004-64450 **(6031)**

2009: 8^{6}G, 10^{4}GF, 10^{4}G, 8^{5}G, 9^{0}SD,

	Starts	1st	2nd	3rd	Win & Pl
Career Total (Turf)	4	0	0	0	192
Career Total (AW)	4	0	0	0	192

Going (Turf): **Sf: 0-0 GS: 0-0 Gd: 0-3 GF: 0-1 Fm: 0-0**
Distance: 5f/6f: 0-0 7f-8f: 0-4 9f-13f: 0-4 14f+: 0-0
Track : LH: 0-6 RH: 0-1 Tight: 0-5 Gall: 0-2
Aids: Bl: 0-0 Vi: 0-0 Tstrap: 0-0 Ckp: 0-0
Best Rating: **64** 8/09 Newb 1m2f6y good

Modest form at up to 1m on Polytrack.

Euston Square

98(99) (83)86

3-y-o b g Oasis Dream-Krisia (Kris)

J H M Gosden K Abdulla

Placings:4-33316 **(6944)**

2009: 7^{3}GF, 7^{3}SD, 7^{3}GF, 7^{1}GF, 7^{6}SD,

	Starts	1st	2nd	3rd	Win & Pl
Career Total (Turf)	4	1	0	2	4612
Career Total (AW)	2	0	0	1	530

71 10/09 Leic 7f9y G-F £2590

Total win prize-money £2590

Going (Turf): Sf: 0-0 GS: 0-0 Gd: 0-0 **GF: 1-4** Fm: 0-0
Distance: 5f/6f: 0-1 **7f-8f: 1-5** 9f-13f: 0-0 14f+: 0-0
Track : LH: 0-1 RH: 0-1 Tight: 0-1 Gall: 0-0
Aids: Bl: 0-0 Vi: 0-0 Tstrap: 0-0 Ckp: 0-0
Best Rating: **86** 4/09 NmkR 7f gd-fm

Fair; stays 7f; acts on fast ground; goes on Polytrack.

Eva's Request (IRE)

111 (81)112

4-y-o ch f Soviet Star (USA)-Ingabelle (Taufan (USA))

M R Channon Liam Mulryan

Placings:0145301/50602251-30011305110 **(7498a)**

2009: 8^{3}G, 8^{0}GF, 8^{0}GF, 8^{1}G, 8^{1}G, 8^{3}GF, 8^{0}G, 8^{5}S, 8^{1}G, 10^{1}GS, 8^{0}F,

	Starts	1st	2nd	3rd	Win & Pl
Career Total (Turf)	24	6	2	3	509874
Career Total (AW)	2	1	0	0	3772

109	10/09	Capa	1m2f		G-S	£167374
111	9/09	Veli	1m		GD	£173611
112	6/09	Epsm	1m114y		GD	£36900
110	5/09	Gdwd	1m		GD	£22708
107	9/08	Asct	1m	(0-110)H	GD	£24978
99	9/07	Curr	7f		YLD	£35189
81	6/07	Kemp	6f		STD	£3562

Total win prize-money £464324

Going (Turf): Sf: 0-1 GS: 1-2 **Gd: 4-12** GF: 0-6 Fm: 0-2
Distance: 5f/6f: 1-2 **7f-8f: 4-18** 9f-13f: 2-6 14f+: 0-0
Track : LH: 1-6 **RH: 5-10** Tight: 1-3 Gall: 1-4
Aids: Bl: 0-0 Vi: 0-0 Tstrap: 0-0 Ckp: 0-0
Best Rating: **112** 6/09 Epsm 1m114y good

Group class; winner in Group 3 company in Britain but higher level abroad; effective over 6f-1m2f; acts on good and easier ground and on Polytrack.

Evasive

111(95) (84)115

3-y-o ch c Elusive Quality (USA)-Canda (USA) (Storm Cat (USA))

Saeed Bin Suroor (Sir Michael Stoute 16/6) Godolphin

Placings:311-646 **(5024)**

2009: 8^{6}GF, 8^{4}GF, 7^{6}GF,

	Starts	1st	2nd	3rd	Win & Pl
Career Total (Turf)	5	2	0	0	55063
Career Total (AW)	1	0	0	1	385

108	10/08	Newb	7f	SFT	£28385
81	10/08	NmkR	7f	G-F	£6152

Total win prize-money £34537

Going (Turf): **Sf: 1-1** GS: 0-0 Gd: 0-0 **GF: 1-4** Fm: 0-0
Distance: 5f/6f: 0-0 **7f-8f: 2-6** 9f-13f: 0-0 14f+: 0-0
Track : LH: 0-0 RH: 0-2 Tight: 0-0 Gall: 0-1
Aids: Bl: 0-0 Vi: 0-0 Tstrap: 0-0 Ckp: 0-0
Best Rating: **115** 6/09 Asct 1m gd-fm

Group class; winner of the 2008 Horris Hill Stakes; effective over 7f-1m; acts on most ground.

Evelith Regent (IRE)

95(88) (31)72

6-y-o b g Imperial Ballet (IRE)-No Avail (IRE) (Imperial Frontier (USA))

J J Davies (G A Swinbank 23/5) J J Davies

Placings:24006202020-5 **(2264)**

2009: 11^{5}G,

	Starts	1st	2nd	3rd	Win & Pl
Career Total (Turf)	11	0	4	0	3307
Career Total (AW)	1	0	0	0	

Going (Turf): Sf: 0-0 GS: 0-2 Gd: 0-6 GF: 0-3 Fm: 0-0
Distance: 5f/6f: 0-0 7f-8f: 0-1 9f-13f: 0-10 14f+: 0-1
Track : LH: 0-7 RH: 0-4 Tight: 0-9 Gall: 0-0
Aids: Bl: 0-0 Vi: 0-0 Tstrap: 0-0 Ckp: 0-0
Best Rating: 72 3/08 Muss 1m4f good

Modest; bumper winner; effective over 1m1f-1m4f; acts on fast ground.

Evelyn May (IRE)

98(105) (81)79
3-y-o b f Acclamation-Lady Eberspacher (IRE) (Royal Abjar (USA))
B W Hills Mrs B W Hills

Placings:2313002-4033066104 (7253)
2009: 5[4]SD, 5[0]GF, 5[3]G, 5[3]GF, 6[0]GF, 5[6]G, 6[6]GF, 5[1]SD, 5[0]GF, 6[4]SD,

	Starts	1st	2nd	3rd	Win & Pl
Career Total (Turf)	11	0	1	3	2813
Career Total (AW)	6	2	1	1	10384

81 9/09 Kemp 5f (0-85)H STD £4727
79 7/08 GrLe 5f STD £3561
Total win prize-money £8289

Going (Turf): Sf: 0-0 GS: 0-0 Gd: 0-5 GF: 0-6 Fm: 0-0
Distance: 5f/6f: 2-15 7f-8f: 0-2 9f-13f: 0-0 14f+: 0-0
Track : LH: 1-4 RH: 1-3 Tight: 0-2 Gall: 1-3
Aids: Bl: 0-0 Vi: 0-0 Tstrap: 0-0 Ckp: 0-0
Best Rating: 81 9/09 Kemp 5f stand

Fair; suited by 5f-6f, acts on most ground and on Polytrack.

Even Bolder

105(109) (88)88
6-y-o ch g Bold Edge-Level Pegging (IRE) (Common Grounds)
E A Wheeler Astrod TA Austin Stroud & Co

Placings:030024020/40451222/63223100233-30000360606110200 (7656)
2009: 5[3]SD, 5[0]GF, 5[0]GF, 5[0]F, 5[0]GF, 5[3]GF, 5[6]G, 5[0]G, 5[6]GF, 5[0]F, 5[6]G, 5[1]GF, 5[1]GS, 5[0]G, 6[2]SD, 5[0]SD, 6[0]SD,

	Starts	1st	2nd	3rd	Win & Pl
Career Total (Turf)	30	3	4	3	24209
Career Total (AW)	15	1	5	4	12398

79 10/09 Asct 5f (0-85)H G-S £6231
76 10/09 Gdwd 5f (0-70)H G-F £3238
88 8/08 Sand 5f6y (0-75)H G-F £4857
75 8/07 Kemp 6f STD £4728
Total win prize-money £19054

Going (Turf): Sf: 0-2 GS: 1-2 Gd: 0-9 GF: 2-13 Fm: 0-4
Distance: 5f/6f: 4-40 7f-8f: 0-3 9f-13f: 0-2 14f+: 0-0
Track : LH: 0-16 RH: 1-3 Tight: 0-13 Gall: 0-3
Aids: Bl: 0-0 Vi: 0-0 Tstrap: 1-7 Ckp: 1-7
Best Rating: 88 11/08 Wolv 5f20y stand

Fair; suited by 5f; acts on most ground on turf; goes on Polytrack.

Evening Glow

79(61) (13)26
2-y-o b f Fantastic Light (USA)-Kartuzy (JPN) (Polish Precedent (USA))
C E Brittain Saif Ali

Placings:00 (5969)
2009: 7[0]SD, 6[0]GF,

	Starts	1st	2nd	3rd	Win & Pl
Career Total (Turf)	1	0	0	0	
Career Total (AW)	1	0	0	0	

Going (Turf): Sf: 0-0 GS: 0-0 Gd: 0-0 GF: 0-1 Fm: 0-0
Distance: 5f/6f: 0-0 7f-8f: 0-2 9f-13f: 0-0 14f+: 0-0
Track : LH: 0-0 RH: 0-1 Tight: 0-0 Gall: 0-0
Aids: Bl: 0-0 Vi: 0-0 Tstrap: 0-0 Ckp: 0-0
Best Rating: 26 9/09 Yarm 6f3y gd-fm

Evening Sunset (GER)

99(97) (62)69
3-y-o b f Dansili-Evening Promise (Aragon)
M G Quinlan (M R Channon 6/8) Liam Mulryan

Placings:406-06534310424 (6784)
2009: 8[0]G, 8[6]GF, 8[5]G, 8[3]S, 8[4]G, 9[3]GF, 8[1]GF, 8[0]G, 8[4]G, 9[2]F, 10[4]SS,

	Starts	1st	2nd	3rd	Win & Pl
Career Total (Turf)	12	1	1	2	4980
Career Total (AW)	2	0	0	0	0

69 7/09 Haml 1m65y (0-65)H G-F £2266
Total win prize-money £2267

Going (Turf): Sf: 0-1 GS: 0-0 Gd: 0-6 GF: 1-3 Fm: 0-1
Distance: 5f/6f: 0-1 7f-8f: 0-3 9f-13f: 1-10 14f+: 0-0
Track : LH: 0-6 RH: 1-3 Tight: 1-6 Gall: 0-0
Aids: Bl: 0-0 Vi: 0-0 Tstrap: 0-0 Ckp: 0-0
Best Rating: 69 9/09 Brig 1m1f209y firm

Modest; stays 1m; acts on most ground.

Evening Tale (IRE)

(83) (59)
2-y-o b f Rock Of Gibraltar (IRE)-Wondrous Story (USA) (Royal Academy (USA))
B J Meehan M Green,Sangster Family,Mrs H Lascelles

Placings:03 (7396)
2009: 7[0]SD, 7[3]SD,

	Starts	1st	2nd	3rd	Win & Pl
Career Total (Turf)	0	0	0	0	
Career Total (AW)	2	0	0	1	578

Going (Turf): Sf: 0-0 GS: 0-0 Gd: 0-0 GF: 0-0 Fm: 0-0
Distance: 5f/6f: 0-0 7f-8f: 0-2 9f-13f: 0-0 14f+: 0-0
Track : LH: 0-2 RH: 0-0 Tight: 0-2 Gall: 0-0
Aids: Bl: 0-0 Vi: 0-0 Tstrap: 0-0 Ckp: 0-0
Best Rating: 59 11/09 Wolv 7f32y stand

Modest; stays 7f; acts on Polytrack.

Evens And Odds (IRE)

109(116) (111)108
5-y-o ch g Johannesburg (USA)-Coeur De La Mer (IRE) (Caerleon (USA))
D Nicholls Dab Hand Racing

Placings:6104/30603003/21050043000-310024 (6091)
2009: 6[3]GF, 6[1]GF, 7[0]GF, 6[0]GF, 6[2]S, 6[4]G,

	Starts	1st	2nd	3rd	Win & Pl
Career Total (Turf)	20	2	1	2	77900
Career Total (AW)	10	1	1	3	21234

106 5/09 NmkR 6f H G-F £31155
111 2/08 Sthl 6f (0-95)H STD £7124
81 7/06 Bevl 5f FRM £4533
Total win prize-money £42814

Going (Turf): Sf: 0-4 GS: 0-2 Gd: 0-7 GF: 1-6 Fm: 1-1
Distance: 5f/6f: 3-19 7f-8f: 0-11 9f-13f: 0-0 14f+: 0-0
Track : LH: 1-10 RH: 0-0 Tight: 0-7 Gall: 0-1
Aids: Bl: 1-13 Vi: 0-0 Tstrap: 0-2 Ckp: 0-2
Best Rating: 111 2/08 Sthl 6f stand

Smart; Listed placed; effective at 5f-7f; acts on fast and easy ground; goes on Polytrack; has worn various head-gear and a tongue tie; likes to race prominently.

Evenstorm (USA)

(98) (50)61
4-y-o ch f Stephen Got Even (USA)-Summer Wind Storm (USA) (Storm Cat (USA))
B Gubby Brian Gubby

Placings:0350600300/4406000-0 (0496)
2009: 7[0]SD,

	Starts	1st	2nd	3rd	Win & Pl
Career Total (Turf)	6	0	0	1	424
Career Total (AW)	12	0	0	1	496

Going (Turf): Sf: 0-0 GS: 0-1 Gd: 0-1 GF: 0-4 Fm: 0-0
Distance: 5f/6f: 0-13 7f-8f: 0-5 9f-13f: 0-0 14f+: 0-0
Track : LH: 0-11 RH: 0-2 Tight: 0-9 Gall: 0-2
Aids: Bl: 0-0 Vi: 0-0 Tstrap: 0-0 Ckp: 0-0
Best Rating: 61 8/07 Ling 5f stand

Modest; effective over 5f-6f; acts on fast ground; also goes on Polytrack.

Ever A Gent

(79) (40)
2-y-o b g Gentleman's Deal (IRE)-Mill End Quest (King's Signet (USA))
M W Easterby W T Allgood

Placings:666 (7705)
2009: 8[6]SD, 8[6]SD, 7[6]SD,

	Starts	1st	2nd	3rd	Win & Pl
Career Total (Turf)	0	0	0	0	
Career Total (AW)	3	0	0	0	0

Going (Turf): Sf: 0-0 GS: 0-0 Gd: 0-0 GF: 0-0 Fm: 0-0
Distance: 5f/6f: 0-0 7f-8f: 0-3 9f-13f: 0-0 14f+: 0-0
Track : LH: 0-3 RH: 0-0 Tight: 0-0 Gall: 0-0
Aids: Bl: 0-0 Vi: 0-0 Tstrap: 0-0 Ckp: 0-0
Best Rating: 40 12/09 Sthl 7f stand

Ever Cheerful

(103) (69)65
8-y-o b g Atraf-Big Story (Cadeaux Genereux)
A B Haynes Abacus Employment Services Ltd

Placings:422220343462/10526003156/1060003055124/12400055454/044523600031223/616125060026-43236020040 (7662)
2009: 7[4]SD, 7[3]SD, 7[2]SD, 7[3]SD, 7[6]SD, 7[0]SD, 7[2]SD, 7[0]SD, 7[0]SD, 7[4]SD, 7[0]SD,

	Starts	1st	2nd	3rd	Win & Pl
Career Total (Turf)	15	0	4	2	6713
Career Total (AW)	72	8	11	8	35109

72 3/08 Ling 7f (0-70)H STD £2331
71 2/08 Ling 7f (0-65)H STD £1876
66 11/07 Ling 7f (0-60)H STD £2047

79 1/06 Ling 5f (0-75)H STD £3238
70 12/05 Ling 7f STD £2921
65 1/05 Wolv 7f32y STD £2667
71 12/04 Wolv 5f216y STD £3052
71 1/04 Ling 6f D STD £3799
Total win prize-money £21935

Going (Turf): **Sf: 0-1 GS: 0-3 Gd: 0-3 GF: 0-6 Fm: 0-2**
Distance: 5f/6f: 3-48 **7f-8f: 5-39** 9f-13f: 0-0 14f+: 0-0
Track : **LH: 8-70** RH: 0-8 **Tight: 8-63** Gall: 0-3
Aids: Bl: 0-0 Vi: 0-2 Tstrap: 6-47 Ckp: 6-47
Best Rating: **80** 1/06 Ling 6f stand

Modest; effective at around 7f and acts on sand; has worn cheekpieces.

Ever So Bold

98(98) (68)**65**
2-y-o b g Reset (AUS)-Bold Byzantium (Bold Arrangement)
W R Muir North Farm Partnership

Placings:5034450144 **(7551)**
2009: 5^{5}GF, 5^{0}GF, 5^{3}GF, 5^{4}G, 7^{4}G, 7^{5}GS, 7^{0}SD, 7^{1}SD, 7^{4}SD, 7^{4}SD,

	Starts	1st	2nd	3rd	Win & Pl
Career Total (Turf)	6	0	0	1	987
Career Total (AW)	4	1	0	0	2576

68 10/09 Kemp 7f (0-65) STD £2047
Total win prize-money £2047

Going (Turf): **Sf: 0-0 GS: 0-1 Gd: 0-2 GF: 0-3 Fm: 0-0**
Distance: 5f/6f: 0-4 **7f-8f: 1-6** 9f-13f: 0-0 14f+: 0-0
Track : LH: 0-5 **RH: 1-1** Tight: 0-4 Gall: 0-0
Aids: **Bl: 1-3** Vi: 0-0 Tstrap: 0-0 Ckp: 0-0
Best Rating: **68** 11/09 Wolv 7f32y stand

Modest; stays 7f; acts on good/fast ground and Polytrack; has worn blinkers.

Everaard (USA)

100(99) (70)**70**
3-y-o ch g Lion Heart (USA)-Via Gras (USA) (Montbrook (USA))
D R C Elsworth Richard Marker

Placings:000-5331304302425 **(6975)**
2009: 8^{5}SD, 7^{3}GF, 8^{3}GS, 8^{1}GF, 8^{3}GF, 8^{0}S, 10^{4}GF, 9^{3}GF, 10^{0}GS, 12^{2}GF, 10^{4}G, 10^{2}SS, 12^{5}SD,

	Starts	1st	2nd	3rd	Win & Pl
Career Total (Turf)	13	1	1	4	5645
Career Total (AW)	3	0	1	0	806

67 5/09 Wwck 1m22y (0-60)H G-F £2047
Total win prize-money £2047

Going (Turf): Sf: 0-1 GS: 0-3 Gd: 0-2 **GF: 1-7** Fm: 0-0
Distance: 5f/6f: 0-1 7f-8f: 0-4 **9f-13f: 1-11** 14f+: 0-0
Track : **LH: 1-4** RH: 0-8 Tight: 0-6 Gall: 0-3
Aids: Bl: 0-0 Vi: 0-0 Tstrap: 0-0 Ckp: 0-0
Best Rating: **70** 10/09 Ling 1m2f std-slw

Fair; stays 1m2f; acts on fast ground and on Polytrack.

Evergreen Dancer (IRE)

86(62) (25)**57**
2-y-o b c Noverre (USA)-Persea (IRE) (Fasliyev (USA))
J R Best Heading For The Rocks Partnership

Placings:400000 **(5967)**
2009: 5^{4}G, 6^{0}GF, 6^{0}GF, 6^{0}SD, 7^{0}GS, 6^{0}GS,

	Starts	1st	2nd	3rd	Win & Pl
Career Total (Turf)	5	0	0	0	264
Career Total (AW)	1	0	0	0	0

Going (Turf): **Sf: 0-0 GS: 0-2 Gd: 0-1 GF: 0-2 Fm: 0-0**
Distance: 5f/6f: 0-5 7f-8f: 0-1 9f-13f: 0-0 14f+: 0-0
Track : LH: 0-2 RH: 0-1 Tight: 0-1 Gall: 0-2
Aids: Bl: 0-0 Vi: 0-1 Tstrap: 0-0 Ckp: 0-0
Best Rating: **57** 7/09 Wind 6f gd-fm

Everybody Knows

105(108) (84)**84**
4-y-o b g King's Best (USA)-Logic (Slip Anchor)
Miss Jo Crowley Mrs Liz Nelson

Placings:6/20124-2510 **(3378)**
2009: 7^{2}SD, 7^{5}SD, 8^{1}GF, 8^{0}GF,

	Starts	1st	2nd	3rd	Win & Pl
Career Total (Turf)	4	2	0	0	8419
Career Total (AW)	6	0	3	0	2433

84 5/09 Wind 1m67y (0-85)H G-F £5180
74 6/08 Folk 1m1f149y (0-70)H G-S £3238
Total win prize-money £8419

Going (Turf): Sf: 0-0 **GS: 1-1** Gd: 0-0 **GF: 1-3** Fm: 0-0
Distance: 5f/6f: 0-0 7f-8f: 0-6 **9f-13f: 2-4** 14f+: 0-0
Track : LH: 0-5 **RH: 2-5 Tight: 2-6** Gall: 0-1
Aids: Bl: 0-0 Vi: 0-0 Tstrap: 0-0 Ckp: 0-0
Best Rating: **84** 5/09 Wind 1m67y gd-fm

Fair; effective over 7f-1m2f; acts on good and easier ground and on Polytrack.

Everyman

99(100) (64)**55**
5-y-o gr g Act One-Maid To Dance (Pyramus (USA))
A W Carroll M Woodall

Placings:3505400/0P50314450/02023120-5054546536 **(4382)**
2009: 9^{5}SD, 10^{0}SD, 11^{5}SD, 12^{4}SD, 10^{5}GF, 12^{4}SD, 11^{6}SD, 8^{5}SD, 10^{3}G, 11^{6}G,

	Starts	1st	2nd	3rd	Win & Pl
Career Total (Turf)	19	1	1	4	6086
Career Total (AW)	16	1	2	0	4062

63 9/08 GrLe 1m2f (0-50)H STD £2590
56 10/07 Leic 1m1f218y SFT £2590
Total win prize-money £5181

Going (Turf): **Sf: 1-5** GS: 0-5 Gd: 0-4 GF: 0-4 Fm: 0-1
Distance: 5f/6f: 0-6 7f-8f: 0-1 **9f-13f: 2-28** 14f+: 0-0
Track : LH: 1-22 RH: 1-9 Tight: 0-15 **Gall: 1-3**
Aids: **Bl: 1-2** Vi: 0-6 Tstrap: 0-2 Ckp: 0-2
Best Rating: **64** 9/08 Kemp 1m2f stand

Moderate; stays 1m4f; acts on good and softer ground and on Polytrack.

Everymanforhimself (IRE)

108(105) (97)**105**
5-y-o b g Fasliyev (USA)-Luisa Demon (IRE) (Barathea (IRE))
K A Ryan J Duddy B McDonald & A Heeney

Placings:1210051230/00540030143/3241060-0322201020623 **(7486)**
2009: 6^{0}GF, 5^{3}GF, 5^{2}G, 6^{2}GF, 5^{2}GF, 6^{0}G, 6^{1}GF, 6^{0}GF, 5^{2}GF, 6^{0}G, 6^{6}GF, 7^{2}G, 7^{3}SD,

	Starts	1st	2nd	3rd	Win & Pl
Career Total (Turf)	39	6	8	5	97512
Career Total (AW)	2	0	0	1	1855

103 8/09 Hayd 6f (0-95)H G-F £9714
101 6/08 Bevl 5f (0-95)H G-F £7123
93 9/07 Leic 5f218y (0-85)H FRM £6309
92 8/06 Nott 6f15y GD £3238
94 5/06 Bevl 5f GD £12464
71 4/06 Bevl 5f G-S £3238
Total win prize-money £42089

Going (Turf): Sf: 0-4 GS: 1-3 **Gd: 2-11 GF: 2-20** Fm: 1-1
Distance: **5f/6f: 5-32** 7f-8f: 1-9 9f-13f: 0-0 14f+: 0-0
Track : LH: 0-5 RH: 0-0 Tight: 0-2 Gall: 0-2
Aids: Bl: 1-12 Vi: 1-8 Tstrap: 0-1 Ckp: 0-1
Best Rating: **105** 9/09 Donc 5f140y gd-fm

Very useful; suited by 5f-6f; acts on most ground; has worn blinkers and a visor.

Everynight (IRE)

101(103) (77)**94**
3-y-o b g Rock Of Gibraltar (IRE)-Rasana (Royal Academy (USA))
M Botti Tenuta Dorna Di Montaltuzzo SRL

Placings:4-106435U **(6004)**
2009: 10^{1}G, 10^{0}GF, 8^{6}G, 8^{4}G, 8^{3}GF, 10^{5}SD, 8^{U}GF,

	Starts	1st	2nd	3rd	Win & Pl
Career Total (Turf)	7	1	0	1	6854
Career Total (AW)	1	0	0	0	0

85 3/09 Donc 1m2f60y GD £4533
Total win prize-money £4533

Going (Turf): Sf: 0-1 GS: 0-0 **Gd: 1-3** GF: 0-3 Fm: 0-0
Distance: 5f/6f: 0-0 7f-8f: 0-1 **9f-13f: 1-7** 14f+: 0-0
Track : **LH: 1-4** RH: 0-1 Tight: 0-1 **Gall: 1-1**
Aids: Bl: 0-0 Vi: 0-0 Tstrap: 0-1 Ckp: 0-1
Best Rating: **94** 5/09 Sand 1m14y good

Useful; stays 1m2f and acts on fast ground.

Everything

(94) (61)**73**
4-y-o bl f Namid-Flight Sequence (Polar Falcon (USA))
P T Midgley Anthony D Copley

Placings:P0443/2351050505-6 **(0095)**
2009: 6^{6}SD,

	Starts	1st	2nd	3rd	Win & Pl
Career Total (Turf)	14	1	1	2	5346
Career Total (AW)	2	0	0	0	0

73 6/08 Ripn 6f GD £2914
Total win prize-money £2914

Going (Turf): Sf: 0-2 GS: 0-5 **Gd: 1-4** GF: 0-3 Fm: 0-0
Distance: **5f/6f: 1-15** 7f-8f: 0-1 9f-13f: 0-0 14f+: 0-0
Track : LH: 0-5 RH: 0-0 Tight: 0-1 Gall: 0-0
Aids: Bl: 0-0 Vi: 0-0 Tstrap: 0-1 Ckp: 0-1
Best Rating: **73** 6/08 Ripn 6f good

Modest; stays 6f; acts on good ground.

Evette

(86) (43)**39**
4-y-o b f Loup Solitaire (USA)-La Scarlet (FR) (Highest Honor (FR))
H J Collingridge Greenstead Hall Racing Ltd

Placings:0605/0-60 **(0587)**
2009: 10^{6}SD, 7^{0}SD,

	Starts	1st	2nd	3rd	Win & Pl
Career Total (Turf)	2	0	0	0	0
Career Total (AW)	5	0	0	0	0

Going (Turf): **Sf: 0-0 GS: 0-0 Gd: 0-2 GF: 0-0 Fm: 0-0**

Distance: 5f/6f: 0-0 7f-8f: 0-5 9f-13f: 0-1 14f+: 0-1
Track : LH: 0-2 RH: 0-3 Tight: 0-1 Gall: 0-1
Aids: Bl: 0-0 Vi: 0-0 Tstrap: 0-0 Ckp: 0-0
Best Rating: 43 11/07 Kemp 1m stand

Evianne

90(70) (23)42
5-y-o b m Lugana Beach-Folk Dance (USA) (Bertrando (USA))
P W Hiatt P W Hiatt

Placings:00006-0060 (5569)
2009: 8[0]GF, 9[0]GF, 7[6]GS, 7[0]F,

	Starts	1st	2nd	3rd	Win & Pl
Career Total (Turf)	8	0	0	0	0
Career Total (AW)	1	0	0	0	

Going (Turf): Sf: 0-0 GS: 0-2 Gd: 0-2 GF: 0-3 Fm: 0-1
Distance: 5f/6f: 0-0 7f-8f: 0-3 9f-13f: 0-5 14f+: 0-1
Track : LH: 0-7 RH: 0-1 Tight: 0-3 Gall: 0-0
Aids: Bl: 0-1 Vi: 0-0 Tstrap: 0-0 Ckp: 0-0
Best Rating: 42 9/08 Brig 7f214y good

Evident Pride (USA)

95(110) (93)73
6-y-o b g Chester House (USA)-Proud Fact (USA) (Known Fact (USA))
B R Johnson Tom Dempsey & Rebecca Middleton

Placings:332112/20142311/200040-10506036436 (7811)
2009: 12[1]SD, 12[0]SD, 11[5]SD, 11[0]SD, 9[6]GF, 8[0]GF, 12[3]SD, 12[6]GS, 12[4]SD, 13[3]SD, 12[6]SD,

	Starts	1st	2nd	3rd	Win & Pl
Career Total (Turf)	6	0	0	1	1011
Career Total (AW)	25	6	5	4	62362

93 1/09 Ling 1m4f (0-100)H STD £11656
102 12/07 Kemp 1m2f (0-95)H STD £6855
94 11/07 Ling 1m2f (0-85)H STD £5181
89 8/07 Kemp 1m (0-90)H STD £6855
83 11/06 Kemp 1m (0-70)H STD £3238
76 9/06 Wolv 1m141y (0-70)H STD £3238
Total win prize-money £37027

Going (Turf): Sf: 0-0 GS: 0-1 Gd: 0-0 GF: 0-5 Fm: 0-0
Distance: 5f/6f: 0-1 7f-8f: 2-10 9f-13f: 4-20 14f+: 0-0
Track : LH: 3-17 RH: 3-13 Tight: 3-18 Gall: 0-2
Aids: Bl: 0-0 Vi: 0-1 Tstrap: 0-0 Ckp: 0-0
Best Rating: 102 12/07 Kemp 1m2f stand

Useful; effective over 1m-1m2f; acts on Polytrack.

Evna (USA)

94(99) (72)65
3-y-o ch f Grand Slam (USA)-Our Josephina (USA) (Tale Of The Cat (USA))
R A Fahey Dr Marwan Koukash

Placings:00130 (4707)
2009: 8[0]GS, 8[0]G, 5[1]SD, 5[3]S, 6[0]GF,

	Starts	1st	2nd	3rd	Win & Pl
Career Total (Turf)	4	0	0	1	1011
Career Total (AW)	1	1	0	0	4777

72 7/09 Sthl 5f STD £4776
Total win prize-money £4777

Going (Turf): Sf: 0-1 GS: 0-1 Gd: 0-1 GF: 0-1 Fm: 0-0
Distance: 5f/6f: 1-3 7f-8f: 0-1 9f-13f: 0-1 14f+: 0-0
Track : LH: 0-2 RH: 0-0 Tight: 0-0 Gall: 0-1
Aids: Bl: 0-0 Vi: 0-0 Tstrap: 0-0 Ckp: 0-0
Best Rating: 72 7/09 Sthl 5f stand

Fair; best effort over 5f but should prove equally effective over 6f; acts on Fibresand; type to win more races.

Ex Gracia

85 25
3-y-o ch f Efisio-Action De Grace (USA) (Riverman (USA))
K A Ryan Guy Reed

Placings:00 (4550)
2009: 6[0]S, 7[0]GS,

	Starts	1st	2nd	3rd	Win & Pl
Career Total (Turf)	2	0	0	0	

Going (Turf): Sf: 0-1 GS: 0-1 Gd: 0-0 GF: 0-0 Fm: 0-0
Distance: 5f/6f: 0-1 7f-8f: 0-1 9f-13f: 0-0 14f+: 0-0
Track : LH: 0-1 RH: 0-0 Tight: 0-1 Gall: 0-0
Aids: Bl: 0-0 Vi: 0-0 Tstrap: 0-0 Ckp: 0-0
Best Rating: 25 8/09 Thsk 7f gd-sft

Exceed Elegance (IRE)

97(100) (59)62
3-y-o b f Exceed And Excel (AUS)-Colleen (IRE) (Sadler's Wells (USA))
D Shaw Market Avenue Racing Club Ltd

Placings:0-05523500260 (7835)
2009: 5[0]G, 5[5]GS, 5[5]SD, 5[2]GS, 6[3]G, 5[5]G, 5[0]SD, 7[0]SD, 5[2]SD, 5[6]SD, 6[0]SD,

	Starts	1st	2nd	3rd	Win & Pl
Career Total (Turf)	5	0	1	1	1610
Career Total (AW)	7	0	1	0	605

Going (Turf): Sf: 0-0 GS: 0-2 Gd: 0-3 GF: 0-0 Fm: 0-0
Distance: 5f/6f: 0-10 7f-8f: 0-2 9f-13f: 0-0 14f+: 0-0
Track : LH: 0-7 RH: 0-2 Tight: 0-5 Gall: 0-1
Aids: Bl: 0-0 Vi: 0-0 Tstrap: 0-0 Ckp: 0-0
Best Rating: 62 7/09 Pont 5f gd-sft

Moderate; handles Polytrack; has worn a tongue tie.

Exceed Power

86(89) (53)54
2-y-o ch f Exceed And Excel (AUS)-Israar (Machiavellian (USA))
D M Simcock Dr Ali Ridha

Placings:0050404 (6938)
2009: 6[0]GF, 6[0]G, 5[5]GF, 5[0]GF, 5[4]SD, 5[0]SD, 5[4]SD,

	Starts	1st	2nd	3rd	Win & Pl
Career Total (Turf)	4	0	0	0	0
Career Total (AW)	3	0	0	0	0

Going (Turf): Sf: 0-0 GS: 0-0 Gd: 0-1 GF: 0-3 Fm: 0-0
Distance: 5f/6f: 0-7 7f-8f: 0-0 9f-13f: 0-0 14f+: 0-0
Track : LH: 0-1 RH: 0-3 Tight: 0-1 Gall: 0-0
Aids: Bl: 0-0 Vi: 0-0 Tstrap: 0-0 Ckp: 0-0
Best Rating: 54 6/09 Folk 6f gd-fm

Exceedingly Bold

98 88
2-y-o b c Exceed And Excel (AUS)-Grey Pearl (Ali-Royal (IRE))
Miss Gay Kelleway Exceedingly Hopeful Partnership

Placings:2310 (7030)
2009: 6[2]GF, 6[3]G, 6[1]G, 7[0]S,

	Starts	1st	2nd	3rd	Win & Pl
Career Total (Turf)	4	1	1	1	15285

85 10/09 Newb 6f110y GD £4857
Total win prize-money £4857

Going (Turf): Sf: 0-1 GS: 0-0 Gd: 1-2 GF: 0-1 Fm: 0-0
Distance: 5f/6f: 0-1 7f-8f: 1-3 9f-13f: 0-0 14f+: 0-0
Track : LH: 0-0 RH: 0-0 Tight: 0-0 Gall: 0-0
Aids: Bl: 0-0 Vi: 0-0 Tstrap: 0-0 Ckp: 0-0
Best Rating: 88 10/09 Newb 7f soft

Useful; stays an extended 6f and acts on good and faster ground.

Exceedingly Good (IRE)

93 67
3-y-o ch f Exceed And Excel (AUS)-Ikan (IRE) (Sri Pekan (USA))
B Smart H E Sheikh Rashid Bin Mohammed

Placings:6303-4005 (5468)
2009: 6[4]GF, 6[0]GF, 6[0]GF, 5[5]GF,

	Starts	1st	2nd	3rd	Win & Pl
Career Total (Turf)	8	0	0	2	1588

Going (Turf): Sf: 0-0 GS: 0-1 Gd: 0-1 GF: 0-6 Fm: 0-0
Distance: 5f/6f: 0-7 7f-8f: 0-1 9f-13f: 0-0 14f+: 0-0
Track : LH: 0-2 RH: 0-0 Tight: 0-2 Gall: 0-0
Aids: Bl: 0-0 Vi: 0-1 Tstrap: 0-0 Ckp: 0-0
Best Rating: 67 6/08 Donc 6f good

Exceedthewildman

93(95) (73)71
2-y-o b c Exceed And Excel (AUS)-Naomi Wildman (USA) (Kingmambo (USA))
J S Moore E Moore & J S Moore

Placings:3306143 (7806)
2009: 6[3]G, 7[3]G, 6[0]G, 8[6]SD, 7[1]SD, 7[4]SD, 7[3]SD,

	Starts	1st	2nd	3rd	Win & Pl
Career Total (Turf)	3	0	0	2	1300
Career Total (AW)	4	1	0	1	3409

73 11/09 Ling 7f (0-75) STD £2590
Total win prize-money £2590

Going (Turf): Sf: 0-0 GS: 0-0 Gd: 0-3 GF: 0-0 Fm: 0-0
Distance: 5f/6f: 0-1 7f-8f: 1-6 9f-13f: 0-0 14f+: 0-0
Track : LH: 1-4 RH: 0-1 Tight: 1-4 Gall: 0-0
Aids: Bl: 0-0 Vi: 0-0 Tstrap: 1-3 Ckp: 1-3
Best Rating: 73 11/09 Ling 7f stand

Fair; stays 7f; acts on good ground; goes on Polytrack.

Excellent Day (IRE)

98 75
2-y-o b f Invincible Spirit (IRE)-Tosca (Be My Guest (USA))
M R Channon Jaber Abdullah

Placings:021 (4711)
2009: 6[0]GF, 5[2]GF, 5[1]GF,

	Starts	1st	2nd	3rd	Win & Pl
Career Total (Turf)	3	1	1	0	4780

75 8/09 Sand 5f6y G-F £3238
Total win prize-money £3238

Going (Turf): Sf: 0-0 GS: 0-0 Gd: 0-0 **GF: 1-3** Fm: 0-0
Distance: **5f/6f: 1-3** 7f-8f: 0-0 9f-13f: 0-0 14f+: 0-0
Track : LH: 0-0 RH: 0-0 Tight: 0-0 Gall: 0-0
Aids: Bl: 0-0 Vi: 0-0 Tstrap: 0-0 Ckp: 0-0
Best Rating: 75 8/09 Sand 5f6y gd-fm

Promise on second start over 5f on fast ground.

Excellent Guest

97 **80**

2-y-o b c Exceed And Excel (AUS)-Princess Speedfit (FR) (Desert Prince (IRE))
G G Margarson John Guest

Placings:44310 (5136)
2009: 6[4]G, 6[4]GF, 7[3]G, 6[1]G, 6[0]GF,

	Starts	1st	2nd	3rd	Win & Pl
Career Total (Turf)	5	1	0	1	5910

80 8/09 Yarm 6f3y GD £4163
Total win prize-money £4163

Going (Turf): Sf: 0-0 GS: 0-0 **Gd: 1-3** GF: 0-2 Fm: 0-0
Distance: 5f/6f: 0-2 **7f-8f: 1-3** 9f-13f: 0-0 14f+: 0-0
Track : LH: 0-0 RH: 0-0 Tight: 0-0 Gall: 0-1
Aids: Bl: 0-0 Vi: 0-0 Tstrap: 0-0 Ckp: 0-0
Best Rating: 80 8/09 Yarm 6f3y good

Useful; effective at 6f; acts on good side.

Excellent Show

105(108) (85)**82**

3-y-o ch f Exceed And Excel (AUS)-Quiz Show (Primo Dominie)
B Smart A Turton, P Langford & S Brown

Placings:210-03533021 (7872)
2009: 6[0]GF, 5[3]GF, 5[5]GF, 5[3]G, 5[3]GF, 5[0]G, 5[2]SD, 5[1]SD,

	Starts	1st	2nd	3rd	Win & Pl
Career Total (Turf)	9	1	1	3	8601
Career Total (AW)	2	1	1	0	6134

12/09 Kemp 5f (0-85)H STD £4727
83 5/08 Muss 5f S GD £3885
Total win prize-money £8613

Going (Turf): Sf: 0-0 GS: 0-0 **Gd: 1-4** GF: 0-5 Fm: 0-0
Distance: **5f/6f: 2-11** 7f-8f: 0-0 9f-13f: 0-0 14f+: 0-0
Track : LH: 0-1 **RH: 1-2** Tight: 0-1 Gall: 0-0
Aids: Bl: 0-0 Vi: 0-0 Tstrap: 0-0 Ckp: 0-0
Best Rating: 85 11/09 Kemp 5f stand

Useful; effective over 5f; acts on good/fast ground and Polytrack.

Excellent Thought

102(99) (74)**70**

2-y-o b f Exceed And Excel (AUS)-Amiata (Pennekamp (USA))
W J Haggas Liam Sheridan

Placings:523223 (7453)
2009: 5[5]GS, 5[2]GF, 6[3]GS, 5[2]G, 5[2]SD, 6[3]SD,

	Starts	1st	2nd	3rd	Win & Pl
Career Total (Turf)	4	0	2	1	2269
Career Total (AW)	2	0	1	1	1541

Going (Turf): **Sf: 0-0 GS: 0-2 Gd: 0-1 GF: 0-1 Fm: 0-0**
Distance: 5f/6f: 0-6 7f-8f: 0-0 9f-13f: 0-0 14f+: 0-0
Track : LH: 0-3 RH: 0-1 Tight: 0-1 Gall: 0-2
Aids: Bl: 0-0 Vi: 0-0 Tstrap: 0-0 Ckp: 0-0
Best Rating: 74 11/09 Kemp 6f stand

Fair; effective over 5f-6f; acts on good ground.

Excellent Vision

90 **70**

2-y-o b c Exceed And Excel (AUS)-Classic Vision (Classic Cliche (IRE))
B Smart H E Sheikh Rashid Bin Mohammed

Placings:43 (6646)
2009: 6[4]G, 6[3]G,

	Starts	1st	2nd	3rd	Win & Pl
Career Total (Turf)	2	0	0	1	1271

Going (Turf): **Sf: 0-0 GS: 0-0 Gd: 0-2 GF: 0-0 Fm: 0-0**
Distance: 5f/6f: 0-1 7f-8f: 0-1 9f-13f: 0-0 14f+: 0-0
Track : LH: 0-0 RH: 0-0 Tight: 0-0 Gall: 0-0
Aids: Bl: 0-0 Vi: 0-0 Tstrap: 0-0 Ckp: 0-0
Best Rating: 70 10/09 York 6f good

Fair; stays 6f; acts on good.

Excellerator (IRE)

107(106) (98)**98**

3-y-o ch f Exceed And Excel (AUS)-Amsicora (Cadeaux Genereux)
George Baker The Excellerators

Placings:13320-3002 (7090)
2009: 6[3]GF, 5[0]GF, 5[0]GF, 5[2]SD,

	Starts	1st	2nd	3rd	Win & Pl
Career Total (Turf)	7	0	1	3	18003
Career Total (AW)	2	1	1	0	5347

74 6/08 Sthl 5f STD £2456
Total win prize-money £2457

Going (Turf): **Sf: 0-0 GS: 0-0 Gd: 0-1 GF: 0-6 Fm: 0-0**
Distance: **5f/6f: 1-8** 7f-8f: 0-1 9f-13f: 0-0 14f+: 0-0
Track : LH: 0-1 RH: 0-0 Tight: 0-1 Gall: 0-0
Aids: Bl: 0-0 Vi: 0-1 Tstrap: 0-0 Ckp: 0-0
Best Rating: 98 10/09 Sthl 5f stand

Very useful; Group 3 placed as a juvenile; effective at 5f-6f; acts on good and faster ground; has worn a tongue tie.

Excelling (IRE)

97(89) (64)**85**

2-y-o b f Exceed And Excel (AUS)-Nojoom (IRE) (Alhaarth (IRE))
P J Makin R P Marchant,D A Poole,G Moss

Placings:01040 (6241)
2009: 5[0]G, 5[1]G, 5[0]GF, 5[4]SD, 6[0]G,

	Starts	1st	2nd	3rd	Win & Pl
Career Total (Turf)	4	1	0	0	8538
Career Total (AW)	1	0	0	0	385

85 7/09 Ling 5f GD £2388
Total win prize-money £2388

Going (Turf): Sf: 0-0 GS: 0-0 **Gd: 1-3** GF: 0-1 Fm: 0-0
Distance: **5f/6f: 1-4** 7f-8f: 0-1 9f-13f: 0-0 14f+: 0-0
Track : LH: 0-1 RH: 0-0 Tight: 0-1 Gall: 0-0
Aids: Bl: 0-0 Vi: 0-0 Tstrap: 0-0 Ckp: 0-0
Best Rating: 85 7/09 Ling 5f good

Useful; effective over 5f; acts on good ground.

Excelsior Academy

103(96) (75)**82**

3-y-o b g Montjeu (IRE)-Birthday Suit (IRE) (Daylami (IRE))
B J Meehan Lady Laidlaw Of Rothiemay

Placings:02420-5301441 (4709)
2009: 10[5]GF, 12[3]GF, 14[0]GF, 14[1]S, 16[4]SD, 13[4]G, 11[1]GS,

	Starts	1st	2nd	3rd	Win & Pl
Career Total (Turf)	9	2	1	1	10006
Career Total (AW)	3	0	1	0	2070

82 8/09 Hayd 1m3f200y (0-80)H G-S £5504
74 6/09 Yarm 1m6f17y (0-70)H SFT £2719
Total win prize-money £8225

Going (Turf): **Sf: 1-1 GS: 1-1** Gd: 0-3 GF: 0-4 Fm: 0-0
Distance: 5f/6f: 0-0 7f-8f: 0-2 9f-13f: 1-7 14f+: 1-3
Track : **LH: 2-7** RH: 0-4 **Tight: 1-5** Gall: 0-2
Aids: Bl: 0-1 Vi: 0-0 Tstrap: 0-0 Ckp: 0-0
Best Rating: 82 8/09 Hayd 1m3f200y gd-sft

Fair; stays 1m6f; acts on most ground on turf; goes on Polytrack.

Exceptional Art

112(98) (71)**105**

3-y-o ch g Exceed And Excel (AUS)-Only In Dreams (Polar Falcon (USA))
D Nicholls (P W Chapple-Hyam 25/6) Middleham Park Racing XXVII

Placings:10-2161 (5420)
2009: 7[2]G, 7[1]HY, 8[6]SD, 5[1]GF,

	Starts	1st	2nd	3rd	Win & Pl
Career Total (Turf)	5	3	1	0	39219
Career Total (AW)	1	0	0	0	0

105 8/09 Bevl 5f G-F £23704
101 5/09 Hayd 7f30y (0-95)H HVY £9066
92 8/08 Wind 6f G-S £4209
Total win prize-money £36979

Going (Turf): **Sf: 1-1 GS: 1-2** Gd: 0-1 **GF: 1-1** Fm: 0-0
Distance: **5f/6f: 2-3** 7f-8f: 1-3 9f-13f: 0-0 14f+: 0-0
Track : **LH: 1-1** RH: 0-2 Tight: 0-0 **Gall: 1-1**
Aids: Bl: 0-0 Vi: 0-0 Tstrap: 0-0 Ckp: 0-0
Best Rating: 105 8/09 Bevl 5f gd-fm

Smart; winner in Listed compnay; effective over 5f-7f; acts on most ground.

Excitable (IRE)

94(97) (52)**54**

3-y-o b f Exceed And Excel (AUS)-Kalwada (USA) (Roberto (USA))
Mrs D J Sanderson R J Budge

Placings:00060-340400 (6553)
2009: 5[3]GF, 5[4]GF, 5[0]GF, 5[4]SD, 5[0]GS, 5[0]GF,

	Starts	1st	2nd	3rd	Win & Pl
Career Total (Turf)	10	0	0	1	519
Career Total (AW)	1	0	0	0	0

Going (Turf): **Sf: 0-2 GS: 0-2 Gd: 0-0 GF: 0-6 Fm: 0-0**
Distance: 5f/6f: 0-11 7f-8f: 0-0 9f-13f: 0-0 14f+: 0-0
Track : LH: 0-1 RH: 0-0 Tight: 0-1 Gall: 0-0
Aids: Bl: 0-0 Vi: 0-0 Tstrap: 0-1 Ckp: 0-1
Best Rating: 54 10/08 Nott 5f13y gd-sft

2,5000euros half-sister to winners in US & Japan; very moderate form so far.

Exclamation

108(104) (97)106

4-y-o br g Acclamation-Summer Siren (FR) (Saint Cyrien (FR))

B J Meehan Raymond Tooth

Placings:511/60-430036 (7394)

2009: 6⁴GF, 6³GF, 6⁰GS, 6⁰GF, 5³SD, 6⁶SD,

	Starts	1st	2nd	3rd	Win & Pl
Career Total (Turf)	8	2	0	1	199047
Career Total (AW)	3	0	0	1	1445

97 10/07 NmkR 6f GD £189390
85 9/07 Hayd 6f SFT £2169
Total win prize-money £191561

Going (Turf): **Sf: 1-1** GS: 0-1 **Gd: 1-2** GF: 0-4 Fm: 0-0
Distance: **5f/6f: 2-8** 7f-8f: 0-3 9f-13f: 0-0 14f+: 0-0
Track : LH: 0-1 RH: 0-1 Tight: 0-1 Gall: 0-0
Aids: Bl: 0-0 Vi: 0-0 Tstrap: 0-0 Ckp: 0-0
Best Rating: **106** 4/09 NmkR 6f gd-fm

Very useful; suited by 6f; acts on good and softer ground and Fibresand.

Excusez Moi (USA)

109(114) (114)101

7-y-o b g Fusaichi Pegasus (USA)-Jiving (Generous (IRE))

Mrs R A Carr S B Clark

Placings:2/03106300024/640241620/**000**022000/**14**00064 050-**56240**015101404530U0026 (7294)

2009: 5⁵SS, 7⁶SD, 7²SD, 5⁴SD, 5⁰SD, 7⁰GF, 7¹GF, 6⁵GF, 6¹GF, 6⁰S, 5¹G, 6⁴GF, 6⁰GF, 6⁴S, 6⁵G, 6³G, 6⁰GF, 6ᵁGS, 6⁰GF, 6⁰G, 5²GS, 7⁶S,

	Starts	1st	2nd	3rd	Win & Pl
Career Total (Turf)	49	5	6	2	144047
Career Total (AW)	13	1	2	1	19993

100 5/09 Bevl 5f GD £11215
97 5/09 Ripn 6f (0-85)H G-F £6476
89 4/09 Muss 7f30y (0-85)H G-F £6231
114 2/08 Ling 6f STD £14762
111 8/06 Ripn 6f (0-105)H SFT £37392
94 4/05 Yarm 7f3y GD £3367
Total win prize-money £79445

Going (Turf): Sf: 1-7 GS: 0-8 **Gd: 2-15 GF: 2-19** Fm: 0-0
Distance: **5f/6f: 4-38** 7f-8f: 2-23 9f-13f: 0-1 14f+: 0-0
Track : LH: 1-17 RH: 1-2 **Tight: 2-9** Gall: 0-6
Aids: Bl: 0-6 Vi: 0-0 Tstrap: 3-17 Ckp: 3-17
Best Rating: **114** 2/08 Ling 6f stand

Very useful; winner of the 2006 Great St Wilfrid and a Listed race in 2008; effective over 5f-7f; acts on most ground and on Polytrack; has worn cheekpieces/blinkers and a tongue tie.

Exearti

(89) (69)

2-y-o b f Exceed And Excel (AUS)-Graffiti Girl (IRE) (Sadler's Wells (USA))

A J McCabe (Paul Mason 15/7) A J McCabe

Placings:05331 (7864)

2009: 6⁰SD, 5⁵SD, 6³SD, 7³SS, 6¹SS,

	Starts	1st	2nd	3rd	Win & Pl
Career Total (Turf)	0	0	0	0	
Career Total (AW)	5	1	0	2	3447

69 12/09 Sthl 6f SS £2590
Total win prize-money £2590

Going (Turf): **Sf: 0-0 GS: 0-0 Gd: 0-0 GF: 0-0 Fm: 0-0**
Distance: **5f/6f: 1-4** 7f-8f: 0-1 9f-13f: 0-0 14f+: 0-0
Track : **LH: 1-5** RH: 0-0 Tight: 0-2 Gall: 0-0
Aids: Bl: 0-0 Vi: 0-0 Tstrap: 0-0 Ckp: 0-0
Best Rating: **69** 12/09 Sthl 6f std-slw

Modest; stays 6f; handles Polytrack and Fibresand.

Execution (IRE)

85(90) (59)64

2-y-o b c Alhaarth (IRE)-Headrest (Habitat)

E A L Dunlop The Serendipity Partnership

Placings:0460630 (6736)

2009: 7⁰SD, 7⁴SD, 7⁶G, 8⁰SD, 8⁶SD, 8³SD, 8⁰GS,

	Starts	1st	2nd	3rd	Win & Pl
Career Total (Turf)	2	0	0	0	0
Career Total (AW)	5	0	0	1	403

Going (Turf): **Sf: 0-0 GS: 0-1 Gd: 0-1 GF: 0-0 Fm: 0-0**
Distance: 5f/6f: 0-0 7f-8f: 0-5 9f-13f: 0-2 14f+: 0-0
Track : LH: 0-3 RH: 0-3 Tight: 0-4 Gall: 0-0
Aids: Bl: 0-1 Vi: 0-0 Tstrap: 0-0 Ckp: 0-0
Best Rating: **64** 7/09 Yarm 7f3y good

Modest; stays 1m and acts on Polytrack.

Exemplary

94(90) (70)79

2-y-o b c Sulamani (IRE)-Epitome (IRE) (Nashwan (USA))

M Johnston Sheikh Hamdan Bin Mohammed Al Maktoum

Placings:431 (6331)

2009: 8⁴SD, 8³SD, 10¹F,

	Starts	1st	2nd	3rd	Win & Pl
Career Total (Turf)	1	1	0	0	2590
Career Total (AW)	2	0	0	1	905

79 9/09 Bath 1m2f46y FRM £2590
Total win prize-money £2590

Going (Turf): Sf: 0-0 GS: 0-0 Gd: 0-0 GF: 0-0 **Fm: 1-1**
Distance: 5f/6f: 0-0 7f-8f: 0-1 **9f-13f: 1-2** 14f+: 0-0
Track : **LH: 1-3** RH: 0-0 **Tight: 1-2** Gall: 0-0
Aids: Bl: 0-0 Vi: 0-0 Tstrap: 0-0 Ckp: 0-0
Best Rating: **79** 9/09 Bath 1m2f46y firm

Fair; stays 1m2f; acts on fast ground.

Exgray (IRE)

93 84

2-y-o ch f Exceed And Excel (AUS)-Mrs Gray (Red Sunset)

X-Thomas Demeaulte (B Smart 30/6) Prime Equestrian SARL

Placings:215

2009: 5²GF, 5¹GF, 5⁵VS,

	Starts	1st	2nd	3rd	Win & Pl
Career Total (Turf)	3	1	1	0	5294

73 6/09 Haml 5f4y G-F £2729
Total win prize-money £2730

Going (Turf): Sf: 0-0 GS: 0-0 Gd: 0-0 **GF: 1-2** Fm: 0-0
Distance: **5f/6f: 1-3** 7f-8f: 0-0 9f-13f: 0-0 14f+: 0-0
Track : LH: 0-0 RH: 0-0 Tight: 0-0 Gall: 0-0
Aids: Bl: 0-0 Vi: 0-0 Tstrap: 0-0 Ckp: 0-0
Best Rating: **84** 5/09 Muss 5f gd-fm

Useful; effective over 5f; acts on fast ground.

Existentialist

94(95) (61)79

2-y-o b f Exceed And Excel (AUS)-Owdbetts (IRE) (High Estate)

A E Price (J G Portman 11/9) Business Development Consultants Limited

Placings:310300510 (6541)

2009: 5³G, 5¹GF, 5⁰GF, 5³GF, 5⁰GS, 5⁰GF, 5⁵F, 5¹SD, 6⁰GF,

	Starts	1st	2nd	3rd	Win & Pl
Career Total (Turf)	8	1	0	2	5831
Career Total (AW)	1	1	0	0	3886

61 9/09 Wolv 5f216y STD £3885
79 5/09 Wind 5f10y G-F £3561
Total win prize-money £7448

Going (Turf): Sf: 0-0 GS: 0-1 Gd: 0-1 **GF: 1-5** Fm: 0-1
Distance: **5f/6f: 2-9** 7f-8f: 0-0 9f-13f: 0-0 14f+: 0-0
Track : **LH: 1-3** RH: 0-0 Tight: 1-1 Gall: 1-4
Aids: Bl: 0-0 Vi: 0-0 Tstrap: 0-0 Ckp: 0-0
Best Rating: **79** 6/09 Wind 5f10y gd-fm

Fair; effective at 5f-6f; acts on fast and easy ground and on Polytrack.

Exit Smiling

106(107) (85)94

7-y-o ch g Dr Fong (USA)-Away To Me (Exit To Nowhere (USA))

P T Midgley Peter Mee

Placings:23050106/**44236**6000/**26U2061**2010400/**031**220 005060/**1216**1042020-**14**0446202321554 (6014)

2009: 8¹SD, 8⁴SD, 8⁰GF, 9⁴GF, 8⁴GF, 8⁶GF, 8²GS, 8⁰GF, 9²GS, 8³GF, 8²GF, 8¹G, 8⁵GF, 8⁵G, 8⁴G,

	Starts	1st	2nd	3rd	Win & Pl
Career Total (Turf)	43	6	7	3	52449
Career Total (AW)	26	3	6	1	15626

88 8/09 Pont 1m4y (0-80)H GD £6476
85 2/09 Sthl 1m (0-85)H STD £4857
91 6/08 Ripn 1m (0-95)H SFT £7885
79 4/08 Newc 1m3y (0-80)H G-S £4415
76 2/08 Sthl 1m (0-70)H SS £2593
80 4/07 Newc 1m3y (0-80)H GD £5608
77 5/06 Pont 1m4y (0-65)H G-S £3238
69 4/06 Sthl 1m (0-60)H STD £2637
68 10/04 Rdcr 7f GD £3556
Total win prize-money £41269

Going (Turf): Sf: 1-6 GS: 2-9 **Gd: 3-13** GF: 0-14 Fm: 0-1
Distance: 5f/6f: 0-8 **7f-8f: 5-43** 9f-13f: 4-18 14f+: 0-0
Track : **LH: 5-34** RH: 1-20 **Tight: 1-25** Gall: 0-2
Aids: Bl: 0-1 Vi: 0-2 Tstrap: 0-0 Ckp: 0-0
Best Rating: **94** 9/08 Bevl 1m100y heavy

Fair; effective at around 1m; handles most types of ground, but well suited by soft, and sand.

Exopuntla

91 55

3-y-o b f Sure Blade (USA)-Opuntia (Rousillon (USA))

R M Whitaker John W Ford

Placings:00-20000 (6217)

2009: 6²GF, 6⁰GF, 6⁰GF, 7⁰GF, 8⁰GF,

	Starts	1st	2nd	3rd	Win & Pl
Career Total (Turf)	7	0	1	0	771

Going (Turf): **Sf: 0-1 GS: 0-1 Gd: 0-0 GF: 0-5 Fm: 0-0**
Distance: 5f/6f: 0-4 7f-8f: 0-3 9f-13f: 0-0 14f+: 0-0
Track : LH: 0-1 RH: 0-0 Tight: 0-0 Gall: 0-0
Aids: Bl: 0-0 Vi: 0-0 Tstrap: 0-1 Ckp: 0-1

Best Rating: 55 6/09 Rdcr 6f gd-fm

Exotic Beauty

105 89

2-y-o b f Barathea (IRE)-Lady Dominatrix (IRE) (Danehill Dancer (IRE))

M R Channon M Al-Qatami & K M Al-Mudhaf

Placings:32101400 **(6486)**

2009: 5^{3}GF, 6^{2}GF, 5^{1}F, 6^{0}G, 6^{1}GF, 6^{4}G, 5^{0}G, 6^{0}GF,

	Starts	1st	2nd	3rd	Win & Pl
Career Total (Turf)	8	2	1	1	15408

89	8/09	Ripn	6f		G-F	£6938
79	6/09	Bath	5f11y		FRM	£5180

Total win prize-money £12120

Going (Turf): Sf: 0-0 GS: 0-0 Gd: 0-3 **GF: 1-4 Fm: 1-1**
Distance: **5f/6f: 2-8** 7f-8f: 0-0 9f-13f: 0-0 14f+: 0-0
Track : **LH: 1-1** RH: 0-0 Tight: 0-0 **Gall: 1-1**
Aids: Bl: 0-0 Vi: 0-1 Tstrap: 0-0 Ckp: 0-0
Best Rating: 89 8/09 Ripn 6f gd-fm

Useful; stays 6f but effective over shorter; acts on fast ground.

Expensive Dinner

78(89) (49)15

3-y-o ch f Dr Fong (USA)-Reservation (IRE) (Common Grounds)

E F Vaughan E F Vaughan

Placings:0-60 **(4981)**

2009: 6^{6}GF, 7^{0}SD,

	Starts	1st	2nd	3rd	Win & Pl
Career Total (Turf)	2	0	0	0	0
Career Total (AW)	1	0	0	0	

Going (Turf): **Sf: 0-0 GS: 0-0 Gd: 0-1 GF: 0-1 Fm: 0-0**
Distance: 5f/6f: 0-0 7f-8f: 0-3 9f-13f: 0-0 14f+: 0-0
Track : LH: 0-0 RH: 0-1 Tight: 0-0 Gall: 0-0
Aids: Bl: 0-0 Vi: 0-0 Tstrap: 0-0 Ckp: 0-0
Best Rating: 49 8/09 Kemp 7f stand

Expensive Legacy

91(85) (42)60

2-y-o ch f Piccolo-American Rouge (IRE) (Grand Lodge (USA))

H J L Dunlop Here Come The Girls

Placings:000606 **(7474)**

2009: 6^{0}GF, 7^{0}SD, 6^{0}GF, 7^{6}GF, 8^{0}G, 10^{6}SD,

	Starts	1st	2nd	3rd	Win & Pl
Career Total (Turf)	4	0	0	0	0
Career Total (AW)	2	0	0	0	0

Going (Turf): **Sf: 0-0 GS: 0-0 Gd: 0-1 GF: 0-3 Fm: 0-0**
Distance: 5f/6f: 0-0 7f-8f: 0-4 9f-13f: 0-2 14f+: 0-0
Track : LH: 0-2 RH: 0-2 Tight: 0-1 Gall: 0-0
Aids: Bl: 0-0 Vi: 0-0 Tstrap: 0-0 Ckp: 0-0
Best Rating: 60 7/09 Sals 6f212y gd-fm

Yet to show much ability so far.

Expensive Problem

95(90) (48)76

6-y-o b g Medicean-Dance Steppe (Rambo Dancer (CAN))

R J Smith F Willson

Placings:045250/16200/400323363/502162541-61600 **(6726)**

2009: 8^{6}G, 8^{1}GF, 10^{6}G, 8^{0}GF, 7^{0}SD,

	Starts	1st	2nd	3rd	Win & Pl
Career Total (Turf)	18	1	0	1	4989
Career Total (AW)	16	3	5	3	24712

76	6/09	Wind	1m67y	(0-70)H	G-F	£2729
	8/08	Mija	1m165y		STD	£3676
	3/08	Mija	1m1f	H	STD	£4044
	3/06	Mija	1m55y		STD	£4965

Total win prize-money £15416

Going (Turf): Sf: 0-1 GS: 0-1 Gd: 0-10 **GF: 1-5** Fm: 0-0
Distance: 5f/6f: 0-2 7f-8f: 0-10 **9f-13f: 4-22** 14f+: 0-0
Track : LH: 0-4 **RH: 1-2 Tight: 1-5** Gall: 0-1
Aids: Bl: 0-0 Vi: 0-1 Tstrap: 0-0 Ckp: 0-0
Best Rating: 76 6/09 Wind 1m67y gd-fm

Fair; effective at around 1m; acts on fast ground; goes on sand.

Explorator (IRE)

(93) (54)

2-y-o b c Whipper (USA)-Certainly Brave (Indian Ridge)

George Baker Kismet Partnership

Placings:04 **(7886)**

2009: 7^{0}SD, 7^{4}SD,

	Starts	1st	2nd	3rd	Win & Pl
Career Total (Turf)	0	0	0	0	
Career Total (AW)	2	0	0	0	0

Going (Turf): **Sf: 0-0 GS: 0-0 Gd: 0-0 GF: 0-0 Fm: 0-0**
Distance: 5f/6f: 0-0 7f-8f: 0-2 9f-13f: 0-0 14f+: 0-0
Track : LH: 0-1 RH: 0-1 Tight: 0-1 Gall: 0-0
Aids: Bl: 0-0 Vi: 0-0 Tstrap: 0-0 Ckp: 0-0
Best Rating: 54 12/09 Kemp 7f stand

Express Wish

108 (77)111

5-y-o b h Danehill Dancer (IRE)-Waffle On (Chief Singer)

J Noseda Peter Mitchell

Placings:0/21100/23015-005045 **(5878)**

2009: 7^{0}Y, 7^{0}G, 7^{5}G, 7^{0}GF, 7^{4}GF, 6^{5}GF,

	Starts	1st	2nd	3rd	Win & Pl
Career Total (Turf)	16	3	1	1	68993
Career Total (AW)	1	0	1	0	867

111	9/08	Gdwd	7f		SFT	£36900
95	6/07	Hayd	6f	(0-95)H	G-F	£9715
88	5/07	Brig	5f213y		GD	£2817

Total win prize-money £49434

Going (Turf): **Sf: 1-2** GS: 0-0 **Gd: 1-6 GF: 1-7** Fm: 0-0
Distance: **5f/6f: 2-9** 7f-8f: 1-8 9f-13f: 0-0 14f+: 0-0
Track : LH: 1-2 RH: 1-3 Tight: 0-1 Gall: 0-0
Aids: Bl: 0-0 Vi: 0-1 Tstrap: 0-0 Ckp: 0-0
Best Rating: 111 9/08 Gdwd 7f soft

Smart; effective over 6f-7f; acts on good and faster ground, but probably best suited by a soft surface; also goes on Polytrack; has worn a visor.

Expressive

(103) (78)

3-y-o b f Falbrav (IRE)-Exclusive (Polar Falcon (USA))

Sir Michael Stoute Cheveley Park Stud

Placings:23221 **(6346)**

2009: 7^{2}SD, 8^{3}SD, 8^{2}SF, 8^{2}SD, 9^{1}SD,

	Starts	1st	2nd	3rd	Win & Pl
Career Total (Turf)	0	0	0	0	
Career Total (AW)	5	1	3	1	7648

78	9/09	Wolv	1m1f103y	(0-80)H	STD	£5046

Total win prize-money £5046

Going (Turf): **Sf: 0-0 GS: 0-0 Gd: 0-0 GF: 0-0 Fm: 0-0**
Distance: 5f/6f: 0-0 7f-8f: 0-2 **9f-13f: 1-3** 14f+: 0-0
Track : **LH: 1-4** RH: 0-1 **Tight: 1-4** Gall: 0-0
Aids: Bl: 0-0 Vi: 0-0 Tstrap: 0-0 Ckp: 0-0
Best Rating: 78 9/09 Wolv 1m1f103y stand

Fair; stays 1m1f; acts on Polytrack.

Expresso Star (USA)

109 113

4-y-o b c War Chant (USA)-Caffe Latte (IRE) (Seattle Dancer (USA))

J H M Gosden H R H Princess Haya Of Jordan

Placings:242111-1300 **(7208a)**

2009: 8^{1}GF, 10^{3}GF, 12^{0}G, 8^{0}VS,

	Starts	1st	2nd	3rd	Win & Pl
Career Total (Turf)	10	4	2	1	104431

113	3/09	Donc	1m	H	G-F	£77887
104	10/08	Nott	1m2f50y	(0-95)H	G-S	£7771
104	10/08	Nott	1m2f50y	(0-85)H	SFT	£6476
88	9/08	Haml	1m1f36y		SFT	£2914

Total win prize-money £95049

Going (Turf): **Sf: 2-2** GS: 1-1 Gd: 0-2 GF: 1-3 Fm: 0-1
Distance: 5f/6f: 0-0 7f-8f: 1-4 **9f-13f: 3-6** 14f+: 0-0
Track : **LH: 2-6** RH: 1-1 **Tight: 1-4** Gall: 0-0
Aids: Bl: 0-0 Vi: 0-0 Tstrap: 0-0 Ckp: 0-0
Best Rating: 113 3/09 Donc 1m gd-fm

Smart; won the 2009 Lincoln at Doncaster; effective at 1m-1m2f; handles fast ground but may be best suited by soft.

Extracurricular (USA)

91(93) (62)48

3-y-o ch f Thunder Gulch (USA)-Frans Lass (USA) (Shanekite (USA))

S Gollings (M Botti 6/8) R C N Davidson

Placings:545640 **(5316)**

2009: 8^{5}SD, 8^{4}SD, 10^{5}SD, 10^{6}GS, 8^{4}G, 7^{0}SD,

	Starts	1st	2nd	3rd	Win & Pl
Career Total (Turf)	2	0	0	0	144
Career Total (AW)	4	0	0	0	0

Going (Turf): **Sf: 0-0 GS: 0-1 Gd: 0-1 GF: 0-0 Fm: 0-0**
Distance: 5f/6f: 0-0 7f-8f: 0-2 9f-13f: 0-4 14f+: 0-0
Track : LH: 0-3 RH: 0-2 Tight: 0-3 Gall: 0-0
Aids: Bl: 0-0 Vi: 0-0 Tstrap: 0-0 Ckp: 0-0
Best Rating: 62 3/09 Kemp 1m stand

Extraterrestrial

109(106) (100)106

5-y-o b g Mind Games-Expectation (IRE) (Night Shift (USA))

R A Fahey G J Paver

Placings:13604210060/021200043042-023100001 **(6094)**

2009: 8^{0}SD, 8^{2}GF, 8^{3}SD, 8^{1}S, 8^{0}G, 8^{0}G, 8^{0}G, 8^{0}GF, 8^{1}G,

	Starts	1st	2nd	3rd	Win & Pl
Career Total (Turf)	28	5	4	2	104706

	Starts	1st	2nd	3rd	Win & Pl
Career Total (AW)	4	0	1	1	5073

106 9/09 Ayr 1m (0-100)H GD £24924
104 4/09 Newb 1m H SFT £24924
101 5/08 Thsk 1m (0-100)H GD £11656
98 7/07 Fair 6f SH £8797
75 4/07 Cork 6f GD £8797
Total win prize-money £79099

Going (Turf): Sf: 1-5 GS: 0-0 **Gd: 3-12** GF: 0-6 Fm: 0-0
Distance: 5f/6f: 2-5 **7f-8f: 3-21** 9f-13f: 0-6 14f+: 0-0
Track : **LH: 2-12** RH: 1-9 **Tight: 1-5** Gall: 0-3
Aids: **Bl: 1-5** Vi: 0-0 Tstrap: 0-5 Ckp: 0-5
Best Rating: 106 9/09 Ayr 1m good

Very useful; ex-Irish; effective over 7f-1m; acts on good and softer ground; goes on Polytrack; has worn blinkers and cheekpieces.

Extreme Green

83 54
2-y-o ch f Motivator-Ventura (IRE) (Spectrum (IRE))
A M Balding George Strawbridge

Placings:00 (6965)
2009: 7^{0}GF, 7^{0}G,

	Starts	1st	2nd	3rd	Win & Pl
Career Total (Turf)	2	0	0	0	

Going (Turf): **Sf: 0-0 GS: 0-0 Gd: 0-1 GF: 0-1 Fm: 0-0**
Distance: 5f/6f: 0-0 7f-8f: 0-2 9f-13f: 0-0 14f+: 0-0
Track : LH: 0-2 RH: 0-0 Tight: 0-0 Gall: 0-0
Aids: Bl: 0-0 Vi: 0-0 Tstrap: 0-0 Ckp: 0-0
Best Rating: 54 9/09 Wwck 7f26y gd-fm

Extreme Pleasure (IRE)

92(92) (63)64
4-y-o b f High Chaparral (IRE)-Height Of Passion (Shirley Heights)
W J Knight W P Churchward

Placings:03300-000 (4935)
2009: 14^{0}GF, 11^{0}GF, 18^{0}G,

	Starts	1st	2nd	3rd	Win & Pl
Career Total (Turf)	5	0	0	2	790
Career Total (AW)	3	0	0	0	

Going (Turf): **Sf: 0-1 GS: 0-1 Gd: 0-1 GF: 0-2 Fm: 0-0**
Distance: 5f/6f: 0-0 7f-8f: 0-0 9f-13f: 0-4 14f+: 0-4
Track : LH: 0-7 RH: 0-1 Tight: 0-5 Gall: 0-1
Aids: Bl: 0-0 Vi: 0-0 Tstrap: 0-0 Ckp: 0-0
Best Rating: 64 9/08 Bath 1m3f144y soft

Extreme Warrior (IRE)

96 82
2-y-o ch g Dubawi (IRE)-Extreme Beauty (USA) (Rahy (USA))
D R Lanigan Saif Ali

Placings:0145 (4086)
2009: 6^{0}G, 6^{1}GF, 6^{4}G, 7^{5}S,

	Starts	1st	2nd	3rd	Win & Pl
Career Total (Turf)	4	1	0	0	6422

82 6/09 NmkJ 6f G-F £5180
Total win prize-money £5181

Going (Turf): Sf: 0-1 GS: 0-0 Gd: 0-2 **GF: 1-1** Fm: 0-0
Distance: **5f/6f: 1-3** 7f-8f: 0-1 9f-13f: 0-0 14f+: 0-0
Track : LH: 0-0 RH: 0-0 Tight: 0-0 Gall: 0-0
Aids: **Bl: 1-3** Vi: 0-0 Tstrap: 0-0 Ckp: 0-0
Best Rating: 82 6/09 NmkJ 6f gd-fm

Useful; effective over 6f; acts on fast ground; has won in blinkers.

Extremely So

99(97) (64)63
3-y-o ch f Kyllachy-Antigua (Selkirk (USA))
P J McBride N Davies

Placings:04430-6026204123 (7608)
2009: 12^{6}SD, 12^{0}GF, 10^{2}GF, 10^{6}GF, 10^{2}GF, 10^{0}G, 12^{4}GF, 11^{1}GF, 12^{2}SD, 16^{3}SD,

	Starts	1st	2nd	3rd	Win & Pl
Career Total (Turf)	9	1	2	0	3609
Career Total (AW)	6	0	1	2	1696

56 10/09 Yarm 1m3f101y G-F £1942
Total win prize-money £1943

Going (Turf): Sf: 0-0 GS: 0-0 Gd: 0-1 **GF: 1-8** Fm: 0-0
Distance: 5f/6f: 0-2 7f-8f: 0-3 **9f-13f: 1-9** 14f+: 0-1
Track : **LH: 1-7** RH: 0-6 **Tight: 1-8** Gall: 0-2
Aids: Bl: 0-0 Vi: 0-0 Tstrap: 0-0 Ckp: 0-0
Best Rating: 64 11/09 Ling 1m4f stand

Moderate; stays 2m; acts on Polytrack.

Eye Candy (IRE)

92 (50)54
8-y-o b g Princely Heir (IRE)-Timissa (IRE) (Kahyasi)
Anthony Mullins (Mrs Sandra McCarthy 5/7) Mrs Sandra McCarthy

Placings:0/25210/6/40000/0/0-604 (5055a)
2009: 14^{6}GF, 13^{0}G, 14^{4}GF,

	Starts	1st	2nd	3rd	Win & Pl
Career Total (Turf)	13	1	2	0	10365
Career Total (AW)	4	0	0	0	241

83 7/04 Naas 1m4f (60-90)H G-F £8272
Total win prize-money £8273

Going (Turf): Sf: 0-0 GS: 0-0 Gd: 0-3 **GF: 1-6** Fm: 0-1
Distance: 5f/6f: 0-0 7f-8f: 0-0 **9f-13f: 1-9** 14f+: 0-8
Track : LH: 0-7 RH: 0-8 Tight: 0-3 Gall: 0-0
Aids: Bl: 0-4 Vi: 0-0 Tstrap: 0-3 Ckp: 0-3
Best Rating: 83 7/04 Naas 1m4f gd-fm

Eye For The Girls

95(72) 58
3-y-o ch g Bertolini (USA)-Aunt Ruby (USA) (Rubiano (USA))
M R Channon Heart Of The South Racing

Placings:0-0005610030 (6787)
2009: 8^{0}S, 8^{0}GF, 7^{0}G, 6^{5}GF, 6^{6}GF, 6^{1}G, 8^{0}G, 7^{0}SD, 7^{3}GF, 7^{0}G,

	Starts	1st	2nd	3rd	Win & Pl
Career Total (Turf)	10	1	0	1	2241
Career Total (AW)	1	0	0	0	

58 7/09 Yarm 6f3y (0-55)H GD £1942
Total win prize-money £1943

Going (Turf): Sf: 0-1 GS: 0-1 **Gd: 1-4** GF: 0-4 Fm: 0-0
Distance: 5f/6f: 0-2 **7f-8f: 1-8** 9f-13f: 0-1 14f+: 0-0
Track : LH: 0-3 RH: 0-1 Tight: 0-1 Gall: 0-0
Aids: Bl: 0-0 Vi: 0-0 Tstrap: 0-0 Ckp: 0-0
Best Rating: 58 9/09 Yarm 7f3y gd-fm

Moderate; effective at 6f on easy ground.

Eye Of Eternity

74 23
2-y-o b f Oratorio (IRE)-Eyeq (IRE) (Cadeaux Genereux)
Rae Guest Light Valley Stud

Placings:0 (7096)
2009: 7^{0}G,

	Starts	1st	2nd	3rd	Win & Pl
Career Total (Turf)	1	0	0	0	

Going (Turf): **Sf: 0-0 GS: 0-0 Gd: 0-1 GF: 0-0 Fm: 0-0**
Distance: 5f/6f: 0-0 7f-8f: 0-1 9f-13f: 0-0 14f+: 0-0
Track : LH: 0-0 RH: 0-0 Tight: 0-0 Gall: 0-0
Aids: Bl: 0-0 Vi: 0-0 Tstrap: 0-0 Ckp: 0-0
Best Rating: 23 10/09 Yarm 7f3y good

Eyeffess (IRE)

(98) (63)57
8-y-o ch g Pasternak-Ben Tack (Lucifer (USA))
P J Rothwell R J Walshe

Placings:300-00006 (7005)
2009: 8^{0}SD, 12^{0}SD, 12^{0}SD, 12^{0}YS, 16^{6}SD,

	Starts	1st	2nd	3rd	Win & Pl
Career Total (Turf)	3	0	0	0	
Career Total (AW)	5	0	0	1	548

Going (Turf): **Sf: 0-1 GS: 0-0 Gd: 0-0 GF: 0-0 Fm: 0-0**
Distance: 5f/6f: 0-0 7f-8f: 0-1 9f-13f: 0-6 14f+: 0-1
Track : LH: 0-7 RH: 0-1 Tight: 0-1 Gall: 0-0
Aids: Bl: 0-0 Vi: 0-0 Tstrap: 0-1 Ckp: 0-1
Best Rating: 68 4/08 Dund 1m4f stand

Eyes Like A Hawk (IRE)

98(51) 61
3-y-o b/br f Diktat-Mexican Hawk (USA) (Silver Hawk (USA))
Tom Dascombe W R B Racing 51

Placings:0-5540 (5806)
2009: 6^{5}GF, 7^{5}GS, 7^{4}GF, 8^{0}SD,

	Starts	1st	2nd	3rd	Win & Pl
Career Total (Turf)	4	0	0	0	0
Career Total (AW)	1	0	0	0	

Going (Turf): **Sf: 0-0 GS: 0-1 Gd: 0-0 GF: 0-3 Fm: 0-0**
Distance: 5f/6f: 0-1 7f-8f: 0-4 9f-13f: 0-0 14f+: 0-0
Track : LH: 0-0 RH: 0-1 Tight: 0-0 Gall: 0-0
Aids: Bl: 0-0 Vi: 0-0 Tstrap: 0-0 Ckp: 0-0
Best Rating: 61 8/09 Ling 7f140y gd-fm

Eyesore

58(84) (32)
3-y-o b f Reel Buddy (USA)-Segretezza (IRE) (Perugino (USA))
S A Harris S A Harris

Placings:000-00 (7796)
2009: 14^{0}GF, 7^{0}SS,

	Starts	1st	2nd	3rd	Win & Pl
Career Total (Turf)	3	0	0	0	
Career Total (AW)	2	0	0	0	

Going (Turf): **Sf: 0-0 GS: 0-1 Gd: 0-1 GF: 0-1 Fm: 0-0**

Distance: 5f/6f: 0-3 7f-8f: 0-1 9f-13f: 0-0 14f+: 0-1
Track : LH: 0-4 RH: 0-0 Tight: 0-1 Gall: 0-0
Aids: Bl: 0-0 Vi: 0-0 Tstrap: 0-0 Ckp: 0-0
Best Rating: **32** 12/09 Sthl 7f std-slw

Ezdeyaad (USA)

102 **87**

5-y-o b g Lemon Drop Kid (USA)-August Storm (USA) (Storm Creek (USA))
G A Swinbank Mrs B Boanson M Wane Mrs J McCann

Placings:3/055145320-0521305635 **(6645)**
2009: 8^{0}GF, 7^{5}GF, 7^{2}GF, 8^{1}GF, 8^{3}G, 8^{0}GF, 8^{5}G, 8^{6}G, 8^{3}GF, 7^{5}G,

	Starts	1st	2nd	3rd	Win & Pl
Career Total (Turf)	**20**	**2**	**2**	**4**	**19285**

87	6/09	Hayd	1m30y	(0-90)H	G-F	£9066
82	6/08	Rdcr	1m	(0-75)H	FRM	£2331

Total win prize-money £11397

Going (Turf): Sf: 0-1 GS: 0-2 Gd: 0-6 **GF: 1-10 Fm: 1-1**
Distance: 5f/6f: 0-0 7f-8f: 1-13 9f-13f: 1-7 14f+: 0-0
Track : **LH: 1-11** RH: 0-2 Tight: 0-3 Gall: 0-1
Aids: Bl: 0-0 Vi: 0-0 Tstrap: 0-0 Ckp: 0-0
Best Rating: **87** 6/09 Hayd 1m30y gd-fm

Useful; effective over 7f-1m; acts on any ground.

Ezdiyaad (IRE)

105 (61)**106**

5-y-o b g Galileo (IRE)-Wijdan (USA) (Mr Prospector (USA))
M P Tregoning Hamdan Al Maktoum

Placings:0013/110354-6053 **(7059)**
2009: 12^{6}S, 9^{0}GF, 10^{5}GS, 11^{3}GF,

	Starts	1st	2nd	3rd	Win & Pl
Career Total (Turf)	**13**	**3**	**0**	**3**	**40802**
Career Total (AW)	**1**	**0**	**0**	**0**	

106	5/08	Donc	1m2f60y	(0-95)H	GD	£9714
98	4/08	Newb	1m2f6y	(0-85)H	SFT	£5180
85	8/07	NmkJ	1m		SFT	£4533

Total win prize-money £19429

Going (Turf): **Sf: 2-5** GS: 0-2 Gd: 1-2 GF: 0-4 Fm: 0-0
Distance: 5f/6f: 0-0 7f-8f: 1-3 **9f-13f: 2-11** 14f+: 0-0
Track : **LH: 2-5** RH: 0-6 Tight: 0-1 **Gall: 2-7**
Aids: Bl: 0-0 Vi: 0-0 Tstrap: 0-0 Ckp: 0-0
Best Rating: **106** 5/08 Donc 1m2f60y good

Smart; effective over 1m2f-1m4f; acts on good and softer ground.

Faasel (IRE)

100 **79**

8-y-o b g Unfuwain (USA)-Waqood (USA) (Riverman (USA))
N G Richards Jim Ennis

Placings:056311/1163421/00 **(3146)**
2009: 16^{0}G, 13^{0}GF,

	Starts	1st	2nd	3rd	Win & Pl
Career Total (Turf)	**15**	**5**	**1**	**2**	**85897**

103	10/04	Naas	1m4f	H	Y-S	£25214
96	7/04	Gway	1m4f	(60-90)H	G-F	£8272
93	3/04	Limk	1m3f	(60-90)H	Y-S	£7785
83	9/03	List	1m		GD	£21103
78	9/03	Gway	7f	(0-80)H	G-Y	£7840

Total win prize-money £70219

Going (Turf): Sf: 0-1 GS: 0-0 **Gd: 1-7 GF: 1-3** Fm: 0-0
Distance: 5f/6f: 0-0 7f-8f: 2-6 **9f-13f: 3-6** 14f+: 0-3
Track : LH: 0-5 **RH: 1-3** Tight: 0-0 Gall: 0-0
Aids: **Bl: 2-6** Vi: 0-0 Tstrap: 0-0 Ckp: 0-0
Best Rating: **103** 10/04 Naas 1m4f yld-sft

Fabled Dancer (IRE)

89 **48**

3-y-o ch g Choisir (AUS)-Age Of Fable (IRE) (Entrepreneur)
E J Alston I L Davies

Placings:050 **(5731)**
2009: 7^{0}G, 8^{5}GF, 8^{0}GS,

	Starts	1st	2nd	3rd	Win & Pl
Career Total (Turf)	3	0	0	0	0

Going (Turf): **Sf: 0-0 GS: 0-1 Gd: 0-1 GF: 0-1 Fm: 0-0**
Distance: 5f/6f: 0-0 7f-8f: 0-2 9f-13f: 0-1 14f+: 0-0
Track : LH: 0-3 RH: 0-0 Tight: 0-1 Gall: 0-1
Aids: Bl: 0-0 Vi: 0-0 Tstrap: 0-0 Ckp: 0-0
Best Rating: **48** 9/09 Newc 1m gd-sft

Fabreze

55(97) (96)**94**

4-y-o ch g Choisir (AUS)-Impulsive Decision (IRE) (Nomination)
P J Makin Weldspec Glasgow Limited

Placings:4/1321-0 **(3795)**
2009: 6^{0}G,

	Starts	1st	2nd	3rd	Win & Pl
Career Total (Turf)	**5**	**1**	**1**	**1**	**4998**
Career Total (AW)	**1**	**1**	**0**	**0**	**4727**

96	7/08	Kemp	6f	(0-85)H	STD	£4727
82	5/08	Nott	6f15y		GD	£2590

Total win prize-money £7317

Going (Turf): Sf: 0-0 GS: 0-0 **Gd: 1-3** GF: 0-2 Fm: 0-0
Distance: 5f/6f: 1-5 7f-8f: 1-1 9f-13f: 0-0 14f+: 0-0
Track : LH: 0-0 **RH: 1-1** Tight: 0-0 Gall: 0-0
Aids: Bl: 0-0 Vi: 0-0 Tstrap: 0-0 Ckp: 0-0
Best Rating: **96** 7/08 Kemp 6f stand

Useful prospect; stays 6f; acts on a sound surface; open to further improvement.

Faintly Hopeful

83(95) (51)**45**

4-y-o b g Marju (IRE)-Twilight Patrol (Robellino (USA))
R A Teal Chris Simpson

Placings:006**50**-**0040**0 **(5018)**
2009: 7^{0}SD, 6^{0}SD, 6^{4}SD, 6^{0}SD, 6^{0}GF,

	Starts	1st	2nd	3rd	Win & Pl
Career Total (Turf)	4	0	0	0	0
Career Total (AW)	6	0	0	0	0

Going (Turf): **Sf: 0-1 GS: 0-2 Gd: 0-0 GF: 0-1 Fm: 0-0**
Distance: 5f/6f: 0-6 7f-8f: 0-4 9f-13f: 0-0 14f+: 0-0
Track : LH: 0-3 RH: 0-3 Tight: 0-3 Gall: 0-0
Aids: Bl: 0-0 Vi: 0-0 Tstrap: 0-4 Ckp: 0-4
Best Rating: **51** 1/09 Ling 6f stand

Fair Along (GER)

89 (67)**90**

7-y-o b g Alkalde (GER)-Fairy Tango (FR) (Acatenango (GER))
P J Hobbs Alan Peterson

Placings:00040001/01043/4114/23/0-0 **(6851)**
2009: 18^{0}G,

	Starts	1st	2nd	3rd	Win & Pl
Career Total (Turf)	**14**	**2**	**1**	**1**	**46383**
Career Total (AW)	**7**	**2**	**0**	**1**	**7022**

94	8/06	Sals	1m6f15y	(0-70)H	GD	£3562
80	8/06	Sals	1m6f15y	(0-70)H	G-S	£3886
67	2/05	Sthl	1m3f	(0-70)H	STD	£3425
63	12/04	Wolv	1m141y		STD	£2968

Total win prize-money £13842

Going (Turf): Sf: 0-1 **GS: 1-4 Gd: 1-5** GF: 0-4 Fm: 0-0
Distance: 5f/6f: 0-2 7f-8f: 0-3 9f-13f: 2-9 14f+: 2-7
Track : LH: 2-10 RH: 2-7 **Tight: 3-12** Gall: 0-4
Aids: Bl: 0-1 Vi: 0-0 Tstrap: 0-2 Ckp: 0-2
Best Rating: **101** 10/07 NmkR 2m2f gd-sft

Very useful; placed in Chester Cup and Cesarewitch in 2007; stays 2m2f; acts on good and softer ground and on sand; has been tried in cheekpieces; high-class hurdler/chaser.

Fair Bunny

92(89) (67)**64**

2-y-o b f Trade Fair-Coney Hills (Beverley Boy)
A D Brown Mrs Susan Johnson

Placings:003466**166** **(7707)**
2009: 5^{0}GS, 6^{0}GF, 5^{3}GF, 6^{4}G, 6^{6}GF, 5^{6}GS, 6^{1}SD, 5^{6}SD, 6^{6}SD,

	Starts	1st	2nd	3rd	Win & Pl
Career Total (Turf)	**6**	**0**	**0**	**1**	**1068**
Career Total (AW)	**3**	**1**	**0**	**0**	**2047**

67	11/09	Sthl	6f	(0-60)	STD	£2047

Total win prize-money £2047

Going (Turf): **Sf: 0-0 GS: 0-2 Gd: 0-1 GF: 0-3 Fm: 0-0**
Distance: **5f/6f: 1-9** 7f-8f: 0-0 9f-13f: 0-0 14f+: 0-0
Track : **LH: 1-3** RH: 0-0 Tight: 0-1 Gall: 0-0
Aids: Bl: 0-0 Vi: 0-0 Tstrap: 0-0 Ckp: 0-0
Best Rating: **67** 11/09 Sthl 6f stand

Modest; effective over 6f; acts on Fibresand.

Fair Nella

89 **65**

2-y-o b f Trade Fair-Zanella (IRE) (Nordico (USA))
J G Portman J G B Portman

Placings:646 **(5096)**
2009: 6^{6}GF, 5^{4}G, 6^{6}GF,

	Starts	1st	2nd	3rd	Win & Pl
Career Total (Turf)	3	0	0	0	164

Going (Turf): **Sf: 0-0 GS: 0-0 Gd: 0-1 GF: 0-2 Fm: 0-0**
Distance: 5f/6f: 0-3 7f-8f: 0-0 9f-13f: 0-0 14f+: 0-0
Track : LH: 0-1 RH: 0-0 Tight: 0-0 Gall: 0-3
Aids: Bl: 0-0 Vi: 0-0 Tstrap: 0-0 Ckp: 0-0
Best Rating: **65** 7/09 Wind 6f gd-fm

Fair Passion

(95) (65)

2-y-o b f Trade Fair-United Passion (Emarati (USA))
D Shaw Derek Shaw

Placings:63 **(7213)**
2009: 5^{6}SD, 5^{3}SD,

	Starts	1st	2nd	3rd	Win & Pl
Career Total (Turf)	0	0	0	0	
Career Total (AW)	2	0	0	1	578

Going (Turf): Sf: 0-0 GS: 0-0 Gd: 0-0 GF: 0-0 Fm: 0-0
Distance: 5f/6f: 0-2 7f-8f: 0-0 9f-13f: 0-0 14f+: 0-0
Track : LH: 0-1 RH: 0-1 Tight: 0-1 Gall: 0-0
Aids: Bl: 0-0 Vi: 0-0 Tstrap: 0-0 Ckp: 0-0
Best Rating: 65 11/09 Wolv 5f20y stand

Modest; effective over 5f; acts on Polytrack.

Fair Trade

103 **85**
2-y-o ch c Trade Fair-Ballet (Sharrood (USA))
D R C Elsworth Raymond Tooth

Placings:2 **(6810)**
2009: 8^{2}G,

	Starts	1st	2nd	3rd	Win & Pl
Career Total (Turf)	1	0	1	0	1734

Going (Turf): Sf: 0-0 GS: 0-0 Gd: 0-1 GF: 0-0 Fm: 0-0
Distance: 5f/6f: 0-0 7f-8f: 0-1 9f-13f: 0-0 14f+: 0-0
Track : LH: 0-0 RH: 0-0 Tight: 0-0 Gall: 0-0
Aids: Bl: 0-0 Vi: 0-0 Tstrap: 0-0 Ckp: 0-0
Best Rating: 85 10/09 NmkR 1m good

Runner-up on debut; effective over 1m; acts on good ground.

Fairly Honest

94(101) (56)**57**
5-y-o b g Alhaarth (IRE)-Miller's Melody (Chief Singer)
P W Hiatt P W Hiatt

Placings:00435/305540060/3002223053300-65601530554 **(3662)**
2009: 10^{6}SD, 9^{5}SD, 8^{6}SD, 8^{0}SD, 8^{1}SD, 8^{5}SD, 8^{3}SD, 6^{0}GF, 7^{5}G, 7^{5}GF, 7^{4}F,

	Starts	1st	2nd	3rd	Win & Pl
Career Total (Turf)	25	0	3	4	3891
Career Total (AW)	13	1	0	3	2888
52 2/09 Kemp 1m	(0-45)		STD		£1619

Total win prize-money £1619

Going (Turf): Sf: 0-0 GS: 0-5 Gd: 0-7 GF: 0-6 Fm: 0-7
Distance: 5f/6f: 0-1 **7f-8f: 1-17** 9f-13f: 0-20 14f+: 0-0
Track : LH: 0-29 **RH: 1-4** Tight: 0-16 Gall: 0-0
Aids: Bl: 0-1 Vi: 0-0 Tstrap: 0-0 Ckp: 0-0
Best Rating: 71 5/07 Wind 1m2f7y gd-sft

Moderate; effective at around 1m-1m2f; acts on fast and easy ground; also goes on Polytrack.

Fairmile

108(110) (101)**107**
7-y-o b g Spectrum (IRE)-Juno Marlowe (IRE) (Danehill (USA))
George Baker (Ian Williams 24/7) The Fairmile Partnership

Placings:3364/110/0012120/133202/2-44251560 **(7465)**
2009: 12^{4}G, 10^{4}GF, 10^{2}SD, 12^{5}GF, 10^{1}G, 12^{5}G, 8^{6}SD, 12^{0}SD,

	Starts	1st	2nd	3rd	Win & Pl
Career Total (Turf)	25	5	5	4	200742
Career Total (AW)	4	1	1	0	10602

92	7/09	Epsm	1m2f18y		GD	£7477
102	1/07	Ndas	1m2f	(90-105)H	GD	£33673
101	7/06	York	1m2f88y	H	G-F	£93480
100	6/06	Kemp	1m2f	(0-95)H	STD	£7790
91	10/05	Wind	1m3f135y	(0-85)H	GD	£6979
91	9/05	Sand	1m2f7y	(0-80)H	SFT	£6086

Total win prize-money £155487

Going (Turf): Sf: 1-4 GS: 0-4 **Gd: 3-11** GF: 1-6 Fm: 0-0
Distance: 5f/6f: 0-0 7f-8f: 0-4 **9f-13f: 6-25** 14f+: 0-0
Track : **LH: 3-18** RH: 2-4 Tight: 2-8 Gall: 2-10
Aids: Bl: 0-1 Vi: 0-0 Tstrap: 1-1 Ckp: 1-1
Best Rating: 117 9/07 Donc 1m2f60y gd-fm

Smart; effective at around 1m2f; acts on most ground, including Polytrack; has worn various headgear.

Fairplaytomyself

90(99) (52)**37**
4-y-o ch f Ballet Master (USA)-Over The Moon (Beveled (USA))
P W Hiatt Eamon Spain

Placings:0650402 **(7814)**
2009: 10^{0}G, 8^{6}SD, 10^{5}F, 9^{0}SD, 8^{4}SF, 8^{0}SD, 8^{2}SD,

	Starts	1st	2nd	3rd	Win & Pl
Career Total (Turf)	2	0	0	0	0
Career Total (AW)	5	0	1	0	403

Going (Turf): Sf: 0-0 GS: 0-0 Gd: 0-1 GF: 0-0 Fm: 0-1
Distance: 5f/6f: 0-0 7f-8f: 0-1 9f-13f: 0-6 14f+: 0-0
Track : LH: 0-7 RH: 0-0 Tight: 0-6 Gall: 0-0
Aids: Bl: 0-0 Vi: 0-0 Tstrap: 0-0 Ckp: 0-0
Best Rating: 52 12/09 Wolv 1m141y stand

Plating-class; stays 1m; acts on Polytrack.

Fairy Flight (USA)

(92) (76)
2-y-o b/br f Fusaichi Pegasus (USA)-La Barberina (USA) (Nijinsky (CAN))
W J Knight Bluehills Racing Limited

Placings:51 **(7622)**
2009: 8^{5}SD, 8^{1}SD,

	Starts	1st	2nd	3rd	Win & Pl
Career Total (Turf)	0	0	0	0	
Career Total (AW)	2	1	0	0	2388
76 12/09 Ling 1m			STD		£2388

Total win prize-money £2388

Going (Turf): Sf: 0-0 GS: 0-0 Gd: 0-0 GF: 0-0 Fm: 0-0
Distance: 5f/6f: 0-0 **7f-8f: 1-1** 9f-13f: 0-1 14f+: 0-0
Track : **LH: 1-2** RH: 0-0 **Tight: 1-2** Gall: 0-0
Aids: Bl: 0-0 Vi: 0-0 Tstrap: 0-0 Ckp: 0-0
Best Rating: 76 12/09 Ling 1m stand

Fair; stays 1m; acts on Polytrack.

Fairy Promises (USA)

90 **77**
2-y-o ch f Brokon Vow (USA)-Fairy Glade (USA) (Gone West (USA))
Pat Eddery K Abdulla

Placings:0140 **(6447)**
2009: 6^{0}GF, 6^{1}HY, 7^{4}GS, 7^{0}GF,

	Starts	1st	2nd	3rd	Win & Pl
Career Total (Turf)	4	1	0	0	4399
75 7/09 Nott 6f15y			HVY		£3885

Total win prize-money £3886

Going (Turf): Sf: 1-1 GS: 0-1 Gd: 0-0 GF: 0-2 Fm: 0-0
Distance: 5f/6f: 0-0 **7f-8f: 1-4** 9f-13f: 0-0 14f+: 0-0
Track : LH: 0-0 RH: 0-1 Tight: 0-0 Gall: 0-0
Aids: Bl: 0-0 Vi: 0-0 Tstrap: 0-0 Ckp: 0-0
Best Rating: 77 10/09 NmkR 7f gd-fm

Fair; effective over 6f; acts on heavy ground.

Fairys In A Storm (IRE)

84 **42**
2-y-o gr f Choisir (AUS)-Fidra (IRE) (Vettori (IRE))
P T Midgley Mrs K L Midgley

Placings:005 **(2414)**
2009: 5^{0}GF, 6^{0}GS, 6^{5}G,

	Starts	1st	2nd	3rd	Win & Pl
Career Total (Turf)	3	0	0	0	0

Going (Turf): Sf: 0-0 GS: 0-1 Gd: 0-1 GF: 0-1 Fm: 0-0
Distance: 5f/6f: 0-2 7f-8f: 0-1 9f-13f: 0-0 14f+: 0-0
Track : LH: 0-0 RH: 0-0 Tight: 0-0 Gall: 0-0
Aids: Bl: 0-0 Vi: 0-0 Tstrap: 0-0 Ckp: 0-0
Best Rating: 42 5/09 Yarm 6f3y good

Fairywater Grey (IRE)

68(71) (27)**32**
2-y-o gr f Swift Gulliver (IRE)-Chilling (Chilibang)
J J Bridger Mrs Susanna Josephine McCaffrey

Placings:000 **(4080)**
2009: 5^{0}SD, 6^{0}SD, 7^{0}G,

	Starts	1st	2nd	3rd	Win & Pl
Career Total (Turf)	1	0	0	0	
Career Total (AW)	2	0	0	0	

Going (Turf): Sf: 0-0 GS: 0-0 Gd: 0-1 GF: 0-0 Fm: 0-0
Distance: 5f/6f: 0-2 7f-8f: 0-1 9f-13f: 0-0 14f+: 0-0
Track : LH: 0-1 RH: 0-1 Tight: 0-1 Gall: 0-0
Aids: Bl: 0-0 Vi: 0-0 Tstrap: 0-0 Ckp: 0-0
Best Rating: 32 7/09 Ling 7f good

Faited To Pretend (IRE)

(87) (60)
2-y-o b f Kheleyf (USA)-Lady Moranbon (USA) (Trempolino (USA))
M L W Bell Joseph Barton

Placings:00 **(7326)**
2009: 7^{0}SD, 7^{0}SD,

	Starts	1st	2nd	3rd	Win & Pl
Career Total (Turf)	0	0	0	0	
Career Total (AW)	2	0	0	0	

Going (Turf): Sf: 0-0 GS: 0-0 Gd: 0-0 GF: 0-0 Fm: 0-0
Distance: 5f/6f: 0-0 7f-8f: 0-2 9f-13f: 0-0 14f+: 0-0
Track : LH: 0-1 RH: 0-1 Tight: 0-1 Gall: 0-0
Aids: Bl: 0-0 Vi: 0-0 Tstrap: 0-0 Ckp: 0-0
Best Rating: 60 10/09 Ling 7f stand

Faith And Reason (USA)

92(90) (72)**73**
6-y-o b g Sunday Silence (USA)-Sheer Reason (USA) (Danzig (USA))
C Grant (B J Curley 27/9) Miss L Horner

Placings:011/425/00600000/521440-6006 (4207)
2009: 14^{6}GF, 16^{0}GF, 10^{0}GF, 10^{6}GF,

	Starts	1st	2nd	3rd	Win & Pl
Career Total (Turf)	21	3	1	0	16723
Career Total (AW)	3	0	1	0	2721

73 7/08 Brig 1m1f209y (0-60)H G-F £2396
85 9/05 NmkR 1m (0-95) GD £8326
73 7/05 Ling 7f G-F £4654
Total win prize-money £15377

Going (Turf): Sf: 0-0 GS: 0-2 Gd: 1-5 **GF: 2-13** Fm: 0-1
Distance: 5f/6f: 0-0 **7f-8f: 2-3** 9f-13f: 1-18 14f+: 0-3
Track : **LH: 1-12** RH: 0-8 Tight: 0-10 Gall: 0-4
Aids: Bl: 0-1 **Vi: 1-4** Tstrap: 0-1 Ckp: 0-1
Best Rating: 89 6/06 Kemp 1m2f stand

Modest sort who was once very useful; effective at around 1m2f at his best for Godolphin; acts on quick ground and Polytrack; has worn a tongue tie and headgear.

Faith Jicaro (IRE)

97 76
2-y-o b f One Cool Cat (USA)-Wings To Soar (USA) (Woodman (USA))
Mrs L Williamson G D Kendrick

Placings:22 (3944)
2009: 6^{2}GF, 5^{2}GF,

	Starts	1st	2nd	3rd	Win & Pl
Career Total (Turf)	2	0	2	0	1794

Going (Turf): **Sf: 0-0 GS: 0-0 Gd: 0-0 GF: 0-2 Fm: 0-0**
Distance: 5f/6f: 0-2 7f-8f: 0-0 9f-13f: 0-0 14f+: 0-0
Track : LH: 0-1 RH: 0-0 Tight: 0-0 Gall: 0-0
Aids: Bl: 0-0 Vi: 0-0 Tstrap: 0-0 Ckp: 0-0
Best Rating: 76 6/09 Hayd 6f gd-fm

Runner-up on debut; effective over 6f; acts on fast ground.

Faithful Duchess (IRE)

88(84) (51)68
2-y-o b f Bachelor Duke (USA)-Portelet (Night Shift (USA))
E A L Dunlop V I Araci

Placings:040 (6069)
2009: 6^{0}GF, 6^{4}GF, 5^{0}SD,

	Starts	1st	2nd	3rd	Win & Pl
Career Total (Turf)	2	0	0	0	321
Career Total (AW)	1	0	0	0	

Going (Turf): **Sf: 0-0 GS: 0-0 Gd: 0-0 GF: 0-2 Fm: 0-0**
Distance: 5f/6f: 0-2 7f-8f: 0-1 9f-13f: 0-0 14f+: 0-0
Track : LH: 0-1 RH: 0-0 Tight: 0-1 Gall: 0-0
Aids: Bl: 0-0 Vi: 0-0 Tstrap: 0-0 Ckp: 0-0
Best Rating: 68 8/09 Yarm 6f3y gd-fm

Faithful One (IRE)

104(94) (73)89
2-y-o b f Dubawi (IRE)-Have Faith (IRE) (Machiavellian (USA))
D R Lanigan Saif Ali

Placings:2220 (7033)
2009: 6^{2}S, 7^{2}SD, 7^{2}GF, 7^{0}S,

	Starts	1st	2nd	3rd	Win & Pl
Career Total (Turf)	3	0	2	0	3372
Career Total (AW)	1	0	1	0	1397

Going (Turf): **Sf: 0-2 GS: 0-0 Gd: 0-0 GF: 0-1 Fm: 0-0**
Distance: 5f/6f: 0-0 7f-8f: 0-4 9f-13f: 0-0 14f+: 0-0
Track : LH: 0-0 RH: 0-1 Tight: 0-0 Gall: 0-0
Aids: Bl: 0-0 Vi: 0-0 Tstrap: 0-0 Ckp: 0-0
Best Rating: 89 10/09 Leic 7f9y gd-fm

Useful; stays 7f; acts on fast and soft ground; goes on Polytrack.

Faithful Ruler (USA)

105(108) (90)95
5-y-o b/br g Elusive Quality (USA)-Fancy Ruler (USA) (Half A Year (USA))
R A Fahey George Murray

Placings:056413/324010-3431032100545 (7789)
2009: 9^{3}SD, 10^{4}SD, 9^{3}SD, 8^{1}SD, 8^{0}SD, 8^{3}GS, 9^{2}S, 8^{1}G, 8^{0}GF, 8^{0}SD, 8^{5}S, 10^{4}SD, 9^{5}SD,

	Starts	1st	2nd	3rd	Win & Pl
Career Total (Turf)	6	1	1	1	8782
Career Total (AW)	19	3	1	4	17407

95 9/09 Ayr 1m (0-85)H GD £6152
83 3/09 Wolv 1m141y (0-90)H STD £9462
77 10/08 Wolv 1m141y (0-65)H STD £2047
67 11/07 Kemp 7f (0-55)H STD £2047
Total win prize-money £19709

Going (Turf): Sf: 0-3 GS: 0-1 **Gd: 1-1** GF: 0-1 Fm: 0-0
Distance: 5f/6f: 0-1 7f-8f: 2-13 9f-13f: 2-11 14f+: 0-0
Track : **LH: 3-19** RH: 1-6 **Tight: 2-13** Gall: 0-0
Aids: Bl: 0-2 Vi: 0-0 Tstrap: 0-0 Ckp: 0-0
Best Rating: 95 9/09 Ayr 1m good

Useful; stays 1m1f; acts on soft ground and on Polytrack.

Fajita

103(90) (51)74
3-y-o b c Lahib (USA)-La Fija (USA) (Dixieland Band (USA))
G L Moore W P Flynn

Placings:5550-602214361344 (6421)
2009: 8^{6}GF, 8^{0}GF, 8^{2}GF, 7^{2}G, 8^{1}GS, 8^{4}G, 8^{3}GS, 8^{6}G, 7^{1}G, 7^{3}GF, 8^{4}GF, 8^{4}GF,

	Starts	1st	2nd	3rd	Win & Pl
Career Total (Turf)	14	2	2	2	11447
Career Total (AW)	2	0	0	0	0

74 8/09 NmkJ 7f GD £3885
65 6/09 NmkJ 1m G-S £3885
Total win prize-money £7772

Going (Turf): Sf: 0-1 **GS: 1-2 Gd: 1-5** GF: 0-6 Fm: 0-0
Distance: 5f/6f: 0-1 **7f-8f: 2-10** 9f-13f: 0-5 14f+: 0-0
Track : LH: 0-2 RH: 0-7 Tight: 0-4 Gall: 0-1
Aids: Bl: 0-1 Vi: 0-0 Tstrap: 1-3 Ckp: 1-3
Best Rating: 74 8/09 NmkJ 7f good

Fair; effective over 1m; acts on easy ground; wears cheekpieces.

Fajr (IRE)

(106) (115)95
7-y-o b g Green Desert (USA)-Ta Rib (USA) (Mr Prospector (USA))
Miss Gay Kelleway The New Dawn Partnership

Placings:0633/112111053/155023230422313/140060000-066 (0388)
2009: 8^{0}SD, 8^{6}SD, 7^{6}SD,

	Starts	1st	2nd	3rd	Win & Pl
Career Total (Turf)	18	1	3	4	33682
Career Total (AW)	22	7	2	3	47618

115 1/08 Ling 1m (0-100)H STD £9971
111 12/07 Ling 1m (0-100)H STD £9971
93 1/07 Ling 1m (0-85)H STD £4857
86 5/06 NmkR 1m (0-95)H GD £9067
85 5/06 Ling 1m (0-85)H STD £6477
82 4/06 Ling 1m (0-70)H STD £3238
71 2/06 Ling 7f (0-58)H STD £2047
69 2/06 Ling 1m (0-60)H STD £2730
Total win prize-money £48362

Going (Turf): Sf: 0-2 GS: 0-3 **Gd: 1-8** GF: 0-5 Fm: 0-0
Distance: 5f/6f: 0-1 **7f-8f: 8-31** 9f-13f: 0-8 14f+: 0-0
Track : **LH: 7-20** RH: 0-7 **Tight: 7-18** Gall: 0-1
Aids: **Bl: 2-9** Vi: 0-3 Tstrap: 0-1 Ckp: 0-1
Best Rating: 115 1/08 Ling 1m stand

Very useful; Group placed; effective over 7f-1m; acts on good and easier ground and on Polytrack; has worn blinkers and a tongue tie.

Falahill

58
2-y-o ch c Selkirk (USA)-Felucca (Green Desert (USA))
R Hannon T Hely-Hutchinson & Lord Donoughmore

Placings:0 (6620)
2009: 8^{0}G,

	Starts	1st	2nd	3rd	Win & Pl
Career Total (Turf)	1	0	0	0	

Going (Turf): **Sf: 0-0 GS: 0-0 Gd: 0-1 GF: 0-0 Fm: 0-0**
Distance: 5f/6f: 0-0 7f-8f: 0-1 9f-13f: 0-0 14f+: 0-0
Track : LH: 0-0 RH: 0-0 Tight: 0-0 Gall: 0-0
Aids: Bl: 0-0 Vi: 0-0 Tstrap: 0-0 Ckp: 0-0

Falakee

80 34
2-y-o b c Sakhee (USA)-Sakhya (IRE) (Barathea (IRE))
P W Chapple-Hyam Ziad A Galadari

Placings:0 (6990)
2009: 7^{0}G,

	Starts	1st	2nd	3rd	Win & Pl
Career Total (Turf)	1	0	0	0	

Going (Turf): **Sf: 0-0 GS: 0-0 Gd: 0-1 GF: 0-0 Fm: 0-0**
Distance: 5f/6f: 0-0 7f-8f: 0-1 9f-13f: 0-0 14f+: 0-0
Track : LH: 0-0 RH: 0-0 Tight: 0-0 Gall: 0-0
Aids: Bl: 0-0 Vi: 0-0 Tstrap: 0-0 Ckp: 0-0
Best Rating: 34 10/09 Donc 7f good

Falasteen (IRE)

104 91
2-y-o ch g Titus Livius (FR)-Law Review (IRE) (Case Law)
D Nicholls Dr Marwan Koukash

Placings:13541 (6275)
2009: 5^{1}GS, 5^{3}GF, 6^{5}GF, 5^{4}GS, 5^{1}GF,

	Starts	1st	2nd	3rd	Win & Pl
Career Total (Turf)	5	2	0	1	25669

91 9/09 Ches 5f16y H G-F £9714
84 6/09 York 5f G-S £6929
Total win prize-money £16643

Going (Turf):	Sf: 0-0 GS: 1-2 Gd: 0-0 GF: 1-3 Fm: 0-0
Distance:	5f/6f: 2-5 7f-8f: 0-0 9f-13f: 0-0 14f+: 0-0
Track :	LH: 1-1 RH: 0-0 Tight: 1-1 Gall: 0-0
Aids:	Bl: 0-0 Vi: 0-0 Tstrap: 0-0 Ckp: 0-0
Best Rating:	91 9/09 Ches 5f16y gd-fm

Useful; effective at 5f; acts on most ground on turf.

Falcativ

105(110) (102)101

4-y-o b g Falbrav (IRE)-Frottola (Muhtarram (USA))

M Botti (L M Cumani 1/8) Dioscuri Srl

Placings:0/05311-150511 (7827)

2009: 11[1]GF, 12[5]GF, 11[0]GF, 10[5]G, 8[1]SD, 8[1]SD,

	Starts	1st	2nd	3rd	Win & Pl
Career Total (Turf)	8	1	0	1	8537
Career Total (AW)	4	4	0	0	26698

102	12/09	Kemp	1m	(0-100)H	STD	£11091
95	12/09	Ling	1m	(0-95)H	STD	£7641
101	5/09	Yarm	1m3f101y	(0-90)H	G-F	£7477
91	10/08	Ling	1m4f	(0-85)H	STD	£4727
81	10/08	Kemp	1m4f	(0-75)H	STD	£3238

Total win prize-money £34175

Going (Turf):	Sf: 0-0 GS: 0-1 Gd: 0-4 GF: 1-3 Fm: 0-0
Distance:	5f/6f: 0-0 7f-8f: 2-4 9f-13f: 3-8 14f+: 0-0
Track :	LH: 3-6 RH: 2-4 Tight: 3-3 Gall: 0-3
Aids:	Bl: 0-0 Vi: 0-0 Tstrap: 0-0 Ckp: 0-0
Best Rating:	102 12/09 Kemp 1m stand

Very useful; stays 1m4f but seems better suited by 1m these days; acts on fast ground; goes on Polytrack.

Falcolnry (IRE)

(88) (39)84

4-y-o b f Hawk Wing (USA)-Fear And Greed (IRE) (Brief Truce (USA))

E F Vaughan E F Vaughan

Placings:610/03000-0 (0128)

2009: 6[0]SD,

	Starts	1st	2nd	3rd	Win & Pl
Career Total (Turf)	8	1	0	1	6985
Career Total (AW)	1	0	0	0	

79	8/07	Donc	7f	G-F	£5829

Total win prize-money £5829

Going (Turf):	Sf: 0-0 GS: 0-0 Gd: 0-7 GF: 1-1 Fm: 0-0
Distance:	5f/6f: 0-2 7f-8f: 1-6 9f-13f: 0-1 14f+: 0-0
Track :	LH: 0-1 RH: 0-2 Tight: 0-0 Gall: 0-1
Aids:	Bl: 0-0 Vi: 0-0 Tstrap: 0-0 Ckp: 0-0
Best Rating:	84 6/08 Sand 7f16y good

Fair; effective over 7f; acts on fast ground.

Falcon Rock (IRE)

113(102) (78)95

4-y-o b g Hawk Wing (USA)-Champaka (IRE) (Caerleon (USA))

S A Callaghan Michael Tabor

Placings:62-3221222 (5865)

2009: 7[3]F, 8[2]G, 10[2]SD, 10[1]G, 11[2]GF, 10[2]GF, 12[2]GF,

	Starts	1st	2nd	3rd	Win & Pl
Career Total (Turf)	8	1	5	1	14247
Career Total (AW)	1	0	1	0	1407

91	7/09	Wind	1m2f7y	(0-75)H	GD	£2729

Total win prize-money £2730

Going (Turf):	Sf: 0-2 GS: 0-0 Gd: 1-2 GF: 0-3 Fm: 0-1
Distance:	5f/6f: 0-0 7f-8f: 0-1 9f-13f: 1-8 14f+: 0-0
Track :	LH: 0-2 RH: 1-4 Tight: 1-3 Gall: 0-2
Aids:	Bl: 0-0 Vi: 0-0 Tstrap: 0-1 Ckp: 0-1
Best Rating:	95 9/09 Donc 1m4f gd-fm

Useful; effective over 1m2f; acts on good ground and on Polytrack.

Falcon's Tribute (IRE)

93 56

7-y-o b m Beneficial-Early Storm (IRE) (Glacial Storm (USA))

P Salmon (P Beaumont 31/8) Falcons Line Ltd

Placings:03 (6390)

2009: 10[0]GF, 8[3]GF,

	Starts	1st	2nd	3rd	Win & Pl
Career Total (Turf)	2	0	0	1	385

Going (Turf):	Sf: 0-0 GS: 0-0 Gd: 0-0 GF: 0-2 Fm: 0-0
Distance:	5f/6f: 0-0 7f-8f: 0-0 9f-13f: 0-2 14f+: 0-0
Track :	LH: 0-2 RH: 0-0 Tight: 0-0 Gall: 0-0
Aids:	Bl: 0-0 Vi: 0-0 Tstrap: 0-0 Ckp: 0-0
Best Rating:	56 9/09 Nott 1m75y gd-fm

Faldal

99(95) (81)85

3-y-o br f Falbrav (IRE)-Tidal (Bin Ajwaad (IRE))

Tom Dascombe Mrs Bernadette Quinn

Placings:651-100 (3968a)

2009: 10[1]G, 9[0]GF, 12[0]GS,

	Starts	1st	2nd	3rd	Win & Pl
Career Total (Turf)	4	1	0	0	9347
Career Total (AW)	2	1	0	0	2737

83	4/09	Pont	1m2f6y	(0-90)H	GD	£9346
81	12/08	GrLe	1m		STD	£2590

Total win prize-money £11937

Going (Turf):	Sf: 0-0 GS: 0-1 Gd: 1-1 GF: 0-1 Fm: 0-0
Distance:	5f/6f: 0-0 7f-8f: 1-2 9f-13f: 1-4 14f+: 0-0
Track :	LH: 2-4 RH: 0-2 Tight: 0-1 Gall: 1-2
Aids:	Bl: 0-0 Vi: 0-0 Tstrap: 0-0 Ckp: 0-0
Best Rating:	85 7/09 Lonc 1m4f gd-sft

Useful; effective over 1m-1m2f; acts on good ground; goes on Polytrack.

Fallen Idol

(98) (81)

2-y-o b c Pivotal-Fallen Star (Brief Truce (USA))

J H M Gosden Normandie Stud Ltd

Placings:1 (5807)

2009: 7[1]SD,

	Starts	1st	2nd	3rd	Win & Pl
Career Total (Turf)	0	0	0	0	
Career Total (AW)	1	1	0	0	2590

81	9/09	Kemp	7f	STD	£2590

Total win prize-money £2590

Going (Turf):	Sf: 0-0 GS: 0-0 Gd: 0-0 GF: 0-0 Fm: 0-0
Distance:	5f/6f: 0-0 7f-8f: 1-1 9f-13f: 0-0 14f+: 0-0
Track :	LH: 0-0 RH: 1-1 Tight: 0-0 Gall: 0-0
Aids:	Bl: 0-0 Vi: 0-0 Tstrap: 0-0 Ckp: 0-0
Best Rating:	81 9/09 Kemp 7f stand

Useful winner over 7f on Polytrack on debut.

Fallen In Love

107 104

3-y-o b f Galileo (IRE)-Fallen Star (Brief Truce (USA))

J L Dunlop Normandie Stud Ltd

Placings:531-23226 (5202)

2009: 9[2]GF, 10[3]GF, 11[2]GF, 12[2]G, 12[6]GF,

	Starts	1st	2nd	3rd	Win & Pl
Career Total (Turf)	8	1	3	2	48896

71	9/08	Hayd	1m30y	G-F	£4533

Total win prize-money £4533

Going (Turf):	Sf: 0-0 GS: 0-0 Gd: 0-2 GF: 1-6 Fm: 0-0
Distance:	5f/6f: 0-0 7f-8f: 0-2 9f-13f: 1-6 14f+: 0-0
Track :	LH: 1-5 RH: 0-1 Tight: 0-1 Gall: 0-3
Aids:	Bl: 0-0 Vi: 0-0 Tstrap: 0-0 Ckp: 0-0
Best Rating:	104 7/09 Hayd 1m3f200y gd-fm

Very useful; Group 2 and Listed placed; stays 1m4f; acts on good and faster ground.

Falling Angel

93 76

2-y-o b f Kylian (USA)-Belle Ile (USA) (Diesis)

P F I Cole C M Budgett

Placings:220 (3086)

2009: 6[2]G, 6[2]GF, 6[0]GF,

	Starts	1st	2nd	3rd	Win & Pl
Career Total (Turf)	3	0	2	0	3025

Going (Turf):	Sf: 0-0 GS: 0-0 Gd: 0-1 GF: 0-2 Fm: 0-0
Distance:	5f/6f: 0-3 7f-8f: 0-0 9f-13f: 0-0 14f+: 0-0
Track :	LH: 0-0 RH: 0-0 Tight: 0-0 Gall: 0-0
Aids:	Bl: 0-0 Vi: 0-0 Tstrap: 0-0 Ckp: 0-0
Best Rating:	76 5/09 York 6f gd-fm

Fair; stays 6f and acts on good ground.

Falpiase (IRE)

92 (75)81

7-y-o b g Montjeu (IRE)-Gift Of The Night (USA) (Slewpy (USA))

J Howard Johnson Andrea & Graham Wylie

Placings:326/2200/0 (2932)

2009: 12[0]G,

	Starts	1st	2nd	3rd	Win & Pl
Career Total (Turf)	7	0	2	1	3757
Career Total (AW)	1	0	1	0	964

Going (Turf):	Sf: 0-1 GS: 0-0 Gd: 0-2 GF: 0-4 Fm: 0-0
Distance:	5f/6f: 0-0 7f-8f: 0-0 9f-13f: 0-4 14f+: 0-4
Track :	LH: 0-7 RH: 0-1 Tight: 0-3 Gall: 0-2
Aids:	Bl: 0-2 Vi: 0-0 Tstrap: 0-0 Ckp: 0-0
Best Rating:	98 8/07 Gdwd 2m good

Useful; stays 2m; acts on fast ground; also goes on Polytrack; has worn blinkers; winning hurdler; very tricky customer.

Fame And Glory

123 131

3-y-o b c Montjeu (IRE)-Gryada (Shirley Heights)

A P O'Brien D Smith, Mrs J Magnier, M Tabor

Placings:11-1121266 (6850)

2009: 10[1]GY, 10[1]G, 12[2]G, 12[1]GY, 10[2]GY, 12[6]G, 10[6]G,

	Starts	1st	2nd	3rd	Win & Pl
Career Total (Turf)	9	5	2	0	1503969

128 6/09 Curr 1m4f G-Y £818446
120 5/09 Leop 1m2f GD £75728
114 4/09 Leop 1m2f G-Y £41082
109 11/08 StCl 1m2f HVY £105037
87 10/08 Navn 1m HVY £6097
Total win prize-money £1046392

Going (Turf): Sf: 2-2 GS: 0-0 Gd: 1-4 GF: 0-0 Fm: 0-0
Distance: 5f/6f: 0-0 7f-8f: 1-1 **9f-13f: 4-8** 14f+: 0-0
Track : **LH: 4-6** RH: 1-2 Tight: 0-1 Gall: 0-0
Aids: Bl: 0-0 Vi: 0-0 Tstrap: 0-0 Ckp: 0-0
Best Rating: 131 9/09 Leop 1m2f gd-yld

High-class colt; runner-up in the Derby and winner of the Irish Derby; effective at 1m2f-1m4f; acts on good or softer ground.

Fame Is The Spur

96 **66**
2-y-o ch f Motivator-Subya (Night Shift (USA))
J W Hills Mrs P De W Johnson

Placings:00 **(6241)**
2009: 6^{0}S, 6^{0}G,

	Starts	1st	2nd	3rd	Win & Pl
Career Total (Turf)	2	0	0	0	

Going (Turf): Sf: 0-1 GS: 0-0 Gd: 0-1 GF: 0-0 Fm: 0-0
Distance: 5f/6f: 0-0 7f-8f: 0-2 9f-13f: 0-0 14f+: 0-0
Track : LH: 0-0 RH: 0-0 Tight: 0-0 Gall: 0-0
Aids: Bl: 0-0 Vi: 0-0 Tstrap: 0-0 Ckp: 0-0
Best Rating: 66 9/09 Sals 6f212y soft

Fan Club

92(87) (53)**41**
5-y-o ch g Zamindar (USA)-Starfan (USA) (Lear Fan (USA))
Mrs R A Carr David W Chapman

Placings:012/556400000/000560600-00000000 **(4034)**
2009: 6^{0}SS, 5^{0}SD, 8^{0}SD, 9^{0}GF, 16^{0}G, 11^{0}GF, 16^{0}S, 9^{0}G,

	Starts	1st	2nd	3rd	Win & Pl
Career Total (Turf)	23	1	1	0	13402
Career Total (AW)	7	0	0	0	1892

88 10/06 MsnL 1m GD £6552
Total win prize-money £6552

Going (Turf): Sf: 0-7 GS: 0-1 **Gd: 1-9** GF: 0-6 Fm: 0-0
Distance: 5f/6f: 0-5 **7f-8f: 1-14** 9f-13f: 0-9 14f+: 0-2
Track : LH: 0-15 RH: 0-7 Tight: 0-10 Gall: 0-1
Aids: Bl: 0-13 Vi: 0-0 Tstrap: 0-0 Ckp: 0-0
Best Rating: 95 3/07 Lonc 1m heavy

Fancy Footsteps (IRE)

95(103) (81)**72**
4-y-o gr f Noverre (USA)-Fancy Intense (Peintre Celebre (USA))
C G Cox John And Anne Soul

Placings:0023-100331406 **(6614)**
2009: 8^{1}SD, 8^{0}GS, 8^{0}G, 7^{3}GF, 8^{3}SD, 8^{1}SD, 8^{4}SD, 8^{0}SD, 8^{6}SD,

	Starts	1st	2nd	3rd	Win & Pl
Career Total (Turf)	5	0	0	1	482
Career Total (AW)	8	2	1	2	10263

81 8/09 Kemp 1m (0-80)H STD £4727
74 1/09 Kemp 1m (0-70)H STD £2590
Total win prize-money £7317

Going (Turf): Sf: 0-1 GS: 0-2 Gd: 0-1 GF: 0-1 Fm: 0-0
Distance: 5f/6f: 0-0 **7f-8f: 2-10** 9f-13f: 0-3 14f+: 0-0
Track : LH: 0-3 **RH: 2-9** Tight: 0-3 Gall: 0-0
Aids: Bl: 0-0 Vi: 0-0 Tstrap: 0-0 Ckp: 0-0
Best Rating: 81 8/09 Kemp 1m stand

Fair; stays 1m and acts on Polytrack.

Fancy Set (IRE)

70(82) (19)
3-y-o b f Reset (AUS)-Crafty Fancy (IRE) (Intikhab (USA))
D J S Ffrench Davis Mrs F Houlihan

Placings:000 **(1652)**
2009: 6^{0}SD, 7^{0}G, 6^{0}SD,

	Starts	1st	2nd	3rd	Win & Pl
Career Total (Turf)	1	0	0	0	
Career Total (AW)	2	0	0	0	

Going (Turf): Sf: 0-0 GS: 0-0 Gd: 0-1 GF: 0-0 Fm: 0-0
Distance: 5f/6f: 0-2 7f-8f: 0-1 9f-13f: 0-0 14f+: 0-0
Track : LH: 0-2 RH: 0-0 Tight: 0-0 Gall: 0-0
Aids: Bl: 0-1 Vi: 0-0 Tstrap: 0-0 Ckp: 0-0
Best Rating: 19 3/09 Sthl 6f stand

Fancy Star

80 **54**
2-y-o b c Starcraft (NZ)-Lorien Hill (IRE) (Danehill (USA))
B W Hills D M James

Placings:00 **(4524)**
2009: 7^{0}S, 7^{0}S,

	Starts	1st	2nd	3rd	Win & Pl
Career Total (Turf)	2	0	0	0	

Going (Turf): Sf: 0-2 GS: 0-0 Gd: 0-0 GF: 0-0 Fm: 0-0
Distance: 5f/6f: 0-0 7f-8f: 0-2 9f-13f: 0-0 14f+: 0-0
Track : LH: 0-0 RH: 0-1 Tight: 0-0 Gall: 0-0
Aids: Bl: 0-0 Vi: 0-0 Tstrap: 0-0 Ckp: 0-0
Best Rating: 54 8/09 Gdwd 7f soft

Fandango Boy

90(105) (76)**68**
8-y-o b g Victory Note (USA)-Dancing Chimes (London Bells (CAN))
J P Broderick (D Carroll 16/2) Miss Aideen Rigney

Placings:60/00464/40534105051300000**2**-3000000002115 **(7672)**
2009: 10^{3}SD, 9^{0}SD, 9^{0}SD, 9^{0}SD, 8^{0}G, 8^{0}G, 6^{0}GF, 7^{0}G, 8^{0}SD, 12^{2}SD, 8^{1}SD, 7^{1}SD, 8^{5}SD,

	Starts	1st	2nd	3rd	Win & Pl
Career Total (Turf)	22	2	0	1	10406
Career Total (AW)	16	2	2	2	11502

76 11/09 Dund 7f (47-65)H STD £4696
71 11/09 Dund 1m (47-65)H STD £3502
60 7/08 Naas 1m (45-60)H G-F £4826
68 5/08 Naas 7f (45-60)H GD £4826
Total win prize-money £17852

Going (Turf): Sf: 0-4 GS: 0-0 **Gd: 1-6 GF: 1-7** Fm: 0-3
Distance: 5f/6f: 0-3 **7f-8f: 4-18** 9f-13f: 0-17 14f+: 0-0
Track : **LH: 4-22** RH: 0-8 Tight: 0-5 Gall: 0-1
Aids: Bl: 0-0 Vi: 0-0 Tstrap: 0-1 Ckp: 0-1
Best Rating: 76 11/09 Dund 7f stand

Fair; stays 1m2f; acts on fast ground, on an easy surface and on Polytrack.

Fanditha (IRE)

107(100) (86)**89**
3-y-o ch f Danehill Dancer (IRE)-Splendid (IRE) (Mujtahid (USA))
R Hannon A P Patey

Placings:5610-2464003133 **(7148)**
2009: 8^{2}SD, 8^{4}GF, 8^{6}GF, 8^{4}S, 9^{0}G, 9^{0}GF, 8^{3}GS, 11^{1}G, 10^{3}G, 12^{3}G,

	Starts	1st	2nd	3rd	Win & Pl
Career Total (Turf)	13	2	0	3	15216
Career Total (AW)	1	0	1	0	1510

87 9/09 Gdwd 1m3f (0-85)H GD £4857
80 9/08 Sals 6f212y GD £6476
Total win prize-money £11333

Going (Turf): Sf: 0-1 GS: 0-2 **Gd: 2-6** GF: 0-3 Fm: 0-0
Distance: 5f/6f: 0-0 7f-8f: 1-7 9f-13f: 1-7 14f+: 0-0
Track : LH: 0-2 **RH: 1-6 Tight: 1-4** Gall: 0-2
Aids: Bl: 0-1 Vi: 0-0 Tstrap: 0-0 Ckp: 0-0
Best Rating: 89 10/09 NmkR 1m4f good

Useful; stays 1m; acts on good ground.

Fangfoss Girls

85(102) (69)**57**
3-y-o ch f Monsieur Bond (IRE)-Bond Shakira (Daggers Drawn (USA))
G L Moore (L Wells 12/2) Stuart Matheson

Placings:1155032-26656 **(1424)**
2009: 5^{2}SD, 6^{6}SD, 5^{6}SD, 5^{5}GF, 5^{6}G,

	Starts	1st	2nd	3rd	Win & Pl
Career Total (Turf)	3	1	0	0	3886
Career Total (AW)	9	1	2	1	5136

69 5/08 Wolv 5f20y STD £2729
57 4/08 Thsk 5f GD £3885
Total win prize-money £6616

Going (Turf): Sf: 0-0 GS: 0-0 **Gd: 1-2** GF: 0-1 Fm: 0-0
Distance: **5f/6f: 2-12** 7f-8f: 0-0 9f-13f: 0-0 14f+: 0-0
Track : **LH: 1-5** RH: 0-5 **Tight: 1-3** Gall: 0-2
Aids: Bl: 0-0 Vi: 0-0 Tstrap: 0-0 Ckp: 0-0
Best Rating: 69 5/08 Wolv 5f20y stand

Modest filly; effective at 5f; handles good ground and Polytrack.

Fanjura (IRE)

109 **111**
4-y-o b g Marju (IRE)-Accelerating (USA) (Lear Fan (USA))
B W Hills Terry Benson

Placings:1500-250011133 **(6202)**
2009: 8^{2}GF, 8^{5}S, 10^{0}GF, 8^{0}G, 10^{1}G, 10^{1}G, 10^{1}GF, 10^{3}G, 9^{3}G,

	Starts	1st	2nd	3rd	Win & Pl
Career Total (Turf)	13	4	1	2	69729

111 8/09 Sand 1m2f7y H G-F £31155
105 7/09 Asct 1m2f (0-105)H GD £11215
102 7/09 Sand 1m2f7y (0-100)H GD £11215
85 4/08 NmkR 1m GD £5990
Total win prize-money £59577

Going (Turf): Sf: 0-1 GS: 0-0 **Gd: 3-7** GF: 1-5 Fm: 0-0
Distance: 5f/6f: 0-0 7f-8f: 1-4 **9f-13f: 3-9** 14f+: 0-0
Track : LH: 0-4 **RH: 3-4** Tight: 0-3 **Gall: 1-3**
Aids: Bl: 0-0 Vi: 0-0 Tstrap: 0-0 Ckp: 0-0
Best Rating: 111 8/09 Sand 1m2f7y gd-fm

Smart; effective at 1m-1m2f; acts on a sound surface.

Fantasia

108 115

3-y-o b f Sadler's Wells (USA)-Blue Symphony (Darshaan)
L M Cumani George Strawbridge

Placings:112-13016 **(6479)**
2009: 7^{1}GF, 8^{3}G, 10^{0}GS, 7^{1}GF, 8^{6}GF,

	Starts	1st	2nd	3rd	Win & Pl
Career Total (Turf)	8	4	1	1	191670
115 9/09 Donc 7f			G-F	£23704	
114 4/09 NmkR 7f			G-F	£36900	
105 8/08 Gdwd 7f			G-S	£31223	
85 7/08 NmkJ 6f			GD	£9714	

Total win prize-money £101543

Going (Turf): Sf: 0-0 GS: 1-2 Gd: 1-3 **GF: 2-3** Fm: 0-0
Distance: 5f/6f: 1-1 **7f-8f: 3-6** 9f-13f: 0-1 14f+: 0-0
Track : LH: 0-0 **RH: 1-3** Tight: 0-0 Gall: 0-1
Aids: Bl: 0-0 Vi: 0-0 Tstrap: 0-0 Ckp: 0-0
Best Rating: **115** 9/09 Donc 7f gd-fm

Group class; winner of the Prestige Stakes and runner-up in the Fillies' Mile in 2008; Listed winner in 2009; stays 1m; acts on good and easy ground.

Fantastic Cuix (FR)

89(89) (71)64

2-y-o gr f Fantastic Light (USA)-Cuixmala (FR) (Highest Honor (FR))
L M Cumani Tsega Horses

Placings:04 **(7450)**
2009: 8^{0}GS, 8^{4}SD,

	Starts	1st	2nd	3rd	Win & Pl
Career Total (Turf)	1	0	0	0	
Career Total (AW)	1	0	0	0	241

Going (Turf): **Sf: 0-0 GS: 0-1 Gd: 0-0 GF: 0-0 Fm: 0-0**
Distance: 5f/6f: 0-0 7f-8f: 0-2 9f-13f: 0-0 14f+: 0-0
Track : LH: 0-1 RH: 0-1 Tight: 0-0 Gall: 0-1
Aids: Bl: 0-0 Vi: 0-0 Tstrap: 0-0 Ckp: 0-0
Best Rating: **71** 11/09 Kemp 1m stand

Fantastic Dubai (USA)

101(101) (76)85

3-y-o b c Storm Cat (USA)-Shy Lady (FR) (Kaldoun (FR))
M R Channon Jaber Abdullah

Placings:5-1222 **(2882)**
2009: 7^{1}SD, 7^{2}SD, 5^{2}G, 6^{2}G,

	Starts	1st	2nd	3rd	Win & Pl
Career Total (Turf)	3	0	2	0	2465
Career Total (AW)	2	1	1	0	3586
66 3/09 Ling 7f		STD	£2729		

Total win prize-money £2730

Going (Turf): **Sf: 0-0 GS: 0-1 Gd: 0-2 GF: 0-0 Fm: 0-0**
Distance: 5f/6f: 0-2 **7f-8f: 1-3** 9f-13f: 0-0 14f+: 0-0
Track : **LH: 1-3** RH: 0-0 **Tight: 1-2** Gall: 0-0
Aids: Bl: 0-0 Vi: 0-0 Tstrap: 0-0 Ckp: 0-0
Best Rating: **85** 6/09 Gdwd 6f good

Fair; stays 7f; acts on Polytrack.

Fantastic Fred (IRE)

57(99) (61)16

3-y-o br g Fantastic Light (USA)-Luxury Launch (USA) (Seeking The Gold (USA))
J A Osborne H R H Prince of Saxe-Weimar

Placings:006-116200 **(1811)**
2009: 8^{1}SD, 8^{1}SD, 9^{6}SD, 8^{2}SD, 8^{0}SD, 10^{0}GF,

	Starts	1st	2nd	3rd	Win & Pl
Career Total (Turf)	2	0	0	0	0
Career Total (AW)	7	2	1	0	5381
61 1/09 Wolv 1m141y (0-60)H			STD	£2388	
56 1/09 Wolv 1m141y (0-55)H			STD	£2388	

Total win prize-money £4776

Going (Turf): **Sf: 0-0 GS: 0-0 Gd: 0-1 GF: 0-1 Fm: 0-0**
Distance: 5f/6f: 0-1 7f-8f: 0-4 **9f-13f: 2-4** 14f+: 0-0
Track : **LH: 2-7** RH: 0-2 **Tight: 2-7** Gall: 0-0
Aids: Bl: 0-0 Vi: 0-0 Tstrap: 0-0 Ckp: 0-0
Best Rating: **61** 3/09 Ling 1m stand

Modest; stays 1m; acts on Polytrack.

Fantastic Morning

83(87) (58)38

5-y-o ch g Fantastic Light (USA)-Gombay Girl (USA) (Woodman (USA))
F Jordan F Jordan

Placings:421/0000-0000 **(6917)**
2009: 11^{0}GF, 9^{0}G, 12^{0}SD, 12^{0}SD,

	Starts	1st	2nd	3rd	Win & Pl
Career Total (Turf)	7	1	1	0	3230
Career Total (AW)	4	0	0	0	241
83 7/07 Bath 1m2f46y			G-S	£2266	

Total win prize-money £2267

Going (Turf): Sf: 0-1 **GS: 1-1** Gd: 0-1 GF: 0-4 Fm: 0-0
Distance: 5f/6f: 0-0 7f-8f: 0-0 **9f-13f: 1-11** 14f+: 0-0
Track : **LH: 1-6** RH: 0-4 **Tight: 1-7** Gall: 0-2
Aids: Bl: 0-2 Vi: 0-0 Tstrap: 0-2 Ckp: 0-2
Best Rating: **83** 7/07 Bath 1m2f46y gd-sft

Useful; suited by 1m2f and will stay further; acts on fast and easy ground.

Fantastic Pick

97 76

2-y-o b g Fantastic Light (USA)-Umlilo (Mtoto)
B J Meehan Raymond Tooth

Placings:6001120 **(6901)**
2009: 6^{6}GS, 7^{0}GF, 6^{0}G, 8^{1}GF, 8^{1}GF, 10^{2}GF, 8^{0}GF,

	Starts	1st	2nd	3rd	Win & Pl
Career Total (Turf)	7	2	1	0	5434
76 9/09 Rdcr 1m (0-65)			G-F	£1942	
62 9/09 Bath 1m5y (0-75)			GD	£2719	

Total win prize-money £4663

Going (Turf): Sf: 0-0 GS: 0-1 **Gd: 1-2 GF: 1-4** Fm: 0-0
Distance: 5f/6f: 0-2 7f-8f: 1-2 9f-13f: 1-3 14f+: 0-0
Track : **LH: 1-4** RH: 0-0 **Tight: 1-2** Gall: 0-1
Aids: Bl: 0-0 Vi: 0-0 Tstrap: 0-0 Ckp: 0-0
Best Rating: **76** 9/09 Rdcr 1m gd-fm

Modest; effective over 1m-1m2f; acts on fast ground.

Fantastic Prince

95 75

2-y-o ch g Cadeaux Genereux-Fantaisiste (Nashwan (USA))
P F I Cole Miss Alfiya Shaykhutdinova

Placings:02305 **(5801)**
2009: 6^{0}G, 6^{2}GF, 6^{3}GF, 6^{0}G, 7^{5}GF,

	Starts	1st	2nd	3rd	Win & Pl
Career Total (Turf)	5	0	1	1	2288

Going (Turf): **Sf: 0-0 GS: 0-0 Gd: 0-2 GF: 0-3 Fm: 0-0**
Distance: 5f/6f: 0-3 7f-8f: 0-2 9f-13f: 0-0 14f+: 0-0
Track : LH: 0-1 RH: 0-0 Tight: 0-1 Gall: 0-0
Aids: Bl: 0-1 Vi: 0-0 Tstrap: 0-0 Ckp: 0-0
Best Rating: **75** 6/09 Ayr 6f gd-fm

Fair; best at 6f on fast ground.

Fantastic Strike (IRE)

95 74

2-y-o b c Noverre (USA)-Hariya (IRE) (Shernazar)
M Johnston Brian Yeardley Continental Ltd

Placings:5024 **(5715)**
2009: 6^{5}GF, 5^{0}G, 6^{2}GF, 8^{4}G,

	Starts	1st	2nd	3rd	Win & Pl
Career Total (Turf)	4	0	1	0	202

Going (Turf): **Sf: 0-0 GS: 0-0 Gd: 0-2 GF: 0-2 Fm: 0-0**
Distance: 5f/6f: 0-2 7f-8f: 0-1 9f-13f: 0-1 14f+: 0-0
Track : LH: 0-1 RH: 0-1 Tight: 0-1 Gall: 0-0
Aids: Bl: 0-0 Vi: 0-0 Tstrap: 0-0 Ckp: 0-0
Best Rating: **74** 8/09 Rdcr 6f gd-fm

Fantastical

87(92) (60)45

3-y-o b f Fantastic Light (USA)-First Musical (First Trump)
C E Brittain Saeed Manana

Placings:400 **(2415)**
2009: 8^{4}SD, 8^{0}SD, 8^{0}G,

	Starts	1st	2nd	3rd	Win & Pl
Career Total (Turf)	1	0	0	0	
Career Total (AW)	2	0	0	0	0

Going (Turf): **Sf: 0-0 GS: 0-0 Gd: 0-1 GF: 0-0 Fm: 0-0**
Distance: 5f/6f: 0-0 7f-8f: 0-2 9f-13f: 0-1 14f+: 0-0
Track : LH: 0-2 RH: 0-0 Tight: 0-2 Gall: 0-0
Aids: Bl: 0-0 Vi: 0-0 Tstrap: 0-0 Ckp: 0-0
Best Rating: **60** 3/09 Ling 1m stand

Fantasy Believer

103 73

11-y-o b g Sure Blade (USA)-Delicious (Dominion)
J J Quinn The Fantasy Fellowship B

Placings:3242216020/045U0142013150101/0040000060 0/00012102041/000004101200263/00005051326305U00 /00605031401011010/00040056002000/6000500-000442 **(3771)**
2009: 5^{0}GF, 6^{0}GF, 6^{0}GF, 5^{4}G, 5^{4}G, 6^{2}G,

	Starts	1st	2nd	3rd	Win & Pl
Career Total (Turf)	126	17	13	6	302988
113 9/06 NmkR 5f			GD	£15898	

110 9/06 York 5f89y H GD £31160
99 8/06 Gdwd 6f (0-95)H GD £11217
97 8/06 Gdwd 6f H G-F £12464
93 7/06 Pont 6f (0-90)H G-F £11217
96 6/05 Epsm 6f (0-95)H G-F £10054
102 7/04 Newc 6f B H GD £11945
99 7/04 Newb 6f8y C(0-95)H G-F £9247
101 10/03 Newc 7f C(0-90) GD £5028
97 7/03 Asct 6f C(0-95)H GD £8688
85 5/03 Ayr 6f D(0-85)H G-S £5720
102 10/01 Donc 5f B(0-100)H HVY £10734
97 9/01 Asct 6f B(0-105)H GD £21320
94 8/01 Ripn 6f D(0-80)H GD £5349
82 7/01 Ling 6f D(0-80)H G-S £4543
76 6/01 Kemp 6f D(0-85)H G-F £4387
76 7/00 Muss 5f E G-S £2808
Total win prize-money £181788

Going (Turf): Sf: 1-20 GS: 3-13 **Gd: 8-46** GF: 5-47 Fm: 0-0
Distance: **5f/6f: 15-112** 7f-8f: 2-14 9f-13f: 0-0 14f+: 0-0
Track : **LH: 2-12** RH: 0-0 **Tight: 1-6** Gall: 0-4
Aids: Bl: 0-0 Vi: 0-0 Tstrap: 0-0 Ckp: 0-0
Best Rating: **113** 9/06 NmkR 5f good

Modest; effective over 5f-7f; acts on most types of ground.

Fantasy Explorer

95(108) (96)91
6-y-o b g Compton Place-Zinzi (Song)
J J Quinn The Fantasy Fellowship E

Placings:005/**21211130**/60/0**2**000020**122**-000**1232** **(7454)**
2009: 6⁰F, 6⁰GF, 5⁰GS, 6¹SD, 5²SD, 5³SD, 6²SD,

	Starts	1st	2nd	3rd	Win & Pl
Career Total (Turf)	25	4	5	1	71971
Career Total (AW)	6	2	3	1	14905

94 10/09 Kemp 6f (0-85)H STD £4727
91 9/08 NmkR 6f (0-85)H G-F £6476
94 7/06 Ayr 5f H FRM £32385
90 6/06 NmkJ 5f (0-85)H G-F £5505
84 6/06 NmkJ 5f (0-75)H G-F £3886
70 5/06 Kemp 5f (0-65)H STD £3238
Total win prize-money £56218

Going (Turf): Sf: 0-1 GS: 0-3 Gd: 0-7 **GF: 3-12** Fm: 1-2
Distance: **5f/6f: 6-31** 7f-8f: 0-0 9f-13f: 0-0 14f+: 0-0
Track : LH: 0-6 **RH: 2-3** Tight: 0-3 Gall: 0-0
Aids: Bl: 0-0 Vi: 0-0 Tstrap: 0-1 Ckp: 0-1
Best Rating: **96** 11/09 Kemp 6f stand

Useful; suited by 5f-6f; handles fast ground; goes on Polytrack; has worn cheekpieces; likes to race prominently.

Fantasy Fighter (IRE)

87(106) (67)39
4-y-o b g Danetime (IRE)-Lady Montekin (Montekin)
J J Quinn The Fantasy Fellowship F

Placings:06/06060032023112-30000351102 **(7735)**
2009: 6³SD, 5⁰SD, 5⁰SD, 5⁰SD, 6⁰GS, 6³SD, 6⁵SD, 5¹SD, 6¹SD, 5⁰SD, 5²SD,

	Starts	1st	2nd	3rd	Win & Pl
Career Total (Turf)	7	0	0	0	47
Career Total (AW)	20	4	4	4	11706

67 11/09 Ling 6f (0-60)H STD £1637
61 11/09 Wolv 5f216y (0-55)H STD £2047
57 12/08 Ling 6f (0-55)H STD £1706
55 12/08 GrLe 6f (0-50)H STD £2266
Total win prize-money £7658

Going (Turf): **Sf: 0-0 GS: 0-2 Gd: 0-3 GF: 0-1 Fm: 0-1**
Distance: **5f/6f: 4-22** 7f-8f: 0-5 9f-13f: 0-0 14f+: 0-0
Track : **LH: 4-21** RH: 0-2 **Tight: 3-14** Gall: 1-5
Aids: Bl: 0-0 Vi: 0-3 Tstrap: 0-0 Ckp: 0-0
Best Rating: **67** 11/09 Ling 6f stand

Moderate; effective over 6f-1m; likes Polytrack.

Fantasy Gladiator

101(105) (81)73
3-y-o b g Ishiguru (USA)-Fancier Bit (Lion Cavern (USA))
R M H Cowell The Fantasy Fellowship

Placings:534-53211 **(6230)**
2009: 5⁵G, 5³GS, 6²G, 6¹SD, 6¹SD,

	Starts	1st	2nd	3rd	Win & Pl
Career Total (Turf)	3	0	1	1	1753
Career Total (AW)	5	2	0	1	6528

81 9/09 Kemp 6f (0-75)H STD £2590
77 8/09 Sthl 6f STD £3070
Total win prize-money £5661

Going (Turf): **Sf: 0-0 GS: 0-1 Gd: 0-2 GF: 0-0 Fm: 0-0**
Distance: **5f/6f: 2-7** 7f-8f: 0-1 9f-13f: 0-0 14f+: 0-0
Track : LH: 1-4 RH: 1-1 Tight: 0-1 Gall: 0-1
Aids: Bl: 0-0 Vi: 0-0 Tstrap: 0-0 Ckp: 0-0
Best Rating: **81** 9/09 Kemp 6f stand

Modest; stays 6f and acts on sand.

Fantasy Land (IRE)

95(91) (54)71
3-y-o ch f Danehill Dancer (IRE)-Wondrous Story (USA) (Royal Academy (USA))
B J Meehan Lady Bamford & The Sangster Family

Placings:033060000 **(6252)**
2009: 7⁰GS, 7³GF, 7³G, 8⁰GF, 6⁶SD, 7⁰G, 7⁰GF, 7⁰GF, 5⁰SD,

	Starts	1st	2nd	3rd	Win & Pl
Career Total (Turf)	7	0	0	2	1295
Career Total (AW)	2	0	0	0	0

Going (Turf): **Sf: 0-0 GS: 0-1 Gd: 0-2 GF: 0-4 Fm: 0-0**
Distance: 5f/6f: 0-2 7f-8f: 0-7 9f-13f: 0-0 14f+: 0-0
Track : LH: 0-2 RH: 0-2 Tight: 0-2 Gall: 0-0
Aids: Bl: 0-3 Vi: 0-0 Tstrap: 0-0 Ckp: 0-0
Best Rating: **71** 5/09 Gdwd 7f good

Fair; stays 7f and acts on good ground.

Fantasy Princess (USA)

75(105) (82)80
4-y-o ch f Johannesburg (USA)-Fantasy (Cadeaux Genereux)
G A Butler A D Spence

Placings:1/4032**2**0-0004 **(7092)**
2009: 9⁰G, 9⁰SD, 12⁰SS, 8⁴SD,

	Starts	1st	2nd	3rd	Win & Pl
Career Total (Turf)	5	0	1	1	4026
Career Total (AW)	6	1	1	0	4683

76 11/07 Ling 7f STD £3141
Total win prize-money £3141

Going (Turf): **Sf: 0-1 GS: 0-0 Gd: 0-2 GF: 0-2 Fm: 0-0**
Distance: 5f/6f: 0-0 **7f-8f: 1-5** 9f-13f: 0-6 14f+: 0-0
Track : **LH: 1-6** RH: 0-2 **Tight: 1-5** Gall: 0-2
Aids: Bl: 0-0 Vi: 0-0 Tstrap: 0-1 Ckp: 0-1
Best Rating: **82** 9/08 GrLe 1m2f stand

Fair; stays 1m1f; acts on most ground and on Polytrack.

Fantasy Ride

103(104) (60)58
7-y-o b g Bahhare (USA)-Grand Splendour (Shirley Heights)
J Pearce Mrs Jennifer Marsh

Placings:0152/000/**5000004355**5620/**125000403**-22050622440020344 **(7888)**
2009: 12²SD, 12²SD, 12⁰SD, 12⁵SD, 9⁰GF, 10⁶GF, 10²G, 10²G, 10⁴GF, 9⁴SD, 12⁰SD, 12⁰SD, 13²SD, 12⁰SD, 12³SD, 12⁴SD, 12⁴SD,

	Starts	1st	2nd	3rd	Win & Pl
Career Total (Turf)	19	1	3	0	12014
Career Total (AW)	28	1	5	3	5838

68 1/08 Wolv 1m4f50y (0-60)H STD £1774
91 8/04 Yarm 1m3y D SFT £3828
Total win prize-money £5604

Going (Turf): **Sf: 1-5** GS: 0-1 Gd: 0-8 GF: 0-4 Fm: 0-1
Distance: 5f/6f: 0-0 7f-8f: 0-1 **9f-13f: 2-42** 14f+: 0-4
Track : **LH: 1-25** RH: 0-18 **Tight: 1-20** Gall: 0-7
Aids: Bl: 0-2 Vi: 0-0 Tstrap: 0-0 Ckp: 0-0
Best Rating: **97** 10/04 NmkR 1m2f gd-sft

Moderate; stays 1m5f; acts on soft ground; also goes on Polytrack.

Fantino

103 70
3-y-o b g Shinko Forest (IRE)-Illustre Inconnue (USA) (Septieme Ciel (USA))
J Mackie Norman A Blyth

Placings:6-055021000 **(6910)**
2009: 8⁰GS, 8⁵G, 8⁵GF, 8⁰G, 10²GF, 11¹GF, 11⁰GF, 14⁰GF, 10⁰G,

	Starts	1st	2nd	3rd	Win & Pl
Career Total (Turf)	10	1	1	0	4070

70 9/09 Leic 1m3f183y (0-70)H G-F £2914
Total win prize-money £2914

Going (Turf): Sf: 0-0 GS: 0-1 Gd: 0-3 **GF: 1-6** Fm: 0-0
Distance: 5f/6f: 0-0 7f-8f: 0-2 **9f-13f: 1-7** 14f+: 0-1
Track : LH: 0-4 **RH: 1-6** Tight: 0-3 Gall: 0-2
Aids: Bl: 0-0 Vi: 0-0 Tstrap: 0-0 Ckp: 0-0
Best Rating: **70** 9/09 Leic 1m3f183y gd-fm

Modest; stays 1m3f; acts on fast ground.

Fanunalter

104(108) (99)102
3-y-o b g Falbrav (IRE)-Step Danzer (IRE) (Desert Prince (IRE))
M Botti Scuderia Rencati Srl

Placings:201203 **(7375)**
2009: 10²G, 10⁰HY, 8¹SD, 8²GF, 8⁰GF, 8³SD,

	Starts	1st	2nd	3rd	Win & Pl
Career Total (Turf)	4	0	2	0	6157
Career Total (AW)	2	1	0	1	4270

90 8/09 Kemp 1m STD £2590
Total win prize-money £2590

Going (Turf): **Sf: 0-1 GS: 0-0 Gd: 0-1 GF: 0-2 Fm: 0-0**
Distance: 5f/6f: 0-0 **7f-8f: 1-2** 9f-13f: 0-4 14f+: 0-0
Track : LH: 0-1 **RH: 1-2** Tight: 0-1 Gall: 0-0
Aids: Bl: 0-0 Vi: 0-0 Tstrap: 0-0 Ckp: 0-0
Best Rating: **102** 9/09 Sand 1m14y gd-fm

Very useful; effective over 1m; acts on fast ground; goes on Polytrack.

Far 'n Wide

75 5

3-y-o ch f Rainbow Quest (USA)-Raspberry Sauce (Niniski (USA))
W J Haggas Mrs Charles Cyzer

Placings:0 (2051)
2009: 12^{0}GF,

	Starts	1st	2nd	3rd	Win & Pl
Career Total (Turf)	1	0	0	0	

Going (Turf): **Sf: 0-0 GS: 0-0 Gd: 0-0 GF: 0-1 Fm: 0-0**
Distance: 5f/6f: 0-0 7f-8f: 0-0 9f-13f: 0-1 14f+: 0-0
Track : LH: 0-0 RH: 0-1 Tight: 0-0 Gall: 0-1
Aids: Bl: 0-0 Vi: 0-0 Tstrap: 0-0 Ckp: 0-0
Best Rating: 5 5/09 NmkR 1m4f gd-fm

Far View (IRE)

(64) (11)

2-y-o b c Oasis Dream-Night Mirage (USA) (Silver Hawk (USA))
J W Hills Gary & Lesley Middlebrook

Placings:0 (7429)
2009: 7^{0}SD,

	Starts	1st	2nd	3rd	Win & Pl
Career Total (Turf)	0	0	0	0	
Career Total (AW)	1	0	0	0	

Going (Turf): **Sf: 0-0 GS: 0-0 Gd: 0-0 GF: 0-0 Fm: 0-0**
Distance: 5f/6f: 0-0 7f-8f: 0-1 9f-13f: 0-0 14f+: 0-0
Track : LH: 0-0 RH: 0-1 Tight: 0-0 Gall: 0-0
Aids: Bl: 0-0 Vi: 0-0 Tstrap: 0-0 Ckp: 0-0
Best Rating: 11 11/09 Kemp 7f stand

Faraday (IRE)

(100) (59)60

6-y-o b g Montjeu (IRE)-Fureau (GER) (Ferdinand (USA))
N P Mulholland The Electric Partnership

Placings:30/464330/01305/232102000-0 (0469)
2009: 10^{0}SD,

	Starts	1st	2nd	3rd	Win & Pl
Career Total (Turf)	11	0	1	3	3273
Career Total (AW)	12	2	2	2	4372
55 3/08 Wolv 1m1f103y	(0-45)	STD	£1365		
59 8/07 Wolv 1m141y	(0-45)	STD	£1706		
			Total win prize-money £3071		

Going (Turf): Sf: 0-6 GS: 0-0 Gd: 0-3 GF: 0-2 Fm: 0-0
Distance: 5f/6f: 0-0 7f-8f: 0-3 **9f-13f: 2-20** 14f+: 0-0
Track : **LH: 2-14** RH: 0-6 **Tight: 2-7** Gall: 0-0
Aids: Bl: 0-3 Vi: 0-0 Tstrap: 0-0 Ckp: 0-0
Best Rating: 60 7/08 Nott 1m2f50y gd-fm

Moderate; ex-German; stays 1m2f; acts on fast ground and on Polytrack.

Faraway Sound (IRE)

91(88) (50)75

3-y-o b g Distant Music (USA)-Queen Consort (Diesis)
P C Haslam Middleham Park Racing XXXIX

Placings:325123400-66 (5626)
2009: 6^{6}GF, 5^{6}S,

	Starts	1st	2nd	3rd	Win & Pl
Career Total (Turf)	9	1	2	2	6476
Career Total (AW)	2	0	0	0	
70 6/08 Muss 5f		G-F	£2266		
			Total win prize-money £2267		

Going (Turf): Sf: 0-1 GS: 0-2 Gd: 0-1 **GF: 1-5** Fm: 0-0
Distance: **5f/6f: 1-10** 7f-8f: 0-1 9f-13f: 0-0 14f+: 0-0
Track : LH: 0-2 RH: 0-1 Tight: 0-1 Gall: 0-1
Aids: Bl: 0-0 Vi: 0-1 Tstrap: 0-2 Ckp: 0-2
Best Rating: 75 7/08 York 5f gd-fm

Fair; effective over 5f-6f; acts on fast ground.

Fardyieh

97(100) (81)77

2-y-o b f King's Best (USA)-Injaaz (Sheikh Albadou)
C E Brittain Saeed Manana

Placings:02100 (6619)
2009: 6^{0}G, 6^{2}GF, 6^{1}SD, 6^{0}G, 6^{0}G,

	Starts	1st	2nd	3rd	Win & Pl
Career Total (Turf)	4	0	1	0	7595
Career Total (AW)	1	1	0	0	3562
81 9/09 Kemp 6f		STD	£3561		
			Total win prize-money £3562		

Going (Turf): **Sf: 0-0 GS: 0-0 Gd: 0-3 GF: 0-1 Fm: 0-0**
Distance: **5f/6f: 1-2** 7f-8f: 0-3 9f-13f: 0-0 14f+: 0-0
Track : LH: 0-0 **RH: 1-1** Tight: 0-0 Gall: 0-0
Aids: Bl: 0-0 Vi: 0-0 Tstrap: 0-0 Ckp: 0-0
Best Rating: 81 9/09 Kemp 6f stand

Fair; effective over 6f and should stay 7f; acts on fast ground and on Polytrack.

Fareeha

(97) (50)61

4-y-o b f King's Best (USA)-Shatarah (Gulch (USA))
J Mackie Ms Lucy Davis

Placings:0000/00406-0 (7152)
2009: 8^{0}SD,

	Starts	1st	2nd	3rd	Win & Pl
Career Total (Turf)	5	0	0	0	0
Career Total (AW)	5	0	0	0	

Going (Turf): **Sf: 0-1 GS: 0-0 Gd: 0-2 GF: 0-1 Fm: 0-1**
Distance: 5f/6f: 0-0 7f-8f: 0-4 9f-13f: 0-6 14f+: 0-0
Track : LH: 0-5 RH: 0-3 Tight: 0-4 Gall: 0-0
Aids: Bl: 0-0 Vi: 0-0 Tstrap: 0-0 Ckp: 0-0
Best Rating: 61 8/07 NmkJ 7f firm

Fareej (USA)

99(100) (92)85

2-y-o b c Kingmambo (USA)-Adonesque (IRE) (Sadler's Wells (USA))
Saeed Bin Suroor Godolphin

Placings:11 (6779)
2009: 8^{1}GF, 8^{1}SS,

	Starts	1st	2nd	3rd	Win & Pl
Career Total (Turf)	1	1	0	0	5181
Career Total (AW)	1	1	0	0	5181
92 10/09 Ling 1m		SS	£5180		
85 10/09 NmkR 1m		G-F	£5180		
			Total win prize-money £10362		

Going (Turf): Sf: 0-0 GS: 0-0 Gd: 0-0 **GF: 1-1** Fm: 0-0
Distance: 5f/6f: 0-0 **7f-8f: 2-2** 9f-13f: 0-0 14f+: 0-0
Track : **LH: 1-1** RH: 0-0 **Tight: 1-1** Gall: 0-0
Aids: Bl: 0-0 Vi: 0-0 Tstrap: 0-0 Ckp: 0-0
Best Rating: 92 10/09 Ling 1m std-slw

Very useful; stays 1m; acts on fast ground and on Polytrack.

Fareer

105 103

3-y-o ch c Bahamian Bounty-Songsheet (Dominion)
E A L Dunlop Hamdan Al Maktoum

Placings:312-3151 (3049)
2009: 7^{3}GS, 7^{1}GF, 8^{5}HY, 8^{1}GF,

	Starts	1st	2nd	3rd	Win & Pl
Career Total (Turf)	7	3	1	2	88844
103 6/09 Asct 1m	(0-105)H	G-F	£62310		
96 5/09 Ches 7f122y	(0-100)H	G-F	£14193		
72 6/08 Donc 6f		G-F	£4857		
			Total win prize-money £81360		

Going (Turf): Sf: 0-1 GS: 0-2 Gd: 0-0 **GF: 3-4** Fm: 0-0
Distance: 5f/6f: 1-2 **7f-8f: 2-4** 9f-13f: 0-1 14f+: 0-0
Track : **LH: 1-2** RH: 0-0 **Tight: 1-1** Gall: 0-0
Aids: Bl: 0-0 Vi: 0-0 Tstrap: 0-0 Ckp: 0-0
Best Rating: 103 6/09 Asct 1m gd-fm

Smart; winner of the Britannia Stakes in 2009; effective over 6f-1m; acts on most ground.

Fareham Town

(84) (58)

2-y-o ch f Cape Town (IRE)-Fareham (Komaite (USA))
S Kirk Brian D Cantle

Placings:030 (7799)
2009: 5^{0}SD, 7^{3}SD, 5^{0}SD,

	Starts	1st	2nd	3rd	Win & Pl
Career Total (Turf)	0	0	0	0	
Career Total (AW)	3	0	0	1	578

Going (Turf): **Sf: 0-0 GS: 0-0 Gd: 0-0 GF: 0-0 Fm: 0-0**
Distance: 5f/6f: 0-2 7f-8f: 0-1 9f-13f: 0-0 14f+: 0-0
Track : LH: 0-3 RH: 0-0 Tight: 0-3 Gall: 0-0
Aids: Bl: 0-0 Vi: 0-0 Tstrap: 0-0 Ckp: 0-0
Best Rating: 58 12/09 Wolv 7f32y stand

Modest; stays 7f and acts on Polytrack.

Farleigh

96(88) (63)74

3-y-o b f Trans Island-Medway (IRE) (Shernazar)
A M Balding Farleigh Partnership

Placings:2-136 (4956)
2009: 8^{1}GF, 8^{3}S, 8^{6}G,

	Starts	1st	2nd	3rd	Win & Pl
Career Total (Turf)	3	1	0	1	4222
Career Total (AW)	1	0	1	0	1156
69 5/09 Wind 1m67y		G-F	£2729		
			Total win prize-money £2730		

Going (Turf): Sf: 0-1 GS: 0-0 Gd: 0-1 **GF: 1-1** Fm: 0-0
Distance: 5f/6f: 0-0 7f-8f: 0-2 **9f-13f: 1-2** 14f+: 0-0
Track : LH: 0-0 **RH: 1-3 Tight: 1-1** Gall: 0-0
Aids: Bl: 0-0 Vi: 0-0 Tstrap: 0-0 Ckp: 0-0
Best Rating: 74 7/09 Sals 1m soft

Fair; effective over 7f-1m; acts on fast ground; goes on Polytrack.

Farleigh House (USA)

99(107) (89)**88**

5-y-o b g Lear Fan (USA)-Verasina (USA) (Woodman (USA))

N B King (Sir Mark Prescott 16/10) The Farleigh House Partnership

Placings:5221/44300/622240-50602312 **(6830)**

2009: 8^{5}GF, 10^{0}GF, 10^{6}GF, 11^{0}SD, 8^{2}SD, 9^{3}GF, 9^{1}SD, 8^{2}SF,

	Starts	1st	2nd	3rd	Win & Pl
Career Total (Turf)	18	1	5	2	27567
Career Total (AW)	5	1	2	0	8067

89 10/09 Wolv 1m1f103y (0-85)H STD £5046
80 9/06 Ling 7f GD £2730
Total win prize-money £7776

Going (Turf): Sf: 0-0 GS: 0-0 **Gd: 1-2** GF: 0-10 Fm: 0-6
Distance: 5f/6f: 0-1 7f-8f: 1-7 9f-13f: 1-15 14f+: 0-0
Track : **LH: 1-5** RH: 0-5 **Tight: 1-5** Gall: 0-1
Aids: Bl: 0-2 Vi: 0-0 Tstrap: 0-0 Ckp: 0-0
Best Rating: 89 10/09 Wolv 1m141y std-fst

Useful; raced in USA in 2008; stays 1m2f; acts on good and faster ground and on Polytrack; has worn blinkers.

Farley Star

104(108) (88)**98**

5-y-o b m Alzao (USA)-Girl Of My Dreams (IRE) (Marju (IRE))

M G Quinlan A Parker (London)

Placings:316/5/301105440-34 **(7032)**

2009: 8^{3}G, 7^{4}S,

	Starts	1st	2nd	3rd	Win & Pl
Career Total (Turf)	11	3	0	1	24225
Career Total (AW)	4	0	0	2	1750

93 6/08 Hayd 1m30y (0-90)H G-F £8095
88 5/08 Leic 7f9y (0-80)H G-F £6231
78 8/06 Folk 7f G-S £3886
Total win prize-money £18212

Going (Turf): Sf: 0-2 GS: 1-2 Gd: 0-3 **GF: 2-4** Fm: 0-0
Distance: 5f/6f: 0-0 **7f-8f: 2-9** 9f-13f: 1-6 14f+: 0-0
Track : **LH: 1-4** RH: 0-6 Tight: 0-5 Gall: 0-0
Aids: Bl: 0-0 Vi: 0-0 Tstrap: 0-0 Ckp: 0-0
Best Rating: 98 7/08 Gdwd 1m1f gd-fm

Very useful; stays 1m2f; acts on fast and soft ground; also goes on Polytrack.

Farmer Giles (IRE)

101(90) (84)**87**

2-y-o b c Danroad (AUS)-Demeter (USA) (Diesis)

M L W Bell R A Green

Placings:6231040340 **(6993)**

2009: 5^{6}GF, 5^{2}GF, 5^{3}F, 5^{1}G, 6^{0}G, 5^{4}SD, 5^{0}GF, 7^{3}GF, 7^{4}GF, 8^{0}GS,

	Starts	1st	2nd	3rd	Win & Pl
Career Total (Turf)	9	1	1	2	6366
Career Total (AW)	1	0	0	0	289

84 6/09 Ripn 5f GD £3238
Total win prize-money £3238

Going (Turf): Sf: 0-0 GS: 0-1 **Gd: 1-2** GF: 0-5 Fm: 0-1
Distance: **5f/6f: 1-7** 7f-8f: 0-3 9f-13f: 0-0 14f+: 0-0
Track : LH: 0-2 RH: 0-0 Tight: 0-1 Gall: 0-1
Aids: Bl: 0-0 Vi: 0-0 Tstrap: 0-0 Ckp: 0-0
Best Rating: 87 9/09 Donc 7f gd-fm

Useful; suited by 5f and good ground.

Farmers Dream (IRE)

75(87) (45)**29**

2-y-o b f Antonius Pius (USA)-Beucaire (IRE) (Entrepreneur)

J L Spearing D J Oseman

Placings:006 **(7234)**

2009: 6^{0}G, 5^{0}GF, 6^{8}SD,

	Starts	1st	2nd	3rd	Win & Pl
Career Total (Turf)	2	0	0	0	
Career Total (AW)	1	0	0	0	0

Going (Turf): Sf: 0-0 GS: 0-0 Gd: 0-1 GF: 0-1 Fm: 0-0
Distance: 5f/6f: 0-2 7f-8f: 0-1 9f-13f: 0-0 14f+: 0-0
Track : LH: 0-0 RH: 0-1 Tight: 0-0 Gall: 0-0
Aids: Bl: 0-0 Vi: 0-0 Tstrap: 0-0 Ckp: 0-0
Best Rating: 45 11/09 Kemp 6f stand

Farmers Wish (IRE)

101(97) (78)**81**

2-y-o b f Val Royal (FR)-Farmers Swing (IRE) (River Falls)

J L Spearing D J Oseman

Placings:421162540 **(7290)**

2009: 6^{4}GF, 6^{2}G, 6^{1}S, 6^{1}GF, 7^{6}GF, 6^{2}G, 6^{5}G, 6^{4}SD, 6^{0}S,

	Starts	1st	2nd	3rd	Win & Pl
Career Total (Turf)	8	2	2	0	12612
Career Total (AW)	1	0	0	0	289

81 8/09 Hayd 6f G-F £6476
69 7/09 Chep 6f16y SFT £2719
Total win prize-money £9196

Going (Turf): Sf: 1-2 GS: 0-0 Gd: 0-3 **GF: 1-3** Fm: 0-0
Distance: 5f/6f: 1-5 7f-8f: 1-4 9f-13f: 0-0 14f+: 0-0
Track : LH: 0-0 RH: 0-1 Tight: 0-0 Gall: 0-0
Aids: Bl: 0-0 Vi: 0-0 Tstrap: 0-0 Ckp: 0-0
Best Rating: 81 8/09 Hayd 6f gd-fm

Useful; stays 6f; acts on a sound surface.

Farncombe (IRE)

96(100) (67)**68**

3-y-o ch f Where Or When (IRE)-Promenade (Primo Dominie)

R A Harris (M P Tregoning 1/11) David Mort

Placings:03363150 **(7665)**

2009: 7^{0}GS, 7^{3}G, 6^{3}G, 7^{6}SD, 9^{3}SD, 10^{1}SD, 10^{5}SD, 12^{0}SD,

	Starts	1st	2nd	3rd	Win & Pl
Career Total (Turf)	3	0	0	2	886
Career Total (AW)	5	1	0	1	2400

67 11/09 Ling 1m2f STD £2047
Total win prize-money £2047

Going (Turf): Sf: 0-0 GS: 0-1 Gd: 0-2 GF: 0-0 Fm: 0-0
Distance: 5f/6f: 0-0 7f-8f: 0-4 **9f-13f: 1-4** 14f+: 0-0
Track : **LH: 1-3** RH: 0-3 **Tight: 1-3** Gall: 0-0
Aids: Bl: 0-0 Vi: 0-0 Tstrap: 0-0 Ckp: 0-0
Best Rating: 68 5/09 Gdwd 7f good

Modest; stays 1m2f; acts on good ground; goes on Polytrack.

Farne Island

98 (62)**59**

6-y-o ch g Arkadian Hero (USA)-Holy Island (Deploy)

Micky Hammond Joe Buzzeo

Placings:053/004421400/026/0060600-245 **(3481)**

2009: 10^{2}F, 10^{4}GF, 9^{5}GF,

	Starts	1st	2nd	3rd	Win & Pl
Career Total (Turf)	24	1	3	0	7280
Career Total (AW)	1	0	0	1	211

65 7/06 Bevl 1m100y (0-65)H G-F £3238
Total win prize-money £3239

Going (Turf): Sf: 0-2 GS: 0-2 Gd: 0-7 **GF: 1-11** Fm: 0-2
Distance: 5f/6f: 0-0 7f-8f: 0-10 **9f-13f: 1-15** 14f+: 0-0
Track : LH: 0-11 **RH: 1-11** Tight: 0-10 Gall: 0-4
Aids: Bl: 0-0 Vi: 0-0 Tstrap: 0-0 Ckp: 0-0
Best Rating: 65 7/06 Bevl 1m100y gd-fm

Moderate sort; stays 1m2f; acts on soft and fast ground.

Farriers Gate

(76) (19)**26**

3-y-o ch f Lomitas-Mountain Stream (FR) (Vettori (IRE))

M E Rimmer E Buddle

Placings:00-00 **(0722)**

2009: 8^{0}SD, 6^{0}SD,

	Starts	1st	2nd	3rd	Win & Pl
Career Total (Turf)	1	0	0	0	
Career Total (AW)	3	0	0	0	

Going (Turf): Sf: 0-0 GS: 0-0 Gd: 0-0 GF: 0-1 Fm: 0-0
Distance: 5f/6f: 0-3 7f-8f: 0-1 9f-13f: 0-0 14f+: 0-0
Track : LH: 0-2 RH: 0-1 Tight: 0-2 Gall: 0-0
Aids: Bl: 0-1 Vi: 0-0 Tstrap: 0-0 Ckp: 0-0
Best Rating: 26 6/08 Yarm 5f43y gd-fm

Farsighted

(97) (42)**72**

4-y-o b f Where Or When (IRE)-Classic Vision (Classic Cliche (IRE))

J M P Eustace Blue Peter Racing 7

Placings:51030/00000-00 **(0186)**

2009: 7^{0}SD, 10^{0}SD,

	Starts	1st	2nd	3rd	Win & Pl
Career Total (Turf)	9	1	0	1	7297
Career Total (AW)	3	0	0	0	

70 7/07 York 7f HVY £6541
Total win prize-money £6542

Going (Turf): Sf: 1-3 GS: 0-2 Gd: 0-1 GF: 0-3 Fm: 0-0
Distance: 5f/6f: 0-1 **7f-8f: 1-6** 9f-13f: 0-4 14f+: 0-1
Track : **LH: 1-5** RH: 0-1 Tight: 0-2 **Gall: 1-2**
Aids: Bl: 0-1 Vi: 0-0 Tstrap: 0-0 Ckp: 0-0
Best Rating: 72 9/07 Yarm 7f3y good

Fascile

53

2-y-o b g Forzando-Frankie Fair (IRE) (Red Sunset)

E J Creighton A S Reid

Placings:0 **(1404)**

2009: 5^{0}GF,

	Starts	1st	2nd	3rd	Win & Pl
Career Total (Turf)	1	0	0	0	

Going (Turf): Sf: 0-0 GS: 0-0 Gd: 0-0 GF: 0-1 Fm: 0-0
Distance: 5f/6f: 0-1 7f-8f: 0-0 9f-13f: 0-0 14f+: 0-0
Track : LH: 0-0 RH: 0-0 Tight: 0-0 Gall: 0-1
Aids: Bl: 0-0 Vi: 0-0 Tstrap: 0-0 Ckp: 0-0

Fasette

84 51

2-y-o b f Fasliyev (USA)-Londonnet (IRE) (Catrail (USA))

M H Tompkins Raceworld

Placings:0 **(2699)**

2009: 6^{0}GS,

	Starts	1st	2nd	3rd	Win & Pl
Career Total (Turf)	1	0	0	0	

Going (Turf): **Sf: 0-0 GS: 0-1 Gd: 0-0 GF: 0-0 Fm: 0-0**
Distance: 5f/6f: 0-1 7f-8f: 0-0 9f-13f: 0-0 14f+: 0-0
Track : LH: 0-0 RH: 0-0 Tight: 0-0 Gall: 0-0
Aids: Bl: 0-0 Vi: 0-0 Tstrap: 0-0 Ckp: 0-0
Best Rating: **51** 6/09 Donc 6f gd-sft

Fashion Icon (USA)

92(98) (59)57

3-y-o ch f Van Nistelrooy (USA)-Los Altos (USA) (Robin Des Pins (USA))

T D Barron Mount Pleasant Farm Racing Partnership

Placings:0056-**5534220440** **(2581)**

2009: 5^{5}SD, 5^{5}SD, 5^{3}SD, 5^{4}SD, 5^{2}SD, 5^{2}GF, 5^{0}F, 5^{4}GF, 5^{4}G, 5^{0}SD,

	Starts	1st	2nd	3rd	Win & Pl
Career Total (Turf)	8	0	1	0	825
Career Total (AW)	6	0	1	1	957

Going (Turf): **Sf: 0-0 GS: 0-1 Gd: 0-3 GF: 0-3 Fm: 0-1**
Distance: 5f/6f: 0-14 7f-8f: 0-0 9f-13f: 0-0 14f+: 0-0
Track : LH: 0-3 RH: 0-0 Tight: 0-3 Gall: 0-0
Aids: Bl: 0-1 Vi: 0-0 Tstrap: 0-0 Ckp: 0-0
Best Rating: **59** 3/09 Sthl 5f stand

Moderate; stays 6f; acts on fast ground and on sand.

Fashion Insider (USA)

86(92) (74)70

2-y-o b/br f Indian Charlie (USA)-Shahalo (USA) (Halo (USA))

B J Meehan Andrew Rosen

Placings:42 **(7624)**

2009: 7^{4}G, 8^{2}SD,

	Starts	1st	2nd	3rd	Win & Pl
Career Total (Turf)	1	0	0	0	361
Career Total (AW)	1	0	1	0	705

Going (Turf): **Sf: 0-0 GS: 0-0 Gd: 0-1 GF: 0-0 Fm: 0-0**
Distance: 5f/6f: 0-0 7f-8f: 0-2 9f-13f: 0-0 14f+: 0-0
Track : LH: 0-1 RH: 0-0 Tight: 0-1 Gall: 0-0
Aids: Bl: 0-0 Vi: 0-0 Tstrap: 0-0 Ckp: 0-0
Best Rating: **74** 12/09 Ling 1m stand

Fashionable Gal (IRE)

84 52

2-y-o b f Galileo (IRE)-Fashion (Bin Ajwaad (IRE))

Sir Mark Prescott W E Sturt-Osborne House V

Placings:0 **(5980)**

2009: 7^{0}GF,

	Starts	1st	2nd	3rd	Win & Pl
Career Total (Turf)	1	0	0	0	

Going (Turf): **Sf: 0-0 GS: 0-0 Gd: 0-0 GF: 0-1 Fm: 0-0**
Distance: 5f/6f: 0-0 7f-8f: 0-1 9f-13f: 0-0 14f+: 0-0
Track : LH: 0-0 RH: 0-1 Tight: 0-0 Gall: 0-0
Aids: Bl: 0-0 Vi: 0-0 Tstrap: 0-0 Ckp: 0-0
Best Rating: **52** 9/09 Bevl 7f100y gd-fm

Fasilight

93(94) (69)69

2-y-o b f Fasliyev (USA)-Rajmata (IRE) (Prince Sabo)

M Botti Giuliano Manfredini

Placings:5230601 **(6494)**

2009: 5^{5}GF, 6^{2}GF, 7^{3}SD, 7^{0}GS, 7^{6}SD, 6^{0}SD, 5^{1}SF,

	Starts	1st	2nd	3rd	Win & Pl
Career Total (Turf)	3	0	1	0	1683
Career Total (AW)	4	1	0	1	2966

65	10/09	Wolv	5f20y	SF	£2388

Total win prize-money £2388

Going (Turf): **Sf: 0-0 GS: 0-1 Gd: 0-0 GF: 0-2 Fm: 0-0**
Distance: **5f/6f: 1-4** 7f-8f: 0-3 9f-13f: 0-0 14f+: 0-0
Track : **LH: 1-2** RH: 0-2 **Tight: 1-2** Gall: 0-0
Aids: Bl: 0-0 Vi: 0-0 Tstrap: 0-0 Ckp: 0-0
Best Rating: **69** 7/09 Kemp 7f stand

Fasliyanne (IRE)

99(91) (52)68

3-y-o b f Fasliyev (USA)-Happy Memories (IRE) (Thatching)

K A Ryan Wooster Partnership

Placings:6430**050-0243**122362025000 **(7838)**

2009: 5^{0}SD, 5^{2}SD, 5^{4}SD, 5^{3}SD, 5^{1}GF, 5^{2}F, 5^{2}GF, 5^{3}GF, 5^{6}G, 5^{2}G, 5^{0}GF, 5^{2}GF, 5^{5}GF, 5^{0}GF, 5^{0}G, 5^{0}SS,

	Starts	1st	2nd	3rd	Win & Pl
Career Total (Turf)	15	1	4	2	6439
Career Total (AW)	8	0	1	1	1099

59	4/09	Catt	5f	(0-60)H	G-F	£2183

Total win prize-money £2184

Going (Turf): Sf: 0-0 GS: 0-1 Gd: 0-5 **GF: 1-8** Fm: 0-1
Distance: **5f/6f: 1-23** 7f-8f: 0-0 9f-13f: 0-0 14f+: 0-0
Track : LH: 0-4 RH: 0-0 Tight: 0-4 Gall: 0-0
Aids: **Bl: 1-12** Vi: 0-1 Tstrap: 0-1 Ckp: 0-1
Best Rating: **68** 8/09 Newc 5f gd-fm

Modest; probably best at 5f; acts on fast ground; goes on Fibresand; has worn blinkers, cheekpieces and a tongue tie.

Fast Elaine (IRE)

74 34

2-y-o ch f Bahamian Bounty Miss A Note (USA) (Miswaki (USA))

Mrs L C Jewell Quintessential Thoroughbreds Solar Syn

Placings:0000 **(6034)**

2009: 5^{0}G, 6^{0}GF, 8^{0}GF, 8^{0}GF,

	Starts	1st	2nd	3rd	Win & Pl
Career Total (Turf)	4	0	0	0	

Going (Turf): **Sf: 0-0 GS: 0-0 Gd: 0-1 GF: 0-3 Fm: 0-0**
Distance: 5f/6f: 0-2 7f-8f: 0-0 9f-13f: 0-2 14f+: 0-0
Track : LH: 0-0 RH: 0-1 Tight: 0-1 Gall: 0-0
Aids: Bl: 0-0 Vi: 0-0 Tstrap: 0-0 Ckp: 0-0
Best Rating: **34** 8/09 Wind 1m67y gd-fm

Fast Freddie

86(104) (76)67

5-y-o b g Agnes World (USA)-Bella Chica (IRE) (Bigstone (IRE))

Mrs A Malzard (S Parr 26/4) Gordon Crawford

Placings:23P/4000**061110/106**40605522400**130-006**602422446 **(5541a)**

2009: 5^{0}SD, 5^{0}SD, 5^{6}SD, 5^{6}GF, 5^{0}GF, 5^{2}G, 7^{4}GF, 5^{2}F, 7^{2}GF, 5^{4}GS, 7^{4}GF, 5^{6}F,

	Starts	1st	2nd	3rd	Win & Pl
Career Total (Turf)	23	0	4	0	2379
Career Total (AW)	19	5	2	2	13902

76	11/08	Wolv	5f20y	(0-70)H	STD	£3238
73	2/08	Kemp	5f	(0-65)H	STD	£2047
69	12/07	Ling	6f	(0-57)H	STD	£1619
66	11/07	Wolv	5f20y	(0-53)H	STD	£2047
61	11/07	Wolv	5f216y	(0-52)H	STD	£1706

Total win prize-money £10659

Going (Turf): **Sf: 0-1 GS: 0-5 Gd: 0-6 GF: 0-8 Fm: 0-3**
Distance: **5f/6f: 5-37** 7f-8f: 0-5 9f-13f: 0-0 14f+: 0-0
Track : **LH: 4-20** RH: 1-4 **Tight: 4-13** Gall: 0-2
Aids: Bl: 0-3 Vi: 0-0 Tstrap: 0-0 Ckp: 0-0
Best Rating: **76** 11/08 Wolv 5f20y stand

Fair; effective at around 5f-6f; acts on Polytrack; has worn blinkers and an eyeshield.

Fast Living

(87) (46)

4-y-o b g Fasliyev (USA)-Fairy Contessa (IRE) (Fairy King (USA))

A M Hales (Ms E L McWilliam 8/8) A M Hales

Placings:50 **(6252)**

2009: 6^{5}SD, 5^{0}SD,

	Starts	1st	2nd	3rd	Win & Pl
Career Total (Turf)	0	0	0	0	
Career Total (AW)	2	0	0	0	0

Going (Turf): **Sf: 0-0 GS: 0-0 Gd: 0-0 GF: 0-0 Fm: 0-0**
Distance: 5f/6f: 0-2 7f-8f: 0-0 9f-13f: 0-0 14f+: 0-0
Track : LH: 0-2 RH: 0-0 Tight: 0-1 Gall: 0-0
Aids: Bl: 0-0 Vi: 0-0 Tstrap: 0-0 Ckp: 0-0
Best Rating: **46** 9/09 Wolv 5f216y stand

Fastnet Storm (IRE)

112 95

3-y-o br g Rock Of Gibraltar (IRE)-Dreams (Rainbow Quest (USA))

T P Tate The Kittywake Partnership

Placings:015521-001103613 **(7185)**

2009: 8^{0}GF, 10^{0}GF, 9^{1}GF, 10^{1}GF, 9^{0}G, 10^{3}GF, 10^{6}GF, 10^{1}S, 8^{3}G,

	Starts	1st	2nd	3rd	Win & Pl
Career Total (Turf)	15	5	1	2	33584

95	10/09	Nott	1m2f50y	(0-95)H	SFT	£7771
95	6/09	Pont	1m2f6y	(0-90)H	G-F	£9346
89	6/09	Ripn	1m1f170y	(0-80)H	G-F	£5180
81	10/08	Pont	1m4y	(0-75)	G-S	£3885
74	6/08	Bevl	7f100y		G-F	£2331

Total win prize-money £28516

Going (Turf): Sf: 1-2 GS: 1-1 Gd: 0-3 **GF: 3-9** Fm: 0-0
Distance: 5f/6f: 0-1 7f-8f: 1-4 **9f-13f: 4-10** 14f+: 0-0
Track : **LH: 3-6** RH: 2-4 **Tight: 1-4** Gall: 0-1
Aids: Bl: 0-0 Vi: 0-0 Tstrap: 0-0 Ckp: 0-0
Best Rating: **95** 10/09 Nott 1m2f50y soft

Useful; stays 1m2f; acts on most ground; likes to race prominently.

Fastrac Boy

(98) (46)**56**

6-y-o b g Bold Edge-Nesyred (IRE) (Paris House)

J R Best P O'Connell

Placings:6166/6002602/000402330-0 **(0046)**

2009: 5^{0}SD,

	Starts	1st	2nd	3rd	Win & Pl
Career Total (Turf)	4	0	1	2	1357
Career Total (AW)	17	1	2	0	4479

60	10/06	Wolv	5f20y	STD	£3238

Total win prize-money £3239

Going (Turf): **Sf: 0-0 GS: 0-1 Gd: 0-0 GF: 0-1 Fm: 0-2**
Distance: **5f/6f: 1-21** 7f-8f: 0-0 9f-13f: 0-0 14f+: 0-0
Track : **LH: 1-12** RH: 0-7 **Tight: 1-10** Gall: 0-0
Aids: Bl: 0-0 Vi: 0-0 Tstrap: 0-0 Ckp: 0-0
Best Rating: **63** 11/06 Wolv 5f20y stand

Moderate; suited by 5f; acts on fast ground; also goes on Polytrack.

Fat Boy (IRE)

98 (77)**116**

4-y-o ch g Choisir (AUS)-Gold Shift (USA) (Night Shift (USA))

P W Chapple-Hyam M Sines

Placings:1060121/211005-000 **(5434)**

2009: 5^{0}GF, 5^{0}G, 6^{0}GF,

	Starts	1st	2nd	3rd	Win & Pl
Career Total (Turf)	15	4	2	0	83014
Career Total (AW)	1	1	0	0	5182

116	5/08	Hayd	6f	GD	£17031
114	5/08	Newb	6f8y	GD	£17031
105	8/07	Ripn	6f	G-F	£17034
98	7/07	NmkJ	6f	G-F	£7772
77	4/07	Kemp	5f	STD	£5181

Total win prize-money £64050

Going (Turf): Sf: 0-0 GS: 0-0 **Gd: 2-5 GF: 2-10** Fm: 0-0
Distance: **5f/6f: 4-14** 7f-8f: 1-2 9f-13f: 0-0 14f+: 0-0
Track : LH: 0-0 **RH: 1-1** Tight: 0-0 Gall: 0-0
Aids: Bl: 0-0 Vi: 0-0 Tstrap: 0-0 Ckp: 0-0
Best Rating: **116** 5/08 Hayd 6f good

Listed-class sprinter; effective over 6f-7f; acts on fast ground; goes on Polytrack.

Fat Chance

75 **54**

3-y-o gr f Linamix (FR)-Hymenee (USA) (Chief's Crown (USA))

Rae Guest The Storm Again Syndicate

Placings:5-000 **(3685)**

2009: 7^{0}GF, 10^{0}GF, 9^{0}G,

	Starts	1st	2nd	3rd	Win & Pl
Career Total (Turf)	4	0	0	0	165

Going (Turf): **Sf: 0-0 GS: 0-0 Gd: 0-2 GF: 0-2 Fm: 0-0**
Distance: 5f/6f: 0-0 7f-8f: 0-2 9f-13f: 0-2 14f+: 0-0
Track : LH: 0-0 RH: 0-2 Tight: 0-1 Gall: 0-1
Aids: Bl: 0-1 Vi: 0-0 Tstrap: 0-0 Ckp: 0-0
Best Rating: **54** 10/08 Yarm 6f3y good

Fatal Attraction

94(96) (50)**59**

4-y-o b f Oasis Dream-Millyant (Primo Dominie)

Rae Guest C J Mills

Placings:443663 **(6856)**

2009: 5^{4}SD, 5^{4}GF, 5^{3}GS, 5^{6}GS, 5^{6}SD, 5^{3}SD,

	Starts	1st	2nd	3rd	Win & Pl
Career Total (Turf)	3	0	0	1	963
Career Total (AW)	3	0	0	1	403

Going (Turf): **Sf: 0-0 GS: 0-2 Gd: 0-0 GF: 0-1 Fm: 0-0**
Distance: 5f/6f: 0-6 7f-8f: 0-0 9f-13f: 0-0 14f+: 0-0
Track : LH: 0-3 RH: 0-0 Tight: 0-3 Gall: 0-0
Aids: Bl: 0-0 Vi: 0-0 Tstrap: 0-0 Ckp: 0-0
Best Rating: **59** 5/09 Muss 5f gd-fm

Moderate half-sister to three winners; effective at 5f; handles fast ground.

Fatanah (IRE)

97(90) (71)**65**

2-y-o b f Green Desert (USA)-Wijdan (USA) (Mr Prospector (USA))

M P Tregoning Hamdan Al Maktoum

Placings:02 **(7390)**

2009: 8^{0}G, 8^{2}SD,

	Starts	1st	2nd	3rd	Win & Pl
Career Total (Turf)	1	0	0	0	
Career Total (AW)	1	0	1	0	1008

Going (Turf): **Sf: 0-0 GS: 0-0 Gd: 0-1 GF: 0-0 Fm: 0-0**
Distance: 5f/6f: 0-0 7f-8f: 0-2 9f-13f: 0-0 14f+: 0-0
Track : LH: 0-1 RH: 0-0 Tight: 0-1 Gall: 0-0
Aids: Bl: 0-0 Vi: 0-0 Tstrap: 0-0 Ckp: 0-0
Best Rating: **71** 11/09 Ling 1m stand

Fair; effective over 1m; acts on Polytrack.

Fateful Attraction

(104) (73)**47**

6-y-o b m Mujahid (USA)-Heavens Above (FR) (Pistolet Bleu (IRE))

I A Wood M I Forbes

Placings:00006015/13003405241005/0003040044010/300006056500560-630 **(0669)**

2009: 16^{6}SD, 12^{3}SD, 11^{0}SD,

	Starts	1st	2nd	3rd	Win & Pl
Career Total (Turf)	16	0	0	1	482
Career Total (AW)	37	4	1	4	10526

73	11/07	Kemp	1m2f	(0-60)H	STD	£1706
74	11/06	Kemp	7f	(0-63)H	STD	£2388
68	2/06	Ling	7f	(0-60)H	STD	£2388
60	10/05	Sthl	7f		STD	£1522

Total win prize-money £8007

Going (Turf): **Sf: 0-2 GS: 0-3 Gd: 0-3 GF: 0-7 Fm: 0-1**
Distance: 5f/6f: 0-6 **7f-8f: 3-23** 9f-13f: 1-22 14f+: 0-2
Track : LH: 2-31 RH: 2-14 **Tight: 1-23** Gall: 0-3
Aids: **Bl: 2-32** Vi: 0-1 Tstrap: 0-0 Ckp: 0-0
Best Rating: **74** 11/06 Kemp 7f stand

Plating class sort; stays 1m2f; acts on Fibresand and Polytrack; has worn a tongue tie.

Father Figure (USA)

(88) (47)

3-y-o gr/ro g Mizzen Mast (USA)-Family (USA) (Danzig (USA))

F J Brennan (Heather Dalton 11/10) David Gibbons

Placings:5000 **(6704)**

2009: 8^{5}GS, 10^{0}GS, 10^{0}SD, 13^{0}SS,

	Starts	1st	2nd	3rd	Win & Pl
Career Total (Turf)	2	0	0	0	1165
Career Total (AW)	2	0	0	0	

Going (Turf): **Sf: 0-0 GS: 0-2 Gd: 0-0 GF: 0-0 Fm: 0-0**
Distance: 5f/6f: 0-0 7f-8f: 0-1 9f-13f: 0-3 14f+: 0-0
Track : LH: 0-1 RH: 0-1 Tight: 0-1 Gall: 0-0
Aids: Bl: 0-0 Vi: 0-0 Tstrap: 0-0 Ckp: 0-0
Best Rating: **47** 9/09 Kemp 1m2f stand

Father Time

113(100) (89)**114**

3-y-o b c Dansili-Clepsydra (Sadler's Wells (USA))

H R A Cecil K Abdulla

Placings:1-3321346 **(7281a)**

2009: 10^{3}GS, 11^{3}GF, 10^{2}GF, 12^{1}GF, 12^{3}GF, 14^{4}GF, 14^{6}FT,

	Starts	1st	2nd	3rd	Win & Pl
Career Total (Turf)	6	1	1	3	154355
Career Total (AW)	2	1	0	0	4362

114	6/09	Asct	1m4f	G-F	£92946
89	11/08	GrLe	1m	STD	£4361

Total win prize-money £97309

Going (Turf): Sf: 0-0 GS: 0-1 Gd: 0-0 **GF: 1-5** Fm: 0-0
Distance: 5f/6f: 0-0 7f-8f: 1-1 9f-13f: 1-5 14f+: 0-2
Track : LH: 1-5 RH: 1-1 Tight: 0-1 **Gall: 2-5**
Aids: Bl: 0-0 Vi: 0-0 Tstrap: 0-0 Ckp: 0-0
Best Rating: **114** 9/09 Donc 1m6f132y gd-fm

Group class; winner of the Group 2 King Edward VII at Royal Ascot; stays 1m4f; acts on most ground and on Polytrack.

Fathey (IRE)

102 **73**

3-y-o ch g Fath (USA)-Christoph's Girl (Efisio)

R A Fahey R M Jeffs & J Potter

Placings:100540-55022000465 **(6755)**

2009: 6^{5}GS, 6^{5}GF, 5^{0}GF, 6^{2}GF, 6^{2}G, 6^{0}G, 6^{0}S, 7^{0}S, 7^{4}G, 8^{6}GF, 7^{5}G,

	Starts	1st	2nd	3rd	Win & Pl
Career Total (Turf)	17	1	2	0	5552

70	5/08	Haml	5f4y	G-F	£2590

Total win prize-money £2590

Going (Turf): Sf: 0-3 GS: 0-3 Gd: 0-4 **GF: 1-7** Fm: 0-0
Distance: **5f/6f: 1-9** 7f-8f: 0-8 9f-13f: 0-0 14f+: 0-0
Track : LH: 0-2 RH: 0-4 Tight: 0-1 Gall: 0-1
Aids: Bl: 0-2 Vi: 0-0 Tstrap: 0-0 Ckp: 0-0
Best Rating: **73** 8/08 Hayd 6f gd-sft

Modest; effective over 5f; acts on fast ground; has worn blinkers.

Fathom Five (IRE)

106 **106**

5-y-o b g Fath (USA)-Ambria (ITY) (Final Straw)

C F Wall Hintlesham Thoroughbreds

Placings:1202630/011120/36524600-1060530 **(7015)**
2009: 5^{1}G, 5^{0}G, 5^{6}GF, 5^{0}GF, 5^{5}GS, 5^{3}G, 5^{0}GS,

	Starts	1st	2nd	3rd	Win & Pl
Career Total (Turf)	**28**	**5**	**4**	**3**	**63700**

103	4/09	Epsm	5f	(0-95)H	GD	£9346
101	6/07	NmkJ	5f	(0-100)H	G-S	£12464
96	6/07	Leic	5f2y	(0-95)H	SFT	£9348
90	5/07	NmkR	5f	(0-80)H	GD	£5181
63	5/06	Muss	5f		G-S	£3238

Total win prize-money £39580

Going (Turf): Sf: 1-5 **GS: 2-8 Gd: 2-10** GF: 0-5 Fm: 0-0
Distance: **5f/6f: 5-26** 7f-8f: 0-2 9f-13f: 0-0 14f+: 0-0
Track : LH: 0-2 RH: 0-0 Tight: 0-2 Gall: 0-0
Aids: Bl: 0-0 Vi: 0-0 Tstrap: 0-0 Ckp: 0-0
Best Rating: **106** 8/08 Curr 5f soft

Very useful; placed in Group 3 company; effective over 5f-6f; acts on most ground; likes to race prominently.

Fathsta (IRE)

107(112) (96)**101**
4-y-o b g Fath (USA)-Kilbride Lass (IRE) (Lahib (USA))
D M Simcock (D Nicholls 21/8) Dr Marwan Koukash

Placings:0632163000**611/1522**1522120004663003**2**0-65320**06421** **(7702)**
2009: 6^{6}GF, 7^{5}SD, 7^{3}GF, 7^{2}G, 7^{0}G, 7^{0}GF, 7^{6}SD, 7^{4}SD, 6^{2}SD, 6^{1}SD,

	Starts	1st	2nd	3rd	Win & Pl
Career Total (Turf)	**32**	**2**	**6**	**5**	**50506**
Career Total (AW)	**14**	**5**	**3**	**0**	**26930**

94	12/09	Kemp	6f	(0-85)H	STD	£4727
101	5/08	York	7f	(0-100)H	G-F	£16190
85	4/08	Kemp	6f	(0-85)H	STD	£4209
79	1/08	Wolv	7f32y	(0-85)H	STD	£4533
77	12/07	Ling	6f	(0-85)	STD	£3886
79	12/07	Ling	7f	(0-85)	STD	£4100
73	8/07	Ches	6f18y		G-F	£4857

Total win prize-money £42505

Going (Turf): Sf: 0-4 GS: 0-0 Gd: 0-12 **GF: 2-16** Fm: 0-0
Distance: 5f/6f: 3-14 **7f-8f: 4-32** 9f-13f: 0-0 14f+: 0-0
Track : **LH: 5-20** RH: 2-8 **Tight: 4-19** Gall: 1-2
Aids: Bl: 0-0 Vi: 0-0 Tstrap: 0-0 Ckp: 0-0
Best Rating: **101** 5/08 York 7f gd-fm

Useful; stays 1m but seems best at shorter; acts on most ground on turf; goes on Polytrack; usually held up.

Fathzo (IRE)

84(99) (49)**57**
5-y-o b g Fath (USA)-Super Zoe (Bustino)
Gerard Keane Patrick O Carr

Placings:065-**00544000** **(6800)**
2009: 9^{0}SD, 17^{0}SW, 10^{5}SD, 10^{4}Y, 7^{4}G, 9^{0}GF, 8^{0}SD, 8^{0}SD,

	Starts	1st	2nd	3rd	Win & Pl
Career Total (Turf)	**6**	**0**	**0**	**0**	**557**
Career Total (AW)	**5**	**0**	**0**	**0**	

Going (Turf): **Sf: 0-0 GS: 0-0 Gd: 0-2 GF: 0-1 Fm: 0-0**
Distance: 5f/6f: 0-0 7f-8f: 0-2 9f-13f: 0-8 14f+: 0-1
Track : LH: 0-7 RH: 0-4 Tight: 0-2 Gall: 0-0
Aids: Bl: 0-0 Vi: 0-0 Tstrap: 0-0 Ckp: 0-0
Best Rating: **57** 7/08 Curr 1m2f gd-yld

Fault

101(104) (91)**97**
3-y-o b g Bahamian Bounty-Trundley Wood (Wassl)

Stef Liddiard David Gilbert

Placings:141**00**303-163000**0025061356** **(7432)**
2009: 5^{1}SD, 5^{6}GF, 5^{3}G, 5^{0}G, 6^{0}G, 5^{0}GF, 5^{0}G, 6^{0}SD, 5^{2}F, 5^{5}F, 5^{0}SS, 5^{6}SD, 6^{1}SD, 7^{3}SD, 6^{5}SD, 7^{6}SD,

	Starts	1st	2nd	3rd	Win & Pl
Career Total (Turf)	**15**	**2**	**1**	**3**	**11799**
Career Total (AW)	**9**	**2**	**0**	**1**	**5941**

91	4/09	Kemp	5f	(0-85)H	STD	£5459
82	7/08	Bath	5f11y		GD	£3885
78	5/08	Wind	5f10y		G-S	£2729

Total win prize-money £12075

Going (Turf): Sf: 0-0 **GS: 1-2 Gd: 1-6** GF: 0-5 Fm: 0-2
Distance: **5f/6f: 4-22** 7f-8f: 0-2 9f-13f: 0-0 14f+: 0-0
Track : LH: 1-10 **RH: 2-3** Tight: 0-7 **Gall: 2-6**
Aids: Bl: 0-0 Vi: 0-2 Tstrap: 0-1 Ckp: 0-1
Best Rating: **97** 5/09 York 5f good

Fair; stays 6f; acts on good ground and on Polytrack; has worn a tongue tie.

Favorite Woods

(86) (67)
2-y-o b c Sakhee (USA)-South Club Hill (Danehill (USA))
W J Haggas Lael Stable

Placings:6 **(5643)**
2009: 8^{6}SD,

	Starts	1st	2nd	3rd	Win & Pl
Career Total (Turf)	**0**	**0**	**0**	**0**	
Career Total (AW)	**1**	**0**	**0**	**0**	**0**

Going (Turf): **Sf: 0-0 GS: 0-0 Gd: 0-0 GF: 0-0 Fm: 0-0**
Distance: 5f/6f: 0-0 7f-8f: 0-1 9f-13f: 0-0 14f+: 0-0
Track : LH: 0-1 RH: 0-0 Tight: 0-1 Gall: 0-0
Aids: Bl: 0-0 Vi: 0-0 Tstrap: 0-0 Ckp: 0-0
Best Rating: **67** 9/09 Ling 1m stand

Favouring (IRE)

82(89) (32)**32**
7-y-o ch g Fayruz-Peace Dividend (IRE) (Alzao (USA))
M C Chapman Mrs M Chapman

Placings:4002406/**00430/10051252**5202530**066542/5262334620**040/**0465-00** **(4372)**
2009: 7^{0}GF, 6^{0}SD,

	Starts	1st	2nd	3rd	Win & Pl
Career Total (Turf)	**20**	**0**	**3**	**1**	**5495**
Career Total (AW)	**32**	**2**	**6**	**3**	**8066**

58	3/06	Sthl	7f	(0-45)	STD	£1876
59	1/06	Sthl	6f		STD	£1365

Total win prize-money £3242

Going (Turf): **Sf: 0-5 GS: 0-0 Gd: 0-4 GF: 0-8 Fm: 0-3**
Distance: 5f/6f: 1-26 7f-8f: 1-25 9f-13f: 0-1 14f+: 0-0
Track : **LH: 2-34** RH: 0-4 Tight: 0-5 Gall: 0-0
Aids: Bl: 0-5 **Vi: 2-33** Tstrap: 0-0 Ckp: 0-0
Best Rating: **69** 8/04 Catt 5f212y soft

Moderate; effective over 6f-7f; acts on soft ground; also goes Fibresand.

Favourite Girl (IRE)

104 **103**
3-y-o b f Refuse To Bend (IRE)-Zuccini Wind (IRE) (Revoque (IRE))
T D Easterby Peter C Bourke

Placings:34213012026-06300000500 **(7083)**
2009: 7^{0}S, 6^{6}F, 6^{3}G, 7^{0}GF, 6^{0}G, 6^{0}G, 5^{0}GF, 6^{0}GF, 6^{5}GF, 5^{0}G, 7^{0}S,

	Starts	1st	2nd	3rd	Win & Pl
Career Total (Turf)	**22**	**2**	**3**	**3**	**78157**

82	8/08	Hayd	5f	HVY	£12952
77	6/08	Carl	5f193y	G-F	£2729

Total win prize-money £15682

Going (Turf): **Sf: 1-4** GS: 0-2 Gd: 0-7 **GF: 1-8** Fm: 0-1
Distance: **5f/6f: 2-18** 7f-8f: 0-4 9f-13f: 0-0 14f+: 0-0
Track : LH: 0-2 **RH: 1-1** Tight: 0-1 Gall: 0-0
Aids: Bl: 0-2 Vi: 0-0 Tstrap: 0-0 Ckp: 0-0
Best Rating: **103** 10/08 Rdcr 6f good

Very useful; placed in Listed company; effective over 5f-6f; acts on most ground.

Favours Brave

100(99) (72)**73**
3-y-o b g Galileo (IRE)-Tuning (Rainbow Quest (USA))
Mrs S Lamyman (J H M Gosden 12/6) Mrs J Bowser

Placings:6-4304400 **(6951)**
2009: 9^{4}GF, 12^{3}SD, 14^{0}F, 14^{4}G, 11^{4}SD, 12^{0}SF, 11^{0}SD,

	Starts	1st	2nd	3rd	Win & Pl
Career Total (Turf)	**4**	**0**	**0**	**0**	**481**
Career Total (AW)	**4**	**0**	**0**	**1**	**698**

Going (Turf): **Sf: 0-0 GS: 0-0 Gd: 0-1 GF: 0-2 Fm: 0-1**
Distance: 5f/6f: 0-0 7f-8f: 0-1 9f-13f: 0-5 14f+: 0-2
Track : LH: 0-4 RH: 0-3 Tight: 0-2 Gall: 0-0
Aids: Bl: 0-0 Vi: 0-0 Tstrap: 0-0 Ckp: 0-0
Best Rating: **73** 4/09 Leic 1m1f218y gd-fm

Fair; stays 1m4f; acts on Polytrack.

Fawley Green

92 **72**
2-y-o b g Shamardal (USA)-Wars (IRE) (Green Desert (USA))
W R Muir Rowland-Clark,Mercer,Jeffery,Clarke

Placings:02440 **(6693)**
2009: 6^{0}GF, 5^{2}F, 6^{4}GF, 5^{4}GF, 7^{0}GS,

	Starts	1st	2nd	3rd	Win & Pl
Career Total (Turf)	**5**	**0**	**1**	**0**	**3808**

Going (Turf): **Sf: 0-0 GS: 0-1 Gd: 0-0 GF: 0-3 Fm: 0-1**
Distance: 5f/6f: 0-3 7f-8f: 0-2 9f-13f: 0-0 14f+: 0-0
Track : LH: 0-1 RH: 0-1 Tight: 0-0 Gall: 0-1
Aids: Bl: 0-0 Vi: 0-0 Tstrap: 0-0 Ckp: 0-0
Best Rating: **72** 6/09 Bath 5f161y firm

Fair; suited by 6f and fast ground.

Fayre Bella

50
2-y-o ch f Zafeen (FR)-Hollybell (Beveled (USA))
J Gallagher R Biggs

Placings:0 **(7182)**
2009: 7^{0}G,

	Starts	1st	2nd	3rd	Win & Pl
Career Total (Turf)	**1**	**0**	**0**	**0**	

Going (Turf): **Sf: 0-0 GS: 0-0 Gd: 0-1 GF: 0-0 Fm: 0-0**
Distance: 5f/6f: 0-0 7f-8f: 0-1 9f-13f: 0-0 14f+: 0-0
Track : LH: 0-0 RH: 0-0 Tight: 0-0 Gall: 0-0
Aids: Bl: 0-0 Vi: 0-0 Tstrap: 0-0 Ckp: 0-0

Fazbee (IRE)

100(101) (86)**85**

3-y-o b f Fasliyev (USA)-Kelpie (IRE) (Kahyasi)

P W D'Arcy Tony Burlton

Placings:2541013-644545026046 **(7739)**

2009: 7^{6}GF, 7^{4}G, 10^{4}GF, 12^{5}SD, 10^{4}GF, 11^{5}SD, 7^{0}GF, 8^{2}GF, 8^{6}GF, 8^{0}SD, 6^{4}SD, 6^{6}SD,

	Starts	1st	2nd	3rd	Win & Pl
Career Total (Turf)	12	1	2	0	7847
Career Total (AW)	7	1	0	1	3973

86 8/08 GrLe 6f STD £2914

75 7/08 Yarm 7f3y G-F £2137

Total win prize-money £5051

Going (Turf): Sf: 0-1 GS: 0-1 Gd: 0-1 **GF: 1-9** Fm: 0-0
Distance: 5f/6f: 1-7 7f-8f: 1-6 9f-13f: 0-6 14f+: 0-0
Track : **LH: 1-6** RH: 0-5 Tight: 0-3 **Gall: 1-4**
Aids: Bl: 0-0 Vi: 0-2 Tstrap: 0-2 Ckp: 0-2
Best Rating: **86** 8/08 GrLe 6f stand

Useful; effective over 5f-7f; acts on most ground; also goes on Polytrack.

Fazza

82(101) (70)**72**

2-y-o ch g Sulamani (IRE)-Markievicz (IRE) (Doyoun)

D W P Arbuthnot Nursery End Syndicate

Placings:025021 **(7886)**

2009: 5^{0}GF, 6^{2}GF, 5^{5}SS, 6^{0}GF, 7^{2}SD, 7^{1}SD,

	Starts	1st	2nd	3rd	Win & Pl
Career Total (Turf)	3	0	1	0	1156
Career Total (AW)	3	1	1	0	2409

12/09 Ling 7f STD £1637

Total win prize-money £1638

Going (Turf): **Sf: 0-0 GS: 0-0 Gd: 0-0 GF: 0-3 Fm: 0-0**
Distance: 5f/6f: 0-3 **7f-8f: 1-3** 9f-13f: 0-0 14f+: 0-0
Track : **LH: 1-3** RH: 0-1 **Tight: 1-2** Gall: 0-0
Aids: Bl: 0-0 Vi: 0-0 Tstrap: 0-0 Ckp: 0-0
Best Rating: **72** 9/09 Nott 6f15y gd-fm

Modest; effective over 6f-7f; acts on fast ground; goes on Polytrack.

Fear Nothing

90(81) (41)**71**

2-y-o ch c Exceed And Excel (AUS)-Galatrix (Be My Guest (USA))

E S McMahon J C Fretwell

Placings:635 **(6556)**

2009: 5^{6}SD, 5^{3}GF, 5^{5}G,

	Starts	1st	2nd	3rd	Win & Pl
Career Total (Turf)	2	0	0	1	578
Career Total (AW)	1	0	0	0	0

Going (Turf): **Sf: 0-0 GS: 0-0 Gd: 0-1 GF: 0-1 Fm: 0-0**
Distance: 5f/6f: 0-3 7f-8f: 0-0 9f-13f: 0-0 14f+: 0-0
Track : LH: 0-1 RH: 0-0 Tight: 0-1 Gall: 0-0
Aids: Bl: 0-0 Vi: 0-0 Tstrap: 0-0 Ckp: 0-0
Best Rating: **71** 9/09 Hayd 5f gd-fm

Promise on second start over 5f on fast.

Feasible

101(99) (67)**69**

4-y-o ch g Efisio-Zoena (Emarati (USA))

J G Portman Berkeley Racing

Placings:4552/6036002300-0422200 **(5905)**

2009: 10^{0}GF, 8^{4}GF, 8^{2}SD, 8^{2}SD, 8^{2}SD, 8^{0}G, 8^{0}F,

	Starts	1st	2nd	3rd	Win & Pl
Career Total (Turf)	12	0	1	1	1812
Career Total (AW)	9	0	4	1	2720

Going (Turf): **Sf: 0-1 GS: 0-2 Gd: 0-3 GF: 0-4 Fm: 0-2**
Distance: 5f/6f: 0-1 7f-8f: 0-11 9f-13f: 0-9 14f+: 0-0
Track : LH: 0-7 RH: 0-12 Tight: 0-12 Gall: 0-0
Aids: Bl: 0-4 Vi: 0-0 Tstrap: 0-0 Ckp: 0-0
Best Rating: **69** 5/08 Wind 1m67y gd-fm

Modest; effective over 1m; acts on fast gound.

Feathered Crown (FR)

100(84) (55)**80**

3-y-o ch c Indian Ridge-Attractive Crown (USA) (Chief's Crown (USA))

H R A Cecil (R Simpson 22/2) H E Sheikh Sultan Bin Khalifa Al Nahyan

Placings:6215 **(6875)**

2009: 8^{6}FT, 10^{2}GF, 10^{1}GF, 14^{5}SD,

	Starts	1st	2nd	3rd	Win & Pl
Career Total (Turf)	2	1	1	0	4849
Career Total (AW)	2	0	0	0	0

80 10/09 Epsm 1m2f18y G-F £3885

Total win prize-money £3886

Going (Turf): Sf: 0-0 GS: 0-0 Gd: 0-0 **GF: 1-2** Fm: 0-0
Distance: 5f/6f: 0-0 7f-8f: 0-1 **9f-13f: 1-2** 14f+: 0-1
Track : **LH: 1-3** RH: 0-0 **Tight: 1-1** Gall: 0-0
Aids: Bl: 0-0 Vi: 0-0 Tstrap: 0-0 Ckp: 0-0
Best Rating: **80** 10/09 Epsm 1m2f18y gd-fm

Modest; stays 1m2f; acts on fast ground.

Featherweight (IRE)

105(94) (73)**85**

3-y-o ch f Fantastic Light (USA)-Dancing Feather (Suave Dancer (USA))

B W Hills Jeremy Gompertz & Patrick Milmo

Placings:3353-1603142 **(7148)**

2009: 10^{1}GF, 9^{6}GF, 10^{0}S, 10^{3}GF, 9^{1}GF, 9^{4}S, 12^{2}G,

	Starts	1st	2nd	3rd	Win & Pl
Career Total (Turf)	9	2	1	2	12250
Career Total (AW)	2	0	0	2	1059

85 9/09 Gdwd 1m1f192y (0-85)H G-F £5180

77 5/09 Wind 1m2f7y G-F £2729

Total win prize-money £7911

Going (Turf): Sf: 0-2 GS: 0-1 Gd: 0-1 **GF: 2-5** Fm: 0-0
Distance: 5f/6f: 0-0 7f-8f: 0-3 **9f-13f: 2-8** 14f+: 0-0
Track : LH: 0-3 **RH: 2-7 Tight: 2-7** Gall: 0-2
Aids: Bl: 0-0 Vi: 0-0 Tstrap: 0-0 Ckp: 0-0
Best Rating: **85** 10/09 NmkR 1m4f good

Fair; stays 1m2f; acts on fast ground; goes on Polytrack.

Federal Reserve

57(43)

2-y-o ch g Central Park (IRE)-Attlongglast (Groom Dancer (USA))

M Madgwick The Bell Boys Krew

Placings:00 **(5119)**

2009: 7^{0}SD, 6^{0}F,

	Starts	1st	2nd	3rd	Win & Pl
Career Total (Turf)	1	0	0	0	
Career Total (AW)	1	0	0	0	

Going (Turf): **Sf: 0-0 GS: 0-0 Gd: 0-0 GF: 0-0 Fm: 0-1**
Distance: 5f/6f: 0-0 7f-8f: 0-2 9f-13f: 0-0 14f+: 0-0
Track : LH: 0-1 RH: 0-1 Tight: 0-0 Gall: 0-0
Aids: Bl: 0-0 Vi: 0-0 Tstrap: 0-0 Ckp: 0-0

Feel The Magic (IRE)

(89) (48)

2-y-o b f Cadeaux Genereux-Triple Green (Green Desert (USA))

S Kirk I A N Wight

Placings:00066500 **(7884)**

2009: 5^{0}SD, 8^{0}SD, 7^{0}SD, 7^{6}SD, 8^{6}SD, 5^{5}SD, 6^{0}SD, 7^{0}SD,

	Starts	1st	2nd	3rd	Win & Pl
Career Total (Turf)	0	0	0	0	
Career Total (AW)	8	0	0	0	0

Going (Turf): **Sf: 0-0 GS: 0-0 Gd: 0-0 GF: 0-0 Fm: 0-0**
Distance: 5f/6f: 0-3 7f-8f: 0-4 9f-13f: 0-1 14f+: 0-0
Track : LH: 0-5 RH: 0-3 Tight: 0-4 Gall: 0-0
Aids: Bl: 0-0 Vi: 0-0 Tstrap: 0-0 Ckp: 0-0
Best Rating: **48** 10/09 Kemp 7f stand

Feelin Foxy

106(105) (87)**85**

5-y-o b m Foxhound (USA)-Charlie Girl (Puissance)

J G Given Danethorpe Racing Partnership

Placings:2363036**43321**/0034336160240152/1330005032 0400-502431212203**226146** **(7511)**

2009: 5^{5}F, 5^{0}GF, 5^{2}GF, 5^{4}GS, 5^{3}GF, 5^{1}GF, 5^{2}G, 5^{1}S, 5^{2}S, 5^{2}GS, 6^{0}G, 5^{3}GS, 5^{2}GF, 5^{2}SD, 5^{6}SD, 5^{1}SD, 5^{4}SD, 5^{6}SD,

	Starts	1st	2nd	3rd	Win & Pl
Career Total (Turf)	46	4	8	10	34811
Career Total (AW)	14	3	3	3	15803

87 10/09 Wolv 5f20y (0-80)H STD £5046

85 7/09 Donc 5f (0-75)H SFT £3238

77 6/09 Ling 5f (0-70)H G-F £3070

81 3/08 Rdcr 5f (0-70)H G-S £2331

73 9/07 Haml 6f5y (0-75)H GD £4533

70 6/07 Wolv 5f20y (0-70)H STD £3071

62 12/06 Kemp 5f STD £2388

Total win prize-money £23681

Going (Turf): **Sf: 1-8 GS: 1-9 Gd: 1-13 GF: 1-14** Fm: 0-2
Distance: **5f/6f: 6-56** 7f-8f: 1-4 9f-13f: 0-0 14f+: 0-0
Track : **LH: 2-17** RH: 1-3 **Tight: 2-12** Gall: 0-4
Aids: Bl: 0-0 **Vi: 2-17** Tstrap: 0-0 Ckp: 0-0
Best Rating: **87** 10/09 Wolv 5f20y stand

Fair; effective over 5f-6f; acts on a most ground and on Polytrack; has worn a visor.

Feeling (IRE)

(95) (46)**45**

5-y-o b g Sadler's Wells (USA)-La Pitie (USA) (Devil's Bag (USA))

D Burchell Heath House Racing

Placings:P0534000/00000-44 **(7719)**

2009: 10^{4}G, 9^{4}SD,

	Starts	1st	2nd	3rd	Win & Pl
Career Total (Turf)	13	0	0	1	748
Career Total (AW)	2	0	0	0	0

Going (Turf): **Sf: 0-2 GS: 0-0 Gd: 0-5 GF: 0-4 Fm: 0-2**

Distance: 5f/6f: 0-0 7f-8f: 0-1 9f-13f: 0-13 14f+: 0-1
Track : LH: 0-11 RH: 0-3 Tight: 0-5 Gall: 0-4
Aids: Bl: 0-2 Vi: 0-1 Tstrap: 0-0 Ckp: 0-0
Best Rating: 75 5/07 Hayd 1m3f200y gd-fm

Fair; effective over 1m4f; acts on good ground.

Feeling Fab (FR)

103(101) (87)91
3-y-o b f Refuse To Bend (IRE)-Les Planches (Tropular)
M Johnston A D Spence

Placings:23141-440303451 **(6311)**
2009: 8^{4}G, 8^{4}GF, 7^{0}GF, 8^{3}GF, 7^{0}GF, 7^{3}SD, 7^{4}GF, 7^{5}SD, 8^{1}GF,

	Starts	1st	2nd	3rd	Win & Pl
Career Total (Turf)	11	2	1	2	37648
Career Total (AW)	3	1	0	1	5546

87 9/09 Muss 1m (0-90)H G-F £10592
91 10/08 NmkR 7f G-F £18693
84 9/08 Ling 7f STD £3885
Total win prize-money £33172

Going (Turf): Sf: 0-0 GS: 0-0 Gd: 0-2 **GF: 2-9** Fm: 0-0
Distance: 5f/6f: 0-0 **7f-8f: 3-12** 9f-13f: 0-2 14f+: 0-0
Track : LH: 1-5 RH: 1-5 **Tight: 2-6** Gall: 0-1
Aids: Bl: 0-0 Vi: 0-0 Tstrap: 0-0 Ckp: 0-0
Best Rating: 91 10/08 NmkR 7f gd-fm

Useful; effective over 7f-1m; acts on fast ground; goes on Polytrack; can pull hard.

Feeling Fragile (IRE)

83(95) (72)53
2-y-o b g Fasliyev (USA)-Boutique (Selkirk (USA))
Pat Eddery Mrs Millicent Mathews

Placings:0462 **(7700)**
2009: 5^{0}G, 7^{4}SD, 7^{6}SD, 7^{2}SD,

	Starts	1st	2nd	3rd	Win & Pl
Career Total (Turf)	1	0	0	0	
Career Total (AW)	3	0	1	0	867

Going (Turf): Sf: 0-0 GS: 0-0 Gd: 0-1 GF: 0-0 Fm: 0-0
Distance: 5f/6f: 0-1 7f-8f: 0-3 9f-13f: 0-0 14f+: 0-0
Track : LH: 0-3 RH: 0-1 Tight: 0-2 Gall: 0-1
Aids: Bl: 0-0 Vi: 0-0 Tstrap: 0-0 Ckp: 0-0
Best Rating: 72 12/09 Kemp 7f stand

Fair; stays 7f; acts on Polytrack; can be keen.

Feeling Fresh (IRE)

97(100) (66)71
4-y-o b c Xaar-Oh'Cecilia (IRE) (Scenic)
Paul Green Paul Green (Oaklea)

Placings:000005414/40140404360-3133 **(4772)**
2009: 5^{3}G, 6^{1}GF, 8^{3}HY, 6^{3}GF,

	Starts	1st	2nd	3rd	Win & Pl
Career Total (Turf)	14	2	0	3	9500
Career Total (AW)	10	1	0	1	3508

64 7/09 Haml 6f5y (0-60)H G-F £2388
71 8/08 Hayd 6f (0-80)H G-S £5504
66 12/07 Wolv 5f216y (0-65) STD £2730
Total win prize-money £10623

Going (Turf): Sf: 0-3 **GS: 1-4** Gd: 0-3 **GF: 1-4** Fm: 0-0
Distance: 5f/6f: 2-15 7f-8f: 1-6 9f-13f: 0 3 14f+: 0-0
Track : LH: 1-15 RH: 0-0 **Tight: 1-10** Gall: 0-0
Aids: Bl: 0-0 Vi: 0-2 Tstrap: 0-0 Ckp: 0-0

Best Rating: 71 9/08 Rdcr 6f gd-sft

Moderate; effective over 6f; acts on fast and easy ground; also goes on Polytrack.

Feeling Peckish (USA)

93(88) (43)42
5-y-o ch g Point Given (USA)-Sunday Bazaar (USA) (Nureyev (USA))
M C Chapman J E Reed

Placings:00060000/025004-640 **(4848)**
2009: 14^{6}GF, 16^{4}GF, 16^{0}G,

	Starts	1st	2nd	3rd	Win & Pl
Career Total (Turf)	12	0	0	0	265
Career Total (AW)	5	0	1	0	564

Going (Turf): Sf: 0-1 GS: 0-1 Gd: 0-5 GF: 0-5 Fm: 0-0
Distance: 5f/6f: 0-0 7f-8f: 0-2 9f-13f: 0-9 14f+: 0-6
Track : LH: 0-14 RH: 0-2 Tight: 0-9 Gall: 0-1
Aids: Bl: 0-0 Vi: 0-0 Tstrap: 0-0 Ckp: 0-0
Best Rating: 43 1/08 Sthl 1m4f stand

Banded class; stays 2m and acts on Fibresand.

Feeling Stylish (IRE)

94(85) (34)48
3-y-o b f Desert Style (IRE)-No Hard Feelings (IRE) (Alzao (USA))
N Tinkler Darling,Dingwall,Lydall,Perkins,Spence

Placings:0460-0040566 **(4812)**
2009: 6^{0}GF, 7^{0}GF, 6^{4}SD, 7^{0}SD, 10^{5}G, 9^{6}G, 7^{6}HY,

	Starts	1st	2nd	3rd	Win & Pl
Career Total (Turf)	9	0	0	0	241
Career Total (AW)	2	0	0	0	0

Going (Turf): Sf: 0-1 GS: 0-2 Gd: 0-3 GF: 0-3 Fm: 0-0
Distance: 5f/6f: 0-3 7f-8f: 0-6 9f-13f: 0-2 14f+: 0-0
Track : LH: 0-4 RH: 0-2 Tight: 0-2 Gall: 0-1
Aids: Bl: 0-0 Vi: 0-0 Tstrap: 0-0 Ckp: 0-0
Best Rating: 48 8/08 Nott 6f15y good

Feet Of Fury

94(93) (56)62
3-y-o b f Deportivo-Fury Dance (USA) (Cryptoclearance (USA))
W M Brisbourne Stratford Bards Racing No 2

Placings:64-40604504 **(6497)**
2009: 7^{4}GF, 7^{0}SD, 7^{6}F, 6^{0}GF, 5^{4}G, 7^{5}GF, 8^{0}GS, 9^{4}SF,

	Starts	1st	2nd	3rd	Win & Pl
Career Total (Turf)	7	0	0	0	673
Career Total (AW)	3	0	0	0	202

Going (Turf): Sf: 0-0 GS: 0-2 Gd: 0-1 GF: 0-3 Fm: 0-1
Distance: 5f/6f: 0-1 7f-8f: 0-7 9f-13f: 0-2 14f+: 0-0
Track : LH: 0-5 RH: 0-0 Tight: 0-4 Gall: 0-0
Aids: Bl: 0-0 Vi: 0-0 Tstrap: 0-0 Ckp: 0-0
Best Rating: 62 3/09 Donc 7f gd-fm

Feisty's Brother

75 28
2-y-o b c Dubawi (IRE)-Hawait Al Barr (Green Desert (USA))
D M Simcock S R Hope

Placings:06 **(3119)**
2009: 6^{0}G, 7^{6}GF,

	Starts	1st	2nd	3rd	Win & Pl
Career Total (Turf)	2	0	0	0	0

Going (Turf): Sf: 0-0 GS: 0-0 Gd: 0-1 GF: 0-1 Fm: 0-0
Distance: 5f/6f: 0-0 7f-8f: 0-2 9f-13f: 0-0 14f+: 0-0
Track : LH: 0-0 RH: 0-0 Tight: 0-0 Gall: 0-0
Aids: Bl: 0-0 Vi: 0-0 Tstrap: 0-0 Ckp: 0-0
Best Rating: 28 6/09 Rdcr 7f gd-fm

Felday

107(107) (97)97
3-y-o b g Bahamian Bounty-Monaiya (Shareef Dancer (USA))
H Morrison Exors Of The Late Mrs R C A Hammond

Placings:0106-40401031 **(7639)**
2009: 7^{4}GS, 6^{0}GF, 6^{4}G, 6^{0}G, 7^{1}G, 7^{0}G, 7^{3}S, 6^{1}SD,

	Starts	1st	2nd	3rd	Win & Pl
Career Total (Turf)	11	2	0	1	16624
Career Total (AW)	1	1	0	0	11354

97 12/09 Sthl 6f (0-100)H STD £11354
97 10/09 York 7f (0-85)H GD £7641
82 8/08 Newb 7f G-S £4209
Total win prize-money £23205

Going (Turf): Sf: 0-1 **GS: 1-2 Gd: 1-6** GF: 0-2 Fm: 0-0
Distance: 5f/6f: 1-4 **7f-8f: 2-8** 9f-13f: 0-0 14f+: 0-0
Track : LH: 2-3 RH: 0-0 Tight: 0-0 **Gall: 1-2**
Aids: Bl: 0-0 Vi: 0-0 Tstrap: 0-0 Ckp: 0-0
Best Rating: 97 12/09 Sthl 6f stand

Very useful; effective over 6f-7f; acts on good and easier ground and on Fibresand.

Felicia

82(97) (56)43
4-y-o b f Diktat-Gracia (Linamix (FR))
J E Long Martin J Gibbs

Placings:00/4044064-00430002 **(7660)**
2009: 10^{0}SD, 9^{0}GF, 10^{4}SD, 12^{3}SD, 12^{0}SD, 12^{0}SD, 12^{0}SD, 10^{2}SD,

	Starts	1st	2nd	3rd	Win & Pl
Career Total (Turf)	3	0	0	0	
Career Total (AW)	14	0	1	1	1123

Going (Turf): Sf: 0-0 GS: 0-1 Gd: 0-1 GF: 0-1 Fm: 0-0
Distance: 5f/6f: 0-3 7f-8f: 0-2 9f-13f: 0-12 14f+: 0-0
Track : LH: 0-11 RH: 0-4 Tight: 0-8 Gall: 0-2
Aids: Bl: 0-0 Vi: 0-0 Tstrap: 0-0 Ckp: 0-0
Best Rating: 58 12/07 Ling 6f stand

Very moderate; suited by 1m2f and Polytrack.

Fell Pack

96 63
5-y-o b g Lake Coniston (IRE)-All On (Dunbeath (USA))
J J Quinn N Hetherton

Placings:400-5415504054 **(6102)**
2009: 9^{5}GF, 12^{4}GF, 10^{1}GS, 12^{5}GF, 10^{5}G, 11^{0}S, 10^{4}G, 12^{0}G, 15^{5}GS, 13^{4}GF,

	Starts	1st	2nd	3rd	Win & Pl
Career Total (Turf)	13	1	0	0	2903

63 5/09 Newc 1m2f32y (0-65)H G-S £2331
Total win prize-money £2331

Going (Turf): Sf: 0-1 **GS: 1-3** Gd: 0-4 GF: 0-5 Fm: 0-0
Distance: 5f/6f: 0-0 7f-8f: 0-2 **9f-13f: 1-9** 14f+: 0-2
Track : **LH: 1-7** RH: 0-6 Tight: 0-9 **Gall: 1-2**
Aids: Bl: 0-0 Vi: 0-0 Tstrap: 0-2 Ckp: 0-2
Best Rating: **63** 5/09 Newc 1m2f32y gd-sft

Moderate; stays 1m4f; acts on fast and easy ground; has worn cheekpieces.

Felsham

101(94) (68)**76**
2-y-o br c Kyllachy-Border Minstral (IRE) (Sri Pekan (USA))
H Candy Six Too Many

Placings:3123 **(7290)**
2009: 5^{3}G, 5^{1}SD, 5^{2}G, 6^{3}S,

	Starts	1st	2nd	3rd	Win & Pl
Career Total (Turf)	**3**	**0**	**1**	**2**	**2986**
Career Total (AW)	**1**	**1**	**0**	**0**	**2590**
68 9/09 Kemp 5f			STD	£2590	

Total win prize-money £2590

Going (Turf): **Sf: 0-1 GS: 0-0 Gd: 0-2 GF: 0-0 Fm: 0-0**
Distance: **5f/6f: 1-4** 7f-8f: 0-0 9f-13f: 0-0 14f+: 0-0
Track : LH: 0-0 **RH: 1-1** Tight: 0-0 Gall: 0-1
Aids: Bl: 0-0 Vi: 0-0 Tstrap: 0-0 Ckp: 0-0
Best Rating: **76** 11/09 Donc 6f soft

Fair; effective at 5f; acts on good and soft ground and Polytrack.

Femme De Fer

99(103) (75)**71**
3-y-o b f Hamas (IRE)-Ajeebah (IRE) (Mujtahid (USA))
C G Cox Ms Liza Judd

Placings:2352330 **(7807)**
2009: 6^{2}GF, 6^{3}G, 5^{5}G, 5^{2}SD, 5^{3}SD, 5^{3}SD, 5^{0}SD,

	Starts	1st	2nd	3rd	Win & Pl
Career Total (Turf)	**3**	**0**	**1**	**1**	**1590**
Career Total (AW)	**4**	**0**	**1**	**2**	**1704**

Going (Turf): **Sf: 0-0 GS: 0-0 Gd: 0-2 GF: 0-1 Fm: 0-0**
Distance: 5f/6f: 0-6 7f-8f: 0-1 9f-13f: 0-0 14f+: 0-0
Track : LH: 0-5 RH: 0-1 Tight: 0-3 Gall: 0-1
Aids: Bl: 0-0 Vi: 0-0 Tstrap: 0-0 Ckp: 0-0
Best Rating: **75** 11/09 Ling 5f stand

Modest; effective over 5f-6f; acts on fast ground and on Polytrack.

Fen Spirit (IRE)

(101) (78)**75**
3-y-o b f Invincible Spirit (IRE)-Irinatinvidio (Rudimentary (USA))
J H M Gosden C J Murfitt

Placings:44321-050 **(7832)**
2009: 7^{0}SD, 6^{5}SD, 6^{0}SD,

	Starts	1st	2nd	3rd	Win & Pl
Career Total (Turf)	**2**	**0**	**0**	**1**	**1140**
Career Total (AW)	**6**	**1**	**1**	**0**	**4886**
78 11/08 GrLe 6f			STD	£3561	

Total win prize-money £3562

Going (Turf): **Sf: 0-1 GS: 0-0 Gd: 0-1 GF: 0-0 Fm: 0-0**
Distance: **5f/6f: 1-4** 7f-8f: 0-4 9f-13f: 0-0 14f+: 0-0
Track : **LH: 1-2** RH: 0-4 Tight: 0-1 **Gall: 1-1**
Aids: Bl: 0-0 Vi: 0-0 Tstrap: 0-0 Ckp: 0-0
Best Rating: **78** 11/08 GrLe 6f stand

Fair; effective over 6f; acts on soft ground; goes on Polytrack.

Fencing Master

111 (86)**117**
2-y-o b c Oratorio (IRE)-Moonlight Dance (USA) (Alysheba (USA))
A P O'Brien D Smith, Mrs J Magnier, M Tabor

Placings:12 **(6849)**
2009: 7^{1}SD, 7^{2}G,

	Starts	1st	2nd	3rd	Win & Pl
Career Total (Turf)	**1**	**0**	**1**	**0**	**68294**
Career Total (AW)	**1**	**1**	**0**	**0**	**9057**
86 9/09 Dund 7f			STD	£9056	

Total win prize-money £9057

Going (Turf): **Sf: 0-0 GS: 0-0 Gd: 0-1 GF: 0-0 Fm: 0-0**
Distance: 5f/6f: 0-0 **7f-8f: 1-2** 9f-13f: 0-0 14f+: 0-0
Track : **LH: 1-1** RH: 0-0 Tight: 0-0 Gall: 0-0
Aids: Bl: 0-0 Vi: 0-0 Tstrap: 0-0 Ckp: 0-0
Best Rating: **117** 10/09 NmkR 7f good

High-class; 400,000 half-brother to winners; effective at 7f; handles Polytrack and good ground; runner-up to stablemate Beetohoven in the Dewhurst Stakes.

Fenella Rose

91 **73**
2-y-o b f Compton Place-Xtrasensory (Royal Applause)
S C Williams Tweenhills Racing XV

Placings:20310 **(6677)**
2009: 5^{2}GF, 5^{0}GF, 5^{3}GF, 6^{1}GF, 6^{0}G,

	Starts	1st	2nd	3rd	Win & Pl
Career Total (Turf)	**5**	**1**	**1**	**1**	**4462**
73 9/09 Epsm 6f			G-F	£3238	

Total win prize-money £3238

Going (Turf): Sf: 0-0 GS: 0-0 Gd: 0-1 **GF: 1-4** Fm: 0-0
Distance: **5f/6f: 1-5** 7f-8f: 0-0 9f-13f: 0-0 14f+: 0-0
Track : **LH: 1-2** RH: 0-0 **Tight: 1-1** Gall: 0-0
Aids: Bl: 0-0 **Vi: 1-2** Tstrap: 0-0 Ckp: 0-0
Best Rating: **73** 9/09 Epsm 6f gd-fm

Fair; stays 6f; acts on fast ground; has worn a visor.

Fenners (USA)

101(102) (66)**66**
6-y-o ch g Pleasant Tap (USA)-Legal Opinion (IRE) (Polish Precedent (USA))
M W Easterby K Wreglesworth

Placings:361/63500/13060353**231**/**2506515500000**40-42255433400 **(6558)**
2009: 12^{4}SD, 13^{2}GF, 12^{2}G, 13^{5}G, 12^{5}G, 12^{4}G, 15^{3}GS, 14^{3}GF, 13^{4}GF, 13^{0}SD, 15^{0}G,

	Starts	1st	2nd	3rd	Win & Pl
Career Total (Turf)	**30**	**2**	**2**	**7**	**10970**
Career Total (AW)	**15**	**2**	**2**	**1**	**6963**
66 6/08 Wolv 1m4f50y (0-70)H			STD	£3238	
62 12/07 Wolv 1m4f50y (0-60)H			STD	£2047	
69 5/07 Newc 1m4f93y (0-60)H			GD	£2914	
73 10/05 Rdcr 1m			G-F	£2922	

Total win prize-money £11124

Going (Turf): Sf: 0-4 GS: 0-3 **Gd: 1-9 GF: 1-12** Fm: 0-2
Distance: 5f/6f: 0-1 7f-8f: 1-2 **9f-13f: 3-31** 14f+: 0-11
Track : **LH: 3-27** RH: 0-16 **Tight: 2-30** Gall: 1-5
Aids: Bl: 0-2 Vi: 0-2 Tstrap: 0-3 Ckp: 0-3
Best Rating: **73** 10/05 Rdcr 1m gd-fm

Moderate; stays 1m4f; acts on a sound surface; also goes on Polytrack.

Fern House (IRE)

93(87) (54)**54**
7-y-o b g Xaar-Certain Impression (USA) (Forli (ARG))
Bruce Hellier J W Barrett

Placings:0/O00/**5526**/00510000**543**/**00**0025060-00005400304000 **(7086)**
2009: 5^{0}SD, 9^{0}GF, 7^{0}GF, 5^{0}GF, 7^{5}GF, 8^{4}GF, 7^{0}GS, 6^{0}G, 5^{3}GF, 5^{0}G, 5^{4}G, 5^{0}GF, 5^{0}GF, 5^{0}S,

	Starts	1st	2nd	3rd	Win & Pl
Career Total (Turf)	**34**	**1**	**2**	**1**	**5408**
Career Total (AW)	**8**	**0**	**0**	**1**	**302**
59 8/07 Catt 5f (0-60)H			FRM	£2730	

Total win prize-money £2730

Going (Turf): Sf: 0-3 GS: 0-5 Gd: 0-13 GF: 0-12 **Fm: 1-1**
Distance: **5f/6f: 1-29** 7f-8f: 0-10 9f-13f: 0-3 14f+: 0-0
Track : LH: 0-11 RH: 0-12 Tight: 0-9 Gall: 0-3
Aids: Bl: 0-4 Vi: 0-2 Tstrap: 0-2 Ckp: 0-2
Best Rating: **59** 8/07 Catt 5f firm

Very moderate; stays 7f and acts on easy ground.

Fernando Torres

93(104) (72)**68**
3-y-o b g Giant's Causeway (USA)-Alstemeria (IRE) (Danehill (USA))
Matthew Salaman (D Nicholls 5/9) Mrs C C Regalado-Gonzalez

Placings:504601332 **(7876)**
2009: 8^{5}GS, 8^{0}G, 8^{4}GF, 8^{6}GF, 8^{0}S, 7^{1}SD, 8^{3}SD, 8^{3}SD, 7^{2}SD,

	Starts	1st	2nd	3rd	Win & Pl
Career Total (Turf)	**5**	**0**	**0**	**0**	**192**
Career Total (AW)	**4**	**1**	**1**	**2**	**3998**
72 11/09 Kemp 7f (0-70)H			STD	£2590	

Total win prize-money £2590

Going (Turf): **Sf: 0-1 GS: 0-1 Gd: 0-1 GF: 0-2 Fm: 0-0**
Distance: 5f/6f: 0-0 **7f-8f: 1-7** 9f-13f: 0-2 14f+: 0-0
Track : LH: 0-3 **RH: 1-6** Tight: 0-3 Gall: 0-1
Aids: Bl: 0-0 Vi: 0-0 Tstrap: 0-1 Ckp: 0-1
Best Rating: **72** 12/09 Kemp 1m stand

Modest; effective at 7f-1m; best on Polytrack.

Ferris Wheel (IRE)

90(94) (78)**71**
2-y-o b f One Cool Cat (USA)-Saffron Crocus (Shareef Dancer (USA))
P F I Cole Fisher,Goldswain,Hunter,Manley,Maynard

Placings:410 **(6055)**
2009: 6^{4}G, 6^{1}SD, 7^{0}GF,

	Starts	1st	2nd	3rd	Win & Pl
Career Total (Turf)	**2**	**0**	**0**	**0**	**241**
Career Total (AW)	**1**	**1**	**0**	**0**	**5181**
78 9/09 Kemp 6f			STD	£5180	

Total win prize-money £5181

Going (Turf): **Sf: 0-0 GS: 0-0 Gd: 0-1 GF: 0-1 Fm: 0-0**
Distance: **5f/6f: 1-2** 7f-8f: 0-1 9f-13f: 0-0 14f+: 0-0
Track : LH: 0-0 **RH: 1-1** Tight: 0-0 Gall: 0-0
Aids: Bl: 0-0 Vi: 0-0 Tstrap: 0-0 Ckp: 0-0
Best Rating: **78** 9/09 Kemp 6f stand

Fair; effective over 6f; acts on Polytrack.

Fesko

103(104) (87)85

3-y-o b f Shinko Forest (IRE)-Young Sue (Local Suitor (USA))

M Johnston C H Greensit & W A Greensit

Placings:4316-13204013000501302 (6879)

2009: 6^{1}SD, 7^{3}SD, 6^{2}SD, 7^{0}GF, 8^{4}G, 8^{0}GF, 8^{1}GF, 8^{3}G, 8^{0}GF, 8^{0}S, 8^{0}GS, 8^{5}GS, 7^{0}G, 5^{1}GF, 6^{3}G, 6^{0}GF, 6^{2}SD,

	Starts	1st	2nd	3rd	Win & Pl
Career Total (Turf)	16	3	0	3	21151
Career Total (AW)	5	1	2	1	8624

85	9/09	Leic	5f218y	(0-85)H	G-F	£5180
82	6/09	Thsk	1m	(0-90)H	G-F	£10102
87	2/09	Sthl	6f	(0-85)H	STD	£4857
79	10/08	Catt	5f		GD	£2266

Total win prize-money £22408

Going (Turf): Sf: 0-1 GS: 0-3 Gd: 1-5 **GF: 2-7** Fm: 0-0
Distance: **5f/6f: 3-9** 7f-8f: 1-10 9f-13f: 0-2 14f+: 0-0
Track : **LH: 2-15** RH: 0-2 **Tight: 1-9** Gall: 0-1
Aids: Bl: 0-0 Vi: 0-0 Tstrap: 0-0 Ckp: 0-0
Best Rating: **87** 10/09 Sthl 6f stand

Fair; effective over 6f-1m; acts on good ground and fast ground; goes on Fibresand and Polytrack.

Festival Dreams

(101) (51)54

4-y-o ch g Largesse-Bright Spangle (IRE) (General Monash (USA))

Miss J S Davis The Three B's

Placings:005/00-5 (0116)

2009: 11^{5}SD,

	Starts	1st	2nd	3rd	Win & Pl
Career Total (Turf)	2	0	0	0	
Career Total (AW)	4	0	0	0	0

Going (Turf): **Sf: 0-0 GS: 0-0 Gd: 0-0 GF: 0-2 Fm: 0-0**
Distance: 5f/6f: 0-0 7f-8f: 0-1 9f-13f: 0-4 14f+: 0-1
Track : LH: 0-3 RH: 0-2 Tight: 0-3 Gall: 0-0
Aids: Bl: 0-0 Vi: 0-0 Tstrap: 0-0 Ckp: 0-0
Best Rating: **54** 8/07 Chep 1m14y gd-fm

Very moderate sort; handles Polytrack.

Festoso (IRE)

107(101) (86)109

4-y-o b f Diesis-Garah (Ajdal (USA))

H J L Dunlop Prince A A Faisal

Placings:10243/30-6165300 (7292)

2009: 8^{6}SD, 6^{1}HY, 7^{6}G, 6^{5}S, 7^{3}GF, 6^{0}GS, 6^{0}S,

	Starts	1st	2nd	3rd	Win & Pl
Career Total (Turf)	13	2	1	3	77624
Career Total (AW)	1	0	0	0	540

109	5/09	Hayd	6f	HVY	£22708
79	5/07	NmkR	6f	GD	£4533

Total win prize-money £27242

Going (Turf): **Sf: 1-4** GS: 0-2 **Gd: 1-5** GF: 0-2 Fm: 0-0
Distance: **5f/6f: 2-8** 7f-8f: 0-6 9f-13f: 0-0 14f+: 0-0
Track : LH: 0-0 RH: 0-2 Tight: 0-0 Gall: 0-0
Aids: Bl: 0-3 Vi: 0-0 Tstrap: 0-0 Ckp: 0-0
Best Rating: **109** 5/09 Hayd 6f heavy

Smart; Listed winner at four; effective over 6-7f; acts on good and softer ground; has worn blinkers.

Fetching

(81) (54)

2-y-o b f Zamindar (USA)-Esplanade (Danehill (USA))

B W Hills K Abdulla

Placings:6 (7325)

2009: 7^{6}SD,

	Starts	1st	2nd	3rd	Win & Pl
Career Total (Turf)	0	0	0	0	
Career Total (AW)	1	0	0	0	0

Going (Turf): **Sf: 0-0 GS: 0-0 Gd: 0-0 GF: 0-0 Fm: 0-0**
Distance: 5f/6f: 0-0 7f-8f: 0-1 9f-13f: 0-0 14f+: 0-0
Track : LH: 0-0 RH: 0-1 Tight: 0-0 Gall: 0-0
Aids: Bl: 0-0 Vi: 0-0 Tstrap: 0-0 Ckp: 0-0
Best Rating: **54** 11/09 Kemp 7f stand

Promise following a slos start on debut in a 7f Polytrack maiden.

Feudal (IRE)

(95) (64)57

3-y-o b c Xaar-Noble Rose (IRE) (Caerleon (USA))

M Johnston Sheikh Hamdan Bin Mohammed Al Maktoum

Placings:5-00 (0917)

2009: 6^{0}SD, 8^{0}SD,

	Starts	1st	2nd	3rd	Win & Pl
Career Total (Turf)	1	0	0	0	0
Career Total (AW)	2	0	0	0	

Going (Turf): **Sf: 0-0 GS: 0-1 Gd: 0-0 GF: 0-0 Fm: 0-0**
Distance: 5f/6f: 0-1 7f-8f: 0-2 9f-13f: 0-0 14f+: 0-0
Track : LH: 0-3 RH: 0-0 Tight: 0-1 Gall: 0-0
Aids: Bl: 0-0 Vi: 0-0 Tstrap: 0-0 Ckp: 0-0
Best Rating: **64** 3/09 Ling 1m stand

Fever Tree

(87) (52)

2-y-o b f Trade Fair-Spielbound (Singspiel (IRE))

P J Makin The Racing Belles

Placings:06 (7663)

2009: 7^{0}SD, 8^{6}SD,

	Starts	1st	2nd	3rd	Win & Pl
Career Total (Turf)	0	0	0	0	
Career Total (AW)	2	0	0	0	0

Going (Turf): **Sf: 0-0 GS: 0-0 Gd: 0-0 GF: 0-0 Fm: 0-0**
Distance: 5f/6f: 0-0 7f-8f: 0-2 9f-13f: 0-0 14f+: 0-0
Track : LH: 0-2 RH: 0-0 Tight: 0-2 Gall: 0-0
Aids: Bl: 0-0 Vi: 0-0 Tstrap: 0-0 Ckp: 0-0
Best Rating: **52** 12/09 Ling 1m stand

Fiamma D'Oro (IRE)

(88) (69)57

3-y-o b/br f Marju (IRE)-Gild (IRE) (Caerleon (USA))

David P Myerscough Goldmine Racing Limited

Placings:4453 (6466a)

2009: 6^{4}SD, 7^{4}Y, 5^{5}SD, 6^{3}SD,

	Starts	1st	2nd	3rd	Win & Pl
Career Total (Turf)	1	0	0	0	
Career Total (AW)	3	0	0	1	1231

Going (Turf): **Sf: 0-0 GS: 0-0 Gd: 0-0 GF: 0-0 Fm: 0-0**
Distance: 5f/6f: 0-3 7f-8f: 0-1 9f-13f: 0-0 14f+: 0-0
Track : LH: 0-3 RH: 0-1 Tight: 0-1 Gall: 0-0
Aids: Bl: 0-0 Vi: 0-0 Tstrap: 0-0 Ckp: 0-0
Best Rating: **69** 10/09 Dund 6f stand

Fiancee (IRE)

84 53

3-y-o b f Pivotal-Name Of Love (IRE) (Petardia)

R Charlton Lady Rothschild

Placings:00 (4057)

2009: 7^{0}GS, 8^{0}S,

	Starts	1st	2nd	3rd	Win & Pl
Career Total (Turf)	2	0	0	0	

Going (Turf): **Sf: 0-1 GS: 0-1 Gd: 0-0 GF: 0-0 Fm: 0-0**
Distance: 5f/6f: 0-0 7f-8f: 0-2 9f-13f: 0-0 14f+: 0-0
Track : LH: 0-0 RH: 0-0 Tight: 0-0 Gall: 0-0
Aids: Bl: 0-0 Vi: 0-0 Tstrap: 0-0 Ckp: 0-0
Best Rating: **53** 4/09 Newb 7f gd-sft

Fibs And Flannel

85 59

2-y-o ch g Tobougg (IRE)-Queens Jubilee (Cayman Kai (IRE))

T D Easterby Jim McGrath

Placings:5640 (5256)

2009: 5^{5}GS, 5^{6}GS, 6^{4}GS, 6^{0}GF,

	Starts	1st	2nd	3rd	Win & Pl
Career Total (Turf)	4	0	0	0	1471

Going (Turf): **Sf: 0-0 GS: 0-3 Gd: 0-0 GF: 0-1 Fm: 0-0**
Distance: 5f/6f: 0-4 7f-8f: 0-0 9f-13f: 0-0 14f+: 0-0
Track : LH: 0-0 RH: 0-0 Tight: 0-0 Gall: 0-0
Aids: Bl: 0-0 Vi: 0-0 Tstrap: 0-0 Ckp: 0-0
Best Rating: **59** 7/09 Hayd 6f gd-sft

Moderate; stays 6f; acts on easy ground.

Fiddlers Ford (IRE)

(98) (61)61

8-y-o b g Sadler's Wells (USA)-Old Domesday Book (High Top)

T Keddy Howard Fielding

Placings:0/32264040105/0066P/0642-5 (0333)

2009: 16^{5}SD,

	Starts	1st	2nd	3rd	Win & Pl
Career Total (Turf)	6	1	0	0	4251
Career Total (AW)	16	0	3	1	4917

64	6/04	Wwck	2m2f	D	G-F	£4251

Total win prize-money £4251

Going (Turf): Sf: 0-2 GS: 0-1 Gd: 0-0 **GF: 1-3** Fm: 0-0
Distance: 5f/6f: 0-0 7f-8f: 0-1 9f-13f: 0-10 **14f+: 1-11**
Track : **LH: 1-14** RH: 0-6 Tight: 0-11 Gall: 0-2
Aids: Bl: 0-0 Vi: 0-1 Tstrap: 0-1 Ckp: 0-1
Best Rating: **77** 6/04 Ling 1m2f stand

Fidler Bay

(57)

3-y-o b g Falbrav (IRE)-Fiddle-Dee-Dee (IRE) (Mujtahid (USA))

H Candy Henry Candy

Placings:0 (2395)
2009: 10^{0}SD,

	Starts	1st	2nd	3rd	Win & Pl
Career Total (Turf)	0	0	0	0	
Career Total (AW)	1	0	0	0	

Going (Turf): **Sf: 0-0 GS: 0-0 Gd: 0-0 GF: 0-0 Fm: 0-0**
Distance: 5f/6f: 0-0 7f-8f: 0-0 9f-13f: 0-1 14f+: 0-0
Track : LH: 0-1 RH: 0-0 Tight: 0-1 Gall: 0-0
Aids: Bl: 0-0 Vi: 0-0 Tstrap: 0-0 Ckp: 0-0

Fiefdom (IRE)

102(106) (80)**78**
7-y-o br g Singspiel (IRE)-Chiquita Linda (IRE) (Mujadil (USA))
I W McInnes Stephen Hackney

Placings:5412430/44/0063140600003050**0**/440246526630 50**523000/0**005202661**1360**-04**2553**0**0063**0**56660** (7587)
2009: 7^{0}GF, 7^{4}GF, 8^{2}SD, 8^{5}SD, 7^{5}SD, 7^{3}GF, 7^{0}GF, 7^{0}SD, 7^{0}SD, 7^{6}SD, 8^{3}SD, 7^{0}GF, 8^{5}SS, 8^{6}SD, 7^{6}SD, 8^{6}SD, 8^{0}SD,

	Starts	1st	2nd	3rd	Win & Pl
Career Total (Turf)	52	2	5	5	33912
Career Total (AW)	25	2	2	3	15855

80 9/08 Ling 7f (0-80)H STD £4604
78 8/08 Ling 7f (0-80)H STD £6308
91 6/06 Ling 7f (0-85)H G-F £6232
77 6/04 Donc 6f E FRM £3649
Total win prize-money £20795

Going (Turf): Sf: 0-2 GS: 0-5 Gd: 0-14 **GF: 1-28 Fm: 1-3**
Distance: 5f/6f: 1-3 **7f-8f: 3-63** 9f-13f: 0-11 14f+: 0-0
Track : **LH: 2-40** RH: 0-19 **Tight: 2-39** Gall: 0-1
Aids: Bl: 0-2 Vi: 0-0 Tstrap: 0-5 Ckp: 0-5
Best Rating: **97** 5/05 Hayd 1m30y good

Modest; effective at around 7f-1m; acts on fast ground; also goes on Polytrack; has worn cheekpieces.

Field Day (IRE)

90 **78**
2-y-o br f Cape Cross (IRE)-Naval Affair (IRE) (Last Tycoon)
B J Meehan Ballymacoll Stud

Placings:1 (7183)
2009: 7^{1}G,

	Starts	1st	2nd	3rd	Win & Pl
Career Total (Turf)	1	1	0	0	4857

78 10/09 NmkR 7f GD £4857
Total win prize-money £4857

Going (Turf): Sf: 0-0 GS: 0-0 **Gd: 1-1** GF: 0-0 Fm: 0-0
Distance: 5f/6f: 0-0 **7f-8f: 1-1** 9f-13f: 0-0 14f+: 0-0
Track : LH: 0-0 RH: 0-0 Tight: 0-0 Gall: 0-0
Aids: Bl: 0-0 Vi: 0-0 Tstrap: 0-0 Ckp: 0-0
Best Rating: **78** 10/09 NmkR 7f good

Fair; stays 7f; acts on good ground.

Field Elect

2-y-o b g Zafeen (FR)-Princess Carranita (IRE) (Desert Sun)
Garry Moss J P Burton

Placings:R (4062)
2009: 6^{R}HY,

	Starts	1st	2nd	3rd	Win & Pl
Career Total (Turf)	1	0	0	0	

Going (Turf): **Sf: 0-1 GS: 0-0 Gd: 0-0 GF: 0-0 Fm: 0-0**
Distance: 5f/6f: 0-0 7f-8f: 0-1 9f-13f: 0-0 14f+: 0-0
Track : LH: 0-0 RH: 0-0 Tight: 0-0 Gall: 0-0
Aids: Bl: 0-0 Vi: 0-0 Tstrap: 0-0 Ckp: 0-0

Field Fantasy

84(92) (43)**37**
3-y-o ch f Bold Edge-Princess Carranita (IRE) (Desert Sun)
Garry Moss J P Burton

Placings:0-6406000 (2577)
2009: 5^{6}SD, 5^{4}SD, 5^{0}SD, 6^{6}GF, 6^{0}G, 5^{0}GF, 7^{0}SD,

	Starts	1st	2nd	3rd	Win & Pl
Career Total (Turf)	3	0	0	0	0
Career Total (AW)	5	0	0	0	0

Going (Turf): **Sf: 0-0 GS: 0-0 Gd: 0-1 GF: 0-2 Fm: 0-0**
Distance: 5f/6f: 0-7 7f-8f: 0-1 9f-13f: 0-0 14f+: 0-0
Track : LH: 0-5 RH: 0-0 Tight: 0-1 Gall: 0-2
Aids: Bl: 0-1 Vi: 0-0 Tstrap: 0-0 Ckp: 0-0
Best Rating: **43** 1/09 Wolv 5f20y stand

Field Of Dream

89 **96**
2-y-o b c Oasis Dream-Field Of Hope (IRE) (Selkirk (USA))
L M Cumani (B Grizzetti 2/6) L Cashman

Placings:110 (5743)
2009: 5^{1}G, 5^{1}S, 7^{0}GF,

	Starts	1st	2nd	3rd	Win & Pl
Career Total (Turf)	3	2	0	0	36893

96 6/09 Capa 5f110y SFT £27184
5/09 Siro 5f GD £9708
Total win prize-money £36893

Going (Turf): **Sf: 1-1** GS: 0-0 **Gd: 1-1** GF: 0-1 Fm: 0-0
Distance: **5f/6f: 2-2** 7f-8f: 0-1 9f-13f: 0-0 14f+: 0-0
Track : LH: 0-0 RH: 0-1 Tight: 0-0 Gall: 0-0
Aids: Bl: 0-0 Vi: 0-0 Tstrap: 0-0 Ckp: 0-0
Best Rating: **96** 6/09 Capa 5f110y soft

Fielder (IRE)

(89) (67)**18**
4-y-o b g Catcher In The Rye (IRE)-Miss Garuda (Persian Bold)
J G Portman Simon Skinner

Placings:00-30 (1073)
2009: 11^{3}SD, 12^{0}SD,

	Starts	1st	2nd	3rd	Win & Pl
Career Total (Turf)	2	0	0	0	
Career Total (AW)	2	0	0	1	302

Going (Turf): **Sf: 0-1 GS: 0-0 Gd: 0-0 GF: 0-1 Fm: 0-0**
Distance: 5f/6f: 0-0 7f-8f: 0-0 9f-13f: 0-4 14f+: 0-0
Track : LH: 0-3 RH: 0-1 Tight: 0-2 Gall: 0-0
Aids: Bl: 0-0 Vi: 0-0 Tstrap: 0-0 Ckp: 0-0
Best Rating: **67** 2/09 Kemp 1m3f stand

Fifer (IRE)

78 **33**
3-y-o b f Soviet Star (USA)-Fife (IRE) (Lomond (USA))
Patrick Morris D Emmerson & Rob Lloyd Racing

Placings:06-00 (3651)
2009: 7^{0}GF, 6^{0}G,

	Starts	1st	2nd	3rd	Win & Pl
Career Total (Turf)	4	0	0	0	0

Going (Turf): **Sf: 0-1 GS: 0-0 Gd: 0-2 GF: 0-1 Fm: 0-0**
Distance: 5f/6f: 0-2 7f-8f: 0-2 9f-13f: 0-0 14f+: 0-0
Track : LH: 0-1 RH: 0-1 Tight: 0-0 Gall: 0-0
Aids: Bl: 0-0 Vi: 0-0 Tstrap: 0-0 Ckp: 0-0
Best Rating: **33** 10/08 Rdcr 6f good

Fifth Amendment

91 **73**
3-y-o ch g Presidium-Lady Magician (Lord Bud)
A Berry J Berry

Placings:02-005060 (5362)
2009: 6^{0}GF, 5^{0}G, 7^{5}G, 7^{0}G, 6^{6}G, 6^{0}S,

	Starts	1st	2nd	3rd	Win & Pl
Career Total (Turf)	8	0	1	0	605

Going (Turf): **Sf: 0-1 GS: 0-1 Gd: 0-5 GF: 0-1 Fm: 0-0**
Distance: 5f/6f: 0-6 7f-8f: 0-2 9f-13f: 0-0 14f+: 0-0
Track : LH: 0-2 RH: 0-1 Tight: 0-1 Gall: 0-0
Aids: Bl: 0-0 Vi: 0-0 Tstrap: 0-0 Ckp: 0-0
Best Rating: **73** 10/08 Catt 5f212y gd-sft

Moderate; stays 6f; acts on soft ground.

Fifth Zak

(93) (47)**41**
5-y-o b g Best Of The Bests (IRE)-Zakuska (Zafonic (USA))
S R Bowring Clark Industrial Services Partnership

Placings:0/305-006 (0399)
2009: 11^{0}SS, 12^{0}SD, 8^{6}SD,

	Starts	1st	2nd	3rd	Win & Pl
Career Total (Turf)	1	0	0	0	
Career Total (AW)	6	0	0	1	302

Going (Turf): **Sf: 0-0 GS: 0-1 Gd: 0-0 GF: 0-0 Fm: 0-0**
Distance: 5f/6f: 0-0 7f-8f: 0-2 9f-13f: 0-5 14f+: 0-0
Track : LH: 0-6 RH: 0-1 Tight: 0-1 Gall: 0-0
Aids: Bl: 0-0 Vi: 0-0 Tstrap: 0-1 Ckp: 0-1
Best Rating: **47** 1/08 Sthl 1m stand

Fifty (IRE)

97(93) (60)**78**
4-y-o b f Fasliyev (USA)-Amethyst (IRE) (Sadler's Wells (USA))
R Hannon Alan Franklin & Neville Poole

Placings:4200**4**/103660-40**0**63**0** (4645)
2009: 6^{4}F, 6^{0}GF, 7^{0}SD, 8^{6}GF, 7^{3}G, 8^{0}SD,

	Starts	1st	2nd	3rd	Win & Pl
Career Total (Turf)	14	1	1	2	7190
Career Total (AW)	3	0	0	0	192

71 5/08 Sals 6f GD £4047
Total win prize-money £4047

Going (Turf): Sf: 0-1 GS: 0-0 **Gd: 1-6** GF: 0-4 Fm: 0-3
Distance: **5f/6f: 1-7** 7f-8f: 0-10 9f-13f: 0-0 14f+: 0-0
Track : LH: 0-1 RH: 0-2 Tight: 0-1 Gall: 0-1
Aids: Bl: 0-0 Vi: 0-0 Tstrap: 0-0 Ckp: 0-0
Best Rating: **78** 6/08 Sals 6f212y good

Fair half-sister to Audit, a dual middle-distance winner at three; best over 6f; acts on good and fast ground.

Fifty Cents

86

5-y-o ch g Diesis-Solaia (USA) (Miswaki (USA))
M F Harris Christopher Shankland

Placings:2/105/3-P **(0017)**
2009: 8^{P}SD,

	Starts	1st	2nd	3rd	Win & Pl
Career Total (Turf)	5	1	1	1	6018
Career Total (AW)	1	0	0	0	

66	5/07	Hayd	1m30y	G-F	£3238

Total win prize-money £3239

Going (Turf): Sf: 0-1 GS: 0-2 Gd: 0-1 **GF: 1-1** Fm: 0-0
Distance: 5f/6f: 0-0 7f-8f: 0-4 **9f-13f: 1-2** 14f+: 0-0
Track : **LH: 1-3** RH: 0-0 Tight: 0-1 Gall: 0-0
Aids: Bl: 0-0 Vi: 0-0 Tstrap: 0-0 Ckp: 0-0
Best Rating: **86** 4/08 Leic 7f9y soft

Useful; stays 1m; likes fast ground.

Fifty Moore

68 **25**

2-y-o b g Selkirk (USA)-Franglais (GER) (Lion Cavern (USA))
Jedd O'Keeffe Colin And Melanie Moore

Placings:0 **(2936)**
2009: 6^{0}G,

	Starts	1st	2nd	3rd	Win & Pl
Career Total (Turf)	1	0	0	0	

Going (Turf): **Sf: 0-0 GS: 0-0 Gd: 0-1 GF: 0-0 Fm: 0-0**
Distance: 5f/6f: 0-1 7f-8f: 0-0 9f-13f: 0-0 14f+: 0-0
Track : LH: 0-0 RH: 0-0 Tight: 0-0 Gall: 0-0
Aids: Bl: 0-0 Vi: 0-0 Tstrap: 0-0 Ckp: 0-0
Best Rating: **25** 6/09 York 6f good

Fiftyfourth Street

93(90) (57)**71**

3-y-o ch g Central Park (IRE)-Retaliator (Rudimentary (USA))
P J Makin Mrs P J Makin

Placings:0445 **(4990)**
2009: 6^{0}GF, 6^{4}GF, 5^{4}SD, 6^{5}GF,

	Starts	1st	2nd	3rd	Win & Pl
Career Total (Turf)	3	0	0	0	433
Career Total (AW)	1	0	0	0	0

Going (Turf): **Sf: 0-0 GS: 0-0 Gd: 0-0 GF: 0-3 Fm: 0-0**
Distance: 5f/6f: 0-1 7f-8f: 0-3 9f-13f: 0-0 14f+: 0-0
Track : LH: 0-0 RH: 0-0 Tight: 0-0 Gall: 0-0
Aids: Bl: 0-0 Vi: 0-0 Tstrap: 0-0 Ckp: 0-0
Best Rating: **71** 8/09 Newb 6f8y gd-fm

Modest; effective over 5f; acts on Fibresand but best effort on fast ground.

Figaro Flyer (IRE)

93(106) (78)**78**

6-y-o b g Mozart (IRE)-Ellway Star (IRE) (Night Shift (USA))
P Howling S J Hammond

Placings:321341126361/2030000500402040612**4**/312404263003405000054100**1**/554562465122032-03354315560224660 **(7739)**
2009: 5^{0}SD, 5^{3}SD, 5^{3}SD, 5^{5}SD, 5^{4}SD, 5^{3}SD, 5^{1}SD, 6^{5}SD, 5^{5}G, 6^{6}SD, 5^{0}S, 5^{2}SD, 5^{2}SD, 5^{4}SD, 5^{6}SD, 6^{6}SD, 6^{0}SD,

	Starts	1st	2nd	3rd	Win & Pl
Career Total (Turf)	36	3	3	3	28215
Career Total (AW)	53	7	10	8	43999

77	4/09	Sthl	5f	(0-80)H	STD	£5180
74	5/08	Sthl	5f	(0-75)H	STD	£3399
73	12/07	Wolv	5f216y	(0-65)H	STD	£2730
71	11/07	Wolv	5f216y	(0-65)H	STD	£2184
84	1/07	Wolv	5f20y	(0-75)H	SS	£3412
81	12/06	Wolv	5f216y	(0-75)H	STD	£3238
72	12/05	Ling	6f		STD	£2504
93	7/05	York	5f		G-F	£8424
66	7/05	York	6f		G-F	£7670
70	6/05	Bath	5f161y		FRM	£3435

Total win prize-money £42181

Going (Turf): Sf: 0-2 GS: 0-3 Gd: 0-7 **GF: 2-22** Fm: 1-2
Distance: **5f/6f: 10-80** 7f-8f: 0-9 9f-13f: 0-0 14f+: 0-0
Track : **LH: 6-41** RH: 0-8 **Tight: 5-35** Gall: 1-7
Aids: Bl: 0-0 Vi: 0-0 Tstrap: 0-0 Ckp: 0-0
Best Rating: **93** 7/05 York 5f gd-fm

Modest; effective over 5f-6f; acts on fast ground and on sand.

Fight Club (GER)

78 **102**

8-y-o b h Lavirco (GER)-Flaming Song (IRE) (Darshaan)
Evan Williams T G Price

Placings:301/1102450/1/1345/006-0 **(6480)**
2009: 9^{0}GF,

	Starts	1st	2nd	3rd	Win & Pl
Career Total (Turf)	19	5	1	2	102201

	5/06	Muni	1m2f	SFT	£8275
113	9/05	Frnk	1m2f	SFT	£28369
111	5/04	Muni	1m2f	GD	£24648
	4/04	Duss	7f110y	GD	£8450
	11/03	Muni	7f	GD	£1948

Total win prize-money £71692

Going (Turf): Sf: 2-9 GS: 0-0 **Gd: 3-6** GF: 0-3 Fm: 0-1
Distance: 5f/6f: 0-1 7f-8f: 2-4 **9f-13f: 3-14** 14f+: 0-0
Track : **LH: 2-7** RH: 0-4 Tight: 0-0 Gall: 0-0
Aids: Bl: 0-1 Vi: 0-0 Tstrap: 0-0 Ckp: 0-0
Best Rating: **114** 7/06 Muni 1m2f good

Fighting Talk (IRE)

85 **56**

2-y-o ch c Shamardal (USA)-Slap Shot (IRE) (Lycius (USA))
M Johnston Sheikh Hamdan Bin Mohammed Al Maktoum

Placings:0 **(6214)**
2009: 7^{0}GF,

	Starts	1st	2nd	3rd	Win & Pl
Career Total (Turf)	1	0	0	0	

Going (Turf): **Sf: 0-0 GS: 0-0 Gd: 0-0 GF: 0-1 Fm: 0-0**
Distance: 5f/6f: 0-0 7f-8f: 0-1 9f-13f: 0-0 14f+: 0-0
Track : LH: 0-0 RH: 0-0 Tight: 0-0 Gall: 0-0
Aids: Bl: 0-0 Vi: 0-0 Tstrap: 0-0 Ckp: 0-0
Best Rating: **56** 9/09 Rdcr 7f gd-fm

Filemot

77(89) (45)**64**

4-y-o ch f Largesse-Hickleton Lady (IRE) (Kala Shikari)
John Berry Mrs Rosemary Moszkowicz

Placings:20506000-0 **(2122)**
2009: 5^{0}GS,

	Starts	1st	2nd	3rd	Win & Pl
Career Total (Turf)	5	0	1	0	771
Career Total (AW)	4	0	0	0	

Going (Turf): **Sf: 0-0 GS: 0-3 Gd: 0-0 GF: 0-2 Fm: 0-0**
Distance: 5f/6f: 0-6 7f-8f: 0-2 9f-13f: 0-1 14f+: 0-0
Track : LH: 0-3 RH: 0-1 Tight: 0-1 Gall: 0-2
Aids: Bl: 0-0 Vi: 0-0 Tstrap: 0-0 Ckp: 0-0
Best Rating: **64** 5/08 Folk 5f gd-sft

Filibuster

55

2-y-o b g Tobougg (IRE)-Blinding Mission (IRE) (Marju (IRE))
Mrs C A Dunnett C R Cawston Ltd & G H Allen (Farms) Ltd

Placings:0 **(6423)**
2009: 8^{0}GF,

	Starts	1st	2nd	3rd	Win & Pl
Career Total (Turf)	1	0	0	0	

Going (Turf): **Sf: 0-0 GS: 0-0 Gd: 0-0 GF: 0-1 Fm: 0-0**
Distance: 5f/6f: 0-0 7f-8f: 0-1 9f-13f: 0-0 14f+: 0-0
Track : LH: 0-0 RH: 0-0 Tight: 0-0 Gall: 0-0
Aids: Bl: 0-0 Vi: 0-0 Tstrap: 0-0 Ckp: 0-0

Filligree (IRE)

105(107) (90)**93**

4-y-o b f Kyllachy-Clunie (Inchinor)
Rae Guest The Filligree Partnership

Placings:356/325114142-06102041005 **(7227)**
2009: 5^{0}GF, 5^{6}GF, 5^{1}F, 5^{0}F, 6^{2}GF, 6^{0}G, 6^{4}GF, 5^{1}F, 6^{0}GF, 6^{0}GF, 6^{5}SD,

	Starts	1st	2nd	3rd	Win & Pl
Career Total (Turf)	20	5	3	1	27526
Career Total (AW)	3	0	0	1	577

93	9/09	Bath	5f161y	(0-85)H	FRM	£6476
88	6/09	Bath	5f161y	(0-85)H	FRM	£4857
87	8/08	Brig	5f213y	(0-75)H	GD	£2964
78	6/08	Yarm	6f3y	(0-65)H	G-F	£2201
72	6/08	Brig	5f213y	(0-65)H	FRM	£2525

Total win prize-money £19026

Going (Turf): Sf: 0-1 GS: 0-1 Gd: 1-5 GF: 1-9 **Fm: 3-4**
Distance: **5f/6f: 4-20** 7f-8f: 1-3 9f-13f: 0-0 14f+: 0-0
Track : **LH: 4-7** RH: 0-1 Tight: 0-2 **Gall: 2-3**
Aids: Bl: 0-0 Vi: 0-0 Tstrap: 0-0 Ckp: 0-0
Best Rating: **93** 9/09 Bath 5f161y firm

Useful; effective over 6f; acts on good and faster ground and on Polytrack.

Film Festival (USA)

97(99) (72)**82**

6-y-o ch g Diesis-To Act (USA) (Roberto (USA))
B Ellison Koo's Racing Club

Placings:3231311/00/400-050 **(2505)**

2009: 10^{0}G, 14^{5}GF, 12^{0}GF,

	Starts	1st	2nd	3rd	Win & Pl
Career Total (Turf)	13	3	1	3	32229
Career Total (AW)	2	0	0	0	

99 10/06 Gowr 1m1f100y (60-90)H SFT £7624
95 9/06 Curr 1m (60-100)H Y-S £13468
86 6/06 Rosc 7f G-F £5718

Total win prize-money £26813

Going (Turf): **Sf: 1-2** GS: 0-0 Gd: 0-3 **GF: 1-5** Fm: 0-1
Distance: 5f/6f: 0-0 **7f-8f: 2-7** 9f-13f: 1-7 14f+: 0-1
Track : LH: 0-7 **RH: 3-7** Tight: 0-2 **Gall: 1-5**
Aids: Bl: 0-0 Vi: 0-0 Tstrap: 0-0 Ckp: 0-0
Best Rating: **99** 10/06 Gowr 1m1f100y soft

Useful; stays 1m2f; acts on most ground.

Film Set (USA)

103(103) (94)**92**

3-y-o b/br c Johar (USA)-Dippers (USA) (Polish Numbers (USA))
F Vermeulen (Saeed Bin Suroor 13/8) J Romel

Placings:213-03264 **(7820a)**

2009: 7^{0}HY, 8^{3}GF, 8^{2}SD, 7^{6}G, 7^{4}SD,

	Starts	1st	2nd	3rd	Win & Pl
Career Total (Turf)	5	1	1	1	8105
Career Total (AW)	3	0	1	1	5632

89 10/08 Newb 6f110y G-S £5504

Total win prize-money £5505

Going (Turf): Sf: 0-1 **GS: 1-1** Gd: 0-1 GF: 0-2 Fm: 0-0
Distance: 5f/6f: 0-2 **7f-8f: 1-5** 9f-13f: 0-1 14f+: 0-0
Track : LH: 0-3 RH: 0-3 Tight: 0-2 Gall: 0-0
Aids: Bl: 0-0 Vi: 0-0 Tstrap: 0-0 Ckp: 0-0
Best Rating: **94** 7/09 Ling 1m stand

Very useful; stays 1m; acts on most ground and on Polytrack; has worn a tongue tie.

Filun

94(102) (71)**67**

4-y-o b g Montjeu (IRE)-Sispre (FR) (Master Willie)
A Middleton R J Matthews

Placings:0035004-21006003500 **(6226)**

2009: 12^{2}SD, 12^{1}SD, 12^{0}SD, 12^{0}GS, 11^{6}GF, 11^{0}GF, 12^{0}S, 10^{3}GS, 12^{5}SF, 11^{0}GF, 12^{0}SD,

	Starts	1st	2nd	3rd	Win & Pl
Career Total (Turf)	11	0	0	2	928
Career Total (AW)	7	1	1	0	3396

71 3/09 Kemp 1m4f (0-75)H STD £2590

Total win prize-money £2590

Going (Turf): **Sf: 0-1** **GS: 0-3** **Gd: 0-2** **GF: 0-5** **Fm: 0-0**
Distance: 5f/6f: 0-0 7f-8f: 0-0 **9f-13f: 1-18** 14f+: 0-0
Track : LH: 0-10 **RH: 1-7** Tight: 0-6 Gall: 0-4
Aids: Bl: 0-2 Vi: 0-0 Tstrap: 0-1 Ckp: 0-1
Best Rating: **71** 3/09 Kemp 1m4f stand

Modest; effective at around 1m4f; acts on Polytrack.

Filwa (IRE)

97 **72**

2-y-o b f Invincible Spirit (IRE)-Capessa (IRE) (Perugino (USA))
B J Meehan Miss A Al-Hejailan

Placings:52202 **(6896)**

2009: 5^{5}F, 6^{2}GF, 5^{2}G, 5^{0}GF, 6^{2}GF,

	Starts	1st	2nd	3rd	Win & Pl
Career Total (Turf)	5	0	3	0	2891

Going (Turf): **Sf: 0-0** **GS: 0-0** **Gd: 0-1** **GF: 0-3** **Fm: 0-1**
Distance: 5f/6f: 0-5 7f-8f: 0-0 9f-13f: 0-0 14f+: 0-0
Track : LH: 0-3 RH: 0-0 Tight: 0-0 Gall: 0-3
Aids: Bl: 0-0 Vi: 0-0 Tstrap: 0-0 Ckp: 0-0
Best Rating: **72** 10/09 Pont 6f gd-fm

Fair efforts in maidens at up to 6f; acts on a sound surface.

Fin Vin De Leu (GER)

106(105) (82)**82**

3-y-o b g Dr Fong (USA)-Fairy Queen (IRE) (Fairy King (USA))
M Johnston R M F Curry

Placings:3542-31200030140226 3 **(6875)**

2009: 8^{3}SD, 12^{1}SD, 12^{2}SD, 12^{0}SD, 12^{0}G, 12^{0}GF, 15^{3}G, 12^{0}G, 16^{1}G, 15^{4}GF, 16^{0}GS, 13^{2}SD, 17^{2}F, 13^{6}SD, 14^{3}SD,

	Starts	1st	2nd	3rd	Win & Pl
Career Total (Turf)	8	1	1	1	7169
Career Total (AW)	11	1	3	3	9514

82 8/09 Bevl 2m35y (0-85)H GD £5180
77 3/09 Sthl 1m4f STD £3070

Total win prize-money £8252

Going (Turf): Sf: 0-0 GS: 0-1 **Gd: 1-4** GF: 0-2 Fm: 0-1
Distance: 5f/6f: 0-0 7f-8f: 0-4 9f-13f: 1-7 14f+: 1-8
Track : LH: 1-11 RH: 1-8 **Tight: 1-10** Gall: 0-3
Aids: Bl: 0-0 Vi: 0-0 Tstrap: 0-0 Ckp: 0-0
Best Rating: **82** 8/09 Bevl 2m35y good

Fair; effective at 1m4f-2m1f; acts on good and fast ground; goes on Fibresand and Polytrack.

Final Answer

95 **80**

2-y-o b c Kyllachy-Valandraud (IRE) (College Chapel)
E S McMahon J C Fretwell

Placings:1 **(4243)**

2009: 5^{1}GF,

	Starts	1st	2nd	3rd	Win & Pl
Career Total (Turf)	1	1	0	0	5181

80 7/09 Sand 5f6y G-F £5180

Total win prize-money £5181

Going (Turf): Sf: 0-0 GS: 0-0 Gd: 0-0 **GF: 1-1** Fm: 0-0
Distance: **5f/6f: 1-1** 7f-8f: 0-0 9f-13f: 0-0 14f+: 0-0
Track : LH: 0-0 RH: 0-0 Tight: 0-0 Gall: 0-0
Aids: Bl: 0-0 Vi: 0-0 Tstrap: 0-0 Ckp: 0-0
Best Rating: **80** 7/09 Sand 5f6y gd-fm

Fair half-brother to several sprinters; winner on debut over 5f on fast ground.

Final Bid (IRE)

(77) (17)**56**

6-y-o b g Mujadil (USA)-Dusky Virgin (Missed Flight)
Mrs Tracey Barfoot-Saunt (A Berry 15/1) A Good Days Racing

Placings:66002/5004/6/00 **(0174)**

2009: 8^{0}SS, 8^{0}SD,

	Starts	1st	2nd	3rd	Win & Pl
Career Total (Turf)	5	0	0	0	0
Career Total (AW)	7	0	1	0	1115

Going (Turf): **Sf: 0-1** **GS: 0-1** **Gd: 0-0** **GF: 0-3** **Fm: 0-0**
Distance: 5f/6f: 0-0 7f-8f: 0-10 9f-13f: 0-2 14f+: 0-0
Track : LH: 0-6 RH: 0-2 Tight: 0-4 Gall: 0-0
Aids: Bl: 0-6 Vi: 0-0 Tstrap: 0-0 Ckp: 0-0
Best Rating: **64** 11/05 Wolv 7f32y std-fst

Final Drive (IRE)

90(98) (72)**41**

3-y-o b g Viking Ruler (AUS)-Forest Delight (IRE) (Shinko Forest (IRE))
E J Creighton Par 4 Racing

Placings:050-0456011 **(7239)**

2009: 10^{0}G, 6^{4}G, 7^{5}SD, 7^{6}SD, 10^{0}SS, 8^{1}SD, 7^{1}SD,

	Starts	1st	2nd	3rd	Win & Pl
Career Total (Turf)	3	0	0	0	144
Career Total (AW)	7	2	0	0	3412

72 11/09 Kemp 7f (0-55)H STD £1706
62 11/09 Ling 1m (0-55)H STD £1706

Total win prize-money £3412

Going (Turf): **Sf: 0-0** **GS: 0-0** **Gd: 0-2** **GF: 0-1** **Fm: 0-0**
Distance: 5f/6f: 0-1 **7f-8f: 2-7** 9f-13f: 0-2 14f+: 0-0
Track : LH: 1-7 RH: 1-3 **Tight: 1-4** Gall: 0-0
Aids: Bl: 0-0 Vi: 0-0 Tstrap: 0-0 Ckp: 0-0
Best Rating: **72** 11/09 Kemp 7f stand

Modest; effective over 7f-1m and acts on Polytrack.

Final Ovation (IRE)

94 **71**

2-y-o b g Acclamation-Last Gasp (Barathea (IRE))
J J Quinn Bellwood Cottage Syndicate I

Placings:4200420 **(6556)**

2009: 5^{4}G, 5^{2}GF, 6^{0}GS, 5^{0}GF, 5^{4}S, 5^{2}GF, 5^{0}G,

	Starts	1st	2nd	3rd	Win & Pl
Career Total (Turf)	7	0	2	0	2505

Going (Turf): **Sf: 0-1** **GS: 0-1** **Gd: 0-2** **GF: 0-3** **Fm: 0-0**
Distance: 5f/6f: 0-7 7f-8f: 0-0 9f-13f: 0-0 14f+: 0-0
Track : LH: 0-0 RH: 0-0 Tight: 0-0 Gall: 0-0
Aids: Bl: 0-0 Vi: 0-0 Tstrap: 0-0 Ckp: 0-0
Best Rating: **71** 5/09 Muss 5f gd-fm

Promise in maidens at 5f on a sound surface.

Final Quest (IRE)

(-12)

6-y-o ch m King Charlemagne (USA)-Tuscaloosa (Robellino (USA))
P J McKenna Platium Starlight Syndicate

Placings:40352/0-0 **(7374)**

2009: 9^{0}SD,

	Starts	1st	2nd	3rd	Win & Pl
Career Total (Turf)	6	0	1	1	1840
Career Total (AW)	1	0	0	0	

Going (Turf): **Sf: 0-2** **GS: 0-0** **Gd: 0-2** **GF: 0-0** **Fm: 0-1**
Distance: 5f/6f: 0-1 7f-8f: 0-4 9f-13f: 0-2 14f+: 0-0
Track : LH: 0-1 RH: 0-4 Tight: 0-1 Gall: 0-0
Aids: Bl: 0-2 Vi: 0-0 Tstrap: 0-0 Ckp: 0-0
Best Rating: **51** 8/05 Slig 6f110y soft

Final Rhapsody

69(101) (64)**37**

3-y-o b f Royal Applause-Rivers Rhapsody (Dominion)
J A Geake David Mead & Exors of Rex Mead

Placings:0062-000 (2632)
2009: 5^{0}F, 6^{0}G, 6^{0}SD,

	Starts	1st	2nd	3rd	Win & Pl
Career Total (Turf)	4	0	0	0	
Career Total (AW)	3	0	1	0	771

Going (Turf): Sf: 0-0 GS: 0-1 Gd: 0-1 GF: 0-1 Fm: 0-1
Distance: 5f/6f: 0-6 7f-8f: 0-1 9f-13f: 0-0 14f+: 0-0
Track : LH: 0-4 RH: 0-2 Tight: 0-1 Gall: 0-3
Aids: Bl: 0-0 Vi: 0-0 Tstrap: 0-0 Ckp: 0-0
Best Rating: 64 11/08 Kemp 5f stand

Modest; suited by 5f and Polytrack.

Final Salute

83(97) (76)72
3-y-o b g Royal Applause-Wildwood Flower (Distant Relative)
B Smart Crossfields Racing & B Smart

Placings:65314-2000 (7870)
2009: 7^{2}SD, 5^{0}S, 7^{0}SD, 6^{0}SS,

	Starts	1st	2nd	3rd	Win & Pl
Career Total (Turf)	6	1	0	1	4956
Career Total (AW)	3	0	1	0	907

72 10/08 Wind 6f (0-70) G-F £3753
Total win prize-money £3753

Going (Turf): Sf: 0-3 GS: 0-0 Gd: 0-0 GF: 1-3 Fm: 0-0
Distance: 5f/6f: 1-7 7f-8f: 0-2 9f-13f: 0-0 14f+: 0-0
Track : LH: 0-4 RH: 0-1 Tight: 0-1 Gall: 1-1
Aids: Bl: 0-0 Vi: 1-6 Tstrap: 0-0 Ckp: 0-0
Best Rating: 76 3/09 Sthl 7f stand

Fair; suited by 7f and fast ground; has worn a visor.

Final Son

93(88) (46)58
4-y-o b g Fourstars Allstar (USA)-Dulzie (Safawan)
A P Jarvis Jarvis Associates

Placings:04500 (5775)
2009: 8^{0}GF, 10^{4}S, 12^{5}SD, 8^{0}SD, 10^{0}SD,

	Starts	1st	2nd	3rd	Win & Pl
Career Total (Turf)	2	0	0	0	241
Career Total (AW)	3	0	0	0	0

Going (Turf): Sf: 0-1 GS: 0-0 Gd: 0-0 GF: 0-1 Fm: 0-0
Distance: 5f/6f: 0-0 7f-8f: 0-1 9f-13f: 0-4 14f+: 0-0
Track : LH: 0-3 RH: 0-2 Tight: 0-2 Gall: 0-0
Aids: Bl: 0-0 Vi: 0-0 Tstrap: 0-0 Ckp: 0-0
Best Rating: 58 5/09 Hayd 1m2f95y soft

Final Tune (IRE)

(102) (75)79
6-y-o ch g Grand Lodge (USA)-Jackie's Opera (FR) (Indian Ridge)
Miss M E Rowland M E Rowland A Corden

Placings:045/055420164512/346423150/66-0 (0618)
2009: 8^{0}SD,

	Starts	1st	2nd	3rd	Win & Pl
Career Total (Turf)	17	2	1	0	9578
Career Total (AW)	10	1	2	2	6867

79 6/07 Ayr 1m1f20y (0-75)H GD £4533
67 10/06 Ling 7f (0-60)H STD £3412
55 7/06 Leic 1m60y G-F £2590
Total win prize-money £10538

Going (Turf): Sf: 0-1 GS: 0-2 Gd: 1-5 GF: 1-9 Fm: 0-0
Distance: 5f/6f: 0-4 7f-8f: 1-13 9f-13f: 2-10 14f+: 0-0
Track : LH: 2-19 RH: 1-3 Tight: 1-14 Gall: 0-0
Aids: Bl: 0-0 Vi: 0-0 Tstrap: 0-0 Ckp: 0-0
Best Rating: 81 3/07 Wolv 7f32y std-fst

Fair sort; suited by around 1m1f; acts on fast ground and Polytrack.

Final Turn

(88) (50)
2-y-o b c Kyllachy-Eveningperformance (Night Shift (USA))
H Candy Mrs David Blackburn

Placings:56 (7843)
2009: 6^{5}SD, 5^{6}SD,

	Starts	1st	2nd	3rd	Win & Pl
Career Total (Turf)	0	0	0	0	
Career Total (AW)	2	0	0	0	0

Going (Turf): Sf: 0-0 GS: 0-0 Gd: 0-0 GF: 0-0 Fm: 0-0
Distance: 5f/6f: 0-2 7f-8f: 0-0 9f-13f: 0-0 14f+: 0-0
Track : LH: 0-2 RH: 0-0 Tight: 0-2 Gall: 0-0
Aids: Bl: 0-0 Vi: 0-0 Tstrap: 0-0 Ckp: 0-0
Best Rating: 50 11/09 Ling 6f stand

Final Verse

106(108) (95)102
6-y-o b g Mark Of Esteem (IRE)-Tamassos (Dance In Time (CAN))
Matthew Salaman (M Salaman 18/7) Mrs N L Young

Placings:1422/610/354416/006500001523-20000000100 (7883)
2009: 8^{2}GF, 8^{0}GF, 8^{0}GF, 10^{0}GS, 8^{0}GF, 9^{0}S, 9^{0}SD, 7^{0}SD, 8^{1}SD, 10^{0}SD, 8^{0}SD,

	Starts	1st	2nd	3rd	Win & Pl
Career Total (Turf)	27	3	4	1	74629
Career Total (AW)	9	2	0	1	8174

87 11/09 Ling 1m (0-75)H STD £2590
88 10/08 Wolv 7f32y STD £3238
109 8/07 NmkJ 1m G-F £12464
106 5/06 Gdwd 1m SFT £17034
79 7/05 Donc 6f GD £5980
Total win prize-money £41306

Going (Turf): Sf: 1-5 GS: 0-5 Gd: 1-8 GF: 1-9 Fm: 0-0
Distance: 5f/6f: 1-3 7f-8f: 4-22 9f-13f: 0-11 14f+: 0-0
Track : LH: 2-12 RH: 1-8 Tight: 2-10 Gall: 0-5
Aids: Bl: 0-0 Vi: 0-0 Tstrap: 0-0 Ckp: 0-0
Best Rating: 113 5/06 NmkR 1m gd-fm

Very useful; former winner in Listed class, stays 1m; acts on most ground and on Polytrack; has worn an eyeshield.

Final Victory

107(94) (86)93
3-y-o ch g Generous (IRE)-Persian Victory (IRE) (Persian Bold)
A M Balding Sir Gordon Brunton

Placings:5-311323030 (7373)
2009: 12^{3}G, 12^{1}GS, 12^{1}SD, 12^{3}GF, 14^{2}GF, 14^{3}G, 14^{0}GF, 12^{3}G, 12^{0}SD,

	Starts	1st	2nd	3rd	Win & Pl
Career Total (Turf)	8	1	1	4	9819
Career Total (AW)	2	1	0	0	4727

86 6/09 Kemp 1m4f (0-85)H STD £4727
80 5/09 Newc 1m4f93y G-S £2590
Total win prize-money £7317

Going (Turf): Sf: 0-0 GS: 1-2 Gd: 0-3 GF: 0-3 Fm: 0-0
Distance: 5f/6f: 0-0 7f-8f: 0-1 9f-13f: 2-6 14f+: 0-3
Track : LH: 1-4 RH: 1-5 Tight: 0-3 Gall: 1-3
Aids: Bl: 0-0 Vi: 0-0 Tstrap: 0-1 Ckp: 0-1
Best Rating: 93 6/09 Sals 1m4f gd-fm

Useful; stays 1m4f; handles fast and easy ground; has worn cheekpieces.

Finch Flyer (IRE)

88(71) (19)49
2-y-o ch c Indian Ridge-Imelda (USA) (Manila (USA))
G L Moore Prix Mature Racing

Placings:006 (6965)
2009: 5^{0}GF, 7^{0}SS, 7^{6}G,

	Starts	1st	2nd	3rd	Win & Pl
Career Total (Turf)	2	0	0	0	102
Career Total (AW)	1	0	0	0	

Going (Turf): Sf: 0-0 GS: 0-0 Gd: 0-1 GF: 0-1 Fm: 0-0
Distance: 5f/6f: 0-1 7f-8f: 0-2 9f-13f: 0-0 14f+: 0-0
Track : LH: 0-2 RH: 0-0 Tight: 0-1 Gall: 0-0
Aids: Bl: 0-0 Vi: 0-0 Tstrap: 0-0 Ckp: 0-0
Best Rating: 49 10/09 Brig 7f214y good

Fine Art Collector (IRE)

72(87) (55)45
3-y-o ch g Choisir (AUS)-New Foundation (IRE) (College Chapel)
G L Moore R A Green

Placings:500 (6430)
2009: 7^{5}GF, 8^{0}SD, 7^{0}SD,

	Starts	1st	2nd	3rd	Win & Pl
Career Total (Turf)	1	0	0	0	0
Career Total (AW)	2	0	0	0	

Going (Turf): Sf: 0-0 GS: 0-0 Gd: 0-0 GF: 0-1 Fm: 0-0
Distance: 5f/6f: 0-0 7f-8f: 0-3 9f-13f: 0-0 14f+: 0-0
Track : LH: 0-1 RH: 0-1 Tight: 0-1 Gall: 0-0
Aids: Bl: 0-0 Vi: 0-0 Tstrap: 0-0 Ckp: 0-0
Best Rating: 55 10/09 Wolv 7f32y stand

Fine Lace (IRE)

91(93) (63)53
2-y-o b f Barathea (IRE)-Fine Detail (IRE) (Shirley Heights)
D J S Ffrench Davis Miss A Jones

Placings:00015035 (7804)
2009: 7^{0}S, 8^{0}SD, 8^{0}GF, 8^{1}SD, 8^{5}S, 8^{0}SD, 10^{3}SD, 8^{5}SD,

	Starts	1st	2nd	3rd	Win & Pl
Career Total (Turf)	3	0	0	0	0
Career Total (AW)	5	1	0	1	3032

63 10/09 Wolv 1m141y (0-65) STD £2729
Total win prize-money £2730

Going (Turf): Sf: 0-2 GS: 0-0 Gd: 0-0 GF: 0-1 Fm: 0-0
Distance: 5f/6f: 0-0 7f-8f: 0-3 9f-13f: 1-5 14f+: 0-0
Track : LH: 1-4 RH: 0-3 Tight: 1-2 Gall: 0-0
Aids: Bl: 0-0 Vi: 0-0 Tstrap: 0-0 Ckp: 0-0
Best Rating: 63 10/09 Wolv 1m141y stand

Modest; stays 1m2f and acts on Polytrack.

Fine Ruler (IRE)

(104) (70)70

5-y-o b g King's Best (USA)-Bint Alajwaad (IRE) (Fairy King (USA))

M R Bosley Mrs Jean M O'Connor

Placings:30/6630542/616665034510-3262600000144 (7586)

2009: 8^{3}SD, 8^{2}SD, 8^{6}SD, 8^{2}SD, 8^{6}SD, 8^{0}SD, 7^{0}SD, 8^{0}SD, 7^{0}SD, 8^{0}SD, 8^{1}SD, 8^{4}SD, 8^{4}SD,

	Starts	1st	2nd	3rd	Win & Pl
Career Total (Turf)	3	0	0	2	1156
Career Total (AW)	31	3	3	2	9530

63 10/09 Kemp 1m (0-60)H STD £1706
66 12/08 GrLe 1m (0-70)H STD £3238
75 2/08 Kemp 7f (0-65)H STD £2047
Total win prize-money £6992

Going (Turf): Sf: 0-0 GS: 0-0 Gd: 0-1 GF: 0-2 Fm: 0-0
Distance: 5f/6f: 0-1 7f-8f: 3-26 9f-13f: 0-7 14f+: 0-0
Track : LH: 1-20 RH: 2-12 Tight: 0-20 Gall: 1-1
Aids: Bl: 0-0 Vi: 0-0 Tstrap: 0-0 Ckp: 0-0
Best Rating: 75 2/08 Kemp 7f stand

Modest; best over 7f and acts on Polytrack.

Fine Sight

102(101) (79)80

2-y-o b c Cape Cross (IRE)-Daring Aim (Daylami (IRE))

R Hannon The Queen

Placings:62221 (7130)

2009: 6^{6}G, 7^{2}GS, 7^{2}G, 8^{2}G, 7^{1}SD,

	Starts	1st	2nd	3rd	Win & Pl
Career Total (Turf)	4	0	3	0	3806
Career Total (AW)	1	1	0	0	4404

79 10/09 Ling 7f STD £4403
Total win prize-money £4404

Going (Turf): Sf: 0-0 GS: 0-1 Gd: 0-3 GF: 0-0 Fm: 0-0
Distance: 5f/6f: 0-1 7f-8f: 1-3 9f-13f: 0-1 14f+: 0-0
Track : LH: 1-3 RH: 0-1 Tight: 1-3 Gall: 0-0
Aids: Bl: 0-0 Vi: 0-0 Tstrap: 0-0 Ckp: 0-0
Best Rating: 80 7/09 Epsm 7f good

Useful; effective over 7f-1m; acts on Polytrack.

Fine Silk (USA)

92 59

3-y-o ch f Rahy (USA)-Meiosis (USA) (Danzig (USA))

B Smart H E Sheikh Rashid Bin Mohammed

Placings:045 (5394)

2009: 7^{0}G, 7^{4}GF, 7^{5}GF,

	Starts	1st	2nd	3rd	Win & Pl
Career Total (Turf)	3	0	0	0	486

Going (Turf): Sf: 0-0 GS: 0-0 Gd: 0-1 GF: 0-2 Fm: 0-0
Distance: 5f/6f: 0-0 7f-8f: 0-3 9f-13f: 0-0 14f+: 0-0
Track : LH: 0-2 RH: 0-0 Tight: 0-0 Gall: 0-1
Aids: Bl: 0-0 Vi: 0-0 Tstrap: 0-0 Ckp: 0-0
Best Rating: 59 7/09 York 7f gd-fm

Modeast; stays 7f; acts on fast ground.

Fine The World

(66)

5-y-o b m Agnes World (USA)-Fine Honor (FR) (Highest Honor (FR))

Mrs J L Le Brocq (G A Ham 4/7) N G Ahier

Placings:00005461

2009: 9^{0}SD, 9^{0}SD, 8^{0}GF, 12^{0}F, 10^{5}GF, 7^{4}GS, 8^{6}GF, 10^{1}F,

	Starts	1st	2nd	3rd	Win & Pl
Career Total (Turf)	6	1	0	0	1460
Career Total (AW)	2	0	0	0	

8/09 LesL 1m2f H FRM £1460
Total win prize-money £1460

Going (Turf): Sf: 0-0 GS: 0-1 Gd: 0-0 GF: 0-3 Fm: 1-2
Distance: 5f/6f: 0-0 7f-8f: 0-2 9f-13f: 1-6 14f+: 0-0
Track : LH: 1-5 RH: 0-0 Tight: 0-2 Gall: 0-0
Aids: Bl: 0-0 Vi: 0-0 Tstrap: 0-0 Ckp: 0-0

Fine Tolerance

96(99) (56)57

3-y-o b f Bertolini (USA)-Sashay (Bishop Of Cashel)

Miss S L Davison (J R Boyle 15/10) Calne Engineering Ltd

Placings:00-P02340603 (7658)

2009: 8^{P}GF, 10^{0}SD, 10^{2}GF, 11^{3}G, 10^{4}SD, 10^{0}SD, 11^{6}G, 12^{0}SD, 12^{3}SD,

	Starts	1st	2nd	3rd	Win & Pl
Career Total (Turf)	4	0	1	1	1209
Career Total (AW)	7	0	0	1	302

Going (Turf): Sf: 0-0 GS: 0-0 Gd: 0-2 GF: 0-2 Fm: 0-0
Distance: 5f/6f: 0-1 7f-8f: 0-2 9f-13f: 0-8 14f+: 0-0
Track : LH: 0-5 RH: 0-5 Tight: 0-5 Gall: 0-1
Aids: Bl: 0-0 Vi: 0-0 Tstrap: 0-0 Ckp: 0-0
Best Rating: 57 7/09 Wind 1m2f7y gd-fm

Moderate; effective over 1m2f-1m4f; acts on fast ground and on Polytrack.

Finest Reserve (IRE)

94 74

2-y-o b c Royal Applause-Red Bandanna (IRE) (Montjeu (IRE))

M R Channon Mrs E F Clarke

Placings:0022 (6235)

2009: 7^{0}G, 7^{0}GF, 8^{2}GF, 8^{2}GF,

	Starts	1st	2nd	3rd	Win & Pl
Career Total (Turf)	4	0	2	0	2987

Going (Turf): Sf: 0-0 GS: 0-0 Gd: 0-1 GF: 0-3 Fm: 0-0
Distance: 5f/6f: 0-0 7f-8f: 0-3 9f-13f: 0-1 14f+: 0-0
Track : LH: 0-1 RH: 0-2 Tight: 0-0 Gall: 0-0
Aids: Bl: 0-0 Vi: 0-0 Tstrap: 0-0 Ckp: 0-0
Best Rating: 74 9/09 Pont 1m4y gd-fm

Fair; stays 1m; acts on fast ground.

Finished Article (IRE)

(94) (48)54

12-y-o b g Indian Ridge-Summer Fashion (Moorestyle)

Mrs D Thomas Mrs D Thomas

Placings:50/46352100/05326612040/3421225052000650 52152204/053000040/00000/024315530040211030605/00 0000-0 (0131)

2009: 8^{0}SD,

	Starts	1st	2nd	3rd	Win & Pl
Career Total (Turf)	63	4	10	5	92717
Career Total (AW)	24	3	2	2	9383

59 1/07 Wolv 1m5f194y STD £2047
61 1/07 Wolv 1m4f50y STD £2388
64 7/06 Wolv 1m4f50y (0-60) STD £2730
95 7/03 Gdwd 1m D(0-85)H GD £11115
94 6/02 Gdwd 1m D(0-85)H G-F £5346
81 8/01 Gdwd 1m1f192yE(0-80)H G-S £4641
75 8/00 Epsm 1m114y D G-F £4095
Total win prize-money £32364

Going (Turf): Sf: 0-8 GS: 1-11 Gd: 1-16 GF: 2-23 Fm: 0-5
Distance: 5f/6f: 0-0 7f-8f: 2-38 9f-13f: 4-38 14f+: 1-11
Track : LH: 4-29 RH: 3-36 Tight: 5-33 Gall: 0-8
Aids: Bl: 0-1 Vi: 0-0 Tstrap: 0-0 Ckp: 0-0
Best Rating: 100 11/03 NmkR 1m gd-sft

Moderate performer; stays 1m6fs; acts on good to firm and good to soft as well as Polytrack; has worn blinkers.

Finjaan

110 118

3-y-o b c Royal Applause-Alhufoof (USA) (Dayjur (USA))

M P Tregoning Hamdan Al Maktoum

Placings:12103-010 (5657)

2009: 8^{0}GF, 7^{1}G, 6^{0}GS,

	Starts	1st	2nd	3rd	Win & Pl
Career Total (Turf)	8	3	1	1	167387

114 7/09 Gdwd 7f GD £87993
108 7/08 Gdwd 5f GD £34062
86 5/08 NmkR 5f G-F £9714
Total win prize-money £131770

Going (Turf): Sf: 0-1 GS: 0-1 Gd: 2-3 GF: 1-3 Fm: 0-0
Distance: 5f/6f: 2-5 7f-8f: 1-3 9f-13f: 0-0 14f+: 0-0
Track : LH: 0-0 RH: 1-1 Tight: 0-0 Gall: 0-0
Aids: Bl: 0-0 Vi: 0-0 Tstrap: 0-0 Ckp: 0-0
Best Rating: 118 10/08 NmkR 7f good

Group class; winner of the Molecomb Stakes and third in the Dewhurst in 2008; winner of the Betfair Cup at Goodwood in 2009; effective over 5f, but stays 7f; acts on most ground.

Finnegan McCool

97(104) (77)89

3-y-o b g Efisio-Royal Jade (Last Tycoon)

R M Beckett Lawrence & Wilkinson

Placings:34120600-00664010 (6976)

2009: 5^{0}G, 5^{0}GF, 6^{6}G, 6^{6}GF, 5^{4}GF, 6^{0}G, 7^{1}SS, 7^{0}SD,

	Starts	1st	2nd	3rd	Win & Pl
Career Total (Turf)	13	1	1	1	6578
Career Total (AW)	3	1	0	0	2914

77 10/09 Ling 7f (0-70)H SS £2914
81 6/08 Wind 5f10y G-F £4403
Total win prize-money £7318

Going (Turf): Sf: 0-0 GS: 0-1 Gd: 0-6 GF: 1-6 Fm: 0-0
Distance: 5f/6f: 1-12 7f-8f: 1-4 9f-13f: 0-0 14f+: 0-0
Track : LH: 1-3 RH: 0-2 Tight: 1-1 Gall: 1-3
Aids: Bl: 0-0 Vi: 0-0 Tstrap: 1-6 Ckp: 1-6
Best Rating: 89 7/08 Newb 5f34y good

Modest; stays 7f; acts on fast ground; goes on Polytrack.

Finnegans Rainbow

91(89) (39)38

7-y-o ch g Spectrum (IRE)-Fairy Story (IRE) (Persian Bold)

M C Chapman J E Reed

Placings:0/000040526024364504660/0005/4000-60 (7817)

2009: 9^{6}GF, 9^{0}SD,

	Starts	1st	2nd	3rd	Win & Pl
Career Total (Turf)	18	0	1	0	1337
Career Total (AW)	14	0	1	1	634

Going (Turf): **Sf: 0-3 GS: 0-2 Gd: 0-5 GF: 0-7 Fm: 0-1**
Distance: 5f/6f: 0-0 7f-8f: 0-2 9f-13f: 0-28 14f+: 0-2
Track : LH: 0-24 RH: 0-6 Tight: 0-18 Gall: 0-1
Aids: Bl: 0-1 Vi: 0-0 Tstrap: 0-0 Ckp: 0-0
Best Rating: **56** 8/06 Bevl 1m1f207y gd-sft

Finney Hill

105 **80**
4-y-o b f Mark Of Esteem (IRE)-Ringing Hill (Charnwood Forest (IRE))
H Candy Major M G Wyatt

Placings:044-2310 **(7148)**
2009: 10^{2}GF, 9^{3}S, 10^{1}G, 12^{0}G,

	Starts	1st	2nd	3rd	Win & Pl
Career Total (Turf)	7	1	1	1	5431

75 10/09 Bath 1m2f46y GD £2590
Total win prize-money £2590

Going (Turf): Sf: 0-2 GS: 0-0 **Gd: 1-4** GF: 0-1 Fm: 0-0
Distance: 5f/6f: 0-0 7f-8f: 0-0 **9f-13f: 1-7** 14f+: 0-0
Track : **LH: 1-3** RH: 0-4 **Tight: 1-3** Gall: 0-2
Aids: Bl: 0-0 Vi: 0-0 Tstrap: 0-0 Ckp: 0-0
Best Rating: **80** 10/09 Sals 1m1f198y soft

Fair; stays 1m2f; acts on good ground.

Finsbury

103(95) (65)**66**
6-y-o gr g Observatory (USA)-Carmela Owen (Owington)
J S Goldie M Mackay & S Bruce

Placings:444/01616366030/0504051306/0450150605-2366040160 **(7172)**
2009: 5^{2}GF, 6^{3}GF, 6^{6}G, 7^{6}G, 6^{0}GF, 7^{4}GF, 7^{0}G, 7^{1}GF, 6^{6}G, 7^{0}S,

	Starts	1st	2nd	3rd	Win & Pl
Career Total (Turf)	29	3	1	2	20018
Career Total (AW)	15	2	0	2	11110

66 10/09 Ayr 7f50y (0-60)H G-F £2388
65 8/08 NmkJ 6f (0-85)H GD £12462
56 8/07 Leic 7f9y FRM £2590
86 7/06 Kemp 7f (0-75)H STD £3238
75 6/06 Kemp 6f (0-80)H STD £5505
Total win prize-money £26185

Going (Turf): Sf: 0-4 GS: 0-4 **Gd: 1-10 GF: 1-9 Fm: 1-2**
Distance: 5f/6f: 2-12 **7f-8f: 3-30** 9f-13f: 0-2 14f+: 0-0
Track : LH: 1-10 **RH: 2-16** Tight: 0-10 Gall: 0-1
Aids: Bl: 0-0 Vi: 0-1 Tstrap: 0-0 Ckp: 0-0
Best Rating: **86** 7/06 Kemp 7f stand

Moderate; effective from 6f-1m; acts on good and faster ground and on Polytrack.

Fire And Rain (FR)

83 **63**
6-y-o b g Galileo (IRE)-Quatre Saisons (FR) (Homme De Loi (IRE))
Miss E C Lavelle Fraser Miller Racing

Placings:1/600/0/0 **(2994)**
2009: 20^{0}GF,

	Starts	1st	2nd	3rd	Win & Pl
Career Total (Turf)	6	1	0	0	8804

98 9/05 NmkR 1m GD £6981
Total win prize-money £6981

Going (Turf): Sf: 0-1 GS: 0-2 **Gd: 1-2** GF: 0-1 Fm: 0-0
Distance: 5f/6f: 0-0 **7f-8f: 1-1** 9f-13f: 0-3 14f+: 0-2
Track : LH: 0-2 RH: 0-3 Tight: 0-0 Gall: 0-4
Aids: Bl: 0-0 Vi: 0-0 Tstrap: 0-0 Ckp: 0-0
Best Rating: **108** 8/06 York 1m4f gd-sft

Fire And Stone (IRE)

91 **66**
2-y-o b g Hawk Wing (USA)-Shinkoh Rose (FR) (Warning)
Tom Dascombe David Coffer

Placings:03400 **(6735)**
2009: 6^{0}GF, 6^{3}GF, 6^{4}G, 7^{0}G, 8^{0}GS,

	Starts	1st	2nd	3rd	Win & Pl
Career Total (Turf)	5	0	0	1	752

Going (Turf): **Sf: 0-0 GS: 0-1 Gd: 0-2 GF: 0-2 Fm: 0-0**
Distance: 5f/6f: 0-2 7f-8f: 0-2 9f-13f: 0-1 14f+: 0-0
Track : LH: 0-0 RH: 0-1 Tight: 0-1 Gall: 0-1
Aids: Bl: 0-0 Vi: 0-0 Tstrap: 0-0 Ckp: 0-0
Best Rating: **66** 6/09 Sals 6f212y good

Fire King

100(100) (61)**65**
3-y-o b g Falbrav (IRE)-Dancing Fire (USA) (Dayjur (USA))
J A Geake Dr J M Leigh

Placings:000-441502406040 **(7587)**
2009: 9^{4}GF, 8^{4}G, 10^{1}GF, 10^{5}G, 9^{0}GS, 7^{2}F, 8^{4}GS, 8^{0}SD, 8^{6}GF, 7^{0}G, 10^{4}SD, 8^{0}SD,

	Starts	1st	2nd	3rd	Win & Pl
Career Total (Turf)	12	1	1	0	3188
Career Total (AW)	3	0	0	0	0

65 7/09 Ling 1m2f (0-65)H G-F £2047
Total win prize-money £2047

Going (Turf): Sf: 0-1 GS: 0-2 Gd: 0-5 **GF: 1-3** Fm: 0-1
Distance: 5f/6f: 0-0 7f-8f: 0-8 **9f-13f: 1-7** 14f+: 0-0
Track : **LH: 1-7** RH: 0-4 **Tight: 1-5** Gall: 0-0
Aids: Bl: 0-0 Vi: 0-1 Tstrap: 0-3 Ckp: 0-3
Best Rating: **65** 8/09 Brig 7f214y firm

Moderate; stays 1m2f and acts on fast and easy ground.

Fire Me Gun

(87) (44)
3-y-o b f Reel Buddy (USA)-Manderina (Mind Games)
M Mullineaux Tom Tuohy & Tony Jafrate

Placings:3-006 **(3954)**
2009: 9^{0}SD, 9^{0}SD, 14^{6}SD,

	Starts	1st	2nd	3rd	Win & Pl
Career Total (Turf)	0	0	0	0	
Career Total (AW)	4	0	0	1	625

Going (Turf): **Sf: 0-0 GS: 0-0 Gd: 0-0 GF: 0-0 Fm: 0-0**
Distance: 5f/6f: 0-0 7f-8f: 0-0 9f-13f: 0-3 14f+: 0-1
Track : LH: 0-4 RH: 0-0 Tight: 0-3 Gall: 0-0
Aids: Bl: 0-0 Vi: 0-0 Tstrap: 0-0 Ckp: 0-0
Best Rating: **44** 12/08 Wolv 1m141y stand

Fire Raiser

87(92) (61)**41**
2-y-o b g Firebreak-Mara River (Efisio)
A M Balding Kingsclere Racing CLub

Placings:50 **(6903)**
2009: 6^{5}SD, 5^{0}G,

	Starts	1st	2nd	3rd	Win & Pl
Career Total (Turf)	1	0	0	0	
Career Total (AW)	1	0	0	0	0

Going (Turf): **Sf: 0-0 GS: 0-0 Gd: 0-1 GF: 0-0 Fm: 0-0**
Distance: 5f/6f: 0-2 7f-8f: 0-0 9f-13f: 0-0 14f+: 0-0
Track : LH: 0-0 RH: 0-1 Tight: 0-0 Gall: 0-1
Aids: Bl: 0-0 Vi: 0-0 Tstrap: 0-0 Ckp: 0-0
Best Rating: **61** 9/09 Kemp 6f stand

Fire Up The Band

79(106) (92)**69**
10-y-o b g Prince Sabo-Green Supreme (Primo Dominie)
A Berry Alan Berry

Placings:1514332/3112023/0034010000/10510431003/50040000/104000500/11530022325500300-60000 **(4192)**
2009: 7^{6}SD, 5^{0}SD, 5^{0}SD, 5^{0}G, 5^{0}S,

	Starts	1st	2nd	3rd	Win & Pl
Career Total (Turf)	65	8	6	9	253108
Career Total (AW)	9	3	0	1	8966

92 4/08 Wolv 5f20y STD £1774
72 3/08 Sthl 5f STD £3238
103 4/07 Nott 5f13y G-F £6477
114 7/05 Gdwd 5f SFT £29000
114 6/05 Epsm 5f H GD £43500
107 5/05 Ches 5f16y (0-100)H G-S £15161
98 7/04 Ches 5f16y A GD £17400
108 5/03 NmkR 6f C(0-95)H GD £29000
97 3/03 Asct 6f C(0-90)H G-F £9805
86 4/02 NmkR 6f C(0-95)H G-F £10530
71 2/02 Ling 7f D STD £2758
Total win prize-money £168644

Going (Turf): Sf: 1-15 GS: 1-10 **Gd: 3-18 GF: 3-20** Fm: 0-2
Distance: **5f/6f: 10-69** 7f-8f: 1-5 9f-13f: 0-0 14f+: 0-0
Track : **LH: 4-16** RH: 0-1 **Tight: 4-13** Gall: 0-0
Aids: Bl: 0-0 Vi: 0-3 Tstrap: 0-0 Ckp: 0-0
Best Rating: **116** 9/03 Ayr 6f good

Modest; effective over 5f-6f; acts well on easy ground; also goes on Fibresand and Polytrack.

Fireback

80 **66**
2-y-o b g Firebreak-So Discreet (Tragic Role (USA))
A M Balding Kennet Valley Thoroughbreds VII

Placings:606 **(6108)**
2009: 6^{6}G, 7^{0}G, 7^{6}GF,

	Starts	1st	2nd	3rd	Win & Pl
Career Total (Turf)	3	0	0	0	0

Going (Turf): **Sf: 0-0 GS: 0-0 Gd: 0-2 GF: 0-1 Fm: 0-0**
Distance: 5f/6f: 0-1 7f-8f: 0-2 9f-13f: 0-0 14f+: 0-0
Track : LH: 0-0 RH: 0-0 Tight: 0-0 Gall: 0-0
Aids: Bl: 0-0 Vi: 0-0 Tstrap: 0-0 Ckp: 0-0
Best Rating: **66** 9/09 Newb 7f gd-fm

Firebet (IRE)

110 112

3-y-o b c Dubai Destination (USA)-Dancing Prize (IRE) (Sadler's Wells (USA))

R A Fahey (Mrs A Duffield 2/5) Mrs H Steel

Placings:1414-2211121 (5508)

2009: 8[2]GF, 7[2]GF, 8[1]G, 8[1]GF, 10[1]G, 12[2]G, 10[1]G,

	Starts	1st	2nd	3rd	Win & Pl
Career Total (Turf)	11	6	3	0	113473

101	8/09	Epsm	1m2f18y		GD	£7477
112	7/09	NmkJ	1m2f	(0-105)H	GD	£49848
109	6/09	Ayr	1m	(0-100)H	G-F	£15577
98	6/09	Nott	1m75y	(0-95)H	GD	£7771
85	9/08	Ches	7f2y	(0-95)	G-S	£9146
77	6/08	Carl	5f193y		SFT	£3885

Total win prize-money £93707

Going (Turf): Sf: 1-1 GS: 1-1 **Gd: 3-6** GF: 1-3 Fm: 0-0
Distance: 5f/6f: 1-1 7f-8f: 2-6 **9f-13f: 3-4** 14f+: 0-0
Track : **LH: 4-5** RH: 2-4 **Tight: 2-5** Gall: 1-1
Aids: Bl: 0-0 Vi: 0-0 Tstrap: 0-0 Ckp: 0-0
Best Rating: **112** 7/09 NmkJ 1m2f good

Smart; stays 1m2f and acts on most ground.

Fireflash (IRE)

84 37

2-y-o b c Noverre (USA)-Miss Langkawi (Daylami (IRE))

Mrs A Duffield Andrew Turton

Placings:0000 (6533)

2009: 6[0]GF, 6[0]GF, 7[0]S, 10[0]GF,

	Starts	1st	2nd	3rd	Win & Pl
Career Total (Turf)	4	0	0	0	

Going (Turf): **Sf: 0-1 GS: 0-0 Gd: 0-0 GF: 0-3 Fm: 0-0**
Distance: 5f/6f: 0-2 7f-8f: 0-1 9f-13f: 0-1 14f+: 0-0
Track : LH: 0-2 RH: 0-0 Tight: 0-1 Gall: 0-0
Aids: Bl: 0-0 Vi: 0-0 Tstrap: 0-1 Ckp: 0-1
Best Rating: **37** 7/09 Rdcr 6f gd-fm

Firefly Mustique

78 39

2-y-o b c Oasis Dream-My Ballerina (USA) (Sir Ivor (USA))

George Baker FireflyMustiquePartnership&Lady Bamford

Placings:400 (7095)

2009: 6[4]G, 7[0]GF, 8[0]G,

	Starts	1st	2nd	3rd	Win & Pl
Career Total (Turf)	3	0	0	0	312

Going (Turf): **Sf: 0-0 GS: 0-0 Gd: 0-2 GF: 0-1 Fm: 0-0**
Distance: 5f/6f: 0-0 7f-8f: 0-2 9f-13f: 0-1 14f+: 0-0
Track : LH: 0-0 RH: 0-0 Tight: 0-0 Gall: 0-0
Aids: Bl: 0-0 Vi: 0-0 Tstrap: 0-0 Ckp: 0-0
Best Rating: **39** 10/09 Yarm 1m3y good

Firehawk

90(88) (51)56

2-y-o b g Firebreak-Distinctly Blu (IRE) (Distinctly North (USA))

J G Portman W Clifford

Placings:566 (6461)

2009: 6[5]G, 6[6]GF, 8[6]SD,

	Starts	1st	2nd	3rd	Win & Pl
Career Total (Turf)	2	0	0	0	0
Career Total (AW)	1	0	0	0	0

Going (Turf): **Sf: 0-0 GS: 0-0 Gd: 0-1 GF: 0-1 Fm: 0-0**
Distance: 5f/6f: 0-0 7f-8f: 0-2 9f-13f: 0-1 14f+: 0-0
Track : LH: 0-1 RH: 0-0 Tight: 0-1 Gall: 0-0
Aids: Bl: 0-0 Vi: 0-0 Tstrap: 0-0 Ckp: 0-0
Best Rating: **56** 8/09 Sals 6f212y gd-fm

Related to several sprint winners; missed the break on debut before showing ability; stays 6f; acts on good.

Firenza Bond

79(103) (63)69

4-y-o b g Captain Rio-Bond Stasia (IRE) (Mukaddamah (USA))

D Flood (G R Oldroyd 20/4) Helshaw Grange Stud Ltd

Placings:061061/06660-360 (2219)

2009: 5[3]SD, 5[6]SD, 5[0]GF,

	Starts	1st	2nd	3rd	Win & Pl
Career Total (Turf)	12	2	0	0	7449
Career Total (AW)	2	0	0	1	302

79	10/07	Catt	5f	GD	£3886
78	7/07	Ches	5f16y	SFT	£3562

Total win prize-money £7448

Going (Turf): **Sf: 1-2** GS: 0-2 **Gd: 1-5** GF: 0-3 Fm: 0-0
Distance: **5f/6f: 2-14** 7f-8f: 0-0 9f-13f: 0-0 14f+: 0-0
Track : **LH: 1-4** RH: 0-0 **Tight: 1-3** Gall: 0-0
Aids: Bl: 0-1 Vi: 0-0 Tstrap: 0-1 Ckp: 0-1
Best Rating: **79** 10/07 Catt 5f good

Fair; effective at 5f; acts on easy ground.

Fireside

96 74

4-y-o b g Dr Fong (USA)-Al Hasnaa (Zafonic (USA))

M A Jarvis Highclere Thoroughbred Racing (VCI)

Placings:61/0-00 (2780)

2009: 8[0]GF, 7[0]GF,

	Starts	1st	2nd	3rd	Win & Pl
Career Total (Turf)	5	1	0	0	11910

90	10/07	NmkR	7f	GD	£5829

Total win prize-money £5829

Going (Turf): Sf: 0-0 GS: 0-0 **Gd: 1-2** GF: 0-3 Fm: 0-0
Distance: 5f/6f: 0-0 **7f-8f: 1-5** 9f-13f: 0-0 14f+: 0-0
Track : LH: 0-1 RH: 0-0 Tight: 0-1 Gall: 0-0
Aids: Bl: 0-0 Vi: 0-0 Tstrap: 0-0 Ckp: 0-0
Best Rating: **92** 9/07 Curr 7f gd-fm

Firestorm (IRE)

87 40

5-y-o b g Celtic Swing-National Ballet (Shareef Dancer (USA))

C W Fairhurst Mrs C A Arnold

Placings:4540/00004000/650000-0000 (6769)

2009: 15[0]GF, 13[0]GF, 15[0]G, 12[0]GS,

	Starts	1st	2nd	3rd	Win & Pl
Career Total (Turf)	22	0	0	0	914

Going (Turf): **Sf: 0-5 GS: 0-3 Gd: 0-5 GF: 0-9 Fm: 0-0**
Distance: 5f/6f: 0-0 7f-8f: 0-2 9f-13f: 0-10 14f+: 0-10
Track : LH: 0-13 RH: 0-8 Tight: 0-13 Gall: 0-2
Aids: Bl: 0-6 Vi: 0-0 Tstrap: 0-1 Ckp: 0-1
Best Rating: **59** 7/06 Rdcr 7f gd-fm

Firetail

57(63) (8)

2-y-o b f Selkirk (USA)-Snow Goose (Polar Falcon (USA))

M L W Bell Sir Thomas Pilkington

Placings:00 (7451)

2009: 8[0]S, 8[0]SD,

	Starts	1st	2nd	3rd	Win & Pl
Career Total (Turf)	1	0	0	0	
Career Total (AW)	1	0	0	0	

Going (Turf): **Sf: 0-1 GS: 0-0 Gd: 0-0 GF: 0-0 Fm: 0-0**
Distance: 5f/6f: 0-0 7f-8f: 0-1 9f-13f: 0-1 14f+: 0-0
Track : LH: 0-1 RH: 0-1 Tight: 0-0 Gall: 0-0
Aids: Bl: 0-0 Vi: 0-0 Tstrap: 0-0 Ckp: 0-0
Best Rating: **8** 11/09 Kemp 1m stand

Firetrap

91 61

2-y-o b g Firebreak-Amber Mill (Doulab (USA))

Mrs A Duffield Mr Buckley & Mr Holdcroft & Mr Addison

Placings:044235 (5358)

2009: 5[0]G, 5[4]G, 5[4]GF, 5[2]G, 5[3]GF, 6[5]S,

	Starts	1st	2nd	3rd	Win & Pl
Career Total (Turf)	6	0	1	1	1637

Going (Turf): **Sf: 0-1 GS: 0-0 Gd: 0-3 GF: 0-2 Fm: 0-0**
Distance: 5f/6f: 0-6 7f-8f: 0-0 9f-13f: 0-0 14f+: 0-0
Track : LH: 0-1 RH: 0-2 Tight: 0-1 Gall: 0-1
Aids: Bl: 0-0 Vi: 0-1 Tstrap: 0-0 Ckp: 0-0
Best Rating: **61** 8/09 Catt 5f212y gd-fm

Firewalker

(92) (59)66

4-y-o b f Bertolini (USA)-Crystal Canyon (Efisio)

P T Dalton L Shillito & Julie Martin & David Martin

Placings:632422/55000005-4000 (1134)

2009: 5[4]SD, 5[0]SD, 5[0]SD, 5[0]SD,

	Starts	1st	2nd	3rd	Win & Pl
Career Total (Turf)	6	0	1	1	1300
Career Total (AW)	12	0	2	0	1411

Going (Turf): **Sf: 0-0 GS: 0-1 Gd: 0-4 GF: 0-1 Fm: 0-0**
Distance: 5f/6f: 0-18 7f-8f: 0-0 9f-13f: 0-0 14f+: 0-0
Track : LH: 0-9 RH: 0-1 Tight: 0-8 Gall: 0-1
Aids: Bl: 0-4 Vi: 0-0 Tstrap: 0-1 Ckp: 0-1
Best Rating: **66** 6/07 Carl 5f good

Modest; best over 5f; acts on good and easy ground and on Polytrack.

Firsaan (IRE)

83(70) 53

3-y-o b g Haafhd-Walayef (USA) (Danzig (USA))

J R Norton Colin Holder

Placings:60-00 (7504)

2009: 8[0]GF, 12[0]SD,

	Starts	1st	2nd	3rd	Win & Pl
Career Total (Turf)	3	0	0	0	
Career Total (AW)	1	0	0	0	

Going (Turf): **Sf: 0-1 GS: 0-0 Gd: 0-0 GF: 0-1 Fm: 0-0**
Distance: 5f/6f: 0-0 7f-8f: 0-3 9f-13f: 0-1 14f+: 0-0

Track : LH: 0-2 RH: 0-1 Tight: 0-1 Gall: 0-0
Aids: Bl: 0-0 Vi: 0-0 Tstrap: 0-0 Ckp: 0-0
Best Rating: **53** 10/08 Navn 1m sft-hvy

First Avenue

102 **96**

4-y-o b g Montjeu (IRE)-Marciala (IRE) (Machiavellian (USA))
G L Moore H R Hunt

Placings:61/3322316-00 **(7293)**
2009: 12^{0}GS, 12^{0}S,

	Starts	1st	2nd	3rd	Win & Pl
Career Total (Turf)	**11**	**2**	**2**	**3**	**23235**

96 10/08 Wwck 1m2f188y (0-95)H SFT £9714
80 10/07 Yarm 1m3y G-S £3141
Total win prize-money £12855

Going (Turf): **Sf: 1-4 GS: 1-2** Gd: 0-3 GF: 0-2 Fm: 0-0
Distance: 5f/6f: 0-0 7f-8f: 0-1 **9f-13f: 2-10** 14f+: 0-0
Track : **LH: 1-6** RH: 0-1 Tight: 0-4 Gall: 0-4
Aids: Bl: 0-0 Vi: 0-0 Tstrap: 1-4 Ckp: 1-4
Best Rating: **96** 10/08 Wwck 1m2f188y soft

Very useful; stays 1m4f but effective at shorter; acts on fast and soft ground.

First Bay (IRE)

105 **83**

3-y-o b g Hawk Wing (USA)-Montmartre (IRE) (Grand Lodge (USA))
J Howard Johnson Andrea & Graham Wylie

Placings:333 **(6137)**
2009: 9^{3}G, 9^{3}HY, 9^{3}G,

	Starts	1st	2nd	3rd	Win & Pl
Career Total (Turf)	**3**	**0**	**0**	**3**	**1926**

Going (Turf): **Sf: 0-1 GS: 0-0 Gd: 0-2 GF: 0-0 Fm: 0-0**
Distance: 5f/6f: 0-0 7f-8f: 0-0 9f-13f: 0-3 14f+: 0-0
Track : LH: 0-0 RH: 0-3 Tight: 0-2 Gall: 0-0
Aids: Bl: 0-0 Vi: 0-0 Tstrap: 0-0 Ckp: 0-0
Best Rating: **83** 9/09 Haml 1m1f36y good

Fair promise in limited starts; stays 1m1f; handles heavy ground.

First Blade

100(101) (66)**66**

3-y-o ch g Needwood Blade-Antonias Melody (Rambo Dancer (CAN))
S R Bowring S R Bowring

Placings:005-36021514363 **(7081)**
2009: 5^{3}SD, 6^{6}SD, 8^{0}GS, 6^{2}GF, 6^{1}SD, 6^{5}SD, 5^{1}SD, 7^{4}SD, 5^{3}GF, 5^{6}SD, 5^{3}S,

	Starts	1st	2nd	3rd	Win & Pl
Career Total (Turf)	**4**	**0**	**1**	**2**	**1266**
Career Total (AW)	**10**	**2**	**0**	**1**	**5281**

64 8/09 Wolv 5f20y (0-60)H STD £2388
61 7/09 Sthl 6f (0-60)H STD £2590
Total win prize-money £4978

Going (Turf): **Sf: 0-1 GS: 0-1 Gd: 0-0 GF: 0-2 Fm: 0-0**
Distance: **5f/6f: 2-8** 7f-8f: 0-5 9f-13f: 0-1 14f+: 0-0
Track : **LH: 2-9** RH: 0-0 **Tight: 1-2** Gall: 0-0
Aids: **Bl: 2-8** Vi: 0-0 Tstrap: 0-0 Ckp: 0-0
Best Rating: **66** 9/09 Nott 5f13y gd-fm

Modest; stays 6f; acts on fast ground; goes on Polytrack and Fibresand; has worn blinkers.

First Cat

96(86) (65)**82**

2-y-o b g One Cool Cat (USA)-Zina La Belle (Mark Of Esteem (IRE))
R Hannon R Barnett

Placings:006132 **(6067)**
2009: 5^{0}GF, 7^{0}SD, 7^{6}SD, 8^{1}G, 8^{3}GS, 9^{2}GF,

	Starts	1st	2nd	3rd	Win & Pl
Career Total (Turf)	**4**	**1**	**1**	**1**	**5478**
Career Total (AW)	**2**	**0**	**0**	**0**	**0**

74 8/09 Sals 1m (0-75) GD £3238
Total win prize-money £3238

Going (Turf): Sf: 0-0 GS: 0-1 **Gd: 1-1** GF: 0-2 Fm: 0-0
Distance: 5f/6f: 0-1 **7f-8f: 1-4** 9f-13f: 0-1 14f+: 0-0
Track : LH: 0-0 RH: 0-2 Tight: 0-0 Gall: 0-0
Aids: Bl: 0-0 Vi: 0-0 Tstrap: 0-0 Ckp: 0-0
Best Rating: **82** 9/09 NmkR 1m1f gd-fm

Fair; stays 1m; acts on good and easier ground.

First City

104 **96**

3-y-o b f Diktat-City Maiden (USA) (Carson City (USA))
D M Simcock Saeed Misleh

Placings:13-3050054 **(6757)**
2009: 7^{3}GF, 8^{0}G, 8^{5}GF, 7^{0}G, 8^{0}G, 7^{5}GF, 8^{4}G,

	Starts	1st	2nd	3rd	Win & Pl
Career Total (Turf)	**9**	**1**	**0**	**2**	**13865**

72 7/08 Ripn 6f HVY £2914
Total win prize-money £2914

Going (Turf): **Sf: 1-2** GS: 0-0 Gd: 0-4 GF: 0-3 Fm: 0-0
Distance: **5f/6f: 1-2** 7f-8f: 0-6 9f-13f: 0-1 14f+: 0-0
Track : LH: 0-0 RH: 0-3 Tight: 0-0 Gall: 0-1
Aids: Bl: 0-0 Vi: 0-0 Tstrap: 0-0 Ckp: 0-0
Best Rating: **96** 9/09 Asct 7f gd-fm

Very useful; effective over 7f-1m; acts on testing and quick ground.

First Fandango

88 **67**

2-y-o b c Hernando (FR)-First Fantasy (Be My Chief (USA))
J W Hills Nick Hubbard & Richard Tufft

Placings:65 **(7034)**
2009: 8^{6}G, 8^{5}S,

	Starts	1st	2nd	3rd	Win & Pl
Career Total (Turf)	**2**	**0**	**0**	**0**	**0**

Going (Turf): **Sf: 0-1 GS: 0-0 Gd: 0-1 GF: 0-0 Fm: 0-0**
Distance: 5f/6f: 0-0 7f-8f: 0-2 9f-13f: 0-0 14f+: 0-0
Track : LH: 0-0 RH: 0-0 Tight: 0-0 Gall: 0-0
Aids: Bl: 0-0 Vi: 0-0 Tstrap: 0-0 Ckp: 0-0
Best Rating: **67** 10/09 Newb 1m good

Ability on debut over 1m on good ground.

First Hand

78(87) (33)

3-y-o b f Act One-Strong Hand (First Trump)
M W Easterby Mrs Jean Turpin

Placings:0-5000 **(6177)**
2009: 8^{5}SD, 7^{0}SD, 11^{0}SD, 12^{0}GF,

	Starts	1st	2nd	3rd	Win & Pl
Career Total (Turf)	**1**	**0**	**0**	**0**	
Career Total (AW)	**4**	**0**	**0**	**0**	**0**

Going (Turf): **Sf: 0-0 GS: 0-0 Gd: 0-0 GF: 0-1 Fm: 0-0**
Distance: 5f/6f: 0-0 7f-8f: 0-3 9f-13f: 0-2 14f+: 0-0
Track : LH: 0-4 RH: 0-1 Tight: 0-1 Gall: 0-0
Aids: Bl: 0-1 Vi: 0-0 Tstrap: 0-0 Ckp: 0-0
Best Rating: **33** 2/09 Sthl 7f stand

First In Command (IRE)

109 (22)**90**

4-y-o b g Captain Rio-Queen Sigi (IRE) (Fairy King (USA))
Daniel Mark Loughnane Raymond Yeung

Placings:0060/02610210-00001203440 **(6315a)**
2009: 6^{0}S, 5^{0}Y, 5^{0}S, 6^{0}HY, 6^{1}GF, 6^{2}GF, 6^{0}HY, 6^{3}GF, 5^{4}G, 5^{4}G, 6^{0}G,

	Starts	1st	2nd	3rd	Win & Pl
Career Total (Turf)	**22**	**3**	**3**	**1**	**30515**
Career Total (AW)	**1**	**0**	**0**	**0**	

86 6/09 Donc 6f (0-85)H G-F £4857
90 9/08 Curr 6f (60-100)H SFT £12206
85 7/08 Naas 6f G-F £6097
Total win prize-money £23160

Going (Turf): Sf: 1-5 GS: 0-0 Gd: 0-8 **GF: 2-6** Fm: 0-0
Distance: **5f/6f: 3-18** 7f-8f: 0-5 9f-13f: 0-0 14f+: 0-0
Track : **LH: 1-5** RH: 0-4 Tight: 0-0 Gall: 0-1
Aids: Bl: 0-0 Vi: 0-0 Tstrap: 0-0 Ckp: 0-0
Best Rating: **90** 9/08 Curr 6f soft

Useful; effective over 6f; acts on a sound surface; usually wears a tongue tie.

First In Show

(98) (49)**42**

4-y-o b f Zamindar (USA)-Rose Show (Belmez (USA))
A M Balding Sir Gordon Brunton

Placings:0/50000-4 **(0114)**
2009: 7^{4}SD,

	Starts	1st	2nd	3rd	Win & Pl
Career Total (Turf)	**1**	**0**	**0**	**0**	
Career Total (AW)	**6**	**0**	**0**	**0**	**0**

Going (Turf): **Sf: 0-0 GS: 0-0 Gd: 0-1 GF: 0-0 Fm: 0-0**
Distance: 5f/6f: 0-1 7f-8f: 0-4 9f-13f: 0-2 14f+: 0-0
Track : LH: 0-2 RH: 0-4 Tight: 0-2 Gall: 0-0
Aids: Bl: 0-1 Vi: 0-0 Tstrap: 0-0 Ckp: 0-0
Best Rating: **49** 10/08 Kemp 1m stand

Moderate; effective at 7f; has worn blinkers and a tongue tie.

First In The Queue (IRE)

98(102) (84)**73**

2-y-o b c Azamour (IRE)-Irina (IRE) (Polar Falcon (USA))
S Kirk Liam Breslin

Placings:02031 **(7277)**
2009: 8^{0}G, 8^{2}G, 8^{0}G, 8^{3}G, 8^{1}SD,

	Starts	1st	2nd	3rd	Win & Pl
Career Total (Turf)	**4**	**0**	**1**	**1**	**1108**
Career Total (AW)	**1**	**1**	**0**	**0**	**3412**

84 11/09 Wolv 1m141y STD £3412
Total win prize-money £3412

Going (Turf): **Sf: 0-0 GS: 0-0 Gd: 0-4 GF: 0-0 Fm: 0-0**
Distance: 5f/6f: 0-0 7f-8f: 0-0 **9f-13f: 1-5** 14f+: 0-0

Track : LH: **1-2** RH: 0-1 **Tight: 1-3** Gall: 0-0
Aids: Bl: 0-0 Vi: 0-0 Tstrap: 0-0 Ckp: 0-0
Best Rating: **84** 11/09 Wolv 1m141y stand

Fair; effective over 1m; acts on good ground.

First Instance

84(90) (71)**71**
2-y-o b c Cape Cross (IRE)-Court Lane (USA) (Machiavellian (USA))
M Johnston Sheikh Hamdan Bin Mohammed Al Maktoum

Placings:054 **(6781)**
2009: 6^{0}GS, 8^{5}GS, 7^{4}SS,

	Starts	1st	2nd	3rd	Win & Pl
Career Total (Turf)	2	0	0	0	0
Career Total (AW)	1	0	0	0	289

Going (Turf): Sf: 0-0 GS: 0-2 Gd: 0-0 GF: 0-0 Fm: 0-0
Distance: 5f/6f: 0-1 7f-8f: 0-1 9f-13f: 0-1 14f+: 0-0
Track : LH: 0-1 RH: 0-1 Tight: 0-1 Gall: 0-0
Aids: Bl: 0-0 Vi: 0-0 Tstrap: 0-0 Ckp: 0-0
Best Rating: **71** 10/09 Ling 7f std-slw

First Maid

92(85) (32)**35**
3-y-o br f First Trump-Angel Maid (Forzando)
A B Haynes Mrs Julie E Palmer

Placings:00000 **(7137)**
2009: 12^{0}SD, 12^{0}G, 11^{0}G, 12^{0}SD, 13^{0}SD,

	Starts	1st	2nd	3rd	Win & Pl
Career Total (Turf)	2	0	0	0	
Career Total (AW)	3	0	0	0	

Going (Turf): Sf: 0-0 GS: 0-0 Gd: 0-2 GF: 0-0 Fm: 0-0
Distance: 5f/6f: 0-0 7f-8f: 0-0 9f-13f: 0-4 14f+: 0-1
Track : LH: 0-4 RH: 0-1 Tight: 0-3 Gall: 0-0
Aids: Bl: 0-0 Vi: 0-0 Tstrap: 0-0 Ckp: 0-0
Best Rating: **35** 8/09 Chep 1m4f23y good

First Order

102(107) (90)**90**
8-y-o b g Primo Dominie-Unconditional Love (IRE) (Polish Patriot (USA))
Miss A Stokell Ms Caron Stokell

Placings:312113/2062/0002540303103/5040002000231/ 436404043105004032150-2445520535000000 4402 **(7819)**

2009: 5^{2}SS, 6^{4}SD, 5^{4}SD, 5^{5}GF, 5^{5}SD, 5^{2}GF, 5^{0}G, 5^{5}GF, 5^{3}G, 5^{5}SD, 5^{0}G, 5^{0}GF, 6^{0}S, 5^{0}GS, 5^{0}G, 5^{0}SD, 5^{4}SD, 5^{4}SD, 5^{0}SD, 5^{2}SD,

	Starts	1st	2nd	3rd	Win & Pl
Career Total (Turf)	46	4	5	7	44141
Career Total (AW)	32	3	5	3	27973

84	12/08	GrLe	6f	(0-85)H	STD	£4857
90	7/08	Newc	5f	(0-85)H	G-F	£7165
90	12/07	Wolv	5f20y	(0-80)H	STD	£4857
94	11/06	Wolv	5f216y	(0-85)H	STD	£5505
99	7/03	Bath	5f11y	D	G-F	£4322
94	7/03	York	5f3y	C	G-F	£8749
75	6/03	Ripn	5f	E	G-F	£3676

Total win prize-money £39134

Going (Turf): Sf: 0-3 GS: 0-4 Gd: 0-19 **GF: 4-19** Fm: 0-1
Distance: **5f/6f: 7-76** 7f-8f: 0-1 9f-13f: 0-1 14f+: 0-0
Track : **LH: 4-30** RH: 0-5 Tight: 2-21 Gall: 2-8
Aids: Bl: 0-0 **Vi: 4-57** Tstrap: 0-0 Ckp: 0-0
Best Rating: **105** 7/04 NmkJ 5f good

Modest; effective over 5f-6f; acts on good and faster ground and on sand; usually wears a visor.

First Post (IRE)

72 **20**
2-y-o b g Celtic Swing-Consignia (IRE) (Definite Article)
D Haydn Jones Llewelyn, Runeckles

Placings:00 **(7029)**
2009: 8^{0}G, 8^{0}S,

	Starts	1st	2nd	3rd	Win & Pl
Career Total (Turf)	2	0	0	0	

Going (Turf): Sf: 0-1 GS: 0-0 Gd: 0-1 GF: 0-0 Fm: 0-0
Distance: 5f/6f: 0-0 7f-8f: 0-1 9f-13f: 0-1 14f+: 0-0
Track : LH: 0-1 RH: 0-0 Tight: 0-1 Gall: 0-0
Aids: Bl: 0-0 Vi: 0-0 Tstrap: 0-0 Ckp: 0-0
Best Rating: **20** 10/09 Newb 1m soft

First Service (IRE)

(98) (68)**60**
3-y-o ch c Intikhab (USA)-Princess Sceptre (Cadeaux Genereux)
R Charlton John Livock

Placings:0-41 **(7464)**
2009: 7^{4}SD, 7^{1}SD,

	Starts	1st	2nd	3rd	Win & Pl
Career Total (Turf)	1	0	0	0	
Career Total (AW)	2	1	0	0	2388

68 11/09 Wolv 7f32y STD £2388
Total win prize-money £2388

Going (Turf): Sf: 0-0 GS: 0-0 Gd: 0-1 GF: 0-0 Fm: 0-0
Distance: 5f/6f: 0-0 **7f-8f: 1-3** 9f-13f: 0-0 14f+: 0-0
Track : **LH: 1-2** RH: 0-0 **Tight: 1-2** Gall: 0-0
Aids: Bl: 0-0 Vi: 0-0 Tstrap: 0-0 Ckp: 0-0
Best Rating: **68** 11/09 Wolv 7f32y stand

Modest; stays 7f and acts on Polytrack.

First Spirit

96(97) (56)**56**
3-y-o ch f First Trump-Flaming Spirt (Blushing Flame (USA))
J S Moore Bill Wyatt

Placings:0-30560013303 **(3588)**
2009: 12^{3}SD, 12^{0}SD, 10^{5}G, 11^{6}GF, 11^{0}GS, 12^{0}GF, 12^{1}SD, 11^{3}G, 12^{3}SD, 12^{0}SD, 10^{3}GF,

	Starts	1st	2nd	3rd	Win & Pl
Career Total (Turf)	6	0	0	2	706
Career Total (AW)	6	1	0	2	2753

56 5/09 Ling 1m4f STD £2047
Total win prize-money £2047

Going (Turf): Sf: 0-0 GS: 0-1 Gd: 0-2 GF: 0-3 Fm: 0-0
Distance: 5f/6f: 0-0 7f-8f: 0-1 **9f-13f: 1-11** 14f+: 0-0
Track : **LH: 1-7** RH: 0-2 **Tight: 1-11** Gall: 0-0
Aids: Bl: 0-0 Vi: 0-0 Tstrap: 1-5 Ckp: 1-5
Best Rating: **56** 5/09 Ling 1m4f stand

Moderate; stays 1m4f; acts on Polytrack; has worn cheek-pieces.

First Swallow

99(100) (68)**64**
4-y-o ch g Bahamian Bounty-Promise Fulfilled (USA) (Bet Twice (USA))
D H Brown (R A Fahey 24/8) The Secret Seven Partnership

Placings:0450100-600300625142 **(7838)**
2009: 5^{6}GF, 5^{0}GF, 5^{0}G, 5^{3}S, 5^{0}S, 5^{0}GS, 5^{6}HY, 6^{2}G, 5^{5}S, 5^{1}SD, 6^{4}SD, 5^{2}SS,

	Starts	1st	2nd	3rd	Win & Pl
Career Total (Turf)	16	1	1	1	3450
Career Total (AW)	3	1	1	0	2551

65	11/09	Sthl	5f	(0-58)H	STD	£2047
64	8/08	Bevl	5f		SFT	£2752

Total win prize-money £4799

Going (Turf): Sf: 1-6 GS: 0-4 Gd: 0-3 GF: 0-2 Fm: 0-1
Distance: **5f/6f: 2-17** 7f-8f: 0-2 9f-13f: 0-0 14f+: 0-0
Track : LH: 0-3 RH: 0-3 Tight: 0-1 Gall: 0-1
Aids: Bl: 0-0 Vi: 0-0 Tstrap: 0-2 Ckp: 0-2
Best Rating: **68** 12/09 Sthl 5f std-slw

Modest; suited by 5f and soft ground, also handles Fibresand; has worn a tongue tie.

First Term

89 **62**
2-y-o b f Acclamation-School Days (Slip Anchor)
R Hannon The Playground Partnership

Placings:54 **(5318)**
2009: 6^{5}G, 6^{4}GF,

	Starts	1st	2nd	3rd	Win & Pl
Career Total (Turf)	2	0	0	0	265

Going (Turf): Sf: 0-0 GS: 0-0 Gd: 0-1 GF: 0-1 Fm: 0-0
Distance: 5f/6f: 0-2 7f-8f: 0-0 9f-13f: 0-0 14f+: 0-0
Track : LH: 0-0 RH: 0-0 Tight: 0-0 Gall: 0-1
Aids: Bl: 0-0 Vi: 0-0 Tstrap: 0-0 Ckp: 0-0
Best Rating: **62** 8/09 Wind 6f gd-fm

Has shown some signs of ability.

First To Call

(100) (74)**83**
5-y-o ch g First Trump-Scarlett Holly (Red Sunset)
P J Makin Mrs P J Makin

Placings:0/51502/30-004 **(7701)**
2009: 10^{0}SD, 12^{0}SD, 16^{4}SD,

	Starts	1st	2nd	3rd	Win & Pl
Career Total (Turf)	4	1	0	0	2073
Career Total (AW)	7	0	1	1	2582

83 6/07 Bath 1m5y GD £2072
Total win prize-money £2073

Going (Turf): Sf: 0-1 GS: 0-2 **Gd: 1-1** GF: 0-0 Fm: 0-0
Distance: 5f/6f: 0-0 7f-8f: 0-2 **9f-13f: 1-8** 14f+: 0-1
Track : **LH: 1-6** RH: 0-4 **Tight: 1-5** Gall: 0-1
Aids: Bl: 0-0 Vi: 0-0 Tstrap: 0-0 Ckp: 0-0
Best Rating: **88** 10/07 Ling 1m4f stand

First Trim (IRE)

(100) (78)**79**
4-y-o b g Acclamation-Spanker (Suave Dancer (USA))
Seamus Fahey J J Bailey

Placings:53300/03160040-60 **(7070a)**
2009: 5^{6}SD, 14^{0}S,

	Starts	1st	2nd	3rd	Win & Pl
Career Total (Turf)	11	1	0	3	5860

	Starts	1st	2nd	3rd	Win & Pl
Career Total (AW)	4	0	0	0	385

79 6/08 NmkJ 5f (0-75)H G-F £3885
Total win prize-money £3886

Going (Turf): Sf: 0-1 GS: 0-3 Gd: 0-1 **GF: 1-6** Fm: 0-0
Distance: **5f/6f: 1-12** 7f-8f: 0-2 9f-13f: 0-0 14f+: 0-1
Track : LH: 0-4 RH: 0-2 Tight: 0-2 Gall: 0-1
Aids: Bl: 0-0 Vi: 0-0 Tstrap: 0-0 Ckp: 0-0
Best Rating: 81 9/07 Gdwd 6f gd-fm

Fair; effective over 5-6f; acts on good/fast ground.

Fisadara

100 69
3-y-o b f Nayef (USA)-Success Story (Sharrood (USA))
Jane Chapple-Hyam (B W Hills 24/6) Wood Hall Stud Ltd & Neil Gilchrist

Placings:0-0201640 (5726)
2009: 10^{0}GS, 10^{2}GF, 10^{0}G, 11^{1}F, 11^{6}G, 10^{4}GF, 12^{0}GF,

	Starts	1st	2nd	3rd	Win & Pl
Career Total (Turf)	8	1	1	0	4454

62 6/09 Bath 1m3f144y FRM £2719
Total win prize-money £2720

Going (Turf): Sf: 0-0 GS: 0-2 Gd: 0-2 GF: 0-3 **Fm: 1-1**
Distance: 5f/6f: 0-0 7f-8f: 0-1 **9f-13f: 1-7** 14f+: 0-0
Track : **LH: 1-5** RH: 0-2 **Tight: 1-4** Gall: 0-2
Aids: Bl: 0-0 Vi: 0-0 Tstrap: 0-0 Ckp: 0-0
Best Rating: 69 5/09 Ling 1m2f gd-fm

Fair; stays 1m3f plus; acts on fast ground.

Fish Called Johnny

(89) (55)76
5-y-o b g Kyllachy-Clare Celeste (Coquelin (USA))
A Berry The Touche Boys

Placings:413000/0310565335**000000**/005**00**-**00** (0277)
2009: 7^{0}SS, 7^{0}SD,

	Starts	1st	2nd	3rd	Win & Pl
Career Total (Turf)	17	2	0	4	22646
Career Total (AW)	12	0	0	0	0

76 5/07 Ayr 6f (0-85)H G-F £6477
85 8/06 Nott 6f15y GD £4533
Total win prize-money £11011

Going (Turf): Sf: 0-5 GS: 0-1 **Gd: 1-6 GF: 1-5** Fm: 0-0
Distance: 5f/6f: 1-20 7f-8f: 1-7 9f-13f: 0-2 14f+: 0-0
Track : LH: 0-11 RH: 0-3 Tight: 0-10 Gall: 0-0
Aids: **Bl: 1-7** Vi: 0-0 Tstrap: 0-0 Ckp: 0-0
Best Rating: 86 8/06 Ripn 6f good

Modest sprinter; suited by 6f-7f; acts on fast and easy ground.

Fishforcompliments

107(104) (80)102
5-y-o b g Royal Applause-Flyfisher (USA) (Riverman (USA))
R A Fahey Mel Roberts and Ms Nicola Meese

Placings:21050/03040/20004000300-20210000200053 (7832)
2009: 7^{2}GF, 7^{0}GF, 7^{2}S, 6^{1}GF, 6^{0}GF, 6^{0}G, 6^{0}S, 8^{0}GF, 9^{2}HY, 6^{0}GF, 7^{0}GF, 7^{0}S, 7^{0}SD, 6^{5}SD, 6^{3}SD,

	Starts	1st	2nd	3rd	Win & Pl
Career Total (Turf)	32	2	5	2	35931
Career Total (AW)	4	0	0	1	770

102 6/09 Haml 6f5y (0-90)H G-F £10361

82 8/06 Hayd 6f G-F £3238
Total win prize-money £13601

Going (Turf): Sf: 0-8 GS: 0-4 Gd: 0-4 **GF: 2-16** Fm: 0-0
Distance: 5f/6f: 1-8 7f-8f: 1-19 9f-13f: 0-9 14f+: 0-0
Track : LH: 0-9 RH: 0-7 Tight: 0-3 Gall: 0-7
Aids: Bl: 0-2 Vi: 0-1 Tstrap: 1-6 Ckp: 1-6
Best Rating: 104 9/06 York 7f good

Fair; Listed placed; stays 1m1f but effective at shorter; acts on most ground; has worn blinkers, cheekpieces and a visor; likes to race prominently.

Fistral

95(92) (43)55
5-y-o b g Piccolo-Fayre Holly (IRE) (Fayruz)
P D Niven Hale Racing Limited

Placings:0600/0442030050/6215-505200306 (5734)
2009: 12^{5}SD, 12^{0}GS, 11^{5}GF, 15^{2}GF, 14^{0}GF, 11^{0}GF, 16^{3}G, 14^{0}GF, 16^{6}GS,

	Starts	1st	2nd	3rd	Win & Pl
Career Total (Turf)	23	1	3	2	5236
Career Total (AW)	4	0	0	0	0

53 7/08 Catt 1m3f214y (0-65)H G-F £2047
Total win prize-money £2047

Going (Turf): Sf: 0-1 GS: 0-6 Gd: 0-6 **GF: 1-10** Fm: 0-0
Distance: 5f/6f: 0-1 7f-8f: 0-10 **9f-13f: 1-10** 14f+: 0-6
Track : **LH: 1-15** RH: 0-6 **Tight: 1-11** Gall: 0-3
Aids: Bl: 0-2 Vi: 0-0 Tstrap: 0-1 Ckp: 0-1
Best Rating: 55 6/09 Ayr 1m7f gd-fm

Modest maiden; effective between 6f and 1m1f; acts on fast and in soft ground.

Fitolini

(88) (41)60
4-y-o ch f Bertolini (USA)-Miss Fit (IRE) (Hamas (IRE))
Mrs G S Rees Mrs G S Rees

Placings:51640006/R0-000 (0474)
2009: 5^{0}SD, 5^{0}SD, 5^{0}SD,

	Starts	1st	2nd	3rd	Win & Pl
Career Total (Turf)	5	0	0	0	1230
Career Total (AW)	8	1	0	0	3179

69 5/07 Wolv 5f20y STD £2914
Total win prize-money £2915

Going (Turf): **Sf: 0-2 GS: 0-1 Gd: 0-1 GF: 0-1 Fm: 0-0**
Distance: **5f/6f: 1-13** 7f-8f: 0-0 9f-13f: 0-0 14f+: 0-0
Track : **LH: 1-8** RH: 0-1 **Tight: 1-7** Gall: 0-1
Aids: Bl: 0-0 Vi: 0-0 Tstrap: 0-0 Ckp: 0-0
Best Rating: 69 7/07 Wolv 5f216y stand

Fair filly; stays 6f; acts on Polytrack.

Fitz

97(94) (62)58
3-y-o b g Mind Games-Timoko (Dancing Spree (USA))
Matthew Salaman (M Salaman 24/8) Mrs Victoria Keen

Placings:040-553105 (6787)
2009: 7^{5}G, 7^{5}GF, 7^{3}SD, 7^{1}SD, 8^{0}SD, 7^{5}G,

	Starts	1st	2nd	3rd	Win & Pl
Career Total (Turf)	3	0	0	0	0
Career Total (AW)	6	1	0	1	2691

62 9/09 Ling 7f (0-55)H STD £2388
Total win prize-money £2388

Going (Turf): **Sf: 0-0 GS: 0-0 Gd: 0-2 GF: 0-1 Fm: 0-0**
Distance: 5f/6f: 0-3 **7f-8f: 1-6** 9f-13f: 0-0 14f+: 0-0
Track : **LH: 1-5** RH: 0-1 **Tight: 1-2** Gall: 0-1
Aids: Bl: 0-0 Vi: 0-0 Tstrap: 0-1 Ckp: 0-1
Best Rating: 62 9/09 Ling 7f stand

Fitz Flyer (IRE)

(107) 88
3-y-o b c Acclamation-Starry Night (Sheikh Albadou)
D H Brown Ron Hull

Placings:22543-1 (7866)
2009: 5^{1}SS,

	Starts	1st	2nd	3rd	Win & Pl
Career Total (Turf)	5	0	2	1	12310
Career Total (AW)	1	1	0	0	7477

12/09 Sthl 5f (0-95)H SS £7477
Total win prize-money £7477

Going (Turf): **Sf: 0-1 GS: 0-1 Gd: 0-2 GF: 0-1 Fm: 0-0**
Distance: **5f/6f: 1-6** 7f-8f: 0-0 9f-13f: 0-0 14f+: 0-0
Track : LH: 0-1 RH: 0-0 Tight: 0-0 Gall: 0-1
Aids: Bl: 0-0 Vi: 0-0 Tstrap: 0-0 Ckp: 0-0
Best Rating: 88 8/08 NmkJ 6f good

Useful; effective over 5f-6f; acts on fast and soft ground, and on Fibresand.

Fitzolini

89(98) (58)70
3-y-o b g Bertolini (USA)-Coney Hills (Beverley Boy)
A D Brown Mrs Susan Johnson

Placings:3056421440-6000061626 (7755)
2009: 6^{6}G, 7^{0}SD, 5^{0}GF, 7^{0}G, 5^{0}G, 6^{6}S, 8^{1}SD, 8^{6}SD, 9^{2}SD, 8^{6}SD,

	Starts	1st	2nd	3rd	Win & Pl
Career Total (Turf)	15	1	1	1	6592
Career Total (AW)	5	1	1	0	2993

53 11/09 Wolv 1m141y (0-65)H STD £2388
70 8/08 Catt 5f212y G-S £3885
Total win prize-money £6274

Going (Turf): Sf: 0-2 **GS: 1-4** Gd: 0-6 GF: 0-3 Fm: 0-0
Distance: 5f/6f: 1-12 7f-8f: 0-5 9f-13f: 1-3 14f+: 0-0
Track : **LH: 2-10** RH: 0-5 **Tight: 2-8** Gall: 0-2
Aids: Bl: 0-0 Vi: 0-2 Tstrap: 2-14 Ckp: 2-14
Best Rating: 70 8/08 Catt 5f212y gd-sft

Moderate; stays 1m1f; acts on easy ground; goes on Polytrack.

Fitzwarren

96(100) (46)49
8-y-o b g Presidium-Coney Hills (Beverley Boy)
A D Brown Mrs Susan Johnson

Placings:202316004402/0300360600/000505000**366**/000 **0060-5000002005** (7666)
2009: 6^{5}SD, 7^{0}GF, 7^{0}G, 5^{0}GF, 7^{0}GF, 6^{0}GF, 9^{2}GF, 10^{0}GF, 9^{0}GS, 10^{5}SD,

	Starts	1st	2nd	3rd	Win & Pl
Career Total (Turf)	42	1	4	3	10378
Career Total (AW)	9	0	0	1	212

67 6/03 Carl 5f E FRM £3822
Total win prize-money £3822

Going (Turf): Sf: 0-1 GS: 0-4 Gd: 0-3 GF: 0-27 **Fm: 1-7**
Distance: **5f/6f: 1-34** 7f-8f: 0-13 9f-13f: 0-4 14f+: 0-0
Track : LH: 0-18 **RH: 1-12** Tight: 0-9 **Gall: 1-4**
Aids: Bl: 0-2 Vi: 0-17 Tstrap: 0-6 Ckp: 0-6
Best Rating: 69 7/04 Rdcr 5f soft

Modest sprinter; best over 5f; handles soft ground but best on firm; has worn most forms of headgear.

Fiulin

111(108) (94)111

4-y-o ch c Galileo (IRE)-Fafinta (IRE) (Indian Ridge)

M Botti Scuderia Rencati Srl

Placings:2/21200123-15560 **(5823)**

2009: 14^{1}GF, 14^{5}GS, 16^{5}G, 13^{6}GF, 14^{0}GF,

	Starts	1st	2nd	3rd	Win & Pl
Career Total (Turf)	13	3	4	1	66540
Career Total (AW)	1	0	0	0	

107 4/09 Nott 1m6f15y G-F £22708
100 9/08 Yarm 1m6f17y (0-100)H GD £11215
90 4/08 Donc 1m4f SFT £4857
Total win prize-money £38781

Going (Turf): **Sf: 1-1** GS: 0-2 **Gd: 1-4 GF: 1-6** Fm: 0-0
Distance: 5f/6f: 0-0 7f-8f: 0-0 9f-13f: 1-6 **14f+: 2-8**
Track : **LH: 3-8** RH: 0-6 Tight: 1-1 Gall: 1-9
Aids: Bl: 0-0 Vi: 0-0 Tstrap: 0-1 Ckp: 0-1
Best Rating: **111** 10/08 NmkR 2m good

Smart; Listed placed; stays 1m6f; acts on most ground.

Fiuntas (IRE)

(90) (53)55

6-y-o b g Lil's Boy (USA)-Scarpetta (USA) (Seattle Dancer (USA))

Shaun Harley Lough Derg Syndicate

Placings:0050000/00/00/**6-40** **(0619)**

2009: 5^{4}SD, 6^{0}SD,

	Starts	1st	2nd	3rd	Win & Pl
Career Total (Turf)	11	0	0	0	
Career Total (AW)	3	0	0	0	0

Going (Turf): **Sf: 0-0 GS: 0-0 Gd: 0-4 GF: 0-3 Fm: 0-0**
Distance: 5f/6f: 0-6 7f-8f: 0-7 9f-13f: 0-1 14f+: 0-0
Track : LH: 0-5 RH: 0-2 Tight: 0-0 Gall: 0-1
Aids: Bl: 0-2 Vi: 0-0 Tstrap: 0-3 Ckp: 0-3
Best Rating: **75** 9/05 Curr 6f good

Five A Side

(82) (28)63

5-y-o b g Lomitas-Fifth Emerald (Formidable (USA))

Evan Williams Irving Struel & David Latte

Placings:12/00206/0 **(0139)**

2009: 12^{0}SD,

	Starts	1st	2nd	3rd	Win & Pl
Career Total (Turf)	7	1	2	0	7393
Career Total (AW)	1	0	0	0	

82 7/06 Epsm 7f G-F £4533
Total win prize-money £4534

Going (Turf): Sf: 0-1 GS: 0-0 Gd: 0-2 **GF: 1-4** Fm: 0-0
Distance: 5f/6f: 0-0 **7f-8f: 1-1** 9f-13f: 0-7 14f+: 0-0
Track : **LH: 1-5** RH: 0-3 **Tight: 1-4** Gall: 0-1
Aids: Bl: 0-1 Vi: 0-0 Tstrap: 0-0 Ckp: 0-0
Best Rating: **84** 8/07 Ripn 1m1f170y gd-fm

Five Cents

95 75

2-y-o b c Exceed And Excel (AUS)-Native Nickel (IRE) (Be My Native (USA))

Saeed Bin Suroor Godolphin

Placings:3155 **(6693)**

2009: 7^{3}G, 7^{1}GF, 6^{5}GF, 7^{5}GS,

	Starts	1st	2nd	3rd	Win & Pl
Career Total (Turf)	4	1	0	1	5951

75 9/09 Epsm 7f G-F £5180
Total win prize-money £5181

Going (Turf): Sf: 0-0 GS: 0-1 Gd: 0-1 **GF: 1-2** Fm: 0-0
Distance: 5f/6f: 0-1 **7f-8f: 1-3** 9f-13f: 0-0 14f+: 0-0
Track : **LH: 1-2** RH: 0-1 **Tight: 1-2** Gall: 0-0
Aids: Bl: 0-0 Vi: 0-0 Tstrap: 0-0 Ckp: 0-0
Best Rating: **75** 9/09 Epsm 7f gd-fm

Five Gold Rings (IRE)

46(92) (63)

3-y-o ch f Captain Rio-Metisse (IRE) (Indian Ridge)

J A Osborne P J D Pottinger & 12 Day Partners

Placings:21000 **(7021)**

2009: 5^{2}SD, 6^{1}SD, 5^{0}SD, 6^{0}GF, 5^{0}SD,

	Starts	1st	2nd	3rd	Win & Pl
Career Total (Turf)	1	0	0	0	
Career Total (AW)	4	1	1	0	3500

63 2/09 Ling 6f STD £2729
Total win prize-money £2730

Going (Turf): **Sf: 0-0 GS: 0-0 Gd: 0-0 GF: 0-1 Fm: 0-0**
Distance: **5f/6f: 1-5** 7f-8f: 0-0 9f-13f: 0-0 14f+: 0-0
Track : **LH: 1-3** RH: 0-1 **Tight: 1-3** Gall: 0-0
Aids: Bl: 0-0 Vi: 0-0 Tstrap: 0-0 Ckp: 0-0
Best Rating: **63** 2/09 Ling 6f stand

Fair; effective over 5f-6f; acts on Polytrack.

Five Star Junior (USA)

105(108) (101)96

3-y-o b g Five Star Day (USA)-Sir Harriett (USA) (Sir Harry Lewis (USA))

Mrs L Stubbs Moyns Park Stud

Placings:304243-11115244344430 **(7862)**

2009: 6^{1}SD, 6^{1}SD, 5^{1}SD, 6^{1}SD, 7^{5}SD, 6^{2}SD, 6^{4}GF, 6^{4}GF, 6^{3}GF, 6^{4}G, 6^{4}GF, 6^{4}GF, 6^{3}SD, 5^{0}SD,

	Starts	1st	2nd	3rd	Win & Pl
Career Total (Turf)	8	0	0	2	8028
Career Total (AW)	12	4	2	2	24480

96 2/09 Ling 6f (0-85)H STD £4857
90 1/09 Wolv 5f216y (0-85)H STD £5180
84 1/09 Ling 6f (0-85)H STD £4857
79 1/09 Kemp 6f STD £2047
Total win prize-money £16942

Going (Turf): **Sf: 0-0 GS: 0-0 Gd: 0-1 GF: 0-6 Fm: 0-1**
Distance: **5f/6f: 4-17** 7f-8f: 0-3 9f-13f: 0-0 14f+: 0-0
Track : **LH: 3-9** RH: 1-4 **Tight: 3-8** Gall: 0-1
Aids: Bl: 0-0 Vi: 0-0 Tstrap: 0-0 Ckp: 0-0
Best Rating: **101** 3/09 Kemp 6f stand

Very useful; effective over 6f-7f; acts on fast ground; goes on Polytrack.

Five Wishes

83 67

5-y-o b m Bahamian Bounty-Due West (Inchinor)

G A Harker Exors of the late Mark Swift

Placings:6/53222000/552642411350-00 **(2264)**

2009: 8^{0}G, 11^{0}G,

	Starts	1st	2nd	3rd	Win & Pl
Career Total (Turf)	23	2	5	2	9732

67 8/08 Haml 1m65y SFT £2388
63 8/08 Haml 1m65y GD £2388
Total win prize-money £4776

Going (Turf): **Sf: 1-4** GS: 0-6 **Gd: 1-7** GF: 0-6 Fm: 0-0
Distance: 5f/6f: 0-4 7f-8f: 0-11 **9f-13f: 2-8** 14f+: 0-0
Track : LH: 0-8 **RH: 2-10 Tight: 2-10** Gall: 0-0
Aids: **Bl: 2-11** Vi: 0-1 Tstrap: 0-0 Ckp: 0-0
Best Rating: **67** 8/08 Haml 1m65y gd-sft

Modest; effective at around 7f-1m; acts on a sound surface and on easy ground.

Fivefold (USA)

(98) (77)

2-y-o b/br c Hennessy (USA)-Calming (USA) (Wild Again (USA))

J Akehurst A D Spence

Placings:020234 **(7685)**

2009: 7^{0}SS, 7^{2}SD, 7^{0}SD, 7^{2}SD, 7^{3}SD, 8^{4}SD,

	Starts	1st	2nd	3rd	Win & Pl
Career Total (Turf)	0	0	0	0	
Career Total (AW)	6	0	2	1	2246

Going (Turf): **Sf: 0-0 GS: 0-0 Gd: 0-0 GF: 0-0 Fm: 0-0**
Distance: 5f/6f: 0-0 7f-8f: 0-6 9f-13f: 0-0 14f+: 0-0
Track : LH: 0-5 RH: 0-1 Tight: 0-5 Gall: 0-0
Aids: Bl: 0-0 Vi: 0-0 Tstrap: 0-0 Ckp: 0-0
Best Rating: **77** 12/09 Kemp 1m stand

Fair; stays 7f and acts on Polytrack.

Fivefootnumberone (IRE)

103(100) (72)84

3-y-o b g Acclamation-Longueville Legend (IRE) (Cajun Cadet)

J J Quinn Maxilead Limited

Placings:31052023-054166624036 **(7219)**

2009: 6^{0}GF, 6^{5}GF, 6^{4}GF, 5^{1}GS, 5^{6}GF, 5^{6}G, 5^{6}S, 5^{2}G, 5^{4}S, 5^{0}G, 5^{3}SD, 5^{6}S,

	Starts	1st	2nd	3rd	Win & Pl
Career Total (Turf)	19	2	3	2	16490
Career Total (AW)	1	0	0	1	353

81 5/09 Hayd 5f (0-85)H G-S £5504
81 5/08 Hayd 5f G-F £2590
Total win prize-money £8095

Going (Turf): Sf: 0-5 **GS: 1-2** Gd: 0-5 **GF: 1-7** Fm: 0-0
Distance: **5f/6f: 2-19** 7f-8f: 0-1 9f-13f: 0-0 14f+: 0-0
Track : LH: 0-4 RH: 0-0 Tight: 0-4 Gall: 0-0
Aids: Bl: 0-1 Vi: 0-6 Tstrap: 0-1 Ckp: 0-1
Best Rating: **84** 10/08 Muss 5f gd-sft

Fair; effective at 5f; acts on fast and soft ground; has worn a visor.

Fiveonthreeforjd

(58)

4-y-o br g Compton Admiral-Patrician Fox (IRE) (Nicolotte)

W J H Ratcliffe The Lord Conyers Racing Partnership

Placings:0-0 **(7723)**

2009: 8^{0}SD,

	Starts	1st	2nd	3rd	Win & Pl
Career Total (Turf)	1	0	0	0	
Career Total (AW)	1	0	0	0	

Going (Turf): **Sf: 0-0 GS: 0-1 Gd: 0-0 GF: 0-0 Fm: 0-0**
Distance: 5f/6f: 0-0 7f-8f: 0-2 9f-13f: 0-0 14f+: 0-0
Track : LH: 0-2 RH: 0-0 Tight: 0-1 Gall: 0-0

Aids: Bl: 0-0 Vi: 0-0 Tstrap: 0-0 Ckp: 0-0

Fixation

90 (66)**45**

5-y-o ch g Observatory (USA)-Fetish (Dancing Brave (USA))

Mrs L C Jewell K Quinn/ C Benham/ I Saunders

Placings:645/05 (3986)

2009: 11^{0}GF, 16^{5}GF,

	Starts	1st	2nd	3rd	Win & Pl
Career Total (Turf)	4	0	0	0	0
Career Total (AW)	1	0	0	0	161

Going (Turf): **Sf: 0-2 GS: 0-0 Gd: 0-0 GF: 0-2 Fm: 0-0**
Distance: 5f/6f: 0-0 7f-8f: 0-1 9f-13f: 0-3 14f+: 0-1
Track : LH: 0-2 RH: 0-2 Tight: 0-5 Gall: 0-0
Aids: Bl: 0-0 Vi: 0-0 Tstrap: 0-0 Ckp: 0-0
Best Rating: **66** 9/07 Ling 1m stand

Fizzlephut (IRE)

95(104) (67)**57**

7-y-o b g Indian Rocket-Cladantom (IRE) (High Estate)

Miss J R Tooth Miss J R Tooth

Placings:0031140065/0045030220360000010240/05146066225/46000400100-60215040063400600 (5900)

2009: 5^{6}SD, 5^{0}SD, 5^{2}SD, 5^{1}SF, 5^{5}SD, 6^{0}SD, 5^{4}SD, 5^{0}SD, 5^{0}SD, 5^{6}GS, 6^{3}GF, 5^{4}F, 5^{0}GF, 5^{0}SD, 5^{6}SD, 5^{0}G, 5^{0}F,

	Starts	1st	2nd	3rd	Win & Pl
Career Total (Turf)	28	2	2	4	17676
Career Total (AW)	44	4	4	0	17462

67	2/09	Wolv	5f20y	(0-60)H	SF	£2047
65	11/08	GrLe	5f	(0-65)H	STD	£2590
79	3/07	Wolv	5f20y	(0-75)H	STD	£4533
77	11/06	Wolv	5f20y	(0-70)H	STD	£3238
87	6/05	Hayd	5f	(0-75)H	GD	£6968
76	5/05	Catt	5f		FRM	£2891

Total win prize-money £22269

Going (Turf): Sf: 0-1 GS: 0-3 **Gd: 1-11** GF: 0-9 **Fm: 1-4**
Distance: **5f/6f: 6-71** 7f-8f: 0-1 9f-13f: 0-0 14f+: 0-0
Track : **LH: 4-37** RH: 0-12 **Tight: 3-25** Gall: 1-5
Aids: **Bl: 1-7** Vi: 0-0 Tstrap: 0-6 Ckp: 0-6
Best Rating: **87** 6/05 Hayd 5f good

Moderate sprinter; acts on a sound surface; goes on Polytrack; has won headgear.

Flag Of Glory

81 **48**

2-y-o b g Trade Fair-Rainbow Sky (Rainbow Quest (USA))

C F Wall Follow The Flag Partnership

Placings:060 (7099)

2009: 7^{0}G, 8^{6}S, 8^{0}G,

	Starts	1st	2nd	3rd	Win & Pl
Career Total (Turf)	3	0	0	0	0

Going (Turf): **Sf: 0-1 GS: 0-0 Gd: 0-2 GF: 0-0 Fm: 0-0**
Distance: 5f/6f: 0-0 7f-8f: 0-1 9f-13f: 0-2 14f+: 0-0
Track : LH: 0-1 RH: 0-0 Tight: 0-0 Gall: 0-0
Aids: Bl: 0-0 Vi: 0-0 Tstrap: 0-0 Ckp: 0-0
Best Rating: **48** 10/09 Yarm 1m3y good

Flagstone (USA)

(90) (46)**57**

5-y-o ch g Distant View (USA)-Navarene (USA) (Known Fact (USA))

Ian Williams Steve Gray

Placings:6340/300-00 (0353)

2009: 7^{0}SD, 9^{0}SD,

	Starts	1st	2nd	3rd	Win & Pl
Career Total (Turf)	6	0	0	2	891
Career Total (AW)	3	0	0	0	

Going (Turf): **Sf: 0-2 GS: 0-0 Gd: 0-2 GF: 0-2 Fm: 0-0**
Distance: 5f/6f: 0-0 7f-8f: 0-1 9f-13f: 0-8 14f+: 0-0
Track : LH: 0-7 RH: 0-2 Tight: 0-6 Gall: 0-2
Aids: Bl: 0-0 Vi: 0-0 Tstrap: 0-0 Ckp: 0-0
Best Rating: **57** 6/07 Nott 1m54y gd-fm

Flam

(100) (68)**75**

4-y-o b f Singspiel (IRE)-Delauncy (Machiavellian (USA))

A M Hales Wood Hall Stud Limited

Placings:56/3254564304-00 (0631)

2009: 12^{0}SD, 13^{0}SD,

	Starts	1st	2nd	3rd	Win & Pl
Career Total (Turf)	8	0	1	1	2841
Career Total (AW)	6	0	0	1	626

Going (Turf): **Sf: 0-0 GS: 0-0 Gd: 0-4 GF: 0-4 Fm: 0-0**
Distance: 5f/6f: 0-0 7f-8f: 0-2 9f-13f: 0-10 14f+: 0-2
Track : LH: 0-9 RH: 0-4 Tight: 0-5 Gall: 0-2
Aids: Bl: 0-0 Vi: 0-0 Tstrap: 0-3 Ckp: 0-3
Best Rating: **75** 7/08 Leic 1m1f218y gd-fm

Fair; stays 1m2f; acts on fast ground; has worn cheek-pieces.

Flambeau

88 **71**

2-y-o b f Oasis Dream-Flavian (Catrail (USA))

H Candy Major M G Wyatt

Placings:5 (6730)

2009: 6^{5}S,

	Starts	1st	2nd	3rd	Win & Pl
Career Total (Turf)	1	0	0	0	0

Going (Turf): **Sf: 0-1 GS: 0-0 Gd: 0-0 GF: 0-0 Fm: 0-0**
Distance: 5f/6f: 0-0 7f-8f: 0-1 9f-13f: 0-0 14f+: 0-0
Track : LH: 0-0 RH: 0-0 Tight: 0-0 Gall: 0-0
Aids: Bl: 0-0 Vi: 0-0 Tstrap: 0-0 Ckp: 0-0
Best Rating: **71** 10/09 Sals 6f212y soft

Flamboyant Red (IRE)

70(95) (44)**28**

3-y-o ch g Redback-Flamboyant (Danzero (AUS))

Miss Gay Kelleway Aggbag Ltd

Placings:0000-30400 (3009)

2009: 6^{3}SD, 6^{0}SD, 6^{4}SD, 5^{0}SD, 7^{0}G,

	Starts	1st	2nd	3rd	Win & Pl
Career Total (Turf)	5	0	0	0	
Career Total (AW)	4	0	0	1	202

Going (Turf): **Sf: 0-0 GS: 0-1 Gd: 0-2 GF: 0-2 Fm: 0-0**
Distance: 5f/6f: 0-5 7f-8f: 0-4 9f-13f: 0-0 14f+: 0-0
Track : LH: 0-0 RH: 0-4 Tight: 0-0 Gall: 0-0
Aids: Bl: 0-0 Vi: 0-0 Tstrap: 0-0 Ckp: 0-0
Best Rating: **44** 1/09 Kemp 6f stand

Flame Creek (IRE)

84(111) (81)**70**

13-y-o b g Shardari-Sheila's Pet (IRE) (Welsh Term)

E J Creighton E J Creighton

Placings:2202115/5606062330/410355515000062660-00055 (3962)

2009: 12^{0}SD, 16^{0}G, 13^{0}GF, 16^{5}S, 14^{5}S,

	Starts	1st	2nd	3rd	Win & Pl
Career Total (Turf)	17	1	2	0	8596
Career Total (AW)	23	3	3	3	12615

70	4/08	Newb	2m	(0-85)H	SFT	£6476
81	1/08	Ling	2m	(0-75)H	STD	£2331
89	12/06	Sthl	1m6f	(0-75)H	STD	£3238
89	12/06	Sthl	1m6f	(0-75)H	STD	£3238

Total win prize-money £15286

Going (Turf): **Sf: 1-8** GS: 0-4 Gd: 0-2 GF: 0-3 Fm: 0-0
Distance: 5f/6f: 0-0 7f-8f: 0-0 9f-13f: 0-7 **14f+: 4-33**
Track : **LH: 4-35** RH: 0-5 **Tight: 1-15** Gall: 0-7
Aids: Bl: 0-0 Vi: 0-0 Tstrap: 0-0 Ckp: 0-0
Best Rating: **89** 12/06 Sthl 1m6f stand

Moderate veteran; stays 1m6f; acts on both All-Weather surfaces.

Flame Of Gibraltar (IRE)

105(110) (93)**103**

3-y-o b f Rock Of Gibraltar (IRE)-Spirit Of Tara (IRE) (Sadler's Wells (USA))

H R A Cecil Rose McKeon,Marie Harris & Tom Gallagher

Placings:21243505 (7131)

2009: 10^{2}GF, 10^{1}GF, 12^{2}GF, 12^{4}G, 12^{3}GF, 10^{5}GF, 12^{0}G, 13^{5}SD,

	Starts	1st	2nd	3rd	Win & Pl
Career Total (Turf)	7	1	2	1	41221
Career Total (AW)	1	0	0	0	1076

85	6/09	Ling	1m2f	G-F	£2729

Total win prize-money £2730

Going (Turf): Sf: 0-0 GS: 0-0 Gd: 0-2 **GF: 1-5** Fm: 0-0
Distance: 5f/6f: 0-0 7f-8f: 0-0 **9f-13f: 1-8** 14f+: 0-0
Track : **LH: 1-4** RH: 0-3 **Tight: 1-3** Gall: 0-4
Aids: Bl: 0-0 Vi: 0-0 Tstrap: 0-0 Ckp: 0-0
Best Rating: **103** 6/09 Asct 1m4f gd-fm

Smart; runner-up in the 2009 Ribblesdale; effective at 1m2f-1m4f; acts on fast ground.

Flame Of Hestia (IRE)

98 **67**

3-y-o ch f Giant's Causeway (USA)-Ellen (IRE) (Machiavellian (USA))

J R Fanshawe Miss Annabelle Condon

Placings:0-32 (3531)

2009: 8^{3}GF, 8^{2}F,

	Starts	1st	2nd	3rd	Win & Pl
Career Total (Turf)	3	0	1	1	1734

Going (Turf): **Sf: 0-0 GS: 0-1 Gd: 0-0 GF: 0-1 Fm: 0-1**

Distance: 5f/6f: 0-0 7f-8f: 0-2 9f-13f: 0-1 14f+: 0-0
Track : LH: 0-1 RH: 0-0 Tight: 0-0 Gall: 0-0
Aids: Bl: 0-0 Vi: 0-0 Tstrap: 0-0 Ckp: 0-0
Best Rating: **67** 7/09 Hayd 1m30y firm

Fair filly; 1,000,000gns purchase; stays 1m; acts on quick ground.

Flamestone

80(108) (56)**52**
5-y-o b g Piccolo-Renee (Wolfhound (USA))
A E Price Mrs H L Price

Placings:03535060/**4**00006330600/F2500-**2**10444230**0** (3269)
2009: 6^2SD, 6^1SD, 5^0SD, 6^4SD, 6^4SD, 8^4SD, 7^2SD, 6^3SD, 8^0F, 8^0SD,

	Starts	1st	2nd	3rd	Win & Pl
Career Total (Turf)	21	0	1	4	2356
Career Total (AW)	14	1	2	1	2869

56 1/09 Kemp 6f (0-45) STD £1364
Total win prize-money £1365

Going (Turf): **Sf: 0-3 GS: 0-2 Gd: 0-5 GF: 0-8 Fm: 0-3**
Distance: **5f/6f: 1-17** 7f-8f: 0-10 9f-13f: 0-8 14f+: 0-0
Track : LH: 0-11 **RH: 1-11** Tight: 0-8 Gall: 0-0
Aids: Bl: 0-5 Vi: 0-0 Tstrap: 0-3 Ckp: 0-3
Best Rating: **58** 5/06 Rdcr 5f firm

Moderate; stays 1m; acts on fast ground; goes on Polytrack.

Flaming Blaze

89(82) (38)**34**
3-y-o b g Tobougg (IRE)-Catch The Flame (USA) (Storm Bird (CAN))
P C Haslam Mark James

Placings:606 (3541)
2009: 7^6SD, 9^0GS, 8^0F,

	Starts	1st	2nd	3rd	Win & Pl
Career Total (Turf)	2	0	0	0	0
Career Total (AW)	1	0	0	0	0

Going (Turf): **Sf: 0-0 GS: 0-1 Gd: 0-0 GF: 0-0 Fm: 0-1**
Distance: 5f/6f: 0-0 7f-8f: 0-2 9f-13f: 0-1 14f+: 0-0
Track : LH: 0-1 RH: 0-1 Tight: 0-1 Gall: 0-0
Aids: Bl: 0-0 Vi: 0-0 Tstrap: 0-0 Ckp: 0-0
Best Rating: **38** 4/09 Sthl 7f stand

Flaming Cat (IRE)

65(42) **49**
6-y-o b/br g Orpen (USA)-Brave Cat (IRE) (Catrail (USA))
F Watson J D Blythe

Placings:005/00/64000/0-0 (3539)
2009: 7^0F,

	Starts	1st	2nd	3rd	Win & Pl
Career Total (Turf)	10	0	0	0	236
Career Total (AW)	2	0	0	0	

Going (Turf): **Sf: 0-1 GS: 0-4 Gd: 0-1 GF: 0-2 Fm: 0-2**
Distance: 5f/6f: 0-4 7f-8f: 0-3 9f-13f: 0-5 14f+: 0-0
Track : LH: 0-6 RH: 0-2 Tight: 0-4 Gall: 0-1
Aids: Bl: 0-0 Vi: 0-0 Tstrap: 0-5 Ckp: 0-5
Best Rating: **49** 8/07 Newc 1m2f32y good

Flaming Miracle

98(98) (74)**76**
2-y-o ch c Firebreak-Sukuma (IRE) (Highest Honor (FR))
A M Balding M A L Evans

Placings:06522621 (6727)
2009: 6^0GF, 6^6SD, 6^5GF, 8^2G, 8^2GF, 8^6G, 8^2SD, 8^1S,

	Starts	1st	2nd	3rd	Win & Pl
Career Total (Turf)	6	1	2	0	5268
Career Total (AW)	2	0	1	0	806

76 10/09 Sals 1m SFT £2914
Total win prize-money £2914

Going (Turf): **Sf: 1-1** GS: 0-0 Gd: 0-2 GF: 0-3 Fm: 0-0
Distance: 5f/6f: 0-3 **7f-8f: 1-3** 9f-13f: 0-2 14f+: 0-0
Track : LH: 0-3 RH: 0-1 Tight: 0-3 Gall: 0-1
Aids: Bl: 0-0 Vi: 0-0 Tstrap: 0-0 Ckp: 0-0
Best Rating: **76** 10/09 Sals 1m soft

Fair; effective over 1m; acts on fast ground.

Flaming Ruby

(84) (28)**43**
3-y-o b f Hunting Lion (IRE)-Floral Spark (Forzando)
N Tinkler Golden Rays

Placings:0000-**6**00 (0964)
2009: 5^6SD, 5^0SD, 8^0SD,

	Starts	1st	2nd	3rd	Win & Pl
Career Total (Turf)	4	0	0	0	
Career Total (AW)	3	0	0	0	0

Going (Turf): **Sf: 0-2 GS: 0-2 Gd: 0-0 GF: 0-0 Fm: 0-0**
Distance: 5f/6f: 0-6 7f-8f: 0-1 9f-13f: 0-0 14f+: 0-0
Track : LH: 0-2 RH: 0-0 Tight: 0-1 Gall: 0-0
Aids: Bl: 0-0 Vi: 0-0 Tstrap: 0-0 Ckp: 0-0
Best Rating: **43** 9/08 Rdcr 5f gd-sft

Flamsteed (IRE)

98(100) (72)**72**
3-y-o b c Clodovil (IRE)-Nautical Gem (IRE) (Alhaarth (IRE))
M Quinn Brian Morton

Placings:5-331232504440 (6914)
2009: 6^3SD, 6^3SD, 5^1SD, 6^2SD, 6^3SD, 5^2G, 5^5SD, 5^0GF, 5^4G, 5^4F, 7^4SD, 6^0SD,

	Starts	1st	2nd	3rd	Win & Pl
Career Total (Turf)	4	0	1	0	2996
Career Total (AW)	9	1	1	3	5334

65 2/09 Ling 5f STD £2729
Total win prize-money £2730

Going (Turf): **Sf: 0-0 GS: 0-0 Gd: 0-2 GF: 0-1 Fm: 0-1**
Distance: **5f/6f: 1-12** 7f-8f: 0-1 9f-13f: 0-0 14f+: 0-0
Track : **LH: 1-12** RH: 0-0 **Tight: 1-8** Gall: 0-1
Aids: Bl: 0-0 Vi: 0-0 Tstrap: 0-0 Ckp: 0-0
Best Rating: **72** 4/09 Brig 5f213y good

Modest; effective at 5f-6f; acts on Polytrack.

Flanders Fields

(50)
4-y-o b g Galileo (IRE)-Vimy Ridge (FR) (Indian Ridge)
G L Moore Wilf Slee

Placings:06-0 (0279)
2009: 12^0SD,

	Starts	1st	2nd	3rd	Win & Pl
Career Total (Turf)	2	0	0	0	0
Career Total (AW)	1	0	0	0	

Going (Turf): **Sf: 0-2 GS: 0-0 Gd: 0-0 GF: 0-0 Fm: 0-0**
Distance: 5f/6f: 0-0 7f-8f: 0-0 9f-13f: 0-3 14f+: 0-0
Track : LH: 0-1 RH: 0-0 Tight: 0-1 Gall: 0-0
Aids: Bl: 0-0 Vi: 0-0 Tstrap: 0-0 Ckp: 0-0

Flaneur

104 **77**
2-y-o b g Chineur (FR)-Tatanka (IRE) (Lear Fan (USA))
T D Easterby Jeremy Gompertz

Placings:0533120035 (7290)
2009: 5^0GF, 6^5S, 5^3GF, 6^3GS, 6^1GS, 6^2GF, 6^0GF, 7^0GF, 6^3G, 6^5S,

	Starts	1st	2nd	3rd	Win & Pl
Career Total (Turf)	10	1	1	3	7523

72 7/09 Newc 6f G-S £3238
Total win prize-money £3238

Going (Turf): Sf: 0-2 **GS: 1-2** Gd: 0-1 GF: 0-5 Fm: 0-0
Distance: **5f/6f: 1-9** 7f-8f: 0-1 9f-13f: 0-0 14f+: 0-0
Track : LH: 0-1 RH: 0-0 Tight: 0-0 Gall: 0-0
Aids: **Bl: 1-9** Vi: 0-0 Tstrap: 0-0 Ckp: 0-0
Best Rating: **77** 8/09 Rdcr 6f gd-fm

Fair; best at 6f; handles fast and soft ground; often blinkered.

Flannel (IRE)

93(85) (58)**68**
3-y-o gr g Clodovil (IRE)-La Captive (IRE) (Selkirk (USA))
J R Fanshawe Chris Van Hoorn

Placings:0-000000 (5011)
2009: 10^0G, 10^0GF, 11^0G, 10^0GS, 12^0SD, 14^0G,

	Starts	1st	2nd	3rd	Win & Pl
Career Total (Turf)	5	0	0	0	
Career Total (AW)	2	0	0	0	

Going (Turf): **Sf: 0-0 GS: 0-1 Gd: 0-3 GF: 0-1 Fm: 0-0**
Distance: 5f/6f: 0-0 7f-8f: 0-1 9f-13f: 0-5 14f+: 0-1
Track : LH: 0-5 RH: 0-2 Tight: 0-4 Gall: 0-1
Aids: Bl: 0-0 Vi: 0-0 Tstrap: 0-0 Ckp: 0-0
Best Rating: **68** 5/09 Wind 1m2f7y gd-fm

Flapjack

90(89) (52)**65**
2-y-o b f Trade Fair-Inya Lake (Whittingham (IRE))
R Hannon R Hannon

Placings:6436550400 (6590)
2009: 5^6G, 5^4GF, 5^3GF, 6^6GF, 5^5G, 7^5GS, 5^0SD, 6^4SD, 6^0SD, 6^0GS,

	Starts	1st	2nd	3rd	Win & Pl
Career Total (Turf)	7	0	0	1	711
Career Total (AW)	3	0	0	0	0

Going (Turf): **Sf: 0-0 GS: 0-2 Gd: 0-2 GF: 0-3 Fm: 0-0**
Distance: 5f/6f: 0-8 7f-8f: 0-2 9f-13f: 0-0 14f+: 0-0
Track : LH: 0-3 RH: 0-2 Tight: 0-1 Gall: 0-1
Aids: Bl: 0-0 Vi: 0-0 Tstrap: 0-0 Ckp: 0-0
Best Rating: **65** 5/09 Wwck 5f110y gd-fm

Flapper (IRE)

98(79) (56)**76**
3-y-o b f Selkirk (USA)-Pure Spin (USA) (Machiavellian (USA))

J W Hills Abbott Racing Partners

Placings:00-440110205 (7149)
2009: 8^{4}GF, 8^{4}G, 10^{0}GF, 8^{1}G, 8^{1}G, 8^{0}GF, 8^{2}GS, 8^{0}GF, 8^{5}G,

	Starts	1st	2nd	3rd	Win & Pl
Career Total (Turf)	10	2	1	0	12158
Career Total (AW)	1	0	0	0	

76 8/09 NmkJ 1m (0-80)H GD £5180
67 7/09 York 1m (0-70)H GD £5051
Total win prize-money £10232

Going (Turf): Sf: 0-1 GS: 0-1 **Gd: 2-4** GF: 0-4 Fm: 0-0
Distance: 5f/6f: 0-0 **7f-8f: 2-9** 9f-13f: 0-2 14f+: 0-0
Track : **LH: 1-4** RH: 0-4 Tight: 0-1 **Gall: 1-4**
Aids: Bl: 0-0 Vi: 0-0 Tstrap: 0-0 Ckp: 0-0
Best Rating: 76 9/09 Sand 1m14y gd-sft

Fair; stays 1m; acts on good ground.

Flash For Freedom (USA)

61(86) (49)
2-y-o b c Essence Of Dubai (USA)-Isathriller (USA) (Buckaroo (USA))
J R Best D Gorton

Placings:00000 (7604)
2009: 6^{0}G, 5^{0}SF, 7^{0}SD, 7^{0}SD, 8^{0}SD,

	Starts	1st	2nd	3rd	Win & Pl
Career Total (Turf)	1	0	0	0	
Career Total (AW)	4	0	0	0	

Going (Turf): **Sf: 0-0 GS: 0-0 Gd: 0-1 GF: 0-0 Fm: 0-0**
Distance: 5f/6f: 0-2 7f-8f: 0-3 9f-13f: 0-0 14f+: 0-0
Track : LH: 0-3 RH: 0-1 Tight: 0-3 Gall: 0-1
Aids: Bl: 0-0 Vi: 0-0 Tstrap: 0-0 Ckp: 0-0
Best Rating: 49 10/09 Wolv 5f216y std-fst

Flash McGahon (IRE)

96(93) (97)100
5-y-o b g Namid-Astuti (IRE) (Waajib)
D Nicholls Dundalk Racing Club

Placings:0214/254500400/353200460-060660 (7758)
2009: 5^{0}GF, 6^{6}GF, 5^{0}G, 5^{6}GS, 5^{6}G, 5^{0}SD,

	Starts	1st	2nd	3rd	Win & Pl
Career Total (Turf)	24	1	3	1	45976
Career Total (AW)	4	0	0	1	1405

98 8/06 Tipp 5f GD £26937
Total win prize-money £26938

Going (Turf): Sf: 0-3 GS: 0-1 **Gd: 1-7** GF: 0-6 Fm: 0-1
Distance: **5f/6f: 1-27** 7f-8f: 0-1 9f-13f: 0-0 14f+: 0-0
Track : **LH: 1-7** RH: 0-1 Tight: 0-0 Gall: 0-0
Aids: Bl: 0-12 Vi: 0-0 Tstrap: 0-2 Ckp: 0-2
Best Rating: 100 5/08 Cork 5f good

Useful former Irish sprinter; acts on most types of ground; wears blinkers/cheekpieces.

Flashgun (USA)

91(88) (49)58
3-y-o b c Lemon Drop Kid (USA)-Tolltally Light (USA) (Majestic Light (USA))
M G Quinlan P C Ashmore

Placings:05000-040 (3358)
2009: 9^{0}SD, 8^{4}GS, 8^{0}GS,

	Starts	1st	2nd	3rd	Win & Pl
Career Total (Turf)	5	0	0	0	241
Career Total (AW)	3	0	0	0	

Going (Turf): **Sf: 0-3 GS: 0-2 Gd: 0-0 GF: 0-0 Fm: 0-0**
Distance: 5f/6f: 0-0 7f-8f: 0-4 9f-13f: 0-4 14f+: 0-0
Track : LH: 0-3 RH: 0-4 Tight: 0-1 Gall: 0-0
Aids: Bl: 0-0 Vi: 0-0 Tstrap: 0-0 Ckp: 0-0
Best Rating: 58 8/08 Gdwd 1m soft

Flashy Lover (IRE)

90 58
2-y-o b f Trans Island-Irish Lover (USA) (Irish River (FR))
M R Channon Mrs T Burns

Placings:06531 (4757)
2009: 6^{0}GF, 6^{6}GF, 5^{5}GF, 6^{3}S, 7^{1}GS,

	Starts	1st	2nd	3rd	Win & Pl
Career Total (Turf)	5	1	0	1	3755

57 8/09 NmkJ 7f G-S £3238
Total win prize-money £3238

Going (Turf): Sf: 0-1 **GS: 1-1** Gd: 0-0 GF: 0-3 Fm: 0-0
Distance: 5f/6f: 0-3 **7f-8f: 1-2** 9f-13f: 0-0 14f+: 0-0
Track : LH: 0-1 RH: 0-0 Tight: 0-0 Gall: 0-0
Aids: Bl: 0-0 Vi: 0-0 Tstrap: 0-0 Ckp: 0-0
Best Rating: 58 6/09 Sals 6f gd-fm

Flashy Max

90(88) (50)55
4-y-o b g Primo Valentino (IRE)-Be Practical (Tragic Role (USA))
Jedd O'Keeffe W R B Racing 50

Placings:0004052/4451100-00000 (4944)
2009: 7^{0}GF, 8^{0}GF, 7^{0}F, 7^{0}GF, 10^{0}GF,

	Starts	1st	2nd	3rd	Win & Pl
Career Total (Turf)	15	2	0	0	4695
Career Total (AW)	4	0	1	0	504

54 7/08 Haml 1m65y (0-65)H GD £2266
55 7/08 Bevl 1m100y (0-65)H GD £1942
Total win prize-money £4210

Going (Turf): Sf: 0-0 GS: 0-1 **Gd: 2-5** GF: 0-8 Fm: 0-1
Distance: 5f/6f: 0-3 7f-8f: 0-8 **9f-13f: 2-8** 14f+: 0-0
Track : LH: 0-9 **RH: 2-7 Tight: 1-9** Gall: 0-1
Aids: Bl: 0-0 Vi: 0-0 Tstrap: 0-1 Ckp: 0-1
Best Rating: 55 7/08 Bevl 1m100y good

Moderate; stays 1m; acts on good ground; also goes on Polytrack.

Flashy Photon

91(88) (48)78
4-y-o b g Compton Place-Showboat (USA) (Theatrical)
H Candy Trolley Action

Placings:01/04-0004000 (6926)
2009: 7^{0}SD, 6^{0}GF, 5^{0}S, 6^{4}GF, 7^{0}G, 6^{0}GS, 6^{0}GF,

	Starts	1st	2nd	3rd	Win & Pl
Career Total (Turf)	10	1	0	0	3403
Career Total (AW)	1	0	0	0	

73 8/07 Folk 6f G-S £2849
Total win prize-money £2850

Going (Turf): Sf: 0-1 **GS: 1-3** Gd: 0-1 GF: 0-5 Fm: 0-0
Distance: **5f/6f: 1-6** 7f-8f: 0-5 9f-13f: 0-0 14f+: 0-0
Track : LH: 0-0 RH: 0-2 Tight: 0-0 Gall: 0-0
Aids: Bl: 0-1 Vi: 0-0 Tstrap: 0-0 Ckp: 0-0
Best Rating: 78 5/08 Leic 5f218y gd-fm

Flawed Genius

106(108) (93)102
4-y-o b g Fasliyev (USA)-Talented (Bustino)
K A Ryan Dubai's Finest

Placings:6140/246040-60661000130460RLR (7520)
2009: 8^{6}SD, 7^{0}SD, 8^{6}GF, 7^{6}F, 8^{1}GF, 7^{0}GF, 10^{0}GF, 8^{0}GF, 8^{1}G, 8^{3}GF, 8^{0}GS, 8^{4}GF, 8^{6}G, 7^{0}SD, 8^{R}GF, 9^{L}GF, 7^{R}SD,

	Starts	1st	2nd	3rd	Win & Pl
Career Total (Turf)	22	3	1	1	34042
Career Total (AW)	5	0	0	0	585

79 7/09 Donc 1m GD £2729
95 5/09 Thsk 1m (0-100)H G-F £12045
78 7/07 Sals 6f212y G-F £3886
Total win prize-money £18661

Going (Turf): Sf: 0-0 GS: 0-1 Gd: 1-6 **GF: 2-14** Fm: 0-1
Distance: 5f/6f: 0-3 **7f-8f: 3-20** 9f-13f: 0-4 14f+: 0-0
Track : **LH: 1-12** RH: 0-3 **Tight: 1-11** Gall: 0-2
Aids: Bl: 0-0 Vi: 0-2 Tstrap: 0-2 Ckp: 0-2
Best Rating: 102 5/08 Hayd 1m30y gd-fm

Useful; stays 1m and acts on fast ground; has worn a tongue tie and a visor and cheekpieces; refused to race last three starts.

Flawless Diamond (IRE)

(100) (57)57
3-y-o ch f Indian Haven-Mystery Hill (USA) (Danehill (USA))
J S Moore Owen Mullen & John Griffin

Placings:000010056664-253 (0267)
2009: 7^{2}SD, 7^{5}SD, 7^{3}SD,

	Starts	1st	2nd	3rd	Win & Pl
Career Total (Turf)	6	0	0	0	551
Career Total (AW)	9	1	1	1	2886

57 8/08 Ling 6f STD £1978
Total win prize-money £1979

Going (Turf): **Sf: 0-1 GS: 0-0 Gd: 0-3 GF: 0-2 Fm: 0-0**
Distance: **5f/6f: 1-8** 7f-8f: 0-6 9f-13f: 0-1 14f+: 0-0
Track : **LH: 1-7** RH: 0-3 **Tight: 1-6** Gall: 0-2
Aids: **Bl: 1-8** Vi: 0-0 Tstrap: 0-3 Ckp: 0-3
Best Rating: 57 8/08 Curr 6f heavy

Moderate; effective at 6-7f; handles Polytrack; has worn blinkers/cheekpieces.

Flaxen Lake

86(95) (70)68
2-y-o b g Sampower Star-Cloudy Reef (Cragador)
R Hollinshead M Johnson

Placings:634364 (7708)
2009: 5^{6}GF, 5^{3}GF, 5^{4}SD, 5^{3}SD, 5^{6}SD, 6^{4}SD,

	Starts	1st	2nd	3rd	Win & Pl
Career Total (Turf)	2	0	0	1	482
Career Total (AW)	4	0	0	1	770

Going (Turf): **Sf: 0-0 GS: 0-0 Gd: 0-0 GF: 0-2 Fm: 0-0**
Distance: 5f/6f: 0-6 7f-8f: 0-0 9f-13f: 0-0 14f+: 0-0
Track : LH: 0-5 RH: 0-0 Tight: 0-3 Gall: 0-0
Aids: Bl: 0-0 Vi: 0-0 Tstrap: 0-1 Ckp: 0-1
Best Rating: 70 10/09 Wolv 5f20y stand

Fair sprinter; effective at 5f; acts on fast turf and Polytrack; has worn cheekpieces.

Fleeting Echo

97(97) (82)85

2-y-o b f Beat Hollow-Sempre Sorriso (Fleetwood (IRE))

R Hannon P J & Mrs J P Haycock

Placings:51413023 (7108)

2009: 5^{5}GF, 5^{1}SD, 6^{4}GF, 6^{1}G, 6^{3}G, 6^{0}GS, 6^{2}G, 6^{3}SD,

	Starts	1st	2nd	3rd	Win & Pl
Career Total (Turf)	6	1	1	1	7054
Career Total (AW)	2	1	0	1	2625

76	7/09	Ling	6f	GD	£3238
68	6/09	Kemp	5f	STD	£2047

Total win prize-money £5285

Going (Turf): Sf: 0-0 GS: 0-1 **Gd: 1-3** GF: 0-2 Fm: 0-0
Distance: **5f/6f: 2-7** 7f-8f: 0-1 9f-13f: 0-0 14f+: 0-0
Track : LH: 0-0 **RH: 1-2** Tight: 0-0 Gall: 0-0
Aids: Bl: 0-0 Vi: 0-0 Tstrap: 0-0 Ckp: 0-0
Best Rating: **85** 10/09 Newb 6f8y good

Fair; suited by 5f-6f; acts on good ground; goes on Polytrack.

Fleeting Spirit (IRE)

116 (109)123

4-y-o b f Invincible Spirit (IRE)-Millennium Tale (FR) (Distant Relative)

J Noseda The Searchers

Placings:11212/1354-21220 (7306a)

2009: 5^{2}GF, 6^{1}GF, 6^{2}GS, 5^{2}G, 6^{0}FT,

	Starts	1st	2nd	3rd	Win & Pl
Career Total (Turf)	13	5	5	1	660624
Career Total (AW)	1	0	0	0	0

123	7/09	NmkJ	6f	G-F	£227080
122	5/08	Hayd	5f	G-F	£56770
111	9/07	Donc	5f	G-F	£42585
110	7/07	Gdwd	5f	GD	£28390
84	6/07	Nott	5f13y	GD	£2914

Total win prize-money £357740

Going (Turf): Sf: 0-0 GS: 0-2 Gd: 2-5 **GF: 3-5** Fm: 0-1
Distance: **5f/6f: 5-13** 7f-8f: 0-1 9f-13f: 0-0 14f+: 0-0
Track : LH: 0-1 RH: 0-0 Tight: 0-0 Gall: 0-0
Aids: Bl: 0-0 Vi: 0-0 Tstrap: 0-0 Ckp: 0-0
Best Rating: **123** 7/09 NmkJ 6f gd-fm

Group class; dual Group winner as a juvenile and runner-up in Group 1 Cheveley Park; winner of the Group 2 Temple Stakes in 2008; runner-up in the King's Stand, Sprint Cup and Abbaye in 2009, but did win her Group 1 in the July Cup; effective over 5f-6f; acts on good and faster ground.

Fleeting Star (USA)

103(101) (78)83

3-y-o gr/ro f Exchange Rate (USA)-Disperse A Star (USA) (Dispersal (USA))

J Noseda The Searchers

Placings:01-60210 (6112)

2009: 7^{6}G, 7^{0}SD, 6^{2}GF, 5^{1}F, 6^{0}GF,

	Starts	1st	2nd	3rd	Win & Pl
Career Total (Turf)	5	1	1	0	5274
Career Total (AW)	2	1	0	0	1706

81	8/09	Brig	5f213y (0-75)H	FRM	£3154
78	8/08	Ling	6f	STD	£1706

Total win prize-money £4860

Going (Turf): Sf: 0-0 GS: 0-0 Gd: 0-2 GF: 0-2 **Fm: 1-1**
Distance: **5f/6f: 2-5** 7f-8f: 0-2 9f-13f: 0-0 14f+: 0-0
Track : **LH: 2-3** RH: 0-1 **Tight: 1-2** Gall: 0-0
Aids: Bl: 0-0 **Vi: 1-3** Tstrap: 0-0 Ckp: 0-0
Best Rating: **83** 7/09 Asct 6f gd-fm

Fair; effective over 6f; acts on Polytrack; has worn a visor.

Fleetwood Flame

85 35

4-y-o ch f Fleetwood (IRE)-Barden Lady (Presidium)

W M Brisbourne D G Blagden

Placings:5-000 (4193)

2009: 10^{0}GF, 9^{0}G, 11^{0}S,

	Starts	1st	2nd	3rd	Win & Pl
Career Total (Turf)	4	0	0	0	0

Going (Turf): **Sf: 0-1 GS: 0-0 Gd: 0-1 GF: 0-2 Fm: 0-0**
Distance: 5f/6f: 0-0 7f-8f: 0-0 9f-13f: 0-4 14f+: 0-0
Track : LH: 0-3 RH: 0-1 Tight: 0-3 Gall: 0-0
Aids: Bl: 0-0 Vi: 0-0 Tstrap: 0-0 Ckp: 0-0
Best Rating: **35** 6/09 Gdwd 1m1f good

Fleetwoodsands (IRE)

55

2-y-o b g Footstepsinthesand-Litchfield Hills (USA) (Relaunch (USA))

P C Haslam Mount Racing Club & Frances Phillips

Placings:0 (3292)

2009: 6^{0}GF,

	Starts	1st	2nd	3rd	Win & Pl
Career Total (Turf)	1	0	0	0	

Going (Turf): **Sf: 0-0 GS: 0-0 Gd: 0-0 GF: 0-1 Fm: 0-0**
Distance: 5f/6f: 0-0 7f-8f: 0-1 9f-13f: 0-0 14f+: 0-0
Track : LH: 0-0 RH: 0-0 Tight: 0-0 Gall: 0-0
Aids: Bl: 0-0 Vi: 0-0 Tstrap: 0-0 Ckp: 0-0

Fleur De'Lion (IRE)

95(97) (65)57

3-y-o ch f Lion Heart (USA)-Viburnum (USA) (El Gran Senor (USA))

S Kirk Mrs John Lee

Placings:00000065-650400036044105206214 (7831)

2009: 8^{6}SD, 7^{5}SD, 7^{0}SD, 9^{4}SF, 12^{0}SD, 12^{0}SD, 11^{0}SD, 9^{3}GS, 10^{6}SD, 8^{0}F, 10^{4}HY, 10^{4}G, 11^{1}GF, 11^{0}F, 9^{5}GF, 9^{2}SF, 11^{0}GS, 10^{6}SD, 12^{2}SD, 12^{1}SD, 12^{4}SD,

	Starts	1st	2nd	3rd	Win & Pl
Career Total (Turf)	12	1	0	1	2530
Career Total (AW)	17	1	2	0	3597

62	12/09	Kemp	1m4f	STD	£2047
57	8/09	Brig	1m3f196y (0-55)H	G-F	£1942

Total win prize-money £3990

Going (Turf): Sf: 0-3 GS: 0-3 Gd: 0-1 **GF: 1-3** Fm: 0-2
Distance: 5f/6f: 0-4 7f-8f: 0-6 **9f-13f: 2-19** 14f+: 0-0
Track : LH: 1-19 RH: 1-6 Tight: 0-12 Gall: 0-4
Aids: Bl: 0-2 Vi: 0-0 Tstrap: 0-0 Ckp: 0-0
Best Rating: **65** 12/09 Kemp 1m4f stand

Moderate; stays 1m4f; acts on most types of ground; has worn blinkers.

Fleurissimo

94 80

3-y-o ch f Dr Fong (USA)-Agnus (IRE) (In The Wings)

J L Dunlop Normandie Stud Ltd

Placings:03-2 (1329)

2009: 10^{2}GS,

	Starts	1st	2nd	3rd	Win & Pl
Career Total (Turf)	3	0	1	1	2264

Going (Turf): **Sf: 0-1 GS: 0-2 Gd: 0-0 GF: 0-0 Fm: 0-0**
Distance: 5f/6f: 0-0 7f-8f: 0-2 9f-13f: 0-1 14f+: 0-0
Track : LH: 0-1 RH: 0-0 Tight: 0-0 Gall: 0-1
Aids: Bl: 0-0 Vi: 0-0 Tstrap: 0-0 Ckp: 0-0
Best Rating: **80** 4/09 Newb 1m2f6y gd-sft

Fair maiden form; effective over 7f; acts on easy ground.

Fleuron

(87) (44)

3-y-o b/br f Diktat-Forthwith (Midyan (USA))

P Howling Longview Stud & Bloodstock Ltd

Placings:0-00 (0503)

2009: 7^{0}SD, 7^{0}SD,

	Starts	1st	2nd	3rd	Win & Pl
Career Total (Turf)	0	0	0	0	
Career Total (AW)	3	0	0	0	

Going (Turf): **Sf: 0-0 GS: 0-0 Gd: 0-0 GF: 0-0 Fm: 0-0**
Distance: 5f/6f: 0-1 7f-8f: 0-2 9f-13f: 0-0 14f+: 0-0
Track : LH: 0-3 RH: 0-0 Tight: 0-2 Gall: 0-1
Aids: Bl: 0-0 Vi: 0-0 Tstrap: 0-0 Ckp: 0-0
Best Rating: **44** 9/08 GrLe 6f stand

Flexible Friend (IRE)

83 25

5-y-o b h Danehill (USA)-Ripple Of Pride (IRE) (Sadler's Wells (USA))

B J Llewellyn B J Llewellyn

Placings:6/25006/0-00 (4264)

2009: 12^{0}GF, 16^{0}S,

	Starts	1st	2nd	3rd	Win & Pl
Career Total (Turf)	9	0	1	0	1632

Going (Turf): **Sf: 0-3 GS: 0-0 Gd: 0-1 GF: 0-4 Fm: 0-0**
Distance: 5f/6f: 0-0 7f-8f: 0-2 9f-13f: 0-5 14f+: 0-2
Track : LH: 0-4 RH: 0-5 Tight: 0-0 Gall: 0-0
Aids: Bl: 0-5 Vi: 0-0 Tstrap: 0-0 Ckp: 0-0
Best Rating: **71** 5/07 Cork 1m2f good

Flighty Fellow (IRE)

(90) (55)85

9-y-o ch g Flying Spur (AUS)-Al Theraab (USA) (Roberto (USA))

B G Powell (Mrs J L Le Brocq 28/11) Mrs J L Le Brocq

Placings:502031015/0062013014322/06106240430/46500 6/606506/61551234200/3041044-35106656 (7803)

2009: 7^{3}G, 8^{5}F, 9^{1}GF, 9^{0}GS, 8^{6}GS, 10^{6}GF, 8^{5}SF, 9^{6}SD,

	Starts	1st	2nd	3rd	Win & Pl
Career Total (Turf)	68	9	7	7	83578

Career Total (AW) 3 0 0 0 0
7/09 LesL 1m1f H G-F £900
6/08 LesL 1m1f H FRM £1790
83 7/07 Pont 1m4y (0-70)H SFT £4533
74 4/07 Pont 1m4y (0-75)H G-F £3886
96 5/04 Bevl 1m100yC(0-95)H G-F £8497
93 8/03 Pont 1m4y C(0-90)H G-F £9349
93 7/03 Bevl 1m100yD(0-85)H G-S £6938
80 10/02 Catt 7f D(0-85) GD £5414
63 8/02 Thsk 7f E GD £5102
Total win prize-money £46415

Going (Turf): Sf: 1-10 GS: 1-8 Gd: 2-20**GF: 4-26** Fm: 1-4
Distance: 5f/6f: 0-2 7f-8f: 2-27 **9f-13f: 7-42** 14f+: 0-0
Track : **LH: 6-42** RH: 2-12 **Tight: 2-12** Gall: 0-9
Aids: **Bl: 6-43** Vi: 0-2 Tstrap: 0-1 Ckp: 0-1
Best Rating: **102** 9/04 Donc 1m firm

Fair; effective at around 1m; acts on any ground; has worn most headgear but usually blinkered.

Flip Flop (IRE)

98(93) (72)**86**
2-y-o b f Footstepsinthesand-Dame Alicia (IRE) (Sadler's Wells (USA))
B W Hills J Acheson

Placings:2**4**15 (7187)
2009: 6^{2}GF, 7^{4}SD, 6^{1}GS, 8^{5}G,

	Starts	1st	2nd	3rd	Win & Pl
Career Total (Turf)	3	1	1	0	4596
Career Total (AW)	1	0	0	0	349

72 10/09 Folk 6f G-S £2729
Total win prize-money £2730

Going (Turf): Sf: 0-0 **GS: 1-1** Gd: 0-1 GF: 0-1 Fm: 0-0
Distance: **5f/6f: 1-2** 7f-8f: 0-2 9f-13f: 0-0 14f+: 0-0
Track : LH: 0-0 RH: 0-1 Tight: 0-0 Gall: 0-1
Aids: Bl: 0-0 Vi: 0-0 Tstrap: 0-0 Ckp: 0-0
Best Rating: **86** 10/09 NmkR 1m good

Fair; suited by 6f-7f and acts on easy ground.

Flipacoin

70(93) (38)**28**
4-y-o b f Josr Algarhoud (IRE)-Eclectic (Emarati (USA))
S Dow T G Parker

Placings:000-05 (1177)
2009: 8^{0}SD, 9^{5}G,

	Starts	1st	2nd	3rd	Win & Pl
Career Total (Turf)	3	0	0	0	0
Career Total (AW)	2	0	0	0	

Going (Turf): **Sf: 0-0 GS: 0-0 Gd: 0-1 GF: 0-2 Fm: 0-0**
Distance: 5f/6f: 0-2 7f-8f: 0-2 9f-13f: 0-1 14f+: 0-0
Track : LH: 0-2 RH: 0-1 Tight: 0-1 Gall: 0-1
Aids: Bl: 0-0 Vi: 0-0 Tstrap: 0-0 Ckp: 0-0
Best Rating: **38** 2/09 Kemp 1m stand

Flipando (IRE)

108(117) (106)**105**
8-y-o b g Sri Pekan (USA)-Magic Touch (Fairy King (USA))
T D Barron Mrs J Hazell

Placings:310/4221531/204556023/024341065/604112030 000/0404660403036**41-21**34600224000000 (6876)
2009: 8^{2}SD, 8^{1}SD, 8^{3}GF, 9^{4}GF, 8^{6}G, 10^{0}GF, 8^{0}G, 8^{2}GF, 8^{2}F, 8^{4}G, 8^{0}GF, 8^{0}G, 8^{0}G, 8^{0}GF, 8^{0}SD,

	Starts	1st	2nd	3rd	Win & Pl
Career Total (Turf)	65	6	8	8	174758
Career Total (AW)	5	2	1	0	47653

103 3/09 Wolv 1m141y (0-105)H STD £31155
99 12/08 GrLe 1m (0-100)H STD £12462
104 5/07 Rdcr 1m2f (0-105)H G-F £32385
99 5/07 Bevl 1m100y (0-90)H GD £7124
99 6/06 Newc 1m3y (0-100)H G-F £18696
93 9/04 Muss 1m (0-100)H GD £15103
90 7/04 Hayd 6f C(0-95)H GD £10270
78 9/03 Newc 6f D GD £3419
Total win prize-money £130615

Going (Turf): Sf: 0-4 GS: 0-5 **Gd: 4-23** GF: 2-28 Fm: 0-5
Distance: 5f/6f: 2-7 7f-8f: 2-43 **9f-13f: 4-20** 14f+: 0-0
Track : **LH: 3-29** RH: 2-9 **Tight: 3-13** Gall: 1-11
Aids: Bl: 0-0 Vi: 0-0 Tstrap: 0-0 Ckp: 0-0
Best Rating: **106** 3/09 Ling 1m stand

Very useful; effective at 1m, but stays 1m2f; acts on most ground and on Polytrack; usually held up.

Flipping

95(95) (77)**79**
2-y-o br g Kheleyf (USA)-Felona (Caerleon (USA))
W S Kittow Reg Gifford

Placings:01445002 (7669)
2009: 6^{0}GF, 6^{1}S, 6^{4}GS, 7^{4}GF, 8^{5}SD, 8^{0}GS, 8^{0}SD, 8^{2}SD,

	Starts	1st	2nd	3rd	Win & Pl
Career Total (Turf)	5	1	0	0	4559
Career Total (AW)	3	0	1	0	806

79 7/09 Hayd 6f SFT £3885
Total win prize-money £3886

Going (Turf): **Sf: 1-1** GS: 0-2 Gd: 0-0 GF: 0-2 Fm: 0-0
Distance: **5f/6f: 1-1** 7f-8f: 0-5 9f-13f: 0-2 14f+: 0-0
Track : LH: 0-4 RH: 0-0 Tight: 0-3 Gall: 0-1
Aids: Bl: 0-0 Vi: 0-0 Tstrap: 0-0 Ckp: 0-0
Best Rating: **79** 7/09 Hayd 6f soft

Modest; effective over 6-7f; acts on soft ground and Polytrack.

Flirty (IRE)

93(94) (45)**46**
3-y-o b f Lujain (USA)-Fifth Edition (Rock Hopper)
Rae Guest Rachel Flynn & Rae Guest

Placings:0-6000030040 (7842)
2009: 6^{6}SS, 7^{0}G, 9^{0}GS, 9^{0}G, 12^{0}SD, 13^{3}GF, 12^{0}SS, 11^{0}GF, 12^{4}SD, 14^{0}SS,

	Starts	1st	2nd	3rd	Win & Pl
Career Total (Turf)	5	0	0	1	302
Career Total (AW)	6	0	0	0	0

Going (Turf): **Sf: 0-0 GS: 0-1 Gd: 0-2 GF: 0-2 Fm: 0-0**
Distance: 5f/6f: 0-1 7f-8f: 0-2 9f-13f: 0-6 14f+: 0-2
Track : LH: 0-9 RH: 0-1 Tight: 0-6 Gall: 0-0
Aids: Bl: 0-0 Vi: 0-0 Tstrap: 0-0 Ckp: 0-0
Best Rating: **46** 9/09 Catt 1m5f175y gd-fm

Flodden Field

83(83) (50)**61**
3-y-o ch g Selkirk (USA)-Sister Bluebird (Bluebird (USA))
P W Chapple-Hyam P W Chapple-Hyam

Placings:00-50 (6806)
2009: 9^{5}GF, 9^{0}SD,

	Starts	1st	2nd	3rd	Win & Pl
Career Total (Turf)	2	0	0	0	0
Career Total (AW)	2	0	0	0	

Going (Turf): **Sf: 0-1 GS: 0-0 Gd: 0-0 GF: 0-1 Fm: 0-0**
Distance: 5f/6f: 0-0 7f-8f: 0-1 9f-13f: 0-3 14f+: 0-0
Track : LH: 0-3 RH: 0-1 Tight: 0-1 Gall: 0-1
Aids: Bl: 0-0 Vi: 0-0 Tstrap: 0-0 Ckp: 0-0
Best Rating: **61** 7/09 Leic 1m1f218y gd-fm

Moderate; stays 1m2f; acts on fast ground.

Floodlit

80(91) (71)**61**
3-y-o b f Fantastic Light (USA)-Westerly Air (USA) (Gone West (USA))
J H M Gosden Cheveley Park Stud

Placings:1-00 (4948)
2009: 11^{0}GF, 12^{0}GF,

	Starts	1st	2nd	3rd	Win & Pl
Career Total (Turf)	2	0	0	0	
Career Total (AW)	1	1	0	0	3886

71 7/08 Kemp 7f STD £3885
Total win prize-money £3886

Going (Turf): **Sf: 0-0 GS: 0-0 Gd: 0-0 GF: 0-2 Fm: 0-0**
Distance: 5f/6f: 0-0 **7f-8f: 1-1** 9f-13f: 0-2 14f+: 0-0
Track : LH: 0-1 **RH: 1-2** Tight: 0-2 Gall: 0-0
Aids: Bl: 0-0 Vi: 0-0 Tstrap: 0-0 Ckp: 0-0
Best Rating: **71** 7/08 Kemp 7f stand

Modest; 7f winner on debut; acts on Polytrack.

Floods Of Tears

80(86) (36)**58**
3-y-o br f Lucky Story (USA)-Lady Natilda (First Trump)
I W McInnes (D Flood 10/6) Barrie Kirby

Placings:500-4600000 (7126)
2009: 6^{4}SD, 7^{6}SD, 8^{0}SD, 7^{0}GF, 10^{0}GS, 6^{0}GF, 8^{0}G,

	Starts	1st	2nd	3rd	Win & Pl
Career Total (Turf)	5	0	0	0	0
Career Total (AW)	5	0	0	0	0

Going (Turf): **Sf: 0-0 GS: 0-2 Gd: 0-1 GF: 0-2 Fm: 0-0**
Distance: 5f/6f: 0-4 7f-8f: 0-4 9f-13f: 0-2 14f+: 0-0
Track : LH: 0-6 RH: 0-2 Tight: 0-4 Gall: 0-0
Aids: Bl: 0-3 Vi: 0-0 Tstrap: 0-0 Ckp: 0-0
Best Rating: **58** 8/08 Hayd 6f gd-sft

Floor Show

95 **86**
3-y-o ch g Bahamian Bounty-Dancing Spirit (IRE) (Ahonoora)
E S McMahon J C Fretwell

Placings:561-1200 (4326)
2009: 7^{1}GF, 7^{2}GS, 7^{0}G, 6^{0}GF,

	Starts	1st	2nd	3rd	Win & Pl
Career Total (Turf)	7	2	1	0	10188

79 4/09 Newc 7f (0-80)H G-F £5180
74 9/08 Rdcr 7f G-S £3561
Total win prize-money £8743

Going (Turf): Sf: 0-0 **GS: 1-2** Gd: 0-1 **GF: 1-4** Fm: 0-0
Distance: 5f/6f: 0-2 **7f-8f: 2-5** 9f-13f: 0-0 14f+: 0-0
Track : LH: 0-0 RH: 0-1 Tight: 0-0 Gall: 0-0
Aids: Bl: 0-0 Vi: 0-0 Tstrap: 0-0 Ckp: 0-0
Best Rating: **86** 5/09 Donc 7f gd-sft

Fair, stays 7f; acts on fast and easy ground.

Flora Trevelyan

102(102) (85)87

3-y-o b f Cape Cross (IRE)-Why So Silent (Mill Reef (USA))

W R Swinburn Pendley Farm

Placings:2-2120 (6813)

2009: 8^{2}SD, 8^{1}G, 10^{2}G, 10^{0}G,

	Starts	1st	2nd	3rd	Win & Pl
Career Total (Turf)	3	1	1	0	4683
Career Total (AW)	2	0	2	0	1927

87 8/09 Sand 1m14y GD £3238

Total win prize-money £3238

Going (Turf): Sf: 0-0 GS: 0-0 **Gd: 1-3** GF: 0-0 Fm: 0-0
Distance: 5f/6f: 0-0 7f-8f: 0-2 **9f-13f: 1-3** 14f+: 0-0
Track : LH: 0-2 **RH: 1-2** Tight: 0-1 Gall: 0-1
Aids: Bl: 0-0 Vi: 0-0 Tstrap: 0-0 Ckp: 0-0
Best Rating: **87** 10/09 Newb 1m2f6y good

Fair; will stay at least 1m; acts on Polytrack; sure to win races.

Flora's Pride

98 58

5-y-o b m Alflora (IRE)-Pennys Pride (IRE) (Pips Pride)

K G Reveley The Eleven O'Clock Club

Placings:6054550055432 (7085)

2009: 11^{6}G, 10^{0}S, 10^{5}GF, 8^{4}G, 8^{5}GF, 10^{5}F, 10^{0}GF, 14^{0}GF, 10^{5}GF, 10^{5}GF, 10^{4}GF, 10^{3}GF, 11^{2}S,

	Starts	1st	2nd	3rd	Win & Pl
Career Total (Turf)	13	0	1	1	1291

Going (Turf): **Sf: 0-2 GS: 0-0 Gd: 0-2 GF: 0-8 Fm: 0-1**
Distance: 5f/6f: 0-0 7f-8f: 0-1 9f-13f: 0-11 14f+: 0-1
Track : LH: 0-11 RH: 0-1 Tight: 0-9 Gall: 0-1
Aids: Bl: 0-0 Vi: 0-0 Tstrap: 0-0 Ckp: 0-0
Best Rating: **58** 10/09 Catt 1m3f214y soft

Moderate; stays 1m4f; acts on soft ground.

Florensky (IRE)

99 67

2-y-o br c Sinndar (IRE)-White Star (IRE) (Darshaan)

Saeed Bin Suroor Godolphin

Placings:46 (7116)

2009: 8^{4}GF, 8^{6}GS,

	Starts	1st	2nd	3rd	Win & Pl
Career Total (Turf)	2	0	0	0	385

Going (Turf): **Sf: 0-0 GS: 0-1 Gd: 0-0 GF: 0-1 Fm: 0-0**
Distance: 5f/6f: 0-0 7f-8f: 0-1 9f-13f: 0-1 14f+: 0-0
Track : LH: 0-1 RH: 0-1 Tight: 0-1 Gall: 0-0
Aids: Bl: 0-0 Vi: 0-0 Tstrap: 0-0 Ckp: 0-0
Best Rating: **67** 10/09 Muss 1m gd-sft

Florentia

97(101) (72)71

3-y-o ch f Medicean-Area Girl (Jareer (USA))

Sir Mark Prescott Neil Greig

Placings:425-0303311303 (7668)

2009: 7^{0}SD, 5^{3}SD, 6^{0}SD, 7^{3}SD, 7^{3}SD, 8^{1}F, 9^{1}GS, 8^{3}SD, 10^{0}SD, 9^{3}SD,

	Starts	1st	2nd	3rd	Win & Pl
Career Total (Turf)	4	2	1	0	6420
Career Total (AW)	9	0	0	5	2326

71 10/09 Folk 1m1f149y (0-65)H G-S £2047
68 9/09 Bath 1m5y (0-70)H FRM £2590

Total win prize-money £4637

Going (Turf): Sf: 0-1 **GS: 1-1** Gd: 0-1 GF: 0-0 **Fm: 1-1**
Distance: 5f/6f: 0-5 7f-8f: 0-3 **9f-13f: 2-5** 14f+: 0-0
Track : LH: 1-7 RH: 1-3 **Tight: 2-6** Gall: 0-1
Aids: Bl: 0-0 Vi: 0-0 Tstrap: 0-0 Ckp: 0-0
Best Rating: **72** 10/09 Wolv 1m141y stand

Modest; stays 1m1f; acts on soft ground and on sand.

Florentine Ruler (USA)

90 67

2-y-o b c Medicean-Follow That Dream (Darshaan)

H R A Cecil Malih L Al Basti

Placings:6 (7121)

2009: 8^{6}GF,

	Starts	1st	2nd	3rd	Win & Pl
Career Total (Turf)	1	0	0	0	0

Going (Turf): **Sf: 0-0 GS: 0-0 Gd: 0-0 GF: 0-1 Fm: 0-0**
Distance: 5f/6f: 0-0 7f-8f: 0-0 9f-13f: 0-1 14f+: 0-0
Track : LH: 0-1 RH: 0-0 Tight: 0-0 Gall: 0-0
Aids: Bl: 0-0 Vi: 0-0 Tstrap: 0-0 Ckp: 0-0
Best Rating: **67** 10/09 Nott 1m75y gd-fm

Flores Sea (USA)

102(110) (86)80

5-y-o ch g Luhuk (USA)-Perceptive (USA) (Capote (USA))

T D Barron T D Barron

Placings:41/01406000/41020330-202123042250 (7854)

2009: 7^{2}SD, 7^{0}SD, 8^{2}SD, 7^{1}SD, 7^{2}SD, 7^{3}G, 7^{0}GF, 7^{4}SD, 9^{2}G, 7^{2}SD, 8^{5}SD, 8^{0}SS,

	Starts	1st	2nd	3rd	Win & Pl
Career Total (Turf)	18	2	2	3	13782
Career Total (AW)	12	2	4	0	9812

86 3/09 Sthl 7f (0-75)H STD £2729
77 1/08 Sthl 7f (0-75)H STD £2593
79 5/07 Thsk 6f (0-75)H G-F £3886
70 10/06 Pont 6f G-S £3238

Total win prize-money £12449

Going (Turf): Sf: 0-2 **GS: 1-1** Gd: 0-7 **GF: 1-8** Fm: 0-0
Distance: 5f/6f: 2-5 7f-8f: 2-21 9f-13f: 0-4 14f+: 0-0
Track : **LH: 3-19** RH: 0-4 Tight: 0-7 Gall: 0-1
Aids: **Bl: 1-7** Vi: 0-0 Tstrap: 0-1 Ckp: 0-1
Best Rating: **86** 4/09 Sthl 7f stand

Fair; effective over 7f-1m; acts on most ground; goes on Fibresand; has worn blinkers.

Florio Vincitore (IRE)

94(97) (80)81

2-y-o b g High Chaparral (IRE)-Salome's Attack (Anabaa (USA))

E J Creighton Murray & Prosser

Placings:20126266 (6063)

2009: 5^{2}G, 7^{0}GF, 6^{1}SD, 6^{2}SD, 6^{6}S, 8^{2}SD, 8^{6}GS, 7^{6}GF,

	Starts	1st	2nd	3rd	Win & Pl
Career Total (Turf)	5	0	1	0	1090
Career Total (AW)	3	1	2	0	4908

75 7/09 Ling 6f STD £2388

Total win prize-money £2388

Going (Turf): **Sf: 0-1 GS: 0-1 Gd: 0-1 GF: 0-2 Fm: 0-0**
Distance: **5f/6f: 1-4** 7f-8f: 0-3 9f-13f: 0-1 14f+: 0-0
Track : **LH: 1-4** RH: 0-0 **Tight: 1-1** Gall: 0-0
Aids: Bl: 0-0 Vi: 0-0 Tstrap: 0-0 Ckp: 0-0
Best Rating: **81** 9/09 Crao 1m55y gd-sft

Useful; stays 1m and acts on sand.

Flotate (USA)

64(82) (57)4

2-y-o b/br f Orientate (USA)-Flo Jo (USA) (Graustark)

Jane Chapple-Hyam Evergreen Stables Partnership

Placings:000 (5722)

2009: 7^{0}SD, 6^{0}SD, 7^{0}F,

	Starts	1st	2nd	3rd	Win & Pl
Career Total (Turf)	1	0	0	0	
Career Total (AW)	2	0	0	0	

Going (Turf): **Sf: 0-0 GS: 0-0 Gd: 0-0 GF: 0-0 Fm: 0-1**
Distance: 5f/6f: 0-1 7f-8f: 0-2 9f-13f: 0-0 14f+: 0-0
Track : LH: 0-1 RH: 0-1 Tight: 0-1 Gall: 0-0
Aids: Bl: 0-0 Vi: 0-0 Tstrap: 0-0 Ckp: 0-0
Best Rating: **57** 8/09 Kemp 7f stand

Flotation (USA)

80 57

2-y-o b/br f Chapel Royal (USA)-Storm Dove (USA) (Storm Bird (CAN))

B W Hills K Abdulla

Placings:0 (7183)

2009: 7^{0}G,

	Starts	1st	2nd	3rd	Win & Pl
Career Total (Turf)	1	0	0	0	

Going (Turf): **Sf: 0-0 GS: 0-0 Gd: 0-1 GF: 0-0 Fm: 0-0**
Distance: 5f/6f: 0-0 7f-8f: 0-1 9f-13f: 0-0 14f+: 0-0
Track : LH: 0-0 RH: 0-0 Tight: 0-0 Gall: 0-0
Aids: Bl: 0-0 Vi: 0-0 Tstrap: 0-0 Ckp: 0-0
Best Rating: **57** 10/09 NmkR 7f good

Flouncing (IRE)

94(100) (77)77

2-y-o b f Barathea (IRE)-Man Eater (Mark Of Esteem (IRE))

W J Haggas Gibson, Goddard, Hamer & Hawkes

Placings:322 (7177)

2009: 7^{3}SD, 8^{2}S, 7^{2}SD,

	Starts	1st	2nd	3rd	Win & Pl
Career Total (Turf)	1	0	1	0	867
Career Total (AW)	2	0	1	1	1469

Going (Turf): **Sf: 0-1 GS: 0-0 Gd: 0-0 GF: 0-0 Fm: 0-0**
Distance: 5f/6f: 0-0 7f-8f: 0-3 9f-13f: 0-0 14f+: 0-0
Track : LH: 0-0 RH: 0-2 Tight: 0-0 Gall: 0-0
Aids: Bl: 0-0 Vi: 0-0 Tstrap: 0-0 Ckp: 0-0
Best Rating: **77** 10/09 Kemp 7f stand

Flow Chart (IRE)

101(93) (70)67

2-y-o b g Acclamation-Free Flow (Mujahid (USA))

T D Barron J Starbuck

Placings:43036061 (7849)

2009: 5^{4}GF, 5^{3}GF, 5^{0}G, 6^{3}GF, 5^{6}GF, 7^{0}GF, 5^{6}GF, 6^{1}SS,

	Starts	1st	2nd	3rd	Win & Pl
Career Total (Turf)	7	0	0	2	1733
Career Total (AW)	1	1	0	0	2730

70 12/09 Sthl 6f (0-75) SS £2729
Total win prize-money £2730

Going (Turf): Sf: 0-0 GS: 0-0 Gd: 0-1 GF: 0-6 Fm: 0-0
Distance: **5f/6f: 1-7** 7f-8f: 0-1 9f-13f: 0-0 14f+: 0-0
Track : **LH: 1-3** RH: 0-0 Tight: 0-1 Gall: 0-0
Aids: **Bl: 1-2** Vi: 0-0 Tstrap: 0-0 Ckp: 0-0
Best Rating: 70 12/09 Sthl 6f std-slw

Modest; effective over 5-7f; acts on fast ground and Fibresand; has worn blinkers.

Flowerbud

79(91) (56)**33**
4-y-o b m Fantastic Light (USA)-Maidment (Insan (USA))
G A Ham (Ms J S Doyle 21/4) Mrs Katrina Hitchins

Placings:4-55000 **(5246)**
2009: 11^{5}SD, 12^{5}SD, 12^{0}GS, 16^{0}SD, 13^{0}F,

	Starts	1st	2nd	3rd	Win & Pl
Career Total (Turf)	2	0	0	0	
Career Total (AW)	4	0	0	0	192

Going (Turf): Sf: 0-0 GS: 0-1 Gd: 0-0 GF: 0-0 Fm: 0-1
Distance: 5f/6f: 0-0 7f-8f: 0-0 9f-13f: 0-3 14f+: 0-3
Track : LH: 0-3 RH: 0-3 Tight: 0-1 Gall: 0-1
Aids: Bl: 0-0 Vi: 0-0 Tstrap: 0-0 Ckp: 0-0
Best Rating: 56 1/09 Kemp 1m3f stand

Moderate form to date.

Flowing Cape (IRE)

(111) (101)**89**
4-y-o b g Cape Cross (IRE)-Jet Lock (USA) (Crafty Prospector (USA))
R Hollinshead John L Marriott

Placings:4202/06-**115300564** **(7862)**
2009: 7^{1}SD, 5^{1}SD, 8^{5}SD, 7^{3}SD, 8^{0}SD, 7^{0}SD, 6^{5}SD, 7^{6}SS, 5^{4}SD,

	Starts	1st	2nd	3rd	Win & Pl
Career Total (Turf)	6	0	2	0	6074
Career Total (AW)	9	2	0	1	26013

101 2/09 Wolv 5f216y (0-100)H STD £12462
96 2/09 Wolv 7f32y (0-90)H STD £9462
Total win prize-money £21924

Going (Turf): Sf: 0-0 GS: 0-0 Gd: 0-2 GF: 0-4 Fm: 0-0
Distance: 5f/6f: 1-4 7f-8f: 1-9 9f-13f: 0-2 14f+: 0-0
Track : **LH: 2-10** RH: 0-1 **Tight: 2-6** Gall: 0-1
Aids: Bl: 0-0 Vi: 0-0 Tstrap: 0-1 Ckp: 0-1
Best Rating: 101 4/09 Kemp 7f stand

Very useful; stays 7f; acts on fast ground and on Polytrack.

Flute Magic

93(93) (44)**72**
3-y-o b g Piccolo-Overcome (Belmez (USA))
W S Kittow Midd Shire Racing

Placings:020-00050060 **(6497)**
2009: 7^{0}SD, 6^{0}F, 7^{0}G, 5^{5}S, 6^{0}GS, 6^{0}G, 6^{6}SD, 9^{0}SF,

	Starts	1st	2nd	3rd	Win & Pl
Career Total (Turf)	8	0	1	0	674
Career Total (AW)	3	0	0	0	0

Going (Turf): Sf: 0-1 GS: 0-1 Gd: 0-2 GF: 0-3 Fm: 0-1
Distance: 5f/6f: 0-4 7f-8f: 0-6 9f-13f: 0-1 14f+: 0-0
Track : LH: 0-6 RH: 0-1 Tight: 0-3 Gall: 0-1
Aids: Bl: 0-2 Vi: 0-0 Tstrap: 0-0 Ckp: 0-0
Best Rating: 72 6/08 Ling 7f gd-fm

Moderate; effective over 7f; acts on fast ground.

Fly Butterfly

80(83) (29)**50**
3-y-o ch f Bahamian Bounty-Aconite (Primo Dominie)
M R Channon Bill Adams

Placings:0000-000 **(2910)**
2009: 6^{0}GF, 5^{0}F, 8^{0}F,

	Starts	1st	2nd	3rd	Win & Pl
Career Total (Turf)	6	0	0	0	1082
Career Total (AW)	1	0	0	0	

Going (Turf): Sf: 0-0 GS: 0-0 Gd: 0-1 GF: 0-3 Fm: 0-2
Distance: 5f/6f: 0-3 7f-8f: 0-3 9f-13f: 0-1 14f+: 0-0
Track : LH: 0-3 RH: 0-0 Tight: 0-1 Gall: 0-2
Aids: Bl: 0-2 Vi: 0-0 Tstrap: 0-0 Ckp: 0-0
Best Rating: 50 8/08 NmkJ 6f gd-fm

Fly By Nelly

99(99) (67)**66**
3-y-o b f Compton Place-Dancing Nelly (Shareef Dancer (USA))
H Morrison Lady Hardy & P W Saunders

Placings:040-23200**204** **(7829)**
2009: 7^{2}GF, 7^{3}GF, 6^{2}GF, 6^{0}GF, 7^{0}G, 7^{2}SD, 7^{0}SD, 7^{4}SD,

	Starts	1st	2nd	3rd	Win & Pl
Career Total (Turf)	7	0	2	1	2497
Career Total (AW)	4	0	1	0	482

Going (Turf): Sf: 0-0 GS: 0-0 Gd: 0-2 GF: 0-5 Fm: 0-0
Distance: 5f/6f: 0-3 7f-8f: 0-8 9f-13f: 0-0 14f+: 0-0
Track : LH: 0-1 RH: 0-3 Tight: 0-1 Gall: 0-2
Aids: Bl: 0-0 Vi: 0-0 Tstrap: 0-0 Ckp: 0-0
Best Rating: 67 10/09 Kemp 7f stand

Modest; effective at 7f; acts on fast ground.

Fly In Johnny (IRE)

91(99) (51)**58**
4-y-o b g Fasliyev (USA)-Goodness Gracious (IRE) (Green Desert (USA))
J J Bridger double-r-racing.com

Placings:440/**5652**2**66**2050**000-0300060000** **(4203)**
2009: 7^{0}SD, 6^{3}SD, 6^{0}SD, 8^{0}GF, 7^{0}GF, 5^{6}GF, 6^{0}GF, 5^{0}S, 6^{0}G, 6^{0}SD,

	Starts	1st	2nd	3rd	Win & Pl
Career Total (Turf)	16	0	3	0	2386
Career Total (AW)	11	0	0	1	302

Going (Turf): Sf: 0-1 GS: 0-4 Gd: 0-2 GF: 0-8 Fm: 0-1
Distance: 5f/6f: 0-12 7f-8f: 0-12 9f-13f: 0-3 14f+: 0-0
Track : LH: 0-14 RH: 0-4 Tight: 0-11 Gall: 0-4
Aids: Bl: 0-1 Vi: 0-1 Tstrap: 0-5 Ckp: 0-5
Best Rating: 68 10/07 Newb 6f110y gd-sft

Moderate; suited by 7f-1m; acts on fast ground.

Fly Silca Fly (IRE)

95 **80**
2-y-o b f Hawk Wing (USA)-Nevis Peak (AUS) (Danehill (USA))
M R Channon Aldridge Racing Partnership

Placings:52021612 **(5208)**
2009: 5^{5}G, 6^{2}GF, 7^{0}GF, 5^{2}F, 5^{1}S, 6^{6}GS, 6^{1}GF, 6^{2}GF,

	Starts	1st	2nd	3rd	Win & Pl
Career Total (Turf)	8	2	3	0	14528

78 8/09 Wind 6f G-F £2729
73 7/09 Ripn 5f SFT £5180
Total win prize-money £7911

Going (Turf): Sf: 1-1 GS: 0-1 Gd: 0-1 **GF: 1-4** Fm: 0-1
Distance: **5f/6f: 2-6** 7f-8f: 0-2 9f-13f: 0-0 14f+: 0-0
Track : LH: 0-2 RH: 0-0 Tight: 0-1 **Gall: 1-1**
Aids: Bl: 0-0 Vi: 0-0 Tstrap: 0-0 Ckp: 0-0
Best Rating: 80 8/09 Ches 6f18y gd-fm

Fair; stays 6f; acts on soft and fast ground.

Fly With The Stars (USA)

76(98) (60)**34**
4-y-o ch g Fusaichi Pegasus (USA)-Forest Key (USA) (Green Forest (USA))
A B Haynes (D E Pipe 13/5) R S Brookhouse

Placings:053/03-00 **(4935)**
2009: 9^{0}S, 18^{0}G,

	Starts	1st	2nd	3rd	Win & Pl
Career Total (Turf)	6	0	0	1	385
Career Total (AW)	1	0	0	1	403

Going (Turf): Sf: 0-3 GS: 0-0 Gd: 0-1 GF: 0-2 Fm: 0-0
Distance: 5f/6f: 0-0 7f-8f: 0-0 9f-13f: 0-6 14f+: 0-1
Track : LH: 0-7 RH: 0-0 Tight: 0-2 Gall: 0-0
Aids: Bl: 0-0 Vi: 0-0 Tstrap: 0-0 Ckp: 0-0
Best Rating: 79 11/07 Nott 1m54y gd-fm

Flyinflyout

94(80) (55)**74**
2-y-o b f Fath (USA)-Hana Dee (Cadeaux Genereux)
M R Channon Racegoers Club Owners Group

Placings:45100500**000** **(6345)**
2009: 6^{4}G, 6^{5}GF, 5^{1}F, 6^{0}GF, 6^{0}G, 5^{5}GF, 7^{0}G, 6^{0}GF, 7^{0}SD, 8^{0}G, 5^{0}SD,

	Starts	1st	2nd	3rd	Win & Pl
Career Total (Turf)	9	1	0	0	2531
Career Total (AW)	2	0	0	0	

74 5/09 Bath 5f161y FRM £2266
Total win prize-money £2267

Going (Turf): Sf: 0-0 GS: 0-0 Gd: 0-4 GF: 0-4 **Fm: 1-1**
Distance: **5f/6f: 1-7** 7f-8f: 0-3 9f-13f: 0-1 14f+: 0-0
Track : **LH: 1-5** RH: 0-1 Tight: 0-3 **Gall: 1-2**
Aids: Bl: 0-0 Vi: 0-0 Tstrap: 0-0 Ckp: 0-0
Best Rating: 74 5/09 Bath 5f161y firm

Fair; effective over 5f-6f; acts on fast ground.

Flying Applause

101(99) (70)**80**
4-y-o b g Royal Applause-Mrs Gray (Red Sunset)
S R Bowring K Nicholls

Placings:0600331/02501066-0460106012650 (4783)
2009: 8⁰SD, 9⁴SD, 11⁶SD, 8⁰SD, 8¹GF, 9⁰GF, 8⁶G, 6⁰G, 6¹G, 5²GF, 6⁶G, 5⁵HY, 6⁰GF,

	Starts	1st	2nd	3rd	Win & Pl
Career Total (Turf)	21	3	2	1	9119
Career Total (AW)	7	1	0	1	4455

74 6/09 Nott 6f15y (0-65)H GD £2047
71 4/09 Nott 1m75y (0-65)H G-F £1942
80 7/08 Wind 1m2f7y (0-75)H G-F £3070
70 11/07 Ling 7f (0-75) STD £3886
Total win prize-money £10947

Going (Turf): Sf: 0-1 GS: 0-1 Gd: 1-7 **GF: 2-12** Fm: 0-0
Distance: 5f/6f: 0-8 7f-8f: 2-9 9f-13f: 2-11 14f+: 0-0
Track : **LH: 2-10** RH: 1-7 **Tight: 2-8** Gall: 0-1
Aids: **Bl: 2-9** Vi: 0-0 Tstrap: 0-0 Ckp: 0-0
Best Rating: 80 7/08 Wind 1m2f7y gd-fm

Modest; effective from 6f-1m2f; acts on fast ground and on Polytrack; has worn blinkers and a tongue tie.

Flying Bantam (IRE)

92(99) (66)78
8-y-o b g Fayruz-Natural Pearl (Petong)
J R Norton The Matthewman Partnership

Placings:22503/2224024041312/1500405653555/U05562 4300/532103616321/2334100400000-066000 (4845)
2009: 6⁰GF, 7⁶F, 8⁶GF, 8⁰G, 8⁰SD, 8⁰G,

	Starts	1st	2nd	3rd	Win & Pl
Career Total (Turf)	54	5	9	5	48262
Career Total (AW)	18	2	2	4	10039

78 6/08 Ayr 7f50y (0-85)H G-F £6476
75 6/07 Bevl 7f100y (0-70)H G-F £3886
69 4/07 Thsk 7f (0-75)H G-F £3886
72 2/07 Sthl 7f (0-70)H STD £3071
89 4/05 Pont 6f (0-90)H SFT £9414
85 10/04 Wolv 5f216y (0-77)H STD £3443
76 9/04 Ripn 6f G-F £4063
Total win prize-money £34242

Going (Turf): Sf: 1-12 GS: 0-6 Gd: 0-7 **GF: 4-23** Fm: 0-6
Distance: 5f/6f: 3-30 **7f-8f: 4-41** 9f-13f: 0-1 14f+: 0-0
Track : **LH: 5-38** RH: 1-9 **Tight: 2-24** Gall: 0-3
Aids: Bl: 0-1 Vi: 0-0 Tstrap: 1-5 Ckp: 1-5
Best Rating: 89 4/05 Pont 6f soft

Fair; effective over 7f; acts on any ground and both All-Weather surfaces.

Flying Cloud (USA)

67(88) (48)44
3-y-o ch f Giant's Causeway (USA)-St Francis Wood (USA) (Irish River (FR))
B J Meehan Joe L Allbritton

Placings:0-000 (3303)
2009: 8⁰SD, 8⁰G, 12⁰SD,

	Starts	1st	2nd	3rd	Win & Pl
Career Total (Turf)	2	0	0	0	
Career Total (AW)	2	0	0	0	

Going (Turf): **Sf: 0-0 GS: 0-1 Gd: 0-1 GF: 0-0 Fm: 0-0**
Distance: 5f/6f: 0-0 7f-8f: 0-3 9f-13f: 0-1 14f+: 0-0
Track : LH: 0-0 RH: 0-3 Tight: 0-0 Gall: 0-0
Aids: Bl: 0-0 Vi: 0-0 Tstrap: 0-0 Ckp: 0-0
Best Rating: 48 6/09 Kemp 1m4f stand

Flying Cloud (IRE)

107 110
3-y-o b f Storming Home-Criquette (Shirley Heights)
Saeed Bin Suroor (A Fabre 1/5) Godolphin

Placings:1116 (7046a)
2009: 10¹GS, 10¹S, 12¹GF, 10⁶GS,

	Starts	1st	2nd	3rd	Win & Pl
Career Total (Turf)	4	3	0	0	127658

110 6/09 Asct 1m4f G-F £77173
102 5/09 StCl 1m2f110y SFT £38835
86 4/09 Lonc 1m2f G-S £11650
Total win prize-money £127658

Going (Turf): **Sf: 1-1 GS: 1-2** Gd: 0-0 **GF: 1-1** Fm: 0-0
Distance: 5f/6f: 0-0 7f-8f: 0-0 **9f-13f: 3-4** 14f+: 0-0
Track : LH: 1-1 **RH: 2-3** Tight: 0-0 **Gall: 1-1**
Aids: Bl: 0-0 Vi: 0-0 Tstrap: 0-0 Ckp: 0-0
Best Rating: 110 6/09 Asct 1m4f gd-fm

Group class; sister to Captain Webb; winner of Group 3 in France and Group 2 Ribblesdale; stays 1m4f; acts on most ground.

Flying Destination

98(95) (72)74
2-y-o ch g Dubai Destination (USA)-Fly For Fame (Shaadi (USA))
W J Knight The Pheasant Rew Partnership

Placings:04025 (6373)
2009: 6⁰G, 7⁴G, 7⁰GF, 8²GF, 8⁵SD,

	Starts	1st	2nd	3rd	Win & Pl
Career Total (Turf)	4	0	1	0	1541
Career Total (AW)	1	0	0	0	0

Going (Turf): **Sf: 0-0 GS: 0-0 Gd: 0-2 GF: 0-2 Fm: 0-0**
Distance: 5f/6f: 0-1 7f-8f: 0-4 9f-13f: 0-0 14f+: 0-0
Track : LH: 0-0 RH: 0-4 Tight: 0-0 Gall: 0-1
Aids: Bl: 0-0 Vi: 0-0 Tstrap: 0-0 Ckp: 0-0
Best Rating: 74 9/09 Gdwd 1m gd-fm

Fair; stays 1m; handles fast ground.

Flying Doctor

(89) (36)37
6-y-o b g Mark Of Esteem (IRE)-Vice Vixen (CAN) (Vice Regent (CAN))
E J Cooper (N G Richards 3/3) Tom McNicholas

Placings:0056/0/0/0 (0252)
2009: 16⁰SD,

	Starts	1st	2nd	3rd	Win & Pl
Career Total (Turf)	6	0	0	0	0
Career Total (AW)	1	0	0	0	

Going (Turf): **Sf: 0-0 GS: 0-0 Gd: 0-2 GF: 0-4 Fm: 0-0**
Distance: 5f/6f: 0-2 7f-8f: 0-1 9f-13f: 0-3 14f+: 0-1
Track : LH: 0-1 RH: 0-4 Tight: 0-4 Gall: 0-0
Aids: Bl: 0-0 Vi: 0-0 Tstrap: 0-0 Ckp: 0-0
Best Rating: 50 6/05 Bevl 7f100y gd-fm

Flying Gazebo (IRE)

95(83) (30)55
3-y-o b g Orpen (USA)-Grand Summit (IRE) (Grand Lodge (USA))
J S Moore Mr & Mrs T Yates & Pier House Stud

Placings:06450 (7687)
2009: 8⁰G, 8⁶GF, 7⁴GS, 8⁵G, 12⁰SD,

	Starts	1st	2nd	3rd	Win & Pl
Career Total (Turf)	4	0	0	0	154
Career Total (AW)	1	0	0	0	

Going (Turf): **Sf: 0-0 GS: 0-1 Gd: 0-2 GF: 0-1 Fm: 0-0**
Distance: 5f/6f: 0-0 7f-8f: 0-2 9f-13f: 0-3 14f+: 0-0
Track : LH: 0-1 RH: 0-1 Tight: 0-0 Gall: 0-0
Aids: Bl: 0-0 Vi: 0-0 Tstrap: 0-0 Ckp: 0-0
Best Rating: 55 7/09 Sals 1m gd-fm

Flying Goose (IRE)

4(99) (86)83
5-y-o ch g Danehill Dancer (IRE)-Top Of The Form (IRE) (Masterclass (USA))
R A Harris Ridge House Stables Ltd

Placings:2/3135303/60506004000-00 (4264)
2009: 12⁰SD, 16⁰S,

	Starts	1st	2nd	3rd	Win & Pl
Career Total (Turf)	13	1	0	3	5811
Career Total (AW)	8	0	1	1	1859

81 7/07 Folk 7f G-F £2914
Total win prize-money £2915

Going (Turf): Sf: 0-2 GS: 0-1 Gd: 0-3 **GF: 1-6** Fm: 0-1
Distance: 5f/6f: 0-5 **7f-8f: 1-12** 9f-13f: 0-3 14f+: 0-1
Track : LH: 0-12 RH: 0-1 Tight: 0-9 Gall: 0-0
Aids: Bl: 0-1 Vi: 0-0 Tstrap: 0-1 Ckp: 0-1
Best Rating: 86 10/07 Wolv 7f32y stand

Fair; effective over 6f-7f; acts on fast ground; also goes on Polytrack.

Flying Indian

(89) (61)65
4-y-o ch f Hawk Wing (USA)-Poppadam (Salse (USA))
J Balding Emilys Birthday Party Racing Partnership

Placings:05206004/210000-0605 (0508)
2009: 5⁰SD, 5⁶SD, 6⁰SD, 5⁵SD,

	Starts	1st	2nd	3rd	Win & Pl
Career Total (Turf)	7	1	1	0	2680
Career Total (AW)	11	0	1	0	838

65 5/08 Bath 5f161y G-F £1813
Total win prize-money £1813

Going (Turf): Sf: 0-1 GS: 0-2 Gd: 0-0 **GF: 1-4** Fm: 0-0
Distance: **5f/6f: 1-18** 7f-8f: 0-0 9f-13f: 0-0 14f+: 0-0
Track : **LH: 1-8** RH: 0-2 Tight: 0-5 **Gall: 1-2**
Aids: Bl: 0-1 Vi: 0-3 Tstrap: 0-1 Ckp: 0-1
Best Rating: 65 5/08 Bath 5f161y gd-fm

Modest; seems best over 6f; acts on most ground and Polytrack; has worn various headgear.

Flying Lady (IRE)

84(106) (70)80
3-y-o b f Hawk Wing (USA)-Lady Nessa (USA) (Al Nasr (FR))
M R Channon M Channon

Placings:4506655-50231256 (1531)
2009: 8⁵SD, 8⁰SD, 8²SD, 8³SD, 10¹SD, 10²G, 9⁵SD, 8⁶SD,

	Starts	1st	2nd	3rd	Win & Pl
Career Total (Turf)	8	0	1	0	2801

Career Total (AW) 7 1 1 1 3156
59 3/09 Ling 1m2f STD £2047
Total win prize-money £2047

Going (Turf): Sf: 0-2 GS: 0-1 Gd: 0-3 GF: 0-2 Fm: 0-0
Distance: 5f/6f: 0-1 7f-8f: 0-7 9f-13f: 1-7 14f+: 0-0
Track : LH: 1-9 RH: 0-2 Tight: 1-7 Gall: 0-0
Aids: Bl: 0-0 Vi: 0-0 Tstrap: 0-0 Ckp: 0-0
Best Rating: 80 6/08 Asct 7f gd-fm

Modest; stays 1m2f; acts on good ground and Polytrack.

Flying Phoebe

100 51
3-y-o b f Sakhee (USA)-Altaweelah (IRE) (Fairy King (USA))
Mrs L Stubbs Des Thurlby

Placings:0504300 (6919)
2009: 10⁰GF, 10⁵GF, 12⁰G, 9⁴F, 12³GF, 12⁰GF, 11⁰GF,

	Starts	1st	2nd	3rd	Win & Pl
Career Total (Turf)	7	0	0	1	590

Going (Turf): Sf: 0-0 GS: 0-0 Gd: 0-1 GF: 0-5 Fm: 0-1
Distance: 5f/6f: 0-0 7f-8f: 0-0 9f-13f: 0-7 14f+: 0-0
Track : LH: 0-3 RH: 0-4 Tight: 0-3 Gall: 0-3
Aids: Bl: 0-0 Vi: 0-0 Tstrap: 0-0 Ckp: 0-0
Best Rating: 51 9/09 Bevl 1m4f16y gd-fm

Flying River (IRE)

(85) (47)
3-y-o b f Bachelor Duke (USA)-Suzuran (Generous (IRE))
Tom Dascombe Oneway Staff

Placings:0-05 (0556)
2009: 8⁰SD, 8⁵SD,

	Starts	1st	2nd	3rd	Win & Pl
Career Total (Turf)	0	0	0	0	
Career Total (AW)	3	0	0	0	0

Going (Turf): Sf: 0-0 GS: 0-0 Gd: 0-0 GF: 0-0 Fm: 0-0
Distance: 5f/6f: 0-1 7f-8f: 0-1 9f-13f: 0-1 14f+: 0-0
Track : LH: 0-3 RH: 0-0 Tight: 0-3 Gall: 0-0
Aids: Bl: 0-0 Vi: 0-0 Tstrap: 0-0 Ckp: 0-0
Best Rating: 47 1/09 Ling 1m stand

Flying Silks (IRE)

105(96) (67)74
3-y-o b g Barathea (IRE)-Future Flight (Polar Falcon (USA))
J R Gask Coffen Construction

Placings:66-4031560 (7246)
2009: 5⁴G, 6⁰GF, 8³S, 8¹G, 8⁵SD, 8⁶GS, 8⁰S,

	Starts	1st	2nd	3rd	Win & Pl
Career Total (Turf)	6	1	0	1	4560
Career Total (AW)	3	0	0	0	0

74 8/09 Pont 1m4y (0-75)H GD £3885
Total win prize-money £3886

Going (Turf): Sf: 0-2 GS: 0-1 Gd: 1-2 GF: 0-1 Fm: 0-0
Distance: 5f/6f: 0-3 7f-8f: 0-3 9f-13f: 1-3 14f+: 0-0
Track : LH: 1-3 RH: 0-3 Tight: 0-0 Gall: 0-0
Aids: Bl: 0-0 Vi: 0-0 Tstrap: 0-0 Ckp: 0-0
Best Rating: 74 8/09 Pont 1m4y good

Fair; stays 1m; suited by good and soft ground.

Flying Squad (UAE)

87(101) (75)39
5-y-o b g Jade Robbery (USA)-Sandova (IRE) (Green Desert (USA))
M F Harris Mick Coulson

Placings:310-00605004 (7354)
2009: 12⁰SD, 8⁰SD, 8⁶SD, 8⁰SD, 8⁵SD, 12⁰SF, 10⁰G, 12⁴SD,

	Starts	1st	2nd	3rd	Win & Pl
Career Total (Turf)	1	0	0	0	
Career Total (AW)	10	1	0	1	3763

75 5/08 Sthl 1m3f STD £3399
Total win prize-money £3400

Going (Turf): Sf: 0-0 GS: 0-0 Gd: 0-1 GF: 0-0 Fm: 0-0
Distance: 5f/6f: 0-0 7f-8f: 0-5 9f-13f: 1-6 14f+: 0-0
Track : LH: 1-8 RH: 0-3 Tight: 0-2 Gall: 0-0
Aids: Bl: 0-0 Vi: 0-0 Tstrap: 0-0 Ckp: 0-0
Best Rating: 75 1/09 Wolv 1m4f50y stand

Fair; stays 1m3f and acts on Fibresand.

Flying Statesman (USA)

101 90
2-y-o b g Johannesburg (USA)-Insomnie (USA) (Seattle Slew (USA))
R A Fahey Hazel Tattersall & G Hyde

Placings:210 (2993)
2009: 6²G, 6¹GF, 6⁰GF,

	Starts	1st	2nd	3rd	Win & Pl
Career Total (Turf)	3	1	1	0	7351

90 6/09 Ayr 6f G-F £5018
Total win prize-money £5019

Going (Turf): Sf: 0-0 GS: 0-0 Gd: 0-1 GF: 1-2 Fm: 0-0
Distance: 5f/6f: 1-3 7f-8f: 0-0 9f-13f: 0-0 14f+: 0-0
Track : LH: 0-0 RH: 0-0 Tight: 0-0 Gall: 0-0
Aids: Bl: 0-0 Vi: 0-0 Tstrap: 0-0 Ckp: 0-0
Best Rating: 90 6/09 Ayr 6f gd-fm

Useful; effective at 6f; acts on fast ground.

Flying Valentino

106(93) (77)83
5-y-o b m Primo Valentino (IRE)-Flying Romance (IRE) (Flying Spur (AUS))
Ian Williams UK Distribution Personnel Ltd

Placings:01/0465302050/6041150-0360313000 (7158)
2009: 5⁰SF, 8³SD, 8⁶GF, 8⁰GF, 9³GF, 8¹GF, 8³G, 7⁰GF, 8⁰GF, 7⁰SD,

	Starts	1st	2nd	3rd	Win & Pl
Career Total (Turf)	25	4	1	3	16384
Career Total (AW)	4	0	0	1	819

83 6/09 Wind 1m67y (0-75)H G-F £3070
83 6/08 Pont 1m4y (0-70)H GD £3238
72 6/08 Carl 7f200y (0-70)H G-F £2590
66 8/06 Newc 6f G-F £2590
Total win prize-money £11490

Going (Turf): Sf: 0-1 GS: 0-3 Gd: 1-6 GF: 3-13 Fm: 0-2
Distance: 5f/6f: 1-7 7f-8f: 1-13 9f-13f: 2-9 14f+: 0-0
Track : LH: 1-16 RH: 2-5 Tight: 1-13 Gall: 0-1
Aids: Bl: 0-0 Vi: 0-0 Tstrap: 0-0 Ckp: 0-0
Best Rating: 83 6/09 Wind 1m67y gd-fm

Useful; effective from 1m-1m2f; acts on good and fast ground.

Flynn's Island (IRE)

88 50
3-y-o b g Trans Island-Cappuccino (IRE) (Mujadil (USA))
M Dods J A Wynn-Williams

Placings:0000005 (3614)
2009: 7⁰GF, 7⁰GF, 8⁰GF, 8⁰GS, 10⁰G, 7⁰GF, 7⁵G,

	Starts	1st	2nd	3rd	Win & Pl
Career Total (Turf)	7	0	0	0	0

Going (Turf): Sf: 0-0 GS: 0-1 Gd: 0-2 GF: 0-4 Fm: 0-0
Distance: 5f/6f: 0-0 7f-8f: 0-5 9f-13f: 0-2 14f+: 0-0
Track : LH: 0-3 RH: 0-2 Tight: 0-4 Gall: 0-0
Aids: Bl: 0-2 Vi: 0-1 Tstrap: 0-0 Ckp: 0-0
Best Rating: 50 5/09 Thsk 7f gd-fm

Focail Eile

104(103) (74)80
4-y-o b g Noverre (USA)-Glittering Image (IRE) (Sadler's Wells (USA))
J Ryan (Miss Gay Kelleway 4/7) Cathal Fegan

Placings:6020-210411400 (7229)
2009: 8²SD, 8¹SD, 8⁰GF, 8⁴G, 8¹HY, 8¹HY, 8⁴GS, 8⁰S, 8⁰SD,

	Starts	1st	2nd	3rd	Win & Pl
Career Total (Turf)	6	2	0	0	7020
Career Total (AW)	7	1	2	0	3817

77 8/09 Leic 1m60y (0-75)H HVY £3885
77 7/09 Nott 1m75y (0-75)H HVY £2590
74 1/09 Wolv 1m141y STD £2047
Total win prize-money £8523

Going (Turf): Sf: 2-3 GS: 0-1 Gd: 0-1 GF: 0-1 Fm: 0-0
Distance: 5f/6f: 0-1 7f-8f: 0-4 9f-13f: 3-8 14f+: 0-0
Track : LH: 2-10 RH: 1-2 Tight: 1-7 Gall: 0-0
Aids: Bl: 0-0 Vi: 0-0 Tstrap: 0-0 Ckp: 0-0
Best Rating: 80 8/09 Nott 1m75y gd-sft

Modest; effective over 1m; acts on Polytrack and good ground.

Fochabers

(76) (65)
2-y-o b g Dr Fong (USA)-Celtic Cross (Selkirk (USA))
R Charlton The Queen

Placings:045 (7865)
2009: 8⁰SD, 8⁴SD, 8⁵SS,

	Starts	1st	2nd	3rd	Win & Pl
Career Total (Turf)	0	0	0	0	
Career Total (AW)	3	0	0	0	0

Going (Turf): Sf: 0-0 GS: 0-0 Gd: 0-0 GF: 0-0 Fm: 0-0
Distance: 5f/6f: 0-0 7f-8f: 0-3 9f-13f: 0-0 14f+: 0-0
Track : LH: 0-3 RH: 0-0 Tight: 0-2 Gall: 0-0
Aids: Bl: 0-0 Vi: 0-0 Tstrap: 0-0 Ckp: 0-0
Best Rating: 65 12/09 Ling 1m stand

Modest; acts on Polytrack.

Fol Hollow (IRE)

108(93) (72)103
4-y-o b g Monashee Mountain (USA)-Constance Do (Risk Me (FR))
D Nicholls Middleham Park Racing Iii

Placings:224231161/30055603530-11604104043304 (6283)

2009: 5^{1}GF, 5^{1}Y, 5^{6}G, 5^{0}GF, 6^{4}GF, 5^{1}GF, 5^{0}HY, 5^{4}GF, 6^{0}S, 5^{4}G, 5^{3}GF, 5^{3}G, 6^{0}G, 5^{4}GF,

	Starts	1st	2nd	3rd	Win & Pl
Career Total (Turf)	32	6	3	6	71112
Career Total (AW)	2	0	0	0	0

103	6/09	Bevl	5f	(0-95)H	G-F	£7641
101	4/09	Naas	5f	(60-95)H	YLD	£9392
97	4/09	Bevl	5f	(0-95)H	G-F	£7641
92	8/07	Ripn	5f		G-F	£6232
88	8/07	Gdwd	6f	H	G-F	£11658
83	7/07	Muss	5f		GD	£2590

Total win prize-money £45158

Going (Turf): Sf: 0-3 GS: 0-6 Gd: 1-10 **GF: 4-11** Fm: 0-1
Distance: **5f/6f: 6-34** 7f-8f: 0-0 9f-13f: 0-0 14f+: 0-0
Track : **LH: 1-3** RH: 0-1 Tight: 0-1 Gall: 0-0
Aids: Bl: 0-0 Vi: 0-0 Tstrap: 0-0 Ckp: 0-0
Best Rating: **103** 9/09 Hayd 5f gd-fm

Very useful; effective at 5f-6f; acts on most ground; likes to race prominently.

Fol Liam

81(99) (69)**81**

3-y-o b g Observatory (USA)-Tide Of Fortune (Soviet Star (USA))
A J McCabe (Ian Williams 7/6) A C Timms

Placings:1120-00**3**0**5**0**5**3 **(5676)**
2009: 10^{0}G, 10^{0}GF, 7^{3}SD, 5^{0}SD, 7^{5}SD, 8^{0}GF, 5^{5}SD, 7^{3}SD,

	Starts	1st	2nd	3rd	Win & Pl
Career Total (Turf)	7	2	1	0	7143
Career Total (AW)	5	0	0	2	784

71	7/08	Hayd	6f	GD	£5504

Total win prize-money £5505

Going (Turf): Sf: 0-1 GS: 0-1 **Gd: 2-3** GF: 0-2 Fm: 0-0
Distance: **5f/6f: 2-5** 7f-8f: 0-4 9f-13f: 0-3 14f+: 0-0
Track : LH: 0-8 RH: 0-0 Tight: 0-4 Gall: 0-2
Aids: Bl: 0-2 Vi: 0-0 Tstrap: 0-4 Ckp: 0-4
Best Rating: **81** 8/08 Hayd 6f gd-sft

Modest; effective over 6-7f; acts on good and easy ground; handles Polytrack; has worn blinkers and cheekpieces.

Fol Wizard

66 **9**

2-y-o ch g Piccolo-Go Go Girl (Pivotal)
P C Haslam Middleham Park Racing XXVII

Placings:00 **(3119)**
2009: 6^{0}G, 7^{0}GF,

	Starts	1st	2nd	3rd	Win & Pl
Career Total (Turf)	2	0	0	0	

Going (Turf): **Sf: 0-0 GS: 0-0 Gd: 0-1 GF: 0-1 Fm: 0-0**
Distance: 5f/6f: 0-1 7f-8f: 0-1 9f-13f: 0-0 14f+: 0-0
Track : LH: 0-0 RH: 0-0 Tight: 0-0 Gall: 0-0
Aids: Bl: 0-0 Vi: 0-0 Tstrap: 0-0 Ckp: 0-0
Best Rating: **9** 6/09 Rdcr 7f gd-fm

Folio (IRE)

94(109) (85)**85**

9-y-o b g Perugino (USA)-Bayleaf (Efisio)
W J Musson Goodey and Broughton

Placings:23211344155/030000/6**0**/**6660**04030220/222143 62031/6000056204/0**41**0**5**00200**060231-114306**006 **(2773)**
2009: **10**^{1}SD, **10**^{1}SD, **10**^{4}SD, **10**^{3}SD, 10^{0}G, **10**^{6}SD, 10^{0}GF, 9^{0}G, 10^{6}G,

	Starts	1st	2nd	3rd	Win & Pl
Career Total (Turf)	59	5	10	6	77429
Career Total (AW)	18	4	1	2	21470

83	1/09	Ling	1m2f	(0-80)H	STD	£4857
78	1/09	GrLe	1m2f	(0-75)H	STD	£3238
77	12/08	GrLe	1m2f	(0-85)H	STD	£4857
85	4/08	GrLe	1m2f	(0-80)H	STD	£4533
93	11/06	Wind	1m2f7y	(0-100)H	G-S	£12954
88	6/06	Ripn	1m1f170y	(0-85)H	G-F	£6309
99	9/02	Yarm	6f3y	C	G-F	£6571
96	7/02	Bath	5f11y	D	FRM	£4017
98	7/02	Wind	5f10y	E	G-F	£3486

Total win prize-money £50822

Going (Turf): Sf: 0-11 GS: 1-5 Gd: 0-20 **GF: 3-21** Fm: 1-2
Distance: 5f/6f: 2-13 7f-8f: 1-14 **9f-13f: 6-50** 14f+: 0-0
Track : **LH: 5-31** RH: 2-25 Tight: 3-23 **Gall: 5-17**
Aids: Bl: 0-0 Vi: 0-0 Tstrap: 0-0 Ckp: 0-0
Best Rating: **101** 10/02 Asct 5f gd-fm

Fair; stays 1m2f; acts on most ground on turf; goes on Polytrack.

Folk Tune (IRE)

93 **75**

6-y-o b h Danehill (USA)-Musk Lime (USA) (Private Account (USA))
J J Quinn (Ferdy Murphy 2/5) J N Blackburn

Placings:5/311016/60 **(6095)**
2009: 12^{6}GF, 13^{0}G,

	Starts	1st	2nd	3rd	Win & Pl
Career Total (Turf)	9	3	0	1	19797

90	8/06	Deau	1m	G-S	£8966
	6/06	Dax	7f110y	GD	£4827
	4/06	Bord	1m	GD	£4482

Total win prize-money £18277

Going (Turf): Sf: 0-0 GS: 1-1 **Gd: 2-4** GF: 0-2 Fm: 0-0
Distance: 5f/6f: 0-0 **7f-8f: 3-7** 9f-13f: 0-1 14f+: 0-1
Track : LH: 0-2 **RH: 1-3** Tight: 0-0 Gall: 0-0
Aids: Bl: 0-0 Vi: 0-0 Tstrap: 0-0 Ckp: 0-0
Best Rating: **90** 8/06 Deau 1m v soft

Folletta (IRE)

92(93) (64)**69**

2-y-o b f Le Vie Dei Colori-Finnine (USA) (Zafonic (USA))
R Hannon H Holmes A Turner J Perry T Dale

Placings:440205020 **(6963)**
2009: 6^{4}G, 6^{4}GF, 6^{0}G, 5^{2}GS, 6^{0}GF, 7^{5}GF, 8^{0}SD, 8^{2}SS, 6^{0}G,

	Starts	1st	2nd	3rd	Win & Pl
Career Total (Turf)	7	0	1	0	1613
Career Total (AW)	2	0	1	0	806

Going (Turf): **Sf: 0-0 GS: 0-1 Gd: 0-3 GF: 0-3 Fm: 0-0**
Distance: 5f/6f: 0-5 7f-8f: 0-4 9f-13f: 0-0 14f+: 0-0
Track : LH: 0-2 RH: 0-1 Tight: 0-1 Gall: 0-1
Aids: Bl: 0-0 Vi: 0-0 Tstrap: 0-1 Ckp: 0-1
Best Rating: **69** 7/09 Leic 5f218y gd-sft

Modest; effective over 6f; acts on easy ground.

Follow The Dream

101(99) (67)**57**

6-y-o b m Double Trigger (IRE)-Aquavita (Kalaglow)
Karen George Eastington Racing Club

Placings:6600**5631221** **(7675)**
2009: **12**^{6}SD, **12**^{6}SD, **12**^{0}SD, 11^{0}G, **12**^{5}SD, **13**^{6}SF, 16^{3}G, 18^{1}G, **16**^{2}SD, **16**^{2}SD, **14**^{1}SD,

	Starts	1st	2nd	3rd	Win & Pl
Career Total (Turf)	3	1	0	1	2670
Career Total (AW)	8	1	2	0	4591

67	12/09	Sthl	1m6f	(0-75)H	STD	£2729
57	8/09	Chep	2m2f	(0-65)H	GD	£2266

Total win prize-money £4997

Going (Turf): Sf: 0-0 GS: 0-0 **Gd: 1-3** GF: 0-0 Fm: 0-0
Distance: 5f/6f: 0-0 7f-8f: 0-0 9f-13f: 0-5 **14f+: 2-6**
Track : **LH: 2-9** RH: 0-2 Tight: 0-7 Gall: 0-0
Aids: Bl: 0-0 Vi: 0-0 Tstrap: 0-0 Ckp: 0-0
Best Rating: **67** 12/09 Sthl 1m6f stand

Moderate; stays 2m; acts on good ground; goes on both AW surfaces.

Follow The Flag (IRE)

103(106) (82)**79**

5-y-o ch g Traditionally (USA)-Iktidar (Green Desert (USA))
A J McCabe S Gillen

Placings:33230/**2550**06**0**/**131234**22000**0612220-531040**2600023**05**21**4205** **(7811)**
2009: **8**^{5}SD, **8**^{3}SD, **8**^{1}SD, **9**^{0}SD, 7^{4}GF, **7**^{0}SD, 8^{2}GF, 8^{6}F, 8^{0}GF, 8^{0}GF, 8^{0}GS, 8^{2}GF, **8**^{3}SD, **8**^{0}SD, 7^{5}SD, 8^{2}GF, 10^{1}GF, 9^{4}G, **12**^{2}SD, 9^{0}SF, **12**^{5}SD,

	Starts	1st	2nd	3rd	Win & Pl
Career Total (Turf)	22	1	6	2	12494
Career Total (AW)	29	4	6	5	17947

79	10/09	Rdcr	1m2f	(0-75)H	G-F	£3238
76	3/09	Wolv	1m141y	(0-75)H	STD	£2729
71	11/08	Wolv	1m141y	(0-65)H	STD	£1706
74	2/08	Wolv	7f32y	(0-65)H	STD	£2047
70	1/08	Ling	6f	(0-60)H	STD	£1876

Total win prize-money £11599

Going (Turf): Sf: 0-1 GS: 0-3 Gd: 0-4 **GF: 1-13** Fm: 0-1
Distance: 5f/6f: 1-7 7f-8f: 1-26 **9f-13f: 3-18** 14f+: 0-0
Track : **LH: 5-33** RH: 0-7 **Tight: 5-28** Gall: 0-1
Aids: Bl: 0-2 Vi: 0-0 Tstrap: 3-22 Ckp: 3-22
Best Rating: **82** 11/09 Wolv 1m4f50y stand

Fair; stays 1m4f; acts on fast ground; goes on Polytrack; has worn cheekpieces.

Follow The Sun (IRE)

95(96) (52)**62**

5-y-o br g Tertullian (USA)-Sun Mate (IRE) (Miller's Mate)
Ronald O'Leary Edward Cooke

Placings:500/001004-43044230 **(7798)**
2009: 12^{4}GF, 11^{3}YS, 9^{0}G, **8**^{4}SD, 9^{4}GF, 10^{2}GF, 11^{3}S, 9^{0}SS,

	Starts	1st	2nd	3rd	Win & Pl
Career Total (Turf)	15	1	1	2	4495
Career Total (AW)	2	0	0	0	0

62	8/08	Rdcr	1m2f	(0-75)H	G-S	£2590

Total win prize-money £2590

Going (Turf): Sf: 0-3 **GS: 1-2** Gd: 0-4 GF: 0-3 Fm: 0-1
Distance: 5f/6f: 0-0 7f-8f: 0-2 **9f-13f: 1-15** 14f+: 0-0
Track : **LH: 1-9** RH: 0-7 **Tight: 1-7** Gall: 0-1
Aids: Bl: 0-0 Vi: 0-0 Tstrap: 0-7 Ckp: 0-7
Best Rating: **62** 8/08 Rdcr 1m2f gd-sft

Moderate; effective over 1m2f but stays 1m4f; acts on easy ground; handles Polytrack; has worn cheekpieces.

Follow Your Spirit

76(91) (53)51

4-y-o b g Compton Place-Ymlaen (IRE) (Desert Prince (IRE))

B Palling Derek And Jean Clee

Placings:000/55004006-00 **(1775)**

2009: 7^{0}SS, 7^{0}GF,

	Starts	1st	2nd	3rd	Win & Pl
Career Total (Turf)	8	0	0	0	0
Career Total (AW)	5	0	0	0	0

Going (Turf): **Sf: 0-1 GS: 0-4 Gd: 0-0 GF: 0-3 Fm: 0-0**
Distance: 5f/6f: 0-0 7f-8f: 0-10 9f-13f: 0-3 14f+: 0-0
Track : LH: 0-3 RH: 0-4 Tight: 0-1 Gall: 0-0
Aids: Bl: 0-0 Vi: 0-0 Tstrap: 0-1 Ckp: 0-1
Best Rating: **53** 3/08 Kemp 7f stand

Folly Bridge

95 82

2-y-o b f Avonbridge-Jalissa (Mister Baileys)

R Charlton D J Deer

Placings:313 **(6397)**

2009: 6^{3}GF, 6^{1}GF, 6^{3}GF,

	Starts	1st	2nd	3rd	Win & Pl
Career Total (Turf)	3	1	0	2	4391
82 9/09 Ling 6f				G-F	£2729

Total win prize-money £2730

Going (Turf): Sf: 0-0 GS: 0-0 Gd: 0-0 **GF: 1-3** Fm: 0-0
Distance: **5f/6f: 1-2** 7f-8f: 0-1 9f-13f: 0-0 14f+: 0-0
Track : LH: 0-0 RH: 0-0 Tight: 0-0 Gall: 0-0
Aids: Bl: 0-0 Vi: 0-0 Tstrap: 0-0 Ckp: 0-0
Best Rating: **82** 9/09 Ling 6f gd-fm

Useful; suited by 6f and fast ground.

Folly Lodge

102(102) (91)91

5-y-o ch m Grand Lodge (USA)-Marika (Marju (IRE))

R M Beckett T D Rootes

Placings:010/106200/4645000-200100 **(4259)**

2009: 8^{2}SD, 7^{0}GF, 7^{0}G, 8^{1}S, 8^{0}GS, 8^{0}G,

	Starts	1st	2nd	3rd	Win & Pl
Career Total (Turf)	18	2	1	0	16767
Career Total (AW)	4	1	1	0	8315
86 7/09 Donc 1m	(0-80)H			SFT	£5118
92 5/07 Newb 7f	(0-85)H			G-S	£6477
75 9/06 Kemp 7f				STD	£4857

Total win prize-money £16453

Going (Turf): **Sf: 1-3 GS: 1-6** Gd: 0-6 GF: 0-3 Fm: 0-0
Distance: 5f/6f: 0-0 **7f-8f: 3-19** 9f-13f: 0-3 14f+: 0-0
Track : LH: 0-4 **RH: 1-6** Tight: 0-0 Gall: 0-3
Aids: Bl: 0-0 Vi: 0-0 Tstrap: 0-0 Ckp: 0-0
Best Rating: **93** 8/07 Newb 7f gd-sft

Useful; stays 1m2f; acts well on easy ground and on Polytrack.

Folsomprisonblues (IRE)

97 83

3-y-o br c Mull Of Kintyre (USA)-Prosaic Star (IRE) (Common Grounds)

E J O'Neill Phil Cunningham

Placings:10-06 **(1677)**

2009: 7^{0}S, 7^{6}GF,

	Starts	1st	2nd	3rd	Win & Pl
Career Total (Turf)	4	1	0	0	2428
78 5/08 Newc 6f				G-F	£2428

Total win prize-money £2428

Going (Turf): Sf: 0-2 GS: 0-0 Gd: 0-0 **GF: 1-2** Fm: 0-0
Distance: **5f/6f: 1-1** 7f-8f: 0-3 9f-13f: 0-0 14f+: 0-0
Track : LH: 0-0 RH: 0-0 Tight: 0-0 Gall: 0-0
Aids: Bl: 0-0 Vi: 0-0 Tstrap: 0-0 Ckp: 0-0
Best Rating: **83** 4/09 Newb 7f soft

Fair; winner at 6f; acts on fast ground; should get further.

Fond

84 39

2-y-o br f Makbul-Favour (Gothenborg (IRE))

Ollie Pears L C Sigsworth

Placings:50 **(6819)**

2009: 6^{5}GF, 7^{0}GF,

	Starts	1st	2nd	3rd	Win & Pl
Career Total (Turf)	2	0	0	0	0

Going (Turf): **Sf: 0-0 GS: 0-0 Gd: 0-0 GF: 0-2 Fm: 0-0**
Distance: 5f/6f: 0-1 7f-8f: 0-1 9f-13f: 0-0 14f+: 0-0
Track : LH: 0-0 RH: 0-0 Tight: 0-0 Gall: 0-0
Aids: Bl: 0-0 Vi: 0-0 Tstrap: 0-0 Ckp: 0-0
Best Rating: **39** 6/09 Thsk 6f gd-fm

Fondant Fancy

100 69

3-y-o b f Falbrav (IRE)-Foodbroker Fancy (IRE) (Halling (USA))

H J L Dunlop Normandie Stud Ltd

Placings:0-3500 **(4303)**

2009: 10^{3}GF, 10^{5}G, 8^{0}G, 7^{0}G,

	Starts	1st	2nd	3rd	Win & Pl
Career Total (Turf)	5	0	0	1	385

Going (Turf): **Sf: 0-0 GS: 0-0 Gd: 0-4 GF: 0-1 Fm: 0-0**
Distance: 5f/6f: 0-1 7f-8f: 0-1 9f-13f: 0-3 14f+: 0-0
Track : LH: 0-2 RH: 0-1 Tight: 0-3 Gall: 0-0
Aids: Bl: 0-0 Vi: 0-0 Tstrap: 0-0 Ckp: 0-0
Best Rating: **69** 4/09 Bath 1m2f46y gd-fm

Modest; stays 1m2f and acts on fast ground.

Fong's Alibi

95(99) (74)68

3-y-o b f Dr Fong (USA)-Alchemy (IRE) (Sadler's Wells (USA))

J S Moore T & Mrs J Cunningham & R Frost

Placings:033000-15001525013 **(5568)**

2009: 8^{1}SD, 10^{5}SD, 9^{0}GF, 8^{0}GF, 9^{1}GF, 12^{5}GF, 10^{2}GF, 10^{5}G, 10^{0}G, 9^{1}GF, 9^{3}F,

	Starts	1st	2nd	3rd	Win & Pl
Career Total (Turf)	15	2	1	3	6569
Career Total (AW)	2	1	0	0	2900
66 8/09 Nott 1m1f				G-F	£2266
63 6/09 Leic 1m1f218y				G-F	£1942
74 2/09 Ling 1m	(0-75)H			STD	£2900

Total win prize-money £7110

Going (Turf): Sf: 0-2 GS: 0-0 Gd: 0-2 **GF: 2-10** Fm: 0-1
Distance: 5f/6f: 0-1 7f-8f: 1-5 **9f-13f: 2-11** 14f+: 0-0
Track : **LH: 2-9** RH: 1-3 **Tight: 1-5** Gall: 0-2
Aids: Bl: 0-0 Vi: 0-0 Tstrap: 2-8 Ckp: 2-8
Best Rating: **74** 3/09 Ling 1m2f stand

Fair; effective at around 1m-1m2f; acts on Polytrack and fast ground; has worn cheekpieces.

Fongoli

96(86) (52)55

3-y-o b f Dr Fong (USA)-Darmagi (IRE) (Desert King (IRE))

B G Powell N Stafford, I Smith & Miss A Bucknall

Placings:620056-0240 **(4470)**

2009: 10^{0}G, 9^{2}GS, 11^{4}GF, 16^{0}HY,

	Starts	1st	2nd	3rd	Win & Pl
Career Total (Turf)	8	0	2	0	2312
Career Total (AW)	2	0	0	0	0

Going (Turf): **Sf: 0-2 GS: 0-2 Gd: 0-2 GF: 0-2 Fm: 0-0**
Distance: 5f/6f: 0-0 7f-8f: 0-3 9f-13f: 0-6 14f+: 0-1
Track : LH: 0-7 RH: 0-2 Tight: 0-3 Gall: 0-0
Aids: Bl: 0-0 Vi: 0-4 Tstrap: 0-0 Ckp: 0-0
Best Rating: **55** 9/08 Leic 1m60y heavy

Fonterutoli (IRE)

95 72

2-y-o gr c Verglas (IRE)-Goldendale (IRE) (Ali-Royal (IRE))

M Botti Scuderia Rencati Srl

Placings:322 **(3376)**

2009: 6^{3}GF, 6^{2}GF, 7^{2}GF,

	Starts	1st	2nd	3rd	Win & Pl
Career Total (Turf)	3	0	2	1	2782

Going (Turf): **Sf: 0-0 GS: 0-0 Gd: 0-0 GF: 0-3 Fm: 0-0**
Distance: 5f/6f: 0-1 7f-8f: 0-2 9f-13f: 0-0 14f+: 0-0
Track : LH: 0-0 RH: 0-0 Tight: 0-0 Gall: 0-0
Aids: Bl: 0-0 Vi: 0-0 Tstrap: 0-0 Ckp: 0-0
Best Rating: **72** 6/09 Donc 7f gd-fm

Fair; stays 7f and acts on fast ground.

Fontley

87 81

2-y-o b f Sadler's Wells (USA)-Horatia (IRE) (Machiavellian (USA))

Eve Johnson Houghton Mrs Virginia Neale

Placings:014 **(7033)**

2009: 6^{0}S, 7^{1}GS, 7^{4}S,

	Starts	1st	2nd	3rd	Win & Pl
Career Total (Turf)	3	1	0	0	8465
81 9/09 Sand 7f16y				G-S	£6854

Total win prize money £6854

Going (Turf): Sf: 0-2 **GS: 1-1** Gd: 0-0 GF: 0-0 Fm: 0-0
Distance: 5f/6f: 0-0 **7f-8f: 1-3** 9f-13f: 0-0 14f+: 0-0
Track : LH: 0-0 **RH: 1-1** Tight: 0-0 Gall: 0-0
Aids: Bl: 0-0 Vi: 0-0 Tstrap: 0-0 Ckp: 0-0
Best Rating: **81** 9/09 Sand 7f16y gd-sft

Useful filly; effective at 7f; acts on easy ground.

Foolin Myself

102(108) (105)98

4-y-o b c Montjeu (IRE)-Friendlier (Zafonic (USA))

M L W Bell W J Gredley

Placings:51/40P02160 (6815)

2009: 10^{4}S, 9^{0}GF, 10^{P}G, 8^{0}G, 8^{2}G, 8^{1}SD, 8^{6}SD, 7^{0}G,

	Starts	1st	2nd	3rd	Win & Pl
Career Total (Turf)	8	1	1	0	7170
Career Total (AW)	2	1	0	0	9347

105 8/09 Sthl 1m (0-90)H STD £9346
83 11/07 NmkR 7f GD £4857
Total win prize-money £14205

Going (Turf): Sf: 0-1 GS: 0-0 **Gd: 1-6** GF: 0-1 Fm: 0-0
Distance: 5f/6f: 0-0 **7f-8f: 2-5** 9f-13f: 0-5 14f+: 0-0
Track : **LH: 1-5** RH: 0-0 Tight: 0-2 Gall: 0-2
Aids: **Bl: 1-3** Vi: 0-0 Tstrap: 0-0 Ckp: 0-0
Best Rating: **105** 8/09 Sthl 1m stand

Useful; stays 1m2f; acts on good ground; goes on Fibresand; has worn blinkers.

Fools Gold

88(103) (82)**43**

4-y-o b g Ishiguru (USA)-Sally Green (IRE) (Common Grounds)
Paul Mason Mick White & Paul Mason

Placings:03/42100020-30500 (4202)

2009: 7^{3}SD, 8^{0}GF, 8^{5}SD, 8^{0}SD, 7^{0}SD,

	Starts	1st	2nd	3rd	Win & Pl
Career Total (Turf)	4	0	0	0	
Career Total (AW)	11	1	2	2	4673

79 6/08 Sthl 7f (0-75)H STD £2456
Total win prize-money £2457

Going (Turf): **Sf: 0-0 GS: 0-1 Gd: 0-1 GF: 0-2 Fm: 0-0**
Distance: 5f/6f: 0-5 **7f-8f: 1-9** 9f-13f: 0-1 14f+: 0-0
Track : **LH: 1-10** RH: 0-2 Tight: 0-2 Gall: 0-1
Aids: Bl: 0-0 Vi: 0-0 Tstrap: 0-0 Ckp: 0-0
Best Rating: **82** 9/08 Sthl 7f stand

Fair; effective at 7f; acts on Fibresand and Polytrack.

Footsie (IRE)

90 **64**

2-y-o b f Footstepsinthesand-Marlene-D (Selkirk (USA))
J G Given Mrs Linda P Fish

Placings:00 (6992)

2009: 7^{0}GF, 8^{0}GS,

	Starts	1st	2nd	3rd	Win & Pl
Career Total (Turf)	2	0	0	0	7840

Going (Turf): **Sf: 0-0 GS: 0-1 Gd: 0-0 GF: 0-1 Fm: 0-0**
Distance: 5f/6f: 0-0 7f-8f: 0-2 9f-13f: 0-0 14f+: 0-0
Track : LH: 0-1 RH: 0-0 Tight: 0-0 Gall: 0-1
Aids: Bl: 0-0 Vi: 0-0 Tstrap: 0-0 Ckp: 0-0
Best Rating: **64** 10/09 NmkR 7f gd-fm

Half-sister to Shanghai Lily, a dual 6f-7f winner at two, and Eden Rock, a dual 7f-1m winner at two and three.

Footstepsofspring (FR)

97(95) (86)**87**

2-y-o b c Footstepsinthesand-Moon West (USA) (Gone West (USA))
R Hannon Mrs J Wood

Placings:6221043466 (6398)

2009: 5^{6}GF, 6^{2}GF, 5^{2}GF, 5^{1}GF, 6^{0}G, 6^{4}GS, 6^{3}GF, 7^{4}SD, 6^{6}GF, 6^{6}GF,

	Starts	1st	2nd	3rd	Win & Pl
Career Total (Turf)	9	1	2	1	9410
Career Total (AW)	1	0	0	0	241

83 6/09 Wind 5f10y G-F £4695
Total win prize-money £4695

Going (Turf): Sf: 0-0 GS: 0-1 Gd: 0-1 **GF: 1-7** Fm: 0-0
Distance: **5f/6f: 1-8** 7f-8f: 0-2 9f-13f: 0-0 14f+: 0-0
Track : LH: 0-2 RH: 0-0 Tight: 0-2 **Gall: 1-2**
Aids: Bl: 0-0 Vi: 0-0 Tstrap: 0-0 Ckp: 0-0
Best Rating: **87** 9/09 Sals 6f gd-fm

Useful; stays 6f but effective at 5f; acts on fast ground.

For Life (IRE)

94(107) (80)**73**

7-y-o b g Bachir (IRE)-Zest (USA) (Zilzal (USA))
J E Long T H Bambridge

Placings:30/34006/00250052405/0012111/54-016600 (7656)

2009: 6^{0}GF, 6^{1}SD, 5^{6}G, 6^{6}SD, 6^{0}SD, 6^{0}SD,

	Starts	1st	2nd	3rd	Win & Pl
Career Total (Turf)	19	3	2	2	12296
Career Total (AW)	14	2	1	0	11454

80 5/09 Ling 6f (0-85)H STD £5828
79 10/07 Ling 6f (0-80)H STD £4728
78 9/07 Brig 5f213y (0-70)H GD £3154
76 9/07 Folk 6f (0-75)H G-F £2817
66 7/07 Yarm 7f3y (0-70)H G-F £2914
Total win prize-money £19443

Going (Turf): Sf: 0-1 GS: 0-1 Gd: 1-8 **GF: 2-8** Fm: 0-1
Distance: **5f/6f: 4-18** 7f-8f: 1-15 9f-13f: 0-0 14f+: 0-0
Track : **LH: 3-15** RH: 0-1 **Tight: 2-10** Gall: 0-1
Aids: Bl: 0-0 Vi: 0-3 Tstrap: 0-6 Ckp: 0-6
Best Rating: **87** 9/04 Donc 6f good

Fair handicapper; effective over 6f-7f; acts on fast ground.

Forbidden (IRE)

103(103) (76)**74**

6-y-o ch g Singspiel (IRE)-Fragrant Oasis (USA) (Rahy (USA))
Daniel Mark Loughnane Lee Suir Syndicate

Placings:63640/00002300/2300060-312600102202405056 (6861)

2009: 8^{3}SD, 8^{1}SD, 8^{2}SD, 8^{6}SD, 8^{0}S, 8^{0}SD, 8^{1}F, 8^{0}GF, 8^{2}G, 8^{2}GF, 8^{0}S, 8^{2}GY, 8^{4}SD, 9^{0}G, 8^{5}SD, 9^{0}GF, 8^{5}SF, 8^{6}SD,

	Starts	1st	2nd	3rd	Win & Pl
Career Total (Turf)	21	1	3	1	6250
Career Total (AW)	17	1	3	3	5162

68 5/09 Nott 1m75y (0-60)H FRM £1942
59 2/09 Wolv 1m141y STD £2047
Total win prize-money £3990

Going (Turf): Sf: 0-3 GS: 0-0 Gd: 0-5 GF: 0-7 **Fm: 1-2**
Distance: 5f/6f: 0-0 7f-8f: 0-15 **9f-13f: 2-22** 14f+: 0-1
Track : **LH: 2-17** RH: 0-17 **Tight: 1-10** Gall: 0-0
Aids: Bl: 0-2 Vi: 0-0 Tstrap: 0-1 Ckp: 0-1
Best Rating: **76** 9/09 Kemp 1m stand

Modest; Irish trained; stays 1m; acts on Polytrack.

Forbidden Paradise (IRE)

93 (73)**68**

2-y-o ch f Chineur (FR)-Villa Nova (IRE) (Petardia)
David Hofmans (K R Burke 25/4) Mr & Mrs Marc C Ferrell

Placings:206 (6531a)

2009: 5^{2}GF, 8^{0}FT, 8^{6}F,

	Starts	1st	2nd	3rd	Win & Pl
Career Total (Turf)	2	0	1	0	1156
Career Total (AW)	1	0	0	0	

Going (Turf): **Sf: 0-0 GS: 0-0 Gd: 0-0 GF: 0-1 Fm: 0-1**
Distance: 5f/6f: 0-1 7f-8f: 0-1 9f-13f: 0-1 14f+: 0-0
Track : LH: 0-2 RH: 0-0 Tight: 0-0 Gall: 0-0
Aids: Bl: 0-0 Vi: 0-0 Tstrap: 0-0 Ckp: 0-0
Best Rating: **73** 10/09 SnAt 1m110y fast

Force Group (IRE)

103(104) (75)**84**

5-y-o b g Invincible Spirit (IRE)-Spicebird (IRE) (Ela-Mana-Mou)
M H Tompkins Construction Horse Racing Club

Placings:000/26/110442-5640362405266 (7475)

2009: 12^{5}GS, 12^{6}GS, 14^{4}G, 12^{0}GF, 12^{3}G, 12^{6}GF, 12^{2}GS, 14^{4}GS, 13^{0}SD, 11^{5}G, 13^{2}SD, 12^{6}SD, 10^{6}SD,

	Starts	1st	2nd	3rd	Win & Pl
Career Total (Turf)	19	2	3	1	12722
Career Total (AW)	5	0	1	0	1542

81 4/08 Pont 1m2f6y (0-75)H HVY £3238
81 4/08 Pont 1m2f6y (0-70)H G-S £3238
Total win prize-money £6476

Going (Turf): **Sf: 1-1 GS: 1-9** Gd: 0-5 GF: 0-4 Fm: 0-0
Distance: 5f/6f: 0-0 7f-8f: 0-3 **9f-13f: 2-18** 14f+: 0-3
Track : **LH: 2-17** RH: 0-5 Tight: 0-6 Gall: 0-9
Aids: Bl: 0-5 Vi: 0-0 Tstrap: 0-0 Ckp: 0-0
Best Rating: **84** 10/08 Bath 1m3f144y gd-sft

Fair; effective at around 1m4f-1m6f; acts easy ground but handles faster.

Force Tradition (IRE)

(90) (57)**47**

4-y-o ch g Traditionally (USA)-Kind Of Loving (Diesis)
M H Tompkins The Force Group

Placings:06000-40 (0346)

2009: 12^{4}SS, 16^{0}SD,

	Starts	1st	2nd	3rd	Win & Pl
Career Total (Turf)	3	0	0	0	0
Career Total (AW)	4	0	0	0	0

Going (Turf): **Sf: 0-0 GS: 0-1 Gd: 0-1 GF: 0-1 Fm: 0-0**
Distance: 5f/6f: 0-0 7f-8f: 0-0 9f-13f: 0-5 14f+: 0-2
Track : LH: 0-6 RH: 0-1 Tight: 0-3 Gall: 0-1
Aids: Bl: 0-1 Vi: 0-0 Tstrap: 0-0 Ckp: 0-0
Best Rating: **57** 5/08 Sthl 1m3f stand

Forced Opinion (USA)

90(92) (61)**47**

4-y-o gr c Distant View (USA)-Kinetic Force (USA) (Holy Bull (USA))
K A Morgan J D M Stables

Placings:05-600 (6998)

2009: 8^{6}SD, 9^{0}G, 9^{0}SD,

	Starts	1st	2nd	3rd	Win & Pl
Career Total (Turf)	1	0	0	0	
Career Total (AW)	4	0	0	0	0

Going (Turf): Sf: 0-0 GS: 0-0 Gd: 0-1 GF: 0-0 Fm: 0-0
Distance: 5f/6f: 0-0 7f-8f: 0-2 9f-13f: 0-3 14f+: 0-0
Track : LH: 0-5 RH: 0-0 Tight: 0-4 Gall: 0-1
Aids: Bl: 0-0 Vi: 0-0 Tstrap: 0-0 Ckp: 0-0
Best Rating: 61 12/08 Ling 1m2f stand

Foreign Investment (IRE)

94(97) (66)**72**

3-y-o ch f Desert Prince (IRE)-Muneera (USA) (Green Dancer (USA))
P D Evans Diamond Racing Ltd

Placings:410120634 (4266)
2009: 5^{4}SD, 7^{1}SD, 8^{0}SD, 8^{1}SD, 7^{2}GF, 8^{0}SD, 7^{6}GF, 8^{3}G, 7^{4}S,

	Starts	1st	2nd	3rd	Win & Pl
Career Total (Turf)	4	0	1	1	1415
Career Total (AW)	5	2	0	0	5459

66 4/09 Wolv 1m141y (0-60)H STD £2388
65 2/09 Wolv 7f32y STD £3070
Total win prize-money £5459

Going (Turf): Sf: 0-1 GS: 0-0 Gd: 0-1 GF: 0-2 Fm: 0-0
Distance: 5f/6f: 0-1 7f-8f: 1-5 9f-13f: 1-3 14f+: 0-0
Track : LH: 2-6 RH: 0-1 Tight: 2-5 Gall: 0-0
Aids: Bl: 0-0 Vi: 0-0 Tstrap: 0-0 Ckp: 0-0
Best Rating: 72 4/09 Catt 7f gd-fm

Modest; stays 1m; acts on Polytrack.

Foreign King (USA)

(108) (64)**66**

5-y-o b g Kingmambo (USA)-Foreign Aid (USA) (Danzig (USA))
J W Mullins John Collins

Placings:600/05416556-0 (0059)
2009: 12^{0}SD,

	Starts	1st	2nd	3rd	Win & Pl
Career Total (Turf)	6	1	0	0	2267
Career Total (AW)	6	0	0	0	0

66 6/08 Brig 1m3f196y (0-65)H FRM £2266
Total win prize-money £2267

Going (Turf): Sf: 0-0 GS: 0-0 Gd: 0-0 GF: 0-4 Fm: 1-2
Distance: 5f/6f: 0-1 7f-8f: 0-2 9f-13f: 1-5 14f+: 0-4
Track : LH: 1-5 RH: 0-4 Tight: 0-5 Gall: 0-0
Aids: Bl: 0-0 Vi: 0-0 Tstrap: 0-0 Ckp: 0-0
Best Rating: 66 6/08 Folk 1m4f gd-fm

Foreign Rhythm (IRE)

98 **56**

4-y-o ch f Distant Music (USA)-Happy Talk (IRE) (Hamas (IRE))
N Tinkler Foreign Rhythm Partnership

Placings:2223360/0506210604400-00015006040660 (7081)
2009: 6^{0}GF, 5^{0}G, 6^{0}G, 5^{1}GF, 5^{5}GF, 5^{0}GF, 5^{0}G, 6^{0}GS, 5^{0}G, 6^{4}GF, 6^{0}GF, 6^{6}GF, 5^{6}GF, 5^{0}S,

	Starts	1st	2nd	3rd	Win & Pl
Career Total (Turf)	34	2	4	2	10157

53 6/09 Bevl 5f (0-55)H G-F £2331
56 7/08 Haml 5f4y G-S £2266
Total win prize-money £4598

Going (Turf): Sf: 0-7 GS: 1-4 Gd: 0-11 GF: 1-12 Fm: 0-0
Distance: 5f/6f: 2-32 7f-8f: 0-2 9f-13f: 0-0 14f+: 0-0
Track : LH: 0-3 RH: 0-1 Tight: 0-2 Gall: 0-2
Aids: Bl: 0-0 Vi: 1-12 Tstrap: 0-1 Ckp: 0-1
Best Rating: 76 7/07 Ches 5f16y soft

Moderate sprinter; acts on fast and soft ground.

Forest Crown

81(101) (76)**69**

2-y-o b f Royal Applause-Wiener Wald (USA) (Woodman (USA))
R M Beckett The Eclipse Partnership

Placings:341 (7234)
2009: 5^{3}GF, 5^{4}SD, 6^{1}SD,

	Starts	1st	2nd	3rd	Win & Pl
Career Total (Turf)	1	0	0	1	698
Career Total (AW)	2	1	0	0	3754

76 11/09 Kemp 6f STD £3561
Total win prize-money £3562

Going (Turf): Sf: 0-0 GS: 0-0 Gd: 0-0 GF: 0-1 Fm: 0-0
Distance: 5f/6f: 1-3 7f-8f: 0-0 9f-13f: 0-0 14f+: 0-0
Track : LH: 0-0 RH: 1-2 Tight: 0-0 Gall: 0-0
Aids: Bl: 0-0 Vi: 0-0 Tstrap: 0-0 Ckp: 0-0
Best Rating: 76 11/09 Kemp 6f stand

Fair; stays 6f; acts on Polytrack.

Forest Dane

101(107) (78)**74**

9-y-o b g Danetime (IRE)-Forest Maid (Thatching)
Mrs N Smith The Ember Partnership

Placings:0064/00/63050050566501/21313341512 2105/10532503200/000064032-532602436032345 (7890)
2009: 6^{5}SD, 6^{3}SD, 6^{2}SD, 6^{6}GF, 5^{0}G, 5^{2}GF, 6^{4}SD, 6^{3}GF, 6^{6}G, 5^{0}G, 6^{3}SD, 6^{2}SD, 6^{3}SD, 6^{4}SD, 6^{5}SD,

	Starts	1st	2nd	3rd	Win & Pl
Career Total (Turf)	39	5	3	3	31959
Career Total (AW)	31	2	6	8	16988

88 4/07 Folk 6f (0-85)H G-F £4857
81 10/06 Ling 5f (0-75)H STD £3886
79 9/06 Sand 5f6y (0-80)H G-F £5505
76 8/06 Sand 5f6y (0-80)H G-F £5505
69 5/06 Brig 5f59y (0-65)H G-F £2590
59 5/06 Kemp 6f (0-45) STD £1706
52 10/05 Brig 5f59y (0-45) GD £1470
Total win prize-money £25521

Going (Turf): Sf: 0-2 GS: 0-1 Gd: 1-17 GF: 4-17 Fm: 0-2
Distance: 5f/6f: 7-53 7f-8f: 0-17 9f-13f: 0-0 14f+: 0-0
Track : LH: 3-32 RH: 1-10 Tight: 1-20 Gall: 0-4
Aids: Bl: 0-0 Vi: 0-0 Tstrap: 0-0 Ckp: 0-0
Best Rating: 88 10/07 Ling 7f stand

Modest; effective over 5f-7f; acts on fast ground; goes on Polytrack.

Forest Runner

87 **75**

2-y-o b c Pivotal-Tiriana (Common Grounds)
Saeed Bin Suroor Godolphin

Placings:2 (5785)
2009: 7^{2}G,

	Starts	1st	2nd	3rd	Win & Pl
Career Total (Turf)	1	0	1	0	1060

Going (Turf): Sf: 0-0 GS: 0-0 Gd: 0-1 GF: 0-0 Fm: 0-0
Distance: 5f/6f: 0-0 7f-8f: 0-1 9f-13f: 0-0 14f+: 0-0
Track : LH: 0-0 RH: 0-0 Tight: 0-0 Gall: 0-0
Aids: Bl: 0-0 Vi: 0-0 Tstrap: 0-0 Ckp: 0-0
Best Rating: 75 9/09 Chep 7f16y good

Fair debut over 7f on good ground.

Forethought

88 **64**

2-y-o b f Lujain (USA)-Flourish (Selkirk (USA))
P Howling Longview Stud & Bloodstock Ltd

Placings:0000 (6821)
2009: 7^{0}G, 8^{0}GF, 8^{0}GF, 8^{0}GF,

	Starts	1st	2nd	3rd	Win & Pl
Career Total (Turf)	4	0	0	0	

Going (Turf): Sf: 0-0 GS: 0-0 Gd: 0-1 GF: 0-3 Fm: 0-0
Distance: 5f/6f: 0-0 7f-8f: 0-4 9f-13f: 0-0 14f+: 0-0
Track : LH: 0-0 RH: 0-1 Tight: 0-0 Gall: 0-0
Aids: Bl: 0-0 Vi: 0-0 Tstrap: 0-0 Ckp: 0-0
Best Rating: 64 8/09 NmkJ 7f good

Forever Changes

(98) (58)

4-y-o gr f Bertolini (USA)-Days Of Grace (Wolfhound (USA))
L Montague Hall Bob Pain & Jeff OWen

Placings:046/520000-0000 (7880)
2009: 6^{0}SD, 6^{0}SD, 5^{0}SD, 7^{0}SD,

	Starts	1st	2nd	3rd	Win & Pl
Career Total (Turf)	1	0	0	0	
Career Total (AW)	12	0	1	0	605

Going (Turf): Sf: 0-0 GS: 0-1 Gd: 0-0 GF: 0-0 Fm: 0-0
Distance: 5f/6f: 0-12 7f-8f: 0-1 9f-13f: 0-0 14f+: 0-0
Track : LH: 0-11 RH: 0-1 Tight: 0-10 Gall: 0-1
Aids: Bl: 0-0 Vi: 0-0 Tstrap: 0-1 Ckp: 0-1
Best Rating: 58 4/08 Ling 6f stand

Forever's Girl

87(108) (76)**48**

3-y-o b f Monsieur Bond (IRE)-Forever Bond (Danetime (IRE))
G R Oldroyd R C Bond

Placings:344032025-1434055611 (7601)
2009: 5^{1}SD, 5^{4}SD, 5^{3}SD, 5^{4}SD, 6^{0}GF, 5^{5}GF, 5^{5}SD, 5^{6}SD, 5^{1}SD, 5^{1}SD,

	Starts	1st	2nd	3rd	Win & Pl
Career Total (Turf)	5	0	0	0	553
Career Total (AW)	14	3	2	3	8965

76 11/09 Wolv 5f20y (0-65)H STD £2047
71 11/09 Wolv 5f20y (0-60)H STD £2388
68 1/09 Wolv 5f216y (0-55)H STD £2047
Total win prize-money £6482

Going (Turf): Sf: 0-1 GS: 0-1 Gd: 0-0 GF: 0-3 Fm: 0-0
Distance: 5f/6f: 3-18 7f-8f: 0-1 9f-13f: 0-0 14f+: 0-0
Track : LH: 3-11 RH: 0-0 Tight: 3-9 Gall: 0-0
Aids: Bl: 0-0 Vi: 0-0 Tstrap: 0-0 Ckp: 0-0
Best Rating: 76 11/09 Wolv 5f20y stand

Modest; suited by 6f; acts on Polytrack.

Forget (IRE)

81(78) (56)**45**

2-y-o b f Tiger Hill (IRE)-Wajina (Rainbow Quest (USA))

C E Brittain Saeed Manana

Placings:30 **(1968)**
2009: 5^{3}SD, 5^{0}GF,

	Starts	1st	2nd	3rd	Win & Pl
Career Total (Turf)	1	0	0	0	
Career Total (AW)	1	0	0	1	578

Going (Turf): **Sf: 0-0 GS: 0-0 Gd: 0-0 GF: 0-1 Fm: 0-0**
Distance: 5f/6f: 0-2 7f-8f: 0-0 9f-13f: 0-0 14f+: 0-0
Track : LH: 0-2 RH: 0-0 Tight: 0-1 Gall: 0-0
Aids: Bl: 0-0 Vi: 0-0 Tstrap: 0-0 Ckp: 0-0
Best Rating: **56** 5/09 Ling 5f stand

Modest; shaped well on debut; will stay 6f; acts on Polytrack.

Forget It

65(97) (71)**65**
4-y-o b g Galileo (IRE)-Queens Way (FR) (Zafonic (USA))
G L Moore The Cockpit Crew

Placings:6/00505220-0 **(6692)**
2009: 16^{0}GS,

	Starts	1st	2nd	3rd	Win & Pl
Career Total (Turf)	8	0	1	0	867
Career Total (AW)	2	0	1	0	605

Going (Turf): **Sf: 0-1 GS: 0-4 Gd: 0-1 GF: 0-2 Fm: 0-0**
Distance: 5f/6f: 0-0 7f-8f: 0-2 9f-13f: 0-3 14f+: 0-5
Track : LH: 0-3 RH: 0-5 Tight: 0-7 Gall: 0-1
Aids: Bl: 0-0 Vi: 0-0 Tstrap: 0-0 Ckp: 0-0
Best Rating: **71** 10/08 Ling 2m stand

Modest; probably stays 2m; acts on good ground and on Polytrack.

Forgotten Army (IRE)

82 **70**
2-y-o b c Arakan (USA)-Brioney (IRE) (Barathea (IRE))
M H Tompkins Miss Clare Hollest

Placings:001 **(6065)**
2009: 7^{0}G, 7^{0}G, 7^{1}GF,

	Starts	1st	2nd	3rd	Win & Pl
Career Total (Turf)	3	1	0	0	5181

70	9/09	NmkR	7f		G-F	£5180

Total win prize-money £5181

Going (Turf): Sf: 0-0 GS: 0-0 Gd: 0-2 **GF: 1-1** Fm: 0-0
Distance: 5f/6f: 0-0 **7f-8f: 1-3** 9f-13f: 0-0 14f+: 0-0
Track : LH: 0-1 RH: 0-0 Tight: 0-0 Gall: 0-0
Aids: Bl: 0-0 Vi: 0-0 Tstrap: 0-0 Ckp: 0-0
Best Rating: **70** 9/09 NmkR 7f gd-fm

Fair; stays 7f; acts on fast ground.

Forgotten Voice (IRE)

110(109) (108)**115**
4-y-o b g Danehill Dancer (IRE)-Asnieres (USA) (Spend A Buck (USA))
J Noseda Mrs Susan Roy

Placings:1/11144530 **(6850)**
2009: 8^{1}SD, 8^{1}SD, 8^{1}GF, 8^{4}GS, 8^{4}G, 8^{5}GF, 8^{3}GF, 10^{0}G,

	Starts	1st	2nd	3rd	Win & Pl
Career Total (Turf)	6	1	0	1	88688
Career Total (AW)	3	3	0	0	15055

115	6/09	Asct	1m	H	G-F	£62310
108	5/09	Kemp	1m	(0-90)H	STD	£7477
95	4/09	Kemp	1m	(0-85)H	STD	£4727
80	10/07	Ling	7f		STD	£2849

Total win prize-money £77364

Going (Turf): Sf: 0-0 GS: 0-1 Gd: 0-2 **GF: 1-3** Fm: 0-0
Distance: 5f/6f: 0-0 **7f-8f: 4-7** 9f-13f: 0-2 14f+: 0-0
Track : LH: 1-2 **RH: 2-3 Tight: 1-1** Gall: 0-1
Aids: Bl: 0-0 Vi: 0-0 Tstrap: 0-0 Ckp: 0-0
Best Rating: **115** 10/09 NmkR 1m gd-fm

Smart; easy winner of 2009 Royal Hunt Cup; effective at around 1m; acts on fast ground; goes on Polytrack.

Foricherforpoorer

72 **17**
2-y-o gr f Where Or When (IRE)-Bridal Path (Groom Dancer (USA))
N Tinkler G Darling,K Lydall,S Perkins,J Marshall

Placings:00600 **(4800)**
2009: 6^{0}GS, 6^{0}GF, 5^{6}G, 7^{0}G, 6^{0}GF,

	Starts	1st	2nd	3rd	Win & Pl
Career Total (Turf)	5	0	0	0	0

Going (Turf): **Sf: 0-0 GS: 0-1 Gd: 0-2 GF: 0-2 Fm: 0-0**
Distance: 5f/6f: 0-4 7f-8f: 0-1 9f-13f: 0-0 14f+: 0-0
Track : LH: 0-1 RH: 0-0 Tight: 0-1 Gall: 0-0
Aids: Bl: 0-0 Vi: 0-1 Tstrap: 0-0 Ckp: 0-0
Best Rating: **17** 5/09 Rdcr 6f gd-fm

Formation (USA)

(117) (99)**91**
4-y-o ch g Van Nistelrooy (USA)-Miss Valedictorian (USA) (With Approval (CAN))
J R Boyle M Khan X2

Placings:63321/24215533563-2113325 **(1642)**
2009: 8^{2}SD, 10^{1}SD, 10^{1}SD, 11^{3}SD, 12^{3}SD, 10^{2}SD, 10^{5}SD,

	Starts	1st	2nd	3rd	Win & Pl
Career Total (Turf)	8	1	1	2	8140
Career Total (AW)	15	3	4	5	39745

95	2/09	Ling	1m2f	(0-100)H	STD	£11656
93	1/09	Ling	1m2f	(0-100)H	STD	£11656
87	6/08	Pont	1m2f6y	(0-85)H	GD	£5180
77	11/07	Wolv	1m141y		STD	£2184

Total win prize-money £30679

Going (Turf): Sf: 0-0 GS: 0-3 **Gd: 1-4** GF: 0-1 Fm: 0-0
Distance: 5f/6f: 0-0 7f-8f: 0-10 **9f-13f: 4-13** 14f+: 0-0
Track : **LH: 4-10** RH: 0-11 **Tight: 3-10** Gall: 0-2
Aids: Bl: 0-0 Vi: 0-0 Tstrap: 0-0 Ckp: 0-0
Best Rating: **99** 4/09 Kemp 1m2f stand

Very useful; effective at around 1m2f-1m4f; acts on good ground; goes on Polytrack.

Formax (FR)

100 **96**
7-y-o gr g Marathon (USA)-Fortuna (FR) (Kaldoun (FR))
M P Tregoning Mr And Mrs A E Pakenham

Placings:213/12351364/021032/1420020/02513536-00 **(1790)**
2009: 12^{0}G, 18^{0}GF,

	Starts	1st	2nd	3rd	Win & Pl
Career Total (Turf)	34	6	7	6	97341

94	5/08	Gdwd	1m4f	(0-90)H	SFT	£7771
	1/07	Cagn	7f110y		GD	£15243
101	6/06	Chan	1m1f		GD	£6897
	6/05	Buch	1m1f		G-S	£8156
	2/05	Toul	1m		GD	£4964
	10/04	Mars	1m1f		GD	£4577

Total win prize-money £47609

Going (Turf): Sf: 1-6 GS: 1-7 **Gd: 4-16** GF: 0-3 Fm: 0-0
Distance: 5f/6f: 0-0 7f-8f: 2-16 **9f-13f: 4-14** 14f+: 0-4
Track : LH: 0-4 **RH: 2-11 Tight: 1-8** Gall: 0-2
Aids: Bl: 0-0 Vi: 0-0 Tstrap: 0-0 Ckp: 0-0
Best Rating: **101** 6/06 Chan 1m1f good

Very useful; ex-French; effective at around 1m4f; best on good ground and softer; usually held up.

Formidable Guest

(105) (74)**25**
5-y-o b m Dilshaan-Fizzy Treat (Efisio)
J Pearce Macniler Racing Partnership

Placings:00123043/310035013034361-2112434350 **(7752)**
2009: 9^{2}SD, 9^{1}SD, 9^{1}SD, 10^{2}SD, 10^{4}SD, 9^{3}SD, 9^{4}SD, 10^{3}SD, 10^{5}SD, 9^{0}SD,

	Starts	1st	2nd	3rd	Win & Pl
Career Total (Turf)	3	0	0	0	
Career Total (AW)	31	6	3	9	18675

71	2/09	Wolv	1m1f103y	(0-65)H	STD	£2047
65	1/09	Wolv	1m1f103y	(0-65)H	STD	£2047
61	12/08	Ling	1m2f	(0-65)H	STD	£2047
62	9/08	Kemp	1m4f	(0-60)H	STD	£2047
59	4/08	Ling	1m2f	(0-60)H	STD	£2047
49	10/07	Ling	1m2f	(0-58)H	STD	£2590

Total win prize-money £12826

Going (Turf): **Sf: 0-0 GS: 0-0 Gd: 0-3 GF: 0-0 Fm: 0-0**
Distance: 5f/6f: 0-0 7f-8f: 0-2 **9f-13f: 6-32** 14f+: 0-0
Track : **LH: 5-22** RH: 1-10 **Tight: 5-22** Gall: 0-0
Aids: Bl: 0-0 Vi: 0-1 Tstrap: 0-0 Ckp: 0-0
Best Rating: **74** 2/09 Kemp 1m2f stand

Modest; effective at around 1m1f-1m4f; handles Polytrack.

Formula (USA)

93(102) (82)**74**
3-y-o b/br g Stormin Fever (USA)-Misty Gallop (USA) (Victory Gallop (CAN))
R Hannon Highclere Thoroughbred Racing-SunChariot

Placings:522-023415340 **(6973)**
2009: 7^{0}GF, 8^{2}GF, 10^{3}GF, 7^{4}G, 8^{1}SD, 8^{5}SD, 10^{3}SD, 12^{4}SS, 10^{0}SD,

	Starts	1st	2nd	3rd	Win & Pl
Career Total (Turf)	5	0	1	1	1209
Career Total (AW)	7	1	2	1	6738

82	8/09	Wolv	1m141y	(0-80)	STD	£3885

Total win prize-money £3886

Going (Turf): **Sf: 0-0 GS: 0-1 Gd: 0-1 GF: 0-3 Fm: 0-0**
Distance: 5f/6f: 0-1 7f-8f: 0-5 **9f-13f: 1-6** 14f+: 0-0
Track : **LH: 1-4** RH: 0-5 **Tight: 1-6** Gall: 0-0
Aids: Bl: 0-0 Vi: 0-0 Tstrap: 0-0 Ckp: 0-0
Best Rating: **82** 9/09 Kemp 1m2f stand

Fair; stays 1m; acts on Polytrack.

Forrest Flyer (IRE)

102 **71**
5-y-o b g Daylami (IRE)-Gerante (USA) (Private Account (USA))
I Semple Mrs Camille Macdonald

Placings:0/0604003/4431230032-51301160500 (7170)
2009: 14^{5}GF, 12^{1}GS, 13^{3}GF, 14^{0}GF, 12^{1}GF, 13^{1}G, 12^{6}G, 12^{0}GS, 14^{5}GS, 17^{0}G, 15^{0}S,

	Starts	1st	2nd	3rd	Win & Pl
Career Total (Turf)	29	4	2	5	16990

71 7/09 Ayr 1m5f13y (0-70)H GD £3238
71 6/09 Muss 1m4f100y (0-70)H G-F £3885
67 5/09 Newc 1m4f93y (0-60)H G-S £2331
65 6/08 Ayr 1m5f13y (0-75)H G-F £3412
Total win prize-money £12867

Going (Turf): Sf: 0-2 GS: 1-11 Gd: 1-8 GF: 2-8 Fm: 0-0
Distance: 5f/6f: 0-0 7f-8f: 0-2 9f-13f: 2-10 14f+: 2-17
Track : LH: 3-17 RH: 1-12 Tight: 1-14 Gall: 1-5
Aids: Bl: 0-0 Vi: 0-1 Tstrap: 0-0 Ckp: 0-0
Best Rating: 71 7/09 Ayr 1m5f13y good

Moderate; stays 2m; acts on good and easy ground.

Forrest Star

78(90) (41)61
4-y-o ch f Fraam-Starfleet (Inchinor)
M Johnston (Miss L A Perratt 27/9) Andrew Forrest

Placings:0/0423240-000000 (7855)
2009: 6^{0}G, 6^{0}GF, 7^{0}G, 6^{0}GF, 6^{0}SD, 8^{0}SS,

	Starts	1st	2nd	3rd	Win & Pl
Career Total (Turf)	11	0	2	1	2408
Career Total (AW)	3	0	0	0	

Going (Turf): Sf: 0-0 GS: 0-2 Gd: 0-5 GF: 0-4 Fm: 0-0
Distance: 5f/6f: 0-5 7f-8f: 0-8 9f-13f: 0-1 14f+: 0-0
Track : LH: 0-3 RH: 0-3 Tight: 0-4 Gall: 0-0
Aids: Bl: 0-0 Vi: 0-0 Tstrap: 0-0 Ckp: 0-0
Best Rating: 61 6/08 Muss 7f30y gd-fm

Moderate sort; stays 7f.

Forshour

90(90) (64)67
2-y-o ch g Forzando-Sharoura (Inchinor)
E S McMahon Manor House Partnership

Placings:2300 (6901)
2009: 7^{2}SD, 7^{3}G, 8^{0}SD, 8^{0}GF,

	Starts	1st	2nd	3rd	Win & Pl
Career Total (Turf)	2	0	0	1	636
Career Total (AW)	2	0	1	0	1060

Going (Turf): Sf: 0-0 GS: 0-0 Gd: 0-1 GF: 0-1 Fm: 0-0
Distance: 5f/6f: 0-0 7f-8f: 0-2 9f-13f: 0-2 14f+: 0-0
Track : LH: 0-4 RH: 0-0 Tight: 0-3 Gall: 0-0
Aids: Bl: 0-0 Vi: 0-0 Tstrap: 0-0 Ckp: 0-0
Best Rating: 67 8/09 Thsk 7f good

Modest; stays 7f; acts on Polytrack.

Fort Churchill (IRE)

98(94) (55)78
8-y-o b g Barathea (IRE)-Brisighella (IRE) (Al Hareb (USA))
Jim Best (B Ellison 5/5) W A Scott

Placings:00/534201020/00002652131501430/056010404 0/000005106-0633 (1765)
2009: 16^{0}SF, 12^{6}GF, 9^{3}SD, 11^{3}GF,

	Starts	1st	2nd	3rd	Win & Pl
Career Total (Turf)	46	6	4	4	39930
Career Total (AW)	5	0	0	1	302

76 9/08 Gdwd 1m3f (0-70)H SFT £3123
94 6/07 Gdwd 1m1f192y (0-80)H GD £5181
87 9/06 Sand 1m2f7y (0-80)H G-S £5505
87 7/06 York 1m4f (0-80)H G-F £8096
74 6/06 Newc 1m4f93y G-F £2590
76 9/04 Sals 1m4f SFT £3497
Total win prize-money £27994

Going (Turf): Sf: 2-11 GS: 1-6 Gd: 1-12 GF: 2-16 Fm: 0-1
Distance: 5f/6f: 0-0 7f-8f: 0-2 9f-13f: 6-44 14f+: 0-5
Track : LH: 2-31 RH: 4-16 Tight: 3-24 Gall: 2-13
Aids: Bl: 6-37 Vi: 0-0 Tstrap: 0-5 Ckp: 0-5
Best Rating: 94 8/07 Gdwd 1m1f gd-fm

Fair; stays 1m3f; acts on most ground; has worn blinkers, cheekpieces and tongue tie.

Forte Dei Marmi

98(87) (64)87
3-y-o b g Selkirk (USA)-Frangy (Sadler's Wells (USA))
L M Cumani Fittocks Stud

Placings:004-10 (2925)
2009: 9^{1}G, 9^{0}G,

	Starts	1st	2nd	3rd	Win & Pl
Career Total (Turf)	4	1	0	0	5027
Career Total (AW)	1	0	0	0	

87 5/09 Gdwd 1m1f (0-85)H GD £4673
Total win prize-money £4673

Going (Turf): Sf: 0-0 GS: 0-1 Gd: 1-3 GF: 0-0 Fm: 0-0
Distance: 5f/6f: 0-0 7f-8f: 0-3 9f-13f: 1-2 14f+: 0-0
Track : LH: 0-1 RH: 1-2 Tight: 1-1 Gall: 0-1
Aids: Bl: 0-0 Vi: 0-0 Tstrap: 0-0 Ckp: 0-0
Best Rating: 87 5/09 Gdwd 1m1f good

Useful; stays 1m1f and acts on good ground.

Fortezza

91 47
3-y-o b f Efisio-Donna Anna (Be My Chief (USA))
C F Wall Lady Juliet Tadgell

Placings:000 (4913)
2009: 6^{0}S, 5^{0}S, 6^{0}G,

	Starts	1st	2nd	3rd	Win & Pl
Career Total (Turf)	3	0	0	0	

Going (Turf): Sf: 0-2 GS: 0-0 Gd: 0-1 GF: 0-0 Fm: 0-0
Distance: 5f/6f: 0-2 7f-8f: 0-1 9f-13f: 0-0 14f+: 0-0
Track : LH: 0-0 RH: 0-0 Tight: 0-0 Gall: 0-0
Aids: Bl: 0-0 Vi: 0-0 Tstrap: 0-0 Ckp: 0-0
Best Rating: 47 8/09 Yarm 6f3y good

Forthe Millionkiss (GER)

101 (24)113
5-y-o b/br h Dashing Blade-Forever Nice (GER) (Greinton)
Uwe Ostmann Reinhard Ubber

Placings:5241/3234020/01121030-05040610 (7704a)
2009: 8^{0}S, 8^{5}G, 8^{0}SD, 8^{4}G, 8^{0}S, 8^{6}S, 8^{1}HY, 9^{0}SD,

	Starts	1st	2nd	3rd	Win & Pl
Career Total (Turf)	25	5	4	3	121189
Career Total (AW)	2	0	0	0	

95 11/09 StCl 1m HVY £16019
111 8/08 Hanv 1m GD £29412
105 6/08 Nant 1m G-S £19117
105 5/08 Chan 1m GD £12132
10/06 Badn 7f110y SFT £3724
Total win prize-money £80405

Going (Turf): Sf: 2-13 GS: 1-2 Gd: 2-10 GF: 0-0 Fm: 0-0
Distance: 5f/6f: 0-0 7f-8f: 5-19 9f-13f: 0-8 14f+: 0-0
Track : LH: 2-7 RH: 1-10 Tight: 0-0 Gall: 0-0
Aids: Bl: 0-0 Vi: 0-0 Tstrap: 0-0 Ckp: 0-0
Best Rating: 113 9/08 Colo 1m soft

Group class; Group 2 winner in Germany; effective over 1m; acts on good and easy ground.

Fortina's Boy (USA)

88(90) (63)56
3-y-o ch c Mr Greeley (USA)-Really Quick (USA) (In Reality (USA))
W R Swinburn C J Collins

Placings:005000 (7484)
2009: 8^{0}G, 8^{0}SD, 8^{5}F, 7^{0}SD, 5^{0}SD, 6^{0}SD,

	Starts	1st	2nd	3rd	Win & Pl
Career Total (Turf)	2	0	0	0	0
Career Total (AW)	4	0	0	0	

Going (Turf): Sf: 0-0 GS: 0-0 Gd: 0-1 GF: 0-0 Fm: 0-1
Distance: 5f/6f: 0-2 7f-8f: 0-2 9f-13f: 0-2 14f+: 0-0
Track : LH: 0-3 RH: 0-2 Tight: 0-3 Gall: 0-0
Aids: Bl: 0-0 Vi: 0-0 Tstrap: 0-0 Ckp: 0-0
Best Rating: 63 5/09 Kemp 1m stand

Fortuitous (IRE)

(92) (43)13
5-y-o ch g Tobougg (IRE)-Shallop (Salse (USA))
S Gollings Colin G R Booth

Placings:0/06-60 (0254)
2009: 7^{6}SD, 9^{0}SD,

	Starts	1st	2nd	3rd	Win & Pl
Career Total (Turf)	1	0	0	0	
Career Total (AW)	4	0	0	0	0

Going (Turf): Sf: 0-0 GS: 0-0 Gd: 0-1 GF: 0-0 Fm: 0-0
Distance: 5f/6f: 0-0 7f-8f: 0-1 9f-13f: 0-4 14f+: 0-0
Track : LH: 0-5 RH: 0-0 Tight: 0-4 Gall: 0-0
Aids: Bl: 0-0 Vi: 0-2 Tstrap: 0-0 Ckp: 0-0
Best Rating: 43 2/08 Wolv 1m4f50y stand

Fortunate Bid (IRE)

105(83) (51)74
3-y-o ch g Modigliani (USA)-Mystery Bid (Auction Ring (USA))
Mrs L Stubbs (B W Hills 6/7) Red Lion Racing Market Bosworth

Placings:043-01524000 (7153)
2009: 7^{0}GF, 8^{1}G, 8^{5}S, 8^{2}GF, 8^{4}GF, 8^{0}G, 8^{0}G, 8^{0}SD,

	Starts	1st	2nd	3rd	Win & Pl
Career Total (Turf)	9	1	1	1	4249
Career Total (AW)	2	0	0	0	

74 7/09 Wind 1m67y (0-70)H GD £2729
Total win prize-money £2730

Going (Turf): Sf: 0-2 GS: 0-0 Gd: 1-4 GF: 0-3 Fm: 0-0
Distance: 5f/6f: 0-3 7f-8f: 0-3 9f-13f: 1-5 14f+: 0-0
Track : LH: 0-5 RH: 1-2 Tight: 1-4 Gall: 0-1
Aids: Bl: 0-0 Vi: 0-0 Tstrap: 0-0 Ckp: 0-0

Best Rating: 74 8/09 Rdcr 1m gd-fm

Fortunate Flame

91(97) (67)56

3-y-o b g Key Of Luck (USA)-Candescent (Machiavellian (USA))

K A Ryan Hambleton Racing Ltd IX

Placings:24350600 (6804)

2009: 8^{2}SD, 7^{4}GF, 7^{3}SD, 7^{5}SD, 7^{0}GF, 8^{6}HY, 7^{0}SD, 9^{0}SD,

	Starts	1st	2nd	3rd	Win & Pl
Career Total (Turf)	3	0	0	0	216
Career Total (AW)	5	0	1	1	1174

Going (Turf): **Sf: 0-1 GS: 0-0 Gd: 0-0 GF: 0-2 Fm: 0-0**
Distance: 5f/6f: 0-0 7f-8f: 0-6 9f-13f: 0-2 14f+: 0-0
Track: LH: 0-6 RH: 0-1 Tight: 0-4 Gall: 0-0
Aids: Bl: 0-0 Vi: 0-1 Tstrap: 0-0 Ckp: 0-0
Best Rating: 67 5/09 Wolv 7f32y stand

Modest; effective over 1m; acts on Fibresand and on Polytrack.

Fortunate Isle (USA)

100 (91)68

7-y-o ch g Swain (IRE)-Isla Del Rey (USA) (Nureyev (USA))

R A Fahey The First Team

Placings:2/1/1000004/30211000/000-500 (2965)

2009: 8^{5}GF, 9^{0}GF, 9^{0}GF,

	Starts	1st	2nd	3rd	Win & Pl
Career Total (Turf)	22	4	2	0	36645
Career Total (AW)	2	0	0	1	1679

95 6/07 Ripn 1m1f (0-90)H SFT £9348
91 5/07 Bevl 1m1f207y (0-85)H GD £4857
95 4/06 Pont 1m4y (0-95)H HVY £11217
80 5/05 Newb 1m FRM £6214
Total win prize-money £31638

Going (Turf): **Sf: 2-7** GS: 0-3 Gd: 1-6 GF: 0-5 Fm: 1-1
Distance: 5f/6f: 0-0 7f-8f: 1-7 **9f-13f: 3-17** 14f+: 0-0
Track: LH: 1-8 **RH: 2-11 Tight: 1-7** Gall: 0-6
Aids: Bl: 0-0 Vi: 0-0 Tstrap: 2-4 Ckp: 2-4
Best Rating: 95 6/07 Ripn 1m1f soft

Useful; stays 1m2f and acts on most ground; has worn cheekpieces.

Fortune Point (IRE)

(98) (51)23

11-y-o ch g Cadeaux Genereux-Mountains Of Mist (IRE) (Shirley Heights)

A W Carroll The T J Racing Partnership

Placings:42/023/000132132040/6220640/402132004062 0/2030000/050451365/000502/0605-5 (0483)

2009: 10^{5}SD,

	Starts	1st	2nd	3rd	Win & Pl
Career Total (Turf)	39	3	7	4	22127
Career Total (AW)	26	1	4	2	7069

63 6/06 Brig 1m1f209y FRM £2266
64 2/04 Ling 1m2f F(0-55)H STD £3010
78 7/02 Kemp 1m E(0-75)H G-S £4699
69 7/02 Chep 1m14y F(0-60)H GD £3080
Total win prize-money £13057

Going (Turf): Sf: 0-6 **GS: 1-3 Gd: 1-13** GF: 0-11 **Fm: 1-6**
Distance: 5f/6f: 0-1 7f-8f: 1-20 **9f-13f: 3-42** 14f+: 0-2
Track: **LH: 2-40** RH: 1-17 Tight: 1-25 Gall: 1-3
Aids: Bl: 0-0 **Vi: 3-35** Tstrap: 0-4 Ckp: 0-4
Best Rating: 84 9/00 Hayd 7f30y heavy

Fortunella

(95) (61)48

4-y-o b f Polish Precedent (USA)-Hazy Heights (Shirley Heights)

Miss Gay Kelleway Miss Gay Kelleway

Placings:0/3001233-2000 (1938)

2009: 14^{2}SS, 16^{0}SD, 11^{0}SD, 12^{0}SD,

	Starts	1st	2nd	3rd	Win & Pl
Career Total (Turf)	3	0	0	1	578
Career Total (AW)	9	1	2	2	4264

56 11/08 Sthl 1m4f (0-52)H STD £2047
Total win prize-money £2047

Going (Turf): **Sf: 0-0 GS: 0-0 Gd: 0-1 GF: 0-2 Fm: 0-0**
Distance: 5f/6f: 0-0 7f-8f: 0-0 **9f-13f: 1-9** 14f+: 0-3
Track: **LH: 1-10** RH: 0-1 Tight: 0-1 Gall: 0-1
Aids: Bl: 0-0 Vi: 0-3 Tstrap: 0-2 Ckp: 0-2
Best Rating: 61 12/08 Sthl 1m3f stand

Moderate; says 1m6f and acts on Fibresand; has worn visor and cheekpieces.

Fortunes Of Fire

95 76

2-y-o ch g Avonbridge-Lucky Arrow (Indian Ridge)

G A Swinbank G H Bell, P Baldwin & Mrs V McGee

Placings:1 (5728)

2009: 6^{1}GS,

	Starts	1st	2nd	3rd	Win & Pl
Career Total (Turf)	1	1	0	0	4289

76 9/09 Newc 6f G-S £4289
Total win prize-money £4289

Going (Turf): Sf: 0-0 **GS: 1-1** Gd: 0-0 GF: 0-0 Fm: 0-0
Distance: **5f/6f: 1-1** 7f-8f: 0-0 9f-13f: 0-0 14f+: 0-0
Track: LH: 0-0 RH: 0-0 Tight: 0-0 Gall: 0-0
Aids: Bl: 0-0 Vi: 0-0 Tstrap: 0-0 Ckp: 0-0
Best Rating: 76 9/09 Newc 6f gd-sft

Made a winning debut over 6f on easy ground.

Fortuni (IRE)

83(113) (96)57

3-y-o b g Montjeu (IRE)-Desert Ease (IRE) (Green Desert (USA))

Sir Mark Prescott Pacific International Management

Placings:521-14 (4103)

2009: 12^{1}SD, 12^{4}S,

	Starts	1st	2nd	3rd	Win & Pl
Career Total (Turf)	1	0	0	0	1168
Career Total (AW)	4	2	1	0	8874

96 5/09 Ling 1m4f (0-80)H STD £5180
73 12/08 Sthl 7f SS £2729
Total win prize-money £7911

Going (Turf): **Sf: 0-1 GS: 0-0 Gd: 0-0 GF: 0-0 Fm: 0-0**
Distance: 5f/6f: 0-0 7f-8f: 1-3 9f-13f: 1-2 14f+: 0-0
Track: **LH: 2-3** RH: 0-2 **Tight: 1-3** Gall: 0-0
Aids: Bl: 0-0 Vi: 0-0 Tstrap: 0-0 Ckp: 0-0
Best Rating: 96 5/09 Ling 1m4f stand

Useful; stays 1m4f; acts on Polytrack and on Fibresand.

Forty Thirty (IRE)

97(95) (66)69

3-y-o b g Poliglote-Ciena (FR) (Gold Away (IRE))

Miss Sheena West (M R Channon 22/5) Janet Menzies,Alan Tappin,Stephen Monks

Placings:42055-56043 (4730)

2009: 11^{5}SD, 11^{6}SD, 8^{0}SD, 9^{4}GF, 6^{3}GS,

	Starts	1st	2nd	3rd	Win & Pl
Career Total (Turf)	6	0	1	1	2083
Career Total (AW)	4	0	0	0	0

Going (Turf): **Sf: 0-1 GS: 0-1 Gd: 0-3 GF: 0-1 Fm: 0-0**
Distance: 5f/6f: 0-0 7f-8f: 0-3 9f-13f: 0-7 14f+: 0-0
Track: LH: 0-5 RH: 0-3 Tight: 0-2 Gall: 0-1
Aids: Bl: 0-0 Vi: 0-0 Tstrap: 0-0 Ckp: 0-0
Best Rating: 69 9/08 Haml 1m65y soft

Fair; stays 1m and acts on soft ground.

Forward Feline (IRE)

93(105) (74)74

3-y-o b f One Cool Cat (USA)-Ymlaen (IRE) (Desert Prince (IRE))

B Palling Derek And Jean Clee

Placings:252523325-520600001 (7729)

2009: 7^{5}SD, 5^{2}SD, 7^{0}GS, 6^{6}G, 6^{0}GF, 6^{0}GS, 5^{0}S, 5^{0}SD, 7^{1}SD,

	Starts	1st	2nd	3rd	Win & Pl
Career Total (Turf)	13	0	3	2	4884
Career Total (AW)	5	1	2	0	2448

Going (Turf): **Sf: 0-3 GS: 0-6 Gd: 0-1 GF: 0-3 Fm: 0-0**
Distance: 5f/6f: 0-9 **7f-8f: 1-9** 9f-13f: 0-0 14f+: 0-0
Track: **LH: 1-7** RH: 0-0 **Tight: 1-6** Gall: 0-1
Aids: Bl: 0-0 Vi: 0-1 Tstrap: 0-2 Ckp: 0-2
Best Rating: 74 4/09 Wolv 5f216y stand

Fair; stays 6f; acts on soft and fast ground and Polytrack.

Forward Planning (USA)

88 47

3-y-o ch f Orientate (USA)-Casa's Kids (USA) (Theatrical)

M Johnston Sheikh Hamdan Bin Mohammed Al Maktoum

Placings:040 (6390)

2009: 7^{0}G, 6^{4}GF, 8^{0}GF,

	Starts	1st	2nd	3rd	Win & Pl
Career Total (Turf)	3	0	0	0	289

Going (Turf): **Sf: 0-0 GS: 0-0 Gd: 0-1 GF: 0-2 Fm: 0-0**
Distance: 5f/6f: 0-0 7f-8f: 0-2 9f-13f: 0-1 14f+: 0-0
Track: LH: 0-2 RH: 0-0 Tight: 0-1 Gall: 0-0
Aids: Bl: 0-0 Vi: 0-0 Tstrap: 0-0 Ckp: 0-0
Best Rating: 47 8/09 Sals 6f212y gd-fm

Forzarzi (IRE)

96(96) (63)63

5-y-o b g Forzando-Zarzi (IRE) (Suave Dancer (USA))

H A McWilliams J D Riches

Placings:063/00/200050100-0600450 (3615)

2009: 8^{0}SD, 7^{6}F, 7^{0}GF, 6^{0}GF, 8^{4}GF, 7^{5}GF, 7^{0}G,

	Starts	1st	2nd	3rd	Win & Pl
Career Total (Turf)	17	0	1	1	1806

Career Total (AW)	4	1	0	0	2388
63 9/08 Wolv 1m141y				STD	£2388

Total win prize-money £2388

Going (Turf): Sf: 0-1 GS: 0-1 Gd: 0-8 GF: 0-6 Fm: 0-1
Distance: 5f/6f: 0-6 7f-8f: 0-10 9f-13f: 1-5 14f+: 0-0
Track : LH: 1-5 RH: 0-7 Tight: 1-6 Gall: 0-0
Aids: Bl: 0-0 Vi: 0-0 Tstrap: 1-6 Ckp: 1-6
Best Rating: 63 9/08 Wolv 1m141y stand

Modest; stays 1m; acts on Polytrack.

Fossgate

105(95) (60)74

8-y-o ch g Halling (USA)-Peryllys (Warning)
J D Bethell Mrs James Bethell

Placings:05/20364440/0410/61421163/02003500/040614 14006-00631536 **(6183)**
2009: 16⁰GF, 12⁰GF, 12⁶GF, 12³GF, 12¹G, 12⁵S, 12³F, 9⁶GF,

	Starts	1st	2nd	3rd	Win & Pl
Career Total (Turf)	44	7	3	4	32390
Career Total (AW)	5	0	0	1	819

58	8/09	Ripn	1m4f10y (0-70)H	GD	£2914
74	8/08	Ripn	1m4f10y (0-70)H	GD	£2914
61	7/08	Bevl	1m4f16y (0-60)H	G-F	£2266
78	8/06	Bevl	1m4f16y (0-75)H	G-S	£5181
77	8/06	Ripn	1m4f10y (0-70)H	GD	£3886
69	6/06	Nott	1m1f213y (0-60)H	G-F	£2730
66	10/05	Leic	1m1f218y (0-70)H	G-F	£4397

Total win prize-money £24290

Going (Turf): Sf: 0-7 GS: 1-7 Gd: 3-7 GF: 3-21 Fm: 0-2
Distance: 5f/6f: 0-0 7f-8f: 0-6 9f-13f: 7-40 14f+: 0-3
Track : LH: 1-18 RH: 6-28 Tight: 5-26 Gall: 0-5
Aids: Bl: 1-4 Vi: 0-1 Tstrap: 0-6 Ckp: 0-6
Best Rating: 81 10/06 Wolv 1m4f50y std-fst

Modest; stays 1m4f; acts on fast and easy ground.

Foundation Room (IRE)

98 95

3-y-o ch f Saffron Walden (FR)-Bellagio Princess (Kris)
A M Balding G W Chong

Placings:1306-305 **(3320)**
2009: 7³GF, 8⁰HY, 7⁵GF,

	Starts	1st	2nd	3rd	Win & Pl
Career Total (Turf)	7	1	0	2	18828
86 5/08 Sals 5f				GD	£6476

Total win prize-money £6476

Going (Turf): Sf: 0-3 GS: 0-0 Gd: 1-2 GF: 0-2 Fm: 0-0
Distance: 5f/6f: 1-2 7f-8f: 0-4 9f-13f: 0-1 14f+: 0-0
Track : LH: 0-3 RH: 0-0 Tight: 0-1 Gall: 0-0
Aids: Bl: 0-0 Vi: 0-0 Tstrap: 0-0 Ckp: 0-0
Best Rating: 95 5/09 Ches 7f122y gd-fm

Useful; Listed placed; stays 7f and acts on most ground.

Four Kicks (IRE)

88 56

3-y-o b f Pyrus (USA)-Dynamo Minsk (IRE) (Polish Precedent (USA))
Muredach Kelly J Clements

Placings:060000 **(5948)**
2009: 7⁰GF, 8⁶G, 7⁰S, 8⁰S, 5⁰S, 7⁰G,

	Starts	1st	2nd	3rd	Win & Pl
Career Total (Turf)	6	0	0	0	

Going (Turf): Sf: 0-3 GS: 0-0 Gd: 0-2 GF: 0-1 Fm: 0-0
Distance: 5f/6f: 0-1 7f-8f: 0-3 9f-13f: 0-2 14f+: 0-0
Track : LH: 0-1 RH: 0-4 Tight: 0-1 Gall: 0-0
Aids: Bl: 0-0 Vi: 0-0 Tstrap: 0-0 Ckp: 0-0
Best Rating: 56 7/09 Wxfd 1m100y good

Four Miracles

97 (64)88

5-y-o b m Vettori (IRE)-North Kildare (USA) (Northjet)
M H Tompkins Pat Swayne and Partners

Placings:633/24210232/2012100-64 **(1878)**
2009: 16⁶GF, 14⁴F,

	Starts	1st	2nd	3rd	Win & Pl
Career Total (Turf)	19	3	6	2	31258
Career Total (AW)	1	0	0	1	282

88	7/08	York	2m2f (0-90)H	G-F	£9066
82	6/08	York	2m88y (0-95)H	G-F	£11009
71	7/07	Brig	1m1f209y	G-S	£2849

Total win prize-money £22925

Going (Turf): Sf: 0-2 GS: 1-4 Gd: 0-5 GF: 2-7 Fm: 0-1
Distance: 5f/6f: 0-0 7f-8f: 0-3 9f-13f: 1-8 14f+: 2-9
Track : LH: 3-12 RH: 0-6 Tight: 0-5 Gall: 2-7
Aids: Bl: 0-0 Vi: 0-0 Tstrap: 0-0 Ckp: 0-0
Best Rating: 88 7/08 York 2m2f gd-fm

Useful; stays 2m2f; acts on a sound surface and on Fibresand; usually held up.

Four Mirrors (CAN)

83(85) (29)44

3-y-o b g Gulch (USA)-Solarity (CAN) (Ascot Knight (CAN))
C R Dore (David P Myerscough 4/10) Sean J Murphy

Placings:040000 **(6771)**
2009: 8⁰G, 8⁴G, 8⁰Y, 8⁰SH, 10⁰SS, 8⁰SD,

	Starts	1st	2nd	3rd	Win & Pl
Career Total (Turf)	4	0	0	0	358
Career Total (AW)	2	0	0	0	

Going (Turf): Sf: 0-0 GS: 0-0 Gd: 0-2 GF: 0-0 Fm: 0-0
Distance: 5f/6f: 0-0 7f-8f: 0-4 9f-13f: 0-2 14f+: 0-0
Track : LH: 0-3 RH: 0-3 Tight: 0-1 Gall: 0-0
Aids: Bl: 0-1 Vi: 0-0 Tstrap: 0-1 Ckp: 0-1
Best Rating: 44 7/09 Cork 1m good

Four Tel

95(93) (63)64

5-y-o gr g Vettori (IRE)-Etienne Lady (IRE) (Imperial Frontier (USA))
Tom Dascombe (N J Vaughan 26/6) Owen Promotions Limited

Placings:03/001021/5-5500 **(6640)**
2009: 7⁵GF, 7⁵GF, 8⁰SD, 9⁰SD,

	Starts	1st	2nd	3rd	Win & Pl
Career Total (Turf)	5	0	0	0	0
Career Total (AW)	8	2	1	1	5419

74	12/07	Wolv	7f32y (0-65)H	STD	£2047
68	9/07	Wolv	7f32y	STD	£2388

Total win prize-money £4437

Going (Turf): Sf: 0-1 GS: 0-0 Gd: 0-1 GF: 0-3 Fm: 0-0
Distance: 5f/6f: 0-0 7f-8f: 2-9 9f-13f: 0-4 14f+: 0-0
Track : LH: 2-10 RH: 0-1 Tight: 2-10 Gall: 0-0
Aids: Bl: 0-0 Vi: 0-0 Tstrap: 0-0 Ckp: 0-0
Best Rating: 74 12/07 Wolv 7f32y stand

Modest; effective over 7f; acts on Polytrack and fast turf.

Four Winds

106 107

3-y-o b g Red Ransom (USA)-Fairy Godmother (Fairy King (USA))
M L W Bell The Queen

Placings:313-21642 **(5141a)**
2009: 10²GS, 8¹GF, 10⁶GF, 8⁴S, 8²GY,

	Starts	1st	2nd	3rd	Win & Pl
Career Total (Turf)	8	2	2	2	34346

103	5/09	NmkR	1m	G-F	£9066
87	9/08	Sand	1m14y	GD	£5180

Total win prize-money £14247

Going (Turf): Sf: 0-1 GS: 0-2 Gd: 1-2 GF: 1-2 Fm: 0-0
Distance: 5f/6f: 0-0 7f-8f: 1-4 9f-13f: 1-4 14f+: 0-0
Track : LH: 0-2 RH: 1-4 Tight: 0-0 Gall: 0-3
Aids: Bl: 0-1 Vi: 0-0 Tstrap: 0-0 Ckp: 0-0
Best Rating: 107 4/09 Newb 1m2f6y gd-sft

Very useful half-brother to several middle-distance winners from the family of Blueprint; stays 1m2f; handles fast and easy ground.

Fourlanends

77 32

2-y-o ch c Dubawi (IRE)-Nova Cyngi (USA) (Kris S (USA))
N Wilson Mrs S L Robinson

Placings:0 **(5668)**
2009: 6⁰S,

	Starts	1st	2nd	3rd	Win & Pl
Career Total (Turf)	1	0	0	0	

Going (Turf): Sf: 0-1 GS: 0-0 Gd: 0-0 GF: 0-0 Fm: 0-0
Distance: 5f/6f: 0-1 7f-8f: 0-0 9f-13f: 0-0 14f+: 0-0
Track : LH: 0-0 RH: 0-0 Tight: 0-0 Gall: 0-0
Aids: Bl: 0-0 Vi: 0-0 Tstrap: 0-0 Ckp: 0-0
Best Rating: 32 9/09 Thsk 6f soft

Fourth Dimension (IRE)

94(86) (53)76

10-y-o b g Entrepreneur-Isle Of Spice (USA) (Diesis)
Miss T Spearing Advantage Chemicals Holdings Ltd

Placings:400/02021115325/6313000/040000/60/013/4353 3350-00 **(2172)**
2009: 11⁰GF, 14⁰GF,

	Starts	1st	2nd	3rd	Win & Pl
Career Total (Turf)	40	5	3	8	28942
Career Total (AW)	2	0	0	0	

73	7/07	Yarm	1m6f17y (0-70)H	G-F	£3238
97	7/03	Sand	1m6f D(0-80)H	GD	£5486
85	7/02	Yarm	1m6f17yE(0-75)H	G-F	£3542
75	6/02	Yarm	1m6f17yE(0-75)H	FRM	£2989
67	6/02	Yarm	1m6f17yE(0-70)H	FRM	£3038

Total win prize-money £18295

Going (Turf): Sf: 0-4 GS: 0-4 Gd: 1-7 GF: 2-20 Fm: 2-5
Distance: 5f/6f: 0-0 7f-8f: 0-2 9f-13f: 0-14 14f+: 5-26
Track : LH: 4-24 RH: 1-15 Tight: 4-16 Gall: 0-13
Aids: Bl: 0-0 Vi: 0-0 Tstrap: 0-0 Ckp: 0-0
Best Rating: 97 7/03 Sand 1m6f good

Modest; best at up to 1m6f; acts best on fast ground.

Fourth Generation (IRE)

95 78

2-y-o ch g Kris Kin (USA)-Merewood Lodge (IRE) (Grand Lodge (USA))

G A Swinbank J V Layton

Placings:02 **(6821)**

2009: 7^{0}S, 8^{2}GF,

	Starts	1st	2nd	3rd	Win & Pl
Career Total (Turf)	2	0	1	0	605

Going (Turf): **Sf: 0-1 GS: 0-0 Gd: 0-0 GF: 0-1 Fm: 0-0**
Distance: 5f/6f: 0-0 7f-8f: 0-2 9f-13f: 0-0 14f+: 0-0
Track : LH: 0-1 RH: 0-0 Tight: 0-1 Gall: 0-0
Aids: Bl: 0-0 Vi: 0-0 Tstrap: 0-0 Ckp: 0-0
Best Rating: **78** 10/09 Rdcr 1m gd-fm

Fair; stays 1m; acts on fast ground.

Fourtowns Flyer (IRE)

85(107) (76)57

5-y-o b g Danetime (IRE)-Music Khan (Music Boy)

Lee Smyth C G Bryson

Placings:0013 **(7398)**

2009: 6^{0}S, 6^{0}G, 5^{1}SD, 5^{3}SD,

	Starts	1st	2nd	3rd	Win & Pl
Career Total (Turf)	2	0	0	0	
Career Total (AW)	2	1	0	1	3211

72 10/09 Wolv 5f20y STD £2729
Total win prize-money £2730

Going (Turf): **Sf: 0-1 GS: 0-0 Gd: 0-1 GF: 0-0 Fm: 0-0**
Distance: **5f/6f: 1-3** 7f-8f: 0-1 9f-13f: 0-0 14f+: 0-0
Track : **LH: 1-2** RH: 0-0 **Tight: 1-2** Gall: 0-0
Aids: Bl: 0-0 Vi: 0-0 Tstrap: 1-2 Ckp: 1-2
Best Rating: **76** 11/09 Wolv 5f20y stand

Fair; effective over 5f; acts on Polytrack; has worn tongue-tie and cheekpieces.

Foxhaven

103 110

7-y-o ch g Unfuwain (USA)-Dancing Mirage (IRE) (Machiavellian (USA))

P R Chamings The Foxford House Partnership

Placings:32216/404251/620140/33560254/051-12 **(6936)**

2009: 11^{1}GF, 11^{2}G,

	Starts	1st	2nd	3rd	Win & Pl
Career Total (Turf)	30	5	6	3	138843

79 8/09 Wind 1m3f135y G-F £2047
110 9/08 Ches 1m4f66y G-S £26074
106 9/06 Ches 1m4f66y G-F £16595
105 7/05 Gdwd 1m4f (0-105)H SFT £49300
93 10/04 Leic 7f9y GD £6148
Total win prize-money £100165

Going (Turf): Sf: 1-4 GS: 1-8 Gd: 1-9 **GF: 2-9** Fm: 0-0
Distance: 5f/6f: 0-0 7f-8f: 1-6 **9f-13f: 4-22** 14f+: 0-2
Track : **LH: 2-10** RH: 1-15 **Tight: 4-13** Gall: 0-8
Aids: Bl: 0-0 **Vi: 1-5** Tstrap: 0-0 Ckp: 0-0
Best Rating: **111** 6/07 Gdwd 1m4f good

Useful; winner in Listed company; stays 1m4f; acts on fast and easy ground; has worn a visor.

Foxholes Lodge

60(65)

4-y-o b f Nasheyt-Duxford Lodge (Dara Monarch)

J D Bethell Graham Scruton

Placings:00 **(5071)**

2009: 5^{0}SD, 8^{0}GF,

	Starts	1st	2nd	3rd	Win & Pl
Career Total (Turf)	1	0	0	0	
Career Total (AW)	1	0	0	0	

Going (Turf): **Sf: 0-0 GS: 0-0 Gd: 0-0 GF: 0-1 Fm: 0-0**
Distance: 5f/6f: 0-1 7f-8f: 0-0 9f-13f: 0-1 14f+: 0-0
Track : LH: 0-1 RH: 0-0 Tight: 0-0 Gall: 0-0
Aids: Bl: 0-0 Vi: 0-0 Tstrap: 0-0 Ckp: 0-0

Foxtrot Alpha (IRE)

84(101) (71)70

3-y-o b f Desert Prince (IRE)-Imelda (USA) (Manila (USA))

P Winkworth P Winkworth

Placings:103-0200300 **(7236)**

2009: 8^{0}GF, 7^{2}SD, 7^{0}SD, 7^{0}G, 6^{3}SD, 6^{0}GS, 8^{0}SD,

	Starts	1st	2nd	3rd	Win & Pl
Career Total (Turf)	6	1	0	1	3706
Career Total (AW)	4	0	1	1	1474

70 6/08 Ling 6f G-F £3302
Total win prize-money £3303

Going (Turf): Sf: 0-0 GS: 0-2 Gd: 0-1 **GF: 1-2** Fm: 0-1
Distance: **5f/6f: 1-5** 7f-8f: 0-5 9f-13f: 0-0 14f+: 0-0
Track : LH: 0-0 RH: 0-5 Tight: 0-0 Gall: 0-2
Aids: Bl: 0-0 Vi: 0-0 Tstrap: 0-0 Ckp: 0-0
Best Rating: **71** 6/09 Kemp 7f stand

Fair; suited by 6f; acts on fast and easy ground.

Foxtrot Bravo (IRE)

88(96) (62)59

3-y-o b g Noverre (USA)-Standcorrected (Shareef Dancer (USA))

Miss S L Davison (P Winkworth 24/2) Miss S L Davison

Placings:0-66260005 **(7652)**

2009: 7^{6}SD, 10^{6}SD, 8^{2}SD, 8^{6}GF, 8^{0}SD, 8^{0}SD, 8^{0}SD, 8^{5}SD,

	Starts	1st	2nd	3rd	Win & Pl
Career Total (Turf)	1	0	0	0	0
Career Total (AW)	8	0	1	0	605

Going (Turf): **Sf: 0-0 GS: 0-0 Gd: 0-0 GF: 0-1 Fm: 0-0**
Distance: 5f/6f: 0-0 7f-8f: 0-7 9f-13f: 0-2 14f+: 0-0
Track : LH: 0-5 RH: 0-3 Tight: 0-4 Gall: 0-0
Aids: Bl: 0-0 Vi: 0-0 Tstrap: 0-0 Ckp: 0-0
Best Rating: **62** 9/09 Kemp 1m stand

Fair; stays 1m; acts on Polytrack.

Foxtrot Charlie

96(105) (73)69

3-y-o b g Lucky Story (USA)-Holy Smoke (Statoblest)

P Winkworth Foxtrot Racing Partnership

Placings:0004-02010 **(6289)**

2009: 8^{0}GF, 10^{2}GF, 8^{0}GF, 10^{1}SD, 10^{0}SD,

	Starts	1st	2nd	3rd	Win & Pl
Career Total (Turf)	6	0	1	0	1157
Career Total (AW)	3	1	0	0	2590

73 9/09 Kemp 1m2f (0-75)H STD £2590
Total win prize-money £2590

Going (Turf): **Sf: 0-1 GS: 0-1 Gd: 0-1 GF: 0-3 Fm: 0-0**
Distance: 5f/6f: 0-0 7f-8f: 0-2 **9f-13f: 1-7** 14f+: 0-0
Track : LH: 0-0 **RH: 1-8** Tight: 0-3 Gall: 0-0
Aids: **Bl: 1-5** Vi: 0-0 Tstrap: 0-0 Ckp: 0-0
Best Rating: **73** 9/09 Kemp 1m2f stand

Modest; stays 1m2f; acts on fast and on easy ground and on Polytrack; has worn blinkers.

Foxtrot Delta (IRE)

(87) (62)

2-y-o ch c Namid-Tarziyana (USA) (Danzig (USA))

P Winkworth Foxtrot Racing Partnership II

Placings:060 **(6627)**

2009: 6^{0}SD, 8^{6}SD, 7^{0}SS,

	Starts	1st	2nd	3rd	Win & Pl
Career Total (Turf)	0	0	0	0	
Career Total (AW)	3	0	0	0	0

Going (Turf): **Sf: 0-0 GS: 0-0 Gd: 0-0 GF: 0-0 Fm: 0-0**
Distance: 5f/6f: 0-1 7f-8f: 0-2 9f-13f: 0-0 14f+: 0-0
Track : LH: 0-2 RH: 0-1 Tight: 0-2 Gall: 0-0
Aids: Bl: 0-0 Vi: 0-0 Tstrap: 0-0 Ckp: 0-0
Best Rating: **62** 9/09 Kemp 1m stand

Foxtrot Foxtrot

60(78) (39)

2-y-o b g Royal Applause-Darmagi (IRE) (Desert King (IRE))

P Winkworth Foxtrot Racing Partnership II

Placings:000 **(6629)**

2009: 6^{0}GF, 8^{0}SD, 7^{0}SS,

	Starts	1st	2nd	3rd	Win & Pl
Career Total (Turf)	1	0	0	0	
Career Total (AW)	2	0	0	0	

Going (Turf): **Sf: 0-0 GS: 0-0 Gd: 0-0 GF: 0-1 Fm: 0-0**
Distance: 5f/6f: 0-1 7f-8f: 0-2 9f-13f: 0-0 14f+: 0-0
Track : LH: 0-1 RH: 0-1 Tight: 0-1 Gall: 0-0
Aids: Bl: 0-0 Vi: 0-0 Tstrap: 0-0 Ckp: 0-0
Best Rating: **39** 10/09 Ling 7f std-slw

Foxy Music

101(99) (74)85

5-y-o b g Foxhound (USA)-Primum Tempus (Primo Dominie)

E J Alston Springs Equestrian, G M & C Baillie

Placings:000052/023304100/4440024-6040200 **(4043)**

2009: 5^{6}SD, 5^{0}SD, 5^{4}HY, 5^{0}G, 5^{2}GF, 5^{0}GF, 5^{0}S,

	Starts	1st	2nd	3rd	Win & Pl
Career Total (Turf)	20	1	3	2	20168
Career Total (AW)	9	0	1	0	1349

85 7/07 Hayd 5f (0-80)H HVY £6477
Total win prize-money £6477

Going (Turf): **Sf: 1-5** GS: 0-3 Gd: 0-6 GF: 0-5 Fm: 0-1
Distance: **5f/6f: 1-29** 7f-8f: 0-0 9f-13f: 0-0 14f+: 0-0
Track : LH: 0-15 RH: 0-3 Tight: 0-14 Gall: 0-2
Aids: Bl: 0-2 Vi: 0-0 Tstrap: 0-0 Ckp: 0-0
Best Rating: **85** 10/08 Pont 5f gd-sft

	Starts	1st	2nd	3rd	Win & Pl
Career Total (Turf)	1	0	0	0	

Going (Turf): Sf: 0-0 GS: 0-0 Gd: 0-0 GF: 0-1 Fm: 0-0
Distance: 5f/6f: 0-1 7f-8f: 0-0 9f-13f: 0-0 14f+: 0-0
Track : LH: 0-0 RH: 0-0 Tight: 0-0 Gall: 0-0
Aids: Bl: 0-0 Vi: 0-0 Tstrap: 0-0 Ckp: 0-0
Best Rating: 3 5/09 Thsk 5f gd-fm

Useful; best over 5f; acts on fast ground and on Polytrack; has worn blinkers; likes to race prominently.

Fraamtaaztiic

74(69) (12)**25**

2-y-o b f Fraam-Dahlawise (IRE) (Caerleon (USA))
R J Hodges Kevin Corcoran Carpets

Placings:600 **(6913)**
2009: 6^{0}GF, 8^{0}SS, 6^{0}SD,

	Starts	1st	2nd	3rd	Win & Pl
Career Total (Turf)	1	0	0	0	0
Career Total (AW)	2	0	0	0	

Going (Turf): Sf: 0-0 GS: 0-0 Gd: 0-0 GF: 0-1 Fm: 0-0
Distance: 5f/6f: 0-2 7f-8f: 0-1 9f-13f: 0-0 14f+: 0-0
Track : LH: 0-2 RH: 0-0 Tight: 0-2 Gall: 0-1
Aids: Bl: 0-0 Vi: 0-0 Tstrap: 0-0 Ckp: 0-0
Best Rating: 25 8/09 Wind 6f gd-fm

Fraizer (IRE)

(99) (53)**51**

5-y-o b g City On A Hill (USA)-She's Our Lady (IRE) (Scenic)
Adrian McGuinness Equine Business Syndicate

Placings:000/04320040-320505 **(3724a)**
2009: 7^{3}SD, 5^{2}SD, 8^{0}SD, 7^{5}HY, 7^{0}GF, 7^{5}S,

	Starts	1st	2nd	3rd	Win & Pl
Career Total (Turf)	8	0	1	1	1450
Career Total (AW)	9	0	1	1	705

Going (Turf): Sf: 0-3 GS: 0-0 Gd: 0-0 GF: 0-2 Fm: 0-0
Distance: 5f/6f: 0-4 7f-8f: 0-12 9f-13f: 0-1 14f+: 0-0
Track : LH: 0-10 RH: 0-6 Tight: 0-6 Gall: 0-1
Aids: Bl: 0-0 Vi: 0-0 Tstrap: 0-1 Ckp: 0-1
Best Rating: 53 2/09 Wolv 5f216y stand

Franali (IRE)

(63) **42**

3-y-o b f Kheleyf (USA)-Christeningpresent (IRE) (Cadeaux Genereux)
R F Fisher Des Johnston

Placings:0000-0 **(4617)**
2009: 15^{0}G,

	Starts	1st	2nd	3rd	Win & Pl
Career Total (Turf)	4	0	0	0	
Career Total (AW)	1	0	0	0	

Going (Turf): Sf: 0-0 GS: 0-1 Gd: 0-2 GF: 0-1 Fm: 0-0
Distance: 5f/6f: 0-1 7f-8f: 0-2 9f-13f: 0-1 14f+: 0-1
Track : LH: 0-3 RH: 0-0 Tight: 0-3 Gall: 0-0
Aids: Bl: 0-0 Vi: 0-0 Tstrap: 0-0 Ckp: 0-0
Best Rating: 42 8/08 Ayr 6f gd-sft

Francesca Conti (IRE)

67 **3**

2-y-o b f Atraf-Gentian Blue (IRE) (Tirol)
K R Burke Mogeely Stud & Mrs Maura Gittins

Placings:0 **(1884)**
2009: 5^{0}GF,

Francesco (FR)

93 **49**

5-y-o gr g Kaldounevees (FR)-Mount Gable (Head For Heights)
Mrs L B Normile Iain A Gauld

Placings:025114/00-5 **(1102)**
2009: 16^{5}GF,

	Starts	1st	2nd	3rd	Win & Pl
Career Total (Turf)	9	2	1	0	16790

73 7/07 Deau 1m7f SFT £7432
6/07 Le L 1m3f110y H G-S £6418
Total win prize-money £13851

Going (Turf): Sf: 1-3 GS: 1-3 Gd: 0-0 GF: 0-1 Fm: 0-0
Distance: 5f/6f: 0-0 7f-8f: 0-0 9f-13f: 1-4 14f+: 1-5
Track : LH: 0-1 RH: 1-5 Tight: 0-2 Gall: 0-0
Aids: Bl: 0-0 Vi: 0-0 Tstrap: 0-0 Ckp: 0-0
Best Rating: 90 7/07 Deau 1m7f soft

Useful; ex-French; stays 1m7f; acts on soft ground.

Franchesca's Gold

(95) (53)**49**

3-y-o b f Monsieur Bond (IRE)-Anita Marie (IRE) (Anita's Prince)
Jane Southcombe The Candlelight Inn Preservation Society

Placings:005356-0006 **(7765)**
2009: 5^{0}SD, 7^{0}SD, 9^{0}SD, 11^{6}SD,

	Starts	1st	2nd	3rd	Win & Pl
Career Total (Turf)	4	0	0	0	0
Career Total (AW)	6	0	0	1	302

Going (Turf): Sf: 0-1 GS: 0-1 Gd: 0-0 GF: 0-1 Fm: 0-1
Distance: 5f/6f: 0-6 7f-8f: 0-2 9f-13f: 0-2 14f+: 0-0
Track : LH: 0-4 RH: 0-2 Tight: 0-4 Gall: 0-0
Aids: Bl: 0-0 Vi: 0-0 Tstrap: 0-0 Ckp: 0-0
Best Rating: 53 8/08 Wolv 5f20y stand

Moderate filly; stays 6f; handles Polytrack.

Francis Albert

92(77) (19)**53**

3-y-o b g Mind Games-Via Dolorosa (Chaddleworth (IRE))
M Mullineaux Peter Danby

Placings:00020 **(6220)**
2009: 5^{0}GS, 6^{0}S, 5^{0}SD, 5^{2}GF, 5^{0}GF,

	Starts	1st	2nd	3rd	Win & Pl
Career Total (Turf)	4	0	1	0	856
Career Total (AW)	1	0	0	0	

Going (Turf): Sf: 0-1 GS: 0-1 Gd: 0-0 GF: 0-2 Fm: 0-0
Distance: 5f/6f: 0-5 7f-8f: 0-0 9f-13f: 0-0 14f+: 0-0
Track : LH: 0-1 RH: 0-0 Tight: 0-1 Gall: 0-0
Aids: Bl: 0-0 Vi: 0-0 Tstrap: 0-0 Ckp: 0-0
Best Rating: 53 8/09 Bevl 5f gd-fm

Moderate; stays 5f and acts on fast ground.

Francis Walsingham (IRE)

98(93) (76)**76**

3-y-o b g Invincible Spirit (IRE)-Web Of Intrigue (Machiavellian (USA))
H Morrison Mrs M Kerr-Dineen & Partners

Placings:0-4014450 **(6396)**
2009: 7^{4}SD, 7^{0}GS, 6^{1}GF, 6^{4}GF, 6^{4}GS, 5^{5}G, 6^{0}GF,

	Starts	1st	2nd	3rd	Win & Pl
Career Total (Turf)	7	1	0	0	3384
Career Total (AW)	1	0	0	0	265

74 6/09 Ripn 6f G-F £2590
Total win prize-money £2590

Going (Turf): Sf: 0-0 GS: 0-2 Gd: 0-2 GF: 1-3 Fm: 0-0
Distance: 5f/6f: 1-5 7f-8f: 0-3 9f-13f: 0-0 14f+: 0-0
Track : LH: 0-1 RH: 0-0 Tight: 0-1 Gall: 0-1
Aids: Bl: 0-0 Vi: 0-0 Tstrap: 0-0 Ckp: 0-0
Best Rating: 76 6/09 Wind 6f gd-fm

Fair; suited by 6f; acts on fast ground; goes on Polytrack.

Franco Is My Name

78(104) (75)**21**

3-y-o b g Namid-Veronica Franco (Darshaan)
P R Hedger P C F Racing Ltd

Placings:0061 **(7392)**
2009: 9^{0}GF, 12^{0}SD, 11^{6}SD, 10^{1}SD,

	Starts	1st	2nd	3rd	Win & Pl
Career Total (Turf)	1	0	0	0	
Career Total (AW)	3	1	0	0	2047

75 11/09 Ling 1m2f (0-60)H STD £2047
Total win prize-money £2047

Going (Turf): Sf: 0-0 GS: 0-0 Gd: 0-0 GF: 0-1 Fm: 0-0
Distance: 5f/6f: 0-0 7f-8f: 0-0 9f-13f: 1-4 14f+: 0-0
Track : LH: 1-1 RH: 0-3 Tight: 1-2 Gall: 0-0
Aids: Bl: 0-0 Vi: 0-0 Tstrap: 0-0 Ckp: 0-0
Best Rating: 75 11/09 Ling 1m2f stand

Modest; effective over 1m2f; acts on Polytrack.

Frank Street

99 **76**

3-y-o ch g Fraam-Pudding Lane (IRE) (College Chapel)
Eve Johnson Houghton R F Johnson Houghton

Placings:325-300 **(2336)**
2009: 5^{3}GF, 7^{0}GF, 5^{0}GF,

	Starts	1st	2nd	3rd	Win & Pl
Career Total (Turf)	6	0	1	2	2312

Going (Turf): Sf: 0-0 GS: 0-1 Gd: 0-0 GF: 0-5 Fm: 0-0
Distance: 5f/6f: 0-5 7f-8f: 0-1 9f-13f: 0-0 14f+: 0-0
Track : LH: 0-2 RH: 0-0 Tight: 0-0 Gall: 0-2
Aids: Bl: 0-0 Vi: 0-0 Tstrap: 0-0 Ckp: 0-0
Best Rating: 76 8/08 Sals 6f gd-sft

Moderate half-brother to his stable's multiple sprint winner Judd Street; stays 6f; acts on fast and easy ground.

Franki J

(89) (64)

2-y-o ch f Barathea (IRE)-Whassup (FR) (Midyan (USA))

D Donovan River Racing

Placings:0005 **(7887)**

2009: 8^0SD, 7^0SD, 8^0SD, 7^5SD,

	Starts	1st	2nd	3rd	Win & Pl
Career Total (Turf)	0	0	0	0	
Career Total (AW)	4	0	0	0	0

Going (Turf): **Sf: 0-0 GS: 0-0 Gd: 0-0 GF: 0-0 Fm: 0-0**
Distance: 5f/6f: 0-0 7f-8f: 0-2 9f-13f: 0-2 14f+: 0-0
Track : LH: 0-4 RH: 0-0 Tight: 0-4 Gall: 0-0
Aids: Bl: 0-0 Vi: 0-0 Tstrap: 0-0 Ckp: 0-0
Best Rating: **64** 10/09 Wolv 1m141y stand

Frankie Falco

(64) (9)

3-y-o br g Bollin Eric-Marsh Marigold (Tina's Pet)

G Fierro G Fierro

Placings:5 **(7725)**

2009: 12^5SD,

	Starts	1st	2nd	3rd	Win & Pl
Career Total (Turf)	0	0	0	0	
Career Total (AW)	1	0	0	0	0

Going (Turf): **Sf: 0-0 GS: 0-0 Gd: 0-0 GF: 0-0 Fm: 0-0**
Distance: 5f/6f: 0-0 7f-8f: 0-0 9f-13f: 0-1 14f+: 0-0
Track : LH: 0-1 RH: 0-0 Tight: 0-0 Gall: 0-0
Aids: Bl: 0-0 Vi: 0-0 Tstrap: 0-0 Ckp: 0-0
Best Rating: **9** 12/09 Sthl 1m4f stand

Franksalot (IRE)

(103) (61)**76**

9-y-o ch g Desert Story (IRE)-Rosie's Guest (IRE) (Be My Guest (USA))

I W McInnes Stephen Hackney

Placings:53052000/05534321222/01454153060033/02460 0253461/64002124646020600/053424110515050060/43 40000020050603-00 **(0277)**

2009: 7^0SD, 7^0SD,

	Starts	1st	2nd	3rd	Win & Pl
Career Total (Turf)	65	6	10	5	38163
Career Total (AW)	35	2	2	5	11267

76	6/07	Pont	6f	(0-70)H	G-F	£3886
71	5/07	Haml	6f5y	(0-70)H	G-F	£3238
67	4/07	Bevl	7f100y	(0-60)H	G-F	£2914
76	5/06	Wind	6f		G-S	£3238
76	12/05	Ling	6f		STD	£2873
81	8/04	Ling	7f	E(0-75)H	STD	£3906
76	6/04	Brig	6f209y	E(0-70)H	FRM	£3415
64	8/03	Brig	6f209y	F(0-60)	FRM	£3150

Total win prize-money £26625

Going (Turf): Sf: 0-1 GS: 1-8 Gd: 0-17 **GF: 3-34** Fm: 2-5
Distance: 5f/6f: 3-32 **7f-8f: 5-63** 9f-13f: 0-5 14f+: 0-0
Track : **LH: 5-58** RH: 1-17 **Tight: 2-45** Gall: 1-8
Aids: Bl: 0-8 Vi: 0-0 Tstrap: 0-5 Ckp: 0-5
Best Rating: **81** 8/04 Ling 7f stand

Moderate handicapper; stays 7f but effective at 6f; acts on most ground including Polytrack; has worn headgear.

Fratellino

101 **100**

2-y-o ch c Auction House (USA)-Vida (IRE) (Wolfhound (USA))

A J McCabe Sale Of The Century

Placings:1401454240 **(6660)**

2009: 5^1GF, 5^4GF, 5^0GF, 5^1GF, 5^4G, 5^5G, 6^4G, 5^2GF, 5^4GF, 5^0GS,

	Starts	1st	2nd	3rd	Win & Pl
Career Total (Turf)	10	2	1	0	26100

92	5/09	York	5f	G-F	£8418
76	4/09	Bevl	5f	G-F	£2590

Total win prize-money £11009

Going (Turf): Sf: 0-0 GS: 0-1 Gd: 0-3 **GF: 2-6** Fm: 0-0
Distance: **5f/6f: 2-10** 7f-8f: 0-0 9f-13f: 0-0 14f+: 0-0
Track : LH: 0-3 RH: 0-0 Tight: 0-3 Gall: 0-0
Aids: Bl: 0-0 Vi: 0-0 Tstrap: 0-0 Ckp: 0-0
Best Rating: **100** 6/09 Asct 5f gd-fm

Very useful; suited by 5f; acts on fast ground.

Fravia

77(76) (27)**12**

3-y-o b f Bertolini (USA)-Alizar (IRE) (Rahy (USA))

B J McMath Mrs Mark Edmondson

Placings:55 **(1045)**

2009: 6^5SD, 6^5G,

	Starts	1st	2nd	3rd	Win & Pl
Career Total (Turf)	1	0	0	0	0
Career Total (AW)	1	0	0	0	0

Going (Turf): **Sf: 0-0 GS: 0-0 Gd: 0-1 GF: 0-0 Fm: 0-0**
Distance: 5f/6f: 0-2 7f-8f: 0-0 9f-13f: 0-0 14f+: 0-0
Track : LH: 0-0 RH: 0-1 Tight: 0-0 Gall: 0-0
Aids: Bl: 0-0 Vi: 0-0 Tstrap: 0-0 Ckp: 0-0
Best Rating: **27** 3/09 Kemp 6f stand

Fred Kennet

(85) (29)

4-y-o ch g Kadastrof (FR)-Evaporate (Insan (USA))

Matthew Salaman (M Salaman 10/8) The Northleach Kennet Connection

Placings:0 **(4838)**

2009: 11^0SD,

	Starts	1st	2nd	3rd	Win & Pl
Career Total (Turf)	0	0	0	0	
Career Total (AW)	1	0	0	0	

Going (Turf): **Sf: 0-0 GS: 0-0 Gd: 0-0 GF: 0-0 Fm: 0-0**
Distance: 5f/6f: 0-0 7f-8f: 0-0 9f-13f: 0-1 14f+: 0-0
Track : LH: 0-1 RH: 0-0 Tight: 0-0 Gall: 0-0
Aids: Bl: 0-0 Vi: 0-0 Tstrap: 0-0 Ckp: 0-0
Best Rating: **29** 8/09 Sthl 1m3f stand

Freda's Rose (IRE)

95(88) (29)**54**

5-y-o b m Rossini (USA)-African Scene (IRE) (Scenic)

J Mackie (O Brennan 17/9) Mrs Pat Brennan

Placings:452460 **(7142)**

2009: 8^4GF, 9^5GF, 8^2GS, 10^4GF, 10^6GF, 9^0SD,

	Starts	1st	2nd	3rd	Win & Pl
Career Total (Turf)	5	0	1	0	1179
Career Total (AW)	1	0	0	0	

Going (Turf): **Sf: 0-0 GS: 0-1 Gd: 0-0 GF: 0-4 Fm: 0-0**
Distance: 5f/6f: 0-0 7f-8f: 0-1 9f-13f: 0-5 14f+: 0-0
Track : LH: 0-5 RH: 0-1 Tight: 0-3 Gall: 0-1
Aids: Bl: 0-0 Vi: 0-0 Tstrap: 0-0 Ckp: 0-0
Best Rating: **54** 8/09 Ripn 1m1f170y gd-fm

Freddie Bolt

76 **19**

3-y-o b c Diktat-Birjand (Green Desert (USA))

F Watson F Watson

Placings:0-0 **(5954)**

2009: 7^0GF,

	Starts	1st	2nd	3rd	Win & Pl
Career Total (Turf)	2	0	0	0	

Going (Turf): **Sf: 0-1 GS: 0-0 Gd: 0-0 GF: 0-1 Fm: 0-0**
Distance: 5f/6f: 0-1 7f-8f: 0-1 9f-13f: 0-0 14f+: 0-0
Track : LH: 0-0 RH: 0-0 Tight: 0-0 Gall: 0-0
Aids: Bl: 0-0 Vi: 0-0 Tstrap: 0-0 Ckp: 0-0
Best Rating: **19** 9/09 Rdcr 7f gd-fm

Freddie's Girl (USA)

85(89) (59)**59**

2-y-o b/br f More Than Ready (USA)-Carib Gal (USA) (Awesome Again (CAN))

Stef Liddiard Mrs Anne & Fred Cowley

Placings:00302 **(7772)**

2009: 6^0SD, 6^0GF, 5^3G, 6^0G, 7^2SD,

	Starts	1st	2nd	3rd	Win & Pl
Career Total (Turf)	3	0	0	1	327
Career Total (AW)	2	0	1	0	1060

Going (Turf): **Sf: 0-0 GS: 0-0 Gd: 0-2 GF: 0-1 Fm: 0-0**
Distance: 5f/6f: 0-4 7f-8f: 0-1 9f-13f: 0-0 14f+: 0-0
Track : LH: 0-3 RH: 0-0 Tight: 0-2 Gall: 0-2
Aids: Bl: 0-0 Vi: 0-0 Tstrap: 0-0 Ckp: 0-0
Best Rating: **59** 12/09 Ling 7f stand

Modest; stays 7f; acts on Polytrack._

Free Agent

108 **103**

3-y-o b g Dr Fong (USA)-Film Script (Unfuwain (USA))

R Hannon The Queen

Placings:11-44434 **(6425)**

2009: 11^4G, 12^4GF, 13^4G, 14^3S, 14^4GF,

	Starts	1st	2nd	3rd	Win & Pl
Career Total (Turf)	7	2	0	1	56392

100	6/08	Asct	7f	G-F	£34062
87	6/08	Leic	5f218y	GD	£3885

Total win prize-money £37948

Going (Turf): Sf: 0-1 GS: 0-0 **Gd: 1-3 GF: 1-3** Fm: 0-0
Distance: 5f/6f: 1-1 7f-8f: 1-1 9f-13f: 0-3 14f+: 0-2
Track : LH: 0-0 RH: 0-5 Tight: 0-2 Gall: 0-3
Aids: Bl: 0-2 Vi: 0-0 Tstrap: 0-0 Ckp: 0-0
Best Rating: **103** 9/09 Sals 1m6f21y soft

Smart; won Chesham Stakes at Royal Ascot in 2008; effective at up to 1m4f; acts on good and fast ground.

Free Falling

84(91) (55)50

3-y-o ch f Selkirk (USA)-Free Flying (Groom Dancer (USA))

A J Lidderdale (L M Cumani 25/6) A C Entertainment Technologies Ltd

Placings:000-00055006 (7842)

2009: 8^{0}SD, 10^{0}SD, 8^{0}SD, 8^{5}GF, 9^{5}GF, 12^{0}SD, 10^{0}SD, 14^{6}SS,

	Starts	1st	2nd	3rd	Win & Pl
Career Total (Turf)	4	0	0	0	0
Career Total (AW)	7	0	0	0	0

Going (Turf): **Sf: 0-1 GS: 0-0 Gd: 0-1 GF: 0-2 Fm: 0-0**
Distance: 5f/6f: 0-0 7f-8f: 0-4 9f-13f: 0-6 14f+: 0-1
Track : LH: 0-5 RH: 0-4 Tight: 0-5 Gall: 0-1
Aids: Bl: 0-1 Vi: 0-0 Tstrap: 0-3 Ckp: 0-3
Best Rating: **55** 4/09 Wolv 1m141y stand

Free For All (IRE)

93 75

2-y-o br c Statue Of Liberty (USA)-Allegorica (IRE) (Alzao (USA))

S Kirk J C Smith

Placings:63 (6616)

2009: 6^{6}GF, 6^{3}G,

	Starts	1st	2nd	3rd	Win & Pl
Career Total (Turf)	2	0	0	1	722

Going (Turf): **Sf: 0-0 GS: 0-0 Gd: 0-1 GF: 0-1 Fm: 0-0**
Distance: 5f/6f: 0-1 7f-8f: 0-1 9f-13f: 0-0 14f+: 0-0
Track : LH: 0-0 RH: 0-0 Tight: 0-0 Gall: 0-0
Aids: Bl: 0-0 Vi: 0-0 Tstrap: 0-0 Ckp: 0-0
Best Rating: **75** 10/09 Newb 6f110y good

Free Grain

88 67

2-y-o b f Sakhee (USA)-All Grain (Polish Precedent (USA))

J L Dunlop R Barnett

Placings:60 (7182)

2009: 6^{6}S, 7^{0}G,

	Starts	1st	2nd	3rd	Win & Pl
Career Total (Turf)	2	0	0	0	0

Going (Turf): **Sf: 0-1 GS: 0-0 Gd: 0-1 GF: 0-0 Fm: 0-0**
Distance: 5f/6f: 0-0 7f-8f: 0-2 9f-13f: 0-0 14f+: 0-0
Track : LH: 0-0 RH: 0-0 Tight: 0-0 Gall: 0-0
Aids: Bl: 0-0 Vi: 0-0 Tstrap: 0-0 Ckp: 0-0
Best Rating: **67** 9/09 Sals 6f212y soft

Free Judgement (USA)

106 (96)108

2-y-o b c Vindication (USA)-South Bay Cove (CAN) (Fusaichi Pegasus (USA))

J S Bolger Mrs June Judd

Placings:5201401 (7072a)

2009: 6^{5}SH, 7^{2}SH, 6^{0}G, 8^{1}SD, 7^{4}SD, 7^{0}G, 7^{1}Y,

	Starts	1st	2nd	3rd	Win & Pl
Career Total (Turf)	5	1	1	0	41609
Career Total (AW)	2	1	0	0	10938
108	10/09	Leop	7f		YLD £39186
90	10/09	Dund	1m		STD £9056

Total win prize-money £48243

Going (Turf): **Sf: 0-0 GS: 0-0 Gd: 0-2 GF: 0-0 Fm: 0-0**
Distance: 5f/6f: 0-2 **7f-8f: 2-5** 9f-13f: 0-0 14f+: 0-0
Track : **LH: 2-3** RH: 0-0 Tight: 0-0 Gall: 0-0
Aids: Bl: 0-0 Vi: 0-0 Tstrap: 0-0 Ckp: 0-0
Best Rating: **108** 10/09 Leop 7f yield

Very useful; effective at 7f-1m; acts on Polytrack and soft ground.

Free Tussy (ARG)

101(103) (84)77

5-y-o b g Freelancer (USA)-Perlada (ARG) (Cipayo (ARG))

G L Moore T Bowley

Placings:311/002060000-4061010232411 (7475)

2009: 7^{4}SD, 7^{0}SD, 7^{6}SD, 10^{1}SD, 10^{0}SD, 10^{1}SD, 11^{0}F, 10^{2}GS, 12^{3}GF, 10^{2}GF, 12^{4}GF, 10^{1}SD, 10^{1}SD,

	Starts	1st	2nd	3rd	Win & Pl
Career Total (Turf)	7	0	2	1	3453
Career Total (AW)	18	6	1	1	19992
84	11/09 Kemp	1m2f	(0-75)H	STD	£2590
78	10/09 Ling	1m2f	(0-75)H	STD	£3412
68	6/09 Ling	1m2f	(0-60)H	STD	£2047
63	4/09 Ling	1m2f	(0-60)H	STD	£2299
	8/07 Plat	1m110y		FST	£4250
	8/07 Plat	7f		SLP	£2833

Total win prize-money £17432

Going (Turf): **Sf: 0-0 GS: 0-1 Gd: 0-0 GF: 0-5 Fm: 0-1**
Distance: 5f/6f: 0-1 7f-8f: 1-10 **9f-13f: 5-14** 14f+: 0-0
Track : **LH: 3-17** RH: 1-4 **Tight: 3-10** Gall: 0-5
Aids: **Bl: 4-14** Vi: 0-0 Tstrap: 0-0 Ckp: 0-0
Best Rating: **84** 11/09 Kemp 1m2f stand

Fair; ex-Argentinian; stays 1m2f; acts on most surfaces; has worn blinkers and a tongue tie.

Freedom Fire (IRE)

100(102) (68)65

3-y-o b g Alhaarth (IRE)-Feel Free (IRE) (Generous (IRE))

G L Moore (J M P Eustace 12/10) The Horse Players Two

Placings:0-44443 (6720)

2009: 8^{4}G, 10^{4}GF, 11^{4}GS, 10^{4}SD, 8^{3}SD,

	Starts	1st	2nd	3rd	Win & Pl
Career Total (Turf)	4	0	0	0	554
Career Total (AW)	2	0	0	1	444

Going (Turf): **Sf: 0-0 GS: 0-2 Gd: 0-1 GF: 0-1 Fm: 0-0**
Distance: 5f/6f: 0-0 7f-8f: 0-2 9f-13f: 0-4 14f+: 0-0
Track : LH: 0-3 RH: 0-2 Tight: 0-2 Gall: 0-0
Aids: Bl: 0-0 Vi: 0-0 Tstrap: 0-0 Ckp: 0-0
Best Rating: **68** 10/09 Kemp 1m stand

Freedom Flying

31

6-y-o b m Kalanisi (IRE)-Free Spirit (IRE) (Caerleon (USA))

P A Kirby (Joss Saville 29/9) Royal Whalley Racing Syndicate

Placings:0-0 (1231)

2009: 12^{0}GF,

	Starts	1st	2nd	3rd	Win & Pl
Career Total (Turf)	2	0	0	0	

Going (Turf): **Sf: 0-1 GS: 0-0 Gd: 0-0 GF: 0-1 Fm: 0-0**
Distance: 5f/6f: 0-0 7f-8f: 0-0 9f-13f: 0-2 14f+: 0-0
Track : LH: 0-1 RH: 0-1 Tight: 0-1 Gall: 0-0
Aids: Bl: 0-0 Vi: 0-0 Tstrap: 0-1 Ckp: 0-1
Best Rating: **31** 4/08 Nott 1m1f213y soft

Freedom Pass (USA)

(85) (52)

2-y-o b f Gulch (USA)-Bold Desire (Cadeaux Genereux)

J A R Toller G B Partnership

Placings:4 (7429)

2009: 7^{4}SD,

	Starts	1st	2nd	3rd	Win & Pl
Career Total (Turf)	0	0	0	0	
Career Total (AW)	1	0	0	0	313

Going (Turf): **Sf: 0-0 GS: 0-0 Gd: 0-0 GF: 0-0 Fm: 0-0**
Distance: 5f/6f: 0-0 7f-8f: 0-1 9f-13f: 0-0 14f+: 0-0
Track : LH: 0-0 RH: 0-1 Tight: 0-0 Gall: 0-0
Aids: Bl: 0-0 Vi: 0-0 Tstrap: 0-0 Ckp: 0-0
Best Rating: **52** 11/09 Kemp 7f stand

Freeforaday (USA)

103(101) (94)86

2-y-o ch c Freefourinternet (USA)-All My Yesterdays (USA) (Wild Again (USA))

J R Best Inside Track Racing Club

Placings:6241411 (7108)

2009: 5^{6}G, 5^{2}GF, 6^{4}GF, 5^{1}GF, 6^{4}GF, 6^{1}G, 6^{1}SD,

	Starts	1st	2nd	3rd	Win & Pl
Career Total (Turf)	6	2	1	0	9005
Career Total (AW)	1	1	0	0	3886
94	10/09 Kemp	6f	(0-90)	STD	£3885
86	10/09 Newb	6f8y	(0-85)	GD	£5180
73	9/09 Folk	5f	(0-75)	G-F	£2729

Total win prize-money £11797

Going (Turf): Sf: 0-0 GS: 0-0 **Gd: 1-2 GF: 1-4** Fm: 0-0
Distance: **5f/6f: 2-6** 7f-8f: 1-1 9f-13f: 0-0 14f+: 0-0
Track : LH: 0-0 **RH: 1-1** Tight: 0-0 Gall: 0-0
Aids: Bl: 0-0 Vi: 0-0 Tstrap: 0-0 Ckp: 0-0
Best Rating: **94** 10/09 Kemp 6f stand

Modest; effective over 5-6f; acts on good and fast ground.

Freeing

94(96) (52)54

3-y-o b f Dansili-Sweeping (Indian King (USA))

J A R Toller G B Partnership

Placings:0-630 (7432)

2009: 6^{6}G, 6^{3}GF, 7^{0}SD,

	Starts	1st	2nd	3rd	Win & Pl
Career Total (Turf)	2	0	0	1	510
Career Total (AW)	2	0	0	0	

Going (Turf): **Sf: 0-0 GS: 0-0 Gd: 0-1 GF: 0-1 Fm: 0-0**
Distance: 5f/6f: 0-1 7f-8f: 0-3 9f-13f: 0-0 14f+: 0-0
Track : LH: 0-1 RH: 0-1 Tight: 0-1 Gall: 0-0
Aids: Bl: 0-0 Vi: 0-0 Tstrap: 0-0 Ckp: 0-0
Best Rating: **54** 8/09 Yarm 6f3y good

Freemantle

113 **115**

3-y-o b c Galileo (IRE)-Patacake Patacake (USA) (Bahri (USA))
A P O'Brien D Smith, Mrs J Magnier, M Tabor

Placings:341-254 **(3970a)**
2009: 10^{2}G, 10^{5}GF, 12^{4}GS,

	Starts	1st	2nd	3rd	Win & Pl
Career Total (Turf)	**6**	**1**	**1**	**1**	**77319**

98	10/08	Tipp	7f100y	HVY	£8637

Total win prize-money £8638

Going (Turf): **Sf: 1-2** GS: 0-1 Gd: 0-2 GF: 0-1 Fm: 0-0
Distance: 5f/6f: 0-0 **7f-8f: 1-3** 9f-13f: 0-3 14f+: 0-0
Track : **LH: 1-2** RH: 0-2 Tight: 0-0 Gall: 0-2
Aids: Bl: 0-0 Vi: 0-0 Tstrap: 0-0 Ckp: 0-0
Best Rating: **115** 7/09 Lonc 1m4f gd-sft

Listed class; runner-up in the 2009 Dante Stakes; probably stays 1m4f; acts on most ground.

Freepressionist

95(96) (70)**60**

3-y-o ch f Compton Place-Sophielu (Rudimentary (USA))
R A Teal Free Press Racing

Placings:02021-045505050 **(6335)**
2009: 5^{0}SD, 6^{4}GF, 6^{5}G, 5^{5}GF, 6^{0}GS, 6^{5}SD, 6^{0}SD, 6^{5}SD, 5^{0}GF,

	Starts	1st	2nd	3rd	Win & Pl
Career Total (Turf)	**6**	**0**	**0**	**0**	**0**
Career Total (AW)	**8**	**1**	**2**	**0**	**4214**

70	11/08	Wolv	5f216y	STD	£2729

Total win prize-money £2730

Going (Turf): **Sf: 0-1 GS: 0-1 Gd: 0-1 GF: 0-3 Fm: 0-0**
Distance: **5f/6f: 1-11** 7f-8f: 0-3 9f-13f: 0-0 14f+: 0-0
Track : **LH: 1-9** RH: 0-1 **Tight: 1-6** Gall: 0-0
Aids: Bl: 0-1 Vi: 0-0 Tstrap: 0-0 Ckp: 0-0
Best Rating: **70** 11/08 Wolv 5f216y stand

Fair; stays 7f and acts on Polytrack.

Fregate Island (IRE)

103(111) (88)**90**

6-y-o gr g Daylami (IRE)-Briery (IRE) (Salse (USA))
A G Newcombe Paul Moulton

Placings:00**131**/0203/310**250**/**0221**242321-6 **(1863)**
2009: 16^{6}GF,

	Starts	1st	2nd	3rd	Win & Pl
Career Total (Turf)	**16**	**2**	**4**	**3**	**24400**
Career Total (AW)	**10**	**3**	**3**	**1**	**14978**

90	9/08	Wwck	1m6f213y	(0-85)H	GD	£5180
79	2/08	Kemp	1m4f		STD	£2047
85	5/07	Gdwd	1m3f	(0-80)H	G-F	£6800
84	11/05	Ling	1m	(0-85)	STD	£5100
71	10/05	Wolv	7f32y		STD	£3094

Total win prize-money £22225

Going (Turf): Sf: 0-1 GS: 0-1 **Gd: 1-7 GF: 1-7** Fm: 0-0
Distance: 5f/6f: 0-1 7f-8f: 2-4 9f-13f: 2-14 14f+: 1-7
Track : **LH: 3-10** RH: 2-14 **Tight: 3-11** Gall: 0-7
Aids: Bl: 0-0 Vi: 0-0 Tstrap: 0-0 Ckp: 0-0
Best Rating: **90** 9/08 Wwck 1m6f213y good

Useful; effective at up to 1m7f; acts on fast ground and on Polytrack; likes to race prominently.

Fremen (USA)

103(108) (90)**93**

9-y-o ch g Rahy (USA)-Northern Trick (USA) (Northern Dancer (CAN))
D Nicholls Miss C King Mrs A Seed Ms Finola Devaney

Placings:23110/000/011055203/**32**060115410/040005000 2432-**1234**162113 **(5944)**
2009: 8^{1}SD, 8^{2}SD, 8^{3}SD, 8^{4}SD, 8^{1}GF, 8^{6}GF, 8^{2}G, 7^{1}GF, 8^{1}GS, 9^{3}G,

	Starts	1st	2nd	3rd	Win & Pl
Career Total (Turf)	**43**	**10**	**4**	**4**	**83076**
Career Total (AW)	**8**	**1**	**3**	**2**	**10238**

88	8/09	Haml	1m65y		G-S	£2388
73	8/09	Muss	7f30y		G-F	£2590
79	6/09	Haml	1m65y		G-F	£2914
90	3/09	Ling	1m	(0-85)H	STD	£6476
104	9/07	Ayr	1m	(0-100)H	G-S	£15580
95	7/07	Gdwd	1m	(0-90)H	GD	£9715
92	7/07	Muss	1m	(0-90)H	GD	£7772
91	7/06	York	1m	(0-90)H	G-F	£9715
78	7/06	Muss	1m1f		GD	£3238
99	8/03	Ripn	1m	C(0-100)H	G-F	£9074
86	8/03	Wind	1m67y D		G-F	£4212

Total win prize-money £73678

Going (Turf): Sf: 0-8 GS: 2-4 Gd: 3-13 **GF: 5-15** Fm: 0-1
Distance: 5f/6f: 0-2 **7f-8f: 7-33** 9f-13f: 4-16 14f+: 0-0
Track : LH: 3-18 **RH: 8-23 Tight: 8-20** Gall: 1-9
Aids: Bl: 0-0 Vi: 0-0 Tstrap: 0-0 Ckp: 0-0
Best Rating: **104** 9/07 Ayr 1m gd-sft

Useful; effective over 7f-1m1f; acts on most ground on turf; also goes on Polytrack.

Fremont (IRE)

99 **101**

2-y-o b c Marju (IRE)-Snow Peak (Arazi (USA))
R Hannon Mrs J Wood

Placings:1041 **(6397)**
2009: 6^{1}G, 6^{0}GF, 6^{4}GF, 6^{1}GF,

	Starts	1st	2nd	3rd	Win & Pl
Career Total (Turf)	**4**	**2**	**0**	**0**	**31289**

96	9/09	Sals	6f212y	G-F	£6476
78	5/09	Gdwd	6f	GD	£6476

Total win prize-money £12952

Going (Turf): Sf: 0-0 GS: 0-0 **Gd: 1-1 GF: 1-3** Fm: 0-0
Distance: 5f/6f: 1-2 7f-8f: 1-2 9f-13f: 0-0 14f+: 0-0
Track : LH: 0-0 RH: 0-0 Tight: 0-0 Gall: 0-0
Aids: Bl: 0-0 Vi: 0-0 Tstrap: 0-0 Ckp: 0-0
Best Rating: **101** 9/09 Donc 6f110y gd-fm

Smart; stays 7f; acts on good/fast ground.

French Applause (IRE)

97 **80**

3-y-o b g Royal Applause-A Ma Guise (USA) (Silver Hawk (USA))
T P Tate T P Tate

Placings:225 **(3566)**
2009: 9^{2}GS, 8^{2}G, 7^{5}G,

	Starts	1st	2nd	3rd	Win & Pl
Career Total (Turf)	**3**	**0**	**2**	**0**	**3006**

Going (Turf): **Sf: 0-0 GS: 0-1 Gd: 0-2 GF: 0-0 Fm: 0-0**
Distance: 5f/6f: 0-0 7f-8f: 0-2 9f-13f: 0-1 14f+: 0-0
Track : LH: 0-1 RH: 0-1 Tight: 0-1 Gall: 0-1
Aids: Bl: 0-0 Vi: 0-0 Tstrap: 0-0 Ckp: 0-0
Best Rating: **80** 6/09 York 1m good

Fair; stays 1m1f; acts on good and easy ground.

French Art

105(101) (71)**88**

4-y-o ch g Peintre Celebre (USA)-Orange Sunset (IRE) (Roanoke (USA))
N Tinkler Nicolas Patsalides

Placings:5/203221-00600064222414 **(7693)**
2009: 8^{0}GF, 8^{0}GS, 8^{6}G, 8^{0}GF, 8^{0}S, 8^{0}GS, 8^{6}GF, 10^{4}GF, 8^{2}GF, 8^{2}SD, 8^{2}G, 9^{4}GS, 8^{1}SD, 8^{4}SD,

	Starts	1st	2nd	3rd	Win & Pl
Career Total (Turf)	**18**	**1**	**5**	**1**	**8419**
Career Total (AW)	**3**	**1**	**1**	**0**	**2311**

71	11/09	Kemp	1m	(0-65)H	STD	£1706
78	8/08	Wind	1m67y		G-S	£2729

Total win prize-money £4436

Going (Turf): Sf: 0-1 **GS: 1-6** Gd: 0-5 GF: 0-6 Fm: 0-0
Distance: 5f/6f: 0-0 7f-8f: 1-13 9f-13f: 1-8 14f+: 0-0
Track : LH: 0-10 **RH: 2-7 Tight: 1-7** Gall: 0-4
Aids: Bl: 0-0 Vi: 0-0 Tstrap: 1-2 Ckp: 1-2
Best Rating: **88** 7/08 Hayd 1m30y good

Moderate; effective over 1m; acts on most ground and on Polytrack; has worn cheekpieces.

French Connexion (IRE)

90(93) (54)**61**

2-y-o b f Chineur (FR)-Hunzy (IRE) (Desert King (IRE))
J S Moore Mrs Evelyn Yates T Yates And J S Moore

Placings:6033000604 **(6292)**
2009: 5^{6}SD, 5^{0}G, 5^{3}GF, 5^{3}F, 6^{0}GF, 6^{0}G, 5^{0}GS, 6^{6}F, 7^{0}SD, 6^{4}SD,

	Starts	1st	2nd	3rd	Win & Pl
Career Total (Turf)	**7**	**0**	**0**	**2**	**713**
Career Total (AW)	**3**	**0**	**0**	**0**	**0**

Going (Turf): **Sf: 0-0 GS: 0-1 Gd: 0-2 GF: 0-2 Fm: 0-2**
Distance: 5f/6f: 0-8 7f-8f: 0-2 9f-13f: 0-0 14f+: 0-0
Track : LH: 0-5 RH: 0-1 Tight: 0-2 Gall: 0-2
Aids: Bl: 0-0 Vi: 0-0 Tstrap: 0-0 Ckp: 0-0
Best Rating: **61** 5/09 Chep 5f16y gd-fm

Modest; effective over 5f; acts on fast ground.

French Fantasy

50(78) (41)

2-y-o ch f Cadeaux Genereux-Footlight Fantasy (USA) (Nureyev (USA))
H Morrison Helena Springfield Ltd

Placings:000 **(7317)**
2009: 8^{0}G, 7^{0}SD, 5^{0}SD,

	Starts	1st	2nd	3rd	Win & Pl
Career Total (Turf)	**1**	**0**	**0**	**0**	
Career Total (AW)	**2**	**0**	**0**	**0**	

Going (Turf): **Sf: 0-0 GS: 0-0 Gd: 0-1 GF: 0-0 Fm: 0-0**
Distance: 5f/6f: 0-1 7f-8f: 0-2 9f-13f: 0-0 14f+: 0-0
Track : LH: 0-2 RH: 0-0 Tight: 0-2 Gall: 0-0
Aids: Bl: 0-0 Vi: 0-0 Tstrap: 0-0 Ckp: 0-0
Best Rating: **41** 10/09 Ling 7f stand

French Hollow

93(97) (71)59
4-y-o b g Beat Hollow-Campaspe (Dominion)
T J Fitzgerald T J Fitzgerald

Placings:342 **(7648)**
2009: 11^{3}S, 12^{4}SD, 12^{2}SD,

	Starts	1st	2nd	3rd	Win & Pl
Career Total (Turf)	1	0	0	1	433
Career Total (AW)	2	0	1	0	806

Going (Turf): **Sf: 0-1 GS: 0-0 Gd: 0-0 GF: 0-0 Fm: 0-0**
Distance: 5f/6f: 0-0 7f-8f: 0-0 9f-13f: 0-3 14f+: 0-0
Track : LH: 0-3 RH: 0-0 Tight: 0-3 Gall: 0-0
Aids: Bl: 0-0 Vi: 0-0 Tstrap: 0-0 Ckp: 0-0
Best Rating: 71 12/09 Wolv 1m4f50y stand

Modest; effective over 1m4f; acts on Polytrack.

French Seventyfive

91 65
2-y-o b g Pursuit Of Love-Miss Tun (Komaite (USA))
T D Walford Francis Argile

Placings:046 **(4652)**
2009: 6^{0}GF, 7^{4}GF, 6^{6}GF,

	Starts	1st	2nd	3rd	Win & Pl
Career Total (Turf)	3	0	0	0	241

Going (Turf): **Sf: 0-0 GS: 0-0 Gd: 0-0 GF: 0-3 Fm: 0-0**
Distance: 5f/6f: 0-2 7f-8f: 0-1 9f-13f: 0-0 14f+: 0-0
Track : LH: 0-0 RH: 0-0 Tight: 0-0 Gall: 0-0
Aids: Bl: 0-0 Vi: 0-0 Tstrap: 0-0 Ckp: 0-0
Best Rating: 65 6/09 Donc 7f gd-fm

French Wind

(77) (45)
2-y-o b c Cadeaux Genereux-Blast (USA) (Roar (USA))
Pat Eddery Brian Goodyear

Placings:0 **(7800)**
2009: 7^{0}SD,

	Starts	1st	2nd	3rd	Win & Pl
Career Total (Turf)	0	0	0	0	
Career Total (AW)	1	0	0	0	

Going (Turf): **Sf: 0-0 GS: 0-0 Gd: 0-0 GF: 0-0 Fm: 0-0**
Distance: 5f/6f: 0-0 7f-8f: 0-1 9f-13f: 0-0 14f+: 0-0
Track : LH: 0-1 RH: 0-0 Tight: 0-1 Gall: 0-0
Aids: Bl: 0-0 Vi: 0-0 Tstrap: 0-0 Ckp: 0-0
Best Rating: 45 12/09 Wolv 7f32y stand

Frequency

89(94) (73)55
2-y-o b c Starcraft (NZ)-Soundwave (Prince Sabo)
E A L Dunlop Thurloe Thoroughbreds XXV

Placings:02 **(6913)**
2009: 6^{0}GS, 6^{2}SD,

	Starts	1st	2nd	3rd	Win & Pl
Career Total (Turf)	1	0	0	0	
Career Total (AW)	1	0	1	0	806

Going (Turf): **Sf: 0-0 GS: 0-1 Gd: 0-0 GF: 0-0 Fm: 0-0**
Distance: 5f/6f: 0-1 7f-8f: 0-1 9f-13f: 0-0 14f+: 0-0
Track : LH: 0-1 RH: 0-0 Tight: 0-1 Gall: 0-0
Aids: Bl: 0-0 Vi: 0-0 Tstrap: 0-0 Ckp: 0-0
Best Rating: 73 10/09 Ling 6f stand

Fair; stays 6f and acts on Polytrack.

Freya's Flight (IRE)

91(72) 55
3-y-o ch f Viking Ruler (AUS)-Polish Saga (Polish Patriot (USA))
K A Ryan Hokey Cokey Partnership

Placings:650 **(7853)**
2009: 6^{6}G, 7^{5}F, 6^{0}SS,

	Starts	1st	2nd	3rd	Win & Pl
Career Total (Turf)	2	0	0	0	0
Career Total (AW)	1	0	0	0	

Going (Turf): **Sf: 0-0 GS: 0-0 Gd: 0-1 GF: 0-0 Fm: 0-1**
Distance: 5f/6f: 0-2 7f-8f: 0-1 9f-13f: 0-0 14f+: 0-0
Track : LH: 0-2 RH: 0-1 Tight: 0-0 Gall: 0-0
Aids: Bl: 0-0 Vi: 0-0 Tstrap: 0-0 Ckp: 0-0
Best Rating: 55 6/09 Bevl 7f100y firm

Friends Hope

97(100) (80)83
8-y-o ch m Docksider (USA)-Stygian (USA) (Irish River (FR))
R Curtis Mrs Joanna Hughes

Placings:0501/01520/5146220000/022344516/11/613312 231406-545265640 **(7761)**
2009: 8^{5}SD, 12^{4}SD, 11^{5}SD, 11^{2}SD, 11^{6}SD, 8^{5}GF, 8^{6}SD, 12^{4}GF, 11^{0}SD,

	Starts	1st	2nd	3rd	Win & Pl
Career Total (Turf)	32	6	5	4	26033
Career Total (AW)	19	3	3	0	10396

83	6/08	Chep	1m2f36y	(0-75)H	G-F	£3238
	5/08	Lanc	1m4f	H	G-F	£1680
69	3/08	Muss	1m1f		GD	£1943
80	12/07	Wolv	1m1f103y	(0-70)H	STD	£2968
76	12/07	Sthl	1m3f	(0-65)H	STD	£2047
61	8/06	Brig	1m1f209y	(0-70)H	FRM	£4210
58	2/05	Wolv	1m141y	(0-55)H	STD	£2948
55	4/04	Sthl	1m2f	F(0-55)H	G-S	£2961
52	9/03	DRoy	7f		FRM	£4480

Total win prize-money £26478

Going (Turf): Sf: 0-4 GS: 1-2 Gd: 1-6 **GF: 2-13 Fm: 2-7**
Distance: 5f/6f: 0-1 7f-8f: 1-10 **9f-13f: 8-40** 14f+: 0-0
Track : **LH: 6-34** RH: 1-11 **Tight: 4-23** Gall: 0-2
Aids: Bl: 0-0 Vi: 0-0 Tstrap: 0-0 Ckp: 0-0
Best Rating: 83 6/08 Chep 1m2f36y gd-fm

Fair; effective at around 1m1f-1m4f; acts on most ground and on sand.

Frightnight (IRE)

(89) (42)
3-y-o ch c Night Shift (USA)-Scared (Royal Academy (USA))
A B Haynes W Clifford

Placings:60 **(0767)**
2009: 8^{6}SD, 9^{0}SD,

	Starts	1st	2nd	3rd	Win & Pl
Career Total (Turf)	0	0	0	0	
Career Total (AW)	2	0	0	0	0

Going (Turf): **Sf: 0-0 GS: 0-0 Gd: 0-0 GF: 0-0 Fm: 0-0**
Distance: 5f/6f: 0-0 7f-8f: 0-0 9f-13f: 0-2 14f+: 0-0
Track : LH: 0-2 RH: 0-0 Tight: 0-2 Gall: 0-0
Aids: Bl: 0-0 Vi: 0-0 Tstrap: 0-0 Ckp: 0-0
Best Rating: 42 2/09 Wolv 1m141y stand

Frill A Minute

78(69) 30
5-y-o b m Lake Coniston (IRE)-Superfrills (Superpower)
Miss L C Siddall Podso Racing

Placings:0000/005000-0000 **(7220)**
2009: 6^{0}G, 6^{0}GF, 7^{0}GF, 7^{0}S,

	Starts	1st	2nd	3rd	Win & Pl
Career Total (Turf)	12	0	0	0	0
Career Total (AW)	2	0	0	0	

Going (Turf): **Sf: 0-2 GS: 0-2 Gd: 0-3 GF: 0-4 Fm: 0-1**
Distance: 5f/6f: 0-7 7f-8f: 0-7 9f-13f: 0-0 14f+: 0-0
Track : LH: 0-5 RH: 0-2 Tight: 0-3 Gall: 0-0
Aids: Bl: 0-1 Vi: 0-0 Tstrap: 0-1 Ckp: 0-1
Best Rating: 30 7/08 Carl 6f192y firm

Fringe Success (IRE)

85(86) (34)61
2-y-o b f Selkirk (USA)-Stage Struck (IRE) (Sadler's Wells (USA))
Sir Michael Stoute Ballymacoll Stud

Placings:06 **(7140)**
2009: 7^{0}GF, 8^{6}SD,

	Starts	1st	2nd	3rd	Win & Pl
Career Total (Turf)	1	0	0	0	
Career Total (AW)	1	0	0	0	0

Going (Turf): **Sf: 0-0 GS: 0-0 Gd: 0-0 GF: 0-1 Fm: 0-0**
Distance: 5f/6f: 0-0 7f-8f: 0-1 9f-13f: 0-1 14f+: 0-0
Track : LH: 0-1 RH: 0-0 Tight: 0-1 Gall: 0-0
Aids: Bl: 0-0 Vi: 0-0 Tstrap: 0-0 Ckp: 0-0
Best Rating: 61 8/09 NmkJ 7f gd-fm

Frisbee

101(99) (64)78
5-y-o b m Efisio-Flying Carpet (Barathea (IRE))
D W Thompson (C J Teague 13/10) G T Carlton

Placings:5/221-020 **(7273)**
2009: 6^{0}G, 5^{2}G, 5^{0}SD,

	Starts	1st	2nd	3rd	Win & Pl
Career Total (Turf)	3	1	1	0	4560
Career Total (AW)	4	0	2	0	1531

78	7/08	Ripn	6f	(0-70)H	GD	£3885

Total win prize-money £3886

Going (Turf): Sf: 0-0 GS: 0-0 **Gd: 1-3** GF: 0-0 Fm: 0-0
Distance: **5f/6f: 1-6** 7f-8f: 0-1 9f-13f: 0-0 14f+: 0-0
Track : LH: 0-4 RH: 0-0 Tight: 0-1 Gall: 0-0
Aids: Bl: 0-0 Vi: 0-0 Tstrap: 0-0 Ckp: 0-0
Best Rating: 78 7/08 Ripn 6f good

Modest; effective over 5f-6f; acts on good ground.

Frisky Queen (IRE)

87(68) (61)**43**

3-y-o b f Val Royal (FR)-Frisky (IRE) (Hamas (IRE))

T G McCourt Mrs R Stewart

Placings:00040-0000066500 (7714)

2009: 5^{0}SD, 5^{0}SD, 5^{0}GF, 5^{0}G, 6^{0}S, 5^{6}GF, 5^{6}GF, 5^{5}S, 5^{0}GF, 5^{0}SD,

	Starts	1st	2nd	3rd	Win & Pl
Career Total (Turf)	10	0	0	0	0
Career Total (AW)	5	0	0	0	377

Going (Turf): Sf: 0-4 GS: 0-0 Gd: 0-2 GF: 0-4 Fm: 0-0
Distance: 5f/6f: 0-15 7f-8f: 0-0 9f-13f: 0-0 14f+: 0-0
Track : LH: 0-8 RH: 0-2 Tight: 0-1 Gall: 0-0
Aids: Bl: 0-0 Vi: 0-0 Tstrap: 0-1 Ckp: 0-1
Best Rating: 61 10/08 Dund 5f stand

Friston Forest (IRE)

104 **112**

5-y-o ch h Barathea (IRE)-Talented (Bustino)

Saeed Bin Suroor Godolphin

Placings:134/31124/01311-123064 (7293)

2009: 13^{1}GF, 14^{2}GF, 16^{3}S, 14^{0}GF, 16^{6}G, 12^{4}S,

	Starts	1st	2nd	3rd	Win & Pl
Career Total (Turf)	19	7	2	4	218946

106	2/09	Ndas	1m5f165y (95-115)H	G-F	£62500
98	10/08	Chan	1m7f	SFT	£19118
98	9/08	StCl	1m4f110y	GD	£12132
94	5/08	StCl	1m7f	G-S	£12132
101	6/07	Toul	1m4f	SFT	£17567
108	5/07	Bord	1m4f	VS	£17567
86	9/06	Lonc	1m	G-S	£6552

Total win prize-money £147570

Going (Turf): Sf: 2-8 GS: 2-3 Gd: 1-4 GF: 1-3 Fm: 0-0
Distance: 5f/6f: 0-0 7f-8f: 1-3 9f-13f: 3-7 14f+: 3-9
Track : LH: 1-8 RH: 3-8 Tight: 0-1 Gall: 0-4
Aids: Bl: 0-0 Vi: 0-0 Tstrap: 0-0 Ckp: 0-0
Best Rating: 112 6/09 Newc 2m19y soft

Smart; ex-French; Listed winner; stays 1m7f; acts on most ground.

Frognal (IRE)

105(99) (81)**91**

3-y-o b g Kheleyf (USA)-Shannon Dore (IRE) (Turtle Island (IRE))

B J Meehan Raymond Tooth

Placings:433166-06433 (6815)

2009: 6^{0}GF, 6^{6}SD, 6^{4}GF, 7^{3}GF, 7^{3}G,

	Starts	1st	2nd	3rd	Win & Pl
Career Total (Turf)	9	0	0	4	40295
Career Total (AW)	2	1	0	0	3562

81	9/08	Kemp	6f	STD	£3561

Total win prize-money £3562

Going (Turf): Sf: 0-0 GS: 0-1 Gd: 0-4 GF: 0-4 Fm: 0-0
Distance: 5f/6f: 1-9 7f-8f: 0-2 9f-13f: 0-0 14f+: 0-0
Track : LH: 0-2 RH: 1-1 Tight: 0-2 Gall: 0-0
Aids: Bl: 0-0 Vi: 0-0 Tstrap: 0-0 Ckp: 0-0
Best Rating: 91 8/08 NmkJ 6f good

Very useful; effective at 7f; acts on good and fast ground, goes on Polytrack.

Fromsong (IRE)

101(113) (88)**77**

11-y-o b g Fayruz-Lindas Delight (Batshoof)

D K Ivory Dean Ivory

Placings:512/140/60002354/030010000/2444400660/0030 1200440001102/42554000/00205410633450660/21124500 5-43633055435600200531 (7807)

2009: 6^{4}SD, 5^{3}SD, 5^{6}SD, 5^{3}SD, 5^{3}SD, 6^{0}SD, 6^{5}G, 6^{5}GF, 5^{4}GS, 5^{3}SD, 5^{5}G, 5^{6}G, 5^{0}GF, 5^{0}S, 6^{2}SD, 6^{0}SD, 6^{0}SD, 5^{5}SD, 5^{3}SD, 5^{1}SD,

	Starts	1st	2nd	3rd	Win & Pl
Career Total (Turf)	65	4	5	4	61022
Career Total (AW)	39	6	5	6	43656

72	12/09	Ling	5f	(0-70)H	STD	£2388
94	2/08	Ling	6f	(0-85)H	STD	£4100
87	1/08	Kemp	5f	(0-85)H	STD	£4210
83	7/07	Kemp	5f	(0-75)H	STD	£2817
97	11/05	Ling	5f	(0-85)H	STD	£5702
92	10/05	Ling	6f	(0-85)H	STD	£7510
95	6/05	Sals	5f	(0-85)H	G-F	£7020
95	6/03	Wind	6f	C(0-90)	G-F	£9886
102	4/01	Nott	5f13y	C	SFT	£7150
103	9/00	Bath	5f161y	D	SFT	£2908

Total win prize-money £53695

Going (Turf): Sf: 2-11 GS: 0-7 Gd: 0-19 GF: 2-26 Fm: 0-2
Distance: 5f/6f: 10-102 7f-8f: 0-2 9f-13f: 0-0 14f+: 0-0
Track : LH: 5-31 RH: 2-9 Tight: 4-25 Gall: 2-16
Aids: Bl: 0-0 Vi: 0-0 Tstrap: 2-12 Ckp: 2-12
Best Rating: 105 6/02 Kemp 5f good

Modest; effective over 5f-6f; acts on most ground; goes on Polytrack; has worn cheekpieces.

Fromthebeginning

87(92) (68)**56**

3-y-o b g Lomitas-Zacchera (Zamindar (USA))

D R C Elsworth Gordon Li

Placings:64-05 (1932)

2009: 10^{0}SD, 8^{5}GF,

	Starts	1st	2nd	3rd	Win & Pl
Career Total (Turf)	1	0	0	0	0
Career Total (AW)	3	0	0	0	337

Going (Turf): Sf: 0-0 GS: 0-0 Gd: 0-0 GF: 0-1 Fm: 0-0
Distance: 5f/6f: 0-0 7f-8f: 0-2 9f-13f: 0-2 14f+: 0-0
Track : LH: 0-3 RH: 0-1 Tight: 0-3 Gall: 0-1
Aids: Bl: 0-0 Vi: 0-0 Tstrap: 0-0 Ckp: 0-0
Best Rating: 68 12/08 GrLe 1m stand

Front Rank (IRE)

96(81) (52)**61**

9-y-o b g Sadler's Wells (USA)-Alignment (IRE) (Alzao (USA))

Mrs Dianne Sayer Andrew Sayer

Placings:0022/30/25/6500/150-4002333 (6768)

2009: 12^{4}SD, 12^{0}GS, 13^{0}GF, 16^{2}G, 13^{3}HY, 16^{3}GS, 12^{3}GS,

	Starts	1st	2nd	3rd	Win & Pl
Career Total (Turf)	18	1	2	4	5349
Career Total (AW)	4	0	2	0	1754

61	6/08	Haml	1m5f9y (0-65)H	GD	£1977

Total win prize-money £1978

Going (Turf): Sf: 0-3 GS: 0-5 Gd: 1-4 GF: 0-6 Fm: 0-0
Distance: 5f/6f: 0-0 7f-8f: 0-0 9f-13f: 0-11 14f+: 1-11
Track : LH: 0-10 RH: 1-12 Tight: 1-14 Gall: 0-4
Aids: Bl: 0-0 Vi: 0-0 Tstrap: 0-0 Ckp: 0-0
Best Rating: 72 9/03 Sthl 1m4f slow

Moderate; stays 1m5f and acts with cut.

Frontline Boy (IRE)

90 **70**

2-y-o b c One Cool Cat (USA)-Diamant (IRE) (Bigstone (IRE))

A P Jarvis Frontline Bathrooms

Placings:0630 (6534)

2009: 7^{0}G, 6^{6}GF, 6^{3}GF, 6^{0}GF,

	Starts	1st	2nd	3rd	Win & Pl
Career Total (Turf)	4	0	0	1	578

Going (Turf): Sf: 0-0 GS: 0-0 Gd: 0-1 GF: 0-3 Fm: 0-0
Distance: 5f/6f: 0-3 7f-8f: 0-1 9f-13f: 0-0 14f+: 0-0
Track : LH: 0-2 RH: 0-0 Tight: 0-1 Gall: 0-0
Aids: Bl: 0-0 Vi: 0-0 Tstrap: 0-0 Ckp: 0-0
Best Rating: 70 9/09 Hayd 6f gd-fm

Modest; stays 6f; acts on fast ground.

Frosted

(96) (60)**60**

3-y-o ch f Dr Fong (USA)-Arctic Air (Polar Falcon (USA))

J H M Gosden Cheveley Park Stud

Placings:0-4 (1532)

2009: 9^{4}SD,

	Starts	1st	2nd	3rd	Win & Pl
Career Total (Turf)	1	0	0	0	
Career Total (AW)	1	0	0	0	0

Going (Turf): Sf: 0-0 GS: 0-1 Gd: 0-0 GF: 0-0 Fm: 0-0
Distance: 5f/6f: 0-0 7f-8f: 0-1 9f-13f: 0-1 14f+: 0-0
Track : LH: 0-1 RH: 0-0 Tight: 0-1 Gall: 0-0
Aids: Bl: 0-0 Vi: 0-0 Tstrap: 0-0 Ckp: 0-0
Best Rating: 60 4/09 Wolv 1m1f103y stand

170,000gns half-sister to Andronikos, who won three times over 6f in Listed company.

Frosty's Gift

66(92) (46)**38**

5-y-o ch m Bold Edge-Coughlan's Gift (Alnasr Alwasheek)

J C Fox Mrs J A Cleary

Placings:000300-600 (2794)

2009: 8^{6}SD, 9^{0}SD, 6^{0}GF,

	Starts	1st	2nd	3rd	Win & Pl
Career Total (Turf)	4	0	0	0	
Career Total (AW)	5	0	0	1	302

Going (Turf): Sf: 0-0 GS: 0-0 Gd: 0-0 GF: 0-3 Fm: 0-1
Distance: 5f/6f: 0-2 7f-8f: 0-6 9f-13f: 0-1 14f+: 0-0
Track : LH: 0-2 RH: 0-4 Tight: 0-1 Gall: 0-0
Aids: Bl: 0-0 Vi: 0-0 Tstrap: 0-0 Ckp: 0-0
Best Rating: 46 9/08 Kemp 1m stand

Frozen Fire (GER)

109 **122**

4-y-o b c Montjeu (IRE)-Flamingo Sea (USA) (Woodman (USA))

A P O'Brien M Tabor, D Smith & Mrs John Magnier

Placings:10/2010-350 (4298)

2009: 13^{3}GF, 12^{5}G, 12^{0}G,

	Starts	1st	2nd	3rd	Win & Pl
Career Total (Turf)	9	2	1	1	674678

122 6/08 Curr 1m4f G-Y £619852
86 8/07 Gowr 7f YLD £7937
Total win prize-money £627790

Going (Turf): Sf: 0-1 GS: 0-0 Gd: 0-4 GF: 0-2 Fm: 0-0
Distance: 5f/6f: 0-0 7f-8f: 1-2 9f-13f: 1-5 14f+: 0-2
Track : LH: 0-5 **RH: 2-3** Tight: 0-3 Gall: 0-3
Aids: Bl: 0-0 Vi: 0-0 Tstrap: 0-0 Ckp: 0-0
Best Rating: 122 6/08 Curr 1m4f gd-yld

Group class; Irish trained; runner-up in the 2008 Dante Stakes and won the Irish Derby; effective over 1m4f; acts on most ground.

Frozen Power (IRE)

97 **102**
2-y-o b c Oasis Dream-Musical Treat (IRE) (Royal Academy (USA))
Saeed Bin Suroor Godolphin

Placings:411100 **(6898)**
2009: 6[4]G, 6[1]GF, 6[1]GF, 7[1]G, 8[0]G, 8[0]GF,

	Starts	1st	2nd	3rd	Win & Pl
Career Total (Turf)	6	3	0	0	35695

102 8/09 Deau 7f GD £26699
92 8/09 Sals 6f212y G-F £3238
78 7/09 Epsm 6f G-F £5180
Total win prize-money £35118

Going (Turf): Sf: 0-0 GS: 0-0 Gd: 1-3 **GF: 2-3** Fm: 0-0
Distance: 5f/6f: 1-2 **7f-8f: 2-3** 9f-13f: 0-1 14f+: 0-0
Track : LH: 1-2 RH: 1-2 **Tight: 1-1** Gall: 0-1
Aids: Bl: 0-0 Vi: 0-0 Tstrap: 0-0 Ckp: 0-0
Best Rating: 102 8/09 Deau 7f good

Very useful, Listed winner; stays 7f; acts on good and faster ground.

Fuel Cell (IRE)

78(85) (59)**24**
8-y-o b g Desert Style (IRE)-Tappen Zee (Sandhurst Prince)
I W McInnes J Morris

Placings:0033013503/**03645060100**5/0000**00**/**405510550**
0/00-0 **(4887)**
2009: 7[0]G,

	Starts	1st	2nd	3rd	Win & Pl
Career Total (Turf)	24	1	0	4	6095
Career Total (AW)	17	2	0	1	6659

59 3/07 Sthl 1m (0-50)H STD £2388
69 8/05 Ling 1m2f STD £3484
73 7/04 Folk 1m1f149y F G-F £2961
Total win prize-money £8834

Going (Turf): Sf: 0-0 GS: 0-5 Gd: 0-10 **GF: 1-8** Fm: 0-1
Distance: 5f/6f: 0-0 7f-8f: 1-12 **9f-13f: 2-28** 14f+: 0-1
Track : **LH: 2-25** RH: 1-12 **Tight: 2-25** Gall: 0-1
Aids: **Bl: 1-18** Vi: 0-0 Tstrap: 0-1 Ckp: 0-1
Best Rating: 75 10/04 Leic 1m1f218y good

Plating-class gelding; probably best over 1m; acts on fast ground and on sand.

Fujin Dancer (FR)

100(106) (75)**78**
4-y-o ch h Storming Home-Badaayer (USA) (Silver Hawk (USA))
K A Ryan (R A Fahey 4/12) John Duddy

Placings:00/314024-4622 **(7776)**
2009: 9[4]GF, 10[6]G, 8[2]SD, 10[2]SD,

	Starts	1st	2nd	3rd	Win & Pl
Career Total (Turf)	8	0	1	0	2472
Career Total (AW)	4	1	2	1	3958

76 4/08 Wolv 1m141y (0-60)H STD £2047
Total win prize-money £2047

Going (Turf): Sf: 0-1 GS: 0-1 Gd: 0-2 GF: 0-4 Fm: 0-0
Distance: 5f/6f: 0-2 7f-8f: 0-1 **9f-13f: 1-9** 14f+: 0-0
Track : **LH: 1-9** RH: 0-2 **Tight: 1-6** Gall: 0-1
Aids: Bl: 0-1 Vi: 0-0 Tstrap: 0-0 Ckp: 0-0
Best Rating: 78 7/08 Haml 1m1f36y good

Modest; stays 1m2f and acts on sand.

Fulfilment (IRE)

88(90) (48)**50**
3-y-o ch f Alhaarth (IRE)-Noble Dane (IRE) (Danehill (USA))
W J Musson Howard Spooner

Placings:000 **(6673)**
2009: 8[0]S, 8[0]SD, 9[0]SD,

	Starts	1st	2nd	3rd	Win & Pl
Career Total (Turf)	1	0	0	0	
Career Total (AW)	2	0	0	0	

Going (Turf): Sf: 0-1 GS: 0-0 Gd: 0-0 GF: 0-0 Fm: 0-0
Distance: 5f/6f: 0-0 7f-8f: 0-1 9f-13f: 0-2 14f+: 0-0
Track : LH: 0-2 RH: 0-0 Tight: 0-2 Gall: 0-0
Aids: Bl: 0-0 Vi: 0-0 Tstrap: 0-0 Ckp: 0-0
Best Rating: 50 7/09 NmkJ 1m soft

Fulford

92(95) (49)**59**
4-y-o ch g Elmaamul (USA)-Last Impression (Imp Society (USA))
M Brittain Mel Brittain

Placings:0203006/1315634050-0000000 **(7680)**
2009: 6[0]SS, 6[0]SD, 6[0]GF, 6[0]G, 8[0]HY, 6[0]GF, 6[0]SD,

	Starts	1st	2nd	3rd	Win & Pl
Career Total (Turf)	16	0	1	2	3275
Career Total (AW)	8	2	0	1	4986

62 1/08 Wolv 5f216y (0-60)H STD £2266
65 1/08 Sthl 6f STD £2457
Total win prize-money £4724

Going (Turf): Sf: 0-4 GS: 0-2 Gd: 0-5 GF: 0-5 Fm: 0-0
Distance: **5f/6f: 2-22** 7f-8f: 0-1 9f-13f: 0-1 14f+: 0-0
Track : **LH: 2-9** RH: 0-2 **Tight: 1-4** Gall: 0-0
Aids: Bl: 0-0 Vi: 0-2 Tstrap: 0-0 Ckp: 0-0
Best Rating: 65 1/08 Sthl 6f stand

Modest sprinter; best over 6f; acts on Polytrack and Fibresand, and on most ground on turf.

Fulham Broadway (IRE)

(105) (91)**70**
3-y-o ch c Exceed And Excel (AUS)-Lomalou (IRE) (Lightning Dealer)
E F Vaughan Trevor C Stewart

Placings:31-2 **(3028)**
2009: 6[2]SD,

	Starts	1st	2nd	3rd	Win & Pl
Career Total (Turf)	1	0	0	1	482
Career Total (AW)	2	1	1	0	5292

74 10/08 Wolv 5f216y STD £3885
Total win prize-money £3886

Going (Turf): Sf: 0-0 GS: 0-0 Gd: 0-0 GF: 0-1 Fm: 0-0
Distance: **5f/6f: 1-3** 7f-8f: 0-0 9f-13f: 0-0 14f+: 0-0
Track : **LH: 1-2** RH: 0-1 **Tight: 1-1** Gall: 0-1
Aids: Bl: 0-0 Vi: 0-0 Tstrap: 0-0 Ckp: 0-0
Best Rating: 91 6/09 Kemp 6f stand

Useful; effective over 6f; acts on Polytrack.

Full Blue

84 **49**
3-y-o gr/b f Falbrav (IRE)-Miss University (USA) (Beau Genius (CAN))
S C Williams D A Shekells

Placings:00-000 **(5011)**
2009: 10[0]GF, 11[0]GS, 14[0]G,

	Starts	1st	2nd	3rd	Win & Pl
Career Total (Turf)	5	0	0	0	

Going (Turf): Sf: 0-0 GS: 0-2 Gd: 0-1 GF: 0-2 Fm: 0-0
Distance: 5f/6f: 0-2 7f-8f: 0-0 9f-13f: 0-2 14f+: 0-1
Track : LH: 0-3 RH: 0-0 Tight: 0-2 Gall: 0-0
Aids: Bl: 0-0 Vi: 0-0 Tstrap: 0-0 Ckp: 0-0
Best Rating: 49 9/08 NmkR 6f gd-fm

Full Mandate (IRE)

100 **98**
2-y-o b f Acclamation-Dani Ridge (IRE) (Indian Ridge)
James Cassidy (R Hannon 27/9) Fontana Racing LLC and Deron Pearson

Placings:412020 **(6317a)**
2009: 5[4]GF, 6[1]GF, 6[2]G, 7[0]G, 6[2]G, 8[0]F,

	Starts	1st	2nd	3rd	Win & Pl
Career Total (Turf)	6	1	2	0	294065

78 7/09 Newb 6f8y G-F £5180
Total win prize-money £5181

Going (Turf): Sf: 0-0 GS: 0-0 Gd: 0-3 **GF: 1-2** Fm: 0-1
Distance: 5f/6f: 0-3 **7f-8f: 1-3** 9f-13f: 0-0 14f+: 0-0
Track : LH: 0-1 RH: 0-1 Tight: 0-0 Gall: 0-0
Aids: Bl: 0-0 Vi: 0-0 Tstrap: 0-0 Ckp: 0-0
Best Rating: 98 9/09 Curr 6f good

Smart; Group placed; stays 6f; acts on fast ground.

Full Of Love (IRE)

103(96) (75)**86**
3-y-o b f Hawk Wing (USA)-Charmingly (USA) (King Of Kings (IRE))
B W Hills Suzanne & Nigel Williams

Placings:0-112320 **(6618)**
2009: 8[1]GF, 8[1]SD, 8[2]G, 8[3]GS, 9[2]G, 10[0]G,

	Starts	1st	2nd	3rd	Win & Pl
Career Total (Turf)	6	1	2	1	9860
Career Total (AW)	1	1	0	0	3886

75 4/09 Wolv 1m141y (0-70)H STD £3885
66 4/09 Newc 1m3y G-F £2719
Total win prize-money £6606

Going (Turf): Sf: 0-0 GS: 0-2 Gd: 0-3 **GF: 1-1** Fm: 0-0
Distance: 5f/6f: 0-0 7f-8f: 0-2 **9f-13f: 2-5** 14f+: 0-0
Track : **LH: 1-3** RH: 0-1 **Tight: 1-2** Gall: 0-1

Aids: Bl: 0-0 Vi: 0-0 Tstrap: 0-0 Ckp: 0-0
Best Rating: **86** 7/09 Gdwd 1m1f good

Useful; stays 1m1f; acts on most ground on turf and on Polytrack.

Full Of Nature

93(96) (73)**76**
3-y-o ch f Monsieur Bond (IRE)-Secret Circle (Magic Ring (IRE))
S Kirk Full Of Nature Partnership

Placings:16400-400304456 **(6460)**
2009: 9^{4}F, 10^{0}SD, 10^{0}G, 8^{3}GS, 8^{0}GF, 10^{4}SD, 9^{4}GF, 12^{5}GF, 9^{6}SD,

	Starts	1st	2nd	3rd	Win & Pl
Career Total (Turf)	11	1	0	1	6862
Career Total (AW)	3	0	0	0	289

76 5/08 NmkR 6f G-S £4533
Total win prize-money £4533

Going (Turf): Sf: 0-1 **GS: 1-3** Gd: 0-3 GF: 0-3 Fm: 0-1
Distance: **5f/6f: 1-4** 7f-8f: 0-1 9f-13f: 0-9 14f+: 0-0
Track : LH: 0-6 RH: 0-4 Tight: 0-9 Gall: 0-1
Aids: Bl: 0-0 Vi: 0-0 Tstrap: 0-0 Ckp: 0-0
Best Rating: **76** 6/08 Epsm 6f good

Fair half-sister to four winners, including Secret Place and Ektimaal; winner on debut; effective over 6f; acts on easy ground.

Full Speed (GER)

105 **89**
4-y-o b g Sholokhov (IRE)-Flagny (FR) (Kaldoun (FR))
G A Swinbank The County Set Three

Placings:025/321504-1000350 **(6681)**
2009: 10^{1}GF, 10^{0}GF, 10^{0}G, 10^{0}GF, 10^{3}GF, 11^{5}GF, 12^{0}G,

	Starts	1st	2nd	3rd	Win & Pl
Career Total (Turf)	16	2	2	2	18015

89 6/09 Ches 1m2f75y (0-85)H G-F £5504
89 5/08 York 1m4f (0-80)H G-F £7123
Total win prize-money £12629

Going (Turf): Sf: 0-2 GS: 0-0 Gd: 0-6 **GF: 2-8** Fm: 0-0
Distance: 5f/6f: 0-0 7f-8f: 0-3 **9f-13f: 2-13** 14f+: 0-0
Track : **LH: 2-13** RH: 0-1 Tight: 1-3 Gall: 1-8
Aids: Bl: 0-0 Vi: 0-0 Tstrap: 0-0 Ckp: 0-0
Best Rating: **89** 6/09 Ches 1m2f75y gd-fm

Useful; stays 1m4f; acts on most ground.

Full Toss

99(106) (92)**99**
3-y-o b g Nayef (USA)-Spinning Top (Alzao (USA))
P D Evans (R Hannon 5/12) J L Guillambert

Placings:2212-000631414 **(7867)**
2009: 8^{0}SD, 10^{0}S, 8^{0}SD, 8^{6}GF, 10^{3}GF, 10^{1}SD, 9^{4}SD, 11^{1}SS, 14^{4}SS,

	Starts	1st	2nd	3rd	Win & Pl
Career Total (Turf)	7	1	3	1	17854
Career Total (AW)	6	2	0	0	8050

92 12/09 Sthl 1m3f (0-85)H SS £4857
82 12/09 Ling 1m2f STD £1978
88 8/08 Ches 7f2y G-F £7317
Total win prize-money £14154

Going (Turf): Sf: 0-1 GS: 0-1 Gd: 0-1 **GF: 1-4** Fm: 0-0
Distance: 5f/6f: 0-0 7f-8f: 1-6 **9f-13f: 2-6** 14f+: 0-1
Track : **LH: 3-6** RH: 0-4 **Tight: 2-3** Gall: 0-1
Aids: Bl: 0-0 Vi: 0-0 Tstrap: 0-0 Ckp: 0-0
Best Rating: **99** 9/08 Newb 1m good

Useful; stays 1m3f; acts on most ground, including both AW surfaces.

Full Victory (IRE)

102(98) (83)**75**
7-y-o b g Imperial Ballet (IRE)-Full Traceability (IRE) (Ron's Victory (USA))
R A Farrant Friends of Saunton Sands

Placings:02330/2600/411045022550/00331524366520400 /4214660500606-510434036 **(6937)**
2009: 7^{5}GF, 8^{1}GS, 8^{0}GF, 8^{4}G, 8^{3}HY, 8^{4}HY, 8^{0}SD, 8^{3}G, 8^{6}G,

	Starts	1st	2nd	3rd	Win & Pl
Career Total (Turf)	52	5	6	7	52383
Career Total (AW)	8	0	1	0	2431

75 5/09 Bath 1m5y (0-70)H G-S £2719
85 5/08 Bevl 1m100y (0-85)H GD £12952
86 5/07 Sand 1m14y (0-80)H G-S £6477
82 6/06 Wind 1m67y (0-65)H G-F £3238
83 5/06 Chep 1m14y (0-70)H G-S £3562
Total win prize-money £28950

Going (Turf): Sf: 0-15 **GS: 3-13** Gd: 1-12 GF: 1-7 Fm: 0-1
Distance: 5f/6f: 0-0 7f-8f: 0-22 **9f-13f: 5-38** 14f+: 0-0
Track : LH: 1-25 **RH: 3-24 Tight: 2-22** Gall: 0-3
Aids: Bl: 0-1 Vi: 0-0 Tstrap: 0-2 Ckp: 0-2
Best Rating: **89** 7/07 York 1m heavy

Fair; effective at around 1m; acts on most ground; usually held up; has looked a difficult ride on occasions.

Fullandby (IRE)

111(110) (105)**111**
7-y-o b g Monashee Mountain (USA)-Ivory Turner (Efisio)
T J Etherington Miss M Greenwood

Placings:2/0231221021/300505152120/50340100100/330 020300140-30200000504110 **(7488)**
2009: 5^{3}GS, 6^{0}GF, 5^{2}G, 5^{0}G, 6^{0}S, 5^{0}G, 5^{0}GF, 5^{0}GF, 6^{5}G, 7^{0}G, 5^{4}GS, 6^{1}SD, 6^{1}S, 6^{0}SD,

	Starts	1st	2nd	3rd	Win & Pl
Career Total (Turf)	53	8	7	6	223170
Career Total (AW)	7	2	2	1	14494

104 11/09 Donc 6f SFT £29630
105 11/09 Kemp 6f (0-95)H STD £7352
103 9/08 Bevl 5f SFT £7477
109 9/07 Donc 5f140y H G-F £46740
104 7/07 Ayr 5f H G-S £29146
98 9/06 Hayd 6f (0-90) HVY £9715
92 7/06 NmkJ 6f (0-90)H G-S £8096
78 10/05 NmkR 6f SFT £5962
87 8/05 Ayr 6f (0-80)H G-F £6716
73 6/05 Wolv 7f32y STD £2583
Total win prize-money £153420

Going (Turf): **Sf: 4-11**GS: 2-14 Gd: 0-14GF: 2-14 Fm: 0-0
Distance: **5f/6f: 9-51** 7f-8f: 1-7 9f-13f: 0-2 14f+: 0-0
Track : LH: 1-6 RH: 1-3 **Tight: 1-4** Gall: 0-2
Aids: Bl: 0-2 Vi: 0-0 Tstrap: 0-0 Ckp: 0-0
Best Rating: **111** 7/08 Ayr 5f good

Very useful; Listed winner; stays 7f, but best over shorter; acts on most ground and on Polytrack; has worn blinkers.

Fullback (IRE)

101(105) (96)**89**
3-y-o ch g Redback-Feet Of Flame (USA) (Theatrical)
J S Moore A J Speyer & R J Lilley

Placings:222212-00024404 **(5648)**
2009: 7^{0}FT, 8^{0}FT, 8^{0}SD, 8^{2}SD, 8^{4}G, 10^{4}GS, 8^{0}SD, 10^{4}SD,

	Starts	1st	2nd	3rd	Win & Pl
Career Total (Turf)	2	0	0	0	2849
Career Total (AW)	12	1	6	0	20032

82 9/08 Wolv 1m141y STD £3885
Total win prize-money £3886

Going (Turf): **Sf: 0-0 GS: 0-1 Gd: 0-1 GF: 0-0 Fm: 0-0**
Distance: 5f/6f: 0-0 7f-8f: 0-10 **9f-13f: 1-4** 14f+: 0-0
Track : **LH: 1-10** RH: 0-3 **Tight: 1-7** Gall: 0-4
Aids: Bl: 0-0 Vi: 0-0 Tstrap: 0-0 Ckp: 0-0
Best Rating: **96** 9/08 GrLe 1m stand

Very useful; stays 1m and acts on Polytrack.

Fun In The Sun

94(104) (63)**57**
5-y-o b g Piccolo-Caught In The Rain (Spectrum (IRE))
A B Haynes WCR V - The Conkwell Connection

Placings:000/020500050063405/21350650020320-201054040 **(5287)**
2009: 7^{2}SD, 8^{0}SD, 7^{1}SD, 7^{0}SD, 8^{5}SD, 7^{4}SD, 6^{0}GF, 6^{4}GF, 7^{0}GF,

	Starts	1st	2nd	3rd	Win & Pl
Career Total (Turf)	26	0	2	2	2264
Career Total (AW)	15	2	3	1	4482

63 2/09 Ling 7f (0-55)H STD £1706
51 3/08 Kemp 7f (0-45) STD £1365
Total win prize-money £3071

Going (Turf): **Sf: 0-4 GS: 0-2 Gd: 0-1 GF: 0-15 Fm: 0-4**
Distance: 5f/6f: 0-2 **7f-8f: 2-31** 9f-13f: 0-8 14f+: 0-0
Track : LH: 1-19 RH: 1-9 **Tight: 1-10** Gall: 0-1
Aids: Bl: 0-3 Vi: 0-8 Tstrap: 0-0 Ckp: 0-0
Best Rating: **63** 2/09 Ling 7f stand

Moderate; effective over 7f-1m; acts on easy ground; goes on Polytrack.

Funday

106 **92**
3-y-o b f Daylami (IRE)-Morina (USA) (Lyphard (USA))
G L Moore Sir Eric Parker

Placings:3134213 **(6452)**
2009: 10^{3}GF, 10^{1}GF, 10^{3}G, 12^{4}GF, 10^{2}G, 12^{1}GF, 12^{3}GF,

	Starts	1st	2nd	3rd	Win & Pl
Career Total (Turf)	7	2	1	3	17806

89 9/09 Epsm 1m4f10y (0-85)H G-F £6476
80 6/09 Ling 1m2f G-F £3070
Total win prize-money £9547

Going (Turf): Sf: 0-0 GS: 0-0 Gd: 0-2 **GF: 2-5** Fm: 0-0
Distance: 5f/6f: 0-0 7f-8f: 0-0 **9f-13f: 2-7** 14f+: 0-0
Track : **LH: 2-5** RH: 0-2 **Tight: 2-4** Gall: 0-2
Aids: Bl: 0-0 Vi: 0-0 Tstrap: 0-0 Ckp: 0-0
Best Rating: **92** 10/09 NmkR 1m4f gd-fm

Fair; Listed placed; stays 1m4f; acts on fast ground.

Funky Munky

101(89) (51)**71**
4-y-o b g Talaash (IRE)-Chilibang Bang (Chilibang)
G A Swinbank The Twelve Munkys

Placings:5050160 **(6349)**
2009: 8^{5}SD, 7^{0}GF, 8^{5}GF, 8^{0}GF, 8^{1}G, 9^{6}G, 8^{0}SD,

	Starts	1st	2nd	3rd	Win & Pl
Career Total (Turf)	5	1	0	0	2979
Career Total (AW)	2	0	0	0	0

71 8/09 Thsk 1m (0-65)H GD £2978
Total win prize-money £2979

Going (Turf): Sf: 0-0 GS: 0-0 **Gd: 1-2** GF: 0-3 Fm: 0-0
Distance: 5f/6f: 0-0 **7f-8f: 1-5** 9f-13f: 0-2 14f+: 0-0
Track : **LH: 1-4** RH: 0-3 **Tight: 1-6** Gall: 0-0

Aids: Bl: 0-0 Vi: 0-0 Tstrap: 0-0 Ckp: 0-0
Best Rating: **71** 8/09 Thsk 1m good

Fair; stays 1m; acts on good ground.

Funky Town (IRE)

66(74) **45**
7-y-o b g Anshan-Dance Rhythm (IRE) (Dancing Dissident (USA))
J Akehurst Simon C Russell

Placings:6045-000 **(1200)**
2009: 12^{0}SD, 8^{0}SD, 12^{0}GF,

	Starts	1st	2nd	3rd	Win & Pl
Career Total (Turf)	5	0	0	0	0
Career Total (AW)	2	0	0	0	

Going (Turf): **Sf: 0-0 GS: 0-1 Gd: 0-0 GF: 0-4 Fm: 0-0**
Distance: 5f/6f: 0-0 7f-8f: 0-1 9f-13f: 0-4 14f+: 0-2
Track : LH: 0-5 RH: 0-2 Tight: 0-6 Gall: 0-0
Aids: Bl: 0-0 Vi: 0-0 Tstrap: 0-0 Ckp: 0-0
Best Rating: **45** 6/08 Rdcr 1m6f19y gd-fm

Furmagiatt

5-y-o b g In The Wings-Sumingasefa (Danehill (USA))
Mrs S Leech Mrs R C Astaire

Placings:R **(0978)**
2009: 12^{R}SD,

	Starts	1st	2nd	3rd	Win & Pl
Career Total (Turf)	0	0	0	0	
Career Total (AW)	1	0	0	0	

Going (Turf): **Sf: 0-0 GS: 0-0 Gd: 0-0 GF: 0-0 Fm: 0-0**
Distance: 5f/6f: 0-0 7f-8f: 0-0 9f-13f: 0-1 14f+: 0-0
Track : LH: 0-1 RH: 0-0 Tight: 0-0 Gall: 0-0
Aids: Bl: 0-0 Vi: 0-0 Tstrap: 0-0 Ckp: 0-0

Furmigadelagiusta

111 (95)**112**
5-y-o ch h Galileo (IRE)-Sispre (FR) (Master Willie)
K R Burke Keep Racing

Placings:003/41301/245-3110 **(3874)**
2009: 12^{3}G, 12^{1}GS, 12^{1}GF, 14^{0}GF,

	Starts	1st	2nd	3rd	Win & Pl
Career Total (Turf)	13	3	1	2	66903
Career Total (AW)	2	1	0	1	7919

112	6/09	Pont	1m4f8y		G-F	£25236
111	5/09	York	1m4f	(0-105)H	G-S	£24924
95	10/07	Wolv	1m4f50y	(0-90)H	STD	£7124
84	7/07	Newb	1m4f5y		HVY	£4533

Total win prize-money £61819

Going (Turf): **Sf: 1-3 GS: 1-2** Gd: 0-2 **GF: 1-5** Fm: 0-1
Distance: 5f/6f: 0-0 7f-8f: 0-3 **9f-13f: 4-9** 14f+: 0-3
Track : **LH: 4-9** RH: 0-4 Tight: 1-2 **Gall: 2-7**
Aids: Bl: 0-0 Vi: 0-0 Tstrap: 0-0 Ckp: 0-0
Best Rating: **112** 6/09 Pont 1m4f8y gd-fm

Smart; Listed winner; stays 1m4f; acts on soft ground and on Polytrack; winning hurdler.

Furnace (IRE)

111(104) (91)**102**
5-y-o b g Green Desert (USA)-Lyrical Dance (USA) (Lear Fan (USA))

Saeed Bin Suroor (M bin Shafya 13/3) Godolphin

Placings:103/304/**36**116-20100 **(2015)**
2009: 8^{2}GF, 7^{0}G, 8^{1}GF, 5^{0}SD, 8^{0}G,

	Starts	1st	2nd	3rd	Win & Pl
Career Total (Turf)	13	4	1	2	185539
Career Total (AW)	3	0	0	1	1260

102	2/09	Ndas	1m		G-F	£41666
100	9/08	Asct	7f	H	GD	£93465
95	8/08	Ches	7f122y	H	G-F	£24924
84	8/06	NmkJ	7f		G-F	£4533

Total win prize-money £164590

Going (Turf): Sf: 0-0 GS: 0-1 Gd: 1-5 **GF: 3-7** Fm: 0-0
Distance: 5f/6f: 0-1 **7f-8f: 4-15** 9f-13f: 0-0 14f+: 0-0
Track : **LH: 2-7** RH: 0-1 Tight: 1-2 Gall: 1-5
Aids: Bl: 0-0 Vi: 0-0 Tstrap: 0-0 Ckp: 0-0
Best Rating: **102** 2/09 Ndas 1m gd-fm

Smart; effective at around 7f-1m; acts on a sound surface; has worn a tongue tie.

Fusaichi Flyer (USA)

(91) (72)
2-y-o b/br g Fusaichi Pegasus (USA)-Songbook (Singspiel (IRE))
R Charlton Peter Webb

Placings:620 **(7859)**
2009: 7^{6}SD, 7^{2}SD, 7^{0}SD,

	Starts	1st	2nd	3rd	Win & Pl
Career Total (Turf)	0	0	0	0	
Career Total (AW)	3	0	1	0	964

Going (Turf): **Sf: 0-0 GS: 0-0 Gd: 0-0 GF: 0-0 Fm: 0-0**
Distance: 5f/6f: 0-0 7f-8f: 0-3 9f-13f: 0-0 14f+: 0-0
Track : LH: 0-3 RH: 0-0 Tight: 0-3 Gall: 0-0
Aids: Bl: 0-0 Vi: 0-0 Tstrap: 0-0 Ckp: 0-0
Best Rating: **72** 12/09 Wolv 7f32y stand

Modest; stays 7f; acts on Polytrack; sure to win a race.

Fusenam

76(92) (63)**43**
2-y-o b g Refuse To Bend (IRE)-Namat (IRE) (Daylami (IRE))
Miss J A Camacho G B Turnbull Ltd

Placings:600 **(7400)**
2009: 8^{6}G, 8^{0}GS, 9^{0}SD,

	Starts	1st	2nd	3rd	Win & Pl
Career Total (Turf)	2	0	0	0	0
Career Total (AW)	1	0	0	0	

Going (Turf): **Sf: 0-0 GS: 0-1 Gd: 0-1 GF: 0-0 Fm: 0-0**
Distance: 5f/6f: 0-0 7f-8f: 0-2 9f-13f: 0-1 14f+: 0-0
Track : LH: 0-3 RH: 0-0 Tight: 0-2 Gall: 0-1
Aids: Bl: 0-0 Vi: 0-0 Tstrap: 0-0 Ckp: 0-0
Best Rating: **63** 11/09 Wolv 1m1f103y stand

Future Gem

99 **67**
3-y-o b f Bertolini (USA)-Georgianna (IRE) (Petardia)
A Dickman Coast To Coast

Placings:000343-0015022511220 **(6824)**
2009: 6^{0}GF, 6^{0}GF, 5^{1}G, 5^{6}GF, 5^{0}GF, 6^{2}G, 5^{2}S, 5^{5}GF, 5^{1}GS, 6^{1}S, 5^{2}S, 6^{2}G, 7^{0}GF,

	Starts	1st	2nd	3rd	Win & Pl
Career Total (Turf)	19	3	4	2	10805

67	8/09	Ayr	6f	(0-60)H	SFT	£2388
59	8/09	Carl	5f193y	(0-55)H	G-S	£1942
55	5/09	Catt	5f		GD	£2388

Total win prize-money £6719

Going (Turf): **Sf: 1-6 GS: 1-1 Gd: 1-5** GF: 0-7 Fm: 0-0
Distance: **5f/6f: 3-16** 7f-8f: 0-3 9f-13f: 0-0 14f+: 0-0
Track : LH: 0-1 **RH: 1-1** Tight: 0-1 Gall: 0-0
Aids: Bl: 0-0 Vi: 0-0 Tstrap: 2-8 Ckp: 2-8
Best Rating: **67** 9/09 Haml 6f5y good

Moderate; stays 6f; acts on good and softer ground; has worn cheekpieces.

Future Regime (IRE)

80(87) (57)**29**
2-y-o b f Xaar-Sadalsud (IRE) (Shaadi (USA))
Patrick Morris Rob Lloyd Racing Limited

Placings:00355 **(7843)**
2009: 5^{0}SD, 5^{0}S, 5^{3}SD, 5^{5}SD, 5^{5}SD,

	Starts	1st	2nd	3rd	Win & Pl
Career Total (Turf)	1	0	0	0	
Career Total (AW)	4	0	0	1	433

Going (Turf): **Sf: 0-1 GS: 0-0 Gd: 0-0 GF: 0-0 Fm: 0-0**
Distance: 5f/6f: 0-5 7f-8f: 0-0 9f-13f: 0-0 14f+: 0-0
Track : LH: 0-5 RH: 0-0 Tight: 0-5 Gall: 0-0
Aids: Bl: 0-0 Vi: 0-0 Tstrap: 0-0 Ckp: 0-0
Best Rating: **57** 11/09 Wolv 5f20y stand

Futurist

92 **79**
2-y-o b c Halling (USA)-Crystal Gazing (USA) (El Gran Senor (USA))
Saeed Bin Suroor Godolphin

Placings:031 **(6533)**
2009: 7^{0}GF, 10^{3}F, 10^{1}GF,

	Starts	1st	2nd	3rd	Win & Pl
Career Total (Turf)	3	1	0	1	5566

79	10/09	Pont	1m2f6y	G-F	£5180

Total win prize-money £5181

Going (Turf): Sf: 0-0 GS: 0-0 Gd: 0-0 **GF: 1-2** Fm: 0-1
Distance: 5f/6f: 0-0 7f-8f: 0-1 **9f-13f: 1-2** 14f+: 0-0
Track : **LH: 1-2** RH: 0-0 Tight: 0-1 Gall: 0-0
Aids: Bl: 0-0 Vi: 0-0 Tstrap: 0-0 Ckp: 0-0
Best Rating: **79** 10/09 Pont 1m2f6y gd-fm

Useful; stays 1m2f as a juvenile; handles quick ground.

Fuzzy Cat

90(100) (58)**48**
3-y-o b g Nayef (USA)-Curfew (Marju (IRE))
T D Barron Richard Barnes, Colin Aitken

Placings:6-00520103 **(7835)**
2009: 7^{0}G, 10^{0}G, 8^{5}GF, 6^{2}SD, 5^{0}GS, 6^{1}SD, 6^{0}GF, 6^{3}SD,

	Starts	1st	2nd	3rd	Win & Pl
Career Total (Turf)	6	0	0	0	0
Career Total (AW)	3	1	1	1	4067

55	8/09	Sthl	6f	(0-60)H	STD	£3043

Total win prize-money £3044

Going (Turf): **Sf: 0-1 GS: 0-1 Gd: 0-2 GF: 0-2 Fm: 0-0**
Distance: **5f/6f: 1-4** 7f-8f: 0-3 9f-13f: 0-2 14f+: 0-0

Track : LH: 1-3 RH: 0-3 Tight: 0-1 Gall: 0-1
Aids: Bl: 1-5 Vi: 0-0 Tstrap: 0-0 Ckp: 0-0
Best Rating: 58 12/09 Kemp 6f stand

Moderate; effective over 6f; acts on Fibresand and Polytrack; has worn blinkers; does not look an easy ride.

Fyelehk (IRE)

107(97) (64)**74**
3-y-o b g Kheleyf (USA)-Opalescent (IRE) (Polish Precedent (USA))
B R Millman The Links Partnership

Placings:5050-444153113001 **(6739)**
2009: 8^{4}SD, 5^{4}SD, 5^{4}SD, 6^{1}SD, 6^{5}GF, 6^{3}GF, 6^{1}F, 6^{1}G, 6^{3}G, 5^{0}GF, 5^{0}SD, 6^{1}GS,

	Starts	1st	2nd	3rd	Win & Pl
Career Total (Turf)	10	3	0	2	11310
Career Total (AW)	6	1	0	0	2408

74	10/09	Wind	6f	(0-70)H	G-S	£2388
69	7/09	Epsm	6f	(0-80)H	GD	£5180
67	7/09	Folk	6f	(0-70)H	FRM	£2729
64	4/09	Kemp	6f	(0-55)	STD	£2047

Total win prize-money £12346

Going (Turf): Sf: 0-1 GS: 1-1 Gd: 1-2 GF: 0-4 Fm: 1-2
Distance: 5f/6f: 4-14 7f-8f: 0-2 9f-13f: 0-0 14f+: 0-0
Track : LH: 1-5 RH: 1-3 Tight: 1-4 Gall: 1-2
Aids: Bl: 0-0 Vi: 0-0 Tstrap: 0-0 Ckp: 0-0
Best Rating: 74 10/09 Wind 6f gd-sft

Modest; stays 6f; acts on fast ground; goes on Polytrack.

Fyodor (IRE)

97(108) (103)**101**
8-y-o b g Fasliyev (USA)-Royale Figurine (IRE) (Dominion Royale)
P D Evans (C R Dore 20/5) R Piff

Placings:2312/06000400/211211/21200043/50500/364025 0030106000316631-006020606060600 **(6670)**
2009: 6^{0}SD, 5^{0}GF, 5^{6}SD, 6^{0}F, 6^{2}SD, 6^{0}GF, 5^{6}GF, 6^{0}GF, 5^{6}GF, 5^{0}G, 5^{6}SD, 5^{0}SD, 5^{0}SD,

	Starts	1st	2nd	3rd	Win & Pl
Career Total (Turf)	38	3	3	3	40688
Career Total (AW)	28	6	5	3	69951

86	12/08	Sthl	5f		STD	£2047
103	11/08	GrLe	6f	(0-95)H	STD	£7477
101	5/08	Hayd	5f	(0-105)H	G-F	£14571
109	2/06	Wolv	5f20y	(0-100)H	STD	£11217
103	1/06	Sthl	5f	(0-100)H	SF	£12954
92	12/05	Sthl	5f	(0-100)H	STD	£13381
87	10/05	Wolv	5f216y	(0-75)H	STD	£3419
80	10/05	Rdcr	5f	(0-70)H	G-F	£3710
83	8/03	Pont	5f	D	G-F	£8716

Total win prize-money £77494

Going (Turf): Sf: 0-2 GS: 0-4 Gd: 0-10 GF: 3-20 Fm: 0-2
Distance: 5f/6f: 9-63 7f-8f: 0-3 9f-13f: 0-0 14f+: 0-0
Track : LH: 4-24 RH: 0-1 Tight: 2-19 Gall: 1-6
Aids: Bl: 0-1 Vi: 1-12 Tstrap: 0-2 Ckp: 0-2
Best Rating: 109 2/06 Wolv 5f20y stand

Very useful; effective over 5f-6f; acts on fast ground and on sand; has worn blinkers, cheekpieces and a visor; can pull hard.

Fyodorovich (USA)

93 **57**
4-y-o b g Stravinsky (USA)-Omnia (USA) (Green Dancer (USA))
J S Wainwright Charles Wentworth

Placings:60010/00-0000400060 **(5730)**
2009: 8^{0}GF, 9^{0}GF, 7^{0}G, 5^{0}GF, 8^{4}G, 7^{0}GF, 8^{0}GF, 6^{0}GF, 8^{6}G, 8^{0}GS,

	Starts	1st	2nd	3rd	Win & Pl
Career Total (Turf)	17	1	0	0	4534

76	8/07	Thsk	6f	G-F	£4533

Total win prize-money £4534

Going (Turf): Sf: 0-0 GS: 0-2 Gd: 0-4 GF: 1-11 Fm: 0-0
Distance: 5f/6f: 1-7 7f-8f: 0-9 9f-13f: 0-1 14f+: 0-0
Track : LH: 0-7 RH: 0-2 Tight: 0-5 Gall: 0-1
Aids: Bl: 0-2 Vi: 1-5 Tstrap: 0-0 Ckp: 0-0
Best Rating: 76 8/07 Thsk 6f gd-fm

Modest; effective at 6f; acts on fast ground; has worn cheekpieces and a visor.

Gabriel's Spirit (IRE)

76 **56**
2-y-o b c Invincible Spirit (IRE)-Over Rating (Desert King (IRE))
Miss Amy Weaver Ms Aine Brodbin

Placings:040 (5527)
2009: 6^{0}G, 6^{4}GF, 7^{0}G,

	Starts	1st	2nd	3rd	Win & Pl
Career Total (Turf)	3	0	0	0	385

Going (Turf): Sf: 0-0 GS: 0-0 Gd: 0-2 GF: 0-1 Fm: 0-0
Distance: 5f/6f: 0-2 7f-8f: 0-1 9f-13f: 0-0 14f+: 0-0
Track : LH: 0-1 RH: 0-0 Tight: 0-0 Gall: 0-0
Aids: Bl: 0-0 Vi: 0-0 Tstrap: 0-0 Ckp: 0-0
Best Rating: 56 8/09 NmkJ 6f gd-fm

Gaditana

85 **26**
3-y-o b f Rainbow Quest (USA)-Armeria (USA) (Northern Dancer (CAN))
Pat Eddery K Abdulla

Placings:0 **(6934)**
2009: 10^{0}G,

	Starts	1st	2nd	3rd	Win & Pl
Career Total (Turf)	1	0	0	0	

Going (Turf): Sf: 0-0 GS: 0-0 Gd: 0-1 GF: 0-0 Fm: 0-0
Distance: 5f/6f: 0-0 7f-8f: 0-0 9f-13f: 0-1 14f+: 0-0
Track : LH: 0-1 RH: 0-0 Tight: 0-1 Gall: 0-0
Aids: Bl: 0-0 Vi: 0-0 Tstrap: 0-0 Ckp: 0-0
Best Rating: 26 10/09 Bath 1m2f46y good

Gadobout Dancer

75 **25**
2-y-o b f Tobougg (IRE)-Delta Tempo (IRE) (Bluebird (USA))
I W McInnes In Memory of the Late Lol Cussons

Placings:000 **(6389)**
2009: 7^{0}G, 7^{0}GF, 8^{0}GF,

	Starts	1st	2nd	3rd	Win & Pl
Career Total (Turf)	3	0	0	0	

Going (Turf): Sf: 0-0 GS: 0-0 Gd: 0-1 GF: 0-2 Fm: 0-0
Distance: 5f/6f: 0-0 7f-8f: 0-2 9f-13f: 0-1 14f+: 0-0
Track : LH: 0-1 RH: 0-2 Tight: 0-0 Gall: 0-0
Aids: Bl: 0-0 Vi: 0-0 Tstrap: 0-1 Ckp: 0-1
Best Rating: 25 9/09 Nott 1m75y gd-fm

Gaelic Rose (IRE)

83(90) (49)**43**
3-y-o b f King Charlemagne (USA)-Harry's Irish Rose (USA) (Sir Harry Lewis (USA))
S Kirk J C Smith

Placings:0-005 **(3157)**
2009: 10^{0}G, 10^{0}GF, 12^{5}SD,

	Starts	1st	2nd	3rd	Win & Pl
Career Total (Turf)	2	0	0	0	
Career Total (AW)	2	0	0	0	0

Going (Turf): Sf: 0-0 GS: 0-0 Gd: 0-1 GF: 0-1 Fm: 0-0
Distance: 5f/6f: 0-0 7f-8f: 0-1 9f-13f: 0-3 14f+: 0-0
Track : LH: 0-3 RH: 0-1 Tight: 0-3 Gall: 0-1
Aids: Bl: 0-0 Vi: 0-0 Tstrap: 0-0 Ckp: 0-0
Best Rating: 49 12/08 GrLe 1m stand

Gaia Prince (USA)

101 **81**
4-y-o b/br g Forestry (USA)-Castlebrook (USA) (Montbrook (USA))
Mrs A J Perrett John Connolly

Placings:5/240-3230 **(2931)**
2009: 9^{3}GF, 10^{2}GF, 12^{3}GF, 14^{0}G,

	Starts	1st	2nd	3rd	Win & Pl
Career Total (Turf)	8	0	2	2	3996

Going (Turf): Sf: 0-0 GS: 0-0 Gd: 0-3 GF: 0-5 Fm: 0-0
Distance: 5f/6f: 0-0 7f-8f: 0-1 9f-13f: 0-6 14f+: 0-1
Track : LH: 0-1 RH: 0-5 Tight: 0-4 Gall: 0-1
Aids: Bl: 0-0 Vi: 0-0 Tstrap: 0-0 Ckp: 0-0
Best Rating: 81 5/09 NmkR 1m2f gd-fm

Fair; effective at 1m2f; acts on fast ground.

Gaily Noble (IRE)

101(104) (84)**86**
3-y-o b c One Cool Cat (USA)-Dream Genie (Puissance)
A B Haynes Athos Racing

Placings:42-1225245414460 **(7759)**
2009: 8^{1}SD, 10^{2}SD, 9^{2}GF, 8^{5}GF, 8^{2}F, 10^{4}F, 8^{5}SD, 9^{4}G, 9^{1}SD, 8^{4}SD, 8^{4}SD, 8^{6}SD, 8^{0}SD,

	Starts	1st	2nd	3rd	Win & Pl
Career Total (Turf)	5	0	2	0	4151
Career Total (AW)	10	2	2	0	9220

79	10/09	Wolv	1m1f103y	STD	£2388
74	2/09	Wolv	1m141y	STD	£2590

Total win prize-money £4978

Going (Turf): Sf: 0-0 GS: 0-0 Gd: 0-1 GF: 0-2 Fm: 0-2
Distance: 5f/6f: 0-0 7f-8f: 0-5 9f-13f: 2-10 14f+: 0-0
Track : LH: 2-9 RH: 0-5 Tight: 2-8 Gall: 0-0
Aids: Bl: 0-0 Vi: 0-0 Tstrap: 0-0 Ckp: 0-0
Best Rating: 86 5/09 Wwck 1m22y firm

Useful; stays 1m2f; acts fast ground and on Polytrack; likes to race prominently.

Gainshare

(103) (72)**68**

4-y-o b g Lend A Hand-Red Shareef (Marju (IRE))

Mrs R A Carr David W Chapman

Placings:46631/50254000120-553 **(0691)**

2009: 5^{5}SD, 6^{5}SD, 5^{3}SD,

	Starts	1st	2nd	3rd	Win & Pl
Career Total (Turf)	10	0	1	1	1902
Career Total (AW)	9	2	1	1	7282

67	11/08	Wolv	5f216y	(0-70)H	STD	£3885
72	11/07	Wolv	5f216y	(0-65)	STD	£2047

Total win prize-money £5934

Going (Turf): Sf: 0-1 GS: 0-0 Gd: 0-6 GF: 0-3 Fm: 0-0
Distance: 5f/6f: 2-17 7f-8f: 0-2 9f-13f: 0-0 14f+: 0-0
Track : LH: 2-11 RH: 0-1 Tight: 2-9 Gall: 0-1
Aids: Bl: 0-0 Vi: 0-0 Tstrap: 0-0 Ckp: 0-0
Best Rating: 72 11/07 Wolv 5f216y stand

Modest; effective over sprint distances; acts on Polytrack; can be headstrong.

Gala Casino Star (IRE)

106(104) (89)**93**

4-y-o ch g Dr Fong (USA)-Abir (Soviet Star (USA))

R A Fahey The Friar Tuck Racing Club

Placings:0520/0110110500-0452364230223 **(7560)**

2009: 8^{0}SD, 10^{4}GF, 9^{5}GF, 8^{2}GF, 9^{3}GS, 8^{6}GF, 8^{4}S, 8^{2}GS, 8^{3}GF, 10^{0}GF, 8^{2}G, 10^{2}S, 8^{3}SD,

	Starts	1st	2nd	3rd	Win & Pl
Career Total (Turf)	24	4	5	2	32785
Career Total (AW)	3	0	0	1	2099

91	7/08	York	1m208y	(0-85)H	G-F	£5180
89	7/08	Bevl	1m100y	(0-80)H	G-S	£5180
76	5/08	Newc	1m3y	(0-85)H	G-F	£4857
73	5/08	Rdcr	1m1f	(0-75)H	G-F	£2331

Total win prize-money £17550

Going (Turf): Sf: 0-3 GS: 1-4 Gd: 0-5 GF: 3-12 Fm: 0-0
Distance: 5f/6f: 0-3 7f-8f: 0-10 9f-13f: 4-14 14f+: 0-0
Track : LH: 2-12 RH: 1-8 Tight: 1-8 Gall: 1-4
Aids: Bl: 0-1 Vi: 0-1 Tstrap: 0-0 Ckp: 0-0
Best Rating: 93 10/09 Nott 1m2f50y soft

Useful; stays 1m1f; acts on most ground.

Gala Evening

96(111) (99)**96**

7-y-o b g Daylami (IRE)-Balleta (USA) (Lyphard (USA))

J A B Old W E Sturt

Placings:402/10/116-204 **(2994)**

2009: 16^{2}SD, 18^{0}GF, 20^{4}GF,

	Starts	1st	2nd	3rd	Win & Pl
Career Total (Turf)	7	0	1	0	4928
Career Total (AW)	4	3	1	0	14692

99	4/08	Kemp	2m	(0-85)H	STD	£4209
92	4/08	Kemp	2m	(0-85)H	STD	£4209
84	5/07	Kemp	2m	(0-75)H	STD	£2914

Total win prize-money £11333

Going (Turf): Sf: 0-0 GS: 0-3 Gd: 0-1 GF: 0-3 Fm: 0-0
Distance: 5f/6f: 0-0 7f-8f: 0-0 9f-13f: 0-3 14f+: 3-8
Track : LH: 0-4 RH: 3-7 Tight: 0-3 Gall: 0-3
Aids: Bl: 0-0 Vi: 0-0 Tstrap: 0-0 Ckp: 0-0
Best Rating: 99 3/09 Kemp 2m stand

Useful; suited by 2m; acts on most ground; goes on Polytrack.

Gala Sunday (USA)

103 (52)**67**

9-y-o b g Lear Fan (USA)-Sunday Bazaar (USA) (Nureyev (USA))

M W Easterby Steve Hull

Placings:22/125100/0000606000/0302050/10441101140 0/06400336612/000022542-0000120565 **(6817)**

2009: 10^{0}GF, 10^{0}F, 10^{0}F, 9^{0}G, 10^{1}GF, 9^{2}GF, 9^{0}GF, 10^{5}GF, 10^{6}GF, 10^{5}GF,

	Starts	1st	2nd	3rd	Win & Pl
Career Total (Turf)	64	8	9	3	48994
Career Total (AW)	4	1	0	0	1536

62	6/09	Pont	1m2f6y	(0-70)H		G-F	£3123
63	10/07	Rdcr	1m2f	(0-60)H		GD	£1977
74	8/06	Yarm	1m2f21y	(0-65)H		G-F	£2186
76	8/06	Bevl	1m1f207y	(0-75)H		G-S	£3578
68	7/06	Bevl	1m1f207y	(0-55)H		G-F	£3123
67	7/06	Nott	1m1f213y	(0-60)H		FRM	£2637
52	5/06	Wolv	1m141y	(0-45)		STD	£1535
100	7/03	Haml	1m1f36y		C	G-F	£10590
73	4/03	Pont	1m2f6yE			G-F	£4114

Total win prize-money £32867

Going (Turf): Sf: 0-10 GS: 1-7 Gd: 1-15GF: 5-25 Fm: 1-6
Distance: 5f/6f: 0-0 7f-8f: 0-7 9f-13f: 9-61 14f+: 0-0
Track : LH: 6-39 RH: 3-26 Tight: 4-20 Gall: 0-7
Aids: Bl: 7-33 Vi: 0-0 Tstrap: 0-0 Ckp: 0-0
Best Rating: 103 4/03 Epsm 1m2f18y good

Moderate; stays 1m4f; acts on fast and soft ground; has worn blinkers.

Galachiya

86 **68**

2-y-o ch f Gulch (USA)-Empress Anna (IRE) (Imperial Ballet (IRE))

C E Brittain Saeed Manana

Placings:0 **(4257)**

2009: 6^{0}G,

	Starts	1st	2nd	3rd	Win & Pl
Career Total (Turf)	1	0	0	0	

Going (Turf): Sf: 0-0 GS: 0-0 Gd: 0-1 GF: 0-0 Fm: 0-0
Distance: 5f/6f: 0-1 7f-8f: 0-0 9f-13f: 0-0 14f+: 0-0
Track : LH: 0-0 RH: 0-0 Tight: 0-0 Gall: 0-0
Aids: Bl: 0-0 Vi: 0-0 Tstrap: 0-0 Ckp: 0-0
Best Rating: 68 7/09 Asct 6f good

Galatian

96 **72**

2-y-o ch g Traditionally (USA)-Easy To Imagine (USA) (Cozzene (USA))

B R Millman Tarka Racing

Placings:045 **(7058)**

2009: 7^{0}GF, 6^{4}G, 5^{5}GF,

	Starts	1st	2nd	3rd	Win & Pl
Career Total (Turf)	3	0	0	0	361

Going (Turf): Sf: 0-0 GS: 0-0 Gd: 0-1 GF: 0-2 Fm: 0-0
Distance: 5f/6f: 0-1 7f-8f: 0-2 9f-13f: 0-0 14f+: 0-0
Track : LH: 0-0 RH: 0-0 Tight: 0-0 Gall: 0-0
Aids: Bl: 0-0 Vi: 0-0 Tstrap: 0-0 Ckp: 0-0
Best Rating: 72 10/09 Leic 5f218y gd-fm

Galeota (IRE)

98(95) (80)**102**

7-y-o b g Mujadil (USA)-Refined (IRE) (Statoblest)

R Hannon R Hannon

Placings:415511/31200/21312031/004010000-0600 **(5900)**

2009: 6^{0}GF, 5^{6}S, 6^{0}S, 5^{0}F,

	Starts	1st	2nd	3rd	Win & Pl
Career Total (Turf)	30	8	3	3	226235
Career Total (AW)	2	0	0	0	

102	9/08	Donc	5f		SFT	£26667
112	11/07	Donc	6f		G-F	£23708
111	9/07	Donc	5f		G-F	£17781
107	8/07	Nott	5f13y		GD	£6232
115	6/05	Epsm	7f		GD	£17400
111	9/04	Newb	6f8y		G-S	£40600
103	9/04	Donc	6f		FRM	£6609
87	7/04	Wind	6f	D	G-S	£5382

Total win prize-money £144379

Going (Turf): Sf: 1-5 GS: 2-6 Gd: 2-7 GF: 2-8 Fm: 1-4
Distance: 5f/6f: 6-27 7f-8f: 2-5 9f-13f: 0-0 14f+: 0-0
Track : LH: 1-4 RH: 0-1 Tight: 1-1 Gall: 1-4
Aids: Bl: 0-0 Vi: 0-0 Tstrap: 0-1 Ckp: 0-1
Best Rating: 117 6/05 York 6f firm

Smart; winner in Listed company and Group placed; gelded after proving to be infertile at stud and returned to action in 2007, effective at 5-7f; acts on any ground; has worn cheekpieces; has a fine record at Doncaster.

Galient (IRE)

87 (97)**90**

6-y-o b g Galileo (IRE)-Endorsement (Warning)

N J Henderson Mr & Mrs Kevan Watts

Placings:0/11250/30040/0-0 **(2994)**

2009: 20^{0}GF,

	Starts	1st	2nd	3rd	Win & Pl
Career Total (Turf)	12	2	1	0	30178
Career Total (AW)	1	0	0	1	1493

101	5/06	Ches	1m4f66y	(0-95)H	G-F	£10039
98	4/06	NmkR	1m4f		G-F	£5181

Total win prize-money £15221

Going (Turf): Sf: 0-0 GS: 0-2 Gd: 0-3 GF: 2-7 Fm: 0-0
Distance: 5f/6f: 0-0 7f-8f: 0-1 9f-13f: 2-3 14f+: 0-9
Track : LH: 1-6 RH: 1-6 Tight: 1-3 Gall: 1-7
Aids: Bl: 0-0 Vi: 0-0 Tstrap: 0-1 Ckp: 0-1
Best Rating: 105 8/06 Newb 1m5f61y gd-sft

Useful; winning hurdler; stays 2m; acts on fast ground; also goes on Polytrack; has worn cheekpieces.

Galilean Moon

102(100) (60)**77**

3-y-o b f Galileo (IRE)-Fascinating Rhythm (Slip Anchor)

Sir Michael Stoute D Smith, Mrs J Magnier, M Tabor

Placings:63150 **(5837)**

2009: 10^{6}G, 12^{3}GF, 12^{1}G, 12^{5}GF, 13^{0}SD,

	Starts	1st	2nd	3rd	Win & Pl
Career Total (Turf)	4	1	0	1	5662
Career Total (AW)	1	0	0	0	

77	7/09	NmkJ	1m4f	GD	£5180

Total win prize-money £5181

Going (Turf): Sf: 0-0 GS: 0-0 Gd: 1-2 GF: 0-2 Fm: 0-0
Distance: 5f/6f: 0-0 7f-8f: 0-0 9f-13f: 1-4 14f+: 0-1
Track : LH: 0-2 RH: 1-3 Tight: 0-2 Gall: 1-1
Aids: Bl: 0-0 Vi: 0-0 Tstrap: 0-0 Ckp: 0-0
Best Rating: 77 7/09 NmkJ 1m4f good

Fair; stays 1m4f; acts on fast and easy ground.

Galiotto (IRE)

99(91) (55)58

3-y-o b g Galileo (IRE)-Welsh Motto (USA) (Mtoto)

C F Wall Archangels 2

Placings:6062253 **(6457)**

2009: 10^6GF, 10^0GF, 11^6GF, 11^2G, 11^2G, 12^5SD, 13^3SD,

	Starts	1st	2nd	3rd	Win & Pl
Career Total (Turf)	5	0	2	0	1233
Career Total (AW)	2	0	0	1	403

Going (Turf): **Sf: 0-0 GS: 0-0 Gd: 0-2 GF: 0-3 Fm: 0-0**
Distance: 5f/6f: 0-0 7f-8f: 0-0 9f-13f: 0-6 14f+: 0-1
Track : LH: 0-4 RH: 0-2 Tight: 0-5 Gall: 0-0
Aids: Bl: 0-0 Vi: 0-0 Tstrap: 0-0 Ckp: 0-0
Best Rating: **58** 8/09 Yarm 1m3f101y good

Moderate handicapper; stays 1m4f; acts on good ground.

Gallagher

107 115

3-y-o ch c Bahamian Bounty-Roo (Rudimentary (USA))

B J Meehan Brimacombe, McNally, Rickman & Sangster

Placings:612224-4105 **(5024)**

2009: 7^4GF, 7^1GF, 8^0S, 7^5GF,

	Starts	1st	2nd	3rd	Win & Pl
Career Total (Turf)	10	2	3	0	122948
108 7/09 Newb 7f				G-F	£7477
88 7/08 Chep 6f16y				G-F	£3561

Total win prize-money £11039

Going (Turf): Sf: 0-1 GS: 0-1 Gd: 0-2 **GF: 2-6** Fm: 0-0
Distance: 5f/6f: 0-3 **7f-8f: 2-7** 9f-13f: 0-0 14f+: 0-0
Track : LH: 0-0 RH: 0-2 Tight: 0-0 Gall: 0-0
Aids: Bl: 0-0 Vi: 0-0 Tstrap: 0-0 Ckp: 0-0
Best Rating: **115** 8/08 Deau 6f gd-sft

Group class; runner-up in the Richmond, Prix Morny and Mill Reef Stakes at two; stays 7f and acts on most ground.

Gallant Eagle (IRE)

95(92) (79)78

2-y-o ch c Hawk Wing (USA)-Generous Gesture (IRE) (Fasliyev (USA))

S Kirk J C Smith

Placings:46431 **(6071)**

2009: 6^4GF, 6^6GF, 6^4GF, 7^3F, 7^1SD,

	Starts	1st	2nd	3rd	Win & Pl
Career Total (Turf)	4	0	0	1	1131
Career Total (AW)	1	1	0	0	3562
79 9/09 Wolv 7f32y (0-75)H				STD	£3561

Total win prize-money £3562

Going (Turf): **Sf: 0-0 GS: 0-0 Gd: 0-0 GF: 0-3 Fm: 0-1**
Distance: 5f/6f: 0-2 **7f-8f: 1-3** 9f-13f: 0-0 14f+: 0-0
Track : **LH: 1-1** RH: 0-0 **Tight: 1-1** Gall: 0-1
Aids: Bl: 0-0 Vi: 0-0 Tstrap: 0-0 Ckp: 0-0
Best Rating: **79** 9/09 Wolv 7f32y stand

Fair; stays 7f; goes on Polytrack.

Gallantian (IRE)

(103) (50)29

7-y-o gr g Turtle Island (IRE)-Galletina (IRE) (Persian Heights)

David Anthony O'Brien Brendan Cawley

Placings:0001/4036/0/30-000 **(5560a)**

2009: 12^0SD, 12^0SD, 7^0SD,

	Starts	1st	2nd	3rd	Win & Pl
Career Total (Turf)	8	0	0	1	1050
Career Total (AW)	6	1	0	1	1762
64 11/04 Wolv 1m1f103y				STD	£1459

Total win prize-money £1460

Going (Turf): **Sf: 0-2 GS: 0-0 Gd: 0-3 GF: 0-2 Fm: 0-0**
Distance: 5f/6f: 0-0 7f-8f: 0-4 **9f-13f: 1-6** 14f+: 0-4
Track : **LH: 1-8** RH: 0-4 **Tight: 1-5** Gall: 0-0
Aids: Bl: 0-0 Vi: 0-0 Tstrap: 0-0 Ckp: 0-0
Best Rating: **75** 8/05 Tral 1m4f yld-sft

Moderate gelding; stays 2m and acts on fast ground and Polytrack.

Gallantry

103(116) (94)91

7-y-o b g Green Desert (USA)-Gay Gallanta (USA) (Woodman (USA))

P Howling The Circle Bloodstock I Limited

Placings:0104/2000510000/441440002402005016/22230 0002106020062100343-6611605020055004005 **(7883)**

2009: 8^6SD, 8^6SD, 7^1SD, 8^1SD, 7^6SD, 7^0F, 8^5GF, 7^0GF, 7^2GF, 8^0SD, 7^0G, 7^5SD, 7^5SD, 8^0SF, 7^0SD, 7^4SD, 7^0SD, 7^0SD, 8^5SD,

	Starts	1st	2nd	3rd	Win & Pl
Career Total (Turf)	37	3	6	0	30721
Career Total (AW)	39	5	4	3	48042
94 2/09 Wolv 1m141y (0-85)H				STD	£4727
90 2/09 Ling 7f (0-85)H				STD	£4857
92 10/08 Ling 7f (0-95)H				STD	£7641
88 6/08 Wwck 7f26y (0-80)H				G-F	£4857
93 10/07 Wolv 7f32y (0-85)H				STD	£4728
91 2/07 Ling 1m (0-95)H				STD	£7478
91 7/06 York 7f (0-85)H				G-F	£6800
74 6/05 Wwck 7f26y				G-F	£3692

Total win prize-money £44782

Going (Turf): Sf: 0-0 GS: 0-2 Gd: 0-12 **GF: 3-20** Fm: 0-3
Distance: 5f/6f: 0-5 **7f-8f: 7-65** 9f-13f: 1-6 14f+: 0-0
Track : **LH: 8-51** RH: 0-11 **Tight: 5-43** Gall: 1-4
Aids: Bl: 0-0 Vi: 0-0 Tstrap: 0-0 Ckp: 0-0
Best Rating: **96** 3/08 Ling 7f stand

Fair; effective over 7f-1m; acts on good and faster ground; goes on Polytrack.

Gallego

99 (62)75

7-y-o br g Danzero (AUS)-Shafir (IRE) (Shaadi (USA))

R J Price My Left Foot Racing Syndicate

Placings:000/004021106222000/0002110000341250150 002033000/46565322145201000/063061256100-06500110266 **(6392)**

2009: 11^0G, 10^6F, 10^5GF, 10^0GF, 10^0GF, 6^1GF, 8^1GF, 10^0G, 8^2GS, 8^6GF, 10^6GF,

	Starts	1st	2nd	3rd	Win & Pl
Career Total (Turf)	62	9	10	2	44136
Career Total (AW)	25	4	2	3	10247
70 7/09 Sals 1m (0-75)H				G-F	£3123
66 6/09 Sals 6f212y (0-65)H				G-F	£2935
73 9/08 Sand 1m2f7y (0-80)H				GD	£6476
68 7/08 Sals 1m (0-75)H				G-F	£3123
70 10/07 Bath 1m2f46y (0-65)H				G-F	£2590
66 8/07 Sals 1m (0-70)H				G-F	£3123
68 7/06 Nott 1m1f213y (0-80)H				FRM	£6477
65 6/06 Hayd 1m2f120y (0-65)H				G-F	£2307
58 3/06 Wolv 1m1f103y (0-45)				STD	£1535
55 3/06 Wolv 1m1f103y (0-60)H				STD	£2047
55 6/05 Wolv 1m141y (0-55)H				STD	£3038
53 5/05 Nott 1m1f213y (0-45)				GD	£1515
51 4/05 Ling 1m (0-40)				STD	£1284

Total win prize-money £39580

Going (Turf): Sf: 0-9 GS: 0-7 Gd: 2-15 **GF: 6-27** Fm: 1-4
Distance: 5f/6f: 0-3 7f-8f: 5-12 **9f-13f: 8-72** 14f+: 0-0
Track : **LH: 8-68** RH: 1-8 **Tight: 5-35** Gall: 0-9
Aids: Bl: 0-1 Vi: 0-1 Tstrap: 0-0 Ckp: 0-0
Best Rating: **75** 9/09 Sals 1m gd-sft

Modest; stays 1m2f; acts on most ground on turf; also goes on Polytrack.

Galley Slave (IRE)

68(95) (62)29

4-y-o b g Spartacus (IRE)-Cimeterre (IRE) (Arazi (USA))

M C Chapman K D Blanch

Placings:4006000000003602/60500-030 **(4519)**

2009: 10^0SD, 12^3SD, 10^0S,

	Starts	1st	2nd	3rd	Win & Pl
Career Total (Turf)	15	0	0	0	241
Career Total (AW)	9	0	1	2	1345

Going (Turf): **Sf: 0-6 GS: 0-1 Gd: 0-5 GF: 0-3 Fm: 0-0**
Distance: 5f/6f: 0-10 7f-8f: 0-10 9f-13f: 0-4 14f+: 0-0
Track : LH: 0-8 RH: 0-1 Tight: 0-2 Gall: 0-3
Aids: Bl: 0-1 Vi: 0-0 Tstrap: 0-0 Ckp: 0-0
Best Rating: **62** 11/07 Wolv 7f32y stand

Moderate gelding; seems to handle most ground; stays 7f.

Gallic Star (IRE)

102 99

2-y-o b f Galileo (IRE)-Oman Sea (USA) (Rahy (USA))

M R Channon Jon and Julia Aisbitt

Placings:014541 **(6898)**

2009: 6^0GF, 5^1GF, 7^4GF, 7^5G, 8^4GF, 8^1GF,

	Starts	1st	2nd	3rd	Win & Pl
Career Total (Turf)	6	2	0	0	31007
93 10/09 Pont 1m4y				G-F	£19869
84 6/09 Leic 5f218y				G-F	£3885

Total win prize-money £23756

Going (Turf): Sf: 0-0 GS: 0-0 Gd: 0-1 **GF: 2-5** Fm: 0-0
Distance: 5f/6f: 1-2 7f-8f: 0-3 9f-13f: 1-1 14f+: 0-0
Track : **LH: 1-1** RH: 0-1 Tight: 0-0 Gall: 0-0
Aids: Bl: 0-0 Vi: 0-0 Tstrap: 0-0 Ckp: 0-0
Best Rating: **99** 9/09 Donc 1m gd-fm

Very useful sister to Racer Forever; effective at 6-7f; acts on fast ground.

Galpin Junior (USA)

104(79) (52)102

3-y-o ch g Hennessy (USA)-Reluctant Diva (Sadler's Wells (USA))

B J Meehan Roldvale Limited

Placings:3100-600 **(6949)**

2009: 6^6GF, 6^0GF, 6^0SD,

	Starts	1st	2nd	3rd	Win & Pl
Career Total (Turf)	6	1	0	1	3805
Career Total (AW)	1	0	0	0	
84 8/08 Folk 6f				G-F	£2590

Total win prize-money £2590

Going (Turf): Sf: 0-0 GS: 0-0 Gd: 0-1 **GF: 1-5** Fm: 0-0
Distance: **5f/6f: 1-6** 7f-8f: 0-1 9f-13f: 0-0 14f+: 0-0
Track : LH: 0-1 RH: 0-0 Tight: 0-0 Gall: 0-0
Aids: Bl: 0-1 Vi: 0-0 Tstrap: 0-0 Ckp: 0-0
Best Rating: 102 10/08 NmkR 6f gd-fm

Smart; stays 6f and acts on fast ground.

Gambling Jack

92(101) (56)**61**
4-y-o b g First Trump-Star Of Flanders (Puissance)
A W Carroll D Lowe

Placings:0/5600**656**-**40**606 (2534)
2009: 7^{4}SD, 8^{0}SD, 6^{6}GF, 8^{0}G, 5^{6}GF,

	Starts	1st	2nd	3rd	Win & Pl
Career Total (Turf)	7	0	0	0	0
Career Total (AW)	6	0	0	0	0

Going (Turf): Sf: 0-1 GS: 0-0 Gd: 0-2 GF: 0-3 Fm: 0-1
Distance: 5f/6f: 0-6 7f-8f: 0-5 9f-13f: 0-2 14f+: 0-0
Track : LH: 0-8 RH: 0-1 Tight: 0-4 Gall: 0-0
Aids: Bl: 0-1 Vi: 0-0 Tstrap: 0-0 Ckp: 0-0
Best Rating: 61 6/08 Wwck 7f26y firm

Moderate; possibly best at 6f; acts on fast ground.

Gambling Queen

81 **28**
2-y-o b f Zafeen (FR)-Pure Speculation (Salse (USA))
Mrs P Sly Mrs R F Knipe

Placings:0 (3248)
2009: 6^{0}GF,

	Starts	1st	2nd	3rd	Win & Pl
Career Total (Turf)	1	0	0	0	

Going (Turf): Sf: 0-0 GS: 0-0 Gd: 0-0 GF: 0-1 Fm: 0-0
Distance: 5f/6f: 0-0 7f-8f: 0-1 9f-13f: 0-0 14f+: 0-0
Track : LH: 0-0 RH: 0-0 Tight: 0-0 Gall: 0-0
Aids: Bl: 0-0 Vi: 0-0 Tstrap: 0-0 Ckp: 0-0
Best Rating: 28 6/09 Newb 6f8y gd-fm

Game Lad

101(77) (28)**89**
7-y-o b g Mind Games-Catch Me (Rudimentary (USA))
T D Easterby T D Easterby

Placings:34030214/0233043116/3400/0000150/03400100-04000 (6361)
2009: 7^{0}GF, 7^{4}GS, 7^{0}S, 7^{0}GS, 7^{0}SD,

	Starts	1st	2nd	3rd	Win & Pl
Career Total (Turf)	39	5	2	6	57452
Career Total (AW)	3	0	0	1	640

89 9/08 Ayr 7f50y (0-95)H HVY £11091
96 6/07 Newc 7f (0-100)H HVY £12464
100 10/05 NmkR 7f (0-85)H SFT £6058
91 10/05 Muss 7f30y (0-80)H GD £5948
73 11/04 Rdcr 7f SFT £4728
Total win prize-money £40291

Going (Turf): **Sf: 4-9** GS: 0-7 Gd: 1-12 GF: 0-10 Fm: 0-1
Distance: 5f/6f: 0-6 **7f-8f: 5-34** 9f-13f: 0-2 14f+: 0-0
Track : LH: 1-14 RH: 1-3 **Tight: 1-7** Gall: 0-4
Aids: Bl: 0-0 Vi: 0-0 Tstrap: 0-0 Ckp: 0-0
Best Rating: 100 10/05 NmkR 7f soft

Useful; effective over 7f, but stays 1m; acts on most ground but goes well in testing conditions; has worn a tongue tie.

Game Roseanna

100(86) (46)**60**
3-y-o b f Mind Games-Rosy Sunset (IRE) (Red Sunset)
W M Brisbourne Mrs C P Lees-Jones & W R Paton-Smith

Placings:03000-3666 (6919)
2009: 10^{3}S, 10^{6}G, 13^{6}GF, 11^{6}GF,

	Starts	1st	2nd	3rd	Win & Pl
Career Total (Turf)	8	0	0	2	1252
Career Total (AW)	1	0	0	0	

Going (Turf): Sf: 0-2 GS: 0-1 Gd: 0-3 GF: 0-2 Fm: 0-0
Distance: 5f/6f: 0-1 7f-8f: 0-3 9f-13f: 0-4 14f+: 0-1
Track : LH: 0-6 RH: 0-1 Tight: 0-5 Gall: 0-0
Aids: Bl: 0-0 Vi: 0-0 Tstrap: 0-0 Ckp: 0-0
Best Rating: 60 7/09 Hayd 1m2f95y soft

Modest efforts in maiden company; stays 7f.

Game Stalker (USA)

93 **79**
3-y-o b/br c Elusive Quality (USA)-Windsharp (USA) (Lear Fan (USA))
Saeed Bin Suroor Godolphin

Placings:41 (6189)
2009: 10^{4}GF, 9^{1}GF,

	Starts	1st	2nd	3rd	Win & Pl
Career Total (Turf)	2	1	0	0	2932

79 9/09 Folk 1m1f149y G-F £2729
Total win prize-money £2730

Going (Turf): Sf: 0-0 GS: 0-0 Gd: 0-0 **GF: 1-2** Fm: 0-0
Distance: 5f/6f: 0-0 7f-8f: 0-0 **9f-13f: 1-2** 14f+: 0-0
Track : LH: 0-1 **RH: 1-1 Tight: 1-1** Gall: 0-0
Aids: Bl: 0-0 Vi: 0-0 Tstrap: 0-0 Ckp: 0-0
Best Rating: 79 9/09 Folk 1m1f149y gd-fm

Fair; stays 1m2f; acts on fast ground.

Gamedor (FR)

(89) (42)**68**
4-y-o ch g Kendor (FR)-Garmeria (FR) (Kadrou (FR))
G L Moore (J-M Capitte 20/6) Mrs Elizabeth Kiernan

Placings:064000611121-3551400300 (6704)
2009: 12^{3}SD, 12^{5}SD, 12^{5}GS, 17^{1}, 13^{4}S, 15^{0}GS, 13^{0}GS, 12^{3}S, 11^{0}GS, 13^{0}SS,

	Starts	1st	2nd	3rd	Win & Pl
Career Total (Turf)	16	5	1	1	30724
Career Total (AW)	6	0	0	1	7127

3/09 Nime 2m1f £6796
11/08 Saln 1m4f GD £5514
Total win prize-money £24443

Going (Turf): Sf: 0-4 GS: 0-4 **Gd: 2-3** GF: 0-0 Fm: 0-0
Distance: 5f/6f: 0-0 7f-8f: 0-0 9f-13f: 2-17 **14f+: 3-5**
Track : LH: 0-1 RH: 0-1 Tight: 0-1 Gall: 0-0
Aids: Bl: 0-1 Vi: 0-0 Tstrap: 0-0 Ckp: 0-0
Best Rating: 68 4/09 Lonc 1m7f110y gd-sft

Gamegear

(70) (9)
4-y-o br f Tomba-Princess Of Hearts (Prince Sabo)
S R Bowring Charterhouse Holdings Plc

Placings:00 (0855)
2009: 7^{0}SD, 8^{0}SD,

	Starts	1st	2nd	3rd	Win & Pl
Career Total (Turf)	0	0	0	0	
Career Total (AW)	2	0	0	0	

Going (Turf): Sf: 0-0 GS: 0-0 Gd: 0-0 GF: 0-0 Fm: 0-0
Distance: 5f/6f: 0-0 7f-8f: 0-2 9f-13f: 0-0 14f+: 0-0
Track : LH: 0-2 RH: 0-0 Tight: 0-0 Gall: 0-0
Aids: Bl: 0-1 Vi: 0-0 Tstrap: 0-0 Ckp: 0-0

Games (IRE)

(50) **27**
8-y-o b g Lord Americo-Anns Run (Deep Run)
C N Kellett (P J Rothwell 11/10) K O Warner

Placings:0/0000060 (7842)
2009: 6^{0}SH, 8^{0}SD, 5^{0}SD, 7^{0}GF, 14^{0}G, 17^{6}Y, 14^{0}SS,

	Starts	1st	2nd	3rd	Win & Pl
Career Total (Turf)	4	0	0	0	
Career Total (AW)	4	0	0	0	

Going (Turf): Sf: 0-0 GS: 0-0 Gd: 0-1 GF: 0-1 Fm: 0-0
Distance: 5f/6f: 0-2 7f-8f: 0-3 9f-13f: 0-0 14f+: 0-3
Track : LH: 0-4 RH: 0-3 Tight: 0-0 Gall: 0-0
Aids: Bl: 0-1 Vi: 0-0 Tstrap: 0-2 Ckp: 0-2
Best Rating: 27 4/09 Cork 6f sft-hvy

Gamesters Lady

96(97) (66)**70**
6-y-o br m Almushtarak (IRE)-Tycoon Tina (Tina's Pet)
W M Brisbourne Gamesters Partnership

Placings:00125212050/5400/**201051**/4524-**6146**00306600 (4861)
2009: 12^{6}SD, 11^{1}SD, 12^{4}SD, 13^{6}SD, 11^{0}GF, 11^{0}F, 10^{3}GF, 12^{0}GF, 11^{6}GF, 10^{6}G, 10^{0}GS, 9^{0}SD,

	Starts	1st	2nd	3rd	Win & Pl
Career Total (Turf)	24	1	4	1	12370
Career Total (AW)	13	4	1	0	11960

66 2/09 Sthl 1m3f (0-75)H STD £2590
70 12/07 Wolv 1m4f50y (0-65)H STD £2218
69 11/07 Wolv 1m4f50y (0-65)H STD £2184
77 8/05 Wolv 7f32y STD £4110
66 5/05 Thsk 6f GD £4065
Total win prize-money £15169

Going (Turf): Sf: 0-4 GS: 0-2 **Gd: 1-5** GF: 0-12 Fm: 0-1
Distance: 5f/6f: 1-3 7f-8f: 1-7 **9f-13f: 3-25** 14f+: 0-2
Track : **LH: 4-29** RH: 0-5 **Tight: 3-24** Gall: 0-2
Aids: Bl: 0-3 Vi: 0-0 Tstrap: 0-3 Ckp: 0-3
Best Rating: 82 8/05 Ches 7f2y gd-fm

Moderate; stays 1m4f; acts on a sound surface, Polytrack and Fibresand.

Gan Amhras (IRE)

113 **119**
3-y-o b c Galileo (IRE)-All's Forgotten (USA) (Darshaan)
J S Bolger Mrs J S Bolger

Placings:312-3060 (6320a)
2009: 8^{3}GF, 12^{0}G, 12^{6}GY, 7^{0}G,

	Starts	1st	2nd	3rd	Win & Pl
Career Total (Turf)	7	1	1	2	280858

89 7/08 Naas 1m G-F £6605
Total win prize-money £6605

Going (Turf): Sf: 0-0 GS: 0-0 Gd: 0-3 **GF: 1-2** Fm: 0-0
Distance: 5f/6f: 0-0 **7f-8f: 1-5** 9f-13f: 0-2 14f+: 0-0
Track : **LH: 1-3** RH: 0-1 Tight: 0-1 Gall: 0-0
Aids: Bl: 0-0 Vi: 0-0 Tstrap: 0-0 Ckp: 0-0
Best Rating: **119** 5/09 NmkR 1m gd-fm

Smart; Irish trained; third in the 2000 Guineas in 2009 and runner-up in a valuable sales race at The Curragh at two; stays 1m; acts on fast and easy ground.

Gandalf

103(112) (77)71
7-y-o b g Sadler's Wells (USA)-Enchant (Lion Cavern (USA))
Miss Amy Weaver (J G Burns 23/7) Colm White

Placings:0106/23300/0510 **(6622)**
2009: 14^{0}YS, 14^{5}GF, 16^{1}SD, 16^{0}G,

	Starts	1st	2nd	3rd	Win & Pl
Career Total (Turf)	**9**	**0**	**1**	**1**	**3131**
Career Total (AW)	**4**	**2**	**0**	**1**	**7203**

77 9/09 Kemp 2m (0-70)H STD £2590
83 7/05 Wolv 1m4f50y STD £3649
Total win prize-money £6240

Going (Turf): **Sf: 0-1 GS: 0-2 Gd: 0-3 GF: 0-2 Fm: 0-0**
Distance: 5f/6f: 0-0 7f-8f: 0-0 9f-13f: 1-4 14f+: 1-9
Track : LH: 1-9 RH: 1-4 **Tight: 1-5** Gall: 0-2
Aids: Bl: 0-0 Vi: 0-0 Tstrap: 0-0 Ckp: 0-0
Best Rating: **83** 7/05 Wolv 1m4f50y stand

Fair; stays 2m; suited by good ground and Polytrack.

Gap Princess (IRE)

101(106) (79)76
5-y-o b m Noverre (USA)-Safe Care (IRE) (Caerleon (USA))
G A Harker (R A Fahey 30/6) Brian Morton

Placings:323240/556134500/0612215234-3302621051 **(7673)**
2009: 5^{3}F, 5^{3}GF, 7^{0}GF, 7^{2}F, 7^{6}GF, 6^{2}GS, 5^{1}GF, 6^{0}G, 5^{5}SD, 5^{1}SD,

	Starts	1st	2nd	3rd	Win & Pl
Career Total (Turf)	**30**	**4**	**7**	**5**	**21334**
Career Total (AW)	**5**	**1**	**0**	**1**	**4008**

79 12/09 Wolv 5f216y (0-70)H STD £3238
64 6/09 Haml 5f4y G-F £2047
74 7/08 Catt 7f (0-80)H G-F £4727
70 5/08 Carl 5f193y (0-70)H G-F £2590
Total win prize-money £12602

Going (Turf): Sf: 0-2 GS: 0-2 Gd: 1-12 **GF: 3-11** Fm: 0-3
Distance: **5f/6f: 4-19** 7f-8f: 1-16 9f-13f: 0-0 14f+: 0-0
Track : **LH: 2-9** RH: 1-4 **Tight: 2-7** Gall: 0-0
Aids: Bl: 0-0 Vi: 0-0 Tstrap: 0-0 Ckp: 0-0
Best Rating: **79** 12/09 Wolv 5f216y stand

Fair; effective over 5-7f; acts on fast and soft ground.

Garden Party

(104) (79)72
5-y-o b g Green Desert (USA)-Tempting Prospect (Shirley Heights)
T J Bougourd (R A Harris 27/2) T J & Mrs R M Bougourd

Placings:00546/134002000-26323441333
2009: 8^{2}SD, 8^{6}SD, 8^{3}SD, 8^{2}SD, 8^{3}GF, 8^{4}G, 10^{4}GF, 8^{1}F, 9^{3}GS, 12^{3}GF, 12^{3}F,

	Starts	1st	2nd	3rd	Win & Pl
Career Total (Turf)	**13**	**1**	**1**	**4**	**3082**
Career Total (AW)	**12**	**1**	**2**	**2**	**4739**

6/09 LesL 1m100y H FRM £600
76 1/08 Ling 1m STD £2331
Total win prize-money £2932

Going (Turf): Sf: 0-1 GS: 0-2 Gd: 0-1 GF: 0-6 **Fm: 1-3**
Distance: 5f/6f: 0-0 7f-8f: 1-12 9f-13f: 1-13 14f+: 0-0
Track : **LH: 2-16** RH: 0-5 **Tight: 1-10** Gall: 0-0
Aids: **Bl: 1-6** Vi: 0-0 Tstrap: 0-3 Ckp: 0-3
Best Rating: **79** 2/08 Ling 1m stand

Modest; effective over 1m; acts on fast ground; goes on Polytrack.

Gardening Leave

100 91
2-y-o b c Selkirk (USA)-Misty Waters (IRE) (Caerleon (USA))
A M Balding Another Bottle Racing 2

Placings:016 **(7404a)**
2009: 8^{0}GF, 8^{1}S, 10^{6}HY,

	Starts	1st	2nd	3rd	Win & Pl
Career Total (Turf)	**3**	**1**	**0**	**0**	**4857**

80 10/09 Newb 1m SFT £4857
Total win prize-money £4857

Going (Turf): **Sf: 1-2** GS: 0-0 Gd: 0-0 GF: 0-1 Fm: 0-0
Distance: 5f/6f: 0-0 **7f-8f: 1-2** 9f-13f: 0-1 14f+: 0-0
Track : LH: 0-1 RH: 0-0 Tight: 0-0 Gall: 0-0
Aids: Bl: 0-0 Vi: 0-0 Tstrap: 0-0 Ckp: 0-0
Best Rating: **91** 11/09 StCl 1m2f heavy

Useful; stays 1m; acts on soft ground.

Garlogs

(105) (84)67
6-y-o b g Hunting Lion (IRE)-Fading (Pharly (FR))
R Hollinshead Peter G Freeman

Placings:210606326/11222134000**4**/3326366/141131440-0000 **(0919)**
2009: 5^{0}SD, 5^{0}SD, 5^{0}SD, 5^{0}SD,

	Starts	1st	2nd	3rd	Win & Pl
Career Total (Turf)	**9**	**2**	**1**	**2**	**8945**
Career Total (AW)	**32**	**6**	**5**	**4**	**24294**

84 5/08 Sthl 5f (0-85)H STD £5180
75 3/08 Sthl 5f (0-70)H STD £2593
73 2/08 Sthl 5f (0-60)H SS £1911
62 1/08 Wolv 5f20y (0-55)H STD £2047
70 3/06 Muss 5f (0-65)H HVY £3412
68 2/06 Sthl 5f (0-60)H STD £2388
57 1/06 Sthl 5f (0-60)H STD £2388
52 4/05 Donc 5f GD £3357
Total win prize-money £23282

Going (Turf): **Sf: 1-3** GS: 0-1 **Gd: 1-3** GF: 0-2 Fm: 0-0
Distance: **5f/6f: 8-40** 7f-8f: 0-1 9f-13f: 0-0 14f+: 0-0
Track : **LH: 1-13** RH: 0-0 **Tight: 1-11** Gall: 0-0
Aids: Bl: 0-1 Vi: 0-1 Tstrap: 0-0 Ckp: 0-0
Best Rating: **84** 5/08 Sthl 5f stand

Modest; suited by 5f; acts on both All-Weather surfaces and on soft turf.

Garnica (FR)

103 112
6-y-o gr g Linamix (FR)-Gueridia (IRE) (Night Shift (USA))
D Nicholls Lady O'Reilly & Eamon Maher

Placings:11/135511/12410/01006-40000 **(7294)**
2009: 7^{4}G, 7^{0}G, 6^{0}G, 7^{0}GS, 7^{0}S,

	Starts	1st	2nd	3rd	Win & Pl
Career Total (Turf)	**23**	**8**	**1**	**1**	**184587**

110 5/08 Lonc 7f SFT £29412
117 8/07 Deau 6f SFT £27027
112 5/07 Lonc 7f HVY £27027
114 10/06 Badn 7f SFT £24138
107 8/06 Deau 5f110y VS £11379
3/06 Bord 1m HVY £10345
12/05 Toul 1m HVY £7446
10/05 Toul 7f GD £4255
Total win prize-money £141030

Going (Turf): **Sf: 6-10** GS: 0-4 Gd: 1-6 GF: 0-1 Fm: 0-0
Distance: 5f/6f: 2-4 **7f-8f: 6-19** 9f-13f: 0-0 14f+: 0-0
Track : LH: 1-3 **RH: 4-10** Tight: 0-0 Gall: 0-0
Aids: Bl: 0-0 Vi: 0-0 Tstrap: 0-0 Ckp: 0-0
Best Rating: **117** 8/07 Deau 6f soft

Group-class sprinter; ex-French; effective at up to 7f; acts well on soft ground.

Garra Molly (IRE)

85(98) (70)70
4-y-o b f Nayef (USA)-Aminata (Glenstal (USA))
G A Swinbank Ballylinch Stud

Placings:456330-**240** **(5035)**
2009: 9^{2}SF, 9^{4}SD, 10^{0}GF,

	Starts	1st	2nd	3rd	Win & Pl
Career Total (Turf)	**7**	**0**	**0**	**2**	**1444**
Career Total (AW)	**2**	**0**	**1**	**0**	**806**

Going (Turf): **Sf: 0-0 GS: 0-2 Gd: 0-3 GF: 0-2 Fm: 0-0**
Distance: 5f/6f: 0-0 7f-8f: 0-0 9f-13f: 0-7 14f+: 0-2
Track : LH: 0-7 RH: 0-2 Tight: 0-5 Gall: 0-2
Aids: Bl: 0-0 Vi: 0-0 Tstrap: 0-0 Ckp: 0-0
Best Rating: **70** 2/09 Wolv 1m1f103y std-fst

Modest; stays 1m6f; acts on good ground.

Garstang

100(104) (86)70
6-y-o ch g Atraf-Approved Quality (IRE) (Persian Heights)
J Balding The Foulrice Twenty

Placings:0023414400/**22101153012641600/00025033006**1641400/600000630-010163220423 **(6632)**
2009: 6^{0}SD, 5^{1}SD, 6^{0}SD, 5^{1}SD, 5^{6}S, 5^{3}S, 5^{2}SD, 5^{2}SD, 5^{0}GF, 5^{4}SD, 5^{2}SD, 5^{3}SS,

	Starts	1st	2nd	3rd	Win & Pl
Career Total (Turf)	**27**	**3**	**2**	**2**	**12372**
Career Total (AW)	**39**	**7**	**6**	**5**	**27704**

83 6/09 Kemp 5f (0-70)H STD £2590
71 4/09 Kemp 5f (0-60)H STD £2047
79 8/07 Wind 5f10y (0-75)H G-F £3238
82 7/06 Ling 6f (0-75)H STD £3238
77 5/06 Ling 6f (0-75)H STD £3238
71 3/06 Ling 7f (0-60)H STD £2388
68 3/06 Ling 6f (0-65)H STD £2388
68 2/06 Wolv 5f216y (0-60)H STD £2388
52 6/05 Muss 5f G-F £2870
Total win prize-money £24391

Going (Turf): Sf: 0-6 GS: 0-2 Gd: 1-7 **GF: 2-12** Fm: 0-0
Distance: **5f/6f: 9-59** 7f-8f: 1-7 9f-13f: 0-0 14f+: 0-0
Track : **LH: 5-31** RH: 2-10 **Tight: 5-28** Gall: 1-3
Aids: **Bl: 9-50** Vi: 0-0 Tstrap: 0-0 Ckp: 0-0
Best Rating: **88** 2/07 Wolv 5f216y stand

Fair; effective over 5f-7f; effective on fast ground; also goes on Polytrack; wears blinkers.

Garter Knight

101(96) (60)73
3-y-o b g Mark Of Esteem (IRE)-Granted (FR) (Cadeaux Genereux)

Mrs P Sly (M L W Bell 18/6) David L Bayliss

Placings:06042023 (7246)
2009: 10^{0}SD, 8^{6}SD, 7^{0}SD, 8^{4}GF, 9^{2}GF, 10^{0}G, 10^{2}G, 8^{3}S,

	Starts	1st	2nd	3rd	Win & Pl
Career Total (Turf)	5	0	2	1	1668
Career Total (AW)	3	0	0	0	0

Going (Turf): Sf: 0-1 GS: 0-0 Gd: 0-2 GF: 0-2 Fm: 0-0
Distance: 5f/6f: 0-0 7f-8f: 0-1 9f-13f: 0-7 14f+: 0-0
Track : LH: 0-6 RH: 0-2 Tight: 0-4 Gall: 0-0
Aids: Bl: 0-0 Vi: 0-0 Tstrap: 0-0 Ckp: 0-0
Best Rating: 73 10/09 Nott 1m2f50y good

Modest; effective over 1m-1m2f; acts on fast and soft ground.

Garter Star

81(90) (54)39
4-y-o b f Mark Of Esteem (IRE)-Palace Affair (Pursuit Of Love)
H Morrison Miss B Swire

Placings:60 (2205)
2009: 7^{6}SD, 6^{0}GF,

	Starts	1st	2nd	3rd	Win & Pl
Career Total (Turf)	1	0	0	0	
Career Total (AW)	1	0	0	0	0

Going (Turf): Sf: 0-0 GS: 0-0 Gd: 0-0 GF: 0-1 Fm: 0-0
Distance: 5f/6f: 0-1 7f-8f: 0-1 9f-13f: 0-0 14f+: 0-0
Track : LH: 0-1 RH: 0-0 Tight: 0-1 Gall: 0-0
Aids: Bl: 0-0 Vi: 0-0 Tstrap: 0-0 Ckp: 0-0
Best Rating: 54 5/09 Ling 7f stand

Gasat (IRE)

96(107) (73)62
8-y-o b h Marju (IRE)-Pechenga (Nureyev (USA))
A B Haynes (F Sheridan 10/1) Danny O'Neill

Placings:031/**2115261312**1/**2531342221**/**21224420413**/24 **1112542111**/**12311**0-**2023122**00400 (6612)
2009: 10^{2}SD, 13^{0}SD, 10^{2}SD, 12^{3}SD, 10^{1}SD, 10^{2}SD, 10^{2}G, 9^{0}GF, 9^{0}GF, 9^{4}F, 10^{0}SD, 12^{0}SD,

	Starts	1st	2nd	3rd	Win & Pl
Career Total (Turf)	51	16	14	6	132677
Career Total (AW)	14	4	5	1	15890

73	3/09	Ling	1m2f		STD	£2047
	10/08	Casc	1m2f		GD	£1471
	9/08	Casc	1m2f		GD	£1471
	5/08	Capa	1m3f		STD	£2574
	12/07	Livo	1m3f55y	H	G-S	£10135
	12/07	Albe	1m3f		STD	£2703
	11/07	Capa	1m4f		G-S	£2703
	5/07	Capa	1m2f110y		GD	£2703
	5/07	Capa	1m3f		STD	£2703
	4/07	Siro	1m3f		GD	£2365
	12/06	Livo	1m3f55y		SFT	£3448
	2/06	Pisa	1m1f		SFT	£4828
	12/05	Livo	1m3f55y		G-S	£3546
	4/05	Casc	1m2f		SFT	£4255
	11/04	Capa	1m110y		SFT	£8803
	8/04	Gros	1m165y	H	GD	£17606
	6/04	Gros	1m165y		GD	£7042
	2/04	Capa	1m2f		G-S	£8803
	2/04	Pisa	1m2f		GD	£7042
	12/03	Livo	1m1f165y		SFT	£3896

Total win prize-money £100144

Going (Turf): Sf: 5-15 GS: 4-9 **Gd: 7-24** GF: 0-2 Fm: 0-1
Distance: 5f/6f: 0-0 7f-8f: 0-1 **9f-13f: 20-64** 14f+: 0-0
Track : **LH: 1-9** RH: 0-4 **Tight: 1-9** Gall: 0-0
Aids: Bl: 0-0 Vi: 0-0 Tstrap: 0-0 Ckp: 0-0
Best Rating: 73 3/09 Ling 1m2f stand

Modest; stays 1m2f; acts on good ground; goes on Polytrack.

Gaselee (USA)

101(100) (71)72
3-y-o b f Toccet (USA)-Vingt Et Une (FR) (Sadler's Wells (USA))
Rae Guest Mrs Paula Smith

Placings:400412422 (6951)
2009: 9^{4}SD, 10^{0}SD, 8^{0}SD, 12^{4}SD, 9^{1}G, 8^{2}GF, 10^{4}G, 12^{2}GS, 11^{2}SD,

	Starts	1st	2nd	3rd	Win & Pl
Career Total (Turf)	4	1	2	0	4613
Career Total (AW)	5	0	1	0	1204

69 7/09 Muss 1m1f GD £2590
Total win prize-money £2590

Going (Turf): Sf: 0-0 GS: 0-1 **Gd: 1-2** GF: 0-1 Fm: 0-0
Distance: 5f/6f: 0-0 7f-8f: 0-1 **9f-13f: 1-8** 14f+: 0-0
Track : LH: 0-6 **RH: 1-3 Tight: 1-5** Gall: 0-1
Aids: Bl: 0-0 Vi: 0-0 Tstrap: 0-0 Ckp: 0-0
Best Rating: 72 10/09 Gdwd 1m4f gd-sft

Modest; stays 1m1f; acts on good and on fast ground.

Gasparilla (IRE)

88(80) (38)47
2-y-o b f Fath (USA)-Tazmeera (IRE) (Priolo (USA))
A J McCabe Sale Of The Century

Placings:353565000 (6354)
2009: 5^{3}GF, 5^{5}GF, 5^{3}F, 6^{5}GS, 5^{6}SF, 6^{5}G, 6^{0}SD, 5^{0}GF, 5^{0}SD,

	Starts	1st	2nd	3rd	Win & Pl
Career Total (Turf)	6	0	0	2	639
Career Total (AW)	3	0	0	0	0

Going (Turf): Sf: 0-0 GS: 0-1 Gd: 0-1 GF: 0-3 Fm: 0-1
Distance: 5f/6f: 0-8 7f-8f: 0-1 9f-13f: 0-0 14f+: 0-0
Track : LH: 0-1 RH: 0-1 Tight: 0-1 Gall: 0-0
Aids: Bl: 0-0 Vi: 0-0 Tstrap: 0-0 Ckp: 0-0
Best Rating: 47 6/09 Bevl 5f firm

Gassin

95(105) (83)69
3-y-o b g Selkirk (USA)-Miss Riviera Golf (Hernando (FR))
M L W Bell J L C Pearce

Placings:56-1500131 (7000)
2009: 8^{1}G, 8^{5}G, 8^{0}HY, 8^{0}G, 7^{1}SD, 7^{3}SS, 7^{1}SD,

	Starts	1st	2nd	3rd	Win & Pl
Career Total (Turf)	5	1	0	0	2767
Career Total (AW)	4	2	0	1	8394

83	10/09	Wolv	7f32y	(0-80)H	STD	£5046
75	10/09	Wolv	7f32y	(0-70)H	STD	£2914
69	6/09	Nott	1m75y	GD	£2590	

Total win prize-money £10550

Going (Turf): Sf: 0-1 GS: 0-0 **Gd: 1-4** GF: 0-0 Fm: 0-0
Distance: 5f/6f: 0-0 **7f-8f: 2-6** 9f-13f: 1-3 14f+: 0-0
Track : **LH: 3-7** RH: 0-0 **Tight: 2-3** Gall: 0-1
Aids: Bl: 0-0 **Vi: 2-3** Tstrap: 0-0 Ckp: 0-0
Best Rating: 83 10/09 Wolv 7f32y stand

Fair; stays 7f and acts on Polytrack.

Gay Mirage (GER)

92 53
2-y-o b f Highest Honor (FR)-Geminiani (IRE) (King Of Kings (IRE))
M A Jarvis B E Nielsen

Placings:6 (7243)
2009: 8^{6}S,

	Starts	1st	2nd	3rd	Win & Pl
Career Total (Turf)	1	0	0	0	0

Going (Turf): Sf: 0-1 GS: 0-0 Gd: 0-0 GF: 0-0 Fm: 0-0
Distance: 5f/6f: 0-0 7f-8f: 0-0 9f-13f: 0-1 14f+: 0-0
Track : LH: 0-1 RH: 0-0 Tight: 0-0 Gall: 0-0
Aids: Bl: 0-0 Vi: 0-0 Tstrap: 0-0 Ckp: 0-0
Best Rating: 53 11/09 Nott 1m75y soft

Gayanula (USA)

(97) (63)
4-y-o b f Yonaguska (USA)-Betamillion Bock (USA) (Bet Twice (USA))
Miss J A Camacho G B Turnbull Ltd

Placings:04/3254012-32046 (2580)
2009: 14^{3}SS, 12^{2}SD, 12^{0}SD, 12^{4}SD, 12^{6}SD,

	Starts	1st	2nd	3rd	Win & Pl
Career Total (Turf)	0	0	0	0	
Career Total (AW)	14	1	3	2	4889

61 12/08 Sthl 1m4f (0-65)H SS £2047
Total win prize-money £2047

Going (Turf): Sf: 0-0 GS: 0-0 Gd: 0-0 GF: 0-0 Fm: 0-0
Distance: 5f/6f: 0-0 7f-8f: 0-3 **9f-13f: 1-10** 14f+: 0-1
Track : **LH: 1-14** RH: 0-0 Tight: 0-3 Gall: 0-0
Aids: Bl: 0-0 Vi: 0-0 Tstrap: 0-2 Ckp: 0-2
Best Rating: 66 2/08 Sthl 1m3f stand

Modest; stays 1m6f; acts on Fibresand.

Gazamali (IRE)

75 36
2-y-o b c Namid-Frond (Alzao (USA))
G A Harker Good Breed Limited

Placings:060 (6842)
2009: 5^{0}GF, 5^{6}GF, 7^{0}G,

	Starts	1st	2nd	3rd	Win & Pl
Career Total (Turf)	3	0	0	0	0

Going (Turf): Sf: 0-0 GS: 0-0 Gd: 0-1 GF: 0-2 Fm: 0-0
Distance: 5f/6f: 0-2 7f-8f: 0-1 9f-13f: 0-0 14f+: 0-0
Track : LH: 0-1 RH: 0-0 Tight: 0-1 Gall: 0-0
Aids: Bl: 0-0 Vi: 0-0 Tstrap: 0-0 Ckp: 0-0
Best Rating: 36 4/09 Bevl 5f gd-fm

Gazboolou

98(106) (79)71
5-y-o b g Royal Applause-Warning Star (Warning)
David Pinder Mrs Angela Pinder

Placings:2222/160536**102**/0044**343110**-**24203602030** (6725)
2009: 8^{2}SD, 8^{4}SD, 7^{2}SD, 7^{0}GF, 7^{3}GF, 7^{6}G, 8^{0}GF, 7^{2}SD, 8^{0}SD, 7^{3}SD, 7^{0}SD,

	Starts	1st	2nd	3rd	Win & Pl
Career Total (Turf)	18	1	4	2	10166

Career Total (AW)	**16**	**3**	**4**	**3**	**14289**

78	10/08	Kemp	7f	(0-70)H	STD	£3238
74	9/08	Kemp	1m	(0-70)H	STD	£2590
78	10/07	Kemp	1m		STD	£2047
72	4/07	Muss	7f30y		G-F	£3238

Total win prize-money £11115

Going (Turf): Sf: 0-1 GS: 0-2 Gd: 0-2 **GF: 1-11** Fm: 0-2
Distance: 5f/6f: 0-1 **7f-8f: 4-29** 9f-13f: 0-4 14f+: 0-0
Track : LH: 0-12 **RH: 4-16 Tight: 1-12** Gall: 0-2
Aids: Bl: 0-0 Vi: 0-0 Tstrap: 0-0 Ckp: 0-0
Best Rating: 80 4/07 Wind 1m67y gd-fm

Fair; stays 1m; acts on fast ground and on Polytrack.

Gearbox (IRE)

79 **41**

3-y-o br g Tillerman-Persian Empress (IRE) (Persian Bold)
R Hannon Mrs J K Powell

Placings:6 **(5010)**
2009: 8^{6}G,

	Starts	1st	2nd	3rd	Win & Pl
Career Total (Turf)	**1**	**0**	**0**	**0**	**0**

Going (Turf): Sf: 0-0 GS: 0-0 Gd: 0-1 GF: 0-0 Fm: 0-0
Distance: 5f/6f: 0-0 7f-8f: 0-0 9f-13f: 0-1 14f+: 0-0
Track : LH: 0-1 RH: 0-0 Tight: 0-0 Gall: 0-0
Aids: Bl: 0-0 Vi: 0-0 Tstrap: 0-0 Ckp: 0-0
Best Rating: 41 8/09 Nott 1m75y good

Gee Dee Nen

99(96) (95)**98**

6-y-o b g Mister Baileys-Special Beat (Bustino)
G L Moore (Jim Best 21/8) Chris Duggan & Brendan Gilligan

Placings:5516/**2333233440/3314051301/515010-500** **(5235)**
2009: 16^{5}SD, 16^{0}GS, 16^{0}GF,

	Starts	1st	2nd	3rd	Win & Pl
Career Total (Turf)	**31**	**6**	**2**	**7**	**89345**
Career Total (AW)	**2**	**0**	**0**	**1**	**901**

98	8/08	Asct	2m	(0-100)H	G-S	£17230
95	5/08	Hayd	2m45y	(0-100)H	G-F	£12462
92	11/07	Muss	1m6f	(0-100)H	GD	£15580
90	9/07	Ches	1m7f195y	(0-85)H	G-F	£5829
87	5/07	Thsk	2m	(0-85)H	G-F	£5181
78	10/05	York	1m		SFT	£7962

Total win prize-money £64247

Going (Turf): Sf: 1-8 GS: 1-8 Gd: 1-7 **GF: 3-8** Fm: 0-0
Distance: 5f/6f: 0-0 7f-8f: 1-3 9f-13f: 0-7 **14f+: 5-23**
Track : **LH: 4-15** RH: 2-17 **Tight: 3-9** Gall: 2-17
Aids: Bl: 0-0 Vi: 0-1 Tstrap: 0-0 Ckp: 0-0
Best Rating: 98 8/08 Asct 2m gd-sft

Very useful; stays 2m; acts on most ground; has worn a visor.

Gee Gina

99 **57**

3-y-o b f Hunting Lion (IRE)-La Thuile (Statoblest)
P T Midgley Mrs M Hills

Placings:500-044251 **(5468)**
2009: 5^{0}GF, 5^{4}G, 5^{4}GF, 5^{2}GF, 5^{5}GF, 5^{1}GF,

	Starts	1st	2nd	3rd	Win & Pl
Career Total (Turf)	**9**	**1**	**1**	**0**	**4220**

56	8/09	Bevl	5f	(0-60)H	G-F	£2900

Total win prize-money £2900

Going (Turf): Sf: 0-1 GS: 0-0 Gd: 0-2 **GF: 1-6** Fm: 0-0
Distance: **5f/6f: 1-8** 7f-8f: 0-1 9f-13f: 0-0 14f+: 0-0
Track : LH: 0-1 RH: 0-0 Tight: 0-1 Gall: 0-0
Aids: Bl: 0-0 Vi: 0-0 Tstrap: 0-0 Ckp: 0-0
Best Rating: 57 8/09 Newc 5f gd-fm

Moderate; suited by 5f and fast ground.

Gee Major

79 **32**

2-y-o b g Reset (AUS)-Polly Golightly (Weldnaas (USA))
Tom Dascombe (N J Vaughan 3/7) David Sykes

Placings:00 **(6591)**
2009: 6^{0}G, 6^{0}GS,

	Starts	1st	2nd	3rd	Win & Pl
Career Total (Turf)	**2**	**0**	**0**	**0**	

Going (Turf): Sf: 0-0 GS: 0-1 Gd: 0-1 GF: 0-0 Fm: 0-0
Distance: 5f/6f: 0-1 7f-8f: 0-1 9f-13f: 0-0 14f+: 0-0
Track : LH: 0-0 RH: 0-0 Tight: 0-0 Gall: 0-0
Aids: Bl: 0-0 Vi: 0-0 Tstrap: 0-0 Ckp: 0-0
Best Rating: 32 10/09 Nott 6f15y gd-sft

Geese A Laying (IRE)

(83) (31)

3-y-o b f Elusive City (USA)-King Of All (IRE) (King Of Clubs)
J A Osborne A D Spence & 12 Day Partners

Placings:050 **(0955)**
2009: 6^{0}SD, 5^{5}SD, 5^{0}SD,

	Starts	1st	2nd	3rd	Win & Pl
Career Total (Turf)	**0**	**0**	**0**	**0**	
Career Total (AW)	**3**	**0**	**0**	**0**	**0**

Going (Turf): Sf: 0-0 GS: 0-0 Gd: 0-0 GF: 0-0 Fm: 0-0
Distance: 5f/6f: 0-3 7f-8f: 0-0 9f-13f: 0-0 14f+: 0-0
Track : LH: 0-3 RH: 0-0 Tight: 0-2 Gall: 0-0
Aids: Bl: 0-0 Vi: 0-0 Tstrap: 0-0 Ckp: 0-0
Best Rating: 31 3/09 Ling 5f stand

Geezers Colours

96(106) (71)**79**

4-y-o b g Fraam-Konica (Desert King (IRE))
J R Weymes (A P Jarvis 26/10) C Waters

Placings:545201121/135500-0006203 **(7845)**
2009: 7^{0}SD, 6^{0}G, 7^{0}G, 6^{6}G, 8^{2}SS, 7^{0}SD, 7^{3}SD,

	Starts	1st	2nd	3rd	Win & Pl
Career Total (Turf)	**8**	**0**	**0**	**0**	**241**
Career Total (AW)	**14**	**4**	**3**	**2**	**24906**

92	1/08	Ling	7f	(0-85)H	STD	£4416
85	12/07	Wolv	7f32y		STD	£2968
78	11/07	Ling	7f		STD	£2047
71	11/07	Ling	7f	(0-85)	STD	£4533

Total win prize-money £13967

Going (Turf): Sf: 0-0 GS: 0-0 Gd: 0-6 GF: 0-1 Fm: 0-1
Distance: 5f/6f: 0-3 **7f-8f: 4-19** 9f-13f: 0-0 14f+: 0-0
Track : **LH: 4-16** RH: 0-2 **Tight: 4-15** Gall: 0-1
Aids: Bl: 0-0 Vi: 0-0 Tstrap: 0-0 Ckp: 0-0
Best Rating: 93 3/08 Ling 7f stand

Fair; Listed placed; effective over 7f-1m and acts on Polytrack; likes to race prominently.

Gelert (IRE)

86(88) (46)**51**

4-y-o b c Acclamation-Game Leader (IRE) (Mukaddamah (USA))
A Berry (Peter Grayson 4/6) Thomas & Susan Blane

Placings:054540552452050-6000005 **(4012)**
2009: 5^{6}SD, 5^{0}F, 5^{0}GF, 5^{0}GF, 5^{0}GF, 5^{0}GF, 5^{5}GF,

	Starts	1st	2nd	3rd	Win & Pl
Career Total (Turf)	**15**	**0**	**2**	**0**	**1542**
Career Total (AW)	**7**	**0**	**0**	**0**	**173**

Going (Turf): Sf: 0-3 GS: 0-3 Gd: 0-2 GF: 0-5 Fm: 0-2
Distance: 5f/6f: 0-22 7f-8f: 0-0 9f-13f: 0-0 14f+: 0-0
Track : LH: 0-5 RH: 0-2 Tight: 0-4 Gall: 0-3
Aids: Bl: 0-11 Vi: 0-0 Tstrap: 0-0 Ckp: 0-0
Best Rating: 51 9/08 Haml 5f4y soft

Moderate; effective over 5f; acts on good ground.

Gems Star

90 **46**

3-y-o b g Elmaamul (USA)-Slipperose (Persepolis (FR))
J J Quinn Mrs Maureen Beddis

Placings:600-0040 **(5145)**
2009: 6^{0}GF, 6^{0}GS, 7^{4}G, 5^{0}GS,

	Starts	1st	2nd	3rd	Win & Pl
Career Total (Turf)	**7**	**0**	**0**	**0**	**192**

Going (Turf): Sf: 0-1 GS: 0-2 Gd: 0-2 GF: 0-2 Fm: 0-0
Distance: 5f/6f: 0-6 7f-8f: 0-1 9f-13f: 0-0 14f+: 0-0
Track : LH: 0-2 RH: 0-2 Tight: 0-1 Gall: 0-0
Aids: Bl: 0-0 Vi: 0-0 Tstrap: 0-0 Ckp: 0-0
Best Rating: 46 8/09 Muss 7f30y good

Genari

(92) (59)**79**

6-y-o b g Generous (IRE)-Sari (Faustus (USA))
Miss S Wheelwright (Gordon Elliott 10/12) M Webb

Placings:215310/53000600/515000/0 **(7402)**
2009: 16^{0}SD,

	Starts	1st	2nd	3rd	Win & Pl
Career Total (Turf)	**17**	**2**	**1**	**2**	**24762**
Career Total (AW)	**4**	**1**	**0**	**0**	**5182**

90	5/07	Sthl	1m	(0-85)H	STD	£5181
93	9/05	Hayd	1m30y		GD	£13386
86	6/05	Sals	6f		G-F	£3874

Total win prize-money £22442

Going (Turf): Sf: 0-1 GS: 0-0 **Gd: 1-8 GF: 1-7** Fm: 0-1
Distance: 5f/6f: 1-1 7f-8f: 1-12 9f-13f: 1-7 14f+: 0-1
Track : **LH: 2-6** RH: 0-8 Tight: 0-4 Gall: 0-1
Aids: Bl: 0-2 Vi: 0-0 Tstrap: 0-0 Ckp: 0-0
Best Rating: 93 9/05 Hayd 1m30y good

Fair gelding; formerly useful; stays 1m3f, but effective over shorter; acts on good or faster ground and Fibresand; has worn blinkers.

Gene Autry (USA)

96 **83**

2-y-o b/br c Zavata (USA)-Total Acceptance (USA) (With Approval (CAN))
R Hannon Mrs J K Powell

Placings:441 **(4851)**
2009: 7^{4}S, 7^{4}G, 6^{1}GF,

	Starts	1st	2nd	3rd	Win & Pl
Career Total (Turf)	3	1	0	0	6239

83 8/09 Wind 6f G-F £5180
Total win prize-money £5181

Going (Turf): Sf: 0-1 GS: 0-0 Gd: 0-1 **GF: 1-1** Fm: 0-0
Distance: **5f/6f: 1-1** 7f-8f: 0-2 9f-13f: 0-0 14f+: 0-0
Track : LH: 0-0 RH: 0-0 Tight: 0-0 **Gall: 1-1**
Aids: Bl: 0-0 Vi: 0-0 Tstrap: 0-0 Ckp: 0-0
Best Rating: 83 8/09 Wind 6f gd-fm

Useful; effective over 6-7f; acts on fast and easy ground.

General Eliott (IRE)

106(102) (73)113
4-y-o b g Rock Of Gibraltar (IRE)-Marlene-D (Selkirk (USA))
P F I Cole Sir George Meyrick

Placings:1/104020-0050303 **(7810)**
2009: 8⁰GF, 8⁰G, 9⁵GF, 9⁰GF, 8³S, 10⁰SD, 8³SD,

	Starts	1st	2nd	3rd	Win & Pl
Career Total (Turf)	11	2	1	1	27082
Career Total (AW)	3	0	0	1	1136

93 4/08 Sand 1m14y G-S £6542
84 10/07 NmkR 1m SFT £5829
Total win prize-money £12372

Going (Turf): **Sf: 1-2 GS: 1-2** Gd: 0-3 GF: 0-4 Fm: 0-0
Distance: 5f/6f: 0-0 7f-8f: 1-7 9f-13f: 1-7 14f+: 0-0
Track : LH: 0-5 **RH: 1-2** Tight: 0-3 Gall: 0-1
Aids: Bl: 0-1 Vi: 0-0 Tstrap: 0-2 Ckp: 0-2
Best Rating: 113 11/08 NmkR 1m gd-sft

Very useful; effective over 1m; acts on most ground; has worn blinkers and cheekpieces.

General Feeling (IRE)

94(106) (75)58
8-y-o b g General Monash (USA)-Kamadara (IRE) (Kahyasi)
Ollie Pears (D Nicholls 15/6) The Hair Of The Dog

Placings:3/33041140/15000005**04015102/4402000000**00606/064356630420032/16616000504600136-211360540000 **(7776)**
2009: 10²SD, 8¹SD, 8¹SD, 10³SD, 12⁶SD, 8⁰GF, 8⁵GF, 8⁴SD, 9⁰G, 9⁰GF, 8⁰SF, 10⁰SD,

	Starts	1st	2nd	3rd	Win & Pl
Career Total (Turf)	39	3	1	4	17371
Career Total (AW)	45	7	4	4	22037

75 1/09 Ling 1m (0-65)H STD £2047
70 1/09 Ling 1m (0-60)H STD £2047
64 11/08 Ling 1m (0-55)H STD £2047
59 3/08 Wolv 1m141y (0-60)H STD £2047
59 1/08 Wolv 1m141y (0-60)H STD £1774
83 12/05 Wolv 7f32y (0-75)H STD £3426
77 11/05 Ling 6f (0-70)H STD £3024
84 4/05 Wind 6f (0-75)H GD £3528
81 8/04 Brig 7f214y E(0-70)H FRM £3993
79 7/04 Gway 7f (40-70)H G-F £6569
Total win prize-money £30507

Going (Turf): Sf: 0-4 GS: 0-5 **Gd: 1-11 GF: 1-17 Fm: 1-2**
Distance: 5f/6f: 2-18 **7f-8f: 6-41** 9f-13f: 2-25 14f+: 0-0
Track : **LH: 8-57** RH: 1-13 **Tight: 7-48** Gall: 1-6
Aids: Bl: 0-1 Vi: 0-0 Tstrap: 1-10 Ckp: 1-10
Best Rating: 84 4/05 Wind 6f good

Modest; stays 1m; acts on a sound surface and on Polytrack; has been tried in cheekpieces.

General Sam (USA)

(89) (47)
3-y-o ch g Trippi (USA)-Milagro Blue (USA) (Cure The Blues (USA))
R Hannon Sir David Seale

Placings:000 **(0343)**
2009: 7⁰SD, 7⁰SD, 10⁰SD,

	Starts	1st	2nd	3rd	Win & Pl
Career Total (Turf)	0	0	0	0	
Career Total (AW)	3	0	0	0	

Going (Turf): **Sf: 0-0 GS: 0-0 Gd: 0-0 GF: 0-0 Fm: 0-0**
Distance: 5f/6f: 0-0 7f-8f: 0-2 9f-13f: 0-1 14f+: 0-0
Track : LH: 0-3 RH: 0-0 Tight: 0-3 Gall: 0-0
Aids: Bl: 0-0 Vi: 0-0 Tstrap: 0-0 Ckp: 0-0
Best Rating: 47 1/09 Ling 7f stand

General Ting (IRE)

99(100) (78)80
4-y-o b c Daylami (IRE)-Luana (Shaadi (USA))
Sir Mark Prescott Lady Katharine Watts

Placings:005/3122-004 **(6822)**
2009: 12⁰SD, 16⁰G, 14⁴GF,

	Starts	1st	2nd	3rd	Win & Pl
Career Total (Turf)	4	1	1	0	7632
Career Total (AW)	6	0	1	1	2071

74 7/08 Nott 1m6f15y (0-80)H G-S £6476
Total win prize-money £6476

Going (Turf): Sf: 0-0 **GS: 1-1** Gd: 0-1 GF: 0-2 Fm: 0-0
Distance: 5f/6f: 0-1 7f-8f: 0-2 9f-13f: 0-2 **14f+: 1-5**
Track : **LH: 1-8** RH: 0-2 Tight: 0-6 Gall: 0-1
Aids: Bl: 0-0 Vi: 0-0 Tstrap: 0-0 Ckp: 0-0
Best Rating: 80 7/08 Sals 1m6f21y gd-fm

Fair; stays 2m; acts on most ground and on Polytrack.

General Tufto

102(106) (73)72
4-y-o b g Fantastic Light (USA)-Miss Pinkerton (Danehill (USA))
C Smith Phil Martin & Trev Sleath

Placings:065/50050004055-**46331112415**2050330105656323030003**3100** **(7854)**
2009: 8⁴SS, 11⁶SD, 8³SD, 12³SD, 12¹SD, 8¹SD, 8¹SD, 8²SD, 8⁴SD, 11¹SD, 12⁵SD, 11²SD, 10⁰GF, 9⁵GF, 8⁰G, 10³F, 10³GF, 12⁰GS, 9¹G, 11⁰G, 9⁵GF, 8⁶GF, 10⁵S,

	Starts	1st	2nd	3rd	Win & Pl
Career Total (Turf)	29	1	1	5	5495
Career Total (AW)	22	5	2	4	13803

71 12/09 Sthl 1m (0-65)H STD £2047
68 5/09 Bevl 1m1f207y (0-70)H GD £2654
70 3/09 Sthl 1m3f (0-70)H STD £2590
66 2/09 Sthl 1m (0-55)H STD £2047
62 2/09 Sthl 1m (0-58)H STD £2047
54 2/09 Sthl 1m4f (0-60)H STD £2047
Total win prize-money £13433

Going (Turf): Sf: 0-5 GS: 0-3 **Gd: 1-6** GF: 0-14 Fm: 0-1
Distance: 5f/6f: 0-0 7f-8f: 3-15 9f-13f: 3-34 14f+: 0-2
Track : **LH: 5-36** RH: 1-12 Tight: 0-12 Gall: 0-4
Aids: **Bl: 6-39** Vi: 0-2 Tstrap: 0-1 Ckp: 0-1
Best Rating: 73 3/09 Sthl 1m3f stand

Modest; effective from 1m-1m4f; acts on fast ground and on Fibresand; sometimes hangs left in his races; has worn blinkers.

General Zhukov

95(90) (51)70
3-y-o b g Largesse-Hickleton Lady (IRE) (Kala Shikari)
J M P Eustace Mrs Rosemary Moszkowicz

Placings:6-0001 **(2357)**
2009: 8⁰G, 8⁰SD, 8⁰GF, 9¹GF,

	Starts	1st	2nd	3rd	Win & Pl
Career Total (Turf)	4	1	0	0	2590
Career Total (AW)	1	0	0	0	

70 5/09 Leic 1m1f218y (0-65)H G-F £2590
Total win prize-money £2590

Going (Turf): Sf: 0-0 GS: 0-1 Gd: 0-1 **GF: 1-2** Fm: 0-0
Distance: 5f/6f: 0-0 7f-8f: 0-2 **9f-13f: 1-3** 14f+: 0-0
Track : LH: 0-1 **RH: 1-2** Tight: 0-2 Gall: 0-0
Aids: Bl: 0-0 Vi: 0-0 Tstrap: 0-0 Ckp: 0-0
Best Rating: 70 5/09 Leic 1m1f218y gd-fm

Modest; stays 1m2f; acts on fast ground.

Generoso (USA)

79 36
2-y-o b c Gone West (USA)-Kentucky Rose (FR) (Hernando (FR))
S C Williams Mad Man Plus One

Placings:060 **(7120)**
2009: 6⁰GF, 7⁶GF, 8⁰GF,

	Starts	1st	2nd	3rd	Win & Pl
Career Total (Turf)	3	0	0	0	117

Going (Turf): **Sf: 0-0 GS: 0-0 Gd: 0-0 GF: 0-3 Fm: 0-0**
Distance: 5f/6f: 0-1 7f-8f: 0-1 9f-13f: 0-1 14f+: 0-0
Track : LH: 0-1 RH: 0-0 Tight: 0-0 Gall: 0-0
Aids: Bl: 0-0 Vi: 0-0 Tstrap: 0-0 Ckp: 0-0
Best Rating: 36 10/09 Nott 1m75y gd-fm

Generous Lad (IRE)

98(103) (77)66
6-y-o b g Generous (IRE)-Tudor Loom (Sallust)
A B Haynes WCR V - The Conkwell Connection

Placings:0100/000**12/43333**2326221**443/44445**0**64230**-**00**205053600 **(5872)**
2009: 13⁰SD, 12⁰SD, 12²SD, 11⁰GF, 9⁵F, 11⁰G, 10⁵G, 12³GF, 12⁶GF, 10⁰GF, 10⁰G,

	Starts	1st	2nd	3rd	Win & Pl
Career Total (Turf)	24	1	4	2	10976
Career Total (AW)	23	2	3	6	13242

77 11/07 Ling 1m4f (0-75)H STD £3238
70 12/06 Kemp 1m2f (0-60)H STD £2388
62 9/05 Chep 1m14y G-F £3125
Total win prize-money £8754

Going (Turf): Sf: 0-1 GS: 0-1 Gd: 0-8 **GF: 1-11** Fm: 0-3
Distance: 5f/6f: 0-0 7f-8f: 0-2 **9f-13f: 3-45** 14f+: 0-0
Track : LH: 1-30 RH: 1-14 **Tight: 1-25** Gall: 0-1
Aids: Bl: 0-1 Vi: 0-0 Tstrap: 2-37 Ckp: 2-37
Best Rating: 77 12/07 Wolv 1m4f50y stand

Modest; effective at around 1m2f-1m4f; acts on fast ground and on Polytrack; has worn cheekpieces.

Generous Star

98(100) (63)**55**

6-y-o ch g Generous (IRE)-Elegant Dance (Statoblest)
J Pearce Mrs Eileen Sheehan

Placings:0044322-3420 **(1426)**
2009: 13^{3}SD, 16^{4}SD, 13^{2}SF, 15^{0}G,

	Starts	1st	2nd	3rd	Win & Pl
Career Total (Turf)	1	0	0	0	
Career Total (AW)	10	0	3	2	3223

Going (Turf): Sf: 0-0 GS: 0-0 Gd: 0-1 GF: 0-0 Fm: 0-0
Distance: 5f/6f: 0-0 7f-8f: 0-0 9f-13f: 0-1 14f+: 0-10
Track : LH: 0-9 RH: 0-2 Tight: 0-4 Gall: 0-6
Aids: Bl: 0-0 Vi: 0-0 Tstrap: 0-1 Ckp: 0-1
Best Rating: **63** 2/09 Wolv 1m5f194y std-fst

Moderate; stays 1m6f; acts on Polytrack.

Geneva Geyser (GER)

108(99) (75)**88**

3-y-o b g One Cool Cat (USA)-Genevra (IRE) (Danehill (USA))
J M P Eustace J C Smith

Placings:F1-505131010P **(6855)**
2009: 7^{5}SD, 8^{0}GF, 8^{5}F, 10^{1}GF, 12^{3}F, 10^{1}F, 9^{0}G, 10^{1}GF, 10^{0}GF, 12^{P}SD,

	Starts	1st	2nd	3rd	Win & Pl
Career Total (Turf)	9	3	0	1	17990
Career Total (AW)	3	1	0	0	3886

88 8/09 Newb 1m2f6y (0-85)H G-F £4857
86 7/09 Rdcr 1m2f (0-85)H FRM £5828
82 5/09 Rdcr 1m2f (0-85)H G-F £6476
75 12/08 GrLe 6f STD £3885
Total win prize-money £21047

Going (Turf): Sf: 0-0 GS: 0-0 Gd: 0-2 **GF: 2-4** Fm: 1-3
Distance: 5f/6f: 1-2 7f-8f: 0-1 **9f-13f: 3-9** 14f+: 0-0
Track : **LH: 4-9** RH: 0-1 Tight: 2-6 Gall: 2-4
Aids: Bl: 0-1 Vi: 0-0 Tstrap: 0-0 Ckp: 0-0
Best Rating: **88** 8/09 Newb 1m2f6y gd-fm

Useful; stays 1m2f; acts on fast ground; goes on Polytrack; has worn blinkers.

Genki (IRE)

109 (53)**109**

5-y-o ch g Shinko Forest (IRE)-Emma's Star (ITY) (Darshaan)
R Charlton Ms Gillian Khosla

Placings:62/1212121/40-5024103 **(6707a)**
2009: 6^{5}GF, 6^{0}GF, 6^{2}GF, 7^{4}G, 6^{1}S, 6^{0}G, 6^{3}S,

	Starts	1st	2nd	3rd	Win & Pl
Career Total (Turf)	17	5	5	1	148264
Career Total (AW)	1	0	0	0	0

109 8/09 Gdwd 6f H SFT £62310
106 9/07 Asct 6f (0-100)H GD £12464
97 8/07 Asct 6f (0-100)H G-F £17234
87 5/07 NmkR 6f (0-105)H G-F £24928
79 4/07 Folk 6f GD £2914
Total win prize-money £119851

Going (Turf): Sf: 1-2 GS: 0-3 **Gd: 2-6 GF: 2-6** Fm: 0-0
Distance: **5f/6f: 5-15** 7f-8f: 0-3 9f-13f: 0-0 14f+: 0-0
Track : LH: 0-3 RH: 0-0 Tight: 0-1 Gall: 0-3
Aids: Bl: 0-0 Vi: 0-0 Tstrap: 0-0 Ckp: 0-0
Best Rating: **109** 8/09 Gdwd 6f soft

Smart; winner of the 2009 Stewards' Cup; effective over 6f; acts on most ground and on Polytrack.

Gentle Beat (IRE)

94 **71**

2-y-o b g Whipper (USA)-Soft (USA) (Lear Fan (USA))
T D Easterby Tri Nations Racing Syndicate

Placings:30635004 **(5942)**
2009: 5^{3}GF, 5^{0}G, 6^{6}GF, 5^{3}G, 6^{5}F, 7^{0}S, 5^{0}GF, 7^{4}G,

	Starts	1st	2nd	3rd	Win & Pl
Career Total (Turf)	8	0	0	2	1454

Going (Turf): Sf: 0-1 GS: 0-0 Gd: 0-3 GF: 0-3 Fm: 0-1
Distance: 5f/6f: 0-6 7f-8f: 0-2 9f-13f: 0-0 14f+: 0-0
Track : LH: 0-2 RH: 0-1 Tight: 0-2 Gall: 0-0
Aids: Bl: 0-0 Vi: 0-0 Tstrap: 0-2 Ckp: 0-2
Best Rating: **71** 6/09 Hayd 5f good

Fair; suited by 5f and fast ground.

Gentle Guru

102(104) (75)**92**

5-y-o b m Ishiguru (USA)-Soft Touch (IRE) (Petorius)
R T Phillips Richard Phillips

Placings:521/221603/0622110-0006064500**1003** **(7870)**
2009: 5^{0}G, 6^{0}HY, 6^{0}G, 6^{6}G, 6^{0}G, 5^{6}G, 5^{4}GF, 6^{5}GS, 7^{0}SD, 6^{0}SD, 6^{1}SD, 6^{0}SD, 6^{0}SD, 6^{3}SS,

	Starts	1st	2nd	3rd	Win & Pl
Career Total (Turf)	24	4	5	1	23615
Career Total (AW)	6	1	0	1	2091

75 11/09 Kemp 6f (0-65)H STD £1706
92 8/08 Newb 6f8y (0-75)H G-S £2914
86 8/08 Folk 5f (0-75)H G-S £2590
81 7/07 Sand 5f6y (0-80)H GD £5181
69 10/06 Wwck 6f21y SFT £3886
Total win prize-money £16278

Going (Turf): Sf: 1-4 **GS: 2-5** Gd: 1-11 GF: 0-4 Fm: 0-0
Distance: **5f/6f: 3-22** 7f-8f: 2-7 9f-13f: 0-1 14f+: 0-0
Track : LH: 1-7 RH: 1-7 Tight: 0-5 Gall: 0-4
Aids: Bl: 0-0 Vi: 0-0 Tstrap: 0-0 Ckp: 0-0
Best Rating: **92** 8/08 Newb 6f8y gd-sft

Modest; effective over 5f-7f; acts on good and easy ground and Polytrack.

Geoffdaw

92(102) (78)**67**

4-y-o b g Vettori (IRE)-Talighta (USA) (Barathea (IRE))
Miss Sheena West (P D Evans 7/8) Michael Moriarty

Placings:3100100/6004110006-60355056 **(4732)**
2009: 6^{6}SD, 7^{0}SD, 7^{3}SD, 5^{5}SD, 5^{5}SD, 6^{0}GF, 6^{5}GF, 5^{6}GS,

	Starts	1st	2nd	3rd	Win & Pl
Career Total (Turf)	7	1	0	0	3019
Career Total (AW)	18	3	0	2	9692

76 9/08 Ling 6f (0-70)H STD £2590
78 8/08 Kemp 6f (0-75)H STD £3238
75 9/07 Ling 6f (0-75) STD £3238
68 4/07 Folk 5f G-F £2730
Total win prize-money £11797

Going (Turf): Sf: 0-0 GS: 0-1 Gd: 0-2 **GF: 1-4** Fm: 0-0
Distance: **5f/6f: 4-18** 7f-8f: 0-7 9f-13f: 0-0 14f+: 0-0
Track : **LH: 2-17** RH: 1-3 **Tight: 2-9** Gall: 0-5
Aids: Bl: 0-0 **Vi: 2-9** Tstrap: 0-4 Ckp: 0-4
Best Rating: **78** 8/08 Kemp 6f stand

Fair; effective over 5f-6f; acts on fast ground; also goes on Fibresand and Polytrack; has worn cheekpieces and a visor.

Geojimali

94 (82)**89**

7-y-o ch g Compton Place-Harrken Heights (IRE) (Belmez (USA))
J S Goldie Fyffees 2

Placings:665/00/**0221**0122**2215313**/10000656260004/510 00146006050-00 **(6764)**
2009: 6^{0}G, 6^{0}G,

	Starts	1st	2nd	3rd	Win & Pl
Career Total (Turf)	44	6	4	2	74998
Career Total (AW)	6	1	3	0	4711

89 6/08 Newc 6f (0-100)H SFT £18693
88 5/08 Donc 6f (0-90)H GD £7123
87 4/07 Muss 5f (0-85)H G-F £6477
89 9/06 Ayr 6f H G-S £21812
78 7/06 Ayr 6f (0-75)H FRM £5181
69 5/06 Carl 5f193y (0-70)H G-S £3238
66 5/06 Wolv 5f216y (0-45) STD £1876
Total win prize-money £64404

Going (Turf): Sf: 1-11 **GS: 2-6** Gd: 1-11 GF: 1-14 Fm: 1-2
Distance: **5f/6f: 7-39** 7f-8f: 0-11 9f-13f: 0-0 14f+: 0-0
Track : LH: 1-15 RH: 1-2 **Tight: 1-7** Gall: 0-0
Aids: Bl: 0-0 Vi: 0-0 Tstrap: 0-1 Ckp: 0-1
Best Rating: **89** 6/08 Newc 6f soft

Fair; suited by 5f-6f; acts on most types of ground and on Polytrack; often misses the break.

Geordie Dancer (IRE)

(97) (46)**46**

7-y-o b g Dansili-Awtaar (USA) (Lyphard (USA))
A Berry Alan Berry

Placings:050/05002520100/**000**6050/00/**0510**000540-0 **(0574)**
2009: 5^{0}SD,

	Starts	1st	2nd	3rd	Win & Pl
Career Total (Turf)	27	1	2	0	4618
Career Total (AW)	8	1	0	0	1775

46 2/08 Wolv 5f20y STD £1774
66 9/05 Carl 5f193y (0-55)H G-F £2987
Total win prize-money £4763

Going (Turf): Sf: 0-1 GS: 0-4 Gd: 0-3 **GF: 1-14** Fm: 0-5
Distance: **5f/6f: 2-20** 7f-8f: 0-15 9f-13f: 0-0 14f+: 0-0
Track : LH: 1-13 RH: 1-8 **Tight: 1-12** Gall: 0-2
Aids: Bl: 1-15 Vi: 0-0 Tstrap: 1-8 Ckp: 1-8
Best Rating: **66** 9/05 Carl 5f193y gd-fm

Plating class; suited by 5f-6f; acts on fast ground and Polytrack; has worn blinkers.

Geordieland (FR)

119 (96)**121**

8-y-o gr h Johann Quatz (FR)-Aerdee (FR) (Highest Honor (FR))
J A Osborne A Taylor, K Conlan & D Carberry

Placings:032/12123123/12105/404240/**2522522**/125-133 **(5824)**
2009: 16^{1}G, 20^{3}GF, 18^{3}GF,

	Starts	1st	2nd	3rd	Win & Pl
Career Total (Turf)	34	7	11	5	536006
Career Total (AW)	1	0	1	0	5595

121 5/09 Sand 2m78y GD £56770
119 5/08 York 1m6f G-F £79478
117 6/05 Chan 1m4f GD £48511
115 4/05 StCl 1m4f HVY £16667
8/04 Claf 1m4f HVY £15845

102 5/04 Chan 1m2f GD £19366
95 3/04 MsnL 1m1f VS £9859
Total win prize-money £246496

Going (Turf): Sf: 2-4 GS: 0-6 **Gd: 3-13** GF: 1-8 Fm: 0-0
Distance: 5f/6f: 0-0 7f-8f: 0-1 **9f-13f: 5-19** 14f+: 2-15
Track : LH: 2-13 **RH: 3-18** Tight: 0-2 **Gall: 1-9**
Aids: Bl: 0-1 Vi: 0-0 Tstrap: 0-0 Ckp: 0-0
Best Rating: **121** 5/09 Sand 2m78y good

Group class; ex-French; winner of the 2008 Group 2 Yorkshire Cup; placed in three Gold Cups; stays 2m4f but effective at 1m6f; can find little off the bridle; acts on most ground; has been tried in blinkers and usually given a very patient ride.

George Adamson (IRE)

91 51

3-y-o b g Where Or When (IRE)-Tactile (Groom Dancer (USA))
G A Swinbank Mrs S Sanbrook

Placings:5005 **(3449)**
2009: 7⁵GF, 10⁰S, 8⁰G, 7⁵GF,

	Starts	1st	2nd	3rd	Win & Pl
Career Total (Turf)	4	0	0	0	0

Going (Turf): **Sf: 0-1 GS: 0-0 Gd: 0-1 GF: 0-2 Fm: 0-0**
Distance: 5f/6f: 0-0 7f-8f: 0-3 9f-13f: 0-1 14f+: 0-0
Track : LH: 0-1 RH: 0-2 Tight: 0-1 Gall: 0-0
Aids: Bl: 0-0 Vi: 0-0 Tstrap: 0-0 Ckp: 0-0
Best Rating: **51** 6/09 Rdcr 1m good

George Baker (IRE)

92(91) (62)80

2-y-o b g Camacho-Petite Maxine (Sharpo)
George Baker Findlay & Bloom

Placings:03003**560** **(6721)**
2009: 5⁰GF, 5³G, 5⁰GF, 7⁰GF, 6³GF, 7⁵SD, 6⁶SD, 8⁰SD,

	Starts	1st	2nd	3rd	Win & Pl
Career Total (Turf)	5	0	0	2	1107
Career Total (AW)	3	0	0	0	0

Going (Turf): **Sf: 0-0 GS: 0-0 Gd: 0-1 GF: 0-4 Fm: 0-0**
Distance: 5f/6f: 0-4 7f-8f: 0-4 9f-13f: 0-0 14f+: 0-0
Track : LH: 0-0 RH: 0-3 Tight: 0-0 Gall: 0-0
Aids: Bl: 0-0 Vi: 0-0 Tstrap: 0-3 Ckp: 0-3
Best Rating: **80** 6/09 Asct 5f gd-fm

Fair; should stay 6f; acts on a sound surface; has worn cheekpieces.

George Benjamin

93 72

2-y-o b g Trade Fair-Unchain My Heart (Pursuit Of Love)
D Nicholls C M & M A Scaife

Placings:233222 **(6646)**
2009: 5²G, 6³GF, 6³G, 7²G, 7²G, 6²G,

	Starts	1st	2nd	3rd	Win & Pl
Career Total (Turf)	6	0	4	2	8564

Going (Turf): **Sf: 0-0 GS: 0-0 Gd: 0-5 GF: 0-1 Fm: 0-0**
Distance: 5f/6f: 0-4 7f-8f: 0-2 9f-13f: 0-0 14f+: 0-0
Track : LH: 0-2 RH: 0-0 Tight: 0-1 Gall: 0-0
Aids: Bl: 0-0 Vi: 0-0 Tstrap: 0-0 Ckp: 0-0
Best Rating: **72** 10/09 York 6f good

Fair; effective over 6f-7f; acts on good ground.

George Rex (USA)

74(50) 69

3-y-o b/br g Johannesburg (USA)-Royal Linkage (USA) (Linkage (USA))
B J Meehan The Tumbleweed Partnership

Placings:540-00 **(3009)**
2009: 8⁰GF, 7⁰G,

	Starts	1st	2nd	3rd	Win & Pl
Career Total (Turf)	4	0	0	0	457
Career Total (AW)	1	0	0	0	

Going (Turf): **Sf: 0-0 GS: 0-0 Gd: 0-2 GF: 0-2 Fm: 0-0**
Distance: 5f/6f: 0-0 7f-8f: 0-5 9f-13f: 0-0 14f+: 0-0
Track : LH: 0-0 RH: 0-2 Tight: 0-0 Gall: 0-0
Aids: Bl: 0-0 Vi: 0-0 Tstrap: 0-0 Ckp: 0-0
Best Rating: **69** 10/08 NmkR 7f gd-fm

George The Best (IRE)

86(84) (28)29

8-y-o b g Imperial Ballet (IRE)-En Retard (IRE) (Petardia)
Micky Hammond Stef Stefanou

Placings:25311000/0640600056/010040**000**/**00**51060605 01014/000304052/**0000-000** **(5309)**
2009: 6⁰SD, 5⁰GF, 5⁰HY,

	Starts	1st	2nd	3rd	Win & Pl
Career Total (Turf)	48	6	2	2	29880
Career Total (AW)	10	0	0	0	

69 10/06 Ayr 6f (0-62)H HVY £2590
63 9/06 Haml 5f4y (0-70)H G-S £3238
69 5/06 Haml 6f5y (0-70)H GD £4533
69 5/05 Haml 6f5y (0-70)H G-S £3666
80 7/03 Haml 6f5y D GD £5655
73 6/03 Pont 5f E G-S £5486
Total win prize-money £25171

Going (Turf): Sf: 1-15 **GS: 3-14** Gd: 2-11 GF: 0-7 Fm: 0-1
Distance: 5f/6f: 3-40 7f-8f: 3-18 9f-13f: 0-0 14f+: 0-0
Track : **LH: 1-12** RH: 0-3 Tight: 0-4 Gall: 0-0
Aids: Bl: 0-0 Vi: 0-1 Tstrap: 0-0 Ckp: 0-0
Best Rating: **80** 7/03 Haml 6f5y good

Modest performer; effective over 5 and 6f; handles fast and easy ground; has won four times at Hamilton.

George Thisby

98(103) (70)78

3-y-o b g Royal Applause-Warning Belle (Warning)
B R Millman Robert Thisby

Placings:24321260 **(6798)**
2009: 7²GF, 7⁴GF, 6³GF, 6²GF, **6¹SD**, 6²GF, 7⁶GF, 6⁰S,

	Starts	1st	2nd	3rd	Win & Pl
Career Total (Turf)	7	0	3	1	4371
Career Total (AW)	1	1	0	0	2730

70 7/09 Sthl 6f STD £2729
Total win prize-money £2730

Going (Turf): **Sf: 0-1 GS: 0-0 Gd: 0-0 GF: 0-6 Fm: 0-0**
Distance: **5f/6f: 1-3** 7f-8f: 0-5 9f-13f: 0-0 14f+: 0-0
Track : **LH: 1-2** RH: 0-0 Tight: 0-0 Gall: 0-0
Aids: Bl: 0-0 Vi: 0-0 Tstrap: 0-0 Ckp: 0-0
Best Rating: **78** 8/09 Newb 6f8y gd-fm

Fair; effective over 6-7f; acts on fast ground; goes on Fibresand.

Georgebernardshaw (IRE)

111 (81)113

4-y-o b c Danehill Dancer (IRE)-Khamseh (Thatching)
A P O'Brien Mrs John Magnier, M Tabor & D Smith

Placings:0436/110032-000302334 **(5135)**
2009: 7⁰Y, 5⁰Y, 6⁰HY, 7³G, 6⁰GY, 7²S, 6³S, 8³Y, 10⁴GF,

	Starts	1st	2nd	3rd	Win & Pl
Career Total (Turf)	16	2	2	4	104673
Career Total (AW)	3	0	0	1	1040

113 4/08 Curr 7f HVY £23933
89 3/08 Curr 6f HVY £7621
Total win prize-money £31555

Going (Turf): **Sf: 2-7** GS: 0-0 Gd: 0-2 GF: 0-2 Fm: 0-0
Distance: 5f/6f: 1-8 7f-8f: 1-10 9f-13f: 0-1 14f+: 0-0
Track : LH: 0-4 RH: 0-2 Tight: 0-0 Gall: 0-1
Aids: Bl: 0-0 Vi: 0-0 Tstrap: 0-0 Ckp: 0-0
Best Rating: **113** 4/08 Curr 7f heavy

Smart; Irish-trained, Listed placed; effective over 6f-7f; acts well on heavy ground; handles Polytrack; has not looked straightforward.

Georgie Bee

96(101) (46)49

3-y-o b f Ishiguru (USA)-Light Of Aragon (Aragon)
T D Walford (D Carroll 18/5) C H Stephenson & Partners

Placings:06-064434000 **(7422)**
2009: 6⁰GF, 7⁶GF, **8⁴SD**, 8⁴GF, 8³GF, 9⁴G, 9⁰F, 8⁰GF, **8⁰SD**,

	Starts	1st	2nd	3rd	Win & Pl
Career Total (Turf)	9	0	0	1	789
Career Total (AW)	2	0	0	0	0

Going (Turf): **Sf: 0-1 GS: 0-0 Gd: 0-1 GF: 0-6 Fm: 0-1**
Distance: 5f/6f: 0-3 7f-8f: 0-2 9f-13f: 0-6 14f+: 0-0
Track : LH: 0-6 RH: 0-3 Tight: 0-1 Gall: 0-0
Aids: Bl: 0-1 Vi: 0-0 Tstrap: 0-0 Ckp: 0-0
Best Rating: **49** 8/09 Bevl 1m1f207y good

Georgina Macrae

(89) (46)

3-y-o b f Bahamian Bounty-Sadly Sober (IRE) (Roi Danzig (USA))
A M Balding Evan M Sutherland

Placings:000 **(0869)**
2009: 7⁰SD, 7⁰SD, 7⁰SD,

	Starts	1st	2nd	3rd	Win & Pl
Career Total (Turf)	0	0	0	0	
Career Total (AW)	3	0	0	0	

Going (Turf): **Sf: 0-0 GS: 0-0 Gd: 0-0 GF: 0-0 Fm: 0-0**
Distance: 5f/6f: 0-0 7f-8f: 0-3 9f-13f: 0-0 14f+: 0-0
Track : LH: 0-3 RH: 0-0 Tight: 0-3 Gall: 0-0
Aids: Bl: 0-0 Vi: 0-0 Tstrap: 0-0 Ckp: 0-0
Best Rating: **46** 2/09 Ling 7f stand

Gertmegalush (IRE)

102 **83**

2-y-o b g One Cool Cat (USA)-Aiming Upwards (Blushing Flame (USA))

J D Bethell (Tom Dascombe 22/4) Business Development Consultants Limited

Placings:4140100230 **(6643)**

2009: 5^{4}GF, 5^{1}GF, 5^{4}GF, 6^{0}GS, 5^{1}GF, 5^{0}G, 5^{0}GF, 5^{2}GF, 6^{3}G, 6^{0}G,

	Starts	1st	2nd	3rd	Win & Pl
Career Total (Turf)	**10**	**2**	**1**	**1**	**14673**

74	7/09	York	5f	H	G-F	£7123
71	5/09	Thsk	5f		G-F	£4274

Total win prize-money £11398

Going (Turf): Sf: 0-0 GS: 0-1 Gd: 0-3 **GF: 2-6** Fm: 0-0
Distance: **5f/6f: 2-10** 7f-8f: 0-0 9f-13f: 0-0 14f+: 0-0
Track : LH: 0-0 RH: 0-0 Tight: 0-0 Gall: 0-0
Aids: Bl: 0-3 Vi: 0-0 Tstrap: 0-0 Ckp: 0-0
Best Rating: **83** 9/09 Ayr 6f good

Useful; effective over 5f; acts on fast ground; has worn blinkers; can miss the break.

Gertrude Bell

98(99) (76)**82**

2-y-o ch f Sinndar (IRE)-Sugar Mill (FR) (Polar Falcon (USA))

J H M Gosden Ms Rachel D S Hood

Placings:332 **(6992)**

2009: 8^{3}GF, 8^{3}SS, 8^{2}GS,

	Starts	1st	2nd	3rd	Win & Pl
Career Total (Turf)	2	0	1	1	2312
Career Total (AW)	1	0	0	1	578

Going (Turf): **Sf: 0-0 GS: 0-1 Gd: 0-0 GF: 0-1 Fm: 0-0**
Distance: 5f/6f: 0-0 7f-8f: 0-3 9f-13f: 0-0 14f+: 0-0
Track : LH: 0-2 RH: 0-0 Tight: 0-1 Gall: 0-1
Aids: Bl: 0-0 Vi: 0-0 Tstrap: 0-0 Ckp: 0-0
Best Rating: **82** 10/09 Donc 1m gd-sft

Useful; stays 1m; acts onfast and easy ground.

Gessabelle

83(74) (4)**38**

2-y-o b f Largesse-Palmstead Belle (IRE) (Wolfhound (USA))

P S McEntee Mrs Rebecca McEntee

Placings:00000 **(6591)**

2009: 5^{0}GF, 6^{0}GS, 6^{0}GF, 5^{0}SD, 6^{0}GS,

	Starts	1st	2nd	3rd	Win & Pl
Career Total (Turf)	4	0	0	0	
Career Total (AW)	1	0	0	0	

Going (Turf): **Sf: 0-0 GS: 0-2 Gd: 0-0 GF: 0-2 Fm: 0-0**
Distance: 5f/6f: 0-4 7f-8f: 0-1 9f-13f: 0-0 14f+: 0-0
Track : LH: 0-0 RH: 0-0 Tight: 0-0 Gall: 0-0
Aids: Bl: 0-0 Vi: 0-0 Tstrap: 0-0 Ckp: 0-0
Best Rating: **38** 7/09 NmkJ 6f gd-sft

Get A Grip (IRE)

89(98) (81)**70**

2-y-o b c Royal Applause-Landela (Alhaarth (IRE))

J A R Toller M Barber

Placings:21 **(6162)**

2009: 7^{2}G, 8^{1}SD,

	Starts	1st	2nd	3rd	Win & Pl
Career Total (Turf)	1	0	1	0	1156
Career Total (AW)	1	1	0	0	5343

81	9/09	Kemp	1m	STD	£5342

Total win prize-money £5343

Going (Turf): **Sf: 0-0 GS: 0-0 Gd: 0-1 GF: 0-0 Fm: 0-0**
Distance: 5f/6f: 0-0 **7f-8f: 1-2** 9f-13f: 0-0 14f+: 0-0
Track : LH: 0-0 **RH: 1-1** Tight: 0-0 Gall: 0-0
Aids: Bl: 0-0 Vi: 0-0 Tstrap: 0-0 Ckp: 0-0
Best Rating: **81** 9/09 Kemp 1m stand

Useful; effective at 1m; acts on good ground and Polytrack.

Getcarter

99(107) (83)**84**

3-y-o b c Fasliyev (USA)-Pourquoi Pas (IRE) (Nordico (USA))

R Hannon Mrs J K Powell

Placings:365-356110310 **(7356)**

2009: 8^{3}GF, 8^{5}GF, 7^{6}GF, 6^{1}GF, 6^{1}GF, 6^{0}G, 6^{3}GF, 6^{1}SD, 7^{0}SD,

	Starts	1st	2nd	3rd	Win & Pl
Career Total (Turf)	10	2	0	3	10183
Career Total (AW)	2	1	0	0	4727

83	9/09	Kemp	6f	(0-85)H	STD	£4727
77	8/09	Newb	6f8y	(0-80)H	G-F	£4857
84	8/09	Sals	6f212y	(0-70)H	G-F	£3238

Total win prize-money £12822

Going (Turf): Sf: 0-1 GS: 0-0 Gd: 0-2 **GF: 2-7** Fm: 0-0
Distance: 5f/6f: 1-5 **7f-8f: 2-6** 9f-13f: 0-1 14f+: 0-0
Track : LH: 0-1 **RH: 1-2** Tight: 0-2 Gall: 0-0
Aids: Bl: 0-0 Vi: 0-0 Tstrap: 0-0 Ckp: 0-0
Best Rating: **84** 8/09 Sals 6f212y gd-fm

Fair; effective at 6f; acts on fast ground and Polytrack.

Ghaayer

67 **27**

3-y-o ch c Nayef (USA)-Valthea (FR) (Antheus (USA))

M P Tregoning Hamdan Al Maktoum

Placings:0-0 **(1355)**

2009: 8^{0}S,

	Starts	1st	2nd	3rd	Win & Pl
Career Total (Turf)	2	0	0	0	

Going (Turf): **Sf: 0-1 GS: 0-0 Gd: 0-1 GF: 0-0 Fm: 0-0**
Distance: 5f/6f: 0-0 7f-8f: 0-2 9f-13f: 0-0 14f+: 0-0
Track : LH: 0-0 RH: 0-0 Tight: 0-0 Gall: 0-0
Aids: Bl: 0-0 Vi: 0-0 Tstrap: 0-0 Ckp: 0-0
Best Rating: **27** 4/09 Newb 1m soft

Ghaill Force

77(92) (45)**16**

7-y-o b g Piccolo-Coir 'A' Ghaill (Jalmood (USA))

P Butler Richard J Wilson

Placings:2/4460005460/0005060/00-0 **(2493)**

2009: 10^{0}GF,

	Starts	1st	2nd	3rd	Win & Pl
Career Total (Turf)	12	0	1	0	726
Career Total (AW)	9	0	0	0	0

Going (Turf): **Sf: 0-2 GS: 0-0 Gd: 0-2 GF: 0-7 Fm: 0-1**
Distance: 5f/6f: 0-0 7f-8f: 0-8 9f-13f: 0-11 14f+: 0-2
Track : LH: 0-9 RH: 0-7 Tight: 0-6 Gall: 0-2
Aids: Bl: 0-1 Vi: 0-1 Tstrap: 0-4 Ckp: 0-4
Best Rating: **59** 9/04 Kemp 1m gd-fm

Ghanaati (USA)

115(97) (87)**120**

3-y-o b f Giant's Causeway (USA)-Sarayir (USA) (Mr Prospector (USA))

B W Hills Hamdan Al Maktoum

Placings:31-1132 **(6479)**

2009: 8^{1}GF, 8^{1}GF, 8^{3}G, 8^{2}GF,

	Starts	1st	2nd	3rd	Win & Pl
Career Total (Turf)	**4**	**2**	**1**	**1**	**457128**
Career Total (AW)	**2**	**1**	**0**	**1**	**4584**

120	6/09	Asct	1m	G-F	£154698
115	5/09	NmkR	1m	G-F	£227080
87	10/08	Kemp	7f	STD	£3885

Total win prize-money £385664

Going (Turf): Sf: 0-0 GS: 0-0 Gd: 0-1 **GF: 2-3** Fm: 0-0
Distance: 5f/6f: 0-0 **7f-8f: 3-6** 9f-13f: 0-0 14f+: 0-0
Track : LH: 0-0 **RH: 2-4** Tight: 0-0 **Gall: 1-1**
Aids: Bl: 0-0 Vi: 0-0 Tstrap: 0-0 Ckp: 0-0
Best Rating: **120** 6/09 Asct 1m gd-fm

High-class; winner of the 1000 Guineas and Coronation Stakes in 2009; effective over 7f-1m; acts on fast ground and Polytrack.

Ghaneema (USA)

98 **77**

3-y-o b f Forestry (USA)-Unify (USA) (Farma Way (USA))

M P Tregoning Hamdan Al Maktoum

Placings:2 **(4955)**

2009: 8^{2}G,

	Starts	1st	2nd	3rd	Win & Pl
Career Total (Turf)	1	0	1	0	964

Going (Turf): **Sf: 0-0 GS: 0-0 Gd: 0-1 GF: 0-0 Fm: 0-0**
Distance: 5f/6f: 0-0 7f-8f: 0-0 9f-13f: 0-1 14f+: 0-0
Track : LH: 0-0 RH: 0-1 Tight: 0-0 Gall: 0-0
Aids: Bl: 0-0 Vi: 0-0 Tstrap: 0-0 Ckp: 0-0
Best Rating: **77** 8/09 Sand 1m14y good

Fair; stays 1m and acts on good ground.

Ghazwah

97(87) (70)**75**

2-y-o b f Shamardal (USA)-Bahja (USA) (Seeking The Gold (USA))

J H M Gosden Hamdan Al Maktoum

Placings:4230 **(7145)**

2009: 6^{4}GF, 7^{2}GS, 7^{3}SD, 6^{0}G,

	Starts	1st	2nd	3rd	Win & Pl
Career Total (Turf)	3	0	1	0	4576
Career Total (AW)	1	0	0	1	578

Going (Turf): **Sf: 0-0 GS: 0-1 Gd: 0-1 GF: 0-1 Fm: 0-0**
Distance: 5f/6f: 0-2 7f-8f: 0-2 9f-13f: 0-0 14f+: 0-0
Track : LH: 0-0 RH: 0-2 Tight: 0-0 Gall: 0-0
Aids: Bl: 0-0 Vi: 0-0 Tstrap: 0-0 Ckp: 0-0
Best Rating: **75** 7/09 Gdwd 7f gd-sft

Promising filly; stays 7f; handles fast and easy ground.

Gheed (IRE)

(84) (42)**53**

4-y-o b f Cape Cross (IRE)-Hareer (Anabaa (USA))

K A Morgan P Doughty

Placings:5-00 **(7826)**
2009: 12^0SD, 8^0SD,

	Starts	1st	2nd	3rd	Win & Pl
Career Total (Turf)	1	0	0	0	0
Career Total (AW)	2	0	0	0	

Going (Turf): Sf: 0-0 GS: 0-0 Gd: 0-1 GF: 0-0 Fm: 0-0
Distance: 5f/6f: 0-0 7f-8f: 0-2 9f-13f: 0-1 14f+: 0-0
Track : LH: 0-2 RH: 0-1 Tight: 0-2 Gall: 0-0
Aids: Bl: 0-0 Vi: 0-0 Tstrap: 0-0 Ckp: 0-0
Best Rating: 53 8/08 Thsk 7f good

Ghent (IRE)

97(94) (62)**63**
3-y-o b g Celtic Swing-Liege (IRE) (Night Shift (USA))
David P Myerscough Mrs P Myerscough

Placings:0-05023254 **(7075a)**
2009: 7^0SD, 6^5S, 7^0G, 9^2YS, 8^3SD, 11^2SD, 12^5SD, 8^4Y,

	Starts	1st	2nd	3rd	Win & Pl
Career Total (Turf)	5	0	1	0	1511
Career Total (AW)	4	0	1	1	1015

Going (Turf): Sf: 0-2 GS: 0-0 Gd: 0-1 GF: 0-0 Fm: 0-0
Distance: 5f/6f: 0-1 7f-8f: 0-5 9f-13f: 0-3 14f+: 0-0
Track : LH: 0-4 RH: 0-3 Tight: 0-1 Gall: 0-0
Aids: Bl: 0-1 Vi: 0-0 Tstrap: 0-5 Ckp: 0-5
Best Rating: 63 10/09 Leop 1m yield

Ghimaar

101 (73)**102**
4-y-o b g Dubai Destination (USA)-Charlecote (IRE) (Caerleon (USA))
D K Weld Hamdan Al Maktoum

Placings:01/20136-0501444 **(6008a)**
2009: 12^0G, 10^5G, 12^0GF, 16^1S, 14^4S, 12^4HY, 12^4Y,

	Starts	1st	2nd	3rd	Win & Pl
Career Total (Turf)	13	3	1	1	73735
Career Total (AW)	1	0	0	0	

99	7/09	Gway	2m	(70-100)H	SFT	£47402
102	7/08	Gway	1m4f	(60-90)H	GD	£8891
81	9/07	Tipp	7f100y		FRM	£7937

Total win prize-money £64232

Going (Turf): Sf: 1-5 GS: 0-0 **Gd: 1-3** GF: 0-3 **Fm: 1-1**
Distance: 5f/6f: 0-1 7f-8f: 1-1 9f-13f: 1-10 14f+: 1-2
Track : LH: 0-5 **RH: 2-8** Tight: 0-0 Gall: 0-2
Aids: Bl: 0-3 Vi: 0-0 Tstrap: 0-0 Ckp: 0-0
Best Rating: 102 7/08 Gway 1m4f good

Smart; effective over 1m4f; acts on fast ground; has worn blinkers.

Ghost (IRE)

97 **79**
2-y-o b g Invincible Spirit (IRE)-Alexander Phantom (IRE) (Soviet Star (USA))
B W Hills The Mystic Mogg Partnership

Placings:4235 **(6231)**
2009: 6^4GF, 6^2G, 6^3G, 6^5GF,

	Starts	1st	2nd	3rd	Win & Pl
Career Total (Turf)	4	0	1	1	2264

Going (Turf): Sf: 0-0 GS: 0-0 Gd: 0-2 GF: 0-2 Fm: 0-0
Distance: 5f/6f: 0-4 7f-8f: 0-0 9f-13f: 0-0 14f+: 0-0
Track : LH: 0-1 RH: 0-0 Tight: 0-0 Gall: 0-2
Aids: Bl: 0-0 Vi: 0-0 Tstrap: 0-0 Ckp: 0-0
Best Rating: 79 7/09 NmkJ 6f good

52,000gns son of Invincible Spirit; promise in maidens 6f on fast and good ground.

Ghost Dancer

105(97) (71)**80**
5-y-o ch g Danehill Dancer (IRE)-Reservation (IRE) (Common Grounds)
J M Bradley E A Hayward

Placings:5240621/03/0106-0003060424122630 **(7203)**
2009: 7^0SD, 7^0GF, 7^0GF, 6^3G, 6^0G, 5^6GF, 6^0GS, 5^4G, 6^2GF, 6^4GF, 6^1G, 6^2GF, 6^2GF, 6^6GS, 6^3SD, 6^0SD,

	Starts	1st	2nd	3rd	Win & Pl
Career Total (Turf)	19	2	4	2	9999
Career Total (AW)	10	1	1	1	11274

71	8/09	Wwck	6f	(0-70)H	GD	£2590
80	9/08	Leic	1m60y	(0-75)H	GD	£2590
75	10/06	Wolv	7f32y		STD	£9348

Total win prize-money £14528

Going (Turf): Sf: 0-0 GS: 0-3 **Gd: 2-6** GF: 0-10 Fm: 0-0
Distance: 5f/6f: 1-15 7f-8f: 1-11 9f-13f: 1-3 14f+: 0-0
Track : **LH: 2-13** RH: 1-3 **Tight: 1-8** Gall: 0-2
Aids: Bl: 0-0 Vi: 0-0 Tstrap: 1-11 Ckp: 1-11
Best Rating: 80 9/08 Leic 1m60y good

Fair; suited by 6f-1m; acts on good and easy ground; goes on Polytrack; has worn cheekpieces.

Ghostwing

100 **89**
2-y-o gr g Kheleyf (USA)-Someone's Angel (USA) (Runaway Groom (CAN))
R A Fahey (Mrs A Duffield 29/4) Mrs H Steel

Placings:3155000 **(6677)**
2009: 5^3G, 6^1GF, 6^5G, 6^5G, 6^0GF, 6^0GF, 6^0G,

	Starts	1st	2nd	3rd	Win & Pl
Career Total (Turf)	7	1	0	1	8960

84	6/09	Ayr	6f	G-F	£3885

Total win prize-money £3886

Going (Turf): Sf: 0-0 GS: 0-0 Gd: 0-4 **GF: 1-3** Fm: 0-0
Distance: **5f/6f: 1-6** 7f-8f: 0-1 9f-13f: 0-0 14f+: 0-0
Track : LH: 0-1 RH: 0-0 Tight: 0-0 Gall: 0-0
Aids: Bl: 0-0 Vi: 0-0 Tstrap: 0-1 Ckp: 0-1
Best Rating: 89 7/09 Gdwd 6f good

Useful; stays 6f; acts on fast ground; has worn cheekpieces.

Ghufa (IRE)

97(105) (73)**66**
5-y-o b g Sakhee (USA)-Hawriyah (USA) (Dayjur (USA))
George Baker Miss Camilla Jenks

Placings:0463453-133420601533112 **(7888)**
2009: 9^1SD, 12^3SD, 10^3SD, 8^4SD, 11^2SD, 12^0G, 10^6GF, 10^0G, 12^1SD, 12^5SD, 12^3SD, 13^3SD, 12^1SD, 9^1SD, 12^2SD,

	Starts	1st	2nd	3rd	Win & Pl
Career Total (Turf)	9	0	0	1	645
Career Total (AW)	13	4	2	5	11466

70	12/09	Wolv	1m1f103y		STD	£2047
65	12/09	Wolv	1m4f50y		STD	£2047
65	9/09	Wolv	1m4f50y		STD	£2388
71	2/09	Wolv	1m1f103y	(0-60)H	STD	£2047

Total win prize-money £8529

Going (Turf): Sf: 0-1 GS: 0-1 Gd: 0-6 GF: 0-1 Fm: 0-0
Distance: 5f/6f: 0-0 7f-8f: 0-1 **9f-13f: 4-20** 14f+: 0-1
Track : **LH: 4-17** RH: 0-4 **Tight: 4-11** Gall: 0-2
Aids: Bl: 0-0 Vi: 0-0 Tstrap: 0-1 Ckp: 0-1
Best Rating: 73 3/09 Sthl 1m3f stand

Modest; probably stays 1m4f; acts on good ground and on Polytrack.

Giant Sequoia (USA)

89(108) (82)**49**
5-y-o ch g Giant's Causeway (USA)-Beware Of The Cat (USA) (Caveat (USA))
Jane Chapple-Hyam (A J Chamberlain 4/8) Mrs Jane Chapple-Hyam

Placings:6/006011301 **(7699)**
2009: 10^0GF, 11^0C, 12^6SD, 12^0HY, 11^1SD, 12^1SD, 12^3SD, 10^0SD, 10^1SD,

	Starts	1st	2nd	3rd	Win & Pl
Career Total (Turf)	4	0	0	0	
Career Total (AW)	6	3	0	1	6646

82	12/09	Kemp	1m2f	(0-70)H	STD	£2590
76	10/09	Ling	1m4f	(0-60)H	STD	£1706
64	9/09	Kemp	1m3f	(0-55)	STD	£2047

Total win prize-money £6343

Going (Turf): Sf: 0-2 GS: 0-0 Gd: 0-1 GF: 0-1 Fm: 0-0
Distance: 5f/6f: 0-0 7f-8f: 0-1 **9f-13f: 3-9** 14f+: 0-0
Track : LH: 1-6 **RH: 2-4 Tight: 1-2** Gall: 0-0
Aids: Bl: 0-0 Vi: 0-0 Tstrap: 0-0 Ckp: 0-0
Best Rating: 82 12/09 Kemp 1m2f stand

Fair; best at around 1m2f-1m4f; goes well on Polytrack; has worn a tongue tie.

Giant Slalom

108(96) (63)**71**
5-y-o b g Tomba-Fallara (FR) (Tropular)
T G McCourt T Manley

Placings:201/2244331515/0000040060506-14000006S650 **(7543a)**
2009: 7^1GF, 7^4SD, 7^0HY, 8^0G, 8^0GF, 7^0Y, 8^0GY, 8^6HY, 7^5GY, 7^6SD, 8^5SD, 7^0SD,

	Starts	1st	2nd	3rd	Win & Pl
Career Total (Turf)	24	2	2	1	17331
Career Total (AW)	14	2	1	1	9383

63	3/09	Leop	7f	(50-75)H	G-F	£6037
88	10/07	Donc	7f	4(0-85)H	GD	£6477
80	9/07	Wolv	7f32y	(0-75)H	STD	£3238
69	11/06	Wolv	7f32y		STD	£3562

Total win prize-money £19316

Going (Turf): Sf: 0-8 GS: 0-2 **Gd: 1-6 GF: 1-3** Fm: 0-0
Distance: 5f/6f: 0-1 **7f-8f: 4-29** 9f-13f: 0-8 14f+: 0-0
Track : **LH: 3-20** RH: 0-10 **Tight: 2-5** Gall: 0-2
Aids: Bl: 0-3 Vi: 0-0 Tstrap: 0-2 Ckp: 0-2
Best Rating: 88 10/07 Donc 7f good

Fair; effective over 7f-1m; acts on soft and fast ground; also goes on Polytrack and Fibresand.

Giant Strides

(92) (59)
3-y-o b f Xaar-Brandish (Warning)
P D Evans The Strangers

Placings:04-45 **(0144)**
2009: 5^4SD, 9^5SD,

	Starts	1st	2nd	3rd	Win & Pl
Career Total (Turf)	0	0	0	0	
Career Total (AW)	4	0	0	0	265

Going (Turf): Sf: 0-0 GS: 0-0 Gd: 0-0 GF: 0-0 Fm: 0-0
Distance: 5f/6f: 0-1 7f-8f: 0-2 9f-13f: 0-1 14f+: 0-0
Track : LH: 0-4 RH: 0-0 Tight: 0-2 Gall: 0-1
Aids: Bl: 0-0 Vi: 0-0 Tstrap: 0-0 Ckp: 0-0
Best Rating: 59 1/09 Wolv 5f216y stand

Giants Play (USA)

96(90) (77)76
2-y-o b f Giant's Causeway (USA)-Playful Act (IRE) (Sadler's Wells (USA))
Sir Michael Stoute Mrs R J Jacobs

Placings:24 **(6992)**
2009: 7^{2}SD, 8^{4}GS,

	Starts	1st	2nd	3rd	Win & Pl
Career Total (Turf)	1	0	0	0	385
Career Total (AW)	1	0	1	0	1156

Going (Turf): Sf: 0-0 GS: 0-1 Gd: 0-0 GF: 0-0 Fm: 0-0
Distance: 5f/6f: 0-0 7f-8f: 0-2 9f-13f: 0-0 14f+: 0-0
Track : LH: 0-1 RH: 0-1 Tight: 0-0 Gall: 0-1
Aids: Bl: 0-0 Vi: 0-0 Tstrap: 0-0 Ckp: 0-0
Best Rating: 77 8/09 Kemp 7f stand

Useful; stays 7f and acts on Polytrack.

Gibb River (IRE)

107 87
3-y-o ch g Mr Greeley (USA)-Laurentine (USA) (Private Account (USA))
P W Chapple-Hyam Favourites Racing

Placings:00-6220225 **(5230)**
2009: 11^{6}GS, 12^{2}GF, 12^{2}G, 16^{0}GF, 12^{2}GS, 14^{2}GS, 14^{5}GF,

	Starts	1st	2nd	3rd	Win & Pl
Career Total (Turf)	9	0	4	0	3507

Going (Turf): Sf: 0-0 GS: 0-3 Gd: 0-3 GF: 0-3 Fm: 0-0
Distance: 5f/6f: 0-0 7f-8f: 0-2 9f-13f: 0-4 14f+: 0-3
Track : LH: 0-5 RH: 0-2 Tight: 0-2 Gall: 0-3
Aids: Bl: 0-1 Vi: 0-0 Tstrap: 0-0 Ckp: 0-0
Best Rating: 87 5/09 Gdwd 1m4f gd-fm

Useful; stays 2m; acts on fast and easy ground; has tried blinkers.

Gibraltar Blue (IRE)

101 94
2-y-o ch f Rock Of Gibraltar (IRE)-Holly Blue (Bluebird (USA))
T Stack M J Jooste

Placings:104 **(6852)**
2009: 6^{1}S, 6^{0}G, 7^{4}G,

	Starts	1st	2nd	3rd	Win & Pl
Career Total (Turf)	3	1	0	0	13353
77 8/09 Fair 6f			SFT	£9056	

Total win prize-money £9057

Going (Turf): Sf: 1-1 GS: 0-0 Gd: 0-2 GF: 0-0 Fm: 0-0
Distance: 5f/6f: 1-2 7f-8f: 0-1 9f-13f: 0-0 14f+: 0-0
Track : LH: 0-0 **RH: 1-1** Tight: 0-0 Gall: 0-0
Aids: Bl: 0-0 Vi: 0-0 Tstrap: 0-0 Ckp: 0-0
Best Rating: 94 10/09 NmkR 7f good

Very useful; stays 7f; handles good and soft ground.

Gibraltar Lass (USA)

(84) (53)
2-y-o ch f Concerto (USA)-Mango Lassie (USA) (Montreal Red (USA))
H J Collingridge Mark Goodridge

Placings:06 **(7582)**
2009: 6^{0}SD, 5^{6}SF,

	Starts	1st	2nd	3rd	Win & Pl
Career Total (Turf)	0	0	0	0	
Career Total (AW)	2	0	0	0	0

Going (Turf): Sf: 0-0 GS: 0-0 Gd: 0-0 GF: 0-0 Fm: 0-0
Distance: 5f/6f: 0-2 7f-8f: 0-0 9f-13f: 0-0 14f+: 0-0
Track : LH: 0-1 RH: 0-1 Tight: 0-1 Gall: 0-0
Aids: Bl: 0-0 Vi: 0-0 Tstrap: 0-0 Ckp: 0-0
Best Rating: 53 10/09 Kemp 6f stand

Gibson Square (USA)

82(86) (47)32
3-y-o b g Gilded Time (USA)-Beyond The Fence (USA) (Grand Slam (USA))
S C Williams J W Parry

Placings:00-6000 **(3474)**
2009: 8^{6}SD, 12^{0}GF, 11^{0}GF, 9^{0}F,

	Starts	1st	2nd	3rd	Win & Pl
Career Total (Turf)	5	0	0	0	
Career Total (AW)	1	0	0	0	0

Going (Turf): Sf: 0-1 GS: 0-0 Gd: 0-1 GF: 0-2 Fm: 0-1
Distance: 5f/6f: 0-1 7f-8f: 0-1 9f-13f: 0-4 14f+: 0-0
Track : LH: 0-4 RH: 0-0 Tight: 0-2 Gall: 0-0
Aids: Bl: 0-0 Vi: 0-1 Tstrap: 0-0 Ckp: 0-0
Best Rating: 47 4/09 Wolv 1m141y stand

Giddywell

(106) (62)58
5-y-o b m Ishiguru (USA)-Understudy (In The Wings)
R Hollinshead The Giddy Gang

Placings:54660400130366/544304455-133000 **(1496)**
2009: 9^{1}SD, 9^{3}SD, 8^{3}SF, 9^{0}SD, 8^{0}SD, 9^{0}SD,

	Starts	1st	2nd	3rd	Win & Pl
Career Total (Turf)	12	1	0	2	3420
Career Total (AW)	17	1	0	3	2652
62 1/09 Wolv 1m1f103y (0-52)H			STD	£2047	
54 7/07 Nott 1m1f213y			HVY	£2388	

Total win prize-money £4436

Going (Turf): Sf: 1-6 GS: 0-0 Gd: 0-3 GF: 0-2 Fm: 0-1
Distance: 5f/6f: 0-0 7f-8f: 0-0 **9f-13f: 2-29** 14f+: 0-0
Track : LH: 2-24 RH: 0-5 **Tight: 1-16** Gall: 0-0
Aids: Bl: 0-0 Vi: 0-0 Tstrap: 1-6 Ckp: 1-6
Best Rating: 62 1/09 Wolv 1m1f103y stand

Moderate; stays 1m4f; acts on soft ground; also goes on Polytrack.

Gift Horse

107(105) (85)96
9-y-o ch g Cadeaux Genereux-Careful Dancer (Gorytus (USA))
P D Evans (D Nicholls 28/5) R Piff

Placings:216/023040/13110/500000/0305005505 0/003603 522024-00210000 4040 **(5788)**
2009: 6^{0}GF, 5^{0}GF, 6^{2}GS, 6^{1}G, 5^{0}GF, 7^{0}GF, 5^{0}GF, 5^{0}GS, 7^{4}G, 7^{0}S, 6^{4}F, 6^{0}G,

	Starts	1st	2nd	3rd	Win & Pl
Career Total (Turf)	53	5	5	5	122752
Career Total (AW)	2	0	1	0	964
74 5/09 Ayr 6f				GD	£3070
115 7/05 Gdwd 6f H				G-S	£58000
101 6/05 Epsm 6f (0-100)H				GD	£23200
97 5/05 Donc 6f (0-85)H				GD	£7241
82 7/03 Sand 1m14y D				G-F	£5577

Total win prize-money £97089

Going (Turf): Sf: 0-10 GS: 1-7 **Gd: 3-19** GF: 1-16 Fm: 0-1
Distance: 5f/6f: 4-38 7f-8f: 0-13 9f-13f: 1-4 14f+: 0-0
Track : LH: 1-12 RH: 1-4 **Tight: 1-5** Gall: 0-4
Aids: Bl: 0-0 Vi: 0-10 Tstrap: 1-14 Ckp: 1-14
Best Rating: 115 7/05 Gdwd 6f gd-sft

Modest; winner of the 2005 Stewards' Cup, best over 6f and acts on any ground; has worn a visor and cheekpieces.

Gift Of Love (IRE)

71 49
2-y-o b f Azamour (IRE)-Spot Prize (USA) (Seattle Dancer (USA))
D R C Elsworth J C Smith

Placings:0 **(4055)**
2009: 7^{0}S,

	Starts	1st	2nd	3rd	Win & Pl
Career Total (Turf)	1	0	0	0	

Going (Turf): Sf: 0-1 GS: 0-0 Gd: 0-0 GF: 0-0 Fm: 0-0
Distance: 5f/6f: 0-0 7f-8f: 0-1 9f-13f: 0-0 14f+: 0-0
Track : LH: 0-0 RH: 0-0 Tight: 0-0 Gall: 0-0
Aids: Bl: 0-0 Vi: 0-0 Tstrap: 0-0 Ckp: 0-0
Best Rating: 49 7/09 NmkJ 7f soft

Gifted Apakay (USA)

(93) (75)
2-y-o ch f Leroidesanimaux (BRZ)-Sentimental Gift (USA) (Green Dancer (USA))
E A L Dunlop V I Araci

Placings:301 **(7624)**
2009: 8^{3}SD, 7^{0}SD, 8^{1}SD,

	Starts	1st	2nd	3rd	Win & Pl
Career Total (Turf)	0	0	0	0	
Career Total (AW)	3	1	0	1	2792
75 12/09 Ling 1m			STD	£2388	

Total win prize-money £2388

Going (Turf): Sf: 0-0 GS: 0-0 Gd: 0-0 GF: 0-0 Fm: 0-0
Distance: 5f/6f: 0-0 **7f-8f: 1-3** 9f-13f: 0-0 14f+: 0-0
Track : LH: 1-3 RH: 0-0 **Tight: 1-3** Gall: 0-0
Aids: Bl: 0-0 Vi: 0-0 Tstrap: 0-0 Ckp: 0-0
Best Rating: 75 12/09 Ling 1m stand

Fair filly; gets 1m and acts on Polytrack.

Gifted Heir (IRE)

96(100) (61)56

5-y-o b g Princely Heir (IRE)-Inzar Lady (IRE) (Inzar (USA))

A Bailey Tregarth Racing & Partner

Placings:005200351/0220562/6132325500000-05002263103000 (7719)

2009: 8^{0}SD, 8^{5}G, 10^{0}G, 8^{0}G, 7^{2}F, 8^{2}GF, 10^{6}GF, 9^{3}SD, 8^{1}SD, 8^{0}SD, 10^{3}SD, 8^{0}SD, 8^{0}SF, 9^{0}SD,

	Starts	1st	2nd	3rd	Win & Pl
Career Total (Turf)	16	0	4	1	3796
Career Total (AW)	27	3	4	4	10269

61 10/09 Wolv 1m141y (0-50)H STD £2183
55 1/08 Wolv 1m1f103y STD £1774
56 11/06 Kemp 7f (0-65) STD £2388
Total win prize-money £6348

Going (Turf):	Sf: 0-0 GS: 0-2 Gd: 0-4 GF: 0-8 Fm: 0-2
Distance:	5f/6f: 0-3 7f-8f: 1-12 9f-13f: 2-27 14f+: 0-1
Track :	LH: 2-28 RH: 1-5 Tight: 2-26 Gall: 0-1
Aids:	Bl: 0-3 Vi: 0-1 Tstrap: 0-2 Ckp: 0-2
Best Rating:	61 11/09 Ling 1m2f stand

Moderate; stays 1m3f; acts on fast ground and Polytrack.

Gifted Leader (USA)

105 90

4-y-o b g Diesis-Zaghruta (USA) (Gone West (USA))

Ian Williams Gifted Leader Partners

Placings:455-5012000 (6995)

2009: 10^{5}GF, 12^{0}GF, 14^{1}GS, 12^{2}G, 12^{0}G, 12^{0}G, 14^{0}GS,

	Starts	1st	2nd	3rd	Win & Pl
Career Total (Turf)	10	1	1	0	7292

85 5/09 Hayd 1m6f (0-70)H G-S £3238
Total win prize-money £3238

Going (Turf):	Sf: 0-1 GS: 1-2 Gd: 0-4 GF: 0-3 Fm: 0-0
Distance:	5f/6f: 0-0 7f-8f: 0-0 9f-13f: 0-8 14f+: 1-2
Track :	LH: 1-7 RH: 0-3 Tight: 0-1 Gall: 0-5
Aids:	Bl: 0-0 Vi: 0-0 Tstrap: 0-0 Ckp: 0-0
Best Rating:	90 6/09 York 1m4f good

Fair; stays 1m6f; acts on good and easy ground.

Giganticus (USA)

109(110) (99)106

6-y-o ch g Giant's Causeway (USA)-Shy Princess (USA) (Irish River (FR))

B W Hills DM James,Cavendish Inv Ltd,Matthew Green

Placings:61/3000/14314100/0505300-500410050 (6815)

2009: 7^{5}SD, 7^{0}GF, 7^{0}GF, 7^{4}GF, 7^{1}GF, 7^{0}GF, 7^{0}G, 7^{5}G, 7^{0}G,

	Starts	1st	2nd	3rd	Win & Pl
Career Total (Turf)	29	5	0	3	158525
Career Total (AW)	1	0	0	0	0

106 6/09 Asct 7f (0-105)H G-F £31155
109 8/07 NmkJ 7f (0-105)H FRM £18696
104 7/07 NmkJ 7f H G-F £62320
94 4/07 Newc 7f (0-100)H GD £9971
91 9/05 Hayd 6f GD £4641
Total win prize-money £126783

Going (Turf):	Sf: 0-0 GS: 0-1 Gd: 2-15 GF: 2-11 Fm: 1-2
Distance:	5f/6f: 1-1 7f-8f: 4-29 9f-13f: 0-0 14f+: 0-0
Track :	LH: 0-4 RH: 0-0 Tight: 0-4 Gall: 0-0
Aids:	Bl: 0-0 Vi: 0-0 Tstrap: 0-0 Ckp: 0-0
Best Rating:	109 8/07 NmkJ 7f firm

Very useful; winner of 2007 Bunbury Cup and 2009 Buckingham Palace Handicap; effective over 7f; acts on a sound surface.

Gilded Age

104(97) (75)79

3-y-o b g Cape Cross (IRE)-Sweet Folly (IRE) (Singspiel (IRE))

A King (M Johnston 4/7) Stennett, Sweeney & Bunter

Placings:521045254 (6203)

2009: 10^{5}SD, 9^{2}F, 12^{1}GF, 12^{0}S, 12^{4}SD, 10^{5}GF, 10^{2}G, 12^{5}GS, 11^{4}G,

	Starts	1st	2nd	3rd	Win & Pl
Career Total (Turf)	7	1	2	0	6655
Career Total (AW)	2	0	0	0	351

72 4/09 Newc 1m4f93y G-F £3885
Total win prize-money £3886

Going (Turf):	Sf: 0-1 GS: 0-1 Gd: 0-2 GF: 1-2 Fm: 0-1
Distance:	5f/6f: 0-0 7f-8f: 0-0 9f-13f: 1-9 14f+: 0-0
Track :	LH: 1-7 RH: 0-2 Tight: 0-5 Gall: 1-2
Aids:	Bl: 0-0 Vi: 0-0 Tstrap: 0-0 Ckp: 0-0
Best Rating:	79 7/09 Nott 1m2f50y good

Fair; stays 1m4f but effective at shorter; acts on fast ground.

Gillburg (USA)

98(98) (73)76

2-y-o ch g Johannesburg (USA)-Bourbon Ball (USA) (Peintre Celebre (USA))

K A Ryan Highbank Syndicate

Placings:3652221250**20** (7551)

2009: 5^{3}GF, 5^{6}GF, 6^{5}G, 5^{2}GF, 6^{2}GS, 6^{2}GS, 6^{1}S, 6^{2}G, 7^{5}GF, 6^{0}GF, 5^{2}SD, 7^{0}SD,

	Starts	1st	2nd	3rd	Win & Pl
Career Total (Turf)	10	1	4	1	9887
Career Total (AW)	2	0	1	0	964

74 8/09 Haml 6f5y SFT £3885
Total win prize-money £3886

Going (Turf):	Sf: 1-1 GS: 0-2 Gd: 0-2 GF: 0-5 Fm: 0-0
Distance:	5f/6f: 0-8 7f-8f: 1-4 9f-13f: 0-0 14f+: 0-0
Track :	LH: 0-3 RH: 0-0 Tight: 0-3 Gall: 0-0
Aids:	Bl: 1-5 Vi: 0-0 Tstrap: 0-3 Ckp: 0-3
Best Rating:	76 9/09 Ripn 6f good

Fair; stays 6f; acts on fast ground; goes on Polytrack; has worn cheekpieces and blinkers.

Gilt Edge Girl

108(110) (96)90

3-y-o ch f Monsieur Bond (IRE)-Tahara (IRE) (Caerleon (USA))

C G Cox Wood Street Syndicate V & C J Harper

Placings:233-2113531 (7414)

2009: 5^{2}SD, 5^{1}GS, 6^{1}GF, 5^{3}GS, 6^{5}G, 5^{3}GF, 5^{1}SD,

	Starts	1st	2nd	3rd	Win & Pl
Career Total (Turf)	8	2	1	4	9646
Career Total (AW)	2	1	1	0	8340

96 11/09 Wolv 5f20y (0-95)H STD £7569
90 5/09 Wind 6f (0-75)H G-F £2914
88 4/09 Nott 5f13y G-S £2729
Total win prize-money £13214

Going (Turf):	Sf: 0-0 GS: 1-5 Gd: 0-1 GF: 1-2 Fm: 0-0
Distance:	5f/6f: 3-10 7f-8f: 0-0 9f-13f: 0-0 14f+: 0-0
Track :	LH: 1-3 RH: 0-1 Tight: 1-1 Gall: 1-1
Aids:	Bl: 0-0 Vi: 0-0 Tstrap: 0-0 Ckp: 0-0
Best Rating:	96 11/09 Wolv 5f20y stand

Useful; effective over 5f-6f; acts on fast and easy ground; goes well on Polytrack.

Ginger Grey (IRE)

97(94) (66)67

2-y-o gr g Bertolini (USA)-Just In Love (FR) (Highest Honor (FR))

S A Callaghan T Mohan & N A Callaghan

Placings:5230022365233 (6963)

2009: 6^{5}GF, 5^{2}G, 5^{3}G, 7^{0}GF, 5^{0}GF, 6^{2}SD, 5^{2}GF, 6^{3}GF, 7^{6}GF, 8^{5}G, 7^{2}GF, 7^{3}SF, 6^{3}G,

	Starts	1st	2nd	3rd	Win & Pl
Career Total (Turf)	11	0	3	3	5075
Career Total (AW)	2	0	1	1	1590

Going (Turf):	Sf: 0-0 GS: 0-0 Gd: 0-4 GF: 0-7 Fm: 0-0
Distance:	5f/6f: 0-7 7f-8f: 0-5 9f-13f: 0-1 14f+: 0-0
Track :	LH: 0-8 RH: 0-1 Tight: 0-3 Gall: 0-0
Aids:	Bl: 0-2 Vi: 0-0 Tstrap: 0-4 Ckp: 0-4
Best Rating:	67 6/09 Brig 5f213y good

Fair 52,000gns half-brother to winners at a mile; showed some ability over 6f on fast ground; has worn blinkers.

Ginger Jack

81(75) (38)56

2-y-o ch g Refuse To Bend (IRE)-Coretta (IRE) (Caerleon (USA))

Saeed Bin Suroor Godolphin

Placings:05 (6382)

2009: 8^{0}SD, 8^{5}GF,

	Starts	1st	2nd	3rd	Win & Pl
Career Total (Turf)	1	0	0	0	0
Career Total (AW)	1	0	0	0	

Going (Turf):	Sf: 0-0 GS: 0-0 Gd: 0-0 GF: 0-1 Fm: 0-0
Distance:	5f/6f: 0-0 7f-8f: 0-2 9f-13f: 0-0 14f+: 0-0
Track :	LH: 0-2 RH: 0-0 Tight: 0-0 Gall: 0-1
Aids:	Bl: 0-0 Vi: 0-0 Tstrap: 0-0 Ckp: 0-0
Best Rating:	56 9/09 Newc 1m gd-fm

Ginger Princess (IRE)

99(106) (74)74

7-y-o b m Pistolet Bleu (IRE)-Palm Lake (IRE) (Spectrum (IRE))

Oliver McKiernan Cavan Developments Bloodstock

Placings:00500003/124013405000-5000 (2732a)

2009: 7^{5}SD, 8^{0}S, 7^{0}GF, 8^{0}S,

	Starts	1st	2nd	3rd	Win & Pl
Career Total (Turf)	17	1	0	0	5651
Career Total (AW)	7	1	1	2	3930

73 4/08 Leop 7f (50-75)H YLD £5080
70 1/08 Sthl 7f (0-65)H STD £2047
Total win prize-money £7129

Going (Turf):	Sf: 0-5 GS: 0-0 Gd: 0-5 GF: 0-2 Fm: 0-0
Distance:	5f/6f: 0-2 7f-8f: 2-20 9f-13f: 0-2 14f+: 0-0
Track :	LH: 2-14 RH: 0-7 Tight: 0-2 Gall: 0-3
Aids:	Bl: 0-3 Vi: 0-0 Tstrap: 0-0 Ckp: 0-0
Best Rating:	74 6/08 Naas 7f gd-fm

Fair; Irish trained; stays 7f and acts well on sand, also handles good ground; often wears tongue tie.

Ginger Ted (IRE)

94(79) (34)76

2-y-o ch g Fath (USA)-Estertide (IRE) (Tagula (IRE))

R C Guest Showhouse Furniture Ltd

Placings:04501010 **(5658)**

2009: 5^{0}GF, 5^{4}GS, 6^{5}G, 5^{0}SD, 6^{1}HY, 5^{0}GS, 6^{1}GS, 6^{0}GS,

	Starts	1st	2nd	3rd	Win & Pl
Career Total (Turf)	7	2	0	0	5902
Career Total (AW)	1	0	0	0	

76 8/09 Nott 6f15y (0-75) G-S £2590
67 7/09 Nott 6f15y HVY £3070
Total win prize-money £5661

Going (Turf): Sf: 1-1 GS: 1-4 Gd: 0-1 GF: 0-1 Fm: 0-0
Distance: 5f/6f: 0-6 7f-8f: 2-2 9f-13f: 0-0 14f+: 0-0
Track : LH: 0-0 RH: 0-0 Tight: 0-0 Gall: 0-0
Aids: Bl: 0-2 Vi: 0-0 Tstrap: 0-1 Ckp: 0-1
Best Rating: 76 8/09 Nott 6f15y gd-sft

Fair; stays 6f; acts on heavy ground; has worn blinkers.

Gingko Lady (USA)

(99) (52)56

4-y-o ch f Mr Greeley (USA)-Highland Tide (USA) (Highland Blade (USA))

J R Boyle J P Foley

Placings:00/0-0006 **(1079)**

2009: 6^{0}SD, 8^{0}SD, 8^{0}SD, 8^{6}SD,

	Starts	1st	2nd	3rd	Win & Pl
Career Total (Turf)	2	0	0	0	
Career Total (AW)	5	0	0	0	0

Going (Turf): Sf: 0-0 GS: 0-0 Gd: 0-0 GF: 0-2 Fm: 0-0
Distance: 5f/6f: 0-2 7f-8f: 0-5 9f-13f: 0-0 14f+: 0-0
Track : LH: 0-6 RH: 0-1 Tight: 0-2 Gall: 0-0
Aids: Bl: 0-0 Vi: 0-1 Tstrap: 0-4 Ckp: 0-4
Best Rating: 56 10/07 Leop 7f gd-fm

Ginobili (IRE)

98(96) (65)96

3-y-o b g Fasliyev (USA)-Imperial Graf (USA) (Blushing John (USA))

Andrew Reid (Stef Liddiard 26/9) A S Reid

Placings:134230-560060100 **(7028)**

2009: 6^{5}GF, 5^{6}G, 5^{0}G, 5^{0}GF, 5^{6}G, 5^{0}F, 6^{1}SD, 7^{0}GF, 6^{0}SD,

	Starts	1st	2nd	3rd	Win & Pl
Career Total (Turf)	13	1	1	2	10552
Career Total (AW)	2	1	0	0	2047

65 9/09 Kemp 6f STD £2047
80 7/08 Sand 5f6y G-F £4986
Total win prize-money £7034

Going (Turf): Sf: 0-1 GS: 0-2 Gd: 0-5 GF: 1-4 Fm: 0-1
Distance: 5f/6f: 2-13 7f-8f: 0-2 9f-13f: 0-0 14f+: 0-0
Track : LH: 0-3 RH: 1-2 Tight: 0-1 Gall: 0-3
Aids: Bl: 1-6 Vi: 0-0 Tstrap: 0-3 Ckp: 0-3
Best Rating: 96 10/08 Sals 6f good

Very useful; effective over 5f-6f; acts on fast and soft ground; has worn blinkers.

Gioacchino (IRE)

97(93) (61)60

4-y-o b g Rossini (USA)-Gareyba (IRE) (Fairy King (USA))

R A Harris Dream Team Syndicate

Placings:30462260-401620000 **(5501)**

2009: 6^{4}GF, 5^{0}GF, 6^{1}SD, 5^{6}F, 6^{2}G, 6^{0}GF, 5^{0}S, 5^{0}SD, 6^{0}G,

	Starts	1st	2nd	3rd	Win & Pl
Career Total (Turf)	14	0	3	1	2956
Career Total (AW)	3	1	0	0	2047

61 6/09 Sthl 6f (0-60)H STD £2047
Total win prize-money £2047

Going (Turf): Sf: 0-2 GS: 0-1 Gd: 0-3 GF: 0-7 Fm: 0-1
Distance: 5f/6f: 1-12 7f-8f: 0-5 9f-13f: 0-0 14f+: 0-0
Track : LH: 1-8 RH: 0-1 Tight: 0-4 Gall: 0-2
Aids: Bl: 0-0 Vi: 0-0 Tstrap: 0-2 Ckp: 0-2
Best Rating: 61 6/09 Sthl 6f stand

Moderate; effective at up to 7f; acts on fast ground.

Giptar (IRE)

85(90) (52)40

2-y-o b g Kheleyf (USA)-Titania (Fairy King (USA))

E F Vaughan Philip Chesterfield

Placings:63 **(7087)**

2009: 5^{6}G, 6^{3}SD,

	Starts	1st	2nd	3rd	Win & Pl
Career Total (Turf)	1	0	0	0	0
Career Total (AW)	1	0	0	1	504

Going (Turf): Sf: 0-0 GS: 0-0 Gd: 0-1 GF: 0-0 Fm: 0-0
Distance: 5f/6f: 0-2 7f-8f: 0-0 9f-13f: 0-0 14f+: 0-0
Track : LH: 0-1 RH: 0-0 Tight: 0-0 Gall: 0-0
Aids: Bl: 0-0 Vi: 0-0 Tstrap: 0-0 Ckp: 0-0
Best Rating: 52 10/09 Sthl 6f stand

Gitano Hernando

110(112) (122)105

3-y-o ch c Hernando (FR)-Gino's Spirits (Perugino (USA))

M Botti Team Valor Intl & Gary Barber

Placings:621-1211 **(6687a)**

2009: 10^{1}G, 10^{2}GF, 8^{1}SD, 9^{1}FT,

	Starts	1st	2nd	3rd	Win & Pl
Career Total (Turf)	4	1	2	0	24497
Career Total (AW)	3	3	0	0	126038

122 10/09 SnAt 1m1f FST £114583
114 9/09 Wolv 1m141y STD £7569
99 3/09 Donc 1m2f60y (0-90)H GD £7771
88 11/08 Wolv 1m1f103y STD £3885
Total win prize-money £133810

Going (Turf): Sf: 0-1 GS: 0-1 Gd: 1-1 GF: 0-1 Fm: 0-0
Distance: 5f/6f: 0-0 7f-8f: 0-1 9f-13f: 4-6 14f+: 0-0
Track : LH: 4-7 RH: 0-0 Tight: 2-3 Gall: 1-1
Aids: Bl: 0-0 Vi: 0-0 Tstrap: 0-0 Ckp: 0-0
Best Rating: 122 10/09 SnAt 1m1f fast

Group-class; Grade 2 winner in USA; effective over 1m1f; acts on easy ground and on synthetics.

Giulietta Da Vinci

96(89) (63)71

2-y-o b f Mujahid (USA)-Gennie Bond (Pivotal)

N Tinkler (R Hannon 14/11) J L Guillambert

Placings:651005145 **(7756)**

2009: 6^{6}GF, 6^{5}GF, 7^{1}GS, 7^{0}G, 7^{0}GS, 6^{5}G, 8^{1}SD, 8^{4}SD, 7^{5}SD,

	Starts	1st	2nd	3rd	Win & Pl
Career Total (Turf)	6	1	0	0	2914
Career Total (AW)	3	1	0	0	1943

63 11/09 Ling 1m STD £1942
71 7/09 Leic 7f9y G-S £2914
Total win prize-money £4857

Going (Turf): Sf: 0-0 GS: 1-2 Gd: 0-2 GF: 0-2 Fm: 0-0
Distance: 5f/6f: 0-1 7f-8f: 2-7 9f-13f: 0-1 14f+: 0-0
Track : LH: 1-3 RH: 0-1 Tight: 1-2 Gall: 0-1
Aids: Bl: 0-0 Vi: 0-0 Tstrap: 0-0 Ckp: 0-0
Best Rating: 71 7/09 Leic 7f9y gd-sft

Fair; stays 1m; acts on fast and easy ground; goes on Polytrack.

Give (IRE)

(88) (48)56

3-y-o b f High Chaparral (IRE)-Generous Gesture (IRE) (Fasliyev (USA))

R A Harris Mrs Ruth M Serrell

Placings:6064606-600 **(0678)**

2009: 8^{6}SD, 10^{0}SD, 9^{0}SF,

	Starts	1st	2nd	3rd	Win & Pl
Career Total (Turf)	5	0	0	0	0
Career Total (AW)	5	0	0	0	0

Going (Turf): Sf: 0-0 GS: 0-1 Gd: 0-1 GF: 0-3 Fm: 0-0
Distance: 5f/6f: 0-3 7f-8f: 0-1 9f-13f: 0-6 14f+: 0-0
Track : LH: 0-4 RH: 0-1 Tight: 0-4 Gall: 0-1
Aids: Bl: 0-0 Vi: 0-0 Tstrap: 0-5 Ckp: 0-5
Best Rating: 56 6/08 Sals 6f gd-fm

Give Us A Song (USA)

68(96) (67)29

3-y-o b/br g Songandaprayer (USA)-Mama G (USA) (Prospector's Bid (USA))

J S Moore John Wells & Ernie Moore

Placings:60361-0640000 **(7845)**

2009: 8^{0}SD, 7^{6}SD, 7^{4}SD, 6^{0}F, 8^{0}SD, 8^{0}SD, 7^{0}SD,

	Starts	1st	2nd	3rd	Win & Pl
Career Total (Turf)	2	0	0	0	
Career Total (AW)	10	1	0	1	3683

66 10/08 Wolv 7f32y STD £2719
Total win prize-money £2720

Going (Turf): Sf: 0-0 GS: 0-0 Gd: 0-1 GF: 0-0 Fm: 0-1
Distance: 5f/6f: 0-2 7f-8f: 1-10 9f-13f: 0-0 14f+: 0-0
Track : LH: 1-10 RH: 0-1 Tight: 1-7 Gall: 0-2
Aids: Bl: 0-0 Vi: 0-0 Tstrap: 0-1 Ckp: 0-1
Best Rating: 67 10/08 GrLe 1m stand

Modest; stays 1m; best efforts on Polytrack.

Given A Choice (IRE)

(108) (70)79

7-y-o b g Trans Island-Miss Audimar (USA) (Mr. Leader (USA))

J Pearce M B Clarke

Placings:405/4310100/0620010050/4203/13212240102634460-0 **(7475)**

2009: 10^{0}SD,

	Starts	1st	2nd	3rd	Win & Pl
Career Total (Turf)	23	2	1	2	18953
Career Total (AW)	19	4	5	2	19601

86 4/08 Ling 1m2f (0-75)H STD £2590
82 2/08 Kemp 1m3f STD £2047
89 1/08 Wolv 1m1f103y (0-75)H SS £2730

92	7/06	Wolv	1m141y	(0-85)H	STD	£6477
88	7/05	Rdcr	1m3f	(0-80)H	G-F	£7273
85	5/05	Rdcr	1m3f	(0-85)H	G-F	£7072

Total win prize-money £28191

Going (Turf): Sf: 0-2 GS: 0-3 Gd: 0-8 **GF: 2-9** Fm: 0-1
Distance: 5f/6f: 0-0 7f-8f: 0-5 **9f-13f: 6-34** 14f+: 0-3
Track : **LH: 5-27** RH: 1-13 **Tight: 5-13** Gall: 0-10
Aids: Bl: 0-0 Vi: 0-1 Tstrap: 1-13 Ckp: 1-13
Best Rating: **93** 5/06 Kemp 1m4f stand

Fair; stays upto 1m4f; acts on fast ground and Polytrack; has worn cheekpieces.

Gizmondo

(100) (61)**65**

6-y-o ch g Lomitas-India Atlanta (Ahonoora)
G L Moore Miss Gill Arthur

Placings:0/**0**66**1**6/**45**20/06**404-6** **(0132)**
2009: 10^6SD,

	Starts	1st	2nd	3rd	Win & Pl
Career Total (Turf)	**8**	**1**	**1**	**0**	**3413**
Career Total (AW)	**8**	**0**	**0**	**0**	**301**

66	7/06	Yarm	1m2f21y	(0-60)H	FRM	£2590

Total win prize-money £2591

Going (Turf): Sf: 0-0 GS: 0-1 Gd: 0-3 GF: 0-2 **Fm: 1-1**
Distance: 5f/6f: 0-0 7f-8f: 0-3 **9f-13f: 1-13** 14f+: 0-0
Track : **LH: 1-10** RH: 0-4 **Tight: 1-7** Gall: 0-1
Aids: Bl: 0-1 Vi: 0-0 Tstrap: 0-0 Ckp: 0-0
Best Rating: **66** 7/06 Yarm 1m2f21y firm

Moderate; stays 1m2f; effective on fast ground.

Gladiatorus (USA)

119 **129**

4-y-o b c Silic (FR)-Gmaasha (IRE) (Kris)
Saeed Bin Suroor (M bin Shafya 28/3) Godolphin

Placings:161112112/11160510 **(7308a)**
2009: 7^1G, 8^1G, 8^1G, 8^6GF, 8^0G, 8^5GS, 8^1S, 8^0F,

	Starts	1st	2nd	3rd	Win & Pl
Career Total (Turf)	**17**	**10**	**2**	**0**	**2562891**

115	10/09	Siro	1m		SFT	£158102
129	3/09	Ndas	1m194y		GD	£2083333
125	2/09	Ndas	1m		GD	£104166
112	1/09	Ndas	7f110y	(100-129)H	GD	£72916
109	9/07	Capa	1m		HVY	£18918
104	9/07	Casc	7f110y		GD	£18918
100	8/07	Var	1m		GD	£18918
94	7/07	Agno	7f110y		GD	£18918
	7/07	Agno	7f110y		GD	£7432
	6/07	Agno	7f		GD	£5743

Total win prize-money £2507370

Going (Turf): Sf: 2-2 GS: 0-2 **Gd: 8-11** GF: 0-1 Fm: 0-1
Distance: 5f/6f: 0-1 **7f-8f: 9-15** 9f-13f: 1-1 14f+: 0-0
Track : LH: 3-4 RH: 3-6 Tight: 0-0 **Gall: 3-3**
Aids: Bl: 0-0 Vi: 0-0 Tstrap: 0-0 Ckp: 0-0
Best Rating: **129** 3/09 Ndas 1m194y good

High-class; formerly trained in Italy; most impressive winner of the Dubai Duty Free at Nad Al Sheba in March 2009; won an Italian Group 1 in Italy in October; acts on good ground and with cut; best at 1m; needs to make the running.

Glamoroso (IRE)

89(96) (47)**35**

4-y-o b g Mull Of Kintyre (USA)-Tuneful (Pivotal)
A Kirtley A Kirtley

Placings:00/00**535-3**00000 **(6177)**
2009: 8^3SD, 9^0SD, 9^0GF, 12^0G, 9^0G, 12^0GF,

	Starts	1st	2nd	3rd	Win & Pl
Career Total (Turf)	**9**	**0**	**0**	**0**	**0**
Career Total (AW)	**4**	**0**	**0**	**2**	**645**

Going (Turf): **Sf: 0-2 GS: 0-1 Gd: 0-4 GF: 0-2 Fm: 0-0**
Distance: 5f/6f: 0-2 7f-8f: 0-1 9f-13f: 0-9 14f+: 0-1
Track : LH: 0-7 RH: 0-4 Tight: 0-8 Gall: 0-2
Aids: Bl: 0-0 Vi: 0-0 Tstrap: 0-0 Ckp: 0-0
Best Rating: **47** 12/08 Wolv 1m1f103y std-fst

Very moderate; stays 1m1f and acts on Polytrack.

Glamorous Spirit (IRE)

107(108) (91)**91**

3-y-o b f Invincible Spirit (IRE)-Glamorous Air (IRE) (Air Express (IRE))
R A Harris Robert Bailey

Placings:1302412-2351501001 **(7605)**
2009: 5^2SD, 5^3G, 5^5GF, 5^1SD, 5^5GF, 5^0GF, 5^1GF, 5^0G, 5^0GF, 5^1SD,

	Starts	1st	2nd	3rd	Win & Pl
Career Total (Turf)	**12**	**2**	**1**	**2**	**20648**
Career Total (AW)	**5**	**3**	**2**	**0**	**10720**

91	12/09	Ling	5f		STD	£1978
91	7/09	Ches	5f16y	(0-95)H	G-F	£9777
91	5/09	Kemp	5f	(0-85)H	STD	£4727
79	11/08	Kemp	5f		STD	£2047
82	5/08	Asct	5f		G-F	£6476

Total win prize-money £25006

Going (Turf): Sf: 0-1 GS: 0-1 Gd: 0-3 **GF: 2-7** Fm: 0-0
Distance: **5f/6f: 5-17** 7f-8f: 0-0 9f-13f: 0-0 14f+: 0-0
Track : LH: 2-5 RH: 2-3 **Tight: 2-4** Gall: 0-0
Aids: Bl: 0-0 Vi: 0-0 Tstrap: 0-0 Ckp: 0-0
Best Rating: **91** 12/09 Ling 5f stand

Useful; effective over 5f; acts on most ground; goes well on Polytrack.

Glamour Profession (IRE)

82(81) (49)**55**

2-y-o ch f Captain Rio-Kriva (Reference Point)
R Hannon Justin Dowley & Michael Pescod

Placings:0606 **(6609)**
2009: 5^0GF, 7^6GF, 8^0GF, 7^6SD,

	Starts	1st	2nd	3rd	Win & Pl
Career Total (Turf)	**3**	**0**	**0**	**0**	**0**
Career Total (AW)	**1**	**0**	**0**	**0**	**0**

Going (Turf): **Sf: 0-0 GS: 0-0 Gd: 0-0 GF: 0-3 Fm: 0-0**
Distance: 5f/6f: 0-1 7f-8f: 0-3 9f-13f: 0-0 14f+: 0-0
Track : LH: 0-0 RH: 0-2 Tight: 0-0 Gall: 0-1
Aids: Bl: 0-0 Vi: 0-0 Tstrap: 0-0 Ckp: 0-0
Best Rating: **55** 7/09 Newb 7f gd-fm

Glan Lady (IRE)

77(88) (56)**58**

3-y-o b f Court Cave (IRE)-Vanished (IRE) (Fayruz)
G J Smith (J L Spearing 2/1) P Voce

Placings:5266015-2305000R **(3054)**
2009: 6^2SS, 6^3SD, 5^0SD, 6^5SD, 7^0SD, 6^0SD, 9^0GF, 9^RGF,

	Starts	1st	2nd	3rd	Win & Pl
Career Total (Turf)	**6**	**0**	**1**	**0**	**1272**
Career Total (AW)	**9**	**1**	**1**	**1**	**2954**

56	12/08	Sthl	6f		STD	£2047

Total win prize-money £2047

Going (Turf): **Sf: 0-3 GS: 0-0 Gd: 0-1 GF: 0-2 Fm: 0-0**
Distance: **5f/6f: 1-8** 7f-8f: 0-5 9f-13f: 0-2 14f+: 0-0
Track : **LH: 1-10** RH: 0-2 Tight: 0-2 Gall: 0-0
Aids: **Bl: 1-7** Vi: 0-0 Tstrap: 0-3 Ckp: 0-3
Best Rating: **58** 8/08 Wwck 7f26y soft

Modest; effective over 6f; acts on soft ground and on Fibresand; has worn cheekpieces.

Glan Y Mor (IRE)

72 **12**

2-y-o b f Mark Of Esteem (IRE)-Molly Mello (GER) (Big Shuffle (USA))
F J Brennan Seasons Holidays

Placings:0 **(5605)**
2009: 6^0S,

	Starts	1st	2nd	3rd	Win & Pl
Career Total (Turf)	**1**	**0**	**0**	**0**	

Going (Turf): **Sf: 0-1 GS: 0-0 Gd: 0-0 GF: 0-0 Fm: 0-0**
Distance: 5f/6f: 0-1 7f-8f: 0-1 9f-13f: 0-0 14f+: 0-0
Track : LH: 0-0 RH: 0-0 Tight: 0-0 Gall: 0-0
Aids: Bl: 0-0 Vi: 0-0 Tstrap: 0-0 Ckp: 0-0
Best Rating: **12** 9/09 Sals 6f212y soft

Glass Harmonium (IRE)

111 **117**

3-y-o gr c Verglas (IRE)-Spring Symphony (IRE) (Darshaan)
Sir Michael Stoute Ballymacoll Stud

Placings:01-56142 **(6812)**
2009: 8^5GF, 10^6G, 10^1GF, 9^4GF, 9^2G,

	Starts	1st	2nd	3rd	Win & Pl
Career Total (Turf)	**7**	**2**	**1**	**0**	**51438**

117	6/09	Asct	1m2f	G-F	£28385
86	9/08	Yarm	7f3y	GD	£4731

Total win prize-money £33116

Going (Turf): Sf: 0-0 GS: 0-0 **Gd: 1-4 GF: 1-3** Fm: 0-0
Distance: 5f/6f: 0-0 7f-8f: 1-3 9f-13f: 1-4 14f+: 0-0
Track : LH: 0-2 **RH: 1-2** Tight: 0-0 **Gall: 1-3**
Aids: Bl: 0-0 Vi: 0-0 Tstrap: 0-0 Ckp: 0-0
Best Rating: **117** 6/09 Asct 1m2f gd-fm

Group class; Listed winner; from the family of Hard Top and Conduit; stays 1m2f; acts on good and fast ground.

Glass Of Red (IRE)

95(74) (28)**66**

2-y-o gr f Verglas (IRE)-Embassy Belle (IRE) (Marju (IRE))
R M Beckett Richard Morecombe and Jamie Perryman

Placings:0601 **(7120)**
2009: 5^0GF, 6^6GF, 7^0SD, 8^1GF,

	Starts	1st	2nd	3rd	Win & Pl
Career Total (Turf)	**3**	**1**	**0**	**0**	**2047**
Career Total (AW)	**1**	**0**	**0**	**0**	

66	10/09	Nott	1m75y	G-F	£2047

Total win prize-money £2047

Going (Turf): Sf: 0-0 GS: 0-0 Gd: 0-0 **GF: 1-3** Fm: 0-0
Distance: 5f/6f: 0-1 7f-8f: 0-2 **9f-13f: 1-1** 14f+: 0-0
Track : **LH: 1-2** RH: 0-0 Tight: 0-1 Gall: 0-1
Aids: Bl: 0-0 Vi: 0-0 Tstrap: 0-0 Ckp: 0-0
Best Rating: **66** 10/09 Nott 1m75y gd-fm

Modest; stays 1m; acts on good ground.

Glasshoughton

99(94) (57)89
6-y-o b g Dansili-Roseum (Lahib (USA))
M Dods Septimus Racing Group

Placings:4224340/04415100/50060143160/423004406504 44-06300000 **(6764)**
2009: 5⁰GF, 5⁶G, 6³GF, 6⁰G, 5⁰GS, 5⁰GF, 7⁰SD, 6⁰G,

	Starts	1st	2nd	3rd	Win & Pl
Career Total (Turf)	**47**	**4**	**3**	**4**	**36323**
Career Total (AW)	**1**	**0**	**0**	**0**	

89	8/07	Carl	5f	(0-80)H	GD	£5181
84	7/07	Bevl	5f	(0-90)H	HVY	£7772
82	6/06	Carl	5f	(0-85)H	GD	£6477
79	6/06	Sand	5f6y	(0-75)H	G-F	£4533

Total win prize-money £23965

Going (Turf): Sf: 1-13 GS: 0-7 **Gd: 2-16** GF: 1-11 Fm: 0-0
Distance: **5f/6f: 4-42** 7f-8f: 0-6 9f-13f: 0-0 14f+: 0-0
Track : LH: 0-6 **RH: 2-6** Tight: 0-3 **Gall: 2-5**
Aids: Bl: 0-1 Vi: 0-0 Tstrap: 0-2 Ckp: 0-2
Best Rating: **89** 6/08 Sand 5f6y soft

Fair; best over 5f but stays 6f; acts on most ground; has worn blinkers and cheekpieces.

Gleaming Spirit (IRE)

86(109) (49)73
5-y-o b g Mujadil (USA)-Gleam (Green Desert (USA))
Peter Grayson E Grayson & Partner

Placings:40/52431500/043504100002006-000006 (7605)
2009: 5⁰G, 5⁰G, 5⁰GS, 5⁰G, 5⁰SD, 5⁶SD,

	Starts	1st	2nd	3rd	Win & Pl
Career Total (Turf)	**18**	**2**	**2**	**1**	**7483**
Career Total (AW)	**13**	**0**	**0**	**1**	**818**

73	7/08	Yarm	5f43y	(0-70)H	G-F	£2719
77	8/07	Yarm	6f3y	(0-65)H	G-F	£1943

Total win prize-money £4663

Going (Turf): Sf: 0-2 GS: 0-5 Gd: 0-4 **GF: 2-7** Fm: 0-0
Distance: 5f/6f: 1-29 7f-8f: 1-2 9f-13f: 0-0 14f+: 0-0
Track : LH: 0-8 RH: 0-4 Tight: 0-6 Gall: 0-1
Aids: Bl: 0-1 **Vi: 1-12** Tstrap: 0-0 Ckp: 0-0
Best Rating: **77** 8/07 Yarm 6f3y gd-fm

Modest; stays 6f and acts on good ground and Polytrack; has worn a visor.

Glen Lass

87(96) (59)59
2-y-o ch f Zafeen (FR)-Welcome Aboard (Be My Guest (USA))
J Pearce (J S Moore 17/9) Ian Bishop

Placings:606323**002111** **(7874)**
2009: 5⁶GS, 5⁰G, 7⁶GF, 7³S, 7²GS, 8³GF, 8⁰SD, 10⁰SD, 8²SD, 9¹SD, 8¹SD, 8¹SD,

	Starts	1st	2nd	3rd	Win & Pl
Career Total (Turf)	**6**	**0**	**1**	**2**	**1541**
Career Total (AW)	**6**	**3**	**1**	**0**	**9267**

	12/09	Kemp	1m		STD	£2047
56	12/09	Wolv	1m141y		STD	£2729
59	12/09	Wolv	1m1f103y		STD	£3885

Total win prize-money £8663

Going (Turf): **Sf: 0-1 GS: 0-2 Gd: 0-1 GF: 0-2 Fm: 0-0**
Distance: 5f/6f: 0-2 7f-8f: 1-5 **9f-13f: 2-5** 14f+: 0-0
Track : **LH: 2-3** RH: 1-4 **Tight: 2-3** Gall: 0-1
Aids: **Bl: 3-4** Vi: 0-0 Tstrap: 0-3 Ckp: 0-3
Best Rating: **59** 12/09 Wolv 1m1f103y stand

Modest; stays 1m; acts on fast and easy ground and Polytrack; has worn blinkers and cheekpieces.

Glen Molly (IRE)

104 96
3-y-o b f Danetime (IRE)-Sonorous (IRE) (Ashkalani (IRE))
B W Hills John C Grant

Placings:21-3241000 **(7294)**
2009: 7³GF, 7²GS, 7⁴GF, 7¹G, 7⁰G, 7⁰S, 7⁰S,

	Starts	1st	2nd	3rd	Win & Pl
Career Total (Turf)	**9**	**2**	**2**	**1**	**19904**

96	8/09	NmkJ	7f	(0-90)H	GD	£9066
76	8/08	Newb	6f8y		G-S	£5828

Total win prize-money £14894

Going (Turf): Sf: 0-2 **GS: 1-2 Gd: 1-3** GF: 0-2 Fm: 0-0
Distance: 5f/6f: 0-0 **7f-8f: 2-9** 9f-13f: 0-0 14f+: 0-0
Track : LH: 0-1 RH: 0-0 Tight: 0-0 Gall: 0-0
Aids: Bl: 0-0 Vi: 0-0 Tstrap: 0-0 Ckp: 0-0
Best Rating: **96** 8/09 NmkJ 7f good

Useful; effective over 6f-7f; acts on good and easy ground.

Glen Shiel (USA)

91 76
2-y-o ch g Whywhywhy (USA)-Staffin (Salse (USA))
M Johnston Sheikh Hamdan Bin Mohammed Al Maktoum

Placings:621 **(5867)**
2009: 5⁶S, 5²GS, 6¹G,

	Starts	1st	2nd	3rd	Win & Pl
Career Total (Turf)	**3**	**1**	**1**	**0**	**5886**

76	9/09	Ffos	6f	GD	£5180

Total win prize-money £5181

Going (Turf): Sf: 0-1 GS: 0-1 **Gd: 1-1** GF: 0-0 Fm: 0-0
Distance: **5f/6f: 1-3** 7f-8f: 0-0 9f-13f: 0-0 14f+: 0-0
Track : LH: 0-0 RH: 0-0 Tight: 0-0 Gall: 0-0
Aids: Bl: 0-0 Vi: 0-0 Tstrap: 0-0 Ckp: 0-0
Best Rating: **76** 9/09 Ffos 6f good

Useful; stays 6f and acts on good ground.

Glencairn Star

73(80) (23)14
8-y-o b g Selkirk (USA)-Bianca Nera (Salse (USA))
F Watson F Watson

Placings:05/0001**141**/**25**00230/001212000000**3**/3/0P**0** **(7503)**
2009: 5⁰S, 6ᴾGF, 5⁰SD,

	Starts	1st	2nd	3rd	Win & Pl
Career Total (Turf)	**25**	**2**	**3**	**3**	**21446**
Career Total (AW)	**8**	**3**	**1**	**0**	**8401**

80	6/06	Ayr	5f	(0-85)H	GD	£6477
74	6/06	Muss	5f	(0-85)H	G-F	£6477
65	12/04	Sthl	7f	(0-62)H	STD	£2935
66	11/04	Sthl	5f	(0-62)H	STD	£2927
61	11/04	Wolv	5f216y	(0-45)	STD	£1484

Total win prize-money £20301

Going (Turf): Sf: 0-5 GS: 0-4 **Gd: 1-7 GF: 1-7** Fm: 0-1
Distance: **5f/6f: 4-23** 7f-8f: 1-9 9f-13f: 0-1 14f+: 0-0
Track : **LH: 2-12** RH: 0-0 **Tight: 1-4** Gall: 0-0
Aids: Bl: 0-0 Vi: 0-0 Tstrap: 0-3 Ckp: 0-3
Best Rating: **83** 7/06 Asct 5f gd-fm

Fair sprinter; best at 5f; acts on both All-Weather surfaces and handles a sound surface on turf.

Glencalvie (IRE)

87(103) (85)39
8-y-o ch g Grand Lodge (USA)-Top Of The Form (IRE) (Masterclass (USA))
J Akehurst Tattenham Corner Racing

Placings:0504110/336410**331**/**5642**00**4**010/**005001630**100 0/00**130250-0500000** **(3159)**
2009: 8⁰SD, 7⁵SD, 8⁰SD, 7⁰SD, 8⁰SD, 7⁰GF, 7⁰GF,

	Starts	1st	2nd	3rd	Win & Pl
Career Total (Turf)	**28**	**5**	**0**	**3**	**28499**
Career Total (AW)	**26**	**3**	**2**	**3**	**16675**

81	6/08	Ling	1m	(0-75)H	STD	£2331
82	8/07	Wind	1m67y	(0-85)H	G-F	£6477
78	5/07	Ling	7f	(0-75)H	STD	£3238
80	9/06	Yarm	1m3y	(0-85)H	G-F	£7478
84	12/05	Ling	1m	(0-80)H	STD	£5754
77	10/05	Wind	1m67y	(0-70)H	GD	£3556
75	9/04	Ling	6f	(0-70)H	G-F	£3675
77	8/04	Yarm	7f3y	E(0-75)H	G-F	£3877

Total win prize-money £36387

Going (Turf): Sf: 0-1 GS: 0-2 Gd: 1-11 **GF: 4-12** Fm: 0-2
Distance: 5f/6f: 1-3 **7f-8f: 4-43** 9f-13f: 3-8 14f+: 0-0
Track : **LH: 3-21** RH: 2-16 **Tight: 5-26** Gall: 0-1
Aids: Bl: 0-0 **Vi: 5-24** Tstrap: 3-23 Ckp: 3-23
Best Rating: **87** 6/06 Kemp 1m stand

Fair; suited by 7f-1m; acts on fast ground and on Polytrack; wears cheekpieces.

Glenlini

97 62
3-y-o b f Bertolini (USA)-Glenhurich (IRE) (Sri Pekan (USA))
J S Goldie John Murphy

Placings:6-25 **(3678)**
2009: 5²GF, 5⁵G,

	Starts	1st	2nd	3rd	Win & Pl
Career Total (Turf)	**3**	**0**	**1**	**0**	**771**

Going (Turf): **Sf: 0-0 GS: 0-1 Gd: 0-1 GF: 0-1 Fm: 0-0**
Distance: 5f/6f: 0-3 7f-8f: 0-0 9f-13f: 0-0 14f+: 0-0
Track : LH: 0-0 RH: 0-0 Tight: 0-0 Gall: 0-0
Aids: Bl: 0-0 Vi: 0-0 Tstrap: 0-0 Ckp: 0-0
Best Rating: **62** 5/09 Muss 5f gd-fm

Modest half-sister to a 5f winner; effective over 5f; acts on fast ground.

Glenluji

94 51
4-y-o b g Lujain (USA)-Glenhurich (IRE) (Sri Pekan (USA))
J S Goldie John Murphy

Placings:6616/0-050000050 **(7174)**
2009: 5⁰GS, 5⁵GF, 5⁰GF, 6⁰GS, 5⁰GS, 5⁰G, 7⁰GF, 7⁵G, 9⁰S,

	Starts	1st	2nd	3rd	Win & Pl
Career Total (Turf)	**14**	**1**	**0**	**0**	**6477**

64	6/07	Muss	5f	GD	£6477

Total win prize-money £6477

Going (Turf): Sf: 0-1 GS: 0-4 **Gd: 1-6** GF: 0-3 Fm: 0-0

Distance: 5f/6f: 1-11 7f-8f: 0-2 9f-13f: 0-1 14f+: 0-0
Track : LH: 0-3 RH: 0-0 Tight: 0-0 Gall: 0-0
Aids: Bl: 0-0 Vi: 0-0 Tstrap: 0-0 Ckp: 0-0
Best Rating: 64 6/07 Muss 5f good

Moderate; lightly raced; best at 5f; effective on fast ground.

Glenmuir (IRE)

102 (46)75
6-y-o b g Josr Algarhoud (IRE)-Beryl (Bering)
J J Quinn (Gordon Elliott 22/7) Jack Syndicate

Placings:122240440/0261060/00300000/0614001002060 4-3004 **(5598)**
2009: 7³Y, 10⁰GF, 8⁰S, 8⁴GF,

	Starts	1st	2nd	3rd	Win & Pl
Career Total (Turf)	41	4	5	2	34625
Career Total (AW)	1	0	0	0	

73	6/08	Fair	1m1f	(50-70)H	G-Y	£5588
67	4/08	Naas	1m	(45-60)H	YLD	£4826
84	7/06	Ches	7f122y	(0-80)H	G-F	£5829
73	4/05	Kemp	5f		G-S	£5395

Total win prize-money £21640

Going (Turf): Sf: 0-7 **GS: 1-4** Gd: 0-8 **GF: 1-13** Fm: 0-0
Distance: 5f/6f: 1-6 **7f-8f: 2-20** 9f-13f: 1-16 14f+: 0-0
Track : **LH: 2-18** RH: 1-12 **Tight: 1-7** Gall: 0-0
Aids: Bl: 0-4 Vi: 0-0 Tstrap: 0-0 Ckp: 0-0
Best Rating: 85 4/06 NmkR 7f good

Fair; effective at around 7f and a mile; acts on any surface.

Glenridding

105(107) (76)83
5-y-o b g Averti (IRE)-Appelone (Emperor Jones (USA))
J G Given Tremousser Partnership

Placings:00/006450201/21120502124654-060011200100000 **(7287)**
2009: 9⁰SD, 8⁰F, 8⁰G, 8⁰G, 7¹GF, 7¹G, 7²GF, 7⁰GF, 7⁰G, 7¹G, 8⁰S, 7⁰SD, 8⁰SD, 7⁰S, 7⁰S,

	Starts	1st	2nd	3rd	Win & Pl
Career Total (Turf)	21	4	3	0	21716
Career Total (AW)	19	3	3	0	9853

83	8/09	Thsk	7f	(0-80)H	GD	£5569
76	6/09	Thsk	7f	(0-75)H	GD	£4274
74	6/09	Ches	7f122y	(0-70)H	G-F	£4209
79	8/08	Thsk	7f	(0-70)H	G-S	£4338
69	1/08	Wolv	1m1f103y	(0-75)H	STD	£2590
73	1/08	Wolv	1m1f103y	(0-70)H	STD	£2590
69	12/07	Wolv	1m141y		STD	£2047

Total win prize-money £25621

Going (Turf): Sf: 0-3 GS: 1-4 **Gd: 2-8** GF: 1-4 Fm: 0-2
Distance: 5f/6f: 0-0 **7f-8f: 4-18** 9f-13f: 3-22 14f+: 0-0
Track : **LH: 7-31** RH: 0-7 **Tight: 7-29** Gall: 0-1
Aids: Bl: 0-5 Vi: 0-0 Tstrap: 3-11 Ckp: 3-11
Best Rating: 83 8/09 Thsk 7f good

Modest; stays 1m1f but effective at 7f; acts good and faster ground and on Polytrack; has worn cheekpieces; suited by forcing tactics.

Glimpse Of Light (IRE)

(90) (65)
3-y-o b f Passing Glance-Sankaty Light (USA) (Summer Squall (USA))
A M Balding Kingsclere Racing CLub

Placings:53-00 **(1563)**
2009: 5⁰SD, 6⁰SD,

	Starts	1st	2nd	3rd	Win & Pl
Career Total (Turf)	0	0	0	0	
Career Total (AW)	4	0	0	1	454

Going (Turf): Sf: 0-0 GS: 0-0 Gd: 0-0 GF: 0-0 Fm: 0-0
Distance: 5f/6f: 0-4 7f-8f: 0-0 9f-13f: 0-0 14f+: 0-0
Track : LH: 0-3 RH: 0-1 Tight: 0-2 Gall: 0-0
Aids: Bl: 0-0 Vi: 0-0 Tstrap: 0-0 Ckp: 0-0
Best Rating: 65 10/08 Wolv 5f216y stand

Global

99(95) (77)88
3-y-o ch g Bahamian Bounty-Tuppenny Blue (Pennekamp (USA))
R Hannon A J Ilsley & G Battocchi

Placings:610-41110504000 **(6731)**
2009: 7⁴SD, 9¹GF, 8¹G, 8¹G, 9⁰G, 8⁵GF, 8⁰S, 8⁴GF, 9⁰GF, 8⁰G, 6⁰S,

	Starts	1st	2nd	3rd	Win & Pl
Career Total (Turf)	10	3	0	0	10194
Career Total (AW)	4	1	0	0	6800

87	5/09	Gdwd	1m	(0-70)H	GD	£3238
88	5/09	Chep	1m14y	(0-70)H	GD	£2914
74	5/09	Sals	1m1f198y	(0-70)H	G-F	£3238
77	11/08	Ling	7f		STD	£6799

Total win prize-money £16190

Going (Turf): Sf: 0-2 GS: 0-0 **Gd: 2-4** GF: 1-4 Fm: 0-0
Distance: 5f/6f: 0-0 7f-8f: 2-9 9f-13f: 2-5 14f+: 0-0
Track : LH: 1-2 **RH: 2-7 Tight: 2-5** Gall: 0-0
Aids: Bl: 0-1 Vi: 0-0 Tstrap: 0-0 Ckp: 0-0
Best Rating: 88 5/09 Chep 1m14y good

Fair; stays 1m; acts on god ground and on Polytrack.

Global City (IRE)

103(111) (102)107
3-y-o b c Exceed And Excel (AUS)-Victory Peak (Shirley Heights)
Saeed Bin Suroor Godolphin

Placings:21061-45100201 **(7394)**
2009: 6⁴GF, 6⁵GF, 6¹GF, 6⁰G, 6⁰S, 6²GF, 6⁰G, 6¹SD,

	Starts	1st	2nd	3rd	Win & Pl
Career Total (Turf)	11	2	2	0	18161
Career Total (AW)	2	2	0	0	12187

102	11/09	Ling	6f		STD	£7771
107	6/09	Hayd	6f	(0-95)H	G-F	£9066
93	10/08	Ling	6f		STD	£4415
80	7/08	Yarm	5f43y		G-F	£3784

Total win prize-money £25038

Going (Turf): Sf: 0-1 GS: 0-0 Gd: 0-4 **GF: 2-6** Fm: 0-0
Distance: **5f/6f: 4-12** 7f-8f: 0-1 9f-13f: 0-0 14f+: 0-0
Track : **LH: 2-3** RH: 0-0 **Tight: 2-3** Gall: 0-0
Aids: Bl: 0-0 Vi: 0-0 Tstrap: 0-0 Ckp: 0-0
Best Rating: 107 6/09 Hayd 6f gd-fm

Very useful; effective over 6f; acts on fast ground; goes on Polytrack; has worn a tongue tie.

Global Conquest (IRE)

97(102) (79)75
3-y-o b f Captain Rio-Triphibious (Zafonic (USA))
Pat Eddery Ms J F Harrison

Placings:224421 **(6784)**
2009: 6²GF, 6²GF, 7⁴G, 7⁴GS, 7²SD, 10¹SS,

	Starts	1st	2nd	3rd	Win & Pl
Career Total (Turf)	4	0	2	0	3087
Career Total (AW)	2	1	1	0	3435

79	10/09	Ling	1m2f	(0-70)H	SS	£2729

Total win prize-money £2730

Going (Turf): Sf: 0-0 GS: 0-1 Gd: 0-1 GF: 0-2 Fm: 0-0
Distance: 5f/6f: 0-1 7f-8f: 0-4 **9f-13f: 1-1** 14f+: 0-0
Track : **LH: 1-3** RH: 0-0 **Tight: 1-3** Gall: 0-0
Aids: Bl: 0-0 Vi: 0-0 Tstrap: 0-0 Ckp: 0-0
Best Rating: 79 10/09 Ling 1m2f std-slw

Fair; stays 1m2f; acts on fast ground and on Polytrack.

Global Strategy

(87) (45)67
6-y-o b g Rainbow Quest (USA)-Pleasuring (Good Times (ITY))
O Sherwood O M C Sherwood

Placings:060/111661600/0 **(0459)**
2009: 16⁰SD,

	Starts	1st	2nd	3rd	Win & Pl
Career Total (Turf)	5	0	0	0	234
Career Total (AW)	8	4	0	0	10238

82	5/07	Sthl	1m6f	(0-75)H	STD	£3071
83	2/07	Sthl	1m6f	(0-65)H	STD	£2388
64	1/07	Sthl	1m4f	(0-60)H	STD	£2388
71	1/07	Sthl	1m4f	(0-55)H	STD	£2388

Total win prize-money £10238

Going (Turf): Sf: 0-0 GS: 0-3 Gd: 0-0 GF: 0-1 Fm: 0-0
Distance: 5f/6f: 0-0 7f-8f: 0-1 9f-13f: 2-6 14f+: 2-6
Track : **LH: 4-10** RH: 0-3 Tight: 0-4 Gall: 0-1
Aids: Bl: 0-0 Vi: 0-0 Tstrap: 0-0 Ckp: 0-0
Best Rating: 83 2/07 Sthl 1m6f stand

Global Traffic

(103) (70)68
5-y-o br g Generous (IRE)-Eyes Wide Open (Fraam)
R Ford D F Price, K Hesketh, A Eyres & R Ford

Placings:0650062452/1115005001665053/30134445-0P **(0627)**
2009: 14⁰SD, 16ᴾSD,

	Starts	1st	2nd	3rd	Win & Pl
Career Total (Turf)	13	1	1	0	2962
Career Total (AW)	23	4	1	3	12126

64	2/08	Sthl	1m4f		STD	£1774
66	7/07	Chep	1m4f23y	(0-65)H	HVY	£1998
70	1/07	Wolv	1m1f103y	(0-60)H	SS	£2388
61	1/07	Wolv	1m1f103y	(0-70)H	STD	£3238
62	1/07	Wolv	1m1f103y	(0-58)H	STD	£2730

Total win prize-money £12132

Going (Turf): **Sf: 1-3** GS: 0-2 Gd: 0-2 GF: 0-5 Fm: 0-1
Distance: 5f/6f: 0-3 7f-8f: 0-5 **9f-13f: 5-25** 14f+: 0-3
Track : **LH: 5-27** RH: 0-4 **Tight: 3-17** Gall: 0-1
Aids: **Bl: 4-13** Vi: 0-8 Tstrap: 0-0 Ckp: 0-0
Best Rating: 70 8/07 Wolv 1m4f50y stand

Moderate; stays 1m4f; acts well on sand and easy ground on turf; has worn blinkers and a visor.

Global Village (IRE)

92(101) (71)68
4-y-o b g Dubai Destination (USA)-Zelding (IRE) (Warning)
Miss D Mountain Mrs Janice Jones

Placings:465231153 **(4824)**

2009: 6^{4}SD, 7^{6}G, 5^{5}GS, 7^{2}G, 5^{3}SD, 7^{1}SD, 7^{1}SD, 7^{5}G, 8^{3}G,

	Starts	1st	2nd	3rd	Win & Pl
Career Total (Turf)	5	0	1	1	1088
Career Total (AW)	4	2	0	1	4930

69 7/09 Kemp 7f (0-65)H STD £2047
71 7/09 Kemp 7f (0-70)H STD £2590
Total win prize-money £4637

Going (Turf): **Sf: 0-0 GS: 0-1 Gd: 0-4 GF: 0-0 Fm: 0-0**
Distance: 5f/6f: 0-3 **7f-8f: 2-5** 9f-13f: 0-1 14f+: 0-0
Track : LH: 0-2 **RH: 2-3** Tight: 0-3 Gall: 0-0
Aids: Bl: 0-0 Vi: 0-0 Tstrap: 0-0 Ckp: 0-0
Best Rating: **71** 7/09 Kemp 7f stand

Fair; stays 7f; acts on Polytrack.

Glorious Dreams (USA)

82(93) (72)**26**
3-y-o b/br f Honour And Glory (USA)-Crissy Aya (USA) (Saros)
T J Pitt O'Donnell, Kelly, Dower

Placings:100-0000 **(3625)**
2009: 5^{0}SD, 5^{0}GS, 6^{0}GS, 5^{0}G,

	Starts	1st	2nd	3rd	Win & Pl
Career Total (Turf)	5	0	0	0	
Career Total (AW)	2	1	0	0	2914

72 5/08 Wolv 5f20y STD £2914
Total win prize-money £2914

Going (Turf): **Sf: 0-0 GS: 0-2 Gd: 0-1 GF: 0-2 Fm: 0-0**
Distance: **5f/6f: 1-7** 7f-8f: 0-0 9f-13f: 0-0 14f+: 0-0
Track : **LH: 1-3** RH: 0-0 **Tight: 1-2** Gall: 0-0
Aids: Bl: 0-0 Vi: 0-0 Tstrap: 0-1 Ckp: 0-1
Best Rating: **72** 5/08 Wolv 5f20y stand

Gloucester

107(100) (71)**80**
6-y-o b g Montjeu (IRE)-Birdlip (USA) (Sanglamore (USA))
M J Scudamore S Smith, K Hunter, P Duffen

Placings:0441/566351/00-4113640 **(6244)**
2009: 10^{4}SD, 11^{1}GF, 11^{1}GF, 11^{3}G, 12^{6}G, 13^{4}GF, 12^{0}G,

	Starts	1st	2nd	3rd	Win & Pl
Career Total (Turf)	16	3	0	2	17203
Career Total (AW)	3	1	0	0	7506

80 6/09 Hayd 1m3f200y (0-75)H G-F £3238
77 6/09 Wind 1m3f135y (0-75)H G-F £3070
77 9/07 Bevl 1m1f207y (0-80)H G-F £6477
77 8/06 Deau 1m4f STD £7241
Total win prize-money £20027

Going (Turf): Sf: 0-1 GS: 0-3 Gd: 0-6 **GF: 3-4** Fm: 0-0
Distance: 5f/6f: 0-0 7f-8f: 0-0 **9f-13f: 4-17** 14f+: 0-2
Track : LH: 1-8 RH: 1-6 **Tight: 1-7** Gall: 0-4
Aids: Bl: 0-1 Vi: 0-0 Tstrap: 0-1 Ckp: 0-1
Best Rating: **80** 7/09 Wind 1m3f135y good

Fair; ex-French; winning hurdler; stays 1m4f; acts on fast ground.

Glow Star (SAF)

110(106) (93)**94**
5-y-o ch g Muhtafal (USA)-Arctic Glow (SAF) (Northern Guest (USA))
G L Moore (H J Brown 13/3) Blue Diamond Racing

Placings:21/4343432/202111-05600033 **(7626)**
2009: 7^{0}G, 7^{5}G, 7^{6}SD, 8^{0}GS, 7^{0}GF, 7^{0}G, 7^{3}SD, 8^{3}SD,

	Starts	1st	2nd	3rd	Win & Pl
Career Total (Turf)	20	4	4	3	25342
Career Total (AW)	3	0	0	2	2292

7/08 Scot 7f GD £3676
5/08 Grey 6f110y H GD £4136
5/08 Grey 6f110y SFT £3676
12/06 Scot 4f GD £2947
Total win prize-money £14436

Going (Turf): Sf: 1-7 GS: 0-1 **Gd: 3-11** GF: 0-1 Fm: 0-0
Distance: 5f/6f: 0-4 **7f-8f: 3-17** 9f-13f: 0-0 14f+: 0-0
Track : LH: 0-4 RH: 0-2 Tight: 0-2 Gall: 0-3
Aids: **Bl: 3-7** Vi: 0-0 Tstrap: 0-0 Ckp: 0-0
Best Rating: **94** 2/09 Ndas 7f110y good

Very useful; ex-South African-trained; effective up to 7f; acts on good, slow ground; has worn blinkers.

Glowing (IRE)

107 (73)**104**
4-y-o b f Dansili-Brightest (Rainbow Quest (USA))
L M Cumani (Charles O'Brien 1/7) William McAlpin

Placings:0510/4300-1410 **(6272)**
2009: 8^{1}SD, 9^{4}G, 7^{1}G, 7^{0}GF,

	Starts	1st	2nd	3rd	Win & Pl
Career Total (Turf)	10	1	0	1	55155
Career Total (AW)	2	2	0	0	20115

104 7/09 Fair 7f GD £51747
73 4/09 Dund 1m STD £12411
77 10/07 Dund 1m STD £7703
Total win prize-money £71863

Going (Turf): Sf: 0-1 GS: 0-0 **Gd: 1-2** GF: 0-4 Fm: 0-1
Distance: 5f/6f: 0-0 **7f-8f: 3-8** 9f-13f: 0-4 14f+: 0-0
Track : LH: 1-5 RH: 1-5 Tight: 0-0 Gall: 0-1
Aids: Bl: 0-0 Vi: 0-0 Tstrap: 0-0 Ckp: 0-0
Best Rating: **104** 7/09 Fair 7f good

Smart; stays 1m; acts on good ground and Polytrack.

Glowing Praise

100 **88**
3-y-o ch g Fantastic Light (USA)-Beading (Polish Precedent (USA))
E S McMahon J C Fretwell

Placings:51-6144041 **(6243)**
2009: 9^{6}G, 8^{1}GF, 8^{4}S, 8^{4}GF, 7^{0}GF, 8^{4}GF, 8^{1}G,

	Starts	1st	2nd	3rd	Win & Pl
Career Total (Turf)	9	3	0	0	14575

88 9/09 Asct 1m (0-85)H GD £7123
82 6/09 Leic 1m60y (0-75)H G-F £3238
71 10/08 Wwck 7f26y SFT £2914
Total win prize-money £13276

Going (Turf): **Sf: 1-2** GS: 0-0 **Gd: 1-2 GF: 1-5** Fm: 0-0
Distance: 5f/6f: 0-1 **7f-8f: 2-5** 9f-13f: 1-3 14f+: 0-0
Track : LH: 1-1 RH: 1-3 Tight: 0-0 Gall: 0-0
Aids: Bl: 0-0 Vi: 0-0 Tstrap: 0-0 Ckp: 0-0
Best Rating: **88** 9/09 Asct 1m good

Useful; stays 1m; acts on fast ground.

Go Alone (IRE)

95(80) (40)**72**
3-y-o b g Elusive City (USA)-Ya Ya (IRE) (Royal Academy (USA))
G A Swinbank B Valentine

Placings:0016240 **(4664)**
2009: 7^{0}SD, 9^{0}GS, 6^{1}GF, 7^{6}GF, 5^{2}G, 6^{4}G, 6^{0}G,

	Starts	1st	2nd	3rd	Win & Pl
Career Total (Turf)	6	1	1	0	3496
Career Total (AW)	1	0	0	0	

72 5/09 Rdcr 6f G-F £2590
Total win prize-money £2590

Going (Turf): Sf: 0-0 GS: 0-1 Gd: 0-3 **GF: 1-2** Fm: 0-0
Distance: **5f/6f: 1-4** 7f-8f: 0-2 9f-13f: 0-1 14f+: 0-0
Track : LH: 0-3 RH: 0-1 Tight: 0-3 Gall: 0-0
Aids: Bl: 0-0 Vi: 0-0 Tstrap: 0-0 Ckp: 0-0
Best Rating: **72** 5/09 Rdcr 6f gd-fm

Fair; effective over 6f; acts on fast ground.

Go Amwell

103(94) (61)**64**
6-y-o b g Kayf Tara-Daarat Alayaam (IRE) (Reference Point)
J R Jenkins Robin Stevens

Placings:00/000050502123/00301130/243410-03045 **(3737)**
2009: 15^{0}G, 18^{3}G, 16^{0}G, 16^{4}SD, 16^{5}SD,

	Starts	1st	2nd	3rd	Win & Pl
Career Total (Turf)	16	2	1	3	10088
Career Total (AW)	18	2	2	2	5987

64 9/08 Gdwd 2m (0-75)H SFT £3238
59 10/07 Kemp 2m (0-65)H STD £2047
55 9/07 Gdwd 2m (0-65)H G-F £3238
46 11/06 Wolv 1m5f194y STD £2730
Total win prize-money £11255

Going (Turf): **Sf: 1-3** GS: 0-2 Gd: 0-5 **GF: 1-4** Fm: 0-2
Distance: 5f/6f: 0-0 7f-8f: 0-4 9f-13f: 0-13 **14f+: 4-17**
Track : LH: 1-18 **RH: 3-15 Tight: 3-21** Gall: 0-1
Aids: Bl: 0-0 Vi: 0-2 Tstrap: 0-0 Ckp: 0-0
Best Rating: **64** 9/08 Gdwd 2m soft

Moderate; stays 2m; acts on fast and soft ground; goes on sand.

Go Blue Chip

74(86) (47)**32**
2-y-o br g More Than Ready (USA)-Bon Vivant (USA) (Salt Lake (USA))
H Candy Blue Chip Feed Ltd

Placings:00 **(7736)**
2009: 5^{0}GF, 6^{0}SD,

	Starts	1st	2nd	3rd	Win & Pl
Career Total (Turf)	1	0	0	0	
Career Total (AW)	1	0	0	0	

Going (Turf): **Sf: 0-0 GS: 0-0 Gd: 0-0 GF: 0-1 Fm: 0-0**
Distance: 5f/6f: 0-2 7f-8f: 0-0 9f-13f: 0-0 14f+: 0-0
Track : LH: 0-0 RH: 0-1 Tight: 0-0 Gall: 0-0
Aids: Bl: 0-0 Vi: 0-0 Tstrap: 0-0 Ckp: 0-0
Best Rating: **47** 12/09 Kemp 6f stand

Go Forth North (USA)

90 **66**
2-y-o ch f North Light (IRE)-Witch Tradition (USA) (Holy Bull (USA))
M L W Bell Leo Baxter & Michael K Schmeling

Placings:344 **(4385)**
2009: 7^{3}GF, 6^{4}GF, 7^{4}G,

	Starts	1st	2nd	3rd	Win & Pl
Career Total (Turf)	3	0	0	1	884

Going (Turf): Sf: 0-0 GS: 0-0 Gd: 0-1 GF: 0-2 Fm: 0-0
Distance: 5f/6f: 0-0 7f-8f: 0-3 9f-13f: 0-0 14f+: 0-0
Track : LH: 0-0 RH: 0-0 Tight: 0-0 Gall: 0-0
Aids: Bl: 0-0 Vi: 0-0 Tstrap: 0-0 Ckp: 0-0
Best Rating: 66 7/09 Sals 6f212y gd-fm

Fair daughter of North Light; stays 7f; acts on fast ground.

Go Free

71 (56)**43**

8-y-o gr g Easycall-Miss Traxdata (Absalom)
J G M O'Shea Pete Smith Car Sales

Placings:00/25050062/63423102500/10/36/0-0 **(5217)**
2009: 14^{0}G,

	Starts	1st	2nd	3rd	Win & Pl
Career Total (Turf)	11	0	1	0	903
Career Total (AW)	16	2	3	3	5555

55 2/06 Ling 1m5f (0-45) STD £1365
53 5/05 Ling 1m5f (0-45) STD £1480
Total win prize-money £2846

Going (Turf): Sf: 0-0 GS: 0-1 Gd: 0-9 GF: 0-1 Fm: 0-0
Distance: 5f/6f: 0-2 7f-8f: 0-7 **9f-13f: 2-14** 14f+: 0-4
Track : **LH: 2-22** RH: 0-4 **Tight: 2-14** Gall: 0-1
Aids: Bl: 0-0 Vi: 0-5 Tstrap: 0-0 Ckp: 0-0
Best Rating: 56 5/07 Sthl 1m4f stand

Go Go Green (IRE)

103(103) (82)**96**

3-y-o b c Acclamation-Preponderance (IRE) (Cyrano De Bergerac)
D H Brown (S Parr 12/2) S Bolland P Holling

Placings:35410114-0450601410 **(7202)**
2009: 5^{0}G, 5^{4}S, 5^{5}G, 6^{0}G, 5^{6}S, 5^{0}GF, 5^{1}GF, 5^{4}G, 5^{1}GF, 5^{0}SD,

	Starts	1st	2nd	3rd	Win & Pl
Career Total (Turf)	16	5	0	1	20973
Career Total (AW)	2	0	0	0	495

96 10/09 Pont 5f (0-85)H G-F £4857
85 9/09 Pont 5f (0-75)H G-F £3238
85 10/08 Bath 5f11y (0-75) G-S £3885
86 10/08 Pont 6f (0-85) GD £3238
73 8/08 Haml 6f5y (0-75) G-S £4209
Total win prize-money £19428

Going (Turf): Sf: 0-3 **GS: 2-2** Gd: 1-6 **GF: 2-5** Fm: 0-0
Distance: **5f/6f: 4-16** 7f-8f: 1-2 9f-13f: 0-0 14f+: 0-0
Track : **LH: 4-7** RH: 0-1 Tight: 0-3 **Gall: 1-1**
Aids: Bl: 0-0 Vi: 0-0 Tstrap: 0-0 Ckp: 0-0
Best Rating: 96 10/09 Pont 5f gd-fm

Fair; effective at 5f-6f; acts on fast and easy ground.

Go Man Go (IRE)

57

7-y-o b g Courtship-Rose Of Summer (IRE) (Taufan (USA))
B Storey (Mrs C Ferguson 28/6) K Ferguson

Placings:0 **(4014)**
2009: 11^{0}GF,

	Starts	1st	2nd	3rd	Win & Pl
Career Total (Turf)	1	0	0	0	

Going (Turf): Sf: 0-0 GS: 0-0 Gd: 0-0 GF: 0-1 Fm: 0-0
Distance: 5f/6f: 0-0 7f-8f: 0-0 9f-13f: 0-1 14f+: 0-0
Track : LH: 0-0 RH: 0-1 Tight: 0-1 Gall: 0-0
Aids: Bl: 0-0 Vi: 0-0 Tstrap: 0-0 Ckp: 0-0

Go Nani Go

92 **82**

3-y-o b c Kyllachy-Go Between (Daggers Drawn (USA))
B Smart H E Sheikh Rashid Bin Mohammed

Placings:1434-0 **(5203)**
2009: 5^{0}GF,

	Starts	1st	2nd	3rd	Win & Pl
Career Total (Turf)	5	1	0	1	5751

81 5/08 Muss 5f G-S £3885
Total win prize-money £3886

Going (Turf): Sf: 0-1 **GS: 1-2** Gd: 0-0 GF: 0-2 Fm: 0-0
Distance: **5f/6f: 1-5** 7f-8f: 0-0 9f-13f: 0-0 14f+: 0-0
Track : LH: 0-1 RH: 0-0 Tight: 0-0 Gall: 0-0
Aids: Bl: 0-0 Vi: 0-0 Tstrap: 0-0 Ckp: 0-0
Best Rating: 82 9/08 Muss 5f soft

Useful; effective over 5f; handles easy ground.

Go Sunshine (IRE)

(72) (20)

3-y-o b g Tagula (IRE)-Taoveret (IRE) (Flash Of Steel)
F Sheridan Frank Sheridan

Placings:00 **(1491)**
2009: 7^{0}SD, 7^{0}SD,

	Starts	1st	2nd	3rd	Win & Pl
Career Total (Turf)	0	0	0	0	
Career Total (AW)	2	0	0	0	

Going (Turf): Sf: 0-0 GS: 0-0 Gd: 0-0 GF: 0-0 Fm: 0-0
Distance: 5f/6f: 0-0 7f-8f: 0-2 9f-13f: 0-0 14f+: 0-0
Track : LH: 0-2 RH: 0-0 Tight: 0-2 Gall: 0-0
Aids: Bl: 0-0 Vi: 0-0 Tstrap: 0-0 Ckp: 0-0
Best Rating: 20 4/09 Wolv 7f32y stand

Go To Dubai

91(88) (47)**55**

2-y-o b f Dubai Destination (USA)-Black Belt Shopper (IRE) (Desert Prince (IRE))
M W Easterby David H Cox

Placings:54224 **(4190)**
2009: 5^{5}SD, 6^{4}G, 7^{2}GF, 7^{2}GF, 7^{4}S,

	Starts	1st	2nd	3rd	Win & Pl
Career Total (Turf)	4	0	2	0	1589
Career Total (AW)	1	0	0	0	0

Going (Turf): Sf: 0-1 GS: 0-0 Gd: 0-1 GF: 0-2 Fm: 0-0
Distance: 5f/6f: 0-2 7f-8f: 0-3 9f-13f: 0-0 14f+: 0-0
Track : LH: 0-1 RH: 0-1 Tight: 0-1 Gall: 0-0
Aids: Bl: 0-0 Vi: 0-0 Tstrap: 0-0 Ckp: 0-0
Best Rating: 55 7/09 Catt 7f soft

Moderate; stays 6f; acts on good ground and on Fibresand.

Go Win Girl

19

2-y-o gr f Mark Of Esteem (IRE)-Grey Again (Unfuwain (USA))
P C Haslam Mason, Stipetic, Beckitt

Placings:0 **(3487)**
2009: 6^{0}G,

	Starts	1st	2nd	3rd	Win & Pl
Career Total (Turf)	1	0	0	0	

Going (Turf): Sf: 0-0 GS: 0-0 Gd: 0-1 GF: 0-0 Fm: 0-0
Distance: 5f/6f: 0-1 7f-8f: 0-0 9f-13f: 0-0 14f+: 0-0
Track : LH: 0-0 RH: 0-0 Tight: 0-0 Gall: 0-0
Aids: Bl: 0-0 Vi: 0-0 Tstrap: 0-0 Ckp: 0-0

Gobama

94(96) (71)**78**

2-y-o br f Dr Fong (USA)-Chine (Inchinor)
J W Hills W Y Chen

Placings:13036 **(7320)**
2009: 6^{1}GF, 7^{3}GF, 7^{0}GF, 7^{3}G, 7^{6}SD,

	Starts	1st	2nd	3rd	Win & Pl
Career Total (Turf)	4	1	0	2	5041
Career Total (AW)	1	0	0	0	0

78 7/09 Sals 6f212y G-F £3885
Total win prize-money £3886

Going (Turf): Sf: 0-0 GS: 0-0 Gd: 0-1 **GF: 1-3** Fm: 0-0
Distance: 5f/6f: 0-0 **7f-8f: 1-5** 9f-13f: 0-0 14f+: 0-0
Track : LH: 0-2 RH: 0-1 Tight: 0-2 Gall: 0-0
Aids: Bl: 0-0 Vi: 0-0 Tstrap: 0-0 Ckp: 0-0
Best Rating: 78 7/09 Sals 6f212y gd-fm

Fair; stays 7f and acts on fast ground.

Goblin

(94) (50)

8-y-o b g Atraf-Forest Fantasy (Rambo Dancer (CAN))
D E Cantillon M Bevington

Placings:3235000/415135130/000/00-40 **(0444)**
2009: 16^{4}SS, 12^{0}SD,

	Starts	1st	2nd	3rd	Win & Pl
Career Total (Turf)	16	2	1	4	13232
Career Total (AW)	7	1	0	0	2947

74 6/04 Wwck 1m2f188yE(0-70)H G-F £4290
72 5/04 Bevl 1m1f207yE(0-75)H G-F £4728
73 4/04 Sthl 1m F(0-60) STD £2947
Total win prize-money £11966

Going (Turf): Sf: 0-0 GS: 0-2 Gd: 0-3 **GF: 2-10** Fm: 0-1
Distance: 5f/6f: 0-6 7f-8f: 1-3 **9f-13f: 2-11** 14f+: 0-3
Track : **LH: 2-12** RH: 1-3 Tight: 0-6 Gall: 0-5
Aids: Bl: 0-0 Vi: 0-0 Tstrap: 0-1 Ckp: 0-1
Best Rating: 75 6/04 Wwck 1m2f188y gd-fm

Goddess Of Light (IRE)

91(99) (73)**45**

2-y-o b f Chineur (FR)-Blues Over (IRE) (Sri Pekan (USA))
Daniel Mark Loughnane M V Kirby

Placings:64321 **(7570)**
2009: 5^{6}G, 6^{4}SD, 5^{3}SF, 5^{2}SD, 5^{1}SD,

	Starts	1st	2nd	3rd	Win & Pl
Career Total (Turf)	1	0	0	0	0
Career Total (AW)	4	1	1	1	4287

73 11/09 Ling 5f (0-70) STD £2590
Total win prize-money £2590

Going (Turf): Sf: 0-0 GS: 0-0 Gd: 0-1 GF: 0-0 Fm: 0-0
Distance: **5f/6f: 1-5** 7f-8f: 0-0 9f-13f: 0-0 14f+: 0-0
Track : **LH: 1-5** RH: 0-0 **Tight: 1-3** Gall: 0-1

Aids: Bl: 0-0 Vi: 0-0 Tstrap: 0-0 Ckp: 0-0
Best Rating: 73 11/09 Ling 5f stand

Fair; stays 6f and acts on Polytrack.

Godfrey Street

100(106) (81)**80**

6-y-o ch g Compton Place-Tahara (IRE) (Caerleon (USA))
A G Newcombe A G Newcombe

Placings:41206312510/0000000402/0010045/41100061P-12654260304 **(7852)**
2009: 5^{1}SD, 5^{2}SD, 5^{6}SD, 5^{5}SD, 5^{4}G, 5^{2}G, 5^{6}SD, 5^{0}SD, 5^{3}S, 5^{0}SD, 5^{4}SS,

	Starts	1st	2nd	3rd	Win & Pl
Career Total (Turf)	28	3	4	2	76163
Career Total (AW)	20	5	1	0	17271

81	1/09	GrLe	5f	(0-75)H	STD	£2590
80	11/08	Catt	5f		HVY	£2047
88	2/08	Sthl	5f	(0-85)H	STD	£4210
84	1/08	Sthl	5f		STD	£1774
88	10/07	Asct	5f	(0-85)H	G-S	£6232
103	9/05	Donc	5f		HVY	£40600
94	8/05	Ling	5f		STD	£4121
81	5/05	Ling	5f		STD	£3081

Total win prize-money £64656

Going (Turf): Sf: 2-6 GS: 1-7 Gd: 0-8 GF: 0-7 Fm: 0-0
Distance: 5f/6f: 8-48 7f-8f: 0-0 9f-13f: 0-0 14f+: 0-0
Track : LH: 3-12 RH: 0-0 Tight: 2-9 Gall: 1-2
Aids: Bl: 4-16 Vi: 0-0 Tstrap: 1-9 Ckp: 1-9
Best Rating: 103 9/05 Donc 5f heavy

Useful sprinter; won the Group 2 Flying Childers as a juvenile; acts on soft ground; also goes on sand; has worn blinkers and cheekpieces.

Going For Gold

101(104) (80)**83**

3-y-o b f Barathea (IRE)-Flash Of Gold (Darshaan)
R Charlton The Queen

Placings:00-31345 **(6613)**
2009: 10^{3}GF, 11^{1}F, 11^{3}GS, 12^{4}GF, 12^{5}SD,

	Starts	1st	2nd	3rd	Win & Pl
Career Total (Turf)	6	1	0	2	5019
Career Total (AW)	1	0	0	0	0

78	7/09	Hayd	1m3f200y	(0-75)H	FRM	£3238

Total win prize-money £3238

Going (Turf): Sf: 0-0 GS: 0-3 Gd: 0-0 GF: 0-2 Fm: 1-1
Distance: 5f/6f: 0-0 7f-8f: 0-2 9f-13f: 1-5 14f+: 0-0
Track : LH: 1-3 RH: 0-2 Tight: 0-1 Gall: 0-1
Aids: Bl: 0-0 Vi: 0-0 Tstrap: 0-0 Ckp: 0-0
Best Rating: 83 9/09 Gdwd 1m4f gd-fm

Useful; stays 1m4f; acts on fast ground.

Going French (IRE)

89(98) (70)**69**

2-y-o ch c Frenchmans Bay (FR)-Easy Going (Hamas (IRE))
R Curtis R P Phillips

Placings:23322024 **(7637)**
2009: 5^{2}GF, 5^{3}SD, 5^{3}F, 7^{2}GF, 6^{2}G, 7^{0}G, 6^{2}SD, 5^{4}SD,

	Starts	1st	2nd	3rd	Win & Pl
Career Total (Turf)	5	0	3	1	3850
Career Total (AW)	3	0	1	1	1704

Going (Turf): Sf: 0-0 GS: 0-0 Gd: 0-2 GF: 0-2 Fm: 0-1
Distance: 5f/6f: 0-6 7f-8f: 0-2 9f-13f: 0-0 14f+: 0-0
Track : LH: 0-2 RH: 0-3 Tight: 0-0 Gall: 0-1
Aids: Bl: 0-0 Vi: 0-0 Tstrap: 0-0 Ckp: 0-0
Best Rating: 70 11/09 Kemp 6f stand

Modest; stays 7f; acts on fast ground, Fibresand and Polytrack.

Gojeri (IRE)

97 **68**

2-y-o ch g Choisir (AUS)-Lady Elysees (USA) (Royal Academy (USA))
M A Jarvis G Moss, J Sims & R Marchant

Placings:06 **(7145)**
2009: 6^{0}S, 6^{6}G,

	Starts	1st	2nd	3rd	Win & Pl
Career Total (Turf)	2	0	0	0	0

Going (Turf): Sf: 0-1 GS: 0-0 Gd: 0-1 GF: 0-0 Fm: 0-0
Distance: 5f/6f: 0-1 7f-8f: 0-1 9f-13f: 0-0 14f+: 0-0
Track : LH: 0-0 RH: 0-0 Tight: 0-0 Gall: 0-0
Aids: Bl: 0-0 Vi: 0-0 Tstrap: 0-0 Ckp: 0-0
Best Rating: 68 10/09 NmkR 6f good

Gold Again (USA)

(96) (60)**54**

4-y-o b f Touch Gold (USA)-Miss Insync (USA) (Miswaki (USA))
W R Swinburn P W Harris

Placings:605-600 **(3224)**
2009: 6^{6}SD, 7^{0}SD, 7^{0}SD,

	Starts	1st	2nd	3rd	Win & Pl
Career Total (Turf)	1	0	0	0	0
Career Total (AW)	5	0	0	0	0

Going (Turf): Sf: 0-0 GS: 0-1 Gd: 0-0 GF: 0-0 Fm: 0-0
Distance: 5f/6f: 0-2 7f-8f: 0-4 9f-13f: 0-0 14f+: 0-0
Track : LH: 0-2 RH: 0-3 Tight: 0-2 Gall: 0-1
Aids: Bl: 0-0 Vi: 0-1 Tstrap: 0-0 Ckp: 0-0
Best Rating: 60 9/08 Kemp 7f stand

Gold Bubbles (USA)

101 **99**

2-y-o b f Street Cry (IRE)-Well Revered (USA) (Red Ransom (USA))
J S Bolger Mrs June Judd

Placings:123466 **(5488a)**
2009: 6^{1}GY, 6^{2}GY, 6^{3}S, 7^{4}GY, 6^{6}GF, 7^{6}HY,

	Starts	1st	2nd	3rd	Win & Pl
Career Total (Turf)	6	1	1	1	26232

87	4/09	Leop	6f	G-Y	£12075

Total win prize-money £12076

Going (Turf): Sf: 0-2 GS: 0-0 Gd: 0-0 GF: 0-1 Fm: 0-0
Distance: 5f/6f: 1-4 7f-8f: 0-2 9f-13f: 0-0 14f+: 0-0
Track : LH: 1-3 RH: 0-0 Tight: 0-0 Gall: 0-0
Aids: Bl: 0-1 Vi: 0-0 Tstrap: 0-2 Ckp: 0-2
Best Rating: 99 8/09 Leop 7f gd-yld

Very useful; Listed placed; stays 6f; acts on soft ground; has worn cheekpieces.

Gold Crusher (USA)

72(92) (63)**57**

2-y-o b g Johannesburg (USA)-Compressed (USA) (Green Forest (USA))
R M H Cowell Stennett/Morley/Warner

Placings:436 **(5311)**
2009: 6^{4}GF, 6^{3}SD, 6^{6}SD,

	Starts	1st	2nd	3rd	Win & Pl
Career Total (Turf)	1	0	0	0	481
Career Total (AW)	2	0	0	1	605

Going (Turf): Sf: 0-0 GS: 0-0 Gd: 0-0 GF: 0-1 Fm: 0-0
Distance: 5f/6f: 0-3 7f-8f: 0-0 9f-13f: 0-0 14f+: 0-0
Track : LH: 0-1 RH: 0-1 Tight: 0-0 Gall: 0-0
Aids: Bl: 0-0 Vi: 0-0 Tstrap: 0-0 Ckp: 0-0
Best Rating: 63 8/09 Kemp 6f stand

Moderate; stays 6f; acts on Fibresand; should improve further.

Gold Diamond (USA)

93(81) (40)**65**

2-y-o b g Seeking The Gold (USA)-Dubai Diamond (Octagonal (NZ))
M Johnston Sheikh Hamdan Bin Mohammed Al Maktoum

Placings:6040000 **(7333)**
2009: 7^{6}GF, 7^{0}G, 7^{4}G, 7^{0}GS, 6^{0}G, 6^{0}G, 6^{0}SD,

	Starts	1st	2nd	3rd	Win & Pl
Career Total (Turf)	6	0	0	0	337
Career Total (AW)	1	0	0	0	

Going (Turf): Sf: 0-0 GS: 0-1 Gd: 0-4 GF: 0-1 Fm: 0-0
Distance: 5f/6f: 0-1 7f-8f: 0-6 9f-13f: 0-0 14f+: 0-0
Track : LH: 0-4 RH: 0-0 Tight: 0-2 Gall: 0-0
Aids: Bl: 0-1 Vi: 0-0 Tstrap: 0-0 Ckp: 0-0
Best Rating: 65 7/09 NmkJ 7f good

Gold Express

108(106) (83)**88**

6-y-o b g Observatory (USA)-Vanishing Point (USA) (Caller I.D. (USA))
P J O'Gorman N S Yong

Placings:0/001/3/453061-600304110 **(5221)**
2009: 6^{6}G, 7^{0}SD, 7^{0}GF, 6^{3}SD, 6^{0}GF, 6^{4}GF, 8^{1}SD, 8^{1}GF, 8^{0}GF,

	Starts	1st	2nd	3rd	Win & Pl
Career Total (Turf)	14	2	0	2	9463
Career Total (AW)	6	2	0	1	8185

88	7/09	Wind	1m67y	(0-75)H	G-F	£2729
83	7/09	Kemp	1m	(0-80)H	STD	£4727
78	11/08	Kemp	7f	(0-75)H	STD	£2590
74	8/06	NmkJ	6f	(0-85)H	GD	£5505

Total win prize-money £15552

Going (Turf): Sf: 0-0 GS: 0-2 Gd: 1-3 GF: 1-9 Fm: 0-0
Distance: 5f/6f: 1-11 7f-8f: 2-7 9f-13f: 1-2 14f+: 0-0
Track : LH: 0-3 RH: 3-5 Tight: 1-3 Gall: 0-4
Aids: Bl: 0-0 Vi: 0-0 Tstrap: 0-0 Ckp: 0-0
Best Rating: 88 7/09 Wind 1m67y gd-fm

Useful; stays 1m; acts on good and fast ground; goes on Polytrack.

Gold Fix (IRE)

101(91) (67)**68**

2-y-o b f Fath (USA)-Gold Blended (IRE) (Goldmark (USA))

M R Channon Mrs T Burns

Placings:00023161226 **(6844)**

2009: 6^{0}GF, 7^{0}GF, 6^{0}S, 7^{2}G, 7^{3}GF, 7^{1}GF, 7^{6}SD, 7^{1}GS, 7^{2}GF, 8^{2}SD, 7^{6}G,

	Starts	1st	2nd	3rd	Win & Pl
Career Total (Turf)	9	2	2	1	9004
Career Total (AW)	2	0	1	0	705

66	9/09	Epsm	7f	(0-70)	G-S £3885
58	8/09	Catt	7f		G-F £2047

Total win prize-money £5933

Going (Turf): Sf: 0-1 **GS: 1-1** Gd: 0-2 **GF: 1-5** Fm: 0-0
Distance: 5f/6f: 0-0 **7f-8f: 2-10** 9f-13f: 0-1 14f+: 0-0
Track : **LH: 2-6** RH: 0-0 **Tight: 2-6** Gall: 0-0
Aids: Bl: 0-0 Vi: 0-0 Tstrap: 0-0 Ckp: 0-0
Best Rating: 68 9/09 Catt 7f gd-fm

Modest; stays 7f; acts on most ground.

Gold Maha

99 **57**

3-y-o b f Diktat-Westwood (FR) (Anabaa (USA))

M E Sowersby (M R Channon 11/6) M E Sowersby

Placings:045400 **(6098)**

2009: 8^{0}G, 10^{4}GF, 10^{5}GS, 14^{4}GF, 10^{0}GF, 13^{0}GF,

	Starts	1st	2nd	3rd	Win & Pl
Career Total (Turf)	6	0	0	0	457

Going (Turf): Sf: 0-0 GS: 0-1 Gd: 0-1 GF: 0-4 Fm: 0-0
Distance: 5f/6f: 0-0 7f-8f: 0-0 9f-13f: 0-4 14f+: 0-2
Track : LH: 0-5 RH: 0-0 Tight: 0-2 Gall: 0-0
Aids: Bl: 0-0 Vi: 0-0 Tstrap: 0-0 Ckp: 0-0
Best Rating: 57 5/09 Wwck 1m2f188y gd-fm

Modest; stays 1m2f; acts on fast ground.

Gold Party

88(94) (70)**63**

2-y-o ch c Bahamian Bounty-West River (USA) (Gone West (USA))

K McAuliffe (Tom Dascombe 7/9) K W J McAuliffe

Placings:50032 **(7865)**

2009: 6^{5}GF, 7^{0}F, 9^{0}SD, 7^{3}SD, 8^{2}SS,

	Starts	1st	2nd	3rd	Win & Pl
Career Total (Turf)	2	0	0	0	0
Career Total (AW)	3	0	1	1	1300

Going (Turf): Sf: 0-0 GS: 0-0 Gd: 0-0 GF: 0-1 Fm: 0-1
Distance: 5f/6f: 0-1 7f-8f: 0-3 9f-13f: 0-1 14f+: 0-0
Track : LH: 0-3 RH: 0-0 Tight: 0-2 Gall: 0-1
Aids: Bl: 0-0 Vi: 0-0 Tstrap: 0-0 Ckp: 0-0
Best Rating: 70 12/09 Sthl 1m std-slw

Modest; stays 1m and acts on both AW surfaces.

Gold Rock (FR)

(93) (59)**90**

4-y-o b g Anabaa (USA)-Golden Sea (FR) (Saint Cyrien (FR))

A W Carroll (H-A Pantall 4/2) Paul Downing

Placings:214/65206-**005540** **(1042)**

2009: 8^{0}SD, 6^{0}SD, 8^{5}SD, 10^{5}SD, 6^{4}SD, 9^{0}SD,

	Starts	1st	2nd	3rd	Win & Pl
Career Total (Turf)	8	1	2	0	20553
Career Total (AW)	6	0	0	0	0

9/07 Fntb 7f G-S £9459

Total win prize-money £9459

Going (Turf): Sf: 0-2 **GS: 1-3** Gd: 0-3 GF: 0-0 Fm: 0-0
Distance: 5f/6f: 0-1 **7f-8f: 1-10** 9f-13f: 0-3 14f+: 0-0
Track : LH: 0-8 RH: 0-3 Tight: 0-4 Gall: 0-0
Aids: Bl: 0-0 Vi: 0-0 Tstrap: 0-0 Ckp: 0-0
Best Rating: 90 9/07 StCl 6f110y gd-sft

Gold Rules

95 **73**

2-y-o ch c Gold Away (IRE)-Raphaela (FR) (Octagonal (NZ))

L M Cumani L Marinopoulos

Placings:002 **(5253)**

2009: 6^{0}GF, 5^{0}S, 6^{2}GF,

	Starts	1st	2nd	3rd	Win & Pl
Career Total (Turf)	3	0	1	0	1156

Going (Turf): Sf: 0-1 GS: 0-0 Gd: 0-0 GF: 0-2 Fm: 0-0
Distance: 5f/6f: 0-3 7f-8f: 0-0 9f-13f: 0-0 14f+: 0-0
Track : LH: 0-0 RH: 0-0 Tight: 0-0 Gall: 0-0
Aids: Bl: 0-0 Vi: 0-0 Tstrap: 0-0 Ckp: 0-0
Best Rating: 73 8/09 Ripn 6f gd-fm

Fair; stays 6f; acts on fast ground.

Gold Story

91 **48**

2-y-o ch g Lucky Story (USA)-Incatinka (Inca Chief (USA))

B Ellison Koo's Racing Club

Placings:6504 **(5595)**

2009: 6^{6}GS, 6^{5}GF, 6^{0}GF, 7^{4}GF,

	Starts	1st	2nd	3rd	Win & Pl
Career Total (Turf)	4	0	0	0	192

Going (Turf): Sf: 0-0 GS: 0-1 Gd: 0-0 GF: 0-3 Fm: 0-0
Distance: 5f/6f: 0-3 7f-8f: 0-1 9f-13f: 0-0 14f+: 0-0
Track : LH: 0-0 RH: 0-0 Tight: 0-0 Gall: 0-0
Aids: Bl: 0-0 Vi: 0-0 Tstrap: 0-0 Ckp: 0-0
Best Rating: 48 9/09 Rdcr 7f gd-fm

Goldan Jess (IRE)

107 (49)**54**

5-y-o b g Golan (IRE)-Bendis (GER) (Danehill (USA))

P A Kirby Druid Sports,Galway Lads & The Jessies

Placings:3000/**560**/600-26252 **(6558)**

2009: 12^{7}GF, 13^{6}G, 14^{2}GF, 14^{5}GF, 15^{2}G,

	Starts	1st	2nd	3rd	Win & Pl
Career Total (Turf)	13	0	3	1	2644
Career Total (AW)	2	0	0	0	0

Going (Turf): Sf: 0-1 GS: 0-1 Gd: 0-3 GF: 0-6 Fm: 0-2
Distance: 5f/6f: 0-4 7f-8f: 0-3 9f-13f: 0-4 14f+: 0-4
Track : LH: 0-11 RH: 0-2 Tight: 0-5 Gall: 0-1
Aids: Bl: 0-1 Vi: 0-1 Tstrap: 0-0 Ckp: 0-0
Best Rating: 72 4/06 Tipp 5f heavy

Moderate; winning hurdler; stays 1m7f; acts on most ground; has worn blinkers and a visor.

Golden Aria (IRE)

99 **79**

2-y-o b f Rakti-Yellow Trumpet (Petong)

R Hannon Thurloe Thoroughbreds XX

Placings:431 **(6062)**

2009: 6^{4}GF, 6^{3}S, 8^{1}GF,

	Starts	1st	2nd	3rd	Win & Pl
Career Total (Turf)	3	1	0	1	6456

79 9/09 NmkR 1m G-F £5180

Total win prize-money £5181

Going (Turf): Sf: 0-1 GS: 0-0 Gd: 0-0 **GF: 1-2** Fm: 0-0
Distance: 5f/6f: 0-0 **7f-8f: 1-3** 9f-13f: 0-0 14f+: 0-0
Track : LH: 0-0 RH: 0-0 Tight: 0-0 Gall: 0-0
Aids: Bl: 0-0 Vi: 0-0 Tstrap: 0-0 Ckp: 0-0
Best Rating: 79 9/09 NmkR 1m gd-fm

Useful; stays 7f and acts on soft ground.

Golden Bishop

(103) (73)**72**

4-y-o ch g Medicean-Hen Harrier (Polar Falcon (USA))

R A Fahey Timeform Betfair Racing Club Ltd

Placings:0002524133-0 **(0105)**

2009: 9^{0}SD,

	Starts	1st	2nd	3rd	Win & Pl
Career Total (Turf)	7	1	2	0	3502
Career Total (AW)	4	0	0	2	1156

69 8/08 Yarm 1m2f21y G-S £2201

Total win prize-money £2202

Going (Turf): Sf: 0-1 **GS: 1-2** Gd: 0-2 GF: 0-2 Fm: 0-0
Distance: 5f/6f: 0-0 7f-8f: 0-1 **9f-13f: 1-10** 14f+: 0-0
Track : **LH: 1-9** RH: 0-1 **Tight: 1-5** Gall: 0-3
Aids: Bl: 0-0 Vi: 0-0 Tstrap: 0-0 Ckp: 0-0
Best Rating: 73 11/08 GrLe 1m2f stand

Modest; stays 1m2f; acts on quick ground and on Polytrack; has broken blood-vessels.

Golden Button (IRE)

99(102) (77)**69**

4-y-o ch f Trans Island-Velvet Appeal (IRE) (Petorius)

Sir Mark Prescott William Charnley & Tweenhills Racing

Placings:21636 **(6648)**

2009: 7^{2}G, 8^{1}SF, 8^{6}G, 9^{3}SD, 10^{6}G,

	Starts	1st	2nd	3rd	Win & Pl
Career Total (Turf)	3	0	1	0	705
Career Total (AW)	2	1	0	1	2802

77 8/09 Wolv 1m141y SF £2047

Total win prize-money £2047

Going (Turf): Sf: 0-0 GS: 0-0 Gd: 0-3 GF: 0-0 Fm: 0-0
Distance: 5f/6f: 0-0 7f-8f: 0-1 **9f-13f: 1-4** 14f+: 0-0
Track : **LH: 1-4** RH: 0-0 **Tight: 1-3** Gall: 0-1
Aids: Bl: 0-0 Vi: 0-0 Tstrap: 0-0 Ckp: 0-0
Best Rating: 77 9/09 Wolv 1m1f103y stand

Fair; stays 1m 1f; acts on Polytrack.

Golden Desert (IRE)

108(93) (94)**109**

5-y-o b g Desert Prince (IRE)-Jules (IRE) (Danehill (USA))

T G Mills S Parker

Placings:00201/265410341/0522331050-3602211000 **(7019)**

2009: 7^{3}GF, 7^{6}GF, 7^{0}G, 7^{2}G, 7^{2}GF, 6^{1}G, 7^{1}GF, 7^{0}G, 6^{0}GS, 7^{0}GS,

	Starts	1st	2nd	3rd	Win & Pl
Career Total (Turf)	25	3	5	3	44309
Career Total (AW)	9	3	1	1	16463

109	9/09	Gdwd	7f	(0-100)H	G-F	£11215
109	8/09	Gdwd	6f	(0-95)H	GD	£7771
94	7/08	Asct	7f	(0-90)H	G-F	£8744
94	11/07	Ling	7f	(0-85)H	STD	£4728
86	8/07	Ling	6f	(0-85)H	STD	£4857
72	11/06	Wolv	5f216y		SF	£3886

Total win prize-money £41203

Going (Turf): Sf: 0-1 GS: 0-4 Gd: 1-9 **GF: 2-11** Fm: 0-0
Distance: 5f/6f: 3-14 7f-8f: 3-20 9f-13f: 0-0 14f+: 0-0
Track : **LH: 3-8** RH: 1-6 **Tight: 3-5** Gall: 0-1
Aids: Bl: 0-0 **Vi: 1-4** Tstrap: 0-0 Ckp: 0-0
Best Rating: **109** 9/09 Gdwd 7f gd-fm

Smart; effective over 6f-7f; acts on a sound surface and on Polytrack.

Golden Destiny (IRE)

105(83) (56)**105**

3-y-o ch f Captain Rio-Dear Catch (IRE) (Bluebird (USA))
P J Makin H J W Davies P Spencer-Jones M H Holland

Placings:0512330-031111 **(5902)**

2009: 7^{0}GS, 6^{3}GF, 5^{1}GF, 5^{1}GF, 5^{1}F, 5^{1}F,

	Starts	1st	2nd	3rd	Win & Pl
Career Total (Turf)	12	5	1	3	55369
Career Total (AW)	1	0	0	0	0

105	9/09	Bath	5f161y	(0-95)H	FRM	£8723
102	8/09	Bath	5f161y	(0-85)H	FRM	£4792
85	8/09	Sand	5f6y	(0-80)H	G-F	£4857
83	7/09	Sand	5f6y	(0-80)H	G-F	£4857
68	8/08	Wind	6f		G-S	£2388

Total win prize-money £25617

Going (Turf): Sf: 0-2 GS: 1-3 Gd: 0-1 **GF: 2-4 Fm: 2-2**
Distance: **5f/6f: 5-9** 7f-8f: 0-4 9f-13f: 0-0 14f+: 0-0
Track : **LH: 2-6** RH: 0-0 Tight: 0-1 **Gall: 3-3**
Aids: Bl: 0-0 Vi: 0-0 Tstrap: 4-4 Ckp: 4-4
Best Rating: **105** 9/09 Bath 5f161y firm

Very useful; effective at 5f-6f; acts on fast ground; has worn cheekpieces.

Golden Dixie (USA)

105(100) (66)**89**

10-y-o ch g Dixieland Band (USA)-Beyrouth (USA) (Alleged (USA))
R A Harris Drag Star On Swan

Placings:110/0240000/0255000**01100/1502**025011365402 2350/**2026**0012003004000/00312000311000**4**/056066000 060-0**44**2003145055040**0006563** **(7834)**

2009: 5^{0}GF, 5^{4}SD, 5^{4}GF, 6^{2}GF, 6^{0}GF, 6^{0}GF, 5^{3}F, 6^{1}G, 6^{4}GF, 6^{5}GS, 6^{0}G, 5^{5}G, 5^{5}S, 5^{0}G, 6^{4}GF, 6^{0}GS, 5^{0}SD, 5^{0}SD, 6^{0}SD, 5^{6}SD, 6^{5}SD, 5^{6}SD, 6^{3}SD,

	Starts	1st	2nd	3rd	Win & Pl
Career Total (Turf)	89	9	8	6	88637
Career Total (AW)	21	3	3	1	15888

76	6/09	Chep	6f16y	(0-70)H	GD	£2914
101	8/07	Gdwd	6f	(0-95)H	GD	£7772
97	8/07	Donc	5f140y	(0-95)H	G-F	£11658
96	6/07	Sals	5f	(0-85)H	GD	£5181
98	6/06	York	5f	(0-95)H	G-F	£8290
84	6/05	Sand	5f6y	(0-85)H	G-F	£6977
81	5/05	Gdwd	5f	(0-70)H	G-S	£4046
62	1/05	Wolv	5f216y		STD	£2996
76	11/04	Wolv	5f20y		STD	£2982
79	11/04	Wolv	5f216y		STD	£2989
93	8/02	Newc	6f	D(0-80)	GD	£4842
83	7/02	Sals	6f	D	G-F	£4160

Total win prize-money £64812

Going (Turf): Sf: 0-6 GS: 1-15 **Gd: 4-27 GF: 4-39** Fm: 0-2
Distance: **5f/6f: 11-98** 7f-8f: 1-12 9f-13f: 0-0 14f+: 0-0
Track : **LH: 3-23** RH: 0-4 **Tight: 3-13** Gall: 0-11
Aids: Bl: 0-0 Vi: 0-0 Tstrap: 0-5 Ckp: 0-5
Best Rating: **101** 8/07 Gdwd 6f good

Moderate; effective over 5f-6f; acts on fast ground; goes on Polytrack; has been tried in cheekpieces.

Golden Emperor (IRE)

96(90) (57)**58**

2-y-o ro g Antonius Pius (USA)-Lily Shing Shang (Spectrum (IRE))
G A Swinbank B Dunn

Placings:034 **(6461)**

2009: 6^{0}GF, 7^{3}GS, 8^{4}SD,

	Starts	1st	2nd	3rd	Win & Pl
Career Total (Turf)	2	0	0	1	337
Career Total (AW)	1	0	0	0	0

Going (Turf): **Sf: 0-0 GS: 0-1 Gd: 0-0 GF: 0-1 Fm: 0-0**
Distance: 5f/6f: 0-1 7f-8f: 0-1 9f-13f: 0-1 14f+: 0-0
Track : LH: 0-1 RH: 0-1 Tight: 0-2 Gall: 0-0
Aids: Bl: 0-0 Vi: 0-0 Tstrap: 0-0 Ckp: 0-0
Best Rating: **58** 8/09 Muss 7f30y gd-sft

Modest; stays 7f and acts on easy ground.

Golden Flight (IRE)

94(89) (55)**64**

3-y-o ch g Hawk Wing (USA)-Cassilis (IRE) (Persian Bold)
J W Hills The Phantom Partnership 1

Placings:00-5405 **(3662)**

2009: 7^{5}G, 8^{4}G, 8^{0}SD, 7^{5}F,

	Starts	1st	2nd	3rd	Win & Pl
Career Total (Turf)	4	0	0	0	216
Career Total (AW)	2	0	0	0	

Going (Turf): **Sf: 0-0 GS: 0-0 Gd: 0-2 GF: 0-1 Fm: 0-1**
Distance: 5f/6f: 0-0 7f-8f: 0-4 9f-13f: 0-2 14f+: 0-0
Track : LH: 0-3 RH: 0-2 Tight: 0-2 Gall: 0-0
Aids: Bl: 0-0 Vi: 0-0 Tstrap: 0-0 Ckp: 0-0
Best Rating: **64** 5/09 Gdwd 7f good

Golden Future

98(93) (48)**58**

6-y-o b g Muhtarram (USA)-Nazca (Zilzal (USA))
P D Niven The Little Ice Club

Placings:60040300/53650/**05**505**1**63**0**3 **(6845)**

2009: 11^{0}SD, 7^{5}SD, 8^{5}G, 10^{0}G, 11^{5}S, 11^{1}G, 11^{6}SD, 12^{3}GS, 16^{0}SD, 13^{3}G,

	Starts	1st	2nd	3rd	Win & Pl
Career Total (Turf)	19	1	0	4	4386
Career Total (AW)	4	0	0	0	0

58	8/09	Carl	1m3f107y	(0-60)H	GD	£2047

Total win prize-money £2047

Going (Turf): Sf: 0-2 GS: 0-1 **Gd: 1-5** GF: 0-6 Fm: 0-3
Distance: 5f/6f: 0-2 7f-8f: 0-11 **9f-13f: 1-8** 14f+: 0-2
Track : LH: 0-11 **RH: 1-8** Tight: 0-3 Gall: 0-1
Aids: Bl: 0-1 Vi: 0-0 Tstrap: 0-3 Ckp: 0-3
Best Rating: **65** 7/06 Gway 7f yield

Golden Games (IRE)

104 **67**

3-y-o b f Montjeu (IRE)-Ski For Gold (Shirley Heights)
D C O'Brien (J L Dunlop 3/7) C Attrell

Placings:040-00224 **(5152)**

2009: 10^{0}GF, 12^{0}GF, 14^{2}GF, 14^{2}G, 12^{4}GF,

	Starts	1st	2nd	3rd	Win & Pl
Career Total (Turf)	8	0	2	0	2124

Going (Turf): **Sf: 0-1 GS: 0-0 Gd: 0-2 GF: 0-5 Fm: 0-0**
Distance: 5f/6f: 0-0 7f-8f: 0-3 9f-13f: 0-3 14f+: 0-2
Track : LH: 0-4 RH: 0-1 Tight: 0-1 Gall: 0-0
Aids: Bl: 0-0 Vi: 0-0 Tstrap: 0-0 Ckp: 0-0
Best Rating: **67** 7/09 Hayd 1m6f good

Modest; stays 7f and acts on fast ground.

Golden Gates (IRE)

88 **67**

2-y-o b g Key Of Luck (USA)-Golden Anthem (USA) (Lion Cavern (USA))
Mrs A Duffield Findlay & Bloom

Placings:4 **(6533)**

2009: 10^{4}GF,

	Starts	1st	2nd	3rd	Win & Pl
Career Total (Turf)	1	0	0	0	385

Going (Turf): **Sf: 0-0 GS: 0-0 Gd: 0-0 GF: 0-1 Fm: 0-0**
Distance: 5f/6f: 0-0 7f-8f: 0-0 9f-13f: 0-1 14f+: 0-0
Track : LH: 0-1 RH: 0-0 Tight: 0-0 Gall: 0-0
Aids: Bl: 0-0 Vi: 0-0 Tstrap: 0-0 Ckp: 0-0
Best Rating: **67** 10/09 Pont 1m2f6y gd-fm

Golden Groom

95 **61**

6-y-o b g Groom Dancer (USA)-Reine De Thebes (FR) (Darshaan)
P Beaumont Colin Stirling

Placings:0500323/534311/1 **(2573)**

2009: 12^{1}GF,

	Starts	1st	2nd	3rd	Win & Pl
Career Total (Turf)	14	3	1	4	11975

61	6/09	Ripn	1m4f10y	(0-70)H	G-F	£3238
64	9/07	Newc	2m19y	(0-65)H	G-F	£3154
57	8/07	Ripn	2m	(0-65)H	G-F	£2590

Total win prize-money £8984

Going (Turf): Sf: 0-1 GS: 0-3 Gd: 0-3 **GF: 3-6** Fm: 0-1
Distance: 5f/6f: 0-0 7f-8f: 0-1 9f-13f: 1-6 **14f+: 2-7**
Track : LH: 1-8 **RH: 2-6 Tight: 2-8** Gall: 1-3
Aids: Bl: 0-0 Vi: 0-0 Tstrap: 0-0 Ckp: 0-0
Best Rating: **64** 9/07 Newc 2m19y gd-fm

Moderate; effective over 1m4f-2m; acts on fast and easy ground.

Golden Kiss

60 **9**

3-y-o b f Golden Snake (USA)-Kiss Me Again (IRE) (Cyrano De Bergerac)

Paul Murphy P Cranney

Placings:5-00 **(2105)**

2009: 7^{0}GF, 9^{0}GS,

	Starts	1st	2nd	3rd	Win & Pl
Career Total (Turf)	3	0	0	0	0

Going (Turf): **Sf: 0-1 GS: 0-1 Gd: 0-0 GF: 0-1 Fm: 0-0**
Distance: 5f/6f: 0-0 7f-8f: 0-2 9f-13f: 0-1 14f+: 0-0
Track : LH: 0-1 RH: 0-2 Tight: 0-3 Gall: 0-0
Aids: Bl: 0-0 Vi: 0-0 Tstrap: 0-0 Ckp: 0-0
Best Rating: **9** 11/08 Muss 7f30y soft

Golden Penny

103(104) (80)**81**

4-y-o b g Xaar-Dog Rose (SAF) (Fort Wood (USA))

M Dods (A G Foster 17/9) J Ross

Placings:0440335/**1**5432210**4**-06100000**0** **(7782)**

2009: 7^{0}GF, 0^{6}G, 7^{1}GS, 7^{0}GF, 8^{0}G, 8^{0}G, 7^{0}G, **8^{0}**SD, **8^{0}**SD,

	Starts	1st	2nd	3rd	Win & Pl
Career Total (Turf)	18	1	2	2	6302
Career Total (AW)	7	2	0	1	8101

81	5/09	Newc	7f	(0-75)H	G-S	£3238
80	8/08	Kemp	1m	(0-85)H	STD	£4727
67	4/08	Sthl	1m		STD	£2456

Total win prize-money £10422

Going (Turf): Sf: 0-3 **GS: 1-4** Gd: 0-4 GF: 0-7 Fm: 0-0
Distance: 5f/6f: 0-2 **7f-8f: 3-17** 9f-13f: 0-6 14f+: 0-0
Track : LH: 1-10 RH: 1-10 Tight: 0-6 Gall: 0-1
Aids: Bl: 0-1 Vi: 0-0 Tstrap: 0-0 Ckp: 0-0
Best Rating: **81** 5/09 Newc 7f gd-sft

Fair; stays 1m; acts on most ground on turf; goes on Fibresand.

Golden Pippin

80(84) (42)**56**

2-y-o b f Medicean-Surf The Net (Cape Cross (IRE))

R Hannon P T Tellwright

Placings:050000 **(7210)**

2009: 6^{0}GF, 6^{5}G, 7^{0}G, 7^{0}SD, 8^{0}SD, 7^{0}SD,

	Starts	1st	2nd	3rd	Win & Pl
Career Total (Turf)	3	0	0	0	0
Career Total (AW)	3	0	0	0	

Going (Turf): **Sf: 0-0 GS: 0-0 Gd: 0-2 GF: 0-1 Fm: 0-0**
Distance: 5f/6f: 0-2 7f-8f: 0-4 9f-13f: 0-0 14f+: 0-0
Track : LH: 0-1 RH: 0-2 Tight: 0-1 Gall: 0-0
Aids: Bl: 0-0 Vi: 0-0 Tstrap: 0-0 Ckp: 0-0
Best Rating: **56** 8/09 NmkJ 7f good

Golden Pool (IRE)

83(94) (55)**48**

3-y-o b f Danetime (IRE)-Miss Megs (IRE) (Croco Rouge (IRE))

S A Callaghan Lord Clinton & Matthew Green

Placings:0064-600 **(2973)**

2009: 7^{6}GF, 7^{0}SD, 6^{0}GS,

	Starts	1st	2nd	3rd	Win & Pl
Career Total (Turf)	3	0	0	0	0
Career Total (AW)	4	0	0	0	202

Going (Turf): **Sf: 0-0 GS: 0-1 Gd: 0-1 GF: 0-1 Fm: 0-0**
Distance: 5f/6f: 0-4 7f-8f: 0-3 9f-13f: 0-0 14f+: 0-0
Track : LH: 0-4 RH: 0-1 Tight: 0-1 Gall: 0-1
Aids: Bl: 0-0 Vi: 0-0 Tstrap: 0-0 Ckp: 0-0
Best Rating: **55** 11/08 Kemp 6f stand

Golden Prospect

105(104) (68)**74**

5-y-o b g Lujain (USA)-Petonellajill (Petong)

Miss J R Tooth (J W Hills 16/10) Miss J R Tooth

Placings:0**50**/1104205/**015**6005405-**400**501530601**35**5000206** **(7861)**

2009: **8^{4}**SD, **8^{0}**SD, 7^{0}SD, 6^{5}GF, 6^{0}GF, 6^{1}G, 6^{5}GF, 6^{3}F, 7^{0}G, 7^{6}F, 7^{0}G, 7^{1}F, 7^{3}SD, 6^{5}GF, 7^{5}SF, **8^{0}**SD, 7^{0}SD, 7^{0}SD, 8^{2}SD, 7^{0}SD, 7^{6}SD,

	Starts	1st	2nd	3rd	Win & Pl
Career Total (Turf)	24	4	1	1	12819
Career Total (AW)	17	1	1	1	3758

63	9/09	Brig	7f214y	(0-60)H	FRM	£2460
61	6/09	Brig	6f209y	(0-75)H	GD	£3280
78	2/08	Wolv	7f32y	(0-75)H	STD	£2457
73	5/07	Thsk	1m	(0-65)H	GD	£2590
66	5/07	Wwck	1m22y	(0-60)H	G-F	£2388

Total win prize-money £13178

Going (Turf): Sf: 0-0 GS: 0-3 **Gd: 2-8** GF: 1-8 Fm: 1-5
Distance: 5f/6f: 0-3 **7f-8f: 4-28** 9f-13f: 1-10 14f+: 0-0
Track : **LH: 5-22** RH: 0-11 **Tight: 2-14** Gall: 0-2
Aids: Bl: 0-3 Vi: 0-0 Tstrap: 0-2 Ckp: 0-2
Best Rating: **78** 2/08 Wolv 7f32y stand

Moderate; stays 1m; acts on fast ground; goes on Polytrack; has worn blinkers.

Golden Ring

76 **42**

3-y-o b c Hawk Wing (USA)-Farhana (Fayruz)

P J O'Gorman Ms Aida Fustoq

Placings:000 **(3168)**

2009: 10^{0}GF, 10^{0}GF, 8^{0}GF,

	Starts	1st	2nd	3rd	Win & Pl
Career Total (Turf)	3	0	0	0	

Going (Turf): **Sf: 0-0 GS: 0-0 Gd: 0-0 GF: 0-3 Fm: 0-0**
Distance: 5f/6f: 0-0 7f-8f: 0-1 9f-13f: 0-2 14f+: 0-0
Track : LH: 0-0 RH: 0-0 Tight: 0-0 Gall: 0-0
Aids: Bl: 0-0 Vi: 0-0 Tstrap: 0-0 Ckp: 0-0
Best Rating: **42** 4/09 NmkR 1m2f gd-fm

Golden Rock (IRE)

102 **77**

3-y-o ch g Rock Of Gibraltar (IRE)-Sister Golden Hair (IRE) (Glint Of Gold)

R Charlton H R H Sultan Ahmad Shah

Placings:562000 **(7248)**

2009: 10^{5}GF, 10^{6}GF, 10^{2}GF, 12^{0}S, 10^{0}G, 10^{0}HY,

	Starts	1st	2nd	3rd	Win & Pl
Career Total (Turf)	6	0	1	0	806

Going (Turf): **Sf: 0-2 GS: 0-0 Gd: 0-1 GF: 0-3 Fm: 0-0**
Distance: 5f/6f: 0-0 7f-8f: 0-0 9f-13f: 0-6 14f+: 0-0
Track : LH: 0 2 RH: 0-2 Tight: 0-2 Gall: 0-1
Aids: Bl: 0-0 Vi: 0-1 Tstrap: 0-0 Ckp: 0-0
Best Rating: **77** 6/09 Wind 1m2f7y gd-fm

Golden Rosie (IRE)

95 **76**

3-y-o ch f Exceed And Excel (AUS)-Kelsey Rose (Most Welcome)

B W Hills John C Grant

Placings:51650-5360 **(6739)**

2009: 7^{5}GF, 7^{3}GF, 5^{6}GF, 6^{0}GS,

	Starts	1st	2nd	3rd	Win & Pl
Career Total (Turf)	9	1	0	1	4936

72	6/08	Donc	6f	G-S	£4533

Total win prize-money £4533

Going (Turf): Sf: 0-1 **GS: 1-2** Gd: 0-2 GF: 0-4 Fm: 0-0
Distance: **5f/6f: 1-6** 7f-8f: 0-3 9f-13f: 0-0 14f+: 0-0
Track : LH: 0-0 RH: 0-0 Tight: 0-0 Gall: 0-1
Aids: Bl: 0-0 Vi: 0-0 Tstrap: 0-0 Ckp: 0-0
Best Rating: **76** 7/08 Leic 5f218y good

Fair; effective at 6f-7f; acts on most ground; has worn a hood.

Golden Run

(82) (24)

6-y-o b m Commanche Run-Goldengirlmichelle (IRE) (Project Manager)

R Hollinshead The Cartmel Syndicate

Placings:0 **(1409)**

2009: 9^{0}SD,

	Starts	1st	2nd	3rd	Win & Pl
Career Total (Turf)	0	0	0	0	
Career Total (AW)	1	0	0	0	

Going (Turf): **Sf: 0-0 GS: 0-0 Gd: 0-0 GF: 0-0 Fm: 0-0**
Distance: 5f/6f: 0-0 7f-8f: 0-0 9f-13f: 0-1 14f+: 0-0
Track : LH: 0-1 RH: 0-0 Tight: 0-1 Gall: 0-0
Aids: Bl: 0-0 Vi: 0-0 Tstrap: 0-0 Ckp: 0-0
Best Rating: **24** 4/09 Wolv 1m1f103y stand

Golden Shaheen (IRE)

92(99) (86)**78**

2-y-o b g Invincible Spirit (IRE)-Cheeky Weeky (Cadeaux Genereux)

Saeed Bin Suroor Godolphin

Placings:2201 **(6943)**

2009: 7^{2}S, 7^{2}SD, 7^{0}GF, 7^{1}SD,

	Starts	1st	2nd	3rd	Win & Pl
Career Total (Turf)	2	0	1	0	11380
Career Total (AW)	2	1	1	0	4656

86	10/09	Kemp	7f	STD	£3885

Total win prize-money £3886

Going (Turf): **Sf: 0-1 GS: 0-0 Gd: 0-0 GF: 0-1 Fm: 0-0**
Distance: 5f/6f: 0-0 **7f-8f: 1-4** 9f-13f: 0-0 14f+: 0-0
Track : LH: 0-1 **RH: 1-2** Tight: 0-0 Gall: 0-0
Aids: Bl: 0-0 **Vi: 1-2** Tstrap: 0-0 Ckp: 0-0
Best Rating: **86** 10/09 Kemp 7f stand

Useful; effective over 7f; acts on soft ground and on Polytrack.

Golden Square

(99) (51)**49**

7-y-o ch g Tomba-Cherish Me (Polar Falcon (USA))
A W Carroll Mr & Mrs J B Bacciochi

Placings:060664/30003020003202032/1401400025/2200 000000000/1060000-0033000 **(7517)**
2009: 8^{0}SD, 8^{0}SD, 10^{3}SD, 8^{3}SD, 10^{0}SD, 8^{0}SD, 7^{0}SD,

	Starts	1st	2nd	3rd	Win & Pl
Career Total (Turf)	23	1	2	2	6264
Career Total (AW)	38	2	5	4	8605

53 1/08 Kemp 1m (0-55)H STD £2047
57 5/06 Wwck 1m22y (0-60)H GD £2388
65 1/06 Sthl 7f (0-55)H STD £2047
Total win prize-money £6485

Going (Turf): Sf: 0-2 GS: 0-5 **Gd: 1-5** GF: 0-7 Fm: 0-4
Distance: 5f/6f: 0-2 **7f-8f: 2-34** 9f-13f: 1-25 14f+: 0-0
Track : **LH: 2-41** RH: 1-14 Tight: 0-22 Gall: 0-1
Aids: Bl: 0-6 Vi: 0-3 Tstrap: 0-4 Ckp: 0-4
Best Rating: **65** 1/07 Kemp 7f stand

Moderate; effective at around 1m; acts on good ground; also goes on Polytrack.

Golden Stream (IRE)

108 **106**

3-y-o b f Sadler's Wells (USA)-Phantom Gold (Machiavellian (USA))
Sir Michael Stoute The Queen

Placings:15-6210310 **(6661)**
2009: 10^{6}GF, 8^{2}GF, 7^{1}GF, 7^{0}G, 8^{3}GF, 7^{1}GF, 6^{0}GS,

	Starts	1st	2nd	3rd	Win & Pl
Career Total (Turf)	9	3	1	1	71396

106 9/09 Asct 7f G-F £22708
102 6/09 Wwck 7f26y G-F £22708
89 8/08 NmkJ 7f GD £4857
Total win prize-money £50273

Going (Turf): Sf: 0-0 GS: 0-1 Gd: 1-3 **GF: 2-5** Fm: 0-0
Distance: 5f/6f: 0-1 **7f-8f: 3-6** 9f-13f: 0-2 14f+: 0-0
Track : **LH: 1-2** RH: 0-2 Tight: 0-1 Gall: 0-1
Aids: Bl: 0-0 Vi: 0-0 Tstrap: 0-0 Ckp: 0-0
Best Rating: **106** 9/09 Asct 7f gd-fm

Very useful; Listed winner; effective over 7f-1m; acts on good/fast ground.

Golden Sword

114 **120**

3-y-o b c High Chaparral (IRE)-Sitara (Salse (USA))
A P O'Brien M Tabor, D Smith & Mrs John Magnier

Placings:3541-41525 **(4298)**
2009: 10^{4}G, 12^{1}GF, 12^{5}G, 12^{2}GY, 12^{5}G,

	Starts	1st	2nd	3rd	Win & Pl
Career Total (Turf)	9	2	1	1	396151

114 5/09 Ches 1m4f66y G-F £39739
85 10/08 Fair 7f SH £6097
Total win prize-money £45836

Going (Turf): Sf: 0-3 GS: 0-0 Gd: 0-3 **GF: 1-1** Fm: 0-0
Distance: 5f/6f: 0-0 7f-8f: 1-4 9f-13f: 1-5 14f+: 0-0
Track : LH: 1-3 RH: 1-5 **Tight: 1-2** Gall: 0-2
Aids: Bl: 0-0 Vi: 0-0 Tstrap: 0-0 Ckp: 0-0
Best Rating: **120** 6/09 Curr 1m4f gd-yld

Group-class; winner of the Chester Vase in 2009; runner-up in the Irish Derby; stays 1m4f and acts on most ground; suited by forcing tactics.

Golden Tiger

(85) (69)

2-y-o br c Kyllachy-Roxy (Rock City)
T P Tate T P Tate

Placings:2 **(7836)**
2009: 7^{2}SS,

	Starts	1st	2nd	3rd	Win & Pl
Career Total (Turf)	0	0	0	0	
Career Total (AW)	1	0	1	0	1108

Going (Turf): **Sf: 0-0 GS: 0-0 Gd: 0-0 GF: 0-0 Fm: 0-0**
Distance: 5f/6f: 0-0 7f-8f: 0-1 9f-13f: 0-0 14f+: 0-0
Track : LH: 0-1 RH: 0-0 Tight: 0-0 Gall: 0-0
Aids: Bl: 0-0 Vi: 0-0 Tstrap: 0-0 Ckp: 0-0
Best Rating: **69** 12/09 Sthl 7f std-slw

Modest half-brother to Night Kiss, a dual winner over 7f; acts on Fibresand.

Golden Waters

86 **65**

2-y-o b f Dubai Destination (USA)-Faraway Waters (Pharly (FR))
Eve Johnson Houghton R Crutchley

Placings:5 **(6393)**
2009: 8^{5}GF,

	Starts	1st	2nd	3rd	Win & Pl
Career Total (Turf)	1	0	0	0	0

Going (Turf): **Sf: 0-0 GS: 0-0 Gd: 0-0 GF: 0-1 Fm: 0-0**
Distance: 5f/6f: 0-0 7f-8f: 0-1 9f-13f: 0-0 14f+: 0-0
Track : LH: 0-0 RH: 0-0 Tight: 0-0 Gall: 0-0
Aids: Bl: 0-0 Vi: 0-0 Tstrap: 0-0 Ckp: 0-0
Best Rating: **65** 9/09 Sals 1m gd-fm

Goldikova (IRE)

125 **131**

4-y-o b f Anabaa (USA)-Born Gold (USA) (Blushing Groom (FR))
F Head Wertheimer & Frere

Placings:11/2231111-011131 **(7308a)**
2009: 9^{0}S, 8^{1}G, 8^{1}S, 8^{1}G, 7^{3}GS, 8^{1}F,

	Starts	1st	2nd	3rd	Win & Pl
Career Total (Turf)	15	10	2	2	2401375

123 11/09 SnAt 1m FRM £750000
131 8/09 Deau 1m GD £332854
124 8/09 Deau 1m SFT £138689
116 7/09 NmkJ 1m GD £113540
125 10/08 SnAt 1m FRM £577990
123 9/08 Lonc 1m G-S £168059
123 8/08 Deau 1m G-S £105037
116 7/08 MsnL 1m G-S £29412
105 10/07 Chan 1m G-S £11486
87 9/07 Chan 1m GD £7095
Total win prize-money £2234162

Going (Turf): Sf: 1-3 **GS: 4-5** Gd: 3-5 GF: 0-0 Fm: 2-2
Distance: 5f/6f: 0-0 **7f-8f: 10-13** 9f-13f: 0-2 14f+: 0-0
Track : LH: 2-2 **RH: 5-8** Tight: 0-0 Gall: 0-0
Aids: Bl: 0-0 Vi: 0-0 Tstrap: 0-0 Ckp: 0-0
Best Rating: **131** 8/09 Deau 1m good

Top-class; multiple Group 1 winner in 2008 and again in 2009; dual winner of the Breeders' Cup Mile; best at 1m; acts on any ground.

Goldtrek (USA)

71(91) (64)**25**

2-y-o b f Medallist (USA)-Traipse (USA) (Digression (USA))
R Charlton AXOM (XVII)

Placings:066 **(7622)**
2009: 8^{0}G, 8^{6}SD, 8^{6}SD,

	Starts	1st	2nd	3rd	Win & Pl
Career Total (Turf)	1	0	0	0	
Career Total (AW)	2	0	0	0	0

Going (Turf): **Sf: 0-0 GS: 0-0 Gd: 0-1 GF: 0-0 Fm: 0-0**
Distance: 5f/6f: 0-0 7f-8f: 0-3 9f-13f: 0-0 14f+: 0-0
Track : LH: 0-2 RH: 0-0 Tight: 0-2 Gall: 0-0
Aids: Bl: 0-0 Vi: 0-0 Tstrap: 0-0 Ckp: 0-0
Best Rating: **64** 12/09 Ling 1m stand

Modest; stays 1m; acts on Polytrack.

Goliaths Boy (IRE)

112 **91**

3-y-o ch g Medecis-Green Belt (FR) (Tirol)
R A Fahey Dr Marwan Koukash

Placings:2314-0002522 **(6733)**
2009: 7^{0}GF, 10^{0}G, 10^{0}G, 8^{2}G, 10^{5}GF, 10^{2}GF, 9^{2}S,

	Starts	1st	2nd	3rd	Win & Pl
Career Total (Turf)	11	1	4	1	19970

88 10/08 Catt 7f G-S £2047
Total win prize-money £2047

Going (Turf): Sf: 0-2 **GS: 1-2** Gd: 0-3 GF: 0-4 Fm: 0-0
Distance: 5f/6f: 0-1 **7f-8f: 1-4** 9f-13f: 0-6 14f+: 0-0
Track : **LH: 1-9** RH: 0-2 **Tight: 1-7** Gall: 0-1
Aids: Bl: 0-0 Vi: 0-0 Tstrap: 0-0 Ckp: 0-0
Best Rating: **91** 11/08 StCl 1m heavy

Useful; effective at around 1m-1m2f; acts on most ground.

Gomrath (IRE)

89 **68**

2-y-o b c Lomitas-Diner De Lune (IRE) (Be My Guest (USA))
M R Channon Jon and Julia Aisbitt

Placings:0 **(4524)**
2009: 7^{0}S,

	Starts	1st	2nd	3rd	Win & Pl
Career Total (Turf)	1	0	0	0	

Going (Turf): **Sf: 0-1 GS: 0-0 Gd: 0-0 GF: 0-0 Fm: 0-0**
Distance: 5f/6f: 0-0 7f-8f: 0-1 9f-13f: 0-0 14f+: 0-0
Track : LH: 0-0 RH: 0-1 Tight: 0-0 Gall: 0-0
Aids: Bl: 0-0 Vi: 0-0 Tstrap: 0-0 Ckp: 0-0
Best Rating: **68** 8/09 Gdwd 7f soft

Gone Hunting

47(101) (85)**81**

3-y-o b g Hunting Lion (IRE)-Arasong (Aragon)
J Pearce (Peter Grayson 14/8) M B Clarke

Placings:6125352122313-3160000 **(7875)**
2009: 7^{3}SD, 5^{1}SD, 6^{6}SD, 7^{0}SD, 6^{0}SD, 6^{0}G, 6^{0}SD,

	Starts	1st	2nd	3rd	Win & Pl
Career Total (Turf)	4	0	1	1	2264
Career Total (AW)	16	4	3	3	16548

85 1/09 Wolv 5f216y STD £2047

84 12/08 GrLe 6f STD £3561
80 9/08 Wolv 5f216y STD £3070
74 4/08 Ling 5f STD £2266
Total win prize-money £10947

Going (Turf): **Sf: 0-0 GS: 0-1 Gd: 0-1 GF: 0-1 Fm: 0-1**
Distance: **5f/6f: 4-18** 7f-8f: 0-2 9f-13f: 0-0 14f+: 0-0
Track : **LH: 4-14** RH: 0-3 **Tight: 3-8** Gall: 1-5
Aids: Bl: 0-1 Vi: 0-0 Tstrap: 0-0 Ckp: 0-0
Best Rating: **85** 1/09 Wolv 5f216y stand

Useful; effective over 5f-6f; acts on easy ground and on Polytrack; has worn a tongue-tie.

Gone'N'Dunnett (IRE)

94(101) (58)**50**
10-y-o b g Petardia-Skerries Bell (Taufan (USA))
Mrs C A Dunnett Christine Dunnett Racing

Placings:056500/0650323100450036124/5500030005022004103/00000066103105V2000031/030002011300100060600002254/030162030060330035046300500/00020001500000545155/6650515605U403000600-050000620 **(4668)**
2009: 6^{0}SD, 6^{5}SD, 6^{0}SD, 7^{0}GF, 5^{0}F, 5^{0}F, 5^{6}S, 5^{2}GS, 6^{0}G,

	Starts	1st	2nd	3rd	Win & Pl
Career Total (Turf)	89	5	6	6	30482
Career Total (AW)	81	8	5	10	31809

58 5/08 GrLe 6f (0-55)H STD £2266
58 12/07 Sthl 5f (0-52)H SS £2047
58 8/07 Yarm 6f3y (0-75)H G-F £2914
74 2/06 Sthl 5f (0-70)H STD £2914
78 5/05 Yarm 6f3y (0-85)H G-S £6845
70 4/05 Wolv 5f216y (0-70)H STD £4106
69 4/05 Yarm 5f43y (0-75)H G-S £3367
66 1/05 Sthl 6f (0-70)H STD £3388
63 7/04 Brig 5f59y E(0-75)H GD £3721
63 6/04 Yarm 6f3y F(0-55)H FRM £3451
74 11/03 Wolv 5f E(0-75)H STD £2051
79 11/02 Sthl 6f F(0-65)H STD £2989
65 7/02 Ling 5f F STD £2765
Total win prize-money £42830

Going (Turf): Sf: 0-8 **GS: 2-6** Gd: 1-24GF: 1-35 Fm: 1-16
Distance: **5f/6f: 10-142**7f-8f: 3-26 9f-13f: 0-214f+: 0-0
Track : **LH: 7-86** RH: 0-6 **Tight: 3-45** Gall: 1-8
Aids: Bl: 0-4 **Vi: 10-122** Tstrap: 3-34 Ckp: 3-34
Best Rating: **79** 11/02 Sthl 6f stand

Moderate sprint handicapper; acts on most surfaces; has worn a visor and cheekpieces; goes well at Yarmouth.

Good Again

110(101) (86)**99**
3-y-o ch f Dubai Destination (USA)-Good Girl (IRE) (College Chapel)
G A Butler Future In Mind Partnership

Placings:213-1414601 **(6535)**
2009: 8^{1}SD, 8^{4}GF, 8^{1}GF, 8^{4}HY, 8^{6}GF, 7^{0}G, 8^{1}GF,

	Starts	1st	2nd	3rd	Win & Pl
Career Total (Turf)	8	3	0	1	47138
Career Total (AW)	2	1	1	0	6203

99 10/09 Pont 1m4y (0-95)H G-F £7477
99 5/09 Asct 1m H G-F £25904
86 4/09 Ling 1m (0-85)H STD £5046
78 7/08 Asct 6f G-F £7123
Total win prize-money £45551

Going (Turf): Sf: 0-1 GS: 0-0 Gd: 0-2 **GF: 3-5** Fm: 0-0
Distance: 5f/6f: 1-1 **7f-8f: 2-7** 9f-13f: 1-2 14f+: 0-0
Track : **LH: 2-3** RH: 0-1 **Tight: 1-1** Gall: 0-0
Aids: Bl: 0-0 Vi: 0-0 Tstrap: 0-0 Ckp: 0-0
Best Rating: **99** 10/09 Pont 1m4y gd-fm

Very useful; stays 1m; acts on fast and heavy ground and on Polytrack.

Good Buy Dubai (USA)

99(103) (63)**62**
3-y-o gr g Essence Of Dubai (USA)-Sofisticada (USA) (Northern Jove (CAN))
J R Best John Keaty

Placings:500-424161033365404 **(6918)**
2009: 10^{4}SD, 10^{2}SD, 12^{4}SD, 12^{1}SD, 12^{6}GF, 11^{1}GS, 14^{0}F, 12^{3}GF, 10^{3}SD, 10^{3}SD, 12^{6}SD, 12^{5}SS, 12^{4}GS, 11^{0}GS, 12^{4}SD,

	Starts	1st	2nd	3rd	Win & Pl
Career Total (Turf)	8	1	0	1	3182
Career Total (AW)	10	1	1	2	3257

62 4/09 Wind 1m3f135y (0-70)H G-S £2729
63 4/09 Kemp 1m4f (0-60)H STD £2047
Total win prize-money £4777

Going (Turf): Sf: 0-0 **GS: 1-3** Gd: 0-0 GF: 0-4 Fm: 0-1
Distance: 5f/6f: 0-2 7f-8f: 0-1 **9f-13f: 2-14** 14f+: 0-1
Track : LH: 0-8 **RH: 1-6 Tight: 1-12** Gall: 0-1
Aids: Bl: 0-0 Vi: 0-1 Tstrap: 0-0 Ckp: 0-0
Best Rating: **63** 5/09 Ling 1m2f stand

Moderate; stays 1m2f and acts on Polytrack; has worn a tongue tie.

Good Cause (IRE)

73(99) (48)**51**
8-y-o b g Simply Great (FR)-Smashing Pet (Mummy's Pet)
Mrs S Lamyman P Lamyman

Placings:560/650606-0 **(4658)**
2009: 10^{0}G,

	Starts	1st	2nd	3rd	Win & Pl
Career Total (Turf)	6	0	0	0	0
Career Total (AW)	4	0	0	0	0

Going (Turf): **Sf: 0-0 GS: 0-1 Gd: 0-3 GF: 0-2 Fm: 0-0**
Distance: 5f/6f: 0-1 7f-8f: 0-1 9f-13f: 0-7 14f+: 0-1
Track : LH: 0-8 RH: 0-2 Tight: 0-1 Gall: 0-1
Aids: Bl: 0-0 Vi: 0-0 Tstrap: 0-0 Ckp: 0-0
Best Rating: **62** 4/07 Leic 1m1f218y gd-fm

Good Effect (USA)

99(98) (65)**73**
5-y-o ch g Woodman (USA)-River Dreams (USA) (Riverman (USA))
Tim Vaughan (C P Morlock 26/6) D Wallis

Placings:034/03114/03040020402340-0300040 **(6025)**
2009: 12^{0}SD, 11^{3}G, 13^{0}SD, 11^{0}GF, 11^{0}F, 12^{4}GF, 13^{0}SD,

	Starts	1st	2nd	3rd	Win & Pl
Career Total (Turf)	16	1	1	2	7609
Career Total (AW)	13	1	1	3	3638

75 8/07 Sand 1m2f7y (0-80)H GD £5181
70 8/07 Kemp 1m (0-65)H STD £2047
Total win prize-money £7230

Going (Turf): Sf: 0-1 GS: 0-4 **Gd: 1-5** GF: 0-5 Fm: 0-1
Distance: 5f/6f: 0-0 7f-8f: 1-4 9f-13f: 1-23 14f+: 0-2
Track : LH: 0-11 **RH: 2-16** Tight: 0-14 Gall: 0-1
Aids: Bl: 0-0 Vi: 0-1 Tstrap: 0-1 Ckp: 0-1
Best Rating: **78** 8/07 Gdwd 1m1f good

Moderate; stays 1m4f; acts on most ground; goes on Polytrack; has worn a tongue tie.

Good For Her

99(85) (51)**69**
3-y-o b f Rock Of Gibraltar (IRE)-Tyranny (Machiavellian (USA))
J L Dunlop Normandie Stud Ltd

Placings:62-634 **(4642)**
2009: 8^{6}GF, 7^{3}G, 7^{4}GF,

	Starts	1st	2nd	3rd	Win & Pl
Career Total (Turf)	4	0	1	1	1734
Career Total (AW)	1	0	0	0	0

Going (Turf): **Sf: 0-0 GS: 0-0 Gd: 0-2 GF: 0-2 Fm: 0-0**
Distance: 5f/6f: 0-1 7f-8f: 0-4 9f-13f: 0-0 14f+: 0-0
Track : LH: 0-2 RH: 0-1 Tight: 0-0 Gall: 0-0
Aids: Bl: 0-0 Vi: 0-0 Tstrap: 0-0 Ckp: 0-0
Best Rating: **69** 8/09 Brig 7f214y gd-fm

Modest; effective at around a mile.

Good Gorsoon (USA)

104(101) (91)**94**
4-y-o b c Stravinsky (USA)-Alwaysinbloom (USA) (Unbridled (USA))
B W Hills Triermore Stud & Partner

Placings:531043/0314060-0600304000100 **(6972)**
2009: 6^{0}GF, 5^{6}GF, 6^{0}GS, 5^{0}GF, 5^{3}SD, 5^{0}G, 6^{4}GS, 5^{0}GS, 5^{0}GF, 6^{0}GF, 6^{1}GF, 6^{0}SS, 5^{0}SD,

	Starts	1st	2nd	3rd	Win & Pl
Career Total (Turf)	22	3	0	2	20930
Career Total (AW)	4	0	0	2	1830

90 9/09 NmkR 6f (0-85)H G-F £5180
92 5/08 Wind 5f10y (0-85)H G-F £4857
83 8/07 Bath 5f161y G-F £2849
Total win prize-money £12888

Going (Turf): Sf: 0-0 GS: 0-6 Gd: 0-3 **GF: 3-13** Fm: 0-0
Distance: **5f/6f: 3-22** 7f-8f: 0-4 9f-13f: 0-0 14f+: 0-0
Track : **LH: 1-7** RH: 0-1 Tight: 0-5 **Gall: 2-4**
Aids: Bl: 0-0 Vi: 0-0 Tstrap: 0-0 Ckp: 0-0
Best Rating: **94** 6/08 York 6f good

Useful; effective at 5f-6f; acts on a sound surface and on Polytrack.

Good Humoured

(101) (63)
3-y-o b g Rock Of Gibraltar (IRE)-Humouresque (Pivotal)
Sir Mark Prescott Charles C Walker - Osborne House II

Placings:2-40503 **(7022)**
2009: 7^{4}SD, 8^{0}SD, 6^{5}SD, 6^{0}SD, 10^{3}SD,

	Starts	1st	2nd	3rd	Win & Pl
Career Total (Turf)	0	0	0	0	
Career Total (AW)	6	0	1	1	1651

Going (Turf): **Sf: 0-0 GS: 0-0 Gd: 0-0 GF: 0-0 Fm: 0-0**
Distance: 5f/6f: 0-3 7f-8f: 0-2 9f-13f: 0-1 14f+: 0-0
Track : LH: 0-4 RH: 0-2 Tight: 0-2 Gall: 0-0
Aids: Bl: 0-0 Vi: 0-0 Tstrap: 0-0 Ckp: 0-0
Best Rating: **63** 10/09 Kemp 1m2f stand

Moderate; stays 1m2f; acts on Polytrack and on Fibresand.

Good Karma (IRE)

(89) (45)

5-y-o b g Shernazar-Kayrava (Irish River (FR))

P J Rothwell J J Leckey

Placings:0 **(7004)**

2009: 9^{0}SD,

	Starts	1st	2nd	3rd	Win & Pl
Career Total (Turf)	0	0	0	0	
Career Total (AW)	1	0	0	0	

Going (Turf): Sf: 0-0 GS: 0-0 Gd: 0-0 GF: 0-0 Fm: 0-0
Distance: 5f/6f: 0-0 7f-8f: 0-0 9f-13f: 0-1 14f+: 0-0
Track : LH: 0-1 RH: 0-0 Tight: 0-1 Gall: 0-0
Aids: Bl: 0-0 Vi: 0-0 Tstrap: 0-0 Ckp: 0-0
Best Rating: 45 10/09 Wolv 1m1f103y stand

Good Queen Best

84 44

3-y-o b f Best Of The Bests (IRE)-Spring Sunrise (Robellino (USA))

B De Haan Mrs D Vaughan

Placings:060-00 **(5384)**

2009: 7^{0}GS, 8^{0}GS,

	Starts	1st	2nd	3rd	Win & Pl
Career Total (Turf)	5	0	0	0	0

Going (Turf): Sf: 0-1 GS: 0-2 Gd: 0-0 GF: 0-2 Fm: 0-0
Distance: 5f/6f: 0-2 7f-8f: 0-1 9f-13f: 0-2 14f+: 0-0
Track : LH: 0-2 RH: 0-0 Tight: 0-1 Gall: 0-0
Aids: Bl: 0-0 Vi: 0-0 Tstrap: 0-0 Ckp: 0-0
Best Rating: 44 7/08 Leic 5f218y gd-fm

Goodbye Cash (IRE)

101(102) (63)66

5-y-o b m Danetime (IRE)-Jellybeen (IRE) (Petardia)

P D Evans Mrs I M Folkes

Placings:2036360215/1014434004/204053536000-10001331505446202550 **(7845)**

2009: 6^{1}GF, 6^{0}GF, 6^{0}GF, 6^{0}GF, 6^{1}GF, 6^{3}F, 6^{3}F, 7^{1}GF, 8^{5}S, 7^{0}G, 7^{5}F, 6^{4}GF, 7^{4}GF, 7^{6}SF, 7^{2}SD, 7^{0}SD, 7^{2}SD, 7^{5}SD, 7^{5}SD, 7^{0}SD,

	Starts	1st	2nd	3rd	Win & Pl
Career Total (Turf)	31	5	2	5	24302
Career Total (AW)	21	1	3	2	7378

62	8/09	Folk	7f	(0-60)H	G-F	£2388
58	7/09	Brig	6f209y		G-F	£1942
	5/09	Lanc	6f	H	G-F	£1680
79	5/07	NmkR	6f	(0-85)H	SFT	£5829
76	5/07	Kemp	5f	(0-85)H	STD	£4728
74	10/06	Ayr	6f	(0-75)	HVY	£3886

Total win prize-money £20454

Going (Turf): Sf: 2-8 GS: 0-2 Gd: 0-6 **GF: 3-11** Fm: 0-3
Distance: 5f/6f: 4-25 7f-8f: 2-27 9f-13f: 0-0 14f+: 0-0
Track : LH: 1-21 RH: 1-9 Tight: 0-10 Gall: 0-2
Aids: Bl: 0-0 Vi: 0-0 Tstrap: 0-1 Ckp: 0-1
Best Rating: 79 5/07 NmkR 6f soft

Moderate; effective over 5f-7f; acts on fast and easy turf; goes on both AW surfaces.

Goodbye Earl (IRE)

98 73

2-y-o b f Bertolini (USA)-Begine (IRE) (Germany (USA))

A Berry Mrs Linda White

Placings:64020634246500 **(5945)**

2009: 5^{6}GF, 5^{4}GF, 5^{0}GS, 5^{2}G, 5^{0}G, 5^{6}G, 5^{3}GS, 5^{4}GF, 5^{2}G, 5^{4}GS, 5^{6}GF, 5^{5}GS, 5^{0}GS, 5^{0}G,

	Starts	1st	2nd	3rd	Win & Pl
Career Total (Turf)	14	0	2	1	5517

Going (Turf): Sf: 0-0 GS: 0-5 Gd: 0-5 GF: 0-4 Fm: 0-0
Distance: 5f/6f: 0-14 7f-8f: 0-0 9f-13f: 0-0 14f+: 0-0
Track : LH: 0-2 RH: 0-0 Tight: 0-2 Gall: 0-0
Aids: Bl: 0-0 Vi: 0-0 Tstrap: 0-0 Ckp: 0-0
Best Rating: 73 7/09 Ches 5f16y gd-fm

Modest half-sister to Tancredi; promise in maidens; acts on good and easy ground.

Goodbye Mr Bond

100 (62)93

9-y-o b g Elmaamul (USA)-Fifth Emerald (Formidable (USA))

E J Alston Peter J Davies

Placings:000/100534045/634341111326106/54362322060 3623/0120154050/051200545550/04120606-00000350 **(4663)**

2009: 8^{0}GF, 8^{0}GF, 9^{0}GS, 8^{0}GS, 7^{0}G, 8^{3}G, 9^{5}S, 8^{0}G,

	Starts	1st	2nd	3rd	Win & Pl
Career Total (Turf)	73	10	8	7	122895
Career Total (AW)	7	0	0	2	709

93	6/08	York	1m208y	(0-80)H	G-F	£6799
91	5/07	Ayr	1m1f20y	(0-85)H	GD	£5019
97	6/06	York	1m208y	(0-105)H	G-F	£16840
95	5/06	Ripn	1m1f170y	(0-85)H	HVY	£7570
83	9/04	Hayd	1m30y	(0-85)H	GD	£7361
76	6/04	Carl	7f200y	D(0-80)H	GD	£17485
79	6/04	Rdcr	1m	E(0-70)H	GD	£3877
68	6/04	Haml	1m65y	D(0-85)H	G-F	£6396
62	6/04	Newc	1m	E(0-75)H	GD	£4192
65	5/03	Haml	1m1f36y	E(0-70)H	G-S	£4212

Total win prize-money £79756

Going (Turf): Sf: 1-11GS: 1-11**Gd: 5-22** GF: 3-28 Fm: 0-1
Distance: 5f/6f: 0-1 7f-8f: 3-27 **9f-13f: 7-52** 14f+: 0-0
Track : LH: 5-44 RH: 4-23 Tight: 3-21 Gall: 3-15
Aids: Bl: 0-0 Vi: 0-1 Tstrap: 0-0 Ckp: 0-0
Best Rating: 97 6/06 York 1m208y gd-fm

Fair; effective from 1m-1m2f; acts on most ground and on Fibresand; usually held up; needs a strong pace.

Goodison Goal (IRE)

79(92) (53)52

2-y-o b f Trade Fair-Chantilly (FR) (Sanglamore (USA))

Patrick Morris Four Boys Racing Club 1

Placings:006603 **(7884)**

2009: 7^{0}G, 6^{0}GF, 5^{6}SD, 6^{6}SD, 7^{0}SF, 7^{3}SD,

	Starts	1st	2nd	3rd	Win & Pl
Career Total (Turf)	2	0	0	0	
Career Total (AW)	4	0	0	1	242

Going (Turf): Sf: 0-0 GS: 0-0 Gd: 0-1 GF: 0-1 Fm: 0-0
Distance: 5f/6f: 0-3 7f-8f: 0-3 9f-13f: 0-0 14f+: 0-0
Track : LH: 0-4 RH: 0-0 Tight: 0-3 Gall: 0-0
Aids: Bl: 0-0 Vi: 0-0 Tstrap: 0-0 Ckp: 0-0
Best Rating: 53 10/09 Wolv 5f216y stand

Goodison Park

77 58

2-y-o ch f Big Shuffle (USA)-Perfect Dream (Emperor Jones (USA))

A G Foster The Toffees Partnership

Placings:040 **(6762)**

2009: 7^{0}GF, 7^{4}GF, 8^{0}GS,

	Starts	1st	2nd	3rd	Win & Pl
Career Total (Turf)	3	0	0	0	241

Going (Turf): Sf: 0-0 GS: 0-1 Gd: 0-0 GF: 0-2 Fm: 0-0
Distance: 5f/6f: 0-0 7f-8f: 0-3 9f-13f: 0-0 14f+: 0-0
Track : LH: 0-1 RH: 0-0 Tight: 0-0 Gall: 0-1
Aids: Bl: 0-0 Vi: 0-0 Tstrap: 0-0 Ckp: 0-0
Best Rating: 58 10/09 Newc 1m gd-sft

Goodwood Diva

80(85) (46)49

2-y-o ch f Kyllachy-Donna Vita (Vettori (IRE))

J L Dunlop Goodwood Racehorse Owners Group (16)

Placings:000 **(6911)**

2009: 6^{0}G, 7^{0}F, 7^{0}SD,

	Starts	1st	2nd	3rd	Win & Pl
Career Total (Turf)	2	0	0	0	
Career Total (AW)	1	0	0	0	

Going (Turf): Sf: 0-0 GS: 0-0 Gd: 0-1 GF: 0-0 Fm: 0-1
Distance: 5f/6f: 0-1 7f-8f: 0-2 9f-13f: 0-0 14f+: 0-0
Track : LH: 0-1 RH: 0-0 Tight: 0-1 Gall: 0-0
Aids: Bl: 0-0 Vi: 0-0 Tstrap: 0-0 Ckp: 0-0
Best Rating: 49 6/09 Gdwd 6f good

Goodwood Maestro

98(85) (71)84

2-y-o b g Piccolo-Madurai (Chilibang)

J L Dunlop Goodwood Racehorse Owners Group(Fifteen)

Placings:150 **(7013)**

2009: 6^{1}GF, 6^{5}SD, 7^{0}GS,

	Starts	1st	2nd	3rd	Win & Pl
Career Total (Turf)	2	1	0	0	3562
Career Total (AW)	1	0	0	0	0

84	5/09	Gdwd	6f	G-F	£3561

Total win prize-money £3562

Going (Turf): Sf: 0-0 GS: 0-1 Gd: 0-0 **GF: 1-1** Fm: 0-0
Distance: 5f/6f: 1-2 7f-8f: 0-1 9f-13f: 0-0 14f+: 0-0
Track : LH: 0-0 RH: 0-1 Tight: 0-0 Gall: 0-0
Aids: Bl: 0-0 Vi: 0-0 Tstrap: 0-0 Ckp: 0-0
Best Rating: 84 5/09 Gdwd 6f gd-fm

Useful; stays 6f and acts on fast ground.

Goodwood Starlight (IRE)

103(104) (94)97

4-y-o br g Mtoto-Starring (FR) (Ashkalani (IRE))

G L Moore Heart Of The South Racing

Placings:11/04110530-0000666640 (6936)
2009: 10^0^GF, 10^0^GF, 12^0^G, 14^0^G, 9^6^GF, 12^6^G, 9^6^GF, 9^6^GF, 12^4^G, 11^0^G,

	Starts	1st	2nd	3rd	Win & Pl
Career Total (Turf)	19	4	0	1	20154
Career Total (AW)	1	0	0	0	280

97 7/08 Asct 1m2f (0-90)H G-S £9066
93 6/08 Gdwd 1m1f192y (0-80)H GD £6476
79 8/07 Sals 6f212y G-S £2590
Total win prize-money £18133

Going (Turf): Sf: 0-2 GS: 2-2 Gd: 1-9 GF: 1-6 Fm: 0-0
Distance: 5f/6f: 0-0 7f-8f: 2-2 9f-13f: 2-17 14f+: 0-1
Track : LH: 0-4 RH: 3-13 Tight: 1-12 Gall: 1-2
Aids: Bl: 0-0 Vi: 0-0 Tstrap: 0-0 Ckp: 0-0
Best Rating: 97 7/08 Asct 1m2f gd-sft

Useful; stays 1m4f; acts on most ground on turf; goes on Polytrack.

Googoobarabajagal (IRE)

95 54
3-y-o b g Almutawakel-Shamah (Unfuwain (USA))
W S Kittow Dr G S Plastow

Placings:500-540305 (6188)
2009: 12^5^GF, 12^4^GF, 11^0^GF, 14^3^G, 16^0^G, 15^5^GF,

	Starts	1st	2nd	3rd	Win & Pl
Career Total (Turf)	9	0	0	1	457

Going (Turf): Sf: 0-1 GS: 0-2 Gd: 0-2 GF: 0-4 Fm: 0-0
Distance: 5f/6f: 0-0 7f-8f: 0-2 9f-13f: 0-4 14f+: 0-3
Track : LH: 0-3 RH: 0-3 Tight: 0-5 Gall: 0-0
Aids: Bl: 0-1 Vi: 0-0 Tstrap: 0-0 Ckp: 0-0
Best Rating: 54 5/09 Chep 1m4f23y gd-fm

Goolagong (IRE)

91 65
2-y-o b f Giant's Causeway (USA)-Maroochydore (IRE) (Danehill (USA))
R M Beckett R A Pegum

Placings:4 (5220)
2009: 7^4^GF,

	Starts	1st	2nd	3rd	Win & Pl
Career Total (Turf)	1	0	0	0	385

Going (Turf): Sf: 0-0 GS: 0-0 Gd: 0-0 GF: 0-1 Fm: 0-0
Distance: 5f/6f: 0-0 7f-8f: 0-1 9f-13f: 0-0 14f+: 0-0
Track : LH: 0-0 RH: 0-1 Tight: 0-0 Gall: 0-0
Aids: Bl: 0-0 Vi: 0-0 Tstrap: 0-0 Ckp: 0-0
Best Rating: 65 8/09 Sand 7f16y gd-fm

Goose Green (IRE)

101(98) (67)69
5-y-o b g Invincible Spirit (IRE)-Narbayda (IRE) (Kahyasi)
R J Hodges Mrs S G Clapp

Placings:3034641451403/0020040420052130/505605040000-0141150 (4300)
2009: 10^0^F, 9^1^GF, 9^4^G, 10^1^F, 9^1^F, 9^5^GF, 10^0^G,

	Starts	1st	2nd	3rd	Win & Pl
Career Total (Turf)	35	5	2	3	19128
Career Total (AW)	13	1	1	1	3640

69 7/09 Brig 1m1f209y (0-65)H FRM £2590
60 6/09 Bath 1m2f46y (0-55)H FRM £2183
57 5/09 Brig 1m1f209y (0-60)H G-F £2460
67 10/07 Wolv 1m141y (0-65)H STD £2115
67 9/06 Wwck 7f26y (0-75) G-S £3238
60 8/06 Muss 1m G-F £3886
Total win prize-money £16476

Going (Turf): Sf: 0-7 GS: 1-7 Gd: 0-6 GF: 2-9 Fm: 2-6
Distance: 5f/6f: 0-4 7f-8f: 2-25 9f-13f: 4-19 14f+: 0-0
Track : LH: 5-23 RH: 1-7 Tight: 3-14 Gall: 0-0
Aids: Bl: 0-0 Vi: 0-0 Tstrap: 0-0 Ckp: 0-0
Best Rating: 69 7/09 Brig 1m1f209y firm

Modest; effective from 7f-1m2f; acts on fast abd easy ground; goes on Polytrack.

Gooseberry Bush

97 65
2-y-o b f Tobougg (IRE)-Away To Me (Exit To Nowhere (USA))
P J Makin Shaun & Claire Woods Maurice Avent M H Holland

Placings:002006 (6903)
2009: 5^0^GF, 6^0^GF, 5^2^GF, 5^0^G, 6^0^G, 5^6^G,

	Starts	1st	2nd	3rd	Win & Pl
Career Total (Turf)	6	0	1	0	6728

Going (Turf): Sf: 0-0 GS: 0-0 Gd: 0-3 GF: 0-3 Fm: 0-0
Distance: 5f/6f: 0-5 7f-8f: 0-1 9f-13f: 0-0 14f+: 0-0
Track : LH: 0-2 RH: 0-0 Tight: 0-0 Gall: 0-4
Aids: Bl: 0-0 Vi: 0-0 Tstrap: 0-0 Ckp: 0-0
Best Rating: 65 9/09 Asct 6f110y good

Gordon Flash

91 62
2-y-o ch c Alhaarth (IRE)-Goslar (In The Wings)
R Hannon Mrs J K Powell

Placings:0535 (6067)
2009: 6^0^GF, 8^5^G, 8^3^GS, 9^5^GF,

	Starts	1st	2nd	3rd	Win & Pl
Career Total (Turf)	4	0	0	1	770

Going (Turf): Sf: 0-0 GS: 0-1 Gd: 0-1 GF: 0-2 Fm: 0-0
Distance: 5f/6f: 0-1 7f-8f: 0-0 9f-13f: 0-3 14f+: 0-0
Track : LH: 0-1 RH: 0-1 Tight: 0-1 Gall: 0-0
Aids: Bl: 0-0 Vi: 0-0 Tstrap: 0-0 Ckp: 0-0
Best Rating: 62 9/09 Epsm 1m114y gd-sft

Gordonsville

109 (81)91
6-y-o b g Generous (IRE)-Kimba (USA) (Kris S (USA))
J S Goldie Thomson & Fyffe Racing

Placings:4/4254/2221/000252224222-10514353461 (7117)
2009: 14^1^GF, 12^0^GS, 12^5^GF, 13^1^GF, 12^4^GF, 16^3^G, 16^5^GF, 13^3^G, 14^4^GF, 18^6^G, 16^1^GS,

	Starts	1st	2nd	3rd	Win & Pl
Career Total (Turf)	29	3	9	2	71188
Career Total (AW)	3	1	2	0	4204

91 10/09 Muss 2m (0-100)H G-S £12462
89 6/09 Ayr 1m5f13y (0-95)H G-F £11009
87 4/09 Muss 1m6f (0-85)H G-F £12462
81 10/07 Wolv 1m4f50y STD £2559
Total win prize-money £38492

Going (Turf): Sf: 0-3 GS: 1-5 Gd: 0-8 GF: 2-13 Fm: 0-0
Distance: 5f/6f: 0-0 7f-8f: 0-1 9f-13f: 1-13 14f+: 3-18
Track : LH: 2-14 RH: 2-17 Tight: 3-18 Gall: 0-8
Aids: Bl: 0-0 Vi: 0-0 Tstrap: 0-0 Ckp: 0-0
Best Rating: 91 10/09 Muss 2m gd-sft

Useful; effective over 1m5f-2m; acts on fast and easy ground; goes on Polytrack; usually held up.

Gordy Bee (USA)

95 71
3-y-o b c More Than Ready (USA)-Honoria (USA) (Danzig (USA))
Pat Eddery Mrs Rita Bailey, Mick White

Placings:6-2003 (5429)
2009: 9^2^F, 8^0^S, 8^0^G, 7^3^G,

	Starts	1st	2nd	3rd	Win & Pl
Career Total (Turf)	5	0	1	1	1501

Going (Turf): Sf: 0-1 GS: 0-1 Gd: 0-2 GF: 0-0 Fm: 0-1
Distance: 5f/6f: 0-0 7f-8f: 0-4 9f-13f: 0-1 14f+: 0-0
Track : LH: 0-2 RH: 0-1 Tight: 0-1 Gall: 0-0
Aids: Bl: 0-0 Vi: 0-0 Tstrap: 0-0 Ckp: 0-0
Best Rating: 71 8/09 Gdwd 7f good

Fair; stays 1m2f but effective at 1m; acts on fast ground.

Gore Hill (IRE)

90(75) (18)51
3-y-o ch g Exceed And Excel (AUS)-Eschasse (USA) (Zilzal (USA))
K R Burke Keep Racing

Placings:00-300 (2970)
2009: 5^3^GF, 5^0^GF, 5^0^GF,

	Starts	1st	2nd	3rd	Win & Pl
Career Total (Turf)	4	0	0	1	337
Career Total (AW)	1	0	0	0	

Going (Turf): Sf: 0-0 GS: 0-0 Gd: 0-1 GF: 0-3 Fm: 0-0
Distance: 5f/6f: 0-5 7f-8f: 0-0 9f-13f: 0-0 14f+: 0-0
Track : LH: 0-2 RH: 0-1 Tight: 0-2 Gall: 0-0
Aids: Bl: 0-0 Vi: 0-0 Tstrap: 0-0 Ckp: 0-0
Best Rating: 51 4/09 Catt 5f212y gd-fm

Moderate; suited by 6f and fast ground.

Gosforth Park

97 61
3-y-o ch c Generous (IRE)-Love And Kisses (Salse (USA))
M Brittain Mel Brittain

Placings:462663545 (6766)
2009: 10^4^GF, 12^6^GF, 12^2^GF, 12^6^S, 14^6^GF, 14^3^GF, 12^5^G, 14^4^HY, 12^5^GS,

	Starts	1st	2nd	3rd	Win & Pl
Career Total (Turf)	9	0	1	1	2263

Going (Turf): Sf: 0-2 GS: 0-1 Gd: 0-1 GF: 0-5 Fm: 0-0
Distance: 5f/6f: 0-0 7f-8f: 0-0 9f-13f: 0-6 14f+: 0-3
Track : LH: 0-8 RH: 0-1 Tight: 0-2 Gall: 0-4
Aids: Bl: 0-0 Vi: 0-0 Tstrap: 0-0 Ckp: 0-0
Best Rating: 61 5/09 Rdcr 1m6f19y gd-fm

Modest; stays 1m6f and should stay 2m; acts on fast ground.

Gospel Spirit

(73) (22)
4-y-o b g Cool Jazz-Churchtown Spirit (Town And Country)

J R Jenkins Robin Stevens & Stephen Bullock

Placings:U0 **(7826)**
2009: 10^{U}GF, 8^{0}SD,

	Starts	1st	2nd	3rd	Win & Pl
Career Total (Turf)	1	0	0	0	
Career Total (AW)	1	0	0	0	

Going (Turf): Sf: 0-0 GS: 0-0 Gd: 0-0 GF: 0-1 Fm: 0-0
Distance: 5f/6f: 0-0 7f-8f: 0-1 9f-13f: 0-1 14f+: 0-0
Track : LH: 0-0 RH: 0-2 Tight: 0-1 Gall: 0-0
Aids: Bl: 0-0 Vi: 0-0 Tstrap: 0-0 Ckp: 0-0
Best Rating: 22 12/09 Kemp 1m stand

Goswick

92 **49**
3-y-o ch f Bertolini (USA)-Holy Island (Deploy)
Micky Hammond G Shiel

Placings:50006006 **(5730)**
2009: 9^{5}GF, 9^{0}GS, 10^{0}GF, 12^{0}F, 12^{6}G, 12^{0}S, 9^{0}G, 8^{6}GS,

	Starts	1st	2nd	3rd	Win & Pl
Career Total (Turf)	8	0	0	0	0

Going (Turf): Sf: 0-1 GS: 0-2 Gd: 0-2 GF: 0-2 Fm: 0-1
Distance: 5f/6f: 0-0 7f-8f: 0-1 9f-13f: 0-7 14f+: 0-0
Track : LH: 0-3 RH: 0-5 Tight: 0-6 Gall: 0-2
Aids: Bl: 0-0 Vi: 0-0 Tstrap: 0-0 Ckp: 0-0
Best Rating: 49 5/09 Newc 1m2f32y gd-fm

Got Flash (FR)

(92) (54)
3-y-o b g Xaar-Wild Flush (USA) (Pine Bluff (USA))
E J O'Neill David Barlow & Lyn Rutherford

Placings:60-460 **(1481)**
2009: 7^{4}SD, 8^{6}SD, 8^{0}SD,

	Starts	1st	2nd	3rd	Win & Pl
Career Total (Turf)	0	0	0	0	
Career Total (AW)	5	0	0	0	0

Going (Turf): Sf: 0-0 GS: 0-0 Gd: 0-0 GF: 0-0 Fm: 0-0
Distance: 5f/6f: 0-0 7f-8f: 0-5 9f-13f: 0-0 14f+: 0-0
Track : LH: 0-4 RH: 0-1 Tight: 0-0 Gall: 0-1
Aids: Bl: 0-0 Vi: 0-0 Tstrap: 0-0 Ckp: 0-0
Best Rating: 54 3/09 Sthl 7f stand

Gouray Girl (IRE)

102(99) (86)**89**
2-y-o b f Redback-Brillano (FR) (Desert King (IRE))
W R Swinburn Alan Le Herissier

Placings:1222 **(7290)**
2009: 5^{1}SD, 6^{2}GF, 6^{2}SD, 6^{2}S,

	Starts	1st	2nd	3rd	Win & Pl
Career Total (Turf)	2	0	2	0	3083
Career Total (AW)	2	1	1	0	4394

73 9/09 Wolv 5f216y STD £3238
Total win prize-money £3238

Going (Turf): Sf: 0-1 GS: 0-0 Gd: 0-0 GF: 0-1 Fm: 0-0
Distance: **5f/6f: 1-4** 7f-8f: 0-0 9f-13f: 0-0 14f+: 0-0
Track : **LH: 1-1** RH: 0-1 **Tight: 1-1** Gall: 0-0
Aids: Bl: 0-0 Vi: 0-0 Tstrap: 0-0 Ckp: 0-0
Best Rating: 89 11/09 Donc 6f soft

Useful; effective over 6f; acts on Polytrack and fast and soft turf.

Govenor Eliott (IRE)

92(89) (45)**41**
4-y-o ch g Rock Of Gibraltar (IRE)-Lac Dessert (USA) (Lac Ouimet (USA))
A J Lockwood Mrs Lynne Lumley

Placings:555/0000-6050 **(7681)**
2009: 8^{6}GF, 10^{0}GF, 7^{5}SD, 6^{0}SD,

	Starts	1st	2nd	3rd	Win & Pl
Career Total (Turf)	7	0	0	0	0
Career Total (AW)	4	0	0	0	0

Going (Turf): Sf: 0-1 GS: 0-1 Gd: 0-1 GF: 0-4 Fm: 0-0
Distance: 5f/6f: 0-2 7f-8f: 0-5 9f-13f: 0-4 14f+: 0-0
Track : LH: 0-5 RH: 0-3 Tight: 0-3 Gall: 0-0
Aids: Bl: 0-1 Vi: 0-0 Tstrap: 0-0 Ckp: 0-0
Best Rating: 69 9/07 York 6f gd-fm

Moderate half-brother to a winner at up to 1m4f.

Govern

98(79) (32)**77**
2-y-o b c Empire Maker (USA)-Imroz (USA) (Nureyev (USA))
H R A Cecil K Abdulla

Placings:230 **(7130)**
2009: 7^{2}GF, 7^{3}G, 7^{0}SD,

	Starts	1st	2nd	3rd	Win & Pl
Career Total (Turf)	2	0	1	1	1914
Career Total (AW)	1	0	0	0	

Going (Turf): Sf: 0-0 GS: 0-0 Gd: 0-1 GF: 0-1 Fm: 0-0
Distance: 5f/6f: 0-0 7f-8f: 0-3 9f-13f: 0-0 14f+: 0-0
Track : LH: 0-1 RH: 0-0 Tight: 0-1 Gall: 0-0
Aids: Bl: 0-0 Vi: 0-0 Tstrap: 0-0 Ckp: 0-0
Best Rating: 77 10/09 Folk 7f good

Useful; suited by 7f and fast ground.

Government (IRE)

(99) (53)**53**
8-y-o b g Great Dane (IRE)-Hidden Agenda (FR) (Machiavellian (USA))
M C Chapman James Gordon-Hall

Placings:0450/**300**/**410600**/**0100421020**0040000/0214000 000050-05005500 **(0748)**
2009: 8^{0}SS, 7^{5}SS, 8^{0}SS, 6^{0}SD, 8^{5}SD, 8^{5}SD, 7^{0}SD, 7^{0}SD,

	Starts	1st	2nd	3rd	Win & Pl
Career Total (Turf)	10	0	0	0	286
Career Total (AW)	41	4	3	1	10248

53 1/08 Sthl 7f (0-45) STD £1706
53 5/07 Sthl 1m (0-50)H STD £2730
53 3/07 Sthl 7f (0-52)H STD £1706
53 3/06 Sthl 7f STD £1365
Total win prize-money £7507

Going (Turf): Sf: 0-1 GS: 0-0 Gd: 0-3 GF: 0-6 Fm: 0-0
Distance: 5f/6f: 0-6 **7f-8f: 4-40** 9f-13f: 0-5 14f+: 0-0
Track : **LH: 4-46** RH: 0-2 Tight: 0-6 Gall: 0-1
Aids: Bl: 0-5 Vi: 0-0 Tstrap: 0-0 Ckp: 0-0
Best Rating: 54 5/07 Sthl 1m stand

Moderate; suited by 7f or a mile; acts well on Fibresand; suited by forcing tactics.

Gower

91(96) (51)**60**
5-y-o b g Averti (IRE)-Alashaan (Darshaan)
R J Price R J Price

Placings:622/1654024000/**350005**-**0005**0000305 **(7839)**
2009: 5^{0}SD, 5^{0}SD, 5^{0}SD, 5^{5}SD, 5^{0}GF, 6^{0}F, 5^{0}GF, 6^{0}SD, 5^{3}SD, 6^{0}SD, 5^{5}SS,

	Starts	1st	2nd	3rd	Win & Pl
Career Total (Turf)	16	0	3	0	4695
Career Total (AW)	14	1	0	2	3256

65 3/07 Wolv 5f216y STD £2218
Total win prize-money £2218

Going (Turf): Sf: 0-1 GS: 0-2 Gd: 0-5 GF: 0-6 Fm: 0-1
Distance: **5f/6f: 1-26** 7f-8f: 0-4 9f-13f: 0-0 14f+: 0-0
Track : **LH: 1-17** RH: 0-2 **Tight: 1-7** Gall: 0-4
Aids: Bl: 0-1 Vi: 0-1 Tstrap: 0-6 Ckp: 0-6
Best Rating: 82 10/06 Bath 5f11y gd-sft

Moderate; stays 6f; handles Polytrack and soft turf; has worn cheekpieces.

Gower Sophia

96(95) (65)**66**
2-y-o b f Captain Rio-Hollow Quaill (IRE) (Entrepreneur)
M Brittain David & Gwyn Joseph

Placings:233040225204 **(7748)**
2009: 5^{2}GF, 5^{3}GF, 5^{3}GS, 5^{0}GF, 5^{4}G, 5^{0}SD, 5^{2}SD, 5^{2}G, 5^{5}SF, 5^{2}S, 5^{0}SD, 5^{4}SD,

	Starts	1st	2nd	3rd	Win & Pl
Career Total (Turf)	7	0	3	2	3380
Career Total (AW)	5	0	1	0	922

Going (Turf): Sf: 0-1 GS: 0-1 Gd: 0-2 GF: 0-3 Fm: 0-0
Distance: 5f/6f: 0-12 7f-8f: 0-0 9f-13f: 0-0 14f+: 0-0
Track : LH: 0-4 RH: 0-1 Tight: 0-4 Gall: 0-1
Aids: Bl: 0-1 Vi: 0-5 Tstrap: 0-0 Ckp: 0-0
Best Rating: 66 4/09 Ripn 5f gd-fm

Modest; stays 6f; handles easy ground; goes on Polytrack and Fibresand; has worn a visor.

Gower Valentine

99 **80**
3-y-o b f Primo Valentino (IRE)-Mania (IRE) (Danehill (USA))
D Nicholls David & Gwyn Joseph & Partner

Placings:53610-000420 **(6824)**
2009: 5^{0}GF, 5^{0}GS, 5^{0}GF, 6^{4}G, 5^{2}GF, 7^{0}GF,

	Starts	1st	2nd	3rd	Win & Pl
Career Total (Turf)	11	1	1	1	21372

80 7/08 Gdwd 6f G-F £12952
Total win prize-money £12952

Going (Turf): Sf: 0-1 GS: 0-1 Gd: 0-2 **GF: 1-7** Fm: 0-0
Distance: **5f/6f: 1-9** 7f-8f: 0-2 9f-13f: 0-0 14f+: 0-0
Track : LH: 0-1 RH: 0-1 Tight: 0-0 Gall: 0-0
Aids: Bl: 0-0 Vi: 0-0 Tstrap: 0-0 Ckp: 0-0
Best Rating: 80 7/08 Gdwd 6f gd-fm

Fair; stays 6f; acts on fast ground.

Gozome (IRE)

57(69) (22)
5-y-o ch g Golan (IRE)-Schonbein (IRE) (Persian Heights)
D G Bridgwater SAB Partnership

Placings:000 **(1087)**

2009: 8^{0}SD, 8^{0}SD, 9^{0}GF,

	Starts	1st	2nd	3rd	Win & Pl
Career Total (Turf)	1	0	0	0	
Career Total (AW)	2	0	0	0	

Going (Turf): Sf: 0-0 GS: 0-0 Gd: 0-0 GF: 0-1 Fm: 0-0
Distance: 5f/6f: 0-0 7f-8f: 0-0 9f-13f: 0-3 14f+: 0-0
Track : LH: 0-2 RH: 0-1 Tight: 0-2 Gall: 0-0
Aids: Bl: 0-0 Vi: 0-0 Tstrap: 0-0 Ckp: 0-0
Best Rating: 22 3/09 Wolv 1m141y stand

Gra Adhmhar (IRE)

(81) (40)
2-y-o b g Mull Of Kintyre (USA)-Enya (Orpen (USA))
D J Coakley John O'Riordan

Placings:6 (7825)
2009: 8^{6}SD,

	Starts	1st	2nd	3rd	Win & Pl
Career Total (Turf)	0	0	0	0	
Career Total (AW)	1	0	0	0	0

Going (Turf): Sf: 0-0 GS: 0-0 Gd: 0-0 GF: 0-0 Fm: 0-0
Distance: 5f/6f: 0-0 7f-8f: 0-1 9f-13f: 0-0 14f+: 0-0
Track : LH: 0-0 RH: 0-1 Tight: 0-0 Gall: 0-0
Aids: Bl: 0-0 Vi: 0-0 Tstrap: 0-0 Ckp: 0-0
Best Rating: 40 12/09 Kemp 1m stand

Grace Jicaro

88 42
2-y-o ch f Firebreak-Anita In Wales (IRE) (Anita's Prince)
Mrs L Williamson G D Kendrick

Placings:0505550 (6932)
2009: 5^{0}GF, 5^{5}GF, 5^{0}GF, 5^{5}G, 5^{5}GF, 5^{5}GF, 5^{0}G,

	Starts	1st	2nd	3rd	Win & Pl
Career Total (Turf)	7	0	0	0	132

Going (Turf): Sf: 0-0 GS: 0-0 Gd: 0-2 GF: 0-5 Fm: 0-0
Distance: 5f/6f: 0-7 7f-8f: 0-0 9f-13f: 0-0 14f+: 0-0
Track : LH: 0-3 RH: 0-0 Tight: 0-0 Gall: 0-1
Aids: Bl: 0-1 Vi: 0-0 Tstrap: 0-0 Ckp: 0-0
Best Rating: 42 8/09 Brig 5f59y gd-fm

Half-sister to a filly placed over 5f as a juvenile; also related to hurdlers; beaten in sellers on fast ground.

Graceandgratitude

67(89) (52)
2-y-o b f Royal Applause-Shararah (Machiavellian (USA))
S C Williams Stuart C Williams

Placings:0606 (7698)
2009: 5^{0}GF, 5^{6}SD, 6^{0}SD, 5^{6}SD,

	Starts	1st	2nd	3rd	Win & Pl
Career Total (Turf)	1	0	0	0	
Career Total (AW)	3	0	0	0	0

Going (Turf): Sf: 0-0 GS: 0-0 Gd: 0-0 GF: 0-1 Fm: 0-0
Distance: 5f/6f: 0-4 7f-8f: 0-0 9f-13f: 0-0 14f+: 0-0
Track : LH: 0-1 RH: 0-2 Tight: 0-1 Gall: 0-0
Aids: Bl: 0-0 Vi: 0-0 Tstrap: 0-0 Ckp: 0-0
Best Rating: 52 10/09 Kemp 5f stand

Gracechurch (IRE)

97(95) (54)67
6-y-o b g Marju (IRE)-Saffron Crocus (Shareef Dancer (USA))
R J Hodges Mrs S G Clapp

Placings:24632100/1100005453520**0**/000064**0**/25033212 20-0004235**000** (6800)
2009: 10^{0}SD, 8^{0}GF, 11^{0}F, 10^{4}F, 10^{2}F, 10^{3}F, 7^{5}GF, 10^{0}GF, 10^{0}SD, 8^{0}SD,

	Starts	1st	2nd	3rd	Win & Pl
Career Total (Turf)	43	4	8	5	34329
Career Total (AW)	6	0	0	0	0

59	8/08	Brig	1m1f209y	(0-70)H	G-F	£3154
82	4/06	Bath	1m2f46y	(0-85)H	GD	£7886
80	3/06	Rdcr	1m2f	(0-80)H	SFT	£6477
66	9/05	Bath	1m5y		HRD	£4065

Total win prize-money £21583

Going (Turf): Sf: 1-4 GS: 0-4 **Gd: 1-14 GF: 1-14 Fm: 1-7**
Distance: 5f/6f: 0-0 7f-8f: 0-9 **9f-13f: 4-39** 14f+: 0-1
Track : **LH: 4-31** RH: 0-14 **Tight: 3-24** Gall: 0-5
Aids: Bl: 0-0 Vi: 0-0 Tstrap: 0-0 Ckp: 0-0
Best Rating: 84 7/05 Gdwd 7f gd-sft

Modest; stays 1m 2f; acts on most ground.

Graceful Descent (FR)

105(101) (74)75
4-y-o b f Hawk Wing (USA)-Itab (USA) (Dayjur (USA))
J S Goldie (R A Fahey 19/8) Eric Nisbet & Stan Moffat

Placings:223210/645404-2222122 (6987)
2009: 9^{2}GF, 9^{2}GF, 9^{2}G, 10^{2}G, 11^{1}S, 12^{2}GF, 9^{2}G,

	Starts	1st	2nd	3rd	Win & Pl
Career Total (Turf)	17	2	8	1	18902
Career Total (AW)	2	0	1	0	1228

58	8/09	Haml	1m3f16y	SFT	£2388
71	9/07	Ayr	1m	G-S	£5829

Total win prize-money £8217

Going (Turf): Sf: 1-5 GS: 1-3 Gd: 0-6 GF: 0-3 Fm: 0-0
Distance: 5f/6f: 0-1 7f-8f: 1-4 9f-13f: 1-13 14f+: 0-1
Track : LH: 1-11 **RH: 1-7 Tight: 1-6** Gall: 0-3
Aids: Bl: 0-0 Vi: 0-0 Tstrap: 0-0 Ckp: 0-0
Best Rating: 75 7/09 Bevl 1m1f207y gd-fm

Modest; stays 1m2f and acts on fast ground.

Gracelightening

88(89) (60)62
2-y-o b f Reset (AUS)-Monica Geller (Komaite (USA))
Paul Green The Haydock Hopefuls

Placings:535 (5839)
2009: 6^{5}HY, 8^{3}G, 8^{5}SD,

	Starts	1st	2nd	3rd	Win & Pl
Career Total (Turf)	2	0	0	1	794
Career Total (AW)	1	0	0	0	0

Going (Turf): Sf: 0-1 GS: 0-0 Gd: 0-1 GF: 0-0 Fm: 0-0
Distance: 5f/6f: 0-0 7f-8f: 0-2 9f-13f: 0-1 14f+: 0-0
Track : LH: 0-2 RH: 0-0 Tight: 0-2 Gall: 0-0
Aids: Bl: 0-0 Vi: 0-0 Tstrap: 0-0 Ckp: 0-0
Best Rating: 62 8/09 Thsk 1m good

Modest; stays 1m; acts on good/easy ground

Gracie's Games

(92) (52)28
3-y-o b f Mind Games-Little Kenny (Warning)
R J Price David Prosser & Keith Warrington

Placings:0030-04000 (7814)
2009: 5^{0}SD, 6^{4}SD, 8^{0}SD, 5^{0}SD, 8^{0}SD,

	Starts	1st	2nd	3rd	Win & Pl
Career Total (Turf)	2	0	0	0	
Career Total (AW)	7	0	0	1	403

Going (Turf): Sf: 0-1 GS: 0-1 Gd: 0-0 GF: 0-0 Fm: 0-0
Distance: 5f/6f: 0-7 7f-8f: 0-1 9f-13f: 0-1 14f+: 0-0
Track : LH: 0-6 RH: 0-1 Tight: 0-6 Gall: 0-0
Aids: Bl: 0-0 Vi: 0-0 Tstrap: 0-0 Ckp: 0-0
Best Rating: 52 11/08 Wolv 5f216y stand

Modest; stays 6f and acts on Polytrack.

Gracie's Gift (IRE)

97(104) (63)65
7-y-o b g Imperial Ballet (IRE)-Settle Petal (IRE) (Roi Danzig (USA))
R C Guest S Hussey

Placings:4430/12056/332441163/02536400/040406-1321062 (7815)
2009: 6^{1}SD, 7^{3}SD, 7^{2}GF, 7^{1}SD, 6^{0}G, 7^{6}SD, 5^{2}SD,

	Starts	1st	2nd	3rd	Win & Pl
Career Total (Turf)	23	2	3	2	11571
Career Total (AW)	16	3	2	4	8747

63	5/09	Sthl	7f	(0-60)H	STD	£2047
59	3/09	Sthl	6f	(0-60)H	STD	£2047
69	10/06	Yarm	7f3y	(0-65)H	SFT	£3238
65	9/06	Gdwd	1m	(0-60)H	GD	£3238
46	5/05	Sthl	6f		STD	£1463

Total win prize-money £12035

Going (Turf): Sf: 1-3 GS: 0-4 **Gd: 1-5** GF: 0-10 Fm: 0-1
Distance: 5f/6f: 2-16 **7f-8f: 3-21** 9f-13f: 0-2 14f+: 0-0
Track : **LH: 3-21** RH: 1-4 Tight: 0-5 Gall: 0-3
Aids: Bl: 0-0 Vi: 0-0 Tstrap: 0-4 Ckp: 0-4
Best Rating: 69 10/06 Yarm 7f3y soft

Moderate; effective over 6f-1m; acts on fast and soft ground; also goes on Fibresand.

Gracious Melange

(102) (78)
2-y-o b f Medicean-Goodness Gracious (IRE) (Green Desert (USA))
M Botti Mrs R J Jacobs

Placings:1 (7763)
2009: 8^{1}SD,

	Starts	1st	2nd	3rd	Win & Pl
Career Total (Turf)	0	0	0	0	
Career Total (AW)	1	1	0	0	3886

78	12/09	Kemp	1m	STD	£3885

Total win prize-money £3886

Going (Turf): Sf: 0-0 GS: 0-0 Gd: 0-0 GF: 0-0 Fm: 0-0
Distance: 5f/6f: 0-0 **7f-8f: 1-1** 9f-13f: 0-0 14f+: 0-0
Track : LH: 0-0 **RH: 1-1** Tight: 0-0 Gall: 0-0
Aids: Bl: 0-0 Vi: 0-0 Tstrap: 0-0 Ckp: 0-0
Best Rating: 78 12/09 Kemp 1m stand

Fair winner on debut over 1m on Polytrack.

Grail Knight

80(84) (37)33

4-y-o ch g Carnival Dancer-Nashkova (Nashwan (USA))

A G Foster A G Foster

Placings:6/6-600 **(2159)**

2009: 10^{6}GF, 14^{0}G, 14^{0}GF,

	Starts	1st	2nd	3rd	Win & Pl
Career Total (Turf)	3	0	0	0	0
Career Total (AW)	2	0	0	0	0

Going (Turf): **Sf: 0-0 GS: 0-0 Gd: 0-1 GF: 0-2 Fm: 0-0**
Distance: 5f/6f: 0-0 7f-8f: 0-1 9f-13f: 0-2 14f+: 0-2
Track : LH: 0-3 RH: 0-2 Tight: 0-3 Gall: 0-1
Aids: Bl: 0-0 Vi: 0-0 Tstrap: 0-0 Ckp: 0-0
Best Rating: **37** 12/07 Sthl 1m std-slw

Gramercy (IRE)

(100) (82)

2-y-o b c Whipper (USA)-Topiary (IRE) (Selkirk (USA))

M L W Bell M B Hawtin

Placings:451 **(7317)**

2009: 5^{4}SF, 7^{5}SD, 5^{1}SD,

	Starts	1st	2nd	3rd	Win & Pl
Career Total (Turf)	0	0	0	0	
Career Total (AW)	3	1	0	0	2970

82 11/09 Wolv 5f216y STD £2729

Total win prize-money £2730

Going (Turf): **Sf: 0-0 GS: 0-0 Gd: 0-0 GF: 0-0 Fm: 0-0**
Distance: **5f/6f: 1-2** 7f-8f: 0-1 9f-13f: 0-0 14f+: 0-0
Track : **LH: 1-3** RH: 0-0 **Tight: 1-3** Gall: 0-0
Aids: Bl: 0-0 Vi: 0-0 Tstrap: 0-0 Ckp: 0-0
Best Rating: **82** 11/09 Wolv 5f216y stand

Useful; suited by 6f and Polytrack.

Grams And Ounces

66(94) (68)4

2-y-o b c Royal Applause-Ashdown Princess (IRE) (King's Theatre (IRE))

Miss Amy Weaver Miss A Weaver

Placings:033 **(7825)**

2009: 7^{0}G, 8^{3}SD, 8^{3}SD,

	Starts	1st	2nd	3rd	Win & Pl
Career Total (Turf)	1	0	0	0	
Career Total (AW)	2	0	0	2	605

Going (Turf): **Sf: 0-0 GS: 0-0 Gd: 0-1 GF: 0-0 Fm: 0-0**
Distance: 5f/6f: 0-0 7f-8f: 0-2 9f-13f: 0-1 14f+: 0-0
Track : LH: 0-1 RH: 0-1 Tight: 0-1 Gall: 0-0
Aids: Bl: 0-0 Vi: 0-0 Tstrap: 0-0 Ckp: 0-0
Best Rating: **68** 12/09 Kemp 1m stand

Moderate; stays 1m; acts on Polytrack.

Granakey (IRE)

(92) (43)

6-y-o b m Key Of Luck (USA)-Grand Morning (IRE) (King Of Clubs)

Ian Williams Tom and Gerry

Placings:005231301/016530050/0-60 **(7555)**

2009: 5^{6}SD, 5^{0}SD,

	Starts	1st	2nd	3rd	Win & Pl
Career Total (Turf)	0	0	0	0	
Career Total (AW)	21	3	1	3	8375

63	2/07	Sthl	1m	(0-58)H	STD	£2388
62	1/07	Sthl	1m	(0-55)H	STD	£2388
59	11/06	Sthl	6f	(0-45)	STD	£1945

Total win prize-money £6723

Going (Turf): **Sf: 0-0 GS: 0-0 Gd: 0-0 GF: 0-0 Fm: 0-0**
Distance: 5f/6f: 1-8 **7f-8f: 2-11** 9f-13f: 0-2 14f+: 0-0
Track : **LH: 3-15** RH: 0-6 Tight: 0-6 Gall: 0-1
Aids: Bl: 0-0 Vi: 0-0 Tstrap: 0-0 Ckp: 0-0
Best Rating: **63** 2/07 Sthl 1m stand

Granary Girl

97(100) (60)65

7-y-o b m Kingsinger (IRE)-Highland Blue (Never So Bold)

J Pearce Mrs P O'Shea

Placings:0060/6506205610140304411/00605436623231 50/0243640003/34433103040612106-123500 **(4498)**

2009: 10^{1}F, 11^{2}G, 10^{3}G, 10^{5}GF, 11^{0}S, 12^{0}G,

	Starts	1st	2nd	3rd	Win & Pl
Career Total (Turf)	33	6	4	5	22916
Career Total (AW)	38	3	2	6	8309

62	5/09	Nott	1m2f50y	(0-60)H	FRM	£2047
54	8/08	NmkJ	1m4f	(0-70)H	G-F	£3885
59	6/08	Folk	1m4f	(0-60)H	G-F	£2047
56	3/08	Kemp	1m4f	(0-60)H	STD	£2047
59	8/06	Leic	1m1f218y	(0-65)H	GD	£3238
56	10/05	Ling	1m2f	(0-45)	STD	£1519
55	10/05	Nott	1m1f213y	(0-55)H	GD	£2678
51	6/05	Bath	1m2f46y	(0-55)H	GD	£3591
49	5/05	Wolv	1m1f103y		STD	£1519

Total win prize-money £22575

Going (Turf): Sf: 0-1 GS: 0-0 **Gd: 3-14** GF: 2-13 Fm: 1-5
Distance: 5f/6f: 0-1 7f-8f: 0-6 **9f-13f: 9-64** 14f+: 0-0
Track : **LH: 5-54** RH: 4-15 **Tight: 4-43** Gall: 1-3
Aids: Bl: 0-0 Vi: 0-0 Tstrap: 0-0 Ckp: 0-0
Best Rating: **65** 5/09 Yarm 1m3f101y good

Moderate; stays 1m4f; acts on good ground; also goes on Polytrack.

Grand Art (IRE)

103 (49)79

5-y-o b g Raise A Grand (IRE)-Mulberry River (IRE) (Bluebird (USA))

P T Midgley (J Howard Johnson 5/5) David Mann

Placings:5350/3251160/350-61311043403522 **(5943)**

2009: 10^{6}F, 11^{1}GF, 12^{3}GS, 12^{1}GF, 12^{1}GF, 12^{0}G, 12^{4}GF, 12^{3}G, 16^{4}GF, 16^{0}G, 11^{3}GF, 12^{5}GF, 12^{2}F, 14^{2}G,

	Starts	1st	2nd	3rd	Win & Pl
Career Total (Turf)	27	5	3	6	25459
Career Total (AW)	1	0	0	0	

79	5/09	York	1m4f	(0-80)H	G-F	£6246
74	5/09	NmkR	1m4f	(0-70)H	G-F	£3123
67	5/09	Catt	1m3f214y		G-F	£2047
81	8/07	Ches	1m2f75y	(0-75)H	G-F	£4095
67	7/07	Yarm	1m1f		G-F	£1943

Total win prize-money £17454

Going (Turf): Sf: 0-0 GS: 0-2 Gd: 0-9 **GF: 5-14** Fm: 0-2
Distance: 5f/6f: 0-2 7f-8f: 0-2 **9f-13f: 5-20** 14f+: 0-4
Track : **LH: 4-16** RH: 1-8 **Tight: 3-15** Gall: 2-6
Aids: Bl: 0-0 Vi: 0-0 Tstrap: 0-0 Ckp: 0-0
Best Rating: **81** 8/07 Ches 1m2f75y gd-fm

Fair; stays 1m6f; acts on fast ground.

Grand Court (IRE)

(95) (38)53

6-y-o b m Grand Lodge (USA)-Nice One Clare (IRE) (Mukaddamah (USA))

George Baker Derek & Cheryl Holder

Placings:0/04/0000/00-0 **(0215)**

2009: 8^{0}SD,

	Starts	1st	2nd	3rd	Win & Pl
Career Total (Turf)	6	0	0	0	250
Career Total (AW)	4	0	0	0	

Going (Turf): **Sf: 0-0 GS: 0-0 Gd: 0-2 GF: 0-4 Fm: 0-0**
Distance: 5f/6f: 0-0 7f-8f: 0-4 9f-13f: 0-6 14f+: 0-0
Track : LH: 0-6 RH: 0-1 Tight: 0-7 Gall: 0-0
Aids: Bl: 0-0 Vi: 0-0 Tstrap: 0-2 Ckp: 0-2
Best Rating: **53** 7/06 Wind 1m67y gd-fm

Grand Diamond (IRE)

102(97) (68)71

5-y-o b g Grand Lodge (USA)-Winona (IRE) (Alzao (USA))

J S Goldie Jim Goldie Racing Club

Placings:550/00330010440/020416334-5502404233O **(7113)**

2009: 7^{5}G, 7^{5}GF, 8^{0}F, 8^{2}GF, 10^{4}GF, 8^{0}GF, 8^{4}G, 8^{2}GF, 8^{3}G, 7^{3}G, 9^{0}GS,

	Starts	1st	2nd	3rd	Win & Pl
Career Total (Turf)	30	2	3	5	11887
Career Total (AW)	4	0	0	1	556

66	7/08	Muss	7f30y	(0-60)H	GD	£2590
58	8/07	Muss	1m	(0-70)H	G-F	£3238

Total win prize-money £5829

Going (Turf): Sf: 0-3 GS: 0-2 **Gd: 1-15 GF: 1-9** Fm: 0-1
Distance: 5f/6f: 0-0 **7f-8f: 2-24** 9f-13f: 0-10 14f+: 0-0
Track : LH: 0-8 **RH: 2-24 Tight: 2-25** Gall: 0-0
Aids: Bl: 0-0 Vi: 0-0 Tstrap: 2-23 Ckp: 2-23
Best Rating: **71** 9/09 Muss 7f30y good

Modest; effective over 7f, but stays 1m; acts on most ground and on Polytrack; has worn cheekpieces.

Grand Exit

(78) (16)

3-y-o b f Exit To Nowhere (USA)-Little Feat (Terimon)

A J McCabe J L Rowsell

Placings:0 **(6375)**

2009: 12^{0}SD,

	Starts	1st	2nd	3rd	Win & Pl
Career Total (Turf)	0	0	0	0	
Career Total (AW)	1	0	0	0	

Going (Turf): **Sf: 0-0 GS: 0-0 Gd: 0-0 GF: 0-0 Fm: 0-0**
Distance: 5f/6f: 0-0 7f-8f: 0-0 9f-13f: 0-1 14f+: 0-0
Track : LH: 0-0 RH: 0-1 Tight: 0-0 Gall: 0-0
Aids: Bl: 0-0 Vi: 0-0 Tstrap: 0-0 Ckp: 0-0
Best Rating: **16** 9/09 Kemp 1m4f stand

Grand Honour (IRE)

92(98) (82)76

3-y-o gr g Verglas (IRE)-Rosy Dudley (IRE) (Grand Lodge (USA))

P Howling Mrs J P Howling

Placings:514401600325-5322000054600 **(7876)**
2009: 7^{5}SD, 7^{3}SD, 7^{2}SD, 7^{2}SD, 7^{0}SD, 7^{0}SD, 7^{0}GF, 8^{0}GF, 6^{5}SD, 7^{4}SD, 7^{6}G, 8^{0}SD, 7^{0}SD,

	Starts	1st	2nd	3rd	Win & Pl
Career Total (Turf)	8	0	0	0	1497
Career Total (AW)	17	2	3	2	10992

82	7/08	Kemp	7f	STD	£3238
69	4/08	Wolv	5f20y	STD	£2590

Total win prize-money £5828

Going (Turf): Sf: 0-0 GS: 0-1 Gd: 0-2 GF: 0-5 Fm: 0-0
Distance: 5f/6f: 1-8 7f-8f: 1-17 9f-13f: 0-0 14f+: 0-0
Track : LH: 1-10 RH: 1-9 **Tight: 1-8** Gall: 0-1
Aids: Bl: 0-0 Vi: 0-0 Tstrap: 0-0 Ckp: 0-0
Best Rating: 82 7/08 Kemp 7f stand

Fair; effective over 5-7f; acts on Polytrack.

Grand Mary (IRE)

81 **43**

2-y-o ch f Kyllachy-Magic Sister (Cadeaux Genereux)
P F I Cole Mrs Fitri Hay

Placings:00 **(5966)**
2009: 5^{0}G, 7^{0}GS,

	Starts	1st	2nd	3rd	Win & Pl
Career Total (Turf)	2	0	0	0	

Going (Turf): Sf: 0-0 GS: 0-1 Gd: 0-1 GF: 0-0 Fm: 0-0
Distance: 5f/6f: 0-1 7f-8f: 0-1 9f-13f: 0-0 14f+: 0-0
Track : LH: 0-1 RH: 0-0 Tight: 0-0 Gall: 0-1
Aids: Bl: 0-0 Vi: 0-0 Tstrap: 0-0 Ckp: 0-0
Best Rating: 43 9/09 Ling 7f gd-sft

Grand Minstrel (IRE)

90 **48**

5-y-o ch m Ashkalani (IRE)-Blushing Minstrel (IRE) (Nicholas (USA))
P J Lally Mrs Christine Kiernan

Placings:45/0/00005 **(4894)**
2009: 6^{0}GY, 8^{0}Y, 8^{0}S, 8^{0}G, 6^{5}GS,

	Starts	1st	2nd	3rd	Win & Pl
Career Total (Turf)	8	0	0	0	481

Going (Turf): Sf: 0-2 GS: 0-1 Gd: 0-1 GF: 0-1 Fm: 0-0
Distance: 5f/6f: 0-3 7f-8f: 0-5 9f-13f: 0-0 14f+: 0-0
Track : LH: 0-5 RH: 0-2 Tight: 0-1 Gall: 0-1
Aids: Bl: 0-0 Vi: 0-0 Tstrap: 0-0 Ckp: 0-0
Best Rating: 60 10/06 Naas 6f yld-sft

Grand Opera (IRE)

(107) (90)**85**

6-y-o b g City On A Hill (USA)-Victoria's Secret (IRE) (Law Society (USA))
Gordon Elliott B D McCormack/J P Clarke

Placings:23345/331/4403/2604101140-410 **(7789)**
2009: 8^{4}SD, 8^{1}SD, 9^{0}SD,

	Starts	1st	2nd	3rd	Win & Pl
Career Total (Turf)	19	2	2	5	13069
Career Total (AW)	6	3	0	0	27386

88	11/09	Dund	1m	H	STD	£13588
84	9/08	Dund	1m	(50-80)H	STD	£6351
76	9/08	Layt	7f	(50-80)H	STD	£6605
76	7/08	Carl	6f192y	(0-75)H	FRM	£2590
59	7/06	Carl	6f192y		FRM	£3238

Total win prize-money £32374

Going (Turf): Sf: 0-0 GS: 0-6 Gd: 0-2 GF: 0-8 **Fm: 2-2**
Distance: 5f/6f: 0-0 **7f-8f: 5-18** 9f-13f: 0-7 14f+: 0-0
Track : **LH: 3-13** RH: 2-8 Tight: 0-9 Gall: 0-2
Aids: Bl: 1-3 Vi: 0-0 Tstrap: 1-2 Ckp: 1-2
Best Rating: 90 12/09 Wolv 1m1f103y stand

Useful; effective from 7f-1m2f; acts on fast ground and with cut; has worn blinkers.

Grand Palace (IRE)

(107) (76)**39**

6-y-o b g Grand Lodge (USA)-Pocket Book (IRE) (Reference Point)
H J Evans (D Shaw 14/3) ownaracehorse.co.uk (Shakespeare)

Placings:005160055320/6312060P0020213212/2013500 0210-4013130600050522 **(7889)**
2009: 5^{4}SD, 6^{0}SD, 5^{1}SD, 5^{3}SD, 6^{1}SD, 6^{3}SD, 5^{0}SD, 6^{5}SD, 5^{0}SD, 5^{0}SD, 5^{0}SD, 6^{5}SD, 6^{0}SD, 6^{5}SD, 6^{2}SD, 5^{2}SD,

	Starts	1st	2nd	3rd	Win & Pl
Career Total (Turf)	3	0	0	0	
Career Total (AW)	54	8	10	6	26911

76	2/09	Kemp	6f	(0-70)H	STD	£2590
74	1/09	Wolv	5f216y	(0-65)H	STD	£2047
71	11/08	Wolv	5f216y	(0-65)H	STD	£2047
71	1/08	Sthl	5f	(0-65)H	STD	£2047
65	12/07	Ling	6f	(0-55)H	STD	£1943
60	11/07	Ling	6f	(0-60)H	STD	£1706
61	1/07	Wolv	7f32y	(0-55)H	SS	£2388
56	6/06	Sthl	7f	(0-60)H	STD	£2730

Total win prize-money £17500

Going (Turf): Sf: 0-1 GS: 0-1 Gd: 0-1 GF: 0-0 Fm: 0-0
Distance: 5f/6f: 6-37 7f-8f: 2-15 9f-13f: 0-4 14f+: 0-1
Track : LH: 6-45 RH: 1-6 **Tight: 5-33** Gall: 0-0
Aids: Bl: 0-0 **Vi: 7-49** Tstrap: 0-0 Ckp: 0-0
Best Rating: 76 2/09 Kemp 6f stand

Moderate; effective over 5f-7f; acts on sand; has worn a visor.

Grand Passion (IRE)

98(113) (109)**89**

9-y-o b g Grand Lodge (USA)-Lovers' Parlour (Beldale Flutter (USA))
C F Wall H H Morriss

Placings:312/310412032/2100421361/004444/612450605 35/20224535012/0560006-5300000 **(5598)**
2009: 12^{5}SD, 11^{3}SD, 11^{0}SD, 10^{0}SD, 10^{0}SD, 12^{0}GF, 8^{0}GF,

	Starts	1st	2nd	3rd	Win & Pl
Career Total (Turf)	35	3	2	6	116013
Career Total (AW)	29	5	8	1	147579

99	11/07	Ling	1m2f		STD	£15614
105	2/06	Ling	1m2f		STD	£15580
110	11/04	Ling	1m2f		STD	£17400
108	6/04	Curr	1m		G-F	£45845
110	2/04	Ling	1m2f	B	STD	£15027
107	7/03	NmkJ	1m	B(0-100)H	G-F	£17400
101	4/03	Sand	1m14y	C(0-100)H	G-F	£12687
89	10/02	Ling	7f	D	STD	£4660

Total win prize-money £144216

Going (Turf): Sf: 0-5 GS: 0-7 Gd: 0-4 **GF: 3-18** Fm: 0-1
Distance: 5f/6f: 0-1 7f-8f: 3-14 **9f-13f: 5-49** 14f+: 0-0
Track : LH: 5-32 RH: 2-22 **Tight: 5-27** Gall: 1-9
Aids: Bl: 0-0 Vi: 0-0 Tstrap: 0-0 Ckp: 0-0
Best Rating: 111 5/05 Sand 1m2f7y gd-fm

Very useful; winner in Listed company and Group placed; stays 1m4f, but effective at 1m; suited by fast ground; goes well on Polytrack; likes to come from off the pace.

Grand Pere

87(86) (43)**52**

3-y-o b g Monsieur Bond (IRE)-Ejay (Emperor Jones (USA))
P D Evans M&R Refurbishments Ltd

Placings:5000 **(4606)**
2009: 8^{5}SD, 9^{0}GF, 8^{0}G, 10^{0}GF,

	Starts	1st	2nd	3rd	Win & Pl
Career Total (Turf)	3	0	0	0	
Career Total (AW)	1	0	0	0	0

Going (Turf): Sf: 0-0 GS: 0-0 Gd: 0-1 GF: 0-2 Fm: 0-0
Distance: 5f/6f: 0-0 7f-8f: 0-0 9f-13f: 0-4 14f+: 0-0
Track : LH: 0-2 RH: 0-2 Tight: 0-4 Gall: 0-0
Aids: Bl: 0-0 Vi: 0-0 Tstrap: 0-0 Ckp: 0-0
Best Rating: 52 8/09 Wind 1m2f7y gd-fm

Grand Sefton

(83) (16)**52**

6-y-o br g Pivotal-Nahlin (Slip Anchor)
N R Mitchell J R Boughey

Placings:003/600/06020/0 **(0872)**
2009: 10^{0}SD,

	Starts	1st	2nd	3rd	Win & Pl
Career Total (Turf)	5	0	1	0	578
Career Total (AW)	7	0	0	1	467

Going (Turf): Sf: 0-1 GS: 0-2 Gd: 0-1 GF: 0-1 Fm: 0-0
Distance: 5f/6f: 0-0 7f-8f: 0-8 9f-13f: 0-4 14f+: 0-0
Track : LH: 0-6 RH: 0-4 Tight: 0-5 Gall: 0-0
Aids: Bl: 0-0 Vi: 0-0 Tstrap: 0-0 Ckp: 0-0
Best Rating: 64 10/05 Sthl 7f stand

Grand Stitch (USA)

59 **67**

3-y-o b g Grand Slam (USA)-Lil Sister Stich (USA) (Seattle Bound (USA))
D Carroll Danny Fantom

Placings:53-0 **(2250)**
2009: 6^{0}G,

	Starts	1st	2nd	3rd	Win & Pl
Career Total (Turf)	3	0	0	1	626

Going (Turf): Sf: 0-1 GS: 0-0 Gd: 0-2 GF: 0-0 Fm: 0-0
Distance: 5f/6f: 0-3 7f-8f: 0-0 9f-13f: 0-0 14f+: 0-0
Track : LH: 0-1 RH: 0-0 Tight: 0-0 Gall: 0-0
Aids: Bl: 0-0 Vi: 0-0 Tstrap: 0-0 Ckp: 0-0
Best Rating: 67 6/08 Ripn 6f soft

Modest; effective over 5f-6f; acts on good and soft ground.

Grand Value (USA)

(93) (52)**63**

4-y-o b f Grand Slam (USA)-Privyet Nadya (USA) (Cure The Blues (USA))

R Ford D W Watson

Placings:562/26300-0 **(0567)**
2009: 12⁰SD,

	Starts	1st	2nd	3rd	Win & Pl
Career Total (Turf)	6	0	2	1	2601
Career Total (AW)	3	0	0	0	

Going (Turf): Sf: 0-2 GS: 0-1 Gd: 0-1 GF: 0-2 Fm: 0-0
Distance: 5f/6f: 0-1 7f-8f: 0-5 9f-13f: 0-3 14f+: 0-0
Track : LH: 0-6 RH: 0-2 Tight: 0-7 Gall: 0-1
Aids: Bl: 0-0 Vi: 0-0 Tstrap: 0-0 Ckp: 0-0
Best Rating: 63 4/08 Muss 7f30y soft

Moderate; stays 7f; effective on fast and on soft ground.

Grand Vista

104(84) (67)**103**
5-y-o b g Danehill (USA)-Revealing (Halling (USA))
G L Moore (H J Brown 20/3) Blue Diamond Racing

Placings:1166/243020/562300-0006000 **(4423)**
2009: 7⁰GS, 7⁰GF, 6⁰GF, 5⁶SD, 6⁰SD, 8⁰SD, 7⁰G,

	Starts	1st	2nd	3rd	Win & Pl
Career Total (Turf)	19	2	3	2	66853
Career Total (AW)	4	0	0	0	
96 7/06 Deau 5f110y			GD		£11379
81 6/06 Chan 6f			G-S		£6552

Total win prize-money £17931

Going (Turf): Sf: 0-1 **GS: 1-3 Gd: 1-11** GF: 0-3 Fm: 0-0
Distance: **5f/6f: 2-8** 7f-8f: 0-15 9f-13f: 0-0 14f+: 0-0
Track : LH: 0-9 RH: 0-7 Tight: 0-1 Gall: 0-8
Aids: Bl: 0-0 Vi: 0-0 Tstrap: 0-0 Ckp: 0-0
Best Rating: 104 8/07 Deau 1m good

Useful; effective at 6f/7f; acts on most ground; has worn tongue tie.

Grand Vizier (IRE)

89(109) (93)**78**
5-y-o b g Desert Style (IRE)-Distant Decree (USA) (Distant View (USA))
C F Wall Hintlesham SP Partners

Placings:01016/1163O100-01056 **(7827)**
2009: 8⁰G, 8¹SD, 8⁰S, 8⁵SD, 8⁶SD,

	Starts	1st	2nd	3rd	Win & Pl
Career Total (Turf)	9	1	0	1	3553
Career Total (AW)	9	5	0	0	19893
93 6/09 Kemp 1m	(0-85)H		STD		£5677
91 9/08 Kemp 1m	(0-85)H		STD		£6231
78 5/08 Yarm 7f3y	(0-70)H		GD		£2590
85 5/08 GrLe 1m	(0-85)H		STD		£4533
67 6/07 Wolv 1m141y			STD		£2968

Total win prize-money £22000

Going (Turf): Sf: 0-1 GS: 0-2 **Gd: 1-5** GF: 0-1 Fm: 0-0
Distance: 5f/6f: 0-0 **7f-8f: 4-9** 9f-13f: 2-9 14f+: 0-0
Track : **LH: 3-7** RH: 2-8 **Tight: 2-5** Gall: 1-3
Aids: Bl: 0-0 Vi: 0-0 Tstrap: 0-0 Ckp: 0-0
Best Rating: 93 12/09 Kemp 1m stand

Useful; suited by 1m and acts on Polytrack.

Grand Zafeen

97 **78**
2-y-o ch f Zafeen (FR)-Majestic Desert (Fraam)
M R Channon Jaber Abdullah

Placings:1202 **(3559)**
2009: 5¹F, 5²GF, 5⁰GF, 5²GF,

	Starts	1st	2nd	3rd	Win & Pl
Career Total (Turf)	4	1	2	0	7392
74 4/09 Pont 5f			FRM		£3238

Total win prize-money £3238

Going (Turf): Sf: 0-0 GS: 0-0 Gd: 0-0 GF: 0-3 **Fm: 1-1**
Distance: **5f/6f: 1-4** 7f-8f: 0-0 9f-13f: 0-0 14f+: 0-0
Track : **LH: 1-1** RH: 0-0 Tight: 0-0 Gall: 0-0
Aids: Bl: 0-0 Vi: 0-0 Tstrap: 0-0 Ckp: 0-0
Best Rating: 78 5/09 Gdwd 5f gd-fm

Fair; effective over 5f; acts on fast ground.

Grandad Bill (IRE)

104(92) (47)**73**
6-y-o ch g Intikhab (USA)-Matikanehanafubuki (IRE) (Caerleon (USA))
J S Goldie C & B Racing Club

Placings:4510/000/0003140/640230414215-0632332126 **(6768)**
2009: 14⁰GF, 13⁶G, 14³GF, 12²GS, 12³GF, 14³G, 12²S, 12¹GS, 12²G, 12⁶GS,

	Starts	1st	2nd	3rd	Win & Pl
Career Total (Turf)	33	5	5	5	30346
Career Total (AW)	3	0	0	0	0
66 9/09 York 1m4f	(0-70)H		G-S		£5051
73 10/08 Muss 1m4f	(0-80)H		G-S		£6476
64 8/08 Ayr 1m2f	(0-70)H		G-S		£3561
55 9/07 Thsk 1m	(0-50)H		G-F		£1943
65 6/05 Thsk 7f			GD		£3750

Total win prize-money £20783

Going (Turf): Sf: 0-4 **GS: 3-9** Gd: 1-10 GF: 1-9 Fm: 0-1
Distance: 5f/6f: 0-2 7f-8f: 2-6 **9f-13f: 3-23** 14f+: 0-5
Track : **LH: 4-21** RH: 1-13 **Tight: 3-17** Gall: 1-4
Aids: Bl: 0-0 Vi: 0-0 Tstrap: 0-0 Ckp: 0-0
Best Rating: 73 10/08 Muss 1m4f gd-sft

Modest; stays 1m4f; acts on most ground.

Grande Caiman (IRE)

100(111) (108)**95**
5-y-o ch g Grand Lodge (USA)-Sweet Retreat (Indian Ridge)
R Hannon I A N Wight

Placings:051/066111/323600303511-2004 **(1709)**
2009: 12²SD, 11⁰SD, 12⁰SD, 14⁴GF,

	Starts	1st	2nd	3rd	Win & Pl
Career Total (Turf)	10	0	0	2	5607
Career Total (AW)	15	6	2	2	41994
107 12/08 GrLe 1m5f66y	(0-95)H		STD		£7477
101 12/08 Ling 1m4f	(0-95)H		STD		£9066
96 12/07 Ling 1m4f	(0-95)H		STD		£6855
86 11/07 Ling 1m5f	(0-75)H		STD		£2817
85 11/07 Ling 1m5f	(0-75)H		STD		£3238
76 12/06 Ling 1m			STD		£3238

Total win prize-money £32693

Going (Turf): **Sf: 0-1 GS: 0-6 Gd: 0-1 GF: 0-2 Fm: 0-0**
Distance: 5f/6f: 0-0 7f-8f: 1-4 **9f-13f: 4-14** 14f+: 1-7
Track : **LH: 6-13** RH: 0-11 **Tight: 5-13** Gall: 1-8
Aids: **Bl: 2-8** Vi: 0-0 Tstrap: 0-3 Ckp: 0-3
Best Rating: 108 1/09 Ling 1m4f stand

Smart; stays 2m; acts on good and easy ground; effective on Polytrack; has worn cheekpieces and blinkers.

Grande Saggio

91 **73**
2-y-o gr c Cape Cross (IRE)-Success Story (Sharrood (USA))
M Botti The Great Partnership

Placings:2 **(7244)**
2009: 8²S,

	Starts	1st	2nd	3rd	Win & Pl
Career Total (Turf)	1	0	1	0	1253

Going (Turf): **Sf: 0-1 GS: 0-0 Gd: 0-0 GF: 0-0 Fm: 0-0**
Distance: 5f/6f: 0-0 7f-8f: 0-0 9f-13f: 0-1 14f+: 0-0
Track : LH: 0-1 RH: 0-0 Tight: 0-0 Gall: 0-0
Aids: Bl: 0-0 Vi: 0-0 Tstrap: 0-0 Ckp: 0-0
Best Rating: 73 11/09 Nott 1m75y soft

Runner-up on debut; effective over 1m; acts on soft ground.

Grange Corner

(84) (26)
4-y-o ch f First Trump-Blennerville (IRE) (General View)
Garry Moss J Pownall

Placings:0-505 **(1778)**
2009: 11⁵SS, 12⁰SD, 8⁵SD,

	Starts	1st	2nd	3rd	Win & Pl
Career Total (Turf)	0	0	0	0	
Career Total (AW)	4	0	0	0	0

Going (Turf): **Sf: 0-0 GS: 0-0 Gd: 0-0 GF: 0-0 Fm: 0-0**
Distance: 5f/6f: 0-0 7f-8f: 0-1 9f-13f: 0-3 14f+: 0-0
Track : LH: 0-4 RH: 0-0 Tight: 0-1 Gall: 0-0
Aids: Bl: 0-0 Vi: 0-0 Tstrap: 0-0 Ckp: 0-0
Best Rating: 26 5/09 Sthl 1m stand

Granite Girl

85 **69**
2-y-o b f Kyllachy-Native Ring (FR) (Bering)
P J McBride P J McBride

Placings:36 **(6920)**
2009: 6³GF, 8⁶GF,

	Starts	1st	2nd	3rd	Win & Pl
Career Total (Turf)	2	0	0	1	770

Going (Turf): **Sf: 0-0 GS: 0-0 Gd: 0-0 GF: 0-2 Fm: 0-0**
Distance: 5f/6f: 0-1 7f-8f: 0-0 9f-13f: 0-1 14f+: 0-0
Track : LH: 0-0 RH: 0-0 Tight: 0-0 Gall: 0-0
Aids: Bl: 0-0 Vi: 0-0 Tstrap: 0-0 Ckp: 0-0
Best Rating: 69 10/09 Yarm 1m3y gd-fm

Fair; suited by 6f and fast ground.

Granny McPhee

96(98) (65)**80**
3-y-o b f Bahri (USA)-Allumette (Rainbow Quest (USA))
A Bailey Middleham Park Racing XXVI & Alan Bailey

Placings:402536-064U041 **(6497)**
2009: 7⁰SD, 6⁶GF, 7⁴GF, 9ᵁF, 7⁰GF, 9⁴GF, 9¹SF,

	Starts	1st	2nd	3rd	Win & Pl
Career Total (Turf)	8	0	1	0	1734
Career Total (AW)	5	1	0	1	3159
63 10/09 Wolv 1m1f103y (0-55)H			SF		£2388

Total win prize-money £2388

Going (Turf): **Sf: 0-0 GS: 0-1 Gd: 0-1 GF: 0-5 Fm: 0-1**

Distance: 5f/6f: 0-1 7f-8f: 0-8 9f-13f: 1-4 14f+: 0-0
Track : LH: 1-8 RH: 0-0 Tight: 1-5 Gall: 0-1
Aids: Bl: 0-0 Vi: 0-0 Tstrap: 0-0 Ckp: 0-0
Best Rating: 80 9/08 Ches 7f2y gd-fm

Fair; best over 7f; acts on fast ground and on Polytrack.

Granski (IRE)

98 (56)68

3-y-o b g Alhaarth (IRE)-Purple Haze (IRE) (Spectrum (IRE))
D M Fogarty (R Hannon 4/7) D M Fogarty

Placings:642000-40004000 (7546a)
2009: 10^{4}GF, 9^{0}GF, 12^{0}GF, 8^{0}GS, 9^{4}G, 10^{0}S, 10^{0}SD, 10^{0}SD,

	Starts	1st	2nd	3rd	Win & Pl
Career Total (Turf)	12	0	1	0	1974
Career Total (AW)	2	0	0	0	

Going (Turf): Sf: 0-1 GS: 0-3 Gd: 0-3 GF: 0-5 Fm: 0-0
Distance: 5f/6f: 0-1 7f-8f: 0-6 9f-13f: 0-7 14f+: 0-0
Track : LH: 0-3 RH: 0-7 Tight: 0-2 Gall: 0-2
Aids: Bl: 0-1 Vi: 0-0 Tstrap: 0-2 Ckp: 0-2
Best Rating: 68 5/09 Wind 1m2f7y gd-fm

Granston (IRE)

106(98) (99)93

8-y-o gr g Revoque (IRE)-Gracious Gretclo (Common Grounds)
J D Bethell The Four Players Partnership

Placings:432055401/316602531/52236661130/22502512 30/03333500/06163630240-221402060 (6480)
2009: 10^{2}G, 10^{2}GF, 9^{1}GF, 10^{4}GF, 8^{0}G, 9^{2}G, 9^{0}GS, 10^{6}GS, 9^{0}GF,

	Starts	1st	2nd	3rd	Win & Pl
Career Total (Turf)	61	8	11	10	119162
Career Total (AW)	6	0	1	2	14038

91	5/09	Ripn	1m1f170y	(0-90)H	G-F	£9714
89	3/08	Donc	1m2f60y	(0-85)H	GD	£6477
93	8/06	Thsk	1m	(0-90)H	G-F	£9067
93	8/05	Ripn	1m	(0-100)H	G-F	£12379
90	8/05	Leic	1m60y	(0-80)H	GD	£7229
85	9/04	Asct	1m	(0-85)H	G-F	£7181
79	4/04	Ripn	1m	C(0-90)H	GD	£8542
74	10/03	Catt	7f	D(0-85)	G-F	£3591

Total win prize-money £64182

Going (Turf): Sf: 0-7 GS: 0-6 Gd: 3-20 GF: 5-25 Fm: 0-3
Distance: 5f/6f: 0-6 7f-8f: 5-34 9f-13f: 3-27 14f+: 0-0
Track : LH: 3-28 RH: 5-19 Tight: 5-14 Gall: 2-16
Aids: Bl: 0-0 Vi: 0-1 Tstrap: 0-1 Ckp: 0-1
Best Rating: 99 5/07 Kemp 1m stand

Useful; suited by 1m-1m2f; acts on most types of ground; has worn a visor and cheekpieces; likes to race prominently.

Grant Me A Wish

39

3-y-o ch g Timeless Times (USA)-Baby Be (Bold Arrangement)
S P Griffiths Miss Emily Grant

Placings:0 (6823)
2009: 6^{0}GF,

	Starts	1st	2nd	3rd	Win & Pl
Career Total (Turf)	1	0	0	0	

Going (Turf): Sf: 0-0 GS: 0-0 Gd: 0-0 GF: 0-1 Fm: 0-0
Distance: 5f/6f: 0-1 7f-8f: 0-0 9f-13f: 0-0 14f+: 0-0
Track : LH: 0-0 RH: 0-0 Tight: 0-0 Gall: 0-0
Aids: Bl: 0-0 Vi: 0-0 Tstrap: 0-0 Ckp: 0-0

Grasp

77(89) (62)48

7-y-o b g Kayf Tara-Circe (Main Reef)
P D Evans (Steve Flook 16/5) S Flook

Placings:400/00441/0031/550/0-50 (4168)
2009: 16^{5}GF, 16^{0}G,

	Starts	1st	2nd	3rd	Win & Pl
Career Total (Turf)	13	1	0	1	5246
Career Total (AW)	5	1	0	0	2389

62	11/06	Kemp	2m	(0-65)H	STD	£2388
64	10/05	Bath	2m1f34y	(0-75)H	G-S	£3899

Total win prize-money £6288

Going (Turf): Sf: 0-3 GS: 1-3 Gd: 0-5 GF: 0-2 Fm: 0-0
Distance: 5f/6f: 0-0 7f-8f: 0-0 9f-13f: 0-3 14f+: 2-15
Track : LH: 1-10 RH: 1-8 Tight: 1-9 Gall: 0-1
Aids: Bl: 0-4 Vi: 2-7 Tstrap: 0-0 Ckp: 0-0
Best Rating: 64 10/05 Bath 2m1f34y gd-sft

Moderate stayer; acts on good ground and Polytrack.

Gratuitous (IRE)

(84) (38)38

5-y-o b g Rudimentary (USA)-Accell (IRE) (Magical Wonder (USA))
L McHugh L McHugh

Placings:000000/0 (0566)
2009: 12^{0}SD,

	Starts	1st	2nd	3rd	Win & Pl
Career Total (Turf)	6	0	0	0	
Career Total (AW)	1	0	0	0	

Going (Turf): Sf: 0-1 GS: 0-0 Gd: 0-3 GF: 0-1 Fm: 0-0
Distance: 5f/6f: 0-0 7f-8f: 0-4 9f-13f: 0-3 14f+: 0-0
Track : LH: 0-3 RH: 0-4 Tight: 0-1 Gall: 0-0
Aids: Bl: 0-0 Vi: 0-0 Tstrap: 0-0 Ckp: 0-0
Best Rating: 71 4/07 Gowr 1m good

Gravitation

102 108

4-y-o b f Galileo (IRE)-Guaranda (Acatenango (GER))
W Jarvis Gillian, Lady Howard De Walden

Placings:5413214-05 (3642)
2009: 11^{0}G, 16^{5}G,

	Starts	1st	2nd	3rd	Win & Pl
Career Total (Turf)	9	2	1	1	64605

108	7/08	Gdwd	1m6f	G-F	£39739
76	6/08	Leic	1m3f183y	GD	£2104

Total win prize-money £41844

Going (Turf): Sf: 0-2 GS: 0-2 Gd: 1-3 GF: 1-1 Fm: 0-1
Distance: 5f/6f: 0-0 7f-8f: 0-0 9f-13f: 1-5 14f+: 1-4
Track : LH: 0-3 RH: 2-6 Tight: 1-1 Gall: 0-5
Aids: Bl: 0-0 Vi: 0-0 Tstrap: 0-0 Ckp: 0-0
Best Rating: 108 7/08 Gdwd 1m6f gd-fm

Smart; winner at Group 3 level; stays at least 1m6f; acts on most ground.

Graycliffe (IRE)

87(100) (64)60

3-y-o gr g Val Royal (FR)-Popiplu (USA) (Cozzene (USA))
Patrick Morris Walsh & Pettigrew

Placings:4055-06103005 (4874)
2009: 8^{0}SD, 9^{6}SF, 10^{1}SD, 10^{0}GF, 12^{3}SD, 11^{0}G, 12^{0}SD, 12^{5}G,

	Starts	1st	2nd	3rd	Win & Pl
Career Total (Turf)	7	0	0	0	253
Career Total (AW)	5	1	0	1	2750

64	4/09	Kemp	1m2f	(0-60)H	STD	£2047

Total win prize-money £2047

Going (Turf): Sf: 0-1 GS: 0-1 Gd: 0-3 GF: 0-2 Fm: 0-0
Distance: 5f/6f: 0-1 7f-8f: 0-4 9f-13f: 1-7 14f+: 0-0
Track : LH: 0-5 RH: 1-5 Tight: 0-4 Gall: 0-2
Aids: Bl: 0-0 Vi: 0-0 Tstrap: 0-0 Ckp: 0-0
Best Rating: 64 4/09 Kemp 1m4f stand

Dam is a sister to Tycoon Todd, a prolific winner in the US; modest form; seems best at around 7f.

Graylyn Ruby (FR)

102(106) (78)74

4-y-o b g Limnos (JPN)-Nandi (IRE) (Mujadil (USA))
J Jay Graham & Lynn Knight

Placings:0005/324504113330-0561526003 (6758)
2009: 12^{0}SD, 12^{5}GF, 12^{6}GS, 11^{1}G, 12^{5}GF, 12^{2}G, 12^{6}SF, 11^{0}GF, 12^{0}GF, 11^{3}G,

	Starts	1st	2nd	3rd	Win & Pl
Career Total (Turf)	17	1	2	2	5170
Career Total (AW)	9	2	0	3	6556

73	5/09	Yarm	1m3f101y	(0-65)H	GD	£2072
76	10/08	Kemp	1m4f	(0-70)H	STD	£2590
71	10/08	Ling	1m4f	(0-60)H	STD	£1942

Total win prize-money £6605

Going (Turf): Sf: 0-1 GS: 0-1 Gd: 1-7 GF: 0-8 Fm: 0-0
Distance: 5f/6f: 0-0 7f-8f: 0-3 9f-13f: 3-20 14f+: 0-3
Track : LH: 2-17 RH: 1-6 Tight: 2-11 Gall: 0-5
Aids: Bl: 0-0 Vi: 0-0 Tstrap: 0-0 Ckp: 0-0
Best Rating: 78 12/08 Kemp 1m4f stand

Modest; stays 1m4f; acts on a sound surface; goes on Polytrack.

Graymalkin (IRE)

99(96) (82)83

2-y-o b c Singspiel (IRE)-Pearl Grey (Gone West (USA))
Saeed Bin Suroor Godolphin

Placings:614 (6805)
2009: 7^{6}G, 8^{1}GF, 8^{4}SD,

	Starts	1st	2nd	3rd	Win & Pl
Career Total (Turf)	2	1	0	0	3886
Career Total (AW)	1	0	0	0	337

83	9/09	Hayd	1m30y	G-F	£3885

Total win prize-money £3886

Going (Turf): Sf: 0-0 GS: 0-0 Gd: 0-1 GF: 1-1 Fm: 0-0
Distance: 5f/6f: 0-0 7f-8f: 0-1 9f-13f: 1-2 14f+: 0-0
Track : LH: 1-2 RH: 0-0 Tight: 0-1 Gall: 0-0
Aids: Bl: 0-0 Vi: 0-0 Tstrap: 0-0 Ckp: 0-0
Best Rating: 83 9/09 Hayd 1m30y gd-fm

Useful sort; stays 1m; handles quick ground.

Graze On And On

93 38

4-y-o ch f Elmaamul (USA)-Laena (Roman Warrior)
J J Quinn J R Rowbottom

Placings:00/00-0 (3486)

2009: 16⁰G,

	Starts	1st	2nd	3rd	Win & Pl
Career Total (Turf)	5	0	0	0	

Going (Turf): Sf: 0-0 GS: 0-0 Gd: 0-3 GF: 0-2 Fm: 0-0
Distance: 5f/6f: 0-1 7f-8f: 0-2 9f-13f: 0-1 14f+: 0-1
Track : LH: 0-4 RH: 0-1 Tight: 0-4 Gall: 0-0
Aids: Bl: 0-0 Vi: 0-0 Tstrap: 0-1 Ckp: 0-1
Best Rating: 38 6/09 Thsk 2m good

Grazeon Gold Blend

107 87

6-y-o ch g Paris House-Thalya (Crofthall)
J J Quinn J R Rowbottom

Placings:411500/6200015502/00/050213324430-001240526 **(6645)**
2009: 6⁰GF, 5⁰G, 6¹GF, 6²GF, 6⁴GF, 6⁰GF, 8⁵GS, 7²GF, 7⁶G,

	Starts	1st	2nd	3rd	Win & Pl
Career Total (Turf)	39	5	6	3	63468

83	6/09	Ripn	6f	(0-95)H	G-F	£8831
85	7/08	Haml	6f5y	(0-75)H	GD	£4533
91	7/06	Ripn	6f	(0-90)H	G-F	£9715
89	8/05	Bevl	5f		G-S	£10627
79	8/05	Pont	5f		GD	£7150

Total win prize-money £40858

Going (Turf): Sf: 0-7 GS: 1-5 **Gd: 2-11 GF: 2-16** Fm: 0-0
Distance: **5f/6f: 4-31** 7f-8f: 1-8 9f-13f: 0-0 14f+: 0-0
Track : **LH: 1-11** RH: 0-1 Tight: 0-5 Gall: 0-1
Aids: Bl: 0-0 Vi: 0-1 Tstrap: 1-8 Ckp: 1-8
Best Rating: 94 8/06 Leic 5f2y good

Fair; suited by 5f-6f; acts on most ground; has worn cheek-pieces and a visor.

Great Art (IRE)

98 83

3-y-o b c One Cool Cat (USA)-Passe Passe (USA) (Lear Fan (USA))
P W Chapple-Hyam Matthew Green

Placings:2-4100 **(6997)**
2009: 7⁴G, 7¹GF, 8⁰G, 7⁰G,

	Starts	1st	2nd	3rd	Win & Pl
Career Total (Turf)	5	1	1	0	5213

71	9/09	Catt	7f	G-F	£3238

Total win prize-money £3238

Going (Turf): Sf: 0-0 GS: 0-0 Gd: 0-4 **GF: 1-1** Fm: 0-0
Distance: 5f/6f: 0-0 **7f-8f: 1-4** 9f-13f: 0-1 14f+: 0-0
Track : **LH: 1-2** RH: 0-0 **Tight: 1-1** Gall: 0-1
Aids: Bl: 0-0 Vi: 0-0 Tstrap: 0-0 Ckp: 0-0
Best Rating: 83 5/08 Newb 6f8y good

Useful 68,000gns half-brother to several winners at up to 1m2f; stays 7f; acts on good/fast ground.

Great Bounder (CAN)

88(96) (64)43

3-y-o b/br g Mr Greeley (USA)-Jo Zak (USA) (Vilzak (USA))
A B Haynes (J R Best 2/12) C Weare & A Pierce

Placings:066-00002206 **(7860)**
2009: 11⁰SD, 12⁰GF, 12⁰SD, 8⁰SD, 9²SD, 8²SD, 7⁰SD, 7⁶SD,

	Starts	1st	2nd	3rd	Win & Pl
Career Total (Turf)	1	0	0	0	
Career Total (AW)	10	0	2	0	1011

Going (Turf): Sf: 0-0 GS: 0-0 Gd: 0-0 GF: 0-1 Fm: 0-0
Distance: 5f/6f: 0-0 7f-8f: 0-6 9f-13f: 0-5 14f+: 0-0
Track : LH: 0-8 RH: 0-3 Tight: 0-7 Gall: 0-1
Aids: Bl: 0-0 Vi: 0-0 Tstrap: 0-0 Ckp: 0-0
Best Rating: 64 11/08 Ling 1m stand

Modest form at up to 1m; acts on Polytrack and Fibresand.

Great Charm (IRE)

95(103) (81)95

4-y-o b g Orpen (USA)-Briery (IRE) (Salse (USA))
E J Alston (M L W Bell 31/10) Mr & Mrs G Middlebrook

Placings:054/011312104030-00000331 **(7506)**
2009: 7⁰SD, 6⁰GF, 6⁰GF, 6⁰G, 5⁰SD, 6³SD, 5³SD, 6¹SD,

	Starts	1st	2nd	3rd	Win & Pl
Career Total (Turf)	16	3	1	2	22826
Career Total (AW)	7	2	0	2	6061

81	11/09	Sthl	6f	(0-75)H	STD	£2729
95	7/08	Hayd	6f	(0-90)H	SFT	£9714
87	6/08	Ripn	6f	(0-85)H	SFT	£4533
72	5/08	Sthl	7f	(0-75)H	GD	£2593
82	4/08	Sthl	7f		STD	£1774

Total win prize-money £21344

Going (Turf): **Sf: 2-4** GS: 0-2 Gd: 1-5 GF: 0-5 Fm: 0-0
Distance: **5f/6f: 3-15** 7f-8f: 2-6 9f-13f: 0-2 14f+: 0-0
Track : **LH: 3-8** RH: 0-1 **Tight: 1-4** Gall: 0-0
Aids: Bl: 0-0 Vi: 0-0 Tstrap: 0-0 Ckp: 0-0
Best Rating: 95 7/08 Hayd 6f soft

Fair; suited by 6f-7f; acts on most ground and on Fibresand; likes to race prominently.

Great Intrigue (IRE)

85 67

2-y-o b g Azamour (IRE)-Bakewell Tart (IRE) (Tagula (IRE))
J S Moore Mrs Fitri Hay

Placings:005 **(6424)**
2009: 6⁰GF, 6⁰GS, 6⁵GF,

	Starts	1st	2nd	3rd	Win & Pl
Career Total (Turf)	3	0	0	0	0

Going (Turf): **Sf: 0-0 GS: 0-1 Gd: 0-0 GF: 0-2 Fm: 0-0**
Distance: 5f/6f: 0-2 7f-8f: 0-1 9f-13f: 0-0 14f+: 0-0
Track : LH: 0-0 RH: 0-0 Tight: 0-0 Gall: 0-0
Aids: Bl: 0-0 Vi: 0-0 Tstrap: 0-0 Ckp: 0-0
Best Rating: 67 6/09 Newb 6f8y gd-fm

Great Knight (IRE)

83(103) (67)67

4-y-o b g Acclamation-Wild Vintage (USA) (Alysheba (USA))
John Joseph Hanlon (S Kirk 21/8) Miss Rachel O'Neill

Placings:322226060-41605150500 **(5225)**
2009: 5⁴SD, 5¹SD, 6⁶SD, 6⁰F, 7⁵SD, 5¹SD, 5⁵SD, 6⁰GS, 6⁵SD, 6⁰GF, 5⁰SD,

	Starts	1st	2nd	3rd	Win & Pl
Career Total (Turf)	8	0	4	0	3950
Career Total (AW)	12	2	0	1	4389

63	6/09	Wolv	5f216y	(0-60)H	STD	£1978
62	2/09	Wolv	5f216y	(0-55)H	STD	£2047

Total win prize-money £4026

Going (Turf): **Sf: 0-0 GS: 0-1 Gd: 0-2 GF: 0-4 Fm: 0-1**
Distance: **5f/6f: 2-13** 7f-8f: 0-6 9f-13f: 0-1 14f+: 0-0
Track : **LH: 2-14** RH: 0-0 **Tight: 2-12** Gall: 0-0
Aids: Bl: 0-2 Vi: 0-1 Tstrap: 0-0 Ckp: 0-0
Best Rating: 67 5/08 Thsk 7f good

Modest; effective from 5f-7f; acts on easy ground and Polytrack; has worn blinkers.

Great Quest (IRE)

97(73) 56

7-y-o b m Montjeu (IRE)-Paparazzi (IRE) (Shernazar)
James Moffatt Arnold Headdock & Mrs Kath Headdock

Placings:323200/600100/0242066/00400 **(5734)**
2009: 13⁰SF, 13⁰G, 14⁴G, 17⁰GF, 16⁰GS,

	Starts	1st	2nd	3rd	Win & Pl
Career Total (Turf)	23	1	4	2	14733
Career Total (AW)	1	0	0	0	

73	7/06	Klny	2m1f	(50-80)H	G-F	£6671

Total win prize-money £6672

Going (Turf): Sf: 0-2 GS: 0-2 Gd: 0-7 **GF: 1-9** Fm: 0-0
Distance: 5f/6f: 0-0 7f-8f: 0-0 9f-13f: 0-12 **14f+: 1-12**
Track : **LH: 1-13** RH: 0-9 Tight: 0-4 Gall: 0-5
Aids: Bl: 0-1 Vi: 0-0 Tstrap: 0-1 Ckp: 0-1
Best Rating: 82 7/05 Limk 1m4f good

Modest; stays 2m1f; acts on fast ground.

Great View (IRE)

100(100) (65)74

10-y-o b g Great Commotion (USA)-Tara View (IRE) (Wassl)
Mrs A L M King All The Kings Horses

Placings:6212400/0060020561020/000402430155432/012 1240230240/050520035233103/311415403100/004551234 00/00451443500-5040 **(4625)**
2009: 11⁵GF, 12⁰GF, 12⁴GF, 12⁰HY,

	Starts	1st	2nd	3rd	Win & Pl
Career Total (Turf)	86	11	12	10	67247
Career Total (AW)	15	1	1	1	5235

74	7/08	Chep	1m4f23y	(0-70)H	SFT	£2590
76	7/07	Newb	1m3f5y	(0-70)H	HVY	£3238
83	10/06	Newb	1m4f5y	(0-75)H	HVY	£4996
83	7/06	Epsm	1m4f10y	(0-80)H	GD	£6477
72	6/06	Newb	1m2f6y	(0-70)H	G-F	£3747
71	5/06	NmkR	1m4f	(0-70)H	G-S	£3747
64	9/05	Carl	1m3f206y	(0-65)H	G-F	£3638
67	4/04	Brig	1m3f196yF	(0-55)H	G-F	£2996
56	3/04	Ling	1m5f	F(0-55)H	STD	£2961
59	8/03	Newb	1m2f6yF	(0-65)H	G-F	£4940
62	8/02	Leic	7f9y	G	G-S	£3143
86	7/01	Chep	6f16y	E	G-F	£2940

Total win prize-money £45417

Going (Turf): Sf: 3-16 GS: 2-13 Gd: 1-22 **GF: 5-32** Fm: 0-3
Distance: 5f/6f: 0-2 7f-8f: 2-19 **9f-13f: 10-75** 14f+: 0-5
Track : **LH: 8-65** RH: 2-23 Tight: 2-33 **Gall: 5-19**
Aids: Bl: 0-12 Vi: 5-38 Tstrap: 6-36 Ckp: 6-36
Best Rating: 91 8/01 York 6f214y good

Modest; effective over 1m5f but stays further; acts on most surfaces, but is suited by soft; has worn cheekpieces and a visor.

Great Western (USA)

76(88) (49)21

3-y-o b/br c Gone West (USA)-Pleasant Temper (USA) (Storm Cat (USA))

P F I Cole John Manley

Placings:000-0 (1594)

2009: 10^{0}GS,

	Starts	1st	2nd	3rd	Win & Pl
Career Total (Turf)	2	0	0	0	
Career Total (AW)	2	0	0	0	

Going (Turf): **Sf: 0-0 GS: 0-2 Gd: 0-0 GF: 0-0 Fm: 0-0**
Distance: 5f/6f: 0-0 7f-8f: 0-2 9f-13f: 0-2 14f+: 0-0
Track : LH: 0-3 RH: 0-0 Tight: 0-0 Gall: 0-2
Aids: Bl: 0-0 Vi: 0-0 Tstrap: 0-0 Ckp: 0-0
Best Rating: **49** 11/08 GrLe 1m stand

Greek Envoy

103

5-y-o br g Diktat-South Shore (Caerleon (USA))

T P Tate T P Tate

Placings:150/1201/405000-P (7018)

2009: 12^{P}GS,

	Starts	1st	2nd	3rd	Win & Pl
Career Total (Turf)	14	3	1	0	26191
109 10/07 NmkR	1m4f	(0-100)H		SFT	£12464
99 6/07 Leic	1m1f218y	(0-85)H		SFT	£5181
78 8/06 Rdcr	7f			GD	£3238

Total win prize-money £20885

Going (Turf): **Sf: 2-8** GS: 0-2 Gd: 1-3 GF: 0-1 Fm: 0-0
Distance: 5f/6f: 0-0 7f-8f: 1-3 **9f-13f: 2-10** 14f+: 0-1
Track : LH: 0-8 **RH: 2-3** Tight: 0-1 **Gall: 1-7**
Aids: Bl: 0-0 Vi: 0-0 Tstrap: 0-0 Ckp: 0-0
Best Rating: **109** 10/07 NmkR 1m4f soft

Useful; stays 1m4f and acts on good and softer ground.

Greek Key (IRE)

90(88) (64)62

2-y-o ch c Selkirk (USA)-Doohulla (USA) (Stravinsky (USA))

M L W Bell M B Hawtin

Placings:006050 (6906)

2009: 7^{0}G, 7^{0}HY, 7^{6}SD, 7^{0}GF, 7^{5}GF, 6^{0}G,

	Starts	1st	2nd	3rd	Win & Pl
Career Total (Turf)	5	0	0	0	0
Career Total (AW)	1	0	0	0	0

Going (Turf): **Sf: 0-1 GS: 0-0 Gd: 0-2 GF: 0-2 Fm: 0-0**
Distance: 5f/6f: 0-1 7f-8f: 0-5 9f-13f: 0-0 14f+: 0-0
Track : LH: 0-2 RH: 0-1 Tight: 0-1 Gall: 0-1
Aids: Bl: 0-0 Vi: 0-0 Tstrap: 0-0 Ckp: 0-0
Best Rating: **64** 8/09 Ling 7f stand

Greek Secret

101(100) (58)63

6-y-o b g Josr Algarhoud (IRE)-Mazurkanova (Song)

J O'Reilly The Boot & Shoe Ackworth Partnership

Placings:023330100/1000552002000**0**/000610000105**0**/0 03406**010-6**0010506**061** (7889)

2009: 7^{6}SD, 6^{0}GF, 7^{0}GF, 5^{1}GF, 6^{U}GF, 6^{5}GF, 5^{0}S, 5^{6}SD, 7^{0}SF, 6^{6}SD, 5^{1}SD,

	Starts	1st	2nd	3rd	Win & Pl
Career Total (Turf)	44	5	3	4	22333
Career Total (AW)	12	2	0	0	3685
12/09 Ling	5f	(0-55)H		STD	£1978
63 7/09 Bevl	5f	(0-60)H		G-F	£2266
58 12/08 Kemp	6f	(0-45)		STD	£1706
61 9/07 Rdcr	6f	(0-70)H		FRM	£2817
64 8/07 Thsk	6f	(0-55)H		G-F	£2498
78 5/06 Thsk	6f	(0-75)H		FRM	£3886
71 9/05 Newc	6f			G-F	£4212

Total win prize-money £19365

Going (Turf): Sf: 0-5 GS: 0-5 Gd: 0-6 **GF: 3-24** Fm: 2-4
Distance: **5f/6f: 7-44** 7f-8f: 0-12 9f-13f: 0-0 14f+: 0-0
Track : LH: 1-18 RH: 1-8 **Tight: 1-12** Gall: 0-4
Aids: **Bl: 3-14** Vi: 0-0 Tstrap: 0-5 Ckp: 0-5
Best Rating: **78** 5/06 Thsk 6f firm

Plater; stays 6f; acts on fast ground and on Polytrack; has worn blinkers.

Greek Theatre (USA)

(99) (64)64

4-y-o ch g Smoke Glacken (USA)-Theatre Flight (USA) (Theatrical)

P S McEntee Eventmaker Racehorses

Placings:55052**U5**/5051-4 (7728)

2009: 8^{4}SD,

	Starts	1st	2nd	3rd	Win & Pl
Career Total (Turf)	4	0	0	0	0
Career Total (AW)	8	1	1	0	2547
64 10/08 GrLe	1m	(0-60)H		STD	£1942

Total win prize-money £1943

Going (Turf): **Sf: 0-0 GS: 0-1 Gd: 0-1 GF: 0-2 Fm: 0-0**
Distance: 5f/6f: 0-2 **7f-8f: 1-7** 9f-13f: 0-2 14f+: 0-1
Track : **LH: 1-6** RH: 0-4 Tight: 0-2 **Gall: 1-2**
Aids: Bl: 0-0 Vi: 0-0 Tstrap: 0-0 Ckp: 0-0
Best Rating: **67** 11/07 Kemp 1m stand

Modest; effective over 1m; acts on Polytrack.

Green Agenda

108(99) (80)81

3-y-o b g Anabaa (USA)-Capistrano Day (USA) (Diesis)

M Johnston The Green Dot Partnership

Placings:000-**112114**4300**2**00**65** (7101)

2009: 7^{1}SD, 8^{1}SD, 8^{2}SD, 7^{1}GF, 8^{1}F, 8^{4}SD, 8^{4}G, 8^{3}G, 8^{0}GF, 8^{0}G, 8^{2}G, 8^{0}GF, 8^{0}SD, 8^{6}GF, 10^{5}G,

	Starts	1st	2nd	3rd	Win & Pl
Career Total (Turf)	13	2	1	1	10288
Career Total (AW)	5	2	1	0	5147
79 4/09 Thsk	1m	(0-75)H		FRM	£4274
81 4/09 Muss	7f30y	(0-70)H		G-F	£3238
67 3/09 Kemp	1m	(0-60)H		STD	£1942
58 3/09 Ling	7f	(0-60)H		STD	£2047

Total win prize-money £11502

Going (Turf): Sf: 0-0 GS: 0-1 Gd: 0-6 **GF: 1-5 Fm: 1-1**
Distance: 5f/6f: 0-0 **7f-8f: 4-14** 9f-13f: 0-4 14f+: 0-0
Track : LH: 2-8 RH: 2-5 **Tight: 3-6** Gall: 0-0
Aids: Bl: 0-0 Vi: 0-0 Tstrap: 0-0 Ckp: 0-0
Best Rating: **81** 4/09 Muss 7f30y gd-fm

Modest; stays 1m; acts on fast ground and sand.

Green Army

79 41

2-y-o b c Sulamani (IRE)-Dowhatjen (Desert Style (IRE))

M R Channon M Channon

Placings:0 (6821)

2009: 8^{0}GF,

	Starts	1st	2nd	3rd	Win & Pl
Career Total (Turf)	1	0	0	0	

Going (Turf): **Sf: 0-0 GS: 0-0 Gd: 0-0 GF: 0-1 Fm: 0-0**
Distance: 5f/6f: 0-0 7f-8f: 0-1 9f-13f: 0-0 14f+: 0-0
Track : LH: 0-0 RH: 0-0 Tight: 0-0 Gall: 0-0
Aids: Bl: 0-0 Vi: 0-0 Tstrap: 0-0 Ckp: 0-0
Best Rating: **41** 10/09 Rdcr 1m gd fm

Green Beret (IRE)

103 101

3-y-o b g Fayruz-Grandel (Owington)

J H M Gosden H R H Princess Haya Of Jordan

Placings:231-1552435 (5203)

2009: 5^{1}G, 6^{5}GF, 5^{5}GF, 5^{2}GF, 5^{4}G, 5^{3}G, 5^{5}GF,

	Starts	1st	2nd	3rd	Win & Pl
Career Total (Turf)	10	2	2	2	19611
98 4/09 Brig	5f213y	(0-90)H		GD	£8418
84 7/08 Wwck	5f			SFT	£2590

Total win prize-money £11009

Going (Turf): **Sf: 1-1** GS: 0-0 **Gd: 1-3** GF: 0-6 Fm: 0-0
Distance: **5f/6f: 2-10** 7f-8f: 0-0 9f-13f: 0-0 14f+: 0-0
Track : **LH: 2-3** RH: 0-0 Tight: 0-1 Gall: 0-1
Aids: Bl: 0-0 Vi: 0-1 Tstrap: 0-0 Ckp: 0-0
Best Rating: **101** 7/09 NmkJ 5f good

Very useful; effective over 5f-6f; acts on any ground.

Green Community (USA)

91(87) (59)65

2-y-o gr/ro f El Prado (IRE)-Dreams (USA) (Silver Hawk (USA))

E F Vaughan Ali Saeed

Placings:4436 (5935)

2009: 5^{4}S, 7^{4}SD, 8^{3}G, 7^{6}GF,

	Starts	1st	2nd	3rd	Win & Pl
Career Total (Turf)	3	0	0	1	842
Career Total (AW)	1	0	0	0	289

Going (Turf): **Sf: 0-1 GS: 0-0 Gd: 0-1 GF: 0-1 Fm: 0-0**
Distance: 5f/6f: 0-1 7f-8f: 0-2 9f-13f: 0-1 14f+: 0-0
Track : LH: 0-1 RH: 0-0 Tight: 0-1 Gall: 0-0
Aids: Bl: 0-0 Vi: 0-0 Tstrap: 0-0 Ckp: 0-0
Best Rating: **65** 8/09 Chep 1m14y good

Moderate; stays 7f; acts on Polytrack.

Green Day Packer (IRE)

69(90) (46)63

5-y-o br g Daylami (IRE)-Durrah Green (Green Desert (USA))

P C Haslam Middleham Park Racing XXX

Placings:500**065**/64040/60 (3499)

2009: 13^{6}SD, 11^{0}GF,

	Starts	1st	2nd	3rd	Win & Pl
Career Total (Turf)	7	0	0	0	265

	Starts	1st	2nd	3rd	Win & Pl
Career Total (AW)	6	0	0	0	0

Going (Turf): **Sf: 0-0 GS: 0-0 Gd: 0-3 GF: 0-4 Fm: 0-0**
Distance: 5f/6f: 0-2 7f-8f: 0-3 9f-13f: 0-6 14f+: 0-2
Track : LH: 0-9 RH: 0-1 Tight: 0-6 Gall: 0-1
Aids: Bl: 0-0 Vi: 0-0 Tstrap: 0-0 Ckp: 0-0
Best Rating: **63** 12/06 Wolv 7f32y stand

Green Dynasty (IRE)

91(91) (64)**55**

3-y-o ch g Giant's Causeway (USA)-Rose Gypsy (Green Desert (USA))
M Johnston The Green Dot Partnership

Placings:4-6540004 **(3480)**
2009: 8^{6}SD, 8^{5}SD, 8^{4}SD, 8^{0}GS, 9^{0}GF, 10^{0}GF, 8^{4}GF,

	Starts	1st	2nd	3rd	Win & Pl
Career Total (Turf)	4	0	0	0	241
Career Total (AW)	4	0	0	0	0

Going (Turf): **Sf: 0-0 GS: 0-1 Gd: 0-0 GF: 0-3 Fm: 0-0**
Distance: 5f/6f: 0-0 7f-8f: 0-3 9f-13f: 0-5 14f+: 0-0
Track : LH: 0-6 RH: 0-2 Tight: 0-6 Gall: 0-0
Aids: Bl: 0-1 Vi: 0-0 Tstrap: 0-0 Ckp: 0-0
Best Rating: **64** 2/09 Ling 1m stand

Moderate; stays 1m; acts on Polytrack.

Green Earth (IRE)

99 **74**

2-y-o b c Cape Cross (IRE)-Inchyre (Shirley Heights)
Mrs A J Perrett The Green Dot Partnership

Placings:0036100 **(6963)**
2009: 6^{0}GF, 7^{0}GF, 6^{3}F, 7^{6}GF, 7^{1}GF, 8^{0}GS, 6^{0}G,

	Starts	1st	2nd	3rd	Win & Pl
Career Total (Turf)	7	1	0	1	3157

74	9/09	Wwck	7f26y	(0-75)	G-F	£2590

Total win prize-money £2590

Going (Turf): Sf: 0-0 GS: 0-1 Gd: 0-1 **GF: 1-4** Fm: 0-1
Distance: 5f/6f: 0-0 **7f-8f: 1-6** 9f-13f: 0-1 14f+: 0-0
Track : **LH: 1-3** RH: 0-2 Tight: 0-1 Gall: 0-0
Aids: Bl: 0-0 Vi: 0-0 Tstrap: 0-0 Ckp: 0-0
Best Rating: **74** 9/09 Wwck 7f26y gd-fm

Fair; stays 7f; acts on fast ground.

Green Endeavour (CAN)

73(84) (44)**20**

3-y-o b g Forestry (USA)-Zuri Ridge (USA) (Cox's Ridge (USA))
Mrs A J Perrett The Green Dot Partnership

Placings:000-00 **(3675)**
2009: 12^{0}SD, 9^{0}F,

	Starts	1st	2nd	3rd	Win & Pl
Career Total (Turf)	2	0	0	0	
Career Total (AW)	3	0	0	0	

Going (Turf): **Sf: 0-0 GS: 0-1 Gd: 0-0 GF: 0-0 Fm: 0-1**
Distance: 5f/6f: 0-0 7f-8f: 0-3 9f-13f: 0-2 14f+: 0-0
Track : LH: 0-3 RH: 0-1 Tight: 0-1 Gall: 0-1
Aids: Bl: 0-1 Vi: 0-0 Tstrap: 0-0 Ckp: 0-0
Best Rating: **44** 11/08 GrLe 1m stand

Green Energy

67 **15**

2-y-o b g Rainbow Quest (USA)-Carambola (IRE) (Danehill (USA))
Mrs A J Perrett The Green Dot Partnership

Placings:00 **(6930)**
2009: 6^{0}G, 8^{0}G,

	Starts	1st	2nd	3rd	Win & Pl
Career Total (Turf)	2	0	0	0	

Going (Turf): **Sf: 0-0 GS: 0-0 Gd: 0-2 GF: 0-0 Fm: 0-0**
Distance: 5f/6f: 0-0 7f-8f: 0-1 9f-13f: 0-1 14f+: 0-0
Track : LH: 0-1 RH: 0-0 Tight: 0-1 Gall: 0-0
Aids: Bl: 0-0 Vi: 0-0 Tstrap: 0-0 Ckp: 0-0
Best Rating: **15** 10/09 Newb 6f110y good

Green For Luck (IRE)

91 **63**

2-y-o b c Key Of Luck (USA)-Kasota (IRE) (Alzao (USA))
S Gollings (T P Tate 27/6) P J Martin

Placings:0630 **(6533)**
2009: 6^{0}GS, 7^{6}GF, 8^{3}GF, 10^{0}GF,

	Starts	1st	2nd	3rd	Win & Pl
Career Total (Turf)	4	0	0	1	755

Going (Turf): **Sf: 0-0 GS: 0-1 Gd: 0-0 GF: 0-3 Fm: 0-0**
Distance: 5f/6f: 0-1 7f-8f: 0-1 9f-13f: 0-2 14f+: 0-0
Track : LH: 0-1 RH: 0-0 Tight: 0-0 Gall: 0-0
Aids: Bl: 0-0 Vi: 0-0 Tstrap: 0-0 Ckp: 0-0
Best Rating: **63** 6/09 Donc 7f gd-fm

Green Lagonda (AUS)

105(102) (61)**75**

7-y-o gr g Crown Jester (AUS)-Fidelis (AUS) (John's Hope (AUS))
P D Evans (Stef Liddiard 23/6) M D Jones

Placings:02312/4000320/530610010/00**00104010**/205033-**5553250**30**3**0203314021**6**0**1**20**3** **(6791)**
2009: **6^{5}**SD, **5^{5}**SD, **5^{5}**SD, **5^{3}**SF, **5^{2}**SD, **6^{5}**SD, **5^{0}**SD, 5^{3}GS, 5^{0}GF, 5^{3}SD, 6^{0}G, 5^{2}GF, 6^{0}GF, 5^{3}GF, 5^{3}G, 5^{1}GF, 5^{4}GF, 5^{0}G, 5^{2}GS, 5^{1}F, 5^{6}G, **6^{0}**SD, 5^{1}F, 5^{2}F, **5^{0}**SD,

	Starts	1st	2nd	3rd	Win & Pl
Career Total (Turf)	45	6	7	9	49728
Career Total (AW)	18	2	1	2	5455

71	9/09	Bath	5f11y		FRM	£2266
67	8/09	Brig	5f59y	(0-65)H	FRM	£2460
61	7/09	Folk	5f	(0-70)H	G-F	£3070
70	12/07	Wolv	5f216y		STD	£2047
66	10/07	Kemp	5f	(0-60)H	STD	£2047
	10/06	EagF	6f		GD	£3611
	9/06	Gcoa	5f		GD	£2777
	11/04	EagF	5f	H	GD	£13445

Total win prize-money £31729

Going (Turf): Sf: 0-5 GS: 0-4 **Gd: 3-23** GF: 1-10 Fm: 2-3
Distance: **5f/6f: 8-60** 7f-8f: 0-2 9f-13f: 0-0 14f+: 0-0
Track : **LH: 3-16** RH: 1-9 Tight: 1-9 Gall: 1-6
Aids: Bl: 0-0 Vi: 0-0 Tstrap: 0-1 Ckp: 0-1
Best Rating: **75** 9/09 Bath 5f11y firm

Modest; best over 5f-6f; handles good and faster ground and Polytrack.

Green Lightning (IRE)

94 **78**

2-y-o b c Montjeu (IRE)-Angelic Song (CAN) (Halo (USA))
M Johnston The Green Dot Partnership

Placings:661 **(7244)**
2009: 7^{6}G, 8^{6}G, 8^{1}S,

	Starts	1st	2nd	3rd	Win & Pl
Career Total (Turf)	3	1	0	0	4209

78	11/09	Nott	1m75y	SFT	£4209

Total win prize-money £4209

Going (Turf): **Sf: 1-1** GS: 0-0 Gd: 0-2 GF: 0-0 Fm: 0-0
Distance: 5f/6f: 0-0 7f-8f: 0-1 **9f-13f: 1-2** 14f+: 0-0
Track : **LH: 1-2** RH: 0-1 Tight: 0-0 Gall: 0-0
Aids: Bl: 0-0 Vi: 0-0 Tstrap: 0-0 Ckp: 0-0
Best Rating: **78** 11/09 Nott 1m75y soft

Fair; effective over 1m; acts on soft ground.

Green Manalishi

109(110) (109)**106**

8-y-o b g Green Desert (USA)-Silca-Cisa (Hallgate)
K A Ryan Mrs S McCarthy, J Brennan & J Smith

Placings:0522551/**42**21031550000/0051142010**44**/**6**61325 6104500/1506010465/6**3**1100-**0**500004314**5140** **(7488)**
2009: **5^{0}**SD, 5^{5}GF, 5^{0}G, 5^{0}GF, 5^{0}GF, 5^{0}GF, 5^{4}GF, 6^{3}G, 5^{1}GF, 6^{4}G, 5^{5}SD, **5^{1}**SD, **6^{4}**SD, **6^{0}**SD,

	Starts	1st	2nd	3rd	Win & Pl
Career Total (Turf)	63	12	5	3	204869
Career Total (AW)	12	2	1	1	26066

109	11/09	Ling	5f	(0-95)H	STD	£9066
102	9/09	Hayd	5f	(0-100)H	G-F	£16190
106	8/08	Ches	6f18y		GD	£24978
87	7/08	Ches	5f16y		GD	£24978
104	8/07	Ches	6f18y		G-F	£14762
113	4/07	Newb	5f34y	(0-110)H	G-F	£9971
106	7/06	Ling	5f	(0-105)H	STD	£12464
106	4/06	Newb	5f34y	(0-110)H	GD	£12464
106	9/05	Hayd	5f	(0-100)H	G-S	£20792
101	8/05	Newb	5f34y	(0-85)H	G-S	£6151
88	8/05	Sand	5f6y	(0-80)H	GD	£5837
94	6/04	NmkJ	5f	B(0-105)H	G-F	£13624
93	5/04	Wind	5f10y	D(0-85)H	G-F	£5622
80	10/03	Ling	5f	D	G-F	£3157

Total win prize-money £180062

Going (Turf): Sf: 0-7 GS: 2-5 Gd: 4-20 **GF: 6-31** Fm: 0-0
Distance: **5f/6f: 12-73** 7f-8f: 2-2 9f-13f: 0-0 14f+: 0-0
Track : **LH: 5-20** RH: 0-1 **Tight: 5-17** Gall: 1-4
Aids: Bl: 0-1 Vi: 0-0 Tstrap: 2-8 Ckp: 2-8
Best Rating: **113** 4/07 Newb 5f34y gd-fm

Smart; winner in Listed company; effective at 5f-6f; acts on most ground on turf; goes on Polytrack; has worn blinkers and cheekpieces.

Green Moon (IRE)

98 **79**

2-y-o b c Montjeu (IRE)-Green Noon (FR) (Green Tune (USA))
H J L Dunlop Mrs Ben Goldsmith

Placings:04 **(7029)**
2009: 8^{0}G, 8^{4}S,

	Starts	1st	2nd	3rd	Win & Pl
Career Total (Turf)	2	0	0	0	361

Going (Turf): **Sf: 0-1 GS: 0-0 Gd: 0-1 GF: 0-0 Fm: 0-0**

Distance: 5f/6f: 0-0 7f-8f: 0-2 9f-13f: 0-0 14f+: 0-0
Track : LH: 0-0 RH: 0-0 Tight: 0-0 Gall: 0-0
Aids: Bl: 0-0 Vi: 0-0 Tstrap: 0-0 Ckp: 0-0
Best Rating: **79** 10/09 Newb 1m soft

Green Onions

99(99) (70)**67**
3-y-o b g Royal Applause-Tremiere (FR) (Anabaa (USA))
A J Lidderdale (D J S Ffrench Davis 27/7) Smart Racing Ltd

Placings:0635-1034626000000 **(7770)**
2009: 6^1SD, 6^0SD, 5^3SD, 5^4SD, 5^6GF, 5^2GS, 5^6G, 5^0S, 6^0SD, 5^0SD, 6^0SD, 8^0SD, 6^0SD,

	Starts	1st	2nd	3rd	Win & Pl
Career Total (Turf)	5	0	1	0	1638
Career Total (AW)	12	1	0	2	3976

69 1/09 GrLe 6f STD £2590
Total win prize-money £2590

Going (Turf): **Sf: 0-1 GS: 0-1 Gd: 0-2 GF: 0-1 Fm: 0-0**
Distance: **5f/6f: 1-15** 7f-8f: 0-2 9f-13f: 0-0 14f+: 0-0
Track : **LH: 1-9** RH: 0-2 Tight: 0-5 **Gall: 1-3**
Aids: Bl: 0-3 Vi: 0-0 Tstrap: 0-1 Ckp: 0-1
Best Rating: **70** 1/09 Wolv 5f20y stand

Fair; effective over 5f-6f; acts on Polytrack and easy ground on turf; has worn cheekpieces.

Green Park (IRE)

100(107) (89)**94**
6-y-o b g Shinko Forest (IRE)-Danccini (IRE) (Dancing Dissident (USA))
D Carroll G A Fixings Ltd

Placings:2110040/021360006040/305301030006/042000 00210360-000346003536**1000061** **(7646)**
2009: 8^0GF, 5^0G, 6^0GF, 5^3GS, 6^4G, 5^6GF, 5^0GF, 6^0GF, 5^3G, 6^5G, 5^3GF, 5^6HY, 5^1SD, 5^0SD, 5^0GF, 5^0SD, 6^0SD, 5^6SD, 5^1SD,

	Starts	1st	2nd	3rd	Win & Pl
Career Total (Turf)	57	5	4	7	80898
Career Total (AW)	7	2	0	1	11441

82 12/09 Wolv 5f20y (0-85)H STD £5046
82 10/09 Wolv 5f216y (0-80)H STD £5046
94 9/08 Ches 5f16y (0-85)H G-S £5504
96 6/07 Newc 5f (0-105)H HVY £18696
96 5/06 Thsk 5f (0-100)H HVY £12954
86 5/05 Wind 5f10y G-F £12006
77 5/05 Ling 5f GD £4225
Total win prize-money £63478

Going (Turf): **Sf: 2-12** GS: 1-8 Gd: 1-18 GF: 1-19 Fm: 0-0
Distance: **5f/6f: 7-63** 7f-8f: 0-1 9f-13f: 0-0 14f+: 0-0
Track : **LH: 3-12** RH: 0-0 **Tight: 3-9** Gall: 1-2
Aids: **Bl: 3-24** Vi: 0-0 Tstrap: 0-0 Ckp: 0-0
Best Rating: **98** 7/07 York 6f heavy

Fair; seems best at 5f; acts on most ground on turf, but probably best with cut; goes on Fibresand and Polytrack; has worn blinkers.

Green Passion (USA)

90(92) (69)**48**
3-y-o b/br g Forestry (USA)-Date Stone (USA) (Forty Niner (USA))
M Johnston The Green Dot Partnership

Placings:0-360 **(6490)**
2009: 9^3SD, 10^6SD, 10^0GF,

	Starts	1st	2nd	3rd	Win & Pl
Career Total (Turf)	2	0	0	0	
Career Total (AW)	2	0	0	1	403

Going (Turf): **Sf: 0-0 GS: 0-0 Gd: 0-0 GF: 0-2 Fm: 0-0**
Distance: 5f/6f: 0-0 7f-8f: 0-1 9f-13f: 0-3 14f+: 0-0
Track : LH: 0-3 RH: 0-0 Tight: 0-3 Gall: 0-0
Aids: Bl: 0-0 Vi: 0-0 Tstrap: 0-0 Ckp: 0-0
Best Rating: **69** 1/09 Ling 1m2f stand

Modest; effective over 1m2f; acts on Polytrack.

Green Poppy

96(89) (34)**63**
3-y-o b f Green Desert (USA)-Vimy Ridge (FR) (Indian Ridge)
B Smart (Eve Johnson Houghton 6/7) Jeffrey Hobby

Placings:43260-605030 **(6856)**
2009: 6^6F, 8^0G, 6^5F, 5^0GF, 5^3GF, 5^0SD,

	Starts	1st	2nd	3rd	Win & Pl
Career Total (Turf)	10	0	1	2	2190
Career Total (AW)	1	0	0	0	

Going (Turf): **Sf: 0-0 GS: 0-1 Gd: 0-2 GF: 0-5 Fm: 0-2**
Distance: 5f/6f: 0-9 7f-8f: 0-2 9f-13f: 0-0 14f+: 0-0
Track : LH: 0-5 RH: 0-1 Tight: 0-1 Gall: 0-2
Aids: Bl: 0-0 Vi: 0-0 Tstrap: 0-0 Ckp: 0-0
Best Rating: **63** 6/08 Wwck 5f gd-fm

Moderate; suited by 5f and fast ground.

Green Shoots

70(66) (7)**2**
2-y-o b f Reset (AUS)-Cryptogam (Zamindar (USA))
M E Sowersby R D Seldon

Placings:0000 **(6821)**
2009: 6^0GF, 6^0GF, 5^0SF, 8^0GF,

	Starts	1st	2nd	3rd	Win & Pl
Career Total (Turf)	3	0	0	0	
Career Total (AW)	1	0	0	0	

Going (Turf): **Sf: 0-0 GS: 0-0 Gd: 0-0 GF: 0-3 Fm: 0-0**
Distance: 5f/6f: 0-2 7f-8f: 0-2 9f-13f: 0-0 14f+: 0-0
Track : LH: 0-1 RH: 0-0 Tight: 0-1 Gall: 0-0
Aids: Bl: 0-0 Vi: 0-0 Tstrap: 0-0 Ckp: 0-0
Best Rating: **7** 10/09 Wolv 5f20y std-fst

Green Spirit (IRE)

56
3-y-o b g Invincible Spirit (IRE)-Randonneur (IRE) (Red Sunset)
Patrick Morris R M Green

Placings:00 **(1400)**
2009: 7^0GF, 6^0F,

	Starts	1st	2nd	3rd	Win & Pl
Career Total (Turf)	2	0	0	0	

Going (Turf): **Sf: 0-0 GS: 0-0 Gd: 0-0 GF: 0-1 Fm: 0-1**
Distance: 5f/6f: 0-1 7f-8f: 0-1 9f-13f: 0-0 14f+: 0-0
Track : LH: 0-1 RH: 0-0 Tight: 0-0 Gall: 0-0
Aids: Bl: 0-0 Vi: 0-0 Tstrap: 0-0 Ckp: 0-0

Green Velvet

96(107) (64)**64**
4-y-o b f Iron Mask (USA)-Scarlett Ribbon (Most Welcome)
P J Makin Mrs P J Makin

Placings:02035-431104252 **(7602)**
2009: 5^4SD, 6^3SD, 5^1SD, 6^1SD, 5^0GF, 5^4GF, 6^2GF, 6^5GF, 6^2SD,

	Starts	1st	2nd	3rd	Win & Pl
Career Total (Turf)	4	0	1	0	964
Career Total (AW)	10	2	2	2	5638

64 3/09 Ling 6f (0-55)H STD £2047
62 3/09 Ling 5f (0-52)H STD £1706
Total win prize-money £3753

Going (Turf): **Sf: 0-0 GS: 0-0 Gd: 0-0 GF: 0-4 Fm: 0-0**
Distance: **5f/6f: 2-14** 7f-8f: 0-0 9f-13f: 0-0 14f+: 0-0
Track : **LH: 2-11** RH: 0-1 **Tight: 2-8** Gall: 0-1
Aids: Bl: 0-0 Vi: 0-0 Tstrap: 0-0 Ckp: 0-0
Best Rating: **64** 12/09 Ling 6f stand

Modest; stays 6f; acts on Polytrack.

Green Wadi

(106) (81)**76**
4-y-o b g Dansili-Peryllys (Warning)
G L Moore Andrew Bradmore

Placings:233/40301-30 **(7684)**
2009: 12^3SD, 10^0SD,

	Starts	1st	2nd	3rd	Win & Pl
Career Total (Turf)	7	1	1	3	5764
Career Total (AW)	3	0	0	1	1057

73 6/08 Bath 1m3f144y FRM £2719
Total win prize-money £2720

Going (Turf): Sf: 0-1 GS: 0-0 Gd: 0-1 GF: 0-4 **Fm: 1-1**
Distance: 5f/6f: 0-0 7f-8f: 0-3 **9f-13f: 1-7** 14f+: 0-0
Track : **LH: 1-6** RH: 0-4 **Tight: 1-5** Gall: 0-0
Aids: Bl: 0-0 Vi: 0-0 Tstrap: 0-0 Ckp: 0-0
Best Rating: **88** 9/07 Gdwd 1m gd-fm

Fair; stays 1m4f; acts on fast ground and on Polytrack.

Greenbelt

93(97) (62)**56**
8-y-o b g Desert Prince (IRE)-Emerald (USA) (El Gran Senor (USA))
G M Moore Mrs A Roddis

Placings:4311/**020213/33124**3020006**060/01200**050/0-320443 **(7093)**
2009: 12^3SD, 12^2SD, 12^0GS, 12^4SD, 12^4GS, 11^3SD,

	Starts	1st	2nd	3rd	Win & Pl
Career Total (Turf)	16	2	1	2	20028
Career Total (AW)	24	3	5	5	15461

65 2/07 Sthl 1m3f (0-75)H STD £3241
77 2/06 Sthl 1m3f (0-70)H STD £3238
64 12/05 Sthl 1m (0-55)H STD £2491
7/04 Claf 1m1f VS £8099
5/04 Lonc 1m110y VS £6690
Total win prize-money £23761

Going (Turf): **Sf: 0-4 GS: 0-5 Gd: 0-4 GF: 0-0 Fm: 0-0**
Distance: 5f/6f: 0-0 7f-8f: 1-9 **9f-13f: 4-29** 14f+: 0-2
Track : **LH: 3-35** RH: 0-2 Tight: 0-5 Gall: 0-4
Aids: Bl: 0-0 Vi: 0-0 Tstrap: 0-1 Ckp: 0-1
Best Rating: **80** 3/04 Lonc 1m holding

Modest; stays 1m4f; acts on Fibresand and Polytrack.

Greenisland (IRE)

107(98) (82)**99**

3-y-o b f Fasliyev (USA)-Green Castle (IRE) (Indian Ridge)

H Morrison Stonethorn Stud Farms Limited

Placings:331-300130030 **(7132)**

2009: 8³S, 8⁰GS, 8⁰GF, 7¹G, 8³G, 7⁰G, 6⁰GF, 7³GF, 8⁰SD,

	Starts	1st	2nd	3rd	Win & Pl
Career Total (Turf)	9	1	0	4	37131
Career Total (AW)	3	1	0	1	5111

95 7/09 NmkJ 7f (0-100)H GD £24924
75 11/08 Kemp 1m STD £4533
Total win prize-money £29457

Going (Turf): Sf: 0-1 GS: 0-1 **Gd: 1-4** GF: 0-3 Fm: 0-0
Distance: 5f/6f: 0-1 **7f-8f: 2-11** 9f-13f: 0-0 14f+: 0-0
Track : LH: 0-4 **RH: 1-4** Tight: 0-2 Gall: 0-2
Aids: Bl: 0-0 Vi: 0-0 Tstrap: 0-0 Ckp: 0-0
Best Rating: **99** 9/09 Asct 7f gd-fm

Useful; Listed placed; stays 1m and acts on Polytrack.

Greenore Gordon

67 **14**

2-y-o ch g Namid-Approaching Storm (IRE) (Entrepreneur)

M S Saunders A P Holland

Placings:00 **(4219)**

2009: 5⁰G, 5⁰G,

	Starts	1st	2nd	3rd	Win & Pl
Career Total (Turf)	2	0	0	0	

Going (Turf): **Sf: 0-0 GS: 0-0 Gd: 0-2 GF: 0-0 Fm: 0-0**
Distance: 5f/6f: 0-2 7f-8f: 0-0 9f-13f: 0-0 14f+: 0-0
Track : LH: 0-1 RH: 0-0 Tight: 0-0 Gall: 0-2
Aids: Bl: 0-0 Vi: 0-0 Tstrap: 0-0 Ckp: 0-0
Best Rating: **14** 7/09 Bath 5f161y good

Greensward

98 **83**

3-y-o b g Green Desert (USA)-Frizzante (Efisio)

B J Meehan Lady Rothschild

Placings:513-624 **(3801)**

2009: 7⁶GF, 7²G, 7⁴GF,

	Starts	1st	2nd	3rd	Win & Pl
Career Total (Turf)	6	1	1	1	9323

79 8/08 NmkJ 6f GD £5180
Total win prize-money £5181

Going (Turf): Sf: 0-0 GS: 0-0 **Gd: 1-4** GF: 0-2 Fm: 0-0
Distance: **5f/6f: 1-1** 7f-8f: 0-5 9f-13f: 0-0 14f+: 0-0
Track : LH: 0-0 RH: 0-1 Tight: 0-0 Gall: 0-0
Aids: Bl: 0-0 Vi: 0-0 Tstrap: 0-0 Ckp: 0-0
Best Rating: **83** 6/09 Sand 7f16y good

Useful; stays 7f; acts on good ground.

Greenwich Meantime

(98) (92)**94**

9-y-o b g Royal Academy (USA)-Shirley Valentine (Shirley Heights)

Mme C Barande-Barbe (F Chappet 17/9) J Phelippon

Placings:3221/0300300560431**313**/2122442511/1131305/10000403/05206604-3621235

2009: 16³SD, 16⁶SD, 14²GS, 12¹SD, 12²G, 12³G, 13⁵VS,

	Starts	1st	2nd	3rd	Win & Pl
Career Total (Turf)	50	8	8	8	179766
Career Total (AW)	10	3	1	3	16779

75 8/09 Deau 1m4f STD £7282
105 5/07 Ches 2m2f147y H G-F £74784
101 6/06 Ayr 1m5f13y (0-95)H GD £9067
93 4/06 Ripn 2m (0-100)H GD £12464
85 4/06 Thsk 1m4f (0-75)H GD £3886
77 8/05 Ripn 2m (0-75)H G-F £4004
74 8/05 Hayd 1m6f (0-70)H G-F £3806
73 3/05 Donc 1m4f (0-70)H GD £3601
74 12/04 Wolv 2m119y (0-77)H STD £3381
75 11/04 Wolv 1m4f50y (0-62)H STD £2609
83 10/03 Newc 1m4f93y D GD £2597
Total win prize-money £127483

Going (Turf): Sf: 0-1 GS: 0-9 **Gd: 5-17** GF: 3-19 Fm: 0-3
Distance: 5f/6f: 0-0 7f-8f: 0-0 9f-13f: 5-15 **14f+: 6-45**
Track : **LH: 8-38** RH: 2-20 **Tight: 6-23** Gall: 2-18
Aids: Bl: 0-0 Vi: 0-0 Tstrap: 0-1 Ckp: 0-1
Best Rating: **105** 5/07 Ches 2m2f147y gd-fm

Useful; winner of the 2007 Chester Cup; stays 2m2f, but effective over shorter; acts on most ground and on sand; usually held up.

Greenwich Village

103(102) (88)**78**

6-y-o b g Mtoto-D'Azy (Persian Bold)

W J Knight Ecurie Franglaise

Placings:0/**3430**/63321101-130 **(3103)**

2009: 16¹SD, 16³SD, 14⁰G,

	Starts	1st	2nd	3rd	Win & Pl
Career Total (Turf)	8	1	1	2	4324
Career Total (AW)	8	3	0	3	16144

88 1/09 Kemp 2m (0-85)H STD £4727
84 12/08 Ling 2m (0-85)H STD £4857
77 8/08 GrLe 1m6f (0-80)H STD £4857
71 7/08 Ling 2m (0-70)H FRM £2590
Total win prize-money £17031

Going (Turf): Sf: 0-0 GS: 0-1 Gd: 0-3 GF: 0-3 **Fm: 1-1**
Distance: 5f/6f: 0-0 7f-8f: 0-1 9f-13f: 0-8 **14f+: 4-7**
Track : **LH: 3-10** RH: 1-6 **Tight: 2-10** Gall: 1-3
Aids: Bl: 0-0 Vi: 0-0 Tstrap: 0-0 Ckp: 0-0
Best Rating: **88** 1/09 Kemp 2m stand

Useful; stays 2m; acts on fast ground; goes on Polytrack.

Gremlin

(87) (66)**72**

5-y-o b g Mujahid (USA)-Fairy Free (Rousillon (USA))

D Burchell (I W McInnes 22/6) Jason Tucker

Placings:24223/120/006-2 **(3223)**

2009: 12²SD,

	Starts	1st	2nd	3rd	Win & Pl
Career Total (Turf)	11	1	4	1	18572
Career Total (AW)	1	0	1	0	608

87 5/07 Sals 1m1f198y (0-80)H G-F £5181
Total win prize-money £5182

Going (Turf): Sf: 0-2 GS: 0-1 Gd: 0-1 **GF: 1-7** Fm: 0-0
Distance: 5f/6f: 0-4 7f-8f: 0-1 **9f-13f: 1-7** 14f+: 0-0
Track : LH: 0-3 **RH: 1-5 Tight: 1-3** Gall: 0-3
Aids: Bl: 0-1 Vi: 0-0 Tstrap: 0-0 Ckp: 0-0
Best Rating: **87** 5/07 Sals 1m1f198y gd-fm

Useful gelding; stays 1m2f; acts on fast but handles easy ground.

Grethel (IRE)

96(88) (35)**65**

5-y-o b m Fruits Of Love (USA)-Stay Sharpe (USA) (Sharpen Up)

A Berry Mrs Linda White

Placings:0560/600000543301043300**1**0/06056013503001 03060030-60066524506506000066**0** **(6840)**

2009: 9⁶GF, 9⁰GF, 8⁰G, 10⁶G, 10⁶GS, 8⁵GF, 9²G, 9⁴GF, 8⁵GF, 9⁰GF, 10⁶HY, 7⁵G, 8⁰G, 12⁶S, 9⁰GF, 12⁰GS, 12⁰G, 11⁰GS, 10⁶GF, 12⁶GF, 11⁰G,

	Starts	1st	2nd	3rd	Win & Pl
Career Total (Turf)	65	4	1	8	19124
Career Total (AW)	2	0	0	0	

65 8/08 Hayd 1m2f120y (0-75)H G-S £3238
55 6/08 Haml 1m1f36y (0-70)H G-F £3238
61 10/07 Ayr 1m1f20y SFT £2914
58 9/07 Bevl 1m100y (0-55) G-F £2730
Total win prize-money £12121

Going (Turf): Sf: 1-13GS: 1-15Gd: 0-18 **GF: 2-18** Fm: 0-1
Distance: 5f/6f: 0-3 7f-8f: 0-13 **9f-13f: 4-51** 14f+: 0-0
Track : LH: 2-34 RH: 2-28 **Tight: 1-24** Gall: 0-2
Aids: Bl: 0-0 Vi: 0-0 Tstrap: 0-0 Ckp: 0-0
Best Rating: **65** 8/08 Haml 1m1f36y soft

Modest; stays 1m2f; acts on a sound and soft surface.

Grey Boy (GER)

104(105) (84)**76**

8-y-o gr g Medaaly-Grey Perri (Siberian Express (USA))

A W Carroll Paul Downing

Placings:0/05/501100300/22110**200**/**4442**0003050/030505 166135-0410363400006566**0** **(7741)**

2009: 8⁰SD, 8⁴G, 7¹SD, 8⁰GF, 7³GF, 7⁶GF, 7³SD, 8⁴G, 8⁰GF, 7⁰G, 6⁰GF, 6⁰GS, 7⁶SD, 8⁵G, 8⁶SD, 8⁶SD, 7⁰SD,

	Starts	1st	2nd	3rd	Win & Pl
Career Total (Turf)	44	5	3	5	37019
Career Total (AW)	16	2	1	1	6707

84 4/09 Kemp 7f (0-70)H STD £2590
79 9/08 Kemp 1m (0-65)H STD £2047
71 7/08 Ling 7f140y (0-65)H FRM £2047
87 6/06 Ripn 1m (0-95)H G-F £9348
87 5/06 Yarm 7f3y (0-85)H GD £6232
77 7/05 Nott 1m54y (0-75)H GD £3628
71 6/05 Newb 1m (0-75)H G-F £4280
Total win prize-money £30172

Going (Turf): Sf: 0-2 GS: 0-6 **Gd: 2-15 GF: 2-17** Fm: 1-4
Distance: 5f/6f: 0-6 **7f-8f: 6-42** 9f-13f: 1-12 14f+: 0-0
Track : LH: 1-24 **RH: 3-13 Tight: 1-16** Gall: 0-4
Aids: Bl: 0-0 Vi: 0-0 Tstrap: 0-0 Ckp: 0-0
Best Rating: **88** 7/06 York 1m gd-fm

Fair; effective over 7f-1m; acts on most ground on turf; also goes on Polytrack.

Grey Bunting

88(90) (57)**63**

2-y-o gr c Oasis Dream-Ribbons And Bows (IRE) (Dr Devious (IRE))

B W Hills The Hon Mrs J M Corbett & C Wright

Placings:64 **(7050)**

2009: 6⁶G, 7⁴SD,

	Starts	1st	2nd	3rd	Win & Pl
Career Total (Turf)	1	0	0	0	0
Career Total (AW)	1	0	0	0	289

Going (Turf): **Sf: 0-0 GS: 0-0 Gd: 0-1 GF: 0-0 Fm: 0-0**
Distance: 5f/6f: 0-0 7f-8f: 0-2 9f-13f: 0-0 14f+: 0-0

Track : LH: 0-0 RH: 0-1 Tight: 0-0 Gall: 0-0
Aids: Bl: 0-0 Vi: 0-0 Tstrap: 0-0 Ckp: 0-0
Best Rating: 63 10/09 Newb 6f110y good

Grey Command (USA)

96(98) (58)74
4-y-o gr c Daylami (IRE)-Shmoose (IRE) (Caerleon (USA))
M Brittain Mel Brittain

Placings:003426200-00520466502 (7719)
2009: 7^{0}GS, 10^{0}GS, 11^{5}GF, 10^{2}G, 12^{0}GS, 12^{4}GS, 10^{6}G, 9^{6}GF, 10^{5}GF, 10^{0}GF, 9^{2}SD,

	Starts	1st	2nd	3rd	Win & Pl
Career Total (Turf)	19	0	3	1	3998
Career Total (AW)	1	0	1	0	605

Going (Turf): Sf: 0-3 GS: 0-5 Gd: 0-3 GF: 0-8 Fm: 0-0
Distance: 5f/6f: 0-0 7f-8f: 0-4 9f-13f: 0-16 14f+: 0-0
Track : LH: 0-12 RH: 0-5 Tight: 0-6 Gall: 0-7
Aids: Bl: 0-0 Vi: 0-0 Tstrap: 0-0 Ckp: 0-0
Best Rating: 74 8/08 Newc 1m1f9y soft

Moderate; effective over 1m2f; acts on good ground and Polytrack.

Grey Garth (IRE)

67 21
2-y-o gr g Verglas (IRE)-Again Royale (IRE) (Royal Academy (USA))
J D Bethell Clarendon Thoroughbred Racing

Placings:6 (3392)
2009: 6^{6}S,

	Starts	1st	2nd	3rd	Win & Pl
Career Total (Turf)	1	0	0	0	117

Going (Turf): Sf: 0-1 GS: 0-0 Gd: 0-0 GF: 0-0 Fm: 0-0
Distance: 5f/6f: 0-1 7f-8f: 0-0 9f-13f: 0-0 14f+: 0-0
Track : LH: 0-0 RH: 0-0 Tight: 0-0 Gall: 0-0
Aids: Bl: 0-0 Vi: 0-0 Tstrap: 0-0 Ckp: 0-0
Best Rating: 21 6/09 Newc 6f soft

Grey Granite (IRE)

103 84
3-y-o gr c Dalakhani (IRE)-Royal Ballerina (IRE) (Sadler's Wells (USA))
W Jarvis Dr J Walker

Placings:6-51 (2199)
2009: 12^{5}GF, 10^{1}S,

	Starts	1st	2nd	3rd	Win & Pl
Career Total (Turf)	3	1	0	0	3238

84 5/09 Hayd 1m2f95y SFT £3238
Total win prize-money £3238

Going (Turf): Sf: 1-2 GS: 0-0 Gd: 0-0 GF: 0-1 Fm: 0-0
Distance: 5f/6f: 0-0 7f-8f: 0-0 9f-13f: 1-3 14f+: 0-0
Track : LH: 1-2 RH: 0-0 Tight: 0-1 Gall: 0-0
Aids: Bl: 0-0 Vi: 0-0 Tstrap: 0-0 Ckp: 0-0
Best Rating: 84 5/09 Hayd 1m2f95y soft

Useful; effective over 1m2f; acts on soft ground.

Grey Gurkha

88(98) (31)42
8-y-o gr h Kasakov-Royal Rebeka (Grey Desire)
I W McInnes Robert E Cook

Placings:606/6001/2450002000-0000000 (7586)
2009: 8^{0}GF, 7^{0}GF, 8^{0}SD, 8^{0}GS, 7^{0}G, 8^{0}GF, 8^{0}SD,

	Starts	1st	2nd	3rd	Win & Pl
Career Total (Turf)	13	0	1	0	578
Career Total (AW)	11	1	1	0	2652

61 12/07 Kemp 1m (0-55)H STD £2047
Total win prize-money £2048

Going (Turf): Sf: 0-1 GS: 0-3 Gd: 0-3 GF: 0-6 Fm: 0-0
Distance: 5f/6f: 0-3 7f-8f: 1-12 9f-13f: 0-9 14f+: 0-0
Track : LH: 0-8 RH: 1-11 Tight: 0-7 Gall: 0-0
Aids: Bl: 0-0 Vi: 0-0 Tstrap: 0-1 Ckp: 0-1
Best Rating: 61 2/08 Kemp 1m stand

Moderate; effective over 1m; acts on good ground.

Greyfriarschorista

85 61
2-y-o ch c King's Best (USA)-Misty Heights (Fasliyev (USA))
M Johnston Greyfriars UK Ltd

Placings:4 (4618)
2009: 7^{4}G,

	Starts	1st	2nd	3rd	Win & Pl
Career Total (Turf)	1	0	0	0	241

Going (Turf): Sf: 0-0 GS: 0-0 Gd: 0-1 GF: 0-0 Fm: 0-0
Distance: 5f/6f: 0-0 7f-8f: 0-1 9f-13f: 0-0 14f+: 0-0
Track : LH: 0-1 RH: 0-0 Tight: 0-1 Gall: 0-0
Aids: Bl: 0-0 Vi: 0-0 Tstrap: 0-0 Ckp: 0-0
Best Rating: 61 8/09 Catt 7f good

Greylami (IRE)

108(110) (95)98
4-y-o gr g Daylami (IRE)-Silent Crystal (USA) (Diesis)
T G Mills J Daniels

Placings:526/143033315-4100203320 (6480)
2009: 11^{4}SD, 11^{1}SD, 10^{0}G, 12^{0}GS, 10^{2}G, 12^{0}G, 10^{3}GF, 9^{3}GF, 10^{2}G, 9^{0}GF,

	Starts	1st	2nd	3rd	Win & Pl
Career Total (Turf)	15	1	2	5	22209
Career Total (AW)	7	2	1	1	30763

95 3/09 Kemp 1m3f (0-105)H STD £24924
92 9/08 Gdwd 1m3f (0-85)H G-F £4857
74 2/08 Kemp 1m2f STD £2590
Total win prize-money £32372

Going (Turf): Sf: 0-1 GS: 0-1 Gd: 0-7 GF: 1-6 Fm: 0-0
Distance: 5f/6f: 0-0 7f-8f: 0-3 9f-13f: 3-19 14f+: 0-0
Track : LH: 0-4 RH: 3-17 Tight: 1-8 Gall: 0-4
Aids: Bl: 0-0 Vi: 0-0 Tstrap: 0-0 Ckp: 0-0
Best Rating: 98 7/09 Sand 1m2f7y good

Very useful; stays 1m3f; handles fast and soft ground; goes on Polytrack.

Greystoke Prince

84(103) (78)52
4-y-o gr g Diktat-Grey Princess (IRE) (Common Grounds)
P S McEntee (W R Swinburn 16/10) Aspen Bloodstock Ltd

Placings:64020/212200-005000000425 (7774)
2009: 7^{0}SD, 7^{0}SD, 7^{5}GF, 7^{0}SD, 7^{0}GF, 7^{0}SD, 7^{0}SF, 6^{0}SD, 7^{0}SD, 10^{4}SD, 8^{2}SD, 6^{5}SD,

	Starts	1st	2nd	3rd	Win & Pl
Career Total (Turf)	7	0	0	0	241
Career Total (AW)	16	1	5	0	6432

72 4/08 Kemp 7f (0-65)H STD £2047
Total win prize-money £2047

Going (Turf): Sf: 0-3 GS: 0-0 Gd: 0-2 GF: 0-2 Fm: 0-0
Distance: 5f/6f: 0-3 7f-8f: 1-19 9f-13f: 0-1 14f+: 0-0
Track : LH: 0-11 RH: 1-7 Tight: 0-9 Gall: 0-0
Aids: Bl: 0-1 Vi: 0-0 Tstrap: 0-6 Ckp: 0-6
Best Rating: 78 8/08 Kemp 7f stand

Moderate; effective at around 7f-1m; acts on Polytrack; has worn a tongue-tie.

Grimes Faith

97(105) (78)69
6-y-o b g Woodborough (USA)-Emma Grimes (IRE) (Nordico (USA))
R C Guest (K A Ryan 14/11) Future Racing (Notts) Limited

Placings:414120/23306502520002000/16006206300/1412362260504001302223-42211631160006004U00 (7852)
2009: 5^{4}SD, 5^{2}SD, 6^{2}SD, 5^{1}SD, 5^{1}SD, 5^{6}SD, 5^{3}SD, 5^{1}SD, 5^{1}SD, 5^{6}G, 5^{0}GS, 5^{0}G, 5^{0}GS, 5^{6}SD, 6^{0}G, 5^{0}S, 5^{4}S, 5^{U}SD, 5^{0}SD, 5^{0}SS,

	Starts	1st	2nd	3rd	Win & Pl
Career Total (Turf)	27	2	2	4	16098
Career Total (AW)	47	8	11	3	32954

77 3/09 Sthl 5f STD £2047
78 3/09 Sthl 5f (0-75)H STD £2729
76 2/09 Sthl 5f STD £1942
76 2/09 Sthl 5f STD £2047
69 9/08 Ayr 5f (0-70)H HVY £5051
79 1/08 Sthl 6f STD £1774
79 1/08 Sthl 5f STD £1774
89 1/07 Ling 7f (0-80)H STD £4857
76 5/05 Bath 5f11y FRM £3750
71 4/05 Ling 5f STD £2926
Total win prize-money £28903

Going (Turf): Sf: 1-7 GS: 0-7 Gd: 0-7 GF: 0-5 Fm: 1-1
Distance: 5f/6f: 9-55 7f-8f: 1-18 9f-13f: 0-1 14f+: 0-0
Track : LH: 4-34 RH: 0-8 Tight: 2-27 Gall: 1-3
Aids: Bl: 3-23 Vi: 0-0 Tstrap: 5-27 Ckp: 5-27
Best Rating: 91 9/06 Gdwd 1m good

Fair; effective from 5f-7f; acts on most ground on turf; goes on sand; has worn cheekpieces.

Gripsholm Castle (USA)

106 105
3-y-o b/br f Dynaformer (USA)-Randaroo (USA) (Gold Case (USA))
H R A Cecil Gestut Ammerland

Placings:1410 (6813)
2009: 10^{1}GF, 10^{4}GF, 10^{1}GF, 10^{0}G,

	Starts	1st	2nd	3rd	Win & Pl
Career Total (Turf)	4	2	0	0	20281

105 9/09 Hayd 1m2f95y (0-90)H G-F £12952
93 5/09 NmkR 1m2f G-F £5180
Total win prize-money £18133

Going (Turf): Sf: 0-0 GS: 0-0 Gd: 0-1 GF: 2-3 Fm: 0-0
Distance: 5f/6f: 0-0 7f-8f: 0-0 9f-13f: 2-4 14f+: 0-0
Track : LH: 1-2 RH: 0-0 Tight: 0-0 Gall: 0-1
Aids: Bl: 0-0 Vi: 0-0 Tstrap: 0-0 Ckp: 0-0
Best Rating: 105 9/09 Hayd 1m2f95y gd-fm

Very useful; effective over 1m2f; acts on fast ground.

Grissom (IRE)

104 **85**

3-y-o b g Desert Prince (IRE)-Misty Peak (IRE) (Sri Pekan (USA))

A Berry Jim & Helen Bowers

Placings:6044431-430105354120224 **(7220)**

2009: 5^4GF, 5^3GF, 5^0GS, 6^1G, 6^0G, 6^5S, 6^3GS, 6^5GS, 6^4GF, 6^1S, 5^2G, 6^0GF, 7^2S, 7^2S, 7^4S,

	Starts	1st	2nd	3rd	Win & Pl
Career Total (Turf)	22	3	3	3	24464

80	8/09	Ayr	6f	(0-75)H	SFT	£2914
75	6/09	Ayr	6f	(0-80)H	GD	£7123
71	11/08	Muss	5f	(0-85)	SFT	£5180

Total win prize-money £15219

Going (Turf): **Sf: 2-10** GS: 0-5 Gd: 1-3 GF: 0-4 Fm: 0-0
Distance: **5f/6f: 3-17** 7f-8f: 0-5 9f-13f: 0-0 14f+: 0-0
Track : LH: 0-6 RH: 0-0 Tight: 0-4 Gall: 0-0
Aids: Bl: 0-0 Vi: 0-0 Tstrap: 0-0 Ckp: 0-0
Best Rating: **85** 10/09 Ayr 7f50y soft

Fair; effective over 5f-6f; acts on good and soft ground.

Gritstone

92 **69**

2-y-o b g Dansili-Cape Trafalgar (IRE) (Cape Cross (IRE))

R A Fahey David W Armstrong

Placings:240 **(6478)**

2009: 7^2G, 7^4G, 7^0GF,

	Starts	1st	2nd	3rd	Win & Pl
Career Total (Turf)	3	0	1	0	1854

Going (Turf): **Sf: 0-0 GS: 0-0 Gd: 0-2 GF: 0-1 Fm: 0-0**
Distance: 5f/6f: 0-0 7f-8f: 0-3 9f-13f: 0-0 14f+: 0-0
Track : LH: 0-1 RH: 0-1 Tight: 0-0 Gall: 0-0
Aids: Bl: 0-0 Vi: 0-0 Tstrap: 0-0 Ckp: 0-0
Best Rating: **69** 10/09 NmkR 7f gd-fm

Cost 70,000gns; dam was a multiple winning juvenile sprinter before enjoying success in the US; effective over 7f; acts on good ground; modest promise in maiden company.

Grizedale (IRE)

92(102) (64)**61**

10-y-o ch g Lake Coniston (IRE)-Zabeta (Diesis)

M J Attwater Canisbay Bloodstock

Placings:23103/250243503/010020/5000006/04001002P/0 0664225302000/146005000/0004**244020000334**-000**65**0 **(5429)**

2009: 6^0SD, 7^0SD, 7^0GF, 7^6SD, 7^5SD, 7^0G,

	Starts	1st	2nd	3rd	Win & Pl
Career Total (Turf)	66	4	8	5	69552
Career Total (AW)	15	0	2	2	2030

83	5/07	NmkR	7f	(0-80)H	GD	£5181
84	8/05	Ling	7f140y	(0-75)H	G-S	£3517
99	5/03	Gdwd	7f	C(0-90)H	G-F	£10523
80	7/01	NmkJ	6f	E	G-F	£4163

Total win prize-money £23386

Going (Turf): Sf: 0-8 GS: 1-19 Gd: 1-18 **GF: 2-20** Fm: 0-1
Distance: 5f/6f: 1-12 **7f-8f: 3-69** 9f-13f: 0-0 14f+: 0-0
Track : LH: 0-10 **RH: 1-24** Tight: 0-6 Gall: 0-5
Aids: Bl: 0-0 Vi: 0-0 Tstrap: 0-18 Ckp: 0-18
Best Rating: **101** 9/03 Asct 7f gd-fm

Moderate; stays 1m; probably best with a little give in the ground; wears a tongue tie; has worn cheekpieces.

Groove Master

84 **57**

2-y-o b g Tobougg (IRE)-Magic Mistress (Magic Ring (IRE))

A King Brian J Griffiths and John Nicholson

Placings:005 **(6331)**

2009: 7^0HY, 8^0G, 10^5F,

	Starts	1st	2nd	3rd	Win & Pl
Career Total (Turf)	3	0	0	0	0

Going (Turf): **Sf: 0-1 GS: 0-0 Gd: 0-1 GF: 0-0 Fm: 0-1**
Distance: 5f/6f: 0-0 7f-8f: 0-1 9f-13f: 0-2 14f+: 0-0
Track : LH: 0-1 RH: 0-0 Tight: 0-1 Gall: 0-0
Aids: Bl: 0-0 Vi: 0-0 Tstrap: 0-0 Ckp: 0-0
Best Rating: **57** 8/09 Leic 7f9y heavy

Gross Prophet

106(101) (77)**82**

4-y-o b g Lujain (USA)-Done And Dusted (IRE) (Up And At 'Em)

A J Lidderdale (Tom Dascombe 15/7) Lambourn Valley Racing

Placings:04313213551/**560000002**0313021-13425020 **(7204)**

2009: 10^1GF, 12^3GF, 9^4GF, 10^2GF, 11^5SD, 12^0G, 9^2G, 10^0SD,

	Starts	1st	2nd	3rd	Win & Pl
Career Total (Turf)	20	3	3	5	18559
Career Total (AW)	15	3	2	1	12323

82	5/09	Chep	1m2f36y		G-F	£1942
72	10/08	Kemp	1m2f		STD	£2047
82	8/08	Wind	1m67y	(0-70)H	G-S	£2729
88	12/07	Wolv	5f216y		STD	£2817
89	9/07	Newb	6f8y	(0-85)	G-F	£4533
81	8/07	Wolv	5f216y		STD	£3886

Total win prize-money £17957

Going (Turf): Sf: 0-1 GS: 1-5 Gd: 0-6 **GF: 2-8** Fm: 0-0
Distance: 5f/6f: 2-11 7f-8f: 1-12 **9f-13f: 3-12** 14f+: 0-0
Track : **LH: 3-14** RH: 2-12 **Tight: 3-11** Gall: 0-3
Aids: Bl: 0-0 Vi: 0-0 Tstrap: 0-0 Ckp: 0-0
Best Rating: **89** 9/07 Newb 6f8y gd-fm

Fair; effective at around 1m2f; acts on fast ground; also goes on Polytrack.

Ground Patrol

84(103) (57)**19**

8-y-o b g Ashkalani (IRE)-Good Grounds (USA) (Alleged (USA))

N R Mitchell Mrs E Mitchell

Placings:0/3436004640/051020/0060/4500-0 **(2516)**

2009: 10^0F,

	Starts	1st	2nd	3rd	Win & Pl
Career Total (Turf)	7	0	1	0	1137
Career Total (AW)	19	1	0	2	4784

64	2/06	Ling	1m4f	(0-60)H	STD	£3238

Total win prize-money £3239

Going (Turf): **Sf: 0-0 GS: 0-1 Gd: 0-2 GF: 0-1 Fm: 0-3**
Distance: 5f/6f: 0-0 7f-8f: 0-5 **9f-13f: 1-21** 14f+: 0-0
Track : **LH: 1-24** RH: 0-2 **Tight: 1-22** Gall: 0-1
Aids: Bl: 0-1 Vi: 0-1 Tstrap: 0-1 Ckp: 0-1
Best Rating: **67** 10/04 Ling 1m2f stand

Moderate handicapper; effective at around 1m2f; acts on Polytrack.

Group Captain

105(104) (92)**96**

7-y-o b g Dr Fong (USA)-Alusha (Soviet Star (USA))

A Fracas (H J Collingridge 10/7) Peter Webb

Placings:54220230/10001410000**15**/0013210/03306100/5 000-05630030

2009: 12^0SD, 12^5G, 12^6G, 16^3SD, 12^0GF, 12^0GS, 15^3VS, 12^0HY,

	Starts	1st	2nd	3rd	Win & Pl
Career Total (Turf)	44	6	4	5	158670
Career Total (AW)	4	1	0	1	7910

116	7/07	Asct	1m4f	(0-105)H	SFT	£37392
110	11/06	Wind	1m3f135y	H	G-S	£31160
98	7/06	NmkJ	1m2f	(0-95)H	G-F	£11217
99	10/05	Donc	1m4f	(0-95)H	HVY	£12675
93	7/05	Gdwd	1m3f	(0-90)H	G-S	£14128
82	7/05	Sand	1m2f7y	(0-85)H	G-F	£8544
75	3/05	Ling	1m2f		STD	£6808

Total win prize-money £121928

Going (Turf): **Sf: 2-10GS: 2-11**Gd: 0-11 **GF: 2-10** Fm: 0-1
Distance: 5f/6f: 0-1 7f-8f: 0-6 **9f-13f: 7-35** 14f+: 0-6
Track : LH: 2-21 **RH: 4-18** Tight: 3-11 Gall: 3-17
Aids: Bl: 0-0 Vi: 0-0 Tstrap: 0-0 Ckp: 0-0
Best Rating: **116** 7/07 Asct 1m4f soft

Very useful; Listed placed; stays 1m5f, but effective at shorter; acts on most ground and Polytrack; very useful hurdler.

Group Leader (IRE)

90(94) (50)**64**

3-y-o ch g Noverre (USA)-Stem The Tide (USA) (Proud Truth (USA))

J R Jenkins D Badham

Placings:60-34000 **(7246)**

2009: 8^3HY, 8^4G, 9^0SD, 10^0G, 8^0S,

	Starts	1st	2nd	3rd	Win & Pl
Career Total (Turf)	5	0	0	1	596
Career Total (AW)	2	0	0	0	

Going (Turf): **Sf: 0-2 GS: 0-0 Gd: 0-2 GF: 0-1 Fm: 0-0**
Distance: 5f/6f: 0-2 7f-8f: 0-0 9f-13f: 0-5 14f+: 0-0
Track : LH: 0-5 RH: 0-1 Tight: 0-2 Gall: 0-0
Aids: Bl: 0-0 Vi: 0-1 Tstrap: 0-0 Ckp: 0-0
Best Rating: **64** 8/09 Nott 1m75y good

Group Therapy

109(95) (72)**109**

4-y-o ch g Choisir (AUS)-Licence To Thrill (Wolfhound (USA))

N P Littmoden Franconson Partners

Placings:6112/0-0050201000 **(6427)**

2009: 5^0GF, 5^0G, 5^5GF, 5^0G, 5^2GF, 5^0GF, 5^1G, 5^0GF, 5^0GF, 5^0GF,

	Starts	1st	2nd	3rd	Win & Pl
Career Total (Turf)	14	3	2	0	34068
Career Total (AW)	1	0	0	0	

109	8/09	Asct	5f	(0-105)H	GD	£17230
93	5/07	Thsk	5f		G-F	£5181
71	4/07	Nott	5f13y		G-F	£2817

Total win prize-money £25230

Going (Turf): Sf: 0-0 GS: 0-0 Gd: 1-4 **GF: 2-9** Fm: 0-1
Distance: **5f/6f: 3-15** 7f-8f: 0-0 9f-13f: 0-0 14f+: 0-0
Track : LH: 0-1 RH: 0-1 Tight: 0-0 Gall: 0-2
Aids: Bl: 0-0 Vi: 0-0 Tstrap: 0-0 Ckp: 0-0
Best Rating: **109** 8/09 Asct 5f good

Smart; suited by 5f; acts on good and faster ground.

Grove View Star

(95) (65)**64**

4-y-o ch g Auction House (USA)-Gracious Imp (USA) (Imp Society (USA))

Patrick Morris (G M Lyons 26/11) D & D Coatings Ltd

Placings:5460/453306-045430 (7766)

2009: 10^{0}SD, 12^{4}GY, 12^{5}SD, 12^{4}SD, 9^{3}SD, 11^{0}SD,

	Starts	1st	2nd	3rd	Win & Pl
Career Total (Turf)	8	0	0	1	1660
Career Total (AW)	8	0	0	2	1155

Going (Turf): **Sf: 0-1 GS: 0-0 Gd: 0-1 GF: 0-2 Fm: 0-0**
Distance: 5f/6f: 0-1 7f-8f: 0-3 9f-13f: 0-12 14f+: 0-0
Track : LH: 0-8 RH: 0-6 Tight: 0-1 Gall: 0-0
Aids: Bl: 0-2 Vi: 0-0 Tstrap: 0-0 Ckp: 0-0
Best Rating: **67** 6/07 Llmk 7f50y yield

Moderate; stays 1m4f; acts on Polytrack.

Grudge

102(106) (74)**74**

4-y-o b g Timeless Times (USA)-Envy (IRE) (Paris House)

Ollie Pears (D W Barker 6/7) K C West

Placings:0525420/63426022100-34020**025212** (7852)

2009: 5^{3}G, 5^{4}G, 5^{0}GF, 5^{2}G, 5^{0}GS, **5^{0}SD**, **5^{2}SD**, 5^{5}S, **5^{2}SD**, **5^{1}SD**, 5^{2}SS,

	Starts	1st	2nd	3rd	Win & Pl
Career Total (Turf)	24	1	6	2	10764
Career Total (AW)	5	1	3	0	3961

71	11/09	Wolv	5f20y	(0-65)H	STD	£2047
74	8/08	Ches	5f16y	(0-65)H	SFT	£2729

Total win prize-money £4777

Going (Turf): **Sf: 1-5** GS: 0-3 Gd: 0-8 GF: 0-8 Fm: 0-0
Distance: **5f/6f: 2-29** 7f-8f: 0-9 9f-13f: 0-0 14f+: 0-0
Track : **LH: 2-7** RH: 0-1 **Tight: 2-6** Gall: 0-1
Aids: Bl: 0-0 Vi: 0-0 Tstrap: 0-1 Ckp: 0-1
Best Rating: **74** 12/09 Sthl 5f std-slw

Modest; effective over 5f; acts on easy ground; goes on Polytrack; looks best going left-handed.

Guarino (GER)

97 **93**

5-y-o b g Acatenango (GER)-Global World (GER) (Big Shuffle (USA))

G L Moore Andrew Bradmore

Placings:1/334/6 (3585)

2009: 10^{6}G,

	Starts	1st	2nd	3rd	Win & Pl
Career Total (Turf)	5	1	0	2	8320

10/06	Dort	1m		GD	£2137

Total win prize-money £2138

Going (Turf): Sf: 0-2 GS: 0-0 **Gd: 1-3** GF: 0-0 Fm: 0-0
Distance: 5f/6f: 0-0 **7f-8f: 1-1** 9f-13f: 0-4 14f+: 0-0
Track : LH: 0-0 RH: 0-3 Tight: 0-0 Gall: 0-0
Aids: Bl: 0-0 Vi: 0-0 Tstrap: 0-0 Ckp: 0-0
Best Rating: **93** 7/09 Sand 1m2f7y good

Guertino (IRE)

93(101) (64)**91**

4-y-o ch g Choisir (AUS)-Isana (JPN) (Sunday Silence (USA))

C J Teague Mrs David Hodgkinson

Placings:5221460/**000**402-05000 (7083)

2009: 6^{0}GF, 5^{5}GF, 5^{0}SD, 5^{0}G, 7^{0}S,

	Starts	1st	2nd	3rd	Win & Pl
Career Total (Turf)	14	1	3	0	9257
Career Total (AW)	4	0	0	0	

86	6/07	Carl	5f193y	G-S	£2968

Total win prize-money £2969

Going (Turf): Sf: 0-1 **GS: 1-1** Gd: 0-4 GF: 0-7 Fm: 0-1
Distance: **5f/6f: 1-16** 7f-8f: 0-2 9f-13f: 0-0 14f+: 0-0
Track : LH: 0-4 **RH: 1-1** Tight: 0-2 Gall: 0-1
Aids: Bl: 0-1 Vi: 0-0 Tstrap: 0-0 Ckp: 0-0
Best Rating: **94** 8/07 York 6f good

Useful; effective at 6f; acts on fast and on easy ground; has worn blinkers.

Guesswork

88(72) (29)**60**

2-y-o ch f Rock Of Gibraltar (IRE)-Show Off (Efisio)

W Jarvis Mrs Susan Davis

Placings:4406 (5992)

2009: 5^{4}G, 6^{4}G, 5^{0}SD, 5^{6}S,

	Starts	1st	2nd	3rd	Win & Pl
Career Total (Turf)	3	0	0	0	779
Career Total (AW)	1	0	0	0	

Going (Turf): **Sf: 0-1 GS: 0-0 Gd: 0-2 GF: 0-0 Fm: 0-0**
Distance: 5f/6f: 0-3 7f-8f: 0-1 9f-13f: 0-0 14f+: 0-0
Track : LH: 0-1 RH: 0-0 Tight: 0-1 Gall: 0-0
Aids: Bl: 0-0 Vi: 0-0 Tstrap: 0-1 Ckp: 0-1
Best Rating: **60** 6/09 Nott 6f15y good

Modest; bred to make her mark at 6-7f.

Guest Book (IRE)

103 **82**

2-y-o b c Green Desert (USA)-Your Welcome (Darshaan)

M Johnston Sheikh Hamdan Bin Mohammed Al Maktoum

Placings:612 (6305)

2009: 6^{6}G, 7^{1}G, 7^{2}GF,

	Starts	1st	2nd	3rd	Win & Pl
Career Total (Turf)	3	1	1	0	5614

81	9/09	Chep	7f16y	GD	£3561

Total win prize-money £3562

Going (Turf): Sf: 0-0 GS: 0-0 **Gd: 1-2** GF: 0-1 Fm: 0-0
Distance: 5f/6f: 0-1 **7f-8f: 1-2** 9f-13f: 0-0 14f+: 0-0
Track : LH: 0-0 RH: 0-0 Tight: 0-0 Gall: 0-0
Aids: Bl: 0-0 Vi: 0-0 Tstrap: 0-0 Ckp: 0-0
Best Rating: **82** 9/09 Asct 7f gd-fm

Useful; effective at 7f; acts on quick ground.

Guest Connections

105 (91)**77**

6-y-o b g Zafonic (USA)-Llyn Gwynant (Persian Bold)

D Nicholls Hall Farm Racing & D Nicholls

Placings:511050/04000560313**000**/00403032200/042262 0110610-6013000 (6489)

2009: 6^{6}GF, 5^{0}GF, 6^{1}G, 6^{3}GF, 6^{0}S, 5^{0}GS, 5^{0}GF,

	Starts	1st	2nd	3rd	Win & Pl
Career Total (Turf)	48	7	5	4	66348
Career Total (AW)	3	0	0	1	1166

77	5/09	Haml	6f5y	(0-70)H	GD	£2590
69	8/08	Catt	5f		G-S	£2388
62	7/08	Haml	5f4y		GD	£2266
77	7/08	Haml	5f4y		GD	£2266
91	8/06	Gdwd	6f	(0-85)H	GD	£5505
97	6/05	Siro	6f		G-F	£30590
87	5/05	Haml	6f5y		GD	£4143

Total win prize-money £49751

Going (Turf): Sf: 0-4 GS: 1-8 **Gd: 5-15** GF: 1-20 Fm: 0-1
Distance: **5f/6f: 5-31** 7f-8f: 2-20 9f-13f: 0-0 14f+: 0-0
Track : LH: 0-13 **RH: 1-5** Tight: 0-9 Gall: 0-2
Aids: Bl: 0-1 **Vi: 5-33** Tstrap: 0-0 Ckp: 0-0
Best Rating: **97** 6/05 Siro 6f gd-fm

Modest; best at 6f; acts on fast and soft ground, also Polytrack; has worn a visor.

Guestofthenation (USA)

98(97) (75)**85**

3-y-o b/br g Gulch (USA)-French Flag (Darshaan)

M Johnston Claire Riordan And Kieran Coughlan

Placings:5120-40300 (4520)

2009: 10^{4}GF, 11^{0}GF, 12^{3}SD, 12^{0}G, 11^{0}G,

	Starts	1st	2nd	3rd	Win & Pl
Career Total (Turf)	6	1	1	0	8335
Career Total (AW)	3	0	0	1	770

76	9/08	Thsk	1m	SFT	£5666

Total win prize-money £5666

Going (Turf): **Sf: 1-2** GS: 0-0 Gd: 0-2 GF: 0-2 Fm: 0-0
Distance: 5f/6f: 0-0 **7f-8f: 1-4** 9f-13f: 0-5 14f+: 0-0
Track : **LH: 1-6** RH: 0-2 **Tight: 1-5** Gall: 0-2
Aids: Bl: 0-1 Vi: 0-0 Tstrap: 0-0 Ckp: 0-0
Best Rating: **85** 9/08 Ayr 1m heavy

Fair; stays 1m4f; acts on fast and soft ground and Polytrack.

Guga (IRE)

91(99) (69)**58**

3-y-o b g Rock Of Gibraltar (IRE)-Attitre (FR) (Mtoto)

Dr R D P Newland (George Baker 6/8) C E Stedman, R J Corsan & J A Provan

Placings:0-600125 (4719)

2009: 5^{6}SD, 7^{0}GF, 6^{0}GF, 8^{1}SD, 12^{2}SD, 8^{5}G,

	Starts	1st	2nd	3rd	Win & Pl
Career Total (Turf)	4	0	0	0	0
Career Total (AW)	3	1	1	0	2652

63	7/09	Sthl	1m	(0-60)H	STD	£2047

Total win prize-money £2047

Going (Turf): **Sf: 0-0 GS: 0-1 Gd: 0-1 GF: 0-2 Fm: 0-0**
Distance: 5f/6f: 0-2 **7f-8f: 1-2** 9f-13f: 0-3 14f+: 0-0
Track : **LH: 1-4** RH: 0-1 Tight: 0-2 Gall: 0-1
Aids: Bl: 0-0 Vi: 0-0 Tstrap: 0-0 Ckp: 0-0
Best Rating: **69** 7/09 Sthl 1m4f stand

Moderate; effective over 1m; acts on Fibresand.

Guidecca Ten

95 **76**

2-y-o b c Peintre Celebre (USA)-Silver Rhapsody (USA) (Silver Hawk (USA))

A M Balding David Brownlow

Placings:43 (6548)

2009: 8^{4}GF, 8^{3}G,

	Starts	1st	2nd	3rd	Win & Pl
Career Total (Turf)	2	0	0	1	987

Going (Turf): Sf: 0-0 GS: 0-0 Gd: 0-1 GF: 0-1 Fm: 0-0
Distance: 5f/6f: 0-0 7f-8f: 0-0 9f-13f: 0-2 14f+: 0-0
Track : LH: 0-0 RH: 0-2 Tight: 0-1 Gall: 0-0
Aids: Bl: 0-0 Vi: 0-0 Tstrap: 0-0 Ckp: 0-0
Best Rating: 76 8/09 Sand 1m14y gd-fm

Fair; stays 1m; acts on good ground.

Guilded Warrior

106(104) (96)94
6-y-o b g Mujahid (USA)-Pearly River (Elegant Air)
W S Kittow The Racing Guild

Placings:61/3344046/131110000/2253235010-306422000 (7060)
2009: 7^{3}SD, 7^{0}GF, 7^{6}GF, 8^{4}GF, 7^{2}GF, 7^{2}G, 7^{0}GF, 7^{0}GF, 8^{0}GF,

	Starts	1st	2nd	3rd	Win & Pl
Career Total (Turf)	26	4	4	4	40062
Career Total (AW)	11	2	1	2	11090

94	9/08	Ches	7f2y	(0-95)H	G-F	£9714
92	7/07	Chep	7f16y	(0-95)H	SFT	£7570
92	7/07	Wwck	7f26y	(0-85)H	SFT	£5181
83	6/07	Chep	7f16y	(0-75)H	SFT	£3238
78	5/07	Kemp	6f	(0-70)H	STD	£2914
70	10/05	Wolv	5f216y		STD	£4299

Total win prize-money £32921

Going (Turf): Sf: 3-7 GS: 0-2 Gd: 0-3 GF: 1-14 Fm: 0-0
Distance: 5f/6f: 2-10 7f-8f: 4-24 9f-13f: 0-3 14f+: 0-0
Track : LH: 3-16 RH: 1-11 Tight: 2-14 Gall: 0-3
Aids: Bl: 0-0 Vi: 0-2 Tstrap: 0-0 Ckp: 0-0
Best Rating: 96 4/08 Kemp 7f stand

Useful; suited by 6f-1m; acts on fast and soft ground; also goes on Polytrack.

Guildenstern (IRE)

95(103) (77)63
7-y-o b g Danetime (IRE)-Lyphard Abu (IRE) (Lyphard's Special (USA))
P Howling Brian Johnson

Placings:045/111320000/053510160/052066004006500005/461524202402040514 4-61162623300000334063004 (7861)
2009: 7^{6}SD, 7^{1}SD, 7^{1}SD, 7^{6}SD, 7^{2}SD, 7^{6}SF, 6^{2}SD, 6^{3}SD, 7^{3}SD, 7^{0}SD, 7^{0}SD, 8^{0}GF, 8^{0}GS, 7^{0}SD, 6^{3}SD, 6^{3}SD, 7^{4}SD, 6^{0}SD, 7^{6}SD, 7^{3}SD, 6^{0}SD, 7^{0}SD,

	Starts	1st	2nd	3rd	Win & Pl
Career Total (Turf)	34	4	3	2	38065
Career Total (AW)	48	5	5	5	17075

72	1/09	Wolv	7f32y	(0-55)H	STD	£1942
67	1/09	Kemp	7f	(0-55)H	STD	£2047
62	11/08	Wolv	7f32y	(0-55)H	STD	£2047
63	2/08	Kemp	7f	(0-55)H	STD	£2047
85	8/06	NmkJ	6f	(0-90)H	G-F	£8096
88	6/06	Sals	6f	(0-75)H	GD	£3591
87	5/05	Ling	6f	(0-80)H	GD	£6412
79	4/05	Ling	6f	(0-70)H	STD	£3460
76	4/05	Folk	6f	(0-70)H	SFT	£3446

Total win prize-money £33092

Going (Turf): Sf: 1-5 GS: 0-6 Gd: 2-11 GF: 1-11 Fm: 0-1
Distance: 5f/6f: 5-37 7f-8f: 4-43 9f-13f: 0-2 14f+: 0-0
Track : LH: 3-32 RH: 2-20 Tight: 3-24 Gall: 0-3
Aids: Bl: 0-0 Vi: 0-1 Tstrap: 0-1 Ckp: 0-1
Best Rating: 91 6/05 Epsm 7f good

Modest; stays 7f; acts on most ground on turf; goes on Polytrack.

Guilin (IRE)

96(90) (46)52
3-y-o b f Giant's Causeway (USA)-Chantress (Peintre Celebre (USA))
P F I Cole D S Lee

Placings:000-0000445 (5430)
2009: 12^{0}SD, 10^{0}G, 10^{0}SD, 10^{0}GF, 12^{4}G, 14^{4}G, 16^{5}G,

	Starts	1st	2nd	3rd	Win & Pl
Career Total (Turf)	7	0	0	0	346
Career Total (AW)	3	0	0	0	

Going (Turf): Sf: 0-0 GS: 0-0 Gd: 0-5 GF: 0-2 Fm: 0-0
Distance: 5f/6f: 0-0 7f-8f: 0-3 9f-13f: 0-5 14f+: 0-2
Track : LH: 0-4 RH: 0-4 Tight: 0-4 Gall: 0-0
Aids: Bl: 0-3 Vi: 0-0 Tstrap: 0-0 Ckp: 0-0
Best Rating: 52 8/09 Gdwd 2m good

Moderate; stays 1m6f plus; acts on a sound surface.

Guiseppe Verdi (USA)

91(100) (60)57
5-y-o ch g Sky Classic (CAN)-Lovington (USA) (Afleet (CAN))
Miss Tor Sturgis Miss Tor Sturgis

Placings:001/011410/15302 (7857)
2009: 10^{1}SD, 11^{5}GF, 10^{3}SD, 12^{0}SD, 9^{2}SD,

	Starts	1st	2nd	3rd	Win & Pl
Career Total (Turf)	7	1	0	0	4415
Career Total (AW)	7	4	1	1	10820

53	7/09	Ling	1m2f		STD	£2047
90	6/07	Kemp	1m2f	(0-85)H	STD	£4728
83	5/07	Bevl	1m1f207y	(0-75)H	GD	£3886
78	10/06	Ling	1m		STD	£3238

Total win prize-money £13900

Going (Turf): Sf: 0-2 GS: 0-0 Gd: 1-1 GF: 0-4 Fm: 0-0
Distance: 5f/6f: 0-0 7f-8f: 1-3 9f-13f: 4-11 14f+: 0-0
Track : LH: 3-7 RH: 2-5 Tight: 3-7 Gall: 0-1
Aids: Bl: 0-0 Vi: 0-0 Tstrap: 0-0 Ckp: 0-0
Best Rating: 90 6/07 Kemp 1m2f stand

Modest; stays 1m2f; acts on good ground and on Polytrack.

Gulf Of Aqaba (USA)

96 60
3-y-o b/br g Mr Greeley (USA)-Ocean Jewel (USA) (Alleged (USA))
D E Pipe (M Johnston 20/7) Mrs S J Brookhouse

Placings:5504 (4139)
2009: 10^{5}GF, 10^{5}GF, 10^{0}G, 9^{4}G,

	Starts	1st	2nd	3rd	Win & Pl
Career Total (Turf)	4	0	0	0	241

Going (Turf): Sf: 0-0 GS: 0-0 Gd: 0-2 GF: 0-2 Fm: 0-0
Distance: 5f/6f: 0-0 7f-8f: 0-0 9f-13f: 0-4 14f+: 0-0
Track : LH: 0-2 RH: 0-2 Tight: 0-1 Gall: 0-1
Aids: Bl: 0-0 Vi: 0-0 Tstrap: 0-0 Ckp: 0-0
Best Rating: 60 7/09 Bevl 1m1f207y good

Gulf President

97(99) (63)64
3-y-o b c Polish Precedent (USA)-Gay Minette (IRE) (Peintre Celebre (USA))
Tim Vaughan (M R Channon 23/7) Diamond Racing Ltd

Placings:5-34005303 (4241)
2009: 8^{3}SD, 10^{4}SD, 11^{0}GS, 8^{0}G, 10^{5}GF, 8^{3}SD, 11^{0}G, 12^{3}GF,

	Starts	1st	2nd	3rd	Win & Pl
Career Total (Turf)	6	0	0	1	302
Career Total (AW)	3	0	0	2	781

Going (Turf): Sf: 0-1 GS: 0-1 Gd: 0-2 GF: 0-2 Fm: 0-0
Distance: 5f/6f: 0-0 7f-8f: 0-1 9f-13f: 0-8 14f+: 0-0
Track : LH: 0-5 RH: 0-3 Tight: 0-6 Gall: 0-2
Aids: Bl: 0-0 Vi: 0-4 Tstrap: 0-0 Ckp: 0-0
Best Rating: 64 5/09 Newb 1m3f5y gd-sft

Moderate; stays 1m2f; acts on heavy ground and on Polytrack.

Gulf Punch

90(87) (56)61
2-y-o b f Dubawi (IRE)-Fruit Punch (IRE) (Barathea (IRE))
M F Harris (R Hannon 7/7) M Harris

Placings:5543640000000 (6367)
2009: 5^{5}GF, 6^{5}GF, 7^{4}SD, 5^{3}SD, 7^{6}SD, 7^{4}G, 7^{0}G, 7^{0}SD, 7^{0}GS, 8^{0}G, 7^{0}GF, 8^{0}GF, 7^{0}GF,

	Starts	1st	2nd	3rd	Win & Pl
Career Total (Turf)	9	0	0	0	322
Career Total (AW)	4	0	0	1	692

Going (Turf): Sf: 0-0 GS: 0-1 Gd: 0-3 GF: 0-5 Fm: 0-0
Distance: 5f/6f: 0-3 7f-8f: 0-9 9f-13f: 0-1 14f+: 0-0
Track : LH: 0-8 RH: 0-2 Tight: 0-5 Gall: 0-0
Aids: Bl: 0-0 Vi: 0-0 Tstrap: 0-2 Ckp: 0-2
Best Rating: 61 5/09 NmkR 6f gd-fm

Modest; stays 6f; acts on fast ground and on Polytrack.

Gulnaz

82(96) (47)29
4-y-o b f Tobougg (IRE)-Hymn Book (IRE) (Darshaan)
C J Teague (Mrs G S Rees 3/8) Richard Underwood

Placings:0004-40006 (7504)
2009: 11^{4}SD, 11^{0}G, 12^{0}GS, 11^{0}S, 12^{6}SD,

	Starts	1st	2nd	3rd	Win & Pl
Career Total (Turf)	5	0	0	0	
Career Total (AW)	4	0	0	0	144

Going (Turf): Sf: 0-2 GS: 0-1 Gd: 0-2 GF: 0-0 Fm: 0-0
Distance: 5f/6f: 0-0 7f-8f: 0-0 9f-13f: 0-9 14f+: 0-0
Track : LH: 0-8 RH: 0-1 Tight: 0-3 Gall: 0-1
Aids: Bl: 0-0 Vi: 0-0 Tstrap: 0-0 Ckp: 0-0
Best Rating: 47 7/09 Sthl 1m3f stand

Very moderate; stays 1m3f; acts on Fibresand.

Gumnd (IRE)

65(87) (63)42
2-y-o b c Selkirk (USA)-Surval (IRE) (Sadler's Wells (USA))
C E Brittain Saeed Manana

Placings:06 (3270)
2009: 7^{0}G, 7^{6}SD,

	Starts	1st	2nd	3rd	Win & Pl
Career Total (Turf)	1	0	0	0	
Career Total (AW)	1	0	0	0	0

Going (Turf): Sf: 0-0 GS: 0-0 Gd: 0-1 GF: 0-0 Fm: 0-0
Distance: 5f/6f: 0-0 7f-8f: 0-2 9f-13f: 0-0 14f+: 0-0

Track : LH: 0-0 RH: 0-2 Tight: 0-0 Gall: 0-0
Aids: Bl: 0-0 Vi: 0-0 Tstrap: 0-0 Ckp: 0-0
Best Rating: 63 6/09 Kemp 7f stand

Gun For Sale (USA)

93(100) (55)**55**
4-y-o b g Quiet American (USA)-Do The Hustle (USA) (Known Fact (USA))
P J Makin Mrs J Carrington

Placings:0000-230540 **(6223)**
2009: 8^{2}SD, 8^{3}GF, 7^{0}GF, 7^{5}G, 8^{4}GF, 8^{0}SD,

	Starts	1st	2nd	3rd	Win & Pl
Career Total (Turf)	6	0	0	1	446
Career Total (AW)	4	0	1	0	504

Going (Turf): **Sf: 0-0 GS: 0-0 Gd: 0-1 GF: 0-5 Fm: 0-0**
Distance: 5f/6f: 0-0 7f-8f: 0-7 9f-13f: 0-3 14f+: 0-0
Track : LH: 0-3 RH: 0-2 Tight: 0-2 Gall: 0-1
Aids: Bl: 0-0 Vi: 0-0 Tstrap: 0-0 Ckp: 0-0
Best Rating: 55 4/09 Bath 1m5y gd-fm

Very moderate; stays 1m; acts on fast ground and on Polytrack.

Gundaroo

92 **70**
2-y-o b f Oasis Dream-Encore My Love (Royal Applause)
J L Dunlop Mrs Mark Burrell

Placings:5236 **(5344)**
2009: 6^{5}GS, 6^{2}GF, 6^{3}HY, 6^{6}GF,

	Starts	1st	2nd	3rd	Win & Pl
Career Total (Turf)	4	0	1	1	1734

Going (Turf): **Sf: 0-1 GS: 0-1 Gd: 0-0 GF: 0-2 Fm: 0-0**
Distance: 5f/6f: 0-2 7f-8f: 0-2 9f-13f: 0-0 14f+: 0-0
Track : LH: 0-1 RH: 0-0 Tight: 0-0 Gall: 0-0
Aids: Bl: 0-0 Vi: 0-0 Tstrap: 0-0 Ckp: 0-0
Best Rating: 70 7/09 Nott 6f15y gd-fm

Fair; stays 6f and acts on fast ground.

Gunfighter (IRE)

(82)**92**
6-y-o ch g Machiavellian (USA)-Reunion (IRE) (Be My Guest (USA))
R A Farrant M Sawers

Placings:3401254114/03LRR-R **(0680)**
2009: 7^{R}SF,

	Starts	1st	2nd	3rd	Win & Pl
Career Total (Turf)	11	2	1	1	11805
Career Total (AW)	5	1	0	1	5892

92 11/07 Donc 7f (0-85)H G-F £5181
82 10/07 Wolv 7f32y (0-85)H STD £4857
78 6/07 Haml 6f5y (0-70)H G-F £3562
Total win prize-money £13602

Going (Turf): Sf: 0-3 GS: 0-1 Gd: 0-1 **GF: 2-6** Fm: 0-0
Distance: 5f/6f: 0-2 **7f-8f: 3-12** 9f-13f: 0-2 14f+: 0-0
Track : **LH: 1-9** RH: 0-1 **Tight: 1-3** Gall: 0-1
Aids: Bl: 0-0 Vi: 0-0 Tstrap: 0-1 Ckp: 0-1
Best Rating: 92 11/07 Donc 7f gd-fm

Gunnadoit (USA)

(96) (66)**62**
4-y-o b/br g Almutawakel-Gharam (USA) (Green Dancer (USA))
N B King Mrs J K Buckle

Placings:600/421044-0 **(0448)**
2009: 13^{0}SD,

	Starts	1st	2nd	3rd	Win & Pl
Career Total (Turf)	5	1	0	0	1684
Career Total (AW)	5	0	1	0	605

62 4/08 Brig 1m1f209y (0-55) G-S £1683
Total win prize-money £1684

Going (Turf): Sf: 0-0 **GS: 1-3** Gd: 0-1 GF: 0-1 Fm: 0-0
Distance: 5f/6f: 0-0 7f-8f: 0-2 **9f-13f: 1-7** 14f+: 0-1
Track : **LH: 1-6** RH: 0-3 Tight: 0-4 Gall: 0-0
Aids: Bl: 0-1 Vi: 0-0 Tstrap: 0-1 Ckp: 0-1
Best Rating: 66 4/08 Kemp 1m4f stand

Modest; stays 1m4f; acts on easy ground; handles Polytrack.

Gunner Be Lucky (IRE)

10
6-y-o b g Key Of Luck (USA)-Iolanta (IRE) (Danehill (USA))
B Palling Terry Gunstone

Placings:0 **(3501)**
2009: 8^{0}GF,

	Starts	1st	2nd	3rd	Win & Pl
Career Total (Turf)	1	0	0	0	

Going (Turf): **Sf: 0-0 GS: 0-0 Gd: 0-0 GF: 0-1 Fm: 0-0**
Distance: 5f/6f: 0-0 7f-8f: 0-0 9f-13f: 0-1 14f+: 0-0
Track : LH: 0-0 RH: 0-0 Tight: 0-0 Gall: 0-0
Aids: Bl: 0-0 Vi: 0-0 Tstrap: 0-1 Ckp: 0-1

Gunner Lindley (IRE)

95 **87**
2-y-o ch c Medicean-Lasso (Indian Ridge)
B W Hills P McNamara, N Browne, S Richards

Placings:421250 **(5864)**
2009: 6^{4}GF, 6^{2}G, 7^{1}GS, 7^{2}G, 7^{5}GF, 8^{0}GF,

	Starts	1st	2nd	3rd	Win & Pl
Career Total (Turf)	6	1	2	0	8440

79 7/09 Hayd 7f30y G-S £3238
Total win prize-money £3238

Going (Turf): Sf: 0-0 **GS: 1-1** Gd: 0-2 GF: 0-3 Fm: 0-0
Distance: 5f/6f: 0-2 **7f-8f: 1-4** 9f-13f: 0-0 14f+: 0-0
Track : **LH: 1-2** RH: 0-1 Tight: 0-1 Gall: 0-0
Aids: Bl: 0-0 Vi: 0-0 Tstrap: 0-0 Ckp: 0-0
Best Rating: 87 7/09 Gdwd 7f good

19,000gns first foal of a 7f winner; showed ability over 6f-7f on good/fast ground.

Gunslinger (FR)

105(88) (80)**81**
4-y-o b g High Chaparral (IRE)-Gamine (IRE) (High Estate)
M J Scudamore S Smith, K Hunter, P Duffen

Placings:54/432-135 **(7841)**
2009: 10^{1}GS, 12^{3}SD, 11^{5}SS,

	Starts	1st	2nd	3rd	Win & Pl
Career Total (Turf)	6	1	1	1	14788
Career Total (AW)	2	0	0	1	703

81 10/09 Nott 1m2f50y (0-80) G-S £2590
Total win prize-money £2590

Going (Turf): Sf: 0-3 **GS: 1-1** Gd: 0-2 GF: 0-0 Fm: 0-0
Distance: 5f/6f: 0-0 7f-8f: 0-3 **9f-13f: 1-5** 14f+: 0-0
Track : **LH: 1-4** RH: 0-1 Tight: 0-1 Gall: 0-0
Aids: Bl: 0-0 Vi: 0-0 Tstrap: 0-0 Ckp: 0-0
Best Rating: 81 10/09 Nott 1m2f50y gd-sft

Fair; effective over 1m2f; acts on easy ground.

Gurtavallig (IRE)

67 **12**
4-y-o ch f Starborough-Alcadia (IRE) (Thatching)
T J Pitt The Gurtavallig Partnership

Placings:65 **(2574)**
2009: 6^{6}F, 6^{5}GF,

	Starts	1st	2nd	3rd	Win & Pl
Career Total (Turf)	2	0	0	0	0

Going (Turf): **Sf: 0-0 GS: 0-0 Gd: 0-0 GF: 0-1 Fm: 0-1**
Distance: 5f/6f: 0-2 7f-8f: 0-0 9f-13f: 0-0 14f+: 0-0
Track : LH: 0-0 RH: 0-0 Tight: 0-0 Gall: 0-0
Aids: Bl: 0-0 Vi: 0-0 Tstrap: 0-0 Ckp: 0-0
Best Rating: 12 6/09 Ripn 6f gd-fm

Gurteen Diamond

98(102) (73)**57**
3-y-o b f Kyllachy-Precious (Danehill (USA))
P D Evans (N J Vaughan 23/2) William Slattery

Placings:04-32301350 **(6725)**
2009: 5^{3}SD, 5^{2}SD, 6^{3}SD, 5^{0}SD, 5^{1}SD, 5^{3}SD, 6^{5}GF, 7^{0}SD,

	Starts	1st	2nd	3rd	Win & Pl
Career Total (Turf)	1	0	0	0	0
Career Total (AW)	9	1	1	3	4725

71 9/09 Wolv 5f216y STD £2729
Total win prize-money £2730

Going (Turf): **Sf: 0-0 GS: 0-0 Gd: 0-0 GF: 0-1 Fm: 0-0**
Distance: **5f/6f: 1-7** 7f-8f: 0-3 9f-13f: 0-0 14f+: 0-0
Track : **LH: 1-8** RH: 0-1 **Tight: 1-7** Gall: 0-0
Aids: Bl: 0-0 Vi: 0-0 Tstrap: 0-0 Ckp: 0-0
Best Rating: 73 9/09 Wolv 5f216y stand

Modest; stays 7f; acts on Polytrack.

Guto

100(103) (74)**78**
6-y-o b g Foxhound (USA)-Mujadilly (Mujadil (USA))
W J H Ratcliffe W J H Ratcliffe

Placings:31212/102006/0000264205/012643260005010005150**1-00324016622411610000** **(7577)**
2009: 5^{0}SD, 5^{0}SD, 5^{3}SD, 5^{2}SD, 5^{4}SD, 5^{0}GF, 5^{1}SD, 5^{6}SD, 5^{6}HY, 6^{2}SD, 5^{2}S, 6^{4}GS, 5^{1}GS, 5^{1}SD, 6^{6}S, 5^{1}G, 5^{0}SD, 5^{0}G, 5^{0}SD, 5^{0}SD,

	Starts	1st	2nd	3rd	Win & Pl
Career Total (Turf)	42	7	7	0	58986
Career Total (AW)	21	4	3	3	16117

78 9/09 Ayr 5f (0-85)H GD £6476
74 8/09 Sthl 5f (0-70)H STD £3885
66 8/09 Nott 5f13y (0-70)H G-S £2590
70 4/09 Sthl 5f STD £2388
67 11/08 Sthl 5f (0-70)H STD £4209
63 10/08 Newc 5f (0-65)H HVY £2266
64 8/08 Catt 5f (0-60)H G-F £2388
66 2/08 Sthl 5f STD £1684

95 4/06 Thsk 5f (0-90)H GD £11658
87 9/05 Ripn 5f (0-85) GD £6942
75 8/05 Ripn 5f G-F £3406
Total win prize-money £47895

Going (Turf): Sf: 1-8 GS: 1-6 **Gd: 3-17** GF: 2-11 Fm: 0-0
Distance: **5f/6f: 11-61** 7f-8f: 0-2 9f-13f: 0-0 14f+: 0-0
Track : LH: 0-9 RH: 0-3 Tight: 0-7 Gall: 0-0
Aids: Bl: 0-2 Vi: 0-0 Tstrap: 0-4 Ckp: 0-4
Best Rating: **99** 5/06 Hayd 6f heavy

Fair; effective over 5f-6f; acts on most ground on turf; goes on Fibresand.

Gwenllian (IRE)

86 **48**
2-y-o b f Royal Dragon (USA)-Desiraka (Kris)
J L Hassett Mrs C Hassett

Placings:0 **(7288)**
2009: 6^{0}S,

	Starts	1st	2nd	3rd	Win & Pl
Career Total (Turf)	1	0	0	0	

Going (Turf): **Sf: 0-1 GS: 0-0 Gd: 0-0 GF: 0-0 Fm: 0-0**
Distance: 5f/6f: 0-1 7f-8f: 0-0 9f-13f: 0-0 14f+: 0-0
Track : LH: 0-0 RH: 0-0 Tight: 0-0 Gall: 0-0
Aids: Bl: 0-0 Vi: 0-0 Tstrap: 0-0 Ckp: 0-0
Best Rating: **48** 11/09 Donc 6f soft

Gwerthybyd

98(96) (53)**44**
3-y-o b f Auction House (USA)-Minette (Bishop Of Cashel)
B Palling Eric Dafydd

Placings:062-603 **(3257)**
2009: 8^{6}SD, 9^{0}SD, 8^{3}F,

	Starts	1st	2nd	3rd	Win & Pl
Career Total (Turf)	2	0	0	1	289
Career Total (AW)	4	0	1	0	907

Going (Turf): **Sf: 0-0 GS: 0-1 Gd: 0-0 GF: 0-0 Fm: 0-1**
Distance: 5f/6f: 0-2 7f-8f: 0-0 9f-13f: 0-4 14f+: 0-0
Track : LH: 0-5 RH: 0-0 Tight: 0-5 Gall: 0-0
Aids: Bl: 0-0 Vi: 0-0 Tstrap: 0-0 Ckp: 0-0
Best Rating: **53** 12/08 Wolv 1m141y stand

Gwilym (GER)

103(105) (76)**74**
6-y-o b g Agnes World (USA)-Glady Rose (GER) (Surumu (GER))
D Haydn Jones S Kon, D Llewelyn and J Runeckles

Placings:00024/00505441254355303/120352320/0005006200-020154430364331P140 **(7478)**
2009: 5^{0}SD, 5^{2}SD, 5^{0}SD, 5^{1}SD, 5^{5}SD, 5^{4}SD, 5^{4}SF, 6^{3}GF, 5^{0}F, 5^{3}GF, 6^{6}GF, 5^{4}G, 5^{3}GF, 6^{1}GF, 5^{P}GF, 5^{1}SD, 5^{4}SD, 6^{0}SD,

	Starts	1st	2nd	3rd	Win & Pl
Career Total (Turf)	39	3	5	5	20146
Career Total (AW)	20	2	2	3	9895

76 10/09 Wolv 5f216y (0-75)H STD £3238
74 8/09 Ling 6f (0-70)H G-F £3412
74 1/09 Wolv 5f20y (0-75)H STD £2590
74 4/07 Wind 6f (0-75)H G-F £3238
68 7/06 Sand 5f6y (0-75)H G-F £3886
Total win prize-money £16365

Going (Turf): Sf: 0-0 GS: 0-2 Gd: 0-10 **GF: 3-26** Fm: 0-1
Distance: **5f/6f: 5-57** 7f-8f: 0-2 9f-13f: 0-0 14f+: 0-0
Track : **LH: 2-17** RH: 0-5 **Tight: 2-15** Gall: 1-15
Aids: Bl: 0-2 Vi: 0-0 Tstrap: 0-1 Ckp: 0-1
Best Rating: **81** 9/07 Sand 5f6y gd-fm

Modest; effective over 5f-6f; acts on fast ground and on Polytrack; has worn blinkers.

Gwynedd (IRE)

96 **70**
2-y-o br f Bertolini (USA)-Bethesda (Distant Relative)
E S McMahon J C Fretwell

Placings:2100 **(4850)**
2009: 6^{2}GF, 5^{1}GF, 6^{0}GF, 6^{0}GF,

	Starts	1st	2nd	3rd	Win & Pl
Career Total (Turf)	4	1	1	0	3828

70 6/09 Ling 5f G-F £2729
Total win prize-money £2730

Going (Turf): Sf: 0-0 GS: 0-0 Gd: 0-0 **GF: 1-4** Fm: 0-0
Distance: **5f/6f: 1-3** 7f-8f: 0-1 9f-13f: 0-0 14f+: 0-0
Track : LH: 0-1 RH: 0-0 Tight: 0-1 Gall: 0-1
Aids: Bl: 0-0 Vi: 0-0 Tstrap: 0-0 Ckp: 0-0
Best Rating: **70** 6/09 Ling 5f gd-fm

Fair; suited by 6f; acts on fast ground.

Gwyre (IRE)

95 **52**
3-y-o b f Mull Of Kintyre (USA)-Boadicea (Celtic Swing)
T D Easterby Habton Farms

Placings:0340 **(5442)**
2009: 10^{0}GS, 10^{3}GF, 10^{4}G, 14^{0}GF,

	Starts	1st	2nd	3rd	Win & Pl
Career Total (Turf)	4	0	0	1	626

Going (Turf): **Sf: 0-0 GS: 0-1 Gd: 0-1 GF: 0-2 Fm: 0-0**
Distance: 5f/6f: 0-0 7f-8f: 0-0 9f-13f: 0-3 14f+: 0-1
Track : LH: 0-4 RH: 0-0 Tight: 0-2 Gall: 0-2
Aids: Bl: 0-0 Vi: 0-0 Tstrap: 0-0 Ckp: 0-0
Best Rating: **52** 5/09 Rdcr 1m2f gd-fm

Gypsy Boy (USA)

(89) (68)
2-y-o b/br c Dixie Union (USA)-Think Fast (USA) (Crafty Prospector (USA))
R Curtis Downs, Smith & Looney

Placings:54 **(5664)**
2009: 6^{5}SD, 7^{4}SD,

	Starts	1st	2nd	3rd	Win & Pl
Career Total (Turf)	0	0	0	0	
Career Total (AW)	2	0	0	0	481

Going (Turf): **Sf: 0-0 GS: 0-0 Gd: 0-0 GF: 0-0 Fm: 0-0**
Distance: 5f/6f: 0-1 7f-8f: 0-1 9f-13f: 0-0 14f+: 0-0
Track : LH: 0-0 RH: 0-2 Tight: 0-0 Gall: 0-0
Aids: Bl: 0-0 Vi: 0-0 Tstrap: 0-0 Ckp: 0-0
Best Rating: **68** 9/09 Kemp 7f stand

Gypsy Jazz (IRE)

96(83) (49)**66**
2-y-o b f Antonius Pius (USA)-Dawn's Folly (IRE) (Bluebird (USA))
Jennie Candlish P and Mrs G A Clarke

Placings:3001 **(6589)**
2009: 5^{3}G, 6^{0}GF, 5^{0}SD, 6^{1}GS,

	Starts	1st	2nd	3rd	Win & Pl
Career Total (Turf)	3	1	0	1	2361
Career Total (AW)	1	0	0	0	

66 10/09 Nott 6f15y (0-60) G-S £1706
Total win prize-money £1706

Going (Turf): Sf: 0-0 **GS: 1-1** Gd: 0-1 GF: 0-1 Fm: 0-0
Distance: 5f/6f: 0-2 **7f-8f: 1-2** 9f-13f: 0-0 14f+: 0-0
Track : LH: 0-1 RH: 0-1 Tight: 0-1 Gall: 0-0
Aids: Bl: 0-0 Vi: 0-0 Tstrap: 0-0 Ckp: 0-0
Best Rating: **66** 10/09 Nott 6f15y gd-sft

Modest; suited by 6f; acts on fast and soft ground.

H Harrison (IRE)

99(102) (68)**80**
9-y-o b g Eagle Eyed (USA)-Penrose (IRE) (Wolfhound (USA))
I W McInnes Stephen Hackney

Placings:23403461560/00655454525111103/064541003500650360000/000543113022220000/6611000464000505326 0/01406024131100015005 00/0604426600452502000-6305060002000000000 **(7787)**
2009: 7^{6}SD, 7^{3}SD, 7^{0}SD, 7^{5}GF, 7^{0}F, 7^{6}GF, 7^{0}GF, 6^{0}GS, 6^{0}G, 7^{2}GF, 7^{0}GF, 7^{0}GF, 7^{0}G, 7^{0}GF, 6^{0}GF, 7^{0}SD, 8^{0}SD, 7^{0}SD,

	Starts	1st	2nd	3rd	Win & Pl
Career Total (Turf)	111	11	10	9	105876
Career Total (AW)	34	3	1	1	10060

90 8/07 Ches 7f2y (0-95)H G-F £9463
86 6/07 Ches 7f2y (0-95)H GD £8832
89 6/07 Muss 7f30y (0-85)H GD £5505
77 5/07 Catt 7f (0-80)H FRM £5181
71 3/07 Wolv 7f32y (0-75)H SF £2590
71 4/06 Ling 6f (0-60)H STD £2730
62 3/06 Ling 6f (0-65)H STD £3238
83 7/05 Muss 7f30y (0-80)H GD £6757
78 7/05 Muss 7f30y (0-80)H G-F £6713
85 6/04 Ches 7f2y C(0-95)H G-F £8720
93 9/03 Muss 7f30y D(0-85)H GD £4959
81 9/03 Yarm 7f3y F(0-75)H G-F £2380
76 9/03 Catt 7f D(0-80)H G-F £3620
73 10/02 Catt 5f D FRM £4095
Total win prize-money £74790

Going (Turf): Sf: 0-4GS: 0-11Gd: 4-31 **GF: 5-54** Fm: 2-11
Distance: 5f/6f: 3-48 **7f-8f: 11-95** 9f-13f: 0-2 14f+: 0-0
Track : **LH: 8-83** RH: 4-27 **Tight: 12-81** Gall: 0-1
Aids: Bl: 0-1 Vi: 0-0 Tstrap: 0-7 Ckp: 0-7
Best Rating: **93** 9/03 Muss 7f30y good

Moderate; effective over 6f-7f; acts on fast ground; also goes on Polytrack.

Haadeeth

98(94) (78)**85**
2-y-o b g Oasis Dream-Musical Key (Key Of Luck (USA))
M P Tregoning Hamdan Al Maktoum

Placings:126 **(7150)**
2009: 6^{1}SD, 6^{2}GF, 6^{6}G,

	Starts	1st	2nd	3rd	Win & Pl
Career Total (Turf)	2	0	1	0	2939
Career Total (AW)	1	1	0	0	

Going (Turf): **Sf: 0-0 GS: 0-0 Gd: 0-1 GF: 0-1 Fm: 0-0**
Distance: **5f/6f: 1-2** 7f-8f: 0-1 9f-13f: 0-0 14f+: 0-0
Track : LH: 0-0 **RH: 1-1** Tight: 0-0 Gall: 0-0
Aids: Bl: 0-0 Vi: 0-0 Tstrap: 0-0 Ckp: 0-0
Best Rating: **85** 10/09 NmkR 6f good

Useful; effective over 6f; acts on fast ground; goes on Polytrack.

Haafhd Time (IRE)

92(107) (64)53

3-y-o b f Haafhd-Amusing Time (IRE) (Sadler's Wells (USA))

Tom Dascombe Mrs Maureen Coxon

Placings:0-036**1**0**1**460 (6376)

2009: 10⁰GS, 12³GF, 12⁶F, **12¹SD**, 14⁰GF, **11¹SD**, **11⁴SD**, 10⁶SD, 12⁰SD,

	Starts	1st	2nd	3rd	Win & Pl
Career Total (Turf)	5	0	0	1	578
Career Total (AW)	5	2	0	0	4884

64	8/09	Kemp	1m3f	(0-75)H	STD	£2590
58	6/09	Kemp	1m4f	(0-55)	STD	£1942

Total win prize-money £4533

Going (Turf): **Sf: 0-0 GS: 0-1 Gd: 0-0 GF: 0-3 Fm: 0-1**
Distance: 5f/6f: 0-0 7f-8f: 0-1 **9f-13f: 2-8** 14f+: 0-1
Track : LH: 0-1 **RH: 2-8** Tight: 0-3 Gall: 0-1
Aids: Bl: 0-0 Vi: 0-0 Tstrap: 0-0 Ckp: 0-0
Best Rating: 64 8/09 Kemp 1m3f stand

Moderate; stays 1m4f; acts on Polytrack.

Haafhds Delight (IRE)

(84) (25)34

3-y-o b f Haafhd-Twitcher's Delight (Polar Falcon (USA))

W M Brisbourne D R B Racing

Placings:000-6 (0555)

2009: 9⁶SD,

	Starts	1st	2nd	3rd	Win & Pl
Career Total (Turf)	2	0	0	0	
Career Total (AW)	2	0	0	0	0

Going (Turf): **Sf: 0-0 GS: 0-1 Gd: 0-0 GF: 0-1 Fm: 0-0**
Distance: 5f/6f: 0-1 7f-8f: 0-1 9f-13f: 0-2 14f+: 0-0
Track : LH: 0-4 RH: 0-0 Tight: 0-4 Gall: 0-0
Aids: Bl: 0-0 Vi: 0-0 Tstrap: 0-0 Ckp: 0-0
Best Rating: 34 10/08 Bath 1m5y gd-sft

Haajes

105(107) (96)100

5-y-o ch g Indian Ridge-Imelda (USA) (Manila (USA))

J Balding (S Parr 8/4) Willie McKay

Placings:5/02001350/0**0**01401211040**0**-00136505603032201**0**0 (6694)

2009: 7⁰SD, 5⁰SD, 5¹SD, 6³SD, 5⁶SD, 5⁵SD, 6⁰GF, 5⁵GF, 5⁶G, 5⁰G, 5³GF, 5⁰GS, 6³GF, 5²S, 6²G, 5⁰GF, 5¹G, 6⁰G, 6⁰GS,

	Starts	1st	2nd	3rd	Win & Pl
Career Total (Turf)	35	6	4	3	42336
Career Total (AW)	7	1	0	1	9346

92	9/09	Ffos	5f	(0-95)H	GD	£9714
92	2/09	Wolv	5f20y	(0-95)H	STD	£7771
100	10/08	Folk	5f	(0-90)H	SFT	£7477
93	10/08	Rdcr	5f	(0-75)H	GD	£3238
85	9/08	Haml	5f4y	(0-80)H	SFT	£6476
82	8/08	Catt	5f	(0-65)H	GD	£2388
78	8/07	Nott	5f13y	(0-70)H	GD	£2914

Total win prize-money £39979

Going (Turf): Sf: 2-9 GS: 0-4 **Gd: 4-10** GF: 0-10 Fm: 0-0
Distance: **5f/6f: 7-38** 7f-8f: 0-4 9f-13f: 0-0 14f+: 0-0
Track : **LH: 1-9** RH: 0-0 **Tight: 1-4** Gall: 0-1
Aids: Bl: 0-3 Vi: 0-1 Tstrap: 0-0 Ckp: 0-0
Best Rating: 100 10/08 Folk 5f soft

Useful; ex-Irish; effective at 5f-6f; acts on most ground on turf; goes on Polytrack; has worn blinkers, a visor and a tongue tie.

Haakima (USA)

86(84) (68)84

3-y-o b/br f Dixieland Band (USA)-Be Fair (BRZ) (Fast Gold (USA))

C E Brittain Saeed Manana

Placings:030-1000 (6614)

2009: 8¹SD, 7⁰S, 8⁰GF, 8⁰SD,

	Starts	1st	2nd	3rd	Win & Pl
Career Total (Turf)	5	0	0	1	578
Career Total (AW)	2	1	0	0	2590

68	3/09	Kemp	1m	STD	£2590

Total win prize-money £2590

Going (Turf): **Sf: 0-2 GS: 0-0 Gd: 0-2 GF: 0-1 Fm: 0-0**
Distance: 5f/6f: 0-0 **7f-8f: 1-7** 9f-13f: 0-0 14f+: 0-0
Track : LH: 0-0 **RH: 1-3** Tight: 0-0 Gall: 0-0
Aids: Bl: 0-0 Vi: 0-0 Tstrap: 0-0 Ckp: 0-0
Best Rating: 84 10/08 NmkR 7f good

Useful; effective over 1m; handles a sound surface, including Polytrack.

Haarth Sovereign (IRE)

105(109) (86)86

5-y-o b g Alhaarth (IRE)-Summer Queen (Robellino (USA))

W R Swinburn The Kingship

Placings:32530/1430646320-102560 (6636)

2009: 12¹SD, 12⁰GF, 14²GF, **16⁵SD**, 14⁶GS, 13⁰SD,

	Starts	1st	2nd	3rd	Win & Pl
Career Total (Turf)	15	0	3	4	7261
Career Total (AW)	6	2	0	0	8117

86	4/09	Kemp	1m4f	(0-80)H	STD	£4727
85	3/08	Kemp	1m2f	(0-75)H	STD	£2730

Total win prize-money £7457

Going (Turf): **Sf: 0-3 GS: 0-2 Gd: 0-5 GF: 0-4 Fm: 0-1**
Distance: 5f/6f: 0-0 7f-8f: 0-0 **9f-13f: 2-14** 14f+: 0-7
Track : LH: 0-9 **RH: 2-11** Tight: 0-6 Gall: 0-4
Aids: Bl: 0-0 Vi: 0-0 Tstrap: 0-1 Ckp: 0-1
Best Rating: 86 7/09 Sand 1m6f gd-fm

Fair; effective over 1m2f-1m4f; acts on Polytrack and on fast ground; has worn a tongue tie and cheekpieces.

Haasem (USA)

79(101) (69)74

6-y-o b g Seeking The Gold (USA)-Thawakib (IRE) (Sadler's Wells (USA))

J R Jenkins Robin Stevens & Stephen Bullock

Placings:6636403**0**100/2220003**0**635-0404 (7860)

2009: 7⁰SD, 8⁴SD, 7⁰GF, 7⁴SD,

	Starts	1st	2nd	3rd	Win & Pl
Career Total (Turf)	15	0	3	3	3618
Career Total (AW)	11	1	0	1	3395

68	11/07	Ling	7f	(0-70)H	STD	£2817

Total win prize-money £2817

Going (Turf): **Sf: 0-1 GS: 0-0 Gd: 0-4 GF: 0-10 Fm: 0-0**
Distance: 5f/6f: 0-0 **7f-8f: 1-16** 9f-13f: 0-10 14f+: 0-0
Track : **LH: 1-16** RH: 0-5 **Tight: 1-9** Gall: 0-2
Aids: Bl: 0-0 Vi: 0-5 Tstrap: 0-0 Ckp: 0-0
Best Rating: 74 6/08 Yarm 1m3y gd-fm

Modest; stays 1m; acts on fast ground; also goes on Polytrack.

Haashed (USA)

(102) (89)

3-y-o ch g Mr Greeley (USA)-Guerre Et Paix (USA) (Soviet Star (USA))

M Johnston Hamdan Al Maktoum

Placings:1-0 (0863)

2009: 9⁰SD,

	Starts	1st	2nd	3rd	Win & Pl
Career Total (Turf)	0	0	0	0	
Career Total (AW)	2	1	0	0	3238

89	11/08	Ling	1m	STD	£3238

Total win prize-money £3238

Going (Turf): **Sf: 0-0 GS: 0-0 Gd: 0-0 GF: 0-0 Fm: 0-0**
Distance: 5f/6f: 0-0 **7f-8f: 1-1** 9f-13f: 0-1 14f+: 0-0
Track : **LH: 1-1** RH: 0-1 **Tight: 1-1** Gall: 0-0
Aids: Bl: 0-0 Vi: 0-0 Tstrap: 0-0 Ckp: 0-0
Best Rating: 89 11/08 Ling 1m stand

Useful; stays 1m and acts on Polytrack.

Haatheq (USA)

89 64

2-y-o b c Seeking The Gold (USA)-Alshadiyah (USA) (Danzig (USA))

J L Dunlop Hamdan Al Maktoum

Placings:005 (6199)

2009: 7⁰S, 7⁰G, 7⁵G,

	Starts	1st	2nd	3rd	Win & Pl
Career Total (Turf)	3	0	0	0	0

Going (Turf): **Sf: 0-1 GS: 0-0 Gd: 0-2 GF: 0-0 Fm: 0-0**
Distance: 5f/6f: 0-0 7f-8f: 0-3 9f-13f: 0-0 14f+: 0-0
Track : LH: 0-0 RH: 0-1 Tight: 0-0 Gall: 0-0
Aids: Bl: 0-0 Vi: 0-0 Tstrap: 0-0 Ckp: 0-0
Best Rating: 64 9/09 Gdwd 7f good

Habaayib

100 105

2-y-o b f Royal Applause-Silver Kestrel (USA) (Silver Hawk (USA))

E A L Dunlop Hamdan Al Maktoum

Placings:31120 (6449)

2009: 5³GF, 5¹GF, 6¹GF, 6²G, 6⁰GF,

	Starts	1st	2nd	3rd	Win & Pl
Career Total (Turf)	5	2	1	1	60316

105	6/09	Asct	6f	G-F	£39739
80	5/09	Nott	5f13y	G-F	£2590

Total win prize-money £42329

Going (Turf): Sf: 0-0 GS: 0-0 Gd: 0-1 **GF: 2-4** Fm: 0-0
Distance: **5f/6f: 2-5** 7f-8f: 0-0 9f-13f: 0-0 14f+: 0-0
Track : LH: 0-0 RH: 0-0 Tight: 0-0 Gall: 0-0
Aids: Bl: 0-0 Vi: 0-0 Tstrap: 0-0 Ckp: 0-0
Best Rating: 105 6/09 Asct 6f gd-fm

Smart; winner of Group 3 Albany Stakes in 2009; suited by 6f and fast ground.

Habshan (USA)

103 (87)90

9-y-o ch g Swain (IRE)-Cambara (Dancing Brave (USA))

C F Wall Alan & Jill Smith

Placings:52/0435103/01425**0**/**0**125112600/0154/464104-3600 **(4262)**

2009: 8^{3}GF, 8^{6}GF, 8^{0}G, 8^{0}G,

	Starts	1st	2nd	3rd	Win & Pl
Career Total (Turf)	**35**	**6**	**4**	**3**	**53712**
Career Total (AW)	**4**	**1**	**0**	**0**	**3797**

90	7/08	NmkJ	1m	(0-90)H	SFT	£9714
92	6/07	Newb	1m	(0-85)H	G-F	£5505
89	7/06	Sand	1m14y	(0-80)H	G-F	£6477
86	7/06	Wwck	1m22y	(0-80)H	FRM	£6477
83	3/06	Ling	1m	(0-75)H	STD	£3412
82	7/05	Donc	1m	(0-85)H	G-F	£7112
75	7/04	NmkJ	1m	D(0-80)H	G-F	£5460

Total win prize-money £44158

Going (Turf): Sf: 1-3 GS: 0-2 Gd: 0-12 **GF: 4-17** Fm: 1-1
Distance: 5f/6f: 0-0 **7f-8f: 5-20** 9f-13f: 2-19 14f+: 0-0
Track : **LH: 2-10** RH: 1-8 **Tight: 1-7** Gall: 0-0
Aids: Bl: 0-0 Vi: 0-0 Tstrap: 0-0 Ckp: 0-0
Best Rating: **92** 9/07 Yarm 1m3y good

Useful; stays 1m; acts on most ground; also goes on Polytrack.

Hachi

92(76) (19)**55**

2-y-o ch f Kyllachy-Milly-M (Cadeaux Genereux)
J L Spearing S Doody

Placings:052300 **(5636)**

2009: 5^{0}GF, 5^{5}GF, 6^{2}GF, 5^{3}G, 6^{0}G, 6^{0}SD,

	Starts	1st	2nd	3rd	Win & Pl
Career Total (Turf)	**5**	**0**	**1**	**1**	**893**
Career Total (AW)	**1**	**0**	**0**	**0**	

Going (Turf): **Sf: 0-0 GS: 0-0 Gd: 0-2 GF: 0-3 Fm: 0-0**
Distance: 5f/6f: 0-5 7f-8f: 0-1 9f-13f: 0-0 14f+: 0-0
Track : LH: 0-0 RH: 0-1 Tight: 0-0 Gall: 0-2
Aids: Bl: 0-1 Vi: 0-0 Tstrap: 0-0 Ckp: 0-0
Best Rating: **55** 6/09 Wind 6f gd-fm

Plating class; stays 6f; acts on a sound surface.

Hada Men (USA)

104(99) (69)**83**

4-y-o b g Dynaformer (USA)-Catchy (USA) (Storm Cat (USA))
L M Cumani Paul Moulton

Placings:053/42-13200 **(5961)**

2009: 12^{1}GF, 11^{3}GS, 14^{2}GS, 16^{0}GF, 14^{0}GS,

	Starts	1st	2nd	3rd	Win & Pl
Career Total (Turf)	**9**	**1**	**2**	**2**	**10597**
Career Total (AW)	**1**	**0**	**0**	**0**	**241**

80	6/09	Folk	1m4f	(0-85)H	G-F	£5828

Total win prize-money £5828

Going (Turf): Sf: 0-0 GS: 0-3 Gd: 0-3 **GF: 1-3** Fm: 0-0
Distance: 5f/6f: 0-0 7f-8f: 0-2 **9f-13f: 1-4** 14f+: 0-4
Track : LH: 0-5 **RH: 1-5 Tight: 1-3** Gall: 0-1
Aids: Bl: 0-0 Vi: 0-0 Tstrap: 0-0 Ckp: 0-0
Best Rating: **83** 8/09 Nott 1m6f15y gd-sft

Fair; stays 1m6f; handles quick ground; goes on Polytrack.

Hadaf (IRE)

97(94) (87)**94**

4-y-o b c Fasliyev (USA)-Elhida (IRE) (Mujtahid (USA))
M P Tregoning Hamdan Al Maktoum

Placings:03011/050100-0000 **(5436)**

2009: 5^{0}GF, 5^{0}GF, 5^{0}GF, 5^{0}GF,

	Starts	1st	2nd	3rd	Win & Pl
Career Total (Turf)	**13**	**2**	**0**	**1**	**10834**
Career Total (AW)	**2**	**1**	**0**	**0**	**3239**

94	6/08	NmkJ	5f	(0-85)H	G-F	£5180
87	10/07	Kemp	5f	(0-85)	STD	£3238
78	8/07	Thsk	5f		G-F	£4533

Total win prize-money £12954

Going (Turf): Sf: 0-0 GS: 0-2 Gd: 0-4 **GF: 2-7** Fm: 0-0
Distance: **5f/6f: 3-15** 7f-8f: 0-0 9f-13f: 0-0 14f+: 0-0
Track : LH: 0-3 **RH: 1-1** Tight: 0-1 Gall: 0-2
Aids: Bl: 0-0 Vi: 0-0 Tstrap: 0-0 Ckp: 0-0
Best Rating: **94** 6/08 NmkJ 5f gd-fm

Useful; suited by 5f; acts on fast ground and Polytrack.

Hafawa (IRE)

104 **93**

2-y-o b f Intikhab (USA)-Banaadir (USA) (Diesis)
M Johnston Hamdan Al Maktoum

Placings:121 **(6756)**

2009: 6^{1}GF, 6^{2}GF, 7^{1}G,

	Starts	1st	2nd	3rd	Win & Pl
Career Total (Turf)	**3**	**2**	**1**	**0**	**12901**

93	10/09	Leic	7f9y	GD	£6938
78	6/09	Pont	6f	G-F	£3885

Total win prize-money £10825

Going (Turf): Sf: 0-0 GS: 0-0 **Gd: 1-1 GF: 1-2** Fm: 0-0
Distance: 5f/6f: 1-2 7f-8f: 1-1 9f-13f: 0-0 14f+: 0-0
Track : **LH: 1-1** RH: 0-0 Tight: 0-0 Gall: 0-0
Aids: Bl: 0-0 Vi: 0-0 Tstrap: 0-0 Ckp: 0-0
Best Rating: **93** 10/09 Leic 7f9y good

Useful; stays 7f and acts on fast ground.

Hail Bold Chief (USA)

91(87) (64)**69**

2-y-o b c Dynaformer (USA)-Yanaseeni (USA) (Trempolino (USA))
G A Swinbank M Fitzpatrick

Placings:05 **(7121)**

2009: 8^{0}SD, 8^{5}GF,

	Starts	1st	2nd	3rd	Win & Pl
Career Total (Turf)	**1**	**0**	**0**	**0**	**0**
Career Total (AW)	**1**	**0**	**0**	**0**	

Going (Turf): **Sf: 0-0 GS: 0-0 Gd: 0-0 GF: 0-1 Fm: 0-0**
Distance: 5f/6f: 0-0 7f-8f: 0-0 9f-13f: 0-2 14f+: 0-0
Track : LH: 0-2 RH: 0-0 Tight: 0-1 Gall: 0-0
Aids: Bl: 0-0 Vi: 0-0 Tstrap: 0-0 Ckp: 0-0
Best Rating: **69** 10/09 Nott 1m75y gd-fm

Hail Caesar (IRE)

108 **103**

3-y-o gr c Montjeu (IRE)-Alabastrine (Green Desert (USA))
A P O'Brien Mrs John Magnier, M Tabor & D Smith

Placings:156-44404010 **(3970a)**

2009: 8^{4}GF, 10^{4}GY, 10^{4}G, 8^{0}HY, 10^{4}GF, 12^{0}GF, 9^{1}Y, 12^{0}GS,

	Starts	1st	2nd	3rd	Win & Pl
Career Total (Turf)	**11**	**2**	**0**	**0**	**28277**

101	7/09	Gowr	1m1f100y	YLD	£11069
91	7/08	Tipp	7f100y	GD	£8637

Total win prize-money £19707

Going (Turf): Sf: 0-2 GS: 0-1 **Gd: 1-2** GF: 0-3 Fm: 0-0
Distance: 5f/6f: 0-0 7f-8f: 1-4 9f-13f: 1-7 14f+: 0-0
Track : LH: 1-6 RH: 1-5 Tight: 0-0 Gall: 0-3
Aids: **Bl: 1-2** Vi: 0-0 Tstrap: 0-0 Ckp: 0-0
Best Rating: **103** 11/08 StCl 1m2f heavy

Very useful; dam is a half-sister to Last Second; winner over extended 7f on debut; acts on good ground.

Hail Promenader (IRE)

101(96) (81)**89**

3-y-o b c Acclamation-Tribal Rite (Be My Native (USA))
B W Hills N Browne,J Clarke,P McNamara,S Richards

Placings:4331-5626220 **(6645)**

2009: 8^{5}GF, 8^{6}SD, 7^{2}GF, 7^{6}G, 6^{2}GF, 7^{2}G, 7^{0}G,

	Starts	1st	2nd	3rd	Win & Pl
Career Total (Turf)	**10**	**1**	**3**	**2**	**12922**
Career Total (AW)	**1**	**0**	**0**	**0**	**0**

79	10/08	Rdcr	7f	GD	£5536

Total win prize-money £5537

Going (Turf): Sf: 0-2 GS: 0-0 **Gd: 1-4** GF: 0-3 Fm: 0-1
Distance: 5f/6f: 0-3 **7f-8f: 1-7** 9f-13f: 0-1 14f+: 0-0
Track : LH: 0-4 RH: 0-3 Tight: 0-2 Gall: 0-2
Aids: Bl: 0-0 Vi: 0-0 Tstrap: 0-0 Ckp: 0-0
Best Rating: **89** 8/09 Sand 7f16y good

Useful; effective at up to 1m; acts on most ground.

Hairs Vital (IRE)

89(85) (61)**70**

2-y-o b g Pearl Of Love (IRE)-Blue Banner (IRE) (Grand Lodge (USA))
E J O'Neill G A Lucas

Placings:445055 **(5371)**

2009: 5^{4}GF, 6^{4}GS, 6^{5}GS, 5^{0}GS, 5^{5}SD, 8^{5}SD,

	Starts	1st	2nd	3rd	Win & Pl
Career Total (Turf)	**4**	**0**	**0**	**0**	**1526**
Career Total (AW)	**2**	**0**	**0**	**0**	**0**

Going (Turf): **Sf: 0-0 GS: 0-3 Gd: 0-0 GF: 0-1 Fm: 0-0**
Distance: 5f/6f: 0-5 7f-8f: 0-1 9f-13f: 0-0 14f+: 0-0
Track : LH: 0-1 RH: 0-0 Tight: 0-0 Gall: 0-0
Aids: Bl: 0-1 Vi: 0-0 Tstrap: 0-0 Ckp: 0-0
Best Rating: **70** 6/09 Pari 6f gd-sft

Hairspray

100 **88**

2-y-o ch f Bahamian Bounty-Quickstyx (Night Shift (USA))
M R Channon John Breslin

Placings:41501600 **(6660)**

2009: 5^{4}GF, 6^{1}GF, 6^{5}G, 6^{0}G, 6^{1}GS, 5^{6}GF, 6^{0}G, 5^{0}GS,

	Starts	1st	2nd	3rd	Win & Pl
Career Total (Turf)	**8**	**2**	**0**	**0**	**13291**

88	7/09	NmkJ	6f	G-S	£9066
75	5/09	Ling	6f	G-F	£2729

Total win prize-money £11796

Going (Turf): Sf: 0-0 **GS: 1-2** Gd: 0-3 **GF: 1-3** Fm: 0-0
Distance: **5f/6f: 2-8** 7f-8f: 0-0 9f-13f: 0-0 14f+: 0-0
Track : LH: 0-1 RH: 0-0 Tight: 0-0 Gall: 0-0
Aids: Bl: 0-0 Vi: 0-0 Tstrap: 0-0 Ckp: 0-0
Best Rating: **88** 7/09 NmkJ 6f gd-sft

Very useful; effective at 6f; acts on fast and easy ground.

Hajar (USA)

99 68

3-y-o gr/ro g Rahy (USA)-Laiyl (IRE) (Nureyev (USA))
M Johnston Sheikh Hamdan Bin Mohammed Al Maktoum

Placings:31 **(3294)**
2009: 8^{3}GF, 9^{1}GF,

	Starts	1st	2nd	3rd	Win & Pl
Career Total (Turf)	2	1	0	1	3072
66 6/09 Haml 1m1f36y				G-F	£2590

Total win prize-money £2590

Going (Turf): Sf: 0-0 GS: 0-0 Gd: 0-0 **GF: 1-2** Fm: 0-0
Distance: 5f/6f: 0-0 7f-8f: 0-1 **9f-13f: 1-1** 14f+: 0-0
Track : LH: 0-0 **RH: 1-2 Tight: 1-2** Gall: 0-0
Aids: Bl: 0-0 Vi: 0-0 Tstrap: 0-0 Ckp: 0-0
Best Rating: 68 6/09 Ripn 1m gd-fm

Fair; effective at around 1m; acts on fast ground.

Hajjaan (USA)

102 79

2-y-o b c Mr Greeley (USA)-Danzig Island (USA) (Danzig (USA))
J L Dunlop Hamdan Al Maktoum

Placings:3 **(7145)**
2009: 6^{3}G,

	Starts	1st	2nd	3rd	Win & Pl
Career Total (Turf)	1	0	0	1	770

Going (Turf): Sf: 0-0 GS: 0-0 Gd: 0-1 GF: 0-0 Fm: 0-0
Distance: 5f/6f: 0-1 7f-8f: 0-0 9f-13f: 0-0 14f+: 0-0
Track : LH: 0-0 RH: 0-0 Tight: 0-0 Gall: 0-0
Aids: Bl: 0-0 Vi: 0-0 Tstrap: 0-0 Ckp: 0-0
Best Rating: 79 10/09 NmkR 6f good

Hajmah (IRE)

100(88) (50)81

3-y-o ch f Singspiel (IRE)-Midnight Line (USA) (Kris S (USA))
Saeed Bin Suroor Godolphin

Placings:3150 **(7066)**
2009: 10^{3}GF, 11^{1}G, 11^{5}G, 12^{0}SD,

	Starts	1st	2nd	3rd	Win & Pl
Career Total (Turf)	3	1	0	1	3201
Career Total (AW)	1	0	0	0	
78 9/09 Bath 1m3f144y				GD	£2719

Total win prize-money £2720

Going (Turf): Sf: 0-0 GS: 0-0 **Gd: 1-2** GF: 0-1 Fm: 0-0
Distance: 5f/6f: 0-0 7f-8f: 0-0 **9f-13f: 1-4** 14f+: 0-0
Track : LH: 1-3 RH: 0-0 **Tight: 1-3** Gall: 0-1
Aids: Bl: 0-0 Vi: 0-0 Tstrap: 0-0 Ckp: 0-0
Best Rating: 81 8/09 Newb 1m2f6y gd-fm

Useful; effective over 1m3f; acts on good ground.

Hajoum (IRE)

104(107) (93)83

3-y-o b c Exceed And Excel (AUS)-Blue Iris (Petong)
Saeed Bin Suroor Godolphin

Placings:42-2124 **(7227)**
2009: 6^{2}GF, 6^{1}G, 6^{2}SD, 6^{4}SD,

	Starts	1st	2nd	3rd	Win & Pl
Career Total (Turf)	4	1	2	0	5514
Career Total (AW)	2	0	1	0	1958
83 10/09 Wind 6f				GD	£2729

Total win prize-money £2730

Going (Turf): Sf: 0-1 GS: 0-0 **Gd: 1-2** GF: 0-1 Fm: 0-0
Distance: 5f/6f: 1-5 7f-8f: 0-1 9f-13f: 0-0 14f+: 0-0
Track : LH: 0-0 RH: 0-2 Tight: 0-0 **Gall: 1-1**
Aids: Bl: 0-0 Vi: 0-0 Tstrap: 0-0 Ckp: 0-0
Best Rating: 93 10/09 Kemp 6f stand

Useful half-brother to smart sprinter Swiss Lake; effective over 6f; acts on good and soft ground.

Halaak (USA)

102(101) (66)66

3-y-o br f Harlan's Holiday (USA)-Henderson Band (USA) (Chimes Band (USA))
D M Simcock Saeed Misleh

Placings:00061-2146532234023 **(6877)**
2009: 6^{2}SS, 5^{1}SD, 6^{4}SD, 5^{6}F, 6^{5}G, 5^{3}GF, 5^{2}F, 6^{2}F, 6^{3}G, 5^{4}SD, 5^{0}SD, 5^{2}GF, 5^{3}SD,

	Starts	1st	2nd	3rd	Win & Pl
Career Total (Turf)	8	0	3	2	3696
Career Total (AW)	10	2	1	1	5588
66 1/09 Sthl 5f (0-60)H				STD	£2047
55 12/08 Sthl 6f (0-60)				STD	£2047

Total win prize-money £4094

Going (Turf): Sf: 0-0 GS: 0-1 Gd: 0-2 GF: 0-2 Fm: 0-3
Distance: 5f/6f: 2-18 7f-8f: 0-0 9f-13f: 0-0 14f+: 0-0
Track : LH: 1-9 RH: 0-3 Tight: 0-3 Gall: 0-2
Aids: Bl: 2-12 Vi: 0-0 Tstrap: 0-0 Ckp: 0-0
Best Rating: 66 9/09 Brig 5f59y gd-fm

Modest; effective over 5f-6f; acts on fast ground; goes on Fibresand; has worn blinkers.

Halam Bankes

(72) 42

2-y-o b c Lucky Owners (NZ)-Grace Bankes (Efisio)
W G M Turner (E Danel 20/10) T Lightbowne

Placings:5610500 **(7410)**
2009: 5^{5}S, 7^{6}G, 5^{1}S, 6^{0}GS, 7^{5}F, 6^{0}GS, 5^{0}SD,

	Starts	1st	2nd	3rd	Win & Pl
Career Total (Turf)	6	1	0	0	6893
Career Total (AW)	1	0	0	0	
8/09 Stma 5f110y				SFT	£5825

Total win prize-money £5825

Going (Turf): Sf: 1-2 GS: 0-2 Gd: 0-1 GF: 0-0 Fm: 0-1
Distance: 5f/6f: 1-5 7f-8f: 0-2 9f-13f: 0-0 14f+: 0-0
Track : LH: 0-1 RH: 0-1 Tight: 0-1 Gall: 0-0
Aids: Bl: 0-0 Vi: 0-0 Tstrap: 0-0 Ckp: 0-0
Best Rating: 42 9/09 Chan 6f gd-sft

Halcyon Dancer

94(90) (48)51

3-y-o ch f Reset (AUS)-Volitant (Ashkalani (IRE))
M Dods J Ellis

Placings:463636 **(6252)**
2009: 7^{4}G, 6^{6}S, 7^{3}G, 6^{6}GF, 6^{3}GF, 5^{6}SD,

	Starts	1st	2nd	3rd	Win & Pl
Career Total (Turf)	5	0	0	2	1261
Career Total (AW)	1	0	0	0	0

Going (Turf): Sf: 0-1 GS: 0-0 Gd: 0-2 GF: 0-2 Fm: 0-0
Distance: 5f/6f: 0-4 7f-8f: 0-2 9f-13f: 0-0 14f+: 0-0
Track : LH: 0-3 RH: 0-0 Tight: 0-2 Gall: 0-0
Aids: Bl: 0-0 Vi: 0-0 Tstrap: 0-0 Ckp: 0-0
Best Rating: 51 7/09 Thsk 7f good

Moderate; effective over 6f-7f; acts on fast and easy ground and on Polytrack.

Halcyon Princess (IRE)

90(88) (30)61

3-y-o b f Barathea (IRE)-Serene Princess (USA) (Louis Quatorze (USA))
D G Bridgwater (Mrs John Harrington 22/5) Building Bridgies

Placings:0-560000 **(6371)**
2009: 8^{5}GY, 8^{6}YS, 8^{0}GF, 8^{0}G, 9^{0}SD, 11^{0}SD,

	Starts	1st	2nd	3rd	Win & Pl
Career Total (Turf)	4	0	0	0	
Career Total (AW)	3	0	0	0	

Going (Turf): Sf: 0-0 GS: 0-0 Gd: 0-1 GF: 0-1 Fm: 0-0
Distance: 5f/6f: 0-1 7f-8f: 0-1 9f-13f: 0-5 14f+: 0-0
Track : LH: 0-4 RH: 0-1 Tight: 0-2 Gall: 0-0
Aids: Bl: 0-0 Vi: 0-0 Tstrap: 0-2 Ckp: 0-2
Best Rating: 61 5/09 Naas 1m gd-yld

Haldibari (IRE)

107(92) (45)57

5-y-o b g Kahyasi-Haladiya (IRE) (Darshaan)
S Lycett Nicholls Family

Placings:400/0-62300 **(6021)**
2009: 12^{6}SD, 21^{2}F, 17^{3}G, 17^{0}GF, 17^{0}GF,

	Starts	1st	2nd	3rd	Win & Pl
Career Total (Turf)	8	0	1	1	3346
Career Total (AW)	1	0	0	0	0

Going (Turf): Sf: 0-3 GS: 0-1 Gd: 0-1 GF: 0-2 Fm: 0-1
Distance: 5f/6f: 0-0 7f-8f: 0-0 9f-13f: 0-5 14f+: 0-4
Track : LH: 0-6 RH: 0-1 Tight: 0-1 Gall: 0-0
Aids: Bl: 0-0 Vi: 0-0 Tstrap: 0-0 Ckp: 0-0
Best Rating: 57 4/09 Pont 2m5f122y firm

Moderate; stays 2m5f; acts on fast ground.

Half A Crown (IRE)

100(78) (17)64

4-y-o b c Compton Place-Penny Ha'Penny (Bishop Of Cashel)
M Dods (D W Barker 14/7) G N Parker

Placings:0340-000060301401 **(6989)**
2009: 6^{0}SD, 5^{0}GF, 5^{0}GF, 5^{0}GF, 5^{6}GF, 6^{0}GF, 6^{3}GS, 6^{0}GF, 5^{1}GS, 5^{4}GF, 5^{0}S, 6^{1}G,

	Starts	1st	2nd	3rd	Win & Pl
Career Total (Turf)	15	2	0	2	6312
Career Total (AW)	1	0	0	0	
64 10/09 Ayr 6f (0-65)H				GD	£1942
64 9/09 Newc 5f				G-S	£3154

Total win prize-money £5097

Going (Turf): Sf: 0-1 **GS: 1-5 Gd: 1-2** GF: 0-7 Fm: 0-0
Distance: 5f/6f: 2-14 7f-8f: 0-2 9f-13f: 0-0 14f+: 0-0
Track : LH: 0-1 RH: 0-2 Tight: 0-0 Gall: 0-1
Aids: Bl: 0-3 **Vi: 2-4** Tstrap: 0-4 Ckp: 0-4
Best Rating: 64 10/09 Ayr 6f good

Moderate; suited by 5f and acts on most ground; has worn a visor.

Half Sister (IRE)

64 **7**

2-y-o b f Oratorio (IRE)-Fifty Five (IRE) (Lake Coniston (IRE))

R Hannon Richard Morecombe & Mrs Anne Ferguson

Placings:0 (5021)

2009: 6^{0}GF,

	Starts	1st	2nd	3rd	Win & Pl
Career Total (Turf)	1	0	0	0	

Going (Turf): Sf: 0-0 GS: 0-0 Gd: 0-0 GF: 0-1 Fm: 0-0
Distance: 5f/6f: 0-0 7f-8f: 0-1 9f-13f: 0-0 14f+: 0-0
Track : LH: 0-0 RH: 0-0 Tight: 0-0 Gall: 0-0
Aids: Bl: 0-0 Vi: 0-0 Tstrap: 0-0 Ckp: 0-0
Best Rating: 7 8/09 Newb 6f8y gd-fm

Halfway House

104(106) (83)**84**

3-y-o b g Dubai Destination (USA)-Zanzibar (IRE) (In The Wings)

M L W Bell Ferguson, Le Gassick, Dawson & Mercer

Placings:050-00112643 (6613)

2009: 11^{0}GS, 9^{0}GF, 9^{1}F, 12^{1}GF, 11^{2}F, 12^{6}G, 12^{4}GF, 12^{3}SD,

	Starts	1st	2nd	3rd	Win & Pl
Career Total (Turf)	10	2	1	0	8183
Career Total (AW)	1	0	0	1	703

79	7/09	Folk	1m4f	(0-65)H	G-F	£2047
67	6/09	Brig	1m1f209y	(0-60)H	FRM	£1942

Total win prize-money £3990

Going (Turf): Sf: 0-1 GS: 0-2 Gd: 0-1 GF: 1-4 Fm: 1-2
Distance: 5f/6f: 0-0 7f-8f: 0-2 9f-13f: 2-9 14f+: 0-0
Track : LH: 1-4 RH: 1-4 Tight: 1-4 Gall: 0-0
Aids: Bl: 0-0 Vi: 0-0 Tstrap: 0-0 Ckp: 0-0
Best Rating: 84 9/09 Epsm 1m4f10y gd-fm

Fair; stays 1m4f; acts on fast ground and Polytrack.

Halfway There

(22)

2-y-o b f Ishiguru (USA)-Hi Ho Silca (Atraf)

J G Given Peter Onslow & Alex Owen

Placings:0 (7816)

2009: 8^{0}SD,

	Starts	1st	2nd	3rd	Win & Pl
Career Total (Turf)	0	0	0	0	
Career Total (AW)	1	0	0	0	

Going (Turf): Sf: 0-0 GS: 0-0 Gd: 0-0 GF: 0-0 Fm: 0-0
Distance: 5f/6f: 0-0 7f-8f: 0-0 9f-13f: 0-1 14f+: 0-0
Track : LH: 0-1 RH: 0-0 Tight: 0-1 Gall: 0-0
Aids: Bl: 0-0 Vi: 0-0 Tstrap: 0-0 Ckp: 0-0

Halicarnassus (IRE)

110(108) (107)**115**

5-y-o b h Cape Cross (IRE)-Launch Time (USA) (Relaunch (USA))

M R Channon Doric Racing

Placings:110/30105012510/450045045000-104461602220503215400 (7031)

2009: 10^{1}G, 12^{0}G, 10^{4}GF, 10^{4}SD, 10^{6}SD, 9^{1}GF, 10^{6}G, 10^{0}GF, 10^{2}GF, 9^{2}GF, 12^{2}GF, 10^{0}GF, 10^{5}G, 10^{0}G, 12^{3}G, 13^{2}GF, 12^{1}GF, 11^{5}GF, 12^{4}G, 12^{0}S,

	Starts	1st	2nd	3rd	Win & Pl
Career Total (Turf)	43	8	5	2	573743
Career Total (AW)	3	0	0	0	5910

114	9/09	Veli	1m4f		G-F	£277778
91	4/09	Ripn	1m1f170y		G-F	£7477
107	2/09	Ndas	1m2f	(95-110)H	GD	£50000
117	9/07	Newb	1m3f5y		G-F	£26686
111	8/07	Hayd	1m2f120y		G-F	£36907
109	5/07	Gdwd	1m3f		GD	£14762
110	7/06	NmkJ	7f		G-F	£39746

Total win prize-money £453358

Going (Turf): Sf: 0-1 GS: 0-2 Gd: 2-16 GF: 6-21 Fm: 0-3
Distance: 5f/6f: 0-0 7f-8f: 2-5 9f-13f: 6-40 14f+: 0-1
Track : LH: 3-20 RH: 3-19 Tight: 2-10 Gall: 2-19
Aids: Bl: 0-0 Vi: 0-2 Tstrap: 0-0 Ckp: 0-0
Best Rating: 117 9/07 Newb 1m3f5y gd-fm

Listed class; winner in Dubai in 2009; stays 1m4f, also effective at 1m2f; acts on fast ground; has worn a visor.

Haling Park (UAE)

98(90) (47)**56**

3-y-o b f Halling (USA)-Friendly (USA) (Lear Fan (USA))

G L Moore The Select Racing Club Limited

Placings:00040605 (7765)

2009: 8^{0}G, 6^{0}GF, 7^{0}GS, 9^{4}GF, 10^{0}SD, 9^{6}GF, 7^{0}G, 11^{5}SD,

	Starts	1st	2nd	3rd	Win & Pl
Career Total (Turf)	6	0	0	0	0
Career Total (AW)	2	0	0	0	0

Going (Turf): Sf: 0-0 GS: 0-1 Gd: 0-2 GF: 0-3 Fm: 0-0
Distance: 5f/6f: 0-0 7f-8f: 0-4 9f-13f: 0-4 14f+: 0-0
Track : LH: 0-2 RH: 0-4 Tight: 0-1 Gall: 0-0
Aids: Bl: 0-0 Vi: 0-0 Tstrap: 0-2 Ckp: 0-2
Best Rating: 56 8/09 Folk 1m1f149y gd-fm

Haljaferia (UAE)

101(94) (70)**78**

3-y-o ch g Halling (USA)-Melisendra (FR) (Highest Honor (FR))

D R C Elsworth The Howarting's Partnership

Placings:03-33410500 (4319)

2009: 8^{3}SD, 10^{3}SD, 12^{4}GF, 12^{1}GF, 12^{0}S, 12^{5}GF, 16^{0}GF, 13^{0}G,

	Starts	1st	2nd	3rd	Win & Pl
Career Total (Turf)	6	1	0	0	4635
Career Total (AW)	4	0	0	3	1336

76	5/09	Thsk	1m4f	G-F	£4274

Total win prize-money £4274

Going (Turf): Sf: 0-1 GS: 0-0 Gd: 0-1 GF: 1-4 Fm: 0-0
Distance: 5f/6f: 0-0 7f-8f: 0-3 9f-13f: 1-6 14f+: 0-1
Track : LH: 1-7 RH: 0-3 Tight: 1-4 Gall: 0-5
Aids: Bl: 0-0 Vi: 0-0 Tstrap: 0-0 Ckp: 0-0
Best Rating: 78 6/09 Newb 1m4f5y gd-fm

Fair; stays 1m and should stay further; acts on Polytrack; should win a race.

Halla San

98(106) (91)**102**

7-y-o b g Halling (USA)-St Radegund (Green Desert (USA))

R A Fahey J J Staunton

Placings:00543/506454211/51410/12000/0220-0330 (3143)

2009: 11^{0}SD, 18^{3}GF, 14^{3}GF, 21^{0}GF,

	Starts	1st	2nd	3rd	Win & Pl
Career Total (Turf)	31	5	4	3	90910
Career Total (AW)	1	0	0	0	

98	4/07	Catt	1m5f175y	(0-85)H	G-F	£5181
88	9/06	Gdwd	1m4f	(0-80)H	GD	£5505
74	8/06	Bevl	1m4f16y	(0-70)H	SFT	£3562
72	9/05	Hayd	1m2f120y	(0-70)H	GD	£4360
68	8/05	Newc	1m2f32y	(0-70)H	SFT	£4451

Total win prize-money £23060

Going (Turf): Sf: 2-8 GS: 0-4 Gd: 2-11 GF: 1-7 Fm: 0-1
Distance: 5f/6f: 0-3 7f-8f: 0-2 9f-13f: 4-17 14f+: 1-10
Track : LH: 3-17 RH: 2-12 Tight: 3-13 Gall: 1-11
Aids: Bl: 0-0 Vi: 0-0 Tstrap: 0-0 Ckp: 0-0
Best Rating: 102 5/09 Ches 2m2f147y gd-fm

Very useful; stays 2m2f and acts on most ground; usually held up.

Halling Gal

94 **76**

3-y-o b f Halling (USA)-Saik (USA) (Riverman (USA))

W R Muir David & Gwyn Joseph

Placings:51 (3100)

2009: 8^{5}G, 9^{1}G,

	Starts	1st	2nd	3rd	Win & Pl
Career Total (Turf)	2	1	0	0	4533

76	6/09	Gdwd	1m1f	GD	£4533

Total win prize-money £4533

Going (Turf): Sf: 0-0 GS: 0-0 Gd: 1-2 GF: 0-0 Fm: 0-0
Distance: 5f/6f: 0-0 7f-8f: 0-1 9f-13f: 1-1 14f+: 0-0
Track : LH: 0-0 RH: 1-2 Tight: 1-1 Gall: 0-0
Aids: Bl: 0-0 Vi: 0-0 Tstrap: 0-0 Ckp: 0-0
Best Rating: 76 6/09 Gdwd 1m1f good

Hallingdal (UAE)

105(105) (85)**77**

4-y-o b m Halling (USA)-Saik (USA) (Riverman (USA))

J J Bridger (Ms J S Doyle 20/4) W Wood

Placings:1/3045134600-2150003365003410524060420 (7823)

2009: 8^{2}SD, 7^{1}SD, 6^{5}SD, 7^{0}SD, 8^{0}SD, 8^{0}GF, 7^{0}G, 8^{3}G, 8^{3}GF, 8^{6}GF, 8^{5}GF, 10^{0}GF, 9^{0}G, 8^{3}G, 9^{4}GF, 9^{1}GF, 8^{0}GS, 9^{5}GF, 9^{2}SD, 10^{4}SD, 10^{0}SD, 10^{6}SD, 12^{0}SD, 10^{4}SD,

	Starts	1st	2nd	3rd	Win & Pl
Career Total (Turf)	17	2	0	4	16564
Career Total (AW)	19	2	3	1	11073

70	8/09	Folk	1m1f149y	(0-90)H	G-F	£9714
81	2/09	Wolv	7f32y	(0-75)H	STD	£2729
81	9/08	Kemp	1m	(0-75)H	STD	£2590
77	10/07	Newc	7f		G-S	£4210

Total win prize-money £19244

Going (Turf): Sf: 0-0 GS: 1-3 Gd: 0-5 GF: 1-9 Fm: 0-0
Distance: 5f/6f: 0-1 7f-8f: 3-15 9f-13f: 1-20 14f+: 0-0
Track : LH: 1-8 RH: 2-24 Tight: 2-13 Gall: 0-2
Aids: Bl: 0-0 Vi: 0-0 Tstrap: 0-0 Ckp: 0-0
Best Rating: 85 10/08 Kemp 7f stand

Fair; effective over 7f-1m2f; acts on fast and soft turf; goes on Polytrack.

Hallingdal Blue (UAE)

84(82) (43)**31**

3-y-o b f Halling (USA)-Blue Melody (USA) (Dayjur (USA))

H R A Cecil The Sticky Wicket Syndicate II

Placings:0-00 (3508)
2009: 11^{0}G, 11^{0}SD,

	Starts	1st	2nd	3rd	Win & Pl
Career Total (Turf)	1	0	0	0	
Career Total (AW)	2	0	0	0	

Going (Turf): **Sf: 0-0 GS: 0-0 Gd: 0-1 GF: 0-0 Fm: 0-0**
Distance: 5f/6f: 0-0 7f-8f: 0-1 9f-13f: 0-2 14f+: 0-0
Track : LH: 0-2 RH: 0-1 Tight: 0-1 Gall: 0-1
Aids: Bl: 0-0 Vi: 0-0 Tstrap: 0-0 Ckp: 0-0
Best Rating: **43** 12/08 GrLe 1m stand

Hallstatt (IRE)

104(100) (77)**83**
3-y-o ch c Halling (USA)-Last Resort (Lahib (USA))
Evan Williams (M Johnston 23/7) R E R Williams

Placings:153226 (4247)
2009: 10^{1}SD, 10^{5}SD, 10^{3}G, 10^{2}GF, 10^{2}G, 10^{6}GF,

	Starts	1st	2nd	3rd	Win & Pl
Career Total (Turf)	4	0	2	1	4094
Career Total (AW)	2	1	0	0	3238

77	5/09	Ling	1m2f	STD	£3238

Total win prize-money £3238

Going (Turf): **Sf: 0-0 GS: 0-0 Gd: 0-2 GF: 0-2 Fm: 0-0**
Distance: 5f/6f: 0-0 7f-8f: 0-0 **9f-13f: 1-6** 14f+: 0-0
Track : **LH: 1-4** RH: 0-2 **Tight: 1-3** Gall: 0-0
Aids: Bl: 0-0 Vi: 0-0 Tstrap: 0-0 Ckp: 0-0
Best Rating: **83** 7/09 Ches 1m2f75y gd-fm

Fair; stays 1m2f; acts on fast ground and on Polytrack.

Hallucinating

71 **10**
2-y-o b g Oasis Dream-Follow Flanders (Pursuit Of Love)
H Candy T A F Frost

Placings:0 (7145)
2009: 6^{0}G,

	Starts	1st	2nd	3rd	Win & Pl
Career Total (Turf)	1	0	0	0	

Going (Turf): **Sf: 0-0 GS: 0-0 Gd: 0-1 GF: 0-0 Fm: 0-0**
Distance: 5f/6f: 0-1 7f-8f: 0-0 9f-13f: 0-0 14f+: 0-0
Track : LH: 0-0 RH: 0-0 Tight: 0-0 Gall: 0-0
Aids: Bl: 0-0 Vi: 0-0 Tstrap: 0-0 Ckp: 0-0
Best Rating: **10** 10/09 NmkR 6f good

Halsion Challenge

(100) (50)**31**
4-y-o b g King's Best (USA)-Zaynah (IRE) (Kahyasi)
J R Best Chris Powell

Placings:000/600000-4234 (0598)
2009: 8^{4}SD, 8^{2}SD, 7^{3}SD, 8^{4}SD,

	Starts	1st	2nd	3rd	Win & Pl
Career Total (Turf)	6	0	0	0	0
Career Total (AW)	7	0	1	1	804

Going (Turf): **Sf: 0-1 GS: 0-0 Gd: 0-0 GF: 0-3 Fm: 0-2**
Distance: 5f/6f: 0-2 7f-8f: 0-8 9f-13f: 0-3 14f+: 0-0
Track : LH: 0-8 RH: 0-2 Tight: 0-6 Gall: 0-1
Aids: Bl: 0-0 Vi: 0-0 Tstrap: 0-1 Ckp: 0-1
Best Rating: **50** 2/09 Kemp 7f stand

PLating-class; stays 1m; acts on Polytrack; has worn a tongue tie and cheekpieces.

Halsion Chancer

103(109) (92)**78**
5-y-o b g Atraf-Lucky Dip (Tirol)
J R Best Halsion Ltd

Placings:11406121/16100040200004-32416600 (5753)
2009: 10^{3}SD, 8^{2}SD, 8^{4}SD, 7^{1}GF, 6^{6}GF, 6^{6}GF, 6^{0}SD, 7^{0}SD,

	Starts	1st	2nd	3rd	Win & Pl
Career Total (Turf)	6	1	0	0	3238
Career Total (AW)	24	6	3	1	28701

78	6/09	Ling	7f	(0-70)H	G-F	£3238
92	2/08	Ling	5f	(0-85)H	STD	£4100
92	1/08	Ling	7f	(0-80)H	STD	£4100
85	12/07	Ling	6f	(0-80)H	STD	£4857
78	11/07	Ling	5f	(0-75)H	STD	£2914
70	2/07	Ling	5f	(0-70)H	STD	£3071
67	2/07	Ling	5f		STD	£2914

Total win prize-money £25199

Going (Turf): Sf: 0-0 GS: 0-1 Gd: 0-1 **GF: 1-4** Fm: 0-0
Distance: **5f/6f: 5-20** 7f-8f: 2-8 9f-13f: 0-2 14f+: 0-0
Track : **LH: 6-23** RH: 0-2 **Tight: 6-22** Gall: 0-3
Aids: Bl: 0-0 Vi: 0-0 Tstrap: 0-0 Ckp: 0-0
Best Rating: **92** 9/08 Ling 6f stand

Useful; effective at 7f-1m2f; acts on Polytrack and fast turf.

Haltela (IRE)

98 **84**
2-y-o b g Namid-Quivala (USA) (Thunder Gulch (USA))
K A Ryan Brendan P Hayes

Placings:0145400 (7013)
2009: 5^{0}GF, 6^{1}G, 6^{4}GS, 6^{5}GF, 8^{4}GS, 6^{0}G, 7^{0}GS,

	Starts	1st	2nd	3rd	Win & Pl
Career Total (Turf)	7	1	0	0	7651

80	6/09	York	6f	GD	£6929

Total win prize-money £6929

Going (Turf): Sf: 0-0 GS: 0-3 **Gd: 1-2** GF: 0-2 Fm: 0-0
Distance: **5f/6f: 1-5** 7f-8f: 0-2 9f-13f: 0-0 14f+: 0-0
Track : LH: 0-1 RH: 0-1 Tight: 0-0 Gall: 0-1
Aids: Bl: 0-1 Vi: 0-1 Tstrap: 0-2 Ckp: 0-2
Best Rating: **84** 9/09 Ayr 1m gd-sft

Halyard (IRE)

86 **65**
2-y-o b c Halling (USA)-Brindisi (Dr Fong (USA))
W R Swinburn Hall Of Fame Partnership

Placings:05 (5966)
2009: 7^{0}G, 7^{5}GS,

	Starts	1st	2nd	3rd	Win & Pl
Career Total (Turf)	2	0	0	0	0

Going (Turf): **Sf: 0-0 GS: 0-1 Gd: 0-1 GF: 0-0 Fm: 0-0**
Distance: 5f/6f: 0-0 7f-8f: 0-2 9f-13f: 0-0 14f+: 0-0
Track : LH: 0-0 RH: 0-1 Tight: 0-0 Gall: 0-0
Aids: Bl: 0-0 Vi: 0-0 Tstrap: 0-0 Ckp: 0-0
Best Rating: **65** 7/09 Sand 7f16y good

Hamaasy

60(103) (68)**53**
8-y-o b g Machiavellian (USA)-Sakha (Wolfhound (USA))
G A Ham (R A Harris 21/4) G A Ham

Placings:0600/50000/01004040600/0502003301**1**/051543 00/016306032-2252600300000 (6256)
2009: 7^{2}SS, 6^{2}SD, 7^{5}SD, 7^{2}SS, 7^{6}SD, 6^{0}SD, 7^{0}SD, 6^{3}SD, 6^{0}SD, 7^{0}SD, 5^{0}G, 5^{0}F, 8^{0}SD,

	Starts	1st	2nd	3rd	Win & Pl
Career Total (Turf)	31	1	1	2	7269
Career Total (AW)	30	4	4	4	12107

70	4/08	Sthl	6f		STD	£1774
78	2/07	Sthl	6f	(0-60)H	STD	£1706
72	1/07	Sthl	6f	(0-70)H	STD	£2914
64	10/06	Sthl	6f	(0-45)	STD	£2013
68	3/05	Muss	7f30y		G-S	£4725

Total win prize-money £13134

Going (Turf): Sf: 0-1 **GS: 1-3** Gd: 0-7 GF: 0-18 Fm: 0-2
Distance: **5f/6f: 4-42** 7f-8f: 1-17 9f-13f: 0-2 14f+: 0-0
Track : **LH: 4-35** RH: 1-6 **Tight: 1-13** Gall: 0-2
Aids: Bl: 0-0 Vi: 0-1 Tstrap: 0-8 Ckp: 0-8
Best Rating: **78** 2/07 Sthl 6f stand

Moderate; effective over 5f-7f; effective on most ground on turf; goes on Fibresand.

Hambledon Hill

98(101) (64)**75**
3-y-o ch g Selkirk (USA)-Dominica (Alhaarth (IRE))
R Hannon Pall Mall Partners

Placings:04046-550403 (4987)
2009: 8^{5}G, 9^{5}G, 9^{0}GF, 11^{4}SD, 13^{0}G, 11^{3}GF,

	Starts	1st	2nd	3rd	Win & Pl
Career Total (Turf)	10	0	0	1	1047
Career Total (AW)	1	0	0	0	351

Going (Turf): **Sf: 0-1 GS: 0-1 Gd: 0-5 GF: 0-3 Fm: 0-0**
Distance: 5f/6f: 0-0 7f-8f: 0-3 9f-13f: 0-8 14f+: 0-0
Track : LH: 0-1 RH: 0-7 Tight: 0-3 Gall: 0-2
Aids: Bl: 0-0 Vi: 0-0 Tstrap: 0-0 Ckp: 0-0
Best Rating: **75** 9/08 Leic 7f9y soft

Fair; out of King's Stand Stakes winner Dominica; stays 7f; acts on good ground.

Hambleton

62(82) (46)**26**
2-y-o b c Monsieur Bond (IRE)-Only Yours (Aragon)
B Smart B Smart

Placings:06 (6356)
2009: 5^{0}G, 6^{6}SD,

	Starts	1st	2nd	3rd	Win & Pl
Career Total (Turf)	1	0	0	0	
Career Total (AW)	1	0	0	0	0

Going (Turf): **Sf: 0-0 GS: 0-0 Gd: 0-1 GF: 0-0 Fm: 0-0**
Distance: 5f/6f: 0-2 7f-8f: 0-0 9f-13f: 0-0 14f+: 0-0
Track : LH: 0-2 RH: 0-0 Tight: 0-0 Gall: 0-0
Aids: Bl: 0-0 Vi: 0-0 Tstrap: 0-0 Ckp: 0-0
Best Rating: **46** 9/09 Sthl 6f stand

Hamish McGonagall

109 **106**
4-y-o b g Namid-Anatase (Danehill (USA))
T D Easterby Reality Partnerships I

Placings:034221/210210010-444432260000 (7015)

2009: 5^{4}G, 5^{4}G, 5^{4}GF, 5^{4}G, 5^{3}G, 5^{2}GF, 5^{2}GF, 5^{6}GF, 5^{0}GS, 5^{0}GF, 6^{0}G, 5^{0}GS,

	Starts	1st	2nd	3rd	Win & Pl
Career Total (Turf)	27	4	6	2	96331

106	10/08	Muss	5f	(0-105)H	G-S	£37386
101	7/08	Ches	5f16y	(0-95)H	G-S	£9462
94	5/08	York	5f	(0-90)H	G-F	£9714
73	11/07	Muss	5f		GD	£3238

Total win prize-money £59801

Going (Turf): Sf: 0-1 **GS: 2-7** Gd: 1-12 GF: 1-7 Fm: 0-0
Distance: **5f/6f: 4-27** 7f-8f: 0-0 9f-13f: 0-0 14f+: 0-0
Track : **LH: 1-1** RH: 0-0 **Tight: 1-1** Gall: 0-0
Aids: Bl: 0-0 Vi: 0-0 Tstrap: 0-0 Ckp: 0-0
Best Rating: **106** 8/09 York 5f89y gd-fm

Very useful; best over 5f; acts on most ground; likes to race prominently.

Hamloola

96 **72**

2-y-o b f Red Ransom (USA)-Dusty Answer (Zafonic (USA))
W J Haggas Hamdan Al Maktoum

Placings:3 **(7288)**
2009: 6^{3}S,

	Starts	1st	2nd	3rd	Win & Pl
Career Total (Turf)	1	0	0	1	915

Going (Turf): **Sf: 0-1 GS: 0-0 Gd: 0-0 GF: 0-0 Fm: 0-0**
Distance: 5f/6f: 0-1 7f-8f: 0-0 9f-13f: 0-0 14f+: 0-0
Track : LH: 0-0 RH: 0-0 Tight: 0-0 Gall: 0-0
Aids: Bl: 0-0 Vi: 0-0 Tstrap: 0-0 Ckp: 0-0
Best Rating: **72** 11/09 Donc 6f soft

Promising third over 6f on soft ground on debut.

Hammer

94(98) (70)**75**

4-y-o b g Beat Hollow-Tranquil Moon (Deploy)
R T Phillips Keweedee

Placings:043245-24606 **(1892)**
2009: 12^{2}SD, 12^{4}SD, 12^{6}SD, 11^{0}GS, 14^{6}GF,

	Starts	1st	2nd	3rd	Win & Pl
Career Total (Turf)	4	0	1	1	2023
Career Total (AW)	7	0	1	0	1374

Going (Turf): **Sf: 0-1 GS: 0-1 Gd: 0-0 GF: 0-2 Fm: 0-0**
Distance: 5f/6f: 0-0 7f-8f: 0-1 9f-13f: 0-8 14f+: 0-2
Track : LH: 0-5 RH: 0-5 Tight: 0-5 Gall: 0-2
Aids: Bl: 0-0 Vi: 0-0 Tstrap: 0-0 Ckp: 0-0
Best Rating: **75** 9/08 NmkR 1m4f gd-fm

Modest; probably stays 1m4f; acts on soft ground and on Polytrack.

Hammer Of The Gods (IRE)

(105) (82)**40**

9-y-o ch g Tagula (IRE)-Bhama (FR) (Habitat)
G C Bravery Graham Newton & Russell Reed

Placings:0500/330**142/21/2424313055020/05446625/1364 4003560-0** **(0590)**
2009: 6^{0}SD,

	Starts	1st	2nd	3rd	Win & Pl
Career Total (Turf)	11	0	0	4	2063
Career Total (AW)	34	4	6	2	25900

82	3/08	Wolv	5f216y	(0-70)H	STD	£3238
85	6/06	Ling	6f	(0-85)H	STD	£7772
73	3/05	Ling	6f	(0-70)H	STD	£3427
68	11/04	Ling	5f	(0-45)	STD	£1519

Total win prize-money £15957

Going (Turf): **Sf: 0-1 GS: 0-2 Gd: 0-3 GF: 0-5 Fm: 0-0**
Distance: **5f/6f: 4-37** 7f-8f: 0-8 9f-13f: 0-0 14f+: 0-0
Track : **LH: 4-31** RH: 0-5 **Tight: 4-24** Gall: 0-5
Aids: **Bl: 4-36** Vi: 0-1 Tstrap: 0-1 Ckp: 0-1
Best Rating: **85** 6/06 Ling 6f stand

Modest; stays 6f; acts well on Polytrack.

Hamoody (USA)

103 **95**

5-y-o ch g Johannesburg (USA)-Northern Gulch (USA) (Gulch (USA))
P W Chapple-Hyam Saleh Al Homaizi & Imad Al Sagar

Placings:110/00**20**/545-0520 **(5799)**
2009: 6^{0}G, 6^{5}GS, 6^{2}G, 6^{0}GF,

	Starts	1st	2nd	3rd	Win & Pl
Career Total (Turf)	12	2	1	0	54703
Career Total (AW)	2	0	1	0	5714

104	8/06	Gdwd	6f	G-F	£39746
83	7/06	NmkJ	6f	G-F	£9715

Total win prize-money £49462

Going (Turf): Sf: 0-0 GS: 0-3 Gd: 0-2 **GF: 2-4** Fm: 0-3
Distance: **5f/6f: 2-8** 7f-8f: 0-6 9f-13f: 0-0 14f+: 0-0
Track : LH: 0-0 RH: 0-0 Tight: 0-0 Gall: 0-0
Aids: Bl: 0-0 Vi: 0-0 Tstrap: 0-0 Ckp: 0-0
Best Rating: **104** 8/06 Gdwd 6f gd-fm

Useful; winner of Group 2 Richmond Stakes at Goodwood in 2006; raced in USA in 2007/8; effective at 6f; acts on fast ground.

Hanbelation (USA)

(85) (51)

2-y-o b/br f Malibu Moon (USA)-Baldellia (FR) (Grape Tree Road)
E F Vaughan Nabil Mourad

Placings:0 **(7585)**
2009: 6^{0}SD,

	Starts	1st	2nd	3rd	Win & Pl
Career Total (Turf)	0	0	0	0	
Career Total (AW)	1	0	0	0	

Going (Turf): **Sf: 0-0 GS: 0-0 Gd: 0-0 GF: 0-0 Fm: 0-0**
Distance: 5f/6f: 0-1 7f-8f: 0-0 9f-13f: 0-0 14f+: 0-0
Track : LH: 0-0 RH: 0-1 Tight: 0-0 Gall: 0-0
Aids: Bl: 0-0 Vi: 0-0 Tstrap: 0-0 Ckp: 0-0
Best Rating: **51** 11/09 Kemp 6f stand

Hanbrin Bhoy (IRE)

(100) (73)**50**

5-y-o b g Cape Cross (IRE)-Sea Of Stone (USA) (Sanglamore (USA))
R Dickin H & E Scaffolding Ltd

Placings:431/004/51-0 **(1604)**
2009: 10^{0}SD,

	Starts	1st	2nd	3rd	Win & Pl
Career Total (Turf)	4	0	0	1	812
Career Total (AW)	5	2	0	0	6682

73	1/08	Ling	1m	(0-80)H	STD	£4100
70	11/06	Kemp	7f		STD	£2388

Total win prize-money £6490

Going (Turf): **Sf: 0-1 GS: 0-2 Gd: 0-0 GF: 0-1 Fm: 0-0**
Distance: 5f/6f: 0-1 **7f-8f: 2-6** 9f-13f: 0-2 14f+: 0-0
Track : LH: 1-2 RH: 1-4 **Tight: 1-2** Gall: 0-0
Aids: Bl: 0-0 Vi: 0-0 Tstrap: 0-0 Ckp: 0-0
Best Rating: **73** 1/08 Ling 1m stand

Fair; stays 7f; acts on Polytrack.

Hand Painted

102(92) (51)**80**

3-y-o b g Lend A Hand-Scarlett Holly (Red Sunset)
P J Makin D A Poole

Placings:445-03112215 **(5937)**
2009: 6^{0}SD, 6^{3}F, 5^{1}G, 5^{1}G, 6^{2}G, 6^{2}GF, 7^{1}GF, 5^{5}GF,

	Starts	1st	2nd	3rd	Win & Pl
Career Total (Turf)	10	3	2	1	16298
Career Total (AW)	1	0	0	0	

80	8/09	Folk	7f	(0-80)H	G-F	£5180
74	6/09	Brig	5f213y	(0-70)H	GD	£3497
75	5/09	Brig	5f213y	(0-75)H	GD	£3406

Total win prize-money £12084

Going (Turf): Sf: 0-0 GS: 0-0 **Gd: 2-3** GF: 1-6 Fm: 0-1
Distance: **5f/6f: 2-9** 7f-8f: 1-2 9f-13f: 0-0 14f+: 0-0
Track : **LH: 2-5** RH: 0-1 Tight: 0-0 Gall: 0-2
Aids: Bl: 0-0 Vi: 0-0 Tstrap: 0-0 Ckp: 0-0
Best Rating: **80** 8/09 Folk 7f gd-fm

Fair; effective over 5f-6f; acts on fast and easy ground.

Handcuff

90(91) (58)**58**

3-y-o br g Lend A Hand-Peruvian Jade (Petong)
I Semple (J Gallagher 13/8) Allan McWilliam/Christopher McWilliam

Placings:5033064-40005500000 **(6380)**
2009: 5^{4}GF, 5^{0}G, 6^{0}F, 6^{0}F, 8^{5}GS, 7^{5}S, 6^{0}G, 5^{0}GS, 5^{0}G, 5^{0}GS, 5^{0}GF,

	Starts	1st	2nd	3rd	Win & Pl
Career Total (Turf)	12	0	0	0	192
Career Total (AW)	6	0	0	2	1111

Going (Turf): **Sf: 0-1 GS: 0-4 Gd: 0-3 GF: 0-2 Fm: 0-2**
Distance: 5f/6f: 0-14 7f-8f: 0-3 9f-13f: 0-1 14f+: 0-0
Track : LH: 0-9 RH: 0-2 Tight: 0-3 Gall: 0-4
Aids: Bl: 0-1 Vi: 0-2 Tstrap: 0-1 Ckp: 0-1
Best Rating: **58** 10/08 Bath 5f11y gd-sft

Moderate; suited by 5f and Polytrack.

Handsinthemist (IRE)

95(101) (67)**57**

4-y-o b f Lend A Hand-Hollow Haze (USA) (Woodman (USA))
P T Midgley J F Wright

Placings:00366**0010**/0430320030-2116**5**550563 **(7709)**
2009: 5^{2}SD, 5^{1}SD, 5^{1}SD, 5^{6}F, 5^{5}SD, 5^{5}SD, 5^{5}GF, 5^{0}GF, 5^{5}G, 5^{6}S, 5^{3}SD,

	Starts	1st	2nd	3rd	Win & Pl
Career Total (Turf)	23	1	1	3	3990
Career Total (AW)	7	2	1	2	5149

67	3/09	Sthl	5f	(0-52)H	STD	£1942
59	3/09	Sthl	5f	(0-60)H	STD	£2047
51	9/07	Rdcr	5f	(0-65)	FRM	£1943

Total win prize-money £5933

Going (Turf):	Sf: 0-4 GS: 0-1 Gd: 0-7 GF: 0-9 **Fm: 1-2**
Distance:	**5f/6f: 3-29** 7f-8f: 0-1 9f-13f: 0-0 14f+: 0-0
Track :	LH: 0-1 RH: 0-2 Tight: 0-1 Gall: 0-2
Aids:	Bl: 0-0 Vi: 0-1 Tstrap: 1-12 Ckp: 1-12
Best Rating:	**67** 3/09 Sthl 5f stand

Moderate; seems best at 5f; acts on firm ground; goes on Fibresand; has worn cheekpieces.

Handsome Cross (IRE)

104(97) (63)**80**

8-y-o b g Cape Cross (IRE)-Snap Crackle Pop (IRE) (Statoblest)

W J Musson McHugh & Partners II

Placings:40321232/5560300/04322156000/**00**024124260654203/242000000/530-4300**0051** **(7890)**

2009: 5^{4}GF, 5^{3}G, 5^{0}GF, 5^{0}GF, 5^{0}SD, 5^{0}SD, 5^{5}SD, 6^{1}SD,

	Starts	1st	2nd	3rd	Win & Pl
Career Total (Turf)	**57**	**3**	**11**	**7**	**73308**
Career Total (AW)	**6**	**1**	**0**	**0**	**1979**

	12/09	Ling	6f	(0-60)H	STD	£1978
89	6/06	Muss	5f	(0-105)H	G-F	£31160
91	6/05	Ches	5f16y	(0-85)H	GD	£8112
89	8/03	Folk	5f	F	G-F	£3248

Total win prize-money £44499

Going (Turf):	Sf: 0-2 GS: 0-10 Gd: 1-16 **GF: 2-27** Fm: 0-2
Distance:	**5f/6f: 4-59** 7f-8f: 0-4 9f-13f: 0-0 14f+: 0-0
Track :	**LH: 2-15** RH: 0-1 **Tight: 2-13** Gall: 0-0
Aids:	Bl: 0-0 **Vi: 1-2** Tstrap: 0-0 Ckp: 0-0
Best Rating:	**94** 5/07 Ayr 5f gd-sft

Modest; effective at around 5f-6f; suited by a sound surface; likes to race prominently.

Handsome Falcon

105(103) (86)**83**

5-y-o b g Kyllachy-Bonne Etoile (Diesis)

R A Fahey B Shaw

Placings:1/00344100/50010425216-5220642202105 **(7194)**

2009: 8^{5}GF, 8^{2}GF, 8^{2}GF, 8^{0}GS, 8^{6}GS, 8^{4}GF, 8^{2}GF, 8^{2}GS, 8^{0}S, 8^{2}GF, 8^{1}SF, 7^{0}G, 9^{5}SD,

	Starts	1st	2nd	3rd	Win & Pl
Career Total (Turf)	**31**	**4**	**7**	**1**	**33908**
Career Total (AW)	**2**	**1**	**0**	**0**	**3520**

86	10/09	Wolv	1m141y	(0-75)H	SF	£3238
79	8/08	Ayr	1m	(0-80)H	SFT	£6476
76	5/08	Newc	7f	(0-80)H	G-F	£4857
79	7/07	Bevl	7f100y	(0-80)H	SFT	£5181
76	9/06	Bevl	5f		G-F	£5181

Total win prize-money £24935

Going (Turf):	**Sf: 2-8** GS: 0-5 Gd: 0-5 **GF: 2-13** Fm: 0-0
Distance:	5f/6f: 1-4 **7f-8f: 3-16** 9f-13f: 1-13 14f+: 0-0
Track :	**LH: 2-10** RH: 1-11 **Tight: 1-5** Gall: 0-2
Aids:	Bl: 0-0 Vi: 0-0 Tstrap: 0-0 Ckp: 0-0
Best Rating:	**86** 10/09 Wolv 1m1f103y stand

Fair; stays 1m; acts on most ground on turf.

Hannah Greeley (USA)

76(78) (33)**22**

2-y-o b/br f Mr Greeley (USA)-Miss Hannah (USA) (Deputy Minister (CAN))

J R Boyle A F O'Callaghan

Placings:00 **(6592)**

2009: 7^{0}SD, 8^{0}GS,

	Starts	1st	2nd	3rd	Win & Pl
Career Total (Turf)	**1**	**0**	**0**	**0**	
Career Total (AW)	**1**	**0**	**0**	**0**	

Going (Turf):	**Sf: 0-0 GS: 0-1 Gd: 0-0 GF: 0-0 Fm: 0-0**
Distance:	5f/6f: 0-0 7f-8f: 0-1 9f-13f: 0-1 14f+: 0-0
Track :	LH: 0-1 RH: 0-1 Tight: 0-0 Gall: 0-0
Aids:	Bl: 0-0 Vi: 0-0 Tstrap: 0-0 Ckp: 0-0
Best Rating:	**33** 9/09 Kemp 7f stand

Hannicean

97(101) (73)**78**

5-y-o ch g Medicean-Hannah's Music (Music Boy)

N B King (R W Price 6/9) Neil King

Placings:5/1000300/32336-40000 **(7416)**

2009: 10^{4}SD, 10^{0}G, 10^{0}GF, 12^{0}GS, 8^{0}SD,

	Starts	1st	2nd	3rd	Win & Pl
Career Total (Turf)	**15**	**1**	**1**	**4**	**7446**
Career Total (AW)	**3**	**0**	**0**	**0**	**351**

75	4/07	Nott	1m1f213y	G-F	£3238

Total win prize-money £3239

Going (Turf):	Sf: 0-1 GS: 0-5 Gd: 0-3 **GF: 1-6** Fm: 0-0
Distance:	5f/6f: 0-0 7f-8f: 0-5 **9f-13f: 1-13** 14f+: 0-0
Track :	**LH: 1-8** RH: 0-6 Tight: 0-3 Gall: 0-4
Aids:	Bl: 0-0 Vi: 0-0 Tstrap: 0-0 Ckp: 0-0
Best Rating:	**78** 7/08 Nott 1m75y good

Fair; effective at around 1m-1m2f; acts on most ground.

Hanoverian Baron

94(97) (85)**92**

4-y-o b g Green Desert (USA)-Josh's Pearl (IRE) (Sadler's Wells (USA))

A G Newcombe (D Nicholls 26/7) Paul Moulton

Placings:02/145-004011 **(6733)**

2009: 7^{0}GF, 7^{0}GF, 7^{4}SD, 6^{0}SD, 10^{1}GS, 9^{1}S,

	Starts	1st	2nd	3rd	Win & Pl
Career Total (Turf)	**7**	**2**	**1**	**0**	**14347**
Career Total (AW)	**4**	**1**	**0**	**0**	**6351**

84	10/09	Sals	1m1f198y	(0-85)H	SFT	£4857
80	9/09	Sand	1m2f7y	(0-80)H	G-S	£4857
85	4/08	Dund	7f		STD	£6351

Total win prize-money £16065

Going (Turf):	**Sf: 1-2 GS: 1-1** Gd: 0-0 GF: 0-3 Fm: 0-0
Distance:	5f/6f: 0-3 7f-8f: 1-6 **9f-13f: 2-2** 14f+: 0-0
Track :	LH: 1-5 **RH: 2-2 Tight: 1-2** Gall: 0-0
Aids:	Bl: 0-1 Vi: 0-0 Tstrap: 0-0 Ckp: 0-0
Best Rating:	**92** 5/08 Curr 7f yld-sft

Useful; effective over 7f-1m2f; acts on Polytrack and on fast and easy ground on turf; has worn blinkers.

Hansomis (IRE)

101 **72**

5-y-o b m Titus Livius (FR)-Handsome Anna (IRE) (Bigstone (IRE))

B Mactaggart Corsby Racing

Placings:6542/02060/40453200646-211220300400 **(6765)**

2009: 6^{2}GF, 5^{1}GF, 5^{1}GF, 6^{2}GF, 6^{2}GF, 5^{0}G, 7^{3}GF, 6^{0}GF, 7^{0}GF, 6^{4}GF, 6^{0}GF, 6^{0}G,

	Starts	1st	2nd	3rd	Win & Pl
Career Total (Turf)	**32**	**2**	**6**	**2**	**10950**

67	6/09	Carl	5f193y	(0-60)H	G-F	£2047
61	6/09	Carl	5f193y	(0-65)H	G-F	£2047

Total win prize-money £4094

Going (Turf):	Sf: 0-5 GS: 0-5 Gd: 0-7 **GF: 2-15** Fm: 0-0
Distance:	**5f/6f: 2-18** 7f-8f: 0-14 9f-13f: 0-0 14f+: 0-0
Track :	LH: 0-6 **RH: 2-4** Tight: 0-0 Gall: 0-0
Aids:	Bl: 0-0 Vi: 0-0 Tstrap: 0-1 Ckp: 0-1
Best Rating:	**72** 8/09 Newc 7f gd-fm

Modest sort; stays 7f but effective at shorter; acts on most ground.

Hanson'D (IRE)

100 **101**

2-y-o ch c Pivotal-Dinka Raja (USA) (Woodman (USA))

K A Ryan Joseph Ogden, J Hanson, John Ogden

Placings:410 **(7017)**

2009: 6^{4}GF, 7^{1}G, 8^{0}GS,

	Starts	1st	2nd	3rd	Win & Pl
Career Total (Turf)	**3**	**1**	**0**	**0**	**6060**

85	9/09	Ayr	7f50y	GD	£4857

Total win prize-money £4857

Going (Turf):	Sf: 0-0 GS: 0-1 **Gd: 1-1** GF: 0-1 Fm: 0-0
Distance:	5f/6f: 0-1 **7f-8f: 1-2** 9f-13f: 0-0 14f+: 0-0
Track :	**LH: 1-1** RH: 0-0 Tight: 0-0 Gall: 0-0
Aids:	Bl: 0-0 Vi: 0-0 Tstrap: 0-0 Ckp: 0-0
Best Rating:	**101** 10/09 Donc 1m gd-sft

Useful; effective over 7f; acts on good ground.

Hanta Yo (IRE)

85(85) (49)**43**

3-y-o ch g Alhaarth (IRE)-Tekindia (FR) (Indian Ridge)

J R Gask Horses First Racing Limited

Placings:6-00 **(4860)**

2009: 6^{0}GF, 5^{0}SD,

	Starts	1st	2nd	3rd	Win & Pl
Career Total (Turf)	**1**	**0**	**0**	**0**	
Career Total (AW)	**2**	**0**	**0**	**0**	**0**

Going (Turf):	**Sf: 0-0 GS: 0-0 Gd: 0-0 GF: 0-1 Fm: 0-0**
Distance:	5f/6f: 0-3 7f-8f: 0-0 9f-13f: 0-0 14f+: 0-0
Track :	LH: 0-2 RH: 0-0 Tight: 0-2 Gall: 0-0
Aids:	Bl: 0-0 Vi: 0-0 Tstrap: 0-0 Ckp: 0-0
Best Rating:	**49** 10/08 Ling 5f stand

Happy And Glorious (IRE)

78(87) (48)**39**

3-y-o ch f Refuse To Bend (IRE)-Wondrous Joy (Machiavellian (USA))

J W Hills M Wauchope, M Baxter, H P Mason

Placings:0-60500 **(5016)**

2009: 7^{6}SD, 9^{0}SF, 8^{5}G, 10^{0}GF, 8^{0}SD,

	Starts	1st	2nd	3rd	Win & Pl
Career Total (Turf)	**3**	**0**	**0**	**0**	**0**
Career Total (AW)	**3**	**0**	**0**	**0**	**0**

Going (Turf):	**Sf: 0-0 GS: 0-1 Gd: 0-1 GF: 0-1 Fm: 0-0**
Distance:	5f/6f: 0-0 7f-8f: 0-4 9f-13f: 0-2 14f+: 0-0

Track : LH: 0-4 RH: 0-0 Tight: 0-4 Gall: 0-0
Aids: Bl: 0-0 Vi: 0-0 Tstrap: 0-0 Ckp: 0-0
Best Rating: 48 1/09 Wolv 7f32y stand

Happy Anniversary (IRE)

103(92) (52)**86**
3-y-o b f Intikhab (USA)-Happy Story (IRE) (Bigstone (IRE))
Mrs D J Sanderson R J Budge

Placings:0233212-3224505 (7287)
2009: 7^{3}G, 7^{2}G, 7^{2}G, 8^{4}GS, 8^{5}GF, 8^{0}GS, 7^{5}S,

	Starts	1st	2nd	3rd	Win & Pl
Career Total (Turf)	**13**	**1**	**5**	**2**	**18820**
Career Total (AW)	**1**	**0**	**0**	**1**	**403**

76 8/08 Ayr 6f SFT £3238
Total win prize-money £3238

Going (Turf): Sf: 1-4 GS: 0-2 Gd: 0-3 GF: 0-4 Fm: 0-0
Distance: 5f/6f: 1-4 7f-8f: 0-9 9f-13f: 0-1 14f+: 0-0
Track : LH: 0-4 RH: 0-1 Tight: 0-0 Gall: 0-3
Aids: Bl: 0-0 Vi: 0-0 Tstrap: 0-0 Ckp: 0-0
Best Rating: 86 7/09 Donc 7f good

Useful; effective over 6f-7f; suited by good and softer ground.

Happy Dubai (IRE)

98 **73**
2-y-o ch c Indian Ridge-Gentle Wind (USA) (Gentlemen (ARG))
B Smart A M A Al Shorafa

Placings:2333 (6214)
2009: 6^{2}GF, 6^{3}S, 7^{3}S, 7^{3}GF,

	Starts	1st	2nd	3rd	Win & Pl
Career Total (Turf)	**4**	**0**	**1**	**3**	**3000**

Going (Turf): Sf: 0-2 GS: 0-0 Gd: 0-0 GF: 0-2 Fm: 0-0
Distance: 5f/6f: 0-2 7f-8f: 0-2 9f-13f: 0-0 14f+: 0-0
Track : LH: 0-1 RH: 0-0 Tight: 0-1 Gall: 0-0
Aids: Bl: 0-0 Vi: 0-1 Tstrap: 0-0 Ckp: 0-0
Best Rating: 73 9/09 Rdcr 7f gd-fm

Fair; stays 7f; acts on soft and fast ground; has worn a tongue tie.

Happy Forever (FR)

100(104) (78)**77**
3-y-o b f Dr Fong (USA)-Happyanunoit (NZ) (Yachtie (AUS))
M Botti Mrs R J Jacobs

Placings:4110-3443 (2949)
2009: 6^{3}SD, 5^{4}SD, 6^{4}SD, 6^{3}GF,

	Starts	1st	2nd	3rd	Win & Pl
Career Total (Turf)	**3**	**1**	**0**	**1**	**4043**
Career Total (AW)	**5**	**1**	**0**	**1**	**5623**

78 10/08 Kemp 5f (0-85) STD £3885
77 8/08 Bath 5f11y G-S £3561
Total win prize-money £7448

Going (Turf): Sf: 0-0 **GS: 1-2** Gd: 0-0 GF: 0-1 Fm: 0-0
Distance: 5f/6f: 2-7 7f-8f: 0-1 9f-13f: 0-0 14f+: 0-0
Track : LH: 1-3 RH: 1-3 Tight: 0-2 **Gall: 1-1**
Aids: Bl: 0-0 Vi: 0-0 Tstrap: 0-0 Ckp: 0-0
Best Rating: 78 10/08 Kemp 5f stand

Fair; stays 7f; acts on Polytrack.

Happy Mood

72 **40**
2-y-o b f Piccolo-Love And Kisses (Salse (USA))
G L Moore Mrs Charles Cyzer

Placings:0 (7182)
2009: 7^{0}G,

	Starts	1st	2nd	3rd	Win & Pl
Career Total (Turf)	**1**	**0**	**0**	**0**	

Going (Turf): Sf: 0-0 GS: 0-0 Gd: 0-1 GF: 0-0 Fm: 0-0
Distance: 5f/6f: 0-0 7f-8f: 0-1 9f-13f: 0-0 14f+: 0-0
Track : LH: 0-0 RH: 0-0 Tight: 0-0 Gall: 0-0
Aids: Bl: 0-0 Vi: 0-0 Tstrap: 0-0 Ckp: 0-0
Best Rating: 40 10/09 NmkR 7f good

Harald Bluetooth (IRE)

(107) (97)**87**
4-y-o b c Danetime (IRE)-Goldthroat (IRE) (Zafonic (USA))
D M Simcock Ahmad Al Shaikh

Placings:6/110-11 (0232)
2009: 8^{1}SD, 8^{1}SD,

	Starts	1st	2nd	3rd	Win & Pl
Career Total (Turf)	**4**	**2**	**0**	**0**	**11009**
Career Total (AW)	**2**	**2**	**0**	**0**	**12658**

97 1/09 Kemp 1m (0-90)H STD £7477
94 1/09 Wolv 1m141y (0-85)H STD £5180
87 7/08 Newb 1m (0-80)H SFT £5828
76 6/08 NmkJ 1m G-F £5180
Total win prize-money £23667

Going (Turf): Sf: 1-1 GS: 0-0 Gd: 0-0 **GF: 1-3** Fm: 0-0
Distance: 5f/6f: 0-1 **7f-8f: 3-4** 9f-13f: 1-1 14f+: 0-0
Track : LH: 1-1 RH: 1-1 **Tight: 1-1** Gall: 0-0
Aids: Bl: 0-0 Vi: 0-0 Tstrap: 0-0 Ckp: 0-0
Best Rating: 97 1/09 Kemp 1m stand

Very useful; stays 1m; acts on most ground and Polytrack.

Harbinger

106 **116**
3-y-o b c Dansili-Penang Pearl (FR) (Bering)
Sir Michael Stoute Highclere Thoroughbred Racing (Adm. Rous)

Placings:21103 (7031)
2009: 8^{2}GF, 10^{1}GF, 12^{1}G, 12^{0}GF, 12^{3}S,

	Starts	1st	2nd	3rd	Win & Pl
Career Total (Turf)	**5**	**2**	**1**	**1**	**55790**

116 7/09 Gdwd 1m4f GD £39739
94 5/09 Ches 1m2f75y G-F £7123
Total win prize-money £46863

Going (Turf): Sf: 0-1 GS: 0-0 **Gd: 1-1 GF: 1-3** Fm: 0-0
Distance: 5f/6f: 0-0 7f-8f: 0-1 **9f-13f: 2-4** 14f+: 0-0
Track : LH: 1-3 RH: 1-1 **Tight: 2-2** Gall: 0-2
Aids: Bl: 0-0 Vi: 0-0 Tstrap: 0-0 Ckp: 0-0
Best Rating: 116 7/09 Gdwd 1m4f good

Group class; stays 1m4f; acts on good/fast ground.

Harbour Blues

100(105) (83)**89**
4-y-o ch c Best Of The Bests (IRE)-Lady Georgia (Arazi (USA))
A W Carroll B Ward

Placings:22604310/6144102000-420 (1668)
2009: 5^{4}GF, 5^{2}SD, 6^{0}G,

	Starts	1st	2nd	3rd	Win & Pl
Career Total (Turf)	**10**	**1**	**3**	**0**	**10280**
Career Total (AW)	**11**	**2**	**1**	**1**	**6594**

89 5/08 Hayd 6f (0-85)H GD £4857
79 1/08 Wolv 5f216y STD £2047
77 11/07 Wolv 5f216y STD £2047
Total win prize-money £8953

Going (Turf): Sf: 0-1 GS: 0-2 **Gd: 1-4** GF: 0-3 Fm: 0-0
Distance: 5f/6f: 3-13 7f-8f: 0-7 9f-13f: 0-1 14f+: 0-0
Track : LH: 2-13 RH: 0-1 **Tight: 2-8** Gall: 0-2
Aids: Bl: 0-0 Vi: 0-0 Tstrap: 0-0 Ckp: 0-0
Best Rating: 89 8/08 Ripn 6f good

Useful; effective over 6f; acts on good and faster ground and on Polytrack; has worn a tongue tie; likes to race prominently.

Harcas (IRE)

108 **65**
7-y-o b g Priolo (USA)-Genetta (Green Desert (USA))
M Todhunter Mr & Mrs Ian Hall

Placings:00651130/000042350/6-4500160 (6102)
2009: 15^{4}GF, 15^{5}GF, 16^{0}GF, 11^{0}GF, 14^{1}GF, 14^{6}G, 13^{0}GF,

	Starts	1st	2nd	3rd	Win & Pl
Career Total (Turf)	**26**	**3**	**1**	**2**	**14153**

63 8/09 Rdcr 1m6f19y (0-60)H G-F £1942
72 8/05 Dpat 1m5f (36-60)H G-F £3920
62 8/05 Tram 1m4f (40-60)H GD £4410
Total win prize-money £10275

Going (Turf): Sf: 0-1 GS: 0-0 Gd: 1-11 **GF: 2-13** Fm: 0-0
Distance: 5f/6f: 0-0 7f-8f: 0-0 **9f-13f: 2-15** 14f+: 1-11
Track : LH: 1-8 **RH: 2-17 Tight: 1-8** Gall: 0-0
Aids: Bl: 0-5 **Vi: 1-2** Tstrap: 0-3 Ckp: 0-3
Best Rating: 78 8/06 Curr 2m gd-fm

Modest; stays 2m; acts on fast ground; has worn cheek-pieces.

Hard Ball

98(100) (57)**74**
3-y-o b g Pivotal-Miss Pinkerton (Danehill (USA))
M Quinn Henry, Blake, Newby, Hesketh & Caypon

Placings:04-0000001 (7727)
2009: 10^{0}SD, 8^{0}GF, 8^{0}S, 11^{0}GS, 10^{0}G, 8^{0}S, 7^{1}SD,

	Starts	1st	2nd	3rd	Win & Pl
Career Total (Turf)	**6**	**0**	**0**	**0**	**467**
Career Total (AW)	**3**	**1**	**0**	**0**	**1706**

57 12/09 Sthl 7f (0-55)H STD £1706
Total win prize-money £1706

Going (Turf): Sf: 0-3 GS: 0-1 Gd: 0-1 GF: 0-1 Fm: 0-0
Distance: 5f/6f: 0-0 **7f-8f: 1-4** 9f-13f: 0-5 14f+: 0-0
Track : LH: 1-5 RH: 0-0 Tight: 0-3 Gall: 0-0
Aids: Bl: 0-0 **Vi: 1-2** Tstrap: 0-0 Ckp: 0-0
Best Rating: 74 9/08 Curr 7f soft

Moderate; stays 7f; handles Fibresand; has worn a visor.

Hard Luck Story

93 **68**
3-y-o br g Lucky Story (USA)-Howards Heroine (IRE) (Danehill Dancer (IRE))
I Semple Gordon McDowall

Placings:6323-4340 (5947)

2009: 9^4GF, 11^3GF, 8^4G, 12^0G,

	Starts	1st	2nd	3rd	Win & Pl
Career Total (Turf)	8	0	1	3	4183

Going (Turf): **Sf: 0-4 GS: 0-0 Gd: 0-2 GF: 0-2 Fm: 0-0**
Distance: 5f/6f: 0-0 7f-8f: 0-3 9f-13f: 0-5 14f+: 0-0
Track : LH: 0-4 RH: 0-4 Tight: 0-5 Gall: 0-1
Aids: Bl: 0-0 Vi: 0-0 Tstrap: 0-1 Ckp: 0-1
Best Rating: **68** 10/08 Newc 1m heavy

Fair; stays 1m and acts on soft ground.

Hardanger (IRE)

85(88) (36)**64**

4-y-o b c Halling (USA)-Naughty Nell (Danehill Dancer (IRE))
T J Fitzgerald R N Cardwell

Placings:300-0005 **(6771)**
2009: 8^0GF, 6^0G, 7^0S, 8^5SD,

	Starts	1st	2nd	3rd	Win & Pl
Career Total (Turf)	6	0	0	1	482
Career Total (AW)	1	0	0	0	0

Going (Turf): **Sf: 0-1 GS: 0-0 Gd: 0-2 GF: 0-3 Fm: 0-0**
Distance: 5f/6f: 0-3 7f-8f: 0-3 9f-13f: 0-1 14f+: 0-0
Track : LH: 0-3 RH: 0-2 Tight: 0-1 Gall: 0-0
Aids: Bl: 0-0 Vi: 0-0 Tstrap: 0-0 Ckp: 0-0
Best Rating: **64** 5/08 Pont 6f gd-fm

Harlech Castle

103(109) (94)**86**

4-y-o b g Royal Applause-Ffestiniog (IRE) (Efisio)
J R Boyle (P F I Cole 14/7) Elite Racing Club

Placings:40213/00040041**1**20-003025000301 **(7870)**
2009: 5^0GF, 5^0GF, 6^3GF, 6^0HY, 6^2GF, 6^5GF, 6^0SD, 6^0SD, 7^0SD, 6^3SD, 6^0SD, 6^1SS,

	Starts	1st	2nd	3rd	Win & Pl
Career Total (Turf)	19	3	2	1	14578
Career Total (AW)	9	1	1	2	6137

	12/09	Sthl	6f	(0-75)H	SS	£2590
86	10/08	Catt	5f212y	(0-75)H	G-S	£2590
78	10/08	Nott	5f13y	(0-75)H	G-S	£3238
87	8/07	Newb	6f8y		GD	£3886

Total win prize-money £12304

Going (Turf): Sf: 0-1 **GS: 2-3** Gd: 1-4 GF: 0-10 Fm: 0-1
Distance: **5f/6f: 3-21** 7f-8f: 1-7 9f-13f: 0-0 14f+: 0-0
Track : **LH: 2-9** RH: 0-3 **Tight: 1-4** Gall: 0-5
Aids: **Bl: 3-15** Vi: 0-0 Tstrap: 0-0 Ckp: 0-0
Best Rating: **94** 11/08 Sthl 6f stand

Fair; effective at up to 7f; acts on good and faster ground, and on Fibresand; has worn blinkers.

Harlequinn Danseur (IRE)

96(83) (45)**57**

4-y-o b g Noverre (USA)-Nassma (IRE) (Sadler's Wells (USA))
N B King (D Burchell 5/5) Neil King

Placings:0560000/000000-1**5**6 **(2294)**
2009: 11^1F, 11^5GF, 12^6GF,

	Starts	1st	2nd	3rd	Win & Pl
Career Total (Turf)	14	1	0	0	3154
Career Total (AW)	2	0	0	0	

57	5/09	Brig	1m3f196y	(0-70)H	FRM	£3154

Total win prize-money £3154

Going (Turf): Sf: 0-0 GS: 0-1 Gd: 0-4 GF: 0-8 **Fm: 1-1**
Distance: 5f/6f: 0-4 7f-8f: 0-5 **9f-13f: 1-7** 14f+: 0-0
Track : **LH: 1-8** RH: 0-4 Tight: 0-3 Gall: 0-4
Aids: Bl: 0-2 Vi: 0-1 Tstrap: 0-0 Ckp: 0-0
Best Rating: **57** 5/09 Brig 1m3f196y firm

Moderate; stays 1m4f and acts on fast ground.

Harlestone Gold

85 **60**

4-y-o b g Golden Snake (USA)-Harlestone Lady (Shaamit (IRE))
J L Dunlop J L Dunlop

Placings:25-0 **(1088)**
2009: 11^0GF,

	Starts	1st	2nd	3rd	Win & Pl
Career Total (Turf)	3	0	1	0	771

Going (Turf): **Sf: 0-1 GS: 0-1 Gd: 0-0 GF: 0-1 Fm: 0-0**
Distance: 5f/6f: 0-0 7f-8f: 0-0 9f-13f: 0-3 14f+: 0-0
Track : LH: 0-0 RH: 0-3 Tight: 0-2 Gall: 0-0
Aids: Bl: 0-0 Vi: 0-0 Tstrap: 0-0 Ckp: 0-0
Best Rating: **60** 4/08 Folk 1m4f gd-sft

Harlestone Snake

102 **79**

3-y-o b g Golden Snake (USA)-Harlestone Lady (Shaamit (IRE))
J L Dunlop J L Dunlop

Placings:500-0316P **(5666)**
2009: 9^0G, 11^3G, 14^1G, 14^6G, 16^PSD,

	Starts	1st	2nd	3rd	Win & Pl
Career Total (Turf)	7	1	0	1	3720
Career Total (AW)	1	0	0	0	

79	6/09	Gdwd	1m6f	(0-75)H	GD	£3238

Total win prize-money £3238

Going (Turf): Sf: 0-0 GS: 0-1 **Gd: 1-5** GF: 0-1 Fm: 0-0
Distance: 5f/6f: 0-0 7f-8f: 0-1 9f-13f: 0-4 **14f+: 1-3**
Track : LH: 0-0 **RH: 1-7 Tight: 1-3** Gall: 0-0
Aids: Bl: 0-0 Vi: 0-0 Tstrap: 0-0 Ckp: 0-0
Best Rating: **79** 6/09 Gdwd 1m6f good

Harlestone Times (IRE)

90 **73**

2-y-o b c Olden Times-Harlestone Lady (Shaamit (IRE))
J L Dunlop J L Dunlop

Placings:0432 **(6786)**
2009: 7^0G, 7^4G, 8^3GF, 7^2G,

	Starts	1st	2nd	3rd	Win & Pl
Career Total (Turf)	4	0	1	1	2116

Going (Turf): **Sf: 0-0 GS: 0-0 Gd: 0-3 GF: 0-1 Fm: 0-0**
Distance: 5f/6f: 0-0 7f-8f: 0-4 9f-13f: 0-0 14f+: 0-0
Track : LH: 0-2 RH: 0-0 Tight: 0-0 Gall: 0-1
Aids: Bl: 0-0 Vi: 0-0 Tstrap: 0-0 Ckp: 0-0
Best Rating: **73** 10/09 Brig 7f214y good

Fair; stays 1m and acts on good ground.

Harley Fern

(77) (25)**5**

3-y-o b f Primo Valentino (IRE)-Its All Relative (Distant Relative)
M E Rimmer M P Murphy

Placings:00-0 **(7278)**
2009: 9^0SD,

	Starts	1st	2nd	3rd	Win & Pl
Career Total (Turf)	1	0	0	0	
Career Total (AW)	2	0	0	0	

Going (Turf): **Sf: 0-1 GS: 0-0 Gd: 0-0 GF: 0-0 Fm: 0-0**
Distance: 5f/6f: 0-0 7f-8f: 0-2 9f-13f: 0-1 14f+: 0-0
Track : LH: 0-1 RH: 0-1 Tight: 0-1 Gall: 0-0
Aids: Bl: 0-0 Vi: 0-0 Tstrap: 0-0 Ckp: 0-0
Best Rating: **25** 11/09 Wolv 1m1f103y stand

Haroldini (IRE)

(108) (71)**16**

7-y-o b g Orpen (USA)-Ciubanga (IRE) (Arazi (USA))
J Balding Tykes And Terriers Racing Club

Placings:04262000/00063030/0014002**1**221/0252336006 51/13150P00045-555256023600 **(3929)**
2009: 7^5SD, 8^5SD, 7^5SD, 7^2SD, 7^5SD, 8^6SD, 8^0SD, 7^2SD, 7^3SD, 8^6SD, 7^0SD, 8^0SF,

	Starts	1st	2nd	3rd	Win & Pl
Career Total (Turf)	19	0	1	2	1854
Career Total (AW)	43	6	8	4	17975

75	1/08	Sthl	1m	(0-65)H	STD	£1911
71	1/08	Sthl	7f	(0-60)H	STD	£1911
62	12/07	Sthl	7f	(0-53)H	SS	£2047
65	12/06	Wolv	7f32y	(0-60)H	STD	£2590
56	12/06	Wolv	7f32y	(0-45)	STD	£1706
64	5/06	Sthl	6f		STD	£1365

Total win prize-money £11532

Going (Turf): **Sf: 0-0 GS: 0-1 Gd: 0-6 GF: 0-8 Fm: 0-4**
Distance: 5f/6f: 1-17 **7f-8f: 5-42** 9f-13f: 0-3 14f+: 0-0
Track : **LH: 6-45** RH: 0-2 **Tight: 2-20** Gall: 0-1
Aids: Bl: 0-3 Vi: 0-5 Tstrap: 6-43 Ckp: 6-43
Best Rating: **75** 1/08 Sthl 1m stand

Modest; stays 7f and acts on Fibresand; has worn blinkers.

Harriet's Girl

101 **77**

3-y-o ch f Choisir (AUS)-Harriet (IRE) (Grand Lodge (USA))
A P Jarvis (K R Burke 24/7) Ray Bailey

Placings:521600-0356210303 **(7149)**
2009: 6^0GF, 7^3GF, 6^5GF, 6^6GF, 8^2G, 8^1G, 8^0GF, 8^3GF, 8^0G, 8^3G,

	Starts	1st	2nd	3rd	Win & Pl
Career Total (Turf)	16	2	2	3	14176

77	8/09	Hayd	1m30y	(0-80)H	GD	£5504
72	6/08	Pont	6f		G-F	£3885

Total win prize-money £9391

Going (Turf): Sf: 0-0 GS: 0-1 **Gd: 1-6 GF: 1-8** Fm: 0-1
Distance: 5f/6f: 1-7 7f-8f: 0-6 9f-13f: 1-3 14f+: 0-0
Track : **LH: 2-7** RH: 0-2 Tight: 0-0 Gall: 0-2
Aids: Bl: 0-0 Vi: 0-0 Tstrap: 0-0 Ckp: 0-0
Best Rating: **77** 10/09 NmkR 1m good

Fair; effective at 6f; acts on fast ground.

Harris Tweed

(86) (65)

2-y-o b c Hernando (FR)-Frog (Akarad (FR))

Sir Mark Prescott B Haggas

Placings:05 **(7276)**
2009: 7^{0}SD, 7^{5}SD,

	Starts	1st	2nd	3rd	Win & Pl
Career Total (Turf)	0	0	0	0	
Career Total (AW)	2	0	0	0	0

Going (Turf): **Sf: 0-0 GS: 0-0 Gd: 0-0 GF: 0-0 Fm: 0-0**
Distance: 5f/6f: 0-0 7f-8f: 0-2 9f-13f: 0-0 14f+: 0-0
Track : LH: 0-1 RH: 0-1 Tight: 0-1 Gall: 0-0
Aids: Bl: 0-0 Vi: 0-0 Tstrap: 0-0 Ckp: 0-0
Best Rating: **65** 11/09 Wolv 7f32y stand

Harrison George (IRE)

110 (73)**101**

4-y-o b g Danetime (IRE)-Dry Lightning (Shareef Dancer (USA))
R A Fahey P D Smith Holdings Ltd

Placings:242434/21311622-4200253615 **(6675)**
2009: 6^{4}GF, 6^{2}S, 7^{0}GF, 6^{0}GF, 6^{2}G, 6^{5}G, 7^{3}GF, 6^{6}GS, 7^{1}G, 7^{5}G,

	Starts	1st	2nd	3rd	Win & Pl
Career Total (Turf)	23	4	7	3	61163
Career Total (AW)	1	0	0	0	168

101	9/09	Ayr	7f50y	(0-95)H	GD	£11091
93	7/08	York	7f	(0-85)H	HVY	£6799
88	6/08	York	6f	(0-80)H	GD	£7123
81	5/08	Donc	6f		G-F	£3238

Total win prize-money £28253

Going (Turf): Sf: 1-6 GS: 0-1 **Gd: 2-8** GF: 1-8 Fm: 0-0
Distance: 5f/6f: 2-15 7f-8f: 2-9 9f-13f: 0-0 14f+: 0-0
Track : **LH: 2-7** RH: 0-1 Tight: 0-1 **Gall: 1-3**
Aids: Bl: 0-0 Vi: 0-0 Tstrap: 0-0 Ckp: 0-0
Best Rating: **101** 9/09 Ayr 7f50y good

Very useful; suited by 6f-7f; acts on any ground.

Harrison's Flyer (IRE)

96(99) (59)**65**

8-y-o b g Imperial Ballet (IRE)-Smart Pet (Petong)
J M Bradley racingshares.co.uk

Placings:4/020202U00111/606134001254100000/0003365323031030046660/246136221562540 0/005055005532004002002 5-00066656 **(5788)**
2009: 7^{0}SD, 7^{0}SD, 7^{0}SD, 6^{6}G, 7^{6}GF, 6^{6}G, 6^{5}GS, 6^{6}G,

	Starts	1st	2nd	3rd	Win & Pl
Career Total (Turf)	78	7	11	9	53371
Career Total (AW)	19	2	1	0	6981

75	6/07	Brig	5f59y	(0-65)H	G-S	£2072
65	5/07	Bath	5f161y	(0-70)H	G-F	£3238
73	9/06	Brig	5f59y	(0-75)H	G-S	£3238
85	10/05	York	5f	(0-75)H	GD	£5268
83	7/05	Sthl	6f		STD	£3146
86	5/05	Muss	5f	H	GD	£10081
86	11/04	Muss	5f	(0-92)H	G-S	£6799
78	10/04	Wolv	5f20y	(0-62)H	STD	£2989
76	10/04	Brig	5f59y	(0-70)H	SFT	£4044

Total win prize-money £40881

Going (Turf): Sf: 1-12 **GS: 3-16** Gd: 2-22 GF: 1-26 Fm: 0-2
Distance: **5f/6f: 9-83** 7f-8f: 0-14 9f-13f: 0-0 14f+: 0-0
Track : **LH: 6-37** RH: 0-4 Tight: 1-18 Gall: 1-10
Aids: Bl: 0-8 Vi: 0-1 Tstrap: 6-71 Ckp: 6-71
Best Rating: **86** 5/05 Muss 5f good

Moderate sprinter; acts on most ground; goes on sand.

Harry Africa (IRE)

67 **21**

3-y-o b g Catcher In The Rye (IRE)-Brave Dance (IRE) (Kris)
Mrs S Leech (Norma Twomey 8/6) R P Behan

Placings:00-0 **(3740)**
2009: 10^{0}GF,

	Starts	1st	2nd	3rd	Win & Pl
Career Total (Turf)	3	0	0	0	

Going (Turf): **Sf: 0-1 GS: 0-0 Gd: 0-0 GF: 0-1 Fm: 0-0**
Distance: 5f/6f: 0-1 7f-8f: 0-1 9f-13f: 0-1 14f+: 0-0
Track : LH: 0-2 RH: 0-1 Tight: 0-1 Gall: 0-0
Aids: Bl: 0-0 Vi: 0-1 Tstrap: 0-0 Ckp: 0-0
Best Rating: **21** 10/08 Naas 6f soft

Harry Days (IRE)

(91) (62)**29**

3-y-o b c Alhaarth (IRE)-Blushing Minstrel (IRE) (Nicholas (USA))
P J Lally Mrs Christine Kiernan

Placings:004 **(7401)**
2009: 7^{0}GF, 10^{0}GY, 8^{4}SD,

	Starts	1st	2nd	3rd	Win & Pl
Career Total (Turf)	2	0	0	0	
Career Total (AW)	1	0	0	0	192

Going (Turf): **Sf: 0-0 GS: 0-0 Gd: 0-0 GF: 0-1 Fm: 0-0**
Distance: 5f/6f: 0-0 7f-8f: 0-1 9f-13f: 0-2 14f+: 0-0
Track : LH: 0-1 RH: 0-2 Tight: 0-1 Gall: 0-0
Aids: Bl: 0-0 Vi: 0-0 Tstrap: 0-0 Ckp: 0-0
Best Rating: **62** 11/09 Wolv 1m141y stand

Harry Paget (IRE)

83 **45**

2-y-o gr c Starcraft (NZ)-True Love (Robellino (USA))
J R Best D Gorton

Placings:000 **(6697)**
2009: 7^{0}S, 9^{0}G, 9^{0}GS,

	Starts	1st	2nd	3rd	Win & Pl
Career Total (Turf)	3	0	0	0	

Going (Turf): **Sf: 0-1 GS: 0-1 Gd: 0-1 GF: 0-0 Fm: 0-0**
Distance: 5f/6f: 0-0 7f-8f: 0-1 9f-13f: 0-2 14f+: 0-0
Track : LH: 0-0 RH: 0-2 Tight: 0-2 Gall: 0-0
Aids: Bl: 0-0 Vi: 0-0 Tstrap: 0-0 Ckp: 0-0
Best Rating: **45** 9/09 Gdwd 1m1f good

Harry Patch

(103) (87)**89**

3-y-o b g Lujain (USA)-Hoh Dancer (Indian Ridge)
M A Jarvis Mrs Gay Jarvis

Placings:11-3 **(1639)**
2009: 6^{3}SD,

	Starts	1st	2nd	3rd	Win & Pl
Career Total (Turf)	2	2	0	0	9547
Career Total (AW)	1	0	0	1	1156

89	11/08	Donc	6f	(0-85)	SFT	£6476
79	10/08	Nott	5f13y		G-S	£3070

Total win prize-money £9547

Going (Turf): **Sf: 1-1 GS: 1-1** Gd: 0-0 GF: 0-0 Fm: 0-0
Distance: **5f/6f: 2-3** 7f-8f: 0-0 9f-13f: 0-0 14f+: 0-0
Track : LH: 0-1 RH: 0-0 Tight: 0-1 Gall: 0-0
Aids: Bl: 0-0 Vi: 0-0 Tstrap: 0-0 Ckp: 0-0
Best Rating: **89** 11/08 Donc 6f soft

Useful brother to Dichoh; winner of both starts on soft ground; stays 6f; acts on Polytrack.

Harry The Hawk

105 **79**

5-y-o b g Pursuit Of Love-Elora Gorge (IRE) (High Estate)
T D Walford David Dickson

Placings:050/36321/133020-205140 **(5622)**
2009: 10^{2}GS, 12^{0}GS, 10^{5}GS, 12^{1}G, 13^{4}G, 11^{0}S,

	Starts	1st	2nd	3rd	Win & Pl
Career Total (Turf)	20	3	3	4	14176

79	7/09	Donc	1m4f	(0-75)H	GD	£3238
76	4/08	Bevl	1m1f207y	(0-70)H	G-S	£2590
71	10/07	Newc	1m4f93y	(0-65)H	G-S	£2307

Total win prize-money £8136

Going (Turf): Sf: 0-6 **GS: 2-7** Gd: 1-4 GF: 0-3 Fm: 0-0
Distance: 5f/6f: 0-1 7f-8f: 0-3 **9f-13f: 3-15** 14f+: 0-1
Track : **LH: 2-13** RH: 1-6 Tight: 0-3 **Gall: 2-9**
Aids: Bl: 0-0 Vi: 0-0 Tstrap: 0-0 Ckp: 0-0
Best Rating: **79** 8/09 Catt 1m5f175y good

Fair; effective over 1m4f; acts on good and easy ground.

Harry Up

97(112) (93)**77**

8-y-o ch g Piccolo-Faraway Lass (Distant Relative)
M J Scudamore (Andrew Reid 6/7) A S Reid

Placings:321612461040/2303400/00200551/00206152500 0014/106060032420325/2201100324223103-411051452114500 **(7646)**
2009: 5^{4}SS, 5^{1}SD, 5^{1}SD, 5^{0}SD, 5^{5}SD, 5^{1}SD, 5^{4}SD, 5^{5}SD, 5^{2}SD, 5^{1}SD, 5^{1}SD, 5^{4}F, 5^{5}G, 5^{0}SD, 5^{0}SD,

	Starts	1st	2nd	3rd	Win & Pl
Career Total (Turf)	50	3	9	5	56837
Career Total (AW)	38	12	6	3	57727

83	5/09	Wolv	5f20y		STD	£2729
86	4/09	Wolv	5f20y		STD	£2047
89	2/09	Wolv	5f20y		STD	£1878
89	1/09	Wolv	5f20y		STD	£2729
93	1/09	Wolv	5f20y		STD	£2047
93	11/08	Wolv	5f20y	(0-85)H	STD	£5828
89	4/08	Wolv	5f20y	(0-85)H	STD	£4209
83	2/08	Kemp	5f		STD	£2331
96	1/07	Wolv	5f20y	(0-85)H	STD	£4857
90	12/06	Kemp	5f	(0-95)H	STD	£7790
93	7/06	Wolv	5f216y	(0-85)H	STD	£6477
86	12/05	Wolv	5f216y	(0-75)H	STD	£2905
80	8/03	Ripn	5f	C	G-F	£7116
89	7/03	Ches	5f16y	D	G-F	£8242
76	6/03	Ling	5f	F	G-F	£3080

Total win prize-money £64271

Going (Turf): Sf: 0-3 GS: 0-4 Gd: 0-16 **GF: 3-21** Fm: 0-6
Distance: **5f/6f: 15-86** 7f-8f: 0-2 9f-13f: 0-0 14f+: 0-0
Track : **LH: 11-38** RH: 2-5 **Tight: 11-32** Gall: 0-7
Aids: Bl: 0-4 Vi: 0-0 Tstrap: 8-29 Ckp: 8-29
Best Rating: **96** 1/07 Wolv 5f20y stand

Fair; effective over 5f-6f; acts on fast ground; also goes on Polytrack; very tough; likes to front-run; has worn blinkers and cheekpieces.

Hart Of Gold

101(104) (71)74

5-y-o b g Foxhound (USA)-Bullion (Sabrehill (USA))

R A Harris Ridge House Stables Ltd

Placings:340123520125/00504120604/6444315633402345100-224340433404000 6602 **(7877)**

2009: 6^2SD, 5^2SD, 6^4SD, 5^3SD, 6^4SD, 6^0G, 6^4GF, 6^3SD, 6^3GF, 5^4F, 6^0GF, 6^4G, 5^0GF, 6^0GF, 6^0SD, 6^6SD, 6^6SD, 6^0SD, 7^2SD,

	Starts	1st	2nd	3rd	Win & Pl
Career Total (Turf)	35	3	5	5	20747
Career Total (AW)	26	2	3	4	10312

71	11/08	Kemp	6f	(0-60)H	STD	£1706
69	4/08	Catt	5f212y	(0-65)H	G-S	£2047
61	9/07	Folk	7f		G-F	£2047
85	9/06	Sthl	7f	(0-85)	GD	£5181
79	6/06	Wolv	5f216y		STD	£3886

Total win prize-money £14869

Going (Turf): Sf: 0-3 **GS: 1-2 Gd: 1-9 GF: 1-18** Fm: 0-3
Distance: **5f/6f: 3-44** 7f-8f: 2-15 9f-13f: 0-2 14f+: 0-0
Track : **LH: 3-26** RH: 1-11 **Tight: 3-22** Gall: 0-3
Aids: Bl: 0-3 Vi: 0-0 Tstrap: 1-22 Ckp: 1-22
Best Rating: **86** 9/06 Ches 7f2y gd-fm

Moderate; effective at 6f-7f; acts on fast and easy ground; goes on Polytrack; has worn cheekpieces.

Harting Hill

98(101) (62)48

4-y-o b g Mujahid (USA)-Mossy Rose (King Of Spain)

M P Tregoning Miss S Sharp

Placings:0/0003030-0456041 **(7614)**

2009: 9^0SD, 10^4SD, 10^5G, 14^6GF, 10^0SD, 8^4SD, 7^1SD,

	Starts	1st	2nd	3rd	Win & Pl
Career Total (Turf)	5	0	0	0	0
Career Total (AW)	10	1	0	2	2735

62	12/09	Kemp	7f	(0-55)	STD	£2047

Total win prize-money £2047

Going (Turf): **Sf: 0-0 GS: 0-0 Gd: 0-4 GF: 0-1 Fm: 0-0**
Distance: 5f/6f: 0-0 **7f-8f: 1-5** 9f-13f: 0-9 14f+: 0-1
Track : LH: 0-7 **RH: 1-7** Tight: 0-6 Gall: 0-1
Aids: Bl: 0-0 Vi: 0-0 Tstrap: 0-0 Ckp: 0-0
Best Rating: **62** 12/09 Kemp 7f stand

Moderate; effective over 7f-1m3f; acts on Polytrack.

Hartley

107 107

3-y-o b g Lucky Story (USA)-Arctic Song (Charnwood Forest (IRE))

J D Bethell Clarendon Thoroughbred Racing

Placings:010-232 **(4521)**

2009: 7^2GF, 7^3GF, 8^2S,

	Starts	1st	2nd	3rd	Win & Pl
Career Total (Turf)	6	1	2	1	18630

92	9/08	Catt	5f212y	G-S	£3561

Total win prize-money £3562

Going (Turf): Sf: 0-1 **GS: 1-1** Gd: 0-1 GF: 0-3 Fm: 0-0
Distance: **5f/6f: 1-2** 7f-8f: 0-4 9f-13f: 0-0 14f+: 0-0
Track : **LH: 1-3** RH: 0-1 **Tight: 1-2** Gall: 0-1
Aids: Bl: 0-0 Vi: 0-0 Tstrap: 0-0 Ckp: 0-0
Best Rating: **107** 8/09 Gdwd 1m soft

Smart; Listed placed; suited by 6f-1m; acts on fast and easy ground.

Hartshead

104 (84)86

10-y-o b g Machiavellian (USA)-Zalitzine (USA) (Zilzal (USA))

W Storey Miss Kay T Thompson

Placings:304460/2061141123/0361230451/625031153/60002000/0530542500-603050 **(6218)**

2009: 6^6G, 8^0G, 7^3GF, 8^0GF, 8^5S, 10^0GF,

	Starts	1st	2nd	3rd	Win & Pl
Career Total (Turf)	57	8	6	7	105582
Career Total (AW)	2	0	0	1	2600

103	7/06	Newc	7f	(0-95)H	G-F	£11217
98	7/06	Catt	7f	(0-90)H	FRM	£9715
98	10/05	York	1m	(0-100)H	GD	£13759
89	6/05	Carl	7f200y	(0-80)H	G-F	£16883
81	9/04	Rdcr	7f	(0-75)	G-F	£6987
83	7/04	Thsk	6f	D(0-80)H	G-F	£5590
81	7/04	Carl	5f193y	E(0-70)	GD	£3623
65	6/04	Rdcr	6f	D	GD	£3474

Total win prize-money £71253

Going (Turf): Sf: 0-2 GS: 0-3 Gd: 3-19 **GF: 4-28** Fm: 1-5
Distance: 5f/6f: 3-10 **7f-8f: 5-35** 9f-13f: 0-14 14f+: 0-0
Track : LH: 2-23 RH: 2-14 Tight: 1-15 Gall: 1-8
Aids: Bl: 0-0 Vi: 0-0 Tstrap: 0-0 Ckp: 0-0
Best Rating: **103** 7/06 Newc 7f gd-fm

Fair; stays 1m and acts on most ground.

Harty Boy (USA)

89(97) (67)48

3-y-o ch g Stravinsky (USA)-Peanut Gallery (USA) (Mister Baileys)

Jim Best (Mrs S Leech 4/5) Miss J S Dollan

Placings:4446006600 **(7658)**

2009: 8^4SD, 8^4SD, 8^4SD, 8^6SD, 7^0SD, 8^0GF, 8^6GF, 8^6SD, 9^0SD, 12^0SD,

	Starts	1st	2nd	3rd	Win & Pl
Career Total (Turf)	2	0	0	0	0
Career Total (AW)	8	0	0	0	332

Going (Turf): **Sf: 0-0 GS: 0-0 Gd: 0-0 GF: 0-2 Fm: 0-0**
Distance: 5f/6f: 0-0 7f-8f: 0-5 9f-13f: 0-5 14f+: 0-0
Track : LH: 0-9 RH: 0-1 Tight: 0-7 Gall: 0-0
Aids: Bl: 0-1 Vi: 0-1 Tstrap: 0-2 Ckp: 0-2
Best Rating: **67** 2/09 Ling 1m stand

Modest; stays 1m; acts on Polytrack.

Harvest Dancer (IRE)

95 79

2-y-o ch c Danehill Dancer (IRE)-Autumnal (IRE) (Indian Ridge)

B J Meehan Paul & Jenny Green

Placings:4 **(4986)**

2009: 7^4GF,

	Starts	1st	2nd	3rd	Win & Pl
Career Total (Turf)	1	0	0	0	361

Going (Turf): **Sf: 0-0 GS: 0-0 Gd: 0-0 GF: 0-1 Fm: 0-0**
Distance: 5f/6f: 0-0 7f-8f: 0-1 9f-13f: 0-0 14f+: 0-0
Track : LH: 0-0 RH: 0-0 Tight: 0-0 Gall: 0-0
Aids: Bl: 0-0 Vi: 0-0 Tstrap: 0-0 Ckp: 0-0
Best Rating: **79** 8/09 Newb 7f gd-fm

Harvest Song (IRE)

70 28

3-y-o b g Sadler's Wells (USA)-La Mouline (IRE) (Nashwan (USA))

Sir Michael Stoute The Queen

Placings:0-0 **(2090)**

2009: 12^0G,

	Starts	1st	2nd	3rd	Win & Pl
Career Total (Turf)	2	0	0	0	

Going (Turf): **Sf: 0-1 GS: 0-0 Gd: 0-1 GF: 0-0 Fm: 0-0**
Distance: 5f/6f: 0-0 7f-8f: 0-0 9f-13f: 0-2 14f+: 0-0
Track : LH: 0-2 RH: 0-0 Tight: 0-1 Gall: 0-0
Aids: Bl: 0-0 Vi: 0-0 Tstrap: 0-0 Ckp: 0-0
Best Rating: **28** 11/08 Nott 1m75y heavy

Hasanpour (IRE)

104 65

9-y-o b g Dr Devious (IRE)-Hasainiya (IRE) (Top Ville)

K J Burke R G Owens

Placings:2/3101/40/0/454/30004/40-0 **(1399)**

2009: 21^0F,

	Starts	1st	2nd	3rd	Win & Pl
Career Total (Turf)	19	2	1	2	26038

101	9/03	Haml	1m5f9y	B(0-105)H	G-S	£12185
70	5/03	Haml	1m3f16y	D	G-S	£5768

Total win prize-money £17955

Going (Turf): Sf: 0-4 **GS: 2-3** Gd: 0-2 GF: 0-6 Fm: 0-1
Distance: 5f/6f: 0-0 7f-8f: 0-1 9f-13f: 1-5 14f+: 1-13
Track : LH: 0-5 **RH: 2-13 Tight: 2-2** Gall: 0-3
Aids: Bl: 0-9 Vi: 0-0 Tstrap: 0-0 Ckp: 0-0
Best Rating: **101** 9/03 Haml 1m5f9y gd-sft

Hassadin

93(88) (61)51

3-y-o ch g Reset (AUS)-Crocolat (Croco Rouge (IRE))

A B Haynes Ms C Berry

Placings:04300-000534 **(5123)**

2009: 10^0SD, 10^0SD, 12^0GF, 11^5GF, 14^3GS, 11^4F,

	Starts	1st	2nd	3rd	Win & Pl
Career Total (Turf)	6	0	0	1	536
Career Total (AW)	5	0	0	1	674

Going (Turf): **Sf: 0-0 GS: 0-1 Gd: 0-0 GF: 0-4 Fm: 0-1**
Distance: 5f/6f: 0-0 7f-8f: 0-2 9f-13f: 0-8 14f+: 0-1
Track : LH: 0-8 RH: 0-2 Tight: 0-6 Gall: 0-1
Aids: Bl: 0-0 Vi: 0-1 Tstrap: 0-2 Ckp: 0-2
Best Rating: **61** 9/08 GrLe 1m2f stand

Hasty (IRE)

97(93) (72)90

2-y-o b f Invincible Spirit (IRE)-Saramacca (IRE) (Kahyasi)

B W Hills Richard Morecombe & James Netherthorpe

Placings:522153 **(6447)**

2009: 6^5G, 6^2GF, 7^2SD, 7^1F, 6^5GF, 7^3GF,

	Starts	1st	2nd	3rd	Win & Pl
Career Total (Turf)	5	1	1	1	10654
Career Total (AW)	1	0	1	0	1156

86	7/09	Folk	7f	FRM	£4209

Total win prize-money £4209

Going (Turf): Sf: 0-0 GS: 0-0 Gd: 0-1 GF: 0-3 **Fm: 1-1**
Distance: 5f/6f: 0-2 **7f-8f: 1-4** 9f-13f: 0-0 14f+: 0-0
Track : LH: 0-0 RH: 0-1 Tight: 0-0 Gall: 0-0
Aids: Bl: 0-0 Vi: 0-0 Tstrap: 0-0 Ckp: 0-0
Best Rating: **90** 10/09 NmkR 7f gd-fm

Useful; effective over 7f; acts on fast ground.

Hatch A Plan (IRE)

98(100) (54)**60**
8-y-o b g Vettori (IRE)-Fast Chick (Henbit (USA))
Mouse Hamilton-Fairley Hamilton-Fairley Racing

Placings:000/**0**U01224005/40645S/**6**064U202414/**000**430 360606**210**/**1400**030**50506**-**65206**552131000 **(7767)**
2009: **11**^{6}SD, **12**^{5}SD, **10**^{2}SD, **12**^{0}SD, **9**^{6}SD, **10**^{5}G, **11**^{5}F, **10**^{2}F, **10**^{1}F, **10**^{3}F, **11**^{1}GF, **10**^{0}GF, **10**^{0}G, **11**^{0}SD,

	Starts	1st	2nd	3rd	Win & Pl
Career Total (Turf)	**48**	**4**	**5**	**4**	**21949**
Career Total (AW)	**23**	**2**	**2**	**0**	**4690**

60	7/09	Newb	1m3f5y	(0-70)H	G-F	£2590
56	6/09	Bath	1m2f46y	(0-70)H	FRM	£2719
63	1/08	Wolv	1m1f103y	(0-60)H	STD	£1774
66	11/07	Kemp	1m2f	(0-60)H	STD	£1706
72	8/06	Wind	1m3f135y	(0-70)H	GD	£3238
74	6/04	Wind	1m2f7yE	(0-65)	GD	£3620

Total win prize-money £15651

Going (Turf): Sf: 0-2 GS: 0-3 **Gd: 2-13** GF: 1-24 Fm: 1-6
Distance: 5f/6f: 0-3 7f-8f: 0-1 **9f-13f: 6-66** 14f+: 0-1
Track : **LH: 3-31** RH: 2-30 **Tight: 4-38** Gall: 1-12
Aids: Bl: 0-0 Vi: 0-0 Tstrap: 0-1 Ckp: 0-1
Best Rating: **77** 8/04 Leic 1m3f183y gd-fm

Moderate; effective over 1m2f-1m4f; acts on fast ground; also goes on Polytrack.

Hathaal (IRE)

87 (74)**25**
10-y-o b g Alzao (USA)-Ballet Shoes (IRE) (Ela-Mana-Mou)
Jim Best Muerren Racing

Placings:21/4015/**14100**/00**506**/**460262**/**43016**/**050220**0021/ 0 **(2634)**
2009: 11^{0}GF,

	Starts	1st	2nd	3rd	Win & Pl
Career Total (Turf)	**19**	**3**	**3**	**0**	**25475**
Career Total (AW)	**18**	**3**	**3**	**1**	**45594**

48	7/07	Wind	1m3f135y		G-S	£3238
	3/06	Mija	1m6f		STD	£3448
	6/03	Mija	1m4f		STD	£33117
	3/03	DosH	1m3f		STD	£2597
93	8/02	Yarm	1m2f21yC	(0-90)	G-F	£9368
93	10/01	NmkR	1m	D	SFT	£5668

Total win prize-money £57437

Going (Turf): **Sf: 1-8 GS: 1-2** Gd: 0-5 **GF: 1-4** Fm: 0-0
Distance: 5f/6f: 0-0 7f-8f: 1-2 **9f-13f: 4-31** 14f+: 1-4
Track : **LH: 1-10** RH: 0-7 **Tight: 2-5** Gall: 0-4
Aids: Bl: 0-1 **Vi: 2-11** Tstrap: 0-0 Ckp: 0-0
Best Rating: **102** 9/02 Donc 1m2f60y gd-fm

Moderate; winner in Spain; effective at around 1m4f; acts on easy ground; also goes on Polytrack.

Hathaway (IRE)

86(86) (48)**51**
2-y-o ch f Redback-Finty (IRE) (Entrepreneur)
W M Brisbourne W M Clare

Placings:5600 **(7799)**
2009: 5^{5}G, 6^{6}GF, 7^{0}GF, 5^{0}SD,

	Starts	1st	2nd	3rd	Win & Pl
Career Total (Turf)	**3**	**0**	**0**	**0**	**0**
Career Total (AW)	**1**	**0**	**0**	**0**	

Going (Turf): **Sf: 0-0 GS: 0-0 Gd: 0-1 GF: 0-2 Fm: 0-0**
Distance: 5f/6f: 0-3 7f-8f: 0-1 9f-13f: 0-0 14f+: 0-0
Track : LH: 0-2 RH: 0-0 Tight: 0-1 Gall: 0-0
Aids: Bl: 0-0 Vi: 0-0 Tstrap: 0-0 Ckp: 0-0
Best Rating: **51** 5/09 Thsk 5f good

Hatman Jack (IRE)

81(98) (66)**32**
3-y-o ch g Bahamian Bounty-Mary Hinge (Dowsing (USA))
B G Powell Mrs Lynn Chapman

Placings:60-44**0000315006** **(7890)**
2009: 6^{4}SD, 6^{4}SD, 7^{0}SD, 5^{0}GF, 10^{0}G, 8^{0}F, 7^{3}SD, 6^{1}SD, 6^{5}SD, 7^{0}SS, 6^{0}SD, 6^{6}SD,

	Starts	1st	2nd	3rd	Win & Pl
Career Total (Turf)	**3**	**0**	**0**	**0**	
Career Total (AW)	**11**	**1**	**0**	**1**	**2542**

64	8/09	Ling	6f	(0-60)H	STD	£2047

Total win prize-money £2047

Going (Turf): **Sf: 0-0 GS: 0-0 Gd: 0-1 GF: 0-1 Fm: 0-1**
Distance: **5f/6f: 1-7** 7f-8f: 0-5 9f-13f: 0-2 14f+: 0-0
Track : **LH: 1-13** RH: 0-1 **Tight: 1-12** Gall: 0-1
Aids: Bl: 0-0 Vi: 0-0 Tstrap: 1-2 Ckp: 1-2
Best Rating: **66** 2/09 Kemp 6f stand

Modest; effective over 6f; acts on Polytrack.

Hatta Diamond (IRE)

100(102) (68)**76**
3-y-o ch c Pivotal-Moonshell (IRE) (Sadler's Wells (USA))
M Johnston Sheikh Hamdan Bin Mohammed Al Maktoum

Placings:516463 **(3543)**
2009: 9^{5}SD, 8^{1}SD, 9^{6}G, 9^{4}GF, 9^{6}GF, 10^{3}F,

	Starts	1st	2nd	3rd	Win & Pl
Career Total (Turf)	**4**	**0**	**0**	**1**	**1227**
Career Total (AW)	**2**	**1**	**0**	**0**	**2730**

68	3/09	Wolv	1m141y	STD	£2729

Total win prize-money £2730

Going (Turf): **Sf: 0-0 GS: 0-0 Gd: 0-1 GF: 0-2 Fm: 0-1**
Distance: 5f/6f: 0-0 7f-8f: 0-0 **9f-13f: 1-6** 14f+: 0-0
Track : **LH: 1-3** RH: 0-3 **Tight: 1-5** Gall: 0-0
Aids: Bl: 0-0 Vi: 0-0 Tstrap: 0-0 Ckp: 0-0
Best Rating: **76** 5/09 Leic 1m1f218y gd-fm

Fair; effective over 1m; acts on Polytrack.

Hatta Fort

111 (109)**112**
4-y-o b c Cape Cross (IRE)-Oshiponga (Barathea (IRE))
Saeed Bin Suroor Godolphin

Placings:513146/**24331413**-6120605 **(5618a)**
2009: 6^{6}G, 6^{1}G, 6^{2}GF, 6^{0}GF, 6^{6}GF, 8^{0}G, 8^{5}GF,

	Starts	1st	2nd	3rd	Win & Pl
Career Total (Turf)	**17**	**4**	**1**	**3**	**200988**
Career Total (AW)	**4**	**1**	**1**	**1**	**82671**

109	2/09	Ndas	6f110y	(100-113)H	GD	£72916
109	10/08	Keen	7f		FST	£62311
	8/08	Sara	5f110y		FRM	£20804
105	7/07	NmkJ	7f		G-F	£39746
94	6/07	Wind	5f10y		G-F	£4533

Total win prize-money £200313

Going (Turf): Sf: 0-0 GS: 0-2 Gd: 1-3 **GF: 2-8** Fm: 1-4
Distance: 5f/6f: 2-10 **7f-8f: 3-10** 9f-13f: 0-1 14f+: 0-0
Track : **LH: 1-5** RH: 0-2 Tight: 0-1 **Gall: 2-4**
Aids: Bl: 0-1 Vi: 0-0 Tstrap: 0-0 Ckp: 0-0
Best Rating: **112** 2/09 Ndas 6f gd-fm

Listed-class; won Group 2 Superlative Stakes at two and Grade 3 winner on sand in the US; effective over 6f-7f; acts on fast ground; has worn a tongue tie.

Hatton Flight

107(107) (93)**102**
5-y-o b g Kahyasi-Platonic (Zafonic (USA))
A M Balding David Brownlow

Placings:064/334516**301**/**41111050**-**111U05** **(5854)**
2009: 12^{1}SD, 12^{1}G, 12^{1}GF, 12^{U}GF, 11^{0}GF, 12^{5}GF,

	Starts	1st	2nd	3rd	Win & Pl
Career Total (Turf)	**17**	**6**	**0**	**2**	**61994**
Career Total (AW)	**9**	**3**	**0**	**1**	**17156**

102	5/09	NmkR	1m4f	(0-105)H	G-F	£31155
99	4/09	Epsm	1m4f10y	(0-95)H	GD	£9346
93	4/09	Ling	1m4f	(0-105)H	STD	£11656
91	7/08	Asct	1m4f	(0-85)H	G-S	£7123
86	6/08	Thsk	1m4f	(0-80)H	FRM	£5180
79	5/08	Gdwd	1m4f	(0-80)H	GD	£5180
72	4/08	Wolv	1m4f50y	(0-65)H	STD	£2388
68	10/07	Kemp	1m4f	(0-60)H	STD	£2047
66	8/07	Bath	1m5f22y	(0-70)H	G-F	£3238

Total win prize-money £77320

Going (Turf): Sf: 0-0 GS: 1-1 **Gd: 2-5 GF: 2-10** Fm: 1-1
Distance: 5f/6f: 0-0 7f-8f: 0-2 **9f-13f: 8-20** 14f+: 1-4
Track : **LH: 5-15** RH: 4-11 **Tight: 6-13** Gall: 2-5
Aids: **Bl: 9-19** Vi: 0-0 Tstrap: 0-3 Ckp: 0-3
Best Rating: **102** 5/09 NmkR 1m4f gd-fm

Very useful; stays 1m6f but best at 1m4f; acts on fast and easy ground and Polytrack; often blinkered.

Haulage Lady (IRE)

95 **64**
3-y-o b f Xaar-Blue Mantle (IRE) (Barathea (IRE))
Karen McLintock J R Adams (Newcastle) Limited

Placings:02504-60640 **(4348)**
2009: 8^{6}GS, 8^{0}GS, 9^{6}GF, 7^{4}G, 9^{0}G,

	Starts	1st	2nd	3rd	Win & Pl
Career Total (Turf)	**10**	**0**	**1**	**0**	**1324**

Going (Turf): **Sf: 0-2 GS: 0-4 Gd: 0-3 GF: 0-1 Fm: 0-0**
Distance: 5f/6f: 0-1 7f-8f: 0-6 9f-13f: 0-3 14f+: 0-0
Track : LH: 0-1 RH: 0-4 Tight: 0-1 Gall: 0-1
Aids: Bl: 0-0 Vi: 0-0 Tstrap: 0-3 Ckp: 0-3
Best Rating: **64** 8/08 Rdcr 7f gd-sft

Fair; effective over 7f; acts on easy ground.

Haunting

79 **16**
3-y-o b f Beat Hollow-Broken Spectre (Rainbow Quest (USA))
A G Foster Stephen Jordan

Placings:00 **(6766)**
2009: 12^{0}G, 12^{0}GS,

	Starts	1st	2nd	3rd	Win & Pl
Career Total (Turf)	2	0	0	0	

Going (Turf): Sf: 0-0 GS: 0-1 Gd: 0-1 GF: 0-0 Fm: 0-0
Distance: 5f/6f: 0-0 7f-8f: 0-0 9f-13f: 0-2 14f+: 0-0
Track : LH: 0-1 RH: 0-1 Tight: 0-1 Gall: 0-1
Aids: Bl: 0-0 Vi: 0-0 Tstrap: 0-0 Ckp: 0-0
Best Rating: 16 10/09 Newc 1m4f93y gd-sft

Have More

76(75) (44)32
2-y-o ch f Haafhd-For More (FR) (Sanglamore (USA))
B J Meehan Paul & Jenny Green

Placings:000 (5284)
2009: 6^{0}GF, 7^{0}SD, 7^{0}GF,

	Starts	1st	2nd	3rd	Win & Pl
Career Total (Turf)	2	0	0	0	
Career Total (AW)	1	0	0	0	

Going (Turf): Sf: 0-0 GS: 0-0 Gd: 0-0 GF: 0-2 Fm: 0-0
Distance: 5f/6f: 0-1 7f-8f: 0-2 9f-13f: 0-0 14f+: 0-0
Track : LH: 0-0 RH: 0-1 Tight: 0-0 Gall: 0-1
Aids: Bl: 0-0 Vi: 0-0 Tstrap: 0-0 Ckp: 0-0
Best Rating: 44 8/09 Kemp 7f stand

Havelock Flyer

76 33
2-y-o b c Mujahid (USA)-Dragon Flyer (IRE) (Tagula (IRE))
C Grant Havelock Racing 2

Placings:000 (3726)
2009: 5^{0}GF, 6^{0}G, 5^{0}G,

	Starts	1st	2nd	3rd	Win & Pl
Career Total (Turf)	3	0	0	0	

Going (Turf): Sf: 0-0 GS: 0-0 Gd: 0-2 GF: 0-1 Fm: 0-0
Distance: 5f/6f: 0-3 7f-8f: 0-0 9f-13f: 0-0 14f+: 0-0
Track : LH: 0-0 RH: 0-0 Tight: 0-0 Gall: 0-0
Aids: Bl: 0-0 Vi: 0-0 Tstrap: 0-0 Ckp: 0-0
Best Rating: 33 5/09 Rdcr 5f gd-fm

Having A Ball

96(103) (71)51
5-y-o b g Mark Of Esteem (IRE)-All Smiles (Halling (USA))
P D Cundell Miss M C Fraser

Placings:0550/6224/42252100023415-51052620 (7481)
2009: 8^{5}SD, 8^{1}SD, 8^{0}SD, 8^{5}SD, 8^{2}SD, 8^{6}G, 8^{2}SD, 8^{0}SD,

	Starts	1st	2nd	3rd	Win & Pl
Career Total (Turf)	8	0	2	1	1761
Career Total (AW)	22	3	6	0	9395

71	4/09	Kemp	1m	(0-65)H	STD	£1942
68	11/08	Sthl	1m	(0-60)H	STD	£1706
60	4/08	Kemp	1m	(0-55)H	STD	£2047

Total win prize-money £5696

Going (Turf): Sf: 0-5 GS: 0-0 Gd: 0-3 GF: 0-0 Fm: 0-0
Distance: 5f/6f: 0-4 **7f-8f: 3-23** 9f-13f: 0-3 14f+: 0-0
Track : LH: 1-12 **RH: 2-13** Tight: 0-5 Gall: 0-0
Aids: Bl: 0-0 Vi: 0-0 Tstrap: 0-0 Ckp: 0-0
Best Rating: 71 11/09 Kemp 1m stand

Modest; effective at around 1m; acts on soft ground; goes on Fibresand and Polytrack.

Hawaana (IRE)

101(108) (85)78
4-y-o b g Bahri (USA)-Congress (IRE) (Dancing Brave (USA))
Miss Gay Kelleway (Eve Johnson Houghton 20/7) Kings Club Syndicate II

Placings:410/000440522-16654414054 (7684)
2009: 8^{1}SD, 7^{6}SD, 8^{6}GF, 8^{5}SD, 8^{4}SD, 8^{4}GF, 8^{1}SS, 8^{4}SD, 8^{0}SD, 8^{5}SD, 10^{4}SD,

	Starts	1st	2nd	3rd	Win & Pl
Career Total (Turf)	13	1	1	0	7091
Career Total (AW)	10	2	1	0	7337

82	10/09	Ling	1m	(0-75)H	SS	£2729
81	3/09	Kemp	1m	(0-75)H	STD	£2590
79	8/07	Leic	7f9y		FRM	£4731

Total win prize-money £10052

Going (Turf): Sf: 0-1 GS: 0-3 Gd: 0-0 GF: 0-8 **Fm: 1-1**
Distance: 5f/6f: 0-1 **7f-8f: 3-12** 9f-13f: 0-10 14f+: 0-0
Track : LH: 1-5 RH: 1-14 **Tight: 1-10** Gall: 0-1
Aids: Bl: 0-0 Vi: 0-0 Tstrap: 0-0 Ckp: 0-0
Best Rating: 85 12/09 Kemp 1m2f stand

Fair; effective at 1m; acts on most ground and on Polytrack.

Hawaass (USA)

101 98
4-y-o b g Seeking The Gold (USA)-Sheroog (USA) (Shareef Dancer (USA))
M Johnston Sheikh Ahmed Al Maktoum

Placings:01/1-20 (1460)
2009: 10^{2}GF, 10^{0}G,

	Starts	1st	2nd	3rd	Win & Pl
Career Total (Turf)	5	2	1	0	13525

96	6/08	NmkJ	1m2f	(0-85)H	G-F	£4984
86	9/07	Sand	1m14y		G-F	£5181

Total win prize-money £10167

Going (Turf): Sf: 0-0 GS: 0-1 Gd: 0-1 **GF: 2-3** Fm: 0-0
Distance: 5f/6f: 0-1 7f-8f: 0-0 **9f-13f: 2-4** 14f+: 0-0
Track : LH: 0-2 **RH: 2-2** Tight: 0-1 **Gall: 1-1**
Aids: Bl: 0-0 Vi: 0-0 Tstrap: 0-0 Ckp: 0-0
Best Rating: 98 4/09 Pont 1m2f6y gd-fm

Very useful; stays 1m2f; acts on fast ground; suited by forcing tactics.

Hawk Mountain (UAE)

105 90
4-y-o b g Halling (USA)-Friendly (USA) (Lear Fan (USA))
J J Quinn P Morrison & N Luck

Placings:40/63122-1421245 (5823)
2009: 14^{1}G, 14^{4}GF, 16^{2}GS, 14^{1}GF, 16^{2}G, 16^{4}GF, 14^{5}GF,

	Starts	1st	2nd	3rd	Win & Pl
Career Total (Turf)	14	3	4	1	21753

85	6/09	Donc	1m6f132y	(0-85)H	G-F	£4857
82	5/09	Donc	1m6f132y	(0-85)H	GD	£4857
70	8/08	Nott	1m6f15y	(0-60)H	GD	£1942

Total win prize-money £11657

Going (Turf): Sf: 0-1 GS: 0-2 **Gd: 2-7** GF: 1-4 Fm: 0-0
Distance: 5f/6f: 0-1 7f-8f: 0-2 9f-13f: 0-2 **14f+: 3-9**
Track : **LH: 3-11** RH: 0-2 Tight: 0-2 **Gall: 2-7**
Aids: Bl: 0-0 Vi: 0-0 Tstrap: 0-0 Ckp: 0-0
Best Rating: 90 8/09 York 2m88y gd-fm

Fair; stays 1m6f and acts on most ground.

Hawk's Eye

107(90) (41)86
3-y-o br g Hawk Wing (USA)-Inchiri (Sadler's Wells (USA))
M F De Kock (E F Vaughan 26/6) Ramsden/Mrs Ramsden/Morecombe/McVeigh

Placings:044-203311 (5366)
2009: 10^{2}GF, 9^{0}GF, 8^{3}GF, 8^{3}GS, 10^{1}GF, 10^{1}F,

	Starts	1st	2nd	3rd	Win & Pl
Career Total (Turf)	8	2	1	2	8295
Career Total (AW)	1	0	0	0	0

83	8/09	Ling	1m2f	(0-75)H	FRM	£3238
86	8/09	Wind	1m2f7y	(0-75)H	G-F	£2729

Total win prize-money £5968

Going (Turf): Sf: 0-1 GS: 0-1 Gd: 0-0 **GF: 1-5 Fm: 1-1**
Distance: 5f/6f: 0-3 7f-8f: 0-2 **9f-13f: 2-4** 14f+: 0-0
Track : LH: 1-2 RH: 1-3 **Tight: 2-4** Gall: 0-1
Aids: Bl: 0-0 Vi: 0-0 Tstrap: 0-2 Ckp: 0-2
Best Rating: 86 8/09 Wind 1m2f7y gd-fm

Useful; stays 1m2f; acts on fast ground; has worn cheek-pieces.

Hawkeyethenoo (IRE)

108(102) (48)78
3-y-o b g Hawk Wing (USA)-Stardance (USA) (Rahy (USA))
J S Goldie (M W Easterby 19/8) J S Goldie, F Connor, G Brown

Placings:0056-435210631214 (7119)
2009: 8^{4}GS, 8^{3}SD, 8^{5}G, 8^{2}GS, 8^{1}GF, 8^{0}SD, 5^{6}G, 6^{3}S, 5^{1}GF, 5^{2}GF, 5^{1}G, 5^{4}GS,

	Starts	1st	2nd	3rd	Win & Pl
Career Total (Turf)	13	3	2	1	9996
Career Total (AW)	3	0	0	1	302

78	10/09	Ayr	5f	(0-70)H	GD	£2914
72	9/09	Muss	5f	(0-65)H	G-F	£2590
57	7/09	Bevl	1m100y	(0-65)H	G-F	£1942

Total win prize-money £7447

Going (Turf): Sf: 0-2 GS: 0-4 Gd: 1-3 **GF: 2-4** Fm: 0-0
Distance: **5f/6f: 2-7** 7f-8f: 0-5 9f-13f: 1-4 14f+: 0-0
Track : LH: 0-4 **RH: 1-4** Tight: 0-4 Gall: 0-1
Aids: Bl: 1-4 Vi: 1-3 Tstrap: 0-0 Ckp: 0-0
Best Rating: 78 10/09 Ayr 5f good

Modest; effective at 5f-1m; acts on fast ground and on Polytrack; has worn blinkers and a visor.

Hawkit (USA)

99 (72)78
8-y-o b g Silver Hawk (USA)-Hey Ghaz (USA) (Ghazi (USA))
P Monteith Allan McLuckie

Placings:232233/52101200500/00024235060/213460325 561264401003/02403031166O2/0632305060-002B43625452 (7174)
2009: 8^{0}G, 9^{0}G, 10^{2}G, 10^{B}GF, 11^{4}GS, 12^{3}GS, 10^{6}S, 12^{2}GS, 11^{5}G, 12^{4}GS, 9^{5}G, 9^{2}S,

	Starts	1st	2nd	3rd	Win & Pl
Career Total (Turf)	60	5	11	7	44013
Career Total (AW)	24	2	5	5	11914

78	8/07	Haml	1m1f36y	(0-80)H	G-S	£6477
76	8/07	Ayr	1m1f20y	(0-75)H	G-S	£3886
74	9/06	Ayr	1m2f		G-S	£6477
78	6/06	Ayr	1m1f20y	(0-75)H	GD	£5181
67	1/06	Sthl	1m3f		STD	£2388
64	5/04	Haml	1m1f36y	E	GD	£3737

67 3/04 Wolv 1m100y D SS £3373
Total win prize-money £31523

Going (Turf): Sf: 0-12 **GS: 3-14** Gd: 2-21 GF: 0-13 Fm: 0-0
Distance: 5f/6f: 0-0 7f-8f: 0-13 **9f-13f: 7-71** 14f+: 0-0
Track : **LH: 5-62** RH: 2-21 **Tight: 3-41** Gall: 0-7
Aids: Bl: 0-0 Vi: 0-0 Tstrap: 0-0 Ckp: 0-0
Best Rating: 81 6/04 Wind 1m2f7y gd-fm

Modest; stays 1m4f; acts on most ground and Fibresand.

Hawkleaf Flier (IRE)

92 **52**
3-y-o b f Hawk Wing (USA)-Flyleaf (FR) (Persian Bold)
T D Easterby Ryedale Partners No 7

Placings:046-050630 **(4995)**
2009: 7^{0}GF, 10^{5}GS, 8^{0}F, 10^{6}G, 7^{3}G, 7^{0}GF,

	Starts	1st	2nd	3rd	Win & Pl
Career Total (Turf)	9	0	0	1	567

Going (Turf): Sf: 0-2 GS: 0-2 Gd: 0-2 GF: 0-2 Fm: 0-1
Distance: 5f/6f: 0-0 7f-8f: 0-7 9f-13f: 0-2 14f+: 0-0
Track : LH: 0-2 RH: 0-3 Tight: 0-1 Gall: 0-0
Aids: Bl: 0-2 Vi: 0-0 Tstrap: 0-0 Ckp: 0-0
Best Rating: 52 9/08 Rdcr 7f gd-sft

Plating-class; stays 1m; acts on good; ahs worn blinkers.

Hawksbury Heights

(93) (30)**35**
7-y-o ch g Nashwan (USA)-Gentle Dame (Kris)
J J Lambe D J McCormack

Placings:200/5300/0-0 **(7751)**
2009: 13^{0}SD,

	Starts	1st	2nd	3rd	Win & Pl
Career Total (Turf)	8	0	1	1	3043
Career Total (AW)	1	0	0	0	

Going (Turf): Sf: 0-0 GS: 0-1 Gd: 0-5 GF: 0-1 Fm: 0-1
Distance: 5f/6f: 0-0 7f-8f: 0-3 9f-13f: 0-4 14f+: 0-2
Track : LH: 0-4 RH: 0-5 Tight: 0-1 Gall: 0-1
Aids: Bl: 0-0 Vi: 0-0 Tstrap: 0-0 Ckp: 0-0
Best Rating: 78 6/06 Curr 1m gd-fm

Hawkspring (IRE)

(99) (70)
3-y-o b c Hawk Wing (USA)-Katavi (USA) (Stravinsky (USA))
S Parr Willie McKay

Placings:510204-4103222412056 **(0924)**
2009: 6^{4}SS, 7^{1}SD, 10^{0}SD, 8^{3}SD, 8^{2}SD, 7^{2}SD, 7^{2}SD, 6^{4}SD, 8^{1}SD, 8^{2}SD, 8^{0}SD, 8^{5}SD, 7^{6}SD,

	Starts	1st	2nd	3rd	Win & Pl
Career Total (Turf)	0	0	0	0	
Career Total (AW)	19	3	5	1	9962

67 2/09 Ling 1m STD £1878
67 1/09 Sthl 7f STD £2047
61 11/08 Sthl 1m STD £2047
Total win prize-money £5972

Going (Turf): Sf: 0-0 GS: 0-0 Gd: 0-0 GF: 0-0 Fm: 0-0
Distance: 5f/6f: 0-2 **7f-8f: 3-13** 9f-13f: 0-4 14f+: 0-0
Track : **LH: 3-17** RH: 0-2 **Tight: 1-7** Gall: 0-1

Aids: Bl: 0-0 **Vi: 1-3** Tstrap: 0-1 Ckp: 0-1
Best Rating: 70 2/09 Sthl 1m stand

Modest; effective over 7f-1m; acts on Fibresand and Polytrack; has worn a tongue tie, visor and cheekpieces.

Hawkstar Express (IRE)

(96) (50)**56**
4-y-o b g Hawk Wing (USA)-Band Of Angels (IRE) (Alzao (USA))
J R Boyle Inside Track Racing Club

Placings:00/0500060-04 **(0169)**
2009: 8^{0}SD, 13^{4}SD,

	Starts	1st	2nd	3rd	Win & Pl
Career Total (Turf)	6	0	0	0	0
Career Total (AW)	5	0	0	0	0

Going (Turf): Sf: 0-2 GS: 0-2 Gd: 0-0 GF: 0-2 Fm: 0-0
Distance: 5f/6f: 0-0 7f-8f: 0-3 9f-13f: 0-7 14f+: 0-1
Track : LH: 0-7 RH: 0-2 Tight: 0-6 Gall: 0-3
Aids: Bl: 0-1 Vi: 0-1 Tstrap: 0-1 Ckp: 0-1
Best Rating: 56 10/07 NmkR 1m soft

-

Hawridge King

110 (65)**85**
7-y-o b g Erhaab (USA)-Sadaka (USA) (Kingmambo (USA))
W S Kittow Eric Gadsden

Placings:35655/335204432/332320/12420/50313350-6651425442 **(7151)**
2009: 11^{6}GS, 14^{6}S, 14^{5}G, 14^{1}F, 14^{4}GF, 15^{2}GF, 16^{5}GF, 14^{4}GF, 14^{4}S, 16^{2}G,

	Starts	1st	2nd	3rd	Win & Pl
Career Total (Turf)	42	3	8	10	32912
Career Total (AW)	1	0	0	0	0

81 7/09 Hayd 1m6f (0-85)H FRM £5180
82 6/08 Sals 1m6f21y (0-85)H G-F £4371
72 8/07 Hayd 1m6f (0-70)H G-F £2817
Total win prize-money £12369

Going (Turf): Sf: 0-4 GS: 0-6 Gd: 0-11 **GF: 2-20** Fm: 1-1
Distance: 5f/6f: 0-1 7f-8f: 0-3 9f-13f: 0-21 **14f+: 3-18**
Track : **LH: 2-24** RH: 1-14 **Tight: 1-19** Gall: 0-2
Aids: Bl: 0-0 Vi: 0-2 Tstrap: 0-0 Ckp: 0-0
Best Rating: 87 10/07 Wwck 2m39y gd-fm

Fair; stays 2m, but probably best over shorter; acts on most ground.

Hawridge Star (IRE)

85 (42)**73**
7-y-o b g Alzao (USA)-Serenity (Selkirk (USA))
W S Kittow Eric Gadsden

Placings:620/40020/504035/1-40 **(6995)**
2009: 16^{4}GS, 14^{0}GS,

	Starts	1st	2nd	3rd	Win & Pl
Career Total (Turf)	16	1	2	1	6275
Career Total (AW)	1	0	0	0	

73 9/08 Hayd 1m6f (0-70)H HVY £3123
Total win prize-money £3123

Going (Turf): Sf: 1-2 GS: 0-7 Gd: 0-3 GF: 0-4 Fm: 0-0
Distance: 5f/6f: 0-0 7f-8f: 0-2 9f-13f: 0-10 **14f+: 1-5**
Track : **LH: 1-7** RH: 0-7 Tight: 0-7 Gall: 0-1
Aids: Bl: 0-0 Vi: 0-2 Tstrap: 0-0 Ckp: 0-0
Best Rating: 82 6/05 Gdwd 1m1f192y good

Modest; stays 1m4f; acts on fast and soft ground.

Hay Fever (IRE)

89(90) (60)**76**
3-y-o b g Namid-Allergy (Alzao (USA))
Eve Johnson Houghton Eden Racing IV

Placings:022222-040200 **(7057)**
2009: 8^{0}SD, 6^{4}GF, 7^{0}GF, 5^{2}SD, 7^{0}SD, 7^{0}GF,

	Starts	1st	2nd	3rd	Win & Pl
Career Total (Turf)	8	0	5	0	4813
Career Total (AW)	4	0	1	0	806

Going (Turf): Sf: 0-1 GS: 0-2 Gd: 0-0 GF: 0-5 Fm: 0-0
Distance: 5f/6f: 0-4 7f-8f: 0-8 9f-13f: 0-0 14f+: 0-0
Track : LH: 0-3 RH: 0-3 Tight: 0-1 Gall: 0-0
Aids: Bl: 0-2 Vi: 0-0 Tstrap: 0-0 Ckp: 0-0
Best Rating: 76 5/08 Brig 5f213y gd-sft

Fair; effective over 6f-7f; acts on any ground and Polytrack; has worn blinkers.

Hayek

85(82) (54)**62**
2-y-o b c Royal Applause-Salagama (IRE) (Alzao (USA))
W Jarvis Dr J Walker

Placings:000 **(6781)**
2009: 7^{0}GS, 6^{0}GF, 7^{0}SS,

	Starts	1st	2nd	3rd	Win & Pl
Career Total (Turf)	2	0	0	0	
Career Total (AW)	1	0	0	0	

Going (Turf): Sf: 0-0 GS: 0-1 Gd: 0-0 GF: 0-1 Fm: 0-0
Distance: 5f/6f: 0-1 7f-8f: 0-2 9f-13f: 0-0 14f+: 0-0
Track : LH: 0-1 RH: 0-0 Tight: 0-1 Gall: 0-0
Aids: Bl: 0-0 Vi: 0-0 Tstrap: 0-0 Ckp: 0-0
Best Rating: 62 8/09 NmkJ 7f gd-sft

Hayley's Girl

89(88) (45)**38**
3-y-o b f Deportivo-Eurolink Artemis (Common Grounds)
S W James B Liversage

Placings:00000-00000 **(7689)**
2009: 5^{0}S, 7^{0}GF, 5^{0}SD, 6^{0}SD, 5^{0}SD,

	Starts	1st	2nd	3rd	Win & Pl
Career Total (Turf)	5	0	0	0	
Career Total (AW)	5	0	0	0	

Going (Turf): Sf: 0-2 GS: 0-0 Gd: 0-1 GF: 0-2 Fm: 0-0
Distance: 5f/6f: 0-6 7f-8f: 0-4 9f-13f: 0-0 14f+: 0-0
Track : LH: 0-4 RH: 0-1 Tight: 0-3 Gall: 0-1
Aids: Bl: 0-2 Vi: 0-0 Tstrap: 0-0 Ckp: 0-0
Best Rating: 45 9/08 GrLe 1m stand

Hayzoom

88 **65**
2-y-o b c Anabaa (USA)-Green Swallow (FR) (Green Tune (USA))
P W Chapple-Hyam Ziad A Galadari

Placings:5 **(7099)**
2009: 8^{5}G,

	Starts	1st	2nd	3rd	Win & Pl
Career Total (Turf)	1	0	0	0	129

Going (Turf): Sf: 0-0 GS: 0-0 Gd: 0-1 GF: 0-0 Fm: 0-0
Distance: 5f/6f: 0-0 7f-8f: 0-0 9f-13f: 0-1 14f+: 0-0
Track : LH: 0-0 RH: 0-0 Tight: 0-0 Gall: 0-0
Aids: Bl: 0-0 Vi: 0-0 Tstrap: 0-0 Ckp: 0-0
Best Rating: 65 10/09 Yarm 1m3y good

Hazelrigg (IRE)

96(104) (78)81
4-y-o b g Namid-Emma's Star (ITY) (Darshaan)
T D Easterby Duncan & Sarah Davidson

Placings:10635-03300 **(7171)**
2009: 5^{0}GS, 5^{3}G, 5^{3}SD, 7^{0}G, 7^{0}S,

	Starts	1st	2nd	3rd	Win & Pl
Career Total (Turf)	9	1	0	2	4989
Career Total (AW)	1	0	0	1	755

81 4/08 Thsk 6f G-S £3399
Total win prize-money £3400

Going (Turf): Sf: 0-1 **GS: 1-4** Gd: 0-3 GF: 0-0 Fm: 0-1
Distance: 5f/6f: 1-8 7f-8f: 0-2 9f-13f: 0-0 14f+: 0-0
Track : LH: 0-3 RH: 0-1 Tight: 0-2 Gall: 0-1
Aids: Bl: 0-0 Vi: 0-0 Tstrap: 0-3 Ckp: 0-3
Best Rating: 81 8/08 Hayd 6f gd-sft

Fair; half-brother to Genki, a multiple 6f winner at three; effective over 6f; acts on easy ground.

Hazy Dancer

84(101) (75)53
3-y-o b f Oasis Dream-Shadow Dancing (Unfuwain (USA))
M P Tregoning Minster Stud & Mrs Hugh Dalgety

Placings:1-60540 **(7238)**
2009: 11^{6}GF, 12^{0}GF, 12^{5}SS, 12^{4}SD, 12^{0}SD,

	Starts	1st	2nd	3rd	Win & Pl
Career Total (Turf)	2	0	0	0	540
Career Total (AW)	4	1	0	0	4078

67 10/08 Ling 1m STD £3885
Total win prize-money £3886

Going (Turf): Sf: 0-0 GS: 0-0 Gd: 0-0 GF: 0-2 Fm: 0-0
Distance: 5f/6f: 0-0 **7f-8f: 1-1** 9f-13f: 0-5 14f+: 0-0
Track : LH: 1-3 RH: 0-3 **Tight: 1-4** Gall: 0-0
Aids: Bl: 0-0 Vi: 0-0 Tstrap: 0-0 Ckp: 0-0
Best Rating: 75 10/09 Ling 1m4f std-slw

Fair; stays 1m and acts on Polytrack.

Hazytoo

101(101) (74)76
5-y-o ch g Sakhee (USA)-Shukran (Hamas (IRE))
P J Makin Wedgewood Estates

Placings:430220/10000610-301000 **(7627)**
2009: 7^{3}SD, 7^{0}SD, 6^{1}GF, 6^{0}GF, 5^{0}GF, 7^{0}SD,

	Starts	1st	2nd	3rd	Win & Pl
Career Total (Turf)	12	1	2	0	4062
Career Total (AW)	8	2	0	2	5548

76 5/09 Wwck 6f (0-65)H G-F £1942
74 7/08 Ling 7f (0-70)H STD £2590
73 4/08 Ling 7f (0-65)H STD £2047
Total win prize-money £6580

Going (Turf): Sf: 0-0 GS: 0-0 Gd: 0-3 **GF: 1-8** Fm: 0-1
Distance: 5f/6f: 1-5 **7f-8f: 2-14** 9f-13f: 0-1 14f+: 0-0
Track : LH: 3-7 RH: 0-4 **Tight: 2-6** Gall: 0-2
Aids: Bl: 0-0 Vi: 0-0 Tstrap: 1-1 Ckp: 1-1
Best Rating: 76 5/09 Wwck 6f gd-fm

Fair; effective over 7f and acts on Polytrack; has worn cheekpieces.

He's A Humbug (IRE)

96(102) (81)91
5-y-o b g Tagula (IRE)-Acidanthera (Alzao (USA))
J O'Reilly J D Walker

Placings:153/1000000/00302150060**454**0206-0000010000 **(7643)**
2009: 6^{0}GF, 5^{0}GF, 6^{0}S, 7^{0}GS, 7^{0}G, 7^{1}G, 6^{0}G, 5^{0}GF, 6^{0}SD, 7^{0}SD,

	Starts	1st	2nd	3rd	Win & Pl
Career Total (Turf)	29	4	1	2	29319
Career Total (AW)	9	0	1	0	2014

75 7/09 Catt 7f (0-65)H GD £2388
91 7/08 Bevl 5f (0-85)H G-S £6476
88 4/07 Leic 5f218y G-F £6232
86 7/06 Thsk 6f G-F £6477
Total win prize-money £21573

Going (Turf): Sf: 0-4 GS: 1-6 Gd: 1-10 **GF: 2-9** Fm: 0-0
Distance: 5f/6f: 3-33 7f-8f: 1-5 9f-13f: 0-0 14f+: 0-0
Track : LH: 1-10 RH: 0-2 **Tight: 1-5** Gall: 0-1
Aids: Bl: 0-2 Vi: 0-2 Tstrap: 1-20 Ckp: 1-20
Best Rating: 91 7/08 Bevl 5f gd-sft

Modest; effective over 5f-7f; acts on most ground; has worn blinkers and cheekpieces.

He's Cool (IRE)

(98) (61)48
4-y-o b g Viking Ruler (AUS)-Miss Progressive (IRE) (Common Grounds)
Aidan Anthony Howard (G M Lyons 27/3) Matthew Mullen

Placings:45000-60010 **(7336)**
2009: 8^{6}SD, 6^{0}SD, 16^{0}YS, 16^{1}SD, 14^{0}SD,

	Starts	1st	2nd	3rd	Win & Pl
Career Total (Turf)	2	0	0	0	
Career Total (AW)	8	1	0	0	2765

61 10/09 Wolv 2m119y (0-60)H STD £2388
Total win prize-money £2388

Going (Turf): Sf: 0-0 GS: 0-0 Gd: 0-1 GF: 0-0 Fm: 0-0
Distance: 5f/6f: 0-2 7f-8f: 0-3 9f-13f: 0-2 **14f+: 1-3**
Track : LH: 1-7 RH: 0-2 **Tight: 1-1** Gall: 0-0
Aids: Bl: 0-0 Vi: 0-0 Tstrap: 1-2 Ckp: 1-2
Best Rating: 63 2/08 Dund 1m stand

Moderate; Irish trained; winning hurdler; stays 2m; acts on Polytrack; has worn cheekpieces.

He's Got Rhythm (IRE)

100 (80)82
4-y-o b g Invincible Spirit (IRE)-Kathy Jet (USA) (Singspiel (IRE))
David Marnane Michael Bealin

Placings:0003203/26210330020-00500360 **(7527a)**
2009: 6^{0}YS, 7^{0}Y, 5^{6}GF, 5^{0}SD, 7^{0}SD, 7^{3}G, 7^{6}GF, 8^{0}SD,

	Starts	1st	2nd	3rd	Win & Pl
Career Total (Turf)	15	1	1	3	12461
Career Total (AW)	11	0	3	2	6115

82 5/08 DRoy 5f FRM £7621
Total win prize-money £7621

Going (Turf): Sf: 0-3 GS: 0-0 Gd: 0-3 GF: 0-4 **Fm: 1-1**
Distance: 5f/6f: 1-16 7f-8f: 0-10 9f-13f: 0-0 14f+: 0-0
Track : LH: 0-12 **RH: 1-5** Tight: 0-1 Gall: 0-0
Aids: Bl: 1-16 Vi: 0-0 Tstrap: 0-0 Ckp: 0-0
Best Rating: 82 6/08 Fair 6f good

Fair; effective at 7f; handles good ground; has worn blinkers.

He's Invincible

81 59
2-y-o b g Invincible Spirit (IRE)-Adamas (IRE) (Fairy King (USA))
B J Meehan Brimacombe,McNally,Vinciguerra,Sangster

Placings:605 **(3792)**
2009: 6^{6}GF, 6^{0}G, 6^{5}G,

	Starts	1st	2nd	3rd	Win & Pl
Career Total (Turf)	3	0	0	0	0

Going (Turf): Sf: 0-0 GS: 0-0 Gd: 0-2 GF: 0-1 Fm: 0-0
Distance: 5f/6f: 0-2 7f-8f: 0-1 9f-13f: 0-0 14f+: 0-0
Track : LH: 0-0 RH: 0-0 Tight: 0-0 Gall: 0-0
Aids: Bl: 0-0 Vi: 0-0 Tstrap: 0-0 Ckp: 0-0
Best Rating: 59 7/09 Asct 6f good

Head Down

100(103) (80)81
3-y-o b g Acclamation-Creese (USA) (Diesis)
Mrs L C Jewell (R Hannon 15/8) Quintessential Thoroughbreds Solar Syn

Placings:502032-3232123034100 **(7883)**
2009: 7^{3}SD, 6^{2}SD, 8^{3}SD, 7^{2}SD, 7^{1}SD, 7^{2}GF, 7^{3}G, 7^{0}G, 7^{3}GF, 8^{4}GF, 8^{1}SD, 8^{0}SD, 8^{0}SD,

	Starts	1st	2nd	3rd	Win & Pl
Career Total (Turf)	8	0	2	2	5250
Career Total (AW)	11	2	3	3	9790

80 8/09 Ling 1m STD £2047
77 3/09 Ling 7f STD £2729
Total win prize-money £4777

Going (Turf): Sf: 0-1 **GS: 0-0 Gd: 0-3 GF: 0-4 Fm: 0-0**
Distance: 5f/6f: 0-4 **7f-8f: 2-14** 9f-13f: 0-1 14f+: 0-0
Track : LH: 2-8 RH: 0-5 **Tight: 2-8** Gall: 0-0
Aids: Bl: 0-0 Vi: 0-0 Tstrap: 0-0 Ckp: 0-0
Best Rating: 81 6/08 NmkJ 6f gd-fm

Fair; effective over 7f-1m; acts on fast ground; goes on Polytrack.

Head First

84(98) (59)44
3-y-o b f Dansili-Break Point (Reference Point)
W Jarvis Mrs Jo Reffo

Placings:05004144 **(7856)**
2009: 8^{0}S, 8^{5}G, 8^{0}GF, 11^{0}SD, 9^{4}SF, 9^{1}SD, 8^{4}SD, 9^{4}SD,

	Starts	1st	2nd	3rd	Win & Pl
Career Total (Turf)	3	0	0	0	0
Career Total (AW)	5	1	0	0	2047

57 11/09 Wolv 1m1f103y (0-55)H STD £2047
Total win prize-money £2047

Going (Turf): Sf: 0-1 GS: 0-0 Gd: 0-1 GF: 0-1 Fm: 0-0
Distance: 5f/6f: 0-0 7f-8f: 0-2 **9f-13f: 1-6** 14f+: 0-0
Track : LH: 1-4 RH: 0-2 **Tight: 1-4** Gall: 0-0
Aids: Bl: 0-0 Vi: 0-0 Tstrap: 0-0 Ckp: 0-0
Best Rating: 59 12/09 Wolv 1m141y stand

Moderate; stays 1m1f; handles Polytrack.

Head Hunted

94 63
2-y-o b g Dubai Destination (USA)-Tropical Breeze (IRE) (Kris)

E A L Dunlop Salem Suhail

Placings:4 (7243)
2009: 8^{4}S,

	Starts	1st	2nd	3rd	Win & Pl
Career Total (Turf)	1	0	0	0	313

Going (Turf): Sf: 0-1 GS: 0-0 Gd: 0-0 GF: 0-0 Fm: 0-0
Distance: 5f/6f: 0-0 7f-8f: 0-0 9f-13f: 0-1 14f+: 0-0
Track : LH: 0-1 RH: 0-0 Tight: 0-0 Gall: 0-0
Aids: Bl: 0-0 Vi: 0-0 Tstrap: 0-0 Ckp: 0-0
Best Rating: 63 11/09 Nott 1m75y soft

Head To Head (IRE)

92(106) (58)56
5-y-o gr g Mull Of Kintyre (USA)-Shoka (FR) (Kaldoun (FR))
A D Brown Mrs M Doherty

Placings:0003/**006345440060**/002000540-315200020036242 (7709)
2009: 6^{3}SS, 6^{1}SD, 6^{5}SD, 5^{2}SD, 6^{0}SD, 5^{0}SD, 5^{0}SD, 6^{2}SD, 6^{0}GS, 5^{0}SD, 5^{3}SD, 6^{6}SD, 5^{2}SD, 6^{4}SD, 5^{2}SD,

	Starts	1st	2nd	3rd	Win & Pl
Career Total (Turf)	5	0	1	0	705
Career Total (AW)	35	1	4	4	6133
56 1/09 Sthl	6f	(0-55)H		STD	£2047

Total win prize-money £2047

Going (Turf): Sf: 0-1 GS: 0-3 Gd: 0-1 GF: 0-0 Fm: 0-0
Distance: **5f/6f: 1-37** 7f-8f: 0-3 9f-13f: 0-0 14f+: 0-0
Track : **LH: 1-23** RH: 0-5 Tight: 0-15 Gall: 0-0
Aids: Bl: 0-10 Vi: 0-0 Tstrap: 1-8 Ckp: 1-8
Best Rating: 58 12/09 Sthl 5f stand

Moderate; stays 6f and acts on Fibresand; has worn blinkers, tongue tie and cheekpieces.

Head To Kerry (IRE)

(91) (52)31
9-y-o b g Eagle Eyed (USA)-The Poachers Lady (IRE) (Salmon Leap (USA))
D J S Ffrench Davis Rochfords

Placings:000/0536213513/0003534245406/4454036/00/6-6 (0065)
2009: 12^{6}SS,

	Starts	1st	2nd	3rd	Win & Pl
Career Total (Turf)	28	2	1	6	13035
Career Total (AW)	9	0	1	0	908
68 9/03 Gdwd	2m	E(0-70)H		G-F	£2989
64 8/03 Gdwd	1m4f	E(0-70)H		G-F	£4176

Total win prize-money £7165

Going (Turf): Sf: 0-3 GS: 0-1 Gd: 0-7 **GF: 2-15** Fm: 0-2
Distance: 5f/6f: 0-0 7f-8f: 0-3 9f-13f: 1-22 14f+: 1-12
Track : LH: 0-22 **RH: 2-12 Tight: 2-18** Gall: 0-2
Aids: Bl: 0-0 Vi: 0-0 Tstrap: 0-1 Ckp: 0-1
Best Rating: 73 10/03 Gdwd 2m gd-fm

Headache

(101) (60)53
4-y-o b g Cape Cross (IRE)-Romantic Myth (Mind Games)
B W Duke Brendan W Duke Racing

Placings:0/000**25**-0455243010 (7796)
2009: 8^{0}SD, 8^{4}SD, 8^{5}SD, 8^{5}SD, 7^{2}SD, 5^{4}SD, 7^{3}SD, 7^{0}SD, 7^{1}SD, 7^{0}SS,

	Starts	1st	2nd	3rd	Win & Pl
Career Total (Turf)	4	0	0	0	
Career Total (AW)	12	1	2	1	1516

Going (Turf): Sf: 0-0 GS: 0-1 Gd: 0-1 GF: 0-2 Fm: 0-0
Distance: 5f/6f: 0-2 **7f-8f: 1-12** 9f-13f: 0-2 14f+: 0-0
Track : **LH: 1-8** RH: 0-5 Tight: 0-5 Gall: 0-0
Aids: **Bl: 1-6** Vi: 0-0 Tstrap: 0-0 Ckp: 0-0
Best Rating: 60 12/09 Sthl 7f stand

Moderate; suited by 7f and Polytrack; has worn a tongue-tie/blinkers.

Headford View (IRE)

113 (92)97
5-y-o b m Bold Fact (USA)-Headfort Rose (IRE) (Desert Style (IRE))
James Halpin J O'r Syndicate

Placings:00/0024630**31**/5406**21113**-4100035 (6516a)
2009: 7^{4}GF, 7^{1}Y, 7^{0}GF, 6^{0}SD, 8^{0}HY, 8^{3}G, 7^{5}SD,

	Starts	1st	2nd	3rd	Win & Pl
Career Total (Turf)	18	1	1	2	50849
Career Total (AW)	9	4	1	2	40202
96 6/09 Curr	7f	H		YLD	£42978
89 11/08 Dund	7f	(60-100)H		STD	£14360
83 9/08 Dund	1m	(60-90)H		STD	£11966
78 8/08 Dund	1m	(50-80)H		STD	£6351
66 12/07 Dund	1m			STD	£5836

Total win prize-money £81493

Going (Turf): Sf: 0-3 GS: 0-0 Gd: 0-6 GF: 0-3 Fm: 0-0
Distance: 5f/6f: 0-5 **7f-8f: 5-20** 9f-13f: 0-2 14f+: 0-0
Track : **LH: 3-10** RH: 0-10 Tight: 0-0 Gall: 0-2
Aids: Bl: 0-0 Vi: 0-0 Tstrap: 5-16 Ckp: 5-16
Best Rating: 97 9/09 Asct 1m good

Very useful; effective at 7f-1m; acts on fast ground and Polytrack; wears cheekpieces.

Heading East (IRE)

91(77) (49)70
3-y-o ch g Dubai Destination (USA)-Nausicaa (USA) (Diesis)
K A Ryan J Duddy A Bailey B McDonald L Duddy

Placings:543-5600 (4822)
2009: 8^{5}SD, 10^{6}S, 8^{0}G, 10^{0}GF,

	Starts	1st	2nd	3rd	Win & Pl
Career Total (Turf)	6	0	0	1	834
Career Total (AW)	1	0	0	0	0

Going (Turf): Sf: 0-2 GS: 0-0 Gd: 0-2 GF: 0-2 Fm: 0-0
Distance: 5f/6f: 0-0 7f-8f: 0-2 9f-13f: 0-5 14f+: 0-0
Track : LH: 0-4 RH: 0-2 Tight: 0-2 Gall: 0-0
Aids: Bl: 0-0 Vi: 0-0 Tstrap: 0-1 Ckp: 0-1
Best Rating: 70 7/08 Bevl 7f100y gd-fm

Fair; effective over 7f-1m; acts on fast and soft ground.

Heading To First

86 67
2-y-o b c Sulamani (IRE)-Bahirah (Ashkalani (IRE))
C E Brittain Saeed Manana

Placings:40 (3750)
2009: 7^{4}GF, 7^{0}G,

	Starts	1st	2nd	3rd	Win & Pl
Career Total (Turf)	2	0	0	0	0

Going (Turf): Sf: 0-0 GS: 0-0 Gd: 0-1 GF: 0-1 Fm: 0-0
Distance: 5f/6f: 0-0 7f-8f: 0-2 9f-13f: 0-0 14f+: 0-0
Track : LH: 0-0 RH: 0-0 Tight: 0-0 Gall: 0-0
Aids: Bl: 0-0 Vi: 0-0 Tstrap: 0-0 Ckp: 0-0
Best Rating: 67 6/09 Ling 7f gd-fm

Cheaply bought; related to winners in Greece; stays 7f; acts on fast ground.

Headline Act

104(102) (84)87
3-y-o ch g Dalakhani (IRE)-Daring Miss (Sadler's Wells (USA))
J H M Gosden K Abdulla

Placings:321-41040 (4319)
2009: 9^{4}GF, **12^{1}SD**, 12^{0}GF, 12^{4}GF, 13^{0}G,

	Starts	1st	2nd	3rd	Win & Pl
Career Total (Turf)	7	1	1	1	9151
Career Total (AW)	1	1	0	0	4727
84 4/09 Kemp	1m4f	(0-85)H		STD	£4727
83 10/08 Brig	7f214y		G-S		£5551

Total win prize-money £10278

Going (Turf): Sf: 0-1 **GS: 1-1** Gd: 0-1 GF: 0-4 Fm: 0-0
Distance: 5f/6f: 0-0 7f-8f: 1-2 9f-13f: 1-6 14f+: 0-0
Track : LH: 1-2 RH: 1-5 Tight: 0-2 Gall: 0-2
Aids: Bl: 0-0 Vi: 0-0 Tstrap: 0-0 Ckp: 0-0
Best Rating: 87 5/09 Ches 1m4f66y gd-fm

Useful; stays 1m4f; acts on any ground and Polytrack.

Heart Of Dubai (USA)

90(95) (69)50
4-y-o b c Outofthebox (USA)-Diablo's Blend (USA) (Diablo (USA))
Micky Hammond Terry Wood

Placings:50/061000-0500 (2237)
2009: 12^{0}F, 9^{5}GF, 8^{0}GF, 10^{0}GS,

	Starts	1st	2nd	3rd	Win & Pl
Career Total (Turf)	7	0	0	0	0
Career Total (AW)	5	1	0	0	2267
69 6/08 Ling	1m4f		STD		£2266

Total win prize-money £2267

Going (Turf): Sf: 0-0 GS: 0-1 Gd: 0-0 GF: 0-5 Fm: 0-1
Distance: 5f/6f: 0-0 7f-8f: 0-3 **9f-13f: 1-9** 14f+: 0-0
Track : **LH: 1-6** RH: 0-5 **Tight: 1-5** Gall: 0-2
Aids: Bl: 0-0 Vi: 0-0 Tstrap: 0-3 Ckp: 0-3
Best Rating: 69 6/08 Ling 1m4f stand

Heart Of Tuscany

91(93) (58)58
3-y-o b f Falbrav (IRE)-Zarma (FR) (Machiavellian (USA))
W J Knight Miss Tracey Dixon

Placings:04-50660 (4640)
2009: 10^{5}GF, 12^{0}GF, 9^{6}GF, 12^{6}SD, 11^{0}GF,

	Starts	1st	2nd	3rd	Win & Pl
Career Total (Turf)	5	0	0	0	0
Career Total (AW)	2	0	0	0	0

Going (Turf): Sf: 0-0 GS: 0-0 Gd: 0-1 GF: 0-4 Fm: 0-0
Distance: 5f/6f: 0-0 7f-8f: 0-2 9f-13f: 0-5 14f+: 0-0
Track : LH: 0-3 RH: 0-3 Tight: 0-3 Gall: 0-0
Aids: Bl: 0-0 Vi: 0-0 Tstrap: 0-2 Ckp: 0-2
Best Rating: 58 5/09 Chep 1m2f36y gd-fm

Heart Shaped (USA)

112 **110**

3-y-o ch f Storm Cat (USA)-Twenty Eight Carat (USA) (Alydar (USA))

A P O'Brien Michael Tabor

Placings:310452-246500 **(5686a)**

2009: 7^{2}GF, 8^{4}GF, 8^{6}GF, 7^{5}G, 6^{0}SH, 8^{0}GY,

	Starts	1st	2nd	3rd	Win & Pl
Career Total (Turf)	12	1	2	1	190488

94 5/08 Curr 5f FRM £26327

Total win prize-money £26327

Going (Turf): Sf: 0-0 GS: 0-1 Gd: 0-2 GF: 0-5 **Fm: 1-2**
Distance: **5f/6f: 1-6** 7f-8f: 0-6 9f-13f: 0-0 14f+: 0-0
Track : LH: 0-4 RH: 0-2 Tight: 0-0 Gall: 0-1
Aids: Bl: 0-0 Vi: 0-0 Tstrap: 0-0 Ckp: 0-0
Best Rating: **110** 10/08 SnAt 1m firm

Group class; Listed winner on second start; runner-up in the Breeders' Cup Juvenile Fillies' Turf; fourth in the 1000 Guineas; effective over 6f-1m; acts on good and fast ground.

Hearts Of Fire

102 **117**

2-y-o b c Firebreak-Alexander Ballet (Mind Games)

Pat Eddery Pat Eddery Racing (Detroit)

Placings:14252111 **(6716a)**

2009: 5^{1}GF, 5^{4}GF, 5^{2}G, 5^{5}GF, 6^{2}S, 7^{1}G, 7^{1}S, 8^{1}S,

	Starts	1st	2nd	3rd	Win & Pl
Career Total (Turf)	8	4	2	0	256552

117 10/09 Siro 1m SFT £178121
112 9/09 Badn 7f SFT £29126
106 8/09 Deau 7f GD £26699
87 3/09 Donc 5f G-F £11333

Total win prize-money £245279

Going (Turf): **Sf: 2-3** GS: 0-0 Gd: 1-2 GF: 1-3 Fm: 0-0
Distance: 5f/6f: 1-4 **7f-8f: 3-4** 9f-13f: 0-0 14f+: 0-0
Track : LH: 1-1 **RH: 2-2** Tight: 0-0 Gall: 0-0
Aids: Bl: 0-0 Vi: 0-0 Tstrap: 0-0 Ckp: 0-0
Best Rating: **117** 10/09 Siro 1m soft

Useful; won Brocklesby on debut; Listed winner in France; effective at 5f-7f; acts on fast and soft ground.

Heartsease

97(74) (23)**62**

3-y-o b f Pursuit Of Love-Balsamita (FR) (Midyan (USA))

J G Portman Mrs R Pease

Placings:0060-3060206 **(4745)**

2009: 10^{3}GF, 9^{0}G, 8^{6}F, 8^{0}G, 9^{2}GF, 10^{0}G, 10^{6}GS,

	Starts	1st	2nd	3rd	Win & Pl
Career Total (Turf)	10	0	1	1	907
Career Total (AW)	1	0	0	0	

Going (Turf): **Sf: 0-1 GS: 0-2 Gd: 0-4 GF: 0-2 Fm: 0-1**
Distance: 5f/6f: 0-2 7f-8f: 0-2 9f-13f: 0-7 14f+: 0-0
Track : LH: 0-7 RH: 0-1 Tight: 0-6 Gall: 0-2
Aids: Bl: 0-0 Vi: 0-0 Tstrap: 0-0 Ckp: 0-0
Best Rating: **62** 7/09 Ling 1m1f gd-fm

Modest; stays 1m1f; acts on fast ground.

Heathyards Junior

(100) (68)

3-y-o b g Beat All (USA)-Heathyards Lady (USA) (Mining (USA))

R Hollinshead L A Morgan

Placings:651 **(7671)**

2009: 9^{6}SD, 9^{5}SD, 8^{1}SD,

	Starts	1st	2nd	3rd	Win & Pl
Career Total (Turf)	0	0	0	0	
Career Total (AW)	3	1	0	0	2730

68 12/09 Wolv 1m141y STD £2729

Total win prize-money £2730

Going (Turf): **Sf: 0-0 GS: 0-0 Gd: 0-0 GF: 0-0 Fm: 0-0**
Distance: 5f/6f: 0-0 7f-8f: 0-0 **9f-13f: 1-3** 14f+: 0-0
Track : **LH: 1-3** RH: 0-0 **Tight: 1-3** Gall: 0-0
Aids: Bl: 0-0 Vi: 0-0 Tstrap: 0-0 Ckp: 0-0
Best Rating: **68** 12/09 Wolv 1m141y stand

Modest; stays 1m, should get 10f; acts on Polytrack.

Heathyards Pride

(107) (89)**84**

9-y-o b g Polar Prince (IRE)-Heathyards Lady (USA) (Mining (USA))

R Hollinshead L A Morgan

Placings:41/045111**1**/0603221032311/**640401253**/313310 **5342**/0531-22 **(0330)**

2009: 12^{2}SD, 12^{2}SD,

	Starts	1st	2nd	3rd	Win & Pl
Career Total (Turf)	20	4	3	2	31075
Career Total (AW)	27	8	4	7	53482

78 12/08 Wolv 1m4f50y SF £2388
84 8/07 Brig 1m3f196y (0-80)H FRM £13934
89 3/07 Wolv 1m4f50y (0-100)H STD £11658
84 10/06 Wolv 1m4f50y (0-85)H SF £5505
83 12/05 Wolv 1m4f50y (0-85)H STD £5704
84 12/05 Sthl 1m6f (0-85)H STD £6661
67 8/05 Bevl 1m4f16y (0-65)H GD £3548
76 11/04 Wolv 1m4f50y (0-60) STD £3542
70 10/04 Wolv 1m4f50y (0-62)H STD £2991
64 10/04 Pont 1m4f8y (0-55)H G-F £3640
58 9/04 Wwck 1m2f188y (0-55)H G-F £2590
57 1/04 Wolv 1m1f79y H STD £1438

Total win prize-money £63605

Going (Turf): Sf: 0-1 GS: 0-0 Gd: 1-10 **GF: 2-7** Fm: 1-2
Distance: 5f/6f: 0-0 7f-8f: 0-1 **9f-13f: 11-42** 14f+: 1-4
Track : **LH: 11-42** RH: 1-5 **Tight: 8-25** Gall: 0-1
Aids: Bl: 0-0 Vi: 0-0 Tstrap: 0-0 Ckp: 0-0
Best Rating: **89** 10/07 Wolv 1m4f50y stand

Fair; effective at around 1m4f-1m6f; acts on fast ground; also goes on well on sand.

Heaven

100(96) (73)**79**

4-y-o ch f Reel Buddy (USA)-Wedgewood Star (Bishop Of Cashel)

P J Makin Wedgewood Estates

Placings:631/32**2**1166**0**-040006 **(5719)**

2009: 5^{0}GF, 5^{4}F, 5^{0}G, 5^{0}GF, 5^{0}GF, 5^{6}G,

	Starts	1st	2nd	3rd	Win & Pl
Career Total (Turf)	15	3	1	2	10988
Career Total (AW)	2	0	1	0	907

79 7/08 Bath 5f11y (0-75)H GD £4403
76 6/08 Wind 5f10y (0-70)H G-F £2729
63 9/07 Bath 5f11y FRM £2072

Total win prize-money £9207

Going (Turf): Sf: 0-0 GS: 0-0 **Gd: 1-7 GF: 1-6 Fm: 1-2**
Distance: **5f/6f: 3-17** 7f-8f: 0-0 9f-13f: 0-0 14f+: 0-0
Track : **LH: 2-10** RH: 0-0 Tight: 0-2 **Gall: 3-11**
Aids: Bl: 0-0 Vi: 0-0 Tstrap: 0-0 Ckp: 0-0
Best Rating: **79** 7/08 Bath 5f11y good

Fair; effective over 5f; acts on fast ground.

Heaven Or Hell (IRE)

89(82) (21)**62**

3-y-o b g Jammaal-Adjasalma (USA) (Lear Fan (USA))

P D Evans J R B Williams

Placings:130230044**4**5-56 **(5872)**

2009: 8^{5}GS, 10^{6}G,

	Starts	1st	2nd	3rd	Win & Pl
Career Total (Turf)	11	1	1	2	3321
Career Total (AW)	1	0	0	0	0

55 4/08 Bath 5f11y GD £1683

Total win prize-money £1684

Going (Turf): Sf: 0-3 GS: 0-2 **Gd: 1-5** GF: 0-1 Fm: 0-0
Distance: **5f/6f: 1-7** 7f-8f: 0-3 9f-13f: 0-2 14f+: 0-0
Track : **LH: 1-4** RH: 0-0 Tight: 0-0 **Gall: 1-2**
Aids: Bl: 0-0 Vi: 0-1 Tstrap: 0-0 Ckp: 0-0
Best Rating: **62** 5/08 Chep 6f16y soft

Moderate; effective over 5f; acts on good ground.

Heaven Sent

112(107) (103)**115**

6-y-o ch m Pivotal-Heavenly Ray (USA) (Rahy (USA))

Sir Michael Stoute Cheveley Park Stud

Placings:03/15613/31223623/**1**12345-122025 **(6479)**

2009: 9^{1}GF, 8^{2}GF, 8^{2}G, 9^{0}S, 8^{2}GY, 8^{5}GF,

	Starts	1st	2nd	3rd	Win & Pl
Career Total (Turf)	26	5	7	6	347321
Career Total (AW)	1	1	0	0	14760

104 5/09 NmkR 1m1f G-F £36900
115 5/08 NmkR 1m1f GD £28385
103 4/08 Kemp 1m STD £14760
103 5/07 Asct 1m H G-S £25908
92 7/06 NmkJ 7f (0-100)H G-F £15580
78 4/06 Wind 1m67y GD £3886

Total win prize-money £125420

Going (Turf): Sf: 0-3 GS: 1-3 **Gd: 2-5 GF: 2-14** Fm: 0-0
Distance: 5f/6f: 0-0 7f-8f: 3-19 9f-13f: 3-8 14f+: 0-0
Track : LH: 0-4 **RH: 2-10 Tight: 1-3** Gall: 0-4
Aids: Bl: 0-0 Vi: 0-0 Tstrap: 0-0 Ckp: 0-0
Best Rating: **115** 7/09 NmkJ 1m good

Group class; effective at 1m-1m2f; acts on fast and easy ground; also goes on Polytrack.

Heavenly Encounter

(86) (28)

4-y-o b f Lujaln (USA)-Inchcoonan (Emperor Jones (USA))

K R Burke Mrs Elaine M Burke

Placings:4650-00 **(0508)**

2009: 6^{0}SD, 5^{0}SD,

	Starts	1st	2nd	3rd	Win & Pl
Career Total (Turf)	1	0	0	0	
Career Total (AW)	5	0	0	0	0

Going (Turf): **Sf: 0-0 GS: 0-1 Gd: 0-0 GF: 0-0 Fm: 0-0**

Distance: 5f/6f: 0-4 7f-8f: 0-2 9f-13f: 0-0 14f+: 0-0
Track : LH: 0-3 RH: 0-2 Tight: 0-1 Gall: 0-0
Aids: Bl: 0-0 Vi: 0-1 Tstrap: 0-0 Ckp: 0-0
Best Rating: **28** 1/08 Sthl 6f stand

Heavenly Saint

99(88) (32)**51**

4-y-o b f Bertolini (USA)-Heavenly Glow (Shavian)
C Roberts F J Ayres

Placings:634**00013**/00-0000**5600** (7152)
2009: 8^{0}GF, 8^{0}GF, 8^{0}G, 10^{0}G, 10^{5}G, 7^{6}SD, 8^{0}SD, 8^{0}SD,

	Starts	1st	2nd	3rd	Win & Pl
Career Total (Turf)	11	1	0	1	3008
Career Total (AW)	7	0	0	1	302

58 10/07 Nott 1m54y G-F £2286
Total win prize-money £2286

Going (Turf): Sf: 0-0 GS: 0-1 Gd: 0-5 **GF: 1-5** Fm: 0-0
Distance: 5f/6f: 0-1 7f-8f: 0-7 **9f-13f: 1-10** 14f+: 0-0
Track : **LH: 1-10** RH: 0-4 Tight: 0-7 Gall: 0-2
Aids: Bl: 0-0 Vi: 0-0 Tstrap: 0-1 Ckp: 0-1
Best Rating: **58** 11/07 Wolv 7f32y stand

Modest; stays 1m; acts on fast ground.

Heavenly Stella (USA)

83 **34**

4-y-o b/br f Wild Wonder (USA)-Nijivision (USA) (Superoyale (USA))
G A Swinbank S Rudolf

Placings:0 (5520)
2009: 8^{0}G,

	Starts	1st	2nd	3rd	Win & Pl
Career Total (Turf)	1	0	0	0	

Going (Turf): **Sf: 0-0 GS: 0-0 Gd: 0-1 GF: 0-0 Fm: 0-0**
Distance: 5f/6f: 0-0 7f-8f: 0-1 9f-13f: 0-0 14f+: 0-0
Track : LH: 0-0 RH: 0-1 Tight: 0-1 Gall: 0-0
Aids: Bl: 0-0 Vi: 0-0 Tstrap: 0-0 Ckp: 0-0
Best Rating: **34** 8/09 Ripn 1m good

Heavens Peak

96(78) (12)**65**

3-y-o ch f Pivotal-Lurina (IRE) (Lure (USA))
M J Grassick Walter J Taylor Jr

Placings:6054400 (6623a)
2009: 8^{6}HY, 9^{0}GF, 9^{5}GF, 8^{4}S, 8^{4}S, 9^{0}SD, 12^{0}G,

	Starts	1st	2nd	3rd	Win & Pl
Career Total (Turf)	6	0	0	0	916
Career Total (AW)	1	0	0	0	

Going (Turf): **Sf: 0-3 GS: 0-0 Gd: 0-1 GF: 0-2 Fm: 0-0**
Distance: 5f/6f: 0-0 7f-8f: 0-2 9f-13f: 0-5 14f+: 0-0
Track : LH: 0-5 RH: 0-2 Tight: 0-1 Gall: 0-0
Aids: Bl: 0-0 Vi: 0-0 Tstrap: 0-0 Ckp: 0-0
Best Rating: **65** 8/09 Naas 1m soft

Hebridean (IRE)

93(104) (95)**114**

4-y-o b g Bach (IRE)-Delphinium (IRE) (Dr Massini (IRE))
L M Cumani (P F Nicholls 2/4) Adrian F Nolan

Placings:05213205/3211030-046 (7589)
2009: 9^{0}G, 10^{4}G, 12^{6}SD,

	Starts	1st	2nd	3rd	Win & Pl
Career Total (Turf)	17	3	3	3	85469
Career Total (AW)	1	0	0	0	540

115 5/08 Curr 1m2f FRM £38294
105 5/08 Gowr 1m4f SFT £10530
76 9/07 Rosc 7f G-F £4668
Total win prize-money £53494

Going (Turf): **Sf: 1-3** GS: 0-0 Gd: 0-7 **GF: 1-3 Fm: 1-2**
Distance: 5f/6f: 0-1 7f-8f: 1-7 **9f-13f: 2-10** 14f+: 0-0
Track : LH: 0-6 **RH: 3-9** Tight: 0-1 Gall: 0-1
Aids: Bl: 0-0 Vi: 0-0 Tstrap: 0-0 Ckp: 0-0
Best Rating: **115** 5/08 Curr 1m2f firm

Group class; Group 3 winner; stays 1m4f; acts on any ground.

Hector Spectre (IRE)

102(100) (72)**64**

3-y-o gr c Verglas (IRE)-Halicardia (Halling (USA))
P D Evans (K M Prendergast 30/9) R Piff

Placings:0330205610**50125342** (7881)
2009: 7^{0}SD, 7^{3}SD, 8^{3}SD, 8^{0}G, 10^{2}GF, 11^{0}S, 8^{5}F, 9^{6}GF, 8^{1}SF, 8^{0}GS, 9^{5}SD, 8^{0}SD, 9^{1}G, 10^{2}SD, 10^{5}SD, 12^{3}SD, 12^{4}SD, 10^{2}SD,

	Starts	1st	2nd	3rd	Win & Pl
Career Total (Turf)	7	1	1	0	2778
Career Total (AW)	11	1	2	3	4787

64 10/09 Brig 1m1f209y (0-60)H GD £2072
72 7/09 Wolv 1m141y (0-60)H SF £2388
Total win prize-money £4460

Going (Turf): Sf: 0-1 GS: 0-1 **Gd: 1-2** GF: 0-2 Fm: 0-1
Distance: 5f/6f: 0-0 7f-8f: 0-3 **9f-13f: 2-15** 14f+: 0-0
Track : **LH: 2-13** RH: 0-4 **Tight: 1-13** Gall: 0-0
Aids: Bl: 0-0 **Vi: 1-5** Tstrap: 0-0 Ckp: 0-0
Best Rating: **72** 7/09 Wolv 1m141y std-fst

Modest; stays 1m4f; acts on Polytrack.

Hector's House

87 **70**

3-y-o b g Tobougg (IRE)-Thrasher (Hector Protector (USA))
Evan Williams (M Dods 24/7) David Brace

Placings:434-5660 (4280)
2009: 10^{5}GF, 10^{6}HY, 8^{6}GF, 12^{0}G,

	Starts	1st	2nd	3rd	Win & Pl
Career Total (Turf)	7	0	0	1	537

Going (Turf): **Sf: 0-3 GS: 0-1 Gd: 0-1 GF: 0-2 Fm: 0-0**
Distance: 5f/6f: 0-0 7f-8f: 0-3 9f-13f: 0-4 14f+: 0-0
Track : LH: 0-4 RH: 0-2 Tight: 0-3 Gall: 0-0
Aids: Bl: 0-0 Vi: 0-0 Tstrap: 0-0 Ckp: 0-0
Best Rating: **70** 10/08 Newc 7f heavy

Hedgerow (IRE)

86 **56**

2-y-o b f Azamour (IRE)-Miss Childrey (IRE) (Dr Fong (USA))
A Dickman The Marooned Crew

Placings:504 (6378)
2009: 7^{5}G, 7^{0}GF, 6^{4}GF,

	Starts	1st	2nd	3rd	Win & Pl
Career Total (Turf)	3	0	0	0	283

Going (Turf): **Sf: 0-0 GS: 0-0 Gd: 0-1 GF: 0-2 Fm: 0-0**
Distance: 5f/6f: 0-1 7f-8f: 0-2 9f-13f: 0-0 14f+: 0-0
Track : LH: 0-1 RH: 0-0 Tight: 0-1 Gall: 0-0
Aids: Bl: 0-0 Vi: 0-0 Tstrap: 0-0 Ckp: 0-0
Best Rating: **56** 8/09 Rdcr 7f gd-fm

Hekaaya (IRE)

67(89) (52)**34**

3-y-o b f Kheleyf (USA)-Victoria Regia (IRE) (Lomond (USA))
M P Tregoning Sheikh Ahmed Al Maktoum

Placings:006-000 (5882)
2009: 7^{0}SD, 8^{0}GF, 5^{0}SD,

	Starts	1st	2nd	3rd	Win & Pl
Career Total (Turf)	3	0	0	0	
Career Total (AW)	3	0	0	0	0

Going (Turf): **Sf: 0-0 GS: 0-1 Gd: 0-1 GF: 0-1 Fm: 0-0**
Distance: 5f/6f: 0-2 7f-8f: 0-3 9f-13f: 0-1 14f+: 0-0
Track : LH: 0-3 RH: 0-0 Tight: 0-3 Gall: 0-0
Aids: Bl: 0-0 Vi: 0-1 Tstrap: 0-0 Ckp: 0-0
Best Rating: **52** 10/08 Ling 6f stand

Hel's Angel (IRE)

103 **76**

3-y-o b f Pyrus (USA)-Any Dream (IRE) (Shernazar)
Mrs A Duffield Mrs H Baines & Middleham Park Racing VII

Placings:3323-1601624503 (6182)
2009: 8^{1}G, 8^{6}GF, 7^{0}GF, 8^{1}GF, 8^{6}GF, 8^{2}G, 8^{4}GF, 7^{5}GF, 8^{0}GF, 8^{3}GF,

	Starts	1st	2nd	3rd	Win & Pl
Career Total (Turf)	14	2	2	4	10320

76 6/09 Pont 1m4y (0-70)H G-F £3238
71 5/09 Thsk 1m (0-65)H GD £2978
Total win prize-money £6217

Going (Turf): Sf: 0-1 GS: 0-0 **Gd: 1-4 GF: 1-9** Fm: 0-0
Distance: 5f/6f: 0-1 7f-8f: 1-7 9f-13f: 1-6 14f+: 0-0
Track : **LH: 2-3** RH: 0-8 **Tight: 1-4** Gall: 0-1
Aids: Bl: 0-0 Vi: 0-0 Tstrap: 0-0 Ckp: 0-0
Best Rating: **76** 9/09 Bevl 1m100y gd-fm

Fair; stays 1m and acts on most ground.

Helaku (IRE)

85 **53**

2-y-o b c Rakti-Saibhreas (IRE) (Last Tycoon)
R Hannon Michael Pescod & Justin Dowley

Placings:00 (6697)
2009: 8^{0}GF, 9^{0}GS,

	Starts	1st	2nd	3rd	Win & Pl
Career Total (Turf)	2	0	0	0	

Going (Turf): **Sf: 0-0 GS: 0-1 Gd: 0-0 GF: 0-1 Fm: 0-0**
Distance: 5f/6f: 0-0 7f-8f: 0-1 9f-13f: 0-1 14f+: 0-0
Track : LH: 0-0 RH: 0-1 Tight: 0-1 Gall: 0-0
Aids: Bl: 0-0 Vi: 0-0 Tstrap: 0-0 Ckp: 0-0
Best Rating: **53** 9/09 NmkR 1m gd-fm

Helieorbea

105(98) (73)**76**

3-y-o b g Reset (AUS)-Rendition (Polish Precedent (USA))

T D Easterby Middleham Park Racing XXXIII

Placings:323216064 (6537)
2009: 7^{3}F, 7^{2}GF, 9^{3}G, 7^{2}GF, 6^{1}S, 7^{6}SD, 8^{0}GF, 8^{6}SD, 8^{4}GF,

	Starts	1st	2nd	3rd	Win & Pl
Career Total (Turf)	7	1	2	2	5475
Career Total (AW)	2	0	0	0	0

73 8/09 Haml 6f5y SFT £2729
Total win prize-money £2730

Going (Turf): **Sf: 1-1** GS: 0-0 Gd: 0-1 GF: 0-4 Fm: 0-1
Distance: 5f/6f: 0-0 **7f-8f: 1-6** 9f-13f: 0-3 14f+: 0-0
Track : LH: 0-4 RH: 0-3 Tight: 0-2 Gall: 0-0
Aids: Bl: 0-0 Vi: 0-0 Tstrap: 0-1 Ckp: 0-1
Best Rating: **76** 8/09 Rdcr 7f gd-fm

Fair; effective at 6f on easy ground; has worn cheekpieces.

Heligoland

75(87) (50)**31**
2-y-o b f Trade Fair-Fine Frenzy (IRE) (Great Commotion (USA))
A G Newcombe Richard J Smith - Paul Nicholas

Placings:0000 (7597)
2009: 5^{0}G, 8^{0}SD, 7^{0}SD, 8^{0}SD,

	Starts	1st	2nd	3rd	Win & Pl
Career Total (Turf)	1	0	0	0	
Career Total (AW)	3	0	0	0	

Going (Turf): **Sf: 0-0 GS: 0-0 Gd: 0-1 GF: 0-0 Fm: 0-0**
Distance: 5f/6f: 0-1 7f-8f: 0-2 9f-13f: 0-1 14f+: 0-0
Track : LH: 0-3 RH: 0-1 Tight: 0-2 Gall: 0-1
Aids: Bl: 0-0 Vi: 0-0 Tstrap: 0-0 Ckp: 0-0
Best Rating: **50** 9/09 Kemp 1m stand

Heliodor (USA)

102(112) (107)**104**
3-y-o b c Scrimshaw (USA)-Playing Footsie (USA) (Valiant Nature (USA))
R Hannon Mrs J Wood

Placings:24624040121-36566614 (7031)
2009: 9^{3}GF, 10^{6}GF, 10^{5}GF, 10^{6}GS, 12^{6}G, 12^{6}SD, 10^{1}SD, 12^{4}S,

	Starts	1st	2nd	3rd	Win & Pl
Career Total (Turf)	17	2	3	1	31735
Career Total (AW)	2	1	0	0	8230

107 9/09 Kemp 1m2f STD £7352
82 11/08 NmkR 1m2f G-S £9346
84 9/08 Gdwd 1m1f G-F £4695
Total win prize-money £21395

Going (Turf): Sf: 0-4 **GS: 1-4** Gd: 0-4 **GF: 1-5** Fm: 0-0
Distance: 5f/6f: 0-5 7f-8f: 0-3 **9f-13f: 3-11** 14f+: 0-0
Track : LH: 0-2 **RH: 2-6 Tight: 1-2** Gall: 0-3
Aids: Bl: 0-1 Vi: 0-0 Tstrap: 0-0 Ckp: 0-0
Best Rating: **107** 9/09 Kemp 1m2f stand

Smart; Listed placed; stays 1m2f; acts on most ground and Polytrack; has worn blinkers.

Hellbender (IRE)

92(106) (86)**61**
3-y-o ch g Exceed And Excel (AUS)-Desert Rose (Green Desert (USA))
S Kirk Mike Newbould

Placings:000621-21235002331166 (7617)
2009: 6^{2}SS, 6^{1}SD, 6^{2}SD, 7^{3}SD, 7^{5}S, 7^{0}S, 5^{0}GF, 5^{2}SD, 6^{3}SS, 5^{3}SD, 6^{1}SD, 7^{1}SD, 7^{6}SD, 7^{6}SD,

	Starts	1st	2nd	3rd	Win & Pl
Career Total (Turf)	7	0	0	0	0
Career Total (AW)	13	4	4	3	18767

86 11/09 Ling 7f (0-90)H STD £7771
70 1/09 Ling 6f (0-70)H STD £2590
65 12/08 Sthl 6f (0-75) STD £2729
Total win prize-money £13091

Going (Turf): **Sf: 0-3 GS: 0-1 Gd: 0-1 GF: 0-2 Fm: 0-0**
Distance: **5f/6f: 3-13** 7f-8f: 1-7 9f-13f: 0-0 14f+: 0-0
Track : **LH: 3-13** RH: 1-1 **Tight: 2-10** Gall: 0-0
Aids: Bl: 0-0 Vi: 0-0 Tstrap: 0-0 Ckp: 0-0
Best Rating: **86** 11/09 Ling 7f stand

Fair; suited by 6f-7f; acts on sand.

Hellenio

89(87) (54)**65**
2-y-o b c Cape Cross (IRE)-Llia (Shirley Heights)
S C Williams R Corona

Placings:0405030 (7097)
2009: 7^{0}GS, 6^{4}GF, 8^{0}SD, 7^{5}GF, 8^{0}SD, 7^{3}GF, 7^{0}G,

	Starts	1st	2nd	3rd	Win & Pl
Career Total (Turf)	5	0	0	1	687
Career Total (AW)	2	0	0	0	

Going (Turf): **Sf: 0-0 GS: 0-1 Gd: 0-1 GF: 0-3 Fm: 0-0**
Distance: 5f/6f: 0-0 7f-8f: 0-7 9f-13f: 0-0 14f+: 0-0
Track : LH: 0-2 RH: 0-2 Tight: 0-0 Gall: 0-0
Aids: Bl: 0-0 Vi: 0-0 Tstrap: 0-0 Ckp: 0-0
Best Rating: **65** 8/09 Brig 6f209y gd-fm

Hello Sunshine

81(76) (4)**33**
3-y-o b g Deportivo-Full English (Perugino (USA))
T J Pitt Recycled Products Limited

Placings:00000 (5105)
2009: 6^{0}GF, 5^{0}GS, 6^{0}GF, 7^{0}S, 5^{0}SD,

	Starts	1st	2nd	3rd	Win & Pl
Career Total (Turf)	4	0	0	0	
Career Total (AW)	1	0	0	0	

Going (Turf): **Sf: 0-1 GS: 0-1 Gd: 0-0 GF: 0-2 Fm: 0-0**
Distance: 5f/6f: 0-3 7f-8f: 0-2 9f-13f: 0-0 14f+: 0-0
Track : LH: 0-1 RH: 0-0 Tight: 0-1 Gall: 0-0
Aids: Bl: 0-0 Vi: 0-0 Tstrap: 0-0 Ckp: 0-0
Best Rating: **33** 4/09 Thsk 6f gd-fm

Helping Hand (IRE)

94(104) (65)**69**
4-y-o b g Lend A Hand-Cardinal Press (Sharrood (USA))
R Hollinshead N Chapman

Placings:5160020000**0561**-000000520 (6119)
2009: 5^{0}SD, 5^{0}SD, 5^{0}F, 5^{0}GF, 5^{0}F, 5^{0}GS, 6^{5}GF, 5^{2}G, 5^{0}SD,

	Starts	1st	2nd	3rd	Win & Pl
Career Total (Turf)	13	0	2	0	1734
Career Total (AW)	10	2	0	0	4400

65 12/08 GrLe 6f (0-55)H STD £1942
67 1/08 Sthl 6f STD £2457
Total win prize-money £4400

Going (Turf): **Sf: 0-0 GS: 0-3 Gd: 0-4 GF: 0-4 Fm: 0-2**
Distance: **5f/6f: 2-21** 7f-8f: 0-2 9f-13f: 0-0 14f+: 0-0
Track : **LH: 2-12** RH: 0-0 Tight: 0-5 **Gall: 1-2**
Aids: Bl: 0-0 Vi: 0-0 Tstrap: 0-0 Ckp: 0-0
Best Rating: **69** 5/08 NmkR 5f gd-fm

Moderate; effective over 6f; acts on fast ground; goes on Fibresand and Polytrack.

Helpmeronda

(89) (49)**61**
3-y-o b f Medicean-Lady Donatella (Last Tycoon)
W M Brisbourne (S A Callaghan 5/2) Stratford Bards Racing No 2

Placings:50440-3050 (7857)
2009: 8^{3}SD, 9^{0}SD, 7^{5}SD, 9^{0}SD,

	Starts	1st	2nd	3rd	Win & Pl
Career Total (Turf)	4	0	0	0	283
Career Total (AW)	5	0	0	1	740

Going (Turf): **Sf: 0-1 GS: 0-0 Gd: 0-1 GF: 0-2 Fm: 0-0**
Distance: 5f/6f: 0-3 7f-8f: 0-3 9f-13f: 0-3 14f+: 0-0
Track : LH: 0-6 RH: 0-0 Tight: 0-4 Gall: 0-0
Aids: Bl: 0-1 Vi: 0-0 Tstrap: 0-0 Ckp: 0-0
Best Rating: **61** 8/08 Brig 6f209y gd-fm

Modest; stays 6f; acts on fast ground; acts on Polytrack.

Helvetio

(90) (57)**72**
7-y-o b g Theatrical-Personal Love (USA) (Diesis)
D E Pipe (Micky Hammond 17/4) Stef Stefanou

Placings:3/221360/025422330/**60**/00-05 (0983)
2009: 13^{0}SD, 13^{5}SD,

	Starts	1st	2nd	3rd	Win & Pl
Career Total (Turf)	19	1	5	4	48966
Career Total (AW)	3	0	0	0	187

95 5/05 Curr 1m2f G-Y £8331
Total win prize-money £8331

Going (Turf): **Sf: 0-3 GS: 0-5 Gd: 0-6 GF: 0-3 Fm: 0-0**
Distance: 5f/6f: 0-0 7f-8f: 0-0 **9f-13f: 1-14** 14f+: 0-8
Track : LH: 0-8 **RH: 1-8** Tight: 0-4 Gall: 0-1
Aids: Bl: 0-1 Vi: 0-0 Tstrap: 0-0 Ckp: 0-0
Best Rating: **106** 6/05 York 1m7f198y gd-fm

Hendersyde (USA)

106(101) (88)**96**
4-y-o ch g Giant's Causeway (USA)-Cimmaron Lady (USA) (Grand Slam (USA))
W R Swinburn P W Harris

Placings:553312-114550 (6273)
2009: 12^{1}SD, 14^{1}GF, 16^{4}S, 16^{5}G, 14^{5}GF, 16^{0}GF,

	Starts	1st	2nd	3rd	Win & Pl
Career Total (Turf)	9	2	1	1	23639
Career Total (AW)	3	1	0	1	5113

96 5/09 NmkR 1m6f (0-85)H G-F £5828
88 4/09 Kemp 1m4f (0-85)H STD £4727
85 8/08 Sand 1m6f (0-80)H G-S £6476
Total win prize-money £17031

Going (Turf): Sf: 0-1 **GS: 1-2** Gd: 0-1 **GF: 1-4** Fm: 0-1
Distance: 5f/6f: 0-0 7f-8f: 0-0 9f-13f: 1-5 **14f+: 2-7**
Track : LH: 0-5 **RH: 3-7** Tight: 0-3 **Gall: 1-4**
Aids: Bl: 0-0 Vi: 0-0 Tstrap: 0-0 Ckp: 0-0
Best Rating: **96** 5/09 NmkR 1m6f gd-fm

Useful; stays 2m; acts on fast and easy ground; goes on Polytrack; has worn a tongue tie.

Hennessy Island (USA)

94(97) (61)43

4-y-o ch g Hennessy (USA)-Heavenly Dawn (USA) (Holy Bull (USA))

T G Mills John Humphreys

Placings:000/225-0006 **(2381)**

2009: 7^{0}SD, 11^{0}SD, 8^{0}GF, 6^{6}GS,

	Starts	1st	2nd	3rd	Win & Pl
Career Total (Turf)	2	0	0	0	0
Career Total (AW)	8	0	2	0	1088

Going (Turf): Sf: 0-0 GS: 0-1 Gd: 0-0 GF: 0-1 Fm: 0-0
Distance: 5f/6f: 0-0 7f-8f: 0-9 9f-13f: 0-1 14f+: 0-0
Track : LH: 0-7 RH: 0-2 Tight: 0-3 Gall: 0-0
Aids: Bl: 0-0 Vi: 0-0 Tstrap: 0-1 Ckp: 0-1
Best Rating: 61 4/08 Sthl 1m stand

Modest; stays mile but may prove better over seven; acts on Fibresand.

Henry Havelock

76 37

2-y-o ch c Noverre (USA)-Burmese Princess (USA) (King Of Kings (IRE))

C Grant Havelock Racing

Placings:600 **(7116)**

2009: 7^{6}GF, 8^{0}GS, 8^{0}GS,

	Starts	1st	2nd	3rd	Win & Pl
Career Total (Turf)	3	0	0	0	0

Going (Turf): Sf: 0-0 GS: 0-2 Gd: 0-0 GF: 0-1 Fm: 0-0
Distance: 5f/6f: 0-0 7f-8f: 0-2 9f-13f: 0-1 14f+: 0-0
Track : LH: 0-1 RH: 0-2 Tight: 0-1 Gall: 0-0
Aids: Bl: 0-0 Vi: 0-0 Tstrap: 0-0 Ckp: 0-0
Best Rating: 37 10/09 Nott 1m75y gd-sft

Henry Holmes

(97) (53)

6-y-o b g Josr Algarhoud (IRE)-Henrietta Holmes (IRE) (Persian Bold)

Mrs L Richards Mrs Judy Seal

Placings:0/4500/004534/5 **(3158)**

2009: 10^{5}SD,

	Starts	1st	2nd	3rd	Win & Pl
Career Total (Turf)	0	0	0	0	
Career Total (AW)	12	0	0	1	735

Going (Turf): Sf: 0-0 GS: 0-0 Gd: 0-0 GF: 0-0 Fm: 0-0
Distance: 5f/6f: 0-0 7f-8f: 0-2 9f-13f: 0-10 14f+: 0-0
Track : LH: 0-8 RH: 0-4 Tight: 0-8 Gall: 0-0
Aids: Bl: 0-0 Vi: 0-0 Tstrap: 0-0 Ckp: 0-0
Best Rating: 63 3/06 Ling 1m stand

Plating-class; stays 1m2f; acts on Polytrack.

Henry San (IRE)

95 74

2-y-o ch c Exceed And Excel (AUS)-Esclava (USA) (Nureyev (USA))

A King Mrs M C Sweeney

Placings:544 **(6548)**

2009: 7^{5}G, 8^{4}GS, 8^{4}G,

	Starts	1st	2nd	3rd	Win & Pl
Career Total (Turf)	3	0	0	0	758

Going (Turf): Sf: 0-0 GS: 0-1 Gd: 0-2 GF: 0-0 Fm: 0-0
Distance: 5f/6f: 0-0 7f-8f: 0-1 9f-13f: 0-2 14f+: 0-0
Track : LH: 0-0 RH: 0-3 Tight: 0-1 Gall: 0-0
Aids: Bl: 0-0 Vi: 0-0 Tstrap: 0-0 Ckp: 0-0
Best Rating: 74 10/09 Wind 1m67y good

Modest form in maidens at up to 1m on good and easy ground.

Herawati

51 16

3-y-o b g Celtic Swing-Lady Of Jakarta (USA) (Procida (USA))

T D Easterby The Fitch Syndicate

Placings:0-0 **(1168)**

2009: 10^{0}GF,

	Starts	1st	2nd	3rd	Win & Pl
Career Total (Turf)	2	0	0	0	

Going (Turf): Sf: 0-1 GS: 0-0 Gd: 0-0 GF: 0-1 Fm: 0-0
Distance: 5f/6f: 0-0 7f-8f: 0-0 9f-13f: 0-2 14f+: 0-0
Track : LH: 0-2 RH: 0-0 Tight: 0-0 Gall: 0-0
Aids: Bl: 0-0 Vi: 0-0 Tstrap: 0-0 Ckp: 0-0
Best Rating: 16 8/08 Hayd 1m30y soft

Herbert Crescent

87(100) (64)75

4-y-o b g Averti (IRE)-With Distinction (Zafonic (USA))

Ollie Pears Keith Taylor

Placings:604344014/50256020560000-140000422206 **(7782)**

2009: 8^{1}SD, 8^{4}SD, 8^{0}SD, 8^{0}GF, 7^{0}GS, 8^{0}SF, 7^{4}SD, 7^{2}SD, 8^{2}SD, 8^{2}SD, 9^{0}SD, 8^{6}SD,

	Starts	1st	2nd	3rd	Win & Pl
Career Total (Turf)	19	1	2	1	10598
Career Total (AW)	16	1	3	0	4042

64 1/09 Ling 1m (0-60)H STD £2047
69 10/07 Curr 7f (52-90) SFT £6069
Total win prize-money £8117

Going (Turf): **Sf: 1-4** GS: 0-1 Gd: 0-4 GF: 0-7 Fm: 0-0
Distance: 5f/6f: 0-5 **7f-8f: 2-24** 9f-13f: 0-6 14f+: 0-0
Track : **LH: 1-23** RH: 0-6 **Tight: 1-10** Gall: 0-0
Aids: Bl: 0-1 Vi: 0-0 Tstrap: 0-2 Ckp: 0-2
Best Rating: 75 9/08 Cork 7f yld-sft

Modest; effective over 1m; acts on Polytrack.

Here Comes Danny

93(102) (75)60

3-y-o b g Kyllachy-Clarice Orsini (Common Grounds)

M Wigham E J Evans

Placings:0-61506 **(6455)**

2009: 5^{6}SD, 5^{1}SD, 6^{5}SD, 7^{0}GF, 7^{6}SD,

	Starts	1st	2nd	3rd	Win & Pl
Career Total (Turf)	2	0	0	0	
Career Total (AW)	4	1	0	0	2730

75 2/09 Wolv 5f216y STD £2729
Total win prize-money £2730

Going (Turf): Sf: 0-0 GS: 0-1 Gd: 0-0 GF: 0-1 Fm: 0-0
Distance: **5f/6f: 1-4** 7f-8f: 0-2 9f-13f: 0-0 14f+: 0-0
Track : **LH: 1-3** RH: 0-1 **Tight: 1-2** Gall: 0-0
Aids: Bl: 0-0 Vi: 0-0 Tstrap: 0-0 Ckp: 0-0
Best Rating: 75 2/09 Wolv 5f216y stand

Fair; effective at sprint trips; handles Polytrack.

Here Now And Why (IRE)

100 87

2-y-o br c Pastoral Pursuits-Why Now (Dansili)

K A Ryan Mrs Sandra McCarthy

Placings:211050300 **(6550)**

2009: 5^{2}GF, 5^{1}GF, 5^{1}GF, 5^{0}GF, 5^{5}GS, 5^{0}G, 5^{3}G, 5^{0}G, 5^{0}G,

	Starts	1st	2nd	3rd	Win & Pl
Career Total (Turf)	9	2	1	1	19529

87 5/09 Thsk 5f G-F £5569
87 4/09 Ripn 5f G-F £4209
Total win prize-money £9778

Going (Turf): Sf: 0-0 GS: 0-1 Gd: 0-4 **GF: 2-4** Fm: 0-0
Distance: **5f/6f: 2-9** 7f-8f: 0-0 9f-13f: 0-0 14f+: 0-0
Track : LH: 0-0 RH: 0-0 Tight: 0-0 Gall: 0-1
Aids: Bl: 0-0 Vi: 0-0 Tstrap: 0-0 Ckp: 0-0
Best Rating: 87 5/09 Thsk 5f gd-fm

Useful; effective over 5f; acts on fast and soft ground.

Herecomesbella

95(95) (51)50

3-y-o b f Lujain (USA)-Blushing Belle (Local Suitor (USA))

P G Murphy (Stef Liddiard 7/6) Mrs Ann Shankland

Placings:000004-434445500 **(4196)**

2009: 8^{4}SD, 9^{3}SD, 9^{4}SF, 10^{4}SD, 10^{4}GF, 8^{5}G, 6^{5}G, 7^{0}GF, 8^{0}GS,

	Starts	1st	2nd	3rd	Win & Pl
Career Total (Turf)	9	0	0	0	0
Career Total (AW)	6	0	0	1	302

Going (Turf): Sf: 0-0 GS: 0-1 Gd: 0-3 GF: 0-5 Fm: 0-0
Distance: 5f/6f: 0-3 7f-8f: 0-5 9f-13f: 0-7 14f+: 0-0
Track : LH: 0-6 RH: 0-5 Tight: 0-5 Gall: 0-0
Aids: Bl: 0-9 Vi: 0-0 Tstrap: 0-0 Ckp: 0-0
Best Rating: 51 1/09 Wolv 1m141y stand

Moderate; stays beyond 1m and acts on sand; has worn blinkers.

Herecomethegirls

87(95) (53)38

3-y-o b f Falbrav (IRE)-Always On My Mind (Distant Relative)

M L W Bell Mascalls Stud

Placings:646605 **(7374)**

2009: 8^{6}HY, 8^{4}G, 8^{6}SD, 8^{6}SD, 8^{0}SD, 9^{5}SD,

	Starts	1st	2nd	3rd	Win & Pl
Career Total (Turf)	2	0	0	0	216
Career Total (AW)	4	0	0	0	0

Going (Turf): Sf: 0-1 GS: 0-0 Gd: 0-1 GF: 0-0 Fm: 0-0
Distance: 5f/6f: 0-0 7f-8f: 0-1 9f-13f: 0-5 14f+: 0-0
Track : LH: 0-5 RH: 0-1 Tight: 0-3 Gall: 0-0
Aids: Bl: 0-0 Vi: 0-0 Tstrap: 0-0 Ckp: 0-0
Best Rating: 53 10/09 Kemp 1m stand

Hereford Boy

101(104) (82)84

5-y-o ch g Tomba-Grown At Rowan (Gabitat)

D K Ivory Recycled Products Limited

Placings:00423231/354402143001010/421400355602664-02500030021014 (7830)
2009: 5^{0}G, 5^{2}G, 5^{5}GF, 5^{0}SD, 5^{0}G, 5^{0}GF, 6^{3}SD, 7^{0}SD, 8^{0}SD, 6^{2}GS, 7^{1}SD, 7^{0}SD, 8^{1}SD, 7^{4}SD,

	Starts	1st	2nd	3rd	Win & Pl
Career Total (Turf)	26	3	5	1	16991
Career Total (AW)	26	4	2	5	17612

72	11/09	Kemp	1m	(0-65)H	STD	£1706
71	10/09	Kemp	7f	(0-60)H	STD	£1706
87	4/08	Folk	5f	(0-80)H	G-S	£4209
82	10/07	Ling	5f	(0-75)H	STD	£2817
77	10/07	Gdwd	5f	(0-70)H	SFT	£3562
73	5/07	Brig	5f59y	(0-75)H	GD	£2775
68	12/06	Sthl	5f		STD	£4533

Total win prize-money £21310

Going (Turf): **Sf: 1-5 GS: 1-6 Gd: 1-7** GF: 0-5 Fm: 0-3
Distance: **5f/6f: 5-46** 7f-8f: 2-6 9f-13f: 0-0 14f+: 0-0
Track : LH: 2-16 RH: 2-12 **Tight: 1-11** Gall: 0-8
Aids: Bl: 0-7 Vi: 0-0 Tstrap: 2-7 Ckp: 2-7
Best Rating: **87** 4/08 Folk 5f gd-sft

Modest; stays 1m; acts on most types of ground and on sand; has worn blinkers and cheekpieces.

Heritage Coast (USA)

100(97) (69)84
4-y-o b f Dynaformer (USA)-Bristol Channel (Generous (IRE))
H Morrison Britannia Thoroughbreds

Placings:422/223-4321000 (7413)
2009: 9^{4}GF, 12^{3}GF, 10^{2}G, 10^{1}GF, 9^{0}S, 10^{0}SD, 12^{0}SD,

	Starts	1st	2nd	3rd	Win & Pl
Career Total (Turf)	9	1	3	2	9395
Career Total (AW)	4	0	2	0	1994

58	8/09	Ches	1m2f75y	G-F	£4047

Total win prize-money £4047

Going (Turf): Sf: 0-1 GS: 0-0 Gd: 0-4 **GF: 1-4** Fm: 0-0
Distance: 5f/6f: 0-0 7f-8f: 0-2 **9f-13f: 1-11** 14f+: 0-0
Track : **LH: 1-6** RH: 0-5 **Tight: 1-8** Gall: 0-1
Aids: Bl: 0-0 Vi: 0-0 Tstrap: 0-0 Ckp: 0-0
Best Rating: **84** 6/08 Sand 1m2f7y good

Fair filly; stays 1m 4f; acts on good ground and Polytrack.

Hermione's Magic

99(93) (71)94
3-y-o ch f Systematic-Eleonor Sympson (Cadeaux Genereux)
Kathy Walsh (P J McBride 5/8) A & S Kirkwood

Placings:1-310 (2001)
2009: 8^{3}GF, 8^{1}F, 9^{0}F,

	Starts	1st	2nd	3rd	Win & Pl
Career Total (Turf)	3	1	0	1	25578
Career Total (AW)	1	1	0	0	3071

	8/09	Delm	1m	FRM	£25000
71	10/08	Wolv	5f216y	STD	£3070

Total win prize-money £28071

Going (Turf): Sf: 0-0 GS: 0-0 Gd: 0-0 GF: 0-1 **Fm: 1-2**
Distance: 5f/6f: 1-1 7f-8f: 1-2 9f-13f: 0-1 14f+: 0-0
Track : **LH: 1-2** RH: 0-0 **Tight: 1-1** Gall: 0-0
Aids: Bl: 0-0 Vi: 0-0 Tstrap: 0-0 Ckp: 0-0
Best Rating: **94** 8/09 Delm 1m1f firm

Hernando's Boy

95 69
8-y-o b g Hernando (FR)-Leave At Dawn (Slip Anchor)
K G Reveley Crack of Dawn Partnership

Placings:000/50002/623631/23/01/4P05-0054 (6845)
2009: 15^{0}S, 13^{0}GF, 15^{5}G, 13^{4}G,

	Starts	1st	2nd	3rd	Win & Pl
Career Total (Turf)	26	2	3	3	14458

74	11/07	Catt	1m5f175y (0-75)H	G-F	£2914
75	11/05	Catt	1m5f175y (0-75)H	SFT	£4264

Total win prize-money £7179

Going (Turf): **Sf: 1-8** GS: 0-5 Gd: 0-5 **GF: 1-6** Fm: 0-2
Distance: 5f/6f: 0-0 7f-8f: 0-3 9f-13f: 0-7 **14f+: 2-16**
Track : **LH: 2-19** RH: 0-5 **Tight: 2-19** Gall: 0-3
Aids: Bl: 0-0 Vi: 0-0 Tstrap: 0-0 Ckp: 0-0
Best Rating: **75** 11/05 Catt 1m5f175y soft

Modest handicapper; winning hurdler; stays 2m; acts on fast and easy ground.

Heroes

101(106) (84)85
5-y-o b g Diktat-Wars (IRE) (Green Desert (USA))
Tim Vaughan M Khan X2

Placings:315/000322250/00552500-155 (4434)
2009: 7^{1}G, 10^{5}G, 10^{5}GF,

	Starts	1st	2nd	3rd	Win & Pl
Career Total (Turf)	19	2	4	2	18726
Career Total (AW)	4	0	0	0	0

81	5/09	Brig	7f214y	GD	£1942
84	10/06	Wind	6f	SFT	£3886

Total win prize-money £5829

Going (Turf): **Sf: 1-7** GS: 0-2 **Gd: 1-6** GF: 0-4 Fm: 0-0
Distance: 5f/6f: 1-2 7f-8f: 1-14 9f-13f: 0-7 14f+: 0-0
Track : **LH: 1-10** RH: 0-4 Tight: 0-6 **Gall: 1-5**
Aids: Bl: 0-0 Vi: 0-1 Tstrap: 1-4 Ckp: 1-4
Best Rating: **95** 10/07 NmkR 1m good

Fair; stays 1m2f, but effective over shorter; acts on fast, but may be best on soft ground; has worn cheekpieces.

Heron Bay

108(107) (103)101
5-y-o b h Hernando (FR)-Wiener Wald (USA) (Woodman (USA))
C F Wall Mollers Racing

Placings:6231000/05405-0004300 (7018)
2009: 9^{0}GF, 10^{0}GF, 12^{0}GF, 10^{4}GS, 12^{3}GS, 11^{0}SD, 12^{0}GS,

	Starts	1st	2nd	3rd	Win & Pl
Career Total (Turf)	17	1	1	2	43591
Career Total (AW)	2	0	0	0	

103	6/07	Asct	1m4f	(0-105)H	G-F	£34276

Total win prize-money £34276

Going (Turf): Sf: 0-0 GS: 0-5 Gd: 0-5 **GF: 1-7** Fm: 0-0
Distance: 5f/6f: 0-0 7f-8f: 0-0 **9f-13f: 1-16** 14f+: 0-3
Track : LH: 0-8 **RH: 1-10** Tight: 0-5 **Gall: 1-9**
Aids: Bl: 0-0 Vi: 0-0 Tstrap: 0-0 Ckp: 0-0
Best Rating: **103** 3/08 Kemp 1m3f stand

Very useful; winner of the 2007 King George V Handicap; stays 1m4f and acts on fast and soft ground.

Heronway (IRE)

(67) (4)
7-y-o b g Heron Island (IRE)-French Willow (IRE) (Un Desperado (FR))
W J Greatrex (Carl Llewellyn 10/5) Malcolm Denmark & Callum Denmark

Placings:0 (7557)
2009: 13^{0}SD,

	Starts	1st	2nd	3rd	Win & Pl
Career Total (Turf)	0	0	0	0	
Career Total (AW)	1	0	0	0	

Going (Turf): **Sf: 0-0 GS: 0-0 Gd: 0-0 GF: 0-0 Fm: 0-0**
Distance: 5f/6f: 0-0 7f-8f: 0-0 9f-13f: 0-0 14f+: 0-1
Track : LH: 0-1 RH: 0-0 Tight: 0-1 Gall: 0-0
Aids: Bl: 0-0 Vi: 0-0 Tstrap: 0-0 Ckp: 0-0
Best Rating: **4** 11/09 Wolv 1m5f194y stand

Herrbee (IRE)

(90) (52)53
4-y-o b g Mark Of Esteem (IRE)-Reematna (Sabrehill (USA))
J L Spearing H James

Placings:000/040002P0000-0 (0215)
2009: 8^{0}SD,

	Starts	1st	2nd	3rd	Win & Pl
Career Total (Turf)	4	0	0	0	
Career Total (AW)	11	0	1	0	524

Going (Turf): **Sf: 0-0 GS: 0-2 Gd: 0-1 GF: 0-1 Fm: 0-0**
Distance: 5f/6f: 0-3 7f-8f: 0-6 9f-13f: 0-6 14f+: 0-0
Track : LH: 0-8 RH: 0-5 Tight: 0-7 Gall: 0-1
Aids: Bl: 0-0 Vi: 0-0 Tstrap: 0-1 Ckp: 0-1
Best Rating: **53** 7/07 Gdwd 6f good

Plating-class; stays 1m 2f; acts on Polytrack.

Herrera (IRE)

103(100) (64)76
4-y-o b f High Chaparral (IRE)-Silk (IRE) (Machiavellian (USA))
R A Fahey Dr Anne J F Gillespie

Placings:022430-1016560140 (6995)
2009: 12^{1}GF, 12^{0}F, 16^{1}G, 16^{6}GF, 16^{5}GS, 13^{6}G, 16^{0}G, 12^{1}S, 12^{4}SD, 14^{0}GS,

	Starts	1st	2nd	3rd	Win & Pl
Career Total (Turf)	15	3	2	1	12182
Career Total (AW)	1	0	0	0	351

74	8/09	Haml	1m4f17y (0-70)H	SFT	£3238
75	5/09	Bevl	2m35y (0-75)H	GD	£2914
76	4/09	Newc	1m4f93y (0-70)H	G-F	£2914

Total win prize-money £9066

Going (Turf): **Sf: 1-2** GS: 0-3 **Gd: 1-3 GF: 1-6** Fm: 0-1
Distance: 5f/6f: 0-0 7f-8f: 0-0 **9f-13f: 2-8** 14f+: 1-8
Track : LH: 1-10 **RH: 2-6 Tight: 2-7** Gall: 1-6
Aids: Bl: 0-0 Vi: 0-0 Tstrap: 0-0 Ckp: 0-0
Best Rating: **76** 4/09 Newc 1m4f93y gd-fm

Fair; effective at up to 2m; acts on good and faster ground.

Herschel (IRE)

94(96) (78)75
3-y-o br g Dr Fong (USA)-Rafting (IRE) (Darshaan)
G L Moore Findlay & Bloom

Placings:066541-004 (2850)
2009: 8^{0}SD, 9^{0}G, 12^{4}GF,

	Starts	1st	2nd	3rd	Win & Pl
Career Total (Turf)	6	0	0	0	241
Career Total (AW)	3	1	0	0	2783

78	11/08	Kemp	1m1f	(0-70)	STD	£2590

Total win prize-money £2590

Going (Turf): Sf: 0-1 GS: 0-1 Gd: 0-2 GF: 0-2 Fm: 0-0
Distance: 5f/6f: 0-0 7f-8f: 0-6 9f-13f: 1-3 14f+: 0-0
Track : LH: 0-2 RH: 1-7 Tight: 0-1 Gall: 0-1
Aids: Bl: 0-0 Vi: 0-0 Tstrap: 0-0 Ckp: 0-0
Best Rating: 78 11/08 Kemp 1m1f stand

Modest; stays 1m; should get further.

Heslington

91(95) (73)67

2-y-o ch c Piccolo-Spice Island (Reprimand)
M Brittain Mel Brittain

Placings:0521 (6355)
2009: 5^{0}GF, 5^{5}GF, 5^{2}GF, 5^{1}SD,

	Starts	1st	2nd	3rd	Win & Pl
Career Total (Turf)	3	0	1	0	771
Career Total (AW)	1	1	0	0	3412

73	9/09	Sthl	5f	(0-70)	STD	£3412

Total win prize-money £3412

Going (Turf): Sf: 0-0 GS: 0-0 Gd: 0-0 GF: 0-3 Fm: 0-0
Distance: 5f/6f: 1-4 7f-8f: 0-0 9f-13f: 0-0 14f+: 0-0
Track : LH: 0-0 RH: 0-0 Tight: 0-0 Gall: 0-0
Aids: Bl: 0-0 Vi: 0-0 Tstrap: 0-0 Ckp: 0-0
Best Rating: 73 9/09 Sthl 5f stand

Fair; suited by 5f; acts on fast ground and on Fibresand.

Hettie Hubble

99 59

3-y-o ch f Dr Fong (USA)-White Rabbit (Zilzal (USA))
D W Thompson Miss E Crozier

Placings:600-0006332244 (5621)
2009: 7^{0}GF, 6^{0}F, 6^{0}G, 7^{6}G, 6^{3}GF, 8^{3}GS, 6^{2}GS, 8^{2}HY, 6^{4}S, 7^{4}S,

	Starts	1st	2nd	3rd	Win & Pl
Career Total (Turf)	13	0	2	2	2151

Going (Turf): Sf: 0-3 GS: 0-3 Gd: 0-2 GF: 0-4 Fm: 0-1
Distance: 5f/6f: 0-4 7f-8f: 0-7 9f-13f: 0-2 14f+: 0-0
Track : LH: 0-4 RH: 0-3 Tight: 0-5 Gall: 0-0
Aids: Bl: 0-0 Vi: 0-0 Tstrap: 0-0 Ckp: 0-0
Best Rating: 59 7/08 Thsk 7f gd-fm

Moderate; stays 1m; handles soft ground.

Heureux (USA)

95 74

6-y-o b g Stravinsky (USA)-Storm West (USA) (Gone West (USA))
J Howard Johnson J Howard Johnson

Placings:3210/44644P0/02000/5342-5031 (2816)
2009: 6^{5}GS, 7^{0}GF, 8^{3}GF, 6^{1}G,

	Starts	1st	2nd	3rd	Win & Pl
Career Total (Turf)	24	2	3	3	23861

	9/09	Ovrl	6f165y	GD	£2830
74	8/05	York	6f	GD	£8528

Total win prize-money £11358

Going (Turf): Sf: 0-2 GS: 0-4 Gd: 2-6 GF: 0-8 Fm: 0-4
Distance: 5f/6f: 1-4 7f-8f: 1-16 9f-13f: 0-4 14f+: 0-0
Track : LH: 0-12 RH: 0-6 Tight: 0-12 Gall: 0-1
Aids: Bl: 0-9 Vi: 0-2 Tstrap: 0-1 Ckp: 0-1
Best Rating: 81 8/05 York 6f good

Modest; effective at around 1m; suited by fast ground; has worn blinkers.

Hevelius

108 97

4-y-o b g Polish Precedent (USA)-Sharp Terms (Kris)
W R Swinburn The Warsaw Pact

Placings:61-26020 (7293)
2009: 10^{2}GF, 11^{6}GF, 12^{0}G, 12^{2}G, 12^{0}S,

	Starts	1st	2nd	3rd	Win & Pl
Career Total (Turf)	7	1	2	0	10551

91	7/08	Pont	1m2f6y	GD	£3885

Total win prize-money £3886

Going (Turf): Sf: 0-1 GS: 0-0 Gd: 1-4 GF: 0-2 Fm: 0-0
Distance: 5f/6f: 0-0 7f-8f: 0-1 9f-13f: 1-6 14f+: 0-0
Track : LH: 1-4 RH: 0-3 Tight: 0-0 Gall: 0-4
Aids: Bl: 0-0 Vi: 0-0 Tstrap: 0-0 Ckp: 0-0
Best Rating: 97 5/09 Donc 1m2f60y gd-fm

Useful; stays 1m4f; acts on good ground.

Hey Presto

87(94) (51)19

9-y-o b g Piccolo-Upping The Tempo (Dunbeath (USA))
R Rowe Richard Rowe

Placings:04204/3012060040/0005610000/30055100/0000 000/0500000/46100-000 (3421)
2009: 6^{0}F, 8^{0}SD, 9^{0}G,

	Starts	1st	2nd	3rd	Win & Pl
Career Total (Turf)	38	3	2	1	29280
Career Total (AW)	17	1	0	1	1885

51	4/08	Kemp	1m	(0-45)	STD	£1364
74	9/05	Sals	6f212y	(0-70)H	FRM	£3720
78	7/04	Asct	7f	C(0-90)H	G-F	£10351
83	5/03	Sals	6f	E(0-75)H	G-F	£3880

Total win prize-money £19318

Going (Turf): Sf: 0-1 GS: 0-2 Gd: 0-7 GF: 2-25 Fm: 1-3
Distance: 5f/6f: 1-18 7f-8f: 3-32 9f-13f: 0-5 14f+: 0-0
Track : LH: 0-14 RH: 1-10 Tight: 0-12 Gall: 0-4
Aids: Bl: 0-2 Vi: 0-0 Tstrap: 0-1 Ckp: 0-1
Best Rating: 88 5/03 NmkR 6f gd-fm

Plating-class; stays 1m; acts on fast ground and Polytrack; has been tried in blinkers.

Hey Up Dad

101 72

3-y-o b g Fantastic Light (USA)-Spanish Quest (Rainbow Quest (USA))
M Dods J N Blackburn

Placings:31-50564050 (6052)
2009: 8^{5}GF, 10^{0}HY, 12^{5}F, 8^{6}G, 8^{4}GS, 10^{0}GS, 9^{5}G, 8^{0}G,

	Starts	1st	2nd	3rd	Win & Pl
Career Total (Turf)	10	1	0	1	5903

72	9/08	Ayr	7f50y	HVY	£5180

Total win prize-money £5181

Going (Turf): Sf: 1-2 GS: 0-3 Gd: 0-3 GF: 0-1 Fm: 0-1
Distance: 5f/6f: 0-1 7f-8f: 1-2 9f-13f: 0-7 14f+: 0-0
Track : LH: 1-8 RH: 0-1 Tight: 0-2 Gall: 0-1
Aids: Bl: 0-3 Vi: 0-0 Tstrap: 0-1 Ckp: 0-1
Best Rating: 72 9/08 Ayr 7f50y heavy

Fair; stays 7f; acts in soft ground.

Hi Dancer

98(96) (72)73

6-y-o b g Medicean-Sea Music (Inchinor)
P C Haslam R Tocher

Placings:5006/14626/0133/64200-1015 (3450)
2009: 16^{1}SS, 12^{0}SD, 13^{1}GF, 10^{5}GF,

	Starts	1st	2nd	3rd	Win & Pl
Career Total (Turf)	16	2	2	2	6585
Career Total (AW)	6	2	0	0	4025

73	6/09	Haml	1m5f9y	(0-65)H	G-F	£2307
72	1/09	Sthl	2m	(0-65)H	SS	£1977
63	6/07	Rdcr	1m6f19y	(0-60)H	SFT	£1943
58	1/06	Sthl	1m	(0-60)H	STD	£2047

Total win prize-money £8277

Going (Turf): Sf: 1-4 GS: 0-1 Gd: 0-3 GF: 1-8 Fm: 0-0
Distance: 5f/6f: 0-3 7f-8f: 1-4 9f-13f: 0-9 14f+: 3-6
Track : LH: 3-15 RH: 1-4 Tight: 2-11 Gall: 0-1
Aids: Bl: 0-0 Vi: 0-0 Tstrap: 0-0 Ckp: 0-0
Best Rating: 73 6/09 Haml 1m5f9y gd-fm

Modest; effective at 1m4f-2m; acts on fast and soft ground and on Fibresand.

Hi Fling

89(102) (63)65

3-y-o b c Oasis Dream-Crafty Buzz (USA) (Crafty Prospector (USA))
B J Meehan Lady Laidlaw Of Rothiemay

Placings:06-0001060 (5286)
2009: 8^{0}SD, 9^{0}GF, 11^{0}S, 12^{1}SD, 11^{0}GS, 11^{6}G, 12^{0}GF,

	Starts	1st	2nd	3rd	Win & Pl
Career Total (Turf)	7	0	0	0	0
Career Total (AW)	2	1	0	0	2047

63	6/09	Ling	1m4f	(0-60)H	STD	£2047

Total win prize-money £2047

Going (Turf): Sf: 0-1 GS: 0-1 Gd: 0-3 GF: 0-2 Fm: 0-0
Distance: 5f/6f: 0-0 7f-8f: 0-3 9f-13f: 1-6 14f+: 0-0
Track : LH: 1-4 RH: 0-3 Tight: 1-6 Gall: 0-0
Aids: Bl: 1-4 Vi: 0-0 Tstrap: 0-0 Ckp: 0-0
Best Rating: 65 10/08 NmkR 1m good

Modest; stays 1m4f; acts on Polytrack; has worn blinkers.

Hi Shinko

105 82

3-y-o b g Shinko Forest (IRE)-Up Front (IRE) (Up And At 'Em)
B R Millman Always Hopeful Partnership

Placings:002220-1601643231250 (6731)
2009: 6^{1}G, 6^{6}GF, 6^{0}F, 5^{1}GF, 5^{6}GF, 6^{4}G, 5^{3}G, 7^{2}S, 7^{3}GF, 7^{1}GS, 7^{2}GF, 7^{5}GF, 6^{0}S,

	Starts	1st	2nd	3rd	Win & Pl
Career Total (Turf)	19	3	5	2	18160

81	9/09	Epsm	7f	(0-80)H	G-S	£5180
73	6/09	Folk	5f	(0-75)H	G-F	£3070
69	3/09	Folk	6f		GD	£2729

Total win prize-money £10982

Going (Turf): Sf: 0-3 GS: 1-2 Gd: 1-3 GF: 1-10 Fm: 0-1
Distance: 5f/6f: 2-13 7f-8f: 1-6 9f-13f: 0-0 14f+: 0-0
Track : LH: 1-6 RH: 0-0 Tight: 1-3 Gall: 0-2
Aids: Bl: 0-1 Vi: 0-0 Tstrap: 0-0 Ckp: 0-0
Best Rating: 82 9/09 Epsm 7f gd-fm

Fair; effective at 7f; acts on fast and soft ground.

Hi Spec (IRE)

91(98) (52)38

6-y-o b m Spectrum (IRE)-Queen Of Fibres (IRE) (Scenic)
Miss M E Rowland Miss M E Rowland

Placings:00/00505/6003602B0/3014056501-00000330 (7719)

2009: 8^{0}SD, 8^{0}SD, 8^{0}SD, 8^{0}SD, 7^{0}GF, 8^{3}SD, 9^{3}SD, 9^{0}SD,

	Starts	1st	2nd	3rd	Win & Pl
Career Total (Turf)	14	0	0	1	408
Career Total (AW)	20	2	1	3	4465

51 12/08 Wolv 1m141y (0-45) STD £1364
51 2/08 Wolv 7f32y (0-45) STD £1365
Total win prize-money £2730

Going (Turf): Sf: 0-3 GS: 0-0 Gd: 0-2 GF: 0-4 Fm: 0-0
Distance: 5f/6f: 0-3 7f-8f: 1-21 9f-13f: 1-10 14f+: 0-0
Track : LH: 2-20 RH: 0-9 Tight: 2-10 Gall: 0-0
Aids: Bl: 0-2 Vi: 0-1 Tstrap: 2-15 Ckp: 2-15
Best Rating: 52 10/09 Kemp 1m stand

Moderate; ex Irish; stays 1m2f; acts on easy ground; goes on Polytrack.

Hibaayeb

108 110
2-y-o b f Singspiel (IRE)-Lady Zonda (Lion Cavern (USA))
C E Brittain Mohammed Al Nabouda

Placings:3221 (6269)
2009: 7^{3}G, 7^{2}GF, 8^{2}GF, 8^{1}G,

	Starts	1st	2nd	3rd	Win & Pl
Career Total (Turf)	4	1	2	1	142998

110 9/09 Asct 1m GD £123758
Total win prize-money £123759

Going (Turf): Sf: 0-0 GS: 0-0 Gd: 1-2 GF: 0-2 Fm: 0-0
Distance: 5f/6f: 0-0 7f-8f: 1-4 9f-13f: 0-0 14f+: 0-0
Track : LH: 0-0 RH: 1-1 Tight: 0-0 Gall: 1-1
Aids: Bl: 0-0 Vi: 0-0 Tstrap: 0-0 Ckp: 0-0
Best Rating: 110 9/09 Asct 1m good

Smart; winner of the Group 1 Fillies' Mile; stays 1m; acts on fast ground.

Hibiki (IRE)

63 85
5-y-o b g Montjeu (IRE)-White Queen (IRE) (Spectrum (IRE))
P J Hobbs R A Green

Placings:321531/1 (5509)
2009: 12^{1}G,

	Starts	1st	2nd	3rd	Win & Pl
Career Total (Turf)	7	3	1	2	16377

85 8/09 Epsm 1m4f10y (0-85)H GD £6246
82 10/07 Bath 1m3f144y (0-80)H GD £4857
71 9/07 Ling 1m3f106y G-F £2817
Total win prize-money £13921

Going (Turf): Sf: 0-1 GS: 0-0 Gd: 2-3 GF: 1-3 Fm: 0-0
Distance: 5f/6f: 0-0 7f-8f: 0-0 9f-13f: 3-7 14f+: 0-0
Track : LH: 3-4 RH: 0-3 Tight: 3-6 Gall: 0-1
Aids: Bl: 0-0 Vi: 0-0 Tstrap: 1-1 Ckp: 1-1
Best Rating: 85 8/09 Epsm 1m4f10y good

Fair colt; generally progressive since winning extended 11f maiden at Lingfield September 2007; landed Class 4 handicap over the same distance at Bath in October; stays 1m3f; acts on fast and easy ground.

Hiccups

104 83
9-y-o b g Polar Prince (IRE)-Simmie's Special (Precocious)
M Dods Andrew Tinkler

Placings:623201010630/203106330/044106050/4200001 510041/136034000/54204420-04020405 (4654)
2009: 7^{0}GF, 7^{4}GF, 7^{0}G, 7^{2}GF, 7^{0}G, 7^{4}G, 6^{0}G, 6^{5}GF,

	Starts	1st	2nd	3rd	Win & Pl
Career Total (Turf)	68	8	7	7	76463

88 4/07 Sthl 7f (0-80)H GD £4857
89 10/06 Catt 7f (0-80)H SFT £6477
82 9/06 Wwck 7f26y (0-85)H GD £6477
77 8/06 Thsk 7f (0-70)H GD £3886
79 6/05 Catt 7f (0-85)H FRM £6862
85 5/04 Donc 6f D(0-80) G-F £5508
86 7/03 Pont 5f D(0-80)H G-F £12412
82 6/03 Carl 5f E(0-75)H FRM £5833
Total win prize-money £52316

Going (Turf): Sf: 1-9 GS: 0-9 Gd: 3-20 GF: 2-26 Fm: 2-4
Distance: 5f/6f: 3-33 7f-8f: 5-35 9f-13f: 0-0 14f+: 0-0
Track : LH: 6-29 RH: 1-4 Tight: 4-22 Gall: 1-2
Aids: Bl: 0-0 Vi: 0-1 Tstrap: 3-15 Ckp: 3-15
Best Rating: 89 5/07 Wwck 7f26y gd-sft

Fair; effective at around 7f; acts on most types of ground.

Hidden Brief

110 94
3-y-o b f Barathea (IRE)-Hazaradjat (IRE) (Darshaan)
M A Jarvis Lordship Stud

Placings:4-24163 (7697a)
2009: 10^{2}G, 11^{4}GF, 10^{1}GF, 10^{6}S, 9^{3}SD,

	Starts	1st	2nd	3rd	Win & Pl
Career Total (Turf)	5	1	1	0	7864
Career Total (AW)	1	0	0	1	8010

73 6/09 Newb 1m2f6y G-F £3885
Total win prize-money £3886

Going (Turf): Sf: 0-2 GS: 0-0 Gd: 0-1 GF: 1-2 Fm: 0-0
Distance: 5f/6f: 0-0 7f-8f: 0-0 9f-13f: 1-6 14f+: 0-0
Track : LH: 1-3 RH: 0-1 Tight: 0-1 Gall: 1-2
Aids: Bl: 0-0 Vi: 0-0 Tstrap: 0-0 Ckp: 0-0
Best Rating: 94 5/09 Ches 1m3f79y gd-fm

Very useful; stays 1m2f and acts on good ground.

Hidden City (IRE)

72 30
2-y-o b c Elusive City (USA)-Lizanne (USA) (Theatrical)
J S Moore The Moore The Merrier

Placings:000 (4384)
2009: 6^{0}GS, 6^{0}GF, 6^{0}G,

	Starts	1st	2nd	3rd	Win & Pl
Career Total (Turf)	3	0	0	0	

Going (Turf): Sf: 0-0 GS: 0-1 Gd: 0-1 GF: 0-1 Fm: 0-0
Distance: 5f/6f: 0-1 7f-8f: 0-2 9f-13f: 0-0 14f+: 0-0
Track : LH: 0-0 RH: 0-0 Tight: 0-0 Gall: 0-0
Aids: Bl: 0-0 Vi: 0-0 Tstrap: 0-1 Ckp: 0-1
Best Rating: 30 7/09 Yarm 6f3y gd-fm

Hidden Door (IRE)

96(98) (64)69
4-y-o b f Montjeu (IRE)-Yaselda (Green Desert (USA))
G Prodromou (Jane Chapple-Hyam 25/5) P Hajipiery

Placings:334-0000205 (7094)
2009: 8^{0}SD, 9^{0}GF, 7^{0}GF, 8^{0}SD, 10^{2}GF, 11^{0}G, 10^{5}G,

	Starts	1st	2nd	3rd	Win & Pl
Career Total (Turf)	8	0	1	2	3155
Career Total (AW)	2	0	0	0	

Going (Turf): Sf: 0-0 GS: 0-0 Gd: 0-5 GF: 0-3 Fm: 0-0
Distance: 5f/6f: 0-0 7f-8f: 0-4 9f-13f: 0-6 14f+: 0-0
Track : LH: 0-6 RH: 0-3 Tight: 0-4 Gall: 0-0
Aids: Bl: 0-0 Vi: 0-0 Tstrap: 0-0 Ckp: 0-0
Best Rating: 69 6/08 Leop 1m good

Modest; stays 1m2f and acts on fast ground.

Hidden Fire

80 54
2-y-o b f Alhaarth (IRE)-Premier Prize (Selkirk (USA))
D R C Elsworth J C Smith

Placings:0 (6730)
2009: 6^{0}S,

	Starts	1st	2nd	3rd	Win & Pl
Career Total (Turf)	1	0	0	0	

Going (Turf): Sf: 0-1 GS: 0-0 Gd: 0-0 GF: 0-0 Fm: 0-0
Distance: 5f/6f: 0-0 7f-8f: 0-1 9f-13f: 0-0 14f+: 0-0
Track : LH: 0-0 RH: 0-0 Tight: 0-0 Gall: 0-0
Aids: Bl: 0-0 Vi: 0-0 Tstrap: 0-0 Ckp: 0-0
Best Rating: 54 10/09 Sals 6f212y soft

Hidden Glory

90(94) (77)74
2-y-o b g Mujahid (USA)-Leominda (Lion Cavern (USA))
Pat Eddery Pat Eddery Racing (Reel Buddy)

Placings:421 (7663)
2009: 7^{4}G, 7^{2}SD, 8^{1}SD,

	Starts	1st	2nd	3rd	Win & Pl
Career Total (Turf)	1	0	0	0	385
Career Total (AW)	2	1	1	0	2653

77 12/09 Ling 1m STD £1978
Total win prize-money £1979

Going (Turf): Sf: 0-0 GS: 0-0 Gd: 0-1 GF: 0-0 Fm: 0-0
Distance: 5f/6f: 0-0 7f-8f: 1-3 9f-13f: 0-0 14f+: 0-0
Track : LH: 1-1 RH: 0-1 Tight: 1-1 Gall: 0-0
Aids: Bl: 0-0 Vi: 0-0 Tstrap: 0-0 Ckp: 0-0
Best Rating: 77 12/09 Ling 1m stand

Fair; stays 1m; handles good ground and Polytrack.

Hidden Horse

(39)
5-y-o b m Fasliyev (USA)-Hopping Higgins (IRE) (Brief Truce (USA))
M R Channon Barry Walters Catering

Placings:0 (0230)
2009: 7^{0}SD,

	Starts	1st	2nd	3rd	Win & Pl
Career Total (Turf)	0	0	0	0	
Career Total (AW)	1	0	0	0	

Going (Turf): Sf: 0-0 GS: 0-0 Gd: 0-0 GF: 0-0 Fm: 0-0
Distance: 5f/6f: 0-0 7f-8f: 0-1 9f-13f: 0-0 14f+: 0-0
Track : LH: 0-0 RH: 0-1 Tight: 0-0 Gall: 0-0
Aids: Bl: 0-0 Vi: 0-0 Tstrap: 0-0 Ckp: 0-0

Hierarch (IRE)

82 60
2-y-o b c Dansili-Danse Classique (IRE) (Night Shift (USA))
R Hannon Highclere Thoroughbred Racing(Emil Adam)

Placings:5 (4336)
2009: 6^{5}GF,

	Starts	1st	2nd	3rd	Win & Pl
Career Total (Turf)	1	0	0	0	0

Going (Turf): Sf: 0-0 GS: 0-0 Gd: 0-0 GF: 0-1 Fm: 0-0
Distance: 5f/6f: 0-1 7f-8f: 0-0 9f-13f: 0-0 14f+: 0-0
Track : LH: 0-0 RH: 0-0 Tight: 0-0 Gall: 0-0
Aids: Bl: 0-0 Vi: 0-0 Tstrap: 0-0 Ckp: 0-0
Best Rating: 60 7/09 Asct 6f gd-fm

Higgy's Ragazzo (FR)

94 77
2-y-o b c Sinndar (IRE)-Super Crusty (IRE) (Namid)
R Hannon I Higginson

Placings:51 (5787)
2009: 8^{5}G, 8^{1}G,

	Starts	1st	2nd	3rd	Win & Pl
Career Total (Turf)	2	1	0	0	2590

77 9/09 Chep 1m14y GD £2590
Total win prize-money £2590

Going (Turf): Sf: 0-0 GS: 0-0 Gd: 1-2 GF: 0-0 Fm: 0-0
Distance: 5f/6f: 0-0 7f-8f: 0-0 9f-13f: 1-2 14f+: 0-0
Track : LH: 0-0 RH: 0-0 Tight: 0-0 Gall: 0-0
Aids: Bl: 0-0 Vi: 0-0 Tstrap: 0-0 Ckp: 0-0
Best Rating: 77 9/09 Chep 1m14y good

High 'n Dry (IRE)

(106) (75)66
5-y-o ch m Halling (USA)-Sisal (IRE) (Danehill (USA))
M A Allen The Hardy Partners

Placings:02/4440510**6504**/**544102343050-0** (1122)
2009: 10^{0}SD,

	Starts	1st	2nd	3rd	Win & Pl
Career Total (Turf)	10	1	0	0	5077
Career Total (AW)	16	1	2	2	4677

73 3/08 Ling 1m (0-60)H STD £2047
57 10/07 Wind 6f GD £2817
Total win prize-money £4865

Going (Turf): Sf: 0-1 GS: 0-0 Gd: 1-2 GF: 0-7 Fm: 0-0
Distance: 5f/6f: 1-3 7f-8f: 1-18 9f-13f: 0-5 14f+: 0-0
Track : LH: 1-15 RH: 0-3 Tight: 1-12 Gall: 1-1
Aids: Bl: 0-0 Vi: 0-0 Tstrap: 1-15 Ckp: 1-15
Best Rating: 75 5/08 Ling 1m stand

Modest; effective over 6f-1m; acts on fast and easy ground; also goes on Polytrack; has worn cheekpieces.

High Achieved

98 76
3-y-o b f Dansili-Achieve (Rainbow Quest (USA))
P W Chapple-Hyam Lady Bamford

Placings:13 (5007)
2009: 6^{1}GF, 6^{3}G,

	Starts	1st	2nd	3rd	Win & Pl
Career Total (Turf)	2	1	0	1	4656

72 7/09 Sals 6f G-F £3885
Total win prize-money £3886

Going (Turf): Sf: 0-0 GS: 0-0 Gd: 0-1 GF: 1-1 Fm: 0-0
Distance: 5f/6f: 1-1 7f-8f: 0-1 9f-13f: 0-0 14f+: 0-0
Track : LH: 0-0 RH: 0-0 Tight: 0-0 Gall: 0-0
Aids: Bl: 0-0 Vi: 0-0 Tstrap: 0-0 Ckp: 0-0
Best Rating: 76 8/09 Nott 6f15y good

Fair; stays 6f; acts on a sound surface.

High Ambition

107(92) (37)84
6-y-o b g High Estate-So Ambitious (Teenoso (USA))
R A Fahey G H Leatham

Placings:46/2010120/001130 (6878)
2009: 7^{0}GF, 8^{0}GF, 10^{1}G, 12^{1}G, 12^{3}GF, 11^{0}SD,

	Starts	1st	2nd	3rd	Win & Pl
Career Total (Turf)	9	4	1	1	20644
Career Total (AW)	6	0	1	0	1069

83 8/09 Pont 1m4f8y (0-90)H GD £9346
78 6/09 Newc 1m2f32y (0-70)H GD £3885
84 5/07 Yarm 7f3y (0-70)H GD £2914
76 4/07 Yarm 7f3y (0-65)H G-F £2266
Total win prize-money £18415

Going (Turf): Sf: 0-0 GS: 0-0 Gd: 3-3 GF: 1-5 Fm: 0-1
Distance: 5f/6f: 0-0 7f-8f: 2-7 9f-13f: 2-8 14f+: 0-0
Track : LH: 2-11 RH: 0-0 Tight: 0-4 Gall: 1-2
Aids: Bl: 0-0 Vi: 2-6 Tstrap: 0-0 Ckp: 0-0
Best Rating: 84 8/09 Pont 1m4f8y gd-fm

Fair; stays 1m4f; acts on fast ground; also goes on Polytrack; has worn a visor.

High Comedy

96 70
2-y-o b c Exceed And Excel (AUS)-Ecstatic (Nashwan (USA))
Saeed Bin Suroor Godolphin

Placings:40 (6922)
2009: 6^{4}GS, 6^{0}GF,

	Starts	1st	2nd	3rd	Win & Pl
Career Total (Turf)	2	0	0	0	385

Going (Turf): Sf: 0-0 GS: 0-1 Gd: 0-0 GF: 0-1 Fm: 0-0
Distance: 5f/6f: 0-0 7f-8f: 0-2 9f-13f: 0-0 14f+: 0-0
Track : LH: 0-0 RH: 0-0 Tight: 0-0 Gall: 0-0
Aids: Bl: 0-0 Vi: 0-0 Tstrap: 0-0 Ckp: 0-0
Best Rating: 70 10/09 Nott 6f15y gd-sft

High Constable

(94) (78)
2-y-o b c Shamardal (USA)-Abbey Strand (USA) (Shadeed (USA))
R Charlton The Queen

Placings:3 (7644)
2009: 7^{3}SD,

	Starts	1st	2nd	3rd	Win & Pl
Career Total (Turf)	0	0	0	0	
Career Total (AW)	1	0	0	1	482

Going (Turf): Sf: 0-0 GS: 0-0 Gd: 0-0 GF: 0-0 Fm: 0-0
Distance: 5f/6f: 0-0 7f-8f: 0-1 9f-13f: 0-0 14f+: 0-0
Track : LH: 0-1 RH: 0-0 Tight: 0-1 Gall: 0-0
Aids: Bl: 0-0 Vi: 0-0 Tstrap: 0-0 Ckp: 0-0
Best Rating: 78 12/09 Wolv 7f32y stand

Beaten at odds on first time out.

High Cross (IRE)

84(103) (82)45
3-y-o b f Cape Cross (IRE)-Overruled (IRE) (Last Tycoon)
Sir Mark Prescott Sir Edmund Loder

Placings:4241320 (1614)
2009: 8^{4}SD, 8^{2}SS, 11^{4}SD, 9^{1}SF, 10^{3}SD, 9^{2}SD, 12^{0}G,

	Starts	1st	2nd	3rd	Win & Pl
Career Total (Turf)	1	0	0	0	
Career Total (AW)	6	1	2	1	5699

72 3/09 Wolv 1m1f103y (0-65)H SF £2388
Total win prize-money £2388

Going (Turf): Sf: 0-0 GS: 0-0 Gd: 0-1 GF: 0-0 Fm: 0-0
Distance: 5f/6f: 0-0 7f-8f: 0-2 9f-13f: 1-5 14f+: 0-0
Track : LH: 1-7 RH: 0-0 Tight: 1-3 Gall: 0-0
Aids: Bl: 0-0 Vi: 0-0 Tstrap: 0-0 Ckp: 0-0
Best Rating: 82 4/09 Wolv 1m1f103y stand

Fair; stays 1m2f; acts on Fibresand and Polytrack.

High Curragh

105(97) (70)91
6-y-o b g Pursuit Of Love-Pretty Poppy (Song)
E J O'Neill (K A Ryan 20/10) David Barlow

Placings:311460/023020/405060313400/2026020000200-14205003523000000 (7822a)
2009: 6^{1}GF, 6^{4}G, 6^{2}GF, 6^{0}GS, 6^{5}GF, 6^{0}GF, 5^{0}G, 5^{3}GF, 6^{5}SD, 5^{2}G, 7^{3}G, 7^{0}G, 6^{0}SD, 5^{0}SD, 8^{0}GF, 15^{0}HY, 7^{0}SD,

	Starts	1st	2nd	3rd	Win & Pl
Career Total (Turf)	48	4	8	6	65076
Career Total (AW)	6	0	0	0	747

85 4/09 Ripn 6f (0-85)H G-F £4857
93 8/07 Hayd 6f (0-90)H G-F £9715
84 7/05 Thsk 5f GD £9548
83 7/05 Ayr 6f GD £3565
Total win prize-money £27687

Going (Turf): Sf: 0-9 GS: 0-5 Gd: 2-18 GF: 2-15 Fm: 0-1
Distance: 5f/6f: 4-43 7f-8f: 0-9 9f-13f: 0-1 14f+: 0-1
Track : LH: 0-9 RH: 0-4 Tight: 0-5 Gall: 0-0
Aids: Bl: 0-2 Vi: 0-1 Tstrap: 1-17 Ckp: 1-17
Best Rating: 96 8/06 Gdwd 7f gd-fm

Useful; effective at 6f-7f; acts on most types of ground; suited by forcing tactics; has worn blinkers and cheekpieces.

High Five Society

97(99) (59)62
5-y-o b g Compton Admiral-Sarah Madeline (Pelder (IRE))
S R Bowring S R Bowring

Placings:0200/060522040/2110400006-60120100 (6074)
2009: 8^{6}SS, 8^{0}SD, 9^{1}SD, 9^{2}SD, 8^{0}SD, 8^{1}GF, 10^{0}G, 9^{0}SD,

	Starts	1st	2nd	3rd	Win & Pl
Career Total (Turf)	15	1	3	0	4818
Career Total (AW)	16	3	2	0	5102

62 5/09 Yarm 1m3y (0-60)H G-F £2072
52 2/09 Wolv 1m1f103y (0-45) STD £1364
64 3/08 Wolv 1m141y (0-45) STD £1365
64 3/08 Wolv 1m141y (0-45) STD £1365
Total win prize-money £6167

Going (Turf): Sf: 0-3 GS: 0-3 Gd: 0-4 GF: 1-5 Fm: 0-0
Distance: 5f/6f: 0-3 7f-8f: 0-12 9f-13f: 4-16 14f+: 0-0
Track : LH: 3-21 RH: 0-2 Tight: 3-13 Gall: 0-1
Aids: Bl: 4-23 Vi: 0-0 Tstrap: 0-1 Ckp: 0-1
Best Rating: 65 9/06 Newc 7f good

Moderate; stays 1m1f; acts on easy ground; goes on Polytrack; has worn a tongue tie and blinkers.

High Heeled (IRE)

111(90) (81)117

3-y-o b f High Chaparral (IRE)-Uncharted Haven (Turtle Island (IRE))

B W Hills Mr And Mrs Steven Jenkins

Placings:2616-14331541 **(7031)**

2009: 10^{1}GS, 10^{4}GF, 12^{3}G, 11^{3}GF, 10^{1}G, 9^{5}S, 12^{4}G, 12^{1}S,

	Starts	1st	2nd	3rd	Win & Pl
Career Total (Turf)	11	3	1	2	127180
Career Total (AW)	1	1	0	0	3562

117 10/09 Newb 1m4f5y SFT £36900
114 7/09 York 1m2f88y GD £22708
106 4/09 Newb 1m2f6y G-S £7477
81 9/08 Kemp 1m STD £3561
Total win prize-money £70648

Going (Turf): **Sf: 1-2 GS: 1-1 Gd: 1-3** GF: 0-4 Fm: 0-0
Distance: 5f/6f: 0-0 7f-8f: 1-4 **9f-13f: 3-8** 14f+: 0-0
Track : **LH: 3-6** RH: 1-4 Tight: 0-2 **Gall: 3-5**
Aids: Bl: 0-0 Vi: 0-0 Tstrap: 0-0 Ckp: 0-0
Best Rating: 117 10/09 Newb 1m4f5y soft

Listed-class; third in the 2009 Epsom Oaks; stays 1m4f but effective at 1m2f; acts on most ground and on Polytrack.

High Holborn (IRE)

88 67

2-y-o b g Danehill Dancer (IRE)-Wedding Morn (IRE) (Sadler's Wells (USA))

B J Meehan Raymond Tooth

Placings:0500 **(5742)**

2009: 7^{0}G, 7^{5}G, 6^{0}GF, 8^{0}GF,

	Starts	1st	2nd	3rd	Win & Pl
Career Total (Turf)	4	0	0	0	0

Going (Turf): **Sf: 0-0 GS: 0-0 Gd: 0-2 GF: 0-2 Fm: 0-0**
Distance: 5f/6f: 0-0 7f-8f: 0-4 9f-13f: 0-0 14f+: 0-0
Track : LH: 0-0 RH: 0-1 Tight: 0-0 Gall: 0-0
Aids: Bl: 0-0 Vi: 0-0 Tstrap: 0-0 Ckp: 0-0
Best Rating: 67 8/09 Sals 6f212y gd-fm

High Importance (USA)

95(92) (69)71

2-y-o b c Arch (USA)-Music Lane (USA) (Miswaki (USA))

J Noseda Saeed Suhail

Placings:43 **(6962)**

2009: 7^{4}SS, 6^{3}G,

	Starts	1st	2nd	3rd	Win & Pl
Career Total (Turf)	1	0	0	1	566
Career Total (AW)	1	0	0	0	265

Going (Turf): **Sf: 0-0 GS: 0-0 Gd: 0-1 GF: 0-0 Fm: 0-0**
Distance: 5f/6f: 0-0 7f-8f: 0-2 9f-13f: 0-0 14f+: 0-0
Track : LH: 0-2 RH: 0-0 Tight: 0-1 Gall: 0-0
Aids: Bl: 0-0 Vi: 0-0 Tstrap: 0-0 Ckp: 0-0
Best Rating: 71 10/09 Brig 6f209y good

High Morning

80 43

3-y-o br f Cape Cross (IRE)-Joharra (USA) (Kris S (USA))

D M Simcock Sultan Ali

Placings:000 **(3278)**

2009: 8^{0}F, 8^{0}G, 6^{0}GF,

	Starts	1st	2nd	3rd	Win & Pl
Career Total (Turf)	3	0	0	0	

Going (Turf): **Sf: 0-0 GS: 0-0 Gd: 0-1 GF: 0-1 Fm: 0-1**
Distance: 5f/6f: 0-0 7f-8f: 0-1 9f-13f: 0-2 14f+: 0-0
Track : LH: 0-1 RH: 0-0 Tight: 0-0 Gall: 0-0
Aids: Bl: 0-0 Vi: 0-0 Tstrap: 0-0 Ckp: 0-0
Best Rating: 43 5/09 Nott 1m75y firm

High Office

96(95) (69)79

3-y-o b g High Chaparral (IRE)-White House (Pursuit Of Love)

R A Fahey R A Fahey

Placings:325-324 **(2571)**

2009: 9^{3}F, 9^{2}GF, 9^{4}GF,

	Starts	1st	2nd	3rd	Win & Pl
Career Total (Turf)	5	0	2	2	3564
Career Total (AW)	1	0	0	0	0

Going (Turf): **Sf: 0-1 GS: 0-1 Gd: 0-0 GF: 0-2 Fm: 0-1**
Distance: 5f/6f: 0-0 7f-8f: 0-3 9f-13f: 0-3 14f+: 0-0
Track : LH: 0-2 RH: 0-3 Tight: 0-2 Gall: 0-0
Aids: Bl: 0-0 Vi: 0-0 Tstrap: 0-0 Ckp: 0-0
Best Rating: 79 5/09 Bevl 1m1f207y gd-fm

Fair; effective over 7f-1m1f; acts on fast and easy ground.

High On A Hill (IRE)

91(86) (52)74

2-y-o b c Val Royal (FR)-Blue Kestrel (IRE) (Bluebird (USA))

S Kirk Seahorse Five & Tim Pearson

Placings:0034 **(7267)**

2009: 8^{0}SD, 8^{0}SD, 8^{3}S, 8^{4}SD,

	Starts	1st	2nd	3rd	Win & Pl
Career Total (Turf)	1	0	0	1	433
Career Total (AW)	3	0	0	0	457

Going (Turf): **Sf: 0-1 GS: 0-0 Gd: 0-0 GF: 0-0 Fm: 0-0**
Distance: 5f/6f: 0-0 7f-8f: 0-4 9f-13f: 0-0 14f+: 0-0
Track : LH: 0-2 RH: 0-1 Tight: 0-1 Gall: 0-0
Aids: Bl: 0-0 Vi: 0-0 Tstrap: 0-0 Ckp: 0-0
Best Rating: 74 10/09 Sals 1m soft

High Point (IRE)

88(99) (81)68

11-y-o b g Ela-Mana-Mou-Top Lady (IRE) (Shirley Heights)

G P Enright The High Point Partnership

Placings:0/01605121/12521500010/00233360513/0550S06505/0250530201001/40505023/5004-0 **(2429)**

2009: 16^{0}G,

	Starts	1st	2nd	3rd	Win & Pl
Career Total (Turf)	38	2	4	5	39633
Career Total (AW)	29	7	3	1	33060

81 11/06 Kemp 2m (0-85)H STD £5505
81 8/06 Kemp 2m (0-75)H STD £3238
81 9/04 Yarm 2m (0-85)H GD £9225
87 11/03 Ling 1m4f C(0-95)H STD £5785
85 6/03 Sand 1m6f D(0-80)H G-F £5557
78 2/03 Ling 1m4f D(0-80)H STD £4173
78 11/02 Ling 2m E(0-75)H STD £3454
75 11/02 Ling 1m5f F(0-75)H STD £2954
68 2/02 Ling 1m5f F STD £2562
Total win prize-money £42456

Going (Turf): Sf: 0-5 GS: 0-6 **Gd: 1-11 GF: 1-16** Fm: 0-0
Distance: 5f/6f: 0-0 7f-8f: 0-0 9f-13f: 4-15 **14f+: 5-52**
Track : **LH: 6-36** RH: 3-31 **Tight: 6-27** Gall: 0-18
Aids: Bl: 0-0 Vi: 0-3 Tstrap: 0-0 Ckp: 0-0
Best Rating: 87 11/03 Ling 1m4f stand

Modest handicapper; stays beyond 2m; acts on most ground and on Polytrack; has worn a visor.

High Profit (IRE)

93(97) (61)58

5-y-o ch g Selkirk (USA)-Spot Prize (USA) (Seattle Dancer (USA))

James Moffatt The Vilprano Partnership

Placings:02/0-650040 **(3499)**

2009: 5^{6}GF, 8^{5}G, 8^{0}GF, 9^{0}G, 12^{4}SD, 11^{0}GF,

	Starts	1st	2nd	3rd	Win & Pl
Career Total (Turf)	5	0	0	0	0
Career Total (AW)	4	0	1	0	1156

Going (Turf): **Sf: 0-0 GS: 0-0 Gd: 0-2 GF: 0-3 Fm: 0-0**
Distance: 5f/6f: 0-1 7f-8f: 0-2 9f-13f: 0-6 14f+: 0-0
Track : LH: 0-8 RH: 0-1 Tight: 0-6 Gall: 0-0
Aids: Bl: 0-0 Vi: 0-3 Tstrap: 0-1 Ckp: 0-1
Best Rating: 71 3/07 Ling 1m stand

Fair colt; should be suited by further than 1m; acts on Polytrack; has worn a visor.

High Ransom

85 51

2-y-o b f Red Ransom (USA)-Shortfall (Last Tycoon)

M A Jarvis Thurloe Thoroughbreds XXIV

Placings:0 **(7034)**

2009: 8^{0}S,

	Starts	1st	2nd	3rd	Win & Pl
Career Total (Turf)	1	0	0	0	

Going (Turf): **Sf: 0-1 GS: 0-0 Gd: 0-0 GF: 0-0 Fm: 0-0**
Distance: 5f/6f: 0-0 7f-8f: 0-1 9f-13f: 0-0 14f+: 0-0
Track : LH: 0-0 RH: 0-0 Tight: 0-0 Gall: 0-0
Aids: Bl: 0-0 Vi: 0-0 Tstrap: 0-0 Ckp: 0-0
Best Rating: 51 10/09 Newb 1m soft

High Resolution

88(89) (54)57

2-y-o ch g Haafhd-Individual Talents (USA) (Distant View (USA))

Miss L A Perratt (S C Williams 18/9) Mrs Helen Perratt

Placings:00033200 **(6983)**

2009: 7^{0}GF, 7^{0}GF, 7^{0}G, 7^{3}SD, 7^{3}SD, 8^{2}GF, 8^{0}SD, 6^{0}G,

	Starts	1st	2nd	3rd	Win & Pl
Career Total (Turf)	5	0	1	0	578
Career Total (AW)	3	0	0	2	885

Going (Turf): **Sf: 0-0 GS: 0-0 Gd: 0-2 GF: 0-3 Fm: 0-0**
Distance: 5f/6f: 0-1 7f-8f: 0-5 9f-13f: 0-2 14f+: 0-0
Track : LH: 0-4 RH: 0-1 Tight: 0-4 Gall: 0-0
Aids: Bl: 0-0 Vi: 0-0 Tstrap: 0-0 Ckp: 0-0

Best Rating: 57 9/09 Yarm 1m3y gd-fm

High Ridge

(85) (29)73

10-y-o ch g Indian Ridge-Change For A Buck (USA) (Time For A Change (USA))

J L Flint M Matthews (Mid-Glamorgan)

Placings:00/50030035360/0151234122400/35110635403 340350040/101600402053303/50400420000/0060-00 (7418)

2009: 6^{0}SD, 6^{0}SD,

	Starts	1st	2nd	3rd	Win & Pl
Career Total (Turf)	70	6	5	11	53634
Career Total (AW)	9	1	0	1	6443

80 5/06 Ling 6f (0-80)H STD £5505
80 5/06 Folk 6f (0-75)H G-F £3238
83 5/05 Wind 6f (0-80)H G-F £7112
76 5/05 Bath 5f161y (0-70)H FRM £4217
75 7/04 Pont 6f E(0-65) G-F £4927
80 6/04 Bath 5f161y D(0-85)H FRM £5990
68 5/04 Bath 5f161y F(0-55)H G-F £3444
Total win prize-money £34435

Going (Turf): Sf: 0-3 GS: 0-4 Gd: 0-16 **GF: 4-41** Fm: 2-6
Distance: **5f/6f: 7-61** 7f-8f: 0-13 9f-13f: 0-5 14f+: 0-0
Track : **LH: 5-25** RH: 0-5 Tight: 1-7 **Gall: 4-22**
Aids: Bl: 0-4 Vi: 0-0 Tstrap: 7-68 Ckp: 7-68
Best Rating: 83 5/05 Wind 6f gd-fm

Modest; best at 6f; acts on fast ground; also effective on Polytrack; wears cheekpieces.

High Rolling

93 63

2-y-o b g Fantastic Light (USA)-Roller Girl (Merdon Melody)

T D Easterby C H Stevens

Placings:063435 (6215)

2009: 6^{0}G, 7^{6}GF, 5^{3}G, 6^{4}GS, 7^{3}GF, 8^{5}GF,

	Starts	1st	2nd	3rd	Win & Pl
Career Total (Turf)	6	0	0	2	1101

Going (Turf): **Sf: 0-0 GS: 0-1 Gd: 0-2 GF: 0-3 Fm: 0-0**
Distance: 5f/6f: 0-2 7f-8f: 0-4 9f-13f: 0-0 14f+: 0-0
Track : LH: 0-0 RH: 0-1 Tight: 0-0 Gall: 0-0
Aids: Bl: 0-0 Vi: 0-0 Tstrap: 0-0 Ckp: 0-0
Best Rating: 63 9/09 Rdcr 7f gd-fm

Modest; says 7f; acts fast ground.

High Severa (IRE)

99 78

3-y-o b c High Chaparral (IRE)-Severa (GER) (Kendor (FR))

A P Jarvis (K R Burke 9/7) Mogeely Stud & Mrs Maura Gittins

Placings:031506 (5333)

2009: 11^{0}GS, 9^{3}G, 8^{1}HY, 8^{5}G, 10^{0}G, 8^{6}S,

	Starts	1st	2nd	3rd	Win & Pl
Career Total (Turf)	6	1	0	1	3720

78 5/09 Hayd 1m30y HVY £3238
Total win prize-money £3238

Going (Turf): **Sf: 1-2** GS: 0-1 Gd: 0-3 GF: 0-0 Fm: 0-0
Distance: 5f/6f: 0-0 7f-8f: 0-1 **9f-13f: 1-5** 14f+: 0-0
Track : **LH: 1-4** RH: 0-2 Tight: 0-1 Gall: 0-2
Aids: Bl: 0-0 Vi: 0-0 Tstrap: 0-0 Ckp: 0-0
Best Rating: 78 5/09 Hayd 1m30y heavy

Fair; effective over 1m; acts on good and softer ground.

High Spice (USA)

98(100) (80)85

2-y-o b f Songandaprayer (USA)-Erin Moor (USA) (Holy Bull (USA))

R M H Cowell Khalifa Dasmal

Placings:16020435 (7108)

2009: 5^{1}GF, 5^{6}G, 5^{0}GF, 5^{2}S, 6^{0}G, 5^{4}GF, 5^{3}SD, 6^{5}SD,

	Starts	1st	2nd	3rd	Win & Pl
Career Total (Turf)	6	1	1	0	11852
Career Total (AW)	2	0	0	1	755

85 5/09 NmkR 5f G-F £9714
Total win prize-money £9714

Going (Turf): Sf: 0-1 GS: 0-0 Gd: 0-2 **GF: 1-3** Fm: 0-0
Distance: **5f/6f: 1-8** 7f-8f: 0-0 9f-13f: 0-0 14f+: 0-0
Track : LH: 0-1 RH: 0-1 Tight: 0-1 Gall: 0-0
Aids: Bl: 0-0 Vi: 0-0 Tstrap: 0-0 Ckp: 0-0
Best Rating: 85 5/09 NmkR 5f gd-fm

Useful; effective over 5f; acts on fast and soft ground.

High Standing (USA)

115(97) (87)118

4-y-o b/br g High Yield (USA)-Nena Maka (Selkirk (USA))

W J Haggas Tony Bloom

Placings:000511/122-111134 (6304)

2009: 6^{1}G, 6^{1}G, 6^{1}GF, 6^{1}S, 6^{3}GS, 6^{4}GF,

	Starts	1st	2nd	3rd	Win & Pl
Career Total (Turf)	11	5	1	1	160957
Career Total (AW)	4	2	1	0	6334

118 7/09 Newb 6f8y SFT £36900
110 6/09 Asct 6f (0-110)H G-F £62310
107 5/09 Gdwd 6f (0-100)H GD £11215
97 5/09 Donc 6f (0-90)H GD £7771
88 5/08 Leic 7f9y (0-80)H G-F £4209
79 10/07 Wolv 5f216y (0-65) STD £2047
78 10/07 Kemp 6f (0-65) STD £2047
Total win prize-money £126503

Going (Turf): Sf: 1-1 GS: 0-1 **Gd: 2-4 GF: 2-5** Fm: 0-0
Distance: **5f/6f: 5-10** 7f-8f: 2-5 9f-13f: 0-0 14f+: 0-0
Track : LH: 1-3 RH: 1-1 **Tight: 1-2** Gall: 0-2
Aids: Bl: 0-0 Vi: 0-0 Tstrap: 0-0 Ckp: 0-0
Best Rating: 118 7/09 Newb 6f8y soft

Very useful; winner of the 2009 Wokingham and a Group 3; effective over 6f-7f; acts on most ground and on Polytrack.

High Tensile

69 24

3-y-o b f Diktat-Shifty Mouse (Night Shift (USA))

J G Given Richard Walker

Placings:00-00 (5010)

2009: 8^{0}G, 8^{0}G,

	Starts	1st	2nd	3rd	Win & Pl
Career Total (Turf)	4	0	0	0	

Going (Turf): **Sf: 0-1 GS: 0-0 Gd: 0-3 GF: 0-0 Fm: 0-0**
Distance: 5f/6f: 0-0 7f-8f: 0-2 9f-13f: 0-2 14f+: 0-0
Track : LH: 0-2 RH: 0-0 Tight: 0-0 Gall: 0-0
Aids: Bl: 0-0 Vi: 0-0 Tstrap: 0-0 Ckp: 0-0
Best Rating: 24 10/08 Newc 7f heavy

High Trail (IRE)

(79) (29)

2-y-o b f Acclamation-Set Trail (IRE) (Second Set (IRE))

Rae Guest Rae Guest

Placings:0 (6228)

2009: 7^{0}SD,

	Starts	1st	2nd	3rd	Win & Pl
Career Total (Turf)	0	0	0	0	
Career Total (AW)	1	0	0	0	

Going (Turf): **Sf: 0-0 GS: 0-0 Gd: 0-0 GF: 0-0 Fm: 0-0**
Distance: 5f/6f: 0-0 7f-8f: 0-1 9f-13f: 0-0 14f+: 0-0
Track : LH: 0-0 RH: 0-1 Tight: 0-0 Gall: 0-0
Aids: Bl: 0-0 Vi: 0-0 Tstrap: 0-0 Ckp: 0-0
Best Rating: 29 9/09 Kemp 7f stand

High Twelve (IRE)

104 103

2-y-o b c Montjeu (IRE)-Much Faster (IRE) (Fasliyev (USA))

J H M Gosden Thomas Barr

Placings:2140 (6849)

2009: 7^{2}GF, 8^{1}GF, 8^{4}G, 7^{0}G,

	Starts	1st	2nd	3rd	Win & Pl
Career Total (Turf)	4	1	1	0	12932

89 8/09 Sand 1m14y G-F £3238
Total win prize-money £3238

Going (Turf): Sf: 0-0 GS: 0-0 Gd: 0-2 **GF: 1-2** Fm: 0-0
Distance: 5f/6f: 0-0 7f-8f: 0-3 **9f-13f: 1-1** 14f+: 0-0
Track : LH: 0-0 **RH: 1-3** Tight: 0-0 Gall: 0-1
Aids: Bl: 0-0 Vi: 0-0 Tstrap: 0-0 Ckp: 0-0
Best Rating: 103 9/09 Asct 1m good

Smart; effective at 1m; acts on fast ground.

Highams Park (IRE)

85(61) 39

3-y-o ch f Redback-Miss Caoimhe (IRE) (Barathea (IRE))

J G Portman Prof C D Green

Placings:00-00400 (5430)

2009: 11^{0}SD, 12^{0}G, 16^{4}HY, 18^{0}G, 16^{0}G,

	Starts	1st	2nd	3rd	Win & Pl
Career Total (Turf)	5	0	0	0	0
Career Total (AW)	2	0	0	0	

Going (Turf): **Sf: 0-1 GS: 0-0 Gd: 0-3 GF: 0-1 Fm: 0-0**
Distance: 5f/6f: 0-0 7f-8f: 0-2 9f-13f: 0-2 14f+: 0-3
Track : LH: 0-4 RH: 0-2 Tight: 0-1 Gall: 0-0
Aids: Bl: 0-0 Vi: 0-0 Tstrap: 0-0 Ckp: 0-0
Best Rating: 39 8/09 Chep 2m2f good

Highcliffe Bridge (IRE)

88(68) (12)53

2-y-o b f Avonbridge-Peig Sayers (IRE) (Royal Academy (USA))

N P Littmoden (P D Evans 14/7) R D Hartshorn

Placings:6533310000 (5935)

2009: 5^{6}F, 6^{5}G, 6^{3}F, 7^{3}S, 7^{3}GF, 7^{1}S, 7^{0}GS, 7^{0}G, 8^{0}SD, 7^{0}GF,

	Starts	1st	2nd	3rd	Win & Pl
Career Total (Turf)	9	1	0	3	3156

	Starts	1st	2nd	3rd	Win & Pl
Career Total (AW)	1	0	0	0	

53 7/09 Yarm 7f3y SFT £1942
Total win prize-money £1943

Going (Turf): **Sf: 1-2** GS: 0-1 Gd: 0-2 GF: 0-2 Fm: 0-2
Distance: 5f/6f: 0-2 **7f-8f: 1-8** 9f-13f: 0-0 14f+: 0-0
Track : LH: 0-1 RH: 0-1 Tight: 0-0 Gall: 0-1
Aids: Bl: 0-2 Vi: 0-0 Tstrap: 0-0 Ckp: 0-0
Best Rating: 53 7/09 Yarm 7f3y soft

Modest; stays 7f and acts on soft ground.

Highest Esteem

(99) (74)55
5-y-o b g Mark Of Esteem (IRE)-For More (FR) (Sanglamore (USA))
G L Moore Paul Green

Placings:500411/4505-2 (1154)
2009: 16^{2}SD,

	Starts	1st	2nd	3rd	Win & Pl
Career Total (Turf)	2	0	0	0	0
Career Total (AW)	9	2	1	0	4873

74 11/07 Kemp 1m4f (0-60)H STD £2047
72 11/07 Kemp 1m3f STD £2047
Total win prize-money £4096

Going (Turf): **Sf: 0-0 GS: 0-1 Gd: 0-0 GF: 0-1 Fm: 0-0**
Distance: 5f/6f: 0-0 7f-8f: 0-2 **9f-13f: 2-7** 14f+: 0-2
Track : LH: 0-4 **RH: 2-6** Tight: 0-4 Gall: 0-1
Aids: Bl: 0-0 Vi: 0-0 Tstrap: 2-8 Ckp: 2-8
Best Rating: 74 1/08 Ling 1m4f stand

Modest; stays 2m; handles Polytrack.

Highgate Cat

87(87) (54)56
3-y-o b g One Cool Cat (USA)-Angry Bark (USA) (Woodman (USA))
B R Millman Mrs Sandra Bell

Placings:5600 (3075)
2009: 7^{5}SD, 7^{6}SD, 7^{0}GS, 7^{0}G,

	Starts	1st	2nd	3rd	Win & Pl
Career Total (Turf)	2	0	0	0	
Career Total (AW)	2	0	0	0	0

Going (Turf): **Sf: 0-0 GS: 0-1 Gd: 0-1 GF: 0-0 Fm: 0-0**
Distance: 5f/6f: 0-0 7f-8f: 0-4 9f-13f: 0-0 14f+: 0-0
Track : LH: 0-3 RH: 0-0 Tight: 0-2 Gall: 0-0
Aids: Bl: 0-0 Vi: 0-0 Tstrap: 0-0 Ckp: 0-0
Best Rating: 56 5/09 Newb 7f gd-sft

Highkingofireland

97 71
3-y-o br g Danehill Dancer (IRE)-Lucky Date (IRE) (Halling (USA))
A P Jarvis (K R Burke 18/7) Cyril Wall

Placings:04106403 (7247)
2009: 7^{0}GF, 9^{4}GF, 9^{1}GS, 9^{0}G, 12^{6}G, 10^{4}S, 10^{0}GS, 10^{3}S,

	Starts	1st	2nd	3rd	Win & Pl
Career Total (Turf)	8	1	0	1	4524

71 5/09 Ripn 1m1f G-S £3561
Total win prize-money £3562

Going (Turf): Sf: 0-2 **GS: 1-2** Gd: 0-2 GF: 0-2 Fm: 0-0
Distance: 5f/6f: 0-0 7f-8f: 0-1 **9f-13f: 1-7** 14f+: 0-0
Track : LH: 0-3 **RH: 1-4 Tight: 1-3** Gall: 0-1
Aids: Bl: 0-0 Vi: 0-0 Tstrap: 0-0 Ckp: 0-0
Best Rating: 71 5/09 Ripn 1m1f gd-sft

Modest; effective at around 1m2f; acts on soft ground.

Highland Bridge

(86) (59)
2-y-o b c Avonbridge-Reciprocal (IRE) (Night Shift (USA))
D R C Elsworth J Wotherspoon

Placings:03 (7429)
2009: 8^{0}SD, 7^{3}SD,

	Starts	1st	2nd	3rd	Win & Pl
Career Total (Turf)	0	0	0	0	
Career Total (AW)	2	0	0	1	626

Going (Turf): **Sf: 0-0 GS: 0-0 Gd: 0-0 GF: 0-0 Fm: 0-0**
Distance: 5f/6f: 0-0 7f-8f: 0-2 9f-13f: 0-0 14f+: 0-0
Track : LH: 0-1 RH: 0-1 Tight: 0-1 Gall: 0-0
Aids: Bl: 0-0 Vi: 0-0 Tstrap: 0-0 Ckp: 0-0
Best Rating: 59 11/09 Kemp 7f stand

Highland Glen

104(112) (101)102
3-y-o b g Montjeu (IRE)-Daring Aim (Daylami (IRE))
Sir Michael Stoute The Queen

Placings:0-16611 (6571)
2009: 10^{1}GF, 11^{6}HY, 12^{6}GF, 12^{1}SD, 11^{1}GF,

	Starts	1st	2nd	3rd	Win & Pl
Career Total (Turf)	5	2	0	0	16892
Career Total (AW)	1	1	0	0	7353

102 10/09 Leic 1m3f183y (0-100)H G-F £11215
101 9/09 Kemp 1m4f (0-95)H STD £7352
88 5/09 Ling 1m2f G-F £4857
Total win prize-money £23426

Going (Turf): Sf: 0-1 GS: 0-0 Gd: 0-1 **GF: 2-3** Fm: 0-0
Distance: 5f/6f: 0-0 7f-8f: 0-1 **9f-13f: 3-5** 14f+: 0-0
Track : LH: 1-2 **RH: 2-3 Tight: 1-1** Gall: 0-1
Aids: Bl: 0-0 Vi: 0-0 Tstrap: 0-0 Ckp: 0-0
Best Rating: 102 10/09 Leic 1m3f183y gd-fm

Very useful; stays 1m4f; acts on a sound surface; goes on Polytrack.

Highland Harvest

103(108) (61)82
5-y-o b g Averti (IRE)-Bee One (IRE) (Catrail (USA))
Jamie Poulton J Wotherspoon

Placings:60333/**1002**0424006/**1314**3-0000**1**020006 (7327)
2009: 8^{0}GF, 8^{0}GF, 7^{0}G, 7^{0}SD, 5^{1}GF, 5^{0}GS, 5^{2}GS, 6^{0}G, 6^{0}GF, 5^{0}G, 7^{6}SD,

	Starts	1st	2nd	3rd	Win & Pl
Career Total (Turf)	20	1	3	2	11707
Career Total (AW)	12	3	0	3	13305

77 7/09 Brig 5f213y (0-75)H G-F £3280
82 2/08 Ling 1m (0-75)H STD £2457
81 1/08 Ling 1m (0-85)H STD £4100
80 1/07 Ling 1m (0-80)H STD £4857
Total win prize-money £14696

Going (Turf): Sf: 0-3 GS: 0-4 Gd: 0-7 **GF: 1-6** Fm: 0-0
Distance: 5f/6f: 1-8 **7f-8f: 3-14** 9f-13f: 0-10 14f+: 0-0
Track : **LH: 4-16** RH: 0-8 **Tight: 3-15** Gall: 0-0
Aids: Bl: 0-0 Vi: 0-0 Tstrap: 0-0 Ckp: 0-0
Best Rating: 85 5/07 Wind 1m67y good

Fair; suited by 1m; acts on soft ground and Polytrack.

Highland Homestead

(104) (69)66
4-y-o b g Makbul-Highland Rossie (Pablond)
M R Hoad (A M Hales 10/5) R P C Hoad

Placings:06/60260501106-00 (7328)
2009: 16^{0}SS, 16^{0}SD,

	Starts	1st	2nd	3rd	Win & Pl
Career Total (Turf)	8	1	0	0	2047
Career Total (AW)	7	1	1	0	2851

69 10/08 GrLe 1m5f66y (0-65)H STD £2266
58 10/08 Wind 1m2f7y G-S £2047
Total win prize-money £4314

Going (Turf): Sf: 0-2 **GS: 1-1** Gd: 0-2 GF: 0-3 Fm: 0-0
Distance: 5f/6f: 0-0 7f-8f: 0-3 9f-13f: 1-8 14f+: 1-4
Track : LH: 1-9 RH: 1-4 Tight: 1-9 Gall: 1-1
Aids: Bl: 0-2 Vi: 0-0 Tstrap: 0-0 Ckp: 0-0
Best Rating: 69 10/08 GrLe 1m5f66y stand

Modest; best at around 1m4f; acts on easy ground and Fibresand.

Highland Jewel (IRE)

85 59
2-y-o b f Azamour (IRE)-Raysiza (IRE) (Alzao (USA))
C G Cox Highland Thoroughbred Ltd

Placings:00 (6730)
2009: 6^{0}S, 6^{0}S,

	Starts	1st	2nd	3rd	Win & Pl
Career Total (Turf)	2	0	0	0	

Going (Turf): **Sf: 0-2 GS: 0-0 Gd: 0-0 GF: 0-0 Fm: 0-0**
Distance: 5f/6f: 0-0 7f-8f: 0-2 9f-13f: 0-0 14f+: 0-0
Track : LH: 0-0 RH: 0-0 Tight: 0-0 Gall: 0-0
Aids: Bl: 0-0 Vi: 0-0 Tstrap: 0-0 Ckp: 0-0
Best Rating: 59 9/09 Sals 6f212y soft

Highland Knight (IRE)

72 57
2-y-o b c Night Shift (USA)-Highland Shot (Selkirk (USA))
A M Balding J C Smith

Placings:0 (6759)
2009: 8^{0}G,

	Starts	1st	2nd	3rd	Win & Pl
Career Total (Turf)	1	0	0	0	

Going (Turf): **Sf: 0-0 GS: 0-0 Gd: 0-1 GF: 0-0 Fm: 0-0**
Distance: 5f/6f: 0-0 7f-8f: 0-0 9f-13f: 0-1 14f+: 0-0
Track : LH: 0-0 RH: 0-1 Tight: 0-0 Gall: 0-0
Aids: Bl: 0-0 Vi: 0-0 Tstrap: 0-0 Ckp: 0-0
Best Rating: 57 10/09 Leic 1m60y good

Highland Lassie (IRE)

96(81) (26)64
3-y-o b f Oasis Dream-Arlesiana (USA) (Woodman (USA))
B J Meehan Lady Laidlaw Of Rothiemay

Placings:06200 (5616)

2009: 8^{0}GF, 8^{6}G, 8^{2}G, 8^{0}GF, 9^{0}SD,

	Starts	1st	2nd	3rd	Win & Pl
Career Total (Turf)	4	0	1	0	806
Career Total (AW)	1	0	0	0	

Going (Turf): Sf: 0-0 GS: 0-0 Gd: 0-2 GF: 0-2 Fm: 0-0
Distance: 5f/6f: 0-0 7f-8f: 0-1 9f-13f: 0-4 14f+: 0-0
Track : LH: 0-2 RH: 0-2 Tight: 0-4 Gall: 0-0
Aids: Bl: 0-0 Vi: 0-0 Tstrap: 0-0 Ckp: 0-0
Best Rating: 64 7/09 Wind 1m67y good

Highland Legacy

104 **95**

5-y-o ch g Selkirk (USA)-Generous Lady (Generous (IRE))
M L W Bell B J Warren

Placings:04/013311/1500-4000 (7293)
2009: 16^{4}G, 14^{0}S, 18^{0}G, 12^{0}S,

	Starts	1st	2nd	3rd	Win & Pl
Career Total (Turf)	16	4	0	2	32505

100 4/08 Ripn 2m (0-100)H GD £12462
95 10/07 Nott 2m9y (0-95)H SFT £7124
88 10/07 Newb 2m (0-75)H G-S £3238
77 4/07 Wind 1m3f135y (0-70)H G-F £3238
Total win prize-money £26065

Going (Turf): Sf: 1-6 GS: 1-3 Gd: 1-6 GF: 1-1 Fm: 0-0
Distance: 5f/6f: 0-0 7f-8f: 0-0 9f-13f: 1-7 14f+: 3-9
Track : LH: 2-8 RH: 1-7 Tight: 2-5 Gall: 0-6
Aids: Bl: 0-0 Vi: 0-3 Tstrap: 0-0 Ckp: 0-0
Best Rating: 100 4/08 Ripn 2m good

Useful; stays 2m; acts on any ground but well suited by soft; has worn a visor.

Highland Love

86(103) (67)**72**

4-y-o b g Fruits Of Love (USA)-Diabaig (Precocious)
Jedd O'Keeffe (J T Stimpson 19/9) John & Susan Robertson

Placings:034/4240121443-00350 (6126)
2009: 10^{0}F, 10^{0}GS, 12^{3}SF, 11^{5}S, 12^{0}SD,

	Starts	1st	2nd	3rd	Win & Pl
Career Total (Turf)	14	2	2	1	10094
Career Total (AW)	4	0	0	2	1372

72 8/08 Bevl 1m1f207y (0-70)H G-S £3076
67 6/08 Ches 1m2f75y (0-70)H GD £3561
Total win prize-money £6638

Going (Turf): Sf: 0-4 GS: 1-4 Gd: 1-3 GF: 0-2 Fm: 0-1
Distance: 5f/6f: 0-3 7f-8f: 0-0 9f-13f: 2-15 14f+: 0-0
Track : LH: 1-13 RH: 1-5 Tight: 1-8 Gall: 0-1
Aids: Bl: 0-0 Vi: 0-0 Tstrap: 0-0 Ckp: 0-0
Best Rating: 72 8/08 Bevl 1m1f207y gd-sft

Modest; stays 1m2f; acts on easy ground.

Highland Quaich

(98) (75)

2-y-o ch c Compton Place-Bee One (IRE) (Catrail (USA))
D R C Elsworth J Wotherspoon

Placings:6146 (7824)
2009: 8^{6}SD, 7^{1}SD, 7^{4}SD, 7^{6}SD,

	Starts	1st	2nd	3rd	Win & Pl
Career Total (Turf)	0	0	0	0	
Career Total (AW)	4	1	0	0	2240

75 10/09 Kemp 7f STD £2047
Total win prize-money £2047

Going (Turf): Sf: 0-0 GS: 0-0 Gd: 0-0 GF: 0-0 Fm: 0-0
Distance: 5f/6f: 0-0 7f-8f: 1-4 9f-13f: 0-0 14f+: 0-0
Track : LH: 0-1 RH: 1-3 Tight: 0-1 Gall: 0-0
Aids: Bl: 0-0 Vi: 0-0 Tstrap: 0-0 Ckp: 0-0
Best Rating: 75 10/09 Kemp 7f stand

Fair; stays 1m; acts on Polytrack.

Highland River

92(98) (63)**55**

3-y-o b g Indian Creek-Bee One (IRE) (Catrail (USA))
A Sadik (D R C Elsworth 13/11) A Sadik

Placings:0002210-000040000 (7855)
2009: 8^{0}GF, 8^{0}G, 10^{0}GF, 11^{0}GF, 8^{4}SD, 8^{0}SD, 9^{0}SD, 7^{0}SD, 8^{0}SS,

	Starts	1st	2nd	3rd	Win & Pl
Career Total (Turf)	7	0	0	0	
Career Total (AW)	9	1	2	0	2627

63 11/08 Kemp 1m (0-65) STD £1619
Total win prize-money £1619

Going (Turf): Sf: 0-0 GS: 0-2 Gd: 0-1 GF: 0-4 Fm: 0-0
Distance: 5f/6f: 0-1 7f-8f: 1-10 9f-13f: 0-5 14f+: 0-0
Track : LH: 0-6 RH: 1-6 Tight: 0-6 Gall: 0-0
Aids: Bl: 0-0 Vi: 0-1 Tstrap: 0-0 Ckp: 0-0
Best Rating: 63 10/09 Kemp 1m stand

Modest; stays 1m and acts on Polytrack.

Highland Song (IRE)

(96) (53)**52**

6-y-o ch g Fayruz-Rose 'n Reason (IRE) (Reasonable (FR))
R F Fisher Des Johnston

Placings:1446064330/4332503001034000/005203300/532 56200-26 (0480)
2009: 6^{2}SD, 7^{6}SD,

	Starts	1st	2nd	3rd	Win & Pl
Career Total (Turf)	30	2	3	7	16937
Career Total (AW)	15	0	2	2	2353

72 8/06 Ayr 5f (0-65)H G-F £2914
60 5/05 Muss 5f GD £6747
Total win prize-money £9662

Going (Turf): Sf: 0-4 GS: 0-6 Gd: 1-8 GF: 1-11 Fm: 0-1
Distance: 5f/6f: 2-42 7f-8f: 0-2 9f-13f: 0-1 14f+: 0-0
Track : LH: 0-17 RH: 0-1 Tight: 0-16 Gall: 0-1
Aids: Bl: 0-0 Vi: 0-0 Tstrap: 0-1 Ckp: 0-1
Best Rating: 73 5/06 Muss 5f gd-fm

Moderate gelding; effective at sprint distances; acts on any ground.

Highland Starlight (USA)

85(95) (63)**47**

3-y-o ch f Dixieland Band (USA)-Fran's Flash (USA) (Star De Naskra (USA))
C G Cox Highland Thoroughbred Ltd

Placings:05-60600 (6771)
2009: 7^{6}G, 7^{0}F, 8^{6}SD, 8^{0}GF, 8^{0}SD,

	Starts	1st	2nd	3rd	Win & Pl
Career Total (Turf)	3	0	0	0	0
Career Total (AW)	4	0	0	0	0

Going (Turf): Sf: 0-0 GS: 0-0 Gd: 0-1 GF: 0-1 Fm: 0-1
Distance: 5f/6f: 0-0 7f-8f: 0-6 9f-13f: 0-1 14f+: 0-0
Track : LH: 0-2 RH: 0-2 Tight: 0-2 Gall: 0-0
Aids: Bl: 0-0 Vi: 0-0 Tstrap: 0-0 Ckp: 0-0
Best Rating: 63 10/08 Ling 1m stand

Highland Storm

98(88) (58)**78**

3-y-o b g Storming Home-Real Emotion (USA) (El Prado (IRE))
B N Pollock (George Baker 3/7) Mrs Linda Pestell

Placings:3261000-406250 (5131)
2009: 10^{4}GS, 12^{0}GF, 11^{6}GF, 10^{2}GF, 10^{5}G, 16^{0}GF,

	Starts	1st	2nd	3rd	Win & Pl
Career Total (Turf)	12	1	2	0	8276
Career Total (AW)	1	0	0	1	539

78 8/08 NmkJ 1m GD £5180
Total win prize-money £5181

Going (Turf): Sf: 0-2 GS: 0-1 Gd: 1-3 GF: 0-6 Fm: 0-0
Distance: 5f/6f: 0-1 7f-8f: 1-5 9f-13f: 0-6 14f+: 0-1
Track : LH: 0-7 RH: 0-1 Tight: 0-3 Gall: 0-2
Aids: Bl: 0-1 Vi: 0-2 Tstrap: 0-3 Ckp: 0-3
Best Rating: 78 8/08 NmkJ 1m good

Fair half-brother to quite useful High Voltage, stays 1m; acts on good ground; has worn various headgear.

Highland Warrior

100(89) (62)**81**

10-y-o b g Makbul-Highland Rowena (Royben)
P T Midgley R Wardlaw

Placings:4000/0625155036/00502000133/3323416004663 026426/102025004005/2100500000/5010401000400/533 0023511143040-60000011050050 (7081)
2009: 5^{6}SD, 5^{0}GF, 5^{0}GF, 5^{0}GF, 5^{0}GF, 5^{0}GS, 5^{1}G, 5^{1}GS, 5^{0}G, 5^{5}GS, 5^{0}GS, 5^{0}GS, 5^{5}G, 5^{0}S,

	Starts	1st	2nd	3rd	Win & Pl
Career Total (Turf)	108	12	9	11	96809
Career Total (AW)	2	0	0	0	0

77 7/09 Donc 5f (0-65)H G-S £2637
75 7/09 York 5f (0-80)H GD £5180
81 8/08 Bevl 5f (0-75)H SFT £2849
67 8/08 Muss 5f SFT £1942
54 7/08 Muss 5f G-S £1942
88 7/07 York 5f (0-90)H SFT £8096
87 6/07 Ripn 5f (0-75)H SFT £3562
88 5/06 Muss 5f (0-90)H G-F £11217
78 4/05 Ripn 5f (0-85)H SFT £6721
78 5/04 Ayr 6f D(0-85)H G-F £5629
67 10/03 Ayr 6f E(0-70)H G-S £3626
77 5/02 Ayr 1m1f20y E(0-70) GD £3080
Total win prize-money £56485

Going (Turf): Sf: 5-27 GS: 3-24 Gd: 2-27 GF: 2-28 Fm: 0-2
Distance: 5f/6f: 11-91 7f-8f: 0-10 9f-13f: 1-9 14f+: 0-0
Track : LH: 1-14 RH: 0-6 Tight: 0-7 Gall: 0-3
Aids: Bl: 0-0 Vi: 0-0 Tstrap: 0-2 Ckp: 0-2
Best Rating: 91 6/06 Muss 5f gd-fm

Modest; effective at 5f-6f and acts on any ground; often starts slowly and likes to come from off the pace.

Highly Acclaimed

95(92) (44)**49**

3-y-o b f Acclamation-Ebba (Elmaamul (USA))
Mrs A Duffield Middleham Park Racing V

Placings:3-600540034 (5336)
2009: 6^{6}GF, 6^{0}F, 7^{0}GF, 6^{5}SD, 8^{4}SD, 8^{0}G, 6^{0}GS, 5^{3}GS, 5^{4}S,

	Starts	1st	2nd	3rd	Win & Pl
Career Total (Turf)	8	0	0	2	867
Career Total (AW)	2	0	0	0	255

Going (Turf): Sf: 0-2 GS: 0-2 Gd: 0-1 GF: 0-2 Fm: 0-1
Distance: 5f/6f: 0-5 7f-8f: 0-5 9f-13f: 0-0 14f+: 0-0
Track : LH: 0-5 RH: 0-2 Tight: 0-1 Gall: 0-0
Aids: Bl: 0-0 Vi: 0-3 Tstrap: 0-1 Ckp: 0-1
Best Rating: 49 8/09 Carl 5f193y gd-sft

Speedily-bred filly; promise on debut over 6f on soft ground.

Highly Regal (IRE)

95(108) (86)77
4-y-o b g High Chaparral (IRE)-Regal Portrait (IRE) (Royal Academy (USA))
R A Teal J Morton

Placings:550/2600000-1111315300155O (7523)
2009: 8^{1}SD, 8^{1}SD, 8^{1}SD, 8^{1}SD, 8^{3}SD, 8^{1}SD, 8^{5}GF, 8^{3}SD, 8^{0}GF, 7^{0}G, 8^{1}SD, 7^{5}SD, 8^{5}SD, 8^{0}SD,

	Starts	1st	2nd	3rd	Win & Pl
Career Total (Turf)	7	0	0	0	0
Career Total (AW)	17	6	1	2	31657

86	9/09	Kemp	1m	H	STD	£18693
83	4/09	Kemp	1m	(0-75)H	STD	£2590
76	3/09	Sthl	1m	(0-75)H	STD	£2729
71	2/09	Kemp	1m	(0-65)H	STD	£2266
65	1/09	Kemp	1m	(0-50)H	STD	£1706
67	1/09	Kemp	1m	(0-50)H	STD	£1978

Total win prize-money £29965

Going (Turf): Sf: 0-1 GS: 0-0 Gd: 0-2 GF: 0-4 Fm: 0-0
Distance: 5f/6f: 0-0 **7f-8f: 6-15** 9f-13f: 0-8 14f+: 0-1
Track : LH: 1-10 **RH: 5-12** Tight: 0-8 Gall: 0-0
Aids: **Bl: 6-14** Vi: 0-0 Tstrap: 0-1 Ckp: 0-1
Best Rating: 86 9/09 Kemp 1m stand

Fair; stays 1m2f and acts on sand; has worn blinkers.

Hightime Heroine (IRE)

107(105) (85)83
3-y-o b f Danetime (IRE)-Esterlina (IRE) (Highest Honor (FR))
J Noseda Cheveley Park Stud

Placings:323212203 (7252)
2009: 6^{3}GF, 7^{2}GF, 6^{3}S, 6^{2}S, 6^{1}GF, 5^{2}GF, 7^{2}SD, 7^{0}SS, 7^{3}SD,

	Starts	1st	2nd	3rd	Win & Pl
Career Total (Turf)	6	1	3	2	7548
Career Total (AW)	3	0	1	1	2666

83	8/09	Yarm	6f3y	G-F	£2901

Total win prize-money £2902

Going (Turf): Sf: 0-2 GS: 0-0 Gd: 0-0 **GF: 1-4** Fm: 0-0
Distance: 5f/6f: 0-3 **7f-8f: 1-6** 9f-13f: 0-0 14f+: 0-0
Track : LH: 0-3 RH: 0-0 Tight: 0-3 Gall: 0-0
Aids: Bl: 0-0 Vi: 0-0 Tstrap: 0-0 Ckp: 0-0
Best Rating: 85 11/09 Ling 7f stand

Fair; effective over 6f-7f; acts best on fast ground; handles Polytrack.

Highway Code (USA)

94 53
3-y-o b g Street Cry (IRE)-Fairy Heights (IRE) (Fairy King (USA))
R Lee (M Johnston 26/7) D E Edwards

Placings:000 (4347)
2009: 10^{0}G, 10^{0}GF, 9^{0}G,

	Starts	1st	2nd	3rd	Win & Pl
Career Total (Turf)	3	0	0	0	

Going (Turf): Sf: 0-0 GS: 0-0 Gd: 0-2 GF: 0-1 Fm: 0-0
Distance: 5f/6f: 0-0 7f-8f: 0-0 9f-13f: 0-3 14f+: 0-0
Track : LH: 0-1 RH: 0-2 Tight: 0-1 Gall: 0-0
Aids: Bl: 0-0 Vi: 0-0 Tstrap: 0-0 Ckp: 0-0
Best Rating: 53 6/09 Sand 1m2f7y good

Highway Magic (IRE)

68(74) (33)66
3-y-o ch c Rainbow Quest (USA)-Adultress (IRE) (Ela-Mana-Mou)
A P Jarvis Philip Milburn

Placings:0500-60 (4389)
2009: 12^{6}GF, 8^{0}G,

	Starts	1st	2nd	3rd	Win & Pl
Career Total (Turf)	5	0	0	0	141
Career Total (AW)	1	0	0	0	

Going (Turf): Sf: 0-0 GS: 0-0 Gd: 0-3 GF: 0-2 Fm: 0-0
Distance: 5f/6f: 0-0 7f-8f: 0-4 9f-13f: 0-2 14f+: 0-0
Track : LH: 0-1 RH: 0-1 Tight: 0-0 Gall: 0-2
Aids: Bl: 0-0 Vi: 0-0 Tstrap: 0-0 Ckp: 0-0
Best Rating: 66 7/08 Yarm 7f3y gd-fm

Hilbre Court (USA)

93(107) (87)75
4-y-o br g Doneraile Court (USA)-Glasgow's Gold (USA) (Seeking The Gold (USA))
B P J Baugh Saddle Up Racing

Placings:111/0400023301450200-0310201000O363012 (7854)
2009: 10^{0}SD, 8^{3}SD, 8^{1}SD, 9^{0}SD, 8^{2}SD, 8^{0}SD, 8^{1}SD, 8^{0}HY, 8^{0}GF, 10^{0}GF, 8^{0}SF, 8^{3}SD, 8^{6}SD, 8^{3}SD, 8^{0}SD, 8^{1}SD, 8^{2}SS,

	Starts	1st	2nd	3rd	Win & Pl
Career Total (Turf)	6	0	1	0	964
Career Total (AW)	30	7	3	5	27664

78	4/09	Sthl	1m	(0-75)H	STD	£2729
73	2/09	Sthl	1m	(0-70)H	STD	£2729
83	8/08	GrLe	1m		STD	£1942
81	12/07	Wolv	1m141y		STD	£6045
80	11/07	Wolv	1m141y		STD	£4533
72	10/07	Ling	1m		STD	£2817

Total win prize-money £20799

Going (Turf): Sf: 0-1 GS: 0-1 Gd: 0-0 GF: 0-4 Fm: 0-0
Distance: 5f/6f: 0-0 **7f-8f: 5-20** 9f-13f: 2-16 14f+: 0-0
Track : **LH: 7-28** RH: 0-6 **Tight: 3-13** Gall: 1-4
Aids: Bl: 0-1 Vi: 0-0 Tstrap: 3-10 Ckp: 3-10
Best Rating: 87 7/08 Kemp 1m stand

Fair; effective over 1m; acts on a sound surface and on sand; has worn blinkers and cheekpieces.

Hilbre Point (USA)

86 61
3-y-o b g Giant's Causeway (USA)-Lady Carla (Caerleon (USA))
B J Meehan E H Jones (paints) Ltd

Placings:0-0000 (2126)
2009: 7^{0}GF, 8^{0}G, 11^{0}GS, 10^{0}GS,

	Starts	1st	2nd	3rd	Win & Pl
Career Total (Turf)	5	0	0	0	

Going (Turf): Sf: 0-0 GS: 0-3 Gd: 0-1 GF: 0-1 Fm: 0-0
Distance: 5f/6f: 0-0 7f-8f: 0-2 9f-13f: 0-3 14f+: 0-0
Track : LH: 0-3 RH: 0-0 Tight: 0-2 Gall: 0-1
Aids: Bl: 0-1 Vi: 0-0 Tstrap: 0-0 Ckp: 0-0
Best Rating: 61 4/09 NmkR 7f gd-fm

48,000gns half-brother to Avalon out of an Oaks winner; Derby entry.

Hill Billy Rock (IRE)

84(92) (57)78
6-y-o b g Halling (USA)-Polska (USA) (Danzig (USA))
Mrs S C Bradburne (G A Swinbank 1/3) W Powrie And Mrs S Sandbrook

Placings:605014/55100-55 (2629)
2009: 14^{5}SS, 13^{5}GF,

	Starts	1st	2nd	3rd	Win & Pl
Career Total (Turf)	10	2	0	0	6634
Career Total (AW)	3	0	0	0	0

78	5/08	Muss	1m6f	(0-70)H	G-S	£3238
72	8/06	Newc	1m4f93y	(0-65)H	G-S	£2914

Total win prize-money £6153

Going (Turf): Sf: 0-0 **GS: 2-3** Gd: 0-2 GF: 0-5 Fm: 0-0
Distance: 5f/6f: 0-0 7f-8f: 0-2 9f-13f: 1-7 14f+: 1-4
Track : LH: 1-8 RH: 1-5 Tight: 1-6 Gall: 1-2
Aids: Bl: 0-0 Vi: 0-0 Tstrap: 0-0 Ckp: 0-0
Best Rating: 78 5/08 Muss 1m6f gd-sft

Modest; effective at 1m4f-1m6f; acts on easy ground.

Hill Cross (IRE)

79 54
3-y-o b g Barathea (IRE)-Darayna (IRE) (Shernazar)
K G Reveley The Well Oiled Partnership

Placings:6000-00 (2340)
2009: 12^{0}GF, 14^{0}GF,

	Starts	1st	2nd	3rd	Win & Pl
Career Total (Turf)	6	0	0	0	0

Going (Turf): Sf: 0-0 GS: 0-3 Gd: 0-1 GF: 0-2 Fm: 0-0
Distance: 5f/6f: 0-2 7f-8f: 0-2 9f-13f: 0-1 14f+: 0-1
Track : LH: 0-1 RH: 0-1 Tight: 0-2 Gall: 0-0
Aids: Bl. 0-0 Vi: 0-0 Tstrap: 0-0 Ckp: 0-0
Best Rating: 54 6/08 Newc 6f gd-sft

Hill Of Clare (IRE)

91(82) (17)51
7-y-o gr m Daylami (IRE)-Sarah-Clare (Reach)
G H Jones Mrs A M McCartney

Placings:0/50/0300/00600/05600-00260 (6692)
2009: 10^{0}GF, 8^{0}G, 16^{7}S, 18^{6}G, 16^{0}GS,

	Starts	1st	2nd	3rd	Win & Pl
Career Total (Turf)	17	0	1	0	617
Career Total (AW)	5	0	0	1	302

Going (Turf): Sf: 0-2 GS: 0-2 Gd: 0-6 GF: 0-5 Fm: 0-1
Distance: 5f/6f: 0-0 7f-8f: 0-5 9f-13f: 0-13 14f+: 0-4
Track : LH: 0-16 RH: 0-4 Tight: 0-7 Gall: 0-1

Aids: Bl: 0-0 Vi: 0-0 Tstrap: 0-0 Ckp: 0-0
Best Rating: 53 7/05 Wind 1m67y gd-sft

–

Hill Of Lujain

68(100) (64)67
5-y-o b g Lujain (USA)-Cinder Hills (Deploy)
Ian Williams J Tredwell

Placings:2154/000**30**/0-0060 (1974)
2009: 5^{0}SD, 7^{0}SD, 8^{6}SF, 10^{0}F,

	Starts	1st	2nd	3rd	Win & Pl
Career Total (Turf)	7	1	1	0	5090
Career Total (AW)	7	0	0	1	438

67 5/06 Haml 5f4y GD £3886
Total win prize-money £3886

Going (Turf): Sf: 0-1 GS: 0-2 **Gd: 1-3** GF: 0-0 Fm: 0-1
Distance: **5f/6f: 1-9** 7f-8f: 0-3 9f-13f: 0-2 14f+: 0-0
Track : LH: 0-8 RH: 0-1 Tight: 0-6 Gall: 0-0
Aids: Bl: 0-0 Vi: 0-0 Tstrap: 0-1 Ckp: 0-1
Best Rating: 67 5/06 Rdcr 5f good

Modest handicapper; acts on good ground and Polytrack; appears to stay 7f.

Hill Of Miller (IRE)

87(98) (75)75
2-y-o b g Indian Ridge-Roshani (IRE) (Kris)
Rae Guest Michael Godfrey Hill

Placings:30406662450 (7871)
2009: 6^{3}G, 5^{0}G, 6^{4}HY, 6^{0}SD, 6^{6}S, 6^{6}GF, 5^{6}F, 6^{2}SD, 6^{4}SD, 5^{5}SD, 5^{0}SD,

	Starts	1st	2nd	3rd	Win & Pl
Career Total (Turf)	6	0	0	1	3586
Career Total (AW)	5	0	1	0	771

Going (Turf): Sf: 0-2 GS: 0-0 Gd: 0-2 GF: 0-1 Fm: 0-1
Distance: 5f/6f: 0-9 7f-8f: 0-2 9f-13f: 0-0 14f+: 0-0
Track : LH: 0-4 RH: 0-5 Tight: 0-3 Gall: 0-1
Aids: Bl: 0-0 Vi: 0-0 Tstrap: 0-0 Ckp: 0-0
Best Rating: 75 11/09 Kemp 6f stand

Fair; stays 6f and acts on good ground.

Hill Tribe

93 77
2-y-o b f Tiger Hill (IRE)-Morning Queen (GER) (Konigsstuhl (GER))
J R Best Findlay & Bloom

Placings:053 (5284)
2009: 6^{0}GS, 6^{5}GF, 7^{3}GF,

	Starts	1st	2nd	3rd	Win & Pl
Career Total (Turf)	3	0	0	1	650

Going (Turf): Sf: 0-0 GS: 0-1 Gd: 0-0 GF: 0-2 Fm: 0-0
Distance: 5f/6f: 0-1 7f-8f: 0-2 9f-13f: 0-0 14f+: 0-0
Track : LH: 0-0 RH: 0-1 Tight: 0-0 Gall: 0-0
Aids: Bl: 0-0 Vi: 0-0 Tstrap: 0-0 Ckp: 0-0
Best Rating: 77 8/09 Folk 7f gd-fm

47,000gns half-sister to winners at 1m-2m2f out of a 1m winning sister to Monsun; showed speed on first two starts over 6f on varying ground.

Hillside Lad

95(98) (71)66
3-y-o b g Tobougg (IRE)-Cumbrian Concerto (Petong)
R M Beckett P Hickey

Placings:0321-064301400 (5628)
2009: 5^{0}SD, 6^{6}F, 5^{4}G, 5^{3}G, 6^{0}SD, 6^{1}GS, 5^{4}G, 6^{0}G, 7^{0}GS,

	Starts	1st	2nd	3rd	Win & Pl
Career Total (Turf)	7	1	0	1	4258
Career Total (AW)	6	1	1	1	4113

66 7/09 Sals 6f (0-75)H G-S £3238
69 12/08 Ling 5f STD £2729
Total win prize-money £5968

Going (Turf): Sf: 0-0 **GS: 1-2** Gd: 0-4 GF: 0-0 Fm: 0-1
Distance: **5f/6f: 2-12** 7f-8f: 0-1 9f-13f: 0-0 14f+: 0-0
Track : **LH: 1-4** RH: 0-3 **Tight: 1-3** Gall: 0-1
Aids: Bl: 0-0 Vi: 0-1 Tstrap: 1-4 Ckp: 1-4
Best Rating: 71 12/08 Ling 6f stand

Modest; effective at 5f-6f; acts on good ground and on Polytrack; has worn cheekpieces.

Hilltop Alchemy

65(77) (27)
3-y-o ch g Zaha (CAN)-Saferjel (Elmaamul (USA))
J R Jenkins G Noble

Placings:00000 (7110)
2009: 8^{0}GF, 9^{0}GS, 12^{0}SD, 12^{0}SD, 8^{0}SD,

	Starts	1st	2nd	3rd	Win & Pl
Career Total (Turf)	2	0	0	0	
Career Total (AW)	3	0	0	0	

Going (Turf): Sf: 0-0 GS: 0-1 Gd: 0-0 GF: 0-1 Fm: 0-0
Distance: 5f/6f: 0-0 7f-8f: 0-2 9f-13f: 0-3 14f+: 0-0
Track : LH: 0-1 RH: 0-3 Tight: 0-1 Gall: 0-0
Aids: Bl: 0-0 Vi: 0-2 Tstrap: 0-0 Ckp: 0-0
Best Rating: 27 9/09 Kemp 1m4f stand

Hilltop Artistry

103(73) (28)65
3-y-o b c Polish Precedent (USA)-Hilltop (Absalom)
S W James S W James

Placings:000-4033 (3708)
2009: 8^{4}G, 8^{0}S, 8^{3}G, 8^{3}GS,

	Starts	1st	2nd	3rd	Win & Pl
Career Total (Turf)	6	0	0	2	1064
Career Total (AW)	1	0	0	0	

Going (Turf): Sf: 0-1 GS: 0-1 Gd: 0-3 GF: 0-1 Fm: 0-0
Distance: 5f/6f: 0-0 7f-8f: 0-3 9f-13f: 0-4 14f+: 0-0
Track : LH: 0-2 RH: 0-0 Tight: 0-1 Gall: 0-0
Aids: Bl: 0-0 Vi: 0-0 Tstrap: 0-0 Ckp: 0-0
Best Rating: 65 6/09 Chep 1m14y good

Hilltop Legacy

96(89) (35)53
6-y-o b m Danzig Connection (USA)-Hilltop (Absalom)
J R Jenkins G Noble

Placings:00-00406 (4665)
2009: 6^{0}SD, 7^{0}SD, 6^{4}G, 6^{0}GS, 7^{6}G,

	Starts	1st	2nd	3rd	Win & Pl
Career Total (Turf)	4	0	0	0	216
Career Total (AW)	3	0	0	0	

Going (Turf): Sf: 0-0 GS: 0-1 Gd: 0-3 GF: 0-0 Fm: 0-0
Distance: 5f/6f: 0-2 7f-8f: 0-5 9f-13f: 0-0 14f+: 0-0
Track : LH: 0-3 RH: 0-1 Tight: 0-2 Gall: 0-0
Aids: Bl: 0-0 Vi: 0-0 Tstrap: 0-0 Ckp: 0-0
Best Rating: 53 8/09 Yarm 7f3y good

Hillview Boy (IRE)

107 100
5-y-o b/br g Bishop Of Cashel-Arandora Star (USA) (Sagace (FR))
J S Goldie Connor & Dunne

Placings:123010322 (7293)
2009: 9^{1}G, 10^{2}G, 12^{3}G, 12^{0}G, 10^{1}S, 10^{0}GF, 10^{3}GS, 12^{2}GS, 12^{2}S,

	Starts	1st	2nd	3rd	Win & Pl
Career Total (Turf)	9	2	3	2	41336

92 8/09 Donc 1m2f60y (0-100)H SFT £12462
86 5/09 Haml 1m1f36y GD £3238
Total win prize-money £15700

Going (Turf): **Sf: 1-2** GS: 0-2 **Gd: 1-4** GF: 0-1 Fm: 0-0
Distance: 5f/6f: 0-0 7f-8f: 0-0 **9f-13f: 2-9** 14f+: 0-0
Track : LH: 1-7 RH: 1-2 Tight: 1-1 Gall: 1-5
Aids: Bl: 0-0 Vi: 0-0 Tstrap: 0-0 Ckp: 0-0
Best Rating: 100 11/09 Donc 1m4f soft

Very useful; stays 1m4f, but effective at shorter; acts on any ground; bumper winner.

Himalya (IRE)

101(110) (106)108
3-y-o b g Danehill Dancer (IRE)-Lady Miletrian (IRE) (Barathea (IRE))
J Noseda Ms Gillian Khosla

Placings:14-66334 (7768)
2009: 7^{6}GF, 5^{6}GF, 6^{3}G, 6^{3}SD, 7^{4}SD,

	Starts	1st	2nd	3rd	Win & Pl
Career Total (Turf)	5	1	0	1	12751
Career Total (AW)	2	0	0	1	6456

88 5/08 Donc 6f GD £3561
Total win prize-money £3562

Going (Turf): Sf: 0-0 GS: 0-0 **Gd: 1-2** GF: 0-3 Fm: 0-0
Distance: **5f/6f: 1-5** 7f-8f: 0-2 9f-13f: 0-0 14f+: 0-0
Track : LH: 0-1 RH: 0-1 Tight: 0-1 Gall: 0-0
Aids: Bl: 0-0 Vi: 0-0 Tstrap: 0-0 Ckp: 0-0
Best Rating: 108 6/08 Asct 6f gd-fm

Smart; fourth in the 2008 Coventry Stakes but then not seen for well over a year; suited by 6f and good ground.

Hindford Oak Sioux

68 62
3-y-o b f Green Card (USA)-Sharp Susy (Beveled (USA))
Mrs L Williamson Hindford Oak Racing

Placings:05-00 (4879)
2009: 10^{0}HY, 7^{0}G,

	Starts	1st	2nd	3rd	Win & Pl
Career Total (Turf)	4	0	0	0	0

Going (Turf): Sf: 0-2 GS: 0-0 Gd: 0-1 GF: 0-1 Fm: 0-0
Distance: 5f/6f: 0-0 7f-8f: 0-3 9f-13f: 0-1 14f+: 0-0
Track : LH: 0-2 RH: 0-2 Tight: 0-2 Gall: 0-0
Aids: Bl: 0-0 Vi: 0-0 Tstrap: 0-0 Ckp: 0-0
Best Rating: 62 9/08 Ches 7f2y gd-fm

Hindu Kush (IRE)

108(78) (47)110

4-y-o b c Sadler's Wells (USA)-Tambora (Darshaan)

D Nicholls Dr Marwan Koukash

Placings:05/4410405-520165000006 (6875)

2009: 12^{5}G, 13^{2}S, 18^{0}GF, 14^{1}G, 20^{6}GF, 12^{5}HY, 14^{0}G, 13^{0}GF, 14^{0}S, 13^{0}G, 12^{0}G, 14^{6}SD,

	Starts	1st	2nd	3rd	Win & Pl
Career Total (Turf)	20	2	1	0	111584
Career Total (AW)	1	0	0	0	0

108 5/09 Leop 1m6f GD £37922
110 6/08 Curr 1m2f FRM £26327
Total win prize-money £64249

Going (Turf): Sf: 0-5 GS: 0-0 **Gd: 1-7** GF: 0-4 **Fm: 1-2**
Distance: 5f/6f: 0-0 **7f-8f: 0-1** 9f-13f: 1-10 **14f+: 1-10**
Track : LH: 1-13 RH: 1-8 Tight: 0-4 Gall: 0-4
Aids: Bl: 0-0 Vi: 0-0 Tstrap: 0-0 Ckp: 0-0
Best Rating: **110** 6/08 Curr 1m2f firm

Useful; stays 1m6f; acts on most ground; likes to race prominently.

Hint Of Honey

79(100) (57)21

3-y-o ch f King Charlemagne (USA)-Jugendliebe (IRE) (Persian Bold)

A G Newcombe A G Newcombe

Placings:0-4040001 (7855)

2009: 6^{4}SD, 7^{0}SD, 7^{4}SD, 6^{0}SD, 6^{0}SD, 6^{0}GF, 8^{1}SS,

	Starts	1st	2nd	3rd	Win & Pl
Career Total (Turf)	1	0	0	0	
Career Total (AW)	7	1	0	0	2240

57 12/09 Sthl 1m (0-60)H SS £2047
Total win prize-money £2047

Going (Turf): **Sf: 0-0 GS: 0-0 Gd: 0-0 GF: 0-1 Fm: 0-0**
Distance: 5f/6f: 0-4 **7f-8f: 1-4** 9f-13f: 0-0 14f+: 0-0
Track : **LH: 1-6** RH: 0-1 Tight: 0-2 Gall: 0-1
Aids: Bl: 0-0 Vi: 0-0 Tstrap: 0-0 Ckp: 0-0
Best Rating: **57** 12/09 Sthl 1m std-slw

Plating-class; stays 1m; acts on Fibresand; handles Polytrack.

Hinton Admiral

104(106) (88)103

5-y-o b g Spectrum (IRE)-Shawanni (Shareef Dancer (USA))

R A Fahey Aidan J Ryan Racing I

Placings:16121/15420/040320000006655-001 (2456)

2009: 7^{0}G, 7^{0}GS, 6^{1}GF,

	Starts	1st	2nd	3rd	Win & Pl
Career Total (Turf)	22	3	3	1	39571
Career Total (AW)	6	2	0	0	58428

77 5/09 Yarm 6f3y G-F £1942
105 3/07 Ling 7f STD £42585
102 10/06 Ling 6f STD £14817
97 9/06 Haml 6f5y H G-S £12464
78 6/06 Haml 6f5y GD £2590
Total win prize-money £74401

Going (Turf): Sf: 0-1 **GS: 1-5 Gd: 1-7 GF: 1-8** Fm: 0-1
Distance: 5f/6f: 1-11 **7f-8f: 4-16** 9f-13f: 0-1 14f+: 0-0
Track : **LH: 2-6** RH: 0-4 **Tight: 2-6** Gall: 0-1
Aids: Bl: 0-0 Vi: 0-0 Tstrap: 0-2 Ckp: 0-2
Best Rating: **106** 4/07 NmkR 7f gd-fm

Very useful; winner in Listed company; suited by 6f-7f; acts on most ground and on Polytrack; has worn cheekpieces.

Hip Hip Hooray

102(100) (68)72

3-y-o ch f Monsieur Bond (IRE)-Birthday Belle (Lycius (USA))

L A Dace M C S D Racing Partnership

Placings:62315240-50320155450000 (6780)

2009: 8^{5}SD, 8^{0}GF, 10^{3}GF, 9^{2}GF, 9^{0}G, 8^{1}GF, 10^{5}G, 9^{5}G, 8^{4}G, 9^{5}SD, 9^{0}GF, 10^{0}SD, 10^{0}G, 8^{0}SS,

	Starts	1st	2nd	3rd	Win & Pl
Career Total (Turf)	15	2	1	2	8224
Career Total (AW)	7	0	2	0	1330

72 6/09 Wind 1m67y (0-70)H G-F £2729
60 8/08 Wind 6f G-S £2729
Total win prize-money £5460

Going (Turf): Sf: 0-0 **GS: 1-4** Gd: 0-5 **GF: 1-6** Fm: 0-0
Distance: 5f/6f: 1-3 7f-8f: 0-6 9f-13f: 1-13 14f+: 0-0
Track : LH: 0-4 **RH: 1-13** Tight: 1-10 Gall: 1-1
Aids: Bl: 0-0 Vi: 0-0 Tstrap: 0-3 Ckp: 0-3
Best Rating: **72** 7/09 Sand 1m1f good

Modest; stays 1m2f; acts on fast and easy ground; goes on Polytrack.

Hippodrome (IRE)

(92) (66)74

7-y-o b g Montjeu (IRE)-Moon Diamond (Unfuwain (USA))

John A Harris Mrs A E Harris

Placings:01202/000002/0-00 (0918)

2009: 14^{0}SD, 11^{0}SD,

	Starts	1st	2nd	3rd	Win & Pl
Career Total (Turf)	9	1	2	0	11387
Career Total (AW)	5	0	1	0	567

82 6/05 Naas 1m2f GD £5880
Total win prize-money £5881

Going (Turf): Sf: 0-0 GS: 0-2 **Gd: 1-2** GF: 0-2 Fm: 0-1
Distance: 5f/6f: 0-0 7f-8f: 0-0 **9f-13f: 1-10** 14f+: 0-4
Track : **LH: 1-7** RH: 0-5 Tight: 0-1 Gall: 0-5
Aids: Bl: 0-5 Vi: 0-1 Tstrap: 0-1 Ckp: 0-1
Best Rating: **101** 10/05 Fair 1m4f yield

Hippolytus

102 81

4-y-o ch g Observatory (USA)-Pasithea (IRE) (Celtic Swing)

J J Quinn Lady Legard

Placings:23343-014265 (5551)

2009: 7^{0}GS, 10^{1}G, 10^{4}GF, 9^{2}S, 9^{6}S, 9^{5}GS,

	Starts	1st	2nd	3rd	Win & Pl
Career Total (Turf)	11	1	2	3	6897

76 6/09 Hayd 1m2f95y (0-75)H GD £3238
Total win prize-money £3238

Going (Turf): Sf: 0-5 GS: 0-2 **Gd: 1-2** GF: 0-2 Fm: 0-0
Distance: 5f/6f: 0-0 7f-8f: 0-3 **9f-13f: 1-8** 14f+: 0-0
Track : **LH: 1-5** RH: 0-4 Tight: 0-3 Gall: 0-1
Aids: Bl: 0-0 Vi: 0-0 Tstrap: 0-0 Ckp: 0-0
Best Rating: **81** 8/09 Haml 1m1f36y soft

Fair; effective over 1m2f; acts on easy ground.

Hisaronu (IRE)

92(99) (69)67

3-y-o b f Stravinsky (USA)-Journey Of Hope (USA) (Slew O'Gold (USA))

H R A Cecil Diamond Racing Ltd

Placings:52 (1532)

2009: 8^{5}G, 9^{2}SD,

	Starts	1st	2nd	3rd	Win & Pl
Career Total (Turf)	1	0	0	0	0
Career Total (AW)	1	0	1	0	806

Going (Turf): **Sf: 0-0 GS: 0-0 Gd: 0-1 GF: 0-0 Fm: 0-0**
Distance: 5f/6f: 0-0 7f-8f: 0-0 9f-13f: 0-2 14f+: 0-0
Track : LH: 0-1 RH: 0-0 Tight: 0-1 Gall: 0-0
Aids: Bl: 0-0 Vi: 0-0 Tstrap: 0-0 Ckp: 0-0
Best Rating: **69** 4/09 Wolv 1m1f103y stand

Fair; stays 1m1f and acts on Polytrack.

Historical Giant (USA)

(96) (49)57

4-y-o ch g Giant's Causeway (USA)-Onima (USA) (Jade Hunter (USA))

E F Vaughan Mrs Lucinda White

Placings:5/600-05 (0444)

2009: 10^{0}SD, 12^{5}SD,

	Starts	1st	2nd	3rd	Win & Pl
Career Total (Turf)	3	0	0	0	0
Career Total (AW)	3	0	0	0	0

Going (Turf): **Sf: 0-2 GS: 0-0 Gd: 0-0 GF: 0-1 Fm: 0-0**
Distance: 5f/6f: 0-0 7f-8f: 0-3 9f-13f: 0-3 14f+: 0-0
Track : LH: 0-3 RH: 0-1 Tight: 0-2 Gall: 0-0
Aids: Bl: 0-0 Vi: 0-0 Tstrap: 0-1 Ckp: 0-1
Best Rating: **57** 5/07 Tipp 7f100y gd-fm

History Lesson

103(94) (82)91

3-y-o ch c Golan (IRE)-Once Upon A Time (Teenoso (USA))

A E Jones (R Hannon 23/10) BPD Ltd

Placings:622-14410023 (6996)

2009: 9^{1}GF, 10^{4}G, 12^{4}GF, 11^{1}G, 12^{0}G, 10^{0}G, 10^{2}GS, 10^{3}GS,

	Starts	1st	2nd	3rd	Win & Pl
Career Total (Turf)	10	2	2	1	14852
Career Total (AW)	1	0	1	0	1156

88 7/09 Wind 1m3f135y (0-85)H GD £5180
79 4/09 Folk 1m1f149y G-F £2729
Total win prize-money £7911

Going (Turf): Sf: 0-0 GS: 0-3 **Gd: 1-5 GF: 1-2** Fm: 0-0
Distance: 5f/6f: 0-0 7f-8f: 0-3 **9f-13f: 2-8** 14f+: 0-0
Track : LH: 0-2 **RH: 1-6 Tight: 2-6** Gall: 0-2
Aids: Bl: 0-0 Vi: 0-0 Tstrap: 0-0 Ckp: 0-0
Best Rating: **91** 10/09 Wind 1m2f7y gd-sft

Useful; stays 1m4f; acts on good and faster ground and on Polytrack.

Hit The Switch

92(103) (65)69

3-y-o b g Reset (AUS)-Scenic Venture (IRE) (Desert King (IRE))

Patrick Morris Rob Lloyd Racing Limited

Placings:610-400006000015316 (7855)

2009: 6^{4}SD, 7^{0}SD, 8^{0}GS, 6^{0}GF, 6^{0}HY, 7^{6}GF, 9^{0}G, 10^{0}GF, 11^{0}GS, 14^{0}HY, 6^{0}SD, 8^{1}SD, 8^{5}SD, 7^{3}SD, 8^{1}SS, 8^{6}SS,

	Starts	1st	2nd	3rd	Win & Pl
Career Total (Turf)	10	1	0	0	3886
Career Total (AW)	9	2	0	1	3998

63	12/09	Sthl	1m	(0-65)H	SS	£2047
65	11/09	Sthl	1m	(0-60)H	STD	£1648
69	9/08	Haml	6f5y		SFT	£3885

Total win prize-money £7581

Going (Turf): **Sf: 1-3** GS: 0-2 Gd: 0-2 GF: 0-3 Fm: 0-0
Distance: 5f/6f: 0-4 **7f-8f: 3-11** 9f-13f: 0-3 14f+: 0-1
Track : **LH: 2-11** RH: 0-5 Tight: 0-4 Gall: 0-1
Aids: Bl: 0-0 Vi: 0-0 Tstrap: 0-1 Ckp: 0-1
Best Rating: **69** 9/08 Haml 6f5y soft

Moderate; effective at 6f-1m; acts on easy ground; goes on Fibresand.

Hitchens (IRE)

108(109) (104)111
4-y-o b g Acclamation-Royal Fizz (IRE) (Royal Academy (USA))
T D Barron Laurence O'Kane

Placings:41325/10003-10600060135 **(6994)**
2009: 6[1]F, 6[0]GF, 5[6]GF, 5[0]G, 5[0]G, 6[0]S, 6[6]GF, 6[0]G, 6[1]GF, 6[3]G, 6[5]G,

	Starts	1st	2nd	3rd	Win & Pl
Career Total (Turf)	20	4	1	2	256185
Career Total (AW)	1	0	0	1	1156

105	9/09	Hayd	6f	(0-100)H	G-F	£12952
109	4/09	Thsk	6f		FRM	£7851
111	6/08	Wind	6f	(0-105)H	G-F	£31155
82	8/07	Folk	6f		G-F	£2817

Total win prize-money £54775

Going (Turf): Sf: 0-1 GS: 0-1 Gd: 0-9 **GF: 3-8** Fm: 1-1
Distance: **5f/6f: 4-18** 7f-8f: 0-3 9f-13f: 0-0 14f+: 0-0
Track : LH: 0-1 RH: 0-0 Tight: 0-0 **Gall: 1-2**
Aids: Bl: 0-0 Vi: 0-0 Tstrap: 0-0 Ckp: 0-0
Best Rating: **111** 6/08 Wind 6f gd-fm

Very useful; effective from 6f-7f; seems best on fast ground.

Hitches Dubai (BRZ)

95 67
4-y-o ch g A Good Reason (BRZ)-Orquidea Vermelha (BRZ) (Lucence (USA))
D Nicholls Michael Reay

Placings:0-410 **(4772)**
2009: 6[4]GF, 5[1]GF, 6[0]GF,

	Starts	1st	2nd	3rd	Win & Pl
Career Total (Turf)	4	1	0	0	3107

67	7/09	Bevl	5f	G-F	£2914

Total win prize-money £2914

Going (Turf): Sf: 0-0 GS: 0-0 Gd: 0-1 **GF: 1-3** Fm: 0-0
Distance: **5f/6f: 1-4** 7f-8f: 0-0 9f-13f: 0-0 14f+: 0-0
Track : LH: 0-0 RH: 0-0 Tight: 0-0 Gall: 0-0
Aids: Bl: 0-0 Vi: 0-0 Tstrap: 0-0 Ckp: 0-0
Best Rating: **67** 7/09 Bevl 5f gd-fm

Hits Only Cash

101(104) (69)70
7-y-o b g Inchinor-Persian Blue (Persian Bold)
J Pearce Oceana racing

Placings:60504**520**/5361**400**/**42030200000**4/**05263224510160**/**550**2030652060**0-342001660100** **(6860)**
2009: 8[3]SD, 8[4]GF, 8[2]G, 8[0]SD, 8[0]SF, 8[1]SD, 9[6]SD, 8[6]S, 8[0]SD, 9[1]SD, 10[0]SD, 9[0]SD,

	Starts	1st	2nd	3rd	Win & Pl
Career Total (Turf)	33	2	4	2	11767
Career Total (AW)	34	3	5	3	14134

67	9/09	Wolv	1m1f103y	(0-65)H	STD	£2729
64	8/09	Kemp	1m	(0-65)H	STD	£2047
73	9/07	Wolv	1m141y	(0-70)H	STD	£3071
70	8/07	Yarm	1m3y	(0-60)H	G-S	£2137
73	5/05	Ayr	7f50y	(0-70)	SFT	£3445

Total win prize-money £13430

Going (Turf): **Sf: 1-12 GS: 1-10** Gd: 0-7 GF: 0-3 Fm: 0-1
Distance: 5f/6f: 0-20 7f-8f: 2-19 **9f-13f: 3-28** 14f+: 0-0
Track : **LH: 3-36** RH: 1-7 **Tight: 2-29** Gall: 0-2
Aids: Bl: 0-1 Vi: 0-0 Tstrap: 2-16 Ckp: 2-16
Best Rating: **77** 4/06 Wolv 7f32y stand

Moderate; effective at around 1m; acts on soft ground; also goes on Polytrack; has worn cheekpieces.

Hits Only Jude (IRE)

95(108) (85)67
6-y-o gr g Bold Fact (USA)-Grey Goddess (Godswalk (USA))
D Carroll Yummy Mummy's Racing Club

Placings:5533622/500500505/500/11213450-20224400204 **(7759)**
2009: 7[2]SD, 6[0]G, 6[2]SD, 6[2]SD, 6[4]G, 5[4]G, 6[0]GF, 6[0]S, 7[2]SD, 7[0]SF, 8[4]SD,

	Starts	1st	2nd	3rd	Win & Pl
Career Total (Turf)	19	0	1	2	4480
Career Total (AW)	19	3	6	1	13826

89	2/08	Sthl	6f	(0-75)H	SS	£2593
78	1/08	Sthl	6f	(0-65)H	STD	£1911
82	1/08	Sthl	6f	(0-55)H	STD	£1911

Total win prize-money £6416

Going (Turf): **Sf: 0-5 GS: 0-3 Gd: 0-9 GF: 0-2 Fm: 0-0**
Distance: **5f/6f: 3-23** 7f-8f: 0-15 9f-13f: 0-0 14f+: 0-0
Track : **LH: 3-24** RH: 0-1 Tight: 0-12 Gall: 0-3
Aids: Bl: 0-1 Vi: 0-1 Tstrap: 0-0 Ckp: 0-0
Best Rating: **89** 2/08 Sthl 6f std-slw

Fair; effective over 6f-7f; seems best on Fibresand but does act on Polytrack; also handles good or softer ground on turf.

Hits Only Time

91(93) (55)50
4-y-o ch g Bertolini (USA)-South Wind (Tina's Pet)
D Carroll Danny Fantom

Placings:0000/460-000 **(3943)**
2009: 6[0]GF, 12[0]GF, 9[0]GF,

	Starts	1st	2nd	3rd	Win & Pl
Career Total (Turf)	8	0	0	0	0
Career Total (AW)	2	0	0	0	0

Going (Turf): **Sf: 0-2 GS: 0-1 Gd: 0-0 GF: 0-5 Fm: 0-0**
Distance: 5f/6f: 0-4 7f-8f: 0-3 9f-13f: 0-3 14f+: 0-0
Track : LH: 0-2 RH: 0-3 Tight: 0-1 Gall: 0-0
Aids: Bl: 0-0 Vi: 0-0 Tstrap: 0-0 Ckp: 0-0
Best Rating: **55** 10/07 Kemp 7f stand

Hits Only Vic (USA)

109 (43)108
5-y-o b/br g Lemon Drop Kid (USA)-Royal Family (USA) (Private Terms (USA))
D Carroll Kell-Stone & Watson

Placings:00000/**003**/521112221105-10130 **(5656)**
2009: 16[1]G, 16[0]S, 14[1]GF, 14[3]GF, 14[0]S,

	Starts	1st	2nd	3rd	Win & Pl
Career Total (Turf)	22	7	4	2	92918
Career Total (AW)	3	0	0	0	

107	7/09	York	1m6f	(0-110)H	G-F	£23704
105	5/09	Hayd	2m45y	(0-100)H	GD	£12462
100	10/08	Ayr	1m5f13y	(0-95)H	HVY	£7771
97	9/08	Hayd	1m6f	(0-85)H	HVY	£5504
89	6/08	Ripn	1m4f10y	(0-75)H	GD	£2914
78	6/08	Donc	1m6f132y	(0-70)H	G-F	£3238
76	6/08	Ripn	1m4f10y	(0-70)H	HVY	£2914

Total win prize-money £58508

Going (Turf): **Sf: 3-7** GS: 0-0 Gd: 2-7 GF: 2-8 Fm: 0-0
Distance: 5f/6f: 0-5 7f-8f: 0-2 9f-13f: 2-7 **14f+: 5-11**
Track : **LH: 5-16** RH: 2-7 Tight: 2-6 Gall: 2-7
Aids: Bl: 0-0 Vi: 0-0 Tstrap: 0-0 Ckp: 0-0
Best Rating: **108** 8/09 York 1m6f gd-fm

Very useful; winner in Listed company; stays 2m but effective at shorter; acts on most ground.

Hobby

97 100
4-y-o b f Robellino (USA)-Wydah (Suave Dancer (USA))
R M Beckett Larksborough Stud Limited

Placings:1320/3340-250 **(3874)**
2009: 12[2]GF, 10[5]GS, 14[0]GF,

	Starts	1st	2nd	3rd	Win & Pl
Career Total (Turf)	11	1	2	3	32430

72	7/07	Wwck	7f26y	GD	£2914

Total win prize-money £2915

Going (Turf): Sf: 0-2 GS: 0-1 **Gd: 1-4** GF: 0-4 Fm: 0-0
Distance: 5f/6f: 0-0 **7f-8f: 1-4** 9f-13f: 0-6 14f+: 0-1
Track : **LH: 1-4** RH: 0-5 Tight: 0-1 Gall: 0-4
Aids: Bl: 0-0 Vi: 0-0 Tstrap: 0-1 Ckp: 0-1
Best Rating: **100** 6/08 Asct 1m4f gd-fm

Very useful; effective at 1m2f-1m4f; acts on good and fast ground; has worn cheekpieces.

Hoboob (USA)

90 58
3-y-o ch f Seeking The Gold (USA)-Bint Salsabil (USA) (Nashwan (USA))
J L Dunlop Hamdan Al Maktoum

Placings:0-0 **(1488)**
2009: 10[0]G,

	Starts	1st	2nd	3rd	Win & Pl
Career Total (Turf)	2	0	0	0	

Going (Turf): **Sf: 0-1 GS: 0-0 Gd: 0-1 GF: 0-0 Fm: 0-0**
Distance: 5f/6f: 0-0 7f-8f: 0-1 9f-13f: 0-1 14f+: 0-0
Track : LH: 0-0 RH: 0-1 Tight: 0-0 Gall: 0-0
Aids: Bl: 0-0 Vi: 0-0 Tstrap: 0-0 Ckp: 0-0
Best Rating: **58** 4/09 Sand 1m2f7y good

Hobson

105(96) (76)76
4-y-o b g Choisir (AUS)-Educating Rita (Emarati (USA))
Eve Johnson Houghton Anthony Pye-Jeary And Mel Smith

Placings:25201654/2005003440-14322555156 **(6562)**
2009: 7[1]GF, 8[4]GF, 6[3]F, 7[2]GF, 7[2]GF, 6[5]GF, 7[5]GF, 7[5]G, 7[1]GF, 7[5]GF, 7[6]GS,

	Starts	1st	2nd	3rd	Win & Pl
Career Total (Turf)	25	3	4	2	13382
Career Total (AW)	4	0	1	0	1011

76 9/09 Leic 7f9y (0-70)H G-F £3238
73 4/09 Yarm 7f3y (0-65)H G-F £1942
67 8/07 Bath 5f11y GD £2072
Total win prize-money £7254

Going (Turf): Sf: 0-0 GS: 0-2 Gd: 1-8 **GF: 2-13** Fm: 0-2
Distance: 5f/6f: 1-15 **7f-8f: 2-13** 9f-13f: 0-1 14f+: 0-0
Track : **LH: 1-8** RH: 0-2 Tight: 0-2 **Gall: 1-4**
Aids: Bl: 0-3 Vi: 0-0 Tstrap: 0-0 Ckp: 0-0
Best Rating: 76 9/09 Leic 7f9y gd-fm

Modest; stays 7f; acts on fast ground.

Hogmaneigh (IRE)

104(106) (106)111
6-y-o b g Namid-Magical Peace (IRE) (Magical Wonder (USA))
J S Goldie (S C Williams 27/6) Mrs Lucille Bone

Placings:14/0131300/3104000/56401034-**2**060000 **(6678)**
2009: 6^{2}SD, 5^{0}GF, 5^{0}HY, 5^{0}GF, 6^{0}GF, 6^{0}G, 6^{0}G,

	Starts	1st	2nd	3rd	Win & Pl
Career Total (Turf)	29	5	0	4	145011
Career Total (AW)	2	0	1	0	2548

110 9/08 Donc 5f140y H SFT £46732
109 6/07 Epsm 5f H GD £46740
106 8/06 Sand 5f6y (0-100)H GD £11217
96 5/06 Nott 6f15y (0-95)H SFT £11658
80 9/05 Ayr 6f G-S £3705
Total win prize-money £120055

Going (Turf): **Sf: 2-8** GS: 1-9 **Gd: 2-7** GF: 0-5 Fm: 0-0
Distance: **5f/6f: 4-30** 7f-8f: 1-1 9f-13f: 0-0 14f+: 0-0
Track : LH: 0-2 RH: 0-1 Tight: 0-1 Gall: 0-1
Aids: Bl: 0-0 Vi: 0-0 Tstrap: 0-0 Ckp: 0-0
Best Rating: 111 10/08 Muss 5f gd-sft

Very useful; Listed placed; winner of the 2007 Vodafone Dash and the 2008 Portland; effective over 5f-6f; acts on good or softer ground and on Polytrack; usually held up.

Hoh Hoh Hoh

109(91) (68)111
7-y-o ch g Piccolo-Nesting (Thatching)
R J Price Multi Lines 2

Placings:1/20/000654160/46051322024303620/02662000 10-0012303600 **(6283)**
2009: 5^{0}SD, 6^{0}GF, 5^{1}GF, 5^{2}GF, 5^{3}G, 5^{0}GF, 5^{3}GF, 6^{6}G, 5^{0}GF, 5^{0}GF,

	Starts	1st	2nd	3rd	Win & Pl
Career Total (Turf)	47	5	8	5	110316
Career Total (AW)	2	0	0	0	

98 4/09 Nott 5f13y G-F £7771
108 8/08 Sand 5f6y (0-100)H GD £12462
93 6/07 Ches 5f16y (0-85)H GD £5505
94 9/06 Sals 6f (0-85)H G-S £6477
94 5/04 Bath 5f161y D FRM £4400
Total win prize-money £36616

Going (Turf): Sf: 0-3 GS: 1-6 **Gd: 2-16** GF: 1-21 Fm: 1-1
Distance: **5f/6f: 5-47** 7f-8f: 0-2 9f-13f: 0-0 14f+: 0-0
Track : **LH: 2-9** RH: 0-1 Tight: 1-6 Gall: 1-4
Aids: Bl: 0-0 Vi: 0-0 Tstrap: 0-0 Ckp: 0-0
Best Rating: 111 5/09 NmkR 5f gd-fm

Smart; placed in Group 3 company; effective over 5f-6f; acts on most ground; likes to race prominently.

Hohrod

78(81) (13)37
3-y-o ch g Tipsy Creek (USA)-Agara (Young Ern)
John A Harris Miss Vivian Pratt

Placings:0000 **(7797)**
2009: 6^{0}SD, 5^{0}S, 8^{0}G, 8^{0}SS,

	Starts	1st	2nd	3rd	Win & Pl
Career Total (Turf)	2	0	0	0	
Career Total (AW)	2	0	0	0	

Going (Turf): Sf: 0-1 GS: 0-0 Gd: 0-1 GF: 0-0 Fm: 0-0
Distance: 5f/6f: 0-2 7f-8f: 0-1 9f-13f: 0-1 14f+: 0-0
Track : LH: 0-3 RH: 0-0 Tight: 0-0 Gall: 0-0
Aids: Bl: 0-0 Vi: 0-0 Tstrap: 0-0 Ckp: 0-0
Best Rating: 37 8/09 Nott 1m75y good

Holbeck Ghyll (IRE)

95(110) (97)99
7-y-o ch g Titus Livius (FR)-Crimada (IRE) (Mukaddamah (USA))
A M Balding D Nicholson

Placings:303/0642111/**5**0510355/40403402455/1121-0 **(1325)**
2009: 5^{0}GS,

	Starts	1st	2nd	3rd	Win & Pl
Career Total (Turf)	29	5	3	4	75493
Career Total (AW)	5	2	0	0	7324

99 6/08 Epsm 5f H GD £31155
97 4/08 Kemp 6f (0-80)H STD £4533
89 3/08 Kemp 5f (0-75)H STD £2590
88 8/06 Gdwd 5f (0-90)H G-F £10363
79 9/05 Sand 5f6y (0-80)H GD £5920
79 9/05 Bath 5f161y (0-75)H FRM £5522
72 9/05 Sals 5f (0-70)H G-F £4889
Total win prize-money £64973

Going (Turf): Sf: 0-0 GS: 0-2 **Gd: 2-14 GF: 2-10** Fm: 1-3
Distance: **5f/6f: 7-30** 7f-8f: 0-4 9f-13f: 0-0 14f+: 0-0
Track : LH: 1-9 **RH: 2-3** Tight: 0-4 **Gall: 1-5**
Aids: Bl: 0-1 Vi: 0-0 Tstrap: 0-5 Ckp: 0-5
Best Rating: 99 6/08 Epsm 5f good

Very useful; effective over 5f-6f; acts on a sound surface and on Polytrack; has worn blinkers and cheekpieces.

Holberg (UAE)

115(102) (82)108
3-y-o b c Halling (USA)-Sweet Willa (USA) (Assert)
M Johnston Sheikh Hamdan Bin Mohammed Al Maktoum

Placings:64511-131 **(3090)**
2009: 11^{1}GF, 11^{3}GF, 16^{1}GF,

	Starts	1st	2nd	3rd	Win & Pl
Career Total (Turf)	6	2	0	1	55366
Career Total (AW)	2	2	0	0	7656

108 6/09 Asct 2m G-F £39739
91 4/09 Leic 1m3f183y (0-95)H G-F £9346
82 12/08 Kemp 1m (0-85) STD £4094
79 11/08 Sthl 7f STD £3561
Total win prize-money £56742

Going (Turf): Sf: 0-1 GS: 0-1 Gd: 0-1 **GF: 2-3** Fm: 0-0
Distance: 5f/6f: 0-1 **7f-8f: 2-4** 9f-13f: 1-2 14f+: 1-1
Track : LH: 1-1 **RH: 3-4** Tight: 0-1 **Gall: 1-1**
Aids: Bl: 0-0 Vi: 0-0 Tstrap: 0-0 Ckp: 0-0
Best Rating: 108 6/09 Asct 2m gd-fm

Smart; Queen's vase winner and Listed placed in 2009; stays 2m; acts on most ground and on sand.

Hold Fire

73(91) (50)21
5-y-o b m Lear Spear (USA)-Kahyasi Moll (IRE) (Brief Truce (USA))
A W Carroll Marita Bayley and Trevor Turner

Placings:0000-000 **(3217)**
2009: 8^{0}G, 10^{0}GF, 10^{0}GF,

	Starts	1st	2nd	3rd	Win & Pl
Career Total (Turf)	4	0	0	0	
Career Total (AW)	3	0	0	0	

Going (Turf): Sf: 0-0 GS: 0-0 Gd: 0-2 GF: 0-2 Fm: 0-0
Distance: 5f/6f: 0-0 7f-8f: 0-2 9f-13f: 0-5 14f+: 0-0
Track : LH: 0-2 RH: 0-4 Tight: 0-1 Gall: 0-1
Aids: Bl: 0-1 Vi: 0-0 Tstrap: 0-0 Ckp: 0-0
Best Rating: 50 3/08 Kemp 1m stand

Hold Me

80(88) (57)37
2-y-o ch f Hold That Tiger (USA)-Sultry Lass (USA) (Private Account (USA))
H R A Cecil Malih L Al Basti

Placings:60 **(6567)**
2009: 8^{6}SD, 7^{0}GF,

	Starts	1st	2nd	3rd	Win & Pl
Career Total (Turf)	1	0	0	0	
Career Total (AW)	1	0	0	0	0

Going (Turf): Sf: 0-0 GS: 0-0 Gd: 0-0 GF: 0-1 Fm: 0-0
Distance: 5f/6f: 0-0 7f-8f: 0-1 9f-13f: 0-1 14f+: 0-0
Track : LH: 0-1 RH: 0-0 Tight: 0-1 Gall: 0-0
Aids: Bl: 0-0 Vi: 0-0 Tstrap: 0-0 Ckp: 0-0
Best Rating: 57 9/09 Wolv 1m141y stand

Hold On Tiger (IRE)

98 75
2-y-o ch c Acclamation-Our Juliette (IRE) (Namid)
I Semple Mrs J Penman

Placings:02156 **(6841)**
2009: 6^{0}GF, 5^{2}GF, 6^{1}S, 6^{5}G, 5^{6}G,

	Starts	1st	2nd	3rd	Win & Pl
Career Total (Turf)	5	1	1	0	3720

75 8/09 Ayr 6f SFT £2914
Total win prize-money £2914

Going (Turf): **Sf: 1-1** GS: 0-0 Gd: 0-2 GF: 0-2 Fm: 0-0
Distance: **5f/6f: 1-4** 7f-8f: 0-1 9f-13f: 0-0 14f+: 0-0
Track : LH: 0-0 RH: 0-1 Tight: 0-0 Gall: 0-0
Aids: Bl: 0-0 Vi: 0-0 Tstrap: 0-0 Ckp: 0-0
Best Rating: 75 8/09 Ayr 6f soft

Fair; stays 6f and acts on most ground.

Hold The Bucks (USA)

92(100) (73)63
3-y-o b g Hold That Tiger (USA)-Buck's Lady (USA) (Alleged (USA))
J S Moore E Moore & J S Moore

Placings:0232002663114-134224041503 (6439)
2009: 8^{1}SD, 8^{3}SD, 8^{4}SD, 8^{2}SD, 8^{2}SD, 8^{4}SD, 10^{0}SD, 10^{4}G, 8^{1}SD, 9^{5}G, 8^{0}SD, 10^{3}SS,

	Starts	1st	2nd	3rd	Win & Pl
Career Total (Turf)	7	0	1	1	886
Career Total (AW)	18	4	4	3	13643

68	4/09	Kemp	1m		STD	£2047
64	1/09	Wolv	1m141y		STD	£2729
66	12/08	Wolv	1m141y	(0-65)	STD	£2729
64	11/08	Ling	1m		STD	£1978

Total win prize-money £9486

Going (Turf): Sf: 0-1 GS: 0-0 Gd: 0-3 GF: 0-3 Fm: 0-0
Distance: 5f/6f: 0-1 7f-8f: 2-15 9f-13f: 2-9 14f+: 0-0
Track : LH: 3-10 RH: 1-12 Tight: 3-10 Gall: 0-3
Aids: Bl: 0-0 Vi: 0-0 Tstrap: 1-3 Ckp: 1-3
Best Rating: 73 1/09 Kemp 1m stand

Fair; effective over 7f-1m2f; acts on good ground; also goes on Polytrack; has worn cheekpieces.

Hold The Star

88(97) (65)51
3-y-o b f Red Ransom (USA)-Sydney Star (Machiavellian (USA))
Miss A Stokell (E F Vaughan 15/10) Ms Caron Stokell

Placings:0-002006004046 (7863)
2009: 9^{0}GF, 9^{0}SD, 7^{2}SD, 6^{0}GF, 7^{0}F, 8^{6}SD, 12^{0}SD, 7^{0}SD, 7^{4}SD, 8^{0}SD, 7^{4}SD, 8^{6}SD,

	Starts	1st	2nd	3rd	Win & Pl
Career Total (Turf)	3	0	0	0	
Career Total (AW)	10	0	1	0	705

Going (Turf): Sf: 0-0 GS: 0-0 Gd: 0-0 GF: 0-2 Fm: 0-1
Distance: 5f/6f: 0-0 7f-8f: 0-7 9f-13f: 0-6 14f+: 0-0
Track : LH: 0-10 RH: 0-2 Tight: 0-9 Gall: 0-0
Aids: Bl: 0-1 Vi: 0-1 Tstrap: 0-0 Ckp: 0-0
Best Rating: 65 5/09 Wolv 7f32y stand

Moderate; stays 7f; acts on Polytrack.

Hold Your Colour (IRE)

97 101
2-y-o br/gr g Verglas (IRE)-Azia (IRE) (Desert Story (IRE))
B J Meehan Sangster Family & Mrs M Findlay

Placings:611 (5521)
2009: 6^{6}GF, 6^{1}GF, 6^{1}G,

	Starts	1st	2nd	3rd	Win & Pl
Career Total (Turf)	3	2	0	0	41651

101	8/09	Ripn	6f	GD	£17031
86	8/09	Ripn	6f	G-F	£24620

Total win prize-money £41651

Going (Turf): Sf: 0-0 GS: 0-0 Gd: 1-1 GF: 1-2 Fm: 0-0
Distance: 5f/6f: 2-3 7f-8f: 0-0 9f-13f: 0-0 14f+: 0-0
Track : LH: 0-0 RH: 0-0 Tight: 0-0 Gall: 0-0
Aids: Bl: 0-0 Vi: 0-0 Tstrap: 0-0 Ckp: 0-0
Best Rating: 101 8/09 Ripn 6f good

Smart; stays 6f; acts on a sound surface.

Holden Eagle

100(97) (62)80
4-y-o b c Catcher In The Rye (IRE)-Bird Of Prey (IRE) (Last Tycoon)
A G Newcombe DXB Bloodstock,Patel,Ryan & Newcombe

Placings:0/64203-0300355 (6941)
2009: 10^{0}S, 10^{3}GF, 12^{0}G, 12^{0}GF, 10^{3}G, 12^{5}G, 12^{5}SD,

	Starts	1st	2nd	3rd	Win & Pl
Career Total (Turf)	12	0	1	3	3917
Career Total (AW)	1	0	0	0	0

Going (Turf): Sf: 0-1 GS: 0-1 Gd: 0-7 GF: 0-3 Fm: 0-0
Distance: 5f/6f: 0-0 7f-8f: 0-2 9f-13f: 0-11 14f+: 0-0
Track : LH: 0-8 RH: 0-3 Tight: 0-2 Gall: 0-4
Aids: Bl: 0-0 Vi: 0-0 Tstrap: 0-0 Ckp: 0-0
Best Rating: 80 8/09 Wwck 1m2f188y good

Fair; effective over 1m-1m2f; acts on good ground.

Holiday Cocktail

81 (69)81
7-y-o b g Mister Baileys-Bermuda Lily (Dunbeath (USA))
J J Quinn Estio Racing

Placings:0/230041/22033004/01201200/030013101130-00 (6648)
2009: 12^{0}S, 10^{0}G,

	Starts	1st	2nd	3rd	Win & Pl
Career Total (Turf)	26	5	2	5	21248
Career Total (AW)	11	2	3	1	7504

81	8/08	Pont	1m2f6y	(0-75)H	GD	£3747
75	7/08	Pont	1m2f6y	(0-70)H	G-F	£4533
73	7/08	Pont	1m2f6y	(0-70)H	GD	£3238
65	6/08	Rdcr	1m2f	(0-70)H	G-F	£2331
69	6/07	Carl	7f200y	(0-65)H	GD	£2047
62	3/07	Wolv	1m141y		STD	£2047
68	12/05	Ling	7f	(0-60)H	STD	£2540

Total win prize-money £20486

Going (Turf): Sf: 0-6 GS: 0-4 Gd: 3-8 GF: 2-8 Fm: 0-0
Distance: 5f/6f: 0-4 7f-8f: 2-6 9f-13f: 5-27 14f+: 0-0
Track : LH: 6-28 RH: 1-3 Tight: 3-17 Gall: 0-2
Aids: Bl: 0-0 Vi: 1-3 Tstrap: 3-7 Ckp: 3-7
Best Rating: 81 8/08 Pont 1m2f6y good

Fair; effective over 1m2f; acts on fast ground; also goes on Polytrack.

Holkham

72(78) (52)33
2-y-o ch g Beat Hollow-Spring Sixpence (Dowsing (USA))
N P Littmoden Franconson Partners

Placings:505 (6026)
2009: 5^{5}GF, 7^{0}G, 5^{5}SD,

	Starts	1st	2nd	3rd	Win & Pl
Career Total (Turf)	2	0	0	0	103
Career Total (AW)	1	0	0	0	0

Going (Turf): Sf: 0-0 GS: 0-0 Gd: 0-1 GF: 0-1 Fm: 0-0
Distance: 5f/6f: 0-2 7f-8f: 0-1 9f-13f: 0-0 14f+: 0-0
Track : LH: 0-2 RH: 0-0 Tight: 0-1 Gall: 0-0
Aids: Bl: 0-0 Vi: 0-0 Tstrap: 0-0 Ckp: 0-0
Best Rating: 52 9/09 Wolv 5f216y stand

Hollins

101 79
5-y-o b g Lost Soldier (USA)-Cutting Reef (IRE) (Kris)
Micky Hammond R D Bickenson

Placings:23250-1400 (6681)
2009: 10^{1}GS, 10^{4}G, 10^{0}S, 12^{0}G,

	Starts	1st	2nd	3rd	Win & Pl
Career Total (Turf)	9	1	2	1	7781

79	7/09	Pont	1m2f6y	(0-85)H	G-S	£5180

Total win prize-money £181

Going (Turf): Sf: 0-3 GS: 1-2 Gd: 0-3 GF: 0-1 Fm: 0-0
Distance: 5f/6f: 0-0 7f-8f: 0-0 9f-13f: 1-7 14f+: 0-2
Track : LH: 1-7 RH: 0-2 Tight: 0-4 Gall: 0-3
Aids: Bl: 0-0 Vi: 0-0 Tstrap: 0-0 Ckp: 0-0
Best Rating: 79 7/09 Pont 1m2f6y gd-sft

Fair; effective at 1m2f-1m4f; acts on good and easy ground.

Hollow Green (IRE)

103(72) (41)88
3-y-o b f Beat Hollow-Three Greens (Niniski (USA))
P D Evans Raymond N R Auld

Placings:00441002000-100161251161340000 (7291)
2009: 10^{1}GF, 12^{0}GF, 12^{0}GF, 11^{1}G, 10^{6}GF, 11^{1}GF, 11^{2}G, 10^{5}GF, 10^{1}G, 11^{1}G, 10^{6}G, 10^{1}S, 10^{3}GF, 12^{4}GF, 10^{0}G, 10^{0}GS, 12^{0}G, 10^{0}S,

	Starts	1st	2nd	3rd	Win & Pl
Career Total (Turf)	25	7	2	1	34135
Career Total (AW)	4	0	0	0	

88	8/09	Ayr	1m2f	(0-85)H	SFT	£6231
78	7/09	Wind	1m3f135y	(0-70)H	GD	£2729
82	7/09	Ffos	1m2f	(0-95)H	GD	£7771
69	6/09	Wind	1m3f135y	(0-70)H	G-F	£2729
56	6/09	Wind	1m3f135y		GD	£2729
60	5/09	Wind	1m2f7y		G-F	£2388
60	9/08	Leic	7f9y		HVY	£1942

Total win prize-money £26523

Going (Turf): Sf: 2-4 GS: 0-4 Gd: 3-7 GF: 2-10 Fm: 0-0
Distance: 5f/6f: 0-1 7f-8f: 1-7 9f-13f: 6-21 14f+: 0-0
Track : LH: 2-13 RH: 1-8 Tight: 4-14 Gall: 1-6
Aids: Bl: 0-0 Vi: 0-2 Tstrap: 0-0 Ckp: 0-0
Best Rating: 88 8/09 Ayr 1m2f soft

Useful; effective at 1m2f-1m4f; acts on good and soft ground.

Hollow Jo

89(108) (69)49
9-y-o b g Most Welcome-Sir Hollow (USA) (Sir Ivor (USA))
J R Jenkins Mrs Wendy Jenkins

Placings:000/2111120/0040/0004004311/1315340303302 511/51000006600100000250/06133600000006036-10613100044542 (7890)
2009: 6^{1}SD, 7^{0}SD, 6^{6}SD, 5^{1}SD, 5^{3}SD, 6^{1}SD, 6^{0}SD, 6^{0}SD, 6^{0}GF, 6^{4}SD, 6^{4}SD, 6^{5}SD, 5^{4}SS, 6^{2}SD,

	Starts	1st	2nd	3rd	Win & Pl
Career Total (Turf)	25	4	2	0	17072
Career Total (AW)	65	12	3	10	33955

69	2/09	Ling	6f	(0-55)H	STD	£1878
64	2/09	Kemp	5f	(0-55)H	STD	£2388
60	1/09	Kemp	6f	(0-54)H	STD	£2047
74	2/08	Kemp	5f	(0-65)H	STD	£2047
74	9/07	Kemp	6f	(0-65)H	STD	£2047
81	1/07	Kemp	5f	(0-70)H	STD	£3238
79	12/06	Ling	6f	(0-65)H	STD	£3238
72	12/06	Kemp	6f	(0-70)H	STD	£3886
68	2/06	Ling	1m	(0-65)H	STD	£2388
62	1/06	Ling	6f	(0-58)H	STD	£2047
61	12/05	Ling	6f	(0-55)H	STD	£2158
56	12/05	Ling	7f	(0-45)	STD	£1457
77	8/03	Wind	6f	F(0-65)H	GD	£3276
67	8/03	Carl	5f193y	F(0-60)H	G-F	£3528
58	6/03	Muss	7f30y	F(0-60)H	G-F	£3339
61	6/03	Thsk	6f	E(0-70)H	FRM	£3623

Total win prize-money £42592

Going (Turf): Sf: 0-2 GS: 0-3 Gd: 1-5 GF: 2-14 Fm: 1-1
Distance: 5f/6f: 13-54 7f-8f: 3-35 9f-13f: 0-1 14f+: 0-0
Track : LH: 6-32 RH: 8-35 Tight: 7-27 Gall: 1-10
Aids: Bl: 0-0 Vi: 2-11 Tstrap: 0-1 Ckp: 0-1

Best Rating: 81 1/07 Kemp 5f stand

Modest; effective from 5f-1m; acts on fast ground, but best on Polytrack; has worn a tongue tie and a visor.

Hollywood George

(96) (57)**55**

5-y-o b g Royal Applause-Aunt Tate (Tate Gallery (USA))

Miss M E Rowland Miss M E Rowland

Placings:331/32461/00064020000360200-0 (0130)

2009: 8^{0}SD,

	Starts	1st	2nd	3rd	Win & Pl
Career Total (Turf)	5	0	1	0	605
Career Total (AW)	21	2	2	4	9628

57	4/07	Wolv	7f32y	STD	£2047
66	12/06	Wolv	5f216y	STD	£3238

Total win prize-money £5287

Going (Turf): Sf: 0-1 GS: 0-0 Gd: 0-2 GF: 0-1 Fm: 0-1
Distance: 5f/6f: 1-11 7f-8f: 1-15 9f-13f: 0-0 14f+: 0-0
Track : LH: 2-17 RH: 0-5 Tight: 2-10 Gall: 0-2
Aids: Bl: 0-1 Vi: 0-0 Tstrap: 1-13 Ckp: 1-13
Best Rating: 73 12/06 Wolv 5f216y stand

Plater; stays 1m and acts on Polytrack.

Holoko Heights

99(94) (61)**65**

4-y-o br g Pivotal-Treble Heights (IRE) (Unfuwain (USA))

Tim Vaughan (N J Vaughan 3/6) Owen Promotions Limited

Placings:0004331 (2592)

2009: 8^{0}SD, 7^{0}SD, 7^{0}SD, 10^{4}GF, 12^{3}SD, 12^{3}GS, 15^{1}GF,

	Starts	1st	2nd	3rd	Win & Pl
Career Total (Turf)	3	1	0	1	2613
Career Total (AW)	4	0	0	1	302

65	6/09	Ayr	1m7f	(0-60)H	G-F	£2266

Total win prize-money £2267

Going (Turf): Sf: 0-0 GS: 0-1 Gd: 0-0 GF: 1-2 Fm: 0-0
Distance: 5f/6f: 0-0 7f-8f: 0-3 9f-13f: 0-3 14f+: 1-1
Track : LH: 1-5 RH: 0-2 Tight: 0-2 Gall: 0-1
Aids: Bl: 0-0 Vi: 0-0 Tstrap: 1-1 Ckp: 1-1
Best Rating: 65 6/09 Ayr 1m7f gd-fm

Moderate; stays 1m7f, also effective at shorter; acts on fast turf; handles Polytrack; has worn cheekpieces.

Holyfield Warrior (IRE)

(99) (65)**28**

5-y-o b g Princely Heir (IRE)-Perugino Lady (IRE) (Perugino (USA))

R J Smith AJ Syndicate

Placings:060006/31-123 (7840)

2009: 8^{1}SD, 9^{2}SD, 12^{3}SS,

	Starts	1st	2nd	3rd	Win & Pl
Career Total (Turf)	3	0	0	0	
Career Total (AW)	8	2	1	2	4622

63	11/09	Ling	1m	(0-55)H	STD	£1637
53	2/08	Ling	1m		STD	£1774

Total win prize-money £3413

Going (Turf): Sf: 0-1 GS: 0-1 Gd: 0-0 GF: 0-1 Fm: 0-0
Distance: 5f/6f: 0-0 7f-8f: 2-6 9f-13f: 0-5 14f+: 0-0
Track : LH: 2-10 RH: 0-1 Tight: 2-7 Gall: 0-0
Aids: Bl: 0-0 Vi: 0-0 Tstrap: 0-1 Ckp: 0-1
Best Rating: 65 12/09 Wolv 1m1f103y stand

Moderate; winning hurdler; effective over 1m; acts on Polytrack.

Holyrood

106 **87**

3-y-o b g Falbrav (IRE)-White Palace (Shirley Heights)

Sir Michael Stoute Cheveley Park Stud

Placings:403-1300 (4767)

2009: 10^{1}G, 10^{3}S, 12^{0}G, 12^{0}GS,

	Starts	1st	2nd	3rd	Win & Pl
Career Total (Turf)	7	1	0	2	8002

79	4/09	Yarm	1m2f21y	GD	£2590

Total win prize-money £2590

Going (Turf): Sf: 0-2 GS: 0-1 Gd: 1-3 GF: 0-1 Fm: 0-0
Distance: 5f/6f: 0-0 7f-8f: 0-3 9f-13f: 1-4 14f+: 0-0
Track : LH: 1-2 RH: 0-3 Tight: 1-2 Gall: 0-2
Aids: Bl: 0-0 Vi: 0-1 Tstrap: 0-0 Ckp: 0-0
Best Rating: 87 8/09 Asct 1m4f gd-sft

Useful; effective over 1m2f; acts on good ground; has worn visor.

Home

100(108) (64)**67**

4-y-o b g Domedriver (IRE)-Swahili (IRE) (Kendor (FR))

C Gordon JFK Partnership

Placings:0300334322/1134120413000-0265003 (7751)

2009: 12^{0}SD, 13^{2}SD, 13^{6}SD, 16^{5}SD, 14^{0}GF, 16^{0}SD, 13^{3}SD,

	Starts	1st	2nd	3rd	Win & Pl
Career Total (Turf)	9	0	0	4	2121
Career Total (AW)	21	4	4	3	9977

70	3/08	Sthl	1m3f	STD	£1774
73	1/08	Sthl	1m	STD	£2047
69	1/08	Sthl	1m	STD	£1774

Total win prize-money £5598

Going (Turf): Sf: 0-0 GS: 0-5 Gd: 0-2 GF: 0-2 Fm: 0-0
Distance: 5f/6f: 0-2 7f-8f: 2-8 9f-13f: 2-15 14f+: 0-5
Track : LH: 4-19 RH: 0-7 Tight: 0-14 Gall: 0-1
Aids: Bl: 0-0 Vi: 0-1 Tstrap: 4-12 Ckp: 4-12
Best Rating: 73 1/08 Sthl 1m stand

Moderate; stays 1m3f; acts on good and easier ground; also goes on sand.

Home Advantage

70 **28**

2-y-o b c Beat Hollow-Houseproud (USA) (Riverman (USA))

R Charlton K Abdulla

Placings:0 (6792)

2009: 8^{0}S,

	Starts	1st	2nd	3rd	Win & Pl
Career Total (Turf)	1	0	0	0	

Going (Turf): Sf: 0-1 GS: 0-0 Gd: 0-0 GF: 0-0 Fm: 0-0
Distance: 5f/6f: 0-0 7f-8f: 0-0 9f-13f: 0-1 14f+: 0-0
Track : LH: 0-1 RH: 0-0 Tight: 0-0 Gall: 0-0
Aids: Bl: 0-0 Vi: 0-0 Tstrap: 0-0 Ckp: 0-0
Best Rating: 28 10/09 Nott 1m75y soft

Home Before Dark

81(80) (39)**48**

3-y-o b g Bertolini (USA)-Compton Girl (Compton Place)

R M Whitaker B D Partnership

Placings:04000-0060 (6219)

2009: 7^{0}GF, 6^{0}S, 7^{6}GF, 10^{0}GF,

	Starts	1st	2nd	3rd	Win & Pl
Career Total (Turf)	7	0	0	0	289
Career Total (AW)	2	0	0	0	

Going (Turf): Sf: 0-2 GS: 0-1 Gd: 0-1 GF: 0-3 Fm: 0-0
Distance: 5f/6f: 0-6 7f-8f: 0-2 9f-13f: 0-1 14f+: 0-0
Track : LH: 0-3 RH: 0-2 Tight: 0-2 Gall: 0-1
Aids: Bl: 0-0 Vi: 0-0 Tstrap: 0-0 Ckp: 0-0
Best Rating: 48 8/08 Ripn 6f gd-sft

Homebred Star

93(97) (47)**40**

8-y-o ch g Safawan-Celtic Chimes (Celtic Cone)

G P Enright Homebred Racing

Placings:000/10/04030000/00006/0400 (5975)

2009: 12^{0}SD, 10^{4}SD, 10^{0}F, 11^{0}GF,

	Starts	1st	2nd	3rd	Win & Pl
Career Total (Turf)	7	0	0	0	0
Career Total (AW)	15	1	0	1	1655

51	11/05	Ling	1m	(0-45)	STD	£1453

Total win prize-money £1454

Going (Turf): Sf: 0-0 GS: 0-2 Gd: 0-0 GF: 0-2 Fm: 0-3
Distance: 5f/6f: 0-0 7f-8f: 1-8 9f-13f: 0-14 14f+: 0-0
Track : LH: 1-15 RH: 0-5 Tight: 1-15 Gall: 0-0
Aids: Bl: 0-1 Vi: 0-0 Tstrap: 0-6 Ckp: 0-6
Best Rating: 51 11/05 Ling 1m stand

Honest Broker (IRE)

86(94) (59)**57**

2-y-o b c Trade Fair-Kashra (IRE) (Dancing Dissident (USA))

M Johnston F Towey

Placings:40343 (7722)

2009: 6^{4}GF, 7^{0}G, 7^{3}S, 7^{4}SD, 8^{3}SD,

	Starts	1st	2nd	3rd	Win & Pl
Career Total (Turf)	3	0	0	1	953
Career Total (AW)	2	0	0	1	680

Going (Turf): Sf: 0-1 GS: 0-0 Gd: 0-1 GF: 0-1 Fm: 0-0
Distance: 5f/6f: 0-1 7f-8f: 0-4 9f-13f: 0-0 14f+: 0-0
Track : LH: 0-4 RH: 0-0 Tight: 0-2 Gall: 0-0
Aids: Bl: 0-0 Vi: 0-0 Tstrap: 0-0 Ckp: 0-0
Best Rating: 59 12/09 Sthl 1m stand

Modest; stays 7f; acts on Polytrack.

Honest Quality (USA)

88 **97**

3-y-o b f Elusive Quality (USA)-Honest Lady (USA) (Seattle Slew (USA))

H R A Cecil K Abdulla

Placings:3116-60 (3320)

2009: 8⁶GF, 7⁰GF,

	Starts	1st	2nd	3rd	Win & Pl
Career Total (Turf)	6	2	0	1	24856

97 7/08 Sand 7f16y G-F £17031
89 5/08 York 6f GD £6605
Total win prize-money £23637

Going (Turf): Sf: 0-1 GS: 0-1 **Gd: 1-1 GF: 1-3** Fm: 0-0
Distance: 5f/6f: 1-2 7f-8f: 1-4 9f-13f: 0-0 14f+: 0-0
Track : LH: 0-1 **RH: 1-2** Tight: 0-0 Gall: 0-1
Aids: Bl: 0-0 Vi: 0-0 Tstrap: 0-0 Ckp: 0-0
Best Rating: 97 7/08 Sand 7f16y gd-fm

Very useful; Listed winner; effective over 6f-7f; acts on fast ground.

Honest Value (IRE)

(97) (57)**56**
4-y-o b g Chevalier (IRE)-Sensimelia (IRE) (Inzar (USA))
Mrs L C Jewell Keith C Bennett

Placings:00060/522500000-1 **(0328)**
2009: 5¹SD,

	Starts	1st	2nd	3rd	Win & Pl
Career Total (Turf)	3	0	0	0	0
Career Total (AW)	12	1	2	0	2929

52 1/09 Wolv 5f20y (0-45) STD £1619
Total win prize-money £1619

Going (Turf): Sf: 0-0 GS: 0-0 Gd: 0-1 GF: 0-1 Fm: 0-1
Distance: 5f/6f: 1-13 7f-8f: 0-2 9f-13f: 0-0 14f+: 0-0
Track : LH: 1-6 RH: 0-6 **Tight: 1-3** Gall: 0-4
Aids: Bl: 0-0 **Vi: 1-1** Tstrap: 0-6 Ckp: 0-6
Best Rating: 57 3/08 Kemp 5f stand

Plating-class; best at sprint trips; has worn cheekpieces and a visor.

Honey Berry (IRE)

100(84) (41)**41**
3-y-o ch f Captain Rio-Daggers At Dawn (IRE) (Daggers Drawn (USA))
Patrick Morris Mrs Helen Jane Lloyd

Placings:600666 **(3498)**
2009: 6⁶SD, 5⁰SD, 6⁰F, 5⁶G, 6⁶F, 5⁶GF,

	Starts	1st	2nd	3rd	Win & Pl
Career Total (Turf)	4	0	0	0	0
Career Total (AW)	2	0	0	0	0

Going (Turf): Sf: 0-0 GS: 0-0 Gd: 0-1 GF: 0-1 Fm: 0-2
Distance: 5f/6f: 0-6 7f-8f: 0-0 9f-13f: 0-0 14f+: 0-0
Track : LH: 0-3 RH: 0-1 Tight: 0-2 Gall: 0-0
Aids: Bl: 0-0 Vi: 0-3 Tstrap: 0-0 Ckp: 0-0
Best Rating: 41 6/09 Ayr 6f firm

Honimiere (IRE)

108 **97**
3-y-o b f Fasliyev (USA)-Sugar (Hernando (FR))
G A Swinbank Gary A Tanaka

Placings:444-4413114210 **(6813)**
2009: 8⁴GF, 7⁴GF, 9¹GF, 8³S, 9¹G, 9¹GF, 8⁴GS, 9²GF, 10¹GF, 10⁰G,

	Starts	1st	2nd	3rd	Win & Pl
Career Total (Turf)	13	4	1	1	38644

97 9/09 NmkR 1m2f (0-100)H G-F £12952
88 7/09 Bevl 1m1f207y (0-85)H G-F £5180
87 7/09 Bevl 1m1f207y (0-75)H GD £3238
73 6/09 Carl 1m1f61y (0-85)H G-F £6476
Total win prize-money £27847

Going (Turf): Sf: 0-2 GS: 0-2 Gd: 1-2 **GF: 3-7** Fm: 0-0
Distance: 5f/6f: 0-2 7f-8f: 0-3 **9f-13f: 4-8** 14f+: 0-0
Track : LH: 0-0 **RH: 3-6** Tight: 0-1 Gall: 0-0
Aids: Bl: 0-0 Vi: 0-0 Tstrap: 0-0 Ckp: 0-0
Best Rating: 97 9/09 NmkR 1m2f gd-fm

Useful; stays 1m2f and acts on fast ground.

Honkey Tonk Tony (IRE)

(93) (34)**78**
4-y-o b c On The Ridge (IRE)-Lisa's Girl (IRE) (Distinctly North (USA))
Luke Comer Luke Comer

Placings:0/050060-000 **(7129)**
2009: 9⁰SD, 12⁰SD, 7⁰SD,

	Starts	1st	2nd	3rd	Win & Pl
Career Total (Turf)	4	0	0	0	
Career Total (AW)	6	0	0	0	0

Going (Turf): Sf: 0-2 GS: 0-0 Gd: 0-0 GF: 0-2 Fm: 0-0
Distance: 5f/6f: 0-4 7f-8f: 0-3 9f-13f: 0-3 14f+: 0-0
Track : LH: 0-8 RH: 0-0 Tight: 0-4 Gall: 0-0
Aids: Bl: 0-1 Vi: 0-0 Tstrap: 0-1 Ckp: 0-1
Best Rating: 78 5/08 Leop 6f gd-fm

Honor In Peace (USA)

50 (90)
2-y-o b c Peace Rules (USA)-Jeanne's Honor (USA) (Honour And Glory (USA))
Wesley A Ward Kenneth L & Sarah K Ramsey

Placings:310 **(3138)**
2009: 4³FT, 5¹FT, 7⁰GF,

	Starts	1st	2nd	3rd	Win & Pl
Career Total (Turf)	1	0	0	0	
Career Total (AW)	2	1	0	1	19472

90 5/09 Chur 5f FST £16416
Total win prize-money £16417

Going (Turf): Sf: 0-0 GS: 0-0 Gd: 0-0 GF: 0-1 Fm: 0-0
Distance: 5f/6f: 1-1 7f-8f: 0-1 9f-13f: 0-0 14f+: 0-0
Track : LH: 0-0 RH: 0-0 Tight: 0-0 Gall: 0-0
Aids: Bl: 1-3 Vi: 0-0 Tstrap: 0-0 Ckp: 0-0
Best Rating: 90 5/09 Chur 5f fast

US-trained juvenile; effective over 5f on dirt; wears blinkers.

Honorable Endeavor

102(97) (63)**61**
3-y-o b g Law Society (USA)-Lilac Dance (Fabulous Dancer (USA))
E F Vaughan A M Pickering

Placings:0045-204202450 **(7635)**
2009: 8²SD, 10⁰SD, 14⁴S, 15²GF, 14⁰G, 16²SD, 12⁴SS, 16⁵SD, 14⁰SD,

	Starts	1st	2nd	3rd	Win & Pl
Career Total (Turf)	6	0	1	0	1392
Career Total (AW)	7	0	2	0	1310

Going (Turf): Sf: 0-1 GS: 0-1 Gd: 0-2 GF: 0-2 Fm: 0-0
Distance: 5f/6f: 0-1 7f-8f: 0-3 9f-13f: 0-3 14f+: 0-6
Track : LH: 0-10 RH: 0-2 Tight: 0-6 Gall: 0-1
Aids: Bl: 0-0 Vi: 0-4 Tstrap: 0-3 Ckp: 0-3
Best Rating: 63 9/09 Kemp 2m stand

Moderate; stays 1m4f; acts on Polytrack; has worn cheekpeices and a visor.

Honoured (IRE)

(81) (49)
2-y-o ch g Mark Of Esteem (IRE)-Traou Mad (IRE) (Barathea (IRE))
Sir Mark Prescott Charles C Walker - Osborne House

Placings:000 **(7522)**
2009: 7⁰SD, 7⁰SD, 8⁰SD,

	Starts	1st	2nd	3rd	Win & Pl
Career Total (Turf)	0	0	0	0	
Career Total (AW)	3	0	0	0	

Going (Turf): Sf: 0-0 GS: 0-0 Gd: 0-0 GF: 0-0 Fm: 0-0
Distance: 5f/6f: 0-0 7f-8f: 0-3 9f-13f: 0-0 14f+: 0-0
Track : LH: 0-3 RH: 0-0 Tight: 0-2 Gall: 0-0
Aids: Bl: 0-0 Vi: 0-0 Tstrap: 0-0 Ckp: 0-0
Best Rating: 49 10/09 Wolv 7f32y stand

Honours Stride (IRE)

101(82) (47)**82**
3-y-o b f Red Ransom (USA)-Dance Parade (USA) (Gone West (USA))
Sir Michael Stoute Saeed Suhail

Placings:03-21 **(2942)**
2009: 9²GF, 10¹GF,

	Starts	1st	2nd	3rd	Win & Pl
Career Total (Turf)	3	1	1	1	4706
Career Total (AW)	1	0	0	0	

82 6/09 Donc 1m2f60y (0-75)H G-F £3238
Total win prize-money £3238

Going (Turf): Sf: 0-0 GS: 0-0 Gd: 0-1 **GF: 1-2** Fm: 0-0
Distance: 5f/6f: 0-0 7f-8f: 0-2 **9f-13f: 1-2** 14f+: 0-0
Track : LH: 1-3 RH: 0-1 Tight: 0-2 **Gall: 1-1**
Aids: Bl: 0-0 Vi: 0-0 Tstrap: 0-0 Ckp: 0-0
Best Rating: 82 6/09 Donc 1m2f60y gd-fm

Fair; stays 1m2f and acts on fast ground.

Hoof It

89 **66**
2-y-o b g Monsieur Bond (IRE)-Forever Bond (Danetime (IRE))
M W Easterby A Chandler & L Westwood

Placings:441 **(4652)**
2009: 6⁴GF, 7⁴G, 6¹GF,

	Starts	1st	2nd	3rd	Win & Pl
Career Total (Turf)	3	1	0	0	3288

66 8/09 Newc 6f G-F £2590
Total win prize-money £2590

Going (Turf): Sf: 0-0 GS: 0-0 Gd: 0-1 **GF: 1-2** Fm: 0-0
Distance: 5f/6f: 1-2 7f-8f: 0-1 9f-13f: 0-0 14f+: 0-0
Track : LH: 0-1 RH: 0-0 Tight: 0-0 Gall: 0-1
Aids: Bl: 0-0 Vi: 0-0 Tstrap: 0-0 Ckp: 0-0
Best Rating: 66 8/09 Newc 6f gd-fm

Fair; should stay 7f but effective at 6f.

Hooligan Sean

92 73

2-y-o ch g Ishiguru (USA)-Sheesha (USA) (Shadeed (USA))

H Candy Henry Candy

Placings:62 **(5722)**

2009: 6^6G, 7^2F,

	Starts	1st	2nd	3rd	Win & Pl
Career Total (Turf)	2	0	1	0	964

Going (Turf): Sf: 0-0 GS: 0-0 Gd: 0-1 GF: 0-0 Fm: 0-1
Distance: 5f/6f: 0-0 7f-8f: 0-2 9f-13f: 0-0 14f+: 0-0
Track : LH: 0-0 RH: 0-0 Tight: 0-0 Gall: 0-0
Aids: Bl: 0-0 Vi: 0-0 Tstrap: 0-0 Ckp: 0-0
Best Rating: 73 9/09 Folk 7f firm

Fair sibling of four winners at 6-7f, including Seamus Shindig; stays 7f; acts on fast ground.

Hope'N'Reason (USA)

78(73) (32)30

2-y-o b/br f Stormy Atlantic (USA)-La Bataille (USA) (Out Of Place (USA))

D M Simcock S R Hope And S W Barrow

Placings:00 **(4711)**

2009: 6^0SD, 5^0GF,

	Starts	1st	2nd	3rd	Win & Pl
Career Total (Turf)	1	0	0	0	
Career Total (AW)	1	0	0	0	

Going (Turf): Sf: 0-0 GS: 0-0 Gd: 0-0 GF: 0-1 Fm: 0-0
Distance: 5f/6f: 0-2 7f-8f: 0-0 9f-13f: 0-0 14f+: 0-0
Track : LH: 0-1 RH: 0-0 Tight: 0-1 Gall: 0-0
Aids: Bl: 0-0 Vi: 0-0 Tstrap: 0-0 Ckp: 0-0
Best Rating: 32 7/09 Ling 6f stand

Hopeful Lady

73 27

3-y-o b f Elmaamul (USA)-Tennessee Star (Teenoso (USA))

I W McInnes Queens Head Racing Club

Placings:04000 **(5972)**

2009: 8^0G, 7^4GF, 7^0GS, 9^0F, 7^0GF,

	Starts	1st	2nd	3rd	Win & Pl
Career Total (Turf)	5	0	0	0	192

Going (Turf): Sf: 0-0 GS: 0-1 Gd: 0-1 GF: 0-2 Fm: 0-1
Distance: 5f/6f: 0-0 7f-8f: 0-4 9f-13f: 0-1 14f+: 0-0
Track : LH: 0-1 RH: 0-2 Tight: 0-1 Gall: 0-0
Aids: Bl: 0-0 Vi: 0-0 Tstrap: 0-0 Ckp: 0-0
Best Rating: 27 6/09 Bevl 7f100y gd-fm

Horatio Carter

107 99

4-y-o b g Bahamian Bounty-Jitterbug (IRE) (Marju (IRE))

K A Ryan T Alderson

Placings:046/00013120-123010000 **(6089)**

2009: 7^1GF, 7^2GS, 7^3G, 7^0GF, 7^1S, 7^0G, 8^0G, 6^0GS, 6^0G,

	Starts	1st	2nd	3rd	Win & Pl
Career Total (Turf)	20	4	2	2	31542

99	6/09	Newc	7f	(0-100)H	SFT	£12462
93	5/09	Thsk	7f	(0-85)H	G-F	£5569
83	8/08	Carl	6f192y	(0-85)H	GD	£4857
80	7/08	Carl	6f192y	(0-70)H	GD	£3238

Total win prize-money £26126

Going (Turf): Sf: 1-4 GS: 0-4 **Gd: 2-7** GF: 1-4 Fm: 0-1
Distance: 5f/6f: 0-6 **7f-8f: 4-14** 9f-13f: 0-0 14f+: 0-0
Track : LH: 1-4 **RH: 2-5 Tight: 1-5** Gall: 0-0
Aids: Bl: 0-0 Vi: 0-0 Tstrap: 3-11 Ckp: 3-11
Best Rating: 99 6/09 Newc 7f soft

Very useful; effective at 6f-7f; handles fast and easy ground; has worn cheekpieces.

Horseford Hill

89(106) (85)90

5-y-o b g In The Wings-Love Of Silver (USA) (Arctic Tern (USA))

Miss J R Tooth (N J Henderson 14/5) Raymond Tooth

Placings:610160/20060-0 **(6851)**

2009: 18^0G,

	Starts	1st	2nd	3rd	Win & Pl
Career Total (Turf)	11	2	1	0	11664
Career Total (AW)	1	0	0	0	0

86	8/07	NmkJ	1m4f	(0-85)H	GD	£5181
68	6/07	NmkJ	1m2f		GD	£5181

Total win prize-money £10364

Going (Turf): Sf: 0-2 GS: 0-0 **Gd: 2-6** GF: 0-3 Fm: 0-0
Distance: 5f/6f: 0-0 7f-8f: 0-0 **9f-13f: 2-7** 14f+: 0-5
Track : LH: 0-2 **RH: 2-9** Tight: 0-1 **Gall: 2-7**
Aids: Bl: 0-1 Vi: 0-0 Tstrap: 0-0 Ckp: 0-0
Best Rating: 90 6/08 Sals 1m4f gd-fm

Useful; winning hurdler; stays 1m4f; acts on good and faster ground; regularly held up.

Horseradish

98(96) (76)77

2-y-o b g Kyllachy-Lihou Island (Beveled (USA))

M L W Bell Mrs G Rowland-Clark

Placings:221 **(6796)**

2009: 6^2GS, 6^2SD, 6^1S,

	Starts	1st	2nd	3rd	Win & Pl
Career Total (Turf)	2	1	1	0	3583
Career Total (AW)	1	0	1	0	1209

77	10/09	Nott	6f15y	SFT	£2388

Total win prize-money £2388

Going (Turf): Sf: 1-1 GS: 0-1 Gd: 0-0 GF: 0-0 Fm: 0-0
Distance: 5f/6f: 0-2 **7f-8f: 1-1** 9f-13f: 0-0 14f+: 0-0
Track : LH: 0-1 RH: 0-0 Tight: 0-0 Gall: 0-0
Aids: Bl: 0-0 Vi: 0-0 Tstrap: 0-0 Ckp: 0-0
Best Rating: 77 10/09 Nott 6f15y soft

Fair; suited by 6f and acts on easy ground.

Horseshoe Reef (AUS)

94(104) (81)70

6-y-o b g Encosta De Lago (AUS)-Christies Beach (AUS) (Naturalism (NZ))

G L Moore (J R Gask 21/7) For Sale

Placings:015052113/103303-**20530030** **(4169)**

2009: 10^2SD, 12^0SD, 13^5SD, 11^3SD, 11^0GF, 10^0SD, 11^3GF, 12^0G,

	Starts	1st	2nd	3rd	Win & Pl
Career Total (Turf)	18	4	1	5	27450
Career Total (AW)	5	0	1	1	1830

1/08	Sann	1m4f	H	GD	£6872
12/07	Moon	1m7f	H	GD	£9008
12/07	Pake	1m4f	H	G-S	£2475
3/07	Arar	1m2f		GD	£2358

Total win prize-money £20715

Going (Turf): Sf: 0-2 GS: 1-2 **Gd: 3-10** GF: 0-2 Fm: 0-0
Distance: 5f/6f: 0-0 7f-8f: 0-2 **9f-13f: 3-16** 14f+: 1-5
Track : LH: 0-8 RH: 0-0 Tight: 0-5 Gall: 0-2
Aids: Bl: 0-0 Vi: 0-0 Tstrap: 0-4 Ckp: 0-4
Best Rating: 81 1/09 Ling 1m2f stand

Modest; stays 1m7f; acts on fast ground; has worn cheek-pieces.

Horsley Warrior

86(101) (71)65

3-y-o b c Alhaarth (IRE)-Polish Lake (Polish Precedent (USA))

E S McMahon Mrs J McMahon

Placings:3-0200 **(3466)**

2009: 10^0GF, 11^2SD, 12^0GF, 12^0SD,

	Starts	1st	2nd	3rd	Win & Pl
Career Total (Turf)	3	0	0	1	433
Career Total (AW)	2	0	1	0	1445

Going (Turf): Sf: 0-1 GS: 0-0 Gd: 0-0 GF: 0-2 Fm: 0-0
Distance: 5f/6f: 0-0 7f-8f: 0-0 9f-13f: 0-5 14f+: 0-0
Track : LH: 0-4 RH: 0-0 Tight: 0-1 Gall: 0-1
Aids: Bl: 0-0 Vi: 0-0 Tstrap: 0-0 Ckp: 0-0
Best Rating: 71 5/09 Sthl 1m3f stand

Fair-looking sort; stays at least 1m3f; acts on soft ground and Fibresand.

Hosanna

96(96) (67)54

3-y-o b f Oasis Dream-Rada's Daughter (Robellino (USA))

J Barclay A Barclay

Placings:000552-0006002 **(6410)**

2009: 8^0G, 6^0G, 6^0S, 7^6G, 5^0GF, 5^0G, 5^2GF,

	Starts	1st	2nd	3rd	Win & Pl
Career Total (Turf)	11	0	1	0	1000
Career Total (AW)	2	0	1	0	781

Going (Turf): Sf: 0-1 GS: 0-1 Gd: 0-4 GF: 0-5 Fm: 0-0
Distance: 5f/6f: 0-8 7f-8f: 0-5 9f-13f: 0-0 14f+: 0-0
Track : LH: 0-2 RH: 0-2 Tight: 0-1 Gall: 0-1
Aids: Bl: 0-1 Vi: 0-0 Tstrap: 0-0 Ckp: 0-0
Best Rating: 67 10/08 Kemp 6f stand

Plating-class; effective at 5f; acts on fast ground and Polytrack.

Hoss Cartwright (IRE)

86 73

2-y-o b g High Chaparral (IRE)-Her Grace (IRE) (Spectrum (IRE))

J Howard Johnson J Howard Johnson

Placings:421 **(4811)**

2009: 7^4G, 7^2GS, 7^1HY,

	Starts	1st	2nd	3rd	Win & Pl
Career Total (Turf)	3	1	1	0	7001

73	8/09	Leic	7f9y	HVY	£5180

Total win prize-money £5181

Going (Turf): Sf: 1-1 GS: 0-1 Gd: 0-1 GF: 0-0 Fm: 0-0

Distance: 5f/6f: 0-0 **7f-8f: 1-3** 9f-13f: 0-0 14f+: 0-0
Track : LH: 0-1 RH: 0-0 Tight: 0-0 Gall: 0-1
Aids: Bl: 0-0 Vi: 0-0 Tstrap: 0-0 Ckp: 0-0
Best Rating: **73** 8/09 Leic 7f9y heavy

Fair; stays 7f; acts on heavy ground.

Hot Chilli

(82) (55)
2-y-o gr f Verglas (IRE)-Hot And Spicy (Grand Lodge (USA))
J R Fanshawe T R G Vestey

Placings:0 **(6372)**
2009: 7^{0}SD,

	Starts	1st	2nd	3rd	Win & Pl
Career Total (Turf)	0	0	0	0	
Career Total (AW)	1	0	0	0	

Going (Turf): **Sf: 0-0 GS: 0-0 Gd: 0-0 GF: 0-0 Fm: 0-0**
Distance: 5f/6f: 0-0 7f-8f: 0-1 9f-13f: 0-0 14f+: 0-0
Track : LH: 0-0 RH: 0-1 Tight: 0-0 Gall: 0-0
Aids: Bl: 0-0 Vi: 0-0 Tstrap: 0-0 Ckp: 0-0
Best Rating: **55** 9/09 Kemp 7f stand

Out of a half-sister to the Italian Oaks winner Zanzibar and the useful middle-distance performer New Guinea.

Hot Diamond

92 (62)80
5-y-o b g Desert Prince (IRE)-Panna (Polish Precedent (USA))
P J Hobbs Louisville Syndicate

Placings:6004614333/5-0 **(2706)**
2009: 12^{0}G,

	Starts	1st	2nd	3rd	Win & Pl
Career Total (Turf)	11	1	0	3	7507
Career Total (AW)	1	0	0	0	0

81 8/07 Sals 1m1f198y (0-70)H G-S £3238
Total win prize-money £3239

Going (Turf): Sf: 0-0 **GS: 1-4** Gd: 0-5 GF: 0-1 Fm: 0-1
Distance: 5f/6f: 0-0 7f-8f: 0-2 **9f-13f: 1-7** 14f+: 0-3
Track : LH: 0-3 **RH: 1-7 Tight: 1-4** Gall: 0-5
Aids: Bl: 0-0 Vi: 0-0 Tstrap: 0-0 Ckp: 0-0
Best Rating: **89** 10/07 Donc 1m6f132y good

Useful gelding; stays 1m6f; acts on good and softer ground but handles fast.

Hot Form

(84) (45)
2-y-o b f Dr Fong (USA)-Hot Tin Roof (IRE) (Thatching)
M Botti Mrs R J Jacobs

Placings:6 **(6913)**
2009: 6^{6}SD,

	Starts	1st	2nd	3rd	Win & Pl
Career Total (Turf)	0	0	0	0	
Career Total (AW)	1	0	0	0	0

Going (Turf): **Sf: 0-0 GS: 0-0 Gd: 0-0 GF: 0-0 Fm: 0-0**
Distance: 5f/6f: 0-1 7f-8f: 0-0 9f-13f: 0-0 14f+: 0-0
Track : LH: 0-1 RH: 0-0 Tight: 0-1 Gall: 0-0
Aids: Bl: 0-0 Vi: 0-0 Tstrap: 0-0 Ckp: 0-0
Best Rating: **45** 10/09 Ling 6f stand

Hot Prospect

107 91
2-y-o b c Motivator-Model Queen (USA) (Kingmambo (USA))
M A Jarvis A D Spence

Placings:216 **(6898)**
2009: 7^{2}G, 8^{1}GF, 8^{6}GF,

	Starts	1st	2nd	3rd	Win & Pl
Career Total (Turf)	3	1	1	0	7195

91 9/09 Sand 1m14y G-F £5180
Total win prize-money £5181

Going (Turf): Sf: 0-0 GS: 0-0 Gd: 0-1 **GF: 1-2** Fm: 0-0
Distance: 5f/6f: 0-0 7f-8f: 0-1 **9f-13f: 1-2** 14f+: 0-0
Track : LH: 0-2 **RH: 1-1** Tight: 0-0 Gall: 0-1
Aids: Bl: 0-0 Vi: 0-0 Tstrap: 0-0 Ckp: 0-0
Best Rating: **91** 9/09 Sand 1m14y gd-fm

Stays 7f; handles good ground; 230,000gn son of Motivator.

Hot Pursuits

99(96) (76)62
2-y-o br f Pastoral Pursuits-Perfect Partner (Be My Chief (USA))
H Morrison Mrs I Eavis

Placings:03301 **(6903)**
2009: 6^{0}G, 6^{3}SD, 6^{3}SD, 7^{0}GF, 5^{1}G,

	Starts	1st	2nd	3rd	Win & Pl
Career Total (Turf)	3	1	0	0	2730
Career Total (AW)	2	0	0	2	931

62 10/09 Wind 5f10y GD £2729
Total win prize-money £2730

Going (Turf): Sf: 0-0 GS: 0-0 **Gd: 1-2** GF: 0-1 Fm: 0-0
Distance: **5f/6f: 1-4** 7f-8f: 0-1 9f-13f: 0-0 14f+: 0-0
Track : LH: 0-1 RH: 0-1 Tight: 0-1 **Gall: 1-1**
Aids: Bl: 0-0 Vi: 0-0 Tstrap: 0-0 Ckp: 0-0
Best Rating: **76** 6/09 Kemp 6f stand

Fair; stays 6f; acts on Polytrack and good ground on turf.

Hot Rod Mamma (IRE)

95(85) (42)58
2-y-o ch f Traditionally (USA)-Try The Air (IRE) (Foxhound (USA))
A Berry Alan Berry

Placings:0564030 **(7331)**
2009: 6^{0}G, 5^{5}GF, 5^{6}G, 5^{4}GF, 5^{0}GF, 5^{3}S, 5^{0}SD,

	Starts	1st	2nd	3rd	Win & Pl
Career Total (Turf)	6	0	0	1	353
Career Total (AW)	1	0	0	0	

Going (Turf): **Sf: 0-1 GS: 0-0 Gd: 0-2 GF: 0-3 Fm: 0-0**
Distance: 5f/6f: 0-7 7f-8f: 0-0 9f-13f: 0-0 14f+: 0-0
Track : LH: 0-3 RH: 0-0 Tight: 0-2 Gall: 0-0
Aids: Bl: 0-0 Vi: 0-0 Tstrap: 0-0 Ckp: 0-0
Best Rating: **58** 7/09 Ches 5f16y gd-fm

Hot Spark

79(91) (75)57
2-y-o b c Firebreak-On The Brink (Mind Games)
K A Ryan T G & Mrs M E Holdcroft

Placings:62 **(6493)**
2009: 6^{6}S, 5^{2}SF,

	Starts	1st	2nd	3rd	Win & Pl
Career Total (Turf)	1	0	0	0	0
Career Total (AW)	1	0	1	0	964

Going (Turf): **Sf: 0-1 GS: 0-0 Gd: 0-0 GF: 0-0 Fm: 0-0**
Distance: 5f/6f: 0-2 7f-8f: 0-0 9f-13f: 0-0 14f+: 0-0
Track : LH: 0-1 RH: 0-0 Tight: 0-1 Gall: 0-0
Aids: Bl: 0-0 Vi: 0-0 Tstrap: 0-0 Ckp: 0-0
Best Rating: **75** 10/09 Wolv 5f216y std-fst

£13,000 half-brother to a 1m-1m2f winner; stays 6f; acts on Polytrack.

Hotgrove Boy

82 44
2-y-o b g Tobougg (IRE)-Tanwir (Unfuwain (USA))
A G Foster S F Cawkwell

Placings:600 **(6763)**
2009: 7^{6}GS, 8^{0}GS, 8^{0}GS,

	Starts	1st	2nd	3rd	Win & Pl
Career Total (Turf)	3	0	0	0	0

Going (Turf): **Sf: 0-0 GS: 0-3 Gd: 0-0 GF: 0-0 Fm: 0-0**
Distance: 5f/6f: 0-0 7f-8f: 0-3 9f-13f: 0-0 14f+: 0-0
Track : LH: 0-2 RH: 0-1 Tight: 0-1 Gall: 0-1
Aids: Bl: 0-0 Vi: 0-0 Tstrap: 0-0 Ckp: 0-0
Best Rating: **44** 9/09 Ayr 1m gd-sft

Hotham

106(102) (85)93
6-y-o b g Komaite (USA)-Malcesine (IRE) (Auction Ring (USA))
N Wilson Far 2 Many Sues

Placings:3653/001430**350**/060164443321**242**/6360245001321000-0000003241525120214 **(6994)**
2009: 5^{0}GF, 6^{0}GF, 5^{0}HY, 5^{0}GF, 6^{0}G, 6^{0}GS, 5^{3}G, 6^{2}G, 6^{4}G, 5^{1}G, 5^{5}GS, 5^{2}GS, 5^{5}GS, 6^{1}GF, 6^{2}GF, 6^{0}G, 5^{2}G, 5^{1}GF, 6^{4}G,

	Starts	1st	2nd	3rd	Win & Pl
Career Total (Turf)	57	8	6	8	63927
Career Total (AW)	6	0	3	1	4682

91 10/09 Pont 5f (0-85)H G-F £4857
83 9/09 Rdcr 6f (0-75)H G-F £2590
75 7/09 Pont 5f (0-70)H GD £3238
90 10/08 Muss 5f H G-S £12462
85 9/08 Ayr 5f (0-85)H HVY £6476
76 9/07 Pont 5f (0-75)H G-F £4533
69 6/07 Pont 5f (0-65)H G-F £3238
73 7/06 Bevl 5f FRM £3562
Total win prize-money £40958

Going (Turf): Sf: 1-9 GS: 1-12 Gd: 1-14 **GF: 4-20** Fm: 1-2
Distance: **5f/6f: 8-60** 7f-8f: 0-3 9f-13f: 0-0 14f+: 0-0
Track : **LH: 4-18** RH: 0-2 Tight: 0-10 Gall: 0-2
Aids: Bl: 0-0 Vi: 0-0 Tstrap: 0-0 Ckp: 0-0
Best Rating: **93** 10/09 Donc 6f good

Useful; effective over 5f-6f; acts on most ground and on Polytrack; can start slowly.

Houda (IRE)

84(71) (35)49
2-y-o ch f Trans Island-Islandagore (IRE) (Indian Ridge)
J G Portman Berkeley Racing

Placings:00 **(4980)**
2009: 6^{0}GF, 7^{0}SD,

	Starts	1st	2nd	3rd	Win & Pl
Career Total (Turf)	1	0	0	0	

	Starts	1st	2nd	3rd	Win & Pl
Career Total (AW)	1	0	0	0	

Going (Turf): **Sf: 0-0 GS: 0-0 Gd: 0-0 GF: 0-1 Fm: 0-0**
Distance: 5f/6f: 0-1 7f-8f: 0-1 9f-13f: 0-0 14f+: 0-0
Track : LH: 0-0 RH: 0-1 Tight: 0-0 Gall: 0-1
Aids: Bl: 0-0 Vi: 0-0 Tstrap: 0-0 Ckp: 0-0
Best Rating: **49** 8/09 Wind 6f gd-fm

Houdella

77 **22**
3-y-o b f Josr Algarhoud (IRE)-Norbella (Nordico (USA))
B W Hills Philip G Harvey

Placings:0-00 **(2151)**
2009: 8^{0}GF, 5^{0}G,

	Starts	1st	2nd	3rd	Win & Pl
Career Total (Turf)	3	0	0	0	

Going (Turf): **Sf: 0-1 GS: 0-0 Gd: 0-1 GF: 0-1 Fm: 0-0**
Distance: 5f/6f: 0-2 7f-8f: 0-0 9f-13f: 0-1 14f+: 0-0
Track : LH: 0-1 RH: 0-0 Tight: 0-0 Gall: 0-0
Aids: Bl: 0-0 Vi: 0-0 Tstrap: 0-0 Ckp: 0-0
Best Rating: **22** 5/09 Leic 5f218y good

Hounds Ditch

(73) (30)**58**
2-y-o b g Avonbridge-Pudding Lane (IRE) (College Chapel)
Eve Johnson Houghton Fighttheban Racing Partnership

Placings:40 **(6356)**
2009: 5^{4}G, 6^{0}SD,

	Starts	1st	2nd	3rd	Win & Pl
Career Total (Turf)	1	0	0	0	289
Career Total (AW)	1	0	0	0	

Going (Turf): **Sf: 0-0 GS: 0-0 Gd: 0-1 GF: 0-0 Fm: 0-0**
Distance: 5f/6f: 0-2 7f-8f: 0-0 9f-13f: 0-0 14f+: 0-0
Track : LH: 0-1 RH: 0-0 Tight: 0-0 Gall: 0-0
Aids: Bl: 0-0 Vi: 0-0 Tstrap: 0-0 Ckp: 0-0
Best Rating: **58** 9/09 Ffos 5f good

Houri (IRE)

97(95) (59)**79**
4-y-o b f Alhaarth (IRE)-Witching Hour (IRE) (Alzao (USA))
J T Stimpson J T Stimpson

Placings:00/0612240**060**-00050 **(6817)**
2009: 9^{0}GF, 10^{0}GF, 10^{0}GF, 12^{5}F, 10^{0}GF,

	Starts	1st	2nd	3rd	Win & Pl
Career Total (Turf)	14	1	2	0	5165
Career Total (AW)	3	0	0	0	0

76 6/08 Nott 1m2f50y (0-75)H G-F £3238
Total win prize-money £3238

Going (Turf): Sf: 0-0 GS: 0-1 Gd: 0-4 **GF: 1-8** Fm: 0-1
Distance: 5f/6f: 0-0 7f-8f: 0-2 **9f-13f: 1-15** 14f+: 0-0
Track : **LH: 1-11** RH: 0-5 Tight: 0-7 Gall: 0-3
Aids: Bl: 0-3 Vi: 0-1 Tstrap: 1-8 Ckp: 1-8
Best Rating: **79** 8/08 Newb 1m2f6y good

Fair; stays 1m2f; acts on fast ground; has worn cheek-pieces.

House Of Frills

90 **61**
2-y-o b f Paris House-Frilly Front (Aragon)
T D Barron M Dalby

Placings:13 **(3559)**
2009: 5^{1}GF, 5^{3}GF,

	Starts	1st	2nd	3rd	Win & Pl
Career Total (Turf)	2	1	0	1	2818

61 4/09 Rdcr 5f G-F £2047
Total win prize-money £2047

Going (Turf): Sf: 0-0 GS: 0-0 Gd: 0-0 **GF: 1-2** Fm: 0-0
Distance: **5f/6f: 1-2** 7f-8f: 0-0 9f-13f: 0-0 14f+: 0-0
Track : LH: 0-0 RH: 0-0 Tight: 0-0 Gall: 0-0
Aids: Bl: 0-0 Vi: 0-0 Tstrap: 0-0 Ckp: 0-0
Best Rating: **61** 4/09 Rdcr 5f gd-fm

Moderate; suited by 5f and fast ground.

House Of Rules

89(73) (24)**60**
2-y-o b g Forzando-Bramble Bear (Beveled (USA))
Miss J A Camacho Miss Julie Camacho

Placings:606 **(6896)**
2009: 6^{6}GF, 6^{0}SD, 6^{6}GF,

	Starts	1st	2nd	3rd	Win & Pl
Career Total (Turf)	2	0	0	0	0
Career Total (AW)	1	0	0	0	

Going (Turf): **Sf: 0-0 GS: 0-0 Gd: 0-0 GF: 0-2 Fm: 0-0**
Distance: 5f/6f: 0-3 7f-8f: 0-0 9f-13f: 0-0 14f+: 0-0
Track : LH: 0-2 RH: 0-0 Tight: 0-0 Gall: 0-0
Aids: Bl: 0-0 Vi: 0-0 Tstrap: 0-0 Ckp: 0-0
Best Rating: **60** 8/09 Rdcr 6f gd-fm

House Point

84 **56**
2-y-o b f Pivotal-Lighthouse (Warning)
S C Williams J W Parry

Placings:0 **(6809)**
2009: 6^{0}G,

	Starts	1st	2nd	3rd	Win & Pl
Career Total (Turf)	1	0	0	0	

Going (Turf): **Sf: 0-0 GS: 0-0 Gd: 0-1 GF: 0-0 Fm: 0-0**
Distance: 5f/6f: 0-1 7f-8f: 0-0 9f-13f: 0-0 14f+: 0-0
Track : LH: 0-0 RH: 0-0 Tight: 0-0 Gall: 0-0
Aids: Bl: 0-0 Vi: 0-0 Tstrap: 0-0 Ckp: 0-0
Best Rating: **56** 10/09 NmkR 6f good

Sister to multiple middle-distance winner Point Of Light, and half-sister to Kehaar, a triple 7f winner at three.

House Red (IRE)

92(101) (67)**73**
2-y-o b g Antonius Pius (USA)-Cindy's Star (IRE) (Dancing Dissident (USA))
B W Hills Richard Morecombe

Placings:050613 **(7359)**
2009: 5^{0}GF, 6^{5}GF, 6^{0}G, 6^{6}GF, 7^{1}GF, 8^{3}SD,

	Starts	1st	2nd	3rd	Win & Pl
Career Total (Turf)	5	1	0	0	2267
Career Total (AW)	1	0	0	1	482

73 10/09 Leic 7f9y (0-65) G-F £2266
Total win prize-money £2267

Going (Turf): Sf: 0-0 GS: 0-0 Gd: 0-1 **GF: 1-4** Fm: 0-0
Distance: 5f/6f: 0-4 **7f-8f: 1-1** 9f-13f: 0-1 14f+: 0-0
Track : LH: 0-1 RH: 0-0 Tight: 0-1 Gall: 0-2
Aids: Bl: 0-0 Vi: 0-0 Tstrap: 0-0 Ckp: 0-0
Best Rating: **73** 10/09 Leic 7f9y gd-fm

Hovering Hawk (IRE)

(74) (39)
2-y-o b f Hawk Wing (USA)-Cause Celebre (IRE) (Peintre Celebre (USA))
B W Hills Triermore Stud

Placings:00 **(7700)**
2009: 7^{0}SD, 7^{0}SD,

	Starts	1st	2nd	3rd	Win & Pl
Career Total (Turf)	0	0	0	0	
Career Total (AW)	2	0	0	0	

Going (Turf): **Sf: 0-0 GS: 0-0 Gd: 0-0 GF: 0-0 Fm: 0-0**
Distance: 5f/6f: 0-0 7f-8f: 0-2 9f-13f: 0-0 14f+: 0-0
Track : LH: 0-1 RH: 0-1 Tight: 0-1 Gall: 0-0
Aids: Bl: 0-0 Vi: 0-0 Tstrap: 0-0 Ckp: 0-0
Best Rating: **39** 11/09 Wolv 7f32y stand

How Many Times (IRE)

(71) (37)**72**
4-y-o b f Okawango (USA)-Blu Tu Miami (USA) (Robin Des Pins (USA))
J R Gask Horses First Racing Limited

Placings:0/332-0 **(0849)**
2009: 8^{0}SD,

	Starts	1st	2nd	3rd	Win & Pl
Career Total (Turf)	3	0	1	2	2752
Career Total (AW)	2	0	0	0	

Going (Turf): **Sf: 0-0 GS: 0-0 Gd: 0-2 GF: 0-0 Fm: 0-0**
Distance: 5f/6f: 0-0 7f-8f: 0-3 9f-13f: 0-2 14f+: 0-0
Track : LH: 0-2 RH: 0-2 Tight: 0-0 Gall: 0-0
Aids: Bl: 0-0 Vi: 0-0 Tstrap: 0-3 Ckp: 0-3
Best Rating: **72** 7/08 Bell 1m good

How's She Cuttin' (IRE)

(107) (99)**93**
6-y-o ch m Shinko Forest (IRE)-Magic Annemarie (IRE) (Dancing Dissident (USA))
T D Barron Christopher McHale

Placings:4012121/1211030/5034305014-3 **(0002)**
2009: 5^{3}SS,

	Starts	1st	2nd	3rd	Win & Pl
Career Total (Turf)	21	6	3	3	46084
Career Total (AW)	4	1	0	1	12624

99 11/08 Sthl 5f (0-95)H STD £8742
94 7/07 Thsk 5f (0-85)H SFT £4857
85 6/07 Muss 5f H GD £9348
85 4/07 Muss 5f (0-70)H G-F £3238
72 11/06 Muss 5f (0-65)H G-S £3238
61 10/06 Muss 5f (0-45) G-S £2218
56 8/06 Ripn 5f HVY £4533
Total win prize-money £36179

Going (Turf): **Sf: 2-4 GS: 2-6** Gd: 1-7 GF: 1-3 Fm: 0-0
Distance: **5f/6f: 7-24** 7f-8f: 0-1 9f-13f: 0-0 14f+: 0-0
Track : LH: 0-3 RH: 0-0 Tight: 0-3 Gall: 0-0
Aids: **Bl: 2-4** Vi: 1-8 Tstrap: 0-0 Ckp: 0-0

Best Rating: 99 11/08 Sthl 5f stand

Very useful; Listed placed; best at 5f and acts on any ground and on sand; has worn blinkers and a visor.

Howard

95 72

3-y-o ch c Haafhd-Dolores (Danehill (USA))

J L Dunlop Normandie Stud Ltd

Placings:650-0045 **(3009)**

2009: 10^{0}G, 10^{0}GF, 8^{4}GF, 7^{5}G,

	Starts	1st	2nd	3rd	Win & Pl
Career Total (Turf)	7	0	0	0	0

Going (Turf): **Sf: 0-0 GS: 0-0 Gd: 0-3 GF: 0-3 Fm: 0-1**
Distance: 5f/6f: 0-0 7f-8f: 0-3 9f-13f: 0-4 14f+: 0-0
Track : LH: 0-1 RH: 0-3 Tight: 0-2 Gall: 0-0
Aids: Bl: 0-0 Vi: 0-0 Tstrap: 0-1 Ckp: 0-1
Best Rating: **72** 6/09 Wind 1m67y gd-fm

Half-brother to smart stayer Samuel; promise in maiden company.

Howards Prince

83 (6)48

6-y-o gr g Bertolini (USA)-Grey Princess (IRE) (Common Grounds)

D A Nolan Miss M McFadyen-Murray

Placings:4641000/6544400/0000/0060054644000-0000600 **(6161)**

2009: 5^{0}GF, 5^{0}F, 5^{0}GF, 5^{0}G, 5^{6}G, 5^{0}S, 5^{0}G,

	Starts	1st	2nd	3rd	Win & Pl
Career Total (Turf)	37	1	0	0	6962
Career Total (AW)	1	0	0	0	
74 7/05 Haml 5f4y			G-F	£4745	

Total win prize-money £4745

Going (Turf): Sf: 0-5 GS: 0-6 Gd: 0-11 **GF: 1-14** Fm: 0-1
Distance: **5f/6f: 1-34** 7f-8f: 0-4 9f-13f: 0-0 14f+: 0-0
Track : LH: 0-1 RH: 0-1 Tight: 0-1 Gall: 0-1
Aids: Bl: 0-2 Vi: 0-0 Tstrap: 1-13 Ckp: 1-13
Best Rating: **74** 7/05 Haml 5f4y gd-fm

Plating-class sprinter; acts on fast and soft ground; successful in cheekpieces.

Howards Tipple

98(99) (66)67

5-y-o b g Diktat-Grey Princess (IRE) (Common Grounds)

I Semple Gordon McDowall

Placings:6333060/43023325133640/10005031354004-0024500040 **(6160)**

2009: 6^{0}GF, 5^{2}GF, 5^{4}G, 6^{5}GF, 6^{0}GF, 6^{0}G, 5^{0}GF, 5^{4}HY, 5^{0}G,

	Starts	1st	2nd	3rd	Win & Pl
Career Total (Turf)	41	2	3	10	13797
Career Total (AW)	4	1	0	0	2218
64 7/08 Haml 5f4y				GD	£2388
66 2/08 Wolv 5f216y (0-60)H				STD	£2218
66 8/07 Ayr 5f (0-65)H				SFT	£2590

Total win prize-money £7197

Going (Turf): **Sf: 1-9** GS: 0-7 **Gd: 1-9** GF: 0-16 Fm: 0-0
Distance: **5f/6f: 3-34** 7f-8f: 0-11 9f-13f: 0-0 14f+: 0-0
Track : **LH: 1-5** RH: 0-2 **Tight: 1-5** Gall: 0-1
Aids: Bl: 0-0 Vi: 0-3 Tstrap: 2-25 Ckp: 2-25
Best Rating: **73** 9/07 Ayr 5f gd-sft

Modest; stays 7f; acts on good and soft ground; has worn a visor, cheekpieces and a tongue tie.

Howards Way

5 62

4-y-o b g Bertolini (USA)-Love Quest (Pursuit Of Love)

D A Nolan Miss M McFadyen-Murray

Placings:4/500-0 **(5727)**

2009: 5^{0}GS,

	Starts	1st	2nd	3rd	Win & Pl
Career Total (Turf)	5	0	0	0	241

Going (Turf): **Sf: 0-1 GS: 0-1 Gd: 0-0 GF: 0-3 Fm: 0-0**
Distance: 5f/6f: 0-4 7f-8f: 0-1 9f-13f: 0-0 14f+: 0-0
Track : LH: 0-0 RH: 0-0 Tight: 0-0 Gall: 0-0
Aids: Bl: 0-0 Vi: 0-0 Tstrap: 0-0 Ckp: 0-0
Best Rating: **62** 5/08 Haml 6f5y gd-fm

Howdigo

104(98) (92)94

4-y-o b g Tobougg (IRE)-Woodrising (Nomination)

J R Best G G Racing

Placings:003332021/601332-03020 **(7018)**

2009: 10^{0}GF, 14^{3}GF, 9^{0}GF, 12^{2}SD, 12^{0}GS,

	Starts	1st	2nd	3rd	Win & Pl
Career Total (Turf)	16	1	2	5	18904
Career Total (AW)	4	1	2	1	5240
85 7/08 Wind 1m3f135y (0-85)H				GD	£5504
78 11/07 Kemp 1m				STD	£2388

Total win prize-money £7894

Going (Turf): Sf: 0-1 GS: 0-1 **Gd: 1-7** GF: 0-6 Fm: 0-1
Distance: 5f/6f: 0-3 7f-8f: 1-5 9f-13f: 1-11 14f+: 0-1
Track : LH: 0-6 **RH: 1-7 Tight: 1-5** Gall: 0-3
Aids: Bl: 0-0 Vi: 0-0 Tstrap: 0-0 Ckp: 0-0
Best Rating: **94** 9/08 Newb 1m4f5y good

Useful; stays 1m6f, but effective over shorter; acts on most ground on turf; goes on Polytrack.

Howdoyalikemenow (IRE)

76 34

2-y-o ch f Captain Rio-Berenice (ITY) (Marouble)

K A Ryan Mrs Gillian Quinn

Placings:0000 **(5942)**

2009: 6^{0}GF, 7^{0}GS, 6^{0}G, 7^{0}G,

	Starts	1st	2nd	3rd	Win & Pl
Career Total (Turf)	4	0	0	0	

Going (Turf): **Sf: 0-0 GS: 0-1 Gd: 0-2 GF: 0-1 Fm: 0-0**
Distance: 5f/6f: 0-1 7f-8f: 0-3 9f-13f: 0-0 14f+: 0-0
Track : LH: 0-0 RH: 0-1 Tight: 0-1 Gall: 0-0
Aids: Bl: 0-2 Vi: 0-0 Tstrap: 0-0 Ckp: 0-0
Best Rating: **34** 5/09 Rdcr 6f gd-fm

Hubble Space

(84) (56)

2-y-o ch f Observatory (USA)-Double Stake (USA) (Kokand (USA))

M Botti Dr Carlini Cozzi & Mrs Sally Doyle

Placings:6040 **(7788)**

2009: 7^{6}SD, 8^{0}SD, 8^{4}SD, 8^{0}SD,

	Starts	1st	2nd	3rd	Win & Pl
Career Total (Turf)	0	0	0	0	
Career Total (AW)	4	0	0	0	0

Going (Turf): **Sf: 0-0 GS: 0-0 Gd: 0-0 GF: 0-0 Fm: 0-0**
Distance: 5f/6f: 0-0 7f-8f: 0-2 9f-13f: 0-2 14f+: 0-0
Track : LH: 0-2 RH: 0-2 Tight: 0-2 Gall: 0-0
Aids: Bl: 0-0 Vi: 0-0 Tstrap: 0-0 Ckp: 0-0
Best Rating: **56** 12/09 Wolv 1m141y stand

Huck Finn (NZ)

(97) (53)

9-y-o b g Foxbay (NZ)-Reckless Spirit (NZ) (Straight Strike (USA))

M Madgwick Collingwood Investment Properties Ltd

Placings:00502/5310000300/00006/00/060 **(0443)**

2009: 10^{0}SD, 16^{6}SD, 12^{0}SD,

	Starts	1st	2nd	3rd	Win & Pl
Career Total (Turf)	23	1	1	2	4282
Career Total (AW)	3	0	0	0	0
2/05 Trap 1m			G-S	£3229	

Total win prize-money £3229

Going (Turf): Sf: 0-2 **GS: 1-10** Gd: 0-11 GF: 0-0 Fm: 0-0
Distance: 5f/6f: 0-6 **7f-8f: 1-14** 9f-13f: 0-5 14f+: 0-1
Track : LH: 0-3 RH: 0-1 Tight: 0-3 Gall: 0-0
Aids: Bl: 0-0 Vi: 0-0 Tstrap: 0-1 Ckp: 0-1
Best Rating: **53** 1/09 Ling 2m stand

Hucking Heat (IRE)

97(105) (84)70

5-y-o b g Desert Sun-Vltava (IRE) (Sri Pekan (USA))

R Hollinshead P & K Swinnerton

Placings:004/6164006200036253/1543214510130305561 10123-634046055654 **(7632)**

2009: 9^{6}SD, 12^{3}SD, 9^{4}SD, 9^{0}SD, 10^{4}GS, 10^{6}GF, 12^{0}SD, 9^{5}GF, 10^{5}GS, 8^{6}SF, 9^{5}SD, 9^{4}SD,

	Starts	1st	2nd	3rd	Win & Pl
Career Total (Turf)	22	2	0	2	6793
Career Total (AW)	33	6	4	5	20546
83 12/08 Wolv 1m1f103y (0-75)H				STD	£3123
73 10/08 Wolv 1m1f103y (0-65)H				STD	£2388
65 10/08 Nott 1m2f50y (0-70)H				SFT	£2637
67 5/08 Hayd 1m2f120y (0-70)H				GD	£2637
70 4/08 Wolv 1m141y (0-65)H				STD	£2388
66 2/08 Sthl 1m4f				SS	£1774
70 1/08 Sthl 1m				STD	£1774
71 3/07 Ling 1m (0-70)H				STD	£2914

Total win prize-money £19638

Going (Turf): **Sf: 1-3** GS: 0-5 **Gd: 1-4** GF: 0-10 Fm: 0-0
Distance: 5f/6f: 0-4 7f-8f: 2-17 **9f-13f: 6-34** 14f+: 0-0
Track : **LH: 8-37** RH: 0-13 **Tight: 4-23** Gall: 0-1
Aids: Bl: 1-1 Vi: 0-5 Tstrap: 5-27 Ckp: 5-27
Best Rating: **84** 12/08 Wolv 1m4f50y stand

Fair; effective at around 1m2f-1m4f; acts on good and soft ground; goes on sand; has been tried in various headgear.

Hucking Hero (IRE)

102(105) (76)73

4-y-o b g Iron Mask (USA)-Selkirk Flyer (Selkirk (USA))

J R Boyle (J R Best 15/5) M Khan X2

Placings:0316301/14430050-240464436435561605 **(7515)**

2009: 8^{2}SD, 10^{4}SD, 8^{0}SD, 4^{4}FZ, 10^{6}FZ, 10^{4}SD, 8^{4}SD, 12^{3}SD, 10^{6}G, 10^{4}SD, 10^{3}GF, 10^{5}GS, 10^{5}GS, 11^{6}G, 13^{1}SD, 13^{6}SD, 12^{0}SD, 16^{5}SD,

	Starts	1st	2nd	3rd	Win & Pl
Career Total (Turf)	8	0	0	2	1059
Career Total (AW)	25	4	1	3	17956

59 10/09 Wolv 1m5f194y STD £1942
76 1/08 Ling 1m (0-85)H STD £4100
74 12/07 Ling 1m (0-95) STD £4731
67 10/07 Ling 7f STD £2169
Total win prize-money £12946

Going (Turf): Sf: 0-0 GS: 0-2 Gd: 0-3 GF: 0-2 Fm: 0-0
Distance: 5f/6f: 0-2 7f-8f: 3-12 9f-13f: 0-16 14f+: 1-2
Track : LH: 4-24 RH: 0-7 Tight: 4-22 Gall: 0-3
Aids: Bl: 0-1 Vi: 0-1 Tstrap: 1-3 Ckp: 1-3
Best Rating: 77 3/08 Ling 1m2f stand

Fair; effective over 7f-1m4f; acts on Polytrack; has worn cheekpieces.

Hudoo

(98) (70)

2-y-o ch f Halling (USA)-Zarara (USA) (Manila (USA))
Saeed Bin Suroor Godolphin

Placings:1 (7157)
2009: 7^{1}SD,

	Starts	1st	2nd	3rd	Win & Pl
Career Total (Turf)	0	0	0	0	
Career Total (AW)	1	1	0	0	2730

70 10/09 Wolv 7f32y STD £2729
Total win prize-money £2730

Going (Turf): Sf: 0-0 GS: 0-0 Gd: 0-0 GF: 0-0 Fm: 0-0
Distance: 5f/6f: 0-0 7f-8f: 1-1 9f-13f: 0-0 14f+: 0-0
Track : LH: 1-1 RH: 0-0 Tight: 1-1 Gall: 0-0
Aids: Bl: 0-0 Vi: 0-0 Tstrap: 0-0 Ckp: 0-0
Best Rating: 70 10/09 Wolv 7f32y stand

Fair winner on debut over 7f on Polytrack.

Huff And Puff

92 69

2-y-o b c Azamour (IRE)-Coyote (Indian Ridge)
Mrs A J Perrett A D Spence

Placings:5 (7146)
2009: 7^{5}G,

	Starts	1st	2nd	3rd	Win & Pl
Career Total (Turf)	1	0	0	0	0

Going (Turf): Sf: 0-0 GS: 0-0 Gd: 0-1 GF: 0-0 Fm: 0-0
Distance: 5f/6f: 0-0 7f-8f: 0-1 9f-13f: 0-0 14f+: 0-0
Track : LH: 0-0 RH: 0-0 Tight: 0-0 Gall: 0-0
Aids: Bl: 0-0 Vi: 0-0 Tstrap: 0-0 Ckp: 0-0
Best Rating: 69 10/09 NmkR 7f good

Hugs Destiny (IRE)

56(94) (64)64

8-y-o b g Victory Note (USA)-Embracing (Reference Point)
M A Barnes Billy Boys Syndicate

Placings:52/60000502660/5054130350/23010200036143 300/00623520304446-0 (1648)
2009: 14^{0}G,

	Starts	1st	2nd	3rd	Win & Pl
Career Total (Turf)	46	2	4	8	14498
Career Total (AW)	9	1	2	0	3966

64 8/07 Catt 1m3f214y (0-75)H GD £3123
64 5/07 Wolv 1m4f50y (0-55)H STD £2307
56 7/06 Catt 1m3f214y (0-55)H FRM £2730
Total win prize-money £8161

Going (Turf): Sf: 0-0 GS: 0-8 Gd: 1-11 GF: 0-24 Fm: 1-3
Distance: 5f/6f: 0-0 7f-8f: 0-1 9f-13f: 3-28 14f+: 0-26
Track : LH: 3-36 RH: 0-18 Tight: 3-35 Gall: 0-7
Aids: Bl: 0-2 Vi: 0-0 Tstrap: 0-1 Ckp: 0-1
Best Rating: 71 6/04 York 7f205y gd-fm

Moderate; suited by 1m4f, but stays further; acts on fast ground; has worn a tongue tie.

Hukba (IRE)

99 (78)78

3-y-o b f Anabaa (USA)-Banaadir (USA) (Diesis)
F Vermeulen (E A L Dunlop 14/6) Ecurie Winning

Placings:2-6231360
2009: 10^{6}GS, 9^{2}GS, 10^{3}GF, 9^{1}SD, 9^{3}G, 10^{6}G, 10^{0}S,

	Starts	1st	2nd	3rd	Win & Pl
Career Total (Turf)	7	0	2	2	2987
Career Total (AW)	1	1	0	0	11650

78 8/09 Deau 1m1f110y STD £11650
Total win prize-money £11650

Going (Turf): Sf: 0-2 GS: 0-2 Gd: 0-2 GF: 0-1 Fm: 0-0
Distance: 5f/6f: 0-0 7f-8f: 0-1 9f-13f: 1-7 14f+: 0-0
Track : LH: 0-2 RH: 0-3 Tight: 0-1 Gall: 0-2
Aids: Bl: 0-0 Vi: 0-0 Tstrap: 0-0 Ckp: 0-0
Best Rating: 78 9/09 Lonc 1m2f110y good

Modest; stays 1m2f; acts on fast ground.

Hulcote Rose (IRE)

71(97) (71)31

2-y-o b f Rock Of Gibraltar (IRE)-Siksikawa (Mark Of Esteem (IRE))
S Kirk The Kathryn Stud

Placings:031 (6942)
2009: 7^{0}GF, 6^{3}SD, 6^{1}SD,

	Starts	1st	2nd	3rd	Win & Pl
Career Total (Turf)	1	0	0	0	
Career Total (AW)	2	1	0	1	3265

71 10/09 Kemp 6f STD £2590
Total win prize-money £2590

Going (Turf): Sf: 0-0 GS: 0-0 Gd: 0-0 GF: 0-1 Fm: 0-0
Distance: 5f/6f: 1-2 7f-8f: 0-1 9f-13f: 0-0 14f+: 0-0
Track : LH: 0-0 RH: 1-2 Tight: 0-0 Gall: 0-0
Aids: Bl: 0-0 Vi: 0-0 Tstrap: 0-0 Ckp: 0-0
Best Rating: 71 10/09 Kemp 6f stand

Hum Again (IRE)

69 19

2-y-o b c Marju (IRE)-Kazatzka (Groom Dancer (USA))
J S Moore Coleman Bloodstock Limited

Placings:0 (4946)
2009: 6^{0}GF,

	Starts	1st	2nd	3rd	Win & Pl
Career Total (Turf)	1	0	0	0	

Going (Turf): Sf: 0-0 GS: 0-0 Gd: 0-0 GF: 0-1 Fm: 0-0
Distance: 5f/6f: 0-0 7f-8f: 0-1 9f-13f: 0-0 14f+: 0-0
Track : LH: 0-0 RH: 0-0 Tight: 0-0 Gall: 0-0
Aids: Bl: 0-0 Vi: 0-0 Tstrap: 0-0 Ckp: 0-0
Best Rating: 19 8/09 Sals 6f212y gd-fm

Humble Opinion

102(105) (95)94

7-y-o br g Singspiel (IRE)-For More (FR) (Sanglamore (USA))
A King Paul Green

Placings:21/02212300/001030/251-344060530 (6059)
2009: 12^{3}SF, 12^{4}SD, 10^{4}SD, 20^{0}GF, 12^{6}GS, 10^{0}S, 10^{5}GF, 9^{3}GF, 10^{0}GF,

	Starts	1st	2nd	3rd	Win & Pl
Career Total (Turf)	23	3	4	3	45510
Career Total (AW)	5	1	1	1	8318

94 5/08 York 1m2f88y (0-90)H GD £11009
93 6/06 Hayd 1m30y (0-90)H G-F £11334
86 6/05 Leic 1m9y (0-85)H G-F £7112
73 12/04 Ling 1m STD £4085
Total win prize-money £33541

Going (Turf): Sf: 0-1 GS: 0-2 Gd: 1-7 GF: 2-13 Fm: 0-0
Distance: 5f/6f: 0-0 7f-8f: 1-6 9f-13f: 3-21 14f+: 0-1
Track : LH: 3-10 RH: 1-14 Tight: 1-10 Gall: 1-7
Aids: Bl: 0-2 Vi: 0-0 Tstrap: 0-0 Ckp: 0-0
Best Rating: 95 4/09 Ling 1m4f stand

Very useful; missed whole of 2007; effective over 1m-1m4f; acts on fast ground; also goes on Polytrack.

Humidor (IRE)

96 78

2-y-o b g Camacho-Miss Indigo (Indian Ridge)
R Charlton Beckhampton Stables Ltd 1

Placings:023 (7058)
2009: 6^{0}G, 6^{2}GS, 5^{3}GF,

	Starts	1st	2nd	3rd	Win & Pl
Career Total (Turf)	3	0	1	1	1927

Going (Turf): Sf: 0-0 GS: 0-1 Gd: 0-1 GF: 0-1 Fm: 0-0
Distance: 5f/6f: 0-3 7f-8f: 0-0 9f-13f: 0-0 14f+: 0-0
Track : LH: 0-0 RH: 0-0 Tight: 0-0 Gall: 0-2
Aids: Bl: 0-0 Vi: 0-0 Tstrap: 0-0 Ckp: 0-0
Best Rating: 78 10/09 Wind 6f gd-sft

Fair; stays 6f; acts on easy ground.

Humourous (IRE)

91 46

7-y-o b g Darshaan-Amusing Time (IRE) (Sadler's Wells (USA))
B Storey Graham & Storey

Placings:510/0/6P0 (4873)
2009: 14^{6}GF, 11^{P}GF, 14^{0}G,

	Starts	1st	2nd	3rd	Win & Pl
Career Total (Turf)	7	1	0	0	5161

86 9/04 Kemp 1m GD £5161
Total win prize-money £5161

Going (Turf): Sf: 0-0 GS: 0-0 Gd: 1-4 GF: 0-3 Fm: 0-0
Distance: 5f/6f: 0-0 7f-8f: 1-2 9f-13f: 0-3 14f+: 0-2
Track : LH: 0-1 RH: 1-4 Tight: 0-3 Gall: 1-1
Aids: Bl: 0-2 Vi: 0-0 Tstrap: 0-0 Ckp: 0-0
Best Rating: 86 9/04 Kemp 1m good

Humungous (IRE)

100(95) (87)104

6-y-o ch g Giant's Causeway (USA)-Doula (USA) (Gone West (USA))
C R Egerton Longmoor Holdings Ltd

Placings:61616/032520/**00**21020403/00541000-005 **(3067)**

2009: 10^{0}GF, 10^{0}GF, 9^{5}GS,

	Starts	1st	2nd	3rd	Win & Pl
Career Total (Turf)	27	3	4	2	78146
Career Total (AW)	5	1	0	0	4329

104 7/08 Asct 1m2f (0-95) G-F £12462
105 6/07 Wind 1m67y (0-95)H GD £7478
96 8/05 Ling 7f STD £4329
87 7/05 Sals 6f212y FRM £4956
Total win prize-money £29225

Going (Turf): Sf: 0-0 GS: 0-2 **Gd: 1-8 GF: 1-14 Fm: 1-3**
Distance: 5f/6f: 0-1 7f-8f: 2-13 9f-13f: 2-18 14f+: 0-0
Track : LH: 1-10 **RH: 2-11 Tight: 2-13** Gall: 1-4
Aids: **Bl: 1-7** Vi: 0-0 Tstrap: 0-5 Ckp: 0-5
Best Rating: **111** 8/07 Gdwd 1m gd-fm

Very useful; effective from 7f-1m2f; acts on fast ground and on Polytrack; has worn blinkers and cheekpieces.

Hunt The Bottle (IRE)

87(97) (58)67

4-y-o b c Bertolini (USA)-Zanoubia (USA) (Our Emblem (USA))
M Mullineaux Michael Mullineaux

Placings:33410/00505000-**0**6536000 **(2245)**

2009: 5^{0}SD, 5^{6}SD, 8^{5}SD, 9^{3}SD, 9^{6}SD, 9^{0}SD, 6^{0}SD, 8^{0}G,

	Starts	1st	2nd	3rd	Win & Pl
Career Total (Turf)	11	1	0	2	4577
Career Total (AW)	10	0	0	1	353

74 9/07 Hayd 6f SFT £2169
Total win prize-money £2170

Going (Turf): **Sf: 1-2** GS: 0-1 Gd: 0-4 GF: 0-4 Fm: 0-0
Distance: **5f/6f: 1-11** 7f-8f: 0-5 9f-13f: 0-5 14f+: 0-0
Track : LH: 0-10 RH: 0-1 Tight: 0-7 Gall: 0-0
Aids: Bl: 0-1 Vi: 0-0 Tstrap: 0-1 Ckp: 0-1
Best Rating: **74** 9/07 Hayd 6f soft

Moderate; effective over 5f-6f; acts on most ground.

Huntdown (USA)

112 111

3-y-o ch c Elusive Quality (USA)-Infinite Spirit (USA) (Maria's Mon (USA))
Saeed Bin Suroor Godolphin

Placings:2130-2520 **(6487)**

2009: 7^{2}G, 7^{5}GF, 7^{2}GF, 7^{0}GF,

	Starts	1st	2nd	3rd	Win & Pl
Career Total (Turf)	8	1	3	1	50870

94 9/08 Newb 6f8y GD £5504
Total win prize-money £5505

Going (Turf): Sf: 0-0 GS: 0-0 **Gd: 1-3** GF: 0-5 Fm: 0-0
Distance: 5f/6f: 0-2 **7f-8f: 1-6** 9f-13f: 0-0 14f+: 0-0
Track : LH: 0-1 RH: 0-0 Tight: 0-0 Gall: 0-1
Aids: Bl: 0-0 Vi: 0-0 Tstrap: 0-0 Ckp: 0-0
Best Rating: **111** 6/09 NmkJ 7f good

Group class; third in the Middle Park Stakes; effective over 6-7f; acts on good and fast ground.

Hunterview

109(106) (96)98

3-y-o ch g Reset (AUS)-Mount Elbrus (Barathea (IRE))
D E Pipe (M A Jarvis 24/10) Mrs Jo Tracey

Placings:310-1466521 **(7018)**

2009: 8^{1}SD, 8^{4}GF, 7^{6}GF, 8^{6}G, 8^{5}SD, 10^{2}GF, 12^{1}GS,

	Starts	1st	2nd	3rd	Win & Pl
Career Total (Turf)	8	2	1	1	12250
Career Total (AW)	2	1	0	0	5132

98 10/09 Donc 1m4f (0-95)H G-S £7771
96 3/09 Sthl 1m (0-80)H STD £4857
Total win prize-money £12628

Going (Turf): **Sf: 1-2 GS: 1-1** Gd: 0-2 GF: 0-3 Fm: 0-0
Distance: 5f/6f: 0-0 **7f-8f: 2-8** 9f-13f: 1-2 14f+: 0-0
Track : **LH: 2-5** RH: 1-3 Tight: 0-3 **Gall: 1-2**
Aids: **Bl: 1-3** Vi: 0-0 Tstrap: 0-0 Ckp: 0-0
Best Rating: **98** 10/09 Donc 1m4f gd-sft

Useful; stays 1m4f; acts on most ground and on Fibresand; has worn blinkers.

Hunting Country

95(104) (90)96

4-y-o b g Cape Cross (IRE)-Steeple (Selkirk (USA))
A bin Huzaim (M Johnston 28/4) Sheikh Hamdan Bin Mohammed Al Maktoum

Placings:4241130033-**6**006

2009: 12^{6}SD, 10^{0}GS, 9^{0}FT, 9^{6}FT,

	Starts	1st	2nd	3rd	Win & Pl
Career Total (Turf)	10	2	1	2	16840
Career Total (AW)	4	0	0	1	1396

96 7/08 Newb 1m2f6y (0-95)H GD £7477
86 7/08 Nott 1m2f50y (0-80)H G-F £5828
Total win prize-money £13305

Going (Turf): Sf: 0-0 GS: 0-1 **Gd: 1-2 GF: 1-7** Fm: 0-0
Distance: 5f/6f: 0-0 7f-8f: 0-0 **9f-13f: 2-14** 14f+: 0-0
Track : **LH: 2-7** RH: 0-5 Tight: 0-5 **Gall: 1-3**
Aids: Bl: 0-0 Vi: 0-0 Tstrap: 0-0 Ckp: 0-0
Best Rating: **96** 7/08 Newb 1m2f6y good

Useful; stays 1m4f; acts on good and faster ground; likes to race prominently.

Hunting Haze

87(96) (51)33

6-y-o b g Foxhound (USA)-Second Affair (IRE) (Pursuit Of Love)
A Crook Mrs D S Wilkinson

Placings:4506/04340/4300/**0000**44-000000 **(7080)**

2009: 15^{0}GF, 14^{0}GF, 11^{0}S, 11^{0}GF, 10^{0}GF, 11^{0}S,

	Starts	1st	2nd	3rd	Win & Pl
Career Total (Turf)	20	0	0	2	2887
Career Total (AW)	5	0	0	0	0

Going (Turf): **Sf: 0-2 GS: 0-2 Gd: 0-4 GF: 0-12 Fm: 0-0**
Distance: 5f/6f: 0-3 7f-8f: 0-1 9f-13f: 0-16 14f+: 0-5
Track : LH: 0-17 RH: 0-5 Tight: 0-10 Gall: 0-4
Aids: Bl: 0-2 Vi: 0-0 Tstrap: 0-4 Ckp: 0-4
Best Rating: **64** 7/06 Ripn 1m4f10y gd-fm

Moderate; effective over 1m6f; acts on fast ground; goes on Fibresand; has worn cheekpieces.

Hunting Tartan

99 92

2-y-o b c Oasis Dream-Delta (Zafonic (USA))
J H M Gosden K Abdulla

Placings:10 **(6426)**

2009: 7^{1}G, 7^{0}GF,

	Starts	1st	2nd	3rd	Win & Pl
Career Total (Turf)	2	1	0	0	3562

87 9/09 Chep 7f16y GD £3561
Total win prize-money £3562

Going (Turf): Sf: 0-0 GS: 0-0 **Gd: 1-1** GF: 0-1 Fm: 0-0
Distance: 5f/6f: 0-0 **7f-8f: 1-2** 9f-13f: 0-0 14f+: 0-0
Track : LH: 0-0 RH: 0-0 Tight: 0-0 Gall: 0-0
Aids: Bl: 0-0 Vi: 0-0 Tstrap: 0-0 Ckp: 0-0
Best Rating: **92** 10/09 NmkR 7f gd-fm

Useful; stays 7f and acts on good ground.

Hunting Tower

99 (86)85

5-y-o b g Sadler's Wells (USA)-Fictitious (Machiavellian (USA))
J J Lambe Mighty Macs Syndicate

Placings:331/20015056/252 **(6412)**

2009: 12^{2}GY, 13^{5}G, 13^{2}GF,

	Starts	1st	2nd	3rd	Win & Pl
Career Total (Turf)	13	2	3	2	17511
Career Total (AW)	1	0	0	0	0

89 7/07 Sals 1m (0-85)H G-F £5181
79 10/06 Brig 7f214y G-S £4533
Total win prize-money £9716

Going (Turf): Sf: 0-0 **GS: 1-3** Gd: 0-3 **GF: 1-6** Fm: 0-0
Distance: 5f/6f: 0-1 **7f-8f: 2-3** 9f-13f: 0-8 14f+: 0-2
Track : **LH: 1-6** RH: 0-6 Tight: 0-3 Gall: 0-1
Aids: Bl: 0-0 Vi: 0-0 Tstrap: 0-0 Ckp: 0-0
Best Rating: **89** 7/07 Sals 1m gd-fm

Useful; stays 1m5f; acts on most ground.

Huntingfortreasure

94 75

2-y-o b g Pastoral Pursuits-Treasure Trove (USA) (The Minstrel (CAN))
M Dods Les Waugh

Placings:22 **(6842)**

2009: 7^{2}G, 7^{2}G,

	Starts	1st	2nd	3rd	Win & Pl
Career Total (Turf)	2	0	2	0	2251

Going (Turf): **Sf: 0-0 GS: 0-0 Gd: 0-2 GF: 0-0 Fm: 0-0**
Distance: 5f/6f: 0-0 7f-8f: 0-2 9f-13f: 0-0 14f+: 0-0
Track : LH: 0-2 RH: 0-0 Tight: 0-1 Gall: 0-0
Aids: Bl: 0-0 Vi: 0-0 Tstrap: 0-0 Ckp: 0-0
Best Rating: **75** 9/09 Ayr 7f50y good

Runner-up on debut; effective over 7f; acts on good ground.

Hurakan (IRE)

91(103) (79)78

3-y-o gr g Daylami (IRE)-Gothic Dream (IRE) (Nashwan (USA))
P D Evans (Mrs A J Perrett 21/10) J L Guillambert

Placings:012-00**213504** **(7823)**

2009: 11^{0}GF, 10^{0}GS, 10^{2}SD, 8^{1}SD, 10^{3}SD, 10^{5}SD, 12^{0}SD, 10^{4}SD,

	Starts	1st	2nd	3rd	Win & Pl
Career Total (Turf)	4	0	1	0	1156
Career Total (AW)	7	2	1	1	6618

78 11/09 Ling 1m (0-75)H STD £2388
76 9/08 Ling 1m STD £2729
Total win prize-money £5118

Going (Turf): **Sf: 0-0 GS: 0-2 Gd: 0-0 GF: 0-2 Fm: 0-0**
Distance: 5f/6f: 0-0 **7f-8f: 2-3** 9f-13f: 0-8 14f+: 0-0
Track : **LH: 2-4** RH: 0-6 **Tight: 2-7** Gall: 0-0
Aids: Bl: 0-0 Vi: 0-0 Tstrap: 0-0 Ckp: 0-0
Best Rating: **79** 12/09 Ling 1m2f stand

Fair; stays 1m; acts on fast ground; goes on Polytrack.

Hurforharmony (IRE)

(98) (47)**51**
6-y-o b m Orpen (USA)-Zolba (IRE) (Classic Secret (USA))
Adrian McGuinness Declan Macpartlin

Placings:0/5400-56 (0255)
2009: 12^{5}SD, 8^{6}SD,

	Starts	1st	2nd	3rd	Win & Pl
Career Total (Turf)	4	0	0	0	286
Career Total (AW)	3	0	0	0	0

Going (Turf): **Sf: 0-0 GS: 0-0 Gd: 0-2 GF: 0-1 Fm: 0-0**
Distance: 5f/6f: 0-0 7f-8f: 0-0 9f-13f: 0-5 14f+: 0-2
Track : LH: 0-4 RH: 0-2 Tight: 0-3 Gall: 0-0
Aids: Bl: 0-0 Vi: 0-0 Tstrap: 0-0 Ckp: 0-0
Best Rating: **51** 6/08 Wxfd 1m4f50y gd-yld

Hurlingham

105(99) (77)**84**
5-y-o b g Halling (USA)-Society (IRE) (Barathea (IRE))
M W Easterby A G Black

Placings:324/1152020/0042511336-04620046600 (7271)
2009: 10^{0}G, 10^{4}GS, 12^{6}G, 12^{2}GF, 11^{0}GF, 10^{0}GS, 10^{4}HY, 9^{6}G, 12^{6}S, 10^{0}G, 8^{0}SD,

	Starts	1st	2nd	3rd	Win & Pl
Career Total (Turf)	25	2	4	3	19327
Career Total (AW)	6	2	1	0	8952

84 9/08 Haml 1m3f16y (0-75)H G-S £4533
81 8/08 Hayd 1m2f120y (0-70)H SFT £3238
89 1/07 Kemp 1m (0-85)H STD £4728
80 1/07 Sthl 1m STD £2817
Total win prize-money £15316

Going (Turf): **Sf: 1-6 GS: 1-4** Gd: 0-9 GF: 0-5 Fm: 0-1
Distance: 5f/6f: 0-0 7f-8f: 2-8 9f-13f: 2-21 14f+: 0-2
Track : LH: 2-20 RH: 2-10 **Tight: 1-7** Gall: 0-6
Aids: Bl: 0-2 Vi: 0-0 Tstrap: 0-2 Ckp: 0-2
Best Rating: **92** 4/07 Wolv 1m1f103y stand

Fair; stays 1m4f; acts on most ground and on Polytrack.

Huroof (IRE)

93(91) (75)**76**
2-y-o ch f Pivotal-Esloob (USA) (Diesis)
Saeed Bin Suroor Godolphin

Placings:241 (7396)
2009: 7^{2}G, 7^{4}GF, 7^{1}SD,

	Starts	1st	2nd	3rd	Win & Pl
Career Total (Turf)	2	0	1	0	1770
Career Total (AW)	1	1	0	0	3886

75 11/09 Wolv 7f32y STD £3885
Total win prize-money £3886

Going (Turf): **Sf: 0-0 GS: 0-0 Gd: 0-1 GF: 0-1 Fm: 0-0**
Distance: 5f/6f: 0-0 **7f-8f: 1-3** 9f-13f: 0-0 14f+: 0-0
Track : **LH: 1-1** RH: 0-0 **Tight: 1-1** Gall: 0-0
Aids: Bl: 0-0 Vi: 0-0 Tstrap: 1-1 Ckp: 1-1
Best Rating: **76** 8/09 Folk 7f gd-fm

Fair; stays 7f; acts on fast ground and on Polytrack; has worn cheekpieces.

Hurricane Coast

87(103) (64)**36**
10-y-o b g Hurricane Sky (AUS)-Tread Carefully (Sharpo)
D Flood Mrs Cheryl Flood

Placings:00330/0004214/0506503020123444/1113132004101664600/0302004010021000000230/4051500354066006/00/00645105405-33105600060 (2441)
2009: 6^{3}SS, 5^{3}SD, 8^{1}SD, 8^{0}SD, 8^{5}SF, 5^{6}SD, 6^{0}SD, 5^{0}SD, 12^{0}SD, 6^{6}SD, 8^{0}GF,

	Starts	1st	2nd	3rd	Win & Pl
Career Total (Turf)	37	3	3	4	19548
Career Total (AW)	70	10	4	7	34404

63 1/09 Sthl 1m (0-55)H STD £2388
64 10/08 Kemp 6f (0-52)H STD £2047
78 1/06 Wolv 1m1f103y STD £2388
79 10/05 Yarm 7f3y (0-70)H HVY £4009
81 4/05 Wolv 7f32y STD £2576
79 4/04 Sthl 7f E(0-75)H G-S £4394
75 1/04 Ling 5f E(0-75)H STD £3370
85 1/04 Ling 6f F STD £2947
69 1/04 Sthl 6f F STD £2891
65 1/04 Sthl 6f H STD £1291
54 11/03 Sthl 7f G STD £2128
67 9/02 Rdcr 7f D FRM £3883
Total win prize-money £34317

Going (Turf): **Sf: 1-5 GS: 1-6** Gd: 0-8 GF: 0-12 **Fm: 1-6**
Distance: 5f/6f: 6-41 7f-8f: 6-46 9f-13f: 1-20 14f+: 0-0
Track : **LH: 10-74** RH: 1-12 **Tight: 6-55** Gall: 0-6
Aids: **Bl: 8-67** Vi: 0-1 Tstrap: 0-2 Ckp: 0-2
Best Rating: **97** 11/05 Ling 1m2f stand

Moderate; stays 1m1f; acts on most ground and on sand; has worn blinkers; a difficult ride.

Hurricane Hymnbook (USA)

98(89) (82)**104**
4-y-o b g Pulpit (USA)-April Squall (USA) (Summer Squall (USA))
Stef Liddiard Bill Hinge & John Searchfield

Placings:12/2000-05 (3431)
2009: 8^{0}GF, 8^{5}GF,

	Starts	1st	2nd	3rd	Win & Pl
Career Total (Turf)	6	1	2	0	9086
Career Total (AW)	2	0	0	0	

78 9/07 Wwck 6f G-F £4533
Total win prize-money £4534

Going (Turf): Sf: 0-0 GS: 0-0 Gd: 0-2 **GF: 1-4** Fm: 0-0
Distance: **5f/6f: 1-1** 7f-8f: 0-3 9f-13f: 0-4 14f+: 0-0
Track : **LH: 1-3** RH: 0-3 Tight: 0-2 Gall: 0-2
Aids: Bl: 0-0 Vi: 0-0 Tstrap: 0-0 Ckp: 0-0
Best Rating: **104** 5/08 Wind 1m67y good

Very useful; stays 1m; acts on fast ground and on Polytrack.

Hurricane Spirit (IRE)

90(106) (88)**97**
5-y-o b h Invincible Spirit (IRE)-Gale Warning (IRE) (Last Tycoon)
J R Best The Little House Partnership

Placings:61111/320/0600340-0500014 (6633)
2009: 7^{0}GF, 6^{5}G, 6^{0}G, 5^{0}SD, 7^{0}SD, 8^{1}SD, 8^{4}SS,

	Starts	1st	2nd	3rd	Win & Pl
Career Total (Turf)	12	0	0	1	3649
Career Total (AW)	10	5	1	1	43304

88 9/09 Kemp 1m (0-85)H STD £4727
89 12/06 Kemp 7f STD £8101
101 12/06 Ling 6f (0-85) STD £4210
87 11/06 Ling 6f STD £4533
79 11/06 Ling 5f STD £3238
Total win prize-money £24812

Going (Turf): **Sf: 0-2 GS: 0-1 Gd: 0-6 GF: 0-3 Fm: 0-0**
Distance: **5f/6f: 3-12** 7f-8f: 2-10 9f-13f: 0-0 14f+: 0-0
Track : **LH: 3-11** RH: 2-3 **Tight: 3-7** Gall: 0-3
Aids: Bl: 0-0 Vi: 0-0 Tstrap: 0-0 Ckp: 0-0
Best Rating: **106** 1/07 Ling 6f stand

Useful; effective over 6f-1m; acts on Polytrack and easy ground on turf.

Hurricane Thomas (IRE)

99 (75)**63**
5-y-o b g Celtic Swing-Viola Royale (IRE) (Royal Academy (USA))
R A Fahey N D Tutty

Placings:0324/4002103/0000550-444401061200 (7127)
2009: 9^{4}G, 12^{4}GF, 12^{4}G, 10^{4}GF, 9^{0}GF, 13^{1}G, 11^{0}GF, 12^{6}GS, 9^{1}GF, 10^{2}GF, 12^{0}GS, 10^{0}G,

	Starts	1st	2nd	3rd	Win & Pl
Career Total (Turf)	29	3	2	2	12386
Career Total (AW)	1	0	1	0	964

58 9/09 Bevl 1m1f207y (0-60)H G-F £2186
55 7/09 Muss 1m5f (0-65)H GD £2498
75 9/07 Muss 1m6f (0-70)H G-F £3886
Total win prize-money £8570

Going (Turf): Sf: 0-4 GS: 0-6 Gd: 1-8 **GF: 2-11** Fm: 0-0
Distance: 5f/6f: 0-0 7f-8f: 0-3 **9f-13f: 2-21** 14f+: 1-6
Track : LH: 0-15 **RH: 3-14 Tight: 2-14** Gall: 0-4
Aids: Bl: 0-0 Vi: 0-2 Tstrap: 0-1 Ckp: 0-1
Best Rating: **75** 9/07 Muss 1m6f good

Moderate; stays 1m6f; acts on fast ground.

Hurstpierpoint (IRE)

(85) (41)**59**
4-y-o b f Night Shift (USA)-Double Gamble (Ela-Mana-Mou)
M G Rimell J & L Wetherald - M & M Glover

Placings:405060220226/022500-0 (4538)
2009: 10^{0}SD,

	Starts	1st	2nd	3rd	Win & Pl
Career Total (Turf)	11	0	2	0	1346
Career Total (AW)	8	0	4	0	2438

Going (Turf): **Sf: 0-1 GS: 0-3 Gd: 0-3 GF: 0-3 Fm: 0-1**
Distance: 5f/6f: 0-1 7f-8f: 0-9 9f-13f: 0-9 14f+: 0-0
Track : LH: 0-11 RH: 0-6 Tight: 0-13 Gall: 0-0
Aids: Bl: 0-0 Vi: 0-0 Tstrap: 0-0 Ckp: 0-0
Best Rating: **62** 9/07 Kemp 7f stand

Moderate; stays 1m; acts on good ground and Polytrack.

Hustle (IRE)

106(105) (89)**91**
4-y-o ch g Choisir (AUS)-Granny Kelly (USA) (Irish River (FR))
Miss Gay Kelleway J Thompson, P Kerridge, Nightmare P'ship

Placings:0314/10423020-**50541000655430655** (7741)
2009: 9^{5}SD, 8^{0}SD, 6^{5}GF, 7^{4}GF, 7^{1}GF, 7^{0}S, 7^{0}GF, 7^{0}SD, 8^{6}HY, 7^{5}GF, 6^{5}SD, 8^{4}GF, 7^{3}SD, 7^{0}SS, 7^{6}SD, 7^{5}SD, 7^{5}SD,

	Starts	1st	2nd	3rd	Win & Pl
Career Total (Turf)	17	2	1	2	9632
Career Total (AW)	12	1	1	1	7631

86 3/08 Ling 7f (0-85)H STD £4100
72 9/07 Ling 7f G-F £2730
Total win prize-money £6831

Going (Turf): Sf: 0-2 GS: 0-1 Gd: 0-1 **GF: 2-12** Fm: 0-1
Distance: 5f/6f: 0-3 **7f-8f: 3-19** 9f-13f: 0-7 14f+: 0-0
Track : **LH: 1-12** RH: 0-6 **Tight: 1-9** Gall: 0-3
Aids: Bl: 0-1 Vi: 0-0 Tstrap: 0-1 Ckp: 0-1
Best Rating: **91** 5/09 NmkR 7f gd-fm

Useful; stays 1m2f, but effective over shorter; acts on fast ground and on Polytrack; has worn a tongue tie and cheek-pieces.

Huygens

99(99) (85)**78**
2-y-o b c Zafeen (FR)-Lindfield Belle (IRE) (Fairy King (USA))
D J Coakley Chris Van Hoorn

Placings:513 (7685)
2009: 5^{5}F, 7^{1}GF, 8^{3}SD,

	Starts	1st	2nd	3rd	Win & Pl
Career Total (Turf)	2	1	0	0	2730
Career Total (AW)	1	0	0	1	578

78 6/09 Folk 7f G-F £2729
Total win prize-money £2730

Going (Turf): Sf: 0-0 GS: 0-0 Gd: 0-0 **GF: 1-1** Fm: 0-1
Distance: 5f/6f: 0-1 **7f-8f: 1-2** 9f-13f: 0-0 14f+: 0-0
Track : LH: 0-1 RH: 0-1 Tight: 0-0 Gall: 0-1
Aids: Bl: 0-0 Vi: 0-0 Tstrap: 0-0 Ckp: 0-0
Best Rating: **85** 12/09 Kemp 1m stand

55,000gns half-brother to Baltic King among others; useful; effective at 7f-1m; acts on fast ground and Polytrack.

Huzzah (IRE)

105 (89)**105**
4-y-o b c Acclamation-Borders Belle (IRE) (Pursuit Of Love)
B W Hills J Gale,J Finch,D Cole,R Dollar,D Powell

Placings:404225134/1106530-50240000 (6732)
2009: 8^{5}GF, 8^{0}S, 8^{2}GF, 8^{4}G, 8^{0}G, 8^{0}GF, 8^{0}GF, 8^{0}S,

	Starts	1st	2nd	3rd	Win & Pl
Career Total (Turf)	22	3	2	1	64098
Career Total (AW)	2	0	1	1	1382

105 5/08 Ches 7f122y (0-100)H G-F £13246
103 4/08 Newb 7f (0-95)H G-S £8723
91 10/07 Sals 1m G-S £4533
Total win prize-money £26504

Going (Turf): Sf: 0-3 **GS: 2-3** Gd: 0-4 GF: 1-12 Fm: 0-0
Distance: 5f/6f: 0-1 **7f-8f: 3-20** 9f-13f: 0-3 14f+: 0-0
Track : **LH: 1-3** RH: 0-6 **Tight: 1-1** Gall: 0-2
Aids: Bl: 0-0 Vi: 0-0 Tstrap: 0-0 Ckp: 0-0
Best Rating: **105** 6/09 Asct 1m gd-fm

Very useful; effective at 7f-1m; acts on fast and easy ground; also goes on Polytrack.

Hyades (USA)

105(100) (96)**95**
3-y-o b/br c Aldebaran (USA)-Lingerie (Shirley Heights)
H R A Cecil Niarchos Family

Placings:2-512666 (5313)
2009: 11^{5}GS, 8^{1}GF, 10^{2}GF, 8^{6}GF, 9^{6}G, 8^{6}SD,

	Starts	1st	2nd	3rd	Win & Pl
Career Total (Turf)	6	1	2	0	9499
Career Total (AW)	1	0	0	0	161

82 4/09 Yarm 1m3y G-F £1942
Total win prize-money £1943

Going (Turf): Sf: 0-0 GS: 0-1 Gd: 0-2 **GF: 1-3** Fm: 0-0
Distance: 5f/6f: 0-0 7f-8f: 0-3 **9f-13f: 1-4** 14f+: 0-0
Track : LH: 0-1 RH: 0-2 Tight: 0-1 Gall: 0-1
Aids: Bl: 0-0 Vi: 0-0 Tstrap: 0-0 Ckp: 0-0
Best Rating: **96** 8/09 Kemp 1m stand

Very useful; stays 1m2f and acts on a sound surface.

Hyde Lea Flyer

90(106) (84)**71**
4-y-o b g Hernando (FR)-Sea Ridge (Slip Anchor)
E S McMahon Mrs J McVay

Placings:402/400**6211-20000054** (7672)
2009: 8^{2}SD, 8^{0}GF, 8^{0}GS, 8^{0}GF, 8^{0}SD, 8^{0}SF, 8^{5}SD, 8^{4}SD,

	Starts	1st	2nd	3rd	Win & Pl
Career Total (Turf)	9	0	1	0	1233
Career Total (AW)	9	2	2	0	12090

80 12/08 Wolv 1m141y (0-80)H SF £5459
76 11/08 Wolv 1m141y (0-70)H STD £3885
Total win prize-money £9345

Going (Turf): **Sf: 0-1 GS: 0-4 Gd: 0-1 GF: 0-3 Fm: 0-0**
Distance: 5f/6f: 0-0 7f-8f: 0-5 **9f-13f: 2-13** 14f+: 0-0
Track : **LH: 2-11** RH: 0-2 **Tight: 2-9** Gall: 0-0
Aids: Bl: 0-0 Vi: 0-0 Tstrap: 0-0 Ckp: 0-0
Best Rating: **84** 1/09 Wolv 1m141y stand

Modest; effective over 1m-1m1f; acts on easy ground; goes on Polytrack.

Hydrant

(91) (55)**65**
3-y-o b g Haafhd-Spring (Sadler's Wells (USA))
P Salmon The Waterboys

Placings:60-3 (7780)
2009: 11^{3}SD,

	Starts	1st	2nd	3rd	Win & Pl
Career Total (Turf)	2	0	0	0	0
Career Total (AW)	1	0	0	1	403

Going (Turf): **Sf: 0-0 GS: 0-0 Gd: 0-2 GF: 0-0 Fm: 0-0**
Distance: 5f/6f: 0-0 7f-8f: 0-2 9f-13f: 0-1 14f+: 0-0
Track : LH: 0-1 RH: 0-1 Tight: 0-0 Gall: 0-0
Aids: Bl: 0-0 Vi: 0-0 Tstrap: 0-0 Ckp: 0-0
Best Rating: **65** 7/08 Newb 7f good

125,000gns half-brother to Inglenook from a family of middle-distance performers; stays 1m3f; acts on Polytrack and on good ground.

Hymnsheet

90 **83**
2-y-o b f Pivotal-Choir Mistress (Chief Singer)
Sir Michael Stoute Cheveley Park Stud

Placings:1 (6920)
2009: 8^{1}GF,

	Starts	1st	2nd	3rd	Win & Pl
Career Total (Turf)	1	1	0	0	4100

83 10/09 Yarm 1m3y G-F £4100
Total win prize-money £4100

Going (Turf): Sf: 0-0 GS: 0-0 Gd: 0-0 **GF: 1-1** Fm: 0-0
Distance: 5f/6f: 0-0 7f-8f: 0-0 **9f-13f: 1-1** 14f+: 0-0
Track : LH: 0-0 RH: 0-0 Tight: 0-0 Gall: 0-0
Aids: Bl: 0-0 Vi: 0-0 Tstrap: 0-0 Ckp: 0-0
Best Rating: **83** 10/09 Yarm 1m3y gd-fm

Exciting half-sister to Chorist; debut winner on quick ground at two; stays 1m, should have no trouble with 1m2f.

Hyper Viper (IRE)

94 (47)**40**
4-y-o b g Atraf-Double Letter (IRE) (M Double M (USA))
C Grant Steve Wilson

Placings:000303200/0 (3313)
2009: 16^{0}GF,

	Starts	1st	2nd	3rd	Win & Pl
Career Total (Turf)	9	0	1	2	1734
Career Total (AW)	1	0	0	0	

Going (Turf): **Sf: 0-2 GS: 0-0 Gd: 0-2 GF: 0-4 Fm: 0-1**
Distance: 5f/6f: 0-3 7f-8f: 0-3 9f-13f: 0-3 14f+: 0-1
Track : LH: 0-6 RH: 0-0 Tight: 0-2 Gall: 0-3
Aids: Bl: 0-4 Vi: 0-0 Tstrap: 0-1 Ckp: 0-1
Best Rating: **58** 9/07 Yarm 1m3y gd-fm

Modest; effective at around 7f-1m; acts on fast ground.

Hypnosis

105(84) (40)**90**
6-y-o b m Mind Games-Salacious (Sallust)
N Wilson R W Snowden

Placings:00020/043212223232/12103/40412400-5320300 (6843)
2009: 5^{5}GF, 5^{3}G, 5^{2}GF, 5^{0}GF, 5^{3}G, 5^{0}SD, 5^{0}G,

	Starts	1st	2nd	3rd	Win & Pl
Career Total (Turf)	35	3	10	6	35415
Career Total (AW)	2	1	0	0	3071

85 7/08 Catt 5f (0-85)H G-F £4857
85 5/07 Catt 5f (0-85)H G-F £4728
79 2/07 Sthl 5f (0-70)H STD £3071
68 6/06 Catt 5f (0-65)H G-F £2730
Total win prize-money £15386

Going (Turf): Sf: 0-3 GS: 0-5 Gd: 0-8 **GF: 3-16** Fm: 0-3
Distance: **5f/6f: 4-37** 7f-8f: 0-0 9f-13f: 0-0 14f+: 0-0
Track : LH: 0-0 RH: 0-4 Tight: 0-0 Gall: 0-4
Aids: Bl: 0-0 Vi: 0-0 Tstrap: 0-0 Ckp: 0-0
Best Rating: **90** 9/08 Donc 5f soft

Fair; seems best over 5f; acts on fast ground; goes on Fibresand.

Hypnotic

104(82) (19)**69**
7-y-o ch g Lomitas-Hypnotize (Machiavellian (USA))
Jim Best Bill Wallace

Placings:411310/00160/000501015/0000/0605-1040200 (7349)
2009: 7^{1}GF, 8^{0}G, 6^{4}F, 7^{0}GF, 7^{2}F, 8^{0}SD, 7^{0}SD,

	Starts	1st	2nd	3rd	Win & Pl
Career Total (Turf)	26	5	1	0	32676
Career Total (AW)	10	2	0	1	8250

69 6/09 Brig 7f214y (0-55)H G-F £2331
87 9/06 Ayr 7f50y (0-70)H G-S £3886
77 8/06 Carl 6f192y (0-65)H G-F £2590
82 8/05 Yarm 1m3y GD £6760
98 9/04 Crao 1m55y G-S £15845
93 8/04 Ling 7f E STD £3857
86 7/04 Ling 7f E STD £3513
Total win prize-money £38784

Going (Turf): Sf: 0-3 **GS: 2-5** Gd: 1-6 **GF: 2-10** Fm: 0-2
Distance: 5f/6f: 0-3 **7f-8f: 5-25** 9f-13f: 2-8 14f+: 0-0
Track: **LH: 4-20** RH: 1-7 **Tight: 2-11** Gall: 0-1
Aids: Bl: 0-1 **Vi: 1-4** Tstrap: 0-0 Ckp: 0-0
Best Rating: 98 9/04 Crao 1m55y gd-sft

Modest; stays 1m; acts on good and fast ground; goes on Polytrack; has worn blinkers.

Hypnotic Gaze (IRE)

101(99) (63)72

3-y-o b g Chevalier (IRE)-Red Trance (IRE) (Soviet Star (USA))

J Mackie W I Bloomfield

Placings:00-3445325 **(4562)**

2009: 8^{3}SD, 8^{4}SD, 8^{4}GF, 8^{5}G, 8^{3}S, 9^{2}G, 10^{5}G,

	Starts	1st	2nd	3rd	Win & Pl
Career Total (Turf)	7	0	1	1	1637
Career Total (AW)	2	0	0	1	454

Going (Turf): Sf: 0-1 GS: 0-1 Gd: 0-4 GF: 0-1 Fm: 0-0
Distance: 5f/6f: 0-0 7f-8f: 0-2 9f-13f: 0-7 14f+: 0-0
Track: LH: 0-6 RH: 0-1 Tight: 0-3 Gall: 0-0
Aids: Bl: 0-0 Vi: 0-0 Tstrap: 0-1 Ckp: 0-1
Best Rating: 72 7/09 Carl 1m1f61y good

Moderate; stays 1m and should stay 1m2f; acts on Polytrack; may do better.

Hypnotist (UAE)

103(97) (73)73

3-y-o b g Halling (USA)-Poised (USA) (Rahy (USA))

C E Brittain Saeed Manana

Placings:4-3325605644 **(6997)**

2009: 8^{3}SD, 10^{3}SD, 7^{2}SD, 8^{5}GF, 9^{6}GF, 10^{0}GF, 10^{5}G, 9^{6}GF, 8^{4}GF, 7^{4}G,

	Starts	1st	2nd	3rd	Win & Pl
Career Total (Turf)	8	0	0	0	986
Career Total (AW)	3	0	1	2	2185

Going (Turf): Sf: 0-0 GS: 0-0 Gd: 0-2 GF: 0-6 Fm: 0-0
Distance: 5f/6f: 0-0 7f-8f: 0-4 9f-13f: 0-7 14f+: 0-0
Track: LH: 0-5 RH: 0-4 Tight: 0-5 Gall: 0-0
Aids: Bl: 0-0 Vi: 0-0 Tstrap: 0-1 Ckp: 0-1
Best Rating: 73 5/09 Gdwd 1m gd-fm

Fair; effective over 1m; acts on fast ground and on Polytrack.

Hypnotized (USA)

88(97) (82)69

2-y-o b c Elusive Quality (USA)-Delighted (IRE) (Danehill (USA))

M L W Bell Ali Saeed

Placings:551 **(7430)**

2009: 7^{5}G, 7^{5}SD, 7^{1}SD,

	Starts	1st	2nd	3rd	Win & Pl
Career Total (Turf)	1	0	0	0	0
Career Total (AW)	2	1	0	0	4209
82 11/09 Kemp 7f			STD	£4209	

Total win prize-money £4209

Going (Turf): Sf: 0-0 GS: 0-0 Gd: 0-1 GF: 0-0 Fm: 0-0
Distance: 5f/6f: 0-0 **7f-8f: 1-3** 9f-13f: 0-0 14f+: 0-0
Track: LH: 0-1 **RH: 1-1** Tight: 0-1 Gall: 0-0
Aids: Bl: 0-0 Vi: 0-0 Tstrap: 0-0 Ckp: 0-0
Best Rating: 82 11/09 Kemp 7f stand

Fair; stays 7f; acts on Polytrack.

Hysterical Lady

99(94) (59)80

3-y-o b f Choisir (AUS)-Royal Mistress (Fasliyev (USA))

D Nicholls Ms Finola Devaney

Placings:24-1316450 **(6642)**

2009: 6^{1}SD, 5^{3}GF, 6^{1}GF, 5^{6}GS, 5^{4}G, 5^{5}GF, 5^{0}SD,

	Starts	1st	2nd	3rd	Win & Pl
Career Total (Turf)	7	1	1	1	6633
Career Total (AW)	2	1	0	0	3071
74 5/09 Thsk 6f		(0-75)H		G-F	£4274
59 3/09 Sthl 6f				STD	£3070

Total win prize-money £7345

Going (Turf): Sf: 0-0 GS: 0-1 Gd: 0-1 **GF: 1-5** Fm: 0-0
Distance: **5f/6f: 2-9** 7f-8f: 0-0 9f-13f: 0-0 14f+: 0-0
Track: **LH: 1-2** RH: 0-1 Tight: 0-1 Gall: 0-1
Aids: Bl: 0-0 Vi: 0-0 Tstrap: 0-0 Ckp: 0-0
Best Rating: 80 5/08 Carl 5f gd-fm

Fair; effective over 5f-6f; acts on fast ground; goes on Fibresand.

I Am That (IRE)

91(87) (76)73

2-y-o b c Statue Of Liberty (USA)-Victory Again (IRE) (Victory Note (USA))

S A Callaghan Mrs C Hassett

Placings:143 **(6585)**

2009: 5^{1}GS, 6^{4}GF, 6^{3}SD,

	Starts	1st	2nd	3rd	Win & Pl
Career Total (Turf)	2	1	0	0	3866
Career Total (AW)	1	0	0	1	385
72 8/09 Carl 5f			G-S	£3865	

Total win prize-money £3866

Going (Turf): Sf: 0-0 **GS: 1-1** Gd: 0-0 GF: 0-1 Fm: 0-0
Distance: **5f/6f: 1-3** 7f-8f: 0-0 9f-13f: 0-0 14f+: 0-0
Track: LH: 0-0 **RH: 1-2** Tight: 0-0 **Gall: 1-2**
Aids: Bl: 0-0 Vi: 0-0 Tstrap: 0-0 Ckp: 0-0
Best Rating: 76 10/09 Kemp 6f stand

Fair; stays 6f; acts on easy and fast ground and on Polytrack.

I Am The Man

(91) (70)

4-y-o b g Auction House (USA)-Sally Gardens (Alzao (USA))

B J McMath B J McMath

Placings:2 **(7694)**

2009: 10^{2}SD,

	Starts	1st	2nd	3rd	Win & Pl
Career Total (Turf)	0	0	0	0	
Career Total (AW)	1	0	1	0	584

Going (Turf): Sf: 0-0 GS: 0-0 Gd: 0-0 GF: 0-0 Fm: 0-0
Distance: 5f/6f: 0-0 7f-8f: 0-0 9f-13f: 0-1 14f+: 0-0
Track: LH: 0-1 RH: 0-0 Tight: 0-1 Gall: 0-0
Aids: Bl: 0-0 Vi: 0-0 Tstrap: 0-0 Ckp: 0-0
Best Rating: 70 12/09 Ling 1m2f stand

Fair; stays 1m2f; goes on Polytrack.

I Certainly May

80(102) (61)33

4-y-o b g Royal Applause-Deep Ravine (USA) (Gulch (USA))

S Dow S Dow

Placings:0000**2**660/0445050000**0**-200000 **(4450)**

2009: 8^{2}SD, 10^{0}SD, 8^{0}SD, 8^{0}SD, 9^{0}GF, 10^{0}G,

	Starts	1st	2nd	3rd	Win & Pl
Career Total (Turf)	9	0	0	0	0
Career Total (AW)	16	0	2	0	1241

Going (Turf): Sf: 0-0 GS: 0-2 Gd: 0-3 GF: 0-3 Fm: 0-1
Distance: 5f/6f: 0-1 7f-8f: 0-11 9f-13f: 0-11 14f+: 0-2
Track: LH: 0-13 RH: 0-10 Tight: 0-12 Gall: 0-0
Aids: Bl: 0-1 Vi: 0-0 Tstrap: 0-5 Ckp: 0-5
Best Rating: 64 8/07 Gdwd 7f gd-fm

Plating-class; stays 1m; acts on Polytrack; has worn cheekpieces.

I Confess

105(106) (85)83

4-y-o br g Fantastic Light (USA)-Vadsagreya (FR) (Linamix (FR))

P D Evans M&R Refurbishments Ltd

Placings:242332/46036460**0**41204212-06531551005253345**00**654635 **(7830)**

2009: 7^{0}SD, 6^{6}GF, 7^{5}GF, 7^{3}GF, 8^{1}SD, 7^{5}GF, 7^{5}GS, 7^{1}SD, 7^{0}G, 8^{0}G, 7^{5}G, 7^{2}GF, 8^{5}F, 7^{3}SD, 8^{3}SD, 7^{4}SD, 6^{5}GF, 7^{0}SS, 7^{0}SD, 6^{6}SD, 7^{5}SD, 8^{4}SD, 7^{6}SD,

	Starts	1st	2nd	3rd	Win & Pl
Career Total (Turf)	26	0	4	4	14294
Career Total (AW)	22	4	3	3	19814
85 6/09 Ling 7f		(0-80)H		STD	£5828
83 5/09 Ling 1m		(0-75)H		STD	£3238
77 12/08 Ling 7f		(0-75)H		STD	£2729
66 10/08 Ling 7f				STD	£1978

Total win prize-money £13775

Going (Turf): Sf: 0-3 GS: 0-2 Gd: 0-6 GF: 0-12 Fm: 0-1
Distance: 5f/6f: 0-9 **7f-8f: 4-36** 9f-13f: 0-3 14f+: 0-0
Track: **LH: 4-29** RH: 0-9 **Tight: 4-24** Gall: 0-0
Aids: **Bl: 4-29** Vi: 0-4 Tstrap: 0-0 Ckp: 0-0
Best Rating: 85 9/09 Wolv 1m141y stand

Fair; effective at 7f-1m; acts on fast ground and on Polytrack; often blinkered.

I See Nice Sea

82 59

3-y-o b f Miesque's Son (USA)-North Sea (IRE) (Selkirk (USA))

Ollie Pears (L M Cumani 28/5) Ian Bishop

Placings:50600 **(5982)**

2009: 8^{5}F, 8^{0}G, 10^{6}GF, 11^{0}GS, 8^{0}GF,

	Starts	1st	2nd	3rd	Win & Pl
Career Total (Turf)	5	0	0	0	0

Going (Turf): Sf: 0-0 GS: 0-1 Gd: 0-1 GF: 0-2 Fm: 0-1
Distance: 5f/6f: 0-0 7f-8f: 0-0 9f-13f: 0-5 14f+: 0-0
Track: LH: 0-3 RH: 0-1 Tight: 0-2 Gall: 0-0
Aids: Bl: 0-1 Vi: 0-0 Tstrap: 0-1 Ckp: 0-1
Best Rating: 59 5/09 Nott 1m75y firm

I'lldoit

66 **16**

2-y-o br g Tamayaz (CAN)-Club Oasis (Forzando)
G A Harker G A Harker

Placings:0 **(4888)**
2009: 7^{0}G,

	Starts	1st	2nd	3rd	Win & Pl
Career Total (Turf)	1	0	0	0	

Going (Turf): **Sf: 0-0 GS: 0-0 Gd: 0-1 GF: 0-0 Fm: 0-0**
Distance: 5f/6f: 0-0 7f-8f: 0-1 9f-13f: 0-0 14f+: 0-0
Track : LH: 0-0 RH: 0-1 Tight: 0-0 Gall: 0-0
Aids: Bl: 0-0 Vi: 0-0 Tstrap: 0-0 Ckp: 0-0
Best Rating: **16** 8/09 Bevl 7f100y good

I'm Agenius

(68) (35)**43**

6-y-o br m Killer Instinct-I'm Sophie (IRE) (Shalford (IRE))
D Burchell (R Curtis 2/1) Three Acres Racing

Placings:0600P0/00-00 **(0793)**
2009: 8^{0}SS, 7^{0}SD,

	Starts	1st	2nd	3rd	Win & Pl
Career Total (Turf)	2	0	0	0	0
Career Total (AW)	8	0	0	0	

Going (Turf): **Sf: 0-0 GS: 0-1 Gd: 0-1 GF: 0-0 Fm: 0-0**
Distance: 5f/6f: 0-0 7f-8f: 0-5 9f-13f: 0-4 14f+: 0-1
Track : LH: 0-6 RH: 0-4 Tight: 0-3 Gall: 0-0
Aids: Bl: 0-0 Vi: 0-0 Tstrap: 0-0 Ckp: 0-0
Best Rating: **43** 8/07 Leic 1m60y gd-sft

I'm In The Pink (FR)

103 **80**

5-y-o b g Garuda (IRE)-Ahwaki (FR) (River Mist (USA))
P D Evans B J Mould

Placings:04361240301 **(7248)**
2009: 10^{0}GF, 12^{4}GF, 10^{3}GF, 10^{6}GF, 10^{1}GS, 10^{2}GF, 10^{4}G, 10^{0}GF, 12^{3}G, 12^{0}GF, 10^{1}HY,

	Starts	1st	2nd	3rd	Win & Pl
Career Total (Turf)	11	2	1	2	9702

80 11/09 Nott 1m2f50y (0-75)H HVY £2914
77 5/09 Hayd 1m2f95y (0-70)H G-S £3296
Total win prize-money £6211

Going (Turf): **Sf: 1-1 GS: 1-1** Gd: 0-2 GF: 0-7 Fm: 0-0
Distance: 5f/6f: 0-0 7f-8f: 0-0 **9f-13f: 2-11** 14f+: 0-0
Track : **LH: 2-10** RH: 0-1 Tight: 0-5 Gall: 0-1
Aids: Bl: 0-0 Vi: 0-0 Tstrap: 0-0 Ckp: 0-0
Best Rating: **80** 11/09 Nott 1m2f50y heavy

Fair; stays 1m2f; acts well on soft ground.

I'm Super Too (IRE)

96 **71**

2-y-o b g Fasliyev (USA)-Congress (IRE) (Dancing Brave (USA))
G A Swinbank David C Young

Placings:025 **(5981)**
2009: 5^{0}G, 6^{2}S, 7^{5}GF,

	Starts	1st	2nd	3rd	Win & Pl
Career Total (Turf)	3	0	1	0	1272

Going (Turf): **Sf: 0-1 GS: 0-0 Gd: 0-1 GF: 0-1 Fm: 0-0**
Distance: 5f/6f: 0-2 7f-8f: 0-1 9f-13f: 0-0 14f+: 0-0
Track : LH: 0-0 RH: 0-2 Tight: 0-0 Gall: 0-0
Aids: Bl: 0-0 Vi: 0-0 Tstrap: 0-0 Ckp: 0-0
Best Rating: **71** 9/09 Thsk 6f soft

Half-brother to Royal Intrigue and United Nations; improved on debut when runner-up over 6f on soft ground.

I'malwaysright (IRE)

87(95) (72)**61**

2-y-o b g Namid-Tashyra (IRE) (Tagula (IRE))
D R C Elsworth Yan Wah Wu

Placings:20240210 **(7156)**
2009: 5^{2}GF, 6^{0}SD, 5^{2}SD, 6^{4}SD, 5^{0}G, 5^{2}SD, 5^{1}SD, 5^{0}SD,

	Starts	1st	2nd	3rd	Win & Pl
Career Total (Turf)	2	0	1	0	1060
Career Total (AW)	6	1	2	0	5130

72 10/09 Wolv 5f216y STD £3561
Total win prize-money £3562

Going (Turf): **Sf: 0-0 GS: 0-0 Gd: 0-1 GF: 0-1 Fm: 0-0**
Distance: **5f/6f: 1-8** 7f-8f: 0-0 9f-13f: 0-0 14f+: 0-0
Track : **LH: 1-3** RH: 0-3 **Tight: 1-3** Gall: 0-0
Aids: Bl: 0-3 Vi: 0-0 Tstrap: 0-0 Ckp: 0-0
Best Rating: **72** 10/09 Wolv 5f216y stand

Fair; suited by 5f; acts on fast ground and on Polytrack.

I'mneverwrong (IRE)

86 **67**

2-y-o ch f Compton Place-Anthyllis (IRE) (Night Shift (USA))
D R C Elsworth D R C Elsworth

Placings:3 **(2238)**
2009: 6^{3}GF,

	Starts	1st	2nd	3rd	Win & Pl
Career Total (Turf)	1	0	0	1	770

Going (Turf): **Sf: 0-0 GS: 0-0 Gd: 0-0 GF: 0-1 Fm: 0-0**
Distance: 5f/6f: 0-1 7f-8f: 0-0 9f-13f: 0-0 14f+: 0-0
Track : LH: 0-0 RH: 0-0 Tight: 0-0 Gall: 0-0
Aids: Bl: 0-0 Vi: 0-0 Tstrap: 0-0 Ckp: 0-0
Best Rating: **67** 5/09 NmkR 6f gd-fm

Iachimo

95(97) (54)**54**

3-y-o ch g Sakhee (USA)-Latin Review (IRE) (Titus Livius (FR))
A P Jarvis (K R Burke 26/7) Philip Richards

Placings:006-100350360 **(5345)**
2009: 5^{1}SD, 5^{0}SD, 5^{0}G, 5^{3}GF, 5^{5}G, 5^{0}GF, 5^{3}G, 5^{6}GF, 5^{0}G,

	Starts	1st	2nd	3rd	Win & Pl
Career Total (Turf)	10	0	0	2	770
Career Total (AW)	2	1	0	0	2047

54 3/09 Ling 5f (0-65)H STD £2047
Total win prize-money £2047

Going (Turf): **Sf: 0-2 GS: 0-0 Gd: 0-4 GF: 0-3 Fm: 0-1**
Distance: **5f/6f: 1-12** 7f-8f: 0-0 9f-13f: 0-0 14f+: 0-0
Track : **LH: 1-3** RH: 0-1 **Tight: 1-2** Gall: 0-1
Aids: Bl: 0-0 Vi: 0-4 Tstrap: 0-1 Ckp: 0-1
Best Rating: **54** 5/09 Muss 5f gd-fm

Moderate; best at 5f on fast ground and Polytrack; has worn a visor, cheekpieces and a tongue tie.

Ialysos (GR)

113 **115**

5-y-o br h So Factual (USA)-Vallota (Polish Precedent (USA))
L M Cumani Mrs M Marinopoulos

Placings:11/111-1110100 **(5233)**
2009: 5^{1}SY, 7^{1}SY, 5^{1}G, 6^{0}GF, 5^{1}G, 5^{0}G, 5^{0}GF,

	Starts	1st	2nd	3rd	Win & Pl
Career Total (Turf)	5	2	0	0	59609
Career Total (AW)	7	7	0	0	100075

115 7/09 Sand 5f6y GD £36900
112 5/09 Hayd 5f GD £22708
2/09 Mkpl 7f SLP £14387
1/09 Mkpl 5f SLP £17293
5/08 Mkpl 5f STD £13097
3/08 Mkpl 7f SLP £20869
1/08 Mkpl 5f STD £16425
10/07 Mkpl 6f STD £9667
2/07 Mkpl 5f STD £8335
Total win prize-money £159684

Going (Turf): Sf: 0-0 GS: 0-0 **Gd: 2-3** GF: 0-2 Fm: 0-0
Distance: **5f/6f: 7-10** 7f-8f: 2-2 9f-13f: 0-0 14f+: 0-0
Track : LH: 0-0 RH: 0-0 Tight: 0-0 Gall: 0-0
Aids: Bl: 0-0 Vi: 0-0 Tstrap: 0-0 Ckp: 0-0
Best Rating: **115** 7/09 Sand 5f6y good

Group class; former mutiple winner in Greece; effective at 5f-7f; acts on good ground and on sand.

Iasia (GR)

105(102) (73)**97**

3-y-o b f One Cool Cat (USA)-Alanis (Warning)
Jane Chapple-Hyam Mrs M Marinopoulos

Placings:1-50102650 **(7431)**
2009: 8^{5}GF, 7^{0}GF, 7^{1}GF, 6^{0}GF, 7^{2}G, 7^{6}GF, 6^{5}G, 7^{0}SD,

	Starts	1st	2nd	3rd	Win & Pl
Career Total (Turf)	7	1	1	0	6688
Career Total (AW)	2	1	0	0	3562

83 7/09 Wwck 7f26y (0-75)H G-F £2914
73 11/08 Kemp 6f STD £3561
Total win prize-money £6476

Going (Turf): Sf: 0-0 GS: 0-0 Gd: 0-2 **GF: 1-5** Fm: 0-0
Distance: 5f/6f: 1-2 7f-8f: 1-7 9f-13f: 0-0 14f+: 0-0
Track : LH: 1-1 RH: 1-3 Tight: 0-0 Gall: 0-0
Aids: Bl: 0-0 Vi: 0-0 Tstrap: 0-0 Ckp: 0-0
Best Rating: **97** 9/09 Donc 7f gd-fm

Fair; suited by 6f-7f; acts on fast ground; goes on Polytrack.

Ibbetson (USA)

95(96) (71)**65**

4-y-o b/br g Street Cry (IRE)-Object Of Virtue (USA) (Partners Hero (USA))
Mrs A M Thorpe (W R Swinburn 5/10) Mrs A M Thorpe

Placings:062-506 **(6547)**
2009: 8^{5}F, 8^{0}G, 8^{6}G,

	Starts	1st	2nd	3rd	Win & Pl
Career Total (Turf)	5	0	0	0	0
Career Total (AW)	1	0	1	0	771

Going (Turf): **Sf: 0-1 GS: 0-1 Gd: 0-2 GF: 0-0 Fm: 0-1**
Distance: 5f/6f: 0-0 7f-8f: 0-2 9f-13f: 0-4 14f+: 0-0
Track : LH: 0-5 RH: 0-1 Tight: 0-1 Gall: 0-2
Aids: Bl: 0-0 Vi: 0-0 Tstrap: 0-0 Ckp: 0-0
Best Rating: **71** 11/08 GrLe 1m stand

Modest; effective over 1m; acts on Polytrack.

Ibmab

92(81) (47)67

2-y-o ch g Deportivo-Kilmovee (Inchinor)

Mrs L Stubbs L Woolams

Placings:6031200 (7098)

2009: 5^{6}G, 6^{0}G, 6^{3}G, 7^{1}G, 7^{2}GF, 7^{0}SD, 7^{0}G,

	Starts	1st	2nd	3rd	Win & Pl
Career Total (Turf)	6	1	1	1	2887
Career Total (AW)	1	0	0	0	

67 8/09 Yarm 7f3y GD £1942

Total win prize-money £1943

Going (Turf): Sf: 0-0 GS: 0-0 **Gd: 1-5** GF: 0-1 Fm: 0-0
Distance: 5f/6f: 0-2 **7f-8f: 1-5** 9f-13f: 0-0 14f+: 0-0
Track : LH: 0-0 RH: 0-1 Tight: 0-0 Gall: 0-0
Aids: Bl: 0-0 Vi: 0-0 Tstrap: 0-0 Ckp: 0-0
Best Rating: **67** 8/09 Yarm 7f3y good

Modest; stays 7f; acts on good/fast ground; has worn a tongue tie.

Ibn Hiyyan (USA)

78(81) (45)59

2-y-o gr/ro g El Prado (IRE)-Lovely Later (USA) (Green Dancer (USA))

M Johnston Sheikh Hamdan Bin Mohammed Al Maktoum

Placings:000 (6772)

2009: 7^{0}G, 8^{0}G, 8^{0}SD,

	Starts	1st	2nd	3rd	Win & Pl
Career Total (Turf)	2	0	0	0	
Career Total (AW)	1	0	0	0	

Going (Turf): **Sf: 0-0 GS: 0-0 Gd: 0-2 GF: 0-0 Fm: 0-0**
Distance: 5f/6f: 0-0 7f-8f: 0-3 9f-13f: 0-0 14f+: 0-0
Track : LH: 0-1 RH: 0-1 Tight: 0-0 Gall: 0-0
Aids: Bl: 0-0 Vi: 0-0 Tstrap: 0-0 Ckp: 0-0
Best Rating: **59** 8/09 NmkJ 1m good

Ibrox (IRE)

101(104) (78)73

4-y-o b g Mujahid (USA)-Ling Lane (Slip Anchor)

A D Brown Rangers Racing

Placings:044/36-**21601034014** (7724)

2009: 11^{2}SD, 12^{1}SD, 14^{6}SD, 12^{0}SD, 10^{1}G, 13^{0}G, 10^{3}GS, 11^{4}HY, 11^{0}GS, 11^{1}SD, 12^{4}SD,

	Starts	1st	2nd	3rd	Win & Pl
Career Total (Turf)	10	1	0	2	4707
Career Total (AW)	6	2	1	0	7115

78 10/09 Sthl 1m3f (0-70)H STD £3238
72 6/09 Ayr 1m2f (0-65)H GD £3070
71 1/09 Sthl 1m4f STD £3070

Total win prize-money £9380

Going (Turf): Sf: 0-2 GS: 0-3 **Gd: 1-4** GF: 0-1 Fm: 0-0
Distance: 5f/6f: 0-0 7f-8f: 0-3 **9f-13f: 3-11** 14f+: 0-2
Track : **LH: 3-14** RH: 0-1 Tight: 0-1 Gall: 0-0
Aids: Bl: 0-0 Vi: 0-0 Tstrap: 1-2 Ckp: 1-2
Best Rating: **78** 10/09 Sthl 1m3f stand

Fair; stays 1m4f; acts on good and softer ground and on Fibresand; has worn cheekpieces.

Ice And Fire

89(101) (53)44

10-y-o b g Cadeaux Genereux-Tanz (IRE) (Sadler's Wells (USA))

J T Stimpson J T Stimpson

Placings:30/0606005/**0**/00**51066**/**3656104454410163**/**000 610/44-50** (1273)

2009: 16^{5}SD, 16^{0}G,

	Starts	1st	2nd	3rd	Win & Pl
Career Total (Turf)	13	0	0	1	758
Career Total (AW)	30	5	0	2	10450

53 12/07 Ling 2m (0-60)H STD £1873
61 11/06 Sthl 1m6f (0-45) STD £1945
57 7/06 Wolv 2m119y (0-55)H STD £2730
54 3/06 Wolv 1m5f194y (0-45) STD £1876
51 11/05 Sthl 1m6f (0-45) SS £1419

Total win prize-money £9846

Going (Turf): **Sf: 0-0 GS: 0-3 Gd: 0-7 GF: 0-3 Fm: 0-0**
Distance: 5f/6f: 0-0 7f-8f: 0-4 9f-13f: 0-11 **14f+: 5-28**
Track : **LH: 5-36** RH: 0-3 **Tight: 3-19** Gall: 0-0
Aids: **Bl: 5-30** Vi: 0-2 Tstrap: 0-1 Ckp: 0-1
Best Rating: **69** 7/01 NmkJ 7f gd-fm

Moderate; stays 2m; acts on Fibresand and Polytrack; often hangs right.

Ice Attack (IRE)

84(60) (38)44

3-y-o gr f Verglas (IRE)-Little Whisper (IRE) (Be My Guest (USA))

Patrick Morris Rob Lloyd Racing Limited

Placings:00-545 (2740)

2009: 6^{5}SD, 5^{4}GF, 5^{5}G,

	Starts	1st	2nd	3rd	Win & Pl
Career Total (Turf)	3	0	0	0	118
Career Total (AW)	2	0	0	0	0

Going (Turf): **Sf: 0-0 GS: 0-0 Gd: 0-1 GF: 0-1 Fm: 0-0**
Distance: 5f/6f: 0-5 7f-8f: 0-0 9f-13f: 0-0 14f+: 0-0
Track : LH: 0-3 RH: 0-2 Tight: 0-0 Gall: 0-1
Aids: Bl: 0-0 Vi: 0-1 Tstrap: 0-0 Ckp: 0-0
Best Rating: **44** 10/08 Fair 6f sft-hvy

Ice Bellini

97(98) (68)58

4-y-o ch f Erhaab (USA)-Peach Sorbet (IRE) (Spectrum (IRE))

Jim Best (Miss Gay Kelleway 12/5) R W Kibble

Placings:0/0001130-2645 (1960)

2009: 14^{2}SD, 13^{6}SF, 12^{4}GS, 11^{5}F,

	Starts	1st	2nd	3rd	Win & Pl
Career Total (Turf)	6	1	0	0	2605
Career Total (AW)	6	1	1	1	5850

66 11/08 Sthl 1m4f (0-70)H STD £4776
58 10/08 Newc 1m4f93y HVY £2266

Total win prize-money £7044

Going (Turf): **Sf: 1-1** GS: 0-1 Gd: 0-3 GF: 0-0 Fm: 0-1
Distance: 5f/6f: 0-0 7f-8f: 0-2 **9f-13f: 2-7** 14f+: 0-3
Track : **LH: 2-8** RH: 0-2 Tight: 0-2 **Gall: 1-3**
Aids: Bl: 0-2 **Vi: 2-6** Tstrap: 0-0 Ckp: 0-0
Best Rating: **68** 11/08 Sthl 1m6f stand

Modest; stays 1m6f; acts on soft ground and on sand; has worn blinkers.

Ice Cool Lady (IRE)

94(95) (62)72

2-y-o gr f Verglas (IRE)-Cafe Creme (IRE) (Catrail (USA))

W R Swinburn London Market Racing Club

Placings:6640140 (7363)

2009: 5^{6}G, 5^{6}SD, 6^{4}GF, 6^{0}GS, 7^{1}GF, 7^{4}GF, 7^{0}SD,

	Starts	1st	2nd	3rd	Win & Pl
Career Total (Turf)	5	1	0	0	3616
Career Total (AW)	2	0	0	0	0

72 9/09 Ling 7f (0-75) G-F £3238

Total win prize-money £3238

Going (Turf): Sf: 0-0 GS: 0-1 Gd: 0-1 **GF: 1-3** Fm: 0-0
Distance: 5f/6f: 0-4 **7f-8f: 1-3** 9f-13f: 0-0 14f+: 0-0
Track : LH: 0-3 RH: 0-0 Tight: 0-2 Gall: 0-1
Aids: Bl: 0-0 Vi: 0-0 Tstrap: 0-0 Ckp: 0-0
Best Rating: **72** 9/09 Ling 7f gd-fm

Fair; stays 7f and acts on fast ground.

Ice Diva

93(100) (70)70

2-y-o gr/b f Verglas (IRE)-La Coqueta (GER) (Kris)

P W D'Arcy Mark & Sue Harniman

Placings:052 (7277)

2009: 7^{0}GF, 8^{5}GS, 8^{2}SD,

	Starts	1st	2nd	3rd	Win & Pl
Career Total (Turf)	2	0	0	0	0
Career Total (AW)	1	0	1	0	1008

Going (Turf): **Sf: 0-0 GS: 0-1 Gd: 0-0 GF: 0-1 Fm: 0-0**
Distance: 5f/6f: 0-0 7f-8f: 0-2 9f-13f: 0-1 14f+: 0-0
Track : LH: 0-2 RH: 0-0 Tight: 0-1 Gall: 0-1
Aids: Bl: 0-0 Vi: 0-0 Tstrap: 0-0 Ckp: 0-0
Best Rating: **70** 11/09 Wolv 1m141y stand

Fair; stays 1m plus; acts on Polytrack.

Ice Planet

100(97) (78)87

8-y-o b g Polar Falcon (USA)-Preference (Efisio)

Mrs R A Carr David W Chapman

Placings:03505/00312412510/425352436/00614404/0005 00340**000-555300** (6596)

2009: 6^{5}SD, 7^{5}SS, 6^{5}G, 6^{3}G, 6^{0}GF, 6^{0}GS,

	Starts	1st	2nd	3rd	Win & Pl
Career Total (Turf)	46	4	4	6	92189
Career Total (AW)	5	0	0	0	0

98 6/07 Rdcr 6f (0-95)H G-S £9715
98 8/05 Ripn 6f (0-105)H G-S £29000
86 6/05 Donc 6f (0-85)H G-F £7107
76 6/05 Thsk 5f (0-70)H G-F £5560

Total win prize-money £51385

Going (Turf): Sf: 0-12 **GS: 2-9**Gd: 0-12 **GF: 2-13** Fm: 0-0
Distance: **5f/6f: 4-41** 7f-8f: 0-10 9f-13f: 0-0 14f+: 0-0
Track : LH: 0-13 RH: 0-1 Tight: 0-5 Gall: 0-2
Aids: Bl: 0-0 Vi: 0-0 Tstrap: 0-0 Ckp: 0-0
Best Rating: **98** 6/07 Rdcr 6f gd-sft

Fair; effective at 6f; acts on most ground.

Ice Viking (IRE)

90(88) (68)68

2-y-o b c Danehill Dancer (IRE)-Maddelina (IRE) (Sadler's Wells (USA))

J G Given Mrs Linda P Fish

Placings:556506 (6793)

2009: 6^{5}G, 6^{5}G, 7^{6}G, 7^{5}SD, 7^{0}GF, 8^{6}S,

	Starts	1st	2nd	3rd	Win & Pl
Career Total (Turf)	5	0	0	0	0
Career Total (AW)	1	0	0	0	0

Going (Turf): Sf: 0-1 GS: 0-0 Gd: 0-3 GF: 0-1 Fm: 0-0
Distance: 5f/6f: 0-1 7f-8f: 0-4 9f-13f: 0-1 14f+: 0-0
Track : LH: 0-3 RH: 0-0 Tight: 0-1 Gall: 0-0
Aids: Bl: 0-0 Vi: 0-0 Tstrap: 0-0 Ckp: 0-0
Best Rating: 68 9/09 Wolv 7f32y stand

Modest; stays 6f; acts on good ground.

Icelandic

111(97) (107)**112**
7-y-o b g Selkirk (USA)-Icicle (Polar Falcon (USA))
F Sheridan Scuderia A4/5

Placings:4/22154551160/043123121/04321331-4362306 (7292)
2009: 5^{4}SD, 6^{3}HY, 6^{6}GF, 5^{2}S, 6^{3}SH, 6^{0}GS, 6^{6}S,

	Starts	1st	2nd	3rd	Win & Pl
Career Total (Turf)	32	7	5	7	160540
Career Total (AW)	4	1	1	0	10912

112 11/08 Donc 6f SFT £26667
104 8/08 Wwck 7f26y SFT £7641
103 11/07 Siro 7f GD £24628
9/07 Siro 7f SH £6317
5/07 Capa 7f110y STD £6317
9/06 Siro 1m HVY £18466
9/06 Siro 1m GD £6448
3/06 Siro 1m110y SFT £6448
Total win prize-money £102934

Going (Turf): Sf: 4-12 GS: 0-1 Gd: 2-12 GF: 0-3 Fm: 0-0
Distance: 5f/6f: 1-10 7f-8f: 6-23 9f-13f: 1-3 14f+: 0-0
Track : LH: 1-2 RH: 2-10 Tight: 0-1 Gall: 0-1
Aids: Bl: 0-0 Vi: 0-0 Tstrap: 0-0 Ckp: 0-0
Best Rating: 112 11/08 Donc 6f soft

Smart; Listed winner in Britain and Group 3 winner in Italy; stays 1m, but effective at shorter; acts on good or softer ground and on sand; often fitted with a tongue tie.

Iceman George

99(95) (62)**66**
5-y-o b g Beat Hollow-Diebiedale (Dominion)
D Morris D & L Racing

Placings:0/01006546/0623000-344050213100 (5035)
2009: 8^{3}SD, 11^{4}SD, 10^{4}G, 12^{0}SD, 10^{5}GF, 10^{0}GF, 10^{2}G, 10^{1}GF, 10^{3}GF, 10^{1}S, 10^{0}G, 10^{0}GF,

	Starts	1st	2nd	3rd	Win & Pl
Career Total (Turf)	22	3	2	2	12030
Career Total (AW)	6	0	0	1	444

66 7/09 NmkJ 1m2f (0-70)H SFT £3885
62 6/09 Newb 1m2f6y (0-70)H G-F £3123
68 7/07 Yarm 1m2f21y SFT £2145
Total win prize-money £9154

Going (Turf): Sf: 2-4 GS: 0-1 Gd: 0-6 GF: 1-11 Fm: 0-0
Distance: 5f/6f: 0-0 7f-8f: 0-2 9f-13f: 3-26 14f+: 0-0
Track : LH: 2-18 RH: 1-7 Tight: 1-11 Gall: 2-10
Aids: Bl: 2-14 Vi: 0-4 Tstrap: 0-4 Ckp: 0-4
Best Rating: 68 7/07 Yarm 1m2f21y soft

Moderate; stays 1m2f; acts on fast and soft ground; has worn blinkers.

Icesolator (IRE)

105(102) (96)**105**
3-y-o b g One Cool Cat (USA)-Zinnia (Zilzal (USA))
R Hannon B Bull

Placings:0111000-0333 (1929)
2009: 7^{0}SD, 8^{3}SD, 7^{3}S, 8^{3}GF,

	Starts	1st	2nd	3rd	Win & Pl
Career Total (Turf)	9	3	0	2	36099
Career Total (AW)	2	0	0	1	4308

101 5/08 Sand 5f6y SFT £12205
91 5/08 Gdwd 5f GD £9346
85 5/08 Gdwd 5f G-S £3238
Total win prize-money £24791

Going (Turf): Sf: 1-2 GS: 1-1 Gd: 1-4 GF: 0-2 Fm: 0-0
Distance: 5f/6f: 3-6 7f-8f: 0-4 9f-13f: 0-1 14f+: 0-0
Track : LH: 0-2 RH: 0-1 Tight: 0-3 Gall: 0-0
Aids: Bl: 0-0 Vi: 0-0 Tstrap: 0-0 Ckp: 0-0
Best Rating: 105 5/09 Wind 1m67y gd-fm

Listed class; winner of the National Stakes at Sandown in 2008; effective over 5f; acts on good and soft ground.

Idealism

73 **35**
2-y-o b c Motivator-Fickle (Danehill (USA))
J H M Gosden H R H Princess Haya Of Jordan

Placings:0 (6792)
2009: 8^{0}S,

	Starts	1st	2nd	3rd	Win & Pl
Career Total (Turf)	1	0	0	0	

Going (Turf): Sf: 0-1 GS: 0-0 Gd: 0-0 GF: 0-0 Fm: 0-0
Distance: 5f/6f: 0-0 7f-8f: 0-0 9f-13f: 0-1 14f+: 0-0
Track : LH: 0-1 RH: 0-0 Tight: 0-0 Gall: 0-0
Aids: Bl: 0-0 Vi: 0-0 Tstrap: 0-0 Ckp: 0-0
Best Rating: 35 10/09 Nott 1m75y soft

Idle Power (IRE)

107(102) (71)**88**
11-y-o b g Common Grounds-Idle Fancy (Mujtahid (USA))
J R Boyle The Idle B's

Placings:2516610/0515300/55020000351/2650000000400 0/0011023002110/01000302105004500/51204240252100 0/000043205303/43155050-0504031260 (7180)
2009: 7^{0}GF, 6^{5}SD, 7^{0}G, 7^{4}SD, 7^{0}G, 7^{3}SD, 6^{1}GS, 6^{2}GS, 5^{6}G, 7^{0}SD,

	Starts	1st	2nd	3rd	Win & Pl
Career Total (Turf)	98	13	10	7	129004
Career Total (AW)	17	1	2	2	14468

80 9/09 Epsm 6f (0-85)H G-S £6476
88 5/08 Gdwd 7f (0-85)H SFT £4533
99 8/06 Wind 6f (0-100)H GD £11658
98 4/06 Folk 6f (0-85)H G-S £5505
96 7/05 Gdwd 6f H G-S £12586
89 9/04 Gdwd 7f (0-85)H GD £6500
89 9/04 Ling 7f (0-85)H STD £6828
82 5/04 Brig 6f209y D(0-85)H FRM £4737
79 5/04 Gdwd 6f D(0-80)H GD £5616
93 10/02 NmkR 7f C(0-90)H FRM £8736
93 7/01 Yarm 6f3y C(0-95)H GD £7345
93 10/00 NmkR 6f C(0-95) SFT £7358
84 6/00 Kemp 5f D G-F £3445
Total win prize-money £91324

Going (Turf): Sf: 2-11 GS: 3-22 Gd: 5-29 GF: 1-33 Fm: 2-3
Distance: 5f/6f: 8-70 7f-8f: 6-45 9f-13f: 0-0 14f+: 0-0
Track : LH: 3-29 RH: 2-16 Tight: 2-23 Gall: 1-9
Aids: Bl: 0-3 Vi: 0-0 Tstrap: 6-36 Ckp: 6-36
Best Rating: 100 8/06 Gdwd 6f gd-fm

Fair; effective over 6f-7f; acts on most types of ground.

If I Were A Boy (IRE)

95(99) (77)**76**
2-y-o b f Invincible Spirit (IRE)-Attymon Lill (IRE) (Marju (IRE))
S Kirk Miss A Jones

Placings:3536253551 (7816)
2009: 6^{3}GF, 7^{5}G, 6^{3}SD, 7^{6}GS, 8^{2}SD, 8^{5}SD, 8^{3}SD, 8^{5}SD, 8^{5}SD, 8^{1}SD,

	Starts	1st	2nd	3rd	Win & Pl
Career Total (Turf)	3	0	0	1	722
Career Total (AW)	7	1	1	2	4950

77 12/09 Wolv 1m141y STD £2590
Total win prize-money £2590

Going (Turf): Sf: 0-0 GS: 0-1 Gd: 0-1 GF: 0-1 Fm: 0-0
Distance: 5f/6f: 0-1 7f-8f: 0-6 9f-13f: 1-3 14f+: 0-0
Track : LH: 1-7 RH: 0-2 Tight: 1-6 Gall: 0-0
Aids: Bl: 0-0 Vi: 0-0 Tstrap: 1-2 Ckp: 1-2
Best Rating: 77 12/09 Wolv 1m141y stand

Fair; stays 1m; acts on Polytrack; has worn cheekpieces.

If Only

96(97) (63)**60**
3-y-o ch g Monsieur Bond (IRE)-La Belle Dominique (Dominion)
J Jay The If Only Team

Placings:30545624 (6340)
2009: 7^{3}SD, 7^{0}SD, 7^{5}G, 6^{4}SD, 6^{5}SD, 7^{6}SD, 6^{2}SD, 5^{4}GF,

	Starts	1st	2nd	3rd	Win & Pl
Career Total (Turf)	2	0	0	0	159
Career Total (AW)	6	0	1	1	907

Going (Turf): Sf: 0-0 GS: 0-0 Gd: 0-1 GF: 0-1 Fm: 0-0
Distance: 5f/6f: 0-4 7f-8f: 0-4 9f-13f: 0-0 14f+: 0-0
Track : LH: 0-6 RH: 0-1 Tight: 0-3 Gall: 0-0
Aids: Bl: 0-1 Vi: 0-0 Tstrap: 0-0 Ckp: 0-0
Best Rating: 63 2/09 Ling 7f stand

Moderate; effective at 6f; acts on Fibresand.

If You Knew Suzy

95(100) (67)**56**
4-y-o b f Efisio-Sioux (Kris)
R E Barr (G A Swinbank 22/5) P Cartmell

Placings:4-25043006 (7853)
2009: 12^{2}SD, 8^{5}SD, 7^{0}GF, 8^{4}SD, 8^{3}SD, 10^{0}G, 8^{0}SD, 6^{6}SS,

	Starts	1st	2nd	3rd	Win & Pl
Career Total (Turf)	2	0	0	0	
Career Total (AW)	7	0	1	1	1863

Going (Turf): Sf: 0-0 GS: 0-0 Gd: 0-1 GF: 0-1 Fm: 0-0
Distance: 5f/6f: 0-1 7f-8f: 0-4 9f-13f: 0-4 14f+: 0-0
Track : LH: 0-9 RH: 0-0 Tight: 0-2 Gall: 0-1
Aids: Bl: 0-0 Vi: 0-0 Tstrap: 0-0 Ckp: 0-0
Best Rating: 67 3/09 Wolv 1m141y stand

Modest; stays 1m4f and acts on sand; has worn a tongue tie.

Ifatfirst (IRE)

99 (65)**70**
6-y-o b g Grand Lodge (USA)-Gaily Grecian (IRE) (Ela-Mana-Mou)
J S Goldie Mrs Janis Macpherson

Placings:000661/1/00-142566130 (6822)
2009: 11^{1}GF, 13^{4}G, 13^{2}G, 11^{5}G, 12^{6}GF, 14^{6}GS, 14^{1}G, 14^{3}GF, 14^{0}GF,

	Starts	1st	2nd	3rd	Win & Pl
Career Total (Turf)	11	2	1	1	9050
Career Total (AW)	7	2	0	0	6477

68 9/09 Muss 1m6f (0-75)H GD £3885
70 6/09 Haml 1m3f16y (0-70)H G-F £3238
65 1/07 Kemp 1m4f (0-65)H STD £3238
61 12/06 Ling 1m4f (0-60)H STD £3238
Total win prize-money £13602

Going (Turf): Sf: 0-0 GS: 0-2 **Gd: 1-5 GF: 1-4** Fm: 0-0
Distance: 5f/6f: 0-0 7f-8f: 0-2 **9f-13f: 3-9** 14f+: 1-7
Track : LH: 1-9 **RH: 3-9 Tight: 3-14** Gall: 0-0
Aids: Bl: 0-2 Vi: 0-0 Tstrap: 0-0 Ckp: 0-0
Best Rating: **70** 6/09 Haml 1m3f16y gd-fm

Modest; stays 1m6f; acts on good ground and on Polytrack; has worn blinkers.

Iffy

95(97) (55)**48**
8-y-o b g Orpen (USA)-Hopesay (Warning)
A B Haynes (R Lee 19/3) C Weare & A Pierce

Placings:050/4041**3020**/6432151600/5050 (7225)
2009: 9^{5}F, 12^{0}SD, 12^{5}SD, 10^{0}SD,

	Starts	1st	2nd	3rd	Win & Pl
Career Total (Turf)	17	3	1	2	18810
Career Total (AW)	8	0	1	0	846

78 7/05 Sand 1m2f7y (0-75)H G-F £3456
77 6/05 Epsm 1m2f18y (0-80)H G-F £6925
66 7/04 Asct 1m2f D(0-80)H G-F £5447
Total win prize-money £15830

Going (Turf): Sf: 0-0 GS: 0-1 Gd: 0-4 **GF: 3-11** Fm: 0-1
Distance: 5f/6f: 0-2 7f-8f: 0-2 **9f-13f: 3-21** 14f+: 0-0
Track : LH: 1-14 **RH: 2-8** Tight: 1-12 Gall: 1-3
Aids: Bl: 0-0 Vi: 0-0 Tstrap: 0-0 Ckp: 0-0
Best Rating: **78** 7/05 Sand 1m2f7y gd-fm

Modest; stays 1m2f; acts on fast ground and Polytrack.

Ignatieff (IRE)

96 **83**
2-y-o b g Fasliyev (USA)-Genial Jenny (IRE) (Danehill (USA))
Mrs L Stubbs P G Shorrock

Placings:5524230115 (5945)
2009: 5^{5}GF, 5^{5}GF, 5^{2}GF, 5^{4}F, 5^{2}G, 5^{3}GF, 5^{0}G, 5^{1}GS, 5^{1}G, 5^{5}G,

	Starts	1st	2nd	3rd	Win & Pl
Career Total (Turf)	10	2	2	1	11828

83 8/09 Muss 5f GD £3885
80 8/09 Thsk 5f G-S £5504
Total win prize-money £9391

Going (Turf): Sf: 0-0 **GS: 1-1 Gd: 1-4** GF: 0-4 Fm: 0-1
Distance: **5f/6f: 2-10** 7f-8f: 0-0 9f-13f: 0-0 14f+: 0-0
Track : LH: 0-0 RH: 0-0 Tight: 0-0 Gall: 0-0
Aids: Bl: 0-0 Vi: 0-0 Tstrap: 0-1 Ckp: 0-1
Best Rating: **83** 8/09 Muss 5f good

Modest; suited by 5f and fast ground.

Igneous

91(74) (30)**48**
3-y-o ch g Lucky Story (USA)-Double Top (IRE) (Thatching)
D W Thompson A J Duffield

Placings:40606-0050 (5730)
2009: 7^{0}GF, 9^{0}G, 8^{5}GF, 8^{0}GS,

	Starts	1st	2nd	3rd	Win & Pl
Career Total (Turf)	8	0	0	0	289
Career Total (AW)	1	0	0	0	

Going (Turf): **Sf: 0-0 GS: 0-3 Gd: 0-2 GF: 0-3 Fm: 0-0**
Distance: 5f/6f: 0-3 7f-8f: 0-3 9f-13f: 0-3 14f+: 0-0
Track : LH: 0-2 RH: 0-2 Tight: 0-2 Gall: 0-1
Aids: Bl: 0-1 Vi: 0-0 Tstrap: 0-1 Ckp: 0-1
Best Rating: **48** 8/08 Ayr 6f gd-sft

Ignition

(94) (46)**34**
7-y-o ch m Rock City-Fire Sprite (Mummy's Game)
A Kirtley M F Hyman

Placings:543400/0301625101/0460**65066**/0010100000/0000000-4 (0056)
2009: 6^{4}SD,

	Starts	1st	2nd	3rd	Win & Pl
Career Total (Turf)	35	5	1	2	21091
Career Total (AW)	8	0	0	0	0

64 7/07 Haml 1m65y (0-65)H G-S £2266
58 6/07 Haml 1m1f36y (0-70)H GD £3886
70 9/05 Ayr 1m (0-70)H GD £4674
65 8/05 Epsm 1m114y (0-75)H GD £4056
63 6/05 Muss 1m (0-55)H G-F £3003
Total win prize-money £17887

Going (Turf): Sf: 0-3 GS: 1-7 **Gd: 3-9** GF: 1-12 Fm: 0-4
Distance: 5f/6f: 0-3 7f-8f: 2-15 **9f-13f: 3-25** 14f+: 0-0
Track : LH: 2-22 **RH: 3-19 Tight: 4-25** Gall: 0-1
Aids: Bl: 0-0 Vi: 0-0 Tstrap: 2-15 Ckp: 2-15
Best Rating: **70** 9/05 Ayr 1m good

Very moderate; stays 1m; acts on fast ground and on Polytrack; suited by forcing tactics; has worn cheekpieces.

Igotim

69(73) (40)**36**
3-y-o b g Umistim-Glistening Silver (Puissance)
J Gallagher L Tomlin

Placings:000-00 (2630)
2009: 8^{0}GF, 7^{0}SD,

	Starts	1st	2nd	3rd	Win & Pl
Career Total (Turf)	3	0	0	0	
Career Total (AW)	2	0	0	0	

Going (Turf): **Sf: 0-0 GS: 0-1 Gd: 0-1 GF: 0-1 Fm: 0-0**
Distance: 5f/6f: 0-2 7f-8f: 0-2 9f-13f: 0-1 14f+: 0-0
Track : LH: 0-2 RH: 0-1 Tight: 0-2 Gall: 0-1
Aids: Bl: 0-0 Vi: 0-0 Tstrap: 0-0 Ckp: 0-0
Best Rating: **40** 8/08 Ling 6f stand

Igoyougo

103 **81**
3-y-o b g Millkom-Club Oasis (Forzando)
G A Harker Miss K Watson

Placings:0005-211421 (7119)
2009: 5^{2}GF, 5^{1}GF, 5^{1}GF, 5^{4}GF, 5^{2}GF, 5^{1}GS,

	Starts	1st	2nd	3rd	Win & Pl
Career Total (Turf)	10	3	2	0	9557

81 10/09 Muss 5f (0-75)H G-S £3238
74 8/09 Newc 5f (0-65)H G-F £2201
73 8/09 Ayr 5f (0-65)H G-F £2388
Total win prize-money £7828

Going (Turf): Sf: 0-0 GS: 1-4 Gd: 0-1 **GF: 2-5** Fm: 0-0
Distance: **5f/6f: 3-10** 7f-8f: 0-0 9f-13f: 0-0 14f+: 0-0
Track : LH: 0-1 RH: 0-0 Tight: 0-0 Gall: 0-0
Aids: Bl: 0-0 Vi: 0-0 Tstrap: 0-0 Ckp: 0-0
Best Rating: **81** 10/09 Muss 5f gd-sft

Fair; effective over 5f; acts on fast and easy ground.

Iguacu

103(100) (58)**58**
5-y-o b g Desert Prince (IRE)-Gay Gallanta (USA) (Woodman (USA))
George Baker Derek & Cheryl Holder

Placings:600/0000-553602**10463210** (7750)
2009: 7^{5}GF, 6^{5}SD, 6^{3}GF, 6^{6}GF, 6^{0}GF, 9^{2}GF, 10^{1}G, 8^{0}SF, 11^{4}G, 10^{6}G, 12^{3}SD, 10^{2}SD, 12^{1}SD, 13^{0}SD,

	Starts	1st	2nd	3rd	Win & Pl
Career Total (Turf)	15	1	1	1	3241
Career Total (AW)	6	1	1	1	2492

58 12/09 Kemp 1m4f (0-55)H STD £1706
58 7/09 Nott 1m2f50y (0-60)H GD £1977
Total win prize-money £3684

Going (Turf): Sf: 0-1 GS: 0-1 **Gd: 1-5** GF: 0-8 Fm: 0-0
Distance: 5f/6f: 0-3 7f-8f: 0-8 **9f-13f: 2-9** 14f+: 0-1
Track : LH: 1-13 RH: 1-1 Tight: 0-4 Gall: 0-1
Aids: Bl: 0-1 Vi: 0-0 Tstrap: 0-0 Ckp: 0-0
Best Rating: **58** 12/09 Kemp 1m4f stand

Moderate; stays 1m4f; acts on fast ground and on sand.

Ike Quebec (FR)

(99) (77)**69**
4-y-o ch g Dr Fong (USA)-Avezia (FR) (Night Shift (USA))
J R Boyle J-P Lim & Keith Marsden

Placings:0322121/1400050000-0300 (0898)
2009: 7^{0}SD, 7^{3}SD, 7^{0}SD, 8^{0}SD,

	Starts	1st	2nd	3rd	Win & Pl
Career Total (Turf)	6	0	0	1	674
Career Total (AW)	15	3	3	1	11160

76 2/08 Kemp 6f STD £2047
74 12/07 Wolv 5f216y STD £3238
78 11/07 Ling 7f (0-75) STD £3238
Total win prize-money £8526

Going (Turf): **Sf: 0-1 GS: 0-1 Gd: 0-1 GF: 0-3 Fm: 0-0**
Distance: **5f/6f: 2-8** 7f-8f: 1-10 9f-13f: 0-3 14f+: 0-0
Track : **LH: 2-8** RH: 1-9 **Tight: 2-8** Gall: 0-1
Aids: Bl: 0-6 Vi: 0-2 Tstrap: 0-0 Ckp: 0-0
Best Rating: **78** 11/07 Ling 7f stand

Modest; won 7f nursery at Lingfield November 2007; effective over 6f-7f; acts on a sound surface; acts on Polytrack.

Iketi (GR)

86(93) (62)**31**
3-y-o b f Filandros (GR)-Eldora (FR) (Highest Honor (FR))
Jane Chapple-Hyam Mrs M Marinopoulos

Placings:3000 (6910)
2009: 10^{3}SD, 10^{0}GS, 10^{0}G, 10^{0}G,

	Starts	1st	2nd	3rd	Win & Pl
Career Total (Turf)	3	0	0	0	
Career Total (AW)	1	0	0	1	385

Going (Turf): **Sf: 0-0 GS: 0-1 Gd: 0-2 GF: 0-0 Fm: 0-0**
Distance: 5f/6f: 0-0 7f-8f: 0-0 9f-13f: 0-4 14f+: 0-0
Track : LH: 0-2 RH: 0-2 Tight: 0-1 Gall: 0-1
Aids: Bl: 0-0 Vi: 0-0 Tstrap: 0-0 Ckp: 0-0

Best Rating: 62 3/09 Kemp 1m2f stand

Il Forno

92(87) (59)72
2-y-o b g Exceed And Excel (AUS)-Fred's Dream (Cadeaux Genereux)
D Nicholls Dr Marwan Koukash

Placings:242502 **(6556)**
2009: 6^{2}GS, 6^{4}GS, 5^{2}G, 5^{5}SF, 7^{0}GF, 5^{2}G,

	Starts	1st	2nd	3rd	Win & Pl
Career Total (Turf)	5	0	3	0	3527
Career Total (AW)	1	0	0	0	0

Going (Turf): Sf: 0-0 GS: 0-2 Gd: 0-2 GF: 0-1 Fm: 0-0
Distance: 5f/6f: 0-5 7f-8f: 0-1 9f-13f: 0-0 14f+: 0-0
Track : LH: 0-2 RH: 0-0 Tight: 0-2 Gall: 0-0
Aids: Bl: 0-0 Vi: 0-0 Tstrap: 0-0 Ckp: 0-0
Best Rating: 72 7/09 Nott 5f13y good

Fair; effective over 5f-6f on good and easy ground.

Il Grande Ardone

(103) (85)
4-y-o br c Dr Fong (USA)-Bombalarina (IRE) (Barathea (IRE))
C Von Der Recke (F Sheridan 20/1) Stall Grimminger

Placings:5065/12023311513421-00 **(0653a)**
2009: 12^{0}SD, 10^{0}FZ,

	Starts	1st	2nd	3rd	Win & Pl
Career Total (Turf)	9	1	2	2	6412
Career Total (AW)	11	4	1	1	14014

85	12/08	Sthl	1m4f	(0-75)H	STD	£2729
	6/08	Tagl	1m2f152y	H	FST	£2941
	4/08	Tagl	1m	H	STD	£3860
	4/08	Tagl	1m		STD	£1471
	1/08	Agno	1m	H	SFT	£2206

Total win prize-money £13208

Going (Turf): Sf: 1-4 GS: 0-0 Gd: 0-4 GF: 0-0 Fm: 0-0
Distance: 5f/6f: 0-0 **7f-8f: 3-9** 9f-13f: 2-11 14f+: 0-0
Track : **LH: 1-3** RH: 0-1 Tight: 0-0 Gall: 0-0
Aids: Bl: 0-0 Vi: 0-0 Tstrap: 2-6 Ckp: 2-6
Best Rating: 85 12/08 Sthl 1m4f stand

Fair; stays 1m4f and acts on Fibresand.

Il Portico

82 47
2-y-o b g Zafeen (FR)-Diddymu (IRE) (Revoque (IRE))
M R Channon Derek And Jean Clee

Placings:060 **(5907)**
2009: 7^{0}S, 6^{6}G, 8^{0}GF,

	Starts	1st	2nd	3rd	Win & Pl
Career Total (Turf)	3	0	0	0	0

Going (Turf): Sf: 0-1 GS: 0-0 Gd: 0-1 GF: 0-1 Fm: 0-0
Distance: 5f/6f: 0-0 7f-8f: 0-3 9f-13f: 0-0 14f+: 0-0
Track : LH: 0-1 RH: 0-0 Tight: 0-0 Gall: 0-1
Aids: Bl: 0-0 Vi: 0-0 Tstrap: 0-0 Ckp: 0-0
Best Rating: 47 9/09 Ffos 1m gd-fm

Ildiko (USA)

84(93) (63)36
2-y-o b f Yes It's True (USA)-Eternity (Suave Dancer (USA))
Sir Mark Prescott Dr Catherine Wills

Placings:000 **(7243)**
2009: 8^{0}SS, 8^{0}GS, 8^{0}S,

	Starts	1st	2nd	3rd	Win & Pl
Career Total (Turf)	2	0	0	0	
Career Total (AW)	1	0	0	0	

Going (Turf): Sf: 0-1 GS: 0-1 Gd: 0-0 GF: 0-0 Fm: 0-0
Distance: 5f/6f: 0-0 7f-8f: 0-2 9f-13f: 0-1 14f+: 0-0
Track : LH: 0-3 RH: 0-0 Tight: 0-1 Gall: 0-1
Aids: Bl: 0-0 Vi: 0-0 Tstrap: 0-0 Ckp: 0-0
Best Rating: 63 10/09 Ling 1m std-slw

Ile Royale

99(94) (54)48
4-y-o b f Royal Applause-Island Destiny (Kris)
W S Kittow Mrs M J Parkhouse

Placings:00000460U330/4000000-450 **(3471)**
2009: 6^{4}GF, 6^{5}G, 5^{0}F,

	Starts	1st	2nd	3rd	Win & Pl
Career Total (Turf)	10	0	0	0	289
Career Total (AW)	13	0	0	2	797

Going (Turf): Sf: 0-0 GS: 0-1 Gd: 0-2 GF: 0-3 Fm: 0-4
Distance: 5f/6f: 0-12 7f-8f: 0-9 9f-13f: 0-2 14f+: 0-0
Track : LH: 0-11 RH: 0-6 Tight: 0-7 Gall: 0-0
Aids: Bl: 0-7 Vi: 0-2 Tstrap: 0-0 Ckp: 0-0
Best Rating: 60 10/07 NmkR 6f good

Plating-class; tried up to 7f to date; seems to act on fast ground; has worn eyeshield and blinkers.

Ilie Nastase (FR)

107(101) (98)96
5-y-o b g Royal Applause-Flying Diva (Chief Singer)
E J O'Neill (D M Simcock 31/10) Dr Marwan Koukash

Placings:35311/43164/624102-004550200000 **(7821a)**
2009: 8^{0}GF, 7^{0}GF, 8^{4}S, 8^{5}GF, 8^{5}SD, 7^{0}GF, 8^{2}S, 8^{0}GS, 10^{0}G, 9^{0}SD, 9^{0}SD, 9^{0}SD,

	Starts	1st	2nd	3rd	Win & Pl
Career Total (Turf)	20	2	2	3	36387
Career Total (AW)	8	2	1	0	31226

80	6/08	MsnL	1m	GD	£8088
98	7/07	Deau	1m1f110y	STD	£11486
	11/06	Deau	7f110y	STD	£10344
90	10/06	MsnL	1m	GD	£7241

Total win prize-money £37159

Going (Turf): Sf: 0-5 GS: 0-3 **Gd: 2-6** GF: 0-4 Fm: 0-0
Distance: 5f/6f: 0-0 **7f-8f: 3-17** 9f-13f: 1-11 14f+: 0-0
Track : LH: 0-8 RH: 0-9 Tight: 0-8 Gall: 0-0
Aids: **Bl: 1-4** Vi: 0-0 Tstrap: 0-2 Ckp: 0-2
Best Rating: 100 5/07 Lonc 1m110y v soft

Useful; ex-French; effective at 1m-1m2f; acts on good ground and on Polytrack; has worn blinkers.

Ilkley

82 44
2-y-o b f Fantastic Light (USA)-Zakuska (Zafonic (USA))
M W Easterby Clark Industrial Services Partnership

Placings:050 **(6181)**
2009: 8^{0}GF, 7^{5}S, 7^{0}GF,

	Starts	1st	2nd	3rd	Win & Pl
Career Total (Turf)	3	0	0	0	0

Going (Turf): Sf: 0-1 GS: 0-0 Gd: 0-0 GF: 0-2 Fm: 0-0
Distance: 5f/6f: 0-0 7f-8f: 0-2 9f-13f: 0-1 14f+: 0-0
Track : LH: 0-1 RH: 0-2 Tight: 0-1 Gall: 0-0
Aids: Bl: 0-0 Vi: 0-0 Tstrap: 0-0 Ckp: 0-0
Best Rating: 44 9/09 Thsk 7f soft

Illicit

79(94) (65)33
4-y-o b g Oasis Dream-Daring Miss (Sadler's Wells (USA))
J R Holt (Paul Mason 27/7) Sean Conway

Placings:32545-0000 **(7512)**
2009: 10^{0}G, 8^{0}SD, 13^{0}SD, 10^{0}SD,

	Starts	1st	2nd	3rd	Win & Pl
Career Total (Turf)	6	0	1	1	9080
Career Total (AW)	3	0	0	0	

Going (Turf): Sf: 0-3 GS: 0-1 Gd: 0-2 GF: 0-0 Fm: 0-0
Distance: 5f/6f: 0-0 7f-8f: 0-0 9f-13f: 0-8 14f+: 0-1
Track : LH: 0-2 RH: 0-3 Tight: 0-3 Gall: 0-0
Aids: Bl: 0-0 Vi: 0-0 Tstrap: 0-1 Ckp: 0-1
Best Rating: 65 10/09 Wolv 1m141y stand

Illuminative (USA)

(102) (74)
3-y-o b g Point Given (USA)-Pretty Clear (USA) (Mr Prospector (USA))
J H M Gosden Malih L Al Basti

Placings:221 **(7004)**
2009: 8^{2}SD, 8^{2}SD, 9^{1}SD,

	Starts	1st	2nd	3rd	Win & Pl
Career Total (Turf)	0	0	0	0	
Career Total (AW)	3	1	2	0	3357

74	10/09	Wolv	1m1f103y	STD	£2047

Total win prize-money £2047

Going (Turf): Sf: 0-0 GS: 0-0 Gd: 0-0 GF: 0-0 Fm: 0-0
Distance: 5f/6f: 0-0 7f-8f: 0-1 **9f-13f: 1-2** 14f+: 0-0
Track : **LH: 1-2** RH: 0-1 **Tight: 1-2** Gall: 0-0
Aids: Bl: 0-0 Vi: 0-0 Tstrap: 0-0 Ckp: 0-0
Best Rating: 74 10/09 Wolv 1m1f103y stand

Fair; stays 1m1f and acts on Polytrack.

Illusive Spirit (IRE)

91(93) (68)70
3-y-o b g Clodovil (IRE)-Poker Dice (Primo Dominie)
J H M Gosden G Strawbridge & Ptnrs

Placings:056010 **(6621)**
2009: 8^{0}GF, 8^{5}SD, 8^{6}G, 8^{0}GF, 8^{1}HY, 8^{0}G,

	Starts	1st	2nd	3rd	Win & Pl
Career Total (Turf)	5	1	0	0	2730
Career Total (AW)	1	0	0	0	0

70	7/09	Nott	1m75y	HVY	£2729

Total win prize-money £2730

Going (Turf): **Sf: 1-1** GS: 0-0 Gd: 0-2 GF: 0-2 Fm: 0-0
Distance: 5f/6f: 0-0 7f-8f: 0-3 **9f-13f: 1-3** 14f+: 0-0
Track : **LH: 1-3** RH: 0-0 Tight: 0-1 Gall: 0-1
Aids: Bl: 0-0 Vi: 0-0 Tstrap: 0-0 Ckp: 0-0
Best Rating: 70 7/09 Nott 1m75y heavy

Illustrious Blue

111(114) (113)114

6-y-o b/br h Dansili-Gipsy Moth (Efisio)

W J Knight Mr & Mrs I H Bendelow

Placings:223224/13351161102/13421403/260250000205-4361500 **(7031)**

2009: 9^{4}GF, 12^{3}GF, 12^{6}GF, 12^{1}G, 12^{5}GF, 12^{0}GF, 12^{0}S,

	Starts	1st	2nd	3rd	Win & Pl
Career Total (Turf)	37	8	6	3	198612
Career Total (AW)	8	0	3	3	36364

114	7/09	Gdwd	1m4f		GD	£39739
113	5/07	Gdwd	1m1f192y		GD	£14762
109	2/07	Ndas	1m194y	(95-115)H	GD	£53571
107	9/06	Gdwd	1m1f	(0-100)H	GD	£13710
101	8/06	Gdwd	7f	(0-105)H	GD	£12464
101	8/06	Gdwd	1m	(0-90)H	GD	£9715
96	7/06	Newb	1m	(0-85)H	GD	£6153
82	5/06	Gdwd	7f		GD	£3562

Total win prize-money £153678

Going (Turf): Sf: 0-6 GS: 0-4 **Gd: 8-16** GF: 0-10 Fm: 0-1
Distance: 5f/6f: 0-0 7f-8f: 4-13 9f-13f: 4-32 14f+: 0-0
Track : LH: 1-11 **RH: 6-27 Tight: 3-10** Gall: 1-12
Aids: Bl: 0-0 Vi: 0-3 Tstrap: 0-0 Ckp: 0-0
Best Rating: 114 7/09 Gdwd 1m4f good

Smart; Listed winner, Group 3 placed; stays 1m4f but effective at shorter; acts on most ground on turf, also Polytrack; goes well at Goodwood; has worn a visor.

Illustrious Prince (IRE)

103(91) (62)81

2-y-o b c Acclamation-Sacred Love (IRE) (Barathea (IRE))

J Noseda Saeed Suhail

Placings:52 **(7145)**

2009: 7^{5}SS, 6^{2}G,

	Starts	1st	2nd	3rd	Win & Pl
Career Total (Turf)	1	0	1	0	1542
Career Total (AW)	1	0	0	0	0

Going (Turf): **Sf: 0-0 GS: 0-0 Gd: 0-1 GF: 0-0 Fm: 0-0**
Distance: 5f/6f: 0-1 7f-8f: 0-1 9f-13f: 0-0 14f+: 0-0
Track : LH: 0-1 RH: 0-0 Tight: 0-1 Gall: 0-0
Aids: Bl: 0-0 Vi: 0-0 Tstrap: 0-0 Ckp: 0-0
Best Rating: 81 10/09 NmkR 6f good

Useful; stays 6f; acts on good ground.

Ilston Lord (IRE)

89 66

2-y-o b c One Cool Cat (USA)-Canouan (IRE) (Sadler's Wells (USA))

M P Tregoning David & Gwyn Joseph

Placings:605 **(5907)**

2009: 6^{6}G, 8^{0}G, 8^{5}GF,

	Starts	1st	2nd	3rd	Win & Pl
Career Total (Turf)	3	0	0	0	0

Going (Turf): **Sf: 0-0 GS: 0-0 Gd: 0-2 GF: 0-1 Fm: 0-0**
Distance: 5f/6f: 0-1 7f-8f: 0-2 9f-13f: 0-0 14f+: 0-0
Track : LH: 0-1 RH: 0-1 Tight: 0-0 Gall: 0-1
Aids: Bl: 0-0 Vi: 0-0 Tstrap: 0-0 Ckp: 0-0
Best Rating: 66 9/09 Ffos 1m gd-fm

Modest form at up to 1m on good ground.

Im Ova Ere Dad (IRE)

108(100) (90)87

6-y-o b g Second Empire (IRE)-Eurolink Profile (Prince Sabo)

D E Cantillon Allan Milton

Placings:0601045/1164011551062/415-25 **(2144)**

2009: 8^{2}GF, 8^{5}SD,

	Starts	1st	2nd	3rd	Win & Pl
Career Total (Turf)	11	2	1	0	8743
Career Total (AW)	14	5	1	0	13096

87	6/08	Gdwd	1m1f	(0-70)H	GD	£3123
81	10/07	Ling	1m	(0-70)H	STD	£2817
77	8/07	Chep	1m14y	(0-70)H	G-F	£3886
76	8/07	Kemp	1m	(0-65)H	STD	£2047
73	2/07	Ling	1m	(0-65)H	STD	£2388
71	1/07	Sthl	1m	(0-60)H	STD	£2047
67	7/06	Sthl	1m	(0-55)H	STD	£2730

Total win prize-money £19041

Going (Turf): Sf: 0-0 GS: 0-1 **Gd: 1-3 GF: 1-7** Fm: 0-0
Distance: 5f/6f: 0-3 **7f-8f: 5-15** 9f-13f: 2-7 14f+: 0-0
Track : **LH: 4-12** RH: 2-7 **Tight: 3-8** Gall: 0-3
Aids: Bl: 0-0 Vi: 0-0 Tstrap: 0-0 Ckp: 0-0
Best Rating: 90 12/07 Sthl 1m std-slw

Fair; effective over 1m-1m1f; acts well on Fibresand and Polytrack, and fast ground on turf.

Imaam

107 87

3-y-o ch c Pivotal-Khulood (USA) (Storm Cat (USA))

J L Dunlop Hamdan Al Maktoum

Placings:2224-15521 **(4814)**

2009: 7^{1}G, 8^{5}G, 8^{5}S, 7^{2}G, 7^{1}HY,

	Starts	1st	2nd	3rd	Win & Pl
Career Total (Turf)	9	2	4	0	22345

87	8/09	Leic	7f9y	(0-100)H	HVY	£12462
75	3/09	Folk	7f		GD	£2729

Total win prize-money £15192

Going (Turf): **Sf: 1-2** GS: 0-0 **Gd: 1-5** GF: 0-1 Fm: 0-1
Distance: 5f/6f: 0-1 **7f-8f: 2-7** 9f-13f: 0-1 14f+: 0-0
Track : LH: 0-1 RH: 0-1 Tight: 0-0 Gall: 0-0
Aids: Bl: 0-0 Vi: 0-0 Tstrap: 0-0 Ckp: 0-0
Best Rating: 87 8/09 Leic 7f9y heavy

Useful; effective over 7f; acts on good ground.

Imaginary Diva

99(99) (67)66

3-y-o b f Lend A Hand-Distant Diva (Distant Relative)

G G Margarson Graham Lodge Partnership

Placings:643662533211-004233335446 **(7100)**

2009: 5^{0}SD, 5^{0}SD, 6^{4}G, 5^{2}GF, 5^{3}GF, 5^{3}G, 5^{3}GF, 5^{3}S, 5^{5}G, 5^{4}SD, 5^{4}GF, 5^{6}G,

	Starts	1st	2nd	3rd	Win & Pl
Career Total (Turf)	14	0	1	5	3437
Career Total (AW)	10	2	2	2	7304

65	12/08	Wolv	5f20y	(0-75)	STD	£3238
67	12/08	Sthl	5f	(0-65)	STD	£2047

Total win prize-money £5285

Going (Turf): **Sf: 0-3 GS: 0-0 Gd: 0-5 GF: 0-6 Fm: 0-0**
Distance: **5f/6f: 2-23** 7f-8f: 0-1 9f-13f: 0-0 14f+: 0-0
Track : **LH: 1-8** RH: 0-2 **Tight: 1-4** Gall: 0-5
Aids: Bl: 0-0 Vi: 0-1 Tstrap: 0-0 Ckp: 0-0
Best Rating: 67 12/08 Sthl 5f stand

Modest; effective at 5f; acts on soft ground, on Polytrack and on Fibresand.

Imbongi (SAF)

113 120

5-y-o ch h Russian Revival (USA)-Garden Verse (SAF) (Foveros)

M F De Kock Sheikh Mohammed Bin Khalifa Al Maktoum

Placings:31120/04151125-244613 **(3841)**

2009: 6^{2}G, 8^{4}G, 8^{4}GF, 8^{6}Y, 7^{1}G, 8^{3}GF,

	Starts	1st	2nd	3rd	Win & Pl
Career Total (Turf)	19	6	3	2	182030

117	6/09	NmkJ	7f	GD	£36900
113	5/08	Grey	7f	GD	£13786
120	4/08	Grey	1m	GD	£13786
	3/08	Turf	1m	GD	£17233
	9/07	Turf	1m	GD	£3623
	9/07	Scot	6f6y	GD	£2717

Total win prize-money £88048

Going (Turf): Sf: 0-1 GS: 0-0 **Gd: 6-15** GF: 0-2 Fm: 0-0
Distance: 5f/6f: 0-1 **7f-8f: 6-15** 9f-13f: 0-3 14f+: 0-0
Track : LH: 0-3 RH: 0-2 Tight: 0-0 Gall: 0-4
Aids: Bl: 0-0 Vi: 0-0 Tstrap: 0-0 Ckp: 0-0
Best Rating: 120 3/09 Ndas 1m194y gd-fm

Smart; South African-trained; winner of Group 3 at Newmarket in 2009; stays 1m; acts on good ground.

Imco Spirit (IRE)

96 (83)85

3-y-o b g Invincible Spirit (IRE)-Treasure Hope (IRE) (Treasure Kay)

G M Lyons Sean Jones

Placings:503-21350 **(4727a)**

2009: 7^{2}SD, 7^{1}SD, 8^{3}SD, 7^{5}GF, 7^{0}GY,

	Starts	1st	2nd	3rd	Win & Pl
Career Total (Turf)	2	0	0	0	529
Career Total (AW)	6	1	1	2	11906

83	4/09	Dund	7f	STD	£7379

Total win prize-money £7380

Going (Turf): **Sf: 0-0 GS: 0-0 Gd: 0-0 GF: 0-1 Fm: 0-0**
Distance: 5f/6f: 0-2 **7f-8f: 1-6** 9f-13f: 0-0 14f+: 0-0
Track : **LH: 1-8** RH: 0-0 Tight: 0-1 Gall: 0-0
Aids: Bl: 0-1 Vi: 0-0 Tstrap: 0-0 Ckp: 0-0
Best Rating: 85 5/09 Ches 7f122y gd-fm

Useful; Irish trained; stays 1m and acts on Polytrack.

Imjin River (IRE)

84(101) (79)59

2-y-o b c Namid-Lady Nasrana (FR) (Al Nasr (FR))

M H Tompkins Roalco Limited

Placings:060113 **(7536)**

2009: 6^{0}G, 5^{6}GS, 7^{0}G, 6^{1}SD, 6^{1}SD, 6^{3}SD,

	Starts	1st	2nd	3rd	Win & Pl
Career Total (Turf)	3	0	0	0	0
Career Total (AW)	3	2	0	1	5693

79	11/09	Kemp	6f	(0-75)	STD	£2590
71	10/09	Sthl	6f	(0-65)	STD	£2524

Total win prize-money £5115

Going (Turf): **Sf: 0-0 GS: 0-1 Gd: 0-2 GF: 0-0 Fm: 0-0**
Distance: **5f/6f: 2-5** 7f-8f: 0-1 9f-13f: 0-0 14f+: 0-0
Track : LH: 1-1 RH: 1-2 Tight: 0-0 Gall: 0-0
Aids: Bl: 0-0 Vi: 0-0 Tstrap: 0-0 Ckp: 0-0
Best Rating: 79 11/09 Kemp 6f stand

Fair; stays 6f and acts on Fibresand and Polytrack.

Immaculate Red

(87) (35)**54**

6-y-o ch g Woodborough (USA)-Primula Bairn (Bairn (USA))

C Roberts A Crowther

Placings:002/660030000/0000/0 (7766)

2009: 11^{0}SD,

	Starts	1st	2nd	3rd	Win & Pl
Career Total (Turf)	11	0	0	0	0
Career Total (AW)	6	0	1	1	997

Going (Turf): **Sf: 0-3 GS: 0-1 Gd: 0-2 GF: 0-5 Fm: 0-0**
Distance: 5f/6f: 0-12 7f-8f: 0-4 9f-13f: 0-1 14f+: 0-0
Track : LH: 0-6 RH: 0-2 Tight: 0-1 Gall: 0-1
Aids: Bl: 0-6 Vi: 0-0 Tstrap: 0-0 Ckp: 0-0
Best Rating: **63** 10/05 Sthl 5f stand

Impeccable Guest (IRE)

(84) (30)**59**

6-y-o b m Orpen (USA)-Perfect Guest (What A Guest)

J Mackie Derbyshire Racing IV

Placings:06304/643F632/0 (1654)

2009: 12^{0}SD,

	Starts	1st	2nd	3rd	Win & Pl
Career Total (Turf)	8	0	0	3	1821
Career Total (AW)	5	0	1	0	504

Going (Turf): **Sf: 0-2 GS: 0-2 Gd: 0-2 GF: 0-2 Fm: 0-0**
Distance: 5f/6f: 0-0 7f-8f: 0-6 9f-13f: 0-5 14f+: 0-2
Track : LH: 0-9 RH: 0-1 Tight: 0-6 Gall: 0-0
Aids: Bl: 0-0 Vi: 0-0 Tstrap: 0-0 Ckp: 0-0
Best Rating: **59** 5/06 Rdcr 1m6f19y good

Imperial Angel (IRE)

76 **54**

3-y-o gr f Tagula (IRE)-New Deal (Rainbow Quest (USA))

D Carroll Imperial Racing

Placings:006-000 (3018)

2009: 12^{0}GF, 14^{0}GF, 8^{0}G,

	Starts	1st	2nd	3rd	Win & Pl
Career Total (Turf)	6	0	0	0	0

Going (Turf): **Sf: 0-0 GS: 0-0 Gd: 0-1 GF: 0-5 Fm: 0-0**
Distance: 5f/6f: 0-0 7f-8f: 0-3 9f-13f: 0-2 14f+: 0-1
Track : LH: 0-3 RH: 0-3 Tight: 0-5 Gall: 0-0
Aids: Bl: 0-2 Vi: 0-0 Tstrap: 0-0 Ckp: 0-0
Best Rating: **54** 7/08 Thsk 7f gd-fm

Imperial Delight

94 **77**

2-y-o b g Royal Applause-Playgirl (IRE) (Caerleon (USA))

H Candy A N Solomons

Placings:430 (7145)

2009: 6^{4}G, 6^{3}GS, 6^{0}G,

	Starts	1st	2nd	3rd	Win & Pl
Career Total (Turf)	3	0	0	1	939

Going (Turf): **Sf: 0-0 GS: 0-1 Gd: 0-2 GF: 0-0 Fm: 0-0**

Distance: 5f/6f: 0-2 7f-8f: 0-1 9f-13f: 0-0 14f+: 0-0
Track : LH: 0-0 RH: 0-0 Tight: 0-0 Gall: 0-1
Aids: Bl: 0-0 Vi: 0-0 Tstrap: 0-0 Ckp: 0-0
Best Rating: **77** 10/09 Wind 6f gd-sft

Out of a sister to the high-class 1m2f performer Stage Gift; promise in maidens over 6f ; acts on good/easy ground.

Imperial Djay (IRE)

98(101) (64)**67**

4-y-o b g Dilshaan-Slayjay (IRE) (Mujtahid (USA))

J R Holt (G J Smith 30/3) Hollinbridge Partnership

Placings:340045406060**-053200563400660** (5633)

2009: 7^{0}SD, 6^{5}SD, 5^{3}SD, 5^{2}SD, 6^{0}SD, 7^{0}SD, 7^{5}SD, 7^{6}SD, 7^{3}SD, 7^{4}GF, 8^{0}SD, 7^{0}G, 6^{6}S, 6^{6}G, 6^{0}GS,

	Starts	1st	2nd	3rd	Win & Pl
Career Total (Turf)	12	0	0	1	539
Career Total (AW)	15	0	1	2	1310

Going (Turf): **Sf: 0-1 GS: 0-3 Gd: 0-5 GF: 0-3 Fm: 0-0**
Distance: 5f/6f: 0-9 7f-8f: 0-16 9f-13f: 0-2 14f+: 0-0
Track : LH: 0-22 RH: 0-0 Tight: 0-17 Gall: 0-0
Aids: Bl: 0-1 Vi: 0-3 Tstrap: 0-5 Ckp: 0-5
Best Rating: **67** 5/08 Catt 7f good

Modest; suited by 7f; acts on fast and easy ground and Polytrack.

Imperial Echo (USA)

99(110) (77)**79**

8-y-o b g Labeeb-Regal Baby (USA) (Northern Baby (CAN))

T D Barron Miss N J Barron

Placings:2421433/0040220341345/00625030606505/0211 0600/20432064060/0000160000006500**-643504** (6415)

2009: 7^{6}GF, 6^{4}GF, 6^{3}GF, 6^{5}GS, 7^{0}GF, 7^{4}GF,

	Starts	1st	2nd	3rd	Win & Pl
Career Total (Turf)	66	5	8	7	86231
Career Total (AW)	9	0	0	0	0

79	4/08	Thsk	6f	(0-75)H	GD	£3885
91	7/06	Newc	7f	(0-100)H	G-F	£12464
88	6/06	York	7f	(0-85)H	G-F	£8096
87	8/04	Ripn	6f	D(0-80)H	G-S	£6201
70	8/03	Ayr	7f50y	E	FRM	£3900

Total win prize-money £34547

Going (Turf): Sf: 0-10 GS: 1-9 Gd: 1-17 **GF: 2-27** Fm: 1-3
Distance: 5f/6f: 2-41 **7f-8f: 3-34** 9f-13f: 0-0 14f+: 0-0
Track : **LH: 2-22** RH: 0-9 Tight: 0-16 **Gall: 1-5**
Aids: Bl: 0-1 Vi: 0-9 Tstrap: 0-0 Ckp: 0-0
Best Rating: **91** 7/07 York 7f heavy

Modest; effective over 6f-7f and acts on most ground.

Imperial Guest

103 **98**

3-y-o ch g Imperial Dancer-Princess Speedfit (FR) (Desert Prince (IRE))

G G Margarson John Guest

Placings:410514031-0005063 (4148)

2009: 8^{0}GF, 8^{0}GF, 6^{0}G, 6^{5}GF, 6^{0}G, 6^{6}G, 6^{3}GF,

	Starts	1st	2nd	3rd	Win & Pl
Career Total (Turf)	16	3	0	2	63091

98	10/08	Donc	6f	GD	£23704
83	8/08	Wind	6f	G-F	£3885
85	5/08	Yarm	6f3y	GD	£3885

Total win prize-money £31476

Going (Turf): Sf: 0-1 GS: 0-2 **Gd: 2-6** GF: 1-7 Fm: 0-0
Distance: **5f/6f: 2-9** 7f-8f: 1-7 9f-13f: 0-0 14f+: 0-0
Track : LH: 0-0 RH: 0-0 Tight: 0-0 **Gall: 1-3**
Aids: Bl: 0-0 Vi: 0-0 Tstrap: 0-0 Ckp: 0-0
Best Rating: **98** 10/08 Donc 6f good

Useful; winner in Listed company; effective at 6f; acts on good and faster ground.

Imperial Harry

80(105) (77)**36**

6-y-o b g Alhaarth (IRE)-Serpentara (Kris)

Jean-Rene Auvray (D E Pipe 11/4) Harrison-Allan, Pike & Waddington

Placings:0/434460/0200023/01030000 (6210)

2009: 12^{0}SD, 12^{1}SD, 12^{0}SD, 12^{3}SD, 12^{0}SD, 12^{0}G, 10^{0}G, 12^{0}SD,

	Starts	1st	2nd	3rd	Win & Pl
Career Total (Turf)	14	0	2	2	4084
Career Total (AW)	8	1	0	1	2673

77	1/09	Kemp	1m4f	(0-65)H	STD	£2047

Total win prize-money £2047

Going (Turf): **Sf: 0-0 GS: 0-3 Gd: 0-6 GF: 0-4 Fm: 0-1**
Distance: 5f/6f: 0-0 7f-8f: 0-4 **9f-13f: 1-17** 14f+: 0-1
Track : LH: 0-7 **RH: 1-10** Tight: 0-7 Gall: 0-4
Aids: Bl: 0-0 Vi: 0-1 Tstrap: 0-1 Ckp: 0-1
Best Rating: **77** 3/09 Kemp 1m4f stand

Fair; stays 1m4f; goes on quick ground; acts on Polytrack.

Imperial House

94(94) (65)**67**

3-y-o b c Imperial Dancer-Cotton House (IRE) (Mujadil (USA))

R A Harris (M R Channon 24/10) Mrs Ruth M Serrell

Placings:6100306 (7645)

2009: 6^{6}GF, 6^{1}GF, 6^{0}GS, 8^{0}S, 7^{3}GF, 7^{0}SD, 5^{6}SD,

	Starts	1st	2nd	3rd	Win & Pl
Career Total (Turf)	5	1	0	1	2976
Career Total (AW)	2	0	0	0	0

63	6/09	Rdcr	6f	G-F	£2590

Total win prize-money £2590

Going (Turf): Sf: 0-1 GS: 0-1 Gd: 0-0 **GF: 1-3** Fm: 0-0
Distance: **5f/6f: 1-3** 7f-8f: 0-4 9f-13f: 0-0 14f+: 0-0
Track : LH: 0-2 RH: 0-1 Tight: 0-2 Gall: 0-0
Aids: Bl: 0-1 Vi: 0-0 Tstrap: 0-0 Ckp: 0-0
Best Rating: **67** 10/09 Rdcr 7f gd-fm

Modest; lightly raced; stays 6f; acts on fast ground; has worn blinkers.

Imperial Skylight

95(98) (68)**64**

3-y-o gr g Imperial Dancer-Sky Light Dreams (Dreams To Reality (USA))

M R Channon Peter Taplin

Placings:34004303043462-324122600606006400456 (7880)

2009: 7^{3}SD, 7^{2}SD, 7^{4}SD, 7^{1}SD, 7^{2}SD, 7^{2}SD, 7^{6}SD, 7^{0}GF, 7^{0}GF, 7^{6}G, 6^{0}G, 6^{6}F, 7^{0}SD, 7^{0}GF, 6^{6}SD, 7^{4}GF, 6^{0}GF, 7^{4}SS, 7^{0}SD, 7^{0}SD, 8^{4}SD, 7^{5}SD, 7^{6}SD,

	Starts	1st	2nd	3rd	Win & Pl
Career Total (Turf)	14	0	0	2	1383
Career Total (AW)	23	1	4	3	6711

66	2/09	Kemp	7f	(0-65)H	STD	£2047

Total win prize-money £2047

Going (Turf): **Sf: 0-1 GS: 0-2 Gd: 0-4 GF: 0-6 Fm: 0-1**

Distance: 5f/6f: 0-9 **7f-8f: 1-28** 9f-13f: 0-0 14f+: 0-0
Track : LH: 0-19 **RH: 1-10** Tight: 0-15 Gall: 0-2
Aids: Bl: 0-0 Vi: 0-3 Tstrap: 0-0 Ckp: 0-0
Best Rating: 68 3/09 Ling 7f stand

Moderate; stays 7f and acts on Polytrack.

Imperial Sword

103(98) (56)73

6-y-o b g Danehill Dancer (IRE)-Hajat (Mujtahid (USA))
T D Barron Mrs Margaret Wilson

Placings:416530/24122000/000006/40546231020022425-01241006062100 **(6989)**
2009: 7^{0}SD, 5^{1}GF, 6^{2}G, 6^{4}GS, 5^{1}HY, 5^{0}GF, 5^{0}GF, 5^{6}GS, 5^{0}G, 6^{6}G, 6^{2}G, 6^{1}GF, 6^{0}GF, 6^{0}G,

	Starts	1st	2nd	3rd	Win & Pl
Career Total (Turf)	44	6	10	2	40756
Career Total (AW)	7	0	0	0	0

72	8/09	Ayr	6f	(0-70)H	G-F	£3885
73	5/09	Hayd	5f	(0-70)H	HVY	£3238
68	4/09	Ripn	5f	(0-70)H	G-F	£3238
61	5/08	Wwck	6f	(0-55)H	G-S	£2047
85	5/06	Haml	6f5y	(0-85)H	GD	£7772
72	5/05	Ripn	6f		SFT	£3477

Total win prize-money £23659

Going (Turf): **Sf: 2-7** GS: 1-10 Gd: 1-14 **GF: 2-12** Fm: 0-1
Distance: **5f/6f: 5-34** 7f-8f: 1-17 9f-13f: 0-0 14f+: 0-0
Track : **LH: 1-11** RH: 0-3 Tight: 0-2 Gall: 0-1
Aids: **Bl: 4-33** Vi: 0-0 Tstrap: 0-0 Ckp: 0-0
Best Rating: 92 6/06 Hayd 6f gd-fm

Modest; suited by 5f-6f; acts on most ground; has worn blinkers.

Imperial Warrior

88(91) (58)72

2-y-o ch g Imperial Dancer-Tribal Lady (Absalom)
H Morrison The End-R-Ways Partnership

Placings:630003 **(6948)**
2009: 6^{6}GF, 6^{3}GF, 6^{0}G, 7^{0}G, 6^{0}G, 7^{3}SD,

	Starts	1st	2nd	3rd	Win & Pl
Career Total (Turf)	5	0	0	1	433
Career Total (AW)	1	0	0	1	819

Going (Turf): **Sf: 0-0 GS: 0-0 Gd: 0-3 GF: 0-2 Fm: 0-0**
Distance: 5f/6f: 0-3 7f-8f: 0-3 9f-13f: 0-0 14f+: 0-0
Track : LH: 0-1 RH: 0-1 Tight: 0-0 Gall: 0-1
Aids: Bl: 0-0 Vi: 0-0 Tstrap: 0-0 Ckp: 0-0
Best Rating: 72 6/09 Sals 6f gd-fm

Fair; stays 6f; acts on fast ground.

Imperium

96(101) (66)65

8-y-o b g Imperial Ballet (IRE)-Partenza (USA) (Red Ransom (USA))
Jean-Rene Auvray The Ultimate Power Partnership

Placings:034620046/402005113000602V30/0000500362030300/2500160440001231212/222562410664002503/52043436630B0350643-130335460000400 **(7688)**
2009: 12^{1}SD, 12^{3}SD, 13^{0}SD, 10^{3}SD, 12^{3}SD, 8^{5}GF, 12^{4}GF, 9^{6}G, 7^{0}G, 10^{0}G, 12^{0}SD, 7^{0}SD, 8^{4}SD, 8^{0}SD, 12^{0}SD,

	Starts	1st	2nd	3rd	Win & Pl
Career Total (Turf)	58	4	4	8	23933
Career Total (AW)	56	4	10	8	16474

65	1/09	Kemp	1m4f	(0-60)H	STD	£1978
68	5/07	Chep	7f16y	(0-70)H	G-F	£3238
64	10/06	Kemp	6f	(0-45)	STD	£2047
56	6/06	Brig	5f59y	(0-60)H	FRM	£2590
55	3/06	Wolv	5f216y		STD	£2388
74	5/04	Brig	5f59y	E(0-75)H	G-F	£4410
68	5/04	Brig	5f59y	E(0-70)H	G-F	£3666

Total win prize-money £20322

Going (Turf): Sf: 0-2GS: 0-3 Gd: 0-14 **GF: 3-29** Fm: 1-10
Distance: **5f/6f: 6-60** 7f-8f: 1-39 9f-13f: 1-15 14f+: 0-0
Track : **LH: 5-65** RH: 2-24 **Tight: 2-36** Gall: 0-7
Aids: Bl: 0-9 Vi: 0-3 Tstrap: 4-42 Ckp: 4-42
Best Rating: 81 7/03 Kemp 6f good

Modest; effective over 6f-1m4f; acts on most ground on turf; goes on Polytrack; has worn cheekpieces.

Implication

104(102) (82)77

3-y-o b f Pivotal-Insinuation (IRE) (Danehill (USA))
E A L Dunlop Cheveley Park Stud

Placings:0-20220221663 **(7092)**
2009: 8^{2}GF, 8^{0}GF, 8^{2}SD, 8^{2}SD, 8^{0}GF, 8^{2}GS, 8^{2}SD, 8^{1}GS, 8^{6}SD, 8^{6}G, 8^{3}SD,

	Starts	1st	2nd	3rd	Win & Pl
Career Total (Turf)	7	1	2	0	5750
Career Total (AW)	5	0	3	1	4691

64	9/09	Newc	1m	G-S	£3784

Total win prize-money £3785

Going (Turf): Sf: 0-1 **GS: 1-2** Gd: 0-1 GF: 0-3 Fm: 0-0
Distance: 5f/6f: 0-0 **7f-8f: 1-7** 9f-13f: 0-5 14f+: 0-0
Track : **LH: 1-5** RH: 0-3 Tight: 0-3 **Gall: 1-2**
Aids: Bl: 0-0 Vi: 0-0 Tstrap: 0-0 Ckp: 0-0
Best Rating: 82 6/09 Kemp 1m stand

Fair; stays 1m; acts on fast and easy ground and on Polytrack.

Imposing

110 96

3-y-o b c Danehill Dancer (IRE)-On Fair Stage (IRE) (Sadler's Wells (USA))
Sir Michael Stoute D Smith, Mrs J Magnier, M Tabor

Placings:210-2 **(1303)**
2009: 10^{2}GF,

	Starts	1st	2nd	3rd	Win & Pl
Career Total (Turf)	4	1	2	0	8965

80	9/08	Hayd	1m30y	G-F	£4533

Total win prize-money £4533

Going (Turf): Sf: 0-1 GS: 0-0 Gd: 0-0 **GF: 1-3** Fm: 0-0
Distance: 5f/6f: 0-0 7f-8f: 0-2 **9f-13f: 1-2** 14f+: 0-0
Track : **LH: 1-1** RH: 0-0 Tight: 0-0 Gall: 0-0
Aids: Bl: 0-0 Vi: 0-0 Tstrap: 0-0 Ckp: 0-0
Best Rating: 96 4/09 NmkR 1m2f gd-fm

Useful; stays 1m2f and acts on fast ground.

Impressible

107(82) (52)96

3-y-o b f Oasis Dream-Imperial Bailiwick (IRE) (Imperial Frontier (USA))
E J Alston Mr & Mrs G Middlebrook

Placings:4505501-21312101052 **(6283)**
2009: 5^{2}GF, 5^{1}GF, 5^{3}GS, 5^{1}GF, 5^{2}GF, 5^{1}GF, 5^{0}GF, 5^{1}S, 5^{0}GF, 5^{5}G, 5^{2}GF,

	Starts	1st	2nd	3rd	Win & Pl
Career Total (Turf)	17	5	3	1	34224
Career Total (AW)	1	0	0	0	

96	8/09	Haml	5f4y	(0-85)H	SFT	£6799
83	6/09	Ches	5f16y	(0-90)H	G-F	£8831
77	6/09	Carl	5f	(0-70)H	G-F	£3412
73	4/09	Hayd	5f	(0-75)H	G-F	£3238
61	10/08	Rdcr	6f		GD	£3561

Total win prize-money £25843

Going (Turf): Sf: 1-2 GS: 0-1 Gd: 1-4 **GF: 3-10** Fm: 0-0
Distance: **5f/6f: 5-17** 7f-8f: 0-1 9f-13f: 0-0 14f+: 0-0
Track : LH: 1-5 RH: 1-1 Tight: 1-4 Gall: 1-2
Aids: Bl: 0-0 Vi: 0-0 Tstrap: 0-0 Ckp: 0-0
Best Rating: 96 8/09 Haml 5f4y soft

Useful sprinter; acts on fast ground and on soft.

Impressionist Art (USA)

99(85) (65)59

3-y-o ch f Giant's Causeway (USA)-Chalamont (IRE) (Kris)
Patrick J Flynn E Fitzpatrick

Placings:0500-000002220 **(7632)**
2009: 7^{0}HY, 7^{0}YS, 10^{0}HY, 10^{0}S, 10^{0}HY, 7^{2}S, 10^{2}SD, 8^{2}SD, 9^{0}SD,

	Starts	1st	2nd	3rd	Win & Pl
Career Total (Turf)	9	0	1	0	1155
Career Total (AW)	4	0	2	0	2188

Going (Turf): **Sf: 0-5 GS: 0-0 Gd: 0-1 GF: 0-2 Fm: 0-0**
Distance: 5f/6f: 0-0 7f-8f: 0-8 9f-13f: 0-5 14f+: 0-0
Track : LH: 0-4 RH: 0-5 Tight: 0-1 Gall: 0-0
Aids: Bl: 0-0 Vi: 0-0 Tstrap: 0-0 Ckp: 0-0
Best Rating: 65 11/09 Dund 1m stand

Imprimis Tagula (IRE)

100(110) (104)71

5-y-o b g Tagula (IRE)-Strelitzia (IRE) (Bluebird (USA))
A Bailey Middleham Park Racing XLI & Alan Bailey

Placings:06542/113/002066-412211662145302006411211 **(7862)**
2009: 7^{4}SD, 6^{1}SD, 5^{2}SD, 7^{2}SD, 5^{1}SD, 6^{1}SD, 6^{6}G, 6^{6}GF, 7^{2}SD, 7^{1}SD, 7^{4}G, 7^{5}SD, 5^{3}GF, 6^{0}SD, 6^{2}SD, 5^{0}GS, 5^{0}SD, 5^{6}SD, 6^{4}SD, 6^{1}SD, 6^{1}SD, 7^{2}SD,

	Starts	1st	2nd	3rd	Win & Pl
Career Total (Turf)	9	0	0	2	3033
Career Total (AW)	29	10	7	0	56865

	12/09	Wolv	5f216y	(0-100)H	STD	£11215
104	12/09	Sthl	7f	(0-100)H	SS	£16241
91	12/09	Ling	6f	(0-80)H	STD	£5180
87	11/09	Sthl	6f	(0-75)H	STD	£2729
87	6/09	Sthl	7f		STD	£2047
87	4/09	Sthl	6f		STD	£2047
73	3/09	Sthl	5f		STD	£2047
84	2/09	Sthl	6f	(0-75)H	STD	£2729
79	2/07	Sthl	6f	(0-75)H	STD	£3238
78	2/07	Sthl	6f		STD	£2968

Total win prize-money £50447

Going (Turf): **Sf: 0-0 GS: 0-1 Gd: 0-3 GF: 0-5 Fm: 0-0**
Distance: **5f/6f: 8-24** 7f-8f: 2-13 9f-13f: 0-1 14f+: 0-0
Track : **LH: 9-30** RH: 0-1 **Tight: 2-16** Gall: 0-1
Aids: Bl: 0-1 **Vi: 8-27** Tstrap: 0-0 Ckp: 0-0
Best Rating: 104 12/09 Sthl 7f std-slw

Smart; seems best suited by 5f-7f; best on Fibresand but handles Polytrack too; has worn a visor.

Impromptu

(100) (73)83

5-y-o b g Mujadil (USA)-Pie In The Sky (Bishop Of Cashel)

P G Murphy The Golden Anorak Partnership

Placings:22542/513150/**60P-30** (1121)
2009: 6^{3}SD, 7^{0}SD,

	Starts	1st	2nd	3rd	Win & Pl
Career Total (Turf)	10	2	3	1	11011
Career Total (AW)	6	0	0	1	385

83 8/07 Bath 5f161y (0-75)H G-S £3076
66 6/07 Wind 6f SFT £3238
Total win prize-money £6316

Going (Turf): **Sf: 1-2 GS: 1-2** Gd: 0-3 GF: 0-2 Fm: 0-1
Distance: **5f/6f: 2-15** 7f-8f: 0-1 9f-13f: 0-0 14f+: 0-0
Track : **LH: 1-4** RH: 0-3 Tight: 0-2 **Gall: 2-4**
Aids: Bl: 0-0 Vi: 0-0 Tstrap: 0-0 Ckp: 0-0
Best Rating: **83** 8/07 Bath 5f161y gd-sft

Fair sort; stays 6f; handles easy ground.

Improper (USA)

82(79) (23)**42**
3-y-o b g Northern Afleet (USA)-Bare It Properly (USA) (Proper Reality (USA))
Mouse Hamilton-Fairley Hamilton-Fairley Racing

Placings:0-00000 (6611)
2009: 8^{0}G, 10^{0}GF, 11^{0}GS, 14^{0}G, 7^{0}SD,

	Starts	1st	2nd	3rd	Win & Pl
Career Total (Turf)	5	0	0	0	
Career Total (AW)	1	0	0	0	

Going (Turf): **Sf: 0-0 GS: 0-1 Gd: 0-3 GF: 0-1 Fm: 0-0**
Distance: 5f/6f: 0-1 7f-8f: 0-1 9f-13f: 0-3 14f+: 0-1
Track : LH: 0-1 RH: 0-3 Tight: 0-2 Gall: 0-1
Aids: Bl: 0-0 Vi: 0-0 Tstrap: 0-0 Ckp: 0-0
Best Rating: **42** 10/08 Wind 6f good

Impure Thoughts

(-3) (42)
4-y-o br g Averti (IRE)-Blooming Lucky (IRE) (Lucky Guest)
D W Thompson J A Moore

Placings:000/0 (7466)
2009: 9^{0}SD,

	Starts	1st	2nd	3rd	Win & Pl
Career Total (Turf)	0	0	0	0	
Career Total (AW)	4	0	0	0	

Going (Turf): **Sf: 0-0 GS: 0-0 Gd: 0-0 GF: 0-0 Fm: 0-0**
Distance: 5f/6f: 0-2 7f-8f: 0-1 9f-13f: 0-1 14f+: 0-0
Track : LH: 0-4 RH: 0-0 Tight: 0-4 Gall: 0-0
Aids: Bl: 0-0 Vi: 0-0 Tstrap: 0-0 Ckp: 0-0
Best Rating: **42** 12/07 Ling 6f stand

In Footlights (USA)

100 **83**
3-y-o b c Elusive Quality (USA)-Triple Act (USA) (Theatrical)
Saeed Bin Suroor Godolphin

Placings:15 (4020)
2009: 8^{1}GF, 9^{5}GF,

	Starts	1st	2nd	3rd	Win & Pl
Career Total (Turf)	2	1	0	0	5463

83 6/09 NmkJ 1m G-F £5180
Total win prize-money £5181

Going (Turf): Sf: 0-0 GS: 0-0 Gd: 0-0 **GF: 1-2** Fm: 0-0
Distance: 5f/6f: 0-0 **7f-8f: 1-1** 9f-13f: 0-1 14f+: 0-0
Track : LH: 0-0 RH: 0-1 Tight: 0-0 Gall: 0-0
Aids: Bl: 0-0 Vi: 0-0 Tstrap: 0-0 Ckp: 0-0
Best Rating: **83** 6/09 NmkJ 1m gd-fm

First foal of a winning half-sister to a couple of useful performers in the USA; won well on belated debut over 1m on fast ground; disappointed over 1m2f next time.

In Secret

104(95) (67)**75**
3-y-o b f Dalakhani (IRE)-Conspiracy (Rudimentary (USA))
J L Dunlop The Earl Cadogan

Placings:0-0330202**022** (7725)
2009: 8^{0}GF, 7^{3}GF, 8^{3}GF, 10^{0}GF, 10^{2}GF, 10^{0}GS, 10^{2}G, 10^{0}SD, 10^{2}SD, 12^{2}SD,

	Starts	1st	2nd	3rd	Win & Pl
Career Total (Turf)	8	0	2	2	4313
Career Total (AW)	3	0	2	0	1814

Going (Turf): **Sf: 0-0 GS: 0-1 Gd: 0-2 GF: 0-5 Fm: 0-0**
Distance: 5f/6f: 0-0 7f-8f: 0-4 9f-13f: 0-7 14f+: 0-0
Track : LH: 0-5 RH: 0-4 Tight: 0-3 Gall: 0-3
Aids: Bl: 0-0 Vi: 0-0 Tstrap: 0-0 Ckp: 0-0
Best Rating: **75** 10/09 Bath 1m2f46y good

Fair; stays at least 1m2f; acts on fast ground and Fibresand.

In Some Respect (IRE)

103(98) (102)**104**
2-y-o b c Indian Haven-Burnin' Memories (USA) (Lit De Justice (USA))
Andrew Oliver R A Pegum

Placings:324241 (6191a)
2009: 5^{3}GF, 6^{2}GY, 6^{4}HY, 6^{2}S, 6^{4}SD, 6^{1}G,

	Starts	1st	2nd	3rd	Win & Pl
Career Total (Turf)	5	1	2	1	92225
Career Total (AW)	1	0	0	0	2685

85 9/09 Fair 6f GD £7044
Total win prize-money £7044

Going (Turf): Sf: 0-2 GS: 0-0 **Gd: 1-1** GF: 0-1 Fm: 0-0
Distance: **5f/6f: 1-6** 7f-8f: 0-0 9f-13f: 0-0 14f+: 0-0
Track : LH: 0-1 **RH: 1-3** Tight: 0-0 Gall: 0-0
Aids: Bl: 0-0 Vi: 0-0 Tstrap: 0-0 Ckp: 0-0
Best Rating: **104** 6/09 Curr 6f gd-yld

Smart; second foal of a 1m winner; effective over 5-6f; acts on most ground.

In Step

(90) (51)**57**
3-y-o b f Montjeu (IRE)-Heart's Harmony (Blushing Groom (FR))
W J Haggas Mrs Denis Haynes

Placings:0060-40 (0205)
2009: 9^{4}SD, 10^{0}SD,

	Starts	1st	2nd	3rd	Win & Pl
Career Total (Turf)	1	0	0	0	
Career Total (AW)	5	0	0	0	0

Going (Turf): **Sf: 0-0 GS: 0-1 Gd: 0-0 GF: 0-0 Fm: 0-0**
Distance: 5f/6f: 0-0 7f-8f: 0-1 9f-13f: 0-5 14f+: 0-0
Track : LH: 0-5 RH: 0-0 Tight: 0-4 Gall: 0-0
Aids: Bl: 0-1 Vi: 0-0 Tstrap: 0-0 Ckp: 0-0
Best Rating: **57** 10/08 Yarm 1m3y gd-sft

In The Mood (IRE)

92(96) (58)**70**
3-y-o ch f Hawk Wing (USA)-Grecian Glory (IRE) (Zafonic (USA))
W Jarvis Kevin Hickman

Placings:00-4200 (7149)
2009: 7^{4}GS, 8^{2}GF, 8^{0}SS, 8^{0}G,

	Starts	1st	2nd	3rd	Win & Pl
Career Total (Turf)	5	0	1	0	809
Career Total (AW)	1	0	0	0	

Going (Turf): **Sf: 0-0 GS: 0-1 Gd: 0-2 GF: 0-1 Fm: 0-0**
Distance: 5f/6f: 0-0 7f-8f: 0-6 9f-13f: 0-0 14f+: 0-0
Track : LH: 0-1 RH: 0-0 Tight: 0-1 Gall: 0-0
Aids: Bl: 0-0 Vi: 0-0 Tstrap: 0-0 Ckp: 0-0
Best Rating: **70** 9/09 Sals 1m gd-fm

Modest; effective at 1m; acts on fast ground.

In The Slips (USA)

104(80) (46)**92**
2-y-o b f More Than Ready (USA)-Tjinouska (USA) (Cozzene (USA))
Jeff Mullins (James Lloyd 6/11) Michael House

Placings:003112 (6232)
2009: 7^{0}SD, 6^{0}GF, 6^{3}GF, 6^{1}GF, 8^{1}GF, 8^{2}F,

	Starts	1st	2nd	3rd	Win & Pl
Career Total (Turf)	5	2	1	1	44904
Career Total (AW)	1	0	0	0	

92 9/09 Pont 1m4y (0-85) G-F £4533
84 9/09 Donc 6f110y H G-F £25904
Total win prize-money £30437

Going (Turf): Sf: 0-0 GS: 0-0 Gd: 0-0 **GF: 2-4** Fm: 0-1
Distance: 5f/6f: 0-2 7f-8f: 1-3 9f-13f: 1-1 14f+: 0-0
Track : **LH: 1-2** RH: 0-1 Tight: 0-0 Gall: 0-2
Aids: Bl: 0-0 Vi: 0-0 Tstrap: 0-0 Ckp: 0-0
Best Rating: **92** 9/09 Pont 1m4y gd-fm

Useful; stays 1m; acts on fast ground.

Inca Slew (IRE)

77(82) (51)**51**
3-y-o ch g City On A Hill (USA)-Con Dancer (Shareef Dancer (USA))
P C Haslam Middleham Park Racing XXXIX

Placings:304-600 (2802)
2009: 8^{6}SD, 9^{0}SD, 12^{0}F,

	Starts	1st	2nd	3rd	Win & Pl
Career Total (Turf)	4	0	0	1	472
Career Total (AW)	2	0	0	0	

Going (Turf): **Sf: 0-0 GS: 0-0 Gd: 0-0 GF: 0-3 Fm: 0-1**
Distance: 5f/6f: 0-2 7f-8f: 0-1 9f-13f: 0-3 14f+: 0-0
Track : LH: 0-2 RH: 0-1 Tight: 0-3 Gall: 0-0
Aids: Bl: 0-1 Vi: 0-2 Tstrap: 0-1 Ckp: 0-1
Best Rating: **51** 1/09 Wolv 1m141y stand

Inca Soldier (FR)

91(103) (66)**62**

6-y-o br g Intikhab (USA)-Chrysalu (Distant Relative)

S A Harris (R C Guest 29/4) Wilf Hobson

Placings:04/0500/000301040310261536**4**/0255**0**000-200600 **(5443)**

2009: 5^{2}SD, 5^{0}SD, 7^{0}G, 8^{6}SD, 7^{0}GF, 6^{0}GF,

	Starts	1st	2nd	3rd	Win & Pl
Career Total (Turf)	22	2	1	2	7151
Career Total (AW)	17	1	2	1	4111

69	8/07	Rdcr	6f	(0-60)H	FRM	£2047
61	6/07	Ayr	6f	(0-70)H	GD	£3238
56	4/07	Wolv	7f32y	(0-50)H	STD	£2047

Total win prize-money £7335

Going (Turf): Sf: 0-2 GS: 0-3 **Gd: 1-7** GF: 0-8 **Fm: 1-2**
Distance: **5f/6f: 2-18** 7f-8f: 1-21 9f-13f: 0-0 14f+: 0-0
Track : **LH: 1-24** RH: 0-4 **Tight: 1-19** Gall: 0-0
Aids: Bl: 0-0 Vi: 0-0 Tstrap: 0-0 Ckp: 0-0
Best Rating: 69 8/07 Rdcr 6f firm

Modest gelding; effective from 6f to 1m; acts on both All-Weather surfaces and a sound surface on turf.

Incendo

99(109) (86)**77**

3-y-o ch g King's Best (USA)-Kindle (Selkirk (USA))

J R Fanshawe Andrew & Julia Turner

Placings:030-66**2**4521 **(6613)**

2009: 8^{6}GS, 8^{6}GF, 12^{2}SD, 12^{4}G, 10^{5}GF, 11^{2}GF, 12^{1}SD,

	Starts	1st	2nd	3rd	Win & Pl
Career Total (Turf)	8	0	1	1	1637
Career Total (AW)	2	1	1	0	5332

86	10/09	Kemp	1m4f	(0-80)H	STD	£4727

Total win prize-money £4727

Going (Turf): **Sf: 0-2 GS: 0-1 Gd: 0-1 GF: 0-4 Fm: 0-0**
Distance: 5f/6f: 0-0 7f-8f: 0-3 **9f-13f: 1-7** 14f+: 0-0
Track : LH: 0-2 **RH: 1-4** Tight: 0-1 Gall: 0-2
Aids: Bl: 0-0 Vi: 0-0 Tstrap: 0-0 Ckp: 0-0
Best Rating: 86 10/09 Kemp 1m4f stand

Modest; stays 1m4f; acts on Polytrack and good ground on turf; has worn a tongue tie.

Inch Lodge

91(109) (70)**66**

7-y-o ch h Grand Lodge (USA)-Legaya (Shirley Heights)

Miss D Mountain Miss Debbie Mountain

Placings:1/0245**0**10151/0/500**0**10**0**4660-0123000100**0**40443 **(7767)**

2009: 10^{0}SD, 10^{1}SD, 10^{2}SD, 11^{3}SD, 11^{0}SD, 9^{0}G, 10^{0}SD, 11^{1}SD, 12^{0}SD, 12^{0}GF, 12^{4}SD, 12^{0}SD, 12^{4}SD, 12^{4}SD, 11^{3}SD,

	Starts	1st	2nd	3rd	Win & Pl
Career Total (Turf)	9	1	1	0	3130
Career Total (AW)	29	6	1	2	23265

70	9/09	Kemp	1m3f	(0-60)H	STD	£2047
67	2/09	Ling	1m2f	(0-70)H	STD	£2729
63	5/08	Yarm	1m3f101y	(0-65)H	GD	£1780
83	12/06	Wolv	1m4f50y	(0-85)H	STD	£5505
80	11/06	Wolv	1m4f50y	(0-75)H	STD	£3238
72	9/06	Wolv	1m4f50y	(0-70)H	STD	£3238
76	11/04	Wolv	7f32y		STD	£4140

Total win prize-money £22682

Going (Turf): Sf: 0-1 GS: 0-0 **Gd: 1-2** GF: 0-4 Fm: 0-2
Distance: 5f/6f: 0-0 7f-8f: 1-4 **9f-13f: 6-34** 14f+: 0-0
Track : **LH: 6-24** RH: 1-12 **Tight: 6-20** Gall: 0-1
Aids: Bl: 0-0 Vi: 0-0 Tstrap: 0-0 Ckp: 0-0
Best Rating: 83 12/06 Wolv 1m4f50y stand

Modest; effective at around 1m2f-1m4f; acts on fast ground; goes on Polytrack; likes Wolverhampton; has worn a tongue-tie.

Inchando (FR)

99(77) (21)**57**

5-y-o ch h Hernando (FR)-Nordican Inch (Inchinor)

A W Carroll Lost The Plot Productions

Placings:30/34/00**0**522 **(4935)**

2009: 9^{0}G, 10^{0}GF, 8^{0}SD, 12^{5}S, 12^{2}HY, 18^{2}G,

	Starts	1st	2nd	3rd	Win & Pl
Career Total (Turf)	9	0	2	2	6197
Career Total (AW)	1	0	0	0	

Going (Turf): **Sf: 0-3 GS: 0-1 Gd: 0-3 GF: 0-1 Fm: 0-0**
Distance: 5f/6f: 0-0 7f-8f: 0-5 9f-13f: 0-4 14f+: 0-1
Track : LH: 0-6 RH: 0-1 Tight: 0-0 Gall: 0-1
Aids: Bl: 0-0 Vi: 0-0 Tstrap: 0-0 Ckp: 0-0
Best Rating: 82 10/07 StCl 1m v soft

Inchnadamph

107(98) (60)**93**

9-y-o b g Inchinor-Pelf (USA) (Al Nasr (FR))

T J Fitzgerald R N Cardwell

Placings:500/00**0**/62211502/34121103/0**0**02/0013051/0003-**0**6053004 **(7117)**

2009: 16^{0}SD, 18^{6}GF, 16^{0}GS, 16^{5}G, 16^{3}G, 16^{0}GF, 18^{0}GF, 16^{4}GS,

	Starts	1st	2nd	3rd	Win & Pl
Career Total (Turf)	42	7	5	5	111517
Career Total (AW)	3	0	0	0	

93	11/07	Donc	2m110y	(0-100)H	G-F	£16192
87	7/07	Catt	1m7f177y	(0-85)H	G-F	£5181
83	8/05	NmkJ	2m24y	(0-90)H	GD	£9626
81	6/05	Hayd	1m6f	(0-85)H	G-F	£7038
74	6/05	Hayd	1m6f	(0-75)H	GD	£3658
70	7/04	Haml	1m5f9yE	(0-75)H	GD	£4143
63	6/04	Haml	1m5f9yE	(0-75)H	GD	£3981

Total win prize-money £49823

Going (Turf): Sf: 0-5 GS: 0-11 **Gd: 4-12** GF: 3-14 Fm: 0-0
Distance: 5f/6f: 0-0 7f-8f: 0-3 9f-13f: 0-10 **14f+: 7-32**
Track : **LH: 4-28** RH: 3-15 **Tight: 3-10** Gall: 2-21
Aids: Bl: 0-0 Vi: 0-0 Tstrap: 0-0 Ckp: 0-0
Best Rating: 93 5/09 Ches 2m2f147y gd-fm

Useful; stays 2m2f; acts on most ground; usually wears a tongue tie.

Inchpast

107(101) (76)**80**

8-y-o ch g Inchinor-Victor Ludorum (Rainbow Quest (USA))

M H Tompkins Marcoe Racing Welwyn

Placings:0**50**/00412111/3511**6**2300/00351**1**/00642000**200**-641160436 **(6115)**

2009: 14^{6}GF, 18^{4}G, 16^{1}G, 16^{1}GF, 17^{6}GF, 16^{0}G, 16^{4}SD, 16^{3}GF, 18^{6}GF,

	Starts	1st	2nd	3rd	Win & Pl
Career Total (Turf)	37	8	3	4	57469
Career Total (AW)	9	2	1	0	7686

76	6/09	Rlpn	2m	(0-75)H	G-F	£3238
74	5/09	Gdwd	2m	(0-70)H	GD	£3238
84	12/07	Wolv	2m119y	(0-75)H	STD	£2968
76	11/07	Wolv	2m119y	(0-75)H	STD	£2968
86	6/05	Sals	1m6f15y	(0-85)H	G-F	£7056
85	6/05	Sand	1m6f	(0-85)H	G-F	£6893
83	9/04	Rdcr	1m6f19y	(0-70)H	FRM	£7553
77	9/04	Catt	1m5f175y	(0-70)H	G-F	£5265
70	8/04	Bevl	1m4f16y	F(0-60)	G-S	£3339
66	7/04	Yarm	1m3f101y	F(0-55)H	GD	£3409

Total win prize-money £45929

Going (Turf): Sf: 0-1 GS: 1-4 Gd: 2-10 **GF: 4-21** Fm: 1-1
Distance: 5f/6f: 0-0 7f-8f: 0-3 9f-13f: 2-7 **14f+: 8-36**
Track : LH: 5-26 RH: 5-18 **Tight: 9-24** Gall: 0-11
Aids: **Bl: 10-40** Vi: 0-0 Tstrap: 0-0 Ckp: 0-0
Best Rating: 89 7/05 York 1m5f197y gd-fm

Fair; stays 2m5f; acts on a sound surface; also goes on Fibresand and Polytrack; usually blinkered.

Incomparable

107(106) (84)**87**

4-y-o ch g Compton Place-Indian Silk (IRE) (Dolphin Street (FR))

J A Glover (A J McCabe 20/3) Paul J Dixon & Brian Morton

Placings:4521/**5**06**0001426-62221**43026140 **(6647)**

2009: 5^{6}SD, 5^{2}SD, 5^{2}SD, 5^{2}SD, 5^{1}SD, 5^{4}SD, 5^{3}SF, 5^{0}GS, 6^{2}GF, 6^{6}GF, 5^{1}GF, 5^{4}GF, 5^{0}G,

	Starts	1st	2nd	3rd	Win & Pl
Career Total (Turf)	12	2	2	0	14324
Career Total (AW)	15	2	4	1	13138

87	9/09	Donc	5f	(0-85)H	G-F	£6152
84	2/09	Wolv	5f20y	(0-80)H	STD	£5180
73	11/08	Sthl	5f	(0-75)H	STD	£2590
77	11/07	Donc	6f		G-F	£4857

Total win prize-money £18781

Going (Turf): Sf: 0-2 GS: 0-1 Gd: 0-3 **GF: 2-6** Fm: 0-0
Distance: **5f/6f: 4-25** 7f-8f: 0-2 9f-13f: 0-0 14f+: 0-0
Track : **LH: 1-10** RH: 0-2 **Tight: 1-9** Gall: 0-0
Aids: Bl: 1-5 Vi: 0-0 Tstrap: 1-8 Ckp: 1-8
Best Rating: 87 9/09 Donc 5f gd-fm

Useful; suited by 5f; acts on fast ground and handles Polytrack; has worn blinkers and cheekpieces.

Inconspicuous Miss (USA)

87(103) (69)**41**

3-y-o b/br f War Chant (USA)-Orissa (USA) (Devil's Bag (USA))

George Baker Jerry Jamgotchian

Placings:531-000100300 **(7524)**

2009: 8^{0}SD, 7^{0}GF, 7^{0}GF, 9^{1}SD, 12^{0}SD, 9^{0}SD, 10^{3}SD, 12^{0}SD, 10^{0}SD,

	Starts	1st	2nd	3rd	Win & Pl
Career Total (Turf)	2	0	0	0	
Career Total (AW)	10	2	0	2	6400

69	9/09	Wolv	1m1f103y	(0-70)H	STD	£2914
66	11/08	Wolv	7f32y		STD	£2729

Total win prize-money £5644

Going (Turf): **Sf: 0-0 GS: 0-0 Gd: 0-0 GF: 0-2 Fm: 0-0**
Distance: 5f/6f: 0-1 7f-8f: 1-4 9f-13f: 1-7 14f+: 0-0
Track : **LH: 2-8** RH: 0-2 **Tight: 2-6** Gall: 0-0
Aids: Bl: 0-0 Vi: 0-0 Tstrap: 0-2 Ckp: 0-2
Best Rating: 69 9/09 Wolv 1m1f103y stand

Modest; effective over 6f-7f; acts on Fibresand and Polytrack; has worn a tongue-tie/cheekpieces.

Incy Wincy

81(91) (39)**31**

3-y-o b g Zahran (IRE)-Miss Money Spider (IRE) (Statoblest)

J M Bradley J M Bradley

Placings:400-5565000 (7719)
2009: 9^5SD, 8^5SD, 8^6SD, 7^5G, 7^0SD, 8^0SD, 9^0SD,

	Starts	1st	2nd	3rd	Win & Pl
Career Total (Turf)	4	0	0	0	0
Career Total (AW)	6	0	0	0	0

Going (Turf): **Sf: 0-0 GS: 0-0 Gd: 0-3 GF: 0-1 Fm: 0-0**
Distance: 5f/6f: 0-3 7f-8f: 0-5 9f-13f: 0-2 14f+: 0-0
Track : LH: 0-5 RH: 0-1 Tight: 0-4 Gall: 0-0
Aids: Bl: 0-1 Vi: 0-0 Tstrap: 0-2 Ckp: 0-2
Best Rating: **39** 12/09 Ling 1m stand

Independent James (IRE)

74(95) (52)31
3-y-o b g Singspiel (IRE)-Massomah (USA) (Seeking The Gold (USA))
S C Williams J W Parry

Placings:50005 (4065)
2009: 8^5SD, 7^0G, 8^0G, 14^0GF, 10^5HY,

	Starts	1st	2nd	3rd	Win & Pl
Career Total (Turf)	4	0	0	0	0
Career Total (AW)	1	0	0	0	0

Going (Turf): **Sf: 0-1 GS: 0-0 Gd: 0-2 GF: 0-1 Fm: 0-0**
Distance: 5f/6f: 0-0 7f-8f: 0-2 9f-13f: 0-2 14f+: 0-1
Track : LH: 0-2 RH: 0-1 Tight: 0-1 Gall: 0-0
Aids: Bl: 0-0 Vi: 0-1 Tstrap: 0-0 Ckp: 0-0
Best Rating: **52** 2/09 Kemp 1m stand

Plating class; has worn a visor.

Indian Art (IRE)

104(104) (81)89
3-y-o b c Choisir (AUS)-Eastern Ember (Indian King (USA))
R Hannon A Al Kathiri

Placings:41230002-052021205O (6731)
2009: 7^0GS, 7^5GF, 6^2SD, 7^0GF, 6^2GF, 6^1GF, 7^2G, 8^0SD, 7^5SS, 6^0S,

	Starts	1st	2nd	3rd	Win & Pl
Career Total (Turf)	13	2	4	1	26327
Career Total (AW)	5	0	1	0	361

84 7/09 Sals 6f212y G-F £3238
79 5/08 Gdwd 6f G-F £3561
Total win prize-money £6800

Going (Turf): Sf: 0-2 GS: 0-1 Gd: 0-5 **GF: 2-5** Fm: 0-0
Distance: 5f/6f: 1-7 7f-8f: 1-11 9f-13f: 0-0 14f+: 0-0
Track : LH: 0-5 RH: 0-3 Tight: 0-3 Gall: 0-0
Aids: Bl: 0-0 Vi: 0-1 Tstrap: 0-0 Ckp: 0-0
Best Rating: **89** 8/09 Chep 7f16y good

Useful; effective at 6-7f; acts on fast ground and Polytrack; has worn a visor.

Indian Days

110(108) (105)108
4-y-o ch c Daylami (IRE)-Cap Coz (IRE) (Indian Ridge)
J G Given D J Fish

Placings:0040100/221031530-050640330 (6303)
2009: 10^0G, 10^5GF, 10^0G, 10^6GF, 12^4G, 12^0G, 12^3SD, 12^3GF, 12^0GF,

	Starts	1st	2nd	3rd	Win & Pl
Career Total (Turf)	24	3	2	3	109805
Career Total (AW)	1	0	0	1	7001

101 7/08 Gdwd 1m1f192y H G-F £62310
92 5/08 Rdcr 1m2f (0-85)H G-F £6476
73 9/07 Sand 7f16y G-F £5181
Total win prize-money £73968

Going (Turf): Sf: 0-4 GS: 0-2 Gd: 0-7 **GF: 3-11** Fm: 0-0
Distance: 5f/6f: 0-1 7f-8f: 1-6 **9f-13f: 2-18** 14f+: 0-0
Track : LH: 1-7 **RH: 2-12 Tight: 2-6** Gall: 0-9
Aids: Bl: 0-0 Vi: 0-0 Tstrap: 0-0 Ckp: 0-0
Best Rating: **108** 7/09 NmkJ 1m4f good

Smart; effective at 1m2f-1m4f; acts on fast ground.

Indian Diva (IRE)

80(108) (86)83
4-y-o b f Indian Danehill (IRE)-Katherine Gorge (USA) (Hansel (USA))
P T Midgley (R Curtis 10/3) P T Midgley

Placings:410/10066-150400000 (5254)
2009: 7^1SD, 8^5SD, 7^0SD, 7^4SD, 7^0SD, 8^0GF, 7^0SD, 6^0GS, 6^0GF,

	Starts	1st	2nd	3rd	Win & Pl
Career Total (Turf)	8	1	0	0	6045
Career Total (AW)	9	2	0	0	5804

86 1/09 Sthl 7f (0-75)H STD £3070
83 5/08 Wwck 7f26y (0-80)H G-S £5828
80 10/07 Ling 6f STD £2266
Total win prize-money £11166

Going (Turf): Sf: 0-1 **GS: 1-2** Gd: 0-2 GF: 0-3 Fm: 0-0
Distance: 5f/6f: 1-4 **7f-8f: 2-12** 9f-13f: 0-1 14f+: 0-0
Track : **LH: 3-10** RH: 0-0 **Tight: 1-4** Gall: 0-1
Aids: **Bl: 1-4** Vi: 0-0 Tstrap: 0-0 Ckp: 0-0
Best Rating: **86** 1/09 Sthl 7f stand

Fair; effective over 7f; acts on easy ground and on sand; has worn blinkers and a tongue tie.

Indian Haze (IRE)

93 (37)44
3-y-o b/br f Indian Haven-Hollow Haze (USA) (Woodman (USA))
Daniel Mark Loughnane F Purcell

Placings:000-0060 (5873)
2009: 10^0GY, 10^0Y, 12^6SH, 10^0G,

	Starts	1st	2nd	3rd	Win & Pl
Career Total (Turf)	6	0	0	0	
Career Total (AW)	1	0	0	0	

Going (Turf): **Sf: 0-0 GS: 0-0 Gd: 0-1 GF: 0-0 Fm: 0-0**
Distance: 5f/6f: 0-0 7f-8f: 0-3 9f-13f: 0-4 14f+: 0-0
Track : LH: 0-5 RH: 0-2 Tight: 0-0 Gall: 0-1
Aids: Bl: 0-0 Vi: 0-0 Tstrap: 0-0 Ckp: 0-0
Best Rating: **44** 7/09 Leop 1m2f yield

Indian Pipe Dream (IRE)

73 20
7-y-o br g Indian Danehill (IRE)-Build A Dream (USA) (Runaway Groom (CAN))
S Gollings The Dreamers

Placings:06/14216115/0 (6281)
2009: 14^0GF,

	Starts	1st	2nd	3rd	Win & Pl
Career Total (Turf)	11	4	1	0	36299

99 10/05 NmkR 2m (0-90)H SFT £8460
96 9/05 Hayd 1m6f (0-90)H G-S £11547
93 5/05 Sand 1m6f (0-85)H G-F £6726
82 4/05 Donc 1m2f60y GD £5408
Total win prize-money £32142

Going (Turf): **Sf: 1-2 GS: 1-4 Gd: 1-2 GF: 1-3** Fm: 0-0
Distance: 5f/6f: 0-0 7f-8f: 0-2 9f-13f: 1-2 **14f+: 3-7**
Track : LH: 2-6 RH: 2-4 Tight: 0-0 **Gall: 2-6**
Aids: Bl: 0-0 Vi: 0-0 Tstrap: 0-0 Ckp: 0-0
Best Rating: **99** 10/05 NmkR 2m soft

Indian Skipper (IRE)

103(105) (89)81
4-y-o b g Indian Danehill (IRE)-Rosy Lydgate (Last Tycoon)
R C Guest (M H Tompkins 13/10) Future Racing (Notts) Limited

Placings:0/10464663-220541602345 (7837)
2009: 10^2GF, 8^2GF, 8^0GS, 8^5GF, 6^4GS, 6^1GF, 6^6GF, 6^0GF, 7^2G, 6^3SD, 8^4SD, 7^5SS,

	Starts	1st	2nd	3rd	Win & Pl
Career Total (Turf)	15	1	3	0	8176
Career Total (AW)	6	1	0	2	4416

81 8/09 Folk 6f (0-75)H G-F £3412
79 3/08 Ling 1m STD £2331
Total win prize-money £5744

Going (Turf): Sf: 0-2 GS: 0-2 Gd: 0-5 **GF: 1-6** Fm: 0-0
Distance: 5f/6f: 1-5 7f-8f: 1-9 9f-13f: 0-7 14f+: 0-0
Track : **LH: 1-8** RH: 0-3 **Tight: 1-2** Gall: 0-3
Aids: Bl: 0-4 Vi: 0-0 Tstrap: 1-4 Ckp: 1-4
Best Rating: **89** 12/09 Sthl 6f stand

Useful; well suited by 6f; acts on fast ground and on sand; has worn an eyeshield and blinkers.

Indian Story (IRE)

(75) (16)
3-y-o b f Indian Ridge-Law Tudor (IRE) (Law Society (USA))
G C Bravery Meddler Bloodstock,R Withers & M Bloor

Placings:0 (0503)
2009: 7^0SD,

	Starts	1st	2nd	3rd	Win & Pl
Career Total (Turf)	0	0	0	0	
Career Total (AW)	1	0	0	0	

Going (Turf): **Sf: 0-0 GS: 0-0 Gd: 0-0 GF: 0-0 Fm: 0-0**
Distance: 5f/6f: 0-0 7f-8f: 0-1 9f-13f: 0-0 14f+: 0-0
Track : LH: 0-1 RH: 0-0 Tight: 0-1 Gall: 0-0
Aids: Bl: 0-0 Vi: 0-0 Tstrap: 0-0 Ckp: 0-0
Best Rating: **16** 2/09 Ling 7f stand

Indian Tonic (IRE)

96(95) (63)73
3-y-o b f Tiger Hill (IRE)-Wellspring (IRE) (Caerleon (USA))
W Jarvis The Indian Tonic Partnership

Placings:0206-05650 (6924)
2009: 8^0S, 7^5GF, 8^6GF, 8^5SD, 8^0GF,

	Starts	1st	2nd	3rd	Win & Pl
Career Total (Turf)	6	0	1	0	1542
Career Total (AW)	3	0	0	0	0

Going (Turf): **Sf: 0-1 GS: 0-0 Gd: 0-1 GF: 0-4 Fm: 0-0**

Distance: 5f/6f: 0-1 7f-8f: 0-6 9f-13f: 0-2 14f+: 0-0
Track : LH: 0-2 RH: 0-2 Tight: 0-1 Gall: 0-1
Aids: Bl: 0-0 Vl: 0-0 Tstrap: 0-0 Ckp: 0-0
Best Rating: **73** 9/08 Leic 7f9y good

Modest; effective at around 7f; acts on good ground and Polytrack.

Indian Trail

108(92) (74)**104**
9-y-o ch g Indian Ridge-Take Heart (Electric)
D Nicholls Martin Lovc

Placings:630/31100/01/160/**6**05616000/0000030033110/6 4004060000000-**4**304165054004 **(5507)**
2009: **6^{4}**SD, 5^{3}G, 6^{0}GF, 5^{4}GF, 5^{1}GF, 5^{6}GS, 5^{5}G, 5^{0}G, 5^{5}GF, 5^{4}GS, 6^{0}G, 5^{0}GF, 5^{4}G,

	Starts	1st	2nd	3rd	Win & Pl
Career Total (Turf)	**60**	**8**	**0**	**6**	**168310**
Career Total (AW)	**2**	**0**	**0**	**0**	**507**

92	6/09	Epsm	5f	H	G-F	£46732
112	9/07	Hayd	5f	(0-100)H	G-F	£18696
108	9/07	Sand	5f6y	(0-100)H	G-F	£11217
110	7/06	Newc	6f	(0-100)H	G-F	£18696
104	4/05	NmkR	6f	H	G-F	£29000
95	7/04	Newb	6f8y	C(0-90)H	GD	£8755
87	6/03	Kemp	6f	D(0-80)	G-F	£5447
88	5/03	Gdwd	7f	D	G-F	£5447

Total win prize-money £143993

Going (Turf): Sf: 0-4 GS: 0-11Gd: 1-20 **GF: 7-25** Fm: 0-0
Distance: **5f/6f: 6-50** 7f-8f: 2-12 9f-13f: 0-0 14f+: 0-0
Track : LH: 0-7 **RH: 1-3** Tight: 0-2 Gall: 0-3
Aids: Bl: 0-1 **Vi: 3-30** Tstrap: 0-0 Ckp: 0-0
Best Rating: **112** 9/07 Hayd 5f gd-fm

Useful; effective over 5f-6f; best on a sound surface; often visored.

Indian Valley (USA)

95(91) (73)**70**
2-y-o b f Cherokee Run (USA)-Shade Dance (USA) (Nureyev (USA))
Rae Guest Triple R Racing

Placings:220 **(7033)**
2009: 7^{2}GF, 7^{2}SD, 7^{0}S,

	Starts	1st	2nd	3rd	Win & Pl
Career Total (Turf)	**2**	**0**	**1**	**0**	**867**
Career Total (AW)	**1**	**0**	**1**	**0**	**771**

Going (Turf): **Sf: 0-1 GS: 0-0 Gd: 0-0 GF: 0-1 Fm: 0-0**
Distance: 5f/6f: 0-0 7f-8f: 0-3 9f-13f: 0-0 14f+: 0-0
Track : LH: 0-0 RH: 0-2 Tight: 0-0 Gall: 0-0
Aids: Bl: 0-0 Vi: 0-0 Tstrap: 0-0 Ckp: 0-0
Best Rating: **73** 9/09 Kemp 7f stand

Fair; stays 7f plus; acts on fast ground and Polytrack.

Indian Violet (IRE)

102(72) (20)**73**
3-y-o b g Indian Ridge-Violet Spring (IRE) (Exactly Sharp (USA))
P F I Cole Mrs Michael Spencer

Placings:00024405 **(6333)**
2009: 7^{0}GF, **8^{0}**SD, 6^{0}GF, 8^{2}GF, 8^{4}GS, 8^{4}GF, 8^{0}G, 8^{5}F,

	Starts	1st	2nd	3rd	Win & Pl
Career Total (Turf)	**7**	**0**	**1**	**0**	**1331**
Career Total (AW)	**1**	**0**	**0**	**0**	**0**

Going (Turf): **Sf: 0-0 GS: 0-1 Gd: 0-1 GF: 0-4 Fm: 0-1**
Distance: 5f/6f: 0-0 7f-8f: 0-4 9f-13f: 0-4 14f+: 0-0
Track : LH: 0-1 RH: 0-2 Tight: 0-2 Gall: 0-0
Aids: Bl: 0-0 Vi: 0-0 Tstrap: 0-0 Ckp: 0-0
Best Rating: **73** 6/09 Wind 1m67y gd-fm

Modest; stays 1m; acts on fast ground.

Indiana Fox

(82) (15)**55**
6-y-o b m Foxhound (USA)-Ridgewood Ruby (IRE) (Indian Ridge)
B G Powell Woodhaven Racing Syndicate

Placings:000-**00** **(0187)**
2009: 10^{0}SD, 12^{0}SD,

	Starts	1st	2nd	3rd	Win & Pl
Career Total (Turf)	**3**	**0**	**0**	**0**	
Career Total (AW)	**2**	**0**	**0**	**0**	

Going (Turf): **Sf: 0-1 GS: 0-1 Gd: 0-1 GF: 0-0 Fm: 0-0**
Distance: 5f/6f: 0-0 7f-8f: 0-0 9f-13f: 0-5 14f+: 0-0
Track : LH: 0-5 RH: 0-0 Tight: 0-3 Gall: 0-0
Aids: Bl: 0-1 Vi: 0-0 Tstrap: 0-0 Ckp: 0-0
Best Rating: **55** 10/08 Nott 1m2f50y soft

Indicible (FR)

90(106) (89)**83**
5-y-o ch g Dyhim Diamond (IRE)-Caslon (FR) (Deep Roots)
A King All The Kings Men

Placings:00021/0331/**2**5030-**00** **(4696)**
2009: 12^{0}SD, 11^{0}F,

	Starts	1st	2nd	3rd	Win & Pl
Career Total (Turf)	**11**	**2**	**1**	**2**	**15904**
Career Total (AW)	**5**	**0**	**1**	**1**	**2052**

4/07	Ponv	1m2f138y	H	SFT	£6081
11/06	Mars	1m1f	G-S		£4482

Total win prize-money £10564

Going (Turf): **Sf: 1-3 GS: 1-4** Gd: 0-1 GF: 0-0 Fm: 0-1
Distance: 5f/6f: 0-2 7f-8f: 0-1 **9f-13f: 2-13** 14f+: 0-0
Track : LH: 0-6 RH: 0-2 Tight: 0-2 Gall: 0-2
Aids: Bl: 0-0 Vi: 0-0 Tstrap: 0-0 Ckp: 0-0
Best Rating: **89** 5/08 GrLe 1m2f stand

Fair; ex-French; effective at around 1m2f; acts in soft ground.

Indigo Belle (IRE)

88(61) **29**
3-y-o b f Mull Of Kintyre (USA)-Frances Canty (USA) (Lear Fan (USA))
Mrs A Duffield D K Barker & Mrs C McMahon

Placings:00-**6**0006 **(4617)**
2009: 11^{6}SD, 10^{0}GS, 10^{0}GF, 7^{0}G, 15^{6}G,

	Starts	1st	2nd	3rd	Win & Pl
Career Total (Turf)	**6**	**0**	**0**	**0**	**0**
Career Total (AW)	**1**	**0**	**0**	**0**	**0**

Going (Turf): **Sf: 0-1 GS: 0-1 Gd: 0-3 GF: 0-1 Fm: 0-0**
Distance: 5f/6f: 0-0 7f-8f: 0-3 9f-13f: 0-3 14f+: 0-1
Track : LH: 0-4 RH: 0-2 Tight: 0-2 Gall: 0-1
Aids: Bl: 0-0 Vi: 0-3 Tstrap: 0-0 Ckp: 0-0
Best Rating: **29** 8/09 Catt 1m7f177y good

Indigo Ink

90(81) (31)**55**
2-y-o b f Rock Of Gibraltar (IRE)-Blue Indigo (FR) (Pistolet Bleu (IRE))
Miss Amy Weaver (S A Callaghan 2/10) Mrs J G Callaghan

Placings:0306 **(7690)**
2009: 7^{0}GF, 8^{3}GF, 8^{0}SD, 7^{6}SD,

	Starts	1st	2nd	3rd	Win & Pl
Career Total (Turf)	**2**	**0**	**0**	**1**	**302**
Career Total (AW)	**2**	**0**	**0**	**0**	**0**

Going (Turf): **Sf: 0-0 GS: 0-0 Gd: 0-0 GF: 0-2 Fm: 0-0**
Distance: 5f/6f: 0-0 7f-8f: 0-3 9f-13f: 0-1 14f+: 0-0
Track : LH: 0-3 RH: 0-0 Tight: 0-2 Gall: 0-0
Aids: Bl: 0-0 Vi: 0-0 Tstrap: 0-0 Ckp: 0-0
Best Rating: **55** 10/09 Nott 1m75y gd-fm

Moderate; effective over 1m; acts on good ground.

Indochina

90 **73**
2-y-o b g Sulamani (IRE)-Lane County (USA) (Rahy (USA))
M Johnston Sheikh Hamdan Bin Mohammed Al Maktoum

Placings:542 **(6533)**
2009: 8^{5}GS, 9^{4}GF, 10^{2}GF,

	Starts	1st	2nd	3rd	Win & Pl
Career Total (Turf)	**3**	**0**	**1**	**0**	**1806**

Going (Turf): **Sf: 0-0 GS: 0-1 Gd: 0-0 GF: 0-2 Fm: 0-0**
Distance: 5f/6f: 0-0 7f-8f: 0-0 9f-13f: 0-3 14f+: 0-0
Track : LH: 0-3 RH: 0-0 Tight: 0-2 Gall: 0-0
Aids: Bl: 0-0 Vi: 0-0 Tstrap: 0-0 Ckp: 0-0
Best Rating: **73** 10/09 Pont 1m2f6y gd-fm

Fair; stays 1m2f; acts on fast ground.

Indonesia

100 (68)**82**
7-y-o ch g Lomitas-Idraak (Kris)
T D Walford G E Dempsey

Placings:005/63/03314/2340210/3-600 **(3313)**
2009: 14^{6}GF, 17^{0}G, 16^{0}GF,

	Starts	1st	2nd	3rd	Win & Pl
Career Total (Turf)	**20**	**2**	**2**	**5**	**11606**
Career Total (AW)	**1**	**0**	**0**	**0**	**0**

80	8/06	Newc	2m19y	(0-70)H	G-F	£3886

Total win prize-money £3886

Going (Turf): Sf: 0-1 GS: 0-3 Gd: 0-5 **GF: 1-9 Fm: 1-2**
Distance: 5f/6f: 0-0 7f-8f: 0-1 9f-13f: 0-4 **14f+: 2-16**
Track : **LH: 2-17** RH: 0-4 Tight: 0-5 **Gall: 1-10**
Aids: Bl: 0-0 Vi: 0-0 Tstrap: 0-0 Ckp: 0-0
Best Rating: **82** 5/08 York 2m88y good

Useful; stays 2m1f; acts on fast ground.

Indy Driver

106(106) (84)**82**
4-y-o ch g Domedriver (IRE)-Condoleezza (USA) (Cozzene (USA))
Matthew Salaman (J R Fanshawe 26/10) Mrs C C Regalado-Gonzalez

Placings:0/245452652-52464011560230 **(7848)**
2009: 8^{5}SD, 10^{2}GF, 10^{4}GF, 12^{6}SD, 9^{4}GF, 8^{0}G, 7^{1}G, 8^{1}G, 8^{5}GF, 7^{6}GF, 8^{0}GS, 8^{2}SD, 10^{3}SD, 9^{0}SD,

	Starts	1st	2nd	3rd	Win & Pl
Career Total (Turf)	14	2	1	0	9196
Career Total (AW)	10	0	4	1	5136

82 8/09 Epsm 1m114y (0-80)H GD £5180
79 7/09 Ling 7f140y (0-65)H GD £2047
Total win prize-money £7228

Going (Turf): Sf: 0-1 GS: 0-1 **Gd: 2-5** GF: 0-7 Fm: 0-0
Distance: 5f/6f: 0-0 7f-8f: 1-10 9f-13f: 1-14 14f+: 0-0
Track : **LH: 1-12** RH: 0-8 **Tight: 1-9** Gall: 0-1
Aids: Bl: 0-0 Vi: 0-1 Tstrap: 2-9 Ckp: 2-9
Best Rating: **84** 12/09 Kemp 1m2f stand

Fair; effective over 7f-1m2f; acts on fast ground; goes on Polytrack; has worn cheekpieces and a visor.

Infamous Angel

108 **103**
3-y-o b f Exceed And Excel (AUS)-Evangeline (Sadler's Wells (USA))
R Hannon Geoff Howard-Spink & Peter Marshall

Placings:61210-046600 **(4489)**
2009: 7^{0}S, 8^{4}G, 7^{6}GF, 8^{6}G, 6^{0}G, 7^{0}G,

	Starts	1st	2nd	3rd	Win & Pl
Career Total (Turf)	11	2	1	0	69658

103 8/08 NmkJ 6f G-F £34062
82 6/08 Bath 5f11y G-F £1942
Total win prize-money £36005

Going (Turf): Sf: 0-2 GS: 0-0 Gd: 0-5 **GF: 2-4** Fm: 0-0
Distance: **5f/6f: 2-5** 7f-8f: 0-5 9f-13f: 0-1 14f+: 0-0
Track : **LH: 1-2** RH: 0-2 Tight: 0-1 **Gall: 1-1**
Aids: Bl: 0-0 Vi: 0-0 Tstrap: 0-0 Ckp: 0-0
Best Rating: **103** 8/08 NmkJ 6f gd-fm

Smart; won the Lowther Stakes at Newmarket at two; effective at 5f-7f; acts on fast ground.

Infanta (IRE)

94 **57**
2-y-o b f Cape Cross (IRE)-Maria Isabella (USA) (Kris)
Saeed Bin Suroor Godolphin

Placings:3 **(7114)**
2009: 7^{3}GS,

	Starts	1st	2nd	3rd	Win & Pl
Career Total (Turf)	1	0	0	1	578

Going (Turf): **Sf: 0-0 GS: 0-1 Gd: 0-0 GF: 0-0 Fm: 0-0**
Distance: 5f/6f: 0-0 7f-8f: 0-1 9f-13f: 0-0 14f+: 0-0
Track : LH: 0-0 RH: 0-1 Tight: 0-1 Gall: 0-0
Aids: Bl: 0-0 Vi: 0-0 Tstrap: 0-0 Ckp: 0-0
Best Rating: **57** 10/09 Muss 7f30y gd-sft

Infinite Patience

(86) (29)**65**
4-y-o b/br f High Chaparral (IRE)-Idma (Midyan (USA))
T D McCarthy Roger Ambrose,Sean Ambrose & Bill Reilly

Placings:050600/0300000-0 **(4084)**
2009: 10^{0}SD,

	Starts	1st	2nd	3rd	Win & Pl
Career Total (Turf)	12	0	0	1	833
Career Total (AW)	2	0	0	0	

Going (Turf): **Sf: 0-2 GS: 0-2 Gd: 0-3 GF: 0-4 Fm: 0-1**
Distance: 5f/6f: 0-3 7f-8f: 0-7 9f-13f: 0-4 14f+: 0-0
Track : LH: 0-4 RH: 0-3 Tight: 0-1 Gall: 0-1
Aids: Bl: 0-1 Vi: 0-0 Tstrap: 0-2 Ckp: 0-2
Best Rating: **65** 10/07 NmkR 7f gd-fm

Infinity Bond

101(92) (56)**68**
4-y-o b g Forzando-Bond Girl (Magic Ring (IRE))
G R Oldroyd R C Bond

Placings:4040614-0426 **(3105)**
2009: 7^{0}GS, 7^{4}GF, 7^{2}GF, 7^{6}GF,

	Starts	1st	2nd	3rd	Win & Pl
Career Total (Turf)	10	1	1	0	3869
Career Total (AW)	1	0	0	0	0

64 7/08 Muss 7f30y GD £1942
Total win prize-money £1943

Going (Turf): Sf: 0-1 GS: 0-1 **Gd: 1-1** GF: 0-7 Fm: 0-0
Distance: 5f/6f: 0-2 **7f-8f: 1-9** 9f-13f: 0-0 14f+: 0-0
Track : LH: 0-1 **RH: 1-5 Tight: 1-6** Gall: 0-0
Aids: Bl: 0-0 Vi: 0-0 Tstrap: 0-0 Ckp: 0-0
Best Rating: **68** 5/09 Muss 7f30y gd-fm

Modest; handles Polytrack; stays 7f.

Infinity World

87(94) (56)**51**
2-y-o b f Lucky Story (USA)-Musical Refrain (IRE) (Dancing Dissident (USA))
G R Oldroyd R C Bond

Placings:0036 **(7799)**
2009: 7^{0}GF, 6^{0}GF, 7^{3}SD, 5^{6}SD,

	Starts	1st	2nd	3rd	Win & Pl
Career Total (Turf)	2	0	0	0	
Career Total (AW)	2	0	0	1	403

Going (Turf): **Sf: 0-0 GS: 0-0 Gd: 0-0 GF: 0-2 Fm: 0-0**
Distance: 5f/6f: 0-2 7f-8f: 0-2 9f-13f: 0-0 14f+: 0-0
Track : LH: 0-2 RH: 0-0 Tight: 0-2 Gall: 0-0
Aids: Bl: 0-0 Vi: 0-0 Tstrap: 0-0 Ckp: 0-0
Best Rating: **56** 11/09 Wolv 7f32y stand

Modest; effective over 7f; acts on Polytrack.

Infiraad

104 **104**
3-y-o ch c Haafhd-Razzle (IRE) (Green Desert (USA))
B W Hills Hamdan Al Maktoum

Placings:3-1100 **(7185)**
2009: 7^{1}GF, 7^{1}GF, 7^{0}GF, 8^{0}G,

	Starts	1st	2nd	3rd	Win & Pl
Career Total (Turf)	5	2	0	1	19048

104 5/09 NmkR 7f (0-100)H G-F £12952
92 4/09 NmkR 7f G-F £5180
Total win prize-money £18133

Going (Turf): Sf: 0-0 GS: 0-0 Gd: 0-1 **GF: 2-4** Fm: 0-0
Distance: 5f/6f: 0-0 **7f-8f: 2-5** 9f-13f: 0-0 14f+: 0-0
Track : LH: 0-0 RH: 0-0 Tight: 0-0 Gall: 0-0
Aids: Bl: 0-0 Vi: 0-0 Tstrap: 0-0 Ckp: 0-0
Best Rating: **104** 5/09 NmkR 7f gd-fm

Smart; effective over 7f; acts on fast ground.

Inflammable

(98) (70)**73**
3-y-o b f Montjeu (IRE)-Flame Valley (USA) (Gulch (USA))
Sir Mark Prescott Cheveley Park Stud

Placings:022-44321 **(7648)**
2009: 11^{4}SD, 16^{4}SD, 12^{3}SD, 13^{2}SD, 12^{1}SD,

	Starts	1st	2nd	3rd	Win & Pl
Career Total (Turf)	1	0	1	0	1156
Career Total (AW)	7	1	2	1	5865

66 12/09 Wolv 1m4f50y STD £2729
Total win prize-money £2730

Going (Turf): **Sf: 0-1 GS: 0-0 Gd: 0-0 GF: 0-0 Fm: 0-0**
Distance: 5f/6f: 0-0 7f-8f: 0-3 **9f-13f: 1-3** 14f+: 0-2
Track : **LH: 1-6** RH: 0-2 **Tight: 1-2** Gall: 0-0
Aids: Bl: 0-0 Vi: 0-0 Tstrap: 0-0 Ckp: 0-0
Best Rating: **73** 11/08 Ayr 7f50y heavy

Modest; stays at least 1m4f; acts on Fibresand and Polytrack.

Informal Affair

84 **49**
3-y-o b g Makbul-Fontaine Lady (Millfontaine)
J D Bethell Peter J Mitchell

Placings:005 **(4974)**
2009: 8^{0}G, 12^{0}G, 11^{5}GF,

	Starts	1st	2nd	3rd	Win & Pl
Career Total (Turf)	3	0	0	0	0

Going (Turf): **Sf: 0-0 GS: 0-0 Gd: 0-2 GF: 0-1 Fm: 0-0**
Distance: 5f/6f: 0-0 7f-8f: 0-1 9f-13f: 0-2 14f+: 0-0
Track : LH: 0-1 RH: 0-2 Tight: 0-3 Gall: 0-0
Aids: Bl: 0-0 Vi: 0-0 Tstrap: 0-0 Ckp: 0-0
Best Rating: **49** 8/09 Ripn 1m4f10y good

Ingenue

100(93) (55)**59**
3-y-o b f Hernando (FR)-I Do (Selkirk (USA))
P Howling (Sir Mark Prescott 14/10) Paul Terry

Placings:00000126 **(7415)**
2009: 10^{0}GF, 12^{0}SD, 11^{0}G, 13^{0}GF, 15^{0}GF, 15^{1}G, 16^{2}SS, 16^{6}SD,

	Starts	1st	2nd	3rd	Win & Pl
Career Total (Turf)	5	1	0	0	2047
Career Total (AW)	3	0	1	0	605

59 10/09 Catt 1m7f177y (0-60)H GD £2047
Total win prize-money £2047

Going (Turf): Sf: 0-0 GS: 0-0 **Gd: 1-2** GF: 0-3 Fm: 0-0
Distance: 5f/6f: 0-0 7f-8f: 0-0 9f-13f: 0-3 **14f+: 1-5**
Track : **LH: 1-5** RH: 0-3 **Tight: 1-7** Gall: 0-0
Aids: **Bl: 1-5** Vi: 0-0 Tstrap: 0-0 Ckp: 0-0
Best Rating: **59** 10/09 Catt 1m7f177y good

Modest; stays 2m and acts on good ground; has worn blinkers.

Ingleby Arch (USA)

107(108) (99)**93**
6-y-o b g Arch (USA)-Inca Dove (USA) (Mr Prospector (USA))
T D Barron Dave Scott

Placings:4431304/1105044000/533030004051/16566006005010-140052603005311 22 **(7837)**
2009: 6^{1}SD, 6^{4}SD, 6^{0}GF, 6^{0}G, 6^{5}GS, 6^{2}HY, 6^{6}GF, 6^{0}G, 6^{3}GS, 6^{0}SD, 6^{0}G, 7^{5}SF, 6^{3}G, 6^{1}SD, 6^{1}SD, 6^{2}SD, 7^{2}SS,

	Starts	1st	2nd	3rd	Win & Pl
Career Total (Turf)	44	3	1	7	45254
Career Total (AW)	16	6	2	0	45976

99	10/09	Sthl	6f	(0-95)H	STD	£9346
96	10/09	Sthl	6f	(0-85)H	STD	£5504
93	2/09	Sthl	6f	(0-90)H	STD	£7771
91	11/08	Sthl	6f	(0-75)H	STD	£2729
95	2/08	Sthl	6f	(0-90)H	STD	£7124
92	12/07	Sthl	6f	(0-85)H	STD	£4728
102	5/06	Haml	6f5y		G-F	£9971
99	4/06	NmkR	6f	(0-100)H	G-F	£11658
79	8/05	Rdcr	6f		GD	£3744

Total win prize-money £62580

Going (Turf): Sf: 0-5 GS: 0-9 Gd: 1-13 **GF: 2-16** Fm: 0-1
Distance: **5f/6f: 8-44** 7f-8f: 1-15 9f-13f: 0-1 14f+: 0-0
Track : **LH: 6-20** RH: 0-0 Tight: 0-4 Gall: 0-1
Aids: Bl: 0-2 Vi: 0-2 Tstrap: 0-0 Ckp: 0-0
Best Rating: **102** 5/06 Haml 6f5y gd-fm

Very useful; stays 6f; acts on most ground and Fibresand.

Ingleby Lady

107 **96**

3-y-o ch f Captain Rio-Petra Nova (First Trump)
T D Barron Dave Scott

Placings:16413102 **(6050)**
2009: 6^{1}GF, 6^{6}GF, 6^{4}G, 5^{1}GF, 5^{3}GS, 6^{1}GF, 6^{0}GF, 6^{2}G,

	Starts	1st	2nd	3rd	Win & Pl
Career Total (Turf)	**8**	**3**	**1**	**1**	**19753**

89	8/09	Rdcr	6f	(0-85)H	G-F	£5180
89	6/09	Rdcr	5f	(0-85)H	G-F	£4857
71	4/09	Pont	6f		G-F	£2914

Total win prize-money £12952

Going (Turf): Sf: 0-0 GS: 0-1 Gd: 0-2 **GF: 3-5** Fm: 0-0
Distance: **5f/6f: 3-8** 7f-8f: 0-0 9f-13f: 0-0 14f+: 0-0
Track : **LH: 1-1** RH: 0-0 Tight: 0-0 Gall: 0-0
Aids: Bl: 0-0 Vi: 0-0 Tstrap: 0-0 Ckp: 0-0
Best Rating: **96** 9/09 Ayr 6f good

Very useful; effective at 6f; acts on fast ground.

Ingleby Princess

100(101) (64)**74**

5-y-o br m Bold Edge-Bob's Princess (Bob's Return (IRE))
T D Barron Dave Scott

Placings:114126/4665005/2663013403466-050403625554466144 **(7678)**
2009: 6^{0}GF, 6^{5}F, 6^{0}GF, 5^{4}GF, 5^{0}GF, 6^{3}GF, 6^{6}GF, 5^{2}GS, 7^{5}SD, 6^{5}GS, 8^{5}G, 8^{4}GS, 10^{4}GF, 7^{6}GF, 9^{6}G, 7^{1}SD, 8^{4}SD, 7^{4}SD,

	Starts	1st	2nd	3rd	Win & Pl
Career Total (Turf)	**40**	**4**	**3**	**4**	**24517**
Career Total (AW)	**4**	**1**	**0**	**0**	**2047**

64	11/09	Sthl	7f		STD	£2047
74	6/08	Haml	6f5y	(0-65)H	GD	£2047
76	8/06	Haml	6f5y		G-F	£5181
66	6/06	Muss	7f30y		FRM	£3886
70	5/06	Newc	5f		G-F	£2590

Total win prize-money £15753

Going (Turf): Sf: 0-4 GS: 0-8 Gd: 1-10 **GF: 2-16** Fm: 1-2
Distance: 5f/6f: 1-22 **7f-8f: 4-20** 9f-13f: 0-2 14f+: 0-0
Track : LH: 1-15 RH: 1-5 **Tight: 1-8** Gall: 0-1
Aids: Bl: 0-2 Vi: 0-0 Tstrap: 0-1 Ckp: 0-1
Best Rating: **78** 5/07 Hayd 6f good

Moderate; effective over 6f-7f; acts on most ground and on Fibresand.

Ingleby Spirit

95(92) (79)**83**

2-y-o b g Avonbridge-Encore Du Cristal (USA) (Quiet American (USA))
R A Fahey Percy/Green Racing

Placings:013034 **(6088)**
2009: 5^{0}GF, 6^{1}S, 6^{3}GF, 7^{0}G, 8^{3}SD, 8^{4}G,

	Starts	1st	2nd	3rd	Win & Pl
Career Total (Turf)	**5**	**1**	**0**	**1**	**4426**
Career Total (AW)	**1**	**0**	**0**	**1**	**655**

80	5/09	Hayd	6f	SFT	£2914

Total win prize-money £2914

Going (Turf): **Sf: 1-1** GS: 0-0 Gd: 0-2 GF: 0-2 Fm: 0-0
Distance: **5f/6f: 1-3** 7f-8f: 0-3 9f-13f: 0-0 14f+: 0-0
Track : LH: 0-2 RH: 0-1 Tight: 0-0 Gall: 0-0
Aids: Bl: 0-0 Vi: 0-0 Tstrap: 0-0 Ckp: 0-0
Best Rating: **83** 9/09 Ayr 1m good

Fair juvenile; stays 6f on soft ground.

Ingleby Star (IRE)

104(97) (67)**79**

4-y-o b g Fath (USA)-Rosy Scintilla (IRE) (Thatching)
N Wilson Renaissance Racing

Placings:01004/06010-00412121406006 **(7758)**
2009: 5^{0}HY, 5^{0}GF, 5^{4}GF, 5^{1}G, 5^{2}GF, 5^{1}G, 5^{2}G, 5^{1}G, 5^{4}G, 5^{0}GF, 5^{6}GF, 5^{0}GF, 5^{0}GS, 5^{8}SD,

	Starts	1st	2nd	3rd	Win & Pl
Career Total (Turf)	**21**	**5**	**2**	**0**	**16279**
Career Total (AW)	**3**	**0**	**0**	**0**	**0**

79	7/09	Muss	5f	(0-65)H	GD	£2266
72	7/09	Ayr	5f	(0-70)H	GD	£2914
67	7/09	Ayr	5f	(0-60)H	GD	£2307
69	9/08	Rdcr	5f	(0-70)H	G-S	£2590
78	5/07	Muss	5f		G-F	£3886

Total win prize-money £13965

Going (Turf): Sf: 0-3 GS: 1-3 **Gd: 3-6** GF: 1-9 Fm: 0-0
Distance: **5f/6f: 5-24** 7f-8f: 0-0 9f-13f: 0-0 14f+: 0-0
Track : LH: 0-3 RH: 0-0 Tight: 0-1 Gall: 0-0
Aids: Bl: 1-3 Vi: 0-0 Tstrap: 3-11 Ckp: 3-11
Best Rating: **79** 7/09 Muss 5f good

Fair; suited by 5f; acts on most ground; has worn blinkers and cheekpieces.

Inheritor (IRE)

103(108) (91)**87**

3-y-o b g Kheleyf (USA)-Miss Devious (IRE) (Dr Devious (IRE))
B Smart Richard Page

Placings:422106-4335160021 **(7734)**
2009: 8^{4}F, 7^{3}GF, 8^{3}GF, 7^{5}G, 6^{1}G, 7^{6}GF, 7^{0}GF, 7^{0}G, 7^{2}SD, 8^{1}SD,

	Starts	1st	2nd	3rd	Win & Pl
Career Total (Turf)	**14**	**2**	**2**	**2**	**14609**
Career Total (AW)	**2**	**1**	**1**	**0**	**7312**

91	12/09	Wolv	1m141y	(0-85)H	STD	£5046
87	8/09	Carl	6f192y	(0-85)H	GD	£6476
81	7/08	Bevl	7f100y		G-F	£3885

Total win prize-money £15408

Going (Turf): Sf: 0-1 GS: 0-0 **Gd: 1-4 GF: 1-8** Fm: 0-1
Distance: 5f/6f: 0-1 **7f-8f: 2-13** 9f-13f: 1-2 14f+: 0-0
Track : LH: 1-6 **RH: 2-6 Tight: 1-5** Gall: 0-1
Aids: Bl: 0-0 Vi: 0-0 Tstrap: 0-0 Ckp: 0-0
Best Rating: **91** 12/09 Wolv 1m141y stand

Useful; effective over an extended 7f; acts on fast ground.

Inhibition

91(103) (84)**86**

3-y-o br f Nayef (USA)-Spurned (USA) (Robellino (USA))
A M Balding Kingsclere Racing CLub

Placings:6-1646 **(3778)**
2009: 12^{1}SD, 11^{6}GF, 11^{4}S, 13^{6}G,

	Starts	1st	2nd	3rd	Win & Pl
Career Total (Turf)	**4**	**0**	**0**	**0**	**6893**
Career Total (AW)	**1**	**1**	**0**	**0**	**2590**

84	4/09	Kemp	1m4f	STD	£2590

Total win prize-money £2590

Going (Turf): **Sf: 0-1 GS: 0-0 Gd: 0-1 GF: 0-2 Fm: 0-0**
Distance: 5f/6f: 0-0 7f-8f: 0-1 **9f-13f: 1-4** 14f+: 0-0
Track : LH: 0-1 **RH: 1-2** Tight: 0-1 Gall: 0-1
Aids: Bl: 0-0 Vi: 0-0 Tstrap: 0-0 Ckp: 0-0
Best Rating: **86** 6/09 Le L 1m3f110y soft

Useful; stays 1m4f; handles Polytrack.

Inis Boffin

97(100) (74)**78**

3-y-o b f Danehill Dancer (IRE)-Windmill (Ezzoud (IRE))
S Kirk M G White

Placings:000-31020025 **(5366)**
2009: 7^{3}SD, 8^{1}SD, 10^{0}G, 8^{2}G, 11^{0}GF, 10^{0}S, 8^{2}GF, 10^{5}F,

	Starts	1st	2nd	3rd	Win & Pl
Career Total (Turf)	**9**	**0**	**2**	**0**	**1715**
Career Total (AW)	**2**	**1**	**0**	**1**	**4220**

74	5/09	Wolv	1m141y	(0-70)H	STD	£3738

Total win prize-money £3739

Going (Turf): **Sf: 0-1 GS: 0-0 Gd: 0-5 GF: 0-2 Fm: 0-1**
Distance: 5f/6f: 0-0 7f-8f: 0-4 **9f-13f: 1-7** 14f+: 0-0
Track : **LH: 1-6** RH: 0-0 **Tight: 1-5** Gall: 0-1
Aids: Bl: 0-0 Vi: 0-0 Tstrap: 0-0 Ckp: 0-0
Best Rating: **78** 8/09 Bath 1m5y gd-fm

Fair; stays 1m; acts on Polytrack; sure to win more races.

Inittowinit

74(68) (16)**37**

2-y-o ch f Trade Fair-Moly (FR) (Anabaa (USA))
W R Muir Linkslade Lottery

Placings:000 **(5543)**
2009: 7^{0}GF, 7^{0}SD, 7^{0}GF,

	Starts	1st	2nd	3rd	Win & Pl
Career Total (Turf)	**2**	**0**	**0**	**0**	
Career Total (AW)	**1**	**0**	**0**	**0**	

Going (Turf): **Sf: 0-0 GS: 0-0 Gd: 0-0 GF: 0-2 Fm: 0-0**
Distance: 5f/6f: 0-0 7f-8f: 0-3 9f-13f: 0-0 14f+: 0-0
Track : LH: 0-1 RH: 0-0 Tight: 0-1 Gall: 0-0
Aids: Bl: 0-1 Vi: 0-0 Tstrap: 0-0 Ckp: 0-0
Best Rating: **37** 6/09 Ling 7f gd-fm

Inka Dancer (IRE)

8(101) (64)**56**

7-y-o ch m Intikhab (USA)-Grannys Reluctance (IRE) (Anita's Prince)
B Palling Bryn Palling

Placings:343/500010/33260012320/0512005626/0060-6240300 **(1741)**
2009: 6^{6}SD, 7^{2}SD, 5^{4}SD, 7^{0}SD, 5^{3}SD, 7^{0}SD, 8^{0}GF,

	Starts	1st	2nd	3rd	Win & Pl
Career Total (Turf)	24	3	3	4	15403
Career Total (AW)	17	0	3	2	2418

66 8/07 Ling 6f (0-60)H G-F £2047
64 9/06 Nott 6f15y (0-70)H GD £4533
56 9/05 Leic 7f9y G-F £3066
Total win prize-money £9648

Going (Turf): Sf: 0-2 GS: 0-4 Gd: 1-10 **GF: 2-8** Fm: 0-0
Distance: 5f/6f: 1-25 **7f-8f: 2-13** 9f-13f: 0-3 14f+: 0-0
Track : LH: 0-21 RH: 0-3 Tight: 0-14 Gall: 0-5
Aids: Bl: 0-0 Vi: 0-0 Tstrap: 0-0 Ckp: 0-0
Best Rating: 70 8/07 Sals 6f gd-sft

Moderate; effective over 6f-7f; acts on good, fast and easy ground; also goes on Polytrack.

Inler (IRE)

99 93
2-y-o br c Red Ransom (USA)-Wedding Gift (FR) (Always Fair (USA))
J R Best Mrs M Findlay

Placings:1 (6809)
2009: 6^{1}G,

	Starts	1st	2nd	3rd	Win & Pl
Career Total (Turf)	1	1	0	0	5828

93 10/09 NmkR 6f GD £5828
Total win prize-money £5828

Going (Turf): Sf: 0-0 GS: 0-0 **Gd: 1-1** GF: 0-0 Fm: 0-0
Distance: **5f/6f: 1-1** 7f-8f: 0-0 9f-13f: 0-0 14f+: 0-0
Track : LH: 0-0 RH: 0-0 Tight: 0-0 Gall: 0-0
Aids: Bl: 0-0 Vi: 0-0 Tstrap: 0-0 Ckp: 0-0
Best Rating: 93 10/09 NmkR 6f good

Very useful; effective over 6f; acts on good ground.

Inlovingmemory (IRE)

91 62
2-y-o br/gr f Dubai Destination (USA)-Oiselina (FR) (Linamix (FR))
R A Fahey The Rumpole Partnership

Placings:2 (2541)
2009: 6^{2}F,

	Starts	1st	2nd	3rd	Win & Pl
Career Total (Turf)	1	0	1	0	1272

Going (Turf): Sf: 0-0 GS: 0-0 Gd: 0-0 GF: 0-0 Fm: 0-1
Distance: 5f/6f: 0-1 7f-8f: 0-0 9f-13f: 0-0 14f+: 0-0
Track : LH: 0-0 RH: 0-0 Tight: 0-0 Gall: 0-0
Aids: Bl: 0-0 Vi: 0-0 Tstrap: 0-0 Ckp: 0-0
Best Rating: 62 6/09 Thsk 6f firm

Promise on debut over 6f on fast ground.

Inn For The Dancer

73(91) (53)20
7-y-o b g Groom Dancer (USA)-Lady Joyce (FR) (Galetto (FR))
J C Fox John Lonergan

Placings:0000/05002/00/46/4-5560 (4263)
2009: 12^{5}SD, 12^{5}SD, 13^{6}SD, 12^{0}S,

	Starts	1st	2nd	3rd	Win & Pl
Career Total (Turf)	6	0	1	0	776
Career Total (AW)	12	0	0	0	0

Going (Turf): Sf: 0-1 GS: 0-1 Gd: 0-3 GF: 0-1 Fm: 0-0
Distance: 5f/6f: 0-0 7f-8f: 0-2 9f-13f: 0-15 14f+: 0-1
Track : LH: 0-14 RH: 0-4 Tight: 0-11 Gall: 0-0
Aids: Bl: 0-0 Vi: 0-0 Tstrap: 0-1 Ckp: 0-1
Best Rating: 56 7/05 Nott 1m54y gd-fm

Plating-class; stays 1m4f; handles fast ground; has worn cheekpieces.

Inn Swinger (IRE)

(86) (42)26
3-y-o b f Makbul-Sheik'n Swing (Celtic Swing)
W G M Turner Barvin Partnership

Placings:620500-00 (0200)
2009: 5^{0}SD, 6^{0}SD,

	Starts	1st	2nd	3rd	Win & Pl
Career Total (Turf)	3	0	0	0	0
Career Total (AW)	5	0	1	0	524

Going (Turf): Sf: 0-0 GS: 0-0 Gd: 0-0 GF: 0-3 Fm: 0-0
Distance: 5f/6f: 0-7 7f-8f: 0-1 9f-13f: 0-0 14f+: 0-0
Track : LH: 0-4 RH: 0-0 Tight: 0-3 Gall: 0-0
Aids: Bl: 0-0 Vi: 0-0 Tstrap: 0-0 Ckp: 0-0
Best Rating: 42 6/08 Ling 5f stand

Plating-class; suited by 5f and Polytrack.

Innactualfact

77(100) (66)57
3-y-o b f Lujain (USA)-Alzianah (Alzao (USA))
L A Dace G Collacott

Placings:63004005-5166000000 (7687)
2009: 10^{5}SD, 10^{1}SD, 11^{6}SD, 10^{6}SD, 8^{0}GF, 10^{0}SD, 10^{0}SS, 12^{0}SD, 10^{0}SD, 12^{0}SD,

	Starts	1st	2nd	3rd	Win & Pl
Career Total (Turf)	5	0	0	1	587
Career Total (AW)	13	1	0	0	2047

66 1/09 Ling 1m2f (0-65)H STD £2047
Total win prize-money £2047

Going (Turf): Sf: 0-2 GS: 0-1 Gd: 0-1 GF: 0-1 Fm: 0-0
Distance: 5f/6f: 0-2 7f-8f: 0-5 **9f-13f: 1-11** 14f+: 0-0
Track : **LH: 1-9** RH: 0-6 **Tight: 1-7** Gall: 0-1
Aids: Bl: 0-1 Vi: 0-0 Tstrap: 0-3 Ckp: 0-3
Best Rating: 66 1/09 Ling 1m2f stand

Moderate; stays 1m2f and acts on Polytrack.

Inner Angel

(92) (72)
2-y-o ch f Motivator-Sea Angel (Nashwan (USA))
M Botti Lucky Seven Stable 1

Placings:32 (7451)
2009: 8^{3}SD, 8^{2}SD,

	Starts	1st	2nd	3rd	Win & Pl
Career Total (Turf)	0	0	0	0	
Career Total (AW)	2	0	1	1	1541

Going (Turf): Sf: 0-0 GS: 0-0 Gd: 0-0 GF: 0-0 Fm: 0-0
Distance: 5f/6f: 0-0 7f-8f: 0-2 9f-13f: 0-0 14f+: 0-0
Track : LH: 0-0 RH: 0-2 Tight: 0-0 Gall: 0-0
Aids: Bl: 0-0 Vi: 0-0 Tstrap: 0-0 Ckp: 0-0
Best Rating: 72 10/09 Kemp 1m stand

Useful; stays 1m and acts on Polytrack.

Inner Voice (USA)

(90) (22)57
6-y-o gr g Cozzene (USA)-Miss Henderson Co (USA) (Silver Hawk (USA))
J J Lambe All Aboard Syndicate

Placings:6/300/024-0 (0627)
2009: 16^{0}SD,

	Starts	1st	2nd	3rd	Win & Pl
Career Total (Turf)	5	0	1	1	1786
Career Total (AW)	3	0	0	0	0

Going (Turf): Sf: 0-0 GS: 0-1 Gd: 0-1 GF: 0-2 Fm: 0-0
Distance: 5f/6f: 0-0 7f-8f: 0-2 9f-13f: 0-2 14f+: 0-4
Track : LH: 0-5 RH: 0-2 Tight: 0-2 Gall: 0-1
Aids: Bl: 0-4 Vi: 0-0 Tstrap: 0-0 Ckp: 0-0
Best Rating: 57 7/08 Ayr 1m5f13y gd-sft

Inpursuitoffreedom

88(87) (49)63
2-y-o b/br f Pastoral Pursuits-Quilt (Terimon)
P J McBride M S Barritt

Placings:35 (6858)
2009: 7^{3}G, 8^{5}SD,

	Starts	1st	2nd	3rd	Win & Pl
Career Total (Turf)	1	0	0	1	578
Career Total (AW)	1	0	0	0	0

Going (Turf): Sf: 0-0 GS: 0-0 Gd: 0-1 GF: 0-0 Fm: 0-0
Distance: 5f/6f: 0-0 7f-8f: 0-1 9f-13f: 0-1 14f+: 0-0
Track : LH: 0-1 RH: 0-0 Tight: 0-1 Gall: 0-0
Aids: Bl: 0-0 Vi: 0-0 Tstrap: 0-0 Ckp: 0-0
Best Rating: 63 8/09 NmkJ 7f good

Inquest

(104) (62)72
4-y-o b g Rainbow Quest (USA)-Katy Nowaitee (Komaite (USA))
Mrs A J Perrett J H Richmond-Watson

Placings:02230-326 (0588)
2009: 10^{3}SD, 10^{2}SD, 10^{6}SD,

	Starts	1st	2nd	3rd	Win & Pl
Career Total (Turf)	4	0	2	1	2573
Career Total (AW)	4	0	1	1	1114

Going (Turf): Sf: 0-2 GS: 0-1 Gd: 0-1 GF: 0-0 Fm: 0-0
Distance: 5f/6f: 0-0 7f-8f: 0-0 9f-13f: 0-8 14f+: 0-0
Track : LH: 0-3 RH: 0-5 Tight: 0-4 Gall: 0-0
Aids: Bl: 0-0 Vi: 0-0 Tstrap: 0-1 Ckp: 0-1
Best Rating: 72 10/08 Brig 1m3f196y good

Modest; effective over 1m2f and acts on soft ground.

Inquisitress

97(104) (66)53
5-y-o b m Hernando (FR)-Caribbean Star (Soviet Star (USA))
J J Bridger C Marshall T Wallace J J Bridger

Placings:506601313/5600030442606305106030/431500 00400-0450565551604561464630 (7880)
2009: 8^{0}SD, 10^{4}SD, 8^{5}SD, 12^{0}SD, 8^{5}SD, 10^{6}SD, 10^{5}SD, 10^{5}SD, 10^{1}SD, 10^{6}F, 11^{0}SD, 8^{4}GS, 9^{5}GS, 7^{6}G, 8^{1}SD, 8^{4}SD, 8^{6}SD, 10^{4}SD, 8^{6}SD, 10^{3}SD, 7^{0}SD,

	Starts	1st	2nd	3rd	Win & Pl
Career Total (Turf)	14	0	0	3	1382
Career Total (AW)	50	6	1	4	16475

56	10/09	Kemp	1m	(0-60)H	STD	£1706
54	8/09	Ling	1m2f	(0-62)H	STD	£2047
66	7/08	Kemp	1m	(0-70)H	STD	£2590
62	9/07	Kemp	1m	(0-60)H	STD	£2047
69	12/06	Kemp	1m	(0-65)	STD	£2388
54	11/06	Ling	1m		STD	£2388

Total win prize-money £13169

Going (Turf): Sf: 0-0 GS: 0-3 Gd: 0-3 GF: 0-5 Fm: 0-3
Distance: 5f/6f: 0-4 7f-8f: 5-44 9f-13f: 1-16 14f+: 0-0
Track : LH: 2-31 RH: 4-28 Tight: 2-26 Gall: 0-0
Aids: Bl: 0-2 Vi: 0-0 Tstrap: 0-0 Ckp: 0-0
Best Rating: 75 8/06 NmkJ 7f gd-fm

Moderate; stays 1m; acts on Polytrack.

Inshaallah

79(82) (49)**43**
2-y-o ch g Doyen (IRE)-Lake Diva (Docksider (USA))
J G Given P B Doyle

Placings:005 (7420)
2009: 8^{0}S, 8^{0}GF, 7^{5}SD,

	Starts	1st	2nd	3rd	Win & Pl
Career Total (Turf)	2	0	0	0	
Career Total (AW)	1	0	0	0	0

Going (Turf): Sf: 0-1 GS: 0-0 Gd: 0-0 GF: 0-1 Fm: 0-0
Distance: 5f/6f: 0-0 7f-8f: 0-1 9f-13f: 0-2 14f+: 0-0
Track : LH: 0-3 RH: 0-0 Tight: 0-0 Gall: 0-0
Aids: Bl: 0-0 Vi: 0-0 Tstrap: 0-0 Ckp: 0-0
Best Rating: 49 11/09 Sthl 7f stand

Inside Knowledge (USA)

97(79) (48)**57**
3-y-o gr/ro g Mizzen Mast (USA)-Kithira (Danehill (USA))
G Woodward Mr & Mrs Bloom

Placings:56-000360 (7080)
2009: 5^{0}SD, 8^{0}F, 8^{0}SD, 10^{3}G, 14^{6}HY, 11^{0}S,

	Starts	1st	2nd	3rd	Win & Pl
Career Total (Turf)	5	0	0	1	482
Career Total (AW)	3	0	0	0	0

Going (Turf): Sf: 0-2 GS: 0-1 Gd: 0-1 GF: 0-0 Fm: 0-1
Distance: 5f/6f: 0-3 7f-8f: 0-1 9f-13f: 0-3 14f+: 0-1
Track : LH: 0-6 RH: 0-0 Tight: 0-2 Gall: 0-2
Aids: Bl: 0-0 Vi: 0-0 Tstrap: 0-1 Ckp: 0-1
Best Rating: 57 5/08 Wind 5f10y gd-sft

Modest; stays 1m2f; acts on good ground.

Inside Story (IRE)

106(108) (70)**75**
7-y-o b g Rossini (USA)-Sliding (Formidable (USA))
C R Dore Chris Marsh

Placings:1043/00041105010133/3053611433564/242036330136050-4402451503134605060600 (7856)
2009: 7^{4}SD, 7^{4}SD, 7^{0}SD, 8^{2}SD, 8^{4}SD, 9^{5}SD, 11^{1}SD, 12^{5}SD, 9^{0}GF, 8^{3}G, 8^{1}GF, 7^{3}GF, 8^{4}GF, 8^{0}S, 7^{0}GF, 8^{5}GS, 8^{0}GF, 8^{6}GS, 8^{0}SD, 8^{6}SD, 10^{0}SD, 9^{0}SD,

	Starts	1st	2nd	3rd	Win & Pl
Career Total (Turf)	40	6	0	10	25607
Career Total (AW)	28	4	3	3	16277

74	5/09	Gdwd	1m	(0-65)H	G-F	£3238
70	2/09	Sthl	1m3f	(0-70)H	STD	£2729
75	8/08	Hayd	1m30y	(0-70)H	G-S	£3238
82	8/07	Hayd	1m30y	(0-70)H	G-F	£3238
76	7/07	Wolv	1m141y		STD	£2730
73	9/06	Leic	1m1f218y		G-F	£2590
61	8/06	Ripn	1m1f170y		G-S	£3238
71	7/06	Hayd	1m30y	(0-65)H	G-F	£3238
65	7/06	Wolv	1m141y	(0-65)H	STD	£2730
72	1/05	Ling	7f		STD	£4238

Total win prize-money £31212

Going (Turf): Sf: 0-3 GS: 2-10 Gd: 0-9 GF: 4-17 Fm: 0-1
Distance: 5f/6f: 0-1 7f-8f: 2-22 9f-13f: 8-45 14f+: 0-0
Track : LH: 7-41 RH: 3-20 Tight: 4-26 Gall: 0-6
Aids: Bl: 9-61 Vi: 0-0 Tstrap: 0-0 Ckp: 0-0
Best Rating: 87 6/05 Donc 7f gd-fm

Modest; stays 1m3f, also effective at 1m; acts on fast and easy ground; also goes on Polytrack and Fibresand; often wears blinkers.

Inside Track (IRE)

101(99) (77)**80**
2-y-o b g Bertolini (USA)-True Crystal (IRE) (Sadler's Wells (USA))
P T Midgley (B J Meehan 9/12) P T Midgley

Placings:022566331 (7781)
2009: 7^{0}GF, 8^{2}GS, 8^{2}SD, 8^{5}S, 7^{6}SD, 7^{6}SD, 8^{3}SD, 7^{3}SD, 7^{1}SD,

	Starts	1st	2nd	3rd	Win & Pl
Career Total (Turf)	3	0	1	0	674
Career Total (AW)	6	1	1	2	3347

69	12/09	Sthl	7f	STD	£2047

Total win prize-money £2047

Going (Turf): Sf: 0-1 GS: 0-1 Gd: 0-0 GF: 0-1 Fm: 0-0
Distance: 5f/6f: 0-0 7f-8f: 1-7 9f-13f: 0-2 14f+: 0-0
Track : LH: 1-4 RH: 0-3 Tight: 0 3 Gall: 0-0
Aids: Bl: 1-4 Vi: 0-0 Tstrap: 0-0 Ckp: 0-0
Best Rating: 80 9/09 Chep 1m14y gd-sft

Fair; stays 1m; acts on sand; has worn blinkers.

Inside Trade (IRE)

93(94) (47)**53**
3-y-o b g Xaar-Azolia (IRE) (Alzao (USA))
N P Mulholland (R M Beckett 27/8) The Insider Traders

Placings:06060000 (7239)
2009: 8^{0}S, 8^{6}GF, 6^{0}GF, 8^{6}SD, 9^{0}F, 8^{0}SD, 7^{0}SD, 7^{0}SD,

	Starts	1st	2nd	3rd	Win & Pl
Career Total (Turf)	4	0	0	0	0
Career Total (AW)	4	0	0	0	0

Going (Turf): Sf: 0-1 GS: 0-0 Gd: 0-0 GF: 0-2 Fm: 0-1
Distance: 5f/6f: 0-0 7f-8f: 0-7 9f-13f: 0-1 14f+: 0-0
Track : LH: 0-2 RH: 0-3 Tight: 0-2 Gall: 0-0
Aids: Bl: 0-0 Vi: 0-1 Tstrap: 0-0 Ckp: 0-0
Best Rating: 53 6/09 Sals 6f212y gd-fm

Insignia (IRE)

(95) (38)**53**
7-y-o b g Royal Applause-Amathea (FR) (Exit To Nowhere (USA))
Mrs K J Tutty (Mrs A M Thorpe 16/5) N D Tutty

Placings:550/50600003/4000404/5306/0 (0443)
2009: 12^{0}SD,

	Starts	1st	2nd	3rd	Win & Pl
Career Total (Turf)	6	0	0	0	0
Career Total (AW)	17	0	0	2	521

Going (Turf): Sf: 0-0 GS: 0-1 Gd: 0-2 GF: 0-3 Fm: 0-0
Distance: 5f/6f: 0-3 7f-8f: 0-4 9f-13f: 0-16 14f+: 0-0
Track : LH: 0-19 RH: 0-2 Tight: 0-15 Gall: 0-0
Aids: Bl: 0-0 Vi: 0-1 Tstrap: 0-7 Ckp: 0-7
Best Rating: 59 6/05 Ches 1m2f75y good

Plating-class gelding; stays 1m; has been tried in cheek-pieces.

Insolence (USA)

103(102) (76)**72**
3-y-o b f Mr Greeley (USA)-Brianda (IRE) (Alzao (USA))
Sir Michael Stoute Ms Nicola Mahoney

Placings:53432431 (7399)
2009: 8^{5}GF, 8^{3}G, 10^{4}GF, 10^{3}GF, 9^{2}SD, 10^{4}G, 9^{3}SD, 9^{1}SD,

	Starts	1st	2nd	3rd	Win & Pl
Career Total (Turf)	5	0	0	2	1558
Career Total (AW)	3	1	1	1	4797

76	11/09	Wolv	1m1f103y	(0-70)H	STD	£3238

Total win prize-money £3238

Going (Turf): Sf: 0-0 GS: 0-0 Gd: 0-2 GF: 0-3 Fm: 0-0
Distance: 5f/6f: 0-0 7f-8f: 0-1 9f-13f: 1-7 14f+: 0-0
Track : LH: 1-6 RH: 0-1 Tight: 1-6 Gall: 0-0
Aids: Bl: 0-0 Vi: 0-0 Tstrap: 0-0 Ckp: 0-0
Best Rating: 76 11/09 Wolv 1m1f103y stand

Fair; stays 1m2f; acts on fast ground and on Polytrack.

Insomnitas

93(92) (54)**54**
4-y-o b g Lomitas-Sleepless (Night Shift (USA))
Seamus Fahey Finbarr Kelly

Placings:0546000/00000-000026300 (7444a)
2009: 7^{0}SD, 7^{0}Y, 5^{0}GF, 8^{0}YS, 7^{2}GF, 7^{6}GY, 8^{3}SD, 9^{0}SD, 8^{0}SD,

	Starts	1st	2nd	3rd	Win & Pl
Career Total (Turf)	13	0	1	0	1070
Career Total (AW)	8	0	0	1	323

Going (Turf): Sf: 0-2 GS: 0-1 Gd: 0-3 GF: 0-3 Fm: 0-1
Distance: 5f/6f: 0-2 7f-8f: 0-14 9f-13f: 0-5 14f+: 0-0
Track : LH: 0-10 RH: 0-7 Tight: 0-4 Gall: 0-0
Aids: Bl: 0-1 Vi: 0-0 Tstrap: 0-0 Ckp: 0-0
Best Rating: 54 10/09 Wolv 1m141y stand

Moderate; effective over 1m; acts on fast ground.

Inspainagain (USA)

81(80) (30)**79**
5-y-o ch g Miswaki (USA)-Counter Cat (USA) (Hennessy (USA))
Paul Mason Mrs S White & Mrs J McCarlie

Placings:62/441200/00010000-00 (3407)
2009: 5^{0}SD, 6^{0}GF,

	Starts	1st	2nd	3rd	Win & Pl
Career Total (Turf)	17	2	2	0	12655
Career Total (AW)	1	0	0	0	

79	7/08	York	5f	(0-90)H	HVY	£8095

68 6/07 Muss 5f (0-65)H G-S £2590
Total win prize-money £10686

Going (Turf): **Sf: 1-4 GS: 1-3** Gd: 0-2 GF: 0-8 Fm: 0-0
Distance: **5f/6f: 2-17** 7f-8f: 0-1 9f-13f: 0-0 14f+: 0-0
Track : LH: 0-0 RH: 0-3 Tight: 0-0 Gall: 0-4
Aids: Bl: 0-0 Vi: 0-0 Tstrap: 0-0 Ckp: 0-0
Best Rating: 79 7/08 York 5f heavy

Fair sprinter; acts on a sound surface.

Inspector Clouseau (IRE)

103(97) (60)81
4-y-o gr g Daylami (IRE)-Claustra (FR) (Green Desert (USA))
T P Tate Allan McLuckie

Placings:421/225450-4025010 (6280)
2009: 12^{4}GF, 10^{0}G, 12^{2}GF, 14^{5}GF, 12^{0}GF, 11^{1}GF, 13^{0}GF,

	Starts	1st	2nd	3rd	Win & Pl
Career Total (Turf)	15	2	4	0	16045
Career Total (AW)	1	0	0	0	

74 8/09 Catt 1m3f214y (0-75)H G-F £2810
68 9/07 Thsk 7f G-F £3562
Total win prize-money £6373

Going (Turf): Sf: 0-1 GS: 0-1 Gd: 0-4 **GF: 2-9** Fm: 0-0
Distance: 5f/6f: 0-0 7f-8f: 1-4 9f-13f: 1-10 14f+: 0-2
Track : **LH: 2-14** RH: 0-1 **Tight: 2-9** Gall: 0-4
Aids: Bl: 0-0 Vi: 0-0 Tstrap: 0-0 Ckp: 0-0
Best Rating: 81 5/08 Thsk 1m good

Fair; stays 1m4f; acts on good and faster ground; likes to race prominently.

Inspirina (IRE)

106(97) (75)79
5-y-o b g Invincible Spirit (IRE)-La Stellina (IRE) (Marju (IRE))
R Ford Miss Gill Quincey

Placings:533/0/**2121**4246050-46151R4442 (7020)
2009: 12^{4}GF, 10^{6}GF, 12^{1}GF, 10^{5}GF, 12^{1}GF, 12^{R}G, 12^{4}G, 12^{4}GF, 11^{4}G, 10^{2}GS,

	Starts	1st	2nd	3rd	Win & Pl
Career Total (Turf)	21	3	2	2	18597
Career Total (AW)	4	1	2	0	3624

75 7/09 Epsm 1m4f10y (0-70)H G-F £3238
72 7/09 Ches 1m4f66y (0-75)H G-F £4047
77 4/08 Wwck 1m2f188y (0-80)H SFT £4533
69 2/08 Kemp 1m3f STD £2047
Total win prize-money £13866

Going (Turf): Sf: 1-3 GS: 0-1 Gd: 0-7 **GF: 2-10** Fm: 0-0
Distance: 5f/6f: 0-2 7f-8f: 0-2 **9f-13f: 4-17** 14f+: 0-4
Track : **LH: 3-19** RH: 1-3 **Tight: 2-13** Gall: 0-4
Aids: Bl: 0-0 Vi: 0-0 Tstrap: 0-0 Ckp: 0-0
Best Rating: 79 6/08 York 1m4f gd-fm

Modest; stays 1m6f; acts on most ground and on Polytrack.

Instalment

101 103
3-y-o b g Cape Cross (IRE)-New Assembly (IRE) (Machiavellian (USA))
R Hannon The Queen

Placings:10602-104 (3621)
2009: 6^{1}GF, 7^{0}GF, 6^{4}GF,

	Starts	1st	2nd	3rd	Win & Pl
Career Total (Turf)	8	2	1	0	21517

103 5/09 Sals 6f (0-100)H G-F £12462
83 5/08 Newb 6f8y GD £5342
Total win prize-money £17805

Going (Turf): Sf: 0-0 GS: 0-0 **Gd: 1-3 GF: 1-5** Fm: 0-0
Distance: 5f/6f: 1-3 7f-8f: 1-5 9f-13f: 0-0 14f+: 0-0
Track : LH: 0-0 RH: 0-2 Tight: 0-0 Gall: 0-0
Aids: Bl: 0-0 Vi: 0-0 Tstrap: 0-0 Ckp: 0-0
Best Rating: 103 5/09 Sals 6f gd-fm

Smart; effective over 6f-7f and acts on good/fast ground.

Instructor

49 (88)69
8-y-o ch g Groom Dancer (USA)-Doctor's Glory (USA) (Elmaamul (USA))
C A Mulhall Keith Sivills

Placings:042/**21**000**665**/**31**0000401131062/00403401300/3400/000-0 (4431)
2009: 10^{0}GF,

	Starts	1st	2nd	3rd	Win & Pl
Career Total (Turf)	36	4	1	4	29629
Career Total (AW)	9	2	2	1	12502

86 7/06 Ches 1m2f75y (0-80)H G-F £5829
83 8/05 Ayr 1m2f (0-75)H G-F £3458
80 7/05 Carl 1m1f61y (0-70)H G-F £3626
77 7/05 Hayd 1m2f120y (0-70)H G-F £5293
89 2/05 Sthl 1m (0-85)H STD £6717
74 4/04 Ling 1m F STD £2898
Total win prize-money £27824

Going (Turf): Sf: 0-4 GS: 0-2 Gd: 0-12 **GF: 4-17** Fm: 0-1
Distance: 5f/6f: 0-1 7f-8f: 2-8 **9f-13f: 4-36** 14f+: 0-0
Track : **LH: 5-28** RH: 1-12 **Tight: 2-14** Gall: 0-11
Aids: Bl: 0-0 Vi: 0-0 Tstrap: 0-0 Ckp: 0-0
Best Rating: 89 2/05 Sthl 1m stand

Useful; stays 1m2f; acts on fast ground and on sand; likes to race prominently.

Intabih (USA)

106(108) (93)86
4-y-o b/br c More Than Ready (USA)-Lookaway Dixieland (USA) (Dixieland Band (USA))
C E Brittain Saeed Manana

Placings:0/5633115-10056 (3213)
2009: 8^{1}SD, 8^{0}GF, 10^{0}SD, 8^{5}G, 10^{6}GF,

	Starts	1st	2nd	3rd	Win & Pl
Career Total (Turf)	6	0	0	0	699
Career Total (AW)	7	3	0	2	12296

93 3/09 Sthl 1m (0-85)H STD £4857
89 10/08 GrLe 1m2f (0-70)H STD £3238
86 10/08 Wolv 1m1f103y (0-70)H SF £3238
Total win prize-money £11333

Going (Turf): **Sf: 0-1 GS: 0-0 Gd: 0-1 GF: 0-4 Fm: 0-0**
Distance: 5f/6f: 0-0 7f-8f: 1-5 **9f-13f: 2-8** 14f+: 0-0
Track : **LH: 3-11** RH: 0-1 Tight: 1-5 Gall: 1-4
Aids: Bl: 0-0 Vi: 0-0 Tstrap: 0-0 Ckp: 0-0
Best Rating: 93 3/09 Sthl 1m stand

Useful; effective over 1m-1m2f and acts on sand.

Intavac Boy

85(86) (13)36
8-y-o ch g Emperor Fountain-Altaia (FR) (Sicyos (USA))
S P Griffiths Ms Elizabeth Grant

Placings:664022/0040530201**240**/03022210/43502450060 22056/000-00000 (7733)
2009: 12^{0}GF, 9^{0}GF, 10^{0}GF, 11^{0}S, 12^{0}SD,

	Starts	1st	2nd	3rd	Win & Pl
Career Total (Turf)	41	2	7	3	18035
Career Total (AW)	10	0	3	0	2159

65 7/06 Bevl 1m4f16y (0-70)H FRM £4857
61 10/05 Newc 1m4f93y (0-60)H G-F £3930
Total win prize-money £8789

Going (Turf): Sf: 0-2 GS: 0-4 Gd: 0-14 **GF: 1-20 Fm: 1-1**
Distance: 5f/6f: 0-4 7f-8f: 0-1 **9f-13f: 2-44** 14f+: 0-2
Track : LH: 1-37 RH: 1-9 Tight: 1-22 Gall: 1-11
Aids: Bl: 0-0 Vi: 0-1 Tstrap: 0-5 Ckp: 0-5
Best Rating: 66 10/04 Pont 1m4y good

Moderate; effective at around 1m4f; acts on good and fast ground; also goes on Polytrack.

Integration

(85) (44)44
9-y-o b g Piccolo-Discrimination (Efisio)
Miss M E Rowland Miss M E Rowland

Placings:000/0052053/033020000/024030/**05**/**04000**/**60-0** (0377)
2009: 11^{0}SD,

	Starts	1st	2nd	3rd	Win & Pl
Career Total (Turf)	24	0	3	4	5064
Career Total (AW)	11	0	0	0	0

Going (Turf): **Sf: 0-1 GS: 0-2 Gd: 0-3 GF: 0-10 Fm: 0-7**
Distance: 5f/6f: 0-0 7f-8f: 0-5 9f-13f: 0-25 14f+: 0-5
Track : LH: 0-21 RH: 0-12 Tight: 0-7 Gall: 0-0
Aids: Bl: 0-0 Vi: 0-0 Tstrap: 0-0 Ckp: 0-0
Best Rating: 56 7/04 Rosc 1m2f gd-fm

Integria

94(101) (74)69
3-y-o b g Intikhab (USA)-Alegria (Night Shift (USA))
J M P Eustace J C Smith

Placings:035-0035100 (6977)
2009: 6^{0}GF, 7^{0}GF, 6^{3}SD, 7^{5}GS, 8^{1}SD, 7^{0}SD, 8^{0}SD,

	Starts	1st	2nd	3rd	Win & Pl
Career Total (Turf)	5	0	0	1	595
Career Total (AW)	5	1	0	1	2432

74 9/09 Kemp 1m (0-65)H STD £2047
Total win prize-money £2047

Going (Turf): **Sf: 0-1 GS: 0-1 Gd: 0-1 GF: 0-2 Fm: 0-0**
Distance: 5f/6f: 0-2 **7f-8f: 1-8** 9f-13f: 0-0 14f+: 0-0
Track : LH: 0-2 **RH: 1-3** Tight: 0-2 Gall: 0-1
Aids: **Bl: 1-5** Vi: 0-0 Tstrap: 0-0 Ckp: 0-0
Best Rating: 74 9/09 Kemp 1m stand

Modest; effective over 7f; acts on good ground.

Intense

102(101) (89)95
3-y-o b f Dansili-Modesta (IRE) (Sadler's Wells (USA))
B W Hills K Abdulla

Placings:210-100 (7132)
2009: 8^{1}GF, 7^{0}GF, 8^{0}SD,

	Starts	1st	2nd	3rd	Win & Pl
Career Total (Turf)	5	2	1	0	18101
Career Total (AW)	1	0	0	0	

95 9/09 NmkR 1m (0-90)H G-F £7771
88 9/08 Sals 6f212y GD £6476
Total win prize-money £14247

Going (Turf): Sf: 0-0 GS: 0-0 **Gd: 1-1 GF: 1-4** Fm: 0-0
Distance: 5f/6f: 0-1 **7f-8f: 2-5** 9f-13f: 0-0 14f+: 0-0

Track : LH: 0-1 RH: 0-0 Tight: 0-1 Gall: 0-0
Aids: Bl: 0-0 Vi: 0-0 Tstrap: 0-0 Ckp: 0-0
Best Rating: 95 9/09 NmkR 1m gd-fm

Useful; stays 7f, will get further; acts on good ground.

Intense Focus (USA)

109 **118**

3-y-o b c Giant's Causeway (USA)-Daneleta (IRE) (Danehill (USA))
J S Bolger Mrs J S Bolger

Placings:412356331-25 (2992)
2009: 8^{2}GF, 8^{5}GF,

	Starts	1st	2nd	3rd	Win & Pl
Career Total (Turf)	11	2	2	3	353135

118 10/08 NmkR 7f GD £163355
89 5/08 Curr 6f FRM £9573
Total win prize-money £172930

Going (Turf): Sf: 0-1 GS: 0-1 Gd: 1-1 GF: 0-3 Fm: 1-1
Distance: 5f/6f: 1-4 7f-8f: 1-7 9f-13f: 0-0 14f+: 0-0
Track : LH: 0-1 RH: 0-2 Tight: 0-0 Gall: 0-1
Aids: Bl: 0-4 Vi: 1-2 Tstrap: 0-0 Ckp: 0-0
Best Rating: 118 10/08 NmkR 7f good

High class; Irish trained; winner of the Dewhurst Stakes in 2008; also runner-up in the Coventry Stakes and third in the Jean-Luc Lagardere; effective at 6f-1m; acts on most ground; has worn blinkers, tongue tie and visor.

Inter Vision (USA)

102 (96)**102**

9-y-o b g Cryptoclearance (USA)-Fateful (USA) (Topsider (USA))
A Dickman Mrs B M Bennett

Placings:2211100/000646012054/005004200066/500406 3110310/000441402/000020061105/004115600-00006066442550 (7220)
2009: 5^{0}G, 6^{0}GF, 6^{0}GF, 6^{0}S, 6^{6}GF, 6^{0}G, 7^{6}GF, 7^{6}GF, 6^{4}GF, 5^{4}S, 7^{2}GF, 5^{5}GF, 7^{5}S, 7^{0}S,

	Starts	1st	2nd	3rd	Win & Pl
Career Total (Turf)	83	12	7	2	104826
Career Total (AW)	5	0	0	0	153

100 5/08 Rdcr 5f (0-85)H G-F £4209
99 5/08 Catt 5f212y (0-85)H G-F £4209
99 9/07 Thsk 6f (0-90)H G-F £7124
93 9/07 Donc 5f (0-85)H G-F £6477
97 8/06 Ches 7f2y (0-95)H GD £9463
94 8/05 Ripn 6f (0-95)H GD £10645
92 6/05 Newc 6f (0-75)H GD £5469
81 6/05 Catt 5f212y (0-75)H FRM £7042
96 8/03 Ripn 6f D(0-80)H G-F £5473
96 7/02 Ches 5f16y B GD £9832
96 6/02 Ripn 5f E G-F £3304
92 6/02 Ches 5f16y D GD £4153
Total win prize-money £77404

Going (Turf): Sf: 0-16GS: 0-4 Gd: 5-23 GF: 6-37 Fm: 1-3
Distance: 5f/6f: 11-71 7f-8f: 1-17 9f-13f: 0-0 14f+: 0-0
Track : LH: 5-25 RH: 0-2 Tight: 5-19 Gall: 0-2
Aids: Bl: 0-0 Vi: 0-0 Tstrap: 0-1 Ckp: 0-1
Best Rating: 102 5/08 Newc 6f gd-fm

Useful; effective over 5f-7f and acts on most ground.

Interactive (IRE)

95(108) (71)**68**

6-y-o b g King's Best (USA)-Forentia (Formidable (USA))
D Burchell (Andrew Turnell 10/10) A G Fear

Placings:00444/042346002050-512260366000 (7496)
2009: 6^{5}SD, 6^{1}SD, 7^{2}SD, 7^{2}SD, 7^{6}SD, 6^{0}GF, 6^{3}G, 5^{6}GF, 5^{6}SD, 5^{0}SD, 7^{0}SD, 5^{0}SD,

	Starts	1st	2nd	3rd	Win & Pl
Career Total (Turf)	9	0	1	1	1095
Career Total (AW)	20	1	3	1	5912

71 1/09 Kemp 6f STD £3070
Total win prize-money £3071

Going (Turf): Sf: 0-0 GS: 0-2 Gd: 0-3 GF: 0-3 Fm: 0-1
Distance: 5f/6f: 1-14 7f-8f: 0-12 9f-13f: 0-3 14f+: 0-0
Track : LH: 0-18 RH: 1-6 Tight: 0-17 Gall: 0-1
Aids: Bl: 0-0 Vi: 0-1 Tstrap: 0-0 Ckp: 0-0
Best Rating: 75 12/07 Ling 7f stand

Modest; effective over 6f; acts on good ground and Polytrack.

Interakt

93 **69**

2-y-o b f Rakti-Amelie Pouliche (FR) (Desert Prince (IRE))
M R Channon Heart Of The South Racing

Placings:523435 (5970)
2009: 7^{5}GF, 7^{2}GF, 6^{3}GF, 7^{4}G, 8^{3}G, 8^{5}GF,

	Starts	1st	2nd	3rd	Win & Pl
Career Total (Turf)	6	0	1	2	3080

Going (Turf): Sf: 0-0 GS: 0-0 Gd: 0-2 GF: 0-4 Fm: 0-0
Distance: 5f/6f: 0-0 7f-8f: 0-4 9f-13f: 0-2 14f+: 0-0
Track : LH: 0-3 RH: 0-0 Tight: 0-2 Gall: 0-0
Aids: Bl: 0-0 Vi: 0-0 Tstrap: 0-0 Ckp: 0-0
Best Rating: 69 7/09 Epsm 7f gd-fm

Fair; stays 7f and acts on fast ground.

Interchoice Star

100(102) (59)**52**

4-y-o b g Josr Algarhoud (IRE)-Blakeshall Girl (Piccolo)
R Hollinshead John P Evitt

Placings:000-325030003446 (7858)
2009: 7^{3}SD, 5^{2}SD, 6^{5}SD, 5^{0}SD, 6^{3}GF, 8^{0}GF, 10^{0}SD, 9^{0}SD, 9^{3}SD, 7^{4}SF, 8^{4}SD, 8^{6}SD,

	Starts	1st	2nd	3rd	Win & Pl
Career Total (Turf)	3	0	0	1	385
Career Total (AW)	12	0	1	2	1310

Going (Turf): Sf: 0-1 GS: 0-0 Gd: 0-0 GF: 0-2 Fm: 0-0
Distance: 5f/6f: 0-4 7f-8f: 0-5 9f-13f: 0-6 14f+: 0-0
Track : LH: 0-14 RH: 0-1 Tight: 0-9 Gall: 0-1
Aids: Bl: 0-0 Vi: 0-0 Tstrap: 0-1 Ckp: 0-1
Best Rating: 59 12/09 Wolv 1m141y stand

Moderate; effective at around 7f; acts on Polytrack; has worn cheekpieces.

Interdiamonds

108(104) (81)**79**

3-y-o b f Montjeu (IRE)-Interpose (Indian Ridge)
M Johnston Syndicate 2007

Placings:221202262 (6360)
2009: 9^{2}GF, 12^{2}GF, 10^{1}GF, 12^{2}S, 12^{0}G, 14^{2}G, 14^{2}GS, 14^{6}S, 12^{2}SD,

	Starts	1st	2nd	3rd	Win & Pl
Career Total (Turf)	8	1	5	0	12816
Career Total (AW)	1	0	1	0	1734

71 6/09 Donc 1m2f60y G-F £4857
Total win prize-money £4857

Going (Turf): Sf: 0-2 GS: 0-1 Gd: 0-2 GF: 1-3 Fm: 0-0
Distance: 5f/6f: 0-0 7f-8f: 0-0 9f-13f: 1-6 14f+: 0-3
Track : LH: 1-6 RH: 0-3 Tight: 0-2 Gall: 1-4
Aids: Bl: 0-0 Vi: 0-0 Tstrap: 0-0 Ckp: 0-0
Best Rating: 81 9/09 Sthl 1m4f stand

Fair; effective at up to 1m6f; handles quick ground.

Interest Free

84 **54**

2-y-o b f Kyllachy-Holly Hayes (IRE) (Alzao (USA))
T D Easterby C H Stevens

Placings:0 (5949)
2009: 6^{0}GF,

	Starts	1st	2nd	3rd	Win & Pl
Career Total (Turf)	1	0	0	0	

Going (Turf): Sf: 0-0 GS: 0-0 Gd: 0-0 GF: 0-1 Fm: 0-0
Distance: 5f/6f: 0-1 7f-8f: 0-0 9f-13f: 0-0 14f+: 0-0
Track : LH: 0-0 RH: 0-0 Tight: 0-0 Gall: 0-0
Aids: Bl: 0-0 Vi: 0-0 Tstrap: 0-0 Ckp: 0-0
Best Rating: 54 9/09 Rdcr 6f gd-fm

Interlace

77(98) (78)**61**

2-y-o ch f Pivotal-Splice (Sharpo)
Sir Mark Prescott Cheveley Park Stud

Placings:0105 (7536)
2009: 6^{0}GF, 6^{1}SD, 7^{0}G, 6^{5}SD,

	Starts	1st	2nd	3rd	Win & Pl
Career Total (Turf)	2	0	0	0	
Career Total (AW)	2	1	0	0	3562

78 9/09 Kemp 6f STD £3561
Total win prize-money £3562

Going (Turf): Sf: 0-0 GS: 0-0 Gd: 0-1 GF: 0-1 Fm: 0-0
Distance: 5f/6f: 1-2 7f-8f: 0-2 9f-13f: 0-0 14f+: 0-0
Track : LH: 0-1 RH: 1-2 Tight: 0-1 Gall: 0-0
Aids: Bl: 0-1 Vi: 0-0 Tstrap: 0-0 Ckp: 0-0
Best Rating: 78 9/09 Kemp 6f stand

Fair; effective over 6f; acts on Polytrack; has worn blinkers.

Internationaldebut (IRE)

109(113) (102)**98**

4-y-o b g High Chaparral (IRE)-Whisper Light (IRE) (Caerleon (USA))
J Balding (S Parr 4/7) W McKay, J Barton

Placings:200/33603311620111-054033060005155030500 0 (6702)
2009: 6^{0}SD, 7^{5}SD, 10^{4}SD, 10^{0}SD, 8^{3}SD, 8^{3}SD, 8^{0}SD, 7^{6}SD, 10^{0}SD, 6^{0}GF, 5^{0}GF, 7^{5}GF, 5^{1}G, 5^{5}G, 5^{5}GF, 6^{0}G, 6^{3}GF, 12^{0}GF, 6^{5}GF, 6^{0}G, 6^{0}GF, 7^{0}SS,

	Starts	1st	2nd	3rd	Win & Pl
Career Total (Turf)	24	2	2	5	26815
Career Total (AW)	15	4	0	2	25689

98 5/09 York 5f (0-100)H GD £12952
101 12/08 Ling 1m (0-95)H STD £7641
102 11/08 Ling 6f (0-85)H STD £4727
90 11/08 Ling 7f (0-85)H STD £4403
85 10/08 Wolv 1m141y (0-80)H STD £5180
77 7/08 Leic 5f218y G-F £3238
Total win prize-money £38141

Going (Turf): Sf: 0-2 GS: 0-1 Gd: 1-10 GF: 1-11 Fm: 0-0

Distance: 5f/6f: 3-12 7f-8f: 2-17 9f-13f: 1-10 14f+: 0-0
Track : LH: 4-23 RH: 0-2 Tight: 4-18 Gall: 0-5
Aids: Bl: 0-0 Vi: 0-0 Tstrap: 0-0 Ckp: 0-0
Best Rating: 102 11/08 Ling 6f stand

Very useful; effective over 5f-1m2f; acts on fast ground; goes on Polytrack; has worn a tongue tie.

Intersky Charm (USA)

101(105) (73)80

5-y-o ch g Lure (USA)-Catala (USA) (Northern Park (USA))
Mrs S C Bradburne (R M Whitaker 9/10) Graham Truscott

Placings:450/1420302505404**6**-061533001 (6640)
2009: 10^{0}GF, 12^{6}SD, 7^{1}GF, 7^{5}G, 7^{3}G, 8^{3}GF, 8^{0}GF, 8^{0}GF, 9^{1}SD,

	Starts	1st	2nd	3rd	Win & Pl
Career Total (Turf)	18	1	1	3	7998
Career Total (AW)	8	2	1	0	8464

73	10/09	Wolv	1m1f103y	(0-70)H	STD	£3238
71	6/09	Carl	7f200y	(0-70)H	G-F	£2914
86	1/08	Sthl	1m	(0-75)H	STD	£3276

Total win prize-money £9428

Going (Turf): Sf: 0-1 GS: 0-1 Gd: 0-8 GF: 1-8 Fm: 0-0
Distance: 5f/6f: 0-0 7f-8f: 2-9 9f-13f: 1-17 14f+: 0-0
Track : LH: 2-16 RH: 1-8 Tight: 1-7 Gall: 0-5
Aids: Bl: 0-0 Vi: 0-1 Tstrap: 0-1 Ckp: 0-1
Best Rating: 86 2/08 Sthl 1m stand

Modest; stays 1m2f; acts on good ground and on sand; has worn a visor.

Intersky Music (USA)

83 48

6-y-o b g Victory Gallop (CAN)-Resounding Grace (USA) (Thunder Gulch (USA))
Jonjo O'Neill Mrs Jonjo O'Neill

Placings:6/606/6 (4263)
2009: 12^{6}S,

	Starts	1st	2nd	3rd	Win & Pl
Career Total (Turf)	5	0	0	0	0

Going (Turf): Sf: 0-1 GS: 0-1 Gd: 0-1 GF: 0-2 Fm: 0-0
Distance: 5f/6f: 0-0 7f-8f: 0-0 9f-13f: 0-4 14f+: 0-1
Track : LH: 0-2 RH: 0-2 Tight: 0-1 Gall: 0-0
Aids: Bl: 0-0 Vi: 0-0 Tstrap: 0-0 Ckp: 0-0
Best Rating: 53 10/06 Wind 1m67y gd-sft

Inthawain

96(106) (62)63

3-y-o b f Bertolini (USA)-Ambassadress (USA) (Alleged (USA))
N Wilson CW Racing Club

Placings:06346-42252606000 (7679)
2009: 8^{4}SD, 6^{2}SD, 6^{2}SD, 7^{5}GF, 6^{2}SD, 6^{6}GF, 6^{0}S, 5^{6}GF, 6^{0}SD, 6^{0}SD, 6^{0}SD,

	Starts	1st	2nd	3rd	Win & Pl
Career Total (Turf)	9	0	0	1	641
Career Total (AW)	7	0	3	0	2015

Going (Turf): Sf: 0-2 GS: 0-1 Gd: 0-3 GF: 0-3 Fm: 0-0
Distance: 5f/6f: 0-12 7f-8f: 0-3 9f-13f: 0-1 14f+: 0-0
Track : LH: 0-9 RH: 0-1 Tight: 0-3 Gall: 0-1
Aids: Bl: 0-0 Vi: 0-0 Tstrap: 0-0 Ckp: 0-0
Best Rating: 63 8/08 Catt 5f good

Modest; effective over 5f; acts on good ground.

Intikama (IRE)

90(80) (23)71

3-y-o ch f Intikhab (USA)-Really Gifted (IRE) (Cadeaux Genereux)
M H Tompkins Vallance, John & Kelly

Placings:533-6453500 (7094)
2009: 8^{6}G, 9^{4}S, 10^{5}G, 10^{3}GF, 11^{5}SD, 11^{0}GF, 10^{0}G,

	Starts	1st	2nd	3rd	Win & Pl
Career Total (Turf)	9	0	0	3	1759
Career Total (AW)	1	0	0	0	0

Going (Turf): Sf: 0-2 GS: 0-1 Gd: 0-4 GF: 0-2 Fm: 0-0
Distance: 5f/6f: 0-2 7f-8f: 0-1 9f-13f: 0-7 14f+: 0-0
Track : LH: 0-7 RH: 0-1 Tight: 0-5 Gall: 0-1
Aids: Bl: 0-2 Vi: 0-0 Tstrap: 0-1 Ckp: 0-1
Best Rating: 71 9/08 Sand 5f6y soft

Modest; stays 6f and acts on soft ground; has worn cheek-pieces.

Intimar (IRE)

79(79) (26)37

3-y-o b f Intikhab (USA)-Genetta (Green Desert (USA))
R J Smith Mrs J King

Placings:63400 (7765)
2009: 6^{6}SD, 8^{3}SD, 8^{4}G, 12^{0}SD, 11^{0}SD,

	Starts	1st	2nd	3rd	Win & Pl
Career Total (Turf)	1	0	0	0	241
Career Total (AW)	4	0	0	1	1165

Going (Turf): Sf: 0-0 GS: 0-0 Gd: 0-1 GF: 0-0 Fm: 0-0
Distance: 5f/6f: 0-0 7f-8f: 0-1 9f-13f: 0-4 14f+: 0-0
Track : LH: 0-0 RH: 0-3 Tight: 0-0 Gall: 0-0
Aids: Bl: 0-0 Vi: 0-0 Tstrap: 0-0 Ckp: 0-0
Best Rating: 37 8/09 Sand 1m14y good

Into Mac

41

3-y-o b g Shinko Forest (IRE)-Efipetite (Efisio)
N Bycroft N Bycroft

Placings:0 (3338)
2009: 6^{0}G,

	Starts	1st	2nd	3rd	Win & Pl
Career Total (Turf)	1	0	0	0	

Going (Turf): Sf: 0-0 GS: 0-0 Gd: 0-1 GF: 0-0 Fm: 0-0
Distance: 5f/6f: 0-1 7f-8f: 0-0 9f-13f: 0-0 14f+: 0-0
Track : LH: 0-0 RH: 0-0 Tight: 0-0 Gall: 0-0
Aids: Bl: 0-0 Vi: 0-0 Tstrap: 0-0 Ckp: 0-0

Into My Arms

83(67) (22)43

3-y-o gr f Kyllachy-True Love (Robellino (USA))
M S Saunders Paul Thorman

Placings:000-0 (1420)
2009: 8^{0}GF,

	Starts	1st	2nd	3rd	Win & Pl
Career Total (Turf)	3	0	0	0	
Career Total (AW)	1	0	0	0	

Going (Turf): Sf: 0-0 GS: 0-1 Gd: 0-1 GF: 0-1 Fm: 0-0
Distance: 5f/6f: 0-2 7f-8f: 0-1 9f-13f: 0-1 14f+: 0-0
Track : LH: 0-3 RH: 0-0 Tight: 0-2 Gall: 0-1
Aids: Bl: 0-0 Vi: 0-0 Tstrap: 0-0 Ckp: 0-0
Best Rating: 43 4/09 Bath 1m5y gd-fm

Into The Light

98(102) (69)71

4-y-o b g Fantastic Light (USA)-Boadicea's Chariot (Commanche Run)
E S McMahon Philip Wilkins

Placings:0055**220**-4526 (4021)
2009: 11^{4}GF, 12^{5}SD, 11^{2}GF, 11^{6}GF,

	Starts	1st	2nd	3rd	Win & Pl
Career Total (Turf)	7	0	1	0	1373
Career Total (AW)	4	0	2	0	1927

Going (Turf): Sf: 0-0 GS: 0-0 Gd: 0-2 GF: 0-5 Fm: 0-0
Distance: 5f/6f: 0-1 7f-8f: 0-0 9f-13f: 0-8 14f+: 0-2
Track : LH: 0-8 RH: 0-2 Tight: 0-5 Gall: 0-0
Aids: Bl: 0-1 Vi: 0-1 Tstrap: 0-0 Ckp: 0-0
Best Rating: 71 6/09 Leic 1m3f183y gd-fm

Modest; effective at 1m4f-1m6f; acts on fast and easy ground; has worn blinkers and a visor.

Intolerable (IRE)

99(98) (62)75

3-y-o b g Intikhab (USA)-Institutrice (IRE) (College Chapel)
R M Beckett Serpentine Racing

Placings:43100 (6630)
2009: 5^{4}GS, 5^{3}GF, 6^{1}GF, 7^{0}SD, 7^{0}SS,

	Starts	1st	2nd	3rd	Win & Pl
Career Total (Turf)	3	1	0	1	3283
Career Total (AW)	2	0	0	0	

75	6/09	Ling	6f	G-F	£2729

Total win prize-money £2730

Going (Turf): Sf: 0-0 GS: 0-1 Gd: 0-0 GF: 1-2 Fm: 0-0
Distance: 5f/6f: 1-3 7f-8f: 0-2 9f-13f: 0-0 14f+: 0-0
Track : LH: 0-2 RH: 0-1 Tight: 0-1 Gall: 0-1
Aids: Bl: 0-0 Vi: 0-0 Tstrap: 0-0 Ckp: 0-0
Best Rating: 75 6/09 Ling 6f gd-fm

Fair; stays 6f'; acts on fast ground.

Intrepid Jack

110 (102)115

7-y-o b h Compton Place-Maria Theresa (Primo Dominie)
H Morrison Michael T Lynch

Placings:01/11420/6020002125/22200/20010400-40020406400 (6091)
2009: 6^{4}G, 6^{0}GF, 6^{0}GF, 6^{2}GF, 6^{0}GF, 7^{4}GF, 6^{0}GF, 6^{6}G, 5^{4}GF, 5^{0}GF, 6^{0}G,

	Starts	1st	2nd	3rd	Win & Pl
Career Total (Turf)	36	4	6	0	137977
Career Total (AW)	5	1	3	0	22411

115	7/08	Newb	6f8y		GD	£36900
107	10/06	Bath	5f11y	(0-95)H	GD	£11217
94	5/05	Hayd	6f	(0-80)H	G-F	£7291
95	5/05	Newb	6f8y	(0-85)H	G-F	£6968
69	11/04	Wolv	5f216y		STD	£5200

Total win prize-money £67579

Going (Turf): Sf: 0-4 GS: 0-4 Gd: 2-9 GF: 2-19 Fm: 0-0
Distance: 5f/6f: 3-30 7f-8f: 2-11 9f-13f: 0-0 14f+: 0-0
Track : LH: 2-7 RH: 0-3 Tight: 1-3 Gall: 1-5
Aids: Bl: 0-3 Vi: 0-2 Tstrap: 0-0 Ckp: 0-0
Best Rating: 115 7/08 Newb 6f8y good

Smart; winner in Group 3 company; effective at 5f-7f; acts on fast ground; goes on Polytrack; has been tried in blinkers and a visor.

Invasian (IRE)

105(104) (96)**92**

8-y-o ch g Desert Prince (IRE)-Jarrayan (Machiavellian (USA))

P W D'Arcy Paul D'Arcy

Placings:0/1200120/000/00310/06103500**631**/**4**00**3**00420 030-100113 **(4288)**

2009: 10^{1}S, 11^{0}SD, 10^{0}SD, 10^{1}S, 11^{1}GF, 12^{3}G,

	Starts	1st	2nd	3rd	Win & Pl
Career Total (Turf)	33	7	3	3	58854
Career Total (AW)	12	1	0	3	12565

82	7/09	Leic	1m3f183y		G-F	£3238
87	7/09	Yarm	1m2f21y		SFT	£1942
86	4/09	Newb	1m2f6y	(0-85)H	SFT	£5180
96	12/07	Wolv	1m4f50y	(0-95)H	STD	£7124
92	8/07	NmkJ	1m4f	(0-85)H	G-F	£5181
92	10/06	Nott	1m1f213y	(0-85)H	SFT	£6477
101	8/04	Folk	1m1f149y	C(0-90)	G-S	£8195
84	6/04	Hayd	1m30y	D	G-S	£6077

Total win prize-money £43419

Going (Turf): **Sf: 3-7** GS: 2-6 Gd: 0-6 GF: 2-14 Fm: 0-0
Distance: 5f/6f: 0-0 7f-8f: 0-4 **9f-13f: 8-38** 14f+: 0-3
Track : **LH: 5-19** RH: 3-22 **Tight: 3-10** Gall: 2-19
Aids: Bl: 0-0 Vi: 0-0 Tstrap: 0-0 Ckp: 0-0
Best Rating: **101** 8/04 Bevl 1m1f207y gd-sft

Useful; stays 1m4f; acts on most ground; goes on Polytrack; has worn an eyeshield/tongue tie.

Invention (USA)

103(102) (65)**75**

6-y-o b g Lear Fan (USA)-Carya (USA) (Northern Dancer (CAN))

Miss E C Lavelle Fraser Miller Racing

Placings:61050/**4**0100/0000 265 **(2429)**

2009: 11^{2}G, 13^{6}SD, 16^{5}G,

	Starts	1st	2nd	3rd	Win & Pl
Career Total (Turf)	14	1	1	0	7114
Career Total (AW)	3	0	0	0	934
89 5/06 NmkR 1m2f			SFT		£5181

Total win prize-money £5182

Going (Turf): **Sf: 1-2** GS: 0-3 Gd: 0-5 GF: 0-4 Fm: 0-0
Distance: 5f/6f: 0-0 7f-8f: 0-2 **9f-13f: 1-14** 14f+: 0-1
Track : LH: 0-6 RH: 0-8 Tight: 0-8 Gall: 0-4
Aids: Bl: 0-0 Vi: 0-1 Tstrap: 0-0 Ckp: 0-0
Best Rating: **93** 8/06 NmkJ 1m2f gd-fm

Modest; effective at 1m2f-1m4f; acts on good and soft ground.

Inventor (IRE)

97(110) (103)**102**

4-y-o b g Alzao (USA)-Magnificent Bell (IRE) (Octagonal (NZ))

D McCain Jnr (B J Meehan 26/10) Jon Glews

Placings:031/16102**2**4-50 **(6662)**

2009: 12^{5}SD, 12^{0}GS,

	Starts	1st	2nd	3rd	Win & Pl
Career Total (Turf)	9	3	0	1	38086
Career Total (AW)	3	0	2	0	6227

100	7/08	Hayd	1m3f200y	(0-100)H	GD	£25904
89	5/08	Wind	1m3f135y	(0-85)H	G-F	£4857
75	10/07	Bath	1m2f46y		G-S	£2914

Total win prize-money £33676

Going (Turf): Sf: 0-1 **GS: 1-3 Gd: 1-2 GF: 1-3** Fm: 0-0
Distance: 5f/6f: 0-0 7f-8f: 0-2 **9f-13f: 3-9** 14f+: 0-1
Track : **LH: 2-4** RH: 0-6 **Tight: 2-2** Gall: 0-2
Aids: Bl: 0-0 Vi: 0-0 Tstrap: 0-0 Ckp: 0-0
Best Rating: **103** 9/09 Kemp 1m4f stand

Very useful; stays 1m4f; acts on fast and easy ground and Polytrack.

Invincible Force (IRE)

121(98) (100)**100**

5-y-o b g Invincible Spirit (IRE)-Highly Respected (IRE) (High Estate)

Paul Green Terry Cummins

Placings:2211411220/00063000150030/06320452001-4000011060 **(6675)**

2009: 6^{4}SD, 8^{0}GF, 6^{0}F, 5^{0}GF, 7^{0}GF, 6^{1}HY, 7^{1}G, 6^{0}G, 7^{6}GF, 7^{0}G,

	Starts	1st	2nd	3rd	Win & Pl
Career Total (Turf)	41	8	6	2	226494
Career Total (AW)	4	0	0	1	2011

98	8/09	Ches	7f122y	(0-95)H	GD	£10037
99	7/09	Curr	6f	H	HVY	£9727
100	11/08	Donc	7f	(0-100)H	SFT	£25904
101	9/07	Curr	5f	H	G-F	£30790
98	8/06	Curr	6f		GD	£101379
85	8/06	Ches	6f18y		G-F	£4728
87	7/06	Ches	5f16y		G-F	£4728
76	6/06	Wwck	5f		G-F	£3238

Total win prize-money £190535

Going (Turf): Sf: 2-9 GS: 0-3 Gd: 2-10 **GF: 4-17** Fm: 0-1
Distance: **5f/6f: 5-34** 7f-8f: 3-11 9f-13f: 0-0 14f+: 0-0
Track : **LH: 4-18** RH: 0-0 **Tight: 3-13** Gall: 0-1
Aids: **Bl: 3-19** Vi: 0-1 Tstrap: 0-0 Ckp: 0-0
Best Rating: **101** 9/07 Curr 5f gd-fm

Very useful; effective over 5f-7f; acts on most ground on turf; goes on Polytrack; has worn a visor, usually blinkered; likes to race prominently, but can miss the break.

Invincible Heart (GR)

100(99) (85)**95**

3-y-o b c Invincible Spirit (IRE)-Flamingo Bay (IRE) (Catrail (USA))

Jane Chapple-Hyam Gordon Li

Placings:4532233-216 **(2049)**

2009: 7^{2}GF, 6^{1}GF, 6^{6}GF,

	Starts	1st	2nd	3rd	Win & Pl
Career Total (Turf)	8	1	3	1	17486
Career Total (AW)	2	0	0	2	2037
95 5/09 Ches 6f18y	(0-90)H		G-F		£10361

Total win prize-money £10362

Going (Turf): Sf: 0-1 GS: 0-1 Gd: 0-2 **GF: 1-4** Fm: 0-0
Distance: 5f/6f: 0-5 **7f-8f: 1-5** 9f-13f: 0-0 14f+: 0-0
Track : **LH: 1-3** RH: 0-0 **Tight: 1-2** Gall: 0-1
Aids: Bl: 0-0 Vi: 0-0 Tstrap: 0-0 Ckp: 0-0
Best Rating: **95** 5/09 Ches 6f18y gd-fm

Useful; stays 6f; acts on most ground and on Polytrack.

Invincible Hero (IRE)

79(80) (43)**68**

2-y-o b c Invincible Spirit (IRE)-Bridelina (FR) (Linamix (FR))

J Noseda Saeed Suhail

Placings:03 **(6065)**

2009: 7^{0}SD, 7^{3}GF,

	Starts	1st	2nd	3rd	Win & Pl
Career Total (Turf)	1	0	0	1	770
Career Total (AW)	1	0	0	0	

Going (Turf): **Sf: 0-0 GS: 0-0 Gd: 0-0 GF: 0-1 Fm: 0-0**
Distance: 5f/6f: 0-0 7f-8f: 0-2 9f-13f: 0-0 14f+: 0-0
Track : LH: 0-0 RH: 0-1 Tight: 0-0 Gall: 0-0
Aids: Bl: 0-0 Vi: 0-0 Tstrap: 0-0 Ckp: 0-0
Best Rating: **68** 9/09 NmkR 7f gd-fm

Invincible Isle (IRE)

101(101) (85)**85**

3-y-o b f Invincible Spirit (IRE)-Ile De France (ITY) (Danehill (USA))

H R A Cecil H E Sheikh Sultan Bin Khalifa Al Nahyan

Placings:2612530**1**45 **(6879)**

2009: 9^{2}GF, 8^{6}SD, 7^{1}GF, 7^{2}S, 7^{5}G, 6^{3}GF, 6^{0}G, 6^{1}GF, 7^{4}SD, 6^{5}SD,

	Starts	1st	2nd	3rd	Win & Pl
Career Total (Turf)	7	2	2	1	17444
Career Total (AW)	3	0	0	0	378

85	9/09	Pont	6f	(0-90)H	G-F	£9346
78	6/09	Donc	7f		G-F	£4209

Total win prize-money £13556

Going (Turf): Sf: 0-1 GS: 0-0 Gd: 0-2 **GF: 2-4** Fm: 0-0
Distance: 5f/6f: 1-3 7f-8f: 1-6 9f-13f: 0-1 14f+: 0-0
Track : **LH: 1-3** RH: 0-2 Tight: 0-2 Gall: 0-0
Aids: Bl: 0-0 Vi: 0-0 Tstrap: 0-0 Ckp: 0-0
Best Rating: **85** 9/09 Wolv 7f32y stand

Useful; effective over 6f-1m1f; acts on most ground.

Invincible Joe (IRE)

85(92) (66)**88**

4-y-o b g Invincible Spirit (IRE)-Abbey Park (USA) (Known Fact (USA))

John Joseph Hanlon Glenview House Stud

Placings:22200/0621**1**0-000000 **(6780)**

2009: 5^{0}HY, 10^{0}HY, 8^{0}S, 8^{0}Y, 7^{0}SH, 8^{0}SS,

	Starts	1st	2nd	3rd	Win & Pl
Career Total (Turf)	15	2	4	0	23309
Career Total (AW)	2	0	0	0	

88	7/08	Gway	1m100y	(60-90)H	YLD	£9573
63	7/08	Fair	7f		GD	£5588

Total win prize-money £15163

Going (Turf): Sf: 0-4 GS: 0-0 **Gd: 1-4** GF: 0-2 Fm: 0-1
Distance: 5f/6f: 0-1 7f-8f: 1-13 9f-13f: 1-3 14f+: 0-0
Track : LH: 0-5 **RH: 2-11** Tight: 0-1 Gall: 0-1
Aids: Bl: 0-2 Vi: 0-0 Tstrap: 2-4 Ckp: 2-4
Best Rating: **88** 7/08 Gway 1m100y yield

Invincible Lad (IRE)

105(107) (98)**93**

5-y-o b g Invincible Spirit (IRE)-Lady Ellen (Horage)

E J Alston Con Harrington

Placings:04200/16051130011-01303606130 **(7015)**

2009: 5^{0}GF, 5^{1}GF, 5^{3}GF, 5^{0}GF, 5^{3}GS, 5^{6}GF, 5^{0}GF, 5^{6}GF, 5^{1}SD, 6^{3}SD, 5^{0}GS,

	Starts	1st	2nd	3rd	Win & Pl
Career Total (Turf)	22	3	1	3	13521
Career Total (AW)	5	4	0	1	22505

98	9/09	Sthl	5f	(0-90)H	STD	£9714
90	5/09	Leic	5f2y	(0-75)H	G-F	£3238
86	10/08	Wolv	5f20y	(0-80)H	STD	£5180
90	10/08	Sthl	5f	(0-70)H	STD	£3753
72	7/08	Ayr	5f	(0-65)H	GD	£2590
70	7/08	Haml	5f4y	(0-75)H	GD	£3238
71	2/08	Wolv	5f216y		STD	£2457

Total win prize-money £30171

Going (Turf): Sf: 0-5 GS: 0-2 **Gd: 2-3** GF: 1-11 Fm: 0-1
Distance: **5f/6f: 7-26** 7f-8f: 0-1 9f-13f: 0-0 14f+: 0-0
Track : **LH: 2-6** RH: 0-2 **Tight: 2-4** Gall: 0-1
Aids: Bl: 0-0 Vi: 0-0 Tstrap: 0-1 Ckp: 0-1
Best Rating: 98 9/09 Sthl 5f stand

Useful; best at 5f; acts on fast ground and on sand; has worn cheekpieces.

Invincible Miss (IRE)

(97) (60)

3-y-o b f Invincible Spirit (IRE)-Saramacca (IRE) (Kahyasi)
M Wigham J M Cullinan

Placings:00-231 **(1492)**
2009: 7^{2}SD, 8^{3}SD, 7^{1}SD,

	Starts	1st	2nd	3rd	Win & Pl
Career Total (Turf)	1	0	0	0	
Career Total (AW)	4	1	1	1	3120

59	4/09	Wolv	7f32y	STD	£2047

Total win prize-money £2047

Going (Turf): **Sf: 0-1 GS: 0-0 Gd: 0-0 GF: 0-0 Fm: 0-0**
Distance: 5f/6f: 0-2 **7f-8f: 1-2** 9f-13f: 0-1 14f+: 0-0
Track : **LH: 1-4** RH: 0-0 **Tight: 1-3** Gall: 0-0
Aids: Bl: 0-0 Vi: 0-0 Tstrap: 0-0 Ckp: 0-0
Best Rating: 60 3/09 Wolv 1m141y stand

Modest; effective over 7f; acts on Polytrack.

Invincible Prince (IRE)

82(94) (78)64

2-y-o b g Invincible Spirit (IRE)-Forest Prize (Charnwood Forest (IRE))
R M Beckett R Roberts

Placings:1055 **(6811)**
2009: 7^{1}SD, 7^{0}G, 8^{5}GS, 8^{5}G,

	Starts	1st	2nd	3rd	Win & Pl
Career Total (Turf)	3	0	0	0	350
Career Total (AW)	1	1	0	0	3886

78	6/09	Kemp	7f	STD	£3885

Total win prize-money £3886

Going (Turf): **Sf: 0-0 GS: 0-1 Gd: 0-2 GF: 0-0 Fm: 0-0**
Distance: 5f/6f: 0-0 **7f-8f: 1-4** 9f-13f: 0-0 14f+: 0-0
Track : LH: 0-0 **RH: 1-1** Tight: 0-0 Gall: 0-0
Aids: Bl: 0-1 Vi: 0-0 Tstrap: 0-0 Ckp: 0-0
Best Rating: 78 6/09 Kemp 7f stand

Useful; stays 7f and acts on Polytrack.

Invincible Soul (IRE)

104 85

2-y-o b c Invincible Spirit (IRE)-Licorne (Sadler's Wells (USA))
R Hannon Patrick J Fahey

Placings:0031 **(6810)**
2009: 7^{0}S, 7^{0}GF, 7^{3}GF, 8^{1}G,

	Starts	1st	2nd	3rd	Win & Pl
Career Total (Turf)	4	1	0	1	6791

85	10/09	NmkR	1m	GD	£5828

Total win prize-money £5828

Going (Turf): Sf: 0-1 GS: 0-0 **Gd: 1-1** GF: 0-2 Fm: 0-0
Distance: 5f/6f: 0-0 **7f-8f: 1-4** 9f-13f: 0-0 14f+: 0-0
Track : LH: 0-0 RH: 0-1 Tight: 0-0 Gall: 0-0
Aids: Bl: 0-0 Vi: 0-0 Tstrap: 0-0 Ckp: 0-0
Best Rating: 85 10/09 NmkR 1m good

Useful; effective over 1m; acts on good ground.

Invisible Man

105(100) (83)99

3-y-o ch c Elusive Quality (USA)-Eternal Reve (USA) (Diesis)
J H M Gosden H R H Princess Haya Of Jordan

Placings:3-44104110 **(5880)**
2009: 7^{4}GF, 8^{4}SD, 8^{1}GF, 8^{0}GF, 7^{4}GF, 8^{1}G, 8^{1}GF, 9^{0}GF,

	Starts	1st	2nd	3rd	Win & Pl
Career Total (Turf)	7	3	0	0	25971
Career Total (AW)	2	0	0	1	809

99	8/09	Pont	1m4y	(0-95)H	G-F	£9346
92	7/09	NmkJ	1m	(0-90)H	GD	£8723
86	5/09	NmkR	1m		G-F	£5180

Total win prize-money £23251

Going (Turf): Sf: 0-0 GS: 0-0 Gd: 1-1 **GF: 2-6** Fm: 0-0
Distance: 5f/6f: 0-0 **7f-8f: 2-7** 9f-13f: 1-2 14f+: 0-0
Track : **LH: 1-2** RH: 0-2 Tight: 0-1 Gall: 0-1
Aids: Bl: 0-0 Vi: 0-0 Tstrap: 0-0 Ckp: 0-0
Best Rating: 99 8/09 Pont 1m4y gd-fm

Useful; stays 1m; acts on fast ground.

Inxile (IRE)

113 111

4-y-o b g Fayruz-Grandel (Owington)
D Nicholls Ian Hewitson

Placings:1/2332312-51313355 **(6427)**
2009: 6^{5}GF, 5^{1}Y, 5^{3}G, 5^{1}GF, 5^{3}GY, 5^{3}G, 5^{5}GF, 5^{5}GF,

	Starts	1st	2nd	3rd	Win & Pl
Career Total (Turf)	16	4	3	6	135447

110	6/09	Naas	5f	G-F	£26861
110	4/09	Naas	5f	YLD	£28441
104	8/08	Deau	5f	SFT	£19118
86	9/07	Hayd	5f	G-F	£3238

Total win prize-money £77661

Going (Turf): Sf: 1-2 GS: 0-0 Gd: 0-5 **GF: 2-6** Fm: 0-0
Distance: **5f/6f: 4-16** 7f-8f: 0-0 9f-13f: 0-0 14f+: 0-0
Track : **LH: 2-2** RH: 1-2 Tight: 0-0 Gall: 0-0
Aids: Bl: 0-0 Vi: 0-0 Tstrap: 0-0 Ckp: 0-0
Best Rating: 111 5/09 Lonc 5f good

Smart; Listed winner and Group placed; effective over 5f-6f; acts on most ground; consistent.

Ionisphere

(88) (45)38

4-y-o b g Vettori (IRE)-Liska's Dance (USA) (Riverman (USA))
W McCreery Ms Mary Mackey

Placings:050-53 **(7545a)**
2009: 14^{5}SD, 12^{3}SD,

	Starts	1st	2nd	3rd	Win & Pl
Career Total (Turf)	3	0	0	0	
Career Total (AW)	2	0	0	1	483

Going (Turf): **Sf: 0-0 GS: 0-0 Gd: 0-2 GF: 0-0 Fm: 0-1**
Distance: 5f/6f: 0-0 7f-8f: 0-1 9f-13f: 0-3 14f+: 0-1
Track : LH: 0-3 RH: 0-2 Tight: 0-0 Gall: 0-1
Aids: Bl: 0-0 Vi: 0-0 Tstrap: 0-0 Ckp: 0-0
Best Rating: 45 11/09 Dund 1m4f stand

Plating-class; point winner; acts on a sound surface.

Ipswich Lad

92(95) (72)69

2-y-o ch c Halling (USA)-Poised (USA) (Rahy (USA))
A M Balding Marcus Evans

Placings:5433 **(7683)**
2009: 8^{5}G, 8^{4}GF, 8^{3}SD, 10^{3}SD,

	Starts	1st	2nd	3rd	Win & Pl
Career Total (Turf)	2	0	0	0	289
Career Total (AW)	2	0	0	2	688

Going (Turf): **Sf: 0-0 GS: 0-0 Gd: 0-1 GF: 0-1 Fm: 0-0**
Distance: 5f/6f: 0-0 7f-8f: 0-2 9f-13f: 0-2 14f+: 0-0
Track : LH: 0-0 RH: 0-2 Tight: 0-0 Gall: 0-0
Aids: Bl: 0-0 Vi: 0-1 Tstrap: 0-0 Ckp: 0-0
Best Rating: 72 10/09 Kemp 1m stand

Modest; stays 1m2f; acts on fast ground and Polytrack.

Iptkaar (USA)

94 72

2-y-o br f Dixie Union (USA)-Low Tolerance (USA) (Proud Truth (USA))
C E Brittain Saeed Manana

Placings:3400 **(6477)**
2009: 5^{3}S, 7^{4}GF, 6^{0}GF, 7^{0}GF,

	Starts	1st	2nd	3rd	Win & Pl
Career Total (Turf)	4	0	0	1	3461

Going (Turf): **Sf: 0-1 GS: 0-0 Gd: 0-0 GF: 0-3 Fm: 0-0**
Distance: 5f/6f: 0-2 7f-8f: 0-2 9f-13f: 0-0 14f+: 0-0
Track : LH: 0-0 RH: 0-0 Tight: 0-0 Gall: 0-0
Aids: Bl: 0-0 Vi: 0-0 Tstrap: 0-0 Ckp: 0-0
Best Rating: 72 9/09 NmkR 6f gd-fm

No more than fair efforts to date.

Ireland Dancer (IRE)

(84) (29)9

5-y-o ch g Trans Island-Come Dancing (Suave Dancer (USA))
John Berry John Berry

Placings:550/0560/00-0 **(7492)**
2009: 8^{0}SD,

	Starts	1st	2nd	3rd	Win & Pl
Career Total (Turf)	5	0	0	0	0

	Starts	1st	2nd	3rd	Win & Pl
Career Total (AW)	5	0	0	0	0

Going (Turf): Sf: 0-0 GS: 0-0 Gd: 0-2 GF: 0-3 Fm: 0-0
Distance: 5f/6f: 0-2 7f-8f: 0-4 9f-13f: 0-4 14f+: 0-0
Track : LH: 0-6 RH: 0-0 Tight: 0-5 Gall: 0-0
Aids: Bl: 0-0 Vi: 0-0 Tstrap: 0-0 Ckp: 0-0
Best Rating: **65** 8/06 Gdwd 6f good

Irish Ballad

(107) (64)**56**
7-y-o b g Singspiel (IRE)-Auenlust (GER) (Surumu (GER))
S Dow Mr & Mrs Chua, Moore & Jurd

Placings:004/001066/0030**2**0**1**/00200**3**25**1**124-642**1**40 **(1378)**
2009: 16^{6}SD, 16^{4}SD, 16^{2}SD, 16^{1}SD, 16^{4}SD, 13^{0}SD,

	Starts	1st	2nd	3rd	Win & Pl
Career Total (Turf)	15	1	1	1	3955
Career Total (AW)	19	4	4	1	14543

64	3/09	Ling	2m	(0-65)H	STD	£1878
57	11/08	Wolv	1m5f194y	(0-65)H	STD	£2388
57	11/08	Ling	2m	(0-70)H	STD	£3238
64	10/06	Wolv	1m5f194y	(0-60)H	SF	£3412
63	7/05	Brig	1m3f196y	(0-60)	FRM	£2877

Total win prize-money £13794

Going (Turf): Sf: 0-1 GS: 0-1 Gd: 0-3 GF: 0-9 **Fm: 1-1**
Distance: 5f/6f: 0-0 7f-8f: 0-0 9f-13f: 1-15 **14f+: 4-19**
Track : **LH: 5-21** RH: 0-11 **Tight: 4-22** Gall: 0-0
Aids: Bl: 0-0 Vi: 0-0 Tstrap: 0-0 Ckp: 0-0
Best Rating: **64** 3/09 Ling 2m stand

Moderate; effective over 1m6f-2m; acts on Polytrack.

Irish Bay (IRE)

(81) (32)**52**
6-y-o b g Brief Passing (IRE)-Echo Bay (IRE) (Barry's Run (IRE))
Luke Comer Brian Comer

Placings:0/00-0 **(7411)**
2009: 5^{0}SD,

	Starts	1st	2nd	3rd	Win & Pl
Career Total (Turf)	3	0	0	0	
Career Total (AW)	1	0	0	0	

Going (Turf): Sf: 0-0 GS: 0-1 Gd: 0-1 GF: 0-0 Fm: 0-0
Distance: 5f/6f: 0-2 7f-8f: 0-0 9f-13f: 0-2 14f+: 0-0
Track : LH: 0-1 RH: 0-2 Tight: 0-2 Gall: 0-1
Aids: Bl: 0-0 Vi: 0-0 Tstrap: 0-0 Ckp: 0-0
Best Rating: **52** 10/08 Wind 6f gd-sft

Irish Eyes

59
2-y-o b g Mark Of Esteem (IRE)-Diabaig (Precocious)
Jedd O'Keeffe Ken And Delia Shaw-KGS Consulting LLP

Placings:00 **(5669)**
2009: 7^{0}GS, 7^{0}S,

	Starts	1st	2nd	3rd	Win & Pl
Career Total (Turf)	2	0	0	0	

Going (Turf): Sf: 0-1 GS: 0-1 Gd: 0-0 GF: 0-0 Fm: 0-0
Distance: 5f/6f: 0-0 7f-8f: 0-2 9f-13f: 0-0 14f+: 0-0
Track : LH: 0-1 RH: 0-0 Tight: 0-1 Gall: 0-0
Aids: Bl: 0-0 Vi: 0-0 Tstrap: 0-0 Ckp: 0-0

Irish Heartbeat (IRE)

113 **92**
4-y-o b g Celtic Swing-She's All Class (USA) (Rahy (USA))
David P Myerscough Philip F Myerscough

Placings:4**1**3-06324**1**140 **(6678)**
2009: 8^{0}S, 5^{6}S, 6^{3}GY, 7^{2}G, 6^{4}HY, 5^{3}S, 5^{1}SH, 6^{4}G, 6^{0}G,

	Starts	1st	2nd	3rd	Win & Pl
Career Total (Turf)	12	2	1	3	46883

91	9/09	Curr	5f	H	SH	£25281
85	7/08	Cork	1m		YLD	£6351

Total win prize-money £31633

Going (Turf): Sf: 0-4 GS: 0-0 Gd: 0-4 GF: 0-0 Fm: 0-0
Distance: 5f/6f: 1-6 7f-8f: 1-5 9f-13f: 0-1 14f+: 0-0
Track : LH: 0-1 **RH: 1-5** Tight: 0-0 Gall: 0-1
Aids: Bl: 0-0 Vi: 0-0 Tstrap: 1-3 Ckp: 1-3
Best Rating: **92** 10/09 York 6f good

Useful; effective at 6f-1m; goes well on easy ground; has worn cheekpieces.

Irish Jugger (USA)

86 **68**
2-y-o ch g Johannesburg (USA)-Jinny's Gold (USA) (Gold Fever (USA))
A P Jarvis (K R Burke 27/6) Mogeely Stud & Mrs Maura Gittins

Placings:355 **(5038)**
2009: 6^{3}GF, 7^{5}G, 6^{5}GF,

	Starts	1st	2nd	3rd	Win & Pl
Career Total (Turf)	3	0	0	1	933

Going (Turf): Sf: 0-0 GS: 0-0 Gd: 0-1 GF: 0-2 Fm: 0-0
Distance: 5f/6f: 0-1 7f-8f: 0-2 9f-13f: 0-0 14f+: 0-0
Track : LH: 0-0 RH: 0-0 Tight: 0-0 Gall: 0-0
Aids: Bl: 0-0 Vi: 0-0 Tstrap: 0-0 Ckp: 0-0
Best Rating: **68** 6/09 NmkJ 7f good

Irish Music (IRE)

85(102) (67)**62**
4-y-o b g Namid-Kelly's Tune (Alhaarth (IRE))
A P Jarvis Mrs Ann Jarvis

Placings:6/32350-54220 **(7819)**
2009: 6^{5}GF, 5^{4}G, 5^{2}SD, 6^{2}SD, 5^{0}SD,

	Starts	1st	2nd	3rd	Win & Pl
Career Total (Turf)	4	0	0	0	154
Career Total (AW)	7	0	3	2	3280

Going (Turf): Sf: 0-0 GS: 0-1 Gd: 0-1 GF: 0-2 Fm: 0-0
Distance: 5f/6f: 0-10 7f-8f: 0-1 9f-13f: 0-0 14f+: 0-0
Track : LH: 0-3 RH: 0-4 Tight: 0-3 Gall: 0-1
Aids: Bl: 0-0 Vi: 0-0 Tstrap: 0-0 Ckp: 0-0
Best Rating: **70** 3/08 Kemp 6f stand

Modest; effective from 5f-7f and acts on Polytrack.

Irish Pearl (IRE)

(113) (104)**89**
4-y-o b f Statue Of Liberty (USA)-Helen Wells (IRE) (Sadler's Wells (USA))
K R Burke M J Halligan

Placings:5106/345062001140-60 **(0086)**
2009: 5^{6}SS, 6^{0}SD,

	Starts	1st	2nd	3rd	Win & Pl
Career Total (Turf)	12	1	1	1	9542
Career Total (AW)	6	2	0	0	13311

104	11/08	Sthl	6f	(0-95)H	STD	£7569
91	10/08	Sthl	6f	(0-85)H	STD	£5180
82	8/07	Wind	6f		SFT	£4533

Total win prize-money £17285

Going (Turf): **Sf: 1-5** GS: 0-3 Gd: 0-3 GF: 0-1 Fm: 0-0
Distance: **5f/6f: 3-16** 7f-8f: 0-2 9f-13f: 0-0 14f+: 0-0
Track : **LH: 2-5** RH: 0-0 Tight: 0-1 **Gall: 1-3**
Aids: Bl: 0-0 Vi: 0-0 Tstrap: 0-0 Ckp: 0-0
Best Rating: **104** 11/08 Sthl 6f stand

Useful; effective over 5f-6f and acts on soft ground.

Irish Saint (IRE)

79(88) (56)**39**
3-y-o ch g Kheleyf (USA)-Tarifana (IRE) (Dr Devious (IRE))
T J Pitt Saintly Racing

Placings:005-00000 **(4664)**
2009: 12^{0}SF, 9^{0}SD, 7^{0}GF, 8^{0}F, 6^{0}G,

	Starts	1st	2nd	3rd	Win & Pl
Career Total (Turf)	5	0	0	0	
Career Total (AW)	3	0	0	0	0

Going (Turf): Sf: 0-1 GS: 0-1 Gd: 0-1 GF: 0-1 Fm: 0-1
Distance: 5f/6f: 0-1 7f-8f: 0-4 9f-13f: 0-3 14f+: 0-0
Track : LH: 0-5 RH: 0-2 Tight: 0-4 Gall: 0-0
Aids: Bl: 0-0 Vi: 0-1 Tstrap: 0-0 Ckp: 0-0
Best Rating: **56** 11/08 Wolv 1m1f103y stand

Irish Stream (USA)

91(96) (56)**39**
11-y-o ch g Irish River (FR)-Euphonic (USA) (The Minstrel (CAN))
N R Mitchell (B G Powell 8/6) Mrs E Mitchell

Placings:326/0P42/000453020/0501**1**000/61600/00000/020/00-400 **(1974)**
2009: 10^{4}SD, 10^{0}GF, 10^{0}F,

	Starts	1st	2nd	3rd	Win & Pl
Career Total (Turf)	38	3	3	2	25648
Career Total (AW)	4	0	1	0	1232

77	7/04	Naas	1m	(50-80)H	FRM	£6569
82	6/03	Leop	1m1f	(0-85)H	GD	£8064
62	6/03	Naas	1m2f	(0 80)H	CD	£5600

Total win prize-money £20235

Going (Turf): Sf: 0-8 GS: 0-0 **Gd: 2-7** GF: 0-11 Fm: 1-4
Distance: 5f/6f: 0-4 7f-8f: 1-10 **9f-13f: 2-27** 14f+: 0-1
Track : **LH: 3-20** RH: 0-6 Tight: 0-0 Gall: 0-1
Aids: Bl: 0-2 Vi: 0-2 Tstrap: 0-5 Ckp: 0-5
Best Rating: **82** 6/03 Leop 1m1f good

Iron Condor

86(87) (60)**63**
2-y-o b g Tobougg (IRE)-Coh Sho No (Old Vic)
J M P Eustace Harold Nass

Placings:4430 **(6993)**
2009: 7^{4}G, 7^{4}G, 7^{3}SD, 8^{0}GS,

	Starts	1st	2nd	3rd	Win & Pl
Career Total (Turf)	3	0	0	0	385
Career Total (AW)	1	0	0	1	482

Going (Turf): Sf: 0-0 GS: 0-1 Gd: 0-2 GF: 0-0 Fm: 0-0
Distance: 5f/6f: 0-0 7f-8f: 0-4 9f-13f: 0-0 14f+: 0-0
Track : LH: 0-2 RH: 0-0 Tight: 0-1 Gall: 0-1
Aids: Bl: 0-0 Vi: 0-0 Tstrap: 0-0 Ckp: 0-0
Best Rating: 63 8/09 Yarm 7f3y good

Fair; stays 7f and acts on Polytrack.

Iron Duke

71 (47)**44**

3-y-o gr c Refuse To Bend (IRE)-Arinaga (Warning)
John Joseph Murphy O Finetto

Placings:000-00506 **(5737a)**
2009: 7^{0}Y, 7^{0}G, 8^{5}S, 7^{0}GF, 10^{6}HY,

	Starts	1st	2nd	3rd	Win & Pl
Career Total (Turf)	7	0	0	0	
Career Total (AW)	1	0	0	0	

Going (Turf): Sf: 0-2 GS: 0-0 Gd: 0-2 GF: 0-1 Fm: 0-0
Distance: 5f/6f: 0-1 7f-8f: 0-5 9f-13f: 0-2 14f+: 0-0
Track : LH: 0-3 RH: 0-2 Tight: 0-0 Gall: 0-0
Aids: Bl: 0-0 Vi: 0-0 Tstrap: 0-0 Ckp: 0-0
Best Rating: 47 9/08 Dund 6f stand

Iron Hague (IRE)

76 **5**

8-y-o b g Among Men (USA)-Conditional Sale (IRE) (Petorius)
O Brennan Mrs Pat Brennan

Placings:000/03601/200200/00/0 **(2337)**
2009: 11^{0}GF,

	Starts	1st	2nd	3rd	Win & Pl
Career Total (Turf)	17	1	2	1	6322

42 8/05 Slig 1m4f (36-60)H SFT £3920
Total win prize-money £3921

Going (Turf): **Sf: 1-4** GS: 0-0 Gd: 0-3 GF: 0-5 Fm: 0-2
Distance: 5f/6f: 0-0 7f-8f: 0-1 **9f-13f: 1-12** 14f+: 0-4
Track : LH: 0-1 **RH: 1-14** Tight: 0-0 Gall: 0-0
Aids: Bl: 0-2 Vi: 0-1 Tstrap: 0-1 Ckp: 0-1
Best Rating: 49 7/06 Wxfd 1m5f gd-fm

Iron Man Of Mersey (FR)

91 (86) (28)**54**

3-y-o b g Poliglote-Miss Echo (Chief Singer)
A W Carroll Seasons Holidays

Placings:0-0000000 **(6399)**
2009: 10^{0}G, 6^{0}GF, 10^{0}GF, 8^{0}S, 7^{0}SD, 8^{0}F, 8^{0}GF,

	Starts	1st	2nd	3rd	Win & Pl
Career Total (Turf)	7	0	0	0	
Career Total (AW)	1	0	0	0	

Going (Turf): Sf: 0-1 GS: 0-1 Gd: 0-1 GF: 0-3 Fm: 0-1
Distance: 5f/6f: 0-0 7f-8f: 0-4 9f-13f: 0-4 14f+: 0-0
Track : LH: 0-4 RH: 0-1 Tight: 0-4 Gall: 0-0
Aids: Bl: 0-1 Vi: 0-0 Tstrap: 0-0 Ckp: 0-0
Best Rating: 54 4/09 Bath 1m2f46y good

Iron Master

70 (43) **42**

3-y-o gr g High Chaparral (IRE)-Blushing Queen (IRE) (Desert King (IRE))
J J Bridger Gayler William Chambers

Placings:0050 **(7576)**
2009: 10^{0}GF, 8^{0}G, 11^{5}GF, 8^{0}SD,

	Starts	1st	2nd	3rd	Win & Pl
Career Total (Turf)	3	0	0	0	0
Career Total (AW)	1	0	0	0	

Going (Turf): Sf: 0-0 GS: 0-0 Gd: 0-1 GF: 0-2 Fm: 0-0
Distance: 5f/6f: 0-0 7f-8f: 0-2 9f-13f: 0-2 14f+: 0-0
Track : LH: 0-1 RH: 0-2 Tight: 0-2 Gall: 0-0
Aids: Bl: 0-0 Vi: 0-0 Tstrap: 0-0 Ckp: 0-0
Best Rating: 42 6/09 Gdwd 1m good

Iron Max (IRE)

88 (71) (21)**46**

3-y-o b g Iron Mask (USA)-Starisa (IRE) (College Chapel)
Tom Dascombe (N J Vaughan 3/6) Deva Racing Iron Mask Partnership

Placings:0-5000 **(7727)**
2009: 6^{5}G, 6^{0}GS, 6^{0}F, 7^{0}SD,

	Starts	1st	2nd	3rd	Win & Pl
Career Total (Turf)	3	0	0	0	0
Career Total (AW)	2	0	0	0	

Going (Turf): Sf: 0-0 GS: 0-1 Gd: 0-1 GF: 0-0 Fm: 0-1
Distance: 5f/6f: 0-4 7f-8f: 0-1 9f-13f: 0-0 14f+: 0-0
Track : LH: 0-2 RH: 0-0 Tight: 0-1 Gall: 0-0
Aids: Bl: 0-0 Vi: 0-0 Tstrap: 0-0 Ckp: 0-0
Best Rating: 46 5/09 Donc 6f good

Iron Out (USA)

103 (108) (89)**76**

3-y-o b g Straight Man (USA)-Fit Fighter (USA) (Fit To Fight (USA))
R Hollinshead John L Marriott

Placings:0-24402012362424222221103 **(7848)**
2009: 6^{2}SD, 7^{4}SD, 7^{4}SD, 9^{0}GF, 7^{2}SD, 5^{0}GF, 7^{1}GF, 8^{2}SD, 8^{3}SD, 8^{6}G, 7^{2}SD, 7^{4}SD, 7^{2}GF, 8^{4}SD, 7^{2}G, 7^{2}GF, 8^{2}S, 8^{2}SD, 9^{1}SD, 9^{1}SD, 10^{0}SD, 9^{3}SD,

	Starts	1st	2nd	3rd	Win & Pl
Career Total (Turf)	9	1	4	0	6126
Career Total (AW)	14	2	5	2	14972

85 12/09 Wolv 1m1f103y (0-75)H STD £2810
79 12/09 Wolv 1m1f103y (0-85)H STD £5046
63 6/09 Leic 7f9y G-F £1942
Total win prize-money £9800

Going (Turf): Sf: 0-1 GS: 0-0 Gd: 0-2 **GF: 1-6** Fm: 0-0
Distance: 5f/6f: 0-2 7f-8f: 1-15 **9f-13f: 2-6** 14f+: 0-0
Track : **LH: 2-14** RH: 0-3 **Tight: 2-6** Gall: 0-1
Aids: Bl: 0-0 Vi: 0-0 Tstrap: 0-0 Ckp: 0-0
Best Rating: 89 12/09 Wolv 1m1f103y stand

Useful; effective over 6f-1m1f; acts on most ground and on sand.

Iron Velvet (USA)

95 **78**

2-y-o b g Dubawi (IRE)-Not For Turning (USA) (Deputy Minister (CAN))
M Johnston Sheikh Hamdan Bin Mohammed Al Maktoum

Placings:020106 **(6099)**
2009: 6^{0}GF, 6^{2}GF, 7^{0}G, 5^{1}GF, 6^{0}G, 7^{6}GF,

	Starts	1st	2nd	3rd	Win & Pl
Career Total (Turf)	6	1	1	0	6518

78 8/09 Catt 5f212y G-F £4533
Total win prize-money £4533

Going (Turf): Sf: 0-0 GS: 0-0 Gd: 0-2 **GF: 1-4** Fm: 0-0
Distance: **5f/6f: 1-3** 7f-8f: 0-3 9f-13f: 0-0 14f+: 0-0
Track : **LH: 1-3** RH: 0-0 **Tight: 1-2** Gall: 0-1
Aids: Bl: 0-0 Vi: 0-0 Tstrap: 0-0 Ckp: 0-0
Best Rating: 78 8/09 Catt 5f212y gd-fm

Fair; stays 6f and acts on fast ground.

Is It Time (IRE)

70 (109) (66)**54**

5-y-o b m Danetime (IRE)-Ishaam (Selkirk (USA))
Mrs P N Dutfield Mrs Nerys Dutfield

Placings:00/5004**0416**/0031400-00 **(3252)**
2009: 7^{0}SD, 5^{0}GF,

	Starts	1st	2nd	3rd	Win & Pl
Career Total (Turf)	7	0	0	0	0
Career Total (AW)	12	2	0	1	5253

66 4/08 Kemp 6f (0-70)H STD £2590
61 12/07 Sthl 5f (0-52)H SS £2047
Total win prize-money £4638

Going (Turf): Sf: 0-1 GS: 0-2 Gd: 0-1 GF: 0-3 Fm: 0-0
Distance: **5f/6f: 2-13** 7f-8f: 0-5 9f-13f: 0-1 14f+: 0-0
Track : LH: 0-4 **RH: 1-9** Tight: 0-3 Gall: 0-2
Aids: Bl: 0-0 Vi: 0-0 Tstrap: 0-0 Ckp: 0-0
Best Rating: 66 4/08 Kemp 6f stand

Moderate sort; stays 6f; handles both sand surfaces.

Isabel's Pet

(78) (20)

3-y-o b f Lucky Story (USA)-Perle D'Azur (Mind Games)
Karen George Mrs Isabel Fraser

Placings:0 **(7411)**
2009: 5^{0}SD,

	Starts	1st	2nd	3rd	Win & Pl
Career Total (Turf)	0	0	0	0	
Career Total (AW)	1	0	0	0	

Going (Turf): Sf: 0-0 GS: 0-0 Gd: 0-0 GF: 0-0 Fm: 0-0
Distance: 5f/6f: 0-1 7f-8f: 0-0 9f-13f: 0-0 14f+: 0-0
Track : LH: 0-1 RH: 0-0 Tight: 0-1 Gall: 0-0
Aids: Bl: 0-0 Vi: 0-0 Tstrap: 0-0 Ckp: 0-0
Best Rating: 20 11/09 Wolv 5f216y stand

Isabella Grey

96 **91**

3-y-o gr f Choisir (AUS)-Karsiyaka (IRE) (Kahyasi)
K A Ryan T G & Mrs M E Holdcroft

Placings:510-400 **(2673)**
2009: 8^{4}GS, 8^{0}HY, 7^{0}G,

	Starts	1st	2nd	3rd	Win & Pl
Career Total (Turf)	6	1	0	0	8624

86 7/08 Hayd 6f GD £6476
Total win prize-money £6476

Going (Turf): Sf: 0-1 GS: 0-1 **Gd: 1-3** GF: 0-1 Fm: 0-0
Distance: **5f/6f: 1-2** 7f-8f: 0-3 9f-13f: 0-1 14f+: 0-0
Track : LH: 0-3 RH: 0-1 Tight: 0-1 Gall: 0-1
Aids: Bl: 0-0 Vi: 0-0 Tstrap: 0-0 Ckp: 0-0
Best Rating: 91 5/09 York 1m gd-sft

Very useful; probably stays 1m; acts on good ground.

Placings:0450 (6965)

2009: 6^{0}G, 8^{4}GF, 8^{5}G, 7^{0}G,

	Starts	1st	2nd	3rd	Win & Pl
Career Total (Turf)	4	0	0	0	289

Going (Turf): Sf: 0-0 GS: 0-0 Gd: 0-3 GF: 0-1 Fm: 0-0
Distance: 5f/6f: 0-1 7f-8f: 0-1 9f-13f: 0-2 14f+: 0-0
Track : LH: 0-2 RH: 0-1 Tight: 0-0 Gall: 0-0
Aids: Bl: 0-1 Vi: 0-0 Tstrap: 0-0 Ckp: 0-0
Best Rating: 66 10/09 Leic 1m60y good

Isabella Romee (IRE)

95(96) (50)**60**

3-y-o gr f Bahri (USA)-Silver Clasp (IRE) (Linamix (FR))
Jane Chapple-Hyam Mrs Jane Chapple-Hyam

Placings:500006-600 **(5031)**
2009: 8^{6}SD, 7^{0}G, 6^{0}GF,

	Starts	1st	2nd	3rd	Win & Pl
Career Total (Turf)	6	0	0	0	0
Career Total (AW)	3	0	0	0	0

Going (Turf): Sf: 0-0 GS: 0-3 Gd: 0-1 GF: 0-2 Fm: 0-0
Distance: 5f/6f: 0-3 7f-8f: 0-6 9f-13f: 0-0 14f+: 0-0
Track : LH: 0-3 RH: 0-0 Tight: 0-0 Gall: 0-1
Aids: Bl: 0-0 Vi: 0-0 Tstrap: 0-1 Ckp: 0-1
Best Rating: 60 8/08 Newb 6f8y gd-sft

Moderate; best at around 6f; acts on Polytrack and fast ground.

Isabella's Fancy

87(97) (57)**45**

4-y-o br f Captain Rio-Princess Of Spain (King Of Spain)
A G Newcombe A G Newcombe

Placings:00550510-0360006 **(5634)**
2009: 7^{0}SS, 7^{3}SD, 8^{6}SD, 8^{0}SD, 6^{0}GF, 7^{0}GF, 7^{6}GS,

	Starts	1st	2nd	3rd	Win & Pl
Career Total (Turf)	8	0	0	0	0
Career Total (AW)	7	1	0	1	3168

57 10/08 Sthl 7f STD £2866
Total win prize-money £2866

Going (Turf): Sf: 0-1 GS: 0-2 Gd: 0-2 GF: 0-3 Fm: 0-0
Distance: 5f/6f: 0-2 **7f-8f: 1-12** 9f-13f: 0-1 14f+: 0-0
Track : **LH: 1-9** RH: 0-1 Tight: 0-0 Gall: 0-1
Aids: Bl: 0-2 **Vi: 1-1** Tstrap: 0-0 Ckp: 0-0
Best Rating: 57 10/08 Sthl 7f stand

Moderate; effective over 7f; acts on Fibresand.

Isabelonabicycle

104(100) (75)**75**

4-y-o b f Helissio (FR)-Santa Isobel (Nashwan (USA))
A M Balding J C & S R Hitchins

Placings:23-21362100 **(4951)**
2009: 12^{2}SD, 15^{1}G, 14^{3}GF, 16^{6}G, 14^{2}GF, 16^{1}SD, 16^{0}GS, 14^{0}GF,

	Starts	1st	2nd	3rd	Win & Pl
Career Total (Turf)	6	1	1	1	4616
Career Total (AW)	4	1	2	1	4482

75 7/09 Kemp 2m (0-75)H STD £2590
75 4/09 Folk 1m7f92y (0-75)H GD £3070
Total win prize-money £5661

Going (Turf): Sf: 0-0 GS: 0-1 **Gd: 1-2** GF: 0-3 Fm: 0-0
Distance: 5f/6f: 0-0 7f-8f: 0-0 9f-13f: 0-3 **14f+: 2-7**
Track : LH: 0-4 **RH: 2-6 Tight: 1-4** Gall: 0-1
Aids: Bl: 0-0 Vi: 0-0 Tstrap: 0-0 Ckp: 0-0
Best Rating: 75 7/09 Kemp 2m stand

Modest; stays 2m; acts on Polytrack and fast turf.

Isdaar (IRE)

89 **66**

2-y-o b g Invincible Spirit (IRE)-Kildare Lady (IRE) (Indian Ridge)
J H M Gosden Hamdan Al Maktoum

Ishe A Lord

82(88) (48)**58**

2-y-o b g Ishiguru (USA)-Lady Killer (IRE) (Daggers Drawn (USA))
W G M Turner Mrs M S Teversham

Placings:2500 **(7661)**
2009: 5^{2}GF, 6^{5}SD, 5^{0}SD, 6^{0}SD,

	Starts	1st	2nd	3rd	Win & Pl
Career Total (Turf)	1	0	1	0	578
Career Total (AW)	3	0	0	0	0

Going (Turf): Sf: 0-0 GS: 0-0 Gd: 0-0 GF: 0-1 Fm: 0-0
Distance: 5f/6f: 0-4 7f-8f: 0-0 9f-13f: 0-0 14f+: 0-0
Track : LH: 0-2 RH: 0-1 Tight: 0-2 Gall: 0-0
Aids: Bl: 0-0 Vi: 0-0 Tstrap: 0-0 Ckp: 0-0
Best Rating: 58 7/09 Leic 5f2y gd-fm

Ishe Mac

100 **81**

3-y-o b f Ishiguru (USA)-Zacinta (USA) (Hawkster (USA))
N Bycroft N Bycroft

Placings:02320-16010 **(5523)**
2009: 7^{1}GF, 7^{6}GF, 7^{0}GF, 6^{1}G, 6^{0}G,

	Starts	1st	2nd	3rd	Win & Pl
Career Total (Turf)	10	2	2	1	13504

81 8/09 Thsk 6f (0-75)H GD £4274
75 5/09 Thsk 7f G-F £5569
Total win prize-money £9843

Going (Turf): Sf: 0-0 GS: 0-0 **Gd: 1-6 GF: 1-4** Fm: 0-0
Distance: 5f/6f: 1-7 7f-8f: 1-3 9f-13f: 0-0 14f+: 0-0
Track : **LH: 1-5** RH: 0-0 **Tight: 1-1** Gall: 0-2
Aids: Bl: 0-0 Vi: 0-0 Tstrap: 0-0 Ckp: 0-0
Best Rating: 81 8/09 Thsk 6f good

Fair; stays 7f and acts on good/fast ground; likes to race prominently.

Ishetoo

109 **103**

5-y-o b g Ishiguru (USA)-Ticcatoo (IRE) (Dolphin Street (FR))
A Dickman John H Sissons

Placings:5650/1114021133/235041000-50160035000530 **(6843)**
2009: 6^{5}F, 6^{0}S, 5^{1}GF, 6^{6}G, 5^{0}G, 6^{0}GF, 5^{3}GF, 6^{5}GF, 6^{0}GF, 5^{0}GF, 6^{0}GS, 5^{5}GF, 5^{3}GF, 5^{0}G,

	Starts	1st	2nd	3rd	Win & Pl
Career Total (Turf)	37	7	2	5	80241

102 5/09 York 5f (0-105)H G-F £24924
103 8/08 Muss 5f (0-95)H GD £9066
92 9/07 Thsk 5f (0-85)H G-F £5505
87 8/07 Thsk 5f (0-85)H GD £5181
75 6/07 Hayd 5f (0-80)H G-F £6477
81 6/07 Catt 5f (0-65)H G-F £2730
64 5/07 Ayr 6f (0-60)H G-S £2590
Total win prize-money £56475

Going (Turf): Sf: 0-5 GS: 1-4 Gd: 2-11 **GF: 4-15** Fm: 0-2
Distance: **5f/6f: 7-35** 7f-8f: 0-2 9f-13f: 0-0 14f+: 0-0
Track : LH: 0-3 RH: 0-0 Tight: 0-2 Gall: 0-0
Aids: Bl: 0-0 Vi: 0-1 Tstrap: 0-4 Ckp: 0-4
Best Rating: 103 8/08 Muss 5f good

Very useful; effective over 5f-6f; acts on most ground; has worn cheekpieces.

Ishiadancer

103(106) (80)**80**

4-y-o b f Ishiguru (USA)-Abaklea (IRE) (Doyoun)
E J Alston Racing Shares Nuppend

Placings:452564-12321640 **(7801)**
2009: 7^{1}GF, 7^{2}S, 7^{3}SD, 7^{2}G, 7^{1}G, 7^{6}S, 7^{4}SD, 7^{0}SD,

	Starts	1st	2nd	3rd	Win & Pl
Career Total (Turf)	8	2	2	0	7194
Career Total (AW)	6	0	1	1	2018

80 10/09 Ayr 7f50y (0-70)H GD £2914
64 7/09 Rdcr 7f (0-70) G-F £2590
Total win prize-money £5504

Going (Turf): Sf: 0-3 GS: 0-1 **Gd: 1-3 GF: 1-1** Fm: 0-0
Distance: 5f/6f: 0-0 **7f-8f: 2-14** 9f-13f: 0-0 14f+: 0-0
Track : **LH: 1-11** RH: 0-0 Tight: 0-7 Gall: 0-0
Aids: Bl: 0-0 Vi: 0-0 Tstrap: 0-0 Ckp: 0-0
Best Rating: 80 11/09 Wolv 7f32y stand

Modest; effective over 7f; acts on most ground; likes to dominate.

Ishibee (IRE)

98(103) (54)**54**

5-y-o b m Ishiguru (USA)-Beauty (IRE) (Alzao (USA))
J J Bridger J J Bridger

Placings:536433315300566/43102401041035055/0000000053-30620056563451000040 **(7239)**
2009: 6^{3}SD, 6^{0}SD, 6^{6}SD, 5^{2}SD, 5^{0}SD, 7^{0}GF, 6^{5}F, 6^{6}GF, 6^{5}GF, 5^{6}GF, 6^{3}GF, 5^{4}F, 7^{5}GS, 6^{1}GF, 6^{0}GF, 7^{0}GF, 5^{0}GF, 7^{0}SD, 6^{4}SD, 7^{0}SD,

	Starts	1st	2nd	3rd	Win & Pl
Career Total (Turf)	38	3	1	7	12483
Career Total (AW)	24	2	1	3	6077

54 8/09 Folk 6f (0-70)H G-F £2729
61 10/07 Kemp 6f (0-55)H STD £2047
54 8/07 Brig 5f213y G-F £1943
55 6/07 Brig 5f213y (0-65)H FRM £2266
60 8/06 Ling 6f STD £2388
Total win prize-money £11377

Going (Turf): Sf: 0-3 GS: 0-6 Gd: 0-6 **GF: 2-17** Fm: 1-6
Distance: **5f/6f: 5-48** 7f-8f: 0-14 9f-13f: 0-0 14f+: 0-0
Track : **LH: 3-20** RH: 1-16 **Tight: 1-12** Gall: 0-0
Aids: Bl: 0-0 Vi: 0-3 Tstrap: 5-52 Ckp: 5-52
Best Rating: 62 8/06 Ripn 6f gd-sft

Moderate filly; effective on most ground and Polytrack; stays 6f but effective at 5f.; has worn cheekpieces.

Ishipink

68 **15**

2-y-o ch f Ishiguru (USA)-Christmas Rose (Absalom)
R J Hodges Miss R Dobson

Placings:450 **(5380)**
2009: 5^{4}G, 5^{5}F, 5^{0}G,

	Starts	1st	2nd	3rd	Win & Pl
Career Total (Turf)	3	0	0	0	265

Going (Turf): Sf: 0-0 GS: 0-0 Gd: 0-2 GF: 0-0 Fm: 0-1
Distance: 5f/6f: 0-3 7f-8f: 0-0 9f-13f: 0-0 14f+: 0-0
Track : LH: 0-3 RH: 0-0 Tight: 0-0 Gall: 0-3
Aids: Bl: 0-0 Vi: 0-0 Tstrap: 0-0 Ckp: 0-0
Best Rating: 15 5/09 Bath 5f11y good

Ishismart

96(93) (52)49
5-y-o ch m Ishiguru (USA)-Smartie Lee (Dominion)
R Hollinshead Mrs Norma Harris

Placings:000/0/320 (7490)
2009: 15^{3}G, 12^{2}SD, 12^{0}SD,

	Starts	1st	2nd	3rd	Win & Pl
Career Total (Turf)	2	0	0	1	302
Career Total (AW)	5	0	1	0	705

Going (Turf): Sf: 0-0 GS: 0-1 Gd: 0-1 GF: 0-0 Fm: 0-0
Distance: 5f/6f: 0-1 7f-8f: 0-2 9f-13f: 0-3 14f+: 0-1
Track : LH: 0-6 RH: 0-1 Tight: 0-6 Gall: 0-0
Aids: Bl: 0-0 Vi: 0-0 Tstrap: 0-0 Ckp: 0-0
Best Rating: 52 11/09 Wolv 1m4f50y stand

Very moderate; stays 1m4f and acts on Polytrack.

Ishtar Gate (USA)

94 87
2-y-o b/br c Gone West (USA)-Sometime (IRE) (Royal Academy (USA))
P F I Cole D S Lee

Placings:105 (6472)
2009: 7^{1}GF, 7^{0}G, 8^{5}GF,

	Starts	1st	2nd	3rd	Win & Pl
Career Total (Turf)	3	1	0	0	4813

76 6/09 Leic 7f9y G-F £4533
Total win prize-money £4533

Going (Turf): Sf: 0-0 GS: 0-0 Gd: 0-1 **GF: 1-2** Fm: 0-0
Distance: 5f/6f: 0-0 **7f-8f: 1-2** 9f-13f: 0-1 14f+: 0-0
Track : LH: 0-1 RH: 0-1 Tight: 0-1 Gall: 0-0
Aids: Bl: 0-0 Vi: 0-0 Tstrap: 0-0 Ckp: 0-0
Best Rating: 87 7/09 Gdwd 7f good

Useful; effective at 7f; acts on Polytrack.

Isintshelovely (IRE)

88 39
6-y-o ch m Broken Hearted-Sarah Blue (IRE) (Bob Back (USA))
B G Powell L Gilbert

Placings:0 (5939)
2009: 11^{0}GF,

	Starts	1st	2nd	3rd	Win & Pl
Career Total (Turf)	1	0	0	0	

Going (Turf): Sf: 0-0 GS: 0-0 Gd: 0-0 GF: 0-1 Fm: 0-0
Distance: 5f/6f: 0-0 7f-8f: 0-0 9f-13f: 0-1 14f+: 0-0
Track : LH: 0-0 RH: 0-1 Tight: 0-0 Gall: 0-0
Aids: Bl: 0-0 Vi: 0-0 Tstrap: 0-0 Ckp: 0-0
Best Rating: 39 9/09 Leic 1m3f183y gd-fm

Isitcozimcool (IRE)

83(91) (52)42
4-y-o b g Shinko Forest (IRE)-Hazarama (IRE) (Kahyasi)
D E Cantillon Michael Davies

Placings:000 (3175)
2009: 7^{0}SD, 6^{0}S, 6^{0}GF,

	Starts	1st	2nd	3rd	Win & Pl
Career Total (Turf)	2	0	0	0	
Career Total (AW)	1	0	0	0	

Going (Turf): Sf: 0-1 GS: 0-0 Gd: 0-0 GF: 0-1 Fm: 0-0
Distance: 5f/6f: 0-1 7f-8f: 0-2 9f-13f: 0-0 14f+: 0-0
Track : LH: 0-1 RH: 0-0 Tight: 0-1 Gall: 0-0
Aids: Bl: 0-0 Vi: 0-0 Tstrap: 0-1 Ckp: 0-1
Best Rating: 52 5/09 Ling 7f stand

Island Chief

100(90) (54)74
3-y-o b g Reel Buddy (USA)-Fisher Island (IRE) (Sri Pekan (USA))
K A Ryan The C H F Partnership

Placings:6436633-020133210040 (7057)
2009: 8^{0}GS, 7^{2}GF, 8^{0}GS, 7^{1}GF, 7^{3}G, 7^{3}GF, 6^{2}G, 8^{1}GS, 8^{0}S, 8^{0}G, 7^{4}G, 7^{0}GF,

	Starts	1st	2nd	3rd	Win & Pl
Career Total (Turf)	15	2	2	3	10256
Career Total (AW)	4	0	0	2	595

74 7/09 Muss 1m (0-65)H G-S £2590
66 5/09 Muss 7f30y (0-70)H G-F £3885
Total win prize-money £6476

Going (Turf): Sf: 0-4 **GS: 1-3** Gd: 0-4 **GF: 1-4** Fm: 0-0
Distance: 5f/6f: 0-0 **7f-8f: 2-18** 9f-13f: 0-1 14f+: 0-0
Track : LH: 0-11 **RH: 2-6 Tight: 2-8** Gall: 0-2
Aids: Bl: 0-8 Vi: 0-0 Tstrap: 2-6 Ckp: 2-6
Best Rating: 74 7/09 Muss 1m gd-sft

Fair; stays 7f; handles soft ground and Fibresand; has worn blinkers/cheekpieces.

Island Express (IRE)

86 58
2-y-o b c Chineur (FR)-Cayman Expresso (IRE) (Fayruz)
Miss A Stokell (J S Moore 13/4) J Miller

Placings:0260605 (2588)
2009: 5^{0}G, 5^{2}GF, 5^{6}G, 5^{0}GF, 5^{6}G, 6^{0}GF, 6^{5}GF,

	Starts	1st	2nd	3rd	Win & Pl
Career Total (Turf)	7	0	1	0	780

Going (Turf): Sf: 0-0 GS: 0-0 Gd: 0-3 GF: 0-4 Fm: 0-0
Distance: 5f/6f: 0-7 7f-8f: 0-0 9f-13f: 0-0 14f+: 0-0
Track : LH: 0-3 RH: 0-0 Tight: 0-0 Gall: 0-0
Aids: Bl: 0-0 Vi: 0-0 Tstrap: 0-2 Ckp: 0-2
Best Rating: 58 4/09 Wwck 5f gd-fm

Runner-up in seller on second start; acts on fast ground.

Island Legend (IRE)

47(102) (73)
3-y-o b g Trans Island-Legand Of Tara (USA) (Gold Legend (USA))
J M Bradley J M Bradley

Placings:3010406 (6635)
2009: 5^{3}SD, 6^{0}GF, 5^{1}SD, 6^{0}G, 5^{4}SD, 5^{0}SD, 5^{6}SD,

	Starts	1st	2nd	3rd	Win & Pl
Career Total (Turf)	2	0	0	0	
Career Total (AW)	5	1	0	1	3974

73 8/09 Wolv 5f20y STD £3238
Total win prize-money £3238

Going (Turf): Sf: 0-0 GS: 0-0 Gd: 0-1 GF: 0-1 Fm: 0-0
Distance: **5f/6f: 1-6** 7f-8f: 0-1 9f-13f: 0-0 14f+: 0-0
Track : **LH: 1-3** RH: 0-2 **Tight: 1-3** Gall: 0-0
Aids: Bl: 0-0 Vi: 0-0 Tstrap: 0-0 Ckp: 0-0
Best Rating: 73 8/09 Wolv 5f20y stand

Fair; suited by 5f and Polytrack.

Island Music (IRE)

96(101) (64)70
4-y-o b f Mujahid (USA)-Ischia (Lion Cavern (USA))
J J Quinn Robert Miller-Bakewell & Mrs A C Robson

Placings:0533/15644043-003065260460 (7403)
2009: 7^{0}GS, 9^{0}GF, 10^{3}G, 10^{0}G, 10^{6}GF, 8^{5}GF, 8^{2}G, 9^{6}GF, 10^{0}GF, 8^{4}SD, 9^{6}GS, 8^{0}SD,

	Starts	1st	2nd	3rd	Win & Pl
Career Total (Turf)	22	1	1	4	8071
Career Total (AW)	2	0	0	0	0

69 5/08 Rdcr 7f (0-85)H G-F £4209
Total win prize-money £4209

Going (Turf): Sf: 0-1 GS: 0-3 Gd: 0-10 **GF: 1-7** Fm: 0-1
Distance: 5f/6f: 0-3 **7f-8f: 1-7** 9f-13f: 0-14 14f+: 0-0
Track : LH: 0-10 RH: 0-8 Tight: 0-12 Gall: 0-1
Aids: Bl: 0-0 Vi: 0-0 Tstrap: 0-5 Ckp: 0-5
Best Rating: 70 7/08 Carl 6f192y good

Fair; stays 1m1f and acts on most ground.

Island Sunset (IRE)

97(93) (70)77
3-y-o ch f Trans Island-Islandagore (IRE) (Indian Ridge)
W R Muir Mrs J M Muir

Placings:1-1 (3574)
2009: 8^{1}G,

	Starts	1st	2nd	3rd	Win & Pl
Career Total (Turf)	1	1	0	0	3238
Career Total (AW)	1	1	0	0	2720

77 7/09 Hayd 1m30y (0-75)H GD £3238
70 10/08 Wolv 7f32y STD £2719
Total win prize-money £5958

Going (Turf): Sf: 0-0 GS: 0-0 **Gd: 1-1** GF: 0-0 Fm: 0-0
Distance: 5f/6f: 0-0 7f-8f: 1-1 9f-13f: 1-1 14f+: 0-0
Track : **LH: 2-2** RH: 0-0 **Tight: 1-1** Gall: 0-0
Aids: Bl: 0-0 Vi: 0-0 Tstrap: 0-0 Ckp: 0-0
Best Rating: 77 7/09 Hayd 1m30y good

Fair; effective at 1m; acts on Polytrack and good ground.

Island Vista

77(73) (6)87
4-y-o b f Montjeu (IRE)-Colorvista (Shirley Heights)
M A Jarvis Helena Springfield Ltd

Placings:2/100-00 (3273)
2009: 12^{0}G, 12^{0}SD,

	Starts	1st	2nd	3rd	Win & Pl
Career Total (Turf)	4	1	0	0	2730

	Starts	1st	2nd	3rd	Win & Pl
Career Total (AW)	2	0	1	0	2239

77 8/08 Wind 1m2f7y G-S £2729
Total win prize-money £2730

Going (Turf): Sf: 0-0 **GS: 1-2** Gd: 0-2 GF: 0-0 Fm: 0-0
Distance: 5f/6f: 0-0 7f-8f: 0-1 **9f-13f: 1-5** 14f+: 0-0
Track : LH: 0-1 **RH: 1-5 Tight: 1-1** Gall: 0-2
Aids: Bl: 0-0 Vi: 0-0 Tstrap: 0-0 Ckp: 0-0
Best Rating: 87 9/08 Asct 1m4f good

Useful; stays 1m2f; acts with ease in the ground and on Polytrack.

Isle De Maurice

(100) (64)**52**
7-y-o b g Sinndar (IRE)-Circe's Isle (Be My Guest (USA))
G L Moore (Mrs D M Grissell 1/5) Ms J Lambert

Placings:2154000/0/62 **(7608)**
2009: 16^{6}SS, 16^{2}SD,

	Starts	1st	2nd	3rd	Win & Pl
Career Total (Turf)	5	0	0	0	278
Career Total (AW)	5	1	2	0	5231

68 3/05 Wolv 1m4f50y STD £3380
Total win prize-money £3380

Going (Turf): Sf: 0-1 GS: 0-2 Gd: 0-2 GF: 0-0 Fm: 0-0
Distance: 5f/6f: 0-0 7f-8f: 0-0 **9f-13f: 1-5** 14f+: 0-5
Track : LH: 1-6 RH: 0-4 **Tight: 1-7** Gall: 0-1
Aids: Bl: 0-3 Vi: 0-0 Tstrap: 0-0 Ckp: 0-0
Best Rating: 69 2/05 Wolv 1m1f103y stand

Moderate; stays 2m; acts well on Polytrack.

Isle Of Ellis (IRE)

66(72) (32)**6**
2-y-o b g Statue Of Liberty (USA)-Fable (Absalom)
A J McCabe Brian Morton

Placings:00 **(1312)**
2009: 5^{0}GF, 5^{0}SD,

	Starts	1st	2nd	3rd	Win & Pl
Career Total (Turf)	1	0	0	0	
Career Total (AW)	1	0	0	0	

Going (Turf): Sf: 0-0 GS: 0-0 Gd: 0-0 GF: 0-1 Fm: 0-0
Distance: 5f/6f: 0-2 7f-8f: 0-0 9f-13f: 0-0 14f+: 0-0
Track : LH: 0-1 RH: 0-0 Tight: 0-1 Gall: 0-0
Aids: Bl: 0-0 Vi: 0-0 Tstrap: 0-0 Ckp: 0-0
Best Rating: 32 4/09 Wolv 5f20y stand

Statue Of Liberty half-brother to four winners including sprinters.

Isphahan

106(98) (77)**93**
6-y-o b g Diktat-Waltzing Star (IRE) (Danehill (USA))
A M Balding Mohamad Rafique

Placings:021/0263640/0060046300/4212141221-600542500 **(7575)**
2009: 8^{6}G, 8^{0}GF, 8^{0}G, 8^{5}G, 8^{4}G, 8^{2}GF, 7^{5}GF, 8^{0}GF, 8^{0}SD,

	Starts	1st	2nd	3rd	Win & Pl
Career Total (Turf)	32	5	6	2	37672
Career Total (AW)	7	0	1	0	964

93 9/08 Asct 1m (0-100)H GD £12462
85 8/08 Sand 1m14y (0-75)H G-S £3885
78 6/08 Sals 6f212y (0-65)H FRM £2914
70 6/08 Chep 7f16y (0-75)H G-F £2719
69 9/05 Brig 6f209y FRM £1508
Total win prize-money £23491

Going (Turf): Sf: 0-0 GS: 1-3 Gd. 1-13 GF: 1-13 **Fm: 2-3**
Distance: 5f/6f: 0-0 **7f-8f: 4-29** 9f-13f: 1-10 14f+: 0-0
Track : LH: 1-7 RH: 1-11 Tight: 0-5 Gall: 0-1
Aids: Bl: 0-0 Vi: 0-12 Tstrap: 0-7 Ckp: 0-7
Best Rating: 93 9/08 Asct 1m good

Useful; effective at 7f-1m; acts on most ground and on Polytrack; has worn cheekpieces and a visor.

Issabella Gem (IRE)

94 **64**
2-y-o b f Marju (IRE)-Robin (Slip Anchor)
C G Cox Dennis Shaw

Placings:0 **(6729)**
2009: 6^{0}S,

	Starts	1st	2nd	3rd	Win & Pl
Career Total (Turf)	1	0	0	0	

Going (Turf): Sf: 0-1 GS: 0-0 Gd: 0-0 GF: 0-0 Fm: 0-0
Distance: 5f/6f: 0-0 7f-8f: 0-1 9f-13f: 0-0 14f+: 0-0
Track : LH: 0-0 RH: 0-0 Tight: 0-0 Gall: 0-0
Aids: Bl: 0-0 Vi: 0-0 Tstrap: 0-0 Ckp: 0-0
Best Rating: 64 10/09 Sals 6f212y soft

Isshe A Lady

(75) (22)
3-y-o b f Ishiguru (USA)-Lady Killer (IRE) (Daggers Drawn (USA))
W G M Turner Mrs M S Teversham

Placings:0 **(0664)**
2009: 6^{0}SD,

	Starts	1st	2nd	3rd	Win & Pl
Career Total (Turf)	0	0	0	0	
Career Total (AW)	1	0	0	0	

Going (Turf): Sf: 0-0 GS: 0-0 Gd: 0-0 GF: 0-0 Fm: 0-0
Distance: 5f/6f: 0-1 7f-8f: 0-0 9f-13f: 0-0 14f+: 0-0
Track : LH: 0-1 RH: 0-0 Tight: 0-1 Gall: 0-0
Aids: Bl: 0-0 Vi: 0-0 Tstrap: 0-0 Ckp: 0-0
Best Rating: 22 2/09 Ling 6f stand

Istidlaal

87 **60**
2-y-o ch c Singspiel (IRE)-On A Soapbox (USA) (Mi Cielo (USA))
Sir Michael Stoute Hamdan Al Maktoum

Placings:0 **(6423)**
2009: 8^{0}GF,

	Starts	1st	2nd	3rd	Win & Pl
Career Total (Turf)	1	0	0	0	

Going (Turf): Sf: 0-0 GS: 0-0 Gd: 0-0 GF: 0-1 Fm: 0-0
Distance: 5f/6f: 0-0 7f-8f: 0-1 9f-13f: 0-0 14f+: 0-0
Track : LH: 0-0 RH: 0-0 Tight. 0-0 Gall: 0-0
Aids: Bl: 0-0 Vi: 0-0 Tstrap: 0-0 Ckp: 0-0
Best Rating: 60 10/09 NmkR 1m gd-fm

Istiqdaam

96(103) (79)**77**
4-y-o b g Pivotal-Auspicious (Shirley Heights)
M W Easterby Two Old Pals

Placings:2-6540056121 **(7715)**
2009: 7^{6}SD, 6^{5}GF, 6^{4}G, 6^{0}G, 5^{0}G, 7^{5}S, 9^{6}S, 7^{1}SD, 7^{2}SD, 7^{1}SD,

	Starts	1st	2nd	3rd	Win & Pl
Career Total (Turf)	7	0	1	0	1011
Career Total (AW)	4	2	1	0	5058

79 12/09 Wolv 7f32y (0-65)H STD £2388
74 11/09 Kemp 7f (0-65)H STD £1706
Total win prize-money £4094

Going (Turf): Sf: 0-2 GS: 0-0 Gd: 0-4 GF: 0-1 Fm: 0-0
Distance: 5f/6f: 0-2 **7f-8f: 2-7** 9f-13f: 0-2 14f+: 0-0
Track : LH: 1-7 RH: 1-1 **Tight: 1-5** Gall: 0-0
Aids: Bl: 2-4 Vi: 0-0 Tstrap: 0-0 Ckp: 0-0
Best Rating: 79 12/09 Wolv 7f32y stand

Fair; effective over 7f; acts on Polytrack; has worn blinkers.

It Must Be Love

52
3-y-o b f Piccolo-True Bird (IRE) (In The Wings)
D Flood Druid Sports & Leisure Limited

Placings:50 **(2199)**
2009: 7^{5}G, 10^{0}S,

	Starts	1st	2nd	3rd	Win & Pl
Career Total (Turf)	2	0	0	0	280

Going (Turf): Sf: 0-1 GS: 0-0 Gd: 0-1 GF: 0-0 Fm: 0-0
Distance: 5f/6f: 0-0 7f-8f: 0-1 9f-13f: 0-1 14f+: 0-0
Track : LH: 0-1 RH: 0-0 Tight: 0-0 Gall: 0-0
Aids: Bl: 0-0 Vi: 0-0 Tstrap: 0-0 Ckp: 0-0

It's A Date

105(70) (28)**89**
4-y-o b g Kyllachy-By Arrangement (IRE) (Bold Arrangement)
A King Horace 5

Placings:0/10655632-21610 **(4988)**
2009: 12^{2}GF, 12^{1}GF, 14^{6}G, 11^{1}GS, 13^{0}GF,

	Starts	1st	2nd	3rd	Win & Pl
Career Total (Turf)	13	3	2	1	18675
Career Total (AW)	1	0	0	0	0

89 7/09 Leic 1m3f183y (0-80)H G-S £4857
84 6/09 Sals 1m4f (0-85)H G-F £4857
82 5/08 Newb 1m2f6y GD £5342
Total win prize-money £15057

Going (Turf): Sf: 0-1 **GS: 1-2 Gd: 1-4 GF: 1-6** Fm: 0-0
Distance: 5f/6f: 0-0 7f-8f: 0-1 **9f-13f: 3-9** 14f+: 0-4
Track : LH: 1-5 **RH: 2-7** Tight: 1-4 Gall: 1-5
Aids: Bl: 0-0 Vi: 0-0 Tstrap: 0-0 Ckp: 0-0
Best Rating: 89 7/09 Leic 1m3f183y gd-sft

Useful; stays 1m4f; acts on fast and easy ground.

It's A Deal (IRE)

81(78) (43)**41**
2-y-o b f Indian Haven-Gold And Blue (IRE) (Bluebird (USA))
P Winkworth Badger's Set

Placings:0006 **(5748)**
2009: 6^{0}G, 7^{0}SD, 7^{0}SD, 7^{6}GF,

	Starts	1st	2nd	3rd	Win & Pl
Career Total (Turf)	2	0	0	0	0
Career Total (AW)	2	0	0	0	

Going (Turf): Sf: 0-0 GS: 0-0 Gd: 0-1 GF: 0-1 Fm: 0-0

Distance: 5f/6f: 0-1 7f-8f: 0-3 9f-13f: 0-0 14f+: 0-0
Track : LH: 0-0 RH: 0-2 Tight: 0-0 Gall: 0-0
Aids: Bl: 0-0 Vi: 0-0 Tstrap: 0-0 Ckp: 0-0
Best Rating: 43 7/09 Kemp 7f stand

It's A Mans World

98(102) (67)68
3-y-o b g Kyllachy-Exhibitor (USA) (Royal Academy (USA))
K M Prendergast (S Dow 13/2) Alchemy Bloodstock

Placings:654-426550620213 **(5391)**
2009: 8^{4}SD, 6^{2}SD, 7^{6}SD, 7^{5}SD, 7^{5}SD, 10^{0}GS, 8^{6}S, 6^{2}SD, 6^{0}GF, 6^{2}GS, 5^{1}G, 6^{3}GF,

	Starts	1st	2nd	3rd	Win & Pl
Career Total (Turf)	7	1	1	1	3323
Career Total (AW)	8	0	2	0	2100

65 8/09 Carl 5f193y (0-60)H GD £2047
Total win prize-money £2047

Going (Turf): Sf: 0-1 GS: 0-2 **Gd: 1-1** GF: 0-3 Fm: 0-0
Distance: **5f/6f: 1-5** 7f-8f: 0-8 9f-13f: 0-2 14f+: 0-0
Track : LH: 0-7 **RH: 1-3** Tight: 0-7 Gall: 0-0
Aids: Bl: 0-0 **Vi: 1-6** Tstrap: 0-0 Ckp: 0-0
Best Rating: 68 9/08 NmkR 1m gd-fm

Moderate; stays 7f; acts on Polytrack and good/fast ground on turf; has worn a visor.

It's Dubai Dolly

99(99) (71)79
3-y-o ch f Dubai Destination (USA)-Betrothal (IRE) (Groom Dancer (USA))
A J Lidderdale Exors Of The Late Mrs Kath Cox

Placings:0243-1001000 **(7291)**
2009: 12^{1}SD, 12^{0}SD, 12^{0}GF, 10^{1}G, 11^{0}SD, 12^{0}GF, 10^{0}S,

	Starts	1st	2nd	3rd	Win & Pl
Career Total (Turf)	7	1	1	1	5146
Career Total (AW)	4	1	0	0	2759

79 8/09 Newb 1m2f6y (0-75)H GD £2590
71 4/09 Kemp 1m4f STD £2590
Total win prize-money £5180

Going (Turf): Sf: 0-2 GS: 0-2 **Gd: 1-1** GF: 0-2 Fm: 0-0
Distance: 5f/6f: 0-1 7f-8f: 0-2 **9f-13f: 2-8** 14f+: 0-0
Track : LH: 1-5 RH: 1-4 Tight: 0-2 **Gall: 1-5**
Aids: Bl: 0-0 Vi: 0-0 Tstrap: 0-0 Ckp: 0-0
Best Rating: 79 8/09 Newb 1m2f6y good

Fair; stays1m4f; acts on soft ground and on Polytrack.

It's Josr

93(106) (58)61
4-y-o b g Josr Algarhoud (IRE)-It's So Easy (Shaadi (USA))
I A Wood G R Jones

Placings:00023/00000015-0500022 **(6918)**
2009: 8^{0}GF, 10^{5}G, 8^{0}G, 8^{0}G, 10^{0}G, 12^{2}SD, 12^{2}SD,

	Starts	1st	2nd	3rd	Win & Pl
Career Total (Turf)	10	1	0	0	2267
Career Total (AW)	10	0	3	1	2278

61 8/08 Bath 1m5y (0-65)H G-S £2266
Total win prize-money £2267

Going (Turf): Sf: 0-0 **GS: 1-3** Gd: 0-6 GF: 0-1 Fm: 0-0
Distance: 5f/6f: 0-0 7f-8f: 0-8 **9f-13f: 1-12** 14f+: 0-0
Track : **LH: 1-11** RH: 0-6 **Tight: 1-7** Gall: 0-2
Aids: **Bl: 1-9** Vi: 0-2 Tstrap: 0-0 Ckp: 0-0
Best Rating: 65 11/07 Wolv 1m141y stand

Moderate; stays 1m4f; acts on easy ground and on sand; has worn blinkers and a visor.

It's My Day (IRE)

93(103) (69)72
4-y-o ch g Soviet Star (USA)-Ezana (Ela-Mana-Mou)
C Gordon Draper Edmonds Draper

Placings:005106/620-50300056 **(5122)**
2009: 10^{5}SD, 10^{0}SD, 10^{3}SD, 10^{0}SD, 11^{0}GF, 11^{0}G, 9^{5}F, 9^{6}F,

	Starts	1st	2nd	3rd	Win & Pl
Career Total (Turf)	8	0	1	0	1025
Career Total (AW)	9	1	0	1	2451

64 9/07 Kemp 7f (0-65) STD £2047
Total win prize-money £2048

Going (Turf): Sf: 0-0 GS: 0-1 Gd: 0-1 GF: 0-4 Fm: 0-2
Distance: 5f/6f: 0-1 **7f-8f: 1-4** 9f-13f: 0-12 14f+: 0-0
Track : LH: 0-9 **RH: 1-4** Tight: 0-7 Gall: 0-1
Aids: Bl: 0-0 Vi: 0-1 Tstrap: 0-1 Ckp: 0-1
Best Rating: 72 5/08 Wind 1m3f135y gd-fm

Modest; stays 1m3f; acts on fast ground; also goes on Polytrack.

Itainteasybeingme

95(87) (57)61
3-y-o ch g Lucky Story (USA)-Concubine (IRE) (Danehill (USA))
J R Boyle John Hopkins (t/a South Hatch Racing)

Placings:054226-50250 **(3693)**
2009: 6^{5}G, 8^{0}G, 7^{2}G, 8^{5}S, 8^{0}G,

	Starts	1st	2nd	3rd	Win & Pl
Career Total (Turf)	10	0	2	0	1676
Career Total (AW)	1	0	1	0	504

Going (Turf): Sf: 0-1 GS: 0-3 Gd: 0-4 GF: 0-2 Fm: 0-0
Distance: 5f/6f: 0-5 7f-8f: 0-3 9f-13f: 0-3 14f+: 0-0
Track : LH: 0-2 RH: 0-2 Tight: 0-2 Gall: 0-1
Aids: Bl: 0-0 Vi: 0-0 Tstrap: 0-0 Ckp: 0-0
Best Rating: 61 5/09 Yarm 7f3y good

Moderate; effective over 5f-7f; acts on good and easy ground.

Italian Dame

86 35
3-y-o b f Bertolini (USA)-Soyalang (FR) (Alydeed (CAN))
J R Turner J R Turner

Placings:005 **(5599)**
2009: 8^{0}G, 6^{0}GF, 6^{5}GF,

	Starts	1st	2nd	3rd	Win & Pl
Career Total (Turf)	3	0	0	0	0

Going (Turf): Sf: 0-0 GS: 0-0 Gd: 0-1 GF: 0-2 Fm: 0-0
Distance: 5f/6f: 0-2 7f-8f: 0-1 9f-13f: 0-0 14f+: 0-0
Track : LH: 0-1 RH: 0-0 Tight: 0-1 Gall: 0-0
Aids: Bl: 0-0 Vi: 0-0 Tstrap: 0-0 Ckp: 0-0
Best Rating: 35 9/09 Rdcr 6f gd-fm

Italian Tom (IRE)

95(98) (80)80
2-y-o b c Le Vie Dei Colori-Brave Cat (IRE) (Catrail (USA))
R A Harris (S A Callaghan 12/8) S & A Mares

Placings:516211006414 **(7793)**
2009: 5^{5}GF, 5^{1}G, 5^{6}SD, 5^{2}G, 5^{1}SD, 5^{1}S, 6^{0}GF, 5^{0}SF, 5^{6}SD, 6^{4}SD, 5^{1}SD, 5^{4}SS,

	Starts	1st	2nd	3rd	Win & Pl
Career Total (Turf)	5	2	1	0	5759
Career Total (AW)	7	2	0	0	5969

80 12/09 Sthl 5f (0-75) STD £2729
80 9/09 Sand 5f6y (0-75) SFT £3238
73 9/09 Kemp 5f (0-70) STD £2590
68 6/09 Chep 5f16y GD £1942
Total win prize-money £10501

Going (Turf): **Sf: 1-1** GS: 0-0 **Gd: 1-2** GF: 0-2 Fm: 0-0
Distance: **5f/6f: 4-12** 7f-8f: 0-0 9f-13f: 0-0 14f+: 0-0
Track : LH: 0-3 **RH: 1-2** Tight: 0-3 Gall: 0-0
Aids: Bl: 0-0 Vi: 0-0 Tstrap: 0-0 Ckp: 0-0
Best Rating: 80 12/09 Sthl 5f stand

Fair; effective at 5f; acts on good and soft ground and on both AW surfaces.

Italiano

90 39
10-y-o b g Emperor Jones (USA)-Elka (USA) (Val De L'Orne (FR))
Mrs Marjorie Fife (P Beaumont 23/6) Mrs Marion Turner

Placings:060 **(3974)**
2009: 9^{0}GF, 12^{6}GF, 11^{0}GS,

	Starts	1st	2nd	3rd	Win & Pl
Career Total (Turf)	3	0	0	0	0

Going (Turf): Sf: 0-0 GS: 0-1 Gd: 0-0 GF: 0-2 Fm: 0-0
Distance: 5f/6f: 0-0 7f-8f: 0-0 9f-13f: 0-3 14f+: 0-0
Track : LH: 0-1 RH: 0-2 Tight: 0-2 Gall: 0-0
Aids: Bl: 0-2 Vi: 0-0 Tstrap: 0-0 Ckp: 0-0
Best Rating: 39 6/09 Bevl 1m4f16y gd-fm

Itcanbedone Again (IRE)

(70) (53)47
10-y-o b g Sri Pekan (USA)-Maradata (IRE) (Shardari)
J W Unett R E Mennell

Placings:4335404/00361450/064/0/11430000/0036640535/0 **(4861)**
2009: 9^{0}SD,

	Starts	1st	2nd	3rd	Win & Pl
Career Total (Turf)	23	1	0	3	7361
Career Total (AW)	15	2	0	3	5216

61 2/06 Wolv 1m1f103y (0-55)H SF £2047
62 1/06 Wolv 1m1f103y (0-45) STD £1706
66 6/02 Rdcr 1m1f E(0-75)H FRM £3668
Total win prize-money £7422

Going (Turf): Sf: 0-5 GS: 0-4 Gd: 0-5 GF: 0-6 **Fm: 1-3**
Distance: 5f/6f: 0-3 7f-8f: 0-5 **9f-13f: 3-30** 14f+: 0-0
Track : **LH: 3-29** RH: 0-3 **Tight: 3-23** Gall: 0-2
Aids: Bl: 0-0 Vi: 0-0 Tstrap: 0-0 Ckp: 0-0
Best Rating: 70 7/01 Donc 7f gd-fm

Moderate; best around 9f but gets further; acts on any ground and Polytrack.

Ithbaat (USA)

104 90
3-y-o b/br c Arch (USA)-Annul (USA) (Conquistador Cielo (USA))
J H M Gosden Hamdan Al Maktoum

Placings:4-21042 **(3535)**
2009: 8^{2}GF, 8^{1}GF, 8^{0}GF, 9^{4}G, 12^{2}GF,

	Starts	1st	2nd	3rd	Win & Pl
Career Total (Turf)	6	1	2	0	6746

76 5/09 Yarm 1m3y G-F £3784
Total win prize-money £3785

Going (Turf): Sf: 0-0 GS: 0-0 Gd: 0-2 **GF: 1-4** Fm: 0-0
Distance: 5f/6f: 0-0 7f-8f: 0-1 **9f-13f: 1-5** 14f+: 0-0
Track : LH: 0-1 RH: 0-2 Tight: 0-0 Gall: 0-1
Aids: Bl: 0-0 Vi: 0-0 Tstrap: 0-0 Ckp: 0-0
Best Rating: 90 7/09 Newb 1m4f5y gd-fm

Useful; stays 1m4f and acts on fast ground.

Ithinkbest

101(105) (91)75
3-y-o b g King's Best (USA)-Monturani (IRE) (Indian Ridge)
Sir Michael Stoute Saeed Suhail

Placings:0-523311 **(6830)**
2009: 8[5]G, 8[2]G, 10[3]GF, 8[3]GF, 8[1]GF, 8[1]SF,

	Starts	1st	2nd	3rd	Win & Pl
Career Total (Turf)	6	1	1	2	4876
Career Total (AW)	1	1	0	0	5046

91 10/09 Wolv 1m141y (0-85)H SF £5046
75 10/09 Pont 1m4y G-F £3238
Total win prize-money £8284

Going (Turf): Sf: 0-0 GS: 0-1 Gd: 0-2 **GF: 1-3** Fm: 0-0
Distance: 5f/6f: 0-0 7f-8f: 0-1 **9f-13f: 2-6** 14f+: 0-0
Track : **LH: 2-5** RH: 0-1 **Tight: 1-3** Gall: 0-0
Aids: Bl: 0-0 Vi: 0-0 Tstrap: 0-0 Ckp: 0-0
Best Rating: 91 10/09 Wolv 1m141y std-fst

Useful; stays 1m2f; acts on good/fast ground.

Itlaaq

102(108) (89)85
3-y-o b c Alhaarth (IRE)-Hathrah (IRE) (Linamix (FR))
J L Dunlop Hamdan Al Maktoum

Placings:0540-0152 **(6613)**
2009: 8[0]GF, 9[1]G, 11[5]G, 12[2]SD,

	Starts	1st	2nd	3rd	Win & Pl
Career Total (Turf)	7	1	0	0	5648
Career Total (AW)	1	0	1	0	1407

85 5/09 Gdwd 1m1f192y (0-80)H GD £4857
Total win prize-money £4857

Going (Turf): Sf: 0-1 GS: 0-2 **Gd: 1-2** GF: 0-2 Fm: 0-0
Distance: 5f/6f: 0-0 7f-8f: 0-4 **9f-13f: 1-4** 14f+: 0-0
Track : LH: 0-1 **RH: 1-6 Tight: 1-2** Gall: 0-0
Aids: Bl: 0-0 Vi: 0-0 Tstrap: 0-0 Ckp: 0-0
Best Rating: 89 10/09 Kemp 1m4f stand

Fair; effective at 1m2f-1m4f; acts on good and soft ground and Polytrack.

Its Alright (IRE)

94 84
2-y-o b f King's Best (USA)-Lightwood Lady (IRE) (Anabaa (USA))
A Bailey Allan McNamee

Placings:1 **(1298)**
2009: 5[1]GF,

	Starts	1st	2nd	3rd	Win & Pl
Career Total (Turf)	1	1	0	0	5181

84 4/09 NmkR 5f G-F £5180
Total win prize-money £5181

Going (Turf): Sf: 0-0 GS: 0-0 Gd: 0-0 **GF: 1-1** Fm: 0-0
Distance: **5f/6f: 1-1** 7f-8f: 0-0 9f-13f: 0-0 14f+: 0-0
Track : LH: 0-0 RH: 0-0 Tight: 0-0 Gall: 0-0
Aids: Bl: 0-0 Vi: 0-0 Tstrap: 0-0 Ckp: 0-0
Best Rating: 84 4/09 NmkR 5f gd-fm

Useful; suited by 5f and fast ground.

Its Beyond Me

48
5-y-o ch g And Beyond (IRE)-Hand On Heart (IRE) (Taufan (USA))
F P Murtagh Mrs M Irving

Placings:0 **(2527)**
2009: 7[0]GF,

	Starts	1st	2nd	3rd	Win & Pl
Career Total (Turf)	1	0	0	0	

Going (Turf): **Sf: 0-0 GS: 0-0 Gd: 0-0 GF: 0-1 Fm: 0-0**
Distance: 5f/6f: 0-0 7f-8f: 0-1 9f-13f: 0-0 14f+: 0-0
Track : LH: 0-0 RH: 0-1 Tight: 0-0 Gall: 0-0
Aids: Bl: 0-0 Vi: 0-0 Tstrap: 0-0 Ckp: 0-0

Its Moon (IRE)

91 69
5-y-o b m Tobougg (IRE)-Shallat (IRE) (Pennekamp (USA))
T D Walford Jaass One Racing

Placings:043/1202610534/435560200-6 **(1767)**
2009: 15[6]GF,

	Starts	1st	2nd	3rd	Win & Pl
Career Total (Turf)	23	2	3	3	15095

76 7/07 Pont 1m4f8y (0-75)H SFT £4533
68 4/07 Bevl 1m4f16y (0-70)H G-F £3238
Total win prize-money £7773

Going (Turf): **Sf: 1-2** GS: 0-3 Gd: 0-10 **GF: 1-8** Fm: 0-0
Distance: 5f/6f: 0-2 7f-8f: 0-1 **9f-13f: 2-13** 14f+: 0-7
Track : LH: 1-12 RH: 1-9 **Tight: 1-12** Gall: 0-4
Aids: Bl: 0-3 Vi: 0-1 Tstrap: 0-0 Ckp: 0-0
Best Rating: 76 7/07 Pont 1m4f8y soft

Modest; effective over 1m2f-1m4f; acts on fast ground.

Itsawindup

79(101) (53)21
5-y-o b g Elnadim (USA)-Topwinder (USA) (Topsider (USA))
Miss Sheena West W R B Racing 46

Placings:00/000000/3163-031650 **(1200)**
2009: 13[0]SD, 12[3]SD, 10[1]SD, 12[6]SD, 10[5]SD, 12[0]GF,

	Starts	1st	2nd	3rd	Win & Pl
Career Total (Turf)	3	0	0	0	
Career Total (AW)	15	2	0	3	4791

53 2/09 Kemp 1m2f (0-50)H STD £2047
50 2/08 Kemp 1m3f STD £2047
Total win prize-money £4095

Going (Turf): **Sf: 0-0 GS: 0-0 Gd: 0-1 GF: 0-2 Fm: 0-0**
Distance: 5f/6f: 0-0 7f-8f: 0-6 **9f-13f: 2-11** 14f+: 0-1
Track : LH: 0-8 **RH: 2-9** Tight: 0-7 Gall: 0-2
Aids: Bl: 0-0 Vi: 0-3 Tstrap: 0-0 Ckp: 0-0
Best Rating: 54 12/06 Ling 7f stand

Very moderate; stays 1m3f and acts on Polytrack; has worn a tongue tie.

Itsher

103(97) (61)75
3-y-o br f Diktat-Shararah (Machiavellian (USA))
S C Williams Itsus

Placings:55043-536422111 **(3663)**
2009: 5[5]SD, 7[3]SD, 7[6]G, 6[4]G, 6[2]GS, 6[2]GF, 5[1]F, 5[1]G, 5[1]F,

	Starts	1st	2nd	3rd	Win & Pl
Career Total (Turf)	10	3	2	0	10375
Career Total (AW)	4	0	0	2	554

75 7/09 Brig 5f59y (0-65)H FRM £2590
75 7/09 Leic 5f218y (0-70)H GD £3885
74 6/09 Brig 5f213y (0-55)H FRM £2331
Total win prize-money £8807

Going (Turf): Sf: 0-0 GS: 0-1 Gd: 1-3 GF: 0-4 **Fm: 2-2**
Distance: **5f/6f: 3-8** 7f-8f: 0-6 9f-13f: 0-0 14f+: 0-0
Track : **LH: 2-5** RH: 0-2 Tight: 0-2 Gall: 0-1
Aids: **Bl: 3-5** Vi: 0-0 Tstrap: 0-0 Ckp: 0-0
Best Rating: 75 7/09 Brig 5f59y firm

Fair; stays 7f, but effective at shorter; acts on fast ground; has worn blinkers.

Itshim

(106) (71)7
3-y-o b g Ishiguru (USA)-Sumitra (Tragic Role (USA))
S C Williams Itsthem

Placings:5000-111 **(0705)**
2009: 5[1]SD, 5[1]SD, 7[1]SD,

	Starts	1st	2nd	3rd	Win & Pl
Career Total (Turf)	4	0	0	0	0
Career Total (AW)	3	3	0	0	6908

69 2/09 Ling 7f (0-70)H STD £2900
71 2/09 Wolv 5f20y (0-60)H STD £2388
55 2/09 Kemp 5f (0-45) STD £1619
Total win prize-money £6907

Going (Turf): **Sf: 0-1 GS: 0-0 Gd: 0-0 GF: 0-3 Fm: 0-0**
Distance: **5f/6f: 2-4** 7f-8f: 1-3 9f-13f: 0-0 14f+: 0-0
Track : **LH: 2-2** RH: 1-1 **Tight: 2-2** Gall: 0-1
Aids: Bl: 0-0 Vi: 0-0 Tstrap: 0-0 Ckp: 0-0
Best Rating: 71 2/09 Wolv 5f20y stand

Progressive sprinter; much improved effort at Wolverhampton in February 2009; likely to prove best over sprint distances; acts on Polytrack.

Itsthursdayalready

93(98) (74)77
2-y-o b g Exceed And Excel (AUS)-Succinct (Hector Protector (USA))
J G Given Danethorpe Racing Partnership

Placings:2100052 **(7846)**
2009: 5[2]GF, 5[1]GF, 5[0]GF, 5[0]GS, 6[0]GF, 5[5]G, 7[2]SD,

	Starts	1st	2nd	3rd	Win & Pl
Career Total (Turf)	6	1	1	0	6311
Career Total (AW)	1	0	1	0	1699

77 6/09 Ches 5f16y G-F £5504
Total win prize-money £5505

Going (Turf): Sf: 0-0 GS: 0-1 Gd: 0-1 **GF: 1-4** Fm: 0-0
Distance: **5f/6f: 1-6** 7f-8f: 0-1 9f-13f: 0-0 14f+: 0-0
Track : **LH: 1-3** RH: 0-0 **Tight: 1-2** Gall: 0-0
Aids: Bl: 0-0 Vi: 0-0 Tstrap: 0-0 Ckp: 0-0
Best Rating: 77 6/09 Ches 5f16y gd-fm

Useful; stays 7f; acts on fast ground and on Polytrack.

Itsy Bitsy

92(94) (47)51
7-y-o b m Danzig Connection (USA)-Cos I Do (IRE) (Double Schwartz)
W J Musson W J Musson

Placings:060/04015050-00060 (4927)
2009: 11^{0}SD, 10^{0}GF, 10^{0}G, 12^{6}G, 12^{0}G,

	Starts	1st	2nd	3rd	Win & Pl
Career Total (Turf)	6	1	0	0	1943
Career Total (AW)	10	0	0	0	0

51 7/08 Yarm 1m2f21y (0-60)H G-F £1942
Total win prize-money £1943

Going (Turf): Sf: 0-0 GS: 0-0 Gd: 0-3 **GF: 1-3** Fm: 0-0
Distance: 5f/6f: 0-0 7f-8f: 0-0 **9f-13f: 1-14** 14f+: 0-2
Track : **LH: 1-10** RH: 0-6 **Tight: 1-6** Gall: 0-3
Aids: Bl: 0-0 Vi: 0-0 Tstrap: 1-6 Ckp: 1-6
Best Rating: **51** 7/08 Yarm 1m2f21y gd-fm

Moderate; effective over 1m2f; acts on fast ground.

Itwasonlyakiss (IRE)

95 **81**
2-y-o b f Exceed And Excel (AUS)-Reem One (IRE) (Rainbow Quest (USA))
J W Hills Gary And Linnet Woodward

Placings:5202 (4147)
2009: 5^{5}GF, 5^{2}GF, 5^{0}GF, 6^{2}GF,

	Starts	1st	2nd	3rd	Win & Pl
Career Total (Turf)	4	0	2	0	3199

Going (Turf): **Sf: 0-0 GS: 0-0 Gd: 0-0 GF: 0-4 Fm: 0-0**
Distance: 5f/6f: 0-4 7f-8f: 0-0 9f-13f: 0-0 14f+: 0-0
Track : LH: 0-0 RH: 0-0 Tight: 0-0 Gall: 0-2
Aids: Bl: 0-0 Vi: 0-0 Tstrap: 0-0 Ckp: 0-0
Best Rating: **81** 5/09 Sand 5f6y gd-fm

Fair; effective over 5f-6f; acts on fast ground.

Iver Bridge Lad

109(103) (104)**108**
2-y-o b c Avonbridge-Fittonia (FR) (Ashkalani (IRE))
J Ryan The Iver Lads

Placings:231102634 (7030)
2009: 5^{2}G, 5^{3}GF, **6^{1}SD**, **5^{1}G**, 5^{0}G, 6^{2}SD, 5^{6}GF, 5^{3}GS, 7^{4}S,

	Starts	1st	2nd	3rd	Win & Pl
Career Total (Turf)	7	1	1	2	27794
Career Total (AW)	2	1	1	0	13350

98 7/09 Sand 5f6y GD £17031
93 6/09 Kemp 6f STD £2590
Total win prize-money £19621

Going (Turf): Sf: 0-1 GS: 0-1 **Gd: 1-3** GF: 0-2 Fm: 0-0
Distance: **5f/6f: 2-8** 7f-8f: 0-1 9f-13f: 0-0 14f+: 0-0
Track : LH: 0-1 **RH: 1-2** Tight: 0-1 Gall: 0-1
Aids: Bl: 0-0 Vi: 0-0 Tstrap: 0-0 Ckp: 0-0
Best Rating: **108** 10/09 Asct 5f gd-sft

Smart; winner in Listed company and Group placed; stays 6f; acts on most ground and on Polytrack; likes to race prominently.

Ivor Novello (IRE)

91(74) (14)**47**
3-y-o b g Noverre (USA)-Pearly Brooks (Efisio)
G A Swinbank Panther Racing Ltd

Placings:00-405 (1926)
2009: 5^{4}GF, 6^{0}SD, 8^{5}F,

	Starts	1st	2nd	3rd	Win & Pl
Career Total (Turf)	4	0	0	0	168
Career Total (AW)	1	0	0	0	

Going (Turf): **Sf: 0-1 GS: 0-0 Gd: 0-0 GF: 0-2 Fm: 0-1**
Distance: 5f/6f: 0-4 7f-8f: 0-1 9f-13f: 0-0 14f+: 0-0
Track : LH: 0-1 RH: 0-1 Tight: 0-1 Gall: 0-0
Aids: Bl: 0-0 Vi: 0-0 Tstrap: 0-0 Ckp: 0-0
Best Rating: **47** 5/09 Rdcr 1m firm

Ivory Jazz

91(78) (39)**67**
2-y-o b c Dubai Destination (USA)-Slow Jazz (USA) (Chief's Crown (USA))
D K Ivory John Khan

Placings:03 (4176)
2009: 7^{0}SD, 6^{3}G,

	Starts	1st	2nd	3rd	Win & Pl
Career Total (Turf)	1	0	0	1	443
Career Total (AW)	1	0	0	0	

Going (Turf): **Sf: 0-0 GS: 0-0 Gd: 0-1 GF: 0-0 Fm: 0-0**
Distance: 5f/6f: 0-0 7f-8f: 0-2 9f-13f: 0-0 14f+: 0-0
Track : LH: 0-1 RH: 0-0 Tight: 0-1 Gall: 0-0
Aids: Bl: 0-0 Vi: 0-0 Tstrap: 0-0 Ckp: 0-0
Best Rating: **67** 7/09 Yarm 6f3y good

Modest; suited by 6f and good ground.

Ivory Lace

104(104) (79)**88**
8-y-o b m Atraf-Miriam (Forzando)
S Woodman Sally Woodman J Lenaghan D Mortimer

Placings:03361500/**5201311**415004/**3620**0250004025/002 261613316**3600/3055**0431133101006**000**/60044060662000-003033354140040 (7575)
2009: 8^{0}G, 7^{0}GF, 7^{3}GF, 7^{0}GF, 6^{3}G, 7^{3}G, 8^{3}G, 7^{5}GF, 6^{4}F, 6^{1}F, 7^{4}GF, 7^{0}GF, 7^{0}SD, 8^{4}SD, 8^{0}SD,

	Starts	1st	2nd	3rd	Win & Pl
Career Total (Turf)	62	12	1	11	63752
Career Total (AW)	38	1	6	4	11226

81 8/09 Brig 6f209y (0-70)H FRM £3027
94 9/07 Gdwd 7f (0-85)H G-F £5181
90 8/07 NmkJ 7f (0-85)H G-F £5181
89 6/07 Gdwd 7f (0-80)H G-F £7124
87 6/07 Ling 7f (0-75)H G-F £2914
85 8/06 Brig 5f213y (0-80)H FRM £6477
83 6/06 Brig 6f209y (0-75)H FRM £3238
76 6/06 Brig 6f209y (0-70)H FRM £3238
77 6/04 Chep 5f16y E(0-75)H GD £3584
69 4/04 Bath 5f11y E(0-70)H GD £3750
68 4/04 Bath 5f11y E(0-70)H GD £3516
60 2/04 Ling 5f G STD £2562
61 5/03 Catt 5f F G-F £3349
Total win prize-money £53152

Going (Turf): Sf: 0-1 GS: 0-5 Gd: 3-18 **GF: 5-29** Fm: 4-9
Distance: 5f/6f: 6-40 **7f-8f: 7-56** 9f-13f: 0-4 14f+: 0-0
Track : **LH: 7-52** RH: 2-18 Tight: 1-37 **Gall: 2-6**
Aids: Bl: 0-1 Vi: 0-0 Tstrap: 0-2 Ckp: 0-2
Best Rating: **94** 9/07 Sand 7f16y good

Fair; effective over 6f-7f; acts on fast ground; also goes on sand.

Ivory Silk

100(110) (93)**84**
4-y-o b f Diktat-Ivory's Joy (Tina's Pet)
J R Gask Resurrection Partners

Placings:33/3000243215411-220053526 (7613)
2009: 5^{2}SD, 5^{2}GF, 5^{0}GF, 5^{0}G, 5^{5}GF, **5^{3}SD**, 5^{5}GF, 5^{2}SD, 6^{6}SD,

	Starts	1st	2nd	3rd	Win & Pl
Career Total (Turf)	12	0	3	1	4373
Career Total (AW)	12	3	2	4	16556

91 12/08 Wolv 5f20y (0-85)H STD £5046
88 11/08 GrLe 5f (0-75)H STD £3238
78 8/08 GrLe 6f STD £2590
Total win prize-money £10874

Going (Turf): **Sf: 0-1 GS: 0-0 Gd: 0-4 GF: 0-6 Fm: 0-1**
Distance: **5f/6f: 3-17** 7f-8f: 0-7 9f-13f: 0-0 14f+: 0-0
Track : **LH: 3-11** RH: 0-2 Tight: 1-6 **Gall: 2-5**
Aids: **Bl: 2-8** Vi: 0-0 Tstrap: 0-0 Ckp: 0-0
Best Rating: **93** 1/09 GrLe 5f stand

Useful; effective over 5f-1m; acts on fast ground; goes on Polytrack; has worn headgear.

Ivy The Terrible

57 **1**
3-y-o b f Bahamian Bounty-Emerald Fire (Pivotal)
Dr J D Scargill Strawberry Fields Stud

Placings:00 (3319)
2009: 6^{0}GF, 7^{0}GF,

	Starts	1st	2nd	3rd	Win & Pl
Career Total (Turf)	2	0	0	0	

Going (Turf): **Sf: 0-0 GS: 0-0 Gd: 0-0 GF: 0-2 Fm: 0-0**
Distance: 5f/6f: 0-0 7f-8f: 0-2 9f-13f: 0-0 14f+: 0-0
Track : LH: 0-1 RH: 0-0 Tight: 0-0 Gall: 0-0
Aids: Bl: 0-0 Vi: 0-0 Tstrap: 0-0 Ckp: 0-0
Best Rating: **1** 6/09 Wwck 7f26y gd-fm

Izaaj (USA)

93 **78**
2-y-o ch c Giant's Causeway (USA)-Miss Coronado (USA) (Coronado's Quest (USA))
Saeed Bin Suroor Godolphin

Placings:310 (3138)
2009: 5^{3}GF, **6^{1}GF**, 7^{0}GF,

	Starts	1st	2nd	3rd	Win & Pl
Career Total (Turf)	3	1	0	1	5229

78 5/09 Yarm 6f3y G-F £3784
Total win prize-money £3785

Going (Turf): Sf: 0-0 GS: 0-0 Gd: 0-0 **GF: 1-3** Fm: 0-0
Distance: 5f/6f: 0-1 **7f-8f: 1-2** 9f-13f: 0-0 14f+: 0-0
Track : LH: 0-0 RH: 0-0 Tight: 0-0 Gall: 0-0
Aids: Bl: 0-0 Vi: 0-0 Tstrap: 0-0 Ckp: 0-0
Best Rating: **78** 5/09 Yarm 6f3y gd-fm

Fair; stays 6f and likes fast ground.

Izuizorizuain't (IRE)

95(85) (44)**57**
2-y-o ch f Johannesburg (USA)-Justly Royal (USA) (Royal Academy (USA))
K A Ryan T Alderson

Placings:236443040 (7616)
2009: 5^{2}G, 5^{3}GF, 7^{6}GF, 7^{4}GF, 6^{4}GS, 7^{3}GF, 7^{0}GF, 7^{4}SD, 8^{0}SD,

	Starts	1st	2nd	3rd	Win & Pl
Career Total (Turf)	7	0	1	2	1533
Career Total (AW)	2	0	0	0	0

Going (Turf): **Sf: 0-0 GS: 0-1 Gd: 0-1 GF: 0-5 Fm: 0-0**
Distance: 5f/6f: 0-2 7f-8f: 0-6 9f-13f: 0-1 14f+: 0-0

Track : LH: 0-3 RH: 0-0 Tight: 0-2 Gall: 0-0
Aids: Bl: 0-2 Vi: 0-0 Tstrap: 0-0 Ckp: 0-0
Best Rating: **57** 9/09 Catt 7f gd-fm

Moderate; effective over 5f; acts on good/fast ground; has worn blinkers.

Izzi Mill (USA)

96(97) (70)**73**

3-y-o gr/ro f Lemon Drop Kid (USA)-Lets Get Cozzy (USA) (Cozzene (USA))
D R C Elsworth J L Rowsell

Placings:4346-24020350 **(6738)**
2009: 7^{2}GF, 6^{4}GF, 7^{0}GF, 7^{2}G, 6^{0}GF, 7^{3}G, 6^{5}SS, 6^{0}GS,

	Starts	1st	2nd	3rd	Win & Pl
Career Total (Turf)	**10**	**0**	**2**	**2**	**3896**
Career Total (AW)	**2**	**0**	**0**	**0**	**0**

Going (Turf): **Sf: 0-0 GS: 0-1 Gd: 0-3 GF: 0-6 Fm: 0-0**
Distance: 5f/6f: 0-5 7f-8f: 0-7 9f-13f: 0-0 14f+: 0-0
Track : LH: 0-4 RH: 0-1 Tight: 0-3 Gall: 0-2
Aids: Bl: 0-0 Vi: 0-0 Tstrap: 0-0 Ckp: 0-0
Best Rating: **73** 6/09 Catt 7f good

Fair; suited by 6-7f and fast ground.

Izzibizzi

94(98) (81)**86**

4-y-o b f Medicean-Sleave Silk (IRE) (Unfuwain (USA))
E A L Dunlop J Weatherby, Champneys

Placings:0222/31140-004550 **(7065)**
2009: 8^{0}GF, 8^{0}GS, 8^{4}G, 7^{5}G, 7^{5}SD, 8^{0}SD,

	Starts	1st	2nd	3rd	Win & Pl
Career Total (Turf)	**9**	**1**	**2**	**1**	**63578**
Career Total (AW)	**6**	**1**	**1**	**0**	**3137**

86	10/08	Newb	7f	(0-95)H	SFT	£9066
63	10/08	Kemp	1m		STD	£2047

Total win prize-money £11113

Going (Turf): **Sf: 1-2** GS: 0-2 Gd: 0-3 GF: 0-2 Fm: 0-0
Distance: 5f/6f: 0-1 **7f-8f: 2-14** 9f-13f: 0-0 14f+: 0-0
Track : LH: 0-5 **RH: 1-2** Tight: 0-3 Gall: 0-1
Aids: Bl: 0-0 Vi: 0-0 Tstrap: 0-4 Ckp: 0-4
Best Rating: **86** 10/08 Newb 7f soft

Useful; stays 1m; acts on good and softer ground and on Polytrack.

Izzy Lou (IRE)

72(51) **71**

3-y-o ch f Spinning World (USA)-High Spot (Shirley Heights)
K A Ryan Highbank Syndicate

Placings:25-00 **(4013)**
2009: 8^{0}SD, 8^{0}GF,

	Starts	1st	2nd	3rd	Win & Pl
Career Total (Turf)	**3**	**0**	**1**	**0**	**1060**
Career Total (AW)	**1**	**0**	**0**	**0**	

Going (Turf): **Sf: 0-1 GS: 0-1 Gd: 0-0 GF: 0-1 Fm: 0-0**
Distance: 5f/6f: 0 0 7f-8f: 0-2 9f-13f: 0-2 14f+: 0-0
Track : LH: 0-1 RH: 0-2 Tight: 0-2 Gall: 0-0
Aids: Bl: 0-1 Vi: 0-0 Tstrap: 0-1 Ckp: 0-1
Best Rating: **71** 8/08 Rdcr 7f gd-sft

J J The Jet Plane (SAF)

116 (80)**121**

5-y-o b g Jet Master (SAF)-Majestic Guest (SAF) (Northern Guest (USA))
R Hannon (M F De Kock 28/7) JJ The Jet Plane Syndicate

Placings:115/3011111-6114300430 **(6304)**
2009: 5^{6}FT, 6^{1}GF, 6^{1}GF, 6^{4}GF, 6^{3}GF, 7^{0}G, 6^{0}GS, 6^{4}GF, 5^{3}GF, 6^{0}GF,

	Starts	1st	2nd	3rd	Win & Pl
Career Total (Turf)	**18**	**8**	**0**	**3**	**311529**
Career Total (AW)	**2**	**1**	**0**	**0**	**4472**

121	6/09	Wind	6f		G-F	£22708
119	2/09	Ndas	6f		G-F	£83333
	7/08	Clai	6f		GD	£22977
	5/08	Scot	6f	H	GD	£22977
	5/08	Turf	5f		SFT	£45955
	4/08	Turf	5f110y		GD	£9191
	3/08	Vaal	6f	H	GD	£17233
	11/07	Turf	7f		GD	£6793
	10/07	Vaas	6f		STD	£2943

Total win prize-money £234114

Going (Turf): Sf: 1-3 GS: 0-1 **Gd: 5-7** GF: 2-7 Fm: 0-0
Distance: **5f/6f: 8-15** 7f-8f: 1-4 9f-13f: 0-1 14f+: 0-0
Track : **LH: 1-1** RH: 0-1 Tight: 0-0 **Gall: 2-2**
Aids: Bl: 0-1 Vi: 0-0 Tstrap: 0-0 Ckp: 0-0
Best Rating: **121** 6/09 Wind 6f gd-fm

Group class; multiple Grade 1 winner in South Africa and winner in Group 3 company in Dubai in 2009; effective over 5f-6f; acts on good and faster ground; has worn blinkers.

Ja One (IRE)

96(94) (68)**67**

3-y-o b f Acclamation-Special Dancer (Shareef Dancer (USA))
B W Hills J Acheson

Placings:000-3044512 **(7025)**
2009: 9^{3}GF, 9^{0}GF, 11^{4}GF, 14^{4}G, 16^{5}G, 16^{1}SS, 16^{2}SD,

	Starts	1st	2nd	3rd	Win & Pl
Career Total (Turf)	**8**	**0**	**0**	**1**	**722**
Career Total (AW)	**2**	**1**	**1**	**0**	**2652**

68	10/09	Ling	2m	(0-65)H	SS	£2047

Total win prize-money £2047

Going (Turf): **Sf: 0-1 GS: 0-0 Gd: 0-3 GF: 0-4 Fm: 0-0**
Distance: 5f/6f: 0-0 7f-8f: 0-3 9f-13f: 0-3 **14f+: 1-4**
Track : **LH: 1-3** RH: 0-4 **Tight: 1-4** Gall: 0-1
Aids: Bl: 0-0 Vi: 0-0 Tstrap: 0-0 Ckp: 0-0
Best Rating: **68** 10/09 Ling 2m std-slw

Modest; stays 2m; acts on fast ground and on Polytrack.

Jabal Tariq

100(109) (91)**90**

4-y-o ch c Rock Of Gibraltar (IRE)-Sueboog (IRE) (Darshaan)
B W Hills Mohamed Obaida

Placings:0563/10144-53204650 **(6239)**
2009: 10^{5}GF, 9^{3}G, 12^{2}SD, 12^{0}GF, 12^{4}G, 11^{6}SD, 12^{5}GF, 10^{0}G,

	Starts	1st	2nd	3rd	Win & Pl
Career Total (Turf)	**15**	**2**	**0**	**2**	**12444**
Career Total (AW)	**2**	**0**	**1**	**0**	**1545**

90	6/08	Ripn	1m4f10y	(0-85)H	SFT	£4857
90	4/08	Ripn	1m1f170y		GD	£2914

Total win prize-money £7771

Going (Turf): **Sf: 1-1** GS: 0-1 **Gd: 1-10** GF: 0-3 Fm: 0-0
Distance: 5f/6f: 0-0 7f-8f: 0-4 **9f-13f: 2-13** 14f+: 0-0
Track : LH: 0-4 **RH: 2-11 Tight: 2-5** Gall: 0-4
Aids: Bl: 0-0 Vi: 0-0 Tstrap: 0-0 Ckp: 0-0
Best Rating: **91** 6/09 Kemp 1m4f stand

Useful; stays 1m4f; acts on good and softer ground; likes to race prominently.

Jabroot (IRE)

92(95) (67)**57**

3-y-o ch f Alhaarth (IRE)-Walesiana (GER) (Star Appeal)
M A Jarvis Sheikh Ahmed Al Maktoum

Placings:4530 **(4498)**
2009: 10^{4}SD, 12^{5}GF, 12^{3}SD, 12^{0}G,

	Starts	1st	2nd	3rd	Win & Pl
Career Total (Turf)	**2**	**0**	**0**	**0**	**0**
Career Total (AW)	**2**	**0**	**0**	**1**	**818**

Going (Turf): **Sf: 0-0 GS: 0-0 Gd: 0-1 GF: 0-1 Fm: 0-0**
Distance: 5f/6f: 0-0 7f-8f: 0-0 9f-13f: 0-4 14f+: 0-0
Track : LH: 0-3 RH: 0-1 Tight: 0-1 Gall: 0-2
Aids: Bl: 0-0 Vi: 0-0 Tstrap: 0-1 Ckp: 0-1
Best Rating: **67** 7/09 Sthl 1m4f stand

Moderate half-sister to Zahrat Dubai; stays 1m4f; acts on Fibresand.

Jachol (IRE)

100(91) (59)**62**

3-y-o b g Bachelor Duke (USA)-Restiv Star (FR) (Soviet Star (USA))
W J Haggas Ian and Christine Beard

Placings:000-202332 **(5838)**
2009: 8^{2}GF, 9^{0}G, 10^{2}G, 12^{3}G, 10^{3}S, 12^{2}SD,

	Starts	1st	2nd	3rd	Win & Pl
Career Total (Turf)	**8**	**0**	**2**	**2**	**2453**
Career Total (AW)	**1**	**0**	**1**	**0**	**806**

Going (Turf): **Sf: 0-2 GS: 0-2 Gd: 0-3 GF: 0-1 Fm: 0-0**
Distance: 5f/6f: 0-3 7f-8f: 0-1 9f-13f: 0-5 14f+: 0-0
Track : LH: 0-3 RH: 0-2 Tight: 0-3 Gall: 0-1
Aids: Bl: 0-0 Vi: 0-0 Tstrap: 0-1 Ckp: 0-1
Best Rating: **62** 8/09 NmkJ 1m4f good

Moderate; stays 1m4f; acts on good and soft ground and Polytrack; has worn cheekpieces.

Jack Cool (IRE)

103(96) (82)**89**

3-y-o b c One Cool Cat (USA)-Rachrush (IRE) (Sadler's Wells (USA))
P W Chapple-Hyam Angus McDonnell

Placings:0-0014200 **(6946)**
2009: 10^{0}GF, 7^{0}GF, 7^{1}G, 7^{4}G, 8^{2}HY, 7^{0}G, 8^{0}SD,

	Starts	1st	2nd	3rd	Win & Pl
Career Total (Turf)	**7**	**1**	**1**	**0**	**5076**
Career Total (AW)	**1**	**0**	**0**	**0**	

84	6/09	Yarm	7f3y	(0-70)	GD	£2849

Total win prize-money £2849

Going (Turf): Sf: 0-1 GS: 0-0 **Gd: 1-4** GF: 0-2 Fm: 0-0
Distance: 5f/6f: 0-0 **7f-8f: 1-6** 9f-13f: 0-2 14f+: 0-0
Track : LH: 0-2 RH: 0-0 Tight: 0-0 Gall: 0-0
Aids: Bl: 0 0 Vi: 0-0 Tstrap: 0-0 Ckp: 0-0
Best Rating: **89** 7/09 Nott 1m75y heavy

Fair; stays 1m but effective at 7f; effective on good and softer ground.

Jack Dawkins (USA)

104 (100)**103**

4-y-o b g Fantastic Light (USA)-Do The Mambo (USA) (Kingmambo (USA))

H R A Cecil Malih L Al Basti

Placings:50411/203-01050 **(5137)**

2009: 8^{0}G, 10^{1}GF, 10^{0}G, 8^{5}G, 10^{0}GF,

	Starts	1st	2nd	3rd	Win & Pl
Career Total (Turf)	12	3	1	0	37425
Career Total (AW)	1	0	0	1	1204
101 5/09 Donc 1m2f60y (0-95)H				G-F	£7771
97 10/07 Donc 1m				GD	£9715
83 9/07 Donc 1m				G-F	£16192

Total win prize-money £33680

Going (Turf): Sf: 0-1 GS: 0-1 Gd: 1-5 **GF: 2-5** Fm: 0-0
Distance: 5f/6f: 0-0 **7f-8f: 2-6** 9f-13f: 1-7 14f+: 0-0
Track : **LH: 2-5** RH: 0-2 Tight: 0-0 **Gall: 2-4**
Aids: Bl: 0-0 Vi: 0-0 Tstrap: 0-0 Ckp: 0-0
Best Rating: **103** 10/08 Pont 1m4y good

Very useful; stays 1m and acts on good and fast ground.

Jack Galvin (IRE)

89(84) (28)**44**

3-y-o b g Danetime (IRE)-Tumbleweed Pearl (Aragon)

J R Gask Horses First Racing Limited

Placings:60 **(6856)**

2009: 6^{6}G, 5^{0}SD,

	Starts	1st	2nd	3rd	Win & Pl
Career Total (Turf)	1	0	0	0	0
Career Total (AW)	1	0	0	0	

Going (Turf): **Sf: 0-0 GS: 0-0 Gd: 0-1 GF: 0-0 Fm: 0-0**
Distance: 5f/6f: 0-2 7f-8f: 0-0 9f-13f: 0-0 14f+: 0-0
Track : LH: 0-1 RH: 0-0 Tight: 0-1 Gall: 0-1
Aids: Bl: 0-0 Vi: 0-0 Tstrap: 0-0 Ckp: 0-0
Best Rating: **44** 10/09 Wind 6f good

Jack Junior (USA)

92(108) (102)**102**

5-y-o b/br g Songandaprayer (USA)-Ra Hydee (USA) (Rahy (USA))

D Nicholls Mrs Jackie Love & D Nicholls

Placings:46/2020/104**530-04006000054** **(6495)**

2009: 7^{0}G, 8^{4}FT, 10^{0}FT, 7^{0}SD, 8^{6}SD, 8^{0}GF, 7^{0}SF, 8^{0}G, 10^{0}GS, 9^{5}G, 7^{4}SF,

	Starts	1st	2nd	3rd	Win & Pl
Career Total (Turf)	13	1	1	0	7061
Career Total (AW)	10	0	1	1	209579
79 6/08 Hayd 1m30y				GD	£2590

Total win prize-money £2590

Going (Turf): Sf: 0-2 GS: 0-2 **Gd: 1-4** GF: 0-5 Fm: 0-0
Distance: 5f/6f: 0-0 7f-8f: 0-13 **9f-13f: 1-10** 14f+: 0-0
Track : **LH: 1-13** RH: 0-6 Tight: 0-4 Gall: 0-10
Aids: Bl: 0-1 Vi: 0-0 Tstrap: 0-0 Ckp: 0-0
Best Rating: **110** 6/07 Asct 1m gd-fm

Very useful; placed at Group level in Dubai; stays 1m1f; acts on most ground and on sand; has worn blinkers.

Jack Kane

63 **8**

2-y-o ch c Ishiguru (USA)-Armada Grove (Fleetwood (IRE))

J A McShane Lothian Recycling Limited

Placings:0 **(4993)**

2009: 7^{0}GF,

	Starts	1st	2nd	3rd	Win & Pl
Career Total (Turf)	1	0	0	0	

Going (Turf): **Sf: 0-0 GS: 0-0 Gd: 0-0 GF: 0-1 Fm: 0-0**
Distance: 5f/6f: 0-0 7f-8f: 0-1 9f-13f: 0-0 14f+: 0-0
Track : LH: 0-0 RH: 0-0 Tight: 0-0 Gall: 0-0
Aids: Bl: 0-0 Vi: 0-0 Tstrap: 0-0 Ckp: 0-0
Best Rating: **8** 8/09 Newc 7f gd-fm

Jack Luey

93(90) (59)**66**

2-y-o b c Danbird (AUS)-Icenaslice (IRE) (Fayruz)

L A Mullaney The Jack Partnership

Placings:463555341 **(7352)**

2009: 5^{4}GF, 5^{6}GF, 5^{3}GS, 5^{5}S, 5^{5}GF, 6^{5}S, 5^{3}S, 5^{4}S, 6^{1}SD,

	Starts	1st	2nd	3rd	Win & Pl
Career Total (Turf)	8	0	0	2	1453
Career Total (AW)	1	1	0	0	2047
59 11/09 Sthl 6f				STD	£2047

Total win prize-money £2047

Going (Turf): **Sf: 0-4 GS: 0-1 Gd: 0-0 GF: 0-3 Fm: 0-0**
Distance: **5f/6f: 1-8** 7f-8f: 0-1 9f-13f: 0-0 14f+: 0-0
Track : **LH: 1-2** RH: 0-2 Tight: 0-1 Gall: 0-2
Aids: Bl: 0-0 Vi: 0-0 Tstrap: 1-3 Ckp: 1-3
Best Rating: **66** 8/09 Carl 5f gd-sft

Modest; effective at 5f-6f; acts on easy ground and on Fibresand; has worn cheekpieces.

Jack My Boy (IRE)

101 **84**

2-y-o b c Tagula (IRE)-Bobanlyn (IRE) (Dance Of Life (USA))

P D Evans Terry Earle

Placings:31101660034 **(7290)**

2009: 5^{3}GF, 5^{1}GF, 6^{1}GS, 6^{0}G, 6^{1}GF, 7^{6}G, 6^{6}GF, 6^{0}GS, 6^{0}GF, 6^{3}G, 6^{4}S,

	Starts	1st	2nd	3rd	Win & Pl
Career Total (Turf)	11	3	0	2	16613
84 6/09 Pont 6f			G-F	£7771	
75 5/09 Newc 6f			G-S	£4209	
77 4/09 Bevl 5f			G-F	£2590	

Total win prize-money £14570

Going (Turf): Sf: 0-1 GS: 1-2 Gd: 0-3 **GF: 2-5** Fm: 0-0
Distance: **5f/6f: 3-9** 7f-8f: 0-2 9f-13f: 0-0 14f+: 0-0
Track : **LH: 1-2** RH: 0-0 Tight: 0-1 Gall: 0-0
Aids: Bl: 0-0 Vi: 0-0 Tstrap: 0-0 Ckp: 0-0
Best Rating: **84** 6/09 Pont 6f gd-fm

Fair; suited by 5-6f; handles fast and easy ground.

Jack O'Lantern

89 **73**

2-y-o b g Shamardal (USA)-Bush Cat (USA) (Kingmambo (USA))

J H M Gosden H R H Princess Haya Of Jordan

Placings:3 **(6991)**

2009: 7^{3}G,

	Starts	1st	2nd	3rd	Win & Pl
Career Total (Turf)	1	0	0	1	674

Going (Turf): **Sf: 0-0 GS: 0-0 Gd: 0-1 GF: 0-0 Fm: 0-0**
Distance: 5f/6f: 0-0 7f-8f: 0-1 9f-13f: 0-0 14f+: 0-0
Track : LH: 0-0 RH: 0-0 Tight: 0-0 Gall: 0-0
Aids: Bl: 0-0 Vi: 0-0 Tstrap: 0-0 Ckp: 0-0
Best Rating: **73** 10/09 Donc 7f good

Fair; stays 7f; acts on good ground.

Jack Rackham

99(102) (78)**75**

5-y-o ch g Kyllachy-Hill Welcome (Most Welcome)

B Smart Mrs F Denniff

Placings:3224/1135300/00000-**250203** **(7739)**

2009: 6^{2}SS, 6^{5}SS, 6^{0}GF, 6^{2}GF, 6^{0}GF, 6^{3}SD,

	Starts	1st	2nd	3rd	Win & Pl
Career Total (Turf)	18	2	3	3	18575
Career Total (AW)	4	0	1	1	1143
88 5/07 Bevl 5f (0-85)H				G-F	£6477
72 4/07 Thsk 5f				FRM	£3886

Total win prize-money £10363

Going (Turf): Sf: 0-2 GS: 0-1 Gd: 0-4 **GF: 1-10 Fm: 1-1**
Distance: **5f/6f: 2-20** 7f-8f: 0-2 9f-13f: 0-0 14f+: 0-0
Track : LH: 0-5 RH: 0-1 Tight: 0-1 Gall: 0-0
Aids: Bl: 0-0 Vi: 0-6 Tstrap: 0-0 Ckp: 0-0
Best Rating: **93** 8/07 Donc 5f140y gd-fm

Modest; effective over 5f-6f; acts on fast ground and on sand; has worn a visor.

Jack Rio (IRE)

(87) (53)**71**

4-y-o gr f Captain Rio-Order Of Success (USA) (With Approval (CAN))

Niall Moran Tom Hunt

Placings:3002000/64602364-500**600** **(7817)**

2009: 12^{5}GF, 12^{0}GF, 10^{0}GF, 10^{6}SD, 10^{0}SD, 9^{0}SD,

	Starts	1st	2nd	3rd	Win & Pl
Career Total (Turf)	18	0	2	2	5063
Career Total (AW)	3	0	0	0	

Going (Turf): **Sf: 0-3 GS: 0-0 Gd: 0-6 GF: 0-4 Fm: 0-0**
Distance: 5f/6f: 0-2 7f-8f: 0-8 9f-13f: 0-11 14f+: 0-0
Track : LH: 0-5 RH: 0-14 Tight: 0-1 Gall: 0-0
Aids: Bl: 0-3 Vi: 0-0 Tstrap: 0-10 Ckp: 0-10
Best Rating: **71** 6/08 Slig 1m2f good

Jack's House (IRE)

96(88) (50)**53**

3-y-o b g Danetime (IRE)-Groupetime (USA) (Gilded Time (USA))

Miss J A Camacho (Jane Chapple-Hyam 29/5) Lee Bolingbroke Racing 3

Placings:00005-3540005 **(5972)**

2009: 7^{3}SD, 7^{5}SD, 6^{4}GF, 6^{0}G, 7^{0}GF, 6^{0}S, 7^{5}GF,

	Starts	1st	2nd	3rd	Win & Pl
Career Total (Turf)	6	0	0	0	144
Career Total (AW)	6	0	0	1	302

Going (Turf): **Sf: 0-2 GS: 0-0 Gd: 0-1 GF: 0-3 Fm: 0-0**

Distance: 5f/6f: 0-2 7f-8f: 0-8 9f-13f: 0-2 14f+: 0-0
Track : LH: 0-7 RH: 0-1 Tight: 0-3 Gall: 0-1
Aids: Bl: 0-0 Vi: 0-0 Tstrap: 0-2 Ckp: 0-2
Best Rating: 53 5/09 Yarm 6f3y gd-fm

Jackday (IRE)

103 **70**

4-y-o b g Daylami (IRE)-Magic Lady (IRE) (Bigstone (IRE))
T D Easterby Mrs Jean P Connew

Placings:0600/064140-3242422414 **(7084)**
2009: 16^{3}G, 16^{2}GF, 16^{4}GF, 16^{2}G, 16^{4}GS, 16^{2}G, 16^{2}GS, 17^{4}GF, 15^{1}G, 15^{4}S,

	Starts	1st	2nd	3rd	Win & Pl
Career Total (Turf)	20	2	4	1	10854

70 10/09 Catt 1m7f177y (0-60)H GD £2047
61 7/08 Bevl 2m35y (0-65)H G-F £2590
Total win prize-money £4637

Going (Turf): Sf: 0-2 GS: 0-3 **Gd: 1-9 GF: 1-6** Fm: 0-0
Distance: 5f/6f: 0-0 7f-8f: 0-4 9f-13f: 0-3 **14f+: 2-13**
Track : LH: 1-11 RH: 1-8 **Tight: 2-13** Gall: 0-2
Aids: Bl: 0-0 Vi: 0-0 Tstrap: 0-0 Ckp: 0-0
Best Rating: **70** 10/09 Catt 1m7f177y good

Modest; stays 2m; acts on most ground.

Jackie Danny

84 **48**

2-y-o b f Mujahid (USA)-Baileys Applause (Royal Applause)
C A Dwyer Mrs Shelley Dwyer

Placings:054 **(2457)**
2009: 5^{0}G, 5^{5}GF, 5^{4}GF,

	Starts	1st	2nd	3rd	Win & Pl
Career Total (Turf)	3	0	0	0	144

Going (Turf): **Sf: 0-0 GS: 0-0 Gd: 0-1 GF: 0-2 Fm: 0-0**
Distance: 5f/6f: 0-3 7f-8f: 0-0 9f-13f: 0-0 14f+: 0-0
Track : LH: 0-0 RH: 0-0 Tight: 0-0 Gall: 0-1
Aids: Bl: 0-0 Vi: 0-0 Tstrap: 0-0 Ckp: 0-0
Best Rating: **48** 5/09 Ling 5f gd-fm

Jackie Kiely

94(107) (69)**68**

8-y-o ch g Vettori (IRE)-Fudge (Polar Falcon (USA))
R Brotherton Mrs Carol Newman

Placings:00/62055421011003040350000/6000503063405012100013402/01116430200320513120 1/2435531005033024/24142335330656-04535022000 2332 **(7840)**
2009: 12^{0}SD, 12^{4}SD, 10^{5}GF, 11^{3}SD, 10^{5}F, 11^{0}G, 12^{2}SD, 12^{2}GS, 12^{0}GF, 16^{0}S, 12^{0}SD, 12^{2}SD, 12^{3}SD, 14^{3}SD, 12^{2}SS,

	Starts	1st	2nd	3rd	Win & Pl
Career Total (Turf)	64	6	6	10	34143
Career Total (AW)	52	8	9	9	31048

79 1/08 Sthl 1m3f (0-70)H STD £2730
76 4/07 Sthl 1m4f (0-75)H STD £3071
77 12/06 Sthl 1m4f (0-75)H STD £3238
70 9/06 Chep 1m2f36y (0-65)H GD £3238
69 8/06 Epsm 1m2f18y (0-70)H GD £3886
67 2/06 Sthl 1m4f (0-65)H STD £2388
60 2/06 Sthl 1m6f (0-45) STD £1706
63 1/06 Sthl 1m4f (0-45) STD £1365
58 11/05 Sthl 1m4f (0-45) STD £1446
69 8/05 Chep 1m2f36y (0-55)H GD £3122
62 8/05 Brig 1m1f209y (0-55)H GD £3068
73 7/04 NmkJ 1m2f E(0-70)H GD £4260
61 7/04 Brig 1m1f209yF(0-55)H G-F £3045
60 6/04 Sthl 1m4f F(0-55)H STD £3304
Total win prize-money £39873

Going (Turf): Sf: 0-4 GS: 0-5 **Gd: 5-21** GF: 1-26 Fm: 0-8
Distance: 5f/6f: 0-0 7f-8f: 0-2 **9f-13f: 13-102** 14f+: 1-12
Track : **LH: 13-98** RH: 1-16 Tight: 1-35 Gall: 1-7
Aids: Bl: 0-0 Vi: 0-0 Tstrap: 0-4 Ckp: 0-4
Best Rating: **82** 5/05 Ches 1m2f75y gd-sft

Moderate; effective over 1m4f-1m6f; handles a sound surface on turf; acts well on sand; has worn blinkers and cheekpieces and often tongue tied.

Jacobite Prince (IRE)

95(81) (6)**65**

3-y-o b g Chevalier (IRE)-Kind Gesture (IRE) (Alzao (USA))
M H Tompkins Raceworld

Placings:0040-000600 **(5750)**
2009: 8^{0}G, 7^{0}G, 8^{0}GS, 10^{6}S, 10^{0}GF, 10^{0}SD,

	Starts	1st	2nd	3rd	Win & Pl
Career Total (Turf)	9	0	0	0	373
Career Total (AW)	1	0	0	0	

Going (Turf): **Sf: 0-1 GS: 0-3 Gd: 0-2 GF: 0-3 Fm: 0-0**
Distance: 5f/6f: 0-1 7f-8f: 0-4 9f-13f: 0-5 14f+: 0-0
Track : LH: 0-6 RH: 0-1 Tight: 0-5 Gall: 0-0
Aids: Bl: 0-1 Vi: 0-0 Tstrap: 0-1 Ckp: 0-1
Best Rating: **65** 8/08 Bevl 7f100y gd-sft

Jaconet (USA)

105(114) (110)**95**

4-y-o ch f Hussonet (USA)-Radiant Rocket (USA) (Peteski (CAN))
T D Barron R G Toes

Placings:350/40011215-111030311001 **(7488)**
2009: 5^{1}SD, 5^{1}GF, 5^{1}GF, 5^{0}G, 6^{3}GF, 5^{0}G, 6^{3}G, 5^{1}SD, 6^{1}SD, 5^{0}GF, 5^{0}GF, 6^{1}SD,

	Starts	1st	2nd	3rd	Win & Pl
Career Total (Turf)	18	5	1	3	27733
Career Total (AW)	5	4	0	0	40778

107 11/09 Ling 6f STD £22708
110 9/09 Ling 6f (0-95)H STD £7771
97 8/09 Wolv 5f216y (0-95)H STD £7569
94 4/09 Rdcr 5f (0-85)H G-F £4857
90 4/09 Muss 5f (0-85)H G-F £6231
83 3/09 Wolv 5f216y (0-75)H STD £2729
76 7/08 York 5f89y (0-80)H G-F £6152
67 7/08 Ayr 6f (0-60)H G-S £2590
49 6/08 Ripn 6f G-F £2590
Total win prize-money £63199

Going (Turf): Sf: 0-1 GS: 1-1 Gd: 0-7 **GF: 4-9** Fm: 0-0
Distance: **5f/6f: 9-22** 7f-8f: 0-1 9f-13f: 0-0 14f+: 0-0
Track : **LH: 4-5** RH: 0-1 **Tight: 4-5** Gall: 0-0
Aids: **Bl: 9-17** Vi: 0-0 Tstrap: 0-0 Ckp: 0-0
Best Rating: **110** 9/09 Ling 6f stand

Smart on Polytrack/very useful on turf; effective over 5f-6f; acts on fast ground on turf; has worn blinkers; likes to race prominently.

Jacqueline Quest (IRE)

104 **90**

2-y-o b f Rock Of Gibraltar (IRE)-Coquette Rouge (IRE) (Croco Rouge (IRE))
H R A Cecil N Martin

Placings:210 **(7033)**
2009: 6^{2}GF, 7^{1}GF, 7^{0}S,

	Starts	1st	2nd	3rd	Win & Pl
Career Total (Turf)	3	1	1	0	6626

90 9/09 Ches 7f2y G-F £5180
Total win prize-money £5181

Going (Turf): Sf: 0-1 GS: 0-0 Gd: 0-0 **GF: 1-2** Fm: 0-0
Distance: 5f/6f: 0-0 **7f-8f: 1-3** 9f-13f: 0-0 14f+: 0-0
Track : **LH: 1-1** RH: 0-0 **Tight: 1-1** Gall: 0-0
Aids: Bl: 0-0 Vi: 0-0 Tstrap: 0-0 Ckp: 0-0
Best Rating: **90** 9/09 Ches 7f2y gd-fm

Very useful; stays 7f; acts on fast ground.

Jadalee (IRE)

105(111) (82)**80**

6-y-o b g Desert Prince (IRE)-Lionne (Darshaan)
D E Pipe (G A Butler 1/11) Stef Stefanou

Placings:021/52216/05/000004-50461521624 **(7201)**
2009: 13^{5}SD, 14^{0}S, 16^{4}SD, 11^{6}SD, 14^{1}G, 12^{5}SD, 16^{2}SD, 13^{1}SD, 13^{6}SD, 13^{2}SS, 13^{4}SD,

	Starts	1st	2nd	3rd	Win & Pl
Career Total (Turf)	16	3	3	0	54342
Career Total (AW)	11	1	2	0	8077

81 9/09 Wolv 1m5f194y (0-80)H STD £5046
80 7/09 NmkJ 1m6f175y (0-85)H GD £5828
107 8/06 Gdwd 1m6f GD £17034
85 9/05 Bath 1m2f46y FRM £3474
Total win prize-money £31382

Going (Turf): Sf: 0-1 GS: 0-0 **Gd: 2-10** GF: 0-4 Fm: 1-1
Distance: 5f/6f: 0-0 7f-8f: 0-2 9f-13f: 1-14 **14f+: 3-11**
Track : LH: 2-15 RH: 2-11 **Tight: 3-9** Gall: 1-10
Aids: Bl: 0-0 Vi: 0-0 Tstrap: 2-9 Ckp: 2-9
Best Rating: **113** 9/06 York 1m5f197y good

Fair; Listed winner and Group placed; stays 1m6f; acts on good and faster ground; goes on Polytrack; has worn cheekpieces.

Jafaru

102(109) (69)**70**

5-y-o b g Silver Hawk (USA)-Rafha (Kris)
G L Moore Miss S Bowles

Placings:000/51123P0/2406604-3122335 **(4170)**
2009: 13^{3}SD, 11^{1}GF, 11^{2}GF, 16^{2}SD, 11^{3}GF, 11^{3}GF, 11^{5}SD,

	Starts	1st	2nd	3rd	Win & Pl
Career Total (Turf)	18	3	3	3	12312
Career Total (AW)	6	0	1	1	884

60 5/09 Brig 1m3f196y (0-55)H G-F £2590
70 5/07 Chep 1m4f23y (0-60)H GD £2266
62 5/07 Haml 1m4f17y (0-70)H GD £3238
Total win prize-money £8096

Going (Turf): Sf: 0-1 GS: 0-4 **Gd: 2-4** GF: 1-9 Fm: 0-0
Distance: 5f/6f: 0-0 7f-8f: 0-3 **9f-13f: 3-16** 14f+: 0-5
Track : **LH: 2-11** RH: 1-11 **Tight: 1-13** Gall: 0-0
Aids: **Bl: 3-15** Vi: 0-0 Tstrap: 0-2 Ckp: 0-2
Best Rating: **70** 5/08 Haml 1m5f9y gd-sft

Moderate; stays 1m4f; acts on most ground; has worn blinkers and cheekpieces.

Jafir (USA)

84 **57**

3-y-o ch c Speightstown (USA)-Day Mate (USA) (Dayjur (USA))
B J Meehan Saleh Al Homaizi & Imad Al Sagar

Placings:0 (6741)
2009: 8^{0}GS,

	Starts	1st	2nd	3rd	Win & Pl
Career Total (Turf)	1	0	0	0	

Going (Turf): **Sf: 0-0 GS: 0-1 Gd: 0-0 GF: 0-0 Fm: 0-0**
Distance: 5f/6f: 0-0 7f-8f: 0-0 9f-13f: 0-1 14f+: 0-0
Track : LH: 0-0 RH: 0-1 Tight: 0-1 Gall: 0-0
Aids: Bl: 0-0 Vi: 0-0 Tstrap: 0-0 Ckp: 0-0
Best Rating: **57** 10/09 Wind 1m67y gd-sft

Jagger

89(107) (94)94
9-y-o gr g Linamix (FR)-Sweetness Herself (Unfuwain (USA))
G A Butler C McFadden

Placings:0/32416011/03040/**U**5036156/6006600/000**5**/353 203153-655 (2146)
2009: 16^{6}SD, 14^{5}GF, 12^{5}SD,

	Starts	1st	2nd	3rd	Win & Pl
Career Total (Turf)	34	3	1	4	102090
Career Total (AW)	11	2	1	3	14846
93	8/08	GrLe	1m6f	(0-95)H	STD £7477
110	8/05	Ches	1m5f89y	(0-110)H	G-F £17400
102	9/03	Asct	1m4f	B H	FRM £34800
99	8/03	York	1m5f197yB(0-100)H		G-F £22066
89	6/03	Ling	1m2f	E(0-70)H	STD £3653

Total win prize-money £85396

Going (Turf): Sf: 0-3 GS: 0-7 Gd: 0-12 **GF: 2-9** Fm: 1-3
Distance: 5f/6f: 0-3 7f-8f: 0-4 9f-13f: 2-19 **14f+: 3-19**
Track : **LH: 4-20** RH: 1-13 Tight: 2-16 **Gall: 3-11**
Aids: Bl: 0-0 Vi: 0-0 Tstrap: 0-6 Ckp: 0-6
Best Rating: **110** 9/05 Donc 2m2f good

Useful; formerly smart; stays 1m6f; acts on fast ground and on Polytrack; has worn a tongue tie and cheekpieces.

Jago (SWI)

95(103) (72)52
6-y-o b g Brief Truce (USA)-Jariyah (USA) (It's The One (USA))
A M Hales Four Counties Partnership

Placings:13/2201504/533**022**/**21**-00040 (2039)
2009: 10^{0}SD, 13^{0}SD, 12^{0}SD, 9^{4}SD, 10^{0}GS,

	Starts	1st	2nd	3rd	Win & Pl
Career Total (Turf)	13	2	2	3	9118
Career Total (AW)	9	1	3	0	4495
72	3/08	Wolv	1m4f50y	(0-65)H	STD £2047
	6/06	Aven	1m2f165y		GD £1699
	6/05	Frau	5f165y		GD £2201

Total win prize-money £5949

Going (Turf): Sf: 0-3 GS: 0-1 **Gd: 2-5** GF: 0-0 Fm: 0-0
Distance: 5f/6f: 1-1 7f-8f: 0-3 **9f-13f: 2-18** 14f+: 0-0
Track : **LH: 1-9** RH: 0-1 **Tight: 1-8** Gall: 0-1
Aids: Bl: 0-0 Vi: 0-0 Tstrap: 0-1 Ckp: 0-1
Best Rating: **72** 3/08 Wolv 1m4f50y stand

Modest; ex-Swiss; stays 1m5f and acts on Polytrack.

Jairzihno

99(98) (82)82
2-y-o b c Royal Applause-Polish Belle (Polish Precedent (USA))
J R Best Findlay & Bloom

Placings:136423 (6693)
2009: 5^{1}GF, 6^{3}GS, 7^{6}G, 8^{4}GF, 8^{2}SD, 7^{3}GS,

	Starts	1st	2nd	3rd	Win & Pl
Career Total (Turf)	5	1	0	2	4923
Career Total (AW)	1	0	1	0	1156
76	6/09	Leic	5f218y		G-F £3238

Total win prize-money £3238

Going (Turf): Sf: 0-0 GS: 0-2 Gd: 0-1 **GF: 1-2** Fm: 0-0
Distance: **5f/6f: 1-2** 7f-8f: 0-3 9f-13f: 0-1 14f+: 0-0
Track : LH: 0-0 RH: 0-4 Tight: 0-1 Gall: 0-0
Aids: Bl: 0-0 Vi: 0-0 Tstrap: 0-0 Ckp: 0-0
Best Rating: **82** 10/09 Gdwd 7f gd-sft

Useful 50,000euros colt; related to the useful sprinter Danehhurst; winner on debut over 6f on fast ground.

Jake The Snake (IRE)

98(107) (85)85
8-y-o ch g Intikhab (USA)-Tilbrook (IRE) (Don't Forget Me)
A W Carroll D Morgan & M B Clarke

Placings:1/0/162063**600023**-**1133131235343** (4502)
2009: 8^{1}SD, 7^{1}SD, 8^{3}SD, 7^{3}SD, 8^{1}SD, 8^{3}SD, 8^{1}SD, 8^{2}SD, 7^{3}SD, 6^{5}GF, 7^{3}SD, 8^{4}SD, 8^{3}G,

	Starts	1st	2nd	3rd	Win & Pl
Career Total (Turf)	8	0	1	2	3179
Career Total (AW)	19	6	2	6	20399
82	4/09	Kemp	1m		STD £1942
81	3/09	Ling	1m		STD £1878
77	2/09	Kemp	7f		STD £2047
82	1/09	Kemp	1m		STD £2047
84	4/08	Kemp	6f	(0-80)H	STD £4209
73	12/03	Ling	1m	D	STD £3146

Total win prize-money £15271

Going (Turf): **Sf: 0-2 GS: 0-1 Gd: 0-1 GF: 0-4 Fm: 0-0**
Distance: 5f/6f: 1-3 **7f-8f: 5-23** 9f-13f: 0-1 14f+: 0-0
Track : LH: 2-7 **RH: 4-13 Tight: 2-6** Gall: 0-0
Aids: Bl: 0-0 Vi: 0-0 Tstrap: 0-0 Ckp: 0-0
Best Rating: **85** 4/09 Kemp 1m stand

Fair; effective from 6f-1m; acts good and easier ground; goes well on Polytrack.

Jalamid (IRE)

86(100) (47)46
7-y-o b g Danehill (USA)-Vignelaure (IRE) (Royal Academy (USA))
M A Barnes M Barnes

Placings:10/16014/000600/0300500/**000**040-00 (1226)
2009: 13^{0}SD, 9^{0}GF,

	Starts	1st	2nd	3rd	Win & Pl
Career Total (Turf)	26	3	0	1	32218
Career Total (AW)	3	0	0	0	
107	8/05	Rdcr	1m	(0-100)H	G-F £14062
103	4/05	Newb	1m	(0-95)H	G-S £10268
73	6/04	Sand	7f16y	D	G-F £4953

Total win prize-money £29284

Going (Turf): Sf: 0-0 GS: 1-7 Gd: 0-2 **GF: 2-16** Fm: 0-1
Distance: 5f/6f: 0-2 **7f-8f: 3-20** 9f-13f: 0-6 14f+: 0-1
Track : LH: 0-11 **RH: 1-5** Tight: 0-6 Gall: 0-7
Aids: Bl: 0-1 Vi: 0-0 Tstrap: 0-0 Ckp: 0-0
Best Rating: **107** 8/05 Rdcr 1m gd-fm

Modest gelding, formerly very useful; effective at 6f-1m; acts on fast and easy ground; usually wears a tongue tie.

Jamaahir (USA)

(75) 66
6-y-o b g Bahri (USA)-Elrehaan (Sadler's Wells (USA))
George Baker The Futures Bright Partnership

Placings:0/06/600600/0 (0107)
2009: 12^{0}SD,

	Starts	1st	2nd	3rd	Win & Pl
Career Total (Turf)	9	0	0	0	0
Career Total (AW)	1	0	0	0	

Going (Turf): **Sf: 0-2 GS: 0-3 Gd: 0-4 GF: 0-0 Fm: 0-0**
Distance: 5f/6f: 0-0 7f-8f: 0-3 9f-13f: 0-6 14f+: 0-1
Track : LH: 0-2 RH: 0-4 Tight: 0-5 Gall: 0-1
Aids: Bl: 0-0 Vi: 0-0 Tstrap: 0-0 Ckp: 0-0
Best Rating: **66** 5/07 Newb 1m2f6y gd-sft

Jamarjo (IRE)

89(82) (51)62
2-y-o b g Marju (IRE)-Athlumney Lady (Lycius (USA))
S Gollings P J Martin

Placings:206 (7491)
2009: 6^{2}HY, 7^{0}S, 8^{6}SD,

	Starts	1st	2nd	3rd	Win & Pl
Career Total (Turf)	2	0	1	0	1156
Career Total (AW)	1	0	0	0	0

Going (Turf): **Sf: 0-2 GS: 0-0 Gd: 0-0 GF: 0-0 Fm: 0-0**
Distance: 5f/6f: 0-0 7f-8f: 0-2 9f-13f: 0-1 14f+: 0-0
Track : LH: 0-2 RH: 0-0 Tight: 0-2 Gall: 0-0
Aids: Bl: 0-0 Vi: 0-0 Tstrap: 0-0 Ckp: 0-0
Best Rating: **62** 7/09 Nott 6f15y heavy

Promising debut over 6f on heavy ground; well beaten next time.

Jamary (IRE)

(31)
2-y-o b/br f Grand Reward (USA)-Datsdawayitis (USA) (Known Fact (USA))
C E Brittain Saeed Manana

Placings:0 (3027)
2009: 7^{0}SD,

	Starts	1st	2nd	3rd	Win & Pl
Career Total (Turf)	0	0	0	0	
Career Total (AW)	1	0	0	0	

Going (Turf): **Sf: 0-0 GS: 0-0 Gd: 0-0 GF: 0-0 Fm: 0-0**
Distance: 5f/6f: 0-0 7f-8f: 0-1 9f-13f: 0-0 14f+: 0-0
Track : LH: 0-0 RH: 0-1 Tight: 0-0 Gall: 0-0
Aids: Bl: 0-0 Vi: 0-0 Tstrap: 0-0 Ckp: 0-0

James Barrymore

94(95) (69)68
2-y-o b c Fraam-Nine Red (Royal Applause)
R Hannon Raymond Tooth

Placings:6343250 (7788)
2009: 8^{6}SD, 7^{3}SD, 8^{4}SD, 7^{3}GF, 6^{2}GF, 7^{5}SD, 8^{0}SD,

	Starts	1st	2nd	3rd	Win & Pl
Career Total (Turf)	2	0	1	1	1312
Career Total (AW)	5	0	0	1	842

Going (Turf): **Sf: 0-0 GS: 0-0 Gd: 0-0 GF: 0-2 Fm: 0-0**
Distance: 5f/6f: 0-0 7f-8f: 0-6 9f-13f: 0-1 14f+: 0-0
Track : LH: 0-5 RH: 0-1 Tight: 0-4 Gall: 0-0
Aids: Bl: 0-0 Vi: 0-0 Tstrap: 0-0 Ckp: 0-0
Best Rating: **69** 8/09 Ling 1m stand

Modest; stays 1m; acts on fast ground and on Polytrack.

James Pollard (IRE)

97(96) (64)61

4-y-o ch g Indian Ridge-Manuetti (IRE) (Sadler's Wells (USA))

B J Llewellyn (D R C Elsworth 9/5) B J Llewellyn

Placings:000030-6000 **(6208)**

2009: 8^{6}GF, 8^{0}SD, 6^{0}GF, 10^{0}SD,

	Starts	1st	2nd	3rd	Win & Pl
Career Total (Turf)	4	0	0	0	0
Career Total (AW)	6	0	0	1	385

Going (Turf): **Sf: 0-0 GS: 0-2 Gd: 0-0 GF: 0-2 Fm: 0-0**
Distance: 5f/6f: 0-1 7f-8f: 0-4 9f-13f: 0-5 14f+: 0-0
Track : LH: 0-5 RH: 0-4 Tight: 0-4 Gall: 0-0
Aids: Bl: 0-0 Vi: 0-0 Tstrap: 0-0 Ckp: 0-0
Best Rating: **64** 10/08 Ling 1m2f stand

Modest; stays 1m2f and acts on Polytrack; can pull hard.

James Street (IRE)

82(95) (46)14

6-y-o b g Fruits Of Love (USA)-Humble Mission (Shack (USA))

Peter Grayson Jasper Partnership

Placings:005030/0155264620/0004000000066/00464060-000 **(4894)**

2009: 7^{0}SD, 7^{0}G, 6^{0}GS,

	Starts	1st	2nd	3rd	Win & Pl
Career Total (Turf)	13	0	1	0	1398
Career Total (AW)	25	1	1	1	5550

74 8/06 Ling 7f (0-70)H STD £3238
Total win prize-money £3239

Going (Turf): **Sf: 0-0 GS: 0-4 Gd: 0-2 GF: 0-7 Fm: 0-0**
Distance: 5f/6f: 0-13 **7f-8f: 1-20** 9f-13f: 0-5 14f+: 0-0
Track : **LH: 1-22** RH: 0-9 **Tight: 1-14** Gall: 0-4
Aids: Bl: 0-9 Vi: 0-10 Tstrap: 0-1 Ckp: 0-1
Best Rating: **77** 9/06 Pont 1m4y gd-sft

Moderate; stays 1m but better at 7f; acts on Polytrack and easy ground.

Jamleson Gold (IRE)

100(87) (59)80

6-y-o b g Desert Style (IRE)-Princess Of Zurich (IRE) (Law Society (USA))

Miss L A Perratt Shatin Racing Group

Placings:22163/044100/0001400/00465652420000-0006225005 **(6411)**

2009: 10^{0}GF, 9^{0}GF, 9^{0}G, 9^{6}G, 7^{2}GF, 8^{2}G, 8^{5}GS, 8^{0}S, 7^{0}G, 8^{5}GF,

	Starts	1st	2nd	3rd	Win & Pl
Career Total (Turf)	40	3	6	1	44424
Career Total (AW)	2	0	0	0	

89 8/07 Sand 7f16y (0-90)H G-S £8420
95 8/06 Newb 7f (0-100)H G-S £12464
82 8/05 Pont 6f GD £5616
Total win prize-money £26500

Going (Turf): Sf: 0-9 **GS: 2-8** Gd: 1-11 GF: 0-12 Fm: 0-0
Distance: 5f/6f: 1-3 **7f-8f: 2-29** 9f-13f: 0-10 14f+: 0-0
Track : LH: 1-16 RH: 1-13 Tight: 0-15 Gall: 0-2
Aids: Bl: 0-2 Vi: 0-0 Tstrap: 0-13 Ckp: 0-13
Best Rating: **95** 8/06 Newb 7f gd-sft

Useful; effective over 7f and stays 1m2f; acts on fast and easier ground; has worn cheekpieces.

Jane Of Arc (FR)

91 57

5-y-o ch m Trempolino (USA)-Aerleon Jane (Caerleon (USA))

J S Goldie C P F Racing

Placings:0120/060650300/043204304610-40445 **(3291)**

2009: 9^{4}GF, 14^{0}G, 13^{4}GF, 12^{4}GF, 13^{5}GF,

	Starts	1st	2nd	3rd	Win & Pl
Career Total (Turf)	30	2	2	3	10320

57 9/08 Muss 1m4f GD £1942
71 6/06 Thsk 7f G-F £3886
Total win prize-money £5829

Going (Turf): Sf: 0-3 GS: 0-4 **Gd: 1-10 GF: 1-13** Fm: 0-0
Distance: 5f/6f: 0-1 7f-8f: 1-5 9f-13f: 1-18 14f+: 0-6
Track : LH: 1-13 RH: 1-13 **Tight: 2-18** Gall: 0-2
Aids: Bl: 0-0 Vi: 0-1 Tstrap: 1-12 Ckp: 1-12
Best Rating: **71** 6/06 Thsk 7f gd-fm

Moderate; stays 1m4f; acts on good and good to firm.

Jane's Payoff (IRE)

(96) (69)61

4-y-o b f Danetime (IRE)-Alimony (IRE) (Groom Dancer (USA))

Mrs L C Jewell Keith C Bennett

Placings:53/31360-00 **(4204)**

2009: 5^{0}SD, 5^{0}SD,

	Starts	1st	2nd	3rd	Win & Pl
Career Total (Turf)	2	0	0	1	482
Career Total (AW)	7	1	0	2	2818

69 4/08 Wolv 5f20y (0-65)H STD £2047
Total win prize-money £2047

Going (Turf): **Sf: 0-1 GS: 0-0 Gd: 0-0 GF: 0-1 Fm: 0-0**
Distance: **5f/6f: 1-8** 7f-8f: 0-1 9f-13f: 0-0 14f+: 0-0
Track : **LH: 1-5** RH: 0-2 **Tight: 1-2** Gall: 0-2
Aids: Bl: 0-0 Vi: 0-0 Tstrap: 0-0 Ckp: 0-0
Best Rating: **69** 4/08 Wolv 5f20y stand

Modest; stays 6f; acts on Polytrack.

Janeiro (IRE)

97(92) (81)87

2-y-o b g Captain Rio-Aspired (IRE) (Mark Of Esteem (IRE))

Tom Dascombe Basing Bellman Newton Stroud

Placings:4322015 **(4901)**

2009: 5^{4}SD, 5^{3}G, 6^{2}SD, 6^{2}GF, 6^{0}SD, 7^{1}G, 6^{5}GF,

	Starts	1st	2nd	3rd	Win & Pl
Career Total (Turf)	4	1	1	1	5387
Career Total (AW)	3	0	1	0	1493

87 7/09 Yarm 7f3y GD £2590
Total win prize-money £2590

Going (Turf): Sf: 0-0 GS: 0-0 **Gd: 1-2** GF: 0-2 Fm: 0-0
Distance: 5f/6f: 0-5 **7f-8f: 1-2** 9f-13f: 0-0 14f+: 0-0
Track : LH: 0-1 RH: 0-1 Tight: 0-1 Gall: 0-0
Aids: Bl: 0-0 Vi: 0-1 Tstrap: 0-0 Ckp: 0-0
Best Rating: **87** 7/09 Yarm 7f3y good

Useful; stays 7f; acts on fast ground and on sand; has worn a visor.

Janshe Gold

86(86) (43)57

4-y-o ch f Bertolini (USA)-Rekindled Flame (IRE) (Kings Lake (USA))

J G Portman Good Connection Ii

Placings:0000-50 **(1974)**

2009: 8^{5}GF, 10^{0}F,

	Starts	1st	2nd	3rd	Win & Pl
Career Total (Turf)	5	0	0	0	0
Career Total (AW)	1	0	0	0	

Going (Turf): **Sf: 0-1 GS: 0-1 Gd: 0-1 GF: 0-1 Fm: 0-1**
Distance: 5f/6f: 0-0 7f-8f: 0-0 9f-13f: 0-6 14f+: 0-0
Track : LH: 0-5 RH: 0-1 Tight: 0-3 Gall: 0-1
Aids: Bl: 0-0 Vi: 0-0 Tstrap: 0-0 Ckp: 0-0
Best Rating: **57** 4/08 Wind 1m67y good

January

(100) (84)70

6-y-o gr g Daylami (IRE)-Noushkey (Polish Precedent (USA))

T M Walsh M A Ryan

Placings:5/562351-60000 **(7382a)**

2009: 8^{6}SD, 10^{0}FZ, 7^{0}SD, 8^{0}SD, 10^{0}SD,

	Starts	1st	2nd	3rd	Win & Pl
Career Total (Turf)	5	0	1	0	1125
Career Total (AW)	7	1	0	1	4355

84 12/08 Wolv 1m141y STD £3885
Total win prize-money £3886

Going (Turf): **Sf: 0-0 GS: 0-0 Gd: 0-1 GF: 0-2 Fm: 0-0**
Distance: 5f/6f: 0-0 7f-8f: 0-4 **9f-13f: 1-6** 14f+: 0-2
Track : **LH: 1-9** RH: 0-3 **Tight: 1-2** Gall: 0-1
Aids: Bl: 0-0 Vi: 0-0 Tstrap: 0-0 Ckp: 0-0
Best Rating: **84** 12/08 Wolv 1m141y stand

Japura (USA)

(95) (56)69

5-y-o ch g Giant's Causeway (USA)-Exchange Place (USA) (Affirmed (USA))

T J Pitt The Camels Back Partnership

Placings:3/00-560 **(0546)**

2009: 9^{5}SD, 13^{6}SD, 12^{0}SD,

	Starts	1st	2nd	3rd	Win & Pl
Career Total (Turf)	1	0	0	1	816
Career Total (AW)	5	0	0	0	0

Going (Turf): **Sf: 0-0 GS: 0-0 Gd: 0-0 GF: 0-0 Fm: 0-0**
Distance: 5f/6f: 0-1 7f-8f: 0-2 9f-13f: 0-2 14f+: 0-1
Track : LH: 0-5 RH: 0-1 Tight: 0-4 Gall: 0-0
Aids: Bl: 0-0 Vi: 0-0 Tstrap: 0-1 Ckp: 0-1
Best Rating: **69** 6/07 Navn 1m yield

Jaq's Sister

68(86) (49)

3-y-o b f Bertolini (USA)-Polly Golightly (Weldnaas (USA))

M Blanshard David Sykes

Placings:60-36000 **(7609)**

2009: 7^{3}SD, 8^{6}SD, 7^{0}SF, 8^{0}GF, 8^{0}SD,

	Starts	1st	2nd	3rd	Win & Pl
Career Total (Turf)	2	0	0	0	0
Career Total (AW)	5	0	0	1	385

Going (Turf): Sf: 0-1 GS: 0-0 Gd: 0-0 GF: 0-1 Fm: 0-0
Distance: 5f/6f: 0-0 7f-8f: 0-6 9f-13f: 0-1 14f+: 0-0
Track : LH: 0-5 RH: 0-1 Tight: 0-5 Gall: 0-0
Aids: Bl: 0-2 Vi: 0-0 Tstrap: 0-0 Ckp: 0-0
Best Rating: 49 1/09 Wolv 7f32y stand

Jargelle (IRE)

108(95) (81)**103**
3-y-o b f Kheleyf (USA)-Winter Tern (USA) (Arctic Tern (USA))
K A Ryan (E Martins 12/2) Abdul Rahman Al Jasmi

Placings:31130-4526032 **(5507)**
2009: 7^{4}SD, 6^{5}G, 5^{2}G, 5^{6}GF, 5^{0}G, 5^{3}GF, 5^{2}G,

	Starts	1st	2nd	3rd	Win & Pl
Career Total (Turf)	11	2	2	3	105949
Career Total (AW)	1	0	0	0	1736

99 7/08 Newb 5f34y GD £79548
82 7/08 Nott 5f13y FRM £3070
Total win prize-money £82619

Going (Turf): Sf: 0-0 GS: 0-0 **Gd: 1-6** GF: 0-4 **Fm: 1-1**
Distance: 5f/6f: 2-10 7f-8f: 0-2 9f-13f: 0-0 14f+: 0-0
Track : LH: 0-3 RH: 0-0 Tight: 0-0 Gall: 0-2
Aids: Bl: 0-0 Vi: 0-0 Tstrap: 0-0 Ckp: 0-0
Best Rating: 103 8/09 Epsm 5f good

Very useful; winner of the 2008 Super Sprint at Newbury and Group placed; effective at 5f; acts on good and faster ground.

Jaroslaw (SAF)

(105) (80)
6-y-o b g Jallad (USA)-Dacha (SAF) (Russian Fox (USA))
D M Simcock H M K Al Mehairi

Placings:22/12053302112/62140050-**41** **(7810)**
2009: 7^{4}SD, 8^{1}SD,

	Starts	1st	2nd	3rd	Win & Pl
Career Total (Turf)	18	4	5	0	25971
Career Total (AW)	5	1	1	2	10439

78 12/09 Ling 1m STD £7641
3/08 Vaal 6f H GD £4825
12/07 Vaal 7f H GD £3623
11/07 Turf 6f H GD £3170
2/07 Vaal 5f GD £2943
Total win prize-money £22205

Going (Turf): Sf: 0-0 GS: 0-0 **Gd: 4-18** GF: 0-0 Fm: 0-0
Distance: 5f/6f: 3-12 7f-8f: 2-11 9f-13f: 0-0 14f+: 0-0
Track : LH: 1-1 RH: 0-1 **Tight: 1-1** Gall: 0-0
Aids: Bl: 0-1 Vi: 0-0 Tstrap: 0-1 Ckp: 0-1
Best Rating: 80 11/09 Kemp 7f stand

Very useful; formerly trained in South Africa; effective at 6f-1m; acts on good ground; goes on Polytrack; has worn cheekpieces.

Jarrah Bay

56(80) (44)**47**
3-y-o b f Mark Of Esteem (IRE)-Wannaplantatree (Niniski (USA))
J G M O'Shea Alan G Craddock

Placings:600-0 **(3803)**
2009: 8^{0}GF,

	Starts	1st	2nd	3rd	Win & Pl
Career Total (Turf)	3	0	0	0	0
Career Total (AW)	1	0	0	0	

Going (Turf): Sf: 0-0 GS: 0-2 Gd: 0-0 GF: 0-1 Fm: 0-0
Distance: 5f/6f: 0-2 7f-8f: 0-1 9f-13f: 0-1 14f+: 0-0
Track : LH: 0-0 RH: 0-1 Tight: 0-0 Gall: 0-0
Aids: Bl: 0-0 Vi: 0-0 Tstrap: 0-0 Ckp: 0-0
Best Rating: 47 8/08 Sals 6f gd-sft

Jarrow (IRE)

97(102) (81)**77**
2-y-o ch c Shamardal (USA)-Wolf Cleugh (IRE) (Last Tycoon)
M Johnston Sheikh Hamdan Bin Mohammed Al Maktoum

Placings:213 **(7552)**
2009: 6^{2}S, 6^{1}SD, 7^{3}SD,

	Starts	1st	2nd	3rd	Win & Pl
Career Total (Turf)	1	0	1	0	1831
Career Total (AW)	2	1	0	1	4698

81 11/09 Ling 6f STD £3561
Total win prize-money £3562

Going (Turf): Sf: 0-1 GS: 0-0 Gd: 0-0 GF: 0-0 Fm: 0-0
Distance: 5f/6f: 1-2 7f-8f: 0-1 9f-13f: 0-0 14f+: 0-0
Track : LH: 1-2 RH: 0-0 **Tight: 1-2** Gall: 0-0
Aids: Bl: 0-0 Vi: 0-0 Tstrap: 0-0 Ckp: 0-0
Best Rating: 81 11/09 Ling 6f stand

Useful; effective over 6f; acts on soft ground; goes on Polytrack.

Jarvo

76(99) (58)**58**
8-y-o b g Pursuit Of Love-Pinkie Rose (FR) (Kenmare (FR))
I W McInnes Mrs Julie Whitehead

Placings:02230/25400230**442**/**05**0450424300/**402**/440211 23060/63151010P6000035-600P00 **(4932)**
2009: 9^{6}SD, 9^{0}SD, 10^{0}GF, 9^{P}GF, 9^{0}GF, 8^{0}G,

	Starts	1st	2nd	3rd	Win & Pl
Career Total (Turf)	36	2	6	4	12259
Career Total (AW)	28	3	3	2	8127

58 5/08 Yarm 1m2f21y (0-55)H GD £1780
58 3/08 Wolv 1m1f103y (0-52)H STD £1774
56 1/08 Wolv 1m1f103y (0-50)H STD £1774
58 5/07 Wolv 1m1f103y (0-50)H STD £2388
57 4/07 Yarm 1m2f21y (0-45) G-F £1295
Total win prize-money £9015

Going (Turf): Sf: 0-1 GS: 0-4 **Gd: 1-6 GF: 1-21** Fm: 0-4
Distance: 5f/6f: 0-2 7f-8f: 0-8 **9f-13f: 5-54** 14f+: 0-0
Track : LH: 5-42 RH: 0-17 **Tight: 5-33** Gall: 0-4
Aids: Bl: 0-3 **Vi: 3-14** Tstrap: 0-2 Ckp: 0-2
Best Rating: 66 8/04 NmkJ 7f soft

Moderate; effective at around 1m2f; acts on fast ground; also goes Polytrack; has worn a visor.

Jaser

101(99) (76)**97**
4-y-o ch c Alhaarth (IRE)-Waafiah (Anabaa (USA))
P W Chapple-Hyam Ziad A Galadari

Placings:001/113003-0600 **(6168)**
2009: 8^{0}S, 10^{6}GS, 10^{0}S, 8^{0}SD,

	Starts	1st	2nd	3rd	Win & Pl
Career Total (Turf)	11	2	0	2	18073
Career Total (AW)	2	1	0	0	2494

96 4/08 Nott 1m54y (0-80)H SFT £4857
87 4/08 Nott 1m54y (0-70)H SFT £2590
68 11/07 Ling 1m STD £2493
Total win prize-money £9941

Going (Turf): Sf: 2-4 GS: 0-3 Gd: 0-1 GF: 0-3 Fm: 0-0
Distance: 5f/6f: 0-0 7f-8f: 1-7 **9f-13f: 2-6** 14f+: 0-0
Track : LH: 3-7 RH: 0-2 **Tight: 1-2** Gall: 0-2
Aids: Bl: 0-0 Vi: 0-0 Tstrap: 0-0 Ckp: 0-0
Best Rating: 97 5/08 Hayd 1m30y gd-fm

Very useful; effective over 1m-1m2f; acts on soft ground and on Polytrack.

Jaslyn (IRE)

(91) (46)**46**
3-y-o b/br f Pyrus (USA)-Ruby Julie (Clantime)
J R Weymes J Wilde

Placings:064543400-6 **(0010)**
2009: 6^{6}SS,

	Starts	1st	2nd	3rd	Win & Pl
Career Total (Turf)	5	0	0	1	770
Career Total (AW)	5	0	0	0	505

Going (Turf): Sf: 0-1 GS: 0-0 Gd: 0-2 GF: 0-1 Fm: 0-1
Distance: 5f/6f: 0-6 7f-8f: 0-4 9f-13f: 0-0 14f+: 0-0
Track : LH: 0-5 RH: 0-2 Tight: 0-4 Gall: 0-2
Aids: Bl: 0-0 Vi: 0-0 Tstrap: 0-0 Ckp: 0-0
Best Rating: 46 11/08 Muss 7f30y soft

Jasmeno

81 61
2-y-o b f Catcher In The Rye (IRE)-Jasmick (IRE) (Definite Article)
H Morrison Melksham Craic

Placings:04 **(6727)**
2009: 8^{0}GF, 8^{4}S,

	Starts	1st	2nd	3rd	Win & Pl
Career Total (Turf)	2	0	0	0	216

Going (Turf): Sf: 0-1 GS: 0-0 Gd: 0-0 GF: 0-1 Fm: 0-0
Distance: 5f/6f: 0-0 7f-8f: 0-2 9f-13f: 0-0 14f+: 0-0
Track : LH: 0-1 RH: 0-0 Tight: 0-0 Gall: 0-1
Aids: Bl: 0-0 Vi: 0-0 Tstrap: 0-0 Ckp: 0-0
Best Rating: 61 10/09 Sals 1m soft

Jasmine Scent (IRE)

66 1
2-y-o ch f Namid-Sky Galaxy (USA) (Sky Classic (CAN))
J A Osborne Liam Mulryan

Placings:00 **(2978)**
2009: 5^{0}GF, 6^{0}GF,

	Starts	1st	2nd	3rd	Win & Pl
Career Total (Turf)	2	0	0	0	

Going (Turf): Sf: 0-0 GS: 0-0 Gd: 0-0 GF: 0-2 Fm: 0-0
Distance: 5f/6f: 0-2 7f-8f: 0-0 9f-13f: 0-0 14f+: 0-0
Track : LH: 0-0 RH: 0-0 Tight: 0-0 Gall: 0-2
Aids: Bl: 0-0 Vi: 0-0 Tstrap: 0-0 Ckp: 0-0

Jasper Cliff

80 39
3-y-o b g Lucky Owners (NZ)-Catmint (Piccolo)
Mark Gillard David Herbert

Placings:00-0000 (3215)
2009: 10^{0}GS, 12^{0}GF, 8^{0}G, 9^{0}GF,

	Starts	1st	2nd	3rd	Win & Pl
Career Total (Turf)	6	0	0	0	

Going (Turf): Sf: 0-0 GS: 0-2 Gd: 0-1 GF: 0-3 Fm: 0-0
Distance: 5f/6f: 0-1 7f-8f: 0-1 9f-13f: 0-4 14f+: 0-0
Track : LH: 0-1 RH: 0-2 Tight: 0-3 Gall: 0-1
Aids: Bl: 0-2 Vi: 0-0 Tstrap: 0-0 Ckp: 0-0
Best Rating: 39 5/09 Chep 1m14y good

Jawaab (IRE)

104(102) (82)**83**
5-y-o ch g King's Best (USA)-Canis Star (Wolfhound (USA))
Mark Buckley C C Buckley

Placings:4042462/50630441342/046163336-430615 (7020)
2009: 8^{4}GF, 10^{3}GF, 12^{0}G, 10^{6}GF, 10^{1}G, 10^{5}GS,

	Starts	1st	2nd	3rd	Win & Pl
Career Total (Turf)	29	3	3	3	19760
Career Total (AW)	4	0	0	3	2053

83	8/09	Wwck	1m2f188y	(0-80)H	GD	£4857
78	9/08	Wwck	1m22y	(0-75)H	GD	£3412
73	9/07	Hayd	1m30y	(0-70)H	G-F	£3011

Total win prize-money £11281

Going (Turf): Sf: 0-2 GS: 0-6 **Gd: 2-11** GF: 1-10 Fm: 0-0
Distance: 5f/6f: 0-1 7f-8f: 0-15 **9f-13f: 3-17** 14f+: 0-0
Track : **LH: 3-14** RH: 0-10 Tight: 0-7 Gall: 0-5
Aids: Bl: 0-0 Vi: 0-0 Tstrap: 0-1 Ckp: 0-1
Best Rating: 83 8/09 Wwck 1m2f188y good

Fair; stays 1m3f; acts on fast and easy ground.

Jawaaher (USA)

70(95) (57)**24**
3-y-o b f Empire Maker (USA)-Winsome (Kris)
M Johnston Sheikh Hamdan Bin Mohammed Al Maktoum

Placings:300 (1128)
2009: 7^{3}SD, 7^{0}SD, 8^{0}GF,

	Starts	1st	2nd	3rd	Win & Pl
Career Total (Turf)	1	0	0	0	
Career Total (AW)	2	0	0	1	385

Going (Turf): Sf: 0-0 GS: 0-0 Gd: 0-0 GF: 0-1 Fm: 0-0
Distance: 5f/6f: 0-0 7f-8f: 0-2 9f-13f: 0-1 14f+: 0-0
Track : LH: 0-2 RH: 0-0 Tight: 0-2 Gall: 0-0
Aids: Bl: 0-0 Vi: 0-0 Tstrap: 0-0 Ckp: 0-0
Best Rating: 57 2/09 Wolv 7f32y stand

70,000gns half-sister to For Criquette, a winner in France at around 1m4f; effective over 7f; acts on Polytrack.

Jay Ell The Trier (IRE)

(77) (36)
5-y-o br g Talkin Man (CAN)-Killoughey Pride (IRE) (Top Of The World)
Tim Vaughan David Lovell

Placings:0 (0501)
2009: 13^{0}SD,

	Starts	1st	2nd	3rd	Win & Pl
Career Total (Turf)	0	0	0	0	
Career Total (AW)	1	0	0	0	

Going (Turf): Sf: 0-0 GS: 0-0 Gd: 0-0 GF: 0-0 Fm: 0-0
Distance: 5f/6f: 0-0 7f-8f: 0-0 9f-13f: 0-1 14f+: 0-0
Track : LH: 0-1 RH: 0-0 Tight: 0-1 Gall: 0-0
Aids: Bl: 0-0 Vi: 0-0 Tstrap: 0-0 Ckp: 0-0
Best Rating: 36 2/09 Ling 1m5f stand

Jay Gee Wigmo

91(89) (35)**53**
4-y-o b g First Trump-Queen Of Shannon (IRE) (Nordico (USA))
A W Carroll J Wigmore Racing Partnership

Placings:0000/006300-000400 (5242)
2009: 8^{0}GF, 8^{0}GF, 8^{0}SD, 11^{4}GF, 8^{0}GF, 8^{0}F,

	Starts	1st	2nd	3rd	Win & Pl
Career Total (Turf)	14	0	0	1	482
Career Total (AW)	2	0	0	0	

Going (Turf): Sf: 0-2 GS: 0-2 Gd: 0-0 GF: 0-9 Fm: 0-1
Distance: 5f/6f: 0-3 7f-8f: 0-6 9f-13f: 0-7 14f+: 0-0
Track : LH: 0-8 RH: 0-1 Tight: 0-5 Gall: 0-2
Aids: Bl: 0-0 Vi: 0-0 Tstrap: 0-0 Ckp: 0-0
Best Rating: 53 7/08 Chep 7f16y gd-fm

Jayyid (IRE)

(94) (53)
4-y-o b g Daylami (IRE)-Mellow Jazz (Lycius (USA))
C E Brittain C E Brittain

Placings:6406-0 (0500)
2009: 10^{0}SD,

	Starts	1st	2nd	3rd	Win & Pl
Career Total (Turf)	0	0	0	0	
Career Total (AW)	5	0	0	0	192

Going (Turf): Sf: 0-0 GS: 0-0 Gd: 0-0 GF: 0-0 Fm: 0-0
Distance: 5f/6f: 0-0 7f-8f: 0-2 9f-13f: 0-3 14f+: 0-0
Track : LH: 0-4 RH: 0-1 Tight: 0-3 Gall: 0-0
Aids: Bl: 0-0 Vi: 0-0 Tstrap: 0-0 Ckp: 0-0
Best Rating: 53 11/08 Kemp 1m4f stand

Jazacosta (USA)

99(93) (64)**81**
3-y-o ch g Dixieland Band (USA)-Dance With Del (USA) (Sword Dance)
Mrs A J Perrett John Connolly

Placings:63213304-00020000 (6784)
2009: 8^{0}SD, 9^{0}GF, 8^{0}GF, 7^{2}GF, 8^{0}G, 8^{0}GF, 8^{0}F, 10^{0}SS,

	Starts	1st	2nd	3rd	Win & Pl
Career Total (Turf)	14	1	2	3	11028
Career Total (AW)	2	0	0	0	

76	6/08	Leic	7f9y	G-F	£4533

Total win prize-money £4533

Going (Turf): Sf: 0-1 GS: 0-0 Gd: 0-4 **GF: 1-8** Fm: 0-1
Distance: 5f/6f: 0-1 **7f-8f: 1-10** 9f-13f: 0-5 14f+: 0-0
Track : LH: 0-3 RH: 0-6 Tight: 0-3 Gall: 0-0
Aids: Bl: 0-1 Vi: 0-0 Tstrap: 0-1 Ckp: 0-1
Best Rating: 81 8/08 NmkJ 1m good

Fair; effective at 7f; acts on good and fast ground.

Jazrawy

(96) (60)**59**
7-y-o b g Dansili-Dalila Di Mare (IRE) (Bob Back (USA))
A J McCabe Mrs B Ramsden

Placings:4412/0054**006**/000000220003403511/11104/05-20 (7840)
2009: 11^{2}SD, 12^{0}SS,

	Starts	1st	2nd	3rd	Win & Pl
Career Total (Turf)	14	0	2	1	3426
Career Total (AW)	24	6	2	1	21108

83	2/07	Sthl	1m4f	(0-70)H	STD	£3071
76	2/07	Sthl	1m4f	(0-65)H	STD	£2388
72	1/07	Sthl	1m4f		STD	£2184
64	12/06	Kemp	1m4f	(0-60)H	STD	£3412
59	12/06	Sthl	1m3f		STD	£2730
73	10/04	Wolv	1m141y		STD	£4270

Total win prize-money £18058

Going (Turf): Sf: 0-2 GS: 0-2 Gd: 0-3 GF: 0-6 Fm: 0-1
Distance: 5f/6f: 0-1 7f-8f: 0-6 **9f-13f: 6-26** 14f+: 0-5
Track : **LH: 5-28** RH: 1-8 **Tight: 1-15** Gall: 0-1
Aids: Bl: 0-0 Vi: 0-0 Tstrap: 0-0 Ckp: 0-0
Best Rating: 83 2/07 Sthl 1m4f stand

Modest; stays 1m6f; acts on sand; suited by forcing tactics.

Jazz Age (IRE)

92(84) (56)**68**
2-y-o b c Shamardal (USA)-Tender Is Thenight (IRE) (Barathea (IRE))
J A Glover (J H M Gosden 21/10) Allan Stennett

Placings:405 (7764)
2009: 8^{4}G, 8^{0}SD, 8^{5}SD,

	Starts	1st	2nd	3rd	Win & Pl
Career Total (Turf)	1	0	0	0	168
Career Total (AW)	2	0	0	0	0

Going (Turf): Sf: 0-0 GS: 0-0 Gd: 0-1 GF: 0-0 Fm: 0-0
Distance: 5f/6f: 0-0 7f-8f: 0-1 9f-13f: 0-2 14f+: 0-0
Track : LH: 0-2 RH: 0-1 Tight: 0-2 Gall: 0-0
Aids: Bl: 0-1 Vi: 0-0 Tstrap: 0-0 Ckp: 0-0
Best Rating: 68 10/09 Bath 1m5y good

Jealous Again (USA)

107 (96)**115**
2-y-o b f Trippi (USA)-Chi Sa (CAN) (Bold Ruckus (USA))
Wesley A Ward R Abrams,R Brewer,M Dutko,W Ward

Placings:121 (3015)
2009: 4^{1}FT, 5^{2}SD, 5^{1}GF,

	Starts	1st	2nd	3rd	Win & Pl
Career Total (Turf)	1	1	0	0	51093
Career Total (AW)	2	1	1	0	34131

115	6/09	Asct	5f	G-F	£51093
96	4/09	Keen	4f110y	FST	£18944

Total win prize-money £70037

Going (Turf): Sf: 0-0 GS: 0-0 Gd: 0-0 **GF: 1-1** Fm: 0-0
Distance: **5f/6f: 1-2** 7f-8f: 0-0 9f-13f: 0-0 14f+: 0-0
Track : LH: 0-0 RH: 0-0 Tight: 0-0 Gall: 0-0
Aids: **Bl: 2-3** Vi: 0-0 Tstrap: 0-0 Ckp: 0-0
Best Rating: 115 6/09 Asct 5f gd-fm

Useful; US trained when winner of the Queen Mary in 2009; since joined Godolphin; stays 5f and acts on dirt and fast ground.

Jean Jeannie

75 **59**
2-y-o b f Giant's Causeway (USA)-Moon Dazzle (USA) (Kingmambo (USA))

W J Haggas Bernard Kantor

Placings:00 **(4542)**
2009: 6⁰GF, 7⁰G,

	Starts	1st	2nd	3rd	Win & Pl
Career Total (Turf)	2	0	0	0	

Going (Turf): **Sf: 0-0 GS: 0-0 Gd: 0-1 GF: 0-1 Fm: 0-0**
Distance: 5f/6f: 0-1 7f-8f: 0-1 9f-13f: 0-0 14f+: 0-0
Track : LH: 0-1 RH: 0-0 Tight: 0-0 Gall: 0-0
Aids: Bl: 0-0 Vi: 0-0 Tstrap: 0-0 Ckp: 0-0
Best Rating: **59** 8/09 NmkJ 7f good

Jeanie Johnston (IRE)

101 **92**
2-y-o b f One Cool Cat (USA)-Bahamamia (Vettori (IRE))
A P Jarvis (K R Burke 25/7) Miss C Wall

Placings:212500 **(7147)**
2009: 6²HY, 6¹GF, 6²G, 6⁵G, 6⁰G, 6⁰G,

	Starts	1st	2nd	3rd	Win & Pl
Career Total (Turf)	6	1	2	0	12330
87 6/09 Hayd 6f			G-F		£3238

Total win prize-money £3238

Going (Turf): Sf: 0-1 GS: 0-0 Gd: 0-4 **GF: 1-1** Fm: 0-0
Distance: **5f/6f: 1-6** 7f-8f: 0-0 9f-13f: 0-0 14f+: 0-0
Track : LH: 0-0 RH: 0-0 Tight: 0-0 Gall: 0-0
Aids: Bl: 0-0 Vi: 0-0 Tstrap: 0-0 Ckp: 0-0
Best Rating: **92** 6/09 NmkJ 6f good

Very useful; effective over 6f; acts on fast and testing ground.

Jeannie (IRE)

77(94) (44)**28**
3-y-o b f Acclamation-Saraluna (IRE) (Mark Of Esteem (IRE))
A Bailey K R Parker

Placings:000 **(6857)**
2009: 7⁰GF, 5⁰SD, 5⁰SD,

	Starts	1st	2nd	3rd	Win & Pl
Career Total (Turf)	1	0	0	0	
Career Total (AW)	2	0	0	0	

Going (Turf): **Sf: 0-0 GS: 0-0 Gd: 0-0 GF: 0-1 Fm: 0-0**
Distance: 5f/6f: 0-2 7f-8f: 0-1 9f-13f: 0-0 14f+: 0-0
Track : LH: 0-3 RH: 0-0 Tight: 0-3 Gall: 0-0
Aids: Bl: 0-0 Vi: 0-0 Tstrap: 0-0 Ckp: 0-0
Best Rating: **44** 10/09 Wolv 5f20y stand

Jeannie Galloway (IRE)

106 **78**
2-y-o b f Bahamian Bounty-Housekeeper (IRE) (Common Grounds)
R A Fahey (A G Foster 14/8) David Renwick

Placings:62311 **(6643)**
2009: 6⁶GF, 7²GS, 7³GF, 6¹GS, 6¹G,

	Starts	1st	2nd	3rd	Win & Pl
Career Total (Turf)	5	2	1	1	6109
71 9/09 Ayr 6f			G-S		£4015

Total win prize-money £4015

Going (Turf): Sf: 0-0 **GS: 1-2 Gd: 1-1** GF: 0-2 Fm: 0-0
Distance: **5f/6f: 2-3** 7f-8f: 0-2 9f-13f: 0-0 14f+: 0-0
Track : LH: 0-0 RH: 0-0 Tight: 0-0 Gall: 0-0
Aids: Bl: 0-0 Vi: 0-0 Tstrap: 0-0 Ckp: 0-0
Best Rating: **78** 10/09 York 6f good

Fair; effective over 6f; acts on good ground.

Jebel Ali (IRE)

(104) (78)**64**
6-y-o b g Fruits Of Love (USA)-Assertive Lass (USA) (Assert)
B Gubby Brian Gubby

Placings:0660/**220165062065/3203**/060150-5 **(1962)**
2009: 10⁵SD,

	Starts	1st	2nd	3rd	Win & Pl
Career Total (Turf)	13	0	1	0	964
Career Total (AW)	14	2	3	2	17131
78 7/08 Kemp 1m2f	(0-80)H		STD		£4727
81 3/06 Ling 1m2f	(0-80)H		STD		£6477

Total win prize-money £11204

Going (Turf): **Sf: 0-1 GS: 0-4 Gd: 0-4 GF: 0-4 Fm: 0-0**
Distance: 5f/6f: 0-0 7f-8f: 0-5 **9f-13f: 2-22** 14f+: 0-0
Track : LH: 1-13 RH: 1-9 **Tight: 1-17** Gall: 0-1
Aids: Bl: 0-1 **Vi: 1-6** Tstrap: 0-1 Ckp: 0-1
Best Rating: **81** 3/06 Ling 1m2f stand

Fair; effective at around 1m2f-1m4f; acts on a sound surface; also goes well on Polytrack.

Jebel Tara

103(106) (71)**83**
4-y-o b g Diktat-Chantilly (FR) (Sanglamore (USA))
A D Brown David J Sturdy

Placings:52100060/**0000**30**00**-**45413400**50 **(4431)**
2009: 7⁴SD, 8⁵SD, 8⁴GF, 8¹F, 8³G, 8⁴GF, 7⁰GF, 7⁰G, 8⁵G, 10⁰GF,

	Starts	1st	2nd	3rd	Win & Pl
Career Total (Turf)	20	2	1	2	10211
Career Total (AW)	6	0	0	0	0
73 4/09 Thsk 1m	(0-70)H		FRM		£4274
77 6/07 Yarm 6f3y			SFT		£2047

Total win prize-money £6322

Going (Turf): **Sf: 1-1** GS: 0-0 Gd: 0-8 GF: 0-10 **Fm: 1-1**
Distance: 5f/6f: 0-6 **7f-8f: 2-16** 9f-13f: 0-4 14f+: 0-0
Track : **LH: 1-9** RH: 0-6 **Tight: 1-4** Gall: 0-2
Aids: **Bl: 1-7** Vi: 0-0 Tstrap: 0-0 Ckp: 0-0
Best Rating: **97** 9/07 Newb 6f8y gd-fm

Modest; stays 1m and acts on most ground; has worn a tongue tie and blinkers.

Jeczmien (POL)

(80) (39)
6-y-o b g Fourth Of June (USA)-Jetka (POL) (Five Star Camp (USA))
N J Gifford Sir Christopher Wates

Placings:5102/41033/540541/0 **(0233)**
2009: 16⁰SD,

	Starts	1st	2nd	3rd	Win & Pl
Career Total (Turf)	15	3	1	2	9924
Career Total (AW)	1	0	0	0	
10/07 MagR 1m55y			GD		£6081
6/06 Brat 1m3f			GD		£1271
8/05 Sluz 5f			G-F		£521

Total win prize-money £7874

Going (Turf): Sf: 0-2 GS: 0-1 **Gd: 2-8** GF: 1-2 Fm: 0-2
Distance: 5f/6f: 1-3 7f-8f: 0-5 **9f-13f: 2-7** 14f+: 0-1
Track : LH: 0-0 RH: 0-1 Tight: 0-0 Gall: 0-0
Aids: **Bl: 1-4** Vi: 0-0 Tstrap: 0-0 Ckp: 0-0
Best Rating: **39** 1/09 Kemp 2m stand

Jedi

101 **89**
3-y-o ch g Pivotal-Threefold (USA) (Gulch (USA))
Sir Michael Stoute Philip Newton

Placings:031-530 **(4520)**
2009: 10⁵G, 12³GF, 11⁰G,

	Starts	1st	2nd	3rd	Win & Pl
Career Total (Turf)	6	1	0	2	6809
78 10/08 Nott 1m75y			HVY		£4533

Total win prize-money £4533

Going (Turf): **Sf: 1-1** GS: 0-1 Gd: 0-2 GF: 0-2 Fm: 0-0
Distance: 5f/6f: 0-0 7f-8f: 0-1 **9f-13f: 1-5** 14f+: 0-0
Track : **LH: 1-3** RH: 0-2 Tight: 0-2 Gall: 0-0
Aids: Bl: 0-0 Vi: 0-0 Tstrap: 0-0 Ckp: 0-0
Best Rating: **89** 5/09 Ches 1m4f66y gd-fm

Useful; gets 1m4f; acts on fast and soft ground.

Jeer (IRE)

104(113) (86)**96**
5-y-o ch g Selkirk (USA)-Purring (USA) (Mountain Cat (USA))
M W Easterby Mrs Jean Turpin

Placings:02/120/542125405033-0054633**363** **(7777)**
2009: 10⁰G, 10⁰GS, 10⁵GF, 10⁴GF, 10⁶GS, 9³GS, 10³GF, **10³SD**, 9⁶SD, **12³SD**,

	Starts	1st	2nd	3rd	Win & Pl
Career Total (Turf)	21	2	4	4	23969
Career Total (AW)	6	0	0	2	1254
94 5/08 NmkR 1m2f	(0-90)H		G-F		£7771
60 4/07 Ripn 1m1f170y			G-F		£3238

Total win prize-money £11010

Going (Turf): Sf: 0-3 GS: 0-5 Gd: 0-4 **GF: 2-9** Fm: 0-0
Distance: 5f/6f: 0-0 7f-8f: 0-2 **9f-13f: 2-25** 14f+: 0-0
Track : LH: 0-18 **RH: 1-7 Tight: 1-8** Gall: 0-9
Aids: Bl: 0-2 Vi: 0-0 Tstrap: 0-0 Ckp: 0-0
Best Rating: **96** 7/08 Sand 1m2f7y gd-fm

Fair; stays 1m2f; acts on most ground.

Jehu

98(89) (74)**81**
2-y-o b c Antonius Pius (USA)-Chalosse (Doyoun)
M R Channon Box 41

Placings:5210154533264 **(6819)**
2009: 6⁵G, 6²G, 7¹GF, 7⁰GF, 7¹S, 7⁵G, 7⁴GF, 8⁵GF, 8³G, 7³GF, 7²SD, 7⁶G, 7⁴GF,

	Starts	1st	2nd	3rd	Win & Pl
Career Total (Turf)	12	2	1	2	10389
Career Total (AW)	1	0	1	0	605
81 7/09 Catt 7f			SFT		£3238
75 6/09 Thsk 7f			G-F		£4274

Total win prize-money £7512

Going (Turf): **Sf: 1-1** GS: 0-0 Gd: 0-5 **GF: 1-6** Fm: 0-0
Distance: 5f/6f: 0-1 **7f-8f: 2-11** 9f-13f: 0-1 14f+: 0-0
Track : **LH: 2-5** RH: 0-2 **Tight: 2-4** Gall: 0-1
Aids: Bl: 0-0 Vi: 0-3 Tstrap: 0-0 Ckp: 0-0
Best Rating: **81** 8/09 Sand 7f16y gd-fm

Useful; stays 7f; acts on most ground.

Jelly Bean

82 52

2-y-o ch f Observatory (USA)-Grandma Lily (IRE) (Bigstone (IRE))

K A Ryan David Fravigar, Kathy Dixon

Placings:00 **(4001)**

2009: 6^{0}GF, 7^{0}GS,

	Starts	1st	2nd	3rd	Win & Pl
Career Total (Turf)	2	0	0	0	

Going (Turf): **Sf: 0-0 GS: 0-1 Gd: 0-0 GF: 0-1 Fm: 0-0**
Distance: 5f/6f: 0-1 7f-8f: 0-1 9f-13f: 0-0 14f+: 0-0
Track : LH: 0-1 RH: 0-0 Tight: 0-0 Gall: 0-0
Aids: Bl: 0-0 Vi: 0-0 Tstrap: 0-0 Ckp: 0-0
Best Rating: **52** 7/09 Donc 7f gd-sft

Jelly Mo

96(102) (70)57

4-y-o b f Royal Applause-Flawless (Warning)

W M Brisbourne P G Evans

Placings:00505/50000010-5560 **(4944)**

2009: 10^{5}F, 12^{5}GF, 10^{6}G, 10^{0}GF,

	Starts	1st	2nd	3rd	Win & Pl
Career Total (Turf)	13	0	0	0	0
Career Total (AW)	4	1	0	0	1979

50 9/08 Ling 1m2f STD £1978
Total win prize-money £1979

Going (Turf): **Sf: 0-0 GS: 0-1 Gd: 0-3 GF: 0-8 Fm: 0-1**
Distance: 5f/6f: 0-3 7f-8f: 0-3 **9f-13f: 1-11** 14f+: 0-0
Track : **LH: 1-11** RH: 0-2 **Tight: 1-8** Gall: 0-1
Aids: Bl: 0-0 Vi: 0-0 Tstrap: 1-2 Ckp: 1-2
Best Rating: **70** 10/07 Ling 7f stand

Moderate; stays 1m2f; acts on fast ground; also goes on Polytrack.

Jellytot (USA)

82(94) (41)48

6-y-o b m Minardi (USA)-Dounine (Kaldoun (FR))

I W McInnes J Morris

Placings:566400/0021013004/500620000/000350000-00 **(4887)**

2009: 6^{0}G, 7^{0}G,

	Starts	1st	2nd	3rd	Win & Pl
Career Total (Turf)	28	2	2	2	8314
Career Total (AW)	9	0	0	0	0

67 7/06 Carl 6f192y (0-70)H G-F £3238
65 6/06 Catt 7f (0-60) G-F £2388
Total win prize-money £5628

Going (Turf): Sf: 0-3 GS: 0-3 Gd: 0-7 **GF: 2-14** Fm: 0-1
Distance: 5f/6f: 0-13 **7f-8f: 2-23** 9f-13f: 0-1 14f+: 0-0
Track : LH: 1-16 RH: 1-6 **Tight: 1-5** Gall: 0-1
Aids: Bl: 0-6 Vi: 0-0 Tstrap: 0-0 Ckp: 0-0
Best Rating: **67** 7/06 Carl 6f192y gd-fm

Moderate filly; acts on fast and soft ground; stays a mile; has worn blinkers.

Jemimaville (IRE)

74 44

2-y-o b f Fasliyev (USA)-Sparkling Isle (Inchinor)

G C Bravery Midbras Group Holdings Ltd

Placings:00 **(7183)**

2009: 6^{0}GF, 7^{0}G,

	Starts	1st	2nd	3rd	Win & Pl
Career Total (Turf)	2	0	0	0	

Going (Turf): **Sf: 0-0 GS: 0-0 Gd: 0-1 GF: 0-1 Fm: 0-0**
Distance: 5f/6f: 0-1 7f-8f: 0-1 9f-13f: 0-0 14f+: 0-0
Track : LH: 0-0 RH: 0-0 Tight: 0-0 Gall: 0-1
Aids: Bl: 0-0 Vi: 0-0 Tstrap: 0-0 Ckp: 0-0
Best Rating: **44** 10/09 NmkR 7f good

Jeninsky (USA)

106(97) (83)95

4-y-o ch f Stravinsky (USA)-Don't Ruffle Me (USA) (Pine Bluff (USA))

Rae Guest J M Beever

Placings:31/056002260-6110 **(6886a)**

2009: 7^{6}G, 7^{1}G, 7^{1}G, 8^{0}S,

	Starts	1st	2nd	3rd	Win & Pl
Career Total (Turf)	12	2	2	1	38482
Career Total (AW)	3	1	0	0	2817

95 8/09 NmkJ 7f (0-105)H GD £24924
91 7/09 Donc 7f (0-90)H GD £7477
77 10/07 Kemp 6f STD £2817
Total win prize-money £35218

Going (Turf): Sf: 0-4 GS: 0-2 **Gd: 2-4** GF: 0-2 Fm: 0-0
Distance: 5f/6f: 1-5 **7f-8f: 2-10** 9f-13f: 0-0 14f+: 0-0
Track : LH: 0-2 **RH: 1-7** Tight: 0-0 Gall: 0-1
Aids: Bl: 0-0 Vi: 0-0 Tstrap: 0-0 Ckp: 0-0
Best Rating: **95** 8/09 NmkJ 7f good

Useful; effective at 6f-1m; acts on good and soft ground; also goes on Polytrack.

Jennerous Blue

(90) (54)

2-y-o b f Generous (IRE)-Jennelle (Nomination)

D K Ivory Mrs J A Cornwell & Cynthia Smith

Placings:0064 **(7597)**

2009: 7^{0}SD, 8^{0}SD, 8^{6}SD, 8^{4}SD,

	Starts	1st	2nd	3rd	Win & Pl
Career Total (Turf)	0	0	0	0	
Career Total (AW)	4	0	0	0	216

Going (Turf): **Sf: 0-0 GS: 0-0 Gd: 0-0 GF: 0-0 Fm: 0-0**
Distance: 5f/6f: 0-0 7f-8f: 0-3 9f-13f: 0-1 14f+: 0-0
Track : LH: 0-2 RH: 0-2 Tight: 0-2 Gall: 0-0
Aids: Bl: 0-0 Vi: 0-0 Tstrap: 0-0 Ckp: 0-0
Best Rating: **54** 9/09 Kemp 7f stand

Jennie Jerome (IRE)

99(105) (79)81

4-y-o br f Pivotal-Colourfast (IRE) (Spectrum (IRE))

C F Wall (V Valiani 5/7) The Honorable Earle I Mack

Placings:0/431345-0024 **(7475)**

2009: 8^{0}G, 11^{0}G, 10^{2}S, 10^{4}SD,

	Starts	1st	2nd	3rd	Win & Pl
Career Total (Turf)	9	1	1	2	5650
Career Total (AW)	2	0	0	0	192

81 8/08 Yarm 7f3y (0-70)H G-S £2719
Total win prize-money £2720

Going (Turf): Sf: 0-3 **GS: 1-1** Gd: 0-4 GF: 0-1 Fm: 0-0
Distance: 5f/6f: 0-1 **7f-8f: 1-5** 9f-13f: 0-5 14f+: 0-0
Track : LH: 0-3 RH: 0-5 Tight: 0-1 Gall: 0-0
Aids: Bl: 0-0 Vi: 0-0 Tstrap: 0-0 Ckp: 0-0
Best Rating: **81** 9/08 Leic 1m60y soft

Fair; stays 1m2f; acts on fast and soft ground.

Jenny Potts

100 74

5-y-o b m Robellino (USA)-Fleeting Vision (IRE) (Vision (USA))

L Lungo Len Lungo Racing Limited

Placings:5461 **(3019)**

2009: 8^{5}GF, 8^{4}GF, 12^{6}G, 9^{1}G,

	Starts	1st	2nd	3rd	Win & Pl
Career Total (Turf)	4	1	0	0	4078

74 6/09 Haml 1m1f36y (0-70)H GD £3885
Total win prize-money £3886

Going (Turf): Sf: 0-0 GS: 0-0 **Gd: 1-2** GF: 0-2 Fm: 0-0
Distance: 5f/6f: 0-0 7f-8f: 0-0 **9f-13f: 1-4** 14f+: 0-0
Track : LH: 0-1 **RH: 1-2 Tight: 1-2** Gall: 0-0
Aids: Bl: 0-0 Vi: 0-0 Tstrap: 0-0 Ckp: 0-0
Best Rating: **74** 6/09 Haml 1m1f36y good

Fair; stays 1m1f; acts on good ground.

Jenny Soba

103(100) (52)68

6-y-o b m Observatory (USA)-Majalis (Mujadil (USA))

Lucinda Featherstone J Roundtree

Placings:4000/060223630/0554061064500035/36401510 22000-4062550005 **(7751)**

2009: 12^{4}GS, 10^{0}GF, 11^{6}S, 12^{2}G, 12^{5}GS, 11^{5}S, 10^{0}S, 13^{0}SD, 12^{0}SD, 13^{5}SD,

	Starts	1st	2nd	3rd	Win & Pl
Career Total (Turf)	41	3	5	2	13585
Career Total (AW)	11	0	0	2	504

63 9/08 Wwck 1m2f188y (0-58)H SFT £2047
55 8/08 Devl 1m1f207y (0-65)H SFT £2752
55 8/07 Rdcr 1m2f G-F £2047
Total win prize-money £6847

Going (Turf): **Sf: 2-14** GS: 0-3 Gd: 0-10 GF: 1-13 Fm: 0-1
Distance: 5f/6f: 0-3 7f-8f: 0-5 **9f-13f: 3-33** 14f+: 0-11
Track : **LH: 2-34** RH: 1-13 **Tight: 1-23** Gall: 0-5
Aids: Bl: 0-0 **Vi: 1-7** Tstrap: 0-3 Ckp: 0-3
Best Rating: **68** 10/08 Wwck 1m4f134y soft

Moderate; stays 1m4f; acts on fast and soft ground.

Jenny's Pride (IRE)

96(91) (53)53

3-y-o ch f Fath (USA)-Softly (IRE) (Grand Lodge (USA))

John A Harris Mrs A E Harris

Placings:5516004 **(7796)**

2009: 8^{5}SD, 8^{5}GF, 7^{1}S, 8^{6}HY, 7^{0}GF, 9^{0}GF, 7^{4}SS,

	Starts	1st	2nd	3rd	Win & Pl
Career Total (Turf)	5	1	0	0	2590
Career Total (AW)	2	0	0	0	144

53 7/09 Leic 7f9y SFT £2590
Total win prize-money £2590

Going (Turf): **Sf: 1-2** GS: 0-0 Gd: 0-0 GF: 0-3 Fm: 0-0
Distance: 5f/6f: 0-0 **7f-8f: 1-3** 9f-13f: 0-4 14f+: 0-0
Track : LH: 0-3 RH: 0-2 Tight: 0-2 Gall: 0-0
Aids: Bl: 0-0 Vi: 0-0 Tstrap: 0-0 Ckp: 0-0

Best Rating: 53 7/09 Leic 7f9y soft

Modesrate; stays 7f; acts on soft.

Jeremiah (IRE)

100(99) (70)**73**

3-y-o ch g Captain Rio-Miss Garuda (Persian Bold)

J G Portman M J Vandenberghe

Placings:03200-420000614600 (7479)

2009: 7^{4}SD, 6^{2}GF, 6^{0}SD, 6^{0}GF, 6^{0}F, 7^{0}G, 6^{6}SD, 6^{1}GS, 7^{4}G, 8^{6}SD, 7^{0}GF, 7^{0}SD,

	Starts	1st	2nd	3rd	Win & Pl
Career Total (Turf)	11	1	2	0	5398
Career Total (AW)	6	0	0	1	353

70 8/09 Brig 6f209y (0-65)H G-S £2901

Total win prize-money £2902

Going (Turf): Sf: 0-1 **GS: 1-1** Gd: 0-3 GF: 0-5 Fm: 0-1
Distance: 5f/6f: 0-9 **7f-8f: 1-8** 9f-13f: 0-0 14f+: 0-0
Track : **LH: 1-5** RH: 0-3 Tight: 0-2 Gall: 0-2
Aids: Bl: 0-0 Vi: 0-1 Tstrap: 0-2 Ckp: 0-2
Best Rating: 73 7/08 Sals 6f gd-fm

Fair; effective over 6f-7f; acts on good and faster ground; has worn cheekpieces.

Jeronimo Joe

99(94) (48)**61**

3-y-o ch g Primo Valentino (IRE)-Yanomami (USA) (Slew O'Gold (USA))

A B Haynes Joe McCarthy

Placings:0-010526 (6570)

2009: 9^{0}GF, 10^{1}GF, 12^{0}SD, 10^{5}GS, 10^{2}GF, 9^{6}GF,

	Starts	1st	2nd	3rd	Win & Pl
Career Total (Turf)	5	1	1	0	2652
Career Total (AW)	2	0	0	0	

58 7/09 Wwck 1m2f188y G-F £2047

Total win prize-money £2047

Going (Turf): Sf: 0-0 GS: 0-1 Gd: 0-0 **GF: 1-4** Fm: 0-0
Distance: 5f/6f: 0-0 7f-8f: 0-1 **9f-13f: 1-6** 14f+: 0-0
Track : **LH: 1-5** RH: 0-2 Tight: 0-4 Gall: 0-0
Aids: Bl: 0-0 Vi: 0-0 Tstrap: 0-0 Ckp: 0-0
Best Rating: 61 8/09 Rdcr 1m2f gd-fm

Moderate; stays 1m2f plus; acts on fast ground.

Jerusalem (IRE)

(81) (50)

3-y-o ch g Indian Haven-Wilrock (IRE) (Docksider (USA))

A Bailey Bridgewater Equine Ltd

Placings:30 (0386)

2009: 6^{3}SD, 8^{0}SD,

	Starts	1st	2nd	3rd	Win & Pl
Career Total (Turf)	0	0	0	0	
Career Total (AW)	2	0	0	1	403

Going (Turf): Sf: 0-0 GS: 0-0 Gd: 0-0 GF: 0-0 Fm: 0-0
Distance: 5f/6f: 0-1 7f-8f: 0-1 9f-13f: 0-0 14f+: 0-0
Track : LH: 0-1 RH: 0-1 Tight: 0-0 Gall: 0-0
Aids: Bl: 0-2 Vi: 0-0 Tstrap: 0-0 Ckp: 0-0
Best Rating: 50 2/09 Sthl 6f stand

Modest; suited by 5f and acts on Fibresand; has worn blinkers.

Jesse James (IRE)

108(101) (80)**92**

3-y-o b g King's Best (USA)-Julie Jalouse (USA) (Kris S (USA))

J H M Gosden H R H Princess Haya Of Jordan

Placings:02-2214 (5914)

2009: 8^{2}SD, 8^{2}GF, 8^{1}GF, 8^{4}GF,

	Starts	1st	2nd	3rd	Win & Pl
Career Total (Turf)	5	1	2	0	5523
Career Total (AW)	1	0	1	0	1445

91 8/09 Wind 1m67y G-F £2729

Total win prize-money £2730

Going (Turf): Sf: 0-0 GS: 0-1 Gd: 0-1 **GF: 1-3** Fm: 0-0
Distance: 5f/6f: 0-0 7f-8f: 0-5 **9f-13f: 1-1** 14f+: 0-0
Track : LH: 0-1 **RH: 1-3 Tight: 1-2** Gall: 0-0
Aids: Bl: 0-0 Vi: 0-0 Tstrap: 0-0 Ckp: 0-0
Best Rating: 92 9/09 Gdwd 1m gd-fm

Fair; stays 1m; acts on fast and easy ground; goes on Polytrack.

Jessica Hayllar (USA)

98 **62**

2-y-o b f Arch (USA)-Pearl Pride (USA) (Theatrical)

G L Moore (M L W Bell 20/7) R A Green

Placings:045203 (6906)

2009: 6^{0}GS, 6^{4}G, 5^{5}GF, 6^{2}G, 6^{0}GF, 6^{3}G,

	Starts	1st	2nd	3rd	Win & Pl
Career Total (Turf)	6	0	1	1	1316

Going (Turf): Sf: 0-0 GS: 0-1 Gd: 0-3 GF: 0-2 Fm: 0-0
Distance: 5f/6f: 0-5 7f-8f: 0-1 9f-13f: 0-0 14f+: 0-0
Track : LH: 0-0 RH: 0-0 Tight: 0-0 Gall: 0-3
Aids: Bl: 0-0 Vi: 0-0 Tstrap: 0-0 Ckp: 0-0
Best Rating: 62 7/09 Yarm 6f3y good

Jessica Wigmo

75(111) (63)**50**

6-y-o b m Bahamian Bounty-Queen Of Shannon (IRE) (Nordico (USA))

A W Carroll J Wigmore Racing Partnership

Placings:0500/00000630/0000**503150**/**22161013040405**-0014535000 (4533)

2009: 8^{0}SD, 7^{0}SD, 6^{1}SD, 8^{4}SD, 7^{5}SD, 6^{3}SD, 7^{5}SD, 7^{0}SD, 8^{0}SD, 7^{0}GS,

	Starts	1st	2nd	3rd	Win & Pl
Career Total (Turf)	16	0	0	1	963
Career Total (AW)	30	5	2	3	12410

63 2/09 Kemp 6f (0-50)H STD £2047
62 4/08 Kemp 7f (0-60)H STD £2047
60 2/08 Kemp 7f (0-50)H STD £2047
56 1/08 Ling 7f (0-60)H STD £1876
52 11/07 Kemp 1m STD £2047

Total win prize-money £10067

Going (Turf): Sf: 0-2 GS: 0-3 Gd: 0-3 GF: 0-8 Fm: 0-0
Distance: 5f/6f: 1-17 **7f-8f: 4-26** 9f-13f: 0-3 14f+: 0-0
Track : LH: 1-19 **RH: 4-15 Tight: 1-16** Gall: 0-4
Aids: Bl: 0-0 Vi: 0-0 Tstrap: 0-0 Ckp: 0-0
Best Rating: 63 2/09 Kemp 6f stand

Moderate; effective over 7f-1m; acts on a sound surface and on Polytrack.

Jet D'Eau (FR)

106(83) (42)**98**

3-y-o b f Numerous (USA)-La Fontainiere (IRE) (Kaldoun (FR))

G L Moore Blue Diamond Racing

Placings:110455-550000 (7486)

2009: 6^{5}GF, 7^{5}GF, 7^{0}GF, 8^{0}G, 7^{0}S, 7^{0}SD,

	Starts	1st	2nd	3rd	Win & Pl
Career Total (Turf)	11	2	0	0	28857
Career Total (AW)	1	0	0	0	

79 6/08 StCl 6f G-S £10662
70 5/08 Wiss 5f GD £4044

Total win prize-money £14706

Going (Turf): Sf: 0-1 **GS: 1-1 Gd: 1-5** GF: 0-3 Fm: 0-1
Distance: **5f/6f: 2-4** 7f-8f: 0-8 9f-13f: 0-0 14f+: 0-0
Track : **LH: 1-2** RH: 0-6 Tight: 0-1 Gall: 0-1
Aids: **Bl: 2-12** Vi: 0-0 Tstrap: 0-0 Ckp: 0-0
Best Rating: 98 8/09 Gdwd 7f gd-fm

Very useful; formerly French trained; effective over 5f-7f; acts on good and easier ground; wears blinkers.

Jethro Bodine (IRE)

101 **56**

3-y-o b g Fath (USA)-John's Ballad (IRE) (Ballad Rock)

W J H Ratcliffe J Sheard & W J S Ratcliffe

Placings:620536-514 (1455)

2009: 5^{5}GF, 5^{1}F, 5^{4}GF,

	Starts	1st	2nd	3rd	Win & Pl
Career Total (Turf)	9	1	1	1	3016

56 4/09 Rdcr 5f (0-60)H FRM £1942

Total win prize-money £1943

Going (Turf): Sf: 0-1 GS: 0-0 Gd: 0-2 GF: 0-5 **Fm: 1-1**
Distance: **5f/6f: 1-9** 7f-8f: 0-0 9f-13f: 0-0 14f+: 0-0
Track : LH: 0-0 RH: 0-0 Tight: 0-0 Gall: 0-0
Aids: Bl: 0-0 Vi: 0-0 Tstrap: 1-3 Ckp: 1-3
Best Rating: 56 4/09 Rdcr 5f firm

Plating-class; effective at 5f; has worn cheekpieces.

Jeu D'Esprit (IRE)

(71)**72**

6-y-o b m Montjeu (IRE)-Cielo Vodkamartini (USA) (Conquistador Cielo (USA))

Mrs L J Mongan Mrs P J Sheen

Placings:0030/150265/P (3737)

2009: 16^{P}SD,

	Starts	1st	2nd	3rd	Win & Pl
Career Total (Turf)	4	0	1	0	1156
Career Total (AW)	7	1	0	1	5339

71 5/07 Sthl 1m3f (0-80)H STD £4857

Total win prize-money £4858

Going (Turf): Sf: 0-1 GS: 0-0 Gd: 0-2 GF: 0-1 Fm: 0-0
Distance: 5f/6f: 0-0 7f-8f: 0-1 **9f-13f: 1-9** 14f+: 0-1
Track : **LH: 1-7** RH: 0-4 Tight: 0-7 Gall: 0-0
Aids: Bl: 0-0 Vi: 0-0 Tstrap: 0-0 Ckp: 0-0
Best Rating: 72 7/07 Ripn 1m heavy

Jeunopse (IRE)

95 **68**

3-y-o b f Hawk Wing (USA)-Innocence (Unfuwain (USA))

X-Thomas Demeaulte (B Smart 16/7) Prime Equestrain Sarl

Placings:4-5256
2009: 7^{5}GF, 8^{2}GF, 11^{5}GF, 10^{6}VS,

	Starts	1st	2nd	3rd	Win & Pl
Career Total (Turf)	5	0	1	0	1035

Going (Turf): Sf: 0-0 GS: 0-0 Gd: 0-1 GF: 0-3 Fm: 0-0
Distance: 5f/6f: 0-1 7f-8f: 0-1 9f-13f: 0-3 14f+: 0-0
Track : LH: 0-1 RH: 0-3 Tight: 0-2 Gall: 0-0
Aids: Bl: 0-0 Vi: 0-0 Tstrap: 0-0 Ckp: 0-0
Best Rating: 68 6/09 Haml 1m65y gd-fm

Fair; stays 1m and acts on fast ground.

Jewelled

99(87) (42)75
3-y-o b f Fantastic Light (USA)-Danemere (IRE) (Danehill (USA))
J W Hills J W Hills

Placings:5554525230 (7356)
2009: 9^{5}G, 9^{5}GF, 9^{5}G, 10^{4}S, 9^{5}GF, 8^{2}GS, 8^{5}G, 8^{2}F, 8^{3}G, 7^{0}SD,

	Starts	1st	2nd	3rd	Win & Pl
Career Total (Turf)	9	0	2	1	1942
Career Total (AW)	1	0	0	0	

Going (Turf): Sf: 0-1 GS: 0-1 Gd: 0-4 GF: 0-2 Fm: 0-1
Distance: 5f/6f: 0-0 7f-8f: 0-2 9f-13f: 0-8 14f+: 0-0
Track : LH: 0-5 RH: 0-5 Tight: 0-8 Gall: 0-1
Aids: Bl: 0-0 Vi: 0-0 Tstrap: 0-0 Ckp: 0-0
Best Rating: 75 10/09 Wind 1m67y good

Modest; effective at 1m plus; handles cut in the ground.

Jewelled Dagger (IRE)

103(99) (82)98
5-y-o b g Daggers Drawn (USA)-Cappadoce (IRE) (General Monash (USA))
I Semple A R M Galbraith

Placings:000/6211120201/22006200-5254600 (5522)
2009: 7^{5}SD, 7^{2}G, 8^{5}GS, 7^{4}GF, 7^{6}G, 6^{0}G, 8^{0}G,

	Starts	1st	2nd	3rd	Win & Pl
Career Total (Turf)	23	4	7	0	33577
Career Total (AW)	5	0	0	0	0

92	10/07	York	1m208y	(0-85)H	G-S	£7772
76	6/07	Muss	1m1f	(0-65)H	GD	£3238
70	5/07	Muss	1m	(0-65)H	G-F	£2590
61	5/07	Muss	1m	(0-60)H	GD	£2047

Total win prize-money £15650

Going (Turf): Sf: 0-2 GS: 1-4 **Gd: 2-10** GF: 1-6 Fm: 0-1
Distance: 5f/6f: 0-0 7f-8f: 2-13 9f-13f: 2-15 14f+: 0-0
Track : LH: 1-12 **RH: 3-15 Tight: 3-16** Gall: 1-3
Aids: **Bl: 4-23** Vi: 0-1 Tstrap: 0-0 Ckp: 0-0
Best Rating: 98 5/08 Ripn 1m gd-fm

Fair; effective at 7f-1m2f; likes fast ground but handles cut; usually wears blinkers; suited by forcing tactics.

Jewelled Reef (IRE)

96 63
3-y-o b f Marju (IRE)-Aqaba (Lake Coniston (IRE))
Eve Johnson Houghton Wood Street Syndicate V

Placings:0640-00250305043300 (6910)
2009: 8^{0}GF, 9^{0}G, 8^{2}F, 8^{5}F, 7^{0}GF, 8^{3}GF, 7^{0}GF, 6^{5}G, 7^{0}G, 7^{4}G, 8^{3}F, 8^{3}F, 7^{0}G, 10^{0}G,

	Starts	1st	2nd	3rd	Win & Pl
Career Total (Turf)	18	0	1	3	2402

Going (Turf): Sf: 0-0 GS: 0-0 Gd: 0-7 GF: 0-7 Fm: 0-4
Distance: 5f/6f: 0-2 7f-8f: 0-8 9f-13f: 0-8 14f+: 0-0
Track : LH: 0-7 RH: 0-2 Tight: 0-6 Gall: 0-2
Aids: Bl: 0-0 Vi: 0-0 Tstrap: 0-0 Ckp: 0-0
Best Rating: 63 5/09 Bath 1m5y firm

Moderate; effective over 1m; acts on fast ground.

Jezza

(102) (52)
3-y-o b g Pentire-Lara (GER) (Sharpo)
Karen George R A Bimson

Placings:060053 (7687)
2009: 10^{0}SD, 8^{6}SF, 8^{0}SD, 12^{0}SD, 13^{5}SD, 12^{3}SD,

	Starts	1st	2nd	3rd	Win & Pl
Career Total (Turf)	0	0	0	0	
Career Total (AW)	6	0	0	1	252

Going (Turf): Sf: 0-0 GS: 0-0 Gd: 0-0 GF: 0-0 Fm: 0-0
Distance: 5f/6f: 0-0 7f-8f: 0-1 9f-13f: 0-4 14f+: 0-1
Track : LH: 0-5 RH: 0-1 Tight: 0-5 Gall: 0-0
Aids: Bl: 0-0 Vi: 0-0 Tstrap: 0-0 Ckp: 0-0
Best Rating: 52 11/09 Wolv 1m5f194y stand

Jhinga Palak (IRE)

62(84) (43)68
3-y-o b f Fath (USA)-Livius Lady (IRE) (Titus Livius (FR))
Mrs K Waldron (P D Evans 2/1) Nick Shutts

Placings:056-000 (3502)
2009: 5^{0}SD, 8^{0}GF, 7^{0}GF,

	Starts	1st	2nd	3rd	Win & Pl
Career Total (Turf)	4	0	0	0	4412
Career Total (AW)	2	0	0	0	0

Going (Turf): Sf: 0-1 GS: 0-0 Gd: 0-1 GF: 0-2 Fm: 0-0
Distance: 5f/6f: 0-3 7f-8f: 0-2 9f-13f: 0-1 14f+: 0-0
Track : LH: 0-4 RH: 0-0 Tight: 0-1 Gall: 0-1
Aids: Bl: 0-0 Vi: 0-0 Tstrap: 0-0 Ckp: 0-0
Best Rating: 68 8/08 Curr 6f heavy

Jibrrya

93 78
2-y-o b c Motivator-Takarna (IRE) (Mark Of Esteem (IRE))
M R Channon Sheikh Ahmed Al Maktoum

Placings:51 (5407)
2009: 8^{5}GF, 8^{1}G,

	Starts	1st	2nd	3rd	Win & Pl
Career Total (Turf)	2	1	0	0	5343

78 8/09 Thsk 1m GD £5342
Total win prize-money £5343

Going (Turf): Sf: 0-0 GS: 0-0 **Gd: 1-1** GF: 0-1 Fm: 0-0
Distance: 5f/6f: 0-0 **7f-8f: 1-1** 9f-13f: 0-1 14f+: 0-0
Track : **LH: 1-1** RH: 0-1 **Tight: 1-1** Gall: 0-0
Aids: Bl: 0-0 Vi: 0-0 Tstrap: 0-0 Ckp: 0-0
Best Rating: 78 8/09 Thsk 1m good

140,000gns yearling; of the mark on second start over 1m on good.

Jigajig

82 26
2-y-o ch g Compton Place-Eau Rouge (Grand Lodge (USA))
N Wilson Mrs Maureen Eason

Placings:06000 (6555)
2009: 5^{0}GF, 6^{6}GF, 5^{0}GS, 5^{0}GF, 5^{0}G,

	Starts	1st	2nd	3rd	Win & Pl
Career Total (Turf)	5	0	0	0	0

Going (Turf): Sf: 0-0 GS: 0-1 Gd: 0-1 GF: 0-3 Fm: 0-0
Distance: 5f/6f: 0-5 7f-8f: 0-0 9f-13f: 0-0 14f+: 0-0
Track : LH: 0-0 RH: 0-0 Tight: 0-0 Gall: 0-0
Aids: Bl: 0-0 Vi: 0-2 Tstrap: 0-0 Ckp: 0-0
Best Rating: 26 9/09 Rdcr 5f gd-fm

Jiggalong

99(92) (55)62
3-y-o ch f Mark Of Esteem (IRE)-Kalamansi (IRE) (Sadler's Wells (USA))
Jim Best (R Ingram 16/9) M&R Refurbishments Ltd

Placings:00-206323000014 (7840)
2009: 6^{2}G, 5^{0}G, 6^{6}GF, 8^{3}G, 8^{2}GF, 8^{3}SD, 11^{0}SD, 12^{0}SD, 8^{0}SD, 8^{0}SD, 12^{1}SD, 12^{4}SS,

	Starts	1st	2nd	3rd	Win & Pl
Career Total (Turf)	7	0	2	1	1915
Career Total (AW)	7	1	0	1	2350

55 12/09 Kemp 1m4f (0-60)H STD £2047
Total win prize-money £2047

Going (Turf): Sf: 0-0 GS: 0-0 Gd: 0-3 GF: 0-3 Fm: 0-1
Distance: 5f/6f: 0-4 7f-8f: 0-6 **9f-13f: 1-4** 14f+: 0-0
Track : LH: 0-5 **RH: 1-5** Tight: 0-2 Gall: 0-0
Aids: Bl: 0-0 Vi: 0-0 Tstrap: 0-0 Ckp: 0-0
Best Rating: 62 8/09 Rdcr 1m gd-fm

Moderate; effective over 1m-1m4f; acts on good ground and on Polytrack.

Jill Le Brocq

89 61
3-y-o b f Reset (AUS)-Our Krissie (Kris)
M Dods J Henderson (co Durham)

Placings:4052 (4589)
2009: 6^{4}GF, 6^{0}GS, 6^{5}S, 7^{2}G,

	Starts	1st	2nd	3rd	Win & Pl
Career Total (Turf)	4	0	1	0	797

Going (Turf): Sf: 0-1 GS: 0-1 Gd: 0-1 GF: 0-1 Fm: 0-0
Distance: 5f/6f: 0-3 7f-8f: 0-1 9f-13f: 0-0 14f+: 0-0
Track : LH: 0-0 RH: 0-1 Tight: 0-0 Gall: 0-0
Aids: Bl: 0-1 Vi: 0-0 Tstrap: 0-0 Ckp: 0-0
Best Rating: 61 8/09 Carl 7f200y good

Moderate; stays 1m; acts on good ground; has worn blinkers.

Jillolini

88 38
3-y-o gr f Bertolini (USA)-Someone's Angel (USA) (Runaway Groom (CAN))
T D Easterby Mrs Jean P Connew

Placings:0-505 (3125)
2009: 6^{5}GF, 6^{0}G, 5^{5}GF,

	Starts	1st	2nd	3rd	Win & Pl
Career Total (Turf)	4	0	0	0	0

Going (Turf): Sf: 0-0 GS: 0-0 Gd: 0-2 GF: 0-2 Fm: 0-0
Distance: 5f/6f: 0-4 7f-8f: 0-0 9f-13f: 0-0 14f+: 0-0
Track : LH: 0-1 RH: 0-0 Tight: 0-0 Gall: 0-0
Aids: Bl: 0-0 Vi: 0-0 Tstrap: 0-0 Ckp: 0-0
Best Rating: 38 4/09 Thsk 6f gd-fm

Jilly Why (IRE)

103(100) (63)**84**
8-y-o b m Mujadil (USA)-Ruwy (Soviet Star (USA))
Paul Green The Lady Birds

Placings:6340/041100240565200/0001400/406064366/0425364342510210344340/430161100000000663036-004364216400540 (7371)
2009: 5^{0}SD, 5^{0}GF, 5^{4}GF, 7^{3}GF, 5^{6}G, 5^{4}GS, 6^{2}G, 5^{1}HY, 6^{6}GF, 5^{4}GS, 5^{0}G, 7^{0}GF, 5^{5}S, 5^{4}G, 5^{0}SD,

	Starts	1st	2nd	3rd	Win & Pl
Career Total (Turf)	49	7	4	4	42477
Career Total (AW)	45	2	2	6	8862

73	7/09	Nott	5f13y	(0-75)H	HVY	£2590
84	5/08	Thsk	5f	(0-85)H	GD	£5180
80	5/08	Nott	5f13y	(0-70)H	GD	£3885
66	4/08	Sthl	5f	(0-60)H	STD	£1774
70	10/07	Wolv	5f216y	(0-55)H	STD	£2047
78	8/07	Curr	7f	(50-80)H	SFT	£6303
78	9/05	Nott	6f15y	(0-70)H	GD	£3694
80	9/04	Ches	5f16y	(0-85)H	GD	£6770
67	9/04	Thsk	6f		FRM	£4114

Total win prize-money £36362

Going (Turf): Sf: 2-9 GS: 0-5 **Gd: 4-16** GF: 0-16 Fm: 1-3
Distance: **5f/6f: 7-77** 7f-8f: 2-15 9f-13f: 0-2 14f+: 0-0
Track : **LH: 2-44** RH: 0-1 **Tight: 2-41** Gall: 0-1
Aids: **Bl: 6-55** Vi: 0-2 Tstrap: 0-0 Ckp: 0-0
Best Rating: 84 5/08 Thsk 5f good

Modest; effective over 5f-7f; seems to act on most types of ground, including sand; often wears blinkers, has worn cheekpieces.

Jim Martin

99(93) (72)**72**
4-y-o b g Auction House (USA)-Folly Finnesse (Joligeneration)
Miss L A Perratt Ken McGarrity

Placings:14/60000100-0400 (7173)
2009: 9^{0}GF, 9^{4}HY, 10^{0}GS, 9^{0}S,

	Starts	1st	2nd	3rd	Win & Pl
Career Total (Turf)	12	2	0	0	12379
Career Total (AW)	2	0	0	0	0

72	9/08	Ayr	1m2f		HVY	£6476
79	7/07	Newc	7f		GD	£5181

Total win prize-money £11658

Going (Turf): **Sf: 1-3** GS: 0-2 **Gd: 1-3** GF: 0-4 Fm: 0-0
Distance: 5f/6f: 0-0 7f-8f: 1-5 9f-13f: 1-9 14f+: 0-0
Track : **LH: 1-8** RH: 0-4 Tight: 0-7 Gall: 0-0
Aids: Bl: 0-0 Vi: 0-0 Tstrap: 0-0 Ckp: 0-0
Best Rating: 79 7/07 Newc 7f good

Modest; effective over 1m2f; acts on good and soft ground.

Jiminor Mack

96(98) (49)**51**
6-y-o bl m Little Jim-Copper Trader (Faustus (USA))
W J H Ratcliffe W J H Ratcliffe

Placings:005040/2400036200/030024662-665630033 (4880)
2009: 10^{6}SD, 10^{6}SD, 9^{5}SD, 12^{6}SD, 11^{3}SD, 12^{0}SD, 10^{0}G, 10^{3}G, 10^{3}GS,

	Starts	1st	2nd	3rd	Win & Pl
Career Total (Turf)	21	0	2	4	2933
Career Total (AW)	13	0	2	1	1461

Going (Turf): **Sf: 0-7 GS: 0-5 Gd: 0-5 GF: 0-4 Fm: 0-0**
Distance: 5f/6f: 0-0 7f-8f: 0-1 9f-13f: 0-33 14f+: 0-0
Track : LH: 0-22 RH: 0-12 Tight: 0-13 Gall: 0-4
Aids: Bl: 0-6 Vi: 0-0 Tstrap: 0-20 Ckp: 0-20
Best Rating: 51 4/08 Bevl 1m100y gd-sft

Moderate; stays 1m2f; acts on soft ground; also goes on Polytrack; has worn cheekpieces.

Jimmy Dean

(95) (46)**49**
4-y-o b g Ishiguru (USA)-Sister Sal (Bairn (USA))
M Wellings Mark Wellings Racing

Placings:00060/00004006006-0 (0133)
2009: 7^{0}SD,

	Starts	1st	2nd	3rd	Win & Pl
Career Total (Turf)	7	0	0	0	241
Career Total (AW)	10	0	0	0	0

Going (Turf): **Sf: 0-1 GS: 0-0 Gd: 0-2 GF: 0-3 Fm: 0-1**
Distance: 5f/6f: 0-4 7f-8f: 0-10 9f-13f: 0-3 14f+: 0-0
Track : LH: 0-11 RH: 0-0 Tight: 0-8 Gall: 0-4
Aids: Bl: 0-4 Vi: 0-1 Tstrap: 0-7 Ckp: 0-7
Best Rating: 49 7/08 Leic 7f9y gd-fm

Jimmy Ryan (IRE)

101 **65**
8-y-o b g Orpen (USA)-Kaysama (FR) (Kenmare (FR))
T D McCarthy Mrs D H McCarthy

Placings:314/00121/2/0030 (7122)
2009: 5^{0}GF, 5^{0}GF, 6^{3}G, 5^{0}G,

	Starts	1st	2nd	3rd	Win & Pl
Career Total (Turf)	13	3	2	2	30417

101	7/04	Gdwd	5f	C(0-90)H	G-F	£9494
92	6/04	NmkJ	5f	D(0-85)H	G-F	£5434
77	9/03	Nott	6f15y	D	G-F	£3622

Total win prize-money £18552

Going (Turf): Sf: 0-0 GS: 0-0 Gd: 0-5 **GF: 3-8** Fm: 0-0
Distance: **5f/6f: 2-10** 7f-8f: 1-3 9f-13f: 0-0 14f+: 0-0
Track : LH: 0-0 RH: 0-0 Tight: 0-0 Gall: 0-1
Aids: Bl: 0-0 Vi: 0-0 Tstrap: 0-0 Ckp: 0-0
Best Rating: 108 5/05 Gdwd 5f good

Very useful handicapper; off the track from 2005 to 2009; effective from 5f-6f; acts on fast ground.

Jimmy Styles

110 **110**
5-y-o ch g Inchinor-Inya Lake (Whittingham (IRE))
C G Cox Gwyn Powell and Peter Ridgers

Placings:241100/15-2105043315 (6661)
2009: 6^{2}GF, 6^{1}GF, 6^{0}GF, 6^{5}GF, 6^{0}S, 6^{4}GF, 6^{3}GF, 6^{3}GF, 6^{1}G, 6^{5}GS,

	Starts	1st	2nd	3rd	Win & Pl
Career Total (Turf)	18	5	2	2	136195

110	9/09	Ayr	6f	H	GD	£93465
108	5/09	NmkR	6f	(0-100)H	G-F	£12952
101	5/08	Asct	6f	(0-95)H	G-F	£7771
97	8/07	Newb	6f8y	(0-80)H	GD	£4857
79	8/07	Wind	6f		G-F	£3238

Total win prize-money £122285

Going (Turf): Sf: 0-1 GS: 0-1 Gd: 2-6 **GF: 3-10** Fm: 0-0
Distance: **5f/6f: 4-15** 7f-8f: 1-3 9f-13f: 0-0 14f+: 0-0
Track : LH: 0-0 RH: 0-0 Tight: 0-0 **Gall: 1-2**
Aids: Bl: 0-0 Vi: 0-0 Tstrap: 1-3 Ckp: 1-3
Best Rating: 110 9/09 Ayr 6f good

Smart; Ayr Gold Cup winner in 2009 and Listed placed; stays 6f; acts on good or faster ground; has worn cheekpieces.

Jimmy The Poacher (IRE)

89(86) (57)**69**
2-y-o gr g Verglas (IRE)-Danish Gem (Danehill (USA))
T D Easterby Stephen Lee & James McDonald

Placings:64300 (6829)
2009: 7^{6}G, 7^{4}G, 7^{3}GF, 7^{0}GS, 7^{0}SF,

	Starts	1st	2nd	3rd	Win & Pl
Career Total (Turf)	4	0	0	1	1473
Career Total (AW)	1	0	0	0	

Going (Turf): **Sf: 0-0 GS: 0-1 Gd: 0-2 GF: 0-1 Fm: 0-0**
Distance: 5f/6f: 0-0 7f-8f: 0-5 9f-13f: 0-0 14f+: 0-0
Track : LH: 0-5 RH: 0-0 Tight: 0-3 Gall: 0-2
Aids: Bl: 0-0 Vi: 0-0 Tstrap: 0-0 Ckp: 0-0
Best Rating: 69 8/09 Ches 7f2y gd-fm

Jimwil (IRE)

101(84) (35)**77**
3-y-o b g One Cool Cat (USA)-Vulnerable (Hector Protector (USA))
M Dods Bill Nelson & Jim Mahony

Placings:6323500-300154000062 (6824)
2009: 6^{3}F, 6^{0}GS, 6^{0}GF, 7^{1}GF, 5^{5}GF, 7^{4}GF, 8^{0}GF, 7^{0}GS, 7^{0}SD, 6^{0}GF, 7^{6}GF, 7^{2}GF,

	Starts	1st	2nd	3rd	Win & Pl
Career Total (Turf)	18	1	2	3	6178
Career Total (AW)	1	0	0	0	

77	6/09	Rdcr	7f	(0-75)H	G-F	£2590

Total win prize-money £2590

Going (Turf): Sf: 0-0 GS: 0-3 Gd: 0-1 **GF: 1-13** Fm: 0-1
Distance: 5f/6f: 0-9 **7f-8f: 1-9** 9f-13f: 0-1 14f+: 0-0
Track : LH: 0-6 RH: 0-1 Tight: 0-3 Gall: 0-0
Aids: **Bl: 1-9** Vi: 0-0 Tstrap: 0-1 Ckp: 0-1
Best Rating: 77 6/09 Rdcr 7f gd-fm

Fair; stays 7f; acts on fast ground.

Jinksy Minx

65(79) (44)**18**
2-y-o b f Piccolo-Medway (IRE) (Shernazar)
Miss Suzy Smith R Gurney & Suzy Smith

Placings:00 (7624)
2009: 7^{0}GF, 8^{0}SD,

	Starts	1st	2nd	3rd	Win & Pl
Career Total (Turf)	1	0	0	0	
Career Total (AW)	1	0	0	0	

Going (Turf): **Sf: 0-0 GS: 0-0 Gd: 0-0 GF: 0-1 Fm: 0-0**
Distance: 5f/6f: 0-0 7f-8f: 0-2 9f-13f: 0-0 14f+: 0-0
Track : LH: 0-1 RH: 0-0 Tight: 0-1 Gall: 0-0
Aids: Bl: 0-0 Vi: 0-0 Tstrap: 0-0 Ckp: 0-0
Best Rating: 44 12/09 Ling 1m stand

Jinto

(89) (62)
2-y-o ch g Halling (USA)-Sweet Willa (USA) (Assert)
R M H Cowell Khalifa Dasmal

Placings:004 (7266)
2009: 8⁰SD, 8⁰SD, 8⁴SD,

	Starts	1st	2nd	3rd	Win & Pl
Career Total (Turf)	0	0	0	0	
Career Total (AW)	3	0	0	0	216

Going (Turf): Sf: 0-0 GS: 0-0 Gd: 0-0 GF: 0-0 Fm: 0-0
Distance: 5f/6f: 0-0 7f-8f: 0-3 9f-13f: 0-0 14f+: 0-0
Track : LH: 0-2 RH: 0-1 Tight: 0-1 Gall: 0-0
Aids: Bl: 0-0 Vi: 0-0 Tstrap: 0-0 Ckp: 0-0
Best Rating: 62 10/09 Kemp 1m stand

Jira

102 96
2-y-o b f Medicean-Time Saved (Green Desert (USA))
C E Brittain Saeed Manana

Placings:410140435 (6477)
2009: 5⁴GF, 5¹GF, 6⁰GF, 6¹G, 6⁴G, 7⁰G, 6⁴S, 6³GF, 7⁵GF,

	Starts	1st	2nd	3rd	Win & Pl
Career Total (Turf)	9	2	0	1	70106
93 6/09 NmkJ 6f			GD		£17031
81 6/09 Leic 5f218y			G-F		£3885

Total win prize-money £20917

Going (Turf): Sf: 0-1 GS: 0-0 **Gd: 1-3 GF: 1-5** Fm: 0-0
Distance: **5f/6f: 2-7** 7f-8f: 0-2 9f-13f: 0-0 14f+: 0-0
Track : LH: 0-0 RH: 0-0 Tight: 0-0 Gall: 0-0
Aids: Bl: 0-0 Vi: 0-0 Tstrap: 0-0 Ckp: 0-0
Best Rating: 96 9/09 Sals 6f soft

Smart; Listed winner; stays 6f; acts on fast ground.

Jo'burg (USA)

105(99) (75)85
5-y-o b g Johannesburg (USA)-La Martina (Atraf)
Lady Herries Seymour Bloodstock (uk) Ltd

Placings:25103/0340606/44030504-041221255 (6470)
2009: 8⁰SD, 10⁴GF, 10¹GF, 9²GF, 9²GF, 10¹GF, 10²GF, 9⁵G, 10⁵GF,

	Starts	1st	2nd	3rd	Win & Pl
Career Total (Turf)	24	3	4	2	23759
Career Total (AW)	5	0	0	1	1926
81 7/09 Newb 1m2f6y (0-70)H			G-F		£3238
71 5/09 NmkR 1m2f (0-70)H			G-F		£3123
79 7/06 Wind 6f			G-F		£4533

Total win prize-money £10895

Going (Turf): Sf: 0-3 GS: 0-1 Gd: 0-4 **GF: 3-15** Fm: 0-1
Distance: 5f/6f: 1-2 7f-8f: 0-12 **9f-13f: 2-15** 14f+: 0-0
Track : **LH: 1-7** RH: 0-13 Tight: 0-6 **Gall: 2-3**
Aids: Bl: 0-3 Vi: 0-0 Tstrap: 0-0 Ckp: 0-0
Best Rating: 99 5/07 Sand 1m14y gd-sft

Modest; stays 1m2f; acts on fast and soft ground.

Joan's Legacy

91(74) (16)53
2-y-o b f Piccolo-CC Canova (Millkom)
J C Fox John Lonergan

Placings:0050 (7050)
2009: 6⁰S, 6⁰GF, 5⁵G, 7⁰SD,

	Starts	1st	2nd	3rd	Win & Pl
Career Total (Turf)	3	0	0	0	0
Career Total (AW)	1	0	0	0	

Going (Turf): **Sf: 0-1 GS: 0-0 Gd: 0-1 GF: 0-1 Fm: 0-0**
Distance: 5f/6f: 0-2 7f-8f: 0-2 9f-13f: 0-0 14f+: 0-0
Track : LH: 0-0 RH: 0-1 Tight: 0-0 Gall: 0-0
Aids: Bl: 0-0 Vi: 0-0 Tstrap: 0-0 Ckp: 0-0
Best Rating: 53 8/09 Sand 5f6y good

Joannadarc (USA)

(95) (69)
3-y-o ch f Johannesburg (USA)-Game Player (USA) (Drumalis)
S A Callaghan R W Kibble

Placings:034-4366 (1183)
2009: 7⁴SD, 7³SD, 7⁶SD, 10⁶SD,

	Starts	1st	2nd	3rd	Win & Pl
Career Total (Turf)	0	0	0	0	
Career Total (AW)	7	0	0	2	1167

Going (Turf): **Sf: 0-0 GS: 0-0 Gd: 0-0 GF: 0-0 Fm: 0-0**
Distance: 5f/6f: 0-0 7f-8f: 0-6 9f-13f: 0-1 14f+: 0-0
Track : LH: 0-6 RH: 0-1 Tight: 0-5 Gall: 0-0
Aids: Bl: 0-0 Vi: 0-0 Tstrap: 0-0 Ckp: 0-0
Best Rating: 69 12/08 Ling 7f stand

Fair; probably stays 7f; handles an all-weather surface.

Jobe (USA)

103(92) (69)104
3-y-o b g Johannesburg (USA)-Bello Cielo (USA) (Conquistador Cielo (USA))
K A Ryan J & L Duddy A Bailey B McDonald A Heeney

Placings:31306-0316000 (5032)
2009: 8⁰SD, 6³GF, 6¹GS, 6⁶G, 7⁰GF, 7⁰GS, 6⁰GF,

	Starts	1st	2nd	3rd	Win & Pl
Career Total (Turf)	11	2	0	3	26571
Career Total (AW)	1	0	0	0	
96 5/09 Haml 6f5y			G-S		£8723
88 8/08 Ayr 6f			G-S		£4015

Total win prize-money £12738

Going (Turf): Sf: 0-1 **GS: 2-4** Gd: 0-2 GF: 0-4 Fm: 0-0
Distance: 5f/6f: 1-6 7f-8f: 1-6 9f-13f: 0-0 14f+: 0-0
Track : LH: 0-1 RH: 0-1 Tight: 0-1 Gall: 0-0
Aids: Bl: 0-0 Vi: 0-0 Tstrap: 0-1 Ckp: 0-1
Best Rating: 104 8/08 Newb 6f8y gd-sft

Very useful; third in the 2008 Gimcrack; stays 6f; acts on good and easy ground; has worn cheekpieces and a tongue tie.

Jobekani (IRE)

98(95) (61)64
3-y-o b g Tagula (IRE)-Lyca Ballerina (Marju (IRE))
Mrs L Williamson Anthony Thomas Sykes

Placings:5500530-030605300 (7818)
2009: 8⁰GF, 8³GF, 8⁰F, 10⁶GF, 10⁰GF, 9⁵G, 9³SD, 9⁰SD, 9⁰SD,

	Starts	1st	2nd	3rd	Win & Pl
Career Total (Turf)	10	0	0	1	302
Career Total (AW)	6	0	0	2	706

Going (Turf): **Sf: 0-1 GS: 0-1 Gd: 0-2 GF: 0-5 Fm: 0-1**
Distance: 5f/6f: 0-2 7f-8f: 0-4 9f-13f: 0-10 14f+: 0-0
Track : LH: 0-11 RH: 0-1 Tight: 0-10 Gall: 0-0
Aids: Bl: 0-0 Vi: 0-0 Tstrap: 0-1 Ckp: 0-1
Best Rating: 64 5/09 Wwck 1m22y gd-fm

Moderate; stays 1m1f and acts on Polytrack.

Jocheski (IRE)

(73) (64)63
5-y-o b g Mull Of Kintyre (USA)-Ludovica (Bustino)
A G Newcombe The Grubbing Well Partnership

Placings:44/2551255/4-0 (0147)
2009: 12⁰SD,

	Starts	1st	2nd	3rd	Win & Pl
Career Total (Turf)	4	1	1	0	2521
Career Total (AW)	7	0	1	0	1108
63 8/07 Yarm 1m2f21y			G-F		£1943

Total win prize-money £1943

Going (Turf): Sf: 0-1 GS: 0-0 Gd: 0-1 **GF: 1-2** Fm: 0-0
Distance: 5f/6f: 0-0 7f-8f: 0-1 **9f-13f: 1-8** 14f+: 0-2
Track : **LH: 1-11** RH: 0-0 **Tight: 1-8** Gall: 0-0
Aids: Bl: 0-0 Vi: 0-1 Tstrap: 0-0 Ckp: 0-0
Best Rating: 65 1/07 Wolv 1m1f103y stand

Modest sort; stays 2m; acts on a sound surface and Polytrack.

Jodawes (USA)

(94)
2-y-o b/br c Burning Roma (USA)-Venetian Peach (USA) (Desert Wine (USA))
J R Best S R Fisher

Placings:4 (7885)
2009: 7⁴SD,

	Starts	1st	2nd	3rd	Win & Pl
Career Total (Turf)	0	0	0	0	
Career Total (AW)	1	0	0	0	0

Going (Turf): **Sf: 0-0 GS: 0-0 Gd: 0-0 GF: 0-0 Fm: 0-0**
Distance: 5f/6f: 0-0 7f-8f: 0-1 9f-13f: 0-0 14f+: 0-0
Track : LH: 0-1 RH: 0-0 Tight: 0-1 Gall: 0-0
Aids: Bl: 0-0 Vi: 0-0 Tstrap: 0-0 Ckp: 0-0

Joe Caster

86(102) (89)87
3-y-o b c Makbul-Oedipus Regina (Fraam)
J M P Eustace The Greek Myths

Placings:23112514-00060 (3469)
2009: 7⁰SD, 6⁰SD, 6⁰SD, 5⁶G, 7⁰SD,

	Starts	1st	2nd	3rd	Win & Pl
Career Total (Turf)	5	1	2	1	7482
Career Total (AW)	8	2	0	0	10941
89 11/08 GrLe 6f (0-85)			STD		£5180
88 10/08 Wolv 5f216y (0-80)			STD		£5180
76 10/08 Nott 5f13y			SFT		£5180

Total win prize-money £15543

Going (Turf): **Sf: 1-3** GS: 0-0 Gd: 0-1 GF: 0-1 Fm: 0-0
Distance: **5f/6f: 3-11** 7f-8f: 0-2 9f-13f: 0-0 14f+: 0-0
Track : **LH: 2-8** RH: 0-1 Tight: 1-6 Gall: 1-3
Aids: Bl: 0-0 Vi: 0-0 Tstrap: 0-0 Ckp: 0-0
Best Rating: 89 11/08 GrLe 6f stand

Useful; effective over 5f-6f; acts on most ground and on Polytrack.

Joe Jo Star

106(100) (58)81
7-y-o b g Piccolo-Zagreb Flyer (Old Vic)

R A Fahey The Ipso Facto Syndicate

Placings:6600/64005006**6410/0213000000/003/11660033-1212100** **(5067)**

2009: 8^{1}SD, 10^{2}SD, 9^{1}F, 9^{2}F, 12^{1}GS, 11^{0}GF, 12^{0}GF,

	Starts	1st	2nd	3rd	Win & Pl
Career Total (Turf)	18	2	1	1	9341
Career Total (AW)	25	5	2	3	10242

81	6/09	York	1m4f	(0-80)H	G-S	£5180
71	6/09	Ayr	1m1f20y	(0-60)H	FRM	£2266
58	1/09	Wolv	1m141y	(0-50)H	STD	£2047
57	2/08	Wolv	1m1f103y	(0-45)	STD	£1365
53	2/08	Wolv	1m1f103y	(0-50)H	STD	£1774
57	2/06	Wolv	1m141y	(0-45)	STD	£1535
50	12/05	Wolv	1m141y	(0-45)	STD	£1429

Total win prize-money £15601

Going (Turf): Sf: 0-1 **GS: 1-2** Gd: 0-6 GF: 0-4 **Fm: 1-5**
Distance: 5f/6f: 0-5 7f-8f: 0-6 **9f-13f: 7-32** 14f+: 0-0
Track : **LH: 7-32** RH: 0-7 **Tight: 5-26** Gall: 1-3
Aids: Bl: 0-0 Vi: 0-0 Tstrap: 2-7 Ckp: 2-7
Best Rating: **81** 6/09 York 1m4f gd-sft

Modest; suited by 1m-2f; acts on Polytrack/fast ground; useful hurdler.

Joe Packet

97 **76**

2-y-o ch c Joe Bear (IRE)-Costa Packet (IRE) (Hussonet (USA))
J G Portman The Joe Packets

Placings:52425 **(6104)**

2009: 6^{5}GF, 6^{2}G, 7^{4}S, 6^{2}GF, 6^{5}GF,

	Starts	1st	2nd	3rd	Win & Pl
Career Total (Turf)	5	0	2	0	2023

Going (Turf): **Sf: 0-1 GS: 0-0 Gd: 0-1 GF: 0-3 Fm: 0-0**
Distance: 5f/6f: 0-2 7f-8f: 0-3 9f-13f: 0-0 14f+: 0-0
Track : LH: 0-0 RH: 0-0 Tight: 0-0 Gall: 0-1
Aids: Bl: 0-0 Vi: 0-0 Tstrap: 0-0 Ckp: 0-0
Best Rating: **76** 7/09 Wind 6f good

Fair; suited by 6f-7f; acts on fast and soft ground.

Joe Rua (USA)

79(83) (36)**53**

2-y-o b/br c Johannesburg (USA)-Red Tulle (USA) (A.P. Indy (USA))
J Ryan A Dee

Placings:06000 **(7685)**

2009: 6^{0}GF, 6^{6}GS, 8^{0}GF, 7^{0}SD, 8^{0}SD,

	Starts	1st	2nd	3rd	Win & Pl
Career Total (Turf)	3	0	0	0	0
Career Total (AW)	2	0	0	0	

Going (Turf): **Sf: 0-0 GS: 0-1 Gd: 0-0 GF: 0-2 Fm: 0-0**
Distance: 5f/6f: 0-2 7f-8f: 0-2 9f-13f: 0-1 14f+: 0-0
Track : LH: 0-1 RH: 0-2 Tight: 0-0 Gall: 0-0
Aids: Bl: 0-0 Vi: 0-2 Tstrap: 0-0 Ckp: 0-0
Best Rating: **53** 10/09 NmkR 6f gd-fm

Moderate; stays 7f; handles Polytrack.

Joel The Mole

79 **31**

2-y-o ch g Reel Buddy (USA)-Fly South (Polar Falcon (USA))
D Nicholls The Three K's

Placings:600 **(5519)**

2009: 6^{6}G, 6^{0}GF, 6^{0}G,

	Starts	1st	2nd	3rd	Win & Pl
Career Total (Turf)	3	0	0	0	0

Going (Turf): **Sf: 0-0 GS: 0-0 Gd: 0-2 GF: 0-1 Fm: 0-0**
Distance: 5f/6f: 0-3 7f-8f: 0-0 9f-13f: 0-0 14f+: 0-0
Track : LH: 0-0 RH: 0-0 Tight: 0-0 Gall: 0-0
Aids: Bl: 0-0 Vi: 0-0 Tstrap: 0-0 Ckp: 0-0
Best Rating: **31** 6/09 Rdcr 6f good

Johann Zoffany

105 **106**

3-y-o b c Galileo (IRE)-Belle Allemande (CAN) (Royal Academy (USA))
A P O'Brien Michael Tabor

Placings:34-611014 **(5685a)**

2009: 10^{6}Y, 10^{1}GY, 10^{1}G, 12^{0}GF, 10^{1}Y, 10^{4}GY,

	Starts	1st	2nd	3rd	Win & Pl
Career Total (Turf)	8	3	0	1	35106

106	6/09	Curr	1m2f	(60-100)H	YLD	£14852
97	5/09	Leop	1m2f	(60-95)H	GD	£9056
89	5/09	Naas	1m2f		G-Y	£8050

Total win prize-money £31960

Going (Turf): Sf: 0-1 GS: 0-0 **Gd: 1-1** GF: 0-1 Fm: 0-0
Distance: 5f/6f: 0-0 7f-8f: 0-2 **9f-13f: 3-6** 14f+: 0-0
Track : **LH: 2-4** RH: 1-3 Tight: 0-0 Gall: 0-1
Aids: Bl: 0-0 Vi: 0-0 Tstrap: 0-0 Ckp: 0-0
Best Rating: **106** 6/09 Curr 1m2f yield

Smart; effective over 1m2f; acts on good and easy ground.

Johannes (IRE)

109(98) (72)**101**

6-y-o b g Mozart (IRE)-Blue Sirocco (Bluebird (USA))
R A Fahey John Nicholls Ltd/David Kilburn

Placings:212/403040/00/303504606-1210110003 **(6994)**

2009: 5^{1}G, 5^{2}GF, 6^{1}GF, 7^{0}G, 6^{1}G, 6^{1}GF, 5^{0}GF, 6^{0}G, 6^{0}G, 6^{3}G,

	Starts	1st	2nd	3rd	Win & Pl
Career Total (Turf)	28	5	3	4	78634
Career Total (AW)	2	0	0	0	0

101	8/09	Ripn	6f	(0-100)H	G-F	£11215
96	7/09	Gdwd	6f	H	GD	£18693
88	6/09	Rdcr	6f	(0-95)H	G-F	£7771
83	5/09	Catt	5f212y	(0-85)H	GD	£5180
86	8/05	York	6f		GD	£17631

Total win prize-money £60492

Going (Turf): Sf: 0-2 GS: 0-1 **Gd: 3-11** GF: 2-13 Fm: 0-1
Distance: **5f/6f: 5-24** 7f-8f: 0-6 9f-13f: 0-0 14f+: 0-0
Track : **LH: 1-7** RH: 0-1 **Tight: 1-4** Gall: 0-1
Aids: Bl: 0-0 Vi: 0-0 Tstrap: 0-0 Ckp: 0-0
Best Rating: **102** 8/05 Ripn 6f gd-fm

Very useful; suited by 5f-6f; acts on good and faster ground; has worn a tongue tie.

Johannesgray (IRE)

97 **70**

2-y-o gr g Verglas (IRE)-Prepare For War (IRE) (Marju (IRE))
D Nicholls Brian Morton

Placings:2 **(6096)**

2009: 5^{2}GF,

	Starts	1st	2nd	3rd	Win & Pl
Career Total (Turf)	1	0	1	0	1156

Going (Turf): **Sf: 0-0 GS: 0-0 Gd: 0-0 GF: 0-1 Fm: 0-0**
Distance: 5f/6f: 0-1 7f-8f: 0-0 9f-13f: 0-0 14f+: 0-0
Track : LH: 0-1 RH: 0-0 Tight: 0-1 Gall: 0-0
Aids: Bl: 0-0 Vi: 0-0 Tstrap: 0-0 Ckp: 0-0
Best Rating: **70** 9/09 Catt 5f212y gd-fm

Fair; stays 6f; acts on fast ground.

John Charles (IRE)

62 (66)**56**

7-y-o b g Fraam-Norwegian Queen (IRE) (Affirmed (USA))
Jim Best (B De Haan 20/8) Alan Clarke

Placings:2/10000/0 **(4053)**

2009: 11^{0}S,

	Starts	1st	2nd	3rd	Win & Pl
Career Total (Turf)	3	0	0	0	
Career Total (AW)	4	1	1	0	3919

66	2/06	Wolv	1m141y	STD	£2914

Total win prize-money £2915

Going (Turf): **Sf: 0-1 GS: 0-0 Gd: 0-1 GF: 0-1 Fm: 0-0**
Distance: 5f/6f: 0-0 7f-8f: 0-0 **9f-13f: 1-7** 14f+: 0-0
Track : **LH: 1-6** RH: 0-1 **Tight: 1-5** Gall: 0-2
Aids: Bl: 0-0 Vi: 0-0 Tstrap: 0-0 Ckp: 0-0
Best Rating: **66** 2/06 Wolv 1m141y stand

Modest; effective at around a mile; acts on Polytrack.

John Dillon (IRE)

(96) (60)**58**

5-y-o ch g Traditionally (USA)-Matikanehanafubuki (IRE) (Caerleon (USA))
P C Haslam Michael Ryan (Bradford)

Placings:4653123/0000-500 **(4403)**

2009: 13^{5}SD, 12^{0}SD, 12^{0}GF,

	Starts	1st	2nd	3rd	Win & Pl
Career Total (Turf)	10	1	1	2	6321
Career Total (AW)	4	0	0	0	209

68	7/07	Haml	1m65y	(0-70)H	SFT	£3238

Total win prize-money £3239

Going (Turf): **Sf: 1-2** GS: 0-2 Gd: 0-3 GF: 0-3 Fm: 0-0
Distance: 5f/6f: 0-0 7f-8f: 0-2 **9f-13f: 1-11** 14f+: 0-1
Track : LH: 0-9 **RH: 1-5 Tight: 1-3** Gall: 0-2
Aids: Bl: 0-1 **Vi: 1-7** Tstrap: 0-0 Ckp: 0-0
Best Rating: **69** 8/07 Hayd 1m3f200y gd-fm

Moderate; stays 1m2f; acts on fast and soft ground.

John Forbes

100(99) (79)**75**

7-y-o b g High Estate-Mavourneen (USA) (Dynaformer (USA))
B Ellison R Wagner

Placings:010000005/341400/**00**1666030/0025213124 **(7170)**

2009: 10^{0}G, 16^{0}GF, 12^{2}G, 14^{5}G, 13^{2}HY, 13^{1}S, 15^{3}S, 16^{1}SD, 16^{2}SD, 15^{4}S,

	Starts	1st	2nd	3rd	Win & Pl
Career Total (Turf)	29	4	2	3	25651
Career Total (AW)	5	1	1	0	4748

76	10/09	Wolv	2m119y	(0-70)H	STD	£3238
71	8/09	Ayr	1m5f13y	(0-65)H	SFT	£2388
69	3/06	Muss	2m	(0-85)H	HVY	£6477
74	5/05	Haml	1m3f16y	(0-70)H	G-S	£4130
78	6/04	Newc	6f	D	SFT	£6825

Total win prize-money £23059

Going (Turf): **Sf: 3-9** GS: 1-5 Gd: 0-9 GF: 0-5 Fm: 0-1
Distance: 5f/6f: 1-3 7f-8f: 0-7 9f-13f: 1-9 **14f+: 3-15**
Track : LH: 2-20 RH: 2-8 **Tight: 3-15** Gall: 0-6
Aids: Bl: 0-2 Vi: 0-0 Tstrap: 0-0 Ckp: 0-0
Best Rating: **87** 7/04 NmkJ 7f gd-sft

Modest; stays 2m; acts well in soft ground.

John Keats

103 (53)**86**

6-y-o b g Bertolini (USA)-Nightingale (Night Shift (USA))
J S Goldie C & B Racing Club

Placings:0101/02550000306/0025204021310**0**/03151330 42000-03520440333300 **(6984)**
2009: 6^{0}HY, 6^{3}GF, 6^{5}GF, 6^{2}F, 6^{0}G, 6^{4}G, 6^{4}G, 6^{0}G, 6^{3}GF, 6^{3}GF, 7^{3}GF, 6^{3}GF, 6^{0}G, 7^{0}G,

	Starts	1st	2nd	3rd	Win & Pl
Career Total (Turf)	55	6	6	10	40653
Career Total (AW)	1	0	0	0	

84	6/08	Donc	6f	(0-85)H	G-F	£4857
76	6/08	Thsk	6f	(0-85)H	FRM	£5180
79	9/07	Rdcr	6f	(0-75)H	G-F	£2817
76	8/07	Newc	6f	(0-65)H	GD	£2266
82	10/05	Pont	6f	(0-75)	GD	£4387
68	8/05	Chep	6f16y		G-F	£3038

Total win prize-money £22548

Going (Turf): Sf: 0-8 GS: 0-3 Gd: 2-21 **GF: 3-21** Fm: 1-2
Distance: **5f/6f: 5-46** 7f-8f: 1-10 9f-13f: 0-0 14f+: 0-0
Track : **LH: 1-9** RH: 0-3 Tight: 0-7 Gall: 0-0
Aids: Bl: 0-2 Vi: 0-0 Tstrap: 0-5 Ckp: 0-5
Best Rating: **86** 7/08 Hayd 6f good

Modest; suited by 6f and acts on good and faster ground; has worn blinkers and cheekpieces.

John Potts

74(98) (57)**27**

4-y-o b g Josr Algarhoud (IRE)-Crown City (USA) (Coronado's Quest (USA))
B P J Baugh Miss J A Price

Placings:000554/04522004005-325000630 **(7857)**
2009: 9^{3}SD, 9^{2}SD, 9^{5}SD, 9^{0}SD, 9^{0}SD, 10^{0}GF, 9^{6}SD, 9^{3}SD, 9^{0}SD,

	Starts	1st	2nd	3rd	Win & Pl
Career Total (Turf)	5	0	0	0	
Career Total (AW)	21	0	3	2	2418

Going (Turf): **Sf: 0-0 GS: 0-1 Gd: 0-0 GF: 0-4 Fm: 0-0**
Distance: 5f/6f: 0-3 7f-8f: 0-4 9f-13f: 0-19 14f+: 0-0
Track : LH: 0-25 RH: 0-0 Tight: 0-22 Gall: 0-2
Aids: Bl: 0-0 Vi: 0-0 Tstrap: 0-6 Ckp: 0-6
Best Rating: **59** 3/08 Wolv 1m1f103y stand

Moderate; stays 1m1f; acts on Polytrack.

John Terry (IRE)

106(115) (100)**97**

6-y-o b g Grand Lodge (USA)-Kardashina (FR) (Darshaan)
Mrs A J Perrett A D Spence

Placings:10/2430/356102050/**143**003003-**5602620** **(2475)**
2009: 10^{5}SD, 12^{6}SD, 10^{0}SD, 11^{2}SD, 11^{6}SD, 12^{2}GF, 12^{0}G,

	Starts	1st	2nd	3rd	Win & Pl
Career Total (Turf)	22	2	3	4	35470
Career Total (AW)	9	1	1	1	17507

97	2/08	Ling	1m4f	(0-100)H	STD	£9971
96	7/07	NmkJ	1m4f	(0-90)H	G-F	£9715
75	5/05	Leic	5f218y		SFT	£5772

Total win prize-money £25459

Going (Turf): **Sf: 1-4** GS: 0-2 Gd: 0-7 **GF: 1-9** Fm: 0-0
Distance: 5f/6f: 1-1 7f-8f: 0-1 **9f-13f: 2-27** 14f+: 0-2
Track : LH: 1-12 RH: 1-15 Tight: 1-15 Gall: 1-8
Aids: Bl: 0-0 Vi: 0-0 Tstrap: 0-1 Ckp: 0-1
Best Rating: **100** 3/08 Kemp 1m3f stand

Useful; stays 1m4f; acts on most ground and on Polytrack; has worn cheekpieces.

Johnmanderville

106(102) (76)**82**

3-y-o b g Kheleyf (USA)-Lady's Walk (IRE) (Charnwood Forest (IRE))
A P Jarvis (K R Burke 25/7) Jet Racing Partnership

Placings:0321415-010020662 **(6804)**
2009: 8^{0}GF, 8^{1}GF, 7^{0}GF, 8^{0}S, 8^{2}G, 8^{0}G, 8^{6}GF, 8^{6}GF, 9^{2}SD,

	Starts	1st	2nd	3rd	Win & Pl
Career Total (Turf)	15	3	2	1	21606
Career Total (AW)	1	0	1	0	705

79	4/09	Newc	1m3y	(0-85)H	G-F	£5180
77	9/08	NmkR	7f	(0-95)	G-F	£9066
73	7/08	Haml	6f5y		GD	£3885

Total win prize-money £18133

Going (Turf): Sf: 0-2 GS: 0-1 Gd: 1-6 **GF: 2-6** Fm: 0-0
Distance: 5f/6f: 0-4 **7f-8f: 2-8** 9f-13f: 1-4 14f+: 0-0
Track : LH: 0-6 RH: 0-1 Tight: 0-4 Gall: 0-1
Aids: Bl: 0-0 Vi: 0-0 Tstrap: 0-2 Ckp: 0-2
Best Rating: **82** 6/09 Thsk 1m good

Fair; effective over 7f-1m; acts on good and faster ground; likes to race prominently.

Johnny Friendly

95(99) (65)**68**

4-y-o b g Auction House (USA)-Quantum Lady (Mujadil (USA))
K R Burke Aricabeau Racing Ltd & Mrs E Burke

Placings:00640/13236340-500604 **(2404)**
2009: 8^{5}SD, 7^{0}SD, 7^{0}GF, 9^{6}GF, 7^{0}GF, 8^{4}GF,

	Starts	1st	2nd	3rd	Win & Pl
Career Total (Turf)	12	0	0	2	1676
Career Total (AW)	7	1	1	1	2933

65	3/08	Ling	7f	(0-60)H	STD	£1876

Total win prize-money £1877

Going (Turf): **Sf: 0-2 GS: 0-1 Gd: 0-3 GF: 0-6 Fm: 0-0**
Distance: 5f/6f: 0-3 **7f-8f: 1-12** 9f-13f: 0-4 14f+: 0-0
Track : **LH: 1-12** RH: 0-5 **Tight: 1-13** Gall: 0-2
Aids: Bl: 0-0 Vi: 0-1 Tstrap: 0-0 Ckp: 0-0
Best Rating: **68** 7/08 Haml 1m65y good

Modest; effective at 7f; acts on most ground and Polytrack.

Johnny Rocket (IRE)

84 **58**

4-y-o ch g Viking Ruler (AUS)-Karen Blixen (Kris)
K A Ryan Mrs D Davenport Tony Rob & Ed Fawcett

Placings:306 **(2232)**
2009: 10^{3}GS, 12^{0}G, 12^{6}GS,

	Starts	1st	2nd	3rd	Win & Pl
Career Total (Turf)	3	0	0	1	404

Going (Turf): **Sf: 0-0 GS: 0-2 Gd: 0-1 GF: 0-0 Fm: 0-0**
Distance: 5f/6f: 0-0 7f-8f: 0-0 9f-13f: 0-3 14f+: 0-0
Track : LH: 0-3 RH: 0-0 Tight: 0-1 Gall: 0-2
Aids: Bl: 0-0 Vi: 0-0 Tstrap: 0-0 Ckp: 0-0
Best Rating: **58** 5/09 Newc 1m2f32y gd-sft

Johnnyleary (IRE)

56 **1**

2-y-o ch g Fayruz-Forgren (IRE) (Thatching)
D Nicholls Dr Marwan Koukash

Placings:00 **(2195)**
2009: 5^{0}GF, 6^{0}S,

	Starts	1st	2nd	3rd	Win & Pl
Career Total (Turf)	2	0	0	0	

Going (Turf): **Sf: 0-1 GS: 0-0 Gd: 0-0 GF: 0-1 Fm: 0-0**
Distance: 5f/6f: 0-2 7f-8f: 0-0 9f-13f: 0-0 14f+: 0-0
Track : LH: 0-1 RH: 0-0 Tight: 0-1 Gall: 0-0
Aids: Bl: 0-0 Vi: 0-0 Tstrap: 0-0 Ckp: 0-0
Best Rating: **1** 5/09 Hayd 6f soft

Johnston's Baby (IRE)

105(100) (65)**68**

7-y-o b m Bob Back (USA)-Mirror Of Flowers (Artaius (USA))
E J Alston The Good Shepherds

Placings:4360223443600 **(5103)**
2009: 8^{4}SD, 12^{3}SD, 8^{6}SD, 11^{0}SD, 8^{2}SD, 10^{2}F, 9^{3}GF, 9^{4}GF, 10^{4}G, 9^{3}GF, 10^{6}GF, 10^{0}G, 9^{0}SD,

	Starts	1st	2nd	3rd	Win & Pl
Career Total (Turf)	7	0	1	2	2001
Career Total (AW)	6	0	1	1	1008

Going (Turf): **Sf: 0-0 GS: 0-0 Gd: 0-2 GF: 0-4 Fm: 0-1**
Distance: 5f/6f: 0-0 7f-8f: 0-1 9f-13f: 0-12 14f+: 0-0
Track : LH: 0-10 RH: 0-3 Tight: 0-6 Gall: 0-0
Aids: Bl: 0-0 Vi: 0-0 Tstrap: 0-0 Ckp: 0-0
Best Rating: **68** 6/09 Carl 1m1f61y gd-fm

Moderate; effective over 1m-1m4f; acts on Polytrack.

Johnston's Glory (IRE)

95(99) (66)**69**

5-y-o b m Desert Sun-Clos De Tart (IRE) (Indian Ridge)
E J Alston The Good Shepherds

Placings:4005**0245**/**54050**3500111-340RR **(4436)**
2009: 6^{3}F, 6^{4}G, 6^{0}GF, 5^{R}GF, 6^{R}GF,

	Starts	1st	2nd	3rd	Win & Pl
Career Total (Turf)	16	3	0	2	8261
Career Total (AW)	9	0	1	0	730

69	7/08	Rdcr	6f	(0-65)H	G-F	£2266
63	7/08	Catt	5f212y	(0-60)H	G-F	£2104
54	7/08	Haml	5f4y		G-S	£2388

Total win prize-money £6760

Going (Turf): Sf: 0-1 GS: 1-1 Gd: 0-1 **GF: 2-11** Fm: 0-2
Distance: **5f/6f: 3-11** 7f-8f: 0-7 9f-13f: 0-7 14f+: 0-0
Track : **LH: 1-12** RH: 0-3 **Tight: 1-9** Gall: 0-1
Aids: Bl: 0-4 Vi: 0-0 Tstrap: 3-7 Ckp: 3-7
Best Rating: **69** 7/08 Rdcr 6f gd-fm

Moderate; effective over 5f; handles fast ground; also goes on Polytrack; has worn headgear.

Johnstown Lad (IRE)

106(108) (89)**89**

5-y-o b g Invincible Spirit (IRE)-Pretext (Polish Precedent (USA))

Daniel Mark Loughnane (Niall Moran 26/6) Leo Cox

Placings:06312040/0401060032/22424000300-6005401350254 **(7646)**

2009: 6^{6}SD, 5^{0}Y, 5^{0}HY, 5^{5}F, 5^{4}GF, 5^{0}S, 5^{1}G, 6^{3}G, 5^{5}Y, 6^{0}SD, 6^{2}SD, 6^{5}SD, 5^{4}SD,

	Starts	1st	2nd	3rd	Win & Pl
Career Total (Turf)	29	3	1	2	31161
Career Total (AW)	14	0	5	2	16794

81 9/09 Bath 5f161y (0-75)H GD £2719
92 7/07 Bell 5f (60-95)H Y-S £10996
78 7/06 Naas 6f G-F £8816
Total win prize-money £22533

Going (Turf): Sf: 0-5 GS: 0-1 **Gd: 1-6 GF: 1-6** Fm: 0-3
Distance: **5f/6f: 3-40** 7f-8f: 0-3 9f-13f: 0-0 14f+: 0-0
Track : **LH: 3-27** RH: 0-3 Tight: 0-5 **Gall: 1-2**
Aids: Bl: 0-1 Vi: 0-0 Tstrap: 0-1 Ckp: 0-1
Best Rating: **94** 2/08 Ling 5f stand

Useful sprinter; Irish-trained; acts well on Polytrack; often wears a tongue tie; has worn blinkers.

Join Up

99(100) (59)**53**

3-y-o b g Green Desert (USA)-Rise (Polar Falcon (USA))

W M Brisbourne P R Kirk

Placings:000605-000463405003212 **(7856)**

2009: 7^{0}SD, 7^{0}G, 5^{0}GF, 7^{4}GF, 8^{6}G, 9^{3}GS, 10^{4}GF, 9^{0}F, 10^{5}SS, 10^{0}SS, 9^{0}SD, 8^{3}SD, 8^{2}SD, 8^{1}SD, 9^{2}SD, 9^{2}SD,

	Starts	1st	2nd	3rd	Win & Pl
Career Total (Turf)	11	0	0	1	707
Career Total (AW)	11	1	3	1	4113

56 12/09 Ling 1m (0-55)H STD £2047
Total win prize-money £2047

Going (Turf): **Sf: 0-0 GS: 0-1 Gd: 0-4 GF: 0-5 Fm: 0-1**
Distance: 5f/6f: 0-4 **7f-8f: 1-9** 9f-13f: 0-9 14f+: 0-0
Track : **LH: 1-11** RH: 0-5 **Tight: 1-10** Gall: 0-1
Aids: Bl: 0-0 Vi: 0-1 Tstrap: 0-1 Ckp: 0-1
Best Rating: **59** 12/09 Wolv 1m1f103y stand

Moderate; effective over 1m-1m2f; acts on Polytrack.

Joinedupwriting

98(94) (46)**70**

4-y-o b g Desert Style (IRE)-Ink Pot (USA) (Green Dancer (USA))

R M Whitaker R C Dollar

Placings:052104/40534500-12100 **(4597)**

2009: 9^{1}GF, 9^{2}GF, 9^{1}GF, 10^{0}GF, 9^{0}G,

	Starts	1st	2nd	3rd	Win & Pl
Career Total (Turf)	18	3	2	1	12137
Career Total (AW)	1	0	0	0	

66 6/09 Ripn 1m1f170y (0-70)H G-F £3238
63 5/09 Ripn 1m1f170y G-F £2590
72 9/07 Rdcr 7f G-F £2817
Total win prize-money £8645

Going (Turf): Sf: 0-0 GS: 0-4 Gd: 0-6 **GF: 3-8** Fm: 0-0
Distance: 5f/6f: 0-3 7f-8f: 1-3 **9f-13f: 2-13** 14f+: 0-0
Track : LH: 0-8 **RH: 2-6 Tight: 2-8** Gall: 0-1
Aids: Bl: 0-0 Vi: 0-0 Tstrap: 0-0 Ckp: 0-0
Best Rating: **77** 10/07 Bath 1m5y gd-fm

Modest; effective at around 1m-1m2f; acts on fast ground.

Jojesse

89(101) (56)**48**

5-y-o ch g Compton Place-Jodeeka (Fraam)

W Storey (G A Swinbank 2/1) W Storey

Placings:0604/2311644303350/650656424-00000000 **(7732)**

2009: 7^{0}SS, 6^{0}F, 9^{0}GF, 8^{0}GF, 7^{0}GF, 7^{0}SD, 8^{0}SD, 12^{0}SD,

	Starts	1st	2nd	3rd	Win & Pl
Career Total (Turf)	21	1	0	3	4341
Career Total (AW)	14	1	2	1	3811

59 4/07 Muss 5f (0-60)H G-F £2590
61 3/07 Kemp 5f (0-55)H STD £2047
Total win prize-money £4639

Going (Turf): Sf: 0-2 GS: 0-1 Gd: 0-3 **GF: 1-14** Fm: 0-1
Distance: **5f/6f: 2-25** 7f-8f: 0-7 9f-13f: 0-3 14f+: 0-0
Track : LH: 0-11 **RH: 1-5** Tight: 0-4 Gall: 0-2
Aids: Bl: 0-3 Vi: 0-0 Tstrap: 0-0 Ckp: 0-0
Best Rating: **61** 3/07 Kemp 5f stand

Moderate; stays 7f and acts on sand.

Jokers Wild

(65) (20)

2-y-o b c Compton Place-Lady Hibernia (Anabaa (USA))

A M Balding Sir Gordon Brunton

Placings:00 **(7571)**

2009: 7^{0}SD, 6^{0}SD,

	Starts	1st	2nd	3rd	Win & Pl
Career Total (Turf)	0	0	0	0	
Career Total (AW)	2	0	0	0	

Going (Turf): **Sf: 0-0 GS: 0-0 Gd: 0-0 GF: 0-0 Fm: 0-0**
Distance: 5f/6f: 0-1 7f-8f: 0-1 9f-13f: 0-0 14f+: 0-0
Track : LH: 0-1 RH: 0-1 Tight: 0-1 Gall: 0-0
Aids: Bl: 0-0 Vi: 0-0 Tstrap: 0-0 Ckp: 0-0
Best Rating: **20** 11/09 Kemp 7f stand

Jolies Dee

(81) (36)

4-y-o br f Diktat-Jolies Eaux (Shirley Heights)

J R Jenkins Ms Joanna Walker

Placings:0-0 **(0102)**

2009: 12^{0}SD,

	Starts	1st	2nd	3rd	Win & Pl
Career Total (Turf)	0	0	0	0	
Career Total (AW)	2	0	0	0	

Going (Turf): **Sf: 0-0 GS: 0-0 Gd: 0-0 GF: 0-0 Fm: 0-0**
Distance: 5f/6f: 0-0 7f-8f: 0-0 9f-13f: 0-2 14f+: 0-0
Track : LH: 0-2 RH: 0-0 Tight: 0-2 Gall: 0-0
Aids: Bl: 0-0 Vi: 0-0 Tstrap: 0-0 Ckp: 0-0
Best Rating: **36** 1/09 Ling 1m4f stand

Jolly Ranch

87(99) (59)**44**

3-y-o gr f Compton Place-How Do I Know (Petong)

A G Newcombe David Bramhill

Placings:63-146003232 **(7651)**

2009: 5^{1}SD, 5^{4}SD, 5^{6}G, 5^{0}SD, 5^{0}G, 5^{3}SD, 5^{2}SD, 5^{3}SD, 5^{2}SD,

	Starts	1st	2nd	3rd	Win & Pl
Career Total (Turf)	2	0	0	0	0
Career Total (AW)	9	1	2	3	4807

53 1/09 Wolv 5f20y STD £2388
Total win prize-money £2388

Going (Turf): **Sf: 0-0 GS: 0-0 Gd: 0-2 GF: 0-0 Fm: 0-0**
Distance: **5f/6f: 1-11** 7f-8f: 0-0 9f-13f: 0-0 14f+: 0-0
Track : **LH: 1-9** RH: 0-1 **Tight: 1-8** Gall: 0-1
Aids: Bl: 0-0 Vi: 0-0 Tstrap: 0-0 Ckp: 0-0
Best Rating: **59** 12/09 Ling 5f stand

Moderate; effective over 5f; acts on Polytrack.

Jonnie Skull (IRE)

98(106) (71)**74**

3-y-o b g Pyrus (USA)-Sovereign Touch (IRE) (Pennine Walk)

P S McEntee (D R C Elsworth 29/1) Mrs Rebecca McEntee

Placings:000024-352223340403651320000142 **(7797)**

2009: 8^{3}SD, 8^{5}SD, 8^{2}SD, 7^{2}SD, 12^{2}SF, 8^{3}SD, 12^{3}SD, 11^{4}SD, 7^{0}G, 7^{4}G, 8^{0}S, 8^{3}SD, 8^{6}G, 7^{5}F, 7^{1}SD, 7^{3}SD, 7^{2}GF, 7^{0}SD, 6^{0}GF, 7^{0}SD, 12^{0}SD, 7^{1}SD, 8^{4}SD,

	Starts	1st	2nd	3rd	Win & Pl
Career Total (Turf)	8	0	1	0	976
Career Total (AW)	22	2	5	5	9450

69 12/09 Sthl 7f (0-60)H STD £2047
59 8/09 Kemp 7f (0-55) STD £2047
Total win prize-money £4094

Going (Turf): **Sf: 0-1 GS: 0-0 Gd: 0-4 GF: 0-2 Fm: 0-1**
Distance: 5f/6f: 0-2 **7f-8f: 2-22** 9f-13f: 0-6 14f+: 0-0
Track : LH: 1-18 RH: 1-7 Tight: 0-6 Gall: 0-2
Aids: Bl: 0-6 **Vi: 2-17** Tstrap: 0-0 Ckp: 0-0
Best Rating: **74** 7/09 NmkJ 1m good

Modest; effective over 7f-1m; acts on Fibresand and Polytrack; has worn headgear.

Jonny Ebeneezer

95 (46)**66**

10-y-o b g Hurricane Sky (AUS)-Leap Of Faith (IRE) (Northiam (USA))

D Flood Mrs Cheryl Flood

Placings:03010/50511002010/0042246402/000202103102 21141100013165/324340006/30000000/0/0526060000-45 **(2436)**

2009: 5^{4}GF, 5^{5}GF,

	Starts	1st	2nd	3rd	Win & Pl
Career Total (Turf)	68	11	9	5	200485
Career Total (AW)	14	1	1	1	4295

106 10/04 York 6f (0-100)H GD £19500
103 9/04 Hayd 5f (0-100)H SFT £20176
92 8/04 Wind 6f C(0-100)H G-S £12504
86 7/04 NmkJ 6f C(0-90)H G-F £9548
81 7/04 NmkJ 6f C(0-90)H G-F £9431
70 7/04 Sand 5f6y D(0-80)H G-F £7036
64 7/04 Sthl 6f F(0-55)H STD £3024
65 5/04 Brig 6f209y G G-F £2590
98 9/02 Gdwd 6f C(0-95)H GD £13746
94 6/02 Epsm 7f C(0-100)H SFT £19500
83 5/02 Wind 5f10y B(0-105)H G-S £29000
82 11/01 Brig 5f213y D G-S £3627
Total win prize-money £149685

Going (Turf): Sf: 2-13GS: 3-13Gd: 2-12 **GF: 4-28** Fm: 0-1
Distance: **5f/6f: 10-48** 7f-8f: 2-33 9f-13f: 0-1 14f+: 0-0
Track : **LH: 4-33** RH: 0-2 Tight: 1-15 **Gall: 2-12**
Aids: **Bl: 7-37** Vi: 0-2 Tstrap: 0-4 Ckp: 0-4
Best Rating: **108** 2/05 Ndas 6f110y gd-fm

Moderate; effective over 5f-7f; acts on most ground on turf, but probably best on an easy surface; also goes on sand; usually wears blinkers or an eyeshield.

Jonny Lesters Hair (IRE)

100(100) (71)**79**

4-y-o b g Danetime (IRE)-Jupiter Inlet (IRE) (Jupiter Island)
T D Easterby Reality Partnerships II

Placings:543/61500532105-6663460025 (7172)
2009: 7F, 7G, 7G, 3GF, 7GF, 7SD, 7SD, 6G, 7G, 7S,

	Starts	1st	2nd	3rd	Win & Pl
Career Total (Turf)	21	2	2	3	13356
Career Total (AW)	3	0	0	0	0

79	9/08	Bevl	7f100y	(0-75)H	SFT	£3238
74	5/08	Thsk	7f		GD	£5180

Total win prize-money £8419

Going (Turf): **Sf: 1-5** GS: 0-3 **Gd: 1-7** GF: 0-5 Fm: 0-1
Distance: 5f/6f: 0-4 **7f-8f: 2-20** 9f-13f: 0-0 14f+: 0-0
Track : LH: 1-11 RH: 1-6 **Tight: 1-9** Gall: 0-0
Aids: Bl: 0-0 Vi: 0-0 Tstrap: 0-0 Ckp: 0-0
Best Rating: **79** 9/08 Bevl 7f100y soft

Fair; stays 7f and acts on easy ground; has worn an eye-shield.

Jonny Mudball

99(108) (98)**66**

3-y-o b c Oasis Dream-Waypoint (Cadeaux Genereux)
Tom Dascombe Woodgate Family

Placings:412 (7486)
2009: 6G, 7SD, 7SD,

	Starts	1st	2nd	3rd	Win & Pl
Career Total (Turf)	1	0	0	0	0
Career Total (AW)	2	1	1	0	6160

91	10/09	Ling	7f	STD	£2729

Total win prize-money £2730

Going (Turf): **Sf: 0-0 GS: 0-0 Gd: 0-1 GF: 0-0 Fm: 0-0**
Distance: 5f/6f: 0-1 **7f-8f: 1-2** 9f-13f: 0-0 14f+: 0-0
Track : **LH: 1-2** RH: 0-0 **Tight: 1-2** Gall: 0-1
Aids: Bl: 0-0 Vi: 0-0 Tstrap: 0-0 Ckp: 0-0
Best Rating: **98** 11/09 Ling 7f stand

Very useful; effective over 7f; acts on Polytrack.

Jonny No Eyebrows

(90) (48)

2-y-o b g Auction House (USA)-She's Expensive (IRE) (Spectrum (IRE))
I A Wood Lewis Caterers

Placings:0L (7749)
2009: 6SD, 5SD,

	Starts	1st	2nd	3rd	Win & Pl
Career Total (Turf)	0	0	0	0	
Career Total (AW)	2	0	0	0	

Going (Turf): **Sf: 0-0 GS: 0-0 Gd: 0-0 GF: 0-0 Fm: 0-0**
Distance: 5f/6f: 0-2 7f-8f: 0-0 9f-13f: 0-0 14f+: 0-0
Track : LH: 0-2 RH: 0-0 Tight: 0-2 Gall: 0-0
Aids: Bl: 0-0 Vi: 0-0 Tstrap: 0-0 Ckp: 0-0
Best Rating: **48** 12/09 Ling 6f stand

Jonquille (IRE)

83(105) (49)**42**

4-y-o ch f Rock Of Gibraltar (IRE)-Moonlight Wish (IRE) (Peintre Celebre (USA))
T J Pitt (R Ford 27/1) Reginald Stephen Blandford

Placings:06/600-00500 (2344)
2009: 9SD, 14SD, 13SD, 11GF, 14GF,

	Starts	1st	2nd	3rd	Win & Pl
Career Total (Turf)	6	0	0	0	0
Career Total (AW)	4	0	0	0	0

Going (Turf): **Sf: 0-3 GS: 0-0 Gd: 0-1 GF: 0-2 Fm: 0-0**
Distance: 5f/6f: 0-0 7f-8f: 0-3 9f-13f: 0-4 14f+: 0-3
Track : LH: 0-7 RH: 0-2 Tight: 0-6 Gall: 0-0
Aids: Bl: 0-3 Vi: 0-0 Tstrap: 0-0 Ckp: 0-0
Best Rating: **50** 8/07 DRoy 7f good

Jord (IRE)

98(104) (73)**53**

5-y-o b m Trans Island-Arcevia (IRE) (Archway (IRE))
J A Glover (A J McCabe 30/5) Paul J Dixon

Placings:420201542/0530310000405054122/6642632500 000-0333121350440020366 (7795)
2009: 7SS, 8SD, 7SD, 7SD, 7SD, 7SD, 5SD, 8SD, 8GF, 7SF, 5S, 8GF, 5SD, 7SD, 7SD, 8SD, 5SD, 7SD, 6SS,

	Starts	1st	2nd	3rd	Win & Pl
Career Total (Turf)	11	0	1	0	1319
Career Total (AW)	49	5	8	8	27201

73	4/09	Wolv	5f216y	(0-80)H	STD	£5180
68	3/09	Wolv	7f32y	(0-60)H	STD	£2047
74	12/07	Sthl	1m	(0-65)H	SS	£2047
75	5/07	Wolv	5f216y	(0-70)H	SF	£3562
71	11/06	Sthl	6f	(0-65)	STD	£2590

Total win prize-money £15429

Going (Turf): **Sf: 0-3 GS: 0-1 Gd: 0-2 GF: 0-5 Fm: 0-0**
Distance: **5f/6f: 3-21** 7f-8f: 2-31 9f-13f: 0-8 14f+: 0-0
Track : **LH: 5-49** RH: 0-4 **Tight: 3-26** Gall: 0-2
Aids: Bl: 0-0 Vi: 0-0 Tstrap: 0-4 Ckp: 0-4
Best Rating: **79** 5/08 Sthl 1m stand

Modest; effective at around 6f-1m2f; acts on sand.

Jordan's Light (USA)

101(81) (11)**65**

6-y-o gr/ro g Aljabr (USA)-Western Friend (USA) (Gone West (USA))
P D Evans (T J Pitt 1/12) J R B Williams

Placings:0600/1660412104/0404/004040-013000 (7425)
2009: 8G, 12GS, 12S, 12GS, 15G, 12SD,

	Starts	1st	2nd	3rd	Win & Pl
Career Total (Turf)	22	2	0	1	7079
Career Total (AW)	8	2	1	0	6521

64	8/09	Haml	1m4f17y	(0-70)H	G-S	£3238
77	11/06	Kemp	1m2f	(0-65)H	STD	£2388
76	11/06	Sthl	1m	(0-66)H	STD	£2730
67	5/06	Muss	1m	(0-60)H	GD	£3071

Total win prize-money £11428

Going (Turf): Sf: 0-3 **GS: 1-5 Gd: 1-5** GF: 0-9 Fm: 0-0
Distance: 5f/6f: 0-1 7f-8f: 2-11 9f-13f: 2-15 14f+: 0-3
Track : LH: 1-15 **RH: 3-11 Tight: 2-9** Gall: 0-2
Aids: Bl: 0-0 **Vi: 2-12** Tstrap: 0-0 Ckp: 0-0
Best Rating: **77** 11/06 Kemp 1m2f stand

Modest gelding; stays ten furlongs; acts on fast ground and Polytrack; has worn a visor.

Jordaura

105(102) (79)**86**

3-y-o br c Primo Valentino (IRE)-Christina's Dream (Spectrum (IRE))
W R Swinburn Carl Hodgson

Placings:333-100244421 (7287)
2009: 6SD, 6SD, 6SD, 5G, 5GF, 5SD, 6S, 7G, 7S,

	Starts	1st	2nd	3rd	Win & Pl
Career Total (Turf)	6	1	2	1	9934
Career Total (AW)	6	1	0	2	3938

86	11/09	Donc	7f	(0-85)H	SFT	£6476
76	4/09	Kemp	6f	(0-70)H	STD	£2590

Total win prize-money £9066

Going (Turf): **Sf: 1-2** GS: 0-0 Gd: 0-2 GF: 0-2 Fm: 0-0
Distance: 5f/6f: 1-9 7f-8f: 1-3 9f-13f: 0-0 14f+: 0-0
Track : LH: 0-3 **RH: 1-4** Tight: 0-2 Gall: 0-2
Aids: Bl: 0-0 Vi: 0-0 Tstrap: 0-0 Ckp: 0-0
Best Rating: **86** 11/09 Donc 7f soft

Fair; stays 7f; acts soft and fast ground and on Polytrack.

Jordi Roper (IRE)

(104) (61)**54**

4-y-o ch g Traditionally (USA)-Xema (Danehill (USA))
S Parr Chris Roper & Jordan Lund

Placings:000000423P-31224606 (0791)
2009: 11SS, 6SD, 8SD, 6SD, 6SD, 8SD, 7SD, 8SD,

	Starts	1st	2nd	3rd	Win & Pl
Career Total (Turf)	6	0	0	0	
Career Total (AW)	12	1	3	2	4566

61	1/09	Sthl	6f	(0-65)H	STD	£2047

Total win prize-money £2047

Going (Turf): **Sf: 0-1 GS: 0-1 Gd: 0-2 GF: 0-2 Fm: 0-0**
Distance: **5f/6f: 1-6** 7f-8f: 0-7 9f-13f: 0-5 14f+: 0-0
Track : **LH: 1-15** RH: 0-1 Tight: 0-3 Gall: 0-0
Aids: Bl: 0-1 Vi: 0-0 Tstrap: 0-3 Ckp: 0-3
Best Rating: **61** 1/09 Sthl 6f stand

Moderate; effective over 6f-1m; acts on Fibresand.

Joseph Henry

108(101) (81)**100**

7-y-o b g Mujadil (USA)-Iris May (Brief Truce (USA))
D Nicholls Billy Hughes

Placings:114435/30400400/000541546/520/24003404330 -001000640000 (6675)
2009: 6GF, 7SD, 7Y, 8G, 7GF, 6GF, 6GY, 7GF, 8G, 6GF, 6G, 7G,

	Starts	1st	2nd	3rd	Win & Pl
Career Total (Turf)	48	4	2	5	66101
Career Total (AW)	1	0	0	0	

100	4/09	Naas	7f	(60-100)H	YLD	£14220
91	7/06	Ayr	1m	(0-85)H	FRM	£7772
98	4/04	Nott	5f13y	F	SFT	£3115
80	4/04	Muss	5f	D	G-F	£4745

Total win prize-money £29853

Going (Turf): **Sf: 1-10**GS: 0-2Gd: 0-17 **GF: 1-16 Fm: 1-1**
Distance: 5f/6f: 2-28 7f-8f: 2-19 9f-13f: 0-2 14f+: 0-0
Track : **LH: 2-12** RH: 0-5 Tight: 0-8 Gall: 0-4
Aids: Bl: 0-1 Vi: 0-0 Tstrap: 0-0 Ckp: 0-0
Best Rating: **100** 7/09 NmkJ 7f gd-fm

Very useful; stays 1m, but effective over shorter; acts on most ground; has worn blinkers; likes to race prominently.

Josephine Malines

97(89) (33)**56**

5-y-o b m Inchinor-Alrisha (IRE) (Persian Bold)

Mrs A Duffield Middleham Park Racing Ix

Placings:0/2600/50510340-06253 **(5364)**

2009: 9^{0}SD, 8^{6}GS, 8^{2}GS, 8^{5}G, 8^{3}S,

	Starts	1st	2nd	3rd	Win & Pl
Career Total (Turf)	16	1	2	2	5163
Career Total (AW)	2	0	0	0	
53 7/08 Nott	1m75y		G-S	£2388	

Total win prize-money £2388

Going (Turf): Sf: 0-3 **GS: 1-6** Gd: 0-1 GF: 0-6 Fm: 0-0
Distance: 5f/6f: 0-0 7f-8f: 0-7 **9f-13f: 1-11** 14f+: 0-0
Track : **LH: 1-7** RH: 0-6 Tight: 0-2 Gall: 0-2
Aids: Bl: 0-0 Vi: 0-0 Tstrap: 0-7 Ckp: 0-7
Best Rating: **78** 9/07 Newb 1m2f6y gd-fm

Moderate; effective at 1m; acts on good or softer ground; has worn cheekpieces.

Josh You Are

84(103) (76)**58**

6-y-o b g Josr Algarhoud (IRE)-Cibenze (Owington)

Ian Williams D Barry

Placings:006/53001/12461320/132365-000000 **(2419)**

2009: 12^{0}SD, 11^{0}SD, 16^{0}SD, 13^{0}SF, 15^{0}GF, 11^{0}G,

	Starts	1st	2nd	3rd	Win & Pl
Career Total (Turf)	12	0	0	2	626
Career Total (AW)	16	4	3	2	11002
75 2/08 Ling	2m	(0-70)H	STD	£2331	
67 7/07 Ling	1m5f	(0-65)H	STD	£2388	
59 1/07 Kemp	2m	(0-50)H	STD	£2047	
58 12/06 Kemp	1m3f		STD	£1365	

Total win prize-money £8134

Going (Turf): **Sf: 0-2 GS: 0-3 Gd: 0-1 GF: 0-6 Fm: 0-0**
Distance: 5f/6f: 0-0 7f-8f: 0-4 9f-13f: 2-9 14f+: 2-15
Track : LH: 2-19 RH: 2-5 **Tight: 2-14** Gall: 0-2
Aids: Bl: 0-0 Vi: 0-0 Tstrap: 0-0 Ckp: 0-0
Best Rating: **76** 6/08 GrLe 1m6f stand

Moderate gelding; has good strike rate on sand with all four of his wins coming on Polytrack; stays 2m; acts on Polytrack.

Joshua Tree (IRE)

109 **112**

2-y-o b c Montjeu (IRE)-Madeira Mist (IRE) (Grand Lodge (USA))

A P O'Brien D Smith, Mrs J Magnier, M Tabor

Placings:121 **(6268)**

2009: 7^{1}S, 8^{2}S, 8^{1}G,

	Starts	1st	2nd	3rd	Win & Pl
Career Total (Turf)	3	2	1	0	102892
112 9/09 Asct	1m		GD	£86188	
83 8/09 Gowr	7f		SFT	£10398	

Total win prize-money £96587

Going (Turf): **Sf: 1-2** GS: 0-0 **Gd: 1-1** GF: 0-0 Fm: 0-0
Distance: 5f/6f: 0-0 **7f-8f: 2-3** 9f-13f: 0-0 14f+: 0-0
Track : LH: 0-1 **RH: 2-2** Tight: 0-0 **Gall: 1-1**
Aids: Bl: 0-0 Vi: 0-0 Tstrap: 0-0 Ckp: 0-0
Best Rating: **112** 9/09 Asct 1m good

Group-class; won the Group 2 Royal Lodge Stakes; effective at 7f-1m; acts on good and soft ground.

Josiah Bartlett (IRE)

88(100) (62)**58**

3-y-o b g Invincible Spirit (IRE)-Princess Caraboo (IRE) (Alzao (USA))

Ian Williams (P S McEntee 23/7) Playboy Kennels

Placings:00062050330-05124000055000260000 **(7877)**

2009: 9^{0}SD, 8^{5}SD, 7^{1}SD, 8^{2}SD, 7^{4}SD, 7^{0}SF, 5^{0}SD, 7^{0}GF, 5^{0}GF, 5^{5}G, 6^{5}F, 5^{0}SD, 8^{0}SD, 7^{0}SD, 5^{2}SD, 7^{6}SD, 6^{0}SD, 8^{0}SD, 7^{0}SD,

	Starts	1st	2nd	3rd	Win & Pl
Career Total (Turf)	8	0	0	0	0
Career Total (AW)	22	1	3	2	4764
62 2/09 Ling	7f	(0-55)H	STD	£2047	

Total win prize-money £2047

Going (Turf): **Sf: 0-0 GS: 0-0 Gd: 0-3 GF: 0-4 Fm: 0-1**
Distance: 5f/6f: 0-11 **7f-8f: 1-14** 9f-13f: 0-5 14f+: 0-0
Track : **LH: 1-17** RH: 0-7 **Tight: 1-15** Gall: 0-0
Aids: **Bl: 1-5** Vi: 0-2 Tstrap: 0-0 Ckp: 0-0
Best Rating: **62** 2/09 Ling 7f stand

Moderate; suited by 7f; acts on Polytrack; has worn blinkers and a tongue-tie.

Josphiel (IRE)

89 **59**

4-y-o b f Okawango (USA)-Indian Honey (Indian King (USA))

A Berry Gerry Callanan

Placings:55/500-043300 **(3498)**

2009: 5^{0}GF, 6^{4}F, 5^{3}G, 6^{3}GF, 6^{0}GF, 5^{0}GF,

	Starts	1st	2nd	3rd	Win & Pl
Career Total (Turf)	11	0	0	2	1027

Going (Turf): **Sf: 0-1 GS: 0-0 Gd: 0-2 GF: 0-5 Fm: 0-1**
Distance: 5f/6f: 0-6 7f-8f: 0-5 9f-13f: 0-0 14f+: 0-0
Track : LH: 0-4 RH: 0-1 Tight: 0-2 Gall: 0-0
Aids: Bl: 0-4 Vi: 0-0 Tstrap: 0-0 Ckp: 0-0
Best Rating: **75** 10/07 Curr 7f gd-yld

Josr's Magic (IRE)

(108) (70)**52**

5-y-o b g Josr Algarhoud (IRE)-Just The Trick (USA) (Phone Trick (USA))

T E Powell Ken Tyre & Lee Tyre

Placings:334521500/36230000530/0310401200045301330 0-00240 **(7693)**

2009: 10^{0}SD, 8^{0}SD, 8^{2}SD, 7^{4}SD, 8^{0}SD,

	Starts	1st	2nd	3rd	Win & Pl
Career Total (Turf)	18	1	2	3	5953
Career Total (AW)	27	3	2	6	9925
70 9/08 Sthl	1m	(0-60)H	STD	£2388	
61 4/08 Wolv	1m1f103y	(0-65)H	STD	£2047	
56 2/08 Ling	1m2f	(0-65)H	STD	£2331	
72 8/06 Carl	5f		G-F	£3238	

Total win prize-money £10006

Going (Turf): Sf: 0-3 GS: 0-3 Gd: 0-1 **GF: 1-10** Fm: 0-1
Distance: 5f/6f: 1-12 7f-8f: 1-14 **9f-13f: 2-19** 14f+: 0-0
Track : **LH: 3-27** RH: 1-8 **Tight: 2-16** Gall: 1-5
Aids: **Bl: 1-7** Vi: 0-1 Tstrap: 0-0 Ckp: 0-0
Best Rating: **73** 5/06 Pont 5f gd-fm

Moderate; effective from 1m-1m4f; acts on fast ground; goes on sand.

Joss Stick

99(102) (69)**65**

4-y-o b g Josr Algarhoud (IRE)-Queen's College (IRE) (College Chapel)

J J Bridger (R A Harris 23/6) Gayler William Chambers

Placings:00603031/10030505320-6136065202450310600200000 **(7240)**

2009: 6^{6}SD, 6^{1}SD, 5^{3}SD, 5^{6}SD, 6^{0}SD, 5^{6}SD, 5^{5}SD, 6^{2}SD, 5^{0}SD, 5^{2}GF, 5^{4}GF, 5^{5}GF, 5^{0}G, 5^{3}GF, 5^{1}GF, 5^{0}GS, 5^{6}SD, 5^{0}F, 5^{0}GF, 6^{2}GF, 6^{0}SD, 5^{0}G, 6^{0}G,

	Starts	1st	2nd	3rd	Win & Pl
Career Total (Turf)	18	1	2	2	4476
Career Total (AW)	26	3	2	4	9100
60 7/09 Brig	5f59y	(0-55)H	G-F	£2072	
68 1/09 Ling	6f	(0-60)H	STD	£2047	
71 4/08 Kemp	5f	(0-70)H	STD	£2590	
66 12/07 Ling	5f		STD	£1943	

Total win prize-money £8652

Going (Turf): Sf: 0-0 GS: 0-1 Gd: 0-6 **GF: 1-9** Fm: 0-2
Distance: **5f/6f: 4-43** 7f-8f: 0-1 9f-13f: 0-0 14f+: 0-0
Track : **LH: 3-23** RH: 1-11 **Tight: 2-13** Gall: 0-7
Aids: Bl: 0-2 Vi: 0-0 Tstrap: 2-22 Ckp: 2-22
Best Rating: **71** 4/08 Kemp 5f stand

Moderate sprinter; acts on fast ground; goes on Polytrack; has worn cheekpieces; not an easy ride.

Jounce (USA)

(84) (60)

2-y-o ch f Gone West (USA)-Shoogle (USA) (A.P. Indy (USA))

J H M Gosden K Abdulla

Placings:2 **(7396)**

2009: 7^{2}SD,

	Starts	1st	2nd	3rd	Win & Pl
Career Total (Turf)	0	0	0	0	
Career Total (AW)	1	0	1	0	1156

Going (Turf): **Sf: 0-0 GS: 0-0 Gd: 0-0 GF: 0-0 Fm: 0-0**
Distance: 5f/6f: 0-0 7f-8f: 0-1 9f-13f: 0-0 14f+: 0-0
Track : LH: 0-1 RH: 0-0 Tight: 0-1 Gall: 0-0
Aids: Bl: 0-0 Vi: 0-0 Tstrap: 0-0 Ckp: 0-0
Best Rating: **60** 11/09 Wolv 7f32y stand

Shaped with promise on debut; should stay 1m; acts on Polytrack; sure to win a race.

Joury

(62)

2-y-o b f Oratorio (IRE)-Contradictive (USA) (Kingmambo (USA))

S A Callaghan Saleh Al Homaizi & Imad Al Sagar

Placings:0 **(6254)**

2009: 7^{0}SD,

	Starts	1st	2nd	3rd	Win & Pl
Career Total (Turf)	0	0	0	0	
Career Total (AW)	1	0	0	0	

Going (Turf): **Sf: 0-0 GS: 0-0 Gd: 0-0 GF: 0-0 Fm: 0-0**
Distance: 5f/6f: 0-0 7f-8f: 0-1 9f-13f: 0-0 14f+: 0-0
Track : LH: 0-1 RH: 0-0 Tight: 0-1 Gall: 0-0
Aids: Bl: 0-0 Vi: 0-0 Tstrap: 0-0 Ckp: 0-0
Best Rating:

Joyeaux

101(99) (67)73

7-y-o b m Mark Of Esteem (IRE)-Divine Secret (Hernando (FR))

Ollie Pears PSB Holdings Ltd

Placings:064260/610103042/16000013545524436/02532 32212046/600032100-04003505240652445 (7555)

2009: 5^{0}GF, 5^{4}G, 5^{0}GF, 6^{0}GF, 5^{3}GF, 5^{5}GF, 6^{0}G, 5^{5}S, 5^{2}G, 5^{4}GF, 5^{0}GS, 5^{6}G, 5^{5}GF, 5^{2}S, 5^{4}S, 5^{4}SD, 5^{5}SD,

	Starts	1st	2nd	3rd	Win & Pl
Career Total (Turf)	50	4	9	5	29449
Career Total (AW)	21	2	2	2	9633

73	10/08	Catt	5f	(0-65)H	G-S	£2047
73	9/07	Haml	5f4y	(0-80)H	GD	£6477
68	6/06	Wolv	5f216y	(0-60)H	STD	£3071
71	1/06	Wolv	5f216y	(0-70)H	STD	£2914
74	4/05	Hayd	5f	(0-75)H	SFT	£3580
72	4/05	Nott	5f13y	(0-70)H	SFT	£3619

Total win prize-money £21710

Going (Turf): Sf: 2-14 GS: 1-15 Gd: 1-9 GF: 0-12 Fm: 0-0
Distance: 5f/6f: 6-56 7f-8f: 0-15 9f-13f: 0-0 14f+: 0-0
Track : LH: 2-26 RH: 0-0 Tight: 2-23 Gall: 0-0
Aids: Bl: 0-0 Vi: 1-15 Tstrap: 0-0 Ckp: 0-0
Best Rating: 74 9/07 Pont 5f gd-fm

Moderate sprinter; effective over 5-6f; acts on good ground and Polytrack but is suited by the soft; has worn a visor.

Jozafeen

101 61

2-y-o ch f Zafeen (FR)-Faithful Beauty (IRE) (Last Tycoon)

R Bastiman Mrs C Steel

Placings:02202 (6797)

2009: 6^{0}G, 5^{2}G, 7^{2}GS, 6^{0}G, 6^{2}S,

	Starts	1st	2nd	3rd	Win & Pl
Career Total (Turf)	5	0	3	0	2151

Going (Turf): Sf: 0-1 GS: 0-1 Gd: 0-3 GF: 0-0 Fm: 0-0
Distance: 5f/6f: 0-2 7f-8f: 0-3 9f-13f: 0-0 14f+: 0-0
Track : LH: 0-0 RH: 0-2 Tight: 0-1 Gall: 0-0
Aids: Bl: 0-0 Vi: 0-0 Tstrap: 0-0 Ckp: 0-0
Best Rating: 61 8/09 Carl 5f193y good

Modest; stays 7f and acts on easy ground.

Jubail (IRE)

85 51

2-y-o ch c Redback-Daneville (IRE) (Danetime (IRE))

A King David Mason

Placings:0 (4945)

2009: 6^{0}GF,

	Starts	1st	2nd	3rd	Win & Pl
Career Total (Turf)	1	0	0	0	

Going (Turf): Sf: 0-0 GS: 0-0 Gd: 0-0 GF: 0-1 Fm: 0-0
Distance: 5f/6f: 0-0 7f-8f: 0-1 9f-13f: 0-0 14f+: 0-0
Track : LH: 0-0 RH: 0-0 Tight: 0-0 Gall: 0-0
Aids: Bl: 0-0 Vi: 0-0 Tstrap: 0-0 Ckp: 0-0
Best Rating: 51 8/09 Sals 6f212y gd-fm

Jubilant Note (IRE)

92(93) (68)69

7-y-o b g Sadler's Wells (USA)-Hint Of Humour (USA) (Woodman (USA))

Michael David Murphy Martry Millers Syndicate

Placings:220414/0440/844/04342-0 (2351)

2009: 10^{0}GF,

	Starts	1st	2nd	3rd	Win & Pl
Career Total (Turf)	17	1	2	1	12943
Career Total (AW)	2	0	1	0	1192

77	8/05	Rosc	1m2f		G-F	£5390

Total win prize-money £5391

Going (Turf): Sf: 0-2 GS: 0-0 Gd: 0-1 GF: 1-7 Fm: 0-3
Distance: 5f/6f: 0-0 7f-8f: 0-6 9f-13f: 1-12 14f+: 0-1
Track : LH: 0-6 RH: 1-11 Tight: 0-1 Gall: 0-2
Aids: Bl: 1-12 Vi: 0-2 Tstrap: 0-0 Ckp: 0-0
Best Rating: 86 5/05 Leop 1m gd-fm

Modest; stays 1m6f; acts on Polytrack.

Jubilee Juggins (IRE)

(91) (64)70

3-y-o b c Clodovil (IRE)-Alleged Touch (USA) (Alleged (USA))

N P Littmoden Miss Vanessa Church

Placings:046621300-5 (0804)

2009: 5^{5}SD,

	Starts	1st	2nd	3rd	Win & Pl
Career Total (Turf)	4	1	1	1	4779
Career Total (AW)	6	0	0	0	265

70	9/08	Gdwd	5f	(0-75)H	SFT	£3238

Total win prize-money £3238

Going (Turf): Sf: 1-2 GS: 0-1 Gd: 0-1 GF: 0-0 Fm: 0-0
Distance: 5f/6f: 1-9 7f-8f: 0-1 9f-13f: 0-0 14f+: 0-0
Track : LH: 0-6 RH: 0-0 Tight: 0-4 Gall: 0-1
Aids: Bl: 0-1 Vi: 0-0 Tstrap: 0-0 Ckp: 0-0
Best Rating: 70 9/08 Gdwd 5f soft

Fair; effective over 5f; acts on easy ground.

Judd Street

111(109) (107)109

7-y-o b g Compton Place-Pudding Lane (IRE) (College Chapel)

Eve Johnson Houghton R F Johnson Houghton

Placings:41/13333122/12300062320/30162031/00600055 15-316234105020 (5657)

2009: 6^{3}GF, 6^{1}G, 6^{6}GF, 5^{2}SD, 5^{3}GF, 5^{4}G, 6^{1}GF, 6^{0}GF, 5^{5}G, 6^{0}S, 6^{2}SD, 6^{0}GS,

	Starts	1st	2nd	3rd	Win & Pl
Career Total (Turf)	39	6	5	9	181487
Career Total (AW)	12	3	3	1	35011

102	6/09	Sals	6f		G-F	£22708
104	2/09	Ndas	6f	(95-110)H	GD	£50000
109	9/08	Hayd	5f	(0-100)H	G-F	£19428
111	10/07	NmkR	5f		GD	£15330
106	8/07	Hayd	5f	(0-100)H	G-F	£16192
94	5/06	Wind	6f	(0-85)H	G-S	£5505
93	8/05	Ling	6f	(0-80)H	STD	£6216
81	3/05	Ling	5f	(0-85)H	STD	£6698
66	12/04	Ling	6f		STD	£3740

Total win prize-money £145822

Going (Turf): Sf: 0-1 GS: 1-4 Gd: 2-10 GF: 3-24 Fm: 0-0
Distance: 5f/6f: 9-50 7f-8f: 0-1 9f-13f: 0-0 14f+: 0-0
Track : LH: 4-18 RH: 0-1 Tight: 3-13 Gall: 2-10
Aids: Bl: 2-9 Vi: 2-10 Tstrap: 0-0 Ckp: 0-0
Best Rating: 111 10/07 NmkR 5f good

Smart; winner in Listed class and Group placed; effective over 5f-6f; acts on most ground and on Polytrack; has worn a visor, blinkers and a tongue tie.

Judge 'n Jury

110(109) (106)111

5-y-o ch g Pivotal-Cyclone Connie (Dr Devious (IRE))

R A Harris Robert & Nina Bailey

Placings:00/316410402312151114-3650064130200 (7015)

2009: 5^{3}SD, 5^{6}VS, 5^{5}Y, 5^{0}GF, 5^{0}GF, 5^{6}GY, 5^{4}GF, 5^{1}GF, 5^{3}G, 6^{0}GF, 5^{2}HY, 5^{0}GF, 5^{0}GS,

	Starts	1st	2nd	3rd	Win & Pl
Career Total (Turf)	26	7	3	2	114026
Career Total (AW)	7	1	0	2	7112

108	7/09	Asct	5f	H	G-F	£31155
111	10/08	Donc	5f	(0-100)H	GD	£31155
110	10/08	Catt	5f	(0-95)H	G-S	£7771
104	10/08	Asct	5f	(0-85)H	G-S	£6231
91	9/08	Donc	5f	(0-85)H	SFT	£6476
87	8/08	Sand	5f6y	(0-80)H	SFT	£5828
81	4/08	Wwck	5f	(0-75)H	SFT	£3070
80	2/08	Ling	5f		STD	£2457

Total win prize-money £94144

Going (Turf): Sf: 3-6 GS: 2-5 Gd: 1-4 GF: 1-7 Fm: 0-1
Distance: 5f/6f: 8-32 7f-8f: 0-1 9f-13f: 0-0 14f+: 0-0
Track : LH: 2-9 RH: 0-0 Tight: 1-6 Gall: 0-2
Aids: Bl: 0-0 Vi: 0-0 Tstrap: 0-0 Ckp: 0-0
Best Rating: 111 10/08 Donc 5f good

Smart; Group and Listed placed; effective over 5f; acts on soft ground and on Polytrack; usually tongue tied; likes to race prominently.

Judgethemoment (USA)

108(102) (92)102

4-y-o br c Judge T C (USA)-Rachael Tennessee (USA) (Matsadoon (USA))

Jane Chapple-Hyam Gordon Li

Placings:63333/15061566-11140000 (7151)

2009: 16^{1}SD, 16^{1}GF, 20^{1}GF, 16^{4}G, 16^{0}G, 16^{0}GF, 18^{0}G, 16^{0}G,

	Starts	1st	2nd	3rd	Win & Pl
Career Total (Turf)	15	3	0	2	50836
Career Total (AW)	6	2	0	2	8889

102	6/09	Asct	2m4f	(0-95)H	G-F	£31155
97	5/09	Asct	2m	(0-90)H	G-F	£7477
92	4/09	Kemp	2m	(0-85)H	STD	£4727
93	7/08	Sand	1m6f	(0-85)H	G-F	£6476
77	4/08	Kemp	1m2f		STD	£2590

Total win prize-money £52425

Going (Turf): Sf: 0-1 GS: 0-2 Gd: 0-4 GF: 3-7 Fm: 0-1
Distance: 5f/6f: 0-0 7f-8f: 0-3 9f-13f: 1-6 14f+: 4-12
Track : LH: 0-4 RH: 5-15 Tight: 0-3 Gall: 2-8
Aids: Bl: 0-0 Vi: 0-0 Tstrap: 0-1 Ckp: 0-1
Best Rating: 102 6/09 Asct 2m4f gd-fm

Very useful; effective at 2m-2m4f; won the Ascot Stakes in 2009; acts on fast and soft ground; goes on Polytrack.

Judiciary (IRE)

96(100) (76)74

2-y-o b c Invincible Spirit (IRE)-Theory Of Law (Generous (IRE))

Saeed Bin Suroor Godolphin

Placings:201 (7266)

2009: 8^{2}GF, 8^{0}G, 8^{1}SD,

	Starts	1st	2nd	3rd	Win & Pl
Career Total (Turf)	2	0	1	0	1503
Career Total (AW)	1	1	0	0	2914

76	11/09	Sthl	1m	STD	£2914

Total win prize-money £2914

Going (Turf): Sf: 0-0 GS: 0-0 Gd: 0-1 GF: 0-1 Fm: 0-0
Distance: 5f/6f: 0-0 7f-8f: 1-3 9f-13f: 0-0 14f+: 0-0
Track : LH: 1-2 RH: 0-0 Tight: 0-0 Gall: 0-1
Aids: Bl: 0-0 Vi: 0-0 Tstrap: 0-0 Ckp: 0-0
Best Rating: 76 11/09 Sthl 1m stand

Fair; stays 1m and acts on fast ground and on Fibresand.

Juicy Pear (IRE)

(91) (75)
2-y-o b g Pyrus (USA)-Cappadoce (IRE) (General Monash (USA))
M L W Bell Billy Maguire

Placings:302 (7325)
2009: 7^{3}SD, 7^{0}SD, 7^{2}SD,

	Starts	1st	2nd	3rd	Win & Pl
Career Total (Turf)	0	0	0	0	
Career Total (AW)	3	0	1	1	977

Going (Turf): Sf: 0-0 GS: 0-0 Gd: 0-0 GF: 0-0 Fm: 0-0
Distance: 5f/6f: 0-0 7f-8f: 0-3 9f-13f: 0-0 14f+: 0-0
Track : LH: 0-2 RH: 0-1 Tight: 0-2 Gall: 0-0
Aids: Bl: 0-0 Vi: 0-0 Tstrap: 0-0 Ckp: 0-0
Best Rating: 75 10/09 Wolv 7f32y stand

Fair; stays 7f and acts on Polytrack.

Jukebox Jury (IRE)

115 120
3-y-o gr c Montjeu (IRE)-Mare Aux Fees (Kenmare (FR))
M Johnston A D Spence

Placings:14312-0614112 (6873a)
2009: 9^{0}G, 10^{6}G, 10^{1}G, 12^{4}GF, 12^{1}G, 12^{1}G, 12^{2}F,

	Starts	1st	2nd	3rd	Win & Pl
Career Total (Turf)	12	5	2	1	633587
120 9/09	Colo	1m4f		GD	£97087
114 8/09	Deau	1m4f110y		GD	£110680
119 8/09	Hayd	1m2f95y		GD	£36900
114 9/08	Asct	1m		GD	£76037
85 8/08	Gdwd	7f		G-F	£12952

Total win prize-money £333658

Going (Turf): Sf: 0-0 GS: 0-2 Gd: 4-7 GF: 1-2 Fm: 0-1
Distance: 5f/6f: 0-0 7f-8f: 2-5 9f-13f: 3-7 14f+: 0-0
Track : LH: 1-3 RH: 4-8 Tight: 0-0 Gall: 1-2
Aids: Bl: 0-0 Vi: 0-0 Tstrap: 0-0 Ckp: 0-0
Best Rating: 120 10/09 Wood 1m4f firm

Group class; winner of the 2008 Royal Lodge and runner-up in the Racing Post Trophy in 2008; winner of a Group 3, the Group 2 Grand Prix de Deauville and the Group 1 Prix Von Europa in 2009; stays 1m4f; acts on fast and easy ground.

Jul's Lad (IRE)

79(94) (68)67
3-y-o b g Modigliani (USA)-Woodenitbenice (USA) (Nasty And Bold (USA))
D Carroll (M Mullineaux 7/7) T & J Tuohy

Placings:0060-2300000 (7784)
2009: 8^{2}SD, 7^{3}SD, 9^{0}GF, 10^{0}GF, 8^{0}SD, 8^{0}SD, 8^{0}SD,

	Starts	1st	2nd	3rd	Win & Pl
Career Total (Turf)	6	0	0	0	0
Career Total (AW)	5	0	1	1	957

Going (Turf): Sf: 0-3 GS: 0-0 Gd: 0-1 GF: 0-2 Fm: 0-0
Distance: 5f/6f: 0-3 7f-8f: 0-3 9f-13f: 0-5 14f+: 0-0
Track : LH: 0-7 RH: 0-1 Tight: 0-5 Gall: 0-0
Aids: Bl: 0-2 Vi: 0-0 Tstrap: 0-1 Ckp: 0-1
Best Rating: 68 3/09 Wolv 1m141y stand

Modest form at up to 7f; handles good or softer.

Julie Mill (IRE)

(88) (38)23
3-y-o b f Apprehension-Ann's Mill (Pelder (IRE))
R A Teal K W Anidjah

Placings:000-0000 (7452)
2009: 12^{0}SD, 8^{0}SD, 10^{0}SD, 8^{0}SD,

	Starts	1st	2nd	3rd	Win & Pl
Career Total (Turf)	2	0	0	0	
Career Total (AW)	5	0	0	0	

Going (Turf): Sf: 0-1 GS: 0-1 Gd: 0-0 GF: 0-0 Fm: 0-0
Distance: 5f/6f: 0-0 7f-8f: 0-5 9f-13f: 0-2 14f+: 0-0
Track : LH: 0-4 RH: 0-2 Tight: 0-3 Gall: 0-0
Aids: Bl: 0-0 Vi: 0-0 Tstrap: 0-0 Ckp: 0-0
Best Rating: 38 9/09 Kemp 1m stand

Julienas (IRE)

(94) (77)
2-y-o b c Cape Cross (IRE)-Dora Carrington (IRE) (Sri Pekan (USA))
W R Swinburn P W Harris

Placings:4 (6943)
2009: 7^{4}SD,

	Starts	1st	2nd	3rd	Win & Pl
Career Total (Turf)	0	0	0	0	
Career Total (AW)	1	0	0	0	289

Going (Turf): Sf: 0-0 GS: 0-0 Gd: 0-0 GF: 0-0 Fm: 0-0
Distance: 5f/6f: 0-0 7f-8f: 0-1 9f-13f: 0-0 14f+: 0-0
Track : LH: 0-0 RH: 0-1 Tight: 0-0 Gall: 0-0
Aids: Bl: 0-0 Vi: 0-0 Tstrap: 0-0 Ckp: 0-0
Best Rating: 77 10/09 Kemp 7f stand

July Days (IRE)

96 (79)78
3-y-o b f Exceed And Excel (AUS)-Tocade (IRE) (Kenmare (FR))
David Marnane July Syndicate

Placings:04034-6160460 (6868a)
2009: 6^{6}SD, 7^{1}GF, 7^{6}GF, 7^{0}GY, 10^{4}SD, 8^{6}GF, 8^{0}G,

	Starts	1st	2nd	3rd	Win & Pl
Career Total (Turf)	7	1	0	0	7243
Career Total (AW)	5	0	0	1	2707
78 6/09	Leop	7f	(50-80)H	G-F	£7044

Total win prize-money £7044

Going (Turf): Sf: 0-1 GS: 0-0 Gd: 0-1 GF: 1-4 Fm: 0-0
Distance: 5f/6f: 0-5 7f-8f: 1-5 9f-13f: 0-2 14f+: 0-0
Track : LH: 1-9 RH: 0-2 Tight: 0-1 Gall: 0-0
Aids: Bl: 0-0 Vi: 0-0 Tstrap: 0-0 Ckp: 0-0
Best Rating: 79 9/09 Dund 1m2f150y stand

July Jasmine (USA)

105 101
3-y-o b f Empire Maker (USA)-Camanoe (USA) (Gone West (USA))
Sir Michael Stoute K Abdulla

Placings:1-2503 (5472)
2009: 11^{2}GF, 12^{5}GF, 11^{0}GF, 9^{3}GF,

	Starts	1st	2nd	3rd	Win & Pl
Career Total (Turf)	5	1	1	1	23582
80 10/08	Leic	7f9y		SFT	£4857

Total win prize-money £4857

Going (Turf): Sf: 1-1 GS: 0-0 Gd: 0-0 GF: 0-4 Fm: 0-0
Distance: 5f/6f: 0-0 7f-8f: 1-1 9f-13f: 0-4 14f+: 0-0
Track : LH: 0-2 RH: 0-2 Tight: 0-2 Gall: 0-1
Aids: Bl: 0-0 Vi: 0-0 Tstrap: 0-0 Ckp: 0-0
Best Rating: 101 8/09 Gdwd 1m1f192y gd-fm

Very useful; stays 1m3f; acts on most ground on turf.

Jumaana (IRE)

97 64
3-y-o b f Selkirk (USA)-Weqaar (USA) (Red Ransom (USA))
J L Dunlop Hamdan Al Maktoum

Placings:50-043 (3661)
2009: 9^{0}F, 11^{4}S, 9^{3}F,

	Starts	1st	2nd	3rd	Win & Pl
Career Total (Turf)	5	0	0	1	626

Going (Turf): Sf: 0-2 GS: 0-0 Gd: 0-0 GF: 0-1 Fm: 0-2
Distance: 5f/6f: 0-0 7f-8f: 0-2 9f-13f: 0-3 14f+: 0-0
Track : LH: 0-2 RH: 0-1 Tight: 0-2 Gall: 0-0
Aids: Bl: 0-0 Vi: 0-0 Tstrap: 0-0 Ckp: 0-0
Best Rating: 64 9/08 NmkR 7f gd-fm

Jung (USA)

(40)
3-y-o b/br g Stroll (USA)-Witching Well (IRE) (Night Shift (USA))
J R Gask For Sale

Placings:0-00 (6670)
2009: 6^{0}GS, 5^{0}SD,

	Starts	1st	2nd	3rd	Win & Pl
Career Total (Turf)	1	0	0	0	
Career Total (AW)	2	0	0	0	

Going (Turf): Sf: 0-0 GS: 0-1 Gd: 0-0 GF: 0-0 Fm: 0-0
Distance: 5f/6f: 0-3 7f-8f: 0-0 9f-13f: 0-0 14f+: 0-0
Track : LH: 0-2 RH: 0-0 Tight: 0-2 Gall: 0-0
Aids: Bl: 0-1 Vi: 0-0 Tstrap: 0-0 Ckp: 0-0

Jupiter Fidius

103 75
2-y-o b c Haafhd-Kyda (USA) (Gulch (USA))
Mrs K Walton Tennant, Sharpe & Boston

Placings:561 (7116)
2009: 5^{5}F, 7^{6}G, 8^{1}GS,

	Starts	1st	2nd	3rd	Win & Pl
Career Total (Turf)	3	1	0	0	3886
75 10/09	Muss	1m		G-S	£3885

Total win prize-money £3886

Going (Turf): Sf: 0-0 GS: 1-1 Gd: 0-1 GF: 0-0 Fm: 0-1
Distance: 5f/6f: 0-1 7f-8f: 1-2 9f-13f: 0-0 14f+: 0-0
Track : LH: 0-1 RH: 1-1 Tight: 1-2 Gall: 0-0
Aids: Bl: 0-0 Vi: 0-0 Tstrap: 0-0 Ckp: 0-0
Best Rating: 75 10/09 Muss 1m gd-sft

Fair colt; effective at 1m; goes well on easy ground.

Just A Monkey

70 38

2-y-o ch c Auction House (USA)-Wedgewood Star (Bishop Of Cashel)

R Curtis Phillips,Downs,Allen,Looney,Hughes

Placings:00 (5319)

2009: 6^{0}G, 8^{0}GF,

	Starts	1st	2nd	3rd	Win & Pl
Career Total (Turf)	2	0	0	0	

Going (Turf): **Sf: 0-0 GS: 0-0 Gd: 0-1 GF: 0-1 Fm: 0-0**
Distance: 5f/6f: 0-1 7f-8f: 0-0 9f-13f: 0-1 14f+: 0-0
Track : LH: 0-0 RH: 0-1 Tight: 0-1 Gall: 0-1
Aids: Bl: 0-0 Vi: 0-0 Tstrap: 0-0 Ckp: 0-0
Best Rating: **38** 8/09 Wind 1m67y gd-fm

Just Bond (IRE)

107(107) (91)89

7-y-o b g Namid-Give Warning (IRE) (Warning)

G R Oldroyd R C Bond

Placings:0063320453/**540313112**/**130**40**1**03**1031062**/024 22302**0**010**04244-53302544**152010**5**00**651340** (7848)

2009: 8^{5}SS, 8^{3}SD, 8^{3}SD, 8^{0}SD, 0^{2}SD, 9^{5}SD, 8^{4}SD, 8^{4}SD, 8^{1}GF, 7^{5}GF, 8^{2}GF, 8^{0}GF, 8^{1}GF, 8^{0}GF, 8^{5}SD, 8^{0}GF, 8^{0}GF, 9^{6}SD, 9^{5}SD, 9^{1}SF, 8^{3}SD, 8^{4}SD, 9^{0}SD,

	Starts	1st	2nd	3rd	Win & Pl
Career Total (Turf)	35	3	6	6	34472
Career Total (AW)	39	8	4	6	48657

86	11/09	Wolv	1m1f103y	(0-85)H	SF	£5046
89	8/09	Rdcr	1m	(0-90)H	G-F	£7771
86	4/09	Muss	1m	(0-85)H	G-F	£5828
88	9/08	Hayd	1m30y	(0-80)H	G-F	£5504
93	10/07	Wolv	1m141y	(0-85)H	STD	£5181
89	8/07	Wolv	1m141y	(0-80)H	STD	£6477
85	6/07	Wolv	1m141y	(0-80)H	STD	£5829
82	1/07	Wolv	1m141y	(0-75)H	STD	£3071
85	12/06	Wolv	1m1f103y	(0-68)H	STD	£3238
79	12/06	Wolv	1m1f103y	(0-65)H	STD	£2590
65	11/06	Wolv	1m141y	(0-53)H	STD	£2388

Total win prize-money £52928

Going (Turf): Sf: 0-2 GS: 0-2 Gd: 0-9 **GF: 3-20** Fm: 0-2
Distance: 5f/6f: 0-0 7f-8f: 2-31 **9f-13f: 9-43** 14f+: 0-0
Track : **LH: 9-56** RH: 1-11 **Tight: 9-53** Gall: 0-2
Aids: Bl: 0-0 Vi: 0-1 Tstrap: 0-1 Ckp: 0-1
Best Rating: **93** 12/07 Wolv 1m1f103y stand

Useful; stays 1m2f; acts on fast ground; goes on Polytrack; has worn cheekpieces and a visor.

Just Call Me Dave (USA)

89(74) (19)45

3-y-o b g Gneiss (USA)-Proud Future (USA) (Proud Birdie (USA))

Paul Green Bluegrass Racing Ltd

Placings:00000 (7500)

2009: 11^{0}GF, 10^{0}G, 11^{0}GF, 16^{0}SD, 8^{0}SD,

	Starts	1st	2nd	3rd	Win & Pl
Career Total (Turf)	3	0	0	0	
Career Total (AW)	2	0	0	0	

Going (Turf): **Sf: 0-0 GS: 0-0 Gd: 0-1 GF: 0-2 Fm: 0-0**
Distance: 5f/6f: 0-0 7f-8f: 0-1 9f-13f: 0-3 14f+: 0-1
Track : LH: 0-4 RH: 0-1 Tight: 0-2 Gall: 0-0
Aids: Bl: 0-0 Vi: 0-0 Tstrap: 0-0 Ckp: 0-0
Best Rating: **45** 9/09 Leic 1m3f183y gd-fm

Just Crystal

82(82) (47)22

5-y-o b m Polar Prince (IRE)-Grandads Dream (Never So Bold)

B P J Baugh C R Watts

Placings:000560/0-50 (2361)

2009: 7^{5}GS, 7^{0}GF,

	Starts	1st	2nd	3rd	Win & Pl
Career Total (Turf)	3	0	0	0	0
Career Total (AW)	6	0	0	0	0

Going (Turf): **Sf: 0-0 GS: 0-1 Gd: 0-0 GF: 0-2 Fm: 0-0**
Distance: 5f/6f: 0-0 7f-8f: 0-6 9f-13f: 0-3 14f+: 0-0
Track : LH: 0-6 RH: 0-1 Tight: 0-5 Gall: 0-0
Aids: Bl: 0-0 Vi: 0-0 Tstrap: 0-0 Ckp: 0-0
Best Rating: **47** 10/07 Wolv 7f32y stand

Just Dan

92(84) (53)43

3-y-o b g Best Of The Bests (IRE)-Scapavia (FR) (Alzao (USA))

R Hollinshead Mrs Dianne E Edwards

Placings:000-044000 (6098)

2009: 14^{0}GF, 10^{4}GF, 14^{4}SD, 12^{0}GF, 11^{0}SD, 13^{0}GF,

	Starts	1st	2nd	3rd	Win & Pl
Career Total (Turf)	5	0	0	0	0
Career Total (AW)	4	0	0	0	187

Going (Turf): **Sf: 0-1 GS: 0-0 Gd: 0-0 GF: 0-4 Fm: 0-0**
Distance: 5f/6f: 0-0 7f-8f: 0-0 9f-13f: 0-6 14f+: 0-3
Track : LH: 0-8 RH: 0-1 Tight: 0-4 Gall: 0-0
Aids: Bl: 0-0 Vi: 0-0 Tstrap: 0-2 Ckp: 0-2
Best Rating: **53** 11/08 Wolv 1m141y stand

Just Dennis

(91) (16)

5-y-o b g Superior Premium-Sweets (IRE) (Persian Heights)

D G Bridgwater R W Neale

Placings:6-00 (0902)

2009: 12^{0}SD, 12^{0}SF,

	Starts	1st	2nd	3rd	Win & Pl
Career Total (Turf)	0	0	0	0	
Career Total (AW)	3	0	0	0	0

Going (Turf): **Sf: 0-0 GS: 0-0 Gd: 0-0 GF: 0-0 Fm: 0-0**
Distance: 5f/6f: 0-0 7f-8f: 0-0 9f-13f: 0-3 14f+: 0-0
Track : LH: 0-3 RH: 0-0 Tight: 0-3 Gall: 0-0
Aids: Bl: 0-0 Vi: 0-0 Tstrap: 0-0 Ckp: 0-0
Best Rating: **48** 3/08 Wolv 1m4f50y stand

Just Five (IRE)

104(102) (69)77

3-y-o b g Olmodavor (USA)-Wildsplash (USA) (Deputy Minister (CAN))

M Dods Just Five Racing Partners

Placings:03U0355-**141210110** (7141)

2009: 8^{1}SD, 8^{4}SD, 8^{1}SD, 7^{2}SD, 8^{1}GS, 7^{0}GF, 7^{1}GF, 8^{1}GF, 8^{0}SD,

	Starts	1st	2nd	3rd	Win & Pl
Career Total (Turf)	11	3	0	2	8847
Career Total (AW)	5	2	1	0	5684

77	9/09	Bevl	1m100y	(0-75)H	G-F	£3238
75	7/09	Bevl	7f100y		G-F	£2590
77	5/09	Newc	1m3y	(0-65)H	G-S	£2331
69	3/09	Sthl	1m	(0-70)H	STD	£2729
60	2/09	Sthl	1m	(0-60)H	STD	£2047

Total win prize-money £12936

Going (Turf): Sf: 0-1 GS: 1-2 Gd: 0-3 **GF: 2-5** Fm: 0-0
Distance: 5f/6f: 0-3 **7f-8f: 3-10** 9f-13f: 2-3 14f+: 0-0
Track : LH: 2-6 RH: 2-4 Tight: 0-3 Gall: 0-0
Aids: Bl: 0-0 Vi: 0-0 Tstrap: 0-0 Ckp: 0-0
Best Rating: **77** 9/09 Bevl 1m100y gd-fm

Fair; stays 1m; acts on Fibresand and on fast and easy ground.

Just For Mary

109(84) (73)88

5-y-o b g Groom Dancer (USA)-Summer Dance (Sadler's Wells (USA))

Daniel Mark Loughnane Andrew Doyle

Placings:50610563/**00160000**-0046041120250 (5889a)

2009: 7^{0}GF, 6^{0}YS, 7^{4}SH, 7^{6}YS, 6^{0}G, 6^{4}GF, 5^{1}S, 5^{1}HY, 5^{2}G, 7^{0}Y, 5^{2}S, 5^{5}S, 5^{0}SH,

	Starts	1st	2nd	3rd	Win & Pl
Career Total (Turf)	21	3	2	1	82379
Career Total (AW)	8	1	0	0	11967

84	7/09	Curr	5f	H	HVY	£52514
73	6/09	Curr	5f	(60-90)H	SFT	£10063
73	3/08	Dund	5f	(60-100)H	STD	£11966
72	7/06	Bell	5f		G-F	£6671

Total win prize-money £81217

Going (Turf): **Sf: 2-6** GS: 0-0 Gd: 0-2 GF: 1-6 Fm: 0-1
Distance: **5f/6f: 4-22** 7f-8f: 0-7 9f-13f: 0-0 14f+: 0-0
Track : **LH: 2-12** RH: 0-6 Tight: 0-3 Gall: 0-0
Aids: **Bl: 1-5** Vi: 0-0 Tstrap: 0-0 Ckp: 0-0
Best Rating: **88** 8/09 Tipp 5f soft

Useful; Irish-trained; effective at 5f; acts on most ground and on Polytrack; has worn blinkers.

Just Jimmy (IRE)

104(103) (64)64

4-y-o b g Ashkalani (IRE)-Berkeley Hall (Saddlers' Hall (IRE))

P D Evans (K M Prendergast 4/9) Richard Edwards

Placings:000000/0**5**1**50**4**353**0**0054-234165**00004200**2**0**41511** (7860)

2009: 8^{2}SD, 8^{3}SD, 7^{4}SD, 7^{1}SD, 8^{6}SD, 7^{5}SD, 7^{0}SD, 6^{0}GF, 8^{0}GF, 8^{0}GF, 7^{4}GF, 6^{2}G, 6^{0}GF, 7^{0}GS, 8^{2}SD, 7^{0}G, 7^{4}SD, 8^{1}SD, 8^{5}SD, 8^{1}SD, 7^{1}SD,

	Starts	1st	2nd	3rd	Win & Pl
Career Total (Turf)	20	1	1	2	4050
Career Total (AW)	21	4	2	1	9433

	12/09	Wolv	7f32y	(0-65)H	STD	£1706
64	12/09	Wolv	1m141y	(0-60)H	STD	£2388
61	11/09	Wolv	1m141y	(0-65)H	STD	£2047
59	2/09	Wolv	7f32y	(0-52)H	STD	£1706
64	5/08	Chep	6f16y	(0-65)H	GD	£2104

Total win prize-money £9952

Going (Turf): Sf: 0-1 GS: 0-4 **Gd: 1-5** GF: 0-8 Fm: 0-2
Distance: 5f/6f: 0-6 **7f-8f: 3-26** 9f-13f: 2-9 14f+: 0-0
Track : **LH: 4-21** RH: 0-6 **Tight: 4-16** Gall: 0-1
Aids: Bl: 0-0 Vi: 0-3 Tstrap: 0-0 Ckp: 0-0
Best Rating: **64** 12/09 Wolv 1m141y stand

Modest; effective over 7f-1m; acts on good ground; goes on Polytrack.

Just Joey

97(93) (52)70

5-y-o b m Averti (IRE)-Fly South (Polar Falcon (USA))

J R Weymes High Moor Racing 4

Placings:120512/030060600/000143246505**600-**0620000446060 **(5341)**

2009: 5^0SD, 5^6SD, 5^2GF, 5^0F, 5^0GF, 5^0F, 5^0GF, 5^4F, 5^4F, 5^6GF, 5^0GF, 5^6G, 5^0GS,

	Starts	1st	2nd	3rd	Win & Pl
Career Total (Turf)	38	3	4	2	21365
Career Total (AW)	5	0	0	0	0

70 5/08 Carl 5f (0-60)H G-F £2047
85 8/06 Hayd 5f G-F £3238
62 4/06 Wwck 5f GD £3238
Total win prize-money £8525

Going (Turf): Sf: 0-0 GS: 0-3 Gd: 1-9 **GF: 2-19** Fm: 0-7
Distance: **5f/6f: 3-43** 7f-8f: 0-0 9f-13f: 0-0 14f+: 0-0
Track : LH: 1-14 RH: 1-4 Tight: 0-5 **Gall: 1-8**
Aids: **Bl: 1-24** Vi: 0-2 Tstrap: 0-0 Ckp: 0-0
Best Rating: **87** 8/06 Bevl 5f gd-sft

Modest sprinter; acts on fast and easy ground.

Just Like Silk (USA)

101(108) (77)93

3-y-o b g Elusive Quality (USA)-Ocean Silk (USA) (Dynaformer (USA))

G A Butler Future In Mind Partnership

Placings:60-5342251 **(5028)**

2009: 8^5SD, 10^3SD, 12^4SD, 9^2G, 9^2G, 10^5S, 12^1GF,

	Starts	1st	2nd	3rd	Win & Pl
Career Total (Turf)	5	1	2	0	8719
Career Total (AW)	4	0	0	1	2417

93 8/09 Newb 1m4f5y (0-80)H G-F £4996
Total win prize-money £4997

Going (Turf): Sf: 0-1 GS: 0-0 Gd: 0-2 **GF: 1-2** Fm: 0-0
Distance: 5f/6f: 0-0 7f-8f: 0-3 **9f-13f: 1-6** 14f+: 0-0
Track : **LH: 1-5** RH: 0-3 Tight: 0-4 **Gall: 1-3**
Aids: Bl: 0-0 Vi: 0-0 Tstrap: 0-0 Ckp: 0-0
Best Rating: **93** 8/09 Newb 1m4f5y gd-fm

Fair; stays 1m4f; acts on fast ground; has worn a tongue tie.

Just Lille (IRE)

109 96

6-y-o b m Mull Of Kintyre (USA)-Tamasriya (IRE) (Doyoun)

Mrs A Duffield Miss Helen Wynne

Placings:54611300/0011115326/21200-36242210321043 **(6536)**

2009: 9^3GF, 10^6G, 9^2GF, 9^4GS, 8^2G, 12^2GF, 8^1GF, 11^0GF, 10^3G, 8^2GS, 14^1G, 14^0GF, 13^4G, 17^3GF,

	Starts	1st	2nd	3rd	Win & Pl
Career Total (Turf)	37	9	7	5	87426

93 8/09 Wwck 1m6f213y (0-95)H GD £7477
93 6/09 Haml 1m65y G-F £11215
91 5/08 Bevl 1m1f207y (0-85)H G-F £4209
82 6/07 Haml 1m65y G-S £9348
84 5/07 Bevl 1m1f207y (0-70)H G-F £3435
87 5/07 Hayd 1m2f120y (0-75)H G-F £3886
75 5/07 Haml 1m65y (0-70)H G-F £3238
77 7/06 Hayd 1m30y (0-70)H G-F £3238
73 7/06 Ayr 7f50y (0-70)H FRM £4533
Total win prize-money £50583

Going (Turf): Sf: 0-2 GS: 1-5 Gd: 1-9 **GF: 6-18** Fm: 1-3
Distance: 5f/6f: 0-1 7f-8f: 1-3 **9f-13f: 7-29** 14f+: 1-4
Track : LH: 4-18 **RH: 5-17 Tight: 3-14** Gall: 0-5
Aids: Bl: 0-0 Vi: 0-0 Tstrap: 7-26 Ckp: 7-26
Best Rating: **96** 9/09 Haml 1m5f9y good

Very useful; stays 1m6f; acts on fast ground but handles cut; usually wears cheekpieces.

Just Mandy (IRE)

86 66

2-y-o ch f Noverre (USA)-Unicamp (Royal Academy (USA))

R A Fahey Dr Marwan Koukash

Placings:3 **(3849)**

2009: 5^3GF,

	Starts	1st	2nd	3rd	Win & Pl
Career Total (Turf)	1	0	0	1	602

Going (Turf): **Sf: 0-0 GS: 0-0 Gd: 0-0 GF: 0-1 Fm: 0-0**
Distance: 5f/6f: 0-1 7f-8f: 0-0 9f-13f: 0-0 14f+: 0-0
Track : LH: 0-1 RH: 0-0 Tight: 0-1 Gall: 0-0
Aids: Bl: 0-0 Vi: 0-0 Tstrap: 0-0 Ckp: 0-0
Best Rating: **66** 7/09 Ches 5f16y gd-fm

Just Mossie

(99) (63)34

4-y-o ch g Ishiguru (USA)-Marinsky (USA) (Diesis)

W G M Turner R A Bracken

Placings:500234/23020-0 **(1496)**

2009: 9^0SD,

	Starts	1st	2nd	3rd	Win & Pl
Career Total (Turf)	3	0	0	0	0
Career Total (AW)	9	0	3	2	2372

Going (Turf): **Sf: 0-0 GS: 0-1 Gd: 0-0 GF: 0-2 Fm: 0-0**
Distance: 5f/6f: 0-2 7f-8f: 0-4 9f-13f: 0-6 14f+: 0-0
Track : LH: 0-10 RH: 0-1 Tight: 0-9 Gall: 0-0
Aids: Bl: 0-0 Vi: 0-0 Tstrap: 0-6 Ckp: 0-6
Best Rating: **63** 10/08 Wolv 1m1f103y stand

Plating-class; stays 1m; acts on Polytrack; has worn cheekpieces.

Just Mustard (USA)

87(95) (65)65

3-y-o gr/ro g Johannesburg (USA)-After All (IRE) (Desert Story (IRE))

G A Butler Keen As Mustard

Placings:5-6040 **(3630)**

2009: 8^6SD, 7^0GF, 6^4GS, 7^0G,

	Starts	1st	2nd	3rd	Win & Pl
Career Total (Turf)	4	0	0	0	192
Career Total (AW)	1	0	0	0	0

Going (Turf): **Sf: 0-0 GS: 0-1 Gd: 0-1 GF: 0-2 Fm: 0-0**
Distance: 5f/6f: 0-0 7f-8f: 0-5 9f-13f: 0-0 14f+: 0-0
Track : LH: 0-1 RH: 0-0 Tight: 0-1 Gall: 0-0
Aids: Bl: 0-0 Vi: 0-0 Tstrap: 0-0 Ckp: 0-0
Best Rating: **65** 3/09 Ling 1m stand

Just Observing

97(101) (74)59

6-y-o ch g Observatory (USA)-Just Speculation (IRE) (Ahonoora)

P T Midgley O R Dukes

Placings:62323/**2150**/23164464/**2606**305554 **(3121)**

2009: 10^2SD, 9^6SD, 9^0SD, 12^6SD, 12^3SD, 10^0G, 12^5GF, 10^5F, 9^5F, 10^4GF,

	Starts	1st	2nd	3rd	Win & Pl
Career Total (Turf)	19	2	2	3	12713
Career Total (AW)	8	0	3	1	3674

81 5/07 Pont 1m2f6y (0-75)H G-F £4533
61 5/06 Folk 1m1f149y G-F £2730
Total win prize-money £7264

Going (Turf): Sf: 0-0 GS: 0-1 Gd: 0-2 **GF: 2-13** Fm: 0-3
Distance: 5f/6f: 0-1 7f-8f: 0-3 **9f-13f: 2-23** 14f+: 0-0
Track : LH: 1-14 RH: 1-11 **Tight: 1-14** Gall: 0-5
Aids: Bl: 0-0 Vi: 0-2 Tstrap: 1-13 Ckp: 1-13
Best Rating: **81** 5/07 Pont 1m2f6y gd-fm

Modest; stays 1m4f but effective at shorter; acts on fast ground and Polytrack; has worn cheekpieces/visor.

Just Oscar (GER)

98(93) (42)58

5-y-o b g Surako (GER)-Jade Chequer (Green Desert (USA))

W M Brisbourne Brisbourne Francis

Placings:0034/040025232050**460**/00032660**000**-55200005 **(4617)**

2009: 7^5SD, 7^5F, 6^2GF, 7^0GF, 8^0GF, 7^0GF, 7^0GF, 15^5G,

	Starts	1st	2nd	3rd	Win & Pl
Career Total (Turf)	28	0	5	2	6463
Career Total (AW)	10	0	0	1	578

Going (Turf): **Sf: 0-2 GS: 0-2 Gd: 0-7 GF: 0-15 Fm: 0-2**
Distance: 5f/6f: 0-3 7f-8f: 0-21 9f-13f: 0-13 14f+: 0-1
Track : LH: 0-28 RH: 0-5 Tight: 0-19 Gall: 0-1
Aids: Bl: 0-2 Vi: 0-1 Tstrap: 0-1 Ckp: 0-1
Best Rating: **68** 8/07 Hayd 1m30y gd-fm

Moderate maiden; effective over 1m; acts on fast ground but handles soft.

Just Pickles

86 30

4-y-o b g Piccolo-Tenderetta (Tender King)

G A Swinbank Mrs H E Aitkin

Placings:00 **(1226)**

2009: 7^0GF, 9^0GF,

	Starts	1st	2nd	3rd	Win & Pl
Career Total (Turf)	2	0	0	0	

Going (Turf): **Sf: 0-0 GS: 0-0 Gd: 0-0 GF: 0-2 Fm: 0-0**
Distance: 5f/6f: 0-0 7f-8f: 0-1 9f-13f: 0-1 14f+: 0-0
Track : LH: 0-1 RH: 0-1 Tight: 0-2 Gall: 0-0
Aids: Bl: 0-0 Vi: 0-0 Tstrap: 0-0 Ckp: 0-0
Best Rating: **30** 4/09 Catt 7f gd-fm

Just Sam (IRE)

106(96) (61)73

4-y-o b f Mull Of Kintyre (USA)-Strawberry Sands (Lugana Beach)

R E Barr P Cartmell

Placings:0500/2223043320040-23010401100210 **(6765)**

2009: 7^2F, 7^3GS, 8^0GF, 6^1GF, 6^0GF, 7^4GF, 5^0S, 6^1GF, 6^1GF, 6^0GF, 6^0GF, 6^2GF, 6^1GF, 6^0G,

	Starts	1st	2nd	3rd	Win & Pl
Career Total (Turf)	30	4	6	3	13164

	Starts	1st	2nd	3rd	Win & Pl
Career Total (AW)	1	0	0	1	302

73 9/09 Rdcr 6f (0-65)H G-F £1706
71 8/09 Rdcr 6f (0-60)H G-F £2047
72 7/09 Rdcr 6f (0-65)H G-F £1942
62 5/09 Rdcr 6f (0-60)H G-F £1977
Total win prize-money £7674

Going (Turf): Sf: 0-3 GS: 0-4 Gd: 0-5 **GF: 4-17** Fm: 0-1
Distance: **5f/6f: 4-12** 7f-8f: 0-10 9f-13f: 0-9 14f+: 0-0
Track : LH: 0-9 RH: 0-8 Tight: 0-10 Gall: 0-0
Aids: Bl: 0-0 Vi: 0-3 Tstrap: 0-0 Ckp: 0-0
Best Rating: 73 9/09 Rdcr 6f gd-fm

Modest; best at around 6f; stays 1m2f; acts on most ground and on Polytrack.

Just Serenade

(95) (39)
10-y-o ch m Factual (USA)-Thimbalina (Salmon Leap (USA))
Mrs Lawney Hill Miss Emma L Owen

Placings:5055306/4063002000000/**20204/00** **(0443)**
2009: 14^{0}SD, 12^{0}SD,

	Starts	1st	2nd	3rd	Win & Pl
Career Total (Turf)	22	0	1	2	2503
Career Total (AW)	6	0	2	0	1812

Going (Turf): Sf: 0-2 GS: 0-4 Gd: 0-11 GF: 0-5 Fm: 0-0
Distance: 5f/6f: 0-6 7f-8f: 0-12 9f-13f: 0-9 14f+: 0-1
Track : LH: 0-10 RH: 0-6 Tight: 0-2 Gall: 0-4
Aids: Bl: 0-1 Vi: 0-4 Tstrap: 0-5 Ckp: 0-5
Best Rating: 69 6/02 Kemp 7f soft

Just Spike

99(98) (48)63
6-y-o ch g Cayman Kai (IRE)-Grandads Dream (Never So Bold)
B P J Baugh C R Watts

Placings:40600/0501300-0004 **(7152)**
2009: 6^{0}G, 6^{0}GF, 8^{0}G, 8^{4}SD,

	Starts	1st	2nd	3rd	Win & Pl
Career Total (Turf)	6	1	0	1	3642
Career Total (AW)	10	0	0	0	0

63 7/08 Leic 5f218y (0-70)H G-F £3238
Total win prize-money £3238

Going (Turf): Sf: 0-0 GS: 0-1 Gd: 0-3 **GF: 1-2** Fm: 0-0
Distance: **5f/6f: 1-9** 7f-8f: 0-5 9f-13f: 0-2 14f+: 0-0
Track : LH: 0-9 RH: 0-1 Tight: 0-8 Gall: 0-0
Aids: Bl: 0-0 Vi: 0-0 Tstrap: 0-0 Ckp: 0-0
Best Rating: 63 7/08 Leic 5f218y gd-fm

Moderate; effective over 6f-1m; acts on fast ground and Polytrack.

Just The Lady

(99) (62)72
3-y-o b f Ishiguru (USA)-Just Run (IRE) (Runnett)
D Nicholls Dr Marwan Koukash

Placings:335511344130-13420665 **(1157)**
2009: 5^{1}SD, 5^{3}SD, 5^{1}SD, 5^{2}SD, 6^{0}SD, 5^{6}SD, 5^{0}SD, 5^{5}SD,

	Starts	1st	2nd	3rd	Win & Pl
Career Total (Turf)	8	2	0	4	8099
Career Total (AW)	12	2	1	1	4728

49 1/09 Kemp 5f STD £2047
72 9/08 Bevl 5f (0-65) SFT £2729
61 6/08 Bevl 5f G-F £1942
60 6/08 Ling 5f STD £1774
Total win prize-money £8494

Going (Turf): Sf: 1-3 GS: 0-1 Gd: 0-1 **GF: 1-3** Fm: 0-0
Distance: **5f/6f: 4-20** 7f-8f: 0-0 9f-13f: 0-0 14f+: 0-0
Track : LH: 1-8 RH: 1-3 **Tight: 1-8** Gall: 0-0
Aids: Bl: 0-0 Vi: 0-0 Tstrap: 0-0 Ckp: 0-0
Best Rating: 72 9/08 Bevl 5f soft

Modest; effective at 5f; acts on easy ground; also goes on Fibresand and Polytrack.

Just The Tonic

97(75) (32)73
2-y-o ch f Medicean-Goodwood Blizzard (Inchinor)
Mrs Marjorie Fife (M R Channon 31/8) R W Fife

Placings:35240020346 **(6215)**
2009: 6^{3}GF, 6^{5}GF, 6^{2}GF, 7^{4}GS, 7^{0}G, 7^{0}G, 6^{2}GF, 7^{0}SD, 6^{3}G, 5^{4}GF, 8^{6}GF,

	Starts	1st	2nd	3rd	Win & Pl
Career Total (Turf)	10	0	2	2	2838
Career Total (AW)	1	0	0	0	

Going (Turf): Sf: 0-0 GS: 0-1 Gd: 0-3 GF: 0-6 Fm: 0-0
Distance: 5f/6f: 0-4 7f-8f: 0-7 9f-13f: 0-0 14f+: 0-0
Track : LH: 0-1 RH: 0-1 Tight: 0-1 Gall: 0-0
Aids: Bl: 0-0 Vi: 0-0 Tstrap: 0-0 Ckp: 0-0
Best Rating: 73 7/09 Sals 6f212y gd-fm

Moderate; stays 7f and acts on fast ground.

Just Timmy Marcus

93(103) (69)59
3-y-o ch g Ishiguru (USA)-Grandads Dream (Never So Bold)
B P J Baugh C R Watts

Placings:110600642343 **(7860)**
2009: 5^{1}SD, 5^{1}SD, 6^{0}GS, 6^{6}GF, 7^{0}G, 6^{0}SD, 7^{6}SD, 7^{4}SD, 7^{2}SD, 7^{3}SD, 7^{4}SD, 7^{3}SD,

	Starts	1st	2nd	3rd	Win & Pl
Career Total (Turf)	3	0	0	0	0
Career Total (AW)	9	2	1	2	6087

68 3/09 Wolv 5f216y (0-65)H STD £2047
62 2/09 Wolv 5f216y STD £2729
Total win prize-money £4777

Going (Turf): Sf: 0-0 GS: 0-1 Gd: 0-1 GF: 0-1 Fm: 0-0
Distance: **5f/6f: 2-5** 7f-8f: 0-7 9f-13f: 0-0 14f+: 0-0
Track : **LH: 2-9** RH: 0-0 **Tight: 2-9** Gall: 0-0
Aids: Bl: 0-0 Vi: 0-0 Tstrap: 0-1 Ckp: 0-1
Best Rating: 69 10/09 Wolv 7f32y stand

Modest; effective over 6f-7f; acts on Polytrack.

Justcallmehandsome

99(107) (81)67
7-y-o ch g Handsome Ridge-Pearl Dawn (IRE) (Jareer (USA))
D J S Ffrench Davis Mrs J E Taylor

Placings:00/401200100303205/20460311403/311431510 31060-402034655065013 **(7812)**
2009: 8^{4}SD, 8^{0}SD, 8^{2}SD, 10^{0}SD, 8^{3}GF, 8^{4}GF, 8^{6}GF, 8^{5}G, 8^{5}GF, 7^{0}SD, 8^{6}SD, 8^{5}SD, 8^{0}SD, 8^{1}SD, 8^{3}SD,

	Starts	1st	2nd	3rd	Win & Pl
Career Total (Turf)	15	0	1	3	2082
Career Total (AW)	42	10	3	6	31831

78 12/09 Wolv 1m141y (60-92)H STD £2590
82 5/08 Wolv 1m141y (0-80)H STD £5046
79 3/08 Wolv 1m141y (0-75)H STD £2730
74 2/08 Wolv 1m141y (0-75)H STD £2590
71 1/08 Wolv 1m141y (0-60)H STD £2388
63 1/08 Wolv 1m141y (0-58)H STD £2047
62 10/07 Kemp 1m (0-55)H STD £2817
58 9/07 Wolv 1m141y (0-45) STD £1911
53 4/06 Kemp 1m2f (0-45) STD £2388
55 1/06 Sthl 7f STD £1365
Total win prize-money £25876

Going (Turf): Sf: 0-3 GS: 0-2 Gd: 0-3 GF: 0-6 Fm: 0-1
Distance: 5f/6f: 0-0 7f-8f: 2-18 **9f-13f: 8-39** 14f+: 0-0
Track : **LH: 8-44** RH: 2-11 **Tight: 7-27** Gall: 0-2
Aids: Bl: 0-0 **Vi: 10-45** Tstrap: 0-0 Ckp: 0-0
Best Rating: 82 5/08 Wolv 1m141y stand

Fair; effective over 1m-1m3f; acts on fast ground and on sand; has worn a visor; goes well for female jockeys.

Justonefortheroad

102(94) (73)75
3-y-o b g Domedriver (IRE)-Lavinia's Grace (USA) (Green Desert (USA))
R A Fahey (N J Vaughan 26/6) The Pontoon Partnership

Placings:36-335100 **(6731)**
2009: 8^{3}GF, 9^{3}F, 8^{5}GF, 7^{1}GF, 7^{0}SD, 6^{0}S,

	Starts	1st	2nd	3rd	Win & Pl
Career Total (Turf)	7	1	0	3	4125
Career Total (AW)	1	0	0	0	

75 9/09 Rdcr 7f G-F £2752
Total win prize-money £2752

Going (Turf): Sf: 0-1 GS: 0-1 Gd: 0-1 **GF: 1-3** Fm: 0-1
Distance: 5f/6f: 0-1 **7f-8f: 1-5** 9f-13f: 0-2 14f+: 0-0
Track : LH: 0-2 RH: 0-1 Tight: 0-1 Gall: 0-0
Aids: Bl: 0-0 Vi: 0-0 Tstrap: 0-0 Ckp: 0-0
Best Rating: 75 9/09 Rdcr 7f gd-fm

Dam was a sprint winner at two in France; promise in maiden company; stays 7f.

Jutland

94 78
2-y-o b g Halling (USA)-Dramatique (Darshaan)
M Johnston Sheikh Hamdan Bin Mohammed Al Maktoum

Placings:4616 **(5265)**
2009: 7^{4}GF, 7^{6}GF, 6^{1}GF, 7^{6}GF,

	Starts	1st	2nd	3rd	Win & Pl
Career Total (Turf)	4	1	0	0	4278

78 8/09 Brig 6f209y G-F £4037
Total win prize-money £4037

Going (Turf): Sf: 0-0 GS: 0-0 Gd: 0-0 **GF: 1-4** Fm: 0-0
Distance: 5f/6f: 0-0 **7f-8f: 1-4** 9f-13f: 0-0 14f+: 0-0
Track : **LH: 1-2** RH: 0-2 Tight: 0-1 Gall: 0-0
Aids: Bl: 0-0 Vi: 0-0 Tstrap: 0-0 Ckp: 0-0
Best Rating: 78 8/09 Brig 6f209y gd-fm

Fair; effective at 7f; handles fast ground.

Juwireya

80 48
2-y-o b f Nayef (USA)-Katayeb (IRE) (Machiavellian (USA))
M P Tregoning Hamdan Al Maktoum

Placings:0 **(5741)**
2009: 8^{0}GF,

	Starts	1st	2nd	3rd	Win & Pl
Career Total (Turf)	1	0	0	0	

Going (Turf): Sf: 0-0 GS: 0-0 Gd: 0-0 GF: 0-1 Fm: 0-0

Distance: 5f/6f: 0-0 7f-8f: 0-1 9f-13f: 0-0 14f+: 0-0
Track : LH: 0-0 RH: 0-1 Tight: 0-0 Gall: 0-0
Aids: Bl: 0-0 Vi: 0-0 Tstrap: 0-0 Ckp: 0-0
Best Rating: 48 9/09 Gdwd 1m gd-fm

K'Gari (USA)

81(100) (57)**40**
3-y-o ch g Fusaichi Pegasus (USA)-To Act (USA) (Roberto (USA))
B Ellison Mrs C L Ellison & C P Lowther

Placings:06-00**610** (7649)
2009: 8^{0}G, 10^{0}GF, 13^{6}SD, 16^{1}SD, 16^{0}SD,

	Starts	1st	2nd	3rd	Win & Pl
Career Total (Turf)	4	0	0	0	0
Career Total (AW)	3	1	0	0	3238
57 11/09 Wolv	2m119y	(0-70)H	STD	£3238	

Total win prize-money £3238

Going (Turf): Sf: 0-1 GS: 0-0 Gd: 0-1 GF: 0-2 Fm: 0-0
Distance: 5f/6f: 0-0 7f-8f: 0-1 9f-13f: 0-3 14f+: 1-3
Track : LH: 1-5 RH: 0-1 Tight: 1-4 Gall: 0-1
Aids: Bl: 1-3 Vi: 0-0 Tstrap: 0-0 Ckp: 0-0
Best Rating: 57 11/09 Wolv 2m119y stand

Moderate; stays 2m; acts on Polytrack; has worn blinkers.

Kaabari (USA)

104(99) (77)**92**
3-y-o b/br f Seeking The Gold (USA)-Cloud Castle (In The Wings)
C E Brittain Saeed Manana

Placings:103050025 (6487)
2009: 7^{1}SD, 7^{0}GF, 7^{3}GF, 9^{0}G, 7^{5}S, 12^{0}G, 8^{0}GF, 7^{2}GF, 7^{5}GF,

	Starts	1st	2nd	3rd	Win & Pl
Career Total (Turf)	8	0	1	1	4342
Career Total (AW)	1	1	0	0	2730
77 3/09 Ling	7f		STD	£2729	

Total win prize-money £2730

Going (Turf): Sf: 0-1 GS: 0-0 Gd: 0-2 GF: 0-5 Fm: 0-0
Distance: 5f/6f: 0-0 7f-8f: 1-6 9f-13f: 0-3 14f+: 0-0
Track : LH: 1-3 RH: 0-1 Tight: 1-3 Gall: 0-1
Aids: Bl: 0-0 Vi: 0-0 Tstrap: 0-0 Ckp: 0-0
Best Rating: 92 10/09 Rdcr 7f gd-fm

Useful; from a fine family including Warrsan, Luso and Needle Gun, all of whom ran in the same colours, and is a half sister to several winners up to 1m4f; winner on debut over 7f on Polytrack.

Kabeer

(111) (98)**47**
11-y-o ch g Unfuwain (USA)-Ta Rib (USA) (Mr Prospector (USA))
A J McCabe Placida Racing

Placings:4300560**65/221010056/002000002212/00001142/1230050506-666500** (0932)
2009: 7^{6}SS, 7^{6}SD, 8^{6}SD, 7^{5}SD, 8^{0}SD, 8^{0}SD,

	Starts	1st	2nd	3rd	Win & Pl
Career Total (Turf)	13	0	0	1	853
Career Total (AW)	41	6	8	1	44220
98 1/08 Sthl	7f	(0-100)H	STD	£10525	
94 12/07 Sthl	1m	(0-75)H	SS	£2968	
89 12/07 Sthl	1m	(0-75)H	SS	£2968	
82 12/06 Ling	1m	(0-75)H	STD	£5505	
85 3/05 Ling	1m	(0-85)H	STD	£6817	
71 2/05 Ling	1m	(0-70)H	STD	£3491	

Total win prize-money £32277

Going (Turf): Sf: 0-0 GS: 0-0 Gd: 0-3 GF: 0-9 Fm: 0-1
Distance: 5f/6f: 0-2 7f-8f: 6-40 9f-13f: 0-12 14f+: 0-0
Track : LH: 6-46 RH: 0-3 Tight: 3-27 Gall: 0-1
Aids: Bl: 0-0 Vi: 0-0 Tstrap: 0-1 Ckp: 0-1
Best Rating: 98 2/08 Sthl 6f stand

Useful; best at 1m, but effective over shorter; acts on Polytrack and Fibresand; has worn a tongue tie; likes to race prominently.

Kabis Amigos

103(103) (67)**76**
7-y-o ch g Nashwan (USA)-River Saint (USA) (Irish River (FR))
Ollie Pears (S T Mason 20/4) Ian W Glenton

Placings:00/504010/00050152/**20111**302061600/3003060 0000**6052-020351350**251366 (4887)
2009: 7^{0}SD, 7^{2}SD, 7^{0}SD, 7^{3}SD, 7^{5}SD, 7^{1}SD, 7^{3}SD, 7^{5}SD, 7^{0}SD, 7^{2}GF, 7^{5}GF, 7^{1}F, 8^{3}GF, 7^{6}GF, 7^{6}G,

	Starts	1st	2nd	3rd	Win & Pl
Career Total (Turf)	39	4	3	3	19045
Career Total (AW)	21	4	3	3	13926
76 6/09 Bevl	7f100y	(0-70)H	FRM	£4209	
63 3/09 Wolv	7f32y		STD	£1706	
76 8/07 Carl	7f200y	(0-70)H	FRM	£2717	
77 3/07 Wolv	7f32y	(0-75)H	SF	£3238	
77 3/07 Wolv	7f32y	(0-75)H	SF	£2590	
72 3/07 Wolv	7f32y	(0-70)H	STD	£3238	
62 8/06 Catt	7f	(0-55)H	G-F	£3412	
76 8/05 Ripn	1m		G-F	£3373	

Total win prize-money £24488

Going (Turf): Sf: 0-4 GS: 0-5 Gd: 0-8 GF: 2-20 Fm: 2-2
Distance: 5f/6f: 0-1 7f-8f: 8-50 9f-13f: 0-9 14f+: 0-0
Track : LH: 5-34 RH: 3-19 Tight: 6-38 Gall: 0-3
Aids: Bl: 2-17 Vi: 0-3 Tstrap: 0-2 Ckp: 0-2
Best Rating: 77 3/07 Wolv 7f32y std-fst

Modest; effective at around 7f; acts on good to firm; goes on Fibresand and Polytrack; has won headgear.

Kabougg

73(80) (30)
3-y-o b f Tobougg (IRE)-Karameg (IRE) (Danehill (USA))
A J McCabe Graham Keith Gordon

Placings:00-000 (7557)
2009: 8^{0}G, 12^{0}SD, 13^{0}SD,

	Starts	1st	2nd	3rd	Win & Pl
Career Total (Turf)	2	0	0	0	
Career Total (AW)	3	0	0	0	

Going (Turf): Sf: 0-1 GS: 0-0 Gd: 0-1 GF: 0-0 Fm: 0-0
Distance: 5f/6f: 0-0 7f-8f: 0-2 9f-13f: 0-2 14f+: 0-1
Track : LH: 0-4 RH: 0-1 Tight: 0-2 Gall: 0-0
Aids: Bl: 0-0 Vi: 0-0 Tstrap: 0-0 Ckp: 0-0
Best Rating: 30 11/09 Wolv 1m5f194y stand

Kahail (USA)

92(89) (56)**61**
2-y-o b c Rahy (USA)-Al Ihsas (IRE) (Danehill (USA))
Miss D Mountain Al-Abdulmalik Hassan

Placings:0555 (4856)
2009: 6^{0}GF, 6^{5}GF, 6^{5}GF, 5^{5}SD,

	Starts	1st	2nd	3rd	Win & Pl
Career Total (Turf)	3	0	0	0	141
Career Total (AW)	1	0	0	0	0

Going (Turf): Sf: 0-0 GS: 0-0 Gd: 0-0 GF: 0-3 Fm: 0-0
Distance: 5f/6f: 0-3 7f-8f: 0-1 9f-13f: 0-0 14f+: 0-0
Track : LH: 0-1 RH: 0-0 Tight: 0-1 Gall: 0-0
Aids: Bl: 0-0 Vi: 0-0 Tstrap: 0-0 Ckp: 0-0
Best Rating: 61 7/09 Yarm 6f3y gd-fm

Kahfre

85(89) (63)**53**
2-y-o ch g Peintre Celebre (USA)-Minerva (IRE) (Caerleon (USA))
E A L Dunlop Ballygallon Stud Limited

Placings:005 (7064)
2009: 8^{0}GF, 8^{0}GS, 8^{5}SD,

	Starts	1st	2nd	3rd	Win & Pl
Career Total (Turf)	2	0	0	0	
Career Total (AW)	1	0	0	0	0

Going (Turf): Sf: 0-0 GS: 0-1 Gd: 0-0 GF: 0-1 Fm: 0-0
Distance: 5f/6f: 0-0 7f-8f: 0-2 9f-13f: 0-1 14f+: 0-0
Track : LH: 0-2 RH: 0-0 Tight: 0-1 Gall: 0-0
Aids: Bl: 0-0 Vi: 0-0 Tstrap: 0-0 Ckp: 0-0
Best Rating: 63 10/09 Ling 1m stand

Kai Broon (IRE)

79 **56**
2-y-o b c Marju (IRE)-Restiv Star (FR) (Soviet Star (USA))
Miss Lucinda V Russell Mrs Elizabeth Ferguson

Placings:035 (5360)
2009: 7^{0}GS, 6^{3}GF, 6^{5}S,

	Starts	1st	2nd	3rd	Win & Pl
Career Total (Turf)	3	0	0	1	597

Going (Turf): Sf: 0-1 GS: 0-1 Gd: 0-0 GF: 0-1 Fm: 0-0
Distance: 5f/6f: 0-2 7f-8f: 0-1 9f-13f: 0-0 14f+: 0-0
Track : LH: 0-0 RH: 0-0 Tight: 0-0 Gall: 0-0
Aids: Bl: 0-0 Vi: 0-0 Tstrap: 0-0 Ckp: 0-0
Best Rating: 56 8/09 Ayr 6f soft

Kai Mer (IRE)

(82) (23)**28**
4-y-o b f Captain Rio-No Shame (Formidable I (USA))
Miss J A Camacho Miss Julie Camacho

Placings:500-00 (0537)
2009: 8^{0}SD, 9^{0}SD,

	Starts	1st	2nd	3rd	Win & Pl
Career Total (Turf)	2	0	0	0	
Career Total (AW)	3	0	0	0	0

Going (Turf): Sf: 0-0 GS: 0-1 Gd: 0-1 GF: 0-0 Fm: 0-0
Distance: 5f/6f: 0-3 7f-8f: 0-1 9f-13f: 0-1 14f+: 0-0
Track : LH: 0-3 RH: 0-0 Tight: 0-1 Gall: 0-0
Aids: Bl: 0-0 Vi: 0-0 Tstrap: 0-1 Ckp: 0-1
Best Rating: 29 4/08 Thsk 6f gd-sft

Kai Mook

85(99) (75)**65**
2-y-o gr/b f Littletown Boy (USA)-Beenaboutabit (Komaite (USA))
R Ingram Miss L McIntosh

Placings:00215 (7824)
2009: 5^{0}SD, 6^{0}S, 7^{2}SD, 7^{1}SD, 7^{5}SD,

	Starts	1st	2nd	3rd	Win & Pl
Career Total (Turf)	1	0	0	0	
Career Total (AW)	4	1	1	0	5042

75 12/09 Ling 7f STD £3885
Total win prize-money £3886

Going (Turf): Sf: 0-1 GS: 0-0 Gd: 0-0 GF: 0-0 Fm: 0-0
Distance: 5f/6f: 0-1 **7f-8f: 1-4** 9f-13f: 0-0 14f+: 0-0
Track : **LH: 1-2** RH: 0-2 **Tight: 1-2** Gall: 0-0
Aids: Bl: 0-0 Vi: 0-0 Tstrap: 0-0 Ckp: 0-0
Best Rating: 75 12/09 Ling 7f stand

Fair; stays 7f; acts on Polytrack.

Kaijai (IRE)

94(57) 41
3-y-o b f Trans Island-Consultant Stylist (IRE) (Desert Style (IRE))
Mrs L C Jewell Field Of Fortune

Placings:0-0000 (5367)
2009: 10^{0}GF, 11^{0}SD, 11^{0}G, 9^{0}F,

	Starts	1st	2nd	3rd	Win & Pl
Career Total (Turf)	3	0	0	0	
Career Total (AW)	2	0	0	0	

Going (Turf): Sf: 0-0 GS: 0-0 Gd: 0-1 GF: 0-1 Fm: 0-1
Distance: 5f/6f: 0-0 7f-8f: 0-1 9f-13f: 0-4 14f+: 0-0
Track : LH: 0-1 RH: 0-3 Tight: 0-3 Gall: 0-0
Aids: Bl: 0-0 Vi: 0-1 Tstrap: 0-0 Ckp: 0-0
Best Rating: 41 8/09 Ling 1m1f firm

Kaikoura

83(78) (34)40
3-y-o br f High Chaparral (IRE)-Landowska (USA) (Langfuhr (CAN))
G Woodward (T D Easterby 16/5) W Lyttle

Placings:00-005 (3569)
2009: 7^{0}GF, 12^{0}G, 7^{5}G,

	Starts	1st	2nd	3rd	Win & Pl
Career Total (Turf)	4	0	0	0	0
Career Total (AW)	1	0	0	0	

Going (Turf): Sf: 0-0 GS: 0-0 Gd: 0-2 GF: 0-2 Fm: 0-0
Distance: 5f/6f: 0-2 7f-8f: 0-2 9f-13f: 0-1 14f+: 0-0
Track : LH: 0-2 RH: 0-1 Tight: 0-2 Gall: 0-1
Aids: Bl: 0-0 Vi: 0-0 Tstrap: 0-0 Ckp: 0-0
Best Rating: 40 7/09 Donc 7f good

Kaiser Willie (IRE)

83(78) (20)47
3-y-o b g Xaar-Miss Bellbird (IRE) (Danehill (USA))
B W Duke Joseph Duke

Placings:000-000 (4351)
2009: 8^{0}SD, 10^{0}GF, 10^{0}G,

	Starts	1st	2nd	3rd	Win & Pl
Career Total (Turf)	5	0	0	0	
Career Total (AW)	1	0	0	0	

Going (Turf): Sf: 0-0 GS: 0-0 Gd: 0-4 GF: 0-1 Fm: 0-0
Distance: 5f/6f: 0-0 7f-8f: 0-4 9f-13f: 0-2 14f+: 0-0
Track : LH: 0-3 RH: 0-0 Tight: 0-2 Gall: 0-0
Aids: Bl: 0-0 Vi: 0-0 Tstrap: 0-0 Ckp: 0-0
Best Rating: 47 9/08 Newb 7f good

Kajima

93 71
2-y-o b g Oasis Dream-Mambo Mistress (USA) (Kingmambo (USA))
R Hannon Miss Yvonne Jacques

Placings:550 (7146)
2009: 6^{5}G, 7^{5}G, 7^{0}G,

	Starts	1st	2nd	3rd	Win & Pl
Career Total (Turf)	3	0	0	0	0

Going (Turf): Sf: 0-0 GS: 0-0 Gd: 0-3 GF: 0-0 Fm: 0-0
Distance: 5f/6f: 0-0 7f-8f: 0-3 9f-13f: 0-0 14f+: 0-0
Track : LH: 0-0 RH: 0-0 Tight: 0-0 Gall: 0-0
Aids: Bl: 0-0 Vi: 0-0 Tstrap: 0-0 Ckp: 0-0
Best Rating: 71 9/09 Chep 7f16y good

Kakapuka

91(68) (52)69
2-y-o br c Shinko Forest (IRE)-No Rehearsal (FR) (Baillamont (USA))
Mrs A L M King Mrs E Mills & A Murphy

Placings:035046 (6534)
2009: 5^{0}F, 5^{3}G, 5^{5}G, 6^{0}SD, 5^{4}GF, 6^{6}GF,

	Starts	1st	2nd	3rd	Win & Pl
Career Total (Turf)	5	0	0	1	644
Career Total (AW)	1	0	0	0	

Going (Turf): Sf: 0-0 GS: 0-0 Gd: 0-2 GF: 0-2 Fm: 0-1
Distance: 5f/6f: 0-6 7f-8f: 0-0 9f-13f: 0-0 14f+: 0-0
Track : LH: 0-3 RH: 0-1 Tight: 0-0 Gall: 0-1
Aids: Bl: 0-0 Vi: 0-0 Tstrap: 0-0 Ckp: 0-0
Best Rating: 69 7/09 Nott 5f13y good

Modest; effective at 5f on good ground.

Kakatosi

89 62
2-y-o br c Pastoral Pursuits-Ladywell Blaise (IRE) (Turtle Island (IRE))
A M Balding Robert E Tillett

Placings:0 (7146)
2009: 7^{0}G,

	Starts	1st	2nd	3rd	Win & Pl
Career Total (Turf)	1	0	0	0	

Going (Turf): Sf: 0-0 GS: 0-0 Gd: 0-1 GF: 0-0 Fm: 0-0
Distance: 5f/6f: 0-0 7f-8f: 0-1 9f-13f: 0-0 14f+: 0-0
Track : LH: 0-0 RH: 0-0 Tight: 0-0 Gall: 0-0
Aids: Bl: 0-0 Vi: 0-0 Tstrap: 0-0 Ckp: 0-0
Best Rating: 62 10/09 NmkR 7f good

Kalahari Desert (IRE)

93(91) (57)64
2-y-o b c Captain Rio-Sally Traffic (River Falls)
R M Whitaker J Barry Pemberton

Placings:4440534 (7088)
2009: 5^{4}GS, 5^{4}GS, 5^{4}GS, 5^{0}GF, 5^{5}SD, 6^{3}S, 6^{4}SD,

	Starts	1st	2nd	3rd	Win & Pl
Career Total (Turf)	5	0	0	1	1267
Career Total (AW)	2	0	0	0	0

Going (Turf): Sf: 0-1 GS: 0-3 Gd: 0-0 GF: 0-1 Fm: 0-0
Distance: 5f/6f: 0-6 7f-8f: 0-1 9f-13f: 0-0 14f+: 0-0
Track : LH: 0-1 RH: 0-1 Tight: 0-0 Gall: 0-1
Aids: Bl: 0-0 Vi: 0-0 Tstrap: 0-0 Ckp: 0-0
Best Rating: 64 10/09 Nott 6f15y soft

Kalam Daleel (IRE)

93 90
2-y-o gr c Clodovil (IRE)-Three Days In May (Cadeaux Genereux)
M R Channon Jaber Abdullah

Placings:316 (5347)
2009: 5^{3}F, 5^{1}G, 7^{6}G,

	Starts	1st	2nd	3rd	Win & Pl
Career Total (Turf)	3	1	0	1	4495

90 5/09 Brig 5f213y GD £3532
Total win prize-money £3532

Going (Turf): Sf: 0-0 GS: 0-0 **Gd: 1-2** GF: 0-0 Fm: 0-1
Distance: **5f/6f: 1-2** 7f-8f: 0-1 9f-13f: 0-0 14f+: 0-0
Track : **LH: 1-2** RH: 0-0 Tight: 0-0 Gall: 0-0
Aids: Bl: 0-0 Vi: 0-0 Tstrap: 0-0 Ckp: 0-0
Best Rating: 90 5/09 Brig 5f213y good

65,000euros second foal of a half-sister to Crazee Mental and Siena Gold; useful juvenile; effective at 6f; acts on easy and fast ground.

Kalasam

101 (82)71
5-y-o ch g Noverre (USA)-Spring Sixpence (Dowsing (USA))
M W Easterby T Bannister, M Hall & G Fawcett

Placings:0330/3064643213322/000002004-00333634046P (5962)
2009: 10^{0}G, 10^{0}G, 10^{3}S, 9^{3}GF, 8^{3}GF, 8^{6}G, 9^{3}GF, 8^{4}GS, 10^{0}G, 9^{4}GF, 12^{6}GS, 11^{P}GS,

	Starts	1st	2nd	3rd	Win & Pl
Career Total (Turf)	36	1	2	10	12512
Career Total (AW)	2	0	2	0	1802

77 9/07 Leic 1m1f218y (0-70)H G-F £3238
Total win prize-money £3239

Going (Turf): Sf: 0-5 GS: 0-5 Gd: 0-12 **GF: 1-14** Fm: 0-0
Distance: 5f/6f: 0-1 7f-8f: 0-10 **9f-13f: 1-26** 14f+: 0-1
Track : LH: 0-20 **RH: 1-12** Tight: 0-10 Gall: 0-5
Aids: Bl: 0-2 Vi: 0-0 Tstrap: 0-0 Ckp: 0-0
Best Rating: 82 10/07 Wolv 1m4f50y stand

Modest; suited by 1m2f; acts on fast and easy ground.

Kaldoun Kingdom (IRE)

109 (47)106
4-y-o b g King's Best (USA)-Bint Kaldoun (IRE) (Kaldoun (FR))
R A Fahey P D Smith Holdings Ltd

Placings:02446131/20023024-0004211 (6678)
2009: 5^{0}G, 5^{0}GF, 6^{0}GF, 6^{4}G, 6^{2}GS, 6^{1}G, 6^{1}G,

	Starts	1st	2nd	3rd	Win & Pl
Career Total (Turf)	22	4	5	2	88634
Career Total (AW)	1	0	0	0	

106 10/09 York 6f (0-105)H GD £25904
99 9/09 Ayr 6f H GD £31155
92 10/07 Ayr 6f (0-75) SFT £3238
72 9/07 Brig 5f213y (0-85) GD £5678
Total win prize-money £65976

Going (Turf): Sf: 1-5 GS: 0-4 Gd: 3-8 GF: 0-5 Fm: 0-0
Distance: 5f/6f: 4-19 7f-8f: 0-4 9f-13f: 0-0 14f+: 0-0
Track : LH: 1-3 RH: 0-1 Tight: 0-0 Gall: 0-2
Aids: Bl: 0-0 Vi: 0-0 Tstrap: 0-0 Ckp: 0-0
Best Rating: 106 10/09 York 6f good

Very useful; effective at 6f and acts on most ground.

Kaleo

107(86) (71)86

5-y-o ch g Lomitas-Kazoo (Shareef Dancer (USA))
S Dow John Robinson and Derek Stubbs

Placings:231/30/3-6060251311 (6470)
2009: 8^{6}SD, 10^{0}G, 10^{6}GF, 12^{0}G, 10^{2}G, 9^{5}S, 10^{1}GF, 10^{3}GF, 10^{1}G, 10^{1}GF,

	Starts	1st	2nd	3rd	Win & Pl
Career Total (Turf)	15	4	2	4	31819
Career Total (AW)	1	0	0	0	0

84 10/09 Epsm 1m2f18y (0-95)H G-F £9714
78 9/09 Ling 1m2f GD £2047
80 8/09 Epsm 1m2f18y G-F £3238
11/06 Brem 1m SFT £2068
Total win prize-money £17068

Going (Turf): Sf: 1-5 GS: 0-0 Gd: 1-6 GF: 2-4 Fm: 0-0
Distance: 5f/6f: 0-0 7f-8f: 1-5 9f-13f: 3-11 14f+: 0-0
Track : LH: 3-9 RH: 0-3 Tight: 3-9 Gall: 0-0
Aids: Bl: 0-0 Vi: 0-0 Tstrap: 0-0 Ckp: 0-0
Best Rating: 100 9/06 Badn 7f soft

Fair; stays 1m2f; acts on fast ground.

Kalhan Sands (IRE)

97(100) (6)74

4-y-o b g Okawango (USA)-Night Spirit (IRE) (Night Shift (USA))
J J Quinn Elsa Crankshaw Gordon Allan

Placings:010/46460-0600355000 (6999)
2009: 7^{0}GF, 7^{6}GS, 7^{0}G, 6^{0}GS, 5^{3}G, 6^{5}GF, 5^{5}GF, 5^{0}G, 5^{0}GF, 8^{0}SD,

	Starts	1st	2nd	3rd	Win & Pl
Career Total (Turf)	15	1	0	1	3986
Career Total (AW)	3	0	0	0	330

82 7/07 Catt 5f212y G-S £2590
Total win prize-money £2591

Going (Turf): Sf: 0-1 GS: 1-4 Gd: 0-6 GF: 0-4 Fm: 0-0
Distance: 5f/6f: 1-11 7f-8f: 0-5 9f-13f: 0-2 14f+: 0-0
Track : LH: 1-5 RH: 0-1 Tight: 1-5 Gall: 0-0
Aids: Bl: 0-0 Vi: 0-0 Tstrap: 0-0 Ckp: 0-0
Best Rating: 82 7/07 Catt 5f212y gd-sft

Fair; suited by 6f; acts on soft ground.

Kalimanka (FR)

(88) (69)66

3-y-o b f Daylami (IRE)-Kalimanta (IRE) (Lake Coniston (IRE))
M Halford Mrs Elaine Merry

Placings:0-2465265 (7790)
2009: 8^{2}SD, 10^{4}GF, 11^{6}GF, 10^{5}SD, 10^{2}SD, 10^{6}SD, 12^{5}SD,

	Starts	1st	2nd	3rd	Win & Pl
Career Total (Turf)	3	0	0	0	577
Career Total (AW)	5	0	2	0	3673

Going (Turf): Sf: 0-0 GS: 0-0 Gd: 0-0 GF: 0-2 Fm: 0-0
Distance: 5f/6f: 0-0 7f-8f: 0-2 9f-13f: 0-6 14f+: 0-0
Track : LH: 0-7 RH: 0-1 Tight: 0-1 Gall: 0-0
Aids: Bl: 0-0 Vi: 0-0 Tstrap: 0-3 Ckp: 0-3
Best Rating: 69 11/09 Dund 1m2f150y stand

Modest; effectiev around 1m2f; acts on most surfaces;has worn cheekpieces and tongue tie.

Kalligal

94(93) (54)68

4-y-o br f Kyllachy-Anytime Baby (Bairn (USA))
R Ingram Mrs C Hallam

Placings:43254/053303030040-46200004 (5566)
2009: 5^{4}SD, 5^{6}GF, 5^{2}G, 5^{0}F, 6^{0}G, 5^{0}G, 5^{0}GF, 5^{4}F,

	Starts	1st	2nd	3rd	Win & Pl
Career Total (Turf)	19	0	2	5	4776
Career Total (AW)	6	0	0	0	0

Going (Turf): Sf: 0-4 GS: 0-4 Gd: 0-4 GF: 0-5 Fm: 0-2
Distance: 5f/6f: 0-24 7f-8f: 0-1 9f-13f: 0-0 14f+: 0-0
Track : LH: 0-11 RH: 0-2 Tight: 0-5 Gall: 0-5
Aids: Bl: 0-4 Vi: 0-0 Tstrap: 0-1 Ckp: 0-1
Best Rating: 73 9/07 Sand 5f6y gd-fm

Modest; effective over 5f-6f; acts on fast and easy ground; also goes on Polytrack.

Kaloni (IRE)

107(97) (75)95

3-y-o b f Kalanisi (IRE)-Santarene (IRE) (Scenic)
Mrs P Sly Alan Speechley & John Watt

Placings:5325-4314105 (6813)
2009: 12^{4}GS, 10^{3}G, 10^{1}G, 10^{4}S, 9^{1}GF, 10^{0}GF, 10^{5}G,

	Starts	1st	2nd	3rd	Win & Pl
Career Total (Turf)	8	2	0	1	11181
Career Total (AW)	3	0	1	1	1134

89 8/09 Ripn 1m1f170y (0-80)H G-F £6308
78 7/09 Nott 1m2f50y (0-75)H GD £2590
Total win prize-money £8898

Going (Turf): Sf: 0-1 GS: 0-2 Gd: 1-3 GF: 1-2 Fm: 0-0
Distance: 5f/6f: 0-0 7f-8f: 0-3 9f-13f: 2-8 14f+: 0-0
Track : LH: 1-6 RH: 1-4 Tight: 1-2 Gall: 0-3
Aids: Bl: 0-0 Vi: 0-0 Tstrap: 0-0 Ckp: 0-0
Best Rating: 95 10/09 NmkR 1m2f good

Fair; stays 1m2f; acts on Polytrack and a sound surface on turf.

Kalypso (IRE)

97(94) (69)65

3-y-o ch f Barathea (IRE)-Russian Waltz (IRE) (Spectrum (IRE))
David P Myerscough Goldmine Racing Limited

Placings:0-530300545 (6123)
2009: 7^{5}SD, 8^{3}SD, 8^{0}Y, 8^{3}G, 7^{0}GF, 8^{0}GY, 7^{5}SH, 7^{4}SD, 7^{5}SD,

	Starts	1st	2nd	3rd	Win & Pl
Career Total (Turf)	6	0	0	1	620
Career Total (AW)	4	0	0	1	1111

Going (Turf): Sf: 0-1 GS: 0-0 Gd: 0-1 GF: 0-1 Fm: 0-0
Distance: 5f/6f: 0-0 7f-8f: 0-8 9f-13f: 0-2 14f+: 0-0
Track : LH: 0-6 RH: 0-0 Tight: 0-1 Gall: 0-0
Aids: Bl: 0-0 Vi: 0-0 Tstrap: 0-0 Ckp: 0-0
Best Rating: 69 9/09 Dund 7f stand

Kalypso King (USA)

103 98

2-y-o ch c Giant's Causeway (USA)-Kalypso Katie (IRE) (Fairy King (USA))
R Hannon Sir David Seale

Placings:3312 (6811)
2009: 6^{3}GF, 6^{3}GF, 8^{1}G, 8^{2}G,

	Starts	1st	2nd	3rd	Win & Pl
Career Total (Turf)	4	1	1	2	9004

98 10/09 Newb 1m GD £4857
Total win prize-money £4857

Going (Turf): Sf: 0-0 GS: 0-0 Gd: 1-2 GF: 0-2 Fm: 0-0
Distance: 5f/6f: 0-1 7f-8f: 1-3 9f-13f: 0-0 14f+: 0-0
Track : LH: 0-0 RH: 0-0 Tight: 0-0 Gall: 0-1
Aids: Bl: 0-0 Vi: 0-0 Tstrap: 0-0 Ckp: 0-0
Best Rating: 98 10/09 Newb 1m good

Useful; effective over 1m; acts on good and easy ground.

Kamanja (UAE)

80(93) (59)40

3-y-o b f Red Ransom (USA)-Nasmatt (Danehill (USA))
M J Attwater (M A Jarvis 1/2) J M Duggan & T P Duggan

Placings:5-433000065604 (7881)
2009: 7^{4}SD, 6^{3}SD, 7^{3}SD, 8^{0}SD, 8^{0}SD, 7^{0}GF, 6^{0}F, 5^{6}SD, 7^{5}SD, 7^{6}SD, 8^{0}SD, 10^{4}SD,

	Starts	1st	2nd	3rd	Win & Pl
Career Total (Turf)	2	0	0	0	
Career Total (AW)	11	0	0	2	832

Going (Turf): Sf: 0-0 GS: 0-0 Gd: 0-0 GF: 0-1 Fm: 0-1
Distance: 5f/6f: 0-2 7f-8f: 0-9 9f-13f: 0-2 14f+: 0-0
Track : LH: 0-10 RH: 0-2 Tight: 0-8 Gall: 0-0
Aids: Bl: 0-0 Vi: 0-0 Tstrap: 0-1 Ckp: 0-1
Best Rating: 59 2/09 Ling 7f stand

Moderate; stays 7f; acts on Polytrack.

Kames Park (IRE)

99(112) (66)72

7-y-o b g Desert Sun-Persian Sally (IRE) (Persian Bold)
R C Guest (I W McInnes 4/1) Future Racing (Notts) Limited

Placings:421/22030/0061300/2110255000/501602405000 0-04003311 (7847)
2009: 12^{0}SS, 12^{4}GF, 11^{0}G, 12^{0}S, 12^{3}SD, 12^{3}SD, 12^{1}SD, 12^{1}SD,

	Starts	1st	2nd	3rd	Win & Pl
Career Total (Turf)	29	2	5	2	32687
Career Total (AW)	17	5	1	2	34487

66 12/09 Wolv 1m4f50y (0-75)H STD £3784
62 12/09 Kemp 1m4f (0-55)H STD £1706
79 3/08 Wolv 1m4f50y STD £2590
98 3/07 Ling 1m4f (0-100)H STD £12464
96 3/07 Ling 1m5f (0-100)H STD £11217
90 6/06 Muss 1m6f (0-85)H G-F £7478
83 10/04 Ayr 7f50y G-S £5605
Total win prize-money £44848

Going (Turf): Sf: 0-2 GS: 1-5 Gd: 0-15 GF: 1-7 Fm: 0-0
Distance: 5f/6f: 0-0 7f-8f: 1-1 9f-13f: 5-36 14f+: 1-9
Track : LH: 5-31 RH: 2-15 Tight: 5-24 Gall: 0-6
Aids: Bl: 0-5 Vi: 0-0 Tstrap: 0-1 Ckp: 0-1
Best Rating: 98 3/07 Ling 1m4f stand

Modest; stays 1m6f, but effective at shorter; acts on most ground and on Polytrack.

Kammaan

100(100) (59)**81**

3-y-o b f Diktat-Qasirah (IRE) (Machiavellian (USA))

M A Jarvis Sheikh Ahmed Al Maktoum

Placings:2-253163 **(4591)**

2009: 6^{2}SD, 7^{5}SD, 8^{3}G, 7^{1}GS, 7^{6}GF, 6^{3}G,

	Starts	1st	2nd	3rd	Win & Pl
Career Total (Turf)	5	1	1	2	6955
Career Total (AW)	2	0	1	0	771

75 6/09 Newc 7f G-S £4533

Total win prize-money £4533

Going (Turf): Sf: 0-0 **GS: 1-1** Gd: 0-2 GF: 0-2 Fm: 0-0
Distance: 5f/6f: 0-2 **7f-8f: 1-5** 9f-13f: 0-0 14f+: 0-0
Track : LH: 0-3 RH: 0-1 Tight: 0-3 Gall: 0-0
Aids: Bl: 0-0 Vi: 0-0 Tstrap: 0-0 Ckp: 0-0
Best Rating: **81** 8/09 Carl 6f192y good

Fair; stays 1m; acts on Polytrack and on most ground on turf.

Kanace

(75) (46)

2-y-o ch c Pastoral Pursuits-Pendulum (Pursuit Of Love)

Ian Williams C Owen

Placings:000 **(6347)**

2009: 5^{0}SD, 5^{0}SD, 5^{0}SD,

	Starts	1st	2nd	3rd	Win & Pl
Career Total (Turf)	0	0	0	0	
Career Total (AW)	3	0	0	0	

Going (Turf): **Sf: 0-0 GS: 0-0 Gd: 0-0 GF: 0-0 Fm: 0-0**
Distance: 5f/6f: 0-3 7f-8f: 0-0 9f-13f: 0-0 14f+: 0-0
Track : LH: 0-3 RH: 0-0 Tight: 0-3 Gall: 0-0
Aids: Bl: 0-0 Vi: 0-0 Tstrap: 0-0 Ckp: 0-0
Best Rating: **46** 9/09 Wolv 5f216y stand

Kanaf (IRE)

91 **74**

2-y-o b c Elnadim (USA)-Catcher Applause (Royal Applause)

E A L Dunlop Hamdan Al Maktoum

Placings:3 **(2853)**

2009: 6^{3}G,

	Starts	1st	2nd	3rd	Win & Pl
Career Total (Turf)	1	0	0	1	578

Going (Turf): **Sf: 0-0 GS: 0-0 Gd: 0-1 GF: 0-0 Fm: 0-0**
Distance: 5f/6f: 0-0 7f-8f: 0-1 9f-13f: 0-0 14f+: 0-0
Track : LH: 0-0 RH: 0-0 Tight: 0-0 Gall: 0-0
Aids: Bl: 0-0 Vi: 0-0 Tstrap: 0-0 Ckp: 0-0
Best Rating: **74** 6/09 Nott 6f15y good

Fair; stays 6f; acts on good ground.

Kandidate

103(115) (113)**108**

7-y-o b h Kabool-Valleyrose (IRE) (Royal Academy (USA))

C E Brittain Mrs E W Richards

Placings:030**621**/**1404**334505005/**16**000**1**15616316/1635 6530/2U10306-61402000000 **(6106)**

2009: 10^{6}SD, 11^{1}SD, 10^{4}SD, 10^{0}SD, 10^{2}SD, 8^{0}G, 10^{0}GF, 10^{0}G, 10^{0}GF, 12^{0}SD, 10^{0}GF,

	Starts	1st	2nd	3rd	Win & Pl
Career Total (Turf)	35	2	0	7	168889
Career Total (AW)	24	8	3	0	270145

111 2/09 Sthl 1m3f (0-100)H STD £11980
110 3/08 Kemp 1m2f STD £14762
118 2/07 Ndas 1m1f FST £61224
115 9/06 Kemp 1m4f STD £28390
118 7/06 Sand 1m2f7y G-F £15898
115 4/06 Kemp 1m2f (0-105)H STD £31160
110 1/06 Ndas 7f110y (90-105)H G-F £41569
100 1/05 Wolv 1m141y STD £12156
91 11/04 Ling 1m (0-85)H STD £5447

Total win prize-money £222590

Going (Turf): Sf: 0-3 GS: 0-4 Gd: 0-9 **GF: 2-18** Fm: 0-0
Distance: 5f/6f: 0-0 7f-8f: 3-23 **9f-13f: 7-36** 14f+: 0-0
Track : **LH: 6-28** RH: 4-19 **Tight: 3-10** Gall: 2-20
Aids: Bl: 0-3 Vi: 0-0 Tstrap: 0-0 Ckp: 0-0
Best Rating: **118** 2/07 Ndas 1m1f fast

Smart; effective over 1m-1m4f; acts on good ground; goes well on dirt, Fibresand and Polytrack; has worn blinkers and a tongue tie.

Kangrina

(102) (65)**67**

7-y-o b m Acatenango (GER)-Kirona (Robellino (USA))

George Baker James, Dean & Partners

Placings:5416/11150/20235600325-50 **(0252)**

2009: 16^{5}SD, 16^{0}SD,

	Starts	1st	2nd	3rd	Win & Pl
Career Total (Turf)	10	3	2	0	12977
Career Total (AW)	12	1	1	2	4805

7/06 Mont 1m3f GD £3103
7/06 Stma 1m1f GD £3793
5/06 Agen 1m1f55y GD £3103
72 10/04 Wolv 1m141y STD £3412

Total win prize-money £13412

Going (Turf): Sf: 0-2 GS: 0-1 **Gd: 3-3** GF: 0-3 Fm: 0-0
Distance: 5f/6f: 0-0 7f-8f: 0-2 **9f-13f: 4-18** 14f+: 0-2
Track : **LH: 1-17** RH: 0-1 **Tight: 1-10** Gall: 0-1
Aids: Bl: 0-0 Vi: 0-0 Tstrap: 0-0 Ckp: 0-0
Best Rating: **75** 11/04 Ling 1m stand

Modest; stays 1m4f; acts on fast ground and on Polytrack.

Kankan Prince (IRE)

68 **11**

2-y-o b c Arakan (USA)-Risanda (Kris)

M G Quinlan W P Flynn

Placings:0 **(4912)**

2009: 5^{0}G,

	Starts	1st	2nd	3rd	Win & Pl
Career Total (Turf)	1	0	0	0	

Going (Turf): **Sf: 0-0 GS: 0-0 Gd: 0-1 GF: 0-0 Fm: 0-0**
Distance: 5f/6f: 0-1 7f-8f: 0-0 9f-13f: 0-0 14f+: 0-0
Track : LH: 0-0 RH: 0-0 Tight: 0-0 Gall: 0-0
Aids: Bl: 0-0 Vi: 0-0 Tstrap: 0-0 Ckp: 0-0
Best Rating: **11** 8/09 Yarm 5f43y good

Kannon

89(98) (62)**69**

4-y-o b f Kyllachy-Violet (IRE) (Mukaddamah (USA))

A J McCabe (I W McInnes 27/10) M Shirley

Placings:0/6002401231303**6** 500000600 **(7795)**

2009: 8^{5}SD, 7^{0}SD, 8^{0}SD, 7^{0}SD, 6^{0}GF, 7^{0}G, 8^{6}SD, 11^{0}S, 6^{0}SS,

	Starts	1st	2nd	3rd	Win & Pl
Career Total (Turf)	12	2	2	1	6533
Career Total (AW)	12	0	0	2	739

68 10/08 Brig 7f214y (0-60)H GD £2331
59 7/08 Folk 7f (0-65)H G-F £2047

Total win prize-money £4378

Going (Turf): Sf: 0-2 GS: 0-2 **Gd: 1-3 GF: 1-5** Fm: 0-0
Distance: 5f/6f: 0-4 **7f-8f: 2-17** 9f-13f: 0-3 14f+: 0-0
Track : **LH: 1-16** RH: 0-2 Tight: 0-9 Gall: 0-2
Aids: Bl: 0-0 Vi: 0-5 Tstrap: 0-2 Ckp: 0-2
Best Rating: **69** 10/08 Brig 7f214y gd-sft

Modest; stays 1m; acts on good and faster ground; has worn a visor.

Kanpai (IRE)

95 **68**

7-y-o br g Trans Island-David's Star (Welsh Saint)

J G M O'Shea Samurai Racing Syndicate

Placings:0/2005/31/20-0 **(6021)**

2009: 17^{0}GF,

	Starts	1st	2nd	3rd	Win & Pl
Career Total (Turf)	10	1	2	1	5530

62 9/06 Gdwd 2m (0-70)H G-F £3238

Total win prize-money £3239

Going (Turf): Sf: 0-0 GS: 0-4 Gd: 0-1 **GF: 1-4** Fm: 0-0
Distance: 5f/6f: 0-0 7f-8f: 0-1 9f-13f: 0-2 **14f+: 1-7**
Track : LH: 0-6 **RH: 1-4 Tight: 1-3** Gall: 0-1
Aids: Bl: 0-0 **Vi: 1-2** Tstrap: 0-0 Ckp: 0-0
Best Rating: **68** 9/08 Pont 2m1f22y gd-sft

Modest chaser/hurdler; stays 2m7f; acts on fast and easy ground; has worn a visor.

Kansai Spirit (IRE)

98(97) (80)**82**

3-y-o ch c Sinndar (IRE)-Daanat Nawal (Machiavellian (USA))

J H M Gosden R Van Gelder

Placings:042-330 **(5649)**

2009: 10^{3}G, 10^{3}GF, 12^{0}SD,

	Starts	1st	2nd	3rd	Win & Pl
Career Total (Turf)	4	0	0	2	2329
Career Total (AW)	2	0	1	0	964

Going (Turf): **Sf: 0-0 GS: 0-0 Gd: 0-1 GF: 0-3 Fm: 0-0**
Distance: 5f/6f: 0-0 7f-8f: 0-3 9f-13f: 0-3 14f+: 0-0
Track : LH: 0-2 RH: 0-2 Tight: 0-2 Gall: 0-2
Aids: Bl: 0-0 Vi: 0-0 Tstrap: 0-0 Ckp: 0-0
Best Rating: **82** 7/09 NmkJ 1m2f good

Fair; effective over 1m; acts on fast ground and on Polytrack.

Kansas Gold

(94) (72)**65**

6-y-o b g Alhaarth (IRE)-Star Tulip (Night Shift (USA))

J Mackie A J Winterton

Placings:0322166/0002131056/600300-0 **(0081)**

2009: 9^{0}SD,

	Starts	1st	2nd	3rd	Win & Pl
Career Total (Turf)	11	1	3	2	9773
Career Total (AW)	13	2	0	1	5450

72 10/07 Wolv 1m1f103y (0-70)H STD £2968
69 9/07 Wolv 1m1f103y (0-65)H STD £2047

70 7/06 Sals 6f G-F £5505
Total win prize-money £10522

Going (Turf): Sf: 0-0 GS: 0-0 Gd: 0-2 **GF: 1-8** Fm: 0-1
Distance: 5f/6f: 1-7 7f-8f: 0-3 **9f-13f: 2-14** 14f+: 0-0
Track : **LH: 2-17** RH: 0-0 **Tight: 2-13** Gall: 0-0
Aids: Bl: 0-0 Vi: 0-2 Tstrap: 0-1 Ckp: 0-1
Best Rating: 72 10/07 Wolv 1m1f103y stand

Modest gelding; effective at around 1m1f; acts on good ground and Polytrack; has worn visor.

Kaolak (USA)

110(101) (78)**100**
3-y-o b/br c Action This Day (USA)-Cerita (USA) (Magesterial (USA))
J Ryan Simon Kerr

Placings:4031-04440542121150 **(6480)**
2009: 8^{0}SD, 8^{4}SD, 8^{4}F, 8^{4}GF, 10^{0}GF, 12^{5}GS, 8^{4}G, 10^{2}G, 8^{1}G, 8^{2}GF, 9^{1}GF, 8^{1}GF, 10^{5}GF, 9^{0}GF,

	Starts	1st	2nd	3rd	Win & Pl
Career Total (Turf)	**14**	**3**	**2**	**0**	**20459**
Career Total (AW)	**4**	**1**	**0**	**1**	**5448**

100 9/09 Gdwd 1m (0-85)H G-F £5180
96 8/09 Gdwd 1m1f (0-85)H G-F £5180
89 8/09 NmkJ 1m (0-75)H GD £3885
78 12/08 GrLe 1m STD £4533
Total win prize-money £18781

Going (Turf): Sf: 0-1 GS: 0-1 Gd: 1-4 **GF: 2-7** Fm: 0-1
Distance: 5f/6f: 0-0 **7f-8f: 3-8** 9f-13f: 1-10 14f+: 0-0
Track : LH: 1-6 **RH: 2-7** Tight: 1-3 Gall: 1-5
Aids: Bl: 0-0 **Vi: 3-8** Tstrap: 0-0 Ckp: 0-0
Best Rating: 100 9/09 Gdwd 1m gd-fm

Very useful; effective over 7f-1m1f; acts on good and fast ground; goes on Polytrack; has worn a visor.

Kapelad Junior (IRE)

94(88) (55)**59**
2-y-o gr g Clodovil (IRE)-Prosaic Star (IRE) (Common Grounds)
Pat Eddery Mrs S White & Mrs J McCarlie

Placings:0150066 **(7419)**
2009: 5^{0}G, 6^{1}GF, 6^{5}SD, 6^{0}GS, 6^{0}GS, 7^{6}SD, 7^{6}SD,

	Starts	1st	2nd	3rd	Win & Pl
Career Total (Turf)	**4**	**1**	**0**	**0**	**2047**
Career Total (AW)	**3**	**0**	**0**	**0**	**0**

59 8/09 Rdcr 6f G-F £2047
Total win prize-money £2047

Going (Turf): Sf: 0-0 GS: 0-2 Gd: 0-1 **GF: 1-1** Fm: 0-0
Distance: **5f/6f: 1-4** 7f-8f: 0-3 9f-13f: 0-0 14f+: 0-0
Track : LH: 0-3 RH: 0-1 Tight: 0-1 Gall: 0-1
Aids: Bl: 0-1 Vi: 0-0 Tstrap: 0-0 Ckp: 0-0
Best Rating: 59 8/09 Rdcr 6f gd-fm

Modest; stays 6f; acts on fast ground and on Polytrack.

Kappalyn (IRE)

(80) (24)**46**
4-y-o b f Marju (IRE)-Miss Tardy (JPN) (Lammtarra (USA))
J R Boyle Mrs Pippa Boyle

Placings:0506-00 **(2184)**
2009: 7^{0}SD, 6^{0}SD,

	Starts	1st	2nd	3rd	Win & Pl
Career Total (Turf)	**4**	**0**	**0**	**0**	**0**
Career Total (AW)	**2**	**0**	**0**	**0**	

Going (Turf): **Sf: 0-2 GS: 0-1 Gd: 0-0 GF: 0-1 Fm: 0-0**
Distance: 5f/6f: 0-1 7f-8f: 0-5 9f-13f: 0-0 14f+: 0-0
Track : LH: 0-2 RH: 0-0 Tight: 0-2 Gall: 0-0
Aids: Bl: 0-0 Vi: 0-0 Tstrap: 0-0 Ckp: 0-0
Best Rating: 46 7/08 Sals 6f212y gd-fm

Kapsiliat (IRE)

91(100) (73)**69**
3-y-o b f Cape Cross (IRE)-Kootenay (IRE) (Selkirk (USA))
J Noseda Capt J Macdonald-Buchanan

Placings:5-3440 **(4822)**
2009: 8^{3}GF, 9^{4}G, 10^{4}SD, 10^{0}GF,

	Starts	1st	2nd	3rd	Win & Pl
Career Total (Turf)	**4**	**0**	**0**	**1**	**1107**
Career Total (AW)	**1**	**0**	**0**	**0**	**0**

Going (Turf): **Sf: 0-0 GS: 0-0 Gd: 0-1 GF: 0-3 Fm: 0-0**
Distance: 5f/6f: 0-1 7f-8f: 0-1 9f-13f: 0-3 14f+: 0-0
Track : LH: 0-2 RH: 0-1 Tight: 0-3 Gall: 0-0
Aids: Bl: 0-0 Vi: 0-0 Tstrap: 0-0 Ckp: 0-0
Best Rating: 73 7/09 Ling 1m2f stand

Fair; stays 1m2f; acts onPolytrack and on fast ground.

Kaptain Kirkup (IRE)

103 **96**
2-y-o ch c Captain Rio-Aquatint (Dansili)
M Dods Kevin Kirkup

Placings:11162 **(6486)**
2009: 6^{1}GS, 6^{1}GF, 6^{1}GS, 6^{6}GS, 6^{2}GF,

	Starts	1st	2nd	3rd	Win & Pl
Career Total (Turf)	**5**	**3**	**1**	**0**	**48168**

96 7/09 Hayd 6f G-S £5504
84 6/09 Newc 6f G-F £3885
79 5/09 Newc 6f G-S £2590
Total win prize-money £11981

Going (Turf): Sf: 0-0 **GS: 2-3** Gd: 0-0 GF: 1-2 Fm: 0-0
Distance: **5f/6f: 3-5** 7f-8f: 0-0 9f-13f: 0-0 14f+: 0-0
Track : LH: 0-0 RH: 0-0 Tight: 0-0 Gall: 0-0
Aids: Bl: 0-0 Vi: 0-0 Tstrap: 0-0 Ckp: 0-0
Best Rating: 96 7/09 Hayd 6f gd-sft

Very useful; effective at 6f; acts on fast and easy ground.

Karaburan (GER)

67 **37**
5-y-o ch g Samum (GER)-Kimora (GER) (Dashing Blade)
P Monteith G M Cowan

Placings:4/0420/000-0 **(5359)**
2009: 13^{0}S,

	Starts	1st	2nd	3rd	Win & Pl
Career Total (Turf)	**9**	**0**	**1**	**0**	**1018**

Going (Turf): **Sf: 0-3 GS: 0-0 Gd: 0-6 GF: 0-0 Fm: 0-0**
Distance: 5f/6f: 0-0 7f-8f: 0-1 9f-13f: 0-7 14f+: 0-1
Track : LH: 0-1 RH: 0-3 Tight: 0-3 Gall: 0-0
Aids: Bl: 0-2 Vi: 0-2 Tstrap: 0-0 Ckp: 0-0
Best Rating: 37 9/08 Muss 1m4f good

Karaka Jack

93(103) (90)**76**
2-y-o ch c Pivotal-Mauri Moon (Green Desert (USA))
M Johnston Sheikh Hamdan Bin Mohammed Al Maktoum

Placings:4011 **(6948)**
2009: 6^{4}GF, 7^{0}GF, 7^{1}G, 7^{1}SD,

	Starts	1st	2nd	3rd	Win & Pl
Career Total (Turf)	**3**	**1**	**0**	**0**	**7703**
Career Total (AW)	**1**	**1**	**0**	**0**	**5505**

90 10/09 Sthl 7f (0-85) STD £5504
76 10/09 York 7f GD £7317
Total win prize-money £12823

Going (Turf): Sf: 0-0 GS: 0-0 **Gd: 1-1** GF: 0-2 Fm: 0-0
Distance: 5f/6f: 0-1 **7f-8f: 2-3** 9f-13f: 0-0 14f+: 0-0
Track : **LH: 2-3** RH: 0-0 Tight: 0-0 **Gall: 1-1**
Aids: Bl: 0-0 Vi: 0-0 Tstrap: 0-0 Ckp: 0-0
Best Rating: 90 10/09 Sthl 7f stand

Useful; stays 7f; can front run; handles Fibresand.

Karamojo Bell

88 **72**
2-y-o b c Selkirk (USA)-Shabby Chic (USA) (Red Ransom (USA))
T P Tate Mrs Fitri Hay

Placings:56P **(6533)**
2009: 8^{5}G, 8^{6}GF, 10^{P}GF,

	Starts	1st	2nd	3rd	Win & Pl
Career Total (Turf)	**3**	**0**	**0**	**0**	**0**

Going (Turf): **Sf: 0-0 GS: 0-0 Gd: 0-1 GF: 0-2 Fm: 0-0**
Distance: 5f/6f: 0-0 7f-8f: 0-2 9f-13f: 0-1 14f+: 0-0
Track : LH: 0-1 RH: 0-0 Tight: 0-0 Gall: 0-0
Aids: Bl: 0-0 Vi: 0-0 Tstrap: 0-0 Ckp: 0-0
Best Rating: 72 9/09 Donc 1m gd-fm

Karashar (IRE)

(99) (71)**67**
4-y-o b g Kalanisi (IRE)-Karaliyfa (IRE) (Kahyasi)
Evan Williams T Hywel Jones

Placings:64-040 **(7461)**
2009: 7^{0}SD, 13^{4}SD, 13^{0}SD,

	Starts	1st	2nd	3rd	Win & Pl
Career Total (Turf)	**2**	**0**	**0**	**0**	**192**
Career Total (AW)	**3**	**0**	**0**	**0**	**0**

Going (Turf): **Sf: 0-1 GS: 0-1 Gd: 0-0 GF: 0-0 Fm: 0-0**
Distance: 5f/6f: 0-0 7f-8f: 0-1 9f-13f: 0-3 14f+: 0-1
Track : LH: 0-4 RH: 0-1 Tight: 0-4 Gall: 0-0
Aids: Bl: 0-0 Vi: 0-0 Tstrap: 0-0 Ckp: 0-0
Best Rating: 71 11/09 Ling 1m5f stand

Karate Queen

83(97) (57)**35**
4-y-o b f King's Best (USA)-Black Belt Shopper (IRE) (Desert Prince (IRE))
R E Barr R E Barr

Placings:004/6004643-000 **(3541)**
2009: 5^{0}GF, 6^{0}GF, 8^{0}F,

	Starts	1st	2nd	3rd	Win & Pl
Career Total (Turf)	**7**	**0**	**0**	**0**	
Career Total (AW)	**6**	**0**	**0**	**1**	**464**

Going (Turf): **Sf: 0-0 GS: 0-1 Gd: 0-0 GF: 0-5 Fm: 0-1**
Distance: 5f/6f: 0-2 7f-8f: 0-9 9f-13f: 0-2 14f+: 0-0
Track : LH: 0-5 RH: 0-2 Tight: 0-5 Gall: 0-0

Aids: Bl: 0-0 Vi: 0-0 Tstrap: 0-0 Ckp: 0-0
Best Rating: 57 10/07 Ling 7f stand

Kargan (IRE)

103(96) (62)**75**

4-y-o b g Intikhab (USA)-Karkiyla (IRE) (Darshaan)
R A Farrant (A G Foster 30/7) M Sawers

Placings:50/2056002-32234413315 **(5997)**
2009: 8^{3}SD, 8^{2}SD, 7^{2}G, 7^{3}G, 7^{4}GF, 7^{4}GF, 7^{1}G, 7^{3}G, 8^{3}GF, 8^{1}GS, 10^{5}GS,

	Starts	1st	2nd	3rd	Win & Pl
Career Total (Turf)	17	2	2	3	9104
Career Total (AW)	3	0	2	1	1753

75	9/09	Chep	1m14y	(0-65)H	G-S	£2266
67	7/09	Ayr	7f50y	(0-70)H	GD	£2914

Total win prize-money £5181

Going (Turf): Sf: 0-5 **GS: 1-2 Gd: 1-5** GF: 0-4 Fm: 0-0
Distance: 5f/6f: 0-0 7f-8f: 1-11 9f-13f: 1-9 14f+: 0-0
Track : **LH: 1-8** RH: 0-7 Tight: 0-11 Gall: 0-1
Aids: Bl: 0-0 Vi: 0-0 Tstrap: 0-0 Ckp: 0-0
Best Rating: 75 9/09 Chep 1m14y gd-sft

Modest; stays 1m; acts on Polytrack; goes on heavy and good ground.

Karky Schultz (GER)

104(100) (66)**64**

4-y-o gr g Diktat-Kazoo (Shareef Dancer (USA))
J M P Eustace Harold Nass

Placings:534000/300000-01203 **(4156)**
2009: 12^{0}SD, 11^{1}SD, 10^{2}G, 16^{0}SD, 11^{3}G,

	Starts	1st	2nd	3rd	Win & Pl
Career Total (Turf)	11	0	1	2	1456
Career Total (AW)	6	1	0	1	2384

59	6/09	Kemp	1m3f	(0-55)H	STD	£2047

Total win prize-money £2047

Going (Turf): **Sf: 0-4 GS: 0-0 Gd: 0-7 GF: 0-0 Fm: 0-0**
Distance: 5f/6f: 0-5 7f-8f: 0-5 **9f-13f: 1-6** 14f+: 0-1
Track : LH: 0-6 **RH: 1-5** Tight: 0-3 Gall: 0-2
Aids: Bl: 0-2 Vi: 0-0 Tstrap: 0-0 Ckp: 0-0
Best Rating: 68 6/07 Yarm 6f3y soft

Moderate; stays 1m3f; acts on good ground; goes on Polytrack.

Karmei

92(93) (51)**59**

4-y-o b g Royal Applause-Lafite (Robellino (USA))
R Curtis Mrs R A Smith

Placings:004/6033400-3000560 **(3348)**
2009: 9^{3}SD, 9^{0}SD, 8^{0}SF, 11^{0}G, 10^{5}GF, 10^{6}GS, 12^{0}GF,

	Starts	1st	2nd	3rd	Win & Pl
Career Total (Turf)	9	0	0	2	775
Career Total (AW)	8	0	0	1	302

Going (Turf): **Sf: 0-0 GS: 0-1 Gd: 0-2 GF: 0-4 Fm: 0-2**
Distance: 5f/6f: 0-3 7f-8f: 0-3 9f-13f: 0-11 14f+: 0-0
Track : LH: 0-13 RH: 0-2 Tight: 0-10 Gall: 0-0
Aids: Bl: 0-0 Vi: 0-0 Tstrap: 0-0 Ckp: 0-0
Best Rating: 61 9/07 Sand 5f6y gd-fm

Karmest

90(106) (78)**73**

5-y-o ch m Best Of The Bests (IRE)-Karmafair (IRE) (Always Fair (USA))
A D Brown David Logan

Placings:6/03010000**4230/1131366416300513**4-0330000 **(4373)**
2009: 12^{0}SD, 12^{3}SD, 11^{3}SD, 12^{0}GF, 9^{0}G, 11^{0}GS, 12^{0}SD,

	Starts	1st	2nd	3rd	Win & Pl
Career Total (Turf)	17	2	0	1	6073
Career Total (AW)	20	4	1	7	10947

78	12/08	Sthl	1m3f	(0-65)H	STD	£2047
73	4/08	Bevl	1m1f207y	(0-70)H	G-S	£2428
69	2/08	Sthl	1m3f	(0-60)H	SS	£1911
62	1/08	Sthl	1m3f	(0-55)H	STD	£1774
54	1/08	Sthl	1m4f	(0-55)H	STD	£1911
59	6/07	Wwck	6f	(0-65)H	SFT	£2730

Total win prize-money £12802

Going (Turf): **Sf: 1-5 GS: 1-4** Gd: 0-7 GF: 0-1 Fm: 0-0
Distance: 5f/6f: 1-4 7f-8f: 0-5 **9f-13f: 5-28** 14f+: 0-0
Track : **LH: 5-28** RH: 1-6 Tight: 0-9 Gall: 0-4
Aids: **Bl: 1-9** Vi: 0-1 Tstrap: 0-0 Ckp: 0-0
Best Rating: 78 12/08 Sthl 1m3f stand

Modest; effective over 1m2f-1m4f; acts on soft ground; goes on Fibresand and Polytrack.

Karoush (USA)

88 **82**

4-y-o b c Gone West (USA)-Victorica (USA) (Exbourne (USA))
Sir Michael Stoute Saleh Al Homaizi & Imad Al Sagar

Placings:32-4 **(5100)**
2009: 8^{4}GF,

	Starts	1st	2nd	3rd	Win & Pl
Career Total (Turf)	3	0	1	1	2023

Going (Turf): **Sf: 0-0 GS: 0-1 Gd: 0-1 GF: 0-1 Fm: 0-0**
Distance: 5f/6f: 0-0 7f-8f: 0-2 9f-13f: 0-1 14f+: 0-0
Track : LH: 0-1 RH: 0-1 Tight: 0-2 Gall: 0-0
Aids: Bl: 0-0 Vi: 0-0 Tstrap: 0-0 Ckp: 0-0
Best Rating: 82 5/08 Newb 7f good

Karta (IRE)

91(99) (64)**75**

3-y-o br f Diktat-Echo River (USA) (Irish River (FR))
H-A Pantall (M Johnston 21/4) Sarl Winning Bloodstock Agency

Placings:624030 **(7386a)**
2009: 7^{6}SD, 8^{2}SD, 7^{4}G, 9^{0}S, 7^{3}, 8^{0}HY,

	Starts	1st	2nd	3rd	Win & Pl
Career Total (Turf)	4	0	0	1	0
Career Total (AW)	2	0	1	0	771

Going (Turf): **Sf: 0-2 GS: 0-0 Gd: 0-1 GF: 0-0 Fm: 0-0**
Distance: 5f/6f: 0-0 7f-8f: 0-5 9f-13f: 0-1 14f+: 0-0
Track : LH: 0-2 RH: 0-0 Tight: 0-0 Gall: 0-0
Aids: Bl: 0-0 Vi: 0-0 Tstrap: 0-0 Ckp: 0-0
Best Rating: 64 3/09 Sthl 1m stand

Fair; stays 1m; acts on Fibresand; handles turf.

Kasaa Ed

84 **66**

3-y-o b f Marju (IRE)-Muwajaha (Night Shift (USA))
M Johnston Hamdan Al Maktoum

Placings:5-000 **(2528)**
2009: 6^{0}GF, 6^{0}F, 9^{0}GF,

	Starts	1st	2nd	3rd	Win & Pl
Career Total (Turf)	4	0	0	0	0

Going (Turf): **Sf: 0-1 GS: 0-0 Gd: 0-0 GF: 0-2 Fm: 0-1**
Distance: 5f/6f: 0-2 7f-8f: 0-1 9f-13f: 0-1 14f+: 0-0
Track : LH: 0-2 RH: 0-1 Tight: 0-0 Gall: 0-0
Aids: Bl: 0-0 Vi: 0-0 Tstrap: 0-0 Ckp: 0-0
Best Rating: 66 10/08 Leic 7f9y soft

Kasban

104 **81**

5-y-o b g Kingmambo (USA)-Ebaraya (IRE) (Sadler's Wells (USA))
Ian Williams Michael H Watt

Placings:0/5034/04100-00140 **(4417)**
2009: 14^{0}GF, 13^{0}GF, 16^{1}GF, 16^{4}G, 21^{0}G,

	Starts	1st	2nd	3rd	Win & Pl
Career Total (Turf)	15	2	0	1	11957

79	6/09	Folk	2m93y	(0-80)H	G-F	£6476
81	6/08	NmkJ	1m6f175y	(0-75)H	G-F	£3885

Total win prize-money £10362

Going (Turf): Sf: 0-3 GS: 0-0 Gd: 0-4 **GF: 2-8** Fm: 0-0
Distance: 5f/6f: 0-0 7f-8f: 0-1 9f-13f: 0-4 **14f+: 2-10**
Track : LH: 0-6 **RH: 2-8** Tight: 1-4 Gall: 1-5
Aids: Bl: 0-0 Vi: 0-0 Tstrap: 1-3 Ckp: 1-3
Best Rating: 81 6/08 NmkJ 1m6f175y gd-fm

Fair; stays 2m; acts on fast and soft ground; has worn blinkers, cheekpieces and a tongue tie.

Kashimin (IRE)

102(102) (82)**85**

4-y-o b g Kyllachy-Oh So Misty (Teenoso (USA))
G A Swinbank Mrs Jean Perratt

Placings:1/002420-335050200 **(7617)**
2009: 5^{3}G, 5^{3}GF, 6^{5}GF, 6^{0}GF, 6^{5}G, 7^{0}G, 7^{2}SD, 7^{0}S, 7^{0}SD,

	Starts	1st	2nd	3rd	Win & Pl
Career Total (Turf)	14	1	2	2	8871
Career Total (AW)	2	0	1	0	1510

77	10/07	Pont	6f	GD	£3886

Total win prize-money £3886

Going (Turf): Sf: 0-2 GS: 0-0 **Gd: 1-8** GF: 0-4 Fm: 0-0
Distance: **5f/6f: 1-9** 7f-8f: 0-7 9f-13f: 0-0 14f+: 0-0
Track : **LH: 1-7** RH: 0-1 Tight: 0-5 Gall: 0-1
Aids: Bl: 0-2 Vi: 0-0 Tstrap: 0-0 Ckp: 0-0
Best Rating: 85 6/09 Catt 5f212y gd-fm

Useful; stays 7f and acts on good ground; has worn blinkers.

Kashmina

99(96) (67)**70**

4-y-o ch m Dr Fong (USA)-Lady Melbourne (IRE) (Indian Ridge)
Miss Sheena West Heart Of The South Racing

Placings:0000**5200/255565-0100**50 **(7873)**
2009: 11^{0}GF, 10^{1}GF, 10^{0}F, 10^{0}SD, 12^{5}SD, 16^{0}SD,

	Starts	1st	2nd	3rd	Win & Pl
Career Total (Turf)	14	1	1	0	3982
Career Total (AW)	6	0	1	0	605

70	6/09	Wind	1m2f7y	(0-70)H	G-F	£2729

Total win prize-money £2730

Going (Turf): Sf: 0-2 GS: 0-1 Gd: 0-5 **GF: 1-5** Fm: 0-1
Distance: 5f/6f: 0-0 7f-8f: 0-9 **9f-13f: 1-10** 14f+: 0-1
Track : LH: 0-10 **RH: 1-6 Tight: 1-9** Gall: 0-0
Aids: Bl: 0-0 Vi: 0-0 Tstrap: 0-0 Ckp: 0-0
Best Rating: **70** 6/09 Wind 1m2f7y gd-fm

Modest maiden; effective over 7f-1m; acts on fast and soft ground; also goes on Polytrack.

Kashubian Quest

73 **11**

3-y-o b g Rainbow Quest (USA)-Kartuzy (JPN) (Polish Precedent (USA))
D R Lanigan Saif Ali

Placings:0 **(6794)**
2009: 10^{0}S,

	Starts	1st	2nd	3rd	Win & Pl
Career Total (Turf)	1	0	0	0	

Going (Turf): **Sf: 0-1 GS: 0-0 Gd: 0-0 GF: 0-0 Fm: 0-0**
Distance: 5f/6f: 0-0 7f-8f: 0-0 9f-13f: 0-1 14f+: 0-0
Track : LH: 0-1 RH: 0-0 Tight: 0-0 Gall: 0-0
Aids: Bl: 0-0 Vi: 0-0 Tstrap: 0-0 Ckp: 0-0
Best Rating: **11** 10/09 Nott 1m2f50y soft

Kaspirit (IRE)

91 **83**

2-y-o b f Invincible Spirit (IRE)-Kathy Kab (IRE) (Intikhab (USA))
G Colella (M Wigham 2/6) Ernesta Micocci

Placings:2130
2009: 5^{2}GF, 5^{1}GF, 5^{3}S, 6^{0}GS,

	Starts	1st	2nd	3rd	Win & Pl
Career Total (Turf)	4	1	1	1	11115

79 5/09 Yarm 5f43y G-F £3784
Total win prize-money £3785

Going (Turf): Sf: 0-1 GS: 0-1 Gd: 0-0 **GF: 1-2** Fm: 0-0
Distance: **5f/6f: 1-4** 7f-8f: 0-0 9f-13f: 0-0 14f+: 0-0
Track : LH: 0-0 RH: 0-2 Tight: 0-0 Gall: 0-0
Aids: Bl: 0-0 Vi: 0-0 Tstrap: 0-0 Ckp: 0-0
Best Rating: **83** 6/09 Capa 5f110y soft

Useful speedy filly; Listed placed; acts on quick ground; handles soft.

Kassuta

98(92) (37)**55**

5-y-o b m Kyllachy-Happy Omen (Warning)
R M H Cowell (M J Gingell 31/3) J Sargeant

Placings:02/4460203000231/00-23303 **(6968)**
2009: 8^{2}GF, 8^{3}GS, 8^{3}GF, 9^{0}SD, 7^{3}G,

	Starts	1st	2nd	3rd	Win & Pl
Career Total (Turf)	13	1	3	5	6769
Career Total (AW)	9	0	1	0	1421

53 10/07 Yarm 1m3y G-S £1943
Total win prize-money £1943

Going (Turf): Sf: 0-5 **GS: 1-4** Gd: 0-1 GF: 0-2 Fm: 0-1
Distance: 5f/6f: 0-5 7f-8f: 0-9 **9f-13f: 1-8** 14f+: 0-0
Track : LH: 0-10 RH: 0-5 Tight: 0-5 Gall: 0-1
Aids: Bl: 0-2 Vi: 0-4 Tstrap: 1-4 Ckp: 1-4
Best Rating: **65** 5/07 Wolv 5f216y std-fst

Modest filly; stays 6f; acts on Polytrack.

Katchmore (IRE)

76(98) (58)**40**

2-y-o br g Catcher In The Rye (IRE)-One For Me (Tragic Role (USA))
Jean-Rene Auvray Miss Sara E Collie

Placings:002 **(7885)**
2009: 8^{0}G, 9^{0}SD, 7^{2}SD,

	Starts	1st	2nd	3rd	Win & Pl
Career Total (Turf)	1	0	0	0	
Career Total (AW)	2	0	1	0	484

Going (Turf): **Sf: 0-0 GS: 0-0 Gd: 0-1 GF: 0-0 Fm: 0-0**
Distance: 5f/6f: 0-0 7f-8f: 0-1 9f-13f: 0-2 14f+: 0-0
Track : LH: 0-2 RH: 0-0 Tight: 0-2 Gall: 0-0
Aids: Bl: 0-0 Vi: 0-0 Tstrap: 0-0 Ckp: 0-0
Best Rating: **58** 11/09 Wolv 1m1f103y stand

Kate Skate

93(88) (55)**65**

2-y-o ch f Mark Of Esteem (IRE)-Saristar (Starborough)
Miss Gay Kelleway (P F I Cole 25/5) Nightmare Partnership, Jon Thompson

Placings:602006650 **(6775)**
2009: 5^{6}GF, 5^{0}GF, 5^{2}GF, 5^{0}GF, 6^{0}GF, 5^{6}SD, 8^{6}GF, 7^{5}SD, 6^{0}SD,

	Starts	1st	2nd	3rd	Win & Pl
Career Total (Turf)	6	0	1	0	578
Career Total (AW)	3	0	0	0	0

Going (Turf): **Sf: 0-0 GS: 0-0 Gd: 0-0 GF: 0-6 Fm: 0-0**
Distance: 5f/6f: 0-7 7f-8f: 0-1 9f-13f: 0-1 14f+: 0-0
Track : LH: 0-3 RH: 0-2 Tight: 0-1 Gall: 0-2
Aids: Bl: 0-0 Vi: 0-0 Tstrap: 0-0 Ckp: 0-0
Best Rating: **65** 5/09 Gdwd 5f gd-fm

Modest; effective over 5f; acts on fast ground.

Kate The Great

75(102) (75)**75**

3-y-o b f Xaar-Ros The Boss (IRE) (Danehill (USA))
C G Cox Anthony Rogers

Placings:1630224-00 **(2915)**
2009: 5^{0}G, 5^{0}GF,

	Starts	1st	2nd	3rd	Win & Pl
Career Total (Turf)	6	0	1	1	1465
Career Total (AW)	3	1	1	0	5462

75 4/08 Ling 5f STD £4209
Total win prize-money £4209

Going (Turf): **Sf: 0-0 GS: 0-0 Gd: 0-4 GF: 0-2 Fm: 0-0**
Distance: **5f/6f: 1-8** 7f-8f: 0-1 9f-13f: 0-0 14f+: 0-0
Track : **LH: 1-4** RH: 0-0 **Tight: 1-2** Gall: 0-1
Aids: Bl: 0-0 Vi: 0-0 Tstrap: 0-0 Ckp: 0-0
Best Rating: **75** 8/08 Brig 5f59y good

Fair; effective over 5f-6f; acts on good ground; also goes on Polytrack.

Katehari (IRE)

100 **71**

2-y-o b f Noverre (USA)-Katariya (IRE) (Barathea (IRE))
A M Balding The Toucan Syndicate

Placings:0163 **(6418)**
2009: 7^{0}G, 6^{1}GF, 5^{6}F, 6^{3}GF,

	Starts	1st	2nd	3rd	Win & Pl
Career Total (Turf)	4	1	0	1	4140

71 8/09 Wind 6f G-F £3561
Total win prize-money £3562

Going (Turf): Sf: 0-0 GS: 0-0 Gd: 0-1 **GF: 1-2** Fm: 0-1
Distance: **5f/6f: 1-3** 7f-8f: 0-1 9f-13f: 0-0 14f+: 0-0
Track : LH: 0-1 RH: 0-0 Tight: 0-0 **Gall: 1-2**
Aids: Bl: 0-0 Vi: 0-0 Tstrap: 0-0 Ckp: 0-0
Best Rating: **71** 10/09 Gdwd 6f gd-fm

Fair; effective over 6f; acts on fast ground.

Kathanikki Girl (IRE)

80(88) (30)**12**

3-y-o b f Tagula (IRE)-Tenalist (IRE) (Tenby)
Mrs L Williamson B & B Hygiene Limited

Placings:00-000 **(3305)**
2009: 8^{0}SD, 8^{0}GF, 7^{0}GF,

	Starts	1st	2nd	3rd	Win & Pl
Career Total (Turf)	2	0	0	0	
Career Total (AW)	3	0	0	0	

Going (Turf): **Sf: 0-0 GS: 0-0 Gd: 0-0 GF: 0-2 Fm: 0-0**
Distance: 5f/6f: 0-1 7f-8f: 0-3 9f-13f: 0-1 14f+: 0-0
Track : LH: 0-4 RH: 0-0 Tight: 0-3 Gall: 0-1
Aids: Bl: 0-0 Vi: 0-0 Tstrap: 0-0 Ckp: 0-0
Best Rating: **30** 4/09 Wolv 1m141y stand

Kathindi (IRE)

80(96) (69)**41**

2-y-o ch c Pearl Of Love (IRE)-Turfcare Flight (IRE) (Mujadil (USA))
J S Moore John Wells

Placings:33033 **(7886)**
2009: 6^{3}SD, 7^{3}SD, 6^{0}G, 8^{3}SD, 7^{3}SD,

	Starts	1st	2nd	3rd	Win & Pl
Career Total (Turf)	1	0	0	0	
Career Total (AW)	4	0	0	4	1351

Going (Turf): **Sf: 0-0 GS: 0-0 Gd: 0-1 GF: 0-0 Fm: 0-0**
Distance: 5f/6f: 0-2 7f-8f: 0-3 9f-13f: 0-0 14f+: 0-0
Track : LH: 0-4 RH: 0-0 Tight: 0-4 Gall: 0-1
Aids: Bl: 0-0 Vi: 0-0 Tstrap: 0-0 Ckp: 0-0
Best Rating: **69** 12/09 Ling 1m stand

Modest; stays 1m; acts on Polytrack.

Kathleen Cox (IRE)

(50) (28)**47**

4-y-o ch f Alhaarth (IRE)-Gintilgalla (IRE) (Grand Lodge (USA))
Daniel Mark Loughnane Leo Cox

Placings:0/0604-0 **(7369)**
2009: 9^{0}SD,

	Starts	1st	2nd	3rd	Win & Pl
Career Total (Turf)	4	0	0	0	332
Career Total (AW)	2	0	0	0	

Going (Turf): **Sf: 0-0 GS: 0-0 Gd: 0-1 GF: 0-0 Fm: 0-1**
Distance: 5f/6f: 0-0 7f-8f: 0-3 9f-13f: 0-3 14f+: 0-0
Track : LH: 0-2 RH: 0-3 Tight: 0-1 Gall: 0-0
Aids: Bl: 0-0 Vi: 0-0 Tstrap: 0-0 Ckp: 0-0
Best Rating: **47** 5/08 Wxfd 1m5f good

Kathleen Frances

86 55

2-y-o b f Sakhee (USA)-Trew Class (Inchinor)

M H Tompkins Russell Trew Ltd

Placings:0 (7099)

2009: 8⁰G,

	Starts	1st	2nd	3rd	Win & Pl
Career Total (Turf)	1	0	0	0	

Going (Turf): Sf: 0-0 GS: 0-0 Gd: 0-1 GF: 0-0 Fm: 0-0
Distance: 5f/6f: 0-0 7f-8f: 0-0 9f-13f: 0-1 14f+: 0-0
Track : LH: 0-0 RH: 0-0 Tight: 0-0 Gall: 0-0
Aids: Bl: 0-0 Vi: 0-0 Tstrap: 0-0 Ckp: 0-0
Best Rating: 55 10/09 Yarm 1m3y good

Katie Girl

94(87) (39)43

3-y-o b f Makbul-Katie Komaite (Komaite (USA))

Mrs G S Rees Red Rose Partnership

Placings:000-560604060040 (7753)

2009: 8⁵SD, 9⁶GS, 9⁰G, 10⁶GF, 11⁰GS, 12⁴G, 9⁰G, 11⁶SD, 12⁰GS, 15⁰G, 9⁴SD, 8⁰SD,

	Starts	1st	2nd	3rd	Win & Pl
Career Total (Turf)	11	0	0	0	322
Career Total (AW)	4	0	0	0	0

Going (Turf): Sf: 0-1 GS: 0-5 Gd: 0-4 GF: 0-1 Fm: 0-0
Distance: 5f/6f: 0-2 7f-8f: 0-1 9f-13f: 0-11 14f+: 0-1
Track : LH: 0-10 RH: 0-3 Tight: 0-10 Gall: 0-1
Aids: Bl: 0-0 Vi: 0-0 Tstrap: 0-9 Ckp: 0-9
Best Rating: 43 8/09 Bevl 1m1f207y good

Moderate; stays 1m2f; acts on fast ground; has worn cheekpieces.

Katie Kingfisher

(97) (46)42

5-y-o b m Fraam-Sonic Sapphire (Royal Academy (USA))

T T Clement Joshua Pearce

Placings:600/00050/4000-00 (0588)

2009: 11⁰SD, 10⁰SD,

	Starts	1st	2nd	3rd	Win & Pl
Career Total (Turf)	5	0	0	0	0
Career Total (AW)	9	0	0	0	0

Going (Turf): Sf: 0-1 GS: 0-2 Gd: 0-1 GF: 0-1 Fm: 0-0
Distance: 5f/6f: 0-3 7f-8f: 0-1 9f-13f: 0-6 14f+: 0-4
Track : LH: 0-10 RH: 0-1 Tight: 0-5 Gall: 0-2
Aids: Bl: 0-2 Vi: 0-0 Tstrap: 0-6 Ckp: 0-6
Best Rating: 46 11/07 Wolv 1m5f194y stand

Katie The Hatter (IRE)

(86) (48)

3-y-o b f Celtic Swing-Kathleen's Dream (USA) (Last Tycoon)

Mike Murphy M P Bass

Placings:00 (7826)

2009: 7⁰SD, 8⁰SD,

	Starts	1st	2nd	3rd	Win & Pl
Career Total (Turf)	0	0	0	0	
Career Total (AW)	2	0	0	0	0

Going (Turf): Sf: 0-0 GS: 0-0 Gd: 0-0 GF: 0-0 Fm: 0-0
Distance: 5f/6f: 0-0 7f-8f: 0-2 9f-13f: 0-0 14f+: 0-0
Track : LH: 0-1 RH: 0-1 Tight: 0-1 Gall: 0-0
Aids: Bl: 0-0 Vi: 0-0 Tstrap: 0-0 Ckp: 0-0
Best Rating: 48 12/09 Kemp 1m stand

Katiyra (IRE)

102 117

4-y-o b f Peintre Celebre (USA)-Katiykha (IRE) (Darshaan)

John M Oxx H H Aga Khan

Placings:1/235113-56 (4522)

2009: 10⁵Y, 9⁶S,

	Starts	1st	2nd	3rd	Win & Pl
Career Total (Turf)	9	3	1	2	179695

110	9/08	Curr	1m2f	SH	£59742
110	8/08	Gowr	1m1f100y	HVY	£23933
85	8/07	Leop	7f	YLD	£8797

Total win prize-money £92474

Going (Turf): Sf: 1-2 GS: 0-1 Gd: 0-3 GF: 0-0 Fm: 0-0
Distance: 5f/6f: 0-0 7f-8f: 1-2 **9f-13f: 2-7** 14f+: 0-0
Track : LH: 1-3 **RH: 2-6** Tight: 0-2 Gall: 0-0
Aids: Bl: 0-0 Vi: 0-0 Tstrap: 0-0 Ckp: 0-0
Best Rating: 117 10/08 Lonc 1m2f gd-sft

Group-class; third in the English Oaks and Prix de L'Opera; probably stays 1m4f but effective at shorter; acts on good ground and softer.

Kattar

83(90) (62)56

3-y-o ch c Singspiel (IRE)-Lady Zonda (Lion Cavern (USA))

D M Simcock Mohammed Al Nabouda

Placings:064-644 (4453)

2009: 10⁶GF, 9⁴GF, 8⁴G,

	Starts	1st	2nd	3rd	Win & Pl
Career Total (Turf)	4	0	0	0	673
Career Total (AW)	2	0	0	0	241

Going (Turf): Sf: 0-0 GS: 0-0 Gd: 0-2 GF: 0-2 Fm: 0-0
Distance: 5f/6f: 0-0 7f-8f: 0-3 9f-13f: 0-3 14f+: 0-0
Track : LH: 0-4 RH: 0-1 Tight: 0-4 Gall: 0-1
Aids: Bl: 0-0 Vi: 0-0 Tstrap: 0-0 Ckp: 0-0
Best Rating: 62 11/08 GrLe 1m stand

Modest; stays 1m and acts on Polytrack; has worn a tongue tie.

Katy's Secret

(94) (66)

2-y-o b f Mind Games-Katy O'Hara (Komaite (USA))

W Jarvis Miss S E Hall

Placings:20 (7799)

2009: 5²SD, 5⁰SD,

	Starts	1st	2nd	3rd	Win & Pl
Career Total (Turf)	0	0	0	0	
Career Total (AW)	2	0	1	0	771

Going (Turf): Sf: 0-0 GS: 0-0 Gd: 0-0 GF: 0-0 Fm: 0-0
Distance: 5f/6f: 0-2 7f-8f: 0-0 9f-13f: 0-0 14f+: 0-0
Track : LH: 0-2 RH: 0-0 Tight: 0-2 Gall: 0-0
Aids: Bl: 0-0 Vi: 0-0 Tstrap: 0-0 Ckp: 0-0
Best Rating: 66 12/09 Wolv 5f216y stand

Speedily-bred; promise on debut over 6f on Polytrack.

Katya Kabanova

74(71) (4)7

3-y-o b f Sadler's Wells (USA)-Kiftsgate Rose (FR) (Nashwan (USA))

J R Fanshawe Miss K Rausing

Placings:060 (5939)

2009: 10⁰S, 12⁶SD, 11⁰GF,

	Starts	1st	2nd	3rd	Win & Pl
Career Total (Turf)	2	0	0	0	
Career Total (AW)	1	0	0	0	0

Going (Turf): Sf: 0-1 GS: 0-0 Gd: 0-0 GF: 0-1 Fm: 0-0
Distance: 5f/6f: 0-0 7f-8f: 0-0 9f-13f: 0-3 14f+: 0-0
Track : LH: 0-1 RH: 0-2 Tight: 0-0 Gall: 0-1
Aids: Bl: 0-0 Vi: 0-0 Tstrap: 0-0 Ckp: 0-0
Best Rating: 7 9/09 Leic 1m3f183y gd-fm

Kavachi (IRE)

108 (67)95

6-y-o b g Cadeaux Genereux-Answered Prayer (Green Desert (USA))

G L Moore Bryan Pennick & Roy Martin

Placings:50/03006152600/00331046231/0114400-402310000 (6665)

2009: 8⁴GF, 10⁰G, 10²GF, 8³G, 8¹G, 8⁰GF, 8⁰G, 10⁰GF, 10⁰GS,

	Starts	1st	2nd	3rd	Win & Pl
Career Total (Turf)	38	6	3	5	54022
Career Total (AW)	2	0	0	0	0

95	6/09	York	1m208y	(0-105)H	GD	£17485
92	5/08	Newb	1m2f6y	(0-85)H	GD	£4209
82	5/08	Folk	1m1f149y	(0-80)H	G-S	£4100
82	10/07	Yarm	1m2f21y	(0-85)H	G-S	£4857
68	6/07	Folk	1m1f149y	(0-75)H	SFT	£3238
71	8/06	Gdwd	1m	(0-80)H	G-F	£5829

Total win prize-money £39720

Going (Turf): Sf: 1-4 **GS: 2-8 Gd: 2-14** GF: 1-10 Fm: 0-2
Distance: 5f/6f: 0-0 7f-8f: 1-12 **9f-13f: 5-28** 14f+: 0-0
Track : LH: 3-19 RH: 3-15 **Tight: 3-14** Gall: 2-7
Aids: Bl: 0-0 Vi: 0-0 Tstrap: 0-0 Ckp: 0-0
Best Rating: 95 6/09 York 1m208y good

Very useful; effective from 1m-1m2f and acts on most ground; usually held up.

Kavak

91(102) (83)70

2-y-o ch c Dubawi (IRE)-Kelang (Kris)

M Botti Grundy Bloodstock Limited

Placings:461 (4790)

2009: 7⁴GF, 7⁶S, 8¹SD,

	Starts	1st	2nd	3rd	Win & Pl
Career Total (Turf)	2	0	0	0	385
Career Total (AW)	1	1	0	0	2730

83	8/09	Ling	1m	STD	£2729

Total win prize-money £2730

Going (Turf): Sf: 0-1 GS: 0-0 Gd: 0-0 GF: 0-1 Fm: 0-0
Distance: 5f/6f: 0-0 **7f-8f: 1-3** 9f-13f: 0-0 14f+: 0-0
Track : **LH: 1-1** RH: 0-0 **Tight: 1-1** Gall: 0-0
Aids: Bl: 0-0 Vi: 0-0 Tstrap: 0-0 Ckp: 0-0
Best Rating: 83 8/09 Ling 1m stand

Promise on debut over 7f on fast ground.

Kavaloti (IRE)

(101) (84)83

5-y-o b g Kahyasi-Just As Good (FR) (Kaldounevees (FR))

G L Moore Graham Gillespie

Placings:6016142/422110 (3510)
2009: 16^{4}SD, 16^{2}SD, 16^{2}SD, 16^{1}SD, 16^{1}SD, 16^{0}SD,

	Starts	1st	2nd	3rd	Win & Pl
Career Total (Turf)	6	2	0	0	11243
Career Total (AW)	7	2	3	0	11446

84 4/09 Kemp 2m (0-85)H STD £4727
82 4/09 Kemp 2m (0-75)H STD £2590
83 6/07 Lonc 1m5f110y GD £7432
Total win prize-money £18127

Going (Turf): Sf: 0-0 GS: 0-1 **Gd: 1-3** GF: 0-0 Fm: 0-0
Distance: 5f/6f: 0-0 7f-8f: 0-0 9f-13f: 1-4 **14f+: 3-9**
Track : LH: 0-0 **RH: 2-9** Tight: 0-0 Gall: 0-0
Aids: **Bl: 4-11** Vi: 0-0 Tstrap: 0-0 Ckp: 0-0
Best Rating: 84 4/09 Kemp 2m stand

Fair; ex French; stays 2m; acts on good ground and on Polytrack; has worn blinkers.

Kay Gee Be (IRE)

108(103) (98)99
5-y-o b g Fasliyev (USA)-Pursuit Of Truth (USA) (Irish River (FR))
W Jarvis Par Jeu Partnership

Placings:321/11051/2563060-30352060 (6480)
2009: 9^{3}GF, 10^{0}GF, 8^{3}GF, 8^{5}GF, 8^{2}G, 8^{0}GF, 8^{6}GF, 9^{0}GF,

	Starts	1st	2nd	3rd	Win & Pl
Career Total (Turf)	17	2	2	4	25176
Career Total (AW)	6	2	1	0	17477

100 10/07 Kemp 1m (0-90)H STD £9348
91 5/07 Wolv 1m141y (0-85)H SF £5829
85 4/07 Nott 1m54y (0-85)H G-F £5829
75 8/06 Thsk 7f G-S £3886
Total win prize-money £24892

Going (Turf): Sf: 0-1 **GS: 1-2** Gd: 0-2 **GF: 1-12** Fm: 0-0
Distance: 5f/6f: 0-2 7f-8f: 2-11 9f-13f: 2-10 14f+: 0-0
Track : **LH: 3-11** RH: 1-4 **Tight: 2-3** Gall: 0-5
Aids: Bl: 0-0 Vi: 0-0 Tstrap: 0-0 Ckp: 0-0
Best Rating: 100 10/07 Kemp 1m stand

Very useful; stays 1m; acts on most ground and on Polytrack.

Kay Two (IRE)

102(102) (87)94
7-y-o ch g Monashee Mountain (USA)-Tricky (Song)
R J Price H McGahon, B Llewellyn

Placings:224151130/465635045/000606000511/2300001 1U00/51064154-520430P (6666)
2009: 5^{5}G, 5^{2}GS, 5^{0}G, 5^{4}S, 5^{3}G, 5^{0}G, 5^{P}GS,

	Starts	1st	2nd	3rd	Win & Pl
Career Total (Turf)	52	9	4	4	118054
Career Total (AW)	5	0	0	0	433

94 10/08 Pont 5f (0-85)H G-S £6476
92 7/08 NmkJ 5f (0-95)H G-S £9714
91 10/07 Bath 5f11y (0-95)H G-F £7570
89 9/07 Leic 5f2y (0-95)H GD £6939
92 10/06 Pont 5f (0-85)H G-S £7772
84 10/06 York 5f (0-75)H SFT £5505
99 10/04 Tipp 5f HVY £27507
94 8/04 Tipp 5f SFT £12378
83 7/04 Tipp 5f G-F £8272
Total win prize-money £92136

Going (Turf): **Sf: 3-9 GS: 3-8** Gd: 1-16 GF: 2-13 Fm: 0-0
Distance: **5f/6f: 9-55** 7f-8f: 0-2 9f-13f: 0-0 14f+: 0-0
Track : **LH: 6-19** RH: 0-0 Tight: 0-8 **Gall: 1-3**
Aids: Bl: 0-1 Vi: 0-0 Tstrap: 4-20 Ckp: 4-20
Best Rating: 105 8/05 Curr 6f good

Useful; ex-Irish; suited by 5f-6f and acts on most ground; has worn blinkers and cheekpieces; likes to race prominently.

Kayak (SAF)

(106) (99)87
7-y-o b g Western Winter (USA)-Donya (SAF) (Elliodor (FR))
D M Simcock Sultan Ali

Placings:00/322221421/031511200/1064230500536-0 (0206)
2009: 8^{0}SD,

	Starts	1st	2nd	3rd	Win & Pl
Career Total (Turf)	19	3	6	2	18206
Career Total (AW)	15	3	1	2	40775

95 1/08 Ndas 1m2f (0-105)H FST £24623
5/07 Vaal 1m4f H GD £3623
4/07 Vaas 1m H STD £3623
3/07 Vaal 1m STD £3849
12/06 Nmkt 1m2f H GD £3045
6/06 Turf 7f GD £3331
Total win prize-money £42097

Going (Turf): Sf: 0-1 GS: 0-0 **Gd: 3-15** GF: 0-3 Fm: 0-0
Distance: 5f/6f: 0-0 7f-8f: 3-15 9f-13f: 3-18 14f+: 0-1
Track : LH: 0-6 RH: 0-4 Tight: 0-4 Gall: 0-4
Aids: Bl: 0-10 Vi: 0-0 Tstrap: 0-0 Ckp: 0-0
Best Rating: 99 6/08 Kemp 1m2f stand

Very useful; multiple winner in South Africa and also successful in Dubai; effective over 1m-1m4f; acted on good and faster ground and on sand; sometimes blinkered; (DEAD).

Kayceebee

80(90) (46)55
3-y-o b g Cyrano De Bergerac-Twice Upon A Time (Primo Dominie)
R M Beckett The Millennium Madness Partnership

Placings:05006-06 (2651)
2009: 5^{0}G, 5^{6}F,

	Starts	1st	2nd	3rd	Win & Pl
Career Total (Turf)	5	0	0	0	0
Career Total (AW)	2	0	0	0	0

Going (Turf): **Sf: 0-0 GS: 0-1 Gd: 0-2 GF: 0-1 Fm: 0-1**
Distance: 5f/6f: 0-7 7f-8f: 0-0 9f-13f: 0-0 14f+: 0-0
Track : LH: 0-1 RH: 0-2 Tight: 0-0 Gall: 0-4
Aids: Bl: 0-2 Vi: 0-0 Tstrap: 0-0 Ckp: 0-0
Best Rating: 55 7/08 Wind 5f10y good

Moderate sort; effective at 6f.

Kayf Aramis

110 (66)94
7-y-o b g Kayf Tara-Ara (Birthright)
N A Twiston-Davies (Miss Venetia Williams 16/6) Mrs Isobel Phipps Coltman

Placings:0/0534406/1215055222522/501032450420/440-156 (2994)
2009: 18^{1}G, 16^{5}G, 20^{6}GF,

	Starts	1st	2nd	3rd	Win & Pl
Career Total (Turf)	38	4	8	2	44279
Career Total (AW)	1	0	0	0	0

94 5/09 York 2m2f (0-80)H GD £6476
79 5/07 York 2m2f (0-80)H G-S £7772
73 5/06 York 2m4f (0-80)H SFT £7772
63 4/06 Bath 2m1f34y (0-75)H SFT £3562
Total win prize-money £25582

Going (Turf): **Sf: 2-7** GS: 1-8 Gd: 1-12 GF: 0-10 Fm: 0-1
Distance: 5f/6f: 0-0 7f-8f: 0-1 9f-13f: 0-2 **14f+: 4-36**
Track : **LH: 4-26** RH: 0-13 Tight: 1-9 **Gall: 3-13**
Aids: Bl: 0-0 Vi: 0-0 Tstrap: 0-11 Ckp: 0-11
Best Rating: 94 5/09 York 2m2f good

Useful; stays 2m4f; suited by soft ground, but handles fast; has worn cheekpieces.

Kayfiar (USA)

95(85) (60)65
3-y-o ch c Lion Heart (USA)-Ivor Jewel (USA) (Sir Ivor (USA))
P F I Cole Mrs Stephanie Smith

Placings:050-6600 (4745)
2009: 9^{6}G, 12^{6}GF, 10^{0}GF, 10^{0}GS,

	Starts	1st	2nd	3rd	Win & Pl
Career Total (Turf)	6	0	0	0	188
Career Total (AW)	1	0	0	0	

Going (Turf): **Sf: 0-0 GS: 0-1 Gd: 0-3 GF: 0-2 Fm: 0-0**
Distance: 5f/6f: 0-0 7f-8f: 0-3 9f-13f: 0-4 14f+: 0-0
Track : LH: 0-4 RH: 0-1 Tight: 0-3 Gall: 0-2
Aids: Bl: 0-1 Vi: 0-0 Tstrap: 0-0 Ckp: 0-0
Best Rating: 65 6/09 Gdwd 1m1f192y good

Half-brother to five winners in the USA; signs of ability on debut over 7f on good ground.

Kayfour (IRE)

(88) (35)55
4-y-o b f Raise A Grand (IRE)-Sunrise (IRE) (Sri Pekan (USA))
M J Grassick Mrs Norman Moore

Placings:030-5500 (2253a)
2009: 12^{5}SF, 11^{5}Y, 15^{0}S, 14^{0}YS,

	Starts	1st	2nd	3rd	Win & Pl
Career Total (Turf)	5	0	0	1	679
Career Total (AW)	2	0	0	0	0

Going (Turf): **Sf: 0-2 GS: 0-0 Gd: 0-0 GF: 0-0 Fm: 0-0**
Distance: 5f/6f: 0-0 7f-8f: 0-0 9f-13f: 0-5 14f+: 0-2
Track : LH: 0-2 RH: 0-4 Tight: 0-1 Gall: 0-0
Aids: Bl: 0-0 Vi: 0-0 Tstrap: 0-0 Ckp: 0-0
Best Rating: 55 4/09 Limk 1m3f70y yield

Kaystar Ridge

93(102) (65)46
4-y-o b g Tumbleweed Ridge-Kayartis (Kaytu)
D K Ivory Mrs J A Cornwell and David G Owen

Placings:0206020/000041-200000306 (6001)
2009: 6^{2}SD, 5^{0}SD, 6^{0}SD, 6^{0}SD, 5^{0}SD, 6^{0}G, 8^{3}G, 9^{0}SD, 10^{6}GF,

	Starts	1st	2nd	3rd	Win & Pl
Career Total (Turf)	6	0	0	1	289
Career Total (AW)	16	1	3	0	3459

64 11/08 Kemp 6f (0-55)H STD £1706
Total win prize-money £1706

Going (Turf): **Sf: 0-0 GS: 0-2 Gd: 0-2 GF: 0-2 Fm: 0-0**
Distance: **5f/6f: 1-17** 7f-8f: 0-2 9f-13f: 0-3 14f+: 0-0
Track : LH: 0-9 **RH: 1-8** Tight: 0-8 Gall: 0-2
Aids: **Bl: 1-6** Vi: 0-0 Tstrap: 0-2 Ckp: 0-2
Best Rating: 65 1/09 Kemp 6f stand

Modest; effective at 6f; acts on Polytrack.

Kazbow (IRE)

95(106) (79)63

3-y-o b g Rainbow Quest (USA)-Kasota (IRE) (Alzao (USA))

L M Cumani Bruce Corman

Placings:00-02221 (7590)

2009: 9^{0}GF, 12^{2}SD, 12^{2}SD, 12^{2}SD, 12^{1}SD,

	Starts	1st	2nd	3rd	Win & Pl
Career Total (Turf)	3	0	0	0	
Career Total (AW)	4	1	3	0	5223

70 11/09 Kemp 1m4f STD £2590

Total win prize-money £2590

Going (Turf): Sf: 0-2 GS: 0-0 Gd: 0-0 GF: 0-1 Fm: 0-0
Distance: 5f/6f: 0-0 7f-8f: 0-0 9f-13f: 1-7 14f+: 0-0
Track : LH: 0-4 RH: 1-3 Tight: 0-3 Gall: 0-0
Aids: Bl: 0-0 Vi: 0-0 Tstrap: 0-0 Ckp: 0-0
Best Rating: 79 11/09 Wolv 1m4f50y stand

Fair; stays 1m4f; acts on Polytrack.

Keelung (USA)

94 83

8-y-o b g Lear Fan (USA)-Miss Universal (IRE) (Lycius (USA))

R Ford D W Watson

Placings:0/4221320000/61156-00 (2766)

2009: 13^{0}G, 17^{0}G,

	Starts	1st	2nd	3rd	Win & Pl
Career Total (Turf)	15	3	2	1	20235
Career Total (AW)	3	0	1	0	1892

79 7/08 Ches 1m7f195y (0-85)H GD £5828
83 7/08 Wwck 1m6f213y (0-75)H SFT £3238
88 4/04 Newc 1m2f32y D HVY £3477

Total win prize-money £12544

Going (Turf): Sf: 2-3 GS: 0-3 Gd: 1-6 GF: 0-3 Fm: 0-0
Distance: 5f/6f: 0-0 7f-8f: 0-3 9f-13f: 1-8 14f+: 2-7
Track : LH: 3-12 RH: 0-5 Tight: 1-8 Gall: 1-5
Aids: Bl: 0-0 Vi: 0-0 Tstrap: 0-1 Ckp: 0-1
Best Rating: 93 6/04 Sand 1m2f7y gd-sft

Fair; stays 2m; acts on good and softer ground; goes on Polytrack; has worn cheekpieces and tongue tie.

Keen As Mustard

84(90) (56)41

4-y-o ch g Keen-Dark Dolores (Inchinor)

M D I Usher M D I Usher

Placings:0505060 (2608)

2009: 9^{0}SD, 8^{5}SD, 8^{0}SD, 8^{5}SD, 8^{0}GF, 9^{6}F, 10^{0}GF,

	Starts	1st	2nd	3rd	Win & Pl
Career Total (Turf)	3	0	0	0	0
Career Total (AW)	4	0	0	0	0

Going (Turf): Sf: 0-0 GS: 0-0 Gd: 0-0 GF: 0-2 Fm: 0-1
Distance: 5f/6f: 0-0 7f-8f: 0-1 9f-13f: 0-6 14f+: 0-0
Track : LH: 0-6 RH: 0-1 Tight: 0-4 Gall: 0-0
Aids: Bl: 0-0 Vi: 0-0 Tstrap: 0-0 Ckp: 0-0
Best Rating: 56 3/09 Kemp 1m stand

Keen Bidder

103 72

2-y-o ch c Auction House (USA)-Lady-Love (Pursuit Of Love)

D M Simcock J M Cook

Placings:004144433 (6993)

2009: 6^{0}S, 6^{0}G, 7^{4}GF, 7^{1}GS, 7^{4}GS, 7^{4}GS, 7^{4}GF, 7^{3}GF, 8^{3}GS,

	Starts	1st	2nd	3rd	Win & Pl
Career Total (Turf)	9	1	0	2	8349

64 7/09 NmkJ 7f G-S £5180

Total win prize-money £5181

Going (Turf): Sf: 0-1 GS: 1-4 Gd: 0-1 GF: 0-3 Fm: 0-0
Distance: 5f/6f: 0-1 7f-8f: 1-8 9f-13f: 0-0 14f+: 0-0
Track : LH: 0-2 RH: 0-0 Tight: 0-1 Gall: 0-1
Aids: Bl: 0-0 Vi: 0-0 Tstrap: 0-0 Ckp: 0-0
Best Rating: 72 10/09 Donc 1m gd-sft

Modest; effective over 7f; acts on easy ground.

Keen Warrior

(74) (12)

9-y-o gr g Keen-Briden (Minster Son)

Mrs S Lamyman R Hill,D Ellis,B Kemp

Placings:0 (0621)

2009: 11^{0}SD,

	Starts	1st	2nd	3rd	Win & Pl
Career Total (Turf)	0	0	0	0	
Career Total (AW)	1	0	0	0	

Going (Turf): Sf: 0-0 GS: 0-0 Gd: 0-0 GF: 0-0 Fm: 0-0
Distance: 5f/6f: 0-0 7f-8f: 0-0 9f-13f: 0-1 14f+: 0-0
Track : LH: 0-1 RH: 0-0 Tight: 0-0 Gall: 0-0
Aids: Bl: 0-0 Vi: 0-0 Tstrap: 0-0 Ckp: 0-0
Best Rating: 12 2/09 Sthl 1m3f stand

Keenes Day (FR)

105(115) (99)100

4-y-o gr g Daylami (IRE)-Key Academy (Royal Academy (USA))

M Johnston Mrs R J Jacobs

Placings:65164/530110-10045440 (6851)

2009: 16^{1}SD, 20^{0}GF, 16^{0}S, 16^{4}GS, 13^{5}GF, 17^{4}F, 16^{4}GF, 18^{0}G,

	Starts	1st	2nd	3rd	Win & Pl
Career Total (Turf)	13	1	0	0	10528
Career Total (AW)	6	3	0	1	20046

99 4/09 Ling 2m (0-95)H STD £7477
96 10/08 Wolv 2m119y (0-80)H STD £5180
94 10/08 Sthl 1m6f (0-85)H STD £6476
76 8/07 Bevl 1m100y G-F £3562

Total win prize-money £22696

Going (Turf): Sf: 0-2 GS: 0-3 Gd: 0-2 GF: 1-5 Fm: 0-1
Distance: 5f/6f: 0-0 7f-8f: 0-4 9f-13f: 1-3 14f+: 3-12
Track : LH: 3-8 RH: 1-10 Tight: 2-6 Gall: 0-5
Aids: Bl: 0-0 Vi: 0-0 Tstrap: 0-0 Ckp: 0-0
Best Rating: 100 9/09 Asct 2m gd-fm

Very useful; effective over 1m6f-2m; acts on fast ground; goes on sand.

Keenes Royale

82 51

2-y-o b f Red Ransom (USA)-Kinnaird (IRE) (Dr Devious (IRE))

P C Haslam Mrs R J Jacobs

Placings:006 (7244)

2009: 7^{0}GS, 7^{0}GF, 8^{6}S,

	Starts	1st	2nd	3rd	Win & Pl
Career Total (Turf)	3	0	0	0	0

Going (Turf): Sf: 0-1 GS: 0-1 Gd: 0-0 GF: 0-1 Fm: 0-0
Distance: 5f/6f: 0-0 7f-8f: 0-2 9f-13f: 0-1 14f+: 0-0
Track : LH: 0-1 RH: 0-0 Tight: 0-0 Gall: 0-0
Aids: Bl: 0-0 Vi: 0-0 Tstrap: 0-0 Ckp: 0-0
Best Rating: 51 7/09 Donc 7f gd-sft

Keep Dancing (IRE)

101(96) (63)73

3-y-o ch f Distant Music (USA)-Miss Indigo (Indian Ridge)

A M Balding The C H F Partnership

Placings:23-3630415600 (6904)

2009: 5^{3}SD, 5^{6}GF, 5^{3}GS, 6^{0}G, 5^{4}GF, 5^{1}G, 6^{5}G, 5^{6}G, 6^{0}SD, 6^{0}G,

	Starts	1st	2nd	3rd	Win & Pl
Career Total (Turf)	10	1	1	2	4517
Career Total (AW)	2	0	0	1	385

73 7/09 Wwck 5f110y (0-70)H GD £2590

Total win prize-money £2590

Going (Turf): Sf: 0-1 GS: 0-1 Gd: 1-5 GF: 0-3 Fm: 0-0
Distance: 5f/6f: 1-11 7f-8f: 0-1 9f-13f: 0-0 14f+: 0-0
Track : LH: 1-3 RH: 0-1 Tight: 0-1 Gall: 0-4
Aids: Bl: 0-0 Vi: 0-0 Tstrap: 1-8 Ckp: 1-8
Best Rating: 73 7/09 Wwck 5f110y good

Moderate; effective over 6f; acts on soft ground and on Polytrack; has worn cheekpieces.

Keep Icy Calm (IRE)

(95) (64)

3-y-o br f One Cool Cat (USA)-Alazima (USA) (Riverman (USA))

W J Haggas Mrs H R Slack

Placings:5-64 (0188)

2009: 5^{6}SD, 5^{4}SD,

	Starts	1st	2nd	3rd	Win & Pl
Career Total (Turf)	0	0	0	0	
Career Total (AW)	3	0	0	0	0

Going (Turf): Sf: 0-0 GS: 0-0 Gd: 0-0 GF: 0-0 Fm: 0-0
Distance: 5f/6f: 0-3 7f-8f: 0-0 9f-13f: 0-0 14f+: 0-0
Track : LH: 0-3 RH: 0-0 Tight: 0-2 Gall: 0-1
Aids: Bl: 0-1 Vi: 0-0 Tstrap: 0-0 Ckp: 0-0
Best Rating: 64 11/08 GrLe 6f stand

Keep Ringing (USA)

(98) (77)

3-y-o b/br f More Than Ready (USA)-No Knocks (USA) (A.P. Indy (USA))

W J Haggas Mrs H R Slack

Placings:6314 (1284)

2009: 6^{6}SD, 7^{3}SD, 8^{1}SD, 8^{4}SD,

	Starts	1st	2nd	3rd	Win & Pl
Career Total (Turf)	0	0	0	0	
Career Total (AW)	4	1	0	1	754

Going (Turf): Sf: 0-0 GS: 0-0 Gd: 0-0 GF: 0-0 Fm: 0-0
Distance: 5f/6f: 0-1 7f-8f: 0-2 9f-13f: 1-1 14f+: 0-0
Track : LH: 1-3 RH: 0-1 Tight: 1-3 Gall: 0-0
Aids: Bl: 0-0 Vi: 0-0 Tstrap: 0-0 Ckp: 0-0
Best Rating: 77 4/09 Kemp 1m stand

Fair; stays 1m; acts on Polytrack.

Keep Silent

71 28

2-y-o gr f Largesse-Not A Word (Batshoof)
W J H Ratcliffe H R Moszkowicz

Placings:00 **(7061)**
2009: 6[0]G, 5[0]GF,

	Starts	1st	2nd	3rd	Win & Pl
Career Total (Turf)	2	0	0	0	

Going (Turf): **Sf: 0-0 GS: 0-0 Gd: 0-1 GF: 0-1 Fm: 0-0**
Distance: 5f/6f: 0-2 7f-8f: 0-0 9f-13f: 0-0 14f+: 0-0
Track : LH: 0-0 RH: 0-0 Tight: 0-0 Gall: 0-0
Aids: Bl: 0-0 Vi: 0-0 Tstrap: 0-0 Ckp: 0-0
Best Rating: **28** 10/09 Leic 5f218y gd-fm

Keepholdin (IRE)

(84) (47)

4-y-o b g King's Best (USA)-Dafariyna (IRE) (Nashwan (USA))
N P Mulholland Sleep Easy Syndicate

Placings:00 **(6974)**
2009: 12[0]SD, 11[0]SD,

	Starts	1st	2nd	3rd	Win & Pl
Career Total (Turf)	0	0	0	0	
Career Total (AW)	2	0	0	0	

Going (Turf): **Sf: 0-0 GS: 0-0 Gd: 0-0 GF: 0-0 Fm: 0-0**
Distance: 5f/6f: 0-0 7f-8f: 0-0 9f-13f: 0-2 14f+: 0-0
Track : LH: 0-0 RH: 0-2 Tight: 0-0 Gall: 0-0
Aids: Bl: 0-0 Vi: 0-0 Tstrap: 0-0 Ckp: 0-0
Best Rating: **47** 10/09 Kemp 1m3f stand

Keepsgettingbetter (IRE)

(98) (64)

4-y-o b g Modigliani (USA)-Adua (IRE) (Kenmare (FR))
J R Gask Horses First Racing Limited

Placings:24-50 **(0478)**
2009: 8[5]SD, 9[0]SD,

	Starts	1st	2nd	3rd	Win & Pl
Career Total (Turf)	0	0	0	0	
Career Total (AW)	4	0	1	0	825

Going (Turf): **Sf: 0-0 GS: 0-0 Gd: 0-0 GF: 0-0 Fm: 0-0**
Distance: 5f/6f: 0-0 7f-8f: 0-1 9f-13f: 0-3 14f+: 0-0
Track : LH: 0-4 RH: 0-0 Tight: 0-3 Gall: 0-1
Aids: Bl: 0-1 Vi: 0-0 Tstrap: 0-0 Ckp: 0-0
Best Rating: **64** 11/08 Wolv 1m141y stand

Keeptheboatafloat (USA)

99(98) (90)90

3-y-o b g Fusaichi Pegasus (USA)-The Perfect Life (IRE) (Try My Best (USA))
A P Jarvis (K R Burke 22/4) Cyril Wall

Placings:01204-00024 **(5186)**
2009: 7[0]FT, 7[0]G, 9[0]SD, 11[2]GF, 10[4]GF,

	Starts	1st	2nd	3rd	Win & Pl
Career Total (Turf)	7	1	2	0	8964
Career Total (AW)	3	0	0	0	

74 6/08 Ripn 6f SFT £4209
Total win prize-money £4209

Going (Turf): **Sf: 1-1** GS: 0-0 Gd: 0-4 GF: 0-2 Fm: 0-0
Distance: **5f/6f: 1-4** 7f-8f: 0-3 9f-13f: 0-3 14f+: 0-0
Track : LH: 0-5 RH: 0-2 Tight: 0-2 Gall: 0-2
Aids: Bl: 0-3 Vi: 0-0 Tstrap: 0-0 Ckp: 0-0
Best Rating: **90** 9/08 Kemp 6f stand

Useful; effective at up to 1m4f; acts on good and soft ground and Polytrack; has worn blinkers.

Kefalonia (USA)

84(100) (71)58

3-y-o gr/ro f Mizzen Mast (USA)-Zante (Zafonic (USA))
B W Hills K Abdulla

Placings:2541 **(4789)**
2009: 8[2]SD, 9[5]F, 8[4]SD, 10[1]SD,

	Starts	1st	2nd	3rd	Win & Pl
Career Total (Turf)	1	0	0	0	0
Career Total (AW)	3	1	1	0	3500

71 8/09 Ling 1m2f STD £2729
Total win prize-money £2730

Going (Turf): **Sf: 0-0 GS: 0-0 Gd: 0-0 GF: 0-0 Fm: 0-1**
Distance: 5f/6f: 0-0 7f-8f: 0-1 **9f-13f: 1-3** 14f+: 0-0
Track : **LH: 1-3** RH: 0-1 **Tight: 1-3** Gall: 0-0
Aids: Bl: 0-0 Vi: 0-0 Tstrap: 0-0 Ckp: 0-0
Best Rating: **71** 8/09 Ling 1m2f stand

Modest filly; stays 1m; acts on Polytrack but does not want the ground too fast.

Keibla Spirit

80(94) (54)36

3-y-o b f Auction House (USA)-Rave On (ITY) (Barathea (IRE))
R Ingram Ann & Elizabeth Buckland

Placings:046000 **(7691)**
2009: 6[0]G, 7[4]SD, 7[6]GF, 6[0]SD, 7[0]SD, 7[0]SD,

	Starts	1st	2nd	3rd	Win & Pl
Career Total (Turf)	2	0	0	0	0
Career Total (AW)	4	0	0	0	265

Going (Turf): **Sf: 0-0 GS: 0-0 Gd: 0-1 GF: 0-1 Fm: 0-0**
Distance: 5f/6f: 0-2 7f-8f: 0-4 9f-13f: 0-0 14f+: 0-0
Track : LH: 0-2 RH: 0-2 Tight: 0-2 Gall: 0-0
Aids: Bl: 0-0 Vi: 0-0 Tstrap: 0-0 Ckp: 0-0
Best Rating: **54** 8/09 Ling 7f stand

Keisha Kayleigh (IRE)

104(92) (47)80

6-y-o b m Almutawakel-Awtaar (USA) (Lyphard (USA))
B Ellison Koo's Racing Club

Placings:0612046253220**4**/5154421262**30**/614212060-0435513431 **(5361)**
2009: 9[0]SD, 8[4]GF, 9[3]GF, 12[5]SD, 9[5]G, 10[1]GF, 10[3]G, 9[4]G, 9[3]HY, 9[1]S,

	Starts	1st	2nd	3rd	Win & Pl
Career Total (Turf)	36	7	7	4	37471
Career Total (AW)	9	0	2	1	1713

76 8/09 Ayr 1m1f20y (0-85)H SFT £6476
69 6/09 Newc 1m2f32y G-F £2849
79 6/08 Newc 1m2f32y (0-70)H G-S £4209
71 5/08 Haml 1m65y (0-70)H G-S £3238
66 9/07 Rdcr 1m2f (0-70)H G-S £2817
50 4/07 Ripn 1m1f170y G-F £2914
48 5/06 Bevl 1m1f207y GD £3400
Total win prize-money £25904

Going (Turf): Sf: 1-6 **GS: 3-7** Gd: 1-12 GF: 2-8 Fm: 0-3
Distance: 5f/6f: 0-0 7f-8f: 0-2 **9f-13f: 7-43** 14f+: 0-0
Track : **LH: 4-27** RH: 3-17 **Tight: 3-25** Gall: 2-6
Aids: Bl: 0-3 **Vi: 4-21** Tstrap: 0-8 Ckp: 0-8
Best Rating: **80** 7/08 Donc 1m2f60y good

Modest; stays 1m 2f; acts on soft ground and on Polytrack.

Keithshazel (IRE)

64(71) (17)3

2-y-o b f Fasliyev (USA)-La Poterie (FR) (Bering)
R C Guest (Garry Moss 7/7) Brooklands Racing

Placings:0000 **(6819)**
2009: 5[0]G, 5[0]G, 5[0]SD, 7[0]GF,

	Starts	1st	2nd	3rd	Win & Pl
Career Total (Turf)	3	0	0	0	
Career Total (AW)	1	0	0	0	

Going (Turf): **Sf: 0-0 GS: 0-0 Gd: 0-2 GF: 0-1 Fm: 0-0**
Distance: 5f/6f: 0-3 7f-8f: 0-1 9f-13f: 0-0 14f+: 0-0
Track : LH: 0-0 RH: 0-0 Tight: 0-0 Gall: 0-0
Aids: Bl: 0-0 Vi: 0-0 Tstrap: 0-0 Ckp: 0-0
Best Rating: **17** 7/09 Sthl 5f stand

Kelamon

73(102) (75)81

5-y-o b g Keltos (FR)-Faraway Moon (Distant Relative)
S C Williams Mr and Mrs M Fairweather

Placings:53253261140046045341354012104501-4000000 **(7424)**
2009: 5[4]SF, 6[0]GF, 6[0]GF, 5[0]G, 6[0]G, 6[0]SD, 6[0]SD,

	Starts	1st	2nd	3rd	Win & Pl
Career Total (Turf)	20	5	2	2	27366
Career Total (AW)	19	1	1	2	6036

81 10/08 Sals 6f (0-85)H GD £5180
81 7/08 Newb 5f34y (0-70)H GD £2590
80 7/08 Wind 6f (0-75)H SFT £2729
77 3/08 Wolv 7f32y (0-70)H STD £2590
77 7/07 Wind 6f (0-85)H HVY £6477
78 6/07 Wind 6f (0-85)H SFT £6477
Total win prize-money £26046

Going (Turf): **Sf: 3-7** GS: 0-5 Gd: 2-6 GF: 0-2 Fm: 0-0
Distance: **5f/6f: 5-30** 7f-8f: 1-9 9f-13f: 0-0 14f+: 0-0
Track : **LH: 1-16** RH: 0-3 Tight: 1-7 **Gall: 3-10**
Aids: Bl: 0-0 Vi: 0-0 Tstrap: 0-0 Ckp: 0-0
Best Rating: **81** 10/08 Sals 6f good

Fair; effective over 5f-7f; suited by good and easy ground; also acts on sand.

Keleyf Byon Belief (IRE)

77(77) (39)34

2-y-o ch f Kheleyf (USA)-Carrozzina (Vettori (IRE))
John C McConnell (Edgar Byrne 8/9) Mrs Eithne Hamilton

Placings:000 **(7071a)**
2009: 8[0]SD, 8[0]GF, 7[0]Y,

	Starts	1st	2nd	3rd	Win & Pl
Career Total (Turf)	2	0	0	0	
Career Total (AW)	1	0	0	0	

Going (Turf): Sf: 0-0 GS: 0-0 Gd: 0-0 GF: 0-1 Fm: 0-0
Distance: 5f/6f: 0-0 7f-8f: 0-3 9f-13f: 0-0 14f+: 0-0
Track : LH: 0-1 RH: 0-2 Tight: 0-0 Gall: 0-0
Aids: Bl: 0-0 Vi: 0-0 Tstrap: 0-0 Ckp: 0-0
Best Rating: 39 8/09 Kemp 1m stand

Kellys Eye (IRE)

95 **76**

2-y-o b g Noverre (USA)-Limit (IRE) (Barathea (IRE))
B Smart Ron Hull

Placings:425 **(6896)**
2009: 6^{4}GS, 6^{2}GF, 6^{5}GF,

	Starts	1st	2nd	3rd	Win & Pl
Career Total (Turf)	3	0	1	0	1188

Going (Turf): **Sf: 0-0 GS: 0-1 Gd: 0-0 GF: 0-2 Fm: 0-0**
Distance: 5f/6f: 0-3 7f-8f: 0-0 9f-13f: 0-0 14f+: 0-0
Track : LH: 0-1 RH: 0-0 Tight: 0-0 Gall: 0-0
Aids: Bl: 0-0 Vi: 0-0 Tstrap: 0-0 Ckp: 0-0
Best Rating: **76** 10/09 Ayr 6f gd-fm

Promise in maidens; stays 6f; acts on fast ground.

Ken's Girl

101 (64)**76**

5-y-o ch m Ishiguru (USA)-There's Two (IRE) (Ashkalani (IRE))
W S Kittow Midd Shire Racing

Placings:0526/120000/0002410-05222060 **(6739)**
2009: 7^{0}GF, 7^{5}GF, 6^{2}GF, 7^{2}GF, 7^{2}S, 7^{0}G, 7^{6}GF, 6^{0}GS,

	Starts	1st	2nd	3rd	Win & Pl
Career Total (Turf)	22	2	6	0	12779
Career Total (AW)	3	0	0	0	0

69 10/08 Leic 7f9y (0-70)H SFT £2590
76 4/07 Bath 5f11y FRM £2914
Total win prize-money £5505

Going (Turf): **Sf: 1-5** GS: 0-2 Gd: 0-3 GF: 0-11 **Fm: 1-1**
Distance: 5f/6f: 1-12 7f-8f: 1-12 9f-13f: 0-1 14f+: 0-0
Track : **LH: 1-8** RH: 0-1 Tight: 0-4 **Gall: 1-5**
Aids: Bl: 0-0 Vi: 0-0 Tstrap: 0-1 Ckp: 0-1
Best Rating: **76** 7/09 Chep 7f16y soft

Modest; stays 7f; acts well on fast and soft ground.

Kenaaya (FR)

93 **58**

3-y-o b/br f Monsun (GER)-Jindy's Dream (USA) (A.P. Indy (USA))
J H M Gosden Hamdan Al Maktoum

Placings:0 **(2847)**
2009: 10^{0}GF,

	Starts	1st	2nd	3rd	Win & Pl
Career Total (Turf)	1	0	0	0	

Going (Turf): **Sf: 0-0 GS: 0-0 Gd: 0-0 GF: 0-1 Fm: 0-0**
Distance: 5f/6f: 0-0 7f-8f: 0-0 9f-13f: 0-1 14f+: 0-0
Track : LH: 0-1 RH: 0-0 Tight: 0-0 Gall: 0-1
Aids: Bl: 0-0 Vi: 0-0 Tstrap: 0-0 Ckp: 0-0
Best Rating: **58** 6/09 Newb 1m2f6y gd-fm

Kenai

(87) (52)**61**

4-y-o ch g Arkadian Hero (USA)-Hicklam Millie (Absalom)
W K Goldsworthy Mrs Susan O'Connor

Placings:0000/5000-05 **(0973)**
2009: 9^{0}SD, 5^{5}SD,

	Starts	1st	2nd	3rd	Win & Pl
Career Total (Turf)	5	0	0	0	
Career Total (AW)	5	0	0	0	0

Going (Turf): **Sf: 0-1 GS: 0-0 Gd: 0-3 GF: 0-0 Fm: 0-0**
Distance: 5f/6f: 0-1 7f-8f: 0-5 9f-13f: 0-4 14f+: 0-0
Track : LH: 0-5 RH: 0-2 Tight: 0-2 Gall: 0-0
Aids: Bl: 0-1 Vi: 0-0 Tstrap: 0-1 Ckp: 0-1
Best Rating: **66** 9/07 Dund 7f stand

Kendalewood

79 **26**

3-y-o b g Viking Ruler (AUS)-Wilsonic (Damister (USA))
T D Walford Mrs J E Morton

Placings:000 **(2042)**
2009: 10^{0}GF, 10^{0}G, 10^{0}GS,

	Starts	1st	2nd	3rd	Win & Pl
Career Total (Turf)	3	0	0	0	

Going (Turf): **Sf: 0-0 GS: 0-1 Gd: 0-1 GF: 0-1 Fm: 0-0**
Distance: 5f/6f: 0-0 7f-8f: 0-0 9f-13f: 0-3 14f+: 0-0
Track : LH: 0-3 RH: 0-0 Tight: 0-0 Gall: 0-1
Aids: Bl: 0-0 Vi: 0-0 Tstrap: 0-0 Ckp: 0-0
Best Rating: **26** 4/09 Nott 1m2f50y gd-fm

Kensei (IRE)

93(91) (69)**73**

2-y-o ch g Peintre Celebre (USA)-Journey Of Hope (USA) (Slew O'Gold (USA))
R M Beckett J C Smith

Placings:3526 **(7003)**
2009: 6^{3}G, 7^{5}S, 7^{2}SD, 8^{6}SD,

	Starts	1st	2nd	3rd	Win & Pl
Career Total (Turf)	2	0	0	1	698
Career Total (AW)	2	0	1	0	964

Going (Turf): **Sf: 0-1 GS: 0-0 Gd: 0-1 GF: 0-0 Fm: 0-0**
Distance: 5f/6f: 0-0 7f-8f: 0-3 9f-13f: 0-1 14f+: 0-0
Track : LH: 0-2 RH: 0-0 Tight: 0-2 Gall: 0-0
Aids: Bl: 0-0 Vi: 0-0 Tstrap: 0-0 Ckp: 0-0
Best Rating: **73** 6/09 Sals 6f212y good

Fair; stays 7f and acts on Polytrack.

Kensington (IRE)

99(106) (79)**80**

8-y-o b g Cape Cross (IRE)-March Star (IRE) (Mac's Imp (USA))
A J McCabe (P D Evans 21/5) Derek Buckley

Placings:33064/63261650/0004013361123/1404400020/5451/32110140360460365046651302-53U03325050530 **(7876)**
2009: 8^{5}SD, 7^{3}SD, 7^{U}SD, 8^{0}SD, 7^{3}SD, 7^{3}SD, 7^{2}SD, 7^{5}SD, 6^{0}G, 7^{5}SD, 6^{0}SD, 7^{5}SD, 7^{3}SD, 7^{0}SD,

	Starts	1st	2nd	3rd	Win & Pl
Career Total (Turf)	35	4	1	7	21306
Career Total (AW)	45	6	5	7	25039

78 12/08 Wolv 7f32y (0-65)H STD £2388
80 4/08 Wind 6f (0-75)H G-S £3070
78 2/08 Wolv 7f32y (0-70)H STD £2730
62 2/08 Sthl 7f (0-70)H STD £2593
64 12/07 Sthl 7f (0-65)H SS £2968
73 1/06 Wolv 5f216y (0-70)H STD £2914
64 10/05 Ling 7f (0-55)H STD £2679
67 9/05 Ayr 5f (0-70)H GD £4932
63 8/05 Bath 5f161y FRM £2695
63 9/04 Ripn 6f G-F £4071
Total win prize-money £31046

Going (Turf): Sf: 0-8 **GS: 1-4 Gd: 1-8 GF: 1-8 Fm: 1-5**
Distance: 5f/6f: 5-28 7f-8f: 5-48 9f-13f: 0-4 14f+: 0-0
Track : **LH: 7-49** RH: 0-6 **Tight: 4-30** Gall: 2-8
Aids: Bl: 1-11 Vi: 1-6 Tstrap: 7-35 Ckp: 7-35
Best Rating: **80** 4/08 Wind 6f gd-sft

Fair; ex-Irish; stays 7f, but effective over shorter; acts on most ground on turf; goes on sand.

Kensington Oval

105(104) (92)**89**

4-y-o b g Sadler's Wells (USA)-Request (Rainbow Quest (USA))
Jonjo O'Neill (Sir Michael Stoute 10/8) John P McManus

Placings:100-332 **(4840)**
2009: 10^{3}G, 12^{3}GS, 12^{2}SD,

	Starts	1st	2nd	3rd	Win & Pl
Career Total (Turf)	5	1	0	2	4656
Career Total (AW)	1	0	1	0	2987

88 6/08 Sand 1m2f7y G-S £3885
Total win prize-money £3886

Going (Turf): Sf: 0-0 **GS: 1-2** Gd: 0-2 GF: 0-1 Fm: 0-0
Distance: 5f/6f: 0-0 7f-8f: 0-0 **9f-13f: 1-6** 14f+: 0-0
Track : LH: 0-1 **RH: 1-5** Tight: 0-0 Gall: 0-3
Aids: Bl: 0-0 Vi: 0-0 Tstrap: 0-0 Ckp: 0-0
Best Rating: **92** 8/09 Sthl 1m4f stand

Very useful; brother to the stable's high-class middle-distance performer Ask; winner on debut over 1m2f; well beaten in Listed comapny next time; acts on easy ground.

Kenswick

85(81) (44)**62**

2-y-o b f Avonbridge-The Jotter (Night Shift (USA))
Pat Eddery The Hill Top Partnership

Placings:460 **(7317)**
2009: 6^{4}S, 5^{6}GF, 5^{0}SD,

	Starts	1st	2nd	3rd	Win & Pl
Career Total (Turf)	2	0	0	0	0
Career Total (AW)	1	0	0	0	

Going (Turf): **Sf: 0-1 GS: 0-0 Gd: 0-0 GF: 0-1 Fm: 0-0**
Distance: 5f/6f: 0-2 7f-8f: 0-1 9f-13f: 0-0 14f+: 0-0
Track : LH: 0-1 RH: 0-0 Tight: 0-1 Gall: 0-0
Aids: Bl: 0-0 Vi: 0-0 Tstrap: 0-0 Ckp: 0-0
Best Rating: **62** 10/09 Nott 6f15y soft

Kentavr's Dream

(77) (47)**23**

6-y-o b m Robellino (USA)-Very Good (Noalto)
P Howling Kentavr (uk) Ltd

Placings:00/0000/4-P **(0145)**
2009: 10^{P}SD,

	Starts	1st	2nd	3rd	Win & Pl
Career Total (Turf)	3	0	0	0	
Career Total (AW)	5	0	0	0	241

Going (Turf): **Sf: 0-1 GS: 0-0 Gd: 0-1 GF: 0-1 Fm: 0-0**

Distance: 5f/6f: 0-2 7f-8f: 0-3 9f-13f: 0-3 14f+: 0-0
Track : LH: 0-4 RH: 0-1 Tight: 0-2 Gall: 0-2
Aids: Bl: 0-0 Vi: 0-0 Tstrap: 0-0 Ckp: 0-0
Best Rating: **47** 11/08 GrLe 1m2f stand

Kenton Street

101(98) (69)**69**
4-y-o ch g Compton Place-Western Applause (Royal Applause)
Michael J Browne Michael J Browne

Placings:4/045434-000000405 **(7587)**
2009: 6^{0}YS, 6^{0}SH, 6^{0}G, 6^{0}GF, 7^{0}SH, 6^{0}S, 7^{4}G, 8^{0}Y, 8^{5}SD,

	Starts	1st	2nd	3rd	Win & Pl
Career Total (Turf)	14	0	0	1	1422
Career Total (AW)	2	0	0	0	192

Going (Turf): Sf: 0-1 GS: 0-2 Gd: 0-4 GF: 0-3 Fm: 0-0
Distance: 5f/6f: 0-8 7f-8f: 0-8 9f-13f: 0-0 14f+: 0-0
Track : LH: 0-3 RH: 0-2 Tight: 0-0 Gall: 0-2
Aids: Bl: 0-1 Vi: 0-0 Tstrap: 0-1 Ckp: 0-1
Best Rating: **69** 10/08 Kemp 6f stand

Modest; effective at around 6f; acts on fast ground.

Kentucky Boy (IRE)

75(72) (10)**60**
5-y-o b g Distant Music (USA)-Delta Town (USA) (Sanglamore (USA))
Jedd O'Keeffe The Kentuckians

Placings:000/32116/40-06 **(1171)**
2009: 14^{0}SD, 17^{6}GF,

	Starts	1st	2nd	3rd	Win & Pl
Career Total (Turf)	10	2	1	0	7344
Career Total (AW)	2	0	0	1	353

65 8/07 Pont 2m1f22y (0-70)H G-S £3886
57 7/07 Bevl 2m35y (0-65)H SFT £2590
Total win prize-money £6477

Going (Turf): Sf: 1-4 GS: 1-3 Gd: 0-2 GF: 0-1 Fm: 0-0
Distance: 5f/6f: 0-0 7f-8f: 0-3 9f-13f: 0-2 **14f+: 2-7**
Track : LH: 1-8 RH: 1-3 **Tight: 1-6** Gall: 0-1
Aids: Bl: 0-0 Vi: 0-0 Tstrap: 0-1 Ckp: 0-1
Best Rating: **65** 8/07 Pont 2m1f22y gd-sft

Moderate; stays 2m; acts on easy ground.

Kentucky Lakes

93 **48**
3-y-o b g Generous (IRE)-Inya Lake (Whittingham (IRE))
Jedd O'Keeffe A Walker

Placings:0600 **(3708)**
2009: 7^{0}GF, 7^{6}GF, 10^{0}G, 8^{0}GS,

	Starts	1st	2nd	3rd	Win & Pl
Career Total (Turf)	4	0	0	0	0

Going (Turf): Sf: 0-0 GS: 0-1 Gd: 0-1 GF: 0-2 Fm: 0-0
Distance: 5f/6f: 0-0 7f-8f: 0-2 9f-13f: 0-2 14f+: 0-0
Track : LH: 0-2 RH: 0-1 Tight: 0-0 Gall: 0-1
Aids: Bl: 0-0 Vi: 0-0 Tstrap: 0-0 Ckp: 0-0
Best Rating: **48** 4/09 Rdcr 7f gd-fm

Kenyan Cat

88 **64**
2-y-o br f One Cool Cat (USA)-Nairobi (FR) (Anabaa (USA))
George Baker David Botterill & John Guest

Placings:343 **(7061)**
2009: 5^{3}GF, 7^{4}GF, 5^{3}GF,

	Starts	1st	2nd	3rd	Win & Pl
Career Total (Turf)	3	0	0	2	1131

Going (Turf): Sf: 0-0 GS: 0-0 Gd: 0-0 GF: 0-3 Fm: 0-0
Distance: 5f/6f: 0-2 7f-8f: 0-1 9f-13f: 0-0 14f+: 0-0
Track : LH: 0-1 RH: 0-0 Tight: 0-0 Gall: 0-0
Aids: Bl: 0-0 Vi: 0-0 Tstrap: 0-0 Ckp: 0-0
Best Rating: **64** 10/09 Leic 5f218y gd-fm

Kerchak (USA)

95 **77**
2-y-o b c Royal Academy (USA)-Traude (USA) (River Special (USA))
W Jarvis The Silverback Partnership

Placings:6636 **(6809)**
2009: 7^{6}G, 7^{6}G, 6^{3}GF, 6^{6}G,

	Starts	1st	2nd	3rd	Win & Pl
Career Total (Turf)	4	0	0	1	578

Going (Turf): Sf: 0-0 GS: 0-0 Gd: 0-3 GF: 0-1 Fm: 0-0
Distance: 5f/6f: 0-2 7f-8f: 0-2 9f-13f: 0-0 14f+: 0-0
Track : LH: 0-1 RH: 0-1 Tight: 0-1 Gall: 0-0
Aids: Bl: 0-0 Vi: 0-0 Tstrap: 0-0 Ckp: 0-0
Best Rating: **77** 9/09 NmkR 6f gd-fm

Kerolad (IRE)

77 **30**
2-y-o ch g Kyllachy-Absolute Precision (USA) (Irish River (FR))
N Wilson D & S L Tanker Transport Limited

Placings:00002 **(4527)**
2009: 6^{0}G, 7^{0}GF, 6^{0}GF, 7^{0}G, 8^{2}GS,

	Starts	1st	2nd	3rd	Win & Pl
Career Total (Turf)	5	0	1	0	1349

Going (Turf): Sf: 0-0 GS: 0-1 Gd: 0-2 GF: 0-2 Fm: 0-0
Distance: 5f/6f: 0-2 7f-8f: 0-2 9f-13f: 0-1 14f+: 0-0
Track : LH: 0-2 RH: 0-1 Tight: 0-2 Gall: 0-1
Aids: Bl: 0-0 Vi: 0-0 Tstrap: 0-0 Ckp: 0-0
Best Rating: **30** 7/09 York 7f good

Kerrys Requiem (IRE)

107 **96**
3-y-o b f King's Best (USA)-Moonlight Wish (IRE) (Peintre Celebre (USA))
M R Channon Findlay & Bloom

Placings:433310260-0526323005620 **(6694)**
2009: 6^{0}GF, 6^{5}GF, 6^{2}G, 5^{6}GF, 6^{3}G, 6^{2}GS, 6^{3}G, 6^{0}G, 5^{0}GF, 5^{5}G, 5^{6}F, 6^{2}G, 6^{0}GS,

	Starts	1st	2nd	3rd	Win & Pl
Career Total (Turf)	22	1	4	5	35789

81 6/08 Wind 5f10y G-F £12462
Total win prize-money £12462

Going (Turf): Sf: 0-1 GS: 0-5 Gd: 0-8 **GF: 1-7** Fm: 0-1
Distance: **5f/6f: 1-21** 7f-8f: 0-1 9f-13f: 0-0 14f+: 0-0
Track : LH: 0-3 RH: 0-0 Tight: 0-0 **Gall: 1-3**
Aids: Bl: 0-0 Vi: 0-0 Tstrap: 0-0 Ckp: 0-0
Best Rating: **96** 7/09 Ripn 6f good

Useful; Listed placed; effective over 5f-6f; acts on most ground.

Kersivay

96(102) (79)**72**
3-y-o b g Royal Applause-Lochmaddy (Selkirk (USA))
Ollie Pears (D W Barker 29/6) Ian Bishop

Placings:0303-3164602553 **(7577)**
2009: 7^{3}GF, 7^{1}GF, 6^{6}GF, 6^{4}GF, 6^{6}G, 7^{0}SD, 7^{2}SD, 7^{5}GF, 7^{5}SD, 5^{3}SD,

	Starts	1st	2nd	3rd	Win & Pl
Career Total (Turf)	9	1	0	2	4251
Career Total (AW)	5	0	1	2	1975

72 4/09 Catt 7f G-F £2914
Total win prize-money £2914

Going (Turf): Sf: 0-1 GS: 0-0 Gd: 0-1 **GF: 1-7** Fm: 0-0
Distance: 5f/6f: 0-2 **7f-8f: 1-12** 9f-13f: 0-0 14f+: 0-0
Track : **LH: 1-10** RH: 0-2 **Tight: 1-8** Gall: 0-0
Aids: Bl: 0-0 Vi: 0-0 Tstrap: 0-0 Ckp: 0-0
Best Rating: **79** 10/09 Wolv 7f32y stand

Modest; effective at 7f; acts on fast ground; handles Polytrack.

Kessraa (IRE)

100(69) (32)**70**
3-y-o b g Kheleyf (USA)-Safe Care (IRE) (Caerleon (USA))
M R Channon Sheikh Ahmed Al Maktoum

Placings:00-24523 **(5773)**
2009: 7^{2}GF, 7^{4}GS, 8^{5}GF, 8^{2}GF, 10^{3}GF,

	Starts	1st	2nd	3rd	Win & Pl
Career Total (Turf)	6	0	2	1	3062
Career Total (AW)	1	0	0	0	

Going (Turf): Sf: 0-0 GS: 0-2 Gd: 0-0 GF: 0-4 Fm: 0-0
Distance: 5f/6f: 0-0 7f-8f: 0-3 9f-13f: 0-4 14f+: 0-0
Track : LH: 0-2 RH: 0-2 Tight: 0-2 Gall: 0-0
Aids: Bl: 0-0 Vi: 0-0 Tstrap: 0-0 Ckp: 0-0
Best Rating: **70** 7/09 Folk 7f gd-fm

Modest; stays 1m; acts on fast ground.

Kestrel Cross (IRE)

(108) (77)**73**
7-y-o b g Cape Cross (IRE)-Lady Rachel (IRE) (Priolo (USA))
A W Carroll Group 1 Racing (1994) Ltd

Placings:432111/230031020/05030/400/000-53P **(0453)**
2009: 10^{5}SD, 10^{3}SD, 9^{P}SD,

	Starts	1st	2nd	3rd	Win & Pl
Career Total (Turf)	25	4	3	4	150379
Career Total (AW)	4	0	0	1	722

101 9/05 Curr 1m H GD £42624
93 9/04 Leop 7f G-F £22922
88 6/04 Curr 6f63y GD £54014
84 6/04 Limk 7f FRM £9169
Total win prize-money £128730

Going (Turf): Sf: 0-2 GS: 0-2 **Gd: 2-8** GF: 1-6 Fm: 1-3
Distance: 5f/6f: 0-3 **7f-8f: 4-11** 9f-13f: 0-15 14f+: 0-0
Track : LH: 1-14 RH: 1-10 Tight: 0-3 **Gall: 1-10**
Aids: Bl: 0-1 Vi: 0-0 Tstrap: 0-0 Ckp: 0-0
Best Rating: **102** 9/05 List 1m1f yield

Fair; stays 1m2f; acts on good and fast ground.

Kevkat (IRE)

96(94) (95)**75**

8-y-o br g Dushyantor (USA)-Diamond Display (IRE) (Shardari)

D E Pipe R Stokes

Placings:531132/5**33**15/005-003 (5244)

2009: 10^{0}SD, 10^{0}GS, 11^{3}F,

	Starts	1st	2nd	3rd	Win & Pl
Career Total (Turf)	9	2	1	3	49215
Career Total (AW)	8	1	0	2	14218

86 11/07 Dund 1m2f150y STD £9237
91 8/06 Gway 1m4f H G-F £31427
78 7/06 Wxfd 1m5f G-F £5242
Total win prize-money £45907

Going (Turf): Sf: 0-0 GS: 0-1 Gd: 0-2 **GF: 2-4** Fm: 0-1
Distance: 5f/6f: 0-0 7f-8f: 0-0 **9f-13f: 3-15** 14f+: 0-2
Track : LH: 0-8 **RH: 2-5** Tight: 0-1 Gall: 0-1
Aids: Bl: 0-0 Vi: 0-0 Tstrap: 0-0 Ckp: 0-0
Best Rating: 101 9/06 Curr 1m2f good

Key Art (IRE)

98(92) (68)**73**

2-y-o b c Kheleyf (USA)-Gift Of Spring (USA) (Gilded Time (USA))

J Noseda The Sangster Family & M Green

Placings:4252244 (6971)

2009: 5^{4}GF, 5^{2}GF, 6^{5}G, 5^{2}G, 5^{2}GF, 5^{4}SS, 5^{4}SD,

	Starts	1st	2nd	3rd	Win & Pl
Career Total (Turf)	5	0	3	0	3083
Career Total (AW)	2	0	0	0	192

Going (Turf): Sf: 0-0 GS: 0-0 Gd: 0-2 GF: 0-3 Fm: 0-0
Distance: 5f/6f: 0-7 7f-8f: 0-0 9f-13f: 0-0 14f+: 0-0
Track : LH: 0-2 RH: 0-1 Tight: 0-1 Gall: 0-0
Aids: Bl: 0-0 Vi: 0-0 Tstrap: 0-0 Ckp: 0-0
Best Rating: 73 8/09 Sand 5f6y good

Fair; effective over 5f; acts on good ground.

Key Breeze

90(85) (60)**66**

2-y-o b c Exceed And Excel (AUS)-Cayman Sound (Turtle Island (IRE))

J H M Gosden H R H Princess Haya Of Jordan

Placings:554 (4537)

2009: 6^{5}GF, 6^{5}GF, 5^{4}SD,

	Starts	1st	2nd	3rd	Win & Pl
Career Total (Turf)	2	0	0	0	0
Career Total (AW)	1	0	0	0	248

Going (Turf): Sf: 0-0 GS: 0-0 Gd: 0-0 GF: 0-2 Fm: 0-0
Distance: 5f/6f: 0-3 7f-8f: 0-0 9f-13f: 0-0 14f+: 0-0
Track : LH: 0-2 RH: 0-0 Tight: 0-2 Gall: 0-0
Aids: Bl: 0-0 Vi: 0-0 Tstrap: 0-0 Ckp: 0-0
Best Rating: 66 5/09 Donc 6f gd-fm

Modest; best effort over 6f on fast on debut.

Key Decision (IRE)

103(102) (75)**80**

5-y-o br g Key Of Luck (USA)-Adalya (IRE) (Darshaan)

Shaun Harley Hard Decisions Syndicate

Placings:5020200000**0**060-1**6**500500001 (6709a)

2009: 11^{1}SD, 10^{6}SD, 11^{5}Y, 12^{0}HY, 12^{0}GF, 10^{5}S, 8^{0}S, 9^{0}YS, 7^{0}SD, 12^{0}GF, 10^{1}S,

	Starts	1st	2nd	3rd	Win & Pl
Career Total (Turf)	16	1	2	0	8878
Career Total (AW)	7	1	0	0	2730

68 10/09 Curr 1m2f (50-70)H SFT £6373
75 2/09 Sthl 1m3f STD £2729
Total win prize-money £9103

Going (Turf): Sf: 1-7 GS: 0-1 Gd: 0-1 GF: 0-4 Fm: 0-0
Distance: 5f/6f: 0-0 7f-8f: 0-5 **9f-13f: 2-18** 14f+: 0-0
Track : LH: 1-11 RH: 1-11 Tight: 0-3 Gall: 0-1
Aids: Bl: 0-0 Vi: 0-0 Tstrap: 0-0 Ckp: 0-0
Best Rating: 80 5/08 Carl 1m3f107y gd-fm

Modest; suited by 1m4lf; acts on easy ground and Fibresand.

Key Light (IRE)

(96) (74)

2-y-o b f Acclamation-Eva Luna (IRE) (Double Schwartz)

J W Hills Mrs P De W Johnson

Placings:41 (7585)

2009: 6^{4}SD, 6^{1}SD,

	Starts	1st	2nd	3rd	Win & Pl
Career Total (Turf)	0	0	0	0	
Career Total (AW)	2	1	0	0	3826

74 11/09 Kemp 6f STD £3561
Total win prize-money £3562

Going (Turf): Sf: 0-0 GS: 0-0 Gd: 0-0 GF: 0-0 Fm: 0-0
Distance: 5f/6f: 1-2 7f-8f: 0-0 9f-13f: 0-0 14f+: 0-0
Track : LH: 0-0 **RH: 1-2** Tight: 0-0 Gall: 0-0
Aids: Bl: 0-0 Vi: 0-0 Tstrap: 0-0 Ckp: 0-0
Best Rating: 74 11/09 Kemp 6f stand

Fair; stays 6f and acts on Polytrack.

Key Of Fortune (IRE)

93(91) (57)**52**

3-y-o b f Key Of Luck (USA)-Alaynia (IRE) (Hamas (IRE))

Jennie Candlish Ms Jennie Candlish

Placings:04-5650505 (4593)

2009: 9^{5}SD, 12^{6}SF, 12^{5}SD, 10^{0}GF, 12^{5}GF, 12^{0}GF, 11^{5}G,

	Starts	1st	2nd	3rd	Win & Pl
Career Total (Turf)	5	0	0	0	0
Career Total (AW)	4	0	0	0	289

Going (Turf): Sf: 0-0 GS: 0-0 Gd: 0-2 GF: 0-3 Fm: 0-0
Distance: 5f/6f: 0-0 7f-8f: 0-1 9f-13f: 0-8 14f+: 0-0
Track : LH: 0-6 RH: 0-3 Tight: 0-5 Gall: 0-0
Aids: Bl: 0-0 Vi: 0-0 Tstrap: 0-0 Ckp: 0-0
Best Rating: 57 2/09 Wolv 1m4f50y std-fst

Key Regard (IRE)

(102) (75)

3-y-o br g Key Of Luck (USA)-Disregard That (IRE) (Don't Forget Me)

P F I Cole (C J Mann 24/9) Jared Sullivan

Placings:2130351 (7578)

2009: 10^{2}SD, 12^{1}SD, 12^{3}SD, 12^{0}SD, 12^{3}SD, 12^{5}SD, 13^{1}SF,

	Starts	1st	2nd	3rd	Win & Pl
Career Total (Turf)	0	0	0	0	
Career Total (AW)	7	2	1	2	7220

70 11/09 Wolv 1m5f194y SF £2914
71 2/09 Ling 1m4f STD £2729
Total win prize-money £5644

Going (Turf): Sf: 0-0 GS: 0-0 Gd: 0-0 GF: 0-0 Fm: 0-0
Distance: 5f/6f: 0-0 7f-8f: 0-0 9f-13f: 1-6 14f+: 1-1
Track : **LH: 2-3** RH: 0-4 **Tight: 2-3** Gall: 0-0
Aids: Bl: 0-0 Vi: 0-0 Tstrap: 0-0 Ckp: 0-0
Best Rating: 75 3/09 Kemp 1m4f stand

Fair; effective up to 1m4f; acts on Polytrack.

Key Signature

106(91) (76)**85**

3-y-o b f Dansili-Musical Key (Key Of Luck (USA))

Pat Eddery Exors of the Late F C T Wilson

Placings:52124-00503002 (6695)

2009: 7^{0}GS, 7^{0}GS, 7^{5}GF, 7^{0}G, 7^{3}G, 7^{0}G, 7^{0}G, 8^{2}GS,

	Starts	1st	2nd	3rd	Win & Pl
Career Total (Turf)	12	0	3	1	7245
Career Total (AW)	1	1	0	0	4533

76 8/08 Kemp 7f STD £4533
Total win prize-money £4533

Going (Turf): Sf: 0-1 GS: 0-4 Gd: 0-5 GF: 0-2 Fm: 0-0
Distance: 5f/6f: 0-0 **7f-8f: 1-13** 9f-13f: 0-0 14f+: 0-0
Track : LH: 0-0 **RH: 1-7** Tight: 0-0 Gall: 0-0
Aids: Bl: 0-4 Vi: 0-0 Tstrap: 0-0 Ckp: 0-0
Best Rating: 85 10/09 Gdwd 1m gd-sft

Fair; stays 7f; acts on fast and soft ground; goes on Polytrack; blinkers.

Key To Love (IRE)

77(96) (64)**69**

3-y-o b f Key Of Luck (USA)-Ski For Me (IRE) (Barathea (IRE))

A J Chamberlain G B Heffaran

Placings:6523514400-6000 (7069)

2009: 7^{6}SF, 5^{0}GF, 6^{0}GF, 6^{0}SD,

	Starts	1st	2nd	3rd	Win & Pl
Career Total (Turf)	5	1	1	1	4205
Career Total (AW)	9	0	0	0	241

69 9/08 Folk 5f (0-65) G-S £2914
Total win prize-money £2914

Going (Turf): Sf: 0-2 **GS: 1-1** Gd: 0-0 GF: 0-2 Fm: 0-0
Distance: 5f/6f: 1-10 7f-8f: 0-4 9f-13f: 0-0 14f+: 0-0
Track : LH: 0-4 RH: 0-5 Tight: 0-3 Gall: 0-1
Aids: Bl: 0-0 Vi: 0-0 Tstrap: 0-1 Ckp: 0-1
Best Rating: 69 9/08 Folk 5f gd-sft

Modest; effective over 5f-6f; acts on soft ground.

Keyala (IRE)

(89) (79)**78**

4-y-o b f Key Of Luck (USA)-Alwiyda (USA) (Trempolino (USA))

David P Myerscough Bull & Bear Syndicate

Placings:40232451-B0600 (7634)

2009: 7^{B}GF, 7^{0}SD, 7^{6}SD, 6^{0}SD, 5^{0}SD,

	Starts	1st	2nd	3rd	Win & Pl
Career Total (Turf)	7	0	2	1	6338
Career Total (AW)	6	1	0	0	6605

79 10/08 Dund 6f STD £6605
Total win prize-money £6605

Going (Turf): Sf: 0-1 GS: 0-0 Gd: 0-1 GF: 0-1 Fm: 0-0
Distance: 5f/6f: 1-4 7f-8f: 0-9 9f-13f: 0-0 14f+: 0-0

Track : LH: 1-10 RH: 0-3 Tight: 0-2 Gall: 0-0
Aids: Bl: 0-0 Vi: 0-0 Tstrap: 0-0 Ckp: 0-0
Best Rating: 79 10/08 Dund 6f stand

Keys Of Cyprus

105(76) (26)86

7-y-o ch g Deploy-Krisia (Kris)
D Nicholls The Beasley Gees

Placings:10/0161162-50100401 (7171)
2009: 7^{5}G, 7^{0}GF, 8^{1}S, 8^{0}GS, 7^{0}G, 8^{4}G, 8^{0}SD, 7^{1}S,

	Starts	1st	2nd	3rd	Win & Pl
Career Total (Turf)	16	6	1	0	27423
Career Total (AW)	1	0	0	0	

84 10/09 Ayr 7f50y (0-80)H SFT £6231
85 7/09 Ripn 1m (0-85)H SFT £6938
83 9/08 Ayr 7f50y (0-75)H HVY £4533
71 9/08 Muss 7f30y (0-65)H SFT £2590
75 8/08 Catt 7f (0-60)H G-S £2388
69 8/05 Catt 5f212y G-F £3513
Total win prize-money £26194

Going (Turf): Sf: **4-5** GS: 1-5 Gd: 0-4 GF: 1-2 Fm: 0-0
Distance: 5f/6f: 1-3 **7f-8f: 5-13** 9f-13f: 0-1 14f+: 0-0
Track : **LH: 4-12** RH: 2-3 **Tight: 4-9** Gall: 0-0
Aids: Bl: 0-0 Vi: 0-0 Tstrap: 0-0 Ckp: 0-0
Best Rating: 86 10/08 Catt 7f gd-sft

Fair; effective at around 7f; acts on fast and soft ground.

Keyta Bonita (IRE)

96 71

2-y-o b f Denon (USA)-Miss Corinne (Mark Of Esteem (IRE))
M G Quinlan Mrs Nicola McGreavy

Placings:402240 (6481)
2009: 6^{4}GS, 7^{0}G, 7^{2}G, 6^{2}GF, 7^{4}GF, 7^{0}GF,

	Starts	1st	2nd	3rd	Win & Pl
Career Total (Turf)	6	0	2	0	2528

Going (Turf): **Sf: 0-0 GS: 0-1 Gd: 0-2 GF: 0-3 Fm: 0-0**
Distance: 5f/6f: 0-2 7f-8f: 0-4 9f-13f: 0-0 14f+: 0-0
Track : LH: 0-0 RH: 0-1 Tight: 0-0 Gall: 0-0
Aids: Bl: 0-0 Vi: 0-0 Tstrap: 0-0 Ckp: 0-0
Best Rating: 71 8/09 Newc 6f gd-fm

Fair, cheaply bought first foal from the family of Sir Percy; effective over 6-7f; acts on good and fast ground.

Khajaaly (IRE)

(93) (69)

2-y-o b c Kheleyf (USA)-Joyfullness (USA) (Dixieland Band (USA))
E A L Dunlop Hamdan Al Maktoum

Placings:5 (6607)
2009: 8^{5}SD,

	Starts	1st	2nd	3rd	Win & Pl
Career Total (Turf)	0	0	0	0	
Career Total (AW)	1	0	0	0	0

Going (Turf): **Sf: 0-0 GS: 0-0 Gd: 0-0 GF: 0-0 Fm: 0-0**
Distance: 5f/6f: 0-0 7f-8f: 0-1 9f-13f: 0-0 14f+: 0-0
Track : LH: 0-0 RH: 0-1 Tight: 0-0 Gall: 0-0
Aids: Bl: 0-0 Vi: 0-0 Tstrap: 0-0 Ckp: 0-0
Best Rating: 69 10/09 Kemp 1m stand

140,000gns as a yearling; promise on debut over 1m on Polytrack.

Khan Tengri (IRE)

75(94) (66)78

3-y-o gr g Sadler's Wells (USA)-Ela Athena (Ezzoud (IRE))
Patrick O Brady (M P Tregoning 24/4) Miss Rita Shah

Placings:033-260 (1489)
2009: 9^{2}SD, 12^{6}SD, 10^{0}G,

	Starts	1st	2nd	3rd	Win & Pl
Career Total (Turf)	4	0	0	2	1445
Career Total (AW)	2	0	1	0	867

Going (Turf): **Sf: 0-1 GS: 0-1 Gd: 0-1 GF: 0-1 Fm: 0-0**
Distance: 5f/6f: 0-0 7f-8f: 0-1 9f-13f: 0-5 14f+: 0-0
Track : LH: 0-1 RH: 0-5 Tight: 0-1 Gall: 0-0
Aids: Bl: 0-1 Vi: 0-0 Tstrap: 0-0 Ckp: 0-0
Best Rating: 78 9/08 Sand 1m14y soft

Fair; effective over 1m; acts on soft ground.

Khanivorous

85(97) (76)55

2-y-o b g Dubai Destination (USA)-Bright Edge (Danehill Dancer (IRE))
J R Boyle M Khan X2

Placings:4415 (7685)
2009: 5^{4}GF, 5^{4}SD, 7^{1}SD, 8^{5}SD,

	Starts	1st	2nd	3rd	Win & Pl
Career Total (Turf)	1	0	0	0	265
Career Total (AW)	3	1	0	0	4209

71 11/09 Kemp 7f STD £4209
Total win prize-money £4209

Going (Turf): **Sf: 0-0 GS: 0-0 Gd: 0-0 GF: 0-1 Fm: 0-0**
Distance: 5f/6f: 0-2 **7f-8f: 1-2** 9f-13f: 0-0 14f+: 0-0
Track : LH: 0-0 **RH: 1-3** Tight: 0-0 Gall: 0-0
Aids: Bl: 0-0 Vi: 0-0 Tstrap: 0-0 Ckp: 0-0
Best Rating: 76 12/09 Kemp 1m stand

Fair; stays 7f; acts on Polytrack.

Khanjar (USA)

89 (81)47

9-y-o ch g Kris S (USA)-Alyssum (USA) (Storm Cat (USA))
J Pearce Arthur Old

Placings:24/22/24012022425/002056432331/3620025003360020/02235/0 (3247)
2009: 11^{0}GF,

	Starts	1st	2nd	3rd	Win & Pl
Career Total (Turf)	25	0	7	2	18227
Career Total (AW)	24	2	8	5	18353

79 12/05 Sthl 1m4f (0-70)H STD £3388
81 8/04 Sthl 7f E(0-70) SF £3360
Total win prize-money £6749

Going (Turf): **Sf: 0-2 GS: 0-3 Gd: 0-6 GF: 0-13 Fm: 0-1**
Distance: 5f/6f: 0-0 7f-8f: 1-11 9f-13f: 1-35 14f+: 0-3
Track : **LH: 2-34** RH: 0-10 Tight: 0-19 Gall: 0-4
Aids: Bl: 0-0 Vi: 0-3 Tstrap: 1-10 Ckp: 1-10
Best Rating: 96 10/02 NmkR 1m gd-fm

Moderate handicapper; stays 1m4f; acts on fast ground and on sand.

Khateeb (IRE)

111(102) (92)112

4-y-o b c King's Best (USA)-Choc Ice (IRE) (Kahyasi)
M A Jarvis Hamdan Al Maktoum

Placings:214403-410140 (6448)
2009: 10^{4}GF, 8^{1}GF, 10^{0}GF, 8^{1}G, 8^{4}GF, 8^{0}GF,

	Starts	1st	2nd	3rd	Win & Pl
Career Total (Turf)	11	2	1	1	50700
Career Total (AW)	1	1	0	0	3724

112 7/09 Pont 1m4y GD £25546
109 6/09 Nott 1m75y G-F £12462
92 5/08 Kemp 1m STD £3723
Total win prize-money £41733

Going (Turf): Sf: 0-1 GS: 0-0 **Gd: 1-3 GF: 1-7** Fm: 0-0
Distance: 5f/6f: 0-0 7f-8f: 1-4 **9f-13f: 2-8** 14f+: 0-0
Track : **LH: 2-3** RH: 1-6 Tight: 0-2 Gall: 0-3
Aids: Bl: 0-0 Vi: 0-0 Tstrap: 0-0 Ckp: 0-0
Best Rating: 112 7/09 Pont 1m4y good

Smart; Listed winner; effective over 1m-1m2f; acts on fast ground; goes on Polytrack; often wears a tongue tie.

Khattaab (USA)

100 94

2-y-o b/br c Dixie Union (USA)-Jemima (Owington)
B W Hills Hamdan Al Maktoum

Placings:16 (6426)
2009: 6^{1}GF, 7^{6}GF,

	Starts	1st	2nd	3rd	Win & Pl
Career Total (Turf)	2	1	0	0	4696

90 8/09 Hayd 6f G-F £3885
Total win prize-money £3886

Going (Turf): Sf: 0-0 GS: 0-0 Gd: 0-0 **GF: 1-2** Fm: 0-0
Distance: **5f/6f: 1-1** 7f-8f: 0-1 9f-13f: 0-0 14f+: 0-0
Track : LH: 0-0 RH: 0-0 Tight: 0-0 Gall: 0-0
Aids: Bl: 0-0 Vi: 0-0 Tstrap: 0-0 Ckp: 0-0
Best Rating: 94 10/09 NmkR 7f gd-fm

Promising, very useful colt; effective at 6f, will get further; acts on quick ground.

Khayar (IRE)

100 67

3-y-o b c Refuse To Bend (IRE)-Khatela (IRE) (Shernazar)
E McNamara (M H Tompkins 21/10) Mrs Margaret Wilmott

Placings:0-64032031 (6543)
2009: 10^{6}G, 12^{4}GF, 11^{0}GS, 11^{3}G, 14^{2}GF, 14^{0}GF, 16^{3}GF, 14^{1}GF,

	Starts	1st	2nd	3rd	Win & Pl
Career Total (Turf)	9	1	1	2	4473

67 10/09 Wwck 1m6f213y (0-75)H G-F £2729
Total win prize-money £2730

Going (Turf): Sf: 0-0 GS: 0-1 Gd: 0-3 **GF: 1-5** Fm: 0-0
Distance: 5f/6f: 0-0 7f-8f: 0-1 9f-13f: 0-4 **14f+: 1-4**
Track : **LH: 1-7** RH: 0-1 Tight: 0-5 Gall: 0-2
Aids: Bl: 0-0 Vi: 0-0 Tstrap: 0-0 Ckp: 0-0
Best Rating: 67 10/09 Wwck 1m6f213y gd-fm

Moderate; stays 1m4f; acts on fast ground; has worn a tongue tie.

Khazara

82(57) 32

2-y-o ch f Starcraft (NZ)-Mystery Lot (IRE) (Revoque (IRE))
A King Barbury Castle Stud

Placings:000 (6930)
2009: 8^{0}SD, 8^{0}S, 8^{0}G,

	Starts	1st	2nd	3rd	Win & Pl
Career Total (Turf)	2	0	0	0	
Career Total (AW)	1	0	0	0	

Going (Turf): Sf: 0-1 GS: 0-0 Gd: 0-1 GF: 0-0 Fm: 0-0
Distance: 5f/6f: 0-0 7f-8f: 0-1 9f-13f: 0-2 14f+: 0-0
Track : LH: 0-2 RH: 0-1 Tight: 0-1 Gall: 0-0
Aids: Bl: 0-0 Vi: 0-0 Tstrap: 0-0 Ckp: 0-0
Best Rating: 32 10/09 Bath 1m5y good

Kheley (IRE)

99(103) (67)**72**
3-y-o b f Kheleyf (USA)-Namesake (Nashwan (USA))
W M Brisbourne W M Clare

Placings:63633533-1211P10304 (7738)
2009: 5[1]SD, 5[2]SD, 6[1]SD, 5[1]SD, 6[P]SD, 5[1]S, 5[0]SD, 5[3]SD, 5[0]SD, 6[4]SD,

	Starts	1st	2nd	3rd	Win & Pl
Career Total (Turf)	8	1	0	4	3591
Career Total (AW)	10	3	1	2	9249

72	9/09	Catt	5f	(0-65)H	SFT	£2388
67	1/09	Wolv	5f20y	(0-55)H	STD	£2729
57	1/09	Kemp	6f	(0-55)H	STD	£3043
51	1/09	Wolv	5f216y		STD	£2047

Total win prize-money £10209

Going (Turf): Sf: 1-2 GS: 0-1 Gd: 0-1 GF: 0-4 Fm: 0-0
Distance: 5f/6f: 4-15 7f-8f: 0-3 9f-13f: 0-0 14f+: 0-0
Track : LH: 2-7 RH: 1-4 **Tight: 2-6** Gall: 0-1
Aids: Bl: 0-0 Vi: 0-0 Tstrap: 0-0 Ckp: 0-0
Best Rating: 72 9/09 Catt 5f soft

Moderate; effective over 6f; acts on Polytrack.

Kheskianto (IRE)

101(101) (63)**83**
3-y-o b f Kheleyf (USA)-Gently (IRE) (Darshaan)
M C Chapman (M Botti 6/2) F A Dickinson

Placings:23233544-1652304025035020005 (7797)
2009: 7[1]SD, 7[6]GF, 6[5]SD, 7[2]GF, 7[3]F, 8[0]GF, 5[4]GF, 6[0]GF, 8[2]GF, 7[5]S, 6[0]G, 8[3]GF, 8[5]GF, 8[0]SD, 7[2]GF, 7[0]GF, 7[0]SD, 7[0]SD, 8[5]SS,

	Starts	1st	2nd	3rd	Win & Pl
Career Total (Turf)	19	0	5	5	10454
Career Total (AW)	8	1	0	0	2336

63	2/09	Sthl	7f	STD	£2047

Total win prize-money £2047

Going (Turf): Sf: 0-2 GS: 0-0 Gd: 0-6 GF: 0-10 Fm: 0-1
Distance: 5f/6f: 0-9 **7f-8f: 1-15** 9f-13f: 0-3 14f+: 0-0
Track : LH: 1-10 RH: 0-6 Tight: 0-3 Gall: 0-0
Aids: Bl: 0-0 Vi: 0-0 Tstrap: 0-0 Ckp: 0-0
Best Rating: 83 8/08 Livo 7f110y good

Modest; effective over 7f; acts on fast ground.

Kheylide (IRE)

98(97) (76)**72**
3-y-o ch g Kheleyf (USA)-Jayzdoll (IRE) (Stravinsky (USA))
Mrs D J Sanderson R J Budge

Placings:00331500-6210545300005650 (6857)
2009: 5[6]GF, 5[2]GF, 5[1]GF, 6[0]HY, 5[5]GF, 5[4]GF, 5[5]GF, 5[3]GF, 5[0]S, 5[0]GF, 5[0]G, 6[0]GF, 5[5]G, 5[6]GF, 5[5]GF, 5[0]SD,

	Starts	1st	2nd	3rd	Win & Pl
Career Total (Turf)	21	1	1	2	6295
Career Total (AW)	3	1	0	1	3527

71	5/09	NmkR	5f	(0-75)H	G-F	£3885
76	7/08	Ling	5f		STD	£3238

Total win prize-money £7124

Going (Turf): Sf: 0-3 GS: 0-0 Gd: 0-4 **GF: 1-14** Fm: 0-0
Distance: 5f/6f: 2-23 7f-8f: 0-1 9f-13f: 0-0 14f+: 0-0
Track : LH: 1-4 RH: 0-1 **Tight: 1-2** Gall: 0-3
Aids: Bl: 0-0 Vi: 0-1 Tstrap: 0-4 Ckp: 0-4
Best Rating: 76 7/08 Ling 5f stand

Fair; effective over 5f-6f; acts on fast ground; also goes on Polytrack.

Khor Dubai (IRE)

107(109) (109)**103**
3-y-o b c Kheleyf (USA)-Dievotchkina (IRE) (Bluebird (USA))
Saeed Bin Suroor Godolphin

Placings:301104641-663301231 (7431)
2009: 8[6]GF, 7[6]G, 7[3]GF, 7[3]GF, 7[0]GS, 7[1]SD, 7[2]G, 8[3]SD, 7[1]SD,

	Starts	1st	2nd	3rd	Win & Pl
Career Total (Turf)	14	3	1	3	35463
Career Total (AW)	4	2	0	1	22262

92	11/09	Kemp	7f		STD	£7352
103	8/09	Kemp	7f	(0-100)H	STD	£11091
86	10/08	NmkR	6f		G-S	£7477
91	7/08	Ling	6f		G-F	£3238
79	7/08	Yarm	6f3y		G-F	£3784

Total win prize-money £32944

Going (Turf): Sf: 0-0 GS: 1-2 Gd: 0-4 **GF: 2-8** Fm: 0-0
Distance: 5f/6f: 2-7 **7f-8f: 3-10** 9f-13f: 0-1 14f+: 0-0
Track : LH: 0-3 **RH: 2-5** Tight: 0-2 Gall: 0-0
Aids: Bl: 0-0 **Vi: 2-8** Tstrap: 0-0 Ckp: 0-0
Best Rating: 109 9/09 Wolv 1m141y stand

Smart; effective over 6-7f; acts on fast and easy ground, and on Polytrack; has worn a visor.

Khun John (IRE)

98(102) (82)**66**
6-y-o b g Marju (IRE)-Kathy Caerleon (IRE) (Caerleon (USA))
W J Musson (V R A Dartnall 9/4) The Strawberries To A Donkey Partnership

Placings:4111/33/5200300 (6640)
2009: 12[5]SD, 10[2]SD, 11[0]GF, 12[0]SD, 10[3]S, 10[0]G, 9[0]SD,

	Starts	1st	2nd	3rd	Win & Pl
Career Total (Turf)	5	0	0	3	1878
Career Total (AW)	8	3	1	0	11974

85	11/06	Kemp	1m2f	(0-75)H	STD	£5181
80	10/06	Ling	1m2f	(0-75)H	STD	£3238
67	10/06	Wolv	1m141y		STD	£2590

Total win prize-money £11012

Going (Turf): Sf: 0-1 GS: 0-0 Gd: 0-1 GF: 0-3 Fm: 0-0
Distance: 5f/6f: 0-0 7f-8f: 0-1 **9f-13f: 3-12** 14f+: 0-0
Track : LH: 2-7 RH: 1-4 **Tight: 2-8** Gall: 0-0
Aids: Bl: 0-0 Vi: 0-0 Tstrap: 0-0 Ckp: 0-0
Best Rating: 87 5/07 NmkR 1m2f gd-fm

Fair performer; stays 1m 2f and acts on Polytrack and on fast ground; can race prominently.

Kiama Bay (IRE)

98 **67**
3-y-o b g Fraam-La Panthere (USA) (Pine Bluff (USA))
J J Quinn Mrs S Quinn

Placings:606-01 (3018)
2009: 7[0]GF, 8[1]G,

	Starts	1st	2nd	3rd	Win & Pl
Career Total (Turf)	5	1	0	0	2267

67	6/09	Haml	1m65y	(0-60)H	GD	£2266

Total win prize-money £2267

Going (Turf): Sf: 0-0 GS: 0-2 **Gd: 1-2** GF: 0-1 Fm: 0-0
Distance: 5f/6f: 0-3 7f-8f: 0-1 **9f-13f: 1-1** 14f+: 0-0
Track : LH: 0-2 **RH: 1-2 Tight: 1-3** Gall: 0-0
Aids: Bl: 0-0 Vi: 0-0 Tstrap: 0-0 Ckp: 0-0
Best Rating: 67 6/09 Haml 1m65y good

Kickahead (USA)

58(95) (55)**65**
7-y-o b g Danzig (USA)-Krissante (USA) (Kris)
Ian Williams Churchill Office Solutions Limited

Placings:4/0000/054/4004 (7688)
2009: 8[4]SD, 8[0]F, 8[0]SD, 12[4]SD,

	Starts	1st	2nd	3rd	Win & Pl
Career Total (Turf)	7	0	0	0	0
Career Total (AW)	5	0	0	0	1271

Going (Turf): Sf: 0-2 GS: 0-0 Gd: 0-2 GF: 0-1 Fm: 0-1
Distance: 5f/6f: 0-1 7f-8f: 0-4 9f-13f: 0-7 14f+: 0-0
Track : LH: 0-4 RH: 0-4 Tight: 0-3 Gall: 0-0
Aids: Bl: 0-0 Vi: 0-0 Tstrap: 0-0 Ckp: 0-0
Best Rating: 72 6/05 Lonc 7f good

Kidlat

101(103) (85)**83**
4-y-o b g Cape Cross (IRE)-Arruhan (IRE) (Mujtahid (USA))
B G Powell John Stocker

Placings:4555-6225001355060 (6973)
2009: 10[6]SD, 10[2]SD, 10[2]SD, 11[5]GF, 10[0]S, 10[0]GF, 10[1]GF, 10[3]GF, 10[5]GS, 10[5]GF, 12[0]GF, 10[6]GF, 10[0]SD,

	Starts	1st	2nd	3rd	Win & Pl
Career Total (Turf)	12	1	0	1	4872
Career Total (AW)	5	0	2	0	2263

78	5/09	Chep	1m2f36y	(0-75)H	G-F	£3885

Total win prize-money £3886

Going (Turf): Sf: 0-1 GS: 0-1 Gd: 0-1 **GF: 1-9** Fm: 0-0
Distance: 5f/6f: 0-0 7f-8f: 0-2 **9f-13f: 1-15** 14f+: 0-0
Track : LH: 1-8 RH: 0-7 Tight: 0-6 Gall: 0-2
Aids: Bl: 0-0 Vi: 0-0 Tstrap: 0-0 Ckp: 0-0
Best Rating: 85 3/09 Kemp 1m2f stand

Fair; stays 1m2f; acts on fast ground; goes on Polytrack; has worn a tongue tie.

Kidnap (IRE)

(79) (31)
2-y-o b c Desert Style (IRE)-Rosalia (USA) (Red Ransom (USA))
M G Quinlan G Morrin

Placings:00 (7749)
2009: 5[0]SD, 5[0]SD,

	Starts	1st	2nd	3rd	Win & Pl
Career Total (Turf)	0	0	0	0	
Career Total (AW)	2	0	0	0	

Going (Turf): Sf: 0-0 GS: 0-0 Gd: 0-0 GF: 0-0 Fm: 0-0
Distance: 5f/6f: 0-2 7f-8f: 0-0 9f-13f: 0-0 14f+: 0-0
Track : LH: 0-2 RH: 0-0 Tight: 0-2 Gall: 0-0
Aids: Bl: 0-0 Vi: 0-0 Tstrap: 0-0 Ckp: 0-0
Best Rating: 31 10/09 Wolv 5f216y stand

Kidson (USA)

96(71) (27)**54**
3-y-o b/br g Lemon Drop Kid (USA)-Solo (USA) (Halo (USA))

George Baker Michael Watt & Happy Valley Syndicate

Placings:000-0223 **(4470)**
2009: 11^{0}G, 14^{2}S, 16^{2}G, 16^{3}HY,

	Starts	1st	2nd	3rd	Win & Pl
Career Total (Turf)	6	0	2	1	1883
Career Total (AW)	1	0	0	0	

Going (Turf): Sf: 0-2 GS: 0-1 Gd: 0-3 GF: 0-0 Fm: 0-0
Distance: 5f/6f: 0-0 7f-8f: 0-3 9f-13f: 0-1 14f+: 0-3
Track : LH: 0-3 RH: 0-2 Tight: 0-3 Gall: 0-0
Aids: Bl: 0-0 Vi: 0-0 Tstrap: 0-0 Ckp: 0-0
Best Rating: 54 7/09 Bevl 2m35y good

Moderate; stays 1m6f and acts on soft ground.

Kielty's Folly

95(100) (59)48
5-y-o gr g Weet-A-Minute (IRE)-Three Sweeties (Cruise Missile)
B P J Baugh Saddle Up Racing

Placings:066/0535-226550251 **(7814)**
2009: 9^{2}SD, 8^{2}SD, 8^{6}SD, 8^{5}GF, 9^{5}G, 8^{0}G, 9^{2}SD, 8^{5}SD, 8^{1}SD,

	Starts	1st	2nd	3rd	Win & Pl
Career Total (Turf)	7	0	0	1	353
Career Total (AW)	9	1	3	0	2977

59 12/09 Wolv 1m141y (0-50)H STD £1364
Total win prize-money £1365

Going (Turf): Sf: 0-1 GS: 0-1 Gd: 0-2 GF: 0-2 Fm: 0-1
Distance: 5f/6f: 0-0 7f-8f: 0-5 **9f-13f: 1-11** 14f+: 0-0
Track : **LH: 1-12** RH: 0-1 **Tight: 1-8** Gall: 0-0
Aids: Bl: 0-0 Vi: 0-0 Tstrap: 0-0 Ckp: 0-0
Best Rating: 59 12/09 Wolv 1m141y stand

Moderate; effective at around 1m-1m2f; acts on easy ground; goes on Polytrack.

Kiho

103(93) (53)66
4-y-o b g Dashing Blade-Krim (GER) (Lagunas)
Eve Johnson Houghton R F Johnson Houghton

Placings:6/02450-6050334 **(3788)**
2009: 12^{6}G, 12^{0}SD, 14^{5}GF, 12^{0}GS, 17^{3}F, 14^{3}GF, 14^{4}GF,

	Starts	1st	2nd	3rd	Win & Pl
Career Total (Turf)	12	0	1	2	2306
Career Total (AW)	1	0	0	0	

Going (Turf): Sf: 0-0 GS: 0-3 Gd: 0-3 GF: 0-5 Fm: 0-1
Distance: 5f/6f: 0-0 7f-8f: 0-1 9f-13f: 0-7 14f+: 0-5
Track : LH: 0-11 RH: 0-1 Tight: 0-6 Gall: 0-3
Aids: Bl: 0-4 Vi: 0-0 Tstrap: 0-0 Ckp: 0-0
Best Rating: 69 10/07 Bath 1m5y good

Modest; stays 2m1f; acts on good/fast ground.

Kilburn

101(104) (76)74
5-y-o b g Grand Lodge (USA)-Lady Lahar (Fraam)
A J Lidderdale Lidderdale Racing LLP

Placings:3015/000006/21306 **(2495)**
2009: 8^{2}SD, 8^{1}SD, 7^{3}SD, 8^{0}GF, 8^{6}GF,

	Starts	1st	2nd	3rd	Win & Pl
Career Total (Turf)	12	1	0	1	11527
Career Total (AW)	3	1	1	1	3355

76 3/09 Ling 1m (0-65)H STD £2047
84 8/06 Gdwd 7f G-F £10363
Total win prize-money £12410

Going (Turf): Sf: 0-0 GS: 0-1 Gd: 0-5 **GF: 1-6** Fm: 0-0
Distance: 5f/6f: 0-1 **7f-8f: 2-9** 9f-13f: 0-5 14f+: 0-0
Track : LH: 1-3 RH: 1-7 **Tight: 1-2** Gall: 0-0
Aids: Bl: 0-0 Vi: 0-0 Tstrap: 0-1 Ckp: 0-1
Best Rating: 84 8/06 Gdwd 7f gd-fm

Fair; stays 7f, should get further; acts on fast ground; has worn cheekpieces.

Kildangan Girl

77(75) (31)43
2-y-o b f Refuse To Bend (IRE)-Paola Maria (Daylami (IRE))
W R Muir Peter C Bourke

Placings:5600 **(5613)**
2009: 5^{5}GF, 5^{6}S, 6^{0}SD, 7^{0}SD,

	Starts	1st	2nd	3rd	Win & Pl
Career Total (Turf)	2	0	0	0	0
Career Total (AW)	2	0	0	0	

Going (Turf): Sf: 0-1 GS: 0-0 Gd: 0-0 GF: 0-1 Fm: 0-0
Distance: 5f/6f: 0-3 7f-8f: 0-1 9f-13f: 0-0 14f+: 0-0
Track : LH: 0-2 RH: 0-0 Tight: 0-2 Gall: 0-0
Aids: Bl: 0-0 Vi: 0-0 Tstrap: 0-0 Ckp: 0-0
Best Rating: 43 7/09 Leic 5f218y soft

Kildare Sun (IRE)

102(108) (79)73
7-y-o b g Desert Sun-Megan's Dream (IRE) (Fayruz)
J Mackie Mrs Barbara Woodworth

Placings:0/040131102/665052000/54120405-03353322300051 **(6806)**
2009: 9^{0}SD, 9^{3}SD, 9^{3}SD, 10^{5}GF, 8^{3}F, 8^{3}GF, 8^{2}G, 8^{2}F, 8^{3}GF, 7^{0}GF, 8^{0}GS, 8^{0}GF, 8^{5}SD, 9^{1}SD,

	Starts	1st	2nd	3rd	Win & Pl
Career Total (Turf)	21	0	2	3	4750
Career Total (AW)	20	5	3	3	22521

74 10/09 Wolv 1m1f103y (0-70)H STD £2914
75 3/08 Wolv 1m141y (0-70)H STD £2331
83 11/06 Wolv 1m1f103y (0-85)H STD £5505
80 11/06 Wolv 1m1f103y (0-70)H STD £3238
72 10/06 Wolv 1m1f103y (0-65)H SF £3238
Total win prize-money £17229

Going (Turf): Sf: 0-1 GS: 0-3 Gd: 0-6 GF: 0-8 Fm: 0-2
Distance: 5f/6f: 0-0 7f-8f: 0-8 **9f-13f: 5-33** 14f+: 0-0
Track : **LH: 5-34** RH: 0-5 **Tight: 5-26** Gall: 0-1
Aids: Bl: 0-0 Vi: 0-4 Tstrap: 1-6 Ckp: 1-6
Best Rating: 83 11/06 Wolv 1m1f103y stand

Modest; stays 1m1f; acts on a sound surface; goes on Polytrack.

Kilkenny Bay

70(84) (57)21
3-y-o b f Tobougg (IRE)-Miss Arizona (IRE) (Sure Blade (USA))
W Jarvis Patrick Swift

Placings:30-0 **(2082)**
2009: 8^{0}GF,

	Starts	1st	2nd	3rd	Win & Pl
Career Total (Turf)	1	0	0	0	
Career Total (AW)	2	0	0	1	433

Going (Turf): Sf: 0-0 GS: 0-0 Gd: 0-0 GF: 0-1 Fm: 0-0
Distance: 5f/6f: 0-1 7f-8f: 0-2 9f-13f: 0-0 14f+: 0-0
Track : LH: 0-2 RH: 0-0 Tight: 0-1 Gall: 0-1
Aids: Bl: 0-0 Vi: 0-0 Tstrap: 0-0 Ckp: 0-0
Best Rating: 57 12/08 GrLe 6f stand

Killer Class

98 70
4-y-o ch f Kyllachy-Class Wan (Safawan)
J S Goldie Frank Brady

Placings:0000/11130320230341 5600-0005030 **(7081)**
2009: 5^{0}G, 5^{0}S, 5^{0}GS, 5^{5}GS, 5^{0}G, 5^{3}GF, 5^{0}S,

	Starts	1st	2nd	3rd	Win & Pl
Career Total (Turf)	29	4	2	5	16977

70 8/08 Ayr 5f (0-80)H SFT £5180
65 4/08 Nott 5f13y (0-70)H SFT £2590
59 4/08 Catt 5f (0-60)H G-S £2047
53 3/08 Rdcr 5f (0-60)H G-S £1943
Total win prize-money £11761

Going (Turf): **Sf: 2-12 GS: 2-8** Gd: 0-3 GF: 0-5 Fm: 0-1
Distance: **5f/6f: 4-29** 7f-8f: 0-0 9f-13f: 0-0 14f+: 0-0
Track : LH: 0-0 RH: 0-2 Tight: 0-0 Gall: 0-2
Aids: Bl: 0-0 Vi: 0-0 Tstrap: 0-0 Ckp: 0-0
Best Rating: 70 9/08 Ayr 5f heavy

Modest sprinter; suited by 5f; acts on soft ground.

Killusty Fancy (IRE)

82(71) (28)65
2-y-o b c Refuse To Bend (IRE)-Crafty Fancy (IRE) (Intikhab (USA))
D J S Ffrench Davis Mrs F Houlihan

Placings:0030 **(6071)**
2009: 6^{0}GS, 7^{0}G, 7^{3}HY, 7^{0}SD,

	Starts	1st	2nd	3rd	Win & Pl
Career Total (Turf)	3	0	0	1	770
Career Total (AW)	1	0	0	0	

Going (Turf): Sf: 0-1 GS: 0-1 Gd: 0-1 GF: 0-0 Fm: 0-0
Distance: 5f/6f: 0-1 7f-8f: 0-3 9f-13f: 0-0 14f+: 0-0
Track : LH: 0-2 RH: 0-0 Tight: 0-2 Gall: 0-1
Aids: Bl: 0-0 Vi: 0-0 Tstrap: 0-0 Ckp: 0-0
Best Rating: 65 8/09 Leic 7f9y heavy

Kilmanseck

86 65
2-y-o b g Royal Applause-Corndavon (USA) (Sheikh Albadou)
Eve Johnson Houghton Anthony Pye-Jeary And Mel Smith

Placings:00020 **(6590)**
2009: 6^{0}GF, 7^{0}G, 6^{0}G, 7^{2}GF, 6^{0}GS,

	Starts	1st	2nd	3rd	Win & Pl
Career Total (Turf)	5	0	1	0	1060

Going (Turf): Sf: 0-0 GS: 0-1 Gd: 0-2 GF: 0-2 Fm: 0-0
Distance: 5f/6f: 0-1 7f-8f: 0-4 9f-13f: 0-0 14f+: 0-0
Track : LH: 0-2 RH: 0-0 Tight: 0-0 Gall: 0-0
Aids: Bl: 0-0 Vi: 0-0 Tstrap: 0-0 Ckp: 0-0
Best Rating: 65 9/09 Wwck 7f26y gd-fm

Kilmeena Dream

68(75) (31)
5-y-o b m Foxhound (USA)-Kilmeena Glen (Beveled (USA))

J C Fox Mrs J A Cleary

Placings:0/000 (3071)
2009: 6⁰SD, 6⁰GF, 6⁰G,

	Starts	1st	2nd	3rd	Win & Pl
Career Total (Turf)	2	0	0	0	
Career Total (AW)	2	0	0	0	

Going (Turf): Sf: 0-0 GS: 0-0 Gd: 0-1 GF: 0-1 Fm: 0-0
Distance: 5f/6f: 0-2 7f-8f: 0-2 9f-13f: 0-0 14f+: 0-0
Track : LH: 0-2 RH: 0-1 Tight: 0-1 Gall: 0-0
Aids: Bl: 0-0 Vi: 0-0 Tstrap: 0-0 Ckp: 0-0
Best Rating: 31 12/07 Kemp 7f stand

Kilmeena Magic

(94) (20)47
7-y-o b m Fumo Di Londra (IRE)-Kilmeena Lady (Inca Chief (USA))
J C Fox Mrs J A Cleary

Placings:0000054056443523/0603506406/260-0 (6612)
2009: 12⁰SD,

	Starts	1st	2nd	3rd	Win & Pl
Career Total (Turf)	9	0	0	0	337
Career Total (AW)	21	0	2	3	1411

Going (Turf): Sf: 0-2 GS: 0-2 Gd: 0-3 GF: 0-1 Fm: 0-1
Distance: 5f/6f: 0-0 7f-8f: 0-6 9f-13f: 0-24 14f+: 0-0
Track : LH: 0-11 RH: 0-16 Tight: 0-10 Gall: 0-1
Aids: Bl: 0-0 Vi: 0-0 Tstrap: 0-1 Ckp: 0-1
Best Rating: 52 1/08 Kemp 1m4f stand

Moderate; stays 1m 2f; acts on Polytrack.

Kilmun

81(84) (18)35
3-y-o b g Zamindar (USA)-Didicoy (USA) (Danzig (USA))
K A Ryan Sunpak Potatoes

Placings:00000 (7796)
2009: 6⁰GF, 8⁰GF, 6⁰GF, 7⁰SD, 7⁰SS,

	Starts	1st	2nd	3rd	Win & Pl
Career Total (Turf)	3	0	0	0	
Career Total (AW)	2	0	0	0	

Going (Turf): Sf: 0-0 GS: 0-0 Gd: 0-0 GF: 0-3 Fm: 0-0
Distance: 5f/6f: 0-2 7f-8f: 0-2 9f-13f: 0-1 14f+: 0-0
Track : LH: 0-2 RH: 0-1 Tight: 0-0 Gall: 0-0
Aids: Bl: 0-1 Vi: 0-0 Tstrap: 0-0 Ckp: 0-0
Best Rating: 35 9/09 Nott 1m75y gd-fm

Kilsyth (IRE)

(77) (16)56
3-y-o b f Marju (IRE)-Easter Song (USA) (Rubiano (USA))
S Parr Willie McKay

Placings:005000-0 (0564)
2009: 8⁰SD,

	Starts	1st	2nd	3rd	Win & Pl
Career Total (Turf)	5	0	0	0	0
Career Total (AW)	2	0	0	0	

Going (Turf): Sf: 0-2 GS: 0-2 Gd: 0-0 GF: 0-1 Fm: 0-0
Distance: 5f/6f: 0-2 7f-8f: 0-3 9f-13f: 0-2 14f+: 0-0
Track : LH: 0-5 RH: 0-0 Tight: 0-2 Gall: 0-0
Aids: Bl: 0-0 Vi: 0-0 Tstrap: 0-0 Ckp: 0-0
Best Rating: 56 9/08 Hayd 1m30y gd-fm

Kilt Rock (IRE)

88(94) (71)60
2-y-o ch g Giant's Causeway (USA)-Eliza (USA) (Mt. Livermore (USA))
T G Mills Mrs L M Askew

Placings:600215 (6829)
2009: 6⁶GF, 7⁰GF, 6⁰GF, 5²SD, 6¹SD, 7⁵SF,

	Starts	1st	2nd	3rd	Win & Pl
Career Total (Turf)	3	0	0	0	0
Career Total (AW)	3	1	1	0	2752

71 10/09 Kemp 6f (0-65) STD £2047
Total win prize-money £2047

Going (Turf): Sf: 0-0 GS: 0-0 Gd: 0-0 GF: 0-3 Fm: 0-0
Distance: **5f/6f: 1-4** 7f-8f: 0-2 9f-13f: 0-0 14f+: 0-0
Track : LH: 0-2 **RH: 1-1** Tight: 0-2 Gall: 0-1
Aids: Bl: 0-0 Vi: 0-0 Tstrap: 0-0 Ckp: 0-0
Best Rating: 71 10/09 Kemp 6f stand

Modest; stays 6f; acts on Polytrack.

Kimberley Downs (USA)

99(104) (90)89
3-y-o gr g Giant's Causeway (USA)-Fountain Lake (USA) (Vigors (USA))
M Johnston Favourites Racing XIX

Placings:41-160010 (6734)
2009: 9¹SD, 12⁶GF, 12⁰GF, 14⁰G, 16¹GF, 14⁰S,

	Starts	1st	2nd	3rd	Win & Pl
Career Total (Turf)	5	1	0	0	7771
Career Total (AW)	3	2	0	0	8336

89 9/09 Asct 2m (0-95)H G-F £7771
90 4/09 Wolv 1m1f103y (0-80)H STD £5180
79 11/08 Wolv 1m141y STD £2914
Total win prize-money £15866

Going (Turf): Sf: 0-1 GS: 0-0 Gd: 0-1 **GF: 1-3** Fm: 0-0
Distance: 5f/6f: 0-0 7f-8f: 0-1 **9f-13f: 2-4** 14f+: 1-3
Track : **LH: 2-5** RH: 1-3 **Tight: 2-4** Gall: 1-4
Aids: Bl: 0-0 **Vi: 1-2** Tstrap: 0-0 Ckp: 0-0
Best Rating: 90 4/09 Wolv 1m1f103y stand

Useful; stays 2m; acts on Polytrack and fast ground; has worn a visor.

Kimberley Rocks (IRE)

95(95) (46)58
3-y-o b f Intikhab (USA)-Kalimar (IRE) (Bigstone (IRE))
R M Beckett P K Gardner

Placings:P53000 (6031)
2009: 8ᴾGF, 8⁵G, 8³G, 8⁰SD, 8⁰GS, 9⁰SD,

	Starts	1st	2nd	3rd	Win & Pl
Career Total (Turf)	4	0	0	1	403
Career Total (AW)	2	0	0	0	

Going (Turf): Sf: 0-0 GS: 0-1 Gd: 0-2 GF: 0-1 Fm: 0-0
Distance: 5f/6f: 0-0 7f-8f: 0-2 9f-13f: 0-4 14f+: 0-0
Track : LH: 0-2 RH: 0-3 Tight: 0-4 Gall: 0-0
Aids: Bl: 0-0 Vi: 0-0 Tstrap: 0-0 Ckp: 0-0
Best Rating: 58 7/09 Wind 1m67y good

Kina Jazz

80(90) (47)10
3-y-o b f Kyllachy-Tapas En Bal (FR) (Mille Balles (FR))
J Ryan (M Botti 22/10) Rothmere Racing Limited

Placings:005-405600 (7462)
2009: 5⁴SD, 6⁰SD, 6⁵SD, 5⁶SF, 7⁰G, 5⁰SD,

	Starts	1st	2nd	3rd	Win & Pl
Career Total (Turf)	2	0	0	0	
Career Total (AW)	7	0	0	0	0

Going (Turf): Sf: 0-0 GS: 0-1 Gd: 0-1 GF: 0-0 Fm: 0-0
Distance: 5f/6f: 0-8 7f-8f: 0-1 9f-13f: 0-0 14f+: 0-0
Track : LH: 0-7 RH: 0-1 Tight: 0-5 Gall: 0-1
Aids: Bl: 0-1 Vi: 0-1 Tstrap: 0-0 Ckp: 0-0
Best Rating: 47 2/09 Ling 6f stand

Kind Heart

104(97) (77)77
3-y-o b f Red Ransom (USA)-Portorosa (USA) (Irish River (FR))
D McCain Jnr (P Howling 6/10) D McCain

Placings:221-43412 (6570)
2009: 12⁴G, 10³G, 11⁴SD, 10¹GF, 9²GF,

	Starts	1st	2nd	3rd	Win & Pl
Career Total (Turf)	4	1	1	1	3520
Career Total (AW)	4	1	2	0	6328

57 9/09 Rdcr 1m2f G-F £2047
77 11/08 Sthl 1m STD £3885
Total win prize-money £5933

Going (Turf): Sf: 0-0 GS: 0-0 Gd: 0-2 **GF: 1-2** Fm: 0-0
Distance: 5f/6f: 0-2 7f-8f: 1-1 9f-13f: 1-5 14f+: 0-0
Track : **LH: 2-7** RH: 0-1 **Tight: 1-2** Gall: 0-2
Aids: Bl: 0-0 Vi: 0-0 Tstrap: 0-0 Ckp: 0-0
Best Rating: 77 7/09 Thsk 1m4f good

Fair; stays 1m2f; acts on decent ground; goes on Fibresand and Polytrack.

Kindest

102 80
3-y-o b f Cadeaux Genereux-Star Profile (IRE) (Sadler's Wells (USA))
C F Wall Peter Botham

Placings:0545122 (4799)
2009: 8⁰GF, 8⁵G, 8⁴G, 8⁵GF, 8¹S, 8²HY, 8²G,

	Starts	1st	2nd	3rd	Win & Pl
Career Total (Turf)	7	1	2	0	5743

77 7/09 Hayd 1m30y (0-70)H SFT £3238
Total win prize-money £3238

Going (Turf): **Sf: 1-2** GS: 0-0 Gd: 0-3 GF: 0-2 Fm: 0-0
Distance: 5f/6f: 0-0 7f-8f: 0-1 **9f-13f: 1-6** 14f+: 0-0
Track : **LH: 1-3** RH: 0-3 Tight: 0-3 Gall: 0-0
Aids: Bl: 0-0 Vi: 0-0 Tstrap: 0-0 Ckp: 0-0
Best Rating: 80 7/09 Nott 1m75y heavy

Fair; stays 1m; acts on good and soft ground.

Kindlelight Blue (IRE)

(105) (80)71
5-y-o gr g Golan (IRE)-Kalimar (IRE) (Bigstone (IRE))
N P Littmoden Kindlelight Ltd

Placings:504/0520401263412/134000-5 (0873)

2009: 10^{5}SD,

	Starts	1st	2nd	3rd	Win & Pl
Career Total (Turf)	11	0	1	0	1348
Career Total (AW)	12	3	2	2	8444

74 11/07 Ling 1m2f (0-75)H STD £2817
69 8/07 Ling 1m2f (0-62)H STD £2047
Total win prize-money £4865

Going (Turf): Sf: 0-0 GS: 0-1 Gd: 0-2 GF: 0-7 Fm: 0-1
Distance: 5f/6f: 0-2 7f-8f: 0-3 **9f-13f: 3-18** 14f+: 0-0
Track : **LH: 3-15** RH: 0-3 **Tight: 3-13** Gall: 0-3
Aids: Bl: 0-0 Vi: 0-0 Tstrap: 0-0 Ckp: 0-0
Best Rating: 80 1/08 Ling 1m2f stand

Fair; stays 1m2f; acts on Polytrack.

Kinetic Art (IRE)

77 **7**

4-y-o b g Mull Of Kintyre (USA)-Sylviani (Ashkalani (IRE))
R M Whitaker Six Iron Partnership

Placings:60 **(6248)**
2009: 13^{6}G, 10^{0}GF,

	Starts	1st	2nd	3rd	Win & Pl
Career Total (Turf)	2	0	0	0	0

Going (Turf): Sf: 0-0 GS: 0-0 Gd: 0-1 GF: 0-1 Fm: 0-0
Distance: 5f/6f: 0-0 7f-8f: 0-0 9f-13f: 0-1 14f+: 0-1
Track : LH: 0-2 RH: 0-0 Tight: 0-1 Gall: 0-0
Aids: Bl: 0-0 Vi: 0-0 Tstrap: 0-0 Ckp: 0-0
Best Rating: 7 7/09 Catt 1m5f175y good

Kinetix

98(92) (59)**74**

3-y-o gr f Linamix (FR)-Kalambara (IRE) (Bluebird (USA))
J H M Gosden Helena Springfield Ltd

Placings:222233 **(7367)**
2009: 8^{2}F, 10^{2}GF, 10^{2}GF, 11^{2}G, 12^{3}SD, 12^{3}SD,

	Starts	1st	2nd	3rd	Win & Pl
Career Total (Turf)	4	0	4	0	3603
Career Total (AW)	2	0	0	2	1106

Going (Turf): Sf: 0-0 GS: 0-0 Gd: 0-1 GF: 0-2 Fm: 0-1
Distance: 5f/6f: 0-0 7f-8f: 0-0 9f-13f: 0-6 14f+: 0-0
Track : LH: 0-5 RH: 0-1 Tight: 0-3 Gall: 0-1
Aids: Bl: 0-0 Vi: 0-0 Tstrap: 0-0 Ckp: 0-0
Best Rating: 74 7/09 Epsm 1m2f18y gd-fm

Fair; stays 1m3f; acts on good ground.

King Bathwick (IRE)

(84) (60)**67**

4-y-o b g Golan (IRE)-Princess Sabaah (IRE) (Desert King (IRE))
A B Haynes W Clifford

Placings:65360455/32000-0 **(0042)**
2009: 8^{0}SD,

	Starts	1st	2nd	3rd	Win & Pl
Career Total (Turf)	12	0	1	2	2023
Career Total (AW)	2	0	0	0	0

Going (Turf): Sf: 0-4 GS: 0-2 Gd: 0-1 GF: 0-5 Fm: 0-0
Distance: 5f/6f: 0-2 7f-8f: 0-6 9f-13f: 0-6 14f+: 0-0
Track : LH: 0-5 RH: 0-3 Tight: 0-5 Gall: 0-0
Aids: Bl: 0-1 Vi: 0-0 Tstrap: 0-0 Ckp: 0-0
Best Rating: 67 4/08 Bath 1m2f46y soft

Modest; effective at around 1m2f; acts on most ground but seems suited to soft; has worn blinkers.

King Charles

106 (88)**105**

5-y-o b g King's Best (USA)-Charlecote (IRE) (Caerleon (USA))
E A L Dunlop Khalifa Sultan

Placings:0050111/4202331/03353600-660415000450 **(7035)**
2009: 9^{6}GF, 12^{6}GS, 10^{0}GF, 10^{4}G, 10^{1}GS, 10^{5}G, 12^{0}GS, 10^{0}GF, 10^{0}GS, 10^{4}GF, 12^{5}G, 10^{0}S,

	Starts	1st	2nd	3rd	Win & Pl
Career Total (Turf)	33	4	2	5	65349
Career Total (AW)	1	1	0	0	3886

101 7/09 Newb 1m2f6y (0-95)H G-S £7477
99 9/07 Asct 1m2f (0-90) G-S £11217
84 9/06 NmkR 1m G-F £12954
88 9/06 Ling 7f (0-75) STD £3886
76 9/06 Ling 7f (0-75) GD £3886
Total win prize-money £39421

Going (Turf): Sf: 0-3 **GS: 2-7** Gd: 1-7 GF: 1-15 Fm: 0-1
Distance: 5f/6f: 0-3 **7f-8f: 3-5** 9f-13f: 2-26 14f+: 0-0
Track : **LH: 2-13** RH: 1-14 Tight: 1-5 **Gall: 2-19**
Aids: Bl: 0-3 Vi: 0-0 Tstrap: 0-1 Ckp: 0-1
Best Rating: 105 6/08 Asct 1m4f gd-fm

Very useful; effective at 1m2f-1m4f and acts on most ground; has worn cheekpieces and blinkers.

King Columbo (IRE)

104(100) (86)**79**

4-y-o ch g King Charlemagne (USA)-Columbian Sand (IRE) (Salmon Leap (USA))
Miss J Feilden Columbian Kings

Placings:515/206003-53461450200 **(7189)**
2009: 8^{5}GF, 10^{3}GF, 10^{4}GF, 8^{6}GF, 8^{1}GS, 8^{4}S, 8^{5}G, 8^{0}G, 8^{2}GF, 7^{0}GF, 7^{0}G,

	Starts	1st	2nd	3rd	Win & Pl
Career Total (Turf)	16	1	1	2	8195
Career Total (AW)	4	1	1	0	3533

74 6/09 NmkJ 1m (0-75)H G-S £3885
70 10/07 Kemp 1m STD £2047
Total win prize-money £5934

Going (Turf): Sf: 0-1 **GS: 1-3** Gd: 0-4 GF: 0-8 Fm: 0-0
Distance: 5f/6f: 0-0 **7f-8f: 2-11** 9f-13f: 0-9 14f+: 0-0
Track : LH: 0-2 **RH: 1-5** Tight: 0-2 Gall: 0-1
Aids: Bl: 0-0 Vi: 0-1 Tstrap: 0-0 Ckp: 0-0
Best Rating: 86 6/08 Kemp 1m stand

Fair; stays at least 1m; handles most ground and Polytrack.

King De Lune (FR)

(98) (63)

7-y-o ch g Muhtathir-Eclipse De Lune (USA) (Shahrastani (USA))
C E Longsdon Transbuild Pack

Placings:001/05/10021/**36** **(0835)**
2009: 13^{3}SF, 16^{6}SD,

	Starts	1st	2nd	3rd	Win & Pl
Career Total (Turf)	10	3	1	0	10920
Career Total (AW)	2	0	0	1	302

9/07 Land 1m5f G-F £2364
5/07 Roya 1m6f110y HVY £3040
9/05 Chat 1m5f G-S £4255
Total win prize-money £9661

Going (Turf): Sf: 1-5 GS: 1-1 Gd: 0-2 **GF: 1-1** Fm: 0-0
Distance: 5f/6f: 0-0 7f-8f: 0-0 **9f-13f: 2-8** 14f+: 1-4
Track : LH: 0-2 RH: 0-2 Tight: 0-2 Gall: 0-0
Aids: **Bl: 2-5** Vi: 0-0 Tstrap: 0-0 Ckp: 0-0
Best Rating: 63 2/09 Wolv 1m5f194y std-fst

Moderate; effective over 1m5f; acts on Polytrack.

King Fernando

81 **44**

6-y-o gr g Silver Patriarch (IRE)-Kastelruth (Midyan (USA))
P Beaumont (S Smrczek 2/5) Mrs C M Clarke

Placings:0012/001100042**315**/**41310**-**6046**551530 **(3068)**
2009: 12^{6}SD, 12^{0}SD, 12^{4}SD, 12^{6}SD, 10^{5}S, 12^{5}HY, 10^{1}SD, 12^{5}G, 12^{3}G, 12^{0}GS,

	Starts	1st	2nd	3rd	Win & Pl
Career Total (Turf)	20	3	1	3	8781
Career Total (AW)	11	4	1	0	4658

4/09 Sons 1m2f STD £583
4/08 Colo 1m3f H HVY £1691
2/08 Dort 1m1f165y H STD £1176
12/07 Dort 1m4f110y H SLW £1351
7/07 Hamb 1m6f H SFT £3378
6/07 Brem 1m3f H GD £1587
11/06 Ghli 5f STD £689
Total win prize-money £10457

Going (Turf): **Sf: 2-10** GS: 0-1 Gd: 1-9 GF: 0-0 Fm: 0-0
Distance: 5f/6f: 1-1 7f-8f: 0-0 **9f-13f: 5-27** 14f+: 1-3
Track : LH: 0-1 RH: 0-1 Tight: 0-1 Gall: 0-0
Aids: **Bl: 1-5** Vi: 0-0 Tstrap: 0-0 Ckp: 0-0
Best Rating: 44 6/09 Ripn 1m4f10y gd-sft

King Fingal (IRE)

104 **85**

4-y-o b g King's Best (USA)-Llia (Shirley Heights)
J J Quinn Geoffrey Van Cutsem

Placings:02441601-4200550 **(6681)**
2009: 12^{4}GF, 12^{2}GS, 11^{0}GF, 12^{0}G, 12^{5}G, 12^{5}S, 12^{0}G,

	Starts	1st	2nd	3rd	Win & Pl
Career Total (Turf)	15	2	2	0	13028

85 10/08 Pont 1m2f6y (0-75)H G-S £3885
79 7/08 Thsk 1m (0-85)H G-F £5569
Total win prize-money £9455

Going (Turf): Sf: 0-1 **GS: 1-3** Gd: 0-4 **GF: 1-6** Fm: 0-1
Distance: 5f/6f: 0-0 7f-8f: 1-6 9f-13f: 1-9 14f+: 0-0
Track : **LH: 2-11** RH: 0-1 **Tight: 1-6** Gall: 0-4
Aids: Bl: 0-0 Vi: 0-0 Tstrap: 0-0 Ckp: 0-0
Best Rating: 85 6/09 Donc 1m4f gd-sft

Fair; stays 1m4f; acts on fast and easy ground; has worn a tongue tie.

King Gabriel (IRE)

(97) (50)**43**

7-y-o b g Desert King (IRE)-Broken Spirit (IRE) (Slip Anchor)
Andrew Turnell Miss A Jones

Placings:06/4000/**54**/60/**55** **(0669)**
2009: 12^{5}SD, 11^{5}SD,

	Starts	1st	2nd	3rd	Win & Pl
Career Total (Turf)	7	0	0	0	284

	Starts	1st	2nd	3rd	Win & Pl
Career Total (AW)	5	0	0	0	0

Going (Turf): Sf: 0-1 GS: 0-1 Gd: 0-2 GF: 0-3 Fm: 0-0
Distance: 5f/6f: 0-0 7f-8f: 0-2 9f-13f: 0-10 14f+: 0-0
Track : LH: 0-7 RH: 0-3 Tight: 0-4 Gall: 0-1
Aids: Bl: 0-0 Vi: 0-0 Tstrap: 0-0 Ckp: 0-0
Best Rating: 64 10/04 Bath 1m5y soft

Modest performer; effective up to an extended 1m1f; acts on most ground.

King In Waiting (IRE)

95(97) (63)68
6-y-o b g Sadler's Wells (USA)-Ballerina (IRE) (Dancing Brave (USA))
J Hetherton (A D Brown 19/2) Akv Cladding Fabrications Ltd

Placings:13/03205/650000525 (6676)
2009: 8^6G, 10^5S, 10^0GS, 12^0G, 16^0GS, 11^0GF, 16^5GS, 16^2SD, 18^5G,

	Starts	1st	2nd	3rd	Win & Pl
Career Total (Turf)	15	1	1	2	21022
Career Total (AW)	1	0	1	0	964
88 3/06 Curr 1m				SH	£8979

Total win prize-money £8979

Going (Turf): Sf: 0-2 GS: 0-3 Gd: 0-5 GF: 0-3 Fm: 0-0
Distance: 5f/6f: 0-0 7f-8f: 1-1 9f-13f: 0-9 14f+: 0-6
Track : LH: 0-11 RH: 1-4 Tight: 0-3 Gall: 1-4
Aids: Bl: 0-3 Vi: 0-5 Tstrap: 0-0 Ckp: 0-0
Best Rating: 101 5/06 Curr 1m2f soft

Modest; stays 2m; seems to go on most ground.

King Jock (USA)

115(105) (82)112
8-y-o b g Ghazi (USA)-Glen Kate (Glenstal (USA))
R J Osborne (A Manuel 26/2) Thistle Bloodstock Limited

Placings:22/100551/0013452066062 0/1545414311/20543 4524315/55200160034-40360006 (6530a)
2009: 7^4GS, 8^0G, 7^3G, 8^6GF, 8^0GY, 7^0GF, 8^0S, 7^6GF,

	Starts	1st	2nd	3rd	Win & Pl
Career Total (Turf)	60	9	7	6	341134
Career Total (AW)	3	0	0	0	1809
112 6/08 Siro 1m				G-S	£42188
106 10/07 Curr 1m				SFT	£9017
102 12/06 AbuD 7f				G-F	£14285
99 12/06 AbuD 1m				G-F	£14285
113 8/06 Leop 1m				G-Y	£31379
113 1/06 Ndas 7f110y		(90-105)H		G-F	£41569
103 2/05 Ndas 7f110y		(90-105)H		G-F	£37239
97 9/04 DRoy 5f		(60-100)H		FRM	£11461
85 5/04 Leop 1m				G-F	£7785

Total win prize-money £209213

Going (Turf): Sf: 1-4 GS: 1-2 Gd: 0-21 GF: 5-23 Fm: 1-3
Distance: 5f/6f: 1-4 7f-8f: 8-57 9f-13f: 0-2 14f+: 0-0
Track : LH: 4-34 RH: 3-12 Tight: 0-2 Gall: 3-25
Aids: Bl: 0-1 Vi: 0-0 Tstrap: 0-0 Ckp: 0-0
Best Rating: 113 1/07 Ndas 7f110y good

Smart Irish-trained performer; effective at around 1m; acts well on fast ground.

King Kenny

79(100) (78)79
4-y-o ch g Lomitas-Salanka (IRE) (Persian Heights)
Mrs A Malzard (S Parr 3/5) Gordon Crawford

Placings:42/3546106305544-0040003404 (5540a)
2009: 8^0SD, 5^0SD, 7^4SD, 7^0F, 7^0GF, 6^0G, 8^3G, 9^4GF, 8^0GS, 8^4F,

	Starts	1st	2nd	3rd	Win & Pl
Career Total (Turf)	19	1	0	3	6311
Career Total (AW)	6	0	1	0	1830
79 6/08 Haml 1m1f36y				GD	£3238

Total win prize-money £3238

Going (Turf): Sf: 0-4 GS: 0-2 Gd: 1-5 GF: 0-6 Fm: 0-2
Distance: 5f/6f: 0-2 7f-8f: 0-8 9f-13f: 1-15 14f+: 0-0
Track : LH: 0-12 RH: 1-6 Tight: 1-9 Gall: 0-2
Aids: Bl: 0-0 Vi: 0-1 Tstrap: 0-0 Ckp: 0-0
Best Rating: 79 6/08 Haml 1m1f36y good

Fair; effective over 6f-1m1f; acts on fast ground and with give; has worn an eyeshield.

King O'The Gypsies (IRE)

57 96
4-y-o b c Sadler's Wells (USA)-Love For Ever (IRE) (Darshaan)
J Howard Johnson Andrea & Graham Wylie

Placings:43215-0 (2471)
2009: 12^0GF,

	Starts	1st	2nd	3rd	Win & Pl
Career Total (Turf)	6	1	1	1	6381
87 8/08 Bath 1m3f144y				G-S	£2590

Total win prize-money £2590

Going (Turf): Sf: 0-2 GS: 1-1 Gd: 0-1 GF: 0-2 Fm: 0-0
Distance: 5f/6f: 0-0 7f-8f: 0-0 9f-13f: 1-6 14f+: 0-0
Track : LH: 1-2 RH: 0-3 Tight: 1-1 Gall: 0-3
Aids: Bl: 0-0 Vi: 0-0 Tstrap: 0-0 Ckp: 0-0
Best Rating: 96 10/08 Leic 1m3f183y soft

Useful; stays 1m3f and acts on most ground.

King Of Axum (IRE)

90 79
2-y-o b c Soviet Star (USA)-Ezana (Ela-Mana-Mou)
Ernesto Tasende (M Johnston 7/7) Dal Pos Amedeo

Placings:14300 (7743a)
2009: 5^1G, 5^4GF, 6^3G, 6^0GS, 7^0GS,

	Starts	1st	2nd	3rd	Win & Pl
Career Total (Turf)	5	1	0	1	4467
78 5/09 Donc 5f				GD	£3238

Total win prize-money £3238

Going (Turf): Sf: 0-0 GS: 0-2 Gd: 1-2 GF: 0-1 Fm: 0-0
Distance: 5f/6f: 1-3 7f-8f: 0-2 9f-13f: 0-0 14f+: 0-0
Track : LH: 0-1 RH: 0-0 Tight: 0-0 Gall: 0-0
Aids: Bl: 0-0 Vi: 0-0 Tstrap: 0-0 Ckp: 0-0
Best Rating: 79 12/09 Pisa 7f110y gd-sft

Fair; effective over 5-6f; acts on good ground.

King Of Cadeaux (IRE)

(99) (54)40
4-y-o br g Cadeaux Genereux-Purple Haze (IRE) (Spectrum (IRE))
M A Magnusson East Wind Racing Ltd

Placings:000/1000004-00 (0746)
2009: 8^0SD, 6^0SD,

	Starts	1st	2nd	3rd	Win & Pl
Career Total (Turf)	3	0	0	0	
Career Total (AW)	9	1	0	0	2047
54 4/08 Ling 6f		(0-60)H		STD	£2047

Total win prize-money £2047

Going (Turf): Sf: 0-0 GS: 0-1 Gd: 0-1 GF: 0-1 Fm: 0-0
Distance: 5f/6f: 1-6 7f-8f: 0-5 9f-13f: 0-1 14f+: 0-0
Track : LH: 1-10 RH: 0-0 Tight: 1-5 Gall: 0-2
Aids: Bl: 0-5 Vi: 0-0 Tstrap: 0-2 Ckp: 0-2
Best Rating: 54 4/08 Ling 6f stand

Very moderate; handles Polytrack, has worn headgear.

King Of Charm (IRE)

(102) (53)42
6-y-o ch g King Charlemagne (USA)-Pumpona (USA) (Sharpen Up)
M Hill Martin Hill

Placings:305000/0654106000606/031550-0 (0022)
2009: 6^0SD,

	Starts	1st	2nd	3rd	Win & Pl
Career Total (Turf)	6	0	0	1	578
Career Total (AW)	20	2	0	1	2932
53 1/08 Kemp 5f		(0-45)		STD	£1365
53 3/07 Kemp 6f		(0-50)H		STD	£1365

Total win prize-money £2730

Going (Turf): Sf: 0-1 GS: 0-0 Gd: 0-1 GF: 0-3 Fm: 0-1
Distance: 5f/6f: 2-21 7f-8f: 0-4 9f-13f: 0-1 14f+: 0-0
Track : LH: 0-14 RH: 2-9 Tight: 0-12 Gall: 0-0
Aids: Bl: 2-18 Vi: 0-0 Tstrap: 0-0 Ckp: 0-0
Best Rating: 62 6/06 Folk 5f good

Moderate sprinter; likes Polytrack; has worn blinkers and a tongue tie.

King Of Connacht

104(102) (64)64
6-y-o b g Polish Precedent (USA)-Lady Melbourne (IRE) (Indian Ridge)
M Wellings Ann Lindsay,Francis Lindsay,Jim O'Connor

Placings:505/0044104033304202-04134004210044016 6 (7856)
2009: 10^0GF, 9^4SD, 10^1GF, 10^3GF, 10^4GF, 11^0GF, 10^0S, 9^4G, 9^2SD, 9^1SD, 8^0GF, 9^0SD, 9^4SD, 9^4SD, 9^0SD, 9^1SD, 9^6SS, 9^6SD,

	Starts	1st	2nd	3rd	Win & Pl
Career Total (Turf)	21	2	0	4	6487
Career Total (AW)	16	2	3	0	6540
64 12/09 Wolv 1m1f103y		(0-60)H		STD	£2047
63 8/09 Wolv 1m1f103y		(0-60)H		STD	£2388
62 5/09 Bath 1m2f46y		(0-65)H		G-F	£2388
64 5/08 Sthl 1m2f		(0-55)H		GD	£1774

Total win prize-money £8597

Going (Turf): Sf: 0-4 GS: 0-1 Gd: 1-4 GF: 1-12 Fm: 0-0
Distance: 5f/6f: 0-0 7f-8f: 0-0 9f-13f: 4-36 14f+: 0-1
Track : LH: 4-32 RH: 0-4 Tight: 4-20 Gall: 0-5
Aids: Bl: 0-0 Vi: 1-3 Tstrap: 3-31 Ckp: 3-31
Best Rating: 64 12/09 Wolv 1m1f103y stand

Moderate; effective over 1m2f; acts on fast ground and on Polytrack; has worn cheekpieces/visor.

King Of Dalyan (IRE)

(24) 26
4-y-o ch g Desert Prince (IRE)-Fawaayid (USA) (Vaguely Noble)

Miss Tracy Waggott B Douglas

Placings:0000/0 **(0405)**
2009: 8^{0}SD,

	Starts	1st	2nd	3rd	Win & Pl
Career Total (Turf)	3	0	0	0	
Career Total (AW)	2	0	0	0	

Going (Turf): **Sf: 0-1 GS: 0-1 Gd: 0-0 GF: 0-1 Fm: 0-0**
Distance: 5f/6f: 0-2 7f-8f: 0-3 9f-13f: 0-0 14f+: 0-0
Track : LH: 0-4 RH: 0-0 Tight: 0-3 Gall: 0-0
Aids: Bl: 0-0 Vi: 0-2 Tstrap: 0-0 Ckp: 0-0
Best Rating: **26** 7/07 Catt 7f gd-sft

King Of Defence

93(103) (74)**63**
3-y-o ch g Kyllachy-Duena (Grand Lodge (USA))
M A Jarvis Barnett, Manasseh & Partners

Placings:000-30**21020** **(7876)**
2009: 7^{3}GF, 6^{0}GF, 7^{2}SS, 7^{1}SD, 7^{0}SD, 7^{2}SD, 7^{0}SD,

	Starts	1st	2nd	3rd	Win & Pl
Career Total (Turf)	5	0	0	1	302
Career Total (AW)	5	1	2	0	3957

74 10/09 Kemp 7f (0-65)H STD £1618
Total win prize-money £1619

Going (Turf): **Sf: 0-1 GS: 0-1 Gd: 0-1 GF: 0-2 Fm: 0-0**
Distance: 5f/6f: 0-0 **7f-8f: 1-10** 9f-13f: 0-0 14f+: 0-0
Track : LH: 0-2 **RH: 1-4** Tight: 0-2 Gall: 0-0
Aids: Bl: 0-0 Vi: 0-0 Tstrap: 0-0 Ckp: 0-0
Best Rating: **74** 10/09 Kemp 7f stand

Modest; effective at 7f; acts on fast ground; goes on Polytrack.

King Of Dixie (USA)

108(110) (111)**115**
5-y-o ch g Kingmambo (USA)-Dixie Accent (USA) (Dixieland Band (USA))
W J Knight Bluehills Racing Limited

Placings:2/113120-1515 **(2476)**
2009: 8^{1}SD, 8^{5}GF, 8^{1}SD, 8^{5}G,

	Starts	1st	2nd	3rd	Win & Pl
Career Total (Turf)	7	1	2	1	29702
Career Total (AW)	4	4	0	0	30683

111 5/09 Ling 1m STD £14331
98 3/09 Kemp 1m STD £7352
115 5/08 York 7f GD £9714
101 4/08 Ling 7f (0-90)H STD £6542
97 1/08 Kemp 7f STD £2457
Total win prize-money £40398

Going (Turf): Sf: 0-0 GS: 0-0 **Gd: 1-3** GF: 0-3 Fm: 0-1
Distance: 5f/6f: 0-0 **7f-8f: 5-11** 9f-13f: 0-0 14f+: 0-0
Track : **LH: 3-4** RH: 2-4 **Tight: 2-2** Gall: 1-2
Aids: Bl: 0-0 Vi: 0-0 Tstrap: 0-0 Ckp: 0-0
Best Rating: **115** 5/08 York 7f good

Smart; Group placed; effective over 7f-1m; acts on fast ground; goes on Polytrack.

King Of Eden (IRE)

92 **49**
3-y-o b g Royal Applause-Moonlight Paradise (USA) (Irish River (FR))
E J Alston The Grumpy Old Geezers

Placings:540050 **(7082)**
2009: 6^{5}GF, 6^{4}S, 8^{0}G, 6^{0}S, 6^{5}GF, 5^{0}S,

	Starts	1st	2nd	3rd	Win & Pl
Career Total (Turf)	6	0	0	0	0

Going (Turf): **Sf: 0-3 GS: 0-0 Gd: 0-1 GF: 0-2 Fm: 0-0**
Distance: 5f/6f: 0-4 7f-8f: 0-2 9f-13f: 0-0 14f+: 0-0
Track : LH: 0-2 RH: 0-0 Tight: 0-2 Gall: 0-0
Aids: Bl: 0-0 Vi: 0-0 Tstrap: 0-0 Ckp: 0-0
Best Rating: **49** 10/09 Rdcr 6f gd-fm

King Of Legend (IRE)

95(103) (70)**59**
5-y-o b g King Charlemagne (USA)-Last Quarry (Handsome Sailor)
D Morris (A G Foster 28/9) M Ferrario

Placings:000/**3413**005-**132**00146**00200** **(7475)**
2009: 8^{1}SD, 8^{3}SD, 8^{2}SD, 8^{0}SD, 8^{0}GF, 8^{1}G, 8^{4}GF, 9^{6}G, 9^{0}G, 8^{0}SD, 8^{2}SD, 8^{0}SD, 10^{0}SD,

	Starts	1st	2nd	3rd	Win & Pl
Career Total (Turf)	11	1	0	0	3107
Career Total (AW)	12	2	2	3	6004

59 6/09 Ayr 1m (0-55)H GD £2914
62 1/09 Wolv 1m141y (0-55)H STD £1577
63 2/08 Wolv 1m141y (0-60)H STD £2047
Total win prize-money £6539

Going (Turf): Sf: 0-2 GS: 0-0 **Gd: 1-5** GF: 0-4 Fm: 0-0
Distance: 5f/6f: 0-0 7f-8f: 1-12 **9f-13f: 2-11** 14f+: 0-0
Track : **LH: 3-12** RH: 0-8 **Tight: 2-13** Gall: 0-0
Aids: Bl: 0-0 Vi: 0-0 Tstrap: 0-1 Ckp: 0-1
Best Rating: **70** 3/09 Sthl 1m stand

Moderate; stays 1m; acts on Polytrack and Fibresand as well as good turf; has worn cheekpieces and a tongue tie.

King Of Reason

95(90) (68)**76**
2-y-o b c King's Best (USA)-Sheer Reason (USA) (Danzig (USA))
D M Simcock Saeed Manana

Placings:343 **(4233)**
2009: 6^{3}SD, 6^{4}GF, 6^{3}GF,

	Starts	1st	2nd	3rd	Win & Pl
Career Total (Turf)	2	0	0	1	1011
Career Total (AW)	1	0	0	1	385

Going (Turf): **Sf: 0-0 GS: 0-0 Gd: 0-0 GF: 0-2 Fm: 0-0**
Distance: 5f/6f: 0-3 7f-8f: 0-0 9f-13f: 0-0 14f+: 0-0
Track : LH: 0-1 RH: 0-1 Tight: 0-1 Gall: 0-0
Aids: Bl: 0-0 Vi: 0-0 Tstrap: 0-0 Ckp: 0-0
Best Rating: **76** 7/09 Epsm 6f gd-fm

King Of Rhythm (IRE)

99(97) (62)**81**
6-y-o b g Imperial Ballet (IRE)-Sharadja (IRE) (Doyoun)
D Carroll Miss C King

Placings:54002/**5**3150/52202632000**0**0-0360000**431** **(7796)**
2009: 8^{0}G, 6^{3}GF, 6^{6}G, 5^{0}GF, 7^{0}GF, 7^{0}G, 9^{0}G, 9^{4}SD, 8^{3}SD, 7^{1}SS,

	Starts	1st	2nd	3rd	Win & Pl
Career Total (Turf)	27	1	5	3	13945
Career Total (AW)	6	1	0	1	2245

62 12/09 Sthl 7f (0-55) SS £1942
75 8/07 Ayr 1m2f (0-85)H G-F £6855
Total win prize-money £8798

Going (Turf): Sf: 0-4 GS: 0-4 Gd: 0-9 **GF: 1-10** Fm: 0-0
Distance: 5f/6f: 0-2 7f-8f: 1-8 9f-13f: 1-23 14f+: 0-0
Track : **LH: 2-23** RH: 0-8 Tight: 0-8 Gall: 0-4
Aids: **Bl: 1-1** Vi: 0-1 Tstrap: 0-2 Ckp: 0-2
Best Rating: **81** 8/08 Thsk 1m good

Moderate; effective over 7f-1m2f; acts on fast ground; goes on Fibresand and Polytrack.

King Of Rome (IRE)

106(106) (102)**114**
4-y-o b c Montjeu (IRE)-Amizette (USA) (Forty Niner (USA))
M F De Kock Sheikh Mohammed Bin Khalifa Al Maktoum

Placings:010/5203611053-0300600 **(7185)**
2009: 8^{0}GF, 12^{3}GF, 12^{0}G, 12^{0}SD, 11^{6}GF, 10^{0}SD, 8^{0}G,

	Starts	1st	2nd	3rd	Win & Pl
Career Total (Turf)	18	3	1	3	150366
Career Total (AW)	2	0	0	0	

114 8/08 Leop 1m2f HVY £56985
112 7/08 Leop 1m2f G-F £33455
89 10/07 Tipp 7f100y GD £7937
Total win prize-money £98378

Going (Turf): **Sf: 1-3** GS: 0-1 **Gd: 1-6 GF: 1-6** Fm: 0-0
Distance: 5f/6f: 0-0 7f-8f: 1-4 **9f-13f: 2-16** 14f+: 0-0
Track : **LH: 2-10** RH: 0-7 Tight: 0-2 Gall: 0-5
Aids: Bl: 0-1 Vi: 0-0 Tstrap: 0-0 Ckp: 0-0
Best Rating: **114** 3/09 Ndas 1m4f gd-fm

Group class; effective at 1m2f-1m4f; acts on good and fast ground; has worn a tongue tie.

King Of Sparta (USA)

81(90) (45)**38**
4-y-o b c Van Nistelrooy (USA)-Selling Sunshine (USA) (Danzig (USA))
T J Fitzgerald N F L Racing

Placings:0050**P**-00 **(3561)**
2009: 10^{0}G, 12^{0}GF,

	Starts	1st	2nd	3rd	Win & Pl
Career Total (Turf)	5	0	0	0	0
Career Total (AW)	2	0	0	0	

Going (Turf): **Sf: 0-0 GS: 0-0 Gd: 0-1 GF: 0-4 Fm: 0-0**
Distance: 5f/6f: 0-0 7f-8f: 0-4 9f-13f: 0-3 14f+: 0-0
Track : LH: 0-4 RH: 0-3 Tight: 0-1 Gall: 0-2
Aids: Bl: 0-0 Vi: 0-0 Tstrap: 0-0 Ckp: 0-0
Best Rating: **45** 8/08 GrLe 1m stand

King Of Swords (IRE)

102(86) (54)**78**
5-y-o b g Desert Prince (IRE)-Okey Dorey (IRE) (Lake Coniston (IRE))
N Tinkler P Alderson & J Raybould

Placings:0216000/02005000/620000031605**5**4-02006000001121260 **(6897)**
2009: 5^{0}GF, 5^{2}F, 5^{0}HY, 5^{0}GF, 5^{6}G, 5^{0}GS, 5^{0}GS, 5^{0}GF, 5^{0}GF, 5^{0}S, 5^{1}G, 5^{1}GF, 5^{2}GF, 5^{1}GF, 5^{2}GF, 5^{6}GS, 5^{0}GF,

	Starts	1st	2nd	3rd	Win & Pl
Career Total (Turf)	45	5	6	1	37422
Career Total (AW)	1	0	0	0	0

69	9/09	Bevl	5f	(0-75)H	G-F	£4209
67	8/09	Pont	5f	(0-70)H	G-F	£3885
66	8/09	Pont	5f	(0-75)H	GD	£4533
76	9/08	Muss	5f	(0-70)H	SFT	£3885
77	6/06	Navn	5f		FRM	£5718

Total win prize-money £22233

Going (Turf): Sf: 1-9 GS: 0-4 Gd: 1-9 **GF: 2-17** Fm: 1-2
Distance: **5f/6f: 5-45** 7f-8f: 0-1 9f-13f: 0-0 14f+: 0-0
Track : **LH: 3-15** RH: 0-1 Tight: 0-1 Gall: 0-0
Aids: Bl: 0-0 Vi: 0-0 Tstrap: 3-7 Ckp: 3-7
Best Rating: **94** 5/07 Tipp 5f gd-fm

Modest; seems best at 5f; acts on fast and soft ground; has worn a tongue tie and cheekpieces.

King Of The Beers (USA)

90(107) (68)54

5-y-o gr/ro g Silver Deputy (CAN)-Pracer (USA) (Lyphard (USA))
R A Harris Dr Simon Clarke

Placings:00000/01656215420140004600256-32304102600003540 (6584)
2009: 10^{3}SD, 8^{2}SD, 11^{3}SD, 9^{0}SD, 8^{4}SD, 11^{1}SD, 10^{0}SD, 12^{2}SD, 11^{6}SD, 10^{0}GF, 10^{0}F, 12^{0}GF, 8^{0}SF, 11^{3}SD, 12^{5}SD, 11^{4}SD, 12^{0}SD,

	Starts	1st	2nd	3rd	Win & Pl
Career Total (Turf)	12	0	0	0	645
Career Total (AW)	33	4	5	3	12529

68	3/09	Sthl	1m3f	(0-60)H	STD	£2047
71	6/07	Wolv	1m4f50y	(0-65)H	STD	£2388
57	3/07	Kemp	1m2f	(0-60)H	STD	£1365
55	1/07	Ling	1m2f	(0-65)H	STD	£2266

Total win prize-money £8068

Going (Turf): **Sf: 0-2 GS: 0-0 Gd: 0-2 GF: 0-6 Fm: 0-2**
Distance: 5f/6f: 0-0 7f-8f: 0-6 **9f-13f: 4-36** 14f+: 0-3
Track : **LH: 3-37** RH: 1-7 **Tight: 2-20** Gall: 0-0
Aids: Bl: 0-2 Vi: 0-0 Tstrap: 4-38 Ckp: 4-38
Best Rating: **71** 6/07 Wolv 1m4f50y stand

Moderate; stays 1m4f; acts well on sand; has worn cheek-pieces.

King Of The Moors (USA)

105(97) (56)77

6-y-o b g King Of Kings (IRE)-Araza (USA) (Arazi (USA))
R C Guest King Treys

Placings:55/13300000/004103256401506/660002564000611040-353630000313130005 (7783)
2009: 9^{3}GF, 9^{5}GF, 9^{3}GS, 8^{6}G, 7^{3}G, 8^{0}GF, 8^{0}GF, 8^{0}GF, 8^{0}G, 8^{3}GS, 9^{1}G, 10^{3}GS, 9^{1}GF, 8^{3}G, 9^{6}G, 10^{0}S, 8^{0}SD, 8^{5}SD,

	Starts	1st	2nd	3rd	Win & Pl
Career Total (Turf)	56	7	2	9	43639
Career Total (AW)	5	0	0	0	0

73	9/09	Muss	1m1f		G-F	£5180
67	9/09	Muss	1m1f		GD	£3885
77	9/08	Haml	1m1f36y	H	G-S	£9714
70	8/08	Muss	1m	(0-65)H	SFT	£2590
81	10/07	Rdcr	1m2f	(0-75)H	GD	£2817
78	5/07	Rdcr	1m1f	(0-70)H	GD	£2817
72	4/06	Muss	7f30y		G-F	£3886

Total win prize-money £30891

Going (Turf): Sf: 1-9 GS: 1-12**Gd: 3-18** GF: 2-17 Fm: 0-0
Distance: 5f/6f: 0-0 7f-8f: 2-25 **9f-13f: 5-35** 14f+: 0-1
Track : LH: 2-27 **RH: 5-25 Tight: 7-33** Gall: 0-1
Aids: Bl: 2-9 Vi: 0-0 Tstrap: 2-12 Ckp: 2-12
Best Rating: **87** 6/06 Epsm 7f good

Modest; effective at around 1m-1m2f; acts on most ground; has worn blinkers and cheekpieces.

King Of Wands

106 103

3-y-o b c Galileo (IRE)-Maid To Treasure (IRE) (Rainbow Quest (USA))
J L Dunlop Normandie Stud Ltd

Placings:043-12115 (5425)
2009: 12^{1}G, 14^{2}GF, 14^{1}GF, 14^{1}GF, 14^{5}G,

	Starts	1st	2nd	3rd	Win & Pl
Career Total (Turf)	8	3	1	1	18929

103	7/09	Sand	1m6f	(0-95)H	G-F	£7771
88	6/09	Sals	1m6f21y	(0-85)H	G-F	£4727
80	4/09	Folk	1m4f		GD	£2729

Total win prize-money £15228

Going (Turf): Sf: 0-1 GS: 0-1 Gd: 1-2 **GF: 2-4** Fm: 0-0
Distance: 5f/6f: 0-0 7f-8f: 0-1 9f-13f: 1-3 **14f+: 2-4**
Track : LH: 0-0 **RH: 3-7 Tight: 2-4** Gall: 0-0
Aids: Bl: 0-0 Vi: 0-0 Tstrap: 0-0 Ckp: 0-0
Best Rating: **103** 7/09 Sand 1m6f gd-fm

Very useful; stays 1m6f and acts on most ground.

King Of Windsor (IRE)

95(90) (66)80

2-y-o b g Intikhab (USA)-Kismah (Machiavellian (USA))
R M Beckett Jones, Healy, Whitehead & Mitchell

Placings:425 (6802)
2009: 6^{4}GF, 6^{2}G, 5^{5}SD,

	Starts	1st	2nd	3rd	Win & Pl
Career Total (Turf)	2	0	1	0	1312
Career Total (AW)	1	0	0	0	0

Going (Turf): **Sf: 0-0 GS: 0-0 Gd: 0-1 GF: 0-1 Fm: 0-0**
Distance: 5f/6f: 0-3 7f-8f: 0-0 9f-13f: 0-0 14f+: 0-0
Track : LH: 0-1 RH: 0-0 Tight: 0-1 Gall: 0-0
Aids: Bl: 0-0 Vi: 0-0 Tstrap: 0-0 Ckp: 0-0
Best Rating: **80** 8/09 Sals 6f good

Fair; stays 6f; acts on good/fast ground.

King Olav (UAE)

101(108) (94)88

4-y-o ch g Halling (USA)-Karamzin (USA) (Nureyev (USA))
A W Carroll Cover Point Racing

Placings:313P-120200502 (7233)
2009: 10^{1}SD, 11^{2}SD, 11^{0}SD, 9^{2}G, 12^{0}GF, 10^{0}GF, 10^{5}G, 12^{0}GS, 10^{2}SD,

	Starts	1st	2nd	3rd	Win & Pl
Career Total (Turf)	8	0	1	2	4868
Career Total (AW)	5	2	2	0	14220

93	2/09	Ling	1m2f	(0-85)H	STD	£4727
82	8/08	Kemp	1m2f		STD	£4727

Total win prize-money £9454

Going (Turf): **Sf: 0-2 GS: 0-2 Gd: 0-2 GF: 0-2 Fm: 0-0**
Distance: 5f/6f: 0-0 7f-8f: 0-0 **9f-13f: 2-13** 14f+: 0-0
Track : LH: 1-5 RH: 1-8 **Tight: 1-2** Gall: 0-5
Aids: Bl: 0-0 Vi: 0-0 Tstrap: 0-0 Ckp: 0-0
Best Rating: **94** 3/09 Kemp 1m3f stand

Useful; effective at around 1m2f; acts easy ground and on Polytrack.

King Pin

104 66

4-y-o b g Pivotal-Danehurst (Danehill (USA))
Miss Tracy Waggott H Conlon

Placings:00221300 (5601)
2009: 7^{0}F, 7^{0}GS, 7^{2}GF, 7^{2}G, 8^{1}GF, 8^{3}GF, 8^{0}GF, 7^{0}GF,

	Starts	1st	2nd	3rd	Win & Pl
Career Total (Turf)	8	1	2	1	4640

66	6/09	Rdcr	1m	(0-75)H	G-F	£2590

Total win prize-money £2590

Going (Turf): Sf: 0-0 GS: 0-1 Gd: 0-1 **GF: 1-5** Fm: 0-1
Distance: 5f/6f: 0-0 **7f-8f: 1-7** 9f-13f: 0-1 14f+: 0-0
Track : LH: 0-0 RH: 0-1 Tight: 0-1 Gall: 0-0
Aids: Bl: 0-0 Vi: 0-0 Tstrap: 0-0 Ckp: 0-0
Best Rating: **66** 6/09 Rdcr 1m gd-fm

Modest; effective at 7f-1m; acts on fast ground.

King Red

(102) (80)

5-y-o ch h King's Best (USA)-Pearl Barley (IRE) (Polish Precedent (USA))
Tom Dascombe John Reed

Placings:411 (7785)
2009: 12^{4}SD, 13^{1}SD, 13^{1}SD,

	Starts	1st	2nd	3rd	Win & Pl
Career Total (Turf)	0	0	0	0	
Career Total (AW)	3	2	0	0	6160

80	12/09	Wolv	1m5f194y	(0-75)H	STD	£3238
67	11/09	Wolv	1m5f194y		STD	£2729

Total win prize-money £5968

Going (Turf): **Sf: 0-0 GS: 0-0 Gd: 0-0 GF: 0-0 Fm: 0-0**
Distance: 5f/6f: 0-0 7f-8f: 0-0 9f-13f: 0-1 **14f+: 2-2**
Track : **LH: 2-2** RH: 0-1 **Tight: 2-2** Gall: 0-0
Aids: Bl: 0-0 Vi: 0-0 Tstrap: 0-0 Ckp: 0-0
Best Rating: **80** 12/09 Wolv 1m5f194y stand

Modest; stays 1m6f; acts on Polytrack.

King Supreme (IRE)

103(109) (82)88

4-y-o b c King's Best (USA)-Oregon Trail (USA) (Gone West (USA))
R Hannon Brian C Oakley

Placings:300100/62332221526400-241620233150641 (7201)
2009: 12^{2}SD, 10^{4}SD, 9^{1}G, 9^{6}G, 11^{2}GF, 12^{0}G, 12^{2}GF, 12^{3}GF, 11^{3}GF, 10^{1}S, 10^{5}G, 11^{0}SD, 11^{6}SD, 11^{4}G, 13^{1}SD,

	Starts	1st	2nd	3rd	Win & Pl
Career Total (Turf)	23	3	7	5	36838
Career Total (AW)	12	2	1	0	8577

79	11/09	Ling	1m5f	(0-85)H	STD	£5180
75	7/09	Hayd	1m2f95y		SFT	£3238
86	4/09	Brig	1m1f209y	(0-80)H	GD	£5504
84	8/08	Brig	1m3f196y	(0-80)H	GD	£13622
68	9/07	Kemp	1m	(0-65)	STD	£2047

Total win prize-money £29594

Going (Turf): Sf: 1-4 GS: 0-1 **Gd: 2-6** GF: 0-12 Fm: 0-0
Distance: 5f/6f: 0-0 7f-8f: 1-6 **9f-13f: 4-29** 14f+: 0-0
Track : **LH: 4-9** RH: 1-18 **Tight: 1-19** Gall: 0-1
Aids: **Bl: 4-24** Vi: 0-0 Tstrap: 0-0 Ckp: 0-0
Best Rating: **88** 6/09 Folk 1m4f gd-fm

Fair; stays 1m5f; acts on fast ground; goes on Polytrack; has been tried in blinkers and a visor.

King's Alchemist

(94) (24)59

4-y-o b g Slickly (FR)-Pure Gold (Dilum (USA))

M D I Usher The Ridgeway Partnership

Placings:0/60040006-0 **(0100)**

2009: 10^{0}SD,

	Starts	1st	2nd	3rd	Win & Pl
Career Total (Turf)	**9**	**0**	**0**	**0**	**241**
Career Total (AW)	**1**	**0**	**0**	**0**	

Going (Turf): **Sf: 0-2 GS: 0-3 Gd: 0-2 GF: 0-2 Fm: 0-0**
Distance: 5f/6f: 0-0 7f-8f: 0-3 9f-13f: 0-6 14f+: 0-1
Track : LH: 0-5 RH: 0-2 Tight: 0-4 Gall: 0-1
Aids: Bl: 0-0 Vi: 0-3 Tstrap: 0-0 Ckp: 0-0
Best Rating: **62** 10/07 Newb 1m gd-sft

King's Apostle (IRE)

117 (89)119

5-y-o b h King's Best (USA)-Politesse (USA) (Barathea (IRE))

W J Haggas Bernard Kantor

Placings:622/**12**011311/530201-02051 **(4837a)**

2009: 5^{0}GF, 6^{2}GF, 6^{0}GF, 6^{5}GF, 6^{1}GS,

	Starts	1st	2nd	3rd	Win & Pl
Career Total (Turf)	**19**	**5**	**4**	**2**	**300574**
Career Total (AW)	**3**	**2**	**1**	**0**	**9206**

117	8/09	Deau	6f110y		G-S	£138689
117	9/08	Asct	6f		GD	£56770
107	9/07	York	6f	(0-100)H	G-F	£12954
96	8/07	NmkJ	6f	(0-105)H	GD	£18696
89	7/07	Kemp	6f	(0-85)H	STD	£4728
84	6/07	Ripn	6f	(0-85)H	G-F	£5047
71	3/07	Ling	7f		STD	£3071

Total win prize-money £239955

Going (Turf): Sf: 0-0 GS: 1-1 **Gd: 2-5 GF: 2-12** Fm: 0-1
Distance: **5f/6f: 5-15** 7f-8f: 2-7 9f-13f: 0-0 14f+: 0-0
Track : LH: 1-4 **RH: 2-3 Tight: 1-3** Gall: 0-0
Aids: Bl: 0-0 **Vi: 1-2** Tstrap: 0-0 Ckp: 0-0
Best Rating: **119** 7/09 NmkJ 6f gd-fm

Group class; winner of the Group 2 Diadem Stakes in 2008; effective over 6f-7f; acts on fast ground and on Polytrack; has won in a visor.

King's Approach (IRE)

92(79) (57)73

2-y-o gr c Fasliyev (USA)-Lady Georgina (Linamix (FR))

R Hannon David & Gwyn Joseph

Placings:313050066 **(6585)**

2009: 5^{3}GF, 5^{1}GF, 6^{3}GF, 6^{0}G, 6^{5}G, 7^{0}G, 6^{0}GF, 5^{6}GF, 6^{6}SD,

	Starts	1st	2nd	3rd	Win & Pl
Career Total (Turf)	**8**	**1**	**0**	**2**	**4577**
Career Total (AW)	**1**	**0**	**0**	**0**	**0**

72	4/09	Leic	5f2y	G-F	£2914

Total win prize-money £2914

Going (Turf): Sf: 0-0 GS: 0-0 Gd: 0-3 **GF: 1-5** Fm: 0-0
Distance: **5f/6f: 1-8** 7f-8f: 0-1 9f-13f: 0-0 14f+: 0-0
Track : LH: 0-2 RH: 0-2 Tight: 0-1 Gall: 0-0
Aids: Bl: 0-0 Vi: 0-0 Tstrap: 0-0 Ckp: 0-0
Best Rating: **73** 6/09 Sals 6f good

Fair; winner over 5f; acts on fast ground.

King's Caprice

93(98) (98)89

8-y-o ch g Pursuit Of Love-Palace Street (USA) (Secreto (USA))

J A Geake Miss B Swire

Placings:523/034104415020/0300003200**420**/0103341001 31/**3**00000006**2206**/4530300-000 **(2883)**

2009: 7^{0}SD, 7^{0}G, 7^{0}G,

	Starts	1st	2nd	3rd	Win & Pl
Career Total (Turf)	**50**	**6**	**3**	**9**	**99695**
Career Total (AW)	**13**	**0**	**3**	**1**	**12704**

108	10/06	NmkR	7f	(0-100)H	G-S	£11217
101	9/06	Gdwd	7f	(0-100)H	GD	£11217
98	7/06	Chep	6f16y	(0-100)H	G-F	£15580
95	4/06	NmkR	7f	(0-105)H	G-F	£11217
94	8/04	Kemp	7f	D(0-85)H	SFT	£7133
78	6/04	Wind	6f	D	G-F	£4290

Total win prize-money £60658

Going (Turf): Sf: 1-8 GS: 1-10 Gd: 1-11 **GF: 3-21** Fm: 0-0
Distance: 5f/6f: 1-20 **7f-8f: 5-43** 9f-13f: 0-0 14f+: 0-0
Track : LH: 0-11 **RH: 2-12** Tight: 0-10 **Gall: 2-7**
Aids: Bl: 0-0 Vi: 0-2 Tstrap: 0-0 Ckp: 0-0
Best Rating: **108** 10/06 NmkR 7f gd-sft

Fair; effective over 6f-7f; acts on most ground; also goes on Polytrack; often wears a tongue tie, has worn a visor; likes to race prominently.

King's Chorister

95(94) (61)61

3-y-o ch g King's Best (USA)-Chorist (Pivotal)

Miss Gay Kelleway K J Holdings Ltd Kingsclub Syndicate

Placings:6062-000663303126 **(4397)**

2009: 8^{0}SD, 8^{0}SD, 8^{0}SD, 10^{6}GF, 10^{6}GS, 9^{3}GF, 12^{3}SD, 12^{0}F, 9^{3}G, 10^{1}GS, 8^{2}G, 12^{6}GF,

	Starts	1st	2nd	3rd	Win & Pl
Career Total (Turf)	**9**	**1**	**1**	**2**	**3521**
Career Total (AW)	**7**	**0**	**1**	**1**	**1459**

55	7/09	Yarm	1m2f21y	G-S	£1942

Total win prize-money £1943

Going (Turf): Sf: 0-0 **GS: 1-2** Gd: 0-3 GF: 0-3 Fm: 0-1
Distance: 5f/6f: 0-0 7f-8f: 0-5 **9f-13f: 1-11** 14f+: 0-0
Track : **LH: 1-13** RH: 0-3 **Tight: 1-10** Gall: 0-0
Aids: Bl: 0-2 Vi: 0-1 Tstrap: 0-0 Ckp: 0-0
Best Rating: **61** 9/08 Wwck 7f26y good

Moderate; stays 1m2f; acts on easy ground and on Polytrack; has worn an eyeshield and a tongue tie.

King's Colour

103(108) (90)85

4-y-o b g King's Best (USA)-Red Garland (Selkirk (USA))

B R Johnson Tann Racing

Placings:060421-3644115212 **(7516)**

2009: 7^{3}SD, 8^{6}SD, 12^{4}SD, 7^{4}G, 7^{1}G, 7^{1}GF, 8^{5}SD, 7^{2}SD, 7^{1}SD, 7^{2}SD,

	Starts	1st	2nd	3rd	Win & Pl
Career Total (Turf)	**5**	**2**	**0**	**0**	**7057**
Career Total (AW)	**11**	**2**	**3**	**1**	**11686**

90	11/09	Ling	7f	(0-85)H	STD	£4727
85	9/09	Epsm	7f	(0-75)H	G-F	£3238
80	8/09	Gdwd	7f	(0-70)H	GD	£3238
74	12/08	GrLe	1m	(0-65)H	STD	£2590

Total win prize-money £13793

Going (Turf): Sf: 0-0 GS: 0-0 **Gd: 1-3 GF: 1-2** Fm: 0-0
Distance: 5f/6f: 0-0 **7f-8f: 4-12** 9f-13f: 0-4 14f+: 0-0
Track : **LH: 3-6** RH: 1-9 **Tight: 2-7** Gall: 1-1
Aids: Bl: 0-0 Vi: 0-0 Tstrap: 0-0 Ckp: 0-0
Best Rating: **90** 11/09 Ling 7f stand

Useful; effective at 7f-1m; acts on good ground; goes on Polytrack.

King's Counsel (IRE)

96(91) (41)63

3-y-o ch g Refuse To Bend (IRE)-Nesaah's Princess (Sinndar (IRE))

J Hetherton R G Fell

Placings:6040-35420606 **(6342)**

2009: 9^{3}GF, 10^{5}GS, 10^{4}G, 10^{2}GF, 10^{0}GF, 8^{6}G, 12^{0}GS, 12^{6}SD,

	Starts	1st	2nd	3rd	Win & Pl
Career Total (Turf)	**11**	**0**	**1**	**1**	**1669**
Career Total (AW)	**1**	**0**	**0**	**0**	**0**

Going (Turf): **Sf: 0-1 GS: 0-3 Gd: 0-3 GF: 0-4 Fm: 0-0**
Distance: 5f/6f: 0-0 7f-8f: 0-4 9f-13f: 0-8 14f+: 0-0
Track : LH: 0-7 RH: 0-2 Tight: 0-5 Gall: 0-2
Aids: Bl: 0-0 Vi: 0-1 Tstrap: 0-0 Ckp: 0-0
Best Rating: **63** 7/09 Rdcr 1m2f gd-fm

Modest; effective over 1m2f; acts on fast ground.

King's Fable (USA)

86(106) (68)65

6-y-o b g Lear Fan (USA)-Fairy Fable (IRE) (Fairy King (USA))

Karen George K George I Bennett P Lyons S Unsworth

Placings:650/**3**4500200010/**331641033300-00256** **(6226)**

2009: 13^{0}SF, 10^{0}SD, 11^{2}GF, 12^{5}SD, 12^{6}SD,

	Starts	1st	2nd	3rd	Win & Pl
Career Total (Turf)	**14**	**1**	**2**	**1**	**5420**
Career Total (AW)	**17**	**2**	**0**	**5**	**6304**

65	3/08	Wolv	1m4f50y	(0-65)H	STD	£1943
60	2/08	Wolv	1m4f50y	(0-65)H	STD	£2047
60	9/06	Catt	1m3f214y	(0-60)H	G-S	£2730

Total win prize-money £6721

Going (Turf): Sf: 0-2 **GS: 1-3** Gd: 0-2 GF: 0-7 Fm: 0-0
Distance: 5f/6f: 0-0 7f-8f: 0-1 **9f-13f: 3-22** 14f+: 0-8
Track : **LH: 3-22** RH: 0-8 **Tight: 3-22** Gall: 0-1
Aids: Bl: 0-0 Vi: 0-0 Tstrap: 2-14 Ckp: 2-14
Best Rating: **68** 6/08 Wolv 1m4f50y stand

Modest handicapper; stays 1m7f; acts on good to firm and good to soft; goes well on Polytrack; has worn cheekpieces.

King's Head (IRE)

90(98) (96)98

6-y-o b g King's Best (USA)-Ustka (Lomond (USA))

Miss L A Perratt (G L Moore 18/2) Ken McGarrity

Placings:4316/1434**34**/**4**/04**P34-15**00036 **(6986)**

2009: 11^{1}SD, 12^{5}SD, 9^{0}GS, 13^{0}G, 14^{0}GF, 13^{3}GF, 10^{6}G,

	Starts	1st	2nd	3rd	Win & Pl
Career Total (Turf)	**15**	**2**	**0**	**4**	**25874**
Career Total (AW)	**8**	**1**	**0**	**1**	**5569**

84	2/09	Kemp	1m3f	STD	£2047
86	9/05	Pont	1m4y	GD	£5629

Total win prize-money £7676

Going (Turf): Sf: 0-0 GS: 0-2 **Gd: 2-7** GF: 0-6 Fm: 0-0
Distance: 5f/6f: 0-0 7f-8f: 0-2 **9f-13f: 3-16** 14f+: 0-5

Track : LH: 1-13 **RH: 2-8** Tight: 0-9 Gall: 0-3
Aids: Bl: 0-0 Vi: 0-0 Tstrap: 1-10 Ckp: 1-10
Best Rating: 103 8/06 Gdwd 1m4f gd fm

Very useful; stays 1m5f; acts on good or faster ground; goes on Polytrack; has worn cheekpieces; winning hurdler.

King's Icon (IRE)

100(104) (74)**70**
4-y-o b g King's Best (USA)-Pink Sovietstaia (FR) (Soviet Star (USA))
M Wigham A Dunmore, John Williams

Placings:2100/**5**3000**4**00**5**0**6**-6**4**23**1**2**222** (5842)
2009: 7^6GF, 7^4G, 8^2G, 8^3G, 8^1GF, 8^2GF, 9^2SD, 8^2SD, 7^2SD,

	Starts	1st	2nd	3rd	Win & Pl
Career Total (Turf)	14	2	3	2	10964
Career Total (AW)	10	0	3	0	2116

59	8/09	Yarm	1m3y	(0-65)H	G-F	£2072
78	6/07	Gdwd	6f		GD	£5019

Total win prize-money £7092

Going (Turf): Sf: 0-1 GS: 0-0 **Gd: 1-7 GF: 1-6** Fm: 0-0
Distance: 5f/6f: 1-4 7f-8f: 0-7 9f-13f: 1-13 14f+: 0-0
Track : LH: 0-9 RH: 0-5 Tight: 0-7 Gall: 0-0
Aids: Bl: 0-1 Vi: 0-1 Tstrap: 1-5 Ckp: 1-5
Best Rating: 78 6/07 Gdwd 6f good

Moderate; stays 1m; acts on good ground and Polytrack; has worn blinkers and cheekpieces.

King's Jester (IRE)

91(98) (54)**51**
7-y-o b g King's Best (USA)-Scent Of Success (USA) (Quiet American (USA))
Lee Smyth (J J Lambe 1/10) Pircan Partnership

Placings:04/521260/0000040**0**/0/**0**-5004 (7818)
2009: 7^5GF, 7^0SF, 8^0SD, 9^4SD,

	Starts	1st	2nd	3rd	Win & Pl
Career Total (Turf)	16	1	2	0	14382
Career Total (AW)	6	0	0	0	1620

92	5/05	Lonc	1m110y	SFT	£7092

Total win prize-money £7092

Going (Turf): **Sf: 1-3** GS: 0-1 Gd: 0-6 GF: 0-2 Fm: 0-1
Distance: 5f/6f: 0-4 7f-8f: 0-6 **9f-13f: 1-11** 14f+: 0-1
Track : LH: 0-11 RH: 0-3 Tight: 0-5 Gall: 0-0
Aids: Bl: 0-3 Vi: 0-0 Tstrap: 0-1 Ckp: 0-1
Best Rating: 94 6/05 Lonc 1m110y good

Moderate; effective over 1m1f; acts on Polytrack.

King's Kazeem

76(92) (56)**64**
4-y-o b f King's Best (USA)-Kazeem (Darshaan)
G L Moore D J Deer

Placings:40/0-50 (3462)
2009: 10^5SD, 11^0GF,

	Starts	1st	2nd	3rd	Win & Pl
Career Total (Turf)	4	0	0	0	841
Career Total (AW)	1	0	0	0	0

Going (Turf): **Sf: 0-1 GS: 0-0 Gd: 0-1 GF: 0-2 Fm: 0-0**
Distance: 5f/6f: 0-0 7f-8f: 0-2 9f-13f: 0-3 14f+: 0-0
Track : LH: 0-1 RH: 0-1 Tight: 0-3 Gall: 0-0
Aids: Bl: 0-0 Vi: 0-0 Tstrap: 0-0 Ckp: 0-0
Best Rating: 73 9/07 Newb 7f gd-fm

King's La Mont (IRE)

102(89) (66)**77**
3-y-o b c King's Best (USA)-La Leuze (IRE) (Caerleon (USA))
Mrs A J Perrett Winterfields Farm, Brooke, Swayne, Black

Placings:046-3500560 (6338)
2009: 10^3GF, 12^5GF, 10^0GS, 8^0G, 10^5GF, 12^6GF, 9^0GF,

	Starts	1st	2nd	3rd	Win & Pl
Career Total (Turf)	9	0	0	1	596
Career Total (AW)	1	0	0	0	0

Going (Turf): **Sf: 0-0 GS: 0-2 Gd: 0-1 GF: 0-6 Fm: 0-0**
Distance: 5f/6f: 0-0 7f-8f: 0-3 9f-13f: 0-7 14f+: 0-0
Track : LH: 0-2 RH: 0-7 Tight: 0-5 Gall: 0-0
Aids: Bl: 0-0 Vi: 0-0 Tstrap: 0-1 Ckp: 0-1
Best Rating: 77 4/09 Wind 1m2f7y gd-fm

King's Majesty (IRE)

89(102) (72)**61**
7-y-o b g King's Best (USA)-Tiavanita (USA) (J O Tobin (USA))
A M Hales The Hexagon Racing Partnership

Placings:021/12/0/0006621/**050-32240** (7888)
2009: 13^3SD, 13^2SD, 13^2SD, 11^4G, 12^0SD,

	Starts	1st	2nd	3rd	Win & Pl
Career Total (Turf)	10	1	2	0	15608
Career Total (AW)	11	2	3	1	10221

72	12/07	Ling	1m2f		STD	£1943
91	8/05	NmkJ	7f	(0-90)H	GD	£9763
88	10/04	Ling	7f		STD	£5135

Total win prize-money £16841

Going (Turf): Sf: 0-1 GS: 0-0 **Gd: 1-5** GF: 0-4 Fm: 0-0
Distance: 5f/6f: 0-0 **7f-8f: 2-9** 9f-13f: 1-12 14f+: 0-0
Track : **LH: 2-12** RH: 0-4 **Tight: 2-9** Gall: 0-0
Aids: Bl: 0-0 Vi: 0-0 Tstrap: 0-1 Ckp: 0-1
Best Rating: 93 9/05 NmkR 1m good

Modest; stays 1m5f; acts on good ground and Polytrack.

King's Masque

98(104) (74)**59**
3-y-o b g Noverre (USA)-Top Flight Queen (Mark Of Esteem (IRE))
W R Muir A Patrick, C Edgington & M Caddy

Placings:40564014 (6968)
2009: 8^4SD, 8^0SD, 8^5SD, 10^6GF, 10^4GS, 8^0G, 8^1SD, 7^4G,

	Starts	1st	2nd	3rd	Win & Pl
Career Total (Turf)	4	0	0	0	337
Career Total (AW)	4	1	0	0	2240

74	9/09	Kemp	1m	(0-70)	STD	£2047

Total win prize-money £2047

Going (Turf): **Sf: 0-0 GS: 0-1 Gd: 0-2 GF: 0-1 Fm: 0-0**
Distance: 5f/6f: 0-0 **7f-8f: 1-5** 9f-13f: 0-3 14f+: 0-0
Track : LH: 0-5 **RH: 1-2** Tight: 0-3 Gall: 0-0
Aids: Bl: 0-0 Vi: 0-0 Tstrap: 0-0 Ckp: 0-0
Best Rating: 74 9/09 Kemp 1m stand

Modest; best at around 1m; suited by Polytrack.

King's Miracle (IRE)

(91) (41)
3-y-o ch f King's Best (USA)-Pretty Sharp (Interrex (CAN))
J R Gask Simon Rowlands

Placings:040 (7826)
2009: 6^0SD, 7^4SD, 8^0SD,

	Starts	1st	2nd	3rd	Win & Pl
Career Total (Turf)	0	0	0	0	
Career Total (AW)	3	0	0	0	0

Going (Turf): **Sf: 0-0 GS: 0-0 Gd: 0-0 GF: 0-0 Fm: 0-0**
Distance: 5f/6f: 0-1 7f-8f: 0-2 9f-13f: 0-0 14f+: 0-0
Track : LH: 0-2 RH: 0-1 Tight: 0-2 Gall: 0-0
Aids: Bl: 0-0 Vi: 0-0 Tstrap: 0-0 Ckp: 0-0
Best Rating: 41 11/09 Wolv 7f32y stand

Moderate; stays 7f and acts on Polytrack.

King's Parade

88(90) (72)**72**
2-y-o b c Dynaformer (USA)-Bay Tree (IRE) (Daylami (IRE))
Sir Michael Stoute Saeed Suhail

Placings:235 (6672)
2009: 7^2HY, 7^3G, 8^5SD,

	Starts	1st	2nd	3rd	Win & Pl
Career Total (Turf)	2	0	1	1	2071
Career Total (AW)	1	0	0	0	0

Going (Turf): **Sf: 0-1 GS: 0-0 Gd: 0-1 GF: 0-0 Fm: 0-0**
Distance: 5f/6f: 0-0 7f-8f: 0-2 9f-13f: 0-1 14f+: 0-0
Track : LH: 0-2 RH: 0-0 Tight: 0-1 Gall: 0-0
Aids: Bl: 0-0 Vi: 0-0 Tstrap: 0-0 Ckp: 0-0
Best Rating: 72 10/09 Wolv 1m141y stand

Fair; stays 7f; acts on good and heavy ground.

King's Ransom

94(105) (78)**70**
6-y-o b g Daylami (IRE)-Luana (Shaadi (USA))
S Gollings Mrs D Dukes

Placings:00/4000P/2100063336166040022/23110133004 0-56030060 (5577)
2009: 8^5SD, 10^6SD, 8^0SD, 10^3G, 8^0GF, 10^0GF, 9^6G, 11^0SD,

	Starts	1st	2nd	3rd	Win & Pl
Career Total (Turf)	17	1	0	4	4102
Career Total (AW)	29	4	4	3	14234

79	3/08	Ling	1m	(0-75)H	STD	£2590
78	2/08	Kemp	1m	(0-70)H	STD	£2590
70	2/08	Wolv	1m1f103y	(0-65)H	STD	£1774
73	8/07	Brig	1m3f196y	(0-65)H	FRM	£1943
67	1/07	Ling	1m4f		STD	£2169

Total win prize-money £11070

Going (Turf): Sf: 0-2 GS: 0-1 Gd: 0-6 GF: 0-7 **Fm: 1-1**
Distance: 5f/6f: 0-0 7f-8f: 2-16 **9f-13f: 3-28** 14f+: 0-2
Track : **LH: 4-35** RH: 1-8 **Tight: 3-23** Gall: 0-3
Aids: **Bl: 1-6** Vi: 0-0 Tstrap: 0-3 Ckp: 0-3
Best Rating: 79 3/08 Ling 1m stand

Modest; stays 1m4f; acts on fast ground; goes on sand.

King's Realm (IRE)

88(76) (34)**52**
2-y-o ch g King's Best (USA)-Sweet Home Alabama (IRE)

(Desert Prince (IRE))
Sir Mark Prescott P J McSwiney - Osborne House

Placings:060 **(6592)**
2009: 8^{0}SD, 8^{6}GF, 8^{0}GS,

	Starts	1st	2nd	3rd	Win & Pl
Career Total (Turf)	2	0	0	0	0
Career Total (AW)	1	0	0	0	

Going (Turf): **Sf: 0-0 GS: 0-1 Gd: 0-0 GF: 0-1 Fm: 0-0**
Distance: 5f/6f: 0-0 7f-8f: 0-1 9f-13f: 0-2 14f+: 0-0
Track : LH: 0-2 RH: 0-1 Tight: 0-0 Gall: 0-0
Aids: Bl: 0-0 Vi: 0-0 Tstrap: 0-0 Ckp: 0-0
Best Rating: **52** 10/09 Nott 1m75y gd-sft

King's Revenge

91(96) (59)**65**
6-y-o br g Wizard King-Retaliator (Rudimentary (USA))
S Lycett (A King 15/5) Nicholls Family

Placings:622030/614650160/6605 **(6342)**
2009: 10^{6}GF, 11^{6}GF, 12^{0}GS, 12^{5}SD,

	Starts	1st	2nd	3rd	Win & Pl
Career Total (Turf)	16	1	2	1	9638
Career Total (AW)	3	1	0	0	3239

79 9/06 Haml 1m65y (0-85)H G-S £6477
57 5/06 Wolv 1m141y STD £3238
Total win prize-money £9716

Going (Turf): Sf: 0-4 **GS: 1-4** Gd: 0-3 GF: 0-5 Fm: 0-0
Distance: 5f/6f: 0-4 7f-8f: 0-3 **9f-13f: 2-12** 14f+: 0-0
Track : LH: 1-12 RH: 1-3 **Tight: 2-6** Gall: 0-4
Aids: **Bl: 1-5** Vi: 0-0 Tstrap: 0-0 Ckp: 0-0
Best Rating: **79** 9/06 Haml 1m65y gd-sft

Fair handicapper; effective from 1m to 1m 2f; suited by good ground or softer.

King's Sabre

95(99) (66)**81**
3-y-o ch g King's Best (USA)-Lightsabre (Polar Falcon (USA))
R C Guest (W R Muir 2/10) Stan Wright & Future Racing Limited

Placings:020-40020402200506002 **(7796)**
2009: 7^{4}SD, 7^{0}G, 7^{0}G, 7^{2}SD, 7^{0}GF, 7^{4}G, 7^{0}SD, 7^{2}GF, 7^{2}SS, 6^{0}SD, 7^{0}GF, 5^{5}S, 5^{0}SD, 6^{6}SD, 5^{0}SD, 5^{0}SD, 7^{2}SS,

	Starts	1st	2nd	3rd	Win & Pl
Career Total (Turf)	9	0	2	0	2505
Career Total (AW)	11	0	3	0	2218

Going (Turf): **Sf: 0-1 GS: 0-0 Gd: 0-4 GF: 0-4 Fm: 0-0**
Distance: 5f/6f: 0-6 7f-8f: 0-14 9f-13f: 0-0 14f+: 0-0
Track : LH: 0-10 RH: 0-1 Tight: 0-8 Gall: 0-0
Aids: Bl: 0-6 Vi: 0-0 Tstrap: 0-2 Ckp: 0-2
Best Rating: **81** 9/08 Newb 7f good

Moderate; effective over 7f; acts on good ground; goes on Fibresand.

King's Salute (USA)

(105) (97)**68**
3-y-o b c Kingmambo (USA)-Imperial Gesture (USA) (Langfuhr (CAN))
M Johnston (A Fabre 17/3) Sheikh Hamdan Bin Mohammed Al Maktoum

Placings:011 **(7573)**
2009: 10^{0}VS, 11^{1}SD, 13^{1}SD,

	Starts	1st	2nd	3rd	Win & Pl
Career Total (Turf)	1	0	0	0	
Career Total (AW)	2	2	0	0	10068

97 11/09 Ling 1m5f (0-90)H STD £7477
77 10/09 Kemp 1m3f STD £2590
Total win prize-money £10067

Going (Turf): **Sf: 0-0 GS: 0-0 Gd: 0-0 GF: 0-0 Fm: 0-0**
Distance: 5f/6f: 0-0 7f-8f: 0-0 **9f-13f: 2-3** 14f+: 0-0
Track : LH: 1-2 RH: 1-1 **Tight: 1-1** Gall: 0-0
Aids: Bl: 0-0 Vi: 0-0 Tstrap: 0-0 Ckp: 0-0
Best Rating: **97** 11/09 Ling 1m5f stand

Useful; stays 1m5f and acts on Polytrack.

King's Siren (IRE)

86(95) (71)**64**
3-y-o b f King's Best (USA)-Blue Siren (Bluebird (USA))
A M Balding J C Smith

Placings:441-00 **(2498)**
2009: 8^{0}GF, 7^{0}GF,

	Starts	1st	2nd	3rd	Win & Pl
Career Total (Turf)	4	0	0	0	409
Career Total (AW)	1	1	0	0	4080

71 10/08 Ling 7f STD £4079
Total win prize-money £4080

Going (Turf): **Sf: 0-0 GS: 0-1 Gd: 0-1 GF: 0-2 Fm: 0-0**
Distance: 5f/6f: 0-0 **7f-8f: 1-5** 9f-13f: 0-0 14f+: 0-0
Track : **LH: 1-2** RH: 0-1 **Tight: 1-1** Gall: 0-0
Aids: Bl: 0-0 Vi: 0-0 Tstrap: 0-0 Ckp: 0-0
Best Rating: **71** 10/08 Ling 7f stand

Fair; stays 7f and acts on Polytrack.

King's Song (IRE)

102(101) (76)**74**
3-y-o ch c Indian Ridge-Alleluia (Caerleon (USA))
Sir Michael Stoute Saeed Suhail

Placings:50-614 **(6059)**
2009: 10^{6}S, 9^{1}SD, 10^{4}GF,

	Starts	1st	2nd	3rd	Win & Pl
Career Total (Turf)	4	0	0	0	361
Career Total (AW)	1	1	0	0	2730

76 9/09 Wolv 1m1f103y (0-75)H STD £2729
Total win prize-money £2730

Going (Turf): **Sf: 0-1 GS: 0-1 Gd: 0-1 GF: 0-1 Fm: 0-0**
Distance: 5f/6f: 0-0 7f-8f: 0-2 **9f-13f: 1-3** 14f+: 0-0
Track : **LH: 1-3** RH: 0-0 **Tight: 1-1** Gall: 0-2
Aids: Bl: 0-0 Vi: 0-0 Tstrap: 0-0 Ckp: 0-0
Best Rating: **76** 9/09 Wolv 1m1f103y stand

Fair; stays 1m1f; acts on Polytrack and fast ground.

King's Starlet

102(105) (87)**95**
3-y-o b f King's Best (USA)-Brightest Star (Unfuwain (USA))
H Morrison Helena Springfield Ltd

Placings:60-16040600 **(6814)**
2009: 8^{1}SD, 10^{6}G, 8^{0}GF, 8^{4}G, 7^{0}G, 8^{6}GF, 7^{0}GF, 6^{0}G,

	Starts	1st	2nd	3rd	Win & Pl
Career Total (Turf)	9	0	0	0	3228
Career Total (AW)	1	1	0	0	2590

87 4/09 Kemp 1m STD £2590
Total win prize-money £2590

Going (Turf): **Sf: 0-0 GS: 0-0 Gd: 0-5 GF: 0-4 Fm: 0-0**
Distance: 5f/6f: 0-1 **7f-8f: 1-6** 9f-13f: 0-3 14f+: 0-0
Track : LH: 0-1 **RH: 1-4** Tight: 0-0 Gall: 0-1
Aids: Bl: 0-0 Vi: 0-0 Tstrap: 0-0 Ckp: 0-0
Best Rating: **95** 7/09 Gdwd 7f good

Very useful; effective over 1m and acts on Polytrack.

King's Warrior (FR)

93 **69**
2-y-o b c King's Best (USA)-Save Me The Waltz (FR) (Halling (USA))
G L Moore Paul Hancock

Placings:4 **(7146)**
2009: 7^{4}G,

	Starts	1st	2nd	3rd	Win & Pl
Career Total (Turf)	1	0	0	0	385

Going (Turf): **Sf: 0-0 GS: 0-0 Gd: 0-1 GF: 0-0 Fm: 0-0**
Distance: 5f/6f: 0-0 7f-8f: 0-1 9f-13f: 0-0 14f+: 0-0
Track : LH: 0-0 RH: 0-0 Tight: 0-0 Gall: 0-0
Aids: Bl: 0-0 Vi: 0-0 Tstrap: 0-0 Ckp: 0-0
Best Rating: **69** 10/09 NmkR 7f good

King's Wonder

105(104) (93)**97**
4-y-o ch g King's Best (USA)-Signs And Wonders (Danehill (USA))
W R Muir D G Clarke & C L A Edginton

Placings:536/30604322120-100565 **(6702)**
2009: 7^{1}G, 7^{0}G, 6^{0}SD, 7^{5}GF, 7^{6}GF, 7^{5}SS,

	Starts	1st	2nd	3rd	Win & Pl
Career Total (Turf)	12	1	1	1	8086
Career Total (AW)	8	1	2	2	5776

97 5/09 Gdwd 7f (0-85)H GD £4857
93 9/08 Kemp 7f (0-75)H STD £2590
Total win prize-money £7447

Going (Turf): Sf: 0-0 GS: 0-1 **Gd: 1-5** GF: 0-6 Fm: 0-0
Distance: 5f/6f: 0-4 **7f-8f: 2-15** 9f-13f: 0-1 14f+: 0-0
Track : LH: 0-5 **RH: 2-8** Tight: 0-5 Gall: 0-1
Aids: Bl: 0-0 Vi: 0-0 Tstrap: 0-0 Ckp: 0-0
Best Rating: **97** 5/09 Gdwd 7f good

Useful; stays 7f; acts on good, fast ground and on Polytrack.

Kingaroo (IRE)

95(98) (67)**57**
3-y-o b g King Charlemagne (USA)-Lady Naomi (USA) (Distant View (USA))
G Woodward (Garry Moss 5/8) J Pownall

Placings:00465501-24320000030 **(7127)**
2009: 8^{2}SD, 8^{4}SD, 8^{3}SD, 8^{2}SD, 7^{0}SD, 8^{0}GF, 9^{0}GF, 8^{0}SD, 7^{0}SD, 10^{3}G, 10^{0}G,

	Starts	1st	2nd	3rd	Win & Pl
Career Total (Turf)	11	0	0	1	520
Career Total (AW)	8	1	2	1	3559

58 12/08 Sthl 7f (0-65) STD £2047
Total win prize-money £2047

Going (Turf): **Sf: 0-3 GS: 0-1 Gd: 0-3 GF: 0-4 Fm: 0-0**
Distance: 5f/6f: 0-1 **7f-8f: 1-11** 9f-13f: 0-7 14f+: 0-0
Track : **LH: 1-13** RH: 0-4 Tight: 0-5 Gall: 0-0
Aids: Bl: 0-0 Vi: 0-0 Tstrap: 0-1 Ckp: 0-1

Best Rating: 67 2/09 Sthl 1m stand

Moderate; effective over 1m and acts on Fibresand.

Kingdom Of Fife

112 **113**

4-y-o b g Kingmambo (USA)-Fairy Godmother (Fairy King (USA))

Sir Michael Stoute The Queen

Placings:5/0361133-21233 **(6303)**

2009: 10^{2}GF, 10^{1}GF, 10^{2}GF, 10^{3}GF, 12^{3}GF,

	Starts	1st	2nd	3rd	Win & Pl
Career Total (Turf)	13	3	2	5	96874

104 5/09 Rdcr 1m2f (0-105)H G-F £32380
84 8/08 Sand 1m2f7y (0-80)H GD £7123
79 8/08 Sand 1m2f7y (0-80)H G-S £6476
Total win prize-money £45980

Going (Turf): Sf: 0-1 **GS: 1-3 Gd: 1-3 GF: 1-6** Fm: 0-0
Distance: 5f/6f: 0-0 7f-8f: 0-2 **9f-13f: 3-11** 14f+: 0-0
Track : LH: 1-5 **RH: 2-6 Tight: 1-6** Gall: 0-2
Aids: Bl: 0-0 **Vi: 1-4** Tstrap: 0-0 Ckp: 0-0
Best Rating: 113 9/09 Asct 1m4f gd-fm

Smart; stays 1m2f; acts on fast ground.

Kingdom Of Light

102 **94**

2-y-o gr c Exceed And Excel (AUS)-Silver Chime (Robellino (USA))

J Howard Johnson Transcend Bloodstock LLP

Placings:2102604 **(6486)**

2009: 5^{2}G, 6^{1}G, 5^{0}GF, 5^{2}GF, 5^{6}GS, 6^{0}GF, 6^{4}GF,

	Starts	1st	2nd	3rd	Win & Pl
Career Total (Turf)	7	1	2	0	22913

86 5/09 Hayd 6f GD £2914
Total win prize-money £2914

Going (Turf): Sf: 0-0 GS: 0-1 **Gd: 1-2** GF: 0-4 Fm: 0-0
Distance: **5f/6f: 1-7** 7f-8f: 0-0 9f-13f: 0-0 14f+: 0-0
Track : LH: 0-1 RH: 0-0 Tight: 0-0 Gall: 0-0
Aids: Bl: 0-0 Vi: 0-0 Tstrap: 0-0 Ckp: 0-0
Best Rating: 94 10/09 Rdcr 6f gd-fm

Useful; effective over 6f; acts on good ground; has worn a tongue tie.

Kings 'n Dreams

95(85) (61)**74**

2-y-o b g Royal Applause-Last Dream (IRE) (Alzao (USA))

D K Ivory PaulBlows, IanRGethin, MrsMelanieDoughty

Placings:044 **(7537)**

2009: 6^{0}G, 6^{4}S, 7^{4}SD,

	Starts	1st	2nd	3rd	Win & Pl
Career Total (Turf)	2	0	0	0	457
Career Total (AW)	1	0	0	0	241

Going (Turf): **Sf: 0-1 GS: 0-0 Gd: 0-1 GF: 0-0 Fm: 0-0**
Distance: 5f/6f: 0-1 7f-8f: 0-2 9f-13f: 0-0 14f+: 0-0
Track : LH: 0-0 RH: 0-1 Tight: 0-0 Gall: 0-0
Aids: Bl: 0-0 Vi: 0-0 Tstrap: 0-0 Ckp: 0-0
Best Rating: 74 11/09 Donc 6f soft

Fair; effective over 6f; should stay 7f; acts on soft ground and on Polytrack.

Kings Ace (IRE)

96(99) (60)**62**

3-y-o b g King's Best (USA)-Full Cream (USA) (Hennessy (USA))

A P Jarvis A B Parr

Placings:54006-100302**0**04460 **(7817)**

2009: 6^{1}SD, 7^{0}GF, 6^{0}SD, 7^{3}G, 6^{0}G, 6^{2}S, 6^{0}G, 6^{0}SD, 7^{4}SD, 8^{4}SD, 7^{6}SD, 9^{0}SD,

	Starts	1st	2nd	3rd	Win & Pl
Career Total (Turf)	10	0	1	1	1446
Career Total (AW)	7	1	0	0	2047

59 4/09 Sthl 6f (0-60)H STD £2047
Total win prize-money £2047

Going (Turf): **Sf: 0-2 GS: 0-0 Gd: 0-4 GF: 0-4 Fm: 0-0**
Distance: **5f/6f: 1-8** 7f-8f: 0-7 9f-13f: 0-2 14f+: 0-0
Track : **LH: 1-5** RH: 0-2 Tight: 0-3 Gall: 0-0
Aids: Bl: 0-0 Vi: 0-7 Tstrap: 0-0 Ckp: 0-0
Best Rating: 62 8/09 Ayr 6f soft

Moderate; suited by 6f and soft ground.

Kings Aphrodite

80 **45**

2-y-o gr g Reset (AUS)-Arctic Queen (Linamix (FR))

Miss Gay Kelleway Winterbeck Kelleway Henderson Joslyn

Placings:000 **(2187)**

2009: 5^{0}GF, 5^{0}GF, 6^{0}GF,

	Starts	1st	2nd	3rd	Win & Pl
Career Total (Turf)	3	0	0	0	

Going (Turf): **Sf: 0-0 GS: 0-0 Gd: 0-0 GF: 0-3 Fm: 0-0**
Distance: 5f/6f: 0-3 7f-8f: 0-0 9f-13f: 0-0 14f+: 0-0
Track : LH: 0-1 RH: 0-0 Tight: 0-0 Gall: 0-0
Aids: Bl: 0-0 Vi: 0-0 Tstrap: 0-0 Ckp: 0-0
Best Rating: 45 4/09 Brig 5f59y gd-fm

Kings Bayonet

92(99) (76)**73**

2-y-o ch g Needwood Blade-Retaliator (Rudimentary (USA))

H R A Cecil W H Ponsonby

Placings:201 **(6254)**

2009: 6^{2}G, 6^{0}GF, 7^{1}SD,

	Starts	1st	2nd	3rd	Win & Pl
Career Total (Turf)	2	0	1	0	886
Career Total (AW)	1	1	0	0	3886

76 9/09 Wolv 7f32y STD £3885
Total win prize-money £3886

Going (Turf): **Sf: 0-0 GS: 0-0 Gd: 0-1 GF: 0-1 Fm: 0-0**
Distance: 5f/6f: 0-1 **7f-8f: 1-2** 9f-13f: 0-0 14f+: 0-0
Track : **LH: 1-1** RH: 0-0 **Tight: 1-1** Gall: 0-0
Aids: Bl: 0-0 Vi: 0-0 Tstrap: 0-0 Ckp: 0-0
Best Rating: 76 9/09 Wolv 7f32y stand

Fair; stays 7f; acts on good ground and on Polytrack.

Kings Destiny

108(103) (86)**106**

3-y-o b g Dubai Destination (USA)-Jalousie (IRE) (Barathea (IRE))

M A Jarvis Dennis Yardy

Placings:2421-1421420 **(7293)**

2009: 9^{1}GF, 12^{4}GF, 12^{2}G, 12^{1}S, 14^{4}S, 12^{2}GS, 12^{0}S,

	Starts	1st	2nd	3rd	Win & Pl
Career Total (Turf)	9	2	3	0	50235
Career Total (AW)	2	1	1	0	3695

102 7/09 Ripn 1m4f10y (0-100)H SFT £15577
91 4/09 Leic 1m1f218y (0-95)H G-F £7569
84 12/08 Ling 1m STD £2388
Total win prize-money £25536

Going (Turf): **Sf: 1-5** GS: 0-1 Gd: 0-1 **GF: 1-2** Fm: 0-0
Distance: 5f/6f: 0-0 7f-8f: 1-3 **9f-13f: 2-7** 14f+: 0-1
Track : LH: 1-6 **RH: 2-4 Tight: 2-4** Gall: 0-3
Aids: Bl: 0-0 Vi: 0-0 Tstrap: 0-0 Ckp: 0-0
Best Rating: 106 10/09 Asct 1m4f gd-sft

Smart; stays 1m4f; acts on fast and soft ground; goes on Polytrack.

Kings Gambit (SAF)

109 **112**

5-y-o ch g Silvano (GER)-Lady Brompton (SAF) (Al Mufti (USA))

T P Tate (H J Brown 28/3) Mrs Fitri Hay

Placings:115211-54503045 **(6644)**

2009: 8^{5}GF, 8^{4}GF, 12^{5}GF, 12^{0}G, 10^{3}G, 13^{0}GF, 10^{4}G, 10^{5}G,

	Starts	1st	2nd	3rd	Win & Pl
Career Total (Turf)	14	4	1	1	136370

5/08 Turf 1m4f55y SFT £45955
4/08 Turf 1m1f GD £55147
2/08 Turf 5f176y GD £3676
1/08 Vaal 6f GD £3216
Total win prize-money £107996

Going (Turf): Sf: 1-2 GS: 0-0 **Gd: 3-8** GF: 0-4 Fm: 0-0
Distance: 5f/6f: 2-2 7f-8f: 0-1 9f-13f: 2-10 14f+: 0-1
Track : LH: 0-8 RH: 0-0 Tight: 0-0 Gall: 0-8
Aids: Bl: 0-0 Vi: 0-0 Tstrap: 0-0 Ckp: 0-0
Best Rating: 112 7/09 York 1m2f88y good

Listed class; dual South African Grade 1 winner; effective over 1m1f-1m4f; acts on good and soft ground; has worn a tongue tie.

Kings Maiden (IRE)

101(111) (65)**68**

6-y-o b m King's Theatre (IRE)-Maidenhair (IRE) (Darshaan)

James Moffatt Mrs S C Huntley

Placings:403-21242 **(4068)**

2009: 10^{2}GF, 13^{1}SD, 12^{2}GS, 14^{4}GF, 12^{2}S,

	Starts	1st	2nd	3rd	Win & Pl
Career Total (Turf)	7	0	3	1	3063
Career Total (AW)	1	1	0	0	2730

65 5/09 Wolv 1m5f194y (0-65)H STD £2729
Total win prize-money £2730

Going (Turf): **Sf: 0-1 GS: 0-3 Gd: 0-0 GF: 0-3 Fm: 0-0**
Distance: 5f/6f: 0-0 7f-8f: 0-0 9f-13f: 0-6 **14f+: 1-2**
Track : **LH: 1-6** RH: 0-2 **Tight: 1-4** Gall: 0-2
Aids: Bl: 0-0 Vi: 0-0 Tstrap: 0-0 Ckp: 0-0
Best Rating: 68 5/09 Newc 1m4f93y gd-sft

Modest; stays 1m6f; acts on fast ground and on Polytrack.

Kings Of Leo

95(102) (65)**83**

2-y-o b f Compton Place-Mrs Brown (Royal Applause)

J R Boyle (R Hannon 16/7) Thompson, Pemberton, Lancaster & Antram

Placings:510320200643 (7871)

2009: 5^{5}G, 5^{1}GF, 5^{0}GF, 5^{3}F, 5^{2}GF, 5^{0}SD, 5^{2}GF, 5^{0}G, 6^{0}SD, 6^{6}SD, 5^{4}SD, 5^{3}SD,

	Starts	1st	2nd	3rd	Win & Pl
Career Total (Turf)	7	1	2	1	9641
Career Total (AW)	5	0	0	1	385

74 5/09 Wwck 5f G-F £3885

Total win prize-money £3886

Going (Turf): Sf: 0-0 GS: 0-0 Gd: 0-2 **GF: 1-4** Fm: 0-1
Distance: **5f/6f: 1-12** 7f-8f: 0-0 9f-13f: 0-0 14f+: 0-0
Track : **LH: 1-5** RH: 0-4 Tight: 0-2 Gall: 0-5
Aids: Bl: 0-0 Vi: 0-0 Tstrap: 0-0 Ckp: 0-0
Best Rating: 83 7/09 Bath 5f11y gd-fm

Fair; best form over 5f, acts on fast ground.

Kings On The Roof

87(92) (55)**49**

3-y-o b c King Charlemagne (USA)-Stylish Clare (IRE) (Desert Style (IRE))

G C Bravery Theresa Fitsall & Sean Gollogly

Placings:06-0444000 (4648)

2009: 6^{0}SD, 7^{4}SD, 6^{4}SD, 7^{4}GF, 7^{0}SD, 6^{0}G, 8^{0}SD,

	Starts	1st	2nd	3rd	Win & Pl
Career Total (Turf)	2	0	0	0	192
Career Total (AW)	7	0	0	0	0

Going (Turf): **Sf: 0-0 GS: 0-0 Gd: 0-1 GF: 0-1 Fm: 0-0**
Distance: 5f/6f: 0-4 7f-8f: 0-5 9f-13f: 0-0 14f+: 0-0
Track : LH: 0-5 RH: 0-2 Tight: 0-2 Gall: 0-2
Aids: Bl: 0-0 Vi: 0-0 Tstrap: 0-1 Ckp: 0-1
Best Rating: 55 3/09 Ling 7f stand

Kings Point (IRE)

105(97) (89)**98**

8-y-o b h Fasliyev (USA)-Rahika Rose (Unfuwain (USA))

D Nicholls W R B Racing 61 (Claire King)

Placings:24116/50530403000/030200516/436602306/600 0040400051/416003125-00640000044 (6217)

2009: 8^{0}GF, 7^{0}GF, 8^{6}GF, 7^{4}GF, 8^{0}GF, 8^{0}GF, 7^{0}S, 7^{0}G, 7^{0}GF, 9^{4}G, 8^{4}GF,

	Starts	1st	2nd	3rd	Win & Pl
Career Total (Turf)	64	6	4	6	134471
Career Total (AW)	3	0	0	0	211

97 9/08 Thsk 7f (0-85)H SFT £5569
90 6/08 Muss 7f30y (0-85)H G-F £6476
82 9/07 Muss 1m1f G-S £2590
109 9/05 Curr 1m G-F £25393
106 7/03 NmkJ 7f A G-F £23200
83 6/03 Gdwd 6f D G-F £4836

Total win prize-money £68066

Going (Turf): Sf: 1-7 GS: 1-7 Gd: 0-15 **GF: 4-33** Fm: 0-2
Distance: 5f/6f: 1-4 **7f-8f: 4-52** 9f-13f: 1-11 14f+: 0-0
Track : LH: 1-30 **RH: 3-16 Tight: 3-17** Gall: 1-17
Aids: Bl: 0-2 Vi: 0-1 Tstrap: 2-16 Ckp: 2-16
Best Rating: 109 8/06 Sals 1m gd-sft

Useful; effective up to 1m1f; suited by fast ground, but handles cut; has worn blinkers, cheekpieces and a visor.

Kings Topic (USA)

(105) (77)**53**

9-y-o ch g Kingmambo (USA)-Topicount (USA) (Private Account (USA))

A B Haynes WCR V - The Conkwell Connection

Placings:000/0/2110/21/65/0300/32222052511005-200100506 (7623)

2009: 10^{2}SD, 9^{0}SD, 10^{0}SD, 10^{1}SD, 10^{0}SD, 9^{0}SD, 10^{5}SD, 10^{0}SD, 10^{6}SD,

	Starts	1st	2nd	3rd	Win & Pl
Career Total (Turf)	5	0	0	0	
Career Total (AW)	34	6	8	2	19425

70 3/09 Ling 1m2f (0-70)H STD £2729
77 8/08 GrLe 1m2f (0-60)H STD £1942
67 8/08 Ling 1m2f (0-60)H STD £2914
66 5/05 Wolv 1m1f103y (0-60)H STD £2660
55 4/04 Ling 1m2f H(0-45) STD £1620
53 4/04 Ling 1m2f H(0-45) STD £1638

Total win prize-money £13506

Going (Turf): **Sf: 0-2 GS: 0-1 Gd: 0-0 GF: 0-2 Fm: 0-0**
Distance: 5f/6f: 0-0 7f-8f: 0-2 **9f-13f: 6-37** 14f+: 0-0
Track : **LH: 6-32** RH: 0-4 **Tight: 5-28** Gall: 1-4
Aids: Bl: 0-3 Vi: 0-0 Tstrap: 3-14 Ckp: 3-14
Best Rating: 77 8/08 GrLe 1m2f stand

Modest; stays 1m2f and acts on Polytrack; has worn blinkers and cheekpieces.

Kings Troop

95(100) (70)**85**

3-y-o ch g Bertolini (USA)-Glorious Colours (Spectrum (IRE))

A King (H R A Cecil 16/9) W H Ponsonby

Placings:561200-50605 (7428)

2009: 7^{5}HY, 8^{0}GF, 8^{6}S, 8^{0}SD, 10^{5}SD,

	Starts	1st	2nd	3rd	Win & Pl
Career Total (Turf)	9	1	1	0	5387
Career Total (AW)	2	0	0	0	0

82 7/08 Wwck 7f26y SFT £3238

Total win prize-money £3238

Going (Turf): **Sf: 1-3** GS: 0-1 Gd: 0-1 GF: 0-4 Fm: 0-0
Distance: 5f/6f: 0-0 **7f-8f: 1-9** 9f-13f: 0-2 14f+: 0-0
Track : **LH: 1-3** RH: 0-3 Tight: 0-1 Gall: 0-1
Aids: Bl: 0-1 Vi: 0-0 Tstrap: 0-0 Ckp: 0-0
Best Rating: 85 8/08 NmkJ 7f gd-sft

Useful; stays 7f and acts on soft ground.

Kingsdale Orion (IRE)

105(103) (82)**91**

5-y-o b/br g Intikhab (USA)-Jinsiyah (USA) (Housebuster (USA))

B Ellison Koo's Racing Club

Placings:03300/036051310/60014306520-6300003135343 (5671)

2009: 9^{6}SD, 10^{3}G, 8^{0}GF, 12^{0}GF, 12^{0}GS, 12^{0}G, 11^{3}GF, 10^{1}S, 11^{3}SD, 9^{5}S, 12^{3}SD, 10^{4}S, 12^{3}S,

	Starts	1st	2nd	3rd	Win & Pl
Career Total (Turf)	35	4	1	8	49998
Career Total (AW)	3	0	0	2	2334

80 6/09 Newc 1m2f32y (0-85)H SFT £4984
91 6/08 Newc 1m3y (0-100)H G-S £15577
99 8/07 Rosc 7f Y-S £7470
93 6/07 Curr 7f (50-80)H SFT £6769

Total win prize-money £34803

Going (Turf): **Sf: 2-13** GS: 1-3 Gd: 0-4 GF: 0-9 Fm: 0-1
Distance: 5f/6f: 0-1 7f-8f: 2-16 9f-13f: 2-21 14f+: 0-0
Track : LH: 1-18 RH: 1-11 Tight: 0-5 **Gall: 1-8**
Aids: Bl: 0-1 Vi: 0-0 Tstrap: 0-1 Ckp: 0-1
Best Rating: 100 5/07 Curr 1m gd-fm

Fair; ex-Irish; effective at 1m2f-1m4f; seems best suited by easy ground.

Kingsdine (IRE)

88 **61**

2-y-o b c King's Best (USA)-Lunadine (FR) (Bering)

M S Saunders M S Saunders

Placings:050 (5499)

2009: 5^{0}S, 6^{5}GF, 8^{0}G,

	Starts	1st	2nd	3rd	Win & Pl
Career Total (Turf)	3	0	0	0	0

Going (Turf): **Sf: 0-1 GS: 0-0 Gd: 0-1 GF: 0-1 Fm: 0-0**
Distance: 5f/6f: 0-1 7f-8f: 0-1 9f-13f: 0-1 14f+: 0-0
Track : LH: 0-0 RH: 0-0 Tight: 0-0 Gall: 0-0
Aids: Bl: 0-0 Vi: 0-0 Tstrap: 0-0 Ckp: 0-0
Best Rating: 61 8/09 Sals 6f212y gd-fm

Kingsgate Castle

100(107) (71)**65**

4-y-o b g Kyllachy-Ella Lamees (Statoblest)

Miss Gay Kelleway Miss Gay Kelleway

Placings:56/315003-5000600424022012 (7834)

2009: 6^{5}SD, 6^{0}GF, 6^{0}G, 7^{0}SD, 7^{6}SD, 6^{0}S, 6^{0}SD, 6^{4}GF, 6^{2}GS, 7^{4}SD, 6^{0}GF, 5^{2}SD, 7^{2}SS, 7^{0}G, 6^{1}SD, 6^{2}SD,

	Starts	1st	2nd	3rd	Win & Pl
Career Total (Turf)	8	0	1	0	1060
Career Total (AW)	16	2	3	2	6876

61 12/09 Kemp 6f (0-55) STD £2047
67 1/08 Ling 6f STD £2331

Total win prize-money £4379

Going (Turf): **Sf: 0-1 GS: 0-1 Gd: 0-3 GF: 0-3 Fm: 0-0**
Distance: **5f/6f: 2-17** 7f-8f: 0-7 9f-13f: 0-0 14f+: 0-0
Track : LH: 1-12 RH: 1-5 **Tight: 1-11** Gall: 0-1
Aids: **Bl: 1-11** Vi: 0-5 Tstrap: 0-0 Ckp: 0-0
Best Rating: 71 10/08 Ling 6f stand

Modest; stays 7f; acts on fast ground; goes on Polytrack; has worn a visor and blinkers.

Kingsgate Choice (IRE)

(96) (76)

2-y-o b c Choisir (AUS)-Kenema (IRE) (Petardia)

J R Best John Mayne

Placings:31 (7556)

2009: 5^{3}SD, 5^{1}SD,

	Starts	1st	2nd	3rd	Win & Pl
Career Total (Turf)	0	0	0	0	
Career Total (AW)	2	1	0	1	3133

76 11/09 Wolv 5f216y STD £2729

Total win prize-money £2730

Going (Turf): **Sf: 0-0 GS: 0-0 Gd: 0-0 GF: 0-0 Fm: 0-0**
Distance: **5f/6f: 1-2** 7f-8f: 0-0 9f-13f: 0-0 14f+: 0-0
Track : **LH: 1-2** RH: 0-0 **Tight: 1-2** Gall: 0-0
Aids: Bl: 0-0 Vi: 0-0 Tstrap: 0-0 Ckp: 0-0
Best Rating: 76 11/09 Wolv 5f216y stand

Fair; suited by 6f and Polytrack.

Kingsgate Native (IRE)

113 **123**

4-y-o b g Mujadil (USA)-Native Force (IRE) (Indian Ridge)
Sir Michael Stoute Cheveley Park Stud

Placings:2212/0153-016 **(5233)**
2009: 6^{0}GF, 5^{1}G, 5^{6}GF,

	Starts	1st	2nd	3rd	Win & Pl
Career Total (Turf)	11	3	3	1	481766

123	7/09	Gdwd	5f	GD	£39739
123	6/08	Asct	6f	G-F	£212887
115	8/07	York	5f	GD	£136158

Total win prize-money £388785

Going (Turf): Sf: 0-0 GS: 0-1 **Gd: 2-5** GF: 1-5 Fm: 0-0
Distance: **5f/6f: 3-11** 7f-8f: 0-0 9f-13f: 0-0 14f+: 0-0
Track : LH: 0-0 RH: 0-0 Tight: 0-0 Gall: 0-0
Aids: Bl: 0-0 Vi: 0-0 Tstrap: 0-0 Ckp: 0-0
Best Rating: **123** 7/09 Gdwd 5f good

High class; winner of the 2007 Nunthorpe Stakes as a juvenile and the Golden Jubilee Stakes in 2008, when trained by John Best; effective at 5f-6f; acts on good and faster ground; returned to training in 2009 after proving infertile at stud and won the King George Stakes at Goodwood.

Kingsgate Storm (IRE)

91(95) (61)**80**

3-y-o gr g Mujadil (USA)-In The Highlands (Petong)
J R Best John Mayne

Placings:0040-40050003 **(7052)**
2009: 5^{4}SD, 7^{0}S, 6^{0}GF, 6^{5}G, 5^{0}G, 5^{0}GF, 5^{0}SD, 7^{3}SD,

	Starts	1st	2nd	3rd	Win & Pl
Career Total (Turf)	6	0	0	0	0
Career Total (AW)	6	0	0	1	661

Going (Turf): **Sf: 0-1 GS: 0-0 Gd: 0-2 GF: 0-3 Fm: 0-0**
Distance: 5f/6f: 0-10 7f-8f: 0-2 9f-13f: 0-0 14f+: 0-0
Track : LH: 0-6 RH: 0-2 Tight: 0-3 Gall: 0-2
Aids: Bl: 0-0 Vi: 0-0 Tstrap: 0-0 Ckp: 0-0
Best Rating: **80** 6/08 Asct 5f gd-fm

Fair; effective at 6f; handles Polytrack.

Kingshill Prince

78(78) (23)**62**

3-y-o b g Mark Of Esteem (IRE)-Trefoil (FR) (Blakeney)
W J Musson James Huckett

Placings:54-000 **(3302)**
2009: 8^{0}G, 8^{0}G, 8^{0}SD,

	Starts	1st	2nd	3rd	Win & Pl
Career Total (Turf)	4	0	0	0	409
Career Total (AW)	1	0	0	0	

Going (Turf): **Sf: 0-2 GS: 0-0 Gd: 0-2 GF: 0-0 Fm: 0-0**
Distance: 5f/6f: 0-1 7f-8f: 0-2 9f-13f: 0-2 14f+: 0-0
Track : LH: 0-1 RH: 0-1 Tight: 0-0 Gall: 0-0
Aids: Bl: 0 0 Vi: 0-0 Tstrap: 0-0 Ckp: 0-0
Best Rating: **62** 11/08 Donc 6f soft

Half-brother to five winners; stays 6f; acts on soft ground.

Kingsholm

93(105) (71)**67**

7-y-o ch g Selkirk (USA)-Putuna (Generous (IRE))
N Wilson Mrs N C Wilson

Placings:630/0261/065**645**1120/005606**V23**/6004004061 1653313-0000600 **(6987)**
2009: 8^{0}SD, 10^{0}G, 8^{0}G, 9^{0}GF, 9^{6}G, 10^{0}GS, 9^{0}G,

	Starts	1st	2nd	3rd	Win & Pl
Career Total (Turf)	31	4	2	1	28683
Career Total (AW)	19	2	1	4	7457

71	12/08	Sthl	1m	(0-65)H	STD	£2047
69	9/08	Wolv	1m141y	(0-55)H	SF	£2388
67	9/08	Bevl	1m1f207y	(0-60)H	SFT	£2498
88	10/06	Bath	1m5y	(0-85)H	GD	£8096
86	9/06	Gdwd	1m	(0-80)H	GD	£5829
82	10/05	Wind	1m2f7y	(0-80)H	GD	£7186

Total win prize-money £28044

Going (Turf): Sf: 1-5 GS: 0-6 **Gd: 3-13** GF: 0-6 Fm: 0-1
Distance: 5f/6f: 0-0 7f-8f: 2-18 **9f-13f: 4-32** 14f+: 0-0
Track : LH: 3-23 RH: 3-25 **Tight: 3-23** Gall: 0-2
Aids: Bl: 0-0 Vi: 0-0 Tstrap: 0-1 Ckp: 0-1
Best Rating: **91** 10/06 Wind 1m2f7y gd-sft

Modest; effective over 1m-1m2f; acts on good ground; goes on Polytrack.

Kingsmaite

94(103) (74)**58**

8-y-o b g Komaite (USA)-Antonias Melody (Rambo Dancer (CAN))
S R Bowring S R Bowring

Placings:60364**212**/0405130502**104**/**15**0000**634**/**65**00004 05316/04043330003000/0225421311405432-31043303601004000 **(7728)**
2009: 7^{3}SD, 5^{1}SD, 7^{0}SS, 6^{4}SD, 6^{3}SD, 6^{3}SD, 7^{0}SD, 6^{3}GF, 7^{6}GF, 7^{0}SD, 6^{1}SD, 6^{0}SD, 7^{0}SD, 7^{4}SF, 7^{0}SD, 5^{0}SD, 8^{0}SD,

	Starts	1st	2nd	3rd	Win & Pl
Career Total (Turf)	25	1	0	3	8355
Career Total (AW)	65	9	7	11	37334

74	6/09	Sthl	6f	(0-60)H	STD	£2047
70	1/09	Wolv	5f216y	(0-60)H	STD	£1648
66	5/08	Wolv	5f216y	(0-65)H	STD	£2047
68	5/08	Sthl	6f	(0-70)H	STD	£3238
62	4/08	Sthl	6f	(0-52)H	STD	£2047
68	12/06	Sthl	1m	(0-65)H	STD	£2590
91	3/05	Wolv	5f216y	(0-85)H	STD	£6669
84	11/04	Wolv	7f32y	(0-77)H	STD	£3393
73	6/04	Rdcr	6f	D(0-80)H	GD	£5638
80	12/03	Sthl	1m	D	STD	£3125

Total win prize-money £32445

Going (Turf): Sf: 0-0 GS: 0-1 **Gd: 1-10** GF: 0-14 Fm: 0-0
Distance: **5f/6f: 7-33** 7f-8f: 3-51 9f-13f: 0-6 14f+: 0-0
Track : **LH: 9-69** RH: 0-3 **Tight: 4-27** Gall: 0-0
Aids: **Bl: 9-68** Vi: 0-5 Tstrap: 0-0 Ckp: 0-0
Best Rating: **91** 3/05 Wolv 5f216y stand

Moderate; effective from 6f-1m; acts on Fibresand and Polytrack; has worn blinkers.

Kingspark Boy (IRE)

11

2-y-o b g Tillerman-Malacca (USA) (Danzig (USA))
W K Goldsworthy E R Clough

Placings:0 **(5907)**
2009: 8^{0}GF,

	Starts	1st	2nd	3rd	Win & Pl
Career Total (Turf)	1	0	0	0	

Going (Turf): **Sf: 0-0 GS: 0-0 Gd: 0-0 GF: 0-1 Fm: 0-0**
Distance: 5f/6f: 0-0 7f-8f: 0-1 9f-13f: 0-0 14f+: 0-0
Track : LH: 0-1 RH: 0-0 Tight: 0-0 Gall: 0-1
Aids: Bl: 0-0 Vi: 0-0 Tstrap: 0-0 Ckp: 0-0
Best Rating: **11** 9/09 Ffos 1m gd-fm

Kingston Acacia

84(92) (63)**46**

2-y-o b f King Of Roses (AUS)-Derartu (AUS) (Last Tycoon)
A M Balding Richard Hains

Placings:0602 **(7389)**
2009: 7^{0}SD, 7^{6}SD, 8^{0}G, 7^{2}SD,

	Starts	1st	2nd	3rd	Win & Pl
Career Total (Turf)	1	0	0	0	
Career Total (AW)	3	0	1	0	560

Going (Turf): **Sf: 0-0 GS: 0-0 Gd: 0-1 GF: 0-0 Fm: 0-0**
Distance: 5f/6f: 0-0 7f-8f: 0-4 9f-13f: 0-0 14f+: 0-0
Track : LH: 0-2 RH: 0-1 Tight: 0-2 Gall: 0-0
Aids: Bl: 0-0 Vi: 0-1 Tstrap: 0-0 Ckp: 0-0
Best Rating: **63** 9/09 Ling 7f stand

Modest; effective over 7f; acts on Polytrack.

Kingston Folly

(65) (60)

2-y-o gr g Septieme Ciel (USA)-Napapijri (FR) (Highest Honor (FR))
A B Haynes Kingston Homes

Placings:5 **(7663)**
2009: 8^{5}SD,

	Starts	1st	2nd	3rd	Win & Pl
Career Total (Turf)	0	0	0	0	
Career Total (AW)	1	0	0	0	0

Going (Turf): **Sf: 0-0 GS: 0-0 Gd: 0-0 GF: 0-0 Fm: 0-0**
Distance: 5f/6f: 0-0 7f-8f: 0-1 9f-13f: 0-0 14f+: 0-0
Track : LH: 0-1 RH: 0-0 Tight: 0-1 Gall: 0-0
Aids: Bl: 0-0 Vi: 0-0 Tstrap: 0-0 Ckp: 0-0
Best Rating: **60** 12/09 Ling 1m stand

Kingswinford (IRE)

104(103) (80)**85**

3-y-o b g Noverre (USA)-Berenica (IRE) (College Chapel)
P D Evans Nick Shutts

Placings:3442440456214102-006642222353130 **(7287)**
2009: 6^{0}G, 6^{0}G, 7^{6}G, 5^{6}GF, 6^{4}G, 5^{2}G, 6^{2}G, 6^{2}S, 7^{2}S, 6^{3}GF, 5^{5}SD, 6^{3}S, 6^{1}G, 7^{3}S, 7^{0}S,

	Starts	1st	2nd	3rd	Win & Pl
Career Total (Turf)	29	3	7	4	29478
Career Total (AW)	2	0	0	0	188

82	10/09	Wind	6f		GD	£2047
81	10/08	Newb	6f8y	(0-85)	G-S	£6476
72	8/08	Newb	6f8y		G-S	£4533

Total win prize-money £13056

Going (Turf): Sf: 0-9 **GS: 2-3** Gd: 1-11 GF: 0-6 Fm: 0-0
Distance: 5f/6f: 1-21 **7f-8f: 2-10** 9f-13f: 0-0 14f+: 0-0
Track : LH: 0-9 RH: 0-0 Tight: 0-6 **Gall: 1-4**

Aids: Bl: 0-0 Vi: 0-1 Tstrap: 0-0 Ckp: 0-0
Best Rating: **85** 11/08 Donc 6f soft

Fair; effective over 5f-7f; acts on most ground on turf; has worn a visor.

Kinian (USA)

58

2-y-o ch c Langfuhr (CAN)-Back It Up (USA) (Mt. Livermore (USA))
J R Best Kent Bloodstock

Placings:0 **(5722)**
2009: 7^{0}F,

	Starts	1st	2nd	3rd	Win & Pl
Career Total (Turf)	1	0	0	0	

Going (Turf): **Sf: 0-0 GS: 0-0 Gd: 0-0 GF: 0-0 Fm: 0-1**
Distance: 5f/6f: 0-0 7f-8f: 0-1 9f-13f: 0-0 14f+: 0-0
Track : LH: 0-0 RH: 0-0 Tight: 0-0 Gall: 0-0
Aids: Bl: 0-0 Vi: 0-0 Tstrap: 0-0 Ckp: 0-0

Kinigi (IRE)

93(99) (60)53

3-y-o gr f Verglas (IRE)-Kamalame (USA) (Souvenir Copy (USA))
R A Harris Brian Hicks

Placings:5451155-3050100044335334 **(7835)**
2009: 7^{3}SD, 8^{0}SD, 7^{5}SD, 8^{0}G, 6^{1}SD, 6^{0}SD, 7^{0}S, 6^{0}SD, 5^{4}G, 7^{4}GF, 5^{3}SD, 5^{3}SD, 5^{5}SD, 6^{3}SD, 7^{3}SD, 6^{4}SD,

	Starts	1st	2nd	3rd	Win & Pl
Career Total (Turf)	6	0	0	0	289
Career Total (AW)	17	3	0	5	8352

59	7/09	Sthl	6f		STD	£2266
56	11/08	Sthl	7f		STD	£2047
57	11/08	Sthl	7f	(0-60)	STD	£2627

Total win prize-money £6941

Going (Turf): **Sf: 0-2 GS: 0-1 Gd: 0-2 GF: 0-1 Fm: 0-0**
Distance: 5f/6f: 1-11 **7f-8f: 2-12** 9f-13f: 0-0 14f+: 0-0
Track : **LH: 3-17** RH: 0-1 Tight: 0-3 Gall: 0-1
Aids: Bl: 0-0 Vi: 0-0 Tstrap: 0-7 Ckp: 0-7
Best Rating: **60** 12/09 Sthl 6f stand

Moderate; effective over 6-7f; acts on heavy ground; handles Fibresand and Polytrack; has worn cheekpieces.

Kinky Afro (IRE)

90(96) (70)61

2-y-o b f Modigliani (USA)-Feet Of Flame (USA) (Theatrical)
J S Moore Phil Cunningham

Placings:04520 **(6481)**
2009: 6^{0}GF, 8^{4}SD, 8^{5}G, 7^{2}SD, 7^{0}GF,

	Starts	1st	2nd	3rd	Win & Pl
Career Total (Turf)	3	0	0	0	0
Career Total (AW)	2	0	1	0	1060

Going (Turf): **Sf: 0-0 GS: 0-0 Gd: 0-1 GF: 0-2 Fm: 0-0**
Distance: 5f/6f: 0-0 7f-8f: 0-5 9f-13f: 0-0 14f+: 0-0
Track : LH: 0-2 RH: 0-1 Tight: 0-2 Gall: 0-0
Aids: Bl: 0-0 Vi: 0-0 Tstrap: 0-0 Ckp: 0-0
Best Rating: **70** 9/09 Wolv 7f32y stand

Modest; stays 1m; acts on Polytrack and good ground on turf.

Kinout (IRE)

(101) (63)74

4-y-o b g Invincible Spirit (IRE)-Kinn (FR) (Suave Dancer (USA))
K A Ryan Mrs J Ryan

Placings:5340350/2103664346500-4006 **(0921)**
2009: 6^{4}SS, 6^{0}SD, 6^{0}SD, 6^{6}SD,

	Starts	1st	2nd	3rd	Win & Pl
Career Total (Turf)	12	0	1	3	3283
Career Total (AW)	12	1	0	1	3356

78	3/08	Wolv	5f20y	(0-75)H	STD	£2730

Total win prize-money £2730

Going (Turf): **Sf: 0-2 GS: 0-0 Gd: 0-6 GF: 0-4 Fm: 0-0**
Distance: **5f/6f: 1-21** 7f-8f: 0-3 9f-13f: 0-0 14f+: 0-0
Track : **LH: 1-10** RH: 0-3 **Tight: 1-5** Gall: 0-1
Aids: Bl: 0-2 Vi: 0-0 Tstrap: 0-1 Ckp: 0-1
Best Rating: **78** 3/08 Wolv 5f20y stand

Modest; effective over 5f-7f; acts on fast ground; also goes on Polytrack.

Kinsman (IRE)

(99) (51)34

12-y-o b g Distant Relative-Besito (Wassl)
T D McCarthy Exors of the late W Weeding

Placings:00006215/30062316010051134 1/4510P0600006 000/040430600/0402605550060 0/2154600052/200040000 610/04060036/563631010/530300-616500 **(7197)**
2009: 8^{6}SD, 8^{1}SD, 8^{6}SD, 8^{5}SD, 8^{0}SD, 8^{0}SD,

	Starts	1st	2nd	3rd	Win & Pl
Career Total (Turf)	35	3	2	0	12730
Career Total (AW)	80	9	4	9	35726

51	1/09	GrLe	1m	(0-45)	STD	£1706
52	10/07	Kemp	1m	(0-45)	STD	£1365
52	4/07	Ling	1m	(0-45)	STD	£2184
53	12/05	Ling	1m	(0-45)	STD	£1433
61	2/04	Ling	7f	F(0-55)H	STD	£2989
96	2/01	Ling	1m	C(0-95)H	SLW	£6695
90	12/00	Ling	7f	D(0-80)H	STD	£3851
86	12/00	Ling	7f	D(0-80)H	STD	£3201
82	11/00	Ling	7f	D(0-80)H	STD	£4078
73	8/00	Epsm	6f	E(0-70)H	GD	£4270
69	6/00	Brig	5f213y	E(0-75)H	FRM	£2899
68	9/99	Brig	5f213y	D(0-85)H	SFT	£3403

Total win prize-money £38077

Going (Turf): **Sf: 1-5** GS: 0-1 **Gd: 1-8** GF: 0-15 **Fm: 1-6**
Distance: 5f/6f: 3-12 **7f-8f: 9-83** 9f-13f: 0-20 14f+: 0-0
Track : **LH: 11-80** RH: 1-22 **Tight: 8-68** Gall: 1-3
Aids: Bl: 1-19 Vi: 3-12 Tstrap: 3-36 Ckp: 3-36
Best Rating: **96** 2/01 Ling 1m slow

Plating class; effective at around 1m-1m2f; acts on Polytrack; has worn headgear.

Kinsya

102(105) (86)95

6-y-o ch g Mister Baileys-Kimono (IRE) (Machiavellian (USA))
M H Tompkins Roalco Limited

Placings:06415/1341401/0205125/5060334650-4020004 **(6695)**
2009: 8^{4}GF, 8^{0}G, 8^{2}G, 8^{0}G, 8^{0}SD, 8^{0}G, 8^{4}GS,

	Starts	1st	2nd	3rd	Win & Pl
Career Total (Turf)	33	5	3	3	57481
Career Total (AW)	3	0	0	0	740

97	10/07	Leic	1m60y	(0-90)H	G-S	£7790
94	10/06	York	1m208y	(0-85)H	SFT	£8096
92	8/06	NmkJ	1m	(0-85)H	GD	£5505
82	4/06	Ripn	1m	(0-90)H	SFT	£9348
73	8/05	NmkJ	1m		G-S	£5629

Total win prize-money £36368

Going (Turf): **Sf: 2-5 GS: 2-11** Gd: 1-13 GF: 0-4 Fm: 0-0
Distance: 5f/6f: 0-0 **7f-8f: 3-18** 9f-13f: 2-18 14f+: 0-0
Track : LH: 1-15 **RH: 2-12** Tight: 1-9 Gall: 1-6
Aids: Bl: 0-0 Vi: 0-0 Tstrap: 0-0 Ckp: 0-0
Best Rating: **100** 11/07 NmkR 1m good

Useful; stays 1m2f and acts on most ground, but probably best on soft.

Kintyre Bay

70 31

2-y-o gr g Mull Of Kintyre (USA)-Dim Ofan (Petong)
T D Barron D Pryde & J Cringan

Placings:00 **(6896)**
2009: 6^{0}S, 6^{0}GF,

	Starts	1st	2nd	3rd	Win & Pl
Career Total (Turf)	2	0	0	0	

Going (Turf): **Sf: 0-1 GS: 0-0 Gd: 0-0 GF: 0-1 Fm: 0-0**
Distance: 5f/6f: 0-2 7f-8f: 0-0 9f-13f: 0-0 14f+: 0-0
Track : LH: 0-1 RH: 0-0 Tight: 0-0 Gall: 0-0
Aids: Bl: 0-0 Vi: 0-0 Tstrap: 0-0 Ckp: 0-0
Best Rating: **31** 10/09 Pont 6f gd-fm

Kipchak (IRE)

104(107) (79)82

4-y-o b/br g Soviet Star (USA)-Khawafi (Kris)
C R Dore (A J McCabe 20/5) Liam Breslin

Placings:023-41134151300140300035 00636136 **(7876)**
2009: 8^{4}SD, 8^{1}SD, 8^{1}SD, 8^{3}SD, 7^{4}SD, 8^{1}SD, 6^{5}GF, 7^{1}F, 5^{3}GF, 7^{0}GF, 6^{0}GS, 7^{1}SD, 7^{4}SD, 7^{0}GF, 6^{3}GF, 8^{0}GF, 7^{0}GS, 6^{0}G, 6^{3}F, 7^{5}G, 7^{0}GF, 5^{0}SD, 6^{6}GS, 6^{3}SD,

	Starts	1st	2nd	3rd	Win & Pl
Career Total (Turf)	14	1	0	3	4257
Career Total (AW)	17	5	1	4	13696

75	12/09	Wolv	7f32y	(0-65)H	STD	£2388
74	5/09	Ling	7f		STD	£2047
82	4/09	Rdcr	7f	(0-70)H	FRM	£2590
67	3/09	Ling	1m		STD	£2047
73	2/09	Ling	1m	(0-70)H	STD	£2729
68	1/09	Ling	1m		STD	£2047

Total win prize-money £13849

Going (Turf): Sf: 0-0 GS: 0-3 Gd: 0-2 GF: 0-7 **Fm: 1-2**
Distance: 5f/6f: 0-8 **7f-8f: 6-20** 9f-13f: 0-3 14f+: 0-0
Track : **LH: 5-22** RH: 0-2 **Tight: 5-11** Gall: 0-3
Aids: Bl: 0-0 Vi: 0-0 Tstrap: 6-26 Ckp: 6-26
Best Rating: **82** 6/09 Brig 6f209y gd-fm

Modest; effective from 7f-1m2f; acts on Polytrack; has worn cheekpieces; best when able to dominate.

Kiribati King (IRE)

104 (62)84

4-y-o b g Kalanisi (IRE)-Everlasting (Desert King (IRE))
M R Channon Bill Adams

Placings:006/214032341113-6064 **(4332)**
2009: 16^{6}S, 18^{0}G, 17^{6}G, 16^{4}G,

	Starts	1st	2nd	3rd	Win & Pl
Career Total (Turf)	18	4	2	3	20782
Career Total (AW)	1	0	0	0	0

84	9/08	Pont	2m1f22y	(0-75)H	G-S	£3885

75	9/08	Wwck	1m6f213y	(0-75)H	SFT	£3238
75	8/08	Hayd	1m6f	(0-70)H	HVY	£4857
73	4/08	Bevl	1m4f16y	(0-70)H	G-S	£2590

Total win prize-money £14571

Going (Turf): **Sf: 2-3 GS: 2-7** Gd: 0-5 GF: 0-3 Fm: 0-0
Distance: 5f/6f: 0-0 7f-8f: 0-2 9f-13f: 1-4 **14f+: 3-13**
Track : **LH: 3-13** RH: 1-4 **Tight: 1-4** Gall: 0-3
Aids: Bl: 0-0 Vi: 0-1 Tstrap: 0-0 Ckp: 0-0
Best Rating: **84** 9/08 Pont 2m1f22y gd-sft

Fair; stays 2m1f; acts on good and softer ground; usually held up.

Kirk Michael

104(98) (89)**89**
5-y-o b g Selkirk (USA)-Pervenche (Latest Model)
H Candy Girsonfield Ltd

Placings:42/51/0-622 **(2883)**
2009: 7^{6}SD, 7^{2}GF, 7^{2}G,

	Starts	1st	2nd	3rd	Win & Pl
Career Total (Turf)	5	0	3	0	4962
Career Total (AW)	3	1	0	0	2969
89 12/07 Wolv 7f32y			STD	£2968	

Total win prize-money £2969

Going (Turf): **Sf: 0-1 GS: 0-1 Gd: 0-1 GF: 0-2 Fm: 0-0**
Distance: 5f/6f: 0-0 **7f-8f: 1-8** 9f-13f: 0-0 14f+: 0-0
Track : **LH: 1-1** RH: 0-4 **Tight: 1-1** Gall: 0-0
Aids: Bl: 0-0 Vi: 0-0 Tstrap: 0-0 Ckp: 0-0
Best Rating: **89** 6/09 Gdwd 7f good

Fair; stays 7f; acts on most ground and on Polytrack.

Kirkby's Gem

88 **48**
2-y-o b f Firebreak-Just A Gem (Superlative)
A Berry Kirkby Lonsdale Racing

Placings:00566300 **(6555)**
2009: 5^{0}GF, 5^{0}G, 5^{5}GF, 5^{6}G, 5^{6}GS, 5^{3}GS, 5^{0}GF, 5^{0}G,

	Starts	1st	2nd	3rd	Win & Pl
Career Total (Turf)	8	0	0	1	433

Going (Turf): **Sf: 0-0 GS: 0-2 Gd: 0-3 GF: 0-3 Fm: 0-0**
Distance: 5f/6f: 0-8 7f-8f: 0-0 9f-13f: 0-0 14f+: 0-0
Track : LH: 0-0 RH: 0-3 Tight: 0-0 Gall: 0-1
Aids: Bl: 0-0 Vi: 0-0 Tstrap: 0-0 Ckp: 0-0
Best Rating: **48** 9/09 Ripn 5f gd-sft

Kirkie (USA)

(100) (68)**27**
4-y-o b/br g Gulch (USA)-Saleela (USA) (Nureyev (USA))
T J Pitt (S Parr 22/3) Willie McKay & Chris Roper

Placings:42500002006-0R05 **(7802)**
2009: 8^{0}SD, 5^{R}SD, 11^{0}SD, 8^{5}SD,

	Starts	1st	2nd	3rd	Win & Pl
Career Total (Turf)	3	0	0	0	
Career Total (AW)	12	0	2	0	1531

Going (Turf): **Sf: 0-1 GS: 0-0 Gd: 0-0 GF: 0-2 Fm: 0-0**
Distance: 5f/6f: 0-2 7f-8f: 0-8 9f-13f: 0-4 14f+: 0-1
Track : LH: 0-12 RH: 0-2 Tight: 0-7 Gall: 0-0
Aids: Bl: 0-1 Vi: 0-1 Tstrap: 0-1 Ckp: 0-1
Best Rating: **68** 11/08 Wolv 7f32y stand

Modest; effective over 6f and acts on sand.

Kirklees (IRE)

113(112) (121)**119**
5-y-o b h Jade Robbery (USA)-Moyesii (USA) (Diesis)
Saeed Bin Suroor Godolphin

Placings:213431/11/32-31**4**01110 **(6871a)**
2009: 8^{3}GF, 10^{1}G, **10**^{4}FT, 12^{0}G, 10^{1}G, 10^{1}G, **12**^{1}SD, 12^{0}GS,

	Starts	1st	2nd	3rd	Win & Pl
Career Total (Turf)	16	7	2	4	445140
Career Total (AW)	2	1	0	0	47317

121	9/09	Kemp	1m4f		STD	£36900
116	7/09	York	1m2f88y		GD	£56770
119	7/09	Sand	1m2f7y		GD	£22708
118	2/09	Ndas	1m2f	(95-119)H	GD	£62500
119	9/07	Gdwd	1m1f192y		G-S	£15898
113	9/07	Donc	1m2f60y		G-F	£12464
110	10/06	Siro	1m		GD	£177480
84	7/06	Catt	7f		FRM	£3886

Total win prize-money £388607

Going (Turf): Sf: 0-0 GS: 1-4 **Gd: 4-7** GF: 1-4 Fm: 1-1
Distance: 5f/6f: 0-0 7f-8f: 2-6 **9f-13f: 6-12** 14f+: 0-0
Track : LH: 4-10 RH: 4-6 Tight: 2-3 **Gall: 3-8**
Aids: Bl: 0-0 Vi: 0-0 Tstrap: 0-0 Ckp: 0-0
Best Rating: **121** 9/09 Kemp 1m4f stand

Group class; Group 3 winner in Britain and Group 1 winner in Italy as a juvenile; stays 1m4f and acts on most ground and Polytrack.

Kirkson

92 **60**
3-y-o ch g Selkirk (USA)-Viva Maria (Hernando (FR))
P W Chapple-Hyam Liggins, Dr M Hone & Mrs K Clark

Placings:0-00255 **(3588)**
2009: 7^{0}GF, 10^{0}GF, 8^{2}GF, 9^{5}G, 10^{5}GF,

	Starts	1st	2nd	3rd	Win & Pl
Career Total (Turf)	6	0	1	0	578

Going (Turf): **Sf: 0-0 GS: 0-1 Gd: 0-1 GF: 0-4 Fm: 0-0**
Distance: 5f/6f: 0-0 7f 8f: 0-2 9f-13f: 0-4 14f+: 0-0
Track : LH: 0-3 RH: 0-1 Tight: 0-2 Gall: 0-0
Aids: Bl: 0-2 Vi: 0-0 Tstrap: 0-0 Ckp: 0-0
Best Rating: **60** 5/09 Yarm 1m3y gd-fm

Modest; stays 1m; acts on fast ground.

Kirsty's Boy (IRE)

97(100) (73)**78**
2-y-o ch g Tagula (IRE)-Mayfair (Green Desert (USA))
J S Moore F J Stephens

Placings:0130600021**2** **(7874)**
2009: 5^{0}SD, 5^{1}G, 5^{3}G, 5^{0}GF, 6^{6}G, 5^{0}GS, 6^{0}GF, 6^{0}GF, 7^{2}SD, 7^{1}SD, 8^{2}SD,

	Starts	1st	2nd	3rd	Win & Pl
Career Total (Turf)	7	1	0	1	9089
Career Total (AW)	4	1	2	0	3168
73 12/09 Ling 7f			STD	£1978	
74 5/09 Gdwd 5f			GD	£3238	

Total win prize-money £5217

Going (Turf): Sf: 0-0 GS: 0-1 **Gd: 1-3** GF: 0-3 Fm: 0-0
Distance: 5f/6f: 1-7 7f-8f: 1-4 9f-13f: 0-0 14f+: 0-0
Track : **LH: 1-2** RH: 0-2 **Tight: 1-2** Gall: 0-1
Aids: Bl: 0-1 Vi: 0-0 Tstrap: 0-0 Ckp: 0-0
Best Rating: **78** 7/09 Newb 5f34y gd-sft

Fair; effective at 5f-7f; acts on good ground; goes on Polytrack; has worn blinkers.

Kirstys Lad

94(100) (65)**59**
7-y-o b g Lake Coniston (IRE)-Killick (Slip Anchor)
M Mullineaux S A Pritchard

Placings:0040**0/4066**0**000**/0123014/000**65**0**135200-6030620**000**006303** **(7814)**
2009: **9**^{6}SD, 8^{0}SD, **8**^{3}SD, 8^{0}SD, **12**^{6}SD, 9^{2}G, 12^{0}GF, 12^{0}GS, 8^{0}SD, 10^{0}GF, **8**^{0}SD, **8**^{0}SD, **9**^{6}SD, **9**^{3}SD, **9**^{0}SS, **8**^{3}SD,

	Starts	1st	2nd	3rd	Win & Pl
Career Total (Turf)	14	0	1	0	1234
Career Total (AW)	34	3	2	5	9533

60	10/08	Wolv	1m141y	(0-55)H	STD	£2866
64	12/07	Wolv	1m141y	(0-57)H	STD	£2047
60	10/07	Wolv	1m1f103y		STD	£2047

Total win prize-money £6962

Going (Turf): **Sf: 0-4 GS: 0-1 Gd: 0-4 GF: 0-5 Fm: 0-0**
Distance: 5f/6f: 0-1 7f-8f: 0-11 **9f-13f: 3-35** 14f+: 0-1
Track : **LH: 3-43** RH: 0-4 **Tight: 3-35** Gall: 0-0
Aids: Bl: 0-5 Vi: 0-0 Tstrap: 0-0 Ckp: 0-0
Best Rating: **65** 11/08 Wolv 1m141y stand

Very moderate; effective at around 7f-1m2f; acts on good ground and on Polytrack.

Kiss 'n Tell

67 **2**
3-y-o ch f Sakhee (USA)-Time For Tea (IRE) (Imperial Frontier (USA))
G L Moore Mrs Charles Cyzer

Placings:0 **(4955)**
2009: 8^{0}G,

	Starts	1st	2nd	3rd	Win & Pl
Career Total (Turf)	1	0	0	0	

Going (Turf): **Sf: 0-0 GS: 0-0 Gd: 0-1 GF: 0-0 Fm: 0-0**
Distance: 5f/6f: 0-0 7f-8f: 0-0 9f-13f: 0-1 14f+: 0-0
Track : LH: 0-0 RH: 0-1 Tight: 0-0 Gall: 0-0
Aids: Bl: 0-0 Vi: 0-0 Tstrap: 0-0 Ckp: 0-0
Best Rating: **2** 8/09 Sand 1m14y good

Kiss A Prince

93(100) (75)**70**
3-y-o b g Fraam-Prancing (Prince Sabo)
D K Ivory A Pryer

Placings:0-**321**00**31**0**4** **(7149)**
2009: 7^{3}SD, 7^{2}SD, 7^{1}SD, 7^{0}GF, 7^{0}SD, 7^{3}SD, 8^{1}SD, 8^{0}SD, 8^{4}G,

	Starts	1st	2nd	3rd	Win & Pl
Career Total (Turf)	3	0	0	0	481
Career Total (AW)	7	2	1	2	7430

75	8/09	Ling	1m	(0-70)H	STD	£3238
69	3/09	Ling	7f	(0-70)H	STD	£2900

Total win prize-money £6138

Going (Turf): **Sf: 0-0 GS: 0-0 Gd: 0-1 GF: 0-2 Fm: 0-0**
Distance: 5f/6f: 0-1 **7f-8f: 2-9** 9f-13f: 0-0 14f+: 0-0
Track : **LH: 2-5** RH: 0-2 **Tight: 2-4** Gall: 0-1
Aids: Bl: 0-0 Vi: 0-0 Tstrap: 0-0 Ckp: 0-0
Best Rating: **75** 8/09 Ling 1m stand

Modest; stays 7f and acts on Polytrack.

Kit Kat

56(61) (7)
2-y-o b g One Cool Cat (USA)-Tanda Tula (IRE) (Alhaarth (IRE))
George Baker The Chocolatiers

Placings:000 (5106)
2009: 7^{0}GF, 7^{0}G, 7^{0}SD,

	Starts	1st	2nd	3rd	Win & Pl
Career Total (Turf)	2	0	0	0	
Career Total (AW)	1	0	0	0	

Going (Turf): Sf: 0-0 GS: 0-0 Gd: 0-1 GF: 0-1 Fm: 0-0
Distance: 5f/6f: 0-0 7f-8f: 0-3 9f-13f: 0-0 14f+: 0-0
Track : LH: 0-2 RH: 0-0 Tight: 0-1 Gall: 0-0
Aids: Bl: 0-0 Vi: 0-0 Tstrap: 0-0 Ckp: 0-0
Best Rating: 7 8/09 Wolv 7f32y stand

Kite Wood (IRE)

111 **121**
3-y-o b c Galileo (IRE)-Kite Mark (Mark Of Esteem (IRE))
Saeed Bin Suroor Godolphin

Placings:211-50112 (5861)
2009: 10^{5}G, 12^{0}G, 13^{1}G, 13^{1}GF, 14^{2}GF,

	Starts	1st	2nd	3rd	Win & Pl
Career Total (Turf)	8	4	2	0	230102

121	8/09	Newb	1m5f61y	G-F	£36900
109	7/09	NmkJ	1m5f	GD	£36900
111	10/08	Asct	1m	G-S	£28385
95	9/08	Donc	1m	SFT	£6152

Total win prize-money £108339

Going (Turf): Sf: 1-1 GS: 1-1 Gd: 1-4 GF: 1-2 Fm: 0-0
Distance: 5f/6f: 0-0 **7f-8f: 2-3** 9f-13f: 1-3 14f+: 1-2
Track : LH: 1-4 **RH: 2-2** Tight: 0-1 **Gall: 3-5**
Aids: Bl: 0-0 Vi: 0-0 Tstrap: 0-0 Ckp: 0-0
Best Rating: 121 8/09 Newb 1m5f61y gd-fm

Group class; triple Group 3 winner; runner-up in St Leger in 2009; stays 1m5f; acts on most ground.

Kithonia (FR)

92 **73**
2-y-o b f Sadler's Wells (USA)-Ratukidul (FR) (Danehill (USA))
H R A Cecil Niarchos Family

Placings:1 (5604)
2009: 6^{1}S,

	Starts	1st	2nd	3rd	Win & Pl
Career Total (Turf)	1	1	0	0	6152

73	9/09	Sals	6f212y	SFT	£6152

Total win prize-money £6152

Going (Turf): Sf: 1-1 GS: 0-0 Gd: 0-0 GF: 0-0 Fm: 0-0
Distance: 5f/6f: 0-0 **7f-8f: 1-1** 9f-13f: 0-0 14f+: 0-0
Track : LH: 0-0 RH: 0-0 Tight: 0-0 Gall: 0-0
Aids: Bl: 0-0 Vi: 0-0 Tstrap: 0-0 Ckp: 0-0
Best Rating: 73 9/09 Sals 6f212y soft

Useful; suited by 7f and soft ground.

Kitty Allen

(85) (54)**44**
3-y-o br f One Cool Cat (USA)-Aly McBe (USA) (Alydeed (CAN))
C N Kellett Dachel Stud

Placings:40250-050 (0812)
2009: 7^{0}SD, 6^{5}SD, 5^{0}SD,

	Starts	1st	2nd	3rd	Win & Pl
Career Total (Turf)	1	0	0	0	
Career Total (AW)	7	0	1	0	964

Going (Turf): Sf: 0-0 GS: 0-0 Gd: 0-0 GF: 0-1 Fm: 0-0
Distance: 5f/6f: 0-7 7f-8f: 0-1 9f-13f: 0-0 14f+: 0-0
Track : LH: 0-4 RH: 0-3 Tight: 0-3 Gall: 0-1
Aids: Bl: 0-1 Vi: 0-0 Tstrap: 0-0 Ckp: 0-0
Best Rating: 54 7/08 Ling 6f stand

Modest; stays 6f and acts on Polytrack.

Kiwi Bay

105(99) (88)**93**
4-y-o b g Mujahid (USA)-Bay Of Plenty (FR) (Octagonal (NZ))
M Dods Kiwi Racing

Placings:2516/05310440355-00532050241322 (7287)
2009: 6^{0}GF, 6^{0}G, 6^{5}G, 7^{3}S, 7^{2}G, 7^{0}GF, 7^{5}G, 7^{0}G, 7^{2}GF, 8^{4}GF, 8^{1}GF, 7^{3}G, 8^{2}G, 7^{2}S,

	Starts	1st	2nd	3rd	Win & Pl
Career Total (Turf)	28	3	5	3	22728
Career Total (AW)	1	0	0	1	963

87	9/09	Pont	1m4y	(0-80)H	G-F	£5180
88	6/08	Rdcr	7f	(0-75)H	G-F	£2331
72	10/07	Newc	7f		GD	£1943

Total win prize-money £9455

Going (Turf): Sf: 0-6 GS: 0-0 Gd: 1-13 **GF: 2-9** Fm: 0-0
Distance: 5f/6f: 0-6 **7f-8f: 2-20** 9f-13f: 1-3 14f+: 0-0
Track : LH: 1-9 RH: 0-1 Tight: 0-1 Gall: 0-3
Aids: Bl: 0-0 Vi: 0-0 Tstrap: 0-0 Ckp: 0-0
Best Rating: 93 11/09 Donc 7f soft

Useful; effective at 7f-1m; acts on most ground on turf; goes on Polytrack.

Kiyari

(95) (63)**36**
3-y-o b f Key Of Luck (USA)-Ashford Castle (USA) (Bates Motel (USA))
M Botti El Catorce

Placings:0063-1245 (1183)
2009: 8^{1}SD, 10^{2}SD, 9^{4}SD, 10^{5}SD,

	Starts	1st	2nd	3rd	Win & Pl
Career Total (Turf)	1	0	0	0	
Career Total (AW)	7	1	1	1	3029

61	1/09	Wolv	1m141y	STD	£1942

Total win prize-money £1943

Going (Turf): Sf: 0-1 GS: 0-0 Gd: 0-0 GF: 0-0 Fm: 0-0
Distance: 5f/6f: 0-0 7f-8f: 0-3 **9f-13f: 1-5** 14f+: 0-0
Track : LH: 1-7 RH: 0-1 **Tight: 1-5** Gall: 0-1
Aids: Bl: 0-0 Vi: 0-0 Tstrap: 0-0 Ckp: 0-0
Best Rating: 63 12/08 Wolv 1m1f103y stand

Modest; suited by around 1m; acts on Polytrack.

Kladester (USA)

82(97) (62)**47**
3-y-o ch g Van Nistelrooy (USA)-Longing To Dance (USA) (Nureyev (USA))
B Smart Prime Equestrian

Placings:000150-60 (2091)
2009: 7^{6}GF, 8^{0}G,

	Starts	1st	2nd	3rd	Win & Pl
Career Total (Turf)	5	0	0	0	0
Career Total (AW)	3	1	0	0	2627

62	11/08	Sthl	7f	(0-60)	STD	£2627

Total win prize-money £2627

Going (Turf): Sf: 0-1 GS: 0-0 Gd: 0-1 GF: 0-2 Fm: 0-1
Distance: 5f/6f: 0-0 **7f-8f: 1-8** 9f-13f: 0-0 14f+: 0-0
Track : LH: 1-5 RH: 0-2 Tight: 0-3 Gall: 0-0
Aids: Bl: 0-0 Vi: 0-0 Tstrap: 0-0 Ckp: 0-0
Best Rating: 62 11/08 Kemp 1m stand

Modest; effective over 7f; acts on Fibresand.

Kleio

(74) (35)
2-y-o b f Sadler's Wells (USA)-Colza (USA) (Alleged (USA))
H R A Cecil Niarchos Family

Placings:0 (7624)
2009: 8^{0}SD,

	Starts	1st	2nd	3rd	Win & Pl
Career Total (Turf)	0	0	0	0	
Career Total (AW)	1	0	0	0	

Going (Turf): Sf: 0-0 GS: 0-0 Gd: 0-0 GF: 0-0 Fm: 0-0
Distance: 5f/6f: 0-0 7f-8f: 0-1 9f-13f: 0-0 14f+: 0-0
Track : LH: 0-1 RH: 0-0 Tight: 0-1 Gall: 0-0
Aids: Bl: 0-0 Vi: 0-0 Tstrap: 0-0 Ckp: 0-0
Best Rating: 35 12/09 Ling 1m stand

Kloof

99(105) (77)**74**
3-y-o b c Cape Cross (IRE)-Ravine (Indian Ridge)
K A Ryan (J H M Gosden 3/7) Abdul Rahman Al Jasmi

Placings:440263040 (6823)
2009: 8^{4}SD, 8^{4}G, 7^{0}SD, 6^{2}GF, 8^{6}GF, 7^{3}SD, 7^{0}SD, 8^{4}GF, 6^{0}GF,

	Starts	1st	2nd	3rd	Win & Pl
Career Total (Turf)	5	0	1	0	1656
Career Total (AW)	4	0	0	1	1116

Going (Turf): Sf: 0-0 GS: 0-0 Gd: 0-1 GF: 0-4 Fm: 0-0
Distance: 5f/6f: 0-1 7f-8f: 0-6 9f-13f: 0-2 14f+: 0-0
Track : LH: 0-5 RH: 0-0 Tight: 0-4 Gall: 0-0
Aids: Bl: 0-0 Vi: 0-0 Tstrap: 0-0 Ckp: 0-0
Best Rating: 77 9/09 Wolv 7f32y stand

Fair; effective over 7f; acts on fast ground.

Klynch

102(99) (92)**87**
3-y-o b g Kyllachy-Inchcoonan (Emperor Jones (USA))
B J Meehan L P R Partnership

Placings:64210645100040-0300103000 (6458)
2009: 6^{0}SD, 6^{3}GF, 6^{0}G, 6^{0}G, 6^{1}S, 6^{0}G, 6^{3}GS, 6^{0}G, 6^{0}SD, 5^{0}SD,

	Starts	1st	2nd	3rd	Win & Pl
Career Total (Turf)	17	1	1	2	8923
Career Total (AW)	7	2	0	0	6414

87	7/09	Hayd	6f	(0-85)H	SFT	£5504
84	8/08	Kemp	6f		STD	£3885
84	6/08	Kemp	5f		STD	£2047

Total win prize-money £11438

Going (Turf): Sf: 1-2 GS: 0-4 Gd: 0-7 GF: 0-4 Fm: 0-0
Distance: 5f/6f: 3-23 7f-8f: 0-1 9f-13f: 0-0 14f+: 0-0
Track : LH: 0-4 **RH: 2-5** Tight: 0-1 Gall: 0-3
Aids: Bl: 2-15 Vi: 0-0 Tstrap: 0-0 Ckp: 0-0
Best Rating: 92 9/08 Kemp 6f stand

Useful; effective over 5f-6f; acts on fast ground but well suited by Polytrack; has worn blinkers.

Knavesmire (IRE)

92 **91**
3-y-o b f One Cool Cat (USA)-Caribbean Escape (Pivotal)
M Brittain Mel Brittain

Placings:33161-P0000 (6645)
2009: 7PGF, 60GF, 60CF, 70G, 70G,

	Starts	1st	2nd	3rd	Win & Pl
Career Total (Turf)	10	2	0	2	16670

91 5/08 Bevl 5f G-F £12205
73 5/08 Rdcr 5f SFT £2331
Total win prize-money £14537

Going (Turf): Sf: 1-1 GS: 0-2 Gd: 0-2 GF: 1-5 Fm: 0-0
Distance: 5f/6f: 2-7 7f-8f: 0-3 9f-13f: 0-0 14f+: 0-0
Track: LH: 0-2 RH: 0-0 Tight: 0-0 Gall: 0-2
Aids: Bl: 0-0 Vi: 0-0 Tstrap: 0-0 Ckp: 0-0
Best Rating: 91 5/08 Bevl 5f gd-fm

Very useful; winner of the Listed Hilary Needler Trophy in 2008; effective at 5f and acts on most ground.

Kneesy Earsy Nosey

89(87) (51)51
3-y-o ch f Compton Place-Evie Hone (IRE) (Royal Academy (USA))
Miss A Stokell David Blythe

Placings:61505000**6526**-603000035060 (5254)
2009: 8⁰SD, 8⁰SD, 9³SD, 12⁰SF, 9⁰SF, 5⁰F, 9⁰G, 8³G, 6⁵GF, 12⁰GF, 8⁰GF, 6⁰GF,

	Starts	1st	2nd	3rd	Win & Pl
Career Total (Turf)	15	1	0	1	3043
Career Total (AW)	9	0	1	1	988

51 5/08 Ripn 6f G-F £2590
Total win prize-money £2590

Going (Turf): Sf: 0-2 GS: 0-1 Gd: 0-5 GF: 1-6 Fm: 0-1
Distance: 5f/6f: 1-8 7f-8f: 0-9 9f-13f: 0-7 14f+: 0-0
Track: LH: 0-11 RH: 0-3 Tight: 0-4 Gall: 0-2
Aids: Bl: 0-0 Vi: 0-1 Tstrap: 0-4 Ckp: 0-4
Best Rating: 51 2/09 Wolv 1m1f103y stand

Plating-class; stays 7f; acts on fast turf and Fibresand; has worn cheekpieces.

Knight's Victory (IRE)

94(95) (53)74
3-y-o b g Cape Cross (IRE)-Diminuendo (USA) (Diesis)
M Johnston Sheikh Hamdan Bin Mohammed Al Maktoum

Placings:610 (5551)
2009: 11⁶SD, 9¹GF, 9⁰GS,

	Starts	1st	2nd	3rd	Win & Pl
Career Total (Turf)	2	1	0	0	3886
Career Total (AW)	1	0	0	0	0

74 8/09 Ripn 1m1f170y G-F £3885
Total win prize-money £3886

Going (Turf): Sf: 0-0 GS: 0-1 Gd: 0-0 GF: 1-1 Fm: 0-0
Distance: 5f/6f: 0-0 7f-8f: 0-0 9f-13f: 1-3 14f+: 0-0
Track: LH: 0-1 RH: 1-2 Tight: 1-2 Gall: 0-0
Aids: Bl: 0-0 Vi: 0-0 Tstrap: 0-0 Ckp: 0-0
Best Rating: 74 8/09 Ripn 1m1f170y gd-fm

Fair; stays 1m2f; acts on fast ground.

Knightfire (IRE)

70(93) (57)34
2-y-o b g Invincible Spirit (IRE)-The Castles (IRE) (Imperial Ballet (IRE))
W R Swinburn The Castle Guards

Placings:65022 (7791)
2009: 5⁶SD, 5⁵G, 5⁰F, 7²SF, 7²SS,

	Starts	1st	2nd	3rd	Win & Pl
Career Total (Turf)	2	0	0	0	0
Career Total (AW)	3	0	2	0	1310

Going (Turf): Sf: 0-0 GS: 0-0 Gd: 0-1 GF: 0-0 Fm: 0-1
Distance: 5f/6f: 0-3 7f-8f: 0-2 9f-13f: 0-0 14f+: 0-0
Track: LH: 0-3 RH: 0-1 Tight: 0-1 Gall: 0-1
Aids: Bl: 0-0 Vi: 0-0 Tstrap: 0-0 Ckp: 0-0
Best Rating: 57 12/09 Sthl 7f std-slw

Moderate; stays 7f; acts on Fibresand and Polytrack.

Knock Three Times (IRE)

105(85) (36)51
3-y-o b f Hernando (FR)-Tawoos (FR) (Rainbow Quest (USA))
W Storey M D Townson

Placings:000-650000460 (5734)
2009: 8⁶GF, 8⁵G, 9⁰GS, 11⁰GF, 8⁰F, 12⁰G, 14⁴GF, 14⁶GF, 16⁰GS,

	Starts	1st	2nd	3rd	Win & Pl
Career Total (Turf)	10	0	0	0	144
Career Total (AW)	2	0	0	0	

Going (Turf): Sf: 0-1 GS: 0-2 Gd: 0-2 GF: 0-4 Fm: 0-1
Distance: 5f/6f: 0-0 7f-8f: 0-2 9f-13f: 0-7 14f+: 0-3
Track: LH: 0-4 RH: 0-5 Tight: 0-6 Gall: 0-1
Aids: Bl: 0-0 Vi: 0-0 Tstrap: 0-0 Ckp: 0-0
Best Rating: 51 4/09 Newc 1m3y gd-fm

Knockback (IRE)

84(82) (45)42
2-y-o b g Redback-Knockanure (USA) (Nureyev (USA))
P R Chamings Funboy Four Partnership

Placings:006000 (7513)
2009: 5⁰G, 7⁰SD, 6⁶GF, 8⁰GS, 8⁰SD, 7⁰SD,

	Starts	1st	2nd	3rd	Win & Pl
Career Total (Turf)	3	0	0	0	0
Career Total (AW)	3	0	0	0	

Going (Turf): Sf: 0-0 GS: 0-1 Gd: 0-1 GF: 0-1 Fm: 0-0
Distance: 5f/6f: 0-2 7f-8f: 0-3 9f-13f: 0-1 14f+: 0-0
Track: LH: 0-2 RH: 0-3 Tight: 0-2 Gall: 0-1
Aids: Bl: 0-0 Vi: 0-0 Tstrap: 0-0 Ckp: 0-0
Best Rating: 45 8/09 Kemp 7f stand

Knockdolian (IRE)

90 67
2-y-o b c Montjeu (IRE)-Doula (USA) (Gone West (USA))
R Charlton Marston Stud & G Stollery

Placings:03 (7034)
2009: 8⁰GF, 8³S,

	Starts	1st	2nd	3rd	Win & Pl
Career Total (Turf)	2	0	0	1	722

Going (Turf): Sf: 0-1 GS: 0-0 Gd: 0-0 GF: 0-1 Fm: 0-0
Distance: 5f/6f: 0-0 7f-8f: 0-2 9f-13f: 0-0 14f+: 0-0
Track: LH: 0-0 RH: 0-0 Tight: 0-0 Gall: 0-0
Aids: Bl: 0-0 Vi: 0-0 Tstrap: 0-0 Ckp: 0-0
Best Rating: 67 10/09 Newb 1m soft

Modest; stays 1m; acts on soft.

Knockenduff

89(91) (59)63
2-y-o b f Oratorio (IRE)-Sewards Folly (Rudimentary (USA))
M R Channon D Brennan

Placings:46364030 (6215)
2009: 6⁴GF, 6⁶GF, 7³G, 7⁶GS, 8⁴G, 8⁰SD, 8³SD, 8⁰GF,

	Starts	1st	2nd	3rd	Win & Pl
Career Total (Turf)	6	0	0	1	1372
Career Total (AW)	2	0	0	1	302

Going (Turf): Sf: 0-0 GS: 0-1 Gd: 0-2 GF: 0-3 Fm: 0-0
Distance: 5f/6f: 0-1 7f-8f: 0-7 9f-13f: 0-0 14f+: 0-0
Track: LH: 0-2 RH: 0-2 Tight: 0-1 Gall: 0-0
Aids: Bl: 0-0 Vi: 0-0 Tstrap: 0-0 Ckp: 0-0
Best Rating: 63 6/09 Pont 6f gd-fm

75,000gns half-sister to Sayif; modest form in maidens on fast and easy ground.

Knot In Wood (IRE)

111(109) (113)115
7-y-o b g Shinko Forest (IRE)-Notley Park (Wolfhound (USA))
R A Fahey Rhodes, Kenyon & Gill

Placings:063/00514411020/43321431522/601300635/020 05441600411-33200014133000 (7232a)
2009: 6³GF, 6³GF, 6²F, 6⁰GF, 6⁰HY, 6⁰GF, 6¹S, 6⁴G, 6¹G, 6³S, 6³G, 6⁰GF, 6⁰GS, 6⁰HO,

	Starts	1st	2nd	3rd	Win & Pl
Career Total (Turf)	58	10	5	10	251693
Career Total (AW)	4	1	1	0	28573

114 7/09 York 6f (0-105)H GD £31155
111 6/09 Newc 6f SFT £37468
113 10/08 Kemp 6f (0-105)H STD £24924
107 9/08 Haml 6f5y SFT £12462
110 7/08 Haml 6f5y (0-105)H GD £21808
110 7/07 Haml 6f5y (0-105)H G-S £21812
93 8/06 York 6f (0-100)H G-S £16192
87 7/06 Hayd 6f (0-85)H G-F £8096
80 7/05 Donc 6f (0-85)H G-F £7046
77 7/05 Haml 6f5y (0-70)H G-F £4241
71 5/05 Carl 5f193y (0-60)H SFT £3066
Total win prize-money £188272

Going (Turf): Sf: 3-11 GS: 2-12 Gd: 2-10 GF: 3-22 Fm: 0-2
Distance: 5f/6f: 7-55 7f-8f: 4-7 9f-13f: 0-0 14f+: 0-0
Track: LH: 0-7 RH: 2-2 Tight: 0-3 Gall: 0-0
Aids: Bl: 0-1 Vi: 0-0 Tstrap: 0-3 Ckp: 0-3
Best Rating: 115 9/09 Ayr 6f good

Smart; Group 3 winner; suited by 6f; acts on most ground but seems best on an easy surface; goes well on Polytrack; has worn blinkers and cheekpieces.

Knotgarden (IRE)

91 55
3-y-o b f Dr Fong (USA)-Eilean Shona (Suave Dancer (USA))
J R Fanshawe Dr Catherine Wills

Placings:4 (3379)
2009: 10⁴GF,

	Starts	1st	2nd	3rd	Win & Pl
Career Total (Turf)	1	0	0	0	361

Going (Turf): Sf: 0-0 GS: 0-0 Gd: 0-0 GF: 0-1 Fm: 0-0

Distance: 5f/6f: 0-0 7f-8f: 0-0 9f-13f: 0-1 14f+: 0-0
Track : LH: 0-1 RH: 0-0 Tight: 0-0 Gall: 0-1
Aids: Bl: 0-0 Vi: 0-0 Tstrap: 0-0 Ckp: 0-0
Best Rating: **55** 6/09 Donc 1m2f60y gd-fm

Know By Now

88(92) (72)**51**
3-y-o b g Piccolo-Addicted To Love (Touching Wood (USA))
T P Tate Mrs Sylvia Clegg and Louise Worthington

Placings:3204000 **(6023)**
2009: 7^{3}SD, 8^{2}SD, 7^{0}SD, 10^{4}GF, 7^{0}G, 8^{0}GF, 8^{0}GF,

	Starts	1st	2nd	3rd	Win & Pl
Career Total (Turf)	4	0	0	0	192
Career Total (AW)	3	0	1	1	1156

Going (Turf): **Sf: 0-0 GS: 0-0 Gd: 0-1 GF: 0-3 Fm: 0-0**
Distance: 5f/6f: 0-0 7f-8f: 0-5 9f-13f: 0-2 14f+: 0-0
Track : LH: 0-3 RH: 0-4 Tight: 0-3 Gall: 0-0
Aids: Bl: 0-1 Vi: 0-0 Tstrap: 0-0 Ckp: 0-0
Best Rating: **72** 2/09 Kemp 1m stand

Know No Fear

75(102) (79)**80**
4-y-o b g Primo Valentino (IRE)-Alustar (Emarati (USA))
A J Lidderdale (D Shaw 3/7) Kachina Racing

Placings:42221/05140-40650000000 **(7768)**
2009: 5^{4}SD, 5^{0}SD, 5^{6}SD, 5^{5}SD, 5^{0}SF, 6^{0}G, 5^{0}SD, 5^{0}GF, 5^{0}SD, 7^{0}SD, 7^{0}SD,

	Starts	1st	2nd	3rd	Win & Pl
Career Total (Turf)	11	2	2	0	17488
Career Total (AW)	10	0	1	0	1348

80 7/08 Catt 5f (0-85)H G-F £4857
75 9/07 Muss 5f (0-95) G-S £9971
Total win prize-money £14828

Going (Turf): Sf: 0-2 **GS: 1-2** Gd: 0-3 **GF: 1-4** Fm: 0-0
Distance: **5f/6f: 2-19** 7f-8f: 0-2 9f-13f: 0-0 14f+: 0-0
Track : LH: 0-9 RH: 0-3 Tight: 0-7 Gall: 0-2
Aids: Bl: 0-0 Vi: 0-0 Tstrap: 0-0 Ckp: 0-0
Best Rating: **80** 7/08 Catt 5f gd-fm

Fair; effective at 5f; acts on easy ground.

Knowledgeable

86 **45**
2-y-o b g Reset (AUS)-Belle's Edge (Danehill Dancer (IRE))
B Palling Lucky Larry Partnership

Placings:0004 **(7055)**
2009: 6^{0}G, 7^{0}GF, 7^{0}G, 7^{4}GF,

	Starts	1st	2nd	3rd	Win & Pl
Career Total (Turf)	4	0	0	0	168

Going (Turf): **Sf: 0-0 GS: 0-0 Gd: 0-2 GF: 0-2 Fm: 0-0**
Distance: 5f/6f: 0-0 7f-8f: 0-4 9f-13f: 0-0 14f+: 0-0
Track : LH: 0-0 RH: 0-0 Tight: 0-0 Gall: 0-0
Aids: Bl: 0-0 Vi: 0-0 Tstrap: 0-0 Ckp: 0-0
Best Rating: **45** 10/09 Leic 7f9y gd-fm

Kochanski (IRE)

99(100) (58)**59**
3-y-o ch f King's Best (USA)-Ascot Cyclone (USA) (Rahy (USA))
J R Weymes (M Johnston 13/8) Highmoor Racing No5 & J Gough

Placings:6-4410235045010250 **(5838)**
2009: 8^{4}SD, 10^{4}SD, 12^{1}SF, 12^{0}SD, 12^{0}GF, 12^{3}F, 12^{5}GS, 11^{0}SD, 11^{4}GF, 14^{5}GF, 12^{0}GF, 12^{1}GF, 11^{0}GF, 12^{2}G, 11^{5}GS, 12^{0}SD,

	Starts	1st	2nd	3rd	Win & Pl
Career Total (Turf)	11	1	2	1	4434
Career Total (AW)	6	1	0	0	2047

57 7/09 Bevl 1m4f16y (0-65)H G-F £2266
56 2/09 Wolv 1m4f50y (0-65)H SF £2047
Total win prize-money £4314

Going (Turf): Sf: 0-0 GS: 0-3 Gd: 0-1 **GF: 1-6** Fm: 0-1
Distance: 5f/6f: 0-0 7f-8f: 0-2 **9f-13f: 2-14** 14f+: 0-1
Track : LH: 1-10 RH: 1-6 **Tight: 2-8** Gall: 0-0
Aids: Bl: 0-0 Vi: 0-0 Tstrap: 0-0 Ckp: 0-0
Best Rating: **59** 8/09 Bevl 1m4f16y good

Moderate; effective over 1m4f; acts on Polytrack.

Kokkokila

92(96) (60)**70**
5-y-o b m Robellino (USA)-Meant To Be (Morston (FR))
Lady Herries Lady Mary Mumford

Placings:4636/02134316-450614 **(7124)**
2009: 16^{4}G, 12^{5}GF, 16^{0}SD, 12^{6}HY, 16^{1}GS, 16^{4}G,

	Starts	1st	2nd	3rd	Win & Pl
Career Total (Turf)	14	3	1	3	10853
Career Total (AW)	4	0	0	0	0

66 10/09 Gdwd 2m (0-70)H G-S £3238
70 10/08 Newb 2m (0-75)H G-S £2590
66 6/08 Wwck 1m4f134y (0-60)H G-F £1977
Total win prize-money £7806

Going (Turf): Sf: 0-4 **GS: 2-3** Gd: 0-3 GF: 1-4 Fm: 0-0
Distance: 5f/6f: 0-0 7f-8f: 0-0 9f-13f: 1-9 **14f+: 2-9**
Track : **LH: 2-9** RH: 1-9 **Tight: 1-11** Gall: 0-1
Aids: Bl: 0-0 Vi: 0-0 Tstrap: 1-4 Ckp: 1-4
Best Rating: **70** 10/08 Newb 2m gd-sft

Modest; stays 2m; acts on fast and soft ground.

Komreyev Star

91(102) (55)**49**
7-y-o b g Komaite (USA)-L'Ancressaan (Dalsaan)
R E Peacock Garry Whittaker

Placings:000/22310063000331/0000001206/0040465265/101000500-00265040066 **(7784)**
2009: 8^{0}SS, 8^{0}SD, 8^{2}SD, 9^{6}SD, 8^{5}SD, 8^{0}SD, 8^{4}GS, 8^{0}G, 8^{0}SD, 8^{6}SD, 8^{6}SD,

	Starts	1st	2nd	3rd	Win & Pl
Career Total (Turf)	28	3	1	3	10078
Career Total (AW)	29	2	4	1	6995

60 2/08 Sthl 1m (0-70)H SS £2593
58 1/08 Sthl 1m (0-50)H STD £2252
52 10/06 Muss 1m1f (0-45) G-S £2047
56 10/05 Ayr 1m1f20y (0-55)H HVY £3324
50 5/05 Bevl 1m100y (0-45) G-F £1603
Total win prize-money £11821

Going (Turf): **Sf: 1-7 GS: 1-4** Gd: 0-7 **GF: 1-10** Fm: 0-0
Distance: 5f/6f: 0-2 7f-8f: 2-19 **9f-13f: 3-35** 14f+: 0-1
Track : **LH: 3-43** RH: 2-9 **Tight: 1-21** Gall: 0-0
Aids: Bl: 0-0 Vi: 0-0 Tstrap: 0-10 Ckp: 0-10
Best Rating: **60** 2/08 Sthl 1m std-slw

Moderate gelding; effective at around 1m1f; acts on fast and heavy ground, Fibresand and Polytrack.

Kona Coast

103 **94**
2-y-o b c Oasis Dream-Macadamia (IRE) (Classic Cliche (IRE))
J H M Gosden H R H Princess Haya Of Jordan

Placings:65102 **(6478)**
2009: 6^{6}G, 7^{5}GF, 6^{1}F, 6^{0}GF, 7^{2}GF,

	Starts	1st	2nd	3rd	Win & Pl
Career Total (Turf)	5	1	1	0	225385

73 9/09 Brig 6f209y FRM £3784
Total win prize-money £3785

Going (Turf): Sf: 0-0 GS: 0-0 Gd: 0-1 GF: 0-3 **Fm: 1-1**
Distance: 5f/6f: 0-2 **7f-8f: 1-3** 9f-13f: 0-0 14f+: 0-0
Track : **LH: 1-1** RH: 0-0 Tight: 0-0 Gall: 0-0
Aids: Bl: 0-2 Vi: 0-0 Tstrap: 0-1 Ckp: 0-1
Best Rating: **94** 10/09 NmkR 7f gd-fm

Fair; stays 7f; acts on quick ground; has worn blinkers.

Konka (USA)

73(76) (20)**15**
3-y-o ch f Johannesburg (USA)-Defining Style (USA) (Out Of Place (USA))
E F Vaughan M Hawkes

Placings:000-66 **(1176)**
2009: 6^{6}SD, 7^{6}G,

	Starts	1st	2nd	3rd	Win & Pl
Career Total (Turf)	4	0	0	0	0
Career Total (AW)	1	0	0	0	0

Going (Turf): **Sf: 0-2 GS: 0-0 Gd: 0-2 GF: 0-0 Fm: 0-0**
Distance: 5f/6f: 0-2 7f-8f: 0-3 9f-13f: 0-0 14f+: 0-0
Track : LH: 0-2 RH: 0-0 Tight: 0-0 Gall: 0-0
Aids: Bl: 0-0 Vi: 0-0 Tstrap: 0-0 Ckp: 0-0
Best Rating: **20** 3/09 Sthl 6f stand

Koo And The Gang (IRE)

90(94) (68)**63**
2-y-o b g Le Vie Dei Colori-Entertain (Royal Applause)
B Ellison Koo's Racing Club

Placings:021000 **(7156)**
2009: 5^{0}GF, 5^{2}SD, 5^{1}SD, 5^{0}G, 5^{0}SD, 5^{0}SD,

	Starts	1st	2nd	3rd	Win & Pl
Career Total (Turf)	2	0	0	0	
Career Total (AW)	4	1	1	0	3536

68 5/09 Sthl 5f STD £2729
Total win prize-money £2730

Going (Turf): **Sf: 0-0 GS: 0-0 Gd: 0-1 GF: 0-1 Fm: 0-0**
Distance: **5f/6f: 1-6** 7f-8f: 0-0 9f-13f: 0-0 14f+: 0-0
Track : LH: 0-1 RH: 0-0 Tight: 0-1 Gall: 0-0
Aids: Bl: 0-0 Vi: 0-0 Tstrap: 0-0 Ckp: 0-0
Best Rating: **68** 5/09 Sthl 5f stand

Modest; suited by 5f; acts on Fibresand.

Kookie

90 **48**
2-y-o b f Makbul-Breakfast Creek (Hallgate)
R E Barr Brian Morton

Placings:06050 **(5595)**
2009: 5^{0}S, 6^{6}GF, 7^{0}GF, 7^{5}GF, 7^{0}GF,

	Starts	1st	2nd	3rd	Win & Pl
Career Total (Turf)	5	0	0	0	0

Going (Turf): **Sf: 0-1 GS: 0-0 Gd: 0-0 GF: 0-4 Fm: 0-0**
Distance: 5f/6f: 0-2 7f-8f: 0-3 9f-13f: 0-0 14f+: 0-0

Track : LH: 0-0 RH: 0-0 Tight: 0-0 Gall: 0-0
Aids: Bl: 0-0 Vi: 0-0 Tstrap: 0-0 Ckp: 0-0
Best Rating: **48** 8/09 Rdcr 7f gd-fm

Kool Katie

100(94) (57)**61**
4-y-o b f Millkom-Katie Komaite (Komaite (USA))
Mrs G S Rees Lancashire Lads Partnership

Placings:2/44005000-0020004020 **(7599)**
2009: 8^{0}HY, 10^{0}GS, 10^{2}GF, 9^{0}GF, 9^{0}G, 9^{0}G, 10^{4}GF, 9^{0}S, 9^{2}SD, 9^{0}SD,

	Starts	1st	2nd	3rd	Win & Pl
Career Total (Turf)	14	0	1	0	1445
Career Total (AW)	6	0	2	0	1502

Going (Turf): **Sf: 0-3 GS: 0-1 Gd: 0-5 GF: 0-5 Fm: 0-0**
Distance: 5f/6f: 0-4 7f-8f: 0-4 9f-13f: 0-12 14f+: 0-0
Track : LH: 0-14 RH: 0-4 Tight: 0-7 Gall: 0-0
Aids: Bl: 0-0 Vi: 0-0 Tstrap: 0-0 Ckp: 0-0
Best Rating: **61** 10/09 Pont 1m2f6y gd-fm

Modest sort; probably best at about a mile.

Koraleva Tectona (IRE)

103 (61)**79**
4-y-o b f Fasliyev (USA)-Miss Teak (USA) (Woodman (USA))
Pat Eddery Pat Eddery Racing (Ramruma)

Placings:60/33301061-0404615000 **(7189)**
2009: 7^{0}GF, 7^{4}GF, 7^{0}GF, 7^{4}G, 6^{6}GF, 7^{1}G, 7^{5}G, 7^{0}GS, 7^{0}GF, 7^{0}G,

	Starts	1st	2nd	3rd	Win & Pl
Career Total (Turf)	19	3	0	3	13639
Career Total (AW)	1	0	0	0	0

79	7/09	Epsm	7f	(0-75)H	GD	£3238
79	9/08	Gdwd	7f	(0-85)H	SFT	£4857
79	6/08	Pont	6f	(0-75)H	G-F	£3238

Total win prize-money £11333

Going (Turf): **Sf: 1-2** GS: 0-3 **Gd: 1-6 GF: 1-8** Fm: 0-0
Distance: 5f/6f: 1-4 **7f-8f: 2-14** 9f-13f: 0-2 14f+: 0-0
Track : **LH: 2-7** RH: 1-6 **Tight: 1-2** Gall: 0-1
Aids: Bl: 0-0 Vi: 0-0 Tstrap: 0-0 Ckp: 0-0
Best Rating: **79** 7/09 Epsm 7f good

Fair; effective over 7f-1m; acts on good and soft ground.

Kostar

100(106) (96)**86**
8-y-o ch g Komaite (USA)-Black And Amber (Weldnaas (USA))
C G Cox Mrs P Scott-Dunn And Mrs F J Ryan

Placings:4104212/30014102/2106420/010001/000-000 **(5424)**
2009: 6^{0}GF, 6^{0}GF, 6^{0}G,

	Starts	1st	2nd	3rd	Win & Pl
Career Total (Turf)	27	6	1	1	112798
Career Total (AW)	7	1	4	0	17111

107	8/07	Ripn	6f	(0-105)H	GD	£37392
109	4/07	Pont	6f	(0-100)H	G-F	£9971
99	5/06	Ling	7f	H	GD	£37392
95	7/05	Hayd	6f	(0-85)H	G-F	£8290
89	6/05	Wind	6f	(0-80)H	G-F	£7038
83	12/04	Wolv	5f216y	(0-75)	STD	£6873
68	7/04	Sals	6f	D	G-F	£5707

Total win prize-money £112665

Going (Turf): Sf: 0-0 GS: 0-4 Gd: 2-6 **GF: 4-17** Fm: 0-0
Distance: **5f/6f: 6-27** 7f-8f: 1-7 9f-13f: 0-0 14f+: 0-0
Track : **LH: 2-8** RH: 0-1 Tight: 1-7 Gall: 1-7
Aids: Bl: 0-0 Vi: 0-0 Tstrap: 0-1 Ckp: 0-1
Best Rating: **109** 4/07 Pont 6f gd-fm

Very useful; winner of the 2007 Great St Wilfrid; best over 6f; acts on good and faster ground and on Polytrack; likes to race prominently.

Kris Kin Line (IRE)

86(101) (76)**76**
3-y-o ch c Kris Kin (USA)-Shell Garland (USA) (Sadler's Wells (USA))
Sir Michael Stoute Saeed Suhail

Placings:5-310 **(3827)**
2009: 9^{3}G, 12^{1}SD, 14^{0}G,

	Starts	1st	2nd	3rd	Win & Pl
Career Total (Turf)	3	0	0	1	482
Career Total (AW)	1	1	0	0	2730

76	6/09	Ling	1m4f	STD	£2729

Total win prize-money £2730

Going (Turf): **Sf: 0-0 GS: 0-1 Gd: 0-2 GF: 0-0 Fm: 0-0**
Distance: 5f/6f: 0-0 7f-8f: 0-0 **9f-13f: 1-3** 14f+: 0-1
Track : **LH: 1-3** RH: 0-1 **Tight: 1-3** Gall: 0-1
Aids: Bl: 0-0 Vi: 0-0 Tstrap: 0-0 Ckp: 0-0
Best Rating: **76** 6/09 Ling 1m4f stand

Fair; stays 1m2f and acts on good ground.

Kristallo (GER)

102 **65**
4-y-o ch g Lando (GER)-Key West (GER) (In The Wings)
P R Webber Iain Russell Watters

Placings:032-430 **(3788)**
2009: 11^{4}GF, 14^{3}GF, 14^{0}GF,

	Starts	1st	2nd	3rd	Win & Pl
Career Total (Turf)	6	0	1	2	1695

Going (Turf): **Sf: 0-1 GS: 0-0 Gd: 0-2 GF: 0-3 Fm: 0-0**
Distance: 5f/6f: 0-0 7f-8f: 0-0 9f-13f: 0-4 14f+: 0-2
Track : LH: 0-2 RH: 0-0 Tight: 0-1 Gall: 0-0
Aids: Bl: 0-1 Vi: 0-0 Tstrap: 0-0 Ckp: 0-0
Best Rating: **65** 7/09 Wwck 1m6f213y gd-fm

Modest; stays 1m7f; acts on good ground.

Kristen Jane (USA)

93 **53**
2-y-o ch f Forest Wildcat (USA)-British Columbia (Selkirk (USA))
Miss L A Perratt Ken McGarrity

Placings:4006400 **(6983)**
2009: 5^{4}G, 5^{0}GF, 6^{0}S, 5^{6}G, 6^{4}G, 5^{0}GF, 6^{0}G,

	Starts	1st	2nd	3rd	Win & Pl
Career Total (Turf)	7	0	0	0	814

Going (Turf): **Sf: 0-1 GS: 0-0 Gd: 0-4 GF: 0-2 Fm: 0-0**
Distance: 5f/6f: 0-6 7f-8f: 0-1 9f-13f: 0-0 14f+: 0-0
Track : LH: 0-0 RH: 0-1 Tight: 0-0 Gall: 0-1
Aids: Bl: 0-0 Vi: 0-0 Tstrap: 0-0 Ckp: 0-0
Best Rating: **53** 8/09 Muss 5f gd-fm

Moderate; effective over 5f; acts on good ground.

Kristopher James (IRE)

97(100) (58)**61**
3-y-o ch g Spartacus (IRE)-Ela Alethia (Kris)
W M Brisbourne Stephen Jones

Placings:46020-05305040041 **(7143)**
2009: 8^{0}SD, 11^{5}SD, 10^{3}GF, 9^{0}GF, 10^{5}S, 10^{0}G, 10^{4}GF, 10^{0}S, 10^{0}SS, 10^{4}SD, 9^{1}SD,

	Starts	1st	2nd	3rd	Win & Pl
Career Total (Turf)	7	0	0	1	1160
Career Total (AW)	9	1	1	0	2823

58	10/09	Wolv	1m1f103y (0-55)H	STD	£2047

Total win prize-money £2047

Going (Turf): **Sf: 0-2 GS: 0-0 Gd: 0-2 GF: 0-3 Fm: 0-0**
Distance: 5f/6f: 0-0 7f-8f: 0-4 **9f-13f: 1-12** 14f+: 0-0
Track : **LH: 1-15** RH: 0-1 **Tight: 1-9** Gall: 0-1
Aids: Bl: 0-0 Vi: 0-0 Tstrap: 0-0 Ckp: 0-0
Best Rating: **61** 8/08 Ches 7f2y good

Moderate; effective over 7f-1m2f; acts on Fibresand; handles fast turf.

Kronful

79 **62**
2-y-o b f Singspiel (IRE)-Albahja (Sinndar (IRE))
M A Jarvis Sheikh Ahmed Al Maktoum

Placings:3 **(5417)**
2009: 7^{3}GF,

	Starts	1st	2nd	3rd	Win & Pl
Career Total (Turf)	1	0	0	1	746

Going (Turf): **Sf: 0-0 GS: 0-0 Gd: 0-0 GF: 0-1 Fm: 0-0**
Distance: 5f/6f: 0-0 7f-8f: 0-1 9f-13f: 0-0 14f+: 0-0
Track : LH: 0-0 RH: 0-1 Tight: 0-0 Gall: 0-0
Aids: Bl: 0-0 Vi: 0-0 Tstrap: 0-0 Ckp: 0-0
Best Rating: **62** 8/09 Bevl 7f100y gd-fm

Modest; stays 7f plus; acts on fast ground.

Krugerrand (USA)

90(106) (77)**75**
10-y-o ch g Gulch (USA)-Nasers Pride (USA) (Al Nasr (FR))
W J Musson The Vale Partnership

Placings:321/00216440/00610054040/000136051500/00 20200001/000302001500/006040006F/0056610463-062232 **(1815)**
2009: 10^{0}SD, 12^{6}SD, 12^{2}SD, 12^{2}SD, 9^{3}SD, 11^{2}GF,

	Starts	1st	2nd	3rd	Win & Pl
Career Total (Turf)	73	8	6	3	108075
Career Total (AW)	10	0	2	2	2119

73	8/08	NmkJ	1m2f	(0-75)H	G-S	£3885
92	9/06	Ayr	1m2f	(0-100)H	G-S	£11658
97	10/05	York	1m208y	(0-85)H	G-S	£10129
93	8/04	Wind	1m67y	D(0-80)	G-S	£5525
89	6/04	York	1m208y	B(0-105)H	G-F	£18281
90	6/03	York	1m208y	B(0-105)H	G-F	£19805
93	7/02	Wwck	7f26y	C(0-90)	G-F	£6919
76	9/01	Wwck	7f26y	D	G-F	£3932

Total win prize-money £80139

Going (Turf): Sf: 0-7**GS: 4-16** Gd: 0-18 **GF: 4-30** Fm: 0-2
Distance: 5f/6f: 0-3 7f-8f: 2-21 **9f-13f: 6-59** 14f+: 0-0
Track : **LH: 6-27** RH: 2-36 Tight: 1-25 **Gall: 4-14**
Aids: Bl: 0-0 Vi: 0-0 Tstrap: 0-0 Ckp: 0-0
Best Rating: **97** 10/05 York 1m208y gd-sft

Modest; stays 1m2f; acts on most ground but suited by cut; usually held up.

Krymian

88(92) (81)**53**

2-y-o gr g Bahamian Bounty-Kryena (Kris)

Sir Michael Stoute Sir Evelyn De Rothschild

Placings:020 **(6592)**

2009: 7^{0}G, 8^{2}SD, 8^{0}GS,

	Starts	1st	2nd	3rd	Win & Pl
Career Total (Turf)	2	0	0	0	
Career Total (AW)	1	0	1	0	1156

Going (Turf): **Sf: 0-0 GS: 0-1 Gd: 0-1 GF: 0-0 Fm: 0-0**
Distance: 5f/6f: 0-0 7f-8f: 0-1 9f-13f: 0-2 14f+: 0-0
Track : LH: 0-2 RH: 0-1 Tight: 0-1 Gall: 0-0
Aids: Bl: 0-0 Vi: 0-0 Tstrap: 0-0 Ckp: 0-0
Best Rating: **81** 9/09 Wolv 1m141y stand

Krysanthe

(73) (32)

2-y-o b f Kyllachy-Aegean Magic (Wolfhound (USA))

J A Geake The Prize Winners

Placings:00 **(7326)**

2009: 6^{0}SD, 7^{0}SD,

	Starts	1st	2nd	3rd	Win & Pl
Career Total (Turf)	0	0	0	0	
Career Total (AW)	2	0	0	0	

Going (Turf): **Sf: 0-0 GS: 0-0 Gd: 0-0 GF: 0-0 Fm: 0-0**
Distance: 5f/6f: 0-1 7f-8f: 0-1 9f-13f: 0-0 14f+: 0-0
Track : LH: 0-0 RH: 0-2 Tight: 0-0 Gall: 0-0
Aids: Bl: 0-0 Vi: 0-0 Tstrap: 0-0 Ckp: 0-0
Best Rating: **32** 10/09 Kemp 6f stand

Kuanyao (IRE)

100(105) (76)**66**

3-y-o b g American Post-Nullarbor (Green Desert (USA))

P J Makin D M Ahier

Placings:60-01332111 **(7729)**

2009: 6^{0}GF, 6^{1}GF, 7^{3}G, 7^{3}GF, 7^{2}SD, 7^{1}SS, 7^{1}SD, 7^{1}SD,

	Starts	1st	2nd	3rd	Win & Pl
Career Total (Turf)	5	1	0	2	3741
Career Total (AW)	5	3	1	0	5124

71 11/09 Kemp 7f (0-65)H STD £1706
68 10/09 Ling 7f (0-70)H SS £2914
66 7/09 Sals 6f (0-65)H G-F £2914
Total win prize-money £7534

Going (Turf): Sf: 0-0 GS: 0-0 Gd: 0-2 **GF: 1-3** Fm: 0-0
Distance: 5f/6f: 1-2 **7f-8f: 3-8** 9f-13f: 0-0 14f+: 0-0
Track : **LH: 2-4** RH: 1-1 **Tight: 2-4** Gall: 0-1
Aids: Bl: 0-0 Vi: 0-0 Tstrap: 0-0 Ckp: 0-0
Best Rating: **76** 12/09 Wolv 7f32y stand

Modest; stays 7f; acts on fast ground; goes on Polytrack.

Kudu Country (IRE)

110 **77**

3-y-o gr g Captain Rio-Nirvavita (FR) (Highest Honor (FR))

T P Tate The Flat Cap Syndicate

Placings:3410-46034 **(5660)**

2009: 12^{4}S, 12^{6}GS, 14^{0}G, 14^{3}GS, 14^{4}S,

	Starts	1st	2nd	3rd	Win & Pl
Career Total (Turf)	9	1	0	2	3345

Going (Turf): **Sf: 1-3** GS: 0-2 Gd: 0-2 GF: 0-1 Fm: 0-1
Distance: 5f/6f: 0-0 **7f-8f: 1-4** 9f-13f: 0-2 14f+: 0-3
Track : LH: 0-6 **RH: 1-2** Tight: 0-2 Gall: 0-3
Aids: Bl: 0-0 Vi: 0-0 Tstrap: 0-0 Ckp: 0-0
Best Rating: **77** 5/09 York 1m4f soft

Fair; stays 1m4f; acts on most ground.

Kumbeshwar

98 **81**

2-y-o b g Doyen (IRE)-Camp Fire (IRE) (Lahib (USA))

P D Evans G E Amey

Placings:061531 **(7218)**

2009: 6^{0}GF, 7^{8}GF, 7^{1}GF, 6^{5}GF, 7^{3}G, 7^{1}S,

	Starts	1st	2nd	3rd	Win & Pl
Career Total (Turf)	6	2	0	1	10644

81 11/09 Catt 7f (0-85) SFT £4209
79 9/09 Ches 7f2y G-F £5828
Total win prize-money £10037

Going (Turf): **Sf: 1-1** GS: 0-0 Gd: 0-1 **GF: 1-4** Fm: 0-0
Distance: 5f/6f: 0-1 **7f-8f: 2-5** 9f-13f: 0-0 14f+: 0-0
Track : **LH: 2-4** RH: 0-0 **Tight: 2-4** Gall: 0-1
Aids: Bl: 0-0 Vi: 0-0 Tstrap: 0-0 Ckp: 0-0
Best Rating: **81** 11/09 Catt 7f soft

Useful; effective over 7f; acts on fast and soft ground.

Kummel Excess (IRE)

(95) (65)

2-y-o ch f Exceed And Excel (AUS)-Ipanema Beach (Lion Cavern (USA))

George Baker Mrs V P Baker & Partners

Placings:04241 **(7748)**

2009: 5^{0}SD, 6^{4}SD, 5^{2}SD, 5^{4}SD, 5^{1}SD,

	Starts	1st	2nd	3rd	Win & Pl
Career Total (Turf)	0	0	0	0	
Career Total (AW)	5	1	1	0	3904

64 12/09 Wolv 5f20y STD £2914
Total win prize-money £2914

Going (Turf): **Sf: 0-0 GS: 0-0 Gd: 0-0 GF: 0-0 Fm: 0-0**
Distance: **5f/6f: 1-5** 7f-8f: 0-0 9f-13f: 0-0 14f+: 0-0
Track : **LH: 1-2** RH: 0-2 **Tight: 1-2** Gall: 0-0
Aids: Bl: 0-0 Vi: 0-0 Tstrap: 0-0 Ckp: 0-0
Best Rating: **65** 11/09 Sthl 5f stand

Modest; effective at 5f; acts on Fibresand and Polytrack.

Kunte Kinteh

84 (69)**69**

5-y-o b g Indian Lodge (IRE)-Summer Siren (FR) (Saint Cyrien (FR))

D Nicholls Warren Smith

Placings:460/2301340/0020000-00 **(7173)**

2009: 6^{0}GF, 9^{0}S,

	Starts	1st	2nd	3rd	Win & Pl
Career Total (Turf)	17	1	1	1	4512
Career Total (AW)	2	0	1	1	1266

58 7/07 Catt 7f GD £2730
Total win prize-money £2730

Going (Turf): Sf: 0-3 GS: 0-3 **Gd: 1-4** GF: 0-7 Fm: 0-0
Distance: 5f/6f: 0-5 **7f-8f: 1-13** 9f-13f: 0-1 14f+: 0-0
Track : **LH: 1-9** RH: 0-3 **Tight: 1-7** Gall: 0-1
Aids: Bl: 0-0 Vi: 0-0 Tstrap: 0-0 Ckp: 0-0
Best Rating: **69** 5/08 Yarm 7f3y good

Modest gelding; stays 7f and acts on Fibresand.

Kurtanella

96(95) (83)**85**

2-y-o b/br f Pastoral Pursuits-Aconite (Primo Dominie)

R Hannon Mrs Philip Snow

Placings:21U01345 **(6471)**

2009: 5^{2}GF, 5^{1}G, 6^{U}GF, 6^{0}G, 6^{1}SD, 7^{3}GF, 7^{4}GF, 7^{5}GF,

	Starts	1st	2nd	3rd	Win & Pl
Career Total (Turf)	7	1	1	1	9697
Career Total (AW)	1	1	0	0	3886

83 8/09 Kemp 6f STD £3885
80 5/09 Newb 5f34y GD £6542
Total win prize-money £10429

Going (Turf): Sf: 0-0 GS: 0-0 **Gd: 1-2** GF: 0-5 Fm: 0-0
Distance: **5f/6f: 2-5** 7f-8f: 0-3 9f-13f: 0-0 14f+: 0-0
Track : LH: 0-2 **RH: 1-2** Tight: 0-2 Gall: 0-0
Aids: Bl: 0-0 Vi: 0-0 Tstrap: 0-0 Ckp: 0-0
Best Rating: **85** 8/09 Epsm 7f gd-fm

Useful; effective over 5f-7f; acts on fast ground.

Kwami Biscuit

83 **46**

2-y-o ch g Clerkenwell (USA)-Singer On The Roof (Chief Singer)

G A Harker Mrs J M Phillips

Placings:500 **(5519)**

2009: 7^{5}S, 7^{0}G, 6^{0}G,

	Starts	1st	2nd	3rd	Win & Pl
Career Total (Turf)	3	0	0	0	0

Going (Turf): **Sf: 0-1 GS: 0-0 Gd: 0-2 GF: 0-0 Fm: 0-0**
Distance: 5f/6f: 0-1 7f-8f: 0-2 9f-13f: 0-0 14f+: 0-0
Track : LH: 0-2 RH: 0-0 Tight: 0-2 Gall: 0-0
Aids: Bl: 0-0 Vi: 0-0 Tstrap: 0-0 Ckp: 0-0
Best Rating: **46** 7/09 Catt 7f soft

Kyber

100(87) (27)**66**

8-y-o ch g First Trump-Mahbob Dancer (FR) (Groom Dancer (USA))

J S Goldie Great Northern Partnership

Placings:543306454/206000/0136461321506/0415102513 4600-5544 **(4873)**

2009: 15^{5}GF, 13^{5}G, 16^{4}GF, 14^{4}G,

	Starts	1st	2nd	3rd	Win & Pl
Career Total (Turf)	40	6	2	5	23858
Career Total (AW)	6	0	1	0	1085

66 8/08 Muss 1m6f (0-65)H SFT £2590
64 6/08 Muss 2m (0-65)H G-F £2498
64 6/08 Muss 2m (0-70)H G-F £3885
62 8/07 Muss 1m6f (0-65)H GD £2590
58 6/07 Ayr 1m5f13y (0-75)H GD £2914
58 4/07 Muss 2m (0-65)H G-F £2590
Total win prize-money £17071

Going (Turf): Sf: 1-6 GS: 0-6 Gd: 2-13 **GF: 3-14** Fm: 0-1
Distance: 5f/6f: 0-0 7f-8f: 0-9 9f-13f: 0-10 **14f+: 6-36**
Track : LH: 1-24 **RH: 5-21 Tight: 5-29** Gall: 0-3
Aids: Bl: 0-0 Vi: 0-0 Tstrap: 0-0 Ckp: 0-0

Best Rating: **66** 9/08 Muss 1m6f soft

Modest sort; stays 2m; handles most ground.

Kyle (IRE)

101(106) (77)**86**

5-y-o ch g Kyllachy-Staylily (IRE) (Grand Lodge (USA))

C R Dore Mrs A N Durkan

Placings:332222/31143304606/40001610-350050164000504430 **(7870)**

2009: 5^{3}G, 5^{5}SD, 6^{0}HY, 7^{0}SD, 6^{5}SD, 6^{0}S, 6^{1}G, 6^{6}GF, 6^{4}G, 6^{0}SD, 5^{0}GF, 5^{0}GF, 5^{5}GF, 5^{0}SD, 5^{4}SD, 6^{4}SD, 5^{3}SD, 6^{0}SS,

	Starts	1st	2nd	3rd	Win & Pl
Career Total (Turf)	29	5	3	4	25937
Career Total (AW)	14	0	1	3	2958

81	8/08	Bath	5f161y		G-S	£2072
86	6/08	Wind	6f	(0-80)H	G-S	£4857
86	5/07	Hayd	6f	(0-80)H	G-F	£5505
74	5/07	Sals	6f		G-F	£4857

Total win prize-money £17292

Going (Turf): Sf: 0-5 **GS: 2-5** Gd: 1-6 **GF: 2-13** Fm: 0-0
Distance: **5f/6f: 4-34** 7f-8f: 1-8 9f-13f: 0-1 14f+: 0-0
Track : **LH: 1-12** RH: 0-8 Tight: 0-7 **Gall: 2-10**
Aids: Bl: 0-0 Vi: 0-0 Tstrap: 0-1 Ckp: 0-1
Best Rating: **88** 7/07 Kemp 6f stand

Modest; stays 7f, but most effective over 6f; acts on any ground; goes on Polytrack; has worn cheekpieces.

Kyle Of Bute

99(87) (50)**67**

3-y-o ch g Kyllachy-Blinding Mission (IRE) (Marju (IRE))

B P J Baugh (J L Dunlop 6/10) J H Chrimes

Placings:000005-0034445225155 **(7127)**

2009: 7^{0}GF, 6^{0}GF, 7^{3}GF, 6^{4}F, 7^{4}F, 9^{4}GS, 10^{5}GF, 9^{2}F, 10^{2}G, 9^{5}GF, 9^{1}GF, 10^{5}G, 10^{5}G,

	Starts	1st	2nd	3rd	Win & Pl
Career Total (Turf)	17	1	2	1	3838
Career Total (AW)	2	0	0	0	

67	10/09	Leic	1m1f218y	G-F	£1942

Total win prize-money £1943

Going (Turf): Sf: 0-0 GS: 0-2 Gd: 0-4 **GF: 1-8** Fm: 0-3
Distance: 5f/6f: 0-2 7f-8f: 0-9 **9f-13f: 1-8** 14f+: 0-0
Track : LH: 0-10 **RH: 1-4** Tight: 0-3 Gall: 0-1
Aids: Bl: 0-2 Vi: 0-3 Tstrap: 0-0 Ckp: 0-0
Best Rating: **67** 10/09 Leic 1m1f218y gd-fm

Moderate; stays 1m2f; acts on fast ground.

Kyleene

(100) (78)**74**

3-y-o b f Kyllachy-Mrs Nash (Night Shift (USA))

J Noseda Lordship Stud

Placings:05-21 **(4859)**

2009: 6^{2}G, 7^{1}SD,

	Starts	1st	2nd	3rd	Win & Pl
Career Total (Turf)	2	0	1	0	964
Career Total (AW)	2	1	0	0	3886

78	8/09	Wolv	7f32y	(0-70)H	STD	£3885

Total win prize-money £3886

Going (Turf): **Sf: 0-0 GS: 0-0 Gd: 0-1 GF: 0-1 Fm: 0-0**
Distance: 5f/6f: 0-2 **7f-8f: 1-2** 9f-13f: 0-0 14f+: 0-0
Track : **LH: 1-1** RH: 0-1 **Tight: 1-1** Gall: 0-0
Aids: Bl: 0-0 Vi: 0-0 Tstrap: 0-0 Ckp: 0-0
Best Rating: **78** 8/09 Wolv 7f32y stand

Fair; stays 7f; acts on good ground and on Polytrack.

Kyllachy King

79 **34**

3-y-o b g Kyllachy-Baileys Dancer (Groom Dancer (USA))

Mrs A J Perrett Cotton, James, Slade, Tracey

Placings:00 **(2930)**

2009: 10^{0}GF, 10^{0}G,

	Starts	1st	2nd	3rd	Win & Pl
Career Total (Turf)	2	0	0	0	

Going (Turf): **Sf: 0-0 GS: 0-0 Gd: 0-1 GF: 0-1 Fm: 0-0**
Distance: 5f/6f: 0-0 7f-8f: 0-0 9f-13f: 0-2 14f+: 0-0
Track : LH: 0-0 RH: 0-2 Tight: 0-1 Gall: 0-0
Aids: Bl: 0-0 Vi: 0-0 Tstrap: 0-0 Ckp: 0-0
Best Rating: **34** 6/09 Wind 1m2f7y gd-fm

Kyllachy Star

105(108) (98)**95**

3-y-o b g Kyllachy-Jaljuli (Jalmood (USA))

R A Fahey Dr Marwan Koukash

Placings:2360210-540116630510 **(7294)**

2009: 6^{5}SD, 7^{4}SD, 6^{0}G, 7^{1}GF, 7^{1}G, 8^{6}GF, 7^{6}GS, 7^{3}HY, 8^{0}HY, 7^{5}G, 7^{1}SS, 7^{0}S,

	Starts	1st	2nd	3rd	Win & Pl
Career Total (Turf)	16	3	2	2	31053
Career Total (AW)	3	1	0	0	9642

98	10/09	Ling	7f	(0-95)H	SS	£8871
95	6/09	Sand	7f16y	(0-90)H	GD	£7771
87	5/09	York	7f	(0-90)H	G-F	£7771
78	9/08	Ayr	6f		HVY	£4015

Total win prize-money £28428

Going (Turf): **Sf: 1-5** GS: 0-2 **Gd: 1-4 GF: 1-5** Fm: 0-0
Distance: 5f/6f: 1-7 **7f-8f: 3-12** 9f-13f: 0-0 14f+: 0-0
Track : **LH: 2-5** RH: 1-6 Tight: 1-2 Gall: 1-3
Aids: Bl: 0-0 Vi: 0-0 Tstrap: 0-1 Ckp: 0-1
Best Rating: **98** 10/09 Ling 7f std-slw

Useful; effective over 6f-7f; acts on fast and soft ground; has worn cheekpieces.

Kyllachy Storm

102(100) (65)**79**

5-y-o b g Kyllachy-Social Storm (USA) (Future Storm (USA))

R J Hodges Mrs Angela Hart

Placings:005660/600620/222350041210-311520502060 **(6915)**

2009: 6^{3}GF, 5^{1}GF, 5^{1}GS, 5^{5}F, 5^{2}F, 6^{0}GF, 5^{5}GF, 5^{0}G, 5^{2}GF, 5^{0}G, 5^{6}F, 6^{0}SD,

	Starts	1st	2nd	3rd	Win & Pl
Career Total (Turf)	30	4	7	2	16906
Career Total (AW)	6	0	0	0	0

77	5/09	Bath	5f161y	(0-70)H	G-S	£2719
74	5/09	Bath	5f11y	(0-65)H	G-F	£2266
69	10/08	Bath	5f161y	(0-58)H	G-S	£1942
64	8/08	Gdwd	6f	(0-70)H	SFT	£3238

Total win prize-money £10168

Going (Turf): Sf: 1-3 **GS: 2-4** Gd: 0-10 GF: 1-9 Fm: 0-4
Distance: **5f/6f: 4-27** 7f-8f: 0-6 9f-13f: 0-2 14f+: 0-1
Track : **LH: 3-24** RH: 0-1 Tight: 0-8 **Gall: 3-15**
Aids: Bl: 0-3 Vi: 0-0 Tstrap: 0-0 Ckp: 0-0
Best Rating: **79** 8/09 Bath 5f161y gd-fm

Fair; effective at 5f-6f; acts on fast and soft ground; has worn blinkers.

Kylladdie

95(97) (72)**78**

2-y-o ch g Kyllachy-Chance For Romance (Entrepreneur)

S Gollings (T P Tate 1/9) P J Martin

Placings:41435534 **(7786)**

2009: 6^{4}G, 6^{1}GS, 6^{4}GF, 6^{3}GS, 6^{5}G, 7^{5}SD, 7^{3}SD, 5^{4}SD,

	Starts	1st	2nd	3rd	Win & Pl
Career Total (Turf)	5	1	0	1	5498
Career Total (AW)	3	0	0	1	1092

78	5/09	Ripn	6f	G-S	£3885

Total win prize-money £3886

Going (Turf): Sf: 0-0 **GS: 1-2** Gd: 0-2 GF: 0-1 Fm: 0-0
Distance: **5f/6f: 1-6** 7f-8f: 0-2 9f-13f: 0-0 14f+: 0-0
Track : LH: 0-4 RH: 0-0 Tight: 0-3 Gall: 0-0
Aids: Bl: 0-0 Vi: 0-0 Tstrap: 0-0 Ckp: 0-0
Best Rating: **78** 5/09 Ripn 6f gd-sft

Fair; stays 7f; acts on easy ground and on Polytrack.

Kyoatee Kilt

(90) (54)

2-y-o ch c Kyllachy-Oatey (Master Willie)

P F I Cole Mrs J M Haines

Placings:005550 **(7887)**

2009: 6^{0}SD, 5^{0}SD, 7^{5}SD, 8^{5}SD, 10^{5}SD, 7^{0}SD,

	Starts	1st	2nd	3rd	Win & Pl
Career Total (Turf)	0	0	0	0	
Career Total (AW)	6	0	0	0	0

Going (Turf): **Sf: 0-0 GS: 0-0 Gd: 0-0 GF: 0-0 Fm: 0-0**
Distance: 5f/6f: 0-2 7f-8f: 0-2 9f-13f: 0-2 14f+: 0-0
Track : LH: 0-4 RH: 0-2 Tight: 0-4 Gall: 0-0
Aids: Bl: 0-1 Vi: 0-0 Tstrap: 0-0 Ckp: 0-0
Best Rating: **54** 12/09 Kemp 1m2f stand

Kyzer Chief

104 **74**

4-y-o b g Rouvres (FR)-Payvashooz (Ballacashtal (CAN))

R E Barr Brian Morton

Placings:0000/5222263-51060254060405 **(6489)**

2009: 5^{5}GF, 5^{1}GF, 5^{0}G, 5^{6}GF, 5^{0}G, 5^{2}G, 5^{5}S, 5^{4}GS, 5^{0}GF, 5^{6}GS, 5^{0}GF, 5^{4}GF, 5^{0}GF, 5^{5}GF,

	Starts	1st	2nd	3rd	Win & Pl
Career Total (Turf)	25	1	5	1	8680

73	4/09	Ripn	5f	(0-75)H	G-F	£3238

Total win prize-money £3238

Going (Turf): Sf: 0-1 GS: 0-5 Gd: 0-5 **GF: 1-14** Fm: 0-0
Distance: **5f/6f: 1-25** 7f-8f: 0-0 9f-13f: 0-0 14f+: 0-0
Track : LH: 0-1 RH: 0-0 Tight: 0-1 Gall: 0-0
Aids: Bl: 0-0 Vi: 0-0 Tstrap: 0-3 Ckp: 0-3
Best Rating: **74** 7/09 York 5f good

Modest sprinter; 5f; acts on fast and easy ground.

L'Arco Baleno (IRE)

85(93) (53)**39**

3-y-o b f Catcher In The Rye (IRE)-Rainbow Java (IRE) (Fairy King (USA))

S A Callaghan Edward M Kirtland

Placings:330000 **(2709)**

2009: 6^{3}SD, 7^{3}SD, 7^{0}SD, 8^{0}GF, 7^{0}G, 10^{0}SD,

	Starts	1st	2nd	3rd	Win & Pl
Career Total (Turf)	2	0	0	0	

Career Total (AW) 4 0 0 2 907

Going (Turf): Sf: 0-0 GS: 0-0 Gd: 0-1 GF: 0-1 Fm: 0-0
Distance: 5f/6f: 0-1 7f-8f: 0-3 9f-13f: 0-2 14f+: 0-0
Track : LH: 0-4 RH: 0-1 Tight: 0-2 Gall: 0-0
Aids: Bl: 0-0 Vi: 0-0 Tstrap: 0-0 Ckp: 0-0
Best Rating: 53 2/09 Ling 6f stand

Moderate filly; stays 7f; acts on Polytrack and Fibresand.

L'Enchanteresse (IRE)

91 72
2-y-o ch f Kyllachy-Enchant (Lion Cavern (USA))
M L W Bell R A Green

Placings:323203 (6820)
2009: 6^3GS, 6^2G, 5^3HY, 6^2GF, 7^0GF, 6^3GF,

	Starts	1st	2nd	3rd	Win & Pl
Career Total (Turf)	6	0	2	3	4701

Going (Turf): Sf: 0-1 GS: 0-1 Gd: 0-1 GF: 0-3 Fm: 0-0
Distance: 5f/6f: 0-5 7f-8f: 0-1 9f-13f: 0-0 14f+: 0-0
Track : LH: 0-1 RH: 0-0 Tight: 0-1 Gall: 0-0
Aids: Bl: 0-0 Vi: 0-0 Tstrap: 0-0 Ckp: 0-0
Best Rating: 72 7/09 York 6f good

Fair; effective at up to 6f; acts on most ground.

L'Hirondelle (IRE)

100(106) (89)89
5-y-o b g Anabaa (USA)-Auratum (USA) (Carson City (USA))
M J Attwater Canisbay Bloodstock

Placings:R15-310040541 (7833)
2009: 8^3SD, 8^1SD, 8^0SD, 7^0GF, 8^4GF, 8^0SD, 8^5SD, 8^4SD, 7^1SD,

	Starts	1st	2nd	3rd	Win & Pl
Career Total (Turf)	3	0	0	0	841
Career Total (AW)	9	3	0	1	14963

89	12/09	Kemp	7f	(0-85)H	STD	£5180
89	1/09	Ling	1m	(0-80)H	STD	£4857
74	11/08	Kemp	1m1f		STD	£3238

Total win prize-money £13276

Going (Turf): Sf: 0-1 GS: 0-0 Gd: 0-0 GF: 0-2 Fm: 0-0
Distance: 5f/6f: 0-0 7f-8f: 2-9 9f-13f: 1-3 14f+: 0-0
Track : LH: 1-4 RH: 2-6 Tight: 1-4 Gall: 0-0
Aids: Bl: 0-0 Vi: 0-0 Tstrap: 0-0 Ckp: 0-0
Best Rating: 89 12/09 Kemp 7f stand

Useful; effective over 7f-1m; acts on Polytrack.

L'Homme De Nuit (GER)

(104) (75)60
5-y-o b g Samum (GER)-La Bouche (GER) (In The Wings)
G L Moore David & Jane George

Placings:312/0003413-3 (7255)
2009: 16^3SD,

	Starts	1st	2nd	3rd	Win & Pl
Career Total (Turf)	5	1	1	1	3736
Career Total (AW)	6	1	0	3	3798

71	11/08	Wolv	1m5f194y	(0-65)H	STD	£2388
	8/07	Hanv	1m3f		GD	£2027

Total win prize-money £4415

Going (Turf): Sf: 0-0 GS: 0-0 Gd: 1-4 GF: 0-1 Fm: 0-0
Distance: 5f/6f: 0-0 7f-8f: 0-0 9f-13f: 1-6 14f+: 1-5
Track : LH: 1-6 RH: 0-2 Tight: 1-6 Gall: 0-1
Aids: Bl: 0-1 Vi: 0-0 Tstrap: 1-3 Ckp: 1-3
Best Rating: 75 12/08 Wolv 2m119y stand

Modest; stays 2m; acts on Polytrack; has worn cheek-pieces.

L'Isle Joyeuse

87(84) (33)38
2-y-o b f Compton Place-Sabalara (IRE) (Mujadil (USA))
P Winkworth D Macham

Placings:0500 (6700)
2009: 5^0G, 5^5GF, 5^0G, 5^0SS,

	Starts	1st	2nd	3rd	Win & Pl
Career Total (Turf)	3	0	0	0	0
Career Total (AW)	1	0	0	0	

Going (Turf): Sf: 0-0 GS: 0-0 Gd: 0-2 GF: 0-1 Fm: 0-0
Distance: 5f/6f: 0-4 7f-8f: 0-0 9f-13f: 0-0 14f+: 0-0
Track : LH: 0-3 RH: 0-0 Tight: 0-1 Gall: 0-2
Aids: Bl: 0-0 Vi: 0-0 Tstrap: 0-0 Ckp: 0-0
Best Rating: 38 8/09 Folk 5f gd-fm

La Adelita (IRE)

84 93
3-y-o b f Anabaa (USA)-Aiming (Highest Honor (FR))
M L W Bell Mrs Melba Bryce

Placings:5120-0 (7032)
2009: 7^0S,

	Starts	1st	2nd	3rd	Win & Pl
Career Total (Turf)	5	1	1	0	5094

76	9/08	Wwck	7f26y	SFT	£3885

Total win prize-money £3886

Going (Turf): Sf: 1-2 GS: 0-2 Gd: 0-1 GF: 0-0 Fm: 0-0
Distance: 5f/6f: 0-0 7f-8f: 1-5 9f-13f: 0-0 14f+: 0-0
Track : LH: 1-1 RH: 0-0 Tight: 0-0 Gall: 0-0
Aids: Bl: 0-0 Vi: 0-0 Tstrap: 0-0 Ckp: 0-0
Best Rating: 93 11/08 NmkR 1m gd-sft

Useful; effective at 7f; acts on good and softer ground.

La Belle Dane

72 6
3-y-o b f Danetime (IRE)-Lindfield Belle (IRE) (Fairy King (USA))
J Noseda Saeed Suhail

Placings:0 (1837)
2009: 7^0GF,

	Starts	1st	2nd	3rd	Win & Pl
Career Total (Turf)	1	0	0	0	

Going (Turf): Sf: 0-0 GS: 0-0 Gd: 0-0 GF: 0-1 Fm: 0-0
Distance: 5f/6f: 0-0 7f-8f: 0-1 9f-13f: 0-0 14f+: 0-0
Track : LH: 0-0 RH: 0-0 Tight: 0-0 Gall: 0-0
Aids: Bl: 0-0 Vi: 0-0 Tstrap: 0-0 Ckp: 0-0
Best Rating: 6 5/09 Ling 7f gd-fm

La Belle Joannie

99(95) (56)60
4-y-o b f Lujain (USA)-Sea Clover (IRE) (Ela-Mana-Mou)
S Curran L M Power

Placings:0352050/6-0330202050 (7422)
2009: 8^0G, 7^3F, 8^3GF, 10^0SD, 7^2HY, 6^0G, 7^2GS, 10^0SD, 7^5SD, 8^0SD,

	Starts	1st	2nd	3rd	Win & Pl
Career Total (Turf)	11	0	3	3	3578
Career Total (AW)	7	0	0	0	0

Going (Turf): Sf: 0-3 GS: 0-2 Gd: 0-2 GF: 0-3 Fm: 0-1
Distance: 5f/6f: 0-3 7f-8f: 0-11 9f-13f: 0-4 14f+: 0-0
Track : LH: 0-8 RH: 0-3 Tight: 0-4 Gall: 0-0
Aids: Bl: 0-0 Vi: 0-0 Tstrap: 0-0 Ckp: 0-0
Best Rating: 60 8/09 Leic 7f9y heavy

Plating-class; suited by 7f; acts on any ground.

La Brigitte

107(91) (75)89
3-y-o ch f Tobougg (IRE)-Bardot (Efisio)
J A Glover (A J McCabe 27/5) Paul Dixon & The White Horse Partnership

Placings:30141014406-620 (7155)
2009: 5^6GF, 5^2G, 5^0SD,

	Starts	1st	2nd	3rd	Win & Pl
Career Total (Turf)	11	2	1	0	15773
Career Total (AW)	3	1	0	1	2036

83	8/08	Rdcr	6f	GD	£6799
79	7/08	Hayd	5f	HVY	£3238
75	6/08	Sthl	5f	STD	£1774

Total win prize-money £11812

Going (Turf): Sf: 1-5 GS: 0-0 Gd: 1-3 GF: 0-3 Fm: 0-0
Distance: 5f/6f: 3-13 7f-8f: 0-1 9f-13f: 0-0 14f+: 0-0
Track : LH: 0-2 RH: 0-0 Tight: 0-1 Gall: 0-0
Aids: Bl: 0-0 Vi: 0-0 Tstrap: 0-0 Ckp: 0-0
Best Rating: 89 8/09 Ripn 5f good

Useful; stays 5f-6f; acts on most ground and on Fibresand.

La Capriosa

99(104) (75)73
3-y-o ch f Kyllachy-La Caprice (USA) (Housebuster (USA))
J A Glover (A J McCabe 22/6) Paul J Dixon

Placings:06433022-135213510212625213330 50 (7223)
2009: 6^1SS, 5^3SD, 6^5SD, 6^2SD, 5^1SD, 6^3SD, 5^5SD, 6^1SD, 5^0SD, 5^2SD, 5^1GF, 6^2GF, 5^6GF, 5^2SD, 5^5S, 5^2G, 5^1S, 5^3G, 6^3G, 5^3GF, 6^0S, 5^5G, 5^0SD,

	Starts	1st	2nd	3rd	Win & Pl
Career Total (Turf)	12	2	2	3	9091
Career Total (AW)	19	3	5	4	12076

69	8/09	Donc	5f	(0-70)H	SFT	£3238
61	4/09	Bevl	5f		G-F	£2590
67	3/09	Sthl	6f		STD	£2137
67	2/09	Sthl	5f		STD	£2047
66	1/09	Sthl	6f	(0-60)H	SS	£2047

Total win prize-money £12059

Going (Turf): Sf: 1-3 GS: 0-1 Gd: 0-4 GF: 1-4 Fm: 0-0
Distance: 5f/6f: 5-30 7f-8f: 0-1 9f-13f: 0-0 14f+: 0-0
Track : LH: 2-15 RH: 0-1 Tight: 0-7 Gall: 0-1
Aids: Bl: 0-0 Vi: 0-0 Tstrap: 0-1 Ckp: 0-1
Best Rating: 75 4/09 Wolv 5f20y stand

Modest; effective over 5f-6f; acts on Fibresand and Polytrack as well as easy and fast turf.

La Columbina

87(98) (70)80
4-y-o ch m Carnival Dancer-Darshay (FR) (Darshaan)
H J Evans (G A Harker 13/10) Mrs J Evans

Placings:03321/6460611-060006 (7779)
2009: 10^{0}G, 10^{6}GF, 9^{0}GF, 9^{0}G, 11^{0}G, 12^{6}SD,

	Starts	1st	2nd	3rd	Win & Pl
Career Total (Turf)	15	2	0	2	9456
Career Total (AW)	3	1	1	0	2583

68 8/08 Newb 1m2f6y G-S £4857
70 8/08 Ling 1m STD £1978
76 10/07 Nott 1m1f213y (0-75) G-F £2914
Total win prize-money £9751

Going (Turf): Sf: 0-0 **GS: 1-3** Gd: 0-5 **GF: 1-7** Fm: 0-0
Distance: 5f/6f: 0-1 7f-8f: 1-2 **9f-13f: 2-15** 14f+: 0-0
Track: **LH: 3-10** RH: 0-6 Tight: 1-5 Gall: 1-5
Aids: Bl: 0-1 **Vi: 2-3** Tstrap: 0-1 Ckp: 0-1
Best Rating: **80** 6/08 Sals 1m1f198y gd-fm

Fair; effective over 1m-1m2f; acts on most ground; also goes on Polytrack; has worn a visor/blinkers.

La Cortezana

(79) (36)
5-y-o ch m Piccolo-Blushing Belle (Local Suitor (USA))
A P Jarvis Christopher Shankland

Placings:5-P (4828)
2009: 10^{P}G,

	Starts	1st	2nd	3rd	Win & Pl
Career Total (Turf)	1	0	0	0	
Career Total (AW)	1	0	0	0	0

Going (Turf): Sf: 0-0 GS: 0-0 Gd: 0-1 GF: 0-0 Fm: 0-0
Distance: 5f/6f: 0-0 7f-8f: 0-0 9f-13f: 0-2 14f+: 0-0
Track: LH: 0-1 RH: 0-1 Tight: 0-1 Gall: 0-0
Aids: Bl: 0-0 Vi: 0-0 Tstrap: 0-0 Ckp: 0-0
Best Rating: **36** 3/08 Sthl 1m4f stand

La Coveta (IRE)

103(102) (77)84
4-y-o b f Marju (IRE)-Colourful Cast (IRE) (Nashwan (USA))
B J Meehan Mrs Wendy English

Placings:01/61044-06431006 (7092)
2009: 8^{0}GF, 8^{6}SD, 8^{4}GF, 8^{3}G, 9^{1}G, 10^{0}G, 10^{0}GF, 8^{6}SD,

	Starts	1st	2nd	3rd	Win & Pl
Career Total (Turf)	13	3	0	1	18995
Career Total (AW)	2	0	0	0	0

82 7/09 Leic 1m1f218y (0-80)H GD £6854
82 7/08 Newb 7f (0-80)H G-F £4857
73 11/07 NmkR 7f GD £4857
Total win prize-money £16569

Going (Turf): Sf: 0-0 GS: 0-0 **Gd: 2-6** GF: 1-7 Fm: 0-0
Distance: 5f/6f: 0-0 **7f-8f: 2-9** 9f-13f: 1-6 14f+: 0-0
Track: LH: 0-5 **RH: 1-3** Tight: 0-4 Gall: 0-1
Aids: Bl: 0-1 Vi: 0-0 Tstrap: 0-0 Ckp: 0-0
Best Rating: **84** 5/09 Newb 1m gd-fm

Useful; stays 1m2f; acts on a sound surface; has been tried in blinkers.

La Creme (IRE)

89 65
3-y-o b f Clodovil (IRE)-Dawiyda (IRE) (Ashkalani (IRE))
M R Channon Jackie & George Smith

Placings:05 (1745)
2009: 7^{0}GS, 8^{5}GF,

	Starts	1st	2nd	3rd	Win & Pl
Career Total (Turf)	2	0	0	0	0

Going (Turf): Sf: 0-0 GS: 0-1 Gd: 0-0 GF: 0-1 Fm: 0-0
Distance: 5f/6f: 0-0 7f-8f: 0-1 9f-13f: 0-1 14f+: 0-0
Track: LH: 0-1 RH: 0-0 Tight: 0-0 Gall: 0-0
Aids: Bl: 0-0 Vi: 0-0 Tstrap: 0-0 Ckp: 0-0
Best Rating: **65** 4/09 Newb 7f gd-sft

La De Two (IRE)

(97) (83)93
3-y-o ch c Galileo (IRE)-Firecrest (IRE) (Darshaan)
Saeed Bin Suroor Godolphin

Placings:2-1 (7278)
2009: 9^{1}SD,

	Starts	1st	2nd	3rd	Win & Pl
Career Total (Turf)	1	0	1	0	1831
Career Total (AW)	1	1	0	0	2590

83 11/09 Wolv 1m1f103y STD £2590
Total win prize-money £2590

Going (Turf): **Sf: 0-1** GS: 0-0 Gd: 0-0 GF: 0-0 Fm: 0-0
Distance: 5f/6f: 0-0 7f-8f: 0-1 **9f-13f: 1-1** 14f+: 0-0
Track: **LH: 1-1** RH: 0-0 **Tight: 1-1** Gall: 0-0
Aids: Bl: 0-0 Vi: 0-0 Tstrap: 0-0 Ckp: 0-0
Best Rating: **93** 9/08 Donc 1m soft

Useful; bred for middle distances at three; stays 1m1f plus; acts on soft ground and Polytrack.

La Di Da

82 57
2-y-o b f Oratorio (IRE)-So Admirable (Suave Dancer (USA))
I Semple Netherfield House Stud

Placings:4 (6982)
2009: 8^{4}G,

	Starts	1st	2nd	3rd	Win & Pl
Career Total (Turf)	1	0	0	0	385

Going (Turf): Sf: 0-0 GS: 0-0 **Gd: 0-1** GF: 0-0 Fm: 0-0
Distance: 5f/6f: 0-0 7f-8f: 0-1 9f-13f: 0-0 14f+: 0-0
Track: LH: 0-1 RH: 0-0 Tight: 0-0 Gall: 0-0
Aids: Bl: 0-0 Vi: 0-0 Tstrap: 0-0 Ckp: 0-0
Best Rating: **57** 10/09 Ayr 1m good

La Diosa (IRE)

85(98) (60)70
3-y-o b f Dansili-El Divino (IRE) (Halling (USA))
Mrs S Lamyman (George Baker 19/3) P Lamyman

Placings:0340-1155000 (6497)
2009: 8^{1}SD, 9^{1}SD, 12^{5}SF, 11^{5}SD, 8^{0}SD, 11^{0}GF, 9^{0}SF,

	Starts	1st	2nd	3rd	Win & Pl
Career Total (Turf)	4	0	0	1	854
Career Total (AW)	7	2	0	0	4094

54 2/09 Wolv 1m1f103y STD £2047
54 1/09 Wolv 1m141y STD £2047
Total win prize-money £4094

Going (Turf): Sf: 0-1 GS: 0-1 Gd: 0-0 GF: 0-2 Fm: 0-0
Distance: 5f/6f: 0-0 7f-8f: 0-3 **9f-13f: 2-8** 14f+: 0-0
Track: **LH: 2-7** RH: 0-3 **Tight: 2-7** Gall: 0-0
Aids: Bl: 0-0 Vi: 0-0 Tstrap: 0-0 Ckp: 0-0
Best Rating: **70** 8/08 Gdwd 1m soft

Modest; effective at around 1m-1m2f; acts on Polytrack.

La Estrella (USA)

(107) (95)92
6-y-o b g Theatrical-Princess Ellen (Tirol)
D E Cantillon Mrs J Hart C Lynas & M Freedman

Placings:056012/55416500040104/30111-1124 (0761)
2009: 12^{1}SS, 13^{1}SD, 11^{2}SD, 12^{4}SF,

	Starts	1st	2nd	3rd	Win & Pl
Career Total (Turf)	14	1	0	0	8517
Career Total (AW)	15	7	2	1	22529

91 1/09 GrLe 1m5f66y STD £1942
87 1/09 Sthl 1m4f SS £2047
87 12/08 Sthl 1m3f STD £2047
93 11/08 Wolv 1m5f194y STD £3070
86 11/08 Sthl 1m4f STD £2047
92 10/07 Wolv 1m4f50y (0-85)H STD £4857
92 5/07 Pont 1m4f8y (0-85)H GD £6477
73 11/06 Wolv 1m1f103y STD £2590
Total win prize-money £25081

Going (Turf): Sf: 0-2 GS: 0-3 **Gd: 1-6** GF: 0-2 Fm: 0-1
Distance: 5f/6f: 0-0 7f-8f: 0-0 **9f-13f: 6-21** 14f+: 2-8
Track: **LH: 8-25** RH: 0-3 **Tight: 3-11** Gall: 1-6
Aids: Bl: 0-2 Vi: 0-0 Tstrap: 0-0 Ckp: 0-0
Best Rating: **95** 2/09 Kemp 1m3f stand

Useful; suited by 1m4f; acts on fast ground and on sand.

La Fortunata

94(100) (72)69
2-y-o b f Lucky Story (USA)-Phantasmagoria (Fraam)
J R Jenkins James Patton

Placings:33345322 (6971)
2009: 5^{3}GF, 5^{3}GF, 5^{3}GF, 5^{4}GF, 5^{5}GF, 5^{3}GF, 5^{2}SD, 5^{2}SD,

	Starts	1st	2nd	3rd	Win & Pl
Career Total (Turf)	6	0	0	4	2227
Career Total (AW)	2	0	2	0	1542

Going (Turf): Sf: 0-0 GS: 0-0 Gd: 0-0 **GF: 0-6** Fm: 0-0
Distance: 5f/6f: 0-8 7f-8f: 0-0 9f-13f: 0-0 14f+: 0-0
Track: LH: 0-1 RH: 0-2 Tight: 0-0 Gall: 0-1
Aids: Bl: 0-0 Vi: 0-0 Tstrap: 0-0 Ckp: 0-0
Best Rating: **72** 10/09 Kemp 5f stand

Fair; effective over 5f; acts on fast ground; goes on Polytrack.

La Gifted

94(103) (72)64
3-y-o b f Fraam-Aileen's Gift (IRE) (Rainbow Quest (USA))
M R Channon Patrick and Simon Trant

Placings:0-3454040000011155011150 (7643)
2009: 7^{3}SD, 8^{4}GF, 7^{5}GF, 8^{4}GF, 7^{0}SD, 8^{4}F, 6^{0}GF, 8^{0}G, 6^{0}S, 5^{0}GF, 6^{0}G, 7^{1}SD, 7^{1}SD, 7^{1}GF, 7^{5}SS, 8^{5}SD, 7^{0}SD, 7^{1}SD, 7^{1}SD, 7^{1}SD, 7^{5}SD, 7^{0}SD,

	Starts	1st	2nd	3rd	Win & Pl
Career Total (Turf)	11	1	0	0	2744
Career Total (AW)	12	5	0	1	11966

72 11/09 Wolv 7f32y (0-62)H STD £2388
70 10/09 Wolv 7f32y (0-75)H STD £3238
70 10/09 Ling 7f (0-60)H STD £2047
64 9/09 Catt 7f (0-60)H G-F £2388
60 9/09 Wolv 7f32y (0-50)H STD £2183
60 9/09 Ling 7f (0-65)H STD £1706
Total win prize-money £13951

Going (Turf): Sf: 0-1 GS: 0-0 Gd: 0-3 **GF: 1-6** Fm: 0-1
Distance: 5f/6f: 0-2 **7f-8f: 6-17** 9f-13f: 0-4 14f+: 0-0
Track: **LH: 6-15** RH: 0-3 **Tight: 6-13** Gall: 0-0
Aids: Bl: 0-0 Vi: 0-0 Tstrap: 0-0 Ckp: 0-0

Best Rating: **72** 11/09 Wolv 7f32y stand

Modest; effective at 7f; acts on Polytrack.

La Marseillaise (IRE)

95(96) (68)**69**

3-y-o ch f Medicean-Saturnalia (Cadeaux Genereux)

B W Hills Ryder Cup Racing Syndicate

Placings:03202 **(7067)**

2009: 7^{0}GS, 7^{3}GF, 7^{2}SD, 7^{0}SD, 7^{2}SD,

	Starts	1st	2nd	3rd	Win & Pl
Career Total (Turf)	2	0	0	1	1059
Career Total (AW)	3	0	2	0	1577

Going (Turf): **Sf: 0-0 GS: 0-1 Gd: 0-0 GF: 0-1 Fm: 0-0**
Distance: 5f/6f: 0-0 7f-8f: 0-5 9f-13f: 0-0 14f+: 0-0
Track : LH: 0-3 RH: 0-1 Tight: 0-3 Gall: 0-0
Aids: Bl: 0-0 Vi: 0-0 Tstrap: 0-0 Ckp: 0-0
Best Rating: **69** 5/09 Ches 7f2y gd-fm

Fair; stays 7f; acts on fast ground and on Polytrack.

La Pantera

96(99) (79)**83**

2-y-o b f Captain Rio-Pantita (Polish Precedent (USA))

R Hannon Ms V O'Sullivan

Placings:31003 **(7320)**

2009: 5^{3}GF, 6^{1}G, 6^{0}GF, 6^{0}G, 7^{3}SD,

	Starts	1st	2nd	3rd	Win & Pl
Career Total (Turf)	4	1	0	1	4091
Career Total (AW)	1	0	0	1	674

83 5/09 Gdwd 6f GD £3561

Total win prize-money £3562

Going (Turf): Sf: 0-0 GS: 0-0 **Gd: 1-2** GF: 0-2 Fm: 0-0
Distance: **5f/6f: 1-2** 7f-8f: 0-3 9f-13f: 0-0 14f+: 0-0
Track : LH: 0-1 RH: 0-0 Tight: 0-1 Gall: 0-1
Aids: Bl: 0-0 Vi: 0-0 Tstrap: 0-0 Ckp: 0-0
Best Rating: **83** 5/09 Gdwd 6f good

Fair; stays 7f; acts on good ground and on Polytrack.

La Polka

96(86) (38)**66**

3-y-o ch f Carnival Dancer-Indubitable (Sharpo)

H Morrison Miss B Swire

Placings:00640 **(5430)**

2009: 10^{0}GF, 10^{0}SD, 11^{6}G, 16^{4}GF, 16^{0}G,

	Starts	1st	2nd	3rd	Win & Pl
Career Total (Turf)	4	0	0	0	168
Career Total (AW)	1	0	0	0	

Going (Turf): **Sf: 0-0 GS: 0-0 Gd: 0-2 GF: 0-2 Fm: 0-0**
Distance: 5f/6f: 0-0 7f-8f: 0-0 9f-13f: 0-3 14f+: 0-2
Track : LH: 0-3 RH: 0-2 Tight: 0-4 Gall: 0-0
Aids: Bl: 0-0 Vi: 0-0 Tstrap: 0-0 Ckp: 0-0
Best Rating: **66** 8/09 Nott 2m9y gd-fm

La Preciosa

(72)

4-y-o b f Arrasas (USA)-Morning Star (Statoblest)

I W McInnes Amaroni

Placings:00 **(7780)**

2009: 8^{0}SD, 11^{0}SD,

	Starts	1st	2nd	3rd	Win & Pl
Career Total (Turf)	0	0	0	0	
Career Total (AW)	2	0	0	0	

Going (Turf): **Sf: 0-0 GS: 0-0 Gd: 0-0 GF: 0-0 Fm: 0-0**
Distance: 5f/6f: 0-0 7f-8f: 0-0 9f-13f: 0-2 14f+: 0-0
Track : LH: 0-2 RH: 0-0 Tight: 0-1 Gall: 0-0
Aids: Bl: 0-0 Vi: 0-0 Tstrap: 0-1 Ckp: 0-1

La Rosa Nostra

99(100) (75)**78**

4-y-o ch f Dr Fong (USA)-Rose Quantas (IRE) (Danehill (USA))

W R Swinburn The Eternal Optimists

Placings:631/256230664 **(6640)**

2009: 10^{2}GF, 9^{5}G, 10^{6}GF, 12^{2}GF, **12^{3}SD**, 10^{0}HY, 8^{6}F, 10^{6}GF, 9^{4}SD,

	Starts	1st	2nd	3rd	Win & Pl
Career Total (Turf)	8	1	2	0	5840
Career Total (AW)	4	0	0	2	1348

75 10/07 Nott 1m54y G-F £3238

Total win prize-money £3239

Going (Turf): Sf: 0-1 GS: 0-0 Gd: 0-1 **GF: 1-5** Fm: 0-1
Distance: 5f/6f: 0-0 7f-8f: 0-2 **9f-13f: 1-10** 14f+: 0-0
Track : **LH: 1-7** RH: 0-5 Tight: 0-3 Gall: 0-3
Aids: Bl: 0-0 Vi: 0-0 Tstrap: 0-1 Ckp: 0-1
Best Rating: **78** 4/09 Donc 1m2f60y gd-fm

Fair; stays 1m4f; acts on a sound surface and on Polytrack; has worn a tongue tie.

La Sylvia (IRE)

97 (76)**98**

4-y-o b f Oasis Dream-Hawas (Mujtahid (USA))

E J O'Neill Frank Cosgrove

Placings:62022/314041600-0014 **(7458a)**

2009: 5^{0}G, 6^{0}F, 6^{1}S, 6^{4}VS,

	Starts	1st	2nd	3rd	Win & Pl
Career Total (Turf)	15	3	2	1	46080
Career Total (AW)	3	0	1	0	1360

98 9/09 Badn 6f SFT £11650
84 7/08 Bell 5f (60-95)H G-F £11966
78 5/08 Cork 5f GD £9573

Total win prize-money £33191

Going (Turf): **Sf: 1-3** GS: 0-0 **Gd: 1-3 GF: 1-2** Fm: 0-3
Distance: **5f/6f: 3-16** 7f-8f: 0-2 9f-13f: 0-0 14f+: 0-0
Track : **LH: 2-8** RH: 0-1 Tight: 0-0 Gall: 0-1
Aids: Bl: 0-0 Vi: 0-0 Tstrap: 0-0 Ckp: 0-0
Best Rating: **98** 9/09 Badn 6f soft

Useful; effective at 5f; acts on fast ground.

La Toya J (IRE)

(93) (60)

2-y-o b f Noverre (USA)-Bevel (USA) (Mr Prospector (USA))

R Curtis (Edgar Byrne 11/11) R P Behan

Placings:035 **(7885)**

2009: 7^{0}SD, 7^{3}SD, 7^{5}SD,

	Starts	1st	2nd	3rd	Win & Pl
Career Total (Turf)	0	0	0	0	
Career Total (AW)	3	0	0	1	433

Going (Turf): **Sf: 0-0 GS: 0-0 Gd: 0-0 GF: 0-0 Fm: 0-0**
Distance: 5f/6f: 0-0 7f-8f: 0-3 9f-13f: 0-0 14f+: 0-0
Track : LH: 0-1 RH: 0-2 Tight: 0-1 Gall: 0-0
Aids: Bl: 0-0 Vi: 0-0 Tstrap: 0-0 Ckp: 0-0
Best Rating: **60** 12/09 Kemp 7f stand

Modest; effective over 7f; acts on Polytrack.

La Verte Rue (USA)

(93) (64)**65**

3-y-o b f Johannesburg (USA)-Settling In (USA) (Green Desert (USA))

Mrs A Malzard (J A Osborne 13/3) A Taylor

Placings:20343-506126 **(5540a)**

2009: 7^{5}SD, 5^{0}F, 9^{6}GS, 8^{1}GS, 7^{2}GF, 8^{6}F,

	Starts	1st	2nd	3rd	Win & Pl
Career Total (Turf)	6	1	2	0	2489
Career Total (AW)	5	0	0	2	834

8/09 LesL 1m110y H G-S £1000

Total win prize-money £1000

Going (Turf): Sf: 0-0 **GS: 1-2** Gd: 0-0 GF: 0-2 Fm: 0-2
Distance: 5f/6f: 0-5 7f-8f: 0-3 **9f-13f: 1-3** 14f+: 0-0
Track : **LH: 1-8** RH: 0-1 Tight: 0-3 Gall: 0-1
Aids: Bl: 0-0 Vi: 0-0 Tstrap: 0-0 Ckp: 0-0
Best Rating: **65** 9/08 Bath 5f161y gd-fm

Modest; stays 7f and acts on Polytrack.

La Ville Lumiere (USA)

94(80) (50)**70**

2-y-o b f Rahy (USA)-La Sylphide (SWI) (Barathea (IRE))

Saeed Bin Suroor Godolphin

Placings:6350 **(6921)**

2009: 6^{6}SD, 8^{3}GF, 8^{5}GF, 8^{0}GF,

	Starts	1st	2nd	3rd	Win & Pl
Career Total (Turf)	3	0	0	1	722
Career Total (AW)	1	0	0	0	0

Going (Turf): **Sf: 0-0 GS: 0-0 Gd: 0-0 GF: 0-3 Fm: 0-0**
Distance: 5f/6f: 0-1 7f-8f: 0-1 9f-13f: 0-2 14f+: 0-0
Track : LH: 0-2 RH: 0-1 Tight: 0-1 Gall: 0-1
Aids: Bl: 0-0 Vi: 0-0 Tstrap: 0-0 Ckp: 0-0
Best Rating: **70** 9/09 Leic 1m60y gd-fm

La Voile Rouge

87(86) (73)**63**

4-y-o ch g Daggers Drawn (USA)-At Amal (IRE) (Astronef)

R M Beckett Malcolm C Denmark

Placings:510/00 **(4500)**

2009: 7^{0}SD, 6^{0}G,

	Starts	1st	2nd	3rd	Win & Pl
Career Total (Turf)	3	0	0	0	0
Career Total (AW)	2	1	0	0	3886

77 6/07 Kemp 7f STD £3886

Total win prize-money £3886

Going (Turf): **Sf: 0-0 GS: 0-0 Gd: 0-2 GF: 0-1 Fm: 0-0**
Distance: 5f/6f: 0-1 **7f-8f: 1-4** 9f-13f: 0-0 14f+: 0-0
Track : LH: 0-1 **RH: 1-2** Tight: 0-1 Gall: 0-0
Aids: Bl: 0-0 Vi: 0-0 Tstrap: 0-0 Ckp: 0-0
Best Rating: **92** 7/07 NmkJ 7f gd-fm

Useful; effective over 7f; acts on Polytrack.

La Zamora

105 85

3-y-o b f Lujain (USA)-Love Quest (Pursuit Of Love)

T D Barron J G Brown

Placings:321515030 **(6051)**

2009: 6^3GF, 6^2G, 5^1GF, 5^5F, 5^1GF, 5^5G, 5^0GF, 5^3S, 5^0G,

	Starts	1st	2nd	3rd	Win & Pl
Career Total (Turf)	9	2	1	2	18315

85 6/09 NmkJ 5f (0-100)H G-F £12462
74 5/09 Muss 5f G-F £2590
Total win prize-money £15052

Going (Turf): Sf: 0-1 GS: 0-0 Gd: 0-3 **GF: 2-4** Fm: 0-1
Distance: **5f/6f: 2-9** 7f-8f: 0-0 9f-13f: 0-0 14f+: 0-0
Track : LH: 0-1 RH: 0-0 Tight: 0-0 Gall: 0-0
Aids: Bl: 0-0 Vi: 0-0 Tstrap: 0-0 Ckp: 0-0
Best Rating: **85** 6/09 NmkJ 5f gd-fm

Fair; effective at 5f; appears to get 6f; acts on fast ground.

Laa Rayb (USA)

111 (87)117

5-y-o b g Storm Cat (USA)-Society Lady (USA) (Mr Prospector (USA))

M Johnston Sheikh Ahmed Al Maktoum

Placings:15100123/6U1651210230-260301304 **(5995)**

2009: 8^2GF, 8^6GF, 7^0G, 8^3GF, 7^0GF, 8^1G, 8^3GF, 8^0G, 8^4GS,

	Starts	1st	2nd	3rd	Win & Pl
Career Total (Turf)	28	6	4	4	316872
Career Total (AW)	1	1	0	0	2591

116 7/09 Gdwd 1m H GD £93465
117 8/08 Deau 1m GD £29412
113 7/08 Asct 7f H G-F £93465
108 5/08 Ripn 1m (0-100)H G-F £10092
101 8/07 Gdwd 7f (0-95) GD £12775
102 6/07 Sand 1m14y (0-85)H GD £6477
87 5/07 Sthl 1m STD £2590
Total win prize-money £248279

Going (Turf): Sf: 0-3 GS: 0-3 **Gd: 4-9** GF: 2-12 Fm: 0-1
Distance: 5f/6f: 0-0 **7f-8f: 6-22** 9f-13f: 1-7 14f+: 0-0
Track : LH: 1-4 **RH: 5-14 Tight: 1-4** Gall: 0-0
Aids: **Bl: 1-4** Vi: 0-0 Tstrap: 0-0 Ckp: 0-0
Best Rating: **117** 8/08 Deau 1m good

Smart; winner in Group 3 company and won the Totesport International Handicap at Ascot in 2008; effective over 7f-1m; acts on most ground and on Fibresand.

Laafet

99(102) (76)76

4-y-o b g Royal Applause-Golden Way (IRE) (Cadeaux Genereux)

K A Morgan J D M Stables

Placings:1503 **(7734)**

2009: 7^1GS, 8^5GS, 10^0SD, 8^3SD,

	Starts	1st	2nd	3rd	Win & Pl
Career Total (Turf)	2	1	0	0	2849
Career Total (AW)	2	0	0	1	755

76 7/09 Yarm 7f3y G-S £2849
Total win prize-money £2849

Going (Turf): Sf: 0-0 **GS: 1-2** Gd: 0-0 GF: 0-0 Fm: 0-0
Distance: 5f/6f: 0-0 **7f-8f: 1-1** 9f-13f: 0-3 14f+: 0-0
Track : LH: 0-2 RH: 0-1 Tight: 0-1 Gall: 0-0
Aids: Bl: 0-0 Vi: 0-0 Tstrap: 0-0 Ckp: 0-0
Best Rating: **76** 12/09 Wolv 1m141y stand

Useful; stays 7f and acts on easy ground.

Laaheb

109 116

3-y-o b g Cape Cross (IRE)-Maskunah (IRE) (Sadler's Wells (USA))

M A Jarvis Hamdan Al Maktoum

Placings:011211 **(7188)**

2009: 10^0GF, 10^1GF, 10^1S, 10^2G, 10^1GF, 10^1G,

	Starts	1st	2nd	3rd	Win & Pl
Career Total (Turf)	6	4	1	0	49990

116 10/09 NmkR 1m2f GD £22708
109 9/09 Pont 1m2f6y (0-100)H G-F £12462
91 7/09 NmkJ 1m2f (0-95)H SFT £9346
91 7/09 Yarm 1m2f21y G-F £2775
Total win prize-money £47293

Going (Turf): Sf: 1-1 GS: 0-0 Gd: 1-2 **GF: 2-3** Fm: 0-0
Distance: 5f/6f: 0-0 7f-8f: 0-0 **9f-13f: 4-6** 14f+: 0-0
Track : **LH: 2-2** RH: 1-3 Tight: 1-1 Gall: 1-3
Aids: Bl: 0-0 Vi: 0-0 Tstrap: 0-0 Ckp: 0-0
Best Rating: **116** 10/09 NmkR 1m2f good

Smart; stays 1m2f; acts on fast and soft ground.

Laazim (USA)

98(94) (57)83

3-y-o b g Seeking The Gold (USA)-Lindy Wells (USA) (A.P. Indy (USA))

M Johnston (A Fabre 1/7) Ali Saeed

Placings:00253620 **(6773)**

2009: 8^0G, 8^0G, 8^2G, 7^5G, 12^3G, 8^6GF, 8^2GF, 8^0SD,

	Starts	1st	2nd	3rd	Win & Pl
Career Total (Turf)	7	0	2	1	7640
Career Total (AW)	1	0	0	0	

Going (Turf): **Sf: 0-0 GS: 0-0 Gd: 0-5 GF: 0-2 Fm: 0-0**
Distance: 5f/6f: 0-0 7f-8f: 0-5 9f-13f: 0-3 14f+: 0-0
Track : LH: 0-2 RH: 0-5 Tight: 0-1 Gall: 0-0
Aids: Bl: 0-2 Vi: 0-0 Tstrap: 0-0 Ckp: 0-0
Best Rating: **83** 7/09 Chan 7f good

Fair; effective 1m; handles quick ground.

Labisa (IRE)

98(106) (77)76

3-y-o b f High Chaparral (IRE)-Damiana (IRE) (Thatching)

H Morrison Michael Kerr-Dineen

Placings:002-221406245 **(7828)**

2009: 8^2GF, 7^2GF, 7^1F, 7^4G, 6^0S, 7^6SD, 7^2SD, 7^4SD, 6^5SD,

	Starts	1st	2nd	3rd	Win & Pl
Career Total (Turf)	7	1	2	0	5164
Career Total (AW)	5	0	2	0	2505

76 5/09 Wwck 7f26y (0-70)H FRM £3238
Total win prize-money £3238

Going (Turf): Sf: 0-1 GS: 0-0 Gd: 0-3 GF: 0-2 **Fm: 1-1**
Distance: 5f/6f: 0-2 **7f-8f: 1-8** 9f-13f: 0-2 14f+: 0-0
Track : **LH: 1-8** RH: 0-3 Tight: 0-4 Gall: 0-1
Aids: Bl: 0-0 Vi: 0-0 Tstrap: 0-0 Ckp: 0-0
Best Rating: **77** 11/09 Wolv 7f32y stand

Modest; effective at 7f-1m; acts on fast ground.

Labretella (IRE)

83(89) (52)50

2-y-o b f Bahamian Bounty-Known Class (USA) (Known Fact (USA))

D W Thompson (M Dods 16/10) Mrs Anna Kenny

Placings:60003330 **(7792)**

2009: 5^6G, 6^0G, 7^0GF, 7^0GF, 8^3SD, 7^3SD, 8^3SD, 8^0SS,

	Starts	1st	2nd	3rd	Win & Pl
Career Total (Turf)	4	0	0	0	0
Career Total (AW)	4	0	0	3	1210

Going (Turf): **Sf: 0-0 GS: 0-0 Gd: 0-2 GF: 0-2 Fm: 0-0**
Distance: 5f/6f: 0-2 7f-8f: 0-6 9f-13f: 0-0 14f+: 0-0
Track : LH: 0-4 RH: 0-0 Tight: 0-0 Gall: 0-0
Aids: Bl: 0-0 Vi: 0-0 Tstrap: 0-0 Ckp: 0-0
Best Rating: **52** 12/09 Sthl 1m stand

Moderate; stays 1m; acts on Fibresand.

Lacrosse

95(87) (68)66

3-y-o b g Cape Cross (IRE)-La Sky (IRE) (Law Society (USA))

M A Jarvis Lordship Stud

Placings:4360 **(4270)**

2009: 10^4SD, 10^3SD, 10^6GF, 12^0G,

	Starts	1st	2nd	3rd	Win & Pl
Career Total (Turf)	2	0	0	0	0
Career Total (AW)	2	0	0	1	403

Going (Turf): **Sf: 0-0 GS: 0-0 Gd: 0-1 GF: 0-1 Fm: 0-0**
Distance: 5f/6f: 0-0 7f-8f: 0-0 9f-13f: 0-4 14f+: 0-0
Track : LH: 0-2 RH: 0-2 Tight: 0-3 Gall: 0-1
Aids: Bl: 0-0 Vi: 0-0 Tstrap: 0-1 Ckp: 0-1
Best Rating: **68** 1/09 Ling 1m2f stand

Ladies Best

108(97) (81)104

5-y-o b g King's Best (USA)-Lady Of The Lake (Caerleon (USA))

B Ellison Koo's Racing Club

Placings:011/3030320/**5**0200500-14450000 **(7720)**

2009: 10^1GF, 10^4G, 12^4G, 10^5GF, 14^0GF, 10^0GS, 12^0S, 12^0SD,

	Starts	1st	2nd	3rd	Win & Pl
Career Total (Turf)	24	3	2	3	51932
Career Total (AW)	2	0	0	0	466

99 4/09 Pont 1m2f6y (0-100)H G-F £11215
92 10/06 NmkR 1m (0-95) G-S £5181
83 9/06 Sals 1m G-S £4210
Total win prize-money £20608

Going (Turf): Sf: 0-3 **GS: 2-8** Gd: 0-5 GF: 1-8 Fm: 0-0
Distance: 5f/6f: 0-0 **7f-8f: 2-3** 9f-13f: 1-22 14f+: 0-1
Track : **LH: 1-13** RH: 0-9 Tight: 0-6 Gall: 0-14
Aids: Bl: 0-0 Vi: 0-0 Tstrap: 0-2 Ckp: 0-2
Best Rating: **104** 6/08 Epsm 1m2f18y good

Very useful; effective from 1m2f-1m4f; acts on most ground; usually held up; has worn cheekpieces and a tongue tie.

Ladies Dancing

79(100) (77)41

3-y-o b g Royal Applause-Queen Of Dance (IRE) (Sadler's Wells (USA))

J A Osborne A D Spence & 12 Day Partners

Placings:130045 **(7794)**

2009: 10^1SD, 10^3SD, 12^0GF, 12^0SD, 9^4SD, 11^5SS,

	Starts	1st	2nd	3rd	Win & Pl
Career Total (Turf)	1	0	0	0	
Career Total (AW)	5	1	0	1	3829

71 2/09 Ling 1m2f STD £2729
Total win prize-money £2730

Going (Turf): Sf: 0-0 GS: 0-0 Gd: 0-0 GF: 0-1 Fm: 0-0
Distance: 5f/6f: 0-0 7f-8f: 0-0 **9f-13f: 1-6** 14f+: 0-0
Track : **LH: 1-5** RH: 0-1 **Tight: 1-5** Gall: 0-0
Aids: Bl: 0-0 Vi: 0-0 Tstrap: 0-0 Ckp: 0-0
Best Rating: 77 3/09 Ling 1m2f stand

Fair; stays 1m2f and acts on Polytrack.

Lady Amberlini

89(95) (62)**42**
4-y-o ch f Bertolini (USA)-Deco Lady (Wolfhound (USA))
C R Dore Miss D L Wisbey & R J Viney

Placings:6/543000200-406000 (7176)
2009: 7^{4}SD, 8^{0}F, 7^{6}SD, 6^{0}SD, 7^{0}SD, 6^{0}SD,

	Starts	1st	2nd	3rd	Win & Pl
Career Total (Turf)	3	0	0	0	
Career Total (AW)	13	0	1	1	1117

Going (Turf): Sf: 0-0 GS: 0-1 Gd: 0-1 GF: 0-0 Fm: 0-1
Distance: 5f/6f: 0-3 7f-8f: 0-11 9f-13f: 0-2 14f+: 0-0
Track : LH: 0-8 RH: 0-8 Tight: 0-6 Gall: 0-0
Aids: Bl: 0-0 Vi: 0-0 Tstrap: 0-1 Ckp: 0-1
Best Rating: 66 2/08 Kemp 1m stand

Modest; effective at around 1m; handles Polytrack.

Lady Anne Nevill

102 **50**
5-y-o b m Nomadic Way (USA)-Prudent Pet (Distant Relative)
C W Fairhurst Mrs C A Arnold

Placings:0000600 (5554)
2009: 12^{0}G, 10^{0}GF, 10^{0}GF, 16^{0}G, 12^{6}GF, 11^{0}G, 16^{0}GS,

	Starts	1st	2nd	3rd	Win & Pl
Career Total (Turf)	7	0	0	0	0

Going (Turf): Sf: 0-0 GS: 0-1 Gd: 0-3 GF: 0-3 Fm: 0-0
Distance: 5f/6f: 0-0 7f-8f: 0-0 9f-13f: 0-5 14f+: 0-2
Track : LH: 0-4 RH: 0-3 Tight: 0-5 Gall: 0-1
Aids: Bl: 0-1 Vi: 0-0 Tstrap: 0-0 Ckp: 0-0
Best Rating: 50 7/09 Bevl 1m4f16y gd-fm

Lady Artemisia (IRE)

109 **94**
3-y-o b f Montjeu (IRE)-Crimson Glory (Lycius (USA))
M L W Bell Marco & Sara Moretti

Placings:02212526 (6594)
2009: 10^{0}GS, 9^{2}F, 10^{2}GF, 12^{1}GF, 12^{5}S, 14^{5}G, 10^{2}GF, 10^{6}GS,

	Starts	1st	2nd	3rd	Win & Pl
Career Total (Turf)	8	1	4	0	16648

81 6/09 Newb 1m4f5y G-F £5180
Total win prize-money £5181

Going (Turf): Sf: 0-1 GS: 0-2 Gd: 0-1 **GF: 1-3** Fm: 0-1
Distance: 5f/6f: 0-0 7f-8f: 0-0 **9f-13f: 1-7** 14f+: 0-1
Track : **LH: 1-4** RH: 0-4 Tight: 0-4 **Gall: 1-3**
Aids: Bl: 0-0 Vi: 0-0 Tstrap: 0-0 Ckp: 0-0
Best Rating: 94 7/09 Gdwd 1m6f good

Useful; effective over 1m2f-1m4f; acts on fast ground.

Lady Asheena

(95) (59)
4-y-o gr f Daylami (IRE)-Star Profile (IRE) (Sadler's Wells (USA))
J Jay K Snell

Placings:04/0-61 (0601)
2009: 11^{6}SD, 12^{1}SD,

	Starts	1st	2nd	3rd	Win & Pl
Career Total (Turf)	0	0	0	0	
Career Total (AW)	5	1	0	0	2267

59 2/09 Kemp 1m4f (0-50)H STD £2266
Total win prize-money £2267

Going (Turf): Sf: 0-0 GS: 0-0 Gd: 0-0 GF: 0-0 Fm: 0-0
Distance: 5f/6f: 0-0 7f-8f: 0-1 **9f-13f: 1-4** 14f+: 0-0
Track : LH: 0-3 **RH: 1-2** Tight: 0-2 Gall: 0-0
Aids: Bl: 0-0 Vi: 0-0 Tstrap: 0-0 Ckp: 0-0
Best Rating: 59 2/09 Kemp 1m4f stand

Lady Aspen (IRE)

89(102) (59)**56**
6-y-o b m Elnadim (USA)-Misty Peak (IRE) (Sri Pekan (USA))
Ian Williams Will Tyrrell Richard Tyrrell Andrew Dick

Placings:0/3025/0240040/02-20166040 (1983)
2009: 8^{2}SD, 7^{0}SD, 8^{1}SD, 8^{6}SD, 8^{6}SD, 10^{0}GF, 9^{4}GF, $10^{\ }$F,

	Starts	1st	2nd	3rd	Win & Pl
Career Total (Turf)	14	0	1	1	3380
Career Total (AW)	8	1	3	0	5384

59 1/09 Wolv 1m141y STD £3238
Total win prize-money £3238

Going (Turf): Sf: 0-5 GS: 0-0 Gd: 0-3 GF: 0-5 Fm: 0-1
Distance: 5f/6f: 0-3 7f-8f: 0-8 **9f-13f: 1-11** 14f+: 0-0
Track : **LH: 1-14** RH: 0-5 **Tight: 1-7** Gall: 0-2
Aids: Bl: 0-1 Vi: 0-0 Tstrap: 0-1 Ckp: 0-1
Best Rating: 80 8/06 Naas 1m gd-fm

Moderate; stays 1m; acts on most ground and on Polytrack; has worn a tongue tie and cheekpieces.

Lady Avon

55
2-y-o ch f Avonbridge-Lady Filly (Atraf)
W G M Turner Mrs M S Teversham

Placings:0 (4689)
2009: 5^{0}G,

	Starts	1st	2nd	3rd	Win & Pl
Career Total (Turf)	1	0	0	0	

Going (Turf): Sf: 0-0 GS: 0-0 Gd: 0-1 GF: 0-0 Fm: 0-0
Distance: 5f/6f: 0-1 7f-8f: 0-0 9f-13f: 0-0 14f+: 0-0
Track : LH: 0-1 RH: 0-0 Tight: 0-0 Gall: 0-1
Aids: Bl: 0-0 Vi: 0-0 Tstrap: 0-0 Ckp: 0-0

Lady Bahia (IRE)

(105) (61)**57**
8-y-o b m Orpen (USA)-Do The Right Thing (Busted)
Peter Grayson Jasper Partnership

Placings:00240/06101/06002100636513010400032000/20064211/3006300635-603 (0467)
2009: 5^{6}SD, 5^{0}SD, 5^{3}SD,

	Starts	1st	2nd	3rd	Win & Pl
Career Total (Turf)	14	2	1	1	14797
Career Total (AW)	43	5	4	6	19004

71 3/07 Kemp 5f (0-70)H STD £2817
68 3/07 Sthl 5f (0-60)H STD £2388
78 8/06 Haml 5f4y (0-85)H G-F £7772
69 6/06 Muss 5f (0-75)H FRM £4533
67 3/06 Ling 5f (0-60)H STD £2388
67 3/04 Wolv 5f F SS £2891
64 2/04 Sthl 6f F(0-60)H SS £2912
Total win prize-money £25704

Going (Turf): Sf: 0-1 GS: 0-0 Gd: 0-4 **GF: 1-8 Fm: 1-1**
Distance: **5f/6f: 7-53** 7f-8f: 0-1 9f-13f: 0-3 14f+: 0-0
Track : **LH: 3-34** RH: 1-5 **Tight: 2-31** Gall: 0-0
Aids: **Bl: 5-40** Vi: 0-0 Tstrap: 0-3 Ckp: 0-3
Best Rating: 78 8/06 Haml 5f4y gd-fm

Moderate; effective from 5f-6f; acts on sand; has worn blinkers; often starts slowly.

Lady Bluesky

90 **50**
6-y-o gr m Cloudings (IRE)-M N L Lady (Polar Falcon (USA))
A C Whillans Mrs S Harrow Mrs L M Whillans

Placings:666 (4347)
2009: 7^{6}G, 7^{6}GS, 9^{6}G,

	Starts	1st	2nd	3rd	Win & Pl
Career Total (Turf)	3	0	0	0	0

Going (Turf): Sf: 0-0 GS: 0-1 Gd: 0-2 GF: 0-0 Fm: 0-0
Distance: 5f/6f: 0-0 7f-8f: 0-2 9f-13f: 0-1 14f+: 0-0
Track : LH: 0-1 RH: 0-1 Tight: 0-0 Gall: 0-0
Aids: Bl: 0-0 Vi: 0-0 Tstrap: 0-0 Ckp: 0-0
Best Rating: 50 6/09 Ayr 7f50y good

Lady Brickhouse

68(87) (45)
2-y-o b f Choisir (AUS)-Music Maid (IRE) (Inzar (USA))
M D Squance Kevin Daniel Crabb

Placings:00054 (7849)
2009: 6^{0}GF, 7^{0}GF, 5^{0}SD, 5^{5}SD, 6^{4}SS,

	Starts	1st	2nd	3rd	Win & Pl
Career Total (Turf)	2	0	0	0	
Career Total (AW)	3	0	0	0	0

Going (Turf): Sf: 0-0 GS: 0-0 Gd: 0-0 GF: 0-2 Fm: 0-0
Distance: 5f/6f: 0-3 7f-8f: 0-2 9f-13f: 0-0 14f+: 0-0
Track : LH: 0-2 RH: 0-0 Tight: 0-1 Gall: 0-0
Aids: Bl: 0-0 Vi: 0-0 Tstrap: 0-0 Ckp: 0-0
Best Rating: 45 11/09 Sthl 5f stand

Plating-class; best effort over 5f on Fibresand.

Lady Brora

104(102) (80)**79**
4-y-o b f Dashing Blade-Tweed Mill (Selkirk (USA))
A M Balding W Aeberhard

Placings:00124-3200440 (6907)
2009: 8^{3}GF, 8^{2}SD, 9^{0}GF, 10^{0}SD, 9^{4}G, 10^{4}GF, 10^{0}G,

	Starts	1st	2nd	3rd	Win & Pl
Career Total (Turf)	7	0	0	1	1371
Career Total (AW)	5	1	2	0	5481

68 8/08 GrLe 1m STD £2590
Total win prize-money £2590

Going (Turf): Sf: 0-0 GS: 0-1 Gd: 0-2 GF: 0-4 Fm: 0-0
Distance: 5f/6f: 0-0 **7f-8f: 1-4** 9f-13f: 0-8 14f+: 0-0
Track : **LH: 1-7** RH: 0-4 Tight: 0-5 **Gall: 1-3**
Aids: Bl: 0-0 Vi: 0-0 Tstrap: 0-0 Ckp: 0-0
Best Rating: 80 9/08 Wolv 1m1f103y std-fst

Fair; stays 1m2f; acts on Polytrack.

Lady Bucket

73(75) (22)**29**

2-y-o b f Avonbridge-Heart Of India (IRE) (Try My Best (USA))

Paul Green Gary Williams

Placings:040000 **(7352)**

2009: 5^{0}GF, 5^{4}GF, 7^{0}GS, 5^{0}GS, 5^{0}GF, 6^{0}SD,

	Starts	1st	2nd	3rd	Win & Pl
Career Total (Turf)	5	0	0	0	289
Career Total (AW)	1	0	0	0	

Going (Turf): **Sf: 0-0 GS: 0-2 Gd: 0-0 GF: 0-3 Fm: 0-0**
Distance: 5f/6f: 0-5 7f-8f: 0-1 9f-13f: 0-0 14f+: 0-0
Track : LH: 0-2 RH: 0-0 Tight: 0-0 Gall: 0-0
Aids: Bl: 0-0 Vi: 0-1 Tstrap: 0-0 Ckp: 0-0
Best Rating: **29** 5/09 Nott 5f13y gd-fm

Lady Calido (USA)

(104) (65)**51**

4-y-o b/br f El Prado (IRE)-Hydro Calido (USA) (Nureyev (USA))

Sir Mark Prescott Lordship Stud

Placings:040/001 **(4861)**

2009: 10^{0}SD, 12^{0}GF, 9^{1}SD,

	Starts	1st	2nd	3rd	Win & Pl
Career Total (Turf)	3	0	0	0	
Career Total (AW)	3	1	0	0	2653
65 8/09 Wolv	1m1f103y (0-60)H			STD	£2388

Total win prize-money £2388

Going (Turf): **Sf: 0-0 GS: 0-2 Gd: 0-0 GF: 0-1 Fm: 0-0**
Distance: 5f/6f: 0-3 7f-8f: 0-0 **9f-13f: 1-3** 14f+: 0-0
Track : **LH: 1-5** RH: 0-1 **Tight: 1-5** Gall: 0-0
Aids: **Bl: 1-1** Vi: 0-0 Tstrap: 0-0 Ckp: 0-0
Best Rating: **65** 8/09 Wolv 1m1f103y stand

Moderate; stays 1m1f and acts on Polytrack; has worn blinkers.

Lady Cavendish (IRE)

88(87) (61)**50**

2-y-o ch f Indian Haven-Madame Marjou (IRE) (Marju (IRE))

A Bailey A Bailey

Placings:600500 **(7474)**

2009: 8^{6}SS, 8^{0}SD, 8^{0}SD, 8^{5}GF, 8^{0}SD, 10^{0}SD,

	Starts	1st	2nd	3rd	Win & Pl
Career Total (Turf)	1	0	0	0	0
Career Total (AW)	5	0	0	0	0

Going (Turf): **Sf: 0-0 GS: 0-0 Gd: 0-0 GF: 0-1 Fm: 0-0**
Distance: 5f/6f: 0-0 7f-8f: 0-3 9f-13f: 0-3 14f+: 0-0
Track : LH: 0-5 RH: 0-1 Tight: 0-3 Gall: 0-0
Aids: Bl: 0-0 Vi: 0-0 Tstrap: 0-3 Ckp: 0-3
Best Rating: **61** 10/09 Ling 1m std-slw

Modest; handles fast ground and Polytrack; has worn cheekpieces.

Lady Champagne

(89) (35)

3-y-o b f Zaha (CAN)-Slavonic Dance (Muhtarram (USA))

Miss J Feilden **(P J McBride 20/10)** Happy Racing

Placings:0 **(7671)**

2009: 8^{0}SD,

	Starts	1st	2nd	3rd	Win & Pl
Career Total (Turf)	0	0	0	0	
Career Total (AW)	1	0	0	0	

Going (Turf): **Sf: 0-0 GS: 0-0 Gd: 0-0 GF: 0-0 Fm: 0-0**
Distance: 5f/6f: 0-0 7f-8f: 0-0 9f-13f: 0-1 14f+: 0-0
Track : LH: 0-1 RH: 0-0 Tight: 0-1 Gall: 0-0
Aids: Bl: 0-0 Vi: 0-0 Tstrap: 0-0 Ckp: 0-0
Best Rating: **35** 12/09 Wolv 1m141y stand

Lady Charlemagne

(89) (50)**11**

4-y-o b f King Charlemagne (USA)-Prospering (Prince Sabo)

N P Littmoden John B Waterfall

Placings:000/00-00 **(0247)**

2009: 8^{0}SD, 8^{0}SD,

	Starts	1st	2nd	3rd	Win & Pl
Career Total (Turf)	2	0	0	0	
Career Total (AW)	5	0	0	0	

Going (Turf): **Sf: 0-0 GS: 0-0 Gd: 0-1 GF: 0-1 Fm: 0-0**
Distance: 5f/6f: 0-1 7f-8f: 0-4 9f-13f: 0-2 14f+: 0-0
Track : LH: 0-2 RH: 0-4 Tight: 0-1 Gall: 0-0
Aids: Bl: 0-1 Vi: 0-2 Tstrap: 0-0 Ckp: 0-0
Best Rating: **50** 10/07 Kemp 1m stand

Lady Christie

82(77) (35)**35**

2-y-o b f Tobougg (IRE)-Atnab (USA) (Riverman (USA))

M Blanshard Chris Buckingham

Placings:00 **(6912)**

2009: 6^{0}S, 7^{0}SD,

	Starts	1st	2nd	3rd	Win & Pl
Career Total (Turf)	1	0	0	0	
Career Total (AW)	1	0	0	0	

Going (Turf): **Sf: 0-1 GS: 0-0 Gd: 0-0 GF: 0-0 Fm: 0-0**
Distance: 5f/6f: 0-0 7f-8f: 0-2 9f-13f: 0-0 14f+: 0-0
Track : LH: 0-1 RH: 0-0 Tight: 0-1 Gall: 0-0
Aids: Bl: 0-0 Vi: 0-0 Tstrap: 0-0 Ckp: 0-0
Best Rating: **35** 10/09 Ling 7f stand

Lady Compton

82 **46**

2-y-o ch f Compton Place-Bright Spells (Salse (USA))

R Bastiman CPM Group Limited

Placings:0000 **(6555)**

2009: 5^{0}G, 5^{0}GS, 6^{0}GF, 5^{0}G,

	Starts	1st	2nd	3rd	Win & Pl
Career Total (Turf)	4	0	0	0	

Going (Turf): **Sf: 0-0 GS: 0-1 Gd: 0-2 GF: 0-1 Fm: 0-0**
Distance: 5f/6f: 0-4 7f-8f: 0-0 9f-13f: 0-0 14f+: 0-0
Track : LH: 0-0 RH: 0-0 Tight: 0-0 Gall: 0-0
Aids: Bl: 0-0 Vi: 0-0 Tstrap: 0-0 Ckp: 0-0
Best Rating: **46** 8/09 Bevl 5f good

Lady Darshaan (IRE)

107 **108**

2-y-o b f High Chaparral (IRE)-Diary (IRE) (Green Desert (USA))

J S Moore Coleman Bloodstock Limited

Placings:3132 **(6269)**

2009: 6^{3}G, 5^{1}GF, 6^{3}G, 8^{2}G,

	Starts	1st	2nd	3rd	Win & Pl
Career Total (Turf)	4	1	1	2	68762
80 6/09 Wind	5f10y			G-F	£12462

Total win prize-money £12462

Going (Turf): Sf: 0-0 GS: 0-0 Gd: 0-3 **GF: 1-1** Fm: 0-0
Distance: **5f/6f: 1-3** 7f-8f: 0-1 9f-13f: 0-0 14f+: 0-0
Track : LH: 0-0 RH: 0-1 Tight: 0-0 **Gall: 1-2**
Aids: Bl: 0-0 Vi: 0-0 Tstrap: 0-0 Ckp: 0-0
Best Rating: **108** 9/09 Asct 1m good

Smart; stays 1m; acts on good and fast ground.

Lady Deauville (FR)

101 **113**

4-y-o gr f Fasliyev (USA)-Mercalle (FR) (Kaldoun (FR))

R Curtis P J Hughes Developments Ltd

Placings:52324121/3045114102014-0646 **(3894a)**

2009: 10^{0}HY, 10^{6}HY, 10^{4}GS, 9^{6}S,

	Starts	1st	2nd	3rd	Win & Pl
Career Total (Turf)	25	6	4	2	199198
111 11/08 Hanv	1m2f			SFT	£23529
110 9/08 Ayr	1m2f			HVY	£34062
113 8/08 Bath	1m5y			G-S	£22708
104 8/08 Sals	1m1f198y			G-S	£28385
101 11/07 Fntb	6f			VS	£17568
99 10/07 Newb	7f			SFT	£12207

Total win prize-money £138460

Going (Turf): **Sf: 3-14** GS: 2-6 Gd: 0-2 GF: 0-2 Fm: 0-0
Distance: 5f/6f: 1-3 7f-8f: 1-8 **9f-13f: 4-14** 14f+: 0-0
Track : **LH: 2-5** RH: 1-11 **Tight: 2-3** Gall: 0-0
Aids: Bl: 0-0 Vi: 0-0 Tstrap: 0-0 Ckp: 0-0
Best Rating: **113** 8/08 Bath 1m5y gd-sft

Listed class; winner in Group 3 company in Germany; stays 1m2f; most effective on soft ground.

Lady Dinsdale (IRE)

88(91) (32)**41**

3-y-o b f Refuse To Bend (IRE)-Lady Digby (IRE) (Petorius)

T Keddy Andrew Duffield

Placings:05-000000006 **(7686)**

2009: 6^{0}S, 6^{0}GF, 6^{0}G, 8^{0}GF, 9^{0}F, 8^{0}GF, 7^{0}SD, 7^{0}SD, 6^{6}SD,

	Starts	1st	2nd	3rd	Win & Pl
Career Total (Turf)	8	0	0	0	0
Career Total (AW)	3	0	0	0	0

Going (Turf): **Sf: 0-1 GS: 0-0 Gd: 0-1 GF: 0-5 Fm: 0-1**
Distance: 5f/6f: 0-1 7f-8f: 0-8 9f-13f: 0-2 14f+: 0-0
Track : LH: 0-2 RH: 0-3 Tight: 0-1 Gall: 0-0
Aids: Bl: 0-1 Vi: 0-0 Tstrap: 0-0 Ckp: 0-0
Best Rating: **41** 7/08 Yarm 6f3y gd-fm

Lady Drac (IRE)

94(90) (62)**73**

3-y-o gr f Hawk Wing (USA)-Cause Celebre (IRE) (Peintre Celebre (USA))

B W Hills F Guerrini-Maraldi,Cavendish,C Hanbury

Placings:05-50 **(3427)**

2009: 10^{5}GF, 8^{0}GF,

	Starts	1st	2nd	3rd	Win & Pl
Career Total (Turf)	3	0	0	0	0
Career Total (AW)	1	0	0	0	0

Going (Turf): **Sf: 0-0 GS: 0-0 Gd: 0-1 GF: 0-2 Fm: 0-0**
Distance: 5f/6f: 0-0 7f-8f: 0-2 9f-13f: 0-2 14f+: 0-0
Track : LH: 0-0 RH: 0-3 Tight: 0-1 Gall: 0-0
Aids: Bl: 0-0 Vi: 0-0 Tstrap: 0-0 Ckp: 0-0
Best Rating: **73** 9/08 Newb 7f good

Lady Dunhill (IRE)

57(95) (54)**46**

3-y-o br f High Chaparral (IRE)-Ribbon Glade (UAE) (Zafonic (USA))

E W Tuer Dunhill Stud Enterprises Ltd

Placings:5000-33300 **(4819)**

2009: 6^{3}SS, 8^{3}SD, 8^{3}SD, 11^{0}SD, 8^{0}GF,

	Starts	1st	2nd	3rd	Win & Pl
Career Total (Turf)	5	0	0	0	0
Career Total (AW)	4	0	0	3	1008

Going (Turf): **Sf: 0-1 GS: 0-2 Gd: 0-1 GF: 0-1 Fm: 0-0**
Distance: 5f/6f: 0-3 7f-8f: 0-5 9f-13f: 0-1 14f+: 0-0
Track : LH: 0-5 RH: 0-1 Tight: 0-1 Gall: 0-0
Aids: Bl: 0-0 Vi: 0-0 Tstrap: 0-0 Ckp: 0-0
Best Rating: **54** 1/09 Sthl 1m stand

Moderate; stays 1m and acts on Fibresand.

Lady Fas (IRE)

(96) (50)**50**

6-y-o b m Fasliyev (USA)-Lady Sheriff (Taufan (USA))

A W Carroll E J Mangan

Placings:00000/00/50500050663000640-0P **(0115)**

2009: 6^{0}SD, 8^{P}SD,

	Starts	1st	2nd	3rd	Win & Pl
Career Total (Turf)	10	0	0	1	302
Career Total (AW)	15	0	0	0	0

Going (Turf): **Sf: 0-0 GS: 0-1 Gd: 0-2 GF: 0-7 Fm: 0-0**
Distance: 5f/6f: 0-18 7f-8f: 0-7 9f-13f: 0-0 14f+: 0-0
Track : LH: 0-7 RH: 0-7 Tight: 0-5 Gall: 0-0
Aids: Bl: 0-0 Vi: 0-0 Tstrap: 0-0 Ckp: 0-0
Best Rating: **50** 10/08 Kemp 6f stand

Lady Florence

102(96) (60)**71**

4-y-o gr f Bollin Eric-Silver Fan (Lear Fan (USA))

A B Coogan A B Coogan

Placings:00/60005600020-30221152014060324000 **(7840)**

2009: 7^{3}SD, 9^{0}GF, 6^{2}G, 7^{2}GF, 7^{1}F, 7^{1}F, 8^{5}SD, 7^{2}G, 8^{0}GF, 6^{1}F, 8^{4}GF, 6^{0}F, 6^{6}F, 7^{0}GF, 6^{3}G, 7^{2}G, 7^{4}GF, 9^{0}SD, 12^{0}SS,

	Starts	1st	2nd	3rd	Win & Pl
Career Total (Turf)	21	3	5	1	12803
Career Total (AW)	11	0	0	1	302

71	8/09	Brig	6f209y	(0-70)H	FRM	£3154
64	7/09	Brig	7f214y	(0-65)H	FRM	£2590
56	6/09	Brig	7f214y		FRM	£1942

Total win prize-money £7687

Going (Turf): Sf: 0-1 GS: 0-3 Gd: 0-6 GF: 0-6 **Fm: 3-5**
Distance: 5f/6f: 0-2 **7f-8f: 3-21** 9f-13f: 0-9 14f+: 0-0
Track : **LH: 3-22** RH: 0-6 Tight: 0-4 Gall: 0-3
Aids: Bl: 0-0 Vi: 0-0 Tstrap: 0-0 Ckp: 0-0
Best Rating: **71** 8/09 Brig 6f209y firm

Moderate; effective over 1m; acts on fast and easy ground.

Lady Francesca

108(99) (80)**99**

3-y-o b f Montjeu (IRE)-Purring (USA) (Mountain Cat (USA))

W R Muir David & Gwyn Joseph

Placings:300-22620103 **(6891a)**

2009: 8^{2}G, 8^{2}G, 8^{6}G, 10^{2}GF, 10^{0}G, 8^{1}SD, 8^{0}G, 9^{3}GS,

	Starts	1st	2nd	3rd	Win & Pl
Career Total (Turf)	10	0	3	2	27811
Career Total (AW)	1	1	0	0	2730

80	9/09	Wolv	1m141y	STD	£2729

Total win prize-money £2730

Going (Turf): **Sf: 0-1 GS: 0-2 Gd: 0-5 GF: 0-2 Fm: 0-0**
Distance: 5f/6f: 0-0 7f-8f: 0-6 **9f-13f: 1-5** 14f+: 0-0
Track : **LH: 1-4** RH: 0-5 **Tight: 1-2** Gall: 0-3
Aids: Bl: 0-0 Vi: 0-0 Tstrap: 0-0 Ckp: 0-0
Best Rating: **99** 10/09 Lonc 1m1f gd-sft

Very useful; effective at 1m-1m2f on good ground and Polytrack.

Lady Gem

(90) (46)**50**

3-y-o b f Captain Rio-Cosmic Song (Cosmonaut)

D H Brown Ron Hull

Placings:5400330-6 **(0246)**

2009: 6^{6}SD,

	Starts	1st	2nd	3rd	Win & Pl
Career Total (Turf)	3	0	0	0	289
Career Total (AW)	5	0	0	2	707

Going (Turf): **Sf: 0-1 GS: 0-2 Gd: 0-0 GF: 0-0 Fm: 0-0**
Distance: 5f/6f: 0-7 7f-8f: 0-1 9f-13f: 0-0 14f+: 0-0
Track : LH: 0-4 RH: 0-1 Tight: 0-2 Gall: 0-1
Aids: Bl: 0-0 Vi: 0-0 Tstrap: 0-1 Ckp: 0-1
Best Rating: **50** 9/08 Rdcr 5f gd-sft

Moderate; stays 6f and acts on sand.

Lady Hestia (USA)

108(100) (49)**73**

4-y-o b f Belong To Me (USA)-Awtaan (USA) (Arazi (USA))

M P Tregoning Mr And Mrs A E Pakenham

Placings:000-211610 **(6822)**

2009: 12^{2}GF, 11^{1}GF, 14^{1}GF, 16^{6}SD, 17^{1}F, 14^{0}GF,

	Starts	1st	2nd	3rd	Win & Pl
Career Total (Turf)	6	3	1	0	8246
Career Total (AW)	3	0	0	0	0

73	9/09	Bath	2m1f34y	(0-75)H	FRM	£2719
72	8/09	Yarm	1m6f17y	(0-60)H	G-F	£2331
61	4/09	Brig	1m3f196y	(0-60)H	G-F	£2590

Total win prize-money £7641

Going (Turf): Sf: 0-0 GS: 0-1 Gd: 0-0 **GF: 2-4** Fm: 1-1
Distance: 5f/6f: 0-0 7f-8f: 0-2 9f-13f: 1-3 **14f+: 2-4**
Track : **LH: 3-5** RH: 0-4 **Tight: 2-5** Gall: 0-0
Aids: Bl: 0-0 Vi: 0-0 Tstrap: 0-0 Ckp: 0-0
Best Rating: **73** 9/09 Bath 2m1f34y firm

Modest; stays 2m1f and acts on good and fast ground.

Lady Hetherington

(86) (59)

2-y-o b f Kyllachy-Silver Top Hat (USA) (Silver Hawk (USA))

Jamie Poulton Miss Emma Wettern

Placings:006 **(7451)**

2009: 7^{0}SD, 7^{0}SS, 8^{6}SD,

	Starts	1st	2nd	3rd	Win & Pl
Career Total (Turf)	0	0	0	0	
Career Total (AW)	3	0	0	0	0

Going (Turf): **Sf: 0-0 GS: 0-0 Gd: 0-0 GF: 0-0 Fm: 0-0**
Distance: 5f/6f: 0-0 7f-8f: 0-3 9f-13f: 0-0 14f+: 0-0
Track : LH: 0-2 RH: 0-1 Tight: 0-2 Gall: 0-0
Aids: Bl: 0-0 Vi: 0-0 Tstrap: 0-0 Ckp: 0-0
Best Rating: **59** 11/09 Kemp 1m stand

Lady Hopeful (IRE)

88(98) (49)**28**

7-y-o b m Lend A Hand-Treble Term (Lion Cavern (USA))

Peter Grayson Peter Grayson Racing Clubs Limited

Placings:54220550406/56536000445114/615004606010002300/432055554464500504/33244255-006200 **(2758)**

2009: 6^{0}SD, 5^{0}SD, 5^{6}SD, 5^{2}SD, 5^{0}GF, 5^{0}GF,

	Starts	1st	2nd	3rd	Win & Pl
Career Total (Turf)	22	1	1	0	5007
Career Total (AW)	54	3	6	5	9591

54	8/06	Folk	5f	(0-65)H	G-S	£3238
57	1/06	Wolv	5f20y	(0-55)H	STD	£2047
54	12/05	Wolv	5f20y	(0-45)	STD	£1446
54	11/05	Wolv	5f20y	(0-45)	STD	£1474

Total win prize-money £8208

Going (Turf): Sf: 0-2 **GS: 1-3** Gd: 0-7 GF: 0-9 Fm: 0-1
Distance: **5f/6f: 4-70** 7f-8f: 0-6 9f-13f: 0-0 14f+: 0-0
Track : **LH: 3-46** RH: 0-11 **Tight: 3-44** Gall: 0-0
Aids: **Bl: 4-60** Vi: 0-1 Tstrap: 0-3 Ckp: 0-3
Best Rating: **61** 6/04 Sthl 7f stand

Moderate; effective at around 5f; acts on Polytrack.

Lady Jane Digby

109(116) (101)**103**

4-y-o b f Oasis Dream-Scandalette (Niniski (USA))

M Johnston Miss K Rausing

Placings:1560/604-3125122311 **(5296a)**

2009: 8^{3}SS, 10^{1}SD, 10^{2}SD, 10^{5}SD, 10^{1}SD, 12^{2}G, 10^{2}GS, 10^{3}GS, 10^{1}GF, 11^{1}G,

	Starts	1st	2nd	3rd	Win & Pl
Career Total (Turf)	11	3	2	1	80327
Career Total (AW)	6	2	1	1	30378

103	8/09	Brem	1m3f		GD	£31068
103	6/09	Newc	1m2f32y		G-F	£22708
101	5/09	Ling	1m2f	(0-105)H	STD	£12952
96	1/09	Ling	1m2f	(0-100)H	STD	£11656
84	8/07	Donc	7f		G-F	£5829

Total win prize-money £84214

Going (Turf): Sf: 0-0 GS: 0-4 Gd: 1-3 **GF: 2-3** Fm: 0-0
Distance: 5f/6f: 0-0 7f-8f: 1-7 **9f-13f: 4-10** 14f+: 0-0
Track : **LH: 3-10** RH: 0-3 **Tight: 2-7** Gall: 1-3
Aids: Bl: 0-0 Vi: 0-0 Tstrap: 0-0 Ckp: 0-0
Best Rating: **103** 8/09 Brem 1m3f good

Smart; effective at 1m2f-1m4f; acts on most ground and on Polytrack.

Lady Jinks

98(91) (50)**64**
4-y-o ch f Kirkwall-Art Deco Lady (Master Willie)
Miss J S Davis (R J Hodges 22/8) Boys Club Racing

Placings:50050/60543310010-00252550 (5246)
2009: 11^{0}GF, 11^{0}GF, 11^{2}F, 12^{5}GF, 12^{2}GF, 17^{5}G, 11^{5}GF, 13^{0}F,

	Starts	1st	2nd	3rd	Win & Pl
Career Total (Turf)	17	2	2	1	5858
Career Total (AW)	7	0	0	1	262

64 8/08 Bath 1m3f144y G-S £1942
53 7/08 Wind 1m3f135y GD £2047
Total win prize-money £3990

Going (Turf): Sf: 0-1 **GS: 1-1 Gd: 1-5** GF: 0-8 Fm: 0-2
Distance: 5f/6f: 0-0 7f-8f: 0-4 **9f-13f: 2-17** 14f+: 0-3
Track : **LH: 1-16** RH: 0-2 **Tight: 2-13** Gall: 0-0
Aids: Bl: 0-1 Vi: 0-0 Tstrap: 0-0 Ckp: 0-0
Best Rating: **64** 8/08 Bath 1m3f144y gd-sft

Moderate; stays 1m4f; acts on a sound surface; goes on Polytrack.

Lady Kingston

(68) **11**
3-y-o ch f Kyllachy-Ash Moon (IRE) (General Monash (USA))
K R Burke Jet Racing Partnership

Placings:3-0 (0982)
2009: 5^{0}SD,

	Starts	1st	2nd	3rd	Win & Pl
Career Total (Turf)	1	0	0	1	698
Career Total (AW)	1	0	0	0	

Going (Turf): **Sf: 0-1 GS: 0-0 Gd: 0-0 GF: 0-0 Fm: 0-0**
Distance: 5f/6f: 0-2 7f-8f: 0-0 9f-13f: 0-0 14f+: 0-0
Track : LH: 0-1 RH: 0-0 Tight: 0-1 Gall: 0-0
Aids: Bl: 0-0 Vi: 0-0 Tstrap: 0-0 Ckp: 0-0
Best Rating: **11** 4/08 Nott 5f13y soft

Lady Lam

89(81) (40)**44**
3-y-o b f Slip Anchor-Tamara (Marju (IRE))
George Baker J B J Richards

Placings:050 (4246)
2009: 8^{0}SD, 7^{5}GF, 8^{0}GF,

	Starts	1st	2nd	3rd	Win & Pl
Career Total (Turf)	2	0	0	0	0
Career Total (AW)	1	0	0	0	

Going (Turf): **Sf: 0-0 GS: 0-0 Gd: 0-0 GF: 0-2 Fm: 0-0**
Distance: 5f/6f: 0-0 7f-8f: 0-2 9f-13f: 0-1 14f+: 0-0
Track : LH: 0-2 RH: 0-1 Tight: 0-1 Gall: 0-0
Aids: Bl: 0-0 Vi: 0-0 Tstrap: 0-0 Ckp: 0-0
Best Rating: **44** 7/09 Wwck 7f26y gd-fm

Lady Laurem

76 **33**
2-y-o b f Avonbridge-Majestic Diva (IRE) (Royal Applause)
D A Nolan Miss M McFadyen-Murray

Placings:000 (6049)
2009: 5^{0}G, 5^{0}S, 5^{0}G,

	Starts	1st	2nd	3rd	Win & Pl
Career Total (Turf)	3	0	0	0	

Going (Turf): **Sf: 0-1 GS: 0-0 Gd: 0-2 GF: 0-0 Fm: 0-0**
Distance: 5f/6f: 0-3 7f-8f: 0-0 9f-13f: 0-0 14f+: 0-0
Track : LH: 0-0 RH: 0-0 Tight: 0-0 Gall: 0-0
Aids: Bl: 0-0 Vi: 0-0 Tstrap: 0-0 Ckp: 0-0
Best Rating: **33** 7/09 Muss 5f good

Lady Lefroy (IRE)

87(95) (47)**60**
2-y-o b f Oratorio (IRE)-Dos Talas (USA) (You And I (USA))
R A Fahey Mrs Una Towell

Placings:60305450 (7168)
2009: 6^{6}GF, 6^{0}G, 5^{3}S, 7^{0}GF, 7^{5}GF, 8^{4}GF, 8^{5}SD, 7^{0}S,

	Starts	1st	2nd	3rd	Win & Pl
Career Total (Turf)	7	0	0	1	915
Career Total (AW)	1	0	0	0	0

Going (Turf): **Sf: 0-2 GS: 0-0 Gd: 0-1 GF: 0-4 Fm: 0-0**
Distance: 5f/6f: 0-3 7f-8f: 0-4 9f-13f: 0-1 14f+: 0-0
Track : LH: 0-2 RH: 0-1 Tight: 0-1 Gall: 0-0
Aids: Bl: 0-1 Vi: 0-0 Tstrap: 0-0 Ckp: 0-0
Best Rating: **60** 7/09 Ripn 5f soft

Modest; stays 6f ; acts on fast and soft ground.

Lady Lion

82(65) (21)**53**
2-y-o b f Hunting Lion (IRE)-Miss Brookie (The West (USA))
W G M Turner Mrs M S Teversham

Placings:01555 (2325)
2009: 5^{0}GF, 5^{1}F, 5^{5}GF, 5^{5}SD, 5^{5}GF,

	Starts	1st	2nd	3rd	Win & Pl
Career Total (Turf)	4	1	0	0	4274
Career Total (AW)	1	0	0	0	0

53 4/09 Thsk 5f FRM £4274
Total win prize-money £4274

Going (Turf): Sf: 0-0 GS: 0-0 Gd: 0-0 GF: 0-3 **Fm: 1-1**
Distance: **5f/6f: 1-5** 7f-8f: 0-0 9f-13f: 0-0 14f+: 0-0
Track : LH: 0-1 RH: 0-0 Tight: 0-1 Gall: 0-0
Aids: Bl: 0-0 Vi: 0-0 Tstrap: 0-1 Ckp: 0-1
Best Rating: **53** 4/09 Thsk 5f firm

Moderate; best at 5f on fast ground.

Lady Llanover

(86) (24)**45**
9-y-o ch m Halling (USA)-Francia (Legend Of France (USA))
P D Evans Mrs I M Folkes

Placings:0/00000/4-00 (0385)
2009: 12^{0}SD, 12^{0}SD,

	Starts	1st	2nd	3rd	Win & Pl
Career Total (Turf)	6	0	0	0	241
Career Total (AW)	3	0	0	0	

Going (Turf): **Sf: 0-1 GS: 0-0 Gd: 0-3 GF: 0-2 Fm: 0-0**
Distance: 5f/6f: 0-0 7f-8f: 0-3 9f-13f: 0-6 14f+: 0-0
Track : LH: 0-2 RH: 0-4 Tight: 0-1 Gall: 0-0
Aids: Bl: 0-0 Vi: 0-1 Tstrap: 0-1 Ckp: 0-1
Best Rating: **59** 8/02 Folk 7f gd-fm

Lady Longcroft

(98) (61)**61**
4-y-o ch f Tobougg (IRE)-Top Of The Morning (Keen)
J Pearce Keith F J Loads

Placings:2-221300 (7857)
2009: 9^{2}SD, 8^{2}SD, 12^{1}SD, 11^{3}SD, 11^{0}SD, 9^{0}SD,

	Starts	1st	2nd	3rd	Win & Pl
Career Total (Turf)	1	0	1	0	867
Career Total (AW)	6	1	2	1	3843

56 2/09 Sthl 1m4f STD £2047
Total win prize-money £2047

Going (Turf): **Sf: 0-0 GS: 0-1 Gd: 0-0 GF: 0-0 Fm: 0-0**
Distance: 5f/6f: 0-0 7f-8f: 0-2 **9f-13f: 1-5** 14f+: 0-0
Track : **LH: 1-7** RH: 0-0 Tight: 0-2 Gall: 0-0
Aids: Bl: 0-0 Vi: 0-0 Tstrap: 0-0 Ckp: 0-0
Best Rating: **61** 2/09 Sthl 1m3f stand

Modest; stays 1m4f and acts on sand.

Lady Lu

(84) (46)**44**
3-y-o b f Lujain (USA)-Noble Story (Last Tycoon)
P F I Cole The Fairy Story Partnership

Placings:000-0 (1465)
2009: 6^{0}SD,

	Starts	1st	2nd	3rd	Win & Pl
Career Total (Turf)	1	0	0	0	
Career Total (AW)	3	0	0	0	

Going (Turf): **Sf: 0-0 GS: 0-1 Gd: 0-0 GF: 0-0 Fm: 0-0**
Distance: 5f/6f: 0-3 7f-8f: 0-1 9f-13f: 0-0 14f+: 0-0
Track : LH: 0-2 RH: 0-1 Tight: 0-2 Gall: 0-1
Aids: Bl: 0-0 Vi: 0-0 Tstrap: 0-0 Ckp: 0-0
Best Rating: **46** 9/08 Wolv 5f216y stand

Lady Luachmhar (IRE)

107 **87**
3-y-o b f Galileo (IRE)-Radhwa (FR) (Shining Steel)
R A Fahey (Mrs A Duffield 17/5) Mrs H Steel

Placings:41136 (6681)
2009: 10^{4}G, 9^{1}GS, 10^{1}S, 11^{3}G, 12^{6}G,

	Starts	1st	2nd	3rd	Win & Pl
Career Total (Turf)	5	2	0	1	8906

87 7/09 Hayd 1m2f95y (0-75)H SFT £3238
76 5/09 Ripn 1m1f G-S £3561
Total win prize-money £6800

Going (Turf): **Sf: 1-1 GS: 1-1** Gd: 0-3 GF: 0-0 Fm: 0-0
Distance: 5f/6f: 0-0 7f-8f: 0-0 **9f-13f: 2-5** 14f+: 0-0
Track : LH: 1-3 RH: 1-2 **Tight: 1-2** Gall: 0-1
Aids: Bl: 0-0 Vi: 0-0 Tstrap: 0-0 Ckp: 0-0
Best Rating: **87** 7/09 Hayd 1m2f95y soft

Useful; stays 1m2f; acts on soft ground.

Lady Lube Rye (IRE)

94 65
2-y-o b f Catcher In The Rye (IRE)-Lady Lucia (IRE) (Royal Applause)
N Wilson D & S L Tanker Transport Limited

Placings:0410634406 **(5358)**
2009: 5⁰GF, 5⁴GF, 5¹GF, 5⁰GF, 6⁶GS, 5³S, 5⁴G, 5⁴G, 6⁰GF, 6⁶S,

	Starts	1st	2nd	3rd	Win & Pl
Career Total (Turf)	10	1	0	1	4154
64 4/09 Rdcr 5f			G-F		£2590

Total win prize-money £2590

Going (Turf): Sf: 0-2 GS: 0-1 Gd: 0-2 **GF: 1-5** Fm: 0-0
Distance: **5f/6f: 1-10** 7f-8f: 0-0 9f-13f: 0-0 14f+: 0-0
Track : LH: 0-1 RH: 0-0 Tight: 0-0 Gall: 0-0
Aids: Bl: 0-0 Vi: 0-0 Tstrap: 0-0 Ckp: 0-0
Best Rating: 65 7/09 Hayd 5f soft

Modest; suited by 5f; acts on fast and soft ground.

Lady Maya

92 (36)47
4-y-o br f Prince Sabo-Monte Mayor Lady (IRE) (Brief Truce (USA))
Paul Henderson Stephen M Cox & Mrs Carol S Cox

Placings:00000/00005-000 **(5217)**
2009: 10⁰GF, 11⁰G, 14⁰G,

	Starts	1st	2nd	3rd	Win & Pl
Career Total (Turf)	12	0	0	0	0
Career Total (AW)	1	0	0	0	

Going (Turf): Sf: 0-0 GS: 0-2 Gd: 0-5 GF: 0-5 Fm: 0-0
Distance: 5f/6f: 0-5 7f-8f: 0-3 9f-13f: 0-4 14f+: 0-1
Track : LH: 0-4 RH: 0-2 Tight: 0-4 Gall: 0-1
Aids: Bl: 0-0 Vi: 0-4 Tstrap: 0-0 Ckp: 0-0
Best Rating: 52 8/07 Sals 6f gd-sft

Lady Meg (IRE)

79 20
3-y-o b f Spartacus (IRE)-Carna (IRE) (Anita's Prince)
B Palling H Perkins

Placings:00-500 **(6170)**
2009: 8⁵G, 7⁰G, 7⁰GF,

	Starts	1st	2nd	3rd	Win & Pl
Career Total (Turf)	5	0	0	0	0

Going (Turf): Sf: 0-0 GS: 0-1 Gd: 0-2 GF: 0-2 Fm: 0-0
Distance: 5f/6f: 0-0 7f-8f: 0-3 9f-13f: 0-2 14f+: 0-0
Track : LH: 0-2 RH: 0-0 Tight: 0-1 Gall: 0-0
Aids: Bl: 0-0 Vi: 0-0 Tstrap: 0-0 Ckp: 0-0
Best Rating: 20 10/08 Bath 1m5y gd-sft

Lady Mickataine (USA)

87(93) (66)65
3-y-o b f Speightstown (USA)-Ivy Leaf (IRE) (Nureyev (USA))
M J Grassick Michael O'Flynn

Placings:3350000 **(7719)**
2009: 10³SD, 12³GF, 10⁵GF, 10⁰GY, 10⁰SD, 12⁰SD, 9⁰SD,

	Starts	1st	2nd	3rd	Win & Pl
Career Total (Turf)	3	0	0	1	724
Career Total (AW)	4	0	0	1	793

Going (Turf): Sf: 0-0 GS: 0-0 Gd: 0-0 GF: 0-2 Fm: 0-0
Distance: 5f/6f: 0-0 7f-8f: 0-0 9f-13f: 0-7 14f+: 0-0
Track : LH: 0-6 RH: 0-1 Tight: 0-1 Gall: 0-0
Aids: Bl: 0-0 Vi: 0-0 Tstrap: 0-0 Ckp: 0-0
Best Rating: 66 4/09 Dund 1m2f150y stand

Lady Micklegate (USA)

96(97) (73)63
3-y-o b f Johar (USA)-Crimson Native (USA) (The Name's Jimmy (USA))
J R Best Kent Bloodstock

Placings:5-4500R **(6783)**
2009: 7⁴SD, 7⁵G, 7⁰GF, 9⁰GF, 7ᴿSS,

	Starts	1st	2nd	3rd	Win & Pl
Career Total (Turf)	3	0	0	0	0
Career Total (AW)	3	0	0	0	0

Going (Turf): Sf: 0-0 GS: 0-0 Gd: 0-1 GF: 0-2 Fm: 0-0
Distance: 5f/6f: 0-0 7f-8f: 0-5 9f-13f: 0-1 14f+: 0-0
Track : LH: 0-3 RH: 0-1 Tight: 0-4 Gall: 0-0
Aids: Bl: 0-0 Vi: 0-0 Tstrap: 0-0 Ckp: 0-0
Best Rating: 73 3/09 Ling 7f stand

Lady Navara (IRE)

67 7
2-y-o b f Trans Island-Changari (USA) (Gulch (USA))
M Brittain David & Gwyn Joseph

Placings:000 **(4226)**
2009: 5⁰GS, 6⁰GF, 7⁰G,

	Starts	1st	2nd	3rd	Win & Pl
Career Total (Turf)	3	0	0	0	

Going (Turf): Sf: 0-0 GS: 0-1 Gd: 0-1 GF: 0-1 Fm: 0-0
Distance: 5f/6f: 0-2 7f-8f: 0-1 9f-13f: 0-0 14f+: 0-0
Track : LH: 0-0 RH: 0-0 Tight: 0-0 Gall: 0-0
Aids: Bl: 0-0 Vi: 0-0 Tstrap: 0-0 Ckp: 0-0
Best Rating: 7 6/09 Donc 6f gd-fm

Lady Norlela

96(77) (33)44
3-y-o b f Reset (AUS)-Lady Netbetsports (IRE) (In The Wings)
T J Fitzgerald (R Hannon 12/1) Paul Moorhouse

Placings:0056-6003 **(5306)**
2009: 5⁶SD, 8⁰GF, 8⁰G, 8³HY,

	Starts	1st	2nd	3rd	Win & Pl
Career Total (Turf)	6	0	0	1	385
Career Total (AW)	2	0	0	0	0

Going (Turf): Sf: 0-2 GS: 0-1 Gd: 0-1 GF: 0-2 Fm: 0-0
Distance: 5f/6f: 0-3 7f-8f: 0-3 9f-13f: 0-2 14f+: 0-0
Track : LH: 0-2 RH: 0-4 Tight: 0-3 Gall: 0-0
Aids: Bl: 0-0 Vi: 0-0 Tstrap: 0-0 Ckp: 0-0
Best Rating: 44 10/08 Brig 6f209y gd-sft

Plating-class; stays 1m; handles soft ground; has worn a tongue tie.

Lady Oaksey

84(90) (55)47
3-y-o b f Tobougg (IRE)-Silk Law (IRE) (Barathea (IRE))
W S Kittow Acorn Racing Partnership

Placings:00500 **(4904)**
2009: 10⁰GS, 12⁰G, 12⁵SD, 12⁰HY, 9⁰GF,

	Starts	1st	2nd	3rd	Win & Pl
Career Total (Turf)	4	0	0	0	
Career Total (AW)	1	0	0	0	0

Going (Turf): Sf: 0-1 GS: 0-1 Gd: 0-1 GF: 0-1 Fm: 0-0
Distance: 5f/6f: 0-0 7f-8f: 0-0 9f-13f: 0-5 14f+: 0-0
Track : LH: 0-3 RH: 0-2 Tight: 0-2 Gall: 0-0
Aids: Bl: 0-0 Vi: 0-0 Tstrap: 0-0 Ckp: 0-0
Best Rating: 55 7/09 Sthl 1m4f stand

Lady Of Akita (USA)

(93) (76)
2-y-o ch f Fantastic Light (USA)-Chancey Squaw (USA) (Chief's Crown (USA))
J H M Gosden Catesby W Clay

Placings:51 **(7630)**
2009: 8⁵SD, 7¹SD,

	Starts	1st	2nd	3rd	Win & Pl
Career Total (Turf)	0	0	0	0	
Career Total (AW)	2	1	0	0	3886
76 12/09 Wolv 7f32y			STD		£3885

Total win prize-money £3886

Going (Turf): Sf: 0-0 GS: 0-0 Gd: 0-0 GF: 0-0 Fm: 0-0
Distance: 5f/6f: 0-0 **7f-8f: 1-2** 9f-13f: 0-0 14f+: 0-0
Track : **LH: 1-2** RH: 0-0 **Tight: 1-2** Gall: 0-0
Aids: Bl: 0-0 Vi: 0-0 Tstrap: 0-0 Ckp: 0-0
Best Rating: 76 12/09 Wolv 7f32y stand

Modest; stays 1m; acts on Polytrack.

Lady Of Garmoran (USA)

75 43
2-y-o b/br f Mr Greeley (USA)-Poetically (CAN) (Silver Deputy (CAN))
P F I Cole Mrs Fitri Hay

Placings:0 **(6730)**
2009: 6⁰S,

	Starts	1st	2nd	3rd	Win & Pl
Career Total (Turf)	1	0	0	0	

Going (Turf): Sf: 0-1 GS: 0-0 Gd: 0-0 GF: 0-0 Fm: 0-0
Distance: 5f/6f: 0-0 7f-8f: 0-1 9f-13f: 0-0 14f+: 0-0
Track : LH: 0-0 RH: 0-0 Tight: 0-0 Gall: 0-0
Aids: Bl: 0-0 Vi: 0-0 Tstrap: 0-0 Ckp: 0-0
Best Rating: 43 10/09 Sals 6f212y soft

Lady Of Namid (IRE)

58
2-y-o ch f Namid-Princess Killeen (IRE) (Sinndar (IRE))
R Curtis Joseph & Mrs Georgina Kinnane

Placings:0 **(5284)**
2009: 7⁰GF,

	Starts	1st	2nd	3rd	Win & Pl
Career Total (Turf)	1	0	0	0	

Going (Turf): Sf: 0-0 GS: 0-0 Gd: 0-0 GF: 0-1 Fm: 0-0
Distance: 5f/6f: 0-0 7f-8f: 0-1 9f-13f: 0-0 14f+: 0-0
Track : LH: 0-0 RH: 0-0 Tight: 0-0 Gall: 0-0
Aids: Bl: 0-0 Vi: 0-0 Tstrap: 0-0 Ckp: 0-0

Lady Of The Desert (USA)

108 **112**
2-y-o ch f Rahy (USA)-Queen's Logic (IRE) (Grand Lodge (USA))
B J Meehan Jaber Abdullah

Placings:16113 (6449)
2009: 5[1]GF, 5[6]GF, 6[1]G, 6[1]GF, 6[3]GF,

	Starts	1st	2nd	3rd	Win & Pl
Career Total (Turf)	5	3	0	1	112375

112	8/09	York	6f	G-F	£56770
103	7/09	Asct	6f	GD	£31223
82	5/09	Leic	5f2y	G-F	£4857

Total win prize-money £92851

Going (Turf): Sf: 0-0 GS: 0-0 Gd: 1-1 **GF: 2-4** Fm: 0-0
Distance: **5f/6f: 3-5** 7f-8f: 0-0 9f-13f: 0-0 14f+: 0-0
Track : LH: 0-0 RH: 0-0 Tight: 0-0 Gall: 0-0
Aids: Bl: 0-0 Vi: 0-0 Tstrap: 0-0 Ckp: 0-0
Best Rating: 112 8/09 York 6f gd-fm

Group class; winner of the 2009 Group 3 Princess Margaret Stakes and the Group 2 Lowther; suited by 5f-6f; acts on fast ground.

Lady Pacha

76 **44**
2-y-o b f Dubai Destination (USA)-St Radegund (Green Desert (USA))
T J Pitt Pacha Bloodstock

Placings:060 (6274)
2009: 7[0]G, 8[6]F, 7[0]GF,

	Starts	1st	2nd	3rd	Win & Pl
Career Total (Turf)	3	0	0	0	0

Going (Turf): Sf: 0-0 GS: 0-0 Gd: 0-1 GF: 0-1 Fm: 0-1
Distance: 5f/6f: 0-0 7f-8f: 0-2 9f-13f: 0-1 14f+: 0-0
Track : LH: 0-2 RH: 0-1 Tight: 0-2 Gall: 0-0
Aids: Bl: 0-0 Vi: 0-0 Tstrap: 0-0 Ckp: 0-0
Best Rating: 44 8/09 Bevl 1m100y firm

Lady Pattern (IRE)

103(95) (67)**79**
2-y-o gr f Verglas (IRE)-Patteness (FR) (General Holme (USA))
P W D'Arcy Stapleford Racing Ltd

Placings:031065335 (6774)
2009: 5[0]G, 6[3]GF, 6[1]GF, 6[0]G, 6[6]G, 7[5]GF, **5[3]SD**, 6[3]SD, 6[5]SD,

	Starts	1st	2nd	3rd	Win & Pl
Career Total (Turf)	6	1	0	1	5634
Career Total (AW)	3	0	0	2	880

79	6/09	Newb	6f8y	G-F	£5180

Total win prize-money £5181

Going (Turf): Sf: 0-0 GS: 0-0 Gd: 0-3 **GF: 1-3** Fm: 0-0
Distance: 5f/6f: 0-7 **7f-8f: 1-2** 9f-13f: 0-0 14f+: 0-0

Track : LH: 0-1 RH: 0-3 Tight: 0-1 Gall: 0-1
Aids: Bl: 0-0 Vi: 0-0 Tstrap: 0-0 Ckp: 0-0
Best Rating: 79 8/09 NmkJ 6f good

Fair; effective over 6f; acts on fast ground and on Polytrack.

Lady Picola

(70) (4)
3-y-o b f Piccolo-Sukuma (IRE) (Highest Honor (FR))
Tom Dascombe M A L Evans

Placings:0 (6255)
2009: 7[0]SD,

	Starts	1st	2nd	3rd	Win & Pl
Career Total (Turf)	0	0	0	0	
Career Total (AW)	1	0	0	0	

Going (Turf): Sf: 0-0 GS: 0-0 Gd: 0-0 GF: 0-0 Fm: 0-0
Distance: 5f/6f: 0-0 7f-8f: 0-1 9f-13f: 0-0 14f+: 0-0
Track : LH: 0-1 RH: 0-0 Tight: 0-1 Gall: 0-0
Aids: Bl: 0-0 Vi: 0-0 Tstrap: 0-0 Ckp: 0-0
Best Rating: 4 9/09 Wolv 7f32y stand

Lady Pilot

101(91) (74)**62**
7-y-o b m Dansili-Mighty Flyer (IRE) (Mujtahid (USA))
Jim Best Odds On Racing

Placings:0060/4220000060302/46533150050064030003/03450111/31-4240 (6188)
2009: 15[4]GF, 14[2]GF, 17[4]F, 15[0]GF,

	Starts	1st	2nd	3rd	Win & Pl
Career Total (Turf)	17	0	1	2	1697
Career Total (AW)	33	5	3	5	18130

74	11/08	Wolv	2m119y	(0-65)H	STD	£2729
74	4/07	Sthl	1m6f	(0-65)H	STD	£2388
71	4/07	Sthl	1m6f	(0-65)H	STD	£3071
58	3/07	Kemp	2m	(0-50)H	STD	£2047
66	3/06	Wolv	2m119y	(0-65)H	STD	£2388

Total win prize-money £12627

Going (Turf): Sf: 0-0 GS: 0-2 Gd: 0-3 GF: 0-9 Fm: 0-3
Distance: 5f/6f: 0-4 7f-8f: 0-9 9f-13f: 0-20 **14f+: 5-17**
Track : **LH: 4-33** RH: 1-11 **Tight: 2-29** Gall: 0-0
Aids: Bl: 0-7 **Vi: 1-6** Tstrap: 0-2 Ckp: 0-2
Best Rating: 82 7/04 Sand 7f16y gd-fm

Modest; stays 2m and acts on sand.

Lady Rangali (IRE)

101 **90**
4-y-o b f Danehill Dancer (IRE)-Promising Lady (Thunder Gulch (USA))
Mrs A Duffield Mrs Sarah E Woodhead

Placings:5121151/32-033626 (4102)
2009: 7[0]G, 8[3]G, 8[3]GF, 8[6]GF, 8[2]GF, 9[6]S,

	Starts	1st	2nd	3rd	Win & Pl
Career Total (Turf)	15	4	3	3	163932

81	9/07	Asct	6f110y		GD	£134354
80	8/07	Hayd	6f		G-F	£5505
81	7/07	York	5f	H	HVY	£7772
68	5/07	Catt	5f		G-F	£2817

Total win prize-money £150448

Going (Turf): Sf: 1-4 GS: 0-1 Gd: 1-3 **GF: 2-6** Fm: 0-1
Distance: **5f/6f: 3-6** 7f-8f: 1-5 9f-13f: 0-4 14f+: 0-0
Track : LH: 0-3 RH: 0-3 Tight: 0-3 Gall: 0-0

Aids: Bl: 0-0 Vi: 0-0 Tstrap: 0-1 Ckp: 0-1
Best Rating: 90 6/08 Donc 1m gd-sft

Useful; winner of the 2007 Watership Down Stud Sales Race at Ascot; effective from 6f-1m; acts on good and softer ground; has worn cheekpieces.

Lady Rockfield (IRE)

(89) (54)**63**
3-y-o b f Rock Of Gibraltar (IRE)-Quiet Mouse (USA) (Quiet American (USA))
M J Grassick Michael O'Flynn

Placings:62050 (7715)
2009: 8[6]GY, 8[2]GF, 8[0]SD, 8[5]SD, 7[0]SD,

	Starts	1st	2nd	3rd	Win & Pl
Career Total (Turf)	2	0	1	0	2267
Career Total (AW)	3	0	0	0	

Going (Turf): Sf: 0-0 GS: 0-0 Gd: 0-0 GF: 0-1 Fm: 0-0
Distance: 5f/6f: 0-0 7f-8f: 0-5 9f-13f: 0-0 14f+: 0-0
Track : LH: 0-5 RH: 0-0 Tight: 0-1 Gall: 0-0
Aids: Bl: 0-2 Vi: 0-0 Tstrap: 0-0 Ckp: 0-0
Best Rating: 63 6/09 Navn 1m gd-fm

Lady Romanov (IRE)

81(88) (30)**57**
6-y-o br m Xaar-Mixremember (FR) (Linamix (FR))
P Butler (Miss M P Bryant 11/6) Miss M Bryant

Placings:601/031/004106/00000 (7608)
2009: 12[0]S, 10[0]G, 12[0]GF, **12[0]SD**, 16[0]SD,

	Starts	1st	2nd	3rd	Win & Pl
Career Total (Turf)	10	1	0	0	3527
Career Total (AW)	7	2	0	1	6249

79	6/07	Yarm	1m2f21y	(0-70)H	G-S	£3238
77	7/06	Ling	1m4f	(0-65)H	STD	£2388
68	10/05	Sthl	7f		STD	£3042

Total win prize-money £8670

Going (Turf): Sf: 0-3 **GS: 1-2** Gd: 0-4 GF: 0-1 Fm: 0-0
Distance: 5f/6f: 0-2 7f-8f: 1-1 **9f-13f: 2-12** 14f+: 0-2
Track : **LH: 3-14** RH: 0-2 **Tight: 2-5** Gall: 0-4
Aids: Bl: 0-0 Vi: 0-1 Tstrap: 0-3 Ckp: 0-3
Best Rating: 79 6/07 Yarm 1m2f21y gd-sft

Fair; stays 1m4f; acts on both All-Weather surfaces and on easy ground on turf.

Lady Rose Anne (IRE)

89 **66**
4-y-o b f Red Ransom (USA)-Surval (IRE) (Sadler's Wells (USA))
T D Barron (Mrs John Harrington 25/6) Miss Rose-Anne Galligan

Placings:0-04000 (4822)
2009: 12[0]GF, 10[4]GF, 12[0]G, 12[0]G, 10[0]GF,

	Starts	1st	2nd	3rd	Win & Pl
Career Total (Turf)	6	0	0	0	438

Going (Turf): Sf: 0-0 GS: 0-0 Gd: 0-2 GF: 0-3 Fm: 0-0
Distance: 5f/6f: 0-0 7f-8f: 0-0 9f-13f: 0-6 14f+: 0-0
Track : LH: 0-5 RH: 0-1 Tight: 0-1 Gall: 0-0
Aids: Bl: 0-0 Vi: 0-0 Tstrap: 0-0 Ckp: 0-0

Best Rating: **66** 6/09 Navn 1m2f gd-fm

Lady Royal Oak (IRE)

89(91) (70)**66**

2-y-o b f Exceed And Excel (AUS)-Enclave (USA) (Woodman (USA))

M Botti Gute Freunde Partnership

Placings:303 **(4746)**

2009: 5^{3}GF, 5^{0}GF, 5^{3}SD,

	Starts	1st	2nd	3rd	Win & Pl
Career Total (Turf)	2	0	0	1	578
Career Total (AW)	1	0	0	1	578

Going (Turf): **Sf: 0-0 GS: 0-0 Gd: 0-0 GF: 0-2 Fm: 0-0**
Distance: 5f/6f: 0-3 7f-8f: 0-0 9f-13f: 0-0 14f+: 0-0
Track : LH: 0-1 RH: 0-0 Tight: 0-1 Gall: 0-0
Aids: Bl: 0-0 Vi: 0-0 Tstrap: 0-0 Ckp: 0-0
Best Rating: **70** 8/09 Ling 5f stand

Fair; suited by 5f and fast ground.

Lady Rusty (IRE)

99(106) (73)**73**

3-y-o gr f Verglas (IRE)-Patteness (FR) (General Holme (USA))

P Winkworth Mrs I Russell

Placings:314-002563 **(6698)**

2009: 9^{0}G, 10^{0}S, 11^{2}SD, 11^{5}SD, 16^{6}SD, 12^{3}GS,

	Starts	1st	2nd	3rd	Win & Pl
Career Total (Turf)	6	1	0	2	5160
Career Total (AW)	3	0	1	0	771

73 9/08 Gdwd 6f SFT £3561

Total win prize-money £3562

Going (Turf): **Sf: 1-2** GS: 0-2 Gd: 0-1 GF: 0-1 Fm: 0-0
Distance: **5f/6f: 1-2** 7f-8f: 0-0 9f-13f: 0-6 14f+: 0-1
Track : LH: 0-1 RH: 0-6 Tight: 0-3 Gall: 0-2
Aids: Bl: 0-0 Vi: 0-0 Tstrap: 0-0 Ckp: 0-0
Best Rating: **73** 8/09 Kemp 1m3f stand

Fair; effective over 6f; acts on soft ground.

Lady Salama

84(92) (58)**64**

3-y-o b f Fasliyev (USA)-Change Of Heart (IRE) (Revoque (IRE))

K R Burke S Marley & S Hyypia

Placings:035165-45000 **(2169)**

2009: 8^{4}SD, 8^{5}SD, 7^{0}GF, 8^{0}SD, 8^{0}GF,

	Starts	1st	2nd	3rd	Win & Pl
Career Total (Turf)	8	1	0	1	4415
Career Total (AW)	3	0	0	0	0

62 8/08 Haml 6f5y SFT £3885

Total win prize-money £3886

Going (Turf): **Sf: 1-1** GS: 0-2 Gd: 0-3 GF: 0-2 Fm: 0-0
Distance: 5f/6f: 0-1 **7f-8f: 1-8** 9f-13f: 0-2 14f+: 0-0
Track : LH: 0-7 RH: 0-0 Tight: 0-4 Gall: 0-0
Aids: Bl: 0-0 Vi: 0-1 Tstrap: 0-0 Ckp: 0-0
Best Rating: **64** 6/08 Ches 7f2y good

Modest; effective over 6f and 7f; acts on soft ground.

Lady Slippers (IRE)

89 **67**

2-y-o ch f Royal Academy (USA)-Woodland Orchid (IRE) (Woodman (USA))

H J L Dunlop Anthony Rogers

Placings:240 **(7058)**

2009: 6^{2}S, 7^{4}GF, 5^{0}GF,

	Starts	1st	2nd	3rd	Win & Pl
Career Total (Turf)	3	0	1	0	1831

Going (Turf): **Sf: 0-1 GS: 0-0 Gd: 0-0 GF: 0-2 Fm: 0-0**
Distance: 5f/6f: 0-1 7f-8f: 0-2 9f-13f: 0-0 14f+: 0-0
Track : LH: 0-1 RH: 0-0 Tight: 0-0 Gall: 0-0
Aids: Bl: 0-0 Vi: 0-0 Tstrap: 0-0 Ckp: 0-0
Best Rating: **67** 9/09 Sals 6f212y soft

Useful; suited by 7f and soft ground.

Lady Sorcerer

99(101) (70)**74**

4-y-o b f Diktat-Silk Law (IRE) (Barathea (IRE))

A P Jarvis The Aston Partnership

Placings:3214/**0066403316000**6-**0604464**02 **(7094)**

2009: 12^{0}G, 12^{6}SD, 16^{0}SD, 11^{4}G, 11^{4}SD, 16^{6}G, 13^{4}S, 13^{0}GF, 10^{2}G,

	Starts	1st	2nd	3rd	Win & Pl
Career Total (Turf)	15	1	2	1	7151
Career Total (AW)	12	1	0	2	3131

74 8/08 Sals 1m6f21y (0-70)H G-S £3238
70 10/07 Kemp 1m STD £2047

Total win prize-money £5286

Going (Turf): Sf: 0-4 **GS: 1-2** Gd: 0-5 GF: 0-4 Fm: 0-0
Distance: 5f/6f: 0-1 7f-8f: 1-6 9f-13f: 0-13 14f+: 1-7
Track : LH: 0-13 **RH: 2-13 Tight: 1-7** Gall: 0-6
Aids: Bl: 0-0 Vi: 0-5 Tstrap: 0-0 Ckp: 0-0
Best Rating: **79** 9/07 Ayr 7f50y soft

Fair; effective at around 1m2f; acts on soft ground and Polytrack.

Lady Splodge

(87) (35)**56**

5-y-o b m Mark Of Esteem (IRE)-La Victoria (GER) (Rousillon (USA))

George Baker N Agran & R Bareham

Placings:30/0 **(0767)**

2009: 9^{0}SD,

	Starts	1st	2nd	3rd	Win & Pl
Career Total (Turf)	2	0	0	1	674
Career Total (AW)	1	0	0	0	

Going (Turf): **Sf: 0-0 GS: 0-1 Gd: 0-1 GF: 0-0 Fm: 0-0**
Distance: 5f/6f: 0-0 7f-8f: 0-0 9f-13f: 0-3 14f+: 0-0
Track : LH: 0-3 RH: 0-0 Tight: 0-3 Gall: 0-0
Aids: Bl: 0-0 Vi: 0-0 Tstrap: 0-0 Ckp: 0-0
Best Rating: **56** 10/07 Bath 1m2f46y gd-sft

Lady Springbank (IRE)

105 **99**

2-y-o gr f Choisir (AUS)-Severa (GER) (Kendor (FR))

P D Deegan (K R Burke 23/7) Mark Gittins

Placings:31361 **(6316a)**

2009: 6^{3}GF, 6^{1}GF, 6^{3}F, 7^{6}GF, 7^{1}G,

	Starts	1st	2nd	3rd	Win & Pl
Career Total (Turf)	5	2	0	2	52464

99 9/09 Curr 7f GD £45506
79 6/09 Donc 6f G-F £4857

Total win prize-money £50364

Going (Turf): Sf: 0-0 GS: 0-0 **Gd: 1-1 GF: 1-3** Fm: 0-1
Distance: 5f/6f: 1-3 7f-8f: 1-2 9f-13f: 0-0 14f+: 0-0
Track : LH: 0-0 RH: 0-1 Tight: 0-0 Gall: 0-0
Aids: Bl: 0-0 Vi: 0-0 Tstrap: 0-0 Ckp: 0-0
Best Rating: **99** 9/09 Curr 7f good

Fair; stays 6f; acts on fast ground.

Lady Trish

(77) (47)

3-y-o b f Red Ransom (USA)-Artifice (Green Desert (USA))

C A Dwyer Mrs Gerry Galligan

Placings:0-000 **(7771)**

2009: 7^{0}SD, 7^{0}SD, 6^{0}SD,

	Starts	1st	2nd	3rd	Win & Pl
Career Total (Turf)	0	0	0	0	
Career Total (AW)	4	0	0	0	

Going (Turf): **Sf: 0-0 GS: 0-0 Gd: 0-0 GF: 0-0 Fm: 0-0**
Distance: 5f/6f: 0-1 7f-8f: 0-3 9f-13f: 0-0 14f+: 0-0
Track : LH: 0-2 RH: 0-2 Tight: 0-2 Gall: 0-0
Aids: Bl: 0-0 Vi: 0-0 Tstrap: 0-0 Ckp: 0-0
Best Rating: **47** 11/08 Kemp 7f stand

Lady Valentino

97(98) (52)**58**

5-y-o b m Primo Valentino (IRE)-Mystery Night (FR) (Fairy King (USA))

B D Leavy Valentino Racing

Placings:404522/3250244-0204350 **(5888)**

2009: 8^{0}G, 9^{2}GF, 10^{0}GF, 11^{4}GF, 10^{3}GF, 12^{5}SD, 9^{0}SD,

	Starts	1st	2nd	3rd	Win & Pl
Career Total (Turf)	17	0	5	2	5121
Career Total (AW)	3	0	0	0	0

Going (Turf): **Sf: 0-1 GS: 0-2 Gd: 0-4 GF: 0-10 Fm: 0-0**
Distance: 5f/6f: 0-1 7f-8f: 0-5 9f-13f: 0-14 14f+: 0-0
Track : LH: 0-10 RH: 0-8 Tight: 0-8 Gall: 0-0
Aids: Bl: 0-0 Vi: 0-0 Tstrap: 0-0 Ckp: 0-0
Best Rating: **58** 10/08 Rdcr 1m2f good

Moderate; effective at around 1m2f; acts on a sound surface.

Lady Valiant

(84) (64)

2-y-o ch f Dr Fong (USA)-Protectorate (Hector Protector (USA))

R M Beckett Lady Cobham & Giles Irwin

Placings:35 **(3507)**

2009: 7^{3}SD, 7^{5}SD,

	Starts	1st	2nd	3rd	Win & Pl
Career Total (Turf)	0	0	0	0	
Career Total (AW)	2	0	0	1	578

Going (Turf): **Sf: 0-0 GS: 0-0 Gd: 0-0 GF: 0-0 Fm: 0-0**
Distance: 5f/6f: 0-0 7f-8f: 0-2 9f-13f: 0-0 14f+: 0-0

Track : LH: 0-0 RH: 0-2 Tight: 0-0 Gall: 0-0
Aids: Bl: 0-0 Vi: 0-0 Tstrap: 0-0 Ckp: 0-0
Best Rating: 64 7/09 Kemp 7f stand

Lady Vivien

90(99) (69)55
3-y-o b f Kyllachy-Elsie Plunkett (Mind Games)
D H Brown Ron Hull

Placings:063-110605050 (6456)
2009: 5^{1}SD, 5^{1}SD, 5^{0}GF, 5^{6}G, 5^{0}GS, 6^{5}GF, 5^{0}SD, 5^{5}SD, 5^{0}SD,

	Starts	1st	2nd	3rd	Win & Pl
Career Total (Turf)	5	0	0	0	0
Career Total (AW)	7	2	0	1	3474

69 1/09 Wolv 5f20y (0-75)H STD £3070
Total win prize-money £3071

Going (Turf): Sf: 0-1 GS: 0-1 Gd: 0-1 GF: 0-2 Fm: 0-0
Distance: **5f/6f: 2-11** 7f-8f: 0-1 9f-13f: 0-0 14f+: 0-0
Track : **LH: 2-7** RH: 0-0 Tight: 1-4 Gall: 1-2
Aids: Bl: 0-0 Vi: 0-0 Tstrap: 0-0 Ckp: 0-0
Best Rating: 69 1/09 Wolv 5f20y stand

Fair sprinter; handles Polytrack; should stay 6f; progressive.

Lady Willa (IRE)

87(85) (67)63
2-y-o b f Footstepsinthesand-Change Partners (IRE) (Hernando (FR))
B W Hills Simon Keswick & Rhydian Morgan-Jones

Placings:06 (6163)
2009: 6^{0}S, 7^{6}SD,

	Starts	1st	2nd	3rd	Win & Pl
Career Total (Turf)	1	0	0	0	
Career Total (AW)	1	0	0	0	0

Going (Turf): Sf: 0-1 GS: 0-0 Gd: 0-0 GF: 0-0 Fm: 0-0
Distance: 5f/6f: 0-0 7f-8f: 0-2 9f-13f: 0-0 14f+: 0-0
Track : LH: 0-0 RH: 0-1 Tight: 0-0 Gall: 0-0
Aids: Bl: 0-0 Vi: 0-0 Tstrap: 0-0 Ckp: 0-0
Best Rating: 67 9/09 Kemp 7f stand

Lady Zena

89(86) (31)36
3-y-o b f Mind Games-Alustar (Emarati (USA))
M W Easterby Bernard Bargh

Placings:000-350 (3651)
2009: 6^{3}SD, 5^{5}SD, 6^{0}G,

	Starts	1st	2nd	3rd	Win & Pl
Career Total (Turf)	4	0	0	0	
Career Total (AW)	2	0	0	1	302

Going (Turf): Sf: 0-1 GS: 0-1 Gd: 0-2 GF: 0-0 Fm: 0-0
Distance: 5f/6f: 0-6 7f-8f: 0-0 9f-13f: 0-0 14f+: 0-0
Track : LH: 0-2 RH: 0-0 Tight: 0-0 Gall: 0-0
Aids: Bl: 0-2 Vi: 0-0 Tstrap: 0-0 Ckp: 0-0
Best Rating: 36 10/08 Pont 6f gd-sft

Lady Zoe (IRE)

44(58)
2-y-o b f Chineur (FR)-Petarga (Petong)
D Donovan Philip Mclaughlin

Placings:000 (6494)
2009: 5^{0}GS, 5^{0}SD, 5^{0}SF,

	Starts	1st	2nd	3rd	Win & Pl
Career Total (Turf)	1	0	0	0	
Career Total (AW)	2	0	0	0	

Going (Turf): Sf: 0-0 GS: 0-1 Gd: 0-0 GF: 0-0 Fm: 0-0
Distance: 5f/6f: 0-3 7f-8f: 0-0 9f-13f: 0-0 14f+: 0-0
Track : LH: 0-1 RH: 0-1 Tight: 0-1 Gall: 0-0
Aids: Bl: 0-0 Vi: 0-1 Tstrap: 0-0 Ckp: 0-0

Lady's Art (FR)

86(99) (64)46
3-y-o gr f Verglas (IRE)-Calithea (IRE) (Marju (IRE))
E F Vaughan Matthew Green

Placings:40501 (6771)
2009: 8^{4}SD, 8^{0}G, 9^{5}G, 10^{0}SS, 8^{1}SD,

	Starts	1st	2nd	3rd	Win & Pl
Career Total (Turf)	2	0	0	0	0
Career Total (AW)	3	1	0	0	2047

62 10/09 Kemp 1m (0-55) STD £2047
Total win prize-money £2047

Going (Turf): Sf: 0-0 GS: 0-0 Gd: 0-2 GF: 0-0 Fm: 0-0
Distance: 5f/6f: 0-0 **7f-8f: 1-2** 9f-13f: 0-3 14f+: 0-0
Track : LH: 0-2 **RH: 1-2** Tight: 0-3 Gall: 0-0
Aids: Bl: 0-0 **Vi: 1-1** Tstrap: 0-0 Ckp: 0-0
Best Rating: 64 1/09 Ling 1m stand

Modest sister to two winners; stays 1m; acts on Polytrack.

Lady's Purse

84 38
2-y-o b f Doyen (IRE)-Jetbeeah (IRE) (Lomond (USA))
Saeed Bin Suroor Godolphin

Placings:0 (5605)
2009: 6^{0}S,

	Starts	1st	2nd	3rd	Win & Pl
Career Total (Turf)	1	0	0	0	

Going (Turf): Sf: 0-1 GS: 0-0 Gd: 0-0 GF: 0-0 Fm: 0-0
Distance: 5f/6f: 0-0 7f-8f: 0-1 9f-13f: 0-0 14f+: 0-0
Track : LH: 0-0 RH: 0-0 Tight: 0-0 Gall: 0-0
Aids: Bl: 0-0 Vi: 0-0 Tstrap: 0-0 Ckp: 0-0
Best Rating: 38 9/09 Sals 6f212y soft

Lagan Handout

79(86) (47)55
3-y-o gr g Lend A Hand-Due To Me (Compton Place)
C Gordon Mrs Sheila Clarke

Placings:45404-500 (2141)
2009: 6^{5}SD, 8^{0}GF, 7^{0}SD,

	Starts	1st	2nd	3rd	Win & Pl
Career Total (Turf)	6	0	0	0	1116
Career Total (AW)	2	0	0	0	0

Going (Turf): Sf: 0-0 GS: 0-1 Gd: 0-3 GF: 0-2 Fm: 0-0
Distance: 5f/6f: 0-5 7f-8f: 0-2 9f-13f: 0-1 14f+: 0-0
Track : LH: 0-5 RH: 0-1 Tight: 0-1 Gall: 0-2
Aids: Bl: 0-0 Vi: 0-0 Tstrap: 0-0 Ckp: 0-0
Best Rating: 55 3/08 Donc 5f gd-sft

Lago Indiano (IRE)

(96) (71)
2-y-o b c Namid-My Potters (USA) (Irish River (FR))
Mrs A J Perrett Lady Clague

Placings:33 (7234)
2009: 6^{3}SD, 6^{3}SD,

	Starts	1st	2nd	3rd	Win & Pl
Career Total (Turf)	0	0	0	0	
Career Total (AW)	2	0	0	2	933

Going (Turf): Sf: 0-0 GS: 0-0 Gd: 0-0 GF: 0-0 Fm: 0-0
Distance: 5f/6f: 0-2 7f-8f: 0-0 9f-13f: 0-0 14f+: 0-0
Track : LH: 0-1 RH: 0-1 Tight: 0-1 Gall: 0-0
Aids: Bl: 0-0 Vi: 0-0 Tstrap: 0-0 Ckp: 0-0
Best Rating: 71 11/09 Kemp 6f stand

Fair; stays 6f and acts on Polytrack.

Lahaleeb (IRE)

109 115
3-y-o b f Redback-Flames (Blushing Flame (USA))
M R Channon M Al-Qatami & K M Al-Mudhaf

Placings:505114321-1025051 (6872a)
2009: 7^{1}S, 8^{0}GF, 8^{2}HY, 8^{5}GF, 8^{0}S, 8^{5}S, 10^{1}F,

	Starts	1st	2nd	3rd	Win & Pl
Career Total (Turf)	16	5	2	1	533377

115 10/09 Wood 1m2f FRM £338983
111 4/09 Newb 7f SFT £36900
111 10/08 NmkR 7f GD £45416
91 8/08 Newc 7f SFT £3784
77 8/08 Newb 7f GD £3885
Total win prize-money £428971

Going (Turf): Sf: 2-7 GS: 0-1 **Gd: 2-2** GF: 0-4 Fm: 1-1
Distance: 5f/6f: 0-0 **7f-8f: 4-15** 9f-13f: 1-1 14f+: 0-0
Track : **LH: 1-1** RH: 0-5 Tight: 0-0 Gall: 0-3
Aids: Bl: 0-0 Vi: 0-0 Tstrap: 0-0 Ckp: 0-0
Best Rating: 115 10/09 Wood 1m2f firm

Group-class; winner of the Rockfel Stakes in 2008 and the Fred Darling in 2009; runner-up in the Irish 1000 Guineas; effective at 7f-1m; best in soft ground.

Laid Bare

45(80) (28)
2-y-o b f Barathea (IRE)-Lady Eberspacher (IRE) (Royal Abjar (USA))
Mrs P N Dutfield Mrs Nerys Dutfield

Placings:00 (7177)
2009: 8^{0}G, 7^{0}SD,

	Starts	1st	2nd	3rd	Win & Pl
Career Total (Turf)	1	0	0	0	
Career Total (AW)	1	0	0	0	

Going (Turf): Sf: 0-0 GS: 0-0 Gd: 0-1 GF: 0-0 Fm: 0-0
Distance: 5f/6f: 0-0 7f-8f: 0-1 9f-13f: 0-1 14f+: 0-0
Track : LH: 0-1 RH: 0-1 Tight: 0-1 Gall: 0-0
Aids: Bl: 0-0 Vi: 0-0 Tstrap: 0-0 Ckp: 0-0
Best Rating: 28 10/09 Kemp 7f stand

Lairy (IRE)

94(87) (46)56
2-y-o ch g Fath (USA)-Akebia (USA) (Trempolino (USA))
M F Harris (D Nicholls 17/5) M Harris

Placings:43363000200**55** (7757)

2009: 5^{4}GF, 6^{3}GS, 5^{3}G, 7^{6}S, 6^{3}HY, 6^{0}GS, 5^{0}G, 6^{0}SD, 6^{2}GS, 7^{0}GF, 5^{0}S, 5^{5}SD, 6^{5}SD,

	Starts	1st	2nd	3rd	Win & Pl
Career Total (Turf)	10	0	1	3	2648
Career Total (AW)	3	0	0	0	0

Going (Turf): Sf: 0-3 GS: 0-3 Gd: 0-2 GF: 0-2 Fm: 0-0
Distance: 5f/6f: 0-9 7f-8f: 0-4 9f-13f: 0-0 14f+: 0-0
Track : LH: 0-4 RH: 0-2 Tight: 0-0 Gall: 0-0
Aids: Bl: 0-0 Vi: 0-0 Tstrap: 0-0 Ckp: 0-0
Best Rating: 56 5/09 Ripn 6f gd-sft

Very moderate; effective at 6f on good and easier ground.

Laish Ya Hajar (IRE)

95(71) (64)**79**

5-y-o ch g Grand Lodge (USA)-Ya Hajar (Lycius (USA))
P R Webber Cream Of The Crop Partnership

Placings:43/3020000/06123010-441 **(2878)**

2009: 10^{4}GF, 9^{4}GF, 10^{1}GF,

	Starts	1st	2nd	3rd	Win & Pl
Career Total (Turf)	16	3	2	2	12857
Career Total (AW)	4	0	0	1	482
79	6/09	Chep	1m2f36y	(0-75)H	G-F £3367
76	7/08	NmkJ	1m2f	(0-70)H	G-F £3747
66	6/08	Wwck	1m2f188y	(0-55)H	FRM £2047

Total win prize-money £9163

Going (Turf): Sf: 0-1 GS: 0-0 Gd: 0-2 **GF: 2-12** Fm: 1-1
Distance: 5f/6f: 0-7 7f-8f: 0-6 **9f-13f: 3-14** 14f+: 0-0
Track : **LH: 2-10** RH: 1-9 Tight: 0-7 **Gall: 1-1**
Aids: Bl: 0-0 Vi: 0-0 Tstrap: 0-0 Ckp: 0-0
Best Rating: 79 6/09 Chep 1m2f36y gd-fm

Modest gelding; stays 1m3f; acts on fast ground.

Lajidaal (USA)

83 **38**

2-y-o b c Dynaformer (USA)-Tayibah (IRE) (Sadler's Wells (USA))
M P Tregoning Hamdan Al Maktoum

Placings:0 **(5831)**

2009: 8^{0}GF,

	Starts	1st	2nd	3rd	Win & Pl
Career Total (Turf)	1	0	0	0	

Going (Turf): Sf: 0-0 GS: 0-0 Gd: 0-0 GF: 0-1 Fm: 0-0
Distance: 5f/6f: 0-0 7f-8f: 0-0 9f-13f: 0-1 14f+: 0-0
Track : LH: 0-0 RH: 0-1 Tight: 0-0 Gall: 0-0
Aids: Bl: 0-0 Vi: 0-0 Tstrap: 0-0 Ckp: 0-0
Best Rating: 38 9/09 Sand 1m14y gd-fm

Lake Chini (IRE)

100(89) (34)**72**

7-y-o b g Raise A Grand (IRE)-Where's The Money (Lochnager)
M W Easterby Mrs Jean Turpin

Placings:0**0**2/0**1010**/**0253**234/**0**35063011226304/6050113 60-04036235**0** **(6877)**

2009: 5^{0}GF, 5^{4}GF, 5^{0}GS, 5^{3}GS, 5^{6}G, 5^{2}GS, 5^{3}HY, 5^{5}GF, 5^{0}SD,

	Starts	1st	2nd	3rd	Win & Pl
Career Total (Turf)	37	4	5	7	24296
Career Total (AW)	11	2	1	1	8035
71	9/08	Bevl	5f	(0-70)H	HVY £4209
72	9/08	Thsk	5f	(0-75)H	SFT £4274
73	8/07	Carl	5f193y	(0-60)H	GD £1977
55	8/07	Ayr	5f		G-S £3238
77	11/05	Ling	6f	(0-70)H	STD £3031
63	10/05	Wolv	5f216y		FST £2989

Total win prize-money £19720

Going (Turf): Sf: 2-9 GS: 1-10 Gd: 1-11 GF: 0-7 Fm: 0-0
Distance: **5f/6f: 6-40** 7f-8f: 0-8 9f-13f: 0-0 14f+: 0-0
Track : **LH: 2-9** RH: 1-1 **Tight: 2-8** Gall: 0-2
Aids: **Bl: 4-34** Vi: 0-0 Tstrap: 1-8 Ckp: 1-8
Best Rating: 82 5/06 Newb 6f8y good

Modest; effective over both 5f and 6f; acts on good to soft and Polytrack; has worn blinkers.

Lake Kalamalka (IRE)

102(92) (69)**73**

3-y-o b f Dr Fong (USA)-Lady Of The Lake (Caerleon (USA))
J L Dunlop Capt J Macdonald-Buchanan

Placings:0000-210**66**36**0** **(6376)**

2009: 9^{2}GS, 10^{1}G, 11^{0}GF, 12^{6}SD, 16^{6}SD, 12^{3}GF, 12^{6}GF, 12^{0}SD,

	Starts	1st	2nd	3rd	Win & Pl
Career Total (Turf)	9	1	1	1	4275
Career Total (AW)	3	0	0	0	0
73	4/09	Bath	1m2f46y	(0-70)H	GD £2914

Total win prize-money £2914

Going (Turf): Sf: 0-1 GS: 0-1 **Gd: 1-3** GF: 0-4 Fm: 0-0
Distance: 5f/6f: 0-0 7f-8f: 0-3 **9f-13f: 1-8** 14f+: 0-1
Track : **LH: 1-1** RH: 0-7 **Tight: 1-5** Gall: 0-0
Aids: Bl: 0-0 Vi: 0-0 Tstrap: 0-0 Ckp: 0-0
Best Rating: 73 4/09 Bath 1m2f46y good

Fair; stays 1m2f; acts on good ground.

Lake Nakuru

65(72) (19)

2-y-o ch f Bahamian Bounty-Social Storm (USA) (Future Storm (USA))
H S Howe Mrs Kate Lindsay-Fynn

Placings:060 **(5096)**

2009: 5^{0}GF, 6^{8}SD, 6^{0}GF,

	Starts	1st	2nd	3rd	Win & Pl
Career Total (Turf)	2	0	0	0	
Career Total (AW)	1	0	0	0	0

Going (Turf): Sf: 0-0 GS: 0-0 Gd: 0-0 GF: 0-2 Fm: 0-0
Distance: 5f/6f: 0-3 7f-8f: 0-0 9f-13f: 0-0 14f+: 0-0
Track : LH: 0-1 RH: 0-0 Tight: 0-1 Gall: 0-1
Aids: Bl: 0-0 Vi: 0-0 Tstrap: 0-0 Ckp: 0-0
Best Rating: 19 8/09 Ling 6f stand

Lake Poet (IRE)

107(98) (71)**104**

6-y-o ch h Galileo (IRE)-Lyric (Lycius (USA))
C E Brittain Mohammed Rashid

Placings:35635/**2305**21346040255**0**/**66**1102060/0055-5422 **(2671)**

2009: 10^{5}SD, 10^{4}GF, 10^{2}G, 10^{2}G,

	Starts	1st	2nd	3rd	Win & Pl
Career Total (Turf)	29	3	5	2	110240
Career Total (AW)	9	0	1	2	3322
104	6/07	Epsm	1m2f18y	H	G-S £46740
99	4/07	Epsm	1m4f10y	(0-95)H	G-F £9348
92	5/06	NmkR	1m2f	(0-100)H	G-S £11658

Total win prize-money £67747

Going (Turf): Sf: 0-2 **GS: 2-7** Gd: 0-10 GF: 1-10 Fm: 0-0
Distance: 5f/6f: 0-0 7f-8f: 0-9 **9f-13f: 3-28** 14f+: 0-1
Track : **LH: 2-20** RH: 0-13 **Tight: 2-14** Gall: 0-12
Aids: Bl: 0-2 Vi: 0-0 Tstrap: 0-0 Ckp: 0-0
Best Rating: 107 7/07 Gdwd 1m1f192y good

Very useful; stays 1m4f, but effective at shorter; acts on most ground; has worn blinkers; likes to race prominently.

Lake Sabina

85(109) (72)**69**

4-y-o b f Diktat-Telori (Muhtarram (USA))
M R Hoad double-r-racing.com

Placings:36233/05445205-00500000 **(1959)**

2009: 5^{0}SD, 5^{0}SD, 6^{5}SD, 7^{0}SD, 6^{0}SD, 6^{0}SD, 5^{0}GF, 7^{0}F,

	Starts	1st	2nd	3rd	Win & Pl
Career Total (Turf)	11	0	1	2	2937
Career Total (AW)	10	0	1	1	1224

Going (Turf): Sf: 0-2 GS: 0-1 Gd: 0-2 GF: 0-4 Fm: 0-2
Distance: 5f/6f: 0-17 7f-8f: 0-4 9f-13f: 0-0 14f+: 0-0
Track : LH: 0-12 RH: 0-2 Tight: 0-7 Gall: 0-1
Aids: Bl: 0-0 Vi: 0-0 Tstrap: 0-0 Ckp: 0-0
Best Rating: 72 10/07 Wolv 5f216y stand

Fair sort; stays 6f; acts on soft ground.

Lake Wakatipu

(33) (65)**27**

7-y-o b m Lake Coniston (IRE)-Lady Broker (Petorius)
R Ford P Clacher

Placings:04366/0543**0040**/**3330666123**66131504/0P0/**0** **(0972)**

2009: 13^{0}SD,

	Starts	1st	2nd	3rd	Win & Pl
Career Total (Turf)	18	2	0	2	9290
Career Total (AW)	17	1	1	5	3973
64	6/06	Haml	1m5f9y	(0-65)H	G-F £3296
61	6/06	Ches	1m4f66y	(0-70)H	GD £3747
58	4/06	Wolv	2m119y	(0-45)	STD £1365

Total win prize-money £8410

Going (Turf): Sf: 0-5 GS: 0-3 **Gd: 1-5 GF: 1-5** Fm: 0-0
Distance: 5f/6f: 0-1 7f-8f: 0-8 9f-13f: 1-12 **14f+: 2-14**
Track : **LH: 2-30** RH: 1-3 **Tight: 3-23** Gall: 0-2
Aids: Bl: 0-0 Vi: 0-0 Tstrap: 0-0 Ckp: 0-0
Best Rating: 65 6/06 Ripn 1m4f10y gd-fm

Lakeman (IRE)

100(95) (72)**81**

3-y-o b g Tillerman-Bishop's Lake (Lake Coniston (IRE))
B Ellison The Country Stayers

Placings:41336220-504550510 **(5598)**

2009: 7^{5}GF, 8^{0}G, 7^{4}SD, 7^{5}GF, 6^{5}GS, 6^{0}G, 7^{5}SD, 8^{1}S, 8^{0}GF,

	Starts	1st	2nd	3rd	Win & Pl
Career Total (Turf)	15	2	2	2	16011
Career Total (AW)	2	0	0	0	0
77	8/09	Muss	1m	(0-70)H	SFT £3238
76	7/08	York	6f		HVY £6670

Total win prize-money £9908

Going (Turf): **Sf: 2-4** GS: 0-4 Gd: 0-4 GF: 0-3 Fm: 0-0
Distance: 5f/6f: 1-5 7f-8f: 1-11 9f-13f: 0-1 14f+: 0-0
Track : LH: 0-5 **RH: 1-4 Tight: 1-3** Gall: 0-0

Aids:	Bl: 0-0 Vi: 0-1 Tstrap: 0-0 Ckp: 0-0				
Best Rating:	**81**	10/08	Catt	7f	good

Fair; stays 1m; acts on good and softer ground.

Lambency (IRE)

94(94) (49)61

6-y-o b m Daylami (IRE)-Triomphale (USA) (Nureyev (USA))

J S Goldie Jim Goldie Racing Club

Placings:000/00050360/50602401530/406020620050250 2465-0000 **(6216)**

2009: 6^{0}GF, 6^{0}GS, 5^{0}G, 6^{0}GF,

	Starts	1st	2nd	3rd	Win & Pl
Career Total (Turf)	43	1	5	2	9346
Career Total (AW)	2	0	0	0	0

61	8/07	Newc	6f	(0-65)H	GD	£2266

Total win prize-money £2267

Going (Turf):	Sf: 0-7 GS: 0-7 **Gd: 1-12** GF: 0-15 Fm: 0-2
Distance:	**5f/6f: 1-30** 7f-8f: 0-9 9f-13f: 0-6 14f+: 0-0
Track :	LH: 0-7 RH: 0-6 Tight: 0-10 Gall: 0-2
Aids:	Bl: 0-0 Vi: 0-0 Tstrap: 0-3 Ckp: 0-3
Best Rating:	**61** 6/08 Haml 6f5y gd-fm

Moderate; effective over 5f-6f; acts on fast and soft ground.

Lambourn Genie (UAE)

93(84) (52)45

3-y-o b g Halling (USA)-Mystery Play (IRE) (Sadler's Wells (USA))

Tom Dascombe Oneway Racers

Placings:000-0046 **(4157)**

2009: 12^{0}GF, 11^{0}F, 8^{4}GF, 10^{6}G,

	Starts	1st	2nd	3rd	Win & Pl
Career Total (Turf)	5	0	0	0	144
Career Total (AW)	2	0	0	0	

Going (Turf):	**Sf: 0-0 GS: 0-1 Gd: 0-1 GF: 0-2 Fm: 0-1**
Distance:	5f/6f: 0-1 7f-8f: 0-2 9f-13f: 0-4 14f+: 0-0
Track :	LH: 0-4 RH: 0-2 Tight: 0-3 Gall: 0-0
Aids:	Bl: 0-0 Vi: 0-0 Tstrap: 0-0 Ckp: 0-0
Best Rating:	**52** 10/08 Ling 7f stand

Lambrini Lace (IRE)

97(91) (33)65

4-y-o b f Namid-Feather 'n Lace (IRE) (Green Desert (USA))

Mrs L Williamson Mrs Judy Halewood

Placings:42000333/10005020-460000 **(7869)**

2009: 7^{4}S, 6^{6}GS, 6^{0}G, 5^{0}SD, 8^{0}SD, 6^{0}SS,

	Starts	1st	2nd	3rd	Win & Pl
Career Total (Turf)	15	1	2	0	4575
Career Total (AW)	7	0	0	3	907

65	6/08	Bath	5f11y	(0-70)H	GD	£2590

Total win prize-money £2590

Going (Turf):	Sf: 0-5 GS: 0-5 **Gd: 1-3** GF: 0-1 Fm: 0-1
Distance:	**5f/6f: 1-19** 7f-8f: 0-2 9f-13f: 0-1 14f+: 0-0
Track :	**LH: 1-14** RH: 0-0 Tight: 0-7 **Gall: 1-4**
Aids:	Bl: 0-0 Vi: 0-1 Tstrap: 0-2 Ckp: 0-2
Best Rating:	**65** 6/08 Bath 5f11y good

Moderate; effective over 5f-6f; acts on good and easy ground; also goes on Polytrack.

Lamh Albasser (USA)

101 96

2-y-o ch g Mr Greeley (USA)-Madame Boulangere (Royal Applause)

Saeed Bin Suroor Godolphin

Placings:4114364 **(6663)**

2009: 5^{4}GF, 7^{1}GF, 7^{1}GF, 7^{4}G, 7^{3}G, 6^{6}GF, 7^{4}GS,

	Starts	1st	2nd	3rd	Win & Pl
Career Total (Turf)	7	2	0	1	28396

94	7/09	NmkJ	7f	G-F	£12952
79	6/09	Rdcr	7f	G-F	£2590

Total win prize-money £15542

Going (Turf):	Sf: 0-0 GS: 0-1 Gd: 0-2 **GF: 2-4** Fm: 0-0
Distance:	5f/6f: 0-1 **7f-8f: 2-6** 9f-13f: 0-0 14f+: 0-0
Track :	LH: 0-1 RH: 0-0 Tight: 0-0 Gall: 0-0
Aids:	Bl: 0-0 Vi: 0-0 Tstrap: 0-2 Ckp: 0-2
Best Rating:	**96** 9/09 Donc 6f110y gd-fm

Very useful; effective over 7f; acts on fast ground.

Laminka

69(86) (44)20

3-y-o b f Intikhab (USA)-Lamees (USA) (Lomond (USA))

G C Bravery Richard Withers And Meddler Bloodstock

Placings:500 **(2082)**

2009: 8^{5}SD, 8^{0}SD, 8^{0}GF,

	Starts	1st	2nd	3rd	Win & Pl
Career Total (Turf)	1	0	0	0	
Career Total (AW)	2	0	0	0	0

Going (Turf):	**Sf: 0-0 GS: 0-0 Gd: 0-0 GF: 0-1 Fm: 0-0**
Distance:	5f/6f: 0-0 7f-8f: 0-2 9f-13f: 0-1 14f+: 0-0
Track :	LH: 0-1 RH: 0-1 Tight: 0-1 Gall: 0-0
Aids:	Bl: 0-0 Vi: 0-0 Tstrap: 0-0 Ckp: 0-0
Best Rating:	**44** 3/09 Kemp 1m stand

Lana's Charm

89(85) (53)42

3-y-o b f Lend A Hand-Eljariha (Unfuwain (USA))

P J Makin Ten Horsepower

Placings:06-56500 **(7002)**

2009: 5^{5}SD, 6^{6}SD, 5^{5}G, 7^{0}SD, 5^{0}SD,

	Starts	1st	2nd	3rd	Win & Pl
Career Total (Turf)	3	0	0	0	0
Career Total (AW)	4	0	0	0	0

Going (Turf):	**Sf: 0-0 GS: 0-1 Gd: 0-2 GF: 0-0 Fm: 0-0**
Distance:	5f/6f: 0-6 7f-8f: 0-1 9f-13f: 0-0 14f+: 0-0
Track :	LH: 0-6 RH: 0-0 Tight: 0-4 Gall: 0-2
Aids:	Bl: 0-0 Vi: 0-0 Tstrap: 0-0 Ckp: 0-0
Best Rating:	**53** 1/09 Ling 5f stand

Lancaster Lad (IRE)

91(98) (58)60

4-y-o b c Piccolo-Ruby Julie (Clantime)

A B Haynes Mrs S M Maine

Placings:0006/6530301101066005-40030005 **(6336)**

2009: 8^{4}SD, 8^{0}SD, 8^{0}GF, 6^{3}G, 7^{0}GF, 7^{0}F, 8^{0}F, 6^{5}GF,

	Starts	1st	2nd	3rd	Win & Pl
Career Total (Turf)	20	3	0	2	7177
Career Total (AW)	8	0	0	1	262

60	7/08	Sals	1m	(0-60)H	G-F	£2914
60	7/08	Brig	7f214y		FRM	£1942
50	6/08	Bath	1m5y	(0-60)H	FRM	£1780

Total win prize-money £6638

Going (Turf):	Sf: 0-0 GS: 0-0 Gd: 0-2 GF: 1-13 **Fm: 2-5**
Distance:	5f/6f: 0-0 **7f-8f: 2-17** 9f-13f: 1-11 14f+: 0-0
Track :	**LH: 2-24** RH: 0-0 **Tight: 1-11** Gall: 0-0
Aids:	Bl: 0-2 Vi: 0-0 Tstrap: 3-18 Ckp: 3-18
Best Rating:	**60** 7/08 Sals 1m gd-fm

Moderate; effective over 1m; acts on fast ground; also goes on Polytrack; has worn cheekpieces.

Lancetto (FR)

98(86) (55)102

4-y-o b g Dubai Destination (USA)-Lanciana (IRE) (Acatenango (GER))

James J Hartnett (K R Burke 24/5) Mark Gittins

Placings:5/3260210-0000 **(7078a)**

2009: 12^{0}G, 12^{0}G, 12^{0}HY, 10^{0}Y,

	Starts	1st	2nd	3rd	Win & Pl
Career Total (Turf)	11	1	2	1	10882
Career Total (AW)	1	0	0	0	

	9/08	Frnk	1m2f	GD	£2205

Total win prize-money £2206

Going (Turf):	Sf: 0-4 GS: 0-0 **Gd: 1-6** GF: 0-0 Fm: 0-0
Distance:	5f/6f: 0-0 7f-8f: 0-2 **9f-13f: 1-10** 14f+: 0-0
Track :	LH: 0-5 RH: 0-2 Tight: 0-2 Gall: 0-1
Aids:	Bl: 0-0 Vi: 0-0 Tstrap: 0-0 Ckp: 0-0
Best Rating:	**102** 7/08 MsnL 1m2f good

Very useful; effective over 1m2f; acts on good ground.

Land 'n Stars

(92) (83)100

9-y-o b g Mtoto-Uncharted Waters (Celestial Storm (USA))

Jamie Poulton Paul Blows

Placings:0/422/01541365/16362216/0155516050/000033 4060/600-00 **(1435)**

2009: 16^{0}SD, 16^{0}SD,

	Starts	1st	2nd	3rd	Win & Pl
Career Total (Turf)	41	5	4	3	197925
Career Total (AW)	4	1	0	1	13356

109	7/06	Sand	2m78y		G-F	£15898
103	2/06	Ndas	1m4f	(95-116)H	G-F	£66133
108	9/05	NmkR	2m		GD	£17400
91	3/05	Ling	1m5f	(0-100)H	STD	£11873
88	9/04	Gdwd	2m	(0-85)H	G-F	£6938
85	5/04	Asct	2m45y	D(0-85)H	G-F	£8323

Total win prize-money £126568

Going (Turf):	Sf: 0-3 GS: 0-7 Gd: 1-14 **GF: 4-17** Fm: 0-0
Distance:	5f/6f: 0-1 7f-8f: 0-0 9f-13f: 2-10 **14f+: 4-34**
Track :	LH: 2-15 **RH: 4-28** Tight: 2-14 **Gall: 3-21**
Aids:	Bl: 0-2 Vi: 0-0 Tstrap: 0-0 Ckp: 0-0
Best Rating:	**109** 7/06 Sand 2m78y gd-fm

Very useful; winner in Listed company and Group placed; stays 2m, but effective over shorter; acts on good and faster ground and Polytrack; has worn a hood.

Land Hawk (IRE)

99(101) (75)70

3-y-o br c Trans Island-Heike (Glenstal (USA))

J Pearce Harley Collins Lee

Placings:5565-555533 **(6365)**

2009: 7^{5}SD, 8^{5}SD, 7^{5}GF, 9^{5}G, 8^{3}SD, 8^{3}GF,

	Starts	1st	2nd	3rd	Win & Pl
Career Total (Turf)	7	0	0	1	621
Career Total (AW)	3	0	0	1	578

Going (Turf): Sf: 0-1 GS: 0-1 Gd: 0-2 GF: 0-3 Fm: 0-0
Distance: 5f/6f: 0-0 7f-8f: 0-5 9f-13f: 0-5 14f+: 0-0
Track : LH: 0-3 RH: 0-3 Tight: 0-2 Gall: 0-0
Aids: Bl: 0-0 Vi: 0-0 Tstrap: 0-0 Ckp: 0-0
Best Rating: 75 4/09 Kemp 7f stand

Fair; 30,000gns half-brother to a 7f-1m juvenile winner out of half sister to Eva Luna and Cois Na Tine; stays 1m; acts on easy ground.

Land Of Plenty (IRE)

77(92) (43)**33**
2-y-o b f Azamour (IRE)-Bring Plenty (USA) (Southern Halo (USA))
E A L Dunlop (M Johnston 14/9) J Shack

Placings:00025 **(7731)**
2009: 8^{0}GS, 7^{0}S, 7^{0}G, 8^{2}SD, 9^{5}SD,

	Starts	1st	2nd	3rd	Win & Pl
Career Total (Turf)	3	0	0	0	
Career Total (AW)	2	0	1	0	806

Going (Turf): Sf: 0-1 GS: 0-1 Gd: 0-1 GF: 0-0 Fm: 0-0
Distance: 5f/6f: 0-0 7f-8f: 0-2 9f-13f: 0-3 14f+: 0-0
Track : LH: 0-4 RH: 0-1 Tight: 0-3 Gall: 0-0
Aids: Bl: 0-0 Vi: 0-0 Tstrap: 0-0 Ckp: 0-0
Best Rating: 43 12/09 Wolv 1m1f103y stand

Very moderate; stays 1m; acts on Polytrack.

Landikhaya (IRE)

(98) (58)**72**
4-y-o ch g Kris Kin (USA)-Montana Lady (IRE) (Be My Guest (USA))
D K Ivory K T Ivory

Placings:5003400/5550016053400-00 **(0213)**
2009: 7^{0}SD, 12^{0}SD,

	Starts	1st	2nd	3rd	Win & Pl
Career Total (Turf)	13	1	0	1	2606
Career Total (AW)	9	0	0	1	302

54 6/08 Leic 1m1f218y G-F £1942
Total win prize-money £1943

Going (Turf): Sf: 0-2 GS: 0-1 Gd: 0-4 GF: 1-6 Fm: 0-0
Distance: 5f/6f: 0-0 7f-8f: 0-9 9f-13f: 1-13 14f+: 0-0
Track : LH: 0-11 RH: 1-8 Tight: 0-13 Gall: 0-0
Aids: Bl: 0-1 Vi: 0-1 Tstrap: 1-7 Ckp: 1-7
Best Rating: 72 10/07 Wwck 7f26y gd-fm

Very moderate; best at around 1m2f; suited by fast ground; has worn blinkers/cheekpieces.

Landofthefourones (USA)

94(91) (57)**68**
3-y-o b c Aldebaran (USA)-Cuanto Es (USA) (Exbourne (USA))
D R Lanigan Niarchos Family

Placings:5424 **(5840)**
2009: 8^{5}S, 8^{4}HY, 8^{2}GF, 8^{4}SD,

	Starts	1st	2nd	3rd	Win & Pl
Career Total (Turf)	3	0	1	0	1445
Career Total (AW)	1	0	0	0	0

Going (Turf): Sf: 0-2 GS: 0-0 Gd: 0-0 GF: 0-1 Fm: 0-0
Distance: 5f/6f: 0-0 7f-8f: 0-1 9f-13f: 0-3 14f+: 0-0
Track : LH: 0-3 RH: 0-0 Tight: 0-1 Gall: 0-0
Aids: Bl: 0-0 Vi: 0-0 Tstrap: 0-0 Ckp: 0-0
Best Rating: 68 7/09 NmkJ 1m soft

Fair; stays 1m; acts on most surfaces.

Landowner

100 **89**
2-y-o b c Shamardal (USA)-Rentless (Zafonic (USA))
Saeed Bin Suroor Godolphin

Placings:4112 **(7097)**
2009: 6^{4}F, 7^{1}GF, 8^{1}GF, 7^{2}G,

	Starts	1st	2nd	3rd	Win & Pl
Career Total (Turf)	4	2	1	0	7723

89 10/09 Pont 1m4y (0-75) G-F £2914
68 9/09 Wwck 7f26y G-F £3561
Total win prize-money £6476

Going (Turf): Sf: 0-0 GS: 0-0 Gd: 0-1 GF: 2-2 Fm: 0-1
Distance: 5f/6f: 0-0 7f-8f: 1-3 9f-13f: 1-1 14f+: 0-0
Track : LH: 2-3 RH: 0-0 Tight: 0-0 Gall: 0-0
Aids: Bl: 0-0 Vi: 0-0 Tstrap: 0-0 Ckp: 0-0
Best Rating: 89 10/09 Pont 1m4y gd-fm

Useful; stays 1m and likes quick ground.

Landucci

106(104) (83)**69**
8-y-o b g Averti (IRE)-Divina Luna (Dowsing (USA))
S Curran (J W Hills 9/1) L M Power

Placings:00/206134026/401311313460/065650014213460/003012205/3015545610005-62044165414341 **(5179)**
2009: 7^{6}SD, 8^{2}SD, 8^{0}SD, 7^{4}SD, 7^{4}SD, 8^{1}SD, 8^{6}F, 7^{5}SD, 7^{4}G, 6^{1}G, 5^{4}GF, 6^{3}GF, 7^{4}F, 8^{1}G,

	Starts	1st	2nd	3rd	Win & Pl
Career Total (Turf)	36	7	1	6	37726
Career Total (AW)	38	6	5	2	32050

69	8/09	Chep	1m14y	(0-60)H	GD	£2217
66	6/09	Brig	6f209y		GD	£1942
73	4/09	Kemp	1m	(0-60)H	STD	£1942
79	8/08	Kemp	7f	(0-75)H	STD	£3238
83	2/08	Wolv	7f32y		STD	£2331
83	8/07	Kemp	7f	(0-75)H	STD	£3238
82	9/06	Kemp	7f	(0-80)H	STD	£5505
78	9/06	Kemp	1m	(0-80)H	STD	£7790
89	7/05	Brig	7f214y	(0-85)H	FRM	£6669
79	6/05	Brig	6f209y	(0-75)H	FRM	£6791
77	6/05	Brig	6f209y	(0-70)H	G-F	£4075
77	5/05	Brig	6f209y	(0-70)H	G-F	£4169
70	8/04	Brig	6f209y	F(0-60)	SFT	£3052

Total win prize-money £52965

Going (Turf): Sf: 1-2 GS: 0-2 Gd: 2-9 GF: 2-14 Fm: 2-9
Distance: 5f/6f: 0-6 7f-8f: 12-61 9f-13f: 1-7 14f+: 0-0
Track : LH: 7-44 RH: 5-22 Tight: 1-25 Gall: 0-2
Aids: Bl: 0-2 Vi: 1-4 Tstrap: 5-23 Ckp: 5-23
Best Rating: 89 8/05 Epsm 1m114y good

Modest; stays 1m; acts on most ground, including Polytrack; has a good record at Brighton; has worn head-gear.

Lang Shining (IRE)

106 **110**
5-y-o ch g Dr Fong (USA)-Dragnet (IRE) (Rainbow Quest (USA))
Sir Michael Stoute Ballymacoll Stud

Placings:3/126/12000206-004600 **(6094)**
2009: 8^{0}G, 10^{0}G, 8^{4}GF, 9^{6}G, 10^{0}GF, 8^{0}G,

	Starts	1st	2nd	3rd	Win & Pl
Career Total (Turf)	18	2	3	1	58585

104 4/08 Newb 1m H SFT £21808
84 7/07 NmkJ 1m GD £5181
Total win prize-money £26991

Going (Turf): Sf: 1-1 GS: 0-3 Gd: 1-7 GF: 0-7 Fm: 0-0
Distance: 5f/6f: 0-0 7f-8f: 2-9 9f-13f: 0-9 14f+: 0-0
Track : LH: 0-4 RH: 0-8 Tight: 0-1 Gall: 0-4
Aids: Bl: 0-0 Vi: 0-0 Tstrap: 0-0 Ckp: 0-0
Best Rating: 110 8/08 Sand 1m2f7y good

Smart; Listed placed; stays 1m2f; acts on good and softer ground.

Langford Decoit (IRE)

92 **60**
3-y-o b c Peintre Celebre (USA)-Litchfield Hills (USA) (Relaunch (USA))
Tim Vaughan (M R Channon 22/6) David Lovell

Placings:06400 **(3222)**
2009: 10^{0}G, 12^{6}GF, 12^{4}G, 11^{0}S, 11^{0}GF,

	Starts	1st	2nd	3rd	Win & Pl
Career Total (Turf)	5	0	0	0	202

Going (Turf): Sf: 0-1 GS: 0-0 Gd: 0-2 GF: 0-2 Fm: 0-0
Distance: 5f/6f: 0-0 7f-8f: 0-0 9f-13f: 0-5 14f+: 0-0
Track : LH: 0-3 RH: 0-1 Tight: 0-3 Gall: 0-0
Aids: Bl: 0-0 Vi: 0-0 Tstrap: 0-0 Ckp: 0-0
Best Rating: 60 5/09 Chep 1m4f23y good

Langham House

(99) (63)**32**
4-y-o ch g Best Of The Bests (IRE)-Dafne (Nashwan (USA))
J R Jenkins Nick Hodge

Placings:0440/0003001-3 **(0118)**
2009: 7^{3}SD,

	Starts	1st	2nd	3rd	Win & Pl
Career Total (Turf)	6	0	0	0	409
Career Total (AW)	6	1	0	2	2652

59 12/08 Kemp 7f STD £2047
Total win prize-money £2047

Going (Turf): Sf: 0-0 GS: 0-3 Gd: 0-1 GF: 0-2 Fm: 0-0
Distance: 5f/6f: 0-1 7f-8f: 1-8 9f-13f: 0-3 14f+: 0-0
Track : LH: 0-2 RH: 1-6 Tight: 0-1 Gall: 0-1
Aids: Bl: 0-0 Vi: 0-1 Tstrap: 0-0 Ckp: 0-0
Best Rating: 63 1/09 Kemp 7f stand

Moderate; effective at around 7f; acts on Polytrack.

Langland Bay

92(94) (45)**58**
3-y-o b f Diktat-Dodo (IRE) (Alzao (USA))
W R Muir Usk Valley Stud

Placings:605000 **(7236)**
2009: 6^{6}SD, 6^{0}GF, 7^{5}GF, 7^{0}SD, 7^{0}SD, 8^{0}SD,

	Starts	1st	2nd	3rd	Win & Pl
Career Total (Turf)	2	0	0	0	0
Career Total (AW)	4	0	0	0	0

Going (Turf): Sf: 0-0 GS: 0-0 Gd: 0-0 GF: 0-2 Fm: 0-0
Distance: 5f/6f: 0-1 7f-8f: 0-5 9f-13f: 0-0 14f+: 0-0
Track : LH: 0-4 RH: 0-1 Tight: 0-2 Gall: 0-1
Aids: Bl: 0-0 Vi: 0-0 Tstrap: 0-0 Ckp: 0-0
Best Rating: 58 6/09 Sals 6f212y gd-fm

Lanizza

66(76) (37)16

2-y-o ch g Alhaarth (IRE)-Cerulean Sky (IRE) (Darshaan)
E A L Dunlop Hamdan Al Maktoum

Placings:00 (5192)
2009: 7^{0}GF, 7^{0}SD,

	Starts	1st	2nd	3rd	Win & Pl
Career Total (Turf)	1	0	0	0	
Career Total (AW)	1	0	0	0	

Going (Turf): Sf: 0-0 GS: 0-0 Gd: 0-0 GF: 0-1 Fm: 0-0
Distance: 5f/6f: 0-0 7f-8f: 0-2 9f-13f: 0-0 14f+: 0-0
Track : LH: 0-1 RH: 0-0 Tight: 0-1 Gall: 0-0
Aids: Bl: 0-1 Vi: 0-0 Tstrap: 0-0 Ckp: 0-0
Best Rating: 37 8/09 Ling 7f stand

Lansdowne Princess

69 42

7-y-o b m Cloudings (IRE)-Premier Princess (Hard Fought)
G A Ham The Lansdowners

Placings:6 (4264)
2009: 16^{6}S,

	Starts	1st	2nd	3rd	Win & Pl
Career Total (Turf)	1	0	0	0	0

Going (Turf): Sf: 0-1 GS: 0-0 Gd: 0-0 GF: 0-0 Fm: 0-0
Distance: 5f/6f: 0-0 7f-8f: 0-0 9f-13f: 0-0 14f+: 0-1
Track : LH: 0-1 RH: 0-0 Tight: 0-0 Gall: 0-0
Aids: Bl: 0-0 Vi: 0-0 Tstrap: 0-0 Ckp: 0-0
Best Rating: 42 7/09 Chep 2m49y soft

Lapina (IRE)

98(98) (70)69

5-y-o ch m Fath (USA)-Alpina (USA) (El Prado (IRE))
A Middleton R J Matthews

Placings:040/01303232643/54153300216-265645 (3593)
2009: 13^{2}SD, 12^{6}SD, 13^{5}SD, 12^{6}GS, 14^{4}G, 14^{5}GF,

	Starts	1st	2nd	3rd	Win & Pl
Career Total (Turf)	21	2	2	5	10257
Career Total (AW)	10	1	2	1	4093

67 12/08 GrLe 1m5f66y (0-60)H STD £2266
69 6/08 Nott 1m6f15y (0-75)H G-F £2914
59 5/07 Bath 1m2f46y (0-70)H FRM £3238
Total win prize-money £8420

Going (Turf): Sf: 0-1 GS: 0-5 Gd: 0-3 GF: 1-10 Fm: 1-2
Distance: 5f/6f: 0-1 7f-8f: 0-2 9f-13f: 1-15 14f+: 2-13
Track : LH: 3-18 RH: 0-12 Tight: 1-20 Gall: 1-3
Aids: Bl: 3-23 Vi: 0-0 Tstrap: 0-4 Ckp: 0-4
Best Rating: 71 10/07 Sals 1m6f21y gd-sft

Modest; stays 1m6f; acts on fast ground; goes on Polytrack; has worn headgear.

Larehaan (USA)

85 54

2-y-o b/br f Smarty Jones (USA)-Wendy Vaala (USA) (Dayjur (USA))
B W Hills Hamdan Al Maktoum

Placings:0 (3820)
2009: 6^{0}GF,

	Starts	1st	2nd	3rd	Win & Pl
Career Total (Turf)	1	0	0	0	

Going (Turf): Sf: 0-0 GS: 0-0 Gd: 0-0 GF: 0-1 Fm: 0-0
Distance: 5f/6f: 0-1 7f-8f: 0-0 9f-13f: 0-0 14f+: 0-0
Track : LH: 0-0 RH: 0-0 Tight: 0-0 Gall: 0-0
Aids: Bl: 0-0 Vi: 0-0 Tstrap: 0-0 Ckp: 0-0
Best Rating: 54 7/09 NmkJ 6f gd-fm

Largem

64(95) (60)25

3-y-o b g Largesse-Jem's Law (Contract Law (USA))
J R Jenkins D Bryans

Placings:0-0514 (6446)
2009: 8^{0}HY, 12^{5}SD, 12^{1}SD, 12^{4}SS,

	Starts	1st	2nd	3rd	Win & Pl
Career Total (Turf)	1	0	0	0	
Career Total (AW)	4	1	0	0	2730

59 9/09 Wolv 1m4f50y (0-55)H STD £2729
Total win prize-money £2730

Going (Turf): Sf: 0-1 GS: 0-0 Gd: 0-0 GF: 0-0 Fm: 0-0
Distance: 5f/6f: 0-0 7f-8f: 0-1 9f-13f: 1-4 14f+: 0-0
Track : LH: 1-4 RH: 0-1 Tight: 1-2 Gall: 0-0
Aids: Bl: 0-0 Vi: 0-0 Tstrap: 0-0 Ckp: 0-0
Best Rating: 60 8/09 Kemp 1m4f stand

Modest; stays 1m4f; acts on Polytrack; should improve.

Larkham (USA)

109(94) (79)92

3-y-o b/br g Action This Day (USA)-La Sarto (USA) (Cormorant (USA))
R M Beckett R A Pegum

Placings:303-11304 (6234)
2009: 8^{1}SD, 9^{1}GF, 9^{3}GF, 10^{0}GF, 10^{4}GF,

	Starts	1st	2nd	3rd	Win & Pl
Career Total (Turf)	7	1	0	3	8028
Career Total (AW)	1	1	0	0	3071

85 5/09 Leic 1m1f218y (0-80)H G-F £4857
79 4/09 Wolv 1m141y STD £3070
Total win prize-money £7928

Going (Turf): Sf: 0-0 GS: 0-0 Gd: 0-2 GF: 1-5 Fm: 0-0
Distance: 5f/6f: 0-2 7f-8f: 0-1 9f-13f: 2-5 14f+: 0-0
Track : LH: 1-4 RH: 1-2 Tight: 1-2 Gall: 0-1
Aids: Bl: 0-0 Vi: 0-0 Tstrap: 0-0 Ckp: 0-0
Best Rating: 92 7/09 Sals 1m1f198y gd-fm

Useful; stays 1m2f; acts on fast ground; goes on Polytrack.

Larkrise Star

87(86) (67)53

2-y-o b f Where Or When (IRE)-Katy Ivory (IRE) (Night Shift (USA))
D K Ivory Dean Ivory

Placings:544 (3979)
2009: 6^{5}GS, 7^{4}SD, 7^{4}SD,

	Starts	1st	2nd	3rd	Win & Pl
Career Total (Turf)	1	0	0	0	0
Career Total (AW)	2	0	0	0	661

Going (Turf): Sf: 0-0 GS: 0-1 Gd: 0-0 GF: 0-0 Fm: 0-0
Distance: 5f/6f: 0-1 7f-8f: 0-2 9f-13f: 0-0 14f+: 0-0
Track : LH: 0-0 RH: 0-2 Tight: 0-0 Gall: 0-1
Aids: Bl: 0-0 Vi: 0-0 Tstrap: 0-0 Ckp: 0-0
Best Rating: 67 7/09 Kemp 7f stand

Lassarina (IRE)

102 98

3-y-o b f Sakhee (USA)-Kalanda (Desert King (IRE))
B W Hills J Hanson

Placings:10-53 (4317)
2009: 7^{5}S, 7^{3}G,

	Starts	1st	2nd	3rd	Win & Pl
Career Total (Turf)	4	1	0	1	15372

88 9/08 Newb 7f GD £11215
Total win prize-money £11216

Going (Turf): Sf: 0-1 GS: 0-0 Gd: 1-3 GF: 0-0 Fm: 0-0
Distance: 5f/6f: 0-0 7f-8f: 1-4 9f-13f: 0-0 14f+: 0-0
Track : LH: 0-0 RH: 0-0 Tight: 0-0 Gall: 0-0
Aids: Bl: 0-0 Vi: 0-0 Tstrap: 0-0 Ckp: 0-0
Best Rating: 98 7/09 NmkJ 7f good

Very useful; effective over 7f and acts on good ground.

Lasso The Moon

105 83

3-y-o b g Sadler's Wells (USA)-Hotelgenie Dot Com (Selkirk (USA))
M R Channon Derek And Jean Clee

Placings:24-024300 (3780)
2009: 11^{0}GS, 12^{2}GF, 10^{4}S, 10^{3}G, 12^{0}GF, 10^{0}G,

	Starts	1st	2nd	3rd	Win & Pl
Career Total (Turf)	8	0	2	1	9621

Going (Turf): Sf: 0-1 GS: 0-3 Gd: 0-2 GF: 0-2 Fm: 0-0
Distance: 5f/6f: 0-0 7f-8f: 0-1 9f-13f: 0-7 14f+: 0-0
Track : LH: 0-5 RH: 0-2 Tight: 0-3 Gall: 0-4
Aids: Bl: 0-0 Vi: 0-0 Tstrap: 0-0 Ckp: 0-0
Best Rating: 83 10/08 Newb 1m gd-sft

Fair; stays 1m4f and acts on most ground; has a tendency to start slowly.

Last Flight (IRE)

103 64

5-y-o b m In The Wings-Fantastic Fantasy (IRE) (Lahib (USA))
P Bowen Mrs Karen Bowen

Placings:004/06212362/0 (4417)
2009: 21^{0}G,

	Starts	1st	2nd	3rd	Win & Pl
Career Total (Turf)	12	1	3	1	7284

76 7/07 Wwck 2m39y (0-75)H HVY £3238
Total win prize-money £3239

Going (Turf): Sf: 1-3 GS: 0-2 Gd: 0-3 GF: 0-3 Fm: 0-1
Distance: 5f/6f: 0-0 7f-8f: 0-0 9f-13f: 0-5 14f+: 1-7
Track : LH: 1-7 RH: 0-5 Tight: 0-5 Gall: 0-1
Aids: Bl: 0-1 Vi: 0-2 Tstrap: 0-0 Ckp: 0-0
Best Rating: 77 10/07 Bath 2m1f34y good

Fair filly; stays 2m2f; goes well in soft ground; acts on firm too; has worn blinkers and cheekpieces.

Last Of The Line

(96) (78)**56**

4-y-o b g Efisio-Dance By Night (Northfields (USA))

B N Pollock Mrs Nicola Pollock

Placings:000216/200004604000-06 **(0545)**

2009: 7^{0}SS, 8^{6}SD,

	Starts	1st	2nd	3rd	Win & Pl
Career Total (Turf)	6	0	0	0	
Career Total (AW)	14	1	2	0	5054

72 11/07 Kemp 1m STD £3238

Total win prize-money £3239

Going (Turf): Sf: 0-1 GS: 0-1 Gd: 0-1 GF: 0-3 Fm: 0-0
Distance: 5f/6f: 0-3 **7f-8f: 1-16** 9f-13f: 0-1 14f+: 0-0
Track : LH: 0-9 **RH: 1-7** Tight: 0-6 Gall: 0-1
Aids: Bl: 0-3 Vi: 0-6 Tstrap: 0-1 Ckp: 0-1
Best Rating: 78 4/08 Kemp 1m stand

Fair; stays 1m; acts on Polytrack.

Last Of The Ravens

(66) (21)

2-y-o b f Zaha (CAN)-Eccentric Dancer (Rambo Dancer (CAN))

J F Coupland J F Coupland

Placings:50 **(7864)**

2009: 7^{5}SS, 6^{0}SS,

	Starts	1st	2nd	3rd	Win & Pl
Career Total (Turf)	0	0	0	0	
Career Total (AW)	2	0	0	0	0

Going (Turf): Sf: 0-0 GS: 0-0 Gd: 0-0 GF: 0-0 Fm: 0-0
Distance: 5f/6f: 0-1 7f-8f: 0-1 9f-13f: 0-0 14f+: 0-0
Track : LH: 0-2 RH: 0-0 Tight: 0-0 Gall: 0-0
Aids: Bl: 0-0 Vi: 0-0 Tstrap: 0-0 Ckp: 0-0
Best Rating: 21 12/09 Sthl 6f std-slw

Last Orders (IRE)

77 **49**

2-y-o gr c Bertolini (USA)-Sassania (IRE) (Persian Bold)

M G Quinlan Liam Mulryan

Placings:500 **(4153)**

2009: 5^{5}GF, 5^{0}GF, 6^{0}G,

	Starts	1st	2nd	3rd	Win & Pl
Career Total (Turf)	3	0	0	0	0

Going (Turf): Sf: 0-0 GS: 0-0 Gd: 0-1 GF: 0-2 Fm: 0-0
Distance: 5f/6f: 0-2 7f-8f: 0-1 9f-13f: 0-0 14f+: 0-0
Track : LH: 0-0 RH: 0-0 Tight: 0-0 Gall: 0-0
Aids: Bl: 0-0 Vi: 0-0 Tstrap: 0-0 Ckp: 0-0
Best Rating: 49 4/09 Folk 5f gd-fm

Last Sovereign

106(106) (88)**86**

5-y-o b g Pivotal-Zayala (Royal Applause)

Jane Chapple-Hyam Howard Spooner

Placings:46/31256/230031-1203643404 **(6564)**

2009: 7^{1}SD, 7^{2}GF, 8^{0}GF, 8^{3}GS, 7^{6}G, 7^{4}G, 6^{3}G, 7^{4}GS, 7^{0}SD, 6^{4}GS,

	Starts	1st	2nd	3rd	Win & Pl
Career Total (Turf)	14	2	1	4	12634
Career Total (AW)	9	1	2	1	4649

88 2/09 Kemp 7f (0-75)H STD £2590
81 8/08 NmkJ 1m (0-75)H GD £3885
80 4/07 Catt 7f (0-65)H G-F £2730

Total win prize-money £9206

Going (Turf): Sf: 0-1 GS: 0-3 **Gd: 1-4 GF: 1-5** Fm: 0-1
Distance: 5f/6f: 0-4 **7f-8f: 3-16** 9f-13f: 0-3 14f+: 0-0
Track : LH: 1-5 RH: 1-11 **Tight: 1-4** Gall: 0-2
Aids: Bl: 0-0 Vi: 0-0 Tstrap: 1-8 Ckp: 1-8
Best Rating: 88 2/09 Kemp 7f stand

Useful; effective at around 7f-1m; acts on fast and soft ground; also goes on Polytrack; has worn cheekpieces.

Last Three Minutes (IRE)

107(104) (89)**98**

4-y-o b g Val Royal (FR)-Circe's Isle (Be My Guest (USA))

E A L Dunlop The Right Angle Club

Placings:4/13060-401366 **(4261)**

2009: 8^{4}GF, 8^{0}GS, 8^{1}SD, 8^{3}G, 8^{6}G, 10^{6}G,

	Starts	1st	2nd	3rd	Win & Pl
Career Total (Turf)	11	1	0	2	7233
Career Total (AW)	1	1	0	0	5828

89 5/09 Ling 1m (0-80)H STD £5828
89 7/08 Yarm 1m1f G-F £2201

Total win prize-money £8030

Going (Turf): Sf: 0-1 GS: 0-2 Gd: 0-5 **GF: 1-3** Fm: 0-0
Distance: 5f/6f: 0-0 7f-8f: 1-6 9f-13f: 1-6 14f+: 0-0
Track : **LH: 2-4** RH: 0-4 **Tight: 2-2** Gall: 0-4
Aids: Bl: 0-0 Vi: 0-0 Tstrap: 0-0 Ckp: 0-0
Best Rating: 98 7/09 NmkJ 1m good

Useful; stays 1m1f; acts on most ground and on Polytrack.

Lastkingofscotland (IRE)

79(80) (62)**92**

3-y-o b g Danehill Dancer (IRE)-Arcade (Rousillon (USA))

G C Bravery (Charles O'Brien 20/9) M&R Refurbishments Ltd

Placings:1262000 **(7759)**

2009: 7^{1}HY, 6^{2}Y, 7^{6}HY, 7^{2}HY, 7^{0}SD, 9^{0}YS, 8^{0}SD,

	Starts	1st	2nd	3rd	Win & Pl
Career Total (Turf)	5	1	2	0	14926
Career Total (AW)	2	0	0	0	

85 4/09 Tipp 7f100y HVY £8721

Total win prize-money £8721

Going (Turf): Sf: 1-3 GS: 0-0 Gd: 0-0 GF: 0-0 Fm: 0-0
Distance: 5f/6f: 0-0 **7f-8f: 1-6** 9f-13f: 0-1 14f+: 0-0
Track : **LH: 1-3** RH: 0-2 Tight: 0-0 Gall: 0-0
Aids: Bl: 0-0 Vi: 0-0 Tstrap: 0-0 Ckp: 0-0
Best Rating: 92 4/09 Limk 6f160y yield

Lastroarofdtiger (USA)

81(98) (78)**54**

3-y-o b g Cherokee Run (USA)-Innocent Affair (IRE) (Night Shift (USA))

J R Weymes (A P Jarvis 11/8) Cyril Wall

Placings:0-1050600 **(7891)**

2009: 8^{1}SD, 7^{0}GF, 8^{5}SD, 8^{0}G, 7^{6}SF, 6^{0}SD, 7^{0}SD,

	Starts	1st	2nd	3rd	Win & Pl
Career Total (Turf)	2	0	0	0	
Career Total (AW)	6	1	0	0	0

Going (Turf): Sf: 0-0 GS: 0-0 Gd: 0-1 GF: 0-1 Fm: 0-0
Distance: 5f/6f: 0-1 7f-8f: 0-5 **9f-13f: 1-2** 14f+: 0-0
Track : **LH: 1-6** RH: 0-1 **Tight: 1-5** Gall: 0-0
Aids: Bl: 0-0 Vi: 0-0 Tstrap: 0-0 Ckp: 0-0
Best Rating: 78 5/09 Ling 1m stand

Fair; stays 1m plus; acts on Polytrack.

Lastroseofsummer (IRE)

90(86) (38)**49**

3-y-o ch f Haafhd-Broken Romance (IRE) (Ela-Mana-Mou)

Rae Guest E P Duggan

Placings:60 **(7648)**

2009: 8^{6}G, 12^{0}SD,

	Starts	1st	2nd	3rd	Win & Pl
Career Total (Turf)	1	0	0	0	0
Career Total (AW)	1	0	0	0	

Going (Turf): Sf: 0-0 GS: 0-0 Gd: 0-1 GF: 0-0 Fm: 0-0
Distance: 5f/6f: 0-0 7f-8f: 0-0 9f-13f: 0-2 14f+: 0-0
Track : LH: 0-2 RH: 0-0 Tight: 0-1 Gall: 0-0
Aids: Bl: 0-0 Vi: 0-0 Tstrap: 0-0 Ckp: 0-0
Best Rating: 49 10/09 Nott 1m75y good

Latansaa

99 **80**

2-y-o b c Indian Ridge-Sahool (Unfuwain (USA))

M P Tregoning Hamdan Al Maktoum

Placings:3 **(7029)**

2009: 8^{3}S,

	Starts	1st	2nd	3rd	Win & Pl
Career Total (Turf)	1	0	0	1	722

Going (Turf): Sf: 0-1 GS: 0-0 Gd: 0-0 GF: 0-0 Fm: 0-0
Distance: 5f/6f: 0-0 7f-8f: 0-1 9f-13f: 0-0 14f+: 0-0
Track : LH: 0-0 RH: 0-0 Tight: 0-0 Gall: 0-0
Aids: Bl: 0-0 Vi: 0-0 Tstrap: 0-0 Ckp: 0-0
Best Rating: 80 10/09 Newb 1m soft

Fair; stays 1m; handles soft ground.

Laterly (IRE)

109(113) (96)**102**

4-y-o b g Tiger Hill (IRE)-La Candela (GER) (Alzao (USA))

S Gollings (T P Tate 19/9) P J Martin

Placings:0F331/3212104-000300350 **(7789)**

2009: 12^{0}GS, 11^{0}GF, 10^{0}GF, 10^{3}G, 10^{0}GF, 10^{0}GF, 12^{3}SD, 12^{5}SD, 9^{0}SD,

	Starts	1st	2nd	3rd	Win & Pl
Career Total (Turf)	18	3	2	4	37753
Career Total (AW)	3	0	0	1	2285

102 7/08 Ripn 1m4f10y (0-100)H GD £11215
91 6/08 Thsk 1m4f (0-85)H G-S £5180
79 11/07 Nott 1m54y G-F £2590

Total win prize-money £18988

Going (Turf): Sf: 0-2 **GS: 1-2 Gd: 1-6 GF: 1-8** Fm: 0-0
Distance: 5f/6f: 0-1 7f-8f: 0-3 **9f-13f: 3-16** 14f+: 0-1
Track : **LH: 2-16** RH: 1-1 **Tight: 2-6** Gall: 0-7
Aids: Bl: 0-0 Vi: 0-0 Tstrap: 0-0 Ckp: 0-0
Best Rating: 102 7/08 Ripn 1m4f10y good

Useful; stays 1m4f; acts on most ground; suited by forcing tactics.

Lathaat

82 **47**

2-y-o b/br f Dubai Destination (USA)-Khulood (USA) (Storm Cat (USA))
J L Dunlop Hamdan Al Maktoum

Placings:0 **(2490)**
2009: 6^{0}GF,

	Starts	1st	2nd	3rd	Win & Pl
Career Total (Turf)	1	0	0	0	

Going (Turf): Sf: 0-0 GS: 0-0 Gd: 0-0 GF: 0-1 Fm: 0-0
Distance: 5f/6f: 0-1 7f-8f: 0-0 9f-13f: 0-0 14f+: 0-0
Track : LH: 0-0 RH: 0-0 Tight: 0-0 Gall: 0-0
Aids: Bl: 0-0 Vi: 0-0 Tstrap: 0-0 Ckp: 0-0
Best Rating: 47 5/09 Ling 6f gd-fm

Latin Connection (IRE)

(85) (25)

3-y-o b g Soviet Star (USA)-Via Verbano (IRE) (Caerleon (USA))
Lee Smyth Pircan Partnership

Placings:0000 **(7863)**
2009: 12^{0}SD, 9^{0}SD, 8^{0}SD, 8^{0}SD,

	Starts	1st	2nd	3rd	Win & Pl
Career Total (Turf)	0	0	0	0	
Career Total (AW)	4	0	0	0	

Going (Turf): Sf: 0-0 GS: 0-0 Gd: 0-0 GF: 0-0 Fm: 0-0
Distance: 5f/6f: 0-0 7f-8f: 0-0 9f-13f: 0-4 14f+: 0-0
Track : LH: 0-4 RH: 0-0 Tight: 0-3 Gall: 0-0
Aids: Bl: 0-0 Vi: 0-0 Tstrap: 0-0 Ckp: 0-0
Best Rating: 25 11/09 Wolv 1m141y stand

Latin Scholar (IRE)

106(96) (78)**80**

4-y-o ch g Titus Livius (FR)-Crimada (IRE) (Mukaddamah (USA))
A King Let's Live Racing

Placings:02600/0320140-1450 **(5532)**
2009: 10^{1}G, 11^{4}SD, 9^{5}G, 10^{0}G,

	Starts	1st	2nd	3rd	Win & Pl
Career Total (Turf)	14	2	2	1	8710
Career Total (AW)	2	0	0	0	351

80 6/09 Chep 1m2f36y O(0-75)H GD £3561
79 7/08 Wind 1m2f7y (0-70)H G-F £2729
Total win prize-money £6292

Going (Turf): Sf: 0-1 GS: 0-2 **Gd: 1-5 GF: 1-5** Fm: 0-1
Distance: 5f/6f: 0-3 7f-8f: 0-2 **9f-13f: 2-11** 14f+: 0-0
Track : **LH: 1-5** RH: 1-7 **Tight: 1-7** Gall: 0-2
Aids: Bl: 0-0 Vi: 0-0 Tstrap: 0-0 Ckp: 0-0
Best Rating: 80 6/09 Chep 1m2f36y good

Fair; stays 1m2f and acts on fast ground.

Latin Tinge (USA)

100(97) (84)**87**

3-y-o gr/ro f King Cugat (USA)-Southern Tradition (USA) (Family Doctor (USA))
P F I Cole Frank Stella

Placings:2014-506000 **(6804)**
2009: 8^{5}SD, 10^{0}G, 11^{6}GF, 10^{0}SD, 10^{0}G, 9^{0}SD,

	Starts	1st	2nd	3rd	Win & Pl
Career Total (Turf)	6	0	1	0	1953
Career Total (AW)	4	1	0	0	2235

84 9/08 Kemp 1m STD £2047
Total win prize-money £2047

Going (Turf): Sf: 0-1 GS: 0-2 Gd: 0-2 GF: 0-1 Fm: 0-0
Distance: 5f/6f: 0-0 **7f-8f: 1-4** 9f-13f: 0-6 14f+: 0-0
Track : LH: 0-4 **RH: 1-3** Tight: 0-3 Gall: 0-1
Aids: Bl: 0-1 Vi: 0-0 Tstrap: 0-0 Ckp: 0-0
Best Rating: 87 9/08 Donc 1m soft

Useful; effective over 7f-1m; acts on easy ground; goes on Polytrack.

Lauberhorn

80 **48**

2-y-o b g Dubai Destination (USA)-Ski Run (Petoski)
Eve Johnson Houghton R F Johnson Houghton

Placings:00 **(5787)**
2009: 7^{0}G, 8^{0}G,

	Starts	1st	2nd	3rd	Win & Pl
Career Total (Turf)	2	0	0	0	

Going (Turf): Sf: 0-0 GS: 0-0 Gd: 0-2 GF: 0-0 Fm: 0-0
Distance: 5f/6f: 0-0 7f-8f: 0-1 9f-13f: 0-1 14f+: 0-0
Track : LH: 0-0 RH: 0-0 Tight: 0-0 Gall: 0-0
Aids: Bl: 0-0 Vi: 0-0 Tstrap: 0-0 Ckp: 0-0
Best Rating: 48 9/09 Chep 1m14y good

Laudatory

100(106) (92)**89**

3-y-o b g Royal Applause-Copy-Cat (Lion Cavern (USA))
W R Swinburn P W Harris

Placings:21-143044426 **(6535)**
2009: 7^{1}SD, 7^{4}GF, 8^{3}GF, 8^{0}G, 7^{4}G, 8^{4}SD, 8^{4}SD, 8^{2}SD, 8^{6}GF,

	Starts	1st	2nd	3rd	Win & Pl
Career Total (Turf)	5	0	0	1	2258
Career Total (AW)	6	2	2	0	12424

86 4/09 Kemp 7f (0-85)H STD £4727
79 11/08 Kemp 7f STD £4209
Total win prize-money £8936

Going (Turf): Sf: 0-0 GS: 0-0 Gd: 0-2 GF: 0-3 Fm: 0-0
Distance: 5f/6f: 0-0 **7f-8f: 2-9** 9f-13f: 0-2 14f+: 0-0
Track : LH: 0-1 **RH: 2-8** Tight: 0-0 Gall: 0-0
Aids: Bl: 0-0 Vi: 0-0 Tstrap: 0-0 Ckp: 0-0
Best Rating: 92 9/09 Kemp 1m stand

Useful; effective over 7f-1m; acts on Polytrack; handles fast turf; has worn a tongue tie.

Laughing Boy (IRE)

99(93) (43)**81**

3-y-o b g Montjeu (IRE)-Mala Mala (IRE) (Brief Truce (USA))
L M Cumani The Honorable Earle I Mack

Placings:442300 **(6878)**
2009: 10^{4}G, 10^{4}GS, 10^{2}GF, 10^{3}GF, 8^{0}G, 11^{0}SD,

	Starts	1st	2nd	3rd	Win & Pl
Career Total (Turf)	5	0	1	1	1738
Career Total (AW)	1	0	0	0	

Going (Turf): Sf: 0-0 GS: 0-1 Gd: 0-2 GF: 0-2 Fm: 0-0
Distance: 5f/6f: 0-0 7f-8f: 0-1 9f-13f: 0-5 14f+: 0-0
Track : LH: 0-2 RH: 0-3 Tight: 0-2 Gall: 0-0
Aids: Bl: 0-0 Vi: 0-0 Tstrap: 0-0 Ckp: 0-0
Best Rating: 81 8/09 Wind 1m2f7y gd-fm

Laughter (IRE)

95 **87**

4-y-o b f Sadler's Wells (USA)-Smashing Review (USA) (Pleasant Tap (USA))
Sir Michael Stoute Highclere Thoroughbred Racing(Petrushka)

Placings:1/0-50 **(3315)**
2009: 10^{5}GS, 10^{0}GF,

	Starts	1st	2nd	3rd	Win & Pl
Career Total (Turf)	4	1	0	0	4210

86 10/07 Leic 7f9y SFT £4210
Total win prize-money £4210

Going (Turf): **Sf: 1-1** GS: 0-1 Gd: 0-1 GF: 0-1 Fm: 0-0
Distance: 5f/6f: 0-0 **7f-8f: 1-1** 9f-13f: 0-3 14f+: 0-0
Track : LH: 0-3 RH: 0-0 Tight: 0-1 Gall: 0-2
Aids: Bl: 0-0 Vi: 0-0 Tstrap: 0-0 Ckp: 0-0
Best Rating: 87 5/08 Ches 1m3f79y good

Very useful; 185,000gns half-sister to a winner over 7f plus in the US; lightly raced; winner over 7f; acts on soft ground.

Laura Land

95(86) (38)**48**

3-y-o b f Lujain (USA)-Perdicula (IRE) (Persian Heights)
W M Brisbourne Law Abiding Citizens

Placings:0600 **(6705)**
2009: 12^{0}GF, 10^{6}GF, 10^{0}G, 10^{0}SS,

	Starts	1st	2nd	3rd	Win & Pl
Career Total (Turf)	3	0	0	0	0
Career Total (AW)	1	0	0	0	

Going (Turf): Sf: 0-0 GS: 0-0 Gd: 0-1 GF: 0-2 Fm: 0-0
Distance: 5f/6f: 0-0 7f-8f: 0-0 9f-13f: 0-4 14f+: 0-0
Track : LH: 0-4 RH: 0-0 Tight: 0-2 Gall: 0-1
Aids: Bl: 0-0 Vi: 0-0 Tstrap: 0-0 Ckp: 0-0
Best Rating: 48 8/09 Wwck 1m2f188y good

Laura's Lady (IRE)

100 **57**

3-y-o b f Namid-Catapila (USA) (Tactical Cat (USA))
G A Swinbank R H Hall

Placings:1543 **(3614)**
2009: 6^{1}F, 6^{5}GF, 7^{4}GF, 7^{3}G,

	Starts	1st	2nd	3rd	Win & Pl
Career Total (Turf)	4	1	0	1	3133

57 5/09 Rdcr 6f FRM £2590
Total win prize-money £2590

Going (Turf): Sf: 0-0 GS: 0-0 Gd: 0-1 GF: 0-2 **Fm: 1-1**
Distance: **5f/6f: 1-2** 7f-8f: 0-2 9f-13f: 0-0 14f+: 0-0
Track : LH: 0-0 RH: 0-1 Tight: 0-0 Gall: 0-0
Aids: Bl: 0-0 Vi: 0-0 Tstrap: 0-0 Ckp: 0-0
Best Rating: 57 5/09 Rdcr 6f firm

Moderate; suited by 6f and fast ground.

Laurel Creek (IRE)

101(113) (93)**82**

4-y-o b g Sakura Laurel (JPN)-Eastern Sky (AUS) (Danehill (USA))

M J Grassick Patrick G McKeon

Placings:06000**221**-**1**10560 **(4729a)**

2009: 12^{1}SD, 16^{1}SF, 16^{0}G, 16^{5}GF, 17^{6}SD, 16^{0}GY,

	Starts	1st	2nd	3rd	Win & Pl
Career Total (Turf)	8	0	0	0	
Career Total (AW)	6	3	2	0	13188

93	3/09	Wolv	2m119y	(0-85)H	SF	£5180
88	2/09	Wolv	1m4f50y	(0-75)H	STD	£2729
74	11/08	Wolv	2m119y	(0-65)H	STD	£2729

Total win prize-money £10641

Going (Turf): Sf: 0-0 GS: 0-0 Gd: 0-3 GF: 0-1 Fm: 0-1
Distance: 5f/6f: 0-0 7f-8f: 0-4 9f-13f: 1-3 **14f+: 2-7**
Track : **LH: 3-9** RH: 0-4 **Tight: 3-4** Gall: 0-1
Aids: Bl: 0-0 Vi: 0-0 Tstrap: 0-0 Ckp: 0-0
Best Rating: 93 3/09 Wolv 2m119y std-fst

Useful; effective over 1m4f-2m and acts on Polytrack; usually held up.

Laureldean Desert

95(78) (40)**58**

2-y-o b f Green Desert (USA)-Heady (Rousillon (USA))

R A Fahey R A Fahey

Placings:6050 **(7389)**

2009: 5^{6}G, 6^{0}GF, 6^{5}GF, 7^{0}SD,

	Starts	1st	2nd	3rd	Win & Pl
Career Total (Turf)	3	0	0	0	141
Career Total (AW)	1	0	0	0	

Going (Turf): Sf: 0-0 GS: 0-0 Gd: 0-1 GF: 0-2 Fm: 0-0
Distance: 5f/6f: 0-2 7f-8f: 0-2 9f-13f: 0-0 14f+: 0-0
Track : LH: 0-1 RH: 0-0 Tight: 0-1 Gall: 0-0
Aids: Bl: 0-0 Vi: 0-0 Tstrap: 0-0 Ckp: 0-0
Best Rating: 58 10/09 Yarm 6f3y gd-fm

Laureldean Spirit (IRE)

93 **73**

2-y-o br f Whipper (USA)-Mise (IRE) (Indian Ridge)

R A Fahey D Brennan

Placings:243 **(5852)**

2009: 7^{2}G, 7^{4}GS, 7^{3}GF,

	Starts	1st	2nd	3rd	Win & Pl
Career Total (Turf)	3	0	1	1	4103

Going (Turf): Sf: 0-0 GS: 0-1 Gd: 0-1 GF: 0-1 Fm: 0-0
Distance: 5f/6f: 0-0 7f-8f: 0-3 9f-13f: 0-0 14f+: 0-0
Track : LH: 0-2 RH: 0-1 Tight: 0-1 Gall: 0-1
Aids: Bl: 0-0 Vi: 0-0 Tstrap: 0-0 Ckp: 0-0
Best Rating: 73 7/09 York 7f good

Useful; stays 7f and acts on good ground.

Laureldeans Best (IRE)

97(93) (59)**67**

3-y-o b f King's Best (USA)-Vanishing River (USA) (Southern Halo (USA))

R A Fahey R A Fahey

Placings:333 **(7648)**

2009: 8^{3}G, 8^{3}SD, 12^{3}SD,

	Starts	1st	2nd	3rd	Win & Pl
Career Total (Turf)	1	0	0	1	482
Career Total (AW)	2	0	0	2	788

Going (Turf): Sf: 0-0 GS: 0-0 Gd: 0-1 GF: 0-0 Fm: 0-0
Distance: 5f/6f: 0-0 7f-8f: 0-0 9f-13f: 0-3 14f+: 0-0
Track : LH: 0-3 RH: 0-0 Tight: 0-2 Gall: 0-0
Aids: Bl: 0-0 Vi: 0-0 Tstrap: 0-0 Ckp: 0-0
Best Rating: 67 7/09 Pont 1m4y good

Modest; seems to stay 1m4f; acts on good ground; goes on Polytrack.

Lauren's Kitty (IRE)

51

2-y-o b f One Cool Cat (USA)-Home Comforts (Most Welcome)

J C Fox Miss Sarah-Jane Durman

Placings:0 **(6729)**

2009: 6^{0}S,

	Starts	1st	2nd	3rd	Win & Pl
Career Total (Turf)	1	0	0	0	

Going (Turf): Sf: 0-1 GS: 0-0 Gd: 0-0 GF: 0-0 Fm: 0-0
Distance: 5f/6f: 0-0 7f-8f: 0-1 9f-13f: 0-0 14f+: 0-0
Track : LH: 0-0 RH: 0-0 Tight: 0-0 Gall: 0-0
Aids: Bl: 0-0 Vi: 0-0 Tstrap: 0-0 Ckp: 0-0

Laurie Grove (IRE)

95(103) (86)**83**

3-y-o b g Danehill Dancer (IRE)-Fragrant (Cadeaux Genereux)

T G Mills Mrs L M Askew

Placings:0**1**-240402003 **(7881)**

2009: 8^{2}SD, 8^{4}SD, 10^{0}GF, 8^{4}G, 6^{0}S, 8^{2}SD, 9^{0}SF, 7^{0}SD, 10^{3}SD,

	Starts	1st	2nd	3rd	Win & Pl
Career Total (Turf)	4	0	0	0	529
Career Total (AW)	7	1	2	1	7008

85	11/08	GrLe	1m	STD	£3238

Total win prize-money £3238

Going (Turf): Sf: 0-1 GS: 0-0 Gd: 0-1 GF: 0-2 Fm: 0-0
Distance: 5f/6f: 0-0 **7f-8f: 1-6** 9f-13f: 0-5 14f+: 0-0
Track : **LH: 1-5** RH: 0-2 Tight: 0-4 **Gall: 1-1**
Aids: Bl: 0-0 Vi: 0-0 Tstrap: 0-1 Ckp: 0-1
Best Rating: 86 10/09 Wolv 1m141y stand

Useful; dam unraced half-sister to high-class triple 1m-1m2f 3yo winner Kissogram, winner of the Sun Chariot; effective over 1m; acts on Polytrack.

Lava Lamp (GER)

97 **74**

2-y-o b c Shamardal (USA)-La Felicita (Shareef Dancer (USA))

G A Harker (M Johnston 5/10) An Englishman, Irishman & Scotsman

Placings:624350 **(7290)**

2009: 6^{6}G, 6^{2}GF, 7^{4}G, 6^{3}GF, 6^{5}GF, 6^{0}S,

	Starts	1st	2nd	3rd	Win & Pl
Career Total (Turf)	6	0	1	1	987

Going (Turf): Sf: 0-1 GS: 0-0 Gd: 0-2 GF: 0-3 Fm: 0-0
Distance: 5f/6f: 0-4 7f-8f: 0-2 9f-13f: 0-0 14f+: 0-0
Track : LH: 0-1 RH: 0-0 Tight: 0-0 Gall: 0-0
Aids: Bl: 0-0 Vi: 0-0 Tstrap: 0-0 Ckp: 0-0
Best Rating: 74 8/09 Nott 6f15y gd-fm

Fair sprinter; best on fast ground; often slowly away.

Lava Steps (USA)

95(104) (77)**59**

3-y-o b c Giant's Causeway (USA)-Miznah (IRE) (Sadler's Wells (USA))

P T Midgley (P F I Cole 28/9) Townville C C Racing Club

Placings:005-40**2**1 **(7725)**

2009: 11^{4}F, 9^{0}GF, 12^{2}SD, 12^{1}SD,

	Starts	1st	2nd	3rd	Win & Pl
Career Total (Turf)	4	0	0	0	255
Career Total (AW)	3	1	1	0	4218

73	12/09	Sthl	1m4f	STD	£3412

Total win prize-money £3412

Going (Turf): Sf: 0-0 GS: 0-1 Gd: 0-0 GF: 0-2 Fm: 0-1
Distance: 5f/6f: 0-0 7f-8f: 0-2 **9f-13f: 1-5** 14f+: 0-0
Track : **LH: 1-5** RH: 0-1 Tight: 0-1 Gall: 0-1
Aids: Bl: 0-0 Vi: 0-0 Tstrap: 0-0 Ckp: 0-0
Best Rating: 77 11/09 Sthl 1m4f stand

Fair; stays 1m4f; handles Fibresand.

Law And Order

92(86) (46)**60**

3-y-o b g Lear Spear (USA)-Sarcita (Primo Dominie)

Miss J R Tooth Raymond Tooth

Placings:000-6000 **(5775)**

2009: 7^{6}GF, 6^{0}GF, 9^{0}GF, 10^{0}SD,

	Starts	1st	2nd	3rd	Win & Pl
Career Total (Turf)	5	0	0	0	0
Career Total (AW)	2	0	0	0	

Going (Turf): Sf: 0-0 GS: 0-1 Gd: 0-0 GF: 0-4 Fm: 0-0
Distance: 5f/6f: 0-2 7f-8f: 0-3 9f-13f: 0-2 14f+: 0-0
Track : LH: 0-3 RH: 0-1 Tight: 0-1 Gall: 0-2
Aids: Bl: 0-0 Vi: 0-0 Tstrap: 0-1 Ckp: 0-1
Best Rating: 60 8/08 Newb 7f gd-sft

Law Of Attraction (IRE)

82 **47**

2-y-o b g Invincible Spirit (IRE)-Karatisa (IRE) (Nishapour (FR))

J R Gask Horses First Racing Limited

Placings:03 **(4062)**

2009: 6^{0}GF, 6^{3}HY,

	Starts	1st	2nd	3rd	Win & Pl
Career Total (Turf)	2	0	0	1	578

Going (Turf): Sf: 0-1 GS: 0-0 Gd: 0-0 GF: 0-1 Fm: 0-0
Distance: 5f/6f: 0-1 7f-8f: 0-1 9f-13f: 0-0 14f+: 0-0
Track : LH: 0-0 RH: 0-0 Tight: 0-0 Gall: 0-1
Aids: Bl: 0-0 Vi: 0-0 Tstrap: 0-0 Ckp: 0-0
Best Rating: 47 7/09 Nott 6f15y heavy

Promise on second start over 6f on heavy ground.

Law Of The Jungle (IRE)

(99) (59)**74**

3-y-o b f Catcher In The Rye (IRE)-Haut Volee (Top Ville)
Tom Dascombe (David Wachman 19/9) Manor House Stables LLP

Placings:0-6000453 **(7857)**
2009: 7^{6}Y, 8^{0}GY, 10^{0}GF, 10^{0}G, 8^{4}G, 8^{5}SD, 9^{3}SD,

	Starts	1st	2nd	3rd	Win & Pl
Career Total (Turf)	6	0	0	0	577
Career Total (AW)	2	0	0	1	252

Going (Turf): Sf: 0-0 GS: 0-0 Gd: 0-2 GF: 0-1 Fm: 0-0
Distance: 5f/6f: 0-0 7f-8f: 0-5 9f-13f: 0-3 14f+: 0-0
Track : LH: 0-4 RH: 0-2 Tight: 0-2 Gall: 0-0
Aids: Bl: 0-0 Vi: 0-0 Tstrap: 0-1 Ckp: 0-1
Best Rating: 74 9/08 Curr 7f yield

Modest; effective over 1m1f; handles good ground and Polytrack; has worn cheekpieces.

Lawyer To World

80(98) (48)**39**

5-y-o gr g Marju (IRE)-Legal Steps (IRE) (Law Society (USA))
Mrs C A Dunnett Ms Julie Green

Placings:6465026/63000501006450/0000000-55000 **(3631)**
2009: 12^{5}SD, 12^{5}SD, 16^{0}G, 10^{0}G, 10^{0}G,

	Starts	1st	2nd	3rd	Win & Pl
Career Total (Turf)	19	1	0	0	2424
Career Total (AW)	14	0	1	1	1523
52 6/07 Brig 1m1f209y G-S					£1943

Total win prize-money £1943

Going (Turf): Sf: 0-0 **GS: 1-2** Gd: 0-11 GF: 0-4 Fm: 0-2
Distance: 5f/6f: 0-3 7f-8f: 0-9 **9f-13f: 1-18** 14f+: 0-3
Track : LH: 1-24 RH: 0-5 Tight: 0-13 Gall: 0-2
Aids: Bl: 0-3 Vi: 0-3 Tstrap: 0-9 Ckp: 0-9
Best Rating: 64 11/06 Kemp 7f stand

Very moderate sort; stays about 1m4f; handles Polytrack; acts on any ground on turf.

Lay Claim (USA)

91(99) (75)**85**

2-y-o b/br c Seeking The Gold (USA)-Promptly (IRE) (Lead On Time (USA))
Sir Michael Stoute J Wigan & G Strawbridge

Placings:244 **(7130)**
2009: 7^{2}GF, 7^{4}G, 7^{4}SD,

	Starts	1st	2nd	3rd	Win & Pl
Career Total (Turf)	2	0	1	0	1542
Career Total (AW)	1	0	0	0	327

Going (Turf): Sf: 0-0 GS: 0-0 Gd: 0-1 GF: 0-1 Fm: 0-0
Distance: 5f/6f: 0-0 7f-8f: 0-3 9f-13f: 0-0 14f+: 0-0
Track : LH: 0-2 RH: 0-0 Tight: 0-1 Gall: 0-1
Aids: Bl: 0-0 Vi: 0-0 Tstrap: 0-0 Ckp: 0-0
Best Rating: 85 9/09 Newb 7f gd-fm

Runner-up on debut; effective over 7f; acts on fast ground.

Layali Al Andalus

105 **105**

2-y-o b c Halling (USA)-Lafite (Robellino (USA))
M Johnston Sheikh Hamdan Bin Mohammed Al Maktoum

Placings:211520 **(7404a)**
2009: 6^{2}GF, 7^{1}GF, 8^{1}GF, 7^{5}GF, 8^{2}G, 10^{0}HY,

	Starts	1st	2nd	3rd	Win & Pl
Career Total (Turf)	6	2	2	0	38605
100 8/09 Newc 1m3y G-F					£9969
92 6/09 Donc 7f G-F					£3238

Total win prize-money £13208

Going (Turf): Sf: 0-1 GS: 0-0 Gd: 0-1 **GF: 2-4** Fm: 0-0
Distance: 5f/6f: 0-1 7f-8f: 1-3 9f-13f: 1-2 14f+: 0-0
Track : LH: 0-1 RH: 0-1 Tight: 0-0 Gall: 0-1
Aids: Bl: 0-0 Vi: 0-0 Tstrap: 0-0 Ckp: 0-0
Best Rating: 105 9/09 Curr 1m good

Very useful; stays 1m; acts on fast ground.

Layer Cake

96(99) (73)**66**

3-y-o b c Monsieur Bond (IRE)-Blue Indigo (FR) (Pistolet Bleu (IRE))
J W Hills Gary And Linnet Woodward

Placings:5240-60220532356 **(6977)**
2009: 8^{6}SD, 6^{0}GF, 8^{2}SD, 8^{2}SD, 10^{0}SD, 8^{5}SF, 8^{3}G, 8^{2}SD, 8^{3}SD, 8^{5}GF, 8^{6}SD,

	Starts	1st	2nd	3rd	Win & Pl
Career Total (Turf)	6	0	0	1	977
Career Total (AW)	9	0	4	1	4043

Going (Turf): Sf: 0-0 GS: 0-0 Gd: 0-2 GF: 0-4 Fm: 0-0
Distance: 5f/6f: 0-1 7f-8f: 0-9 9f-13f: 0-5 14f+: 0-0
Track : LH: 0-8 RH: 0-4 Tight: 0-7 Gall: 0-0
Aids: Bl: 0-0 Vi: 0-0 Tstrap: 0-1 Ckp: 0-1
Best Rating: 73 8/08 Wolv 5f216y stand

Fair; stays 1m; acts on Polytrack.

Layla's Boy

92(98) (75)**79**

2-y-o ch g Sakhee (USA)-Gay Romance (Singspiel (IRE))
R A Fahey Dr Marwan Koukash

Placings:4220443 **(6727)**
2009: 6^{4}G, 7^{2}G, 7^{2}GS, 7^{0}GF, 8^{4}SD, 8^{4}G, 8^{3}S,

	Starts	1st	2nd	3rd	Win & Pl
Career Total (Turf)	6	0	2	1	2745
Career Total (AW)	1	0	0	0	378

Going (Turf): Sf: 0-1 GS: 0-1 Gd: 0-3 GF: 0-1 Fm: 0-0
Distance: 5f/6f: 0-0 7f-8f: 0-5 9f-13f: 0-2 14f+: 0-0
Track : LH: 0-3 RH: 0-1 Tight: 0-3 Gall: 0-0
Aids: Bl: 0-0 Vi: 0-0 Tstrap: 0-0 Ckp: 0-0
Best Rating: 79 7/09 Ayr 7f50y good

Fair; stays 7f; acts on good and easy ground.

Layla's Dancer

99 **81**

2-y-o b c Danehill Dancer (IRE)-Crumpetsfortea (IRE) (Henbit (USA))
R A Fahey Dr Marwan Koukash

Placings:14 **(6993)**
2009: 7^{1}S, 8^{4}GS,

	Starts	1st	2nd	3rd	Win & Pl
Career Total (Turf)	2	1	0	0	5920
79 9/09 Thsk 7f SFT					£5342

Total win prize-money £5343

Going (Turf): Sf: 1-1 GS: 0-1 Gd: 0-0 GF: 0-0 Fm: 0-0
Distance: 5f/6f: 0-0 **7f-8f: 1-2** 9f-13f: 0-0 14f+: 0-0
Track : LH: 1-2 RH: 0-0 **Tight: 1-1** Gall: 0-1
Aids: Bl: 0-0 Vi: 0-0 Tstrap: 0-0 Ckp: 0-0
Best Rating: 81 10/09 Donc 1m gd-sft

Useful 130,000gns brother to Prohibition; winner on debut over 7f on soft; stays 1m.

Layla's Hero (IRE)

110 **105**

2-y-o b g One Cool Cat (USA)-Capua (USA) (Private Terms (USA))
D Nicholls Dr Marwan Koukash

Placings:41210111 **(7016)**
2009: 6^{4}G, 5^{1}GF, 6^{2}S, 6^{1}GF, 6^{0}GF, 6^{1}GS, 6^{1}G, 6^{1}GS,

	Starts	1st	2nd	3rd	Win & Pl
Career Total (Turf)	8	5	1	0	73882
105 10/09 Donc 6f G-S					£20741
103 10/09 York 6f GD					£17778
101 9/09 Hayd 6f G-S					£15577
80 8/09 Hayd 6f (0-80) G-F					£5504
72 7/09 Haml 5f4y G-F					£2729

Total win prize-money £62332

Going (Turf): Sf: 0-1 **GS: 2-2** Gd: 1-2 **GF: 2-3** Fm: 0-0
Distance: 5f/6f: 5-8 7f-8f: 0-0 9f-13f: 0-0 14f+: 0-0
Track : LH: 0-0 RH: 0-0 Tight: 0-0 Gall: 0-0
Aids: Bl: 0-0 Vi: 0-0 Tstrap: 0-0 Ckp: 0-0
Best Rating: 105 10/09 Donc 6f gd-sft

Smart; winner in Listed company; suited by 5f-6f; acts on most ground.

Layla's Lad (USA)

(90) (61)

2-y-o b c Dixieland Band (USA)-Requesting More (USA) (Norquestor (CAN))
R A Fahey Dr Marwan Koukash

Placings:6045 **(7791)**
2009: 5^{6}SD, 7^{0}SD, 5^{4}SF, 7^{5}SS,

	Starts	1st	2nd	3rd	Win & Pl
Career Total (Turf)	0	0	0	0	
Career Total (AW)	4	0	0	0	241

Going (Turf): Sf: 0-0 GS: 0-0 Gd: 0-0 GF: 0-0 Fm: 0-0
Distance: 5f/6f: 0-2 7f-8f: 0-2 9f-13f: 0-0 14f+: 0-0
Track : LH: 0-4 RH: 0-0 Tight: 0-3 Gall: 0-0
Aids: Bl: 0-0 Vi: 0-0 Tstrap: 0-0 Ckp: 0-0
Best Rating: 61 11/09 Wolv 7f32y stand

Modest; stays 6f; acts on Polytrack.

Layla's Lexi

88 **53**

2-y-o b f Reset (AUS)-Tricoteuse (Kris)
D Nicholls Dr Marwan Koukash

Placings:30 **(5977)**
2009: 5^{3}S, 5^{0}GF,

	Starts	1st	2nd	3rd	Win & Pl
Career Total (Turf)	2	0	0	1	504

Going (Turf): Sf: 0-1 GS: 0-0 Gd: 0-0 GF: 0-1 Fm: 0-0
Distance: 5f/6f: 0-2 7f-8f: 0-0 9f-13f: 0-0 14f+: 0-0
Track : LH: 0-0 RH: 0-0 Tight: 0-0 Gall: 0-0

Aids: Bl: 0-0 Vi: 0-0 Tstrap: 0-0 Ckp: 0-0
Best Rating: 53 9/09 Catt 5f soft

Layla's Prince (IRE)

81 50

2-y-o b g Statue Of Liberty (USA)-Nihonpillow Mirai (IRE) (Zamindar (USA))
D Nicholls Dr Marwan Koukash

Placings:60 (6646)
2009: 6^{6}GF, 6^{0}G,

	Starts	1st	2nd	3rd	Win & Pl
Career Total (Turf)	2	0	0	0	0

Going (Turf): Sf: 0-0 GS: 0-0 Gd: 0-1 GF: 0-1 Fm: 0-0
Distance: 5f/6f: 0-2 7f-8f: 0-0 9f-13f: 0-0 14f+: 0-0
Track : LH: 0-0 RH: 0-0 Tight: 0-0 Gall: 0-0
Aids: Bl: 0-0 Vi: 0-0 Tstrap: 0-0 Ckp: 0-0
Best Rating: 50 8/09 Ripn 6f gd-fm

Moderate half-brother to the quirky Mt Kintyre out of a half-sister to five winners.

Layline (IRE)

104 92

2-y-o b g King's Best (USA)-Belle Reine (King Of Kings (IRE))
R M Beckett Mrs M E Slade

Placings:130 (6993)
2009: 8^{1}GS, 8^{3}GF, 8^{0}GS,

	Starts	1st	2nd	3rd	Win & Pl
Career Total (Turf)	3	1	0	1	3386
85 9/09 Chep 1m14y			G-S		£2266

Total win prize-money £2267

Going (Turf): Sf: 0-0 **GS: 1-2** Gd: 0-0 GF: 0-1 Fm: 0-0
Distance: 5f/6f: 0-0 7f-8f: 0-1 **9f-13f: 1-2** 14f+: 0-0
Track : LH: 0-2 RH: 0-0 Tight: 0-1 Gall: 0-1
Aids: Bl: 0-0 Vi: 0-0 Tstrap: 0-0 Ckp: 0-0
Best Rating: 92 10/09 Epsm 1m114y gd-fm

Useful; effective at 7f but stays 1m; acts on easy ground but handles fast.

Lazy Darren

99 (79)70

5-y-o b g Largesse-Palmstead Belle (IRE) (Wolfhound (USA))
C Grant Woodgate Family

Placings:01/**644**010300504533/0 (2666)
2009: 10^{0}GF,

	Starts	1st	2nd	3rd	Win & Pl
Career Total (Turf)	14	1	0	3	8420
Career Total (AW)	4	1	0	0	4901
87 5/07 Chep 1m14y (0-80)H			G-F		£4857
77 12/06 Wolv 1m141y			STD		£3886

Total win prize-money £8744

Going (Turf): Sf: 0-1 GS: 0-1 Gd: 0-3 **GF: 1-9** Fm: 0-0
Distance: 5f/6f: 0-0 7f-8f: 0-8 **9f-13f: 2-10** 14f+: 0-0
Track : **LH: 1-6** RH: 0-4 **Tight: 1-4** Gall: 0-1
Aids: Bl: 0-1 Vi: 0-1 Tstrap: 0-0 Ckp: 0-0
Best Rating: 87 5/07 Chep 1m14y gd-fm

Le Chiffre (IRE)

(102) (76)67

7-y-o br g Celtic Swing-Implicit View (Persian Bold)
Miss Sheena West Michael Moriarty

Placings:3/13/4501146001**0**/3505105431313260/0236101 5513412-00 (7664)
2009: 8^{0}SD, 8^{0}SD,

	Starts	1st	2nd	3rd	Win & Pl
Career Total (Turf)	15	4	0	1	16531
Career Total (AW)	31	7	3	7	24373
72 10/08 GrLe 1m (0-70)H			STD		£2590
72 9/08 Wolv 7f32y			STD		£3238
64 8/08 Bevl 7f100y			G-S		£2590
65 7/08 Wolv 1m141y			STD		£2388
77 8/07 Kemp 1m (0-70)H			STD		£2817
71 7/07 Wolv 1m141y (0-65)H			STD		£2047
67 4/07 Brig 5f213y			G-F		£1943
67 11/06 Sthl 6f			STD		£2047
75 7/06 Hayd 7f30y (0-70)H			G-F		£5505
62 7/06 Wolv 7f32y			STD		£2730
80 10/05 Pont 1m4y			GD		£5707

Total win prize-money £33604

Going (Turf): Sf: 0-1 GS: 1-2 Gd: 1-3 **GF: 2-9** Fm: 0-0
Distance: 5f/6f: 2-8 **7f-8f: 6-31** 9f-13f: 3-7 14f+: 0-0
Track : **LH: 9-26** RH: 2-13 **Tight: 4-19** Gall: 1-2
Aids: Bl: 1-8 Vi: 0-0 Tstrap: 9-33 Ckp: 9-33
Best Rating: 80 10/05 Pont 1m4y good

Modest; effective over 1m; acts on fast and soft ground; also goes on sand.

Le Corvee (IRE)

102(97) (73)57

7-y-o b g Rossini (USA)-Elupa (IRE) (Mtoto)
A W Carroll A W Carroll

Placings:1342/5405**0**/00/**00**100/**00**206-00064536 (5246)
2009: 10^{0}GF, 10^{0}GF, 10^{0}GF, 11^{6}GF, 10^{4}G, 12^{5}GF, 12^{3}GF, 13^{6}F,

	Starts	1st	2nd	3rd	Win & Pl
Career Total (Turf)	23	2	1	2	13562
Career Total (AW)	6	0	1	0	1532
81 5/07 NmkR 1m2f (0-70)H			G-F		£3747
91 7/04 Donc 7f D			G-F		£4992

Total win prize-money £8740

Going (Turf): Sf: 0-0 GS: 0-2 Gd: 0-6 **GF: 2-13** Fm: 0-2
Distance: 5f/6f: 0-0 7f-8f: 1-2 9f-13f: 1-25 14f+: 0-2
Track : LH: 0-20 RH: 0-4 Tight: 0-13 Gall: 0-3
Aids: Bl: 0-0 Vi: 0-0 Tstrap: 0-0 Ckp: 0-0
Best Rating: 95 5/05 Newb 1m3f5y firm

Fair performer; stays 1m2f; acts on fast ground and Polytrack.

Le Petit Vigier

(98) (49)47

3-y-o b f Groom Dancer (USA)-Fallujah (Dr Fong (USA))
P Beaumont Mrs J M Plummer

Placings:004320-42366 (1054)
2009: 8^{4}SD, 8^{2}SD, 8^{3}SD, 7^{6}SD, 8^{6}SD,

	Starts	1st	2nd	3rd	Win & Pl
Career Total (Turf)	4	0	0	1	302
Career Total (AW)	7	0	2	1	1683

Going (Turf): **Sf: 0-3 GS: 0-1 Gd: 0-0 GF: 0-0 Fm: 0-0**
Distance: 5f/6f: 0-0 7f-8f: 0-11 9f-13f: 0-0 14f+: 0-0
Track : LH: 0-9 RH: 0-2 Tight: 0-2 Gall: 0-0
Aids: Bl: 0-0 Vi: 0-0 Tstrap: 0-0 Ckp: 0-0
Best Rating: 49 11/08 Sthl 7f stand

Moderate; effective over 7f and acts on Fibresand; has worn a tongue tie.

Le Reve Royal

98(91) (44)58

3-y-o ch f Monsieur Bond (IRE)-Bond Royale (Piccolo)
G R Oldroyd Bond, Hart & Oldroyd

Placings:306-0030000 (7814)
2009: 6^{0}GS, 8^{0}G, 7^{3}GS, 8^{0}SD, 10^{0}GS, 5^{0}SD, 8^{0}SD,

	Starts	1st	2nd	3rd	Win & Pl
Career Total (Turf)	6	0	0	2	1420
Career Total (AW)	4	0	0	0	

Going (Turf): **Sf: 0-1 GS: 0-3 Gd: 0-2 GF: 0-0 Fm: 0-0**
Distance: 5f/6f: 0-4 7f-8f: 0-4 9f-13f: 0-2 14f+: 0-0
Track : LH: 0-6 RH: 0-0 Tight: 0-3 Gall: 0-2
Aids: Bl: 0-0 Vi: 0-1 Tstrap: 0-2 Ckp: 0-2
Best Rating: 58 8/08 Bevl 5f soft

Modest; best effort over 5f on soft ground.

Le Toreador

105(105) (99)97

4-y-o ch g Piccolo-Peggy Spencer (Formidable (USA))
K A Ryan Guy Reed

Placings:544/04**11**1462-5320**11**502361100 (6843)
2009: 5^{5}GF, 5^{3}GF, 5^{2}GF, 5^{0}GS, 5^{1}GF, 5^{1}G, 5^{5}GS, 5^{0}GF, 5^{2}GF, 5^{3}GF, 5^{6}GF, 5^{1}GF, 5^{1}SD, 6^{0}G, 5^{0}G,

	Starts	1st	2nd	3rd	Win & Pl
Career Total (Turf)	23	5	3	2	30658
Career Total (AW)	3	2	0	0	7637
99 10/09 Wolv 5f20y (0-85)H			STD		£5046
97 9/09 Leic 5f2y (0-85)H			G-F		£4857
90 6/09 Thsk 5f (0-85)H			GD		£5569
90 6/09 Ayr 5f (0-85)H			G-F		£6476
82 7/08 Pont 5f (0-75)H			GD		£3885
83 7/08 Kemp 5f (0-75)H			STD		£2590
69 6/08 Rdcr 5f (0-70)H			FRM		£2331

Total win prize-money £30755

Going (Turf): Sf: 0-1 GS: 0-3 **Gd: 2-6 GF: 2-12** Fm: 1-1
Distance: **5f/6f: 7-26** 7f-8f: 0-0 9f-13f: 0-0 14f+: 0-0
Track : **LH: 2-5** RH: 1-1 **Tight: 1-4** Gall: 0-0
Aids: Bl: 0-0 Vi: 0-0 Tstrap: 2-5 Ckp: 2-5
Best Rating: 99 10/09 Wolv 5f20y stand

Very useful; suited by 5f; acts on most ground and on Polytrack; has worn a tongue tie and cheekpieces.

Leadenhall Lass (IRE)

101(94) (70)76

3-y-o ch f Monsieur Bond (IRE)-Zest (USA) (Zilzal (USA))
P M Phelan The Lime Street Syndicate

Placings:130-503443120 (6731)
2009: 6^{5}GF, 6^{0}SD, 6^{3}GF, 5^{4}GF, 5^{4}G, 6^{3}G, 6^{1}GF, 7^{2}GF, 6^{0}S,

	Starts	1st	2nd	3rd	Win & Pl
Career Total (Turf)	10	2	1	2	12881
Career Total (AW)	2	0	0	1	433
73 9/09 Epsm 6f (0-80)H			G-F		£5180
70 7/08 Wind 5f10y			G-F		£4209

Total win prize-money £9390

Going (Turf): Sf: 0-1 GS: 0-0 Gd: 0-3 **GF: 2-6** Fm: 0-0
Distance: **5f/6f: 2-9** 7f-8f: 0-3 9f-13f: 0-0 14f+: 0-0
Track : **LH: 1-5** RH: 0-0 Tight: 1-4 Gall: 1-3
Aids: Bl: 0-0 **Vi: 1-4** Tstrap: 0-1 Ckp: 0-1

Best Rating: **76** 10/09 Epsm 7f gd-fm

Fair; stays 7f and acts on fast ground.

Leader Of The Land (IRE)

80(95) (59)**48**

2-y-o ch c Halling (USA)-Cheerleader (Singspiel (IRE))

D R Lanigan Saeed H Altayer

Placings:004 **(7721)**

2009: 8^{0}S, 8^{0}SD, 8^{4}SD,

	Starts	1st	2nd	3rd	Win & Pl
Career Total (Turf)	1	0	0	0	
Career Total (AW)	2	0	0	0	289

Going (Turf): **Sf: 0-1 GS: 0-0 Gd: 0-0 GF: 0-0 Fm: 0-0**
Distance: 5f/6f: 0-0 7f-8f: 0-2 9f-13f: 0-1 14f+: 0-0
Track : LH: 0-3 RH: 0-0 Tight: 0-1 Gall: 0-0
Aids: Bl: 0-0 Vi: 0-0 Tstrap: 0-0 Ckp: 0-0
Best Rating: **59** 12/09 Sthl 1m stand

Leading Edge (IRE)

99(108) (76)**78**

4-y-o gr f Clodovil (IRE)-Ja Ganhou (Midyan (USA))

M R Channon M Channon

Placings:665040**5**6160**134**/022526**2**0201500000**3**1-**2532**5**00**0**343510** **(7828)**

2009: 6^{2}SD, 6^{5}SD, 7^{3}SD, 5^{2}SD, 5^{5}GF, 6^{0}S, 6^{0}SD, 5^{0}GF, 6^{3}GS, 6^{4}G, 5^{3}SD, 5^{5}SD, 5^{1}SD, 6^{0}SD,

	Starts	1st	2nd	3rd	Win & Pl
Career Total (Turf)	32	3	4	1	18400
Career Total (AW)	15	2	3	4	8881

74 11/09 Wolv 5f216y (0-65)H STD £2047
74 12/08 GrLe 6f (0-75)H STD £2590
76 7/08 Donc 6f (0-80)H G-F £4857
70 11/07 Nott 5f13y (0-65) G-F £2914
63 10/07 Gdwd 6f (0-80) SFT £4857
Total win prize-money £17267

Going (Turf): Sf: 1-6 GS: 0-4 Gd: 0-7 **GF: 2-15** Fm: 0-0
Distance: **5f/6f: 5-41** 7f-8f: 0-6 9f-13f: 0-0 14f+: 0-0
Track : **LH: 2-20** RH: 0-4 Tight: 1-9 Gall: 1-8
Aids: Bl: 0-0 Vi: 0-0 Tstrap: 0-0 Ckp: 0-0
Best Rating: **79** 6/08 Ling 6f stand

Modest; stays 6f; acts on most ground; goes on Polytrack.

Leaf Hollow

67 **25**

3-y-o ch f Beat Hollow-Lauren (GER) (Lightning (FR))

M Madgwick Miss E M L Coller

Placings:000-5 **(5963)**

2009: 10^{5}G,

	Starts	1st	2nd	3rd	Win & Pl
Career Total (Turf)	4	0	0	0	0

Going (Turf): **Sf: 0-0 GS: 0-0 Gd: 0-2 GF: 0-2 Fm: 0-0**
Distance: 5f/6f: 0-2 7f-8f: 0-1 9f-13f: 0-1 14f+: 0-0
Track : LH: 0-1 RH: 0-0 Tight: 0-1 Gall: 0-1
Aids: Bl: 0-0 Vi: 0-0 Tstrap: 0-0 Ckp: 0-0
Best Rating: **25** 6/08 Ling 7f gd-fm

Leahurst (IRE)

101(109) (109)**92**

3-y-o gr g Verglas (IRE)-Badee'A (IRE) (Marju (IRE))

J Noseda Mrs Susan Roy

Placings:0-121 **(5615)**

2009: 7^{1}SD, 7^{2}HY, 7^{1}SD,

	Starts	1st	2nd	3rd	Win & Pl
Career Total (Turf)	2	0	1	0	2698
Career Total (AW)	2	2	0	0	10715

109 9/09 Wolv 7f32y (0-95)H STD £7477
95 4/09 Wolv 7f32y STD £3238
Total win prize-money £10715

Going (Turf): **Sf: 0-1 GS: 0-0 Gd: 0-1 GF: 0-0 Fm: 0-0**
Distance: 5f/6f: 0-0 **7f-8f: 2-4** 9f-13f: 0-0 14f+: 0-0
Track : **LH: 2-3** RH: 0-0 **Tight: 2-2** Gall: 0-0
Aids: Bl: 0-0 Vi: 0-0 Tstrap: 0-0 Ckp: 0-0
Best Rating: **109** 9/09 Wolv 7f32y stand

Smart; stays 7f; acts on testing ground, goes on Polytrack.

Lean Burn (USA)

86(82) (40)**56**

3-y-o b g Johannesburg (USA)-Anthelion (USA) (Stop The Music (USA))

A G Newcombe C S Pike

Placings:500 **(7278)**

2009: 7^{5}GS, 8^{0}GS, 9^{0}SD,

	Starts	1st	2nd	3rd	Win & Pl
Career Total (Turf)	2	0	0	0	0
Career Total (AW)	1	0	0	0	

Going (Turf): **Sf: 0-0 GS: 0-2 Gd: 0-0 GF: 0-0 Fm: 0-0**
Distance: 5f/6f: 0-0 7f-8f: 0-1 9f-13f: 0-2 14f+: 0-0
Track : LH: 0-1 RH: 0-1 Tight: 0-2 Gall: 0-0
Aids: Bl: 0-0 Vi: 0-0 Tstrap: 0-0 Ckp: 0-0
Best Rating: **56** 10/09 Wind 1m67y gd-sft

Lean Machine

95 **77**

2-y-o b c Exceed And Excel (AUS)-Al Corniche (IRE) (Bluebird (USA))

R Hannon Thurloe Thoroughbreds XXIV

Placings:2224 **(5867)**

2009: 7^{2}GF, 6^{2}S, 6^{2}G, 6^{4}G,

	Starts	1st	2nd	3rd	Win & Pl
Career Total (Turf)	4	0	3	0	4865

Going (Turf): **Sf: 0-1 GS: 0-0 Gd: 0-2 GF: 0-1 Fm: 0-0**
Distance: 5f/6f: 0-2 7f-8f: 0-2 9f-13f: 0-0 14f+: 0-0
Track : LH: 0-0 RH: 0-0 Tight: 0-0 Gall: 0-0
Aids: Bl: 0-0 Vi: 0-0 Tstrap: 0-0 Ckp: 0-0
Best Rating: **77** 8/09 NmkJ 6f good

Fair; stays 7f and acts on most ground.

Leandros (FR)

107 (102)**109**

4-y-o br g Invincible Spirit (IRE)-Logjam (IRE) (Royal Academy (USA))

G M Lyons Sean Jones

Placings:35**1**03/**16**04**521**-264001200 **(5045a)**

2009: 6^{2}G, 6^{6}G, 7^{4}G, 6^{0}GF, 7^{0}GF, 7^{1}GF, 6^{2}GF, 7^{0}G, 6^{0}SD,

	Starts	1st	2nd	3rd	Win & Pl
Career Total (Turf)	13	1	2	1	51271
Career Total (AW)	8	3	1	1	30489

109 6/09 Naas 7f G-F £12746
102 10/08 Dund 7f (60-95)H STD £7875
87 3/08 Dund 6f STD £9812
83 8/07 Dund 7f STD £7937
Total win prize-money £38372

Going (Turf): Sf: 0-1 GS: 0-0 Gd: 0-6 **GF: 1-6** Fm: 0-0
Distance: 5f/6f: 1-8 **7f-8f: 3-13** 9f-13f: 0-0 14f+: 0-0
Track : **LH: 3-15** RH: 0-1 Tight: 0-1 Gall: 0-4
Aids: **Bl: 1-5** Vi: 0-0 Tstrap: 0-1 Ckp: 0-1
Best Rating: **109** 6/09 Naas 7f gd-fm

Smart; Irish trained; stays 7f; acts on good ground and on Polytrack; sometimes blinkered.

Leap The Liffey (IRE)

(55) (61)**57**

6-y-o ch g Carrowkeel (IRE)-Golden Leap (Salmon Leap (USA))

Mrs Valerie Keatley Royal Kerry Syndicate

Placings:044/0443/00**5**0/0**506-5332400** **(7444a)**

2009: 10^{5}SD, 10^{3}GF, 8^{3}SD, 8^{2}GY, 8^{4}SD, 8^{0}SD, 8^{0}SD,

	Starts	1st	2nd	3rd	Win & Pl
Career Total (Turf)	13	0	1	2	3849
Career Total (AW)	9	0	0	1	816

Going (Turf): **Sf: 0-1 GS: 0-0 Gd: 0-3 GF: 0-5 Fm: 0-0**
Distance: 5f/6f: 0-0 7f-8f: 0-12 9f-13f: 0-10 14f+: 0-0
Track : LH: 0-11 RH: 0-7 Tight: 0-1 Gall: 0-0
Aids: Bl: 0-1 Vi: 0-0 Tstrap: 0-1 Ckp: 0-1
Best Rating: **72** 6/06 Baln 1m1f gd-fm

Modest sort; effective at mile.

Learo Dochais (USA)

94(96) (74)**76**

3-y-o b g Mutakddim (USA)-Brush With The Law (USA) (Broad Brush (USA))

M A Jarvis Mrs Lynn Mernagh

Placings:25-6513060 **(7891)**

2009: 7^{6}SD, 5^{5}GF, 7^{1}G, 7^{3}S, 8^{0}GF, 7^{6}SD, 7^{0}SD,

	Starts	1st	2nd	3rd	Win & Pl
Career Total (Turf)	4	1	0	1	2870
Career Total (AW)	5	0	1	0	1156

76 7/09 Ling 7f GD £2388
Total win prize-money £2388

Going (Turf): Sf: 0-1 GS: 0-0 **Gd: 1-1** GF: 0-2 Fm: 0-0
Distance: 5f/6f: 0-1 **7f-8f: 1-7** 9f-13f: 0-1 14f+: 0-0
Track : LH: 0-3 RH: 0-3 Tight: 0-4 Gall: 0-0
Aids: Bl: 0-0 Vi: 0-0 Tstrap: 0-0 Ckp: 0-0
Best Rating: **76** 7/09 Ling 7f good

Fair; effective over 6f-7f; acts on good ground; goes on Polytrack.

Leaving Alone (USA)

95(91) (75)**66**

2-y-o ch f Mr Greeley (USA)-Spankin' (USA) (A.P. Indy (USA))

R Hannon Malih L Al Basti

Placings:6325 **(7772)**

2009: 6^{6}S, 8^{3}SD, 8^{2}SD, 7^{5}SD,

	Starts	1st	2nd	3rd	Win & Pl
Career Total (Turf)	1	0	0	0	0
Career Total (AW)	3	0	1	1	1187

Going (Turf): Sf: 0-1 GS: 0-0 Gd: 0-0 GF: 0-0 Fm: 0-0
Distance: 5f/6f: 0-0 7f-8f: 0-4 9f-13f: 0-0 14f+: 0-0
Track : LH: 0-2 RH: 0-1 Tight: 0-2 Gall: 0-0
Aids: Bl: 0-0 Vi: 0-0 Tstrap: 0-0 Ckp: 0-0
Best Rating: **75** 12/09 Ling 1m stand

Fair; stays 1m and acts on Polytrack.

Leceile (USA)

105(91) (64)**91**
3-y-o b f Forest Camp (USA)-Summerwood (USA) (Boston Harbor (USA))
W J Haggas Brian Wallace

Placings:63-112 **(5472)**
2009: 10^{1}GS, 10^{1}G, 9^{2}GF,

	Starts	1st	2nd	3rd	Win & Pl
Career Total (Turf)	3	2	1	0	18646
Career Total (AW)	2	0	0	1	482

91 8/09 Nott 1m2f50y (0-85)H GD £6476
76 5/09 Newc 1m2f32y G-S £3561
Total win prize-money £10038

Going (Turf): Sf: 0-0 **GS: 1-1 Gd: 1-1** GF: 0-1 Fm: 0-0
Distance: 5f/6f: 0-0 7f-8f: 0-2 **9f-13f: 2-3** 14f+: 0-0
Track : **LH: 2-4** RH: 0-1 Tight: 0-3 **Gall: 1-1**
Aids: Bl: 0-0 Vi: 0-0 Tstrap: 0-0 Ckp: 0-0
Best Rating: **91** 8/09 Nott 1m2f50y good

Very useful; $160,000 purchase; stays 1m2f; acts on fast and easy ground; goes on Polytrack.

Ledgerwood

86(96) (64)**54**
4-y-o b g Royal Applause-Skies Are Blue (Unfuwain (USA))
A J Chamberlain The Runaway Boys

Placings:0003000/16255150600-00 **(3215)**
2009: 6^{0}SD, 9^{0}GF,

	Starts	1st	2nd	3rd	Win & Pl
Career Total (Turf)	11	1	0	1	2204
Career Total (AW)	9	1	1	0	2648

54 5/08 Yarm 1m1f G-F £1683
62 1/08 Ling 1m (0-60)H STD £1876
Total win prize-money £3561

Going (Turf): Sf: 0-0 GS: 0-2 Gd: 0-3 **GF: 1-5** Fm: 0-1
Distance: 5f/6f: 0-4 7f-8f: 1-6 9f-13f: 1-10 14f+: 0-0
Track : **LH: 2-14** RH: 0-3 **Tight: 2-10** Gall: 0-2
Aids: Bl: 0-1 Vi: 0-0 Tstrap: 2-8 Ckp: 2-8
Best Rating: **64** 3/08 Wolv 1m141y stand

Modest; stays 1m; acts on good ground and Polytrack.

Leelu

70(103) (66)**13**
3-y-o b f Largesse-Strat's Quest (Nicholas (USA))
D W P Arbuthnot Philip Banfield

Placings:452-000502031334 **(7591)**
2009: 8^{0}SD, 7^{0}GF, 9^{0}GF, 8^{5}SD, 10^{0}SD, 8^{2}SD, 6^{0}SD, 8^{3}SD, 7^{1}SD, 7^{3}SD, 7^{3}SD, 7^{4}SD,

	Starts	1st	2nd	3rd	Win & Pl
Career Total (Turf)	2	0	0	0	
Career Total (AW)	13	1	2	3	6063

62 10/09 Kemp 7f STD £2590
Total win prize-money £2590

Going (Turf): **Sf: 0-0 GS: 0-0 Gd: 0-0 GF: 0-2 Fm: 0-0**
Distance: 5f/6f: 0-1 **7f-8f: 1-11** 9f-13f: 0-3 14f+: 0-0
Track : LH: 0-8 **RH: 1-6** Tight: 0-7 Gall: 0-0
Aids: Bl: 0-0 Vi: 0-0 Tstrap: 0-0 Ckp: 0-0
Best Rating: **66** 12/08 Ling 7f stand

Moderate; stays 7f; acts on Polytrack.

Lees Anthem

85(87) (53)**79**
2-y-o b g Mujahid (USA)-Lady Rock (Mistertopogigo (IRE))
C J Teague A Rice

Placings:O3000400 **(7088)**
2009: 5^{0}GF, 5^{3}G, 5^{0}G, 5^{0}G, 5^{0}GF, 5^{4}SD, 5^{0}G, 6^{0}SD,

	Starts	1st	2nd	3rd	Win & Pl
Career Total (Turf)	6	0	0	1	482
Career Total (AW)	2	0	0	0	0

Going (Turf): **Sf: 0-0 GS: 0-0 Gd: 0-4 GF: 0-2 Fm: 0-0**
Distance: 5f/6f: 0-8 7f-8f: 0-0 9f-13f: 0-0 14f+: 0-0
Track : LH: 0-1 RH: 0-0 Tight: 0-0 Gall: 0-0
Aids: Bl: 0-0 Vi: 0-2 Tstrap: 0-0 Ckp: 0-0
Best Rating: **79** 4/09 Newc 5f gd-fm

Modest; suited by 5f and fast ground; has worn a visor.

LeftonthesheIf (IRE)

99(97) (85)**80**
3-y-o ch f Namid-Corryvreckan (IRE) (Night Shift (USA))
Miss T Spearing (J L Spearing 31/7) Advantage Chemicals Holdings Ltd

Placings:213334-4235003 **(7136)**
2009: 7^{4}F, 6^{2}GF, 6^{3}G, 5^{5}GF, 5^{0}G, 5^{0}GF, 5^{3}SD,

	Starts	1st	2nd	3rd	Win & Pl
Career Total (Turf)	9	1	2	2	5790
Career Total (AW)	4	0	0	3	2263

80 7/08 Yarm 5f43y G-F £2137
Total win prize-money £2137

Going (Turf): Sf: 0-0 GS: 0-0 Gd: 0-3 **GF: 1-4** Fm: 0-2
Distance: **5f/6f: 1-11** 7f-8f: 0-2 9f-13f: 0-0 14f+: 0-0
Track : LH: 0-8 RH: 0-0 Tight: 0-1 Gall: 0-5
Aids: Bl: 0-0 Vi: 0-0 Tstrap: 0-4 Ckp: 0-4
Best Rating: **85** 8/08 GrLe 5f stand

Useful; effective over 5f and acts on fast ground.

Legal Eagle (IRE)

107(104) (82)**86**
4-y-o b g Invincible Spirit (IRE)-Lupulina (CAN) (Saratoga Six (USA))
Paul Green (D Nicholls 6/6) Paul Boyers

Placings:310/450-222015033200030265 **(7269)**
2009: 5^{2}SD, 5^{2}GF, 6^{2}G, 6^{0}HY, 6^{1}GF, 6^{5}GF, 6^{0}GF, 5^{3}GF, 5^{3}G, 5^{2}S, 5^{0}GF, 6^{0}GF, 5^{0}GS, 5^{3}GF, 6^{0}GF, 5^{2}SD, 5^{6}G, 5^{5}SD,

	Starts	1st	2nd	3rd	Win & Pl
Career Total (Turf)	20	2	3	4	19232
Career Total (AW)	4	0	2	0	1542

82 6/09 Haml 6f5y G-F £2388
84 7/07 Newb 6f8y HVY £6477
Total win prize-money £8865

Going (Turf): **Sf: 1-4** GS: 0-1 Gd: 0-4 **GF: 1-11** Fm: 0-0
Distance: 5f/6f: 0-19 **7f-8f: 2-5** 9f-13f: 0-0 14f+: 0-0
Track : LH: 0-6 RH: 0-1 Tight: 0-6 Gall: 0-1
Aids: Bl: 0-1 Vi: 0-0 Tstrap: 0-0 Ckp: 0-0
Best Rating: **86** 7/09 Hayd 5f soft

Fair; effective over 6f; acts on most ground and on Polytrack.

Legal Legacy

100 **84**
3-y-o ch g Beat Hollow-Dans Delight (Machiavellian (USA))
M Dods D Vic Roper

Placings:055-4111240 **(6645)**
2009: 6^{4}GF, 7^{1}GF, 7^{1}G, 7^{1}G, 6^{2}G, 7^{4}GF, 7^{0}G,

	Starts	1st	2nd	3rd	Win & Pl
Career Total (Turf)	10	3	1	0	13279

83 6/09 Donc 7f (0-80)H GD £4857
81 6/09 Muss 7f30y (0-70)H GD £3238
71 5/09 Muss 7f30y (0-65)H G-F £2266
Total win prize-money £10362

Going (Turf): Sf: 0-1 GS: 0-1 **Gd: 2-4** GF: 1-4 Fm: 0-0
Distance: 5f/6f: 0-3 **7f-8f: 3-7** 9f-13f: 0-0 14f+: 0-0
Track : LH: 0-3 **RH: 2-3 Tight: 2-3** Gall: 0-1
Aids: Bl: 0-0 Vi: 0-0 Tstrap: 0-0 Ckp: 0-0
Best Rating: **84** 8/09 Carl 6f192y good

Useful; stays 7f; handles quick ground.

Legal Lover (IRE)

89(86) (29)**59**
7-y-o b g Woodborough (USA)-Victoria's Secret (IRE) (Law Society (USA))
R Hollinshead Tim Leadbeater

Placings:05000000**011645/444152401521022/561020/000 00** **(4376)**
2009: 7^{0}SD, 8^{0}SD, 8^{0}GF, 9^{0}F, 8^{0}SD,

	Starts	1st	2nd	3rd	Win & Pl
Career Total (Turf)	18	2	2	0	6504
Career Total (AW)	22	4	3	0	8784

68 5/07 Brig 7f214y (0-60)H GD £2849
63 11/06 Sthl 1m (0-45) STD £1945
64 9/06 Bath 1m5y G-F £2266
53 4/06 Sthl 1m (0-45) STD £1876
59 11/05 Sthl 1m (0-45) SS £1433
53 11/05 Sthl 1m (0-45) STD £1412
Total win prize-money £11785

Going (Turf): Sf: 0-0 GS: 0-3 **Gd: 1-6 GF: 1-8** Fm: 0-1
Distance: 5f/6f: 0-2 **7f-8f: 5-25** 9f-13f: 1-13 14f+: 0-0
Track : **LH: 6-34** RH: 0-2 **Tight: 1-4** Gall: 0-0
Aids: Bl: 0-0 Vi: 0-0 Tstrap: 0-1 Ckp: 0-1
Best Rating: **71** 8/07 Brig 7f214y gd-fm

Moderate; suited by a mile; acts on Fibresand and fast ground on turf.

Legend Of Greece (IRE)

87 **43**
3-y-o b g Danetime (IRE)-Lodema (IRE) (Lycius (USA))
Mrs N Smith Team Supreme

Placings:0-0046 **(6789)**
2009: 8^{0}GF, 10^{0}G, 9^{4}GF, 11^{6}G,

	Starts	1st	2nd	3rd	Win & Pl
Career Total (Turf)	5	0	0	0	0

Going (Turf): **Sf: 0-1 GS: 0-0 Gd: 0-2 GF: 0-2 Fm: 0-0**
Distance: 5f/6f: 0-0 7f-8f: 0-1 9f-13f: 0-4 14f+: 0-0
Track : LH: 0-2 RH: 0-3 Tight: 0-2 Gall: 0-0
Aids: Bl: 0-0 Vi: 0-0 Tstrap: 0-0 Ckp: 0-0
Best Rating: **43** 9/09 Folk 1m1f149y gd-fm

Legendary Guest

89(78) (17)73

4-y-o b g Bahamian Bounty-Legend Of Aragon (Aragon)

D W Barker Stef Stefanou

Placings:26410306455/01040404200-600 **(1243)**

2009: 6⁶SD, 7⁰GF, 7⁰F,

	Starts	1st	2nd	3rd	Win & Pl
Career Total (Turf)	24	2	2	1	10274
Career Total (AW)	1	0	0	0	0

71	4/08	Sthl	6f	(0-70)H	G-F	£2456
76	8/07	Rdcr	6f		GD	£1808

Total win prize-money £4266

Going (Turf): Sf: 0-3 GS: 0-1 **Gd: 1-4 GF: 1-14** Fm: 0-2
Distance: **5f/6f: 2-16** 7f-8f: 0-9 9f-13f: 0-0 14f+: 0-0
Track: **LH: 1-6** RH: 0-3 Tight: 0-5 Gall: 0-2
Aids: Bl: 0-0 Vi: 0-5 Tstrap: 0-4 Ckp: 0-4
Best Rating: 78 4/07 Newb 5f34y gd-fm

Fair; seems best over 6f; acts on good ground; has worn a visor/cheekpieces.

Legion D'Honneur (UAE)

106 79

4-y-o b g Halling (USA)-Renowned (IRE) (Darshaan)

L Lungo Len Lungo Racing Limited

Placings:03/41-35 **(2018)**

2009: 13³G, 18⁵G,

	Starts	1st	2nd	3rd	Win & Pl
Career Total (Turf)	6	1	0	2	4131

79	5/08	Haml	1m4f17y	(0-70)H	G-F	£2590

Total win prize-money £2590

Going (Turf): Sf: 0-1 GS: 0-1 Gd: 0-2 **GF: 1-2** Fm: 0-0
Distance: 5f/6f: 0-0 7f-8f: 0-1 **9f-13f: 1-3** 14f+: 0-2
Track: LH: 0-3 **RH: 1-3 Tight: 1-3** Gall: 0-1
Aids: Bl: 0-0 Vi: 0-0 Tstrap: 0-0 Ckp: 0-0
Best Rating: 79 5/08 Haml 1m4f17y gd-fm

Fair; stays 1m4f; acts on fast and on soft ground.

Legislate

109(102) (80)91

3-y-o b c Dansili-Shining Water (Kalaglow)

B W Hills K Abdulla

Placings:03-130362 **(6429)**

2009: 8¹SD, 10³GF, 10⁰S, 10³GF, 9⁶GS, 8²GF,

	Starts	1st	2nd	3rd	Win & Pl
Career Total (Turf)	7	0	1	3	6436
Career Total (AW)	1	1	0	0	4857

80	3/09	Ling	1m	STD	£4857

Total win prize-money £4857

Going (Turf): **Sf: 0-1 GS: 0-1 Gd: 0-2 GF: 0-3 Fm: 0-0**
Distance: 5f/6f: 0-0 **7f-8f: 1-4** 9f-13f: 0-4 14f+: 0-0
Track: **LH: 1-2** RH: 0-2 **Tight: 1-3** Gall: 0-1
Aids: Bl: 0-0 Vi: 0-0 Tstrap: 0-0 Ckp: 0-0
Best Rating: 91 10/09 NmkR 1m gd-fm

Useful; stays 1m2f; acts on fast ground and on Polytrack.

Legnani

81 (77)14

3-y-o b f Fasliyev (USA)-Top Sauce (Hector Protector (USA))

George Baker Orbit Performance

Placings:04500-00 **(4812)**

2009: 9⁰G, 7⁰HY,

	Starts	1st	2nd	3rd	Win & Pl
Career Total (Turf)	2	0	0	0	
Career Total (AW)	5	0	0	0	479

Going (Turf): **Sf: 0-1 GS: 0-0 Gd: 0-1 GF: 0-0 Fm: 0-0**
Distance: 5f/6f: 0-0 7f-8f: 0-6 9f-13f: 0-1 14f+: 0-0
Track: LH: 0-5 RH: 0-1 Tight: 0-1 Gall: 0-0
Aids: Bl: 0-0 Vi: 0-1 Tstrap: 0-2 Ckp: 0-2
Best Rating: 77 9/08 Dund 7f stand

Leitzu (IRE)

94(88) (64)69

2-y-o b f Barathea (IRE)-Ann's Annie (IRE) (Alzao (USA))

M R Channon Upsan Downs Racing

Placings:06145 **(6391)**

2009: 7⁰GS, 8⁶SD, 8¹G, 9⁴GF, 10⁵GF,

	Starts	1st	2nd	3rd	Win & Pl
Career Total (Turf)	4	1	0	0	4270
Career Total (AW)	1	0	0	0	0

69	8/09	Chep	1m14y	GD	£3885

Total win prize-money £3886

Going (Turf): Sf: 0-0 GS: 0-1 **Gd: 1-1** GF: 0-2 Fm: 0-0
Distance: 5f/6f: 0-0 7f-8f: 0-2 **9f-13f: 1-3** 14f+: 0-0
Track: LH: 0-1 RH: 0-2 Tight: 0-0 Gall: 0-0
Aids: Bl: 0-0 Vi: 0-0 Tstrap: 0-0 Ckp: 0-0
Best Rating: 69 8/09 Chep 1m14y good

Modest; stays 1m; acts on good ground.

Lekita

101(104) (76)77

4-y-o b f Kyllachy-Tender Moment (IRE) (Caerleon (USA))

W R Swinburn Mrs A M Richards

Placings:5/61663042-50 **(3030)**

2009: 7⁵GF, 7⁰SD,

	Starts	1st	2nd	3rd	Win & Pl
Career Total (Turf)	5	1	0	1	3529
Career Total (AW)	6	0	1	0	1011

77	6/08	Wind	6f	G-F	£2729

Total win prize-money £2730

Going (Turf): Sf: 0-1 GS: 0-1 Gd: 0-0 **GF: 1-3** Fm: 0-0
Distance: **5f/6f: 1-3** 7f-8f: 0-7 9f-13f: 0-1 14f+: 0-0
Track: LH: 0-2 RH: 0-6 Tight: 0-3 **Gall: 1-1**
Aids: Bl: 0-0 Vi: 0-0 Tstrap: 0-1 Ckp: 0-1
Best Rating: 77 6/08 Wind 6f gd-fm

Fair filly; stays 6f and acts on fast ground.

Leleyf (IRE)

94(101) (78)77

2-y-o b f Kheleyf (USA)-Titchwell Lass (Lead On Time (USA))

M R Channon Box 41

Placings:11030550061642046 **(6827)**

2009: 5¹SD, 5¹GF, 5⁰GS, 5³GF, 6⁰GF, 5⁵GF, 6⁵GF, 5⁰GS, 6⁰S, 7⁶GF, 5¹G, 6⁶G, 5⁴GF, 5²SD, 5⁰CF, 5⁴G, 5⁶SF,

	Starts	1st	2nd	3rd	Win & Pl
Career Total (Turf)	14	2	0	1	15397
Career Total (AW)	3	1	1	0	4240

77	8/09	Wwck	5f110y	(0-75)	GD	£2914
77	5/09	Sals	5f		G-F	£6799
71	3/09	Ling	5f		STD	£2729

Total win prize-money £12444

Going (Turf): Sf: 0-1 GS: 0-2 **Gd: 1-3 GF: 1-8** Fm: 0-0
Distance: **5f/6f: 3-15** 7f-8f: 0-2 9f-13f: 0-0 14f+: 0-0
Track: **LH: 2-7** RH: 0-0 **Tight: 1-6** Gall: 0-2
Aids: Bl: 0-0 Vi: 0-0 Tstrap: 0-0 Ckp: 0-0
Best Rating: 78 9/09 Wolv 5f20y stand

Fair; effective over 5f plus; acts on fast ground; goes on Polytrack.

Lemon N Sugar (USA)

108(102) (92)88

4-y-o b f Lemon Drop Kid (USA)-Altos De Chavon (USA) (Polish Numbers (USA))

J Noseda The Searchers

Placings:03/02-131141 **(6631)**

2009: 6¹SS, 6³SD, 6¹SD, 6¹G, 6⁴G, 6¹SS,

	Starts	1st	2nd	3rd	Win & Pl
Career Total (Turf)	4	1	0	0	10291
Career Total (AW)	6	3	1	2	16215

92	10/09	Ling	6f	(0-90)H	SS	£8418
88	6/09	Gdwd	6f	(0-95)H	GD	£9714
85	5/09	Ling	6f	(0-70)H	STD	£3070
80	1/09	Sthl	6f		SS	£2729

Total win prize-money £23934

Going (Turf): Sf: 0-0 GS: 0-0 **Gd: 1-4** GF: 0-0 Fm: 0-0
Distance: **5f/6f: 4-6** 7f-8f: 0-3 9f-13f: 0-1 14f+: 0-0
Track: **LH: 3-6** RH: 0-2 **Tight: 2-6** Gall: 0-0
Aids: Bl: 0-0 Vi: 0-0 Tstrap: 0-0 Ckp: 0-0
Best Rating: 92 10/09 Ling 6f std-slw

Fair; effective over 6-7f; acts on Polytrack and Fibresand.

Lend A Grand (IRE)

89(103) (79)64

5-y-o br g Lend A Hand-Grand Madam (Grand Lodge (USA))

Miss Jo Crowley Mrs Liz Nelson

Placings:0056100/000153505/6000506-2400250 **(2330)**

2009: 7²SD, 7⁴SD, 7⁰SD, 7⁰SD, 8²SD, 8⁵SD, 8⁰GF,

	Starts	1st	2nd	3rd	Win & Pl
Career Total (Turf)	17	2	0	1	10155
Career Total (AW)	13	0	2	0	1627

81	6/07	DRoy	7f	GD	£5836
77	9/06	DRoy	7f	SFT	£3812

Total win prize-money £9648

Going (Turf): **Sf: 1-3** GS: 0-0 **Gd: 1-5** GF: 0-4 Fm: 0-1
Distance: 5f/6f: 0-5 **7f-8f: 2-21** 9f-13f: 0-4 14f+: 0-0
Track: LH: 0-14 **RH: 2-11** Tight: 0-8 Gall: 0-0
Aids: **Bl: 2-12** Vi: 0-0 Tstrap: 0-0 Ckp: 0-0
Best Rating: 81 6/07 DRoy 7f good

Modest; stays 1m; acts on Polytrack.

Lend A Light

(84) (46)55

3-y-o b c Lend A Hand-No Candles Tonight (Star Appeal)

I W McInnes Skeltools Ltd

Placings:000-0 **(0667)**

2009: 7⁰SD,

	Starts	1st	2nd	3rd	Win & Pl
Career Total (Turf)	1	0	0	0	
Career Total (AW)	3	0	0	0	

Going (Turf): **Sf: 0-1 GS: 0-0 Gd: 0-0 GF: 0-0 Fm: 0-0**

Distance: 5f/6f: 0-0 7f-8f: 0-1 9f-13f: 0-3 14f+: 0-0
Track : LH: 0-4 RH: 0-0 Tight: 0-3 Gall: 0-0
Aids: Bl: 0-0 Vi: 0-0 Tstrap: 0-0 Ckp: 0-0
Best Rating: **55** 10/08 Nott 1m75y soft

Lenkiewicz

100 **76**
2-y-o gr f Oratorio (IRE)-Philadelphie (IRE) (Anabaa (USA))
B R Millman The Lenkiewicz Partnership

Placings:65530 **(6727)**
2009: 5^{6}GF, 6^{5}GF, 6^{5}S, 6^{3}G, 8^{0}S,

	Starts	1st	2nd	3rd	Win & Pl
Career Total (Turf)	5	0	0	1	24625

Going (Turf): Sf: 0-2 GS: 0-0 Gd: 0-1 GF: 0-2 Fm: 0-0
Distance: 5f/6f: 0-1 7f-8f: 0-4 9f-13f: 0-0 14f+: 0-0
Track : LH: 0-0 RH: 0-0 Tight: 0-0 Gall: 0-0
Aids: Bl: 0-0 Vi: 0-0 Tstrap: 0-0 Ckp: 0-0
Best Rating: **76** 9/09 Asct 6f110y good

Fair; stays 6f plus; acts on good ground.

Lennie Briscoe (IRE)

96(94) (52)**67**
3-y-o b g Rock Of Gibraltar (IRE)-Tammany Hall (IRE) (Petorius)
S Kirk Sylvester Kirk

Placings:00-06006360 **(6358)**
2009: 10^{0}SD, 10^{6}GF, 9^{0}G, 7^{0}GF, 7^{6}F, 7^{3}GF, 8^{6}F, 8^{0}SD,

	Starts	1st	2nd	3rd	Win & Pl
Career Total (Turf)	8	0	0	1	353
Career Total (AW)	2	0	0	0	

Going (Turf): Sf: 0-1 GS: 0-1 Gd: 0-1 GF: 0-3 Fm: 0-2
Distance: 5f/6f: 0-0 7f-8f: 0-5 9f-13f: 0-5 14f+: 0-0
Track : LH: 0-6 RH: 0-2 Tight: 0-5 Gall: 0-0
Aids: Bl: 0-1 Vi: 0-0 Tstrap: 0-0 Ckp: 0-0
Best Rating: **67** 10/08 Newb 1m soft

Modest; stays 1m2f; acts on fast ground; has worn blinkers.

Lenny Bee

105(106) (81)**89**
3-y-o gr/ro g Kyllachy-Smart Hostess (Most Welcome)
D H Brown Ron Hull

Placings:21222634136 **(6283)**
2009: 5^{2}SD, 5^{1}SD, 5^{2}SD, 6^{2}G, 5^{2}GF, 5^{6}GF, 5^{3}GF, 5^{4}G, 5^{1}GF, 5^{3}GF, 5^{6}GF,

	Starts	1st	2nd	3rd	Win & Pl
Career Total (Turf)	8	1	2	2	13033
Career Total (AW)	3	1	2	0	4803

89 8/09 NmkJ 5f (0-85)H G-F £5180
64 4/09 Kemp 5f STD £2590
Total win prize-money £7771

Going (Turf): Sf: 0-0 GS: 0-0 Gd: 0-2 **GF: 1-6** Fm: 0-0
Distance: **5f/6f: 2-11** 7f-8f: 0-0 9f-13f: 0-0 14f+: 0-0
Track : LH: 0-2 **RH: 1-2** Tight: 0-2 Gall: 0-0
Aids: Bl: 0-0 Vi: 0-0 Tstrap: 0-0 Ckp: 0-0
Best Rating: **89** 9/09 Gdwd 5f gd-fm

Useful; suited by 5f-6f; acts on fast ground and on Polytrack; likes to race prominently, but can miss the break.

Leo The Lion (IRE)

24(89) (64)
3-y-o b g Sulamani (IRE)-Sail Away (GER) (Platini (GER))
M Johnston Claire Riordan And Kieran Coughlan

Placings:3410 **(1614)**
2009: 11^{3}SD, 11^{4}SD, 12^{1}SD, 12^{0}G,

	Starts	1st	2nd	3rd	Win & Pl
Career Total (Turf)	1	0	0	0	
Career Total (AW)	3	1	0	1	3115

61 2/09 Ling 1m4f STD £2729
Total win prize-money £2730

Going (Turf): **Sf: 0-0 GS: 0-0 Gd: 0-1 GF: 0-0 Fm: 0-0**
Distance: 5f/6f: 0-0 7f-8f: 0-0 **9f-13f: 1-4** 14f+: 0-0
Track : **LH: 1-2** RH: 0-2 **Tight: 1-1** Gall: 0-0
Aids: Bl: 0-0 Vi: 0-0 Tstrap: 0-0 Ckp: 0-0
Best Rating: **64** 2/09 Kemp 1m3f stand

Fair half-brother to quite useful 6f-7f winner Shinko's Best; stays 1m4f; acts on Polytrack.

Leoballero

40 (83)**82**
9-y-o ch g Lion Cavern (USA)-Ball Gown (Jalmood (USA))
K M Prendergast M Matthews (Mid-Glamorgan)

Placings:352231/5354020/000/446/00 **(2876)**
2009: 7^{0}G, 7^{0}GF,

	Starts	1st	2nd	3rd	Win & Pl
Career Total (Turf)	16	0	3	3	10689
Career Total (AW)	5	1	0	0	2792

69 10/03 Ling 7f D STD £2383
Total win prize-money £2384

Going (Turf): **Sf: 0-1 GS: 0-1 Gd: 0-4 GF: 0-10 Fm: 0-0**
Distance: 5f/6f: 0-0 **7f-8f: 1-15** 9f-13f: 0-6 14f+: 0-0
Track : **LH: 1-7** RH: 0-5 **Tight: 1-6** Gall: 0-1
Aids: Bl: 0-1 Vi: 0-0 Tstrap: 0-1 Ckp: 0-1
Best Rating: **93** 10/04 NmkR 7f good

Leocorno (IRE)

107 **108**
3-y-o br f Pivotal-Highland Gift (IRE) (Generous (IRE))
Sir Michael Stoute Ballymacoll Stud

Placings:1-1420 **(6813)**
2009: 9^{1}GF, 12^{4}GF, 12^{2}GF, 10^{0}G,

	Starts	1st	2nd	3rd	Win & Pl
Career Total (Turf)	5	2	1	0	26626

104 5/09 Sand 1m1f (0-80)H G-F £5180
80 10/08 Donc 1m GD £5180
Total win prize-money £10362

Going (Turf): Sf: 0-0 GS: 0-0 **Gd: 1-2 GF: 1-3** Fm: 0-0
Distance: 5f/6f: 0-0 7f-8f: 1-1 9f-13f: 1-4 14f+: 0-0
Track : LH: 1-2 RH: 1-2 Tight: 0-0 **Gall: 1-3**
Aids: Bl: 0-0 Vi: 0-0 Tstrap: 0-0 Ckp: 0-0
Best Rating: **108** 8/09 York 1m4f gd-fm

Smart; Listed placed; stays 1m4f and acts on fast ground.

Leonaldo (USA)

(107) (83)**74**
4-y-o b g Silver Deputy (CAN)-Electric Talent (USA) (Capote (USA))
J R Gask Horses First Racing Limited

Placings:1165200-32450 **(5884)**
2009: 8^{3}SD, 8^{2}SD, 7^{4}SD, 8^{5}SD, 7^{0}SD,

	Starts	1st	2nd	3rd	Win & Pl
Career Total (Turf)	5	2	0	0	10662
Career Total (AW)	7	0	2	1	6414

3/08 Tarb 7f110y VS £5514
2/08 Bord 1m GD £5147
Total win prize-money £10662

Going (Turf): Sf: 0-2 GS: 0-0 **Gd: 1-2** GF: 0-0 Fm: 0-0
Distance: 5f/6f: 0-0 **7f-8f: 2-9** 9f-13f: 0-3 14f+: 0-0
Track : LH: 0-5 RH: 0-2 Tight: 0-4 Gall: 0-0
Aids: Bl: 0-0 Vi: 0-0 Tstrap: 0-1 Ckp: 0-1
Best Rating: **83** 3/09 Kemp 7f stand

Fair; effective over 7f-1m; acts on Polytrack.

Leonid Glow

105(97) (70)**82**
4-y-o b f Hunting Lion (IRE)-On Till Morning (IRE) (Never So Bold)
M Dods Mrs G C Stanley

Placings:554213214-0030354226200 **(7287)**
2009: 6^{0}GF, 7^{0}GF, 6^{3}GS, 6^{0}G, 6^{3}G, 7^{5}GF, 7^{4}GF, 7^{2}GF, 7^{2}G, 7^{6}SD, 6^{2}G, 7^{0}S, 7^{0}S,

	Starts	1st	2nd	3rd	Win & Pl
Career Total (Turf)	21	2	5	3	14529
Career Total (AW)	1	0	0	0	0

81 7/08 Ayr 6f (0-70)H GD £3885
76 6/08 Wwck 6f (0-65)H G-F £2729
Total win prize-money £6616

Going (Turf): Sf: 0-2 GS: 0-4 **Gd: 1-6 GF: 1-9** Fm: 0-0
Distance: **5f/6f: 2-12** 7f-8f: 0-10 9f-13f: 0-0 14f+: 0-0
Track : **LH: 1-8** RH: 0-1 Tight: 0-3 Gall: 0-0
Aids: Bl: 0-0 Vi: 0-0 Tstrap: 0-0 Ckp: 0-0
Best Rating: **82** 8/08 Hayd 6f gd-sft

Fair; effective over 6f-7f; acts on most ground.

Leopard Hills (IRE)

98 **66**
2-y-o b g Acclamation-Sadler's Park (USA) (Sadler's Wells (USA))
J Howard Johnson Transcend Bloodstock LLP

Placings:466 **(4187)**
2009: 6^{4}GS, 7^{6}GF, 5^{6}S,

	Starts	1st	2nd	3rd	Win & Pl
Career Total (Turf)	3	0	0	0	313

Going (Turf): **Sf: 0-1 GS: 0-1 Gd: 0-0 GF: 0-1 Fm: 0-0**
Distance: 5f/6f: 0-2 7f-8f: 0-1 9f-13f: 0-0 14f+: 0-0
Track : LH: 0-1 RH: 0-0 Tight: 0-1 Gall: 0-0
Aids: Bl: 0-0 Vi: 0-0 Tstrap: 0-0 Ckp: 0-0
Best Rating: **66** 5/09 Newc 6f gd-sft

£90,000 gelded half-brother to two winners in Greece; promise on debut over 6f on easy ground.

Leptis Magna

75(92) (59)**68**
5-y-o ch g Danehill Dancer (IRE)-Dark Eyed Lady (IRE) (Exhibitioner)
R H York (T E Powell 5/8) E George

Placings:504/10023000/0006412300-000 **(6968)**
2009: 8^{0}SD, 8^{0}SD, 7^{0}G,

	Starts	1st	2nd	3rd	Win & Pl
Career Total (Turf)	21	2	2	2	9537

	Starts	1st	2nd	3rd	Win & Pl
Career Total (AW)	4	0	0	0	

66	8/08	Yarm	1m3y	(0-65)H	GD	£1942
82	5/07	Wind	1m67y	(0-70)H	G-S	£3238

Total win prize-money £5182

Going (Turf): Sf: 0-3 **GS: 1-5 Gd: 1-5** GF: 0-7 Fm: 0-1
Distance: 5f/6f: 0-2 7f-8f: 0-14 **9f-13f: 2-9** 14f+: 0-0
Track : LH: 0-4 **RH: 1-11 Tight: 1-7** Gall: 0-0
Aids: Bl: 0-0 Vi: 0-0 Tstrap: 0-0 Ckp: 0-0
Best Rating: 82 5/07 Wind 1m67y gd-sft

Modest; effective at 1m; acts on good and easy ground.

Les Fazzani (IRE)

113(112) (107)109
5-y-o b m Intikhab (USA)-Massada (Most Welcome)
K A Ryan Dr Marwan Koukash

Placings:1/501161/0U43512-6201341 **(7589)**
2009: 10^{6}GY, 11^{2}G, 12^{0}G, 12^{1}GY, 10^{3}GS, 10^{4}S, **12^{1}SD**,

	Starts	1st	2nd	3rd	Win & Pl
Career Total (Turf)	16	4	1	2	179514
Career Total (AW)	5	3	1	0	39711

107	11/09	Kemp	1m4f		STD	£22708
109	9/09	Leop	1m4f	H	G-Y	£56883
109	11/08	Donc	1m2f60y		SFT	£26667
104	11/07	Capa	1m2f		SFT	£18919
98	7/07	York	1m208y	(0-85)H	HVY	£5181
89	7/07	Kemp	1m	(0-85)H	STD	£4728
74	12/06	Ling	1m		STD	£2590

Total win prize-money £137678

Going (Turf): Sf: 3-5 GS: 0-1 Gd: 0-6 GF: 0-0 Fm: 0-0
Distance: 5f/6f: 0-0 7f-8f: 2-3 **9f-13f: 5-18** 14f+: 0-0
Track : LH: 4-9 RH: 3-12 Tight: 1-4 **Gall: 2-4**
Aids: Bl: 0-0 Vi: 0-0 Tstrap: 0-0 Ckp: 0-0
Best Rating: 109 9/09 Leop 1m4f gd-yld

Smart; Listed winner; stays 1m4f; acts on soft ground and on Polytrack.

Lesley's Choice

94(107) (97)76
3-y-o b g Lucky Story (USA)-Wathbat Mtoto (Mtoto)
R Curtis B C Allen

Placings:236160103-5221360060620111 **(7676)**
2009: 5^{5}SD, 5^{2}SD, 5^{2}SD, 5^{1}SD, 6^{3}SD, 5^{6}SD, 5^{0}GF, 5^{0}G, 5^{6}GS, 5^{0}GS, 5^{6}F, 5^{2}SD, 6^{0}SD, 5^{1}SD, 5^{1}SD, 5^{1}SD,

	Starts	1st	2nd	3rd	Win & Pl
Career Total (Turf)	11	1	1	1	5226
Career Total (AW)	14	5	3	2	34179

97	12/09	Sthl	5f	(0-95)H	STD	£7771
92	11/09	Kemp	5f	(0-85)H	STD	£4727
93	11/09	Sthl	5f	(0-80)H	STD	£5828
84	3/09	Kemp	5f	(0-85)H	STD	£4548
76	9/08	Sand	5f6y	(0-75)	GD	£3885
76	7/08	Sthl	5f		STD	£3885

Total win prize-money £30647

Going (Turf): Sf: 0-2 GS: 0-2 **Gd: 1-2** GF: 0-4 Fm: 0-1
Distance: 5f/6f: 6-24 7f-8f: 0-1 9f-13f: 0-0 14f+: 0-0
Track : LH: 0-8 **RH: 2-4** Tight: 0-3 Gall: 0-1
Aids: Bl: 1-3 **Vi: 2-2** Tstrap: 0-1 Ckp: 0-1
Best Rating: 97 12/09 Sthl 5f stand

Very useful; effective over 5f-6f; acts on fast ground and on sand; has worn blinkers and a visor.

Leslingtaylor (IRE)

100(104) (73)76
7-y-o b g Orpen (USA)-Rite Of Spring (Niniski (USA))
J J Quinn Mrs Marie Taylor

Placings:53150/00000515150/00330411013/0020/05-544 **(5698)**
2009: 12^{5}SD, 12^{4}SD, 12^{4}GS,

	Starts	1st	2nd	3rd	Win & Pl
Career Total (Turf)	35	6	1	4	32997
Career Total (AW)	2	0	0	0	216

85	10/06	York	1m4f	(60-92)H	SFT	£5829
81	9/06	Hayd	1m3f200y	(0-75)H	HVY	£5505
72	8/06	Leic	1m3f183y	(0-70)H	GD	£5505
73	10/05	Catt	1m3f214y	(0-75)H	G-F	£3554
66	9/05	Pont	1m2f6y	(0-60)H	G-S	£3684
70	9/04	Catt	5f212y		FRM	£4212

Total win prize-money £28290

Going (Turf): Sf: 2-8 GS: 1-10 Gd: 1-10 GF: 1-6 Fm: 1-1
Distance: 5f/6f: 1-6 7f-8f: 0-3 **9f-13f: 5-24** 14f+: 0-4
Track : LH: 5-28 RH: 1-4 **Tight: 2-11** Gall: 1-9
Aids: Bl: 0-0 Vi: 0-0 Tstrap: 0-0 Ckp: 0-0
Best Rating: 85 10/06 York 1m4f soft

Fair; stays 1m4f; acts on any ground.

Lesoto Diamond (IRE)

104(95) (79)79
7-y-o b m Darnay Fallon (IRE) (Arcane (USA))
P A Fahy M Foley

Placings:0040/0351600550-4610060546 **(7701)**
2009: 10^{4}SD, 16^{6}G, 12^{1}GF, 13^{0}GF, 12^{0}GY, 10^{6}GY, 12^{0}GY, 12^{5}SD, 10^{4}SD, 16^{5}SD,

	Starts	1st	2nd	3rd	Win & Pl
Career Total (Turf)	16	2	0	1	13924
Career Total (AW)	8	0	0	0	1654

76	6/09	Fair	1m4f	(50-80)H	G-F	£7044
73	6/08	Leop	1m6f		GD	£6097

Total win prize-money £13141

Going (Turf): Sf: 0-1 GS: 0-0 **Gd: 1-5 GF: 1-3** Fm: 0-1
Distance: 5f/6f: 0-0 7f-8f: 0-1 9f-13f: 1-16 14f+: 1-7
Track : LH: 1-13 RH: 1-9 Tight: 0-0 Gall: 0-0
Aids: Bl: 0-0 Vi: 0-0 Tstrap: 0-0 Ckp: 0-0
Best Rating: 79 11/09 Dund 1m2f150y stand

Lessing (FR)

104 (99)106
4-y-o b f Orpen (USA)-Lady Morgane (IRE) (Medaaly)
X-Thomas Demeaulte (X Nakkachdji 20/2) Prime Equestrian

Placings:1521/13065-200152
2009: 7^{2}GS, 7^{0}GF, 6^{0}GF, 7^{1}VS, 7^{5}G, 8^{2}G,

	Starts	1st	2nd	3rd	Win & Pl
Career Total (Turf)	12	2	3	1	58793
Career Total (AW)	3	2	0	0	23599

95	5/09	MsnL	7f	VS	£12621
99	3/08	Deau	6f110y	STD	£20221
	11/07	Madr	7f	GD	£8108
	6/07	Madr	5f110y	STD	£3378

Total win prize-money £44328

Going (Turf): Sf: 0-1 GS: 0-2 **Gd: 1-5** GF: 0-2 Fm: 0-0
Distance: 5f/6f: 1-2 **7f-8f: 3-13** 9f-13f: 0-0 14f+: 0-0
Track : LH: 0-3 RH: 0-4 Tight: 0-0 Gall: 0-3
Aids: Bl: 0-0 Vi: 0-0 Tstrap: 0-0 Ckp: 0-0
Best Rating: 106 4/08 Lonc 1m heavy

Smart filly; effectivc at sprint trips.

Lesson In Humility (IRE)

116 115
4-y-o b f Mujadil (USA)-Vanity (IRE) (Thatching)
A P Jarvis (K R Burke 10/7) M Nelmes-Crocker

Placings:1244/5212116-113234 **(5493a)**
2009: 6^{1}F, 6^{1}GF, 6^{3}GF, 6^{2}G, 6^{3}GS, 6^{4}G,

	Starts	1st	2nd	3rd	Win & Pl
Career Total (Turf)	17	6	4	2	249669

109	6/09	Leop	6f		G-F	£41019
112	5/09	Nott	6f15y		FRM	£23704
110	9/08	Gdwd	6f		SFT	£24978
109	7/08	York	6f	(0-105)H	G-F	£31155
97	5/08	Donc	6f	(0-95)	GD	£11656
65	7/07	Carl	5f		G-F	£2817

Total win prize-money £135331

Going (Turf): Sf: 1-2 GS: 0-2 Gd: 1-5 **GF: 3-7** Fm: 1-1
Distance: 5f/6f: 5-14 7f-8f: 1-3 9f-13f: 0-0 14f+: 0-0
Track : LH: 1-3 RH: 1-2 Tight: 0-0 **Gall: 1-1**
Aids: Bl: 0-0 Vi: 0-0 Tstrap: 0-0 Ckp: 0-0
Best Rating: 115 7/09 York 6f good

Smart; winner in Group 3 company and Group 1 placed; effective at 6f-7f; consistent sort; acts on any ground.

Let It Rock (IRE)

68 52
2-y-o b f Noverre (USA)-Green Life (Green Desert (USA))
K R Burke Mrs Elaine M Burke

Placings:0 **(1841)**
2009: 5^{0}GF,

	Starts	1st	2nd	3rd	Win & Pl
Career Total (Turf)	1	0	0	0	

Going (Turf): Sf: 0-0 GS: 0-0 Gd: 0-0 GF: 0-1 Fm: 0-0
Distance: 5f/6f: 0-1 7f-8f: 0-0 9f-13f: 0-0 14f+: 0-0
Track : LH: 0-0 RH: 0-0 Tight: 0-0 Gall: 0-0
Aids: Bl: 0-0 Vi: 0-0 Tstrap: 0-0 Ckp: 0-0
Best Rating: 52 5/09 Nott 5f13y gd-fm

Related to several juvenile winners; showed some ability on debut.

Let Them Eat Cake

76(87) (52)29
2-y-o b f Danehill Dancer (IRE)-Lady Adnil (IRE) (Stravinsky (USA))
R A Fahey Netherfield House Stud

Placings:603 **(6874)**
2009: 7^{6}GF, 8^{0}SD, 7^{3}SD,

	Starts	1st	2nd	3rd	Win & Pl
Career Total (Turf)	1	0	0	0	0
Career Total (AW)	2	0	0	1	578

Going (Turf): Sf: 0-0 GS: 0-0 Gd: 0-0 GF: 0-1 Fm: 0-0
Distance: 5f/6f: 0-0 7f-8f: 0-2 9f-13f: 0-1 14f+: 0-0
Track : LH: 0-3 RH: 0-0 Tight: 0-2 Gall: 0-0
Aids: Bl: 0-0 Vi: 0-0 Tstrap: 0-0 Ckp: 0-0
Best Rating: 52 10/09 Wolv 1m141y stand

Lethal

103(106) (71)**78**

6-y-o ch g Nashwan (USA)-Ipanema Beach (Lion Cavern (USA))

M J Scudamore (Andrew Reid 26/10) A S Reid

Placings:0431/013130300000/40542252450146-316611606502254321 6 **(7738)**

2009: 6^{3}SS, 7^{1}SD, 6^{6}SD, 5^{6}SD, 6^{1}SD, 6^{1}G, 7^{6}SD, 7^{0}GS, 7^{6}SD, 5^{5}F, 6^{0}GF, 6^{2}SD, 6^{2}SD, 7^{5}SD, 5^{4}SD, 6^{3}SD, 6^{2}SD, 6^{1}SD, 6^{6}SD,

	Starts	1st	2nd	3rd	Win & Pl
Career Total (Turf)	17	2	1	2	7098
Career Total (AW)	32	6	5	4	27560

71 11/09 Kemp 6f STD £1706
75 4/09 Yarm 6f3y GD £1942
63 3/09 Sthl 6f (0-60) STD £2047
64 1/09 Sthl 7f STD £2047
61 7/08 Catt 5f212y G-F £2047
96 3/07 Kemp 7f (0-85)H STD £4728
91 1/07 Kemp 6f (0-80)H STD £4728
85 12/06 Ling 6f (0-70)H STD £3238
Total win prize-money £22485

Going (Turf): Sf: 0-1 GS: 0-1 **Gd: 1-7 GF: 1-7** Fm: 0-1
Distance: **5f/6f: 5-35** 7f-8f: 3-14 9f-13f: 0-0 14f+: 0-0
Track : **LH: 4-24** RH: 3-12 **Tight: 2-13** Gall: 0-3
Aids: Bl: 0-0 Vi: 0-0 Tstrap: 0-0 Ckp: 0-0
Best Rating: **96** 3/07 Kemp 7f stand

Modest; suited by 5f-7f; acts on good ground and on sand; has worn an eyeshield.

Lethal Combination (USA)

101(94) (76)**84**

2-y-o b g Broken Vow (USA)-Yard (USA) (Boundary (USA))

W J Haggas Findlay & Bloom

Placings:03161 **(6067)**

2009: 6^{0}G, 7^{3}G, 7^{1}SD, 8^{6}GF, 9^{1}GF,

	Starts	1st	2nd	3rd	Win & Pl
Career Total (Turf)	4	1	0	1	6042
Career Total (AW)	1	1	0	0	3238

84 9/09 NmkR 1m1f (0-85)H G-F £5180
76 8/09 Ling 7f STD £3238
Total win prize-money £8419

Going (Turf): Sf: 0-0 GS: 0-0 Gd: 0-2 **GF: 1-2** Fm: 0-0
Distance: 5f/6f: 0-1 7f-8f: 1-2 9f-13f: 1-2 14f+: 0-0
Track : **LH: 1-2** RH: 0-0 **Tight: 1-2** Gall: 0-0
Aids: Bl: 0-0 Vi: 0-0 Tstrap: 0-0 Ckp: 0-0
Best Rating: **84** 9/09 NmkR 1m1f gd-fm

Fair; stays 7f and acts on Polytrack.

Lethal Glaze (IRE)

109(107) (100)**96**

3-y-o gr g Verglas (IRE)-Sticky Green (Lion Cavern (USA))

R Hannon Nigel Morris

Placings:00411-10511005 **(7151)**

2009: 11^{1}G, 16^{0}GF, 11^{5}GF, 14^{1}S, 12^{1}SD, 14^{0}G, 12^{0}GS, 16^{5}G,

	Starts	1st	2nd	3rd	Win & Pl
Career Total (Turf)	12	4	0	0	17702
Career Total (AW)	1	1	0	0	7353

100 8/09 Kemp 1m4f (0-95)H STD £7352
94 7/09 Hayd 1m6f (0-85)H SFT £5504
86 5/09 Wind 1m3f135y (0-80)H GD £4857
82 10/08 Nott 1m2f50y (0-75) SFT £3238
70 9/08 Gdwd 1m (0-85)H SFT £3885
Total win prize-money £24839

Going (Turf): **Sf: 3-3** GS: 0-2 Gd: 1-5 GF: 0-2 Fm: 0-0
Distance: 5f/6f: 0-1 7f-8f: 1-3 **9f-13f: 3-5** 14f+: 1-4
Track : LH: 2-4 RH: 2-5 **Tight: 1-1** Gall: 0-4
Aids: Bl: 0-0 Vi: 0-0 Tstrap: 0-0 Ckp: 0-0
Best Rating: **100** 8/09 Kemp 1m4f stand

Very useful; stays 1m6f; acts on good and soft ground; also handles Polytrack.

Letham Island (IRE)

53 (44)**77**

5-y-o b m Trans Island-Common Cause (Polish Patriot (USA))

R M Stronge Tim Whiting

Placings:4221/230006/0 **(4301)**

2009: 16^{0}G,

	Starts	1st	2nd	3rd	Win & Pl
Career Total (Turf)	7	0	1	1	2191
Career Total (AW)	4	1	2	0	5337

57 12/06 Sthl 1m STD £3238
Total win prize-money £3239

Going (Turf): **Sf: 0-0 GS: 0-3 Gd: 0-2 GF: 0-2 Fm: 0-0**
Distance: 5f/6f: 0-0 **7f-8f: 1-4** 9f-13f: 0-5 14f+: 0-2
Track : **LH: 1-6** RH: 0-5 Tight: 0-5 Gall: 0-1
Aids: Bl: 0-0 Vi: 0-0 Tstrap: 0-1 Ckp: 0-1
Best Rating: **77** 4/07 Bevl 1m1f207y gd-fm

Lets Get Cracking (FR)

(83) (51)**70**

5-y-o b h Anabaa Blue-Queenhood (FR) (Linamix (FR))

A E Jones BPD Ltd

Placings:63510/0/0 **(0017)**

2009: 8^{0}SD,

	Starts	1st	2nd	3rd	Win & Pl
Career Total (Turf)	5	0	0	1	578
Career Total (AW)	2	1	0	0	2730

72 10/06 Wolv 1m1f103y SF £2730
Total win prize-money £2730

Going (Turf): **Sf: 0-2 GS: 0-3 Gd: 0-0 GF: 0-0 Fm: 0-0**
Distance: 5f/6f: 0-0 7f-8f: 0-3 **9f-13f: 1-4** 14f+: 0-0
Track : **LH: 1-5** RH: 0-2 **Tight: 1-4** Gall: 0-2
Aids: Bl: 0-0 Vi: 0-0 Tstrap: 0-0 Ckp: 0-0
Best Rating: **72** 10/06 Wolv 1m1f103y std-fst

Lets Move It

(86) (46)

2-y-o b c Piccolo-Park Star (Gothenberg (IRE))

D Shaw Mrs Lyndsey Shaw

Placings:00030 **(7871)**

2009: 5^{0}SD, 5^{0}SD, 5^{0}SF, 5^{3}SD, 5^{0}SD,

	Starts	1st	2nd	3rd	Win & Pl
Career Total (Turf)	0	0	0	0	
Career Total (AW)	5	0	0	1	302

Going (Turf): **Sf: 0-0 GS: 0-0 Gd: 0-0 GF: 0-0 Fm: 0-0**
Distance: 5f/6f: 0-5 7f-8f: 0-0 9f-13f: 0-0 14f+: 0-0
Track : LH: 0-3 RH: 0-1 Tight: 0-3 Gall: 0-0
Aids: Bl: 0-0 Vi: 0-3 Tstrap: 0-0 Ckp: 0-0
Best Rating: **46** 11/09 Wolv 5f20y std-fst

Moderate; suited by 5f and acts on Fibresand.

Lets Roll

105 **83**

8-y-o b g Tamure (IRE)-Miss Petronella (Petoski)

C W Thornton A Crute and Partners

Placings:02251/2622311524/0341035106/6523203051504/2636060424/0000206-0052556505 **(7124)**

2009: 14^{0}GF, 14^{0}GF, 14^{5}GF, 16^{2}GF, 16^{5}GF, 14^{5}G, 16^{6}GS, 17^{5}G, 16^{0}GS, 16^{5}G,

	Starts	1st	2nd	3rd	Win & Pl
Career Total (Turf)	65	6	12	6	104565

97 9/06 Ayr 1m5f13y (0-90)H G-S £11658
96 9/05 Ayr 1m5f13y (0-85)H GD £8346
89 6/05 Ayr 1m5f13y (0-95)H G-S £9376
87 7/04 Ripn 1m4f60yD(0-85)H SFT £13780
80 7/04 Rdcr 1m3f D(0-80)H SFT £14365
68 10/03 Newc 7f F GD £2219
Total win prize-money £59746

Going (Turf): **Sf: 2-13 GS: 2-18 Gd: 2-19** GF: 0-15 Fm: 0-0
Distance: 5f/6f: 0-2 7f-8f: 1-5 9f-13f: 2-20 **14f+: 3-38**
Track : **LH: 4-28** RH: 1-31 **Tight: 2-19** Gall: 0-21
Aids: Bl: 0-0 Vi: 0-0 Tstrap: 0-0 Ckp: 0-0
Best Rating: **97** 9/06 Ayr 1m5f13y gd-sft

Fair; stays 1m6f; acts on most types of ground, but well suited by soft.

Leulahleulahlay

95(100) (75)**75**

3-y-o ch g Dr Fong (USA)-Fidelio's Miracle (USA) (Mountain Cat (USA))

Evan Williams (M Johnston 3/8) Mad Vic Partnership

Placings:5-4235 **(7873)**

2009: 11^{4}SD, 12^{2}G, 12^{3}SD, 16^{5}SD,

	Starts	1st	2nd	3rd	Win & Pl
Career Total (Turf)	1	0	1	0	867
Career Total (AW)	4	0	0	1	495

Going (Turf): **Sf: 0-0 GS: 0-0 Gd: 0-1 GF: 0-0 Fm: 0-0**
Distance: 5f/6f: 0-0 7f-8f: 0-1 9f-13f: 0-3 14f+: 0-1
Track : LH: 0-0 RH: 0-5 Tight: 0-1 Gall: 0-0
Aids: Bl: 0-0 Vi: 0-0 Tstrap: 0-1 Ckp: 0-1
Best Rating: **75** 8/09 Ripn 1m4f10y good

Fair; effective on Polytrack; best at around 1m4f; has worn cheekpieces.

Leverage (IRE)

104(100) (81)**89**

3-y-o b c Xaar-She Looks On High (USA) (Secreto (USA))

L M Cumani Ron Levi & Stuart Roden

Placings:21204 **(7027)**

2009: 6^{2}G, 6^{1}GF, 6^{2}GF, 7^{0}SD, 7^{4}SD,

	Starts	1st	2nd	3rd	Win & Pl
Career Total (Turf)	3	1	2	0	8334
Career Total (AW)	2	0	0	0	351

79 7/09 Newb 6f8y G-F £5828
Total win prize-money £5828

Going (Turf): Sf: 0-0 GS: 0-0 Gd: 0-1 **GF: 1-2** Fm: 0-0
Distance: 5f/6f: 0-2 **7f-8f: 1-3** 9f-13f: 0-0 14f+: 0-0
Track : LH: 0-1 RH: 0-2 Tight: 0-0 Gall: 0-0
Aids: Bl: 0-0 Vi: 0-0 Tstrap: 0-0 Ckp: 0-0
Best Rating: **89** 10/09 Wwck 6f gd-fm

Useful; stays 7f; acts on Polytrack and on fast ground.

Leviathan

99 90

2-y-o b c Dubawi (IRE)-Gipsy Moth (Efisio)
T P Tate Paul Moulton

Placings:15301 (7013)
2009: 6^{1}GF, 6^{5}GF, 7^{3}GS, 7^{0}GS, 7^{1}GS,

	Starts	1st	2nd	3rd	Win & Pl
Career Total (Turf)	5	2	0	1	15018
90 10/09 Donc 7f				G-S	£9714
77 6/09 Haml 6f5y				G-F	£4533

Total win prize-money £14247

Going (Turf): Sf: 0-0 **GS: 1-3** Gd: 0-0 **GF: 1-2** Fm: 0-0
Distance: 5f/6f: 0-1 **7f-8f: 2-4** 9f-13f: 0-0 14f+: 0-0
Track : LH: 0-1 RH: 0-0 Tight: 0-0 Gall: 0-1
Aids: Bl: 0-0 Vi: 0-0 Tstrap: 0-0 Ckp: 0-0
Best Rating: **90** 10/09 Donc 7f gd-sft

Useful; stays 7f and acts on most ground.

Levitation (IRE)

103(102) (67)73

3-y-o b f Vettori (IRE)-Uplifting (Magic Ring (IRE))
W S Kittow Philip Gibbs

Placings:0-6200**641** (7863)
2009: 8^{6}G, 8^{2}GF, 10^{0}S, 8^{0}GF, **10**^{6}SD, **8**^{4}SD, **8**^{1}SD,

	Starts	1st	2nd	3rd	Win & Pl
Career Total (Turf)	5	0	1	0	1156
Career Total (AW)	3	1	0	0	2730
12/09 Wolv 1m141y				STD	£2729

Total win prize-money £2730

Going (Turf): **Sf: 0-1 GS: 0-1 Gd: 0-1 GF: 0-2 Fm: 0-0**
Distance: 5f/6f: 0-0 7f-8f: 0-3 **9f-13f: 1-5** 14f+: 0-0
Track : **LH: 1-3** RH: 0-1 **Tight: 1-2** Gall: 0-1
Aids: Bl: 0-0 Vi: 0-0 Tstrap: 0-0 Ckp: 0-0
Best Rating: **73** 6/09 Sals 1m gd-fm

Fair; stays 1m; acts on Polytrack.

Lewyn

91(99) (72)65

2-y-o b f Exceed And Excel (AUS)-Panoramic View (Polar Falcon (USA))
K A Ryan N Cable & M Smith

Placings:0342**31**0**00** (7372)
2009: 5^{0}GF, 5^{3}G, 5^{4}GF, 5^{2}GF, **5**^{3}SD, **5**^{1}SF, 5^{0}GS, **5**^{0}SD, **5**^{0}SD,

	Starts	1st	2nd	3rd	Win & Pl
Career Total (Turf)	5	0	1	1	1454
Career Total (AW)	4	1	0	1	4390
72 10/09 Wolv 5f20y (0-85)				SF	£3885

Total win prize-money £3886

Going (Turf): **Sf: 0-0 GS: 0-1 Gd: 0-1 GF: 0-3 Fm: 0-0**
Distance: **5f/6f: 1-9** 7f-8f: 0-0 9f-13f: 0-0 14f+: 0-0
Track : **LH: 1-3** RH: 0-0 **Tight: 1-3** Gall: 0-0
Aids: Bl: 0-2 Vi: 0-1 Tstrap: 0-0 Ckp: 0-0
Best Rating: **72** 10/09 Wolv 5f20y std-fst

Modest; suited by 5f and good ground; has worn blinkers.

Lexi's Layla (IRE)

88(93) (64)68

2-y-o ch f Kheleyf (USA)-Woodstamp (IRE) (Woodborough (USA))
D M Simcock Dr Marwan Koukash

Placings:2203 (6971)
2009: 5^{2}S, 5^{2}HY, 5^{0}G, 5^{3}SD,

	Starts	1st	2nd	3rd	Win & Pl
Career Total (Turf)	3	0	2	0	1869
Career Total (AW)	1	0	0	1	385

Going (Turf): **Sf: 0-2 GS: 0-0 Gd: 0-1 GF: 0-0 Fm: 0-0**
Distance: 5f/6f: 0-4 7f-8f: 0-0 9f-13f: 0-0 14f+: 0-0
Track : LH: 0-1 RH: 0-1 Tight: 0-0 Gall: 0-1
Aids: Bl: 0-0 Vi: 0-0 Tstrap: 0-0 Ckp: 0-0
Best Rating: **68** 7/09 Leic 5f218y soft

Modest sprint maiden; best at 5f on soft ground.

Lexlenos (IRE)

(97) (80)105

3-y-o ch f Intikhab (USA)-Blazing Glory (IRE) (Glow (USA))
Patrick Gallagher (D R C Elsworth 14/1) Frank Scardino and Alex Solis II

Placings:121-26330 (0158)
2009: 7^{2}SD, 8^{6}F, 9^{3}F, 10^{3}F, 9^{0}F,

	Starts	1st	2nd	3rd	Win & Pl
Career Total (Turf)	4	0	0	2	70833
Career Total (AW)	4	2	2	0	8727
73 12/08 Kemp 7f (0-75)				STD	£2047
65 11/08 Kemp 6f				STD	£3885

Total win prize-money £5933

Going (Turf): **Sf: 0-0 GS: 0-0 Gd: 0-0 GF: 0-0 Fm: 0-4**
Distance: 5f/6f: 1-1 7f-8f: 1-4 9f-13f: 0-3 14f+: 0-0
Track : LH: 0-4 **RH: 2-3** Tight: 0-1 Gall: 0-0
Aids: Bl: 0-0 Vi: 0-0 Tstrap: 0-0 Ckp: 0-0
Best Rating: **105** 7/09 Holl 1m2f firm

Useful; stays 7f and acts on Polytrack.

Leyte Gulf (USA)

99(105) (70)61

6-y-o b g Cozzene (USA)-Gabacha (USA) (Woodman (USA))
C C Bealby Robert Jenkinson

Placings:0323**4**0564/3450145/**54**23**20**22300-05**1**01**25123** (7675)
2009: **14**^{0}SD, 16^{5}G, 14^{1}G, 16^{0}GS, **13**^{1}SD, **13**^{2}SD, **13**^{5}SD, **13**^{1}SD, 13^{2}SD, **14**^{3}SD,

	Starts	1st	2nd	3rd	Win & Pl
Career Total (Turf)	19	2	1	3	19034
Career Total (AW)	18	2	6	3	13789
66 11/09 Wolv 1m5f194y (0-60)H				STD	£2388
66 9/09 Wolv 1m5f194y (0-60)H				STD	£2047
61 8/09 Hayd 1m6f (0-70)H				GD	£3238
5/07 Bord 1m1f110y				SFT	£3378

Total win prize-money £11051

Going (Turf): **Sf: 1-6** GS: 0-3 **Gd: 1-6** GF: 0-0 Fm: 0-0
Distance: 5f/6f: 0-0 7f-8f: 0-1 9f-13f: 1-18 **14f+: 3-18**
Track : **LH: 3-18** RH: 0-7 **Tight: 2-8** Gall: 0-1
Aids: Bl: 0-0 Vi: 0-0 Tstrap: 0-0 Ckp: 0-0
Best Rating: **83** 6/06 Lonc 1m2f good

Modest; probably best at around 1m4f-1m5f; acts on good and softer ground; goes on sand.

Lhashan

55(81) (39)

3-y-o b f Green Desert (USA)-Society Lady (USA) (Mr Prospector (USA))
M A Jarvis Sheikh Ahmed Al Maktoum

Placings:00 (5882)
2009: 7^{0}G, 5^{0}SD,

	Starts	1st	2nd	3rd	Win & Pl
Career Total (Turf)	1	0	0	0	
Career Total (AW)	1	0	0	0	

Going (Turf): **Sf: 0-0 GS: 0-0 Gd: 0-1 GF: 0-0 Fm: 0-0**
Distance: 5f/6f: 0-1 7f-8f: 0-1 9f-13f: 0-0 14f+: 0-0
Track : LH: 0-1 RH: 0-0 Tight: 0-1 Gall: 0-0
Aids: Bl: 0-0 Vi: 0-0 Tstrap: 0-0 Ckp: 0-0
Best Rating: **39** 9/09 Wolv 5f216y stand

Libel Law

111 111

3-y-o ch c Kingmambo (USA)-Innuendo (IRE) (Caerleon (USA))
M A Jarvis Sheikh Ahmed Al Maktoum

Placings:4-1621 (4781)
2009: 10^{1}GF, 10^{6}GF, 9^{2}GF, 10^{1}G,

	Starts	1st	2nd	3rd	Win & Pl
Career Total (Turf)	5	2	1	0	46802
111 8/09 Hayd 1m2f95y (0-105)H				GD	£40501
89 4/09 Wind 1m2f7y				G-F	£2729

Total win prize-money £43232

Going (Turf): Sf: 0-0 GS: 0-1 **Gd: 1-1 GF: 1-3** Fm: 0-0
Distance: 5f/6f: 0-0 7f-8f: 0-1 **9f-13f: 2-4** 14f+: 0-0
Track : LH: 1-2 RH: 1-2 **Tight: 1-2** Gall: 0-0
Aids: Bl: 0-0 Vi: 0-0 Tstrap: 0-0 Ckp: 0-0
Best Rating: **111** 8/09 Hayd 1m2f95y good

Very useful; stays 1m2f and acts on fast ground.

Liberally (IRE)

105(90) (53)87

4-y-o b f Statue Of Liberty (USA)-Specifically (USA) (Sky Classic (CAN))
B J Meehan Andrew Rosen

Placings:002611-64106 (6618)
2009: 10^{6}S, 9^{4}GS, 10^{1}G, 10^{0}GS, 10^{6}G,

	Starts	1st	2nd	3rd	Win & Pl
Career Total (Turf)	10	3	1	0	12213
Career Total (AW)	1	0	0	0	
87 7/09 Nott 1m2f50y (0-80)H				GD	£5504
81 8/08 Ling 1m2f (0-75)H				GD	£2590
81 8/08 Bath 1m5y (0-70)H				G-S	£2914

Total win prize-money £11009

Going (Turf): Sf: 0-1 GS: 1-3 **Gd: 2-4** GF: 0-2 Fm: 0-0
Distance: 5f/6f: 0-0 7f-8f: 0-0 **9f-13f: 3-11** 14f+: 0-0
Track : **LH: 3-7** RH: 0-3 **Tight: 2-4** Gall: 0-2
Aids: Bl: 0-0 Vi: 0-0 Tstrap: 0-0 Ckp: 0-0
Best Rating: **87** 7/09 Nott 1m2f50y good

Useful; effective over 1m-1m2f; acts on good ground.

Liberate

74 (88)93

6-y-o ch g Lomitas-Eversince (USA) (Foolish Pleasure (USA))
P J Hobbs Mrs Diana L Whateley

Placings:000/412122113/30-0 (2994)
2009: 20^{0}GF,

	Starts	1st	2nd	3rd	Win & Pl
Career Total (Turf)	12	3	2	2	21491
Career Total (AW)	3	1	1	0	4009
94 7/06 Ling 1m3f106y (0-75)H				G-F	£3238
88 7/06 Ling 2m (0-75)H				STD	£3238
75 6/06 Haml 1m3f16y (0-60)H				G-F	£3071

67 5/06 Bevl 1m4f16y (0-70)H GD £3562
Total win prize-money £13111

Going (Turf): Sf: 0-2 GS: 0-0 Gd: 1-2 **GF: 2-8** Fm: 0-0
Distance: 5f/6f: 0-0 7f-8f: 0-3 **9f-13f: 3-5** 14f+: 1-7
Track : LH: 2-5 RH: 2-8 **Tight: 4-7** Gall: 0-4
Aids: Bl: 0-0 Vi: 0-0 Tstrap: 0-2 Ckp: 0-2
Best Rating: 94 7/06 Ling 1m3f106y gd-fm

Useful; stays 2m4f and acts on fast ground; has worn cheekpieces; likes to race prominently; winning hurdler.

Liberation (IRE)

104 **108**

3-y-o b c Refuse To Bend (IRE)-Mosaique Bleue (Shirley Heights)
Saeed Bin Suroor Godolphin

Placings:3114-206 **(7185)**
2009: 7²G, 10⁰GF, 8⁶G,

	Starts	1st	2nd	3rd	Win & Pl
Career Total (Turf)	7	2	1	1	81706

108 9/08 Asct 7f GD £6854
80 9/08 Brig 6f209y SFT £3885
Total win prize-money £10740

Going (Turf): **Sf: 1-1** GS: 0-0 **Gd: 1-4** GF: 0-2 Fm: 0-0
Distance: 5f/6f: 0-0 **7f-8f: 2-6** 9f-13f: 0-1 14f+: 0-0
Track : **LH: 1-2** RH: 0-1 Tight: 0-0 Gall: 0-1
Aids: Bl: 0-0 Vi: 0-0 Tstrap: 0-0 Ckp: 0-0
Best Rating: 108 9/08 Asct 7f good

Smart; suited by 7f; acts on fast and soft ground.

Libertino (IRE)

88(86) (67)**69**

2-y-o ch c Bertolini (USA)-Villafranca (IRE) (In The Wings)
B J Meehan The Chain Gang

Placings:524 **(7430)**
2009: 6⁵GF, 6²GF, 7⁴SD,

	Starts	1st	2nd	3rd	Win & Pl
Career Total (Turf)	2	0	1	0	1253
Career Total (AW)	1	0	0	0	313

Going (Turf): Sf: 0-0 GS: 0-0 Gd: 0-0 GF: 0-2 Fm: 0-0
Distance: 5f/6f: 0-2 7f-8f: 0-1 9f-13f: 0-0 14f+: 0-0
Track : LH: 0-1 RH: 0-1 Tight: 0-0 Gall: 0-0
Aids: Bl: 0-0 Vi: 0-0 Tstrap: 0-0 Ckp: 0-0
Best Rating: 69 10/09 Wwck 6f gd-fm

Modest; effective over 6f; acts on fast ground.

Liberty Beau (IRE)

(97) (59)

3-y-o b g Statue Of Liberty (USA)-La Shalak (IRE) (Shalford (IRE))
D R C Elsworth D R C Elsworth

Placings:550-3 **(0205)**
2009: 10³SD,

	Starts	1st	2nd	3rd	Win & Pl
Career Total (Turf)	0	0	0	0	
Career Total (AW)	4	0	0	1	302

Going (Turf): Sf: 0-0 GS: 0-0 Gd: 0-0 GF: 0-0 Fm: 0-0
Distance: 5f/6f: 0-0 7f-8f: 0-2 9f-13f: 0-2 14f+: 0-0
Track : LH: 0-3 RH: 0-1 Tight: 0-2 Gall: 0-1
Aids: Bl: 0-0 Vi: 0-0 Tstrap: 0-0 Ckp: 0-0
Best Rating: 59 12/08 Kemp 1m2f stand

Moderate; stays 1m2f and acts on Polytrack.

Liberty Diamond

86 **72**

3-y-o br f Needwood Blade-Take Liberties (Warning)
K R Burke David and Nicola Leggate

Placings:522-00 **(2028)**
2009: 6⁰GF, 6⁰GF,

	Starts	1st	2nd	3rd	Win & Pl
Career Total (Turf)	5	0	2	0	2023

Going (Turf): Sf: 0-3 GS: 0-0 Gd: 0-0 GF: 0-2 Fm: 0-0
Distance: 5f/6f: 0-4 7f-8f: 0-1 9f-13f: 0-0 14f+: 0-0
Track : LH: 0-0 RH: 0-0 Tight: 0-0 Gall: 0-0
Aids: Bl: 0-0 Vi: 0-0 Tstrap: 0-0 Ckp: 0-0
Best Rating: 72 9/08 Hayd 6f heavy

Modest; effective over 6f; acts on testing ground.

Liberty Estelle (IRE)

77(73) (19)**17**

3-y-o gr f Statue Of Liberty (USA)-Bella Estella (GER) (Sternkoenig (IRE))
P D Evans Andrew Longman

Placings:U0-00 **(1793)**
2009: 7⁰SD, 10⁰GF,

	Starts	1st	2nd	3rd	Win & Pl
Career Total (Turf)	3	0	0	0	
Career Total (AW)	1	0	0	0	

Going (Turf): Sf: 0-2 GS: 0-0 Gd: 0-0 GF: 0-1 Fm: 0-0
Distance: 5f/6f: 0-0 7f-8f: 0-3 9f-13f: 0-1 14f+: 0-0
Track : LH: 0-2 RH: 0-0 Tight: 0-2 Gall: 0-0
Aids: Bl: 0-0 Vi: 0-0 Tstrap: 0-0 Ckp: 0-0
Best Rating: 19 4/09 Wolv 7f32y stand

Liberty Island (IRE)

(98) (80)**63**

4-y-o b g Statue Of Liberty (USA)-Birthday (IRE) (Singspiel (IRE))
W McCreery Iona Equine Syndicate

Placings:60/5000-02313415120 **(7566a)**
2009: 6⁰SD, 5²SD, 5³SD, 5¹GF, 5³G, 5⁴G, 5¹SD, 6⁵SD, 5¹SD, 5²SD, 6⁰SD,

	Starts	1st	2nd	3rd	Win & Pl
Career Total (Turf)	7	1	0	1	5477
Career Total (AW)	10	2	2	1	14261

80 10/09 Wolv 5f20y (0-70)H STD £3238
71 7/09 Dund 5f (50-80)H STD £7379
61 6/09 DRoy 5f (47-65)H G-F £4696
Total win prize-money £15314

Going (Turf): Sf: 0-1 GS: 0-0 Gd: 0-4 **GF: 1-2** Fm: 0-0
Distance: **5f/6f: 3-16** 7f-8f: 0-1 9f-13f: 0-0 14f+: 0-0
Track : **LH: 2-13** RH: 1-2 **Tight: 1-1** Gall: 0-0
Aids: Bl: 0-2 Vi: 0-0 Tstrap: 0-0 Ckp: 0-0
Best Rating: 80 10/09 Dund 5f stand

Fair; suited by 5f; acts on fast ground and on Polytrack; has worn blinkers.

Liberty Lady (IRE)

(93) (62)

2-y-o b f Statue Of Liberty (USA)-Crossed Wire (Lycius (USA))
D Donovan Mark Jones

Placings:226 **(7736)**
2009: 5²SD, 5²SF, 6⁶SD,

	Starts	1st	2nd	3rd	Win & Pl
Career Total (Turf)	0	0	0	0	
Career Total (AW)	3	0	2	0	1734

Going (Turf): Sf: 0-0 GS: 0-0 Gd: 0-0 GF: 0-0 Fm: 0-0
Distance: 5f/6f: 0-3 7f-8f: 0-0 9f-13f: 0-0 14f+: 0-0
Track : LH: 0-1 RH: 0-2 Tight: 0-1 Gall: 0-0
Aids: Bl: 0-0 Vi: 0-0 Tstrap: 0-0 Ckp: 0-0
Best Rating: 62 9/09 Kemp 5f stand

Modest; effective at 5f; acts on Polytrack.

Liberty Lodge (IRE)

(65) **19**

3-y-o b g Statue Of Liberty (USA)-Lady Justice (Compton Place)
G A Swinbank G H Bell

Placings:6-5P **(1950)**
2009: 11⁵SD, 7ᴾGF,

	Starts	1st	2nd	3rd	Win & Pl
Career Total (Turf)	2	0	0	0	0
Career Total (AW)	1	0	0	0	0

Going (Turf): Sf: 0-0 GS: 0-0 Gd: 0-1 GF: 0-1 Fm: 0-0
Distance: 5f/6f: 0-1 7f-8f: 0-1 9f-13f: 0-1 14f+: 0-0
Track : LH: 0-1 RH: 0-2 Tight: 0-0 Gall: 0-1
Aids: Bl: 0-0 Vi: 0-0 Tstrap: 0-0 Ckp: 0-0
Best Rating: 19 8/08 Carl 5f good

Liberty Power (IRE)

66 **12**

2-y-o b g Statue Of Liberty (USA)-Shaydeylaydeh (IRE) (Shaddad (USA))
Garry Moss Brooklands Racing

Placings:6 **(3634)**
2009: 5⁶G,

	Starts	1st	2nd	3rd	Win & Pl
Career Total (Turf)	1	0	0	0	0

Going (Turf): Sf: 0-0 GS: 0-0 Gd: 0-1 GF: 0-0 Fm: 0-0
Distance: 5f/6f: 0-1 7f-8f: 0-0 9f-13f: 0-0 14f+: 0-0
Track : LH: 0-0 RH: 0-0 Tight: 0-0 Gall: 0-0
Aids: Bl: 0-0 Vi: 0-0 Tstrap: 0-0 Ckp: 0-0
Best Rating: 12 7/09 Nott 5f13y good

Liberty Seeker (FR)

91(86) (36)**42**

10-y-o ch g Machiavellian (USA)-Samara (IRE) (Polish Patriot (USA))
John A Harris Mrs A E Harris

Placings:033/0000/002/24105/134/000-00 (3486)
2009: 12^{0}GS, 16^{0}G,

	Starts	1st	2nd	3rd	Win & Pl
Career Total (Turf)	19	2	2	2	11522
Career Total (AW)	4	0	0	1	541

73 4/06 Catt 1m7f177y (0-65)H G-S £2730
71 8/05 Ayr 1m2f (0-75)H G-F £3631
Total win prize-money £6362

Going (Turf): Sf: 0-3 **GS: 1-5** Gd: 0-3 **GF: 1-8** Fm: 0-0
Distance: 5f/6f: 0-0 7f-8f: 0-1 9f-13f: 1-16 14f+: 1-6
Track : **LH: 2-17** RH: 0-5 **Tight: 1-9** Gall: 0-4
Aids: Bl: 0-0 Vi: 0-0 Tstrap: 0-2 Ckp: 0-2
Best Rating: 79 10/02 Newb 1m2f6y soft

Liberty Ship

105(102) (66)**77**
4-y-o b g Statue Of Liberty (USA)-Flag (Selkirk (USA))
J D Bethell M W Territt

Placings:3225/53425-36215222 (3607)
2009: 5^{3}SD, 5^{6}SD, 5^{2}GF, 5^{1}GF, 5^{5}G, 5^{2}GF, 5^{2}GS, 5^{2}GF,

	Starts	1st	2nd	3rd	Win & Pl
Career Total (Turf)	12	1	6	2	9914
Career Total (AW)	5	0	1	1	1073

74 5/09 Catt 5f (0-70)H G-F £3070
Total win prize-money £3071

Going (Turf): Sf: 0-0 GS: 0-3 Gd: 0-2 **GF: 1-6** Fm: 0-1
Distance: **5f/6f: 1-16** 7f-8f: 0-1 9f-13f: 0-0 14f+: 0-0
Track : LH: 0-3 RH: 0-2 Tight: 0-3 Gall: 0-2
Aids: **Bl: 1-5** Vi: 0-0 Tstrap: 0-3 Ckp: 0-3
Best Rating: 77 6/09 Ripn 5f gd-sft

Modest; suited by 5f; acts on most ground and on Fibresand; has worn a tongue tie, cheekpieces and blinkers.

Liberty Square (USA)

96 **67**
2-y-o ch c Street Cry (IRE)-Gracious Hope (USA) (Rahy (USA))
Saeed Bin Suroor Godolphin

Placings:044 (6930)
2009: 7^{0}GF, 8^{4}GS, 8^{4}G,

	Starts	1st	2nd	3rd	Win & Pl
Career Total (Turf)	3	0	0	0	385

Going (Turf): **Sf: 0-0 GS: 0-1 Gd: 0-1 GF: 0-1 Fm: 0-0**
Distance: 5f/6f: 0-0 7f-8f: 0-1 9f-13f: 0-2 14f+: 0-0
Track : LH: 0-2 RH: 0-0 Tight: 0-1 Gall: 0-0
Aids: Bl: 0-0 Vi: 0-0 Tstrap: 0-0 Ckp: 0-0
Best Rating: 67 10/09 Bath 1m5y good

Liberty Trail (IRE)

98(97) (70)**74**
3-y-o b g Statue Of Liberty (USA)-Karinski (USA) (Palace Music (USA))
I Semple G L S Partnership

Placings:026-2023021651006 (7496)
2009: 7^{2}GF, 7^{0}G, 7^{2}G, 8^{3}GF, 7^{0}G, 6^{2}GF, 6^{1}HY, 6^{6}G, 6^{5}GF, 7^{1}GF, 7^{0}S, 7^{0}SD, 5^{6}SD,

	Starts	1st	2nd	3rd	Win & Pl
Career Total (Turf)	14	2	4	1	10094
Career Total (AW)	2	0	0	0	0

74 10/09 Rdcr 7f (0-70)H G-F £2590
65 8/09 Haml 6f5y HVY £2590
Total win prize-money £5180

Going (Turf): **Sf: 1-3** GS: 0-0 Gd: 0-6 **GF: 1-5** Fm: 0-0
Distance: 5f/6f: 0-6 **7f-8f: 2-9** 9f-13f: 0-1 14f+: 0-0
Track : LH: 0-4 RH: 0-4 Tight: 0-6 Gall: 0-0
Aids: Bl: 0-1 Vi: 0-0 Tstrap: 0-1 Ckp: 0-1
Best Rating: 74 10/09 Rdcr 7f gd-fm

Modest; effective over 6-7f; acts on most ground.

Liberty Valance (IRE)

(105) (71)**67**
4-y-o b g Statue Of Liberty (USA)-Tabdea (USA) (Topsider (USA))
P M Phelan (S Kirk 27/2) P Wheatley

Placings:53/1206540340000-523050 (3269)
2009: 7^{5}SD, 7^{2}SD, 7^{3}SD, 7^{0}SD, 6^{5}SD, 8^{0}SD,

	Starts	1st	2nd	3rd	Win & Pl
Career Total (Turf)	3	0	0	1	482
Career Total (AW)	18	1	2	2	4787

74 2/08 Ling 7f STD £2331
Total win prize-money £2332

Going (Turf): **Sf: 0-0 GS: 0-0 Gd: 0-0 GF: 0-3 Fm: 0-0**
Distance: 5f/6f: 0-8 **7f-8f: 1-12** 9f-13f: 0-1 14f+: 0-0
Track : **LH: 1-11** RH: 0-7 **Tight: 1-10** Gall: 0-0
Aids: Bl: 0-0 Vi: 0-0 Tstrap: 0-0 Ckp: 0-0
Best Rating: 79 2/08 Kemp 6f stand

Moderate; effective over 7f; acts on Polytrack; has worn a tongue-tie.

Libre

96(101) (56)**67**
9-y-o b g Bahamian Bounty-Premier Blues (FR) (I aw Society (USA))
F Jordan On The Up Partnership

Placings:60502220/000231040140/05400010001121/402 2332256501/06022440430300/004224120O/50034041622 060-0053500625003026 (7857)
2009: 9^{0}GF, 8^{0}GF, 8^{5}GF, 7^{3}G, 8^{5}G, 8^{0}GF, 8^{0}G, 8^{6}G, 8^{2}GS, 9^{5}SD, 10^{0}SD, 9^{0}SD, 9^{3}SD, 9^{0}SD, 8^{2}SD, 9^{6}SD,

	Starts	1st	2nd	3rd	Win & Pl
Career Total (Turf)	74	5	13	7	41372
Career Total (AW)	27	4	5	1	17608

64 7/08 Chep 1m14y (0-70)H SFT £3238
69 9/07 Chep 1m14y (0-65)H G-F £2590
62 12/05 Ling 1m2f STD £2893
80 12/04 Wolv 1m141y (0-77)H STD £4089
67 12/04 Wolv 1m1f103y (0-62)H STD £2942
69 11/04 Wolv 7f32y (0-62)H STD £2952
62 6/04 Bevl 7f100y E(0-75)H GD £4719
78 9/03 Bath 1m5y E(0-75)H FRM £2856
71 5/03 Ayr 1m1f20y E(0-70) G-S £4186
Total win prize-money £30469

Going (Turf): **Sf: 1-10GS: 1-11Gd: 1-23GF: 1-27Fm: 1-3**
Distance: 5f/6f: 0-2 7f-8f: 2-20 **9f-13f: 7-79** 14f+: 0-0
Track : **LH: 6-64** RH: 1-15 **Tight: 5-37** Gall: 0-5
Aids: Bl: 1-7 Vi: 0-0 Tstrap: 1-13 Ckp: 1-13
Best Rating: 83 6/05 Wwck 1m22y gd-fm

Moderate; effective at around 1m-1m2f; acts on most ground and on Polytrack.

Licence To Till (USA)

95(99) (82)**68**
2-y-o b c War Chant (USA)-With A Wink (USA) (Clever Trick (USA))
M Johnston The Vine Accord

Placings:032313 (7846)
2009: 5^{0}GF, 5^{3}S, 5^{2}GF, 5^{3}GF, 7^{1}SD, 7^{3}SD,

	Starts	1st	2nd	3rd	Win & Pl
Career Total (Turf)	4	0	1	2	3246
Career Total (AW)	2	1	0	1	4411

82 12/09 Ling 7f STD £3561
Total win prize-money £3562

Going (Turf): **Sf: 0-1 GS: 0-0 Gd: 0-0 GF: 0-3 Fm: 0-0**
Distance: 5f/6f: 0-4 **7f-8f: 1-2** 9f-13f: 0-0 14f+: 0-0
Track : **LH: 1-4** RH: 0-0 **Tight: 1-3** Gall: 0-0
Aids: Bl: 0-0 Vi: 0-0 Tstrap: 0-0 Ckp: 0-0
Best Rating: 82 12/09 Wolv 7f32y stand

Useful; stays 7f and acts on Polytrack.

Liebelei (USA)

81(82) (35)**46**
2-y-o b/br f Royal Academy (USA)-Part With Pride (USA) (Executive Pride)
H J L Dunlop William Armitage

Placings:000 (6931)
2009: 7^{0}G, 7^{0}SD, 8^{0}G,

	Starts	1st	2nd	3rd	Win & Pl
Career Total (Turf)	2	0	0	0	
Career Total (AW)	1	0	0	0	

Going (Turf): **Sf: 0-0 GS: 0-0 Gd: 0-2 GF: 0-0 Fm: 0-0**
Distance: 5f/6f: 0-0 7f-8f: 0-2 9f-13f: 0-1 14f+: 0-0
Track : LH: 0-2 RH: 0-0 Tight: 0-2 Gall: 0-0
Aids: Bl: 0-0 Vi: 0-0 Tstrap: 0-0 Ckp: 0-0
Best Rating: 46 7/09 Donc 7f good

Lieu Day Louie (IRE)

95 **64**
2-y-o b g Bahamian Bounty-Nebraska Lady (IRE) (Lujain (USA))
N Wilson Hogans Bar Flies

Placings:02045 (7115)
2009: 5^{0}G, 5^{2}G, 5^{0}GF, 6^{4}G, 5^{5}GS,

	Starts	1st	2nd	3rd	Win & Pl
Career Total (Turf)	5	0	1	0	1300

Going (Turf): **Sf: 0-0 GS: 0-1 Gd: 0-3 GF: 0-1 Fm: 0-0**
Distance: 5f/6f: 0-5 7f-8f: 0-0 9f-13f: 0-0 14f+: 0-0
Track : LH: 0-0 RH: 0-0 Tight: 0-0 Gall: 0-0
Aids: Bl: 0-0 Vi: 0-0 Tstrap: 0-0 Ckp: 0-0
Best Rating: 64 8/09 Bevl 5f good

Lieutenant Pigeon

(108) (80)**73**
4-y-o ch g Captain Rio-Blue Velvet (Formidable (USA))
Paul Mason P A Mason

Placings:1060025/1102266000-0606 (4203)

2009: 6[0]SD, 6[6]SD, 5[0]SD, 6[6]SD,

	Starts	1st	2nd	3rd	Win & Pl
Career Total (Turf)	10	1	2	0	5598
Career Total (AW)	11	2	1	0	6303

77	3/08	Kemp	6f	(0-75)H	STD	£2457
80	3/08	Sthl	6f	(0-70)H	STD	£2593
73	5/07	Haml	5f4y		GD	£3886

Total win prize-money £8937

Going (Turf): Sf: 0-2 GS: 0-2 **Gd: 1-3** GF: 0-3 Fm: 0-0
Distance: **5f/6f: 3-20** 7f-8f: 0-1 9f-13f: 0-0 14f+: 0-0
Track : LH: 1-12 RH: 1-3 Tight: 0-6 Gall: 0-1
Aids: Bl: 0-2 Vi: 0-0 Tstrap: 0-0 Ckp: 0-0
Best Rating: **80** 6/08 Kemp 6f stand

Fair; effective over 6f, acts on good and easy ground; also goes Fibresand and Polytrack.

Life And Soul (IRE)

91(94) (72)75

2-y-o b c Azamour (IRE)-Way For Life (GER) (Platini (GER))
Mrs A J Perrett A D Spence

Placings:022 (7064)
2009: 7[0]G, 8[2]GS, 8[2]SD,

	Starts	1st	2nd	3rd	Win & Pl
Career Total (Turf)	2	0	1	0	867
Career Total (AW)	1	0	1	0	806

Going (Turf): **Sf: 0-0 GS: 0-1 Gd: 0-1 GF: 0-0 Fm: 0-0**
Distance: 5f/6f: 0-0 7f-8f: 0-2 9f-13f: 0-1 14f+: 0-0
Track : LH: 0-2 RH: 0-1 Tight: 0-1 Gall: 0-0
Aids: Bl: 0-0 Vi: 0-0 Tstrap: 0-0 Ckp: 0-0
Best Rating: **75** 10/09 Nott 1m75y gd-sft

Fair; effective over 1m; acts on easy ground.

Life's Challenge (USA)

100(97) (72)82

3-y-o ch f Mr Greeley (USA)-Danse Du Diable (IRE) (Sadler's Wells (USA))
M Johnston Sheikh Hamdan Bin Mohammed Al Maktoum

Placings:1300 (7769)
2009: 8[1]GF, 10[3]GF, 8[0]SD, 8[0]SD,

	Starts	1st	2nd	3rd	Win & Pl
Career Total (Turf)	2	1	0	1	5579
Career Total (AW)	2	0	0	0	

78	8/09	Pont	1m4y	G-F	£4857

Total win prize-money £4857

Going (Turf): Sf: 0-0 GS: 0-0 Gd: 0-0 **GF: 1-2** Fm: 0-0
Distance: 5f/6f: 0-0 7f-8f: 0-2 **9f-13f: 1-2** 14f+: 0-0
Track : **LH: 1-2** RH: 0-2 Tight: 0-0 Gall: 0-0
Aids: Bl: 0-0 Vi: 0-0 Tstrap: 0-0 Ckp: 0-0
Best Rating: **82** 9/09 Sand 1m2f7y gd-fm

Fair; stays 1m2f; acts on fast ground.

Lifetime Endeavour

90 33

5-y-o b g Aragon-Musical Star (Music Boy)
R E Barr D Thomson

Placings:000-00000 (3123)
2009: 5[0]GF, 6[0]G, 6[0]F, 7[0]GF, 10[0]GF,

	Starts	1st	2nd	3rd	Win & Pl
Career Total (Turf)	8	0	0	0	

Going (Turf): **Sf: 0-0 GS: 0-2 Gd: 0-2 GF: 0-3 Fm: 0-1**
Distance: 5f/6f: 0-5 7f-8f: 0-2 9f-13f: 0-1 14f+: 0-0
Track : LH: 0-3 RH: 0-0 Tight: 0-3 Gall: 0-0
Aids: Bl: 0-0 Vi: 0-0 Tstrap: 0-0 Ckp: 0-0
Best Rating: **33** 4/09 Catt 5f212y gd-fm

Light Dubai (IRE)

98(87) (68)77

3-y-o b f Fantastic Light (USA)-Seeking A Way (USA) (Seeking The Gold (USA))
M R Channon Mrs M Findlay

Placings:6-2320544 (4166)
2009: 10[2]SD, 10[3]GS, 9[2]GF, 9[0]F, 12[5]G, 9[4]G, 10[4]G,

	Starts	1st	2nd	3rd	Win & Pl
Career Total (Turf)	7	0	1	1	3086
Career Total (AW)	1	0	1	0	1445

Going (Turf): **Sf: 0-0 GS: 0-1 Gd: 0-4 GF: 0-1 Fm: 0-1**
Distance: 5f/6f: 0-0 7f-8f: 0-1 9f-13f: 0-7 14f+: 0-0
Track : LH: 0-3 RH: 0-4 Tight: 0-5 Gall: 0-2
Aids: Bl: 0-0 Vi: 0-0 Tstrap: 0-0 Ckp: 0-0
Best Rating: **77** 4/09 Newb 1m2f6y gd-sft

Modest; effective at 1m2f; acts on fast and easy ground, and Polytrack.

Light From Mars

109 106

4-y-o gr g Fantastic Light (USA)-Hylandra (USA) (Bering)
B R Millman R K Arrowsmith

Placings:331106-120033216 (7019)
2009: 8[1]G, 8[2]G, 8[0]G, 8[0]GF, 7[3]G, 8[3]GF, 8[2]GF, 7[1]G, 7[6]GS,

	Starts	1st	2nd	3rd	Win & Pl
Career Total (Turf)	15	4	2	4	34572

106	10/09	York	7f	(0-100)H	GD	£11656
92	4/09	Wind	1m67y	(0-85)H	GD	£5180
88	7/08	Sand	1m14y	(0-80)H	G-F	£5828
81	6/08	Chep	1m14y		G-F	£2590

Total win prize-money £25256

Going (Turf): Sf: 0-1 GS: 0-3 **Gd: 2-5 GF: 2-6** Fm: 0-0
Distance: 5f/6f: 0-0 7f-8f: 1-5 **9f-13f: 3-10** 14f+: 0-0
Track : LH: 1-3 **RH: 2-6** Tight: 1-1 Gall: 1-1
Aids: Bl: 0-0 Vi: 0-0 Tstrap: 0-0 Ckp: 0-0
Best Rating: **106** 10/09 York 7f good

Very useful; effective at 1m; acts on fast ground.

Light Nights (IRE)

71(56) 38

2-y-o b f Acclamation-Grecian Grail (IRE) (Rainbow Quest (USA))
T D Easterby Habton Farms

Placings:060 (7419)
2009: 7[0]GF, 5[6]S, 7[0]SD,

	Starts	1st	2nd	3rd	Win & Pl
Career Total (Turf)	2	0	0	0	0
Career Total (AW)	1	0	0	0	

Going (Turf): **Sf: 0-1 GS: 0-0 Gd: 0-0 GF: 0-1 Fm: 0-0**
Distance: 5f/6f: 0-1 7f-8f: 0-2 9f-13f: 0-0 14f+: 0-0
Track : LH: 0-2 RH: 0-1 Tight: 0-1 Gall: 0-0
Aids: Bl: 0-0 Vi: 0-0 Tstrap: 0-0 Ckp: 0-0
Best Rating: **38** 8/09 Bevl 7f100y gd-fm

Light Sleeper

92(98) (71)75

3-y-o b c Kyllachy-Snoozy (Cadeaux Genereux)
P W Chapple-Hyam J C Fretwell

Placings:2-435 (7610)
2009: 8[4]G, 7[3]SD, 7[5]SD,

	Starts	1st	2nd	3rd	Win & Pl
Career Total (Turf)	2	0	1	0	1397
Career Total (AW)	2	0	0	1	353

Going (Turf): **Sf: 0-1 GS: 0-0 Gd: 0-1 GF: 0-0 Fm: 0-0**
Distance: 5f/6f: 0-0 7f-8f: 0-3 9f-13f: 0-1 14f+: 0-0
Track : LH: 0-3 RH: 0-1 Tight: 0-1 Gall: 0-0
Aids: Bl: 0-0 Vi: 0-0 Tstrap: 0-0 Ckp: 0-0
Best Rating: **75** 6/09 Hayd 1m30y good

Fair; effective over 7f; acts on soft ground and on Polytrack.

Light The City (IRE)

73 29

2-y-o b g Fantastic Light (USA)-Marine City (JPN) (Carnegie (IRE))
C E Brittain Saif Ali

Placings:6 (6033)
2009: 8[6]GF,

	Starts	1st	2nd	3rd	Win & Pl
Career Total (Turf)	1	0	0	0	0

Going (Turf): **Sf: 0-0 GS: 0-0 Gd: 0-0 GF: 0-1 Fm: 0-0**
Distance: 5f/6f: 0-0 7f-8f: 0-0 9f-13f: 0-1 14f+: 0-0
Track : LH: 0-0 RH: 0-0 Tight: 0-0 Gall: 0-0
Aids: Bl: 0-0 Vi: 0-0 Tstrap: 0-0 Ckp: 0-0
Best Rating: **29** 9/09 Yarm 1m3y gd-fm

Light The Light (IRE)

65(90) (55)

4-y-o ch f King Charlemagne (USA)-Saana (IRE) (Erins Isle)
M D Squance (Rae Guest 28/1) Richard T Golding

Placings:43-600 (2806)
2009: 7[6]SD, 7[0]SD, 6[0]G,

	Starts	1st	2nd	3rd	Win & Pl
Career Total (Turf)	1	0	0	0	
Career Total (AW)	4	0	0	1	674

Going (Turf): **Sf: 0-0 GS: 0-0 Gd: 0-1 GF: 0-0 Fm: 0-0**
Distance: 5f/6f: 0-1 7f-8f: 0-4 9f-13f: 0-0 14f+: 0-0
Track : LH: 0-4 RH: 0-1 Tight: 0-1 Gall: 0-2
Aids: Bl: 0-0 Vi: 0-1 Tstrap: 0-0 Ckp: 0-0
Best Rating: **55** 12/08 GrLe 1m stand

Light The Way

86(89) (54)54

2-y-o b c Fantastic Light (USA)-Monteleone (IRE) (Montjeu (IRE))

P J Makin J Malins

Placings:050630 (7698)
2009: 6⁰GF, 6⁵F, 6⁰GF, 7⁶SD, 6³SD, 5⁰SD,

	Starts	1st	2nd	3rd	Win & Pl
Career Total (Turf)	3	0	0	0	141
Career Total (AW)	3	0	0	1	385

Going (Turf): **Sf: 0-0 GS: 0-0 Gd: 0-0 GF: 0-2 Fm: 0-1**
Distance: 5f/6f: 0-2 7f-8f: 0-4 9f-13f: 0-0 14f+: 0-0
Track : LH: 0-3 RH: 0-2 Tight: 0-1 Gall: 0-0
Aids: Bl: 0-2 Vi: 0-0 Tstrap: 0-0 Ckp: 0-0
Best Rating: **54** 10/09 Ling 7f stand

Modest; effective over 6f; acts on Polytrack.

Lighterman

65 **25**
2-y-o ch g Firebreak-Manuka Too (IRE) (First Trump)
E J Alston Brian Chambers

Placings:000 (4557)
2009: 6⁰G, 7⁰GS, 7⁰G,

	Starts	1st	2nd	3rd	Win & Pl
Career Total (Turf)	3	0	0	0	

Going (Turf): **Sf: 0-0 GS: 0-1 Gd: 0-2 GF: 0-0 Fm: 0-0**
Distance: 5f/6f: 0-1 7f-8f: 0-2 9f-13f: 0-0 14f+: 0-0
Track : LH: 0-1 RH: 0-0 Tight: 0-1 Gall: 0-0
Aids: Bl: 0-0 Vi: 0-0 Tstrap: 0-0 Ckp: 0-0
Best Rating: **25** 7/09 Newc 7f gd-sft

Lighthearted (FR)

101(94) (68)**68**
3-y-o ch f Fantastic Light (USA)-My Heart's Deelite (USA) (Afternoon Deelites (USA))
C G Cox H E Sheikh Sultan Bin Khalifa Al Nahyan

Placings:00-241600 (3387)
2009: 6²SD, 6⁴SD, 7¹GF, 8⁶G, 7⁰SD, 7⁰GF,

	Starts	1st	2nd	3rd	Win & Pl
Career Total (Turf)	5	1	0	0	4857
Career Total (AW)	3	0	1	0	1599

68 5/09 Ling 7f (0-70)H G-F £4857
Total win prize-money £4857

Going (Turf): Sf: 0-1 GS: 0-1 Gd: 0-1 **GF: 1-2** Fm: 0-0
Distance: 5f/6f: 0-2 **7f-8f: 1-6** 9f-13f: 0-0 14f+: 0-0
Track : LH: 0-0 RH: 0-4 Tight: 0-0 Gall: 0-0
Aids: Bl: 0-0 Vi: 0-0 Tstrap: 0-0 Ckp: 0-0
Best Rating: **68** 5/09 Ling 7f gd-fm

Modest; stays 7f; acts on fast ground and on Polytrack.

Like For Like (IRE)

94(91) (66)**72**
3-y-o ch f Kheleyf (USA)-Just Like Annie (IRE) (Mujadil (USA))
R J Hodges Richard Prince

Placings:33323512-054026000 (7427)
2009: 5⁰GF, 5⁵F, 6⁴GS, 8⁰F, 7²GF, 5⁶G, 8⁰GS, 5⁰G, 5⁰SD,

	Starts	1st	2nd	3rd	Win & Pl
Career Total (Turf)	15	1	3	3	5414
Career Total (AW)	2	0	0	1	385

58 8/08 Bath 5f11y G-S £1942
Total win prize-money £1943

Going (Turf): Sf: 0-0 **GS: 1-3** Gd: 0-4 GF: 0-6 Fm: 0-2
Distance: **5f/6f: 1-14** 7f-8f: 0-1 9f-13f: 0-2 14f+: 0-0
Track : **LH: 1-10** RH: 0-2 Tight: 0-3 **Gall: 1-8**
Aids: Bl: 0-0 Vi: 0-0 Tstrap: 0-0 Ckp: 0-0
Best Rating: **72** 6/08 Bath 5f161y good

Modest; effective over 5f; acts on fast and easy ground.

Lilac Moon (GER)

99(104) (67)**71**
5-y-o b m Dr Fong (USA)-Luna De Miel (Shareef Dancer (USA))
Tom Dascombe (N J Vaughan 20/6) A Black

Placings:0/66413320/0111-04530 (7699)
2009: 10⁰SD, 10⁴G, 10⁵GF, 12³SD, 10⁰SD,

	Starts	1st	2nd	3rd	Win & Pl
Career Total (Turf)	10	3	0	0	9621
Career Total (AW)	8	1	1	3	4378

71	8/08	NmkJ	1m2f	(0-70)H	GD	£3885
67	7/08	Donc	1m4f	(0-75)H	G-F	£3238
67	7/08	Ling	1m2f	(0-55)H	STD	£2590
57	8/07	Carl	7f200y		FRM	£2047

Total win prize-money £11762

Going (Turf): Sf: 0-0 GS: 0-0 **Gd: 1-4 GF: 1-5 Fm: 1-1**
Distance: 5f/6f: 0-1 7f-8f: 1-4 **9f-13f: 3-13** 14f+: 0-0
Track : LH: 2-11 RH: 2-6 Tight: 1-8 **Gall: 2-2**
Aids: Bl: 0-0 Vi: 0-0 Tstrap: 0-0 Ckp: 0-0
Best Rating: **71** 8/08 NmkJ 1m2f good

Modest; effective at 1m2f-1m4f; acts on good and faster ground; goes on Polytrack.

Lilac Wine

93(98) (54)**45**
6-y-o ch m Dancing Spree (USA)-Stay With Me Baby (Nicholas Bill)
D J S Ffrench Davis G H Black

Placings:5-050466 (5579)
2009: 12⁰SD, 12⁵SD, 17⁰GS, 16⁴SD, 14⁶G, 16⁶GF,

	Starts	1st	2nd	3rd	Win & Pl
Career Total (Turf)	3	0	0	0	0
Career Total (AW)	4	0	0	0	0

Going (Turf): **Sf: 0-0 GS: 0-1 Gd: 0-1 GF: 0-1 Fm: 0-0**
Distance: 5f/6f: 0-0 7f-8f: 0-0 9f-13f: 0-3 14f+: 0-4
Track : LH: 0-4 RH: 0-3 Tight: 0-5 Gall: 0-0
Aids: Bl: 0-1 Vi: 0-1 Tstrap: 0-1 Ckp: 0-1
Best Rating: **54** 9/08 Kemp 1m4f stand

Lileo (IRE)

89 **64**
2-y-o b g Galileo (IRE)-Jabali (FR) (Shirley Heights)
L M Cumani Tsega Horses

Placings:4 (7096)
2009: 7⁴G,

	Starts	1st	2nd	3rd	Win & Pl
Career Total (Turf)	1	0	0	0	297

Going (Turf): **Sf: 0-0 GS: 0-0 Gd: 0-1 GF: 0-0 Fm: 0-0**
Distance: 5f/6f: 0-0 7f-8f: 0-1 9f-13f: 0-0 14f+: 0-0
Track : LH: 0-0 RH: 0-0 Tight: 0-0 Gall: 0-0
Aids: Bl: 0-0 Vi: 0-0 Tstrap: 0-0 Ckp: 0-0
Best Rating: **64** 10/09 Yarm 7f3y good

Lilleput

88(83) (19)**47**
4-y-o b f High Estate-A Little Hot (Petong)
E A Wheeler (Ms J S Doyle 14/2) G W Witheford

Placings:0064600 (7200)
2009: 6⁰SD, 8⁰SD, 10⁶GF, 11⁴F, 11⁶GF, 11⁰GF, 8⁰SD,

	Starts	1st	2nd	3rd	Win & Pl
Career Total (Turf)	4	0	0	0	202
Career Total (AW)	3	0	0	0	

Going (Turf): **Sf: 0-0 GS: 0-0 Gd: 0-0 GF: 0-3 Fm: 0-1**
Distance: 5f/6f: 0-1 7f-8f: 0-2 9f-13f: 0-4 14f+: 0-0
Track : LH: 0-3 RH: 0-3 Tight: 0-4 Gall: 0-1
Aids: Bl: 0-0 Vi: 0-0 Tstrap: 0-0 Ckp: 0-0
Best Rating: **47** 6/09 Wind 1m2f7y gd-fm

Lillie Langtry (IRE)

105 (96)**107**
2-y-o b/br f Danehill Dancer (IRE)-Hoity Toity (Darshaan)
A P O'Brien M Tabor, D Smith & Mrs John Magnier

Placings:2121310 (7282a)
2009: 6²GY, 6¹GF, 6²GF, 7¹GY, 7³HY, 7¹GF, 8⁰F,

	Starts	1st	2nd	3rd	Win & Pl
Career Total (Turf)	7	3	2	1	608331

99	10/09	NmkR	7f	G-F	£433360
107	8/09	Leop	7f	G-Y	£72572
100	6/09	Naas	6f	G-F	£63203

Total win prize-money £569137

Going (Turf): Sf: 0-1 GS: 0-0 Gd: 0-0 **GF: 2-3** Fm: 0-1
Distance: 5f/6f: 1-3 **7f-8f: 2-4** 9f-13f: 0-0 14f+: 0-0
Track : **LH: 2-4** RH: 0-0 Tight: 0-0 Gall: 0-0
Aids: Bl: 0-0 Vi: 0-0 Tstrap: 0-0 Ckp: 0-0
Best Rating: **107** 8/09 Leop 7f gd-yld

Smart; Group 2 winner; effective over 6-7f; acts on fast and easy ground.

Lillie Le Quesne

57 (57)**38**
6-y-o b m Desert Prince (IRE)-Bathe In Light (USA) (Sunshine Forever (USA))
Jane Southcombe Mark Savill

Placings:000/0 (2322)
2009: 12⁰G,

	Starts	1st	2nd	3rd	Win & Pl
Career Total (Turf)	3	0	0	0	
Career Total (AW)	1	0	0	0	

Going (Turf): **Sf: 0-0 GS: 0-1 Gd: 0-1 GF: 0-1 Fm: 0-0**
Distance: 5f/6f: 0-0 7f-8f: 0-2 9f-13f: 0-2 14f+: 0-0
Track : LH: 0-2 RH: 0-1 Tight: 0-1 Gall: 0-0
Aids: Bl: 0-0 Vi: 0-0 Tstrap: 0-0 Ckp: 0-0
Best Rating: **56** 10/05 Ling 7f stand

Lilly Be (IRE)

(94) (81)**74**
6-y-o ch m Titus Livius (FR)-Mystery Hill (USA) (Danehill (USA))
Paul Magnier Ms Kate Kelly

Placings:5436000/005433211520/002010/0603200404-12630000 (7646)

2009: 5^{1}SD, 5^{2}SD, 5^{6}GF, 5^{3}GF, 5^{0}SD, 5^{0}SD, 5^{0}SD, 5^{0}SD,

	Starts	1st	2nd	3rd	Win & Pl
Career Total (Turf)	30	2	4	5	16945
Career Total (AW)	13	2	1	0	13156

73	4/09	Dund	5f	(50-70)H	STD	£6373
73	9/07	Layt	6f	(50-70)H	STD	£4902
73	8/06	Bell	5f	(40-60)H	FRM	£4288
58	8/06	Naas	6f	(40-60)H	G-F	£3812

Total win prize-money £19376

Going (Turf): Sf: 0-1 GS: 0-0 Gd: 0-6 **GF: 1-10 Fm: 1-6**
Distance: **5f/6f: 4-41** 7f-8f: 0-2 9f-13f: 0-0 14f+: 0-0
Track : **LH: 4-28** RH: 0-9 Tight: 0-1 Gall: 0-0
Aids: **Bl: 2-26** Vi: 0-0 Tstrap: 1-6 Ckp: 1-6
Best Rating: 81 4/09 Dund 5f stand

Lilly Blue (IRE)

95(96) (60)86
3-y-o b f Hawk Wing (USA)-Holly Blue (Bluebird (USA))
R Brotherton (M R Channon 5/6) Arthur Clayton

Placings:0566-6550020550 (7211)
2009: 12^{6}SD, 9^{5}GS, 12^{5}F, 9^{0}G, 8^{0}G, 9^{2}SD, 12^{0}SD, 7^{5}G, 8^{5}GS, 8^{0}SD,

	Starts	1st	2nd	3rd	Win & Pl
Career Total (Turf)	9	0	0	0	807
Career Total (AW)	5	0	1	0	806

Going (Turf): Sf: 0-1 GS: 0-3 Gd: 0-3 GF: 0-1 Fm: 0-1
Distance: 5f/6f: 0-0 7f-8f: 0-5 9f-13f: 0-9 14f+: 0-0
Track : LH: 0-7 RH: 0-5 Tight: 0-6 Gall: 0-1
Aids: Bl: 0-0 Vi: 0-0 Tstrap: 0-0 Ckp: 0-0
Best Rating: 86 9/08 Gdwd 1m soft

Modest; stays 1m; acts on a sound surface.

Lilly Grove

(96) (56)45
4-y-o b m Mtoto-Armada Grove (Fleetwood (IRE))
G A Swinbank Lothian Recycling Limited

Placings:2-62 (7004)
2009: 9^{6}SD, 9^{2}SD,

	Starts	1st	2nd	3rd	Win & Pl
Career Total (Turf)	1	0	1	0	867
Career Total (AW)	2	0	1	0	605

Going (Turf): Sf: 0-1 GS: 0-0 Gd: 0-0 GF: 0-0 Fm: 0-0
Distance: 5f/6f: 0-0 7f-8f: 0-0 9f-13f: 0-3 14f+: 0-0
Track : LH: 0-2 RH: 0-1 Tight: 0-3 Gall: 0-0
Aids: Bl: 0-0 Vi: 0-0 Tstrap: 0-0 Ckp: 0-0
Best Rating: 56 10/09 Wolv 1m1f103y stand

Modest; stays 1m1f and acts on Polytrack.

Lilly Royal (IRE)

101 69
3-y-o b f Tillerman-Ervedya (IRE) (Doyoun)
B Palling Wayne Brackstone

Placings:026450 (7246)
2009: 8^{0}GF, 8^{2}HY, 7^{6}G, 10^{4}GS, 11^{5}G, 8^{0}S,

	Starts	1st	2nd	3rd	Win & Pl
Career Total (Turf)	6	0	1	0	1125

Going (Turf): Sf: 0-2 GS: 0-1 Gd: 0-2 GF: 0-1 Fm: 0-0
Distance: 5f/6f: 0-0 7f-8f: 0-1 9f-13f: 0-5 14f+: 0-0
Track : LH: 0-4 RH: 0-1 Tight: 0-0 Gall: 0-0
Aids: Bl: 0-0 Vi: 0-0 Tstrap: 0-0 Ckp: 0-0
Best Rating: 69 10/09 Nott 1m2f50y gd-sft

Modest; stays 1m2f; acts on soft ground.

Lily Eva

(88) (34)
3-y-o ch f Definite Article-Avanindra (Zamindar (USA))
D Donovan The Ellis Harriet Clark Syndicate

Placings:00 (7882)
2009: 8^{0}SD, 10^{0}SD,

	Starts	1st	2nd	3rd	Win & Pl
Career Total (Turf)	0	0	0	0	
Career Total (AW)	2	0	0	0	

Going (Turf): Sf: 0-0 GS: 0-0 Gd: 0-0 GF: 0-0 Fm: 0-0
Distance: 5f/6f: 0-0 7f-8f: 0-0 9f-13f: 0-2 14f+: 0-0
Track : LH: 0-2 RH: 0-0 Tight: 0-2 Gall: 0-0
Aids: Bl: 0-0 Vi: 0-0 Tstrap: 0-0 Ckp: 0-0
Best Rating: 34 12/09 Wolv 1m141y stand

Lily In The Pond

(93) (60)
2-y-o br f Kyllachy-Tidal (Bin Ajwaad (IRE))
Miss Gay Kelleway Mrs Bernadette Quinn

Placings:400 (7886)
2009: 7^{4}SD, 8^{0}SD, 7^{0}SD,

	Starts	1st	2nd	3rd	Win & Pl
Career Total (Turf)	0	0	0	0	
Career Total (AW)	3	0	0	0	192

Going (Turf): Sf: 0-0 GS: 0-0 Gd: 0-0 GF: 0-0 Fm: 0-0
Distance: 5f/6f: 0-0 7f-8f: 0-3 9f-13f: 0-0 14f+: 0-0
Track : LH: 0-2 RH: 0-1 Tight: 0-2 Gall: 0-0
Aids: Bl: 0-0 Vi: 0-0 Tstrap: 0-0 Ckp: 0-0
Best Rating: 60 12/09 Ling 1m stand

Lily Jicaro (IRE)

93(82) (21)60
3-y-o ch f Choisir (AUS)-Mourir D'Aimer (USA) (Trempolino (USA))
Mrs L Williamson G D Kendrick

Placings:25-003002000000 (6824)
2009: 7^{0}GF, 7^{0}SD, 6^{3}GF, 6^{0}GS, 7^{0}GF, 5^{2}GF, 5^{0}GF, 5^{0}GS, 5^{0}GS, 5^{0}GF, 5^{0}SD, 7^{0}GF,

	Starts	1st	2nd	3rd	Win & Pl
Career Total (Turf)	12	0	2	1	2062
Career Total (AW)	2	0	0	0	

Going (Turf): Sf: 0-1 GS: 0-3 Gd: 0-1 GF: 0-7 Fm: 0-0
Distance: 5f/6f: 0-9 7f-8f: 0-5 9f-13f: 0-0 14f+: 0-0
Track : LH: 0-6 RH: 0-4 Tight: 0-4 Gall: 0-0
Aids: Bl: 0-0 Vi: 0-1 Tstrap: 0-0 Ckp: 0-0
Best Rating: 60 10/08 Rdcr 6f good

Modest; stays 6f; should improve.

Lily Lenor (IRE)

84 52
2-y-o b f Bertolini (USA)-Mosaique Beauty (IRE) (Sadler's Wells (USA))
B Ellison S Hawe

Placings:0040 (2936)
2009: 5^{0}GF, 5^{0}GF, 5^{4}GF, 6^{0}G,

	Starts	1st	2nd	3rd	Win & Pl
Career Total (Turf)	4	0	0	0	144

Going (Turf): Sf: 0-0 GS: 0-0 Gd: 0-1 GF: 0-3 Fm: 0-0
Distance: 5f/6f: 0-4 7f-8f: 0-0 9f-13f: 0-0 14f+: 0-0
Track : LH: 0-0 RH: 0-0 Tight: 0-0 Gall: 0-0
Aids: Bl: 0-0 Vi: 0-0 Tstrap: 0-0 Ckp: 0-0
Best Rating: 52 5/09 Bevl 5f gd-fm

Lily Lily

(95) (60)
2-y-o b f Efisio-Bel Tempo (Petong)
K McAuliffe (Tom Dascombe 20/10) K W J McAuliffe

Placings:6021 (7792)
2009: 8^{6}SD, 9^{0}SD, 8^{2}SD, 8^{1}SS,

	Starts	1st	2nd	3rd	Win & Pl
Career Total (Turf)	0	0	0	0	
Career Total (AW)	4	1	1	0	3308

60	12/09	Sthl	1m	SS	£2729

Total win prize-money £2730

Going (Turf): Sf: 0-0 GS: 0-0 Gd: 0-0 GF: 0-0 Fm: 0-0
Distance: 5f/6f: 0-0 **7f-8f: 1-2** 9f-13f: 0-2 14f+: 0-0
Track : **LH: 1-4** RH: 0-0 Tight: 0-2 Gall: 0-0
Aids: **Bl: 1-2** Vi: 0-0 Tstrap: 0-0 Ckp: 0-0
Best Rating: 60 12/09 Sthl 1m std-slw

Modest; stays 1m; acts on Fibresand; has worn blinkers.

Lily Of The Nile (UAE)

82 38
3-y-o ch f Halling (USA)-Covet (Polish Precedent (USA))
J G Portman Prof C D Green

Placings:00-000 (6172)
2009: 12^{0}G, 10^{0}G, 9^{0}GF,

	Starts	1st	2nd	3rd	Win & Pl
Career Total (Turf)	5	0	0	0	

Going (Turf): Sf: 0-1 GS: 0-0 Gd: 0-2 GF: 0-2 Fm: 0-0
Distance: 5f/6f: 0-0 7f-8f: 0-2 9f-13f: 0-3 14f+: 0-0
Track : LH: 0-1 RH: 0-3 Tight: 0-1 Gall: 0-0
Aids: Bl: 0-0 Vi: 0-1 Tstrap: 0-1 Ckp: 0-1
Best Rating: 38 8/09 Wind 1m2f7y good

Lily Rio (IRE)

70 29
2-y-o b/br f Marju (IRE)-Jinsiyah (USA) (Housebuster (USA))
W R Muir Mrs J M Muir

Placings:00 (6729)
2009: 8^{0}GF, 6^{0}S,

	Starts	1st	2nd	3rd	Win & Pl
Career Total (Turf)	2	0	0	0	

Going (Turf): Sf: 0-1 GS: 0-0 Gd: 0-0 GF: 0-1 Fm: 0-0
Distance: 5f/6f: 0-0 7f-8f: 0-1 9f-13f: 0-1 14f+: 0-0
Track : LH: 0-1 RH: 0-0 Tight: 0-0 Gall: 0-0
Aids: Bl: 0-0 Vi: 0-0 Tstrap: 0-0 Ckp: 0-0
Best Rating: 29 9/09 Hayd 1m30y gd-fm

Lily Wood

53(94) (48)

3-y-o ch f Central Park (IRE)-Lady Castanea (Superlative)

J W Unett Mrs Shirley Downes

Placings:006 (7753)

2009: 8^{0}G, 8^{0}SD, 8^{6}SD,

	Starts	1st	2nd	3rd	Win & Pl
Career Total (Turf)	1	0	0	0	
Career Total (AW)	2	0	0	0	0

Going (Turf): Sf: 0-0 GS: 0-0 Gd: 0-1 GF: 0-0 Fm: 0-0
Distance: 5f/6f: 0-0 7f-8f: 0-0 9f-13f: 0-3 14f+: 0-0
Track : LH: 0-3 RH: 0-0 Tight: 0-2 Gall: 0-0
Aids: Bl: 0-0 Vi: 0-0 Tstrap: 0-0 Ckp: 0-0
Best Rating: 48 12/09 Wolv 1m141y stand

Lilyannabanana

86 68

2-y-o ch f Avonbridge-Bundle (Cadeaux Genereux)

P D Evans (A B Haynes 13/6) Bathwick Gold Partnership

Placings:0026 (5852)

2009: 5^{0}GF, 6^{0}GF, 6^{2}S, 7^{6}GF,

	Starts	1st	2nd	3rd	Win & Pl
Career Total (Turf)	4	0	1	0	867

Going (Turf): Sf: 0-1 GS: 0-0 Gd: 0-0 GF: 0-3 Fm: 0-0
Distance: 5f/6f: 0-3 7f-8f: 0-1 9f-13f: 0-0 14f+: 0-0
Track : LH: 0-1 RH: 0-0 Tight: 0-1 Gall: 0-0
Aids: Bl: 0-0 Vi: 0-0 Tstrap: 0-0 Ckp: 0-0
Best Rating: 68 8/09 Ayr 6f soft

Fair; suited by 6f and soft ground.

Lilymay

55 33

9-y-o b m Sovereign Water (FR)-Maysimp (IRE) (Mac's Imp (USA))

B P J Baugh J H Chrimes

Placings:0006/50 (4742)

2009: 11^{5}F, 14^{0}G,

	Starts	1st	2nd	3rd	Win & Pl
Career Total (Turf)	6	0	0	0	0

Going (Turf): Sf: 0-0 GS: 0-0 Gd: 0-1 GF: 0-4 Fm: 0-1
Distance: 5f/6f: 0-0 7f-8f: 0-0 9f-13f: 0-5 14f+: 0-1
Track : LH: 0-6 RH: 0-0 Tight: 0-1 Gall: 0-0
Aids: Bl: 0-0 Vi: 0-0 Tstrap: 0-0 Ckp: 0-0
Best Rating: 33 8/07 Ches 1m2f75y gd-fm

Limelight (USA)

(102) (53)58

4-y-o gr f Dalakhani (IRE)-Last Second (IRE) (Alzao (USA))

Sir Mark Prescott Faisal Salman

Placings:000/334550-2362 (0918)

2009: 13^{2}SD, 12^{3}SD, 16^{6}SD, 11^{2}SD,

	Starts	1st	2nd	3rd	Win & Pl
Career Total (Turf)	6	0	0	2	828
Career Total (AW)	7	0	2	1	1360

Going (Turf): Sf: 0-1 GS: 0-1 Gd: 0-2 GF: 0-2 Fm: 0-0
Distance: 5f/6f: 0-2 7f-8f: 0-1 9f-13f: 0-6 14f+: 0-4
Track : LH: 0-10 RH: 0-1 Tight: 0-6 Gall: 0-3
Aids: Bl: 0-1 Vi: 0-0 Tstrap: 0-1 Ckp: 0-1
Best Rating: 58 8/08 Brig 1m3f196y gd-sft

Moderate, stays 1m4f and acts on soft ground.

Linby (IRE)

88(88) (31)57

4-y-o b g Dr Fong (USA)-Dubious (Darshaan)

Miss Tor Sturgis Miss Tor Sturgis

Placings:05604100-00 (3561)

2009: 12^{0}GF, 12^{0}GF,

	Starts	1st	2nd	3rd	Win & Pl
Career Total (Turf)	9	1	0	0	2267
Career Total (AW)	1	0	0	0	

57 7/08 Bevl 1m4f16y (0-65)H G-F £2266

Total win prize-money £2267

Going (Turf): Sf: 0-0 GS: 0-2 Gd: 0-2 **GF: 1-5** Fm: 0-0
Distance: 5f/6f: 0-0 7f-8f: 0-0 **9f-13f: 1-10** 14f+: 0-0
Track : LH: 0-5 **RH: 1-5 Tight: 1-6** Gall: 0-1
Aids: Bl: 0-0 Vi: 0-0 Tstrap: 0-0 Ckp: 0-0
Best Rating: 57 7/08 Bevl 1m4f16y gd-fm

Lindoro

105(105) (93)93

4-y-o b g Marju (IRE)-Floppie (FR) (Law Society (USA))

M G Quinlan (W R Swinburn 3/10) Mrs J Quinlan

Placings:1050500/031206634-664061P0 (7645)

2009: 7^{6}GF, 7^{6}S, 7^{4}SF, 7^{0}G, 7^{6}SD, 7^{1}GF, 7^{P}SD, 5^{0}SD,

	Starts	1st	2nd	3rd	Win & Pl
Career Total (Turf)	18	3	1	1	27910
Career Total (AW)	6	0	0	1	2237

93 10/09 Epsm 7f (0-85)H G-F £6476
91 6/08 Thsk 7f (0-85)H G-S £5180
81 5/07 Gdwd 6f GD £2914

Total win prize-money £14572

Going (Turf): Sf: 0-1 **GS: 1-3 Gd: 1-6 GF: 1-8** Fm: 0-0
Distance: 5f/6f: 1-8 **7f-8f: 2-16** 9f-13f: 0-0 14f+: 0-0
Track : **LH: 2-6** RH: 0-7 **Tight: 2-5** Gall: 0-0
Aids: Bl: 0-1 Vi: 0-1 Tstrap: 0-1 Ckp: 0-1
Best Rating: 93 10/09 Epsm 7f gd-fm

Useful; stays 7f; acts on fast and easy ground; has worn a tongue tie.

Lindy Hop (IRE)

94(96) (64)65

3-y-o b f Danehill Dancer (IRE)-Healing Music (FR) (Bering)

K A Ryan (W R Swinburn 21/11) T G & Mrs M E Holdcroft

Placings:66-6566065 (7863)

2009: 6^{6}GF, 7^{5}GF, 7^{6}SS, 7^{6}SD, 8^{0}SD, 8^{6}SS, 8^{5}SD,

	Starts	1st	2nd	3rd	Win & Pl
Career Total (Turf)	3	0	0	0	0
Career Total (AW)	6	0	0	0	0

Going (Turf): Sf: 0-0 GS: 0-0 Gd: 0-0 GF: 0-3 Fm: 0-0
Distance: 5f/6f: 0-1 7f-8f: 0-7 9f-13f: 0-1 14f+: 0-0
Track : LH: 0-7 RH: 0-2 Tight: 0-4 Gall: 0-0
Aids: Bl: 0-0 Vi: 0-0 Tstrap: 0-0 Ckp: 0-0
Best Rating: 65 5/09 Wwck 7f26y gd-fm

Moderate; stays 7f; acts on Polytrack.

Lion Mountain

93 77

2-y-o b c Tiger Hill (IRE)-Cal Norma's Lady (IRE) (Lyphard's Special (USA))

Saeed Bin Suroor Godolphin

Placings:2 (7099)

2009: 8^{2}G,

	Starts	1st	2nd	3rd	Win & Pl
Career Total (Turf)	1	0	1	0	1038

Going (Turf): Sf: 0-0 GS: 0-0 Gd: 0-1 GF: 0-0 Fm: 0-0
Distance: 5f/6f: 0-0 7f-8f: 0-0 9f-13f: 0-1 14f+: 0-0
Track : LH: 0-0 RH: 0-0 Tight: 0-0 Gall: 0-0
Aids: Bl: 0-0 Vi: 0-0 Tstrap: 0-0 Ckp: 0-0
Best Rating: 77 10/09 Yarm 1m3y good

Lion Road (USA)

64 5

3-y-o ch g Lion Heart (USA)-Elusive Road (USA) (Elusive Quality (USA))

A B Haynes R S Brookhouse

Placings:00 (6789)

2009: 9^{0}G, 11^{0}G,

	Starts	1st	2nd	3rd	Win & Pl
Career Total (Turf)	2	0	0	0	

Going (Turf): Sf: 0-0 GS: 0-0 Gd: 0-2 GF: 0-0 Fm: 0-0
Distance: 5f/6f: 0-0 7f-8f: 0-0 9f-13f: 0-2 14f+: 0-0
Track : LH: 0-1 RH: 0-1 Tight: 0-1 Gall: 0-0
Aids: Bl: 0-0 Vi: 0-0 Tstrap: 0-0 Ckp: 0-0
Best Rating: 5 9/09 Haml 1m1f36y good

Liquid Asset (FR)

86 73

2-y-o ch g Refuse To Bend (IRE)-Lilyfoot (IRE) (Sanglamore (USA))

A M Balding Mick and Janice Mariscotti

Placings:20 (3750)

2009: 7^{2}G, 7^{0}G,

	Starts	1st	2nd	3rd	Win & Pl
Career Total (Turf)	2	0	1	0	1542

Going (Turf): Sf: 0-0 GS: 0-0 Gd: 0-2 GF: 0-0 Fm: 0-0
Distance: 5f/6f: 0-0 7f-8f: 0-2 9f-13f: 0-0 14f+: 0-0
Track : LH: 0-0 RH: 0-1 Tight: 0-0 Gall: 0-0
Aids: Bl: 0-0 Vi: 0-0 Tstrap: 0-0 Ckp: 0-0
Best Rating: 73 6/09 Sand 7f16y good

Out of a half-sister to Lingfield Derby Trial winner Linda's Lad, from the family of Arc winner Rail Link; promise on debut over 7f on good.

Lis Pendens

81(90) (57)63

2-y-o b g Tobougg (IRE)-In Good Faith (USA) (Dynaformer (USA))

W R Muir Raymond Tooth

Placings:000 (7400)

2009: 8^{0}GS, 9^{0}GS, 9^{0}SD,

	Starts	1st	2nd	3rd	Win & Pl
Career Total (Turf)	2	0	0	0	
Career Total (AW)	1	0	0	0	

Going (Turf): **Sf: 0-0 GS: 0-2 Gd: 0-0 GF: 0-0 Fm: 0-0**
Distance: 5f/6f: 0-0 7f-8f: 0-0 9f-13f: 0-3 14f+: 0-0
Track : LH: 0-1 RH: 0-2 Tight: 0-2 Gall: 0-0
Aids: Bl: 0-0 Vi: 0-0 Tstrap: 0-0 Ckp: 0-0
Best Rating: **63** 9/09 Sand 1m14y gd-sft

Lisahane Bog

84(98) (69)55
2-y-o b c Royal Applause-Veronica Franco (Darshaan)
P R Hedger P C F Racing Ltd

Placings:0000111 (7654)
2009: 7^{0}G, 7^{0}SD, 8^{0}GF, 9^{0}GS, 7^{1}SD, 7^{1}SD, 7^{1}SD,

	Starts	1st	2nd	3rd	Win & Pl
Career Total (Turf)	3	0	0	0	
Career Total (AW)	4	3	0	0	6813

69 12/09 Ling 7f (0-75) STD £3238
65 11/09 Kemp 7f (0-65) STD £1706
61 11/09 Ling 7f (0-60) STD £1869
Total win prize-money £6813

Going (Turf): **Sf: 0-0 GS: 0-1 Gd: 0-1 GF: 0-1 Fm: 0-0**
Distance: 5f/6f: 0-0 **7f-8f: 3-6** 9f-13f: 0-1 14f+: 0-0
Track : **LH: 2-3** RH: 1-3 **Tight: 2-3** Gall: 0-0
Aids: Bl: 0-0 Vi: 0-0 Tstrap: 3-4 Ckp: 3-4
Best Rating: **69** 12/09 Ling 7f stand

Modest; effective over 7f; acts on Polytrack; has worn cheekpieces.

Lisbon Lion (IRE)

94(99) (62)62
4-y-o br/gr g Mull Of Kintyre (USA)-Ludovica (Bustino)
James Moffatt (N J Vaughan 20/2) David And Nicky Robinson

Placings:60430-346 (7085)
2009: 12^{3}SD, 12^{4}GS, 11^{6}S,

	Starts	1st	2nd	3rd	Win & Pl
Career Total (Turf)	7	0	0	1	1299
Career Total (AW)	1	0	0	1	302

Going (Turf): **Sf: 0-3 GS: 0-2 Gd: 0-1 GF: 0-1 Fm: 0-0**
Distance: 5f/6f: 0-0 7f-8f: 0-0 9f-13f: 0-6 14f+: 0-2
Track : LH: 0-8 RH: 0-0 Tight: 0-2 Gall: 0-2
Aids: Bl: 0-0 Vi: 0-0 Tstrap: 0-0 Ckp: 0-0
Best Rating: **62** 2/09 Sthl 1m4f stand

Moderate; stays 1m4f; acts on good and soft ground; handles Fibresand.

Listen Carefully (IRE)

85 (42)23
5-y-o ch m Lil's Boy (USA)-Join The Party (Be My Guest (USA))
Patrick Morris (P J Rothwell 26/4) L Walsh

Placings:0-000000 (2806)
2009: 12^{0}SD, 12^{0}SW, 8^{0}SD, 5^{0}S, 5^{0}G, 6^{0}G,

	Starts	1st	2nd	3rd	Win & Pl
Career Total (Turf)	3	0	0	0	
Career Total (AW)	4	0	0	0	

Going (Turf): **Sf: 0-1 GS: 0-0 Gd: 0-2 GF: 0-0 Fm: 0-0**
Distance: 5f/6f: 0-2 7f-8f: 0-3 9f-13f: 0-2 14f+: 0-0
Track : LH: 0-7 RH: 0-0 Tight: 0-2 Gall: 0-0
Aids: Bl: 0-0 Vi: 0-0 Tstrap: 0-1 Ckp: 0-1
Best Rating: **42** 11/08 Dund 1m stand

Listillo (USA)

95(95) (72)72
2-y-o ch c More Than Ready (USA)-Dowry (USA) (Belong To Me (USA))
H J L Dunlop William Armitage

Placings:642222002 (5611)
2009: 6^{6}G, 5^{4}GF, 5^{2}SD, 5^{2}SF, 5^{2}G, 5^{2}G, 5^{0}SD, 5^{0}G, 5^{2}SD,

	Starts	1st	2nd	3rd	Win & Pl
Career Total (Turf)	5	0	2	0	2842
Career Total (AW)	4	0	3	0	3219

Going (Turf): **Sf: 0-0 GS: 0-0 Gd: 0-4 GF: 0-1 Fm: 0-0**
Distance: 5f/6f: 0-8 7f-8f: 0-1 9f-13f: 0-0 14f+: 0-0
Track : LH: 0-5 RH: 0-0 Tight: 0-4 Gall: 0-1
Aids: Bl: 0-0 Vi: 0-1 Tstrap: 0-0 Ckp: 0-0
Best Rating: **72** 9/09 Wolv 5f20y stand

Modest; effective at 5f on good ground.

Litenup (IRE)

(102) (58)39
3-y-o b f Trans Island-Common Cause (Polish Patriot (USA))
A J Lidderdale A C Entertainment Technologies Ltd

Placings:004-2020004 (7882)
2009: 8^{2}SD, 8^{0}SD, 10^{2}SD, 10^{0}SD, 12^{0}SD, 8^{0}SD, 10^{4}SD,

	Starts	1st	2nd	3rd	Win & Pl
Career Total (Turf)	1	0	0	0	
Career Total (AW)	9	0	2	0	1450

Going (Turf): **Sf: 0-0 GS: 0-1 Gd: 0-0 GF: 0-0 Fm: 0-0**
Distance: 5f/6f: 0-0 7f-8f: 0-5 9f-13f: 0-5 14f+: 0-0
Track : LH: 0-4 RH: 0-5 Tight: 0-3 Gall: 0-0
Aids: Bl: 0-0 Vi: 0-0 Tstrap: 0-0 Ckp: 0-0
Best Rating: **58** 2/09 Sthl 1m stand

Moderate; stays 1m2f and acts on sand.

Liteup My World (USA)

92(92) (61)58
3-y-o ch g Hennessy (USA)-Liteup My Life (USA) (Green Dancer (USA))
B Ellison Carr, Marucci, Amin, Duggan, Gilligan

Placings:060-50 (4436)
2009: 7^{5}GF, 6^{0}GF,

	Starts	1st	2nd	3rd	Win & Pl
Career Total (Turf)	2	0	0	0	0
Career Total (AW)	3	0	0	0	0

Going (Turf): **Sf: 0-0 GS: 0-0 Gd: 0-0 GF: 0-2 Fm: 0-0**
Distance: 5f/6f: 0-3 7f-8f: 0-2 9f-13f: 0-0 14f+: 0-0
Track : LH: 0-3 RH: 0-1 Tight: 0-1 Gall: 0-2
Aids: Bl: 0-0 Vi: 0-0 Tstrap: 0-0 Ckp: 0-0
Best Rating: **61** 10/08 GrLe 5f stand

Lithaam (IRE)

100(104) (77)73
5-y-o ch g Elnadim (USA)-Elhida (IRE) (Mujtahid (USA))
J M Bradley JMB Racing.co.uk

Placings:06000/000010000306365121-6540030366141413005156522 (7807)
2009: 5^{6}SD, 5^{5}SD, 5^{4}SD, 5^{0}SD, 5^{0}SD, 5^{3}GF, 5^{0}F, 5^{3}GF, 5^{6}GS, 5^{6}GS, 5^{1}G, 5^{4}G, 5^{1}G, 5^{4}SD, 5^{1}G, 5^{3}G, 5^{0}GF, 5^{0}SD, 5^{5}G, 5^{1}SD, 5^{5}SD, 5^{6}SD, 5^{5}SD, 5^{2}SD,

	Starts	1st	2nd	3rd	Win & Pl
Career Total (Turf)	24	4	0	5	10584
Career Total (AW)	24	3	3	0	8798

74 10/09 Wolv 5f20y (0-70)H STD £3238
73 9/09 Chep 5f16y (0-65)H GD £2072
66 8/09 Chep 5f16y (0-60)H GD £2266
61 8/09 Nott 5f13y (0-55)H GD £2047
64 12/08 Ling 5f (0-55)H STD £1706
57 12/08 Sthl 5f (0-55)H SS £1706
61 6/08 Folk 5f G-F £2590
Total win prize-money £15626

Going (Turf): Sf: 0-1 GS: 0-2 **Gd: 3-12** GF: 1-8 Fm: 0-1
Distance: **5f/6f: 7-46** 7f-8f: 0-2 9f-13f: 0-0 14f+: 0-0
Track : **LH: 2-23** RH: 0-3 **Tight: 2-15** Gall: 0-3
Aids: Bl: 0-0 Vi: 0-0 Tstrap: 7-41 Ckp: 7-41
Best Rating: **77** 12/09 Ling 5f stand

Modest; effective at 5f; acts on fast ground; goes on Fibresand and Polytrack; has worn cheekpieces.

Little Arrows (IRE)

77(103) (84)83
3-y-o b c Danehill Dancer (IRE)-Lovers Walk (USA) (Diesis)
W McCreery Mrs Catherine O'Flynn

Placings:21040-0053002 (7192)
2009: 7^{0}HY, 6^{0}GY, 5^{5}G, 5^{3}SD, 5^{0}SD, 8^{0}S, 7^{2}SD,

	Starts	1st	2nd	3rd	Win & Pl
Career Total (Turf)	7	1	1	0	11954
Career Total (AW)	5	0	1	1	2603

83 7/08 Naas 6f YLD £9145
Total win prize-money £9146

Going (Turf): **Sf: 0-3 GS: 0-0 Gd: 0-2 GF: 0-0 Fm: 0-0**
Distance: **5f/6f: 1-8** 7f-8f: 0-4 9f-13f: 0-0 14f+: 0-0
Track : **LH: 1-11** RH: 0-0 Tight: 0-2 Gall: 0-0
Aids: Bl: 0-4 Vi: 0-0 Tstrap: 0-2 Ckp: 0-2
Best Rating: **84** 11/08 Dund 6f stand

Little Billie

64
3-y-o b f Efisio-Kembla (Known Fact (USA))
Mike Murphy M Murphy

Placings:0 (6794)
2009: 10^{0}S,

	Starts	1st	2nd	3rd	Win & Pl
Career Total (Turf)	1	0	0	0	

Going (Turf): **Sf: 0-1 GS: 0-0 Gd: 0-0 GF: 0-0 Fm: 0-0**
Distance: 5f/6f: 0-0 7f-8f: 0-0 9f-13f: 0-1 14f+: 0-0
Track : LH: 0-1 RH: 0-0 Tight: 0-0 Gall: 0-0
Aids: Bl: 0-0 Vi: 0-0 Tstrap: 0-0 Ckp: 0-0

Little Blacknumber

(90) (51)
3-y-o b f Superior Premium-The Synergist (Botanic (USA))
R Hannon Mrs Sue Brendish

Placings:6645-66 (0707)
2009: 6^{6}SD, 8^{6}SD,

	Starts	1st	2nd	3rd	Win & Pl
Career Total (Turf)	1	0	0	0	0
Career Total (AW)	5	0	0	0	0

Going (Turf): **Sf: 0-0 GS: 0-0 Gd: 0-0 GF: 0-1 Fm: 0-0**
Distance: 5f/6f: 0-4 7f-8f: 0-2 9f-13f: 0-0 14f+: 0-0
Track : LH: 0-4 RH: 0-1 Tight: 0-4 Gall: 0-1
Aids: Bl: 0-0 Vi: 0-0 Tstrap: 0-0 Ckp: 0-0
Best Rating: **51** 11/08 Wolv 5f216y stand

Little Bones

65(73) (53)**54**
4-y-o ch f Tobougg (IRE)-City Gambler (Rock City)
J F Coupland J F Coupland

Placings:0030254/0460-0 (5254)
2009: 6^{0}GF,

	Starts	1st	2nd	3rd	Win & Pl
Career Total (Turf)	10	0	1	1	1239
Career Total (AW)	2	0	0	0	0

Going (Turf): **Sf: 0-1 GS: 0-0 Gd: 0-1 GF: 0-8 Fm: 0-0**
Distance: 5f/6f: 0-6 7f-8f: 0-6 9f-13f: 0-0 14f+: 0-0
Track : LH: 0-4 RH: 0-0 Tight: 0-3 Gall: 0-1
Aids: Bl: 0-0 Vi: 0-0 Tstrap: 0-0 Ckp: 0-0
Best Rating: **56** 8/07 Ripn 6f gd-fm

Little Brazilien

97(87) (58)**60**
2-y-o ch f Kyllachy-Girl From Ipanema (Salse (USA))
Mme G Rarick (P F I Cole 29/9) Mme G Rarick

Placings:4403300
2009: 5^{4}G, 5^{4}G, 5^{0}G, 5^{3}SD, 5^{3}G, 7^{0}GF, 7^{0}HY,

	Starts	1st	2nd	3rd	Win & Pl
Career Total (Turf)	6	0	0	1	597
Career Total (AW)	1	0	0	1	302

Going (Turf): **Sf: 0-1 GS: 0-0 Gd: 0-4 GF: 0-1 Fm: 0-0**
Distance: 5f/6f: 0-5 7f-8f: 0-2 9f-13f: 0-0 14f+: 0-0
Track : LH: 0-5 RH: 0-1 Tight: 0-0 Gall: 0-4
Aids: Bl: 0-2 Vi: 0-0 Tstrap: 0-0 Ckp: 0-0
Best Rating: **60** 9/09 Bath 5f11y good

Modest; effective over 5f; acts on good ground.

Little Buddy

56
2-y-o ch g Reel Buddy (USA)-Little Kenny (Warning)
R J Price David Prosser & Keith Warrington

Placings:000 (6386)
2009: 6^{0}GF, 7^{0}GF, 6^{0}GF,

	Starts	1st	2nd	3rd	Win & Pl
Career Total (Turf)	3	0	0	0	

Going (Turf): **Sf: 0-0 GS: 0-0 Gd: 0-0 GF: 0-3 Fm: 0-0**
Distance: 5f/6f: 0-0 7f-8f: 0-3 9f-13f: 0-0 14f+: 0-0
Track : LH. 0-1 RH: 0-0 Tight: 0-0 Gall: 0-0
Aids: Bl: 0-0 Vi: 0-0 Tstrap: 0-0 Ckp: 0-0

Little Calla (IRE)

94(95) (55)**59**
3-y-o ch f Indian Ridge-Queen Of Palms (IRE) (Desert Prince (IRE))
E A L Dunlop St Albans Bloodstock LLP

Placings:44-200 (4174)
2009: 7^{2}GF, 6^{0}G, 5^{0}SD,

	Starts	1st	2nd	3rd	Win & Pl
Career Total (Turf)	2	0	1	0	705
Career Total (AW)	3	0	0	0	577

Going (Turf): **Sf: 0-0 GS: 0-0 Gd: 0-1 GF: 0-1 Fm: 0-0**
Distance: 5f/6f: 0-4 7f-8f: 0-1 9f-13f: 0-0 14f+: 0-0
Track : LH: 0-2 RH: 0-0 Tight: 0-0 Gall: 0-3
Aids: Bl: 0-0 Vi: 0-0 Tstrap: 0-0 Ckp: 0-0
Best Rating: **59** 5/09 Ling 7f gd-fm

Modest; stays 7f and acts on fast ground.

Little Carmela

99(101) (69)**65**
5-y-o gr m Beat Hollow-Carmela Owen (Owington)
S C Williams O Pointing

Placings:00/0022**160/126-145662045002** (7750)
2009: 14^{1}SD, 12^{4}SD, 13^{5}SD, 16^{8}SD, 13^{6}GS, 14^{2}GF, 13^{0}SD, 13^{4}SS, 16^{5}SD, 16^{0}SD, 12^{0}SD, 13^{2}SD,

	Starts	1st	2nd	3rd	Win & Pl
Career Total (Turf)	9	0	3	0	2374
Career Total (AW)	15	3	2	0	8686

69	1/09	GrLe	1m6f	(0-65)H	STD	£2590
69	11/08	Kemp	1m4f	(0-60)H	STD	£2047
69	9/07	Kemp	1m3f	(0 60)H	STD	£2047

Total win prize-money £6685

Going (Turf): **Sf: 0-2 GS: 0-4 Gd: 0-1 GF: 0-2 Fm: 0-0**
Distance: 5f/6f: 0-3 7f-8f: 0-9 **9f-13f: 2-11** 14f+: 1-10
Track : LH: 1-15 **RH: 2-5** Tight: 0-12 **Gall: 1-5**
Aids: Bl: 0-0 Vi: 0-2 Tstrap: 0-2 Ckp: 0-2
Best Rating: **69** 1/09 GrLe 1m6f stand

Moderate; stays 1m6f; acts on most ground; goes on Polytrack.

Little Eden (IRE)

92(95) (67)**59**
4-y-o b g Piccolo-Paradise Eve (Bahamian Bounty)
T D Barron Clive Washbourn

Placings:12-000 (1846)
2009: 5^{0}SD, 5^{0}GF, 6^{0}F,

	Starts	1st	2nd	3rd	Win & Pl
Career Total (Turf)	3	0	1	0	674
Career Total (AW)	2	1	0	0	2915

67	3/08	Sthl	5f	STD	£2914

Total win prize-money £2915

Going (Turf): **Sf: 0-0 GS: 0-1 Gd: 0-0 GF: 0-1 Fm: 0-1**
Distance: **5f/6f: 1-4** 7f-8f: 0-1 9f-13f: 0-0 14f+: 0-0
Track : LH: 0-0 RH: 0-0 Tight: 0-0 Gall: 0-0
Aids: Bl: 0-0 Vi: 0-0 Tstrap: 0-0 Ckp: 0-0
Best Rating: **67** 3/08 Sthl 5f stand

Moderate gelding; best at 5f; acts on Fibresand and handles easy ground on turf.

Little Edward

96(110) (98)**96**
11-y-o gr g King's Signet (USA)-Cedar Lady (Telsmoss)
R J Hodges J W Mursell

Placings:21/01102000/32010010225/50500500056460/06000/100**321115/6004121020360/160640022142-23201050** (2474)
2009: 6^{2}SD, 5^{3}SD, 5^{2}SD, 5^{0}SD, 5^{1}SD, 6^{0}SD, 5^{5}GF, 6^{0}G,

	Starts	1st	2nd	3rd	Win & Pl
Career Total (Turf)	55	7	6	2	73510
Career Total (AW)	28	7	7	2	56749

98	3/09	Wolv	5f20y	(0-90)H	STD	£9462
88	12/08	Ling	6f		STD	£2729
96	6/08	Ling	5f	(0-90)H	STD	£7477
98	9/07	Bath	5f161y	(0-85)H	FRM	£4857
88	8/07	Ling	6f	(0-80)H	STD	£4857
88	11/06	Kemp	5f	(0-75)H	STD	£3886
91	11/06	Ling	5f	(0-85)H	STD	£5505
86	11/06	Ling	5f	(0-75)H	STD	£5181
84	7/06	Sand	5f6y	(0-75)H	G-F	£4533
94	7/03	Bath	5f161y	C	HRD	£9002
104	6/03	Sand	5f6y	C	G-F	£8568
101	7/02	Wwck	5f110y	C(0-95)H	G-F	£12180
89	7/02	Wwck	5f	D(0-85)H	G-F	£5746
77	8/01	Sand	5f6y	D	G-S	£4329

Total win prize-money £88317

Going (Turf): Sf: 0-4 GS: 1-5 Gd: 0-17 **GF: 4-23** Fm: 2-6
Distance: **5f/6f: 14-80** 7f-8f: 0-3 9f-13f: 0-0 14f+: 0-0
Track : **LH: 10-35** RH: 1-4 **Tight: 6-23** Gall: 2-12
Aids: Bl: 0-0 Vi: 0-0 Tstrap: 0-1 Ckp: 0-1
Best Rating: **104** 9/03 Curr 5f good

Very useful; suited by 5f-6f; acts on most ground and on Polytrack.

Little Finch (IRE)

(91) (32)**54**
4-y-o b f Acclamation-Hard To Lay (IRE) (Dolphin Street (FR))
S Curran D M Barry

Placings:0601045050U**62000/25200-0** (6940)
2009: 10^{0}SD,

	Starts	1st	2nd	3rd	Win & Pl
Career Total (Turf)	11	1	0	0	3019
Career Total (AW)	11	0	3	0	1814

54	5/07	Catt	5f212y	G-F	£2730

Total win prize-money £2730

Going (Turf): Sf: 0-0 GS: 0-0 Gd: 0-4 **GF: 1-6** Fm: 0-1
Distance: **5f/6f: 1-18** 7f-8f: 0-2 9f-13f: 0-2 14f+: 0-0
Track : **LH: 1-8** RH: 0-5 **Tight: 1-6** Gall: 0-1
Aids: **Bl: 1-16** Vi: 0-1 Tstrap: 0-1 Ckp: 0-1
Best Rating: **54** 5/07 Catt 5f212y gd-fm

Modest filly; stays 6f; acts on fast ground; has worn blinkers.

Little Firecracker

(96) (61)**62**
4-y-o b f Cadeaux Genereux-El Hakma (Shareef Dancer (USA))
N B King (Tim Vaughan 8/11) B Bell N J Catterwell

Placings:10605633/21460000000-0 (0537)
2009: 9^{0}SD,

	Starts	1st	2nd	3rd	Win & Pl
Career Total (Turf)	5	1	0	0	3886
Career Total (AW)	15	1	1	2	2994

61	1/08	Wolv	1m1f103y	(0-60)H	STD	£1774
60	6/07	Thsk	6f		G-S	£3886

Total win prize-money £5661

Going (Turf): Sf: 0-0 **GS: 1-2** Gd: 0-3 GF: 0-0 Fm: 0-0
Distance: 5f/6f: 1-5 7f-8f: 0-5 9f-13f: 1-10 14f+: 0-0
Track : **LH: 1-16** RH: 0-1 **Tight: 1-9** Gall: 0-2
Aids: Bl: 0-1 Vi: 0-0 Tstrap: 0-2 Ckp: 0-2
Best Rating: **62** 9/07 Leic 5f218y good

Moderate; effective at around 1m; acts on good to soft and both All-Weather surfaces.

Little Garcon (USA)

89(101) (82)64
2-y-o b g Bernstein (USA)-Demure (Machiavellian (USA))
M Botti Joseph Barton

Placings:001 **(7001)**
2009: 6^0GF, 5^0SF, 5^1SD,

	Starts	1st	2nd	3rd	Win & Pl
Career Total (Turf)	1	0	0	0	
Career Total (AW)	2	1	0	0	3238

82 10/09 Wolv 5f216y STD £3238
Total win prize-money £3238

Going (Turf): **Sf: 0-0 GS: 0-0 Gd: 0-0 GF: 0-1 Fm: 0-0**
Distance: **5f/6f: 1-3** 7f-8f: 0-0 9f-13f: 0-0 14f+: 0-0
Track : **LH: 1-2** RH: 0-0 **Tight: 1-2** Gall: 0-0
Aids: Bl: 0-0 Vi: 0-0 Tstrap: 0-0 Ckp: 0-0
Best Rating: **82** 10/09 Wolv 5f216y stand

Useful; suited by 6f and Polytrack.

Little Knickers

(98) (71)66
4-y-o b f Prince Sabo-Pants (Pivotal)
E J Creighton A S Reid

Placings:610005/40333514256660-050 **(1074)**
2009: 8^0SD, 7^5SD, 7^0SD,

	Starts	1st	2nd	3rd	Win & Pl
Career Total (Turf)	5	1	0	0	3412
Career Total (AW)	18	1	1	3	4452

67 4/08 Ling 7f (0-70)H STD £2590
74 7/07 Bath 5f11y G-S £3238
Total win prize-money £5829

Going (Turf): Sf: 0-2 **GS: 1-3** Gd: 0-0 GF: 0-0 Fm: 0-0
Distance: 5f/6f: 1-10 7f-8f: 1-12 9f-13f: 0-1 14f+: 0-0
Track : **LH: 1-12** RH: 0-7 Tight: 0-10 **Gall: 1-1**
Aids: **Bl: 1-10** Vi: 0-0 Tstrap: 0-0 Ckp: 0-0
Best Rating: **74** 7/07 Bath 5f11y gd-sft

Modest; effective at around 7f; acts on easy ground; also goes on Polytrack.

Little Lost (IRE)

(93) (41)
3-y-o b f Tagula (IRE)-Prima Marta (Primo Dominie)
Karen George (J A Osborne 25/3) Mrs Isabel Fraser

Placings:00500 **(6641)**
2009: 5^0SD, 5^0SF, 5^5SD, 5^0SD, 5^0SD,

	Starts	1st	2nd	3rd	Win & Pl
Career Total (Turf)	0	0	0	0	
Career Total (AW)	5	0	0	0	0

Going (Turf): **Sf: 0-0 GS: 0-0 Gd: 0-0 GF: 0-0 Fm: 0-0**
Distance: 5f/6f: 0-5 7f-8f: 0-0 9f-13f: 0-0 14f+: 0-0
Track : LH: 0-5 RH: 0-0 Tight: 0-5 Gall: 0-0
Aids: Bl: 0-0 Vi: 0-0 Tstrap: 0-1 Ckp: 0-1
Best Rating: **41** 3/09 Ling 5f stand

Little Meadow (IRE)

70(88) (46)15
2-y-o b f Antonius Pius (USA)-Cresalin (Coquelin (USA))
Miss J Feilden R J Creese

Placings:005 **(7792)**
2009: 7^0GF, 8^0SD, 8^5SS,

	Starts	1st	2nd	3rd	Win & Pl
Career Total (Turf)	1	0	0	0	
Career Total (AW)	2	0	0	0	0

Going (Turf): **Sf: 0-0 GS: 0-0 Gd: 0-0 GF: 0-1 Fm: 0-0**
Distance: 5f/6f: 0-0 7f-8f: 0-3 9f-13f: 0-0 14f+: 0-0
Track : LH: 0-2 RH: 0-0 Tight: 0-1 Gall: 0-0
Aids: Bl: 0-0 Vi: 0-0 Tstrap: 0-0 Ckp: 0-0
Best Rating: **46** 12/09 Sthl 1m std-slw

Little Miss Ginger

(72) (3)
5-y-o ch m Whittingham (IRE)-Miss Tress (IRE) (Salse (USA))
P S McEntee Eventmaker Racehorses

Placings:0 **(0286)**
2009: 5^0SD,

	Starts	1st	2nd	3rd	Win & Pl
Career Total (Turf)	0	0	0	0	
Career Total (AW)	1	0	0	0	

Going (Turf): **Sf: 0-0 GS: 0-0 Gd: 0-0 GF: 0-0 Fm: 0-0**
Distance: 5f/6f: 0-1 7f-8f: 0-0 9f-13f: 0-0 14f+: 0-0
Track : LH: 0-1 RH: 0-0 Tight: 0-1 Gall: 0-0
Aids: Bl: 0-0 Vi: 0-0 Tstrap: 0-0 Ckp: 0-0
Best Rating: **3** 1/09 Wolv 5f20y stand

Little Opera (IRE)

(57) 59
3-y-o b f Fasliyev (USA)-El Opera (IRE) (Sadler's Wells (USA))
Aidan Anthony Howard Mrs Ann D Coogan

Placings:000-00000 **(7143)**
2009: 8^0HY, 9^0S, 7^0G, 12^0GF, 9^0SD,

	Starts	1st	2nd	3rd	Win & Pl
Career Total (Turf)	7	0	0	0	
Career Total (AW)	1	0	0	0	

Going (Turf): **Sf: 0-2 GS: 0-0 Gd: 0-2 GF: 0-1 Fm: 0-0**
Distance: 5f/6f: 0-3 7f-8f: 0-2 9f-13f: 0-3 14f+: 0-0
Track : LH: 0-4 RH: 0-3 Tight: 0-1 Gall: 0-0
Aids: Bl: 0-0 Vi: 0-0 Tstrap: 0-0 Ckp: 0-0
Best Rating: **59** 4/08 Leop 6f gd-yld

Little Oz (IRE)

88 68
2-y-o br f Red Ransom (USA)-Australie (IRE) (Sadler's Wells (USA))
E A L Dunlop Ballygallon Stud Limited

Placings:604 **(7244)**
2009: 8^6GF, 8^0GS, 8^4S,

	Starts	1st	2nd	3rd	Win & Pl
Career Total (Turf)	3	0	0	0	313

Going (Turf): **Sf: 0-1 GS: 0-1 Gd: 0-0 GF: 0-1 Fm: 0-0**
Distance: 5f/6f: 0-0 7f-8f: 0-2 9f-13f: 0-1 14f+: 0-0
Track : LH: 0-2 RH: 0-0 Tight: 0-0 Gall: 0-1
Aids: Bl: 0-0 Vi: 0-0 Tstrap: 0-0 Ckp: 0-0
Best Rating: **68** 9/09 NmkR 1m gd-fm

Little Pandora

84(87) (32)39
5-y-o b m Komaite (USA)-Little Talitha (Lugana Beach)
L R James The Casma Pandora Syndicate

Placings:000-00000 **(5309)**
2009: 7^0SD, 7^0GS, 5^0GS, 6^0G, 5^0HY,

	Starts	1st	2nd	3rd	Win & Pl
Career Total (Turf)	6	0	0	0	
Career Total (AW)	2	0	0	0	

Going (Turf): **Sf: 0-1 GS: 0-2 Gd: 0-2 GF: 0-1 Fm: 0-0**
Distance: 5f/6f: 0-5 7f-8f: 0-3 9f-13f: 0-0 14f+: 0-0
Track : LH: 0-3 RH: 0-0 Tight: 0-2 Gall: 0-0
Aids: Bl: 0-0 Vi: 0-0 Tstrap: 0-0 Ckp: 0-0
Best Rating: **39** 6/09 Newc 7f gd-sft

Little Perc (IRE)

54
2-y-o ch c Pearl Of Love (IRE)-Bitter Sweet (Deploy)
G L Moore C S C Hancock

Placings:00 **(1783)**
2009: 5^0GF, 5^0GF,

	Starts	1st	2nd	3rd	Win & Pl
Career Total (Turf)	2	0	0	0	

Going (Turf): **Sf: 0-0 GS: 0-0 Gd: 0-0 GF: 0-2 Fm: 0-0**
Distance: 5f/6f: 0-2 7f-8f: 0-0 9f-13f: 0-0 14f+: 0-0
Track : LH: 0-1 RH: 0-0 Tight: 0-0 Gall: 0-1
Aids: Bl: 0-1 Vi: 0-0 Tstrap: 0-0 Ckp: 0-0

Little Perisher

97(96) (75)88
2-y-o b c Desert Sun-Sasperella (Observatory (USA))
A P Jarvis Mrs Ann Jarvis

Placings:02316066400500105 **(7410)**
2009: 5^0GS, 5^2GF, 5^3GF, 5^1GF, 6^6G, 5^0GF, 5^6G, 5^6GF, 6^4G, 6^0GF, 6^0G, 6^5G, 6^0GF, 6^0G, 6^1SD, 7^0SD, 5^5SD,

	Starts	1st	2nd	3rd	Win & Pl
Career Total (Turf)	14	1	1	1	11352
Career Total (AW)	3	1	0	0	2047

75 10/09 Kemp 6f STD £2047
88 5/09 Asct 5f G-F £7771
Total win prize-money £9818

Going (Turf): Sf: 0-0 GS: 0-1 Gd: 0-6 **GF: 1-7** Fm: 0-0
Distance: **5f/6f: 2-15** 7f-8f: 0-2 9f-13f: 0-0 14f+: 0-0
Track : LH: 0-6 **RH: 1-1** Tight: 0-4 Gall: 0-2
Aids: Bl: 0-0 Vi: 0-1 Tstrap: 0-0 Ckp: 0-0
Best Rating: **88** 5/09 Asct 5f gd-fm

Useful; effective at 5f; acts on fast ground.

Little Pete (IRE)

102(111) (89)97
4-y-o ch g City On A Hill (USA)-Full Traceability (IRE) (Ron's Victory (USA))
I W McInnes (A M Balding 12/10) Keith Brown Properties (hull) Ltd

Placings:01205/31233302604-0230050052030 **(7702)**
2009: 5^0G, 5^2G, 5^3GF, 5^0GF, 6^0GF, 5^5G, 5^0GS, 6^0G, 5^5SD, 6^2SD, 6^0SD, 6^3SD, 6^0SD,

	Starts	1st	2nd	3rd	Win & Pl
Career Total (Turf)	23	1	4	5	25346
Career Total (AW)	6	1	1	1	4345

95 5/08 Hayd 5f (0-85)H GD £6476
67 5/07 Kemp 5f STD £2047
Total win prize-money £8524

Going (Turf): Sf: 0-2 GS: 0-3 **Gd: 1-7** GF: 0-11 Fm: 0-0
Distance: **5f/6f: 2-29** 7f-8f: 0-0 9f-13f: 0-0 14f+: 0-0
Track : LH: 0-6 **RH: 1-4** Tight: 0-5 Gall: 0-3
Aids: Bl: 0-0 Vi: 0-2 Tstrap: 0-1 Ckp: 0-1
Best Rating: **97** 8/08 Gdwd 5f gd-fm

Useful; suited by 5f; acts on good ground; also goes on Polytrack; has worn a tongue-tie/visor.

Little Prudence

100 **68**
3-y-o ch f Generous (IRE)-Redgrave Devil (Tug Of War)
R M Beckett Mrs Sandra Fox

Placings:34550 **(5430)**
2009: 10^{3}GF, 12^{4}GF, 12^{5}GF, 11^{5}GF, 16^{0}G,

	Starts	1st	2nd	3rd	Win & Pl
Career Total (Turf)	5	0	0	1	963

Going (Turf): Sf: 0-0 GS: 0-0 Gd: 0-1 GF: 0-4 Fm: 0-0
Distance: 5f/6f: 0-0 7f-8f: 0-0 9f-13f: 0-4 14f+: 0-1
Track : LH: 0-3 RH: 0-1 Tight: 0-3 Gall: 0-0
Aids: Bl: 0-0 Vi: 0-0 Tstrap: 0-0 Ckp: 0-0
Best Rating: **68** 8/09 Gdwd 2m good

Little Richard (IRE)

(106) (66)**59**
10-y-o b g Alhaarth (IRE)-Intricacy (Formidable (USA))
M Wellings Mark Wellings Racing

Placings:0303023120600/22230000/0043140235400/02432131000232/11352360466121/2000463515/14542210301-34036042 **(7847)**
2009: 12^{3}SD, 12^{4}SD, 12^{0}SD, 13^{3}SD, 12^{6}SD, 13^{0}SD, 12^{4}SD, 12^{2}SD,

	Starts	1st	2nd	3rd	Win & Pl
Career Total (Turf)	8	0	2	0	1600
Career Total (AW)	83	12	14	15	38532

65 12/08 Wolv 1m4f50y (0-60)H STD £2388
68 3/08 Wolv 1m5f194y (0-65)H STD £2047
64 1/08 Kemp 1m4f (0 55)H STD £2047
61 12/07 Wolv 1m5f194y (0-55)H SS £2047
66 12/06 Wolv 1m5f194y (0-60)H STD £2730
58 12/06 Wolv 1m5f194y (0-55)H STD £2730
60 1/06 Wolv 1m4f50y (0-55)H STD £2388
53 1/06 Wolv 1m5f194y (0-45) STD £1365
56 3/05 Wolv 1m4f50y (0-45) STD £1477
49 3/05 Wolv 1m4f50y (0-40) STD £1494
42 2/04 Ling 2m H(0-40) STD £1463
55 5/02 Wolv 1m4f F STD £2331
Total win prize-money £24512

Going (Turf): **Sf: 0-0 GS: 0-2 Gd: 0-2 GF: 0-2 Fm: 0-2**
Distance: 5f/6f: 0-0 7f-8f: 0-1 9f-13f: 6-51 14f+: 6-39
Track : **LH: 11-86** RH: 1-5 **Tight: 11-74** Gall: 0-1
Aids: Bl: 0-4 Vi: 1-10 Tstrap: 11-71 Ckp: 11-71
Best Rating: **68** 3/08 Wolv 1m5f194y stand

Moderate; effective at around 1m4f-2m and acts on Polytrack; was worn cheekpieces.

Little Rococoa

(82) (39)**8**
4-y-o b g Killer Instinct-Little Kenny (Warning)
R J Price David Prosser & Keith Warrington

Placings:00006000-00 **(0857)**
2009: 8^{0}SD, 11^{0}SD,

	Starts	1st	2nd	3rd	Win & Pl
Career Total (Turf)	4	0	0	0	
Career Total (AW)	6	0	0	0	0

Going (Turf): **Sf: 0-1 GS: 0-2 Gd: 0-0 GF: 0-1 Fm: 0-0**
Distance: 5f/6f: 0-0 7f-8f: 0-1 9f-13f: 0-9 14f+: 0-0
Track : LH: 0-6 RH: 0-4 Tight: 0-4 Gall: 0-0
Aids: Bl: 0-0 Vi: 0-0 Tstrap: 0-0 Ckp: 0-0
Best Rating: **39** 11/08 Kemp 1m1f stand

Little Roxy (IRE)

(79) (43)
4-y-o b f Dilshaan-Brunswick (Warning)
Miss A M Newton-Smith The Ash Tree Inn Racing Club

Placings:00 **(0455)**
2009: 11^{0}SD, 11^{0}SD,

	Starts	1st	2nd	3rd	Win & Pl
Career Total (Turf)	0	0	0	0	
Career Total (AW)	2	0	0	0	

Going (Turf): Sf: 0-0 GS: 0-0 Gd: 0-0 GF: 0-0 Fm: 0-0
Distance: 5f/6f: 0-0 7f-8f: 0-0 9f-13f: 0-2 14f+: 0-0
Track : LH: 0-0 RH: 0-2 Tight: 0-0 Gall: 0-0
Aids: Bl: 0-0 Vi: 0-0 Tstrap: 0-0 Ckp: 0-0
Best Rating: **43** 1/09 Kemp 1m3f stand

Little Rufus

81 **62**
2-y-o b c Lujain (USA)-Compendium (Puissance)
K A Morgan P Doughty

Placings:4 **(4349)**
2009: 5^{4}G,

	Starts	1st	2nd	3rd	Win & Pl
Career Total (Turf)	1	0	0	0	337

Going (Turf): **Sf: 0-0 GS: 0-0 Gd: 0-1 GF: 0-0 Fm: 0-0**
Distance: 5f/6f: 0-1 7f-8f: 0-0 9f-13f: 0-0 14f+: 0-0
Track : LH: 0-1 RH: 0-0 Tight: 0-0 Gall: 0-0
Aids: Bl: 0-0 Vi: 0-0 Tstrap: 0-0 Ckp: 0-0
Best Rating: **62** 7/09 Pont 5f good

Little Sark (IRE)

97 (102) (60)**55**
4-y-o b g Singspiel (IRE)-Notenqueen (GER) (Turfkonig (GER))
P D Evans Trevor Gallienne

Placings:0-00630004120 **(7336)**
2009: 10^{0}GF, 11^{0}G, 10^{6}GF, 12^{3}GF, 16^{0}GF, 12^{0}HY, 12^{0}SD, 12^{4}SD, 12^{1}SD, 12^{2}SD, 14^{0}SD,

	Starts	1st	2nd	3rd	Win & Pl
Career Total (Turf)	7	0	0	1	337
Career Total (AW)	5	1	1	0	2652

57 10/09 Kemp 1m4f (0-50)H STD £2047
Total win prize-money £2047

Going (Turf): **Sf: 0-1 GS: 0-0 Gd: 0-2 GF: 0-4 Fm: 0-0**
Distance: 5f/6f: 0-0 7f-8f: 0-0 **9f-13f: 1-10** 14f+: 0-2
Track : LH: 0-8 **RH: 1-4** Tight: 0-3 Gall: 0-1
Aids: Bl: 0-0 Vi: 0-0 Tstrap: 0-1 Ckp: 0-1
Best Rating: **60** 10/09 Kemp 1m4f stand

Moderate sort; stays 1m4f; acts on Polytrack.

Little Scotland

96 **91**
2-y-o b f Acclamation-Belladera (IRE) (Alzao (USA))
T D Easterby David W Armstrong

Placings:235400 **(5199)**
2009: 5^{2}G, 5^{3}GS, 5^{5}GF, 5^{4}GF, 6^{0}G, 6^{0}GF,

	Starts	1st	2nd	3rd	Win & Pl
Career Total (Turf)	6	0	1	1	7816

Going (Turf): **Sf: 0-0 GS: 0-1 Gd: 0-2 GF: 0-3 Fm: 0-0**
Distance: 5f/6f: 0-6 7f-8f: 0-0 9f-13f: 0-0 14f+: 0-0
Track : LH: 0-0 RH: 0-0 Tight: 0-0 Gall: 0-0
Aids: Bl: 0-0 Vi: 0-0 Tstrap: 0-0 Ckp: 0-0
Best Rating: **91** 5/09 York 5f gd-sft

Useful; Listed placed; suited by 5f; acts on good ground.

Little Weed (IRE)

(58)
2-y-o b/br g Statue Of Liberty (USA)-Carna (IRE) (Anita's Prince)
B Palling The Bill & Ben Partnership

Placings:4 **(7190)**
2009: 5^{4}SD,

	Starts	1st	2nd	3rd	Win & Pl
Career Total (Turf)	0	0	0	0	
Career Total (AW)	1	0	0	0	216

Going (Turf): **Sf: 0-0 GS: 0-0 Gd: 0-0 GF: 0-0 Fm: 0-0**
Distance: 5f/6f: 0-1 7f-8f: 0-0 9f-13f: 0-0 14f+: 0-0
Track : LH: 0-1 RH: 0-0 Tight: 0-1 Gall: 0-0
Aids: Bl: 0-0 Vi: 0-0 Tstrap: 0-0 Ckp: 0-0

Littledodayno (IRE)

(106) (70)**63**
6-y-o b m Mujadil (USA)-Perfect Welcome (Taufan (USA))
M Wigham John Williams Partnership, M Wigham

Placings:212/060000631123/006000004502421/61000402100614-040 **(0861)**
2009: 5^{0}SD, 6^{4}SD, 6^{0}SD,

	Starts	1st	2nd	3rd	Win & Pl
Career Total (Turf)	22	3	4	2	18006
Career Total (AW)	24	4	2	0	9932

70 11/08 Kemp 6f (0-65)H STD £2047
70 8/08 Wolv 5f216y (0-60)H STD £2388
70 2/08 Kemp 6f (0-60)H STD £2047
65 11/07 Kemp 6f (0-55)H STD £2047
74 9/06 Folk 6f (0-65)H G-F £3238
69 8/06 Ling 6f (0-70)H GD £3238
63 5/05 Rdcr 6f FRM £4143
Total win prize-money £19153

Going (Turf): Sf: 0-2 GS: 0-3 **Gd: 1-4 GF: 1-10 Fm: 1-3**
Distance: **5f/6f: 7-37** 7f-8f: 0-8 9f-13f: 0-1 14f+: 0-0
Track : LH: 1-16 **RH: 3-13 Tight: 1-13** Gall: 0-2
Aids: Bl: 0-0 Vi: 0-0 Tstrap: 0-1 Ckp: 0-1
Best Rating: **78** 7/05 Thsk 5f good

Modest; suited by 6f; acts on most ground and on Polytrack.

Littlemisssunshine (IRE)

101(106) (74)73

4-y-o b m Oasis Dream-Sharp Catch (IRE) (Common Grounds)

J S Moore Albert Conneally

Placings:422615005/20606-04315**434** **(7872)**

2009: 5^{0}GF, 5^{4}S, 5^{3}F, 5^{1}G, 5^{5}GF, 5^{4}SD, 5^{3}SD, 5^{4}SD,

	Starts	1st	2nd	3rd	Win & Pl
Career Total (Turf)	18	2	3	1	14583
Career Total (AW)	4	0	0	1	704

73	8/09	Chep	5f16y	(0-65)H	GD	£2388
69	7/07	Folk	5f		G-F	£3886

Total win prize-money £6274

Going (Turf): Sf: 0-3 GS: 0-1 **Gd: 1-3 GF: 1-9** Fm: 0-2
Distance: **5f/6f: 2-22** 7f-8f: 0-0 9f-13f: 0-0 14f+: 0-0
Track : LH: 0-8 RH: 0-2 Tight: 0-2 Gall: 0-1
Aids: Bl: 0-0 Vi: 0-0 Tstrap: 2-16 Ckp: 2-16
Best Rating: **96** 6/07 Asct 5f gd-fm

Modest; suited by 5f; handles fast ground; goes on Polytrack; has worn cheekpieces.

Lively Blade

(91) (46)

3-y-o ch g Needwood Blade-Breezy Day (Day Is Done)

E S McMahon R L Bedding

Placings:50 **(0425)**

2009: 6^{5}SD, 7^{0}SD,

	Starts	1st	2nd	3rd	Win & Pl
Career Total (Turf)	0	0	0	0	
Career Total (AW)	2	0	0	0	0

Going (Turf): **Sf: 0-0 GS: 0-0 Gd: 0-0 GF: 0-0 Fm: 0-0**
Distance: 5f/6f: 0-1 7f-8f: 0-1 9f-13f: 0-0 14f+: 0-0
Track : LH: 0-2 RH: 0-0 Tight: 0-0 Gall: 0-0
Aids: Bl: 0-0 Vi: 0-0 Tstrap: 0-0 Ckp: 0-0
Best Rating: **46** 2/09 Sthl 7f stand

Lively Fling (USA)

104 91

3-y-o b g Dynaformer (USA)-Creaking Board (Night Shift (USA))

Miss Venetia Williams (J H M Gosden 5/10) John Nicholls (Trading) Ltd

Placings:0-120031 **(6552)**

2009: 11^{1}GF, 11^{2}GF, 14^{0}GF, 12^{0}S, 12^{3}GF, 11^{1}G,

	Starts	1st	2nd	3rd	Win & Pl
Career Total (Turf)	7	2	1	1	12181

90	10/09	Wind	1m3f135y	(0-85)H	GD	£5180
78	4/09	Leic	1m3f183y		G-F	£3238

Total win prize-money £8419

Going (Turf): Sf: 0-2 GS: 0-0 **Gd: 1-1 GF: 1-4** Fm: 0-0
Distance: 5f/6f: 0-0 7f-8f: 0-1 **9f-13f: 2-5** 14f+: 0-1
Track : LH: 0-2 **RH: 1-3 Tight: 1-2** Gall: 0-1
Aids: **Bl: 1-1** Vi: 0-1 Tstrap: 0-0 Ckp: 0-0
Best Rating: **91** 9/09 Epsm 1m4f10y gd-fm

Fair; stays 1m4f; acts on good and fast ground; has worn a visor and blinkers.

Living It Large (FR)

99(104) (89)78

2-y-o ch c Bertolini (USA)-Dilag (IRE) (Almutawakel)

R F Fisher Des Johnston

Placings:2161114 **(7536)**

2009: 6^{2}GF, 5^{1}G, 7^{6}G, 6^{1}G, 5^{1}SD, 5^{1}SD, 6^{4}SD,

	Starts	1st	2nd	3rd	Win & Pl
Career Total (Turf)	4	2	1	0	7798
Career Total (AW)	3	2	0	0	8573

89	11/09	Wolv	5f20y	(0-85)	STD	£5046
81	10/09	Wolv	5f20y	(0-75)	STD	£3238
78	10/09	Ayr	6f	(0-75)	GD	£3238
69	7/09	Muss	5f		GD	£3885

Total win prize-money £15408

Going (Turf): Sf: 0-0 GS: 0-0 **Gd: 2-3** GF: 0-1 Fm: 0-0
Distance: **5f/6f: 4-5** 7f-8f: 0-2 9f-13f: 0-0 14f+: 0-0
Track : **LH: 2-3** RH: 0-1 **Tight: 2-3** Gall: 0-0
Aids: Bl: 0-0 Vi: 0-0 Tstrap: 0-0 Ckp: 0-0
Best Rating: **89** 11/09 Wolv 5f20y stand

Very useful; effective over 5f-6f; acts on good ground and Polytrack.

Living The Dream

71(91) (46)

7-y-o b g Double Trigger (IRE)-Aquavita (Kalaglow)

Karen George Eastington Racing Club

Placings:0000 **(2221)**

2009: 12^{0}SD, 12^{0}SD, 12^{0}SD, 9^{0}GF,

	Starts	1st	2nd	3rd	Win & Pl
Career Total (Turf)	1	0	0	0	
Career Total (AW)	3	0	0	0	

Going (Turf): **Sf: 0-0 GS: 0-0 Gd: 0-0 GF: 0-1 Fm: 0-0**
Distance: 5f/6f: 0-0 7f-8f: 0-0 9f-13f: 0-4 14f+: 0-0
Track : LH: 0-3 RH: 0-1 Tight: 0-2 Gall: 0-0
Aids: Bl: 0-0 Vi: 0-0 Tstrap: 0-2 Ckp: 0-2
Best Rating: **46** 3/09 Wolv 1m4f50y stand

Lizard Island (USA)

87(105) (94)81

4-y-o b c Danehill Dancer (IRE)-Add (USA) (Spectacular Bid (USA))

P F I Cole Mrs Fitri Hay

Placings:21246/**4300-0** **(2015)**

2009: 8^{0}G,

	Starts	1st	2nd	3rd	Win & Pl
Career Total (Turf)	7	1	2	0	78895
Career Total (AW)	3	0	0	1	2261

102	7/07	Curr	6f	SH	£54898

Total win prize-money £54899

Going (Turf): **Sf: 0-1 GS: 0-0 Gd: 0-3 GF: 0-1 Fm: 0-0**
Distance: **5f/6f: 1-2** 7f-8f: 0-8 9f-13f: 0-0 14f+: 0-0
Track : LH: 0-4 RH: 0-3 Tight: 0-0 Gall: 0-4
Aids: Bl: 0-0 Vi: 0-0 Tstrap: 0-0 Ckp: 0-0
Best Rating: **110** 9/07 Curr 7f gd-fm

Useful, formerly smart; won the Group 2 Railway Stakes at the Curragh as a juvenile; stays 7f and acts on soft ground.

Llandovery

87(100) (68)65

2-y-o b c Auction House (USA)-Sweet Coincidence (Mujahid (USA))

P J McBride S A Douch

Placings:0336140 **(6993)**

2009: 7^{0}GF, 7^{3}SD, 7^{3}G, 8^{6}GF, 8^{1}SD, 8^{4}SD, 8^{0}GS,

	Starts	1st	2nd	3rd	Win & Pl
Career Total (Turf)	4	0	0	1	385
Career Total (AW)	3	1	0	1	5954

68	9/09	Wolv	1m141y	(0-80)	STD	£5046

Total win prize-money £5046

Going (Turf): **Sf: 0-0 GS: 0-1 Gd: 0-1 GF: 0-2 Fm: 0-0**
Distance: 5f/6f: 0-0 7f-8f: 0-4 **9f-13f: 1-3** 14f+: 0-0
Track : **LH: 1-4** RH: 0-1 **Tight: 1-4** Gall: 0-1
Aids: Bl: 0-0 Vi: 0-0 Tstrap: 0-0 Ckp: 0-0
Best Rating: **68** 10/09 Wolv 1m141y stand

Moderate half-brother to a middle-distance performer; stays 1m; acts on fast ground and Polytrack.

Loaded

(87) (61)

2-y-o b c Tobougg (IRE)-Missed Again (High Top)

P Winkworth P Winkworth

Placings:0 **(5191)**

2009: 7^{0}SD,

	Starts	1st	2nd	3rd	Win & Pl
Career Total (Turf)	0	0	0	0	
Career Total (AW)	1	0	0	0	

Going (Turf): **Sf: 0-0 GS: 0-0 Gd: 0-0 GF: 0-0 Fm: 0-0**
Distance: 5f/6f: 0-0 7f-8f: 0-1 9f-13f: 0-0 14f+: 0-0
Track : LH: 0-1 RH: 0-0 Tight: 0-1 Gall: 0-0
Aids: Bl: 0-0 Vi: 0-0 Tstrap: 0-0 Ckp: 0-0
Best Rating: **61** 8/09 Ling 7f stand

Local Hero (GER)

78 65

2-y-o b c Lomitas-Lolli Pop (GER) (Cagliostro (GER))

T P Tate P J Martin

Placings:5 **(2997)**

2009: 7^{5}GF,

	Starts	1st	2nd	3rd	Win & Pl
Career Total (Turf)	1	0	0	0	0

Going (Turf): **Sf: 0-0 GS: 0-0 Gd: 0-0 GF: 0-1 Fm: 0-0**
Distance: 5f/6f: 0-0 7f-8f: 0-1 9f-13f: 0-0 14f+: 0-0
Track : LH: 0-1 RH: 0-0 Tight: 0-1 Gall: 0-0
Aids: Bl: 0-0 Vi: 0-0 Tstrap: 0-0 Ckp: 0-0
Best Rating: **65** 6/09 Thsk 7f gd-fm

Localiser (IRE)

94 68

3-y-o b g Iron Mask (USA)-Becada (GER) (Cadeaux Genereux)

D Nicholls Clipper Logistics

Placings:330 **(6823)**

2009: 7^{3}GF, 8^{3}GF, 6^{0}GF,

	Starts	1st	2nd	3rd	Win & Pl
Career Total (Turf)	3	0	0	2	867

Going (Turf): **Sf: 0-0 GS: 0-0 Gd: 0-0 GF: 0-3 Fm: 0-0**

Distance: 5f/6f: 0-1 7f-8f: 0-1 9f-13f: 0-1 14f+: 0-0
Track : LH: 0-1 RH: 0-0 Tight: 0-0 Gall: 0-0
Aids: Bl: 0-0 Vi: 0-0 Tstrap: 0-0 Ckp: 0-0
Best Rating: **68** 10/09 Pont 1m4y gd-fm

Location

97(102) (61)**63**
3-y-o b f Dansili-Well Away (IRE) (Sadler's Wells (USA))
P D Evans (Evan Williams 15/8) R Edwards, S Howell & J Swinnerton

Placings:4-**6014426**0425444033**140** **(7250)**
2009: 5^{6}SD, 8^{0}SD, 7^{1}SF, 7^{4}GF, 8^{4}SD, 10^{2}G, 9^{6}GF, 10^{0}G, 11^{4}GF, 9^{2}G, 11^{5}G, 9^{4}GF, 8^{4}F, 10^{4}GF, 9^{0}GF, 10^{3}SS, 11^{3}G, 10^{1}SD, 9^{4}SD, 10^{0}SD,

	Starts	1st	2nd	3rd	Win & Pl
Career Total (Turf)	13	0	2	1	2973
Career Total (AW)	8	2	0	1	4672

61 10/09 Kemp 1m2f (0-60)H STD £2047
58 3/09 Wolv 7f32y (0-60)H SF £2047
Total win prize-money £4094

Going (Turf): **Sf: 0-0 GS: 0-0 Gd: 0-5 GF: 0-7 Fm: 0-1**
Distance: 5f/6f: 0-1 7f-8f: 1-3 9f-13f: 1-17 14f+: 0-0
Track : LH: 1-13 RH: 1-6 **Tight: 1-11** Gall: 0-0
Aids: Bl: 0-0 Vi: 0-0 Tstrap: 0-0 Ckp: 0-0
Best Rating: **63** 5/09 Pont 1m2f6y good

Moderate; stays 1m2f; acts on Polytrack.

Loch Jipp (USA)

88 **84**
4-y-o b f Belong To Me (USA)-Miss Keyonna (USA) (Septieme Ciel (USA))
J S Wainwright I Barran & P Rhodes

Placings:16104400/00000-000 **(5978)**
2009: 6^{0}G, 5^{0}G, 5^{0}GF,

	Starts	1st	2nd	3rd	Win & Pl
Career Total (Turf)	16	2	0	0	23988

96 5/07 Bevl 5f GD £14195
71 4/07 Pont 5f G-F £3886
Total win prize-money £18081

Going (Turf): Sf: 0-1 GS: 0-4 **Gd: 1-8 GF: 1-3** Fm: 0-0
Distance: **5f/6f: 2-16** 7f-8f: 0-0 9f-13f: 0-0 14f+: 0-0
Track : **LH: 1-2** RH: 0-0 Tight: 0-0 Gall: 0-1
Aids: Bl: 0-1 Vi: 0-2 Tstrap: 0-1 Ckp: 0-1
Best Rating: **98** 7/07 NmkJ 6f good

Useful; winner of the Hilary Needler in 2007; effective over 5f-6f; acts on good and fast ground.

Loch Linnhe (USA)

104 **104**
3-y-o b g Elusive Quality (USA)-Firth Of Lorne (IRE) (Danehill (USA))
J H M Gosden H R H Princess Haya Of Jordan

Placings:1030 **(4296)**
2009: 8^{1}GF, 7^{0}GF, 8^{3}G, 8^{0}G,

	Starts	1st	2nd	3rd	Win & Pl
Career Total (Turf)	4	1	0	1	7047

89 5/09 NmkR 1m G-F £5180
Total win prize-money £5181

Going (Turf): Sf: 0-0 GS: 0-0 Gd: 0-2 **GF: 1-2** Fm: 0-0
Distance: 5f/6f: 0-0 **7f-8f: 1-4** 9f-13f: 0-0 14f+: 0-0
Track : LH: 0-0 RH: 0-0 Tight: 0-0 Gall: 0-0
Aids: Bl: 0-0 Vi: 0-0 Tstrap: 0-0 Ckp: 0-0
Best Rating: **104** 7/09 NmkJ 1m good

Very useful prospect; effective at 1m; acts on fast ground.

Lochan Mor

103(106) (86)**86**
3-y-o b g Kyllachy-Bright Moll (Mind Games)
M L W Bell A Buxton

Placings:2124223 **(7155)**
2009: 6^{2}GS, 6^{1}GF, 6^{2}SD, 6^{4}S, 5^{2}SD, 5^{2}G, 5^{3}SD,

	Starts	1st	2nd	3rd	Win & Pl
Career Total (Turf)	4	1	2	0	6606
Career Total (AW)	3	0	2	1	2266

75 5/09 Yarm 6f3y G-F £2590
Total win prize-money £2590

Going (Turf): Sf: 0-1 GS: 0-1 Gd: 0-1 **GF: 1-1** Fm: 0-0
Distance: 5f/6f: 0-6 **7f-8f: 1-1** 9f-13f: 0-0 14f+: 0-0
Track : LH: 0-3 RH: 0-1 Tight: 0-2 Gall: 0-0
Aids: Bl: 0-0 Vi: 0-0 Tstrap: 0-0 Ckp: 0-0
Best Rating: **86** 10/09 Brig 5f213y good

Fair; stays 6f and acts on easy ground.

Lochbroom Sunset

86(90) (64)**53**
2-y-o b c Firebreak-Woore Lass (IRE) (Persian Bold)
S C Williams Essex Racing Club et al

Placings:000020400 **(6586)**
2009: 6^{0}SD, 6^{0}G, 7^{0}G, 6^{0}G, 6^{2}SD, 7^{0}SD, 7^{4}SD, 6^{0}SD, 7^{0}SD,

	Starts	1st	2nd	3rd	Win & Pl
Career Total (Turf)	3	0	0	0	
Career Total (AW)	6	0	1	0	605

Going (Turf): **Sf: 0-0 GS: 0-0 Gd: 0-3 GF: 0-0 Fm: 0-0**
Distance: 5f/6f: 0-3 7f-8f: 0-6 9f-13f: 0-0 14f+: 0-0
Track : LH: 0-3 RH: 0-3 Tight: 0-3 Gall: 0-0
Aids: Bl: 0-0 Vi: 0-0 Tstrap: 0-0 Ckp: 0-0
Best Rating: **64** 9/09 Ling 6f stand

Plating-class; stays 6f; acts on good; has worn a tongue tie.

Lochiel

106(107) (91)**96**
5-y-o b g Mind Games-Summerhill Special (IRE) (Roi Danzig (USA))
G A Swinbank G Hawkes & Partner

Placings:40233/12101652**312-4**532U**0**110 **(7018)**
2009: 12^{4}SD, 12^{5}GF, 12^{3}GF, 12^{2}G, 12^{U}GS, 12^{0}SD, 14^{1}GF, 12^{1}GF, 12^{0}GS,

	Starts	1st	2nd	3rd	Win & Pl
Career Total (Turf)	19	5	3	3	55735
Career Total (AW)	6	1	2	1	10218

96 10/09 NmkR 1m4f (0-95)H G-F £8723
93 9/09 Hayd 1m6f (0-90)H G-F £11215
88 12/08 Wolv 1m4f50y (0-80)H STD £5180
82 6/08 Carl 1m3f107y (0-80)H SFT £19428
78 5/08 Muss 1m4f (0-70)H GD £3238
63 5/08 Haml 1m3f16y G-S £2047
Total win prize-money £49833

Going (Turf): Sf: 1-3 GS: 1-6 Gd: 1-4 **GF: 2-6** Fm: 0-0
Distance: 5f/6f: 0-0 7f-8f: 0-0 **9f-13f: 5-21** 14f+: 1-4
Track : LH: 2-10 **RH: 4-15 Tight: 3-14** Gall: 1-6
Aids: Bl: 0-0 Vi: 0-0 Tstrap: 0-0 Ckp: 0-0
Best Rating: **96** 10/09 NmkR 1m4f gd-fm

Very useful; effective at 1m4f-1m6f; acts on most ground and on Polytrack.

Lochstar

100(106) (92)**78**
5-y-o b g Anabaa (USA)-Lochsong (Song)
A M Balding J C Smith

Placings:51/025-6104606 **(6972)**
2009: 5^{6}GF, 5^{1}SD, 5^{0}GS, 5^{4}SD, 5^{6}G, 5^{0}GF, 5^{6}SD,

	Starts	1st	2nd	3rd	Win & Pl
Career Total (Turf)	7	0	0	0	233
Career Total (AW)	5	2	1	0	11137

92 5/09 Ling 5f (0-85)H STD £5828
78 5/07 Ling 6f STD £3238
Total win prize-money £9067

Going (Turf): **Sf: 0-0 GS: 0-2 Gd: 0-2 GF: 0-2 Fm: 0-1**
Distance: **5f/6f: 2-12** 7f-8f: 0-0 9f-13f: 0-0 14f+: 0-0
Track : **LH: 2-5** RH: 0-1 **Tight: 2-3** Gall: 0-3
Aids: Bl: 0-0 Vi: 0-0 Tstrap: 0-0 Ckp: 0-0
Best Rating: **92** 5/09 Ling 5f stand

Useful; effective over 6f; acts on fast ground; also goes on Polytrack.

Lock 'N' Load (IRE)

78 **69**
3-y-o b f Johannesburg (USA)-Margay (IRE) (Marju (IRE))
B Smart Steve Macdonald

Placings:040-0 **(6311)**
2009: 8^{0}GF,

	Starts	1st	2nd	3rd	Win & Pl
Career Total (Turf)	4	0	0	0	414

Going (Turf): **Sf: 0-0 GS: 0-1 Gd: 0-0 GF: 0-3 Fm: 0-0**
Distance: 5f/6f: 0-1 7f-8f: 0-3 9f-13f: 0-0 14f+: 0-0
Track : LH: 0-2 RH: 0-2 Tight: 0-3 Gall: 0-0
Aids: Bl: 0-0 Vi: 0-0 Tstrap: 0-0 Ckp: 0-0
Best Rating: **69** 7/08 Thsk 7f gd-fm

Fair; stays 7f; acts on fast ground.

Locksley Hall (USA)

102(95) (78)**91**
2-y-o ch g Songandaprayer (USA)-Wonderously (USA) (Awesome Again (CAN))
E F Vaughan Gold Rush Thoroughbreds

Placings:22 **(6054)**
2009: 6^{2}SD, 6^{2}GF,

	Starts	1st	2nd	3rd	Win & Pl
Career Total (Turf)	1	0	1	0	1638
Career Total (AW)	1	0	1	0	771

Going (Turf): **Sf: 0-0 GS: 0-0 Gd: 0-0 GF: 0-1 Fm: 0-0**
Distance: 5f/6f: 0-1 7f-8f: 0-1 9f-13f: 0-0 14f+: 0-0
Track : LH: 0-0 RH: 0-1 Tight: 0-0 Gall: 0-0
Aids: Bl: 0-0 Vi: 0-0 Tstrap: 0-0 Ckp: 0-0
Best Rating: **91** 9/09 Newb 6f8y gd-fm

Promising colt; runner-up over 6f on Polytrackand fast turf.

Locum

103(100) (73)**72**
4-y-o ch g Dr Fong (USA)-Exhibitor (USA) (Royal Academy (USA))

M H Tompkins Ray Smith and Partners

Placings:052/30246433224-1304624440 (6473)
2009: 10^{1}GF, 9^{3}GF, 12^{0}SD, 10^{4}GF, 10^{6}GF, 10^{2}G, 12^{4}GF, 12^{4}G, 12^{4}G, 12^{0}GF,

	Starts	1st	2nd	3rd	Win & Pl
Career Total (Turf)	15	1	1	1	6777
Career Total (AW)	9	0	4	3	4012

72 5/09 Yarm 1m2f21y (0-70)H G-F £3238
Total win prize-money £3238

Going (Turf): Sf: 0-0 GS: 0-1 Gd: 0-4 **GF: 1-10** Fm: 0-0
Distance: 5f/6f: 0-1 7f-8f: 0-3 **9f-13f: 1-20** 14f+: 0-0
Track : **LH: 1-15** RH: 0-8 **Tight: 1-14** Gall: 0-3
Aids: Bl: 0-0 Vi: 0-0 Tstrap: 0-0 Ckp: 0-0
Best Rating: **73** 6/08 Wolv 1m1f103y stand

Modest; stays 1m4f; acts on Polytrack and fast turf.

Loden

83(80) (48)**66**
2-y-o b c Barathea (IRE)-Tentpole (USA) (Rainbow Quest (USA))
L M Cumani Fittocks Stud

Placings:040 (6291)
2009: 7^{0}G, 8^{4}GF, 8^{0}SD,

	Starts	1st	2nd	3rd	Win & Pl
Career Total (Turf)	2	0	0	0	385
Career Total (AW)	1	0	0	0	

Going (Turf): Sf: 0-0 GS: 0-0 Gd: 0-1 GF: 0-1 Fm: 0-0
Distance: 5f/6f: 0-0 7f-8f: 0-3 9f-13f: 0-0 14f+: 0-0
Track : LH: 0-1 RH: 0-1 Tight: 0-0 Gall: 0-1
Aids: Bl: 0-0 Vi: 0-0 Tstrap: 0-0 Ckp: 0-0
Best Rating: **66** 9/09 Ffos 1m gd-fm

Lodi (IRE)

103(105) (85)**91**
4-y-o ch g Bertolini (USA)-Lady Of Leisure (USA) (Diesis)
J Akehurst Tattenham Corner Racing 3

Placings:43105/346103052005-0001000033424 (6726)
2009: 7^{0}SD, 6^{0}GS, 7^{0}GF, 7^{1}GF, 7^{0}G, 7^{0}GF, 7^{0}GF, 8^{0}GF, 6^{3}G, 7^{3}GF, 7^{4}GF, 7^{2}GS, 7^{4}SD,

	Starts	1st	2nd	3rd	Win & Pl
Career Total (Turf)	25	2	2	5	15218
Career Total (AW)	5	1	0	0	2898

83 5/09 Ling 7f (0-75)H G-F £3238
86 6/08 Wind 6f (0-85)H G-F £5180
79 9/07 Kemp 6f STD £2730
Total win prize-money £11149

Going (Turf): Sf: 0-1 GS: 0-4 Gd: 0-7 **GF: 2-13** Fm: 0-0
Distance: **5f/6f: 2-10** 7f-8f: 1-19 9f-13f: 0-1 14f+: 0-0
Track : LH: 0-6 **RH: 1-4** Tight: 0-5 **Gall: 1-4**
Aids: Bl: 0-0 Vi: 0-0 Tstrap: 0-0 Ckp: 0-0
Best Rating: **91** 9/08 Newb 7f good

Fair; effective over 6f-7f; acts on fast ground and on Polytrack; has worn a tongue tie.

Lofthouse

83(91) (59)**56**
2-y-o b g Hunting Lion (IRE)-Noble Destiny (Dancing Brave (USA))
M R Channon Ray Angels

Placings:003005660 (7363)
2009: 5^{0}GS, 5^{0}G, 6^{3}G, 6^{0}GF, 6^{0}GF, 6^{5}SD, 7^{6}G, 7^{6}SD, 7^{0}SD,

	Starts	1st	2nd	3rd	Win & Pl
Career Total (Turf)	6	0	0	1	722
Career Total (AW)	3	0	0	0	0

Going (Turf): Sf: 0-0 GS: 0-1 Gd: 0-3 GF: 0-2 Fm: 0-0
Distance: 5f/6f: 0-5 7f-8f: 0-4 9f-13f: 0-0 14f+: 0-0
Track : LH: 0-4 RH: 0-2 Tight: 0-3 Gall: 0-0
Aids: Bl: 0-0 Vi: 0-0 Tstrap: 0-0 Ckp: 0-0
Best Rating: **59** 10/09 Kemp 7f stand

Modest half-brother to several sprint winners; stays 7f; acts on Polytrack and good ground on turf.

Logic Way (USA)

104 **108**
5-y-o b g Freud (USA)-Just A Ginny (USA) (Go For Gin (USA))
Miss D Mountain (Trainer Unknown 26/3) Al-Abdulmalik Hassan

Placings:00450/51232343/12151132-015000 (6106)
2009: 12^{0}G, 11^{1}G, 9^{5}GF, 10^{0}GF, 12^{0}GS, 10^{0}GF,

	Starts	1st	2nd	3rd	Win & Pl
Career Total (Turf)	23	6	4	4	220128
Career Total (AW)	4	0	0	0	2038

3/09 Dohr 1m3f GD £54389
99 10/08 Belm 1m1f H FRM £45226
10/08 Belm 1m110y FRM £16884
7/08 Sara 1m FRM £19296
5/08 Belm 1m110y YLD £15075
5/07 Belm 1m110y FRM £12857
Total win prize-money £163727

Going (Turf): Sf: 0-1 GS: 0-1 Gd: 1-4 GF: 0-3 **Fm: 4-10**
Distance: 5f/6f: 0-0 7f-8f: 1-5 **9f-13f: 5-22** 14f+: 0-0
Track : **LH: 1-5** RH: 0-0 Tight: 0-1 Gall: 0-2
Aids: **Bl: 1-7** Vi: 0-1 Tstrap: 0-0 Ckp: 0-0
Best Rating: **108** 12/08 Cald 1m4f firm

Very useful; formerly trained in Qatar and the US; stays 1m3f; acts on good and faster ground; has worn blinkers and a tongue tie.

Logos Astra (USA)

93(97) (73)**72**
2-y-o b c Elusive Quality (USA)-Wild Planet (USA) (Nureyev (USA))
D R Lanigan Niarchos Family

Placings:4325 (5682)
2009: 7^{4}G, 7^{3}GF, 7^{2}SD, 8^{5}SD,

	Starts	1st	2nd	3rd	Win & Pl
Career Total (Turf)	2	0	0	1	1251
Career Total (AW)	2	0	1	0	1344

Going (Turf): Sf: 0-0 GS: 0-0 Gd: 0-1 GF: 0-1 Fm: 0-0
Distance: 5f/6f: 0-0 7f-8f: 0-3 9f-13f: 0-1 14f+: 0-0
Track : LH: 0-2 RH: 0-2 Tight: 0-2 Gall: 0-0
Aids: Bl: 0-0 Vi: 0-0 Tstrap: 0-0 Ckp: 0-0
Best Rating: **73** 9/09 Wolv 1m141y stand

Fair; stays 7f; acts on good ground and on Polytrack.

Lois Darlin (IRE)

73(92) (54)**43**
3-y-o ch f Indian Haven-Miriana (IRE) (Bluebird (USA))
R A Harris The Digging Club Racing

Placings:0300450433-402500 (1956)
2009: 6^{4}SS, 7^{0}SD, 5^{2}SD, 5^{5}SD, 5^{0}SD, 5^{0}F,

	Starts	1st	2nd	3rd	Win & Pl
Career Total (Turf)	4	0	0	0	0
Career Total (AW)	12	0	1	3	1695

Going (Turf): Sf: 0-0 GS: 0-1 Gd: 0-0 GF: 0-2 Fm: 0-1
Distance: 5f/6f: 0-12 7f-8f: 0-3 9f-13f: 0-1 14f+: 0-0
Track : LH: 0-12 RH: 0-2 Tight: 0-8 Gall: 0-3
Aids: Bl: 0-9 Vi: 0-1 Tstrap: 0-4 Ckp: 0-4
Best Rating: **54** 12/08 GrLe 6f stand

Modest; stays 1m; acts on Polytrack and fast turf; has worn cheekpieces and blinkers.

Lombok

99 **77**
3-y-o b c Hernando (FR)-Miss Rinjani (Shirley Heights)
M L W Bell J L C Pearce

Placings:0-56541 (3861)
2009: 12^{5}GF, 10^{6}G, 11^{5}G, 14^{4}GF, 14^{1}GF,

	Starts	1st	2nd	3rd	Win & Pl
Career Total (Turf)	6	1	0	0	6668

77 7/09 Nott 1m6f15y (0-80)H G-F £6476
Total win prize-money £6476

Going (Turf): Sf: 0-0 GS: 0-0 Gd: 0-3 **GF: 1-3** Fm: 0-0
Distance: 5f/6f: 0-0 7f-8f: 0-1 9f-13f: 0-3 **14f+: 1-2**
Track : **LH: 1-4** RH: 0-1 Tight: 0-0 Gall: 0-1
Aids: Bl: 0-0 Vi: 0-0 Tstrap: 0-0 Ckp: 0-0
Best Rating: **77** 7/09 Nott 1m6f15y gd-fm

Modest; stays 1m6f; acts on fast ground.

Lomica

91(91) (32)**56**
3-y-o ch f Lomitas-Ecstatic (Nashwan (USA))
Miss J A Camacho Miss Julie Camacho

Placings:040-004340 (4818)
2009: 8^{0}SD, 11^{0}SD, 9^{4}GF, 9^{3}G, 12^{4}GF, 10^{0}GF,

	Starts	1st	2nd	3rd	Win & Pl
Career Total (Turf)	6	0	0	1	1311
Career Total (AW)	3	0	0	0	

Going (Turf): Sf: 0-2 GS: 0-0 Gd: 0-1 GF: 0-3 Fm: 0-0
Distance: 5f/6f: 0-0 7f-8f: 0-3 9f-13f: 0-6 14f+: 0-0
Track : LH: 0-5 RH: 0-4 Tight: 0-4 Gall: 0-0
Aids: Bl: 0-0 Vi: 0-0 Tstrap: 0-4 Ckp: 0-4
Best Rating: **56** 9/08 Thsk 1m soft

London Bridge

100 **82**
3-y-o br g Beat Hollow-Cantanta (Top Ville)
Noel Meade (J H M Gosden 12/8) R J Bagnall

Placings:2-41000 (4910)
2009: 10^{4}G, 10^{1}GF, 10^{0}G, 12^{0}GF, 10^{0}G,

	Starts	1st	2nd	3rd	Win & Pl
Career Total (Turf)	6	1	1	0	7155

82 5/09 NmkR 1m2f G-F £5180
Total win prize-money £5181

Going (Turf): Sf: 0-0 GS: 0-1 Gd: 0-3 **GF: 1-2** Fm: 0-0
Distance: 5f/6f: 0-0 7f-8f: 0-1 **9f-13f: 1-5** 14f+: 0-0
Track : LH: 0-2 RH: 0-2 Tight: 0-1 Gall: 0-2
Aids: Bl: 0-0 Vi: 0-0 Tstrap: 0-0 Ckp: 0-0
Best Rating: **82** 5/09 NmkR 1m2f gd-fm

Useful; stays 1m2f and acts on soft and fast ground.

London Girl (IRE)

79(79) (43)36

2-y-o b f Trans Island-Sweet As A Nut (IRE) (Pips Pride)

A J McCabe Sale Of The Century

Placings:006600 **(5835)**

2009: 5^{0}GF, 5^{0}SD, 5^{6}SD, 7^{6}GF, 5^{0}SF, 5^{0}SD,

	Starts	1st	2nd	3rd	Win & Pl
Career Total (Turf)	2	0	0	0	0
Career Total (AW)	4	0	0	0	0

Going (Turf): **Sf: 0-0 GS: 0-0 Gd: 0-0 GF: 0-2 Fm: 0-0**
Distance: 5f/6f: 0-5 7f-8f: 0-1 9f-13f: 0-0 14f+: 0-0
Track : LH: 0-3 RH: 0-0 Tight: 0-3 Gall: 0-0
Aids: Bl: 0-0 Vi: 0-0 Tstrap: 0-2 Ckp: 0-2
Best Rating: **43** 6/09 Sthl 5f stand

London Gold

100 78

2-y-o b c Fraam-Princess Londis (Interrex (CAN))

H Candy John Simms

Placings:421 **(7289)**

2009: 6^{4}GF, 6^{2}GS, 6^{1}S,

	Starts	1st	2nd	3rd	Win & Pl
Career Total (Turf)	3	1	1	0	7525

78 11/09 Donc 6f SFT £6152

Total win prize-money £6152

Going (Turf): **Sf: 1-1** GS: 0-1 Gd: 0-0 GF: 0-1 Fm: 0-0
Distance: **5f/6f: 1-2** 7f-8f: 0-1 9f-13f: 0-0 14f+: 0-0
Track : LH: 0-0 RH: 0-0 Tight: 0-0 Gall: 0-0
Aids: Bl: 0-0 Vi: 0-0 Tstrap: 0-0 Ckp: 0-0
Best Rating: **78** 11/09 Donc 6f soft

Fair; acts well in soft ground; effective at 6f.

London Stripe (IRE)

96 79

2-y-o ch c Rock Of Gibraltar (IRE)-Agenda (IRE) (Sadler's Wells (USA))

Sir Michael Stoute Takashi Watanabe

Placings:51 **(7096)**

2009: 8^{5}G, 7^{1}G,

	Starts	1st	2nd	3rd	Win & Pl
Career Total (Turf)	2	1	0	0	3974

79 10/09 Yarm 7f3y GD £3974

Total win prize-money £3974

Going (Turf): Sf: 0-0 GS: 0-0 **Gd: 1-2** GF: 0-0 Fm: 0-0
Distance: 5f/6f: 0-0 **7f-8f: 1-2** 9f-13f: 0-0 14f+: 0-0
Track : LH: 0-0 RH: 0-0 Tight: 0-0 Gall: 0-0
Aids: Bl: 0-0 Vi: 0-0 Tstrap: 0-0 Ckp: 0-0
Best Rating: **79** 10/09 Yarm 7f3y good

Ffirst foal of a 1m2f winner; ability on debut over 1m on good ground before scoring over 7f.

Lone Wolfe

(111) (97)100

5-y-o b g Foxhound (USA)-Fleet Hill (IRE) (Warrshan (USA))

Jane Chapple-Hyam Gordon Li

Placings:13342300/000**233313-6** **(0123)**

2009: 6^{6}SD,

	Starts	1st	2nd	3rd	Win & Pl
Career Total (Turf)	10	0	1	3	9828

Career Total (AW)	**8**	**2**	**1**	**4**	**20654**

97 12/08 GrLe 6f (0-100)H STD £11354
70 1/07 Kemp 7f STD £4728

Total win prize-money £16082

Going (Turf): **Sf: 0-2 GS: 0-0 Gd: 0-5 GF: 0-3 Fm: 0-0**
Distance: 5f/6f: 1-6 7f-8f: 1-11 9f-13f: 0-1 14f+: 0-0
Track : LH: 1-6 RH: 1-6 Tight: 0-2 **Gall: 1-4**
Aids: Bl: 0-0 Vi: 0-0 Tstrap: 0-0 Ckp: 0-0
Best Rating: **100** 8/07 Deau 1m good

Very useful; Listed placed; effective over 6f-1m; acts on good ground; goes on Polytrack.

Lonely Star (IRE)

96(83) (49)78

3-y-o b f Bachelor Duke (USA)-Soviet Belle (IRE) (Soviet Star (USA))

D R Lanigan Saeed H Altayer

Placings:5030-325 **(3100)**

2009: 8^{3}G, 10^{2}G, 9^{5}G,

	Starts	1st	2nd	3rd	Win & Pl
Career Total (Turf)	6	0	1	2	2938
Career Total (AW)	1	0	0	0	

Going (Turf): **Sf: 0-1 GS: 0-1 Gd: 0-4 GF: 0-0 Fm: 0-0**
Distance: 5f/6f: 0-0 7f-8f: 0-2 9f-13f: 0-5 14f+: 0-0
Track : LH: 0-2 RH: 0-4 Tight: 0-2 Gall: 0-0
Aids: Bl: 0-0 Vi: 0-0 Tstrap: 0-0 Ckp: 0-0
Best Rating: **78** 5/09 Nott 1m2f50y good

Fair; effective over 1m; acts on good and easier ground.

Long Distance (FR)

42(103) (79)52

4-y-o b/br g Storming Home-Lovers Luck (IRE) (Anabaa (USA))

Miss Lucinda V Russell (J R Fanshawe 19/4) Mr And Mrs T P Winnell

Placings:022/103-20 **(6681)**

2009: 12^{2}SD, 12^{0}G,

	Starts	1st	2nd	3rd	Win & Pl
Career Total (Turf)	5	0	2	0	1411
Career Total (AW)	3	1	1	1	3256

76 8/08 Wolv 1m1f103y STD £2047

Total win prize-money £2047

Going (Turf): **Sf: 0-1 GS: 0-0 Gd: 0-4 GF: 0-0 Fm: 0-0**
Distance: 5f/6f: 0-0 7f-8f: 0-3 **9f-13f: 1-5** 14f+: 0-0
Track : **LH: 1-4** RH: 0-2 **Tight: 1-4** Gall: 0-1
Aids: Bl: 0-0 Vi: 0-1 Tstrap: 0-0 Ckp: 0-0
Best Rating: **79** 1/09 Wolv 1m4f50y stand

Fair; stays 1m4f; acts on a sound surface; goes on Polytrack.

Long Lashes (USA)

107 107

2-y-o b f Rock Hard Ten (USA)-Border Dispute (USA) (Boundary (USA))

Saeed Bin Suroor (Mrs John Harrington 26/6) Godolphin

Placings:1140 **(6269)**

2009: 6^{1}S, 7^{1}G, 7^{4}HY, 8^{0}G,

	Starts	1st	2nd	3rd	Win & Pl
Career Total (Turf)	4	2	0	0	65785

107 8/09 NmkJ 7f GD £28385
102 6/09 Curr 6f SFT £30021

Total win prize-money £58407

Going (Turf): **Sf: 1-2** GS: 0-0 **Gd: 1-2** GF: 0-0 Fm: 0-0
Distance: 5f/6f: 1-1 7f-8f: 1-3 9f-13f: 0-0 14f+: 0-0
Track : LH: 0-0 RH: 0-1 Tight: 0-0 Gall: 0-1
Aids: Bl: 0-0 Vi: 0-0 Tstrap: 0-0 Ckp: 0-0
Best Rating: **107** 8/09 NmkJ 7f good

Smart; Listed and Group 3 winner; effective over 6f-7f; acts on good and soft.

Longboat Key

104(89) (64)77

3-y-o b g Dr Fong (USA)-You Are The One (Unfuwain (USA))

M Johnston Mrs Christine Brown

Placings:03-5**203**3352250 **(4793)**

2009: 8^{5}SD, **10^{2}SD, 11^{0}SD**, 12^{3}GF, 14^{3}F, 12^{5}GF, 14^{2}GF, 16^{2}GF, 14^{5}G, 16^{0}G,

	Starts	1st	2nd	3rd	Win & Pl
Career Total (Turf)	8	0	2	3	6474
Career Total (AW)	4	0	1	0	964

Going (Turf): **Sf: 0-0 GS: 0-1 Gd: 0-2 GF: 0-4 Fm: 0-1**
Distance: 5f/6f: 0-0 7f-8f: 0-1 9f-13f: 0-6 14f+: 0-5
Track : LH: 0-7 RH: 0-5 Tight: 0-5 Gall: 0-1
Aids: Bl: 0-4 Vi: 0-0 Tstrap: 0-0 Ckp: 0-0
Best Rating: **77** 7/09 Bevl 2m35y gd-fm

Fair; stays 2m; acts on fast and easy ground; goes on Polytrack; has worn blinkers.

Longliner

94 77

2-y-o gr c Dalakhani (IRE)-Ive Gota Bad Liver (USA) (Mt. Livermore (USA))

Sir Michael Stoute Rick Barnes

Placings:32 **(7095)**

2009: 8^{3}GF, 8^{2}G,

	Starts	1st	2nd	3rd	Win & Pl
Career Total (Turf)	2	0	1	1	1737

Going (Turf): **Sf: 0-0 GS: 0-0 Gd: 0-1 GF: 0-1 Fm: 0-0**
Distance: 5f/6f: 0-0 7f-8f: 0-1 9f-13f: 0-1 14f+: 0-0
Track : LH: 0-0 RH: 0-0 Tight: 0-0 Gall: 0-0
Aids: Bl: 0-0 Vi: 0-0 Tstrap: 0-0 Ckp: 0-0
Best Rating: **77** 10/09 Yarm 1m3y good

Fair; stays 1m; acts on a sound surface.

Longspur

71 (75)79

5-y-o br g Singspiel (IRE)-Bunting (Shaadi (USA))

M W Easterby M W Easterby

Placings:321/060505-P00 **(7247)**

2009: 12^{P}G, 10^{0}GF, 10^{0}S,

	Starts	1st	2nd	3rd	Win & Pl
Career Total (Turf)	11	0	1	1	2023
Career Total (AW)	1	1	0	0	3239

75 8/07 Kemp 1m4f STD £3238

Total win prize-money £3239

Going (Turf): **Sf: 0-2 GS: 0-3 Gd: 0-3 GF: 0-2 Fm: 0-1**
Distance: 5f/6f: 0-0 7f-8f: 0-0 **9f-13f: 1-12** 14f+: 0-0
Track : LH: 0-9 **RH: 1-3** Tight: 0-1 Gall: 0-6
Aids: Bl: 0-0 Vi: 0-0 Tstrap: 0-0 Ckp: 0-0

Best Rating: 84 8/07 NmkJ 1m4f firm

Fair; stays 1m4f; acts on fast ground.

Lonsdale Lad

(78) (27)**14**
3-y-o b g Elusive City (USA)-Winchcombe (Danehill (USA))
R C Guest Lonsdales Racing

Placings:6000000-0 **(0037)**
2009: 7^{0}SS,

	Starts	1st	2nd	3rd	Win & Pl
Career Total (Turf)	2	0	0	0	
Career Total (AW)	6	0	0	0	0

Going (Turf): Sf: 0-1 GS: 0-0 Gd: 0-1 GF: 0-0 Fm: 0-0
Distance: 5f/6f: 0-5 7f-8f: 0-3 9f-13f: 0-0 14f+: 0-0
Track : LH: 0-6 RH: 0-1 Tight: 0-1 Gall: 0-3
Aids: Bl: 0-3 Vi: 0-0 Tstrap: 0-1 Ckp: 0-1
Best Rating: 27 12/08 Wolv 5f20y stand

Looby Loo

(101) (56)
3-y-o b f Kyllachy-Halland Park Lass (IRE) (Spectrum (IRE))
P W Chapple-Hyam A Black

Placings:26 **(7107)**
2009: 5^{2}SD, 6^{6}SD,

	Starts	1st	2nd	3rd	Win & Pl
Career Total (Turf)	0	0	0	0	
Career Total (AW)	2	0	1	0	605

Going (Turf): Sf: 0-0 GS: 0-0 Gd: 0-0 GF: 0-0 Fm: 0-0
Distance: 5f/6f: 0-2 7f-8f: 0-0 9f-13f: 0-0 14f+: 0-0
Track : LH: 0-0 RH: 0-2 Tight: 0-0 Gall: 0-0
Aids: Bl: 0-0 Vi: 0-0 Tstrap: 0-0 Ckp: 0-0
Best Rating: 56 9/09 Kemp 5f stand

Modest; stays 5f; acts on Polytrack.

Look Busy (IRE)

110 **111**
4-y-o b f Danetime (IRE)-Unfortunate (Komaite (USA))
A Berry A Underwood

Placings:P423311224235/41114161124-131360052 **(6499a)**
2009: 5^{1}G, 6^{3}F, 5^{1}HY, 6^{3}G, 5^{6}G, 5^{0}GF, 5^{0}HY, 5^{5}GF, 5^{2}G,

	Starts	1st	2nd	3rd	Win & Pl
Career Total (Turf)	33	10	6	5	269825

108	5/09	Hayd	5f		HVY	£56770
98	4/09	Bath	5f11y		GD	£22708
111	8/08	Curr	5f		SFT	£35882
109	8/08	Bevl	5f		SFT	£23704
110	7/08	Ayr	5f	H	GD	£25904
93	6/08	Ayr	5f		G-F	£17031
104	5/08	Bevl	5f		G-F	£12462
104	5/08	Ches	5f16y	(0-100)H	GD	£13246
88	8/07	Thsk	5f		G-F	£7772
76	7/07	Muss	5f2y		GD	£2590

Total win prize-money £218071

Going (Turf): Sf: 3-8 GS: 0-3 **Gd: 4-11** GF: 3-10 Fm: 0-1
Distance: **5f/6f: 10-29** 7f-8f: 0-4 9f-13f: 0-0 14f+: 0-0
Track : **LH: 2-7** RH: 0-1 Tight: 1-6 Gall: 1-1
Aids: Bl: 0-0 Vi: 0-0 Tstrap: 0-0 Ckp: 0-0
Best Rating: 111 8/08 Curr 5f soft

Smart; winner of the 2009 Temple Stakes; also winner in Group 3 and Listed company; acts on most ground.

Look Here

110 **121**
4-y-o b f Hernando (FR)-Last Look (Rainbow Quest (USA))
R M Beckett J H Richmond-Watson

Placings:1/213-33620 **(6872a)**
2009: 12^{3}G, 10^{3}Y, 12^{6}G, 11^{2}GF, 10^{0}F,

	Starts	1st	2nd	3rd	Win & Pl
Career Total (Turf)	9	2	2	3	349705

121	6/08	Epsm	1m4f10y	GD	£208118
81	10/07	Sals	1m	G-S	£4533

Total win prize-money £212653

Going (Turf): Sf: 0-1 **GS: 1-1 Gd: 1-3** GF: 0-2 Fm: 0-1
Distance: 5f/6f: 0-0 7f-8f: 1-1 9f-13f: 1-7 14f+: 0-1
Track : **LH: 1-6** RH: 0-2 **Tight: 1-3** Gall: 0-3
Aids: Bl: 0-0 Vi: 0-0 Tstrap: 0-0 Ckp: 0-0
Best Rating: 121 6/08 Epsm 1m4f10y good

High class filly; won the 2008 Epsom Oaks; subsequently third in the St Leger; narrowly beaten in Comonation Cup and Irish St Leger at four; stays 1m6f, seems best at 1m4f; best on ground good or softer.

Look Officer (USA)

(90) (63)**66**
3-y-o b f Officer (USA)-Inn Between (USA) (Quiet American (USA))
Tom Dascombe (David Wachman 20/9) Grant Thornton Racing Club

Placings:6003400-6203 **(7694)**
2009: 8^{6}GF, 10^{2}GF, 9^{0}YS, 10^{3}SD,

	Starts	1st	2nd	3rd	Win & Pl
Career Total (Turf)	10	0	1	1	2176
Career Total (AW)	1	0	0	1	292

Going (Turf): Sf: 0-1 GS: 0-0 Gd: 0-3 GF: 0-3 Fm: 0-0
Distance: 5f/6f: 0-2 7f-8f: 0-6 9f-13f: 0-3 14f+: 0-0
Track : LH: 0-6 RH: 0-4 Tight: 0-1 Gall: 0-0
Aids: Bl: 0-3 Vi: 0-0 Tstrap: 0-0 Ckp: 0-0
Best Rating: 66 6/09 DRoy 1m2f100y gd-fm

Modest; stays 1m2f; goes on Polytrack.

Look To This Day

97(86) (46)**79**
4-y-o ch f In The Wings-Yanka (USA) (Blushing John (USA))
R Charlton A Parker (London)

Placings:006100-3036 **(4098)**
2009: 11^{3}GF, 16^{0}G, 14^{3}G, 14^{6}G,

	Starts	1st	2nd	3rd	Win & Pl
Career Total (Turf)	9	1	0	2	4860
Career Total (AW)	1	0	0	0	

79	8/08	Bath	1m5f22y (0-70)H	G-S	£3367

Total win prize-money £3368

Going (Turf): Sf: 0-1 **GS: 1-1** Gd: 0-4 GF: 0-3 Fm: 0-0
Distance: 5f/6f: 0-0 7f-8f: 0-0 9f-13f: 0-5 **14f+: 1-5**
Track : **LH: 1-4** RH: 0-5 **Tight: 1-7** Gall: 0-2
Aids: Bl: 0-0 Vi: 0-0 Tstrap: 0-1 Ckp: 0-1
Best Rating: 79 8/08 Bath 1m5f22y gd-sft

Look Whos Next

92(99) (75)**71**
2-y-o ch c Compton Place-Look Here's Carol (IRE) (Safawan)

E S McMahon S L Edwards

Placings:334321 **(6347)**
2009: 5^{3}G, 5^{3}G, 5^{4}G, 6^{3}GS, 5^{2}G, 5^{1}SD,

	Starts	1st	2nd	3rd	Win & Pl
Career Total (Turf)	5	0	1	3	2612
Career Total (AW)	1	1	0	0	3886

75	9/09	Wolv	5f20y	STD	£3885

Total win prize-money £3886

Going (Turf): Sf: 0-0 GS: 0-1 Gd: 0-4 GF: 0-0 Fm: 0-0
Distance: **5f/6f: 1-5** 7f-8f: 0-1 9f-13f: 0-0 14f+: 0-0
Track : **LH: 1-3** RH: 0-0 **Tight: 1-1** Gall: 0-1
Aids: Bl: 0-0 Vi: 0-0 Tstrap: 0-0 Ckp: 0-0
Best Rating: 75 9/09 Wolv 5f20y stand

Fair; suited by 5f; acts on Polytrack and good ground.

Looks Like Slim

91(77) (35)**55**
2-y-o b c Passing Glance-Slims Lady (Theatrical Charmer)
P F I Cole Martyn Butler

Placings:00402 **(5935)**
2009: 6^{0}GF, 6^{0}GF, 5^{4}G, 7^{0}SD, 7^{2}GF,

	Starts	1st	2nd	3rd	Win & Pl
Career Total (Turf)	4	0	1	0	1541
Career Total (AW)	1	0	0	0	

Going (Turf): Sf: 0-0 GS: 0-0 Gd: 0-1 GF: 0-3 Fm: 0-0
Distance: 5f/6f: 0-3 7f-8f: 0-2 9f-13f: 0-0 14f+: 0-0
Track : LH: 0-0 RH: 0-1 Tight: 0-0 Gall: 0-1
Aids: Bl: 0-0 Vi: 0-0 Tstrap: 0-0 Ckp: 0-0
Best Rating: 55 9/09 Leic 7f9y gd-fm

Moderate; effective over 7f; acts on fast ground.

Looks The Business (IRE)

105(104) (64)**61**
8-y-o b g Marju (IRE)-Business Centre (IRE) (Digamist (USA))
A B Haynes Mould, Harrold, Drewett & Drewett

Placings:445/245000/24351325/21330/6621/03332430315 00-0410100 **(7214)**
2009: 11^{0}GF, 14^{4}GF, 12^{1}GF, 14^{0}GF, 13^{1}F, 16^{0}SD, 13^{0}SD,

	Starts	1st	2nd	3rd	Win & Pl
Career Total (Turf)	25	3	3	5	11926
Career Total (AW)	21	3	3	4	11231

61	8/09	Bath	1m5f22y (0-55)H	FRM	£1942
61	7/09	Wwck	1m4f134y (0-60)H	G-F	£2047
64	6/08	Ling	1m5f (0-65)H	STD	£1942
66	1/08	Wolv	1m4f50y	STD	£2047
66	7/06	Yarm	1m3f101y (0-60)H	FRM	£2590
69	7/05	Wolv	1m4f50y	STD	£3041

Total win prize-money £13614

Going (Turf): Sf: 0-2 GS: 0-2 Gd: 0-4 GF: 1-10 **Fm: 2-7**
Distance: 5f/6f: 0-0 7f-8f: 0-2 **9f-13f: 5-37** 14f+: 1-7
Track : **LH: 6-38** RH: 0-5 **Tight: 5-34** Gall: 0-1
Aids: Bl: 0-0 Vi: 0-0 Tstrap: 2-9 Ckp: 2-9
Best Rating: 69 8/07 Ling 1m4f stand

Moderate; stays 1m5f; acts on fast ground; goes on Polytrack; suited by forcing tactics.

Looping The Loop (USA)

(89) (49)**56**
4-y-o gr/ro g Alphabet Soup (USA)-Citidance Missy (USA) (Citidancer (USA))

J G Portman A S B Portman

Placings:00050-60 (3275)
2009: 12^{6}SD, 16^{0}SD,

	Starts	1st	2nd	3rd	Win & Pl
Career Total (Turf)	2	0	0	0	
Career Total (AW)	5	0	0	0	0

Going (Turf): Sf: 0-0 GS: 0-1 Gd: 0-0 GF: 0-1 Fm: 0-0
Distance: 5f/6f: 0-0 7f-8f: 0-2 9f-13f: 0-3 14f+: 0-2
Track : LH: 0-2 RH: 0-4 Tight: 0-2 Gall: 0-1
Aids: Bl: 0-0 Vi: 0-0 Tstrap: 0-0 Ckp: 0-0
Best Rating: 56 5/08 Wind 1m2f7y gd-fm

Loose Caboose (IRE)

103(103) (76)71
4-y-o b f Tagula (IRE)-Tama (IRE) (Indian Ridge)
A J McCabe McCabe And Timms

Placings:00015224154/43622101230055000-00206201515002000 4405 (7852)
2009: 6^{0}SS, 5^{0}SD, 5^{2}SD, 5^{0}SD, 5^{6}SD, 6^{2}GF, 6^{0}F, 5^{1}SD, 5^{5}GF, 5^{1}GF, 5^{5}GF, 5^{0}F, 5^{0}GF, 5^{2}SD, 5^{0}SD, 5^{0}SD, 5^{0}SD, 5^{4}SD, 6^{4}SD, 5^{0}SD, 5^{5}SS,

	Starts	1st	2nd	3rd	Win & Pl
Career Total (Turf)	14	1	2	0	4729
Career Total (AW)	35	5	6	2	21131

71	5/09	Donc	5f	(0-75)H	G-F	£3238
73	5/09	Sthl	5f	(0-60)H	STD	£2388
76	4/08	GrLe	6f	(0-85)H	STD	£4533
74	3/08	Sthl	5f	(0-70)H	STD	£2457
67	11/07	Wolv	5f20y	(0-65)	STD	£2047
56	8/07	Ling	6f		STD	£2047

Total win prize-money £16712

Going (Turf): Sf: 0-0 GS: 0-2 Gd: 0-4 **GF: 1-6** Fm: 0-2
Distance: **5f/6f: 6-44** 7f-8f: 0-5 9f-13f: 0-0 14f+: 0-0
Track : **LH: 3-30** RH: 0-3 **Tight: 2-18** Gall: 1-5
Aids: Bl: 2-15 Vi: 0-3 Tstrap: 3-23 Ckp: 3-23
Best Rating: 78 5/08 GrLe 6f stand

Modest; effective from 5f-7f; acts on most ground on turf; goes on sand; has worn cheekpieces, a visor, eyeshield and blinkers.

Looter (FR)

65(94) (56)55
4-y-o b g Red Ransom (USA)-Water Echo (USA) (Mr Prospector (USA))
P Butler Christopher W Wilson

Placings:056/0350566-000060 (2675)
2009: 8^{0}SD, 13^{0}SD, 12^{0}SD, 8^{0}SD, 9^{6}G, 9^{0}GF,

	Starts	1st	2nd	3rd	Win & Pl
Career Total (Turf)	10	0	0	0	0
Career Total (AW)	6	0	0	1	302

Going (Turf): Sf: 0-1 GS: 0-1 Gd: 0-3 GF: 0-5 Fm: 0-0
Distance: 5f/6f: 0-0 7f-8f: 0-6 9f-13f: 0-10 14f+: 0-0
Track : LH: 0-10 RH: 0-4 Tight: 0-8 Gall: 0-0
Aids: Bl: 0-2 Vi: 0-1 Tstrap: 0-6 Ckp: 0-6
Best Rating: 56 5/08 Ling 1m2f stand

Modest; stays 1m2f and acts on Polytrack.

Lopinot (IRE)

(102) (73)77
6-y-o br g Pursuit Of Love-La Suquet (Puissance)
M R Bosley Mrs Jean M O'Connor

Placings:030/022/2111000000/66003010000-1315654000006 (7587)
2009: 8^{1}SD, 8^{3}SD, 8^{1}SD, 8^{5}SD, 8^{6}SD, 8^{5}SD, 8^{4}SD, 8^{0}SD, 8^{0}SD, 8^{0}SD, 8^{0}SD, 8^{0}SD, 8^{6}SD,

	Starts	1st	2nd	3rd	Win & Pl
Career Total (Turf)	13	1	0	2	3446
Career Total (AW)	28	5	3	1	19002

72	3/09	Ling	1m	(0-65)H	STD	£2388
69	1/09	Kemp	1m	(0-65)H	STD	£2047
61	8/08	Brig	7f214y	(0-60)H	GD	£2396
90	3/07	Ling	1m	(0-85)H	STD	£6477
81	3/07	Ling	1m	(0-75)H	STD	£3238
70	1/07	Kemp	7f		STD	£2047

Total win prize-money £18595

Going (Turf): Sf: 0-0 GS: 0-0 **Gd: 1-5** GF: 0-8 Fm: 0-0
Distance: 5f/6f: 0-1 **7f-8f: 6-37** 9f-13f: 0-3 14f+: 0-0
Track : **LH: 4-19** RH: 2-17 **Tight: 3-13** Gall: 0-1
Aids: Bl: 0-0 **Vi: 2-14** Tstrap: 1-7 Ckp: 1-7
Best Rating: 90 3/07 Ling 1m stand

Modest; stays 1m; acts on good to firm ground and Polytrack; has worn cheekpieces/visor.

Lord Admiral (USA)

113 (103)113
8-y-o b h El Prado (IRE)-Lady Ilsley (USA) (Trempolino (USA))
Charles O'Brien Mrs M V O'Brien

Placings:510/325625220/14245/2233322332/66225134321/1310225400-0526552 (7565a)
2009: 8^{0}G, 7^{5}G, 10^{2}YS, 8^{6}GF, 10^{5}GY, 10^{5}SD, 7^{2}SD,

	Starts	1st	2nd	3rd	Win & Pl
Career Total (Turf)	52	6	16	9	532809
Career Total (AW)	3	0	1	0	2579

116	3/08	Ndas	1m194y	GD	£75376
112	1/08	Ndas	1m194y	GD	£60301
108	11/07	Leop	7f	G-F	£21993
113	6/07	Leop	7f	GD	£30743
112	6/05	Leop	1m	G-F	£23085
86	8/03	Naas	7f	GD	£8441

Total win prize-money £219942

Going (Turf): Sf: 0-2 GS: 0-0 **Gd: 4-16** GF: 2-21 Fm: 0-5
Distance: 5f/6f: 0-0 **7f-8f: 4-26** 9f-13f: 2-29 14f+: 0-0
Track : **LH: 6-44** RH: 0-7 Tight: 0-0 **Gall: 2-12**
Aids: **Bl: 4-26** Vi: 0-1 Tstrap: 0-0 Ckp: 0-0
Best Rating: 116 3/08 Ndas 1m194y good

Smart performer; winner in Group 3 company; effective from 7f-1m2f; suited by good or faster ground; usually wears blinkers.

Lord Aeryn (IRE)

95 72
2-y-o b g Antonius Pius (USA)-White Paper (IRE) (Marignan (USA))
R A Fahey Mrs H Steel

Placings:5101 (6471)
2009: 6^{5}GF, 6^{1}GF, 6^{0}GF, 7^{1}GF,

	Starts	1st	2nd	3rd	Win & Pl
Career Total (Turf)	4	2	0	0	10685

72	10/09	Epsm	7f	(0-90)	G-F	£7771
69	7/09	Ayr	6f		G-F	£2914

Total win prize-money £10685

Going (Turf): Sf: 0-0 GS: 0-0 Gd: 0-0 **GF: 2-4** Fm: 0-0
Distance: 5f/6f: 1-3 7f-8f: 1-1 9f-13f: 0-0 14f+: 0-0
Track : **LH: 1-1** RH: 0-0 **Tight: 1-1** Gall: 0-0
Aids: Bl: 0-0 Vi: 0-0 Tstrap: 0-0 Ckp: 0-0
Best Rating: 72 10/09 Epsm 7f gd-fm

Fair; stays 7f; acts on fast ground.

Lord Chancellor (IRE)

(103) (93)79
3-y-o b c King's Best (USA)-Summer Serenade (Sadler's Wells (USA))
M Johnston Sheikh Hamdan Bin Mohammed Al Maktoum

Placings:342-131 (0755)
2009: 10^{1}SD, 10^{3}SD, 10^{1}SD,

	Starts	1st	2nd	3rd	Win & Pl
Career Total (Turf)	1	0	0	1	770
Career Total (AW)	5	2	1	1	9706

93	3/09	Ling	1m2f	(0-85)H	STD	£4857
83	1/09	Ling	1m2f		STD	£2729

Total win prize-money £7587

Going (Turf): Sf: 0-0 GS: 0-0 Gd: 0-1 GF: 0-0 Fm: 0-0
Distance: 5f/6f: 0-0 7f-8f: 0-2 **9f-13f: 2-4** 14f+: 0-0
Track : **LH: 2-5** RH: 0-1 **Tight: 2-4** Gall: 0-0
Aids: Bl: 0-0 Vi: 0-0 Tstrap: 0-0 Ckp: 0-0
Best Rating: 93 3/09 Ling 1m2f stand

Useful; stays 1m2f and acts on Polytrack.

Lord Deevert

99(102) (68)66
4-y-o br g Averti (IRE)-Dee-Lady (Deploy)
W G M Turner Mrs M S Teversham

Placings:00431301040203 3/124640241161306-520535052 (7606)
2009: 7^{5}SD, 7^{2}SD, 6^{0}G, 6^{5}SD, 6^{3}GS, 6^{5}G, 6^{0}SD, 6^{5}SD, 6^{2}SD,

	Starts	1st	2nd	3rd	Win & Pl
Career Total (Turf)	13	1	2	2	5577
Career Total (AW)	26	5	3	4	15664

68	10/08	Ling	6f	(0-70)H	STD	£2590
64	7/08	Ling	6f	(0-75)H	STD	£2590
59	7/08	Sals	6f	(0-65)H	G-F	£2914
65	1/08	Ling	6f		STD	£1774
62	8/07	Wolv	5f216y		STD	£3238
61	6/07	Ling	5f		STD	£2047

Total win prize-money £15156

Going (Turf): Sf: 0-1 GS: 0-1 Gd: 0-2 **GF: 1-7** Fm: 0-2
Distance: **5f/6f: 6-26** 7f-8f: 0-12 9f-13f: 0-1 14f+: 0-0
Track : **LH: 5-29** RH: 0-3 **Tight: 5-22** Gall: 0-2
Aids: Bl: 0-2 **Vi: 1-5** Tstrap: 0-6 Ckp: 0-6
Best Rating: 68 11/08 Wolv 5f216y stand

Modest; effective over 6f; acts on fast ground; goes on Polytrack.

Lord Fidelio (IRE)

97(101) (71)70
3-y-o b g Xaar-Rekindled Affair (IRE) (Rainbow Quest (USA))
A M Balding J B Munz

Placings:003041 (7610)
2009: 8^{0}GF, 8^{0}SD, 6^{3}GF, 6^{0}GF, 7^{4}SD, 7^{1}SD,

	Starts	1st	2nd	3rd	Win & Pl
Career Total (Turf)	3	0	0	1	578
Career Total (AW)	3	1	0	0	2783

61	12/09	Kemp	7f	STD	£2590

Total win prize-money £2590

Going (Turf): **Sf: 0-0 GS: 0-0 Gd: 0-0 GF: 0-3 Fm: 0-0**
Distance: 5f/6f: 0-0 **7f-8f: 1-6** 9f-13f: 0-0 14f+: 0-0
Track : LH: 0-0 **RH: 1-3** Tight: 0-0 Gall: 0-0
Aids: Bl: 0-0 Vi: 0-0 Tstrap: 0-0 Ckp: 0-0
Best Rating: **71** 11/09 Kemp 7f stand

Modest; effective over 7f; acts on Polytrack.

Lord High Admiral (IRE)

103 **103**
2-y-o b c Galileo (IRE)-Splendid (IRE) (Mujtahid (USA))
A P O'Brien Michael Tabor

Placings:1002 (7072a)
2009: 7^1G, 8^0G, 7^0G, 7^2Y,

	Starts	1st	2nd	3rd	Win & Pl
Career Total (Turf)	4	1	1	0	22231
84 5/09 Gowr 7f			GD	£10733	

Total win prize-money £10734

Going (Turf): Sf: 0-0 GS: 0-0 **Gd: 1-3** GF: 0-0 Fm: 0-0
Distance: 5f/6f: 0-0 **7f-8f: 1-4** 9f-13f: 0-0 14f+: 0-0
Track : LH: 0-1 **RH: 1-2** Tight: 0-0 Gall: 0-1
Aids: Bl: 0-0 Vi: 0-0 Tstrap: 0-0 Ckp: 0-0
Best Rating: **103** 10/09 Leop 7f yield

Smart half-brother to 2yo winners Fanditha (7f) and Packing Hero (6f) and two winners in the US, including fairly useful sprinter Bohunk; effective at 7f on good ground.

Lord Laing (USA)

(94) (53)**46**
6-y-o b/br g Chester House (USA)-Johanna Keene (USA) (Raise A Cup (USA))
H J Collingridge Maynard Durrant Partnership II

Placings:05/0004/400005610/3000000-0 (0059)
2009: 12^0SD,

	Starts	1st	2nd	3rd	Win & Pl
Career Total (Turf)	7	0	0	0	
Career Total (AW)	16	1	0	1	2480
53 11/07 Wolv 1m4f50y (0-50)H			STD	£2047	

Total win prize-money £2048

Going (Turf): **Sf: 0-0 GS: 0-0 Gd: 0-1 GF: 0-6 Fm: 0-0**
Distance: 5f/6f: 0-0 7f-8f: 0-3 **9f-13f: 1-18** 14f+: 0-2
Track : **LH: 1-11** RH: 0-12 **Tight: 1-11** Gall: 0-1
Aids: Bl: 0-0 Vi: 0-2 Tstrap: 0-0 Ckp: 0-0
Best Rating: **65** 1/07 Kemp 1m4f stand

Moderate; stays 1m4f; acts on Polytrack.

Lord Of The Dance (IRE)

98(101) (66)**59**
3-y-o ch c Indian Haven-Maine Lobster (USA) (Woodman (USA))
J M P Eustace Bridgewater Equine Ltd

Placings:0-3363262 (7610)
2009: 7^3SD, 7^3SD, 10^6G, 8^3SD, 8^2SD, 8^6SD, 7^2SD,

	Starts	1st	2nd	3rd	Win & Pl
Career Total (Turf)	1	0	0	0	0
Career Total (AW)	7	0	2	3	2632

Going (Turf): **Sf: 0-0 GS: 0-0 Gd: 0-1 GF: 0-0 Fm: 0-0**
Distance: 5f/6f: 0-0 7f-8f: 0-6 9f-13f: 0-2 14f+: 0-0
Track : LH: 0-4 RH: 0-4 Tight: 0-3 Gall: 0-1
Aids: Bl: 0-2 Vi: 0-1 Tstrap: 0-0 Ckp: 0-0
Best Rating: **66** 11/09 Kemp 1m stand

Modest; effective over 7f-1m; acts on Polytrack.

Lord Of The Flame

58 **13**
3-y-o br g Largesse-Maylan (IRE) (Lashkari)
W De Best-Turner De Best racing

Placings:6-0 (3090)
2009: 16^0GF,

	Starts	1st	2nd	3rd	Win & Pl
Career Total (Turf)	2	0	0	0	211

Going (Turf): **Sf: 0-0 GS: 0-0 Gd: 0-1 GF: 0-1 Fm: 0-0**
Distance: 5f/6f: 0-0 7f-8f: 0-1 9f-13f: 0-0 14f+: 0-1
Track : LH: 0-0 RH: 0-1 Tight: 0-0 Gall: 0-1
Aids: Bl: 0-0 Vi: 0-0 Tstrap: 0-0 Ckp: 0-0
Best Rating: **13** 9/08 Newb 1m good

Lord Of The Reins (IRE)

101(106) (80)**91**
5-y-o b g Imperial Ballet (IRE)-Waroonga (IRE) (Brief Truce (USA))
J G Given Danethorpe Racing Partnership

Placings:0030151132300/5136301123306021000-000600403001010 (7872)
2009: 5^0GF, 5^0G, 5^0HY, 5^6G, 6^0GF, 5^0G, 5^4G, 5^0G, 5^3GF, 5^0S, 5^0G, 5^1SD, 5^0SD, 5^1SD, 5^0SD,

	Starts	1st	2nd	3rd	Win & Pl
Career Total (Turf)	25	2	2	2	16394
Career Total (AW)	22	7	1	6	22672
80 12/09 Kemp 5f	(0-75)H		STD	£2590	
73 11/09 Kemp 5f	(0-70)H		STD	£2266	
91 8/08 NmkJ 5f	(0-85)H		GD	£6476	
81 4/08 GrLe 5f	(0-85)H		STD	£4533	
75 4/08 Kemp 5f	(0-70)H		STD	£2590	
72 1/08 Wolv 5f20y	(0-70)H		STD	£2590	
68 9/07 Ling 6f	(0-70)H		STD	£2817	
67 8/07 Ling 6f	(0-60)H		STD	£2047	
55 7/07 Leic 5f2y			SFT	£3562	

Total win prize-money £29474

Going (Turf): **Sf: 1-4** GS: 0-6 **Gd: 1-8** GF: 0-7 Fm: 0-0
Distance: **5f/6f: 9-47** 7f-8f: 0-0 9f-13f: 0-0 14f+: 0-0
Track : **LH: 4-16** RH: 3-7 **Tight: 3-10** Gall: 1-2
Aids: Bl: 0-0 Vi: 0-0 Tstrap: 0-0 Ckp: 0-0
Best Rating: **91** 8/08 NmkJ 5f good

Modest; effective over 5f-6f; acts on most ground and on Polytrack.

Lord Oroko

104(76) (58)**65**
5-y-o ch g Lord Of Men-Wannaplantatree (Niniski (USA))
J G M O'Shea Alan G Craddock

Placings:4422/0401223/004100 (3997)
2009: 12^0SD, 17^0GF, 11^4GF, 17^1F, 14^0F, 17^0G,

	Starts	1st	2nd	3rd	Win & Pl
Career Total (Turf)	12	2	2	1	8423
Career Total (AW)	5	0	2	0	2164
65 5/09 Bath 2m1f34y (0-60)H			FRM	£2072	
71 9/07 Bath 1m5f22y (0-70)H			FRM	£2810	

Total win prize-money £4883

Going (Turf): Sf: 0-2 GS: 0-0 Gd: 0-3 GF: 0-4 **Fm: 2-3**
Distance: 5f/6f: 0-0 7f-8f: 0-1 9f-13f: 0-8 **14f+: 2-8**
Track : **LH: 2-14** RH: 0-3 **Tight: 2-10** Gall: 0-1
Aids: Bl: 0-0 Vi: 0-0 Tstrap: 0-0 Ckp: 0-0
Best Rating: **76** 10/07 Nott 2m9y gd-fm

Modest; stays 2m1f; acts on fast ground; goes on sand.

Lord Orpen (IRE)

87(94) (41)**36**
5-y-o b g Orpen (USA)-Kenyane (IRE) (Kahyasi)
Patrick Morris W J Crosbie

Placings:000/000000/60-00 (6612)
2009: 6^0G, 12^0SD,

	Starts	1st	2nd	3rd	Win & Pl
Career Total (Turf)	9	0	0	0	
Career Total (AW)	4	0	0	0	0

Going (Turf): **Sf: 0-2 GS: 0-0 Gd: 0-1 GF: 0-3 Fm: 0-0**
Distance: 5f/6f: 0-0 7f-8f: 0-6 9f-13f: 0-7 14f+: 0-0
Track : LH: 0-4 RH: 0-6 Tight: 0-0 Gall: 0-0
Aids: Bl: 0-3 Vi: 0-2 Tstrap: 0-1 Ckp: 0-1
Best Rating: **51** 4/07 Navn 1m2f sft-hvy

Lord Raglan (IRE)

87(85) (48)**62**
2-y-o b g Noverre (USA)-Raglan Rose (USA) (Giant's Causeway (USA))
A P Jarvis (K R Burke 20/7) John A Duffy

Placings:3300 (7210)
2009: 6^3G, 6^3G, 6^0GS, 7^0SD,

	Starts	1st	2nd	3rd	Win & Pl
Career Total (Turf)	3	0	0	2	1565
Career Total (AW)	1	0	0	0	

Going (Turf): **Sf: 0-0 GS: 0-1 Gd: 0-2 GF: 0-0 Fm: 0-0**
Distance: 5f/6f: 0-3 7f-8f: 0-1 9f-13f: 0-0 14f+: 0-0
Track : LH: 0-1 RH: 0-0 Tight: 0-1 Gall: 0-0
Aids: Bl: 0-0 Vi: 0-0 Tstrap: 0-0 Ckp: 0-0
Best Rating: **62** 7/09 Ayr 6f good

Modest; stays 6f; acts on good ground.

Lord Shanakill (USA)

114 **119**
3-y-o b/br c Speightstown (USA)-Green Room (USA) (Theatrical)
Richard E Mandella (A P Jarvis 29/7) Mogeely Stud & Mark T Gittins

Placings:31323512-03150 (7305a)
2009: 8^0GF, 8^3GF, 8^1G, 8^5G, 6^0F,

	Starts	1st	2nd	3rd	Win & Pl
Career Total (Turf)	13	3	2	4	433415
119 7/09 Chan 1m			GD	£221845	
116 9/08 Newb 6f8y			GD	£45416	
91 5/08 York 6f			G-F	£7835	

Total win prize-money £275097

Going (Turf): Sf: 0-1 GS: 0-2 **Gd: 2-4** GF: 1-5 Fm: 0-1
Distance: 5f/6f: 1-5 **7f-8f: 2-8** 9f-13f: 0-0 14f+: 0-0
Track : LH: 0-0 **RH: 1-5** Tight: 0-0 Gall: 0-1
Aids: Bl: 0-0 Vi: 0-0 Tstrap: 0-0 Ckp: 0-0
Best Rating: **119** 7/09 Chan 1m good

High class; winner of the 2008 Group 2 Mill Reef Stakes; runner-up in the Dewhurst in 2008 and winner of the Prix

Jean Prat in 2009; effective up to 1m; acts on fast and easy ground.

Lord Theo

107(108) (81)**86**

5-y-o b g Averti (IRE)-Love You Too (Be My Chief (USA))

N P Littmoden Mrs Karen Graham

Placings:031/01640663203/40236203306000001260-460335005256111210050 **(6795)**

2009: 8^{4}SD, 10^{6}SD, 8^{0}SD, 8^{3}SD, 8^{3}SD, 8^{5}GF, 8^{0}SD, 10^{0}GS, 8^{5}GF, 8^{2}GS, 10^{5}GF, 9^{6}S, 10^{1}GS, 10^{1}GF, 12^{2}GF, 10^{1}GF, 14^{0}S, 10^{0}GF, 12^{5}GF, 10^{0}S,

	Starts	1st	2nd	3rd	Win & Pl
Career Total (Turf)	35	5	4	3	36913
Career Total (AW)	19	1	2	5	7920

86	8/09	NmkJ	1m2f	(0-95)H	G-F	£9066
85	8/09	NmkJ	1m2f	(0-70)H	G-F	£3885
75	8/09	NmkJ	1m2f	(0-75)H	G-S	£3885
68	10/08	GrLe	1m2f	(0-70)H	STD	£3238
80	5/07	Wwck	7f26y	(0-80)H	G-F	£6477
73	7/06	Wind	6f		G-F	£3886

Total win prize-money £30439

Going (Turf): Sf: 0-5 GS: 1-3 Gd: 0-5 **GF: 4-21** Fm: 0-1
Distance: 5f/6f: 1-7 7f-8f: 1-14 **9f-13f: 4-32** 14f+: 0-1
Track : LH: 2-28 **RH: 3-14** Tight: 0-15 **Gall: 5-9**
Aids: Bl: 0-3 Vi: 0-1 Tstrap: 0-0 Ckp: 0-0
Best Rating: **86** 8/09 NmkJ 1m2f gd-fm

Useful; effective 7f-1m4f; acts on fast ground; goes on Polytrack.

Lord Victor

80(103) (66)**34**

2-y-o ch c Needwood Blade-La Victoria (GER) (Rousillon (USA))

A J McCabe Khalifa Dasmal

Placings:60030204131 **(7868)**

2009: 8^{6}SD, 8^{0}SD, 6^{0}GS, 7^{3}SD, 7^{0}SD, 6^{2}SD, 7^{0}SD, 5^{4}SD, 7^{1}SD, 6^{3}SS, 7^{1}SS,

	Starts	1st	2nd	3rd	Win & Pl
Career Total (Turf)	1	0	0	0	
Career Total (AW)	10	2	1	2	6137

66	12/09	Sthl	7f	SS	£2729
63	12/09	Sthl	7f	STD	£2047

Total win prize-money £4777

Going (Turf): **Sf: 0-0 GS: 0-1 Gd: 0-0 GF: 0-0 Fm: 0-0**
Distance: 5f/6f: 0-3 **7f-8f: 2-7** 9f-13f: 0-1 14f+: 0-0
Track : **LH: 2-9** RH: 0-1 Tight: 0-4 Gall: 0-0
Aids: Bl: 0-1 Vi: 0-0 Tstrap: 0-1 Ckp: 0-1
Best Rating: **66** 12/09 Sthl 7f std-slw

Modest; stays 7f; acts on Fibresand and Polytrack; has worn cheekpieces.

Lord Wheathill

73 **49**

2-y-o b g Tobougg (IRE)-Classic Quartet (Classic Cliche (IRE))

Mrs L Williamson K C Hire & Sales Ltd

Placings:000 **(7121)**

2009: 7^{0}GS, 7^{0}G, 8^{0}GF,

	Starts	1st	2nd	3rd	Win & Pl
Career Total (Turf)	3	0	0	0	

Going (Turf): **Sf: 0-0 GS: 0-1 Gd: 0-1 GF: 0-1 Fm: 0-0**
Distance: 5f/6f: 0-0 7f-8f: 0-2 9f-13f: 0-1 14f+: 0-0
Track : LH: 0-3 RH: 0-0 Tight: 0-1 Gall: 0-0

Aids: Bl: 0-0 Vi: 0-0 Tstrap: 0-0 Ckp: 0-0
Best Rating: **49** 7/09 Hayd 7f30y gd-sft

Lord Zenith

101 **98**

2-y-o b c Zamindar (USA)-Lady Donatella (Last Tycoon)

A M Balding Mrs M E Wates

Placings:615 **(3817)**

2009: 6^{6}GF, 6^{1}G, 7^{5}GF,

	Starts	1st	2nd	3rd	Win & Pl
Career Total (Turf)	3	1	0	0	6847

89	6/09	Sals	6f212y	GD	£4695

Total win prize-money £4695

Going (Turf): Sf: 0-0 GS: 0-0 **Gd: 1-1** GF: 0-2 Fm: 0-0
Distance: 5f/6f: 0-0 **7f-8f: 1-3** 9f-13f: 0-0 14f+: 0-0
Track : LH: 0-0 RH: 0-0 Tight: 0-0 Gall: 0-0
Aids: Bl: 0-0 Vi: 0-0 Tstrap: 0-0 Ckp: 0-0
Best Rating: **98** 7/09 NmkJ 7f gd-fm

Very useful; effective over 7f; acts on good/fast ground.

Lord's Seat

88(86) (33)**53**

2-y-o b g Trade Fair-Clashfern (Smackover)

A Berry A B Parr

Placings:6406300550 **(7335)**

2009: 5^{6}G, 5^{4}GF, 5^{0}GF, 5^{6}GF, 5^{3}G, 5^{0}G, 6^{0}HY, 7^{5}S, 7^{5}S, 8^{0}SD,

	Starts	1st	2nd	3rd	Win & Pl
Career Total (Turf)	9	0	0	1	674
Career Total (AW)	1	0	0	0	

Going (Turf): **Sf: 0-3 GS: 0-0 Gd: 0-3 GF: 0-3 Fm: 0-0**
Distance: 5f/6f: 0-6 7f-8f: 0-4 9f-13f: 0-0 14f+: 0-0
Track : LH: 0-3 RH: 0-2 Tight: 0-1 Gall: 0-1
Aids: Bl: 0-0 Vi: 0-0 Tstrap: 0-0 Ckp: 0-0
Best Rating: **53** 5/09 Haml 5f4y gd-fm

Lords A Leaping (IRE)

91(97) (72)**69**

3-y-o b c Bahamian Bounty-Joonayh (Warning)

J A Osborne P J D Pottinger & 12 Day Partners

Placings:332 **(2659)**

2009: 9^{3}SD, 10^{3}SD, 11^{2}G,

	Starts	1st	2nd	3rd	Win & Pl
Career Total (Turf)	1	0	1	0	964
Career Total (AW)	2	0	0	2	885

Going (Turf): **Sf: 0-0 GS: 0-0 Gd: 0-1 GF: 0-0 Fm: 0-0**
Distance: 5f/6f: 0-0 7f-8f: 0-0 9f-13f: 0-3 14f+: 0-0
Track : LH: 0-3 RH: 0-0 Tight: 0-3 Gall: 0-0
Aids: Bl: 0-0 Vi: 0-0 Tstrap: 0-0 Ckp: 0-0
Best Rating: **72** 5/09 Ling 1m2f stand

Lordship (IRE)

105(89) (63)**76**

5-y-o b g King's Best (USA)-Rahika Rose (Unfuwain (USA))

A W Carroll Group 1 Racing (1994) Ltd

Placings:000/002313003100660/043302020606004-004506031100150 **(7350)**

2009: 8^{0}GF, 7^{0}GF, 8^{4}G, 8^{5}GF, 7^{0}G, 7^{6}GS, 8^{0}G, 7^{3}S, 8^{1}S, 7^{1}GS, 8^{0}GF, 8^{0}G, 7^{1}S, 7^{5}S, 7^{0}SD,

	Starts	1st	2nd	3rd	Win & Pl
Career Total (Turf)	46	5	3	6	23160
Career Total (AW)	2	0	0	0	

76	10/09	Ayr	7f50y	(0-75)H	SFT	£3885
69	9/09	Chep	7f16y	(0-60)H	G-S	£2460
64	8/09	Ayr	1m	(0-60)H	SFT	£2590
73	8/07	Folk	7f	(0-80)H	HVY	£4605
64	7/07	Wwck	7f26y	(0-75)H	GD	£2914

Total win prize-money £16458

Going (Turf): **Sf: 3-13**GS: 1-13 Gd: 1-11 GF: 0-7 Fm: 0-2
Distance: 5f/6f: 0-1 **7f-8f: 5-29** 9f-13f: 0-18 14f+: 0-0
Track : **LH: 3-23** RH: 0-8 Tight: 0-4 Gall: 0-0
Aids: Bl: 0-0 Vi: 0-0 Tstrap: 0-0 Ckp: 0-0
Best Rating: **76** 10/09 Ayr 7f50y soft

Moderate; stays 1m; acts on good and softer ground.

Los Nadis (GER)

100 **78**

5-y-o ch g Hernando (FR)-La Estrella (GER) (Desert King (IRE))

P Monteith Ian G M Dalgleish

Placings:2010063/0230-4605 **(2044)**

2009: 16^{4}GF, 14^{6}GF, 14^{0}G, 16^{5}GS,

	Starts	1st	2nd	3rd	Win & Pl
Career Total (Turf)	15	1	2	2	8074

5/07	Vann	1m4f	GD	£3040

Total win prize-money £3041

Going (Turf): Sf: 0-3 GS: 0-4 **Gd: 1-6** GF: 0-2 Fm: 0-0
Distance: 5f/6f: 0-0 7f-8f: 0-0 **9f-13f: 1-5** 14f+: 0-10
Track : LH: 0-3 RH: 0-8 Tight: 0-8 Gall: 0-1
Aids: Bl: 0-0 Vi: 0-0 Tstrap: 0-0 Ckp: 0-0
Best Rating: **78** 8/08 Haml 1m4f17y soft

Modest; better known as a hurdler; stays 2m; acts on good or softer ground.

Loss Leader (IRE)

75 **30**

2-y-o ch g Captain Rio-Nenagh (IRE) (Barathea (IRE))

T D Easterby C H Stevens

Placings:00 **(6018)**

2009: 5^{0}GF, 5^{0}GF,

	Starts	1st	2nd	3rd	Win & Pl
Career Total (Turf)	2	0	0	0	

Going (Turf): **Sf: 0-0 GS: 0-0 Gd: 0-0 GF: 0-2 Fm: 0-0**
Distance: 5f/6f: 0-2 7f-8f: 0-0 9f-13f: 0-0 14f+: 0-0
Track : LH: 0-1 RH: 0-0 Tight: 0-0 Gall: 0-0
Aids: Bl: 0-0 Vi: 0-0 Tstrap: 0-0 Ckp: 0-0
Best Rating: **30** 9/09 Pont 5f gd-fm

Lost Cause

89(85) (60)**59**

2-y-o b c Dubawi (IRE)-Crystal (IRE) (Danehill (USA))

R Charlton B E Nielsen

Placings:06640 **(6793)**

2009: 7^{0}G, 7^{6}HY, 6^{6}GF, 7^{4}SD, 8^{0}S,

	Starts	1st	2nd	3rd	Win & Pl
Career Total (Turf)	4	0	0	0	0
Career Total (AW)	1	0	0	0	0

Going (Turf): Sf: 0-2 GS: 0-0 Gd: 0-1 GF: 0-1 Fm: 0-0
Distance: 5f/6f: 0-1 7f-8f: 0-3 9f-13f: 0-1 14f+: 0-0
Track : LH: 0-1 RH: 0-1 Tight: 0-0 Gall: 0-1
Aids: Bl: 0-0 Vi: 0-0 Tstrap: 0-0 Ckp: 0-0
Best Rating: 60 10/09 Kemp 7f stand

Modest; best effort over 7f on Polytrack.

Lost Horizon (IRE)

98 **82**
2-y-o b f Elusive City (USA)-Souvenir Souvenir (Highest Honor (FR))
R Hannon Mrs J Wood

Placings:020 (6730)
2009: 6^{0}S, 7^{2}GF, 6^{0}S,

	Starts	1st	2nd	3rd	Win & Pl
Career Total (Turf)	3	0	1	0	3359

Going (Turf): Sf: 0-2 GS: 0-0 Gd: 0-0 GF: 0-1 Fm: 0-0
Distance: 5f/6f: 0-0 7f-8f: 0-3 9f-13f: 0-0 14f+: 0-0
Track : LH: 0-0 RH: 0-0 Tight: 0-0 Gall: 0-0
Aids: Bl: 0-0 Vi: 0-0 Tstrap: 0-0 Ckp: 0-0
Best Rating: 82 9/09 Newb 7f gd-fm

Useful; stays 7f; acts on fast ground.

Lost In France (IRE)

84 (48)**37**
4-y-o ch f Atraf-Sharply's Gift (IRE) (Nicolotte)
T G McCourt Twenty Seventh Time Syndicate

Placings:0/0030-000 (6558)
2009: 14^{0}Y, 12^{0}SD, 15^{0}G,

	Starts	1st	2nd	3rd	Win & Pl
Career Total (Turf)	5	0	0	0	
Career Total (AW)	3	0	0	1	444

Going (Turf): Sf: 0-0 GS: 0-0 Gd: 0-3 GF: 0-0 Fm: 0-0
Distance: 5f/6f: 0-0 7f-8f: 0-1 9f-13f: 0-5 14f+: 0-2
Track : LH: 0-7 RH: 0-1 Tight: 0-1 Gall: 0-0
Aids: Bl: 0-1 Vi: 0-1 Tstrap: 0-0 Ckp: 0-0
Best Rating: 48 9/08 Dund 1m2f150y stand

Lost In Paris (IRE)

101(106) (70)**71**
3-y-o b g Elusive City (USA)-Brazilia (Forzando)
T D Easterby W H Ponsonby

Placings:50440-50330533214 (7398)
2009: 8^{5}GF, 8^{0}GF, 7^{3}GF, 7^{3}GF, 7^{0}G, 6^{5}S, 7^{3}S, 6^{3}G, 5^{2}GF, 5^{1}GF, 5^{4}SD,

	Starts	1st	2nd	3rd	Win & Pl
Career Total (Turf)	15	1	1	4	5971
Career Total (AW)	1	0	0	0	241

70 10/09 Ayr 5f (0-58)H G-F £2729
Total win prize-money £2730

Going (Turf): Sf: 0-5 GS: 0-2 Gd: 0-2 **GF: 1-6** Fm: 0-0
Distance: **5f/6f: 1-6** 7f-8f: 0-8 9f-13f: 0-2 14f+: 0-0
Track : LH: 0-5 RH: 0-1 Tight: 0-4 Gall: 0-0
Aids: **Bl: 1-9** Vi: 0-0 Tstrap: 0-0 Ckp: 0-0
Best Rating: 71 9/09 Muss 5f gd-fm

Moderate; effective at 5f on fast ground; has worn blinkers.

Lost In The Desert (IRE)

95 **64**
3-y-o b g Nayef (USA)-Desert Harmony (Green Desert (USA))
M Botti Effevi Snc Di Villa Felice & C

Placings:0040 (4284)
2009: 10^{0}GF, 8^{0}G, 8^{4}F, 8^{0}G,

	Starts	1st	2nd	3rd	Win & Pl
Career Total (Turf)	4	0	0	0	241

Going (Turf): Sf: 0-0 GS: 0-0 Gd: 0-2 GF: 0-1 Fm: 0-1
Distance: 5f/6f: 0-0 7f-8f: 0-1 9f-13f: 0-3 14f+: 0-0
Track : LH: 0-3 RH: 0-1 Tight: 0-0 Gall: 0-1
Aids: Bl: 0-2 Vi: 0-0 Tstrap: 0-0 Ckp: 0-0
Best Rating: 64 7/09 Hayd 1m30y firm

Lost In The Forest

88 **43**
2-y-o ch f Trade Fair-Fallujah (Dr Fong (USA))
A P Jarvis Malih L Al Basti

Placings:05 (5669)
2009: 7^{0}GF, 7^{5}S,

	Starts	1st	2nd	3rd	Win & Pl
Career Total (Turf)	2	0	0	0	0

Going (Turf): Sf: 0-1 GS: 0-0 Gd: 0-0 GF: 0-1 Fm: 0-0
Distance: 5f/6f: 0-0 7f-8f: 0-2 9f-13f: 0-0 14f+: 0-0
Track : LH: 0-1 RH: 0-0 Tight: 0-1 Gall: 0-0
Aids: Bl: 0-0 Vi: 0-0 Tstrap: 0-0 Ckp: 0-0
Best Rating: 43 9/09 Thsk 7f soft

Some promise in maidens; stays 7f; acts on soft.

Lost In The Moment (IRE)

83 **55**
2-y-o b c Danehill Dancer (IRE)-Streetcar (IRE) (In The Wings)
J Noseda M Tabor & Mrs Susan Roy

Placings:6 (6679)
2009: 7^{6}G,

	Starts	1st	2nd	3rd	Win & Pl
Career Total (Turf)	1	0	0	0	0

Going (Turf): Sf: 0-0 GS: 0-0 Gd: 0-1 GF: 0-0 Fm: 0-0
Distance: 5f/6f: 0-0 7f-8f: 0-1 9f-13f: 0-0 14f+: 0-0
Track : LH: 0-1 RH: 0-0 Tight: 0-0 Gall: 0-1
Aids: Bl: 0-0 Vi: 0-0 Tstrap: 0-0 Ckp: 0-0
Best Rating: 55 10/09 York 7f good

Lost Soldier Three (IRE)

104(107) (79)**98**
8-y-o b g Barathea (IRE)-Donya (Mill Reef (USA))
D Nicholls Eamon Maher

Placings:61542114/610630/3353/50063/05014-0044035022222 (7760)
2009: 12^{0}G, 16^{0}SD, 12^{4}G, 12^{4}GF, 15^{0}GF, 11^{3}GF, 14^{5}GF, 12^{0}G, 11^{2}G, 12^{2}GS, 12^{2}SD, 12^{2}SD, 16^{2}SD,

	Starts	1st	2nd	3rd	Win & Pl
Career Total (Turf)	37	5	3	6	112612
Career Total (AW)	4	0	3	0	2217

98 9/08 Catt 1m3f214y (0-90)H G-S £7771
111 7/05 York 1m5f197y (0-110)H GD £20300
106 9/04 Donc 1m6f132y (0-110)H G-F £23200
104 8/04 York 1m5f197yB(0-100)H SFT £12945
86 6/04 Chep 1m2f36y D GD £3571
Total win prize-money £67789

Going (Turf): Sf: 1-3 GS: 1-6 **Gd: 2-19** GF: 1-9 Fm: 0-0
Distance: 5f/6f: 0-0 7f-8f: 0-1 9f-13f: 2-21 **14f+: 3-19**
Track : **LH: 5-31** RH: 0-9 Tight: 1-10 **Gall: 3-21**
Aids: Bl: 0-0 Vi: 0-1 Tstrap: 0-0 Ckp: 0-0
Best Rating: 112 9/05 Donc 1m6f132y gd-sft

Fair, formerly useful; stays 2m, but effective over 1m4f; acts on most ground; has worn a visor.

Lou Bear (IRE)

(89) (63)
2-y-o b c Lujain (USA)-Dream Of Dubai (IRE) (Vettori (IRE))
J Akehurst Georgia Partnership

Placings:40 (7886)
2009: 7^{4}SD, 7^{0}SD,

	Starts	1st	2nd	3rd	Win & Pl
Career Total (Turf)	0	0	0	0	
Career Total (AW)	2	0	0	0	216

Going (Turf): Sf: 0-0 GS: 0-0 Gd: 0-0 GF: 0-0 Fm: 0-0
Distance: 5f/6f: 0-0 7f-8f: 0-2 9f-13f: 0-0 14f+: 0-0
Track : LH: 0-1 RH: 0-1 Tight: 0-1 Gall: 0-0
Aids: Bl: 0-0 Vi: 0-0 Tstrap: 0-0 Ckp: 0-0
Best Rating: 63 12/09 Kemp 7f stand

Lough Beg (IRE)

(101) (65)**49**
6-y-o b g Close Conflict (USA)-Mia Gigi (Hard Fought)
Miss Tor Sturgis M M McGrogan

Placings:42050/006/506051/**144150-600** (1463)
2009: 12^{6}SD, 16^{0}SD, 12^{0}SD,

	Starts	1st	2nd	3rd	Win & Pl
Career Total (Turf)	14	0	1	0	1865
Career Total (AW)	9	3	0	0	5460

65 4/08 Kemp 1m4f (0-55)H STD £2047
59 1/08 Kemp 1m2f (0-52)H STD £2047
52 1/08 Kemp 1m2f (0-45) STD £1365
Total win prize-money £5460

Going (Turf): Sf: 0-4 GS: 0-0 Gd: 0-3 GF: 0-3 Fm: 0-0
Distance: 5f/6f: 0-2 7f-8f: 0-6 **9f-13f: 3-14** 14f+: 0-1
Track : LH: 0-10 **RH: 3-10** Tight: 0-3 Gall: 0-0
Aids: Bl: 0-2 Vi: 0-0 Tstrap: 0-0 Ckp: 0-0
Best Rating: 65 4/08 Kemp 1m4f stand

Moderate sort; stays 1m4f; handles Polytrack; wears a tongue tie and has worn blinkers.

Louidor

85(90) (56)**70**
3-y-o b g Lujain (USA)-Simonida (IRE) (Royal Academy (USA))
M R Bosley I H Stephenson

Placings:200-000 (2683)
2009: 8^{0}GS, 8^{0}G, 5^{0}SD,

	Starts	1st	2nd	3rd	Win & Pl
Career Total (Turf)	4	0	1	0	1253
Career Total (AW)	2	0	0	0	

Going (Turf): Sf: 0-0 GS: 0-2 Gd: 0-1 GF: 0-1 Fm: 0-0
Distance: 5f/6f: 0-4 7f-8f: 0-0 9f-13f: 0-2 14f+: 0-0
Track : LH: 0-2 RH: 0-1 Tight: 0-3 Gall: 0-2
Aids: Bl: 0-0 Vi: 0-0 Tstrap: 0-0 Ckp: 0-0
Best Rating: 70 7/08 Wind 5f10y gd-fm

Louie's Lad

101(79) (20)**54**

3-y-o gr g Compton Place-Silver Louie (IRE) (Titus Livius (FR))
J J Bridger Mr & Mrs K Finch

Placings:60000405-000322425604000 **(5877)**
2009: 5^{0}GF, 5^{0}F, 5^{0}SD, 5^{3}G, 5^{2}G, 5^{2}G, 5^{4}GF, 5^{2}F, 5^{5}F, 5^{6}GF, 5^{0}GF, 5^{4}GS, 5^{0}F, 6^{0}GF, 5^{0}GF,

	Starts	1st	2nd	3rd	Win & Pl
Career Total (Turf)	22	0	3	1	4239
Career Total (AW)	1	0	0	0	

Going (Turf): Sf: 0-2 GS: 0-4 Gd: 0-3 GF: 0-9 Fm: 0-4
Distance: 5f/6f: 0-21 7f-8f: 0-2 9f-13f: 0-0 14f+: 0-0
Track : LH: 0-9 RH: 0-0 Tight: 0-1 Gall: 0-4
Aids: Bl: 0-0 Vi: 0-0 Tstrap: 0-14 Ckp: 0-14
Best Rating: 54 6/09 Brig 5f59y firm

Moderate; suited by 5f-6f and fast ground; has worn cheek-pieces.

Louisa (GER)

97 **56**

5-y-o b m Seattle Dancer (USA)-La Ola (GER) (Dashing Blade)
P Monteith G M Cowan

Placings:53213/4666000 **(5734)**
2009: 9^{4}G, 11^{6}G, 11^{6}G, 12^{6}GS, 12^{0}S, 13^{0}S, 16^{0}GS,

	Starts	1st	2nd	3rd	Win & Pl
Career Total (Turf)	12	1	1	2	2939

7/07 Aabe 1m2f GD £1418
Total win prize-money £1419

Going (Turf): Sf: 0-4 GS: 0-2 **Gd: 1-6** GF: 0-0 Fm: 0-0
Distance: 5f/6f: 0-0 7f-8f: 0-0 **9f-13f: 1-10** 14f+: 0-2
Track : LH: 0-2 RH: 0-5 Tight: 0-3 Gall: 0-1
Aids: Bl: 0-0 Vi: 0-0 Tstrap: 0-0 Ckp: 0-0
Best Rating: 56 8/09 Carl 1m3f107y good

Louise Bonne (USA)

94 **79**

3-y-o b/br f Yes It's True (USA)-Blushing Issue (USA) (Blushing John (USA))
C G Cox Old Peartree Stud

Placings:0-10 **(2925)**
2009: 8^{1}G, 9^{0}G,

	Starts	1st	2nd	3rd	Win & Pl
Career Total (Turf)	3	1	0	0	3238

79 5/09 Gdwd 1m GD £3238
Total win prize-money £3238

Going (Turf): Sf: 0-0 GS: 0-0 **Gd: 1-2** GF: 0-1 Fm: 0-0
Distance: 5f/6f: 0-1 **7f-8f: 1-1** 9f-13f: 0-1 14f+: 0-0
Track : LH: 0-0 **RH: 1-2** Tight: 0-0 Gall: 0-1
Aids: Bl: 0-0 Vi: 0-0 Tstrap: 0-0 Ckp: 0-0
Best Rating: 79 5/09 Gdwd 1m good

Fair; stays 1m; acts on good ground.

Louise Sauvage

93(87) (49)**53**

3-y-o b f Loup Sauvage (USA)-Breezy Louise (Dilum (USA))
M D I Usher Champagne And Shambles

Placings:U5500 **(6551)**
2009: 6^{U}GF, 6^{5}G, 7^{5}SD, 7^{0}G, 6^{0}G,

	Starts	1st	2nd	3rd	Win & Pl
Career Total (Turf)	4	0	0	0	0
Career Total (AW)	1	0	0	0	0

Going (Turf): Sf: 0-0 GS: 0-0 Gd: 0-3 GF: 0-1 Fm: 0-0
Distance: 5f/6f: 0-3 7f-8f: 0-2 9f-13f: 0-0 14f+: 0-0
Track : LH: 0-1 RH: 0-0 Tight: 0-1 Gall: 0-1
Aids: Bl: 0-0 Vi: 0-0 Tstrap: 0-0 Ckp: 0-0
Best Rating: 53 8/09 Ling 6f good

Louisiade (IRE)

93(104) (59)**64**

8-y-o b g Tagula (IRE)-Titchwell Lass (Lead On Time (USA))
R C Guest (M C Chapman 17/9) Future Racing (Notts) Limited

Placings:6120000/03003300555/52110134400006/64060402352/4021151510/13121234060000000063450043-050320000006540250 **(7855)**
2009: 8^{0}SS, 8^{5}SS, 8^{0}SD, 8^{3}SD, 7^{2}SD, 8^{0}SD, 7^{0}SD, 7^{0}SD, 7^{0}F, 7^{6}SD, 7^{5}SD, 5^{4}G, 6^{0}GF, 8^{2}SD, 7^{5}SD, 8^{0}SS,

	Starts	1st	2nd	3rd	Win & Pl
Career Total (Turf)	40	2	1	3	16487
Career Total (AW)	54	9	8	7	29385

65	2/08	Sthl	1m		STD	£1774
69	1/08	Sthl	7f		STD	£2047
62	1/08	Sthl	7f		STD	£1774
61	4/07	Wolv	1m141y		STD	£2307
67	3/07	Sthl	7f	(0-70)H	STD	£3071
58	2/07	Sthl	7f		STD	£2184
60	2/07	Wolv	7f32y		STD	£2047
71	5/05	Rdcr	6f	(0-60)H	G-F	£4091
69	4/05	Wolv	7f32y	(0-60)H	STD	£3042
58	4/05	Wolv	7f32y	(0-60)H	STD	£2629
71	6/03	Hayd	5f	D	G-F	£5281

Total win prize-money £30253

Going (Turf): Sf: 0-3 GS: 0-3 Gd: 0-12 **GF: 2-21** Fm: 0-1
Distance: 5f/6f: 2-18 **7f-8f: 8-69** 9f-13f: 1-7 14f+: 0-0
Track : **LH: 9-61** RH: 0-8 **Tight: 4-25** Gall: 0-4
Aids: Bl: 0-10 Vi: 0-1 Tstrap: 7-40 Ckp: 7-40
Best Rating: 74 10/03 York 6f3y gd-fm

Moderate; effective from 6f-1m; acts on fast ground; goes on sand; has worn cheekpieces.

Louisiana Gift (IRE)

(91) (67)

2-y-o b g Cadeaux Genereux-Southern Queen (Anabaa (USA))
J W Hills Nick Hubbard and Partners

Placings:560 **(6911)**
2009: 7^{5}SD, 7^{6}SD, 7^{0}SD,

	Starts	1st	2nd	3rd	Win & Pl
Career Total (Turf)	0	0	0	0	
Career Total (AW)	3	0	0	0	0

Going (Turf): Sf: 0-0 GS: 0-0 Gd: 0-0 GF: 0-0 Fm: 0-0
Distance: 5f/6f: 0-0 7f-8f: 0-3 9f-13f: 0-0 14f+: 0-0
Track : LH: 0-2 RH: 0-1 Tight: 0-2 Gall: 0-0
Aids: Bl: 0-0 Vi: 0-0 Tstrap: 0-0 Ckp: 0-0
Best Rating: 67 9/09 Kemp 7f stand

Modest; stays 7f; acts on Polytrack.

Loulou (USA)

93(85) (59)**62**

3-y-o ch f El Prado (IRE)-Hatoof (USA) (Irish River (FR))
S A Callaghan Saleh Al Homaizi & Imad Al Sagar

Placings:5600-130 **(2380)**
2009: 10^{1}GS, 12^{3}GF, 9^{0}GS,

	Starts	1st	2nd	3rd	Win & Pl
Career Total (Turf)	3	1	0	1	2432
Career Total (AW)	4	0	0	0	0

62 4/09 Nott 1m2f50y (0-60)H G-S £2047
Total win prize-money £2047

Going (Turf): Sf: 0-0 **GS: 1-2** Gd: 0-0 GF: 0-1 Fm: 0-0
Distance: 5f/6f: 0-0 7f-8f: 0-4 **9f-13f: 1-3** 14f+: 0-0
Track : **LH: 1-4** RH: 0-3 Tight: 0-1 Gall: 0-2
Aids: Bl: 0-0 Vi: 0-0 Tstrap: 0-0 Ckp: 0-0
Best Rating: 62 5/09 Bevl 1m4f16y gd-fm

Modest; stays 1m2f; acts on easy ground.

Louphole

98(105) (84)**75**

7-y-o ch g Loup Sauvage (USA)-Goodwood Lass (IRE) (Alzao (USA))
J R Jenkins Miss K McManus

Placings:341003101/000050655004/42003331212/1166424055/42055264316-22005106432626 **(7203)**
2009: 6^{2}SD, 6^{2}SD, 6^{0}SD, 6^{0}G, 6^{5}GF, 5^{1}GF, 6^{0}GF, 6^{6}GF, 6^{4}GF, 5^{3}F, 6^{2}SD, 6^{6}SD, 6^{2}GF, 6^{6}SD,

	Starts	1st	2nd	3rd	Win & Pl
Career Total (Turf)	34	5	3	6	34918
Career Total (AW)	33	4	7	1	23945

70	5/09	Brig	5f213y	(0-70)H	G-F	£3154
72	10/08	Ling	6f	(0-75)H	STD	£2590
81	2/07	Ling	6f	(0-75)H	STD	£3238
78	1/07	Kemp	6f	(0-70)H	STD	£3238
76	7/06	Leic	5f218y	(0-70)H	FRM	£5181
75	6/06	Bath	5f161y	(0-70)H	G-F	£3886
89	11/04	Wolv	5f216y	(0-85)	STD	£6841
85	10/04	Epsm	5f	(0-85)	GD	£10348
81	7/04	Brig	5f59y	F	G-F	£2905

Total win prize-money £41384

Going (Turf): Sf: 0-1 GS: 0-0 Gd: 1-10 **GF: 3-21** Fm: 1-2
Distance: **5f/6f: 9-58** 7f-8f: 0-7 9f-13f: 0-2 14f+: 0-0
Track : **LH: 6-40** RH: 1-7 **Tight: 3-30** Gall: 1-10
Aids: Bl: 0-0 Vi: 0-1 Tstrap: 0-1 Ckp: 0-1
Best Rating: 89 11/04 Wolv 5f216y stand

Modest; effective at around 6f-7f; acts on fast ground and on Polytrack; goes well on sharp/switchback tracks.

Love Action (IRE)

92(88) (68)**72**

2-y-o b f Motivator-Speciale (USA) (War Chant (USA))
R Hannon Mrs R Ablett

Placings:406 **(7450)**
2009: 7^{4}GF, 7^{0}GF, 8^{6}SD,

	Starts	1st	2nd	3rd	Win & Pl
Career Total (Turf)	2	0	0	0	385
Career Total (AW)	1	0	0	0	0

Going (Turf): **Sf: 0-0 GS: 0-0 Gd: 0-0 GF: 0-2 Fm: 0-0**
Distance: 5f/6f: 0-0 7f-8f: 0-3 9f-13f: 0-0 14f+: 0-0
Track : LH: 0-0 RH: 0-1 Tight: 0-0 Gall: 0-0
Aids: Bl: 0-0 Vi: 0-0 Tstrap: 0-0 Ckp: 0-0
Best Rating: **72** 6/09 Newb 7f gd-fm

Love Allowed

91(88) (47)55

3-y-o br f Diktat-Love Song (Kris)

Jamie Poulton Michael Ogburn

Placings:00330000000 **(6783)**

2009: 6^{0}SD, 7^{0}SD, 7^{3}G, 7^{3}G, 7^{0}GF, 8^{0}G, 7^{0}GF, 7^{0}G, 7^{0}SD, 7^{0}SS, 7^{0}SS,

	Starts	1st	2nd	3rd	Win & Pl
Career Total (Turf)	6	0	0	2	756
Career Total (AW)	5	0	0	0	

Going (Turf): **Sf: 0-0 GS: 0-0 Gd: 0-4 GF: 0-2 Fm: 0-0**
Distance: 5f/6f: 0-1 7f-8f: 0-9 9f-13f: 0-1 14f+: 0-0
Track : LH: 0-6 RH: 0-2 Tight: 0-6 Gall: 0-0
Aids: Bl: 0-0 Vi: 0-0 Tstrap: 0-0 Ckp: 0-0
Best Rating: **55** 4/09 Folk 7f good

Love And Devotion

90 62

2-y-o b f Shamardal (USA)-Romantic Myth (Mind Games)

Saeed Bin Suroor Godolphin

Placings:5065 **(6378)**

2009: 6^{5}GF, 6^{0}GF, 5^{6}G, 6^{5}GF,

	Starts	1st	2nd	3rd	Win & Pl
Career Total (Turf)	4	0	0	0	141

Going (Turf): **Sf: 0-0 GS: 0-0 Gd: 0-1 GF: 0-3 Fm: 0-0**
Distance: 5f/6f: 0-3 7f-8f: 0-1 9f-13f: 0-0 14f+: 0-0
Track : LH: 0-1 RH: 0-0 Tight: 0-0 Gall: 0-2
Aids: Bl: 0-0 Vi: 0-0 Tstrap: 0-0 Ckp: 0-0
Best Rating: **62** 8/09 Wind 6f gd-fm

Modest; failed to build on debut when beaten favourite on second start; all runs at 5-6f on a sound surface.

Love Angel (USA)

(95) (51)51

7-y-o b/br g Woodman (USA)-Omnia (USA) (Green Dancer (USA))

J J Bridger J J Bridger

Placings:43/42402626011425/**0**00600004**5**/**000**/06550-R **(0825)**

2009: 10^{R}SD,

	Starts	1st	2nd	3rd	Win & Pl
Career Total (Turf)	27	2	4	1	16347
Career Total (AW)	8	0	0	0	0

75 9/05 Bath 1m2f46y (0-65)H HRD £2804
81 9/05 York 1m2f88y (0-70)H G-F £5323
Total win prize-money £8128

Going (Turf): Sf: 0-4 GS: 0-4 Gd: 0-7 **GF: 1-11 Fm: 1-1**
Distance: 5f/6f: 0-2 7f-8f: 0-4 **9f-13f: 2-23** 14f+: 0-6
Track : **LH: 2-15** RH: 0-16 Tight: 1-17 Gall: 1-2
Aids: Bl: 0-3 Vi: 0-5 Tstrap: 0-0 Ckp: 0-0
Best Rating: **81** 9/05 York 1m2f88y gd-fm

Fair handicapper; stays ten furlongs; handles soft, but well suited by fast ground; has worn blinkers and a visor.

Love Call (IRE)

97(90) (39)62

3-y-o ch f Indian Haven-Cap And Gown (IRE) (Royal Academy (USA))

W R Muir Mrs C Henley

Placings:661 **(5348)**

2009: 8^{6}GF, 12^{6}SD, 8^{1}G,

	Starts	1st	2nd	3rd	Win & Pl
Career Total (Turf)	2	1	0	0	2914
Career Total (AW)	1	0	0	0	0

62 8/09 Wwck 1m22y GD £2914
Total win prize-money £2914

Going (Turf): Sf: 0-0 GS: 0-0 **Gd: 1-1** GF: 0-1 Fm: 0-0
Distance: 5f/6f: 0-0 7f-8f: 0-1 **9f-13f: 1-2** 14f+: 0-0
Track : **LH: 1-2** RH: 0-0 Tight: 0-1 Gall: 0-0
Aids: Bl: 0-0 Vi: 0-0 Tstrap: 0-0 Ckp: 0-0
Best Rating: **62** 8/09 Wwck 1m22y good

Modest; stays 1m; acts on good ground.

Love Delta (USA)

92(90) (57)76

2-y-o b/br c Seeking The Gold (USA)-Delta Princess (USA) (A.P. Indy (USA))

M Johnston Crone Stud Farms Ltd

Placings:5360 **(7763)**

2009: 7^{5}S, 7^{3}G, 6^{6}GS, 8^{0}SD,

	Starts	1st	2nd	3rd	Win & Pl
Career Total (Turf)	3	0	0	1	746
Career Total (AW)	1	0	0	0	

Going (Turf): **Sf: 0-1 GS: 0-1 Gd: 0-1 GF: 0-0 Fm: 0-0**
Distance: 5f/6f: 0-1 7f-8f: 0-3 9f-13f: 0-0 14f+: 0-0
Track : LH: 0-0 RH: 0-3 Tight: 0-0 Gall: 0-0
Aids: Bl: 0-0 Vi: 0-0 Tstrap: 0-0 Ckp: 0-0
Best Rating: **76** 8/09 Gdwd 7f soft

Fair; stays 7f; acts on good or softer ground.

Love Galore (IRE)

102(88) (60)106

4-y-o b g Galileo (IRE)-Lobmille (Mill Reef (USA))

M Johnston Crone Stud Farms Ltd

Placings:41/2304210500-030**6**5000 **(3873)**

2009: 12^{0}G, 12^{3}GF, 10^{0}G, 12^{6}G, **12^{5}SD**, 12^{0}G, 11^{0}GF, 10^{0}GF,

	Starts	1st	2nd	3rd	Win & Pl
Career Total (Turf)	19	2	2	2	88115
Career Total (AW)	1	0	0	0	1076

106 7/08 Gdwd 1m4f (0-105)H G-F £52963
88 9/07 Haml 1m65y GD £3886
Total win prize-money £56850

Going (Turf): Sf: 0-0 GS: 0-1 **Gd: 1-9 GF: 1-9** Fm: 0-0
Distance: 5f/6f: 0-0 7f-8f: 0-2 **9f-13f: 2-18** 14f+: 0-0
Track : LH: 0-8 **RH: 2-9 Tight: 2-4** Gall: 0-9
Aids: Bl: 0-0 Vi: 0-0 Tstrap: 0-0 Ckp: 0-0
Best Rating: **106** 9/08 Veli 1m4f good

Very useful; Listed placed; stays 1m4f; acts on good and faster ground.

Love In The Park

106(88) (51)75

4-y-o b f Pivotal-Naughty Crown (USA) (Chief's Crown (USA))

R Brotherton Arthur Clayton

Placings:30002131166 **(5964)**

2009: 6^{3}SD, 7^{0}SD, 7^{0}F, 8^{0}GF, 7^{2}GF, 9^{1}GF, 10^{3}GF, 10^{1}G, 10^{1}GS, 10^{6}G, 11^{6}GS,

	Starts	1st	2nd	3rd	Win & Pl
Career Total (Turf)	9	3	1	1	7569
Career Total (AW)	2	0	0	1	385

75 8/09 Ling 1m2f (0-65)H G-S £2047
69 7/09 Ling 1m2f (0-65)H GD £2047
65 6/09 Ling 1m1f (0-55)H G-F £2388
Total win prize-money £6482

Going (Turf): Sf: 0-0 **GS: 1-2 Gd: 1-2 GF: 1-4** Fm: 0-1
Distance: 5f/6f: 0-1 7f-8f: 0-3 **9f-13f: 3-7** 14f+: 0-0
Track : **LH: 3-8** RH: 0-1 **Tight: 3-4** Gall: 0-1
Aids: Bl: 0-0 Vi: 0-0 Tstrap: 0-0 Ckp: 0-0
Best Rating: **75** 8/09 Ling 1m2f gd-sft

Fair; stays 1m2f; acts on fast and easy ground.

Love In The West (IRE)

98 60

3-y-o b f Fruits Of Love (USA)-Sandhill (IRE) (Danehill (USA))

G A Swinbank John P Jones

Placings:0412530 **(5947)**

2009: 8^{0}G, 10^{4}GF, 9^{1}G, 7^{2}GF, 12^{5}GS, 11^{3}GS, 12^{0}G,

	Starts	1st	2nd	3rd	Win & Pl
Career Total (Turf)	7	1	1	1	4238

54 7/09 Ripn 1m1f170y GD £2729
Total win prize-money £2730

Going (Turf): Sf: 0-0 GS: 0-2 **Gd: 1-3** GF: 0-2 Fm: 0-0
Distance: 5f/6f: 0-0 7f-8f: 0-2 **9f-13f: 1-5** 14f+: 0-0
Track : LH: 0-3 **RH: 1-4 Tight: 1-5** Gall: 0-1
Aids: Bl: 0-0 Vi: 0-0 Tstrap: 0-0 Ckp: 0-0
Best Rating: **60** 8/09 Catt 1m3f214y gd-sft

Moderate; stays 1m2f; acts on good ground; may progress further.

Love Lockdown (IRE)

100(101) (109)99

2-y-o gr g Verglas (IRE)-Out Of Thanks (IRE) (Sadler's Wells (USA))

G M Lyons Sean Jones

Placings:3111631 **(5661)**

2009: 5^{3}Y, 6^{1}G, 6^{1}GF, 6^{1}G, 6^{6}GY, 5^{3}GF, 6^{1}SD,

	Starts	1st	2nd	3rd	Win & Pl
Career Total (Turf)	6	3	0	2	61314
Career Total (AW)	1	1	0	0	28385

109 9/09 Kemp 6f STD £28385
99 6/09 Cork 6f GD £30021
97 6/09 Naas 6f G-F £13588
88 5/09 Leop 6f GD £12075
Total win prize-money £84072

Going (Turf): Sf: 0-0 GS: 0-0 **Gd: 2-2** GF: 1-2 Fm: 0-0
Distance: **5f/6f: 4-7** 7f-8f: 0-0 9f-13f: 0-0 14f+: 0-0
Track : **LH: 2-3** RH: 1-1 Tight: 0-0 Gall: 0-0
Aids: Bl: 0-0 Vi: 0-0 Tstrap: 0-0 Ckp: 0-0
Best Rating: **109** 9/09 Kemp 6f stand

Smart; Listed winner; stays 6f; acts on good/fast ground.

Love Match

94(89) (64)69

2-y-o b f Danehill Dancer (IRE)-Name Of Love (IRE) (Petardia)

R Charlton Lady Rothschild

Placings:553024 (6775)

2009: 6[5]GS, 6[5]S, 6[3]GF, 6[0]SD, 5[2]GF, 6[4]SD,

	Starts	1st	2nd	3rd	Win & Pl
Career Total (Turf)	4	0	1	1	1158
Career Total (AW)	2	0	0	0	0

Going (Turf): Sf: 0-1 GS: 0-1 Gd: 0-0 GF: 0-2 Fm: 0-0
Distance: 5f/6f: 0-5 7f-8f: 0-1 9f-13f: 0-0 14f+: 0-0
Track : LH: 0-0 RH: 0-2 Tight: 0-0 Gall: 0-0
Aids: Bl: 0-1 Vi: 0-1 Tstrap: 0-0 Ckp: 0-0
Best Rating: 69 10/09 Catt 5f gd-fm

Modest; stays 6f; acts on fast ground and Polytrack; has worn blinkers.

Love Pegasus (USA)

90(105) (96)71

3-y-o b c Fusaichi Pegasus (USA)-Take Charge Lady (USA) (Dehere (USA))

Niall O'Callaghan (M Johnston 11/6) Kilmichael Racing Syndicate

Placings:64-1106 (7531a)

2009: 8[1]SD, 8[1]SD, 8[0]G, 10[6]SD,

	Starts	1st	2nd	3rd	Win & Pl
Career Total (Turf)	2	0	0	0	0
Career Total (AW)	4	2	0	0	7318
96 6/09 Kemp 1m	(0-80)H			STD	£4727
77 2/09 Kemp 1m				STD	£2590

Total win prize-money £7317

Going (Turf): Sf: 0-0 GS: 0-1 Gd: 0-1 GF: 0-0 Fm: 0-0
Distance: 5f/6f: 0-0 7f-8f: 2-4 9f-13f: 0-2 14f+: 0-0
Track : LH: 0-3 RH: 2-3 Tight: 0-2 Gall: 0-0
Aids: Bl: 0-0 Vi: 0-0 Tstrap: 0-0 Ckp: 0-0
Best Rating: 96 6/09 Kemp 1m stand

Useful; stays 1m and acts on Polytrack.

Love You Louis

92(102) (76)75

3-y-o b g Mark Of Esteem (IRE)-Maddie's A Jem (Emperor Jones (USA))

J R Jenkins J Pepper

Placings:361035632-6015003005 (7738)

2009: 6[6]SD, 5[0]SD, 5[1]SD, 5[5]SD, 5[0]G, 5[0]G, 5[3]SD, 5[0]SD, 5[0]SD, 6[5]SD,

	Starts	1st	2nd	3rd	Win & Pl
Career Total (Turf)	8	1	0	2	4867
Career Total (AW)	11	1	1	2	8618
76 2/09 Kemp 5f	(0-85)H			STD	£5828
75 6/08 Sand 5f6y				SFT	£3885

Total win prize-money £9714

Going (Turf): Sf: 1-2 GS: 0-2 Gd: 0-4 GF: 0-0 Fm: 0-0
Distance: 5f/6f: 2-19 7f-8f: 0-0 9f-13f: 0-0 14f+: 0-0
Track : LH: 0-7 RH: 1-3 Tight: 0-5 Gall: 0-5
Aids: Bl: 1-6 Vi: 0-3 Tstrap: 0-2 Ckp: 0-2
Best Rating: 76 2/09 Kemp 5f stand

Fair; suited by 5f; acts on soft ground; goes on Polytrack; has worn cheekpieces.

Loveinthesand (IRE)

90 76

2-y-o b c Footstepsinthesand-Love Emerald (USA) (Mister Baileys)

M Johnston M Doyle

Placings:240 (5763)

2009: 6[2]GF, 6[4]G, 6[0]GF,

	Starts	1st	2nd	3rd	Win & Pl
Career Total (Turf)	3	0	1	0	1844

Going (Turf): Sf: 0-0 GS: 0-0 Gd: 0-1 GF: 0-2 Fm: 0-0
Distance: 5f/6f: 0-2 7f-8f: 0-1 9f-13f: 0-0 14f+: 0-0
Track : LH: 0-0 RH: 0-0 Tight: 0-0 Gall: 0-0
Aids: Bl: 0-0 Vi: 0-0 Tstrap: 0-0 Ckp: 0-0
Best Rating: 76 6/09 Haml 6f5y gd-fm

Lovelace

108(109) (112)118

5-y-o b h Royal Applause-Loveleaves (Polar Falcon (USA))

M Johnston Hamad Suhail

Placings:1/53111100/3000012160-4646050 (5200)

2009: 7[4]Y, 0[6]C, 0[4]O, 0[6]O, 0[0]GF, 0[5]O, 0[0]GF,

	Starts	1st	2nd	3rd	Win & Pl
Career Total (Turf)	25	7	1	1	204372
Career Total (AW)	1	0	0	1	2800
113 9/08 Badn 1m				SFT	£40401
115 7/08 Sand 1m14y	H			G-F	£62310
112 9/07 Gdwd 7f				G-F	£28390
102 8/07 Newb 7f	(0-100)H			G-S	£12464
97 8/07 Leic 7f9y	(0-100)H			FRM	£9971
86 5/07 Hayd 7f30y	(0-95)H			G-F	£9715
78 4/06 Thsk 5f				G-S	£7772

Total win prize-money £171024

Going (Turf): Sf: 1-1 GS: 2-6 Gd: 0-7 GF: 3-7 Fm: 1-3
Distance: 5f/6f: 1-4 7f-8f: 5-18 9f-13f: 1-4 14f+: 0-0
Track : LH: 2-7 RH: 2-5 Tight: 0-3 Gall: 0-2
Aids: Bl: 0-0 Vi: 0-0 Tstrap: 0-0 Ckp: 0-0
Best Rating: 118 7/08 NmkJ 7f good

Smart; winner in Group 2 company in Germany; stays 1m and acts on most ground; usually held up.

Lovely Eyes (IRE)

91 67

2-y-o b f Red Ransom (USA)-Polygueza (FR) (Be My Guest (USA))

D M Simcock Dr Ali Ridha

Placings:44 (6331)

2009: 8[4]GF, 10[4]F,

	Starts	1st	2nd	3rd	Win & Pl
Career Total (Turf)	2	0	0	0	577

Going (Turf): Sf: 0-0 GS: 0-0 Gd: 0-0 GF: 0-1 Fm: 0-1
Distance: 5f/6f: 0-0 7f-8f: 0-1 9f-13f: 0-1 14f+: 0-0
Track : LH: 0-2 RH: 0-0 Tight: 0-1 Gall: 0-1
Aids: Bl: 0-0 Vi: 0-0 Tstrap: 0-0 Ckp: 0-0
Best Rating: 67 9/09 Bath 1m2f46y firm

Modest; stay 1m2f; acts on fast ground.

Lovely Steps (USA)

(93) (53)

3-y-o b/br f Gone West (USA)-Magicalmysterycat (USA) (Storm Cat (USA))

D M Simcock Ali Saeed

Placings:05-026 (0673)

2009: 8[0]SD, 6[2]SD, 6[6]SD,

	Starts	1st	2nd	3rd	Win & Pl
Career Total (Turf)	0	0	0	0	
Career Total (AW)	5	0	1	0	605

Going (Turf): Sf: 0-0 GS: 0-0 Gd: 0-0 GF: 0-0 Fm: 0-0
Distance: 5f/6f: 0-2 7f-8f: 0-3 9f-13f: 0-0 14f+: 0-0
Track : LH: 0-3 RH: 0-2 Tight: 0-3 Gall: 0-0
Aids: Bl: 0-2 Vi: 0-0 Tstrap: 0-0 Ckp: 0-0
Best Rating: 53 2/09 Kemp 6f stand

Moderate; suited by 6f and acts on Polytrack; has worn blinkers.

Lovely Thought

108 94

3-y-o b f Dubai Destination (USA)-Fairy Flight (IRE) (Fairy King (USA))

W J Haggas Liam Sheridan

Placings:0061-13000013 (7292)

2009: 6[1]G, 7[3]GS, 6[0]GS, 7[0]G, 6[0]GF, 6[0]S, 5[1]S, 6[3]S,

	Starts	1st	2nd	3rd	Win & Pl
Career Total (Turf)	12	3	0	2	15953
89 10/09 Catt 5f212y	(0-75)H			SFT	£2914
87 4/09 Yarm 6f3y	(0-70)H			GD	£3238
66 10/08 Yarm 7f3y	(0-70)			SFT	£3238

Total win prize-money £9390

Going (Turf): Sf: 2-4 GS: 0-3 Gd: 1-3 GF: 0-2 Fm: 0-0
Distance: 5f/6f: 1-6 7f-8f: 2-6 9f-13f: 0-0 14f+: 0-0
Track : LH: 1-1 RH: 0-0 Tight: 1-1 Gall: 0-2
Aids: Bl: 3-8 Vi: 0-0 Tstrap: 0-1 Ckp: 0-1
Best Rating: 94 11/09 Donc 6f soft

Useful; suited by 6f-7f; acts on good and easier ground; has worn blinkers.

Lovers Causeway (USA)

(94) (74)32

2-y-o b c Giant's Causeway (USA)-Heeremandi (IRE) (Royal Academy (USA))

M Johnston Crone Stud Farms Ltd

Placings:02 (7844)

2009: 8[0]GF, 8[2]SD,

	Starts	1st	2nd	3rd	Win & Pl
Career Total (Turf)	1	0	0	0	
Career Total (AW)	1	0	1	0	1156

Going (Turf): Sf: 0-0 GS: 0-0 Gd: 0-0 GF: 0-1 Fm: 0-0
Distance: 5f/6f: 0-0 7f-8f: 0-1 9f-13f: 0-1 14f+: 0-0
Track : LH: 0-2 RH: 0-0 Tight: 0-1 Gall: 0-1
Aids: Bl: 0-0 Vi: 0-0 Tstrap: 0-0 Ckp: 0-0
Best Rating: 74 12/09 Wolv 1m141y stand

Fair; stays 1m and acts on Polytrack.

Lowdown (IRE)

104 90

2-y-o ch c Shamardal (USA)-Mood Swings (IRE) (Shirley Heights)

M Johnston Sheikh Hamdan Bin Mohammed Al Maktoum

Placings:521004 **(6478)**

2009: 6^{5}S, 7^{2}S, 6^{1}G, 6^{0}GF, 6^{0}GF, 7^{4}GF,

	Starts	1st	2nd	3rd	Win & Pl
Career Total (Turf)	**6**	**1**	**1**	**0**	**65968**

90	7/09	Gdwd	6f	GD	£12952

Total win prize-money £12952

Going (Turf): Sf: 0-2 GS: 0-0 **Gd: 1-1** GF: 0-3 Fm: 0-0
Distance: **5f/6f: 1-3** 7f-8f: 0-3 9f-13f: 0-0 14f+: 0-0
Track : LH: 0-0 RH: 0-0 Tight: 0-0 Gall: 0-0
Aids: Bl: 0-0 Vi: 0-0 Tstrap: 0-0 Ckp: 0-0
Best Rating: **90** 7/09 Gdwd 6f good

Very useful; effective at 6f on good ground.

Lowther

108(98) (89)101

4-y-o b c Beat All (USA)-Ever So Lonely (Headin' Up)

A Bailey L J Barratt

Placings:1160202500 **(6994)**

2009: 8^{1}G, 7^{1}GF, 7^{6}GF, 8^{0}G, 7^{2}GF, 6^{0}GF, 6^{2}G, 7^{5}GF, 8^{0}SD, 6^{0}G,

	Starts	1st	2nd	3rd	Win & Pl
Career Total (Turf)	**9**	**2**	**2**	**0**	**28151**
Career Total (AW)	**1**	**0**	**0**	**0**	

95	6/09	Ches	7f2y	(0-95)H	G-F	£8831
91	5/09	Yarm	1m3y		GD	£2525

Total win prize-money £11357

Going (Turf): Sf: 0-0 GS: 0-0 **Gd: 1-4 GF: 1-5** Fm: 0-0
Distance: 5f/6f: 0-2 7f-8f: 1-6 9f-13f: 1-2 14f+: 0-0
Track : **LH: 1-5** RH: 0-0 **Tight: 1-3** Gall: 0-0
Aids: Bl: 0-4 Vi: 0-0 Tstrap: 0-0 Ckp: 0-0
Best Rating: **101** 9/09 Ayr 6f good

Very useful; effective over 6f-1m; acts on good ground; has worn blinkers and eyeshield.

Loyal Royal (IRE)

95(104) (69)68

6-y-o b g King Charlemagne (USA)-Supportive (IRE) (Nashamaa)

J M Bradley JMB Racing.co.uk

Placings:22302/5140605/0000/003000050331-4432526000630205201 4063 **(7876)**

2009: 6^{4}SD, 7^{4}SD, 5^{3}SD, 7^{2}SD, 7^{5}SD, 7^{2}SD, 7^{6}SD, 7^{0}SD, 7^{0}GF, 7^{0}G, 7^{6}SD, 7^{3}SD, 7^{0}GF, 5^{2}SD, 5^{0}SD, 5^{5}SD, 7^{2}SF, 7^{0}SD, 5^{1}SD, 6^{4}SD, 7^{0}SD, 7^{6}SD,

	Starts	1st	2nd	3rd	Win & Pl
Career Total (Turf)	**23**	**1**	**3**	**2**	**15288**
Career Total (AW)	**28**	**2**	**4**	**5**	**8411**

69	10/09	Wolv	5f216y	(0-65)H	STD	£2388
61	12/08	Ling	7f	(0-52)H	STD	£1706
88	5/06	Sals	6f		FRM	£5505

Total win prize-money £9599

Going (Turf): Sf: 0-2 GS: 0-3 Gd: 0-9 GF: 0-7 **Fm: 1-2**
Distance: **5f/6f: 2-28** 7f-8f: 1-23 9f-13f: 0-0 14f+: 0-0
Track : **LH: 2-26** RH: 0-8 **Tight: 2-20** Gall: 0-4
Aids: **Bl: 2-28** Vi: 0-0 Tstrap: 0-2 Ckp: 0-2
Best Rating: **96** 5/06 Newb 6f8y good

Modest; formerly very useful; effective over 6f-7f; acts on most ground including Polytrack; has worn blinkers.

Loyaliste (FR)

85 66

2-y-o ch c Green Tune (USA)-Whitby (FR) (Gold Away (IRE))

R Hannon Mrs Sue Brendish

Placings:36 **(6533)**

2009: 9^{3}G, 10^{6}GF,

	Starts	1st	2nd	3rd	Win & Pl
Career Total (Turf)	**2**	**0**	**0**	**1**	**698**

Going (Turf): **Sf: 0-0 GS: 0-0 Gd: 0-1 GF: 0-1 Fm: 0-0**
Distance: 5f/6f: 0-0 7f-8f: 0-0 9f-13f: 0-2 14f+: 0-0
Track : LH: 0-1 RH: 0-1 Tight: 0-1 Gall: 0-0
Aids: Bl: 0-0 Vi: 0-0 Tstrap: 0-0 Ckp: 0-0
Best Rating: **66** 9/09 Gdwd 1m1f good

Luberon

(116) (88)101

6-y-o b g Fantastic Light (USA)-Luxurious (USA) (Lyphard (USA))

M Johnston H Kronseder

Placings:212410/**5411540/000100000**0/**22130052-45** **(7640)**

2009: 12^{4}SD, 11^{5}SD,

	Starts	1st	2nd	3rd	Win & Pl
Career Total (Turf)	**26**	**5**	**3**	**1**	**79155**
Career Total (AW)	**7**	**1**	**2**	**0**	**34826**

97	5/08	York	1m4f	(0-105)H	G-F	£31155
109	4/07	Kemp	1m3f	(0-105)H	STD	£24928
108	7/06	York	1m4f	(0-100)H	G-F	£11658
104	7/06	Wind	1m3f135y	(0-100)H	G-F	£12464
92	9/05	Ayr	1m		GD	£6084
80	6/05	Muss	7f30y		FRM	£3341

Total win prize-money £89631

Going (Turf): Sf: 0-2 GS: 0-0 Gd: 1-14 **GF: 3-9** Fm: 1-1
Distance: 5f/6f: 0-0 7f-8f: 2-7 **9f-13f: 4-25** 14f+: 0-1
Track : **LH: 3-17** RH: 2-14 Tight: 2-9 Gall: 2-12
Aids: Bl: 0-0 Vi: 0-0 Tstrap: 0-0 Ckp: 0-0
Best Rating: **109** 4/07 Kemp 1m3f stand

Very useful; stays 1m4f; acts on good ground and faster, also goes on Polytrack; likes to race prominently.

Luc Jordan

103(103) (84)92

3-y-o b c Intikhab (USA)-Saphila (IRE) (Sadler's Wells (USA))

L M Cumani Equibreed S.R.L.

Placings:222632111 **(6996)**

2009: 8^{2}GF, 8^{2}G, 8^{2}G, 10^{6}GF, 7^{3}GS, 7^{2}G, 8^{1}SD, 10^{1}SD, 10^{1}GS,

	Starts	1st	2nd	3rd	Win & Pl
Career Total (Turf)	**7**	**1**	**4**	**1**	**10169**
Career Total (AW)	**2**	**2**	**0**	**0**	**6775**

92	10/09	Donc	1m2f60y	(0-85)H	G-S	£6476
84	9/09	Kemp	1m2f	(0-85)H	STD	£4727
79	9/09	Wolv	1m141y		STD	£2047

Total win prize-money £13250

Going (Turf): Sf: 0-0 **GS: 1-2** Gd: 0-3 GF: 0-2 Fm: 0-0
Distance: 5f/6f: 0-0 7f-8f: 0-3 **9f-13f: 3-6** 14f+: 0-0
Track : **LH: 2-3** RH: 1-1 Tight: 1-2 Gall: 1-1
Aids: Bl: 0-0 Vi: 0-0 Tstrap: 0-0 Ckp: 0-0
Best Rating: **92** 10/09 Donc 1m2f60y gd-sft

Useful; stays 1m2f; acts on fast ground and Polytrack.

Lucayan Dancer

105(102) (77)77

9-y-o b g Zieten (USA)-Tittle Tattle (IRE) (Soviet Lad (USA))

D Nicholls James E Greaves

Placings:21260232/06206600026640334/6550141234/200130103230/2002601235106/03300005100500/**0135230055131150-6**202124132260 **(6012)**

2009: 9^{6}SD, 9^{2}GF, 10^{0}F, 11^{2}GF, 9^{1}GF, 7^{2}GF, 9^{4}G, 10^{1}GF, 11^{3}GF, 10^{2}GF, 9^{2}GF, 10^{6}GF, 10^{0}GS,

	Starts	1st	2nd	3rd	Win & Pl
Career Total (Turf)	**98**	**13**	**18**	**13**	**105461**
Career Total (AW)	**5**	**1**	**0**	**1**	**2893**

68	6/09	Rdcr	1m2f	G-F	£2047
60	5/09	Muss	1m1f	G-F	£1942
76	8/08	Catt	1m3f214y	G-F	£2388
76	7/08	Rdcr	1m2f	G-F	£2388
77	6/08	Ches	1m2f75y	GD	£3432
77	3/08	Wolv	1m1f103y	STD	£2590
86	7/07	Ches	1m2f75y (0-80)H	SFT	£5829
89	8/06	Gdwd	1m1f (0-90)H	G-F	£9715
82	6/06	Ches	1m2f75y (0-85)H	GD	£6153
81	6/05	Ches	1m2f75y (0-85)H	G-F	£6942
77	5/05	Rdcr	1m2f (0-70)H	G-F	£3867
68	9/04	Pont	1m2f6y (0-60)	FRM	£4202
63	8/04	Brig	1m1f209yF(0-55)H	SFT	£3038
88	5/02	Brig	5f213y E	GD	£3474

Total win prize-money £58011

Going (Turf): Sf: 2-13GS: 0-10Gd: 3-26 **GF: 7-43** Fm: 1-6
Distance: 5f/6f: 1-1 7f-8f: 0-14 **9f-13f: 13-88** 14f+: 0-0
Track : **LH: 12-67** RH: 2-30 **Tight: 11-53** Gall: 0-14
Aids: Bl: 0-3 Vi: 0-0 Tstrap: 0-4 Ckp: 0-4
Best Rating: **92** 8/02 Gdwd 7f gd-fm

Modest; effective at up to 1m4f; acts on any ground; has worn blinkers and cheekpieces.

Luck Of The Draw (IRE)

(84) (52)

2-y-o b g Key Of Luck (USA)-Sarifa (IRE) (Kahyasi)

Sir Mark Prescott L A Larratt - Osborne House

Placings:060 **(6627)**

2009: 7^{0}SD, 5^{6}SD, 7^{0}SS,

	Starts	1st	2nd	3rd	Win & Pl
Career Total (Turf)	**0**	**0**	**0**	**0**	
Career Total (AW)	**3**	**0**	**0**	**0**	**0**

Going (Turf): **Sf: 0-0 GS: 0-0 Gd: 0-0 GF: 0-0 Fm: 0-0**
Distance: 5f/6f: 0-1 7f-8f: 0-2 9f-13f: 0-0 14f+: 0-0
Track : LH: 0-2 RH: 0-1 Tight: 0-2 Gall: 0-0
Aids: Bl: 0-0 Vi: 0-0 Tstrap: 0-0 Ckp: 0-0
Best Rating: **52** 9/09 Kemp 7f stand

Luck Will Come (IRE)

102(103) (77)79

5-y-o b m Desert Style (IRE)-Petite Maxine (Sharpo)

H J Collingridge Greenstead Hall Racing Ltd

Placings:20/51432/021332100-412202203 **(6496)**

2009: 8^{4}GF, 8^{1}SD, 8^{2}GF, 8^{2}GF, 9^{0}G, 10^{2}SD, 9^{2}G, 8^{0}G, 8^{3}SF,

	Starts	1st	2nd	3rd	Win & Pl
Career Total (Turf)	**14**	**2**	**4**	**2**	**13072**
Career Total (AW)	**11**	**2**	**4**	**2**	**14657**

75	5/09	Wolv	1m141y	(0-80)H	STD	£5046
72	8/08	Ling	1m2f	(0-85)H	STD	£5677

67	6/08	Pont	1m4y	(0-70)H	G-F	£3238
57	8/07	Haml	6f5y		G-F	£2914

Total win prize-money £16876

Going (Turf): Sf: 0-0 GS: 0-1 Gd: 0-5 **GF: 2-8** Fm: 0-0
Distance: 5f/6f: 0-2 7f-8f: 1-10 **9f-13f: 3-13** 14f+: 0-0
Track : **LH: 3-14** RH: 0-5 **Tight: 2-10** Gall: 0-2
Aids: Bl: 0-0 Vi: 0-0 Tstrap: 0-0 Ckp: 0-0
Best Rating: **79** 7/09 Sand 1m1f good

Modest; effective at 1m; acts on fast ground and on Polytrack.

Luckette

83 **32**
3-y-o b f Lucky Story (USA)-Thea (USA) (Marju (IRE))
M Brittain Mel Brittain

Placings:00-06060 **(3498)**
2009: 7^{0}GF, 9^{6}GF, 12^{0}F, 6^{6}G, 5^{0}GF,

	Starts	1st	2nd	3rd	Win & Pl
Career Total (Turf)	7	0	0	0	0

Going (Turf): **Sf: 0-0 GS: 0-0 Gd: 0-2 GF: 0-4 Fm: 0-1**
Distance: 5f/6f: 0-4 7f-8f: 0-1 9f-13f: 0-2 14f+: 0-0
Track : LH: 0-2 RH: 0-2 Tight: 0-3 Gall: 0-0
Aids: Bl: 0-0 Vi: 0-2 Tstrap: 0-0 Ckp: 0-0
Best Rating: **32** 5/09 Bevl 1m1f207y gd-fm

Luckier (IRE)

86(99) (75)**51**
3-y-o gr f Key Of Luck (USA)-Ibiza (GER) (Linamix (FR))
S Kirk The Hon Mrs J M Corbett & C Wright

Placings:021-2400020 **(7027)**
2009: 8^{2}SD, 8^{4}SD, 8^{0}GF, 7^{0}GF, 7^{0}SD, 7^{2}SD, 7^{0}SD,

	Starts	1st	2nd	3rd	Win & Pl
Career Total (Turf)	2	0	0	0	
Career Total (AW)	8	1	3	0	7027

73	12/08	Ling	7f		STD	£3561

Total win prize-money £3562

Going (Turf): **Sf: 0-0 GS: 0-0 Gd: 0-0 GF: 0-2 Fm: 0-0**
Distance: 5f/6f: 0-0 **7f-8f: 1-9** 9f-13f: 0-1 14f+: 0-0
Track : **LH: 1-7** RH: 0-1 **Tight: 1-5** Gall: 0-1
Aids: Bl: 0-0 Vi: 0-0 Tstrap: 0-0 Ckp: 0-0
Best Rating: **75** 4/09 Ling 1m stand

Fair; effective over 1m; acts on Polytrack.

Lucky Art (USA)

104(92) (59)**85**
3-y-o b g Johannesburg (USA)-Syrian Summer (USA) (Damascus (USA))
Mrs R A Carr (J Howard Johnson 22/7) Brian Morton

Placings:54106-05002431503300 **(7506)**
2009: 5^{0}F, 5^{5}G, 5^{0}GF, 5^{0}G, 5^{2}S, 5^{4}G, 5^{3}GF, 5^{1}G, 5^{5}GF, 5^{0}GF, 6^{3}S, 5^{3}S, 5^{0}SD, 6^{0}SD,

	Starts	1st	2nd	3rd	Win & Pl
Career Total (Turf)	17	2	1	3	13843
Career Total (AW)	2	0	0	0	

78	8/09	Thsk	5f	(0-85)H	GD	£5569
85	8/08	Thsk	5f		GD	£5504

Total win prize-money £11074

Going (Turf): Sf: 0-3 GS: 0-2 **Gd: 2-6** GF: 0-5 Fm: 0-1
Distance: **5f/6f: 2-18** 7f-8f: 0-1 9f-13f: 0-0 14f+: 0-0
Track : LH: 0-3 RH: 0-0 Tight: 0-2 Gall: 0-0
Aids: Bl: 0-0 Vi: 0-0 Tstrap: 0-1 Ckp: 0-1
Best Rating: **85** 8/08 Thsk 5f good

Fair; effective at 5f-6f; acts on good ground.

Lucky Bid

61(83) (34)**19**
3-y-o b g Josr Algarhoud (IRE)-Double Fault (IRE) (Zieten (USA))
J M Bradley J M Bradley

Placings:0000-50 **(1982)**
2009: 6^{5}SD, 5^{0}F,

	Starts	1st	2nd	3rd	Win & Pl
Career Total (Turf)	5	0	0	0	
Career Total (AW)	1	0	0	0	0

Going (Turf): **Sf: 0-0 GS: 0-0 Gd: 0-1 GF: 0-1 Fm: 0-3**
Distance: 5f/6f: 0-6 7f-8f: 0-0 9f-13f: 0-0 14f+: 0-0
Track : LH: 0-3 RH: 0-1 Tight: 0-0 Gall: 0-3
Aids: Bl: 0-0 Vi: 0-0 Tstrap: 0-0 Ckp: 0-0
Best Rating: **34** 4/09 Kemp 6f stand

Lucky Breeze (IRE)

(61) (46)
2-y-o b f Key Of Luck (USA)-Lasting Chance (USA) (American Chance (USA))
W J Knight Mrs Sheila Mitchell

Placings:0 **(7663)**
2009: 8^{0}SD,

	Starts	1st	2nd	3rd	Win & Pl
Career Total (Turf)	0	0	0	0	
Career Total (AW)	1	0	0	0	

Going (Turf): **Sf: 0-0 GS: 0-0 Gd: 0-0 GF: 0-0 Fm: 0-0**
Distance: 5f/6f: 0-0 7f-8f: 0-1 9f-13f: 0-0 14f+: 0-0
Track : LH: 0-1 RH: 0-0 Tight: 0-1 Gall: 0-0
Aids: Bl: 0-0 Vi: 0-0 Tstrap: 0-0 Ckp: 0-0
Best Rating: **46** 12/09 Ling 1m stand

Lucky Buddha

102 **59**
3-y-o gr g Kyllachy-Heaven-Liegh-Grey (Grey Desire)
Jedd O'Keeffe Ken And Delia Shaw-KGS Consulting LLP

Placings:005-5306030 **(6161)**
2009: 5^{5}GF, 6^{3}GS, 6^{0}F, 6^{6}G, 5^{0}G, 5^{3}G, 5^{0}G,

	Starts	1st	2nd	3rd	Win & Pl
Career Total (Turf)	10	0	0	2	726

Going (Turf): **Sf: 0-0 GS: 0-2 Gd: 0-5 GF: 0-2 Fm: 0-1**
Distance: 5f/6f: 0-10 7f-8f: 0-0 9f-13f: 0-0 14f+: 0-0
Track : LH: 0-2 RH: 0-1 Tight: 0-1 Gall: 0-0
Aids: Bl: 0-0 Vi: 0-0 Tstrap: 0-0 Ckp: 0-0
Best Rating: **59** 5/09 Newc 6f gd-sft

Moderate; best at 6f on good ground.

Lucky Character

(89) (47)**42**
4-y-o br g Key Of Luck (USA)-Gay Heroine (Caerleon (USA))
N J Vaughan Aykroyd And Sons Ltd

Placings:06002650-40 **(0587)**
2009: 7^{4}SD, 7^{0}SD,

	Starts	1st	2nd	3rd	Win & Pl
Career Total (Turf)	3	0	1	0	674
Career Total (AW)	7	0	0	0	0

Going (Turf): **Sf: 0-0 GS: 0-0 Gd: 0-1 GF: 0-2 Fm: 0-0**
Distance: 5f/6f: 0-1 7f-8f: 0-6 9f-13f: 0-3 14f+: 0-0
Track : LH: 0-5 RH: 0-4 Tight: 0-6 Gall: 0-0
Aids: Bl: 0-2 Vi: 0-2 Tstrap: 0-0 Ckp: 0-0
Best Rating: **47** 2/08 Wolv 1m141y stand

Lucky Dan (IRE)

100(104) (77)**72**
3-y-o b g Danetime (IRE)-Katherine Gorge (USA) (Hansel (USA))
Paul Green B & B Hygiene Limited

Placings:U045**662**-**665**00100042230 **(6798)**
2009: 6^{6}SD, 7^{6}SD, 5^{5}GF, 5^{0}GF, 7^{0}GF, 6^{1}GF, 5^{0}G, 6^{0}GS, 6^{0}GF, 5^{4}GF, 6^{2}G, 5^{2}SD, 5^{3}GF, 6^{0}S,

	Starts	1st	2nd	3rd	Win & Pl
Career Total (Turf)	15	1	1	1	6216
Career Total (AW)	6	0	2	0	1927

69	7/09	Haml	6f5y	(0-75)H	G-F	£3885

Total win prize-money £3886

Going (Turf): Sf: 0-1 GS: 0-3 Gd: 0-3 **GF: 1-8** Fm: 0-0
Distance: 5f/6f: 0-15 **7f-8f: 1-6** 9f-13f: 0-0 14f+: 0-0
Track : LH: 0-7 RH: 0-2 Tight: 0-6 Gall: 0-1
Aids: Bl: 0-0 Vi: 0-0 Tstrap: 0-0 Ckp: 0-0
Best Rating: **77** 9/09 Wolv 5f216y stand

Modest; effective over 6f; seems to act best on fast ground.

Lucky Dance (BRZ)

106(102) (80)**98**
7-y-o b h Mutakddim (USA)-Linda Francesa (ARG) (Equalize (USA))
A G Foster Joshua Snellings

Placings:22104**021**/**213346**/00362/00500606410-0503000666404 **(7810)**
2009: 8^{0}SD, 8^{5}GF, 8^{0}S, 7^{3}GF, 8^{0}GF, 8^{0}GF, 8^{0}GF, 7^{6}GS, 8^{6}GF, 8^{6}SD, 8^{4}G, 10^{0}SD, 8^{4}SD,

	Starts	1st	2nd	3rd	Win & Pl
Career Total (Turf)	34	3	3	4	39136
Career Total (AW)	9	1	2	0	2153

96	11/08	NmkR	1m	(0-100)H	G-S	£12462
	3/06	Cida	1m		HVY	£1356
	12/05	Cida	1m		FST	£906
	7/05	Cida	1m		SFT	£906

Total win prize-money £15633

Going (Turf): **Sf: 2-10** GS: 1-5 Gd: 0-9 GF: 0-9 Fm: 0-1
Distance: 5f/6f: 0-0 **7f-8f: 4-34** 9f-13f: 0-8 14f+: 0-0
Track : LH: 0-14 RH: 0-2 Tight: 0-5 Gall: 0-7
Aids: Bl: 0-1 Vi: 0-0 Tstrap: 0-0 Ckp: 0-0
Best Rating: **98** 3/09 Donc 1m gd-fm

Useful; formerly trained in Brazil and Dubai; stays 1m and acts on most ground; likes to race prominently; has worn blinkers.

Lucky Dancer

91(95) (62)**57**
4-y-o ch g Selkirk (USA)-Spot Prize (USA) (Seattle Dancer (USA))
Evan Williams (D R C Elsworth 17/6) Gold Bloodstock

Placings:56-665250 (3029)
2009: 12^{6}SD, 10^{6}SD, 16^{5}G, 16^{2}SD, 16^{5}GF, 16^{0}SD,

	Starts	1st	2nd	3rd	Win & Pl
Career Total (Turf)	2	0	0	0	0
Career Total (AW)	6	0	1	0	578

Going (Turf): **Sf: 0-0 GS: 0-0 Gd: 0-1 GF: 0-1 Fm: 0-0**
Distance: 5f/6f: 0-0 7f-8f: 0-1 9f-13f: 0-3 14f+: 0-4
Track : LH: 0-5 RH: 0-3 Tight: 0-5 Gall: 0-1
Aids: Bl: 0-2 Vi: 0-0 Tstrap: 0-0 Ckp: 0-0
Best Rating: **62** 4/09 Kemp 2m stand

Modearate; stays well; handles Polytrack.

Lucky Diva

89 **41**

2-y-o ch f Lucky Story (USA)-Cosmic Countess (IRE) (Lahib (USA))
Rae Guest Gracelands Stud Partnership

Placings:0 (5714)
2009: 5^{0}G,

	Starts	1st	2nd	3rd	Win & Pl
Career Total (Turf)	1	0	0	0	

Going (Turf): **Sf: 0-0 GS: 0-0 Gd: 0-1 GF: 0-0 Fm: 0-0**
Distance: 5f/6f: 0-1 7f-8f: 0-0 9f-13f: 0-0 14f+: 0-0
Track : LH: 0-1 RH: 0-0 Tight: 0-0 Gall: 0-1
Aids: Bl: 0-0 Vi: 0-0 Tstrap: 0-0 Ckp: 0-0
Best Rating: **41** 9/09 Bath 5f11y good

Lucky Flyer

74 **17**

2-y-o br f Lucky Story (USA)-Fly Like The Wind (Cyrano De Bergerac)
Rae Guest Gracelands Stud Partnership

Placings:0 (2636)
2009: 5^{0}GF,

	Starts	1st	2nd	3rd	Win & Pl
Career Total (Turf)	1	0	0	0	

Going (Turf): **Sf: 0-0 GS: 0-0 Gd: 0-0 GF: 0-1 Fm: 0-0**
Distance: 5f/6f: 0-1 7f-8f: 0-0 9f-13f: 0-0 14f+: 0-0
Track : LH: 0-0 RH: 0-0 Tight: 0-0 Gall: 0-0
Aids: Bl: 0-0 Vi: 0-0 Tstrap: 0-0 Ckp: 0-0
Best Rating: **17** 6/09 Sand 5f6y gd-fm

Lucky Forteen

56(88) (31)

6-y-o b m Forzando-Grey Blade (Dashing Blade)
P W Hiatt Mrs D Mitchell

Placings:00-000 (1743)
2009: 8^{0}SD, 6^{0}SD, 7^{0}GF,

	Starts	1st	2nd	3rd	Win & Pl
Career Total (Turf)	1	0	0	0	
Career Total (AW)	4	0	0	0	

Going (Turf): **Sf: 0-0 GS: 0-0 Gd: 0-0 GF: 0-1 Fm: 0-0**
Distance: 5f/6f: 0-1 7f-8f: 0-3 9f-13f: 0-1 14f+: 0-0
Track : LH: 0-4 RH: 0-1 Tight: 0-3 Gall: 0-0
Aids: Bl: 0-0 Vi: 0-0 Tstrap: 0-0 Ckp: 0-0
Best Rating: **31** 4/09 Kemp 6f stand

Lucky Fortune (IRE)

62(93) (58)

3-y-o ch g Lucky Story (USA)-Majborah (IRE) (Entrepreneur)
Miss Amy Weaver Peter Joyner

Placings:004-30360 (1746)
2009: 7^{3}SD, 7^{0}SD, 8^{3}SD, 8^{6}SD, 8^{0}GF,

	Starts	1st	2nd	3rd	Win & Pl
Career Total (Turf)	1	0	0	0	
Career Total (AW)	7	0	0	2	688

Going (Turf): **Sf: 0-0 GS: 0-0 Gd: 0-0 GF: 0-1 Fm: 0-0**
Distance: 5f/6f: 0-2 7f-8f: 0-5 9f-13f: 0-1 14f+: 0-0
Track : LH: 0-7 RH: 0-1 Tight: 0-4 Gall: 0-2
Aids: Bl: 0-4 Vi: 0-0 Tstrap: 0-0 Ckp: 0-0
Best Rating: **58** 1/09 Kemp 7f stand

Moderate stays 1m; acts on Polytrack; has worn blinkers.

Lucky General (IRE)

103 **108**

2-y-o b c Hawk Wing (USA)-Dress Code (IRE) (Barathea (IRE))
R Hannon Mrs J Wood

Placings:51401431 (6317a)
2009: 6^{5}GF, 6^{1}GF, 7^{4}GF, 7^{0}G, 6^{1}G, 7^{4}GF, 6^{3}GF, 6^{1}G,

	Starts	1st	2nd	3rd	Win & Pl
Career Total (Turf)	8	3	0	1	1008829

108	9/09	Curr	6f	GD	£956310
93	8/09	Wind	6f	GD	£7512
93	6/09	Wind	6f	G-F	£2388

Total win prize-money £966211

Going (Turf): Sf: 0-0 GS: 0-0 **Gd: 2-3** GF: 1-5 Fm: 0-0
Distance: **5f/6f: 3-3** 7f-8f: 0-5 9f-13f: 0-0 14f+: 0-0
Track : LH: 0-0 RH: 0-1 Tight: 0-0 **Gall: 2-2**
Aids: Bl: 0-0 Vi: 0-0 Tstrap: 0-0 Ckp: 0-0
Best Rating: **108** 9/09 Curr 6f good

Very useful; effective at 6f; acts on good/fast ground.

Lucky Leigh

100(101) (81)**95**

3-y-o b f Piccolo-Solmorin (Fraam)
M R Channon R Flintoff, J Channon & K Baker

Placings:14520-000200051065 (7634)
2009: 5^{0}G, 5^{0}G, 6^{0}S, 5^{2}GF, 6^{0}GF, 5^{0}GF, 5^{0}SD, 5^{5}GF, 5^{1}SS, 5^{0}GF, 6^{6}SD, 5^{5}SD,

	Starts	1st	2nd	3rd	Win & Pl
Career Total (Turf)	13	1	2	0	11574
Career Total (AW)	4	1	0	0	6476

81	10/09	Ling	5f	(0-80)H	SS	£6476
77	5/08	Rdcr	5f		G-F	£2047

Total win prize-money £8523

Going (Turf): Sf: 0-1 GS: 0-2 Gd: 0-2 **GF: 1-7** Fm: 0-1
Distance: **5f/6f: 2-16** 7f-8f: 0-1 9f-13f: 0-0 14f+: 0-0
Track : **LH: 1-6** RH: 0-1 **Tight: 1-3** Gall: 0-2
Aids: Bl: 0-0 Vi: 0-1 Tstrap: 0-0 Ckp: 0-0
Best Rating: **95** 6/08 Asct 5f gd-fm

Fair; effective over 5f and acts on fast ground; has worn a visor.

Lucky Like (FR)

109 **104**

2-y-o b/br c Lucky Story (USA)-Land Bound (USA) (Boundary (USA))
E J O'Neill Victory Racing & Partners

Placings:524151 (6486)
2009: 5^{5}GS, 6^{2}S, 6^{4}G, 5^{1}G, 7^{5}G, 6^{1}GF,

	Starts	1st	2nd	3rd	Win & Pl
Career Total (Turf)	6	2	1	0	120638

104	10/09	Rdcr	6f	G-F	£94692
93	8/09	Chat	5f110y	GD	£11650

Total win prize-money £106342

Going (Turf): Sf: 0-1 GS: 0-1 **Gd: 1-3 GF: 1-1** Fm: 0-0
Distance: **5f/6f: 2-5** 7f-8f: 0-1 9f-13f: 0-0 14f+: 0-0
Track : LH: 0-0 RH: 0-2 Tight: 0-0 Gall: 0-0
Aids: Bl: 0-0 Vi: 0-0 Tstrap: 0-0 Ckp: 0-0
Best Rating: **104** 10/09 Rdcr 6f gd-fm

Useful; has raced mainly in France; winner of the Redcar 2-y-o Trophy in 2009; stays 7f but effective at 6f; handles soft but may be better on good/fast ground.

Lucky Mellor

98(98) (84)**71**

2-y-o b c Lucky Story (USA)-Lady Natilda (First Trump)
D K Ivory L M Baker

Placings:0145203243321 (7793)
2009: 5^{0}GF, 5^{1}SD, 5^{4}GF, 6^{5}SD, 5^{2}SD, 5^{0}GF, 5^{3}SD, 5^{2}SD, 5^{4}SD, 6^{3}G, 5^{3}SD, 5^{2}SD, 5^{1}SS,

	Starts	1st	2nd	3rd	Win & Pl
Career Total (Turf)	4	0	0	1	714
Career Total (AW)	9	2	3	2	14015

84	12/09	Sthl	5f	(0-85)	SS	£6152
67	5/09	Sthl	5f		STD	£2729

Total win prize-money £8882

Going (Turf): **Sf: 0-0 GS: 0-0 Gd: 0-1 GF: 0-3 Fm: 0-0**
Distance: **5f/6f: 2-13** 7f-8f: 0-0 9f-13f: 0-0 14f+: 0-0
Track : LH: 0-5 RH: 0-1 Tight: 0-4 Gall: 0-2
Aids: **Bl: 1-6** Vi: 0-0 Tstrap: 0-0 Ckp: 0-0
Best Rating: **84** 12/09 Sthl 5f std-slw

Fair; suited by 5f; acts on Fibresand; has worn blinkers.

Lucky Numbers (IRE)

103 **90**

3-y-o b c Key Of Luck (USA)-Pure Folly (IRE) (Machiavellian (USA))
Paul Green Men Behaving Badly Two

Placings:0431013-5220606202635 (5959)
2009: 6^{5}GF, 6^{2}GF, 6^{2}GF, 5^{0}GF, 6^{6}G, 7^{0}GF, 6^{6}GF, 6^{2}S, 6^{0}GF, 6^{2}GF, 5^{6}GF, 6^{3}G, 6^{5}GF,

	Starts	1st	2nd	3rd	Win & Pl
Career Total (Turf)	20	2	4	3	19022

83	11/08	Catt	5f212y	(0-85)	HVY	£3885
70	8/08	Thsk	5f		SFT	£4274

Total win prize-money £8160

Going (Turf): **Sf: 2-4** GS: 0-0 Gd: 0-5 GF: 0-11 Fm: 0-0
Distance: **5f/6f: 2-18** 7f-8f: 0-2 9f-13f: 0-0 14f+: 0-0
Track : **LH: 1-6** RH: 0-1 **Tight: 1-6** Gall: 0-1
Aids: Bl: 0-1 Vi: 0-0 Tstrap: 0-0 Ckp: 0-0
Best Rating: **90** 4/09 Donc 6f gd-fm

Useful; stays 6f; acts on most ground but well suited by soft.

Lucky Punt

98(109) (99)58
3-y-o ch g Auction House (USA)-Sweet Coincidence (Mujahid (USA))
B G Powell I S Smith

Placings:44006005206-41101211 (7640)
2009: 10^4G, 11^1SD, 12^1SD, 12^0GS, 12^1SD, 11^2SD, 14^1SD, 11^1SD,

	Starts	1st	2nd	3rd	Win & Pl
Career Total (Turf)	7	0	0	0	654
Career Total (AW)	12	5	2	0	29356

99	12/09	Sthl	1m3f	(0-95)H	STD	£7477
91	10/09	Sthl	1m6f	(0-95)H	STD	£9714
84	9/09	Sthl	1m4f	(0-85)H	STD	£5828
83	6/09	Sthl	1m4f	(0-65)H	STD	£2047
68	5/09	Sthl	1m3f	(0-60)H	STD	£2047

Total win prize-money £27113

Going (Turf): Sf: 0-1 GS: 0-2 Gd: 0-1 GF: 0-3 Fm: 0-0
Distance: 5f/6f: 0-4 7f-8f: 0-3 **9f-13f: 4-11** 14f+: 1-1
Track : **LH: 5-9** RH: 0-7 Tight: 0-4 Gall: 0-1
Aids: Bl: 0-0 Vi: 0-0 Tstrap: 0-0 Ckp: 0-0
Best Rating: 99 12/09 Sthl 1m3f stand

Useful; effective at 1m3f-1m6f; acts on Fibresand.

Lucky Quay (IRE)

(83) (44)
2-y-o b g Key Of Luck (USA)-Lakatoi (Saddlers' Hall (IRE))
W R Swinburn M H Dixon & Cinque Ports Syndicate

Placings:0 (7522)
2009: 8^0SD,

	Starts	1st	2nd	3rd	Win & Pl
Career Total (Turf)	0	0	0	0	
Career Total (AW)	1	0	0	0	

Going (Turf): Sf: 0-0 GS: 0-0 Gd: 0-0 GF: 0-0 Fm: 0-0
Distance: 5f/6f: 0-0 7f-8f: 0-1 9f-13f: 0-0 14f+: 0-0
Track : LH: 0-1 RH: 0-0 Tight: 0-1 Gall: 0-0
Aids: Bl: 0-0 Vi: 0-0 Tstrap: 0-0 Ckp: 0-0
Best Rating: 44 11/09 Ling 1m stand

Lucky Rave

95(97) (93)94
2-y-o b c Lucky Story (USA)-Rave On (ITY) (Barathea (IRE))
Peter Eurton (D H Brown 9/9) Mr & Mrs Marc C Ferrell

Placings:3421103
2009: 6^3G, 6^4GF, 5^2G, 5^1SF, 7^1SD, 8^0FT, 8^3F,

	Starts	1st	2nd	3rd	Win & Pl
Career Total (Turf)	4	0	1	2	9778
Career Total (AW)	3	2	0	0	5800

89	8/09	Ling	7f	(0-75)	STD	£2729
76	7/09	Wolv	5f216y		SF	£3070

Total win prize-money £5801

Going (Turf): Sf: 0-0 GS: 0-0 Gd: 0-2 GF: 0-1 Fm: 0-1
Distance: 5f/6f: 1-4 7f-8f: 1-2 9f-13f: 0-1 14f+: 0-0
Track : **LH: 2-4** RH: 0-1 **Tight: 2-2** Gall: 0-0
Aids: Bl: 0-0 Vi: 0-0 Tstrap: 0-0 Ckp: 0-0
Best Rating: 94 11/09 Holl 1m firm

Useful; effective over 6f-7f; acts on fast ground; goes on Polytrack.

Lucky Score (IRE)

94(100) (66)68
3-y-o b f Lucky Story (USA)-Musical Score (Blushing Flame (USA))
Mouse Hamilton-Fairley Mrs Richard Plummer & Partners

Placings:0305-3523556 (7829)
2009: 9^3G, 9^5GF, 8^2SD, 8^3SD, 9^5SD, 8^5SD, 7^6SD,

	Starts	1st	2nd	3rd	Win & Pl
Career Total (Turf)	6	0	0	2	1156
Career Total (AW)	5	0	1	1	907

Going (Turf): Sf: 0-0 GS: 0-2 Gd: 0-3 GF: 0-1 Fm: 0-0
Distance: 5f/6f: 0-1 7f-8f: 0-5 9f-13f: 0-5 14f+: 0-0
Track : LH: 0-3 RH: 0-7 Tight: 0-5 Gall: 0-1
Aids: Bl: 0-0 Vi: 0-0 Tstrap: 0-2 Ckp: 0-2
Best Rating: 68 5/09 Sals 1m1f198y gd-fm

Modest; stays 1m2f; acts on most ground on turf; goes on Polytrack.

Lucky Traveller

79 44
2-y-o b g Lucky Story (USA)-Bollin Sophie (Efisio)
T D Easterby Middleham Park Racing Xxi

Placings:550 (5253)
2009: 5^5G, 6^5GF, 6^0GF,

	Starts	1st	2nd	3rd	Win & Pl
Career Total (Turf)	3	0	0	0	0

Going (Turf): Sf: 0-0 GS: 0-0 Gd: 0-1 GF: 0-2 Fm: 0-0
Distance: 5f/6f: 0-3 7f-8f: 0-0 9f-13f: 0-0 14f+: 0-0
Track : LH: 0-0 RH: 0-1 Tight: 0-0 Gall: 0-0
Aids: Bl: 0-0 Vi: 0-0 Tstrap: 0-0 Ckp: 0-0
Best Rating: 44 8/09 Newc 6f gd-fm

Lucky Windmill

84 54
2-y-o b g Lucky Story (USA)-Windmill Princess (Gorytus (USA))
G A Swinbank Porter, Watson, Valentine

Placings:40 (6646)
2009: 6^4S, 6^0G,

	Starts	1st	2nd	3rd	Win & Pl
Career Total (Turf)	2	0	0	0	467

Going (Turf): Sf: 0-1 GS: 0-0 Gd: 0-1 GF: 0-0 Fm: 0-0
Distance: 5f/6f: 0-2 7f-8f: 0-0 9f-13f: 0-0 14f+: 0-0
Track : LH: 0-0 RH: 0-0 Tight: 0-0 Gall: 0-0
Aids: Bl: 0-0 Vi: 0-0 Tstrap: 0-0 Ckp: 0-0
Best Rating: 54 10/09 York 6f good

Luckydolly (IRE)

(96) (66)57
3-y-o ch f Daggers Drawn (USA)-Dolly Dimpler (IRE) (Nordico (USA))
F Costello F Costello

Placings:00003452-4000405 (7730)
2009: 7^4SD, 7^0GF, 5^0YS, 6^0S, 7^4SD, 7^0SD, 7^5SD,

	Starts	1st	2nd	3rd	Win & Pl
Career Total (Turf)	7	0	0	0	
Career Total (AW)	8	0	1	1	2644

Going (Turf): Sf: 0-2 GS: 0-0 Gd: 0-0 GF: 0-2 Fm: 0-0
Distance: 5f/6f: 0-6 7f-8f: 0-9 9f-13f: 0-0 14f+: 0-0
Track : LH: 0-11 RH: 0-0 Tight: 0-4 Gall: 0-0
Aids: Bl: 0-0 Vi: 0-0 Tstrap: 0-0 Ckp: 0-0
Best Rating: 66 12/08 Wolv 5f216y stand

Modest; stays 7f; acts on Polytrack.

Lucullus

(102) (73)51
4-y-o b g Bertolini (USA)-Calcavella (Pursuit Of Love)
M Blanshard Messrs Oliver, Gale, Ward & Roberts

Placings:010-4 (1186)
2009: 7^4SD,

	Starts	1st	2nd	3rd	Win & Pl
Career Total (Turf)	1	0	0	0	
Career Total (AW)	3	1	0	0	2683

70	3/08	Ling	7f	STD	£2331

Total win prize-money £2332

Going (Turf): Sf: 0-1 GS: 0-0 Gd: 0-0 GF: 0-0 Fm: 0-0
Distance: 5f/6f: 0-0 **7f-8f: 1-4** 9f-13f: 0-0 14f+: 0-0
Track : **LH: 1-3** RH: 0-1 **Tight: 1-2** Gall: 0-0
Aids: Bl: 0-0 Vi: 0-0 Tstrap: 0-0 Ckp: 0-0
Best Rating: 73 4/09 Kemp 7f stand

Modest; effective over 7f; acts on Polytrack.

Lucy Brown

99(96) (67)77
3-y-o br f Compton Place-Harambee (IRE) (Robellino (USA))
R Hannon J T Brown

Placings:00-42014260 (7327)
2009: 6^4GF, 7^2GF, 6^0G, 6^1GF, 6^4G, 6^2GF, 7^6SD, 7^0SD,

	Starts	1st	2nd	3rd	Win & Pl
Career Total (Turf)	8	1	2	0	6272
Career Total (AW)	2	0	0	0	0

77	8/09	Sals	6f	(0-70)H	G-F	£3238

Total win prize-money £3238

Going (Turf): Sf: 0-0 GS: 0-2 Gd: 0-2 **GF: 1-4** Fm: 0-0
Distance: **5f/6f: 1-5** 7f-8f: 0-5 9f-13f: 0-0 14f+: 0-0
Track : LH: 0-2 RH: 0-2 Tight: 0-2 Gall: 0-1
Aids: Bl: 0-0 Vi: 0-0 Tstrap: 0-0 Ckp: 0-0
Best Rating: 77 9/09 NmkR 6f gd-fm

Fair; stays 7f but effective at 6f; acts on fast ground.

Lucy Gliters

87 45
2-y-o ch f Observatory (USA)-Bombay Sapphire (Be My Chief (USA))
T P Tate T P Tate

Placings:6603 (5976)
2009: 5^6G, 5^6GS, 6^0S, 5^3GF,

	Starts	1st	2nd	3rd	Win & Pl
Career Total (Turf)	4	0	0	1	403

Going (Turf): Sf: 0-1 GS: 0-1 Gd: 0-1 GF: 0-1 Fm: 0-0
Distance: 5f/6f: 0-4 7f-8f: 0-0 9f-13f: 0-0 14f+: 0-0
Track : LH: 0-0 RH: 0-0 Tight: 0-0 Gall: 0-0
Aids: Bl: 0-0 Vi: 0-0 Tstrap: 0-0 Ckp: 0-0
Best Rating: 45 9/09 Bevl 5f gd-fm

Moderate sprinter; best on fast ground.

Lucy's Perfect

102 59

3-y-o ch f Systematic-Water Flower (Environment Friend)
B R Millman Avalon Surfacing Ltd

Placings:04034610 **(6910)**
2009: 10^{0}GF, 12^{4}GF, 12^{0}G, 11^{3}F, 11^{4}G, 13^{6}G, 10^{1}G, 10^{0}G,

	Starts	1st	2nd	3rd	Win & Pl
Career Total (Turf)	8	1	0	1	2933

59	10/09	Wind	1m2f7y	GD	£2047

Total win prize-money £2047

Going (Turf): Sf: 0-0 GS: 0-0 **Gd: 1-5** GF: 0-2 Fm: 0-1
Distance: 5f/6f: 0-0 7f-8f: 0-0 **9f-13f: 1-7** 14f+: 0-1
Track : LH: 0-5 **RH: 1-3 Tight: 1-7** Gall: 0-0
Aids: **Bl: 1-2** Vi: 0-0 Tstrap: 0-0 Ckp: 0-0
Best Rating: **59** 10/09 Wind 1m2f7y good

Plating-class; stays 1m2f; acts on good ground; has worn blinkers.

Ludwigshafen (IRE)

102(97) (74)72

5-y-o b m Cape Cross (IRE)-Cape Clear (Slip Anchor)
John Geoghegan Mrs R Bean

Placings:0/323002204/P504500-243516660 **(3081a)**
2009: 8^{2}SD, 8^{4}SD, 10^{3}SD, 10^{5}GY, 8^{1}SD, 8^{6}SD, 8^{6}SD, 10^{6}GF, 8^{0}G,

	Starts	1st	2nd	3rd	Win & Pl
Career Total (Turf)	16	0	2	2	5188
Career Total (AW)	10	1	2	1	9713

71	4/09	Dund	1m	STD	£6037

Total win prize-money £6038

Going (Turf): **Sf: 0-5 GS: 0-0 Gd: 0-5 GF: 0-3 Fm: 0-0**
Distance: 5f/6f: 0-0 **7f-8f: 1-9** 9f-13f: 0-17 14f+: 0-0
Track : **LH: 1-16** RH: 0-5 Tight: 0-2 Gall: 0-0
Aids: Bl: 0-2 Vi: 0-0 Tstrap: 0-1 Ckp: 0-1
Best Rating: **77** 7/07 Leop 1m soft

Lugato (GER)

95(90) (42)54

7-y-o br g Winged Love (IRE)-Lugano (GER) (Orofino (GER))
Lee Smyth (J J Lambe 16/7) JMCL Construction Limited

Placings:5/513112500/0/3-000 **(6519a)**
2009: 14^{0}GF, 12^{0}SD, 10^{0}SD,

	Starts	1st	2nd	3rd	Win & Pl
Career Total (Turf)	13	3	1	2	7092
Career Total (AW)	2	0	0	0	

	7/06	BDob	1m5f	H	GD	£1793
	7/06	Dres	1m3f110y	H	GD	£1517
	5/06	Hopp	1m3f		GD	£1517

Total win prize-money £4827

Going (Turf): Sf: 0-1 GS: 0-0 **Gd: 3-10** GF: 0-2 Fm: 0-0
Distance: 5f/6f: 0-0 7f-8f: 0-0 **9f-13f: 3-13** 14f+: 0-2
Track : LH: 0-3 RH: 0-1 Tight: 0-1 Gall: 0-0
Aids: Bl: 0-0 Vi: 0-0 Tstrap: 0-2 Ckp: 0-2
Best Rating: **54** 5/08 Dpat 1m4f110y good

Luisa Tetrazzini (IRE)

67(96) (55)

3-y-o b f Hawk Wing (USA)-Break Of Day (USA) (Favorite Trick (USA))
John A Harris (K A Ryan 4/12) Miss Nicola Carroll

Placings:0553334 **(7797)**
2009: 5^{0}S, 8^{5}SD, 7^{5}SD, 7^{3}SD, 7^{3}SD, 5^{3}SD, 8^{4}SS,

	Starts	1st	2nd	3rd	Win & Pl
Career Total (Turf)	1	0	0	0	
Career Total (AW)	6	0	0	3	1512

Going (Turf): **Sf: 0-1 GS: 0-0 Gd: 0-0 GF: 0-0 Fm: 0-0**
Distance: 5f/6f: 0-2 7f-8f: 0-4 9f-13f: 0-1 14f+: 0-0
Track : LH: 0-6 RH: 0-0 Tight: 0-4 Gall: 0-0
Aids: Bl: 0-0 Vi: 0-0 Tstrap: 0-1 Ckp: 0-1
Best Rating: **55** 11/09 Wolv 7f32y stand

Moderate; stays 7f and acts on Fibresand and Polytrack.

Luisant

114 (105)106

6-y-o ch g Pivotal-La Legere (USA) (Lit De Justice (USA))
J A Nash J A McCarthy

Placings:0211135/3265042/34-3053116263 **(7259a)**
2009: 8^{3}G, 8^{0}GF, 7^{5}YS, 6^{3}HY, 6^{1}SD, 6^{1}SD, 7^{6}G, 6^{2}S, 5^{6}SD, 7^{3}HY,

	Starts	1st	2nd	3rd	Win & Pl
Career Total (Turf)	22	3	4	6	74897
Career Total (AW)	4	2	0	0	42876

105	8/09	Dund	6f	H	STD	£13588
100	8/09	Dund	6f	H	STD	£26861
97	10/06	Deau	6f	H	SFT	£18476
93	8/06	Claf	7f		SFT	£7241
	7/06	Seno	6f165y		GD	£4827

Total win prize-money £70996

Going (Turf): **Sf: 2-10** GS: 0-3 Gd: 1-6 GF: 0-1 Fm: 0-0
Distance: **5f/6f: 3-10** 7f-8f: 2-16 9f-13f: 0-0 14f+: 0-0
Track : LH: 2-6 RH: 2-5 Tight: 0-0 Gall: 0-0
Aids: Bl: 0-2 Vi: 0-0 Tstrap: 0-0 Ckp: 0-0
Best Rating: **113** 10/06 MsnL 6f soft

Very useful Irish-trained handicapper; ex-French; unsuccessful over hurdles; stays 1m; acts with cut; has worn blinkers.

Lujano

98(100) (71)74

4-y-o b g Lujain (USA)-Latch Key Lady (USA) (Tejano (USA))
Ollie Pears David Scott and Co (Pattern Makers) Ltd

Placings:013/40160065321-000301100 **(7322)**
2009: 7^{0}SD, 6^{0}GF, 8^{0}GS, 8^{3}GF, 8^{0}GS, 8^{1}SD, 8^{1}GF, 8^{0}SD, 8^{0}SD,

	Starts	1st	2nd	3rd	Win & Pl
Career Total (Turf)	9	2	0	1	6247
Career Total (AW)	14	3	1	2	9513

74	9/09	Newc	1m	(0-70)H	G-F	£2978
71	9/09	Wolv	1m141y	(0-70)H	STD	£4209
71	12/08	Sthl	1m	(0-60)H	STD	£2047
65	7/08	Thsk	1m	(0-65)H	G-F	£2978
60	12/07	Wolv	5f216y		STD	£2047

Total win prize-money £14262

Going (Turf): Sf: 0-1 GS: 0-2 Gd: 0-2 **GF: 2-4** Fm: 0-0
Distance: 5f/6f: 1-4 **7f-8f: 3-11** 9f-13f: 1-8 14f+: 0-0
Track : **LH: 5-18** RH: 0-4 **Tight: 3-16** Gall: 1-1
Aids: Bl: 0-0 Vi: 0-0 Tstrap: 0-0 Ckp: 0-0
Best Rating: **74** 9/09 Newc 1m gd-fm

Modest; stays 1m; acts on fast ground and on sand.

Lujeanie

103(107) (78)80

3-y-o br g Lujain (USA)-Ivory's Joy (Tina's Pet)
D K Ivory K T Ivory

Placings:040434-5140101 **(7875)**
2009: 7^{5}GF, 6^{1}SD, 6^{4}SD, 7^{0}G, 6^{1}G, 6^{0}SD, 6^{1}SD,

	Starts	1st	2nd	3rd	Win & Pl
Career Total (Turf)	6	1	0	0	3335
Career Total (AW)	7	2	0	1	8789

	12/09	Kemp	6f	(0-85)H	STD	£4727
80	8/09	Ling	6f	(0-75)H	GD	£3070
78	6/09	Kemp	6f	(0-70)H	STD	£3469

Total win prize-money £11267

Going (Turf): Sf: 0-1 GS: 0-0 **Gd: 1-2** GF: 0-3 Fm: 0-0
Distance: **5f/6f: 3-9** 7f-8f: 0-4 9f-13f: 0-0 14f+: 0-0
Track : LH: 0-2 **RH: 2-5** Tight: 0-1 Gall: 0-2
Aids: Bl: 0-0 Vi: 0-0 Tstrap: 3-6 Ckp: 3-6
Best Rating: **80** 8/09 Ling 6f good

Fair; effective from 6f-1m; acts on sand; handles fast turf; has worn cheekpieces.

Lujiana

88(100) (41)66

4-y-o b f Lujain (USA)-Compact Disc (IRE) (Royal Academy (USA))
M Brittain Mel Brittain

Placings:503/132500015400-0000 **(7561)**
2009: 6^{0}G, 6^{0}GF, 5^{0}GF, 5^{0}SD,

	Starts	1st	2nd	3rd	Win & Pl
Career Total (Turf)	14	1	0	0	3145
Career Total (AW)	5	1	1	2	3443

66	7/08	Donc	5f	(0-60)H	GD	£2729
64	2/08	Sthl	5f	(0-65)H	STD	£1911

Total win prize-money £4641

Going (Turf): Sf: 0-2 GS: 0-3 **Gd: 1-5** GF: 0-4 Fm: 0-0
Distance: **5f/6f: 2-17** 7f-8f: 0-2 9f-13f: 0-0 14f+: 0-0
Track : LH: 0-4 RH: 0-0 Tight: 0-3 Gall: 0-0
Aids: Bl: 0-0 Vi: 0-0 Tstrap: 0-0 Ckp: 0-0
Best Rating: **66** 7/08 Donc 5f good

Moderate; suited by 5f-6f; acts on good ground; also goes on sand.

Lukatara (USA)

(79) (21)

4-y-o b g Kayrawan (USA)-Hey Winnie (USA) (Hey Big Spender (USA))
Miss Sheena West Michael Moriarty

Placings:0-00 **(0663)**
2009: 12^{0}SD, 7^{0}SD,

	Starts	1st	2nd	3rd	Win & Pl
Career Total (Turf)	0	0	0	0	
Career Total (AW)	3	0	0	0	

Going (Turf): **Sf: 0-0 GS: 0-0 Gd: 0-0 GF: 0-0 Fm: 0-0**
Distance: 5f/6f: 0-0 7f-8f: 0-2 9f-13f: 0-1 14f+: 0-0
Track : LH: 0-3 RH: 0-0 Tight: 0-2 Gall: 0-1
Aids: Bl: 0-0 Vi: 0-0 Tstrap: 0-0 Ckp: 0-0
Best Rating: **21** 2/09 Ling 7f stand

Luluti (IRE)

(85) (58)

2-y-o b f Kheleyf (USA)-Amsicora (Cadeaux Genereux)
S A Callaghan Saleh Al Homaizi & Imad Al Sagar

Placings:6 **(3987)**
2009: 6^{6}SD,

	Starts	1st	2nd	3rd	Win & Pl
Career Total (Turf)	0	0	0	0	

Career Total (AW) 1 0 0 0 0

Going (Turf): Sf: 0-0 GS: 0-0 Gd: 0-0 GF: 0-0 Fm: 0-0
Distance: 5f/6f: 0-1 7f-8f: 0-0 9f-13f: 0-0 14f+: 0-0
Track : LH: 0-1 RH: 0-0 Tight: 0-1 Gall: 0-0
Aids: Bl: 0-0 Vi: 0-0 Tstrap: 0-0 Ckp: 0-0
Best Rating: 58 7/09 Ling 6f stand

Luminosa

(78) (27)
2-y-o ch f Zaha (CAN)-Lightning Blaze (Cosmonaut)
D Donovan Ms Clare Sharp

Placings:0 (7580)
2009: 7⁰SF,

	Starts	1st	2nd	3rd	Win & Pl
Career Total (Turf)	0	0	0	0	
Career Total (AW)	1	0	0	0	

Going (Turf): Sf: 0-0 GS: 0-0 Gd: 0-0 GF: 0-0 Fm: 0-0
Distance: 5f/6f: 0-0 7f-8f: 0-1 9f-13f: 0-0 14f+: 0-0
Track : LH: 0-1 RH: 0-0 Tight: 0-1 Gall: 0-0
Aids: Bl: 0-0 Vi: 0-0 Tstrap: 0-0 Ckp: 0-0
Best Rating: 27 11/09 Wolv 7f32y std-fst

Luminous Gold

103(95) (72)79
4-y-o b f Fantastic Light (USA)-Nasaieb (IRE) (Fairy King (USA))
C F Wall Dr Philip Brown

Placings:062/16600-01443330 (6666)
2009: 6⁰GF, 6¹G, 6⁴GF, 6⁴G, 6³G, 6³GF, 5³GF, 5⁰GS,

	Starts	1st	2nd	3rd	Win & Pl
Career Total (Turf)	15	2	1	3	8595
Career Total (AW)	1	0	0	0	
79 5/09 Yarm	6f3y	(0-70)H		GD	£2719
77 5/08 Folk	6f	(0-70)H		G-S	£2331

Total win prize-money £5051

Going (Turf): Sf: 0-3 GS: 1-3 Gd: 1-4 GF: 0-5 Fm: 0-0
Distance: 5f/6f: 1-10 7f-8f: 1-6 9f-13f: 0-0 14f+: 0-0
Track : LH: 0-0 RH: 0-2 Tight: 0-0 Gall: 0-2
Aids: Bl: 0-0 Vi: 0-0 Tstrap: 0-0 Ckp: 0-0
Best Rating: 79 8/09 Ling 6f good

Fair; effective over 6f-7f; acts on most ground.

Luminous Star (USA)

94(98) (77)76
2-y-o b/br g Aldebaran (USA)-Best Of Memories (USA) (Halo (USA))
R M Beckett Sheikh Khaled Duaij Al Sabah

Placings:562135 (6491)
2009: 6⁵GF, 6⁶GF, 6²GF, 6¹F, 8³SD, 8⁵SD,

	Starts	1st	2nd	3rd	Win & Pl
Career Total (Turf)	4	1	1	0	4867
Career Total (AW)	2	0	0	1	943
76 8/09 Brig	6f209y		FRM	£3658	

Total win prize-money £3659

Going (Turf): Sf: 0-0 GS: 0-0 Gd: 0-0 GF: 0-3 Fm: 1-1
Distance: 5f/6f: 0-2 7f-8f: 1-2 9f-13f: 0-2 14f+: 0-0
Track : LH: 1-4 RH: 0-0 Tight: 0-2 Gall: 0-1
Aids: Bl: 0-0 Vi: 0-0 Tstrap: 0-0 Ckp: 0-0
Best Rating: 77 9/09 Wolv 1m141y stand

Fair; stays 1m; acts on fast ground and Polytrack.

Luna Landing

103 (74)82
6-y-o ch g Allied Forces (USA)-Macca Luna (IRE) (Kahyasi)
Jedd O'Keeffe W R B Racing 47

Placings:0213000/336134100/501025056/0430-043660 (5252)
2009: 16⁰GF, 14⁴GF, 17³GF, 15⁶G, 16⁶G, 15⁰GF,

	Starts	1st	2nd	3rd	Win & Pl
Career Total (Turf)	32	4	2	6	32917
Career Total (AW)	3	0	0	0	0
84 6/07 Thsk	1m4f	(0-90)H	G-F	£7772	
84 10/06 Catt	1m3f214y	(0-75)H	GD	£3886	
78 7/06 Pont	1m2f6y	(0-85)H	G-F	£6477	
76 7/05 Newc	7f		GD	£3841	

Total win prize-money £21977

Going (Turf): Sf: 0-1 GS: 0-3 Gd: 2-11 GF: 2-16 Fm: 0-1
Distance: 5f/6f: 0-1 7f-8f: 1-6 9f-13f: 3-20 14f+: 0-8
Track : LH: 3-21 RH: 0-9 Tight: 2-17 Gall: 0-3
Aids: Bl: 0-0 Vi: 0-0 Tstrap: 0-0 Ckp: 0-0
Best Rating: 85 8/07 Ches 1m4f66y gd-fm

Fair; winning hurdler; stays 1m4f; acts on fast and easy ground.

Lunar Limelight

(104) (67)53
4-y-o b g Royal Applause-Moon Magic (Polish Precedent (USA))
P J Makin Mrs Jacqueline McColl

Placings:0500/00-403011 (7754)
2009: 10⁴SD, 10⁰GS, 8³SD, 9⁰SD, 10¹SD, 8¹SD,

	Starts	1st	2nd	3rd	Win & Pl
Career Total (Turf)	4	0	0	0	0
Career Total (AW)	8	2	0	1	4008
67 12/09 Wolv	1m141y	(0-55)H	STD	£2047	
57 12/09 Ling	1m2f	(0-52)H	STD	£1637	

Total win prize-money £3685

Going (Turf): Sf: 0-2 GS: 0-1 Gd: 0-1 GF: 0-0 Fm: 0-0
Distance: 5f/6f: 0-2 7f-8f: 0-2 9f-13f: 2-8 14f+: 0-0
Track : LH: 2-8 RH: 0-1 Tight: 2-7 Gall: 0-1
Aids: Bl: 0-0 Vi: 0-0 Tstrap: 0-0 Ckp: 0-0
Best Rating: 67 12/09 Wolv 1m141y stand

Very moderate; stays 1m2f and acts on Polytrack.

Lunar River (FR)

96(105) (73)67
6-y-o b m Muhtathir-Moon Gorge (Pursuit Of Love)
David Pinder The Little Farm Partnership

Placings:055/5232361/0041003053030/4546231064256 2 0-6103246206240 (7399)
2009: 10⁶SD, 10¹SD, 10⁰GS, 10³SD, 10²GF, 9⁴GF, 10⁶G, 10²SD, 8⁰SD, 9⁶SD, 9²SD, 10⁴SD, 9⁰SD,

	Starts	1st	2nd	3rd	Win & Pl
Career Total (Turf)	23	1	3	1	6777
Career Total (AW)	28	3	5	6	15651
71 5/09 Ling	1m2f	(0-70)H	STD	£3070	
71 7/08 Wolv	1m141y	(0-60)H	STD	£2388	
71 5/07 Ling	1m2f	(0-65)H	STD	£3230	
66 10/06 Bath	1m2f46y		GD	£3238	

Total win prize-money £11937

Going (Turf): Sf: 0-2 GS: 0-6 Gd: 1-7 GF: 0-8 Fm: 0-0
Distance: 5f/6f: 0-0 7f-8f: 0-4 9f-13f: 4-47 14f+: 0-0
Track : LH: 4-39 RH: 0-12 Tight: 4-34 Gall: 0-4
Aids: Bl: 0-0 Vi: 0-1 Tstrap: 0-0 Ckp: 0 0
Best Rating: 73 10/09 Wolv 1m1f103y stand

Modest; stays 1m2f; acts on good and faster ground and on Polytrack; has worn a tongue tie.

Lunar Romance

(79) (31)50
3-y-o b f Royal Applause-Witness (Efisio)
T J Pitt The Hatfield Connection

Placings:0400-00 (7353)
2009: 9⁰SF, 7⁰SD,

	Starts	1st	2nd	3rd	Win & Pl
Career Total (Turf)	4	0	0	0	265
Career Total (AW)	2	0	0	0	

Going (Turf): Sf: 0-1 GS: 0-0 Gd: 0-3 GF: 0-0 Fm: 0-0
Distance: 5f/6f: 0-2 7f-8f: 0-3 9f-13f: 0-1 14f+: 0-0
Track : LH: 0-4 RH: 0-0 Tight: 0-3 Gall: 0-0
Aids: Bl: 0-0 Vi: 0-0 Tstrap: 0-0 Ckp: 0-0
Best Rating: 50 6/08 Ches 7f2y good

Lunar Storm (IRE)

79(86) (44)15
5-y-o b g Machiavellian (USA)-Moonshell (IRE) (Sadler's Wells (USA))
Mrs R A Carr David W Chapman

Placings:060000 (4656)
2009: 12⁰SD, 8⁶SD, 9⁰GF, 10⁰GF, 14⁰GF, 8⁰GF,

	Starts	1st	2nd	3rd	Win & Pl
Career Total (Turf)	4	0	0	0	
Career Total (AW)	2	0	0	0	0

Going (Turf): Sf: 0-0 GS: 0-0 Gd: 0-0 GF: 0-4 Fm: 0-0
Distance: 5f/6f: 0-0 7f-8f: 0-1 9f-13f: 0-4 14f+: 0-1
Track : LH: 0-4 RH: 0-1 Tight: 0-3 Gall: 0-1
Aids: Bl: 0-1 Vi: 0-0 Tstrap: 0-1 Ckp: 0-1
Best Rating: 44 3/09 Sthl 1m stand

Lunar Victory (USA)

104 80
2-y-o b c Speightstown (USA)-Lunar Colony (USA) (A.P. Indy (USA))
J H M Gosden K Abdulla

Placings:34 (6620)
2009: 8³GF, 8⁴G,

	Starts	1st	2nd	3rd	Win & Pl
Career Total (Turf)	2	0	0	1	2040

Going (Turf): Sf: 0-0 GS: 0-0 Gd: 0-1 GF: 0-1 Fm: 0-0
Distance: 5f/6f: 0-0 7f-8f: 0-2 9f-13f: 0-0 14f+: 0-0
Track : LH: 0-0 RH: 0-0 Tight: 0-0 Gall: 0-0
Aids: Bl: 0-0 Vi: 0-0 Tstrap: 0-0 Ckp: 0-0
Best Rating: 80 9/09 Newb 1m gd-fm

Promising debut over 1m on fast ground; disappointed on easier surface next time.

Lunaticus

(77) (10)
3-y-o b f Lujain (USA)-Steppin Out (First Trump)
M J Attwater Canisbay Bloodstock

Placings:00 (7829)
2009: 6^{0}SD, 7^{0}SD,

	Starts	1st	2nd	3rd	Win & Pl
Career Total (Turf)	0	0	0	0	
Career Total (AW)	2	0	0	0	

Going (Turf): **Sf: 0-0 GS: 0-0 Gd: 0-0 GF: 0-0 Fm: 0-0**
Distance: 5f/6f: 0-1 7f-8f: 0-1 9f-13f: 0-0 14f+: 0-0
Track : LH: 0-0 RH: 0-2 Tight: 0-0 Gall: 0-0
Aids: Bl: 0-0 Vi: 0-0 Tstrap: 0-0 Ckp: 0-0
Best Rating: **10** 11/09 Kemp 6f stand

Lunces Lad (IRE)

96(107) (86)**81**
5-y-o gr g Xaar-Bridelina (FR) (Linamix (FR))
G Brown Athos Racing

Placings:01604/0640244030/**6**4635100060-6000 **(7179)**
2009: 6^{6}GF, 5^{0}F, 5^{0}GF, 7^{0}SD,

	Starts	1st	2nd	3rd	Win & Pl
Career Total (Turf)	26	2	1	2	17578
Career Total (AW)	4	0	0	0	1021
81 6/08 Bath	5f161y	(0-80)H	G-F	£4209	
77 8/06 Newb	7f		G-S	£5829	

Total win prize-money £10038

Going (Turf): Sf: 0-3 **GS: 1-6** Gd: 0-4 **GF: 1-12** Fm: 0-1
Distance: 5f/6f: 1-10 7f-8f: 1-20 9f-13f: 0-0 14f+: 0-0
Track : **LH: 1-9** RH: 0-6 Tight: 0-3 **Gall: 1-3**
Aids: Bl: 0-0 **Vi: 1-5** Tstrap: 0-0 Ckp: 0-0
Best Rating: **86** 4/08 Ling 7f stand

Fair; effective over 6f-7f; acts on most ground; has worn a visor.

Lupita (IRE)

95 **63**
5-y-o ch m Intikhab (USA)-Sarah (IRE) (Hernando (FR))
D D Scott (B G Powell 31/5) Mrs D D Scott

Placings:000/511400/100-00 **(2519)**
2009: 15^{0}G, 17^{0}F,

	Starts	1st	2nd	3rd	Win & Pl
Career Total (Turf)	14	3	0	0	11230
63 4/08 Bath	2m1f34y	(0-75)H	GD	£2590	
63 8/07 Wxfd	1m5f	(42-60)H	GD	£4435	
53 7/07 Wxfd	1m5f		YLD	£3968	

Total win prize-money £10994

Going (Turf): Sf: 0-1 GS: 0-1 **Gd: 2-5** GF: 0-3 Fm: 0-1
Distance: 5f/6f: 0-1 7f-8f: 0-2 **9f-13f: 2-4** 14f+: 1-7
Track : LH: 1-4 **RH: 2-9 Tight: 1-4** Gall: 0-0
Aids: Bl: 0-0 Vi: 0-0 Tstrap: 0-1 Ckp: 0-1
Best Rating: **63** 4/08 Bath 2m1f34y good

Modest filly; stays 2m1f; handles good ground.

Luscivious

101(111) (93)**89**
5-y-o ch g Kyllachy-Lloc (Absalom)
J A Glover (A J McCabe 8/6) Paul J Dixon & Brian Morton

Placings:6050511/425000060/6100130000000060250-00302012016000 **(6359)**
2009: 6^{0}SS, 5^{0}SF, 5^{3}SD, 5^{0}SD, 5^{2}HY, 5^{0}G, 6^{1}SD, 5^{2}GS, 5^{0}GS, 5^{1}SD, 5^{6}SD, 5^{0}S, 5^{0}G, 5^{0}SD,

	Starts	1st	2nd	3rd	Win & Pl
Career Total (Turf)	30	3	3	0	22307
Career Total (AW)	18	3	1	2	27633
93 8/09 Sthl	5f	(0-95)H	STD	£9066	
91 7/09 Sthl	6f	(0-85)H	STD	£5180	
92 5/08 Sthl	5f	(0-90)H	STD	£9066	
90 4/08 Bevl	5f	(0-95)H	G-S	£6799	
94 10/06 Catt	5f		SFT	£4210	
82 10/06 Catt	5f		GD	£3238	

Total win prize-money £37562

Going (Turf): **Sf: 1-6 GS: 1-8 Gd: 1-11** GF: 0-4 Fm: 0-1
Distance: **5f/6f: 6-47** 7f-8f: 0-1 9f-13f: 0-0 14f+: 0-0
Track : **LH: 1-14** RH: 0-1 Tight: 0-8 Gall: 0-1
Aids: **Bl: 4-32** Vi: 0-0 Tstrap: 2-8 Ckp: 2-8
Best Rating: **94** 10/06 Catt 5f soft

Useful sprinter; seems best over 5f; suited by good and easier ground; goes on Fibresand; often wears blinkers; has worn cheekpieces.

Lush (IRE)

98(97) (69)**75**
4-y-o b f Fasliyev (USA)-Our Hope (Dancing Brave (USA))
R Hannon Mrs R Ablett

Placings:35/440340020-40020 **(6074)**
2009: 12^{4}G, 9^{0}GF, 10^{0}GF, 10^{2}F, 9^{0}SD,

	Starts	1st	2nd	3rd	Win & Pl
Career Total (Turf)	13	0	1	2	2818
Career Total (AW)	3	0	1	0	1599

Going (Turf): **Sf: 0-1 GS: 0-2 Gd: 0-5 GF: 0-4 Fm: 0-1**
Distance: 5f/6f: 0-1 7f-8f: 0-3 9f-13f: 0-12 14f+: 0-0
Track : LH: 0-6 RH: 0-7 Tight: 0-6 Gall: 0-3
Aids: Bl: 0-0 Vi: 0-0 Tstrap: 0-1 Ckp: 0-1
Best Rating: **76** 5/07 Gdwd 6f good

Modest; stays 1m2f; acts on good ground.

Lush Lashes

102 **121**
4-y-o b f Galileo (IRE)-Dance For Fun (Anabaa (USA))
J S Bolger Mrs J S Bolger

Placings:1/0615121120-364 **(3412a)**
2009: 10^{3}HY, 8^{6}GF, 10^{4}Y,

	Starts	1st	2nd	3rd	Win & Pl
Career Total (Turf)	14	5	2	1	1199713
117 9/08 Leop	1m		YLD	£119485	
119 8/08 NmkJ	1m4f		GD	£93670	
121 6/08 Asct	1m		FRM	£154698	
113 5/08 York	1m2f88y		G-F	£34062	
95 9/07 Curr	7f		G-F	£665540	

Total win prize-money £1067457

Going (Turf): Sf: 0-2 GS: 0-1 Gd: 1-3 **GF: 2-5** Fm: 1-1
Distance: 5f/6f: 0-0 **7f-8f: 3-6** 9f-13f: 2-8 14f+: 0-0
Track : LH: 2-3 RH: 2-8 Tight: 0-2 **Gall: 3-4**
Aids: Bl: 0-0 Vi: 0-0 Tstrap: 0-0 Ckp: 0-0
Best Rating: **121** 6/08 Asct 1m firm

High class; fast-finishing sixth in the 1000 Guineas, then won the Musidora; fifth in the Oaks; won the Group 1 Coronation Stakes; unlucky runner-up in the Nassau before winning the Yorkshire Oaks and Matron Stakes; effective over 1m-1m4f; acts really well on fast ground; handles easy ground too.

Luthien (IRE)

92(95) (66)**56**
3-y-o b f Polish Precedent (USA)-Triplemoon (USA) (Trempolino (USA))
A M Hales (W R Swinburn 14/8) David Taylor

Placings:4-5006**0**0600 **(7369)**
2009: 9^{5}SD, 9^{0}F, 11^{0}GF, 12^{6}GF, 14^{0}G, 11^{0}SD, 9^{6}SF, 7^{0}G, 9^{0}SD,

	Starts	1st	2nd	3rd	Win & Pl
Career Total (Turf)	5	0	0	0	0
Career Total (AW)	5	0	0	0	289

Going (Turf): **Sf: 0-0 GS: 0-0 Gd: 0-2 GF: 0-2 Fm: 0-1**
Distance: 5f/6f: 0-0 7f-8f: 0-2 9f-13f: 0-7 14f+: 0-1
Track : LH: 0-6 RH: 0-3 Tight: 0-6 Gall: 0-1
Aids: Bl: 0-0 Vi: 0-0 Tstrap: 0-4 Ckp: 0-4
Best Rating: **66** 10/08 GrLe 1m stand

Lutine Bell

76(87) (61)**52**
2-y-o ch g Starcraft (NZ)-Satin Bell (Midyan (USA))
Sir Mark Prescott Tom Wilson/Nicholas Jones

Placings:545 **(4200)**
2009: 7^{5}GF, 7^{4}SD, 7^{5}SD,

	Starts	1st	2nd	3rd	Win & Pl
Career Total (Turf)	1	0	0	0	0
Career Total (AW)	2	0	0	0	265

Going (Turf): **Sf: 0-0 GS: 0-0 Gd: 0-0 GF: 0-1 Fm: 0-0**
Distance: 5f/6f: 0-0 7f-8f: 0-3 9f-13f: 0-0 14f+: 0-0
Track : LH: 0-2 RH: 0-1 Tight: 0-3 Gall: 0-0
Aids: Bl: 0-0 Vi: 0-0 Tstrap: 0-0 Ckp: 0-0
Best Rating: **61** 7/09 Ling 7f stand

Modest; effective over 7f; acts on Polytrack; should improve.

Lutine Charlie (IRE)

97(99) (84)**77**
2-y-o b g Kheleyf (USA)-Silvery Halo (USA) (Silver Ghost (USA))
P Winkworth P Morris

Placings:22405 **(7243)**
2009: 6^{2}S, 6^{2}SD, 6^{4}SD, 6^{0}G, 8^{5}S,

	Starts	1st	2nd	3rd	Win & Pl
Career Total (Turf)	3	0	1	0	1445
Career Total (AW)	2	0	1	0	1252

Going (Turf): **Sf: 0-2 GS: 0-0 Gd: 0-1 GF: 0-0 Fm: 0-0**
Distance: 5f/6f: 0-3 7f-8f: 0-1 9f-13f: 0-1 14f+: 0-0
Track : LH: 0-1 RH: 0-2 Tight: 0-0 Gall: 0-0
Aids: Bl: 0-0 Vi: 0-0 Tstrap: 0-0 Ckp: 0-0
Best Rating: **84** 9/09 Kemp 6f stand

Fair; stays 6f; acts on soft ground and on Polytrack; sure to win a race.

Lutine Lady

76 **43**
2-y-o b f Exceed And Excel (AUS)-Hillside Girl (IRE) (Tagula (IRE))
P Winkworth Lutine Syndicate

Placings:00 **(2135)**
2009: 5^{0}GF, 5^{0}G,

	Starts	1st	2nd	3rd	Win & Pl
Career Total (Turf)	2	0	0	0	

Going (Turf): **Sf: 0-0 GS: 0-0 Gd: 0-1 GF: 0-1 Fm: 0-0**
Distance: 5f/6f: 0-2 7f-8f: 0-0 9f-13f: 0-0 14f+: 0-0
Track : LH: 0-0 RH: 0-0 Tight: 0-0 Gall: 0-1

Aids: Bl: 0-0 Vi: 0-0 Tstrap: 0-0 Ckp: 0-0
Best Rating: 43 5/09 Wind 5f10y good

Luv U Noo

87(78) (44)60
2-y-o b f Needwood Blade-Lady Suesanne (IRE) (Cape Cross (IRE))
A P Jarvis (K R Burke 28/7) Phones Direct Partnership

Placings:5355 (7089)
2009: 5^{5}GF, 5^{3}GF, 5^{5}GS, 6^{5}SD,

	Starts	1st	2nd	3rd	Win & Pl
Career Total (Turf)	3	0	0	1	302
Career Total (AW)	1	0	0	0	0

Going (Turf): Sf: 0-0 GS: 0-1 Gd: 0-0 GF: 0-2 Fm: 0-0
Distance: 5f/6f: 0-4 7f-8f: 0-0 9f-13f: 0-0 14f+: 0-0
Track : LH: 0-1 RH: 0-0 Tight: 0-0 Gall: 0-0
Aids: Bl: 0-0 Vi: 0-0 Tstrap: 0-0 Ckp: 0-0
Best Rating: 60 8/09 Ayr 5f gd-fm

Moderate; effective at 5f on fast ground.

Lyceana

100(106) (85)79
4-y-o ch f Medicean-Wax Lyrical (Safawan)
M A Jarvis Cromhall Stud

Placings:44132-55200 (5997)
2009: 8^{5}GF, 8^{5}G, 12^{2}GF, 10^{0}G, 10^{0}GS,

	Starts	1st	2nd	3rd	Win & Pl
Career Total (Turf)	7	0	1	0	2480
Career Total (AW)	3	1	1	1	4632

76 11/08 GrLe 1m STD £2590
Total win prize-money £2590

Going (Turf): Sf: 0-1 GS: 0-2 Gd: 0-2 GF: 0-2 Fm: 0-0
Distance: 5f/6f: 0-0 7f-8f: 1-4 9f-13f: 0-6 14f+: 0-0
Track : LH: 1-5 RH: 0-3 Tight: 0-3 Gall: 1-2
Aids: Bl: 0-0 Vi: 0-0 Tstrap: 0-0 Ckp: 0-0
Best Rating: 85 12/08 GrLe 1m2f stand

Fair; effective up to 1m2f; acts on easy ground and on Polytrack.

Lydia's Legacy

88 34
4-y-o b f Bahamian Bounty-Lydia's Look (IRE) (Distant View (USA))
T J Etherington Training At Wold House

Placings:006-000 (2603)
2009: 5^{0}F, 6^{0}GF, 5^{0}GF,

	Starts	1st	2nd	3rd	Win & Pl
Career Total (Turf)	6	0	0	0	0

Going (Turf): Sf: 0-0 GS: 0-2 Gd: 0-0 GF: 0-3 Fm: 0-1
Distance: 5f/6f: 0-6 7f-8f: 0-0 9f-13f: 0-0 14f+: 0-0
Track : LH: 0-0 RH: 0-0 Tight: 0-0 Gall: 0-0
Aids: Bl: 0-0 Vi: 0-0 Tstrap: 0-0 Ckp: 0-0
Best Rating: 34 4/09 Rdcr 5f firm

Lyra's Daemon

96(101) (79)74
3-y-o b f Singspiel (IRE)-Seven Of Nine (IRE) (Alzao (USA))
W R Muir M J Caddy

Placings:01-1606150 (7811)
2009: 10^{1}GF, 9^{6}GF, 9^{0}G, 10^{6}SD, 12^{1}SD, 12^{5}SD, 12^{0}SD,

	Starts	1st	2nd	3rd	Win & Pl
Career Total (Turf)	5	2	0	0	6002
Career Total (AW)	4	1	0	0	3238

79 11/09 Wolv 1m4f50y (0-75)H STD £3238
74 4/09 Bath 1m2f46y (0-70)H G-F £2590
70 9/08 Wwck 7f26y GD £3412
Total win prize-money £9240

Going (Turf): Sf: 0-0 GS: 0-0 Gd: 1-3 GF: 1-2 Fm: 0-0
Distance: 5f/6f: 0-0 7f-8f: 1-2 9f-13f: 2-7 14f+: 0-0
Track : LH: 3-4 RH: 0-4 Tight: 2-3 Gall: 0-0
Aids: Bl: 0-0 Vi: 0-0 Tstrap: 0-0 Ckp: 0-0
Best Rating: 79 11/09 Wolv 1m4f50y stand

Fair; stays 1m4f; acts on a sound surface; goes on Polytrack.

Lyric Art (USA)

99(99) (61)61
3-y-o b f Red Ransom (USA)-String Quartet (IRE) (Sadler's Wells (USA))
B Smart H E Sheikh Rashid Bin Mohammed

Placings:06-2340614 (6358)
2009: 7^{2}SD, 8^{3}SD, 7^{4}GF, 7^{0}GF, 8^{6}GF, 7^{1}S, 8^{4}SD,

	Starts	1st	2nd	3rd	Win & Pl
Career Total (Turf)	6	1	0	0	2629
Career Total (AW)	3	0	1	1	1191

58 9/09 Catt 7f (0-60) SFT £2388
Total win prize-money £2388

Going (Turf): Sf: 1-1 GS: 0-2 Gd: 0-0 GF: 0-3 Fm: 0-0
Distance: 5f/6f: 0-1 7f-8f: 1-7 9f-13f: 0-1 14f+: 0-0
Track : LH: 1-5 RH: 0-1 Tight: 1-2 Gall: 0-0
Aids: Bl: 0-0 Vi: 0-1 Tstrap: 0-0 Ckp: 0-0
Best Rating: 61 2/09 Sthl 7f stand

Modest; stays 1m; acts on Fibresand.

Lyric Poet (USA)

88 51
2-y-o b/br c Distorted Humor (USA)-Baltic Nations (USA) (Seattle Slew (USA))
Saeed Bin Suroor Godolphin

Placings:06 (5831)
2009: 7^{0}G, 8^{6}GF,

	Starts	1st	2nd	3rd	Win & Pl
Career Total (Turf)	2	0	0	0	0

Going (Turf): Sf: 0-0 GS: 0-0 Gd: 0-1 GF: 0-1 Fm: 0-0
Distance: 5f/6f: 0-0 7f-8f: 0-1 9f-13f: 0-1 14f+: 0-0
Track : LH: 0-0 RH: 0-1 Tight: 0-0 Gall: 0-0
Aids: Bl: 0-0 Vi: 0-0 Tstrap: 0-0 Ckp: 0-0
Best Rating: 51 9/09 Sand 1m14y gd-fm

Lyrical Intent

(98) (57)
3-y-o ch g Imperial Dancer-Magical Flute (Piccolo)
P Howling Ajaz Ahmed

Placings:5040000064 (7814)
2009: 7^{5}SD, 8^{0}SD, 8^{4}SD, 7^{0}SD, 8^{0}SD, 9^{0}SD, 10^{0}SD, 12^{0}SD, 11^{6}SD, 8^{4}SD,

	Starts	1st	2nd	3rd	Win & Pl
Career Total (Turf)	0	0	0	0	
Career Total (AW)	10	0	0	0	241

Going (Turf): Sf: 0-0 GS: 0-0 Gd: 0-0 GF: 0-0 Fm: 0-0
Distance: 5f/6f: 0-0 7f-8f: 0-4 9f-13f: 0-6 14f+: 0-0
Track : LH: 0-6 RH: 0-4 Tight: 0-6 Gall: 0-0
Aids: Bl: 0-0 Vi: 0-0 Tstrap: 0-0 Ckp: 0-0
Best Rating: 57 2/09 Kemp 1m stand

Moderate; effective at around 1m; acts on Polytrack.

Lytham (IRE)

102(106) (67)66
8-y-o b g Spectrum (IRE)-Nousaiyra (IRE) (Be My Guest (USA))
A W Carroll Morgan, Clarke & Parris

Placings:040003201/544/00410/05-11103302035040 0 (5888)
2009: 11^{1}SD, 10^{1}SD, 11^{1}SD, 9^{0}SD, 12^{3}SD, 12^{3}G, 10^{0}SD, 10^{2}SD, 8^{0}G, 10^{3}GF, 12^{5}SD, 10^{0}G, 9^{4}SD, 11^{0}SD, 9^{0}SD,

	Starts	1st	2nd	3rd	Win & Pl
Career Total (Turf)	13	0	0	3	2480
Career Total (AW)	21	5	2	1	13647

63 2/09 Kemp 1m3f (0-55)H STD £2047
59 2/09 Kemp 1m2f (0-55)H STD £2047
57 1/09 Kemp 1m3f (0-52)H STD £1706
56 7/07 Ling 1m2f (0-45) STD £2252
69 11/04 Wolv 1m1f103y STD £3438
Total win prize-money £11491

Going (Turf): Sf: 0-2 GS: 0-0 Gd: 0-6 GF: 0-3 Fm: 0-0
Distance: 5f/6f: 0-0 7f-8f: 0-4 9f-13f: 5-30 14f+: 0-0
Track : LH: 2-21 RH: 3-11 Tight: 2-13 Gall: 0-3
Aids: Bl: 0-0 Vi: 0-0 Tstrap: 0-0 Ckp: 0-0
Best Rating: 71 11/04 Wolv 1m141y stand

Modest; effective at around 1m2f-1m3f; suited by easy ground on turf; acts well on Polytrack.

Lytton

102(101) (76)86
4-y-o b g Royal Applause-Dora Carrington (IRE) (Sri Pekan (USA))
R Ford Tarporley Turf Club

Placings:105/U0000030-0002100 (6103)
2009: 5^{0}SD, 6^{0}SD, 6^{0}SD, 7^{2}GF, 7^{1}GF, 7^{0}SD, 7^{0}GF,

	Starts	1st	2nd	3rd	Win & Pl
Career Total (Turf)	8	2	1	0	7729
Career Total (AW)	10	0	0	1	302

67 4/09 Bevl 7f100y (0-60)H G-F £1942
79 8/07 Wind 6f G-F £5181
Total win prize-money £7125

Going (Turf): Sf: 0-0 GS: 0-2 Gd: 0-1 GF: 2-5 Fm: 0-0
Distance: 5f/6f: 1-11 7f-8f: 1-7 9f-13f: 0-0 14f+: 0-0
Track : LH: 0-9 RH: 1-4 Tight: 0-6 Gall: 1-2
Aids: Bl: 0-1 Vi: 1-5 Tstrap: 0-1 Ckp: 0-1
Best Rating: 93 9/07 Kemp 6f stand

Modest; effective over 6f-7f; acts on fast ground and on Polytrack; has worn a visor.

M'Lady Rousseur (IRE)

80(96) (61)59
3-y-o ch f Selkirk (USA)-Millay (Polish Precedent (USA))
D R C Elsworth Wyddial Racing

Placings:03506241 (7025)
2009: 8^{0}SD, 10^{3}SD, 10^{5}SD, 10^{0}S, 11^{6}SD, 12^{2}SS, 12^{4}SD, 16^{1}SD,

	Starts	1st	2nd	3rd	Win & Pl
Career Total (Turf)	1	0	0	0	
Career Total (AW)	7	1	1	1	2954

61 10/09 Kemp 2m (0-65)H STD £2047
Total win prize-money £2047

Going (Turf): Sf: 0-1 GS: 0-0 Gd: 0-0 GF: 0-0 Fm: 0-0
Distance: 5f/6f: 0-0 7f-8f: 0-1 9f-13f: 0-6 **14f+: 1-1**
Track : LH: 0-3 **RH: 1-5** Tight: 0-3 Gall: 0-1
Aids: Bl: 0-0 Vi: 0-0 Tstrap: 0-0 Ckp: 0-0
Best Rating: **61** 10/09 Kemp 2m stand

Modest; effective up to 2m; acts on Polytrack.

Ma Patrice

90(87) (46)38
3-y-o ch f Tumbleweed Ridge-Ma Barnicle (IRE) (Al Hareb (USA))
T D McCarthy Mrs D H McCarthy

Placings:0000-00000 (6289)
2009: 11^{0}SD, 9^{0}G, 9^{0}GF, 8^{0}SD, 10^{0}SD,

	Starts	1st	2nd	3rd	Win & Pl
Career Total (Turf)	3	0	0	0	
Career Total (AW)	6	0	0	0	

Going (Turf): Sf: 0-0 GS: 0-0 Gd: 0-2 GF: 0-1 Fm: 0-0
Distance: 5f/6f: 0-0 7f-8f: 0-5 9f-13f: 0-4 14f+: 0-0
Track : LH: 0-3 RH: 0-5 Tight: 0-5 Gall: 0-0
Aids: Bl: 0-0 Vi: 0-0 Tstrap: 0-0 Ckp: 0-0
Best Rating: **46** 11/08 Ling 1m stand

Ma Ridge

99(100) (57)48
5-y-o ch g Tumbleweed Ridge-Ma Barnicle (IRE) (Al Hareb (USA))
T D McCarthy Mrs D H McCarthy

Placings:000/04U0/5040650600005-500626060 (3525)
2009: 8^{5}SD, 8^{0}SD, 8^{0}SD, 8^{6}SD, 10^{2}SD, 10^{6}SD, 10^{0}G, 9^{6}GF, 8^{0}GF,

	Starts	1st	2nd	3rd	Win & Pl
Career Total (Turf)	11	0	0	0	0
Career Total (AW)	18	0	1	0	482

Going (Turf): Sf: 0-0 GS: 0-1 Gd: 0-2 GF: 0-6 Fm: 0-2
Distance: 5f/6f: 0-2 7f-8f: 0-20 9f-13f: 0-7 14f+: 0-0
Track : LH: 0-19 RH: 0-5 Tight: 0-16 Gall: 0-1
Aids: Bl: 0-1 Vi: 0-0 Tstrap: 0-1 Ckp: 0-1
Best Rating: **57** 1/08 Ling 1m stand

Plating-class; stays 1m2f; acts on Polytrack.

Maadraa (IRE)

91(103) (81)79
4-y-o br g Josr Algarhoud (IRE)-Del Deya (IRE) (Caerleon (USA))
B J Llewellyn Terry Warner

Placings:2231-0164 (4042)
2009: 16^{0}S, 11^{1}GF, 11^{6}GF, 10^{4}S,

	Starts	1st	2nd	3rd	Win & Pl
Career Total (Turf)	4	1	0	0	3155
Career Total (AW)	4	1	2	1	4140

79 5/09 Wind 1m3f135y (0-75)H G-F £2914
81 3/08 Ling 1m4f STD £2457
Total win prize-money £5371

Going (Turf): Sf: 0-2 GS: 0-0 Gd: 0-0 **GF: 1-2** Fm: 0-0
Distance: 5f/6f: 0-0 7f-8f: 0-1 **9f-13f: 2-6** 14f+: 0-1
Track : **LH: 1-5** RH: 0-1 **Tight: 2-5** Gall: 0-0
Aids: Bl: 0-0 Vi: 0-0 Tstrap: 0-1 Ckp: 0-1
Best Rating: **81** 3/08 Ling 1m4f stand

Useful; effective at around 1m4f; acts on Polytrack and fast turf.

Maany (USA)

78 51
2-y-o ch f Mr Greeley (USA)-Dixie Card (USA) (Dixieland Band (USA))
M A Jarvis Hamdan Al Maktoum

Placings:0 (4797)
2009: 7^{0}G,

	Starts	1st	2nd	3rd	Win & Pl
Career Total (Turf)	1	0	0	0	

Going (Turf): Sf: 0-0 GS: 0-0 Gd: 0-1 GF: 0-0 Fm: 0-0
Distance: 5f/6f: 0-0 7f-8f: 0-1 9f-13f: 0-0 14f+: 0-0
Track : LH: 0-0 RH: 0-0 Tight: 0-0 Gall: 0-0
Aids: Bl: 0-0 Vi: 0-0 Tstrap: 0-0 Ckp: 0-0
Best Rating: **51** 8/09 NmkJ 7f good

Maashooq

90(83) (55)74
2-y-o ch g Observatory (USA)-Chatifa (IRE) (Titus Livius (FR))
M P Tregoning Hamdan Al Maktoum

Placings:03 (6809)
2009: 6^{0}SD, 6^{3}G,

	Starts	1st	2nd	3rd	Win & Pl
Career Total (Turf)	1	0	0	1	867
Career Total (AW)	1	0	0	0	

Going (Turf): Sf: 0-0 GS: 0-0 Gd: 0-1 GF: 0-0 Fm: 0-0
Distance: 5f/6f: 0-2 7f-8f: 0-0 9f-13f: 0-0 14f+: 0-0
Track : LH: 0-0 RH: 0-1 Tight: 0-0 Gall: 0-0
Aids: Bl: 0-0 Vi: 0-0 Tstrap: 0-0 Ckp: 0-0
Best Rating: **74** 10/09 NmkR 6f good

Fair; stays 6f; acts on good ground.

Mabait

107(107) (91)97
3-y-o b c Kyllachy-Czarna Roza (Polish Precedent (USA))
L M Cumani Sheikh Mohammed Obaid Al Maktoum

Placings:544013-1000111 (7060)
2009: 6^{1}GF, 6^{0}GF, 7^{0}G, 6^{0}G, 7^{1}SD, 7^{1}SD, 8^{1}GF,

	Starts	1st	2nd	3rd	Win & Pl
Career Total (Turf)	9	3	0	0	20119
Career Total (AW)	4	2	0	1	10863

97 10/09 Leic 1m60y (0-90)H G-F £7788
91 9/09 Wolv 7f32y (0-85)H STD £5046
88 9/09 Wolv 7f32y (0-85)H STD £5046
85 6/09 Ripn 6f (0-85)H G-F £5180
78 9/08 Hayd 6f (0-80) G-F £6476
Total win prize-money £29538

Going (Turf): Sf: 0-0 GS: 0-1 Gd: 0-3 **GF: 3-5** Fm: 0-0
Distance: 5f/6f: 2-7 7f-8f: 2-5 9f-13f: 1-1 14f+: 0-0
Track : **LH: 2-4** RH: 1-1 **Tight: 2-3** Gall: 0-1
Aids: Bl: 0-0 Vi: 0-0 Tstrap: 0-0 Ckp: 0-0
Best Rating: **97** 10/09 Leic 1m60y gd-fm

Useful; effective over 6-7f; acts on fast ground and on Polytrack.

Mabuya (UAE)

103 91
3-y-o b g Halling (USA)-City Of Gold (IRE) (Sadler's Wells (USA))
P J Makin R A Henley

Placings:55-22312003 (6203)
2009: 7^{2}G, 10^{2}GS, 9^{3}G, 9^{1}GF, 10^{2}GF, 12^{0}GS, 9^{0}GF, 11^{3}G,

	Starts	1st	2nd	3rd	Win & Pl
Career Total (Turf)	10	1	3	2	9946

84 6/09 Sals 1m1f198y (0-75)H G-F £3238
Total win prize-money £3238

Going (Turf): Sf: 0-0 GS: 0-3 Gd: 0-3 **GF: 1-4** Fm: 0-0
Distance: 5f/6f: 0-0 7f-8f: 0-3 **9f-13f: 1-7** 14f+: 0-0
Track : LH: 0-1 **RH: 1-8 Tight: 1-5** Gall: 0-2
Aids: Bl: 0-0 Vi: 0-0 Tstrap: 0-0 Ckp: 0-0
Best Rating: **91** 7/09 Asct 1m2f gd-fm

Useful; stays 1m2f; acts on most ground.

Mac Dalia

(101) (68)70
4-y-o b f Namid-Maugwenna (Danehill (USA))
A J McCabe Paul J Dixon & Brian Morton

Placings:5016031/6151453026100-0 (0146)
2009: 5^{0}SD,

	Starts	1st	2nd	3rd	Win & Pl
Career Total (Turf)	6	1	0	0	2730
Career Total (AW)	15	4	1	2	10024

68 7/08 GrLe 5f (0-70)H STD £3238
55 2/08 Sthl 5f SS £1774
60 1/08 Sthl 5f STD £1774
68 12/07 Sthl 5f STD £2047
70 7/07 Ling 5f GD £2730
Total win prize-money £11566

Going (Turf): Sf: 0-1 GS: 0-2 **Gd: 1-2** GF: 0-1 Fm: 0-0
Distance: **5f/6f: 5-20** 7f-8f: 0-1 9f-13f: 0-0 14f+: 0-0
Track : **LH: 1-7** RH: 0-0 Tight: 0-2 **Gall: 1-3**
Aids: Bl: 0-0 Vi: 0-0 Tstrap: 3-12 Ckp: 3-12
Best Rating: **70** 7/07 Ling 5f good

Modest; effective over 5f; acts on good ground and on sand; suited by forcing tactics.

Mac Don (IRE)

(98) (64)74
5-y-o b g Soviet Star (USA)-Sharena (IRE) (Kahyasi)
G J Smith Graham Smith

Placings:0654/0000/0060222050-0 (0805)
2009: 11^{0}SD,

	Starts	1st	2nd	3rd	Win & Pl
Career Total (Turf)	17	0	3	0	4419
Career Total (AW)	2	0	0	0	

Going (Turf): Sf: 0-4 GS: 0-0 Gd: 0-4 GF: 0-2 Fm: 0-1
Distance: 5f/6f: 0-0 7f-8f: 0-8 9f-13f: 0-11 14f+: 0-0
Track : LH: 0-9 RH: 0-10 Tight: 0-1 Gall: 0-2
Aids: Bl: 0-5 Vi: 0-0 Tstrap: 0-3 Ckp: 0-3
Best Rating: **74** 8/08 NmkJ 1m2f good

Modest; stays 1m2f and acts on good and softer ground.

Mac Gille Eoin

112(100) (93)112
5-y-o b h Bertolini (USA)-Peruvian Jade (Petong)
J Gallagher M C S D Racing Partnership

Placings:64005164251/253211002510/014056000-060241520 (6091)
2009: 6^{0}GF, 6^{6}GF, 6^{0}GF, 6^{2}G, 6^{4}GF, 6^{1}GF, 6^{5}S, 6^{2}GF, 6^{0}G,

	Starts	1st	2nd	3rd	Win & Pl
Career Total (Turf)	31	5	5	0	75384

	Starts	1st	2nd	3rd	Win & Pl
Career Total (AW)	10	2	1	1	11685

103	7/09	Epsm	6f	(0-95)H	G-F	£7771
105	6/08	Epsm	6f	(0-100)H	GD	£15577
100	9/07	Gdwd	6f	(0-100)H	G-F	£11217
93	6/07	Kemp	6f	(0-80)H	STD	£4728
85	6/07	Gdwd	6f	(0-85)H	GD	£7124
73	11/06	Wolv	5f216y	(0-75)	STD	£4533
66	8/06	Bath	5f161y		G-F	£3886

Total win prize-money £54840

Going (Turf): Sf: 0-1 GS: 0-3 Gd: 2-10 **GF: 3-17** Fm: 0-0
Distance: **5f/6f: 7-38** 7f-8f: 0-3 9f-13f: 0-0 14f+: 0-0
Track : **LH: 4-13** RH: 1-5 **Tight: 3-8** Gall: 1-7
Aids: Bl: 0-1 Vi: 0-0 Tstrap: 0-0 Ckp: 0-0
Best Rating: **112** 9/09 Gdwd 6f gd-fm

Very useful; stays 6f; acts on fast ground; goes on Polytrack; likes to race prominently; has worn blinkers.

Mac Love

112(115) (109)**116**

8-y-o b g Cape Cross (IRE)-My Lass (Elmaamul (USA))
Stef Liddiard Vimal Khosla

Placings:6231366113363232/54226610101/425450056/23230450/2543066450/0210-410141 **(5875)**
2009: 8^{4}G, 8^{1}G, 8^{0}GF, 8^{1}GF, 8^{4}G, 9^{1}GF,

	Starts	1st	2nd	3rd	Win & Pl
Career Total (Turf)	60	9	9	9	350817
Career Total (AW)	4	1	1	0	26197

97	9/09	Gdwd	1m1f192y		G-F	£36900
116	8/09	Sals	1m		G-F	£36900
112	6/09	Epsm	1m114y		GD	£36900
109	11/08	Kemp	1m		STD	£22708
115	9/04	Gdwd	7f		GD	£29000
114	9/04	Epsm	7f		G-F	£20300
107	7/04	Donc	6f	C	G-F	£8631
88	8/03	Kemp	5f	D	G-F	£4849
88	8/03	Hayd	5f	E	G-F	£3744
82	4/03	Nott	5f13y	D	G-F	£3584

Total win prize-money £203521

Going (Turf): Sf: 0-5 GS: 0-4 Gd: 2-23 **GF: 7-24** Fm: 0-4
Distance: 5f/6f: 4-23 7f-8f: 4-38 9f-13f: 2-3 14f+: 0-0
Track : LH: 2-12 **RH: 3-11 Tight: 3-6** Gall: 0-6
Aids: Bl: 0-0 Vi: 0-0 Tstrap: 0-0 Ckp: 0-0
Best Rating: **116** 8/09 Sals 1m gd-fm

Group class; winner at Group 3 level and runner-up in the 2005 Lockinge Stakes; effective over 6f-1m; acts well on good and faster ground and on Polytrack.

Mac Wolf

89(82) (48)**55**

3-y-o b c Polish Precedent (USA)-Herminoe (Rainbow Quest (USA))
M G Quinlan Dr Angelo Macchi

Placings:04060 **(5988)**
2009: 10^{0}GF, 9^{4}GF, 8^{0}GF, 10^{6}G, 12^{0}SD,

	Starts	1st	2nd	3rd	Win & Pl
Career Total (Turf)	4	0	0	0	0
Career Total (AW)	1	0	0	0	

Going (Turf): **Sf: 0-0 GS: 0-0 Gd: 0-1 GF: 0-3 Fm: 0-0**
Distance: 5f/6f: 0-0 7f-8f: 0-0 9f-13f: 0-5 14f+: 0-0
Track : LH: 0-0 RH: 0-3 Tight: 0-1 Gall: 0-1
Aids: Bl: 0-0 Vi: 0-0 Tstrap: 0-0 Ckp: 0-0
Best Rating: **55** 4/09 NmkR 1m2f gd-fm

Mac's Power (IRE)

72(106) (93)**14**

3-y-o b g Exceed And Excel (AUS)-Easter Girl (Efisio)
P J O'Gorman Michael McDonnell

Placings:4-40451336214 **(6229)**
2009: 5^{4}SD, 5^{0}GS, 5^{4}SD, 6^{5}SD, 6^{1}SD, 6^{3}SD, 7^{3}SD, 7^{6}SD, 7^{2}SD, 8^{1}SD, 8^{4}SD,

	Starts	1st	2nd	3rd	Win & Pl
Career Total (Turf)	1	0	0	0	
Career Total (AW)	11	2	1	2	13797

93	9/09	Kemp	1m	(0-85)H	STD	£4727
77	6/09	Kemp	6f	(0-85)H	STD	£4727

Total win prize-money £9454

Going (Turf): **Sf: 0-0 GS: 0-1 Gd: 0-0 GF: 0-0 Fm: 0-0**
Distance: 5f/6f: 1-7 7f-8f: 1-5 9f-13f: 0-0 14f+: 0-0
Track : LH: 0-1 **RH: 2-10** Tight: 0-0 Gall: 0-1
Aids: Bl: 0-0 Vi: 0-0 Tstrap: 0-0 Ckp: 0-0
Best Rating: **93** 9/09 Kemp 1m stand

Fair; effective over 6-7f; acts on Polytrack; wears a tongue tie.

Macademy Royal (USA)

(99) (14)**34**

6-y-o b g Royal Academy (USA)-Garden Folly (USA) (Pine Bluff (USA))
Miss N A Lloyd-Beavis Miss Wendy Gill

Placings:3/20/160002202/346000-0 **(7521)**
2009: 7^{0}SD,

	Starts	1st	2nd	3rd	Win & Pl
Career Total (Turf)	4	0	0	0	
Career Total (AW)	15	1	4	2	6636

75	3/07	Ling	5f	STD	£3071

Total win prize-money £3071

Going (Turf): **Sf: 0-1 GS: 0-0 Gd: 0-1 GF: 0-2 Fm: 0-0**
Distance: **5f/6f: 1-16** 7f-8f: 0-3 9f-13f: 0-0 14f+: 0-0
Track : **LH: 1-11** RH: 0-4 **Tight: 1-9** Gall: 0-1
Aids: Bl: 0-0 Vi: 0-0 Tstrap: 0-0 Ckp: 0-0
Best Rating: **75** 3/07 Ling 5f stand

Modest gelding; effective over sprint trips; acts on Polytrack; has worn a tongue tie.

Macarthur

103 **122**

5-y-o b g Montjeu (IRE)-Out West (USA) (Gone West (USA))
M F De Kock Sheikh Mohammed Bin Khalifa Al Maktoum

Placings:1/3336/01310-0000 **(6303)**
2009: 8^{0}GF, 12^{0}GF, 12^{0}G, 12^{0}GF,

	Starts	1st	2nd	3rd	Win & Pl
Career Total (Turf)	14	3	0	4	188662

121	6/08	Asct	1m4f	G-F	£85155
116	5/08	Ches	1m5f89y	GD	£42577
97	10/06	Navn	1m	HVY	£5718

Total win prize-money £133452

Going (Turf): **Sf: 1-2** GS: 0-0 **Gd: 1-4 GF: 1-8** Fm: 0-0
Distance: 5f/6f: 0-0 7f-8f: 1-1 9f-13f: 1-11 14f+: 1-2
Track : **LH: 2-10** RH: 1-4 Tight: 1-2 Gall: 1-8
Aids: Bl: 0-1 Vi: 0-0 Tstrap: 0-0 Ckp: 0-0
Best Rating: **122** 6/08 Epsm 1m4f10y good

High class; Irish trained; winner of the Group 3 Ormonde Stakes at Chester and the Group 2 Hardwicke Stakes at Ascot in 2008; effective at around 1m4f; acts on most ground; has worn blinkers.

Macdillon

105(106) (89)**96**

3-y-o b g Acclamation-Dilys (Efisio)
W S Kittow The Macdillon Partnership

Placings:41-204065 **(7202)**
2009: 6^{2}GF, 6^{0}G, 5^{4}GF, 6^{0}G, 6^{6}SS, 5^{5}SD,

	Starts	1st	2nd	3rd	Win & Pl
Career Total (Turf)	6	1	1	0	8839
Career Total (AW)	2	0	0	0	0

84	6/08	Sand	5f6y	GD	£4533

Total win prize-money £4533

Going (Turf): Sf: 0-0 GS: 0-0 **Gd: 1-4** GF: 0-2 Fm: 0-0
Distance: **5f/6f: 1-8** 7f-8f: 0-0 9f-13f: 0-0 14f+: 0-0
Track : LH: 0-2 RH: 0-0 Tight: 0-2 Gall: 0-0
Aids: Bl: 0-0 Vi: 0-0 Tstrap: 0-0 Ckp: 0-0
Best Rating: **96** 5/09 NmkR 6f gd-fm

Very useful; effective at 5f-6f; acts on good and fast ground.

Machinate (USA)

75(104) (72)**29**

7-y-o b/br g Machiavellian (USA)-Dancing Sea (USA) (Storm Cat (USA))
W M Brisbourne D Slingsby

Placings:010465/00/002402020365050262612201/314633314400065054-546000500 **(5465)**
2009: 8^{5}SD, 8^{4}SD, 8^{6}SD, 8^{0}SD, 8^{0}SF, 7^{0}SD, 8^{5}SD, 8^{0}SD, 7^{0}GF,

	Starts	1st	2nd	3rd	Win & Pl
Career Total (Turf)	12	1	0	1	3773
Career Total (AW)	47	4	7	4	14533

72	3/08	Wolv	1m141y	(0-70)H	STD	£2730
64	1/08	Wolv	1m141y		STD	£2047
65	12/07	Wolv	1m141y	(0-60)H	STD	£2218
62	11/07	Wolv	1m141y	(0-60)H	STD	£2047
65	9/05	Catt	7f		GD	£3484

Total win prize-money £12528

Going (Turf): Sf: 0-4 GS: 0-0 **Gd: 1-2** GF: 0-5 Fm: 0-1
Distance: 5f/6f: 0-0 7f-8f: 1-16 **9f-13f: 4-43** 14f+: 0-0
Track : **LH: 5-53** RH: 0-5 **Tight: 5-46** Gall: 0-0
Aids: Bl: 0-0 Vi: 0-1 Tstrap: 0-0 Ckp: 0-0
Best Rating: **72** 3/08 Wolv 1m141y stand

Modest; effective at around 1m; acts on good ground and Polytrack.

Machine Gun Kelly (IRE)

95 **66**

2-y-o b g Johannesburg (USA)-West Brooklyn (USA) (Gone West (USA))
G L Moore Findlay & Bloom

Placings:034060 **(6963)**
2009: 6^{0}G, 6^{3}GF, 5^{4}GF, 7^{0}GF, 8^{6}GS, 6^{0}G,

	Starts	1st	2nd	3rd	Win & Pl
Career Total (Turf)	6	0	0	1	914

Going (Turf): **Sf: 0-0 GS: 0-1 Gd: 0-2 GF: 0-3 Fm: 0-0**
Distance: 5f/6f: 0-3 7f-8f: 0-2 9f-13f: 0-1 14f+: 0-0
Track : LH: 0-1 RH: 0-1 Tight: 0-1 Gall: 0-0
Aids: Bl: 0-0 Vi: 0-0 Tstrap: 0-0 Ckp: 0-0
Best Rating: **66** 8/09 Ling 6f gd-fm

Modest; suited by 6f and acts on fast ground.

Machinist (IRE)

108(103) (95)106

9-y-o br g Machiavellian (USA)-Athene (IRE) (Rousillon (USA))

D Nicholls Berry & Gould Partnership

Placings:31/040/00012450/410005012/**5**0021020/0**4**53001100/52030240004-001 **(2093)**

2009: 6^{0}GF, 6^{0}GF, 6^{1}G,

	Starts	1st	2nd	3rd	Win & Pl
Career Total (Turf)	47	7	6	2	193500
Career Total (AW)	7	1	0	1	9157

98	5/09	Thsk	6f	(0-90)H	GD	£8159
106	7/07	Curr	6f63y	H	SH	£43986
101	6/07	Haml	6f5y	(0-90)H	GD	£10363
97	7/06	Asct	5f	H	G-F	£43624
95	9/05	Ayr	6f	H	GD	£17400
89	5/05	Donc	6f	(0-80)	G-F	£6808
92	7/04	Ayr	6f	D(0-80)H	G-F	£7038
83	10/02	Ling	7f	D	STD	£4660

Total win prize-money £142041

Going (Turf): Sf: 0-5 GS: 0-1 **Gd: 3-20 GF: 3-19** Fm: 0-1
Distance: **5f/6f: 5-40** 7f-8f: 3-13 9f-13f: 0-1 14f+: 0-0
Track : **LH: 1-14** RH: 0-3 **Tight: 1-5** Gall: 0-7
Aids: Bl: 0-0 Vi: 0-0 Tstrap: 0-0 Ckp: 0-0
Best Rating: **106** 5/08 Hayd 6f good

Very useful; effective over 5f-6f; seems best on a sound surface.

Mackintosh (IRE)

88(95) (54)55

3-y-o ch g Kyllachy-Louhossoa (USA) (Trempolino (USA))

Patrick Morris (G M Lyons 11/11) D & D Coatings Ltd

Placings:000000634 **(7857)**

2009: 7^{0}SD, 7^{0}HY, 8^{0}G, 8^{0}GF, 8^{0}SD, 10^{0}SD, 12^{6}SD, 9^{3}SD, 9^{4}SD,

	Starts	1st	2nd	3rd	Win & Pl
Career Total (Turf)	3	0	0	0	
Career Total (AW)	6	0	0	1	302

Going (Turf): **Sf: 0-1 GS: 0-0 Gd: 0-1 GF: 0-1 Fm: 0-0**
Distance: 5f/6f: 0-0 7f-8f: 0-5 9f-13f: 0-4 14f+: 0-0
Track : LH: 0-7 RH: 0-1 Tight: 0-2 Gall: 0-0
Aids: Bl: 0-2 Vi: 0-0 Tstrap: 0-0 Ckp: 0-0
Best Rating: **55** 5/09 Leop 1m good

Moderate; effective over 1m2f; acts on Polytrack; has worn blinkers.

Mackten

97(93) (72)70

3-y-o b g Makbul-Tender (IRE) (Zieten (USA))

W J Knight Mrs Felicity Ashfield

Placings:310 **(2399)**

2009: 7^{3}G, 7^{1}GF, 8^{0}SD,

	Starts	1st	2nd	3rd	Win & Pl
Career Total (Turf)	2	1	0	1	2741
Career Total (AW)	1	0	0	0	

70	5/09	Ling	7f	G-F	£2388

Total win prize-money £2388

Going (Turf): Sf: 0-0 GS: 0-0 Gd: 0-1 **GF: 1-1** Fm: 0-0
Distance: 5f/6f: 0-0 **7f-8f: 1-3** 9f-13f: 0-0 14f+: 0-0
Track : LH: 0-1 RH: 0-0 Tight: 0-1 Gall: 0-0
Aids: Bl: 0-0 Vi: 0-0 Tstrap: 0-0 Ckp: 0-0
Best Rating: **72** 5/09 Ling 1m stand

Fair; stays 7f and acts on fast ground

Macorville (USA)

85 90

6-y-o b g Diesis-Desert Jewel (USA) (Caerleon (USA))

G M Moore Geoff & Sandra Turnbull

Placings:302/24141110/6662240/000 **(5656)**

2009: 10^{0}G, 16^{0}GS, 14^{0}S,

	Starts	1st	2nd	3rd	Win & Pl
Career Total (Turf)	21	4	4	1	89113

98	9/06	Haml	1m5f9y	(0-95)H	G-S	£11217
95	9/06	Hayd	1m2f120y	(0-85)H	HVY	£8096
89	8/06	Ripn	1m1f170y	(0-90)H	G-S	£9348
81	5/06	Ripn	1m1f		HVY	£4210

Total win prize-money £32872

Going (Turf): **Sf: 2-6 GS: 2-5** Gd: 0-6 GF: 0-4 Fm: 0-0
Distance: 5f/6f: 0-0 7f-8f: 0-1 **9f-13f: 3-12** 14f+: 1-8
Track : LH: 1-11 **RH: 3-10 Tight: 3-8** Gall: 0-9
Aids: Bl: 0-0 Vi: 0-0 Tstrap: 0-0 Ckp: 0-0
Best Rating: **113** 9/07 Curr 1m6f gd-fm

Smart; placed in Listed company; stays 2m; best in soft ground; likes to race prominently.

Macroy

78 62

2-y-o b g Makbul-Royal Orchid (IRE) (Shalford (IRE))

B R Millman The Macroy Partnership

Placings:604 **(6386)**

2009: 5^{6}G, 5^{0}G, 6^{4}GF,

	Starts	1st	2nd	3rd	Win & Pl
Career Total (Turf)	3	0	0	0	289

Going (Turf): **Sf: 0-0 GS: 0-0 Gd: 0-2 GF: 0-1 Fm: 0-0**
Distance: 5f/6f: 0-2 7f-8f: 0-1 9f-13f: 0-0 14f+: 0-0
Track : LH: 0-1 RH: 0-0 Tight: 0-0 Gall: 0-0
Aids: Bl: 0-0 Vi: 0-0 Tstrap: 0-0 Ckp: 0-0
Best Rating: **62** 9/09 Nott 6f15y gd-fm

Mactrac

64(84) (48)34

2-y-o b g Marju (IRE)-Zanna (FR) (Soviet Star (USA))

R Hannon Exors Of The Late Mrs R McArdle

Placings:06000 **(7884)**

2009: 5^{0}GF, 6^{6}SD, 6^{0}G, 10^{0}SD, 7^{0}SD,

	Starts	1st	2nd	3rd	Win & Pl
Career Total (Turf)	2	0	0	0	
Career Total (AW)	3	0	0	0	0

Going (Turf): **Sf: 0-0 GS: 0-0 Gd: 0-1 GF: 0-1 Fm: 0-0**
Distance: 5f/6f: 0-3 7f-8f: 0-1 9f-13f: 0-1 14f+: 0-0
Track : LH: 0-1 RH: 0-2 Tight: 0-1 Gall: 0-0
Aids: Bl: 0-0 Vi: 0-0 Tstrap: 0-0 Ckp: 0-0
Best Rating: **48** 11/09 Kemp 1m2f stand

Mad Existence (IRE)

(97) (58)57

5-y-o b m Val Royal (FR)-Hanzala (FR) (Akarad (FR))

Mrs Valerie Keatley (H Rogers 29/8) J A Moran

Placings:50301430/450000**614**-000002452 **(7732)**

2009: 8^{0}SD, 10^{0}SD, 12^{0}GF, 14^{0}GF, 12^{0}SD, 12^{2}SD, 12^{4}SD, 12^{5}SD, 12^{2}SD,

	Starts	1st	2nd	3rd	Win & Pl
Career Total (Turf)	15	1	0	2	8962
Career Total (AW)	11	1	2	0	6961

53	11/08	Dund	1m2f150y	(45-60)H	STD	£4572
69	6/07	Clon	1m2f		YLD	£7003

Total win prize-money £11576

Going (Turf): **Sf: 0-0 GS: 0-0 Gd: 0-3 GF: 0-3 Fm: 0-3**
Distance: 5f/6f: 0-0 7f-8f: 0-4 **9f-13f: 2-21** 14f+: 0-1
Track : LH: 1-16 RH: 1-9 Tight: 0-1 Gall: 0-0
Aids: **Bl: 2-22** Vi: 0-0 Tstrap: 0-0 Ckp: 0-0
Best Rating: **71** 5/07 Klny 1m100y good

Mad Millie (IRE)

97(84) (47)69

2-y-o b f Pyrus (USA)-Tipsy Lady (Intikhab (USA))

J Hetherton R Fell & K Everitt

Placings:6220U00 **(6354)**

2009: 6^{6}G, 7^{2}G, 6^{2}G, 6^{0}GF, 5^{U}S, 7^{0}GF, 5^{0}SD,

	Starts	1st	2nd	3rd	Win & Pl
Career Total (Turf)	6	0	2	0	2939
Career Total (AW)	1	0	0	0	

Going (Turf): **Sf: 0-1 GS: 0-0 Gd: 0-3 GF: 0-2 Fm: 0-0**
Distance: 5f/6f: 0-5 7f-8f: 0-2 9f-13f: 0-0 14f+: 0-0
Track : LH: 0-1 RH: 0-1 Tight: 0-1 Gall: 0-0
Aids: Bl: 0-0 Vi: 0-0 Tstrap: 0-0 Ckp: 0-0
Best Rating: **69** 7/09 Thsk 7f good

Modest form in maidens at 6-7f; acts on fast and easy ground.

Mad Rush (USA)

111 117

5-y-o b g Lemon Drop Kid (USA)-Revonda (IRE) (Sadler's Wells (USA))

L M Cumani The Honorable Earle I Mack

Placings:3122/221240-15 **(3413a)**

2009: 12^{1}GF, 14^{5}Y,

	Starts	1st	2nd	3rd	Win & Pl
Career Total (Turf)	12	3	5	1	228727

112	6/09	Gdwd	1m4f		G-F	£23704
117	7/08	Hayd	1m3f200y	H	SFT	£62310
80	5/07	Hayd	1m2f120y		GD	£2817

Total win prize-money £88831

Going (Turf): **Sf: 1-2** GS: 0-2 **Gd: 1-3 GF: 1-4** Fm: 0-0
Distance: 5f/6f: 0-0 7f-8f: 0-0 **9f-13f: 3-9** 14f+: 0-3
Track : **LH: 2-5** RH: 1-7 **Tight: 1-2** Gall: 0-2
Aids: Bl: 0-0 Vi: 0-0 Tstrap: 0-0 Ckp: 0-0
Best Rating: **117** 7/08 Hayd 1m3f200y soft

Group class; winner in Listed company and Group placed; effective at 1m4f-2m; acts on most ground.

Madam Isshe

94 56

2-y-o b f Ishiguru (USA)-Lucky Dip (Tirol)

M S Saunders M S Saunders

Placings:05034 **(5714)**

2009: 6^{0}S, 5^{5}G, 5^{0}G, 5^{3}G, 5^{4}G,

	Starts	1st	2nd	3rd	Win & Pl
Career Total (Turf)	5	0	0	1	539

Going (Turf): **Sf: 0-1 GS: 0-0 Gd: 0-4 GF: 0-0 Fm: 0-0**
Distance: 5f/6f: 0-4 7f-8f: 0-1 9f-13f: 0-0 14f+: 0-0
Track : LH: 0-4 RH: 0-0 Tight: 0-0 Gall: 0-4
Aids: Bl: 0-0 Vi: 0-0 Tstrap: 0-0 Ckp: 0-0
Best Rating: **56** 9/09 Bath 5f11y good

Moderate; stays an extended 5f; acts on good ground.

Madam Macie (IRE)

98 77

2-y-o ch f Bertolini (USA)-Dictatrice (FR) (Anabaa (USA))

J Hetherton R Fell & K Everitt

Placings:15 (7033)

2009: 7¹G, 7⁵S,

	Starts	1st	2nd	3rd	Win & Pl
Career Total (Turf)	2	1	0	0	3537

77 10/09 Catt 7f GD £2729

Total win prize-money £2730

Going (Turf): Sf: 0-1 GS: 0-0 **Gd: 1-1** GF: 0-0 Fm: 0-0
Distance: 5f/6f: 0-0 **7f-8f: 1-2** 9f-13f: 0-0 14f+: 0-0
Track : **LH: 1-1** RH: 0-0 **Tight: 1-1** Gall: 0-0
Aids: Bl: 0-0 Vi: 0-0 Tstrap: 0-0 Ckp: 0-0
Best Rating: 77 10/09 Catt 7f good

Fair winner on debut; effective over 7f; acts on good ground.

Madam President

93(102) (74)71

4-y-o b f Royal Applause-White House (Pursuit Of Love)

W R Swinburn Mrs Doreen M Swinburn

Placings:3650-10050 (6566)

2009: 10¹SD, 10⁰GF, 10⁰SD, 11⁵GF, 12⁰GS,

	Starts	1st	2nd	3rd	Win & Pl
Career Total (Turf)	6	0	0	1	403
Career Total (AW)	3	1	0	0	2047

74 4/09 Kemp 1m2f (0-65)H STD £2047

Total win prize-money £2047

Going (Turf): Sf: 0-0 GS: 0-2 Gd: 0-0 GF: 0-4 Fm: 0-0
Distance: 5f/6f: 0-0 7f-8f: 0-0 **9f-13f: 1-9** 14f+: 0-0
Track : LH: 0-4 **RH: 1-4** Tight: 0-7 Gall: 0-0
Aids: Bl: 0-0 Vi: 0-0 Tstrap: 0-0 Ckp: 0-0
Best Rating: 74 4/09 Kemp 1m2f stand

Fair; effective over 1m2f; acts on Polytrack.

Madam Ruby (IRE)

89 59

2-y-o ch f Observatory (USA)-Azur (IRE) (Brief Truce (USA))

A King Mrs L Field

Placings:606 (6931)

2009: 8⁶G, 6⁰S, 8⁶G,

	Starts	1st	2nd	3rd	Win & Pl
Career Total (Turf)	3	0	0	0	0

Going (Turf): Sf: 0-1 GS: 0-0 Gd: 0-2 GF: 0-0 Fm: 0-0
Distance: 5f/6f: 0-0 7f-8f: 0-1 9f-13f: 0-2 14f+: 0-0
Track : LH: 0-1 RH: 0-0 Tight: 0-1 Gall: 0-0
Aids: Bl: 0-0 Vi: 0-0 Tstrap: 0-0 Ckp: 0-0
Best Rating: 59 8/09 Chep 1m14y good

Madam'X

98(89) (50)46

3-y-o b f Xaar-Bonne Etoile (Diesis)

Mrs A Duffield C M Budgett

Placings:0040-446 (6384)

2009: 9⁴G, 12⁴GF, 16⁶GF,

	Starts	1st	2nd	3rd	Win & Pl
Career Total (Turf)	4	0	0	0	409
Career Total (AW)	3	0	0	0	192

Going (Turf): Sf: 0-0 GS: 0-1 Gd: 0-1 GF: 0-2 Fm: 0-0
Distance: 5f/6f: 0-0 7f-8f: 0-3 9f-13f: 0-3 14f+: 0-1
Track : LH: 0-5 RH: 0-2 Tight: 0-5 Gall: 0-2
Aids: Bl: 0-0 Vi: 0-0 Tstrap: 0-0 Ckp: 0-0
Best Rating: 50 12/08 GrLe 1m stand

Madame Boot (FR)

86 53

2-y-o b f Diktat-Esprit Libre (Daylami (IRE))

P J Makin Mrs B J Carrington

Placings:00 (5604)

2009: 6⁰GF, 6⁰S,

	Starts	1st	2nd	3rd	Win & Pl
Career Total (Turf)	2	0	0	0	

Going (Turf): Sf: 0-1 GS: 0-0 Gd: 0-0 GF: 0-1 Fm: 0-0
Distance: 5f/6f: 0-1 7f-8f: 0-1 9f-13f: 0-0 14f+: 0-0
Track : LH: 0-0 RH: 0-0 Tight: 0-0 Gall: 0-1
Aids: Bl: 0-0 Vi: 0-0 Tstrap: 0-0 Ckp: 0-0
Best Rating: 53 8/09 Wind 6f gd-fm

Madame Excelerate

83(97) (70)43

2-y-o b f Pursuit Of Love-Skovshoved (IRE) (Danetime (IRE))

W M Brisbourne Equiform Nutrition Limited

Placings:502 (7157)

2009: 7⁵GF, 7⁰G, 7²SD,

	Starts	1st	2nd	3rd	Win & Pl
Career Total (Turf)	2	0	0	0	0
Career Total (AW)	1	0	1	0	806

Going (Turf): Sf: 0-0 GS: 0-0 Gd: 0-1 GF: 0-1 Fm: 0-0
Distance: 5f/6f: 0-0 7f-8f: 0-3 9f-13f: 0-0 14f+: 0-0
Track : LH: 0-3 RH: 0-0 Tight: 0-3 Gall: 0-0
Aids: Bl: 0-0 Vi: 0-0 Tstrap: 0-0 Ckp: 0-0
Best Rating: 70 10/09 Wolv 7f32y stand

Madame Guillotine (USA)

98(91) (45)62

3-y-o gr/ro f Proud Citizen (USA)-Paris Gem (USA) (Rubiano (USA))

R M Beckett The Hon Mrs J M Corbett & C Wright

Placings:005 (6611)

2009: 8⁰GF, 8⁰SD, 7⁵SD,

	Starts	1st	2nd	3rd	Win & Pl
Career Total (Turf)	1	0	0	0	
Career Total (AW)	2	0	0	0	0

Going (Turf): Sf: 0-0 GS: 0-0 Gd: 0-0 GF: 0-1 Fm: 0-0
Distance: 5f/6f: 0-0 7f-8f: 0-3 9f-13f: 0-0 14f+: 0-0
Track : LH: 0-0 RH: 0-2 Tight: 0-0 Gall: 0-0
Aids: Bl: 0-0 Vi: 0-0 Tstrap: 0-0 Ckp: 0-0
Best Rating: 62 6/09 Sals 1m gd-fm

Madame Jourdain (IRE)

90 64

3-y-o b f Beckett (IRE)-Cladantom (IRE) (High Estate)

S A Harris (A Berry 4/9) A B Parr

Placings:06122400-0006500 (7246)

2009: 5⁰GF, 5⁰GF, 5⁰GS, 5⁶S, 6⁵S, 5⁰G, 8⁰S,

	Starts	1st	2nd	3rd	Win & Pl
Career Total (Turf)	15	1	2	0	6872

62 6/08 Thsk 6f G-S £3885

Total win prize-money £3886

Going (Turf): Sf: 0-3 **GS: 1-4** Gd: 0-4 GF: 0-4 Fm: 0-0
Distance: **5f/6f: 1-13** 7f-8f: 0-1 9f-13f: 0-1 14f+: 0-0
Track : LH: 0-3 RH: 0-1 Tight: 0-1 Gall: 0-0
Aids: **Bl: 1-4** Vi: 0-0 Tstrap: 0-0 Ckp: 0-0
Best Rating: 64 7/08 Pont 6f good

Modest; effective over 6f; acts on good ground.

Madame McManus

(69) (4)

3-y-o ch f Needwood Blade-Madame Jones (IRE) (Lycius (USA))

P D Evans J E Abbey

Placings:000 (7753)

2009: 8⁰SD, 7⁰SD, 8⁰SD,

	Starts	1st	2nd	3rd	Win & Pl
Career Total (Turf)	0	0	0	0	
Career Total (AW)	3	0	0	0	

Going (Turf): Sf: 0-0 GS: 0-0 Gd: 0-0 GF: 0-0 Fm: 0-0
Distance: 5f/6f: 0-0 7f-8f: 0-2 9f-13f: 0-1 14f+: 0-0
Track : LH: 0-3 RH: 0-0 Tight: 0-3 Gall: 0-0
Aids: Bl: 0-0 Vi: 0-1 Tstrap: 0-0 Ckp: 0-0
Best Rating: 4 11/09 Ling 1m stand

Madame Rio (IRE)

46 (26)42

4-y-o b f Captain Rio-Glenviews Purchase (IRE) (Desert Story (IRE))

E J Cooper Cumberland Lodge Racing & Leisure Co Ltd

Placings:06400/60000-0 (3296)

2009: 6⁰GF,

	Starts	1st	2nd	3rd	Win & Pl
Career Total (Turf)	9	0	0	0	337
Career Total (AW)	2	0	0	0	

Going (Turf): Sf: 0-2 GS: 0-2 Gd: 0-3 GF: 0-2 Fm: 0-0
Distance: 5f/6f: 0-7 7f-8f: 0-3 9f-13f: 0-1 14f+: 0-0
Track : LH: 0-5 RH: 0-1 Tight: 0-4 Gall: 0-0
Aids: Bl: 0-0 Vi: 0-1 Tstrap: 0-0 Ckp: 0-0
Best Rating: 61 9/07 Ches 7f2y good

Madame Roulin (IRE)

77(85) (68)57

2-y-o b f Xaar-Cradle Rock (IRE) (Desert Sun)

M L W Bell Three To One Racing

Placings:405 (7277)

2009: 8^{4}SS, 8^{0}S, 8^{5}SD,

	Starts	1st	2nd	3rd	Win & Pl
Career Total (Turf)	1	0	0	0	
Career Total (AW)	2	0	0	0	0

Going (Turf): Sf: 0-1 GS: 0-0 Gd: 0-0 GF: 0-0 Fm: 0-0
Distance: 5f/6f: 0-0 7f-8f: 0-2 9f-13f: 0-1 14f+: 0-0
Track : LH: 0-2 RH: 0-0 Tight: 0-2 Gall: 0-0
Aids: Bl: 0-0 Vi: 0-0 Tstrap: 0-0 Ckp: 0-0
Best Rating: 68 10/09 Ling 1m std-slw

Madame Trop Vite (IRE)

107 (82)104

3-y-o b f Invincible Spirit (IRE)-Gladstone Street (IRE) (Waajib)

K A Ryan Mrs T Marnane

Placings:152411-0600000 (7007a)

2009: 6^{0}G, 5^{6}G, 5^{0}G, 6^{0}S, 6^{0}G, 6^{0}G, 5^{0}SD,

	Starts	1st	2nd	3rd	Win & Pl
Career Total (Turf)	12	3	1	0	71533
Career Total (AW)	1	0	0	0	

104 9/08 Donc 5f SFT £45416
103 8/08 Newb 5f34y G-S £17031
72 6/08 Ches 5f16y G-F £5180
Total win prize-money £67628

Going (Turf): Sf: 1-3 GS: 1-2 Gd: 0-5 GF: 1-1 Fm: 0-1
Distance: 5f/6f: 3-12 7f-8f: 0-1 9f-13f: 0-0 14f+: 0-0
Track : LH: 1-3 RH: 0-0 Tight: 1-2 Gall: 0-0
Aids: Bl: 0-1 Vi: 0-0 Tstrap: 0-0 Ckp: 0-0
Best Rating: 104 9/08 Donc 5f soft

Smart; winner of the Group 2 Flying Childers in 2008; effective over 5f; acts on most ground.

Madamlily (IRE)

99(92) (71)74

3-y-o b f Refuse To Bend (IRE)-Rainbow Dream (Rainbow Quest (USA))

J J Quinn Bob McMillan

Placings:521-00440226 (6313)

2009: 10^{0}G, 12^{0}S, 12^{4}GS, 12^{4}G, 12^{0}S, 12^{2}G, 12^{2}SD, 14^{6}GF,

	Starts	1st	2nd	3rd	Win & Pl
Career Total (Turf)	10	1	2	0	8398
Career Total (AW)	1	0	1	0	1060

74 10/08 Pont 1m2f6y GD £5180
Total win prize-money £5181

Going (Turf): Sf: 0-3 GS: 0-2 Gd: 1-4 GF: 0-1 Fm: 0-0
Distance: 5f/6f: 0-0 7f-8f: 0-2 9f-13f: 1-8 14f+: 0-1
Track : LH: 1-6 RH: 0-4 Tight: 0-5 Gall: 0-2
Aids: Bl: 0-0 Vi: 0-0 Tstrap: 0-0 Ckp: 0-0
Best Rating: 74 10/08 Pont 1m2f6y good

Fair; effective at 1m2f-1m4f; acts on good and easy ground.

Maddy

97(102) (62)60

4-y-o b f Daggers Drawn (USA)-Summer Lightning (IRE) (Tamure (IRE))

George Baker Collings, Powner, Sword & Partners

Placings:514050/4336141500026-064303336040 (4667)

2009: 8^{0}SD, 12^{6}SD, 10^{4}SD, 9^{3}GF, 11^{0}SD, 8^{3}G, 9^{3}GF, 9^{3}GF, 9^{6}G, 7^{0}F, 10^{4}S, 8^{0}G,

	Starts	1st	2nd	3rd	Win & Pl
Career Total (Turf)	18	2	0	5	7130
Career Total (AW)	13	1	1	1	3374

54 8/08 Yarm 1m2f21y SFT £1942
49 7/08 Leic 1m1f218y G-F £3238
63 7/07 Ling 6f STD £2047
Total win prize-money £7229

Going (Turf): Sf: 1-3 GS: 0-3 Gd: 0-6 GF: 1-5 Fm: 0-1
Distance: 5f/6f: 1-5 7f-8f: 0-4 9f-13f: 2-22 14f+: 0-0
Track : LH: 2-21 RH: 1-7 Tight: 2-13 Gall: 0-2
Aids: Bl: 0-0 Vi: 0-0 Tstrap: 2-24 Ckp: 2-24
Best Rating: 63 10/07 Pont 6f good

Plating class; stays 1m2f; acts on most ground and on Polytrack; has worn cheekpieces.

Made To Ransom

102 94

4-y-o b g Red Ransom (USA)-Maid For The Hills (Indian Ridge)

J H M Gosden Normandie Stud Ltd

Placings:3/10 (2327)

2009: 10^{1}GF, 9^{0}GF,

	Starts	1st	2nd	3rd	Win & Pl
Career Total (Turf)	3	1	0	1	3683

94 5/09 Chep 1m2f36y G-F £2719
Total win prize-money £2720

Going (Turf): Sf: 0-0 GS: 0-0 Gd: 0-1 GF: 1-2 Fm: 0-0
Distance: 5f/6f: 0-0 7f-8f: 0-1 9f-13f: 1-2 14f+: 0-0
Track : LH: 1-1 RH: 0-1 Tight: 0-1 Gall: 0-0
Aids: Bl: 0-0 Vi: 0-0 Tstrap: 0-0 Ckp: 0-0
Best Rating: 94 5/09 Chep 1m2f36y gd-fm

Useful; stays 1m2f; acts on fast ground.

Madhaaq (IRE)

84 66

2-y-o b f Medicean-Winsa (USA) (Riverman (USA))

J L Dunlop Hamdan Al Maktoum

Placings:5 (7183)

2009: 7^{5}G,

	Starts	1st	2nd	3rd	Win & Pl
Career Total (Turf)	1	0	0	0	0

Going (Turf): Sf: 0-0 GS: 0-0 Gd: 0-1 GF: 0-0 Fm: 0-0
Distance: 5f/6f: 0-0 7f-8f: 0-1 9f-13f: 0-0 14f+: 0-0
Track : LH: 0-0 RH: 0-0 Tight: 0-0 Gall: 0-0
Aids: Bl: 0-0 Vi: 0-0 Tstrap: 0-0 Ckp: 0-0
Best Rating: 66 10/09 NmkR 7f good

Madhal

93(89) (56)55

3-y-o b g First Trump-Jane Grey (Tragic Role (USA))

Matthew Salaman (M Salaman 5/6) A A Byrne

Placings:3005600 (7787)

2009: 5^{3}F, 8^{0}G, 8^{0}F, 7^{5}SD, 5^{6}SD, 7^{0}SD, 7^{0}SD,

	Starts	1st	2nd	3rd	Win & Pl
Career Total (Turf)	3	0	0	1	566
Career Total (AW)	4	0	0	0	0

Going (Turf): Sf: 0-0 GS: 0-0 Gd: 0-1 GF: 0-0 Fm: 0-2
Distance: 5f/6f: 0-2 7f-8f: 0-3 9f-13f: 0-2 14f+: 0-0
Track : LH: 0-4 RH: 0-2 Tight: 0-3 Gall: 0-0
Aids: Bl: 0-0 Vi: 0-0 Tstrap: 0-0 Ckp: 0-0
Best Rating: 56 10/09 Kemp 7f stand

Moderate; stays 7f; acts on fast ground and Polytrack.

Madison Belle

(101) (72)53

3-y-o ch f Bahamian Bounty-Indian Flag (IRE) (Indian Ridge)

J R Weymes (K R Burke 1/5) Mrs Elaine M Burke

Placings:55000465160-31121320 (7870)

2009: 8^{3}SD, 7^{1}SS, 6^{1}SD, 6^{2}SD, 7^{1}SD, 6^{3}SD, 6^{2}SD, 6^{0}SS,

	Starts	1st	2nd	3rd	Win & Pl
Career Total (Turf)	5	0	0	0	245
Career Total (AW)	14	4	2	2	10473

72 2/09 Sthl 7f STD £2047
72 2/09 Sthl 6f STD £2047
69 1/09 Sthl 7f SS £2047
69 11/08 Sthl 6f (0-60) STD £2047
Total win prize-money £8188

Going (Turf): Sf: 0-0 GS: 0-0 Gd: 0-2 GF: 0-3 Fm: 0-0
Distance: 5f/6f: 2-15 7f-8f: 2-3 9f-13f: 0-1 14f+: 0-0
Track : LH: 4-15 RH: 0-0 Tight: 0-3 Gall: 0-3
Aids: Bl: 0-0 Vi: 0-0 Tstrap: 0-0 Ckp: 0-0
Best Rating: 72 2/09 Sthl 7f stand

Modest; best at around 6f-7f; handles fast ground and sand.

Madison Park (IRE)

86(101) (68)65

3-y-o b c Montjeu (IRE)-Crystal Gaze (IRE) (Rainbow Quest (USA))

H R A Cecil Ballygallon Stud Limited

Placings:0040 (4650)

2009: 10^{0}GF, 10^{0}GF, 12^{4}SD, 11^{0}SD,

	Starts	1st	2nd	3rd	Win & Pl
Career Total (Turf)	2	0	0	0	
Career Total (AW)	2	0	0	0	0

Going (Turf): Sf: 0-0 GS: 0-0 Gd: 0-0 GF: 0-2 Fm: 0-0
Distance: 5f/6f: 0-0 7f-8f: 0-0 9f-13f: 0-4 14f+: 0-0
Track : LH: 0-1 RH: 0-2 Tight: 0-1 Gall: 0-1
Aids: Bl: 0-2 Vi: 0-1 Tstrap: 0-0 Ckp: 0-0
Best Rating: 68 7/09 Ling 1m4f stand

Madj's Baby

84 57

2-y-o b f Footstepsinthesand-Madamoiselle Jones (Emperor Jones (USA))

H S Howe Horses Away Racing Club

Placings:000 (5212)

2009: 6^{0}GF, 7^{0}GF, 6^{0}G,

	Starts	1st	2nd	3rd	Win & Pl
Career Total (Turf)	3	0	0	0	

Going (Turf): Sf: 0-0 GS: 0-0 Gd: 0-1 GF: 0-2 Fm: 0-0
Distance: 5f/6f: 0-2 7f-8f: 0-1 9f-13f: 0-0 14f+: 0-0
Track : LH: 0-0 RH: 0-0 Tight: 0-0 Gall: 0-0
Aids: Bl: 0-0 Vi: 0-0 Tstrap: 0-0 Ckp: 0-0
Best Rating: 57 6/09 Sals 6f gd-fm

Madman (FR)

(66)

5-y-o br g Kaldou Star-Shirlauges (FR) (Port Lyautey (FR))

C N Kellett (P J Rothwell 2/8) G C Chipman

Placings:0 **(6673)**

2009: 9^{0}SD,

	Starts	1st	2nd	3rd	Win & Pl
Career Total (Turf)	0	0	0	0	
Career Total (AW)	1	0	0	0	

Going (Turf): **Sf: 0-0 GS: 0-0 Gd: 0-0 GF: 0-0 Fm: 0-0**
Distance: 5f/6f: 0-0 7f-8f: 0-0 9f-13f: 0-1 14f+: 0-0
Track : LH: 0-1 RH: 0-0 Tight: 0-1 Gall: 0-0
Aids: Bl: 0-0 Vi: 0-0 Tstrap: 0-0 Ckp: 0-0

Mae Cigan (FR)

98(94) (55)73

6-y-o gr g Medaaly-Concert (Polar Falcon (USA))

M Blanshard A D Jones

Placings:34000/24301004013 0/0245644261 56/33150526 4545-02500 **(6936)**

2009: 16^{0}SD, 12^{2}G, 11^{5}G, 13^{0}SD, 11^{0}G,

	Starts	1st	2nd	3rd	Win & Pl
Career Total (Turf)	34	4	3	5	19579
Career Total (AW)	12	0	2	0	1568

73	5/08	Newb	1m4f5y	(0-75)H	GD	£2590
69	9/07	Hayd	1m3f200y	(0-75)H	SFT	£2817
71	9/06	Hayd	1m2f120y	(0-70)H	HVY	£3886
69	5/06	Bath	1m2f46y	(0-75)H	SFT	£3562

Total win prize-money £12855

Going (Turf): **Sf: 3-13** GS: 0-6 Gd: 1-12 GF: 0-3 Fm: 0-0
Distance: 5f/6f: 0-3 7f-8f: 0-2 **9f-13f: 4-35** 14f+: 0-6
Track : **LH: 4-33** RH: 0-10 Tight: 1-18 Gall: 1-6
Aids: Bl: 0-0 Vi: 0-1 Tstrap: 0-0 Ckp: 0-0
Best Rating: 74 9/06 Hayd 1m3f200y good

Modest; stays 1m4f; goes well on soft ground.

Mafaaz

(104) (102)99

3-y-o ch c Medicean-Complimentary Pass (Danehill (USA))

J H M Gosden Hamdan Al Maktoum

Placings:15-10 **(1225a)**

2009: 9^{1}SD, 9^{0}FT,

	Starts	1st	2nd	3rd	Win & Pl
Career Total (Turf)	1	0	0	0	24600
Career Total (AW)	3	2	0	0	52438

102	3/09	Kemp	1m1f	STD	£49848
86	9/08	Kemp	7f	STD	£2590

Total win prize-money £52438

Going (Turf): **Sf: 0-0 GS: 0-0 Gd: 0-0 GF: 0-1 Fm: 0-0**
Distance: 5f/6f: 0-0 7f-8f: 1-2 9f-13f: 1-2 14f+: 0-0
Track : LH: 0-0 **RH: 2-2** Tight: 0-0 Gall: 0-0
Aids: **Bl: 1-2** Vi: 0-0 Tstrap: 0-0 Ckp: 0-0
Best Rating: 102 3/09 Kemp 1m1f stand

Smart; effective over 7f-1m1f; acts on Polytrack.

Mafaheem

87(103) (76)77

7-y-o b g Mujahid (USA)-Legend Of Aragon (Aragon)

A B Haynes WCR V - The Conkwell Connection

Placings:1/23236/0060115541041/1154300316030305-160440000 **(5225)**

2009: 6^{1}SD, 6^{6}SD, 6^{0}SD, 5^{4}SD, 5^{4}SD, 6^{0}S, 5^{0}SD, 6^{0}GS, 5^{0}SD,

	Starts	1st	2nd	3rd	Win & Pl
Career Total (Turf)	20	4	2	3	25384
Career Total (AW)	24	5	0	3	11592

70	1/09	GrLe	6f		STD	£2590
77	8/08	Yarm	6f3y	(0-70)H	GD	£2719
70	1/08	Wolv	5f216y		STD	£1774
66	1/08	Wolv	5f216y		STD	£2047
70	1/08	Wolv	5f216y		STD	£1774
73	10/07	Wolv	5f216y		STD	£2047
65	7/07	Wind	6f		HVY	£3886
59	6/07	Bath	5f161y		G-S	£1943
82	10/04	York	6f		GD	£5489

Total win prize-money £24274

Going (Turf): Sf: 1-7 GS: 1-6 **Gd: 2-6** GF: 0-1 Fm: 0-0
Distance: **5f/6f: 8-34** 7f-8f: 1-10 9f-13f: 0-0 14f+: 0-0
Track : **LH: 6-25** RH: 0-2 **Tight: 4-20** Gall: 3-5
Aids: **Bl: 1-12** Vi: 0-0 Tstrap: 0-1 Ckp: 0-1
Best Rating: 91 6/05 Epsm 7f good

Fair; suited by 6f; acts on good and softer ground; also goes on Polytrack.

Mafasina (USA)

(99) (70)24

4-y-o b f Orientate (USA)-Money Madam (USA) (A.P. Indy (USA))

B Smart Prime Equestrian

Placings:14/3000-33 **(2133)**

2009: 8^{3}SD, 7^{3}SD,

	Starts	1st	2nd	3rd	Win & Pl
Career Total (Turf)	1	0	0	0	
Career Total (AW)	7	1	0	3	5297

70	11/07	Ling	7f	STD	£3141

Total win prize-money £3141

Going (Turf): **Sf: 0-0 GS: 0-0 Gd: 0-1 GF: 0-0 Fm: 0-0**
Distance: 5f/6f: 0-1 **7f-8f: 1-6** 9f-13f: 0-1 14f+: 0-0
Track : **LH: 1-6** RH: 0-1 **Tight: 1-4** Gall: 0-0
Aids: Bl: 0-0 Vi: 0-0 Tstrap: 0-0 Ckp: 0-0
Best Rating: 70 1/08 Kemp 7f stand

Modest; stays 7f; acts on Fibresand and Polytrack.

Mafeking (UAE)

98(107) (92)84

5-y-o b g Jade Robbery (USA)-Melisendra (FR) (Highest Honor (FR))

M R Hoad Mrs J E Taylor

Placings:013/2504323231/31064254-600222P22 **(7775)**

2009: 12^{6}SD, 10^{0}G, 10^{0}G, 11^{2}SD, 10^{2}GS, 10^{2}SD, 10^{P}SD, 10^{2}SD, 10^{2}SD,

	Starts	1st	2nd	3rd	Win & Pl
Career Total (Turf)	5	0	1	0	1445
Career Total (AW)	25	3	8	5	37403

93	1/08	Ling	1m2f	(0-100)H	STD	£9971
88	12/07	Ling	1m2f	(0-85)H	STD	£4605
74	11/06	Kemp	1m		STD	£2388

Total win prize-money £16966

Going (Turf): **Sf: 0-0 GS: 0-1 Gd: 0-3 GF: 0-1 Fm: 0-0**
Distance: 5f/6f: 0-0 7f-8f: 1-4 **9f-13f: 2-26** 14f+: 0-0
Track : **LH: 2-16** RH: 1-14 **Tight: 2-15** Gall: 0-3
Aids: Bl: 0-0 Vi: 0-0 Tstrap: 0-0 Ckp: 0-0
Best Rating: 93 1/08 Ling 1m2f stand

Useful; stays 1m2f; acts on Polytrack.

Magaling (IRE)

97 92

3-y-o ch c Medicean-Fling (Pursuit Of Love)

L M Cumani Sheikh Mohammed Obaid Al Maktoum

Placings:24210-100 **(3049)**

2009: 7^{1}GS, 8^{0}S, 8^{0}GF,

	Starts	1st	2nd	3rd	Win & Pl
Career Total (Turf)	8	2	2	0	17206

92	5/09	Donc	7f	(0-85)H	G-S	£4857
83	9/08	Yarm	6f3y		GD	£3238

Total win prize-money £8095

Going (Turf): Sf: 0-1 **GS: 1-2 Gd: 1-2** GF: 0-3 Fm: 0-0
Distance: 5f/6f: 0-2 **7f-8f: 2-6** 9f-13f: 0-0 14f+: 0-0
Track : LH: 0-0 RH: 0-0 Tight: 0-0 Gall: 0-0
Aids: Bl: 0-0 Vi: 0-0 Tstrap: 0-0 Ckp: 0-0
Best Rating: 92 5/09 Donc 7f gd-sft

Useful; stays 7f and acts on good and softer ground.

Magenta Strait

(95) (60)

2-y-o b f Sampower Star-Vermilion Creek (Makbul)

R Hollinshead M Johnson

Placings:01 **(7749)**

2009: 5^{0}SD, 5^{1}SD,

	Starts	1st	2nd	3rd	Win & Pl
Career Total (Turf)	0	0	0	0	
Career Total (AW)	2	1	0	0	2388

60	12/09	Wolv	5f216y	STD	£2388

Total win prize-money £2388

Going (Turf): **Sf: 0-0 GS: 0-0 Gd: 0-0 GF: 0-0 Fm: 0-0**
Distance: **5f/6f: 1-2** 7f-8f: 0-0 9f-13f: 0-0 14f+: 0-0
Track : **LH: 1-2** RH: 0-0 **Tight: 1-2** Gall: 0-0
Aids: Bl: 0-0 Vi: 0-0 Tstrap: 0-0 Ckp: 0-0
Best Rating: 60 12/09 Wolv 5f216y stand

Modest; effective over 6f; acts on Polytrack.

Maggie Kate

101(102) (66)69

4-y-o b m Auction House (USA)-Perecapa (IRE) (Archway (IRE))

R Ingram Tommy Tighe

Placings:62/4022034241420360-000000511 **(5629)**

2009: 6^{0}SD, 6^{0}SD, 5^{0}GF, 5^{0}GF, 5^{0}G, 6^{0}GS, 5^{0}F, 5^{5}GF, 5^{1}GS, 5^{1}GS,

	Starts	1st	2nd	3rd	Win & Pl
Career Total (Turf)	14	2	2	1	8038
Career Total (AW)	14	1	3	1	5061

57	9/09	Chep	5f16y	(0-52)H	G-S	£2460
58	8/09	Brig	5f59y	(0-60)H	G-S	£2590
66	5/08	GrLe	5f	(0-60)H	STD	£2047

Total win prize-money £7098

Going (Turf): Sf: 0-0 **GS: 2-4** Gd: 0-4 GF: 0-5 Fm: 0-1
Distance: **5f/6f: 3-23** 7f-8f: 0-5 9f-13f: 0-0 14f+: 0-0
Track : **LH: 2-14** RH: 0-5 Tight: 0-6 **Gall: 1-5**
Aids: **Bl: 2-3** Vi: 0-0 Tstrap: 0-11 Ckp: 0-11
Best Rating: 69 6/08 Sand 5f6y good

Modest; effective at 5f-7f; acts on good and easy ground; also goes on Polytrack.

Maggie Lou (IRE)

94(86) (50)86

3-y-o b f Red Ransom (USA)-Triomphale (USA) (Nureyev (USA))

K A Ryan Highbank Syndicate

Placings:12400-**0**44500 **(5335)**
2009: 5^{0}SD, 6^{4}G, 7^{4}S, 7^{5}G, 7^{0}S, 6^{0}S,

	Starts	1st	2nd	3rd	Win & Pl
Career Total (Turf)	10	1	1	0	9514
Career Total (AW)	1	0	0	0	

77 4/08 Hayd 5f G-S £3399
Total win prize-money £3400

Going (Turf): Sf: 0-4 **GS: 1-1** Gd: 0-3 GF: 0-1 Fm: 0-0
Distance: **5f/6f: 1-8** 7f-8f: 0-3 9f-13f: 0-0 14f+: 0-0
Track : LH: 0-1 RH: 0-2 Tight: 0-0 Gall: 0-0
Aids: Bl: 0-0 Vi: 0-1 Tstrap: 0-0 Ckp: 0-0
Best Rating: **86** 7/08 Vich 5f holding

Fair; effective at 6f; acts on good and softer ground.

Maggie Maggie May (IRE)

67 **5**
7-y-o b m Spectrum (IRE)-Liberty Song (IRE) (Last Tycoon)
P C Haslam Henry Cafferty

Placings:5054/R60/0/0 **(2366)**
2009: 6^{0}GF,

	Starts	1st	2nd	3rd	Win & Pl
Career Total (Turf)	9	0	0	0	433

Going (Turf): **Sf: 0-0 GS: 0-0 Gd: 0-4 GF: 0-3 Fm: 0-1**
Distance: 5f/6f: 0-3 7f-8f: 0-2 9f-13f: 0-4 14f+: 0-0
Track : LH: 0-1 RH: 0-4 Tight: 0-0 Gall: 0-0
Aids: Bl: 0-1 Vi: 0-0 Tstrap: 0-3 Ckp: 0-3
Best Rating: **55** 9/04 DRoy 7f good

Magic Amigo

84(101) (54)**18**
8-y-o ch g Zilzal (USA)-Emaline (FR) (Empery (USA))
J R Jenkins Mrs Wendy Jenkins

Placings:05420/**2**10**2**30436**2**60/401/630650**3**/**2**00050445**5** 4403/25340-3060 **(4158)**
2009: 11^{3}SD, 10^{0}SD, 9^{6}SD, 10^{0}G,

	Starts	1st	2nd	3rd	Win & Pl
Career Total (Turf)	28	2	3	3	15141
Career Total (AW)	22	0	3	4	3719

78 11/05 Yarm 1m2f21y (0-70)H HVY £3906
64 5/04 Folk 1m1f149y F SFT £2954
Total win prize-money £6860

Going (Turf): **Sf: 2-5** GS: 0-4 Gd: 0-5 GF: 0-12 Fm: 0-2
Distance: 5f/6f: 0-3 7f-8f: 0-3 **9f-13f: 2-43** 14f+: 0-1
Track : LH: 1-22 RH: 1-23 **Tight: 2-19** Gall: 0-7
Aids: Bl: 0-6 Vi: 0-6 Tstrap: 0-2 Ckp: 0-2
Best Rating: **79** 8/04 Folk 1m1f149y gd-sft

Moderate; stays 1m4f; acts on most ground and on Polytrack; has worn blinkers.

Magic Cat

84 **101**
3-y-o b g One Cool Cat (USA)-Magic Music (IRE) (Magic Ring (IRE))
A P Jarvis (K R Burke 30/5) Ray Bailey

Placings:2110-0000 **(6678)**
2009: 6^{0}GF, 6^{0}G, 6^{0}G, 6^{0}G,

	Starts	1st	2nd	3rd	Win & Pl
Career Total (Turf)	8	2	1	0	27954

101 9/08 Ayr 5f HVY £19869
97 8/08 Ripn 5f G-S £6542
Total win prize-money £26413

Going (Turf): **Sf: 1-1 GS: 1-2** Gd: 0-3 GF: 0-2 Fm: 0-0
Distance: **5f/6f: 2-8** 7f-8f: 0-0 9f-13f: 0-0 14f+: 0-0
Track : LH: 0-1 RH: 0-0 Tight: 0-0 Gall: 0-0
Aids: Bl: 0-0 Vi: 0-0 Tstrap: 0-1 Ckp: 0-1
Best Rating: **101** 9/08 Ayr 5f heavy

Very useful; Listed winner; effective over 5f and acts on soft ground; has worn cheekpieces.

Magic Cloud

99(94) (61)**66**
4-y-o b g Cloudings (IRE)-Magic Orb (Primo Dominie)
John Joseph Hanlon Magestic Syndicate

Placings:60635/**555**15400**0**-30600 **(6783)**
2009: 7^{3}SD, 8^{0}G, 7^{6}GF, 6^{0}G, 7^{0}SS,

	Starts	1st	2nd	3rd	Win & Pl
Career Total (Turf)	12	1	0	1	5251
Career Total (AW)	7	0	0	1	551

63 5/08 Gowr 7f (45-65)H G-F £4318
Total win prize-money £4319

Going (Turf): Sf: 0-1 GS: 0-0 Gd: 0-4 **GF: 1-3** Fm: 0-1
Distance: 5f/6f: 0-1 **7f-8f: 1-15** 9f-13f: 0-3 14f+: 0-0
Track : LH: 0-11 **RH: 1-7** Tight: 0-1 Gall: 0-0
Aids: Bl: 0-4 Vi: 0-0 Tstrap: 0-4 Ckp: 0-4
Best Rating: **66** 6/08 Leop 7f gd-fm

Magic Doll (USA)

95(96) (78)**72**
2-y-o ch f Elusive Quality (USA)-Meniatarra (USA) (Zilzal (USA))
Saeed Bin Suroor Godolphin

Placings:31 **(6164)**
2009: 7^{3}G, 7^{1}SD,

	Starts	1st	2nd	3rd	Win & Pl
Career Total (Turf)	1	0	0	1	722
Career Total (AW)	1	1	0	0	4695

78 9/09 Kemp 7f STD £4695
Total win prize-money £4695

Going (Turf): **Sf: 0-0 GS: 0-0 Gd: 0-1 GF: 0-0 Fm: 0-0**
Distance: 5f/6f: 0-0 **7f-8f: 1-2** 9f-13f: 0-0 14f+: 0-0
Track : LH: 0-0 **RH: 1-1** Tight: 0-0 Gall: 0-0
Aids: Bl: 0-0 Vi: 0-0 Tstrap: 0-0 Ckp: 0-0
Best Rating: **78** 9/09 Kemp 7f stand

Half-sister to the smart miler Menokee; effective at 7f; acts on good ground and Polytrack.

Magic Echo

104(100) (88)**92**
5-y-o b m Wizard King-Sunday News'N'Echo (USA) (Trempolino (USA))
M Dods D C Batey

Placings:16/33115026/**514**134620-002406550 **(6986)**
2009: 10^{0}GF, 9^{0}GF, 8^{2}GS, 10^{4}GS, 10^{0}G, 9^{6}HY, 7^{5}S, 8^{5}G, 10^{0}G,

	Starts	1st	2nd	3rd	Win & Pl
Career Total (Turf)	26	4	3	3	29061
Career Total (AW)	2	1	0	0	5546

92 6/08 Donc 1m2f60y (0-85)H G-S £6476
88 4/08 Sthl 1m (0-85)H STD £5180
82 6/07 Bevl 1m1f207y (0-85)H G-S £6477
82 6/07 Nott 1m1f213y (0-75)H G-F £3238
69 10/06 Newc 7f SFT £3238
Total win prize-money £24612

Going (Turf): Sf: 1-9 **GS: 2-7** Gd: 0-6 GF: 1-4 Fm: 0-0
Distance: 5f/6f: 0-0 7f-8f: 2-8 **9f-13f: 3-20** 14f+: 0-0
Track : **LH: 3-18** RH: 1-7 Tight: 0-5 **Gall: 1-8**
Aids: Bl: 0-0 Vi: 0-0 Tstrap: 0-0 Ckp: 0-0
Best Rating: **92** 6/08 Donc 1m2f60y gd-sft

Useful; effective over 1m-1m2f; acts on most ground, including sand.

Magic Footsteps

90 **72**
2-y-o b c Footstepsinthesand-Dayville (USA) (Dayjur (USA))
Jedd O'Keeffe Ken And Delia Shaw-KGS Consulting LLP

Placings:02 **(2623)**
2009: 6^{0}G, 6^{2}GF,

	Starts	1st	2nd	3rd	Win & Pl
Career Total (Turf)	2	0	1	0	771

Going (Turf): **Sf: 0-0 GS: 0-0 Gd: 0-1 GF: 0-1 Fm: 0-0**
Distance: 5f/6f: 0-1 7f-8f: 0-1 9f-13f: 0-0 14f+: 0-0
Track : LH: 0-0 RH: 0-0 Tight: 0-0 Gall: 0-0
Aids: Bl: 0-0 Vi: 0-0 Tstrap: 0-0 Ckp: 0-0
Best Rating: **72** 6/09 Haml 6f5y gd-fm

Magic Glade

67(102) (74)**72**
10-y-o b g Magic Ring (IRE)-Ash Glade (Nashwan (USA))
Peter Grayson Peter Grayson Racing Clubs Limited

Placings:31323/**00**/**0121**300**356213**/**23**00240400**0006**/**6600** 61003/**1351**1003140003**211300**/**5005**000**053-66006**00 **(3386)**
2009: 6^{6}SD, 5^{6}SD, 5^{0}SD, 5^{0}SD, 5^{6}SD, 5^{0}SD, 5^{0}GF,

	Starts	1st	2nd	3rd	Win & Pl
Career Total (Turf)	32	3	2	7	63790
Career Total (AW)	47	8	4	6	47752

80 11/07 Wolv 5f216y STD £1943
72 10/07 Kemp 6f STD £2047
93 5/07 Thsk 5f (0-100)H GD £11658
94 2/07 Ling 5f (0-85)H STD £4857
87 2/07 Sthl 6f SLW £2184
87 1/07 Sthl 5f (0-85)H STD £4857
88 6/06 Ches 5f16y (0-85)H GD £6153
90 12/04 Sthl 5f (0-92)H STD £6734
93 4/04 Muss 5f C(0-100)H G-F £13754
85 2/04 Sthl 5f D(0-80)H STD £4017
89 7/02 Wolv 6f F STD £2786
Total win prize-money £60994

Going (Turf): Sf: 0-4 GS: 0-1 **Gd: 2-11** GF: 1-16 Fm: 0-0
Distance: **5f/6f: 11-78** 7f-8f: 0-1 9f-13f: 0-0 14f+: 0-0
Track : **LH: 5-33** RH: 1-4 **Tight: 4-29** Gall: 0-1
Aids: Bl: 0-6 Vi: 0-0 Tstrap: 0-4 Ckp: 0-4
Best Rating: **95** 8/07 Gdwd 5f good

Modest; effective over 5f-6f; acts on fast ground; also goes on sand.

Magic Haze

94 **58**
3-y-o b g Makbul-Turn Back (Pivotal)
Miss S E Hall Mrs Joan Hodgson

Placings:604-600 **(6217)**
2009: 7^{6}GF, 9^{0}G, 8^{0}GF,

	Starts	1st	2nd	3rd	Win & Pl
Career Total (Turf)	6	0	0	0	265

Going (Turf): **Sf: 0-1 GS: 0-1 Gd: 0-2 GF: 0-2 Fm: 0-0**

Distance: 5f/6f: 0-2 7f-8f: 0-3 9f-13f: 0-1 14f+: 0-0
Track : LH: 0-1 RH: 0-1 Tight: 0-1 Gall: 0-0
Aids: Bl: 0-0 Vi: 0-0 Tstrap: 0-0 Ckp: 0-0
Best Rating: 58 7/09 Rdcr 7f gd-fm

Magic Kahyasi (IRE)

(97) (53)**68**
6-y-o b g Kahyasi-Magic Play (IRE) (Deploy)
G L Moore R Henderson

Placings:0/34004060006/066120130000/00 **(0502)**
2009: 16^{0}SD, 16^{0}SD,

	Starts	1st	2nd	3rd	Win & Pl
Career Total (Turf)	23	2	1	2	12602
Career Total (AW)	3	0	0	0	

Total win prize-money £6419

Going (Turf): Sf: 0-10 GS: 0-3 Gd: 0-4 GF: 0-0 Fm: 0-0
Distance: 5f/6f: 0-0 7f-8f: 0-0 **9f-13f: 2-19** 14f+: 0-7
Track : LH: 0-3 RH: 0-1 Tight: 0-2 Gall: 0-0
Aids: Bl: 0-4 Vi: 0-0 Tstrap: 0-1 Ckp: 0-1
Best Rating: 68 7/06 Deau 1m7f soft

Magic Lantern

96(94) (76)**75**
2-y-o ch f Halling (USA)-Papabile (USA) (Chief's Crown (USA))
R Hannon John Manley

Placings:022005 **(6722)**
2009: 6^{0}GF, 7^{2}SD, 6^{2}GF, 8^{0}G, 6^{0}G, 6^{5}SD,

	Starts	1st	2nd	3rd	Win & Pl
Career Total (Turf)	4	0	1	0	867
Career Total (AW)	2	0	1	0	1493

Going (Turf): Sf: 0-0 GS: 0-0 Gd: 0-2 GF: 0-2 Fm: 0-0
Distance: 5f/6f: 0-1 7f-8f: 0-5 9f-13f: 0-0 14f+: 0-0
Track : LH: 0-0 RH: 0-3 Tight: 0-0 Gall: 0-0
Aids: Bl: 0-0 Vi: 0-0 Tstrap: 0-0 Ckp: 0-0
Best Rating: 76 7/09 Kemp 7f stand

Fair; stays 7f; acts on fast ground and Polytrack.

Magic Millie (IRE)

89 **52**
2-y-o b/br f Marju (IRE)-Fille De La Terre (IRE) (Namaqualand (USA))
J Hetherton R Fell & K Everitt

Placings:0000 **(5981)**
2009: 7^{0}G, 6^{0}GF, 7^{0}GF, 7^{0}GF,

	Starts	1st	2nd	3rd	Win & Pl
Career Total (Turf)	4	0	0	0	

Going (Turf): Sf: 0-0 GS: 0-0 Gd: 0-1 GF: 0-3 Fm: 0-0
Distance: 5f/6f: 0-1 7f-8f: 0-3 9f-13f: 0-0 14f+: 0-0
Track : LH: 0-0 RH: 0-1 Tight: 0-0 Gall: 0-0
Aids: Bl: 0-0 Vi: 0-0 Tstrap: 0-0 Ckp: 0-0
Best Rating: 52 7/09 Donc 7f good

Magic Place

2-y-o b c Compton Place-Michelle Shift (Night Shift (USA))
R Hannon I A N Wight

Placings:0 **(7289)**
2009: 6^{0}S,

	Starts	1st	2nd	3rd	Win & Pl
Career Total (Turf)	1	0	0	0	

Going (Turf): Sf: 0-1 GS: 0-0 Gd: 0-0 GF: 0-0 Fm: 0-0
Distance: 5f/6f: 0-1 7f-8f: 0-0 9f-13f: 0-0 14f+: 0-0
Track : LH: 0-0 RH: 0-0 Tight: 0-0 Gall: 0-0
Aids: Bl: 0-0 Vi: 0-0 Tstrap: 0-0 Ckp: 0-0

Magic Queen (IRE)

84(88) (52)**39**
3-y-o b f Aptitude (USA)-Second Wind (USA) (Hennessy (USA))
A P Jarvis Philip Milburn

Placings:56000 **(7240)**
2009: 7^{5}GF, 7^{6}SD, 7^{0}SD, 9^{0}SD, 7^{0}SD,

	Starts	1st	2nd	3rd	Win & Pl
Career Total (Turf)	1	0	0	0	0
Career Total (AW)	4	0	0	0	0

Going (Turf): Sf: 0-0 GS: 0-0 Gd: 0-0 GF: 0-1 Fm: 0-0
Distance: 5f/6f: 0-0 7f-8f: 0-4 9f-13f: 0-1 14f+: 0-0
Track : LH: 0-3 RH: 0-2 Tight: 0-3 Gall: 0-0
Aids: Bl: 0-0 Vi: 0-0 Tstrap: 0-0 Ckp: 0-0
Best Rating: 52 10/09 Wolv 7f32y stand

Magic Rush

92(106) (78)**71**
7-y-o b g Almaty (IRE)-Magic Legs (Reprimand)
Norma Twomey Kine,Antell,Donovan,Twomey

Placings:323156030/6020/44-62253 **(5095)**
2009: 8^{6}SD, 7^{2}SD, 9^{2}GF, 8^{5}F, 8^{3}SD,

	Starts	1st	2nd	3rd	Win & Pl
Career Total (Turf)	5	0	1	1	1252
Career Total (AW)	15	1	3	3	9167

88	8/06	Wolv	7f32y	(0-75)H	STD	£3238

Total win prize-money £3239

Going (Turf): Sf: 0-1 GS: 0-0 Gd: 0-1 GF: 0-2 Fm: 0-1
Distance: 5f/6f: 0-3 **7f-8f: 1-14** 9f-13f: 0-3 14f+: 0-0
Track : **LH: 1-12** RH: 0-6 **Tight: 1-10** Gall: 0-0
Aids: Bl: 0-0 Vi: 0-0 Tstrap: 0-0 Ckp: 0-0
Best Rating: 88 8/06 Wolv 7f32y stand

Modest; stays 7f; acts on Polytrack.

Magic Spirit

(85) (62)
2-y-o ch f Kirkwall-Flaming Spirt (Blushing Flame (USA))
J S Moore Bill Wyatt

Placings:0 **(7622)**
2009: 8^{0}SD,

	Starts	1st	2nd	3rd	Win & Pl
Career Total (Turf)	0	0	0	0	
Career Total (AW)	1	0	0	0	

Going (Turf): Sf: 0-0 GS: 0-0 Gd: 0-0 GF: 0-0 Fm: 0-0
Distance: 5f/6f: 0-0 7f-8f: 0-1 9f-13f: 0-0 14f+: 0-0
Track : LH: 0-1 RH: 0-0 Tight: 0-1 Gall: 0-0
Aids: Bl: 0-0 Vi: 0-0 Tstrap: 0-0 Ckp: 0-0
Best Rating: 62 12/09 Ling 1m stand

Magic Warrior

92(99) (69)**53**
9-y-o b g Magic Ring (IRE)-Clarista (USA) (Riva Ridge (USA))
J C Fox John Lonergan

Placings:6060136/500505/346000/606111040/602124134 10501041/005322365560053614/54303505425-350020P650 **(5211)**
2009: 10^{3}SD, 8^{5}SD, 9^{0}SD, 8^{0}SD, 9^{2}SD, 10^{0}SD, 10^{P}F, 9^{6}GF, 9^{5}GF, 8^{0}G,

	Starts	1st	2nd	3rd	Win & Pl
Career Total (Turf)	22	2	0	0	5261
Career Total (AW)	63	8	6	9	26175

69	12/07	Wolv	1m1f103y	(0-65)H	STD	£2218
73	12/06	Kemp	1m	(0-70)H	STD	£3886
69	11/06	Kemp	1m	(0-63)H	STD	£2388
69	8/06	Kemp	1m	(0-65)H	STD	£3238
61	6/06	Leic	1m60y	(0-60)H	G-F	£3238
65	5/06	Wolv	1m141y	(0-45)	STD	£1876
62	9/05	Ling	1m2f	(0-45)	STD	£1494
59	9/05	Wolv	1m141y	(0-45)	STD	£1508
53	8/05	Leic	1m60y	(0-45)	GD	£1491
65	11/02	Ling	6f	G	STD	£2240

Total win prize-money £23583

Going (Turf): Sf: 0-1 GS: 0-3 **Gd: 1-6 GF: 1-9** Fm: 0-3
Distance: 5f/6f: 1-6 7f-8f: 3-34 **9f-13f: 6-45** 14f+: 0-0
Track : LH: 5-47 RH: 5-31 **Tight: 5-42** Gall: 0-4
Aids: Bl: 0-1 Vi: 0-0 Tstrap: 0-0 Ckp: 0-0
Best Rating: 74 4/07 Ling 1m stand

Moderate; effective over 1m-1m2f; acts on good ground; also goes on Polytrack.

Magical Destiny (IRE)

(95) (69)
3-y-o b g Exceed And Excel (AUS)-Magic Lady (IRE) (Bigstone (IRE))
B Smart Alan Zheng

Placings:53-4 **(0855)**
2009: 8^{4}SD,

	Starts	1st	2nd	3rd	Win & Pl
Career Total (Turf)	0	0	0	0	
Career Total (AW)	3	0	0	1	596

Going (Turf): Sf: 0-0 GS: 0-0 Gd: 0-0 GF: 0-0 Fm: 0-0
Distance: 5f/6f: 0-0 7f-8f: 0-3 9f-13f: 0-0 14f+: 0-0
Track : LH: 0-3 RH: 0-0 Tight: 0-0 Gall: 0-0
Aids: Bl: 0-0 Vi: 0-0 Tstrap: 0-0 Ckp: 0-0
Best Rating: 69 11/08 Sthl 7f stand

Modest; effective over 7f; acts on Fibresand.

Magical Macey (USA)

92 **80**
2-y-o ch g Rossini (USA)-Spring's Glory (USA) (Honour And Glory (USA))
T D Barron K J Alderson

Placings:0210 **(7115)**
2009: 5^{0}GF, 5^{2}S, 5^{1}GF, 5^{0}GS,

	Starts	1st	2nd	3rd	Win & Pl
Career Total (Turf)	4	1	1	0	4893

80	9/09	Hayd	5f	G-F	£3885

Total win prize-money £3886

Going (Turf): Sf: 0-1 GS: 0-1 Gd: 0-0 **GF: 1-2** Fm: 0-0
Distance: **5f/6f: 1-4** 7f-8f: 0-0 9f-13f: 0-0 14f+: 0-0
Track : LH: 0-0 RH: 0-0 Tight: 0-0 Gall: 0-0
Aids: **Bl: 1-3** Vi: 0-0 Tstrap: 0-0 Ckp: 0-0
Best Rating: **80** 9/09 Hayd 5f gd-fm

Useful; effective at 5f on fast ground; has worn blinkers.

Magical Mimi

(86) (30)
8-y-o b m Magic Ring (IRE)-Naval Dispatch (Slip Anchor)
K G Wingrove L T Woodhouse

Placings:5130/00045050/**006000/16000/0000** (0682)
2009: 5^{0}SD, 5^{0}SD, 9^{0}SD, 8^{0}SF,

	Starts	1st	2nd	3rd	Win & Pl
Career Total (Turf)	14	1	0	1	13484
Career Total (AW)	13	1	0	0	2389

55	3/06	Wolv	5f216y		STD	£2388
71	9/03	Nott	6f15y	D	G-F	£3087

Total win prize-money £5476

Going (Turf): Sf: 0-0 GS: 0-1 Gd: 0-3 **GF: 1-9** Fm: 0-1
Distance: 5f/6f: 1-9 7f-8f: 1-10 9f-13f: 0-8 14f+: 0-0
Track : **LH: 1-20** RH: 0-2 **Tight: 1-15** Gall: 0-1
Aids: Bl: 0-3 Vi: 0-0 Tstrap: 0-0 Ckp: 0-0
Best Rating: **72** 10/03 Newb 7f gd-fm

Magical Molecule

2-y-o b g Whittingham (IRE)-Fontaine House (Pyramus (USA))
G D Blake G Blake

Placings:6 (2887)
2009: 5^{6}G,

	Starts	1st	2nd	3rd	Win & Pl
Career Total (Turf)	1	0	0	0	0

Going (Turf): **Sf: 0-0 GS: 0-0 Gd: 0-1 GF: 0-0 Fm: 0-0**
Distance: 5f/6f: 0-1 7f-8f: 0-0 9f-13f: 0-0 14f+: 0-0
Track : LH: 0-0 RH: 0-0 Tight: 0-0 Gall: 0-0
Aids: Bl: 0-0 Vi: 0-0 Tstrap: 0-0 Ckp: 0-0

Magical Song

100(99) (59)58
4-y-o ch g Forzando-Classical Song (IRE) (Fayruz)
J Balding (R Curtis 20/1) Peter Balding

Placings:6000/61016020056060243306422 (3852)
2009: 7^{0}SS, 7^{2}SD, 7^{4}SD, 8^{3}SD, 8^{3}SD, 7^{0}SD, 7^{6}SD, 7^{4}GF, 6^{2}GF, 6^{2}GF,

	Starts	1st	2nd	3rd	Win & Pl
Career Total (Turf)	7	0	3	0	2236
Career Total (AW)	20	2	1	2	4981

56	2/08	Sthl	7f	(0-65)H	SS	£1911
49	1/08	Sthl	1m	(0-60)H	STD	£1911

Total win prize-money £3822

Going (Turf): **Sf: 0-2 GS: 0-1 Gd: 0-0 GF: 0-3 Fm: 0-1**
Distance: 5f/6f: 0-4 **7f-8f: 2-19** 9f-13f: 0-4 14f+: 0-0
Track : **LH: 2-24** RH: 0-0 Tight: 0-7 Gall: 0-0
Aids: Bl: 0-9 Vi: 0-0 Tstrap: 0-4 Ckp: 0-4
Best Rating: **59** 3/09 Sthl 1m stand

Moderate; effective at around 7f-1m; acts on soft ground; also goes on Fibresand.

Magical Speedfit (IRE)

104(99) (77)78
4-y-o ch g Bold Fact (USA)-Magical Peace (IRE) (Magical Wonder (USA))
G G Margarson John Guest

Placings:220234200/2610404205020440-100400302426313 (7123)
2009: 5^{1}G, 5^{0}GF, 5^{0}GF, 5^{4}GF, 5^{0}G, 5^{0}G, 5^{3}GF, 6^{0}GF, 5^{2}GF, 5^{4}GF, 5^{2}F, 5^{6}GF, 5^{3}GS, 5^{1}G, 5^{3}G,

	Starts	1st	2nd	3rd	Win & Pl
Career Total (Turf)	38	3	9	4	24026
Career Total (AW)	2	0	0	0	192

76	10/09	Brig	5f59y	(0-75)H	GD	£3280
78	4/09	Brig	5f59y	(0-85)H	GD	£5504
76	5/08	Brig	5f59y	(0-75)H	G-F	£2784

Total win prize-money £11570

Going (Turf): Sf: 0-2 GS: 0-2 **Gd: 2-10** GF: 1-22 Fm: 0-2
Distance: **5f/6f: 3-40** 7f-8f: 0-0 9f-13f: 0-0 14f+: 0-0
Track : **LH: 3-11** RH: 0-1 Tight: 0-1 Gall: 0-7
Aids: Bl: 0-1 Vi: 0-0 Tstrap: 0-0 Ckp: 0-0
Best Rating: **78** 4/09 Brig 5f59y good

Fair; effective over 5f; acts on good and softer ground.

Magicalmysterytour (IRE)

105 106
6-y-o b g Sadler's Wells (USA)-Jude (Darshaan)
W J Musson Broughton Thermal Insulation

Placings:221600/03201/100-52300060 (7293)
2009: 13^{5}S, 11^{2}GF, 14^{3}GF, 14^{0}GF, 14^{0}S, 12^{0}GS, 12^{6}GS, 12^{0}S,

	Starts	1st	2nd	3rd	Win & Pl
Career Total (Turf)	22	3	4	2	42036

104	9/08	Donc	1m4f	(0-105)H	SFT	£12952
97	8/07	Newb	1m5f61y	(0-90)H	GD	£7124
84	6/06	Leop	1m4f		G-F	£7148

Total win prize-money £27225

Going (Turf): **Sf: 1-6** GS: 0-4 **Gd: 1-3 GF: 1-7** Fm: 0-0
Distance: 5f/6f: 0-0 7f-8f: 0-0 **9f-13f: 2-17** 14f+: 1-5
Track : **LH: 3-11** RH: 0-9 Tight: 0-3 **Gall: 2-13**
Aids: Bl: 0-0 Vi: 0-0 Tstrap: 0-0 Ckp: 0-0
Best Rating: **106** 7/09 York 1m6f gd-fm

Very useful; Listed placed; stays 1m6f; seems to act on most ground.

Magician's Cape (IRE)

94(96) (85)79
2-y-o b c Montjeu (IRE)-Seven Magicians (USA) (Silver Hawk (USA))
Sir Michael Stoute Niarchos Family

Placings:13 (6779)
2009: 7^{1}GS, 8^{3}SS,

	Starts	1st	2nd	3rd	Win & Pl
Career Total (Turf)	1	1	0	0	3562
Career Total (AW)	1	0	0	1	770

79	9/09	Ling	7f	G-S	£3561

Total win prize-money £3562

Going (Turf): Sf: 0-0 **GS: 1-1** Gd: 0-0 GF: 0-0 Fm: 0-0
Distance: 5f/6f: 0-0 **7f-8f: 1-2** 9f-13f: 0-0 14f+: 0-0
Track : LH: 0-1 RH: 0-0 Tight: 0-1 Gall: 0-0
Aids: Bl: 0-0 Vi: 0-0 Tstrap: 0-0 Ckp: 0-0
Best Rating: **85** 10/09 Ling 1m std-slw

Useful; stays 7f and acts on easy ground.

Magistrate (IRE)

(95) (60)
4-y-o b g Nayef (USA)-Alabastrine (Green Desert (USA))
Andrew Turnell Miss S Douglas-Pennant

Placings:05 (7367)
2009: 9^{0}SD, 12^{5}SD,

	Starts	1st	2nd	3rd	Win & Pl
Career Total (Turf)	0	0	0	0	
Career Total (AW)	2	0	0	0	0

Going (Turf): **Sf: 0-0 GS: 0-0 Gd: 0-0 GF: 0-0 Fm: 0-0**
Distance: 5f/6f: 0-0 7f-8f: 0-0 9f-13f: 0-2 14f+: 0-0
Track : LH: 0-2 RH: 0-0 Tight: 0-2 Gall: 0-0
Aids: Bl: 0-0 Vi: 0-0 Tstrap: 0-0 Ckp: 0-0
Best Rating: **60** 11/09 Ling 1m4f stand

Magners Hill (IRE)

100(99) (69)53
5-y-o b g Desert Sun-Tropicana (IRE) (Imperial Frontier (USA))
Gerard Keane Yes We Can Syndicate

Placings:42-36060000 (7733)
2009: 8^{3}SD, 12^{6}SW, 10^{0}SD, 10^{6}HY, 10^{0}HY, 10^{0}GF, 9^{0}SD, 12^{0}SD,

	Starts	1st	2nd	3rd	Win & Pl
Career Total (Turf)	3	0	0	0	
Career Total (AW)	7	0	1	1	1486

Going (Turf): **Sf: 0-2 GS: 0-0 Gd: 0-0 GF: 0-1 Fm: 0-0**
Distance: 5f/6f: 0-0 7f-8f: 0-0 9f-13f: 0-10 14f+: 0-0
Track : LH: 0-8 RH: 0-2 Tight: 0-4 Gall: 0-0
Aids: Bl: 0-0 Vi: 0-0 Tstrap: 0-0 Ckp: 0-0
Best Rating: **69** 11/08 Dund 1m2f150y stand

Modest; stays 1m2f; acts on Polytrack.

Magnetic Force (IRE)

93(94) (73)73
2-y-o gr g Verglas (IRE)-Upperville (IRE) (Selkirk (USA))
Sir Michael Stoute Saeed Suhail

Placings:632 (6607)
2009: 7^{6}GF, 8^{3}GF, 8^{2}SD,

	Starts	1st	2nd	3rd	Win & Pl
Career Total (Turf)	2	0	0	1	722
Career Total (AW)	1	0	1	0	605

Going (Turf): **Sf: 0-0 GS: 0-0 Gd: 0-0 GF: 0-2 Fm: 0-0**
Distance: 5f/6f: 0-0 7f-8f: 0-3 9f-13f: 0-0 14f+: 0-0
Track : LH: 0-0 RH: 0-3 Tight: 0-0 Gall: 0-0
Aids: Bl: 0-0 Vi: 0-0 Tstrap: 0-0 Ckp: 0-0
Best Rating: **73** 10/09 Kemp 1m stand

Fair; stays 1m and acts on fast ground.

Magneto (IRE)

87(92) (60)53
2-y-o b g Fasliyev (USA)-Shashana (IRE) (King's Best (USA))
E J Creighton The Vixens

Placings:00604043060 (7235)
2009: 5^{0}SD, 5^{0}SD, 5^{6}GF, 5^{0}F, 6^{4}GF, 6^{0}SD, 7^{4}SD, 8^{3}SD, 7^{0}SF, 8^{6}GF, 8^{0}SD,

	Starts	1st	2nd	3rd	Win & Pl
Career Total (Turf)	4	0	0	0	144
Career Total (AW)	7	0	0	1	403

Going (Turf): Sf: 0-0 GS: 0-0 Gd: 0-0 GF: 0-3 Fm: 0-1
Distance: 5f/6f: 0-5 7f-8f: 0-4 9f-13f: 0-2 14f+: 0-0
Track : LH: 0-5 RH: 0-2 Tight: 0-3 Gall: 0-1
Aids: Bl: 0-0 Vi: 0-0 Tstrap: 0-0 Ckp: 0-0
Best Rating: 60 10/09 Wolv 1m141y stand

Magnificence

91(84) (55)60
2-y-o gr f Sadler's Wells (USA)-Doctor's Glory (USA) (Elmaamul (USA))
Sir Michael Stoute Cheveley Park Stud

Placings:60555 (6923)
2009: 7^{6}S, 6^{0}S, 6^{5}GF, 7^{5}SD, 8^{5}GF,

	Starts	1st	2nd	3rd	Win & Pl
Career Total (Turf)	4	0	0	0	150
Career Total (AW)	1	0	0	0	0

Going (Turf): Sf: 0-2 GS: 0-0 Gd: 0-0 GF: 0-2 Fm: 0-0
Distance: 5f/6f: 0-0 7f-8f: 0-4 9f-13f: 0-1 14f+: 0-0
Track : LH: 0-0 RH: 0-1 Tight: 0-0 Gall: 0-0
Aids: Bl: 0-0 Vi: 0-0 Tstrap: 0-0 Ckp: 0-0
Best Rating: 60 9/09 Sals 6f212y soft

Modest; stays 7f; acts on Polytrack and fast ground.

Magnifico (FR)

(76) (28)
8-y-o b g Solid Illusion (USA)-Born For Run (FR) (Pharly (FR))
P D Evans (Mrs K Waldron 27/7) Nick Shutts

Placings:4/6/00 (1439)
2009: 9^{0}SD, 16^{0}SD,

	Starts	1st	2nd	3rd	Win & Pl
Career Total (Turf)	1	0	0	0	638
Career Total (AW)	3	0	0	0	0

Going (Turf): Sf: 0-1 GS: 0-0 Gd: 0-0 GF: 0-0 Fm: 0-0
Distance: 5f/6f: 0-0 7f-8f: 0-0 9f-13f: 0-1 14f+: 0-3
Track : LH: 0-3 RH: 0-0 Tight: 0-2 Gall: 0-0
Aids: Bl: 0-0 Vi: 0-0 Tstrap: 0-1 Ckp: 0-1
Best Rating: 33 1/07 Wolv 1m5f194y std-slw

Magnitude

97(103) (71)84
4-y-o ch g Pivotal-Miswaki Belle (USA) (Miswaki (USA))
M E Rimmer (G L Moore 28/4) Ady Boughen

Placings:1104-504003540040 (7695)
2009: 8^{5}SD, 8^{0}SD, 8^{4}SD, 10^{0}G, 10^{0}GF, 7^{3}GF, 8^{5}G, 8^{4}GS, 9^{0}S, 8^{0}G, 6^{4}F, 12^{0}SD,

	Starts	1st	2nd	3rd	Win & Pl
Career Total (Turf)	12	2	0	1	9424
Career Total (AW)	4	0	0	0	0

84 4/08 Yarm 7f3y (0-85)H G-F £4533
82 3/08 Wwck 7f26y SFT £3412
Total win prize-money £7946

Going (Turf): Sf: 1-2 GS: 0-2 Gd: 0-3 GF: 1-4 Fm: 0-1
Distance: 5f/6f: 0-0 7f-8f: 2-10 9f-13f: 0-6 14f+: 0-0
Track : LH: 1-8 RH: 0-3 Tight: 0-7 Gall: 0-0
Aids: Bl: 0-3 Vi: 0-0 Tstrap: 0-2 Ckp: 0-2
Best Rating: 84 4/08 Yarm 7f3y gd-fm

Useful; effective over 7f; acts on fast and soft ground.

Magnus Thrax (USA)

97(99) (81)81
2-y-o b c Roman Ruler (USA)-Wild Catseye (USA) (Forest Wildcat (USA))
R Hannon Michael Pescod

Placings:01064 (7063)
2009: 6^{0}GF, 6^{1}G, 6^{0}GF, 7^{6}GF, 6^{4}SD,

	Starts	1st	2nd	3rd	Win & Pl
Career Total (Turf)	4	1	0	0	14970
Career Total (AW)	1	0	0	0	289

76 8/09 Chep 6f16y GD £2719
Total win prize-money £2720

Going (Turf): Sf: 0-0 GS: 0-0 Gd: 1-1 GF: 0-3 Fm: 0-0
Distance: 5f/6f: 0-2 7f-8f: 1-3 9f-13f: 0-0 14f+: 0-0
Track : LH: 0-1 RH: 0-0 Tight: 0-1 Gall: 0-0
Aids: Bl: 0-0 Vi: 0-0 Tstrap: 0-0 Ckp: 0-0
Best Rating: 81 10/09 Ling 6f stand

Fair; effective at 6f on a sound surface.

Magroom

103(97) (72)75
5-y-o b g Compton Place-Fudge (Polar Falcon (USA))
R J Hodges Mrs A Hart Mrs A Hodges Mrs C Penny

Placings:00001124350142120/0232004200-06266210212444 (7153)
2009: 7^{0}GF, 8^{6}GF, 8^{2}F, 8^{6}GF, 6^{8}GF, 8^{2}GF, 9^{1}GF, 10^{0}GF, 8^{2}GS, 8^{1}G, 7^{2}GF, 8^{4}G, 8^{4}GS, 8^{4}SD,

	Starts	1st	2nd	3rd	Win & Pl
Career Total (Turf)	33	5	9	2	23717
Career Total (AW)	8	1	1	0	845

73 9/09 Chep 1m14y (0-65)H GD £2072
69 8/09 Newb 1m1f (0-70)H G-F £2590
64 10/07 Bath 1m5y (0-70)H G-F £3886
58 6/07 Brig 6f209y G-F £1943
54 5/07 Brig 6f209y GD £1943
Total win prize-money £12434

Going (Turf): Sf: 0-2 GS: 0-5 Gd: 2-7 GF: 3-15 Fm: 0-4
Distance: 5f/6f: 0-1 7f-8f: 3-20 9f-13f: 3-20 14f+: 0-0
Track : LH: 5-28 RH: 0-6 Tight: 2-18 Gall: 1-1
Aids: Bl: 0-0 Vi: 2-5 Tstrap: 0-1 Ckp: 0-1
Best Rating: 75 8/08 Bath 1m5y good

Modest; effective over 7f-1m; acts on most ground on turf; goes on Polytrack.

Mahadee (IRE)

97(109) (105)86
4-y-o br g Cape Cross (IRE)-Rafiya (Halling (USA))
C E Brittain Saeed Manana

Placings:00200/4400216121410-1404013000 (5863)
2009: 8^{1}SD, 8^{4}SD, 7^{0}SD, 8^{4}SD, 10^{0}SD, 8^{1}SD, 8^{3}SD, 8^{0}GF, 8^{0}GS, 8^{0}GF,

	Starts	1st	2nd	3rd	Win & Pl
Career Total (Turf)	13	1	2	0	4939
Career Total (AW)	15	5	1	1	45504

105 4/09 Kemp 1m (0-105)H STD £11527
101 1/09 Wolv 1m141y STD £12462
95 11/08 GrLe 1m (0-85)H STD £5180
85 10/08 GrLe 1m2f (0-85)H STD £4857
79 9/08 Sthl 1m (0-75)H STD £3691
71 7/08 Ling 1m2f (0-65)H G-F £2047
Total win prize-money £39765

Going (Turf): Sf: 0-1 GS: 0-1 Gd: 0-1 GF: 1-10 Fm: 0-0
Distance: 5f/6f: 0-0 7f-8f: 3-16 9f-13f: 3-12 14f+: 0-0
Track : LH: 5-15 RH: 1-10 Tight: 2-11 Gall: 2-5
Aids: Bl: 6-20 Vi: 0-0 Tstrap: 0-0 Ckp: 0-0
Best Rating: 105 4/09 Kemp 1m stand

Very useful; effective over 1m-1m2f; acts on fast ground and on sand; often wears blinkers.

Mahiki

87(92) (71)55
2-y-o ch f Compton Place-Sound Of Sleat (Primo Dominie)
S A Callaghan The Mahiki Partnership

Placings:56511006 (6494)
2009: 5^{5}GF, 5^{6}GF, 5^{5}G, 5^{1}SD, 5^{1}SD, 5^{0}SD, 5^{0}GF, 5^{6}SF,

	Starts	1st	2nd	3rd	Win & Pl
Career Total (Turf)	4	0	0	0	0
Career Total (AW)	4	2	0	0	4777

71 7/09 Sthl 5f STD £2729
63 7/09 Sthl 5f STD £2047
Total win prize-money £4777

Going (Turf): Sf: 0-0 GS: 0-0 Gd: 0-1 GF: 0-3 Fm: 0-0
Distance: 5f/6f: 2-8 7f-8f: 0-0 9f-13f: 0-0 14f+: 0-0
Track : LH: 0-3 RH: 0-0 Tight: 0-2 Gall: 0-0
Aids: Bl: 0-0 Vi: 0-0 Tstrap: 0-0 Ckp: 0-0
Best Rating: 71 7/09 Sthl 5f stand

Modest; effective over 5f; acts on Fibresand.

Mahjong Girl

89 62
2-y-o ch f Kirkwall-Gulchina (USA) (Gulch (USA))
R M Beckett J C Smith

Placings:004 (5498)
2009: 7^{0}GF, 7^{0}C, 8^{4}C,

	Starts	1st	2nd	3rd	Win & Pl
Career Total (Turf)	3	0	0	0	289

Going (Turf): Sf: 0-0 GS: 0-0 Gd: 0-2 GF: 0-1 Fm: 0-0
Distance: 5f/6f: 0-0 7f-8f: 0-2 9f-13f: 0-1 14f+: 0-0
Track : LH: 0-0 RH: 0-1 Tight: 0-0 Gall: 0-0
Aids: Bl: 0-0 Vi: 0-0 Tstrap: 0-0 Ckp: 0-0
Best Rating: 62 8/09 Chep 1m14y good

Mahlak (IRE)

80 50
2-y-o ch f Pastoral Pursuits-Bint Al Hammour (IRE) (Grand Lodge (USA))
C E Brittain Saeed Manana

Placings:0 (5397)
2009: 7^{0}GF,

	Starts	1st	2nd	3rd	Win & Pl
Career Total (Turf)	1	0	0	0	

Going (Turf): Sf: 0-0 GS: 0-0 Gd: 0-0 GF: 0-1 Fm: 0-0
Distance: 5f/6f: 0-0 7f-8f: 0-1 9f-13f: 0-0 14f+: 0-0
Track : LH: 0-0 RH: 0-0 Tight: 0-0 Gall: 0-0
Aids: Bl: 0-0 Vi: 0-0 Tstrap: 0-0 Ckp: 0-0
Best Rating: 50 8/09 NmkJ 7f gd-fm

Maid In Heaven (IRE)

(87) (58)
2-y-o b f Clodovil (IRE)-Serious Delight (Lomond (USA))
W R Swinburn Delightful Dozen

Placings:5 **(7326)**
2009: 7⁵SD,

	Starts	1st	2nd	3rd	Win & Pl
Career Total (Turf)	0	0	0	0	
Career Total (AW)	1	0	0	0	0

Going (Turf): **Sf: 0-0 GS: 0-0 Gd: 0-0 GF: 0-0 Fm: 0-0**
Distance: 5f/6f: 0-0 7f-8f: 0-1 9f-13f: 0-0 14f+: 0-0
Track : LH: 0-0 RH: 0-1 Tight: 0-0 Gall: 0-0
Aids: Bl: 0-0 Vi: 0-0 Tstrap: 0-0 Ckp: 0-0
Best Rating: **58** 11/09 Kemp 7f stand

Promising debut over 7f on Polytrack.

Maid Of Stone (IRE)

90(90) (54)**50**
3-y-o ch f Rock Of Gibraltar (IRE)-Gold Flair (Tap On Wood)
D R C Elsworth Ten Green Bottles Racing

Placings:40000 **(5403)**
2009: 10⁴GF, 11⁰SD, 8⁰S, 12⁰G, 7⁰G,

	Starts	1st	2nd	3rd	Win & Pl
Career Total (Turf)	4	0	0	0	0
Career Total (AW)	1	0	0	0	

Going (Turf): **Sf: 0-1 GS: 0-0 Gd: 0-2 GF: 0-1 Fm: 0-0**
Distance: 5f/6f: 0-0 7f-8f: 0-2 9f-13f: 0-3 14f+: 0-0
Track : LH: 0-1 RH: 0-2 Tight: 0-1 Gall: 0-1
Aids: Bl: 0-0 Vi: 0-0 Tstrap: 0-0 Ckp: 0-0
Best Rating: **54** 7/09 Kemp 1m3f stand

Maidanni (USA)

(81) (64)
7-y-o b/br g Private Terms (USA)-Carley's Birthday (USA) (Marfa (USA))
J R Gask Resurrection Partners

Placings:410/0/000 **(0823)**
2009: 9⁰SD, 13⁰SD, 8⁰SD,

	Starts	1st	2nd	3rd	Win & Pl
Career Total (Turf)	3	1	0	0	5682
Career Total (AW)	4	0	0	0	

77 10/04 York 7f205y GD £5346
Total win prize-money £5346

Going (Turf): Sf: 0-1 GS: 0-0 **Gd: 1-1** GF: 0-1 Fm: 0-0
Distance: 5f/6f: 0-0 **7f-8f: 1-5** 9f-13f: 0-2 14f+: 0-0
Track : **LH: 1-6** RH: 0-0 Tight: 0-3 **Gall: 1-2**
Aids: Bl: 0-1 Vi: 0-0 Tstrap: 0-0 Ckp: 0-0
Best Rating: **78** 9/04 NmkR 1m gd-fm

Maidtorun (IRE)

91 **67**
2-y-o ch f Rakti-Bayletta (IRE) (Woodborough (USA))
R A Fahey Mrs H Steel

Placings:5100 **(2800)**
2009: 5⁵GF, 5¹GF, 6⁰G, 5⁰F,

	Starts	1st	2nd	3rd	Win & Pl
Career Total (Turf)	4	1	0	0	1943

67 5/09 Bevl 5f G-F £1942
Total win prize-money £1943

Going (Turf): Sf: 0-0 GS: 0-0 Gd: 0-1 **GF: 1-2** Fm: 0-1
Distance: **5f/6f: 1-4** 7f-8f: 0-0 9f-13f: 0-0 14f+: 0-0
Track : LH: 0-1 RH: 0-0 Tight: 0-0 Gall: 0-0
Aids: Bl: 0-0 Vi: 0-0 Tstrap: 0-0 Ckp: 0-0
Best Rating: **67** 5/09 Bevl 5f gd-fm

Maigh Eo (IRE)

77(92) (51)**20**
3-y-o b g Elusive City (USA)-Princess Magdalena (Pennekamp (USA))
Patrick Morris Rob Lloyd Racing Limited

Placings:0-40006 **(4777)**
2009: 5⁴SD, 6⁰G, 5⁰GF, 5⁰SD, 5⁶GF,

	Starts	1st	2nd	3rd	Win & Pl
Career Total (Turf)	4	0	0	0	0
Career Total (AW)	2	0	0	0	192

Going (Turf): **Sf: 0-1 GS: 0-0 Gd: 0-1 GF: 0-2 Fm: 0-0**
Distance: 5f/6f: 0-6 7f-8f: 0-0 9f-13f: 0-0 14f+: 0-0
Track : LH: 0-1 RH: 0-1 Tight: 0-1 Gall: 0-0
Aids: Bl: 0-0 Vi: 0-0 Tstrap: 0-0 Ckp: 0-0
Best Rating: **51** 4/09 Kemp 5f stand

Main Aim

114 **123**
4-y-o b c Oasis Dream-Orford Ness (Selkirk (USA))
Sir Michael Stoute K Abdulla

Placings:113100-1142004 **(6848)**
2009: 6¹GS, 7¹G, 8⁴GF, 6²GF, 7⁰G, 6⁰GS, 7⁴G,

	Starts	1st	2nd	3rd	Win & Pl
Career Total (Turf)	13	5	1	1	183492

121 5/09 Hayd 7f30y GD £39739
119 5/09 Newb 6f8y (0-100)H G-S £12462
108 9/08 Donc 6f (0-90)H SFT £9714
96 7/08 Sand 7f16y (0-95)H G-F £9346
84 6/08 Sals 6f212y G-F £3399
Total win prize-money £74662

Going (Turf): Sf: 1-2 GS: 1-2 Gd: 1-3 **GF: 2-6** Fm: 0-0
Distance: 5f/6f: 1-5 **7f-8f: 4-8** 9f-13f: 0-0 14f+: 0-0
Track : LH: 1-1 RH: 1-3 Tight: 0-0 Gall: 0-0
Aids: Bl: 0-0 Vi: 0-0 Tstrap: 0-0 Ckp: 0-0
Best Rating: **123** 7/09 NmkJ 6f gd-fm

Group class; winner in Group 3 company and runner-up in the 2009 July Cup; effective over 6f-7f and acts on most ground.

Main Spring

(78) (41)
2-y-o b f Pivotal-Fairy Godmother (Fairy King (USA))
Sir Michael Stoute The Queen

Placings:0 **(7388)**
2009: 8⁰SD,

	Starts	1st	2nd	3rd	Win & Pl
Career Total (Turf)	0	0	0	0	
Career Total (AW)	1	0	0	0	

Going (Turf): **Sf: 0-0 GS: 0-0 Gd: 0-0 GF: 0-0 Fm: 0-0**
Distance: 5f/6f: 0-0 7f-8f: 0-1 9f-13f: 0-0 14f+: 0-0
Track : LH: 0-1 RH: 0-0 Tight: 0-1 Gall: 0-0
Aids: Bl: 0-0 Vi: 0-0 Tstrap: 0-0 Ckp: 0-0
Best Rating: **41** 11/09 Ling 1m stand

Mainstay

(99) (66)
3-y-o b f Elmaamul (USA)-Felucca (Green Desert (USA))
J H M Gosden Ms Rachel D S Hood

Placings:2 **(7452)**
2009: 8²SD,

	Starts	1st	2nd	3rd	Win & Pl
Career Total (Turf)	0	0	0	0	
Career Total (AW)	1	0	1	0	771

Going (Turf): **Sf: 0-0 GS: 0-0 Gd: 0-0 GF: 0-0 Fm: 0-0**
Distance: 5f/6f: 0-0 7f-8f: 0-1 9f-13f: 0-0 14f+: 0-0
Track : LH: 0-0 RH: 0-1 Tight: 0-0 Gall: 0-0
Aids: Bl: 0-0 Vi: 0-0 Tstrap: 0-0 Ckp: 0-0
Best Rating: **66** 11/09 Kemp 1m stand

Modest; stays 1m and acts on Polytrack.

Maison Brillet (IRE)

96 **74**
2-y-o b g Pyrus (USA)-Stormchaser (IRE) (Titus Livius (FR))
J Howard Johnson J Howard Johnson

Placings:313406 **(6048)**
2009: 5³GF, 6¹G, 6³G, 6⁴GF, 8⁰GF, 6⁶G,

	Starts	1st	2nd	3rd	Win & Pl
Career Total (Turf)	6	1	0	2	6776

74 5/09 Ayr 6f GD £5018
Total win prize-money £5019

Going (Turf): Sf: 0-0 GS: 0-0 **Gd: 1-3** GF: 0-3 Fm: 0-0
Distance: **5f/6f: 1-4** 7f-8f: 0-1 9f-13f: 0-1 14f+: 0-0
Track : LH: 0-0 RH: 0-0 Tight: 0-0 Gall: 0-0
Aids: Bl: 0-0 Vi: 0-0 Tstrap: 0-0 Ckp: 0-0
Best Rating: **74** 5/09 Ayr 6f good

Fairly cheap purchase and already gelded; promise on debut over 5f on fast ground.

Maison D'Or

88(92) (57)**38**
3-y-o b g Auction House (USA)-Figura (Rudimentary (USA))
R Ingram The Stargazers

Placings:64-0600000 **(4934)**
2009: 8⁰SD, 10⁶SD, 8⁰SD, 8⁰SD, 8⁰G, 9⁰GF, 12⁰G,

	Starts	1st	2nd	3rd	Win & Pl
Career Total (Turf)	3	0	0	0	
Career Total (AW)	6	0	0	0	192

Going (Turf): **Sf: 0-0 GS: 0-0 Gd: 0-2 GF: 0-1 Fm: 0-0**
Distance: 5f/6f: 0-0 7f-8f: 0-5 9f-13f: 0-4 14f+: 0-0
Track : LH: 0-8 RH: 0-1 Tight: 0-6 Gall: 0-1
Aids: Bl: 0-0 Vi: 0-0 Tstrap: 0-0 Ckp: 0-0
Best Rating: **57** 12/08 GrLe 1m stand

Modest; stays 1m; acts on Polytrack.

Maison Dieu

102(99) (58)**66**
6-y-o b/br g King Charlemagne (USA)-Shining Desert (IRE) (Green Desert (USA))

E J Alston Whitehills Racing Syndicate

Placings:00/01220050/13650002040003/344016060-02333414405260 (6825)
2009: 6⁰SD, 7²F, 7³G, 5³GF, 6³GF, 5⁴G, 6¹GF, 5⁴GF, 7⁴GF, 7⁰G, 7⁵G, 6²GF, 6⁶GF, 5⁰SD,

	Starts	1st	2nd	3rd	Win & Pl
Career Total (Turf)	40	4	5	3	17389
Career Total (AW)	7	0	0	3	1043

66 6/09 Ayr 6f (0-70)H G-F £2914
65 6/08 Ayr 6f (0-70)H G-F £3238
67 4/07 Sthl 6f (0-60)H GD £2388
61 5/06 Ripn 6f GD £2590
Total win prize-money £11132

Going (Turf): Sf: 0-0 GS: 0-6 Gd: 2-11 GF: 2-19 Fm: 0-4
Distance: 5f/6f: 4-28 7f-8f: 0-19 9f-13f: 0-0 14f+: 0-0
Track : LH: 1-19 RH: 0-7 Tight: 0-18 Gall: 0-1
Aids: Bl: 0-3 Vi: 0-0 Tstrap: 0-1 Ckp: 0-1
Best Rating: 67 4/07 Sthl 6f good

Moderate; suited by 5-6f; acts on good/fast ground; also goes on Polytrack; has worn blinkers.

Maiwand

80(73) (30)38
2-y-o b f Reset (AUS)-Iris May (Brief Truce (USA))
Mrs R A Carr (Sir Mark Prescott 31/7) David W Chapman

Placings:00006000 (7088)
2009: 6⁰SD, 7⁰S, 7⁰G, 7⁰G, 7⁶GF, 7⁰GF, 6⁰G, 6⁰SD,

	Starts	1st	2nd	3rd	Win & Pl
Career Total (Turf)	6	0	0	0	0
Career Total (AW)	2	0	0	0	

Going (Turf): Sf: 0-1 GS: 0-0 Gd: 0-3 GF: 0-2 Fm: 0-0
Distance: 5f/6f: 0-3 7f-8f: 0-5 9f-13f: 0-0 14f+: 0-0
Track : LH: 0-3 RH: 0-3 Tight: 0-2 Gall: 0-0
Aids: Bl: 0-1 Vi: 0-0 Tstrap: 0-0 Ckp: 0-0
Best Rating: 38 7/09 Catt 7f soft

Majaji

53
5-y-o b m Bal Harbour-Petaz (Petong)
P Salmon Ann And Eric Lumley

Placings:0 (1769)
2009: 7⁰GF,

	Starts	1st	2nd	3rd	Win & Pl
Career Total (Turf)	1	0	0	0	

Going (Turf): Sf: 0-0 GS: 0-0 Gd: 0-0 GF: 0-1 Fm: 0-0
Distance: 5f/6f: 0-0 7f-8f: 0-1 9f-13f: 0-0 14f+: 0-0
Track : LH: 0-1 RH: 0-0 Tight: 0-1 Gall: 0-0
Aids: Bl: 0-0 Vi: 0-0 Tstrap: 0-0 Ckp: 0-0

Majd Aljazeera

81(90) (61)45
3-y-o b g King's Best (USA)-Tegwen (USA) (Nijinsky (CAN))
D M Simcock Abdullah Saeed Belhab

Placings:00-46000 (5775)
2009: 10⁴SD, 11⁶F, 12⁰SD, 8⁰SD, 10⁰SD,

	Starts	1st	2nd	3rd	Win & Pl
Career Total (Turf)	1	0	0	0	0
Career Total (AW)	6	0	0	0	0

Going (Turf): Sf: 0-0 GS: 0-0 Gd: 0-0 GF: 0-0 Fm: 0-1
Distance: 5f/6f: 0-0 7f-8f: 0-3 9f-13f: 0-4 14f+: 0-0
Track : LH: 0-5 RH: 0-2 Tight: 0-3 Gall: 0-1
Aids: Bl: 0-0 Vi: 0-0 Tstrap: 0-0 Ckp: 0-0
Best Rating: 61 2/09 Ling 1m2f stand

Majehar

92(105) (76)62
7-y-o b g Marju (IRE)-Joonayh (Warning)
E J O'Neill (A G Newcombe 11/11) Geoffrey Lucas

Placings:45/00000004/323205051314/215304411413/032-101066214 (7332)
2009: 10¹SD, 10⁰SD, 11¹SD, 10⁰GF, 12⁶S, 11⁶SD, 12²SD, 12¹SD, 12⁴SD,

	Starts	1st	2nd	3rd	Win & Pl
Career Total (Turf)	13	0	0	0	731
Career Total (AW)	33	9	5	6	23708

73 11/09 Sthl 1m4f STD £2047
76 3/09 Sthl 1m3f (0-75)H STD £2590
66 1/09 Ling 1m2f (0-70)H STD £2590
67 10/07 Kemp 1m2f (0-60)H STD £2047
64 7/07 Ling 1m2f (0-65)H STD £2047
64 2/07 Sthl 1m (0-55)H SS £2388
58 12/06 Kemp 1m (0-45) STD £1365
54 10/06 Kemp 1m2f (0-45) STD £2047
Total win prize-money £17125

Going (Turf): Sf: 0-1 GS: 0-3 Gd: 0-1 GF: 0-6 Fm: 0-0
Distance: 5f/6f: 0-5 7f-8f: 2-12 9f-13f: 7-29 14f+: 0-0
Track : LH: 6-31 RH: 3-11 Tight: 3-19 Gall: 0-2
Aids: Bl: 0-0 Vi: 0-0 Tstrap: 0-0 Ckp: 0-0
Best Rating: 76 3/09 Sthl 1m3f stand

Modest; effective over 1m-1m4f; acts well on Fibresand and Polytrack.

Majestic Cheer

95(95) (67)60
5-y-o b g Royal Applause-Muwasim (USA) (Meadowlake (USA))
John A Harris Mrs A E Harris

Placings:6061/36040000/R3000000004000-56650 (3401)
2009: 6⁵SS, 7⁶SD, 6⁶SD, 5⁵GF, 7⁰G,

	Starts	1st	2nd	3rd	Win & Pl
Career Total (Turf)	20	0	0	1	863
Career Total (AW)	12	1	0	1	4589

73 11/06 Wolv 7f32y SF £3886
Total win prize-money £3886

Going (Turf): Sf: 0-3 GS: 0-1 Gd: 0-7 GF: 0-6 Fm: 0-0
Distance: 5f/6f: 0-14 7f-8f: 1-11 9f-13f: 0-7 14f+: 0-0
Track : LH: 1-9 RH: 0-9 Tight: 1-2 Gall: 0-0
Aids: Bl: 0-1 Vi: 0-0 Tstrap: 0-6 Ckp: 0-6
Best Rating: 73 11/06 Wolv 7f32y std-fst

Moderate; effective over 5f; acts on soft ground; goes on Polytrack.

Majestic Chief

93 (61)44
5-y-o b g Xaar-Grand Splendour (Shirley Heights)
Miss Lucinda V Russell Mr And Mrs T P Winnell

Placings:00/40652/00 (2233)
2009: 12⁰GS, 12⁰GS,

	Starts	1st	2nd	3rd	Win & Pl
Career Total (Turf)	7	0	1	0	1403
Career Total (AW)	2	0	0	0	0

Going (Turf): Sf: 0-2 GS: 0-2 Gd: 0-0 GF: 0-3 Fm: 0-0
Distance: 5f/6f: 0-0 7f-8f: 0-2 9f-13f: 0-7 14f+: 0-0
Track : LH: 0-7 RH: 0-1 Tight: 0-1 Gall: 0-3
Aids: Bl: 0-0 Vi: 0-0 Tstrap: 0-4 Ckp: 0-4
Best Rating: 66 7/07 NmkJ 1m2f gd-fm

Majestic Lady (IRE)

93(96) (55)59
3-y-o b f Royal Applause-Kiris World (Distant Relative)
Mlle C Comte (B W Hills 9/10) Mlle C Comte

Placings:405-55264340 (7385a)
2009: 5⁵G, 6⁵GS, 5²GF, 6⁶G, 5⁴SD, 6³SD, 5⁴SD, 6⁰HY,

	Starts	1st	2nd	3rd	Win & Pl
Career Total (Turf)	8	0	1	0	1252
Career Total (AW)	3	0	0	1	693

Going (Turf): Sf: 0-2 GS: 0-1 Gd: 0-3 GF: 0-2 Fm: 0-0
Distance: 5f/6f: 0-11 7f-8f: 0-0 9f-13f: 0-0 14f+: 0-0
Track : LH: 0-5 RH: 0-0 Tight: 0-2 Gall: 0-2
Aids: Bl: 0-0 Vi: 0-0 Tstrap: 0-0 Ckp: 0-0
Best Rating: 59 9/08 Sand 5f6y soft

Moderate; stays 6f; acts on fast ground and on sand.

Major Cadeaux

106 119
5-y-o ch h Cadeaux Genereux-Maine Lobster (USA) (Woodman (USA))
R A Fahey (R Hannon 16/5) T G & Mrs M E Holdcroft

Placings:12/1625/21133200-535 (6718a)
2009: 8⁵S, 6³G, 8⁵S,

	Starts	1st	2nd	3rd	Win & Pl
Career Total (Turf)	17	4	4	3	278105

119 5/08 Hayd 7f30y G-F £28385
115 4/08 Sand 1m14y GD £45416
117 4/07 Newb 7f G-F £27254
89 5/06 Newb 6f8y SFT £6477
Total win prize-money £107532

Going (Turf): Sf: 1-6 GS: 0-1 Gd: 1-5 GF: 2-5 Fm: 0-0
Distance: 5f/6f: 0-1 7f-8f: 3-15 9f-13f: 1-1 14f+: 0-0
Track : LH: 1-1 RH: 1-6 Tight: 0-0 Gall: 0-0
Aids: Bl: 0-0 Vi: 0-0 Tstrap: 0-0 Ckp: 0-0
Best Rating: 119 5/08 Hayd 7f30y gd-fm

Group class; winner in Group 2 and Group 3 company and Group 1 placed; effective over 6f-1m; handles most ground.

Major Eazy (IRE)

104(80) (35)99
4-y-o b g Fasliyev (USA)-Castilian Queen (USA) (Diesis)
B J Meehan The Comic Strip Heroes

Placings:345010010/50-5 (2474)
2009: 6⁵G,

	Starts	1st	2nd	3rd	Win & Pl
Career Total (Turf)	11	2	0	1	19050
Career Total (AW)	1	0	0	0	

103 10/07 Sals 6f G-S £11217
93 6/07 Ling 5f SFT £3562
Total win prize-money £14780

Going (Turf): Sf: 1-1 GS: 1-4 Gd: 0-3 GF: 0-3 Fm: 0-0
Distance: 5f/6f: 2-12 7f-8f: 0-0 9f-13f: 0-0 14f+: 0-0
Track : LH: 0-1 RH: 0-0 Tight: 0-0 Gall: 0-1
Aids: Bl: 0-0 Vi: 0-0 Tstrap: 0-0 Ckp: 0-0
Best Rating: 103 10/07 Sals 6f gd-sft

Very useful; effective over 5f-6f; acts on fast, but may prefer soft ground.

Major Lawrence (IRE)

96(97) (67)77
3-y-o b c Fasliyev (USA)-Ziffany (Taufan (USA))
J Noseda Mrs Susan Roy

Placings:234043 **(7863)**
2009: 6^{2}GF, 6^{3}G, 7^{4}SD, 7^{0}SD, 6^{4}SD, 8^{3}SD,

	Starts	1st	2nd	3rd	Win & Pl
Career Total (Turf)	2	0	1	1	2138
Career Total (AW)	4	0	0	1	788

Going (Turf): Sf: 0-0 GS: 0-0 Gd: 0-1 GF: 0-1 Fm: 0-0
Distance: 5f/6f: 0-2 7f-8f: 0-3 9f-13f: 0-1 14f+: 0-0
Track : LH: 0-2 RH: 0-2 Tight: 0-2 Gall: 0-0
Aids: Bl: 0-0 Vi: 0-0 Tstrap: 0-0 Ckp: 0-0
Best Rating: 77 7/09 Newb 6f8y gd-fm

Modest; stays 7f; acts on fast ground and on Polytrack.

Major Magpie (IRE)

99 89
7-y-o b g Rossini (USA)-Picnic Basket (Pharly (FR))
M Dods Mrs Patsy Monk

Placings:33620565/616000223610/21/330361410-00000000 **(5333)**
2009: 8^{0}GF, 8^{0}GF, 8^{0}GS, 7^{0}GF, 7^{0}G, 6^{0}G, 8^{0}G, 8^{0}S,

	Starts	1st	2nd	3rd	Win & Pl
Career Total (Turf)	39	5	4	6	37005

89	9/08	Pont	1m4y	(0-80)H	G-S	£6476
87	8/08	Pont	1m4y	(0-80)H	GD	£5180
89	4/07	Hayd	1m30y	(0-85)H	GD	£6477
81	9/06	Pont	1m4y	(0-75)H	G-S	£3886
78	4/06	Pont	1m4y	(0-75)H	GD	£4533

Total win prize-money £26554

Going (Turf): Sf: 0-3 GS: 2-8 **Gd: 3-11** GF: 0-15 Fm: 0-2
Distance: 5f/6f: 0-0 7f-8f: 0-17 **9f-13f: 5-22** 14f+: 0-0
Track : **LH: 5-31** RH: 0-6 Tight: 0-8 Gall: 0-3
Aids: Bl: 0-0 Vi: 0-0 Tstrap: 0-1 Ckp: 0-1
Best Rating: 89 9/08 Pont 1m4y gd-sft

Useful; effective at around 1m-1m2f; acts on fast and easy ground; goes well at Pontefract.

Major Maximus

(94) (73)
2-y-o br c Domedriver (IRE)-Madame Maxine (USA) (Dayjur (USA))
George Baker Mrs Susan Roy

Placings:34453 **(7874)**
2009: 7^{3}SD, 7^{4}SD, 5^{4}SF, 6^{5}SD, 8^{3}SD,

	Starts	1st	2nd	3rd	Win & Pl
Career Total (Turf)	0	0	0	0	
Career Total (AW)	5	0	0	2	880

Going (Turf): Sf: 0-0 GS: 0-0 Gd: 0-0 GF: 0-0 Fm: 0-0
Distance: 5f/6f: 0-2 7f-8f: 0-3 9f-13f: 0-0 14f+: 0-0
Track : LH: 0-4 RH: 0-1 Tight: 0-3 Gall: 0-0
Aids: Bl: 0-0 Vi: 0-0 Tstrap: 0-0 Ckp: 0-0
Best Rating: 73 10/09 Wolv 7f32y stand

Modest; stays 7f; acts on Polytrack.

Major Monty (IRE)

(89) (52)
2-y-o b g Orpen (USA)-Mari-Ela (IRE) (River Falls)
Tom Dascombe Deva Racing Orpen Partnership

Placings:05 **(7637)**
2009: 5^{0}SD, 5^{5}SD,

	Starts	1st	2nd	3rd	Win & Pl
Career Total (Turf)	0	0	0	0	
Career Total (AW)	2	0	0	0	0

Going (Turf): Sf: 0-0 GS: 0-0 Gd: 0-0 GF: 0-0 Fm: 0-0
Distance: 5f/6f: 0-2 7f-8f: 0-0 9f-13f: 0-0 14f+: 0-0
Track : LH: 0-1 RH: 0-0 Tight: 0-1 Gall: 0-0
Aids: Bl: 0-0 Vi: 0-0 Tstrap: 0-0 Ckp: 0-0
Best Rating: 52 12/09 Sthl 5f stand

Major Phil (IRE)

92(101) (81)77
3-y-o b c Captain Rio-Choral Sundown (Night Shift (USA))
L M Cumani L Marinopoulos

Placings:51-50015 **(3996)**
2009: 6^{5}SD, 7^{0}S, 7^{0}GF, 7^{1}SD, 8^{5}GF,

	Starts	1st	2nd	3rd	Win & Pl
Career Total (Turf)	3	0	0	0	235
Career Total (AW)	4	2	0	0	7642

81	6/09	Wolv	7f32y	(0-85)H	STD	£4727
78	12/08	GrLe	6f		STD	£2914

Total win prize-money £7641

Going (Turf): Sf: 0-1 GS: 0-0 Gd: 0-0 GF: 0-2 Fm: 0-0
Distance: 5f/6f: 1-3 7f-8f: 1-3 9f-13f: 0-1 14f+: 0-0
Track : **LH: 2-6** RH: 0-1 Tight: 1-3 Gall: 1-2
Aids: Bl: 0-0 Vi: 0-0 Tstrap: 0-0 Ckp: 0-0
Best Rating: 81 6/09 Wolv 7f32y stand

Fair; stays 7f and acts on Polytrack.

Major Promise

(102) (59)63
4-y-o b g Lomitas-Distant Diva (Distant Relative)
Jane Chapple-Hyam Norcroft Park Stud

Placings:60406-502 **(7733)**
2009: 13^{5}SD, 14^{0}SD, 12^{2}SD,

	Starts	1st	2nd	3rd	Win & Pl
Career Total (Turf)	5	0	0	0	248
Career Total (AW)	3	0	1	0	605

Going (Turf): Sf: 0-1 GS: 0-2 Gd: 0-1 GF: 0-1 Fm: 0-0
Distance: 5f/6f: 0-0 7f-8f: 0-0 9f-13f: 0-5 14f+: 0-3
Track : LH: 0-7 RH: 0-1 Tight: 0-6 Gall: 0-0
Aids: Bl: 0-0 Vi: 0-0 Tstrap: 0-0 Ckp: 0-0
Best Rating: 63 8/08 Bath 1m3f144y gd-sft

Modest; stays 1m3f; acts on good to soft.

Major Value

91(75) (30)54
3-y-o b c Tobougg (IRE)-Surrealist (ITY) (Night Shift (USA))
C G Cox Duncan Jones & Dr Sosie Kassab

Placings:0-50300 **(6910)**
2009: 8^{5}GF, 8^{0}GF, 9^{3}HY, 10^{0}G, 10^{0}G,

	Starts	1st	2nd	3rd	Win & Pl
Career Total (Turf)	5	0	0	1	578
Career Total (AW)	1	0	0	0	

Going (Turf): Sf: 0-1 GS: 0-0 Gd: 0-2 GF: 0-2 Fm: 0-0
Distance: 5f/6f: 0-0 7f-8f: 0-1 9f-13f: 0-5 14f+: 0-0
Track : LH: 0-1 RH: 0-5 Tight: 0-2 Gall: 0-0
Aids: Bl: 0-1 Vi: 0-0 Tstrap: 0-1 Ckp: 0-1
Best Rating: 54 6/09 Wind 1m67y gd-fm

Majuro (IRE)

104(113) (106)100
5-y-o b g Danetime (IRE)-First Fling (IRE) (Last Tycoon)
K A Ryan N Cable & M Smith

Placings:012131/166605523505/000013-222233040 **(1861)**
2009: 8^{2}SS, 7^{2}SD, 8^{2}SD, 7^{2}SD, 5^{3}SD, 8^{3}GF, 8^{0}S, 8^{4}GF, 7^{0}GF,

	Starts	1st	2nd	3rd	Win & Pl
Career Total (Turf)	19	2	1	2	18741
Career Total (AW)	14	3	5	3	37757

93	9/08	Sthl	1m	(0-85)H	STD	£5180
93	4/07	Ling	7f		STD	£7570
87	10/06	Leic	7f9y		G-S	£4533
90	9/06	Wolv	1m141y		SF	£3238
81	8/06	Folk	7f		G-F	£3238

Total win prize-money £23764

Going (Turf): Sf: 0-3 **GS: 1-2** Gd: 0-6 **GF: 1-8** Fm: 0-0
Distance: 5f/6f: 0-6 **7f-8f: 4-25** 9f-13f: 1-2 14f+: 0-0
Track : **LH: 3-15** RH: 0-5 **Tight: 2-10** Gall: 0-0
Aids: Bl: 0-0 Vi: 0-0 Tstrap: 0-0 Ckp: 0-0
Best Rating: 106 3/09 Wolv 5f216y stand

Very useful; effective over 6f-1m; acts on most ground on turf; goes well on sand.

Makaam (USA)

95(96) (82)62
3-y-o ch c Giant's Causeway (USA)-Elaflaak (USA) (Gulch (USA))
M P Tregoning Hamdan Al Maktoum

Placings:220400 **(6374)**
2009: 7^{2}SD, 7^{2}SD, 6^{0}S, 7^{4}GF, 8^{0}SD, 7^{0}SD,

	Starts	1st	2nd	3rd	Win & Pl
Career Total (Turf)	2	0	0	0	216
Career Total (AW)	4	0	2	0	2023

Going (Turf): Sf: 0-1 GS: 0-0 Gd: 0-0 GF: 0-1 Fm: 0-0
Distance: 5f/6f: 0-0 7f-8f: 0-6 9f-13f: 0-0 14f+: 0-0
Track : LH: 0-2 RH: 0-3 Tight: 0-1 Gall: 0-0
Aids: Bl: 0-0 Vi: 0-0 Tstrap: 0-0 Ckp: 0-0
Best Rating: 82 5/09 Ling 7f stand

Fair; stays 7f; acts on Polytrack.

Makaamen

103 100
3-y-o ch g Selkirk (USA)-Bird Key (Cadeaux Genereux)
B W Hills Hamdan Al Maktoum

Placings:2-1100 **(6675)**
2009: 7^{1}GF, 7^{1}GS, 7^{0}HY, 7^{0}G,

	Starts	1st	2nd	3rd	Win & Pl
Career Total (Turf)	5	2	1	0	14489

100	4/09	Newb	7f	(0-95)H	G-S	£7477
83	3/09	Donc	7f		G-F	£5180

Total win prize-money £12658

Going (Turf): Sf: 0-1 **GS: 1-1** Gd: 0-1 **GF: 1-2** Fm: 0-0
Distance: 5f/6f: 0-0 **7f-8f: 2-5** 9f-13f: 0-0 14f+: 0-0
Track : LH: 0-2 RH: 0-0 Tight: 0-0 Gall: 0-1

Aids: Bl: 0-0 Vi: 0-0 Tstrap: 0-0 Ckp: 0-0
Best Rating: **100** 4/09 Newb 7f gd-sft

Very useful; lightly raced; effective over 7f; acts on most ground.

Makarthy

(41)
2-y-o b c Makbul-Royal Shepley (Royal Applause)
H A McWilliams Seven Stars Racing

Placings:0 (7749)
2009: 5^{0}SD,

	Starts	1st	2nd	3rd	Win & Pl
Career Total (Turf)	0	0	0	0	
Career Total (AW)	1	0	0	0	

Going (Turf): **Sf: 0-0 GS: 0-0 Gd: 0-0 GF: 0-0 Fm: 0-0**
Distance: 5f/6f: 0-1 7f-8f: 0-0 9f-13f: 0-0 14f+: 0-0
Track : LH: 0-1 RH: 0-0 Tight: 0-1 Gall: 0-0
Aids: Bl: 0-0 Vi: 0-0 Tstrap: 0-0 Ckp: 0-0

Makaykla

88 58
3-y-o b f Makbul-Primum Tempus (Primo Dominie)
E J Alston Springs Equestrian, G M & C Baillie

Placings:530-05 (4137)
2009: 5^{0}GF, 5^{5}G,

	Starts	1st	2nd	3rd	Win & Pl
Career Total (Turf)	5	0	0	1	530

Going (Turf): **Sf: 0-1 GS: 0-1 Gd: 0-2 GF: 0-1 Fm: 0-0**
Distance: 5f/6f: 0-5 7f-8f: 0-0 9f-13f: 0-0 14f+: 0-0
Track : LH: 0-0 RH: 0-0 Tight: 0-0 Gall: 0-0
Aids: Bl: 0-0 Vi: 0-0 Tstrap: 0-0 Ckp: 0-0
Best Rating: **58** 10/08 Rdcr 6f good

Moderate; should stay 7f.

Makbullet

93 79
2-y-o gr g Makbul-Gold Belt (IRE) (Bellypha)
J Howard Johnson Transcend Bloodstock LLP

Placings:6334210 (5198)
2009: 5^{6}F, 5^{3}GF, 6^{3}G, 5^{4}F, 5^{2}S, 6^{1}G, 6^{0}GF,

	Starts	1st	2nd	3rd	Win & Pl
Career Total (Turf)	7	1	1	2	7301

79 8/09 Ripn 6f GD £4209
Total win prize-money £4209

Going (Turf): Sf: 0-1 GS: 0-0 **Gd: 1-2** GF: 0-2 Fm: 0-2
Distance: **5f/6f: 1-7** 7f-8f: 0-0 9f-13f: 0-0 14f+: 0-0
Track : LH: 0-1 RH: 0-0 Tight: 0-1 Gall: 0-0
Aids: Bl: 0-0 Vi: 0-0 Tstrap: 0-0 Ckp: 0-0
Best Rating: **79** 8/09 Ripn 6f good

Fair; best at 6f; acts on most ground.

Make Amends (IRE)

102(97) (61)69
4-y-o b m Indian Ridge-Chill Seeking (USA) (Theatrical)
R J Hodges Miss R Dobson

Placings:0100-**0030**26452615300**1** (7856)
2009: 12^{0}SD, 9^{0}SD, 8^{3}SF, 12^{0}SD, 10^{2}SD, 10^{6}GF, 13^{4}GS, 12^{5}GF, 10^{2}F, 10^{6}G, 9^{1}GF, 8^{5}GF, 8^{3}G, 11^{0}GF, 9^{0}SD, 9^{1}SD,

	Starts	1st	2nd	3rd	Win & Pl
Career Total (Turf)	13	2	1	1	7122
Career Total (AW)	7	1	1	1	2385

	12/09	Wolv	1m1f103y	(0-60)H	STD	£1706
65	7/09	Folk	1m1f149y	(0-70)H	G-F	£3070
69	8/08	Chep	7f16y		HVY	£2719

Total win prize-money £7497

Going (Turf): **Sf: 1-1** GS: 0-2 Gd: 0-3 **GF: 1-6** Fm: 0-1
Distance: 5f/6f: 0-0 7f-8f: 1-3 **9f-13f: 2-16** 14f+: 0-1
Track : LH: 1-13 RH: 1-4 **Tight: 2-15** Gall: 0-0
Aids: Bl: 0-0 Vi: 0-0 Tstrap: 0-0 Ckp: 0-0
Best Rating: **69** 8/08 Chep 7f16y heavy

Modest; effective over 7f-1m; acts on soft ground and on Polytrack.

Make My Dream

105(104) (77)80
6-y-o b g My Best Valentine-Sandkatoon (IRE) (Archway (IRE))
J Gallagher Mrs Irene Clifford

Placings:0054400/30203002**2025**/00223245241**6004**/4132 4523225-442003051**632260** (7739)
2009: 5^{4}G, 5^{4}GF, 5^{2}F, 5^{0}GF, 5^{0}GF, 6^{3}GF, 6^{0}G, 6^{5}G, 5^{1}GF, 5^{6}GF, 5^{3}SS, 5^{2}G, 6^{2}SD, 5^{6}SD, 6^{0}SD,

	Starts	1st	2nd	3rd	Win & Pl
Career Total (Turf)	42	3	11	6	26128
Career Total (AW)	17	0	3	1	2440

74	9/09	Sand	5f6y	(0-80)H	G-F	£4857
73	7/08	Wind	5f10y	(0-75)H	GD	£3070
69	10/07	Nott	5f13y	(0-70)H	G-F	£3238

Total win prize-money £11167

Going (Turf): Sf: 0-3 GS: 0-4 Gd: 1-14 **GF: 2-17** Fm: 0-4
Distance: **5f/6f: 3-53** 7f-8f: 0-6 9f-13f: 0-0 14f+: 0-0
Track : LH: 0-24 RH: 0-5 Tight: 0-12 **Gall: 1-6**
Aids: Bl: 0-2 Vi: 0-1 Tstrap: 0-0 Ckp: 0-0
Best Rating: **80** 10/08 Nott 5f13y heavy

Fair; effective at 5f-6f; acts on most ground and on Polytrack.

Makhaaleb (IRE)

96(91) (73)73
3-y-o b g Haafhd-Summerhill Parkes (Zafonic (USA))
Paul Stafford (B W Hills 2/7) Sean F Gallagher

Placings:0603-43430 (4635a)
2009: 10^{4}SD, 8^{3}G, 8^{4}GF, 8^{3}F, 10^{0}HY,

	Starts	1st	2nd	3rd	Win & Pl
Career Total (Turf)	7	0	0	2	1550
Career Total (AW)	2	0	0	1	939

Going (Turf): **Sf: 0-2 GS: 0-0 Gd: 0-3 GF: 0-1 Fm: 0-1**
Distance: 5f/6f: 0-0 7f-8f: 0-6 9f-13f: 0-3 14f+: 0-0
Track : LH: 0-4 RH: 0-1 Tight: 0-2 Gall: 0-1
Aids: Bl: 0-1 Vi: 0-0 Tstrap: 0-0 Ckp: 0-0
Best Rating: **73** 5/09 Thsk 1m good

Fair; cost 190,000gns as a foal; stays 1m; acts on good/fast ground.

Making Music

90 58
6-y-o b m Makbul-Crofters Ceilidh (Scottish Reel)
T D Easterby Jonathan Gill

Placings:020422010/00233366605/00041114/00000-060 (3445)
2009: 5^{0}GF, 5^{6}GF, 5^{0}GF,

	Starts	1st	2nd	3rd	Win & Pl
Career Total (Turf)	37	4	4	3	21638

66	9/07	Bevl	5f	(0-70)H	G-F	£3886
63	8/07	Haml	5f4y	(0-55)H	G-F	£2730
56	8/07	Newc	5f	(0-60)H	GD	£2590
63	9/05	Carl	5f		FRM	£2982

Total win prize-money £12189

Going (Turf): Sf: 0-6 GS: 0-5 Gd: 1-7 **GF: 2-17** Fm: 1-2
Distance: **5f/6f: 4-34** 7f-8f: 0-3 9f-13f: 0-0 14f+: 0-0
Track : LH: 0-5 **RH: 1-5** Tight: 0-1 **Gall: 1-3**
Aids: **Bl: 3-12** Vi: 0-0 Tstrap: 0-6 Ckp: 0-6
Best Rating: **72** 7/06 Leic 5f218y good

Makshoof (IRE)

100(101) (85)87
5-y-o b g Kyllachy-Tres Sage (Reprimand)
I W McInnes (K A Ryan 11/5) Stephen Hackney

Placings:2310/10606/54551543123**050**-350500000430 (7774)
2009: 6^{3}G, 6^{5}F, 6^{0}HY, 6^{5}G, 6^{0}SD, 5^{0}GF, 6^{0}G, 7^{0}G, 7^{0}SD, 6^{4}SD, 6^{3}SD, 6^{0}SD,

	Starts	1st	2nd	3rd	Win & Pl
Career Total (Turf)	24	4	2	2	26150
Career Total (AW)	11	0	0	3	1995

87	9/08	Hayd	6f	(0-85)H	HVY	£5504
82	7/08	Hayd	6f	(0-80)H	GD	£5504
87	5/07	Hayd	6f	(0-85)H	GD	£5505
73	9/06	Hayd	6f		HVY	£3886

Total win prize-money £20401

Going (Turf): **Sf: 2-6** GS: 0-3 **Gd: 2-9** GF: 0-4 Fm: 0-2
Distance: **5f/6f: 4-26** 7f-8f: 0-9 9f-13f: 0-0 14f+: 0-0
Track : LH: 0-13 RH: 0-2 Tight: 0-7 Gall: 0-1
Aids: Bl: 0-1 Vi: 0-0 Tstrap: 1-13 Ckp: 1-13
Best Rating: **87** 9/08 Hayd 6f heavy

Moderate; effective at around 6f; acts on good and softer ground; goes on Fibresand and Polytrack; has worn cheek-pieces.

Mal And Dave (IRE)

96 69
2-y-o b g Redback-Louvolite (IRE) (Fayruz)
D Nicholls Dr Marwan Koukash

Placings:465221 (3446)
2009: 5^{4}G, 6^{6}G, 5^{5}GF, 5^{2}F, 5^{2}G, 5^{1}GF,

	Starts	1st	2nd	3rd	Win & Pl
Career Total (Turf)	6	1	2	0	5956

69 6/09 Muss 5f G-F £3885
Total win prize-money £3886

Going (Turf): Sf: 0-0 GS: 0-0 Gd: 0-3 **GF: 1-2** Fm: 0-1
Distance: **5f/6f: 1-6** 7f-8f: 0-0 9f-13f: 0-0 14f+: 0-0
Track : LH: 0-0 RH: 0-1 Tight: 0-0 Gall: 0-1
Aids: Bl: 0-0 Vi: 0-0 Tstrap: 0-0 Ckp: 0-0
Best Rating: **69** 6/09 Muss 5f gd-fm

Modest; best at 5f on fast ground.

Malapropism

99(97) (60)86
9-y-o ch g Compton Place-Mrs Malaprop (Night Shift (USA))
M R Channon Michael A Foy

Placings:02332120523/000614333243100300**1**/6000604 066106110**0/0402**0004300540053005052**35**/06000142245

1242050000/6600033421233535411100046/250440064343 020004-00030040003**2100000** **(7889)**
2009: 5^{0}GF, 5^{0}GF, 5^{0}G, 5^{3}F, 5^{0}S, 5^{0}F, 5^{4}GF, 5^{0}GF, 5^{0}F, 5^{0}G, 5^{3}SD, 6^{2}SD, 6^{1}SD, 6^{0}SD, 5^{0}SD, 5^{0}SD, 6^{0}SD, 5^{0}SD,

	Starts	1st	2nd	3rd	Win & Pl
Career Total (Turf)	**142**	**13**	**14**	**20**	**132751**
Career Total (AW)	**12**	**1**	**2**	**1**	**16465**

60	10/09	Ling	6f	(0-55)H	STD	£1706
89	9/07	Gdwd	5f	(0-70)H	G-S	£3238
89	9/07	NmkR	5f	(0-75)H	FRM	£3886
86	9/07	Bevl	5f	(0-75)H	G-F	£3562
78	7/07	Wind	5f10y	(0-75)H	G-F	£3238
88	7/06	York	5f	(0-90)H	G-F	£8096
82	6/06	Sand	5f6y	(0-80)H	G-F	£5505
98	10/04	Muss	5f	(0-107)H	SFT	£12082
93	10/04	Catt	5f	(0-92)H	G-S	£13942
87	9/04	Donc	5f	(0-85)H	G-F	£6500
97	11/03	Muss	5f	D(0-85)H	G-F	£4420
90	8/03	Gdwd	5f	D(0-80)H	GD	£5356
72	5/03	Bath	5f161y	E(0-75)H	FRM	£4163
83	7/02	Rdcr	5f	E	G-F	£3458

Total win prize-money £79156

Going (Turf): Sf: 1-15GS: 2-19Gd: 1-36**GF: 7-61**Fm: 2-11
Distance: **5f/6f: 14-150** 7f-8f: 0-4 9f-13f: 0-0 14f+: 0-0
Track : **LH: 2-36** RH: 0-2 Tight: 1-17 **Gall: 2-15**
Aids: Bl: 0-0 **Vi: 3-12** Tstrap: 0-0 Ckp: 0-0
Best Rating: **98** 2/05 Ndas 5f fast

Modest; seems best at 5f-6f; acts on any ground; has worn a visor.

Malcheek (IRE)

109(104) (75)87
7-y-o br g Lend A Hand-Russland (GER) (Surumu (GER))
T D Easterby Mrs Susie Dicker

Placings:4/113430/21030005**010**/310500014200/5660000-1400000**241000** **(7558)**
2009: 7^{1}GF, 7^{4}F, 6^{0}GF, 7^{0}G, 6^{0}GF, 7^{0}GF, 6^{0}G, 7^{2}G, 7^{4}SD, 7^{1}GF, 7^{0}G, 7^{0}S, 7^{0}SD,

	Starts	1st	2nd	3rd	Win & Pl
Career Total (Turf)	**46**	**7**	**3**	**4**	**59134**
Career Total (AW)	**4**	**1**	**0**	**0**	**5883**

87	9/09	Muss	7f30y	(0-80)H	G-F	£5180
81	4/09	Catt	7f	(0-75)H	G-F	£2590
96	8/07	Ripn	6f	(0-95)H	G-F	£10906
93	5/07	Thsk	7f	(0-85)H	G-F	£5181
92	10/06	Wolv	7f32y	(0-85)H	SF	£5505
88	5/06	Thsk	7f	(0-85)H	FRM	£8096
83	6/05	Thsk	7f	(0-75)H	G-F	£5474
85	6/05	Thsk	7f		G-F	£5538

Total win prize-money £48473

Going (Turf): Sf: 0-1 GS: 0-5 Gd: 0-14 **GF: 6-23** Fm: 1-3
Distance: 5f/6f: 1-15 **7f-8f: 7-34** 9f-13f: 0-1 14f+: 0-0
Track : **LH: 6-26** RH: 1-2 **Tight: 7-23** Gall: 0-3
Aids: Bl: 0-0 Vi: 0-0 Tstrap: 0-0 Ckp: 0-0
Best Rating: **96** 9/07 Ripn 6f gd-fm

Fair; effective over 6f-7f; acts on fast ground and on Polytrack; likes to race prominently.

Maldon Prom (IRE)

94(98) (73)66
2-y-o br g Kheleyf (USA)-Misty Peak (IRE) (Sri Pekan (USA))
C A Dwyer The Super Four

Placings:6030021 **(7786)**
2009: 6^{6}GS, 6^{0}G, 5^{3}SD, 5^{0}SD, 6^{0}S, 5^{2}SD, 5^{1}SD,

	Starts	1st	2nd	3rd	Win & Pl
Career Total (Turf)	**3**	**0**	**0**	**0**	**0**
Career Total (AW)	**4**	**1**	**1**	**1**	**5737**

73	12/09	Wolv	5f216y	(0-90)	STD	£4533

Total win prize-money £4533

Going (Turf): **Sf: 0-1 GS: 0-1 Gd: 0-1 GF: 0-0 Fm: 0-0**
Distance: **5f/6f: 1-7** 7f-8f: 0-0 9f-13f: 0-0 14f+: 0-0
Track : **LH: 1-3** RH: 0-0 **Tight: 1-3** Gall: 0-0
Aids: Bl: 0-0 Vi: 0-1 Tstrap: 0-0 Ckp: 0-0
Best Rating: **73** 12/09 Wolv 5f216y stand

Fair; stays 6f; acts on Polytrack; has worn a visor.

Malguru

82 59
5-y-o b g Ishiguru (USA)-Vento Del Oreno (FR) (Lando (GER))
J A McShane Lothian Recycling Limited

Placings:00600/0051416-0 **(4876)**
2009: 8^{0}G,

	Starts	1st	2nd	3rd	Win & Pl
Career Total (Turf)	**13**	**2**	**0**	**0**	**5505**

59	7/08	Newc	1m2f32y	(0-60)H	G-F	£2590
53	5/08	Ayr	1m1f20y	(0-60)H	G-F	£2914

Total win prize-money £5504

Going (Turf): Sf: 0-2 GS: 0-1 Gd: 0-1 **GF: 2-9** Fm: 0-0
Distance: 5f/6f: 0-0 7f-8f: 0-4 **9f-13f: 2-7** 14f+: 0-2
Track : **LH: 2-7** RH: 0-5 Tight: 0-7 **Gall: 1-1**
Aids: Bl: 0-1 Vi: 0-0 Tstrap: 2-6 Ckp: 2-6
Best Rating: **59** 7/08 Newc 1m2f32y gd-fm

Modest performer; stays 1m2f; acts on fast ground.

Malibu Bay (USA)

106 99
3-y-o b c El Prado (IRE)-Favorite Funtime (USA) (Seeking The Gold (USA))
A P O'Brien Mrs John Magnier, M Tabor & D Smith

Placings:1-30000 **(4419)**
2009: 10^{3}G, 10^{0}G, 10^{0}G, 10^{0}YS, 8^{0}G,

	Starts	1st	2nd	3rd	Win & Pl
Career Total (Turf)	**6**	**1**	**0**	**1**	**15638**

87	10/08	Navn	1m	SH	£8637

Total win prize-money £8638

Going (Turf): **Sf: 0-0 GS: 0-0 Gd: 0-4 GF: 0-0 Fm: 0-0**
Distance: 5f/6f: 0-0 **7f-8f: 1-2** 9f-13f: 0-4 14f+: 0-0
Track : **LH: 1-2** RH: 0-4 Tight: 0-0 Gall: 0-0
Aids: Bl: 0-0 Vi: 0-0 Tstrap: 0-0 Ckp: 0-0
Best Rating: **99** 4/09 Sand 1m2f7y good

Very useful; Group placed; effective over 1m; acts on good and softer ground.

Malinsa Blue (IRE)

94(91) (63)63
7-y-o b m Desert Style (IRE)-Talina's Law (IRE) (Law Society (USA))
B Ellison Mrs Andrea M Mallinson

Placings:6226210/025435602600/500500/04115600310/0 05563420**100**-05056 **(2968)**
2009: 9^{0}GF, 7^{5}GF, 9^{0}GF, 8^{5}GF, 7^{6}GF,

	Starts	1st	2nd	3rd	Win & Pl
Career Total (Turf)	**51**	**4**	**6**	**3**	**35631**
Career Total (AW)	**3**	**1**	**0**	**0**	**2866**

63	10/08	Wolv	1m141y	(0-55)H	STD	£2866
72	9/07	Pont	1m4y	(0-75)H	FRM	£5181
70	5/07	Bevl	1m1f207y	(0-70)H	G-F	£3238
69	5/07	Pont	1m4y	(0-70)H	G-F	£4533
80	9/04	Donc	7f	(0-85)	FRM	£7280

Total win prize-money £23101

Going (Turf): Sf: 0-3 GS: 0-5 Gd: 0-13 **GF: 2-27 Fm: 2-3**
Distance: 5f/6f: 0-4 7f-8f: 1-22 **9f-13f: 4-28** 14f+: 0-0
Track : **LH: 3-25** RH: 1-14 **Tight: 1-15** Gall: 0-1
Aids: Bl: 0-6 Vi: 0-0 Tstrap: 2-12 Ckp: 2-12
Best Rating: **86** 5/05 Thsk 1m gd-fm

Moderate; effective at around 1m; acts well on fast ground.

Mallorey

(87) (54)64
3-y-o ch g Medicean-In Luck (In The Wings)
A M Hales (T Stack 5/8) John Findlay

Placings:04003400 **(7831)**
2009: 7^{0}SD, 8^{4}HY, 7^{0}YS, 10^{0}SD, 11^{3}YS, 9^{4}S, 11^{0}SD, 12^{0}SD,

	Starts	1st	2nd	3rd	Win & Pl
Career Total (Turf)	**4**	**0**	**0**	**1**	**1397**
Career Total (AW)	**4**	**0**	**0**	**0**	

Going (Turf): **Sf: 0-2 GS: 0-0 Gd: 0-0 GF: 0-0 Fm: 0-0**
Distance: 5f/6f: 0-0 7f-8f: 0-3 9f-13f: 0-5 14f+: 0-0
Track : LH: 0-3 RH: 0-5 Tight: 0-0 Gall: 0-0
Aids: Bl: 0-0 Vi: 0-0 Tstrap: 0-0 Ckp: 0-0
Best Rating: **64** 7/09 Klny 1m3f yld-sft

Malt Empress (IRE)

(93) (52)
4-y-o b f Second Empire (IRE)-Sunset Malt (IRE) (Red Sunset)
B W Duke Brendan W Duke Racing

Placings:0/U060-0 **(0248)**
2009: 12^{0}SD,

	Starts	1st	2nd	3rd	Win & Pl
Career Total (Turf)	**1**	**0**	**0**	**0**	
Career Total (AW)	**5**	**0**	**0**	**0**	**0**

Going (Turf): **Sf: 0-0 GS: 0-0 Gd: 0-1 GF: 0-0 Fm: 0-0**
Distance: 5f/6f: 0-0 7f-8f: 0-2 9f-13f: 0-4 14f+: 0-0
Track : LH: 0-5 RH: 0-1 Tight: 0-5 Gall: 0-0
Aids: Bl: 0-0 Vi: 0-0 Tstrap: 0-0 Ckp: 0-0
Best Rating: **52** 3/08 Ling 1m2f stand

Malt Or Mash (USA)

102(109) (68)108
5-y-o gr h Black Minnaloushe (USA)-Southern Tradition (USA) (Family Doctor (USA))
R Hannon A P Patey

Placings:633/2114011/1065-00154606 **(7332)**
2009: 11^{0}GF, 10^{0}G, 11^{1}GF, 10^{5}GS, 12^{4}GF, 14^{6}S, 14^{0}GS, 12^{6}SD,

	Starts	1st	2nd	3rd	Win & Pl
Career Total (Turf)	**19**	**5**	**0**	**2**	**73335**
Career Total (AW)	**3**	**1**	**1**	**0**	**16170**

79	8/09	Newb	1m3f5y		G-F	£2590
109	3/08	Kemp	1m4f		STD	£14762
108	11/07	Donc	1m4f	H	G-F	£46740
105	10/07	NmkR	1m4f	(0-95)H	G-F	£9348
85	6/07	Gdwd	1m1f192y	(0-80)H	G-F	£7124

Total win prize-money £80566

Going (Turf): Sf: 0-3 GS: 0-3 Gd: 1-6 **GF: 4-7** Fm: 0-0

Distance:	5f/6f: 0-0 7f-8f: 0-4 **9f-13f: 6-14** 14f+: 0-4
Track :	LH: 2-10 **RH: 4-10** Tight: 1-3 **Gall: 3-11**
Aids:	Bl: 0-0 Vi: 0-0 Tstrap: 0-0 Ckp: 0-0
Best Rating:	**109** 3/08 Kemp 1m4f stand

Useful; Listed winner; stays 1m4f; best on fast ground and acts on Polytrack.

Mambo Spirit (IRE)

100(105) (86)86

5-y-o b g Invincible Spirit (IRE)-Mambodorga (USA) (Kingmambo (USA))

Stef Liddiard (J G Given 18/6) That's The Spirit

Placings:0420110/1042204660/0333006260-55544040 **(7682)**

2009: 5^{5}GF, 5^{5}GF, 5^{5}GF, 5^{4}GF, 5^{4}GF, 5^{0}GS, 6^{4}SD, 5^{0}SD,

	Starts	1st	2nd	3rd	Win & Pl
Career Total (Turf)	**27**	**3**	**2**	**3**	**17517**
Career Total (AW)	**8**	**0**	**2**	**0**	**3808**

82	9/06	Ches	5f16y	(0-85)	G-F	£6477
78	9/06	Wwck	5f110y	(0-75)	GD	£3238

Total win prize-money £9716

Going (Turf):	Sf: 0-2 GS: 0-3 Gd: 1-7 **GF: 2-15** Fm: 0-0
Distance:	**5f/6f: 3-35** 7f-8f: 0-0 9f-13f: 0-0 14f+: 0-0
Track :	**LH: 2-11** RH: 0-3 **Tight: 1-8** Gall: 0-1
Aids:	Bl: 0-1 Vi: 0-0 Tstrap: 0-0 Ckp: 0-0
Best Rating:	**91** 7/07 Kemp 6f stand

Modest; stays 6f; handles most ground and Polytrack.

Mambo Sun

(103) (72)70

6-y-o ro g Superior Premium-The Manx Touch (IRE) (Petardia)

R Curtis Market Avenue Racing Club Ltd

Placings:644006231/4433220522/0054/4323-1433 **(0622)**

2009: 8^{1}SS, 8^{4}SD, 9^{3}SD, 11^{3}SD,

	Starts	1st	2nd	3rd	Win & Pl
Career Total (Turf)	**10**	**0**	**4**	**0**	**4802**
Career Total (AW)	**21**	**2**	**2**	**7**	**11151**

70	1/09	Sthl	1m	(0-60)H	SS	£2047
68	12/05	Sthl	7f	(0-75)	STD	£4090

Total win prize-money £6137

Going (Turf):	**Sf: 0-0 GS: 0-2 Gd: 0-2 GF: 0-3 Fm: 0-3**
Distance:	5f/6f: 0-2 **7f-8f: 2-17** 9f-13f: 0-12 14f+: 0-0
Track :	**LH: 2-25** RH: 0-4 Tight: 0-10 Gall: 0-1
Aids:	Bl: 0-1 Vi: 0-0 Tstrap: 1-4 Ckp: 1-4
Best Rating:	**72** 2/09 Sthl 1m3f stand

Modest; effective at around 1m-1m2f; acts on Fibresand and Polytrack.

Mamlakati (IRE)

100 81

3-y-o b f Invincible Spirit (IRE)-Elba (IRE) (Ela-Mana-Mou)

R Hannon Malih L Al Basti

Placings:14-40500641010 **(6798)**

2009: 7^{4}GF, 6^{0}GF, 7^{5}GF, 7^{0}G, 6^{0}GF, 5^{6}G, 5^{4}G, 5^{1}G, 5^{0}GF, 5^{1}GF, 6^{0}S,

	Starts	1st	2nd	3rd	Win & Pl
Career Total (Turf)	**13**	**3**	**0**	**0**	**11405**

71	9/09	Brig	5f213y	(0-58)H	G-F	£2137
56	8/09	Chep	5f16y		GD	£1942
74	7/08	Wind	6f		G-F	£5569

Total win prize-money £9649

Going (Turf):	Sf: 0-1 GS: 0-0 Gd: 1-5 **GF: 2-7** Fm: 0-0
Distance:	**5f/6f: 3-9** 7f-8f: 0-4 9f-13f: 0-0 14f+: 0-0
Track :	**LH: 1-4** RH: 0-0 Tight: 0-1 **Gall: 1-3**
Aids:	Bl: 0-0 Vi: 0-0 Tstrap: 0-0 Ckp: 0-0
Best Rating:	**81** 10/08 Sals 6f good

Useful; effective over 6f and acts on fast ground.

Mamlook (IRE)

109 100

5-y-o br g Key Of Luck (USA)-Cradle Brief (IRE) (Brief Truce (USA))

D E Pipe P A Deal & G Lowe

Placings:23/43120/23-2 **(6851)**

2009: 18^{2}G,

	Starts	1st	2nd	3rd	Win & Pl
Career Total (Turf)	**10**	**1**	**4**	**3**	**67318**

87	5/07	Wxfd	1m5f	GD	£5135

Total win prize-money £5136

Going (Turf):	Sf: 0-2 GS: 0-0 **Gd: 1-4** GF: 0-1 Fm: 0-0
Distance:	5f/6f: 0-0 7f-8f: 0-4 **9f-13f: 1-3** 14f+: 0-3
Track :	LH: 0-1 **RH: 1-8** Tight: 0-0 Gall: 0-4
Aids:	Bl: 0-0 Vi: 0-0 Tstrap: 0-0 Ckp: 0-0
Best Rating:	**100** 10/09 NmkR 2m2f good

Useful; stays 2m4f; acts on good and easier ground.

Man In The Mirror (IRE)

88(83) (31)49

2-y-o b g Captain Rio-Shyshiyra (IRE) (Kahyasi)

P L Gilligan Treasure Seekers

Placings:00056 **(7722)**

2009: 7^{0}SD, 8^{0}SD, 8^{0}GS, 7^{5}G, 8^{6}SD,

	Starts	1st	2nd	3rd	Win & Pl
Career Total (Turf)	**2**	**0**	**0**	**0**	**0**
Career Total (AW)	**3**	**0**	**0**	**0**	**0**

Going (Turf):	**Sf: 0-0 GS: 0-1 Gd: 0-1 GF: 0-0 Fm: 0-0**
Distance:	5f/6f: 0-0 7f-8f: 0-4 9f-13f: 0-1 14f+: 0-0
Track :	LH: 0-3 RH: 0-0 Tight: 0-1 Gall: 0-0
Aids:	Bl: 0-0 Vi: 0-2 Tstrap: 0-0 Ckp: 0-0
Best Rating:	**49** 10/09 Yarm 7f3y good

Man Of Action (USA)

95 74

2-y-o ch c Elusive Quality (USA)-Dixie Melody I (USA) (Dixieland Band (USA))

J H M Gosden H R H Princess Haya Of Jordan

Placings:3 **(7146)**

2009: 7^{3}G,

	Starts	1st	2nd	3rd	Win & Pl
Career Total (Turf)	**1**	**0**	**0**	**1**	**770**

Going (Turf):	**Sf: 0-0 GS: 0-0 Gd: 0-1 GF: 0-0 Fm: 0-0**
Distance:	5f/6f: 0-0 7f-8f: 0-1 9f-13f: 0-0 14f+: 0-0
Track :	LH: 0-0 RH: 0-0 Tight: 0-0 Gall: 0-0
Aids:	Bl: 0-0 Vi: 0-0 Tstrap: 0-0 Ckp: 0-0
Best Rating:	**74** 10/09 NmkR 7f good

Fair debut over 7f on good ground.

Man Of Gwent (UAE)

91(105) (87)79

5-y-o b g In The Wings-Welsh Valley (USA) (Irish River (FR))

P D Evans R Piff

Placings:0/12060403004050512-0553042000 **(3847)**

2009: 12^{0}SD, 10^{5}SD, 10^{5}SD, 10^{3}SD, 12^{0}SD, 9^{4}GF, 10^{2}GF, 10^{0}GF, 9^{0}GF, 10^{0}GF,

	Starts	1st	2nd	3rd	Win & Pl
Career Total (Turf)	**14**	**0**	**1**	**1**	**2316**
Career Total (AW)	**14**	**2**	**2**	**1**	**9119**

69	12/08	Kemp	1m2f	(0-75)H	STD	£3238
74	2/08	Wolv	1m1f103y		STD	£2457

Total win prize-money £5695

Going (Turf):	**Sf: 0-2 GS: 0-1 Gd: 0-3 GF: 0-8 Fm: 0-0**
Distance:	5f/6f: 0-0 7f-8f: 0-2 **9f-13f: 2-25** 14f+: 0-1
Track :	LH: 1-17 RH: 1-10 **Tight: 1-11** Gall: 0-3
Aids:	Bl: 0-1 Vi: 0-0 Tstrap: 0-2 Ckp: 0-2
Best Rating:	**87** 2/08 Kemp 1m3f stand

Modest; stays 1m3f; acts on fast ground and on Polytrack.

Manana Manana

95(95) (65)63

3-y-o b g Tobougg (IRE)-Midnight Allure (Aragon)

J Balding (S Parr 23/5) W McKay,D Kilpatrick,D Mcivor,R Mcivor

Placings:520-0305 **(7853)**

2009: 8^{0}SD, 6^{3}G, 7^{0}GF, 6^{5}SS,

	Starts	1st	2nd	3rd	Win & Pl
Career Total (Turf)	**2**	**0**	**0**	**1**	**482**
Career Total (AW)	**5**	**0**	**1**	**0**	**907**

Going (Turf):	**Sf: 0-0 GS: 0-0 Gd: 0-1 GF: 0-1 Fm: 0-0**
Distance:	5f/6f: 0-3 7f-8f: 0-4 9f-13f: 0-0 14f+: 0-0
Track :	LH: 0-5 RH: 0-1 Tight: 0-3 Gall: 0-0
Aids:	Bl: 0-2 Vi: 0-0 Tstrap: 0-0 Ckp: 0-0
Best Rating:	**65** 12/08 Sthl 7f stand

Modest; best on All-Weather; acts on fast turf; stays 7f; has worn blinkers.

Manarah (USA)

95 51

3-y-o ch f Giant's Causeway (USA)-Ishtak (Nashwan (USA))

J H M Gosden Hamdan Al Maktoum

Placings:00 **(2051)**

2009: 10^{0}G, 12^{0}GF,

	Starts	1st	2nd	3rd	Win & Pl
Career Total (Turf)	**2**	**0**	**0**	**0**	

Going (Turf):	**Sf: 0-0 GS: 0-0 Gd: 0-1 GF: 0-1 Fm: 0-0**
Distance:	5f/6f: 0-0 7f-8f: 0-0 9f-13f: 0-2 14f+: 0-0
Track :	LH: 0-0 RH: 0-2 Tight: 0-0 Gall: 0-1
Aids:	Bl: 0-0 Vi: 0-0 Tstrap: 0-0 Ckp: 0-0
Best Rating:	**51** 5/09 NmkR 1m4f gd-fm

Manassas (IRE)

109 104

4-y-o b g Cape Cross (IRE)-Monnavanna (IRE) (Machiavellian (USA))

B J Meehan Mrs R Philipps

Placings:310/5-10001 **(5863)**
2009: 8^{1}GF, 8^{0}S, 8^{0}GF, 8^{0}GF, 8^{1}GF,

	Starts	1st	2nd	3rd	Win & Pl
Career Total (Turf)	9	3	0	1	52439

104	9/09	Donc	1m	(0-110)H	G-F	£16190
102	3/09	Donc	1m	H	G-F	£31155
85	9/07	Yarm	6f3y		G-F	£3886

Total win prize-money £51231

Going (Turf): Sf: 0-1 GS: 0-2 Gd: 0-1 **GF: 3-5** Fm: 0-0
Distance: 5f/6f: 0-1 **7f-8f: 3-6** 9f-13f: 0-2 14f+: 0-0
Track : LH: 0-0 RH: 0-3 Tight: 0-1 Gall: 0-0
Aids: Bl: 0-0 Vi: 0-0 Tstrap: 0-0 Ckp: 0-0
Best Rating: 104 9/09 Donc 1m gd-fm

Smart; won Spring Mile at Doncaster in 2009; effective over 6f-1m; acts on good ground.

Manchestermaverick (USA)

99(101) (65)63
4-y-o ch g Van Nistelrooy (USA)-Lydia Louise (USA) (Southern Halo (USA))
Dr J R J Naylor (H Morrison 18/8) Cleeve Stables Racing Partnership

Placings:4224204-034200100 **(7861)**
2009: 9^{0}SD, 7^{3}SD, 7^{4}SD, 6^{2}GF, 6^{0}GF, 6^{0}GF, 6^{1}F, 7^{0}F, 7^{0}SD,

	Starts	1st	2nd	3rd	Win & Pl
Career Total (Turf)	7	1	3	0	4213
Career Total (AW)	9	0	1	1	1108

62	8/09	Brig	6f209y		FRM	£1942

Total win prize-money £1943

Going (Turf): Sf: 0-0 GS: 0-0 Gd: 0-0 GF: 0-4 **Fm: 1-3**
Distance: 5f/6f: 0-1 **7f-8f: 1-12** 9f-13f: 0-3 14f+: 0-0
Track : **LH: 1-11** RH: 0-1 Tight: 0-8 Gall: 0-0
Aids: Bl: 0-0 **Vi: 1-6** Tstrap: 0-0 Ckp: 0-0
Best Rating: 65 2/09 Ling 7f stand

Modest; stays 7f; acts on fast turf and on Polytrack.

Mandalay King (IRE)

105(70) (49)76
4-y-o b g King's Best (USA)-Mahamuni (IRE) (Sadler's Wells (USA))
Mrs Marjorie Fife R W Fife

Placings:00/4041311225-510056021260 **(5623)**
2009: 7^{5}F, 5^{1}GF, 7^{0}G, 5^{0}GF, 6^{5}GF, 5^{6}GF, 5^{0}GF, 6^{2}G, 6^{1}G, 5^{2}G, 5^{6}GS, 5^{0}S,

	Starts	1st	2nd	3rd	Win & Pl
Career Total (Turf)	21	5	4	1	19594
Career Total (AW)	3	0	0	0	

76	7/09	York	6f	(0-80)H	GD	£5180
75	4/09	Catt	5f212y	(0-65)H	G-F	£2183
67	7/08	Carl	5f	(0-70)H	FRM	£2590
65	7/08	Haml	6f5y	(0-60)H	G-S	£2388
54	7/08	Rdcr	6f	(0-60)H	G-F	£2388

Total win prize-money £14731

Going (Turf): Sf: 0-2 GS: 1-4 Gd: 1-5 **GF: 2-8** Fm: 1-2
Distance: **5f/6f: 4-15** 7f-8f: 1-9 9f-13f: 0-0 14f+: 0-0
Track : LH: 1-6 RH: 1-8 Tight: 1-7 Gall: 1-3
Aids: Bl: 0-0 Vi: 0-0 Tstrap: 0-0 Ckp: 0-0
Best Rating: 76 8/09 Catt 5f212y good

Modest; stays 6f and acts on most ground.

Mandarin Express

88(78) (39)53
2-y-o ch g Dubai Destination (USA)-Hsi Wang Mu (IRE) (Dr Fong (USA))
B J Meehan Catesby W Clay

Placings:00500 **(6034)**
2009: 7^{0}S, 6^{0}G, 6^{5}GF, 8^{0}SD, 8^{0}GF,

	Starts	1st	2nd	3rd	Win & Pl
Career Total (Turf)	4	0	0	0	0
Career Total (AW)	1	0	0	0	

Going (Turf): Sf: 0-1 GS: 0-0 Gd: 0-1 GF: 0-2 Fm: 0-0
Distance: 5f/6f: 0-2 7f-8f: 0-2 9f-13f: 0-1 14f+: 0-0
Track : LH: 0-0 RH: 0-1 Tight: 0-0 Gall: 0-1
Aids: Bl: 0-0 Vi: 0-0 Tstrap: 0-0 Ckp: 0-0
Best Rating: 53 8/09 Ling 6f gd-fm

Mandarin Spirit (IRE)

102(101) (75)76
9-y-o b g Primo Dominie-Lithe Spirit (IRE) (Dancing Dissident (USA))
Miss L A Perratt Peter Tsim

Placings:605/64211041**1000/0550514301**6**/641134**316250 506/**0100050526**0**6461312/33515**0**5044606400/55**2430221 504100435-001005020 **(7735)**
2009: 8^{0}GF, 8^{0}SD, 5^{1}G, 7^{0}GF, 5^{0}GF, 5^{5}SD, 7^{0}G, 5^{2}GS, 5^{0}SD,

	Starts	1st	2nd	3rd	Win & Pl
Career Total (Turf)	52	8	7	4	41780
Career Total (AW)	50	8	1	4	35789

73	9/09	Haml	5f4y	(0-80)H	GD	£5180
76	8/08	Folk	6f	(0-75)H	G-F	£2590
71	7/08	Brig	5f213y	(0-75)H	G-F	£2775
87	2/07	Sthl	7f	(0-85)H	STD	£4857
84	12/06	Wolv	7f32y	(0-75)H	STD	£3238
76	11/06	Kemp	6f	(0-75)H	STD	£3238
77	3/06	Wolv	7f32y	(0-75)H	STD	£2914
76	5/05	Folk	6f	(0-70)H	SFT	£3597
77	2/05	Wolv	7f32y	(0-70)H	STD	£3387
74	1/05	Ling	6f	(0-70)	STD	£3454
78	12/04	Wolv	7f32y		STD	£3399
71	9/04	Epsm	7f	(0-70)H	G-F	£5683
82	9/03	Epsm	7f	D(0-80)H	GD	£3581
78	9/03	Folk	7f	E(0-70)H	G-F	£2142
68	7/03	Wolv	1m100y	E(0-70)H	STD	£4163
65	7/03	Catt	7f	E(0-75)H	G-F	£3877

Total win prize-money £58086

Going (Turf): Sf: 1-5 GS: 0-4 Gd: 2-8 **GF: 5-32** Fm: 0-3
Distance: 5f/6f: 6-50 **7f-8f: 9-48** 9f-13f: 1-4 14f+: 0-0
Track : **LH: 11-64** RH: 1-10 **Tight: 9-54** Gall: 0-4
Aids: **Bl: 15-78** Vi: 0-1 Tstrap: 0-4 Ckp: 0-4
Best Rating: 87 2/07 Sthl 7f stand

Modest; effective over 6f-7f; acts on fast ground and easy ground; also goes on sand; has worn blinkers and a visor.

Mandelieu (IRE)

96(87) (59)73
4-y-o b g Acclamation-Notley Park (Wolfhound (USA))
Ollie Pears Ian Bishop

Placings:026445/4351000-0000460440 **(4192)**
2009: 5^{0}SD, 5^{0}SD, 6^{0}GF, 5^{0}GS, 5^{4}F, 5^{6}GF, 5^{0}GF, 5^{4}F, 5^{4}GS, 5^{0}S, 5^{0}SD,

	Starts	1st	2nd	3rd	Win & Pl
Career Total (Turf)	18	1	1	1	4956
Career Total (AW)	5	0	0	0	0

73	7/08	Brig	5f213y	(0-75)H	G-F	£2784

Total win prize-money £2785

Going (Turf): Sf: 0-2 GS: 0-4 Gd: 0-3 **GF: 1-7** Fm: 0-2
Distance: **5f/6f: 1-21** 7f-8f: 0-2 9f-13f: 0-0 14f+: 0-0
Track : **LH: 1-10** RH: 0-2 Tight: 0-6 Gall: 0-2
Aids: Bl: 0-3 Vi: 0-0 Tstrap: 0-0 Ckp: 0-0
Best Rating: 73 7/08 Brig 5f213y gd-fm

Modest; effective at around 5f; enjoys a sound surface; has worn blinkers.

Mandhooma

94(95) (54)63
3-y-o b f Oasis Dream-Shatarah (Gulch (USA))
P W Hiatt P W Hiatt

Placings:054-201000 **(7795)**
2009: 6^{2}SD, 6^{0}GS, 5^{1}GF, 5^{0}GF, 5^{0}SD, 6^{0}SS,

	Starts	1st	2nd	3rd	Win & Pl
Career Total (Turf)	3	1	0	0	2590
Career Total (AW)	6	0	1	0	1035

63	8/09	Brig	5f213y	(0-55)H	G-F	£2590

Total win prize-money £2590

Going (Turf): Sf: 0-0 GS: 0-1 Gd: 0-0 **GF: 1-2** Fm: 0-0
Distance: **5f/6f: 1-8** 7f-8f: 0-1 9f-13f: 0-0 14f+: 0-0
Track : **LH: 1-8** RH: 0-0 Tight: 0-3 Gall: 0-3
Aids: Bl: 0-0 Vi: 0-0 Tstrap: 0-0 Ckp: 0-0
Best Rating: 63 8/09 Brig 5f213y gd-fm

Moderate; effective at 6f; acts on Polytrack and fast ground.

Mandrake (IRE)

58 2
2-y-o b c Bertolini (USA)-Aquaba (USA) (Damascus (USA))
M Johnston Sheikh Hamdan Bin Mohammed Al Maktoum

Placings:0 **(2311)**
2009: 5^{0}GF,

	Starts	1st	2nd	3rd	Win & Pl
Career Total (Turf)	1	0	0	0	

Going (Turf): Sf: 0-0 GS: 0-0 Gd: 0-0 GF: 0-1 Fm: 0-0
Distance: 5f/6f: 0-1 7f-8f: 0-0 9f-13f: 0-0 14f+: 0-0
Track : LH: 0-0 RH: 0-1 Tight: 0-0 Gall: 0-1
Aids: Bl: 0-0 Vi: 0-0 Tstrap: 0-0 Ckp: 0-0
Best Rating: 2 5/09 Carl 5f gd-fm

Mandurah (IRE)

105(106) (70)94
5-y-o b g Tagula (IRE)-Fearfully Grand (Grand Lodge (USA))
B P J Baugh (D Nicholls 8/8) Martin Hignett

Placings:036/31201334120/00014401300-4010011000504 **(6902)**
2009: 5^{4}SD, 5^{0}GF, 5^{1}GF, 5^{0}G, 5^{0}GF, 5^{1}GF, 5^{1}GF, 5^{0}GF, 5^{0}GS, 5^{0}G, 5^{5}GF, 5^{0}G, 5^{4}GF,

	Starts	1st	2nd	3rd	Win & Pl
Career Total (Turf)	36	8	2	4	39653
Career Total (AW)	2	0	0	1	812

94	7/09	Asct	5f	(0-85)H	G-F	£6476
90	6/09	Hayd	5f	(0-80)H	G-F	£5180
87	5/09	Thsk	5f	(0-80)H	G-F	£5569
77	7/08	Hayd	5f	(0-75)H	GD	£3238
74	5/08	Hayd	5f	(0-75)H	G-F	£3043
74	7/07	Carl	5f	(0-70)H	G-F	£2817
70	4/07	Hayd	5f	(0-75)H	GD	£2817
55	4/07	Sthl	6f	(0-60)H	GD	£2388

Total win prize-money £31531

Going (Turf): Sf: 0-1 GS: 0-2 Gd: 3-14 **GF: 5-18** Fm: 0-1
Distance: **5f/6f: 8-35** 7f-8f: 0-3 9f-13f: 0-0 14f+: 0-0
Track : LH: 1-9 RH: 1-2 Tight: 0-7 **Gall: 1-1**
Aids: Bl: 0-0 Vi: 0-0 Tstrap: 0-0 Ckp: 0-0
Best Rating: **94** 7/09 Asct 5f gd-fm

Useful; effective over 5f-6f; acts on fast ground and on Polytrack.

Manere Bay

98 **73**

4-y-o b f Olden Times-Madurai (Chilibang)
J L Dunlop J L Dunlop

Placings:442-53320 **(6909)**
2009: 7^{5}G, 7^{3}GF, 8^{3}S, 7^{2}G, 8^{0}G,

	Starts	1st	2nd	3rd	Win & Pl
Career Total (Turf)	**8**	**0**	**2**	**2**	**2986**

Going (Turf): **Sf: 0-2 GS: 0-0 Gd: 0-4 GF: 0-2 Fm: 0-0**
Distance: 5f/6f: 0-0 7f-8f: 0-4 9f-13f: 0-4 14f+: 0-0
Track : LH: 0-1 RH: 0-3 Tight: 0-3 Gall: 0-0
Aids: Bl: 0-0 Vi: 0-0 Tstrap: 0-0 Ckp: 0-0
Best Rating: **73** 8/09 Chep 7f16y good

Modest maiden form to datestays 1m; handles most ground.

Mangano

89 (41)**42**

5-y-o b g Mujadil (USA)-Secret Dance (Sadler's Wells (USA))
A Berry Anthony White

Placings:500**65/024**00204360220352515406/000000000-005 **(4750)**
2009: 7^{0}GF, 7^{0}G, 7^{5}GF,

	Starts	1st	2nd	3rd	Win & Pl
Career Total (Turf)	**35**	**1**	**4**	**2**	**7500**
Career Total (AW)	**5**	**0**	**1**	**0**	**877**
55 8/07 Muss 7f30y	(0-65)H	SFT	£2590		

Total win prize-money £2591

Going (Turf): **Sf: 1-4** GS: 0-9 Gd: 0-7 GF: 0-14 Fm: 0-1
Distance: 5f/6f: 0-22 **7f-8f: 1-14** 9f-13f: 0-4 14f+: 0-0
Track : LH: 0-13 **RH: 1-11 Tight: 1-10** Gall: 0-1
Aids: Bl: 0-0 Vi: 0-0 Tstrap: 0-0 Ckp: 0-0
Best Rating: **55** 8/07 Muss 7f30y soft

Moderate; stays 1m and acts on most ground.

Mangham (IRE)

102(80) (41)**101**

4-y-o b g Montjeu (IRE)-Lovisa (USA) (Gone West (USA))
D H Brown Ron Hull

Placings:253/13231012-006**000** **(6168)**
2009: 8^{0}GF, 8^{0}GF, 8^{6}GS, 8^{0}GF, 8^{0}SD, 8^{0}SD,

	Starts	1st	2nd	3rd	Win & Pl
Career Total (Turf)	**15**	**3**	**3**	**3**	**29742**
Career Total (AW)	**2**	**0**	**0**	**0**	
100 10/08 Pont 1m4y	(0-95)H	GD	£9346		
88 8/08 Hayd 1m30y	(0-95)H	SFT	£9714		
81 5/08 Ripn 1m1f		G-F	£3561		

Total win prize-money £22623

Going (Turf): **Sf: 1-2** GS: 0-5 **Gd: 1-3 GF: 1-5** Fm: 0-0
Distance: 5f/6f: 0-0 7f-8f: 0-10 **9f-13f: 3-7** 14f+: 0-0
Track : **LH: 2-6** RH: 1-8 **Tight: 1-9** Gall: 0-0
Aids: Bl: 0-0 Vi: 0-0 Tstrap: 0-0 Ckp: 0-0
Best Rating: **101** 10/08 Leic 1m60y gd-sft

Very useful; effective over 1m-1m2f; acts on easy ground.

Mango Music

103(98) (62)**91**

6-y-o ch m Distant Music (USA)-Eurolink Sundance (Night Shift (USA))
M Quinn Brian Morton

Placings:166220510104/0500234**030/011**63166042436-36621000020 **(7679)**
2009: 5^{3}SD, 5^{6}GF, 6^{6}GF, 5^{2}GF, 6^{1}G, 6^{0}GF, 6^{0}G, 5^{0}GF, 5^{0}GF, 6^{2}G, 6^{0}SD,

	Starts	1st	2nd	3rd	Win & Pl
Career Total (Turf)	**41**	**7**	**6**	**3**	**53692**
Career Total (AW)	**6**	**0**	**0**	**2**	**1059**
84 6/09 Hayd 6f	(0-75)H	GD	£3238		
91 6/08 Pont 6f	(0-90)H	GD	£9346		
87 5/08 NmkR 6f	(0-75)H	G-S	£3885		
81 5/08 Folk 6f	(0-75)H	G-S	£2331		
87 9/06 Sand 5f6y	(0-85)H	G-F	£5505		
87 8/06 Brig 5f213y	(0-80)H	FRM	£8096		
75 3/06 Folk 6f		SFT	£3238		

Total win prize-money £35642

Going (Turf): Sf: 1-7 **GS: 2-9 Gd: 2-10** GF: 1-12 Fm: 1-3
Distance: **5f/6f: 7-43** 7f-8f: 0-4 9f-13f: 0-0 14f+: 0-0
Track : **LH: 2-14** RH: 0-0 Tight: 0-5 Gall: 0-4
Aids: Bl: 0-0 Vi: 0-0 Tstrap: 0-0 Ckp: 0-0
Best Rating: **91** 6/08 Pont 6f good

Useful; effective over 5f-6f; acts on fast and soft ground; goes on Polytrack.

Manhattan Fox (USA)

99 **92**

2-y-o ch c Elusive Quality (USA)-Safeen (USA) (Storm Cat (USA))
B J Meehan Catesby W Clay

Placings:02100 **(6849)**
2009: 7^{0}GF, 8^{2}G, 8^{1}GF, 7^{0}GF, 7^{0}G,

	Starts	1st	2nd	3rd	Win & Pl
Career Total (Turf)	**5**	**1**	**1**	**0**	**6447**
77 9/09 Gdwd 1m	G-F	£4857			

Total win prize-money £4857

Going (Turf): Sf: 0-0 GS: 0-0 Gd: 0-2 **GF: 1-3** Fm: 0-0
Distance: 5f/6f: 0-0 **7f-8f: 1-5** 9f-13f: 0-0 14f+: 0-0
Track : LH: 0-1 **RH: 1-1** Tight: 0-1 Gall: 0-0
Aids: Bl: 0-0 Vi: 0-0 Tstrap: 0-0 Ckp: 0-0
Best Rating: **92** 10/09 NmkR 7f gd-fm

Useful; stays 1m and acts on a sound surface.

Manhattan Sunrise (USA)

(83) (53)

3-y-o ch f Hold That Tiger (USA)-Sellsey (USA) (Pulpit (USA))
Paul Mason P A Mason & Mick White

Placings:000-0 **(2577)**
2009: 7^{0}SD,

	Starts	1st	2nd	3rd	Win & Pl
Career Total (Turf)	**0**	**0**	**0**	**0**	
Career Total (AW)	**4**	**0**	**0**	**0**	

Going (Turf): **Sf: 0-0 GS: 0-0 Gd: 0-0 GF: 0-0 Fm: 0-0**
Distance: 5f/6f: 0-1 7f-8f: 0-3 9f-13f: 0-0 14f+: 0-0
Track : LH: 0-2 RH: 0-2 Tight: 0-0 Gall: 0-0
Aids: Bl: 0-0 Vi: 0-0 Tstrap: 0-0 Ckp: 0-0
Best Rating: **53** 7/08 Kemp 7f stand

Manifest

110 **107**

3-y-o b c Rainbow Quest (USA)-Modena (USA) (Roberto (USA))
H R A Cecil K Abdulla

Placings:213 **(6425)**
2009: 10^{2}G, 12^{1}G, 14^{3}GF,

	Starts	1st	2nd	3rd	Win & Pl
Career Total (Turf)	**3**	**1**	**1**	**1**	**12379**
107 8/09 NmkJ 1m4f	GD	£5180			

Total win prize-money £5181

Going (Turf): Sf: 0-0 GS: 0-0 **Gd: 1-2** GF: 0-1 Fm: 0-0
Distance: 5f/6f: 0-0 7f-8f: 0-0 **9f-13f: 1-2** 14f+: 0-1
Track : LH: 0-0 **RH: 1-3** Tight: 0-0 **Gall: 1-3**
Aids: Bl: 0-0 Vi: 0-0 Tstrap: 0-0 Ckp: 0-0
Best Rating: **107** 8/09 NmkJ 1m4f good

Smart; Listed placed; effective over 1m4f; acts on good ground.

Mannello

86(92) (61)**59**

6-y-o b m Mamalik (USA)-Isle Of Sodor (Cyrano De Bergerac)
S W Hall Eagle Bloodstock & Racing

Placings:000/62520/000226**000524550**/01501266-3060 **(1958)**
2009: 6^{3}SD, 6^{0}G, 5^{6}GF, 6^{0}F,

	Starts	1st	2nd	3rd	Win & Pl
Career Total (Turf)	**27**	**2**	**5**	**0**	**8102**
Career Total (AW)	**9**	**0**	**1**	**1**	**907**
59 7/08 Brig 6f209y	G-F	£1942			
59 6/08 Brig 6f209y	G-F	£1748			

Total win prize-money £3692

Going (Turf): Sf: 0-4 GS: 0-3 Gd: 0-8 **GF: 2-9** Fm: 0-3
Distance: 5f/6f: 0-14 **7f-8f: 2-22** 9f-13f: 0-0 14f+: 0-0
Track : **LH: 2-14** RH: 0-3 Tight: 0-6 Gall: 0-0
Aids: **Bl: 2-8** Vi: 0-2 Tstrap: 0-7 Ckp: 0-7
Best Rating: **61** 12/07 Ling 6f stand

Moderate; effective over 6f; acts on fast and soft ground; has worn headgear.

Mannlichen

94(107) (86)**77**

3-y-o ch g Selkirk (USA)-Robe Chinoise (Robellino (USA))
M Johnston Graham Mezzone

Placings:52201-0444122 **(7628)**
2009: 10^{0}GF, 10^{4}G, 9^{4}SD, 11^{4}SD, 12^{1}SD, 12^{2}SD, 12^{2}SD,

	Starts	1st	2nd	3rd	Win & Pl
Career Total (Turf)	**6**	**0**	**2**	**0**	**2553**
Career Total (AW)	**6**	**2**	**2**	**0**	**9752**
81 11/09 Kemp 1m4f	(0-75)H	STD	£2590		
75 11/08 GrLe 1m		STD	£3561		

Total win prize-money £6152

Going (Turf): **Sf: 0-1 GS: 0-0 Gd: 0-2 GF: 0-3 Fm: 0-0**
Distance: 5f/6f: 0-0 7f-8f: 1-5 9f-13f: 1-7 14f+: 0-0
Track : LH: 1-7 RH: 1-3 Tight: 0-2 **Gall: 1-2**
Aids: Bl: 0-0 Vi: 0-0 Tstrap: 0-0 Ckp: 0-0
Best Rating: **86** 11/09 Kemp 1m4f stand

Fair; stays 1m4f; acts on fast ground and on Polytrack.

Manolito Montoya (IRE)

88(97) (65)66

3-y-o b g High Chaparral (IRE)-Queens Wharf (IRE) (Ela-Mana-Mou)

J W Hills Gary & Linnet Woodward (2)

Placings:060-500005 **(3629)**

2009: 8^{5}SD, 10^{0}GF, 9^{0}GF, 10^{0}G, 12^{0}SD, 9^{5}G,

	Starts	1st	2nd	3rd	Win & Pl
Career Total (Turf)	7	0	0	0	0
Career Total (AW)	2	0	0	0	0

Going (Turf): **Sf: 0-0 GS: 0-1 Gd: 0-3 GF: 0-3 Fm: 0-0**
Distance: 5f/6f: 0-0 7f-8f: 0-3 9f-13f: 0-6 14f+: 0-0
Track : LH: 0-1 RH: 0-8 Tight: 0-3 Gall: 0-0
Aids: Bl: 0-2 Vi: 0-4 Tstrap: 0-1 Ckp: 0-1
Best Rating: **66** 9/08 Gdwd 7f gd-fm

Manshoor (IRE)

92(104) (85)83

4-y-o gr g Linamix (FR)-Lady Wells (IRE) (Sadler's Wells (USA))

Mrs L Wadham Tim Wood

Placings:0310-11402 **(3361)**

2009: 12^{1}SD, 10^{1}SD, 13^{4}SD, 10^{0}G, 10^{2}GS,

	Starts	1st	2nd	3rd	Win & Pl
Career Total (Turf)	6	1	1	1	8370
Career Total (AW)	3	2	0	0	8442

84 4/09 Ling 1m2f (0-80)H STD £5180
79 4/09 Ling 1m4f (0-75)H STD £2900
5/08 Cros 1m2f110y SFT £5147
Total win prize-money £13228

Going (Turf): **Sf: 1-2** GS: 0-2 Gd: 0-1 GF: 0-0 Fm: 0-0
Distance: 5f/6f: 0-0 7f-8f: 0-0 **9f-13f: 3-8** 14f+: 0-1
Track : **LH: 2-4** RH: 0-2 **Tight: 2-4** Gall: 0-1
Aids: Bl: 0-0 Vi: 0-0 Tstrap: 0-0 Ckp: 0-0
Best Rating: **85** 5/09 Ling 1m5f stand

Useful; effective over 1m2f-1m5f; acts on soft ground; goes on Polytrack.

Mansii

99(108) (65)63

4-y-o b g Dr Fong (USA)-Enclave (USA) (Woodman (USA))

P J McBride P J McBride

Placings:53042462/00500-660043023 **(6674)**

2009: 6^{6}SD, 6^{6}SD, 8^{0}SD, 7^{0}GF, 5^{4}GS, 6^{3}G, 6^{0}GF, 7^{2}SD, 7^{3}SD,

	Starts	1st	2nd	3rd	Win & Pl
Career Total (Turf)	14	0	2	2	5307
Career Total (AW)	8	0	1	1	967

Going (Turf): **Sf: 0-1 GS: 0-3 Gd: 0-2 GF: 0-8 Fm: 0-0**
Distance: 5f/6f: 0-12 7f-8f: 0-9 9f-13f: 0-1 14f+: 0-0
Track : LH: 0-7 RH: 0-3 Tight: 0-5 Gall: 0-0
Aids: Bl: 0-0 Vi: 0-0 Tstrap: 0-0 Ckp: 0-0
Best Rating: **79** 10/07 Nott 6f15y gd-fm

Modest; stays 7f; acts on fast ground and on Polytrack; has worn a tongue tie.

Manx Miss (USA)

83 (78)56

2-y-o b/br f El Corredor (USA)-Final Legacy (USA) (Boston Harbor (USA))

David P Myerscough Peter M O'Shea

Placings:210 **(7147)**

2009: 7^{2}SD, 7^{1}SD, 6^{0}G,

	Starts	1st	2nd	3rd	Win & Pl
Career Total (Turf)	1	0	0	0	
Career Total (AW)	2	1	1	0	11167

78 10/09 Dund 7f STD £9056
Total win prize-money £9057

Going (Turf): **Sf: 0-0 GS: 0-0 Gd: 0-1 GF: 0-0 Fm: 0-0**
Distance: 5f/6f: 0-1 **7f-8f: 1-2** 9f-13f: 0-0 14f+: 0-0
Track : **LH: 1-2** RH: 0-0 Tight: 0-0 Gall: 0-0
Aids: Bl: 0-0 Vi: 0-0 Tstrap: 0-0 Ckp: 0-0
Best Rating: **78** 10/09 Dund 7f stand

Many A Slip

97 76

2-y-o gr g Verglas (IRE)-Tri Pac (IRE) (Fairy King (USA))

J L Dunlop J L Dunlop

Placings:02415 **(5399)**

2009: 6^{0}GF, 6^{2}GF, 7^{4}GF, 6^{1}GF, 8^{5}G,

	Starts	1st	2nd	3rd	Win & Pl
Career Total (Turf)	5	1	1	0	3973

76 8/09 Sals 6f212y G-F £2914
Total win prize-money £2914

Going (Turf): Sf: 0-0 GS: 0-0 Gd: 0-1 **GF: 1-4** Fm: 0-0
Distance: 5f/6f: 0-2 **7f-8f: 1-3** 9f-13f: 0-0 14f+: 0-0
Track : LH: 0-1 RH: 0-0 Tight: 0-0 Gall: 0-1
Aids: Bl: 0-0 Vi: 0-0 Tstrap: 0-0 Ckp: 0-0
Best Rating: **76** 8/09 Sals 6f212y gd-fm

Fair; effective at 7f on fast ground.

Many Welcomes

101(100) (57)62

4-y-o ch f Young Ern-Croeso Cynnes (Most Welcome)

B P J Baugh Gang Of Four

Placings:5034615-1335U12022 **(6925)**

2009: 5^{1}SD, 5^{3}SD, 6^{3}F, 6^{5}GF, 7^{U}GF, 7^{1}GF, 7^{2}G, 7^{0}GF, 7^{2}GF, 7^{2}GF,

	Starts	1st	2nd	3rd	Win & Pl
Career Total (Turf)	13	2	3	1	8877
Career Total (AW)	4	1	0	2	3044

61 7/09 Ches 7f122y (0-70)H G-F £4047
57 2/09 Wolv 5f216y (0-50)H STD £2388
52 8/08 Haml 6f5y (0-55)H G-S £2388
Total win prize-money £8823

Going (Turf): Sf: 0-1 **GS: 1-3** Gd: 0-1 **GF: 1-7** Fm: 0-1
Distance: 5f/6f: 1-7 **7f-8f: 2-10** 9f-13f: 0-0 14f+: 0-0
Track : **LH: 2-8** RH: 0-0 **Tight: 2-6** Gall: 0-0
Aids: Bl: 0-0 Vi: 0-0 Tstrap: 0-0 Ckp: 0-0
Best Rating: **62** 10/09 Yarm 7f3y gd-fm

Moderate; stays 7f and acts on fast ground.

Manyriverstocross (IRE)

111 104

4-y-o b g Cape Cross (IRE)-Alexandra S (IRE) (Sadler's Wells (USA))

A King Mrs M C Sweeney

Placings:5/2421440-302162 **(5823)**

2009: 12^{3}G, 12^{0}G, 12^{2}GF, 14^{1}G, 14^{6}GF, 14^{2}GF,

	Starts	1st	2nd	3rd	Win & Pl
Career Total (Turf)	14	2	4	1	35524

99 7/09 Gdwd 1m6f (0-105)H GD £12462
86 6/08 Chep 1m4f23y G-F £2590
Total win prize-money £15052

Going (Turf): Sf: 0-3 GS: 0-3 **Gd: 1-3 GF: 1-5** Fm: 0-0
Distance: 5f/6f: 0-0 7f-8f: 0-1 9f-13f: 1-8 14f+: 1-5
Track : LH: 1-8 RH: 1-5 **Tight: 1-3** Gall: 0-6
Aids: Bl: 0-0 Vi: 0-0 Tstrap: 0-0 Ckp: 0-0
Best Rating: **104** 9/09 Donc 1m6f132y gd-fm

Very useful; stays 1m6f; acts on most ground; likes to race prominently.

Manzila (FR)

101 107

6-y-o ch m Cadeaux Genereux-Mannsara (IRE) (Royal Academy (USA))

Mme C Barande-Barbe (D Nicholls 28/4) Michel Guerriche

Placings:615413320/50166000/610550344-000604

2009: 5^{0}GF, 5^{0}G, 6^{0}G, 5^{6}G, 6^{0}S, 5^{4}GS,

	Starts	1st	2nd	3rd	Win & Pl
Career Total (Turf)	32	4	1	3	73897

107 5/08 Thsk 5f (0-100)H GD £11656
102 4/07 Chan 6f GD £27027
88 6/06 Chan 5f110y H G-S £8276
4/06 Roya 1m GD £3103
Total win prize-money £50063

Going (Turf): Sf: 0-7 GS: 1-9 **Gd: 3-8** GF: 0-6 Fm: 0-0
Distance: **5f/6f: 3-26** 7f-8f: 1-6 9f-13f: 0-0 14f+: 0-0
Track : LH: 0-3 RH: 0-4 Tight: 0-1 Gall: 0-1
Aids: Bl: 0-2 Vi: 0-0 Tstrap: 0-1 Ckp: 0-1
Best Rating: **107** 5/08 Thsk 5f good

Very useful; ex-French; Listed placed; has won at up to 1m, but most effective over sprint trips these days; acts on good or softer ground.

Maoi Chinn Tire (IRE)

101(95) (68)63

2-y-o b g Mull Of Kintyre (USA)-Primrose And Rose (Primo Dominie)

J S Moore W Adams & J S Moore

Placings:66234426 **(7625)**

2009: 5^{6}G, 5^{6}GF, 6^{2}G, 7^{3}G, 6^{4}GS, 7^{4}SD, 7^{2}SD, 6^{6}SD,

	Starts	1st	2nd	3rd	Win & Pl
Career Total (Turf)	5	0	1	1	2408
Career Total (AW)	3	0	1	0	605

Going (Turf): **Sf: 0-0 GS: 0-1 Gd: 0-3 GF: 0-1 Fm: 0-0**
Distance: 5f/6f: 0-4 7f-8f: 0-4 9f-13f: 0-0 14f+: 0-0
Track : LH: 0-2 RH: 0-1 Tight: 0-2 Gall: 0-1
Aids: Bl: 0-0 Vi: 0-0 Tstrap: 0-2 Ckp: 0-2
Best Rating: **68** 10/09 Kemp 7f stand

Modest third foal of a dual sprint winner; stays 7f; acts on good ground and Polytrack; has worn cheekpieces.

Maoineach (USA)

107 105

3-y-o ch f Congaree (USA)-Trepidation (USA) (Seeking The Gold (USA))

J S Bolger Mrs J S Bolger

Placings:10-10030 **(3516a)**

2009: 7^{1}GF, 7^{0}S, 7^{0}HY, 6^{3}GF, 7^{0}G,

	Starts	1st	2nd	3rd	Win & Pl
Career Total (Turf)	7	2	0	1	85056

105	3/09	Leop	7f	G-F	£41082
98	8/08	Curr	6f	SFT	£38294

Total win prize-money £79377

Going (Turf): **Sf: 1-3** GS: 0-1 Gd: 0-1 **GF: 1-2** Fm: 0-0
Distance: 5f/6f: 1-2 7f-8f: 1-5 9f-13f: 0-0 14f+: 0-0
Track : **LH: 1-2** RH: 0-1 Tight: 0-0 Gall: 0-0
Aids: Bl: 0-0 Vi: 0-0 Tstrap: 0-0 Ckp: 0-0
Best Rating: **105** 6/09 Leop 6f gd-fm

Group class; twice a winner in Group 3 company; stays 7f, should get further; acts on fast and easy ground; has worn a tongue tie.

Maqaam

88 **74**

3-y-o b g Dubai Destination (USA)-Desert Lynx (IRE) (Green Desert (USA))
M Johnston Hamdan Al Maktoum

Placings:1 **(2364)**
2009: 10^{1}GF,

	Starts	1st	2nd	3rd	Win & Pl
Career Total (Turf)	**1**	**1**	**0**	**0**	**2590**

74 5/09 Rdcr 1m2f G-F £2590
Total win prize-money £2590

Going (Turf): Sf: 0-0 GS: 0-0 Gd: 0-0 **GF: 1-1** Fm: 0-0
Distance: 5f/6f: 0-0 7f-8f: 0-0 **9f-13f: 1-1** 14f+: 0-0
Track : **LH: 1-1** RH: 0-0 **Tight: 1-1** Gall: 0-0
Aids: Bl: 0-0 Vi: 0-0 Tstrap: 0-0 Ckp: 0-0
Best Rating: **74** 5/09 Rdcr 1m2f gd-fm

Fair; stays 1m2f and acts on fast ground.

Maraased

50(98) (64)**91**

4-y-o b g Alhaarth (IRE)-Fleeting Rainbow (Rainbow Quest (USA))
S Gollings P J Martin

Placings:53-02 **(7790)**
2009: 11^{0}S, 12^{2}SD,

	Starts	1st	2nd	3rd	Win & Pl
Career Total (Turf)	**3**	**0**	**0**	**1**	**1059**
Career Total (AW)	**1**	**0**	**1**	**0**	**605**

Going (Turf): **Sf: 0-1 GS: 0-0 Gd: 0-2 GF: 0-0 Fm: 0-0**
Distance: 5f/6f: 0-0 7f-8f: 0-0 9f-13f: 0-4 14f+: 0-0
Track : LH: 0-3 RH: 0-0 Tight: 0-3 Gall: 0-0
Aids: Bl: 0-0 Vi: 0-0 Tstrap: 0-0 Ckp: 0-0
Best Rating: **91** 5/08 Ches 1m2f75y good

Moderate; stays 1m4f; acts on good ground and Polytrack.

Marafong

87(88) (60)**83**

2-y-o ch g Dr Fong (USA)-Marakabei (Hernando (FR))
Miss J Feilden Hoofbeats Racing Club

Placings:55520 **(5166)**
2009: 6^{5}SD, 7^{5}SD, 7^{5}G, 6^{2}GS, 7^{0}SD,

	Starts	1st	2nd	3rd	Win & Pl
Career Total (Turf)	**2**	**0**	**1**	**0**	**1156**
Career Total (AW)	**3**	**0**	**0**	**0**	**0**

Going (Turf): **Sf: 0-0 GS: 0-1 Gd: 0-1 GF: 0-0 Fm: 0-0**
Distance: 5f/6f: 0-1 7f-8f: 0-4 9f-13f: 0-0 14f+: 0-0
Track : LH: 0-1 RH: 0-2 Tight: 0-1 Gall: 0-0
Aids: Bl: 0-0 Vi: 0-0 Tstrap: 0-0 Ckp: 0-0
Best Rating: **83** 8/09 Nott 6f15y gd-sft

Modest; stays 7f; acts on a sound surface.

Maragna (IRE)

87(87) (39)**51**

2-y-o b c Invincible Spirit (IRE)-Bradwell (IRE) (Taufan (USA))
Paul Green Celeb Style Racing

Placings:65455 **(7619)**
2009: 6^{6}S, 6^{5}GF, 6^{4}GF, 6^{5}SD, 5^{5}SD,

	Starts	1st	2nd	3rd	Win & Pl
Career Total (Turf)	**3**	**0**	**0**	**0**	**241**
Career Total (AW)	**2**	**0**	**0**	**0**	**0**

Going (Turf): **Sf: 0-1 GS: 0-0 Gd: 0-0 GF: 0-2 Fm: 0-0**
Distance: 5f/6f: 0-5 7f-8f: 0-0 9f-13f: 0-0 14f+: 0-0
Track : LH: 0-2 RH: 0-0 Tight: 0-1 Gall: 0-0
Aids: Bl: 0-0 Vi: 0-0 Tstrap: 0-0 Ckp: 0-0
Best Rating: **51** 9/09 Thsk 6f soft

Moderate; speedily-bred; promise on debut over 6f on soft; handles Fibresand.

Marajaa (IRE)

106(102) (83)**94**

7-y-o b g Green Desert (USA)-Ghyraan (IRE) (Cadeaux Genereux)
W J Musson John D Jacques

Placings:6/4641510/0600012/464550030550/05P-6136215100 **(6480)**
2009: 8^{6}SD, 8^{1}SD, 8^{3}SD, 8^{6}GF, 8^{2}GF, 8^{1}G, 8^{5}G, 8^{1}G, 8^{0}GF, 9^{0}GF,

	Starts	1st	2nd	3rd	Win & Pl
Career Total (Turf)	**26**	**4**	**1**	**1**	**42716**
Career Total (AW)	**14**	**2**	**1**	**1**	**20747**

94	7/09	Gdwd	1m	(0-90)H	GD	£12952
88	6/09	Yarm	1m3y	(0-85)H	GD	£4667
82	4/09	Kemp	1m	(0-80)H	STD	£4727
92	11/06	Kemp	7f	(0-90)H	STD	£7790
92	9/05	MsnL	6f	H	GD	£8511
	6/05	Comp	1m		GD	£8510

Total win prize-money £47159

Going (Turf): Sf: 0-5 GS: 0-1 **Gd: 4-10** GF: 0-9 Fm: 0-0
Distance: 5f/6f: 1-3 **7f-8f: 4-29** 9f-13f: 1-8 14f+: 0-0
Track : LH: 0-7 **RH: 3-16** Tight: 0-7 Gall: 0-0
Aids: Bl: 0-0 Vi: 0-0 Tstrap: 0-0 Ckp: 0-0
Best Rating: **97** 1/07 Ling 1m stand

Useful; stays 1m; acts on good ground; goes on Polytrack; usually held up.

Maranda (IRE)

88 (59)**46**

5-y-o b m Spectrum (IRE)-Mariyba (IRE) (Be My Guest (USA))
Liam P Cusack Mrs F Hughes

Placings:0000-000 **(3092)**
2009: 7^{0}SD, 7^{0}SD, 8^{0}G,

	Starts	1st	2nd	3rd	Win & Pl
Career Total (Turf)	**3**	**0**	**0**	**0**	
Career Total (AW)	**4**	**0**	**0**	**0**	

Going (Turf): **Sf: 0-1 GS: 0-0 Gd: 0-2 GF: 0-0 Fm: 0-0**
Distance: 5f/6f: 0-0 7f-8f: 0-5 9f-13f: 0-2 14f+: 0-0
Track : LH: 0-5 RH: 0-2 Tight: 0-0 Gall: 0-0
Aids: Bl: 0-0 Vi: 0-0 Tstrap: 0-0 Ckp: 0-0
Best Rating: **59** 9/08 Dund 1m stand

Marbled Cat (USA)

(90) (66)**69**

3-y-o b c Cherokee Run (USA)-Catstar (USA) (Storm Cat (USA))
Niall O'Callaghan (M Johnston 28/1) Kilmichael Racing Syndicate

Placings:30404-5000 **(7527a)**
2009: 6^{5}SD, 8^{0}SD, 10^{0}SD, 8^{0}SD,

	Starts	1st	2nd	3rd	Win & Pl
Career Total (Turf)	**2**	**0**	**0**	**1**	**963**
Career Total (AW)	**7**	**0**	**0**	**0**	**289**

Going (Turf): **Sf: 0-0 GS: 0-0 Gd: 0-1 GF: 0-1 Fm: 0-0**
Distance: 5f/6f: 0-6 7f-8f: 0-2 9f-13f: 0-1 14f+: 0-0
Track : LH: 0-4 RH: 0-2 Tight: 0-1 Gall: 0-0
Aids: Bl: 0-0 Vi: 0-0 Tstrap: 0-0 Ckp: 0-0
Best Rating: **69** 7/08 Asct 6f gd-fm

Modest; effective at around 6f; acts on fast ground; goes on Polytrack.

March Mate

(96) (66)**61**

5-y-o b g Warningford-Daira (Daring March)
B Ellison Ronald McCulloch

Placings:5635/0022200-1 **(0554)**
2009: 8^{1}SD,

	Starts	1st	2nd	3rd	Win & Pl
Career Total (Turf)	**11**	**0**	**3**	**1**	**3376**
Career Total (AW)	**1**	**1**	**0**	**0**	**1978**

66 2/09 Wolv 1m141y (0-60)H STD £1977
Total win prize-money £1978

Going (Turf): **Sf: 0-0 GS: 0-0 Gd: 0-4 GF: 0-7 Fm: 0-0**
Distance: 5f/6f: 0-0 7f-8f: 0-7 **9f-13f: 1-5** 14f+: 0-0
Track : **LH: 1-7** RH: 0-5 **Tight: 1-8** Gall: 0-2
Aids: Bl: 0-0 Vi: 0-0 Tstrap: 0-1 Ckp: 0-1
Best Rating: **66** 2/09 Wolv 1m141y stand

Moderate; effective over 7f-1m; acts on fast ground; also goes on Polytrack.

Marchin Star (IRE)

92 **53**

2-y-o ch c Chineur (FR)-March Star (IRE) (Mac's Imp (USA))
M Brittain Northgate White

Placings:46000 **(5595)**
2009: 5^{4}GF, 6^{6}GS, 5^{0}GF, 6^{0}GF, 7^{0}GF,

	Starts	1st	2nd	3rd	Win & Pl
Career Total (Turf)	**5**	**0**	**0**	**0**	**414**

Going (Turf): **Sf: 0-0 GS: 0-1 Gd: 0-0 GF: 0-4 Fm: 0-0**
Distance: 5f/6f: 0-4 7f-8f: 0-1 9f-13f: 0-0 14f+: 0-0
Track : LH: 0-0 RH: 0-0 Tight: 0-0 Gall: 0-0
Aids: Bl: 0-0 Vi: 0-0 Tstrap: 0-0 Ckp: 0-0
Best Rating: **53** 5/09 Newc 6f gd-sft

Moderate form at up to 7f.

Marching Time

109 **101**

3-y-o b g Sadler's Wells (USA)-Marching West (USA) (Gone West (USA))

Sir Michael Stoute K Abdulla

Placings:610-6541104 (6732)
2009: 10^{6}GF, 10^{5}G, 10^{4}G, 8^{1}GF, 7^{1}GF, 7^{0}G, 8^{4}S,

	Starts	1st	2nd	3rd	Win & Pl
Career Total (Turf)	**10**	**3**	**0**	**0**	**25114**

98 8/09 Gdwd 7f (0-105)H G-F £12462
92 8/09 Sals 1m (0-85)H G-F £4857
80 9/08 Yarm 7f3y GD £4731
Total win prize-money £22050

Going (Turf): Sf: 0-1 GS: 0-0 Gd: 1-5 **GF: 2-4** Fm: 0-0
Distance: 5f/6f: 0-0 **7f-8f: 3-7** 9f-13f: 0-3 14f+: 0-0
Track : LH: 0-3 **RH: 1-2** Tight: 0-1 Gall: 0-2
Aids: Bl: 0-0 Vi: 0-0 Tstrap: 0-0 Ckp: 0-0
Best Rating: **101** 10/09 Sals 1m soft

Very useful; effective over 7f-1m; acts on fast ground.

Marcus Cicero (IRE)

99 **86**
2-y-o b g Le Vie Dei Colori-Stroke Of Six (IRE) (Woodborough (USA))
P Winkworth Kennet Valley Thoroughbreds VIII

Placings:41014 (6398)
2009: 6^{4}GF, 6^{1}G, 6^{0}GS, 6^{1}GF, 6^{4}GF,

	Starts	1st	2nd	3rd	Win & Pl
Career Total (Turf)	**5**	**2**	**0**	**0**	**12971**

86 9/09 Newb 6f8y H G-F £9346
78 8/09 Wind 6f GD £2729
Total win prize-money £12077

Going (Turf): Sf: 0-0 GS: 0-1 **Gd: 1-1 GF: 1-3** Fm: 0-0
Distance: 5f/6f: 1-3 7f-8f: 1-2 9f-13f: 0-0 14f+: 0-0
Track : LH: 0-0 RH: 0-0 Tight: 0-0 **Gall: 1-1**
Aids: Bl: 0-0 Vi: 0-0 Tstrap: 0-0 Ckp: 0-0
Best Rating: **86** 9/09 Sals 6f gd-fm

Useful; effective at 6f; acts on good and fast ground.

Mared (USA)

98(99) (85)**87**
3-y-o ch c Speightstown (USA)-Unbridled Lady (USA) (Unbridled (USA))
J Noseda Sheikh Mohammed Bin Khalifa Al-Thani

Placings:632 (2710)
2009: 8^{6}SD, 10^{3}GF, 8^{2}SD,

	Starts	1st	2nd	3rd	Win & Pl
Career Total (Turf)	**1**	**0**	**0**	**1**	**770**
Career Total (AW)	**2**	**0**	**1**	**0**	**806**

Going (Turf): **Sf: 0-0 GS: 0-0 Gd: 0-0 GF: 0-1 Fm: 0-0**
Distance: 5f/6f: 0-0 7f-8f: 0-2 9f-13f: 0-1 14f+: 0-0
Track : LH: 0-1 RH: 0-1 Tight: 0-1 Gall: 0-0
Aids: Bl: 0-0 Vi: 0-0 Tstrap: 0-0 Ckp: 0-0
Best Rating: **87** 5/09 NmkR 1m2f gd-fm

Useful; stays 1m2f; acts fast ground and Polytrack.

Mareva

47
3-y-o ch f Reel Buddy (USA)-Margarets First (Puissance)
Ollie Pears Ollie Pears

Placings:00 (4654)
2009: 7^{0}GS, 6^{0}GF,

	Starts	1st	2nd	3rd	Win & Pl
Career Total (Turf)	**2**	**0**	**0**	**0**	

Going (Turf): **Sf: 0-0 GS: 0-1 Gd: 0-0 GF: 0-1 Fm: 0-0**
Distance: 5f/6f: 0-1 7f-8f: 0-1 9f-13f: 0-0 14f+: 0-0
Track : LH: 0-1 RH: 0-0 Tight: 0-1 Gall: 0-0
Aids: Bl: 0-0 Vi: 0-0 Tstrap: 0-0 Ckp: 0-0

Margarets John (IRE)

59 **4**
2-y-o b g Kalanisi (IRE)-Tarrara (UAE) (Lammtarra (USA))
G A Swinbank J J Hamilton

Placings:0 (7167)
2009: 7^{0}S,

	Starts	1st	2nd	3rd	Win & Pl
Career Total (Turf)	**1**	**0**	**0**	**0**	

Going (Turf): **Sf: 0-1 GS: 0-0 Gd: 0-0 GF: 0-0 Fm: 0-0**
Distance: 5f/6f: 0-0 7f-8f: 0-1 9f-13f: 0-0 14f+: 0-0
Track : LH: 0-1 RH: 0-0 Tight: 0-0 Gall: 0-0
Aids: Bl: 0-0 Vi: 0-0 Tstrap: 0-0 Ckp: 0-0
Best Rating: **4** 10/09 Ayr 7f50y soft

Margarita (IRE)

97(94) (63)**69**
3-y-o b f Marju (IRE)-Kalinka (IRE) (Soviet Star (USA))
J R Fanshawe Elite Racing Club

Placings:0-503600 (6925)
2009: 7^{5}G, 7^{0}GF, 8^{3}GF, 8^{6}SD, 8^{0}G, 7^{0}GF,

	Starts	1st	2nd	3rd	Win & Pl
Career Total (Turf)	**6**	**0**	**0**	**1**	**520**
Career Total (AW)	**1**	**0**	**0**	**0**	**0**

Going (Turf): **Sf: 0-0 GS: 0-0 Gd: 0-2 GF: 0-4 Fm: 0-0**
Distance: 5f/6f: 0-1 7f-8f: 0-3 9f-13f: 0-3 14f+: 0-0
Track : LH: 0-1 RH: 0-3 Tight: 0-3 Gall: 0-0
Aids: Bl: 0-0 Vi: 0-1 Tstrap: 0-0 Ckp: 0-0
Best Rating: **69** 8/09 Wind 1m67y gd-fm

Maria Antonia (IRE)

(101) (61)**60**
6-y-o ch m King's Best (USA)-Annieirwin (IRE) (Perugino (USA))
Mrs A M Thorpe (D G Bridgwater 29/4) Clear Racing

Placings:0050110151/2040006023650/12304-46 (0918)
2009: 11^{4}SD, 11^{6}SD,

	Starts	1st	2nd	3rd	Win & Pl
Career Total (Turf)	**11**	**2**	**1**	**1**	**6597**
Career Total (AW)	**19**	**3**	**2**	**1**	**7925**

61 1/08 Sthl 1m4f STD £1774
64 1/07 Sthl 1m4f (0-60)H STD £2266
66 11/06 Sthl 1m4f STD £2388
59 10/06 Catt 1m3f214y SFT £2730
51 10/06 Leic 1m1f218y SFT £2590
Total win prize-money £11752

Going (Turf): **Sf: 2-2** GS: 0-2 Gd: 0-4 GF: 0-3 Fm: 0-0
Distance: 5f/6f: 0-1 7f-8f: 0-0 **9f-13f: 5-26** 14f+: 0-3
Track : **LH: 4-23** RH: 1-6 **Tight: 1-10** Gall: 0-0
Aids: Bl: 0-0 Vi: 0-0 Tstrap: 0-0 Ckp: 0-0
Best Rating: **66** 11/06 Sthl 1m4f stand

Moderate; suited 1m4f; acts on soft ground; also goes Fibresand.

Maria Di Scozia

96(98) (74)**83**
4-y-o ch f Selkirk (USA)-Viva Maria (Hernando (FR))
P W Chapple-Hyam Miss K Rausing

Placings:522101-0604 (7841)
2009: 9^{0}GF, 10^{6}GS, 10^{0}SD, 11^{4}SS,

	Starts	1st	2nd	3rd	Win & Pl
Career Total (Turf)	**7**	**2**	**2**	**0**	**8644**
Career Total (AW)	**3**	**0**	**0**	**0**	**361**

83 10/08 Rdcr 1m2f (0-75)H GD £3238
75 6/08 Leic 1m3f183y G-F £3238
Total win prize-money £6476

Going (Turf): Sf: 0-0 GS: 0-3 **Gd: 1-2 GF: 1-2** Fm: 0-0
Distance: 5f/6f: 0-0 7f-8f: 0-0 **9f-13f: 2-9** 14f+: 0-1
Track : LH: 1-5 RH: 1-5 **Tight: 1-3** Gall: 0-2
Aids: Bl: 0-0 Vi: 0-0 Tstrap: 0-0 Ckp: 0-0
Best Rating: **83** 10/08 Rdcr 1m2f good

Fair; stays 1m4f; acts on fast ground.

Maria Nunziata

98(97) (73)**75**
3-y-o b f Green Desert (USA)-Napoleon's Sister (IRE) (Alzao (USA))
J Noseda Normandie Stud Ltd

Placings:3331 (7401)
2009: 8^{3}GF, 10^{3}GF, 10^{3}GF, 8^{1}SD,

	Starts	1st	2nd	3rd	Win & Pl
Career Total (Turf)	**3**	**0**	**0**	**3**	**1338**
Career Total (AW)	**1**	**1**	**0**	**0**	**2590**

73 11/09 Wolv 1m141y STD £2590
Total win prize-money £2590

Going (Turf): **Sf: 0-0 GS: 0-0 Gd: 0-0 GF: 0-3 Fm: 0-0**
Distance: 5f/6f: 0-0 7f-8f: 0-1 **9f-13f: 1-3** 14f+: 0-0
Track : **LH: 1-2** RH: 0-2 **Tight: 1-3** Gall: 0-0
Aids: Bl: 0-0 Vi: 0-0 Tstrap: 0-0 Ckp: 0-0
Best Rating: **75** 6/09 Wind 1m2f7y gd-fm

Fair; stays 1m; acts on fast ground and on Polytrack.

Marie Cuddy (IRE)

92 **63**
2-y-o b f Galileo (IRE)-Corrine (IRE) (Spectrum (IRE))
M R Channon Findlay & Bloom

Placings:3 (6274)
2009: 7^{3}GF,

	Starts	1st	2nd	3rd	Win & Pl
Career Total (Turf)	**1**	**0**	**0**	**1**	**770**

Going (Turf): **Sf: 0-0 GS: 0-0 Gd: 0-0 GF: 0-1 Fm: 0-0**
Distance: 5f/6f: 0-0 7f-8f: 0-1 9f-13f: 0-0 14f+: 0-0
Track : LH: 0-1 RH: 0-0 Tight: 0-1 Gall: 0-0
Aids: Bl: 0-0 Vi: 0-0 Tstrap: 0-0 Ckp: 0-0
Best Rating: **63** 9/09 Ches 7f2y gd-fm

Modest debut over 7f on fast ground.

Marie De Medici (USA)

107 **104**
2-y-o ch f Medicean-Mare Nostrum (Caerleon (USA))
M Johnston Sheikh Hamdan Bin Mohammed Al Maktoum

Placings:33124 (7187)
2009: 6^{3}GF, 7^{3}G, 7^{1}GF, 8^{2}GS, 8^{4}G,

	Starts	1st	2nd	3rd	Win & Pl
Career Total (Turf)	5	1	1	2	8410

94 10/09 Leic 7f9y G-F £5180
Total win prize-money £5181

Going (Turf): Sf: 0-0 GS: 0-1 Gd: 0-2 **GF: 1-2** Fm: 0-0
Distance: 5f/6f: 0-1 **7f-8f: 1-4** 9f-13f: 0-0 14f+: 0-0
Track: LH: 0-1 RH: 0-1 Tight: 0-0 Gall: 0-1
Aids: Bl: 0-0 Vi: 0-0 Tstrap: 0-0 Ckp: 0-0
Best Rating: 104 10/09 Deau 1m gd-sft

Smart; stays 1m; acts acts on easy and fast ground.

Marie Louise

87(94) (57)59
4-y-o b f Helissio (FR)-Self Esteem (Suave Dancer (USA))
L A Dace Mrs Diane Simpson

Placings:556-060 (3029)
2009: 12^{0}GS, 12^{6}GF, 16^{0}SD,

	Starts	1st	2nd	3rd	Win & Pl
Career Total (Turf)	4	0	0	0	0
Career Total (AW)	2	0	0	0	0

Going (Turf): **Sf: 0-0 GS: 0-2 Gd: 0-1 GF: 0-1 Fm: 0-0**
Distance: 5f/6f: 0-0 7f-8f: 0-0 9f-13f: 0-4 14f+: 0-2
Track: LH: 0-3 RH: 0-3 Tight: 0-3 Gall: 0-1
Aids: Bl: 0-0 Vi: 0-0 Tstrap: 0-0 Ckp: 0-0
Best Rating: 59 4/08 Leic 1m1f218y gd-sft

Marie Tempest

99(98) (55)48
4-y-o b f Act One-Hakkaniyah (Machiavellian (USA))
M R Bosley Mrs Jean M O'Connor

Placings:0/00345324-6005 (3215)
2009: 8^{0}SD, 10^{0}SD, 9^{0}GF, 9^{5}GF,

	Starts	1st	2nd	3rd	Win & Pl
Career Total (Turf)	6	0	0	0	241
Career Total (AW)	7	0	1	2	1247

Going (Turf): **Sf: 0-0 GS: 0-2 Gd: 0-2 GF: 0-2 Fm: 0-0**
Distance: 5f/6f: 0-0 7f-8f: 0-1 9f-13f: 0-12 14f+: 0-0
Track: LH: 0-10 RH: 0-2 Tight: 0-3 Gall: 0-5
Aids: Bl: 0-0 Vi: 0-1 Tstrap: 0-0 Ckp: 0-0
Best Rating: 55 10/08 GrLe 1m2f stand

Very moderate; stays 1m2f; acts on good ground and on sand.

Marieschi (USA)

(91) (51)68
5-y-o b g Maria's Mon (USA)-Pennygown (Rainbow Quest (USA))
R F Fisher A Kerr

Placings:404/00656-06 (1442)
2009: 12^{0}SD, 12^{6}SD,

	Starts	1st	2nd	3rd	Win & Pl
Career Total (Turf)	8	0	0	0	481
Career Total (AW)	2	0	0	0	0

Going (Turf): **Sf: 0-0 GS: 0-3 Gd: 0-2 GF: 0-3 Fm: 0-0**
Distance: 5f/6f: 0-0 7f-8f: 0-1 9f-13f: 0-8 14f+: 0-1
Track: LH: 0-7 RH: 0-3 Tight: 0-7 Gall: 0-0
Aids: Bl: 0-0 Vi: 0-0 Tstrap: 0-0 Ckp: 0-0
Best Rating: 68 5/07 Ling 1m2f gd-sft

Marillos Proterras

97(67) (7)61
3-y-o b f Fraam-Legend Of Aragon (Aragon)
Mrs A Duffield Stephen Everatt

Placings:00-600205 (4142)
2009: 10^{6}GF, 12^{0}GF, 8^{0}GS, 13^{2}G, 11^{0}GS, 16^{5}G,

	Starts	1st	2nd	3rd	Win & Pl
Career Total (Turf)	7	0	1	0	964
Career Total (AW)	1	0	0	0	

Going (Turf): **Sf: 0-0 GS: 0-2 Gd: 0-3 GF: 0-2 Fm: 0-0**
Distance: 5f/6f: 0-0 7f-8f: 0-2 9f-13f: 0-4 14f+: 0-2
Track: LH: 0-5 RH: 0-2 Tight: 0-4 Gall: 0-1
Aids: Bl: 0-0 Vi: 0-1 Tstrap: 0-1 Ckp: 0-1
Best Rating: 61 10/08 Donc 1m good

Marina Walk

85(92) (53)39
3-y-o ch f Compton Place-Raindrop (Primo Dominie)
H Morrison Lord Margadale, G Doyle & H Lawrence

Placings:650000 (4479)
2009: 6^{6}SD, 6^{5}SD, 6^{0}SD, 6^{0}GF, 6^{0}GF, 5^{0}G,

	Starts	1st	2nd	3rd	Win & Pl
Career Total (Turf)	3	0	0	0	
Career Total (AW)	3	0	0	0	0

Going (Turf): **Sf: 0-0 GS: 0-0 Gd: 0-1 GF: 0-2 Fm: 0-0**
Distance: 5f/6f: 0-6 7f-8f: 0-0 9f-13f: 0-0 14f+: 0-0
Track: LH: 0-4 RH: 0-0 Tight: 0-2 Gall: 0-1
Aids: Bl: 0-0 Vi: 0-0 Tstrap: 0-0 Ckp: 0-0
Best Rating: 53 1/09 Ling 6f stand

Sister to triple 6f-7f winner Glencal.

Marina's Ocean

89(84) (46)47
5-y-o b m Beat All (USA)-Ocean Song (Savahra Sound)
S R Bowring S R Bowring

Placings:006000 (7726)
2009: 8^{0}SD, 8^{0}SD, 8^{6}GF, 11^{0}S, 9^{0}SD, 7^{0}SD,

	Starts	1st	2nd	3rd	Win & Pl
Career Total (Turf)	2	0	0	0	0
Career Total (AW)	4	0	0	0	

Going (Turf): **Sf: 0-1 GS: 0-0 Gd: 0-0 GF: 0-1 Fm: 0-0**
Distance: 5f/6f: 0-0 7f-8f: 0-1 9f-13f: 0-5 14f+: 0-0
Track: LH: 0-6 RH: 0-0 Tight: 0-4 Gall: 0-0
Aids: Bl: 0-0 Vi: 0-0 Tstrap: 0-0 Ckp: 0-0
Best Rating: 47 9/09 Nott 1m75y gd-fm

Marine Boy (IRE)

104 104
3-y-o b g One Cool Cat (USA)-Bahamamia (Vettori (IRE))
Tom Dascombe A Black

Placings:105-504052 (7150)
2009: 7^{5}GF, 6^{0}GF, 6^{4}G, 7^{0}GF, 7^{5}G, 6^{2}G,

	Starts	1st	2nd	3rd	Win & Pl
Career Total (Turf)	9	1	1	0	13998

99 8/08 Newb 6f8y GD £5828
Total win prize-money £5828

Going (Turf): Sf: 0-0 GS: 0-1 **Gd: 1-5** GF: 0-3 Fm: 0-0
Distance: 5f/6f: 0-2 **7f-8f: 1-7** 9f-13f: 0-0 14f+: 0-0
Track: LH: 0-1 RH: 0-0 Tight: 0-0 Gall: 0-1
Aids: Bl: 0-0 Vi: 0-0 Tstrap: 0-0 Ckp: 0-0
Best Rating: 104 9/08 Newb 6f8y good

Very useful; effective over 6f; acts on good ground.

Marine Spirit (GER)

101(92) (71)84
2-y-o b c Big Shuffle (USA)-Molly Dancer (GER) (Shareef Dancer (USA))
Saeed Bin Suroor Godolphin

Placings:431260 (7108)
2009: 6^{4}G, 6^{3}G, 6^{1}GF, 6^{2}GF, 6^{6}G, 6^{0}SD,

	Starts	1st	2nd	3rd	Win & Pl
Career Total (Turf)	5	1	1	1	6517
Career Total (AW)	1	0	0	0	

84 8/09 Folk 6f GF £3723
Total win prize-money £3724

Going (Turf): Sf: 0-0 GS: 0-0 Gd: 0-3 **GF: 1-2** Fm: 0-0
Distance: **5f/6f: 1-6** 7f-8f: 0-0 9f-13f: 0-0 14f+: 0-0
Track: LH: 0-1 RH: 0-1 Tight: 0-0 Gall: 0-0
Aids: Bl: 0-1 Vi: 0-0 Tstrap: 0-0 Ckp: 0-0
Best Rating: 84 8/09 Wwck 6f gd-fm

Usful; effective over 6f; acts on fast ground.

Marino Prince (FR)

96(94) (54)47
4-y-o b g Dr Fong (USA)-Hula Queen (USA) (Irish River (FR))
T Wall Derek & Mrs Marie Dean

Placings:6001113/55000000-060 (4861)
2009: 10^{0}G, 8^{6}GF, 9^{0}SD,

	Starts	1st	2nd	3rd	Win & Pl
Career Total (Turf)	3	0	0	0	0
Career Total (AW)	15	3	0	1	6581

70 11/07 Wolv 1m141y STD £2047
64 11/07 Wolv 1m141y STD £2047
62 11/07 Wolv 7f32y STD £2047
Total win prize-money £6144

Going (Turf): **Sf: 0-1 GS: 0-0 Gd: 0-1 GF: 0-1 Fm: 0-0**
Distance: 5f/6f: 0-0 7f-8f: 1-4 **9f-13f: 2-14** 14f+: 0-0
Track: **LH: 3-16** RH: 0-1 **Tight: 3-14** Gall: 0-0
Aids: Bl: 0-0 Vi: 0-0 Tstrap: 0-2 Ckp: 0-2
Best Rating: 70 12/07 Wolv 1m1f103y stand

Mariol (FR)

116 116
6-y-o b g Munir-La Bastoche (IRE) (Kaldoun (FR))
Robert Collet Family Vidal

Placings:641352212304445/00016511233/2555033103400-23642100 (6503a)
2009: 6^{2}G, 7^{3}G, 7^{6}G, 6^{4}G, 6^{2}GS, 6^{1}G, 6^{0}GF, 7^{0}GS,

	Starts	1st	2nd	3rd	Win & Pl
Career Total (Turf)	47	7	7	8	334849

116 8/09 Deau 6f GD £38835
116 7/08 Deau 6f SFT £29412
101 10/07 Chan 6f H SFT £18419
102 9/07 Chan 6f H GD £18419
7/07 Vich 5f VS £6756
93 7/05 MsnL 7f G-S £10993
72 5/05 Chan 5f GD £6383
Total win prize-money £129218

Going (Turf): Sf: 2-10 GS: 1-12 **Gd: 3-19** GF: 0-2 Fm: 0-0
Distance: **5f/6f: 6-33** 7f-8f: 1-13 9f-13f: 0-1 14f+: 0-0
Track : LH: 0-5 **RH: 2-16** Tight: 0-0 Gall: 0-4
Aids: Bl: 0-0 Vi: 0-0 Tstrap: 0-0 Ckp: 0-0
Best Rating: **116** 8/09 Deau 6f good

Group class; effective over 6f; acts on soft ground.

Maristar (USA)

95(97) (77)**77**

2-y-o b f Giant's Causeway (USA)-Jewel Princess (USA) (Key To The Mint (USA))
G A Butler M V Deegan

Placings:351 **(6947)**
2009: 7^{3}GF, 8^{5}SS, 7^{1}SD,

	Starts	1st	2nd	3rd	Win & Pl
Career Total (Turf)	1	0	0	1	1679
Career Total (AW)	2	1	0	0	3886

77 10/09 Sthl 7f STD £3885
Total win prize-money £3886

Going (Turf): **Sf: 0-0 GS: 0-0 Gd: 0-0 GF: 0-1 Fm: 0-0**
Distance: 5f/6f: 0-0 **7f-8f: 1-3** 9f-13f: 0-0 14f+: 0-0
Track : **LH: 1-2** RH: 0-0 Tight: 0-1 Gall: 0-0
Aids: Bl: 0-0 Vi: 0-0 Tstrap: 0-0 Ckp: 0-0
Best Rating: **77** 10/09 Sthl 7f stand

Fair; handles Fibresand; stays 7f.

Marius Maximus (IRE)

84 **41**

2-y-o b c Kheleyf (USA)-Marju Guest (IRE) (Marju (IRE))
M Johnston Sheikh Hamdan Bin Mohammed Al Maktoum

Placings:03 **(6246)**
2009: 5^{0}GS, 6^{3}GF,

	Starts	1st	2nd	3rd	Win & Pl
Career Total (Turf)	2	0	0	1	482

Going (Turf): **Sf: 0-0 GS: 0-1 Gd: 0-0 GF: 0-1 Fm: 0-0**
Distance: 5f/6f: 0-2 7f-8f: 0-0 9f-13f: 0-0 14f+: 0-0
Track : LH: 0-0 RH: 0-0 Tight: 0-0 Gall: 0-0
Aids: Bl: 0-0 Vi: 0-0 Tstrap: 0-0 Ckp: 0-0
Best Rating: **41** 9/09 Hayd 6f gd-fm

Marjolly (IRE)

80(87) (54)**40**

2-y-o b c Marju (IRE)-Lost Icon (IRE) (Intikhab (USA))
M Botti Giuliano Manfredini

Placings:63553 **(7757)**
2009: 6^{6}GF, 6^{3}SD, 6^{5}SD, 7^{5}SD, 6^{3}SD,

	Starts	1st	2nd	3rd	Win & Pl
Career Total (Turf)	1	0	0	0	0
Career Total (AW)	4	0	0	2	977

Going (Turf): **Sf: 0-0 GS: 0-0 Gd: 0-0 GF: 0-1 Fm: 0-0**
Distance: 5f/6f: 0-3 7f-8f: 0-2 9f-13f: 0-0 14f+: 0-0
Track : LH: 0-4 RH: 0-0 Tight: 0-1 Gall: 0-0
Aids: Bl: 0-0 Vi: 0-0 Tstrap: 0-1 Ckp: 0-1
Best Rating: **54** 9/09 Sthl 6f stand

Moderate; suited by 6f and acts on Fibresand.

Marju King (IRE)

104 **70**

3-y-o b c Marju (IRE)-Blue Reema (IRE) (Bluebird (USA))
W S Kittow Chris & David Stam

Placings:00-503 **(5223)**
2009: 10^{5}G, 10^{0}G, 10^{3}G,

	Starts	1st	2nd	3rd	Win & Pl
Career Total (Turf)	5	0	0	1	770

Going (Turf): **Sf: 0-0 GS: 0-0 Gd: 0-5 GF: 0-0 Fm: 0-0**
Distance: 5f/6f: 0-0 7f-8f: 0-2 9f-13f: 0-3 14f+: 0-0
Track : LH: 0-1 RH: 0-2 Tight: 0-1 Gall: 0-0
Aids: Bl: 0-0 Vi: 0-0 Tstrap: 0-0 Ckp: 0-0
Best Rating: **70** 7/09 Bath 1m2f46y good

Marjury Daw (IRE)

(98) (59)**56**

3-y-o b f Marju (IRE)-The Stick (Singspiel (IRE))
J G Given Danethorpe Racing Partnership

Placings:000-00200 **(7600)**
2009: 10^{0}SD, 10^{0}SD, 9^{2}SD, 8^{0}SD, 9^{0}SD,

	Starts	1st	2nd	3rd	Win & Pl
Career Total (Turf)	3	0	0	0	
Career Total (AW)	5	0	1	0	605

Going (Turf): **Sf: 0-1 GS: 0-1 Gd: 0-1 GF: 0-0 Fm: 0-0**
Distance: 5f/6f: 0-0 7f-8f: 0-2 9f-13f: 0-6 14f+: 0-0
Track : LH: 0-6 RH: 0-2 Tight: 0-3 Gall: 0-1
Aids: Bl: 0-0 Vi: 0-0 Tstrap: 0-0 Ckp: 0-0
Best Rating: **59** 10/09 Wolv 1m1f103y stand

Mark Anthony (IRE)

95 **78**

2-y-o b g Antonius Pius (USA)-Zuniga's Date (USA) (Diesis)
K A Ryan J Nattrass

Placings:531 **(5036)**
2009: 7^{5}G, 8^{3}GS, 6^{1}GF,

	Starts	1st	2nd	3rd	Win & Pl
Career Total (Turf)	3	1	0	1	5015

78 8/09 Ripn 6f G-F £4533
Total win prize-money £4533

Going (Turf): Sf: 0-0 GS: 0-1 Gd: 0-1 **GF: 1-1** Fm: 0-0
Distance: **5f/6f: 1-1** 7f-8f: 0-1 9f-13f: 0-1 14f+: 0-0
Track : LH: 0-2 RH: 0-0 Tight: 0-0 Gall: 0-1
Aids: Bl: 0-0 Vi: 0-0 Tstrap: 0-0 Ckp: 0-0
Best Rating: **78** 8/09 Ripn 6f gd-fm

Fair; stays 1m but seems most effective at around 6f; acts on fast and easy ground.

Mark Carmers

77 **38**

2-y-o b g Mark Of Esteem (IRE)-Queen Lea (FR) (Alzao (USA))
T D Barron D Pryde & J Cringan

Placings:00 **(5728)**
2009: 6^{0}G, 6^{0}GS,

	Starts	1st	2nd	3rd	Win & Pl
Career Total (Turf)	2	0	0	0	

Going (Turf): **Sf: 0-0 GS: 0-1 Gd: 0-1 GF: 0-0 Fm: 0-0**
Distance: 5f/6f: 0-2 7f-8f: 0-0 9f-13f: 0-0 14f+: 0-0
Track : LH: 0-0 RH: 0-0 Tight: 0-0 Gall: 0-0
Aids: Bl: 0-0 Vi: 0-0 Tstrap: 0-0 Ckp: 0-0
Best Rating: **38** 5/09 Ayr 6f good

Mark Of Meydan

104(107) (81)**79**

4-y-o ch g Mark Of Esteem (IRE)-Rose Bounty (Polar Falcon (USA))
M Dods The Bounty Hunters

Placings:32-350100320 **(6630)**
2009: 6^{3}SD, 7^{5}GS, 6^{0}G, 6^{1}GS, 6^{0}GS, 6^{0}G, 7^{3}SD, 7^{2}SD, 7^{0}SS,

	Starts	1st	2nd	3rd	Win & Pl
Career Total (Turf)	7	1	1	1	5331
Career Total (AW)	4	0	1	2	2870

79 6/09 Newc 6f (0-75)H G-S £3885
Total win prize-money £3886

Going (Turf): Sf: 0-0 **GS: 1-4** Gd: 0-2 GF: 0-1 Fm: 0-0
Distance: **5f/6f: 1-7** 7f-8f: 0-4 9f-13f: 0-0 14f+: 0-0
Track : LH: 0-7 RH: 0-0 Tight: 0-3 Gall: 0-0
Aids: Bl: 0-0 Vi: 0-0 Tstrap: 0-0 Ckp: 0-0
Best Rating: **81** 9/09 Wolv 7f32y stand

Fair; effective over 6f; acts on most ground and on Polytrack.

Markab

112(110) (107)**108**

6-y-o b g Green Desert (USA)-Hawafiz (Nashwan (USA))
H Candy Tight Lines Partnership

Placings:613323/P0/06115400122-644105 **(6661)**
2009: 7^{6}GF, 6^{4}GF, 6^{4}S, 6^{1}GF, 5^{0}GF, 6^{5}GS,

	Starts	1st	2nd	3rd	Win & Pl
Career Total (Turf)	16	3	1	3	76920
Career Total (AW)	9	2	2	0	22702

108 8/09 Ripn 6f H G-F £37386
101 11/08 Ling 7f (0-90)H STD £9714
99 4/08 Newc 7f (0-100)H G-S £9969
92 3/08 Kemp 7f (0-85)H STD £4210
94 3/06 MsnL 1m HVY £6552
Total win prize-money £67832

Going (Turf): **Sf: 1-5 GS: 1-3** Gd: 0-3 **GF: 1-5** Fm: 0-0
Distance: 5f/6f: 1-8 **7f-8f: 4-17** 9f-13f: 0-0 14f+: 0-0
Track : LH: 1-9 RH: 1-4 **Tight: 1-7** Gall: 0-0
Aids: Bl: 0-0 Vi: 0-0 Tstrap: 0-0 Ckp: 0-0
Best Rating: **108** 8/09 Ripn 6f gd-fm

Smart; winner of the 2009 Great St Wilfrid; effective over 6f-1m; acts on good and softer ground and on Polytrack; suited by forcing tactics.

Markadam

93(96) (43)**60**

3-y-o b g Mark Of Esteem (IRE)-Elucidate (Elmaamul (USA))
Miss S E Hall Mrs Joan Hodgson

Placings:026-0064000 **(7751)**
2009: 8^{0}GF, 12^{0}GF, 10^{6}GF, 14^{4}GF, 15^{0}G, 12^{0}SD, 13^{0}SD,

	Starts	1st	2nd	3rd	Win & Pl
Career Total (Turf)	7	0	1	0	1325
Career Total (AW)	3	0	0	0	0

Going (Turf): **Sf: 0-2 GS: 0-0 Gd: 0-1 GF: 0-4 Fm: 0-0**
Distance: 5f/6f: 0-0 7f-8f: 0-3 9f-13f: 0-4 14f+: 0-3

Track : LH: 0-6 RH: 0-3 Tight: 0-7 Gall: 0-0
Aids: Bl: 0-0 Vi: 0-0 Tstrap: 0-1 Ckp: 0-1
Best Rating: 60 11/08 Muss 1m soft

Modest; stays 1m and acts on soft ground.

Markazzi

103 88

2-y-o b c Dansili-Bandanna (Bandmaster (USA))
Sir Michael Stoute Hamdan Al Maktoum

Placings:210 (6478)
2009: 7^{2}GF, 7^{1}GF, 7^{0}GF,

	Starts	1st	2nd	3rd	Win & Pl
Career Total (Turf)	3	1	1	0	6302

88	9/09	Leic	7f9y		G-F	£4857

Total win prize-money £4857

Going (Turf): Sf: 0-0 GS: 0-0 Gd: 0-0 **GF: 1-3** Fm: 0-0
Distance: 5f/6f: 0-0 **7f-8f: 1-3** 9f-13f: 0-0 14f+: 0-0
Track : LH: 0-0 RH: 0-0 Tight: 0-0 Gall: 0-0
Aids: Bl: 0-0 Vi: 0-0 Tstrap: 0-0 Ckp: 0-0
Best Rating: 88 9/09 Leic 7f9y gd-fm

Useful; effective over 7f; acts on fast ground.

Market Watcher (USA)

(99) (60)56

8-y-o b g Boundary (USA)-Trading (USA) (A.P. Indy (USA))
Seamus Fahey J J Bailey

Placings:002/60100/00200/52311/300300000/034-1060 (7578)
2009: 16^{1}SD, 16^{0}GF, 16^{6}SD, 13^{0}SF,

	Starts	1st	2nd	3rd	Win & Pl
Career Total (Turf)	23	1	3	3	16225
Career Total (AW)	11	3	0	1	7888

60	1/09	Wolv	2m119y	(0-65)H	STD	£1706
80	12/06	Wolv	2m119y	(0-65)H	STD	£2730
68	11/06	Wolv	2m119y	(0-65)H	SF	£2730
72	10/04	Cork	1m		SFT	£7785

Total win prize-money £14952

Going (Turf): **Sf: 1-6** GS: 0-0 Gd: 0-5 GF: 0-6 Fm: 0-0
Distance: 5f/6f: 0-0 7f-8f: 1-7 9f-13f: 0-12 **14f+: 3-15**
Track : **LH: 3-14** RH: 1-16 **Tight: 3-10** Gall: 0-2
Aids: Bl: 0-4 Vi: 0-0 Tstrap: 0-0 Ckp: 0-0
Best Rating: 80 12/06 Wolv 2m119y stand

Moderate; Irish trained; stays 2m; acts on Polytrack.

Markhesa

97(95) (60)64

3-y-o b f Sakhee (USA)-Marciala (IRE) (Machiavellian (USA))
J R Boyle (C F Wall 13/10) The Brignon Strollers

Placings:6-0303510 (7149)
2009: 8^{0}G, 8^{3}GF, 8^{0}GS, 8^{3}SD, 7^{5}SD, 7^{1}G, 8^{0}G,

	Starts	1st	2nd	3rd	Win & Pl
Career Total (Turf)	6	1	0	1	2232
Career Total (AW)	2	0	0	1	385

64	10/09	Leic	7f9y		GD	£1942

Total win prize-money £1943

Going (Turf): Sf: 0-0 GS: 0-1 **Gd: 1-4** GF: 0-1 Fm: 0-0
Distance: 5f/6f: 0-0 **7f-8f: 1-6** 9f-13f: 0-2 14f+: 0-0
Track : LH: 0-1 RH: 0-1 Tight: 0-1 Gall: 0-0
Aids: Bl: 0-0 Vi: 0-0 Tstrap: 0-0 Ckp: 0-0
Best Rating: 64 10/09 Leic 7f9y good

Modest; stays 1m; acts on fast ground.

Markington

106 (74)76

6-y-o b g Medicean-Nemesia (Mill Reef (USA))
P Bowen Ron Stepney

Placings:40/2445332150/45300-111020 (7151)
2009: 14^{1}GF, 17^{1}GF, 16^{1}GF, 21^{0}G, 17^{2}GF, 16^{0}G,

	Starts	1st	2nd	3rd	Win & Pl
Career Total (Turf)	19	4	2	3	24374
Career Total (AW)	4	0	1	0	1674

72	6/09	Newc	2m19y	(0-80)H	G-F	£5046
76	6/09	Pont	2m1f216y	(0-85)H	G-F	£5180
70	6/09	Donc	1m6f132y	(0-70)H	G-F	£3238
78	7/06	Rdcr	1m3f	(0-80)H	G-F	£5505

Total win prize-money £18970

Going (Turf): Sf: 0-2 GS: 0-0 Gd: 0-5 **GF: 4-11** Fm: 0-1
Distance: 5f/6f: 0-0 7f-8f: 0-0 9f-13f: 1-13 **14f+: 3-10**
Track : **LH: 4-18** RH: 0-5 Tight: 1-12 **Gall: 2-3**
Aids: **Bl: 3-8** Vi: 0-0 Tstrap: 0-4 Ckp: 0-4
Best Rating: 78 7/06 Rdcr 1m3f gd-fm

Fair; stays 2m2f; acts on fast ground and on Polytrack; has worn blinkers/cheekpieces.

Markyg (USA)

97(101) (95)90

3-y-o b/br c Fusaichi Pegasus (USA)-Spring Pitch (USA) (Storm Cat (USA))
K R Burke Mogeely Stud & Mrs Maura Gittins

Placings:4341-10460 (3049)
2009: 7^{1}SD, 9^{0}SD, 8^{4}SD, 8^{6}HY, 8^{0}GF,

	Starts	1st	2nd	3rd	Win & Pl
Career Total (Turf)	5	0	0	1	8274
Career Total (AW)	4	2	0	0	10761

94	2/09	Kemp	7f	(0-85)H	STD	£4727
82	10/08	Kemp	1m		STD	£3885

Total win prize-money £8613

Going (Turf): **Sf: 0-1 GS: 0-1 Gd: 0-0 GF: 0-3 Fm: 0-0**
Distance: 5f/6f: 0-0 **7f-8f: 2-7** 9f-13f: 0-2 14f+: 0-0
Track : LH: 0-1 **RH: 2-4** Tight: 0-0 Gall: 0-0
Aids: Bl: 0-0 Vi: 0-1 Tstrap: 0-0 Ckp: 0-0
Best Rating: 95 4/09 Kemp 1m stand

Very useful; effective over 7f-1m; acts on most ground and on Polytrack.

Marmooq

93(106) (73)62

6-y-o ch g Cadeaux Genereux-Portelet (Night Shift (USA))
M J Attwater The Attwater Partnership

Placings:35/2013534160/06001052366043400000/456112 31424646151-5143220150000053513 (7699)
2009: 7^{5}SD, 7^{1}SD, 7^{4}SD, 7^{3}SD, 8^{2}SD, 7^{2}SD, 8^{0}SD, 8^{1}SD, 8^{5}SD, 7^{0}SD, 8^{0}SD, 7^{0}G, 8^{0}GF, 8^{0}SD, 8^{0}SD, 8^{5}SD, 8^{3}SD, 8^{5}SD, 10^{1}SD, 10^{3}SD,

	Starts	1st	2nd	3rd	Win & Pl
Career Total (Turf)	21	1	2	4	8174
Career Total (AW)	47	10	4	5	25948

69	11/09	Ling	1m2f	(0-65)H	STD	£1978
73	3/09	Kemp	1m	(0-75)H	STD	£2590
68	1/09	Kemp	7f	(0-65)H	STD	£2047
67	12/08	Ling	7f	(0-65)H	STD	£2388
62	11/08	Wolv	7f32y	(0-55)H	STD	£2047
58	4/08	Kemp	6f	(0-52)H	STD	£2047
56	2/08	Kemp	1m	(0-45)	STD	£1295
47	2/08	Kemp	1m	(0-45)	STD	£1365
64	3/07	Ling	7f		STD	£2184
63	9/06	Wolv	7f32y		SF	£3238
76	6/06	Ayr	7f50y	(0-70)	GD	£3238

Total win prize-money £24420

Going (Turf): Sf: 0-2 GS: 0-0 **Gd: 1-8** GF: 0-8 Fm: 0-3
Distance: 5f/6f: 1-4 **7f-8f: 9-57** 9f-13f: 1-7 14f+: 0-0
Track : **LH: 6-35** RH: 5-19 **Tight: 5-29** Gall: 0-1
Aids: Bl: 0-0 Vi: 0-5 Tstrap: 0-2 Ckp: 0-2
Best Rating: 80 8/06 NmkJ 6f good

Modest; effective at around 6f-1m2f; acts on good ground; also goes on Polytrack; has worn an eyeshield.

Marning Star

106(93) (67)83

4-y-o b g Diktat-Mustique Dream (Don't Forget Me)
Ian Williams N Martin

Placings:020035/2314130-530003100 (6357)
2009: 8^{5}SD, 8^{3}SD, 10^{0}GF, 8^{0}GF, 8^{0}G, 8^{3}HY, 8^{1}GS, 8^{0}GF, 8^{0}SD,

	Starts	1st	2nd	3rd	Win & Pl
Career Total (Turf)	19	3	2	4	18062
Career Total (AW)	3	0	0	1	770

76	8/09	Nott	1m75y	(0-80)H	G-S	£4727
83	6/08	Hayd	1m30y	(0-80)H	GD	£4533
71	5/08	Muss	1m		G-F	£2590

Total win prize-money £11850

Going (Turf): Sf: 0-3 **GS: 1-3 Gd: 1-4 GF: 1-9** Fm: 0-0
Distance: 5f/6f: 0-1 7f-8f: 1-12 **9f-13f: 2-9** 14f+: 0-0
Track : **LH: 2-11** RH: 1-6 **Tight: 1-9** Gall: 0-1
Aids: Bl: 0-0 Vi: 0-0 Tstrap: 0-0 Ckp: 0-0
Best Rating: 83 6/08 Hayd 1m30y good

Fair; stays 1m and acts on most ground; suited by forcing tactics.

Maroon Machine (IRE)

102 98

2-y-o ch c Muhtathir-Mediaeval (FR) (Medaaly)
E J O'Neill G A Lucas & A E Hunt

Placings:132102 (7346a)
2009: 7^{1}S, 7^{3}GS, 8^{2}G, 8^{1}G, 7^{0}G, 8^{2}VS,

	Starts	1st	2nd	3rd	Win & Pl
Career Total (Turf)	6	2	2	1	62621

95	10/09	StCl	1m		GD	£16505
77	7/09	Diep	7f		SFT	£6796

Total win prize-money £23301

Going (Turf): **Sf: 1-1** GS: 0-1 **Gd: 1-3** GF: 0-0 Fm: 0-0
Distance: 5f/6f: 0-0 **7f-8f: 2-6** 9f-13f: 0-0 14f+: 0-0
Track : LH: 1-1 RH: 1-4 Tight: 0-0 Gall: 0-0
Aids: Bl: 0-0 Vi: 0-0 Tstrap: 0-0 Ckp: 0-0
Best Rating: 98 11/09 Toul 1m v soft

Very useful; effective at 7f-1m on good or soft ground.

Marosh (FR)

69(82) (46)61

2-y-o b c American Post-Madragoa (FR) (Kaldoun (FR))
R M H Cowell Le Deauville Racers

Placings:4440 (3925)
2009: 5^{4}G, 5^{4}GF, 6^{4}SD, 5^{0}SF,

	Starts	1st	2nd	3rd	Win & Pl
Career Total (Turf)	2	0	0	0	2619
Career Total (AW)	2	0	0	0	373

Going (Turf): **Sf: 0-0 GS: 0-0 Gd: 0-1 GF: 0-1 Fm: 0-0**

Distance: 5f/6f: 0-4 7f-8f: 0-0 9f-13f: 0-0 14f+: 0-0
Track : LH: 0-1 RH: 0-1 Tight: 0-1 Gall: 0-0
Aids: Bl: 0-0 Vi: 0-0 Tstrap: 0-1 Ckp: 0-1
Best Rating: **61** 5/09 NmkR 5f gd-fm

Marrayah

99 **80**
2-y-o b f Fraam-Mania (IRE) (Danehill (USA))
M A Jarvis Hamdan Al Maktoum

Placings:1 **(5109)**
2009: 6^{1}GF,

	Starts	1st	2nd	3rd	Win & Pl
Career Total (Turf)	1	1	0	0	2590

80 8/09 Yarm 6f3y G-F £2590
Total win prize-money £2590

Going (Turf): Sf: 0-0 GS: 0-0 Gd: 0-0 **GF: 1-1** Fm: 0-0
Distance: 5f/6f: 0-0 **7f-8f: 1-1** 9f-13f: 0-0 14f+: 0-0
Track : LH: 0-0 RH: 0-0 Tight: 0-0 Gall: 0-0
Aids: Bl: 0-0 Vi: 0-0 Tstrap: 0-0 Ckp: 0-0
Best Rating: **80** 8/09 Yarm 6f3y gd-fm

Useful prospect; stays 6f, should get further; acts on quick ground.

Marsam (IRE)

(99) (33)**95**
6-y-o gr g Daylami (IRE)-Dancing Prize (IRE) (Sadler's Wells (USA))
M G Quinlan L Mulryan & M C Fahy

Placings:223/14350/50**02/5-0** **(7761)**
2009: 11^{0}SD,

	Starts	1st	2nd	3rd	Win & Pl
Career Total (Turf)	10	1	2	2	12288
Career Total (AW)	4	0	1	0	877

86 5/06 Baln 1m1f GD £5003
Total win prize-money £5004

Going (Turf): Sf: 0-1 GS: 0-1 **Gd: 1-3** GF: 0-2 Fm: 0-2
Distance: 5f/6f: 0-0 7f-8f: 0-5 **9f-13f: 1-8** 14f+: 0-1
Track : LH: 0-7 **RH: 1-5** Tight: 0-3 Gall: 0-3
Aids: Bl: 0-1 Vi: 0-0 Tstrap: 0-0 Ckp: 0-0
Best Rating: **95** 8/06 Slig 1m2f soft

Marsh Warbler

98 **82**
2-y-o ch g Barathea (IRE)-Echo River (USA) (Irish River (FR))
M Johnston Sheikh Hamdan Bin Mohammed Al Maktoum

Placings:100 **(4488)**
2009: 6^{1}GF, 6^{0}GF, 7^{0}G,

	Starts	1st	2nd	3rd	Win & Pl
Career Total (Turf)	3	1	0	0	2590

82 6/09 Rdcr 6f G-F £2590
Total win prize-money £2590

Going (Turf): Sf: 0-0 GS: 0-0 Gd: 0-1 **GF: 1-2** Fm: 0-0
Distance: **5f/6f: 1-2** 7f-8f: 0-1 9f-13f: 0-0 14f+: 0-0
Track : LH: 0-0 RH: 0-1 Tight: 0-0 Gall: 0-0
Aids: Bl: 0-0 Vi: 0-0 Tstrap: 0-0 Ckp: 0-0
Best Rating: **82** 6/09 Rdcr 6f gd-fm

Useful; stays 6f and should stay 7f; acts on fast ground; sure to improve and win more races.

Marshal Plat Club

(86) (44)
2-y-o b f Monsieur Bond (IRE)-Bond May Day (Among Men (USA))
G R Oldroyd R C Bond

Placings:6 **(7331)**
2009: 5^{6}SD,

	Starts	1st	2nd	3rd	Win & Pl
Career Total (Turf)	0	0	0	0	
Career Total (AW)	1	0	0	0	0

Going (Turf): **Sf: 0-0 GS: 0-0 Gd: 0-0 GF: 0-0 Fm: 0-0**
Distance: 5f/6f: 0-1 7f-8f: 0-0 9f-13f: 0-0 14f+: 0-0
Track : LH: 0-0 RH: 0-0 Tight: 0-0 Gall: 0-0
Aids: Bl: 0-0 Vi: 0-0 Tstrap: 0-0 Ckp: 0-0
Best Rating: **44** 11/09 Sthl 5f stand

Promise on debut over 5f on Fibresand; has worn an eye-shield.

Marsool

85 **60**
3-y-o br g Key Of Luck (USA)-Chatifa (IRE) (Titus Livius (FR))
D McCain Jnr (M P Tregoning 30/6) Timeform Betfair Racing Club Ltd

Placings:0-4 **(3472)**
2009: 9^{4}F,

	Starts	1st	2nd	3rd	Win & Pl
Career Total (Turf)	2	0	0	0	255

Going (Turf): **Sf: 0-0 GS: 0-0 Gd: 0-1 GF: 0-0 Fm: 0-1**
Distance: 5f/6f: 0-0 7f-8f: 0-1 9f-13f: 0-1 14f+: 0-0
Track : LH: 0-1 RH: 0-0 Tight: 0-0 Gall: 0-0
Aids: Bl: 0-0 Vi: 0-0 Tstrap: 0-0 Ckp: 0-0
Best Rating: **60** 6/09 Brig 1m1f209y firm

Martha's Girl (USA)

67(86) (27)**56**
3-y-o ch f E Dubai (USA)-Blue Stream (USA) (King Of Kings (IRE))
D Carroll (D H Brown 20/4) Dreams

Placings:50-00**500** **(7782)**
2009: 10^{0}G, 12^{0}F, 12^{5}SD, 14^{0}SD, 8^{0}SD,

	Starts	1st	2nd	3rd	Win & Pl
Career Total (Turf)	4	0	0	0	0
Career Total (AW)	3	0	0	0	0

Going (Turf): **Sf: 0-1 GS: 0-0 Gd: 0-2 GF: 0-0 Fm: 0-1**
Distance: 5f/6f: 0-0 7f-8f: 0-2 9f-13f: 0-4 14f+: 0-1
Track : LH: 0-7 RH: 0-0 Tight: 0-0 Gall: 0-2
Aids: Bl: 0-0 Vi: 0-1 Tstrap: 0-0 Ckp: 0-0
Best Rating: **56** 10/08 Donc 1m good

Martin's Friend (USA)

41(88) (43)
4-y-o b g Grand Slam (USA)-Dans La Ville (CHI) (Winning (USA))
Mrs L Wadham Ron Davies

Placings:5110401-00 **(4054)**
2009: 10^{0}SD, 10^{0}S,

	Starts	1st	2nd	3rd	Win & Pl
Career Total (Turf)	8	3	0	0	6838
Career Total (AW)	1	0	0	0	

9/08 Fmk 1m2f H GD £2205
5/08 Fmk 1m2f GD £2205
5/08 Fmk 1m2f GD £2205
Total win prize-money £6618

Going (Turf): Sf: 0-2 GS: 0-0 **Gd: 3-6** GF: 0-0 Fm: 0-0
Distance: 5f/6f: 0-0 7f-8f: 0-0 **9f-13f: 3-9** 14f+: 0-0
Track : LH: 0-0 RH: 0-2 Tight: 0-0 Gall: 0-1
Aids: Bl: 0-1 Vi: 0-0 Tstrap: 0-0 Ckp: 0-0
Best Rating: **43** 6/09 Kemp 1m2f stand

Martingrange Boy (IRE)

81(97) (64)**23**
4-y-o b g Danetime (IRE)-Coloma (JPN) (Forty Niner (USA))
J Balding John Howard Wilson

Placings:02120/5000 **(1587)**
2009: 5^{5}SD, 5^{0}SD, 5^{0}GF, 6^{0}SD,

	Starts	1st	2nd	3rd	Win & Pl
Career Total (Turf)	1	0	0	0	
Career Total (AW)	8	1	2	0	3152

69 12/07 Ling 6f STD £1943
Total win prize-money £1943

Going (Turf): **Sf: 0-0 GS: 0-0 Gd: 0-0 GF: 0-1 Fm: 0-0**
Distance: **5f/6f: 1-9** 7f-8f: 0-0 9f-13f: 0-0 14f+: 0-0
Track : **LH: 1-6** RH: 0-0 **Tight: 1-5** Gall: 0-0
Aids: Bl: 0-0 Vi: 0-0 Tstrap: 0-0 Ckp: 0-0
Best Rating: **69** 12/07 Sthl 5f stand

Modest sort; effective over 6f; acts on Fibresand; has worn a tongue tie.

Martingrange Lass (IRE)

(97) (46)**49**
4-y-o b f Chevalier (IRE)-Jellybeen (IRE) (Petardia)
S Parr Willie McKay

Placings:05040400**466-00404** **(0920)**
2009: 11^{0}SS, 7^{0}SD, 6^{4}SD, 5^{0}SD, 6^{4}SD,

	Starts	1st	2nd	3rd	Win & Pl
Career Total (Turf)	6	0	0	0	192
Career Total (AW)	10	0	0	0	0

Going (Turf): **Sf: 0-1 GS: 0-2 Gd: 0-2 GF: 0-1 Fm: 0-0**
Distance: 5f/6f: 0-4 7f-8f: 0-2 9f-13f: 0-10 14f+: 0-0
Track : LH: 0-11 RH: 0-4 Tight: 0-4 Gall: 0-3
Aids: Bl: 0-3 Vi: 0-1 Tstrap: 0-2 Ckp: 0-2
Best Rating: **49** 7/08 Newc 1m2f32y gd-fm

Plating-class; stays 1m4f; acts on Polytrack; has worn a tongue tie.

Martyr

107(100) (91)**96**
4-y-o b g Cape Cross (IRE)-Sudeley (Dancing Brave (USA))
R Hannon Highclere Thoroughbred Racing (Delilah)

Placings:0021/2146-011330 **(3826)**
2009: 10^{0}S, 10^{1}GF, 12^{1}GF, 12^{3}G, 12^{3}GF, 12^{0}G,

	Starts	1st	2nd	3rd	Win & Pl
Career Total (Turf)	8	2	0	2	20778
Career Total (AW)	6	2	2	0	9786

93 5/09 NmkR 1m4f (0-90)H G-F £9066
91 5/09 Wind 1m2f7y (0-85)H G-F £5180
86 2/08 Ling 1m2f (0-85)H STD £4100
79 12/07 Wolv 1m1f103y (0-75) STD £2968
Total win prize-money £21317

Going (Turf): Sf: 0-1 GS: 0-1 Gd: 0-3 **GF: 2-3** Fm: 0-0
Distance: 5f/6f: 0-0 7f-8f: 0-2 **9f-13f: 4-12** 14f+: 0-0
Track : LH: 2-8 RH: 2-4 **Tight: 3-6** Gall: 1-5
Aids: Bl: 0-0 Vi: 0-0 Tstrap: 0-0 Ckp: 0-0
Best Rating: 96 6/09 Asct 1m4f gd-fm

Very useful; stays 1m4f; acts on fast ground; goes well on Polytrack; likes to race prominently.

Marvin Gardens

(104) (56)**47**
6-y-o b g Largesse-En Grisaille (Mystiko (USA))
P S McEntee H R Moszkowicz

Placings:00/600300/30/050000**601-0040** **(0646)**
2009: 5^{0}SD, 6^{0}SD, 5^{4}SD, 6^{0}SD,

	Starts	1st	2nd	3rd	Win & Pl
Career Total (Turf)	13	0	0	2	626
Career Total (AW)	10	1	0	0	2388

56 11/08 Wolv 5f216y STD £2388
Total win prize-money £2388

Going (Turf): Sf: 0-2 GS: 0-2 Gd: 0-2 GF: 0-7 Fm: 0-0
Distance: 5f/6f: 1-8 7f-8f: 0-11 9f-13f: 0-4 14f+: 0-0
Track : LH: 1-10 RH: 0-3 **Tight: 1-5** Gall: 0-3
Aids: Bl: 1-4 Vi: 0-1 Tstrap: 0-0 Ckp: 0-0
Best Rating: 56 11/08 Wolv 5f216y stand

Very moderate; suited by 6f and Polytrack; has worn blinkers.

Marvo

107(97) (62)**89**
5-y-o b g Bahamian Bounty-Mega (IRE) (Petardia)
M H Tompkins M P Bowring

Placings:01/34032030020-0**6**11401050 **(7185)**
2009: 8^{0}G, 7^{6}SD, 8^{1}G, 8^{1}G, 8^{4}GF, 7^{0}GF, 9^{1}S, 10^{0}GS, 10^{5}S, 8^{0}G,

	Starts	1st	2nd	3rd	Win & Pl
Career Total (Turf)	22	4	2	3	26983
Career Total (AW)	1	0	0	0	0

89 8/09 Haml 1m1f36y H SFT £9714
81 6/09 Donc 1m (0-85)H GD £4857
79 5/09 Pont 1m4y (0-70)H GD £3238
76 10/06 Newc 7f SFT £2914
Total win prize-money £20724

Going (Turf): Sf: 2-5 GS: 0-4 **Gd: 2-10** GF: 0-3 Fm: 0-0
Distance: 5f/6f: 0-1 7f-8f: 2-6 9f-13f: 2-16 14f+: 0-0
Track : LH: 2-10 RH: 1-9 Tight: 1-8 Gall: 1-2
Aids: Bl: 0-1 Vi: 0-1 Tstrap: 0-0 Ckp: 0-0
Best Rating: 89 8/09 Haml 1m1f36y soft

Useful; effective at around 1m-1m2f; acts on good and softer ground.

Mary Celest (IRE)

85(83) (41)**53**
2-y-o b f Barathea (IRE)-Rack And Ruin (IRE) (King's Best (USA))
K A Ryan John Duddy

Placings:0030000 **(7210)**
2009: 6^{0}G, 6^{0}GF, 7^{3}GF, 8^{0}SD, 10^{0}GF, 9^{0}SD, 7^{0}SD,

	Starts	1st	2nd	3rd	Win & Pl
Career Total (Turf)	4	0	0	1	347
Career Total (AW)	3	0	0	0	

Going (Turf): Sf: 0-0 GS: 0-0 Gd: 0-1 GF: 0-3 Fm: 0-0
Distance: 5f/6f: 0-2 7f-8f: 0-3 9f-13f: 0-2 14f+: 0-0
Track : LH: 0-3 RH: 0-2 Tight: 0-2 Gall: 0-0
Aids: Bl: 0-0 Vi: 0-0 Tstrap: 0-3 Ckp: 0-3
Best Rating: 53 5/09 Rdcr 6f gd-fm

Mary Goodnight

101(95) (63)**84**
3-y-o b f King's Best (USA)-Disco Volante (Sadler's Wells (USA))
J Noseda Capt J Macdonald-Buchanan

Placings:130 **(6634)**
2009: 10^{1}GF, 10^{3}G, **12^{0}SS,**

	Starts	1st	2nd	3rd	Win & Pl
Career Total (Turf)	2	1	0	1	3500
Career Total (AW)	1	0	0	0	

78 7/09 Wind 1m2f7y G-F £2729
Total win prize-money £2730

Going (Turf): Sf: 0-0 GS: 0-0 Gd: 0-1 **GF: 1-1** Fm: 0-0
Distance: 5f/6f: 0-0 7f-8f: 0-0 **9f-13f: 1-3** 14f+: 0-0
Track : LH: 0-1 **RH: 1-2 Tight: 1-3** Gall: 0-0
Aids: Bl: 0-0 Vi: 0-0 Tstrap: 0-0 Ckp: 0-0
Best Rating: 84 8/09 Wind 1m2f7y good

Winner on debut; effective over 1m2f; acts on fast ground.

Mary Helen

95(95) (64)**54**
2-y-o b f Dandoun-Hotel California (IRE) (Last Tycoon)
W M Brisbourne P Mort & Mark Brisbourne

Placings:0431624**4112** **(7731)**
2009: 5^{0}GF, 6^{4}GS, 6^{3}G, 7^{1}S, 7^{6}S, 7^{2}G, 7^{4}G, **8^{4}**SD, **9^{1}**SD, **10^{1}**SD, 9^{2}SD,

	Starts	1st	2nd	3rd	Win & Pl
Career Total (Turf)	7	1	1	1	3956
Career Total (AW)	4	2	1	0	5592

54 11/09 Kemp 1m2f STD £2047
53 10/09 Wolv 1m1f103y STD £2388
54 6/09 Yarm 7f3y SFT £1942
Total win prize-money £6378

Going (Turf): Sf: 1-2 GS: 0-1 Gd: 0-3 GF: 0-1 Fm: 0-0
Distance: 5f/6f: 0-2 7f-8f: 1-6 **9f-13f: 2-3** 14f+: 0-0
Track : LH: 1-4 RH: 1-3 **Tight: 1-4** Gall: 0-0
Aids: Bl: 0-0 Vi: 0-0 Tstrap: 0-0 Ckp: 0-0
Best Rating: 64 12/09 Wolv 1m1f103y stand

Modest; stays 1m2f; acts on soft ground and on Polytrack.

Mary Mason

81(90) (34)**71**
3-y-o b f Hunting Lion (IRE)-Kalarram (Muhtarram (USA))
James Moffatt (M Hill 5/6) R R Whitton

Placings:610-00 **(2321)**
2009: 6^{0}SD, 6^{0}G,

	Starts	1st	2nd	3rd	Win & Pl
Career Total (Turf)	4	1	0	0	3562
Career Total (AW)	1	0	0	0	

71 8/08 Ripn 6f GD £3561
Total win prize-money £3562

Going (Turf): Sf: 0-1 GS: 0-0 **Gd: 1-2** GF: 0-1 Fm: 0-0
Distance: 5f/6f: 1-4 7f-8f: 0-1 9f-13f: 0-0 14f+: 0-0
Track : LH: 0-0 RH: 0-1 Tight: 0-0 Gall: 0-0
Aids: Bl: 0-0 Vi: 0-0 Tstrap: 0-0 Ckp: 0-0
Best Rating: 71 8/08 Ripn 6f good

Mary West (IRE)

73(78) (18)**52**
3-y-o b f Pyrus (USA)-Pivot D'Amour (Pivotal)
Patrick Morris Mrs Pamela MacDonald

Placings:540-00 **(4137)**
2009: 5^{0}SD, 5^{0}G,

	Starts	1st	2nd	3rd	Win & Pl
Career Total (Turf)	4	0	0	0	168
Career Total (AW)	1	0	0	0	

Going (Turf): Sf: 0-0 GS: 0-0 Gd: 0-2 GF: 0-2 Fm: 0-0
Distance: 5f/6f: 0-5 7f-8f: 0-0 9f-13f: 0-0 14f+: 0-0
Track : LH: 0-2 RH: 0-0 Tight: 0-1 Gall: 0-1
Aids: Bl: 0-0 Vi: 0-0 Tstrap: 0-0 Ckp: 0-0
Best Rating: 52 9/08 Pont 6f gd-fm

Modest; probably best over 6f; acts on good ground.

Marygate (IRE)

82 **54**
3-y-o b f Spartacus (IRE)-Thorn Tree (Zafonic (USA))
M Brittain Mel Brittain

Placings:3000-00 **(1949)**
2009: 5^{0}GF, 5^{0}GF,

	Starts	1st	2nd	3rd	Win & Pl
Career Total (Turf)	6	0	0	1	578

Going (Turf): Sf: 0-1 GS: 0-1 Gd: 0-1 GF: 0-3 Fm: 0-0
Distance: 5f/6f: 0-6 7f-8f: 0-0 9f-13f: 0-0 14f+: 0-0
Track : LH: 0-0 RH: 0-0 Tight: 0-0 Gall: 0-0
Aids: Bl: 0-0 Vi: 0-0 Tstrap: 0-0 Ckp: 0-0
Best Rating: 54 4/08 Donc 5f soft

Maryolini

93(97) (73)**76**
4-y-o b f Bertolini (USA)-Mary Jane (Tina's Pet)
Tom Dascombe (N J Vaughan 2/3) K Warth, I Smith, P Jones

Placings:612**531**/2**5**40**4**0**0-603000** **(6939)**
2009: 5^{6}SD, **5^{0}**SD, **5^{3}**SD, 6^{0}GF, **5^{0}**SD, **5^{0}**SD,

	Starts	1st	2nd	3rd	Win & Pl
Career Total (Turf)	7	0	2	0	2697
Career Total (AW)	12	2	0	2	6196

79 12/07 Wolv 5f216y (0-75) STD £2047
64 7/07 Wolv 5f216y STD £3071
Total win prize-money £5119

Going (Turf): Sf: 0-0 GS: 0-0 Gd: 0-1 GF: 0-6 Fm: 0-0
Distance: 5f/6f: 2-18 7f-8f: 0-1 9f-13f: 0-0 14f+: 0-0
Track : LH: 2-10 RH: 0-4 **Tight: 2-10** Gall: 0-1
Aids: Bl: 0-0 Vi: 0-1 Tstrap: 0-0 Ckp: 0-0
Best Rating: 79 12/07 Wolv 5f216y stand

Fair; effective over 6f; acts on Polytrack.

Marzy

(87) (44)
3-y-o br f Kyllachy-Amarella (FR) (Balleroy (USA))

M Botti Dachel Stud

Placings:600 **(2683)**
2009: 5^{6}SD, 6^{0}SD, 5^{0}SD,

	Starts	1st	2nd	3rd	Win & Pl
Career Total (Turf)	0	0	0	0	
Career Total (AW)	3	0	0	0	0

Going (Turf): **Sf: 0-0 GS: 0-0 Gd: 0-0 GF: 0-0 Fm: 0-0**
Distance: 5f/6f: 0-3 7f-8f: 0-0 9f-13f: 0-0 14f+: 0-0
Track : LH: 0-2 RH: 0-1 Tight: 0-2 Gall: 0-0
Aids: Bl: 0-0 Vi: 0-0 Tstrap: 0-0 Ckp: 0-0
Best Rating: **44** 4/09 Kemp 5f stand

Masafi (IRE)

(26)
8-y-o b g Desert King (IRE)-Mrs Fisher (IRE) (Salmon Leap (USA))
E J Cooper Cumberland Lodge Racing & Leisure Co Ltd

Placings:000/211111111150/0221/0 **(3223)**
2009: 12^{0}SD,

	Starts	1st	2nd	3rd	Win & Pl
Career Total (Turf)	11	6	2	0	39486
Career Total (AW)	7	2	1	0	7631

101	9/05	DRoy	1m4f195y		FRM	£7351
89	7/04	Carl	1m1f61y	E(0-70)	G-F	£3558
96	7/04	Muss	1m1f	E(0-75)H	G-F	£5424
77	7/04	Sthl	1m	E(0-75)H	STD	£3779
75	7/04	Folk	1m1f149y	D(0-80)H	G-F	£5508
82	7/04	Brig	1m1f209y	F(0-55)H	G-F	£2975
69	7/04	Carl	1m1f61y	E(0-70)H	G-F	£3753
77	7/04	Sthl	1m	F(0-55)H	STD	£3017

Total win prize-money £35369

Going (Turf): Sf: 0-0 GS: 0-1 Gd: 0-1 **GF: 5-6** Fm: 1-3
Distance: 5f/6f: 0-3 7f-8f: 2-4 **9f-13f: 6-10** 14f+: 0-1
Track : LH: 3-12 RH: 3-4 **Tight: 1-7** Gall: 0-0
Aids: Bl: 0-0 Vi: 0-0 Tstrap: 0-0 Ckp: 0-0
Best Rating: **104** 8/05 Pont 1m4f8y good

Masai Moon

105(107) (101)101
5-y-o b g Lujain (USA)-Easy To Imagine (USA) (Cozzene (USA))
B R Millman C Roper

Placings:0453242/431200140/541010042200-2604603435 **(6949)**
2009: 6^{2}SD, 6^{6}GF, 7^{0}GF, 7^{4}GF, 7^{6}G, 7^{0}G, 7^{3}GF, 7^{4}SD, 6^{3}GF, 6^{5}SD,

	Starts	1st	2nd	3rd	Win & Pl
Career Total (Turf)	34	3	5	4	42837
Career Total (AW)	4	1	1	0	8293

98	6/08	NmkJ	7f	(0-95)H	G-F	£9066
97	5/08	Sthl	7f	(0-85)H	STD	£5180
92	10/07	Sals	6f	(0-85)H	G-S	£6477
86	5/07	Leic	7f9y	(0-80)H	G-F	£5047

Total win prize-money £25771

Going (Turf): Sf: 0-10 GS: 1-4 Gd: 0-7 **GF: 2-13** Fm: 0-0
Distance: 5f/6f: 1-16 **7f-8f: 3-20** 9f-13f: 0-2 14f+: 0-0
Track : **LH: 1-4** RH: 0-4 Tight: 0-1 Gall: 0-2
Aids: Bl: 0-0 Vi: 0-0 Tstrap: 0-1 Ckp: 0-1
Best Rating: **101** 4/09 Kemp 6f stand

Very useful; effective over 6f-7f; acts on most ground and on both sand surfaces; likes to race prominently.

Masamah (IRE)

87(99) (97)87
3-y-o gr g Exceed And Excel (AUS)-Bethesda (Distant Relative)
E A L Dunlop Hamdan Al Maktoum

Placings:110-002 **(6631)**
2009: 6^{0}GF, 5^{0}GF, 6^{2}SS,

	Starts	1st	2nd	3rd	Win & Pl
Career Total (Turf)	4	1	0	0	8419
Career Total (AW)	2	1	1	0	6391

97	8/08	Ling	5f	STD	£3885
87	5/08	York	5f	G-F	£8418

Total win prize-money £12305

Going (Turf): Sf: 0-0 GS: 0-0 Gd: 0-1 **GF: 1-3** Fm: 0-0
Distance: **5f/6f: 2-5** 7f-8f: 0-1 9f-13f: 0-0 14f+: 0-0
Track : **LH: 1-3** RH: 0-0 **Tight: 1-3** Gall: 0-0
Aids: **Bl: 1-2** Vi: 0-0 Tstrap: 0-0 Ckp: 0-0
Best Rating: **97** 8/08 Ling 5f stand

Very useful; cost 60,000gns; effective at 5f; acts on fast ground and Polytrack.

Maskan

84 61
2-y-o ch g Starcraft (NZ)-Silence Is Golden (Danehill Dancer (IRE))
W J Haggas Hamdan Al Maktoum

Placings:5 **(6786)**
2009: 7^{5}G,

	Starts	1st	2nd	3rd	Win & Pl
Career Total (Turf)	1	0	0	0	132

Going (Turf): **Sf: 0-0 GS: 0-0 Gd: 0-1 GF: 0-0 Fm: 0-0**
Distance: 5f/6f: 0-0 7f-8f: 0-1 9f-13f: 0-0 14f+: 0-0
Track : LH: 0-1 RH: 0-0 Tight: 0-0 Gall: 0-0
Aids: Bl: 0-0 Vi: 0-0 Tstrap: 0-0 Ckp: 0-0
Best Rating: **61** 10/09 Brig 7f214y good

Maskateer (IRE)

84 46
3-y-o b g Iron Mask (USA)-Indescent Blue (Bluebird (USA))
Mrs A M Thorpe Mrs T Brown

Placings:06 **(3205)**
2009: 12^{0}G, 12^{6}G,

	Starts	1st	2nd	3rd	Win & Pl
Career Total (Turf)	2	0	0	0	0

Going (Turf): **Sf: 0-0 GS: 0-0 Gd: 0-2 GF: 0-0 Fm: 0-0**
Distance: 5f/6f: 0-0 7f-8f: 0-0 9f-13f: 0-2 14f+: 0-0
Track : LH: 0-2 RH: 0-0 Tight: 0-0 Gall: 0-0
Aids: Bl: 0-0 Vi: 0-0 Tstrap: 0-0 Ckp: 0-0
Best Rating: **46** 5/09 Chep 1m4f23y good

Masked Dance (IRE)

99(82) (47)77
2-y-o gr g Captain Rio-Brooks Masquerade (Absalom)
K A Ryan Mrs L D Edwards

Placings:4554332152 **(7168)**
2009: 5^{4}GF, 5^{5}SD, 5^{5}GS, 6^{4}HY, 5^{3}G, 5^{3}S, 6^{2}HY, 6^{1}G, 6^{5}G, 7^{2}S,

	Starts	1st	2nd	3rd	Win & Pl
Career Total (Turf)	9	1	2	2	5330

	Starts	1st	2nd	3rd	Win & Pl
Career Total (AW)	1	0	0	0	0

77	8/09	Ripn	6f	GD	£2729

Total win prize-money £2730

Going (Turf): Sf: 0-4 GS: 0-1 **Gd: 1-3** GF: 0-1 Fm: 0-0
Distance: **5f/6f: 1-7** 7f-8f: 0-3 9f-13f: 0-0 14f+: 0-0
Track : LH: 0-1 RH: 0-0 Tight: 0-0 Gall: 0-1
Aids: Bl: 0-0 Vi: 0-3 Tstrap: 1-3 Ckp: 1-3
Best Rating: **77** 10/09 Ayr 7f50y soft

Fair; effective at 5f-6f; handles cut in the ground; has worn a visor.

Masking Baldini (IRE)

75(97) (47)12
5-y-o b g Iron Mask (USA)-Royal Baldini (USA) (Green Dancer (USA))
J Hetherton R G Fell

Placings:00406/00/40-060 **(4600)**
2009: 10^{0}GF, 12^{6}GS, 12^{0}G,

	Starts	1st	2nd	3rd	Win & Pl
Career Total (Turf)	11	0	0	0	428
Career Total (AW)	1	0	0	0	0

Going (Turf): **Sf: 0-1 GS: 0-1 Gd: 0-3 GF: 0-3 Fm: 0-2**
Distance: 5f/6f: 0-0 7f-8f: 0-4 9f-13f: 0-7 14f+: 0-1
Track : LH: 0-5 RH: 0-6 Tight: 0-4 Gall: 0-0
Aids: Bl: 0-0 Vi: 0-0 Tstrap: 0-0 Ckp: 0-0
Best Rating: **56** 7/06 Tipp 7f100y firm

Maslak (IRE)

109(111) (88)92
5-y-o b g In The Wings-Jeed (IRE) (Mujtahid (USA))
P W Hiatt Clive Roberts

Placings:552/2330236224301 3/1311010060-0546340210224 00622 **(7777)**
2009: 12^{0}SD, 12^{5}SF, 12^{4}SD, 11^{6}SD, 12^{3}GS, 14^{4}G, 12^{0}GF, 12^{2}G, 11^{1}GF, 12^{0}GF, 11^{2}HY, 12^{2}SD, 13^{4}SD, 12^{0}G, 11^{0}G, 12^{6}SD, 12^{2}SD, 12^{2}SD,

	Starts	1st	2nd	3rd	Win & Pl
Career Total (Turf)	21	2	3	3	15490
Career Total (AW)	24	4	7	4	26647

79	8/09	Wind	1m3f135y	(0-75)H	G-F	£2637
92	5/08	Ches	1m4f66y	(0-85)H	GD	£7123
94	2/08	Ling	1m4f	(0-85)H	STD	£4100
90	2/08	Ling	1m4f	(0-95)H	STD	£4100
94	1/08	Sthl	1m4f	(0-85)H	STD	£4210
75	12/07	Sthl	1m4f		SS	£2968

Total win prize-money £25142

Going (Turf): Sf: 0-3 GS: 0-2 **Gd: 1-10 GF: 1-6** Fm: 0-0
Distance: 5f/6f: 0-0 7f-8f: 0-3 **9f-13f: 6-38** 14f+: 0-4
Track : **LH: 5-34** RH: 0-9 **Tight: 4-24** Gall: 0-6
Aids: Bl: 0-0 Vi: 0-0 Tstrap: 0-0 Ckp: 0-0
Best Rating: **94** 2/08 Ling 1m4f stand

Fair; effective at around 1m4f; acts on fast ground; also goes on Fibresand and Polytrack.

Mason Hindmarsh

100 70
2-y-o ch g Dr Fong (USA)-Sierra Virgen (USA) (Stack (USA))
Karen McLintock Equiname Ltd

Placings:060425 **(7116)**

2009: 6^{0}G, 5^{6}GF, 7^{0}GF, 8^{4}GF, 8^{2}GF, 8^{5}GS,

	Starts	1st	2nd	3rd	Win & Pl
Career Total (Turf)	6	0	1	0	1011

Going (Turf): **Sf: 0-0 GS: 0-1 Gd: 0-1 GF: 0-4 Fm: 0-0**
Distance: 5f/6f: 0-2 7f-8f: 0-3 9f-13f: 0-1 14f+: 0-0
Track : LH: 0-1 RH: 0-1 Tight: 0-1 Gall: 0-0
Aids: Bl: 0-0 Vi: 0-0 Tstrap: 0-0 Ckp: 0-0
Best Rating: **70** 10/09 Muss 1m gd-sft

Mass Rally (IRE)

95(99) (89)78
2-y-o b c Kheleyf (USA)-Reunion (IRE) (Be My Guest (USA))
J H M Gosden H R H Princess Haya Of Jordan

Placings:052211 **(7494)**
2009: 7^{0}G, 8^{5}GF, 7^{2}SS, 7^{2}G, 7^{1}SD, 7^{1}SD,

	Starts	1st	2nd	3rd	Win & Pl
Career Total (Turf)	3	0	1	0	1189
Career Total (AW)	3	2	1	0	8469

89	11/09	Wolv	7f32y	(0-85)	STD	£5046
84	11/09	Kemp	7f		STD	£2266

Total win prize-money £7313

Going (Turf): **Sf: 0-0 GS: 0-0 Gd: 0-2 GF: 0-1 Fm: 0-0**
Distance: 5f/6f: 0-0 **7f-8f: 2-6** 9f-13f: 0-0 14f+: 0-0
Track : LH: 1-2 RH: 1-2 **Tight: 1-2** Gall: 0-0
Aids: Bl: 0-0 Vi: 0-0 Tstrap: 0-0 Ckp: 0-0
Best Rating: **89** 11/09 Wolv 7f32y stand

Useful; stays 7f and acts on Polytrack; has worn a tongue-tie.

Massilah

95(89) (57)69
3-y-o b f Namid-Loveleaves (Polar Falcon (USA))
B W Hills Hamdan Al Maktoum

Placings:643 **(7067)**
2009: 7^{6}GS, 7^{4}GF, 7^{3}SD,

	Starts	1st	2nd	3rd	Win & Pl
Career Total (Turf)	2	0	0	0	529
Career Total (AW)	1	0	0	1	403

Going (Turf): **Sf: 0-0 GS: 0-1 Gd: 0-0 GF: 0-1 Fm: 0-0**
Distance: 5f/6f: 0-0 7f-8f: 0-3 9f-13f: 0-0 14f+: 0-0
Track : LH: 0-2 RH: 0-0 Tight: 0-2 Gall: 0-0
Aids: Bl: 0-0 Vi: 0-0 Tstrap: 0-0 Ckp: 0-0
Best Rating: **69** 5/09 Ches 7f2y gd-fm

Masta Plasta (IRE)

111(99) (111)114
6-y-o b g Mujadil (USA)-Silver Arrow (USA) (Shadeed (USA))
D Nicholls Lady O'Reilly

Placings:211002/50560/0043432000/3152125213-2003230440 **(5420)**
2009: 5^{2}SD, 5^{0}S, 5^{0}HY, 5^{3}G, 5^{2}G, 5^{3}G, 5^{0}GF, 5^{4}G, 5^{4}GS, 5^{0}GF,

	Starts	1st	2nd	3rd	Win & Pl
Career Total (Turf)	39	5	7	5	231353
Career Total (AW)	2	0	1	1	5547

109	10/08	Chan	5f110y		SFT	£19118
114	7/08	Curr	5f	H	G-Y	£53029
111	5/08	York	5f	(0-105)H	GD	£31155
108	6/05	York	5f		G-F	£34800
92	6/05	Newc	5f		GD	£3542

Total win prize-money £141645

Going (Turf): Sf: 1-7 GS: 0-6 **Gd: 2-14** GF: 1-9 Fm: 0-1
Distance: **5f/6f: 5-38** 7f-8f: 0-3 9f-13f: 0-0 14f+: 0-0
Track : LH: 0-6 RH: 0-2 Tight: 0-3 Gall: 0-0
Aids: Bl: 0-0 Vi: 0-1 Tstrap: 0-0 Ckp: 0-0
Best Rating: **114** 7/08 Gdwd 5f gd-fm

Smart; winner of the 2005 Norfolk Stakes at Royal Ascot at York; Listed winner in 2008; effective at 5f-6f and acts on any ground; has worn a visor; likes to race prominently.

Master At Arms

97(109) (85)78
6-y-o ch g Grand Lodge (USA)-L'Ideale (USA) (Alysheba (USA))
Daniel Mark Loughnane M V Kirby

Placings:054/0000640033**1**/03001206**2**15-03000 **(5706a)**
2009: 16^{0}Y, 13^{3}GF, 16^{0}GY, 16^{0}GF, 16^{0}SD,

	Starts	1st	2nd	3rd	Win & Pl
Career Total (Turf)	20	0	0	2	2862
Career Total (AW)	10	3	2	2	10972

85	12/08	Wolv	2m119y	(0-75)H	STD	£3238
79	8/08	Wolv	2m119y	(0-65)H	STD	£2388
68	11/07	Wolv	1m4f50y	(0-65)H	STD	£2047

Total win prize-money £7674

Going (Turf): **Sf: 0-2 GS: 0-0 Gd: 0-6 GF: 0-8 Fm: 0-1**
Distance: 5f/6f: 0-0 7f-8f: 0-3 9f-13f: 1-17 **14f+: 2-10**
Track : **LH: 3-11** RH: 0-14 **Tight: 3-7** Gall: 0-0
Aids: Bl: 0-0 Vi: 0-0 Tstrap: 0-0 Ckp: 0-0
Best Rating: **85** 12/08 Wolv 2m119y stand

Fair; Irish trained; stays 2m; acts on Polytrack.

Master Fong (IRE)

107(100) (80)77
3-y-o b g Dr Fong (USA)-Last Cry (FR) (Peintre Celebre (USA))
D McCain Jnr (B W Hills 26/10) Woodland Racings

Placings:5010-00461542 **(7048)**
2009: 7^{0}GF, 8^{0}SD, 10^{4}S, 10^{6}G, 10^{1}G, 9^{5}GF, 11^{4}G, 10^{2}SD,

	Starts	1st	2nd	3rd	Win & Pl
Career Total (Turf)	8	2	0	0	9180
Career Total (AW)	4	0	1	0	771

76	8/09	Sand	1m2f7y	(0-80)H	GD	£5180
77	9/08	Gdwd	7f		G-F	£2914

Total win prize-money £8095

Going (Turf): Sf: 0-1 GS: 0-0 **Gd: 1-3 GF: 1-4** Fm: 0-0
Distance: 5f/6f: 0-0 7f-8f: 1-6 9f-13f: 1-6 14f+: 0-0
Track : LH: 0-3 **RH: 2-8** Tight: 0-4 Gall: 0-2
Aids: Bl: 0-0 Vi: 0-0 Tstrap: 0-0 Ckp: 0-0
Best Rating: **80** 10/09 Kemp 1m2f stand

Fair; stays 1m2f; acts on good and fast ground; goes on Polytrack.

Master Leon

100(99) (70)71
2-y-o b c Monsieur Bond (IRE)-Bollin Rita (Rambo Dancer (CAN))
B Smart Alan Zheng

Placings:0034322 **(7721)**
2009: 7^{0}GS, 7^{0}GF, 8^{3}GF, 8^{4}GS, 7^{3}SD, 8^{2}SD, 8^{2}SD,

	Starts	1st	2nd	3rd	Win & Pl
Career Total (Turf)	4	0	0	1	591
Career Total (AW)	3	0	2	1	2839

Going (Turf): **Sf: 0-0 GS: 0-2 Gd: 0-0 GF: 0-2 Fm: 0-0**
Distance: 5f/6f: 0-0 7f-8f: 0-7 9f 13f: 0-0 14f+: 0-0
Track : LH: 0-3 RH: 0-2 Tight: 0-1 Gall: 0-0
Aids: Bl: 0-0 Vi: 0-2 Tstrap: 0-0 Ckp: 0-0
Best Rating: **71** 10/09 Rdcr 1m gd-fm

Fair; stays 1m; acts on most ground and Fibresand; has worn a visor.

Master Lightfoot

(103) (80)65
3-y-o b c Kyllachy-Two Step (Mujtahid (USA))
W R Swinburn P W Harris & Miss V Palmer

Placings:6242-00140 **(7828)**
2009: 5^{0}SS, 5^{0}SD, 5^{1}SD, 5^{4}SD, 6^{0}SD,

	Starts	1st	2nd	3rd	Win & Pl
Career Total (Turf)	2	0	0	0	289
Career Total (AW)	7	1	2	0	4630

68	11/09	Ling	5f	STD	£2729

Total win prize-money £2730

Going (Turf): **Sf: 0-0 GS: 0-1 Gd: 0-0 GF: 0-1 Fm: 0-0**
Distance: **5f/6f: 1-9** 7f-8f: 0-0 9f-13f: 0-0 14f+: 0-0
Track : **LH: 1-5** RH: 0-2 **Tight: 1-5** Gall: 0-0
Aids: Bl: 0-0 Vi: 0-0 Tstrap: 0-0 Ckp: 0-0
Best Rating: **80** 10/08 Kemp 5f stand

Fair; effective over 5f-6f; acts on Polytrack.

Master Mahogany

100(93) (63)69
8-y-o b g Bandmaster (USA)-Impropriety (Law Society (USA))
R J Hodges Villagers Five

Placings:0400654603016/212362244/4530/6036042210-6050404400 **(5179)**
2009: 8^{6}SD, 9^{0}SD, 10^{5}GF, 10^{0}GF, 8^{4}GS, 8^{0}GF, 8^{4}F, 8^{4}F, 8^{0}G, 8^{0}G,

	Starts	1st	2nd	3rd	Win & Pl
Career Total (Turf)	40	3	6	3	31789
Career Total (AW)	6	0	0	1	482

69	8/08	Gdwd	1m1f	(0-75)H	SFT	£6246
71	5/05	Bath	1m5y	(0-70)H	FRM	£4554
63	9/04	Bath	1m5y	(0-70)H	GD	£3701

Total win prize-money £14503

Going (Turf): **Sf: 1-6** GS: 0-2 **Gd: 1-16** GF: 0-13 **Fm: 1-3**
Distance: 5f/6f: 0-1 7f-8f: 0-6 **9f-13f: 3-39** 14f+: 0-0
Track : **LH: 2-32** RH: 1-9 **Tight: 3-32** Gall: 0-2
Aids: Bl: 0-0 Vi: 0-0 Tstrap: 0-0 Ckp: 0-0
Best Rating: **83** 8/05 Wind 1m67y good

Modest; stays 1m2f; acts on most ground.

Master Mylo (IRE)

95 58
2-y-o ch c Bertolini (USA)-Sheboygan (IRE) (Grand Lodge (USA))
D K Ivory (Mrs L C Jewell 6/8) K Quinn/ C Benham/ I Saunders

Placings:455004 **(6903)**
2009: 5^{4}G, 5^{5}GF, 6^{5}GF, 6^{0}GF, 7^{0}GF, 5^{4}G,

	Starts	1st	2nd	3rd	Win & Pl
Career Total (Turf)	6	0	0	0	0

Going (Turf): **Sf: 0-0 GS: 0-0 Gd: 0-2 GF: 0-4 Fm: 0-0**

Distance: 5f/6f: 0-5 7f-8f: 0-1 9f-13f: 0-0 14f+: 0-0
Track : LH: 0-0 RH: 0-0 Tight: 0-0 Gall: 0-3
Aids: Bl: 0-1 Vi: 0-0 Tstrap: 0-0 Ckp: 0-0
Best Rating: **58** 10/09 Wind 5f10y good

Master Nimbus

106 (53)**69**

9-y-o b g Cloudings (IRE)-Miss Charlie (Pharly (FR))
J J Quinn J H Hewitt

Placings:040/000000/0/02/621/432/143132-2411360 **(5600)**
2009: 14^{2}GF, 14^{4}GF, 14^{1}GF, 14^{1}F, 12^{3}G, 14^{6}G, 14^{0}GF,

	Starts	1st	2nd	3rd	Win & Pl
Career Total (Turf)	**30**	**5**	**4**	**4**	**21193**
Career Total (AW)	**1**	**0**	**1**	**0**	**605**

69	7/09	Rdcr	1m6f19y	(0-70)H	FRM	£3885
65	6/09	Rdcr	1m6f19y	(0-60)H	G-F	£1942
64	7/08	Pont	1m4f8y	(0-70)H	G-F	£3885
68	6/08	Ripn	1m4f10y	(0-65)H	SFT	£2810
52	8/06	Rdcr	1m6f19y	(0-60)H	G-F	£2590

Total win prize-money £15117

Going (Turf): Sf: 1-2 GS: 0-5 Gd: 0-7 **GF: 3-12** Fm: 1-4
Distance: 5f/6f: 0-7 7f-8f: 0-3 9f-13f: 2-13 **14f+: 3-8**
Track : **LH: 4-13** RH: 1-11 **Tight: 4-16** Gall: 0-1
Aids: Bl: 0-0 Vi: 0-0 Tstrap: 0-0 Ckp: 0-0
Best Rating: **69** 7/09 Rdcr 1m6f19y firm

Modest; hurdles winner; stays 1m6f; acts on fast and soft ground.

Master Of Dance (IRE)

99(99) (83)**78**

2-y-o ch c Noverre (USA)-Shambodia (IRE) (Petardia)
R Hannon P D Merritt

Placings:6431504440226 **(7685)**
2009: 5^{6}GF, 6^{4}GF, 5^{3}G, 5^{1}F, 7^{5}GF, 7^{0}GS, 6^{4}GF, 6^{4}GF, 7^{4}GS, 7^{0}SD, 7^{2}SD, 7^{2}SD, 8^{6}SD,

	Starts	1st	2nd	3rd	Win & Pl
Career Total (Turf)	**9**	**1**	**0**	**1**	**6043**
Career Total (AW)	**4**	**0**	**2**	**0**	**3430**

76	6/09	Bath	5f161y	FRM	£3561

Total win prize-money £3562

Going (Turf): Sf: 0-0 GS: 0-2 Gd: 0-1 GF: 0-5 **Fm: 1-1**
Distance: **5f/6f: 1-5** 7f-8f: 0-8 9f-13f: 0-0 14f+: 0-0
Track : **LH: 1-4** RH: 0-3 Tight: 0-3 **Gall: 1-1**
Aids: Bl: 0-0 Vi: 0-0 Tstrap: 0-0 Ckp: 0-0
Best Rating: **83** 12/09 Kemp 7f stand

Fair; stays 7f; act on a sound surface; goes on Polytrack.

Master Of Disguise

104 **101**

3-y-o b c Kyllachy-St James's Antigua (IRE) (Law Society (USA))
C G Cox Courtenay Club

Placings:201-1040 **(6089)**
2009: 5^{1}GF, 6^{0}G, 5^{4}G, 6^{0}G,

	Starts	1st	2nd	3rd	Win & Pl
Career Total (Turf)	**7**	**2**	**1**	**0**	**16791**

101	4/09	Sand	5f6y	(0-100)H	G-F	£11215
83	10/08	Bath	5f11y		G-S	£3561

Total win prize-money £14778

Going (Turf): Sf: 0-0 **GS: 1-1** Gd: 0-3 **GF: 1-3** Fm: 0-0

Distance: **5f/6f: 2-7** 7f-8f: 0-0 9f-13f: 0-0 14f+: 0-0
Track : **LH: 1-2** RH: 0-0 Tight: 0-0 **Gall: 1-2**
Aids: Bl: 0-0 Vi: 0-0 Tstrap: 0-0 Ckp: 0-0
Best Rating: **101** 4/09 Sand 5f6y gd-fm

Very useful; suited by 5f; acts on most ground.

Master Of Song

83(79) (29)**44**

2-y-o ch g Ballet Master (USA)-Ocean Song (Savahra Sound)
S R Bowring S R Bowring

Placings:0000 **(7757)**
2009: 8^{0}S, 5^{0}GF, 8^{0}SD, 6^{0}SD,

	Starts	1st	2nd	3rd	Win & Pl
Career Total (Turf)	**2**	**0**	**0**	**0**	
Career Total (AW)	**2**	**0**	**0**	**0**	

Going (Turf): **Sf: 0-1 GS: 0-0 Gd: 0-0 GF: 0-1 Fm: 0-0**
Distance: 5f/6f: 0-2 7f-8f: 0-0 9f-13f: 0-2 14f+: 0-0
Track : LH: 0-3 RH: 0-0 Tight: 0-1 Gall: 0-0
Aids: Bl: 0-2 Vi: 0-0 Tstrap: 0-0 Ckp: 0-0
Best Rating: **44** 10/09 Leic 5f218y gd-fm

Master Pegasus

(106) (86)**89**

6-y-o b g Lujain (USA)-Seeking Utopia (Wolfhound (USA))
J R Boyle Mrs J Roberts

Placings:02/1063/4625**0036135/0406**00043040-5 **(0047)**
2009: 10^{5}SD,

	Starts	1st	2nd	3rd	Win & Pl
Career Total (Turf)	**13**	**1**	**1**	**1**	**8488**
Career Total (AW)	**17**	**1**	**1**	**3**	**8602**

89	11/07	Wolv	1m141y	(0-85)H	STD	£4857
88	5/06	Newb	7f		SFT	£4857

Total win prize-money £9716

Going (Turf): **Sf: 1-1** GS: 0-5 Gd: 0-4 GF: 0-3 Fm: 0-0
Distance: 5f/6f: 0-0 7f-8f: 1-13 9f-13f: 1-17 14f+: 0-0
Track : **LH: 1-14** RH: 0-11 **Tight: 1-11** Gall: 0-3
Aids: Bl: 0-0 Vi: 0-0 Tstrap: 0-0 Ckp: 0-0
Best Rating: **90** 8/06 Wind 1m67y good

Modest; effective over 7f-1m2f; acts well on soft ground; also goes on Polytrack.

Master Rooney (IRE)

98 **93**

3-y-o b/br c Cape Cross (IRE)-Wimple (USA) (Kingmambo (USA))
B Smart H E Sheikh Rashid Bin Mohammed

Placings:2241-03 **(6897)**
2009: 6^{0}GS, 5^{3}GF,

	Starts	1st	2nd	3rd	Win & Pl
Career Total (Turf)	**6**	**1**	**2**	**1**	**8673**

88	10/08	Leic	5f218y	G-S	£5180

Total win prize-money £5181

Going (Turf): Sf: 0-0 **GS: 1-3** Gd: 0-1 GF: 0-2 Fm: 0-0
Distance: **5f/6f: 1-3** 7f-8f: 0-3 9f-13f: 0-0 14f+: 0-0
Track : LH: 0-1 RH: 0-0 Tight: 0-0 Gall: 0-0
Aids: Bl: 0-0 Vi: 0-0 Tstrap: 0-0 Ckp: 0-0
Best Rating: **93** 10/09 Pont 5f gd-fm

Useful; effective over 6f; acts on fast and easy ground.

Mastercraftsman (IRE)

122 (121)**129**

3-y-o gr c Danehill Dancer (IRE)-Starlight Dreams (USA) (Black Tie Affair)
A P O'Brien D Smith, Mrs J Magnier, M Tabor

Placings:11114-5112314 **(7309a)**
2009: 8^{5}GF, 8^{1}HY, 8^{1}GF, 10^{2}GF, 10^{3}GY, 10^{1}SD, 8^{4}FT,

	Starts	1st	2nd	3rd	Win & Pl
Career Total (Turf)	**10**	**6**	**1**	**1**	**937819**
Career Total (AW)	**2**	**1**	**0**	**0**	**80793**

121	10/09	Dund	1m2f150y	STD	£39126
124	6/09	Asct	1m	G-F	£141925
124	5/09	Curr	1m	HVY	£221844
117	9/08	Curr	7f	HVY	£130441
120	7/08	Curr	6f	G-F	£137205
109	6/08	Curr	6f	G-Y	£55147
83	5/08	Curr	6f	Y-S	£9573

Total win prize-money £735264

Going (Turf): **Sf: 2-2** GS: 0-1 Gd: 0-0 **GF: 2-4** Fm: 0-0
Distance: 5f/6f: 3-3 7f-8f: 3-6 9f-13f: 1-3 14f+: 0-0
Track : LH: 1-3 **RH: 2-3** Tight: 0-0 **Gall: 2-3**
Aids: Bl: 0-0 Vi: 0-0 Tstrap: 0-0 Ckp: 0-0
Best Rating: **129** 8/09 York 1m2f88y gd-fm

High class; winner of the Group 1 Phoenix and National Stakes at two; won the Irish 2000 Guineas in 2009 and followed up in the St James's Palace Stakes; far from disgraced against Sea The Stars in the Juddmonte International at York; effective at 1m-1m2f; acts on any ground and Polytrack; tough sort.

Masterful Act (USA)

65(91) (71)**9**

2-y-o ch g Pleasantly Perfect (USA)-Catnip (USA) (Flying Paster (USA))
J R Best Hungerford Park Stud

Placings:0630 **(6211)**
2009: 7^{0}S, 7^{6}SD, 8^{3}SD, 8^{0}SD,

	Starts	1st	2nd	3rd	Win & Pl
Career Total (Turf)	**1**	**0**	**0**	**0**	
Career Total (AW)	**3**	**0**	**0**	**1**	**433**

Going (Turf): **Sf: 0-1 GS: 0-0 Gd: 0-0 GF: 0-0 Fm: 0-0**
Distance: 5f/6f: 0-0 7f-8f: 0-3 9f-13f: 0-1 14f+: 0-0
Track : LH: 0-2 RH: 0-1 Tight: 0-2 Gall: 0-0
Aids: Bl: 0-0 Vi: 0-0 Tstrap: 0-0 Ckp: 0-0
Best Rating: **71** 9/09 Wolv 1m141y stand

Modest; stays 1m; acts on Polytrack.

Masterofceremonies

101(98) (68)**70**

6-y-o ch g Definite Article-Darakah (Doulab (USA))
W M Brisbourne (James Moffatt 30/7) Paul Murphy

Placings:62521/0-**55103546610** **(5438)**
2009: 8^{5}SD, 12^{5}SD, 9^{1}GF, 10^{0}G, 12^{3}GF, 10^{5}G, 11^{4}GF, 9^{6}GF, 12^{6}SD, 9^{1}G, 10^{0}GF,

	Starts	1st	2nd	3rd	Win & Pl
Career Total (Turf)	**14**	**3**	**2**	**1**	**12016**
Career Total (AW)	**3**	**0**	**0**	**0**	**0**

70	7/09	Muss	1m1f	GD	£1942
66	4/09	Muss	1m1f	G-F	£1942
72	9/07	Clon	1m2f	G-F	£4668

Total win prize-money £8555

Going (Turf): Sf: 0-1 GS: 0-0 Gd: 1-4 **GF: 2-7** Fm: 0-0
Distance: 5f/6f: 0-0 7f-8f: 0-1 **9f-13f: 3-16** 14f+: 0-0
Track : LH: 0-11 **RH: 3-5 Tight: 2-9** Gall: 0-0
Aids: Bl: 1-5 Vi: 0-2 Tstrap: 2-5 Ckp: 2-5
Best Rating: 77 7/07 Naas 1m2f soft

Modest; effective at around 1m1f; acts on fast ground.

Masterofthehorse (IRE)

112 **120**

3-y-o b c Sadler's Wells (USA)-Shouk (Shirley Heights)
Miss D Mountain (A P O'Brien 28/6) Al-Abdulmalik Hassan

Placings:2130-23400 **(6303)**
2009: 12²GF, 12³G, 12⁴GY, 12⁰G, 12⁰GF,

	Starts	1st	2nd	3rd	Win & Pl
Career Total (Turf)	**9**	**1**	**2**	**2**	**212199**

84	8/08	Gowr	1m	G-Y	£6097

Total win prize-money £6097

Going (Turf): **Sf: 0-0 GS: 0-0 Gd: 0-3 GF: 0-3 Fm: 0-0**
Distance: 5f/6f: 0-0 **7f-8f: 1-4** 9f-13f: 0-5 14f+: 0-0
Track : LH: 0-3 **RH: 1-5** Tight: 0-3 Gall: 0-2
Aids: Bl: 0-0 Vi: 0-0 Tstrap: 0-0 Ckp: 0-0
Best Rating: 120 6/09 Epsm 1m4f10y good

Group-class; Group 2 placed and third in the Derby when trained by Aidan O'Brien; stays 1m4f and acts on most ground.

Masters House (IRE)

77 **16**

6-y-o b g Indian Lodge (IRE)-Aster Aweke (IRE) (Alzao (USA))
Mrs J C McGregor Mrs Jean McGregor

Placings:0 **(2965)**
2009: 9⁰GF,

	Starts	1st	2nd	3rd	Win & Pl
Career Total (Turf)	**1**	**0**	**0**	**0**	

Going (Turf): **Sf: 0-0 GS: 0-0 Gd: 0-0 GF: 0-1 Fm: 0-0**
Distance: 5f/6f: 0-0 7f-8f: 0-0 9f-13f: 0-1 14f+: 0-0
Track : LH: 0-0 RH: 0-1 Tight: 0-0 Gall: 0-0
Aids: Bl: 0-0 Vi: 0-0 Tstrap: 0-0 Ckp: 0-0
Best Rating: 16 6/09 Carl 1m1f61y gd-fm

Mastership (IRE)

107(107) (101)**102**

5-y-o ch g Best Of The Bests (IRE)-Shady Point (IRE) (Unfuwain (USA))
J J Quinn Dark Horse Racing Partnership Two

Placings:55001221/21440400000/02403000-04644160040 **(6675)**
2009: 6⁰GF, 7⁴SD, 8⁶G, 7⁴GF, 8⁴G, 7¹GS, 7⁶G, 7⁰G, 8⁰SD, 6⁴G, 7⁰G,

	Starts	1st	2nd	3rd	Win & Pl
Career Total (Turf)	**25**	**2**	**2**	**0**	**29296**
Career Total (AW)	**13**	**2**	**2**	**1**	**17367**

98	7/09	Newc	7f	(0-95)H	G-S	£9346
101	2/07	Ling	6f	(0-85)H	STD	£4857
80	12/06	Wolv	1m141y	(0-75)	STD	£3238
66	9/06	Rdcr	1m	(0-65)	FRM	£3238

Total win prize-money £20683

Going (Turf): Sf: 0-2 **GS: 1-3** Gd: 0-11 GF: 0-8 **Fm: 1-1**
Distance: 5f/6f: 1-10 **7f-8f: 2-24** 9f-13f: 1-4 14f+: 0-0

Track : **LH: 2-13** RH: 0-5 **Tight: 2-10** Gall: 0-2
Aids: **Bl: 2-16** Vi: 0-1 Tstrap: 1-7 Ckp: 1-7
Best Rating: 102 6/08 Donc 6f gd-fm

Very useful; stays 1m, but best at shorter; seems to act on most ground; goes on Polytrack; has worn blinkers, cheek-pieces and a visor.

Mastery

113(103) (116)**119**

3-y-o b c Sulamani (IRE)-Moyesii (USA) (Diesis)
Saeed Bin Suroor (M Johnston 18/3) Godolphin

Placings:13-4133213 **(7281a)**
2009: 9⁴SD, 11¹GF, 16³GF, 12³GS, 12²GF, 14¹GF, 14³FT,

	Starts	1st	2nd	3rd	Win & Pl
Career Total (Turf)	**7**	**3**	**1**	**3**	**776085**
Career Total (AW)	**2**	**0**	**0**	**1**	**38111**

119	9/09	Donc	1m6f132y	G-F	£306586
107	5/09	Capa	1m3f	G-F	£359223
83	10/08	Nott	1m75y	SFT	£2914

Total win prize-money £668723

Going (Turf): Sf: 1-1 GS: 0-1 Gd: 0-1 **GF: 2-4** Fm: 0-0
Distance: 5f/6f: 0-0 7f-8f: 0-1 **9f-13f: 2-5** 14f+: 1-3
Track : **LH: 2-3** RH: 1-4 Tight: 0-0 **Gall: 1-3**
Aids: Bl: 0-0 Vi: 0-0 Tstrap: 0-0 Ckp: 0-0
Best Rating: 119 9/09 Donc 1m6f132y gd-fm

Group-class; winner of the Italian Derby and 2009 St Leger; effective at 1m3f-2m; acts on most ground.

Mastoora (IRE)

98 **83**

3-y-o b f Acclamation-Sacred Love (IRE) (Barathea (IRE))
W J Haggas Hamdan Al Maktoum

Placings:1060 **(3746)**
2009: 7¹G, 7⁰G, 7⁶GF, 7⁰G,

	Starts	1st	2nd	3rd	Win & Pl
Career Total (Turf)	**4**	**1**	**0**	**0**	**2388**

83	4/09	Folk	7f	GD	£2388

Total win prize-money £2388

Going (Turf): Sf: 0-0 GS: 0-0 **Gd: 1-3** GF: 0-1 Fm: 0-0
Distance: 5f/6f: 0-0 **7f-8f: 1-4** 9f-13f: 0-0 14f+: 0-0
Track : LH: 0-1 RH: 0-0 Tight: 0-1 Gall: 0-0
Aids: Bl: 0-0 Vi: 0-0 Tstrap: 0-0 Ckp: 0-0
Best Rating: 83 6/09 NmkJ 7f gd-fm

Useful; effective at 7f on good ground.

Maswerte (IRE)

104(98) (76)**85**

3-y-o b c Fraam-Rose Chime (IRE) (Tirol)
L M Cumani Sheikh Mohammed Obaid Al Maktoum

Placings:052-124030 **(6773)**
2009: 7¹GF, 7²G, 8⁴G, 7⁰G, 7³GF, 8⁰SD,

	Starts	1st	2nd	3rd	Win & Pl
Career Total (Turf)	**5**	**1**	**1**	**1**	**7182**
Career Total (AW)	**4**	**0**	**1**	**0**	**605**

85	6/09	Newb	7f	(0-75)H	G-F	£3238

Total win prize-money £3238

Going (Turf): Sf: 0-0 GS: 0-0 Gd: 0-3 **GF: 1-2** Fm: 0-0
Distance: 5f/6f: 0-2 **7f-8f: 1-7** 9f-13f: 0-0 14f+: 0-0
Track : LH: 0-2 RH: 0-4 Tight: 0-2 Gall: 0-0
Aids: Bl: 0-0 Vi: 0-0 Tstrap: 0-0 Ckp: 0-0
Best Rating: 85 9/09 Folk 7f gd-fm

Useful; effective over 7f; acts on good and faster ground and on Polytrack.

Mata Hari Blue

98(96) (46)**64**

3-y-o ch f Monsieur Bond (IRE)-Feeling Blue (Missed Flight)
J R Holt Mrs Hilary Morrish

Placings:6243 **(5477)**
2009: 5⁶SF, 5²S, 6⁴G, 6³GF,

	Starts	1st	2nd	3rd	Win & Pl
Career Total (Turf)	**3**	**0**	**1**	**1**	**1349**
Career Total (AW)	**1**	**0**	**0**	**0**	**0**

Going (Turf): **Sf: 0-1 GS: 0-0 Gd: 0-1 GF: 0-1 Fm: 0-0**
Distance: 5f/6f: 0-4 7f-8f: 0-0 9f-13f: 0-0 14f+: 0-0
Track : LH: 0-1 RH: 0-0 Tight: 0-1 Gall: 0-0
Aids: Bl: 0-0 Vi: 0-0 Tstrap: 0-0 Ckp: 0-0
Best Rating: 64 8/09 Gdwd 6f gd-fm

Mata Keranjang (USA)

103 **106**

2-y-o b/br c More Than Ready (USA)-Love Sick (USA) (Salt Lake (USA))
P F I Cole Mrs Fitri Hay

Placings:326233 **(6716a)**
2009: 5³GS, 7²G, 7⁶GF, 7²GF, 7³GF, 8³S,

	Starts	1st	2nd	3rd	Win & Pl
Career Total (Turf)	**6**	**0**	**2**	**3**	**93127**

Going (Turf): **Sf: 0-1 GS: 0-1 Gd: 0-1 GF: 0-3 Fm: 0-0**
Distance: 5f/6f: 0-1 7f-8f: 0-5 9f-13f: 0-0 14f+: 0-0
Track : LH: 0-1 RH: 0-4 Tight: 0-0 Gall: 0-1
Aids: Bl: 0-0 Vi: 0-0 Tstrap: 0-0 Ckp: 0-0
Best Rating: 106 7/09 Gdwd 7f good

Smart; runner-up in Group 2 Vintage Stakes on second start; effective at 7f; acts on good ground.

Mataaleb

69 **51**

2-y-o b c Dalakhani (IRE)-Elfaslah (IRE) (Green Desert (USA))
M A Jarvis Hamdan Al Maktoum

Placings:0 **(6759)**
2009: 8⁰G,

	Starts	1st	2nd	3rd	Win & Pl
Career Total (Turf)	**1**	**0**	**0**	**0**	

Going (Turf): **Sf: 0-0 GS: 0-0 Gd: 0-1 GF: 0-0 Fm: 0-0**
Distance: 5f/6f: 0-0 7f-8f: 0-0 9f-13f: 0-1 14f+: 0-0
Track : LH: 0-0 RH: 0-1 Tight: 0-0 Gall: 0-0
Aids: Bl: 0-0 Vi: 0-0 Tstrap: 0-0 Ckp: 0-0
Best Rating: 51 10/09 Leic 1m60y good

Mataram (USA)

(110) (89)**71**

6-y-o b g Matty G (USA)-Kalinka (USA) (Mr Prospector (USA))
W Jarvis Sales Race 2001 Syndicate

Placings:006/1201034/130230064/221042400-20 **(0550)**
2009: 8²SD, 10⁰SD,

	Starts	1st	2nd	3rd	Win & Pl
Career Total (Turf)	**6**	**0**	**0**	**0**	**0**

Career Total (AW)	24	4	6	3	30247	
89	2/08	Ling	1m2f	(0-85)H	STD	£4100
85	1/07	Ling	1m2f	(0-85)H	STD	£4857
79	9/06	Kemp	1m	(0-80)H	STD	£7478
70	6/06	Ling	7f	(0-65)H	STD	£3238

Total win prize-money £19676

Going (Turf): **Sf: 0-1 GS: 0-3 Gd: 0-0 GF: 0-2 Fm: 0-0**
Distance: 5f/6f: 0-0 7f-8f: 2-15 9f-13f: 2-15 14f+: 0-0
Track : **LH: 3-15** RH: 1-10 **Tight: 3-13** Gall: 0-2
Aids: Bl: 0-0 Vi: 0-0 Tstrap: 0-0 Ckp: 0-0
Best Rating: **90** 2/07 Kemp 1m3f stand

Useful; effective at around 1m2f; acts well on Polytrack.

Mater Mater

(86) (64)
2-y-o gr f Silver Patriarch (IRE)-Emily-Mou (IRE) (Cadeaux Genereux)
M J Scudamore (Andrew Reid 10/6) A S Reid

Placings:000 **(7624)**
2009: 6^{0}SD, 8^{0}SD, 8^{0}SD,

	Starts	1st	2nd	3rd	Win & Pl
Career Total (Turf)	0	0	0	0	
Career Total (AW)	3	0	0	0	

Going (Turf): **Sf: 0-0 GS: 0-0 Gd: 0-0 GF: 0-0 Fm: 0-0**
Distance: 5f/6f: 0-1 7f-8f: 0-2 9f-13f: 0-0 14f+: 0-0
Track : LH: 0-1 RH: 0-2 Tight: 0-1 Gall: 0-0
Aids: Bl: 0-0 Vi: 0-0 Tstrap: 0-0 Ckp: 0-0
Best Rating: **64** 11/09 Kemp 1m stand

Mathaaq

104(102) (82)**75**
3-y-o b c Nayef (USA)-Mouwadh (USA) (Nureyev (USA))
E McNamara (M A Jarvis 31/8) Gigginstown House Stud

Placings:021 **(5531)**
2009: 10^{0}S, 10^{2}SD, 10^{1}G,

	Starts	1st	2nd	3rd	Win & Pl	
Career Total (Turf)	2	1	0	0	2914	
Career Total (AW)	1	0	1	0	1407	
75	8/09	Wwck	1m2f188y		GD	£2914

Total win prize-money £2914

Going (Turf): Sf: 0-1 GS: 0-0 **Gd: 1-1** GF: 0-0 Fm: 0-0
Distance: 5f/6f: 0-0 7f-8f: 0-0 **9f-13f: 1-3** 14f+: 0-0
Track : **LH: 1-2** RH: 0-1 Tight: 0-0 Gall: 0-1
Aids: Bl: 0-0 Vi: 0-0 Tstrap: 0-0 Ckp: 0-0
Best Rating: **82** 8/09 Kemp 1m2f stand

Fair; stays 1m2f plus; acts on good ground and Polytrack.

Matilda Poliport

92(100) (52)**59**
3-y-o b f Mind Games-Poppy Carew (IRE) (Danehill (USA))
W R Swinburn Pendley Farm

Placings:0-000 **(4569)**
2009: 8^{0}SD, 8^{0}S, 10^{0}G,

	Starts	1st	2nd	3rd	Win & Pl
Career Total (Turf)	2	0	0	0	
Career Total (AW)	2	0	0	0	

Going (Turf): **Sf: 0-1 GS: 0-0 Gd: 0-1 GF: 0-0 Fm: 0-0**
Distance: 5f/6f: 0-0 7f-8f: 0-3 9f-13f: 0-1 14f+: 0-0
Track : LH: 0-3 RH: 0-0 Tight: 0-2 Gall: 0-1
Aids: Bl: 0-0 Vi: 0-0 Tstrap: 0-0 Ckp: 0-0
Best Rating: **59** 7/09 NmkJ 1m soft

Matinee Idol

(92) (45)**49**
6-y-o ch m In The Wings-Bibliotheque (USA) (Woodman (USA))
Mrs S Lamyman Mrs S Lamyman

Placings:55360400/0035004/26502300040-000 **(0603)**
2009: 14^{0}SS, 16^{0}SD, 12^{0}SD,

	Starts	1st	2nd	3rd	Win & Pl
Career Total (Turf)	16	0	0	2	1305
Career Total (AW)	13	0	2	1	1189

Going (Turf): **Sf: 0-1 GS: 0-1 Gd: 0-6 GF: 0-5 Fm: 0-3**
Distance: 5f/6f: 0-0 7f-8f: 0-0 9f-13f: 0-14 14f+: 0-15
Track : LH: 0-28 RH: 0-1 Tight: 0-13 Gall: 0-0
Aids: Bl: 0-13 Vi: 0-0 Tstrap: 0-1 Ckp: 0-1
Best Rating: **63** 9/06 Pont 2m1f216y gd-sft

Moderate; stays 2m and acts on good ground and sand.

Matjar (IRE)

(103) (68)**55**
6-y-o ch g Grand Lodge (USA)-Tajawuz (Kris)
Joseph Quinn Ms Aine Brodbin

Placings:6/00661612-000232 **(7798)**
2009: 8^{0}Y, 6^{0}GF, 8^{0}G, 8^{2}SD, 8^{3}SD, 9^{2}SS,

	Starts	1st	2nd	3rd	Win & Pl	
Career Total (Turf)	9	1	0	0	4827	
Career Total (AW)	6	1	3	1	7645	
58	10/08	Dund	1m	(45-60)H	STD	£4572
55	7/08	Klny	1m100y	(45-60)H	GD	£4826

Total win prize-money £9400

Going (Turf): Sf: 0-2 GS: 0-0 **Gd: 1-3** GF: 0-1 Fm: 0-1
Distance: 5f/6f: 0-0 7f-8f: 1-9 9f-13f: 1-6 14f+: 0-0
Track : **LH: 2-9** RH: 0-3 Tight: 0-1 Gall: 0-0
Aids: Bl: 0-0 Vi: 0-0 Tstrap: 0-0 Ckp: 0-0
Best Rating: **68** 11/08 Dund 1m stand

Modest; stays 1m1f; acts on Polytrack.

Matraash (USA)

106 **92**
3-y-o b c Elusive Quality (USA)-Min Alhawa (USA) (Riverman (USA))
M Johnston Hamdan Al Maktoum

Placings:0-2211006 **(5865)**
2009: 8^{2}GF, 9^{2}G, 10^{1}G, 9^{1}GF, 12^{0}G, 10^{0}GF, 12^{6}GF,

	Starts	1st	2nd	3rd	Win & Pl	
Career Total (Turf)	8	2	2	0	10022	
92	6/09	Leic	1m1f218y	(0-85)H	G-F	£4857
79	6/09	Newc	1m2f32y		GD	£3238

Total win prize-money £8095

Going (Turf): Sf: 0-0 GS: 0-1 **Gd: 1-3 GF: 1-4** Fm: 0-0
Distance: 5f/6f: 0-0 7f-8f: 0-1 **9f-13f: 2-7** 14f+: 0-0
Track : LH: 1-4 RH: 1-4 Tight: 0-3 **Gall: 1-3**
Aids: Bl: 0-0 Vi: 0-0 Tstrap: 0-0 Ckp: 0-0
Best Rating: **92** 6/09 Leic 1m1f218y gd-fm

Useful; stays 1m3f; acts on good/fast ground.

Matsunosuke

110(116) (117)**109**
7-y-o b g Magic Ring (IRE)-Lon Isa (Grey Desire)
A B Coogan A B Coogan

Placings:F0/10503000103/41000136U202/500006001023 1231164/240005006404334503432213-013111000003400004003 **(7862)**
2009: 5^{0}SS, 6^{1}SD, 6^{3}SD, 5^{1}SD, 5^{1}SD, 6^{1}SD, 5^{0}SD, 5^{0}SD, 6^{0}GF, 5^{0}GF, 6^{0}SD, 6^{3}GF, 5^{4}G, 5^{0}GF, 5^{0}G, 6^{0}GF, 6^{0}SD, 5^{4}GF, 5^{0}GF, 5^{0}GS, 5^{3}SD,

	Starts	1st	2nd	3rd	Win & Pl	
Career Total (Turf)	64	6	4	6	59256	
Career Total (AW)	25	7	3	7	102347	
112	2/09	Ling	6f		STD	£22708
117	2/09	Ling	5f	(0-100)H	STD	£11527
112	1/09	Ling	5f	(0-100)H	STD	£11656
109	1/09	GrLe	6f	(0-95)H	STD	£7352
100	12/08	GrLe	6f	(0-90)H	STD	£7477
104	10/07	Ling	5f	(0-85)H	STD	£5362
104	10/07	Wolv	5f20y	(0-90)H	STD	£9715
88	9/07	Sand	5f6y	(0-80)H	G-F	£5181
82	8/07	Sand	5f6y	(0-80)H	GD	£5181
85	7/06	NmkJ	5f	(0-85)H	G-F	£8096
82	5/06	Thsk	5f	(0-80)H	FRM	£6477
78	8/05	Sand	5f6y	(0-75)H	G-F	£3437
66	4/05	Catt	5f212y		GD	£3367

Total win prize-money £107542

Going (Turf): Sf: 0-2 GS: 0-4 Gd: 2-23 **GF: 3-31** Fm: 1-4
Distance: **5f/6f: 13-87** 7f-8f: 0-2 9f-13f: 0-0 14f+: 0-0
Track : **LH: 8-27** RH: 0-1 **Tight: 6-17** Gall: 2-10
Aids: Bl: 0-0 Vi: 0-0 Tstrap: 0-0 Ckp: 0-0
Best Rating: **117** 2/09 Ling 5f stand

Very useful; effective over 5f-6f; acts on good and faster ground on grass; usually held up.

Mattamia (IRE)

103 **99**
3-y-o b g Makbul-Lady Dominatrix (IRE) (Danehill Dancer (IRE))
B R Millman C Roper

Placings:0505-102112240 **(5654)**
2009: 5^{1}GF, 5^{0}GS, 5^{2}G, 5^{1}GF, 5^{1}GS, 5^{2}G, 5^{2}G, 5^{4}GF, 5^{0}GS,

	Starts	1st	2nd	3rd	Win & Pl	
Career Total (Turf)	13	3	3	0	24093	
94	6/09	NmkJ	5f	(0-85)H	G-S	£5828
95	6/09	Leic	5f2y	(0-80)H	G-F	£6308
81	4/09	Nott	5f13y	(0-70)H	G-F	£2590

Total win prize-money £14726

Going (Turf): Sf: 0-0 GS: 1-3 Gd: 0-7 **GF: 2-3** Fm: 0-0
Distance: **5f/6f: 3-12** 7f-8f: 0-1 9f-13f: 0-0 14f+: 0-0
Track : LH: 0-0 RH: 0-0 Tight: 0-0 Gall: 0-1
Aids: Bl: 0-0 Vi: 0-0 Tstrap: 0-0 Ckp: 0-0
Best Rating: **99** 7/09 Gdwd 5f good

Very useful sprinter; best at 5f; acts on fast but handles easy ground.

Matterofact (IRE)

102(98) (67)**75**
6-y-o b m Bold Fact (USA)-Willow Dale (IRE) (Danehill (USA))
M S Saunders Prempro Racing

Placings:604320122/006603056/0213165000640/2335312 32122653030-4522122063263 **(6329)**
2009: 5^{4}GF, 5^{5}F, 5^{2}GF, 5^{2}GF, 5^{1}GF, 5^{2}G, 5^{2}G, 5^{0}S, 5^{6}GF, 5^{3}S, 5^{2}GF, 5^{6}S, 5^{3}F,

	Starts	1st	2nd	3rd	Win & Pl	
Career Total (Turf)	53	6	14	10	37368	
Career Total (AW)	9	0	0	1	403	
75	6/09	Ling	5f	(0-75)H	G-F	£3070
73	9/08	Brig	5f59y	(0-65)H	SFT	£2072
72	8/08	Wind	5f10y	(0-75)H	G-S	£2934
73	6/07	Ling	5f	(0-70)H	G-F	£2817
66	5/07	Gdwd	5f	(0-65)H	GD	£3238
69	9/05	Bath	5f11y		FRM	£2940

Total win prize-money £17073

Going (Turf): Sf: 1-8 GS: 1-7 Gd: 1-10 **GF: 2-23** Fm: 1-5
Distance: **5f/6f: 6-61** 7f-8f: 0-1 9f-13f: 0-0 14f+: 0-0
Track : **LH: 2-26** RH: 0-1 Tight: 0-8 **Gall: 2-21**
Aids: Bl: 0-0 Vi: 0-0 Tstrap: 0-0 Ckp: 0-0
Best Rating: 77 10/05 Bath 5f11y gd-fm

Modest; effective at 5f; acts on most ground.

Matuza (IRE)

98 (92)70
6-y-o ch h Cadeaux Genereux-Aoife (IRE) (Thatching)
P R Chamings P R Chamings

Placings:11/0324301354/530102040/106 (6904)
2009: 6^{1}GF, 6^{0}GF, 6^{6}G,

	Starts	1st	2nd	3rd	Win & Pl
Career Total (Turf)	14	2	1	2	11528
Career Total (AW)	10	3	1	2	21286

60	6/09	Wind	6f		G-F	£2047
86	6/07	Bath	5f161y	(0-85)H	GD	£4857
87	11/06	Ling	6f	(0-85)H	STD	£7478
77	12/05	Sthl	5f		STD	£4022
69	11/05	Ling	6f		STD	£4158

Total win prize-money £22563

Going (Turf): Sf: 0-1 GS: 0-0 **Gd: 1-3 GF: 1-10** Fm: 0-0
Distance: **5f/6f: 5-21** 7f-8f: 0-2 9f-13f: 0-1 14f+: 0-0
Track : **LH: 3-6** RH: 0-3 Tight: 2-5 Gall: 2-8
Aids: Bl: 0-1 Vi: 0-0 Tstrap: 0-0 Ckp: 0-0
Best Rating: 92 6/07 Wolv 5f216y stand

Modest; effective at around 5f-6f; acts on good and fast ground; goes on Fibresand and Polytrack.

Mausin (IRE)

80 51
2-y-o b f Monsun (GER)-Cote Quest (USA) (Green Desert (USA))
H Morrison Mrs B Oppenheimer

Placings:4 (6389)
2009: 8^{4}GF,

	Starts	1st	2nd	3rd	Win & Pl
Career Total (Turf)	1	0	0	0	289

Going (Turf): **Sf: 0-0 GS: 0-0 Gd: 0-0 GF: 0-1 Fm: 0-0**
Distance: 5f/6f: 0-0 7f-8f: 0-0 9f-13f: 0-1 14f+: 0-0
Track : LH: 0-1 RH: 0-0 Tight: 0-0 Gall: 0-0
Aids: Bl: 0-0 Vi: 0-0 Tstrap: 0-0 Ckp: 0-0
Best Rating: 51 9/09 Nott 1m75y gd-fm

Mavalenta (IRE)

77 38
2-y-o b f Montjeu (IRE)-Velouette (Darshaan)
J W Hills CGA Racing Partnership 4

Placings:0 (6055)
2009: 7^{0}GF,

	Starts	1st	2nd	3rd	Win & Pl
Career Total (Turf)	1	0	0	0	

Going (Turf): **Sf: 0-0 GS: 0-0 Gd: 0-0 GF: 0-1 Fm: 0-0**
Distance: 5f/6f: 0-0 7f-8f: 0-1 9f-13f: 0-0 14f+: 0-0
Track : LH: 0-0 RH: 0-0 Tight: 0-0 Gall: 0-0
Aids: Bl: 0-0 Vi: 0-0 Tstrap: 0-0 Ckp: 0-0
Best Rating: 38 9/09 Newb 7f gd-fm

Maverick's Magic

(92)
3-y-o ch g Karinga Bay-Magical Day (Halling (USA))
W G M Turner M J B Racing

Placings:0-0 (7888)
2009: 12^{0}SD,

	Starts	1st	2nd	3rd	Win & Pl
Career Total (Turf)	1	0	0	0	
Career Total (AW)	1	0	0	0	

Going (Turf): **Sf: 0-1 GS: 0-0 Gd: 0-0 GF: 0-0 Fm: 0-0**
Distance: 5f/6f: 0-0 7f-8f: 0-1 9f-13f: 0-1 14f+: 0-0
Track : LH: 0-1 RH: 0-0 Tight: 0-1 Gall: 0-0
Aids: Bl: 0-0 Vi: 0-0 Tstrap: 0-0 Ckp: 0-0

Maverin (IRE)

100(94) (77)77
3-y-o b c King's Best (USA)-Minerva (IRE) (Caerleon (USA))
Tom Dascombe (J Noseda 29/6) M A Al-Attiyah

Placings:4-3432310 (6396)
2009: 8^{3}G, 8^{4}SD, 8^{3}G, 6^{2}S, 6^{3}GS, 6^{1}GF, 6^{0}GF,

	Starts	1st	2nd	3rd	Win & Pl
Career Total (Turf)	7	1	1	3	5335
Career Total (AW)	1	0	0	0	327

77	6/09	Wind	6f	G-F	£2729

Total win prize-money £2730

Going (Turf): Sf: 0-1 GS: 0-1 Gd: 0-3 **GF: 1-2** Fm: 0-0
Distance: **5f/6f: 1-3** 7f-8f: 0-3 9f-13f: 0-2 14f+: 0-0
Track : LH: 0-0 RH: 0-1 Tight: 0-0 **Gall: 1-1**
Aids: Bl: 0-0 Vi: 0-0 Tstrap: 0-0 Ckp: 0-0
Best Rating: 77 6/09 Wind 6f gd-fm

Fair; effective over 6f-1m; acts on good ground.

Mawaddah (IRE)

99(93) (75)75
2-y-o b c Intikhab (USA)-Handsome Anna (IRE) (Bigstone (IRE))
R Hannon Malih L Al Basti

Placings:06333 (7326)
2009: 6^{0}GF, 8^{6}GS, 8^{3}GS, 8^{3}S, 7^{3}SD,

	Starts	1st	2nd	3rd	Win & Pl
Career Total (Turf)	4	0	0	2	988
Career Total (AW)	1	0	0	1	337

Going (Turf): **Sf: 0-1 GS: 0-2 Gd: 0-0 GF: 0-1 Fm: 0-0**
Distance: 5f/6f: 0-1 7f-8f: 0-1 9f-13f: 0-3 14f+: 0-0
Track : LH: 0-2 RH: 0-2 Tight: 0-0 Gall: 0-0
Aids: Bl: 0-0 Vi: 0-0 Tstrap: 0-0 Ckp: 0-0
Best Rating: 75 11/09 Kemp 7f stand

Fair; effective at 7f-1m; acts on easy ground and Polytrack.

Mawatheeq (USA)

118(98) (83)122
4-y-o b c Danzig (USA)-Sarayir (USA) (Mr Prospector (USA))
M P Tregoning Hamdan Al Maktoum

Placings:2116-0112 (6850)
2009: 8^{0}S, 10^{1}G, 12^{1}GF, 10^{2}G,

	Starts	1st	2nd	3rd	Win & Pl
Career Total (Turf)	7	4	1	0	146648
Career Total (AW)	1	0	1	0	771

119	9/09	Asct	1m4f		G-F	£36900
111	9/09	Donc	1m2f60y	(0-110)H	GD	£16190
106	9/08	Asct	1m	(0-85)H	GD	£6476
90	8/08	NmkJ	1m		G-F	£5180

Total win prize-money £64748

Going (Turf): Sf: 0-1 GS: 0-0 **Gd: 2-4 GF: 2-2** Fm: 0-0
Distance: 5f/6f: 0-0 7f-8f: 2-4 9f-13f: 2-4 14f+: 0-0
Track : LH: 1-1 RH: 1-2 Tight: 0-0 **Gall: 2-2**
Aids: Bl: 0-0 Vi: 0-0 Tstrap: 0-0 Ckp: 0-0
Best Rating: 122 10/09 NmkR 1m2f good

Group class; runner-up in the 2009 Champion Stakes; effective at 1m2f-1m4f; acts on a sound surface; handles Polytrack.

Mawzoon (IRE)

101 75
2-y-o ch c Pivotal-Two Clubs (First Trump)
M A Jarvis Hamdan Al Maktoum

Placings:4 (7145)
2009: 6^{4}G,

	Starts	1st	2nd	3rd	Win & Pl
Career Total (Turf)	1	0	0	0	385

Going (Turf): **Sf: 0-0 GS: 0-0 Gd: 0-1 GF: 0-0 Fm: 0-0**
Distance: 5f/6f: 0-1 7f-8f: 0-0 9f-13f: 0-0 14f+: 0-0
Track : LH: 0-0 RH: 0-0 Tight: 0-0 Gall: 0-0
Aids: Bl: 0-0 Vi: 0-0 Tstrap: 0-0 Ckp: 0-0
Best Rating: 75 10/09 NmkR 6f good

Max One Two Three (IRE)

107 99
4-y-o b f Princely Heir (IRE)-Dakota Sioux (IRE) (College Chapel)
Tom Dascombe A Black

Placings:131/0-60463 (2536)
2009: 6^{6}GF, 5^{0}GS, 6^{4}F, 6^{6}HY, 7^{3}GF,

	Starts	1st	2nd	3rd	Win & Pl
Career Total (Turf)	9	2	0	2	24921

99	10/07	York	6f	G-S	£14817
75	8/07	Sals	6f	G-F	£3238

Total win prize-money £18057

Going (Turf): Sf: 0-1 **GS: 1-2** Gd: 0-0 **GF: 1-5** Fm: 0-1
Distance: **5f/6f: 2-5** 7f-8f: 0-4 9f-13f: 0-0 14f+: 0-0
Track : LH: 0-0 RH: 0-0 Tight: 0-0 Gall: 0-0
Aids: Bl: 0-0 Vi: 0-0 Tstrap: 0-0 Ckp: 0-0
Best Rating: 99 5/09 Nott 6f15y firm

Very useful; winner in Listed company at two; effective over 6f-7f; acts on most ground.

Maxijack (IRE)

(83) (48)
2-y-o b g Governor Brown (USA)-Aster Fields (IRE) (Common Grounds)
G Brown Michael James Burke

Placings:00 (7885)
2009: 7^{0}SD, 7^{0}SD,

	Starts	1st	2nd	3rd	Win & Pl
Career Total (Turf)	0	0	0	0	

	Starts	1st	2nd	3rd	Win & Pl
Career Total (AW)	2	0	0	0	

Going (Turf): Sf: 0-0 GS: 0-0 Gd: 0-0 GF: 0-0 Fm: 0-0
Distance: 5f/6f: 0-0 7f-8f: 0-2 9f-13f: 0-0 14f+: 0-0
Track : LH: 0-2 RH: 0-0 Tight: 0-2 Gall: 0-0
Aids: Bl: 0-0 Vi: 0-0 Tstrap: 0-0 Ckp: 0-0
Best Rating: 48 12/09 Ling 7f stand

Maximix

(94) (57)**57**
6-y-o gr g Linamix (FR)-Time Will Show (FR) (Exit To Nowhere (USA))
G L Moore Wilf Slee

Placings:0/500601/00/0-05 (1609)
2009: 12^{0}SD, 16^{5}SD,

	Starts	1st	2nd	3rd	Win & Pl
Career Total (Turf)	5	0	0	0	0
Career Total (AW)	7	1	0	0	2389

70 10/06 Ling 1m4f (0-60)H STD £2388
Total win prize-money £2389

Going (Turf): **Sf: 0-0 GS: 0-1 Gd: 0-0 GF: 0-4 Fm: 0-0**
Distance: 5f/6f: 0-0 7f-8f: 0-3 **9f-13f: 1-7** 14f+: 0-2
Track : **LH: 1-5** RH: 0-5 **Tight: 1-7** Gall: 0-0
Aids: Bl: 0-0 Vi: 0-0 Tstrap: 0-0 Ckp: 0-0
Best Rating: 70 10/06 Ling 1m4f stand

Maximus Aurelius (IRE)

76(103) (76)**73**
4-y-o b g Night Shift (USA)-Dame's Violet (IRE) (Groom Dancer (USA))
J Jay K Snell

Placings:603100/23020020-00 (6640)
2009: 9^{0}S, 9^{0}SD,

	Starts	1st	2nd	3rd	Win & Pl
Career Total (Turf)	12	1	2	2	9195
Career Total (AW)	4	0	1	0	1156

73 9/07 Catt 7f (0-85) GD £5181
Total win prize-money £5182

Going (Turf): Sf: 0-2 GS: 0-3 **Gd: 1-3** GF: 0-4 Fm: 0-0
Distance: 5f/6f: 0-3 **7f-8f: 1-4** 9f-13f: 0-8 14f+: 0-1
Track : **LH: 1-7** RH: 0-4 **Tight: 1-7** Gall: 0-3
Aids: Bl: 0-0 Vi: 0-0 Tstrap: 0-0 Ckp: 0-0
Best Rating: 76 11/08 Wolv 1m141y stand

Modest; effective at around 1m-1m2f; acts on fast and easy ground; goes on Polytrack.

Maxwell Hawke (IRE)

100 **79**
3-y-o br g Rock Of Gibraltar (IRE)-Twice The Ease (Green Desert (USA))
P W Chapple-Hyam The Comic Strip Heroes

Placings:5-100000 (6111)
2009: 7^{1}GF, 7^{0}GS, 7^{0}GF, 6^{0}G, 6^{0}GF, 7^{0}GF,

	Starts	1st	2nd	3rd	Win & Pl
Career Total (Turf)	7	1	0	0	3071

79 4/09 Wwck 7f26y G-F £3070
Total win prize-money £3071

Going (Turf): Sf: 0-0 GS: 0-2 Gd: 0-1 **GF: 1-4** Fm: 0-0
Distance: 5f/6f: 0-3 **7f-8f: 1-4** 9f-13f: 0-0 14f+: 0-0
Track : **LH: 1-2** RH: 0-0 Tight: 0-0 Gall: 0-1
Aids: Bl: 0-0 Vi: 0-0 Tstrap: 0-0 Ckp: 0-0
Best Rating: 79 4/09 Wwck 7f26y gd-fm

Fair; stays 7f; acts on fast ground.

Maxwil

101(105) (78)**90**
4-y-o b g Storming Home-Lady Donatella (Last Tycoon)
P M Phelan (G L Moore 13/4) H R Hunt

Placings:0641/236-00400 (6634)
2009: 11^{0}SD, 7^{0}G, 10^{4}G, 10^{0}GF, 12^{0}SS,

	Starts	1st	2nd	3rd	Win & Pl
Career Total (Turf)	10	1	1	1	6764
Career Total (AW)	2	0	0	0	

78 10/07 Brig 6f209y GD £2849
Total win prize-money £2850

Going (Turf): Sf: 0-0 GS: 0-1 **Gd: 1-5** GF: 0-4 Fm: 0-0
Distance: 5f/6f: 0-0 **7f-8f: 1-4** 9f-13f: 0-8 14f+: 0-0
Track : **LH: 1-5** RH: 0-7 Tight: 0-3 Gall: 0-2
Aids: Bl: 0-1 Vi: 0-0 Tstrap: 0-0 Ckp: 0-0
Best Rating: 90 6/08 Sand 1m1f good

Useful; stays 1m3f and acts on good and faster ground; has worn blinkers.

May Chorus (IRE)

86(89) (67)**38**
2-y-o b f Night Shift (USA)-Chorus (USA) (Darshaan)
J R Boyle Darks Racing Partnership

Placings:0300 (7824)
2009: 6^{0}SD, 6^{3}SD, 6^{0}G, 7^{0}SD,

	Starts	1st	2nd	3rd	Win & Pl
Career Total (Turf)	1	0	0	0	
Career Total (AW)	3	0	0	1	385

Going (Turf): **Sf: 0-0 GS: 0-0 Gd: 0-1 GF: 0-0 Fm: 0-0**
Distance: 5f/6f: 0-3 7f-8f: 0-1 9f-13f: 0-0 14f+: 0-0
Track : LH: 0-0 RH: 0-3 Tight: 0-0 Gall: 0-0
Aids: Bl: 0-0 Vi: 0-0 Tstrap: 0-0 Ckp: 0-0
Best Rating: 67 10/09 Kemp 6f stand

May Martin

85(95) (59)**44**
3-y-o b f Monsieur Bond (IRE)-Calcavella (Pursuit Of Love)
Rae Guest Mrs A Shone

Placings:10300 (7068)
2009: 5^{1}SD, 5^{0}SD, 6^{3}G, 6^{0}G, 6^{0}SD,

	Starts	1st	2nd	3rd	Win & Pl
Career Total (Turf)	2	0	0	1	482
Career Total (AW)	3	1	0	0	2590

59 2/09 Sthl 5f STD £2590
Total win prize-money £2590

Going (Turf): **Sf: 0-0 GS: 0-0 Gd: 0-2 GF: 0-0 Fm: 0-0**
Distance: **5f/6f: 1-4** 7f-8f: 0-1 9f-13f: 0-0 14f+: 0-0
Track : LH: 0-1 RH: 0-0 Tight: 0-1 Gall: 0-1
Aids: Bl: 0-0 Vi: 0-0 Tstrap: 0-0 Ckp: 0-0
Best Rating: 59 2/09 Sthl 5f stand

Half-sister to those multiple sprint winners Skhilling Spirit and Bertoliver; winner on debut over 5f on Fibresand.

May Need A Spell

63(79) (55)**51**
3-y-o b g Needwood Blade-Under My Spell (Wizard King)
J G M O'Shea J R Salter

Placings:600-000 (3743)
2009: 8^{0}GF, 5^{0}GF, 6^{0}SD,

	Starts	1st	2nd	3rd	Win & Pl
Career Total (Turf)	3	0	0	0	
Career Total (AW)	3	0	0	0	0

Going (Turf): **Sf: 0-0 GS: 0-1 Gd: 0-0 GF: 0-2 Fm: 0-0**
Distance: 5f/6f: 0-5 7f-8f: 0-0 9f-13f: 0-1 14f+: 0-0
Track : LH: 0-5 RH: 0-0 Tight: 0-3 Gall: 0-0
Aids: Bl: 0-1 Vi: 0-0 Tstrap: 0-0 Ckp: 0-0
Best Rating: 55 8/08 Ling 6f stand

May Parkin (IRE)

(94) (48)**1**
4-y-o b f Acclamation-Pretext (Polish Precedent (USA))
M Wigham D Hassan

Placings:006-05 (7240)
2009: 8^{0}SD, 7^{5}SD,

	Starts	1st	2nd	3rd	Win & Pl
Career Total (Turf)	2	0	0	0	
Career Total (AW)	3	0	0	0	0

Going (Turf): **Sf: 0-2 GS: 0-0 Gd: 0-0 GF: 0-0 Fm: 0-0**
Distance: 5f/6f: 0-1 7f-8f: 0-3 9f-13f: 0-1 14f+: 0-0
Track : LH: 0-1 RH: 0-3 Tight: 0-1 Gall: 0-1
Aids: Bl: 0-1 Vi: 0-0 Tstrap: 0-0 Ckp: 0-0
Best Rating: 48 11/09 Kemp 7f stand

Moderate; stays 7f; acts on Polytrack; has worn tongue-tie/blinkers.

Mayadeen (IRE)

90(99) (57)**61**
7-y-o b g King's Best (USA)-Inaaq (Lammtarra (USA))
R A Fahey James Gaffney

Placings:31/020/55000/00634016065401/035120-40036 (3444)
2009: 16^{4}SD, 14^{0}SD, 11^{0}G, 14^{3}GF, 16^{6}GF,

	Starts	1st	2nd	3rd	Win & Pl
Career Total (Turf)	29	2	2	4	12402
Career Total (AW)	6	2	0	0	3754

57 10/08 Kemp 1m4f (0-55)H STD £1706
53 12/07 Wolv 1m4f50y STD £2047
59 7/07 Haml 1m1f36y (0-75)H SFT £3238
68 10/04 Bath 1m5y G-S £3965
Total win prize-money £10958

Going (Turf): **Sf: 1-3 GS: 1-7** Gd: 0-8 GF: 0-11 Fm: 0-0
Distance: 5f/6f: 0-0 7f-8f: 0-4 **9f-13f: 4-25** 14f+: 0-6
Track : LH: 2-14 RH: 2-19 **Tight: 3-20** Gall: 0-5
Aids: **Bl: 2-13** Vi: 0-7 Tstrap: 0-1 Ckp: 0-1
Best Rating: 85 5/05 Donc 1m2f60y gd-fm

Moderate; effective at around 1m4f; acts on soft ground; also goes on Polytrack.

Maybe I Will (IRE)

99 (70)**73**
4-y-o b f Hawk Wing (USA)-Canterbury Lace (USA) (Danehill (USA))
S Dow Mrs Alicia Aldis

Placings:6410600/01160010-036 (2518)
2009: 10^{0}GF, 9^{3}GF, 8^{6}F,

	Starts	1st	2nd	3rd	Win & Pl
Career Total (Turf)	16	3	0	1	8338
Career Total (AW)	2	1	0	0	4743

73 9/08 Brig 1m1f209y (0-70)H GD £2775
71 6/08 Bath 1m5y (0-70)H G-F £2719
66 6/08 Bath 1m5y (0-60)H GD £2072
70 7/07 Kemp 7f STD £4533
Total win prize-money £12102

Going (Turf): Sf: 0-0 GS: 0-1 **Gd: 2-5** GF: 1-9 Fm: 0-1
Distance: 5f/6f: 0-2 7f-8f: 1-7 **9f-13f: 3-9** 14f+: 0-0
Track : LH: 3-7 RH: 1-7 **Tight: 2-7** Gall: 0-0
Aids: Bl: 0-0 Vi: 0-0 Tstrap: 0-0 Ckp: 0-0
Best Rating: 73 9/08 Brig 1m1f209y good

Modest; stays 1m; acts on a sound surface and Polytrack.

Maybe I Wont

105(101) (72)70
4-y-o b g Kyllachy-Surprise Surprise (Robellino (USA))
Lucinda Featherstone J Roundtree

Placings:03224060600416522l2/322104600-40053001103020 (5532)
2009: 5[4]SD, 6[0]SD, 8[0]SD, 8[5]SD, 10[3]F, 10[0]GF, 8[0]G, 10[1]G, 10[1]G, 11[0]SD, 9[3]G, 12[0]G, 10[2]GS, 10[0]G,

	Starts	1st	2nd	3rd	Win & Pl
Career Total (Turf)	17	2	3	3	8574
Career Total (AW)	25	3	5	1	10016

69 6/09 Wwck 1m2f188y (0-55)H GD £2047
70 6/09 Nott 1m2f50y (0-60)H GD £2047
72 2/08 Wolv 7f32y STD £2388
64 12/07 Ling 6f STD £1943
68 10/07 Ling 6f STD £2047
Total win prize-money £10474

Going (Turf): Sf: 0-0 GS: 0-3 **Gd: 2-9** GF: 0-4 Fm: 0-1
Distance: 5f/6f: 2-21 7f-8f: 1-10 9f-13f: 2-11 14f+: 0-0
Track : **LH: 5-30** RH: 0-5 **Tight: 3-22** Gall: 0-3
Aids: Bl: 0-0 Vi: 0-0 Tstrap: 2-5 Ckp: 2-5
Best Rating: 72 2/08 Wolv 7f32y stand

Modest; stays 1m2f; acts on good ground; also goes on Polytrack; has worn cheekpieces.

Maybeme

104 71
3-y-o b f Lujain (USA)-Malvadilla (IRE) (Doyoun)
N Bycroft Cavalier Racing

Placings:00-4524456 (7014)
2009: 9[4]GS, 8[5]G, 9[2]GF, 9[4]GF, 12[4]GF, 10[5]GF, 10[6]GS,

	Starts	1st	2nd	3rd	Win & Pl
Career Total (Turf)	9	0	1	0	4115

Going (Turf): **Sf: 0-1 GS: 0-3 Gd: 0-1 GF: 0-4 Fm: 0-0**
Distance: 5f/6f: 0-0 7f-8f: 0-3 9f-13f: 0-6 14f+: 0-0
Track : LH: 0-3 RH: 0-4 Tight: 0-2 Gall: 0-2
Aids: Bl: 0-0 Vi: 0-0 Tstrap: 0-0 Ckp: 0-0
Best Rating: 71 9/09 Bevl 1m4f16y gd-fm

Fair; stays 1m2f.

Mayfair's Future

93(100) (64)59
4-y-o b c High Estate-Riva La Belle (Ron's Victory (USA))
J R Jenkins G D I Markets Ltd

Placings:0000215-00300260 (4745)
2009: 10[0]SD, 10[0]SD, 9[3]GF, 10[0]F, 9[0]GF, 12[2]SD, 8[6]SF, 10[0]GS,

	Starts	1st	2nd	3rd	Win & Pl
Career Total (Turf)	5	0	0	1	385
Career Total (AW)	10	1	2	0	3808

64 11/08 GrLe 1m2f STD £2266
Total win prize-money £2267

Going (Turf): **Sf: 0-0 GS: 0-2 Gd: 0-0 GF: 0-2 Fm: 0-1**
Distance: 5f/6f: 0-0 7f-8f: 0-2 **9f-13f: 1-13** 14f+: 0-0
Track : **LH: 1-9** RH: 0-6 Tight: 0-5 **Gall: 1-2**
Aids: Bl: 0-0 Vi: 0-1 Tstrap: 0-0 Ckp: 0-0
Best Rating: 64 11/08 GrLe 1m2f stand

Modest; effective over 1m2f and acts on Polytrack.

Mayolynn (USA)

95(98) (73)64
3-y-o ch f Johannesburg (USA)-Civilynn (USA) (Lost Code (USA))
H R A Cecil Mr & Mrs R Scott

Placings:034230 (5570)
2009: 8[0]G, 11[3]SD, 9[4]GF, 9[2]HY, 9[3]GF, 10[0]SD,

	Starts	1st	2nd	3rd	Win & Pl
Career Total (Turf)	4	0	1	1	1559
Career Total (AW)	2	0	0	1	385

Going (Turf): **Sf: 0-1 GS: 0-0 Gd: 0-1 GF: 0-2 Fm: 0-0**
Distance: 5f/6f: 0-0 7f-8f: 0-0 9f-13f: 0-6 14f+: 0-0
Track : LH: 0-1 RH: 0-4 Tight: 0-2 Gall: 0-0
Aids: Bl: 0-0 Vi: 0-2 Tstrap: 0-0 Ckp: 0-0
Best Rating: 73 7/09 Kemp 1m3f stand

Fair; stays 1m3f; acts on fast ground and Polytrack.

Mayoman (IRE)

101(100) (64)70
4-y-o b g Namid-America Lontana (FR) (King's Theatre (IRE))
D Carroll (M Mullineaux 14/7) Tom Tuohy

Placings:1000260-0646431610 (7138)
2009: 5[0]SD, 5[6]SD, 7[4]GF, 9[6]GF, 7[4]GF, 5[3]GS, 6[1]GS, 7[6]GF, 5[1]SD, 5[0]SD,

	Starts	1st	2nd	3rd	Win & Pl
Career Total (Turf)	10	2	0	1	5627
Career Total (AW)	7	1	1	0	3352

64 10/09 Wolv 5f216y (0-60)H STD £2388
64 9/09 Newc 6f (0-55)H G-S £2914
70 5/08 Catt 5f G-F £2047
Total win prize-money £7349

Going (Turf): Sf: 0-2 **GS: 1-2** Gd: 0-0 **GF: 1-6** Fm: 0-0
Distance: **5f/6f: 3-12** 7f-8f: 0-4 9f-13f: 0-1 14f+: 0-0
Track : **LH: 1-10** RH: 0-1 **Tight: 1-10** Gall: 0-0
Aids: **Bl: 2-4** Vi: 0-0 Tstrap: 0-0 Ckp: 0-0
Best Rating: 70 5/08 Catt 5f gd-fm

Moderate; stays 7f; acts on fast and easy ground and on Polytrack; has worn blinkers.

Mayorstone (IRE)

73 10
3-y-o ch f Exceed And Excel (AUS)-Coolrain Lady (IRE) (Common Grounds)
B Smart H E Sheikh Rashid Bin Mohammed

Placings:0-0 (5599)
2009: 6[0]GF,

	Starts	1st	2nd	3rd	Win & Pl
Career Total (Turf)	2	0	0	0	

Going (Turf): **Sf: 0-0 GS: 0-0 Gd: 0-1 GF: 0-1 Fm: 0-0**
Distance: 5f/6f: 0-2 7f-8f: 0-0 9f-13f: 0-0 14f+: 0-0
Track : LH: 0-0 RH: 0-0 Tight: 0-0 Gall: 0-0
Aids: Bl: 0-0 Vi: 0-0 Tstrap: 0-0 Ckp: 0-0
Best Rating: 10 8/08 Thsk 5f good

Mays Louise

80(88) (64)15
5-y-o ch m Sir Harry Lewis (USA)-Maysimp (IRE) (Mac's Imp (USA))
B P J Baugh J H Chrimes

Placings:0000/60-004000 (2843)
2009: 8[0]SS, 8[0]SD, 8[4]SD, 8[0]SF, 8[0]GF, 10[0]GF,

	Starts	1st	2nd	3rd	Win & Pl
Career Total (Turf)	2	0	0	0	
Career Total (AW)	10	0	0	0	0

Going (Turf): **Sf: 0-0 GS: 0-0 Gd: 0-0 GF: 0-2 Fm: 0-0**
Distance: 5f/6f: 0-0 7f-8f: 0-6 9f-13f: 0-6 14f+: 0-0
Track : LH: 0-11 RH: 0-0 Tight: 0-8 Gall: 0-0
Aids: Bl: 0-0 Vi: 0-0 Tstrap: 0-0 Ckp: 0-0
Best Rating: 64 2/09 Wolv 1m141y stand

Mayta Capac (USA)

(86) (57)
3-y-o ch c Thunder Gulch (USA)-Yvecrique (FR) (Epervier Bleu)
D M Simcock El Catorce

Placings:4-65 (7694)
2009: 8[6]SD, 10[5]SD,

	Starts	1st	2nd	3rd	Win & Pl
Career Total (Turf)	0	0	0	0	
Career Total (AW)	3	0	0	0	192

Going (Turf): **Sf: 0-0 GS: 0-0 Gd: 0-0 GF: 0-0 Fm: 0-0**
Distance: 5f/6f: 0-0 7f-8f: 0-1 9f-13f: 0-2 14f+: 0-0
Track : LH: 0-2 RH: 0-1 Tight: 0-2 Gall: 0-0
Aids: Bl: 0-0 Vi: 0-0 Tstrap: 0-0 Ckp: 0-0
Best Rating: 57 8/08 Kemp 7f stand

Mazamorra (USA)

(88) (44)
2-y-o b/br f Orientate (USA)-Mumbo Jumbo (USA) (Kingmambo (USA))
M Botti El Catorce

Placings:6 (7199)
2009: 8[6]SD,

	Starts	1st	2nd	3rd	Win & Pl
Career Total (Turf)	0	0	0	0	
Career Total (AW)	1	0	0	0	0

Going (Turf): **Sf: 0-0 GS: 0-0 Gd: 0-0 GF: 0-0 Fm: 0-0**
Distance: 5f/6f: 0-0 7f-8f: 0-1 9f-13f: 0-0 14f+: 0-0
Track : LH: 0-1 RH: 0-0 Tight: 0-1 Gall: 0-0
Aids: Bl: 0-0 Vi: 0-0 Tstrap: 0-0 Ckp: 0-0
Best Rating: 44 11/09 Ling 1m stand

Maze (IRE)

105(99) (72)95
4-y-o ch g Dr Fong (USA)-Aryadne (Rainbow Quest (USA))
B Smart Pinnacle Dr Fong Partnership

Placings:116020/50056-4040000 (6830)
2009: 6^{4}F, 7^{0}GF, 6^{4}GF, 6^{0}GF, 6^{0}GS, 8^{0}GS, 8^{0}SF,

	Starts	1st	2nd	3rd	Win & Pl
Career Total (Turf)	17	2	1	0	43789
Career Total (AW)	1	0	0	0	

96 6/07 Asct 7f GD £31229
85 6/07 Newc 6f GD £3368
Total win prize-money £34597

Going (Turf): Sf: 0-1 GS: 0-3 **Gd: 2-6** GF: 0-5 Fm: 0-2
Distance: 5f/6f: 1-7 7f-8f: 1-10 9f-13f: 0-1 14f+: 0-0
Track : LH: 0-4 RH: 0-1 Tight: 0-2 Gall: 0-0
Aids: Bl: 0-0 Vi: 0-0 Tstrap: 0-0 Ckp: 0-0
Best Rating: **101** 10/07 York 6f gd-sft

Very useful; winner in Listed company; stays 7f; acts on most ground.

Mazzola

103(100) (80)**82**
3-y-o b g Bertolini (USA)-Elegant Dance (Statoblest)
M R Channon M Channon

Placings:3412532410**360-4433230005260**3600453323 (7122)
2009: 6^{4}SD, 5^{4}SD, 5^{3}SD, 5^{3}G, 6^{2}GF, 6^{3}G, 5^{0}GS, 5^{0}GF, 5^{0}G, 5^{5}G, 5^{2}GF, 6^{6}G, 5^{0}G, 5^{3}SD, 5^{6}GF, 5^{0}GF, 5^{0}GF, 5^{4}G, 5^{5}GF, 5^{3}SD, 5^{3}S, 5^{2}G, 5^{3}G,

	Starts	1st	2nd	3rd	Win & Pl
Career Total (Turf)	28	2	5	6	21386
Career Total (AW)	8	0	0	4	2828

82 8/08 Haml 6f5y GD £3885
75 5/08 Brig 5f213y G-F £3626
Total win prize-money £7513

Going (Turf): Sf: 0-2 GS: 0-1 **Gd: 1-15 GF: 1-10** Fm: 0-0
Distance: 5f/6f: 1-34 7f-8f: 1-2 9f-13f: 0-0 14f+: 0-0
Track : **LH: 1-11** RH: 0-5 Tight: 0-6 Gall: 0-3
Aids: Bl: 0-0 Vi: 0-0 Tstrap: 0-0 Ckp: 0-0
Best Rating: **82** 8/08 Haml 6f5y good

Fair; effective over 5f-6f; acts on most ground and on Polytrack.

McCartney (GER)

107 **104**
4-y-o b/br c In The Wings-Messina (GER) (Dashing Blade)
Saeed Bin Suroor Godolphin

Placings:31110/6-05 (2953a)
2009: 7^{0}GF, 8^{5}GS,

	Starts	1st	2nd	3rd	Win & Pl
Career Total (Turf)	8	3	0	1	80768

114 9/07 Donc 7f G-F £56780
99 8/07 Sals 1m G-F £12775
94 8/07 Haml 1m65y G-S £4533
Total win prize-money £74090

Going (Turf): Sf: 0-0 GS: 1-3 Gd: 0-1 **GF: 2-4** Fm: 0-0
Distance: 5f/6f: 0-0 **7f-8f: 2-6** 9f-13f: 1-2 14f+: 0-0
Track : LH: 0-2 **RH: 1-3 Tight: 1-1** Gall: 0-2
Aids: Bl: 0-0 Vi: 0-0 Tstrap: 0-0 Ckp: 0-0
Best Rating: **114** 9/07 Donc 7f gd-fm

Group class; winner of Champagne Stakes at Doncaster and seventh in the Dewhurst when trained by M.Johnston; stays 1m; acts on most ground.

Mcconnell (USA)

88(109) (91)**82**
4-y-o ch g Petionville (USA)-Warsaw Girl (IRE) (Polish Precedent (USA))
G L Moore Joe McCarthy

Placings:4542/23015430-0140014521 (7782)
2009: 10^{0}SD, 8^{1}SD, 8^{4}SD, 8^{0}SD, 10^{0}GS, 8^{1}SD, 8^{4}SD, 8^{5}SD, 8^{2}SD, 8^{1}SD,

	Starts	1st	2nd	3rd	Win & Pl
Career Total (Turf)	9	1	0	1	5998
Career Total (AW)	13	3	3	1	15316

85 12/09 Sthl 1m STD £2047
86 9/09 Sthl 1m (0-85)H STD £5828
84 1/09 Sthl 1m (0-75)H STD £2729
82 5/08 Gdwd 1m1f (0-85)H GD £4361
Total win prize-money £14967

Going (Turf): Sf: 0-1 GS: 0-1 **Gd: 1-3** GF: 0-4 Fm: 0-0
Distance: 5f/6f: 0-1 **7f-8f: 3-13** 9f-13f: 1-8 14f+: 0-0
Track : **LH: 3-11** RH: 1-8 **Tight: 1-9** Gall: 0-0
Aids: Bl: 0-0 Vi: 0-0 Tstrap: 0-0 Ckp: 0-0
Best Rating: **91** 11/09 Sthl 1m stand

Useful; stays 1m1f; acts on a sound surface and sand.

McCormack (IRE)

97 (7)**54**
7-y-o b g Desert Story (IRE)-La Loba (IRE) (Treasure Kay)
Miss T Jackson R D Bickenson

Placings:006/0050000/000/100340060 (6184)
2009: 10^{1}GF, 8^{0}F, 12^{0}GS, 10^{3}GF, 11^{4}GF, 9^{0}GF, 9^{0}GF, 8^{6}GF, 9^{0}GF,

	Starts	1st	2nd	3rd	Win & Pl
Career Total (Turf)	21	1	0	1	2705
Career Total (AW)	1	0	0	0	

54 4/09 Newc 1m2f32y (0-60)H G-F £2320
Total win prize-money £2320

Going (Turf): Sf: 0-1 GS: 0-2 Gd: 0-1 **GF: 1-14** Fm: 0-3
Distance: 5f/6f: 0-0 7f-8f: 0-3 **9f-13f: 1-19** 14f+: 0-0
Track : **LH: 1-11** RH: 0-11 Tight: 0-9 **Gall: 1-2**
Aids: Bl: 0-0 Vi: 0-1 Tstrap: 0-1 Ckp: 0-1
Best Rating: **54** 4/09 Newc 1m2f32y gd-fm

Moderate; effective over 1m2f; acts on fast ground.

McEldowney

92(86) (44)**50**
7-y-o b g Zafonic (USA)-Ayodhya (IRE) (Astronef)
M C Chapman Mrs M Chapman

Placings:3222300251/00U040160111600/4021011425054 26450/23003/0000-4050 (7332)
2009: 16^{4}GF, 18^{0}G, 13^{5}GF, 12^{0}SD,

	Starts	1st	2nd	3rd	Win & Pl
Career Total (Turf)	52	7	8	4	62238
Career Total (AW)	4	1	0	0	3239

86 6/06 Catt 1m3f214y (0-70)H G-F £5181
81 5/06 Catt 1m5f175y (0-80)H G-S £6477
76 5/06 Sthl 1m3f (0-70)H STD £3238
79 8/05 Brig 1m3f196y (0-70)H SFT £5423
75 8/05 Haml 1m3f16y (0-75)H G-F £3523
75 8/05 Haml 1m4f17y (0-70)H G-F £3480
66 7/05 Haml 1m65y (0-65) G-F £4208
71 11/04 Catt 7f SFT £2926
Total win prize-money £34461

Going (Turf): Sf: 2-10 GS: 1-5 Gd: 0-16 **GF: 4-19** Fm: 0-2
Distance: 5f/6f: 0-1 7f-8f: 1-13 **9f-13f: 6-20** 14f+: 1-22
Track : **LH: 5-30** RH: 3-19 **Tight: 6-21** Gall: 0-12
Aids: Bl: 0-3 Vi: 0-0 Tstrap: 0-1 Ckp: 0-1
Best Rating: **94** 9/06 Hayd 1m6f heavy

Fair; stays 2m and acts on any ground; likes to race prominently.

McQueen (IRE)

95 (53)**65**
9-y-o ch g Barathea (IRE)-Bibliotheque (USA) (Woodman (USA))
B D Leavy Moorland Racing & Mrs Laura Leavy

Placings:0/33203310/06006021105112/00060/**00**/2540610/0260-00 (4806)
2009: 14^{0}GS, 14^{0}GF,

	Starts	1st	2nd	3rd	Win & Pl
Career Total (Turf)	29	5	5	0	24715
Career Total (AW)	14	1	0	4	4090

60 10/07 Catt 1m5f175y (0-60)H GD £2590
81 11/04 Rdcr 1m2f (0-77)H SFT £5380
79 10/04 Newb 1m1f (0-77)H SFT £4032
75 8/04 Chep 1m2f36y F(0-55)H SFT £3507
75 8/04 Gdwd 1m F(0-55)H G-S £3591
84 11/03 Sthl 1m E(0-70)H STD £2086
Total win prize-money £21189

Going (Turf): **Sf: 3-7** GS: 1-6 Gd: 1-9 GF: 0-7 Fm: 0-0
Distance: 5f/6f: 0-0 7f-8f: 2-5 **9f-13f: 3-25** 14f+: 1-13
Track : **LH: 5-39** RH: 1-3 **Tight: 2-20** Gall: 1-4
Aids: Bl: 0-0 Vi: 0-1 Tstrap: 0-0 Ckp: 0-0
Best Rating: **84** 11/03 Sthl 1m stand

Moderate; stays 1m 5f; suited by Fibresand and soft ground on turf.

Mdawee (IRE)

95 **86**
2-y-o b c Choisir (AUS)-Its All Eurs (IRE) (Barathea (IRE))
Tom Dascombe Khalifa Al Attiyah

Placings:10205 (6541)
2009: 5^{1}GF, 5^{0}G, 5^{2}GF, 5^{0}G, 6^{5}GF,

	Starts	1st	2nd	3rd	Win & Pl
Career Total (Turf)	5	1	1	0	5997

77 6/09 Wwck 5f G-F £3070
Total win prize-money £3071

Going (Turf): Sf: 0-0 GS: 0-0 Gd: 0-2 **GF: 1-3** Fm: 0-0
Distance: **5f/6f: 1-5** 7f-8f: 0-0 9f-13f: 0-0 14f+: 0-0
Track : **LH: 1-3** RH: 0-0 Tight: 0-1 Gall: 0-0
Aids: Bl: 0-0 Vi: 0-0 Tstrap: 0-0 Ckp: 0-0
Best Rating: **86** 7/09 Ches 5f16y gd-fm

Useful; suited by 5f and fast ground.

Mean Machine (IRE)

(88) (49)**36**
7-y-o b g Idris (IRE)-Date Mate (USA) (Thorn Dance (USA))
J W Unett Guyzance Hall Ltd

Placings:050/005500/2056/000000-60 (4862)
2009: 11^{6}SD, 16^{0}SD,

	Starts	1st	2nd	3rd	Win & Pl
Career Total (Turf)	16	0	1	0	1033
Career Total (AW)	5	0	0	0	0

Going (Turf): **Sf: 0-3 GS: 0-0 Gd: 0-5 GF: 0-3 Fm: 0-0**
Distance: 5f/6f: 0-1 7f-8f: 0-3 9f-13f: 0-13 14f+: 0-4
Track : LH: 0-12 RH: 0-7 Tight: 0-6 Gall: 0-0
Aids: Bl: 0-5 Vi: 0-0 Tstrap: 0-2 Ckp: 0-2
Best Rating: **66** 10/04 Curr 7f soft

65	2/09	Ling	1m5f		STD	£2047

Total win prize-money £2047

Going (Turf): Sf: 0-1 GS: 0-2 Gd: 0-0 GF: 0-5 Fm: 0-0
Distance: 5f/6f: 0-0 7f-8f: 0-3 9f-13f: 1-11 14f+: 0-0
Track : LH: 1-11 RH: 0-3 Tight: 1-6 Gall: 0-4
Aids: Bl: 0-2 Vi: 0-0 Tstrap: 0-2 Ckp: 0-2
Best Rating: 65 2/09 Ling 1m5f stand

Modest; stays 1m5f; acts on Polytrack.

Mean Mr Mustard (IRE)

(95) (56)44

3-y-o b g Invincible Spirit (IRE)-White Lavender (USA) (Mt. Livermore (USA))

J A Osborne J A Osborne

Placings:003040-335 (0348)

2009: 5^{3}SD, 6^{3}SD, 6^{5}SD,

	Starts	1st	2nd	3rd	Win & Pl
Career Total (Turf)	4	0	0	0	
Career Total (AW)	5	0	0	3	1453

Going (Turf): Sf: 0-0 GS: 0-0 Gd: 0-4 GF: 0-0 Fm: 0-0
Distance: 5f/6f: 0-9 7f-8f: 0-0 9f-13f: 0-0 14f+: 0-0
Track : LH: 0-6 RH: 0-1 Tight: 0-4 Gall: 0-0
Aids: Bl: 0-4 Vi: 0-0 Tstrap: 0-0 Ckp: 0-0
Best Rating: 56 6/08 Ling 5f stand

Moderate; suited by 5f-6f; acts on Polytrack.

Mecox Bay (IRE)

91 65

2-y-o b c Noverre (USA)-Birdsong (IRE) (Dolphin Street (FR))

A M Balding E N Kronfeld

Placings:03 (4953)

2009: 7^{0}GF, 8^{3}G,

	Starts	1st	2nd	3rd	Win & Pl
Career Total (Turf)	2	0	0	1	770

Going (Turf): Sf: 0-0 GS: 0-0 Gd: 0-1 GF: 0-1 Fm: 0-0
Distance: 5f/6f: 0-0 7f-8f: 0-1 9f-13f: 0-1 14f+: 0-0
Track : LH: 0-0 RH: 0-2 Tight: 0-0 Gall: 0-0
Aids: Bl: 0-0 Vi: 0-0 Tstrap: 0-0 Ckp: 0-0
Best Rating: 65 7/09 Sand 7f16y gd-fm

Media Jury

82 42

2-y-o b g Lucky Owners (NZ)-Landofheartsdesire (IRE) (Up And At 'Em)

J S Wainwright S Enwright

Placings:00 (6646)

2009: 5^{0}GF, 6^{0}G,

	Starts	1st	2nd	3rd	Win & Pl
Career Total (Turf)	2	0	0	0	

Going (Turf): Sf: 0-0 GS: 0-0 Gd: 0-1 GF: 0-1 Fm: 0-0
Distance: 5f/6f: 0-2 7f-8f: 0-0 9f-13f: 0-0 14f+: 0-0
Track : LH: 0-0 RH: 0-0 Tight: 0-0 Gall: 0-0
Aids: Bl: 0-0 Vi: 0-0 Tstrap: 0-0 Ckp: 0-0
Best Rating: 42 9/09 Bevl 5f gd-fm

Media Stars

97(104) (65)55

4-y-o gr g Green Desert (USA)-Starine (FR) (Mendocino (USA))

R Johnson (J A Osborne 4/2) Barry Robson

Placings:6/30055-60160000 (7080)

2009: 8^{6}SD, 10^{0}SD, 13^{1}SD, 12^{6}GF, 10^{0}GF, 8^{0}GF, 12^{0}GS, 11^{0}S,

	Starts	1st	2nd	3rd	Win & Pl
Career Total (Turf)	8	0	0	0	103
Career Total (AW)	6	1	0	1	2601

Medicea Sidera

106(106) (96)99

5-y-o br m Medicean-Broughtons Motto (Mtoto)

E F Vaughan M A Whelton

Placings:02261150**5**/026122-5060 (6272)

2009: 6^{5}SD, 7^{0}GF, 7^{6}GF, 7^{0}GF,

	Starts	1st	2nd	3rd	Win & Pl
Career Total (Turf)	15	3	4	0	61599
Career Total (AW)	4	0	1	0	1253

96	7/08	NmkJ	7f	(0-105)H	G-F	£25904
87	8/07	NmkJ	7f	(0-95)H	G-F	£7772
78	7/07	NmkJ	7f		GD	£5181

Total win prize-money £38858

Going (Turf): Sf: 0-0 GS: 0-0 Gd: 1-6 GF: 2-9 Fm: 0-0
Distance: 5f/6f: 0-3 7f-8f: 3-16 9f-13f: 0-0 14f+: 0-0
Track : LH: 0-4 RH: 0-4 Tight: 0-3 Gall: 0-1
Aids: Bl: 0-0 Vi: 0-0 Tstrap: 0-0 Ckp: 0-0
Best Rating: 99 10/08 NmkR 6f good

Very useful; Listed placed; seems best at 7f; acts on good and faster ground; goes very well on the Newmarket July course.

Medicean Man

102 87

3-y-o ch g Medicean-Kalindi (Efisio)

J R Gask Stuart Dobb & Miss Kate Dobb

Placings:04131414 (6645)

2009: 6^{0}GF, 6^{4}GS, 6^{1}G, 6^{3}S, 6^{1}GS, 6^{4}GF, 6^{1}G, 7^{4}G,

	Starts	1st	2nd	3rd	Win & Pl
Career Total (Turf)	8	3	0	1	15900

87	8/09	Ripn	6f	(0-85)H	GD	£4857
84	7/09	Hayd	6f	(0-80)H	G-S	£5504
77	6/09	Donc	6f		GD	£3238

Total win prize-money £13600

Going (Turf): Sf: 0-1 GS: 1-2 Gd: 2-3 GF: 0-2 Fm: 0-0
Distance: 5f/6f: 3-5 7f-8f: 0-3 9f-13f: 0-0 14f+: 0-0
Track : LH: 0-1 RH: 0-0 Tight: 0-0 Gall: 0-1
Aids: Bl: 0-0 Vi: 0-0 Tstrap: 0-0 Ckp: 0-0
Best Rating: 87 8/09 Ripn 6f good

Fair; stays 6f; acts on good ground.

Medici Pearl

108 (39)97

5-y-o b m Medicean-In Love Again (IRE) (Prince Rupert (FR))

T D Easterby Ryedale Partners No 3

Placings:3421444100000/611501130-03000306100 (6675)

2009: 8^{0}GF, 8^{3}S, 8^{0}GF, 8^{0}G, 8^{0}G, 10^{3}GF, 10^{0}GF, 10^{6}G, 8^{1}GS, 8^{0}G, 7^{0}G,

	Starts	1st	2nd	3rd	Win & Pl
Career Total (Turf)	32	7	1	3	56624
Career Total (AW)	1	0	0	1	438

92	8/09	Haml	1m65y	(0-95)H	G-S	£11009
92	9/08	Ayr	1m	(0-85)H	HVY	£6476
86	9/08	Rdcr	1m	(0-85)H	G-S	£4857
87	6/08	Carl	6f192y	(0-85)H	SFT	£6476
79	6/08	Catt	7f	(0-75)H	G-S	£2590
85	7/07	Bevl	7f100y	(0-85)H	HVY	£7772
78	5/07	Bevl	7f100y		GD	£3238

Total win prize-money £42419

Going (Turf): Sf: 3-9 GS: 3-4 Gd: 1-11 GF: 0-7 Fm: 0-1
Distance: 5f/6f: 0-1 7f-8f: 6-22 9f-13f: 1-10 14f+: 0-0
Track : LH: 2-20 RH: 4-7 Tight: 2-8 Gall: 0-7
Aids: Bl: 0-0 Vi: 0-0 Tstrap: 0-0 Ckp: 0-0
Best Rating: 97 4/09 Newb 1m soft

Useful; effective over 1m-1m2f; acts on good or softer ground.

Medici Time

104 77

4-y-o gr g Medicean-Pendulum (Pursuit Of Love)

T D Easterby Mrs C A Hodgetts

Placings:0050/4030010-2600321010 (6647)

2009: 6^{2}F, 6^{6}GF, 5^{0}GF, 6^{0}G, 5^{3}GF, 5^{2}G, 6^{1}GF, 6^{0}GF, 5^{1}GS, 5^{0}G,

	Starts	1st	2nd	3rd	Win & Pl
Career Total (Turf)	21	3	2	2	16238

77	9/09	Ayr	5f	(0-70)H	G-S	£5051
76	8/09	Hayd	6f	(0-70)H	G-F	£4857
70	10/08	Rdcr	6f		GD	£2590

Total win prize-money £12498

Going (Turf): Sf: 0-2 GS: 1-3 Gd: 1-7 GF: 1-8 Fm: 0-1
Distance: 5f/6f: 3-11 7f-8f: 0-7 9f-13f: 0-3 14f+: 0-0
Track : LH: 0-4 RH: 0-3 Tight: 0-3 Gall: 0-0
Aids: Bl: 0-1 Vi: 3-12 Tstrap: 0-1 Ckp: 0-1
Best Rating: 77 9/09 Ayr 5f gd-sft

Modest; effective over 6f-7f; acts on fast ground; often visored.

Medicinal Compound

96 78

2-y-o b g Dr Fong (USA)-Liska's Dance (USA) (Riverman (USA))

K A Ryan Hambleton Racing Ltd XIII

Placings:321 (6821)

2009: 8^{3}G, 7^{2}GF, 8^{1}GF,

	Starts	1st	2nd	3rd	Win & Pl
Career Total (Turf)	3	1	1	1	4576

78	10/09	Rdcr	1m	G-F	£2047

Total win prize-money £2047

Going (Turf): Sf: 0-0 GS: 0-0 Gd: 0-1 GF: 1-2 Fm: 0-0
Distance: 5f/6f: 0-0 7f-8f: 1-3 9f-13f: 0-0 14f+: 0-0
Track : LH: 0-2 RH: 0-0 Tight: 0-2 Gall: 0-0
Aids: Bl: 0-0 Vi: 0-0 Tstrap: 0-0 Ckp: 0-0
Best Rating: 78 10/09 Rdcr 1m gd-fm

£21,000 half-brother to numerous winners in France out of a winner over 1m-1m2f; fair form; effective over 1m on fast ground.

Medieval Maiden

100(103) (62)56

6-y-o gr m Zaha (CAN)-Brillante (FR) (Green Dancer (USA))

Mrs L J Mongan Condover Racing

Placings:200/6555103060605/3561236522060000-022156000 (6770)

2009: 13^{0}SD, 11^{2}GF, 11^{2}GF, 12^{1}SD, 12^{5}GF, 11^{6}SD, 16^{0}SD,

12^{0}SD, 12^{0}SD,

	Starts	1st	2nd	3rd	Win & Pl
Career Total (Turf)	12	0	3	0	2698
Career Total (AW)	29	3	3	3	9587

53 6/09 Ling 1m4f STD £2047
62 2/08 Kemp 1m4f (0-55)H STD £1943
70 5/07 Wolv 1m4f50y (0-60)H STD £2730
Total win prize-money £6720

Going (Turf): **Sf: 0-1 GS: 0-1 Gd: 0-2 GF: 0-8 Fm: 0-0**
Distance: 5f/6f: 0-0 7f-8f: 0-1 **9f-13f: 3-36** 14f+: 0-4
Track : **LH: 2-19** RH: 1-19 **Tight: 2-19** Gall: 0-1
Aids: Bl: 0-0 Vi: 0-0 Tstrap: 0-4 Ckp: 0-4
Best Rating: **70** 5/07 Wolv 1m4f50y stand

Moderate handicapper; stays 1m4f; acts on Polytrack; has worn cheekpieces.

Mediterranean Sea (IRE)

92(91) (53)61
3-y-o b f Medecis-High Glider (High Top)
J R Jenkins Mrs Wendy Jenkins

Placings:0040003 (7324)
2009: 8^{0}G, 8^{0}G, 10^{4}G, 11^{0}SD, 12^{0}SD, 11^{0}SD, 12^{3}SD,

	Starts	1st	2nd	3rd	Win & Pl
Career Total (Turf)	3	0	0	0	0
Career Total (AW)	4	0	0	1	302

Going (Turf): **Sf: 0-0 GS: 0-0 Gd: 0-3 GF: 0-0 Fm: 0-0**
Distance: 5f/6f: 0-0 7f-8f: 0-1 9f-13f: 0-6 14f+: 0-0
Track : LH: 0-0 RH: 0-7 Tight: 0-2 Gall: 0-0
Aids: Bl: 0-0 Vi: 0-0 Tstrap: 0-0 Ckp: 0-0
Best Rating: **61** 8/09 Wind 1m2f7y good

Moderate; seems best at around 1m4f; acts well on Polytrack.

Meer Und Wind (GER)

81(76) (62)52
2-y-o b f Xaar-Moneypenny (GER) (Neshad (USA))
P R Webber Shully Liebermann

Placings:6000 (6441)
2009: 6^{6}G, 7^{0}GF, 7^{0}G, 8^{0}SS,

	Starts	1st	2nd	3rd	Win & Pl
Career Total (Turf)	3	0	0	0	0
Career Total (AW)	1	0	0	0	

Going (Turf): **Sf: 0-0 GS: 0-0 Gd: 0-2 GF: 0-1 Fm: 0-0**
Distance: 5f/6f: 0-1 7f-8f: 0-3 9f-13f: 0-0 14f+: 0-0
Track : LH: 0-3 RH: 0-0 Tight: 0-1 Gall: 0-0
Aids: Bl: 0-1 Vi: 0-0 Tstrap: 0-0 Ckp: 0-0
Best Rating: **62** 10/09 Ling 1m std-slw

Meethaaq (USA)

108 93
4-y-o b g Kingmambo (USA)-New Harmony (USA) (A.P. Indy (USA))
Sir Michael Stoute Hamdan Al Maktoum

Placings:21-6200 (6816)
2009: 10^{6}GF, 12^{2}GF, 16^{0}S, 12^{0}G,

	Starts	1st	2nd	3rd	Win & Pl
Career Total (Turf)	6	1	2	0	8464

89 6/08 Leic 1m3f183y GD £2104
Total win prize-money £2105

Going (Turf): **Sf: 0-1 GS: 0-0 Gd: 1-2 GF: 0-3 Fm: 0-0**
Distance: 5f/6f: 0-0 7f-8f: 0-0 **9f-13f: 1-5** 14f+: 0-1
Track : LH: 0-3 **RH: 1-2** Tight: 0-0 Gall: 0-4
Aids: Bl: 0-0 Vi: 0-0 Tstrap: 0-0 Ckp: 0-0
Best Rating: **93** 5/09 Donc 1m4f gd-fm

Useful; stays 1m4f; acts on good and faster ground.

Meetings Man (IRE)

85 55
2-y-o br c Footstepsinthesand-Missella (IRE) (Danehill (USA))
Micky Hammond Largo, Legal & Receivables

Placings:06060 (6679)
2009: 6^{0}GF, 6^{6}S, 6^{0}GS, 8^{6}GF, 7^{0}G,

	Starts	1st	2nd	3rd	Win & Pl
Career Total (Turf)	5	0	0	0	0

Going (Turf): **Sf: 0-1 GS: 0-1 Gd: 0-1 GF: 0-2 Fm: 0-0**
Distance: 5f/6f: 0-3 7f-8f: 0-1 9f-13f: 0-1 14f+: 0-0
Track : LH: 0-3 RH: 0-0 Tight: 0-0 Gall: 0-1
Aids: Bl: 0-0 Vi: 0-0 Tstrap: 0-0 Ckp: 0-0
Best Rating: **55** 7/09 Pont 6f soft

Meezaan (IRE)

85(96) (84)62
2-y-o b c Medicean-Varenka (IRE) (Fasliyev (USA))
J H M Gosden Hamdan Al Maktoum

Placings:01 (6781)
2009: 7^{0}GF, 7^{1}SS,

	Starts	1st	2nd	3rd	Win & Pl
Career Total (Turf)	1	0	0	0	
Career Total (AW)	1	1	0	0	3886

84 10/09 Ling 7f SS £3885
Total win prize-money £3886

Going (Turf): **Sf: 0-0 GS: 0-0 Gd: 0-0 GF: 0-1 Fm: 0-0**
Distance: 5f/6f: 0-0 **7f-8f: 1-2** 9f-13f: 0-0 14f+: 0-0
Track : **LH: 1-1** RH: 0-0 **Tight: 1-1** Gall: 0-0
Aids: Bl: 0-0 Vi: 0-0 Tstrap: 0-0 Ckp: 0-0
Best Rating: **84** 10/09 Ling 7f std-slw

Useful; suited by 7f and acts on Polytrack.

Meeznah (USA)

100 76
2-y-o b f Dynaformer (USA)-String Quartet (IRE) (Sadler's Wells (USA))
D R Lanigan Saif Ali & Saeed H Altayer

Placings:33 (6921)
2009: 7^{3}G, 8^{3}GF,

	Starts	1st	2nd	3rd	Win & Pl
Career Total (Turf)	2	0	0	2	1336

Going (Turf): **Sf: 0-0 GS: 0-0 Gd: 0-1 GF: 0-1 Fm: 0-0**
Distance: 5f/6f: 0-0 7f-8f: 0-1 9f-13f: 0-1 14f+: 0-0
Track : LH: 0-0 RH: 0-0 Tight: 0-0 Gall: 0-0
Aids: Bl: 0-0 Vi: 0-0 Tstrap: 0-0 Ckp: 0-0
Best Rating: **76** 10/09 Yarm 1m3y gd-fm

Mefraas (IRE)

107(103) (79)79
3-y-o b g King's Best (USA)-Khaizarana (Alhaarth (IRE))
E A L Dunlop Hamdan Al Maktoum

Placings:430-223323 (6475)
2009: 9^{2}GF, 8^{2}GF, 9^{3}G, 10^{3}SD, 9^{2}GF, 10^{3}GF,

	Starts	1st	2nd	3rd	Win & Pl
Career Total (Turf)	8	0	3	3	6233
Career Total (AW)	1	0	0	1	385

Going (Turf): **Sf: 0-1 GS: 0-0 Gd: 0-1 GF: 0-6 Fm: 0-0**
Distance: 5f/6f: 0-0 7f-8f: 0-3 9f-13f: 0-6 14f+: 0-0
Track : LH: 0-3 RH: 0-5 Tight: 0-3 Gall: 0-2
Aids: Bl: 0-0 Vi: 0-0 Tstrap: 0-0 Ckp: 0-0
Best Rating: **79** 10/09 Epsm 1m2f18y gd-fm

Fair; effective over 1m-1m2f; acts on fast ground and on Polytrack.

Meg Jicaro

75(89) (41)62
3-y-o b f Reel Buddy (USA)-Anita In Wales (IRE) (Anita's Prince)
Mrs L Williamson G D Kendrick

Placings:326500505-**0036000** (1848)
2009: 5^{0}SD, 7^{0}SD, 6^{3}SD, 6^{6}SD, 5^{0}GF, 6^{0}SD, 9^{0}GF,

	Starts	1st	2nd	3rd	Win & Pl
Career Total (Turf)	10	0	1	1	1566
Career Total (AW)	6	0	0	1	302

Going (Turf): **Sf: 0-4 GS: 0-2 Gd: 0-2 GF: 0-2 Fm: 0-0**
Distance: 5f/6f: 0-12 7f-8f: 0-3 9f-13f: 0-1 14f+: 0-0
Track : LH: 0-8 RH: 0-2 Tight: 0-5 Gall: 0-0
Aids: Bl: 0-0 Vi: 0-0 Tstrap: 0-1 Ckp: 0-1
Best Rating: **62** 4/08 Ripn 5f good

Fair; hung left fourth start when shaping as though she is ready for a step up to 6f; acts on good and soft ground.

Mega Dame (IRE)

(69) (12)
5-y-o b m Iron Mask (USA)-Easter Girl (Efisio)
D Haydn Jones R T Drage

Placings:062P00/00 (2859)
2009: 8^{0}SD, 10^{0}G,

	Starts	1st	2nd	3rd	Win & Pl
Career Total (Turf)	2	0	0	0	
Career Total (AW)	6	0	1	0	705

Going (Turf): **Sf: 0-0 GS: 0-0 Gd: 0-1 GF: 0-1 Fm: 0-0**
Distance: 5f/6f: 0-0 7f-8f: 0-0 9f-13f: 0-8 14f+: 0-0
Track : LH: 0-8 RH: 0-0 Tight: 0-6 Gall: 0-1
Aids: Bl: 0-1 Vi: 0-0 Tstrap: 0-0 Ckp: 0-0
Best Rating: **62** 7/07 Wolv 1m141y stand

Mega Steps (IRE)

(94) (36)43
5-y-o b g Groom Dancer (USA)-Marmaga (IRE) (Shernazar)
Jennie Candlish P and Mrs G A Clarke

Placings:00000/00-**00** (0566)
2009: 13^{0}SD, 12^{0}SD,

	Starts	1st	2nd	3rd	Win & Pl
Career Total (Turf)	7	0	0	0	
Career Total (AW)	2	0	0	0	

Going (Turf): **Sf: 0-1 GS: 0-2 Gd: 0-4 GF: 0-0 Fm: 0-0**
Distance: 5f/6f: 0-0 7f-8f: 0-2 9f-13f: 0-4 14f+: 0-3

Track : LH: 0-5 RH: 0-2 Tight: 0-4 Gall: 0-0
Aids: Bl: 0-0 Vi: 0-0 Tstrap: 0-2 Ckp: 0-2
Best Rating: 65 4/07 Gowr 1m good

Mega Watt (IRE)

102(67) 81

4-y-o b g Acclamation-Kilshanny (Groom Dancer (USA))
W Jarvis The Mega Watt Partnership

Placings:03/21544655-3305 **(4207)**
2009: 10³GF, 10³GF, 12⁰SD, 10⁵GF,

	Starts	1st	2nd	3rd	Win & Pl
Career Total (Turf)	13	1	1	3	8986
Career Total (AW)	1	0	0	0	

78 5/08 Chep 1m14y (0-80)H GD £4533
Total win prize-money £4533

Going (Turf): Sf: 0-1 GS: 0-3 **Gd: 1-4** GF: 0-5 Fm: 0-0
Distance: 5f/6f: 0-1 7f-8f: 0-2 **9f-13f: 1-11** 14f+: 0-0
Track : LH: 0-3 RH: 0-6 Tight: 0-4 Gall: 0-1
Aids: Bl: 0-2 Vi: 0-0 Tstrap: 0-1 Ckp: 0-1
Best Rating: 81 7/08 Wind 1m3f135y good

Fair; effective over 1m; acts on good ground.

Megalala (IRE)

101(101) (64)68

8-y-o b g Petardia-Avionne (Derrylin)
J J Bridger Tommy Ware

Placings:0/0040006400041/00004020/112625352633010 0-013100150606 **(7225)**
2009: 11⁰G, 10¹SD, 10³GS, 11¹GS, 9⁰GF, 10⁰GF, 9¹GF, 11⁵G, 12⁰SD, 7⁶G, 12⁰S, 10⁶SD,

	Starts	1st	2nd	3rd	Win & Pl
Career Total (Turf)	29	4	2	3	14662
Career Total (AW)	21	3	2	1	6304

68 7/09 Brig 1m1f209y (0-60)H G-F £2590
64 5/09 Brig 1m3f196y (0-75)H G-S £3406
64 5/09 Kemp 1m2f (0-65)H STD £2047
62 8/08 Newb 1m3f5y (0-70)H G-S £2590
56 1/08 Kemp 1m2f (0-45) STD £1365
53 1/08 Kemp 1m2f (0-45) STD £1365
59 9/06 Brig 6f209y G-S £2590
Total win prize-money £15954

Going (Turf): Sf: 0-3 **GS: 3-5** Gd: 0-10 GF: 1-8 Fm: 0-3
Distance: 5f/6f: 0-1 7f-8f: 1-14 **9f-13f: 6-35** 14f+: 0-0
Track : **LH: 4-24** RH: 3-23 Tight: 0-14 **Gall: 1-5**
Aids: Bl: 0-0 Vi: 0-0 Tstrap: 0-1 Ckp: 0-1
Best Rating: 68 7/09 Brig 1m1f209y gd-fm

Modest; effective at up to 1m4f; acts on easy ground and Polytrack.

Megalo Maniac

(100) (63)62

6-y-o b g Efisio-Sharanella (Shareef Dancer (USA))
R A Fahey A Long

Placings:00000224/1130404150/00552011250-0035400 **(7834)**
2009: 5⁰SD, 5⁰SD, 6³SD, 5⁵SD, 6⁴SD, 7⁰SF, 6⁰SD,

	Starts	1st	2nd	3rd	Win & Pl
Career Total (Turf)	17	0	3	0	2523
Career Total (AW)	21	5	1	2	15566

58 11/08 Sthl 7f (0-50)H STD £3070
63 10/08 Sthl 6f (0-50)H STD £2388
72 9/07 Wolv 7f32y STD £3071
73 5/07 Sthl 7f (0-50)H STD £3071
61 4/07 Sthl 6f (0-50)H STD £2730
Total win prize-money £14331

Going (Turf): **Sf: 0-4 GS: 0-2 Gd: 0-4 GF: 0-5 Fm: 0-2**
Distance: 5f/6f: 2-15 **7f-8f: 3-20** 9f-13f: 0-3 14f+: 0-0
Track : **LH: 5-24** RH: 0-10 **Tight: 1-15** Gall: 0-0
Aids: Bl: 0-0 Vi: 0-4 Tstrap: 2-8 Ckp: 2-8
Best Rating: 73 5/07 Sthl 7f stand

Moderate; suited by 7f; acts on fast ground; also goes on Polytrack and Fibresand; has worn cheekpieces.

Megasecret

99(89) (64)70

3-y-o b c Falbrav (IRE)-Silver Quest (Rainbow Quest (USA))
R Hannon Carmel Stud

Placings:02420-44006 **(4947)**
2009: 5⁴GF, 7⁴GF, 7⁰GF, 7⁰G, 6⁶GF,

	Starts	1st	2nd	3rd	Win & Pl
Career Total (Turf)	8	0	1	0	1998
Career Total (AW)	2	0	1	0	1060

Going (Turf): **Sf: 0-1 GS: 0-1 Gd: 0-1 GF: 0-5 Fm: 0-0**
Distance: 5f/6f: 0-6 7f-8f: 0-4 9f-13f: 0-0 14f+: 0-0
Track : LH: 0-3 RH: 0-0 Tight: 0-1 Gall: 0-3
Aids: Bl: 0-0 Vi: 0-0 Tstrap: 0-0 Ckp: 0-0
Best Rating: 70 5/09 Ling 7f gd-fm

Fair; stays 6f and acts on most ground.

Megavista (USA)

72(87) (30)53

3-y-o gr/ro f Medaglia D'Oro (USA)-Bodhavista (USA) (Pass The Tab (USA))
Paul Mason Seven Plus Seven

Placings:00 **(4205)**
2009: 10⁰GF, 12⁰SD,

	Starts	1st	2nd	3rd	Win & Pl
Career Total (Turf)	1	0	0	0	
Career Total (AW)	1	0	0	0	

Going (Turf): **Sf: 0-0 GS: 0-0 Gd: 0-0 GF: 0-1 Fm: 0-0**
Distance: 5f/6f: 0-0 7f-8f: 0-0 9f-13f: 0-2 14f+: 0-0
Track : LH: 0-2 RH: 0-0 Tight: 0-1 Gall: 0-1
Aids: Bl: 0-0 Vi: 0-0 Tstrap: 0-0 Ckp: 0-0
Best Rating: 53 6/09 Newb 1m2f6y gd-fm

Meglio Ancora

95 81

2-y-o ch g Best Of The Bests (IRE)-May Fox (Zilzal (USA))
J G Portman Anthony Boswood

Placings:100 **(4565)**
2009: 6¹G, 7⁰GF, 7⁰G,

	Starts	1st	2nd	3rd	Win & Pl
Career Total (Turf)	3	1	0	0	4857

81 5/09 Newb 6f8y GD £4857
Total win prize-money £4857

Going (Turf): Sf: 0-0 GS: 0-0 **Gd: 1-2** GF: 0-1 Fm: 0-0
Distance: 5f/6f: 0-0 **7f-8f: 1-3** 9f-13f: 0-0 14f+: 0-0
Track : LH: 0-0 RH: 0-0 Tight: 0-0 Gall: 0-0
Aids: Bl: 0-0 Vi: 0-0 Tstrap: 0-0 Ckp: 0-0
Best Rating: 81 5/09 Newb 6f8y good

Cheap buy; made winning debut over 6f; acts on good.

Mehendi (IRE)

87(98) (64)73

3-y-o b g Indian Danehill (IRE)-Wedding Cake (IRE) (Groom Dancer (USA))
B Ellison (B J Meehan 4/7) Koo's Racing Club

Placings:42-000035 **(6769)**
2009: 8⁰G, 9⁰GF, 10⁰G, 8⁰S, 12³SD, 12⁵GS,

	Starts	1st	2nd	3rd	Win & Pl
Career Total (Turf)	7	0	1	0	1122
Career Total (AW)	1	0	0	1	353

Going (Turf): **Sf: 0-1 GS: 0-3 Gd: 0-2 GF: 0-1 Fm: 0-0**
Distance: 5f/6f: 0-0 7f-8f: 0-2 9f-13f: 0-6 14f+: 0-0
Track : LH: 0-6 RH: 0-1 Tight: 0-4 Gall: 0-1
Aids: Bl: 0-1 Vi: 0-0 Tstrap: 0-0 Ckp: 0-0
Best Rating: 73 10/08 Newb 1m gd-sft

Modest; stays 1m4f; acts on Polytrack and easy ground on turf.

Meikle Barfil

94(104) (54)51

7-y-o b g Compton Place-Oare Sparrow (Night Shift (USA))
J M Bradley J M Bradley

Placings:0523450/0000051000/000050200/5641300006 056600606 **(7689)**
2009: 5⁵SD, 5⁶SD, 5⁴SD, 5¹SD, 5³SD, 5⁰SD, 5⁰SD, 5⁰GF, 5⁶G, 5⁰GF, 5⁵G, 5⁶F, 5⁶G, 5⁰G, 5⁰GS, 5⁶G, 5⁰SD, 5⁶SD,

	Starts	1st	2nd	3rd	Win & Pl
Career Total (Turf)	29	1	0	1	5201
Career Total (AW)	17	1	2	1	3971

53 3/09 Kemp 5f (0-45) STD £1706
67 8/06 Sals 5f (0-70)H G-F £3886
Total win prize-money £5592

Going (Turf): Sf: 0-1 GS: 0-3 Gd: 0-11 **GF: 1-12** Fm: 0-2
Distance: **5f/6f: 2-45** 7f-8f: 0-1 9f-13f: 0-0 14f+: 0-0
Track : LH: 0-18 **RH: 1-5** Tight: 0-11 Gall: 0-5
Aids: Bl: 0-1 Vi: 0-0 Tstrap: 2-33 Ckp: 2-33
Best Rating: 79 10/05 York 5f good

Moderate; effective over 5f; acts on easy ground; also goes on Polytrack.

Meirig's Dream (IRE)

86(94) (57)54

3-y-o b g Golan (IRE)-Women In Love (IRE) (Danehill (USA))
Miss N A Lloyd-Beavis Miss V Dunn H Davies

Placings:500-0032 **(7873)**
2009: 11⁰GS, 10⁰SD, 12³SD, 16²SD,

	Starts	1st	2nd	3rd	Win & Pl
Career Total (Turf)	4	0	0	0	0
Career Total (AW)	3	0	1	1	1023

Going (Turf): **Sf: 0-0 GS: 0-2 Gd: 0-0 GF: 0-2 Fm: 0-0**
Distance: 5f/6f: 0-1 7f-8f: 0-2 9f-13f: 0-3 14f+: 0-1
Track : LH: 0-1 RH: 0-2 Tight: 0-2 Gall: 0-1
Aids: Bl: 0-0 Vi: 0-0 Tstrap: 0-0 Ckp: 0-0
Best Rating: 57 12/09 Kemp 1m4f stand

Modest; stays 2m; acts on Polytrack.

Mejala (IRE)

101 74

3-y-o b f Red Ransom (USA)-Wissal (USA) (Woodman (USA))

J L Dunlop Hamdan Al Maktoum

Placings:50-061052 (5128)
2009: 8^{0}GF, 9^{6}GF, 9^{1}G, 9^{0}G, 10^{5}G, 10^{2}GF,

	Starts	1st	2nd	3rd	Win & Pl
Career Total (Turf)	8	1	1	0	5331

74 6/09 Gdwd 1m1f192y (0-70)H GD £3885
Total win prize-money £3886

Going (Turf): Sf: 0-0 GS: 0-0 **Gd: 1-5** GF: 0-3 Fm: 0-0
Distance: 5f/6f: 0-0 7f-8f: 0-3 **9f-13f: 1-5** 14f+: 0-0
Track : LH: 0-2 **RH: 1-4 Tight: 1-2** Gall: 0-1
Aids: Bl: 0-1 Vi: 0-0 Tstrap: 0-0 Ckp: 0-0
Best Rating: **74** 6/09 Gdwd 1m1f192y good

Fair sort; stays a 1m2f; acts on good.

Mejd (IRE)

75 **22**
2-y-o b c Desert Style (IRE)-Rainstone (Rainbow Quest (USA))
M R Channon M Al-Qatami & K M Al-Mudhaf

Placings:0 (6810)
2009: 8^{0}G,

	Starts	1st	2nd	3rd	Win & Pl
Career Total (Turf)	1	0	0	0	

Going (Turf): **Sf: 0-0 GS: 0-0 Gd: 0-1 GF: 0-0 Fm: 0-0**
Distance: 5f/6f: 0-0 7f-8f: 0-1 9f-13f: 0-0 14f+: 0-0
Track : LH: 0-0 RH: 0-0 Tight: 0-0 Gall: 0-0
Aids: Bl: 0-0 Vi: 0-0 Tstrap: 0-0 Ckp: 0-0
Best Rating: **22** 10/09 NmkR 1m good

Mekong Miss

(101) (61)**58**
3-y-o ch f Mark Of Esteem (IRE)-Missouri (Charnwood Forest (IRE))
J Jay Mrs J Martin & K Snell

Placings:0300-**20420** (7840)
2009: 12^{2}SD, 12^{0}SD, 11^{4}SD, 12^{2}SD, 12^{0}SS,

	Starts	1st	2nd	3rd	Win & Pl
Career Total (Turf)	4	0	0	1	385
Career Total (AW)	5	0	2	0	1209

Going (Turf): **Sf: 0-2 GS: 0-1 Gd: 0-0 GF: 0-1 Fm: 0-0**
Distance: 5f/6f: 0-0 7f-8f: 0-3 9f-13f: 0-6 14f+: 0-0
Track : LH: 0-5 RH: 0-3 Tight: 0-0 Gall: 0-0
Aids: Bl: 0-0 Vi: 0-0 Tstrap: 0-0 Ckp: 0-0
Best Rating: **61** 3/09 Kemp 1m4f stand

Modest; stays 1m4f; acts on soft ground and Polytrack.

Melange (USA)

95(96) (69)**62**
3-y-o b g Alphabet Soup (USA)-Garendare (Vacarme (USA))
G A Charlton (P F I Cole 8/6) Northumbria Leisure Ltd/ G A Charlton

Placings:00-010500 (2772)
2009: 7^{0}SD, 11^{1}SD, 12^{0}GF, 12^{5}GF, 14^{0}GF, 11^{0}G,

	Starts	1st	2nd	3rd	Win & Pl
Career Total (Turf)	6	0	0	0	0
Career Total (AW)	2	1	0	0	2047

69 4/09 Sthl 1m3f STD £2047
Total win prize-money £2047

Going (Turf): **Sf: 0-0 GS: 0-1 Gd: 0-1 GF: 0-4 Fm: 0-0**
Distance: 5f/6f: 0-1 7f-8f: 0-2 **9f-13f: 1-4** 14f+: 0-1
Track : **LH: 1-4** RH: 0-2 Tight: 0-2 Gall: 0-0
Aids: Bl: 0-0 Vi: 0-0 Tstrap: 0-0 Ckp: 0-0
Best Rating: **69** 4/09 Sthl 1m3f stand

Melkatant

100 **53**
3-y-o b f Rock City-Change Of Image (Spectrum (IRE))
N Bycroft Sybil's Legacy

Placings:000-0306343 (6766)
2009: 7^{0}GF, 8^{3}GF, 9^{0}GF, 9^{6}G, 10^{3}GF, 10^{4}GF, 12^{3}GS,

	Starts	1st	2nd	3rd	Win & Pl
Career Total (Turf)	10	0	0	3	990

Going (Turf): **Sf: 0-1 GS: 0-1 Gd: 0-2 GF: 0-6 Fm: 0-0**
Distance: 5f/6f: 0-2 7f-8f: 0-3 9f-13f: 0-5 14f+: 0-0
Track : LH: 0-5 RH: 0-3 Tight: 0-5 Gall: 0-1
Aids: Bl: 0-0 Vi: 0-0 Tstrap: 0-0 Ckp: 0-0
Best Rating: **53** 10/09 Newc 1m4f93y gd-sft

Moderate; stays 1m4f; acts on most ground.

Mellifera

91(93) (68)**73**
2-y-o b f Leporello (IRE)-Christina's Dream (Spectrum (IRE))
W R Swinburn Pendley Farm

Placings:44560 (7453)
2009: 6^{4}SD, 6^{4}SD, 7^{5}GF, 7^{6}SD, 6^{0}SD,

	Starts	1st	2nd	3rd	Win & Pl
Career Total (Turf)	1	0	0	0	0
Career Total (AW)	4	0	0	0	553

Going (Turf): **Sf: 0-0 GS: 0-0 Gd: 0-0 GF: 0-1 Fm: 0-0**
Distance: 5f/6f: 0-3 7f-8f: 0-2 9f-13f: 0-0 14f+: 0-0
Track : LH: 0-2 RH: 0-2 Tight: 0-2 Gall: 0-0
Aids: Bl: 0-0 Vi: 0-0 Tstrap: 0-0 Ckp: 0-0
Best Rating: **73** 8/09 Folk 7f gd-fm

Mellifluous (IRE)

95(76) (33)**43**
4-y-o b f Noverre (USA)-Danestar (Danehill (USA))
W S Kittow (Mrs P N Dutfield 6/3) Mrs P De W Johnson

Placings:00/000-6 (5367)
2009: 9^{6}F,

	Starts	1st	2nd	3rd	Win & Pl
Career Total (Turf)	4	0	0	0	0
Career Total (AW)	2	0	0	0	

Going (Turf): **Sf: 0-0 GS: 0-0 Gd: 0-1 GF: 0-2 Fm: 0-1**
Distance: 5f/6f: 0-0 7f-8f: 0-3 9f-13f: 0-3 14f+: 0-0
Track : LH: 0-3 RH: 0-2 Tight: 0-2 Gall: 0-0
Aids: Bl: 0-0 Vi: 0-0 Tstrap: 0-0 Ckp: 0-0
Best Rating: **43** 8/09 Ling 1m1f firm

Mellow Mixture

97(100) (78)**72**
3-y-o b c Marju (IRE)-Night Owl (Night Shift (USA))
S Kirk (R Hannon 12/6) Ben CM Wong

Placings:0625-22063060051 (6705)
2009: 10^{2}SD, 10^{2}SD, 12^{0}SD, 10^{6}GS, 9^{3}GF, 10^{0}G, 7^{6}G, 11^{0}SD, 10^{0}GF, 12^{5}SD, 10^{1}SS,

	Starts	1st	2nd	3rd	Win & Pl
Career Total (Turf)	6	0	0	1	454
Career Total (AW)	9	1	3	0	4260

65 10/09 Ling 1m2f (0-60)H SS £1942
Total win prize-money £1943

Going (Turf): **Sf: 0-0 GS: 0-2 Gd: 0-2 GF: 0-2 Fm: 0-0**
Distance: 5f/6f: 0-0 7f-8f: 0-4 **9f-13f: 1-11** 14f+: 0-0
Track : **LH: 1-7** RH: 0-6 **Tight: 1-9** Gall: 0-0
Aids: Bl: 0-0 Vi: 0-0 Tstrap: 0-0 Ckp: 0-0
Best Rating: **78** 1/09 Ling 1m2f stand

Modest; stays 1m2f; acts on Polytrack.

Melody In The Mist (FR)

97 **72**
2-y-o b f Intikhab (USA)-She's All Class (USA) (Rahy (USA))
T D Barron P D Savill

Placings:62311 (5292)
2009: 5^{6}GF, 5^{2}GF, 5^{3}GF, 5^{1}GF, 5^{1}S,

	Starts	1st	2nd	3rd	Win & Pl
Career Total (Turf)	5	2	1	1	5199

61 8/09 Muss 5f SFT £1942
69 8/09 Ayr 5f G-F £2047
Total win prize-money £3990

Going (Turf): **Sf: 1-1** GS: 0-0 Gd: 0-0 **GF: 1-4** Fm: 0-0
Distance: **5f/6f: 2-5** 7f-8f: 0-0 9f-13f: 0-0 14f+: 0-0
Track : LH: 0-0 RH: 0-0 Tight: 0-0 Gall: 0-0
Aids: Bl: 0-0 Vi: 0-0 Tstrap: 0-0 Ckp: 0-0
Best Rating: **72** 6/09 Haml 5f4y gd-fm

Fair; suited by 5f; acts on most ground.

Melt (IRE)

100(103) (65)**61**
4-y-o b f Intikhab (USA)-Kindle (Selkirk (USA))
R Hannon J T Brown

Placings:5620/65200253-05212346 (1710)
2009: 8^{0}SD, 7^{5}SD, 7^{2}SD, 8^{1}SD, 7^{2}SD, 7^{3}SD, 8^{4}GF, 6^{6}GF,

	Starts	1st	2nd	3rd	Win & Pl
Career Total (Turf)	9	0	1	0	1002
Career Total (AW)	11	1	4	2	5825

63 3/09 Ling 1m (0-70)H STD £2752
Total win prize-money £2752

Going (Turf): **Sf: 0-2 GS: 0-2 Gd: 0-1 GF: 0-4 Fm: 0-0**
Distance: 5f/6f: 0-4 **7f-8f: 1-15** 9f-13f: 0-1 14f+: 0-0
Track : **LH: 1-10** RH: 0-4 **Tight: 1-8** Gall: 0-1
Aids: **Bl: 1-6** Vi: 0-0 Tstrap: 0-1 Ckp: 0-1
Best Rating: **65** 4/09 Ling 7f stand

Moderate; stays 1m; acts on soft ground; goes on Polytrack; has worn blinkers.

Melting Bob (USA)

(87) (51)
3-y-o gr/ro f Johannesburg (USA)-Dancingonice (USA) (Robyn Dancer (USA))
Dr J D Scargill Strawberry Fields Stud

Placings:0 (7826)
2009: 8^{0}SD,

	Starts	1st	2nd	3rd	Win & Pl
Career Total (Turf)	0	0	0	0	
Career Total (AW)	1	0	0	0	

Going (Turf): **Sf: 0-0 GS: 0-0 Gd: 0-0 GF: 0-0 Fm: 0-0**
Distance: 5f/6f: 0-0 7f-8f: 0-1 9f-13f: 0-0 14f+: 0-0
Track : LH: 0-0 RH: 0-1 Tight: 0-0 Gall: 0-0
Aids: Bl: 0-0 Vi: 0-0 Tstrap: 0-0 Ckp: 0-0
Best Rating: 51 12/09 Kemp 1m stand

Melundy

95 **69**

2-y-o b f Best Of The Bests (IRE)-Nova Zembla (Young Ern)
Mrs L Stubbs Ian Murray Tough

Placings:25 (5949)
2009: 6^2GF, 6^5GF,

	Starts	1st	2nd	3rd	Win & Pl
Career Total (Turf)	2	0	1	0	0

Going (Turf): **Sf: 0-0 GS: 0-0 Gd: 0-0 GF: 0-2 Fm: 0-0**
Distance: 5f/6f: 0-2 7f-8f: 0-0 9f-13f: 0-0 14f+: 0-0
Track : LH: 0-0 RH: 0-0 Tight: 0-0 Gall: 0-0
Aids: Bl: 0-0 Vi: 0-0 Tstrap: 0-0 Ckp: 0-0
Best Rating: 69 8/09 Rdcr 6f gd-fm

Modest; stays 6f; acts on fast ground.

Meml

92(92) (47)**47**

3-y-o b f Mark Of Esteem (IRE)-Matisse (Shareef Dancer (USA))
J D Bethell Clarendon Thoroughbred Racing

Placings:60640 (7318)
2009: 8^6G, 8^0G, 9^6GF, 9^4SD, 12^0SD,

	Starts	1st	2nd	3rd	Win & Pl
Career Total (Turf)	3	0	0	0	0
Career Total (AW)	2	0	0	0	0

Going (Turf): **Sf: 0-0 GS: 0-0 Gd: 0-2 GF: 0-1 Fm: 0-0**
Distance: 5f/6f: 0-0 7f-8f: 0-2 9f-13f: 0-3 14f+: 0-0
Track : LH: 0-3 RH: 0-2 Tight: 0-5 Gall: 0-0
Aids: Bl: 0-0 Vi: 0-0 Tstrap: 0-0 Ckp: 0-0
Best Rating: 47 10/09 Wolv 1m1f103y stand

Memorandum

100(108) (75)**65**

2-y-o b f Oasis Dream-Marani (Ashkalani (IRE))
R Charlton K Abdulla

Placings:53153 (7878)
2009: 5^5F, 5^3G, $5^1$3D, $5^6$3D, 6^3SD,

	Starts	1st	2nd	3rd	Win & Pl
Career Total (Turf)	2	0	0	1	530
Career Total (AW)	3	1	0	1	4140

75 11/09 Ling 5f STD £3561
Total win prize-money £3562

Going (Turf): **Sf: 0-0 GS: 0-0 Gd: 0-1 GF: 0-0 Fm: 0-1**
Distance: **5f/6f: 1-5** 7f-8f: 0-0 9f-13f: 0-0 14f+: 0-0
Track : **LH: 1-5** RH: 0-0 **Tight: 1-3** Gall: 0-2
Aids: Bl: 0-0 Vi: 0-0 Tstrap: 0-0 Ckp: 0-0
Best Rating: 75 11/09 Ling 5f stand

Fair; effective over 5f; acts on good ground and on Polytrack.

Memory And Magic (USA)

95(92) (66)**63**

2-y-o b f Sahm (USA)-Aljawza (USA) (Riverman (USA))
C G Cox Miss Bridgette Egan

Placings:20440 (7363)
2009: 5^2GF, 5^0GF, 6^4SD, 7^4GF, 7^0SD,

	Starts	1st	2nd	3rd	Win & Pl
Career Total (Turf)	3	0	1	0	1252
Career Total (AW)	2	0	0	0	265

Going (Turf): **Sf: 0-0 GS: 0-0 Gd: 0-0 GF: 0-3 Fm: 0-0**
Distance: 5f/6f: 0-3 7f-8f: 0-2 9f-13f: 0-0 14f+: 0-0
Track : LH: 0-2 RH: 0-1 Tight: 0-1 Gall: 0-0
Aids: Bl: 0-0 Vi: 0-0 Tstrap: 0-0 Ckp: 0-0
Best Rating: 66 9/09 Kemp 6f stand

Memphis Man

107(104) (81)**86**

6-y-o b g Bertolini (USA)-Something Blue (Petong)
P D Evans M D Jones

Placings:160200/5536000152350060/0330065001411301024/32362503342044553035651522033150065-55066541253535230000 (7083)
2009: 6^5SD, 5^5SD, 5^0G, 6^6GS, 7^6GS, 6^5HY, 6^4GF, 6^1GF, 5^2G, 6^5GF, 5^3G, 6^5G, 6^3G, 6^5GF, 6^2G, 7^3S, 6^0GF, 6^0GF, 5^0G, 7^0S,

	Starts	1st	2nd	3rd	Win & Pl
Career Total (Turf)	66	8	7	12	45567
Career Total (AW)	30	1	3	4	7742

79	6/09	Wind	6f	(0-80)H	G-F	£4857
86	9/08	Wind	6f	(0-75)H	G-F	£2729
81	8/08	Hayd	6f	(0-70)H	HVY	£4857
76	11/07	Wolv	5f216y	(0-58)H	STD	£2047
75	10/07	Ayr	6f	(0-65)H	SFT	£2266
70	10/07	Yarm	6f3y	(0-60)H	SFT	£2914
62	10/07	Brig	5f213y	(0-60)H	G-S	£2590
69	8/06	Sand	5f6y	(0-85)H	GD	£5505
69	4/05	Muss	5f		GD	£3396

Total win prize-money £31166

Going (Turf): **Sf: 3-12**GS: 1-12Gd: 2-20GF: 2-22 Fm: 0-0
Distance: **5f/6f: 8-65** 7f-8f: 1-28 9f-13f: 0-3 14f+: 0-0
Track : **LH: 2-38** RH: 0-4 Tight: 1-20 **Gall: 2-16**
Aids: Bl: 0-0 Vi: 0-0 Tstrap: 0-3 Ckp: 0-3
Best Rating: 86 9/08 Wind 6f gd-fm

Fair; effective over 5f-7f; acts on fast and soft ground; also goes on Polytrack.

Memphis Marie

88 (60)**39**

5-y-o b m Desert Sun-Spirito Libro (USA) (Lear Fan (USA))
P J McBride C R Souter

Placings:0/6400160/060 (5998)
2009: 8^0GS, 8^6GF, 7^0GF,

	Starts	1st	2nd	3rd	Win & Pl
Career Total (Turf)	7	0	0	0	0
Career Total (AW)	4	1	0	0	3886

60 8/07 Wolv 7f32y STD £3886
Total win prize-money £3886

Going (Turf): **Sf: 0-1 GS: 0-1 Gd: 0-0 GF: 0-5 Fm: 0-0**
Distance: 5f/6f: 0-1 **7f-8f: 1-4** 9f-13f: 0-6 14f+: 0-0
Track : **LH: 1-7** RH: 0-0 **Tight: 1-7** Gall: 0-0
Aids: Bl: 0-0 Vi: 0-0 Tstrap: 0-0 Ckp: 0-0
Best Rating: 60 8/07 Wolv 7f32y stand

Modest; effective over 7f; acts on Polytrack.

Mena Rl

(54)

2-y-o b f Sulamani (IRE)-Natalie (Dushyantor (USA))
Karen George Adam Richard Wilson

Placings:0 (7451)
2009: 8^0SD,

	Starts	1st	2nd	3rd	Win & Pl
Career Total (Turf)	0	0	0	0	
Career Total (AW)	1	0	0	0	

Going (Turf): **Sf: 0-0 GS: 0-0 Gd: 0-0 GF: 0-0 Fm: 0-0**
Distance: 5f/6f: 0-0 7f-8f: 0-1 9f-13f: 0-0 14f+: 0-0
Track : LH: 0-0 RH: 0-1 Tight: 0-0 Gall: 0-0
Aids: Bl: 0-0 Vi: 0-0 Tstrap: 0-0 Ckp: 0-0

Mendip (USA)

(94) (84)

2-y-o b/br c Harlan's Holiday (USA)-Well Spring (USA) (Coronado's Quest (USA))
Saeed Bin Suroor Godolphin

Placings:1 (5637)
2009: 8^1SD,

	Starts	1st	2nd	3rd	Win & Pl
Career Total (Turf)	0	0	0	0	
Career Total (AW)	1	1	0	0	5181

84 9/09 Kemp 1m STD £5180
Total win prize-money £5181

Going (Turf): **Sf: 0-0 GS: 0-0 Gd: 0-0 GF: 0-0 Fm: 0-0**
Distance: 5f/6f: 0-0 **7f-8f: 1-1** 9f-13f: 0-0 14f+: 0-0
Track : LH: 0-0 **RH: 1-1** Tight: 0-0 Gall: 0-0
Aids: Bl: 0-0 Vi: 0-0 Tstrap: 0-0 Ckp: 0-0
Best Rating: 84 9/09 Kemp 1m stand

Useful; stays 1m; acts on Polytrack; sure to improve and win more races.

Menediva

84 **42**

2-y-o b f Danbird (AUS)-Princess Ismene (Sri Pekan (USA))
L A Mullaney K Humphries & Sons Roofing Contractors

Placings:00440 (4800)
2009: 5^0F, 6^0GF, 5^4G, 5^4G, 6^0GF,

	Starts	1st	2nd	3rd	Win & Pl
Career Total (Turf)	5	0	0	0	0

Going (Turf): **Sf: 0-0 GS: 0-0 Gd: 0-2 GF: 0-2 Fm: 0-1**
Distance: 5f/6f: 0-5 7f-8f: 0-0 9f-13f: 0-0 14f+: 0-0
Track : LH: 0-1 RH: 0-0 Tight: 0-0 Gall: 0-0
Aids: Bl: 0-0 Vi: 0-0 Tstrap: 0-0 Ckp: 0-0
Best Rating: 42 6/09 Bevl 5f firm

Menelaus

70(89) (39)**50**

8-y-o b g Machiavellian (USA)-Mezzogiorno (Unfuwain (USA))
K A Morgan Rex Norton

Placings:6/30/0/00/40 (6859)
2009: 16^4S, 16^0SD,

	Starts	1st	2nd	3rd	Win & Pl
Career Total (Turf)	6	0	0	1	708
Career Total (AW)	2	0	0	0	

Going (Turf): Sf: 0-1 GS: 0-0 Gd: 0-4 GF: 0-1 Fm: 0-0
Distance: 5f/6f: 0-0 7f-8f: 0-0 9f-13f: 0-3 14f+: 0-5
Track : LH: 0-5 RH: 0-3 Tight: 0-2 Gall: 0-0
Aids: Bl: 0-0 Vi: 0-0 Tstrap: 0-6 Ckp: 0-6
Best Rating: 56 8/07 Chep 2m2f good

Menhir Bay

(85) (52)
3-y-o b g Sure Blade (USA)-Turkish Delight (Prince Sabo)
D K Ivory John Khan

Placings:66-6 (0188)
2009: 5^6SD,

	Starts	1st	2nd	3rd	Win & Pl
Career Total (Turf)	0	0	0	0	
Career Total (AW)	3	0	0	0	0

Going (Turf): Sf: 0-0 GS: 0-0 Gd: 0-0 GF: 0-0 Fm: 0-0
Distance: 5f/6f: 0-3 7f-8f: 0-0 9f-13f: 0-0 14f+: 0-0
Track : LH: 0-3 RH: 0-0 Tight: 0-3 Gall: 0-0
Aids: Bl: 0-0 Vi: 0-0 Tstrap: 0-0 Ckp: 0-0
Best Rating: 52 12/08 Ling 5f stand

Menkaura

(74) (37)79
6-y-o b g Pivotal-Nekhbet (Artaius (USA))
John R Upson Mrs Diane Upson

Placings:56/0300/00/0-0 (0147)
2009: 12^0SD,

	Starts	1st	2nd	3rd	Win & Pl
Career Total (Turf)	6	0	0	1	2361
Career Total (AW)	4	0	0	0	

Going (Turf): Sf: 0-0 GS: 0-0 Gd: 0-1 GF: 0-3 Fm: 0-0
Distance: 5f/6f: 0-1 7f-8f: 0-3 9f-13f: 0-6 14f+: 0-0
Track : LH: 0-4 RH: 0-3 Tight: 0-3 Gall: 0-0
Aids: Bl: 0-2 Vi: 0-1 Tstrap: 0-0 Ckp: 0-0
Best Rating: 79 6/06 Rosc 7f gd-fm

Meohmy

(96) (49)48
6-y-o b m Marju (IRE)-Meshhed (USA) (Gulch (USA))
M R Channon M Channon

Placings:0/0060000/40504052000-03 (0484)
2009: 12^0SD, 10^3SD,

	Starts	1st	2nd	3rd	Win & Pl
Career Total (Turf)	15	0	1	0	605
Career Total (AW)	6	0	0	1	3231

Going (Turf): Sf: 0-0 GS: 0-1 Gd: 0-4 GF: 0-8 Fm: 0-2
Distance: 5f/6f: 0-1 7f-8f: 0-1 9f-13f: 0-18 14f+: 0-1
Track : LH: 0-14 RH: 0-5 Tight: 0-13 Gall: 0-4
Aids: Bl: 0-0 Vi: 0-2 Tstrap: 0-0 Ckp: 0-0
Best Rating: 55 5/06 Newb 1m2f6y good

Moderate mare; probably stays 1m4f but effective at shorter; acts on fast ground.

Mercers Row

95 69
2-y-o b g Bahamian Bounty-Invincible (Slip Anchor)
A Dickman Allan Dickman - Keith Fitzsimons

Placings:4203634 (6408)
2009: 5^4GF, 5^2GF, 5^0G, 5^3G, 5^6S, 5^3GF, 6^4GF,

	Starts	1st	2nd	3rd	Win & Pl
Career Total (Turf)	7	0	1	2	2672

Going (Turf): Sf: 0-1 GS: 0-0 Gd: 0-2 GF: 0-4 Fm: 0-0
Distance: 5f/6f: 0-7 7f-8f: 0-0 9f-13f: 0-0 14f+: 0-0
Track : LH: 0-0 RH: 0-1 Tight: 0-0 Gall: 0-1
Aids: Bl: 0-0 Vi: 0-0 Tstrap: 0-0 Ckp: 0-0
Best Rating: 69 9/09 Bevl 5f gd-fm

Modest; stays 6f; acts on fast ground.

Merchant Man

97(91) (46)60
3-y-o b g Mark Of Esteem (IRE)-Birsay (Bustino)
J D Bethell L B Holliday

Placings:450355 (6027)
2009: 9^4GS, 8^5F, 9^0G, 9^3G, 14^5GF, 13^5SD,

	Starts	1st	2nd	3rd	Win & Pl
Career Total (Turf)	5	0	0	1	746
Career Total (AW)	1	0	0	0	0

Going (Turf): Sf: 0-0 GS: 0-1 Gd: 0-2 GF: 0-1 Fm: 0-1
Distance: 5f/6f: 0-0 7f-8f: 0-0 9f-13f: 0-4 14f+: 0-2
Track : LH: 0-3 RH: 0-3 Tight: 0-3 Gall: 0-0
Aids: Bl: 0-2 Vi: 0-0 Tstrap: 0-1 Ckp: 0-1
Best Rating: 60 5/09 Ripn 1m1f gd-sft

Merchant Of Dubai

104(114) (103)102
4-y-o b g Dubai Destination (USA)-Chameleon (Green Desert (USA))
G A Swinbank Highland Racing 2

Placings:6214/32014115-312061 (7465)
2009: 10^3G, 14^1G, 13^2G, 12^0S, 12^6S, 12^1SD,

	Starts	1st	2nd	3rd	Win & Pl
Career Total (Turf)	16	4	3	2	34630
Career Total (AW)	2	2	0	0	17643

103	11/09	Wolv	1m4f50y	(0-100)H	STD	£12462
98	10/08	Muss	1m6f	(0-100)H	G-S	£15577
99	9/08	Sthl	1m4f	(0-85)H	STD	£5180
88	9/08	Muss	1m6f	(0-75)H	SFT	£3885
76	7/07	Ayr	6f		G-S	£3886

Total win prize-money £40993

Going (Turf): Sf: 1-6 GS: 2-2 Gd: 1-6 GF: 0-2 Fm: 0-0
Distance: 5f/6f: 1-2 7f-8f: 0-2 9f-13f: 2-7 14f+: 3-7
Track : LH: 2-7 RH: 3-7 Tight: 3-6 Gall: 1-4
Aids: Bl: 0-0 Vi: 0-0 Tstrap: 0-0 Ckp: 0-0
Best Rating: 103 11/09 Wolv 1m4f50y stand

Very useful; effective over 1m4f-1m6f plus; acts on good and soft ground; goes well on Fibresand and on Polytrack.

Merchant Of Medici

88(96) (73)68
2-y-o b g Medicean-Regal Rose (Danehill (USA))
W R Muir Jones, Haim, Kennedy

Placings:320430 (7359)
2009: 6^3G, 5^2GF, 6^0GS, 7^4SD, 8^3SD, 8^0SD,

	Starts	1st	2nd	3rd	Win & Pl
Career Total (Turf)	3	0	1	1	1493
Career Total (AW)	3	0	0	1	482

Going (Turf): Sf: 0-0 GS: 0-1 Gd: 0-1 GF: 0-1 Fm: 0-0
Distance: 5f/6f: 0-2 7f-8f: 0-2 9f-13f: 0-2 14f+: 0-0
Track : LH: 0-3 RH: 0-0 Tight: 0-3 Gall: 0-0
Aids: Bl: 0-2 Vi: 0-0 Tstrap: 0-0 Ckp: 0-0
Best Rating: 73 10/09 Wolv 1m141y stand

Modest; effective over 6f; acts on fast ground.

Mercoliano

(94) (68)
2-y-o b g Medicean-Mega (IRE) (Petardia)
M Botti Giuliano Manfredini

Placings:45 (7400)
2009: 8^4SD, 9^5SD,

	Starts	1st	2nd	3rd	Win & Pl
Career Total (Turf)	0	0	0	0	
Career Total (AW)	2	0	0	0	241

Going (Turf): Sf: 0-0 GS: 0-0 Gd: 0-0 GF: 0-0 Fm: 0-0
Distance: 5f/6f: 0-0 7f-8f: 0-0 9f-13f: 0-2 14f+: 0-0
Track : LH: 0-2 RH: 0-0 Tight: 0-2 Gall: 0-0
Aids: Bl: 0-0 Vi: 0-0 Tstrap: 0-0 Ckp: 0-0
Best Rating: 68 10/09 Wolv 1m141y stand

Modest; stays 1m1f; acts on Polytrack.

Merdaam

94 81
3-y-o ch g Dubai Destination (USA)-Faydah (USA) (Bahri (USA))
J L Dunlop Hamdan Al Maktoum

Placings:0-32360 (6595)
2009: 8^3S, 8^2GF, 9^3GF, 8^6G, 10^0GS,

	Starts	1st	2nd	3rd	Win & Pl
Career Total (Turf)	6	0	1	2	2745

Going (Turf): Sf: 0-1 GS: 0-1 Gd: 0-2 GF: 0-2 Fm: 0-0
Distance: 5f/6f: 0-0 7f-8f: 0-3 9f-13f: 0-3 14f+: 0-0
Track : LH: 0-2 RH: 0-1 Tight: 0-1 Gall: 0-0
Aids: Bl: 0-0 Vi: 0-0 Tstrap: 0-0 Ckp: 0-0
Best Rating: 81 5/09 NmkR 1m gd-fm

Useful; stays 1m; acts on most ground.

Merlin's Dancer

102(112) (91)95
9-y-o b g Magic Ring (IRE)-La Piaf (FR) (Fabulous Dancer (USA))
S Dow Miss Helen Chamberlain & Tom Parker

Placings:0323/4562011000400/051000410/155400/441040000/165000560300/30432000-43630040 (4232)
2009: 5^4SD, 5^3G, 5^6G, 5^3GF, 5^0GF, 6^0GF, 6^4GF, 5^0GF,

	Starts	1st	2nd	3rd	Win & Pl
Career Total (Turf)	60	6	3	6	89426
Career Total (AW)	9	1	0	1	13369

103	3/07	Ling	5f	(0-100)H	STD	£11217
103	5/06	Ches	5f16y	(0-100)H	G-F	£15141
96	3/05	Donc	6f	(0-100)H	GD	£12098
94	7/04	Gdwd	6f	B H	G-F	£13108
87	5/04	Ripn	6f	E(0-70)	G-F	£4056
84	6/03	NmkJ	6f	C(0-95)H	G-F	£9529
66	6/03	Ling	6f	D	G-F	£3877

Total win prize-money £69029

Going (Turf): Sf: 0-2 GS: 0-5 Gd: 1-17 GF: 5-36 Fm: 0-0
Distance: 5f/6f: 7-64 7f-8f: 0-5 9f-13f: 0-0 14f+: 0-0
Track : LH: 2-14 RH: 0-0 Tight: 2-10 Gall: 0-5

Aids: Bl: 0-2 Vi: 0-0 Tstrap: 0-0 Ckp: 0-0
Best Rating: **104** 6/06 Muss 5f gd-fm

Useful; effective over 5f-6f; effective on fast ground; also goes on Polytrack.

Merrion Tiger (IRE)

96(105) (74)**69**
4-y-o ch g Choisir (AUS)-Akita (IRE) (Foxhound (USA))
A G Foster A G Foster

Placings:50040304-1102034000012 (7842)
2009: 12[1]SD, 16[1]SD, 16[0]SF, 14[2]G, 16[0]GS, 14[3]GF, 13[4]G, 12[0]G, 13[0]G, 17[0]G, 16[0]GS, 14[1]SD, 14[2]SS,

	Starts	1st	2nd	3rd	Win & Pl
Career Total (Turf)	15	0	1	2	2870
Career Total (AW)	6	3	1	0	6318

69	12/09	Sthl	1m6f	(0-60)H	STD	£1619
74	2/09	Sthl	2m	(0-65)H	STD	£2047
72	1/09	Sthl	1m4f	(0-60)H	STD	£2047

Total win prize-money £5713

Going (Turf): **Sf: 0-0 GS: 0-5 Gd: 0-6 GF: 0-4 Fm: 0-0**
Distance: 5f/6f: 0-1 7f-8f: 0-6 9f-13f: 1-4 **14f+: 2-10**
Track : **LH: 3-14** RH: 0-4 Tight: 0-8 Gall: 0-2
Aids: Bl: 0-1 Vi: 0-1 Tstrap: 0-1 Ckp: 0-1
Best Rating: **74** 2/09 Sthl 2m stand

Moderate; stays 2m; acts on fast ground and on sand.

Merry Diva

100(93) (66)**76**
3-y-o b f Bahamian Bounty-Merry Rous (Rousillon (USA))
C F Wall Mrs Barry Green

Placings:61-0023423 (5968)
2009: 6[0]GF, 6[0]SD, 6[2]GF, 6[3]G, 6[4]G, 6[2]G, 6[3]GS,

	Starts	1st	2nd	3rd	Win & Pl
Career Total (Turf)	8	1	2	2	7759
Career Total (AW)	1	0	0	0	

76	10/08	Yarm	6f3y	GD	£4415

Total win prize-money £4416

Going (Turf): Sf: 0-0 GS: 0-1 **Gd: 1-4** GF: 0-3 Fm: 0-0
Distance: 5f/6f: 0-8 **7f-8f: 1-1** 9f-13f: 0-0 14f+: 0-0
Track : LH: 0-4 RH: 0-0 Tight: 0-2 Gall: 0-2
Aids: Bl: 0-0 Vi: 0-0 Tstrap: 0-0 Ckp: 0-0
Best Rating: **76** 9/09 Ling 6f gd-sft

Fair; effective over 6f and acts on most ground.

Merry May

84(82) (33)**34**
3-y-o b f Compton Place-Swift Dame (IRE) (Montjeu (IRE))
S Kirk Miss J A Challen

Placings:0000-000 (5632)
2009: 6[0]SD, 6[0]GF, 6[0]GS,

	Starts	1st	2nd	3rd	Win & Pl
Career Total (Turf)	4	0	0	0	
Career Total (AW)	3	0	0	0	

Going (Turf): **Sf: 0-0 GS: 0-1 Gd: 0-1 GF: 0-2 Fm: 0-0**
Distance: 5f/6f: 0-4 7f-8f: 0-3 9f-13f: 0-0 14f+: 0-0
Track : LH: 0-2 RH: 0-1 Tight: 0-1 Gall: 0-1
Aids: Bl: 0-0 Vi: 0-0 Tstrap: 0-0 Ckp: 0-0
Best Rating: **34** 8/09 Sals 6f gd-fm

Merrymadcap (IRE)

103(103) (79)**74**
7-y-o b g Lujain (USA)-Carina Clare (Slip Anchor)
Matthew Salaman (M Salaman 22/8) Mrs N L Young

Placings:05660600/3020003420**1**/**111**0332200453645**3**/4 342050604014/235425441500-210051643342 (7475)
2009: 8[2]G, 9[1]G, 10[0]GF, 8[0]G, 9[5]GF, 11[1]F, 12[6]GF, 11[4]GS, 9[3]SD, 12[3]SS, 10[4]SD, 10[2]SD,

	Starts	1st	2nd	3rd	Win & Pl
Career Total (Turf)	47	4	6	3	23605
Career Total (AW)	26	4	3	7	19907

74	8/09	Bath	1m3f144y	(0-80)H	FRM	£4727
74	6/09	Sals	1m1f198y	(0-70)H	GD	£3238
73	8/08	Newb	1m1f	(0-70)H	G-S	£2590
76	9/07	Wolv	1m1f103y	(0-75)H	SF	£2914
81	3/06	Wolv	1m141y	(0-75)H	STD	£3238
78	2/06	Wolv	1m1f103y	(0-70)H	STD	£3238
75	2/06	Wolv	1m1f103y	(0-65)H	STD	£2388
64	9/05	Bath	1m5y	(0-55)H	FRM	£2711

Total win prize-money £25049

Going (Turf): Sf: 0-10 GS: 1-3Gd: 1-19 GF: 0-12 **Fm: 2-3**
Distance: 5f/6f: 0-2 7f-8f: 0-14 **9f-13f: 8-57** 14f+: 0-0
Track : **LH: 7-44** RH: 1-15 **Tight: 7-44** Gall: 1-4
Aids: Bl: 0-2 Vi: 0-0 Tstrap: 0-0 Ckp: 0-0
Best Rating: **84** 5/06 Ling 1m stand

Fair; effective over 1m-1m2f; acts on most types of ground on turf; goes on Polytrack.

Merseyside Star (IRE)

97 **71**
2-y-o ch c Kheleyf (USA)-The Oldladysays No (IRE) (Perugino (USA))
A P Jarvis (K R Burke 25/7) Mogeely Stud & Mrs Maura Gittins

Placings:6414364 (5187)
2009: 6[6]S, 6[4]GF, 5[1]G, 6[4]GS, 6[3]GF, 5[6]G, 7[4]GF,

	Starts	1st	2nd	3rd	Win & Pl
Career Total (Turf)	7	1	0	1	6377

71	6/09	Carl	5f193y	GD	£4403

Total win prize-money £4404

Going (Turf): Sf: 0-1 GS: 0-1 **Gd: 1-2** GF: 0-3 Fm: 0-0
Distance: **5f/6f: 1-6** 7f-8f: 0-1 9f-13f: 0-0 14f+: 0-0
Track : LH: 0-2 **RH: 1-1** Tight: 0-1 Gall: 0-0
Aids: Bl: 0-0 Vi: 0-0 Tstrap: 0-0 Ckp: 0-0
Best Rating: **71** 6/09 Carl 5f193y good

Modest; suited by 6f and fast ground.

Merton Lad

(97) (67)**38**
3-y-o ch g Fantastic Light (USA)-Artistic Blue (USA) (Diesis)
T G Mills J Daniels

Placings:0463-350 (1408)
2009: 12[3]SD, 12[5]SD, 11[0]GF,

	Starts	1st	2nd	3rd	Win & Pl
Career Total (Turf)	2	0	0	0	
Career Total (AW)	5	0	0	2	1185

Going (Turf): **Sf: 0-1 GS: 0-0 Gd: 0-0 GF: 0-1 Fm: 0-0**
Distance: 5f/6f: 0-0 7f-8f: 0-3 9f-13f: 0-4 14f+: 0-0
Track : LH: 0-2 RH: 0-3 Tight: 0-3 Gall: 0-0
Aids: Bl: 0-0 Vi: 0-0 Tstrap: 0-1 Ckp: 0-1

Best Rating: **67** 3/09 Wolv 1m4f50y stand

Bred for middle distances at three; modest maiden form to date.

Merton Matriarch

(89) (67)
2-y-o ch f Cadeaux Genereux-Tesary (Danehill (USA))
P Winkworth P Winkworth

Placings:2 (6942)
2009: 6[2]SD,

	Starts	1st	2nd	3rd	Win & Pl
Career Total (Turf)	0	0	0	0	
Career Total (AW)	1	0	1	0	771

Going (Turf): **Sf: 0-0 GS: 0-0 Gd: 0-0 GF: 0-0 Fm: 0-0**
Distance: 5f/6f: 0-1 7f-8f: 0-0 9f-13f: 0-0 14f+: 0-0
Track : LH: 0-0 RH: 0-1 Tight: 0-0 Gall: 0-0
Aids: Bl: 0-0 Vi: 0-0 Tstrap: 0-0 Ckp: 0-0
Best Rating: **67** 10/09 Kemp 6f stand

Mesbaah (IRE)

95(102) (87)**91**
5-y-o b g Noverre (USA)-Deyaajeer (USA) (Dayjur (USA))
R A Fahey P D Smith Holdings Ltd

Placings:4615/30356/**6**00022026000-000000 (7085)
2009: 12[0]GF, 7[0]G, 7[0]GF, 8[0]GF, 9[0]GF, 11[0]S,

	Starts	1st	2nd	3rd	Win & Pl
Career Total (Turf)	24	1	3	2	19136
Career Total (AW)	3	0	0	0	328

91	8/06	Bevl	7f100y	GD	£5829

Total win prize-money £5829

Going (Turf): Sf: 0-3 GS: 0-1 **Gd: 1-8** GF: 0-11 Fm: 0-1
Distance: 5f/6f: 0-2 **7f-8f: 1-13** 9f-13f: 0-12 14f+: 0-0
Track : LH: 0-12 **RH: 1-7** Tight: 0-4 Gall: 0-8
Aids: Bl: 0-3 Vi: 0-2 Tstrap: 1-3 Ckp: 1-3
Best Rating: **102** 8/07 Donc 1m gd-fm

Useful: stays 1m1f; acts on good and faster ground; has worn blinkers, cheekpieces and visor.

Meshtri (IRE)

97(104) (106)**100**
4-y-o ch g Dalakhani (IRE)-Arctic Hunt (IRE) (Bering)
M A Jarvis Sheikh Ahmed Al Maktoum

Placings:212051-30 (3390)
2009: 16[3]SD, 16[0]S,

	Starts	1st	2nd	3rd	Win & Pl
Career Total (Turf)	6	2	2	0	37407
Career Total (AW)	2	0	0	1	1679

100	9/08	Hayd	1m6f	(0-105)H	G-F	£31155
85	4/08	Hayd	1m3f200y		G-S	£2590

Total win prize-money £33745

Going (Turf): Sf: 0-4 **GS: 1-1** Gd: 0-0 **GF: 1-1** Fm: 0-0
Distance: 5f/6f: 0-0 7f-8f: 0-0 9f-13f: 1-4 14f+: 1-4
Track : **LH: 2-5** RH: 0-3 Tight: 0-0 Gall: 0-2
Aids: Bl: 0-0 Vi: 0-0 Tstrap: 0-0 Ckp: 0-0
Best Rating: **106** 3/09 Kemp 2m stand

Very useful; effective over 1m4f-2m; acts on most ground and on Polytrack.

Metal Guru

88(104) (69)**70**
5-y-o ch m Ishiguru (USA)-Gemtastic (Tagula (IRE))

R Hollinshead Moores Metals Ltd

Placings:54/2510030**460**/00100025**2**05-050**110**326 **(7852)**
2009: 5^{0}SD, 5^{5}F, 5^{0}G, 5^{1}SD, 5^{1}SD, 5^{0}SD, 5^{3}SD, 5^{2}SS, 5^{6}SS,

	Starts	1st	2nd	3rd	Win & Pl
Career Total (Turf)	18	1	2	1	4522
Career Total (AW)	14	3	2	1	8677

67	10/09	Wolv	5f20y	(0-60)H	STD	£2729
66	9/09	Wolv	5f20y	(0-60)H	STD	£2047
70	6/08	Bevl	5f	(0-65)H	G-F	£2266
70	7/07	Wolv	5f216y	(0-65)H	STD	£2388

Total win prize-money £9433

Going (Turf): Sf: 0-2 GS: 0-3 Gd: 0-5 **GF: 1-6** Fm: 0-2
Distance: **5f/6f: 4-31** 7f-8f: 0-1 9f-13f: 0-0 14f+: 0-0
Track : **LH: 3-19** RH: 0-0 **Tight: 3-12** Gall: 0-4
Aids: Bl: 0-0 Vi: 0-0 Tstrap: 3-18 Ckp: 3-18
Best Rating: **71** 10/07 Leic 5f218y soft

Moderate; effective over 5f-6f; acts on fast ground; goes on both AW surfaces; has worn cheekpieces.

Metal Madness (IRE)

99(104) (67)74
4-y-o b g Acclamation-Dosha (Touching Wood (USA))
Paul Cashman (M G Quinlan 24/1) Patrick Bohan

Placings:550/1625130-**6**000030 **(7070a)**
2009: 10^{6}SD, 10^{0}SD, 10^{0}HY, 8^{0}S, 9^{0}G, 7^{3}S, 14^{0}S,

	Starts	1st	2nd	3rd	Win & Pl
Career Total (Turf)	15	2	1	2	11606
Career Total (AW)	2	0	0	0	0

68	8/08	Gway	1m100y	(50-70)H	YLD	£7621
66	5/08	Thsk	1m	(0-65)H	GD	£2590

Total win prize-money £10211

Going (Turf): Sf: 0-6 GS: 0-1 **Gd: 1-3** GF: 0-2 Fm: 0-1
Distance: 5f/6f: 0-1 7f-8f: 1-6 9f-13f: 1-9 14f+: 0-1
Track : LH: 1-5 RH: 1-6 **Tight: 1-2** Gall: 0-1
Aids: Bl: 0-2 Vi: 0-0 Tstrap: 0-1 Ckp: 0-1
Best Rating: **74** 8/08 Gowr 1m gd-yld

Modest; effective over 1m; acts on fast and easy surface.

Metal Soldier (IRE)

90 74
2-y-o b g Antonius Pius (USA)-Shenkara (IRE) (Night Shift (USA))
J J Quinn The Clay Family

Placings:1 **(1802)**
2009: 5^{1}GF,

	Starts	1st	2nd	3rd	Win & Pl
Career Total (Turf)	1	1	0	0	8419

74	5/09	Ches	5f16y	G-F	£8418

Total win prize-money £8419

Going (Turf): Sf: 0-0 GS: 0-0 Gd: 0-0 **GF: 1-1** Fm: 0-0
Distance: **5f/6f: 1-1** 7f-8f: 0-0 9f-13f: 0-0 14f+: 0-0
Track : **LH: 1-1** RH: 0-0 **Tight: 1-1** Gall: 0-0
Aids: Bl: 0-0 Vi: 0-0 Tstrap: 0-0 Ckp: 0-0
Best Rating: **74** 5/09 Ches 5f16y gd-fm

Fair; suited by 5f and acts on fast ground.

Methaaly (IRE)

108(110) (92)89
6-y-o b g Red Ransom (USA)-Santorini (USA) (Spinning World (USA))
M Mullineaux A Jones

Placings:16/**0531450261210305035332/5003510642**3040 0111203030-**2524**0006014560000**5010035** **(7875)**
2009: 5^{2}SD, 7^{5}SD, 5^{2}SD, 5^{4}SD, 5^{0}SD, 7^{0}GF, 6^{0}GF, 5^{6}GF, 7^{0}GF, 6^{1}GS, 5^{4}GF, 6^{5}G, 7^{6}GF, 6^{0}F, 5^{0}GS, 6^{0}G, 6^{0}GF, 6^{5}GF, 6^{0}GF, 6^{1}GF, 6^{0}SD, 5^{0}SD, 6^{3}SD, 6^{5}SD,

	Starts	1st	2nd	3rd	Win & Pl
Career Total (Turf)	37	6	3	2	37334
Career Total (AW)	35	4	4	8	22174

84	10/09	Wwck	6f	(0-85)H	G-F	£5180
84	5/09	Donc	6f	(0-80)H	G-S	£4857
89	7/08	York	6f	(0-80)H	G-F	£6476
81	7/08	Ayr	6f	(0-80)H	GD	£6476
78	7/08	Wolv	7f32y	(0-75)H	STD	£3238
73	3/08	Wolv	5f216y	(0-75)H	STD	£2730
77	8/07	Muss	5f	(0-70)H	G-F	£3238
77	7/07	Wolv	5f216y		STD	£2047
74	3/07	Kemp	6f	(0-65)H	STD	£2590
73	6/06	Hayd	6f		G-F	£3238

Total win prize-money £40075

Going (Turf): Sf: 0-3 GS: 1-4 Gd: 1-9 **GF: 4-20** Fm: 0-1
Distance: **5f/6f: 9-57** 7f-8f: 1-15 9f-13f: 0-0 14f+: 0-0
Track : **LH: 4-40** RH: 1-6 **Tight: 3-37** Gall: 0-1
Aids: **Bl: 5-29** Vi: 0-0 Tstrap: 0-0 Ckp: 0-0
Best Rating: **92** 2/09 Wolv 5f216y stand

Fair; effective over 5f-7f; acts on fast ground; goes on Polytrack; has worn blinkers and an eyeshield; can miss the break.

Metroland

101 76
3-y-o b f Royal Applause-Chetwynd (IRE) (Exit To Nowhere (USA))
D Nicholls Dr Marwan Koukash

Placings:3523116-022465 **(3479)**
2009: 5^{0}F, 5^{2}GF, 6^{2}G, 6^{4}GF, 5^{6}F, 5^{5}GF,

	Starts	1st	2nd	3rd	Win & Pl
Career Total (Turf)	13	2	3	2	10146

75	7/08	Bevl	5f	G-F	£2729
68	7/08	Carl	5f	GD	£2590

Total win prize-money £5320

Going (Turf): Sf: 0-0 GS: 0-2 **Gd: 1-2 GF: 1-7** Fm: 0-2
Distance: **5f/6f: 2-13** 7f-8f: 0-0 9f-13f: 0-0 14f+: 0-0
Track : LH: 0-0 **RH: 1-2** Tight: 0-0 **Gall: 1-1**
Aids: Bl: 0-0 Vi: 0-0 Tstrap: 0-0 Ckp: 0-0
Best Rating: **76** 5/09 Hayd 6f good

Fair; suited by 6f; acts on fast ground.

Metropolitan Chief

92(101) (47)41
5-y-o b g Compton Place-Miss Up N Go (Gorytus (USA))
P Burgoyne L Tomlin

Placings:00/**550534531630/502406400-006006006000030** **(7770)**
2009: 7^{0}SD, 6^{0}SD, 6^{6}SD, 5^{0}SD, 5^{0}SD, 6^{6}SD, 5^{0}GF, 7^{0}SD, 5^{6}GF, 6^{0}SD, 5^{0}GS, 6^{0}GF, 7^{0}SD, 7^{3}SD, 6^{0}SD,

	Starts	1st	2nd	3rd	Win & Pl
Career Total (Turf)	15	0	0	2	1168
Career Total (AW)	23	1	1	2	3705

66	9/07	Wolv	7f32y	(0-60)H	STD	£2388

Total win prize-money £2389

Going (Turf): **Sf: 0-0 GS: 0-4 Gd: 0-1 GF: 0-9 Fm: 0-1**
Distance: 5f/6f: 0-13 **7f-8f: 1-25** 9f-13f: 0-0 14f+: 0-0
Track : **LH: 1-18** RH: 0-9 **Tight: 1-13** Gall: 0-1
Aids: **Bl: 1-7** Vi: 0-0 Tstrap: 0-7 Ckp: 0-7
Best Rating: **66** 9/07 Wolv 7f32y stand

Moderate; stays 1m; acts on fast ground; also goes on Polytrack; has worn blinkers.

Metropolitan Man

(102) (91)113
6-y-o ch g Dr Fong (USA)-Preceder (Polish Precedent (USA))
D M Simcock The Metropolitans

Placings:315/225124/3002426/52330-0 **(6030)**
2009: 8^{0}SD,

	Starts	1st	2nd	3rd	Win & Pl
Career Total (Turf)	21	2	6	4	101268
Career Total (AW)	1	0	0	0	

104	7/06	Haml	1m65y	G-F	£9971
83	9/05	York	6f	G-F	£7800

Total win prize-money £17771

Going (Turf): Sf: 0-2 GS: 0-1 Gd: 0-8 **GF: 2-10** Fm: 0-0
Distance: 5f/6f: 1-2 7f-8f: 0-12 9f-13f: 1-8 14f+: 0-0
Track : LH: 0-8 **RH: 1-5 Tight: 1-4** Gall: 0-6
Aids: Bl: 0-0 Vi: 0-0 Tstrap: 0-0 Ckp: 0-0
Best Rating: **113** 4/08 Sand 1m14y good

Smart; Group and Listed placed; stays 1m; acts on most ground.

Mexican Bob

101(97) (67)70
6-y-o b g Atraf-Eskimo Nel (IRE) (Shy Groom (USA))
C E Longsdon First Chance Racing

Placings:6465326/624/0103 **(7847)**
2009: 10^{0}GF, 12^{1}G, 14^{0}G, 12^{3}SD,

	Starts	1st	2nd	3rd	Win & Pl
Career Total (Turf)	11	1	2	1	5332
Career Total (AW)	3	0	0	1	566

70	8/09	Bevl	1m4f16y	(0-65)H	GD	£2590

Total win prize-money £2590

Going (Turf): Sf: 0-0 GS: 0-1 **Gd: 1-4** GF: 0-4 Fm: 0-2
Distance: 5f/6f: 0-0 7f-8f: 0-0 **9f-13f: 1-12** 14f+: 0-2
Track : LH: 0-9 **RH: 1-4 Tight: 1-7** Gall: 0-1
Aids: Bl: 0-0 Vi: 0-0 Tstrap: 0-0 Ckp: 0-0
Best Rating: **71** 8/07 Hayd 1m2f120y gd-fm

Modest; effective over 1m2f; acts on fast and easy ground.

Mexican Jay (USA)

84 56
3-y-o b f Elusive Quality (USA)-Mistle Song (Nashwan (USA))
B Smart H E Sheikh Rashid Bin Mohammed

Placings:3 **(2403)**
2009: 10^{3}GF,

	Starts	1st	2nd	3rd	Win & Pl
Career Total (Turf)	1	0	0	1	482

Going (Turf): **Sf: 0-0 GS: 0-0 Gd: 0-0 GF: 0-1 Fm: 0-0**
Distance: 5f/6f: 0-0 7f-8f: 0-0 9f-13f: 0-1 14f+: 0-0
Track : LH: 0-1 RH: 0-0 Tight: 0-0 Gall: 0-1
Aids: Bl: 0-0 Vi: 0-0 Tstrap: 0-0 Ckp: 0-0
Best Rating: **56** 5/09 Newc 1m2f32y gd-fm

Mexican Milly (IRE)

91(84) (47)56

2-y-o ch f Noverre (USA)-Forest Bride (USA) (Woodman (USA))

B W Hills Suzanne & Nigel Williams

Placings:0336 **(6343)**

2009: 5[0]GF, 6[3]S, 6[3]GF, 5[6]SD,

	Starts	1st	2nd	3rd	Win & Pl
Career Total (Turf)	3	0	0	2	1396
Career Total (AW)	1	0	0	0	0

Going (Turf): **Sf: 0-1 GS: 0-0 Gd: 0-0 GF: 0-2 Fm: 0-0**
Distance: 5f/6f: 0-4 7f-8f: 0-0 9f-13f: 0-0 14f+: 0-0
Track : LH: 0-1 RH: 0-0 Tight: 0-1 Gall: 0-0
Aids: Bl: 0-0 Vi: 0-0 Tstrap: 0-0 Ckp: 0-0
Best Rating: **56** 8/09 Ripn 6f gd-fm

Half-sister to a winner over 1m2f in Italy; modest form to date.

Mexican Pete

(107) (79)83

9-y-o b g Atraf-Eskimo Nel (IRE) (Shy Groom (USA))

A King First Chance Racing

Placings:00605/6122421103/03020443260/54024666/031 0/3/3-25 **(1069)**

2009: 16[2]SD, 16[5]SD,

	Starts	1st	2nd	3rd	Win & Pl
Career Total (Turf)	36	4	6	4	33169
Career Total (AW)	6	0	1	2	1791

83	7/06	Wwck	1m4f134y	(0-70)H	FRM	£3123
79	8/03	Sals	1m4f	E(0-75)H	GD	£3926
72	8/03	Rdcr	1m3f	E(0-70)H	G-F	£4176
63	7/03	Wwck	1m2f188y	F(0-65)H	G-F	£3794

Total win prize-money £15019

Going (Turf): Sf: 0-1 GS: 0-3 Gd: 1-8 **GF: 2-18** Fm: 1-6
Distance: 5f/6f: 0-2 7f-8f: 0-2 **9f-13f: 4-35** 14f+: 0-3
Track : **LH: 3-27** RH: 1-13 **Tight: 2-17** Gall: 0-9
Aids: Bl: 0-0 Vi: 0-0 Tstrap: 0-0 Ckp: 0-0
Best Rating: **84** 7/05 Donc 1m4f gd-fm

Fair; best over 1m4f; suited by fast ground; winning hurdler.

Mey Blossom

102(102) (78)92

4-y-o ch f Captain Rio-Petra Nova (First Trump)

R M Whitaker Waz Developments Ltd

Placings:6214060/14404000404-55452020000 **(7191)**

2009: 7[5]F, 7[5]GF, 5[4]GF, 7[5]GF, 6[2]GF, 7[0]G, 6[2]S, 5[0]G, 5[0]SD, 6[0]G, 5[0]SD,

	Starts	1st	2nd	3rd	Win & Pl
Career Total (Turf)	25	2	3	0	21728
Career Total (AW)	4	0	0	0	481

92	4/08	Thsk	5f	(0-90)H	GD	£7771
77	8/07	Bevl	5f		GD	£5181

Total win prize-money £12953

Going (Turf): Sf: 0-2 GS: 0-4 **Gd: 2-9** GF: 0-9 Fm: 0-1
Distance: **5f/6f: 2-21** 7f-8f: 0-8 9f-13f: 0-0 14f+: 0-0
Track : LH: 0-11 RH: 0-2 Tight: 0-6 Gall: 0-2
Aids: Bl: 0-0 Vi: 0-0 Tstrap: 0-4 Ckp: 0-4
Best Rating: **92** 4/08 Thsk 5f good

Useful; effective over 5f but stays 7f; acts on good ground; has worn cheekpieces.

Meydan Dubai (IRE)

(95) (72)91

4-y-o b h Alzao (USA)-Rorkes Drift (IRE) (Royal Abjar (USA))

J R Best John Best

Placings:3632/5060062044-00 **(7699)**

2009: 8[0]SD, 10[0]SD,

	Starts	1st	2nd	3rd	Win & Pl
Career Total (Turf)	12	0	2	2	6251
Career Total (AW)	4	0	0	0	241

Going (Turf): **Sf: 0-0 GS: 0-2 Gd: 0-5 GF: 0-3 Fm: 0-2**
Distance: 5f/6f: 0-3 7f-8f: 0-9 9f-13f: 0-4 14f+: 0-0
Track : LH: 0-3 RH: 0-7 Tight: 0-6 Gall: 0-3
Aids: Bl: 0-0 Vi: 0-3 Tstrap: 0-0 Ckp: 0-0
Best Rating: **91** 5/08 NmkR 1m good

Fair maiden; stays 7f, should get 1m; acts on good and softer ground.

Meydan Groove

98(91) (66)67

3-y-o b f Reset (AUS)-In The Groove (Night Shift (USA))

R Johnson Robert Johnson

Placings:0531362000**0**-66000030 **(4594)**

2009: 8[6]SD, 7[6]GF, 6[0]GS, 6[0]F, 6[0]GF, 7[0]GF, 6[3]G, 5[0]G,

	Starts	1st	2nd	3rd	Win & Pl
Career Total (Turf)	13	1	0	2	3243
Career Total (AW)	6	0	1	1	1182

67	7/08	Leic	5f218y	G-F	£1942

Total win prize-money £1943

Going (Turf): Sf: 0-0 GS: 0-4 Gd: 0-2 **GF: 1-6** Fm: 0-1
Distance: **5f/6f: 1-7** 7f-8f: 0-10 9f-13f: 0-2 14f+: 0-0
Track : LH: 0-6 RH: 0-5 Tight: 0-5 Gall: 0-1
Aids: Bl: 0-0 Vi: 0-0 Tstrap: 0-0 Ckp: 0-0
Best Rating: **67** 7/08 Leic 5f218y gd-fm

Modest; stays 7f; acts on fast ground and on Polytrack.

Meydan Style (USA)

70(86) (52)37

3-y-o b g Essence Of Dubai (USA)-Polish Ruby (USA) (Polish Pro (USA))

J Balding The Style Council

Placings:0600-6600506 **(6950)**

2009: 5[6]SD, 5[6]SD, 8[0]SD, 7[0]G, 6[5]SD, 7[0]SD, 8[6]SD,

	Starts	1st	2nd	3rd	Win & Pl
Career Total (Turf)	3	0	0	0	0
Career Total (AW)	8	0	0	0	0

Going (Turf): **Sf: 0-0 GS: 0-0 Gd: 0-2 GF: 0-0 Fm: 0-1**
Distance: 5f/6f: 0-7 7f-8f: 0-4 9f-13f: 0-0 14f+: 0-0
Track : LH: 0-7 RH: 0-1 Tight: 0-3 Gall: 0-0
Aids: Bl: 0-2 Vi: 0-0 Tstrap: 0-3 Ckp: 0-3
Best Rating: **52** 11/08 Wolv 5f20y stand

Meyyal (USA)

100(98) (72)78

3-y-o b c War Chant (USA)-Tamgeed (USA) (Woodman (USA))

B W Hills Hamdan Al Maktoum

Placings:3-335 **(6595)**

2009: 10[3]SD, 10[3]SD, 10[5]GS,

	Starts	1st	2nd	3rd	Win & Pl
Career Total (Turf)	2	0	0	1	722
Career Total (AW)	2	0	0	2	1088

Going (Turf): **Sf: 0-0 GS: 0-1 Gd: 0-1 GF: 0-0 Fm: 0-0**
Distance: 5f/6f: 0-0 7f-8f: 0-1 9f-13f: 0-3 14f+: 0-0
Track : LH: 0-1 RH: 0-2 Tight: 0-0 Gall: 0-0
Aids: Bl: 0-0 Vi: 0-0 Tstrap: 0-0 Ckp: 0-0
Best Rating: **78** 10/08 Donc 7f good

Fair; stays 1m2f and acts on Polytrack.

Mezenah

105 86

3-y-o b f Cape Cross (IRE)-Saytarra (USA) (Seeking The Gold (USA))

Saeed Bin Suroor Godolphin

Placings:232-21 **(4955)**

2009: 8[2]GF, 8[1]G,

	Starts	1st	2nd	3rd	Win & Pl
Career Total (Turf)	5	1	3	1	8777

78	8/09	Sand	1m14y	GD	£3238

Total win prize-money £3238

Going (Turf): Sf: 0-1 GS: 0-1 **Gd: 1-2** GF: 0-1 Fm: 0-0
Distance: 5f/6f: 0-0 7f-8f: 0-3 **9f-13f: 1-2** 14f+: 0-0
Track : LH: 0-0 **RH: 1-1** Tight: 0-0 Gall: 0-0
Aids: Bl: 0-0 Vi: 0-0 Tstrap: 0-0 Ckp: 0-0
Best Rating: **86** 7/09 Asct 1m gd-fm

Fair; stays 1m; acts on good and softer ground.

Mezuzah

(59) (57)89

9-y-o b g Barathea (IRE)-Mezzogiorno (Unfuwain (USA))

Miss J E Foster R Batty & Partners

Placings:51/630406/050000/240100354/1006025601013/ 530004262000206/600-0 **(7711)**

2009: 8[0]SD,

	Starts	1st	2nd	3rd	Win & Pl
Career Total (Turf)	53	5	5	4	54809
Career Total (AW)	2	0	0	0	

92	10/06	Nott	1m54y	(0-80)H	SFT	£6477
84	3/06	Rdcr	1m	H	SFT	£15580
84	6/05	Haml	1m1f36y	(0-70)H	SFT	£4270
94	11/02	Donc	7f	D	HVY	£5411

Total win prize-money £31739

Going (Turf): **Sf: 5-20** GS: 0-5 Gd: 0-16 GF: 0-12 Fm: 0-0
Distance: 5f/6f: 0-1 **7f-8f: 3-28** 9f-13f: 2-26 14f+: 0-0
Track : LH: 1-25 **RH: 2-12 Tight: 2-14** Gall: 0-7
Aids: Bl: 0-1 Vi: 0-0 Tstrap: 0-0 Ckp: 0-0
Best Rating: **95** 8/03 Gdwd 1m1f192y good

Fair; effective over 7f-1m2f; acts on most ground, but seems ideally suited by plenty of give underfoot.

Mezzanisi (IRE)

108(110) (94)96

4-y-o b g Kalanisi (IRE)-Mezzanine (Sadler's Wells (USA))

M L W Bell T Redman And P Philipps

Placings:03/52201233322-213 **(3620)**

2009: 12[2]G, 12[1]SD, 11[3]GF,

	Starts	1st	2nd	3rd	Win & Pl
Career Total (Turf)	12	0	5	5	20523

Career Total (AW)	4	2	1	0	8855

94 5/09 Wolv 1m4f50y (0-85)H STD £5046
71 6/08 Ling 1m2f STD £2266
Total win prize-money £7313

Going (Turf): **Sf: 0-4 GS: 0-0 Gd: 0-5 GF: 0-3 Fm: 0-0**
Distance: 5f/6f: 0-0 7f-8f: 0-2 **9f-13f: 2-14** 14f+: 0-0
Track : **LH: 2-9** RH: 0-5 **Tight: 2-10** Gall: 0-1
Aids: Bl: 0-0 Vi: 0-0 Tstrap: 0-0 Ckp: 0-0
Best Rating: 96 7/09 Hayd 1m3f200y gd-fm

Very useful; stays 1m4f; acts on a sound surface and on Fibresand.

Mia's Boy

108(110) (110)113
5-y-o b h Pivotal-Bint Zamayem (IRE) (Rainbow Quest (USA))
C A Dwyer Iraj Parvizi

Placings:6/3616/1111316550-46232300212 **(7294)**
2009: 8^{4}GF, 8^{6}S, 7^{2}GF, 8^{3}G, 7^{2}GF, 8^{3}GF, 8^{0}G, 8^{0}GF, 8^{2}SD, 7^{1}GS, 7^{2}S,

	Starts	1st	2nd	3rd	Win & Pl
Career Total (Turf)	20	5	3	2	83517
Career Total (AW)	6	2	1	2	9991

111 10/09 Donc 7f G-S £12462
111 5/08 York 1m (0-110)H G-F £20741
95 4/08 Yarm 1m3y (0-90)H GD £6854
92 3/08 Donc 1m (0-90)H SFT £6800
85 3/08 Wolv 1m141y (0-75)H STD £2730
80 2/08 Ling 1m (0-75)H STD £2590
74 6/07 Thsk 7f G-S £3886
Total win prize-money £56065

Going (Turf): Sf: 1-4 **GS: 2-2** Gd: 1-5 GF: 1-9 Fm: 0-0
Distance: 5f/6f: 0-0 **7f-8f: 5-19** 9f-13f: 2-7 14f+: 0-0
Track : **LH: 4-12** RH: 0-2 **Tight: 3-7** Gall: 1-6
Aids: Bl: 0-0 Vi: 0-0 Tstrap: 0-0 Ckp: 0-0
Best Rating: 113 11/09 Donc 7f soft

Smart; stays 1m; acts on any ground and on Polytrack.

Miacarla

88(85) (33)61
6-y-o b m Forzando-Zarzi (IRE) (Suave Dancer (USA))
H A McWilliams J D Riches

Placings:0/036/0041330002541000/0600040150-000000000 **(7136)**
2009: 5^{0}SD, 5^{0}F, 5^{0}GS, 5^{0}G, 5^{0}G, 5^{0}GF, 5^{0}HY, 5^{0}GF, 5^{0}SD,

	Starts	1st	2nd	3rd	Win & Pl
Career Total (Turf)	34	3	1	3	10431
Career Total (AW)	5	0	0	0	

61 8/08 Haml 5f4y (0-55)H G-S £2388
64 9/07 Thsk 5f (0-65)H G-F £2047
56 6/07 Rdcr 5f (0-70)H G-S £2817
Total win prize-money £7253

Going (Turf): Sf: 0-7 **GS: 2-9** Gd: 0-4 GF: 1-12 Fm: 0-2
Distance: **5f/6f: 3-38** 7f-8f: 0-1 9f-13f: 0-0 14f+: 0-0
Track : LH: 0-5 RH: 0-2 Tight: 0-4 Gall: 0-2
Aids: Bl: 0-0 Vi: 0-0 Tstrap: 0-1 Ckp: 0-1
Best Rating: 66 9/07 Bevl 5f gd-fm

Moderate; best over 5f; acts on fast and easy ground; has worn a tongue tie.

Miami Gator (IRE)

89(94) (61)59
2-y-o ch g Titus Livius (FR)-Lovere (St Jovite (USA))
J R Weymes (A P Jarvis 31/10) Mrs Elaine M Burke

Placings:01456051 **(7884)**
2009: 5^{0}GF, 6^{1}G, 6^{4}GS, 6^{5}G, 6^{6}GS, 7^{0}S, 6^{5}SD, 7^{1}SD,

	Starts	1st	2nd	3rd	Win & Pl
Career Total (Turf)	6	1	0	0	2528
Career Total (AW)	2	1	0	0	1638

12/09 Ling 7f (0-60) STD £1637
59 6/09 Rdcr 6f GD £2047
Total win prize-money £3685

Going (Turf): Sf: 0-1 GS: 0-2 **Gd: 1-2** GF: 0-1 Fm: 0-0
Distance: 5f/6f: 1-5 7f-8f: 1-3 9f-13f: 0-0 14f+: 0-0
Track : **LH: 1-3** RH: 0-0 **Tight: 1-2** Gall: 0-0
Aids: Bl: 0-0 Vi: 0-0 Tstrap: 0-0 Ckp: 0-0
Best Rating: 61 12/09 Ling 6f stand

Moderate; stays 6f; acts on good ground.

Miami Mix

43(78) (42)
3-y-o gr c Fair Mix (IRE)-Granma (Little Wolf)
B N Pollock Alan Hunt

Placings:0500 **(1363)**
2009: 10^{0}SD, 9^{5}SD, 10^{0}SD, 10^{0}GF,

	Starts	1st	2nd	3rd	Win & Pl
Career Total (Turf)	1	0	0	0	
Career Total (AW)	3	0	0	0	0

Going (Turf): **Sf: 0-0 GS: 0-0 Gd: 0-0 GF: 0-1 Fm: 0-0**
Distance: 5f/6f: 0-0 7f-8f: 0-0 9f-13f: 0-4 14f+: 0-0
Track : LH: 0-4 RH: 0-0 Tight: 0-3 Gall: 0-0
Aids: Bl: 0-0 Vi: 0-0 Tstrap: 0-0 Ckp: 0-0
Best Rating: 42 3/09 Ling 1m2f stand

Miccolo

83 59
2-y-o b c Piccolo-Ashkernazy (IRE) (Salt Dome (USA))
P T Midgley Anthony D Copley

Placings:60050 **(4282)**
2009: 5^{6}GF, 5^{0}GF, 5^{0}GF, 5^{5}GS, 5^{0}G,

	Starts	1st	2nd	3rd	Win & Pl
Career Total (Turf)	5	0	0	0	0

Going (Turf): **Sf: 0-0 GS: 0-1 Gd: 0-1 GF: 0-3 Fm: 0-0**
Distance: 5f/6f: 0-5 7f-8f: 0-0 9f-13f: 0-0 14f+: 0-0
Track : LH: 0-0 RH: 0-0 Tight: 0-0 Gall: 0-0
Aids: Bl: 0-0 Vi: 0-0 Tstrap: 0-0 Ckp: 0-0
Best Rating: 59 6/09 York 5f gd-sft

Michael Collins (IRE)

70(94) (66)57
3-y-o b g Oasis Dream-West Virginia (IRE) (Gone West (USA))
G J Smith (Ms Maria Kelly 29/9) K G Kitchen

Placings:00-42000000 **(7349)**
2009: 7^{4}SD, 8^{2}SD, 8^{0}S, 7^{0}HY, 8^{0}G, 8^{0}HY, 8^{0}SD, 7^{0}SD,

	Starts	1st	2nd	3rd	Win & Pl
Career Total (Turf)	5	0	0	0	
Career Total (AW)	5	0	1	0	806

Going (Turf): **Sf: 0-3 GS: 0-0 Gd: 0-1 GF: 0-0 Fm: 0-0**
Distance: 5f/6f: 0-1 7f-8f: 0-8 9f-13f: 0-1 14f+: 0-0
Track : LH: 0-6 RH: 0-3 Tight: 0-2 Gall: 0-1
Aids: Bl: 0-0 Vi: 0-0 Tstrap: 0-3 Ckp: 0-3
Best Rating: 66 1/09 Sthl 1m stand

Michael Laskey

84(92) (50)49
3-y-o b g Lujain (USA)-Enchanted Ocean (USA) (Royal Academy (USA))
B R Millman Graham J Richards

Placings:50000 **(7818)**
2009: 8^{5}SD, 10^{0}G, 10^{0}GF, 12^{0}SD, 9^{0}SD,

	Starts	1st	2nd	3rd	Win & Pl
Career Total (Turf)	2	0	0	0	
Career Total (AW)	3	0	0	0	0

Going (Turf): **Sf: 0-0 GS: 0-0 Gd: 0-1 GF: 0-1 Fm: 0-0**
Distance: 5f/6f: 0-0 7f-8f: 0-1 9f-13f: 0-4 14f+: 0-0
Track : LH: 0-3 RH: 0-2 Tight: 0-3 Gall: 0-0
Aids: Bl: 0-0 Vi: 0-0 Tstrap: 0-0 Ckp: 0-0
Best Rating: 50 3/09 Ling 1m stand

Michaelmas Daisy

93(94) (55)67
2-y-o b f Camacho-Desert Daisy (IRE) (Desert Prince (IRE))
P Howling (Miss Amy Weaver 27/10) Paul Howling

Placings:5031260066 **(7410)**
2009: 5^{5}SD, 5^{0}GF, 5^{3}GF, 6^{1}GF, 6^{2}GF, 6^{6}G, 7^{0}SD, 7^{0}SD, 6^{6}SD, 5^{6}SD,

	Starts	1st	2nd	3rd	Win & Pl
Career Total (Turf)	5	1	1	1	6718
Career Total (AW)	5	0	0	0	0

67 7/09 Sals 6f G-F £4695
Total win prize-money £4695

Going (Turf): Sf: 0-0 GS: 0-0 Gd: 0-1 **GF: 1-4** Fm: 0-0
Distance: **5f/6f: 1-6** 7f-8f: 0-4 9f-13f: 0-0 14f+: 0-0
Track : LH: 0-6 RH: 0-2 Tight: 0-4 Gall: 0-1
Aids: Bl: 0-1 Vi: 0-0 Tstrap: 0-0 Ckp: 0-0
Best Rating: 67 7/09 Sals 6f gd-fm

Modest; suited by 6f and fast ground.

Michaels Dream (IRE)

(77) (39)35
10-y-o b g Spectrum (IRE)-Stormswept (USA) (Storm Bird (CAN))
N Wilson Mrs Michael John Paver

Placings:055300500/00004425330331321 42/4205000000 300/6330400/00310/0000/0/0 **(0249)**
2009: 16^{0}SD,

	Starts	1st	2nd	3rd	Win & Pl
Career Total (Turf)	48	2	3	9	19826
Career Total (AW)	11	1	1	1	2861

49 12/05 Wolv 1m5f194y (0-45) STD £1443
64 10/02 Catt 1m3f214yE(0-70)H FRM £4160
59 9/02 Bevl 1m4f16y E(0-70)H G-F £5239
Total win prize-money £10842

Going (Turf): Sf: 0-5 GS: 0-6 Gd: 0-7 **GF: 1-20 Fm: 1-10**
Distance: 5f/6f: 0-3 7f-8f: 0-4 **9f-13f: 2-36** 14f+: 1-16
Track : **LH: 2-38** RH: 1-15 **Tight: 3-31** Gall: 0-5
Aids: Bl: 1-25 **Vi: 2-18** Tstrap: 0-1 Ckp: 0-1
Best Rating: 71 1/03 Sthl 1m3f stand

Michelle (IRE)

(98) (48)

3-y-o b f Marju (IRE)-Bel Sole (ITY) (Spectrum (IRE))

P Butler (J A Osborne 7/2) Miss M Bryant

Placings:3500 **(1036)**

2009: 8^{3}SD, 8^{5}SD, 10^{0}SD, 8^{0}SD,

	Starts	1st	2nd	3rd	Win & Pl
Career Total (Turf)	0	0	0	0	
Career Total (AW)	4	0	0	1	302

Going (Turf): **Sf: 0-0 GS: 0-0 Gd: 0-0 GF: 0-0 Fm: 0-0**
Distance: 5f/6f: 0-0 7f-8f: 0-3 9f-13f: 0-1 14f+: 0-0
Track : LH: 0-4 RH: 0-0 Tight: 0-4 Gall: 0-0
Aids: Bl: 0-0 Vi: 0-0 Tstrap: 0-0 Ckp: 0-0
Best Rating: **48** 2/09 Ling 1m stand

Modest; stays 1m and acts on Polytrack.

Michevious Spirit (IRE)

88 **70**

2-y-o ch f Dalakhani (IRE)-Roseanna (FR) (Anabaa (USA))

K A Ryan L M Rutherford

Placings:526 **(6762)**

2009: 7^{5}GF, 8^{2}GF, 8^{6}GS,

	Starts	1st	2nd	3rd	Win & Pl
Career Total (Turf)	3	0	1	0	1156

Going (Turf): **Sf: 0-0 GS: 0-1 Gd: 0-0 GF: 0-2 Fm: 0-0**
Distance: 5f/6f: 0-0 7f-8f: 0-2 9f-13f: 0-1 14f+: 0-0
Track : LH: 0-2 RH: 0-1 Tight: 0-0 Gall: 0-1
Aids: Bl: 0-0 Vi: 0-0 Tstrap: 0-0 Ckp: 0-0
Best Rating: **70** 9/09 Nott 1m75y gd-fm

Fair; effective over 1m; acts on fast ground.

Mick Is Back

103(97) (53)**65**

5-y-o b g Diktat-Classy Cleo (IRE) (Mujadil (USA))

G G Margarson M Jenner & G Margarson

Placings:460/**2453634122**61115104**460/004**03302100030 0012542-05223100**5**6**0**000 **(7127)**

2009: 9^{0}GF, 10^{5}GF, 7^{2}G, 9^{2}G, 7^{3}G, 7^{1}GF, 8^{0}G, 8^{0}G, 9^{5}G, 9^{6}SD, 10^{0}SD, 6^{0}G, 9^{0}G, 10^{0}G,

	Starts	1st	2nd	3rd	Win & Pl
Career Total (Turf)	43	7	7	4	25440
Career Total (AW)	16	1	1	2	3637

65	7/09	Brig	7f214y	(0-60)H	G-F	£2590
58	5/08	Brig	7f214y		G-S	£1683
63	8/07	Sand	7f16y		GD	£4533
61	6/07	NmkJ	1m		G-S	£3886
55	6/07	Chep	7f16y		SFT	£1943
62	5/07	Leic	7f9y		SFT	£3238
57	3/07	Wolv	7f32y		STD	£2047

Total win prize-money £19924

Going (Turf): **Sf: 3-7** GS: 2-6 Gd: 1-16 GF: 1-14 Fm: 0-0
Distance: 5f/6f: 0-3 **7f-8f: 7-30** 9f-13f: 1-26 14f+: 0-0
Track : **LH: 4-32** RH: 1-11 **Tight: 2-21** Gall: 0-1
Aids: Bl: 0-7 Vi: 2-23 Tstrap: 0-24 Ckp. 6-24
Best Rating: **65** 7/09 Brig 7f214y gd-fm

Moderate; effective over 7f-1m2f; acts on good and soft ground; also goes on Polytrack; has worn a visor.

Mick's Dancer

112(103) (79)**89**

4-y-o b g Pivotal-La Piaf (FR) (Fabulous Dancer (USA))

W R Muir Perspicacious Punters Racing Club

Placings:04/000062**122**-260113124 **(6546)**

2009: 10^{2}GF, 10^{6}GF, 10^{0}G, 9^{1}GF, 10^{1}GF, 10^{3}G, 10^{1}GF, 9^{2}GF, 10^{4}GF,

	Starts	1st	2nd	3rd	Win & Pl
Career Total (Turf)	15	3	3	1	20109
Career Total (AW)	5	1	2	0	5952

85	8/09	Bath	1m2f46y	(0-80)H	G-F	£4857
86	7/09	Ches	1m2f75y	(0-80)H	G-F	£5828
75	6/09	Folk	1m1f149y	(0-75)H	G-F	£3885
73	10/08	Wolv	1m1f103y	(0-70)H	STD	£3238

Total win prize-money £17809

Going (Turf): Sf: 0-1 GS: 0-1 Gd: 0-5 **GF: 3-8** Fm: 0-0
Distance: 5f/6f: 0-0 7f-8f: 0-6 **9f-13f: 4-14** 14f+: 0-0
Track : **LH: 3-11** RH: 1-6 **Tight: 4-12** Gall: 0-3
Aids: Bl: 0-1 Vi: 0-0 Tstrap: 0-0 Ckp: 0-0
Best Rating: **89** 9/09 Folk 1m1f149y gd-fm

Fair; stays 1m2f; acts on fast ground and on Polytrack.

Micky Mac (IRE)

99(103) (66)**70**

5-y-o b g Lend A Hand-Gazette It Tonight (Merdon Melody)

C J Teague A M McArdle

Placings:0040/**54/6213**316005-03203020 **(7555)**

2009: 7^{0}G, 6^{3}GF, 6^{2}GF, 7^{0}GF, 6^{3}GS, 7^{0}G, 5^{2}SD, 5^{0}SD,

	Starts	1st	2nd	3rd	Win & Pl
Career Total (Turf)	15	1	1	3	4600
Career Total (AW)	9	1	2	1	3387

70	7/08	Catt	7f	(0-65)H	GD	£2217
64	2/08	Wolv	1m1f103y	(0-60)H	STD	£1774

Total win prize-money £3993

Going (Turf): Sf: 0-1 GS: 0-2 **Gd: 1-4** GF: 0-7 Fm: 0-1
Distance: 5f/6f: 0-9 7f-8f: 1-12 9f-13f: 1-3 14f+: 0-0
Track : **LH: 2-12** RH: 0-5 **Tight: 2-12** Gall: 0-1
Aids: Bl: 0-2 Vi: 0-0 Tstrap: 0-0 Ckp: 0-0
Best Rating: **70** 7/08 Catt 7f good

Moderate; stays 1m1f but effective at 6f; acts on good/fast ground and Polytrack.

Micky P

83 **57**

2-y-o gr c Dr Fong (USA)-Carmela Owen (Owington)

S C Williams O Pointing

Placings:00 **(7146)**

2009: 6^{0}GS, 7^{0}G,

	Starts	1st	2nd	3rd	Win & Pl
Career Total (Turf)	2	0	0	0	

Going (Turf): **Sf: 0-0 GS: 0-1 Gd: 0-1 GF: 0-0 Fm: 0-0**
Distance: 5f/6f: 0-1 7f-8f: 0-1 9f-13f: 0-0 14f+: 0-0
Track : LH: 0-0 RH: 0-0 Tight: 0-0 Gall: 0-1
Aids: Bl: 0-0 Vi: 0-0 Tstrap: 0-0 Ckp: 0-0
Best Rating: **57** 10/09 Wind 6f gd-sft

Micky's Bird

89(79) (28)**53**

2-y-o ch f Needwood Blade-Silver Peak (FR) (Sillery (USA))

R C Guest Future Racing (Notts) Limited

Placings:00200000 **(7706)**

2009: 5^{0}GF, 5^{0}SD, 6^{2}G, 7^{0}GS, 6^{0}G, 6^{0}SD, 7^{0}SD, 8^{0}SD,

	Starts	1st	2nd	3rd	Win & Pl
Career Total (Turf)	4	0	1	0	578
Career Total (AW)	4	0	0	0	

Going (Turf): **Sf: 0-0 GS: 0-1 Gd: 0-2 GF: 0-1 Fm: 0-0**
Distance: 5f/6f: 0-3 7f-8f: 0-5 9f-13f: 0-0 14f+: 0-0
Track : LH: 0-3 RH: 0-1 Tight: 0-1 Gall: 0-0
Aids: Bl: 0-0 Vi: 0-0 Tstrap: 0-0 Ckp: 0-0
Best Rating: **53** 5/09 Yarm 6f3y good

Micky's Knock Off (IRE)

101(98) (66)**78**

2-y-o b g Camacho-La Grace (Lahib (USA))

R C Guest Miss Alison Ibbotson

Placings:00251603540 **(7636)**

2009: 6^{0}S, 5^{0}G, 5^{2}S, 5^{5}GF, 5^{1}G, 5^{6}G, 5^{0}SF, 5^{3}GS, 5^{5}SD, 5^{4}SD, 5^{0}SD,

	Starts	1st	2nd	3rd	Win & Pl
Career Total (Turf)	7	1	1	1	8826
Career Total (AW)	4	0	0	0	429

78	9/09	Muss	5f	(0-90)	GD	£7477

Total win prize-money £7477

Going (Turf): Sf: 0-2 GS: 0-1 **Gd: 1-3** GF: 0-1 Fm: 0-0
Distance: **5f/6f: 1-11** 7f-8f: 0-0 9f-13f: 0-0 14f+: 0-0
Track : LH: 0-4 RH: 0-0 Tight: 0-3 Gall: 0-1
Aids: Bl: 0-0 Vi: 0-0 Tstrap: 0-0 Ckp: 0-0
Best Rating: **78** 9/09 Muss 5f good

Modest; suited by 5f; acts on good and softer ground.

Mickys Mate

84(75) (13)**39**

4-y-o b g Choisir (AUS)-Adept (Efisio)

A Crook Columber Lads Partnership

Placings:00-00600 **(1628)**

2009: 8^{0}SD, 7^{0}SD, 5^{6}GF, 7^{0}F, 6^{0}GF,

	Starts	1st	2nd	3rd	Win & Pl
Career Total (Turf)	3	0	0	0	0
Career Total (AW)	4	0	0	0	

Going (Turf): **Sf: 0-0 GS: 0-0 Gd: 0-0 GF: 0-2 Fm: 0-1**
Distance: 5f/6f: 0-3 7f-8f: 0-3 9f-13f: 0-1 14f+: 0-0
Track : LH: 0-4 RH: 0-0 Tight: 0-3 Gall: 0-0
Aids: Bl: 0-0 Vi: 0-0 Tstrap: 0-1 Ckp: 0-1
Best Rating: **39** 4/09 Catt 5f212y gd-fm

Mid Valley

95(106) (52)**58**

6-y-o ch g Zilzal (USA)-Isabella D'Este (IRE) (Irish River (FR))

J R Jenkins M Ng

Placings:000/0135060300**626/026014520600004024/241 202420005-400005400**0 **(7888)**

2009: 12^{4}SD, 12^{0}SD, 13^{0}SD, 10^{0}SD, 11^{0}GF, 11^{5}GF, 14^{4}S, 16^{0}G, 10^{0}SD, 12^{0}SD,

	Starts	1st	2nd	3rd	Win & Pl
Career Total (Turf)	16	0	1	1	1288
Career Total (AW)	40	3	7	1	9324

59	2/08	Sthl	1m4f	(0-60)H	SS	£1911
61	2/07	Sthl	1m	(0-45)	SS	£1876
53	2/06	Sthl	7f	(0-45)	STD	£1365

Total win prize-money £5153

Going (Turf): **Sf: 0-1 GS: 0-1 Gd: 0-3 GF: 0-8 Fm: 0-3**
Distance: 5f/6f: 0-3 **7f-8f: 2-21** 9f-13f: 1-30 14f+: 0-2
Track : **LH: 3-37** RH: 0-15 Tight: 0-24 Gall: 0-1
Aids: Bl: 0-0 **Vi: 1-17** Tstrap: 0-2 Ckp: 0-2
Best Rating: **63** 4/08 Sthl 1m3f stand

Moderate; effective at around 1m4f; acts on sand.

Mid Wicket (USA)

85(95) (52)**50**

3-y-o b g Strong Hope (USA)-Sunday Bazaar (USA) (Nureyev (USA))
Mouse Hamilton-Fairley (B W Hills 1/6) Hamilton-Fairley Racing

Placings:0-600 **(7755)**
2009: 10^{6}GF, 10^{0}GF, 8^{0}SD,

	Starts	1st	2nd	3rd	Win & Pl
Career Total (Turf)	3	0	0	0	0
Career Total (AW)	1	0	0	0	

Going (Turf): **Sf: 0-0 GS: 0-0 Gd: 0-0 GF: 0-3 Fm: 0-0**
Distance: 5f/6f: 0-0 7f-8f: 0-1 9f-13f: 0-3 14f+: 0-0
Track : LH: 0-1 RH: 0-2 Tight: 0-3 Gall: 0-0
Aids: Bl: 0-0 Vi: 0-0 Tstrap: 0-0 Ckp: 0-0
Best Rating: **52** 12/09 Wolv 1m141y stand

Midas Way

91 (81)**84**

9-y-o ch g Halling (USA)-Arietta's Way (IRE) (Darshaan)
P R Chamings Mrs Alexandra J Chandris

Placings:01/616320/2030/3202560/665/**50**/0 **(2994)**
2009: 20^{0}GF,

	Starts	1st	2nd	3rd	Win & Pl
Career Total (Turf)	**24**	**2**	**4**	**3**	**57560**
Career Total (AW)	**1**	**0**	**0**	**0**	**466**
97 6/03 Sals	1m4f	C(0-95)H	G-F	£15457	
88 10/02 Newb	1m	D	SFT	£5193	

Total win prize-money £20651

Going (Turf): **Sf: 1-4** GS: 0-6 Gd: 0-5 **GF: 1-9** Fm: 0-0
Distance: 5f/6f: 0-0 7f-8f: 1-2 9f-13f: 1-8 14f+: 0-15
Track : LH: 0-9 **RH: 1-13 Tight: 1-10** Gall: 0-12
Aids: Bl: 0-0 Vi: 0-1 Tstrap: 0-0 Ckp: 0-0
Best Rating: **106** 7/05 Sand 2m78y gd-fm

Very useful; Listed placed; stays 2m, but effective at shorter; acts on most types of ground; has worn a visor; likes to race prominently; winning hurdler.

Midday

112 **120**

3-y-o b f Oasis Dream-Midsummer (Kingmambo (USA))
H R A Cecil K Abdulla

Placings:0314-2123131 **(7284a)**
2009: 10^{2}G, 11^{1}GF, 12^{2}G, 12^{3}HY, 9^{1}S, 10^{3}G, 10^{1}F,

	Starts	1st	2nd	3rd	Win & Pl
Career Total (Turf)	**11**	**4**	**2**	**3**	**1051704**
119 11/09 SnAt	1m2f		FRM	£750000	
120 8/09 Gdwd	1m1f192y		SFT	£113540	
106 5/09 Ling	1m3f106y		G-F	£28385	
84 9/08 NmkR	1m		G-F	£6476	

Total win prize-money £898401

Going (Turf): Sf: 1-2 GS: 0-1 Gd: 0-4 **GF: 2-3** Fm: 1-1
Distance: 5f/6f: 0-0 7f-8f: 1-4 **9f-13f: 3-7** 14f+: 0-0
Track : **LH: 2-4** RH: 1-4 **Tight: 2-4** Gall: 0-0
Aids: Bl: 0-0 Vi: 0-0 Tstrap: 0-0 Ckp: 0-0
Best Rating: **120** 8/09 Gdwd 1m1f192y soft

High class; winner of Lingfield Oaks Trial and runner-up in the Epsom Oaks; won the Nassau Stakes and the Breeders' Cup Filly & Mare Turf in 2009; effective over 1m2f-1m4f; acts on any ground.

Middle Club

99 **103**

2-y-o b f Fantastic Light (USA)-Anna Oleanda (IRE) (Old Vic)
R Hannon R J McCreery

Placings:3121 **(6045a)**
2009: 7^{3}GF, 7^{1}GF, 7^{2}GF, 8^{1}G,

	Starts	1st	2nd	3rd	Win & Pl
Career Total (Turf)	**4**	**2**	**1**	**1**	**51242**
103 9/09 Chan	1m		GD	£38835	
83 7/09 Newb	7f		G-F	£5180	

Total win prize-money £44016

Going (Turf): Sf: 0-0 GS: 0-0 **Gd: 1-1 GF: 1-3** Fm: 0-0
Distance: 5f/6f: 0-0 **7f-8f: 2-4** 9f-13f: 0-0 14f+: 0-0
Track : LH: 0-0 **RH: 1-2** Tight: 0-0 Gall: 0-0
Aids: Bl: 0-0 Vi: 0-0 Tstrap: 0-0 Ckp: 0-0
Best Rating: **103** 9/09 Chan 1m good

Useful; Listed placed; stays 7f and acts on fast ground.

Middle Of Nowhere (USA)

(111) (79)**11**

4-y-o b c Carson City (USA)-Ivy Leaf (IRE) (Nureyev (USA))
M A Magnusson Eastwind Racing Ltd and Martha Trussell

Placings:00-221 **(0493)**
2009: 10^{2}SD, 10^{2}SD, 12^{1}SD,

	Starts	1st	2nd	3rd	Win & Pl
Career Total (Turf)	**1**	**0**	**0**	**0**	
Career Total (AW)	**4**	**1**	**2**	**0**	**3458**
79 2/09 Sthl	1m4f	(0-65)H	STD	£2047	

Total win prize-money £2047

Going (Turf): **Sf: 0-0 GS: 0-0 Gd: 0-1 GF: 0-0 Fm: 0-0**
Distance: 5f/6f: 0-0 7f-8f: 0-0 **9f-13f: 1-5** 14f+: 0-0
Track : **LH: 1-5** RH: 0-0 Tight: 0-3 Gall: 0-0
Aids: Bl: 0-0 Vi: 0-0 Tstrap: 0-0 Ckp: 0-0
Best Rating: **79** 2/09 Sthl 1m4f stand

Modest half-brother to Distinction; should stay well.

Middlemarch (IRE)

108(94) (64)**79**

9-y-o ch g Grand Lodge (USA)-Blanche Dubois (Nashwan (USA))
J S Goldie W M Johnstone

Placings:12325016/04050/00050000050/0225253136**216**/005656110/40600000610**0**-53040050100 **(7014)**
2009: 7^{5}GF, 7^{3}GF, 8^{0}GF, 8^{4}GS, 7^{0}G, 7^{0}G, 8^{5}GS, 8^{0}GF, 10^{1}GS, 10^{0}GS, 10^{0}GS,

	Starts	1st	2nd	3rd	Win & Pl
Career Total (Turf)	**65**	**7**	**5**	**4**	**77002**
Career Total (AW)	**4**	**1**	**1**	**0**	**5139**
77 9/09 York	1m2f88y		G-S	£6540	
79 9/08 Rdcr	1m		G-S	£4857	
86 8/07 Newc	7f	(0-85)H	GD	£5047	
81 7/07 Asct	7f	(0-90)H	GD	£8744	
81 10/06 Wolv	1m141y	(0-75)H	SF	£3886	
78 8/06 Haml	1m65y	(0-85)H	GD	£6477	
98 10/03 Curr	1m		GD	£10551	
93 6/03 Curr	1m		GD	£8441	

Total win prize-money £54546

Going (Turf): Sf: 0-7 GS: 2-13 **Gd: 5-22** GF: 0-22 Fm: 0-0
Distance: 5f/6f: 0-0 **7f-8f: 5-37** 9f-13f: 3-32 14f+: 0-0
Track : LH: 2-25 **RH: 3-17** Tight: 2-12 **Gall: 3-13**
Aids: Bl: 3-14 Vi: 3-20 Tstrap: 0-16 Ckp: 0-16
Best Rating: **113** 10/03 Lonc 1m1f165y holding

Modest; effective at up to 1m2f; acts on most ground on turf; goes on Polytrack; has worn blinkers, a visor and cheekpieces.

Midfielder (USA)

(85) (54)

2-y-o ch c Smart Strike (CAN)-Quiet Weekend (USA) (Quiet American (USA))
J H M Gosden H R H Princess Haya Of Jordan

Placings:0 **(6772)**
2009: 8^{0}SD,

	Starts	1st	2nd	3rd	Win & Pl
Career Total (Turf)	**0**	**0**	**0**	**0**	
Career Total (AW)	**1**	**0**	**0**	**0**	

Going (Turf): **Sf: 0-0 GS: 0-0 Gd: 0-0 GF: 0-0 Fm: 0-0**
Distance: 5f/6f: 0-0 7f-8f: 0-1 9f-13f: 0-0 14f+: 0-0
Track : LH: 0-0 RH: 0-1 Tight: 0-0 Gall: 0-0
Aids: Bl: 0-0 Vi: 0-0 Tstrap: 0-0 Ckp: 0-0
Best Rating: **54** 10/09 Kemp 1m stand

Midget

90 **59**

2-y-o b f Invincible Spirit (IRE)-Sharp Mode (USA) (Diesis)
M A Magnusson East Wind Racing Ltd

Placings:1 **(2800)**
2009: 5^{1}F,

	Starts	1st	2nd	3rd	Win & Pl
Career Total (Turf)	**1**	**1**	**0**	**0**	**2267**
59 6/09 Bevl	5f		FRM	£2266	

Total win prize-money £2267

Going (Turf): Sf: 0-0 GS: 0-0 Gd: 0-0 GF: 0-0 **Fm: 1-1**
Distance: **5f/6f: 1-1** 7f-8f: 0-0 9f-13f: 0-0 14f+: 0-0
Track : LH: 0-0 RH: 0-0 Tight: 0-0 Gall: 0-0
Aids: Bl: 0-0 Vi: 0-0 Tstrap: 0-0 Ckp: 0-0
Best Rating: **59** 6/09 Bevl 5f firm

Claiming winner on her debut over 5f; handles quick ground.

Midnight Bay

94(99) (65)**66**

3-y-o br g Domedriver (IRE)-Serriera (FR) (Highest Honor (FR))
P D Evans (Mrs K J Stephens 25/10) Jeremiah Coffey

Placings:506-**46**00000350 **(7888)**
2009: 8^{4}SD, 12^{6}SD, 12^{0}SD, 8^{0}F, 7^{0}GF, 8^{0}GF, 8^{0}G, 12^{3}SD, 11^{5}SD, 12^{0}SD,

	Starts	1st	2nd	3rd	Win & Pl
Career Total (Turf)	**6**	**0**	**0**	**0**	**0**
Career Total (AW)	**7**	**0**	**0**	**1**	**403**

Going (Turf): **Sf: 0-0 GS: 0-2 Gd: 0-1 GF: 0-2 Fm: 0-1**
Distance: 5f/6f: 0-0 7f-8f: 0-3 9f-13f: 0-10 14f+: 0-0
Track : LH: 0-9 RH: 0-2 Tight: 0-8 Gall: 0-0
Aids: Bl: 0-0 Vi: 0-2 Tstrap: 0-0 Ckp: 0-0
Best Rating: **66** 10/08 Newb 1m gd-sft

Plating-class; stays 1m4f; acts on Polytrack.

Midnight Cruiser (IRE)

105(90) (69)99

3-y-o ch c Captain Rio-Kriva (Reference Point)

M bin Shafya (R Hannon 31/8) Sheikh Mansoor bin Mohammed al Maktoum

Placings:31440-03310020

2009: 8^{0}SD, 8^{3}G, 8^{3}G, 10^{1}GF, 10^{0}GF, 9^{0}G, 10^{2}G, 8^{0}FT,

	Starts	1st	2nd	3rd	Win & Pl
Career Total (Turf)	11	2	1	3	21084
Career Total (AW)	2	0	0	0	

96 6/09 Wind 1m2f7y (0-95)H G-F £8742
81 8/08 Newb 7f G-S £4209
Total win prize-money £12952

Going (Turf): Sf: 0-1 **GS: 1-2** Gd: 0-6 **GF: 1-2** Fm: 0-0
Distance: 5f/6f: 0-0 7f-8f: 1-7 9f-13f: 1-6 14f+: 0-0
Track : LH: 0-3 **RH: 1-4 Tight: 1-4** Gall: 0-1
Aids: Bl: 0-0 Vi: 0-0 Tstrap: 0-0 Ckp: 0-0
Best Rating: 99 8/09 Epsm 1m2f18y good

Very useful; effective over 7f-1m2f; acts on most ground.

Midnight Fantasy

103(101) (76)79

3-y-o b f Oasis Dream-Midnight Shift (IRE) (Night Shift (USA))

Rae Guest C J Mills

Placings:0023-15510120 (6765)

2009: 6^{1}GF, 6^{5}GF, 6^{5}G, 6^{1}SD, 6^{0}G, 6^{1}GF, 7^{2}GS, 6^{0}G,

	Starts	1st	2nd	3rd	Win & Pl
Career Total (Turf)	11	2	2	1	9287
Career Total (AW)	1	1	0	0	4727

79 8/09 Newc 6f (0-70)H G-F £2978
76 6/09 Kemp 6f (0-80)H STD £4727
74 5/09 Ripn 6f G-F £3238
Total win prize-money £10944

Going (Turf): Sf: 0-1 GS: 0-2 Gd: 0-5 **GF: 2-3** Fm: 0-0
Distance: 5f/6f: 3-9 7f-8f: 0-3 9f-13f: 0-0 14f+: 0-0
Track : LH: 0-2 **RH: 1-1** Tight: 0-1 Gall: 0-2
Aids: Bl: 0-0 Vi: 0-0 Tstrap: 0-0 Ckp: 0-0
Best Rating: 79 9/09 Epsm 7f gd-sft

Fair; stays 7f; acts on fast and soft ground and Polytrack.

Midnight In May (IRE)

100 78

3-y-o b g Mull Of Kintyre (USA)-Birthday (IRE) (Singspiel (IRE))

W R Muir C L A Edginton

Placings:531-3 (1462)

2009: 8^{3}G,

	Starts	1st	2nd	3rd	Win & Pl
Career Total (Turf)	4	1	0	2	4350

73 10/08 Brig 6f209y G-S £3108
Total win prize-money £3108

Going (Turf): Sf: 0-0 **GS: 1-1** Gd: 0-2 GF: 0-1 Fm: 0-0
Distance: 5f/6f: 0-0 **7f-8f: 1-3** 9f-13f: 0-1 14f+: 0-0
Track : LH: 1-3 RH: 0-1 Tight: 0-1 Gall: 0-0
Aids: Bl: 0-0 Vi: 0-0 Tstrap: 0-0 Ckp: 0-0
Best Rating: 78 10/08 Brig 7f214y good

Fair; effective over 7f-1m; acts on good and easy ground.

Midnight Martini

98 90

2-y-o b f Night Shift (USA)-Shaken And Stirred (Cadeaux Genereux)

T D Easterby D A West

Placings:441112 (6090)

2009: 5^{4}G, 6^{4}G, 5^{1}G, 5^{1}GS, 6^{1}GF, 6^{2}G,

	Starts	1st	2nd	3rd	Win & Pl
Career Total (Turf)	6	3	1	0	174711

89 8/09 York 6f G-F £147720
83 8/09 Thsk 5f G-S £8159
73 6/09 Carl 5f GD £3238
Total win prize-money £159118

Going (Turf): Sf: 0-0 **GS: 1-1 Gd: 1-4 GF: 1-1** Fm: 0-0
Distance: 5f/6f: 3-6 7f-8f: 0-0 9f-13f: 0-0 14f+: 0-0
Track : LH: 0-1 **RH: 1-1** Tight: 0-0 **Gall: 1-1**
Aids: Bl: 0-0 Vi: 0-0 Tstrap: 0-0 Ckp: 0-0
Best Rating: 90 9/09 Ayr 6f good

Very useful; suited by 5f-6f; acts on fast and easy ground.

Midnight Strider (IRE)

(100) (71)

3-y-o br c Golan (IRE)-Danish Gem (Danehill (USA))

Tom Dascombe Owen Promotions Limited

Placings:22 (7863)

2009: 7^{2}SD, 8^{2}SD,

	Starts	1st	2nd	3rd	Win & Pl
Career Total (Turf)	0	0	0	0	
Career Total (AW)	2	0	2	0	1612

Going (Turf): Sf: 0-0 GS: 0-0 Gd: 0-0 GF: 0-0 Fm: 0-0
Distance: 5f/6f: 0-0 7f-8f: 0-1 9f-13f: 0-1 14f+: 0-0
Track : LH: 0-2 RH: 0-0 Tight: 0-2 Gall: 0-0
Aids: Bl: 0-0 Vi: 0-0 Tstrap: 0-0 Ckp: 0-0
Best Rating: 71 12/09 Wolv 7f32y stand

Modest; should be suited by further than 1m; acts on Polytrack.

Midnight Uno

84(83) (51)55

2-y-o b g Desert Style (IRE)-Carati (Selkirk (USA))

W G M Turner Mrs Tracy Turner

Placings:43300 (3925)

2009: 5^{4}SD, 5^{3}GS, 5^{3}GF, 7^{0}GF, 5^{0}SF,

	Starts	1st	2nd	3rd	Win & Pl
Career Total (Turf)	3	0	0	2	952
Career Total (AW)	2	0	0	0	0

Going (Turf): Sf: 0-0 GS: 0-1 Gd: 0-0 GF: 0-2 Fm: 0-0
Distance: 5f/6f: 0-4 7f-8f: 0-1 9f-13f: 0-0 14f+: 0-0
Track : LH: 0-2 RH: 0-0 Tight: 0-1 Gall: 0-0
Aids: Bl: 0-0 Vi: 0-1 Tstrap: 0-0 Ckp: 0-0
Best Rating: 55 5/09 Haml 5f4y gd-sft

Modest; stays 6f and acts on fast ground.

Midnite Blews (IRE)

87 (29)61

4-y-o gr g Trans Island-Felicita (IRE) (Catrail (USA))

M A Barnes Minstrel's Double Racing

Placings:4425500/3401503565-60 (3291)

2009: 12^{6}GS, 13^{0}GF,

	Starts	1st	2nd	3rd	Win & Pl
Career Total (Turf)	18	1	1	2	3842
Career Total (AW)	1	0	0	0	

61 6/08 Bath 5f11y GD £1748
Total win prize-money £1749

Going (Turf): Sf: 0-3 GS: 0-3 **Gd: 1-2** GF: 0-8 Fm: 0-2
Distance: 5f/6f: 1-12 7f-8f: 0-4 9f-13f: 0-2 14f+: 0-1
Track : LH: 1-12 RH: 0-2 Tight: 0-4 **Gall: 1-5**
Aids: Bl: 0-1 Vi: 0-0 Tstrap: 0-1 Ckp: 0-1
Best Rating: 66 8/07 Brig 6f209y firm

Moderate; off the mark in 5f claimer at Bath June 2008; effective at 6f; acts on fast ground.

Midsummer Madness (IRE)

68(83) (49)7

3-y-o b f Alhaarth (IRE)-Robalana (USA) (Wild Again (USA))

David Pinder Ambermarley Partnership

Placings:000-0 (1148)

2009: 10^{0}G,

	Starts	1st	2nd	3rd	Win & Pl
Career Total (Turf)	1	0	0	0	
Career Total (AW)	3	0	0	0	

Going (Turf): Sf: 0-0 GS: 0-0 Gd: 0-1 GF: 0-0 Fm: 0-0
Distance: 5f/6f: 0-0 7f-8f: 0-3 9f-13f: 0-1 14f+: 0-0
Track : LH: 0-2 RH: 0-2 Tight: 0-2 Gall: 0-1
Aids: Bl: 0-0 Vi: 0-0 Tstrap: 0-0 Ckp: 0-0
Best Rating: 49 10/08 Ling 1m stand

Midwestern (USA)

98 71

2-y-o b/br g Tiznow (USA)-She's Enough (USA) (Exploit (USA))

M L W Bell H E Sheikh Rashid Bin Mohammed

Placings:604 (6922)

2009: 6^{6}GF, 6^{0}GS, 6^{4}GF,

	Starts	1st	2nd	3rd	Win & Pl
Career Total (Turf)	3	0	0	0	283

Going (Turf): Sf: 0-0 GS: 0-1 Gd: 0-0 GF: 0-2 Fm: 0-0
Distance: 5f/6f: 0-0 7f-8f: 0-3 9f-13f: 0-0 14f+: 0-0
Track : LH: 0-0 RH: 0-0 Tight: 0-0 Gall: 0-0
Aids: Bl: 0-0 Vi: 0-0 Tstrap: 0-0 Ckp: 0-0
Best Rating: 71 10/09 Yarm 6f3y gd-fm

Miesko (USA)

73(92) (55)42

4-y-o b g Quiet American (USA)-Polish Style (USA) (Danzig (USA))

M G Quinlan (Adrian McGuinness 1/9) T Manning

Placings:2602511/0000-00005 (7605)

2009: 6^{0}S, 7^{0}SH, 6^{0}SD, 6^{0}SD, 5^{5}SD,

	Starts	1st	2nd	3rd	Win & Pl
Career Total (Turf)	10	2	1	0	8300
Career Total (AW)	6	0	1	0	867

86 10/07 Bath 5f11y (0-85) G-F £4857
75 10/07 Catt 5f GD £2266
Total win prize-money £7125

Going (Turf):	Sf: 0-1 GS: 0-0 **Gd: 1-5 GF: 1-2** Fm: 0-1
Distance:	**5f/6f: 2-11** 7f-8f: 0-4 9f-13f: 0-1 14f+: 0-0
Track :	**LH: 1-8** RH: 0-3 Tight: 0-3 **Gall: 1-1**
Aids:	Bl: 0-1 Vi: 0-0 Tstrap: 0-0 Ckp: 0-0
Best Rating:	**86** 10/07 Bath 5f11y gd-fm

Useful; effective at 5f and acts on good and faster ground.

Mighty Aphrodite

79 **46**

2-y-o b f Observatory (USA)-Sahara Rose (Green Desert (USA))

Rae Guest Mrs Paula Smith

Placings:0 **(6797)**

2009: 6^{0}S,

	Starts	1st	2nd	3rd	Win & Pl
Career Total (Turf)	1	0	0	0	

Going (Turf):	**Sf: 0-1 GS: 0-0 Gd: 0-0 GF: 0-0 Fm: 0-0**
Distance:	5f/6f: 0-0 7f-8f: 0-1 9f-13f: 0-0 14f+: 0-0
Track :	LH: 0-0 RH: 0-0 Tight: 0-0 Gall: 0-0
Aids:	Bl: 0-0 Vi: 0-0 Tstrap: 0-0 Ckp: 0-0
Best Rating:	**46** 10/09 Nott 6f15y soft

Mighty Clarets (IRE)

90 **65**

2-y-o br g Whipper (USA)-Collected (IRE) (Taufan (USA))

R A Fahey Dale Scaffolding Co Ltd

Placings:00343 **(6895)**

2009: 6^{0}GS, 6^{0}GF, 6^{3}G, 7^{4}GF, 8^{3}GF,

	Starts	1st	2nd	3rd	Win & Pl
Career Total (Turf)	5	0	0	2	1382

Going (Turf):	**Sf: 0-0 GS: 0-1 Gd: 0-1 GF: 0-3 Fm: 0-0**
Distance:	5f/6f: 0-3 7f-8f: 0-1 9f-13f: 0-1 14f+: 0-0
Track :	LH: 0-1 RH: 0-0 Tight: 0-0 Gall: 0-0
Aids:	Bl: 0-0 Vi: 0-0 Tstrap: 0-0 Ckp: 0-0
Best Rating:	**65** 9/09 Leic 7f9y gd-fm

Fair; stays 6f and acts on good ground.

Mighty Kitchener (USA)

(94) (54)**55**

6-y-o br g Mighty (USA)-Libeccio (NZ) (Danzatore (CAN))

P Howling Paul Howling

Placings:20/04500432/30123200041105000060/00566-50 **(0877)**

2009: 14^{5}SD, 12^{0}SD,

	Starts	1st	2nd	3rd	Win & Pl
Career Total (Turf)	6	0	0	0	0
Career Total (AW)	30	3	4	3	12486

72	8/07	Wolv	1m4f50y	(0-70)H	STD	£3562
67	8/07	Wolv	1m5f194y	(0-65)H	STD	£2559
61	1/07	Wolv	1m5f194y		SS	£2388

Total win prize-money £8510

Going (Turf):	**Sf: 0-0 GS: 0-1 Gd: 0-1 GF: 0-4 Fm: 0-0**
Distance:	5f/6f: 0-0 7f-8f: 0-2 9f-13f: 1-24 **14f+: 2-10**
Track :	**LH: 3-28** RH: 0-8 **Tight: 3-22** Gall: 0-3
Aids:	Bl: 0-0 Vi: 0-0 Tstrap: 0-0 Ckp: 0-0
Best Rating:	**72** 8/07 Wolv 1m4f50y stand

Modest; effective over 1m4f-1m6f; acts on Polytrack.

Mighty Mambo

(93) (66)

2-y-o b c Fantastic Light (USA)-Mambo's Melody (Kingmambo (USA))

Jane Chapple-Hyam Norcroft Park Stud

Placings:2 **(7502)**

2009: 8^{2}SD,

	Starts	1st	2nd	3rd	Win & Pl
Career Total (Turf)	0	0	0	0	
Career Total (AW)	1	0	1	0	771

Going (Turf):	**Sf: 0-0 GS: 0-0 Gd: 0-0 GF: 0-0 Fm: 0-0**
Distance:	5f/6f: 0-0 7f-8f: 0-1 9f-13f: 0-0 14f+: 0-0
Track :	LH: 0-1 RH: 0-0 Tight: 0-0 Gall: 0-0
Aids:	Bl: 0-0 Vi: 0-0 Tstrap: 0-0 Ckp: 0-0
Best Rating:	**66** 11/09 Sthl 1m stand

A half-brother to AW winner Keenes Day; promise on debut over 1m at Southwell.

Mighty Moon

107(91) (78)**85**

6-y-o gr g Daylami (IRE)-Moon Magic (Polish Precedent (USA))

R A Fahey Enda Hunston

Placings:4000/001231**625**/45600543240402/210502-016 **(2085)**

2009: 16^{0}SD, 16^{1}S, 14^{6}GF,

	Starts	1st	2nd	3rd	Win & Pl
Career Total (Turf)	32	4	5	2	32564
Career Total (AW)	4	0	1	0	3009

85	4/09	Newb	2m	(0-85)H	SFT	£6476
82	5/08	York	2m2f	(0-80)H	G-F	£7123
89	10/06	Catt	1m5f175y	(0-75)H	SFT	£3886
71	7/06	NmkJ	1m2f	(0-70)H	G-S	£3747

Total win prize-money £21234

Going (Turf):	**Sf: 2-6** GS: 1-4 Gd: 0-9 GF: 1-11 Fm: 0-1
Distance:	5f/6f: 0-1 7f-8f: 0-2 9f-13f: 1-12 **14f+: 3-21**
Track :	**LH: 3-23** RH: 1-12 Tight: 1-17 **Gall: 2-8**
Aids:	**Bl: 2-13** Vi: 0-0 Tstrap: 0-3 Ckp: 0-3
Best Rating:	**90** 12/06 Sthl 1m4f stand

Useful; stays 2m2f; acts on most ground and on Fibresand; has worn a tongue tie and blinkers.

Mighty Mover (IRE)

97(102) (59)**57**

7-y-o ch g Bahhare (USA)-Ericeira (IRE) (Anita's Prince)

B Palling Bryn Palling

Placings:6/0/00042120/0022000540-33160 **(7600)**

2009: 8^{3}GS, 8^{3}GF, 8^{1}SD, 8^{6}SD, 9^{0}SD,

	Starts	1st	2nd	3rd	Win & Pl
Career Total (Turf)	6	0	0	2	742
Career Total (AW)	19	2	4	0	6468

59	10/09	Wolv	1m141y	(0-50)H	STD	£2183
60	11/07	Wolv	1m1f103y	(0-55)H	STD	£2047

Total win prize-money £4232

Going (Turf):	**Sf: 0-0 GS: 0-2 Gd: 0-3 GF: 0-1 Fm: 0-0**
Distance:	5f/6f: 0-0 7f-8f: 0-2 **9f-13f: 2-22** 14f+: 0-1
Track :	**LH: 2-23** RH: 0-0 **Tight: 2-21** Gall: 0-0
Aids:	Bl: 0-0 Vi: 0-0 Tstrap: 0-0 Ckp: 0-0
Best Rating:	**66** 2/08 Wolv 1m1f103y stand

Moderate; effective at around 1m2f; acts on Polytrack.

Migliori

95(73) (14)**55**

3-y-o b g Royal Applause-Millyant (Primo Dominie)

Rae Guest Bradmill Ltd

Placings:5045060 **(6755)**

2009: 5^{5}SD, 6^{0}S, 5^{4}S, 6^{5}G, 6^{0}G, 5^{6}G, 7^{0}G,

	Starts	1st	2nd	3rd	Win & Pl
Career Total (Turf)	6	0	0	0	216
Career Total (AW)	1	0	0	0	0

Going (Turf):	**Sf: 0-2 GS: 0-0 Gd: 0-4 GF: 0-0 Fm: 0-0**
Distance:	5f/6f: 0-4 7f-8f: 0-3 9f-13f: 0-0 14f+: 0-0
Track :	LH: 0-1 RH: 0-0 Tight: 0-0 Gall: 0-1
Aids:	Bl: 0-0 Vi: 0-0 Tstrap: 0-0 Ckp: 0-0
Best Rating:	**55** 8/09 Yarm 6f3y good

Cost 40,000gns and is a half-brother to three sprint winners; promise on debut over 5f on Fibresand.

Mijas Playa

95 **78**

2-y-o b f Avonbridge-Rainbow Spectrum (FR) (Spectrum (IRE))

C A Dwyer R S G Jones

Placings:2522010050 **(6841)**

2009: 5^{2}GF, 5^{5}GF, 5^{2}G, 5^{2}GF, 5^{0}G, 5^{1}G, 5^{0}GS, 5^{0}GF, 5^{5}GF, 5^{0}G,

	Starts	1st	2nd	3rd	Win & Pl
Career Total (Turf)	10	1	3	0	10389

78	7/09	Ffos	5f	GD	£4857

Total win prize-money £4857

Going (Turf):	Sf: 0-0 GS: 0-1 **Gd: 1-4** GF: 0-5 Fm: 0-0
Distance:	**5f/6f: 1-10** 7f-8f: 0-0 9f-13f: 0-0 14f+: 0-0
Track :	LH: 0-1 RH: 0-0 Tight: 0-1 Gall: 0-0
Aids:	Bl: 0-0 Vi: 0-0 Tstrap: 0-0 Ckp: 0-0
Best Rating:	**78** 7/09 Ffos 5f good

Fair; suited by 5f and fast ground.

Mik

50

3-y-o b g Baryshnikov (AUS)-Daphne's Doll (IRE) (Polish Patriot (USA))

Dr J R J Naylor Mrs S P Elphick

Placings:0 **(3425)**

2009: 9^{0}G,

	Starts	1st	2nd	3rd	Win & Pl
Career Total (Turf)	1	0	0	0	

Going (Turf):	**Sf: 0-0 GS: 0-0 Gd: 0-1 GF: 0-0 Fm: 0-0**
Distance:	5f/6f: 0-0 7f-8f: 0-0 9f-13f: 0-1 14f+: 0-0
Track :	LH: 0-0 RH: 0-1 Tight: 0-1 Gall: 0-0
Aids:	Bl: 0-0 Vi: 0-0 Tstrap: 0-0 Ckp: 0-0

Mikado

(88) (44)**74**

8-y-o b g Sadler's Wells (USA)-Free At Last (Shirley Heights)

Jonjo O'Neill John P McManus

Placings:211/44351/0000-6 **(0003)**

2009: 14^{6}SS,

	Starts	1st	2nd	3rd	Win & Pl
Career Total (Turf)	11	3	1	1	80717
Career Total (AW)	2	0	0	0	0

114	10/04	Curr	1m2f	Y-S	£25214

98 11/03 Leop 1m1f GD £21103
85 9/03 List 1m GD £8441
Total win prize-money £54761

Going (Turf): Sf: 0-2 GS: 0-0 Gd: 2-6 GF: 0-2 Fm: 0-0
Distance: 5f/6f: 0-0 7f-8f: 1-1 9f-13f: 2-4 14f+: 0-8
Track : LH: 1-8 RH: 1-3 Tight: 0-2 Gall: 0-4
Aids: Bl: 0-0 Vi: 0-1 Tstrap: 0-3 Ckp: 0-3
Best Rating: 118 9/04 Donc 1m6f132y gd-fm

Mikhail Glinka (IRE)

107 106
2-y-o b c Galileo (IRE)-Lady Karr (Mark Of Esteem (IRE))
A P O'Brien Mrs John Magnier, M Tabor & D Smith

Placings:12612 (7404a)
2009: 8^{1}YS, 8^{2}GY, 8^{6}G, 9^{1}HY, 10^{2}HY,

	Starts	1st	2nd	3rd	Win & Pl
Career Total (Turf)	5	2	2	0	102441

104 11/09 Leop 1m1f HVY £26861
81 8/09 Gway 1m100y Y-S £11740
Total win prize-money £38602

Going (Turf): Sf: 1-2 GS: 0-0 Gd: 0-1 GF: 0-0 Fm: 0-0
Distance: 5f/6f: 0-0 7f-8f: 0-1 9f-13f: 2-4 14f+: 0-0
Track : LH: 1-3 RH: 1-2 Tight: 0-0 Gall: 0-1
Aids: Bl: 0-0 Vi: 0-0 Tstrap: 0-0 Ckp: 0-0
Best Rating: 106 11/09 StCl 1m2f heavy

Very useful; effective at 1m; acts on easy ground.

Mildoura (FR)

102(108) (91)88
4-y-o b f Sendawar (IRE)-Miliana (IRE) (Polar Falcon (USA))
Mrs L J Mongan Mrs P J Sheen

Placings:52126-5120011 (7811)
2009: 12^{5}SD, 12^{1}GS, 10^{2}S, 10^{0}G, 13^{0}SD, 12^{1}SD, 12^{1}SD,

	Starts	1st	2nd	3rd	Win & Pl
Career Total (Turf)	8	2	3	0	17254
Career Total (AW)	4	2	0	0	9455

91 12/09 Ling 1m4f (0-85)H STD £4727
89 11/09 Kemp 1m4f (0-80)H STD £4727
81 3/09 Folk 1m4f (0-75)H G-S £3070
10/08 Claf 1m3f G-S £5514
Total win prize-money £18040

Going (Turf): Sf: 0-3 GS: 2-2 Gd: 0-1 GF: 0-2 Fm: 0-0
Distance: 5f/6f: 0-0 7f-8f: 0-0 9f-13f: 4-12 14f+: 0-0
Track : LH: 1-5 RH: 2-2 Tight: 2-4 Gall: 0-2
Aids: Bl: 0-0 Vi: 0-0 Tstrap: 0-0 Ckp: 0-0
Best Rating: 91 12/09 Ling 1m4f stand

Useful; stays 1m4f; acts on soft ground; goes on Polytrack.

Mile High Lad (USA)

94(103) (74)53
3-y-o b/br g Sky Mesa (USA)-Thunder Warmth (USA) (Thunder Gulch (USA))
George Baker Jerry Jamgotchian

Placings:002-33404500 (7576)
2009: 10^{3}SD, 11^{3}SD, 10^{4}G, 11^{0}SD, 10^{4}G, 9^{5}SD, 12^{0}SD, 8^{0}SD,

	Starts	1st	2nd	3rd	Win & Pl
Career Total (Turf)	2	0	0	0	433
Career Total (AW)	9	0	1	2	2070

Going (Turf): Sf: 0-0 GS: 0-0 Gd: 0-2 GF: 0-0 Fm: 0-0
Distance: 5f/6f: 0-0 7f-8f: 0-2 9f-13f: 0-9 14f+: 0-0
Track : LH: 0-7 RH: 0-4 Tight: 0-5 Gall: 0-1
Aids: Bl: 0-0 Vi: 0-1 Tstrap: 0-3 Ckp: 0-3
Best Rating: 74 1/09 Ling 1m2f stand

Fair; effective over 1m2f; acts on Polytrack.

Milemilia (IRE)

96(94) (63)49
3-y-o b f Milan-Emilia Romagna (GER) (Acatenango (GER))
H Morrison Mrs G C Maxwell & Partners

Placings:003000060 (4142)
2009: 8^{0}SD, 10^{0}SD, 12^{3}SD, 11^{0}GF, 14^{0}F, 12^{0}SD, 12^{0}SD, 11^{6}GF, 16^{0}G,

	Starts	1st	2nd	3rd	Win & Pl
Career Total (Turf)	4	0	0	0	0
Career Total (AW)	5	0	0	1	403

Going (Turf): Sf: 0-0 GS: 0-0 Gd: 0-1 GF: 0-2 Fm: 0-1
Distance: 5f/6f: 0-0 7f-8f: 0-1 9f-13f: 0-6 14f+: 0-2
Track : LH: 0-6 RH: 0-3 Tight: 0-5 Gall: 0-0
Aids: Bl: 0-2 Vi: 0-0 Tstrap: 0-0 Ckp: 0-0
Best Rating: 63 3/09 Ling 1m4f stand

Fair; stays 1m4f and acts on Polytrack.

Militarist (USA)

101(89) (63)92
3-y-o b g War Chant (USA)-Season's Greetings (IRE) (Ezzoud (IRE))
J H M Gosden H R H Princess Haya Of Jordan

Placings:126540 (5986)
2009: 8^{1}GF, 8^{2}G, 8^{6}GF, 8^{5}G, 7^{4}G, 8^{0}SD,

	Starts	1st	2nd	3rd	Win & Pl
Career Total (Turf)	5	1	1	0	9619
Career Total (AW)	1	0	0	0	

81 4/09 NmkR 1m G-F £6476
Total win prize-money £6476

Going (Turf): Sf: 0-0 GS: 0-0 Gd: 0-3 GF: 1-2 Fm: 0-0
Distance: 5f/6f: 0-0 7f-8f: 1-5 9f-13f: 0-1 14f+: 0-0
Track : LH: 0-0 RH: 0-3 Tight: 0-0 Gall: 0-0
Aids: Bl: 0-1 Vi: 0-0 Tstrap: 0-0 Ckp: 0-0
Best Rating: 92 4/09 Sand 1m14y good

Useful; won the Wood Ditton on debut; stays 1m; acts on fast ground.

Military Call

101 74
2-y-o b c Royal Applause-Trump Street (First Trump)
E S McMahon J C Fretwell

Placings:425156 (4739)
2009: 5^{4}GF, 5^{2}GS, 5^{5}GF, 6^{1}F, 5^{5}GS, 6^{6}GF,

	Starts	1st	2nd	3rd	Win & Pl
Career Total (Turf)	6	1	1	0	3544

74 7/09 Rdcr 6f FRM £2388
Total win prize-money £2388

Going (Turf): Sf: 0-0 GS: 0-2 Gd: 0-0 GF: 0-3 Fm: 1-1
Distance: 5f/6f: 1-6 7f-8f: 0-0 9f-13f: 0-0 14f+: 0-0
Track : LH: 0-0 RH: 0-0 Tight: 0-0 Gall: 0-0
Aids: Bl: 0-0 Vi: 0-0 Tstrap: 0-0 Ckp: 0-0
Best Rating: 74 7/09 Rdcr 6f firm

Modest form in maidens at 5f on fast and easy ground.

Military Power

105(97) (104)100
4-y-o b c Dubai Destination (USA)-Susun Kelapa (USA) (St Jovite (USA))
Saeed Bin Suroor (M bin Shafya 13/3) Godolphin

Placings:35/2311240-2050014 (2342)
2009: 8^{2}FT, 10^{0}G, 10^{5}G, 9^{0}FT, 8^{0}FT, 9^{1}SD, 10^{4}GF,

	Starts	1st	2nd	3rd	Win & Pl
Career Total (Turf)	10	2	1	2	41299
Career Total (AW)	6	1	2	0	23157

104 3/09 Jebl 1m1f (75-100)H STD £10227
85 6/08 York 1m2f88y (0-100)H GD £14247
86 5/08 Rdcr 1m2f G-F £2331
Total win prize-money £26805

Going (Turf): Sf: 0-0 GS: 0-0 Gd: 1-4 GF: 1-6 Fm: 0-0
Distance: 5f/6f: 0-0 7f-8f: 0-5 9f-13f: 3-11 14f+: 0-0
Track : LH: 2-9 RH: 0-3 Tight: 1-4 Gall: 1-6
Aids: Bl: 0-0 Vi: 0-0 Tstrap: 0-0 Ckp: 0-0
Best Rating: 104 3/09 Jebl 1m1f stand

Very useful; stays 1m2f; acts on good and faster ground and on sand; likes to race prominently.

Mill Beattie

(91) (45)54
4-y-o b f Beat All (USA)-Step On Degas (Superpower)
J Mackie M T Bloore & Mrs J E Lockwood

Placings:0450304-050 (0857)
2009: 12^{0}SD, 9^{5}SF, 11^{0}SD,

	Starts	1st	2nd	3rd	Win & Pl
Career Total (Turf)	7	0	0	1	751
Career Total (AW)	3	0	0	0	0

Going (Turf): Sf: 0-2 GS: 0-1 Gd: 0-1 GF: 0-3 Fm: 0-0
Distance: 5f/6f: 0-0 7f-8f: 0-1 9f-13f: 0-9 14f+: 0-0
Track : LH: 0-6 RH: 0-4 Tight: 0-4 Gall: 0-0
Aids: Bl: 0-0 Vi: 0-0 Tstrap: 0-0 Ckp: 0-0
Best Rating: 54 8/08 Ripn 1m1f170y gd-sft

Moderate; stays 1m2f; acts on fast and easy ground.

Millagros (IRE)

87(86) (26)47
9-y-o b m Pennekamp (USA)-Grey Galava (Generous (IRE))
I Semple James A Cringan

Placings:20250143510641 0/044633133400/05541043342 /10040/5/0003 (2592)
2009: 13^{0}SF, 9^{0}SD, 12^{0}GS, 15^{3}GF,

	Starts	1st	2nd	3rd	Win & Pl
Career Total (Turf)	40	5	3	8	42196
Career Total (AW)	8	1	0	0	3239

70 1/06 Wolv 1m4f50y (0-70)H STD £3238
74 7/05 Haml 1m3f16y (0-70)H G-F £3575
77 8/04 Ayr 1m E(0-70) SFT £3516
85 10/03 Muss 1m D(0-85)H G-F £5200
81 8/03 Carl 7f200y E(0-70)H FRM £3734
74 6/03 Haml 1m1f36y D FRM £7441
Total win prize-money £26707

Going (Turf): Sf: 1-4 GS: 0-11 Gd: 0-9 GF: 2-13 Fm: 2-3
Distance: 5f/6f: 0-0 7f-8f: 3-8 9f-13f: 3-34 14f+: 0-6
Track : LH: 2-23 RH: 4-24 Tight: 4-33 Gall: 0-2
Aids: Bl: 0-0 Vi: 0-2 Tstrap: 1-6 Ckp: 1-6
Best Rating: 87 11/03 Donc 1m2f60y good

Millden

(90) (55)

2-y-o b g Compton Place-Pretty Poppy (Song)

H Candy Thurloe Thoroughbreds XVIII

Placings:0 (7736)

2009: 6^{0}SD,

	Starts	1st	2nd	3rd	Win & Pl
Career Total (Turf)	0	0	0	0	
Career Total (AW)	1	0	0	0	

Going (Turf): Sf: 0-0 GS: 0-0 Gd: 0-0 GF: 0-0 Fm: 0-0
Distance: 5f/6f: 0-1 7f-8f: 0-0 9f-13f: 0-0 14f+: 0-0
Track : LH: 0-0 RH: 0-1 Tight: 0-0 Gall: 0-0
Aids: Bl: 0-1 Vi: 0-0 Tstrap: 0-0 Ckp: 0-0
Best Rating: 55 12/09 Kemp 6f stand

Milldown Story

99(102) (71)71

3-y-o b f Lucky Story (USA)-Barnacla (IRE) (Bluebird (USA))

B R Millman Mrs J E & J F S Laws

Placings:63332310 (7138)

2009: 6^{6}GF, 6^{3}GF, 6^{3}G, 7^{3}G, 6^{2}SD, 5^{3}G, 5^{1}SD, 5^{0}SD,

	Starts	1st	2nd	3rd	Win & Pl
Career Total (Turf)	5	0	0	4	2215
Career Total (AW)	3	1	1	0	3636

62 9/09 Wolv 5f216y STD £2729

Total win prize-money £2730

Going (Turf): Sf: 0-0 GS: 0-0 Gd: 0-3 GF: 0-2 Fm: 0-0
Distance: **5f/6f: 1-6** 7f-8f: 0-2 9f-13f: 0-0 14f+: 0-0
Track : **LH: 1-4** RH: 0-0 **Tight: 1-2** Gall: 0-1
Aids: Bl: 0-0 Vi: 0-0 Tstrap: 0-0 Ckp: 0-0
Best Rating: 71 8/09 Sthl 6f stand

Modest; suited by 6f; suited by fast ground, Fibresand and Polytrack.

Millers Crossing

90 61

3-y-o b g Tobougg (IRE)-Tweed Mill (Selkirk (USA))

W J H Ratcliffe W J H Ratcliffe

Placings:450 (3175)

2009: 7^{4}GF, 6^{5}S, 6^{0}GF,

	Starts	1st	2nd	3rd	Win & Pl
Career Total (Turf)	3	0	0	0	493

Going (Turf): Sf: 0-1 GS: 0-0 Gd: 0-0 GF: 0-2 Fm: 0-0
Distance: 5f/6f: 0-1 7f-8f: 0-2 9f-13f: 0-0 14f+: 0-0
Track : LH: 0-0 RH: 0-0 Tight: 0-0 Gall: 0-0
Aids: Bl: 0-0 Vi: 0-0 Tstrap: 0-0 Ckp: 0-0
Best Rating: 61 6/09 Yarm 6f3y soft

Millfield (IRE)

97(107) (81)79

6-y-o br g Elnadim (USA)-Eschasse (USA) (Zilzal (USA))

P R Chamings Inhurst Players

Placings:013130/0560000/40661200031312З/0223151060 5210035001-62605000035121435 (7575)

2009: 8^{6}SD, 7^{2}SD, 8^{6}SD, 8^{0}SD, 8^{5}SD, 8^{0}SD, 9^{0}GF, 8^{0}GF, 8^{0}GF, 8^{3}SD, 6^{5}F, 8^{1}SD, 7^{2}SD, 7^{1}SD, 7^{4}SD, 7^{3}SD, 8^{5}SD,

	Starts	1st	2nd	3rd	Win & Pl
Career Total (Turf)	27	4	1	2	16241
Career Total (AW)	38	7	6	7	23583

80	10/09	Kemp	7f	(0-75)H	STD	£2266
74	9/09	Kemp	1m		STD	£2047
79	11/08	Kemp	1m	(0-70)H	STD	£2266
81	7/08	Kemp	1m	(0-70)H	STD	£3238
79	4/08	Brig	7f214y	(0-70)H	GD	£2460
77	3/08	Ling	1m	(0-70)H	STD	£2590
73	12/07	Kemp	7f	(0-65)H	STD	£2047
64	11/07	Ling	7f	(0-60)H	STD	£1706
63	8/07	Brig	6f209y	(0-70)H	G-F	£2775
79	7/05	Catt	7f		FRM	£3493
69	6/05	Catt	5f		FRM	£4180

Total win prize-money £29076

Going (Turf): Sf: 0-1 GS: 0-3 Gd: 1-4 GF: 1-13 **Fm: 2-6**
Distance: 5f/6f: 1-12 **7f-8f: 10-46** 9f-13f: 0-7 14f+: 0-0
Track : LH: 5-29 RH: 5-25 **Tight: 3-21** Gall: 0-1
Aids: Bl: 0-1 Vi: 0-0 Tstrap: 0-0 Ckp: 0-0
Best Rating: 81 7/08 Kemp 1m stand

Fair; effective over 7f-1m; suited by fast ground; also goes on sand.

Millfields Dreams

103(102) (72)76

10-y-o b g Dreams End-Millfields Lady (Sayf El Arab (USA))

G C Bravery Mrs Theresa Fitsall

Placings:0/0404604/1000060005/1523222000446614/103 5400430/0224603120000-243522604600 (5182)

2009: 7^{2}GF, 6^{4}GF, 8^{3}GF, 7^{5}GF, 7^{2}GF, 10^{2}G, 6^{6}S, 8^{0}G, 6^{4}GF, 6^{6}G, 8^{0}G, 7^{0}G,

	Starts	1st	2nd	3rd	Win & Pl
Career Total (Turf)	53	2	9	3	26174
Career Total (AW)	16	3	1	2	9405

72	7/08	Kemp	7f	(0-70)H	STD	£2590
73	1/07	Wolv	5f216y	(0-65)H	STD	£2388
66	12/06	Kemp	6f	(0-53)H	STD	£2590
58	6/06	Folk	5f	(0-60)H	G-F	£2730
63	6/04	Chep	6f16y	E(0-70)H	G-F	£3926

Total win prize-money £14226

Going (Turf): Sf: 0-3 GS: 0-6 Gd: 0-13 **GF: 2-30** Fm: 0-1
Distance: **5f/6f: 3-39** 7f-8f: 2-23 9f-13f: 0-7 14f+: 0-0
Track : LH: 1-21 **RH: 2-7 Tight: 1-11** Gall: 0-5
Aids: Bl: 0-0 Vi: 0-0 Tstrap: 1-26 Ckp: 1-26
Best Rating: 76 6/09 Newc 6f soft

Fair; effective over 7f-1m2f; acts on most ground and on Polytrack; often wears cheekpieces.

Millharbour (IRE)

98(96) (56)69

3-y-o b g Nayef (USA)-My Funny Valentine (IRE) (Mukaddamah (USA))

B W Hills C J O'Shea And Co Ltd

Placings:00-404466 (6475)

2009: 10^{4}G, 12^{0}GF, 12^{4}GF, 10^{4}GF, 8^{6}SD, 10^{6}GF,

	Starts	1st	2nd	3rd	Win & Pl
Career Total (Turf)	7	0	0	0	313
Career Total (AW)	1	0	0	0	0

Going (Turf): Sf: 0-1 GS: 0-1 Gd: 0-1 GF: 0-4 Fm: 0-0
Distance: 5f/6f: 0-0 7f-8f: 0-2 9f-13f: 0-6 14f+: 0-0
Track : LH: 0-4 RH: 0-2 Tight: 0-4 Gall: 0-2
Aids: Bl: 0-1 Vi: 0-0 Tstrap: 0-0 Ckp: 0-0
Best Rating: 69 4/09 Wind 1m2f7y good

Millie's Rock (IRE)

86(108) (78)71

4-y-o b f Rock Of Gibraltar (IRE)-Miletrian (IRE) (Marju (IRE))

K A Ryan Mrs J Ryan

Placings:0/43012154-120400000 (7399)

2009: 10^{1}SD, 10^{2}SD, 12^{0}SD, 8^{4}SD, 8^{0}GF, 9^{0}G, 6^{0}G, 8^{0}G, 9^{0}SD,

	Starts	1st	2nd	3rd	Win & Pl
Career Total (Turf)	9	2	0	0	5051
Career Total (AW)	9	1	2	1	5898

74	1/09	Ling	1m2f	(0-70)H	STD	£2900
71	7/08	Bevl	1m1f207y	(0-70)H	G-F	£3238
64	5/08	Yarm	1m2f21y	(0-55)H	G-S	£1813

Total win prize-money £7951

Going (Turf): Sf: 0-0 **GS: 1-1** Gd: 0-3 **GF: 1-5** Fm: 0-0
Distance: 5f/6f: 0-3 7f-8f: 0-4 **9f-13f: 3-11** 14f+: 0-0
Track : **LH: 2-11** RH: 1-3 **Tight: 2-11** Gall: 0-0
Aids: Bl: 0-0 Vi: 0-0 Tstrap: 0-0 Ckp: 0-0
Best Rating: 78 1/09 Ling 1m2f stand

Fair; stays 1m2f; acts on easy ground; also goes on Polytrack.

Million Dollars (USA)

83(93) (63)56

2-y-o ch f Pleasant Tap (USA)-Six Zeroes (USA) (Hold For Gold (USA))

Saeed Bin Suroor Godolphin

Placings:04 (5984)

2009: 7^{0}GF, 8^{4}SD,

	Starts	1st	2nd	3rd	Win & Pl
Career Total (Turf)	1	0	0	0	
Career Total (AW)	1	0	0	0	0

Going (Turf): Sf: 0-0 GS: 0-0 Gd: 0-0 GF: 0-1 Fm: 0-0
Distance: 5f/6f: 0-0 7f-8f: 0-2 9f-13f: 0-0 14f+: 0-0
Track : LH: 0-0 RH: 0-1 Tight: 0-0 Gall: 0-0
Aids: Bl: 0-0 Vi: 0-0 Tstrap: 0-0 Ckp: 0-0
Best Rating: 63 9/09 Kemp 1m stand

Milloaks (IRE)

(68)

4-y-o b f Tamayaz (CAN)-Jaldini (IRE) (Darshaan)

Paul W Flynn Sean Dalton

Placings:0/00000-0 (0304)

2009: 6^{0}SD,

	Starts	1st	2nd	3rd	Win & Pl
Career Total (Turf)	4	0	0	0	
Career Total (AW)	3	0	0	0	

Going (Turf): Sf: 0-2 GS: 0-0 Gd: 0-0 GF: 0-2 Fm: 0-0
Distance: 5f/6f: 0-3 7f-8f: 0-2 9f-13f: 0-2 14f+: 0-0
Track : LH: 0-4 RH: 0-1 Tight: 0-1 Gall: 0-0
Aids: Bl: 0-2 Vi: 0-0 Tstrap: 0-0 Ckp: 0-0

Millville

93(114) (115)91

9-y-o ch g Millkom-Miss Top Ville (FR) (Top Ville)

M A Jarvis T G Warner

Placings:10110545020/55221003**3**/1305**162**/**25**005**34**/**141**
361-30 (1458)
2009: 12^{3}SD, 12^{0}G,

	Starts	1st	2nd	3rd	Win & Pl
Career Total (Turf)	24	2	3	2	38798
Career Total (AW)	18	7	2	4	85755

114	11/08	Wolv	1m4f50y	(0-100)H	STD	£12616
113	2/08	Wolv	1m4f50y	(0-100)H	STD	£10363
111	1/08	Ling	1m4f	(0-100)H	STD	£9971
111	10/06	Ling	1m4f	(0-95)H	STD	£11658
101	5/06	York	1m4f	(0-95)H	G-S	£9067
101	8/05	Pont	1m4f8y	(0-90)H	GD	£10277
87	3/04	Ling	1m5f	C(0-95)H	STD	£12383
87	2/04	Ling	1m4f	D(0-80)H	STD	£4160
72	1/04	Ling	1m2f	D	STD	£3828

Total win prize-money £84327

Going (Turf): Sf: 0-2 **GS: 1-9 Gd: 1-9** GF: 0-4 Fm: 0-0
Distance: 5f/6f: 0-0 7f-8f: 0-1 **9f-13f: 9-35** 14f+: 0-6
Track : **LH: 9-31** RH: 0-10 **Tight: 7-22** Gall: 1-12
Aids: Bl: 0-0 Vi: 0-0 Tstrap: 0-0 Ckp: 0-0
Best Rating: 115 1/09 Ling 1m4f stand

Smart on sand; Listed placed; effective over 1m2f-2m; acts on most ground on turf; suited by Polytrack.

Millway Beach (IRE)

95(101) (69)**72**
3-y-o b g Diktat-Cape Cod (IRE) (Unfuwain (USA))
Pat Eddery Pat Eddery Racing (Toulon)

Placings:4000-**1**44040000 (6376)
2009: 7^{1}SD, 8^{4}SD, 8^{4}SD, 7^{0}GF, 9^{4}GF, 11^{0}GF, 10^{0}G, 10^{0}SD, 12^{0}SD,

	Starts	1st	2nd	3rd	Win & Pl
Career Total (Turf)	8	0	0	0	397
Career Total (AW)	5	1	0	0	3297
69	1/09 Ling	7f	(0-75)H	STD	£2900

Total win prize-money £2900

Going (Turf): Sf: 0-0 GS: 0-0 Gd: 0-3 GF: 0-5 Fm: 0-0
Distance: 5f/6f: 0-1 **7f-8f: 1-7** 9f-13f: 0-5 14f+: 0-0
Track : **LH: 1-3** RH: 0-5 **Tight: 1-5** Gall: 0-0
Aids: Bl: 0-0 Vi: 0-0 Tstrap: 0-3 Ckp: 0-3
Best Rating: 72 7/08 Newb 7f good

Modest; effective over 7f; acts on Polytrack.

Milly Rose

78(83) (44)**56**
3-y-o br f Diktat-Milly Fleur (Primo Dominie)
George Baker Jeremy Gompertz & Patrick Milmo

Placings:060-00 (3474)
2009: 6^{0}GS, 9^{0}F,

	Starts	1st	2nd	3rd	Win & Pl
Career Total (Turf)	4	0	0	0	0
Career Total (AW)	1	0	0	0	

Going (Turf): Sf: 0-1 GS: 0-1 Gd: 0-0 GF: 0-1 Fm: 0-1
Distance: 5f/6f: 0-2 7f-8f: 0-2 9f-13f: 0-1 14f+: 0-0
Track : LH: 0-3 RH: 0-0 Tight: 0-1 Gall: 0-0
Aids: Bl: 0-0 Vi: 0-0 Tstrap: 0-0 Ckp: 0-0
Best Rating: 56 5/08 Newb 6f8y soft

Milnagavie

97(94) (77)**67**
2-y-o ch f Tobougg (IRE)-Abyaan (IRE) (Ela-Mana-Mou)
R Hannon Mrs R Ablett

Placings:346 (6607)
2009: 8^{3}SD, 8^{4}GS, 8^{6}SD,

	Starts	1st	2nd	3rd	Win & Pl
Career Total (Turf)	1	0	0	0	168
Career Total (AW)	2	0	0	1	674

Going (Turf): Sf: 0-0 GS: 0-1 Gd: 0-0 GF: 0-0 Fm: 0-0
Distance: 5f/6f: 0-0 7f-8f: 0-2 9f-13f: 0-1 14f+: 0-0
Track : LH: 0-0 RH: 0-2 Tight: 0-0 Gall: 0-0
Aids: Bl: 0-0 Vi: 0-0 Tstrap: 0-0 Ckp: 0-0
Best Rating: 77 8/09 Kemp 1m stand

Milne Bay (IRE)

94(106) (79)**78**
4-y-o b g Tagula (IRE)-Fiction (Dominion)
D M Simcock DXB Bloodstock Ltd

Placings:0/004**1**46**11**-16532260 (6642)
2009: 6^{1}SD, 7^{6}SD, 6^{5}SD, 5^{3}SD, 6^{2}GF, 7^{2}SD, 5^{6}SD, 5^{0}SD,

	Starts	1st	2nd	3rd	Win & Pl
Career Total (Turf)	2	0	1	0	1156
Career Total (AW)	15	4	1	1	12146

79	1/09	GrLe	6f	(0-75)H	STD	£2590
78	12/08	Wolv	7f32y	(0-65)H	STD	£2388
68	12/08	GrLe	6f	(0-75)H	STD	£3238
64	10/08	GrLe	6f	(0-55)H	STD	£2388

Total win prize-money £10604

Going (Turf): Sf: 0-1 GS: 0-0 Gd: 0-0 GF: 0-1 Fm: 0-0
Distance: **5f/6f: 3-10** 7f-8f: 1-7 9f-13f: 0-0 14f+: 0-0
Track : **LH: 4-10** RH: 0-5 Tight: 1-6 **Gall: 3-4**
Aids: Bl: 0-0 Vi: 0-0 Tstrap: 0-0 Ckp: 0-0
Best Rating: 79 1/09 GrLe 6f stand

Fair; stays 7f and acts on Polytrack; has worn a tongue tie.

Milton Of Campsie

102(101) (60)**79**
4-y-o ch f Medicean-La Caprice (USA) (Housebuster (USA))
J Balding (S Parr 27/6) Willie McKay

Placings:6**41**005-5000531**11**0 (6764)
2009: 7^{5}SD, 6^{0}SD, 8^{0}GF, 5^{0}SD, 7^{5}GF, 5^{3}GF, 5^{1}GF, 5^{1}G, 6^{1}GF, 6^{0}G,

	Starts	1st	2nd	3rd	Win & Pl
Career Total (Turf)	12	4	0	1	10420
Career Total (AW)	4	0	0	0	0

79	10/09	Ayr	6f	(0-70)H	G-F	£2914
75	9/09	Haml	5f4y	(0-65)H	GD	£1942
67	9/09	Ffos	5f	(0-60)H	G-F	£2590
69	5/08	Rdcr	6f		G-F	£2331

Total win prize-money £9778

Going (Turf): Sf: 0-0 GS: 0-2 Gd: 1-3 **GF: 3-6** Fm: 0-1
Distance: **5f/6f: 4-10** 7f-8f: 0-5 9f-13f: 0-1 14f+: 0-0
Track : LH: 0-6 RH: 0-1 Tight: 0-2 Gall: 0-1
Aids: Bl: 0-0 Vi: 0-0 Tstrap: 0-0 Ckp: 0-0
Best Rating: 79 10/09 Ayr 6f gd-fm

Modest; effective at 5f-6f; acts on fast ground.

Miltons Choice

88(92) (57)**64**
6-y-o b g Diktat-Starosta (Soviet Star (USA))
J M Bradley racingshares.co.uk

Placings:430645/10000/0/1-003 (1528)
2009: 6^{0}GF, 6^{0}G, 5^{3}SD,

	Starts	1st	2nd	3rd	Win & Pl
Career Total (Turf)	14	2	0	1	6760
Career Total (AW)	2	0	0	1	304

64	4/08	Folk	6f	(0-60)H	G-S	£2047
64	4/06	Nott	5f13y	(0-70)H	SFT	£3238

Total win prize-money £5286

Going (Turf): Sf: 1-2 GS: 1-2 Gd: 0-6 GF: 0-4 Fm: 0-0
Distance: **5f/6f: 2-12** 7f-8f: 0-4 9f-13f: 0-0 14f+: 0-0
Track : LH: 0-3 RH: 0-2 Tight: 0-1 Gall: 0-1
Aids: Bl: 0-0 Vi: 0-0 Tstrap: 0-0 Ckp: 0-0
Best Rating: 64 4/08 Folk 6f gd-sft

Mind Alert

(106) (68)**41**
8-y-o b g Mind Games-Bombay Sapphire (Be My Chief (USA))
D Shaw M Shirley

Placings:44521006/02000051**540**/0000600**540410341**/04
230160600520060523/22334002330000450/1130206035
000423-4005 (0461)
2009: 6^{4}SD, 7^{0}SD, 6^{0}SD, 6^{5}SD,

	Starts	1st	2nd	3rd	Win & Pl
Career Total (Turf)	21	1	2	0	9463
Career Total (AW)	72	6	8	10	19486

68	1/08	Kemp	6f	(0-52)H	STD	£2047
65	1/08	Sthl	6f	(0-52)H	STD	£1399
62	2/06	Ling	6f	(0-60)H	STD	£2047
58	12/05	Sthl	6f	(0-45)	STD	£1433
53	11/05	Sthl	6f	(0-45)	SS	£1429
66	10/04	Ling	7f	(0-62)H	STD	£3022
73	8/03	Ripn	6f	D	G-F	£4865

Total win prize-money £16247

Going (Turf): Sf: 0-1 GS: 0-3 Gd: 0-7 **GF: 1-10** Fm: 0-0
Distance: **5f/6f: 6-72** 7f-8f: 1-20 9f-13f: 0-1 14f+: 0-0
Track : **LH: 5-61** RH: 1-14 **Tight: 2-39** Gall: 0-1
Aids: Bl: 0-3 **Vi: 5-63** Tstrap: 0-3 Ckp: 0-3
Best Rating: 73 8/03 Ripn 6f gd-fm

Moderate; effective at around 6f; acts on a sound surface; also goes on Fibresand and Polytrack; usually wears a visor; suited by a strong pace.

Mind Of Her Own

84(92) (56)**57**
2-y-o b f Pastoral Pursuits-Mindfulness (Primo Dominie)
P D Evans Mrs I M Folkes

Placings:6204000400 (7757)
2009: 5^{6}GF, 5^{2}F, 5^{0}GF, 7^{4}SD, 8^{0}SD, 7^{0}SD, 5^{0}SD, 6^{4}SD, 5^{0}SD, 6^{0}SD,

	Starts	1st	2nd	3rd	Win & Pl
Career Total (Turf)	3	0	1	0	1272
Career Total (AW)	7	0	0	0	0

Going (Turf): Sf: 0-0 GS: 0-0 Gd: 0-0 GF: 0-2 Fm: 0-1
Distance: 5f/6f: 0-7 7f-8f: 0-3 9f-13f: 0-0 14f+: 0-0
Track : LH: 0-6 RH: 0-1 Tight: 0-4 Gall: 0-0
Aids: Bl: 0-0 Vi: 0-1 Tstrap: 0-0 Ckp: 0-0
Best Rating: 57 4/09 Thsk 5f firm

Moderate; stays 6f; acts on fast ground; handles Fibresand; has worn a visor.

Mind The Monarch

86(92) (54)**61**
2-y-o b f Mind Games-Enford Princess (Pivotal)

R A Teal J Morton

Placings:44056360254 (7884)
2009: 5^{4}SD, 5^{4}GF, 6^{0}GF, 5^{5}SD, 5^{6}SD, 6^{3}SD, 6^{6}SD, 8^{0}SD, 5^{2}SD, 6^{5}SD, 7^{4}SD,

	Starts	1st	2nd	3rd	Win & Pl
Career Total (Turf)	2	0	0	0	385
Career Total (AW)	9	0	1	1	907

Going (Turf): **Sf: 0-0 GS: 0-0 Gd: 0-0 GF: 0-2 Fm: 0-0**
Distance: 5f/6f: 0-9 7f-8f: 0-2 9f-13f: 0-0 14f+: 0-0
Track : LH: 0-6 RH: 0-2 Tight: 0-6 Gall: 0-0
Aids: Bl: 0-0 Vi: 0-0 Tstrap: 0-0 Ckp: 0-0
Best Rating: **61** 5/09 Sand 5f6y gd-fm

Moderate; effective over 5f; acts on Polytrack.

Minder

97(86) (57)**63**
3-y-o b g Mind Games-Exotic Forest (Dominion)
J G Portman M J Vandenberghe

Placings:44000-56 (2320)
2009: 8^{5}GF, 8^{6}G,

	Starts	1st	2nd	3rd	Win & Pl
Career Total (Turf)	6	0	0	0	481
Career Total (AW)	1	0	0	0	

Going (Turf): **Sf: 0-1 GS: 0-0 Gd: 0-2 GF: 0-2 Fm: 0-1**
Distance: 5f/6f: 0-3 7f-8f: 0-2 9f-13f: 0-2 14f+: 0-0
Track : LH: 0-2 RH: 0-2 Tight: 0-0 Gall: 0-1
Aids: Bl: 0-0 Vi: 0-0 Tstrap: 0-0 Ckp: 0-0
Best Rating: **63** 5/08 Gdwd 6f soft

Fair; stays 6f and acts on fast ground.

Mine Behind

86(102) (71)**49**
9-y-o b g Sheikh Albadou-Arapi (IRE) (Arazi (USA))
J R Best John Best

Placings:0160032263/1622000100014045/00001160/4040300/00030002664/0055404-00 (1421)
2009: 6^{0}G, 6^{0}G,

	Starts	1st	2nd	3rd	Win & Pl
Career Total (Turf)	47	6	2	3	56416
Career Total (AW)	14	0	3	1	5027

95	8/05	NmkJ	6f	(0-85)H	GD	£6422
90	7/05	Newb	7f	(0-90)H	G-F	£9914
93	9/04	Yarm	5f43y	(0-85)H	GD	£9331
88	7/04	Bath	5f161y	D(0-85)H	GD	£6864
82	4/04	Wind	6f	E(0-85)H	G-S	£4329
78	6/03	Newb	6f8y	D	G-F	£5772

Total win prize-money £42632

Going (Turf): Sf: 0-0 GS: 1-7 **Gd: 3-20** GF: 2-19 Fm: 0-1
Distance: **5f/6f: 4-46** 7f-8f: 2-14 9f-13f: 0-1 14f+: 0-0
Track : **LH: 1-23** RH: 0-3 Tight: 0-20 **Gall: 2-10**
Aids: Bl: 0-0 Vi: 0-0 Tstrap: 0-1 Ckp: 0-1
Best Rating: **95** 8/05 NmkJ 6f good

Modest; stays 7f, but effective over shorter; acts on fast ground; handles Polytrack.

Ming Master (FR)

(98) (75)
2-y-o b g Tobougg (IRE)-Sakura Queen (IRE) (Woodman (USA))
W J Haggas Lok Ho Ting

Placings:044 (7763)
2009: 6^{0}SD, 7^{4}SD, 8^{4}SD,

	Starts	1st	2nd	3rd	Win & Pl
Career Total (Turf)	0	0	0	0	
Career Total (AW)	3	0	0	0	529

Going (Turf): **Sf: 0-0 GS: 0-0 Gd: 0-0 GF: 0-0 Fm: 0-0**
Distance: 5f/6f: 0-1 7f-8f: 0-2 9f-13f: 0-0 14f+: 0-0
Track : LH: 0-2 RH: 0-1 Tight: 0-2 Gall: 0-0
Aids: Bl: 0-0 Vi: 0-0 Tstrap: 0-0 Ckp: 0-0
Best Rating: **75** 12/09 Kemp 1m stand

Ming Vase

104(99) (55)**54**
7-y-o b g Vettori (IRE)-Minstrel's Dance (CAN) (Pleasant Colony (USA))
P T Midgley Michael Ng

Placings:6256053/60050002004/050020656606166350/60445530340003/41025030400303-46305006205400 (5730)
2009: 8^{4}SD, 8^{6}SD, 11^{3}SD, 11^{0}SD, 8^{5}GF, 8^{0}F, 9^{0}G, 9^{6}GF, 10^{2}GF, 10^{0}GF, 10^{5}G, 10^{4}GF, 10^{0}GS, 8^{0}GS,

	Starts	1st	2nd	3rd	Win & Pl
Career Total (Turf)	48	1	1	7	7272
Career Total (AW)	30	1	4	2	6014

55	3/08	Sthl	1m3f	STD	£1774
50	7/06	Nott	1m1f213y (0-60)H	G-F	£2730

Total win prize-money £4505

Going (Turf): Sf: 0-11 GS: 0-9 Gd: 0-9 **GF: 1-16** Fm: 0-3
Distance: 5f/6f: 0-4 7f-8f: 0-28 **9f-13f: 2-46** 14f+: 0-0
Track : **LH: 2-59** RH: 0-15 Tight: 0-19 Gall: 0-3
Aids: Bl: 0-2 Vi: 0-1 Tstrap: 0-3 Ckp: 0-3
Best Rating: **60** 4/05 Wind 1m67y gd-sft

Moderate; stays 1m3f; acts on firm and easy ground; also goes on Fibresand.

Mingun Bell (USA)

94(97) (92)**79**
2-y-o b c Mingun (USA)-Miss Tippins (USA) (Squadron Leader (USA))
H R A Cecil Niarchos Family

Placings:331146 (7184)
2009: 6^{3}GF, 7^{3}GF, 7^{1}GF, 8^{1}SD, 8^{4}GF, 10^{6}G,

	Starts	1st	2nd	3rd	Win & Pl
Career Total (Turf)	5	1	0	2	5424
Career Total (AW)	1	1	0	0	4404

92	8/09	Sthl	1m	STD	£4403
79	7/09	Wwck	7f26y	G-F	£3399

Total win prize-money £7804

Going (Turf): Sf: 0-0 GS: 0-0 Gd: 0-1 **GF: 1-4** Fm: 0-0
Distance: 5f/6f: 0-1 **7f-8f: 2-3** 9f-13f: 0-2 14f+: 0-0
Track : **LH: 2-3** RH: 0-0 Tight: 0-1 Gall: 0-0
Aids: Bl: 0-0 Vi: 0-0 Tstrap: 0-0 Ckp: 0-0
Best Rating: **92** 8/09 Sthl 1m stand

Useful; stays 1m; acts on fast ground and on Fibresand.

Mini Max

85(85) (63)**58**
2-y-o b f Tobougg (IRE)-Maxilla (IRE) (Lahib (USA))
B W Duke K B Hodges

Placings:0504 (7056)
2009: 7^{0}GF, 7^{5}SD, 6^{0}S, 7^{4}GF,

	Starts	1st	2nd	3rd	Win & Pl
Career Total (Turf)	3	0	0	0	168
Career Total (AW)	1	0	0	0	280

Going (Turf): **Sf: 0-1 GS: 0-0 Gd: 0-0 GF: 0-2 Fm: 0-0**
Distance: 5f/6f: 0-0 7f-8f: 0-4 9f-13f: 0-0 14f+: 0-0
Track : LH: 0-0 RH: 0-1 Tight: 0-0 Gall: 0-0
Aids: Bl: 0-0 Vi: 0-0 Tstrap: 0-0 Ckp: 0-0
Best Rating: **63** 9/09 Kemp 7f stand

Modest; stays 7f; acts on Polytrack.

Minibuzz

57(84) (35)
3-y-o b g Superior Premium-Amy Leigh (IRE) (Imperial Frontier (USA))
Mrs G S Rees Mr & Mrs Furby & Mrs G Rees

Placings:00-040 (1451)
2009: 5^{0}SD, 6^{4}SD, 7^{0}GF,

	Starts	1st	2nd	3rd	Win & Pl
Career Total (Turf)	1	0	0	0	
Career Total (AW)	4	0	0	0	192

Going (Turf): **Sf: 0-0 GS: 0-0 Gd: 0-0 GF: 0-1 Fm: 0-0**
Distance: 5f/6f: 0-3 7f-8f: 0-2 9f-13f: 0-0 14f+: 0-0
Track : LH: 0-5 RH: 0-0 Tight: 0-4 Gall: 0-0
Aids: Bl: 0-0 Vi: 0-3 Tstrap: 0-0 Ckp: 0-0
Best Rating: **35** 3/09 Sthl 6f stand

Minimum Fuss (IRE)

89(81) (28)**50**
5-y-o b m Second Empire (IRE)-Jamis (IRE) (Be My Guest (USA))
M C Chapman Mrs M Chapman

Placings:046623014403003/5030006000000/0000-0560 (2534)
2009: 6^{0}SD, 6^{5}SD, 5^{6}F, 5^{0}GF,

	Starts	1st	2nd	3rd	Win & Pl
Career Total (Turf)	24	0	1	3	3600
Career Total (AW)	12	1	0	1	2870

51	7/06	Sthl	5f	STD	£2388

Total win prize-money £2389

Going (Turf): **Sf: 0-2 GS: 0-4 Gd: 0-2 GF: 0-13 Fm: 0-3**
Distance: **5f/6f: 1-33** 7f-8f: 0-3 9f-13f: 0-0 14f+: 0-0
Track : LH: 0-7 RH: 0-0 Tight: 0-1 Gall: 0-0
Aids: **Bl: 1-14** Vi: 0-0 Tstrap: 0-0 Ckp: 0-0
Best Rating: **58** 9/06 Leic 5f218y gd-fm

Modest; effective over 5f-6f; has worn blinkers; acts on fast ground; also goes on Fibresand.

Minimusic

(76) (32)
2-y-o b f Distant Music (USA)-Minette (Bishop Of Cashel)
B Palling Flying Eight Partnership

Placings:0 (7491)
2009: 8^{0}SD,

	Starts	1st	2nd	3rd	Win & Pl
Career Total (Turf)	0	0	0	0	
Career Total (AW)	1	0	0	0	

Going (Turf): **Sf: 0-0 GS: 0-0 Gd: 0-0 GF: 0-0 Fm: 0-0**
Distance: 5f/6f: 0-0 7f-8f: 0-0 9f-13f: 0-1 14f+: 0-0
Track : LH: 0-1 RH: 0-0 Tight: 0-1 Gall: 0-0
Aids: Bl: 0-0 Vi: 0-0 Tstrap: 0-0 Ckp: 0-0
Best Rating: **32** 11/09 Wolv 1m141y stand

Ministerofinterior

89(101) (60)65

4-y-o b g Nayef (USA)-Maureen's Hope (USA) (Northern Baby (CAN))

B D Leavy (G L Moore 12/7) D E Simpson & R Farrington-Kirkham

Placings:0/50565154-445 **(3382)**

2009: 12^{4}SD, 9^{4}G, 12^{5}SD,

	Starts	1st	2nd	3rd	Win & Pl
Career Total (Turf)	7	1	0	0	2087
Career Total (AW)	5	0	0	0	0

53 9/08 Brig 1m1f209y SFT £1942

Total win prize-money £1943

Going (Turf): **Sf: 1-2** GS: 0-0 Gd: 0-1 GF: 0-3 Fm: 0-1
Distance: 5f/6f: 0-0 7f-8f: 0-1 **9f-13f: 1-11** 14f+: 0-0
Track : **LH: 1-8** RH: 0-3 Tight: 0-6 Gall: 0-0
Aids: Bl: 0-3 Vi: 0-1 Tstrap: 0-0 Ckp: 0-0
Best Rating: 65 6/08 Wind 1m2f7y gd-fm

Moderate; best over 1m2f; acts on soft ground and on Polytrack; has worn blinkers and an eyeshield.

Miniyamba (IRE)

98 69

2-y-o b f Sadler's Wells (USA)-Atlantide (USA) (Southern Halo (USA))

J L Dunlop Benny Andersson

Placings:0600 **(6993)**

2009: 7^{0}G, 6^{6}S, 8^{0}GF, 8^{0}GS,

	Starts	1st	2nd	3rd	Win & Pl
Career Total (Turf)	4	0	0	0	0

Going (Turf): Sf: 0-1 GS: 0-1 Gd: 0-1 GF: 0-1 Fm: 0-0
Distance: 5f/6f: 0-0 7f-8f: 0-4 9f-13f: 0-0 14f+: 0-0
Track : LH: 0-1 RH: 0-0 Tight: 0-0 Gall: 0-1
Aids: Bl: 0-0 Vi: 0-0 Tstrap: 0-0 Ckp: 0-0
Best Rating: 69 9/09 Sals 6f212y soft

Minnie Rocket

76(51) 8

2-y-o ch f Monsieur Bond (IRE)-Real Popcorn (IRE) (Jareer (USA))

R C Guest Shaun Taylor

Placings:00000 **(5950)**

2009: 5^{0}GF, 5^{0}SD, 6^{0}G, 5^{0}S, 5^{0}GF,

	Starts	1st	2nd	3rd	Win & Pl
Career Total (Turf)	4	0	0	0	
Career Total (AW)	1	0	0	0	

Going (Turf): Sf: 0-1 GS: 0-0 Gd: 0-1 GF: 0-2 Fm: 0-0
Distance: 5f/6f: 0-4 7f-8f: 0-1 9f-13f: 0-0 14f+: 0-0
Track : LH: 0-0 RH: 0-0 Tight: 0-0 Gall: 0-0
Aids: Bl: 0-0 Vi: 0-0 Tstrap: 0-0 Ckp: 0-0
Best Rating: 8 8/09 Muss 5f soft

Minnola

98(95) (52)58

4-y-o b f Royal Applause-Miss Anabaa (Anabaa (USA))

Rae Guest C J Mills

Placings:30-5300400640 **(7877)**

2009: 5^{5}SD, 6^{3}S, 6^{0}GS, 7^{0}SD, 6^{4}G, 7^{0}S, 7^{0}SD, 5^{6}SD, 7^{4}SD, 7^{0}SD,

	Starts	1st	2nd	3rd	Win & Pl
Career Total (Turf)	6	0	0	2	1155
Career Total (AW)	6	0	0	0	0

Going (Turf): Sf: 0-3 GS: 0-2 Gd: 0-1 GF: 0-0 Fm: 0-0
Distance: 5f/6f: 0-6 7f-8f: 0-6 9f-13f: 0-0 14f+: 0-0
Track : LH: 0-4 RH: 0-3 Tight: 0-4 Gall: 0-0
Aids: Bl: 0-3 Vi: 0-0 Tstrap: 0-0 Ckp: 0-0
Best Rating: 58 7/09 Ripn 6f soft

Minority Report

102(96) (57)88

9-y-o b g Rainbow Quest (USA)-Queen Sceptre (IRE) (Fairy King (USA))

K A Ryan (D Nicholls 28/7) R J Stevenson & S C B Limited

Placings:3020/21221/101300/30300030/000030001-3050046000 **(5780)**

2009: 7^{3}GF, 8^{0}GF, 7^{5}F, 8^{0}GF, 8^{0}GF, 8^{4}G, 8^{6}GF, 8^{0}GS, 8^{0}GF, 8^{0}SD,

	Starts	1st	2nd	3rd	Win & Pl
Career Total (Turf)	41	5	4	7	62873
Career Total (AW)	1	0	0	0	

84 9/08 Muss 7f30y (0-80)H GD £5180
103 8/06 Gdwd 7f (0-95) G-F £12464
100 5/06 Thsk 1m (0-100)H FRM £16192
91 10/05 Newb 7f (0-85)H G-F £6939
75 9/05 Newc 1m G-F £3474

Total win prize-money £44251

Going (Turf): Sf: 0-1 GS: 0-7 Gd: 1-10 **GF: 3-21** Fm: 1-2
Distance: 5f/6f: 0-0 **7f-8f: 5-30** 9f-13f: 0-12 14f+: 0-0
Track : LH: 2-12 RH: 2-14 **Tight: 2-12** Gall: 1-1
Aids: Bl: 0-0 Vi: 0-1 Tstrap: 0-0 Ckp: 0-0
Best Rating: 108 9/07 Gdwd 7f gd-fm

Useful; effective over 7f-1m; acts on fast ground.

Minortransgression (USA)

(93) (66)

2-y-o ch g Yes It's True (USA)-Casting Pearls (USA) (Fusaichi Pegasus (USA))

G L Moore G L Moore

Placings:4 **(7806)**

2009: 7^{4}SD,

	Starts	1st	2nd	3rd	Win & Pl
Career Total (Turf)	0	0	0	0	
Career Total (AW)	1	0	0	0	289

Going (Turf): Sf: 0-0 GS: 0-0 Gd: 0-0 GF: 0-0 Fm: 0-0
Distance: 5f/6f: 0-0 7f-8f: 0-1 9f-13f: 0-0 14f+: 0-0
Track : LH: 0-1 RH: 0-0 Tight: 0-1 Gall: 0-0
Aids: Bl: 0-0 Vi: 0-0 Tstrap: 0-0 Ckp: 0-0
Best Rating: 66 12/09 Ling 7f stand

Minotaurious (IRE)

82(93) (66)79

3-y-o b f Acclamation-Bella Vie (IRE) (Sadler's Wells (USA))

K R Burke Ms L Durcan

Placings:0220-2320 **(1062)**

2009: 5^{2}SD, 5^{3}SD, 5^{2}SD, 5^{0}GF,

	Starts	1st	2nd	3rd	Win & Pl
Career Total (Turf)	5	0	2	0	2698
Career Total (AW)	3	0	2	1	2199

Going (Turf): Sf: 0-1 GS: 0-0 Gd: 0-1 GF: 0-3 Fm: 0-0
Distance: 5f/6f: 0-8 7f-8f: 0-0 9f-13f: 0-0 14f+: 0-0
Track : LH: 0-4 RH: 0-0 Tight: 0-3 Gall: 0-1
Aids: Bl: 0-0 Vi: 0-0 Tstrap: 0-0 Ckp: 0-0
Best Rating: 79 9/08 Ayr 6f heavy

Fair filly; stays 6f; acts on quick ground and on Polytrack.

Minstalad

91 44

5-y-o ch g Minster Son-Denby Wood (Lord Bud)

G R Oldroyd Tony Longbottom

Placings:3 **(4974)**

2009: 11^{3}GF,

	Starts	1st	2nd	3rd	Win & Pl
Career Total (Turf)	1	0	0	1	482

Going (Turf): Sf: 0-0 GS: 0-0 Gd: 0-0 GF: 0-1 Fm: 0-0
Distance: 5f/6f: 0-0 7f-8f: 0-0 9f-13f: 0-1 14f+: 0-0
Track : LH: 0-1 RH: 0-0 Tight: 0-1 Gall: 0-0
Aids: Bl: 0-0 Vi: 0-0 Tstrap: 0-0 Ckp: 0-0
Best Rating: 44 8/09 Catt 1m3f214y gd-fm

Mint Whip (IRE)

94(84) (51)64

2-y-o b f Whipper (USA)-Aminata (Glenstal (USA))

R Hannon Ballylinch Stud

Placings:66 **(7317)**

2009: 5^{6}GF, 5^{6}SD,

	Starts	1st	2nd	3rd	Win & Pl
Career Total (Turf)	1	0	0	0	0
Career Total (AW)	1	0	0	0	0

Going (Turf): Sf: 0-0 GS: 0-0 Gd: 0-0 GF: 0-1 Fm: 0-0
Distance: 5f/6f: 0-2 7f-8f: 0-0 9f-13f: 0-0 14f+: 0-0
Track : LH: 0-1 RH: 0-0 Tight: 0-1 Gall: 0-0
Aids: Bl: 0-0 Vi: 0-0 Tstrap: 0-0 Ckp: 0-0
Best Rating: 64 10/09 Licc 5f218y gd-fm

Mintoe

98(89) (58)63

3-y-o b g Noverre (USA)-West One (Gone West (USA))

K A Ryan David Fravigar, Kathy Dixon

Placings:5600-060 **(4279)**

2009: 5^{0}G, 7^{6}G, 8^{0}G,

	Starts	1st	2nd	3rd	Win & Pl
Career Total (Turf)	6	0	0	0	0
Career Total (AW)	1	0	0	0	

Going (Turf): Sf: 0-1 GS: 0-0 Gd: 0-4 GF: 0-1 Fm: 0-0
Distance: 5f/6f: 0-5 7f-8f: 0-2 9f-13f: 0-0 14f+: 0-0
Track : LH: 0-4 RH: 0-0 Tight: 0-4 Gall: 0-0
Aids: Bl: 0-0 Vi: 0-0 Tstrap: 0-2 Ckp: 0-2
Best Rating: 63 6/08 York 6f good

Moderate; stays 7f; acts on good ground; has worn cheek-pieces.

Minturno (USA)

101 74

3-y-o b g Ten Most Wanted (USA)-Panama Jane (USA) (Perrault)

Mrs A Duffield Trevor Wilson

Placings:5-4420124310540 (6178)
2009: 5^4GF, 6^4GF, 7^2GF, 6^0F, 6^1GF, 7^2GF, 7^4GF, 5^3G, 6^1G, 6^0GF, 7^5GS, 6^4GF, 7^0GF,

				Starts	1st	2nd	3rd	Win & Pl
Career Total (Turf)				14	2	2	1	8586
68	7/09	Ayr	6f		(0-70)H		GD	£3070
62	5/09	Rdcr	6f		(0-70)H		G-F	£2590

Total win prize-money £5661

Going (Turf): Sf: 0-0 GS: 0-2 **Gd: 1-2 GF: 1-9** Fm: 0-1
Distance: **5f/6f: 2-8** 7f-8f: 0-6 9f-13f: 0-0 14f+: 0-0
Track : LH: 0-4 RH: 0-2 Tight: 0-4 Gall: 0-0
Aids: Bl: 0-0 Vi: 0-0 Tstrap: 1-5 Ckp: 1-5
Best Rating: **74** 9/09 Rdcr 6f gd-fm

Modest; stays 7f and acts on fast ground.

Minwir (IRE)

(96) (59)**68**
4-y-o b g Green Desert (USA)-Elshamms (Zafonic (USA))
W M Brisbourne (M Quinn 13/2) K Bennett

Placings:0603/**0**5000**1**0000-0600 (6800)
2009: 8^0SD, 5^6SD, 7^0SD, 8^0SD,

				Starts	1st	2nd	3rd	Win & Pl
Career Total (Turf)				8	0	0	1	722
Career Total (AW)				10	1	0	0	1943
59	6/08	GrLe	6f		(0-55)H		STD	£1942

Total win prize-money £1943

Going (Turf): Sf: 0-2 GS: 0-2 Gd: 0-1 GF: 0-3 Fm: 0-0
Distance: **5f/6f: 1-9** 7f-8f: 0-6 9f-13f: 0-3 14f+: 0-0
Track : **LH: 1-10** RH: 0-2 Tight: 0-6 **Gall: 1-1**
Aids: Bl: 0-0 **Vi: 1-5** Tstrap: 0-0 Ckp: 0-0
Best Rating: **68** 10/07 Gdwd 6f soft

Modest; effective at around 6f; acts on good ground and Polytrack.

Mirabella (IRE)

(105) (83)
2-y-o b f Motivator-Anayid (A.P. Indy (USA))
R Hannon The Royal Ascot Racing Club

Placings:4021 (7363)
2009: 7^4SD, 8^0SS, 7^2SD, 7^1SD,

				Starts	1st	2nd	3rd	Win & Pl
Career Total (Turf)				0	0	0	0	
Career Total (AW)				4	1	1	0	4249
83	11/09	Ling	7f		(0-75)		STD	£2590

Total win prize-money £2590

Going (Turf): Sf: 0-0 GS: 0-0 Gd: 0-0 GF: 0-0 Fm: 0-0
Distance: 5f/6f: 0-0 **7f-8f: 1-4** 9f-13f: 0-0 14f+: 0-0
Track : **LH: 1-3** RH: 0-1 **Tight: 1-3** Gall: 0-0
Aids: Bl: 0-0 Vi: 0-0 Tstrap: 0-0 Ckp: 0-0
Best Rating: **83** 11/09 Ling 7f stand

Fair; effective over 7f; acts on Polytrack.

Miracle Baby

81(96) (56)**50**
7-y-o b m Atraf-Musica (Primo Dominie)
J A Geake Kimpton Down Racing Club

Placings:0/6400/**0000/00/2**04560-6006 (6782)
2009: 6^6SD, 7^0SD, 6^0GF, 7^6SS,

	Starts	1st	2nd	3rd	Win & Pl
Career Total (Turf)	10	0	0	0	237
Career Total (AW)	11	0	1	0	524

Going (Turf): Sf: 0-1 GS: 0-0 Gd: 0-4 GF: 0-4 Fm: 0-1
Distance: 5f/6f: 0-8 7f-8f: 0-10 9f-13f: 0-3 14f+: 0-0
Track : LH: 0-12 RH: 0-1 Tight: 0-10 Gall: 0-1
Aids: Bl: 0-0 Vi: 0-0 Tstrap: 0-0 Ckp: 0-0
Best Rating: **56** 6/08 Ling 7f stand

Plating-class; probably best over 7f and acts on Polytrack.

Miracle Seeker

101 **103**
4-y-o br f Rainbow Quest (USA)-Miracle (Ezzoud (IRE))
C G Cox D J Burke

Placings:23/31043-0 (3619)
2009: 11^0GF,

				Starts	1st	2nd	3rd	Win & Pl
Career Total (Turf)				8	1	1	3	41920
100	5/08	Ling	1m3f106y				G-F	£25546

Total win prize-money £25547

Going (Turf): Sf: 0-1 GS: 0-2 Gd: 0-2 **GF: 1-3** Fm: 0-0
Distance: 5f/6f: 0-0 7f-8f: 0-1 **9f-13f: 1-6** 14f+: 0-1
Track : **LH: 1-7** RH: 0-1 **Tight: 1-3** Gall: 0-2
Aids: Bl: 0-0 Vi: 0-0 Tstrap: 0-0 Ckp: 0-0
Best Rating: **103** 7/08 Gdwd 1m6f gd-fm

Smart; winner of 2008 Lingfield Oaks Trial; stays 1m4f and acts on most ground; likes to race prominently.

Miracle Wish (IRE)

71 **17**
2-y-o b f One Cool Cat (USA)-Bentley's Bush (IRE) (Barathea (IRE))
R M Beckett F & N Syndicate

Placings:0 (2494)
2009: 6^0GF,

	Starts	1st	2nd	3rd	Win & Pl
Career Total (Turf)	1	0	0	0	

Going (Turf): Sf: 0-0 GS: 0-0 Gd: 0-0 GF: 0-1 Fm: 0-0
Distance: 5f/6f: 0-0 7f-8f: 0-1 9f-13f: 0-0 14f+: 0-0
Track : LH: 0-0 RH: 0-0 Tight: 0-0 Gall: 0-0
Aids: Bl: 0-0 Vi: 0-0 Tstrap: 0-0 Ckp: 0-0
Best Rating: **17** 5/09 Newb 6f8y gd-fm

Miranda's Girl (IRE)

101(100) (89)**96**
4-y-o b f Titus Livius (FR)-Ela Tina (IRE) (Ela-Mana-Mou)
Thomas Cleary Moyclear Syndicate

Placings:03002626/3551**0**2042301**1**4300-000421060000**5500330** (7801)
2009: 8^0S, 7^0SH, 8^0G, 7^4GF, 7^2S, 7^1HY, 8^0SH, 7^6Y, 7^0GY, 7^0Y, 7^0SD, 7^5SD, 8^5SD, 7^0SD, 7^0SD, 8^3SD, 7^3SD, 7^0SD,

				Starts	1st	2nd	3rd	Win & Pl
Career Total (Turf)				31	3	4	3	53185
Career Total (AW)				12	1	1	3	9830
96	7/09	Rosc	7f		(50-80)H		HVY	£12075
82	7/08	Gway	7f		H		YLD	£19147
85	7/08	Gway	7f		(50-70)H		GD	£7621
75	4/08	Dund	6f		(45-65)H		STD	£4572

Total win prize-money £43417

Going (Turf): Sf: 1-10 GS: 0-0 **Gd: 1-6** GF: 0-4 Fm: 0-1
Distance: 5f/6f: 1-8 **7f-8f: 3-33** 9f-13f: 0-2 14f+: 0-0
Track : LH: 1-18 **RH: 3-19** Tight: 0-1 Gall: 0-3
Aids: Bl: 0-0 Vi: 0-0 Tstrap: 4-33 Ckp: 4-33
Best Rating: **96** 7/09 Rosc 7f heavy

Mirjan (IRE)

87 **79**
13-y-o b g Tenby-Mirana (IRE) (Ela-Mana-Mou)
L Lungo Len Lungo Racing Limited

Placings:132404/310/0000/5403100/3015/600-0 (2044)
2009: 16^0GS,

				Starts	1st	2nd	3rd	Win & Pl
Career Total (Turf)				28	4	1	4	138032
96	8/07	Newc	2m19y		(0-95)H		GD	£7790
98	8/06	Newc	2m19y		(0-95)H		G-S	£7790
96	6/04	Newc	2m19y		B H		SFT	£104400
93	4/99	NmkJ	1m2f		D		GD	£4500

Total win prize-money £124480

Going (Turf): Sf: 1-7 GS: 1-9 **Gd: 2-6** GF: 0-6 Fm: 0-0
Distance: 5f/6f: 0-0 7f-8f: 0-0 9f-13f: 1-8 **14f+: 3-20**
Track : **LH: 3-14** RH: 1-14 Tight: 0-5 **Gall: 4-20**
Aids: **Bl: 3-18** Vi: 0-0 Tstrap: 0-0 Ckp: 0-0
Best Rating: **106** 6/99 Asct 1m4f gd-fm

Mirror Lake

(89) (65)
2-y-o b f Dubai Destination (USA)-Reflections (Sadler's Wells (USA))
Mrs A J Perrett K Abdulla

Placings:5 (7135)
2009: 7^5SD,

	Starts	1st	2nd	3rd	Win & Pl
Career Total (Turf)	0	0	0	0	
Career Total (AW)	1	0	0	0	0

Going (Turf): Sf: 0-0 GS: 0-0 Gd: 0-0 GF: 0-0 Fm: 0-0
Distance: 5f/6f: 0-0 7f-8f: 0-1 9f-13f: 0-0 14f+: 0-0
Track : LH: 0-1 RH: 0-0 Tight: 0-1 Gall: 0-0
Aids: Bl: 0-0 Vi: 0-0 Tstrap: 0-0 Ckp: 0-0
Best Rating: **65** 10/09 Ling 7f stand

Mirrored

108(99) (86)**105**
3-y-o b g Dansili-Reflections (Sadler's Wells (USA))
Sir Michael Stoute K Abdulla

Placings:643-1133304 (6277)
2009: 8^1SD, 8^1GF, 8^3GF, 8^3G, 9^3G, 8^0GF, 10^4GF,

				Starts	1st	2nd	3rd	Win & Pl
Career Total (Turf)				8	1	0	3	32033
Career Total (AW)				2	1	0	1	5305
86	5/09	Sand	1m14y		(0-85)H		G-F	£5180
86	4/09	Kemp	1m		(0-80)H		STD	£4727

Total win prize-money £9908

Going (Turf): Sf: 0-0 GS: 0-0 Gd: 0-2 **GF: 1-6** Fm: 0-0
Distance: 5f/6f: 0-0 7f-8f: 1-6 9f-13f: 1-4 14f+: 0-0
Track : LH: 0-3 **RH: 2-4** Tight: 0-3 Gall: 0-1
Aids: Bl: 0-0 Vi: 0-0 Tstrap: 0-0 Ckp: 0-0
Best Rating: **105** 7/09 Gdwd 1m1f192y good

Very useful; stays 1m; acts on fast ground and on Polytrack.

Misaro (GER)

102(105) (86)**96**
8-y-o b g Acambaro (GER)-Misniniski (Niniski (USA))
R A Harris Messrs Criddle Davies Dawson & Villa

Placings:351/05624**001**/003**212**/**3031**1005124000**0060/22 5**5311130140004050**0/534302**421311140604300-00436155064036**101304** (7832)

2009: 5^{0}G, 5^{0}G, 6^{4}GF, 5^{3}F, 5^{6}F, 5^{1}G, 5^{5}G, 5^{5}GF, 5^{0}GF, 5^{6}GF, 5^{4}GF, 5^{0}S, 5^{3}F, 5^{6}F, 5^{1}SD, 5^{0}SD, 6^{1}SD, 5^{3}SD, 6^{0}SD, 6^{4}SD,

	Starts	1st	2nd	3rd	Win & Pl
Career Total (Turf)	62	12	4	7	64014
Career Total (AW)	34	5	4	6	25011

74	11/09	Kemp	6f		STD	£1706
84	10/09	Wolv	5f20y	(0-75)H	STD	£3238
88	6/09	Sals	5f	(0-80)H	GD	£6476
96	7/08	Bath	5f161y	(0-80)H	GD	£6572
89	7/08	Donc	5f	(0-75)H	GD	£3561
84	6/08	Sals	5f	(0-80)H	G-F	£6476
80	6/08	Ches	5f16y	(0-85)H	G-F	£5180
93	7/07	Kemp	6f	(0-85)H	STD	£6477
88	5/07	Haml	5f4y	(0-75)H	GD	£3886
82	5/07	Wwck	5f110y	(0-65)H	G-S	£2590
75	4/07	Brig	5f59y	(0-70)H	G-F	£2849
80	6/06	Ling	5f	(0-75)H	G-F	£3238
67	4/06	Brig	5f59y	(0-70)H	FRM	£3886
73	4/06	Folk	6f	(0-60)H	G-F	£2730
71	10/05	Wolv	5f20y	(0-58)H	FST	£3014
64	12/04	Wolv	5f216y		STD	£2660
78	11/03	Nott	6f15y	D	G-S	£2968

Total win prize-money £67513

Going (Turf): Sf: 0-5 GS: 2-1 Gd: 4-12 **GF: 5-27** Fm: 1-7
Distance: **5f/6f: 16-87** 7f-8f: 1-8 9f-13f: 0-1 14f+: 0-0
Track : **LH: 8-51** RH: 2-7 **Tight: 4-25** Gall: 1-15
Aids: **Bl: 14-77** Vi: 2-7 Tstrap: 0-0 Ckp: 0-0
Best Rating: **96** 7/08 Bath 5f161y good

Fair; effective over 5f-6f; acts on most ground on turf; goes on sand; usually wears blinkers/visor.

Misbehaviour

70 (32)10

10-y-o b g Tragic Role (USA)-Exotic Forest (Dominion)
P Butler (Jim Best 27/4) J Sabitini

Placings:03300/0S0040000/0/000/3/43/0 **(5028)**
2009: 12^{0}GF,

	Starts	1st	2nd	3rd	Win & Pl
Career Total (Turf)	15	0	0	3	1114
Career Total (AW)	7	0	0	1	302

Going (Turf): **Sf: 0-1 GS: 0-2 Gd: 0-6 GF: 0-6 Fm: 0-0**
Distance: 5f/6f: 0-7 7f-8f: 0-8 9f-13f: 0-5 14f+: 0-2
Track : LH: 0-10 RH: 0-2 Tight: 0-5 Gall: 0-1
Aids: Bl: 0-0 Vi: 0-1 Tstrap: 0-4 Ckp: 0-4
Best Rating: **70** 8/01 Folk 6f good

Mischief Making (USA)

110(110) (99)102

4-y-o b/br f Lemon Drop Kid (USA)-Fraulein (Acatenango (GER))
E A L Dunlop Cliveden Stud

Placings:0/521116016-20030 **(6854)**
2009: 16^{2}GF, 16^{0}G, 16^{0}S, 12^{3}G, 16^{0}G,

	Starts	1st	2nd	3rd	Win & Pl
Career Total (Turf)	8	1	1	1	25782
Career Total (AW)	7	3	1	0	29143

99	10/08	Ling	1m5f		STD	£22708
91	4/08	Catt	1m3f214y		G-S	£6542
84	3/08	Wolv	1m1f103y	(0-75)H	STD	£2752
79	2/08	Sthl	1m3f	(0-70)H	STD	£2593

Total win prize-money £34598

Going (Turf): Sf: 0-2 **GS: 1-1** Gd: 0-3 GF: 0-2 Fm: 0-0
Distance: 5f/6f: 0-0 7f-8f: 0-2 **9f-13f: 4-9** 14f+: 0-4
Track : **LH: 4-9** RH: 0-5 **Tight: 3-6** Gall: 0-4
Aids: Bl: 0-0 Vi: 0-0 Tstrap: 0-0 Ckp: 0-0
Best Rating: **102** 4/09 Asct 2m gd-fm

Smart; Listed winner; stays 1m4f; acts on fast and easy ground; goes on sand.

Misdaqeya

99(87) (84)94

3-y-o br f Red Ransom (USA)-Crystal Power (USA) (Pleasant Colony (USA))
B W Hills Hamdan Al Maktoum

Placings:02120-0030 **(7291)**
2009: 7^{0}GF, 8^{0}GF, 9^{3}GF, 10^{0}S,

	Starts	1st	2nd	3rd	Win & Pl
Career Total (Turf)	8	0	2	1	13338
Career Total (AW)	1	1	0	0	3886

84	6/08	Kemp	7f	STD	£3885

Total win prize-money £3886

Going (Turf): **Sf: 0-1 GS: 0-1 Gd: 0-1 GF: 0-5 Fm: 0-0**
Distance: 5f/6f: 0-2 **7f-8f: 1-5** 9f-13f: 0-2 14f+: 0-0
Track : LH: 0-1 **RH: 1-2** Tight: 0-0 Gall: 0-1
Aids: Bl: 0-0 Vi: 0-0 Tstrap: 0-0 Ckp: 0-0
Best Rating: **94** 8/08 NmkJ 7f gd-sft

Very useful; placed in Group 3 company; stays 1m2f; acts on fast and easy ground; goes on Polytrack.

Misheer

105 109

2-y-o b f Oasis Dream-All For Laura (Cadeaux Genereux)
C E Brittain Saeed Manana

Placings:112102 **(6449)**
2009: 5^{1}GF, 5^{1}GS, 5^{2}GF, 6^{1}G, 5^{0}GF, 6^{2}GF,

	Starts	1st	2nd	3rd	Win & Pl
Career Total (Turf)	6	3	2	0	122773

108	7/09	NmkJ	6f	GD	£45416
95	5/09	York	5f	G-S	£17778
91	4/09	Yarm	5f43y	G-F	£3626

Total win prize-money £66821

Going (Turf): Sf: 0-0 **GS: 1-1 Gd: 1-1 GF: 1-4** Fm: 0-0
Distance: **5f/6f: 3-6** 7f-8f: 0-0 9f-13f: 0-0 14f+: 0-0
Track : LH: 0-0 RH: 0-0 Tight: 0-0 Gall: 0-0
Aids: Bl: 0-0 Vi: 0-0 Tstrap: 0-0 Ckp: 0-0
Best Rating: **109** 10/09 NmkR 6f gd-fm

Smart; Cherry Hinton winner; suited by 5f-6f; acts on fast and easy ground.

Mishrif (USA)

98(102) (98)94

3-y-o b/br g Arch (USA)-Peppy Priscilla (USA) (Latin American (USA))
J R Jenkins (P W Chapple-Hyam 18/6) Sheik Ahmad Yousuf Al Sabah

Placings:512-3650**600000** **(6996)**
2009: 8^{3}SD, 10^{6}G, 7^{5}G, 8^{0}GF, 8^{6}GS, 7^{0}SD, 8^{0}SD, 8^{0}SD, 8^{0}GS, 10^{0}GS,

	Starts	1st	2nd	3rd	Win & Pl
Career Total (Turf)	9	1	1	0	13476
Career Total (AW)	4	0	0	1	4308

91	9/08	Folk	7f	SFT	£2914

Total win prize-money £2914

Going (Turf): **Sf: 1-1** GS: 0-5 Gd: 0-2 GF: 0-1 Fm: 0-0
Distance: 5f/6f: 0-0 **7f-8f: 1-9** 9f-13f: 0-4 14f+: 0-0
Track : LH: 0-5 RH: 0-5 Tight: 0-1 Gall: 0-1
Aids: Bl: 0-0 Vi: 0-1 Tstrap: 0-0 Ckp: 0-0
Best Rating: **98** 4/09 Kemp 1m stand

Very useful; effective over 7f-1m; acts well on soft ground.

Miskin Flyer

93(86) (58)40

3-y-o b f Lend A Hand-Sipsi Fach (Prince Sabo)
B Palling Welsh Pack Racing

Placings:04-000 **(5617)**
2009: 8^{0}G, 8^{0}G, 9^{0}SD,

	Starts	1st	2nd	3rd	Win & Pl
Career Total (Turf)	3	0	0	0	
Career Total (AW)	2	0	0	0	241

Going (Turf): **Sf: 0-0 GS: 0-0 Gd: 0-2 GF: 0-1 Fm: 0-0**
Distance: 5f/6f: 0-1 7f-8f: 0-1 9f-13f: 0-3 14f+: 0-0
Track : LH: 0-3 RH: 0-1 Tight: 0-3 Gall: 0-1
Aids: Bl: 0-0 Vi: 0-0 Tstrap: 0-0 Ckp: 0-0
Best Rating: **58** 11/08 Wolv 7f32y stand

Miskin Nights

96 68

2-y-o b f Zafeen (FR)-Risalah (Marju (IRE))
B Palling Maywood Racing

Placings:035 **(4163)**
2009: 6^{0}GS, 6^{3}GF, 6^{5}G,

	Starts	1st	2nd	3rd	Win & Pl
Career Total (Turf)	3	0	0	1	530

Going (Turf): **Sf: 0-0 GS: 0-1 Gd: 0-1 GF: 0-1 Fm: 0-0**
Distance: 5f/6f: 0-2 7f-8f: 0-1 9f-13f: 0-0 14f+: 0-0
Track : LH: 0-0 RH: 0-0 Tight: 0-0 Gall: 0-1
Aids: Bl: 0-0 Vi: 0-0 Tstrap: 0-0 Ckp: 0-0
Best Rating: **68** 7/09 Chep 6f16y gd-fm

Miskin Spirit

81(82) (40)43

3-y-o b f Bertolini (USA)-Risalah (Marju (IRE))
B Palling Maywood Racing

Placings:0000 **(7459)**
2009: 8^{0}GS, 7^{0}SD, 9^{0}SD, 7^{0}SD,

	Starts	1st	2nd	3rd	Win & Pl
Career Total (Turf)	1	0	0	0	
Career Total (AW)	3	0	0	0	

Going (Turf): **Sf: 0-0 GS: 0-1 Gd: 0-0 GF: 0-0 Fm: 0-0**
Distance: 5f/6f: 0-0 7f-8f: 0-2 9f-13f: 0-2 14f+: 0-0
Track : LH: 0-3 RH: 0-1 Tight: 0-4 Gall: 0-0
Aids: Bl: 0-1 Vi: 0-0 Tstrap: 0-1 Ckp: 0-1
Best Rating: **43** 10/09 Wind 1m67y gd-sft

Misphire

98 85

6-y-o b m Mister Baileys-Bombay Sapphire (Be My Chief (USA))
M Dods Transpennine Partnership

Placings:04302441/00425/053013530/056010021-0055000 **(7172)**
2009: 6^{0}GS, 6^{0}G, 7^{5}G, 7^{5}G, 7^{0}S, 7^{0}G, 7^{0}S,

	Starts	1st	2nd	3rd	Win & Pl
Career Total (Turf)	38	4	3	4	47342

85	11/08	Donc	7f	(0-85)H	SFT	£5180
84	7/08	Wwck	7f26y	(0-80)H	SFT	£6799
82	6/07	Hayd	6f	(0-75)H	HVY	£2817
85	10/05	Pont	6f		G-S	£3649

Total win prize-money £18448

Going (Turf): **Sf: 3-11** GS: 1-6 Gd: 0-17 GF: 0-4 Fm: 0-0
Distance: 5f/6f: 2-25 7f-8f: 2-13 9f-13f: 0-0 14f+: 0-0
Track : **LH: 2-9** RH: 0-0 Tight: 0-1 Gall: 0-0
Aids: Bl: 0-5 Vi: 0-1 Tstrap: 1-8 Ckp: 1-8
Best Rating: **85** 11/08 Donc 7f soft

Fair; effective over 6f-7f and acts on most ground; has worn cheekpieces, blinkers and a visor; usually held up.

Misplaced Fortune

105(83) (46)**84**
4-y-o b f Compton Place-Tide Of Fortune (Soviet Star (USA))
N Tinkler W F Burton

Placings:654303/32056002-011243462153 **(7287)**
2009: 7^{0}F, 6^{1}F, 5^{1}GF, 5^{2}GF, 6^{4}GS, 6^{3}G, 6^{4}G, 7^{6}GS, 6^{2}GF, 6^{1}G, 7^{5}G, 7^{3}S,

	Starts	1st	2nd	3rd	Win & Pl
Career Total (Turf)	**25**	**3**	**4**	**5**	**18654**
Career Total (AW)	**1**	**0**	**0**	**0**	

84	10/09	Newc	6f	(0-75)H	GD	£2525
78	5/09	Carl	5f193y	(0-70)H	G-F	£2590
68	5/09	Nott	6f15y	(0-60)H	FRM	£2047

Total win prize-money £7163

Going (Turf): Sf: 0-1 GS: 0-5 **Gd: 1-5 GF: 1-12 Fm: 1-2**
Distance: **5f/6f: 2-13** 7f-8f: 1-11 9f-13f: 0-2 14f+: 0-0
Track : LH: 0-8 **RH: 1-1** Tight: 0-1 Gall: 0-3
Aids: Bl: 0-0 **Vi: 3-7** Tstrap: 0-0 Ckp: 0-0
Best Rating: **84** 10/09 Newc 6f good

Fair; effective at 6f, but stays 1m; acts on most ground; has worn a visor.

Miss Antonia (IRE)

88(90) (69)**75**
2-y-o b f Antonius Pius (USA)-Masharik (IRE) (Caerleon (USA))
H R A Cecil Gestut Ammerland

Placings:344 **(6920)**
2009: 7^{3}SD, 8^{4}GF, 8^{4}GF,

	Starts	1st	2nd	3rd	Win & Pl
Career Total (Turf)	**2**	**0**	**0**	**0**	**595**
Career Total (AW)	**1**	**0**	**0**	**1**	**578**

Going (Turf): **Sf: 0-0 GS: 0-0 Gd: 0-0 GF: 0-2 Fm: 0-0**
Distance: 5f/6f: 0-0 7f-8f: 0-1 9f-13f: 0-2 14f+: 0-0
Track : LH: 0-2 RH: 0-0 Tight: 0-1 Gall: 0-0
Aids: Bl: 0-0 Vi: 0-0 Tstrap: 0-0 Ckp: 0-0
Best Rating: **75** 10/09 Yarm 1m3y gd-fm

Useful; stays 7f and acts on Polytrack.

Miss Beat (IRE)

96(96) (73)**89**
3-y-o b f Beat Hollow-Bolas (Unfuwain (USA))
B J Meehan Coleman Bloodstock Limited

Placings:221-30506 **(3870)**
2009: 9^{3}SD, 8^{0}GF, 9^{5}GF, 10^{0}GF, 8^{6}S,

	Starts	1st	2nd	3rd	Win & Pl
Career Total (Turf)	**5**	**0**	**1**	**0**	**1632**
Career Total (AW)	**3**	**1**	**1**	**1**	**4862**

68	12/08	Wolv	7f32y	STD	£3561

Total win prize-money £3562

Going (Turf): **Sf: 0-1 GS: 0-1 Gd: 0-0 GF: 0-3 Fm: 0-0**
Distance: 5f/6f: 0-0 **7f-8f: 1-4** 9f-13f: 0-4 14f+: 0-0
Track : **LH: 1-4** RH: 0-1 **Tight: 1-4** Gall: 0-1
Aids: Bl: 0-0 Vi: 0-0 Tstrap: 0-0 Ckp: 0-0
Best Rating: **89** 5/09 Gdwd 1m1f192y gd-fm

Fair; stays 1m1f; acts on easy ground and on Polytrack.

Miss Blueandblack (IRE)

3-y-o ch f Hawkeye (IRE)-Don't Tell Trigger (IRE) (Mujadil (USA))
Jean-Rene Auvray Mrs C Worsley

Placings:0 **(6941)**
2009: 12^{0}SD,

	Starts	1st	2nd	3rd	Win & Pl
Career Total (Turf)	**0**	**0**	**0**	**0**	
Career Total (AW)	**1**	**0**	**0**	**0**	

Going (Turf): **Sf: 0-0 GS: 0-0 Gd: 0-0 GF: 0-0 Fm: 0-0**
Distance: 5f/6f: 0-0 7f-8f: 0-0 9f-13f: 0-1 14f+: 0-0
Track : LH: 0-0 RH: 0-1 Tight: 0-0 Gall: 0-0
Aids: Bl: 0-0 Vi: 0-0 Tstrap: 0-0 Ckp: 0-0

Miss Bootylishes

101(96) (64)**76**
4-y-o b f Mujahid (USA)-Moxby (Efisio)
A B Haynes Mrs H Adams & Miss C Berry

Placings:1435005/0005550-6100**264** **(7762)**
2009: 8^{6}G, 7^{1}S, 7^{0}F, 6^{0}G, 7^{2}S, 6^{6}SD, 7^{4}SD,

	Starts	1st	2nd	3rd	Win & Pl
Career Total (Turf)	**19**	**2**	**1**	**1**	**10349**
Career Total (AW)	**2**	**0**	**0**	**0**	**0**

74	7/09	Chep	7f16y	(0-70)H	SFT	£4533
61	6/07	Brig	5f213y		G-S	£2914

Total win prize-money £7448

Going (Turf): **Sf: 1-7 GS: 1-4** Gd: 0-3 GF: 0-4 Fm: 0-1
Distance: 5f/6f: 1-4 7f-8f: 1-13 9f-13f: 0-4 14f+: 0-0
Track : **LH: 1-7** RH: 0-3 Tight: 0-1 Gall: 0-1
Aids: Bl: 0-0 Vi: 0-0 Tstrap: 0-0 Ckp: 0-0
Best Rating: **86** 5/08 Gdwd 1m gd-sft

Modest; effective over 6f-1m; acts on easy ground.

Miss California

78 **31**
2-y-o b f Mtoto-Lightning Princess (Puissance)
Miss Tor Sturgis Miss Tor Sturgis

Placings:0 **(6567)**
2009: 7^{0}GF,

	Starts	1st	2nd	3rd	Win & Pl
Career Total (Turf)	**1**	**0**	**0**	**0**	

Going (Turf): **Sf: 0-0 GS: 0-0 Gd: 0-0 GF: 0-1 Fm: 0-0**
Distance: 5f/6f: 0-0 7f-8f: 0-1 9f-13f: 0-0 14f+: 0-0
Track : LH: 0-0 RH: 0-0 Tight: 0-0 Gall: 0-0
Aids: Bl: 0-0 Vi: 0-0 Tstrap: 0-0 Ckp: 0-0
Best Rating: **31** 10/09 Leic 7f9y gd-fm

Miss Cameo (USA)

96(93) (50)**56**
3-y-o b f Mizzen Mast (USA)-Angela Niner (USA) (Forty Niner (USA))
R M Whitaker One-Six-One Partnership

Placings:0003-332P **(1725)**
2009: 9^{3}SD, 7^{3}GF, 8^{2}SD, 7^{P}GF,

	Starts	1st	2nd	3rd	Win & Pl
Career Total (Turf)	**4**	**0**	**0**	**1**	**385**
Career Total (AW)	**4**	**0**	**1**	**2**	**1209**

Going (Turf): **Sf: 0-0 GS: 0-0 Gd: 0-2 GF: 0-2 Fm: 0-0**
Distance: 5f/6f: 0-1 7f-8f: 0-6 9f-13f: 0-1 14f+: 0-0
Track : LH: 0-4 RH: 0-2 Tight: 0-2 Gall: 0-0
Aids: Bl: 0-0 Vi: 0-0 Tstrap: 0-0 Ckp: 0-0
Best Rating: **56** 4/09 Bevl 7f100y gd-fm

Moderate; stays an extended 1m1f; acts on Fibresand and Polytrack.

Miss Chamanda (IRE)

102(98) (78)**89**
3-y-o ch f Choisir (AUS)-Smandar (USA) (Sahm (USA))
P D Evans E A R Morgans

Placings:21-300103155 **(5856)**
2009: 6^{3}SD, 6^{0}GF, 7^{0}GF, 6^{1}GF, 6^{0}G, 6^{3}G, 5^{1}GF, 5^{5}GF, 5^{5}GF,

	Starts	1st	2nd	3rd	Win & Pl
Career Total (Turf)	**10**	**3**	**1**	**1**	**14619**
Career Total (AW)	**1**	**0**	**0**	**1**	**703**

89	8/09	Wind	5f10y	(0-85)H	G-F	£5180
83	6/09	Wind	6f	(0-85)H	G-F	£5180
73	4/08	Wind	5f10y		GD	£2729

Total win prize-money £13092

Going (Turf): Sf: 0-0 GS: 0-1 Gd: 1-3 **GF: 2-6** Fm: 0-0
Distance: **5f/6f: 3-10** 7f-8f: 0-1 9f-13f: 0-0 14f+: 0-0
Track : LH: 0-1 RH: 0-1 Tight: 0-1 **Gall: 3-5**
Aids: Bl: 0-0 Vi: 0-0 Tstrap: 0-0 Ckp: 0-0
Best Rating: **89** 8/09 Wind 5f10y gd-fm

Fair; effective over 5f-6f; acts on good ground; goes on Polytrack.

Miss Chaumiere

38
2-y-o b f Selkirk (USA)-Miss Corniche (Hernando (FR))
M L W Bell J L C Pearce

Placings:0 **(4460)**
2009: 7^{0}GS,

	Starts	1st	2nd	3rd	Win & Pl
Career Total (Turf)	**1**	**0**	**0**	**0**	

Going (Turf): **Sf: 0-0 GS: 0-1 Gd: 0-0 GF: 0-0 Fm: 0-0**
Distance: 5f/6f: 0-0 7f-8f: 0-1 9f-13f: 0-0 14f+: 0-0
Track : LH: 0-0 RH: 0-1 Tight: 0-0 Gall: 0-0
Aids: Bl: 0-0 Vi: 0-0 Tstrap: 0-0 Ckp: 0-0

Miss Christophene (IRE)

94(100) (73)**67**
3-y-o bl f Christophene (USA)-Lotus Flower (IRE) (Grand Lodge (USA))

Mrs S Lamyman P Lamyman

Placings:0-2110500 (5329)
2009: 8[2]SD, 8[1]SS, 8[1]SD, 9[0]GF, 8[5]G, 12[0]GF, 8[0]SD,

	Starts	1st	2nd	3rd	Win & Pl
Career Total (Turf)	3	0	0	0	0
Career Total (AW)	5	2	1	0	6126

73 2/09 Sthl 1m (0-75)H STD £2590
69 2/09 Sthl 1m SS £2729
Total win prize-money £5320

Going (Turf): Sf: 0-0 GS: 0-0 Gd: 0-1 GF: 0-2 Fm: 0-0
Distance: 5f/6f: 0-0 7f-8f: 2-6 9f-13f: 0-2 14f+: 0-0
Track : LH: 2-5 RH: 0-2 Tight: 0-0 Gall: 0-2
Aids: Bl: 0-0 Vi: 0-0 Tstrap: 0-0 Ckp: 0-0
Best Rating: 73 2/09 Sthl 1m stand

Modest; stays 1m; acts on Fibresand.

Miss Clarice (USA)

(94) (49)56
4-y-o b/br f Mr Greeley (USA)-Mutton Maniac (USA) (Wolf Power (SAF))
J R Jenkins Ahmed Hamdam

Placings:0500006-30 (0867)
2009: 8[3]SF, 8[0]SD,

	Starts	1st	2nd	3rd	Win & Pl
Career Total (Turf)	6	0	0	0	0
Career Total (AW)	3	0	0	1	353

Going (Turf): Sf: 0-1 GS: 0-1 Gd: 0-2 GF: 0-2 Fm: 0-0
Distance: 5f/6f: 0-0 7f-8f: 0-5 9f-13f: 0-4 14f+: 0-0
Track : LH: 0-5 RH: 0-1 Tight: 0-3 Gall: 0-0
Aids: Bl: 0-0 Vi: 0-0 Tstrap: 0-2 Ckp: 0-2
Best Rating: 56 6/08 Sals 6f212y gd-fm

Miss Cracklinrosie

75(87) (54)60
3-y-o b f Tobougg (IRE)-Anatase (Danehill (USA))
J R Weymes J Weymes

Placings:34362-50400 (2528)
2009: 9[5]SD, 12[0]SF, 8[4]SD, 7[0]GF, 9[0]GF,

	Starts	1st	2nd	3rd	Win & Pl
Career Total (Turf)	6	0	1	2	1712
Career Total (AW)	4	0	0	0	0

Going (Turf): Sf: 0-4 GS: 0-0 Gd: 0-0 GF: 0-2 Fm: 0-0
Distance: 5f/6f: 0-0 7f-8f: 0-5 9f-13f: 0-5 14f+: 0-0
Track : LH: 0-5 RH: 0-4 Tight: 0-5 Gall: 0-0
Aids: Bl: 0-0 Vi: 0-0 Tstrap: 0-1 Ckp: 0-1
Best Rating: 60 11/08 Catt 7f heavy

Modest; stays 1m and acts on soft ground.

Miss Daawe

104(95) (58)74
5-y-o b m Daawe (USA)-Feiticeira (USA) (Deposit Ticket (USA))
B Ellison Mrs Andrea M Mallinson

Placings:00/660553433324/20122411646-045335506250000 (6799)
2009: 5[0]GF, 5[4]SD, 5[5]GS, 5[3]GF, 6[3]G, 6[5]GS, 5[5]GF, 5[0]G, 5[6]G, 5[2]G, 5[5]GF, 5[0]SD, 5[0]GS, 5[0]GF, 5[0]S,

	Starts	1st	2nd	3rd	Win & Pl
Career Total (Turf)	37	3	5	6	19588
Career Total (AW)	3	0	0	0	385

74 7/08 Thsk 5f (0-75)H G-F £4274
74 7/08 Carl 5f193y (0-75)H GD £3070
61 6/08 Thsk 5f (0-75)H G-S £3885
Total win prize-money £11231

Going (Turf): Sf: 0-4 GS: 1-7 Gd: 1-14 GF: 1-11 Fm: 0-1
Distance: 5f/6f: 3-37 7f-8f: 0-2 9f-13f: 0-1 14f+: 0-0
Track : LH: 0-7 RH: 1-3 Tight: 0-3 Gall: 0-0
Aids: Bl: 0-2 Vi: 0-0 Tstrap: 0-0 Ckp: 0-0
Best Rating: 74 7/08 Thsk 5f gd-fm

Modest; stays 6f; acts on most ground; has worn a tongue tie.

Miss Dee Lady (IRE)

77 19
3-y-o ch f Captain Rio-Windomen (IRE) (Forest Wind (USA))
Patrick Morris Chester Racing Club Ltd

Placings:00 (3614)
2009: 7[0]GF, 7[0]G,

	Starts	1st	2nd	3rd	Win & Pl
Career Total (Turf)	2	0	0	0	

Going (Turf): Sf: 0-0 GS: 0-0 Gd: 0-1 GF: 0-1 Fm: 0-0
Distance: 5f/6f: 0-0 7f-8f: 0-2 9f-13f: 0-0 14f+: 0-0
Track : LH: 0-0 RH: 0-2 Tight: 0-1 Gall: 0-0
Aids: Bl: 0-0 Vi: 0-0 Tstrap: 0-0 Ckp: 0-0
Best Rating: 19 4/09 Muss 7f30y gd-fm

Miss Doodle

99(85) (39)62
3-y-o ch f Dubai Destination (USA)-Running Flame (IND) (Steinbeck (USA))
Eve Johnson Houghton Mrs Virginia Neale

Placings:03660 (5430)
2009: 10[0]SD, 12[3]GF, 12[6]G, 14[6]G, 16[0]G,

	Starts	1st	2nd	3rd	Win & Pl
Career Total (Turf)	4	0	0	1	626
Career Total (AW)	1	0	0	0	

Going (Turf): Sf: 0-0 GS: 0-0 Gd: 0-3 GF: 0-1 Fm: 0-0
Distance: 5f/6f: 0-0 7f-8f: 0-0 9f-13f: 0-3 14f+: 0-2
Track : LH: 0-1 RH: 0-4 Tight: 0-1 Gall: 0-2
Aids: Bl: 0-0 Vi: 0-0 Tstrap: 0-0 Ckp: 0-0
Best Rating: 62 7/09 NmkJ 1m4f good

Modest; stays 1m4f; acts on fast ground.

Miss Dreamy

30
2-y-o b f Whipper (USA)-Highest Dream (IRE) (Highest Honor (FR))
P C Haslam Blue Lion Racing VIII

Placings:0 (1623)
2009: 5[0]GF,

	Starts	1st	2nd	3rd	Win & Pl
Career Total (Turf)	1	0	0	0	

Going (Turf): Sf: 0-0 GS: 0-0 Gd: 0-0 GF: 0-1 Fm: 0-0
Distance: 5f/6f: 0-1 7f-8f: 0-0 9f-13f: 0-0 14f+: 0-0
Track : LH: 0-0 RH: 0-0 Tight: 0-0 Gall: 0-0
Aids: Bl: 0-0 Vi: 0-0 Tstrap: 0-0 Ckp: 0-0

Miss Eze

95(99) (78)81
3-y-o b f Danehill Dancer (IRE)-Miss Corniche (Hernando (FR))
M L W Bell J L C Pearce

Placings:16-006025 (7362)
2009: 7[0]GS, 7[0]HY, 8[6]SD, 6[0]S, 7[2]SD, 8[5]SD,

	Starts	1st	2nd	3rd	Win & Pl
Career Total (Turf)	5	1	0	0	3319
Career Total (AW)	3	0	1	0	964

71 10/08 Folk 6f SFT £2914
Total win prize-money £2914

Going (Turf): Sf: 1-3 GS: 0-2 Gd: 0-0 GF: 0-0 Fm: 0-0
Distance: 5f/6f: 1-2 7f-8f: 0-6 9f-13f: 0-0 14f+: 0-0
Track : LH: 0-3 RH: 0-1 Tight: 0-2 Gall: 0-0
Aids: Bl: 0-0 Vi: 0-0 Tstrap: 0-0 Ckp: 0-0
Best Rating: 81 10/08 NmkR 6f gd-sft

Useful; probably stays 7f; acts on easy ground.

Miss Ferney

102 62
5-y-o ch m Cayman Kai (IRE)-Jendorcet (Grey Ghost)
A Kirtley Mrs P J Taylor-Garthwaite

Placings:0060-00611362 (6218)
2009: 10[0]G, 8[0]G, 12[6]S, 10[1]GF, 10[1]GF, 9[3]GF, 12[6]GS, 10[2]GF,

	Starts	1st	2nd	3rd	Win & Pl
Career Total (Turf)	12	2	1	1	5227

60 8/09 Newc 1m2f32y (0-52)H G-F £2072
59 8/09 Rdcr 1m2f G-F £2047
Total win prize-money £4119

Going (Turf): Sf: 0-1 GS: 0-3 Gd: 0-3 GF: 2-5 Fm: 0-0
Distance: 5f/6f: 0-0 7f-8f: 0-2 9f-13f: 2-10 14f+: 0-0
Track : LH: 2-10 RH: 0-2 Tight: 1-6 Gall: 1-3
Aids: Bl: 0-0 Vi: 0-0 Tstrap: 0-0 Ckp: 0-0
Best Rating: 62 9/09 Rdcr 1m2f gd-fm

Moderate; effective at 1m2f; acts on fast ground.

Miss Firefly

100(100) (66)65
4-y-o b m Compton Place-Popocatepetl (FR) (Nashwan (USA))
R J Hodges R J Hodges

Placings:326405300/503622153000-026602336302040 (7771)
2009: 5[0]GF, 5[2]G, 5[6]GF, 6[6]GF, 5[0]F, 5[2]SF, 5[3]GF, 5[3]GS, 5[6]GF, 6[3]GS, 5[0]G, 5[2]SD, 7[0]SD, 5[4]SD, 6[0]SD,

	Starts	1st	2nd	3rd	Win & Pl
Career Total (Turf)	26	1	3	7	8715
Career Total (AW)	10	0	3	0	2015

63 7/08 Bath 5f11y (0-70)H FRM £2719
Total win prize-money £2720

Going (Turf): Sf: 0-1 GS: 0-4 Gd: 0-4 GF: 0-15 Fm: 1-2
Distance: 5f/6f: 1-29 7f-8f: 0-7 9f-13f: 0-0 14f+: 0-0
Track : LH: 1-23 RH: 0-2 Tight: 0-8 Gall: 1-7
Aids: Bl: 0-1 Vi: 0-0 Tstrap: 0-0 Ckp: 0-0
Best Rating: 70 8/07 Gdwd 7f gd-fm

Moderate; effective over 5f-6f; acts on good ground; goes on Polytrack.

Miss Frangipane (IRE)

100(99) (67)70

3-y-o b f Acclamation-Snap Crackle Pop (IRE) (Statoblest)

J Noseda Netherfield House Stud

Placings:432213 (6701)

2009: 6^{4}G, 6^{3}GF, 6^{2}G, 6^{2}GF, 6^{1}GF, 7^{3}SS,

	Starts	1st	2nd	3rd	Win & Pl
Career Total (Turf)	5	1	2	1	5805
Career Total (AW)	1	0	0	1	433

57 9/09 Yarm 6f3y G-F £3406

Total win prize-money £3406

Going (Turf): Sf: 0-0 GS: 0-0 Gd: 0-2 **GF: 1-3** Fm: 0-0
Distance: 5f/6f: 0-3 **7f-8f: 1-3** 9f-13f: 0-0 14f+: 0-0
Track : LH: 0-1 RH: 0-0 Tight: 0-1 Gall: 0-0
Aids: Bl: 0-0 Vi: 0-0 Tstrap: 0-0 Ckp: 0-0
Best Rating: **70** 9/09 Rdcr 6f gd-fm

Modest; effective over 6f; acts on fast ground.

Miss Fritton (IRE)

(95) (67)66

3-y-o b f Refuse To Bend (IRE)-Golly Gosh (IRE) (Danehill (USA))

M Botti Giuseppe Piccinni

Placings:60400-10 (0450)

2009: 8^{1}SD, 9^{0}SD,

	Starts	1st	2nd	3rd	Win & Pl
Career Total (Turf)	4	0	0	0	216
Career Total (AW)	3	1	0	0	3071

67 1/09 Sthl 1m (0-70)H STD £3070

Total win prize-money £3071

Going (Turf): **Sf: 0-0 GS: 0-1 Gd: 0-0 GF: 0-3 Fm: 0-0**
Distance: 5f/6f: 0-3 **7f-8f: 1-2** 9f-13f: 0-2 14f+: 0-0
Track : **LH: 1-2** RH: 0-1 Tight: 0-1 Gall: 0-0
Aids: Bl: 0-0 Vi: 0-0 Tstrap: 0-0 Ckp: 0-0
Best Rating: **67** 1/09 Sthl 1m stand

Fair; effective at 1m and Fibresand.

Miss Gibboa (IRE)

92 50

3-y-o ch f Spartacus (IRE)-Ludovica (Bustino)

P C Haslam Andrew Sparks

Placings:006-0000 (4142)

2009: 7^{0}GF, 12^{0}GF, 10^{0}G, 16^{0}G,

	Starts	1st	2nd	3rd	Win & Pl
Career Total (Turf)	7	0	0	0	0

Going (Turf): **Sf: 0-1 GS: 0-1 Gd: 0-2 GF: 0-3 Fm: 0-0**
Distance: 5f/6f: 0-3 7f-8f: 0-1 9f-13f: 0-2 14f+: 0-1
Track : LH: 0-1 RH: 0-3 Tight: 0-3 Gall: 0-0
Aids: Bl: 0-0 Vi: 0-0 Tstrap: 0-0 Ckp: 0-0
Best Rating: **50** 9/08 Rdcr 5f gd-sft

Miss Gibbs

79 34

2-y-o b f Needwood Blade-Katy-Q (IRE) (Taufan (USA))

P D Evans Diamond Racing Ltd

Placings:0 (1577)

2009: 5^{0}G,

	Starts	1st	2nd	3rd	Win & Pl
Career Total (Turf)	1	0	0	0	

Going (Turf): **Sf: 0-0 GS: 0-0 Gd: 0-1 GF: 0-0 Fm: 0-0**
Distance: 5f/6f: 0-1 7f-8f: 0-0 9f-13f: 0-0 14f+: 0-0
Track : LH: 0-1 RH: 0-0 Tight: 0-0 Gall: 0-1
Aids: Bl: 0-0 Vi: 0-0 Tstrap: 0-0 Ckp: 0-0
Best Rating: **34** 4/09 Bath 5f11y good

Miss Glitters (IRE)

101(105) (91)78

4-y-o b f Chevalier (IRE)-Geht Schnell (Fairy King (USA))

H Morrison Mrs M D W Morrison

Placings:4121066012 (7759)

2009: 7^{4}SD, 7^{1}SD, 6^{2}F, 7^{1}SD, 8^{0}GF, 8^{6}SD, 6^{6}G, 8^{0}SD, 8^{1}SD, 8^{2}SD,

	Starts	1st	2nd	3rd	Win & Pl
Career Total (Turf)	3	0	1	0	964
Career Total (AW)	7	3	1	0	13628

87 10/09 Sthl 1m (0-85)H STD £6824
84 5/09 Sthl 7f (0-70)H STD £3070
82 4/09 Sthl 7f STD £2047

Total win prize-money £11942

Going (Turf): **Sf: 0-0 GS: 0-0 Gd: 0-1 GF: 0-1 Fm: 0-1**
Distance: 5f/6f: 0-0 **7f-8f: 3-9** 9f-13f: 0-1 14f+: 0-0
Track : **LH: 3-5** RH: 0-4 Tight: 0-0 Gall: 0-0
Aids: Bl: 0-0 Vi: 0-0 Tstrap: 0-0 Ckp: 0-0
Best Rating: **91** 12/09 Sthl 1m stand

Useful; effective at around 7f-1m; acts on Fibresand and Polytrack.

Miss Hollybell

98(88) (53)74

3-y-o b f Umistim-Hollybell (Beveled (USA))

J Gallagher Gallagher Partnership

Placings:242020-06150000 (7518)

2009: 6^{0}GF, 6^{6}HY, 6^{1}G, 6^{5}G, 6^{0}GF, 7^{0}G, 7^{0}SD, 6^{0}SD,

	Starts	1st	2nd	3rd	Win & Pl
Career Total (Turf)	11	1	3	0	5537
Career Total (AW)	3	0	0	0	

74 6/09 Wind 6f (0-70)H GD £2729

Total win prize-money £2730

Going (Turf): Sf: 0-2 GS: 0-0 **Gd: 1-4** GF: 0-5 Fm: 0-0
Distance: **5f/6f: 1-12** 7f-8f: 0-2 9f-13f: 0-0 14f+: 0-0
Track : LH: 0-5 RH: 0-1 Tight: 0-1 **Gall: 1-5**
Aids: Bl: 0-0 Vi: 0-0 Tstrap: 0-0 Ckp: 0-0
Best Rating: **74** 6/09 Wind 6f good

Fair; stays 6f; acts on good and softer ground.

Miss Isle Control

53(73) (32)

2-y-o ch f Monsieur Bond (IRE)-Sea Isle (Selkirk (USA))

A J McCabe The Rocket Partnership

Placings:00P0 (6874)

2009: 6^{0}SD, 7^{0}GF, 7^{P}GF, 7^{0}SD,

	Starts	1st	2nd	3rd	Win & Pl
Career Total (Turf)	2	0	0	0	
Career Total (AW)	2	0	0	0	

Going (Turf): **Sf: 0-0 GS: 0-0 Gd: 0-0 GF: 0-2 Fm: 0-0**
Distance: 5f/6f: 0-1 7f-8f: 0-1 7f-8f: 0-3 9f-13f: 0-0 14f+: 0-0
Track : LH: 0-1 RH: 0-2 Tight: 0-0 Gall: 0-0
Aids: Bl: 0-0 Vi: 0-0 Tstrap: 0-0 Ckp: 0-0
Best Rating: **32** 9/09 Kemp 6f stand

Miss Jabba (IRE)

95(85) (40)43

3-y-o b f Bertolini (USA)-Najaaba (USA) (Bahhare (USA))

Miss J Feilden Mrs Judith Sparks

Placings:000-00300 (7653)

2009: 7^{0}GF, 7^{0}SD, 7^{3}G, 8^{0}SD, 8^{0}SD,

	Starts	1st	2nd	3rd	Win & Pl
Career Total (Turf)	3	0	0	1	385
Career Total (AW)	5	0	0	0	

Going (Turf): **Sf: 0-0 GS: 0-1 Gd: 0-1 GF: 0-1 Fm: 0-0**
Distance: 5f/6f: 0-2 7f-8f: 0-6 9f-13f: 0-0 14f+: 0-0
Track : LH: 0-6 RH: 0-1 Tight: 0-2 Gall: 0-1
Aids: Bl: 0-1 Vi: 0-0 Tstrap: 0-0 Ckp: 0-0
Best Rating: **43** 10/09 Brig 7f214y good

Very moderate; stays 1m and acts on good ground.

Miss Jodarah (USA)

75(83) (47)16

3-y-o b f Action This Day (USA)-Suzie Diamond (USA) (Secreto (USA))

J R Best Simon Malcolm

Placings:00-000005 (6417)

2009: 10^{0}SD, 7^{0}SD, 8^{0}SD, 9^{0}GF, 12^{0}SD, 14^{5}GF,

	Starts	1st	2nd	3rd	Win & Pl
Career Total (Turf)	3	0	0	0	0
Career Total (AW)	5	0	0	0	

Going (Turf): **Sf: 0-0 GS: 0-1 Gd: 0-0 GF: 0-2 Fm: 0-0**
Distance: 5f/6f: 0-0 7f-8f: 0-3 9f-13f: 0-4 14f+: 0-1
Track : LH: 0-3 RH: 0-4 Tight: 0-5 Gall: 0-0
Aids: Bl: 0-4 Vi: 0-0 Tstrap: 0-0 Ckp: 0-0
Best Rating: **47** 9/09 Kemp 1m4f stand

Miss Kadee

89(87) (44)55

3-y-o ch f Needwood Blade-Deco Lady (Wolfhound (USA))

J S Moore Miss D L Wisbey & R J Viney

Placings:0466P-006 (2630)

2009: 6^{0}GF, 6^{0}F, 7^{6}SD,

	Starts	1st	2nd	3rd	Win & Pl
Career Total (Turf)	4	0	0	0	178
Career Total (AW)	4	0	0	0	0

Going (Turf): **Sf: 0-0 GS: 0-1 Gd: 0-0 GF: 0-2 Fm: 0-1**
Distance: 5f/6f: 0-1 7f-8f: 0-5 9f-13f: 0-2 14f+: 0-0
Track : LH: 0-5 RH: 0-0 Tight: 0-4 Gall: 0-1
Aids: Bl: 0-0 Vi: 0-1 Tstrap: 0-0 Ckp: 0-0
Best Rating: **55** 10/08 Bath 1m5y gd-sft

Miss Keck

103(99) (63)73

5-y-o b m Inchinor-En Vacances (IRE) (Old Vic)

G A Swinbank Alan Wright

Placings:343560143145 (5625)

2009: 11[3]SD, 12[4]SD, 12[3]SD, 16[5]F, 14[6]G, 14[0]GF, 16[1]G, 17[4]GF, 16[3]GF, 16[1]GS, 16[4]G, 15[5]S,

	Starts	1st	2nd	3rd	Win & Pl
Career Total (Turf)	9	2	0	1	9172
Career Total (AW)	3	0	0	2	857

73 8/09 Thsk 2m (0-75)H G-S £4274
71 6/09 Newc 2m19y (0-65)H GD £2201
Total win prize-money £6476

Going (Turf): Sf: 0-1 **GS: 1-1 Gd: 1-3** GF: 0-3 Fm: 0-1
Distance: 5f/6f: 0-0 7f-8f: 0-0 9f-13f: 0-3 **14f+: 2-9**
Track : **LH: 2-9** RH: 0-3 Tight: 1-8 Gall: 1-1
Aids: Bl: 0-0 Vi: 0-0 Tstrap: 0-0 Ckp: 0-0
Best Rating: **73** 8/09 Thsk 2m gd-sft

Modest; ex-bumper performer; stays 2m; acts on good ground and Fibresand.

Miss Kitty Grey (IRE)

81 **50**

2-y-o gr f One Cool Cat (USA)-Nortolixa (FR) (Linamix (FR))
J R Boyle Inside Track Racing Club

Placings:60 (4688)

2009: 5[0]G, 5[0]G,

	Starts	1st	2nd	3rd	Win & Pl
Career Total (Turf)	2	0	0	0	0

Going (Turf): **Sf: 0-0 GS: 0-0 Gd: 0-2 GF: 0-0 Fm: 0-0**
Distance: 5f/6f: 0-2 7f-8f: 0-0 9f-13f: 0-0 14f+: 0-0
Track : LH: 0-1 RH: 0-0 Tight: 0-0 Gall: 0-1
Aids: Bl: 0-0 Vi: 0-0 Tstrap: 0-0 Ckp: 0-0
Best Rating: **50** 7/09 Ling 5f good

Miss Kittyhawk (IRE)

95 **66**

3-y-o b f Hawk Wing (USA)-Canterbury Lace (USA) (Danehill (USA))
Rae Guest Scott Fish Metcalf Hirschfeld Gough

Placings:34040 (6787)

2009: 8[3]GF, 7[4]F, 7[0]G, 7[4]GF, 7[0]G,

	Starts	1st	2nd	3rd	Win & Pl
Career Total (Turf)	5	0	0	1	1275

Going (Turf): **Sf: 0-0 GS: 0-0 Gd: 0-2 GF: 0-2 Fm: 0-1**
Distance: 5f/6f: 0-0 7f-8f: 0-5 9f-13f: 0-0 14f+: 0-0
Track : LH: 0-3 RH: 0-0 Tight: 0-1 Gall: 0-0
Aids: Bl: 0-0 Vi: 0-0 Tstrap: 0-0 Ckp: 0-0
Best Rating: **66** 6/09 NmkJ 1m gd-fm

Modest sister to a winner at up to 1m2f; stays 1m; acts on fast ground.

Miss Lauz

78 **34**

2-y-o b f Whipper (USA)-Absolve (USA) (Diesis)
R Hannon Pat Gorman

Placings:505 (3626)

2009: 5[5]GF, 5[0]GF, 5[5]G,

	Starts	1st	2nd	3rd	Win & Pl
Career Total (Turf)	3	0	0	0	0

Going (Turf): **Sf: 0-0 GS: 0-0 Gd: 0-1 GF: 0-2 Fm: 0-0**
Distance: 5f/6f: 0-3 7f-8f: 0-0 9f-13f: 0-0 14f+: 0-0
Track : LH: 0-0 RH: 0-0 Tight: 0-0 Gall: 0-0
Aids: Bl: 0-0 Vi: 0-0 Tstrap: 0-0 Ckp: 0-0
Best Rating: **34** 6/09 Nott 5f13y gd-fm

Miss Leona

76 **28**

3-y-o b f Kyllachy-Feather Circle (IRE) (Indian Ridge)
J M Bradley J M Bradley

Placings:000-0 (5500)

2009: 5[0]G,

	Starts	1st	2nd	3rd	Win & Pl
Career Total (Turf)	4	0	0	0	

Going (Turf): **Sf: 0-0 GS: 0-0 Gd: 0-1 GF: 0-2 Fm: 0-1**
Distance: 5f/6f: 0-4 7f-8f: 0-0 9f-13f: 0-0 14f+: 0-0
Track : LH: 0-1 RH: 0-0 Tight: 0-0 Gall: 0-1
Aids: Bl: 0-0 Vi: 0-0 Tstrap: 0-0 Ckp: 0-0
Best Rating: **28** 7/08 Nott 5f13y firm

Miss Lesley

94(99) (75)**78**

2-y-o b f Needwood Blade-You Found Me (Robellino (USA))
D K Ivory Mrs L A Ivory

Placings:532215000415 (7871)

2009: 5[5]G, 5[3]G, 5[2]SD, 6[2]SD, 6[1]GF, 6[5]G, 6[0]G, 6[0]S, 7[0]SD, 6[4]SD, 6[1]SD, 6[5]SD,

	Starts	1st	2nd	3rd	Win & Pl
Career Total (Turf)	6	1	0	1	6147
Career Total (AW)	6	1	2	0	3941

70 12/09 Ling 6f STD £1978
78 7/09 Wind 6f G-F £5569
Total win prize-money £7548

Going (Turf): Sf: 0-1 GS: 0-0 Gd: 0-4 **GF: 1-1** Fm: 0-0
Distance: **5f/6f: 2-10** 7f-8f: 0-2 9f-13f: 0-0 14f+: 0-0
Track : **LH: 1-3** RH: 0-2 Tight: 1-3 Gall: 1-3
Aids: **Bl: 1-3** Vi: 0-0 Tstrap: 0-0 Ckp: 0-0
Best Rating: **78** 7/09 Wind 6f gd-fm

Fair; effective over 5f-6f; acts on good and fast ground; goes on Fibresand and Polytrack.

Miss Marani (IRE)

72(68) (12)**20**

2-y-o b f Statue Of Liberty (USA)-Countess Bankes (Son Pardo)
W G M Turner T Lightbowne

Placings:00 (1783)

2009: 5[0]SD, 5[0]GF,

	Starts	1st	2nd	3rd	Win & Pl
Career Total (Turf)	1	0	0	0	
Career Total (AW)	1	0	0	0	

Going (Turf): **Sf: 0-0 GS: 0-0 Gd: 0-0 GF: 0-1 Fm: 0-0**
Distance: 5f/6f: 0-2 7f-8f: 0-0 9f-13f: 0-0 14f+: 0-0
Track : LH: 0-1 RH: 0-0 Tight: 0-0 Gall: 0-1
Aids: Bl: 0-0 Vi: 0-0 Tstrap: 0-0 Ckp: 0-0
Best Rating: **20** 5/09 Bath 5f11y gd-fm

Miss Medusa

(74) (16)

4-y-o b f Medicean-College Night (IRE) (Night Shift (USA))
Mrs C A Dunnett Mrs S E A Burton

Placings:000-0 (0626)

2009: 7[0]SD,

	Starts	1st	2nd	3rd	Win & Pl
Career Total (Turf)	1	0	0	0	
Career Total (AW)	3	0	0	0	

Going (Turf): **Sf: 0-1 GS: 0-0 Gd: 0-0 GF: 0-0 Fm: 0-0**
Distance: 5f/6f: 0-0 7f-8f: 0-3 9f-13f: 0-1 14f+: 0-0
Track : LH: 0-4 RH: 0-0 Tight: 0-2 Gall: 0-1
Aids: Bl: 0-0 Vi: 0-0 Tstrap: 0-0 Ckp: 0-0
Best Rating: **16** 10/08 Ling 7f stand

Miss Minnies (IRE)

92(105) (84)**76**

3-y-o b/br f Fraam-Gold Majesty (Josr Algarhoud (IRE))
David P Myerscough David K Kelly

Placings:410-40004211520 (7010a)

2009: 8[4]SD, 8[0]S, 8[0]G, 7[0]G, 7[4]GY, 9[2]G, 8[1]SD, 8[1]SD, 7[5]SD, 7[2]SD, 7[0]SD,

	Starts	1st	2nd	3rd	Win & Pl
Career Total (Turf)	8	1	1	0	7692
Career Total (AW)	6	2	1	0	11426

84 9/09 Kemp 1m (0-75)H STD £2590
73 8/09 Dund 1m (50-70)H STD £4202
74 8/08 DRoy 7f YLD £5080
Total win prize-money £11874

Going (Turf): **Sf: 0-2 GS: 0-0 Gd: 0-3 GF: 0-0 Fm: 0-0**
Distance: 5f/6f: 0-1 **7f-8f: 3-12** 9f-13f: 0-1 14f+: 0-0
Track : LH: 1-9 **RH: 2-4** Tight: 0-1 Gall: 0-1
Aids: Bl: 0-0 Vi: 0-0 Tstrap: 0-0 Ckp: 0-0
Best Rating: **84** 9/09 Kemp 1m stand

Fair; effective at around 1m; acts on Polytrack and good ground.

Miss Miracle

88 **68**

2-y-o gr f Motivator-Miracle (Ezzoud (IRE))
C G Cox D J Burke & Peter Alderson

Placings:45 (6062)

2009: 7[4]GF, 8[5]GF,

	Starts	1st	2nd	3rd	Win & Pl
Career Total (Turf)	2	0	0	0	361

Going (Turf): **Sf: 0-0 GS: 0-0 Gd: 0-0 GF: 0-2 Fm: 0-0**
Distance: 5f/6f: 0-0 7f-8f: 0-2 9f-13f: 0-0 14f+: 0-0
Track : LH: 0-0 RH: 0-0 Tight: 0-0 Gall: 0-0
Aids: Bl: 0-0 Vi: 0-0 Tstrap: 0-0 Ckp: 0-0
Best Rating: **68** 9/09 NmkR 1m gd-fm

Miss Mittagong (USA)

89(79) (54)**75**

2-y-o b f Pleasantly Perfect (USA)-Go Go (USA) (Falstaff (USA))
R M Beckett R A Pegum

Placings:03 (7182)
2009: 7⁰SD, 7³G,

	Starts	1st	2nd	3rd	Win & Pl
Career Total (Turf)	1	0	0	1	722
Career Total (AW)	1	0	0	0	

Going (Turf): **Sf: 0-0 GS: 0-0 Gd: 0-1 GF: 0-0 Fm: 0-0**
Distance: 5f/6f: 0-0 7f-8f: 0-2 9f-13f: 0-0 14f+: 0-0
Track : LH: 0-0 RH: 0-1 Tight: 0-0 Gall: 0-0
Aids: Bl: 0-0 Vi: 0-0 Tstrap: 0-0 Ckp: 0-0
Best Rating: **75** 10/09 NmkR 7f good

Miss Mojito (IRE)

100(98) (66)73
3-y-o ch f Lucky Story (USA)-Lamanka Lass (USA) (Woodman (USA))
J W Hills Gary & Linnet Woodward (2)

Placings:060-**26**205**1**240**1**0 (6243)
2009: 7²SD, 7⁶SD, 8²SD, 7⁰GF, 8⁵F, 8¹GF, 8²SD, 8⁴GF, 8⁰SD, 8¹GS, 8⁰G,

	Starts	1st	2nd	3rd	Win & Pl
Career Total (Turf)	8	2	0	0	6859
Career Total (AW)	6	0	3	0	1761
73	9/09	Sals	1m	(0-70)H	G-S £3238
66	6/09	Sals	1m	(0-65)H	G-F £3043

Total win prize-money £6282

Going (Turf): Sf: 0-0 **GS: 1-1** Gd: 0-2 **GF: 1-4** Fm: 0-1
Distance: 5f/6f: 0-2 **7f-8f: 2-11** 9f-13f: 0-1 14f+: 0-0
Track : LH: 0-5 RH: 0-4 Tight: 0-4 Gall: 0-0
Aids: Bl: 0-0 Vi: 0-0 Tstrap: 0-0 Ckp: 0-0
Best Rating: **73** 9/09 Sals 1m gd-sft

Modest; effective over 7f-1m; acts on most ground and on Polytrack; has worn a tongue tie.

Miss Moloney (IRE)

69(80) (45)46
3-y-o b f Sesaro (USA)-Mickey Towbar (IRE) (Mujadil (USA))
Mrs S Lamyman P Lamyman

Placings:55550-00 (3305)
2009: 8⁰SD, 7⁰GF,

	Starts	1st	2nd	3rd	Win & Pl
Career Total (Turf)	4	0	0	0	0
Career Total (AW)	3	0	0	0	0

Going (Turf): **Sf: 0-0 GS: 0-2 Gd: 0-0 GF: 0-2 Fm: 0-0**
Distance: 5f/6f: 0-4 7f-8f: 0-3 9f-13f: 0-0 14f+: 0-0
Track : LH: 0-3 RH: 0-0 Tight: 0-0 Gall: 0-0
Aids: Bl: 0-0 Vi: 0-0 Tstrap: 0-0 Ckp: 0-0
Best Rating: **46** 8/08 NmkJ 7f gd-sft

Plating-class form at up to 7f on Fibresand and turf.

Miss Mujanna

102(106) (77)73
4-y-o b f Mujahid (USA)-Robanna (Robellino (USA))
J Akehurst Green Pastures Partnership

Placings:322/230140504-4015560 (5810)
2009: 7⁴SD, 7⁰SD, 6¹GF, 8⁵GF, 8⁵S, 8⁶G, 7⁰SD,

	Starts	1st	2nd	3rd	Win & Pl
Career Total (Turf)	7	1	0	0	3238
Career Total (AW)	12	1	3	2	6341
73	6/09	Sals	6f212y	(0-75)H	G-F £3238
74	3/08	Kemp	7f	(0-70)H	STD £2590

Total win prize-money £5829

Going (Turf): Sf: 0-2 GS: 0-0 Gd: 0-2 **GF: 1-3** Fm: 0-0
Distance: 5f/6f: 0-2 **7f-8f: 2-16** 9f-13f: 0-1 14f+: 0-0
Track : LH: 0-6 **RH: 1-7** Tight: 0-6 Gall: 0-1
Aids: Bl: 0-0 Vi: 0-0 Tstrap: 0-1 Ckp: 0-1
Best Rating: **77** 1/09 Ling 7f stand

Fair; effective at around 7f-1m; acts on Polytrack.

Miss Pelling (IRE)

103(98) (69)73
4-y-o b f Danehill Dancer (IRE)-Morningsurprice (USA) (Future Storm (USA))
J G Burns (B J Meehan 18/6) Michael O'Callaghan

Placings:0651-2210 (4961a)
2009: 10²F, 9²GF, 8¹G, 8⁰G,

	Starts	1st	2nd	3rd	Win & Pl
Career Total (Turf)	7	1	2	0	5358
Career Total (AW)	1	1	0	0	1943
73	6/09	Wwck	1m22y	(0-75)H	GD £3238
69	10/08	Ling	1m2f	(0-65)H	STD £1942

Total win prize-money £5181

Going (Turf): Sf: 0-0 GS: 0-1 **Gd: 1-3** GF: 0-2 Fm: 0-1
Distance: 5f/6f: 0-0 7f-8f: 0-2 **9f-13f: 2-6** 14f+: 0-0
Track : **LH: 2-6** RH: 0-1 **Tight: 1-1** Gall: 0-1
Aids: Bl: 0-0 Vi: 0-0 Tstrap: 0-0 Ckp: 0-0
Best Rating: **73** 6/09 Wwck 1m22y good

Modest; effective over 1m-1m2f; acts on fast ground; goes on Polytrack.

Miss Perfectionist

(96) (67)43
3-y-o b f Invincible Spirit (IRE)-To The Woods (IRE) (Woodborough (USA))
P Howling Andrew Baker

Placings:004-0606400 (7818)
2009: 6⁰SD, 8⁶SD, 7⁰SD, 10⁶SD, 9⁴SD, 9⁰SD, 9⁰SD,

	Starts	1st	2nd	3rd	Win & Pl
Career Total (Turf)	1	0	0	0	
Career Total (AW)	9	0	0	0	385

Going (Turf): **Sf: 0-0 GS: 0-0 Gd: 0-0 GF: 0-1 Fm: 0-0**
Distance: 5f/6f: 0-3 7f-8f: 0-3 9f-13f: 0-4 14f+: 0-0
Track : LH: 0-7 RH: 0-2 Tight: 0-3 Gall: 0-2
Aids: Bl: 0-0 Vi: 0-0 Tstrap: 0-0 Ckp: 0-0
Best Rating: **67** 11/08 GrLe 6f stand

Miss Polly Plum

(79) (36)
2-y-o b f Doyen (IRE)-Mrs Plum (Emarati (USA))
C A Dwyer Mrs J Hughes & Miss C Hughes

Placings:0 (7772)
2009: 7⁰SD,

	Starts	1st	2nd	3rd	Win & Pl
Career Total (Turf)	0	0	0	0	
Career Total (AW)	1	0	0	0	

Going (Turf): **Sf: 0-0 GS: 0-0 Gd: 0-0 GF: 0-0 Fm: 0-0**
Distance: 5f/6f: 0-0 7f-8f: 0-1 9f-13f: 0-0 14f+: 0-0
Track : LH: 0-1 RH: 0-0 Tight: 0-1 Gall: 0-0
Aids: Bl: 0-0 Vi: 0-0 Tstrap: 0-0 Ckp: 0-0
Best Rating: **36** 12/09 Ling 7f stand

Miss Porky

90 61
3-y-o b f Deportivo-Carati (Selkirk (USA))
R Hollinshead Edenbrook Partnership

Placings:5505 (2950)
2009: 6⁵GF, 7⁵GF, 6⁰GF, 8⁵GF,

	Starts	1st	2nd	3rd	Win & Pl
Career Total (Turf)	4	0	0	0	0

Going (Turf): **Sf: 0-0 GS: 0-0 Gd: 0-0 GF: 0-4 Fm: 0-0**
Distance: 5f/6f: 0-1 7f-8f: 0-3 9f-13f: 0-0 14f+: 0-0
Track : LH: 0-2 RH: 0-0 Tight: 0-1 Gall: 0-0
Aids: Bl: 0-0 Vi: 0-0 Tstrap: 0-0 Ckp: 0-0
Best Rating: **61** 4/09 Pont 6f gd-fm

Miss Pusey Street

99(99) (43)51
3-y-o ch f Compton Place-Pusey Street Girl (Gildoran)
P D Evans (J Gallagher 7/8) Nick Shutts

Placings:0-40024300**0**50 (7838)
2009: 6⁴G, 6⁰GF, 5⁰GF, 5²GS, 6⁴GF, 5³S, 6⁰S, 5⁰GS, 5⁰SD, 6⁵SD, 5⁰SS,

	Starts	1st	2nd	3rd	Win & Pl
Career Total (Turf)	9	0	1	1	931
Career Total (AW)	3	0	0	0	0

Going (Turf): **Sf: 0-2 GS: 0-2 Gd: 0-1 GF: 0-4 Fm: 0-0**
Distance: 5f/6f: 0-11 7f-8f: 0-1 9f-13f: 0-0 14f+: 0-0
Track : LH: 0-3 RH: 0-1 Tight: 0-1 Gall: 0-0
Aids: Bl: 0-0 Vi: 0-2 Tstrap: 0-0 Ckp: 0-0
Best Rating: **51** 8/09 Ayr 5f soft

Miss Roma (IRE)

76(75) (34)35
2-y-o b f Le Vie Dei Colori-Saffa Garden (IRE) (King's Best (USA))
R A Harris Mrs Ruth M Serrell

Placings:06040 (6328)
2009: 5⁰GF, 5⁶S, 5⁰SD, 5⁴G, 5⁰F,

	Starts	1st	2nd	3rd	Win & Pl
Career Total (Turf)	4	0	0	0	144
Career Total (AW)	1	0	0	0	

Going (Turf): **Sf: 0-1 GS: 0-0 Gd: 0-1 GF: 0-1 Fm: 0-1**
Distance: 5f/6f: 0-5 7f-8f: 0-0 9f-13f: 0-0 14f+: 0-0
Track : LH: 0-3 RH: 0-0 Tight: 0-0 Gall: 0-2
Aids: Bl: 0-0 Vi: 0-0 Tstrap: 0-1 Ckp: 0-1
Best Rating: **35** 7/09 Ripn 5f soft

Miss Sampower (IRE)

(58)
3-y-o b f Sampower Star-Miss Mimosa (IRE) (Salmon Leap (USA))
D Carroll J F O'Sullivan

Placings:0 (0251)
2009: 7^{0}SD,

	Starts	1st	2nd	3rd	Win & Pl
Career Total (Turf)	0	0	0	0	
Career Total (AW)	1	0	0	0	

Going (Turf): Sf: 0-0 GS: 0-0 Gd: 0-0 GF: 0-0 Fm: 0-0
Distance: 5f/6f: 0-0 7f-8f: 0-1 9f-13f: 0-0 14f+: 0-0
Track : LH: 0-1 RH: 0-0 Tight: 0-1 Gall: 0-0
Aids: Bl: 0-0 Vi: 0-0 Tstrap: 0-0 Ckp: 0-0

Miss Scarlet

39 **64**

3-y-o b f Red Ransom (USA)-Give Warning (IRE) (Warning)
K A Ryan J Nattrass

Placings:024-00 (3305)
2009: 8^{0}G, 7^{0}GF,

	Starts	1st	2nd	3rd	Win & Pl
Career Total (Turf)	5	0	1	0	1445

Going (Turf): Sf: 0-1 GS: 0-0 Gd: 0-2 GF: 0-2 Fm: 0-0
Distance: 5f/6f: 0-1 7f-8f: 0-4 9f-13f: 0-0 14f+: 0-0
Track : LH: 0 1 RH: 0 1 Tight: 0-1 Gall: 0-1
Aids: Bl: 0-0 Vi: 0-0 Tstrap: 0-0 Ckp: 0-0
Best Rating: 64 7/08 Nott 6f15y gd-fm

Modest form at 6f; acts on fast does not handle soft.

Miss Serena

69(101) (75)**76**

4-y-o gr f Singspiel (IRE)-Valnerina (IRE) (Caerleon (USA))
Mrs P Sly Erik Amlie

Placings:003050112-5450 (2163)
2009: 16^{5}SD, 16^{4}SF, 16^{5}SD, 16^{0}G,

	Starts	1st	2nd	3rd	Win & Pl
Career Total (Turf)	8	0	1	1	1638
Career Total (AW)	5	2	0	0	5022

72 10/08 GrLe 2m (0-65)H STD £2590
64 9/08 Kemp 2m (0-65)H STD £2047
Total win prize-money £4637

Going (Turf): Sf: 0-0 GS: 0-2 Gd: 0-4 GF: 0-2 Fm: 0-0
Distance: 5f/6f: 0-0 7f-8f: 0-0 9f-13f: 0-4 **14f+: 2-9**
Track : LH: 1-10 RH: 1-3 Tight: 0-4 **Gall: 1-2**
Aids: Bl: 0-0 Vi: 0-0 Tstrap: 0-0 Ckp: 0-0
Best Rating: 76 10/08 Pont 2m1f216y gd-sft

Modest; stays 2m; acts on Polytrack.

Miss Smilla

98(98) (74)**77**

2-y-o b f Red Ransom (USA)-Snowing (Tate Gallery (USA))
K A Ryan Findlay & Bloom

Placings:415443 (7003)
2009: 5^{4}GF, 6^{1}GF, 6^{5}GS, 7^{4}GF, 8^{4}GF, 8^{3}SD,

	Starts	1st	2nd	3rd	Win & Pl
Career Total (Turf)	5	1	0	0	5232
Career Total (AW)	1	0	0	1	626

77 7/09 Nott 6f15y G-F £3885
Total win prize-money £3886

Going (Turf): Sf: 0-0 GS: 0-1 Gd: 0-0 **GF: 1-4** Fm: 0-0
Distance: 5f/6f: 0-2 **7f-8f: 1-2** 9f-13f: 0-2 14f+: 0-0
Track : LH: 0-2 RH: 0-0 Tight: 0-1 Gall: 0-0
Aids: Bl: 0-0 Vi: 0-0 Tstrap: 0-0 Ckp: 0-0
Best Rating: 77 9/09 Donc 7f gd-fm

Fair; stays 7f and acts on fast ground.

Miss Sophisticat

105(102) (76)**77**

3-y-o b f Alhaarth (IRE)-She's Classy (USA) (Boundary (USA))
W J Knight Mrs Sheila Mitchell

Placings:502323-065252041100 (7399)
2009: 12^{0}SD, 11^{6}G, 10^{5}GF, 8^{2}GS, 9^{5}GS, 8^{2}G, 8^{0}GF, 8^{4}SD, 8^{1}G, 10^{1}SD, 10^{0}HY, 9^{0}SD,

	Starts	1st	2nd	3rd	Win & Pl
Career Total (Turf)	14	1	4	2	7976
Career Total (AW)	4	1	0	0	2730

76 11/09 Ling 1m2f (0-75)H STD £2729
77 10/09 Wind 1m67y (0-70)H GD £2388
Total win prize-money £5118

Going (Turf): Sf: 0-3 GS: 0-5 **Gd: 1-3** GF: 0-3 Fm: 0-0
Distance: 5f/6f: 0-0 7f-8f: 0-4 **9f-13f: 2-14** 14f+: 0-0
Track : LH: 1-8 RH: 1-7 **Tight: 2-7** Gall: 0-1
Aids: Bl: 0-0 **Vi: 2-8** Tstrap: 0-2 Ckp: 0-2
Best Rating: 77 10/09 Wind 1m67y good

Fair; stays 1m2f; acts on easy ground; goes on Polytrack; has worn a visor.

Miss Starlight

92(93) (78)**66**

2-y-o b f Trade Fair-Redeem (IRE) (Doyoun)
P J McBride Maelor Racing

Placings:610 (7434)
2009: 7^{6}G, 8^{1}SD, 8^{0}SD,

	Starts	1st	2nd	3rd	Win & Pl
Career Total (Turf)	1	0	0	0	0
Career Total (AW)	2	1	0	0	3886

78 9/09 Wolv 1m141y STD £3885
Total win prize-money £3886

Going (Turf): Sf: 0-0 GS: 0-0 Gd: 0-1 GF: 0-0 Fm: 0-0
Distance: 5f/6f: 0-0 7f-8f: 0-2 **9f-13f: 1-1** 14f+: 0-0
Track : **LH: 1-2** RH: 0-0 **Tight: 1-2** Gall: 0-0
Aids: Bl: 0-0 Vi: 0-0 Tstrap: 0-0 Ckp: 0-0
Best Rating: 78 9/09 Wolv 1m141y stand

Fair; effective over 1m; acts on Polytrack.

Miss Taken (IRE)

89(92) (55)**67**

2-y-o b f Dubai Destination (USA)-Miss Takeortwo (IRE) (Danehill Dancer (IRE))
D Carroll K & D Racing Partnership

Placings:23506054420335 (7868)
2009: 6^{2}S, 5^{3}GF, 6^{5}G, 8^{0}GF, 8^{6}GF, 8^{0}SD, 6^{5}SD, 6^{4}SD, 6^{4}SD, 7^{2}SD, 7^{0}SF, 7^{3}SD, 7^{3}SS, 7^{5}SS,

	Starts	1st	2nd	3rd	Win & Pl
Career Total (Turf)	5	0	1	1	1782
Career Total (AW)	9	0	1	2	1209

Going (Turf): Sf: 0-1 GS: 0-0 Gd: 0-1 GF: 0-3 Fm: 0-0
Distance: 5f/6f: 0-6 7f-8f: 0-5 9f-13f: 0-3 14f+: 0-0
Track : LH: 0-12 RH: 0-0 Tight: 0-2 Gall: 0-0
Aids: Bl: 0-8 Vi: 0-0 Tstrap: 0-0 Ckp: 0-0
Best Rating: 67 7/09 Pont 6f soft

Moderate; stays 7f; handles Fibresand; has worn blinkers.

Miss Tango Hotel

96 **73**

3-y-o b f Green Desert (USA)-Inchyre (Shirley Heights)
J H M Gosden Michael O'Flynn

Placings:02-26 (2179)
2009: 7^{2}GF, 7^{6}G,

	Starts	1st	2nd	3rd	Win & Pl
Career Total (Turf)	4	0	2	0	3720

Going (Turf): Sf: 0-0 GS: 0-0 Gd: 0-3 GF: 0-1 Fm: 0-0
Distance: 5f/6f: 0-1 7f-8f: 0-3 9f-13f: 0-0 14f+: 0-0
Track : LH: 0-1 RH: 0-1 Tight: 0-1 Gall: 0-0
Aids: Bl: 0-0 Vi: 0-0 Tstrap: 0-0 Ckp: 0-0
Best Rating: 73 8/08 NmkJ 6f good

Fair; suited by 6f and good ground.

Miss Thippawan (USA)

83(93) (43)**43**

3-y-o b/br f Street Cry (IRE)-Sheathanna (USA) (Mr. Leader (USA))
P T Midgley R Fell & K Everitt

Placings:60545-006 (2454)
2009: 5^{0}SD, 5^{0}GF, 5^{6}GF,

	Starts	1st	2nd	3rd	Win & Pl
Career Total (Turf)	5	0	0	0	168
Career Total (AW)	3	0	0	0	0

Going (Turf): Sf: 0-0 GS: 0-2 Gd: 0-1 GF: 0-2 Fm: 0-0
Distance: 5f/6f: 0-8 7f-8f: 0-0 9f-13f: 0-0 14f+: 0-0
Track : LH: 0-2 RH: 0-1 Tight: 0-1 Gall: 0-1
Aids: Bl: 0-0 Vi: 0-0 Tstrap: 0-1 Ckp: 0-1
Best Rating: 43 10/08 Catt 5f good

Moderate sprinter; acts on good ground.

Miss Tikitiboo (IRE)

96(97) (59)**60**

3-y-o b f Elusive City (USA)-Sabindra (Magic Ring (IRE))
E F Vaughan A M Pickering

Placings:0063-635P (4749)
2009: 8^{6}SD, 7^{3}SD, 5^{5}GF, 7^{P}SD,

	Starts	1st	2nd	3rd	Win & Pl
Career Total (Turf)	2	0	0	0	0
Career Total (AW)	6	0	0	2	655

Going (Turf): Sf: 0-0 GS: 0-1 Gd: 0-0 GF: 0-1 Fm: 0-0
Distance: 5f/6f: 0-3 7f-8f: 0-5 9f-13f: 0-0 14f+: 0-0
Track : LH: 0-4 RH: 0-2 Tight: 0-4 Gall: 0-1
Aids: Bl: 0-0 Vi: 0-0 Tstrap: 0-0 Ckp: 0-0
Best Rating: 60 6/09 Leic 5f218y gd-fm

Moderate; suited by 6f and Polytrack.

Miss Totnes

79 **29**

5-y-o b m Bandmaster (USA)-Kingston Black (Shaab)
M Hill Martin Hill

Placings:0 (4828)
2009: 10^{0}G,

	Starts	1st	2nd	3rd	Win & Pl
Career Total (Turf)	1	0	0	0	

Going (Turf): Sf: 0-0 GS: 0-0 Gd: 0-1 GF: 0-0 Fm: 0-0
Distance: 5f/6f: 0-0 7f-8f: 0-0 9f-13f: 0-1 14f+: 0-0
Track : LH: 0-0 RH: 0-1 Tight: 0-1 Gall: 0-0
Aids: Bl: 0-0 Vi: 0-0 Tstrap: 0-0 Ckp: 0-0
Best Rating: 29 8/09 Wind 1m2f7y good

Miss Understanding

64(97) (47)44

4-y-o br f Dansili-Crossed Wire (Lycius (USA))
J R Weymes C E Giblett

Placings:0600405452-3046000 (1848)
2009: 10^{3}SD, 12^{0}SD, 9^{4}SD, 10^{6}SD, 8^{0}SD, 9^{0}GF, 9^{0}GF,

	Starts	1st	2nd	3rd	Win & Pl
Career Total (Turf)	11	0	0	0	418
Career Total (AW)	6	0	1	1	867

Going (Turf): Sf: 0-0 GS: 0-1 Gd: 0-4 GF: 0-6 Fm: 0-0
Distance: 5f/6f: 0-0 7f-8f: 0-8 9f-13f: 0-9 14f+: 0-0
Track : LH: 0-11 RH: 0-6 Tight: 0-11 Gall: 0-2
Aids: Bl: 0-6 Vi: 0-3 Tstrap: 0-1 Ckp: 0-1
Best Rating: 47 2/09 Wolv 1m1f103y stand

Moderate; looks to need further than 1m; acts on Polytrack; has worn blinkers and a visor.

Miss Wendy

72(85) (58)36

2-y-o b f Where Or When (IRE)-Grove Dancer (Reprimand)
M H Tompkins Miss Clare Hollest

Placings:03 (5637)
2009: 5^{0}S, 8^{3}SD,

	Starts	1st	2nd	3rd	Win & Pl
Career Total (Turf)	1	0	0	0	
Career Total (AW)	1	0	0	1	770

Going (Turf): Sf: 0-1 GS: 0-0 Gd: 0-0 GF: 0-0 Fm: 0-0
Distance: 5f/6f: 0-1 7f-8f: 0-1 9f-13f: 0-0 14f+: 0-0
Track : LH: 0-0 RH: 0-1 Tight: 0-0 Gall: 0-0
Aids: Bl: 0-0 Vi: 0-0 Tstrap: 0-0 Ckp: 0-0
Best Rating: 58 9/09 Kemp 1m stand

Modest; stays 1m; acts on Polytrack.

Miss Whippy

99 58

2-y-o b f Whipper (USA)-Glorious (Nashwan (USA))
M L W Bell D W & L Y Payne

Placings:413 (6232)
2009: 7^{4}GS, 8^{1}GF, 8^{3}GF,

	Starts	1st	2nd	3rd	Win & Pl
Career Total (Turf)	3	1	0	1	2962

56 8/09 Wind 1m67y G-F £2047
Total win prize-money £2047

Going (Turf): Sf: 0-0 GS: 0-1 Gd: 0-0 GF: 1-2 Fm: 0-0
Distance: 5f/6f: 0-0 7f-8f: 0-1 9f-13f: 1-2 14f+: 0-0
Track : LH: 0-1 RH: 1-1 Tight: 1-1 Gall: 0-0
Aids: Bl: 0-0 Vi: 0-0 Tstrap: 0-0 Ckp: 0-0
Best Rating: 58 9/09 Pont 1m4y gd-fm

Moderate; effective over 1m; acts on fast ground.

Miss Xu Xia

(92) (45)41

3-y-o b f Monsieur Bond (IRE)-Bond Girl (Magic Ring (IRE))
G R Oldroyd R C Bond

Placings:0400500510-3 (0005)
2009: 8^{3}SS,

	Starts	1st	2nd	3rd	Win & Pl
Career Total (Turf)	6	0	0	0	481
Career Total (AW)	5	1	0	1	2350

45 11/08 Sthl 7f STD £2047
Total win prize-money £2047

Going (Turf): Sf: 0-2 GS: 0-1 Gd: 0-2 GF: 0-1 Fm: 0-0
Distance: 5f/6f: 0-6 7f-8f: 1-5 9f-13f: 0-0 14f+: 0-0
Track : LH: 1-6 RH: 0-0 Tight: 0-2 Gall: 0-0
Aids: Bl: 0-0 Vi: 0-0 Tstrap: 1-7 Ckp: 1-7
Best Rating: 45 11/08 Sthl 7f stand

Moderate; effective over 7f and acts on Fibresand; has worn cheekpieces.

Miss Zooter (IRE)

95 80

2-y-o b f Intikhab (USA)-Laraissa (Machiavellian (USA))
R M Beckett Timeform Betfair Racing Club Ltd

Placings:561 (7061)
2009: 5^{5}G, 7^{6}GF, 5^{1}GF,

	Starts	1st	2nd	3rd	Win & Pl
Career Total (Turf)	3	1	0	0	2590

80 10/09 Leic 5f218y G-F £2590
Total win prize-money £2590

Going (Turf): Sf: 0-0 GS: 0-0 Gd: 0-1 GF: 1-2 Fm: 0-0
Distance: 5f/6f: 1-2 7f-8f: 0-1 9f-13f: 0-0 14f+: 0-0
Track : LH: 0-2 RH: 0-0 Tight: 0-0 Gall: 0-1
Aids: Bl: 0-0 Vi: 0-0 Tstrap: 0-0 Ckp: 0-0
Best Rating: 80 10/09 Leic 5f218y gd-fm

Useful; stays 6f; acts on fast ground.

Missed Mondays

100(90) (53)42

3-y-o ch f Distant Music (USA)-Lilting Prose (IRE) (Indian Ridge)
Patrick Morris Monday Club

Placings:00-500650 (7069)
2009: 7^{5}SD, 5^{0}SD, 6^{0}SD, 6^{6}SD, 6^{5}F, 6^{0}SD,

	Starts	1st	2nd	3rd	Win & Pl
Career Total (Turf)	1	0	0	0	0
Career Total (AW)	7	0	0	0	0

Going (Turf): Sf: 0-0 GS: 0-0 Gd: 0-0 GF: 0-0 Fm: 0-1
Distance: 5f/6f: 0-5 7f-8f: 0-3 9f-13f: 0-0 14f+: 0-0
Track : LH: 0-6 RH: 0-1 Tight: 0-5 Gall: 0-0
Aids: Bl: 0-0 Vi: 0-1 Tstrap: 0-0 Ckp: 0-0
Best Rating: 53 11/08 Wolv 7f32y stand

Mission Control (IRE)

(103) (83)73

4-y-o ch g Dubai Destination (USA)-Stage Manner (In The Wings)
Tim Vaughan (J R Boyle 20/3) M Khan X2

Placings:01/134441-612354 (7515)
2009: 12^{6}SD, 13^{1}SD, 16^{2}SD, 16^{3}SD, 16^{5}SF, 16^{4}SD,

	Starts	1st	2nd	3rd	Win & Pl
Career Total (Turf)	4	0	0	1	1549
Career Total (AW)	10	4	1	1	11850

78 1/09 Ling 1m5f (0-75)H STD £2900
75 12/08 Kemp 1m4f (0-65)H STD £2047
65 3/08 Wolv 1m1f103y (0-65)H STD £2047
60 12/07 Wolv 1m141y STD £2047
Total win prize-money £9043

Going (Turf): Sf: 0-0 GS: 0-1 Gd: 0-0 GF: 0-3 Fm: 0-0
Distance: 5f/6f: 0-0 7f-8f: 0-1 9f-13f: 4-9 14f+: 0-4
Track : LH: 3-8 RH: 1-6 Tight: 3-11 Gall: 0-0
Aids: Bl: 0-0 Vi: 0-0 Tstrap: 0-0 Ckp: 0-0
Best Rating: 83 2/09 Kemp 2m stand

Fair; stays 2m; acts on Polytrack.

Mission Impossible

89(93) (70)80

4-y-o gr g Kyllachy-Eastern Lyric (Petong)
Miss Tracy Waggott (P C Haslam 8/9) H Conlon

Placings:243500214/12300-00000001 (7241)
2009: 5^{0}SD, 6^{0}SD, 7^{0}GF, 5^{0}GS, 6^{0}GS, 6^{0}GF, 7^{0}G, 5^{1}S,

	Starts	1st	2nd	3rd	Win & Pl
Career Total (Turf)	17	2	2	2	8543
Career Total (AW)	5	1	1	0	3335

59 11/09 Nott 5f13y (0-55)H SFT £2047
81 4/08 Nott 5f13y (0-70)H SFT £2590
70 12/07 Wolv 5f216y STD £2730
Total win prize-money £7367

Going (Turf): Sf: 2-4 GS: 0-4 Gd: 0-4 GF: 0-5 Fm: 0-0
Distance: 5f/6f: 3-17 7f-8f: 0-5 9f-13f: 0-0 14f+: 0-0
Track : LH: 1-10 RH: 0-0 Tight: 1-6 Gall: 0-0
Aids: Bl: 0-0 Vi: 0-0 Tstrap: 0-1 Ckp: 0-1
Best Rating: 81 4/08 Nott 5f13y soft

Moderate; effective over 5f-6f; suited by soft ground; goes on Polytrack.

Mission Lodge

79 22

3-y-o b f Selkirk (USA)-Hiddendale (IRE) (Indian Ridge)
B J Meehan Mrs Susan Roy

Placings:00 (2847)
2009: 8^{0}G, 10^{0}GF,

	Starts	1st	2nd	3rd	Win & Pl
Career Total (Turf)	2	0	0	0	

Going (Turf): Sf: 0-0 GS: 0-0 Gd: 0-1 GF: 0-1 Fm: 0-0
Distance: 5f/6f: 0-0 7f-8f: 0-0 9f-13f: 0-2 14f+: 0-0
Track : LH: 0-1 RH: 0-1 Tight: 0-1 Gall: 0-1
Aids: Bl: 0-0 Vi: 0-0 Tstrap: 0-0 Ckp: 0-0
Best Rating: 22 6/09 Newb 1m2f6y gd-fm

Missionaire (USA)

101 82

2-y-o b/br c El Corredor (USA)-Fapindy (USA) (A.P. Indy (USA))
W J Knight Bluehills Racing Limited

Placings:2154 (5399)
2009: 6^{2}GS, 7^{1}G, 7^{5}G, 8^{4}G,

	Starts	1st	2nd	3rd	Win & Pl
Career Total (Turf)	4	1	1	0	7179

82 6/09 NmkJ 7f GD £5180
Total win prize-money £5181

Going (Turf): Sf: 0-0 GS: 0-1 **Gd: 1-3** GF: 0-0 Fm: 0-0
Distance: 5f/6f: 0-1 **7f-8f: 1-3** 9f-13f: 0-0 14f+: 0-0
Track : LH: 0-0 RH: 0-0 Tight: 0-0 Gall: 0-1
Aids: Bl: 0-0 Vi: 0-0 Tstrap: 0-0 Ckp: 0-0
Best Rating: 82 6/09 NmkJ 7f good

Useful; stays 7f and acts on good and easy ground.

Mississippian (IRE)

94(92) (63)**54**

5-y-o b g Montjeu (IRE)-Swilly (USA) (Irish River (FR))
C J Mann (James Cassidy 1/2) Gordian Troeller

Placings:1/00000036-000000 **(6909)**
2009: 10^{0}F, 9^{0}F, 10^{0}G, 8^{0}SD, 10^{0}SD, 8^{0}G,

	Starts	1st	2nd	3rd	Win & Pl
Career Total (Turf)	11	1	0	1	11451
Career Total (AW)	4	0	0	0	479

82 10/07 Navn 1m2f FRM £7236
Total win prize-money £7237

Going (Turf): Sf: 0-0 GS: 0-0 Gd: 0-2 GF: 0-0 **Fm: 1-9**
Distance: 5f/6f: 0-0 7f-8f: 0-3 **9f-13f: 1-12** 14f+: 0-0
Track : **LH: 1-3** RH: 0-4 Tight: 0-2 Gall: 0-0
Aids: Bl: 0-5 Vi: 0-0 Tstrap: 0-0 Ckp: 0-0
Best Rating: 82 10/07 Navn 1m2f firm

Missoula (IRE)

90 **92**

6-y-o b m Kalanisi (IRE)-Medway (IRE) (Shernazar)
Miss Suzy Smith M J Weaver & Pollards Bloodstock

Placings:013/3/00062141/041000-00 **(2994)**
2009: 16^{0}G, 20^{0}GF,

	Starts	1st	2nd	3rd	Win & Pl
Career Total (Turf)	20	4	1	2	65787

92 6/08 Asct 2m4f (0-95)H G-F £37386
90 10/07 York 2m2f (0-95)H G-S £8096
76 9/07 Ches 1m7f195y (0-80)H G-F £5829
73 8/05 York 1m G-F £7800
Total win prize-money £59111

Going (Turf): Sf: 0-2 GS: 1-3 Gd: 0-6 **GF: 3-8** Fm: 0-1
Distance: 5f/6f: 0-0 7f-8f: 1-2 9f-13f: 0-6 **14f+: 3-12**
Track : **LH: 3-13** RH: 1-6 Tight: 1-3 **Gall: 3-9**
Aids: Bl: 0-0 Vi: 0-0 Tstrap: 0-0 Ckp: 0-0
Best Rating: 92 6/08 Newc 2m19y soft

Useful; stays 2m4f; acts on most ground.

Missprint

2-y-o b f Ishiguru (USA)-Miss Up N Go (Gorytus (USA))
B P J Baugh Miss S M Potts

Placings:0 **(7556)**
2009: 5^{0}SD,

	Starts	1st	2nd	3rd	Win & Pl
Career Total (Turf)	0	0	0	0	
Career Total (AW)	1	0	0	0	

Going (Turf): Sf: 0-0 GS: 0-0 Gd: 0-0 GF: 0-0 Fm: 0-0
Distance: 5f/6f: 0-1 7f-8f: 0-0 9f-13f: 0-0 14f+: 0-0
Track : LH: 0-1 RH: 0-0 Tight: 0-1 Gall: 0-0
Aids: Bl: 0-0 Vi: 0-0 Tstrap: 0-0 Ckp: 0-0

Missrepresentation

89 **55**

3-y-o b f Intikhab (USA)-Fairy Story (IRE) (Persian Bold)
J C Fox The Fairy Story Partnership

Placings:6060P **(5602)**
2009: 7^{6}GS, 8^{0}GF, 6^{6}GF, 7^{0}S, 8^{P}GS,

	Starts	1st	2nd	3rd	Win & Pl
Career Total (Turf)	5	0	0	0	0

Going (Turf): Sf: 0-1 GS: 0-2 Gd: 0-0 GF: 0-2 Fm: 0-0
Distance: 5f/6f: 0-0 7f-8f: 0-5 9f-13f: 0-0 14f+: 0-0
Track : LH: 0-0 RH: 0-0 Tight: 0-0 Gall: 0-0
Aids: Bl: 0-0 Vi: 0-0 Tstrap: 0-0 Ckp: 0-0
Best Rating: 55 6/09 Sals 6f212y gd-fm

Mista Rossa

103(101) (75)**75**

4-y-o br g Red Ransom (USA)-Cloud Hill (Danehill (USA))
Jamie Snowden (H Morrison 24/10) The Mista Rossa Racing Partnership

Placings:000/103022646-1250035102 **(7036)**
2009: 12^{1}SD, 12^{2}GF, 14^{5}GF, 13^{0}GF, 12^{0}SD, 11^{3}SD, 16^{5}SD, 12^{1}SD, 11^{0}G, 12^{2}S,

	Starts	1st	2nd	3rd	Win & Pl
Career Total (Turf)	11	0	2	1	2317
Career Total (AW)	11	3	2	1	9122

72 9/09 Kemp 1m4f STD £2047
75 4/09 Kemp 1m4f (0-70)H STD £2590
71 4/08 Kemp 1m2f (0-65)H STD £2047
Total win prize-money £6684

Going (Turf): Sf: 0-2 GS: 0-2 Gd: 0-3 GF: 0-4 Fm: 0-0
Distance: 5f/6f: 0-0 7f-8f: 0-2 **9f-13f: 3-16** 14f+: 0-4
Track : LH: 0-6 **RH: 3-14** Tight: 0-3 Gall: 0-4
Aids: Bl: 0-2 Vi: 0-0 Tstrap: 0-0 Ckp: 0-0
Best Rating: 75 5/09 NmkR 1m6f gd-fm

Fair; stays 1m4f; acts on fast ground; goes on Polytrack.

Mister Angry (IRE)

99(99) (84)**87**

2-y-o b c Cape Cross (IRE)-Yaya (USA) (Rahy (USA))
M Johnston The Originals

Placings:2111001 **(7717)**
2009: 7^{2}GF, 7^{1}SD, 7^{1}GS, 8^{1}GS, 8^{0}GF, 8^{0}GS, 8^{1}SD,

	Starts	1st	2nd	3rd	Win & Pl
Career Total (Turf)	5	2	1	0	8446
Career Total (AW)	2	2	0	0	11320

84 12/09 Wolv 1m141y STD £7758
87 8/09 Haml 1m65y G-S £4533
79 7/09 Catt 7f G-S £3238
84 7/09 Wolv 7f32y STD £3561
Total win prize-money £19091

Going (Turf): Sf: 0-0 **GS: 2-3** Gd: 0-0 GF: 0-2 Fm: 0-0
Distance: 5f/6f: 0-0 7f-8f: 2-5 9f-13f: 2-2 14f+: 0-0
Track : **LH: 3-4** RH: 1-2 **Tight: 4-5** Gall: 0-1
Aids: Bl: 0-0 Vi: 0-0 Tstrap: 0-0 Ckp: 0-0
Best Rating: 87 8/09 Haml 1m65y gd-sft

Useful; effective over 7f-1m; acts on fast ground and on Polytrack.

Mister Arjay (USA)

95 (60)**81**

9-y-o b g Mister Baileys-Crystal Stepper (USA) (Fred Astaire (USA))
B Ellison Keith Middleton

Placings:1/42104535200/0600/004513006/003312342123 50/144412003610 0/50221051000-400 **(2262)**
2009: 12^{4}GF, 12^{0}GF, 16^{0}G,

	Starts	1st	2nd	3rd	Win & Pl
Career Total (Turf)	62	9	8	7	67779
Career Total (AW)	4	1	0	0	4862

81 7/08 Catt 1m7f177y (0-85)H GD £4857
78 5/08 Bevl 2m35y (0-75)H G-F £2752
81 9/07 York 2m88y (0-85)H G-F £7772
80 5/07 Rdcr 1m6f19y (0-75)H G-F £2817
78 4/07 Catt 1m3f214y (0-70)H G-F £3238
71 8/06 Pont 2m1f22y (0-70)H GD £4533
68 6/06 Newc 2m19y (0-80)H G-F £6232
68 6/05 Newc 1m2f32y (0-75)H GD £3395
84 5/03 York 7f205y C(0-95)H G-F £10419
74 12/02 Ling 6f D STD £4862
Total win prize-money £50881

Going (Turf): Sf: 0-1 GS: 0-9 Gd: 3-20 **GF: 6-30** Fm: 0-2
Distance: 5f/6f: 1-1 7f-8f: 1-11 9f-13f: 2-18 **14f+: 6-36**
Track : **LH: 9-43** RH: 1-21 **Tight: 5-32** Gall: 4-18
Aids: Bl: 0-3 Vi: 0-0 Tstrap: 0-0 Ckp: 0-0
Best Rating: 85 7/03 Kemp 1m good

Fair; stays 2m plus, but still effective over as short as 1m4f; acts on fast ground; has worn blinkers; only won going left-handed.

Mister Benedictine

(97) (58)**81**

6-y-o b g Mister Baileys-Cultural Role (Night Shift (USA))
B W Duke Noel Horan

Placings:522251150/052663650/0620/0 **(3734)**
2009: 11^{0}SD,

	Starts	1st	2nd	3rd	Win & Pl
Career Total (Turf)	18	2	5	1	19579
Career Total (AW)	5	0	0	0	88

81 8/05 Bevl 7f100y G-F £3838
72 8/05 Brig 6f209y GD £4109
Total win prize-money £7947

Going (Turf): Sf: 0-0 GS: 0-0 **Gd: 1-9 GF: 1-7** Fm: 0-2
Distance: 5f/6f: 0-5 **7f-8f: 2-14** 9f-13f: 0-4 14f+: 0-0
Track : LH: 1-10 RH: 1-5 Tight: 0-7 Gall: 0-2
Aids: Bl: 0-0 Vi: 0-0 Tstrap: 0-0 Ckp: 0-0
Best Rating: 83 8/05 Ling 7f stand

Fair; suited by 7f; acts on fast ground.

Mister Benji

(102) (54)**31**

10-y-o b g Catrail (USA)-Katy-Q (IRE) (Taufan (USA))
B P J Baugh J H Chrimes And Mr & Mrs G W Hannam

Placings:110050/00004000/0003540001 0/0503303/12600 05/2331604003004 5/3100504005 5/32605066006066-3043040 **(1131)**
2009: 7^{3}SS, 7^{0}SD, 8^{4}SD, 8^{3}SD, 7^{0}SD, 8^{4}SD, 8^{0}SD,

	Starts	1st	2nd	3rd	Win & Pl
Career Total (Turf)	23	2	0	0	9715
Career Total (AW)	62	4	3	11	16053

63 2/07 Wolv 7f32y (0-58)H STD £1706
67 2/06 Wolv 1m141y (0-60)H STD £2388

61	1/05	Sthl	7f	(0-55)H	STD	£2936
63	11/03	Sthl	1m	G(0-60)H	STD	£2107
74	5/01	Pont	6f	C	FRM	£6119
77	4/01	Muss	5f	E	G-S	£2926

Total win prize-money £18184

Going (Turf): Sf: 0-3 **GS: 1-4** Gd: 0-7 GF: 0-8 **Fm: 1-1**
Distance: 5f/6f: 2-18 **7f-8f: 3-49** 9f-13f: 1-18 14f+: 0-0
Track : **LH: 5-66** RH: 0-4 **Tight: 2-36** Gall: 0-2
Aids: Bl: 0-2 Vi: 0-2 Tstrap: 2-28 Ckp: 2-28
Best Rating: 87 9/01 Donc 6f good

Moderate sort; stays 1m and acts on sand; has worn cheek-pieces.

Mister Biscuit (USA)

85 **24**

3-y-o b g Proud Citizen (USA)-Nouvelle (USA) (Hazaam (USA))
Miss L A Perratt Ken McGarrity

Placings:00060 **(6414)**
2009: 7^{0}G, 6^{0}S, 6^{0}S, 9^{6}G, 7^{0}GF,

	Starts	1st	2nd	3rd	Win & Pl
Career Total (Turf)	5	0	0	0	0

Going (Turf): Sf: 0-2 GS: 0-0 Gd: 0-2 GF: 0-1 Fm: 0-0
Distance: 5f/6f: 0-0 7f-8f: 0-4 9f-13f: 0-1 14f+: 0-0
Track : LH: 0-2 RH: 0-1 Tight: 0-2 Gall: 0-0
Aids: Bl: 0-0 Vi: 0-0 Tstrap: 0-0 Ckp: 0-0
Best Rating: 24 10/09 Ayr 7f50y gd-fm

Mister Bombastic (IRE)

98 **61**

3-y-o ch c Monsieur Bond (IRE)-Sheen Falls (IRE) (Prince Rupert (FR))
N J Vaughan Andrew Tinkler

Placings:055-0 **(2779)**
2009: 10^{0}GF,

	Starts	1st	2nd	3rd	Win & Pl
Career Total (Turf)	4	0	0	0	0

Going (Turf): Sf: 0-1 GS: 0-0 Gd: 0-1 GF: 0-2 Fm: 0-0
Distance: 5f/6f: 0-0 7f-8f: 0-3 9f-13f: 0-1 14f+: 0-0
Track : LH: 0-2 RH: 0-0 Tight: 0-1 Gall: 0-0
Aids: Bl: 0-0 Vi: 0-0 Tstrap: 0-0 Ckp: 0-0
Best Rating: 61 10/08 Rdcr 7f good

Mister Completely (IRE)

53(105) (73)**62**

8-y-o b g Princely Heir (IRE)-Blue Goose (Belmez (USA))
Ms J S Doyle Ms J S Doyle

Placings:03640/265000001601053350/0442441/43113510 0600061/1303120501521632502300 5/1636450502304200 0-05 **(3029)**
2009: 16^{0}G, 16^{5}SD,

	Starts	1st	2nd	3rd	Win & Pl
Career Total (Turf)	36	3	4	6	13650
Career Total (AW)	51	9	4	5	25494

73	1/08	Wolv	2m119y	(0-75)H	STD	£2457
76	8/07	Wolv	2m119y	(0-65)H	STD	£2388
70	7/07	Ling	2m	(0-75)H	G-F	£2817
68	6/07	Wolv	1m5f194y		STD	£2047
58	1/07	Kemp	2m	(0-65)H	STD	£1706
56	12/06	Kemp	2m	(0-45)	STD	£1365
56	5/06	Nott	1m6f15y	(0-60)H	G-F	£2388
61	1/06	Wolv	2m119y	(0-45)	STD	£1365
59	1/06	Ling	2m		STD	£2388
51	12/05	Ling	1m2f	(0-45)	STD	£1453
52	8/04	Ling	1m2f	F(0-55)H	STD	£3066
49	6/04	Bath	1m5y	G(0-55)H	FRM	£2597

Total win prize-money £26042

Going (Turf): Sf: 0-7 GS: 0-3 Gd: 0-8 **GF: 2-15** Fm: 1-3
Distance: 5f/6f: 0-6 7f-8f: 0-6 9f-13f: 3-22 **14f+: 9-53**
Track : **LH: 10-59** RH: 2-22 **Tight: 9-42** Gall: 0-4
Aids: Bl: 0-1 **Vi: 3-32** Tstrap: 0-0 Ckp: 0-0
Best Rating: 76 8/07 Wolv 2m119y stand

Moderate; stays 2m; acts on most ground; also goes on Polytrack; often wears a visor.

Mister Dee Bee (IRE)

105(84) (53)**96**

3-y-o b g Orpen (USA)-Acidanthera (Alzao (USA))
B W Hills South Bank Thoroughbred Racing

Placings:60326-11142 **(4409)**
2009: 8^{1}GF, 8^{1}F, 9^{1}GF, 10^{4}G, 8^{2}G,

	Starts	1st	2nd	3rd	Win & Pl
Career Total (Turf)	9	3	2	1	25614
Career Total (AW)	1	0	0	0	0

91	6/09	Leic	1m1f218y	(0-85)H	G-F	£4857
85	5/09	Wwck	1m22y	(0-85)H	FRM	£6476
79	4/09	Ripn	1m		G-F	£3238

Total win prize-money £14571

Going (Turf): Sf: 0-1 GS: 0-1 Gd: 0-4 **GF: 2-2** Fm: 1-1
Distance: 5f/6f: 0-0 7f-8f: 1-7 **9f-13f: 2-3** 14f+: 0-0
Track : LH: 1-1 **RH: 2-5 Tight: 1-1** Gall: 0-1
Aids: Bl: 0-0 Vi: 0-0 Tstrap: 0-0 Ckp: 0-0
Best Rating: 96 7/09 Gdwd 1m good

Useful; stays 1m2f; acts on fast and easy ground and on Polytrack.

Mister Fantastic

92 **69**

3-y-o ch g Green Tune (USA)-Lomapamar (Nashwan (USA))
M Dods (N J Vaughan 11/6) Andrew Tinkler

Placings:35-3000 **(5672)**
2009: 7^{3}GF, 8^{0}GF, 6^{0}S, 8^{0}S,

	Starts	1st	2nd	3rd	Win & Pl
Career Total (Turf)	6	0	0	2	1031

Going (Turf): Sf: 0-3 GS: 0-0 Gd: 0-1 GF: 0-2 Fm: 0-0
Distance: 5f/6f: 0-3 7f-8f: 0-3 9f-13f: 0-0 14f+: 0-0
Track : LH: 0-2 RH: 0-1 Tight: 0-1 Gall: 0-0
Aids: Bl: 0-0 Vi: 0-0 Tstrap: 0-0 Ckp: 0-0
Best Rating: 69 4/09 Wwck 7f26y gd-fm

Fair; stays 7f; acts on fast and soft ground.

Mister Fizzbomb (IRE)

100(93) (62)**73**

6-y-o b g Lend A Hand-Crocus (IRE) (Mister Baileys)
T D Walford S Enwright

Placings:000/02214/0021014/002325340340-12605 **(6236)**
2009: 12^{1}GF, 12^{2}G, 12^{6}GF, 12^{0}F, 10^{5}GF,

	Starts	1st	2nd	3rd	Win & Pl
Career Total (Turf)	30	4	6	3	18625
Career Total (AW)	2	0	0	0	0

72	8/09	Muss	1m4f100y	(0-65)H	G-F	£2590
59	10/07	Catt	1m3f214y		GD	£2730
59	9/07	Bevl	1m4f16y		GD	£2914
61	6/06	Bevl	1m4f16y	(0-55)H	G-F	£3238

Total win prize-money £11474

Going (Turf): Sf: 0-3 GS: 0-3 **Gd: 2-7 GF: 2-15** Fm: 0-2
Distance: 5f/6f: 0-2 7f-8f: 0-1 **9f-13f: 4-28** 14f+: 0-1
Track : LH: 1-16 **RH: 3-14 Tight: 4-20** Gall: 0-1
Aids: Bl: 1-6 **Vi: 3-19** Tstrap: 0-1 Ckp: 0-1
Best Rating: 73 8/09 Bevl 1m4f16y good

Modest; suited by around 1m4f; acts on fast and easy ground; has worn a visor.

Mister Frosty (IRE)

92(100) (55)**57**

3-y-o gr g Verglas (IRE)-La Chinampina (FR) (Darshaan)
G Prodromou Matt Bartram

Placings:0-000000325 **(7851)**
2009: 7^{0}SD, 8^{0}G, 8^{0}S, 9^{0}GF, 12^{0}SD, 10^{0}SD, 11^{3}SD, 11^{2}SS, 11^{5}SS,

	Starts	1st	2nd	3rd	Win & Pl
Career Total (Turf)	3	0	0	0	
Career Total (AW)	7	0	1	1	1058

Going (Turf): Sf: 0-1 GS: 0-0 Gd: 0-1 GF: 0-1 Fm: 0-0
Distance: 5f/6f: 0-0 7f-8f: 0-2 9f-13f: 0-8 14f+: 0-0
Track : LH: 0-7 RH: 0-1 Tight: 0-4 Gall: 0-0
Aids: Bl: 0-0 Vi: 0-0 Tstrap: 0-0 Ckp: 0-0
Best Rating: 57 5/09 Yarm 1m3y good

Moderate; stays 1m3f; acts on Fibresand.

Mister Green (FR)

88(108) (81)**88**

3-y-o b g Green Desert (USA)-Summertime Legacy (Darshaan)
K McAuliffe (D Flood 17/6) K W J McAuliffe

Placings:1423000-002 **(7664)**
2009: 6^{0}GF, 6^{0}SD, 8^{2}SD,

	Starts	1st	2nd	3rd	Win & Pl
Career Total (Turf)	4	0	1	0	1637
Career Total (AW)	6	1	1	1	4477

82	5/08	GrLe	6f	STD	£3238

Total win prize-money £3238

Going (Turf): Sf: 0-0 GS: 0-0 Gd: 0-3 GF: 0-1 Fm: 0-0
Distance: **5f/6f: 1-7** 7f-8f: 0-3 9f-13f: 0-0 14f+: 0-0
Track : **LH: 1-4** RH: 0-3 Tight: 0-3 **Gall: 1-1**
Aids: Bl: 0-2 Vi: 0-1 Tstrap: 0-0 Ckp: 0-0
Best Rating: 88 7/08 Leic 5f218y good

Fair; stays 1m; acts on good ground and on Polytrack.

Mister Hardy

108(108) (93)**103**

4-y-o b g Kyllachy-Balladonia (Primo Dominie)
R A Fahey The Cosmic Cases

Placings:11035050/654054260010023-1110060640 **(7294)**
2009: 7^{1}GF, 7^{1}GF, 7^{1}GF, 7^{0}GF, 7^{0}GF, 7^{6}G, 6^{0}G, 7^{6}G, 7^{4}G, 7^{0}S,

	Starts	1st	2nd	3rd	Win & Pl
Career Total (Turf)	30	6	1	1	95707
Career Total (AW)	3	0	1	1	3559

103	5/09	Ches	7f122y	(0-105)H	G-F	£25232
95	4/09	Newc	7f	(0-100)H	G-F	£11215
103	3/09	Donc	7f	(0-85)H	G-F	£5180
89	8/08	Haml	6f5y	(0-80)H	SFT	£7123
89	4/07	Newc	5f		GD	£4533
85	3/07	Newc	5f		G-S	£7478

Total win prize-money £60765

Going (Turf): Sf: 1-6 GS: 1-2 Gd: 1-13 **GF: 3-8** Fm: 0-1
Distance: 5f/6f: 2-17 **7f-8f: 4-16** 9f-13f: 0-0 14f+: 0-0
Track : **LH: 1-6** RH: 0-2 **Tight: 1-4** Gall: 0-1
Aids: Bl: 0-0 Vi: 0-0 Tstrap: 0-0 Ckp: 0-0
Best Rating: **103** 5/09 Ches 7f122y gd-fm

Very useful; effective over 6f-7f; acts on most ground.

Mister Hughie (IRE)

102 **92**

2-y-o b c Elusive City (USA)-Bonne Mere (FR) (Stepneyev (IRE))
M R Channon Liam Mulryan

Placings:6335112215 **(6486)**
2009: 5^{6}F, 5^{3}GF, 5^{3}G, 5^{5}G, 5^{1}G, 5^{1}GF, 5^{2}G, 6^{2}G, 6^{1}GF, 6^{5}GF,

	Starts	1st	2nd	3rd	Win & Pl
Career Total (Turf)	10	3	2	2	22705

86	9/09	Hayd	6f	(0-80)	G-F	£4857
81	8/09	NmkJ	5f		G-F	£5180
69	8/09	Bath	5f11y		GD	£1942

Total win prize-money £11981

Going (Turf): Sf: 0-0 GS: 0-0 Gd: 1-5 **GF: 2-4** Fm: 0-1
Distance: **5f/6f: 3-10** 7f-8f: 0-0 9f-13f: 0-0 14f+: 0-0
Track : **LH: 1-2** RH: 0-0 Tight: 0-0 **Gall: 1-3**
Aids: Bl: 0-0 Vi: 0-0 Tstrap: 0-0 Ckp: 0-0
Best Rating: **92** 10/09 Rdcr 6f gd-fm

Useful; suited by 5f-6f; acts on good and faster ground.

Mister Incredible

67(100) (56)**3**

6-y-o b g Wizard King-Judiam (Primo Dominie)
J M Bradley racingshares.co.uk

Placings:040054341/30042300006/0031105623051400/5005262252-645302300 **(1781)**
2009: 6^{6}SS, 5^{4}SD, 5^{5}SD, **5^{3}SD**, **5^{0}SD**, 6^{2}SD, 5^{3}SD, 6^{0}G, 6^{0}SD,

	Starts	1st	2nd	3rd	Win & Pl
Career Total (Turf)	13	1	0	0	3256
Career Total (AW)	42	3	7	7	13423

57	6/07	Bevl	5f	(0-45)	G-S	£2266
58	2/07	Sthl	6f	(0-60)	STD	£2184
55	2/07	Sthl	7f		STD	£2184
64	1/06	Sthl	6f	(0-65)H	STD	£2388

Total win prize-money £9024

Going (Turf): Sf: 0-3 **GS: 1-4** Gd: 0-4 GF: 0-2 Fm: 0-0
Distance: **5f/6f: 3-49** 7f-8f: 1-6 9f-13f: 0-0 14f+: 0-0
Track : **LH: 3-34** RH: 0-4 Tight: 0-14 Gall: 0-2
Aids: Bl: 0-1 **Vi: 3-34** Tstrap: 1-10 Ckp: 1-10
Best Rating: **64** 1/06 Sthl 6f stand

Moderate; effective over 6f-7f; acts on soft ground; goes on Fibresand; usually wears headgear.

Mister Jingles

101(101) (61)**66**

6-y-o ch g Desert Story (IRE)-Fairy Free (Rousillon (USA))
R M Whitaker James Marshall & Mrs Susan Marshall

Placings:00500**26**/0**33**60**1131**000/00**61**0**36**0-336553003**120** **(7348)**
2009: 7^{3}GF, 7^{3}GF, 6^{6}GF, 7^{5}F, 8^{5}GF, 8^{3}G, 7^{0}G, 8^{0}GF, 7^{3}GF, 7^{1}SD, 7^{2}SD, 7^{0}SD,

	Starts	1st	2nd	3rd	Win & Pl
Career Total (Turf)	28	4	0	6	13934
Career Total (AW)	11	1	2	2	4000

61	10/09	Wolv	7f32y	(0-50)H	STD	£2183
66	6/08	Bevl	7f100y	(0-70)H	G-F	£2914
66	8/07	Bevl	7f100y	(0-75)H	G-F	£3886
64	8/07	Carl	6f192y	(0-60)H	FRM	£2047
59	7/07	Muss	7f30y		GD	£2590

Total win prize-money £13623

Going (Turf): Sf: 0-4 GS: 0-1 Gd: 1-8 **GF: 2-11** Fm: 1-4
Distance: 5f/6f: 0-7 **7f-8f: 5-29** 9f-13f: 0-3 14f+: 0-0
Track : LH: 1-16 **RH: 4-19 Tight: 2-13** Gall: 0-0
Aids: Bl: 0-2 **Vi: 4-10** Tstrap: 0-4 Ckp: 0-4
Best Rating: **66** 6/08 Bevl 7f100y gd-fm

Moderate; suited by 7f; acts on fast ground and on Polytrack; likes to race prominently; has worn a visor.

Mister Laurel

105 **88**

3-y-o b g Diktat-Balladonia (Primo Dominie)
R A Fahey The Cosmic Cases

Placings:13000-10056310 **(4598)**
2009: 6^{1}GF, 6^{0}GF, 6^{0}HY, 5^{5}GF, 5^{6}G, 5^{3}G, 6^{1}GS, 6^{0}G,

	Starts	1st	2nd	3rd	Win & Pl
Career Total (Turf)	13	3	0	2	26327

88	7/09	Newc	6f	(0-90)H	G-S	£7477
83	4/09	Ripn	6f	(0-85)H	G-F	£4857
77	6/08	Haml	6f5y		GD	£4857

Total win prize-money £17191

Going (Turf): Sf: 0-3 **GS: 1-1 Gd: 1-5 GF: 1-4** Fm: 0-0
Distance: **5f/6f: 2-11** 7f-8f: 1-2 9f-13f: 0-0 14f+: 0-0
Track : LH: 0-0 RH: 0-0 Tight: 0-0 Gall: 0-0
Aids: Bl: 0-2 Vi: 0-0 Tstrap: 0-0 Ckp: 0-0
Best Rating: **88** 7/09 Newc 6f gd-sft

Fair; effective at 6f; acts on good/fast ground; has worn blinkers.

Mister Manannan (IRE)

108 **110**

2-y-o b c Desert Style (IRE)-Cover Girl (IRE) (Common Grounds)
D Nicholls Mrs Maureen Quayle

Placings:3102231 **(6049)**
2009: 5^{3}GF, 5^{1}G, 5^{0}GF, 5^{2}G, 5^{2}GF, 5^{3}GF, 5^{1}G,

	Starts	1st	2nd	3rd	Win & Pl
Career Total (Turf)	7	2	2	2	53927

110	9/09	Ayr	5f	GD	£19869
97	4/09	Pont	5f	GD	£5180

Total win prize-money £25051

Going (Turf): Sf: 0-0 GS: 0-0 **Gd: 2-3** GF: 0-4 Fm: 0-0
Distance: **5f/6f: 2-7** 7f-8f: 0-0 9f-13f: 0-0 14f+: 0-0
Track : **LH: 1-1** RH: 0-0 Tight: 0-0 Gall: 0-0
Aids: Bl: 0-0 Vi: 0-0 Tstrap: 0-0 Ckp: 0-0
Best Rating: **110** 9/09 Ayr 5f good

Smart; Group placed; Listed winner; effective over 5f; acts on good and fast ground.

Mister Maq

98(87) (27)**48**

6-y-o b g Namaqualand (USA)-Nordico Princess (Nordico (USA))
A Crook Lerigo Family

Placings:0020/540451240**0060**/035060400/0600-64005 **(2965)**
2009: 12^{6}SD, 8^{4}GF, 10^{0}GF, 8^{0}G, 9^{5}GF,

	Starts	1st	2nd	3rd	Win & Pl
Career Total (Turf)	27	1	2	0	5921
Career Total (AW)	9	0	0	1	202

64	7/06	Thsk	1m	(0-60)H	FRM	£3238

Total win prize-money £3239

Going (Turf): Sf: 0-5 GS: 0-1 Gd: 0-9 GF: 0-11 **Fm: 1-1**
Distance: 5f/6f: 0-0 **7f-8f: 1-11** 9f-13f: 0-24 14f+: 0-1
Track : **LH: 1-16** RH: 0-14 **Tight: 1-11** Gall: 0-2
Aids: **Bl: 1-26** Vi: 0-5 Tstrap: 0-3 Ckp: 0-3
Best Rating: **64** 7/06 Thsk 1m firm

Moderate; seems best over 1m; acts on fast ground.

Mister New York (USA)

94(114) (89)**68**

4-y-o b c Forest Wildcat (USA)-Shebane (USA) (Alysheba (USA))
Noel T Chance Chance, Talbot & Taylor

Placings:044/211020000012164-4434000531024 **(7811)**
2009: 8^{4}SD, 7^{4}SD, 8^{3}SD, 7^{4}SD, 8^{0}G, 8^{0}SD, 8^{0}S, 12^{5}SD, 12^{3}SD, 12^{1}SD, 10^{0}SD, 12^{2}SD, 12^{4}SD,

	Starts	1st	2nd	3rd	Win & Pl
Career Total (Turf)	4	0	0	0	
Career Total (AW)	27	5	4	2	35451

89	10/09	Ling	1m4f	(0-85)H	STD	£5180
89	11/08	Ling	1m	(0-85)H	STD	£4727
85	11/08	Wolv	7f32y	(0-75)H	STD	£3885
81	2/08	Wolv	5f216y	(0-85)H	STD	£4533
76	2/08	Ling	6f	(0-85)H	STD	£4100

Total win prize-money £22429

Going (Turf): **Sf: 0-2 GS: 0-0 Gd: 0-2 GF: 0-0 Fm: 0-0**
Distance: 5f/6f: 2-6 7f-8f: 2-17 9f-13f: 1-8 14f+: 0-0
Track : **LH: 5-22** RH: 0-7 **Tight: 5-20** Gall: 0-2
Aids: **Bl: 1-9** Vi: 0-0 Tstrap: 0-0 Ckp: 0-0
Best Rating: **89** 12/09 Wolv 1m4f50y stand

Useful; stays 1m4f; acts on Polytrack; usually held up; has worn blinkers.

Mister Pete (IRE)

98 **66**

6-y-o b g Piccolo-Whistfilly (First Trump)
C Grant (W Storey 18/6) David Armstrong

Placings:0/4040/2164013322-66350 **(3068)**
2009: 15^{6}GF, 16^{6}F, 16^{3}GS, 16^{5}GF, 12^{0}GS,

	Starts	1st	2nd	3rd	Win & Pl
Career Total (Turf)	20	2	3	3	8479

64	9/08	Haml	1m5f9y	(0-65)H	G-S	£2307
56	7/08	Carl	2m1f52y	(0-65)H	GD	£2047

Total win prize-money £4355

Going (Turf): Sf: 0-5 **GS: 1-7 Gd: 1-4** GF: 0-3 Fm: 0-1
Distance: 5f/6f: 0-0 7f-8f: 0-3 9f-13f: 0-5 **14f+: 2-12**
Track : LH: 0-10 **RH: 2-9** Tight: 1-16 Gall: 1-3
Aids: Bl: 0-0 Vi: 0-0 Tstrap: 0-0 Ckp: 0-0
Best Rating: **66** 11/08 Catt 1m5f175y heavy

Mister Ross

91(101) (84)89

4-y-o b g Medicean-Aqualina (IRE) (King's Theatre (IRE))

G L Moore Mrs Patricia Pink

Placings:034110-00 **(2188)**

2009: 8^{0}GF, 7^{0}GF,

	Starts	1st	2nd	3rd	Win & Pl
Career Total (Turf)	6	1	0	1	4397
Career Total (AW)	2	1	0	0	2730

84 10/08 Ling 1m (0-70)H STD £2729

89 10/08 Wind 1m67y (0-70)H G-S £3753

Total win prize-money £6483

Going (Turf): Sf: 0-1 **GS: 1-2** Gd: 0-0 GF: 0-3 Fm: 0-0

Distance: 5f/6f: 0-0 7f-8f: 1-4 9f-13f: 1-4 14f+: 0-0

Track : LH: 1-1 RH: 1-6 **Tight: 2-4** Gall: 0-0

Aids: Bl: 0-0 Vi: 0-0 Tstrap: 0-0 Ckp: 0-0

Best Rating: 89 10/08 Wind 1m67y gd-sft

Fair; stays 1m; acts on easy ground and on Polytrack.

Mister Standfast

(78) (50)58

3-y-o b g Haafhd-Off The Blocks (Salse (USA))

J M P Eustace The Macdougall Partnership

Placings:000-P **(1594)**

2009: 10^{P}GS,

	Starts	1st	2nd	3rd	Win & Pl
Career Total (Turf)	3	0	0	0	
Career Total (AW)	1	0	0	0	

Going (Turf): Sf: 0-1 GS: 0-1 Gd: 0-1 GF: 0-0 Fm: 0-0

Distance: 5f/6f: 0-0 7f-8f: 0-3 9f-13f: 0-1 14f+: 0-0

Track : LH: 0-1 RH: 0-1 Tight: 0-0 Gall: 0-0

Aids: Bl: 0-0 Vi: 0-0 Tstrap: 0-0 Ckp: 0-0

Best Rating: 58 10/08 Yarm 7f3y soft

Mister Tinktastic (IRE)

105 84

3-y-o ch g Noverre (USA)-Psychic (IRE) (Alhaarth (IRE))

M Dods Andrew Tinkler

Placings:43-206113130 **(5148)**

2009: 5^{2}GF, 6^{0}GS, 7^{6}GF, 5^{1}GF, 6^{1}GF, 7^{3}G, 6^{1}G, 6^{3}GF, 5^{0}GS,

	Starts	1st	2nd	3rd	Win & Pl
Career Total (Turf)	11	3	1	3	11734

84 8/09 Pont 6f (0-75)H GD £3238

74 6/09 Pont 6f (0-75)H G-F £3238

71 6/09 Carl 5f193y (0-75)H G-F £2590

Total win prize-money £9066

Going (Turf): Sf: 0-2 GS: 0-2 Gd: 1-2 **GF: 2-5** Fm: 0-0

Distance: 5f/6f: 3-9 7f-8f: 0-2 9f-13f: 0-0 14f+: 0-0

Track : LH: 2-4 RH: 1-2 Tight: 0-2 Gall: 0-1

Aids: Bl: 0-0 Vi: 0-0 Tstrap: 3-7 Ckp: 3-7

Best Rating: 84 8/09 Pont 6f good

Fair; suited by 6f; acts on fast ground; has worn cheek-pieces.

Mister Trickster (IRE)

100(104) (61)61

8-y-o b g Woodborough (USA)-Tinos Island (IRE) (Alzao (USA))

R Dickin The Tricksters

Placings:046650/60010003/**4-202363060** **(6909)**

2009: 7^{2}SD, 8^{0}SD, 9^{2}GF, 8^{3}SD, 9^{6}GF, 11^{3}SD, 8^{0}SD, 8^{6}SD, 8^{0}G,

	Starts	1st	2nd	3rd	Win & Pl
Career Total (Turf)	17	1	1	1	5151
Career Total (AW)	7	0	1	2	1196

64 6/04 Chep 7f16y E(0-70)H GD £3721

Total win prize-money £3721

Going (Turf): Sf: 0-1 GS: 0-3 **Gd: 1-4** GF: 0-7 Fm: 0-2

Distance: 5f/6f: 0-0 **7f-8f: 1-13** 9f-13f: 0-11 14f+: 0-0

Track : LH: 0-6 RH: 0-11 Tight: 0-4 Gall: 0-0

Aids: Bl: 0-0 Vi: 0-0 Tstrap: 0-0 Ckp: 0-0

Best Rating: 64 6/04 Chep 7f16y good

Moderate; stays 1m1f; acts on good and softer ground and on Polytrack.

Mister Wilberforce

55(58)

3-y-o b g Paris House-She's A Breeze (Crofthall)

M Mullineaux Mrs Stella Pearson

Placings:500-00 **(5987)**

2009: 5^{0}GF, 12^{0}SD,

	Starts	1st	2nd	3rd	Win & Pl
Career Total (Turf)	3	0	0	0	0
Career Total (AW)	2	0	0	0	

Going (Turf): Sf: 0-2 GS: 0-0 Gd: 0-0 GF: 0-1 Fm: 0-0

Distance: 5f/6f: 0-1 7f-8f: 0-2 9f-13f: 0-2 14f+: 0-0

Track : LH: 0-4 RH: 0-1 Tight: 0-3 Gall: 0-0

Aids: Bl: 0-1 Vi: 0-1 Tstrap: 0-1 Ckp: 0-1

Misterisland (IRE)

(89) (29)46

4-y-o b c Spectrum (IRE)-Carranita (IRE) (Anita's Prince)

M Mullineaux (A Bailey 6/3) D J P Turner

Placings:0/50-**00000** **(7858)**

2009: 8^{0}SD, 7^{0}SD, 5^{0}SD, 5^{0}SD, 8^{0}SD,

	Starts	1st	2nd	3rd	Win & Pl
Career Total (Turf)	3	0	0	0	0
Career Total (AW)	5	0	0	0	

Going (Turf): Sf: 0-1 GS: 0-0 Gd: 0-1 GF: 0-1 Fm: 0-0

Distance: 5f/6f: 0-2 7f-8f: 0-3 9f-13f: 0-3 14f+: 0-0

Track : LH: 0-6 RH: 0-1 Tight: 0-6 Gall: 0-0

Aids: Bl: 0-4 Vi: 0-0 Tstrap: 0-0 Ckp: 0-0

Best Rating: 46 5/08 Rdcr 7f soft

Mistic Academy (IRE)

81 26

4-y-o ch m Royal Academy (USA)-Mistic Sun (Dashing Blade)

Miss J E Foster Howdale Bloodstock Ltd

Placings:0600 **(6390)**

2009: 12^{0}G, 11^{6}GF, 10^{0}GF, 8^{0}GF,

	Starts	1st	2nd	3rd	Win & Pl
Career Total (Turf)	4	0	0	0	0

Going (Turf): Sf: 0-0 GS: 0-0 Gd: 0-1 GF: 0-3 Fm: 0-0

Distance: 5f/6f: 0-0 7f-8f: 0-0 9f-13f: 0-4 14f+: 0-0

Track : LH: 0-3 RH: 0-1 Tight: 0-2 Gall: 0-0

Aids: Bl: 0-0 Vi: 0-0 Tstrap: 0-0 Ckp: 0-0

Best Rating: 26 9/09 Nott 1m75y gd-fm

Mistic Magic (IRE)

98 87

2-y-o b f Orpen (USA)-Mistic Sun (Dashing Blade)

P F I Cole Stan James Syndicate 2

Placings:41040 **(7033)**

2009: 5^{4}GF, 7^{1}GF, 7^{0}GF, 7^{4}GF, 7^{0}S,

	Starts	1st	2nd	3rd	Win & Pl
Career Total (Turf)	5	1	0	0	6582

81 6/09 Newb 7f G-F £5180

Total win prize-money £5181

Going (Turf): Sf: 0-1 GS: 0-0 Gd: 0-0 **GF: 1-4** Fm: 0-0

Distance: 5f/6f: 0-1 **7f-8f: 1-4** 9f-13f: 0-0 14f+: 0-0

Track : LH: 0-0 RH: 0-1 Tight: 0-0 Gall: 0-0

Aids: Bl: 0-0 Vi: 0-0 Tstrap: 0-1 Ckp: 0-1

Best Rating: 87 10/09 NmkR 7f gd-fm

Useful; stays 7f; acts on fast ground.

Mistoffelees

80(95) (64)29

3-y-o b c Tiger Hill (IRE)-Auenlust (GER) (Surumu (GER))

L M Cumani Mrs Luca Cumani

Placings:065 **(6287)**

2009: 10^{0}GF, 12^{6}SD, 10^{5}SD,

	Starts	1st	2nd	3rd	Win & Pl
Career Total (Turf)	1	0	0	0	
Career Total (AW)	2	0	0	0	0

Going (Turf): Sf: 0-0 GS: 0-0 Gd: 0-0 GF: 0-1 Fm: 0-0

Distance: 5f/6f: 0-0 7f-8f: 0-0 9f-13f: 0-3 14f+: 0-0

Track : LH: 0-0 RH: 0-3 Tight: 0-1 Gall: 0-0

Aids: Bl: 0-0 Vi: 0-0 Tstrap: 0-0 Ckp: 0-0

Best Rating: 64 9/09 Kemp 1m2f stand

Mistress Cooper

(101) (65)68

4-y-o b/br f Kyllachy-Litewska (IRE) (Mujadil (USA))

W J Musson Mrs Rita Brown

Placings:0566221/3405044-03 **(0461)**

2009: 7^{0}SD, 6^{3}SD,

	Starts	1st	2nd	3rd	Win & Pl
Career Total (Turf)	12	1	2	1	7375
Career Total (AW)	4	0	0	1	252

71 9/07 Sand 5f6y (0-75) G-F £4533

Total win prize-money £4534

Going (Turf): Sf: 0-1 GS: 0-1 Gd: 0-3 **GF: 1-7** Fm: 0-0

Distance: 5f/6f: 1-13 7f-8f: 0-3 9f-13f: 0-0 14f+: 0-0

Track : LH: 0-3 RH: 0-3 Tight: 0-1 Gall: 0-2

Aids: Bl: 0-0 Vi: 0-0 Tstrap: 0-0 Ckp: 0-0

Best Rating: 71 9/07 Sand 5f6y gd-fm

Modest; best at sprint trips; acts on fast ground.

Mistress Eva

(92) (62)76

4-y-o br f Diktat-Foreign Mistress (Darshaan)

Mrs S Leech (L Corcoran 9/3) John Cocks

Placings:16/0543516-0 (0142)
2009: 14[0]SD,

	Starts	1st	2nd	3rd	Win & Pl
Career Total (Turf)	9	2	0	1	6054
Career Total (AW)	1	0	0	0	

76 10/08 Newb 1m3f5y (0-75)H G-S £2590
67 8/07 Folk 7f HVY £2817
Total win prize-money £5407

Going (Turf): Sf: 1-2 GS: 1-4 Gd: 0-1 GF: 0-2 Fm: 0-0
Distance: 5f/6f: 0-0 7f-8f: 1-2 9f-13f: 1-7 14f+: 0-1
Track : **LH: 1-5** RH: 0-4 Tight: 0-5 **Gall: 1-3**
Aids: Bl: 0-0 Vi: 0-0 Tstrap: 0-0 Ckp: 0-0
Best Rating: 76 10/08 Newb 1m3f5y gd-sft

Modest; stays 1m3f; acts on soft ground.

Mistress Greeley (USA)

(95) (64)**85**
4-y-o ch f Mr Greeley (USA)-My Reem (USA) (Chief's Crown (USA))
M Botti Newsells Park Stud

Placings:16/60-0 (0694)
2009: 8[0]SD,

	Starts	1st	2nd	3rd	Win & Pl
Career Total (Turf)	4	1	0	0	4480
Career Total (AW)	1	0	0	0	

74 8/07 Nott 6f15y GD £3562
Total win prize-money £3562

Going (Turf): Sf: 0-0 GS: 0-0 **Gd: 1-2** GF: 0-2 Fm: 0-0
Distance: 5f/6f: 0-0 **7f-8f: 1-4** 9f-13f: 0-1 14f+: 0-0
Track : LH: 0-2 RH: 0-1 Tight: 0-1 Gall: 0-1
Aids: Bl: 0-0 Vi: 0-0 Tstrap: 0-0 Ckp: 0-0
Best Rating: 85 5/08 York 1m gd-fm

Misty Dancer

94 **87**
10-y-o gr g Vettori (IRE)-Light Fantastic (Deploy)
Miss Venetia Williams Exit 36 Racing Club

Placings:32/3300/1030/414/421430/0-00 (6734)
2009: 12[0]GF, 14[0]S,

	Starts	1st	2nd	3rd	Win & Pl
Career Total (Turf)	22	3	2	5	49031

91 6/07 Ayr 1m5f13y (0-95)H GD £11658
85 6/05 Epsm 1m4f10y (0-85)H G-F £6711
81 5/03 Newb 1m2f6yD(0-80)H G-F £6188
Total win prize-money £24558

Going (Turf): Sf: 0-2 GS: 0-2 Gd: 1-7 **GF: 2-11** Fm: 0-0
Distance: 5f/6f: 0-0 7f-8f: 0-3 **9f-13f: 2-16** 14f+: 1-3
Track : **LH: 3-11** RH: 0-10 Tight: 1-8 Gall: 1-4
Aids: Bl: 0-0 Vi: 0-0 Tstrap: 0-0 Ckp: 0-0
Best Rating: 97 8/07 Hayd 1m3f200y gd-fm

Useful; stays 1m5f; acts on most ground; winner over hurdles and fences.

Misty Kit

(78) (18)
4-y-o b f Umistim-River Ensign (River God (USA))
W M Brisbourne Mrs Mary Brisbourne

Placings:00 (7670)
2009: 12[0]SD, 12[0]SD,

	Starts	1st	2nd	3rd	Win & Pl
Career Total (Turf)	0	0	0	0	
Career Total (AW)	2	0	0	0	

Going (Turf): Sf: 0-0 GS: 0-0 Gd: 0-0 GF: 0-0 Fm: 0-0
Distance: 5f/6f: 0-0 7f-8f: 0-0 9f-13f: 0-2 14f+: 0-0
Track : LH: 0-2 RH: 0-0 Tight: 0-2 Gall: 0-0
Aids: Bl: 0-0 Vi: 0-0 Tstrap: 0-0 Ckp: 0-0
Best Rating: 18 12/09 Wolv 1m4f50y stand

Misyaar (IRE)

(92) (65)
3-y-o b f Dubai Destination (USA)-Saafeya (IRE) (Sadler's Wells (USA))
M A Jarvis Sheikh Ahmed Al Maktoum

Placings:3-654 (0356)
2009: 9[6]SD, 8[5]SD, 7[4]SD,

	Starts	1st	2nd	3rd	Win & Pl
Career Total (Turf)	0	0	0	0	
Career Total (AW)	4	0	0	1	530

Going (Turf): Sf: 0-0 GS: 0-0 Gd: 0-0 GF: 0-0 Fm: 0-0
Distance: 5f/6f: 0-0 7f-8f: 0-3 9f-13f: 0-1 14f+: 0-0
Track : LH: 0-4 RH: 0-0 Tight: 0-4 Gall: 0-0
Aids: Bl: 0-0 Vi: 0-0 Tstrap: 0-0 Ckp: 0-0
Best Rating: 65 12/08 Ling 7f stand

Mith Hill

101 **83**
8-y-o b g Daylami (IRE)-Delirious Moment (IRE) (Kris)
Ian Williams P J Vogt

Placings:01110/014064/40/633330-132 (6676)
2009: 15[1]GF, 16[3]GF, 18[2]G,

	Starts	1st	2nd	3rd	Win & Pl
Career Total (Turf)	19	3	1	5	28933
Career Total (AW)	3	2	0	0	7196

77 9/09 Ches 1m7f195y (0-80)H G-F £5504
84 4/05 Haml 1m4f17y (0-80)H G-S £6832
80 10/04 Ling 1m4f (0-77)H STD £3515
74 10/04 Ling 1m4f (0-70)H STD £3680
77 8/04 Bevl 1m1f207y D G-S £4392
Total win prize-money £23926

Going (Turf): Sf: 0-5 **GS: 2-4** Gd: 0-5 GF: 1-5 Fm: 0-0
Distance: 5f/6f: 0-0 7f-8f: 0-0 **9f-13f: 4-8** 14f+: 1-14
Track : **LH: 3-16** RH: 2-6 **Tight: 4-8** Gall: 0-6
Aids: Bl: 0-0 **Vi: 1-2** Tstrap: 0-3 Ckp: 0-3
Best Rating: 85 9/05 Nott 1m6f15y good

Fair; winning hurdler; stays 2m5f; acts on most ground on turf; goes on Polytrack; has worn cheekpieces, tongue tie and visor.

Mito

96 **47**
8-y-o b m Mtoto-Shibui (Shirley Heights)
B R Millman Mrs Jenny Willment

Placings:5635555/2052200/6P02000/06P (3798)
2009: 12[0]GF, 12[6]GF, 12[P]GF,

	Starts	1st	2nd	3rd	Win & Pl
Career Total (Turf)	24	0	4	1	5811

Going (Turf): Sf: 0-2 GS: 0-3 Gd: 0-5 GF: 0-3 Fm: 0-0
Distance: 5f/6f: 0-0 7f-8f: 0-0 9f-13f: 0-24 14f+: 0-0
Track : LH: 0-3 RH: 0-1 Tight: 0-0 Gall: 0-0
Aids: Bl: 0-0 Vi: 0-0 Tstrap: 0-0 Ckp: 0-0
Best Rating: 47 7/09 Chep 1m4f23y gd-fm

Mitra Jaan (IRE)

101(85) (71)**67**
3-y-o b f Diktat-Persian Lass (IRE) (Grand Lodge (USA))
W R Swinburn Dr Jamal Ahmadzadeh

Placings:045-6650 (5806)
2009: 8[6]GS, 10[6]G, 8[5]G, 8[0]SD,

	Starts	1st	2nd	3rd	Win & Pl
Career Total (Turf)	5	0	0	0	0
Career Total (AW)	2	0	0	0	265

Going (Turf): Sf: 0-0 GS: 0-2 Gd: 0-2 GF: 0-1 Fm: 0-0
Distance: 5f/6f: 0-0 7f-8f: 0-3 9f-13f: 0-4 14f+: 0-0
Track : LH: 0-0 RH: 0-6 Tight: 0-3 Gall: 0-0
Aids: Bl: 0-0 Vi: 0-0 Tstrap: 0-0 Ckp: 0-0
Best Rating: 71 9/08 Kemp 1m stand

Modest; should stay 1m; acts on Polytrack.

Mix N Match

88(106) (59)**35**
5-y-o b g Royal Applause-South Wind (Tina's Pet)
J D Frost (R M Stronge 24/9) Share My Dream

Placings:000460/3200240006-31350 (4300)
2009: 10[3]SD, 10[1]SD, 10[3]SD, 11[5]SD, 10[0]G,

	Starts	1st	2nd	3rd	Win & Pl
Career Total (Turf)	7	0	0	0	192
Career Total (AW)	14	1	2	3	4015

56 1/09 Ling 1m2f (0-55)H STD £1706
Total win prize-money £1706

Going (Turf): Sf: 0-0 GS: 0-1 Gd: 0-4 GF: 0-2 Fm: 0-0
Distance: 5f/6f: 0-1 7f-8f: 0-5 **9f-13f: 1-15** 14f+: 0-0
Track : **LH: 1-10** RH: 0-9 **Tight: 1-9** Gall: 0-0
Aids: Bl: 0-0 Vi: 0-0 Tstrap: 0-0 Ckp: 0-0
Best Rating: 59 2/09 Kemp 1m2f stand

Moderate; effective at around 1m2f; acts on Polytrack.

Mixing

94(104) (65)**57**
7-y-o gr g Linamix (FR)-Tuning (Rainbow Quest (USA))
M J Attwater Canisbay Bloodstock

Placings:033051000/604045060/00014220/61230253241 21064-004051260**0P0000** (7766)
2009: 12[0]SD, 12[0]SD, 12[4]GF, 12[0]SD, 11[5]G, 12[1]SD, 11[2]GF, 12[6]GF, 12[0]GF, 11[0]SD, 12[P]SD, 13[0]SS, 13[0]SD, 12[0]SD, 11[0]SD,

	Starts	1st	2nd	3rd	Win & Pl
Career Total (Turf)	29	2	1	2	7825
Career Total (AW)	28	4	6	2	12857

62 6/09 Kemp 1m4f (0-65)H STD £2047
65 9/08 Kemp 1m4f (0-75)H STD £2590
63 9/08 Kemp 1m3f (0-60)H STD £2047
58 1/08 Kemp 1m4f (0-60)H STD £1774
60 10/07 Brig 1m3f196y (0-55)H GD £1943
70 8/05 Wind 1m2f7y G-S £3493
Total win prize-money £13896

Going (Turf): Sf: 0-7 **GS: 1-6 Gd: 1-11** GF: 0-5 Fm: 0-0
Distance: 5f/6f: 0-0 7f-8f: 0-3 **9f-13f: 6-53** 14f+: 0-1
Track : LH: 1-23 **RH: 5-30 Tight: 1-20** Gall: 0-5
Aids: Bl: 0-2 Vi: 0-0 Tstrap: 0-0 Ckp: 0-0
Best Rating: 70 8/05 Wind 1m2f7y gd-sft

Modest; effective at around 1m4f; acts on good and softer ground and on Polytrack.

Miyasaki (CHI)

93 (91)**90**

7-y-o b g Memo (CHI)-Cantame Al Oido (CHI) (Yendaka (USA))

Rune Haugen Fun Trip Racing

Placings:110133126/230055/1015050300/52300335-30424040 (7185)

2009: 6^{3}SD, 6^{0}G, 6^{4}G, 6^{2}HY, 6^{4}FT, 5^{0}G, 6^{4}SD, 8^{0}G,

	Starts	1st	2nd	3rd	Win & Pl
Career Total (Turf)	20	1	1	3	19460
Career Total (AW)	21	5	3	5	54917

Date	Course	Dist		Going	Prize
5/07	Ovrl	1m	H	GD	£2461
4/07	Ovrl	1m	H	STD	£2461
10/05	HipC	1m1f110y		GD	£20619
7/05	HipC	7f110y		GD	£3186
5/05	HipC	6f		GD	£3092
2/05	HipC	5f		GD	£2905

Total win prize-money £34726

Going (Turf): Sf: 0-6 GS: 0-1 **Gd: 5-17** GF: 0-1 Fm: 0-2
Distance: 5f/6f: 2-15 **7f-8f: 3-19** 9f-13f: 1-7 14f+: 0-0
Track : **LH: 1-15** RH: 0-0 Tight: 0-0 Gall: 0-0
Aids: **Bl: 1-20** Vi: 0-1 Tstrap: 0-0 Ckp: 0-0
Best Rating: 94 9/07 Newb 7f gd-fm

Useful; a winner in Chile and Norway; stays 1m but effective at shorter; acts on fast ground and dirt; has worn blinkers, a visor and a tongue tie.

Mizair Nouvair (IRE)

67(69) (14)**18**

2-y-o b g Noverre (USA)-Arzachena (FR) (Grand Lodge (USA))

J R Weymes T A Scothern

Placings:000 (5224)

2009: 7^{0}G, 7^{0}GF, 7^{0}SD,

	Starts	1st	2nd	3rd	Win & Pl
Career Total (Turf)	2	0	0	0	
Career Total (AW)	1	0	0	0	

Going (Turf): **Sf: 0-0 GS: 0-0 Gd: 0-1 GF: 0-1 Fm: 0-0**
Distance: 5f/6f: 0-0 7f-8f: 0-3 9f-13f: 0-0 14f+: 0-0
Track : LH: 0-2 RH: 0-0 Tight: 0-2 Gall: 0-0
Aids: Bl: 0-0 Vi: 0-2 Tstrap: 0-0 Ckp: 0-0
Best Rating: 18 8/09 Newc 7f gd-fm

Mme De Stael

84 **53**

2-y-o ch f Selkirk (USA)-Scandalette (Niniski (USA))

Sir Mark Prescott Miss K Rausing

Placings:0003 (7244)

2009: 8^{0}GF, 8^{0}G, 8^{0}GF, 8^{3}S,

	Starts	1st	2nd	3rd	Win & Pl
Career Total (Turf)	4	0	0	1	626

Going (Turf): **Sf: 0-1 GS: 0-0 Gd: 0-1 GF: 0-2 Fm: 0-0**
Distance: 5f/6f: 0-0 7f-8f: 0-0 9f-13f: 0-4 14f+: 0-0
Track : LH: 0-2 RH: 0-1 Tight: 0-0 Gall: 0-0
Aids: Bl: 0-0 Vi: 0-0 Tstrap: 0-0 Ckp: 0-0
Best Rating: 53 11/09 Nott 1m75y soft

Mnarani (IRE)

91(92) (61)**66**

2-y-o b g Oasis Dream-Finity (USA) (Diesis)

J S Moore T Wilkinson E Moore J S Moore

Placings:004000 (7604)

2009: 6^{0}G, 6^{0}GF, 6^{4}GF, 6^{0}GF, 6^{0}S, 8^{0}SD,

	Starts	1st	2nd	3rd	Win & Pl
Career Total (Turf)	5	0	0	0	385
Career Total (AW)	1	0	0	0	

Going (Turf): **Sf: 0-1 GS: 0-0 Gd: 0-1 GF: 0-3 Fm: 0-0**
Distance: 5f/6f: 0-3 7f-8f: 0-3 9f-13f: 0-0 14f+: 0-0
Track : LH: 0-1 RH: 0-1 Tight: 0-1 Gall: 0-0
Aids: Bl: 0-0 Vi: 0-0 Tstrap: 0-0 Ckp: 0-0
Best Rating: 66 6/09 Chep 6f16y gd-fm

Mnasikia (USA)

(95) (66)

2-y-o b f Rahy (USA)-Entendu (USA) (Diesis)

L M Cumani William McAlpin

Placings:032 (7859)

2009: 5^{0}SD, 7^{3}SD, 7^{2}SD,

	Starts	1st	2nd	3rd	Win & Pl
Career Total (Turf)	0	0	0	0	
Career Total (AW)	3	0	1	1	1493

Going (Turf): **Sf: 0-0 GS: 0-0 Gd: 0-0 GF: 0-0 Fm: 0-0**
Distance: 5f/6f: 0-1 7f-8f: 0-2 9f-13f: 0-0 14f+: 0-0
Track : LH: 0-3 RH: 0-0 Tight: 0-3 Gall: 0-0
Aids: Bl: 0-0 Vi: 0-0 Tstrap: 0-0 Ckp: 0-0
Best Rating: 66 12/09 Wolv 7f32y stand

Modest; stays 7f; acts on Polytrack.

Mo Mhuirnin (IRE)

102(92) (63)**84**

3-y-o b f Danetime (IRE)-Cotton Grace (IRE) (Case Law)

R A Fahey Gone West Syndicate

Placings:40323-333211200 (5607)

2009: 5^{3}GS, 6^{3}GS, 5^{3}GF, 7^{2}GF, 6^{1}GF, 7^{1}GF, 7^{2}G, 8^{0}GF, 6^{0}S,

	Starts	1st	2nd	3rd	Win & Pl
Career Total (Turf)	13	2	3	4	14090
Career Total (AW)	1	0	0	1	770

Rating	Date	Course	Dist	Race	Going	Prize
84	6/09	Donc	7f	(0-70)H	G-F	£3238
73	6/09	Carl	6f192y	(0-80)H	G-F	£6476

Total win prize-money £9714

Going (Turf): Sf: 0-3 GS: 0-2 Gd: 0-2 **GF: 2-6** Fm: 0-0
Distance: 5f/6f: 0-7 **7f-8f: 2-7** 9f-13f: 0-0 14f+: 0-0
Track : LH: 0-2 **RH: 1-1** Tight: 0-0 Gall: 0-2
Aids: Bl: 0-0 Vi: 0-0 Tstrap: 0-0 Ckp: 0-0
Best Rating: 84 7/09 NmkJ 7f good

Fair; effective over 5f-7f; acts on quick and soft ground.

Moandei

(86) (53)**54**

5-y-o b m Silver Wizard (USA)-Its All Too Much (Chaddleworth (IRE))

R Ingram Stuart Higgins

Placings:00-0 (0455)

2009: 11^{0}SD,

	Starts	1st	2nd	3rd	Win & Pl
Career Total (Turf)	2	0	0	0	
Career Total (AW)	1	0	0	0	

Going (Turf): **Sf: 0-0 GS: 0-0 Gd: 0-1 GF: 0-1 Fm: 0-0**
Distance: 5f/6f: 0-0 7f-8f: 0-0 9f-13f: 0-3 14f+: 0-0
Track : LH: 0-0 RH: 0-3 Tight: 0-2 Gall: 0-0
Aids: Bl: 0-0 Vi: 0-0 Tstrap: 0-0 Ckp: 0-0
Best Rating: 54 9/08 Wind 1m67y gd-fm

Moayed

(100) (70)**67**

10-y-o b g Selkirk (USA)-Song Of Years (IRE) (Shareef Dancer (USA))

N P Littmoden Nigel Shields

Placings:0210/520000/111500/1263310401221001/12520002000000020005353/1650206460000/0005400000/3442356-45402 (1153)

2009: 8^{4}SD, 8^{5}SD, 8^{4}SD, 8^{0}SD, 8^{2}SD,

	Starts	1st	2nd	3rd	Win & Pl
Career Total (Turf)	34	2	4	1	64037
Career Total (AW)	57	9	8	5	111345

Rating	Date	Course	Dist	Race	Going	Prize
82	1/06	Ling	6f		STD	£12464
95	1/05	Wolv	1m141y		STD	£11901
109	12/04	Ling	7f	(0-107)H	STD	£12058
107	11/04	Wolv	5f216y	(0-107)H	STD	£13488
98	10/04	Ling	6f	(0-92)H	STD	£7034
94	5/04	NmkR	6f	C(0-95)H	GD	£29000
74	2/04	Ling	1m	G	STD	£2660
91	2/03	Ling	1m	D(0-80)H	STD	£4160
79	1/03	Ling	7f	F	STD	£3073
62	1/03	Ling	1m	F	STD	£2919
89	10/01	Tipp	1m1f		HVY	£7790

Total win prize-money £106549

Going (Turf): **Sf: 1-4** GS: 0-5 **Gd: 1-7** GF: 0-15 Fm: 0-1
Distance: 5f/6f: 4-20 **7f-8f: 5-51** 9f-13f: 2-20 14f+: 0-0
Track : **LH: 9-58** RH: 0-7 **Tight: 9-52** Gall: 0-3
Aids: **Bl: 11-82** Vi: 0-0 Tstrap: 0-0 Ckp: 0-0
Best Rating: 109 12/04 Ling 7f stand

Moderate; effective over 1m; goes on Polytrack; usually wears blinkers or a tongue tie; can start slowly and likes to come late.

Mocha Java

84(109) (69)**46**

6-y-o b g Bertolini (USA)-Coffee Cream (Common Grounds)

Matthew Salaman (M Salaman 27/7) R H Brookes

Placings:430030/4546121000000/0000/32-534151000100346420 (7845)

2009: 7^{5}SD, 8^{3}SD, 8^{4}SD, 6^{1}SD, 7^{5}SD, 7^{1}SD, 6^{0}GF, 6^{0}G, 7^{0}GF, 7^{1}SD, 7^{0}SD, 7^{0}SD, 7^{0}GS, 5^{3}SD, 7^{4}SD, 7^{6}SD, 7^{4}SD, 6^{2}SD, 7^{0}SD,

	Starts	1st	2nd	3rd	Win & Pl
Career Total (Turf)	19	2	1	1	7816
Career Total (AW)	23	3	2	4	8726

Rating	Date	Course	Dist	Race	Going	Prize
64	6/09	Wolv	7f32y		STD	£2047
69	2/09	Sthl	7f	(0-65)H	STD	£2047
61	1/09	Sthl	6f	(0-50)H	STD	£2047
74	8/06	Yarm	7f3y	(0-70)H	SFT	£3562
55	7/06	Chep	7f16y		GD	£2266

Total win prize-money £11970

Going (Turf): **Sf: 1-3** GS: 0-3 **Gd: 1-4** GF: 0-9 Fm: 0-0
Distance: 5f/6f: 1-5 **7f-8f: 4-32** 9f-13f: 0-5 14f+: 0-0
Track : **LH: 3-21** RH: 0-10 **Tight: 1-13** Gall: 0-2
Aids: Bl: 0-6 Vi: 0-0 Tstrap: 0-1 Ckp: 0-1
Best Rating: 74 8/06 Yarm 7f3y soft

Moderate; stays 7f; acts on most ground and on sand; has worn blinkers.

Mochua (IRE)

(67) **33**

5-y-o ch g Moscow Society (USA)-Devilabit (IRE) (Buckskin (FR))

Adrian Sexton S Buggy

Placings:0-0 **(0621)**
2009: 11^{0}SD,

	Starts	1st	2nd	3rd	Win & Pl
Career Total (Turf)	1	0	0	0	
Career Total (AW)	1	0	0	0	

Going (Turf): **Sf: 0-0 GS: 0-0 Gd: 0-0 GF: 0-0 Fm: 0-0**
Distance: 5f/6f: 0-0 7f-8f: 0-0 9f-13f: 0-2 14f+: 0-0
Track : LH: 0-1 RH: 0-1 Tight: 0-0 Gall: 0-0
Aids: Bl: 0-0 Vi: 0-0 Tstrap: 0-0 Ckp: 0-0
Best Rating: **33** 9/08 Rosc 1m4f yield

Modeyra

99 **83**
2-y-o br f Shamardal (USA)-Zahrat Dubai (Unfuwain (USA))
Saeed Bin Suroor Godolphin

Placings:1 **(6992)**
2009: 8^{1}GS,

	Starts	1st	2nd	3rd	Win & Pl
Career Total (Turf)	1	1	0	0	5181

83 10/09 Donc 1m G-S £5180
Total win prize-money £5181

Going (Turf): Sf: 0-0 **GS: 1-1** Gd: 0-0 GF: 0-0 Fm: 0-0
Distance: 5f/6f: 0-0 **7f-8f: 1-1** 9f-13f: 0-0 14f+: 0-0
Track : **LH: 1-1** RH: 0-0 Tight: 0-0 **Gall: 1-1**
Aids: Bl: 0-0 Vi: 0-0 Tstrap: 0-0 Ckp: 0-0
Best Rating: **83** 10/09 Donc 1m gd-sft

Well-bred daughter of Shamardal out of a mare who won the Musidora, was third in the Oaks and then won the Nassau; effective over 1m; acts on easy ground.

Moggy (IRE)

95(85) (50)**54**
3-y-o br f One Cool Cat (USA)-Termania (IRE) (Shirley Heights)
G A Harker (M L W Bell 17/7) Brian Morton

Placings:060-02204360 **(7324)**
2009: 10^{0}GF, 9^{2}G, 10^{2}HY, 10^{0}GF, 13^{4}GF, 10^{3}GF, 11^{6}G, 12^{0}SD,

	Starts	1st	2nd	3rd	Win & Pl
Career Total (Turf)	9	0	2	1	1870
Career Total (AW)	2	0	0	0	

Going (Turf): **Sf: 0-2 GS: 0-0 Gd: 0-3 GF: 0-4 Fm: 0-0**
Distance: 5f/6f: 0-0 7f-8f: 0-3 9f-13f: 0-7 14f+: 0-1
Track : LH: 0-7 RH: 0-2 Tight: 0-4 Gall: 0-2
Aids: Bl: 0-0 Vi: 0-0 Tstrap: 0-0 Ckp: 0-0
Best Rating: **54** 7/09 Nott 1m2f50y heavy

Moderate; stays 1m2f; acts on good and soft ground.

Mogok Ruby

98(106) (86)**82**
5-y-o gr g Bertolini (USA)-Days Of Grace (Wolfhound (USA))
L Montague Hall The Ruby Partnership

Placings:306333015/**5434**/3133500350443-51313630000000 **(7702)**
2009: 6^{5}SD, 6^{1}SD, 6^{3}SD, 6^{1}SD, 5^{3}SD, 6^{6}SD, 6^{3}G, 6^{0}GF, 6^{0}GF, 6^{0}GF, 6^{0}G, 6^{0}SD, 6^{0}SD, 6^{0}SD,

	Starts	1st	2nd	3rd	Win & Pl
Career Total (Turf)	14	1	0	3	7604
Career Total (AW)	26	3	0	10	20694

86 2/09 Kemp 6f (0-85)H STD £6476
83 1/09 Kemp 6f (0-85)H STD £4727
82 1/08 Kemp 6f (0-70)H STD £2590
71 9/06 Sand 5f6y (0-75) GD £4533
Total win prize-money £18328

Going (Turf): Sf: 0-0 GS: 0-1 **Gd: 1-7** GF: 0-6 Fm: 0-0
Distance: **5f/6f: 4-38** 7f-8f: 0-2 9f-13f: 0-0 14f+: 0-0
Track : LH: 0-12 **RH: 3-15** Tight: 0-10 Gall: 0-3
Aids: Bl: 0-0 Vi: 0-1 Tstrap: 0-0 Ckp: 0-0
Best Rating: **86** 2/09 Kemp 6f stand

Useful; effective at 6f; acts on Polytrack and fast ground.

Mohanad (IRE)

91(91) (71)**76**
3-y-o b g Invincible Spirit (IRE)-Irish Design (IRE) (Alhaarth (IRE))
Miss Sheena West (M R Channon 3/7) Heart Of The South Racing

Placings:6230-**44**606 **(3575)**
2009: 8^{4}SD, 12^{4}SD, 12^{6}G, 9^{0}GF, 14^{6}G,

	Starts	1st	2nd	3rd	Win & Pl
Career Total (Turf)	7	0	1	1	2712
Career Total (AW)	2	0	0	0	0

Going (Turf): **Sf: 0-0 GS: 0-0 Gd: 0-5 GF: 0-2 Fm: 0-0**
Distance: 5f/6f: 0-2 7f-8f: 0-3 9f-13f: 0-3 14f+: 0-1
Track : LH: 0-4 RH: 0-1 Tight: 0-3 Gall: 0-0
Aids: Bl: 0-0 Vi: 0-0 Tstrap: 0-0 Ckp: 0-0
Best Rating: **76** 6/08 Sals 6f212y gd-fm

70,000gns colt out of a half-sister to the high-class Idris; showed promise in maidens over 6f on good ground.

Mohathab (IRE)

81(107) (83)**86**
4-y-o b g Cadeaux Genereux-Zeiting (IRE) (Zieten (USA))
Tim Vaughan (J R Boyle 9/9) M Khan X2

Placings:0422-1002606 **(7734)**
2009: 8^{1}SD, 9^{0}GF, 9^{0}S, 8^{2}SD, 10^{6}GF, 10^{0}SD, 8^{6}SD,

	Starts	1st	2nd	3rd	Win & Pl
Career Total (Turf)	7	0	2	0	2168
Career Total (AW)	4	1	1	0	3997

77 4/09 Ling 1m STD £2590
Total win prize-money £2590

Going (Turf): **Sf: 0-1 GS: 0-1 Gd: 0-1 GF: 0-4 Fm: 0-0**
Distance: 5f/6f: 0-0 **7f-8f: 1-4** 9f-13f: 0-7 14f+: 0-0
Track : **LH: 1-5** RH: 0-4 **Tight: 1-6** Gall: 0-0
Aids: Bl: 0-2 Vi: 0-1 Tstrap: 0-0 Ckp: 0-0
Best Rating: **86** 6/08 Gdwd 1m1f gd-fm

Useful; stays 1m1f; acts on good and faster ground and on Polytrack; has worn blinkers.

Mohawk Ridge

103(96) (53)**68**
3-y-o b g Storming Home-Ipsa Loquitur (Unfuwain (USA))
M Dods Doug Graham

Placings:300-02341530 **(6860)**
2009: 9^{0}GF, 8^{2}G, 8^{3}G, 8^{4}GS, 8^{1}HY, 8^{5}S, 8^{3}G, 9^{0}SD,

	Starts	1st	2nd	3rd	Win & Pl
Career Total (Turf)	10	1	1	3	5277
Career Total (AW)	1	0	0	0	

68 8/09 Haml 1m65y (0-60)H HVY £2590
Total win prize-money £2590

Going (Turf): **Sf: 1-4** GS: 0-2 Gd: 0-3 GF: 0-1 Fm: 0-0
Distance: 5f/6f: 0-3 7f-8f: 0-4 **9f-13f: 1-4** 14f+: 0-0
Track : LH: 0-5 **RH: 1-4 Tight: 1-6** Gall: 0-0
Aids: Bl: 0-0 Vi: 0-0 Tstrap: 0-1 Ckp: 0-1
Best Rating: **68** 8/09 Haml 1m65y heavy

Modest; stays 1m; acts on good and soft ground.

Mohawk Star (IRE)

99(108) (75)**69**
8-y-o ch g Indian Ridge-Searching Star (Rainbow Quest (USA))
I A Wood Richard Abbott & Mario Stavrou

Placings:03/3102363/0/0**444**00**5**/**0601160324**-06240 **(4951)**
2009: 16^{0}SD, 16^{6}SD, 16^{2}GF, 16^{4}G, 14^{0}GF,

	Starts	1st	2nd	3rd	Win & Pl
Career Total (Turf)	20	1	2	4	15775
Career Total (AW)	12	2	1	1	7093

73 9/08 Kemp 2m (0-60)H STD £2047
63 9/08 Kemp 2m (0-70)H STD £2590
87 3/04 Leop 1m (60-90)H YLD £7299
Total win prize-money £11936

Going (Turf): **Sf: 0-6 GS: 0-1 Gd: 0-6 GF: 0-5 Fm: 0-0**
Distance: 5f/6f: 0-3 7f-8f: 1-10 9f-13f: 0-6 **14f+: 2-13**
Track : LH: 1-10 **RH: 2-16** Tight: 0-9 Gall: 0-2
Aids: Bl: 0-5 **Vi: 2-11** Tstrap: 0-0 Ckp: 0-0
Best Rating: **88** 7/04 Gway 1m100y good

Modest; ex-Irish; stays 2m; acts on good ground or softer and on Polytrack; has worn a visor.

Moheebb (IRE)

107 (63)**98**
5-y-o b g Machiavellian (USA)-Rockerlong (Deploy)
Mrs R A Carr Michael Hill

Placings:0/2050210**5**0**11**00**4**/03230240400502013505-456123403110300 **(6013)**
2009: 8^{4}GF, 8^{5}GF, 8^{6}GS, 8^{1}HY, 9^{2}GF, 8^{3}GS, 7^{4}GF, 8^{0}GF, 9^{3}S, 8^{1}GS, 9^{1}G, 9^{0}G, 10^{3}GF, 10^{0}GF, 10^{0}GS,

	Starts	1st	2nd	3rd	Win & Pl
Career Total (Turf)	46	7	6	6	47950
Career Total (AW)	4	0	0	0	0

97 8/09 Ripn 1m1f170y (0-85)H GD £4731
92 8/09 Thsk 1m (0-90)H G-S £8159
89 5/09 Hayd 1m30y (0-80)H HVY £6476
81 9/08 Haml 1m1f36y (0-70)H SFT £3238
78 10/07 Ayr 1m1f20y (0-65)H G-S £2730
72 9/07 Bevl 1m100y (0-75)H GD £3238
63 8/07 Carl 7f200y (0-75)H GD £2817
Total win prize-money £31391

Going (Turf): Sf: 2-16 GS: 2-9 **Gd: 3-11**GF: 0-10 Fm: 0-0
Distance: 5f/6f: 0-2 7f-8f: 2-20 **9f-13f: 5-28** 14f+: 0-0
Track : LH: 3-22 **RH: 4-21 Tight: 3-19** Gall: 0-7
Aids: **Bl: 4-33** Vi: 0-0 Tstrap: 0-0 Ckp: 0-0
Best Rating: **98** 8/09 York 1m2f88y gd-fm

Very useful; effective over 1m-1m2f; acts on good and heavy ground; usually blinkered.

Mohtashem (IRE)

100(102) (87)**85**
3-y-o b c Haafhd-Showering (Danehill (USA))
Sir Michael Stoute Hamdan Al Maktoum

Placings:3310030 **(5665)**
2009: 8^{3}SD, 8^{3}G, 8^{1}G, 8^{0}GF, 8^{0}GS, 8^{3}GF, 7^{0}SD,

	Starts	1st	2nd	3rd	Win & Pl
Career Total (Turf)	5	1	0	2	5023

Career Total (AW)	2	0	0	1	655

84 6/09 Gdwd 1m GD £3238

Total win prize-money £3238

Going (Turf): Sf: 0-0 GS: 0-1 **Gd: 1-2** GF: 0-2 Fm: 0-0
Distance: 5f/6f: 0-0 **7f-8f: 1-5** 9f-13f: 0-2 14f+: 0-0
Track : LH: 0-3 **RH: 1-3** Tight: 0-1 Gall: 0-0
Aids: Bl: 0-0 Vi: 0-1 Tstrap: 0-0 Ckp: 0-0
Best Rating: 87 5/09 Kemp 1m stand

Very useful; stays 1m; acts on Polytrack and on good ground.

Moi Mel

43

2-y-o b f Danbird (AUS)-Lady Double U (Sheikh Albadou)
L A Mullaney D A Flavell

Placings:0 (4396)
2009: 7^{0}GF,

	Starts	1st	2nd	3rd	Win & Pl
Career Total (Turf)	1	0	0	0	

Going (Turf): **Sf: 0-0 GS: 0-0 Gd: 0-0 GF: 0-1 Fm: 0-0**
Distance: 5f/6f: 0-0 7f-8f: 0-1 9f-13f: 0-0 14f+: 0-0
Track : LH: 0-0 RH: 0-1 Tight: 0-0 Gall: 0-0
Aids: Bl: 0-0 Vi: 0-0 Tstrap: 0-0 Ckp: 0-0

Mojeerr

93(97) (55)54

3-y-o b g Royal Applause-Princess Miletrian (IRE) (Danehill (USA))
A J McCabe A J McCabe

Placings:000-0363303 (7796)
2009: 8^{0}GF, 9^{3}GF, 11^{6}SD, 9^{3}SD, 9^{3}SD, 8^{0}SD, 7^{3}SS,

	Starts	1st	2nd	3rd	Win & Pl
Career Total (Turf)	4	0	0	1	339
Career Total (AW)	6	0	0	3	843

Going (Turf): **Sf: 0-0 GS: 0-0 Gd: 0-2 GF: 0-2 Fm: 0-0**
Distance: 5f/6f: 0-1 7f-8f: 0-4 9f-13f: 0-5 14f+: 0-0
Track : LH: 0-5 RH: 0-4 Tight: 0-3 Gall: 0-1
Aids: Bl: 0-0 Vi: 0-0 Tstrap: 0-4 Ckp: 0-4
Best Rating: 55 11/09 Wolv 1m1f103y stand

Moderate; stays 1m2f; handles Fibresand and Polytrack.

Molly The Witch (IRE)

96(87) (59)59

3-y-o b f Rock Of Gibraltar (IRE)-Tree Peony (Woodman (USA))
W J Musson (M P Tregoning 6/8) West, Weaver, Huckett & Eliades

Placings:00-0100 (6705)
2009: 10^{0}GF, 8^{1}G, 8^{0}SD, 10^{0}SS,

	Starts	1st	2nd	3rd	Win & Pl
Career Total (Turf)	2	1	0	0	1943
Career Total (AW)	4	0	0	0	

59 8/09 Yarm 1m3y GD £1942

Total win prize-money £1943

Going (Turf): Sf: 0-0 GS: 0-0 **Gd: 1-1** GF: 0-1 Fm: 0-0
Distance: 5f/6f: 0-0 7f-8f: 0-2 **9f-13f: 1-4** 14f+: 0-0
Track : LH: 0-2 RH: 0-3 Tight: 0-3 Gall: 0-0
Aids: Bl: 0-0 Vi: 0-0 Tstrap: 0-0 Ckp: 0-0
Best Rating: 59 8/09 Yarm 1m3y good

Moderate; best at 1m on good ground.

Molly Two

101(95) (53)71

4-y-o ch f Muhtarram (USA)-Rum Lass (Distant Relative)
L A Mullaney N Bulmer

Placings:05405-1060000000 (6877)
2009: 5^{1}GS, 5^{0}GS, 5^{6}GF, 5^{0}G, 5^{0}G, 5^{0}GS, 5^{0}GS, 5^{0}GF, 5^{0}GF, 5^{0}SD,

	Starts	1st	2nd	3rd	Win & Pl
Career Total (Turf)	13	1	0	0	2252
Career Total (AW)	2	0	0	0	0

71 4/09 Nott 5f13y (0-60)H G-S £2047

Total win prize-money £2047

Going (Turf): Sf: 0-2 **GS: 1-6** Gd: 0-2 GF: 0-3 Fm: 0-0
Distance: **5f/6f: 1-15** 7f-8f: 0-0 9f-13f: 0-0 14f+: 0-0
Track : LH: 0-2 RH: 0-1 Tight: 0-1 Gall: 0-1
Aids: Bl: 0-0 Vi: 0-1 Tstrap: 0-1 Ckp: 0-1
Best Rating: 71 4/09 Nott 5f13y gd-sft

Moderate; effective over 5f; acts on Polytrack.

Molon Labe (IRE)

99 73

2-y-o ch g Footstepsinthesand-Pillars Of Society (IRE) (Caerleon (USA))
T P Tate Mrs Fitri Hay

Placings:062 (7243)
2009: 7^{0}G, 8^{6}GS, 8^{2}S,

	Starts	1st	2nd	3rd	Win & Pl
Career Total (Turf)	3	0	1	0	1253

Going (Turf): **Sf: 0-1 GS: 0-1 Gd: 0-1 GF: 0-0 Fm: 0-0**
Distance: 5f/6f: 0-0 7f-8f: 0-2 9f-13f: 0-1 14f+: 0-0
Track : LH: 0-2 RH: 0-0 Tight: 0-0 Gall: 0-1
Aids: Bl: 0-0 Vi: 0-0 Tstrap: 0-0 Ckp: 0-0
Best Rating: 73 11/09 Nott 1m75y soft

Fair; effective over 1m; acts on soft ground.

Moment Of Clarity

(102) (71)66

7-y-o b g Lujain (USA)-Kicka (Shirley Heights)
R C Guest Andrew Shedden

Placings:0036/0035420455112/640001000000310-5020 (0554)
2009: 9^{5}SD, 10^{0}SD, 8^{2}SD, 8^{0}SD,

	Starts	1st	2nd	3rd	Win & Pl
Career Total (Turf)	18	1	1	2	5001
Career Total (AW)	18	3	2	1	7654

63 12/08 Wolv 1m141y (0-55)H STD £2047
66 6/08 Hayd 1m2f120y (0-75)H GD £2590
69 12/07 Wolv 1m1f103y (0-65)H STD £2047
63 11/07 Wolv 1m4f50y (0-55)H STD £2047

Total win prize-money £8733

Going (Turf): Sf: 0-2 GS: 0-1 **Gd: 1-7** GF: 0-5 Fm: 0-3
Distance: 5f/6f: 0-0 7f-8f: 0-1 **9f-13f: 4-34** 14f+: 0-1
Track : **LH: 4-33** RH: 0-3 **Tight: 3-21** Gall: 0-1
Aids: Bl: 0-0 Vi: 0-0 Tstrap: 4-25 Ckp: 4-25
Best Rating: 71 12/07 Wolv 1m1f103y stand

Moderate stays 1m4f; acts on good ground and on Polytrack; has worn cheekpieces.

Momtaz

90(83) (44)70

2-y-o b f Motivator-Sahra Alsalam (USA) (Gone West (USA))
C E Brittain Saeed Manana

Placings:400 (6628)
2009: 8^{4}GF, 7^{0}SD, 8^{0}SS,

	Starts	1st	2nd	3rd	Win & Pl
Career Total (Turf)	1	0	0	0	265
Career Total (AW)	2	0	0	0	

Going (Turf): **Sf: 0-0 GS: 0-0 Gd: 0-0 GF: 0-1 Fm: 0-0**
Distance: 5f/6f: 0-0 7f-8f: 0-3 9f-13f: 0-0 14f+: 0-0
Track : LH: 0-1 RH: 0-2 Tight: 0-1 Gall: 0-0
Aids: Bl: 0-0 Vi: 0-0 Tstrap: 0-0 Ckp: 0-0
Best Rating: 70 9/09 Gdwd 1m gd-fm

Mon Brav

96 76

2-y-o b c Sampower Star-Danehill Princess (IRE) (Danehill (USA))
D Carroll D Wallis

Placings:104 (3871)
2009: 5^{1}G, 6^{0}G, 5^{4}GF,

	Starts	1st	2nd	3rd	Win & Pl
Career Total (Turf)	3	1	0	0	4415

71 5/09 Bevl 5f GD £3885

Total win prize-money £3886

Going (Turf): Sf: 0-0 GS: 0-0 **Gd: 1-2** GF: 0-1 Fm: 0-0
Distance: **5f/6f: 1-3** 7f-8f: 0-0 9f-13f: 0-0 14f+: 0-0
Track : LH: 0-1 RH: 0-0 Tight: 0-1 Gall: 0-0
Aids: Bl: 0-0 Vi: 0-0 Tstrap: 0-0 Ckp: 0-0
Best Rating: 76 6/09 Epsm 6f good

Fair; suited by 5f and good ground.

Mon Cadeaux

99 99

2-y-o b c Cadeaux Genereux-Ushindi (IRE) (Montjeu (IRE))
A M Balding Mick and Janice Mariscotti

Placings:2101 (6398)
2009: 6^{2}G, 6^{1}GF, 7^{0}GF, 6^{1}GF,

	Starts	1st	2nd	3rd	Win & Pl
Career Total (Turf)	4	2	1	0	14456

99 9/09 Sals 6f G-F £8411
89 8/09 Sals 6f G-F £4695

Total win prize-money £13107

Going (Turf): Sf: 0-0 GS: 0-0 Gd: 0-1 **GF: 2-3** Fm: 0-0
Distance: **5f/6f: 2-3** 7f-8f: 0-1 9f-13f: 0-0 14f+: 0-0
Track : LH: 0-0 RH: 0-1 Tight: 0-0 Gall: 0-0
Aids: Bl: 0-0 Vi: 0-0 Tstrap: 0-0 Ckp: 0-0
Best Rating: 99 9/09 Sals 6f gd-fm

Useful; effective at 6f; acts on good and fast ground.

Mon Mon (IRE)

(79) (30)

2-y-o b f Refuse To Bend (IRE)-Adaja (Cadeaux Genereux)
G A Swinbank Mrs V Birnie

Placings:0 (7638)
2009: 8^{0}SD,

	Starts	1st	2nd	3rd	Win & Pl
Career Total (Turf)	0	0	0	0	
Career Total (AW)	1	0	0	0	

Going (Turf): Sf: 0-0 GS: 0-0 Gd: 0-0 GF: 0-0 Fm: 0-0
Distance: 5f/6f: 0-0 7f-8f: 0-1 9f-13f: 0-0 14f+: 0-0
Track : LH: 0-1 RH: 0-0 Tight: 0-0 Gall: 0-0
Aids: Bl: 0-0 Vi: 0-0 Tstrap: 0-0 Ckp: 0-0
Best Rating: 30 12/09 Sthl 1m stand

Monaadema (IRE)

105 **81**

4-y-o b f Elnadim (USA)-Suhaad (Unfuwain (USA))
W J Haggas Hamdan Al Maktoum

Placings:21-1 **(2565)**
2009: 7^{1}GF,

	Starts	1st	2nd	3rd	Win & Pl
Career Total (Turf)	3	2	1	0	9436

81	6/09	Folk	7f	(0-80)H	G-F	£5828
79	6/08	Wwck	7f26y		FRM	£2914

Total win prize-money £8742

Going (Turf): Sf: 0-0 GS: 0-0 Gd: 0-0 **GF: 1-2 Fm: 1-1**
Distance: 5f/6f: 0-1 **7f-8f: 2-2** 9f-13f: 0-0 14f+: 0-0
Track : **LH: 1-1** RH: 0-0 Tight: 0-0 Gall: 0-0
Aids: Bl: 0-0 Vi: 0-0 Tstrap: 0-0 Ckp: 0-0
Best Rating: 81 6/09 Folk 7f gd-fm

Fair; effective over 7f; acts on fast ground.

Monaadi (IRE)

94(105) (68)**56**

4-y-o b g Singspiel (IRE)-Bint Albaadiya (USA) (Woodman (USA))
F E Sutherland (R Hollinshead 20/8) Miss H P J Scheffers

Placings:002-4133652000 **(3594)**
2009: 12^{4}SD, 13^{1}SD, 13^{3}SD, 16^{3}SD, 16^{6}SF, 17^{5}GF, 11^{2}GF, 14^{0}GS, 12^{0}GF, 12^{0}GF,

	Starts	1st	2nd	3rd	Win & Pl
Career Total (Turf)	7	0	1	0	771
Career Total (AW)	6	1	1	2	3351

68	2/09	Wolv	1m5f194y	(0-60)H	STD	£1706

Total win prize-money £1706

Going (Turf): Sf: 0-0 GS: 0-2 Gd: 0-1 GF: 0-4 Fm: 0-0
Distance: 5f/6f: 0-0 7f-8f: 0-0 9f-13f: 0-7 **14f+: 1-6**
Track : **LH: 1-10** RH: 0-2 **Tight: 1-5** Gall: 0-0
Aids: Bl: 0-0 Vi: 0-3 Tstrap: 1-6 Ckp: 1-6
Best Rating: 68 2/09 Wolv 1m5f194y stand

Modest; stays 1m6f; acts on Polytrack; said not to handle Fibresand; has worn cheekpieces.

Monaco (GER)

(98) (76)

3-y-o b c Monsun (GER)-Miss Holsten (USA) (Diesis)
L M Cumani Andy Macdonald & Chris Wright

Placings:2 **(5840)**
2009: 8^{2}SD,

	Starts	1st	2nd	3rd	Win & Pl
Career Total (Turf)	0	0	0	0	
Career Total (AW)	1	0	1	0	806

Going (Turf): Sf: 0-0 GS: 0-0 Gd: 0-0 GF: 0-0 Fm: 0-0
Distance: 5f/6f: 0-0 7f-8f: 0-0 9f-13f: 0-1 14f+: 0-0
Track : LH: 0-1 RH: 0-0 Tight: 0-1 Gall: 0-0
Aids: Bl: 0-0 Vi: 0-0 Tstrap: 0-0 Ckp: 0-0
Best Rating: 76 9/09 Wolv 1m141y stand

Fair; stays 1m; acts on Polytrack; sure to improve.

Monaco Dream (IRE)

99(93) (71)**74**

3-y-o b f Hawk Wing (USA)-Parvenue (FR) (Ezzoud (IRE))
W Jarvis Monaco Dream Partnership

Placings:3024 **(3056)**
2009: 8^{3}SD, 8^{0}GF, 10^{2}GF, 11^{4}GF,

	Starts	1st	2nd	3rd	Win & Pl
Career Total (Turf)	3	0	1	0	1047
Career Total (AW)	1	0	0	1	403

Going (Turf): Sf: 0-0 GS: 0-0 Gd: 0-0 GF: 0-3 Fm: 0-0
Distance: 5f/6f: 0-0 7f-8f: 0-2 9f-13f: 0-2 14f+: 0-0
Track : LH: 0-2 RH: 0-2 Tight: 0-2 Gall: 0-0
Aids: Bl: 0-0 Vi: 0-0 Tstrap: 0-0 Ckp: 0-0
Best Rating: 74 6/09 Ling 1m2f gd-fm

Fair; stays 1m2f and acts on Polytrack and fast ground.

Monaco Mistress (IRE)

84(77) **55**

3-y-o b f Acclamation-Bendis (GER) (Danehill (USA))
N Tinkler (P C Haslam 8/7) Team Fashion Rocks

Placings:045-0000 **(7425)**
2009: 7^{0}GF, 7^{0}G, 9^{0}S, 12^{0}SD,

	Starts	1st	2nd	3rd	Win & Pl
Career Total (Turf)	6	0	0	0	373
Career Total (AW)	1	0	0	0	

Going (Turf): Sf: 0-2 GS: 0-0 Gd: 0-3 GF: 0-1 Fm: 0-0
Distance: 5f/6f: 0-3 7f-8f: 0-2 9f-13f: 0-2 14f+: 0-0
Track : LH: 0-3 RH: 0-1 Tight: 0-1 Gall: 0-0
Aids: Bl: 0-0 Vi: 0-0 Tstrap: 0-0 Ckp: 0-0
Best Rating: 55 8/08 Bevl 5f soft

Monagasque (IRE)

85(74) (34)**37**

3-y-o ch f King Charlemagne (USA)-Amiela (FR) (Mujtahid (USA))
S Kirk R J Brennan and D Boocock

Placings:06600 **(5328)**
2009: 8^{0}G, 8^{6}F, 8^{6}SD, 10^{0}GF, 11^{0}SD,

	Starts	1st	2nd	3rd	Win & Pl
Career Total (Turf)	3	0	0	0	0
Career Total (AW)	2	0	0	0	0

Going (Turf): Sf: 0-0 GS: 0-0 Gd: 0-1 GF: 0-1 Fm: 0-1
Distance: 5f/6f: 0-0 7f-8f: 0-0 9f-13f: 0-5 14f+: 0-0
Track : LH: 0-4 RH: 0-0 Tight: 0-2 Gall: 0-1
Aids: Bl: 0-0 Vi: 0-0 Tstrap: 0-0 Ckp: 0-0
Best Rating: 37 6/09 Bath 1m5y firm

Monahullan Prince

106(100) (76)**68**

8-y-o b g Pyramus (USA)-Classic Artiste (USA) (Arctic Tern (USA))
Gerard Keane Mrs E Keane

Placings:00/00040/6000053/65522131560/0211404040/405664-403131210 **(7261a)**
2009: 16^{4}YS, 17^{0}S, 16^{3}YS, 16^{1}GY, 16^{3}GF, 14^{1}SH, 16^{2}GY, 16^{1}SD, 16^{0}HY,

	Starts	1st	2nd	3rd	Win & Pl
Career Total (Turf)	48	6	4	4	36649
Career Total (AW)	2	1	0	0	5363

76	10/09	Wolv	2m119y	(0-85)H	STD	£5046
66	8/09	Klny	1m6f	(50-70)H	SH	£6037
56	8/09	Wxfd	2m	(47-65)H	G-Y	£4696
71	6/07	Tram	1m6f	(50-70)H	GD	£4668
61	5/07	Wxfd	1m5f	(42-60)H	GD	£3968
61	7/06	Klny	2m1f	(40-60)H	G-F	£4288
52	7/06	Bell	1m6f	(40-60)H	FRM	£4288

Total win prize-money £32996

Going (Turf): Sf: 0-5 GS: 0-0 **Gd: 2-12** GF: 1-10 Fm: 1-6
Distance: 5f/6f: 0-1 7f-8f: 0-4 9f-13f: 1-18 **14f+: 6-27**
Track : **LH: 4-12** RH: 3-34 **Tight: 1-1** Gall: 0-0
Aids: Bl: 0-0 Vi: 0-0 Tstrap: 1-4 Ckp: 1-4
Best Rating: 76 10/09 Wolv 2m119y stand

Monalini (IRE)

94 **76**

2-y-o b g Bertolini (USA)-Mona Em (IRE) (Catrail (USA))
B Smart Pinnacle Bertolini Partnership

Placings:15000 **(6534)**
2009: 5^{1}GF, 5^{5}GF, 6^{0}GF, 5^{0}GF, 6^{0}GF,

	Starts	1st	2nd	3rd	Win & Pl
Career Total (Turf)	5	1	0	0	3886

72	4/09	Muss	5f	G-F	£3885

Total win prize-money £3886

Going (Turf): Sf: 0-0 GS: 0-0 Gd: 0-0 **GF: 1-5** Fm: 0-0
Distance: **5f/6f: 1-5** 7f-8f: 0-0 9f-13f: 0-0 14f+: 0-0
Track : LH: 0-1 RH: 0-0 Tight: 0-0 Gall: 0-0
Aids: Bl: 0-0 Vi: 0-0 Tstrap: 0-0 Ckp: 0-0
Best Rating: 76 8/09 Muss 5f gd-fm

Fair; suited by 5f and fast ground.

Monashee Rock (IRE)

101(101) (71)**76**

4-y-o b f Monashee Mountain (USA)-Polar Rock (Polar Falcon (USA))
Matthew Salaman (M Salaman 29/8) Mrs P G Lewin & D Grieve

Placings:33532/001014405050-233634401244 **(7716)**
2009: 8^{2}F, 7^{3}F, 8^{3}GF, 8^{6}GF, 7^{3}GF, 8^{4}SD, 7^{4}SS, 8^{0}SD, 7^{1}SD, 7^{2}SD, 7^{4}SD, 7^{4}SD,

	Starts	1st	2nd	3rd	Win & Pl
Career Total (Turf)	16	2	1	6	11777
Career Total (AW)	13	1	2	0	3468

71	11/09	Wolv	7f32y		STD	£2047
76	7/08	Chep	7f16y	(0-75)H	G-F	£3238
75	6/08	Sals	6f212y	(0-75)H	GD	£3238

Total win prize-money £8523

Going (Turf): Sf: 0-2 GS: 0-3 **Gd: 1-2 GF: 1-7** Fm: 0-2
Distance: 5f/6f: 0-1 **7f-8f: 3-19** 9f-13f: 0-9 14f+: 0-0
Track : **LH: 1-14** RH: 0-6 **Tight: 1-13** Gall: 0-1
Aids: Bl: 0-0 Vi: 0-0 Tstrap: 0-0 Ckp: 0-0
Best Rating: 76 7/08 Chep 7f16y gd-fm

Modest; effective over 7f-1m; acts on fast and easy ground; goes on Polytrack.

Mondego (GER)

(91) (69)

7-y-o b g Big Shuffle (USA)-Molto In Forma (GER) (Surumu (GER))

George Baker Lady Forwood & Partners

Placings:64/100/11 **(6917)**

2009: 9^{1}SF, 12^{1}SD,

	Starts	1st	2nd	3rd	Win & Pl
Career Total (Turf)	4	0	0	0	211
Career Total (AW)	3	3	0	0	5313

69	10/09	Ling	1m4f	(0-60)H	STD	£1706
56	10/09	Wolv	1m1f103y	(0-55)	SF	£2047
	2/05	Neus	7f110y		STD	£1560

Total win prize-money £5313

Going (Turf): **Sf: 0-1 GS: 0-0 Gd: 0-2 GF: 0-1 Fm: 0-0**
Distance: 5f/6f: 0-0 7f-8f: 1-4 **9f-13f: 2-3** 14f+: 0-0
Track : **LH: 2-3** RH: 0-3 **Tight: 2-2** Gall: 0-0
Aids: Bl: 0-0 Vi: 0-0 Tstrap: 0-0 Ckp: 0-0
Best Rating: **69** 10/09 Ling 1m4f stand

Modest; stays 1m4f and handles Polytrack.

Mondovi

95(104) (96)95

5-y-o b m Kyllachy-Branston Fizz (Efisio)

Tom Dascombe K Dyer & C Bellamy

Placings:11521/61605-1000 **(7676)**

2009: 5^{1}SD, 5^{0}G, 5^{0}SD, 5^{0}SD,

	Starts	1st	2nd	3rd	Win & Pl
Career Total (Turf)	9	3	1	0	15606
Career Total (AW)	5	2	0	0	8704

96	9/09	Wolv	5f20y	(0-85)H	STD	£5046
95	5/08	Hayd	5f	(0-90)H	G-F	£10167
	8/07	Badn	5f		GD	£3378
	7/07	Kref	6f110y		GD	£1790
	6/07	Hanv	7f		GD	£2027

Total win prize-money £22409

Going (Turf): Sf: 0-1 GS: 0-0 **Gd: 3-6** GF: 1-3 Fm: 0-0
Distance: **5f/6f: 3-11** 7f-8f: 2-3 9f-13f: 0-0 14f+: 0-0
Track : **LH: 2-4** RH: 0-0 **Tight: 1-3** Gall: 0-0
Aids: Bl: 0-0 Vi: 0-0 Tstrap: 0-0 Ckp: 0-0
Best Rating: **96** 9/09 Wolv 5f20y stand

Useful ex-German performer; effective from 5f-7f; acts on good ground and Polytrack.

Monetary Fund (USA)

103(110) (88)83

3-y-o b g Montjeu (IRE)-Maddie G (USA) (Blush Rambler (USA))

G A Butler A D Spence

Placings:03-625532130 **(6613)**

2009: 10^{6}GF, 8^{2}GF, 8^{5}G, 14^{5}S, 11^{3}SD, 9^{2}GF, 10^{1}GF, 12^{3}SD, 12^{0}SD,

	Starts	1st	2nd	3rd	Win & Pl
Career Total (Turf)	8	1	2	1	6581
Career Total (AW)	3	0	0	2	1493

83	9/09	Epsm	1m2f18y	G-F	£3238

Total win prize-money £3238

Going (Turf): Sf: 0-1 GS: 0-0 Gd: 0-2 **GF: 1-5** Fm: 0-0
Distance: 5f/6f: 0-0 7f-8f: 0-3 **9f-13f: 1-7** 14f+: 0-1
Track : **LH: 1-5** RH: 0-3 **Tight: 1-3** Gall: 0-0
Aids: Bl: 0-0 Vi: 0-0 Tstrap: 0-0 Ckp: 0-0
Best Rating: **88** 8/09 Sthl 1m3f stand

Fair; effective at 1m-1m3f; acts on fast ground; has worn a tongue tie.

Money Lender

80 45

3-y-o b c Lend A Hand-Ellen Mooney (Efisio)

N J Vaughan Manor House Stables LLP

Placings:5 **(1611)**

2009: 10^{5}G,

	Starts	1st	2nd	3rd	Win & Pl
Career Total (Turf)	1	0	0	0	0

Going (Turf): **Sf: 0-0 GS: 0-0 Gd: 0-1 GF: 0-0 Fm: 0-0**
Distance: 5f/6f: 0-0 7f-8f: 0-0 9f-13f: 0-1 14f+: 0-0
Track : LH: 0-1 RH: 0-0 Tight: 0-0 Gall: 0-0
Aids: Bl: 0-0 Vi: 0-0 Tstrap: 0-0 Ckp: 0-0
Best Rating: **45** 4/09 Pont 1m2f6y good

Money Money Money

97(85) (64)62

3-y-o b f Generous (IRE)-Shi Shi (Alnasr Alwasheek)

P Winkworth Mrs Jenny Willment

Placings:400-66 **(2204)**

2009: 10^{6}G, 12^{6}GF,

	Starts	1st	2nd	3rd	Win & Pl
Career Total (Turf)	4	0	0	0	0
Career Total (AW)	1	0	0	0	337

Going (Turf): **Sf: 0-0 GS: 0-0 Gd: 0-1 GF: 0-3 Fm: 0-0**
Distance: 5f/6f: 0-0 7f-8f: 0-2 9f-13f: 0-3 14f+: 0-0
Track : LH: 0-1 RH: 0-3 Tight: 0-3 Gall: 0-0
Aids: Bl: 0-0 Vi: 0-0 Tstrap: 0-0 Ckp: 0-0
Best Rating: **64** 8/08 Kemp 7f stand

Moneycantbuymelove (IRE)

108 115

3-y-o b f Pivotal-Sabreon (Caerleon (USA))

M L W Bell Wright,Stanley,Marsh,Lascelles & Harris

Placings:344-531134 **(6510a)**

2009: 10^{5}GF, 10^{3}GF, 9^{1}GF, 8^{1}GF, 9^{3}S, 10^{4}S,

	Starts	1st	2nd	3rd	Win & Pl
Career Total (Turf)	9	2	0	3	110830

108	6/09	Asct	1m	(0-110)H	G-F	£28385
99	5/09	Gdwd	1m1f192y		G-F	£23704

Total win prize-money £52089

Going (Turf): Sf: 0-3 GS: 0-0 Gd: 0-1 **GF: 2-5** Fm: 0-0
Distance: 5f/6f: 0-0 7f-8f: 1-4 9f-13f: 1-5 14f+: 0-0
Track : LH: 0-1 **RH: 1-3 Tight: 1-2** Gall: 0-0
Aids: Bl: 0-0 Vi: 0-0 Tstrap: 0-0 Ckp: 0-0
Best Rating: **115** 8/09 Gdwd 1m1f192y soft

Group class; winner in Listed company; third in the 2009 Nassau Stakes; effective at around 1m2f; acts on fast and soft ground.

Moneysupermarket (IRE)

92(86) (43)51

3-y-o b f Acclamation-Almaviva (IRE) (Grand Lodge (USA))

Patrick Morris Lloyd & Mcleod Partnership

Placings:504564600 **(7051)**

2009: 6^{5}SD, 7^{0}GF, 5^{4}GS, 6^{5}G, 5^{6}G, 5^{4}GF, 6^{6}S, 5^{0}SD, 7^{0}SD,

	Starts	1st	2nd	3rd	Win & Pl
Career Total (Turf)	6	0	0	0	385
Career Total (AW)	3	0	0	0	0

Going (Turf): **Sf: 0-1 GS: 0-1 Gd: 0-2 GF: 0-2 Fm: 0-0**
Distance: 5f/6f: 0-6 7f-8f: 0-3 9f-13f: 0-0 14f+: 0-0
Track : LH: 0-3 RH: 0-2 Tight: 0-3 Gall: 0-1
Aids: Bl: 0-0 Vi: 0-0 Tstrap: 0-0 Ckp: 0-0
Best Rating: **51** 6/09 Donc 5f gd-sft

Monfils Monfils (USA)

103(99) (74)83

7-y-o b g Sahm (USA)-Sorpresa (USA) (Pleasant Tap (USA))

R E Barr (A J McCabe 30/5) Northumbria Leisure Ltd & B Morton

Placings:2325/0021301042/650231500000-336102500600016000 **(7851)**

2009: 9^{3}SD, 9^{3}SD, 8^{6}SD, 12^{1}G, 12^{0}GF, 12^{2}GF, 12^{5}F, 14^{0}G, 12^{0}GS, 12^{6}GF, 12^{0}GS, 10^{0}G, 11^{0}G, 9^{1}GF, 11^{6}GF, 10^{0}GF, 12^{0}GS, 11^{0}SS,

	Starts	1st	2nd	3rd	Win & Pl
Career Total (Turf)	35	5	6	3	53813
Career Total (AW)	9	0	0	2	1125

73	7/09	Bevl	1m1f207y	(0-65)H	G-F	£2729
75	3/09	Donc	1m4f	(0-70)H	GD	£3412
83	8/08	Leic	1m3f183y	(0-75)H	GD	£4533
86	7/06	MsnL	1m2f110y	H	GD	£15559
	4/06	Mtne	1m110y		GD	£2758

Total win prize-money £28993

Going (Turf): Sf: 0-4 GS: 0-6 **Gd: 4-13** GF: 1-10 Fm: 0-1
Distance: 5f/6f: 0-0 7f-8f: 0-2 **9f-13f: 5-39** 14f+: 0-3
Track : LH: 1-25 **RH: 2-8** Tight: 0-12 **Gall: 1-10**
Aids: Bl: 0-2 Vi: 0-0 Tstrap: 0-2 Ckp: 0-2
Best Rating: **89** 8/06 Deau 1m2f good

Modest; stays 1m4f; acts on most types of ground; has worn blinkers.

Monitor Closely (IRE)

112 117

3-y-o b c Oasis Dream-Independence (Selkirk (USA))

P W Chapple-Hyam Lawrie Inman

Placings:361-2043513 **(5861)**

2009: 10^{2}GF, 8^{0}GF, 10^{4}G, 10^{3}GF, 10^{5}G, 12^{1}GF, 14^{3}GF,

	Starts	1st	2nd	3rd	Win & Pl
Career Total (Turf)	10	2	1	3	262117

117	8/09	York	1m4f	G-F	£82964
79	10/08	Newb	1m	G-S	£5504

Total win prize-money £88469

Going (Turf): Sf: 0-1 **GS: 1-1** Gd: 0-2 **GF: 1-6** Fm: 0-0
Distance: 5f/6f: 0-0 7f-8f: 1-4 9f-13f: 1-5 14f+: 0-1
Track : **LH: 1-4** RH: 0-1 Tight: 0-0 **Gall: 1-5**
Aids: Bl: 0-0 Vi: 0-0 Tstrap: 0-0 Ckp: 0-0
Best Rating: **117** 8/09 York 1m4f gd-fm

Group class; winner of the Group 2 Great Voltigeur; stays 1m4f and acts on most ground.

Monkey Glas (IRE)

(116) (97)**76**

5-y-o b h Mull Of Kintyre (USA)-Maura's Pet (IRE) (Prince Of Birds (USA))

J R Gask Horses First Racing Limited

Placings:3513103/0050130656**3**/11333100132-00 (0452)

2009: 7^{0}SD, 8^{0}SD,

	Starts	1st	2nd	3rd	Win & Pl
Career Total (Turf)	14	3	0	2	13835
Career Total (AW)	17	4	1	7	26620

74 11/08 Ling 7f STD £1978
97 3/08 Wolv 7f32y (0-100)H STD £9971
94 1/08 Kemp 1m (0-85)H STD £4210
85 1/08 Ling 1m (0-75)H STD £2590
76 8/07 Pont 1m4y (0-75)H G-F £4533
72 8/06 Newc 7f G-F £3238
72 6/06 Rdcr 6f FRM £3238
Total win prize-money £29763

Going (Turf): Sf: 0-0 GS: 0-0 Gd: 0-5 **GF: 2-8** Fm: 1-1
Distance: 5f/6f: 1-4 **7f-8f: 5-21** 9f-13f: 1-6 14f+: 0-0
Track : **LH: 4-20** RH: 1-7 **Tight: 3-15** Gall: 0-0
Aids: Bl: 0-1 **Vi: 4-12** Tstrap: 0-0 Ckp: 0-0
Best Rating: 97 3/08 Wolv 7f32y stand

Useful; effective between 6f-1m; acts on fast ground and Polytrack; suited by forcing tactics; often wears headgear.

Monkton Vale (IRE)

90 **65**

2-y-o b g Catcher In The Rye (IRE)-Byproxy (IRE) (Mujtahid (USA))

N Wilson B Plows P M Watson J Owen

Placings:36 (6982)

2009: 7^{3}G, 8^{6}G,

	Starts	1st	2nd	3rd	Win & Pl
Career Total (Turf)	2	0	0	1	722

Going (Turf): **Sf: 0-0 GS: 0-0 Gd: 0-2 GF: 0-0 Fm: 0-0**
Distance: 5f/6f: 0-0 7f-8f: 0-2 9f-13f: 0-0 14f+: 0-0
Track : LH: 0-2 RH: 0-0 Tight: 0-0 Gall: 0-0
Aids: Bl: 0-0 Vi: 0-0 Tstrap: 0-0 Ckp: 0-0
Best Rating: 65 9/09 Ayr 7f50y good

Monmouthshire

85(35) (49)**64**

6-y-o b g Singspiel (IRE)-Croeso Cariad (Most Welcome)

R J Price Dick's Neighbours

Placings:6600600/0006015600/0-00 (3631)

2009: 10^{0}F, 10^{0}G,

	Starts	1st	2nd	3rd	Win & Pl
Career Total (Turf)	11	1	0	0	2733
Career Total (AW)	9	0	0	0	0

53 4/07 Bath 1m2f46y (0-50)H FRM £2733
Total win prize-money £2733

Going (Turf): Sf: 0-2 GS: 0-1 Gd: 0-2 GF: 0-2 **Fm: 1-4**
Distance: 5f/6f: 0-0 7f-8f: 0-0 **9f-13f: 1-18** 14f+: 0-2
Track : **LH: 1-17** RH: 0-2 **Tight: 1-13** Gall: 0-0
Aids: Bl: 0-0 **Vi: 1-11** Tstrap: 0-0 Ckp: 0-0
Best Rating: 64 5/06 Wind 1m2f7y soft

Moderate; effective at around 1m2f; acts on fast ground; has worn a visor.

Mono's Only

72(83) (55)**18**

3-y-o br f Red Ransom (USA)-Mono Lady (IRE) (Polish Patriot (USA))

Paul Mason Mrs R E Mason

Placings:50 (1198)

2009: 10^{5}SD, 9^{0}GF,

	Starts	1st	2nd	3rd	Win & Pl
Career Total (Turf)	1	0	0	0	
Career Total (AW)	1	0	0	0	0

Going (Turf): **Sf: 0-0 GS: 0-0 Gd: 0-0 GF: 0-1 Fm: 0-0**
Distance: 5f/6f: 0-0 7f-8f: 0-0 9f-13f: 0-2 14f+: 0-0
Track : LH: 0-1 RH: 0-1 Tight: 0-2 Gall: 0-0
Aids: Bl: 0-0 Vi: 0-0 Tstrap: 0-0 Ckp: 0-0
Best Rating: 55 3/09 Ling 1m2f stand

Monograph

82(90) (61)**51**

2-y-o b g Kyllachy-Beading (Polish Precedent (USA))

J W Hills Longview Stud & Bloodstock Ltd

Placings:000 (7859)

2009: 6^{0}GF, 6^{0}G, 7^{0}SD,

	Starts	1st	2nd	3rd	Win & Pl
Career Total (Turf)	2	0	0	0	
Career Total (AW)	1	0	0	0	

Going (Turf): **Sf: 0-0 GS: 0-0 Gd: 0-1 GF: 0-1 Fm: 0-0**
Distance: 5f/6f: 0-0 7f-8f: 0-3 9f-13f: 0-0 14f+: 0-0
Track : LH: 0-1 RH: 0-0 Tight: 0-1 Gall: 0-0
Aids: Bl: 0-0 Vi: 0-0 Tstrap: 0-0 Ckp: 0-0
Best Rating: 61 12/09 Wolv 7f32y stand

Monopole (IRE)

89 **55**

5-y-o b g Montjeu (IRE)-Pretty (IRE) (Darshaan)

D E Pipe (P R Webber 27/6) M C Pipe

Placings:50 (3374)

2009: 10^{5}GF, 10^{0}GF,

	Starts	1st	2nd	3rd	Win & Pl
Career Total (Turf)	2	0	0	0	0

Going (Turf): **Sf: 0-0 GS: 0-0 Gd: 0-0 GF: 0-2 Fm: 0-0**
Distance: 5f/6f: 0-0 7f-8f: 0-0 9f-13f: 0-2 14f+: 0-0
Track : LH: 0-1 RH: 0-1 Tight: 0-2 Gall: 0-0
Aids: Bl: 0-0 Vi: 0-0 Tstrap: 0-0 Ckp: 0-0
Best Rating: 55 6/09 Wind 1m2f7y gd-fm

Monreale (GER)

99 **74**

5-y-o b g Silvano (GER)-Maratea (USA) (Fast Play (USA))

G Brown (D E Pipe 18/7) Inglethorpe

Placings:46/255015/11000-04 (7248)

2009: 10^{0}GS, 10^{4}HY,

	Starts	1st	2nd	3rd	Win & Pl
Career Total (Turf)	15	3	1	0	15049

5/08 Badn 1m H GD £8823
4/08 Hanv 1m3f SFT £1507
7/07 Mulh 1m2f SFT £1756
Total win prize-money £12088

Going (Turf): **Sf: 2-5** GS: 0-1 Gd: 1-7 GF: 0-2 Fm: 0-0
Distance: 5f/6f: 0-0 7f-8f: 1-3 **9f-13f: 2-12** 14f+: 0-0
Track : LH: 0-3 RH: 0-6 Tight: 0-1 Gall: 0-2
Aids: Bl: 0-0 Vi: 0-0 Tstrap: 0-0 Ckp: 0-0
Best Rating: 85 8/07 Badn 1m2f good

Useful performer; stays 1m3f; acts on good and softer ground.

Monroe Gold

84(77) (42)**20**

9-y-o ch g Pivotal-Golden Daring (IRE) (Night Shift (USA))

Jennie Candlish Ms Jennie Candlish

Placings:000002/6001500/00**600**/0/50 (3233)

2009: 12^{5}SD, 12^{0}GF,

	Starts	1st	2nd	3rd	Win & Pl
Career Total (Turf)	17	1	1	0	5956
Career Total (AW)	4	0	0	0	0

42 7/04 Bell 1m (33-60)H GD £4866
Total win prize-money £4866

Going (Turf): Sf: 0-1 GS: 0-0 **Gd: 1-7** GF: 0-7 Fm: 0-1
Distance: 5f/6f: 0-1 **7f-8f: 1-7** 9f-13f: 0-11 14f+: 0-2
Track : **LH: 1-10** RH: 0-8 Tight: 0-5 Gall: 0-0
Aids: **Bl: 1-7** Vi: 0-3 Tstrap: 0-4 Ckp: 0-4
Best Rating: 42 2/09 Wolv 1m4f50y stand

Mons Calpe (IRE)

99(98) (65)**74**

3-y-o b g Rock Of Gibraltar (IRE)-Taking Liberties (IRE) (Royal Academy (USA))

P F I Cole H R H Sultan Ahmad Shah

Placings:0630-041105 (3321)

2009: 10^{0}GF, 12^{4}G, 9^{1}GF, 9^{1}GF, 10^{0}GF, 10^{5}GF,

	Starts	1st	2nd	3rd	Win & Pl
Career Total (Turf)	9	2	0	0	6226
Career Total (AW)	1	0	0	1	794

74 6/09 Folk 1m1f149y (0-70)H G-F £3070
73 5/09 Bevl 1m1f207y (0-70)H G-F £2914
Total win prize-money £5985

Going (Turf): Sf: 0-0 GS: 0-0 Gd: 0-3 **GF: 2-6** Fm: 0-0
Distance: 5f/6f: 0-0 7f-8f: 0-3 **9f-13f: 2-7** 14f+: 0-0
Track : LH: 0-3 **RH: 2-6 Tight: 1-4** Gall: 0-0
Aids: **Bl: 2-4** Vi: 0-0 Tstrap: 0-0 Ckp: 0-0
Best Rating: 74 6/09 Wind 1m2f7y gd-fm

Fair; stays 1m2f; acts on fast ground; goes on Polytrack.

Monsieur Chevalier (IRE)

110(98) (106)**108**

2-y-o b c Chevalier (IRE)-Blue Holly (IRE) (Blues Traveller (IRE))

R Hannon Mrs Valerie Hubbard & Ian Higginson

Placings:111511330 (6522a)

2009: 5^{1}GF, 5^{1}GF, 5^{1}G, 5^{1}G, 5^{5}GF, 5^{1}GS, 5^{1}G, 6^{3}GF, 6^{3}SD, 5^{0}G,

	Starts	1st	2nd	3rd	Win & Pl
Career Total (Turf)	9	6	0	1	191127
Career Total (AW)	1	0	0	1	5385

108 7/09 Gdwd 5f GD £34062
105 7/09 Newb 5f34y G-S £98480
105 5/09 Sand 5f6y GD £17031
100 5/09 Wind 5f10y GD £11656
100 4/09 NmkR 5f G-F £9066
96 4/09 Folk 5f G-F £2729
Total win prize-money £173026

Going (Turf): Sf: 0-0 GS: 1-1 **Gd: 3-4** GF: 2-4 Fm: 0-0

Distance: **5f/6f: 6-10** 7f-8f: 0-0 9f-13f: 0-0 14f+: 0-0
Track : LH: 0-0 RH: 0-1 Tight: 0-0 **Gall: 1-1**
Aids: Bl: 0-0 Vi: 0-0 Tstrap: 0-0 Ckp: 0-0
Best Rating: **108** 8/09 York 6f gd-fm

Group class; winner of the National Stakes, Super Sprint and Molecomb in 2009; suited by 5f but stays 6f; acts on most ground.

Monsieur Fillioux (USA)

(104) (79)
3-y-o ch g Hennessy (USA)-Eventually (USA) (Affirmed (USA))
J R Fanshawe Mrs J Fanshawe

Placings:31-02 **(7830)**
2009: 7^0SD, 7^2SD,

	Starts	1st	2nd	3rd	Win & Pl
Career Total (Turf)	0	0	0	0	
Career Total (AW)	4	1	1	1	4096

73 12/08 Ling 6f STD £2729
Total win prize-money £2730

Going (Turf): **Sf: 0-0 GS: 0-0 Gd: 0-0 GF: 0-0 Fm: 0-0**
Distance: **5f/6f: 1-1** 7f-8f: 0-3 9f-13f: 0-0 14f+: 0-0
Track : **LH: 1-3** RH: 0-1 **Tight: 1-3** Gall: 0-0
Aids: Bl: 0-0 Vi: 0-0 Tstrap: 0-0 Ckp: 0-0
Best Rating: **79** 12/09 Kemp 7f stand

Fair; effective over 7f; acts on Polytrack.

Monsieur Harvey

76 37
3-y-o ch g Monsieur Bond (IRE)-Annie Harvey (Fleetwood (IRE))
B Smart B Smart

Placings:500 **(2343)**
2009: 6^5GF, 6^0GS, 6^0GF,

	Starts	1st	2nd	3rd	Win & Pl
Career Total (Turf)	3	0	0	0	0

Going (Turf): **Sf: 0-0 GS: 0-1 Gd: 0-0 GF: 0-2 Fm: 0-0**
Distance: 5f/6f: 0-3 7f-8f: 0-0 9f-13f: 0-0 14f+: 0-0
Track : LH: 0-0 RH: 0-0 Tight: 0-0 Gall: 0-0
Aids: Bl: 0-0 Vi: 0-0 Tstrap: 0-0 Ckp: 0-0
Best Rating: **37** 5/09 Rdcr 6f gd-fm

Monsieur Joe (IRE)

99(103) (83)85
2-y-o b c Choisir (AUS)-Pascali (Compton Place)
W R Swinburn Mrs Helen Checkley

Placings:231150 **(6660)**
2009: 5^2GF, 5^3GF, 5^1GF, 5^1SD, 5^5G, 5^0GS,

	Starts	1st	2nd	3rd	Win & Pl
Career Total (Turf)	5	1	1	1	4691
Career Total (AW)	1	1	0	0	5046

83 9/09 Wolv 5f20y (0-85)H STD £5046
79 8/09 Folk 5f G-F £2729
Total win prize-money £7776

Going (Turf): Sf: 0-0 GS: 0-1 Gd: 0-1 **GF: 1-3** Fm: 0-0
Distance: **5f/6f: 2-6** 7f-8f: 0-0 9f-13f: 0-0 14f+: 0-0
Track : **LH: 1-1** RH: 0-0 **Tight: 1-1** Gall: 0-2
Aids: Bl: 0-0 Vi: 0-0 Tstrap: 0-0 Ckp: 0-0
Best Rating: **85** 10/09 Asct 5f gd-sft

Fair; effective over 5f; acts on fast ground.

Monsieur Jourdain (IRE)

80 50
3-y-o b g Royal Applause-Palwina (FR) (Unfuwain (USA))
T D Easterby C H Stevens

Placings:50000-0 **(4105)**
2009: 6^0S,

	Starts	1st	2nd	3rd	Win & Pl
Career Total (Turf)	6	0	0	0	0

Going (Turf): **Sf: 0-3 GS: 0-1 Gd: 0-1 GF: 0-1 Fm: 0-0**
Distance: 5f/6f: 0-4 7f-8f: 0-2 9f-13f: 0-0 14f+: 0-0
Track : LH: 0-0 RH: 0-0 Tight: 0-0 Gall: 0-0
Aids: Bl: 0-0 Vi: 0-0 Tstrap: 0-0 Ckp: 0-0
Best Rating: **50** 7/08 Bevl 5f good

Monsieur Kiss Kiss

79 59
3-y-o b c Monsieur Bond (IRE)-Known Class (USA) (Known Fact (USA))
R J Osborne William Hitchen

Placings:00-0500 **(5019)**
2009: 7^0GF, 8^5Y, 8^0SH, 7^0GF,

	Starts	1st	2nd	3rd	Win & Pl
Career Total (Turf)	6	0	0	0	

Going (Turf): **Sf: 0-1 GS: 0-1 Gd: 0-0 GF: 0-2 Fm: 0-0**
Distance: 5f/6f: 0-2 7f-8f: 0-2 9f-13f: 0-2 14f+: 0-0
Track : LH: 0-1 RH: 0-2 Tight: 0-0 Gall: 0-0
Aids: Bl: 0-0 Vi: 0-0 Tstrap: 0-0 Ckp: 0-0
Best Rating: **59** 10/08 NmkR 6f gd-sft

Monsieur Pontaven

72 28
2-y-o b c Avonbridge-Take Heart (Electric)
R Bastiman Ms M Austerfield

Placings:00 **(6896)**
2009: 5^0GF, 6^0GF,

	Starts	1st	2nd	3rd	Win & Pl
Career Total (Turf)	2	0	0	0	

Going (Turf): **Sf: 0-0 GS: 0-0 Gd: 0-0 GF: 0-2 Fm: 0-0**
Distance: 5f/6f: 0-2 7f-8f: 0-0 9f-13f: 0-0 14f+: 0-0
Track : LH: 0-1 RH: 0-0 Tight: 0-0 Gall: 0-0
Aids: Bl: 0-0 Vi: 0-0 Tstrap: 0-0 Ckp: 0-0
Best Rating: **28** 10/09 Pont 6f gd-fm

Monsieur Reynard

100(107) (72)82
4-y-o ch g Compton Place-Tell Tale Fox (Tel Quel (FR))
J M Bradley E A Hayward

Placings:300/342052134000002060-0050002053220032 **(7651)**
2009: 5^0F, 5^0GS, 5^5SD, 5^0F, 5^0GF, 5^0GS, 5^2G, 5^0G, 5^5G, 5^3G, 5^2SD, 5^2SD, 5^0GF, 5^0SD, 5^3SD, 5^2SD, 5^5SD,

	Starts	1st	2nd	3rd	Win & Pl
Career Total (Turf)	25	1	3	3	11603

	Starts	1st	2nd	3rd	Win & Pl
Career Total (AW)	13	0	4	2	3869

82 6/08 Wind 5f10y (0-80)H G-F £4857
Total win prize-money £4857

Going (Turf): Sf: 0-5 GS: 0-4 Gd: 0-6 **GF: 1-8** Fm: 0-2
Distance: **5f/6f: 1-36** 7f-8f: 0-2 9f-13f: 0-0 14f+: 0-0
Track : LH: 0-14 RH: 0-4 Tight: 0-9 **Gall: 1-5**
Aids: Bl: 0-3 Vi: 0-0 Tstrap: 0-2 Ckp: 0-2
Best Rating: **82** 6/08 Wind 5f10y gd-fm

Moderate; suited by 5f; acts on fast ground; goes on Polytrack.

Mont Agel

100 89
2-y-o b c Danehill Dancer (IRE)-Miss Riviera Golf (Hernando (FR))
M L W Bell J L C Pearce

Placings:31 **(6548)**
2009: 7^3GF, 8^1G,

	Starts	1st	2nd	3rd	Win & Pl
Career Total (Turf)	2	1	0	1	5774

89 10/09 Wind 1m67y GD £5018
Total win prize-money £5019

Going (Turf): Sf: 0-0 GS: 0-0 **Gd: 1-1** GF: 0-1 Fm: 0-0
Distance: 5f/6f: 0-0 7f-8f: 0-1 **9f-13f: 1-1** 14f+: 0-0
Track : LH: 0-0 **RH: 1-1 Tight: 1-1** Gall: 0-0
Aids: Bl: 0-0 Vi: 0-0 Tstrap: 0-0 Ckp: 0-0
Best Rating: **89** 10/09 Wind 1m67y good

Useful; stays 1m; acts on good and fast ground.

Mont Cervin

72(95) (58)74
4-y-o b g Sakhee (USA)-Daylight Dreams (Indian Ridge)
Mrs R A Carr David W Chapman

Placings:6610000-040000 **(2722)**
2009: 8^0SD, 8^4SD, 8^0SD, 7^0SD, 8^0SF, 7^0G,

	Starts	1st	2nd	3rd	Win & Pl
Career Total (Turf)	6	1	0	0	2267
Career Total (AW)	7	0	0	0	0

74 6/08 Folk 1m1f149y G-F £2266
Total win prize-money £2267

Going (Turf): Sf: 0-1 GS: 0-1 Gd: 0-2 **GF: 1-2** Fm: 0-0
Distance: 5f/6f: 0-0 7f-8f: 0-4 **9f-13f: 1-9** 14f+: 0-0
Track : LH: 0-8 **RH: 1-2 Tight: 1-7** Gall: 0-0
Aids: Bl: 0-5 Vi: 0-0 Tstrap: 0-0 Ckp: 0-0
Best Rating: **74** 6/08 Folk 1m1f149y gd-fm

Modest; stays 1m2f; acts on quick ground.

Montaff

107 107
3-y-o b c Montjeu (IRE)-Meshhed (USA) (Gulch (USA))
M R Channon Barry Walters Catering

Placings:21-2005204 **(6202)**
2009: 11^2GF, 12^0G, 12^0GF, 12^5G, 10^2GS, 10^0GF, 9^4G,

	Starts	1st	2nd	3rd	Win & Pl
Career Total (Turf)	9	1	3	0	27727

70 10/08 Newc 1m HVY £5180
Total win prize-money £5181

Going (Turf): **Sf: 1-2** GS: 0-1 Gd: 0-3 GF: 0-3 Fm: 0-0
Distance: 5f/6f: 0-0 **7f-8f: 1-1** 9f-13f: 0-8 14f+: 0-0
Track : **LH: 1-4** RH: 0-5 Tight: 0-4 **Gall: 1-4**
Aids: Bl: 0-0 Vi: 0-4 Tstrap: 0-0 Ckp: 0-0
Best Rating: **107** 5/09 Ling 1m3f106y gd-fm

Smart; effective at 1m2f-1m4f; acts on quick and soft ground; has worn a visor.

Montbretia

102(109) (92)98

4-y-o b f Montjeu (IRE)-Bayswater (Caerleon (USA))

H R A Cecil K Abdulla

Placings:4/2123-46 (2482)

2009: 10^4SD, 11^6G,

	Starts	1st	2nd	3rd	Win & Pl
Career Total (Turf)	6	1	2	1	10141
Career Total (AW)	1	0	0	0	962

79 7/08 Nott 1m2f50y GD £3238

Total win prize-money £3238

Going (Turf): Sf: 0-1 GS: 0-1 **Gd: 1-2** GF: 0-2 Fm: 0-0
Distance: 5f/6f: 0-0 7f-8f: 0-0 **9f-13f: 1-7** 14f+: 0-0
Track : **LH: 1-4** RH: 0-2 Tight: 0-2 Gall: 0-2
Aids: Bl: 0-0 Vi: 0-0 Tstrap: 0-0 Ckp: 0-0
Best Rating: 98 9/08 NmkR 1m4f gd-fm

Very useful; stays 1m4f; acts on good and fast ground.

Montchara (IRE)

87 (75)47

6-y-o b g Montjeu (IRE)-Mochara (Last Fandango)

M Todhunter Gill and Bill Hazeldean

Placings:0/40/3100060/60 (3023)

2009: 14^6GF, 12^0G,

	Starts	1st	2nd	3rd	Win & Pl
Career Total (Turf)	10	0	0	0	265
Career Total (AW)	2	1	0	1	2742

75 4/07 Wolv 1m4f50y (0-65)H STD £2388

Total win prize-money £2389

Going (Turf): **Sf: 0-3 GS: 0-1 Gd: 0-3 GF: 0-3 Fm: 0-0**
Distance: 5f/6f: 0-0 7f-8f: 0-1 **9f-13f: 1-10** 14f+: 0-1
Track : **LH: 1-4** RH: 0-7 **Tight: 1-8** Gall: 0-2
Aids: Bl: 0-0 Vi: 0-0 Tstrap: 0-0 Ckp: 0-0
Best Rating: 75 4/07 Wolv 1m4f50y stand

Monte Cassino (IRE)

92(102) (64)64

4-y-o ch g Choisir (AUS)-Saucy Maid (IRE) (Sure Blade (USA))

J O'Reilly Woodcock Electrical Limited

Placings:00/00040005333-05420300000 (7834)

2009: 5^0GF, 6^5GF, 5^4GF, 5^2SD, 5^0SD, 5^3G, 5^0GF, 5^0GF, 5^0SD, 5^0SD, 6^0SD,

	Starts	1st	2nd	3rd	Win & Pl
Career Total (Turf)	13	0	0	1	866
Career Total (AW)	11	0	1	3	1675

Going (Turf): **Sf: 0-0 GS: 0-1 Gd: 0-3 GF: 0-9 Fm: 0-0**
Distance: 5f/6f: 0-17 7f-8f: 0-7 9f-13f: 0-0 14f+: 0-0
Track : LH: 0-9 RH: 0-6 Tight: 0-6 Gall: 0-0
Aids: Bl: 0-1 Vi: 0-0 Tstrap: 0-0 Ckp: 0-0
Best Rating: 64 7/09 Pont 5f good

Modest; effective over 6f; acts on Polytrack.

Monte Major (IRE)

78(107) (67)42

8-y-o b g Docksider (USA)-Danalia (IRE) (Danehill (USA))

D Shaw Derek Shaw

Placings:063/42120/000000/01003004300343/013452013 061325030232/620460400230432534-332105053060 (7484)

2009: 5^3SD, 5^3SD, 5^2SD, 5^1SD, 5^0SD, 5^5SF, 5^0SD, 5^5SD, 5^3SD, 5^0G, 5^6SD, 6^0SD,

	Starts	1st	2nd	3rd	Win & Pl
Career Total (Turf)	22	0	2	3	3895
Career Total (AW)	57	6	8	13	27439

67 2/09 Wolv 5f20y (0-60)H STD £2047
75 6/07 Wolv 5f20y (0-60)H STD £2388
65 4/07 Wolv 5f20y STD £2388
61 1/07 Wolv 5f20y (0-52)H STD £1318
59 2/06 Wolv 5f20y (0-65)H STD £2388
70 3/04 Ling 7f D STD £5200

Total win prize-money £15733

Going (Turf): **Sf: 0-4 GS: 0-6 Gd: 0-9 GF: 0-3 Fm: 0-0**
Distance: **5f/6f: 5-72** 7f-8f: 1-7 9f-13f: 0-0 14f+: 0-0
Track : **LH: 6-52** RH: 0-7 **Tight: 6-40** Gall: 0-7
Aids: Bl: 0-0 **Vi: 5-59** Tstrap: 0-0 Ckp: 0-0
Best Rating: 75 12/07 Wolv 5f20y stand

Moderate; effective at around 5f-6f; acts well on Fibresand and Polytrack; has worn a visor.

Monte Mayor Eagle

90(99) (56)39

3-y-o ch f Captain Rio-Ink Pot (USA) (Green Dancer (USA))

D Haydn Jones Miss Gillian Byrne

Placings:00014-0500022000 (7350)

2009: 5^0SD, 5^5SD, 8^0GF, 6^0SD, 7^0HY, 6^2SD, 6^2SD, 6^0GS, 5^0SD, 7^0SD,

	Starts	1st	2nd	3rd	Win & Pl
Career Total (Turf)	5	0	0	0	
Career Total (AW)	11	1	2	0	3557

55 11/08 Sthl 6f STD £2047

Total win prize-money £2047

Going (Turf): **Sf: 0-1 GS: 0-1 Gd: 0-1 GF: 0-2 Fm: 0-0**
Distance: **5f/6f: 1-9** 7f-8f: 0-6 9f-13f: 0-1 14f+: 0-0
Track : **LH: 1-12** RH: 0-2 Tight: 0-3 Gall: 0-1
Aids: **Bl: 1-7** Vi: 0-0 Tstrap: 0-0 Ckp: 0-0
Best Rating: 56 8/09 Sthl 6f stand

Moderate; suited by 6f and Fibresand; has worn blinkers.

Monte Mayor One

91(82) (38)65

2-y-o b f Lujain (USA)-Alvarinho Lady (Royal Applause)

D Haydn Jones R Phillips

Placings:56001600 (7156)

2009: 5^5GF, 5^6G, 5^0GS, 6^0SD, 5^1HY, 5^6GF, 6^0G, 5^0SD,

	Starts	1st	2nd	3rd	Win & Pl
Career Total (Turf)	6	1	0	0	2720
Career Total (AW)	2	0	0	0	

65 8/09 Chep 5f16y HVY £2719

Total win prize-money £2720

Going (Turf): **Sf: 1-1** GS: 0-1 Gd: 0-2 GF: 0-2 Fm: 0-0
Distance: **5f/6f: 1-7** 7f-8f: 0-1 9f-13f: 0-0 14f+: 0-0
Track : LH: 0-2 RH: 0-1 Tight: 0-1 Gall: 0-1
Aids: Bl: 0-0 Vi: 0-0 Tstrap: 0-0 Ckp: 0-0
Best Rating: 65 8/09 Chep 5f16y heavy

Modest; effective at 5f; acts on heavy ground.

Monte Pattino (USA)

100(100) (51)64

5-y-o ch g Rahy (USA)-Jood (USA) (Nijinsky (CAN))

C J Teague Collins Chauffeur Driven Executive Cars

Placings:00000050-5412310 (3940)

2009: 11^5SD, 11^4SD, 14^1GF, 14^2GF, 14^3G, 16^1GF, 16^0GF,

	Starts	1st	2nd	3rd	Win & Pl
Career Total (Turf)	13	2	1	1	6052
Career Total (AW)	2	0	0	0	361

64 6/09 Muss 2m (0-65)H G-F £2498
64 5/09 Muss 1m6f (0-65)H G-F £2590

Total win prize-money £5088

Going (Turf): Sf: 0-1 GS: 0-1 Gd: 0-3 **GF: 2-7** Fm: 0-1
Distance: 5f/6f: 0-0 7f-8f: 0-0 9f-13f: 0-5 **14f+: 2-10**
Track : LH: 0-9 **RH: 2-6 Tight: 2-9** Gall: 0-2
Aids: Bl: 0-0 **Vi: 2-10** Tstrap: 0-0 Ckp: 0-0
Best Rating: 64 6/09 Muss 2m gd-fm

Moderate; stays 1m6f; acts on fast ground; has worn a tongue tie and visor.

Montego Breeze

87(92) (46)51

3-y-o b f Tipsy Creek (USA)-Mofeyda (IRE) (Mtoto)

John A Harris Miss Vivian Pratt

Placings:304 (7853)

2009: 7^3GF, 8^0G, 6^4SS,

	Starts	1st	2nd	3rd	Win & Pl
Career Total (Turf)	2	0	0	1	385
Career Total (AW)	1	0	0	0	0

Going (Turf): **Sf: 0-0 GS: 0-0 Gd: 0-1 GF: 0-1 Fm: 0-0**
Distance: 5f/6f: 0-1 7f-8f: 0-1 9f-13f: 0-1 14f+: 0-0
Track : LH: 0-2 RH: 0-0 Tight: 0-0 Gall: 0-0
Aids: Bl: 0-0 Vi: 0-0 Tstrap: 0-0 Ckp: 0-0
Best Rating: 51 10/09 Leic 7f9y gd-fm

Moderate; stays 6f; acts on fast ground; handles Fibresand.

Montelissima (IRE)

82 62

2-y-o b f Montjeu (IRE)-Issa (Pursuit Of Love)

E A L Dunlop Mrs G A Rupert

Placings:06 (7183)

2009: 7^0F, 7^6G,

	Starts	1st	2nd	3rd	Win & Pl
Career Total (Turf)	2	0	0	0	0

Going (Turf): **Sf: 0-0 GS: 0-0 Gd: 0-1 GF: 0-0 Fm: 0-1**
Distance: 5f/6f: 0-0 7f-8f: 0-2 9f-13f: 0-0 14f+: 0-0
Track : LH: 0-0 RH: 0-0 Tight: 0-0 Gall: 0-0
Aids: Bl: 0-0 Vi: 0-0 Tstrap: 0-0 Ckp: 0-0
Best Rating: 62 10/09 NmkR 7f good

Monterey (IRE)

83(92) (68)40

2-y-o b c Montjeu (IRE)-Magnificient Style (USA) (Silver Hawk (USA))

T G Mills T G Mills, J Humphreys, Mrs S Ecclestone

Placings:04 (6772)
2009: 8^{0}GF, 8^{4}SD,

	Starts	1st	2nd	3rd	Win & Pl
Career Total (Turf)	1	0	0	0	
Career Total (AW)	1	0	0	0	289

Going (Turf): **Sf: 0-0 GS: 0-0 Gd: 0-0 GF: 0-1 Fm: 0-0**
Distance: 5f/6f: 0-0 7f-8f: 0-1 9f-13f: 0-1 14f+: 0-0
Track : LH: 0-0 RH: 0-2 Tight: 0-0 Gall: 0-0
Aids: Bl: 0-0 Vi: 0-0 Tstrap: 0-0 Ckp: 0-0
Best Rating: **68** 10/09 Kemp 1m stand

Monterosso

(87) (59)
2-y-o b c Dubawi (IRE)-Porto Roca (AUS) (Barathea (IRE))
M Johnston Sheikh Hamdan Bin Mohammed Al Maktoum

Placings:5 (7376)
2009: 7^{5}SD,

	Starts	1st	2nd	3rd	Win & Pl
Career Total (Turf)	0	0	0	0	
Career Total (AW)	1	0	0	0	0

Going (Turf): **Sf: 0-0 GS: 0-0 Gd: 0-0 GF: 0-0 Fm: 0-0**
Distance: 5f/6f: 0-0 7f-8f: 0-1 9f-13f: 0-0 14f+: 0-0
Track : LH: 0-1 RH: 0-0 Tight: 0-1 Gall: 0-0
Aids: Bl: 0-0 Vi: 0-0 Tstrap: 0-0 Ckp: 0-0
Best Rating: **59** 11/09 Wolv 7f32y stand

Montiboli (IRE)

103(104) (76)76
4-y-o ch f Bahamian Bounty-Aunt Sadie (Pursuit Of Love)
K A Ryan Dales Homes Ltd

Placings:23300/4254141233336-06460441142 (4496)
2009: 7^{0}SD, 7^{6}SD, 7^{4}SD, 8^{6}SD, 8^{0}F, 7^{4}SD, 8^{4}F, 8^{1}GS, 8^{1}G, 6^{4}G, 8^{2}HY,

	Starts	1st	2nd	3rd	Win & Pl
Career Total (Turf)	15	3	2	4	12835
Career Total (AW)	14	1	2	2	5971

72	7/09	Ripn	1m	(0-70)H	GD	£3238
70	6/09	Ripn	1m	(0-65)H	G-S	£2590
76	5/08	Sthl	1m	(0-70)H	STD	£3275
74	4/08	Catt	7f	(0-65)H	G-S	£2047

Total win prize-money £11151

Going (Turf): Sf: 0-3 **GS: 2-3** Gd: 1-6 GF: 0-1 Fm: 0-2
Distance: 5f/6f: 0-9 **7f-8f: 4-18** 9f-13f: 0-2 14f+: 0-0
Track : LH: 2-19 RH: 2-5 **Tight: 3-13** Gall: 0-0
Aids: Bl: 0-1 Vi: 0-0 Tstrap: 2-6 Ckp: 2-6
Best Rating: **76** 7/09 Hayd 1m30y heavy

Modest; suited by 7f-1m; acts on good and easy ground and sand; has worn cheekpieces.

Montiyra (IRE)

(57) 68
5-y-o b g Montjeu (IRE)-Shiyra (Darshaan)
Miss L C Siddall Stonebridge Racing

Placings:300/00 (7495)
2009: 14^{0}SD, 12^{0}SD,

	Starts	1st	2nd	3rd	Win & Pl
Career Total (Turf)	3	0	0	1	624
Career Total (AW)	2	0	0	0	

Going (Turf): **Sf: 0-1 GS: 0-0 Gd: 0-1 GF: 0-0 Fm: 0-0**
Distance: 5f/6f: 0-0 7f-8f: 0-0 9f-13f: 0-4 14f+: 0-1
Track : LH: 0-4 RH: 0-1 Tight: 0-1 Gall: 0-0
Aids: Bl: 0-0 Vi: 0-0 Tstrap: 0-0 Ckp: 0-0
Best Rating: **68** 5/07 Naas 1m2f gd-yld

Montmartre (USA)

102(87) (36)62
3-y-o b g Awesome Again (CAN)-Sacre Coeur (USA) (Saint Ballado (CAN))
David Pinder (B J Meehan 25/6) Miss N M Haine

Placings:45-564100000 (6787)
2009: 8^{5}G, 8^{6}GF, 7^{4}GF, 8^{1}F, 7^{0}GF, 8^{0}GS, 8^{0}F, 10^{0}SS, 7^{0}G,

	Starts	1st	2nd	3rd	Win & Pl
Career Total (Turf)	10	1	0	0	2448
Career Total (AW)	1	0	0	0	

57	6/09	Bath	1m5y	FRM	£1942

Total win prize-money £1943

Going (Turf): Sf: 0-0 GS: 0-1 Gd: 0-3 GF: 0-4 **Fm: 1-2**
Distance: 5f/6f: 0-0 7f-8f: 0-6 **9f-13f: 1-5** 14f+: 0-0
Track : **LH: 1-8** RH: 0-0 **Tight: 1-5** Gall: 0-1
Aids: Bl: 0-0 Vi: 0-0 Tstrap: 0-0 Ckp: 0-0
Best Rating: **62** 5/09 Nott 1m75y good

Modest; stays 1m; acts on fast ground.

Monyati

(57) (42)
2-y-o ch c Kyllachy-Mustique Dream (Don't Forget Me)
D M Simcock Saleh Al Homaizi & Imad Al Sagar

Placings:0 (7663)
2009: 8^{0}SD,

	Starts	1st	2nd	3rd	Win & Pl
Career Total (Turf)	0	0	0	0	
Career Total (AW)	1	0	0	0	

Going (Turf): **Sf: 0-0 GS: 0-0 Gd: 0-0 GF: 0-0 Fm: 0-0**
Distance: 5f/6f: 0-0 7f-8f: 0-1 9f-13f: 0-0 14f+: 0-0
Track : LH: 0-1 RH: 0-0 Tight: 0-1 Gall: 0-0
Aids: Bl: 0-0 Vi: 0-0 Tstrap: 0-0 Ckp: 0-0
Best Rating: **42** 12/09 Ling 1m stand

Mooakada (IRE)

107(111) (105)100
3-y-o gr f Montjeu (IRE)-Sulaalah (IRE) (Darshaan)
J H M Gosden Hamdan Al Maktoum

Placings:1-4002022 (7589)
2009: 10^{4}G, 12^{0}GF, 12^{0}G, 10^{2}GF, 10^{0}G, 10^{2}S, 12^{2}SD,

	Starts	1st	2nd	3rd	Win & Pl
Career Total (Turf)	7	1	2	0	25804
Career Total (AW)	1	0	1	0	8608

83	10/08	NmkR	1m	GD	£6152

Total win prize-money £6152

Going (Turf): Sf: 0-1 GS: 0-0 **Gd: 1-4** GF: 0-2 Fm: 0-0
Distance: 5f/6f: 0-0 **7f-8f: 1-1** 9f-13f: 0-7 14f+: 0-0
Track : LH: 0-3 RH: 0-3 Tight: 0-1 Gall: 0-4
Aids: Bl: 0-0 Vi: 0-0 Tstrap: 0-0 Ckp: 0-0
Best Rating: **105** 11/09 Kemp 1m4f stand

Very useful; Listed placed; stays 1m4f; acts on good ground and on Polytrack.

Moobeyn

75(88) (71)19
2-y-o ch g Selkirk (USA)-Key Academy (Royal Academy (USA))
M P Tregoning Sheikh Ahmed Al Maktoum

Placings:003 (7276)
2009: 7^{0}SS, 7^{0}G, 7^{3}SD,

	Starts	1st	2nd	3rd	Win & Pl
Career Total (Turf)	1	0	0	0	
Career Total (AW)	2	0	0	1	482

Going (Turf): **Sf: 0-0 GS: 0-0 Gd: 0-1 GF: 0-0 Fm: 0-0**
Distance: 5f/6f: 0-0 7f-8f: 0-3 9f-13f: 0-0 14f+: 0-0
Track : LH: 0-3 RH: 0-0 Tight: 0-2 Gall: 0-0
Aids: Bl: 0-0 Vi: 0-0 Tstrap: 0-1 Ckp: 0-1
Best Rating: **71** 11/09 Wolv 7f32y stand

Mood Music

111(105) (100)109
5-y-o b g Kyllachy-Something Blue (Petong)
Mario Hofer WH Sport International

Placings:212626332/6100150/10320023310-102150 (3908a)
2009: 6^{1}SD, 5^{0}SD, 5^{2}HY, 5^{1}G, 5^{5}G, 6^{0}G,

	Starts	1st	2nd	3rd	Win & Pl
Career Total (Turf)	30	5	7	5	155036
Career Total (AW)	3	2	0	0	3413

109	5/09	Lonc	5f	GD	£38835
	3/09	Dort	6f	STD	£1942
109	10/08	Badn	5f	SFT	£11029
	1/08	Dort	6f	STD	£1470
99	9/07	Siro	5f	GD	£18918
99	5/07	Badn	6f	GD	£10135
85	5/06	Haml	5f4y	G-F	£3886

Total win prize-money £86217

Going (Turf): Sf: 1-9 GS: 0-1 **Gd: 3-15** GF: 1-4 Fm: 0-0
Distance: **5f/6f: 7-32** 7f-8f: 0-1 9f-13f: 0-0 14f+: 0-0
Track : **LH: 2-6** RH: 0-5 Tight: 0-1 Gall: 0-1
Aids: **Bl: 2-12** Vi: 0-0 Tstrap: 0-0 Ckp: 0-0
Best Rating: **109** 5/09 Lonc 5f good

Very useful half-brother to the useful Steel Blue; has won in Listed company; effective at 5f-6f; handles most ground and acts on an artificial surface.

Moody Tunes

105(86) (58)86
6-y-o b g Merdon Melody-Lady-Love (Pursuit Of Love)
A P Jarvis (K R Burke 26/7) Geoffrey Hamilton

Placings:5460064/01112400/024101204000/00060260102-240211403 (7169)
2009: 8^{2}GF, 8^{4}G, 7^{0}G, 7^{2}GS, 7^{1}G, 7^{1}G, 8^{4}GS, 8^{0}G, 8^{3}S,

	Starts	1st	2nd	3rd	Win & Pl
Career Total (Turf)	45	8	7	1	51316
Career Total (AW)	2	0	0	0	0

85	8/09	Carl	7f200y	(0-70)H	GD	£2498
76	7/09	Carl	7f200y		GD	£2047
75	8/08	Haml	1m1f36y		SFT	£6476
91	6/07	Hayd	1m30y	(0-90)H	HVY	£9715
88	5/07	Yarm	1m3y	(0-80)H	GD	£4731
88	5/06	Ayr	7f50y	(0-65)H	SFT	£3238
78	5/06	Thsk	1m	(0-65)H	HVY	£2590

Total win prize-money £31299

Going (Turf): **Sf: 4-14** GS: 0-8 Gd: 3-16 GF: 1-6 Fm: 0-0
Distance: 5f/6f: 0-4 7f-8f: 4-26 9f-13f: 4-17 14f+: 0-0
Track : LH: 3-19 RH: 3-12 **Tight: 2-7** Gall: 0-4
Aids: Bl: 0-1 Vi: 0-0 Tstrap: 0-0 Ckp: 0-0
Best Rating: **91** 7/07 Gway 1m100y gd-yld

Fair; stays 1m 1f; acts on most ground; has worn blinkers.

Mooinooi

88 64

2-y-o b f Kyllachy-Amused (Prince Sabo)

T D Walford D R Brotherton

Placings:0020 (6245)

2009: 6^{0}G, 5^{0}S, 6^{2}GF, 6^{0}GF,

	Starts	1st	2nd	3rd	Win & Pl
Career Total (Turf)	4	0	1	0	1060

Going (Turf): **Sf: 0-1 GS: 0-0 Gd: 0-1 GF: 0-2 Fm: 0-0**
Distance: 5f/6f: 0-4 7f-8f: 0-0 9f-13f: 0-0 14f+: 0-0
Track : LH: 0-0 RH: 0-0 Tight: 0-0 Gall: 0-0
Aids: Bl: 0-0 Vi: 0-0 Tstrap: 0-2 Ckp: 0-2
Best Rating: **64** 9/09 Rdcr 6f gd-fm

Modest half-sister to good sprinters Bishops Court, Astonished and Cape Royal; stays 6f; acts on fast ground.

Moojeh (IRE)

(105) (79)

3-y-o ch f King's Best (USA)-Bahareeya (USA) (Riverman (USA))

M Botti (E A L Dunlop 17/6) Can Artam

Placings:041001 (7830)

2009: 8^{0}SD, 10^{4}SD, 7^{1}SD, 7^{0}SD, 8^{0}SD, 7^{1}SD,

	Starts	1st	2nd	3rd	Win & Pl
Career Total (Turf)	0	0	0	0	
Career Total (AW)	6	2	0	0	6021

79 12/09 Kemp 7f (0-75)H STD £3238
74 9/09 Kemp 7f STD £2590
Total win prize-money £5828

Going (Turf): **Sf: 0-0 GS: 0-0 Gd: 0-0 GF: 0-0 Fm: 0-0**
Distance: 5f/6f: 0-0 **7f-8f: 2-5** 9f-13f: 0-1 14f+: 0-0
Track : LH: 0-2 **RH: 2-4** Tight: 0-2 Gall: 0-0
Aids: Bl: 0-0 Vi: 0-0 Tstrap: 0-0 Ckp: 0-0
Best Rating: **79** 12/09 Kemp 7f stand

Fair; suited by 7f; acts on Polytrack.

Moon Crystal

(104) (76)

4-y-o b f Fasliyev (USA)-Sabreon (Caerleon (USA))

E A L Dunlop Geoffrey Bishop

Placings:613404202-4312423 (0945)

2009: 8^{4}SD, 8^{3}SD, 8^{1}SD, 8^{2}SD, 5^{4}SD, 8^{2}SD, 7^{3}SD,

	Starts	1st	2nd	3rd	Win & Pl
Career Total (Turf)	0	0	0	0	
Career Total (AW)	16	2	4	3	11200

72 2/09 Kemp 1m (0-75)H STD £3238
57 3/08 Kemp 1m STD £2590
Total win prize-money £5829

Going (Turf): **Sf: 0-0 GS: 0-0 Gd: 0-0 GF: 0-0 Fm: 0-0**
Distance: 5f/6f: 0-1 **7f-8f: 2-11** 9f-13f: 0-4 14f+: 0-0
Track : LH: 0-10 **RH: 2-6** Tight: 0-7 Gall: 0-2
Aids: Bl: 0-1 Vi: 0-0 Tstrap: 0-0 Ckp: 0-0
Best Rating: **76** 3/09 Ling 1m stand

Modest; effective over 1m-1m2f and acts on Polytrack; has worn a tongue-tie and blinkers.

Moon Lightning (IRE)

95(91) (76)73

3-y-o b g Desert Prince (IRE)-Moon Tango (IRE) (Last Tycoon)

M H Tompkins David P Noblett

Placings:001-005340060 (7246)

2009: 8^{0}GF, 7^{0}GF, 9^{5}GF, 8^{3}G, 10^{4}G, 8^{0}G, 9^{0}G, 8^{6}G, 8^{0}S,

	Starts	1st	2nd	3rd	Win & Pl
Career Total (Turf)	11	0	0	1	751
Career Total (AW)	1	1	0	0	2047

76 11/08 Sthl 7f STD £2047
Total win prize-money £2047

Going (Turf): **Sf: 0-2 GS: 0-0 Gd: 0-6 GF: 0-3 Fm: 0-0**
Distance: 5f/6f: 0-1 **7f-8f: 1-6** 9f-13f: 0-5 14f+: 0-0
Track : **LH: 1-8** RH: 0-2 Tight: 0-3 Gall: 0-2
Aids: Bl: 0-1 Vi: 0-0 Tstrap: 0-1 Ckp: 0-1
Best Rating: **76** 11/08 Sthl 7f stand

Fair; stays 7f and acts on Fibresand.

Moon Mix (FR)

97(96) (88)76

6-y-o gr g Linamix (FR)-Cherry Moon (USA) (Quiet American (USA))

J R Jenkins Mrs T McCoubrey

Placings:261210/3050/**200**0450006-0560000 (4388)

2009: 12^{0}SD, 10^{5}SD, 9^{6}GF, 11^{0}GF, 9^{0}S, 11^{0}G, 16^{0}G,

	Starts	1st	2nd	3rd	Win & Pl
Career Total (Turf)	21	2	2	1	26188
Career Total (AW)	6	0	1	0	1253

87 9/06 MsnL 1m4f110y G-S £8966
90 6/06 Lonc 1m2f GD £6552
Total win prize-money £15518

Going (Turf): Sf: 0-3 **GS: 1-5 Gd: 1-5** GF: 0-6 Fm: 0-0
Distance: 5f/6f: 0-0 7f-8f: 0-0 **9f-13f: 2-19** 14f+: 0-8
Track : LH: 0-16 **RH: 2-10** Tight: 0-10 Gall: 0-3
Aids: Bl: 0-0 Vi: 0-4 Tstrap: 0-1 Ckp: 0-1
Best Rating: **98** 5/06 StCl 1m2f good

Modest; winning hurdler; stays 2m; acts on Polytrack.

Moon Money (IRE)

92(93) (51)60

3-y-o b g King's Theatre (IRE)-Last Drama (IRE) (Last Tycoon)

K A Ryan Mrs J Ryan

Placings:62600540 (7425)

2009: 12^{6}GF, 9^{2}G, 11^{6}GF, 7^{0}GF, 9^{0}GF, 15^{5}G, 16^{4}SD, 12^{0}SD,

	Starts	1st	2nd	3rd	Win & Pl
Career Total (Turf)	6	0	1	0	771
Career Total (AW)	2	0	0	0	0

Going (Turf): **Sf: 0-0 GS: 0-0 Gd: 0-2 GF: 0-4 Fm: 0-0**
Distance: 5f/6f: 0-0 7f-8f: 0-1 9f-13f: 0-5 14f+: 0-2
Track : LH: 0-3 RH: 0-4 Tight: 0-3 Gall: 0-1
Aids: Bl: 0-0 Vi: 0-0 Tstrap: 0-0 Ckp: 0-0
Best Rating: **60** 6/09 Donc 1m4f gd-fm

Moderate; stays 2m; acts on Polytrack.

Moon Sister (IRE)

100 103

4-y-o b f Cadeaux Genereux-Tanz (IRE) (Sadler's Wells (USA))

W Jarvis Abdullah Saeed Belhab

Placings:0/35413120-40046 (5004)

2009: 9^{4}GF, 8^{0}G, 10^{0}GF, 10^{4}G, 10^{6}G,

	Starts	1st	2nd	3rd	Win & Pl
Career Total (Turf)	14	2	1	2	29500

86 8/08 Folk 1m1f149y (0-90)H G-F £9346
79 7/08 Wwck 1m2f188y SFT £3238
Total win prize-money £12585

Going (Turf): **Sf: 1-2** GS: 0-1 Gd: 0-7 **GF: 1-4** Fm: 0-0
Distance: 5f/6f: 0-1 7f-8f: 0-2 **9f-13f: 2-11** 14f+: 0-0
Track : LH: 1-7 RH: 1-4 **Tight: 1-4** Gall: 0-5
Aids: Bl: 0-0 Vi: 0-0 Tstrap: 0-0 Ckp: 0-0
Best Rating: **103** 9/08 Yarm 1m2f21y good

Smart; Listed placed; stays 1m2f; acts on most ground; likes to race prominently.

Moon Warrior

60(84) (28)16

3-y-o b g Yoshka-Lunalux (Emarati (USA))

C Smith Oh No Not Again

Placings:0600**600000**-0 (2104)

2009: 9^{0}GS,

	Starts	1st	2nd	3rd	Win & Pl
Career Total (Turf)	5	0	0	0	176
Career Total (AW)	6	0	0	0	0

Going (Turf): **Sf: 0-2 GS: 0-1 Gd: 0-1 GF: 0-1 Fm: 0-0**
Distance: 5f/6f: 0-3 7f-8f: 0-6 9f-13f: 0-2 14f+: 0-0
Track : LH: 0-6 RH: 0-1 Tight: 0-2 Gall: 0-0
Aids: Bl: 0-0 Vi: 0-1 Tstrap: 0-0 Ckp: 0-0
Best Rating: **28** 11/08 Sthl 7f stand

Moonage Daydream (IRE)

102(92) (61)73

4-y-o b g Captain Rio-Thelma (Blakeney)

T D Easterby Rio Grande Partnership

Placings:6200165230100-00060104430 (6761)

2009: 6^{0}GF, 7^{0}GS, 6^{0}F, 7^{6}F, 8^{0}GF, 7^{1}G, 7^{0}G, 7^{4}GF, 9^{4}G, 8^{3}GF, 9^{0}G,

	Starts	1st	2nd	3rd	Win & Pl
Career Total (Turf)	22	3	1	2	14075
Career Total (AW)	2	0	1	0	524

66 7/09 Bevl 7f100y (0-75)H GD £4533
73 8/08 Rdcr 6f (0-85)H G-S £4857
63 5/08 Rdcr 6f (0-70)H G-F £2331
Total win prize-money £11721

Going (Turf): Sf: 0-0 **GS: 1-7 Gd: 1-7 GF: 1-6** Fm: 0-2
Distance: **5f/6f: 2-11** 7f-8f: 1-10 9f-13f: 0-3 14f+: 0-0
Track : LH: 0-8 **RH: 1-6** Tight: 0-3 Gall: 0-0
Aids: **Bl: 3-19** Vi: 0-0 Tstrap: 0-0 Ckp: 0-0
Best Rating: **73** 8/08 Rdcr 6f gd-sft

Modest; effective over 7f-1m; acts on fast and easy ground; also goes on Fibresand; has worn blinkers.

Moonbalej

85 57

2-y-o ch g Motivator-Glam Rock (Nashwan (USA))

M Johnston Sheikh Hamdan Bin Mohammed Al Maktoum

Placings:000 (6930)

2009: 7^{0}G, 8^{0}G, 8^{0}G,

	Starts	1st	2nd	3rd	Win & Pl
Career Total (Turf)	3	0	0	0	

Going (Turf): **Sf: 0-0 GS: 0-0 Gd: 0-3 GF: 0-0 Fm: 0-0**

Distance: 5f/6f: 0-0 7f-8f: 0-1 9f-13f: 0-2 14f+: 0-0
Track : LH: 0-1 RH: 0-1 Tight: 0-2 Gall: 0-0
Aids: Bl: 0-0 Vi: 0-0 Tstrap: 0-0 Ckp: 0-0
Best Rating: **57** 9/09 Haml 1m65y good

Moonbeam Dancer (USA)

100(102) (80)**65**
3-y-o b/br f Singspiel (IRE)-Shepherd's Moon (USA) (Silver Hawk (USA))
D M Simcock Dr Ali Ridha

Placings:442-24331012 **(7701)**
2009: 12^{2}SD, 12^{4}SD, 11^{3}GF, 10^{3}F, 13^{1}SD, 13^{0}SD, 16^{1}SD, 16^{2}SD,

	Starts	1st	2nd	3rd	Win & Pl
Career Total (Turf)	2	0	0	2	1059
Career Total (AW)	9	2	3	0	11055

73 11/09 Kemp 2m (0-85)H STD £4727
71 11/09 Ling 1m5f (0-70)H STD £2729
Total win prize-money £7457

Going (Turf): **Sf: 0-0 GS: 0-0 Gd: 0-0 GF: 0-1 Fm: 0-1**
Distance: 5f/6f: 0-0 7f-8f: 0-1 9f-13f: 1-7 14f+: 1-3
Track : LH: 1-6 RH: 1-5 **Tight: 1-5** Gall: 0-1
Aids: Bl: 0-0 Vi: 0-0 Tstrap: 0-0 Ckp: 0-0
Best Rating: **80** 4/09 Kemp 1m4f stand

Fair; stays 2m; acts on Polytrack.

Moondarra Blade

67 **10**
2-y-o b g Needwood Blade-Beechy Bank (IRE) (Shareef Dancer (USA))
J R Weymes Thoroughbred Partners

Placings:00 **(4188)**
2009: 7^{0}GF, 7^{0}S,

	Starts	1st	2nd	3rd	Win & Pl
Career Total (Turf)	2	0	0	0	

Going (Turf): **Sf: 0-1 GS: 0-0 Gd: 0-0 GF: 0-1 Fm: 0-0**
Distance: 5f/6f: 0-0 7f-8f: 0-2 9f-13f: 0-0 14f+: 0-0
Track : LH: 0-1 RH: 0-0 Tight: 0-1 Gall: 0-0
Aids: Bl: 0-0 Vi: 0-1 Tstrap: 0-0 Ckp: 0-0
Best Rating: **10** 6/09 Rdcr 7f gd-fm

Moonlife (IRE)

109(109) (107)**104**
3-y-o b f Invincible Spirit (IRE)-Marania (IRE) (Marju (IRE))
Saeed Bin Suroor Godolphin

Placings:6125-2011 **(7132)**
2009: 8^{2}GS, 8^{0}GF, 8^{1}G, 8^{1}SD,

	Starts	1st	2nd	3rd	Win & Pl
Career Total (Turf)	6	1	2	0	29090
Career Total (AW)	2	2	0	0	30185

107 10/09 Ling 1m STD £22708
102 10/09 Leic 1m60y GD £7569
85 9/08 Kemp 7f STD £7477
Total win prize-money £37755

Going (Turf): Sf: 0-0 GS: 0-2 **Gd: 1-2** GF: 0-2 Fm: 0-0
Distance: 5f/6f: 0-1 **7f-8f: 2-6** 9f-13f: 1-1 14f+: 0-0
Track : LH: 1-2 **RH: 2-2 Tight: 1-1** Gall: 0-2
Aids: Bl: 0-0 Vi: 0-0 Tstrap: 0-0 Ckp: 0-0
Best Rating: **107** 10/09 Ling 1m stand

Smart; Listed winner; effective over 7f-1m; acts on fast and easy ground; goes on Polytrack; has worn a tongue tie.

Moonlight Affair (IRE)

99 **75**
3-y-o b f Distant Music (USA)-Petite Maxine (Sharpo)
E S McMahon D J Allen S E Allen/ G A Weetman

Placings:210-6204 **(4198)**
2009: 6^{6}GF, 6^{2}HY, 7^{0}G, 7^{4}S,

	Starts	1st	2nd	3rd	Win & Pl
Career Total (Turf)	7	1	2	0	6408

71 8/08 Hayd 6f G-S £3238
Total win prize-money £3238

Going (Turf): Sf: 0-2 **GS: 1-1** Gd: 0-3 GF: 0-1 Fm: 0-0
Distance: **5f/6f: 1-5** 7f-8f: 0-2 9f-13f: 0-0 14f+: 0-0
Track : LH: 0-0 RH: 0-0 Tight: 0-0 Gall: 0-0
Aids: Bl: 0-0 Vi: 0-0 Tstrap: 0-0 Ckp: 0-0
Best Rating: **75** 6/08 Donc 6f good

Fair; effective over 6f; acts on easy ground.

Moonlight Babe (USA)

77 **32**
2-y-o b f Thunder Gulch (USA)-Autumn Moon (USA) (Mr Prospector (USA))
I W McInnes Mrs Ann Milburn

Placings:0000 **(5417)**
2009: 5^{0}GF, 5^{0}GF, 5^{0}G, 7^{0}GF,

	Starts	1st	2nd	3rd	Win & Pl
Career Total (Turf)	4	0	0	0	

Going (Turf): **Sf: 0-0 GS: 0-0 Gd: 0-1 GF: 0-3 Fm: 0-0**
Distance: 5f/6f: 0-3 7f-8f: 0-1 9f-13f: 0-0 14f+: 0-0
Track : LH: 0-0 RH: 0-1 Tight: 0-0 Gall: 0-0
Aids: Bl: 0-0 Vi: 0-0 Tstrap: 0-0 Ckp: 0-0
Best Rating: **32** 8/09 Bevl 7f100y gd-fm

Moonlight Blaze

87 **59**
2-y-o b g Barathea (IRE)-Moonlight (IRE) (Night Shift (USA))
C W Fairhurst The PQD Partnership

Placings:00500 **(6901)**
2009: 6^{0}GF, 7^{0}G, 7^{5}G, 8^{0}GF, 8^{0}GF,

	Starts	1st	2nd	3rd	Win & Pl
Career Total (Turf)	5	0	0	0	0

Going (Turf): **Sf: 0-0 GS: 0-0 Gd: 0-2 GF: 0-3 Fm: 0-0**
Distance: 5f/6f: 0-1 7f-8f: 0-2 9f-13f: 0-2 14f+: 0-0
Track : LH: 0-2 RH: 0-1 Tight: 0-0 Gall: 0-1
Aids: Bl: 0-0 Vi: 0-0 Tstrap: 0-0 Ckp: 0-0
Best Rating: **59** 8/09 Bevl 7f100y good

Moonlight Man

(108) (86)**86**
8-y-o ch g Night Shift (USA)-Fleeting Rainbow (Rainbow Quest (USA))
C R Dore Liam Breslin

Placings:341113/220024260/300031204/00/054424600/0 551642500000412332000520-246 **(7854)**
2009: 8^{2}SD, 10^{4}SD, 8^{6}SS,

	Starts	1st	2nd	3rd	Win & Pl
Career Total (Turf)	40	5	7	5	93647
Career Total (AW)	24	1	4	1	8733

81 7/08 Bevl 1m100y (0-75)H G-F £2914
83 2/08 Wolv 1m141y (0-75)H STD £2457
101 7/05 Chep 7f16y (0-95)H G-F £10863
102 10/03 York 6f217y B G-F £8986
91 9/03 NmkR 6f D(0-85) G-F £4231
84 8/03 Kemp 6f D G-F £4979
Total win prize-money £34432

Going (Turf): Sf: 0-3 GS: 0-6 Gd: 0-9 **GF: 5-22** Fm: 0-0
Distance: 5f/6f: 2-12 7f-8f: 2-35 9f-13f: 2-17 14f+: 0-0
Track : **LH: 2-24** RH: 1-15 Tight: 1-15 Gall: 1-8
Aids: Bl: 0-2 Vi: 0-0 Tstrap: 0-1 Ckp: 0-1
Best Rating: **104** 7/05 Newb 1m gd-fm

Fair; effective over 7f-1m2f; acts on most ground and on Polytrack; has been tried in blinkers, cheekpieces and a tongue tie.

Moonlight Serenade

83(92) (49)**58**
2-y-o b f Mind Games-Rasseem (IRE) (Fasliyev (USA))
W G M Turner P & M Racing

Placings:0406443 **(7887)**
2009: 5^{0}GF, 5^{4}F, 6^{0}G, 6^{6}SD, 5^{4}SD, 7^{4}SS, 7^{3}SD,

	Starts	1st	2nd	3rd	Win & Pl
Career Total (Turf)	3	0	0	0	289
Career Total (AW)	4	0	0	1	242

Going (Turf): **Sf: 0-0 GS: 0-0 Gd: 0-1 GF: 0-1 Fm: 0-1**
Distance: 5f/6f: 0-4 7f-8f: 0-3 9f-13f: 0-0 14f+: 0-0
Track : LH: 0-6 RH: 0-0 Tight: 0-3 Gall: 0-1
Aids: Bl: 0-0 Vi: 0-0 Tstrap: 0-0 Ckp: 0-0
Best Rating: **58** 5/09 Bath 5f11y firm

Moonline Dancer (FR)

97 **78**
2-y-o b f Royal Academy (USA)-Tulipe Noire (USA) (Alleged (USA))
R Hannon Malih L Al Basti

Placings:3156 **(6619)**
2009: 7^{3}G, 6^{1}GF, 7^{5}GF, 6^{6}G,

	Starts	1st	2nd	3rd	Win & Pl
Career Total (Turf)	4	1	0	1	6047

78 8/09 Newb 6f8y G-F £4857
Total win prize-money £4857

Going (Turf): Sf: 0-0 GS: 0-0 Gd: 0-2 **GF: 1-2** Fm: 0-0
Distance: 5f/6f: 0-0 **7f-8f: 1-4** 9f-13f: 0-0 14f+: 0-0
Track : LH: 0-0 RH: 0-0 Tight: 0-0 Gall: 0-0
Aids: Bl: 0-0 Vi: 0-0 Tstrap: 0-0 Ckp: 0-0
Best Rating: **78** 9/09 Newb 7f gd-fm

160,000gns half-sister to four winners; promising debut over 7f on good and scored over 6f on fast next time.

Moonquake (USA)

111(107) (104)**109**
4-y-o b/br c Mr Greeley (USA)-Beaming Meteor (USA) (Pleasant Colony (USA))
Saeed Bin Suroor (M bin Shafya 13/3) Godolphin

Placings:621300-13262120 **(3873)**
2009: 10^{1}FT, 12^{3}GF, 10^{2}FT, 10^{6}FT, 9^{2}SD, 10^{1}GF, 10^{2}GF, 10^{0}GF,

	Starts	1st	2nd	3rd	Win & Pl
Career Total (Turf)	10	2	2	2	36126
Career Total (AW)	4	1	2	0	25896

105 5/09 York 1m2f88y (0-100)H G-F £12952
79 1/09 Ndas 1m2f FST £5681
78 6/08 Newc 1m2f32y G-S £3238
Total win prize-money £21872

Going (Turf): Sf: 0-2 **GS: 1-1** Gd: 0-2 **GF: 1-5** Fm: 0-0
Distance: 5f/6f: 0-0 7f-8f: 0-1 **9f-13f: 3-13** 14f+: 0-0
Track : **LH: 2-7** RH: 0-3 Tight: 0-1 **Gall: 2-8**
Aids: Bl: 0-0 Vi: 0-0 Tstrap: 0-0 Ckp: 0-0
Best Rating: **109** 6/09 Asct 1m2f gd-fm

Smart; effective over 1m2f-1m4f; acted on fast and easy ground; acted on sand; (DEAD).

Moonraker's Choice (IRE)

84 61
2-y-o ch f Choisir (AUS)-Staploy (Deploy)
R Hannon The Moonrakers

Placings:00 (4478)
2009: 6⁰GF, 5⁰G,

	Starts	1st	2nd	3rd	Win & Pl
Career Total (Turf)	2	0	0	0	

Going (Turf): **Sf: 0-0 GS: 0-0 Gd: 0-1 GF: 0-1 Fm: 0-0**
Distance: 5f/6f: 0-1 7f-8f: 0-1 9f-13f: 0-0 14f+: 0-0
Track : LH: 0-1 RH: 0-0 Tight: 0-0 Gall: 0-1
Aids: Bl: 0-0 Vi: 0-0 Tstrap: 0-0 Ckp: 0-0
Best Rating: **61** 7/09 Sals 6f212y gd-fm

Moonshine Beach

93(100) (66)64
11-y-o b g Lugana Beach-Monongelia (Welsh Pageant)
P W Hiatt Mrs Kerry Lewis

Placings:3620/6105/4063654P1103110311/06421306420 06/00/**0044055**/3155323-0 (2262)
2009: 16⁰G,

	Starts	1st	2nd	3rd	Win & Pl
Career Total (Turf)	45	8	2	6	42508
Career Total (AW)	11	1	2	2	4518

64 6/08 Kemp 2m (0-65)H STD £2047
84 7/05 Wwck 2m39y (0-75)H G-S £3645
81 10/04 Pont 2m1f216y (0-77)H GD £4120
78 10/04 Pont 2m1f22y (0-70)H G-F £4182
77 8/04 Wwck 2m39y E(0-70)H G-S £4855
75 8/04 Bevl 2m35y E(0-75)H G-S £4134
65 7/04 Bath 2m1f34yF(0-55)H GD £3601
69 7/04 Wwck 2m39y E(0-75)H GD £4348
71 7/03 Chep 2m2f E(0-70)H G-F £3887
Total win prize-money £34822

Going (Turf): Sf: 0-5 **GS: 3-7 Gd: 3-13** GF: 2-18 Fm: 0-2
Distance: 5f/6f: 0-0 7f-8f: 0-0 9f-13f: 0-4 **14f+: 9-52**
Track : **LH: 7-37** RH: 2-19 **Tight: 2-22** Gall: 0-2
Aids: Bl: 0-0 Vi: 0-1 Tstrap: 0-4 Ckp: 0-4
Best Rating: **86** 7/05 Wwck 1m6f213y gd-fm

Fair handicapper on turf; stays 2m2f; acts on most types of ground; has won twice at Pontefract and three times at Warwick.

Moonshine Creek

103(99) (70)70
7-y-o b g Pyramus (USA)-Monongelia (Welsh Pageant)
P W Hiatt P W Hiatt

Placings:000/2034000/521462134-01106264122 (7779)
2009: 12⁰SD, 11¹G, 11¹G, 11⁰GF, 13⁶GF, 11²GF, 12⁶SF, 12⁴SD, 12¹SD, 12²SD, 12²SD,

	Starts	1st	2nd	3rd	Win & Pl
Career Total (Turf)	22	4	3	2	15682
Career Total (AW)	8	1	3	0	5142

67 11/09 Ling 1m4f (0-70)H STD £2637
68 4/09 Bath 1m3f144y (0-75)H GD £3043
65 4/09 Brig 1m3f196y (0-85)H GD £2590
64 8/08 Bath 1m3f144y (0-55)H GD £2914
61 7/08 Wwck 1m4f134y (0-75)H GD £3238
Total win prize-money £14423

Going (Turf): Sf: 0-4 GS: 0-1 **Gd: 4-10** GF: 0-7 Fm: 0-0
Distance: 5f/6f: 0-0 7f-8f: 0-0 **9f-13f: 5-27** 14f+: 0-3
Track : **LH: 5-24** RH: 0-5 **Tight: 3-15** Gall: 0-1
Aids: Bl: 0-0 Vi: 0-0 Tstrap: 0-0 Ckp: 0-0
Best Rating: **70** 12/09 Ling 1m4f stand

Modest; stays 1m4f; acts on most ground and on sand.

Moonstreaker

93(104) (73)70
6-y-o b g Foxhound (USA)-Ling Lane (Slip Anchor)
C T Pogson (R M Whitaker 25/6) Wordingham Plant Hire

Placings:0053/54500**031**/040002**024**/313510022035-60054 (3314)
2009: 9⁰GF, 10⁰G, 10⁰GS, 7⁵GF, 10⁴GF,

	Starts	1st	2nd	3rd	Win & Pl
Career Total (Turf)	30	2	3	2	11152
Career Total (AW)	8	1	1	3	4671

70 6/08 Ripn 1m1f170y (0-70)H SFT £2914
66 4/08 Bevl 7f100y (0-60)H G-S £1942
66 12/06 Sthl 1m (0-62)H STD £2730
Total win prize-money £7587

Going (Turf): **Sf: 1-4 GS: 1-7** Gd: 0-4 GF: 0-14 Fm: 0-1
Distance: 5f/6f: 0-1 **7f-8f: 2-17** 9f-13f: 1-20 14f+: 0-0
Track : LH: 1-20 **RH: 2-11 Tight: 1-10** Gall: 0-4
Aids: Bl: 0-0 Vi: 0-0 Tstrap: 0-0 Ckp: 0-0
Best Rating: **73** 11/08 Sthl 1m4f stand

Modest; effective at around 7f-1m; acts on easy ground; also goes on Fibresand and Polytrack.

Moonwalking

101(89) (34)63
5-y-o b g Danehill Dancer (IRE)-Macca Luna (IRE) (Kahyasi)
Jedd O'Keeffe W R B Racing 38

Placings:0152060/433000/006-505 (4600)
2009: 12⁵G, 14⁰GS, 12⁵G,

	Starts	1st	2nd	3rd	Win & Pl
Career Total (Turf)	18	1	1	2	7433
Career Total (AW)	1	0	0	0	

75 6/06 Ayr 6f GD £3886
Total win prize-money £3886

Going (Turf): Sf: 0-0 GS: 0-3 **Gd: 1-8** GF: 0-7 Fm: 0-0
Distance: **5f/6f: 1-2** 7f-8f: 0-5 9f-13f: 0-11 14f+: 0-1
Track : LH: 0-9 RH: 0-5 Tight: 0-5 Gall: 0-3
Aids: Bl: 0-0 Vi: 0-0 Tstrap: 0-0 Ckp: 0-0
Best Rating: **78** 5/07 York 1m4f good

Modest handicapper; stays 1m4f, but effective at shorter; acts on a sound surface.

Moorhouse Girl

96 70
2-y-o b f Makbul-Record Time (Clantime)
D H Brown Ron Hull

Placings:23 (5693)
2009: 5²G, 5³GS,

	Starts	1st	2nd	3rd	Win & Pl
Career Total (Turf)	2	0	1	1	2505

Going (Turf): **Sf: 0-0 GS: 0-1 Gd: 0-1 GF: 0-0 Fm: 0-0**
Distance: 5f/6f: 0-2 7f-8f: 0-0 9f-13f: 0-0 14f+: 0-0
Track : LH: 0-0 RH: 0-0 Tight: 0-0 Gall: 0-0
Aids: Bl: 0-0 Vi: 0-0 Tstrap: 0-0 Ckp: 0-0
Best Rating: **70** 9/09 York 5f89y gd-sft

Fair; suited by 5f and good ground.

Moorhouse Lad

109 (91)116
6-y-o b g Bertolini (USA)-Record Time (Clantime)
B Smart Ron Hull

Placings:3200/0144156**621**/03220110/0063120-0000 (5765)
2009: 5⁰GF, 5⁰G, 5⁰GF, 5⁰GF,

	Starts	1st	2nd	3rd	Win & Pl
Career Total (Turf)	29	5	4	3	162489
Career Total (AW)	4	1	1	0	13744

104 9/08 Newb 5f34y GD £36900
116 8/07 Gdwd 5f GD £28390
106 7/07 NmkJ 5f (0-95)H G-F £9715
91 1/07 Sthl 5f (0-100)H STD £11334
87 6/06 NmkJ 5f (0-100)H G-F £12464
86 5/06 Newc 5f GD £2590
Total win prize-money £101397

Going (Turf): Sf: 0-1 GS: 0-2 **Gd: 3-12** GF: 2-14 Fm: 0-0
Distance: **5f/6f: 6-33** 7f-8f: 0-0 9f-13f: 0-0 14f+: 0-0
Track : LH: 0-3 RH: 0-0 Tight: 0-3 Gall: 0-0
Aids: Bl: 0-0 Vi: 0-0 Tstrap: 0-0 Ckp: 0-0
Best Rating: **116** 10/08 Lonc 5f gd sft

Group class; winner at Group 3 level and runner-up in the 2008 Prix de l'Abbaye; best at 5f; acts on good and faster ground but handles and easy surface and Fibresand.

Moorside Diamond

(94) (53)53
5-y-o b m Elmaamul (USA)-Dispol Diamond (Sharpo)
A D Brown Mrs M Doherty

Placings:0053605023030-00020 (0792)
2009: 8⁰SD, 8⁰SD, 10⁰SD, 7²SD, 8⁰SD,

	Starts	1st	2nd	3rd	Win & Pl
Career Total (Turf)	2	0	1	0	705
Career Total (AW)	16	0	1	3	1159

Going (Turf): **Sf: 0-0 GS: 0-1 Gd: 0-1 GF: 0-0 Fm: 0-0**
Distance: 5f/6f: 0-0 7f-8f: 0-10 9f-13f: 0-8 14f+: 0-0
Track : LH: 0-12 RH: 0-6 Tight: 0-5 Gall: 0-0
Aids: Bl. 0-6 Vi: 0-0 Tstrap: 0-1 Ckp: 0-1
Best Rating: **53** 11/08 Kemp 1m stand

Moderate; effective over 1m-1m2f; acts on Polytrack; has worn blinkers.

Moose Moran (USA)

(90) (66)

2-y-o gr/ro c Lemon Drop Kid (USA)-After All (IRE) (Desert Story (IRE))

H R A Cecil Raymond Tooth

Placings:5 **(6629)**

2009: 7^{5}SS,

	Starts	1st	2nd	3rd	Win & Pl
Career Total (Turf)	0	0	0	0	
Career Total (AW)	1	0	0	0	0

Going (Turf): **Sf: 0-0 GS: 0-0 Gd: 0-0 GF: 0-0 Fm: 0-0**
Distance: 5f/6f: 0-0 7f-8f: 0-1 9f-13f: 0-0 14f+: 0-0
Track : LH: 0-1 RH: 0-0 Tight: 0-1 Gall: 0-0
Aids: Bl: 0-0 Vi: 0-0 Tstrap: 0-0 Ckp: 0-0
Best Rating: **66** 10/09 Ling 7f std-slw

Mooted (UAE)

96(98) (71)**75**

4-y-o b g Mtoto-Assraar (Cadeaux Genereux)

Miss J A Camacho Axom (XII)

Placings:6100003-021 **(3447)**

2009: 9^{0}GF, 12^{2}GS, 12^{1}GF,

	Starts	1st	2nd	3rd	Win & Pl
Career Total (Turf)	6	2	1	0	7579
Career Total (AW)	4	0	0	1	403

66 6/09 Muss 1m4f100y (0-70)H G-F £3885
75 5/08 Wind 1m67y GD £2729
Total win prize-money £6616

Going (Turf): Sf: 0-0 GS: 0-3 **Gd: 1-1 GF: 1-2** Fm: 0-0
Distance: 5f/6f: 0-0 7f-8f: 0-4 **9f-13f: 2-6** 14f+: 0-0
Track : LH: 0-4 **RH: 2-4 Tight: 2-5** Gall: 0-1
Aids: Bl: 0-0 Vi: 0-0 Tstrap: 0-0 Ckp: 0-0
Best Rating: **75** 5/08 Wind 1m67y good

Fair; stays 1m1f and acts on good ground and on Polytrack; has worn an eyeshield.

Mooteeah (IRE)

94(99) (68)**71**

3-y-o b f Sakhee (USA)-Cerulean Sky (IRE) (Darshaan)

M A Jarvis Hamdan Al Maktoum

Placings:50-13 **(4068)**

2009: 10^{1}SD, 12^{3}S,

	Starts	1st	2nd	3rd	Win & Pl
Career Total (Turf)	3	0	0	1	482
Career Total (AW)	1	1	0	0	2730

68 5/09 Ling 1m2f STD £2729
Total win prize-money £2730

Going (Turf): **Sf: 0-2 GS: 0-0 Gd: 0-1 GF: 0-0 Fm: 0-0**
Distance: 5f/6f: 0-0 7f-8f: 0-2 **9f-13f: 1-2** 14f+: 0-0
Track : **LH: 1-2** RH: 0-0 **Tight: 1-1** Gall: 0-0
Aids: Bl: 0-0 Vi: 0-0 Tstrap: 0-0 Ckp: 0-0
Best Rating: **71** 7/09 Pont 1m4f8y soft

Half-sister to Honolulu out of the top-class Cerulean Sky; modest filly; effective at 7f; acts on Polytrack.

Mootriba

92(92) (72)**67**

3-y-o ch f Nayef (USA)-Tarbiyah (Singspiel (IRE))

W J Haggas Ms Nicola Mahoney

Placings:452-33 **(3358)**

2009: 7^{3}GF, 8^{3}GS,

	Starts	1st	2nd	3rd	Win & Pl
Career Total (Turf)	2	0	0	2	963
Career Total (AW)	3	0	1	0	1120

Going (Turf): **Sf: 0-0 GS: 0-1 Gd: 0-0 GF: 0-1 Fm: 0-0**
Distance: 5f/6f: 0-0 7f-8f: 0-5 9f-13f: 0-0 14f+: 0-0
Track : LH: 0-1 RH: 0-3 Tight: 0-0 Gall: 0-1
Aids: Bl: 0-4 Vi: 0-0 Tstrap: 0-0 Ckp: 0-0
Best Rating: **72** 11/08 GrLe 1m stand

Modest; effective over 1m; acts on Polytrack.

Moral Duty (USA)

91 **69**

4-y-o ch c Silver Deputy (CAN)-Shoogle (USA) (A.P. Indy (USA))

J S Moore D Gerza

Placings:5651/000-300 **(5502)**

2009: 5^{3}GF, 5^{0}S, 7^{0}G,

	Starts	1st	2nd	3rd	Win & Pl
Career Total (Turf)	10	1	0	1	3395

75 10/07 Wind 6f SFT £2817
Total win prize-money £2817

Going (Turf): **Sf: 1-2** GS: 0-1 Gd: 0-1 GF: 0-3 Fm: 0-0
Distance: **5f/6f: 1-6** 7f-8f: 0-2 9f-13f: 0-2 14f+: 0-0
Track : LH: 0-1 RH: 0-0 Tight: 0-0 **Gall: 1-2**
Aids: Bl: 0-0 Vi: 0-0 Tstrap: 0-0 Ckp: 0-0
Best Rating: **75** 10/07 Wind 6f soft

Fair; effective over 6f; acts on fast and soft ground.

Moran Gra (USA)

102 **93**

2-y-o ch g Rahy (USA)-Super Supreme (IND) (Zafonic (USA))

Ms Joanna Morgan M A Ryan

Placings:614000 **(6317a)**

2009: 5^{6}S, 6^{1}GF, 6^{4}GF, 6^{0}G, 7^{0}S, 6^{0}G,

	Starts	1st	2nd	3rd	Win & Pl
Career Total (Turf)	6	1	0	0	17110

84 6/09 Leop 6f G-F £11740
Total win prize-money £11740

Going (Turf): Sf: 0-2 GS: 0-0 Gd: 0-2 **GF: 1-2** Fm: 0-0
Distance: **5f/6f: 1-5** 7f-8f: 0-1 9f-13f: 0-0 14f+: 0-0
Track : **LH: 1-2** RH: 0-1 Tight: 0-0 Gall: 0-0
Aids: Bl: 0-1 Vi: 0-0 Tstrap: 0-0 Ckp: 0-0
Best Rating: **93** 6/09 Asct 6f gd-fm

Useful; Irish-trained; effective at 6f on fast ground.

Morana (IRE)

105 **108**

2-y-o b c Alhaarth (IRE)-Blushing Barada (USA) (Blushing Groom (FR))

P W Chapple-Hyam A Black

Placings:2215 **(7017)**

2009: 8^{2}GF, 7^{2}GF, 8^{1}GS, 8^{5}GS,

	Starts	1st	2nd	3rd	Win & Pl
Career Total (Turf)	4	1	2	0	36270

108 10/09 Asct 1m G-S £28385
Total win prize-money £28385

Going (Turf): Sf: 0-0 **GS: 1-2** Gd: 0-0 GF: 0-2 Fm: 0-0
Distance: 5f/6f: 0-0 **7f-8f: 1-3** 9f-13f: 0-1 14f+: 0-0
Track : LH: 0-0 **RH: 1-3** Tight: 0-0 **Gall: 1-1**
Aids: Bl: 0-0 Vi: 0-0 Tstrap: 0-0 Ckp: 0-0
Best Rating: **108** 10/09 Asct 1m gd-sft

Smart; Group 3 winner at two; stays 1m; acts on most ground; can be keen.

Morbick

(110) (78)**55**

5-y-o ch g Kyllachy-Direcvil (Top Ville)

J G M O'Shea (W M Brisbourne 2/3) J R Salter

Placings:4500053/1121535023033-03324 **(0734)**

2009: 9^{0}SD, 12^{3}SD, 12^{3}SD, 12^{2}SD, 13^{4}SD,

	Starts	1st	2nd	3rd	Win & Pl
Career Total (Turf)	4	0	0	0	0
Career Total (AW)	21	3	3	7	13338

77 2/08 Wolv 1m1f103y (0-75)H STD £2730
77 1/08 Wolv 1m1f103y (0-58)H STD £2047
69 1/08 Wolv 1m1f103y (0-55)H STD £1249
Total win prize-money £6027

Going (Turf): **Sf: 0-1 GS: 0-0 Gd: 0-1 GF: 0-2 Fm: 0-0**
Distance: 5f/6f: 0-1 7f-8f: 0-2 **9f-13f: 3-21** 14f+: 0-1
Track : **LH: 3-23** RH: 0-2 **Tight: 3-22** Gall: 0-0
Aids: Bl: 0-0 Vi: 0-0 Tstrap: 0-0 Ckp: 0-0
Best Rating: **78** 11/08 Wolv 1m141y stand

Fair; effective at around 1m4f; acts on Polytrack.

More For Less

81 **50**

2-y-o b g Danbird (AUS)-Patricia Philomena (IRE) (Prince Of Birds (USA))

T D Barron Dovebrace Ltd Air-Conditioning-Projects

Placings:550 **(2788)**

2009: 5^{5}GF, 5^{5}GF, 6^{0}G,

	Starts	1st	2nd	3rd	Win & Pl
Career Total (Turf)	3	0	0	0	0

Going (Turf): **Sf: 0-0 GS: 0-0 Gd: 0-1 GF: 0-2 Fm: 0-0**
Distance: 5f/6f: 0-3 7f-8f: 0-0 9f-13f: 0-0 14f+: 0-0
Track : LH: 0-0 RH: 0-0 Tight: 0-0 Gall: 0-0
Aids: Bl: 0-0 Vi: 0-0 Tstrap: 0-0 Ckp: 0-0
Best Rating: **50** 5/09 Bevl 5f gd-fm

More Lashes (USA)

97(91) (55)**74**

2-y-o ch f More Than Ready (USA)-Red Piano (USA) (Red Ransom (USA))

M G Quinlan EHR Partnership

Placings:05032050 **(6068)**

2009: 5^{0}G, 5^{5}S, 6^{0}GF, 5^{3}G, 5^{2}GF, 5^{0}GF, 6^{5}GF, 5^{0}SD,

	Starts	1st	2nd	3rd	Win & Pl
Career Total (Turf)	7	0	1	1	1638
Career Total (AW)	1	0	0	0	

Going (Turf): **Sf: 0-1 GS: 0-0 Gd: 0-2 GF: 0-4 Fm: 0-0**
Distance: 5f/6f: 0-8 7f-8f: 0-0 9f-13f: 0-0 14f+: 0-0
Track : LH: 0-3 RH: 0-0 Tight: 0-2 Gall: 0-0
Aids: Bl: 0-0 Vi: 0-0 Tstrap: 0-0 Ckp: 0-0
Best Rating: **74** 8/09 Sand 5f6y gd-fm

Fair; effective over 5f; acts on fast ground.

More Tea Vicar (IRE)

86(91) (63)45

3-y-o b f Bahhare (USA)-Grand Splendour (Shirley Heights)

Patrick Morris Mrs Janet McLeod

Placings:5355-606500 (5647)

2009: 9^{6}SD, 9^{0}GS, 8^{6}GF, 7^{5}G, 8^{0}HY, 7^{0}SD,

	Starts	1st	2nd	3rd	Win & Pl
Career Total (Turf)	4	0	0	0	0
Career Total (AW)	6	0	0	1	588

Going (Turf): **Sf: 0-1 GS: 0-1 Gd: 0-1 GF: 0-1 Fm: 0-0**
Distance: 5f/6f: 0-0 7f-8f: 0-6 9f-13f: 0-4 14f+: 0-0
Track : LH: 0-6 RH: 0-4 Tight: 0-7 Gall: 0-2
Aids: Bl: 0-0 Vi: 0-1 Tstrap: 0-0 Ckp: 0-0
Best Rating: **63** 11/08 GrLe 1m stand

Modest; effective over 1m; acts on Polytrack.

More Than Many (USA)

103 76

3-y-o b/br c More Than Ready (USA)-Slewnami (AUS) (Seattle Slew (USA))

R A Fahey The Rumpole Partnership

Placings:10-1 (1281)

2009: 7^{1}GF,

	Starts	1st	2nd	3rd	Win & Pl
Career Total (Turf)	3	2	0	0	6476

76 4/09 Bevl 7f100y (0-70)H G-F £2590
61 8/08 Ripn 6f G-S £3885
Total win prize-money £6476

Going (Turf): Sf: 0-0 **GS: 1-2** Gd: 0-0 **GF: 1-1** Fm: 0-0
Distance: 5f/6f: 1-1 7f-8f: 1-2 9f-13f: 0-0 14f+: 0-0
Track : LH: 0-0 **RH: 1-1** Tight: 0-0 Gall: 0-0
Aids: Bl: 0-0 Vi: 0-0 Tstrap: 0-0 Ckp: 0-0
Best Rating: **76** 4/09 Bevl 7f100y gd-fm

Modest; stays 7f and acts on most ground.

More Time Tim (IRE)

103(108) (93)78

4-y-o b g Namid-Lady Nasrana (FR) (Al Nasr (FR))

J R Boyle M Khan X2

Placings:0/052330-32111016130 (6876)

2009: 8^{3}SD, 8^{2}SD, 8^{1}SD, 8^{1}SD, 8^{1}SD, 8^{0}SD, 8^{1}SD, 8^{6}G, 7^{1}SF, 7^{3}SD, 8^{0}SD,

	Starts	1st	2nd	3rd	Win & Pl
Career Total (Turf)	8	0	1	2	2795
Career Total (AW)	10	5	1	2	21777

93 7/09 Wolv 7f32y (0-95)H SF £7443
89 5/09 Ling 1m (0-80)H STD £4857
84 2/09 Sthl 1m (0-75)H STD £2590
82 2/09 Sthl 1m (0-70)H STD £2729
77 1/09 Sthl 1m STD £2047
Total win prize-money £19667

Going (Turf): **Sf: 0-1 GS: 0-0 Gd: 0-3 GF: 0-3 Fm: 0-0**
Distance: 5f/6f: 0-0 **7f-8f: 5-12** 9f-13f: 0-6 14f+: 0-0
Track : **LH: 5-11** RH: 0-7 **Tight: 2-5** Gall: 0-0
Aids: Bl: 0-0 Vi: 0-0 Tstrap: 0-0 Ckp: 0-0
Best Rating: **93** 7/09 Wolv 7f32y std-fst

Useful; ex-Irish; effective over 7f-1m; acts on Fibresand and Polytrack.

Mores Wells

108 118

5-y-o b h Sadler's Wells (USA)-Endorsement (Warning)

R Gibson Mrs Catherine O'Flynn

Placings:2/11450136/34213460-46532032 (7497a)

2009: 10^{4}GS, 15^{6}S, 10^{5}GF, 12^{3}S, 12^{2}G, 10^{0}S, 12^{3}VS, 12^{2}VS,

	Starts	1st	2nd	3rd	Win & Pl
Career Total (Turf)	25	4	4	5	282934

118 8/08 Leop 1m4f HVY £33455
115 8/07 Leop 1m4f YLD £30743
111 4/07 Leop 1m2f G-F £30790
79 4/07 Leop 1m2f GD £7937
Total win prize-money £102927

Going (Turf): **Sf: 1-5** GS: 0-1 **Gd: 1-4 GF: 1-4** Fm: 0-1
Distance: 5f/6f: 0-0 7f-8f: 0-1 **9f-13f: 4-19** 14f+: 0-5
Track : **LH: 4-10** RH: 0-13 Tight: 0-1 Gall: 0-1
Aids: Bl: 0-8 Vi: 0-0 Tstrap: 0-0 Ckp: 0-0
Best Rating: **118** 9/08 Leop 1m2f yield

Smart; Irish trained; winner in Group 3 company; stays 1m6f; acts on most ground; has worn blinkers, often wears a tongue tie.

Moresco

97(97) (71)76

3-y-o gr g Dalakhani (IRE)-Majoune (FR) (Take Risks (FR))

W R Swinburn P W Harris

Placings:46-5630 (4911)

2009: 10^{5}G, 12^{6}SD, 13^{3}G, 14^{0}G,

	Starts	1st	2nd	3rd	Win & Pl
Career Total (Turf)	5	0	0	1	1155
Career Total (AW)	1	0	0	0	0

Going (Turf): **Sf: 0-0 GS: 0-0 Gd: 0-5 GF: 0-0 Fm: 0-0**
Distance: 5f/6f: 0-0 7f-8f: 0-0 9f-13f: 0-5 14f+: 0-1
Track : LH: 0-0 RH: 0-6 Tight: 0-1 Gall: 0-1
Aids: Bl: 0-0 Vi: 0-0 Tstrap: 0-0 Ckp: 0-0
Best Rating: **76** 7/09 NmkJ 1m5f good

Fair; stays 1m5f; acts on good ground and Polytrack.

Morestead (IRE)

88(80) (14)54

4-y-o ch g Traditionally (USA)-Itsy Bitsy Betsy (USA) (Beau Genius (CAN))

B G Powell L Gilbert

Placings:0060/66400-0 (4935)

2009: 18^{0}G,

	Starts	1st	2nd	3rd	Win & Pl
Career Total (Turf)	9	0	0	0	241
Career Total (AW)	1	0	0	0	

Going (Turf): **Sf: 0-1 GS: 0-1 Gd: 0-3 GF: 0-4 Fm: 0-0**
Distance: 5f/6f: 0-0 7f-8f: 0-4 9f-13f: 0-5 14f+: 0-1
Track : LH: 0-4 RH: 0-2 Tight: 0-2 Gall: 0-2
Aids: Bl: 0-0 Vi: 0-1 Tstrap: 0-0 Ckp: 0-0
Best Rating: **71** 7/07 Asct 7f gd-sft

Morgans Choice

89(81) (37)73

2-y-o b g Namid-Polar Dawn (Polar Falcon (USA))

J L Spearing G M Eales

Placings:02310 (6827)

2009: 6^{0}GF, 5^{2}G, 5^{3}GF, 5^{1}G, 5^{0}SF,

	Starts	1st	2nd	3rd	Win & Pl
Career Total (Turf)	4	1	1	1	4880
Career Total (AW)	1	0	0	0	

70 9/09 Ffos 5f GD £3885
Total win prize-money £3886

Going (Turf): Sf: 0-0 GS: 0-0 **Gd: 1-2** GF: 0-2 Fm: 0-0
Distance: **5f/6f: 1-5** 7f-8f: 0-0 9f-13f: 0-0 14f+: 0-0
Track : LH: 0-2 RH: 0-0 Tight: 0-1 Gall: 0-2
Aids: Bl: 0-0 Vi: 0-0 Tstrap: 0-0 Ckp: 0-0
Best Rating: **73** 7/09 Ling 5f good

Modest; suited by 5f and good ground.

Mormeatmic

92(92) (51)58

6-y-o b g Orpen (USA)-Mimining (Tower Walk)

M W Easterby M Broad & Mrs M E Attwood

Placings:330000/4101101600/0006/000343000-400 (4552)

2009: 6^{4}G, 5^{0}GF, 6^{0}GS,

	Starts	1st	2nd	3rd	Win & Pl
Career Total (Turf)	30	4	0	3	18178
Career Total (AW)	2	0	0	1	262

80 6/06 Ayr 5f (0-85)H GD £6477
77 6/06 Ayr 5f (0-70)H GD £3368
69 5/06 Carl 5f (0-70)H G-S £3886
61 4/06 Catt 5f (0-65)H G-S £2730
Total win prize-money £16461

Going (Turf): Sf: 0-4 **GS: 2-7 Gd: 2-11** GF: 0-8 Fm: 0-0
Distance: **5f/6f: 4-29** 7f-8f: 0-3 9f-13f: 0-0 14f+: 0-0
Track : LH: 0-4 **RH: 1-1** Tight: 0-1 **Gall: 1-1**
Aids: Bl: 0-2 Vi: 0-0 Tstrap: 0-0 Ckp: 0-0
Best Rating: **80** 6/06 Ayr 5f good

Morning Calm

103 65

3-y-o b f Montjeu (IRE)-Tempting Prospect (Shirley Heights)

R Charlton The Queen

Placings:00-0605 (4241)

2009: 9^{0}F, 14^{6}G, 14^{0}G, 12^{5}GF,

	Starts	1st	2nd	3rd	Win & Pl
Career Total (Turf)	6	0	0	0	0

Going (Turf): **Sf: 0-0 GS: 0-0 Gd: 0-4 GF: 0-1 Fm: 0-1**
Distance: 5f/6f: 0-0 7f-8f: 0-2 9f-13f: 0-2 14f+: 0-2
Track : LH: 0-2 RH: 0-3 Tight: 0-3 Gall: 0-1
Aids: Bl: 0-0 Vi: 0-2 Tstrap: 0-0 Ckp: 0-0
Best Rating: **65** 5/09 Sals 1m1f198y firm

Morning Dress (USA)

83(81) (28)40

3-y-o gr/ro g Smart Strike (CAN)-Black Tie Kiss (USA) (Danzig (USA))

M Johnston Sheikh Hamdan Bin Mohammed Al Maktoum

Placings:000 (5322)

2009: 7^{0}G, 10^{0}SD, 10^{0}GF,

	Starts	1st	2nd	3rd	Win & Pl
Career Total (Turf)	2	0	0	0	
Career Total (AW)	1	0	0	0	

Going (Turf): **Sf: 0-0 GS: 0-0 Gd: 0-1 GF: 0-1 Fm: 0-0**

Distance: 5f/6f: 0-0 7f-8f: 0-1 9f-13f: 0-2 14f+: 0-0
Track : LH: 0-1 RH: 0-2 Tight: 0-2 Gall: 0-0
Aids: Bl: 0-0 Vi: 0-0 Tstrap: 0-0 Ckp: 0-0
Best Rating: **40** 7/09 Thsk 7f good

Morning Drive

(79) (54)
2-y-o ch f Motivator-Bright Hope (IRE) (Danehill (USA))
W R Swinburn Pendley Farm

Placings:0 **(6163)**
2009: 7^{0}SD,

	Starts	1st	2nd	3rd	Win & Pl
Career Total (Turf)	0	0	0	0	
Career Total (AW)	1	0	0	0	

Going (Turf): **Sf: 0-0 GS: 0-0 Gd: 0-0 GF: 0-0 Fm: 0-0**
Distance: 5f/6f: 0-0 7f-8f: 0-1 9f-13f: 0-0 14f+: 0-0
Track : LH: 0-0 RH: 0-1 Tight: 0-0 Gall: 0-0
Aids: Bl: 0-0 Vi: 0-0 Tstrap: 0-0 Ckp: 0-0
Best Rating: **54** 9/09 Kemp 7f stand

Morning Queen (IRE)

98(82) (47)60
3-y-o b f Night Shift (USA)-Woodland Glade (Mark Of Esteem (IRE))
C G Cox J T & K M Thomas

Placings:00-5255 **(4164)**
2009: 5^{5}GS, 5^{2}GF, 6^{5}GF, 6^{5}G,

	Starts	1st	2nd	3rd	Win & Pl
Career Total (Turf)	5	0	1	0	964
Career Total (AW)	1	0	0	0	

Going (Turf): **Sf: 0-0 GS: 0-1 Gd: 0-1 GF: 0-3 Fm: 0-0**
Distance: 5f/6f: 0-6 7f-8f: 0-0 9f-13f: 0-0 14f+: 0-0
Track : LH: 0-2 RH: 0-1 Tight: 0-0 Gall: 0-2
Aids: Bl: 0-0 Vi: 0-0 Tstrap: 0-1 Ckp: 0-1
Best Rating: **60** 6/09 Leic 5f218y gd-fm

Morning Sir Alan

104(101) (72)78
3-y-o b c Diktat-Menhoubah (USA) (Dixieland Band (USA))
S A Callaghan Gallagher Equine Ltd

Placings:0-42320215 **(3222)**
2009: 8^{4}SD, 8^{2}SD, 8^{3}SD, 9^{2}G, 9^{0}GF, 10^{2}SD, 9^{1}GF, 11^{5}GF,

	Starts	1st	2nd	3rd	Win & Pl
Career Total (Turf)	5	1	1	0	3636
Career Total (AW)	4	0	2	1	2015

78 6/09 Folk 1m1f149y G-F £2729
Total win prize-money £2730

Going (Turf): Sf: 0-0 GS: 0-0 Gd: 0-1 **GF: 1-4** Fm: 0-0
Distance: 5f/6f: 0-0 7f-8f: 0-1 **9f-13f: 1-8** 14f+: 0-0
Track : LH: 0-4 **RH: 1-3 Tight: 1-8** Gall: 0-0
Aids: Bl: 0-0 Vi: 0-0 Tstrap: 0-1 Ckp: 0-1
Best Rating: **78** 6/09 Folk 1m1f149y gd-fm

Fair; effective over 1m; acts on Polytrack.

Morning Spring

(73)
4-y-o b f Montjoy (USA)-Dino's Girl (Sabrehill (USA))
D Shaw John Branson

Placings:0 **(7863)**
2009: 8^{0}SD,

	Starts	1st	2nd	3rd	Win & Pl
Career Total (Turf)	0	0	0	0	
Career Total (AW)	1	0	0	0	

Going (Turf): **Sf: 0-0 GS: 0-0 Gd: 0-0 GF: 0-0 Fm: 0-0**
Distance: 5f/6f: 0-0 7f-8f: 0-0 9f-13f: 0-1 14f+: 0-0
Track : LH: 0-1 RH: 0-0 Tight: 0-1 Gall: 0-0
Aids: Bl: 0-0 Vi: 0-0 Tstrap: 0-0 Ckp: 0-0

Morning View (USA)

(65) (12)
2-y-o b f North Light (IRE)-Vignette (USA) (Diesis)
J H M Gosden George Strawbridge

Placings:0 **(7451)**
2009: 8^{0}SD,

	Starts	1st	2nd	3rd	Win & Pl
Career Total (Turf)	0	0	0	0	
Career Total (AW)	1	0	0	0	

Going (Turf): **Sf: 0-0 GS: 0-0 Gd: 0-0 GF: 0-0 Fm: 0-0**
Distance: 5f/6f: 0-0 7f-8f: 0-1 9f-13f: 0-0 14f+: 0-0
Track : LH: 0-0 RH: 0-1 Tight: 0-0 Gall: 0-0
Aids: Bl: 0-0 Vi: 0-0 Tstrap: 0-0 Ckp: 0-0
Best Rating: **12** 11/09 Kemp 1m stand

Morocchius (USA)

103(94) (65)70
4-y-o b g Black Minnaloushe (USA)-Shakespearean (USA) (Theatrical)
Miss J A Camacho Lee Bolingbroke Currie & Partners

Placings:540/660002030-003121135 **(6908)**
2009: 7^{0}GS, 7^{0}G, 7^{3}GS, 7^{1}G, 8^{2}G, 8^{1}GS, 8^{1}GF, 8^{3}G, 8^{5}G,

	Starts	1st	2nd	3rd	Win & Pl
Career Total (Turf)	15	3	2	2	12382
Career Total (AW)	6	0	0	1	302

64 8/09 Newc 1m (0-70)H G-F £3885
69 8/09 Muss 1m (0-60)H G-S £2590
62 7/09 Muss 7f30y (0-70)H GD £3238
Total win prize-money £9714

Going (Turf): Sf: 0-0 **GS: 1-6 Gd: 1-7 GF: 1-2** Fm: 0-0
Distance: 5f/6f: 0-1 **7f-8f: 3-17** 9f-13f: 0-3 14f+: 0-0
Track : LH: 1-8 **RH: 2-9 Tight: 2-8** Gall: 1-2
Aids: Bl: 0-0 Vi: 0-0 Tstrap: 3-14 Ckp: 3-14
Best Rating: **70** 9/09 Ffos 1m good

Moderate; stays 1m; acts on most ground; has worn cheek-pieces.

Morristown Music (IRE)

83 51
5-y-o b m Distant Music (USA)-Tongabezi (IRE) (Shernazar)
J S Wainwright J S Wainwright

Placings:226/4401000051/0000306-00 **(2046)**
2009: 7^{0}GS, 5^{0}GS,

	Starts	1st	2nd	3rd	Win & Pl
Career Total (Turf)	23	2	2	1	10101

67 10/07 Ayr 5f (0-70)H SFT £3238
69 6/07 Newc 5f (0-75)H HVY £3886
Total win prize-money £7125

Going (Turf): **Sf: 2-9** GS: 0-4 Gd: 0-4 GF: 0-6 Fm: 0-0
Distance: **5f/6f: 2-22** 7f-8f: 0-1 9f-13f: 0-0 14f+: 0-0
Track : LH: 0-0 RH: 0-0 Tight: 0-0 Gall: 0-0
Aids: Bl: 0-0 Vi: 0-3 Tstrap: 0-1 Ckp: 0-1
Best Rating: **69** 6/07 Newc 5f heavy

Moderate sprinter; seems best in testing ground; may be capable of better.

Morse (IRE)

(101) (65)62
8-y-o b g Shinko Forest (IRE)-Auriga (Belmez (USA))
J A Osborne Morsethehorse Syndicate

Placings:011050336/022312006000102 5/2416650550026/200501/236000/060562544220-5656 **(0984)**
2009: 6^{5}SD, 5^{6}SD, 6^{5}SD, 7^{6}SD,

	Starts	1st	2nd	3rd	Win & Pl
Career Total (Turf)	43	5	6	2	65871
Career Total (AW)	23	1	5	2	12694

79 12/06 Kemp 6f (0-75)H STD £5505
73 9/04 Wwck 7f26y G-S £3753
90 5/04 Ling 6f B(0-105)H SFT £34800
78 6/03 Wind 6f E G-F £3614
78 5/03 Nott 6f15y E G-S £4290
Total win prize-money £51963

Going (Turf): Sf: 1-11 **GS: 2-9** Gd: 1-17 GF: 1-5 Fm: 0-1
Distance: **5f/6f: 4-40** 7f-8f: 2-23 9f-13f: 0-3 14f+: 0-0
Track : LH: 1-18 RH: 1-16 Tight: 0-13 **Gall: 1-4**
Aids: Bl: 0-0 Vi: 0-0 Tstrap: 0-12 Ckp: 0-12
Best Rating: **92** 5/04 Nott 6f15y good

Moderate; effective over 6f-7f; acts well on Polytrack.

Mosa Mine

92(99) (58)54
2-y-o b f Exceed And Excel (AUS)-Baldemosa (FR) (Lead On Time (USA))
D H Brown Norton Common Farm Racing

Placings:445 **(7365)**
2009: 5^{4}S, 5^{4}SD, 5^{5}SD,

	Starts	1st	2nd	3rd	Win & Pl
Career Total (Turf)	1	0	0	0	289
Career Total (AW)	2	0	0	0	289

Going (Turf): **Sf: 0-1 GS: 0-0 Gd: 0-0 GF: 0-0 Fm: 0-0**
Distance: 5f/6f: 0-3 7f-8f: 0-0 9f-13f: 0-0 14f+: 0-0
Track : LH: 0-2 RH: 0-0 Tight: 0-2 Gall: 0-0
Aids: Bl: 0-0 Vi: 0-0 Tstrap: 0-0 Ckp: 0-0
Best Rating: **58** 11/09 Wolv 5f20y stand

Moderate half-sister to Caustic Wit; effective at 5f; handles soft ground and Polytrack.

Moscow Ali (IRE)

62
9-y-o ch g Moscow Society (USA)-Down The Bog (IRE) (Down The Hatch)
J A McShane Lothian Recycling Limited

Placings:0 **(2030)**
2009: 9^{0}G,

	Starts	1st	2nd	3rd	Win & Pl
Career Total (Turf)	1	0	0	0	

Going (Turf): **Sf: 0-0 GS: 0-0 Gd: 0-1 GF: 0-0 Fm: 0-0**

Distance: 5f/6f: 0-0 7f-8f: 0-0 9f-13f: 0-1 14f+: 0-0
Track : LH: 0-0 RH: 0-1 Tight: 0-1 Gall: 0-0
Aids: Bl: 0-0 Vi: 0-0 Tstrap: 0-0 Ckp: 0-0

Moscow Eight (IRE)

89(99) (80)**92**
3-y-o b c Elusive City (USA)-Hurricane Lily (IRE) (Ali-Royal (IRE))
E J O'Neill (Tom Dascombe 17/10) David Barlow

Placings:51024-000522332 **(7820a)**
2009: 6^{0}GF, 6^{0}SD, 5^{0}SD, 5^{5}SD, 6^{2}HY, 6^{2}HY, 6^{3}HY, 6^{3}SD, 7^{2}SD,

	Starts	1st	2nd	3rd	Win & Pl
Career Total (Turf)	6	0	2	1	13544
Career Total (AW)	8	1	2	1	10846

80 10/08 Ling 5f STD £2266
Total win prize-money £2267

Going (Turf): **Sf: 0-3 GS: 0-1 Gd: 0-0 GF: 0-2 Fm: 0-0**
Distance: **5f/6f: 1-10** 7f-8f: 0-4 9f-13f: 0-0 14f+: 0-0
Track : **LH: 1-6** RH: 0-2 **Tight: 1-4** Gall: 0-3
Aids: Bl: 0-0 Vi: 0-0 Tstrap: 0-0 Ckp: 0-0
Best Rating: **92** 11/09 Bord 6f heavy

Useful; effective over 5-6f; acts on fast ground; goes on Polytrack.

Moscow Oznick

97(100) (66)**63**
4-y-o b/br g Auction House (USA)-Cozette (IRE) (Danehill Dancer (IRE))
D Donovan (Tom Dascombe 13/10) W P Flynn

Placings:00/55602-0045203 **(7790)**
2009: 10^{0}GS, 10^{0}G, 9^{4}GF, 10^{5}GF, 11^{2}G, 11^{0}SD, 12^{3}SD,

	Starts	1st	2nd	3rd	Win & Pl
Career Total (Turf)	8	0	1	0	915
Career Total (AW)	6	0	1	1	1008

Going (Turf): **Sf: 0-0 GS: 0-3 Gd: 0-3 GF: 0-2 Fm: 0-0**
Distance: 5f/6f: 0-0 7f-8f: 0-4 9f-13f: 0-10 14f+: 0-0
Track : LH: 0-11 RH: 0-2 Tight: 0-6 Gall: 0-2
Aids: Bl: 0-1 Vi: 0-3 Tstrap: 0-1 Ckp: 0-1
Best Rating: **66** 12/08 Wolv 1m1f103y stand

Modest; stays 1m2f; acts on good to soft and Polytrack; has worn cheekpieces and a visor.

Mosqueras Romance

74(104) (86)**33**
3-y-o gr f Rock Of Gibraltar (IRE)-Mosquera (GER) (Acatenango (GER))
M Botti Mrs R J Jacobs

Placings:3201 **(3981)**
2009: 7^{3}SD, 8^{2}SD, 8^{0}GF, 8^{1}SD,

	Starts	1st	2nd	3rd	Win & Pl
Career Total (Turf)	1	0	0	0	
Career Total (AW)	3	1	1	1	6588

86 7/09 Kemp 1m (0-85)H STD £4727
Total win prize-money £4727

Going (Turf): **Sf: 0-0 GS: 0-0 Gd: 0-0 GF: 0-1 Fm: 0-0**
Distance: 5f/6f: 0-0 **7f-8f: 1-3** 9f-13f: 0-1 14f+: 0-0
Track : LH: 0-1 **RH: 1-2** Tight: 0-1 Gall: 0-0
Aids: Bl: 0-0 Vi: 0-0 Tstrap: 0-0 Ckp: 0-0
Best Rating: **86** 7/09 Kemp 1m stand

Fair; stays 1m; acts on Polytrack; should improve.

Mosqueta

78(91) (56)**16**
2-y-o b f Doyen (IRE)-Arantxa (Sharpo)
P D Evans Diamond Racing Ltd

Placings:005 **(7213)**
2009: 5^{0}SF, 5^{0}G, 5^{5}SD,

	Starts	1st	2nd	3rd	Win & Pl
Career Total (Turf)	1	0	0	0	
Career Total (AW)	2	0	0	0	0

Going (Turf): **Sf: 0-0 GS: 0-0 Gd: 0-1 GF: 0-0 Fm: 0-0**
Distance: 5f/6f: 0-3 7f-8f: 0-0 9f-13f: 0-0 14f+: 0-0
Track : LH: 0-2 RH: 0-0 Tight: 0-2 Gall: 0-1
Aids: Bl: 0-0 Vi: 0-0 Tstrap: 0-0 Ckp: 0-0
Best Rating: **56** 11/09 Wolv 5f20y stand

Mossmann Gorge

101(102) (46)**56**
7-y-o b g Lujain (USA)-North Pine (Import)
A Middleton Mrs C Middleton

Placings:065244/0002100600063/0560114505223300024 0/300/010540 **(5246)**
2009: 12^{0}SD, 11^{1}G, 10^{0}G, 12^{5}GF, 12^{4}HY, 13^{0}F,

	Starts	1st	2nd	3rd	Win & Pl
Career Total (Turf)	24	2	4	2	11932
Career Total (AW)	24	2	1	2	6807

56 5/09 Ling 1m3f106y (0-60)H GD £2047
63 3/06 Sthl 1m3f STD £2388
53 2/06 Sthl 1m4f SF £2388
73 5/05 Chep 1m14y (0-70)H GD £3877
Total win prize-money £10702

Going (Turf): Sf: 0-3 GS: 0-4 **Gd: 2-7** GF: 0-8 Fm: 0-2
Distance: 5f/6f: 0-5 7f-8f: 0-6 **9f-13f: 4-35** 14f+: 0-2
Track : **LH: 3-39** RH: 0-3 **Tight: 1-15** Gall: 0-2
Aids: Bl: 0-9 **Vi: 2-15** Tstrap: 1-8 Ckp: 1-8
Best Rating: **73** 6/05 Sand 1m14y gd-fm

Moderate; stays a 1m4; suited by good or soft ground and Fibresand; has worn cheekpieces.

Most Definitely (IRE)

(105) (71)**63**
9-y-o b g Definite Article-Unbidden Melody (USA) (Chieftain)
R M Stronge Tim Whiting

Placings:5500/400322222/206232212/13010105043/6056 00062030620/03556054/33235250-0 **(0497)**
2009: 12^{0}SD,

	Starts	1st	2nd	3rd	Win & Pl
Career Total (Turf)	51	4	11	5	59578
Career Total (AW)	14	0	3	4	5793

96 7/05 Ripn 1m4f10y (0-95)H G-F £11113
91 6/05 Donc 1m6f132y (0-85)H G-F £6831
81 4/05 Muss 1m6f (0-85)H GD £6747
74 10/04 Rdcr 1m6f19y (0-70)H G-S £7787
Total win prize-money £32479

Going (Turf): Sf: 0-3 GS: 1-11Gd: 1-13 **GF: 2-20** Fm: 0-4
Distance: 5f/6f: 0-1 7f-8f: 0-3 9f-13f: 1-24 **14f+: 3-37**
Track : LH: 2-34 RH: 2-28 **Tight: 3-28** Gall: 1-15
Aids: Bl: 0-8 Vi: 0-0 Tstrap: 0-4 Ckp: 0-4
Best Rating: **96** 7/05 Ripn 1m4f10y gd-fm

Modest; stays 2m, but effective at shorter; handles any ground and Polytrack; does not always find a lot off the bridle.

Mostofitleft (IRE)

73 **12**
2-y-o ch f Pastoral Pursuits-Gold Majesty (Josr Algarhoud (IRE))
A Berry Alan Berry

Placings:0660 **(2996)**
2009: 5^{0}GF, 5^{6}GF, 5^{6}GF, 6^{0}GF,

	Starts	1st	2nd	3rd	Win & Pl
Career Total (Turf)	4	0	0	0	0

Going (Turf): **Sf: 0-0 GS: 0-0 Gd: 0-0 GF: 0-4 Fm: 0-0**
Distance: 5f/6f: 0-4 7f-8f: 0-0 9f-13f: 0-0 14f+: 0-0
Track : LH: 0-0 RH: 0-0 Tight: 0-0 Gall: 0-0
Aids: Bl: 0-0 Vi: 0-0 Tstrap: 0-0 Ckp: 0-0
Best Rating: **12** 4/09 Catt 5f gd-fm

Motafarred (IRE)

105 (72)**86**
7-y-o ch g Machiavellian (USA)-Thurayya (Nashwan (USA))
Micky Hammond R D Bickenson

Placings:6160/6060060/00251241260/16635240-2020030 **(6648)**
2009: 7^{2}GF, 8^{0}G, 8^{2}G, 8^{0}GF, 8^{0}GF, 10^{3}GF, 10^{0}G,

	Starts	1st	2nd	3rd	Win & Pl
Career Total (Turf)	35	3	5	2	35399
Career Total (AW)	2	1	1	0	3656

82 5/08 Pont 1m4y (0-70)H G-F £3238
76 8/07 Leic 1m60y (0-75)H FRM £4533
69 7/07 Kemp 7f (0-70)H STD £2817
86 7/05 Gway 1m4f G-F £11542
Total win prize-money £22132

Going (Turf): Sf: 0-3 GS: 0-2 Gd: 0-10 **GF: 2-18** Fm: 1-2
Distance: 5f/6f: 0-0 7f-8f: 1-12 **9f-13f: 3-22** 14f+: 0-3
Track : LH: 1-12 **RH: 3-20** Tight: 0-5 Gall: 0-7
Aids: Bl: 0-0 Vi: 0-1 Tstrap: 0-0 Ckp: 0-0
Best Rating: **86** 8/09 Pont 1m4y good

Fair; has won at up to 1m4f, but is effective at 1m; acts on fast ground; suited by Polytrack; has worn a visor.

Motarjm (USA)

(107) (76)**84**
5-y-o br g Elusive Quality (USA)-Agama (USA) (Nureyev (USA))
J Pearce P D Band

Placings:00065452/251113545-000 **(7539)**
2009: 10^{0}SD, 10^{0}SD, 12^{0}SD,

	Starts	1st	2nd	3rd	Win & Pl
Career Total (Turf)	7	0	0	0	209
Career Total (AW)	13	3	2	1	12849

88 3/08 Wolv 1m5f194y (0-85)H STD £4533
87 2/08 Wolv 1m4f50y (0-75)H STD £2730
72 2/08 Wolv 1m4f50y STD £2457
Total win prize-money £9721

Going (Turf): **Sf: 0-0 GS: 0-1 Gd: 0-1 GF: 0-5 Fm: 0-0**
Distance: 5f/6f: 0-0 7f-8f: 0-3 **9f-13f: 2-15** 14f+: 1-2
Track : **LH: 3-12** RH: 0-7 **Tight: 3-9** Gall: 0-1
Aids: Bl: 0-0 Vi: 0-0 Tstrap: 0-0 Ckp: 0-0
Best Rating: **89** 4/08 Ling 1m4f stand

Useful; completed a hat-trick on sand early in 2008; stays 1m5f and acts well on Polytrack; wears tongue tie.

Motivated Choice

(103) (69)**67**

4-y-o b f Compton Place-Makhsusah (IRE) (Darshaan)

Miss Amy Weaver D Redvers

Placings:4516-053356 **(0737)**

2009: 7^{0}SD, 7^{5}SD, 8^{3}SD, 7^{3}SD, 7^{5}SD, 9^{6}SD,

	Starts	1st	2nd	3rd	Win & Pl
Career Total (Turf)	2	1	0	0	2730
Career Total (AW)	8	0	0	2	976

67 10/08 Wind 6f G-S £2729

Total win prize-money £2730

Going (Turf): Sf: 0-0 **GS: 1-2** Gd: 0-0 GF: 0-0 Fm: 0-0
Distance: **5f/6f: 1-4** 7f-8f: 0-5 9f-13f: 0-1 14f+: 0-0
Track : LH: 0-6 RH: 0-2 Tight: 0-4 **Gall: 1-2**
Aids: Bl: 0-0 Vi: 0-0 Tstrap: 0-1 Ckp: 0-1
Best Rating: **69** 2/09 Kemp 1m stand

Modest; stays 6f; acts on easy ground and Polytrack.

Motivational (IRE)

87(88) (69)**68**

2-y-o ch c Motivator-Park Romance (IRE) (Dr Fong (USA))

D R Lanigan Saif Ali & Saeed H Altayer

Placings:303300 **(6071)**

2009: 5^{3}GF, 6^{0}G, 7^{3}SD, 7^{3}SD, 5^{0}GF, 7^{0}SD,

	Starts	1st	2nd	3rd	Win & Pl
Career Total (Turf)	3	0	0	1	578
Career Total (AW)	3	0	0	2	981

Going (Turf): **Sf: 0-0 GS: 0-0 Gd: 0-1 GF: 0-2 Fm: 0-0**
Distance: 5f/6f: 0-2 7f-8f: 0-4 9f-13f: 0-0 14f+: 0-0
Track : LH: 0-4 RH: 0-0 Tight: 0-3 Gall: 0-0
Aids: Bl: 0-0 Vi: 0-0 Tstrap: 0-0 Ckp: 0-0
Best Rating: **69** 6/09 Wolv 7f32y stand

Modest; stays 7f; acts on Polytrack.

Motor Home

99(81) (37)**77**

3-y-o b g Tobougg (IRE)-Desert Dawn (Belfort (FR))

A M Balding David Brownlow

Placings:03130000-000260000 **(6333)**

2009: 8^{0}G, 8^{0}GF, 7^{0}GF, 6^{2}F, 7^{6}GF, 7^{0}SD, 6^{0}F, 7^{0}SD, 8^{0}F,

	Starts	1st	2nd	3rd	Win & Pl
Career Total (Turf)	15	1	1	2	6443
Career Total (AW)	2	0	0	0	

77 6/08 Thsk 7f FRM £3885

Total win prize-money £3886

Going (Turf): Sf: 0-2 GS: 0-1 Gd: 0-4 GF: 0-4 **Fm: 1-4**
Distance: 5f/6f: 0-1 **7f-8f: 1-13** 9f-13f: 0-3 14f+: 0-0
Track : **LH: 1-7** RH: 0-3 **Tight: 1-4** Gall: 0-0
Aids: Bl: 0-0 Vi: 0-2 Tstrap: 0-2 Ckp: 0-2
Best Rating: **77** 6/08 Thsk 7f firm

Moderate; stays 7f and acts on fast ground.

Motrice

83(90) (63)**40**

2-y-o gr f Motivator-Entente Cordiale (USA) (Affirmed (USA))

Sir Mark Prescott Miss K Rausing

Placings:0000 **(6921)**

2009: 7^{0}SD, 7^{0}SD, 7^{0}SD, 8^{0}GF,

	Starts	1st	2nd	3rd	Win & Pl
Career Total (Turf)	1	0	0	0	
Career Total (AW)	3	0	0	0	

Going (Turf): **Sf: 0-0 GS: 0-0 Gd: 0-0 GF: 0-1 Fm: 0-0**
Distance: 5f/6f: 0-0 7f-8f: 0-3 9f-13f: 0-1 14f+: 0-0
Track : LH: 0-2 RH: 0-1 Tight: 0-2 Gall: 0-0
Aids: Bl: 0-0 Vi: 0-0 Tstrap: 0-0 Ckp: 0-0
Best Rating: **63** 10/09 Wolv 7f32y stand

Motty's Gift

76(80) (48)**42**

2-y-o ch g Lucky Story (USA)-Oatcake (Selkirk (USA))

W R Swinburn Mrs A Motson

Placings:6000 **(7513)**

2009: 5^{6}GF, 6^{0}GF, 6^{0}SD, 7^{0}SD,

	Starts	1st	2nd	3rd	Win & Pl
Career Total (Turf)	2	0	0	0	0
Career Total (AW)	2	0	0	0	

Going (Turf): **Sf: 0-0 GS: 0-0 Gd: 0-0 GF: 0-2 Fm: 0-0**
Distance: 5f/6f: 0-3 7f-8f: 0-1 9f-13f: 0-0 14f+: 0-0
Track : LH: 0-0 RH: 0-2 Tight: 0-0 Gall: 0-1
Aids: Bl: 0-0 Vi: 0-0 Tstrap: 0-0 Ckp: 0-0
Best Rating: **48** 8/09 Kemp 6f stand

Moderate; stays 6f; acts on Polytrack.

Mount Athos (IRE)

85 **59**

2-y-o b c Montjeu (IRE)-Ionian Sea (Slip Anchor)

J W Hills Corinthian

Placings:00 **(7029)**

2009: 8^{0}G, 8^{0}S,

	Starts	1st	2nd	3rd	Win & Pl
Career Total (Turf)	2	0	0	0	

Going (Turf): **Sf: 0-1 GS: 0-0 Gd: 0-1 GF: 0-0 Fm: 0-0**
Distance: 5f/6f: 0-0 7f-8f: 0-2 9f-13f: 0-0 14f+: 0-0
Track : LH: 0-0 RH: 0-0 Tight: 0-0 Gall: 0-0
Aids: Bl: 0-0 Vi: 0-0 Tstrap: 0-0 Ckp: 0-0
Best Rating: **59** 10/09 Newb 1m good

Mount Ella

85(83) (34)**55**

3-y-o b f Royal Applause-Hiraeth (Petong)

J R Boyle (J A Osborne 8/6) Cavendish Star Racing

Placings:060-400060 **(5188)**

2009: 7^{4}GF, 7^{0}SD, 6^{0}G, 7^{0}GS, 6^{6}GF, 7^{0}GF,

	Starts	1st	2nd	3rd	Win & Pl
Career Total (Turf)	7	0	0	0	0
Career Total (AW)	2	0	0	0	

Going (Turf): **Sf: 0-0 GS: 0-1 Gd: 0-1 GF: 0-5 Fm: 0-0**
Distance: 5f/6f: 0-5 7f-8f: 0-4 9f-13f: 0-0 14f+: 0-0
Track : LH: 0-2 RH: 0-1 Tight: 0-2 Gall: 0-3
Aids: Bl: 0-1 Vi: 0-0 Tstrap: 0-0 Ckp: 0-0
Best Rating: **55** 4/09 Folk 7f gd-fm

Mount Hadley (USA)

105(100) (85)**93**

5-y-o b g Elusive Quality (USA)-Fly To The Moon (USA) (Blushing Groom (FR))

G A Butler Stef Stefanou

Placings:01/313/60006-261001504 **(7271)**

2009: 8^{2}GF, 8^{6}SD, 7^{1}G, 8^{0}G, 8^{0}GF, 7^{1}GF, 10^{5}GF, 8^{0}GF, 8^{4}SD,

	Starts	1st	2nd	3rd	Win & Pl
Career Total (Turf)	13	4	1	1	30600
Career Total (AW)	6	0	0	1	1988

93 8/09 Bevl 7f100y (0-80)H G-F £4857
89 7/09 Carl 7f200y (0-80)H GD £6476
101 3/07 Ndas 7f110y GD £9183
92 10/06 Leic 7f9y G-S £4533

Total win prize-money £25051

Going (Turf): Sf: 0-1 GS: 1-1 **Gd: 2-4** GF: 1-7 Fm: 0-0
Distance: 5f/6f: 0-0 **7f-8f: 4-15** 9f-13f: 0-4 14f+: 0-0
Track : LH: 1-8 **RH: 2-6** Tight: 0-4 **Gall: 1-5**
Aids: Bl: 0-3 Vi: 0-3 Tstrap: 0-0 Ckp: 0-0
Best Rating: **101** 3/07 Ndas 7f110y good

Useful; effective at around 7f-1m; acts on good ground; has worn blinkers, tongue tie and visor.

Mount Hermon (IRE)

102(102) (85)**79**

5-y-o b g Golan (IRE)-Machudi (Bluebird (USA))

H Morrison Wood Street Syndicate III

Placings:320/1610/040610240-062402 **(6488)**

2009: 8^{0}G, 8^{6}GF, 10^{2}GF, 10^{4}GS, 10^{0}GF, 10^{2}GF,

	Starts	1st	2nd	3rd	Win & Pl
Career Total (Turf)	14	0	3	1	3864
Career Total (AW)	8	3	1	0	10505

83 7/08 GrLe 1m (0-70)H STD £3238
81 9/07 Ling 1m (0-75)H STD £3071
64 3/07 Sthl 7f STD £2184

Total win prize-money £8493

Going (Turf): **Sf: 0-1 GS: 0-4 Gd: 0-3 GF: 0-6 Fm: 0-0**
Distance: 5f/6f: 0-1 **7f-8f: 3-12** 9f-13f: 0-9 14f+: 0-0
Track : **LH: 3-11** RH: 0-6 Tight: 1-5 Gall: 1-6
Aids: **Bl: 1-10** Vi: 0-0 Tstrap: 0-0 Ckp: 0-0
Best Rating: **85** 8/08 GrLe 1m stand

Fair; stays 1m2f; acts on good ground and on sand; has worn blinkers.

Mount Juliet (IRE)

95(96) (65)**62**

2-y-o b f Danehill Dancer (IRE)-Stylist (IRE) (Sadler's Wells (USA))

S A Callaghan Joseph Barton

Placings:002 **(6347)**

2009: 6^{0}SD, 6^{0}S, 5^{2}SD,

	Starts	1st	2nd	3rd	Win & Pl
Career Total (Turf)	1	0	0	0	
Career Total (AW)	2	0	1	0	1156

Going (Turf): **Sf: 0-1 GS: 0-0 Gd: 0-0 GF: 0-0 Fm: 0-0**
Distance: 5f/6f: 0-2 7f-8f: 0-1 9f-13f: 0-0 14f+: 0-0
Track : LH: 0-1 RH: 0-1 Tight: 0-1 Gall: 0-0
Aids: Bl: 0-0 Vi: 0-0 Tstrap: 0-0 Ckp: 0-0
Best Rating: **65** 9/09 Wolv 5f20y stand

Fair; effective at 5f; acts on Polytrack.

Mount Usher

(98) (61)**77**

7-y-o br g Polar Falcon (USA)-Division Bell (Warning)

Miss Diana Weeden (M J Gingell 31/3) M Hole

Placings:35500/156412546/0234/**000-05506** (7754)

2009: 7^{0}SS, 8^{5}SD, 8^{5}SD, 10^{0}SD, 8^{6}SD,

	Starts	1st	2nd	3rd	Win & Pl
Career Total (Turf)	18	2	2	2	12717
Career Total (AW)	8	0	0	0	0

71	6/06	Newc	1m2f32y	(0-75)H	G-F	£3562
64	4/06	Bevl	7f100y	(0-60)H	G-F	£3335

Total win prize-money £6898

Going (Turf): Sf: 0-0 GS: 0-3 Gd: 0-6 **GF: 2-8** Fm: 0-1
Distance: 5f/6f: 0-0 7f-8f: 1-8 9f-13f: 1-18 14f+: 0-0
Track : LH: 1-15 RH: 1-10 Tight: 0-11 **Gall: 1-2**
Aids: Bl: 0-3 Vi: 0-1 Tstrap: 0-0 Ckp: 0-0
Best Rating: **80** 7/06 Bevl 1m1f207y firm

Fair handicapper; stays 1m2f; acts on fast ground.

Mountain Cat (IRE)

105(108) (91)**91**

5-y-o b g Red Ransom (USA)-Timewee (USA) (Romanov (IRE))

G A Swinbank S Rudolf

Placings:00/**51011100**/0000-**6211152130** (6485)

2009: 7^{6}G, 6^{2}GF, 8^{1}GF, 6^{1}G, 8^{1}GF, 8^{5}GF, 9^{2}S, 8^{1}SD, 8^{3}GF, 8^{0}GF,

	Starts	1st	2nd	3rd	Win & Pl
Career Total (Turf)	15	3	2	1	14222
Career Total (AW)	9	5	0	0	15636

91	9/09	Wolv	1m141y	(0-85)H	STD	£5046
79	6/09	Muss	1m	(0-70)H	G-F	£3252
76	6/09	Brig	6f209y	(0-65)H	GD	£2590
69	6/09	Haml	1m65y	(0-70)H	G-F	£3561
80	9/07	Wolv	1m141y	(0-75)H	STD	£2914
78	8/07	Wolv	1m141y	(0-70)H	STD	£3238
76	7/07	Kemp	1m	(0-65)H	STD	£2047
65	6/07	Wolv	1m141y	(0-65)H	STD	£2388

Total win prize-money £25042

Going (Turf): Sf: 0-4 GS: 0-1 Gd: 1-4 **GF: 2-6** Fm: 0-0
Distance: 5f/6f: 0-2 7f-8f: 3-13 **9f-13f: 5-9** 14f+: 0-0
Track : **LH: 5-9** RH: 3-7 **Tight: 6-10** Gall: 0-1
Aids: Bl: 0-0 Vi: 0-0 Tstrap: 0-0 Ckp: 0-0
Best Rating: **91** 9/09 NmkR 1m gd-fm

Useful; stays an extended 1m; acts on fast ground and on Polytrack; can make all.

Mountain Fairy

(81) (8)**71**

6-y-o gr m Daylami (IRE)-Mountain Spirit (IRE) (Royal Academy (USA))

M W Easterby M W Easterby

Placings:0640533/**0P/6** (0743)

2009: 14^{0}SD,

	Starts	1st	2nd	3rd	Win & Pl
Career Total (Turf)	7	0	0	2	7103
Career Total (AW)	3	0	0	0	0

Going (Turf): **Sf: 0-3 GS: 0-0 Gd: 0-2 GF: 0-0 Fm: 0-0**
Distance: 5f/6f: 0-0 7f-8f: 0-0 9f-13f: 0-7 14f+: 0-3
Track : LH: 0-3 RH: 0-2 Tight: 0-1 Gall: 0-0
Aids: Bl: 0-4 Vi: 0-1 Tstrap: 0-0 Ckp: 0-0
Best Rating: **71** 6/06 Chan 1m4f110y good

Mountain Forest (GER)

84(96) (49)**52**

3-y-o b g Tiger Hill (IRE)-Moricana (GER) (Konigsstuhl (GER))

H Morrison H Morrison

Placings:000-**06644563** (7740)

2009: 11^{0}SD, 14^{6}GF, 9^{6}F, 8^{4}SD, 8^{4}SD, 8^{5}SD, 10^{6}SD, 12^{3}SD,

	Starts	1st	2nd	3rd	Win & Pl
Career Total (Turf)	4	0	0	0	0
Career Total (AW)	7	0	0	1	302

Going (Turf): **Sf: 0-0 GS: 0-1 Gd: 0-1 GF: 0-1 Fm: 0-1**
Distance: 5f/6f: 0-0 7f-8f: 0-5 9f-13f: 0-5 14f+: 0-1
Track : LH: 0-7 RH: 0-3 Tight: 0-3 Gall: 0-1
Aids: Bl: 0-0 Vi: 0-0 Tstrap: 0-0 Ckp: 0-0
Best Rating: **52** 10/08 Sals 1m good

Mountain Pass (USA)

96(101) (66)**65**

7-y-o b g Stravinsky (USA)-Ribbony (USA) (Dayjur (USA))

B J Llewellyn B J Llewellyn

Placings:03/34533304/**10000465**44401130**425305**/14650 0515/**61541406305-04302**060260 (3501)

2009: 7^{0}SD, 8^{4}SD, 8^{3}SD, 8^{0}SD, 7^{2}SD, 8^{0}SD, 7^{6}GF, 8^{0}GF, 6^{2}G, 7^{6}G, 8^{0}GF,

	Starts	1st	2nd	3rd	Win & Pl
Career Total (Turf)	31	3	1	6	13627
Career Total (AW)	32	4	2	3	11880

59	6/08	Brig	7f214y		FRM	£2266
66	3/08	Wolv	1m141y		STD	£1483
63	12/07	Wolv	7f32y		STD	£2047
66	1/07	Ling	7f	(0-60)H	STD	£2388
63	9/06	Yarm	7f3y	(0-60)H	G-F	£3238
58	8/06	Brig	6f209y		G-F	£2388
70	2/06	Ling	5f		STD	£3886

Total win prize-money £17701

Going (Turf): Sf: 0-1 GS: 0-1 Gd: 0-10 **GF: 2-14** Fm: 1-4
Distance: 5f/6f: 1-14 **7f-8f: 5-40** 9f-13f: 1-9 14f+: 0-0
Track : **LH: 6-41** RH: 0-8 **Tight: 4-31** Gall: 0-2
Aids: Bl: 0-5 Vi: 1-7 Tstrap: 6-45 Ckp: 6-45
Best Rating: **72** 8/05 Bell 1m gd-fm

Moderate handicapper; suited by 7f; acts on good to firm and Polytrack; has worn cheekpieces.

Mountain Pride (IRE)

107 **97**

4-y-o b g High Chaparral (IRE)-Lioness (Lion Cavern (USA))

J L Dunlop Ian Cameron

Placings:351/5016065-5014326 (6665)

2009: 8^{5}GF, 7^{0}GF, 10^{1}G, 10^{4}G, 10^{3}G, 9^{2}S, 10^{6}GS,

	Starts	1st	2nd	3rd	Win & Pl
Career Total (Turf)	17	3	1	2	22561

91	5/09	Sand	1m2f7y	(0-85)H	GD	£5180
90	6/08	Sand	1m14y	(0-85)H	GD	£6476
87	10/07	Leic	1m60y		G-S	£4857

Total win prize-money £16515

Going (Turf): Sf: 0-3 GS: 1-5 **Gd: 2-6** GF: 0-3 Fm: 0-0
Distance: 5f/6f: 0-0 7f-8f: 0-6 **9f-13f: 3-11** 14f+: 0-0
Track : LH: 0-1 **RH: 3-12** Tight: 0-4 Gall: 0-3
Aids: Bl: 0-1 Vi: 0-0 Tstrap: 0-0 Ckp: 0-0
Best Rating: **97** 8/09 Gdwd 1m1f soft

Useful; stays 1m2f; acts on good and softer ground; has worn blinkers.

Mountain Quest

91 **68**

2-y-o b c Hernando (FR)-Miss Katmandu (IRE) (Rainbow Quest (USA))

M L W Bell J L C Pearce

Placings:50 (7121)

2009: 8^{5}GF, 8^{0}GF,

	Starts	1st	2nd	3rd	Win & Pl
Career Total (Turf)	2	0	0	0	0

Going (Turf): **Sf: 0-0 GS: 0-0 Gd: 0-0 GF: 0-2 Fm: 0-0**
Distance: 5f/6f: 0-0 7f-8f: 0-1 9f-13f: 0-1 14f+: 0-0
Track : LH: 0-1 RH: 0-0 Tight: 0-0 Gall: 0-0
Aids: Bl: 0-0 Vi: 0-0 Tstrap: 0-0 Ckp: 0-0
Best Rating: **68** 10/09 Rdcr 1m gd-fm

Mountrath

95(72) (31)**76**

2-y-o b g Dubai Destination (USA)-Eurolink Sundance (Night Shift (USA))

B R Johnson David Phelan

Placings:055322 (6735)

2009: 7^{0}SD, 7^{5}GF, 6^{5}G, 7^{3}GS, 8^{2}GF, 8^{2}GS,

	Starts	1st	2nd	3rd	Win & Pl
Career Total (Turf)	5	0	2	1	2439
Career Total (AW)	1	0	0	0	

Going (Turf): **Sf: 0-0 GS: 0-2 Gd: 0-1 GF: 0-2 Fm: 0-0**
Distance: 5f/6f: 0-0 7f-8f: 0-5 9f-13f: 0-1 14f+: 0-0
Track : LH: 0-2 RH: 0-2 Tight: 0-3 Gall: 0-0
Aids: Bl: 0-0 Vi: 0-0 Tstrap: 0-1 Ckp: 0-1
Best Rating: **76** 10/09 Wind 1m67y gd-sft

Moderate; effective at 6f-7f; acts on most ground; has worn a tongue tie.

Mourayan (IRE)

113 **118**

3-y-o b c Alhaarth (IRE)-Mouramara (IRE) (Kahyasi)

John M Oxx H H Aga Khan

Placings:0121-32325 (5861)

2009: 10^{3}GY, 10^{2}G, 12^{3}GY, 12^{2}G, 14^{5}GF,

	Starts	1st	2nd	3rd	Win & Pl
Career Total (Turf)	9	2	3	2	238794

109	11/08	Leop	1m1f	SFT	£23933
87	7/08	Leop	1m	GD	£9573

Total win prize-money £33508

Going (Turf): **Sf: 1-1** GS: 0-0 **Gd: 1-4** GF: 0-1 Fm: 0-0
Distance: 5f/6f: 0-0 7f-8f: 1-3 9f-13f: 1-5 14f+: 0-1
Track : **LH: 2-6** RH: 0-3 Tight: 0-0 Gall: 0-2
Aids: Bl: 0-3 Vi: 0-0 Tstrap: 0-0 Ckp: 0-0
Best Rating: **118** 6/09 Curr 1m4f gd-yld

Group class; third in the Irish Derby; stays 1m4f; acts on good and easy ground.

Mourilyan (IRE)

118(109) (107)**119**

5-y-o b h Desert Prince (IRE)-Mouramara (IRE) (Kahyasi)
H J Brown (G L Moore 29/8) Ramzan Kadyrov

Placings:3/311/11200360-3202413 **(7215a)**
2009: 13^{3}GF, 16^{2}GF, 12^{0}GF, 16^{2}G, 13^{4}GF, 14^{1}G, 16^{3}GS,

	Starts	1st	2nd	3rd	Win & Pl
Career Total (Turf)	**18**	**5**	**3**	**4**	**403960**
Career Total (AW)	**1**	**0**	**0**	**1**	**7001**

110	8/09	Gdwd	1m6f		GD	£22708
111	2/08	Ndas	1m4f	(95-110)H	GD	£36180
107	1/08	Ndas	1m4f	(95-110)H	GD	£36180
93	11/07	Leop	1m1f		G-F	£5602
89	10/07	Curr	1m2f		G-Y	£7470

Total win prize-money £108143

Going (Turf): Sf: 0-0 GS: 0-1 **Gd: 3-9** GF: 1-5 Fm: 0-1
Distance: 5f/6f: 0-0 7f-8f: 0-1 **9f-13f: 4-12** 14f+: 1-6
Track : **LH: 3-12** RH: 2-5 Tight: 1-2 **Gall: 2-6**
Aids: Bl: 0-0 Vi: 0-1 Tstrap: 0-1 Ckp: 0-1
Best Rating: **119** 11/09 Flem 2m gd-sft

Listed class; Listed winner in 2009 and placed in Group 2 company; winner in Dubai in 2008; effective at 1m4f-2m; acts on fast and easy ground; has worn cheekpieces and a visor.

Moves Goodenough

98(95) (70)**87**

6-y-o ch g Woodborough (USA)-Rekindled Flame (IRE) (Kings Lake (USA))
A G Foster (Andrew Turnell 28/5) D Goodenough Removals & Transport

Placings:340330/300124000/203464111-300000 **(6014)**
2009: 10^{3}S, 10^{0}G, 10^{0}GS, 9^{0}G, 8^{0}GF, 8^{0}G,

	Starts	1st	2nd	3rd	Win & Pl
Career Total (Turf)	**23**	**4**	**2**	**4**	**15862**
Career Total (AW)	**7**	**0**	**0**	**2**	**1027**

84	10/08	Bath	1m5y	(0-75)H	G-S	£2719
74	10/08	Nott	1m75y	(0-70)H	SFT	£3238
73	10/08	Sals	1m	(0-65)H	GD	£2810
70	6/07	Bath	1m5y	(0-70)H	GD	£2914

Total win prize-money £11684

Going (Turf): Sf: 1-3 GS: 1-3 **Gd: 2-10** GF: 0-6 Fm: 0-1
Distance: 5f/6f: 0-0 7f-8f: 1-14 **9f-13f: 3-16** 14f+: 0-0
Track : **LH: 3-20** RH: 0-4 **Tight: 2-15** Gall: 0-2
Aids: **Bl: 4-13** Vi: 0-0 Tstrap: 0-1 Ckp: 0-1
Best Rating: **87** 4/09 Newb 1m2f6y soft

Modest; stays 1m; acts on good and soft ground; handles Polytrack; has worn blinkers.

Moyenne Corniche

106 **107**

4-y-o ch g Selkirk (USA)-Miss Corniche (Hernando (FR))
M L W Bell J L C Pearce

Placings:4/1250420-630420 **(7208a)**
2009: 8^{6}GS, 8^{3}GS, 9^{0}G, 8^{4}S, 10^{2}VS, 8^{0}VS,

	Starts	1st	2nd	3rd	Win & Pl
Career Total (Turf)	**14**	**1**	**3**	**1**	**31808**

94	4/08	Newb	1m		G-S	£5828

Total win prize-money £5828

Going (Turf): Sf: 0-2 **GS: 1-3** Gd: 0-3 GF: 0-4 Fm: 0-0
Distance: 5f/6f: 0-0 **7f-8f: 1-9** 9f-13f: 0-5 14f+: 0-0
Track : LH: 0-5 RH: 0-4 Tight: 0-1 Gall: 0-1
Aids: Bl: 0-1 Vi: 0-1 Tstrap: 0-0 Ckp: 0-0
Best Rating: **107** 9/08 Donc 1m soft

Smart; effective over 1m; acts on most ground; has worn blinkers and a visor.

Moynahan (USA)

107(107) (103)**103**

4-y-o ch g Johannesburg (USA)-Lakab (USA) (Manila (USA))
P F I Cole D S Lee

Placings:41/60030**234**-022400**5**0 **(7375)**
2009: 8^{0}G, 7^{2}G, 8^{2}GS, 8^{4}G, 9^{0}GF, 8^{0}SD, 8^{5}G, 8^{0}SD,

	Starts	1st	2nd	3rd	Win & Pl
Career Total (Turf)	**13**	**1**	**2**	**1**	**34229**
Career Total (AW)	**5**	**0**	**1**	**1**	**5879**

94	8/07	York	6f	GD	£16192

Total win prize-money £16193

Going (Turf): Sf: 0-0 GS: 0-2 **Gd: 1-8** GF: 0-3 Fm: 0-0
Distance: **5f/6f: 1-2** 7f-8f: 0-10 9f-13f: 0-6 14f+: 0-0
Track : LH: 0-5 RH: 0-6 Tight: 0-3 Gall: 0-4
Aids: Bl: 0-1 Vi: 0-0 Tstrap: 0-0 Ckp: 0-0
Best Rating: **103** 11/08 Kemp 1m2f stand

Very useful; probably stays 1m; acts on good ground.

Moyoko (IRE)

99(101) (61)**57**

6-y-o b m Mozart (IRE)-Kayoko (IRE) (Shalford (IRE))
M Salaman Mrs N L Young

Placings:00000/6024231**6**/40605445**1000**/4025260-424045300 **(1959)**
2009: 9^{4}SD, 8^{2}SD, 9^{4}SD, 10^{0}SD, 8^{4}SD, 9^{5}SD, 9^{3}GF, 11^{0}GF, 7^{0}F,

	Starts	1st	2nd	3rd	Win & Pl
Career Total (Turf)	**19**	**0**	**3**	**1**	**3953**
Career Total (AW)	**22**	**2**	**2**	**1**	**5002**

56	9/07	Wolv	1m1f103y	(0-50)H	STD	£2047
58	12/06	Kemp	1m	(0-52)H	STD	£1706

Total win prize-money £3754

Going (Turf): **Sf: 0-1 GS: 0-3 Gd: 0-5 GF: 0-8 Fm: 0-2**
Distance: 5f/6f: 0-2 7f-8f: 1-18 9f-13f: 1-21 14f+: 0-0
Track : LH: 1-21 RH: 1-10 **Tight: 1-17** Gall: 0-0
Aids: Bl: 0-3 Vi: 0-0 Tstrap: 0-2 Ckp: 0-2
Best Rating: **62** 1/07 Kemp 1m stand

Moderate; stays 1m1f; acts on most ground and on Polytrack; has worn blinkers.

Mozayada (USA)

104(107) (85)**71**

5-y-o ch m Street Cry (IRE)-Fatina (Nashwan (USA))
M Brittain Mel Brittain

Placings:054/**0**000504002**1111**-41345040601000**05423** **(7783)**
2009: 8^{4}SS, 8^{1}SD, 7^{3}SD, 8^{4}SD, 8^{5}SD, 8^{0}GF, 8^{4}SD, 8^{0}GF, 7^{6}G, 8^{0}S, 8^{1}GS, 8^{0}S, 7^{0}GF, 8^{0}SD, 7^{0}G, 8^{5}SD, 6^{4}SD, 8^{2}SD, 8^{3}SD,

	Starts	1st	2nd	3rd	Win & Pl
Career Total (Turf)	**19**	**1**	**0**	**0**	**4851**
Career Total (AW)	**17**	**5**	**2**	**2**	**19570**

71	8/09	Thsk	1m	(0-75)H	G-S	£4274
85	1/09	Sthl	1m	(0-80)H	STD	£5118
79	12/08	Sthl	1m	(0-75)H	STD	£2729
84	12/08	Sthl	1m	(0-75)H	SS	£2729
75	11/08	Sthl	7f	(0-60)H	STD	£1706
69	11/08	Sthl	1m	(0-60)H	STD	£1706

Total win prize-money £18264

Going (Turf): Sf: 0-3 **GS: 1-3** Gd: 0-4 GF: 0-9 Fm: 0-0
Distance: 5f/6f: 0-2 **7f-8f: 6-25** 9f-13f: 0-7 14f+: 0-2
Track : **LH: 6-27** RH: 0-6 **Tight: 1-10** Gall: 0-1
Aids: Bl: 0-0 Vi: 0-0 Tstrap: 0-0 Ckp: 0-0
Best Rating: **85** 1/09 Sthl 1m stand

Fair; stays 1m and acts on Fibresand; suited by forcing tactics.

Mr Aitch (IRE)

86(104) (82)**63**

7-y-o b g Soviet Star (USA)-Welsh Mist (Damister (USA))
E McNamara (R T Phillips 26/6) Bellflower Racing Limited

Placings:244/66001/00415130/50/**2-4412320** **(3346)**
2009: 12^{4}SD, 11^{4}SD, 16^{1}SD, 16^{2}SD, 16^{3}SF, 16^{2}SD, 16^{0}GF,

	Starts	1st	2nd	3rd	Win & Pl
Career Total (Turf)	**16**	**3**	**1**	**1**	**17994**
Career Total (AW)	**10**	**1**	**3**	**1**	**10014**

78	2/09	Ling	2m	(0-85)H	STD	£4857
81	8/06	Ches	1m4f66y	(0-85)H	G-F	£5829
78	6/06	Leic	1m3f183y	(0-75)H	G-F	£5181
73	9/05	Bath	1m5y	(0-70)H	FRM	£3951

Total win prize-money £19819

Going (Turf): Sf: 0-0 GS: 0-2 Gd: 0-1 **GF: 2-12** Fm: 1-1
Distance: 5f/6f: 0-0 7f-8f: 0-3 **9f-13f: 3-18** 14f+: 1-5
Track : **LH: 3-21** RH: 1-4 **Tight: 3-17** Gall: 0-1
Aids: Bl: 0-0 Vi: 0-0 Tstrap: 0-0 Ckp: 0-0
Best Rating: **84** 8/06 Hayd 1m3f200y gd-fm

Fair; stays 2m; acts on fast ground and on sand; wears a tongue tie.

Mr Burton

(91) (55)**61**

5-y-o gr g Thethingaboutitis (USA)-Quay Four (IRE) (Barathea (IRE))
M Mullineaux C A Oats

Placings:3550060-0 **(0567)**
2009: 12^{0}SD,

	Starts	1st	2nd	3rd	Win & Pl
Career Total (Turf)	**3**	**0**	**0**	**1**	**563**
Career Total (AW)	**5**	**0**	**0**	**0**	**0**

Going (Turf): **Sf: 0-2 GS: 0-0 Gd: 0-0 GF: 0-1 Fm: 0-0**
Distance: 5f/6f: 0-0 7f-8f: 0-5 9f-13f: 0-3 14f+: 0-0
Track : LH: 0-7 RH: 0-1 Tight: 0-6 Gall: 0-0
Aids: Bl: 0-0 Vi: 0-0 Tstrap: 0-1 Ckp: 0-1
Best Rating: **61** 7/08 Thsk 7f gd-fm

Mr Chocolate Drop (IRE)

(98) (62)**34**

5-y-o b g Danetime (IRE)-Forest Blade (IRE) (Charnwood Forest (IRE))
Miss M E Rowland Dean R Mitchell

Placings:00052/0410440000050/233311040**1**-20044225 **(0979)**
2009: 7^{2}SD, 8^{0}SD, 7^{0}SD, 8^{4}SD, 9^{4}SD, 8^{2}SD, 7^{2}SD, 8^{5}SD,

	Starts	1st	2nd	3rd	Win & Pl
Career Total (Turf)	**5**	**0**	**0**	**0**	
Career Total (AW)	**31**	**4**	**5**	**3**	**10822**

56	12/08	Wolv	1m141y	(0-55)H	STD	£2047
55	2/08	Kemp	7f	(0-45)	STD	£1365
53	2/08	Kemp	7f	(0-45)	STD	£1365
56	2/07	Sthl	7f		SLW	£2184

Total win prize-money £6961

Going (Turf): **Sf: 0-0 GS: 0-2 Gd: 0-2 GF: 0-1 Fm: 0-0**
Distance: 5f/6f: 0-0 **7f-8f: 3-28** 9f-13f: 1-8 14f+: 0-0
Track : LH: 2-30 RH: 2-4 **Tight: 1-13** Gall: 0-0
Aids: **Bl: 3-16** Vi: 0-3 Tstrap: 0-2 Ckp: 0-2
Best Rating: 62 1/09 Kemp 7f stand

Moderate; effective over 7f-1m; goes on Polytrack.

Mr Corby (IRE)

92(93) (69)**71**
2-y-o b c Camacho-Clochette (IRE) (Namaqualand (USA))
M R Channon Findlay & Bloom

Placings:343**2**00 **(6905)**
2009: 6^{3}G, 7^{4}GF, 7^{3}GF, **6^{2}**SD, 6^{0}G, 6^{0}G,

	Starts	1st	2nd	3rd	Win & Pl
Career Total (Turf)	5	0	0	2	2199
Career Total (AW)	1	0	1	0	771

Going (Turf): **Sf: 0-0 GS: 0-0 Gd: 0-3 GF: 0-2 Fm: 0-0**
Distance: 5f/6f: 0-2 7f-8f: 0-4 9f-13f: 0-0 14f+: 0-0
Track : LH: 0-1 RH: 0-1 Tight: 0-1 Gall: 0-1
Aids: Bl: 0-0 Vi: 0-0 Tstrap: 0-0 Ckp: 0-0
Best Rating: 71 8/09 Newc 7f gd-fm

Out of a half-sister to Cheveley Park Stakes winner Capricciosa, and a half-brother to a couple of winning sprinters; fair form; stays 7f; acts on fast ground.

Mr Crystal (FR)

108 (41)**84**

5-y-o ch g Trempolino (USA)-Iyrbila (FR) (Lashkari)
Micky Hammond Champagne Ascent Partnership

Placings:00/60**6**1633/123251-122043 **(6676)**
2009: 21^{1}F, 17^{2}G, 17^{2}GF, 16^{0}G, 17^{4}GF, 18^{3}G,

	Starts	1st	2nd	3rd	Win & Pl
Career Total (Turf)	18	4	4	4	22657
Career Total (AW)	3	0	0	0	0

75	4/09	Pont	2m5f122y (0-75)H		FRM	£3885
77	10/08	Pont	2m1f216y (0-75)H		G-S	£3885
72	5/08	Newc	2m19y (0-70)H		G-F	£3885
60	6/07	Bevl	1m4f16y (0-55)H		G-F	£2914

Total win prize-money £14573

Going (Turf): Sf: 0-1 GS: 1-2 Gd: 0-6 **GF: 2-7** Fm: 1-2
Distance: 5f/6f: 0-0 7f-8f: 0-2 9f-13f: 1-5 **14f+: 3-14**
Track : **LH: 3-15** RH: 1-6 Tight: 1-9 Gall: 1-3
Aids: Bl: 0-0 Vi: 0-0 Tstrap: 0-0 Ckp: 0-0
Best Rating: 84 6/09 Pont 2m1f216y gd-fm

Fair; stays 2m5f; acts on fast and easy ground; also goes on Fibresand.

Mr David (USA)

101 **103**
2-y-o b c Sky Mesa (USA)-Dancewiththebride (USA) (Belong To Me (USA))
B J Meehan Gold Group International Ltd

Placings:414 **(5172)**
2009: 6^{4}GF, 6^{1}G, 6^{4}GF,

	Starts	1st	2nd	3rd	Win & Pl
Career Total (Turf)	3	1	0	0	13021

83	7/09	NmkJ	6f	GD	£5180

Total win prize-money £5181

Going (Turf): Sf: 0-0 GS: 0-0 **Gd: 1-1** GF: 0-2 Fm: 0-0
Distance: **5f/6f: 1-3** 7f-8f: 0-0 9f-13f: 0-0 14f+: 0-0
Track : LH: 0-0 RH: 0-0 Tight: 0-0 Gall: 0-1
Aids: Bl: 0-0 Vi: 0-0 Tstrap: 0-0 Ckp: 0-0
Best Rating: 103 8/09 York 6f gd-fm

Useful; effective at 6f; acts on good ground.

Mr Deal

89(97) (55)**51**
3-y-o b g King's Best (USA)-One Of The Family (Alzao (USA))
Eve Johnson Houghton Osborne, Davies & Mercer

Placings:500-060**45** **(7660)**
2009: 12^{0}SD, 10^{6}G, 11^{0}GS, **10^{4}**SD, **10^{5}**SD,

	Starts	1st	2nd	3rd	Win & Pl
Career Total (Turf)	4	0	0	0	0
Career Total (AW)	4	0	0	0	165

Going (Turf): **Sf: 0-0 GS: 0-1 Gd: 0-2 GF: 0-1 Fm: 0-0**
Distance: 5f/6f: 0-0 7f-8f: 0-2 9f-13f: 0-6 14f+: 0-0
Track : LH: 0-5 RH: 0-3 Tight: 0-6 Gall: 0-0
Aids: Bl: 0-1 Vi: 0-0 Tstrap: 0-0 Ckp: 0-0
Best Rating: 55 11/09 Kemp 1m2f stand

Mr Emirati (USA)

84 **66**
2-y-o ch c Mr Greeley (USA)-Kathy K D (USA) (Saint Ballado (CAN))
B Smart H E Sheikh Rashid Bin Mohammed

Placings:3 **(6982)**
2009: 8^{3}G,

	Starts	1st	2nd	3rd	Win & Pl
Career Total (Turf)	1	0	0	1	770

Going (Turf): **Sf: 0-0 GS: 0-0 Gd: 0-1 GF: 0-0 Fm: 0-0**
Distance: 5f/6f: 0-0 7f-8f: 0-1 9f-13f: 0-0 14f+: 0-0
Track : LH: 0-1 RH: 0-0 Tight: 0-0 Gall: 0-0
Aids: Bl: 0-0 Vi: 0-0 Tstrap: 0-0 Ckp: 0-0
Best Rating: 66 10/09 Ayr 1m good

Fair; stays 1m and acts on good ground.

Mr Fantozzi (IRE)

100(91) (66)**67**
4-y-o br g Statue Of Liberty (USA)-Indian Sand (Indian King (USA))
D Donovan Mrs Rita Cioffi

Placings:400/**6**053**1006-0**12000**00** **(7855)**
2009: 10^{0}SD, 7^{1}F, 6^{2}GS, 8^{0}GF, 8^{0}GS, 7^{0}F, 8^{0}S, **9^{0}**SD, 8^{0}SS,

	Starts	1st	2nd	3rd	Win & Pl
Career Total (Turf)	12	1	1	1	3761
Career Total (AW)	8	1	0	0	1979

63	5/09	Brig	7f214y	(0-60)H	FRM	£2460
66	7/08	Sthl	1m	(0-65)H	SS	£1978

Total win prize-money £4440

Going (Turf): Sf: 0-1 GS: 0-3 Gd: 0-3 GF: 0-3 **Fm: 1-2**
Distance: 5f/6f: 0-1 **7f-8f: 2-14** 9f-13f: 0-5 14f+: 0-0
Track : **LH: 2-11** RH: 0-2 Tight: 0-4 Gall: 0-2
Aids: Bl: 1-6 Vi: 0-0 Tstrap: 1-6 Ckp: 1-6
Best Rating: 67 5/09 Brig 6f209y gd-sft

Moderate; best over 1m; acts on most ground and on Fibresand; has worn blinkers; suited by forcing tactics.

Mr Flannegan

97 **65**
3-y-o ch g Forzando-Star Of Flanders (Puissance)
H Candy Henry Candy

Placings:04503-06200500 **(5120)**
2009: 8^{0}GF, 8^{6}GF, 6^{2}F, 6^{0}GF, 8^{0}F, 6^{5}GF, 7^{0}S, 6^{0}F,

	Starts	1st	2nd	3rd	Win & Pl
Career Total (Turf)	13	0	1	1	1843

Going (Turf): **Sf: 0-2 GS: 0-2 Gd: 0-0 GF: 0-6 Fm: 0-3**
Distance: 5f/6f: 0-5 7f-8f: 0-6 9f-13f: 0-2 14f+: 0-0
Track : LH: 0-4 RH: 0-1 Tight: 0-1 Gall: 0-2
Aids: Bl: 0-0 Vi: 0-2 Tstrap: 0-0 Ckp: 0-0
Best Rating: 65 10/08 Wind 6f gd-fm

Cheaply bought gelding from a family of sprinters; modest form; stays 6f; acts on easy ground; has worn a visor.

Mr Forthright

97(83) (24)**51**
5-y-o b g Fraam-Form At Last (Formidable (USA))
J M Bradley E A Hayward

Placings:0660/0001641566**000**/00002000-3005660 **(4982)**
2009: 5^{3}GF, 5^{0}GS, 5^{0}G, 5^{5}GF, 5^{6}G, 5^{6}G, 6^{0}SD,

	Starts	1st	2nd	3rd	Win & Pl
Career Total (Turf)	28	2	1	1	6474
Career Total (AW)	4	0	0	0	

56	7/07	Bath	5f11y	(0-70)H	SFT	£3044
56	5/07	Bath	5f11y		G-F	£2266

Total win prize-money £5311

Going (Turf): **Sf: 1-4** GS: 0-4 Gd: 0-10 **GF: 1-8** Fm: 0-2
Distance: **5f/6f: 2-27** 7f-8f: 0-4 9f-13f: 0-1 14f+: 0-0
Track : **LH: 2-18** RH: 0-2 Tight: 0-1 **Gall: 2-14**
Aids: Bl: 0-4 Vi: 0-1 Tstrap: 0-4 Ckp: 0-4
Best Rating: 56 7/07 Bath 5f11y soft

Moderate sprinter; best at 5f; acts on fast ground; has worn blinkers.

Mr Freddy (IRE)

105 **77**
3-y-o b g Intikhab (USA)-Bubble N Squeak (IRE) (Catrail (USA))
R A Fahey R F White

Placings:050-621323 **(4518)**
2009: 8^{6}G, 8^{2}GS, 8^{1}GF, 8^{3}G, 9^{2}S, 12^{3}S,

	Starts	1st	2nd	3rd	Win & Pl
Career Total (Turf)	9	1	2	2	4504

Going (Turf): Sf: 0-4 GS: 0-2 Gd: 0-2 **GF: 1-1** Fm: 0-0
Distance: 5f/6f: 0-3 7f-8f: 0-1 **9f-13f: 1-5** 14f+: 0-0
Track : LH: 0-5 **RH: 1-2** Tight: 0-3 Gall: 0-2
Aids: Bl: 0-0 Vi: 0-0 Tstrap: 0-0 Ckp: 0-0
Best Rating: 77 6/09 Hayd 1m30y good

Fair; effective 1m-1m4f; acts on most ground on turf and synthetics.

Mr Funshine

83(99) (62)**51**
4-y-o b g Namid-Sunrise Girl (King's Signet (USA))
D Shaw (R J Hodges 11/12) Unity Farm Holiday Centre Ltd

Placings:000**040**/05104**4**000-00**606631** **(7838)**
2009: 7^{0}GF, 5^{0}F, **6^{6}**SD, **5^{0}**SD, **5^{6}**SD, **6^{6}**SD, **5^{3}**SD, **5^{1}**SS,

	Starts	1st	2nd	3rd	Win & Pl
Career Total (Turf)	13	0	0	0	168
Career Total (AW)	10	2	0	1	3937

56 12/09 Sthl 5f (0-60)H SS £1706
62 7/08 Sthl 5f (0-65)H SS £1978
Total win prize-money £3685

Going (Turf): Sf: 0-1 GS: 0-3 Gd: 0-4 GF: 0-4 Fm: 0-1
Distance: **5f/6f: 2-22** 7f-8f: 0-1 9f-13f: 0-0 14f+: 0-0
Track : LH: 0-10 RH: 0-2 Tight: 0-4 Gall: 0-8
Aids: Bl: 0-0 Vi: 0-0 Tstrap: 0-0 Ckp: 0-0
Best Rating: 62 7/08 Sthl 5f std-slw

Plating-class; suited by 5f and Fibresand.

Mr Garston

(100) (79)**91**
6-y-o b g Mull Of Kintyre (USA)-Ninfa Of Cisterna (Polish Patriot (USA))
J R Boyle A R O'Donnell

Placings:1/5/20/05000305-0 **(0155)**
2009: 7^{0}SD,

	Starts	1st	2nd	3rd	Win & Pl
Career Total (Turf)	4	1	1	0	5304
Career Total (AW)	9	0	0	1	543

74 8/05 Sand 5f6y GD £3376
Total win prize-money £3377

Going (Turf): Sf: 0-1 GS: 0-1 **Gd: 1-2** GF: 0-0 Fm: 0-0
Distance: **5f/6f: 1-2** 7f-8f: 0-11 9f-13f: 0-0 14f+: 0-0
Track : LH: 0-2 RH: 0-9 Tight: 0-0 Gall: 0-0
Aids: Bl: 0-1 Vi: 0-0 Tstrap: 0-0 Ckp: 0-0
Best Rating: 91 5/07 Wwck 7f26y gd-sft

Useful; stays 7f; acts on good and softer ground.

Mr Grinch (IRE)

97 **88**
2-y-o b g Green Tune (USA)-Flyamore (FR) (Sanglamore (USA))
M Dods M J K Dods

Placings:110 **(5762)**
2009: 5^{1}G, 6^{1}GF, 7^{0}GF,

	Starts	1st	2nd	3rd	Win & Pl
Career Total (Turf)	3	2	0	0	6476

88 8/09 Newc 6f G-F £3885
70 8/09 Carl 5f193y GD £2590
Total win prize-money £6476

Going (Turf): Sf: 0-0 GS: 0-0 **Gd: 1-1 GF: 1-2** Fm: 0-0
Distance: **5f/6f: 2-2** 7f-8f: 0-1 9f-13f: 0-0 14f+: 0-0
Track : LH: 0-0 **RH: 1-1** Tight: 0-0 Gall: 0-0
Aids: Bl: 0-0 Vi: 0-0 Tstrap: 0-0 Ckp: 0-0
Best Rating: 88 8/09 Newc 6f gd-fm

Fair; 12,500gns already gelded half-brother to a few middle-distance winners; winner on debut over 6f on good ground and followed up on fast.

Mr Harmoosh (IRE)

90 **62**
2-y-o b g Noverre (USA)-Polish Affair (IRE) (Polish Patriot (USA))
E F Vaughan Salem Rashid

Placings:0640 **(7056)**
2009: 7^{0}G, 8^{6}G, 6^{4}GF, 7^{0}GF,

	Starts	1st	2nd	3rd	Win & Pl
Career Total (Turf)	4	0	0	0	208

Going (Turf): Sf: 0-0 GS: 0-0 Gd: 0-2 GF: 0-2 Fm: 0-0
Distance: 5f/6f: 0-0 7f-8f: 0-3 9f-13f: 0-1 14f+: 0-0
Track : LH: 0-1 RH: 0-0 Tight: 0-0 Gall: 0-0
Aids: Bl: 0-0 Vi: 0-0 Tstrap: 0-0 Ckp: 0-0
Best Rating: 62 8/09 NmkJ 7f good

Mr Hichens

98(100) (84)**91**
4-y-o b g Makbul-Lake Melody (Sizzling Melody)
Karen George Adam Richard Wilson

Placings:4005224111456-560000010 **(7664)**
2009: 8^{5}SD, 8^{6}S, 10^{0}G, 9^{0}HY, 8^{0}GF, 8^{0}G, 8^{0}SD, 8^{1}SD, 8^{0}SD,

	Starts	1st	2nd	3rd	Win & Pl
Career Total (Turf)	18	3	2	0	18376
Career Total (AW)	4	1	0	0	2870

74 11/09 Kemp 1m (0-70)H STD £2590
91 9/08 Folk 1m1f149y (0-85)H SFT £5361
86 8/08 Gdwd 1m1f (0-85)H SFT £6476
77 7/08 Nott 1m75y G-F £3070
Total win prize-money £17499

Going (Turf): Sf: 2-6 GS: 0-3 Gd: 0-4 GF: 1-5 Fm: 0-0
Distance: 5f/6f: 0-0 7f-8f: 1-9 **9f-13f: 3-13** 14f+: 0-0
Track : LH: 1-4 **RH: 3-13 Tight: 2-7** Gall: 0-0
Aids: Bl: 0-2 Vi: 0-2 Tstrap: 1-3 Ckp: 1-3
Best Rating: 91 10/08 Nott 1m2f50y gd-sft

Modest; effective at around 1m-1m2f; acts on fast and soft ground, and on Polytrack; has worn blinkers.

Mr Irons (USA)

98 **80**
2-y-o ch c Mr Greeley (USA)-Jive Talk (USA) (Kingmambo (USA))
Sir Michael Stoute Mrs Elizabeth Moran

Placings:01 **(6484)**
2009: 7^{0}GF, 7^{1}GF,

	Starts	1st	2nd	3rd	Win & Pl
Career Total (Turf)	2	1	0	0	5181

80 10/09 Rdcr 7f G-F £5180
Total win prize-money £5181

Going (Turf): Sf: 0-0 GS: 0-0 Gd: 0-0 **GF: 1-2** Fm: 0-0
Distance: 5f/6f: 0-0 **7f-8f: 1-2** 9f-13f: 0-0 14f+: 0-0
Track : LH: 0-0 RH: 0-0 Tight: 0-0 Gall: 0-0
Aids: Bl: 0-0 Vi: 0-0 Tstrap: 0-0 Ckp: 0-0
Best Rating: 80 10/09 Rdcr 7f gd-fm

Fair; stays 7f; acts on fast ground.

Mr Kartoffel (IRE)

82 **33**
4-y-o b g Night Shift (USA)-Diamant (IRE) (Bigstone (IRE))
H Candy Henry Candy

Placings:000 **(3205)**
2009: 8^{0}G, 10^{0}GF, 12^{0}G,

	Starts	1st	2nd	3rd	Win & Pl
Career Total (Turf)	3	0	0	0	

Going (Turf): Sf: 0-0 GS: 0-0 Gd: 0-2 GF: 0-1 Fm: 0-0
Distance: 5f/6f: 0-0 7f-8f: 0-0 9f-13f: 0-3 14f+: 0-0
Track : LH: 0-1 RH: 0-1 Tight: 0-1 Gall: 0-0
Aids: Bl: 0-0 Vi: 0-0 Tstrap: 0-0 Ckp: 0-0
Best Rating: 33 5/09 Chep 1m14y good

Mr Lambros

(114) (99)**78**
8-y-o ch g Pivotal-Magical Veil (Majestic Light (USA))
Miss Gay Kelleway Winterbeck Manor Stud

Placings:31/2000/10360400/01210005/P000051/1152600-602 **(0282)**
2009: 6^{6}SD, 6^{0}SD, 7^{2}SD,

	Starts	1st	2nd	3rd	Win & Pl
Career Total (Turf)	13	0	0	1	6470
Career Total (AW)	26	7	4	1	43583

98 1/08 Wolv 7f32y (0-85)H STD £4533
89 1/08 Kemp 6f (0-75)H STD £2590
84 12/07 Wolv 5f216y (0-75)H STD £2914
98 4/06 Ling 7f STD £5297
102 2/06 Ling 7f (0-85)H STD £6477
94 1/05 Ling 7f (0-85)H STD £6269
82 1/04 Ling 7f D STD £3552
Total win prize-money £31636

Going (Turf): Sf: 0-1 GS: 0-1 Gd: 0-6 GF: 0-5 Fm: 0-0
Distance: 5f/6f: 2-15 **7f-8f: 5-24** 9f-13f: 0-0 14f+: 0-0
Track : **LH: 6-23** RH: 1-5 **Tight: 6-21** Gall: 0-2
Aids: Bl: 0-0 **Vi: 2-12** Tstrap: 0-0 Ckp: 0-0
Best Rating: 103 3/06 Ling 7f stand

Useful; effective at around 6f-7f; acts on good ground and on Polytrack; has worn a visor and a tongue tie.

Mr Loire

90(100) (55)**44**
5-y-o b g Bertolini (USA)-Miss Sancerre (Last Tycoon)
A J Chamberlain (K G Wingrove 16/3) Miss J M Foran

Placings:3230133/351004256610600005/0522144000-002535000050 **(3947)**
2009: 6^{0}SD, 5^{0}SD, 6^{2}SD, 5^{5}SD, 5^{3}SD, 5^{5}SD, 5^{0}SD, 5^{0}GF, 5^{0}F, 6^{0}G, 5^{5}F, 5^{0}GF,

	Starts	1st	2nd	3rd	Win & Pl
Career Total (Turf)	17	1	2	1	4801
Career Total (AW)	31	3	3	5	13371

55 1/08 Wolv 5f20y (0-45) STD £1365
66 8/07 Bath 5f161y FRM £2072
76 3/07 Wolv 5f216y (0-85)H STD £5505
68 11/06 Kemp 6f STD £2388
Total win prize-money £11332

Going (Turf): Sf: 0-2 GS: 0-2 Gd: 0-4 GF: 0-5 **Fm: 1-4**
Distance: **5f/6f: 4-44** 7f-8f: 0-4 9f-13f: 0-0 14f+: 0-0
Track : **LH: 3-33** RH: 1-9 **Tight: 2-21** Gall: 1-7
Aids: **Bl: 2-31** Vi: 0-1 Tstrap: 0-0 Ckp: 0-0
Best Rating: 76 6/07 Brig 5f59y gd-fm

Plating-class sprinter; acts on Polytrack and firm ground; has not always looked straightforward; has worn blinkers.

Mr Lu

99(98) (64)**69**
4-y-o b g Lujain (USA)-Libretta (Highest Honor (FR))
J S Goldie (A G Foster 25/7) The Greens Committee

Placings:603/0041226-0004600061U **(6984)**
2009: 8^{0}GF, 7^{0}G, 7^{0}GS, 6^{4}GF, 6^{6}GF, 7^{0}GS, 7^{0}GS, 8^{0}GS, 7^{6}GF, 7^{1}GF, 7^{U}G,

	Starts	1st	2nd	3rd	Win & Pl
Career Total (Turf)	20	2	2	1	9140
Career Total (AW)	1	0	0	0	0

61 10/09 Ayr 7f50y (0-60)H G-F £2388
63 7/08 Muss 7f30y (0-75)H G-F £3885
Total win prize-money £6274

Going (Turf): Sf: 0-3 GS: 0-5 Gd: 0-4 **GF: 2-8** Fm: 0-0
Distance: 5f/6f: 0-5 **7f-8f: 2-13** 9f-13f: 0-3 14f+: 0-0

Track : LH: 1-5 RH: 1-7 Tight: 1-8 Gall: 0-1
Aids: Bl: 0-0 Vi: 0-0 Tstrap: 0-1 Ckp: 0-1
Best Rating: 69 9/08 Muss 7f30y soft

Modest; effective at around 7f-1m; acts on fast and soft ground.

Mr Macattack

103(105) (91)85
4-y-o b c Machiavellian (USA)-Aunty Rose (IRE) (Caerleon (USA))
N J Vaughan Owen Promotions Limited

Placings:10-511040 (3091)
2009: 7SD, 7SF, 7SD, 7GF, 7GF, 7GF,

	Starts	1st	2nd	3rd	Win & Pl
Career Total (Turf)	4	0	0	0	1168
Career Total (AW)	4	3	0	0	10385

91 3/09 Wolv 7f32y (0-70)H STD £3070
88 2/09 Wolv 7f32y (0-85)H SF £4857
68 1/08 Wolv 7f32y STD £2457
Total win prize-money £10385

Going (Turf): Sf: 0-0 GS: 0-0 Gd: 0-0 GF: 0-4 Fm: 0-0
Distance: 5f/6f: 0-0 7f-8f: 3-8 9f-13f: 0-0 14f+: 0-0
Track : LH: 3-5 RH: 0-0 Tight: 3-4 Gall: 0-0
Aids: Bl: 0-0 Vi: 0-0 Tstrap: 0-0 Ckp: 0-0
Best Rating: 91 3/09 Wolv 7f32y stand

Useful; effective over 7f; acts on Polytrack; has worn tongue tie.

Mr Mahoganeigh

(94) (85)
2-y-o b c Mark Of Esteem (IRE)-Sweet Cando (IRE) (Royal Applause)
M L W Bell Mrs Lucille Bone

Placings:1 (5643)
2009: 8SD,

	Starts	1st	2nd	3rd	Win & Pl
Career Total (Turf)	0	0	0	0	
Career Total (AW)	1	1	0	0	2730

85 9/09 Ling 1m STD £2729
Total win prize-money £2730

Going (Turf): Sf: 0-0 GS: 0-0 Gd: 0-0 GF: 0-0 Fm: 0-0
Distance: 5f/6f: 0-0 7f-8f: 1-1 9f-13f: 0-0 14f+: 0-0
Track : LH: 1-1 RH: 0-0 Tight: 1-1 Gall: 0-0
Aids: Bl: 0-0 Vi: 0-0 Tstrap: 0-0 Ckp: 0-0
Best Rating: 85 9/09 Ling 1m stand

Mr Maximas

84 50
2-y-o ch g Auction House (USA)-Cashiki (IRE) (Case Law)
B Palling Nigel Thomas

Placings:006 (6331)
2009: 0G, 7G, 10F,

	Starts	1st	2nd	3rd	Win & Pl
Career Total (Turf)	3	0	0	0	0

Going (Turf): Sf: 0-0 GS: 0-0 Gd: 0-2 GF: 0-0 Fm: 0-1
Distance: 5f/6f: 0-0 7f-8f: 0-1 9f-13f: 0-2 14f+: 0-0
Track : LH: 0-1 RH: 0-0 Tight: 0-1 Gall: 0-0
Aids: Bl: 0-0 Vi: 0-0 Tstrap: 0-1 Ckp: 0-1
Best Rating: 50 9/09 Bath 1m2f46y firm

Mr Mischief

82(94) (72)44
9-y-o b g Millkom-Snow Huntress (Shirley Heights)
C Gordon R A Gadd

Placings:011/0050211/3010/3222/2100605353234413/6-0000 (2127)
2009: 12SD, 12SD, 16SD, 17GS,

	Starts	1st	2nd	3rd	Win & Pl
Career Total (Turf)	23	0	5	3	7191
Career Total (AW)	16	7	1	3	27994

73 10/07 Wolv 1m5f194y (0-65)H STD £2115
61 5/07 Sthl 1m4f STD £2184
95 3/04 Wolv 1m4f C(0-100)H SLW £8398
73 12/03 Sthl 1m3f F STD £2044
93 11/03 Wolv 1m6f166yG(0-80)H STD £2247
84 12/02 Wolv 1m100y E(0-75) STD £3532
79 11/02 Wolv 1m100y F STD £2968
Total win prize-money £23489

Going (Turf): Sf: 0-3 GS: 0-5 Gd: 0-6 GF: 0-9 Fm: 0-0
Distance: 5f/6f: 0-1 7f-8f: 0-1 9f-13f: 5-23 14f+: 2-14
Track : LH: 7-30 RH: 0-6 Tight: 5-21 Gall: 0-3
Aids: Bl: 0-0 Vi: 0-0 Tstrap: 0-0 Ckp: 0-0
Best Rating: 95 3/04 Wolv 1m4f slow

Moderate handicapper; stays 2m; acts on sound turf and Fibresand; winning hurdler.

Mr Mohican (IRE)

81 47
2-y-o b g Barathea (IRE)-Tipi Squaw (King's Best (USA))
Mrs A Duffield Mrs Ann Starkie & David Darlow

Placings:000 (6842)
2009: 7S, 8GF, 7G,

	Starts	1st	2nd	3rd	Win & Pl
Career Total (Turf)	3	0	0	0	

Going (Turf): Sf: 0-1 GS: 0-0 Gd: 0-1 GF: 0-1 Fm: 0-0
Distance: 5f/6f: 0-0 7f-8f: 0-3 9f-13f: 0-0 14f+: 0-0
Track : LH: 0-3 RH: 0-0 Tight: 0-2 Gall: 0-1
Aids: Bl: 0-0 Vi: 0-0 Tstrap: 0-1 Ckp: 0-1
Best Rating: 47 10/09 Catt 7f good

Mr Money Maker

94 57
2-y-o ch c Ishiguru (USA)-Ellopassoff (Librate)
Tom Dascombe E R Griffiths

Placings:5 (6903)
2009: 5G,

	Starts	1st	2nd	3rd	Win & Pl
Career Total (Turf)	1	0	0	0	0

Going (Turf): Sf: 0-0 GS: 0-0 Gd: 0-1 GF: 0-0 Fm: 0-0
Distance: 5f/6f: 0-1 7f-8f: 0-0 9f-13f: 0-0 14f+: 0-0
Track : LH: 0-0 RH: 0-0 Tight: 0-0 Gall: 0-1
Aids: Bl: 0-0 Vi: 0-0 Tstrap: 0-0 Ckp: 0-0
Best Rating: 57 10/09 Wind 5f10y good

Mr Napoleon (IRE)

(107) (74)69
7-y-o gr g Daylami (IRE)-Dathuil (IRE) (Royal Academy (USA))
G L Moore Jason Gibbons

Placings:0/50/050003030011/42541053-65 (0726)
2009: 11SD, 12SD,

	Starts	1st	2nd	3rd	Win & Pl
Career Total (Turf)	12	0	0	1	318
Career Total (AW)	14	3	1	2	8955

73 9/08 Ling 1m4f (0-70)H STD £3238
70 12/07 Ling 1m2f (0-65)H STD £1943
63 12/07 Kemp 1m2f (0-55)H STD £2047
Total win prize-money £7229

Going (Turf): Sf: 0-1 GS: 0-1 Gd: 0-6 GF: 0-3 Fm: 0-0
Distance: 5f/6f: 0-2 7f-8f: 0-1 9f-13f: 3-23 14f+: 0-0
Track : LH: 2-17 RH: 1-8 Tight: 2-11 Gall: 0-3
Aids: Bl: 0-2 Vi: 0-0 Tstrap: 0-1 Ckp: 0-1
Best Rating: 74 12/08 GrLe 1m2f stand

Modest; effective over 1m2f-1m4f; acts well on Polytrack.

Mr Plod

(101) (65)53
4-y-o ch g Silver Patriarch (IRE)-Emily-Mou (IRE) (Cadeaux Genereux)
M J Scudamore (Andrew Reid 14/10) A S Reid

Placings:0/00-034410 (7767)
2009: 12SD, 10G, 11SD, 12SD, 12SD, 11SD,

	Starts	1st	2nd	3rd	Win & Pl
Career Total (Turf)	1	0	0	1	337
Career Total (AW)	8	1	0	0	2047

65 12/09 Ling 1m4f (0-50)H STD £2047
Total win prize-money £2047

Going (Turf): Sf: 0-0 GS: 0-0 Gd: 0-1 GF: 0-0 Fm: 0-0
Distance: 5f/6f: 0-0 7f-8f: 0-1 9f-13f: 1-8 14f+: 0-0
Track : LH: 1-4 RH: 0-5 Tight: 1-3 Gall: 0-1
Aids: Bl: 0-0 Vi: 0-3 Tstrap: 0-1 Ckp: 0-1
Best Rating: 65 12/09 Ling 1m4f stand

Moderate; stays 1m4f and acts on good ground and on Polytrack.

Mr Prize Fighter

84 45
2-y-o b g Piccolo-Lv Girl (IRE) (Mukaddamah (USA))
I W McInnes P Kershaw

Placings:605 (6246)
2009: 6G, 7S, 5GF,

	Starts	1st	2nd	3rd	Win & Pl
Career Total (Turf)	3	0	0	0	0

Going (Turf): Sf: 0-1 GS: 0-0 Gd: 0-1 GF: 0-1 Fm: 0-0
Distance: 5f/6f: 0-1 7f-8f: 0-2 9f-13f: 0-0 14f+: 0-0
Track : LH: 0-1 RH: 0-0 Tight: 0-1 Gall: 0-0
Aids: Bl: 0-0 Vi: 0-0 Tstrap: 0-0 Ckp: 0-0
Best Rating: 45 8/09 Nott 6f15y good

Mr Prolific

88 54
3-y-o b g Haafhd-Rumpipumpy (Shirley Heights)
N A Twiston-Davies (B W Hills 26/5) H R Mould

Placings:000-200 (2350)
2009: 10GF, 10G, 12GF,

	Starts	1st	2nd	3rd	Win & Pl
Career Total (Turf)	6	0	1	0	605

Going (Turf): Sf: 0-0 GS: 0-1 Gd: 0-2 GF: 0-3 Fm: 0-0
Distance: 5f/6f: 0-1 7f-8f: 0-2 9f-13f: 0-3 14f+: 0-0

Track : LH: 0-3 RH: 0-0 Tight: 0-1 Gall: 0-1
Aids: Bl: 0-0 Vi: 0-0 Tstrap: 0-0 Ckp: 0-0
Best Rating: 54 4/09 Nott 1m2f50y gd-fm

Mr Rainbow

101(98) (79)**90**
3-y-o ch g Efisio-Blossom (Warning)
G A Swinbank Guy Reed

Placings:12 (6731)
2009: 7^{1}SD, 6^{2}S,

	Starts	1st	2nd	3rd	Win & Pl
Career Total (Turf)	1	0	1	0	1445
Career Total (AW)	1	1	0	0	3238
79 10/09 Wolv 7f32y			STD		£3238

Total win prize-money £3238

Going (Turf): Sf: 0-1 GS: 0-0 Gd: 0-0 GF: 0-0 Fm: 0-0
Distance: 5f/6f: 0-0 **7f-8f: 1-2** 9f-13f: 0-0 14f+: 0-0
Track : **LH: 1-1** RH: 0-0 **Tight: 1-1** Gall: 0-0
Aids: Bl: 0-0 Vi: 0-0 Tstrap: 0-0 Ckp: 0-0
Best Rating: 90 10/09 Sals 6f212y soft

Winner over 7f on belated debut; acts on Polytrack.

Mr Rev

94(107) (55)**53**
6-y-o b g Foxhound (USA)-Branston Berry (IRE) (Mukaddamah (USA))
J M Bradley J M Bradley

Placings:43302500003000-02366054434356650 (5283)
2009: 7^{0}SD, 6^{2}SD, 8^{3}SD, 7^{6}SD, 8^{6}SD, 7^{0}SD, 8^{5}SD, 7^{4}G, 5^{4}GF, 5^{3}GF, 6^{4}GF, 6^{3}GF, 6^{5}GF, 6^{6}GF, 6^{6}GS, 6^{5}F, 7^{0}GF,

	Starts	1st	2nd	3rd	Win & Pl
Career Total (Turf)	13	0	0	2	954
Career Total (AW)	18	0	2	4	2350

Going (Turf): Sf: 0-0 GS: 0-1 Gd: 0-2 GF: 0-9 Fm: 0-1
Distance: 5f/6f: 0-14 7f-8f: 0-17 9f-13f: 0-0 14f+: 0-0
Track : LH: 0-14 RH: 0-11 Tight: 0-5 Gall: 0-2
Aids: Bl: 0-18 Vi: 0-0 Tstrap: 0-3 Ckp: 0-3
Best Rating: 65 3/08 Kemp 6f stand

Moderate; effective at around 6f; acts on Polytrack; has worn cheekpieces and blinkers.

Mr Rio (IRE)

93(97) (58)**58**
4-y-o b g Captain Rio-Amoras (IRE) (Hamas (IRE))
A P Jarvis Mrs Ann Jarvis

Placings:605-3000604550 (7834)
2009: 6^{3}SD, 6^{0}G, 5^{0}GS, 6^{0}G, 6^{6}SD, 6^{0}G, 7^{4}SD, 7^{5}SD, 6^{5}SD, 6^{0}SD,

	Starts	1st	2nd	3rd	Win & Pl
Career Total (Turf)	6	0	0	0	0
Career Total (AW)	7	0	0	1	403

Going (Turf): Sf: 0-1 GS: 0-1 Gd: 0-4 GF: 0-0 Fm: 0-0
Distance: 5f/6f: 0-10 7f-8f: 0-3 9f-13f: 0-0 14f+: 0-0
Track : LH: 0-2 RH: 0-6 Tight: 0-0 Gall: 0-2
Aids: Bl: 0-0 Vi: 0-1 Tstrap: 0-0 Ckp: 0-0
Best Rating: 58 7/09 Sthl 6f stand

Moderate; stays 7f; acts on Polytrack and on Fibresand.

Mr Rooney (IRE)

91(101) (59)**65**
6-y-o b g Mujadil (USA)-Desert Bride (USA) (Key To The Kingdom (USA))
A Berry Alan Berry

Placings:6130334/60050/0260006422O/0442350551O360 50-5410000000060000 (7219)
2009: 5^{5}SD, 5^{4}SD, 5^{1}SD, 5^{0}SF, 5^{0}GF, 5^{0}G, 5^{0}GF, 5^{0}GF, 5^{0}G, 5^{6}GF, 5^{0}G, 5^{0}S, 5^{0}G, 5^{0}S,

	Starts	1st	2nd	3rd	Win & Pl
Career Total (Turf)	46	2	4	6	17511
Career Total (AW)	8	1	0	0	2047
59 2/09 Sthl 5f	(0-55)H		STD		£2047
65 7/08 Muss 5f	(0-70)H		G-F		£3885
80 4/05 Bevl 5f			GD		£3623

Total win prize-money £9557

Going (Turf): Sf: 0-7 GS: 0-6 **Gd: 1-12 GF: 1-20** Fm: 0-1
Distance: **5f/6f: 3-51** 7f-8f: 0-3 9f-13f: 0-0 14f+: 0-0
Track : LH: 0-8 RH: 0-4 Tight: 0-7 Gall: 0-4
Aids: Bl: 0-0 Vi: 0-0 Tstrap: 0-0 Ckp: 0-0
Best Rating: 87 7/05 NmkJ 6f gd-fm

Moderate; stays 6f, acts on most ground, but look best on fast; likes to race prominently.

Mr Skipiton (IRE)

104(104) (65)**73**
4-y-o b g Statue Of Liberty (USA)-Salty Air (IRE) (Singspiel (IRE))
B J McMath Steve & Ros Chaplin-Brown

Placings:0050-00411562140 (5576)
2009: 7^{0}SD, 5^{0}SD, 5^{4}SD, 6^{1}SD, 6^{1}SD, 5^{5}GF, 6^{6}GF, 6^{2}GF, 6^{1}GS, 6^{4}S, 6^{0}SD,

	Starts	1st	2nd	3rd	Win & Pl
Career Total (Turf)	5	1	1	0	2747
Career Total (AW)	10	2	0	0	3753
73 7/09 Yarm 6f3y	(0-60)H		G-S		£2072
65 4/09 Ling 6f	(0-60)H		STD		£2047
60 3/09 Kemp 6f	(0-55)H		STD		£1706

Total win prize-money £5825

Going (Turf): Sf: 0-1 **GS: 1-1** Gd: 0-0 GF: 0-3 Fm: 0-0
Distance: **5f/6f: 2-8** 7f-8f: 1-7 9f-13f: 0-0 14f+: 0-0
Track : LH: 1-7 RH: 1-3 **Tight: 1-6** Gall: 0-1
Aids: Bl: 0-0 Vi: 0-1 Tstrap: 0-0 Ckp: 0-0
Best Rating: 73 7/09 Yarm 6f3y gd-sft

Moderate; effective over 6f; acts on easy ground and on Polytrack.

Mr Smithson (IRE)

91(87) (65)**68**
2-y-o br g Xaar-Amanda Louise (IRE) (Perugino (USA))
B Ellison Koo's Racing Club

Placings:2032003500 (6345)
2009: 5^{2}GF, 5^{0}GF, 5^{3}GF, 5^{2}GF, 5^{0}G, 5^{0}GF, 5^{3}SD, 6^{5}SD, 5^{0}GF, 5^{0}SD,

	Starts	1st	2nd	3rd	Win & Pl
Career Total (Turf)	7	0	2	1	2635
Career Total (AW)	3	0	0	1	403

Going (Turf): Sf: 0-0 GS: 0-0 Gd: 0-1 GF: 0-6 Fm: 0-0
Distance: 5f/6f: 0-10 7f-8f: 0-0 9f-13f: 0-0 14f+: 0-0
Track : LH: 0-2 RH: 0-1 Tight: 0-1 Gall: 0-1
Aids: Bl: 0-0 Vi: 0-1 Tstrap: 0-0 Ckp: 0-0
Best Rating: 68 5/09 Carl 5f gd-fm

Modest; effective at 5f but shapes as though step up to 6f will suit; acts on fast ground and Fibresand.

Mr Snowballs

(80) (43)**58**
3-y-o gr g Monsieur Bond (IRE)-Swissmatic (Petong)
R A Farrant Snowballs Partnership

Placings:400-0 (1322)
2009: 6^{0}SD,

	Starts	1st	2nd	3rd	Win & Pl
Career Total (Turf)	2	0	0	0	289
Career Total (AW)	2	0	0	0	

Going (Turf): Sf: 0-2 GS: 0-0 Gd: 0-0 GF: 0-0 Fm: 0-0
Distance: 5f/6f: 0-3 7f-8f: 0-1 9f-13f: 0-0 14f+: 0-0
Track : LH: 0-0 RH: 0-2 Tight: 0-0 Gall: 0-1
Aids: Bl: 0-0 Vi: 0-0 Tstrap: 0-0 Ckp: 0-0
Best Rating: 58 7/08 Wind 6f soft

Mr Toshiwonka

52(79) (14)**69**
5-y-o b g Compton Place-Victoria (Old Vic)
D Nicholls Warren Smith

Placings:00210-004 (2842)
2009: 7^{0}SD, 7^{0}GF, 8^{4}GF,

	Starts	1st	2nd	3rd	Win & Pl
Career Total (Turf)	7	1	1	0	4070
Career Total (AW)	1	0	0	0	
69 8/08 Bevl 7f100y	(0-75)H		SFT		£2914

Total win prize-money £2914

Going (Turf): **Sf: 1-2** GS: 0-0 Gd: 0-1 GF: 0-4 Fm: 0-0
Distance: 5f/6f: 0-1 **7f-8f: 1-6** 9f-13f: 0-1 14f+: 0-0
Track : LH: 0-3 **RH: 1-3** Tight: 0-2 Gall: 0-0
Aids: Bl: 0-0 Vi: 0-0 Tstrap: 0-0 Ckp: 0-0
Best Rating: 69 8/08 Bevl 7f100y soft

Modest; suited by 7f and good or softer ground.

Mr Udagawa

102(90) (70)**76**
3-y-o b g Bahamian Bounty-Untold Riches (USA) (Red Ransom (USA))
R M Beckett B R Ingram

Placings:5453-3022310 (6907)
2009: 8^{3}GF, 8^{0}G, 8^{2}GF, 8^{2}GS, 8^{3}SD, 8^{1}GF, 10^{0}G,

	Starts	1st	2nd	3rd	Win & Pl
Career Total (Turf)	8	1	2	2	6005
Career Total (AW)	3	0	0	1	353
76 9/09 Nott 1m75y			G-F		£2590

Total win prize-money £2590

Going (Turf): Sf: 0-1 GS: 0-2 Gd: 0-2 **GF: 1-3** Fm: 0-0
Distance: 5f/6f: 0-0 7f-8f: 0-6 **9f-13f: 1-5** 14f+: 0-0
Track : **LH: 1-5** RH: 0-3 Tight: 0-5 Gall: 0-0
Aids: Bl: 0-0 Vi: 0-0 Tstrap: 1-2 Ckp: 1-2
Best Rating: 76 9/09 Nott 1m75y gd-fm

Fair; effective at around 7f-1m; acts on fast and easy ground.

Mr Willis

(106) (96)**51**
3-y-o b g Desert Sun-Santiburi Girl (Casteddu)
J R Best Miss Sara Furnival

Placings:00651-113112 (7789)
2009: 7^{1}SD, 7^{1}SD, 7^{3}SD, 8^{1}SD, 8^{1}SD, 9^{2}SD,

	Starts	1st	2nd	3rd	Win & Pl
Career Total (Turf)	2	0	0	0	

Career Total (AW)	9	5	1	1	20853
93	12/09 Ling	1m	(0-80)H	STD	£4727
89	11/09 Ling	1m	(0-85)H	STD	£4727
79	4/09 Ling	7f	(0-70)H	STD	£2900
74	3/09 Ling	7f	(0-70)H	STD	£2729
64	12/08 Ling	7f	(0-60)	STD	£1706

Total win prize-money £16790

Going (Turf): Sf: 0-0 GS: 0-0 Gd: 0-0 GF: 0-2 Fm: 0-0
Distance: 5f/6f: 0-3 **7f-8f: 5-7** 9f-13f: 0-1 14f+: 0-0
Track : **LH: 5-8** RH: 0-1 **Tight: 5-8** Gall: 0-2
Aids: Bl: 0-0 Vi: 0-0 Tstrap: 0-0 Ckp: 0-0
Best Rating: **96** 12/09 Wolv 1m1f103y stand

Useful; effective over 1m2f; acts on Polytrack; goes well at Lingfield.

Mr Wolf

102(101) (77)**81**

8-y-o b g Wolfhound (USA)-Madam Millie (Milford)
J J Quinn (D W Barker 17/7) Andrew Turton & David Barker

Placings:04500/221166000526/0060051113100020 3/000 1001105606 0/2000530500/005052653203313 3-60616002030 **(6847)**
2009: 5^{6}GF, 6^{0}GF, 5^{0}G, 5^{1}G, 5^{6}GF, 6^{0}GS, 5^{0}G, 5^{4}GS, 5^{0}GF, 5^{3}GF, 7^{0}G,

	Starts	1st	2nd	3rd	Win & Pl
Career Total (Turf)	83	11	8	8	88838
Career Total (AW)	2	0	0	1	482

81	6/09 Pont	5f	(0-75)H	GD	£3238
79	9/08 Pont	5f	(0-75)H	G-F	£3885
99	7/06 Pont	6f	(0-90)H	G-F	£8101
100	7/06 Pont	5f	(0-90)H	FRM	£11217
85	6/06 Catt	5f212y	(0-85)H	G-F	£6477
101	8/05 Pont	5f	(0-75)H	GD	£5636
88	7/05 Pont	6f	(0-90)H	G-F	£9405
84	7/05 Pont	6f	(0-65)	G-F	£4862
75	7/05 Ayr	6f	(0-65)H	G-F	£3590
79	5/04 Thsk	6f	E(0-70)	GD	£3604
72	4/04 Newc	5f	F	SFT	£3234

Total win prize-money £63254

Going (Turf): Sf: 1-10 GS: 0-9Gd: 3-29 **GF: 6-30** Fm: 1-5
Distance: **5f/6f: 11-81** 7f-8f: 0-4 9f-13f: 0-0 14f+: 0-0
Track : **LH: 8-34** RH: 0-0 **Tight: 1-14** Gall: 0-0
Aids: Bl: 0-0 Vi: 0-0 Tstrap: 9-54 Ckp: 9-54
Best Rating: **101** 8/05 Pont 5f good

Fair; effective over 5f-6f; acts on all types of ground, but well suited by a sound surface; often wears cheekpieces; has a fine record at Pontefract.

Mrs Beeton (IRE)

104(91) (66)**74**

3-y-o b f Dansili-Eliza Acton (Shirley Heights)
W R Swinburn Pendley Farm

Placings:4-10 **(3627)**
2009: 8^{1}GF, 9^{0}G,

	Starts	1st	2nd	3rd	Win & Pl
Career Total (Turf)	2	1	0	0	3886
Career Total (AW)	1	0	0	0	289
74	6/09 Sals	1m		G-F	£3885

Total win prize-money £3886

Going (Turf): Sf: 0-0 GS: 0-0 Gd: 0-1 **GF: 1-1** Fm: 0-0
Distance: 5f/6f: 0-0 **7f-8f: 1-2** 9f-13f: 0-1 14f+: 0-0
Track : LH: 0-0 RH: 0-2 Tight: 0-0 Gall: 0-0
Aids: Bl: 0-0 Vi: 0-0 Tstrap: 0-0 Ckp: 0-0
Best Rating: **74** 6/09 Sals 1m gd-fm

Fair; half-sister to multiple 1m2f winner Stotsfold; stays 1m.

Mrs Boss

99(90) (71)**78**

2-y-o b f Makbul-Chorus (Bandmaster (USA))
B R Millman Mrs L S Millman

Placings:03033040 **(6241)**
2009: 5^{0}GF, 5^{3}GF, 5^{0}GS, 6^{3}GF, 5^{3}SD, 5^{0}G, 5^{4}F, 6^{0}G,

	Starts	1st	2nd	3rd	Win & Pl
Career Total (Turf)	7	0	0	2	8021
Career Total (AW)	1	0	0	1	530

Going (Turf): Sf: 0-0 GS: 0-1 Gd: 0-2 GF: 0-3 Fm: 0-1
Distance: 5f/6f: 0-7 7f-8f: 0-1 9f-13f: 0-0 14f+: 0-0
Track : LH: 0-2 RH: 0-0 Tight: 0-1 Gall: 0-2
Aids: Bl: 0-0 Vi: 0-1 Tstrap: 0-0 Ckp: 0-0
Best Rating: **78** 5/09 Sals 5f gd-fm

Useful; effective at 5f on fast ground.

Mrs Bun

(108) (75)**52**

4-y-o b f Efisio-Card Games (First Trump)
K A Ryan Guy Reed

Placings:604620103-11240 **(0934)**
2009: 8^{1}SS, 7^{1}SD, 8^{2}SD, 7^{4}SD, 7^{0}SD,

	Starts	1st	2nd	3rd	Win & Pl
Career Total (Turf)	5	0	0	0	216
Career Total (AW)	9	3	2	1	8246
69	1/09 Sthl	7f	(0-70)H	STD	£2729
69	1/09 Sthl	1m	(0-55)H	SS	£2047
61	11/08 Sthl	7f	(0-60)H	STD	£1706

Total win prize-money £6483

Going (Turf): Sf: 0-2 GS: 0-2 Gd: 0-1 GF: 0-0 Fm: 0-0
Distance: 5f/6f: 0-5 **7f-8f: 3-9** 9f-13f: 0-0 14f+: 0-0
Track : **LH: 3-9** RH: 0-0 Tight: 0-1 Gall: 0-0
Aids: **Bl: 2-4** Vi: 0-1 Tstrap: 1-3 Ckp: 1-3
Best Rating: **75** 1/09 Sthl 1m stand

Modest, stays 1m and acts on Fibresand; has worn blinkers and cheekpieces.

Mrs E

81 **55**

2-y-o b f Doyen (IRE)-Fille De Bucheron (USA) (Woodman (USA))
M W Easterby Clark Industrial Services Partnership

Placings:05 **(6982)**
2009: 8^{0}GF, 8^{5}G,

	Starts	1st	2nd	3rd	Win & Pl
Career Total (Turf)	2	0	0	0	0

Going (Turf): Sf: 0-0 GS: 0-0 Gd: 0-1 GF: 0-1 Fm: 0-0
Distance: 5f/6f: 0-0 7f-8f: 0-1 9f-13f: 0-1 14f+: 0-0
Track : LH: 0-2 RH: 0-0 Tight: 0-0 Gall: 0-0
Aids: Bl: 0-0 Vi: 0-0 Tstrap: 0-0 Ckp: 0-0
Best Rating: **55** 10/09 Ayr 1m good

Mrs Jones And Me (IRE)

84(85) (56)**59**

2-y-o b f Namid-Meadow (Green Desert (USA))
P T Midgley Anthony D Copley

Placings:505640400 **(5372)**
2009: 5^{5}G, 5^{0}GF, 6^{5}GF, 6^{6}GS, 5^{4}GF, 5^{0}G, 5^{4}SD, 5^{0}SF, 5^{0}SD,

	Starts	1st	2nd	3rd	Win & Pl
Career Total (Turf)	6	0	0	0	289
Career Total (AW)	3	0	0	0	289

Going (Turf): Sf: 0-0 GS: 0-1 Gd: 0-2 GF: 0-3 Fm: 0-0
Distance: 5f/6f: 0-9 7f-8f: 0-0 9f-13f: 0-0 14f+: 0-0
Track : LH: 0-1 RH: 0-0 Tight: 0-1 Gall: 0-0
Aids: Bl: 0-1 Vi: 0-2 Tstrap: 0-0 Ckp: 0-0
Best Rating: **59** 5/09 York 6f gd-fm

Mrs Medley

39(82) (27)

3-y-o b f Rambling Bear-Animal Cracker (Primo Dominie)
D Shaw J Medley

Placings:0000000 **(7829)**
2009: 6^{0}G, 5^{0}SD, 5^{0}SD, 5^{0}SD, 5^{0}SD, 5^{0}SD, 7^{0}SD,

	Starts	1st	2nd	3rd	Win & Pl
Career Total (Turf)	1	0	0	0	
Career Total (AW)	6	0	0	0	

Going (Turf): Sf: 0-0 GS: 0-0 Gd: 0-1 GF: 0-0 Fm: 0-0
Distance: 5f/6f: 0-6 7f-8f: 0-1 9f-13f: 0-0 14f+: 0-0
Track : LH: 0-4 RH: 0-2 Tight: 0-3 Gall: 0-0
Aids: Bl: 0-0 Vi: 0-0 Tstrap: 0-0 Ckp: 0-0
Best Rating: **27** 10/09 Wolv 5f20y stand

Mrs Mogg

70 **52**

2-y-o b f Green Desert (USA)-Maybe Forever (Zafonic (USA))
N J Vaughan Money Never Sleeps Racing

Placings:6 **(3633)**
2009: 5^{6}G,

	Starts	1st	2nd	3rd	Win & Pl
Career Total (Turf)	1	0	0	0	0

Going (Turf): Sf: 0-0 GS: 0-0 Gd: 0-1 GF: 0-0 Fm: 0-0
Distance: 5f/6f: 0-1 7f-8f: 0-0 9f-13f: 0-0 14f+: 0-0
Track : LH: 0-0 RH: 0-0 Tight: 0-0 Gall: 0-0
Aids: Bl: 0-0 Vi: 0-0 Tstrap: 0-0 Ckp: 0-0
Best Rating: **52** 7/09 Nott 5f13y good

Mrs Penny (AUS)

(107) (91)**92**

5-y-o br m Planchet (AUS)-Respective (AUS) (Noalcoholic (FR))
J R Gask Horses First Racing Limited

Placings:321/1664-10450 **(7862)**
2009: 5^{1}SD, 5^{0}SD, 5^{4}SD, 5^{5}SD, 5^{0}SD,

	Starts	1st	2nd	3rd	Win & Pl
Career Total (Turf)	6	2	1	1	13302
Career Total (AW)	6	1	0	0	6587
91	1/09 Wolv	5f216y	(0-80)H	STD	£5180
	1/08 Morp	5f55y	H	GD	£5903
	12/07 Morp	5f55y	H	G-S	£5403

Total win prize-money £16487

Going (Turf): Sf: 0-0 **GS: 1-1 Gd: 1-5** GF: 0-0 Fm: 0-0
Distance: **5f/6f: 3-11** 7f-8f: 0-1 9f-13f: 0-0 14f+: 0-0
Track : **LH: 1-6** RH: 0-0 **Tight: 1-6** Gall: 0-0
Aids: Bl: 0-1 Vi: 0-0 Tstrap: 1-2 Ckp: 1-2
Best Rating: **92** 3/08 Morp 6f good

Useful ex-Australian trained mare; dual 5f winner on good

ground down under; stays 6f; acts on Polytrack; has worn cheekpieces.

Mrs Puff (IRE)

91(93) (48)46

2-y-o gr f Trans Island-Canosa (IRE) (Catrail (USA))

P D Evans (A B Haynes 3/4) Bathwick Gold Partnership

Placings:0000050456 (7334)

2009: 5⁰GF, 7⁰G, 6⁰G, 7⁰GF, 6⁰GS, 5⁵GF, 8⁰SD, 7⁴G, 7⁵SD, 8⁶SD,

	Starts	1st	2nd	3rd	Win & Pl
Career Total (Turf)	7	0	0	0	144
Career Total (AW)	3	0	0	0	0

Going (Turf): Sf: 0-0 GS: 0-1 Gd: 0-3 GF: 0-3 Fm: 0-0
Distance: 5f/6f: 0-4 7f-8f: 0-6 9f-13f: 0-0 14f+: 0-0
Track: LH: 0-3 RH: 0-2 Tight: 0-1 Gall: 0-2
Aids: Bl: 0-0 Vi: 0-0 Tstrap: 0-0 Ckp: 0-0
Best Rating: 48 11/09 Wolv 7f32y stand

Mrs Slocombe (IRE)

99(90) (51)78

3-y-o b f Masterful (USA)-Mrs Beatty (Cadeaux Genereux)

Mrs N S Evans (J Akehurst 8/7) John Berry (Gwent)

Placings:0206-4300450 (5063)

2009: 7⁴SD, 6³GF, 7⁰GF, 8⁰G, 10⁴GF, 11⁵G, 8⁰GF,

	Starts	1st	2nd	3rd	Win & Pl
Career Total (Turf)	9	0	1	1	2583
Career Total (AW)	2	0	0	0	192

Going (Turf): Sf: 0-0 GS: 0-0 Gd: 0-2 GF: 0-4 Fm: 0-0
Distance: 5f/6f: 0-1 7f-8f: 0-6 9f-13f: 0-4 14f+: 0-0
Track: LH: 0-5 RH: 0-2 Tight: 0-4 Gall: 0-0
Aids: Bl: 0-0 Vi: 0-0 Tstrap: 0-1 Ckp: 0-1
Best Rating: 78 7/08 Naas 6f yield

Fair; stays 6f; acts on most ground; has worn cheekpieces and a tongue tie.

Ms Sophie Eleanor (USA)

96 68

3-y-o b/br f Grand Slam (USA)-Population (IRE) (General Assembly (USA))

T D Barron J Browne

Placings:0120 (5941)

2009: 6⁰GF, 7¹G, 7²G, 7⁰G,

	Starts	1st	2nd	3rd	Win & Pl
Career Total (Turf)	4	1	1	0	4721

66 7/09 Thsk 7f GD £3950
Total win prize-money £3950

Going (Turf): Sf: 0-0 GS: 0-0 Gd: 1-3 GF: 0-1 Fm: 0-0
Distance: 5f/6f: 0-1 7f-8f: 1-3 9f-13f: 0-0 14f+: 0-0
Track: LH: 1-1 RH: 0-2 Tight: 1-3 Gall: 0-0
Aids: Bl: 0-0 Vi: 0-0 Tstrap: 0-0 Ckp: 0-0
Best Rating: 68 8/09 Muss 7f30y good

$140,000 half-sister to lots of winners including Saratoga Springs; winner on second start over 7f on easy ground.

Mt Desert

(89) (24)70

7-y-o b g Rainbow Quest (USA)-Chief Bee (Chief's Crown (USA))

E W Tuer Far Distant Partnership

Placings:66/01520/0/40002-0 (7505)

2009: 12⁰SD,

	Starts	1st	2nd	3rd	Win & Pl
Career Total (Turf)	13	1	2	0	6938
Career Total (AW)	1	0	0	0	

80 4/05 Hayd 1m2f120y (0-75)H SFT £3424
Total win prize-money £3424

Going (Turf): Sf: 1-1 GS: 0-3 Gd: 0-8 GF: 0-1 Fm: 0-0
Distance: 5f/6f: 0-0 7f-8f: 0-2 9f-13f: 1-4 14f+: 0-8
Track: LH: 1-9 RH: 0-3 Tight: 0-3 Gall: 0-0
Aids: Bl: 0-1 Vi: 0-1 Tstrap: 0-0 Ckp: 0-0
Best Rating: 80 9/05 Hayd 1m3f200y gd-sft

Modest; stays 2m; acts well in soft ground; has worn a visor.

Mt Kintyre (IRE)

103(87) (39)76

3-y-o b g Mull Of Kintyre (USA)-Nihonpillow Mirai (IRE) (Zamindar (USA))

M H Tompkins Jackie & George Smith

Placings:560-22403006 (7101)

2009: 10²GF, 10²GF, 11⁴G, 8⁰G, 9³GS, 12⁰SD, 10⁰G, 10⁶G,

	Starts	1st	2nd	3rd	Win & Pl
Career Total (Turf)	10	0	2	1	2531
Career Total (AW)	1	0	0	0	

Going (Turf): Sf: 0-1 GS: 0-1 Gd: 0-4 GF: 0-3 Fm: 0-0
Distance: 5f/6f: 0-0 7f-8f: 0-3 9f-13f: 0-8 14f+: 0-0
Track: LH: 0-7 RH: 0-3 Tight: 0-4 Gall: 0-1
Aids: Bl: 0-0 Vi: 0-0 Tstrap: 0-0 Ckp: 0-0
Best Rating: 76 4/09 Pont 1m2f6y gd-fm

Useful Mull Of Kintyre colt; stays 1m2f; acts on fast ground; has shown quirks.

Mtoto Girl

(100) (53)36

5-y-o b m Mtoto-Shalati (FR) (High Line)

J J Bridger Gayler William Chambers

Placings:000/56P566055600040-0 (0598)

2009: 8⁰SD,

	Starts	1st	2nd	3rd	Win & Pl
Career Total (Turf)	4	0	0	0	0
Career Total (AW)	15	0	0	0	192

Going (Turf): Sf: 0-1 GS: 0-2 Gd: 0-1 GF: 0-0 Fm: 0-0
Distance: 5f/6f: 0-0 7f-8f: 0-7 9f-13f: 0-12 14f+: 0-0
Track: LH: 0-5 RH: 0-13 Tight: 0-6 Gall: 0-0
Aids: Bl: 0-0 Vi: 0-0 Tstrap: 0-0 Ckp: 0-0
Best Rating: 53 4/08 Ling 1m2f stand

Mubrook (USA)

102(103) (82)90

4-y-o b g Alhaarth (IRE)-Zomaradah (Deploy)

L M Cumani Sheikh Mohammed Obaid Al Maktoum

Placings:422-04422 (6995)

2009: 10⁰G, 12⁴G, 12⁴G, 12²SD, 14²GS,

	Starts	1st	2nd	3rd	Win & Pl
Career Total (Turf)	7	0	3	0	5002
Career Total (AW)	1	0	1	0	771

Going (Turf): Sf: 0-1 GS: 0-2 Gd: 0-4 GF: 0-0 Fm: 0-0
Distance: 5f/6f: 0-0 7f-8f: 0-0 9f-13f: 0-7 14f+: 0-1
Track: LH: 0-5 RH: 0-3 Tight: 0-1 Gall: 0-3
Aids: Bl: 0-0 Vi: 0-0 Tstrap: 0-0 Ckp: 0-0
Best Rating: 90 10/09 Donc 1m6f132y gd-sft

Useful; stays 1m4f; acts on good and easy ground.

Much Acclaimed (IRE)

98 75

2-y-o b g Sulamani (IRE)-Much Commended (Most Welcome)

T P Tate T P Tate

Placings:26 (6991)

2009: 7²GF, 7⁶G,

	Starts	1st	2nd	3rd	Win & Pl
Career Total (Turf)	2	0	1	0	1156

Going (Turf): Sf: 0-0 GS: 0-0 Gd: 0-1 GF: 0-1 Fm: 0-0
Distance: 5f/6f: 0-0 7f-8f: 0-2 9f-13f: 0-0 14f+: 0-0
Track: LH: 0-0 RH: 0-0 Tight: 0-0 Gall: 0-0
Aids: Bl: 0-0 Vi: 0-0 Tstrap: 0-0 Ckp: 0-0
Best Rating: 75 9/09 Rdcr 7f gd-fm

Mucho Loco (IRE)

(96) (48)64

6-y-o ch g Tagula (IRE)-Mousseux (IRE) (Jareer (USA))

R Curtis Guildings Racing Club

Placings:003/022642065032/600066/66-62 (0385)

2009: 12⁶SD, 10²GF,

	Starts	1st	2nd	3rd	Win & Pl
Career Total (Turf)	13	0	4	1	4409
Career Total (AW)	12	0	1	1	957

Going (Turf): Sf: 0-3 GS: 0-2 Gd: 0-2 GF: 0-6 Fm: 0-0
Distance: 5f/6f: 0-1 7f-8f: 0-10 9f-13f: 0-14 14f+: 0-0
Track: LH: 0-12 RH: 0-6 Tight: 0-9 Gall: 0-1
Aids: Bl: 0-15 Vi: 0-1 Tstrap: 0-2 Ckp: 0-2
Best Rating: 64 7/06 Wind 1m67y gd-fm

Modest maiden who has had plenty of chances; stays a mile; acts on most types of ground; has worn blinkers/cheekpieces.

Mudaaraah

100 103

2-y-o b f Cape Cross (IRE)-Wissal (USA) (Woodman (USA))

J L Dunlop Hamdan Al Maktoum

Placings:10120 (6269)

2009: 6¹GF, 6⁰G, 7¹GF, 7²G, 8⁰G,

	Starts	1st	2nd	3rd	Win & Pl
Career Total (Turf)	5	2	1	0	30862

101 7/09 Sand 7f16y G-F £17031
84 6/09 Folk 6f G-F £3070
Total win prize-money £20102

Going (Turf): Sf: 0-0 GS: 0-0 Gd: 0-3 GF: 2-2 Fm: 0-0
Distance: 5f/6f: 1-2 7f-8f: 1-3 9f-13f: 0-0 14f+: 0-0
Track: LH: 0-0 RH: 1-3 Tight: 0-0 Gall: 0-1
Aids: Bl: 0-0 Vi: 0-0 Tstrap: 0-0 Ckp: 0-0
Best Rating: 103 8/09 Gdwd 7f good

Very useful; Listed winner and Group 3 placed; effective over 6f-7f; acts on good and fast ground.

Mudawin (IRE)

106 (99)93

8-y-o b g Intikhab (USA)-Fida (IRE) (Persian Heights)

James Moffatt John Macgregor

Placings:5/01010/36013101302/0635050/0000-05321 **(4332)**

2009: 16^{0}G, 13^{5}GF, 14^{3}F, 14^{2}S, 16^{1}G,

	Starts	1st	2nd	3rd	Win & Pl
Career Total (Turf)	31	5	1	5	173007
Career Total (AW)	2	1	1	0	13816

84	7/09	York	2m88y	(0-90)H	GD	£9066
101	8/06	York	1m5f197y	H	G-S	£124640
92	7/06	Sand	1m6f	(0-85)H	G-F	£6477
92	5/06	Kemp	1m4f	(0-85)H	STD	£7790
98	5/04	Asct	1m2f	C(0-90)H	G-F	£9850
89	4/04	Newb	1m	D	GD	£6240

Total win prize-money £164064

Going (Turf): Sf: 0-5 GS: 1-4 **Gd: 2-13 GF: 2-7** Fm: 0-1
Distance: 5f/6f: 0-0 7f-8f: 1-4 9f-13f: 2-8 **14f+: 3-21**
Track : LH: 2-11 **RH: 3-18** Tight: 0-5 **Gall: 3-14**
Aids: Bl: 0-0 Vi: 0-0 Tstrap: 0-0 Ckp: 0-0
Best Rating: 101 8/06 York 1m5f197y gd-sft

Fair now; formerly very useful; surprise winner of the 2006 Ebor; stays 2m, but effective at shorter; acts on fast and soft ground; goes on Polytrack.

Mudhish (IRE)

99(103) (73)75

4-y-o b g Lujain (USA)-Silver Satire (Dr Fong (USA))

C E Brittain C E Brittain

Placings:62410033/00060-**1450022**203424 **(6175)**

2009: 8^{1}SD, 7^{4}SD, 8^{5}SD, 7^{0}SD, 5^{0}SD, 6^{2}SD, 6^{2}SD, 7^{2}GF, 7^{0}GF, 7^{3}SD, 7^{4}GF, 7^{2}G, 7^{4}GF,

	Starts	1st	2nd	3rd	Win & Pl
Career Total (Turf)	15	1	2	1	6113
Career Total (AW)	11	1	3	2	5953

72	2/09	Sthl	1m	(0-60)H	STD	£2047
76	8/07	Brig	6f209y		FRM	£2839

Total win prize-money £4886

Going (Turf): Sf: 0-1 GS: 0-1 Gd: 0-4 GF: 0-8 **Fm: 1-1**
Distance: 5f/6f: 0-12 **7f-8f: 2-14** 9f-13f: 0-0 14f+: 0-0
Track : **LH: 2-13** RH: 0-1 Tight: 0-8 Gall: 0-1
Aids: Bl: 0-16 Vi: 0-0 Tstrap: 0-0 Ckp: 0-0
Best Rating: 77 12/07 Ling 6f stand

Modest; stays 1m; acts on fast ground and on sand; has been tried in blinkers.

Mufarrh (IRE)

97 89

2-y-o b c Marju (IRE)-What A Picture (FR) (Peintre Celebre (USA))

J L Dunlop Hamdan Al Maktoum

Placings:321 **(6754)**

2009: 7^{3}GF, 7^{2}GF, 7^{1}G,

	Starts	1st	2nd	3rd	Win & Pl
Career Total (Turf)	3	1	1	1	7493

89	10/09	Leic	7f9y	GD	£5180

Total win prize-money £5181

Going (Turf): Sf: 0-0 GS: 0-0 **Gd: 1-1** GF: 0-2 Fm: 0-0
Distance: 5f/6f: 0-0 **7f-8f: 1-3** 9f-13f: 0-0 14f+: 0-0
Track : LH: 0-0 RH: 0-1 Tight: 0-0 Gall: 0-0
Aids: Bl: 0-0 Vi: 0-0 Tstrap: 0-0 Ckp: 0-0
Best Rating: 89 10/09 Leic 7f9y good

Useful; effective over 7f; acts on fast ground.

Muffett's Dream

97(94) (45)52

5-y-o b m Fraam-Loveless Carla (Pursuit Of Love)

J J Bridger Mr & Mrs K Finch

Placings:000/0000/06066001000500-00044 **(3739)**

2009: 11^{0}F, 11^{0}GF, 11^{0}GF, 11^{4}GF, 11^{4}GF,

	Starts	1st	2nd	3rd	Win & Pl
Career Total (Turf)	21	1	0	0	2240
Career Total (AW)	5	0	0	0	0

52	8/08	Ling	1m2f	(0-65)H	GD	£2047

Total win prize-money £2047

Going (Turf): Sf: 0-1 GS: 0-3 **Gd: 1-5** GF: 0-11 Fm: 0-1
Distance: 5f/6f: 0-0 7f-8f: 0-3 **9f-13f: 1-22** 14f+: 0-1
Track : **LH: 1-14** RH: 0-8 **Tight: 1-16** Gall: 0-3
Aids: Bl: 0-0 Vi: 0-0 Tstrap: 0-0 Ckp: 0-0
Best Rating: 57 9/06 Newb 7f good

Moderate; stays 1m2f; handles good ground.

Muftarres (IRE)

102(104) (81)89

4-y-o b c Green Desert (USA)-Ghazal (USA) (Gone West (USA))

G A Butler Beetle N Wedge Partnership

Placings:611350-0663126 **(7233)**

2009: 6^{0}GS, 6^{6}GS, 6^{6}SD, 7^{3}SD, 8^{1}GF, 9^{2}G, 10^{6}SD,

	Starts	1st	2nd	3rd	Win & Pl
Career Total (Turf)	10	3	1	1	12016
Career Total (AW)	3	0	0	1	385

77	10/09	Wwck	1m22y	(0-75)H	G-F	£3885
79	8/08	Bath	5f11y	(0-75)H	G-S	£4209
73	6/08	Rdcr	6f		G-F	£2331

Total win prize-money £10426

Going (Turf): Sf: 0-1 GS: 1-5 Gd: 0-2 **GF: 2-2** Fm: 0-0
Distance: **5f/6f: 2-7** 7f-8f: 0-3 9f-13f: 1-3 14f+: 0-0
Track : **LH: 2-4** RH: 0-3 Tight: 0-1 **Gall: 1-1**
Aids: Bl: 0-0 Vi: 0-0 Tstrap: 0-1 Ckp: 0-1
Best Rating: 89 10/09 Leic 1m1f218y good

Fair; stays 1m2f and acts on most ground; has worn a tongue tie.

Mufti (IRE)

86 75

2-y-o b c Noverre (USA)-Dark Indian (IRE) (Indian Ridge)

B J Meehan Saleh Al Homaizi & Imad Al Sagar

Placings:46 **(5527)**

2009: 8^{4}G, 7^{6}G,

	Starts	1st	2nd	3rd	Win & Pl
Career Total (Turf)	2	0	0	0	385

Going (Turf): Sf: 0-0 GS: 0-0 Gd: 0-2 GF: 0-0 Fm: 0-0
Distance: 5f/6f: 0-0 7f-8f: 0-2 9f-13f: 0-0 14f+: 0-0
Track : LH: 0-1 RH: 0-0 Tight: 0-0 Gall: 0-0
Aids: Bl: 0-0 Vi: 0-0 Tstrap: 0-0 Ckp: 0-0
Best Rating: 75 8/09 NmkJ 1m good

Fair; stays 1m; acts on good ground.

Mugeba

82(65) (49)49

8-y-o b m Primo Dominie-Ella Lamees (Statoblest)

C A Dwyer M M Foulger

Placings:02/5512206305/30232234031540001/60001453 5/346023144200 2201/54600034-0000 **(7100)**

2009: 7^{0}G, 7^{0}SD, 6^{0}GS, 5^{0}G,

	Starts	1st	2nd	3rd	Win & Pl
Career Total (Turf)	55	6	9	7	34171
Career Total (AW)	11	0	1	2	1693

65	11/07	Ayr	7f50y	(0-70)H	HVY	£3238
65	6/07	NmkJ	7f	(0-70)H	SFT	£3886
62	8/06	Yarm	7f3y	(0-75)H	G-F	£3562
68	11/05	Yarm	6f3y	(0-58)H	HVY	£3106
64	8/05	Yarm	7f3y	(0-70)H	GD	£4178
52	6/04	Yarm	7f3y	G	FRM	£2583

Total win prize-money £20556

Going (Turf): Sf: 3-14 GS: 0-10 Gd: 1-14 GF: 1-16 Fm: 1-1
Distance: 5f/6f: 0-17 **7f-8f: 6-47** 9f-13f: 0-2 14f+: 0-0
Track : **LH: 1-16** RH: 0-1 Tight: 0-10 Gall: 0-2
Aids: Bl: 0-1 Vi: 0-2 Tstrap: 0-2 Ckp: 0-2
Best Rating: 68 11/05 Yarm 6f3y heavy

Moderate; effective over 6f-7f; acts on fast and soft ground; also goes on Polytrack; likes Yarmouth.

Muhannak (IRE)

109(113) (112)113

5-y-o b g Chester House (USA)-Opera (Forzando)

R M Beckett R A Pegum

Placings:0/**213140013**/10**1110**-**500P055** **(7281a)**

2009: 10^{5}FT, 10^{0}FT, 12^{0}G, 12^{P}SD, 8^{0}SD, 12^{5}GF, 14^{5}FT,

	Starts	1st	2nd	3rd	Win & Pl
Career Total (Turf)	10	2	0	0	19778
Career Total (AW)	13	5	1	2	211089

112	10/08	SnAt	1m4f		FST	£153317
101	9/08	Dund	1m2f150y		STD	£23933
101	8/08	Kemp	1m3f	(0-90)H	STD	£7477
96	6/08	Ches	1m2f75y	(0-85)H	G-F	£5180
87	10/07	Kemp	1m4f	(0-80)H	STD	£5181
84	8/07	Wind	1m2f7y	(0-85)H	G-F	£12464
70	7/07	Wolv	1m141y		STD	£2388

Total win prize-money £209944

Going (Turf): Sf: 0-1 GS: 0-1 Gd: 0-3 **GF: 2-5** Fm: 0-0
Distance: 5f/6f: 0-0 7f-8f: 0-2 **9f-13f: 7-20** 14f+: 0-1
Track : LH: 3-10 RH: 3-10 **Tight: 3-9** Gall: 0-4
Aids: **Bl: 1-4** Vi: 0-0 Tstrap: 0-0 Ckp: 0-0
Best Rating: 113 12/08 ShTn 1m4f good

Smart; winner of 2008 Breeders' Cup Marathon; stays 1m4f; acts on fast ground, Polytrack and Pro-Ride; has worn blinkers.

Mujaadel (USA)

105(102) (88)83

4-y-o ch g Street Cry (IRE)-Quiet Rumour (USA) (Alleged (USA))

D Nicholls W R B Racing 49

Placings:2416/60620-5003001601 **(6847)**

2009: 7^{5}G, 8^{0}GS, 7^{0}GF, 8^{3}F, 10^{0}GF, 8^{0}GS, 7^{1}GF, 7^{6}G, 7^{0}G, 7^{1}G,

	Starts	1st	2nd	3rd	Win & Pl
Career Total (Turf)	16	3	1	1	14734
Career Total (AW)	3	0	1	0	1535

80	10/09	Catt	7f	(0-75)H	GD	£2914
80	8/09	Rdcr	7f	(0-80)H	G-F	£5180
82	9/07	Ling	7f		G-F	£2730

Total win prize-money £10825

Going (Turf): Sf: 0-0 GS: 0-3 Gd: 1-7 **GF: 2-5** Fm: 0-1
Distance: 5f/6f: 0-0 **7f-8f: 3-15** 9f-13f: 0-4 14f+: 0-0
Track : **LH: 1-7** RH: 0-5 **Tight: 1-7** Gall: 0-1
Aids: Bl: 0-0 Vi: 0-0 Tstrap: 2-3 Ckp: 2-3
Best Rating: 88 9/08 Kemp 1m stand

Useful, stays 1m; acts on fast ground and on Polytrack.

Mujada

81(90) (52)**39**

4-y-o b f Mujahid (USA)-Catriona (Bustino)

M Brittain Mel Brittain

Placings:2066/5400000-000 **(4995)**

2009: 7^{0}SD, 6^{0}SD, 7^{0}GF,

	Starts	1st	2nd	3rd	Win & Pl
Career Total (Turf)	7	0	0	0	0
Career Total (AW)	7	0	1	0	645

Going (Turf): **Sf: 0-0 GS: 0-3 Gd: 0-1 GF: 0-3 Fm: 0-0**
Distance: 5f/6f: 0-8 7f-8f: 0-6 9f-13f: 0-0 14f+: 0-0
Track : LH: 0-6 RH: 0-2 Tight: 0-2 Gall: 0-0
Aids: Bl: 0-1 Vi: 0-0 Tstrap: 0-0 Ckp: 0-0
Best Rating: **52** 2/08 Sthl 6f stand

Mujamead

(101) (71)**28**

5-y-o b g Mujahid (USA)-Island Mead (Pharly (FR))

J R Holt (A W Carroll 10/1) J T Billson

Placings:450/00/2111-0 **(0112)**

2009: 16^{0}SD,

	Starts	1st	2nd	3rd	Win & Pl
Career Total (Turf)	1	0	0	0	
Career Total (AW)	9	3	1	0	5236

71	2/08	Sthl	2m	(0-65)H	STD	£1911
68	1/08	Wolv	2m119y	(0-45)	STD	£1365
55	1/08	Wolv	1m5f194y	(0-45)	STD	£1365

Total win prize-money £4641

Going (Turf): **Sf: 0-0 GS: 0-0 Gd: 0-1 GF: 0-0 Fm: 0-0**
Distance: 5f/6f: 0-1 7f-8f: 0-3 9f-13f: 0-1 **14f+: 3-5**
Track : **LH: 3-7** RH: 0-2 **Tight: 2-4** Gall: 0-0
Aids: Bl: 0-0 Vi: 0-1 Tstrap: 2-4 Ckp: 2-4
Best Rating: **71** 2/08 Sthl 2m stand

Moderate; winning hurdler; stays 2m; acts on Polytrack.

Mujdeya

99 **79**

2-y-o gr f Linamix (FR)-Majhud (IRE) (Machiavellian (USA))

J H M Gosden Hamdan Al Maktoum

Placings:5 **(6921)**

2009: 8^{5}GF,

	Starts	1st	2nd	3rd	Win & Pl
Career Total (Turf)	1	0	0	0	153

Going (Turf): **Sf: 0-0 GS: 0-0 Gd: 0-0 GF: 0-1 Fm: 0-0**
Distance: 5f/6f: 0-0 7f-8f: 0-0 9f-13f: 0-1 14f+: 0-0
Track : LH: 0-0 RH: 0-0 Tight: 0-0 Gall: 0-0
Aids: Bl: 0-0 Vi: 0-0 Tstrap: 0-0 Ckp: 0-0
Best Rating: **79** 10/09 Yarm 1m3y gd-fm

Mujma

89(101) (60)**49**

5-y-o gr/b g Indian Ridge-Farfala (FR) (Linamix (FR))

S Parr Willie McKay

Placings:06/5030/0002400-6612300 **(1695)**

2009: 8^{6}SD, 8^{6}SD, 5^{1}SD, 5^{2}SD, 5^{3}SD, 5^{0}GS, 5^{0}G,

	Starts	1st	2nd	3rd	Win & Pl
Career Total (Turf)	13	0	0	1	530
Career Total (AW)	8	1	2	1	3197

60	3/09	Ling	5f	(0-52)H	STD	£1706

Total win prize-money £1706

Going (Turf): **Sf: 0-2 GS: 0-5 Gd: 0-3 GF: 0-3 Fm: 0-0**
Distance: **5f/6f: 1-7** 7f-8f: 0-7 9f-13f: 0-7 14f+: 0-0
Track : **LH: 1-13** RH: 0-2 **Tight: 1-7** Gall: 0-2
Aids: **Bl: 1-4** Vi: 0-3 Tstrap: 0-1 Ckp: 0-1
Best Rating: **67** 6/07 Ches 1m2f75y good

Moderate; effective over 5f-1m2f; acts on fast ground; goes on Fibresand and Polytrack.

Mujood

110(98) (79)**98**

6-y-o b g Mujahid (USA)-Waqood (USA) (Riverman (USA))

Eve Johnson Houghton Eden Racing

Placings:553130250/045203542415631 6/0361604406060 06200/351112004602620 40-050122023000611 00 **(6694)**

2009: 8^{0}SD, 7^{5}GF, 6^{0}GF, 8^{1}GF, 8^{2}G, 8^{2}GF, 8^{0}GF, 8^{2}GF, 8^{3}G, 8^{0}G, 7^{0}G, 7^{0}G, 6^{6}G, 7^{1}GF, 7^{1}GF, 7^{0}GF, 6^{0}GS,

	Starts	1st	2nd	3rd	Win & Pl
Career Total (Turf)	64	10	9	5	89190
Career Total (AW)	13	0	1	2	4035

96	9/09	Gdwd	7f	(0-85)H	G-F	£5180
92	9/09	Gdwd	7f	(0-85)H	G-F	£4857
91	5/09	Gdwd	1m	(0-85)H	G-F	£4857
94	5/08	Bevl	7f100y	(0-85)H	G-F	£4209
94	5/08	Yarm	1m3y	(0-90)H	G-F	£7477
92	5/08	Gdwd	6f	(0-85)H	G-S	£5828
96	5/07	Gdwd	6f	(0-85)H	GD	£7772
89	10/06	Brig	5f213y	(0-85)H	G-S	£5505
82	8/06	Folk	7f	(0-75)H	G-S	£4533
78	7/05	Pont	6f		G-F	£5817

Total win prize-money £56038

Going (Turf): Sf: 0-3 GS: 3-14 Gd: 1-17 **GF: 6-25** Fm: 0-5
Distance: 5f/6f: 4-28 **7f-8f: 5-40** 9f-13f: 1-9 14f+: 0-0
Track : LH: 2-16 **RH: 4-26** Tight: 0-7 Gall: 0-1
Aids: Bl: 2-22 **Vi: 3-16** Tstrap: 0-2 Ckp: 0-2
Best Rating: **98** 7/08 Gdwd 7f gd-fm

Useful; effective at up to 1m; acts on most ground; goes on Polytrack; has worn blinkers and a visor; likes to race prominently.

Muktasb (USA)

(110) (73)**52**

8-y-o b g Bahri (USA)-Maghaarb (Machiavellian (USA))

D Shaw Miss Claire Comery

Placings:002/03003/520004/500324201500 20224/434534 634560002261 3031/1120660000523250-451334344300 **(3227)**

2009: 6^{4}SD, 5^{5}SD, 5^{1}SD, 6^{3}SD, 6^{3}SD, 5^{4}SF, 5^{3}SD, 5^{4}SD, 5^{4}SD, 5^{3}SD, 6^{0}SD, 5^{0}SD,

	Starts	1st	2nd	3rd	Win & Pl
Career Total (Turf)	7	0	0	0	
Career Total (AW)	74	6	12	13	22949

65	1/09	Wolv	5f216y	(0-60)H	STD	£1648
71	1/08	Kemp	6f	(0-70)H	STD	£2590
65	1/08	Kemp	6f	(0-58)H	STD	£2047
63	12/07	Ling	6f	(0-52)H	STD	£1943
58	11/07	Kemp	5f	(0-45)	STD	£1365
59	4/06	Wolv	5f20y	(0-45)	STD	£1365

Total win prize-money £10960

Going (Turf): **Sf: 0-1 GS: 0-2 Gd: 0-1 GF: 0-3 Fm: 0-0**
Distance: **5f/6f: 6-79** 7f-8f: 0-2 9f-13f: 0-0 14f+: 0-0
Track : LH: 3-52 RH: 3-17 **Tight: 3-44** Gall: 0-4
Aids: Bl: 0-2 **Vi: 6-67** Tstrap: 0-1 Ckp: 0-1
Best Rating: **73** 1/08 Ling 6f stand

Moderate; effective over 5f-6f; acts on Polytrack; has worn headgear.

Mulaazem

(100) (62)**69**

6-y-o b g King's Best (USA)-Harayir (USA) (Gulch (USA))

A M Hales Brick Farm Racing

Placings:0/21/000520/060-450 **(0668)**

2009: 16^{4}SD, 16^{5}SD, 16^{0}SD,

	Starts	1st	2nd	3rd	Win & Pl
Career Total (Turf)	12	1	2	0	5237
Career Total (AW)	4	0	0	0	0

83	8/06	Hayd	1m2f120y	G-F	£3238

Total win prize-money £3239

Going (Turf): Sf: 0-0 GS: 0-1 Gd: 0-2 **GF: 1-9** Fm: 0-0
Distance: 5f/6f: 0-0 7f-8f: 0-1 **9f-13f: 1-11** 14f+: 0-4
Track : **LH: 1-13** RH: 0-2 Tight: 0-5 Gall: 0-0
Aids: Bl: 0-3 Vi: 0-0 Tstrap: 0-0 Ckp: 0-0
Best Rating: **85** 7/06 Sand 1m14y gd-fm

Modest; stays 10f; likes a sound surface.

Mulazem (USA)

76 **16**

3-y-o gr/ro c El Prado (IRE)-Muwakleh (Machiavellian (USA))

W J Haggas Hamdan Al Maktoum

Placings:0 **(1941)**

2009: 8^{0}GF,

	Starts	1st	2nd	3rd	Win & Pl
Career Total (Turf)	1	0	0	0	

Going (Turf): **Sf: 0-0 GS: 0-0 Gd: 0-0 GF: 0-1 Fm: 0-0**
Distance: 5f/6f: 0-0 7f-8f: 0-0 9f-13f: 0-1 14f+: 0-0
Track : LH: 0-0 RH: 0-0 Tight: 0-0 Gall: 0-0
Aids: Bl: 0-0 Vi: 0-0 Tstrap: 0-0 Ckp: 0-0
Best Rating: **16** 5/09 Yarm 1m3y gd-fm

Mull Of Dubai

105 (49)**102**

6-y-o b g Mull Of Kintyre (USA)-Enlisted (IRE) (Sadler's Wells (USA))

T P Tate Mrs Fitri Hay

Placings:22000600/4635213421014/34311240/601024400 -5014 **(4517)**

2009: 10^{5}GS, 10^{0}GF, 12^{1}G, 10^{4}S,

	Starts	1st	2nd	3rd	Win & Pl
Career Total (Turf)	41	7	6	4	81812
Career Total (AW)	1	0	0	0	

101	6/09	York	1m4f	(0-95)H	GD	£12492
97	5/08	Ches	1m2f75y	(0-100)H	G-F	£13246
91	7/07	Wwck	1m2f188y	(0-85)H	SFT	£5181
83	7/07	Wind	1m2f7y	(0-80)H	HVY	£5181
74	10/06	Wind	1m3f135y	(0-70)H	SFT	£3886
71	9/06	Bevl	1m4f16y	(0-80)H	G-F	£6477
69	7/06	Bath	1m3f144y	(0-75)H	GD	£3562

Total win prize-money £50028

Going (Turf): **Sf: 3-10** GS: 0-8 Gd: 2-9 GF: 2-13 Fm: 0-1
Distance: 5f/6f: 0-6 7f-8f: 0-5 **9f-13f: 7-27** 14f+: 0-4
Track : **LH: 4-21** RH: 2-9 **Tight: 5-14** Gall: 1-12
Aids: Bl: 0-1 Vi: 0-0 Tstrap: 0-0 Ckp: 0-0
Best Rating: **102** 7/08 York 1m4f heavy

Very useful; stays 1m4f, but effective at shorter; acts on most ground; usually held up.

Mull Of Killough (IRE)

105 102

3-y-o b g Mull Of Kintyre (USA)-Sun Shower (IRE) (Indian Ridge)

J L Spearing Noel B Lawless

Placings:112301 **(6249)**

2009: 7^{1}GF, 8^{1}G, 8^{2}G, 8^{3}GS, 9^{0}GF, 8^{1}GF,

	Starts	1st	2nd	3rd	Win & Pl
Career Total (Turf)	**6**	**3**	**1**	**1**	**20880**

102	9/09	Hayd	1m30y	(0-95)H	G-F	£8723
86	5/09	Thsk	1m	(0-85)H	GD	£5569
80	4/09	Wwck	7f26y		G-F	£3070

Total win prize-money £17363

Going (Turf): Sf: 0-0 GS: 0-1 Gd: 1-2 **GF: 2-3** Fm: 0-0
Distance: 5f/6f: 0-0 **7f-8f: 2-2** 9f-13f: 1-4 14f+: 0-0
Track : **LH: 3-5** RH: 0-1 **Tight: 1-1** Gall: 0-0
Aids: Bl: 0-0 Vi: 0-0 Tstrap: 0-0 Ckp: 0-0
Best Rating: 102 9/09 Hayd 1m30y gd-fm

Very useful; stays 1m; acts on good or faster ground.

Mullein

111(108) (102)108

4-y-o b f Oasis Dream-Gipsy Moth (Efisio)

R M Beckett Landmark Racing Limited

Placings:0/1462101-10301330 **(6661)**

2009: 6^{1}SD, 6^{0}HY, 6^{3}GS, 6^{0}G, 6^{1}GF, 6^{3}GF, 6^{3}GF, 6^{0}GS,

	Starts	1st	2nd	3rd	Win & Pl
Career Total (Turf)	**14**	**3**	**1**	**3**	**57764**
Career Total (AW)	**2**	**2**	**0**	**0**	**11563**

106	8/09	Pont	6f		G-F	£25546
102	4/09	Kemp	6f	(0-95)H	STD	£7352
97	10/08	Wwck	6f	(0-85)H	SFT	£5180
92	8/08	Wind	6f	(0-95)H	G-S	£8418
79	3/08	Kemp	6f		STD	£4210

Total win prize-money £50710

Going (Turf): **Sf: 1-3 GS: 1-5** Gd: 0-2 **GF: 1-4** Fm: 0-0
Distance: **5f/6f: 5-16** 7f-8f: 0-0 9f-13f: 0-0 14f+: 0-0
Track : LH: 2-2 RH: 2-2 Tight: 0-0 **Gall: 1-2**
Aids: Bl: 0-0 Vi: 0-0 Tstrap: 0-0 Ckp: 0-0
Best Rating: 108 9/09 Asct 6f gd-fm

Very useful; winner in Listed company; effective over 5f-6f; acts on most ground and on Polytrack.

Mullglen

102 83

3-y-o b g Mull Of Kintyre (USA)-However (IRE) (Hector Protector (USA))

T D Easterby Richard Taylor & Philip Hebdon

Placings:52110-600160366 **(6902)**

2009: 6^{6}GF, 5^{0}GS, 5^{0}GF, 5^{1}GS, 6^{6}GS, 5^{0}G, 5^{3}G, 6^{6}G, 5^{6}GF,

	Starts	1st	2nd	3rd	Win & Pl
Career Total (Turf)	**14**	**3**	**1**	**1**	**18945**

81	7/09	Catt	5f	(0-85)H	G-S	£5180
83	7/08	York	5f	H	HVY	£7771
79	5/08	Muss	5f		G-F	£3885

Total win prize-money £16838

Going (Turf): **Sf: 1-2 GS: 1-3** Gd: 0-5 **GF: 1-4** Fm: 0-0
Distance: **5f/6f: 3-14** 7f-8f: 0-0 9f-13f: 0-0 14f+: 0-0
Track : LH: 0-2 RH: 0-0 Tight: 0-0 Gall: 0-0
Aids: Bl: 0-3 Vi: 0-0 Tstrap: 0-0 Ckp: 0-0
Best Rating: 83 7/08 York 5f heavy

Useful colt; winner over 5f on fast and heavy ground.

Mullitovermaurice

(99) (65)

3-y-o ch g Pursuit Of Love-Ellovamul (Elmaamul (USA))

J G Given Joseph Hogan

Placings:4501-22360 **(7798)**

2009: 8^{2}SD, 9^{2}SD, 8^{3}SD, 8^{6}SD, 9^{0}SS,

	Starts	1st	2nd	3rd	Win & Pl
Career Total (Turf)	**0**	**0**	**0**	**0**	
Career Total (AW)	**9**	**1**	**2**	**1**	**5101**

59	12/08	Wolv	1m141y		STD	£3070

Total win prize-money £3071

Going (Turf): **Sf: 0-0 GS: 0-0 Gd: 0-0 GF: 0-0 Fm: 0-0**
Distance: 5f/6f: 0-0 7f-8f: 0-4 **9f-13f: 1-5** 14f+: 0-0
Track : **LH: 1-9** RH: 0-0 **Tight: 1-6** Gall: 0-1
Aids: Bl: 0-0 Vi: 0-0 Tstrap: 0-0 Ckp: 0-0
Best Rating: 65 2/09 Wolv 1m141y stand

Modest; stays 1m2f; handles Polytrack.

Multahab

101(109) (62)69

10-y-o b/br g Zafonic (USA)-Alumisiyah (USA) (Danzig (USA))

M Wigham Dave Anderson

Placings:20555/24240000V060002/012002555304/01501 100/5042001030/415000005015-3030214440 **(7280)**

2009: 5^{3}SD, 5^{0}GF, 5^{3}F, 5^{0}SD, 5^{2}GF, 5^{1}F, 5^{4}F, 5^{4}GF, 5^{4}GF, 5^{0}SD,

	Starts	1st	2nd	3rd	Win & Pl
Career Total (Turf)	**42**	**6**	**4**	**1**	**21117**
Career Total (AW)	**30**	**2**	**4**	**3**	**10000**

69	7/09	Brig	5f59y	(0-65)H	FRM	£2590
68	9/08	Brig	5f59y	(0-65)H	G-F	£2396
74	2/08	Wolv	5f20y	(0-65)H	STD	£2218
73	9/07	Wolv	5f20y	(0-60)H	SF	£1943
71	8/06	Brig	5f59y	(0-65)H	G-F	£2590
72	8/06	Catt	5f	(0-55)H	G-F	£3412
69	6/06	Brig	5f59y	(0-65)H	FRM	£2590
52	7/05	Brig	5f59y	(0-55)H	FRM	£2975

Total win prize-money £20717

Going (Turf): Sf: 0-1 GS: 0-1 Gd: 0-9 **GF: 3-19 Fm: 3-12**
Distance: **5f/6f: 8-70** 7f-8f: 0-2 9f-13f: 0-0 14f+: 0-0
Track : **LH: 7-48** RH: 0-3 **Tight: 2-25** Gall: 0-4
Aids: Bl: 0-1 Vi: 0-0 Tstrap: 0-5 Ckp: 0-5
Best Rating: 74 2/08 Wolv 5f20y stand

Modest; effective over 5f-6f; acts on fast ground; goes on Polytrack; usually wears a tongue-tie.

Multakka (IRE)

(108) (96)54

6-y-o b g Alhaarth (IRE)-Elfaslah (IRE) (Green Desert (USA))

M P Tregoning Hamdan Al Maktoum

Placings:533/332204/21/0115-200 **(6633)**

2009: 8^{2}SD, 8^{0}SD, 8^{0}SS,

	Starts	1st	2nd	3rd	Win & Pl
Career Total (Turf)	**9**	**0**	**2**	**3**	**13422**
Career Total (AW)	**9**	**3**	**2**	**1**	**16822**

89	10/08	GrLe	1m	(0-80)H	STD	£5180
85	9/08	Kemp	1m	(0-85)H	STD	£4727
74	11/07	Llng	7f		STD	£2832

Total win prize-money £12740

Going (Turf): **Sf: 0-1 GS: 0-4 Gd: 0-1 GF: 0-3 Fm: 0-0**
Distance: 5f/6f: 0-0 **7f-8f: 3-15** 9f-13f: 0-3 14f+: 0-0
Track : **LH: 2-5** RH: 1-10 Tight: 1-5 Gall: 1-1
Aids: Bl: 0-1 Vi: 0-0 Tstrap: 0-0 Ckp: 0-0
Best Rating: 96 5/09 Kemp 1m stand

Useful; stays 1m1f; acts on Polytrack and on fast ground and with cut on turf.

Multames (IRE)

105 93

2-y-o b c Cape Cross (IRE)-Elutrah (Darshaan)

Saeed Bin Suroor Godolphin

Placings:01 **(7029)**

2009: 7^{0}GF, 8^{1}S,

	Starts	1st	2nd	3rd	Win & Pl
Career Total (Turf)	**2**	**1**	**0**	**0**	**4857**

93	10/09	Newb	1m	SFT	£4857

Total win prize-money £4857

Going (Turf): **Sf: 1-1** GS: 0-0 Gd: 0-0 GF: 0-1 Fm: 0-0
Distance: 5f/6f: 0-0 **7f-8f: 1-2** 9f-13f: 0-0 14f+: 0-0
Track : LH: 0-0 RH: 0-0 Tight: 0-0 Gall: 0-0
Aids: Bl: 0-0 Vi: 0-0 Tstrap: 0-0 Ckp: 0-0
Best Rating: 93 10/09 Newb 1m soft

Useful; effective at 1m; acts in soft ground.

Multi Tasker

(92) (52)49

3-y-o b c Lear Spear (USA)-Lola Lola (IRE) (Piccolo)

Miss J R Tooth Raymond Tooth

Placings:0554000-0 **(0135)**

2009: 5^{0}SD,

	Starts	1st	2nd	3rd	Win & Pl
Career Total (Turf)	**1**	**0**	**0**	**0**	**0**
Career Total (AW)	**7**	**0**	**0**	**0**	**0**

Going (Turf): **Sf: 0-0 GS: 0-1 Gd: 0-0 GF: 0-0 Fm: 0-0**
Distance: 5f/6f: 0-7 7f-8f: 0-1 9f-13f: 0-0 14f+: 0-0
Track : LH: 0-4 RH: 0-3 Tight: 0-4 Gall: 0-0
Aids: Bl: 0-1 Vi: 0-0 Tstrap: 0-0 Ckp: 0-0
Best Rating: 57 4/08 Kemp 5f stand

Multiplication

106 82

3-y-o b f Marju (IRE)-Lunda (IRE) (Soviet Star (USA))

W J Knight (R Charlton 17/7) D G Hardisty Bloodstock

Placings:430-1406 **(6757)**

2009: 10^{1}GF, 9^{4}GF, 12^{0}G, 8^{6}G,

	Starts	1st	2nd	3rd	Win & Pl
Career Total (Turf)	**7**	**1**	**0**	**1**	**4599**

73	5/09	Wwck	1m2f188y	G-F	£2914

Total win prize-money £2914

Going (Turf): Sf: 0-0 GS: 0-0 Gd: 0-5 **GF: 1-2** Fm: 0-0
Distance: 5f/6f: 0-0 7f-8f: 0-3 **9f-13f: 1-4** 14f+: 0-0
Track : **LH: 1-1** RH: 0-3 Tight: 0-0 Gall: 0-1
Aids: Bl: 0-0 Vi: 0-0 Tstrap: 0-0 Ckp: 0-0
Best Rating: 82 10/09 Leic 1m60y good

110,000gns yearling is a half-sister to several winners, including Black Monday; stays 7f on good ground.

Mumaathel (IRE)

(89) (58)86

6-y-o b g Alhaarth (IRE)-Alhufoof (USA) (Dayjur (USA))

W R Muir C C Buckley

Placings:322032/000/0-0 **(0087)**

2009: 6^{0}SD,

	Starts	1st	2nd	3rd	Win & Pl
Career Total (Turf)	5	0	1	2	2071
Career Total (AW)	6	0	2	0	2120

Going (Turf): Sf: 0-0 GS: 0-0 Gd: 0-4 GF: 0-1 Fm: 0-0
Distance: 5f/6f: 0-4 7f-8f: 0-7 9f-13f: 0-0 14f+: 0-0
Track : LH: 0-6 RH: 0-3 Tight: 0-3 Gall: 0-2
Aids: Bl: 0-0 Vi: 0-0 Tstrap: 0-0 Ckp: 0-0
Best Rating: 86 5/06 Gdwd 7f good

Fair; dam a useful juvenile winner over 6f; stays 7f; acts on a sound surface and Polytrack.

Mumtaz Begum

69(66) **32**
4-y-o ch f Kyllachy-Indian Gift (Cadeaux Genereux)
J E Long Amaroni

Placings:000 **(5747)**
2009: 7^0GS, 7^0SD, 7^0GF,

	Starts	1st	2nd	3rd	Win & Pl
Career Total (Turf)	2	0	0	0	
Career Total (AW)	1	0	0	0	

Going (Turf): Sf: 0-0 GS: 0-1 Gd: 0-0 GF: 0-1 Fm: 0-0
Distance: 5f/6f: 0-0 7f-8f: 0-3 9f-13f: 0-0 14f+: 0-0
Track : LH: 0-1 RH: 0-0 Tight: 0-1 Gall: 0-0
Aids: Bl: 0-0 Vi: 0-0 Tstrap: 0-0 Ckp: 0-0
Best Rating: 32 7/09 Yarm 7f3y gd-sft

Muncaster Castle (IRE)

(96) (57)**58**
5-y-o b g Johannesburg (USA)-Eubee (FR) (Common Grounds)
R F Fisher Des Johnston

Placings:555206/**5**61**0**6330/**5**004533**0**500-**1**0 **(0608)**
2009: 8^1SD, 8^0SD,

	Starts	1st	2nd	3rd	Win & Pl
Career Total (Turf)	15	0	1	4	2958
Career Total (AW)	12	2	0	0	4436
54 2/09 Sthl	1m	(0-50)H		STD	£1706
60 3/07 Wolv	1m141y	(0-65)H		STD	£2730

Total win prize-money £4436

Going (Turf): Sf: 0-1 GS: 0-5 Gd: 0-2 GF: 0-7 Fm: 0-0
Distance: 5f/6f: 0-4 7f-8f: 1-6 9f-13f: 1-16 14f+: 0-1
Track : **LH: 2-17** RH: 0-9 **Tight: 1-15** Gall: 0-1
Aids: Bl: 0-1 Vi: 0-0 Tstrap: 0-0 Ckp: 0-0
Best Rating: 60 3/07 Wolv 1m141y stand

Moderate; stays 1m and acts on sand.

Munching Mike (IRE)

(92) (34)**60**
6-y-o br g Orpen (USA)-Stargard (Polish Precedent (USA))
K M Prendergast Wye Diamonds

Placings:004/00400/020/**2**-000 **(3927)**
2009: 12^0SD, 16^0SD, 13^0SF,

	Starts	1st	2nd	3rd	Win & Pl
Career Total (Turf)	11	0	1	0	2115
Career Total (AW)	4	0	1	0	524

Going (Turf): Sf: 0-2 GS: 0-0 Gd: 0-4 GF: 0-2 Fm: 0-0
Distance: 5f/6f: 0-1 7f-8f: 0-3 9f-13f: 0-9 14f+: 0-2
Track : LH: 0-10 RH: 0-4 Tight: 0-1 Gall: 0-0
Aids: Bl: 0-0 Vi: 0-1 Tstrap: 0-2 Ckp: 0-2
Best Rating: 65 9/05 List 1m gd-yld

Moderate; ex-Irish; stays 1m3f and acts on soft ground and Fibresand.

Mundo's Magic

88(87) (38)**58**
5-y-o b g Foxhound (USA)-Amber's Bluff (Mind Games)
N Wilson Fishing 4 Fun

Placings:001505/23254060360/00000-04 **(4818)**
2009: 8^0GF, 10^4GF,

	Starts	1st	2nd	3rd	Win & Pl
Career Total (Turf)	23	1	2	2	11320
Career Total (AW)	1	0	0	0	
73 7/06 Pont	6f			FRM	£4533

Total win prize-money £4534

Going (Turf): Sf: 0-1 GS: 0-3 Gd: 0-3 GF: 0-14 **Fm: 1-2**
Distance: **5f/6f: 1-17** 7f-8f: 0-6 9f-13f: 0-1 14f+: 0-0
Track : **LH: 1-8** RH: 0-1 Tight: 0-5 Gall: 0-1
Aids: Bl: 0-1 Vi: 0-0 Tstrap: 0-3 Ckp: 0-3
Best Rating: 76 5/07 Bevl 5f gd-fm

Munich (IRE)

91(97) (78)**78**
5-y-o b g Noverre (USA)-Mayara (IRE) (Ashkalani (IRE))
Mrs S Leech (Norma Twomey 3/6) R P Behan

Placings:0340/30**6**14**1**0005-0024504 **(4389)**
2009: 12^0SD, 7^0SD, 8^2SD, 7^4SD, 7^5SD, 7^0SD, 8^4G,

	Starts	1st	2nd	3rd	Win & Pl
Career Total (Turf)	11	1	0	2	8678
Career Total (AW)	10	1	1	0	5913
78 9/08 Layt	7f			STD	£5334
78 5/08 Curr	7f	(50-80)H		Y-S	£6351

Total win prize-money £11686

Going (Turf): Sf: 0-5 GS: 0-0 Gd: 0-2 GF: 0-1 Fm: 0-0
Distance: 5f/6f: 0-2 **7f-8f: 2-15** 9f-13f: 0-4 14f+: 0-0
Track : **LH: 1-9** RH: 0-7 Tight: 0-3 Gall: 0-3
Aids: Bl: 0-0 Vi: 0-0 Tstrap: 0-0 Ckp: 0-0
Best Rating: 78 9/08 Layt 7f stand

Modest; effective at 1m; acts on good.

Munlochy Bay

106(92) (57)**75**
5-y-o b m Karinga Bay-Meghdoot (Celestial Storm (USA))
M Sheppard (W S Kittow 18/6) The Blues Partnership

Placings:606421-20620 **(2931)**
2009: 12^2GS, 16^0SD, 17^6GS, 16^2G, 14^0G,

	Starts	1st	2nd	3rd	Win & Pl
Career Total (Turf)	8	1	3	0	6162
Career Total (AW)	3	0	0	0	0
64 10/08 Gdwd	2m	(0-70)H		G-S	£3238

Total win prize-money £3238

Going (Turf): Sf: 0-2 **GS: 1-4** Gd: 0-2 GF: 0-0 Fm: 0-0
Distance: 5f/6f: 0-0 7f-8f: 0-0 9f-13f: 0-4 **14f+: 1-7**
Track : LH: 0-5 **RH: 1-6 Tight: 1-7** Gall: 0-0
Aids: Bl: 0-0 Vi: 0-0 Tstrap: 0-1 Ckp: 0-1
Best Rating: 75 5/09 Gdwd 2m good

Modest; stays 2m; acts on soft ground.

Munsarim (IRE)

101 **80**
2-y-o b c Shamardal (USA)-Etizaaz (USA) (Diesis)
J L Dunlop Hamdan Al Maktoum

Placings:343 **(6810)**
2009: 7^3GS, 8^4GF, 8^3G,

	Starts	1st	2nd	3rd	Win & Pl
Career Total (Turf)	3	0	0	2	2142

Going (Turf): Sf: 0-0 GS: 0-1 Gd: 0-1 GF: 0-1 Fm: 0-0
Distance: 5f/6f: 0-0 7f-8f: 0-3 9f-13f: 0-0 14f+: 0-0
Track : LH: 0-0 RH: 0-0 Tight: 0-0 Gall: 0-0
Aids: Bl: 0-0 Vi: 0-0 Tstrap: 0-0 Ckp: 0-0
Best Rating: 80 10/09 NmkR 1m good

Useful; effective over 1m; acts on good ground.

Munsef

111 **111**
7-y-o b g Zafonic (USA)-Mazaya (IRE) (Sadler's Wells (USA))
Ian Williams (D Nicholls 19/2) Dr Marwan Koukash

Placings:03/21113/220325/3613022/5220-000121120 **(7215a)**
2009: 10^0G, 10^0G, 12^0G, 10^1GF, 11^2GF, 12^1G, 13^1GF, 12^2G, 16^0GS,

	Starts	1st	2nd	3rd	Win & Pl
Career Total (Turf)	33	7	10	5	233388
110 8/09 Ches	1m5f89y	(0-110)H		G-F	£22708
110 7/09 Asct	1m4f	(0-105)H		GD	£24924
87 6/09 Ches	1m2f75y			G-F	£4047
111 6/07 Gdwd	1m4f			G-F	£9815
116 9/05 NmkR	1m4f			G-S	£16240
102 6/05 York	1m4f	(0-105)H		G-F	£29000
71 5/05 Ripn	1m1f			G-F	£5096

Total win prize-money £111830

Going (Turf): Sf: 0-6 GS: 1-5 Gd: 1-11 **GF: 5-11** Fm: 0-0
Distance: 5f/6f: 0-1 7f-8f: 0-2 **9f-13f: 6-24** 14f+: 1-6
Track : LH: 3-16 **RH: 4-14 Tight: 4-7** Gall: 3-19
Aids: **Bl: 1-5** Vi: 0-0 Tstrap: 0-0 Ckp: 0-0
Best Rating: 116 5/06 NmkR 1m4f soft

Smart; Listed winner and Group placed; stays 1m6f but effective at shorter; best on a sound surface; has worn blinkers.

Muntami (IRE)

83(95) (41)**59**
8-y-o gr g Daylami (IRE)-Bashashah (IRE) (Kris)
John A Harris Chris Owens & Mrs A E Harris

Placings:0/510/000002/**5**40/**11**063244/065606-06064 **(7642)**
2009: 14^0SS, 16^6S, 14^0GF, 16^6G, 14^4SD,

	Starts	1st	2nd	3rd	Win & Pl
Career Total (Turf)	20	1	2	1	10732
Career Total (AW)	12	2	0	0	4898
74 3/07 Sthl	1m4f	(0-65)H		STD	£3071
68 2/07 Sthl	1m3f	(0-60)H		STD	£1706
80 8/04 Gowr	1m1f130y			YLD	£6326

Total win prize-money £11103

Going (Turf): Sf: 0-5 GS: 0-2 Gd: 0-5 GF: 0-7 Fm: 0-0
Distance: 5f/6f: 0-0 7f-8f: 0-3 **9f-13f: 3-13** 14f+: 0-16
Track : **LH: 2-23** RH: 0-7 Tight: 0-4 Gall: 0-4
Aids: Bl: 0-1 Vi: 0-2 Tstrap: 0-2 Ckp: 0-2
Best Rating: 80 8/04 Gowr 1m1f130y yield

Modest; effective over 1m4f; acts on Fibresand; has worn blinkers.

Muraco

(94) (58)74

5-y-o b g Bertolini (USA)-Miss Honeypenny (IRE) (Old Vic)

A M Hales Brick Farm Racing

Placings:0030150/0600-0 **(0320)**

2009: 10^{0}SD,

	Starts	1st	2nd	3rd	Win & Pl
Career Total (Turf)	9	1	0	1	3299
Career Total (AW)	3	0	0	0	

74	8/07	Ling	1m3f106y (0-70)H	G-F	£2817

Total win prize-money £2817

Going (Turf): Sf: 0-0 GS: 0-4 Gd: 0-2 **GF: 1-3** Fm: 0-0
Distance: 5f/6f: 0-0 7f-8f: 0-0 **9f-13f: 1-11** 14f+: 0-1
Track : **LH: 1-10** RH: 0-2 **Tight: 1-8** Gall: 0-1
Aids: Bl: 0-0 Vi: 0-0 Tstrap: 0-0 Ckp: 0-0
Best Rating: **74** 8/07 Ling 1m3f106y gd-fm

Muraweg (IRE)

108(98) (80)88

3-y-o b c Kheleyf (USA)-Lady Moranbon (USA) (Trempolino (USA))

J H M Gosden Hamdan Al Maktoum

Placings:5-145550 **(6594)**

2009: 8^{1}SD, 10^{4}GF, 10^{5}GF, 10^{5}GF, 11^{5}G, 10^{0}GS,

	Starts	1st	2nd	3rd	Win & Pl
Career Total (Turf)	6	0	0	0	1071
Career Total (AW)	1	1	0	0	2730

80	3/09	Ling	1m	STD	£2729

Total win prize-money £2730

Going (Turf): **Sf: 0-0 GS: 0-1 Gd: 0-2 GF: 0-3 Fm: 0-0**
Distance: 5f/6f: 0-0 **7f-8f: 1-2** 9f-13f: 0-5 14f+: 0-0
Track : **LH: 1-4** RH: 0-2 **Tight: 1-2** Gall: 0-2
Aids: Bl: 0-2 Vi: 0-0 Tstrap: 0-0 Ckp: 0-0
Best Rating: **88** 5/09 York 1m2f88y gd-fm

Useful; stays 1m2f; acts on fast ground and on Polytrack.

Murcar

105(110) (82)79

4-y-o ch g Medicean-In Luck (In The Wings)

C G Cox Peter J Skinner

Placings:641033-551642341 **(7005)**

2009: 12^{5}SD, 14^{5}S, 13^{1}GF, 14^{6}G, 14^{4}GF, 13^{2}SD, 14^{3}GF, 18^{4}G, 16^{1}SD,

	Starts	1st	2nd	3rd	Win & Pl
Career Total (Turf)	11	2	0	3	9449
Career Total (AW)	4	1	1	0	6557

82	10/09	Wolv	2m119y (0-80)H	STD	£5046
77	5/09	Newb	1m5f61y (0-75)H	G-F	£2590
60	5/08	Chep	1m2f36y	GD	£2590

Total win prize-money £10226

Going (Turf): Sf: 0-1 GS: 0-3 **Gd: 1-4 GF: 1-3** Fm: 0-0
Distance: 5f/6f: 0-0 7f-8f: 0-1 9f-13f: 1-4 **14f+: 2-10**
Track : **LH: 3-12** RH: 0-3 Tight: 1-3 Gall: 1-3
Aids: **Bl: 2-7** Vi: 0-0 Tstrap: 0-0 Ckp: 0-0
Best Rating: **82** 10/09 Wolv 2m119y stand

Fair; stays 1m6f; acts on good and faster ground and on Polytrack; has worn blinkers.

Mureb (USA)

(102) (71)

2-y-o b c Elusive Quality (USA)-Sumoto (Mtoto)

Saeed Bin Suroor Godolphin

Placings:3 **(7209)**

2009: 7^{3}SD,

	Starts	1st	2nd	3rd	Win & Pl
Career Total (Turf)	0	0	0	0	
Career Total (AW)	1	0	0	1	482

Going (Turf): **Sf: 0-0 GS: 0-0 Gd: 0-0 GF: 0-0 Fm: 0-0**
Distance: 5f/6f: 0-0 7f-8f: 0-1 9f-13f: 0-0 14f+: 0-0
Track : LH: 0-1 RH: 0-0 Tight: 0-1 Gall: 0-0
Aids: Bl: 0-0 Vi: 0-0 Tstrap: 0-0 Ckp: 0-0
Best Rating: **71** 11/09 Wolv 7f32y stand

Fair debut over 7f on Polytrack.

Murfreesboro

(111) (98)90

6-y-o b g Bahamian Bounty-Merry Rous (Rousillon (USA))

A E Jones (D Shaw 15/1) BPD Ltd

Placings:0121/0200/0400064/303550230204-33 **(0171)**

2009: 8^{3}SD, 10^{3}SD,

	Starts	1st	2nd	3rd	Win & Pl
Career Total (Turf)	13	2	2	0	135312
Career Total (AW)	16	0	2	5	9006

95	9/05	NmkR	6f	GD	£125300
87	6/05	Rdcr	6f	G-F	£3932

Total win prize-money £129233

Going (Turf): Sf: 0-0 GS: 0-0 **Gd: 1-5 GF: 1-6** Fm: 0-1
Distance: **5f/6f: 2-9** 7f-8f: 0-10 9f-13f: 0-10 14f+: 0-0
Track : LH: 0-12 RH: 0-6 Tight: 0-9 Gall: 0-3
Aids: Bl: 0-4 Vi: 0-6 Tstrap: 0-0 Ckp: 0-0
Best Rating: **98** 1/08 Wolv 1m141y stand

Useful; effective at up to 1m4f; acts on fast ground and Polytrack; has worn various headgear.

Murhee (USA)

91(102) (62)62

3-y-o b c Rahy (USA)-Grand Ogygia (USA) (Ogygian (USA))

D R Lanigan Saif Ali & Saeed H Altayer

Placings:00-560 **(5035)**

2009: 8^{5}SD, 8^{6}GF, 10^{0}GF,

	Starts	1st	2nd	3rd	Win & Pl
Career Total (Turf)	3	0	0	0	0
Career Total (AW)	2	0	0	0	0

Going (Turf): **Sf: 0-0 GS: 0-1 Gd: 0-0 GF: 0-2 Fm: 0-0**
Distance: 5f/6f: 0-0 7f-8f: 0-3 9f-13f: 0-2 14f+: 0-0
Track : LH: 0-1 RH: 0-3 Tight: 0-2 Gall: 0-1
Aids: Bl: 0-1 Vi: 0-0 Tstrap: 0-0 Ckp: 0-0
Best Rating: **62** 6/09 Wind 1m67y gd-fm

Signs of ability on debut over 7f on easy ground.

Murrays Magic (IRE)

90(46) 43

3-y-o b f Bahri (USA)-Fiina (Most Welcome)

D Nicholls T Murray

Placings:004-00 **(1481)**

2009: 7^{0}GF, 8^{0}SD,

	Starts	1st	2nd	3rd	Win & Pl
Career Total (Turf)	4	0	0	0	0
Career Total (AW)	1	0	0	0	

Going (Turf): **Sf: 0-2 GS: 0-0 Gd: 0-1 GF: 0-1 Fm: 0-0**
Distance: 5f/6f: 0-1 7f-8f: 0-4 9f-13f: 0-0 14f+: 0-0
Track : LH: 0-2 RH: 0-1 Tight: 0-2 Gall: 0-0
Aids: Bl: 0-0 Vi: 0-0 Tstrap: 0-0 Ckp: 0-0
Best Rating: **43** 10/08 Rdcr 1m good

Murrin (IRE)

100(105) (81)74

5-y-o b/br g Trans Island-Flimmering (Dancing Brave (USA))

T G Mills Miss J A Leighs

Placings:65154/461000/26053401555006-132344054206 **(7362)**

2009: 8^{1}SD, 8^{3}SD, 8^{2}SD, 8^{3}SD, 7^{4}GF, 8^{4}SD, 8^{0}GF, 8^{5}GF, 7^{4}GF, 8^{2}SS, 8^{0}SD, 8^{6}SD,

	Starts	1st	2nd	3rd	Win & Pl
Career Total (Turf)	15	1	0	0	4034
Career Total (AW)	22	3	3	3	14199

74	1/09	GrLe	1m	(0-75)H	STD	£2590
81	8/08	Ling	1m	(0-70)H	STD	£3238
83	6/07	Gdwd	1m	(0-75)H	G-F	£3562
73	9/06	Ling	7f		STD	£3238

Total win prize-money £12629

Going (Turf): Sf: 0-2 GS: 0-0 Gd: 0-4 **GF: 1-9** Fm: 0-0
Distance: 5f/6f: 0-0 **7f-8f: 4-31** 9f-13f: 0-6 14f+: 0-0
Track : **LH: 3-19** RH: 1-16 **Tight: 2-18** Gall: 1-1
Aids: Bl: 0-1 Vi: 0-0 Tstrap: 0-3 Ckp: 0-3
Best Rating: **83** 6/07 Gdwd 1m gd-fm

Modest; effective over 1m; acts on fast ground and on Polytrack; has worn cheekpieces.

Murrumbidgee (IRE)

103 (61)60

6-y-o gr g Bluebird (USA)-Blanche Neige (USA) (Lit De Justice (USA))

Mike Murphy D J Ellis

Placings:0000/542660216530360/4225450004/441 **(2608)**

2009: 9^{4}GF, 10^{4}GF, 10^{1}GF,

	Starts	1st	2nd	3rd	Win & Pl
Career Total (Turf)	23	2	4	2	10795
Career Total (AW)	9	0	0	0	241

60	6/09	Nott	1m2f50y (0-60)H	G-F	£2047
68	6/06	Sals	1m (0-70)H	GD	£3562

Total win prize-money £5609

Going (Turf): Sf: 0-0 GS: 0-2 **Gd: 1-7 GF: 1-11** Fm: 0-3
Distance: 5f/6f: 0-0 7f-8f: 1-17 9f-13f: 1-15 14f+: 0-0
Track : **LH: 1-18** RH: 0-9 Tight: 0-14 Gall: 0-1
Aids: Bl: 0-0 Vi: 0-3 Tstrap: 0-1 Ckp: 0-1
Best Rating: **68** 7/06 NmkJ 1m gd-sft

Moderate gelding; stays 1m2f; acts on fast ground; has worn a visor, tongue tie and cheekpieces.

Musaafer (IRE)

100(91) (76)98

2-y-o b c Marju (IRE)-Alexander Icequeen (IRE) (Soviet Star (USA))

M A Jarvis Hamdan Al Maktoum

Placings:210 **(7017)**

2009: 8^{2}SD, 8^{1}GF, 8^{0}GS,

	Starts	1st	2nd	3rd	Win & Pl
Career Total (Turf)	2	1	0	0	5181
Career Total (AW)	1	0	1	0	1542

92 9/09 Pont 1m4y G-F £5180
Total win prize-money £5181

Going (Turf): Sf: 0-0 GS: 0-1 Gd: 0-0 **GF: 1-1** Fm: 0-0
Distance: 5f/6f: 0-0 7f-8f: 0-2 **9f-13f: 1-1** 14f+: 0-0
Track : **LH: 1-1** RH: 0-1 Tight: 0-0 Gall: 0-0
Aids: Bl: 0-0 Vi: 0-0 Tstrap: 0-0 Ckp: 0-0
Best Rating: 98 10/09 Donc 1m gd-sft

Very useful; stays 1m; acts on fast ground and on Polytrack.

Musaalem (USA)

107 110
5-y-o gr g Aljabr (USA)-Atyab (USA) (Mr Prospector (USA))
W J Haggas Hamdan Al Maktoum

Placings:1/1100-501041 **(6487)**
2009: 6^5GF, 7^0GF, 7^1G, 7^0G, 6^4GF, 7^1GF,

	Starts	1st	2nd	3rd	Win & Pl
Career Total (Turf)	11	5	0	0	43422

110 10/09 Rdcr 7f G-F £22708
105 7/09 Donc 7f (0-95)H GD £7771
101 6/08 Donc 6f (0-95)H G-F £6799
95 5/08 Yarm 7f3y (0-75)H G-F £2590
58 8/07 Wwck 7f26y G-F £2590
Total win prize-money £42460

Going (Turf): Sf: 0-0 GS: 0-0 Gd: 1-2 **GF: 4-9** Fm: 0-0
Distance: 5f/6f: 1-3 **7f-8f: 4-8** 9f-13f: 0-0 14f+: 0-0
Track : **LH: 1-1** RH: 0-0 Tight: 0-0 Gall: 0-0
Aids: Bl: 0-0 Vi: 0-0 Tstrap: 0-0 Ckp: 0-0
Best Rating: 110 10/09 Rdcr 7f gd-fm

Smart; effective over 6f-7f and acts on fast ground.

Musashi (IRE)

92(105) (75)56
4-y-o ch g Hawk Wing (USA)-Soubrette (USA) (Opening Verse (USA))
Mrs L J Mongan (T P Tate 18/5) Mrs P J Sheen

Placings:06404/623-5460050 **(7549)**
2009: 11^5SD, 9^4GF, 12^6SD, 10^0SD, 10^0SD, 11^5G, 12^0SD,

	Starts	1st	2nd	3rd	Win & Pl
Career Total (Turf)	6	0	0	0	625
Career Total (AW)	9	0	1	1	1621

Going (Turf): Sf: 0-1 GS: 0-1 Gd: 0-1 GF: 0-3 Fm: 0-0
Distance: 5f/6f: 0-1 7f-8f: 0-3 9f-13f: 0-11 14f+: 0-0
Track : LH: 0-8 RH: 0-2 Tight: 0-7 Gall: 0-2
Aids: Bl: 0-1 Vi: 0-0 Tstrap: 0-1 Ckp: 0-1
Best Rating: 75 12/08 GrLe 1m2f stand

Modest; stays 1m2f; acts on fast ground; goes on Polytrack.

Musca (IRE)

82 78
5-y-o b g Tendulkar (USA)-Canary Bird (IRE) (Catrail (USA))
J Wade John Wade

Placings:21/364460/3560-00 **(2235)**
2009: 6^0G, 7^0GS,

	Starts	1st	2nd	3rd	Win & Pl
Career Total (Turf)	14	1	1	2	8231

83 10/06 Catt 7f SFT £2730
Total win prize-money £2730

Going (Turf): Sf: 1-4 GS: 0-1 Gd: 0-5 GF: 0-4 Fm: 0-0
Distance: 5f/6f: 0-2 **7f-8f: 1-11** 9f-13f: 0-1 14f+: 0-0
Track : **LH: 1-6** RH: 0-2 **Tight: 1-2** Gall: 0-2
Aids: Bl: 0-0 Vi: 0-0 Tstrap: 0-0 Ckp: 0-0
Best Rating: 84 5/07 York 7f good

Mushagak (IRE)

(83) (58)
2-y-o b f Oratorio (IRE)-Tetou (IRE) (Peintre Celebre (USA))
E A L Dunlop Mrs Susan Roy

Placings:0 **(7622)**
2009: 8^0SD,

	Starts	1st	2nd	3rd	Win & Pl
Career Total (Turf)	0	0	0	0	
Career Total (AW)	1	0	0	0	

Going (Turf): Sf: 0-0 GS: 0-0 Gd: 0-0 GF: 0-0 Fm: 0-0
Distance: 5f/6f: 0-0 7f-8f: 0-1 9f-13f: 0-0 14f+: 0-0
Track : LH: 0-1 RH: 0-0 Tight: 0-1 Gall: 0-0
Aids: Bl: 0-0 Vi: 0-0 Tstrap: 0-0 Ckp: 0-0
Best Rating: 58 12/09 Ling 1m stand

Mushreq (USA)

91 69
2-y-o b c Distorted Humor (USA)-Casual Look (USA) (Red Ransom (USA))
Sir Michael Stoute Hamdan Al Maktoum

Placings:45 **(6451)**
2009: 7^4G, 7^5GF,

	Starts	1st	2nd	3rd	Win & Pl
Career Total (Turf)	2	0	0	0	361

Going (Turf): Sf: 0-0 GS: 0-0 Gd: 0-1 GF: 0-1 Fm: 0-0
Distance: 5f/6f: 0-0 7f-8f: 0-2 9f-13f: 0-0 14f+: 0-0
Track : LH: 0-0 RH: 0-0 Tight: 0-0 Gall: 0-0
Aids: Bl: 0-0 Vi: 0-0 Tstrap: 0-0 Ckp: 0-0
Best Rating: 69 10/09 NmkR 7f gd-fm

Modest son of the Oaks winner Casual Look; ordinary form at 7f but will stay much further.

Musiara

85 49
2-y-o b f Hunting Lion (IRE)-Search Party (Rainbow Quest (USA))
M R Channon Dave and Gill Hedley

Placings:463204000 **(6215)**
2009: 5^4GF, 5^6GF, 5^3GF, 5^2GF, 6^0GS, 5^4GF, 7^0G, 8^0G, 8^0GF,

	Starts	1st	2nd	3rd	Win & Pl
Career Total (Turf)	9	0	1	1	2104

Going (Turf): Sf: 0-0 GS: 0-1 Gd: 0-2 GF: 0-6 Fm: 0-0
Distance: 5f/6f: 0-6 7f-8f: 0-2 9f-13f: 0-1 14f+: 0-0
Track : LH: 0-1 RH: 0-0 Tight: 0-1 Gall: 0-0
Aids: Bl: 0-0 Vi: 0-0 Tstrap: 0-0 Ckp: 0-0
Best Rating: 49 4/09 Donc 5f gd-fm

Plating-class; effective at 5f on fast ground.

Music Box Express

99(105) (70)76
5-y-o b g Tale Of The Cat (USA)-Aly McBe (USA) (Alydeed (CAN))
George Baker The Betfair Radioheads

Placings:0313/035265150055220414100-44300034230000 **(7819)**
2009: 6^4SD, 5^4SD, 5^3SD, 6^0GF, 6^0GF, 6^0G, 5^3GS, 6^4GF, 5^2GF, 5^3GF, 6^0GF, 5^0GF, 6^0SD, 5^0SD,

	Starts	1st	2nd	3rd	Win & Pl
Career Total (Turf)	18	2	3	2	7594
Career Total (AW)	21	2	1	4	7412

76 9/08 Wwck 6f (0-65)H GD £2047
66 9/08 Ling 6f (0-50)H GD £2729
69 3/08 Wolv 5f216y (0-65)H STD £2047
61 12/07 Wolv 5f20y STD £2968
Total win prize-money £9794

Going (Turf): Sf: 0-1 GS: 0-2 **Gd: 2-6** GF: 0-8 Fm: 0-1
Distance: **5f/6f: 4-37** 7f-8f: 0-2 9f-13f: 0-0 14f+: 0-0
Track : **LH: 3-26** RH: 0-2 **Tight: 2-15** Gall: 0-3
Aids: Bl: 0-1 Vi: 0-0 Tstrap: 0-1 Ckp: 0-1
Best Rating: 76 9/08 Wwck 6f good

Moderate; effective over 5f-6f; acts on fast ground; also goes on Polytrack; has worn a tongue tie.

Music Maestro (IRE)

93(105) (77)74
2-y-o b g Oratorio (IRE)-Adjalisa (IRE) (Darshaan)
B W Hills Triermore Stud

Placings:6242 **(7209)**
2009: 7^6S, 7^2S, 8^4SD, 7^2SD,

	Starts	1st	2nd	3rd	Win & Pl
Career Total (Turf)	2	0	1	0	1590
Career Total (AW)	2	0	1	0	964

Going (Turf): Sf: 0-2 GS: 0-0 Gd: 0-0 GF: 0-0 Fm: 0-0
Distance: 5f/6f: 0-0 7f-8f: 0-3 9f-13f: 0-1 14f+: 0-0
Track : LH: 0-3 RH: 0-1 Tight: 0-3 Gall: 0-0
Aids: Bl: 0-0 Vi: 0-0 Tstrap: 0-0 Ckp: 0-0
Best Rating: 77 11/09 Wolv 7f32y stand

Fair; effective over 7f; acts on Polytrack.

Music Of The Moor (IRE)

97 76
2-y-o ch g Rock Of Gibraltar (IRE)-A La Longue (GER) (Mtoto)
T P Tate The Ivy Syndicate

Placings:4420503 **(7218)**
2009: 6^4G, 7^4GF, 8^2GS, 8^0G, 8^5GF, 8^0GF, 7^3S,

	Starts	1st	2nd	3rd	Win & Pl
Career Total (Turf)	7	0	1	1	2482

Going (Turf): Sf: 0-1 GS: 0-1 Gd: 0-2 GF: 0-3 Fm: 0-0
Distance: 5f/6f: 0-1 7f-8f: 0-3 9f-13f: 0-3 14f+: 0-0
Track : LH: 0-6 RH: 0-0 Tight: 0-2 Gall: 0-0
Aids: Bl: 0-1 Vi: 0-0 Tstrap: 0-0 Ckp: 0-0
Best Rating: 76 8/09 Hayd 1m30y gd-sft

Modest; stays 1m; acts on easy ground.

Music Show (IRE)

110 110
2-y-o b f Noverre (USA)-Dreamboat (USA) (Mr Prospector (USA))
M R Channon Jaber Abdullah

Placings:1101 **(6852)**

2009: 5^{1}G, 5^{1}F, 6^{0}G, 7^{1}G,

	Starts	1st	2nd	3rd	Win & Pl
Career Total (Turf)	4	3	0	0	51568

110 10/09 NmkR 7f GD £45416
93 8/09 Bath 5f161y FRM £3950
80 8/09 Bath 5f161y GD £2201
Total win prize-money £51568

Going (Turf): Sf: 0-0 GS: 0-0 **Gd: 2-3** GF: 0-0 Fm: 1-1
Distance: **5f/6f: 2-3** 7f-8f: 1-1 9f-13f: 0-0 14f+: 0-0
Track : **LH: 2-2** RH: 0-0 Tight: 0-0 **Gall: 2-2**
Aids: Bl: 0-0 Vi: 0-0 Tstrap: 0-0 Ckp: 0-0
Best Rating: **110** 10/09 NmkR 7f good

Very useful; won the Group 2 Rockfel Stakes; effective over 7f; acts on fast ground.

Musical Bridge

101(94) (62)**78**
3-y-o b g Night Shift (USA)-Carrie Pooter (Tragic Role (USA))
Mrs L Williamson John Conway

Placings:2623620-21533030 **(7355)**
2009: 5^{2}GS, 5^{1}GF, 6^{5}G, 5^{3}GS, 5^{3}GF, 5^{0}GF, 5^{3}G, 5^{0}SD,

	Starts	1st	2nd	3rd	Win & Pl
Career Total (Turf)	13	1	4	4	8672
Career Total (AW)	2	0	0	0	

71 6/09 Nott 5f13y G-F £2590
Total win prize-money £2590

Going (Turf): Sf: 0-1 GS: 0-3 Gd: 0-3 **GF: 1-6** Fm: 0-0
Distance: **5f/6f: 1-15** 7f-8f: 0-0 9f-13f: 0-0 14f+: 0-0
Track : LH: 0-6 RH: 0-0 Tight: 0-2 Gall: 0-3
Aids: Bl: 0-0 Vi: 0-0 Tstrap: 0-0 Ckp: 0-0
Best Rating: **78** 10/08 Muss 5f gd-sft

Fair; effective over 5f; acts on most ground.

Musical Delight

75(55) **23**
2-y-o b g Oratorio (IRE)-Living Daylights (IRE) (Night Shift (USA))
A P Jarvis Geoffrey Bishop

Placings:000 **(6047)**
2009: 6^{0}SD, 6^{0}G, 7^{0}G,

	Starts	1st	2nd	3rd	Win & Pl
Career Total (Turf)	2	0	0	0	
Career Total (AW)	1	0	0	0	

Going (Turf): **Sf: 0-0 GS: 0-0 Gd: 0-2 GF: 0-0 Fm: 0-0**
Distance: 5f/6f: 0-1 7f-8f: 0-2 9f-13f: 0-0 14f+: 0-0
Track : LH: 0-1 RH: 0-1 Tight: 0-0 Gall: 0-0
Aids: Bl: 0-0 Vi: 0-0 Tstrap: 0-0 Ckp: 0-0
Best Rating: **23** 8/09 Newb 6f8y good

Musical Maze

100(89) (57)**66**
3-y-o b f Distant Music (USA)-Maze Garden (USA) (Riverman (USA))
W M Brisbourne The Nelson Pigs Might Fly Racing Club

Placings:32341240-003245630P **(4562)**
2009: 8^{0}SD, 8^{0}G, 9^{3}GF, 10^{2}GF, 9^{4}G, 10^{5}GF, 12^{6}GF, 10^{3}S, 12^{0}G, 10^{P}G,

	Starts	1st	2nd	3rd	Win & Pl
Career Total (Turf)	17	1	3	4	9205
Career Total (AW)	1	0	0	0	

66 8/08 Bevl 7f100y (0-75) SFT £2752
Total win prize-money £2752

Going (Turf): **Sf: 1-4** GS: 0-1 Gd: 0-5 GF: 0-7 Fm: 0-0
Distance: 5f/6f: 0-1 **7f-8f: 1-5** 9f-13f: 0-12 14f+: 0-0
Track : LH: 0-13 **RH: 1-3** Tight: 0-11 Gall: 0-0
Aids: Bl: 0-0 Vi: 0-0 Tstrap: 0-0 Ckp: 0-0
Best Rating: **66** 6/09 Ches 1m2f75y gd-fm

Modest; stays 1m and best on soft ground.

Musical Script (USA)

95(108) (80)**55**
6-y-o b g Stravinsky (USA)-Cyrillic (USA) (Irish River (FR))
Mouse Hamilton-Fairley The Composers

Placings:52300330021**2**/0553000635022246**25**/35231600 636421130135**1**-3203006500053240**6** **(7828)**
2009: 6^{3}SD, 6^{2}SD, 5^{0}SD, 6^{3}SD, 6^{0}SD, 6^{0}GS, 7^{6}SD, 7^{5}SD, 6^{0}SS, 7^{0}SD, 6^{0}SD, 6^{5}SD, 6^{3}SD, 7^{2}SD, 6^{4}SD, 6^{0}SD, 6^{6}SD,

	Starts	1st	2nd	3rd	Win & Pl
Career Total (Turf)	24	0	3	4	4816
Career Total (AW)	44	6	8	9	23715

79 12/08 Kemp 6f (0-70)H STD £3238
79 12/08 Kemp 6f (0-70)H STD £2590
74 10/08 Kemp 7f (0-60)H STD £2047
66 10/08 Kemp 5f (0-55)H STD £2047
65 2/08 Ling 6f (0-65)H STD £1876
67 10/06 Wolv 5f216y (0-60)H SF £2388
Total win prize-money £14188

Going (Turf): **Sf: 0-3 GS: 0-7 Gd: 0-4 GF: 0-10 Fm: 0-0**
Distance: **5f/6f: 5-54** 7f-8f: 1-13 9f-13f: 0-1 14f+: 0-0
Track : LH: 2-22 **RH: 4-30 Tight: 2-14** Gall: 0-3
Aids: **Bl: 5-42** Vi: 0-0 Tstrap: 0-7 Ckp: 0-7
Best Rating: **80** 1/09 Kemp 6f stand

Modest; effective over 5f-7f; seems to act on any ground on turf; goes on Polytrack; has worn headgear.

Musigny (USA)

100(95) (62)**65**
3-y-o b/br g Forest Wildcat (USA)-Water Rights (USA) (Kris S (USA))
Miss S E Hall (W Jarvis 20/10) Mrs J Hodgson,Miss S E Hall,C Platts

Placings:05040-00222 **(6924)**
2009: 8^{0}S, 8^{0}SD, 7^{0}GF, 7^{2}GF, 8^{2}GF,

	Starts	1st	2nd	3rd	Win & Pl
Career Total (Turf)	7	0	2	0	1253
Career Total (AW)	3	0	0	0	216

Going (Turf): **Sf: 0-3 GS: 0-0 Gd: 0-1 GF: 0-3 Fm: 0-0**
Distance: 5f/6f: 0-0 7f-8f: 0-6 9f-13f: 0-4 14f+: 0-0
Track : LH: 0-4 RH: 0-1 Tight: 0-2 Gall: 0-0
Aids: Bl: 0-0 Vi: 0-0 Tstrap: 0-0 Ckp: 0-0
Best Rating: **65** 10/08 Nott 1m75y soft

Plating-class; stays 1m and acts on quick ground.

Musleh (USA)

(105) (98)
3-y-o b c Forestry (USA)-Lucifer's Stone (USA) (Horse Chestnut (SAF))
Saeed Bin Suroor Godolphin

Placings:21-1103 **(6229)**
2009: 8^{1}SD, 8^{1}SD, 8^{0}SD, 8^{3}SD,

	Starts	1st	2nd	3rd	Win & Pl
Career Total (Turf)	0	0	0	0	
Career Total (AW)	6	3	1	1	17706

98 8/09 Kemp 1m (0-95)H STD £7352
92 8/09 Kemp 1m (0-85)H STD £4727
77 10/08 Ling 7f STD £3561
Total win prize-money £15642

Going (Turf): **Sf: 0-0 GS: 0-0 Gd: 0-0 GF: 0-0 Fm: 0-0**
Distance: 5f/6f: 0-0 **7f-8f: 3-6** 9f-13f: 0-0 14f+: 0-0
Track : LH: 1-2 **RH: 2-4 Tight: 1-2** Gall: 0-0
Aids: Bl: 0-0 Vi: 0-0 Tstrap: 0-0 Ckp: 0-0
Best Rating: **98** 8/09 Kemp 1m stand

Very useful; stays 1m and acts on Polytrack.

Mustajed

93(107) (79)**86**
8-y-o b g Alhaarth (IRE)-Jasarah (IRE) (Green Desert (USA))
B R Millman Mrs L S Millman

Placings:1/60/0062132301/3/**0**023641004**140**/6035450020250**63**-**611**650323304 **(7761)**
2009: 12^{6}SD, 12^{1}SD, 11^{1}SD, 10^{6}S, 12^{5}GF, 10^{0}GF, 12^{3}G, 12^{2}S, 12^{3}G, 11^{3}GF, 11^{0}GF, 11^{4}SD,

	Starts	1st	2nd	3rd	Win & Pl
Career Total (Turf)	39	4	4	8	48042
Career Total (AW)	15	3	2	1	14789

79 2/09 Sthl 1m3f (0-70)H STD £2729
79 1/09 Ling 1m4f (0-70)H STD £2472
85 8/07 Kemp 1m3f (0-90)H STD £6855
91 6/07 Sals 1m4f (0-85)H G-F £5181
90 10/05 Bath 1m3f144y (0-85)H G-F £6123
87 7/05 Sand 1m2f7y (0-90)H G-F £8847
83 5/03 Newb 5f34y D GD £7247
Total win prize-money £39458

Going (Turf): Sf: 0-4 GS: 0-7 Gd: 1-11 **GF: 3-17** Fm: 0-0
Distance: 5f/6f: 1-1 7f-8f: 0-4 **9f-13f: 6-46** 14f+: 0-3
Track : LH: 3-25 RH: 3-24 **Tight: 3-19** Gall: 0-15
Aids: Bl: 0-4 Vi: 0-4 Tstrap: 0-1 Ckp: 0-1
Best Rating: **92** 8/07 Asct 1m4f gd-fm

Fair; effective at around 1m4f; acts on most ground on turf and on sand; has worn blinkers

Mustakhlas (USA)

(80) (9)**46**
8-y-o ch g Diesis-Katiba (USA) (Gulch (USA))
B P J Baugh Miss S M Potts

Placings:0/0050600/0510000054/30000/0 **(7842)**
2009: 14^{0}SS,

	Starts	1st	2nd	3rd	Win & Pl
Career Total (Turf)	6	0	0	0	0
Career Total (AW)	18	1	0	1	1647

54 3/06 Wolv 1m4f50y (0-45) STD £1365
Total win prize-money £1365

Going (Turf): **Sf: 0-0 GS: 0-0 Gd: 0-4 GF: 0-2 Fm: 0-0**
Distance: 5f/6f: 0-0 7f-8f: 0-2 **9f-13f: 1-14** 14f+: 0-8
Track : **LH: 1-20** RH: 0-3 **Tight: 1-18** Gall: 0-0
Aids: Bl: 0-0 Vi: 0-0 Tstrap: 0-1 Ckp: 0-1
Best Rating: **54** 12/06 Wolv 1m5f194y stand

Mustakmil (IRE)

99(104) (83)**76**
3-y-o b c Haafhd-Elfaslah (IRE) (Green Desert (USA))
S Dow (E A L Dunlop 12/9) Simon Caunce

Placings:3023411 **(7769)**
2009: 8^{3}G, 10^{0}S, 8^{2}G, 8^{3}G, 10^{4}GF, 8^{1}SD, 8^{1}SD,

	Starts	1st	2nd	3rd	Win & Pl
Career Total (Turf)	5	0	1	2	1986
Career Total (AW)	2	2	0	0	7318

83 12/09 Kemp 1m (0-85)H STD £4727
76 11/09 Ling 1m STD £2590
Total win prize-money £7317

Going (Turf): **Sf: 0-1 GS: 0-0 Gd: 0-3 GF: 0-1 Fm: 0-0**
Distance: 5f/6f: 0-0 **7f-8f: 2-4** 9f-13f: 0-3 14f+: 0-0
Track : LH: 1-4 RH: 1-3 **Tight: 1-4** Gall: 0-1
Aids: Bl: 0-0 Vi: 0-0 Tstrap: 0-0 Ckp: 0-0
Best Rating: **83** 12/09 Kemp 1m stand

Fair; stays 1m; acts on good ground and on Polytrack.

Mustaqer (IRE)

98 **90**
3-y-o b g Dalakhani (IRE)-Al Ihtithar (IRE) (Barathea (IRE))
B W Hills Hamdan Al Maktoum

Placings:251-00 **(2935)**
2009: 10^{0}G, 10^{0}G,

	Starts	1st	2nd	3rd	Win & Pl
Career Total (Turf)	5	1	1	0	12608

83 10/08 NmkR 1m GD £6152
Total win prize-money £6152

Going (Turf): Sf: 0-1 GS: 0-1 **Gd: 1-3** GF: 0-0 Fm: 0-0
Distance: 5f/6f: 0-0 **7f-8f: 1-3** 9f-13f: 0-2 14f+: 0-0
Track : LH: 0-2 RH: 0-0 Tight: 0-1 Gall: 0-1
Aids: Bl: 0-0 Vi: 0-0 Tstrap: 0-0 Ckp: 0-0
Best Rating: **90** 8/08 Newb 7f gd-sft

Useful; placed in Listed company; stays 1m; acts on good and easier ground; likes to race prominently.

Mut'Ab (USA)

105(103) (90)**93**
4-y-o b g Alhaarth (IRE)-Mistle Song (Nashwan (USA))
C E Brittain Saeed Manana

Placings:320/051000-0020 **(2402)**
2009: 7^{0}SD, 8^{0}G, 6^{2}GF, 7^{0}GF,

	Starts	1st	2nd	3rd	Win & Pl
Career Total (Turf)	9	1	2	1	7838
Career Total (AW)	4	0	0	0	

87 7/08 Yarm 7f3y G-F £2719
Total win prize-money £2720

Going (Turf): Sf: 0-0 GS: 0-1 Gd: 0-5 **GF: 1-3** Fm: 0-0
Distance: 5f/6f: 0-0 **7f-8f: 1-11** 9f-13f: 0-2 14f+: 0-0
Track : LH: 0-4 RH: 0-5 Tight: 0-2 Gall: 0-2
Aids: **Bl: 1-7** Vi: 0-0 Tstrap: 0-0 Ckp: 0-0
Best Rating: **93** 4/08 Sand 1m2f7y good

Useful; stays 1m; acts on good or softer ground and on Polytrack; has worn blinkers; likes to race prominently.

Mutafajer

88(99) (78)**64**
2-y-o b/br c Oasis Dream-Shahaamah (IRE) (Red Ransom (USA))
Saeed Bin Suroor Godolphin

Placings:532 **(7234)**
2009: 6^{5}G, 7^{3}SD, 6^{2}SD,

	Starts	1st	2nd	3rd	Win & Pl
Career Total (Turf)	1	0	0	0	0
Career Total (AW)	2	0	1	1	1638

Going (Turf): **Sf: 0-0 GS: 0-0 Gd: 0-1 GF: 0-0 Fm: 0-0**
Distance: 5f/6f: 0-1 7f-8f: 0-2 9f-13f: 0-0 14f+: 0-0
Track : LH: 0-0 RH: 0-2 Tight: 0-0 Gall: 0-0
Aids: Bl: 0-0 Vi: 0-0 Tstrap: 0-0 Ckp: 0-0
Best Rating: **78** 11/09 Kemp 6f stand

Fair; stays 6f; acts on Polytrack.

Mutajaaser (USA)

70(98) (63)**11**
4-y-o b g War Chant (USA)-Hazimah (USA) (Gone West (USA))
K A Morgan P Doughty

Placings:05 **(7671)**
2009: 7^{0}G, 8^{5}SD,

	Starts	1st	2nd	3rd	Win & Pl
Career Total (Turf)	1	0	0	0	
Career Total (AW)	1	0	0	0	0

Going (Turf): **Sf: 0-0 GS: 0-0 Gd: 0-1 GF: 0-0 Fm: 0-0**
Distance: 5f/6f: 0-0 7f-8f: 0-1 9f-13f: 0-1 14f+: 0-0
Track : LH: 0-2 RH: 0-0 Tight: 0-2 Gall: 0-0
Aids: Bl: 0-0 Vi: 0-0 Tstrap: 0-0 Ckp: 0-0
Best Rating: **63** 12/09 Wolv 1m141y stand

Well bred; got upset in stalls and well beaten on belated debut.

Mutajarred

91(112) (113)**108**
5-y-o ch g Alhaarth (IRE)-Bedara (Barathea (IRE))
W J Haggas Hamdan Al Maktoum

Placings:4/11142/21020-00 **(4543)**
2009: 10^{0}GS, 8^{0}G,

	Starts	1st	2nd	3rd	Win & Pl
Career Total (Turf)	12	3	3	0	37359
Career Total (AW)	1	1	0	0	6939

113 5/08 GrLe 1m2f STD £6938
105 7/07 Nott 1m54y (0-85)H HVY £5608
97 7/07 York 1m (0-90)H SFT £9715
78 6/07 Hayd 1m30y HVY £2817
Total win prize-money £25081

Going (Turf): **Sf: 3-5** GS: 0-5 Gd: 0-2 GF: 0-0 Fm: 0-0
Distance: 5f/6f: 0-1 7f-8f: 1-3 **9f-13f: 3-9** 14f+: 0-0
Track : **LH: 4-8** RH: 0-1 Tight: 0-0 **Gall: 2-5**
Aids: Bl: 0-1 Vi: 0-0 Tstrap: 0-0 Ckp: 0-0
Best Rating: **113** 5/08 GrLe 1m2f stand

Smart; effective from 1m-1m2f; acts well in soft ground and on Polytrack; has worn a visor and blinkers; likes to race prominently.

Mutamaashi

104(107) (94)**99**
3-y-o b g Sakhee (USA)-Almahab (USA) (Danzig (USA))
W J Haggas Hamdan Al Maktoum

Placings:12303213 **(6665)**
2009: 8^{1}SD, 8^{2}GF, 10^{3}GF, 8^{0}GF, 10^{3}S, 10^{2}SD, 10^{1}GF, 10^{3}GS,

	Starts	1st	2nd	3rd	Win & Pl
Career Total (Turf)	6	1	1	3	33200
Career Total (AW)	2	1	1	0	5042

94 9/09 Ches 1m2f75y (0-105)H G-F £28195
82 2/09 Ling 1m STD £2729
Total win prize-money £30925

Going (Turf): Sf: 0-1 GS: 0-1 Gd: 0-0 **GF: 1-4** Fm: 0-0
Distance: 5f/6f: 0-0 7f-8f: 1-3 9f-13f: 1-5 14f+: 0-0
Track : **LH: 2-3** RH: 0-3 **Tight: 2-4** Gall: 0-2
Aids: Bl: 0-0 Vi: 0-0 Tstrap: 0-0 Ckp: 0-0
Best Rating: **99** 10/09 Asct 1m2f gd-sft

Very useful; stays 1m2f; acts on fast ground; goes on Polytrack.

Mutamared (USA)

101(111) (94)**99**
9-y-o ch g Nureyev (USA)-Alydariel (USA) (Alydar (USA))
M J Scudamore (Andrew Reid 24/10) A S Reid

Placings:226/130/461010/110021/00352000600/00003421 31-111125430502064160000 **(7656)**
2009: 6^{1}SD, 6^{1}SD, 7^{1}SD, 6^{1}SD, 5^{2}SD, 7^{5}SD, 7^{4}SD, 6^{3}SD, 6^{0}GF, 6^{5}G, 6^{0}GS, 6^{2}GF, 5^{0}SD, 6^{6}G, 7^{4}SD, 6^{1}GF, 6^{6}SD, 6^{0}SS, 6^{0}SD, 6^{0}SD, 6^{0}SD,

	Starts	1st	2nd	3rd	Win & Pl
Career Total (Turf)	33	5	5	1	89931
Career Total (AW)	27	8	2	4	62261

82 9/09 Gdwd 6f (0-85)H G-F £4984
89 2/09 Ling 6f (0-85)H STD £4857
84 1/09 Ling 7f STD £2047
83 1/09 Ling 6f STD £2047
81 1/09 Kemp 6f STD £1978
85 12/08 Ling 6f STD £2047
79 10/08 Kemp 6f STD £2047
110 9/06 Kemp 6f (0-100)H STD £24928
106 5/06 NmkR 6f H G-F £31160
97 4/06 Ling 6f (0-100)H STD £12464
96 9/05 Sals 6f (0-85)H GD £7472
92 9/05 NmkJ 6f (0-85)H G-F £7159
87 5/04 Thsk 7f D FRM £5512
Total win prize-money £108705

Going (Turf): Sf: 0-1 GS: 0-4 Gd: 1-10 **GF: 3-16** Fm: 1-1
Distance: **5f/6f: 11-46** 7f-8f: 2-14 9f-13f: 0-0 14f+: 0-0
Track : **LH: 6-21** RH: 3-11 **Tight: 6-16** Gall: 0-6
Aids: Bl: 0-0 Vi: 0-0 Tstrap: 0-0 Ckp: 0-0
Best Rating: **110** 9/06 Kemp 6f stand

Useful; formerly smart; effective over 6f-7f; acts on fast ground and on sand; usually held up; has worn a tongue tie.

Mutamayez

(100) (77)
3-y-o b c Dalakhani (IRE)-Blue Oasis (IRE) (Sadler's Wells (USA))
M A Jarvis Hamdan Al Maktoum

Placings:1 **(6287)**
2009: 10^{1}SD,

	Starts	1st	2nd	3rd	Win & Pl
Career Total (Turf)	0	0	0	0	
Career Total (AW)	1	1	0	0	2590

77 9/09 Kemp 1m2f STD £2590
Total win prize-money £2590

Going (Turf): **Sf: 0-0 GS: 0-0 Gd: 0-0 GF: 0-0 Fm: 0-0**
Distance: 5f/6f: 0-0 7f-8f: 0-0 **9f-13f: 1-1** 14f+: 0-0
Track : LH: 0-0 **RH: 1-1** Tight: 0-0 Gall: 0-0
Aids: Bl: 0-0 Vi: 0-0 Tstrap: 0-0 Ckp: 0-0
Best Rating: **77** 9/09 Kemp 1m2f stand

Fair winning debut over 1m2f on Polytrack.

Mutawarath (IRE)

102(94) (72)**87**
3-y-o b c Marju (IRE)-Castlerahan (IRE) (Thatching)
W J Haggas Hamdan Al Maktoum

Placings:041404 **(6474)**
2009: 8^{0}GF, 8^{4}G, 8^{1}G, 7^{4}S, 8^{0}SD, 8^{4}GF,

	Starts	1st	2nd	3rd	Win & Pl
Career Total (Turf)	5	1	0	0	7787
Career Total (AW)	1	0	0	0	

83 6/09 York 1m GD £6540
Total win prize-money £6541

Going (Turf): Sf: 0-1 GS: 0-0 **Gd: 1-2** GF: 0-2 Fm: 0-0
Distance: 5f/6f: 0-0 **7f-8f: 1-4** 9f-13f: 0-2 14f+: 0-0
Track : **LH: 1-3** RH: 0-2 Tight: 0-1 **Gall: 1-1**
Aids: Bl: 0-0 Vi: 0-0 Tstrap: 0-0 Ckp: 0-0
Best Rating: 87 10/09 Epsm 1m114y gd-fm

Useful; brother to German Guineas winner Brunel; effective over 1m; acts on good ground.

Mutayam

83 46
9-y-o b g Compton Place-Final Shot (Dalsaan)
D A Nolan Miss M McFadyen-Murray

Placings:000/460520000/6060100/00050060/00000/0006 00500/000000500-060 (3445)
2009: 5[0]GF, 5[6]GF, 5[0]GF,

	Starts	1st	2nd	3rd	Win & Pl
Career Total (Turf)	53	1	1	0	5488

55 9/04 Newc 5f GD £3454
Total win prize-money £3455

Going (Turf): Sf: 0-3 GS: 0-13 **Gd: 1-14** GF: 0-18 Fm: 0-5
Distance: **5f/6f: 1-49** 7f-8f: 0-4 9f-13f: 0-0 14f+: 0-0
Track : LH: 0-1 RH: 0-1 Tight: 0-0 Gall: 0-4
Aids: Bl: 0-0 Vi: 0-0 Tstrap: 0-5 Ckp: 0-5
Best Rating: 58 7/05 Muss 5f gd-fm

Moderate sprinter; best at 5f; wears a tongue tie; has worn cheekpieces.

Mutheeb (USA)

108(111) (105)109
4-y-o b c Danzig (USA)-Magicalmysterykate (USA) (Woodman (USA))
Saeed Bin Suroor Godolphin

Placings:1-1343 (3818)
2009: 7[1]GF, 6[3]SD, 7[4]GF, 7[3]GF,

	Starts	1st	2nd	3rd	Win & Pl
Career Total (Turf)	3	1	0	1	17896
Career Total (AW)	2	1	0	1	4035

109 4/09 Yarm 7f3y G-F £6231
77 9/08 Ling 7f STD £2590
Total win prize-money £8821

Going (Turf): Sf: 0-0 GS: 0-0 Gd: 0-0 **GF: 1-3** Fm: 0-0
Distance: 5f/6f: 0-1 **7f-8f: 2-4** 9f-13f: 0-0 14f+: 0-0
Track : **LH: 1-2** RH: 0-0 **Tight: 1-2** Gall: 0-0
Aids: Bl: 0-0 Vi: 0-0 Tstrap: 0-0 Ckp: 0-0
Best Rating: 109 4/09 Yarm 7f3y gd-fm

Smart; effective over 7f; acts on fast ground; goes on Polytrack.

Mutually Mine (USA)

97(100) (69)68
3-y-o ch f Golden Missile (USA)-Gal Of Mine (USA) (Mining (USA))
Mrs P Sly Team Speciosa

Placings:530-62363056300 (7667)
2009: 10[6]SD, 8[2]F, 8[3]GF, 8[6]GF, 7[3]GF, 7[0]GF, 8[5]GF, 8[6]GF, 9[3]SD, 10[0]SD, 9[0]SD,

	Starts	1st	2nd	3rd	Win & Pl
Career Total (Turf)	10	0	1	3	2639
Career Total (AW)	4	0	0	1	482

Going (Turf): **Sf: 0-1 GS: 0-0 Gd: 0-0 GF: 0-8 Fm: 0-1**
Distance: 5f/6f: 0-2 7f-8f: 0-5 9f-13f: 0-7 14f+: 0-0
Track : LH: 0-6 RH: 0-3 Tight: 0-5 Gall: 0-0
Aids: Bl: 0-0 Vi: 0-0 Tstrap: 0-2 Ckp: 0-2
Best Rating: 69 3/09 Ling 1m2f stand

Modest; stays 1m and acts on fast ground and on Polytrack.

Muwakaba (USA)

(91) (82)
2-y-o ch f Elusive Quality (USA)-Saleela (USA) (Nureyev (USA))
Sir Michael Stoute Hamdan Al Maktoum

Placings:1 (6163)
2009: 7[1]SD,

	Starts	1st	2nd	3rd	Win & Pl
Career Total (Turf)	0	0	0	0	
Career Total (AW)	1	1	0	0	4695

82 9/09 Kemp 7f STD £4695
Total win prize-money £4695

Going (Turf): **Sf: 0-0 GS: 0-0 Gd: 0-0 GF: 0-0 Fm: 0-0**
Distance: 5f/6f: 0-0 **7f-8f: 1-1** 9f-13f: 0-0 14f+: 0-0
Track : LH: 0-0 **RH: 1-1** Tight: 0-0 Gall: 0-0
Aids: Bl: 0-0 Vi: 0-0 Tstrap: 0-0 Ckp: 0-0
Best Rating: 82 9/09 Kemp 7f stand

Promising filly; effective at 7f; acts on Polytrack.

Muwalla

98 80
2-y-o b c Bahri (USA)-Easy Sunshine (IRE) (Sadler's Wells (USA))
C E Brittain Saeed Manana

Placings:4032 (6173)
2009: 7[4]G, 7[0]G, 8[3]GF, 7[2]GF,

	Starts	1st	2nd	3rd	Win & Pl
Career Total (Turf)	4	0	1	1	2926

Going (Turf): **Sf: 0-0 GS: 0-0 Gd: 0-2 GF: 0-2 Fm: 0-0**
Distance: 5f/6f: 0-0 7f-8f: 0-4 9f-13f: 0-0 14f+: 0-0
Track : LH: 0-1 RH: 0-1 Tight: 0-0 Gall: 0-0
Aids: Bl: 0-0 Vi: 0-0 Tstrap: 0-0 Ckp: 0-0
Best Rating: 80 9/09 Leic 7f9y gd-fm

Fair; stays 1m; acts on fast ground.

Muzmin (USA)

97 60
4-y-o b/br g Seeking The Gold (USA)-In On The Secret (CAN) (Secretariat (USA))
E A L Dunlop Hamdan Al Maktoum

Placings:5/505 (3150)
2009: 7[5]G, 8[0]G, 10[5]GF,

	Starts	1st	2nd	3rd	Win & Pl
Career Total (Turf)	4	0	0	0	0

Going (Turf): **Sf: 0-0 GS: 0-0 Gd: 0-2 GF: 0-2 Fm: 0-0**
Distance: 5f/6f: 0-0 7f-8f: 0-2 9f-13f: 0-2 14f+: 0-0
Track : LH: 0-2 RH: 0-0 Tight: 0-1 Gall: 0-0
Aids: Bl: 0-0 Vi: 0-0 Tstrap: 0-0 Ckp: 0-0
Best Rating: 72 9/07 Thsk 1m gd-fm

Modest; stays 1m2f; acts on fast ground.

Muzo (USA)

(96) (70)
3-y-o b c Gone West (USA)-Bowl Of Emeralds (USA) (A.P. Indy (USA))
J Noseda Mrs Susan Roy

Placings:43 (6974)
2009: 9[4]SD, 11[3]SD,

	Starts	1st	2nd	3rd	Win & Pl
Career Total (Turf)	0	0	0	0	
Career Total (AW)	2	0	0	1	385

Going (Turf): **Sf: 0-0 GS: 0-0 Gd: 0-0 GF: 0-0 Fm: 0-0**
Distance: 5f/6f: 0-0 7f-8f: 0-0 9f-13f: 0-2 14f+: 0-0
Track : LH: 0-1 RH: 0-1 Tight: 0-1 Gall: 0-0
Aids: Bl: 0-0 Vi: 0-0 Tstrap: 0-0 Ckp: 0-0
Best Rating: 70 10/09 Kemp 1m3f stand

My Arch

99 74
7-y-o b g Silver Patriarch (IRE)-My Desire (Grey Desire)
Ollie Pears J D Spensley & Mrs M A Spensley

Placings:3432210/0010400/0 (6681)
2009: 12[0]G,

	Starts	1st	2nd	3rd	Win & Pl
Career Total (Turf)	15	2	2	2	16402

89 5/07 Ripn 1m1f170y (0-85)H GD £5678
83 8/06 Bevl 1m1f207y G-S £3562
Total win prize-money £9240

Going (Turf): Sf: 0-0 **GS: 1-2 Gd: 1-7** GF: 0-5 Fm: 0-0
Distance: 5f/6f: 0-0 7f-8f: 0-2 **9f-13f: 2-13** 14f+: 0-0
Track : LH: 0-5 **RH: 2-9 Tight: 1-7** Gall: 0-3
Aids: **Bl: 1-1** Vi: 0-0 Tstrap: 0-2 Ckp: 0-2
Best Rating: 91 7/07 Curr 1m4f sft-hvy

Useful; stays 1m2f; acts on fast and easy ground; has worn blinkers and cheekpieces.

My Aunt Fanny

106 (71)92
4-y-o b f Nayef (USA)-Putuna (Generous (IRE))
A M Balding J C & S R Hitchins

Placings:3/43211640-560 (6106)
2009: 9[5]G, 9[6]GF, 10[0]GF,

	Starts	1st	2nd	3rd	Win & Pl
Career Total (Turf)	11	2	1	1	17856
Career Total (AW)	1	0	0	1	1120

92 7/08 Ches 1m2f75y (0-85)H G-S £5828
72 6/08 Ches 1m2f75y GD £5180
Total win prize-money £11009

Going (Turf): Sf: 0-2 **GS: 1-1 Gd: 1-2** GF: 0-6 Fm: 0-0
Distance: 5f/6f: 0-0 7f-8f: 0-2 **9f-13f: 2-10** 14f+: 0-0
Track : **LH: 2-4** RH: 0-8 **Tight: 2-8** Gall: 0-2
Aids: Bl: 0-0 Vi: 0-0 Tstrap: 0-0 Ckp: 0-0
Best Rating: 92 7/08 Ches 1m2f75y gd-sft

Useful; stays 1m2f and acts on fast and easy ground; likes to race prominently.

My Best Bet

102(102) (87)78
3-y-o ch f Best Of The Bests (IRE)-Cibenze (Owington)
Stef Liddiard (M R Channon 31/10) Ownaracehorse Ltd (ownaracehorse.co.uk)

Placings:53315-3310602253142565313 (7769)

2009: 6^{3}SD, 6^{3}SD, 6^{1}SD, 7^{0}GS, 7^{6}F, 6^{0}GF, 7^{2}GF, 7^{2}GF, 7^{5}GF, 7^{3}S, 7^{1}GF, 7^{4}GF, 7^{2}SD, 6^{5}GS, 7^{6}SD, 7^{5}SD, 7^{3}G, 8^{1}SD, 8^{3}SD,

	Starts	1st	2nd	3rd	Win & Pl
Career Total (Turf)	13	1	2	3	5908
Career Total (AW)	11	3	1	4	13111

82 11/09 Ling 1m (0-85)H STD £4727
78 8/09 Folk 7f (0-75)H G-F £2729
76 1/09 Kemp 6f (0-75)H STD £2590
71 11/08 Wolv 5f216y (0-65) STD £2388
Total win prize-money £12435

Going (Turf): Sf: 0-3 GS: 0-2 Gd: 0-1 **GF: 1-6** Fm: 0-1
Distance: 5f/6f: 2-6 7f-8f: 2-18 9f-13f: 0-0 14f+: 0-0
Track : **LH: 2-8** RH: 1-6 **Tight: 2-7** Gall: 0-0
Aids: Bl: 0-0 Vi: 0-0 Tstrap: 0-0 Ckp: 0-0
Best Rating: **87** 12/09 Kemp 1m stand

Fair; effective at 6f-7f; acts on fast and easy ground; goes on Polytrack.

My Best Man

97(93) (67)68
3-y-o b g Forzando-Victoria Sioux (Ron's Victory (USA))
B R Millman D Lowe

Placings:03230400-**53334366560** (5184)
2009: 5^{5}SD, 6^{3}SD, 8^{3}SD, 7^{3}SD, 8^{4}GF, 8^{3}G, 6^{6}GF, 8^{6}G, 5^{5}S, 6^{6}G, 5^{0}G,

	Starts	1st	2nd	3rd	Win & Pl
Career Total (Turf)	14	0	1	3	2499
Career Total (AW)	5	0	0	3	1501

Going (Turf): **Sf: 0-2 GS: 0-1 Gd: 0-4 GF: 0-7 Fm: 0-0**
Distance: 5f/6f: 0-10 7f-8f: 0-7 9f-13f: 0-2 14f+: 0-0
Track : LH: 0-7 RH: 0-0 Tight: 0-2 Gall: 0-2
Aids: Bl: 0-1 Vi: 0-0 Tstrap: 0-2 Ckp: 0-2
Best Rating: **68** 7/08 Chep 6f16y gd-fm

Modest; effective at 6f; handles Polytrack.

My Bodyguard (FR)

78(85) (33)36
3-y-o b c Alhaarth (IRE)-Hollow Dynasty (USA) (Deputy Commander (USA))
H J L Dunlop H E Sheikh Sultan Bin Khalifa Al Nahyan

Placings:000 (2743)
2009: 10^{0}GS, 12^{0}G, 12^{0}SD,

	Starts	1st	2nd	3rd	Win & Pl
Career Total (Turf)	2	0	0	0	
Career Total (AW)	1	0	0	0	

Going (Turf): **Sf: 0-0 GS: 0-1 Gd: 0-1 GF: 0-0 Fm: 0-0**
Distance: 5f/6f: 0-0 7f-8f: 0-0 9f-13f: 0-3 14f+: 0-0
Track : LH: 0-2 RH: 0-1 Tight: 0-2 Gall: 0-0
Aids: Bl: 0-1 Vi: 0-0 Tstrap: 0-0 Ckp: 0-0
Best Rating: **36** 4/09 Wind 1m2f7y gd-sft

My Boy Nick

(70)
7-y-o b g Bold Fort-Suelizelle (Carnival Dancer)
D L Williams R Williams

Placings:0 (1530)
2009: 8^{0}SD,

	Starts	1st	2nd	3rd	Win & Pl
Career Total (Turf)	0	0	0	0	
Career Total (AW)	1	0	0	0	

Going (Turf): **Sf: 0-0 GS: 0-0 Gd: 0-0 GF: 0-0 Fm: 0-0**
Distance: 5f/6f: 0-0 7f-8f: 0-0 9f-13f: 0-1 14f+: 0-0
Track : LH: 0-1 RH: 0-0 Tight: 0-1 Gall: 0-0
Aids: Bl: 0-0 Vi: 0-0 Tstrap: 0-0 Ckp: 0-0

My Chestnut Girl (USA)

100 81
3-y-o ch f Horse Chestnut (SAF)-Mien (USA) (Nureyev (USA))
H R A Cecil Malih L Al Basti

Placings:0-043421 (4599)
2009: 10^{0}G, 9^{4}GF, 9^{3}GF, 10^{4}GF, 11^{2}F, 12^{1}G,

	Starts	1st	2nd	3rd	Win & Pl
Career Total (Turf)	7	1	1	1	4577

81 8/09 Ripn 1m4f10y GD £2914
Total win prize-money £2914

Going (Turf): Sf: 0-1 GS: 0-0 **Gd: 1-2** GF: 0-3 Fm: 0-1
Distance: 5f/6f: 0-0 7f-8f: 0-0 **9f-13f: 1-7** 14f+: 0-0
Track : LH: 0-3 **RH: 1-4 Tight: 1-4** Gall: 0-0
Aids: Bl: 0-0 Vi: 0-0 Tstrap: 0-0 Ckp: 0-0
Best Rating: **81** 8/09 Ripn 1m4f10y good

Modest; stays 1m4f; acts on fast ground.

My Choice

(76) (34)27
3-y-o b g Groom Dancer (USA)-Beleza (IRE) (Revoque (IRE))
A P Jarvis Mrs Ann Jarvis

Placings:000-0 (1440)
2009: 11^{0}SD,

	Starts	1st	2nd	3rd	Win & Pl
Career Total (Turf)	2	0	0	0	
Career Total (AW)	2	0	0	0	

Going (Turf): **Sf: 0-1 GS: 0-0 Gd: 0-0 GF: 0-1 Fm: 0-0**
Distance: 5f/6f: 0-0 7f-8f: 0-3 9f-13f: 0-1 14f+: 0-0
Track : LH: 0-1 RH: 0-2 Tight: 0-0 Gall: 0-0
Aids: Bl: 0-0 Vi: 0-0 Tstrap: 0-0 Ckp: 0-0
Best Rating: **34** 8/08 Kemp 7f stand

My Condor (IRE)

(67)
8-y-o b g Beneficial-Margellen's Castle (IRE) (Castle Keep)
D McCain Jnr D McCain

Placings:0 (4857)
2009: 12^{0}SD,

	Starts	1st	2nd	3rd	Win & Pl
Career Total (Turf)	0	0	0	0	
Career Total (AW)	1	0	0	0	

Going (Turf): **Sf: 0-0 GS: 0-0 Gd: 0-0 GF: 0-0 Fm: 0-0**
Distance: 5f/6f: 0-0 7f-8f: 0-0 9f-13f: 0-1 14f+: 0-0
Track : LH: 0-1 RH: 0-0 Tight: 0-1 Gall: 0-0
Aids: Bl: 0-0 Vi: 0-0 Tstrap: 0-0 Ckp: 0-0

My Flame

102(94) (59)62
4-y-o b g Cool Jazz-Suselja (IRE) (Mon Tresor)
J R Jenkins Smart K Syndicate

Placings:0000**0**/2455500-26150004005 (7614)
2009: 7^{2}G, 7^{6}G, 6^{1}GF, 7^{5}F, 6^{0}GF, 7^{0}G, 7^{0}GF, 7^{4}SD, 7^{0}SD, 8^{0}SD, 7^{5}SD,

	Starts	1st	2nd	3rd	Win & Pl
Career Total (Turf)	14	1	2	0	4145
Career Total (AW)	9	0	0	0	0

62 4/09 Brig 6f209y (0-55)H G-F £2590
Total win prize-money £2590

Going (Turf): Sf: 0-1 GS: 0-4 Gd: 0-5 **GF: 1-3** Fm: 0-1
Distance: 5f/6f: 0-6 **7f-8f: 1-17** 9f-13f: 0-0 14f+: 0-0
Track : **LH: 1-7** RH: 0-6 Tight: 0-3 Gall: 0-1
Aids: Bl: 0-1 Vi: 0-2 Tstrap: 0-1 Ckp: 0-1
Best Rating: **62** 4/09 Brig 6f209y gd-fm

Moderate; stays 7f; acts on easy ground and Polytrack.

My Friend Fritz

(104) (75)
9-y-o ch g Safawan-Little Scarlett (Mazilier (USA))
P W Hiatt P W Hiatt

Placings:63/212143-**1404100** (2129)
2009: 14^{1}SS, 12^{4}SS, 14^{0}SD, 12^{4}SD, 12^{1}SD, 16^{0}SD, 12^{0}SD,

	Starts	1st	2nd	3rd	Win & Pl
Career Total (Turf)	0	0	0	0	
Career Total (AW)	15	4	2	2	10298

69 3/09 Sthl 1m4f STD £2047
73 1/09 Sthl 1m6f (0-75)H SS £2590
75 3/08 Sthl 1m4f (0-65)H STD £1911
62 2/08 Sthl 1m4f STD £1774
Total win prize-money £8323

Going (Turf): **Sf: 0-0 GS: 0-0 Gd: 0-0 GF: 0-0 Fm: 0-0**
Distance: 5f/6f: 0-0 7f-8f: 0-0 **9f-13f: 3-11** 14f+: 1-4
Track : **LH: 4-14** RH: 0-1 Tight: 0-1 Gall: 0-0
Aids: Bl: 0-0 Vi: 0-0 Tstrap: 0-0 Ckp: 0-0
Best Rating: **75** 3/08 Sthl 1m4f stand

Modest; effective over 1m4f-1m6f; acts on Fibresand.

My Gacho (IRE)

107(107) (96)96
7-y-o b g Shinko Forest (IRE)-Floralia (Auction Ring (USA))
M Johnston Grant Mercer

Placings:033033/**141**0223540**625**/**0**10124653/100000/020 0100**041031506-55**000611110000 (7837)
2009: 7^{5}SD, 7^{5}SD, 7^{0}F, 6^{0}GF, 7^{0}GF, 5^{6}GF, 7^{1}GF, 7^{1}GF, 7^{1}GF, 7^{1}GF, 6^{0}G, 7^{0}GF, 6^{0}G, 7^{0}SS,

	Starts	1st	2nd	3rd	Win & Pl
Career Total (Turf)	44	8	4	4	82261
Career Total (AW)	20	4	1	3	26042

96 8/09 Ches 7f2y (0-95)H G-F £9462
89 8/09 Newc 7f (0-85)H G-F £4792
88 8/09 Brig 7f214y (0-80)H G-F £16099
80 7/09 Leic 7f9y (0-80)H G-F £4857
96 11/08 Ling 7f (0-85)H STD £4403
91 10/08 Sthl 6f (0-85)H STD £5957
89 7/08 Leic 5f218y (0-85)H G-F £6854
88 5/07 Thsk 6f (0-90)H GD £7772
86 6/06 Thsk 6f (0-85)H G-F £6477
82 6/06 Hayd 6f (0-75)H G-F £3238
76 2/05 Ling 6f (0-85)H STD £6643
70 1/05 Sthl 6f STD £3484
Total win prize-money £80041

Going (Turf): Sf: 0-1 GS: 0-3 Gd: 1-9 **GF: 7-27** Fm: 0-4
Distance: **5f/6f: 7-40** 7f-8f: 5-24 9f-13f: 0-0 14f+: 0-0
Track : **LH: 6-27** RH: 0-2 **Tight: 3-15** Gall: 0-2
Aids: Bl: 4-30 **Vi: 8-28** Tstrap: 0-0 Ckp: 0-0
Best Rating: **96** 8/09 Ches 7f2y gd-fm

Very useful; effective over 6f-1m; handles fast ground and sand; usually wears blinkers or a visor; likes to race prominently.

My Girl Jode

102(100) (66)**68**

3-y-o ch f Haafhd-Brush Strokes (Cadeaux Genereux)

M H Tompkins Jackie & George Smith

Placings:40-05125030 **(7524)**

2009: 8^{0}G, 10^{5}G, 10^{1}G, 10^{2}G, 11^{5}G, 10^{0}G, 10^{3}SD, 10^{0}SD,

	Starts	1st	2nd	3rd	Win & Pl
Career Total (Turf)	8	1	1	0	3300
Career Total (AW)	2	0	0	1	403

68 7/09 Yarm 1m2f21y (0-65)H GD £2072

Total win prize-money £2072

Going (Turf): Sf: 0-0 GS: 0-1 **Gd: 1-7** GF: 0-0 Fm: 0-0
Distance: 5f/6f: 0-0 7f-8f: 0-1 **9f-13f: 1-9** 14f+: 0-0
Track : **LH: 1-5** RH: 0-2 **Tight: 1-5** Gall: 0-1
Aids: Bl: 0-0 Vi: 0-0 Tstrap: 0-0 Ckp: 0-0
Best Rating: **68** 7/09 Yarm 1m2f21y good

Moderate; stays 1m2f on good ground.

My Grand Duke (USA)

(88) (52)

2-y-o b c Johannesburg (USA)-Hit It Here Cafe (USA) (Grand Slam (USA))

J A Osborne H R H Prince of Saxe-Weimar

Placings:060 **(7865)**

2009: 7^{0}SF, 8^{6}SD, 8^{0}SS,

	Starts	1st	2nd	3rd	Win & Pl
Career Total (Turf)	0	0	0	0	
Career Total (AW)	3	0	0	0	0

Going (Turf): **Sf: 0-0 GS: 0-0 Gd: 0-0 GF: 0-0 Fm: 0-0**
Distance: 5f/6f: 0-0 7f-8f: 0-3 9f-13f: 0-0 14f+: 0-0
Track : LH: 0-3 RH: 0-0 Tight: 0-1 Gall: 0-0
Aids: Bl: 0-0 Vi: 0-0 Tstrap: 0-0 Ckp: 0-0
Best Rating: **52** 11/09 Wolv 7f32y std-fst

My Immortal

101 **79**

7-y-o b g Monsun (GER)-Dame Kiri (FR) (Old Vic)

J J Quinn Major & Mrs P Arkwright & Mrs IC Sellars

Placings:323110/0450 **(3728)**

2009: 14^{0}GF, 14^{4}G, 17^{5}GF, 15^{0}G,

	Starts	1st	2nd	3rd	Win & Pl
Career Total (Turf)	9	2	0	2	12049
Career Total (AW)	1	0	1	0	1123

91 8/05 Ches 1m7f195y (0-85)H G-F £6821
87 8/05 Ling 1m6f SFT £3139

Total win prize-money £9962

Going (Turf): **Sf: 1-2** GS: 0-1 Gd: 0-2 **GF: 1-4** Fm: 0-0
Distance: 5f/6f: 0-0 7f-8f: 0-0 9f-13f: 0-3 **14f+: 2-7**
Track : **LH: 2-6** RH: 0-4 **Tight: 2-6** Gall: 0-2
Aids: Bl: 0-0 Vi: 0-0 Tstrap: 0-0 Ckp: 0-0
Best Rating: **91** 8/05 Ches 1m7f195y gd-fm

My Jeanie (IRE)

95(87) (36)**49**

5-y-o ch m King Charlemagne (USA)-Home Comforts (Most Welcome)

J C Fox R E Kavanagh

Placings:0032/51/0-0050 **(7660)**

2009: 8^{0}G, 7^{0}SD, 8^{5}GF, 10^{0}SD,

	Starts	1st	2nd	3rd	Win & Pl
Career Total (Turf)	3	0	0	0	0
Career Total (AW)	8	1	1	1	2803

55 12/07 Kemp 1m (0-55)H STD £2047

Total win prize-money £2048

Going (Turf): **Sf: 0-0 GS: 0-0 Gd: 0-1 GF: 0-2 Fm: 0-0**
Distance: 5f/6f: 0-0 **7f-8f: 1-9** 9f-13f: 0-2 14f+: 0-0
Track : LH: 0-5 **RH: 1-4** Tight: 0-4 Gall: 0-0
Aids: Bl: 0-0 Vi: 0-0 Tstrap: 0-0 Ckp: 0-0
Best Rating: **55** 12/07 Kemp 1m stand

Moderate; effective over 1m; acts on Polytrack.

My Kaiser Chief

(102) (58)**72**

4-y-o bl g Paris House-So Tempted (So Factual (USA))

W J H Ratcliffe T B Tarn

Placings:44056/612000004-00 **(0803)**

2009: 6^{0}SD, 7^{0}SD,

	Starts	1st	2nd	3rd	Win & Pl
Career Total (Turf)	11	1	1	0	5374
Career Total (AW)	5	0	0	0	0

72 4/08 Thsk 6f G-S £3399

Total win prize-money £3400

Going (Turf): Sf: 0-1 **GS: 1-3** Gd: 0-5 GF: 0-2 Fm: 0-0
Distance: **5f/6f: 1-13** 7f-8f: 0-3 9f-13f: 0-0 14f+: 0-0
Track : LH: 0-1 RH: 0-2 Tight: 0-0 Gall: 0-1
Aids: Bl: 0-0 Vi: 0-0 Tstrap: 0-0 Ckp: 0-0
Best Rating: **72** 5/08 Thsk 6f good

Modest; effective over 6f; acts on easy ground.

My Kingdom (IRE)

106(96) (82)**90**

3-y-o b g King's Best (USA)-Nebraas (Green Desert (USA))

H Morrison Wood Street Syndicate V

Placings:00102-4404213046 **(6723)**

2009: 7^{4}GF, 8^{4}SD, 7^{0}GF, 6^{4}G, 6^{2}G, 5^{1}GS, 6^{3}GS, 6^{0}GF, 6^{4}GF, 6^{6}SD,

	Starts	1st	2nd	3rd	Win & Pl
Career Total (Turf)	12	2	2	1	14869
Career Total (AW)	3	0	0	0	433

89 8/09 Brig 5f213y (0-80)H G-S £6231
75 9/08 Brig 6f209y GD £3784

Total win prize-money £10016

Going (Turf): Sf: 0-0 **GS: 1-3 Gd: 1-5** GF: 0-4 Fm: 0-0
Distance: 5f/6f: 1-6 7f-8f: 1-9 9f-13f: 0-0 14f+: 0-0
Track : **LH: 2-9** RH: 0-2 Tight: 0-5 Gall: 0-0
Aids: Bl: 0-0 Vi: 0-0 Tstrap: 0-0 Ckp: 0-0
Best Rating: **90** 9/09 Epsm 6f gd-sft

Fair; effective over 7f; acts on fast and easy ground and Polytrack; wears a tongue tie.

My Learned Friend (IRE)

105(102) (72)**83**

5-y-o b g Marju (IRE)-Stately Princess (Robellino (USA))

A M Balding DR E Harris

Placings:0513/60005/011500545-4021060 **(6476)**

2009: 7^{4}GF, 7^{0}GF, 6^{2}GF, 6^{1}F, 7^{0}G, 7^{6}G, 7^{0}GF,

	Starts	1st	2nd	3rd	Win & Pl
Career Total (Turf)	21	4	1	1	16014
Career Total (AW)	4	0	0	0	0

80 7/09 Brig 6f209y (0-75)H FRM £3406
83 6/08 Ling 7f (0-75)H G-F £2331
72 5/08 Ling 7f (0-75)H G-S £2331
82 8/06 Ling 7f GD £4533

Total win prize-money £12602

Going (Turf): Sf: 0-1 **GS: 1-3 Gd: 1-8 GF: 1-8 Fm: 1-1**
Distance: 5f/6f: 0-1 **7f-8f: 4-23** 9f-13f: 0-1 14f+: 0-0
Track : **LH: 1-6** RH: 0-6 Tight: 0-4 Gall: 0-1
Aids: Bl: 0-0 Vi: 0-1 Tstrap: 0-0 Ckp: 0-0
Best Rating: **84** 9/06 Asct 7f gd-sft

Fair; effective over 7f; acts on most ground and on Polytrack; has worn a visor.

My Legal Eagle (IRE)

69 (40)**49**

15-y-o b g Law Society (USA)-Majestic Nurse (On Your Mark)

E G Bevan E G Bevan

Placings:65004/030041304/06533304250021304053204/032222213606004006400/624222050/5/1421112/606322600356500400/340345/4320620503256/0303-0 **(2222)**

2009: 11^{0}GF,

	Starts	1st	2nd	3rd	Win & Pl
Career Total (Turf)	89	6	14	14	45157
Career Total (AW)	27	1	5	3	5641

61 6/04 Newb 1m5f61yE(0-75)H G-F £4712
54 6/04 Nott 1m6f15yE(0-70)H G-F £3750
49 5/04 York 1m5f197yF(0-55)H G-F £3094
51 5/04 Wolv 1m6f166y H(0-40) STD £1421
67 4/00 Nott 1m6f15yE(0-70)H SFT £3157
66 9/99 Sals 1m1f198yF(0-70)H HVY £2708
52 7/98 Thsk 7f F(0-70)H GD £2550

Total win prize-money £21395

Going (Turf): Sf: 2-26 GS: 0-13 Gd: 1-18 **GF: 3-29** Fm: 0-2
Distance: 5f/6f: 0-1 7f-8f: 1-7 9f-13f: 1-41 **14f+: 5-67**
Track : **LH: 6-102** RH: 1-12 **Tight: 3-46** Gall: 2-5
Aids: Bl: 0-11 Vi: 0-0 Tstrap: 0-0 Ckp: 0-0
Best Rating: **75** 4/00 Sand 2m78y soft

Plating class veteran; stayed 2m; acted on most types of ground, including Fibresand; (DEAD).

My Les

101(106) (60)**65**

3-y-o b f Josr Algarhoud (IRE)-Ashantiana (Ashkalani (IRE))

Jim Best (J R Best 18/8) SN Racing II

Placings:000-5013 **(6918)**

2009: 12^{5}SD, 16^{0}GF, 11^{1}G, 12^{3}SD,

	Starts	1st	2nd	3rd	Win & Pl
Career Total (Turf)	3	1	0	0	1943
Career Total (AW)	4	0	0	1	252

65 10/09 Brig 1m3f196y GD £1942

Total win prize-money £1943

Going (Turf): Sf: 0-0 GS: 0-0 **Gd: 1-1** GF: 0-2 Fm: 0-0
Distance: 5f/6f: 0-0 7f-8f: 0-3 **9f-13f: 1-3** 14f+: 0-1
Track : **LH: 1-6** RH: 0-0 Tight: 0-3 Gall: 0-1
Aids: Bl: 0-0 Vi: 0-0 Tstrap: 0-0 Ckp: 0-0
Best Rating: **65** 10/09 Brig 1m3f196y good

Very moderate; stays 1m4f and acts on good ground.

My Mandy (IRE)

94(96) (62)69

2-y-o b f Xaar-Ikan (IRE) (Sri Pekan (USA))

Ian Williams Dr Marwan Koukash

Placings:432642345334 **(6913)**

2009: 5^{4}SD, 5^{3}GF, 5^{2}GF, 5^{6}GF, 5^{4}GF, 5^{2}GF, 5^{3}G, 5^{4}GS, 5^{5}GF, 5^{3}SD, 5^{3}SS, 6^{4}SD,

	Starts	1st	2nd	3rd	Win & Pl
Career Total (Turf)	8	0	2	2	4074
Career Total (AW)	4	0	0	2	986

Going (Turf): Sf: 0-0 GS: 0-1 Gd: 0-1 GF: 0-6 Fm: 0-0
Distance: 5f/6f: 0-12 7f-8f: 0-0 9f-13f: 0-0 14f+: 0-0
Track : LH: 0-6 RH: 0-0 Tight: 0-5 Gall: 0-0
Aids: Bl: 0-0 Vi: 0-0 Tstrap: 0-3 Ckp: 0-3
Best Rating: 69 4/09 Hayd 5f gd-fm

Modest; suited by 5f and fast ground.

My Mate Granite (USA)

(93) (45)

5-y-o ch g High Yield (USA)-Fellwaati (USA) (Alydar (USA))

H J Collingridge (M E Rimmer 27/3) Stephen Wilsher

Placings:0-26P **(3275)**

2009: 12^{2}SD, 12^{6}SD, 16^{P}SD,

	Starts	1st	2nd	3rd	Win & Pl
Career Total (Turf)	0	0	0	0	
Career Total (AW)	4	0	1	0	605

Going (Turf): Sf: 0-0 GS: 0-0 Gd: 0-0 GF: 0-0 Fm: 0-0
Distance: 5f/6f: 0-0 7f-8f: 0-0 9f-13f: 0-2 14f+: 0-2
Track : LH: 0-3 RH: 0-1 Tight: 0-0 Gall: 0-1
Aids: Bl: 0-0 Vi: 0-0 Tstrap: 0-0 Ckp: 0-0
Best Rating: 45 2/09 Sthl 1m4f stand

My Mate Mal

101(100) (67)68

5-y-o b g Daawe (USA)-Kandymal (IRE) (Prince Of Birds (USA))

B Ellison Koo's Racing Club

Placings:045310-062610260302503 **(7761)**

2009: 8^{0}SD, 8^{6}GF, 8^{2}SD, 7^{6}GF, 8^{1}GF, 8^{0}GS, 8^{2}GS, 8^{6}SD, 7^{0}GS, 9^{3}S, 10^{0}GS, 12^{2}SD, 8^{5}SD, 9^{0}SD, 11^{3}SD,

	Starts	1st	2nd	3rd	Win & Pl
Career Total (Turf)	11	2	1	1	6746
Career Total (AW)	10	0	2	2	2036

63 5/09 Newc 1m G-F £1942
68 10/08 Yarm 1m3y SFT £2137
Total win prize-money £4080

Going (Turf): Sf: 1-2 GS: 0-6 Gd: 0-0 GF: 1-3 Fm: 0-0
Distance: 5f/6f: 0-0 7f-8f: 1-9 9f-13f: 1-12 14f+: 0-0
Track : LH: 1-14 RH: 0-3 Tight: 0-9 Gall: 1-1
Aids: Bl: 0-0 Vi: 0-0 Tstrap: 0-0 Ckp: 0-0
Best Rating: 68 8/09 Ayr 1m1f20y soft

Modest; stays 1m4f; acts on soft ground and on Fibresand.

My Mate Max

104(100) (79)79

4-y-o b g Fraam-Victory Flip (IRE) (Victory Note (USA))

R Hollinshead Tim Leadbeater

Placings:1/25640245-02260314 **(7151)**

2009: 12^{0}SD, 14^{2}GF, 14^{2}G, 14^{6}GF, 15^{0}GF, 14^{3}G, 14^{1}GF, 16^{4}G,

	Starts	1st	2nd	3rd	Win & Pl
Career Total (Turf)	12	1	3	1	10189
Career Total (AW)	5	1	1	0	3840

76 9/09 Wwck 1m6f213y (0-85)H G-F £5180
72 12/07 Wolv 7f32y STD £2730
Total win prize-money £7911

Going (Turf): Sf: 0-0 GS: 0-3 Gd: 0-4 GF: 1-5 Fm: 0-0
Distance: 5f/6f: 0-0 7f-8f: 1-2 9f-13f: 0-6 14f+: 1-9
Track : LH: 2-16 RH: 0-1 Tight: 1-7 Gall: 0-4
Aids: Bl: 0-0 Vi: 0-0 Tstrap: 1-10 Ckp: 1-10
Best Rating: 79 10/08 Wolv 1m5f194y stand

Fair; stays 1m6f; acts on good ground and Polytrack; has worn cheekpieces.

My Mentor (IRE)

(109) (83)

5-y-o b g Golan (IRE)-Vanille (IRE) (Selkirk (USA))

Sir Mark Prescott Mr And Mrs Arthur Finn

Placings:000210/24425104462130-4246000 **(4373)**

2009: 8^{4}SD, 11^{2}SD, 11^{4}SD, 10^{6}SD, 7^{0}SD, 11^{0}SD, 12^{0}SD,

	Starts	1st	2nd	3rd	Win & Pl
Career Total (Turf)	0	0	0	0	
Career Total (AW)	27	3	5	1	12075

83 7/08 Sthl 7f (0-70)H SS £2729
75 3/08 Sthl 1m4f (0-75)H STD £2593
69 6/07 Ling 1m (0-60)H STD £2047
Total win prize-money £7372

Going (Turf): Sf: 0-0 GS: 0-0 Gd: 0-0 GF: 0-0 Fm: 0-0
Distance: 5f/6f: 0-0 7f-8f: 2-13 9f-13f: 1-13 14f+: 0-1
Track : LH: 3-22 RH: 0-5 Tight: 1-8 Gall: 0-2
Aids: Bl: 1-10 Vi: 0-0 Tstrap: 0-1 Ckp: 0-1
Best Rating: 83 7/08 Sthl 7f std-slw

Fair; effective from 7f-1m4f and acts on sand; has worn blinkers.

My Mirasol

(104) (68)65

5-y-o ch m Primo Valentino (IRE)-Distinctly Blu (IRE) (Distinctly North (USA))

D E Cantillon J A Bailie

Placings:22300541/42221600 5030/512133203240-360 **(0623)**

2009: 12^{3}SS, 11^{6}SD, 12^{0}SD,

	Starts	1st	2nd	3rd	Win & Pl
Career Total (Turf)	7	0	2	1	2698
Career Total (AW)	28	4	6	5	14922

64 2/08 Wolv 1m1f103y (0-60)H STD £2218
57 1/08 Wolv 1m141y (0-45) STD £1365
63 2/07 Wolv 1m141y STD £2047
61 12/06 Wolv 1m141y SS £2730
Total win prize-money £8361

Going (Turf): Sf: 0-1 GS: 0-0 Gd: 0-3 GF: 0-2 Fm: 0-1
Distance: 5f/6f: 0-5 7f-8f: 0-4 9f-13f: 4-26 14f+: 0-0
Track : LH: 4-29 RH: 0-1 Tight: 4-21 Gall: 0-1
Aids: Bl: 0-0 Vi: 0-0 Tstrap: 4-22 Ckp: 4-22
Best Rating: 68 9/08 Wolv 1m1f103y stand

Modest; effective at around 1m-1m2f; acts well on Polytrack; has worn cheekpieces.

My One Weakness (IRE)

103(97) (69)75

2-y-o ch g Bertolini (USA)-Lucina (Machiavellian (USA))

B Ellison Koo's Racing Club

Placings:3301401 **(6048)**

2009: 6^{3}GS, 6^{3}S, 5^{0}GF, 7^{1}SD, 6^{4}GF, 8^{0}GF, 6^{1}G,

	Starts	1st	2nd	3rd	Win & Pl
Career Total (Turf)	6	1	0	2	11828
Career Total (AW)	1	1	0	0	2730

75 9/09 Ayr 6f (0-95)H GD £9066
69 7/09 Sthl 7f STD £2729
Total win prize-money £11796

Going (Turf): Sf: 0-1 GS: 0-1 Gd: 1-1 GF: 0-3 Fm: 0-0
Distance: 5f/6f: 1-5 7f-8f: 1-1 9f-13f: 0-1 14f+: 0-0
Track : LH: 1-1 RH: 0-0 Tight: 0-0 Gall: 0-0
Aids: Bl: 0-0 Vi: 0-0 Tstrap: 0-0 Ckp: 0-0
Best Rating: 75 9/09 Ayr 6f good

Fair; effective over 6f-7f; acts on good and easy ground; goes on Fibresand.

My Paris

(84) (38)94

8-y-o b g Paris House-My Desire (Grey Desire)

Ollie Pears J D Spensley & Mrs M A Spensley

Placings:0/3222522111/0524601013/003530000/0501265 00000/4303300060-0 **(1479)**

2009: 8^{0}SD,

	Starts	1st	2nd	3rd	Win & Pl
Career Total (Turf)	47	6	6	6	122684
Career Total (AW)	6	0	1	1	1300

99 5/07 Thsk 1m (0-100)H G-F £11658
109 9/05 Donc 1m (0-110)H SFT £17400
105 8/05 NmkJ 7f (0-105)H GD £17400
99 8/04 NmkJ 7f C(0-90)H G-S £14170
90 8/04 Leic 7f9y B(0-100)H G-F £12414
63 7/04 Ripn 1m1f F SFT £4225
Total win prize-money £77268

Going (Turf): Sf: 2-8 GS: 1-9 Gd: 1-12 GF: 2-17 Fm: 0-1
Distance: 5f/6f: 0-0 7f-8f: 5-32 9f-13f: 1-21 14f+: 0-0
Track : LH: 1-26 RH: 1-10 Tight: 2-15 Gall: 0-7
Aids: Bl: 0-2 Vi: 0-2 Tstrap: 0-2 Ckp: 0-2
Best Rating: 109 5/06 NmkR 1m1f good

Formerly useful; stays 1m2f, but probably better over shorter; handles most ground, but best on an easy surface; likes to race prominently; has worn blinkers and cheekpieces.

My Red Kite

84(85) (53)60

2-y-o ch g Avonbridge-Cup Of Love (USA) (Behrens (USA))

G D Blake Adrian Smith

Placings:5006 **(7235)**

2009: 5^{5}GF, 7^{0}G, 7^{0}G, 8^{6}SD,

	Starts	1st	2nd	3rd	Win & Pl
Career Total (Turf)	3	0	0	0	0
Career Total (AW)	1	0	0	0	0

Going (Turf): Sf: 0-0 GS: 0-0 Gd: 0-2 GF: 0-1 Fm: 0-0
Distance: 5f/6f: 0-1 7f-8f: 0-3 9f-13f: 0-0 14f+: 0-0
Track : LH: 0-1 RH: 0-2 Tight: 0-1 Gall: 0-0
Aids: Bl: 0-0 Vi: 0-0 Tstrap: 0-1 Ckp: 0-1
Best Rating: 60 6/09 Sand 7f16y good

My Shadow

98(102) (83)75

4-y-o b g Zamindar (USA)-Reflections (Sadler's Wells (USA))

S Dow Tom Parker, Nigel Scandrett, John Taylor

Placings:4004/22011046000366-102251300 (5780)
2009: 10¹SD, 10⁰SD, 8²SD, 10²SD, 10⁵F, 8¹G, 10³GF, 8⁰GF, 8⁰SD,

	Starts	1st	2nd	3rd	Win & Pl
Career Total (Turf)	9	1	2	1	10196
Career Total (AW)	18	3	2	1	11157

75 6/09 Gdwd 1m (0-70)H GD £3885
77 2/09 Kemp 1m2f (0-70)H STD £3561
83 4/08 Kemp 1m (0-65)H STD £2047
77 3/08 Ling 1m (0-65)H STD £2047
Total win prize-money £11543

Going (Turf): Sf: 0-0 GS: 0-0 **Gd: 1-3** GF: 0-3 Fm: 0-1
Distance: 5f/6f: 0-0 **7f-8f: 3-20** 9f-13f: 1-7 14f+: 0-0
Track : LH: 1-15 **RH: 3-12 Tight: 1-12** Gall: 0-2
Aids: Bl: 0-0 Vi: 0-0 Tstrap: 0-0 Ckp: 0-0
Best Rating: 83 4/08 Kemp 1m stand

Fair; effective over 1m; acts well on Polytrack.

My Sister

92(85) (52)63
2-y-o b f Royal Applause-Mysistra (FR) (Machiavellian (USA))
M D I Usher Itchen Valley Stud & Partners

Placings:045056 (6735)
2009: 6⁰GF, 6⁴G, 6⁵G, 6⁰GF, 5⁵SD, 8⁶GS,

	Starts	1st	2nd	3rd	Win & Pl
Career Total (Turf)	5	0	0	0	0
Career Total (AW)	1	0	0	0	0

Going (Turf): **Sf: 0-0 GS: 0-1 Gd: 0-2 GF: 0-2 Fm: 0-0**
Distance: 5f/6f: 0-3 7f-8f: 0-2 9f-13f: 0-1 14f+: 0-0
Track : LH: 0-1 RH: 0-1 Tight: 0-2 Gall: 0-1
Aids: Bl: 0-0 Vi: 0-0 Tstrap: 0-0 Ckp: 0-0
Best Rating: 63 8/09 Wind 6f good

My Sweet Georgia (IRE)

(99) (73)76
3-y-o b f Royal Applause-Harda Arda (USA) (Nureyev (USA))
Stef Liddiard (S A Callaghan 12/3) Higgi's In The Wings

Placings:52220500-1521240001003 (7797)
2009: 6¹SD, 8⁵SD, 7²SD, 6¹SD, 7²SD, 6⁴SD, 6⁰SD, 8⁰SD, 7⁰SS, 7¹SD, 5⁰SD, 7⁰SD, 8³SS,

	Starts	1st	2nd	3rd	Win & Pl
Career Total (Turf)	5	0	3	0	3334
Career Total (AW)	16	3	2	1	8153

72 11/09 Sthl 7f (0-60)H STD £1706
71 2/09 Sthl 6f STD £2047
73 1/09 Sthl 6f (0-70)H STD £2729
Total win prize-money £6483

Going (Turf): **Sf: 0-1 GS: 0-0 Gd: 0-2 GF: 0-2 Fm: 0-0**
Distance: **5f/6f: 2-10** 7f-8f: 1-10 9f-13f: 0-1 14f+: 0-0
Track : **LH: 3-13** RH: 0-3 Tight: 0-5 Gall: 0-3
Aids: **Bl: 3-6** Vi: 0-1 Tstrap: 0-2 Ckp: 0-2
Best Rating: 76 9/08 Ling 7f soft

Modest; stays 7f; acts on most ground and on Fibresand; has worn blinkers and a visor.

My Verse

104(92) (72)83
3 y o b f Exceed And Excel (AUS)-Reematna (Sabrehill (USA))
M A Jarvis Sheikh Ahmed Al Maktoum

Placings:3-114 (6535)
2009: 8¹G, 8¹GS, 8⁴GF,

	Starts	1st	2nd	3rd	Win & Pl
Career Total (Turf)	3	2	0	0	8332
Career Total (AW)	1	0	0	1	607

83 9/09 Sand 1m14y (0-85)H G-S £4857
75 8/09 Ripn 1m GD £2914
Total win prize-money £7771

Going (Turf): Sf: 0-0 **GS: 1-1 Gd: 1-1** GF: 0-1 Fm: 0-0
Distance: 5f/6f: 0-0 7f-8f: 1-2 9f-13f: 1-2 14f+: 0-0
Track : LH: 0-2 **RH: 2-2 Tight: 1-2** Gall: 0-0
Aids: Bl: 0-0 Vi: 0-0 Tstrap: 0-0 Ckp: 0-0
Best Rating: 83 9/09 Sand 1m14y gd-sft

Useful; stays 1m; acts on good and easy ground and Polytrack.

Mycana (IRE)

(68) (1)
3-y-o b g Tikkanen (USA)-Amme Enaek (IRE) (Wolverlife)
Lee Smyth Mrs M A McNeice

Placings:0000 (6750a)
2009: 10⁰Y, 8⁰HY, 5⁰SD, 10⁰S,

	Starts	1st	2nd	3rd	Win & Pl
Career Total (Turf)	3	0	0	0	
Career Total (AW)	1	0	0	0	

Going (Turf): **Sf: 0-2 GS: 0-0 Gd: 0-0 GF: 0-0 Fm: 0-0**
Distance: 5f/6f: 0-1 7f-8f: 0-1 9f-13f: 0-2 14f+: 0-0
Track : LH: 0-2 RH: 0-1 Tight: 0-1 Gall: 0-0
Aids: Bl: 0-0 Vi: 0-0 Tstrap: 0-2 Ckp: 0-2
Best Rating: 1 10/09 Wolv 5f20y stand

Mycenean Prince (USA)

91(89) (47)41
6-y-o b g Swain (IRE)-Nijinsky's Beauty (USA) (Nijinsky (CAN))
S A Harris (G Woodward 12/6) Wilf Hobson

Placings:000/0000605/000440/00-000 (6184)
2009: 8⁰SD, 11⁰GF, 9⁰GF,

	Starts	1st	2nd	3rd	Win & Pl
Career Total (Turf)	12	0	0	0	0
Career Total (AW)	9	0	0	0	0

Going (Turf): **Sf: 0-0 GS: 0-2 Gd: 0-3 GF: 0-7 Fm: 0-0**
Distance: 5f/6f: 0-2 7f-8f: 0-8 9f-13f: 0-10 14f+: 0-1
Track : LH: 0-12 RH: 0-6 Tight: 0-10 Gall: 0-0
Aids: Bl: 0-5 Vi: 0-4 Tstrap: 0-0 Ckp: 0-0
Best Rating: 49 9/05 Catt 5f212y good

Mydy Easy (USA)

90 60
3-y-o b/br g Speightstown (USA)-Eze (USA) (Williamstown (USA))
P W Chapple-Hyam Joy And Valentine Feerick

Placings:55 (6573)
2009: 8⁵GF, 7⁵GF,

	Starts	1st	2nd	3rd	Win & Pl
Career Total (Turf)	2	0	0	0	0

Going (Turf): **Sf: 0-0 GS: 0-0 Gd: 0-0 GF: 0-2 Fm: 0-0**
Distance: 5f/6f: 0-0 7f-8f: 0-1 9f-13f: 0-1 14f+: 0-0
Track : LH: 0-0 RH: 0-1 Tight: 0-1 Gall: 0-0
Aids: Bl: 0-0 Vi: 0-0 Tstrap: 0-0 Ckp: 0-0
Best Rating: 60 8/09 Wind 1m67y gd-fm

Mykingdomforahorse

105 81
3-y-o b c Fantastic Light (USA)-Charlecote (IRE) (Caerleon (USA))
M R Channon C C Buckley

Placings:64021-042413210 (6676)
2009: 8⁰GF, 9⁴G, 9²GF, 10⁴GS, 10¹G, 10³GF, 12²GF, 14¹GF, 18⁰G,

	Starts	1st	2nd	3rd	Win & Pl
Career Total (Turf)	14	3	3	1	12928

81 9/09 Sals 1m6f21y (0-75)H G-F £3238
70 8/09 Yarm 1m2f21y (0-70)H GD £2590
69 10/08 Yarm 1m3y (0-75) G-S £3367
Total win prize-money £9196

Going (Turf): Sf: 0-1 **GS: 1-4 Gd: 1-3 GF: 1-6** Fm: 0-0
Distance: 5f/6f: 0-0 7f-8f: 0-3 **9f-13f: 2-9** 14f+: 1-2
Track : LH: 1-6 RH: 1-5 **Tight: 2-6** Gall: 0-3
Aids: Bl: 0-0 **Vi: 1-3** Tstrap: 0-0 Ckp: 0-0
Best Rating: 81 9/09 Sals 1m6f21y gd-fm

Fair; effective over 1m2f-1m6f; acts on easy and fast ground.

Mymateeric

95(97) (55)69
3-y-o b g Reset (AUS)-Ewenny (Warrshan (USA))
J Pearce B Lee

Placings:03040460-00052043400 (7025)
2009: 9⁰G, 9⁰GF, 8⁰SD, 9⁵G, 11²GS, 11⁰G, 11⁴G, 16³SD, 16⁴SD, 16⁰SS, 16⁰SD,

	Starts	1st	2nd	3rd	Win & Pl
Career Total (Turf)	13	0	1	1	3214
Career Total (AW)	6	0	0	1	543

Going (Turf): **Sf: 0-2 GS: 0-1 Gd: 0-6 GF: 0-4 Fm: 0-0**
Distance: 5f/6f: 0-3 7f-8f: 0-5 9f-13f: 0-7 14f+: 0-4
Track : LH: 0-8 RH: 0-6 Tight: 0-8 Gall: 0-0
Aids: Bl: 0-8 Vi: 0-2 Tstrap: 0-1 Ckp: 0-1
Best Rating: 69 9/08 Yarm 1m3y good

Modest; stays 1m3f; acts on most ground; has worn blinkers.

Mymumsaysimthebest

103(87) (64)86
4-y-o b g Reel Buddy (USA)-Night Gypsy (Mind Games)
G L Moore Mrs M J George

Placings:0246/026 (2980)
2009: 7⁰SD, 6²GF, 6⁶GF,

	Starts	1st	2nd	3rd	Win & Pl
Career Total (Turf)	6	0	2	0	12313
Career Total (AW)	1	0	0	0	

Going (Turf): **Sf: 0-0 GS: 0-0 Gd: 0-3 GF: 0-3 Fm: 0-0**
Distance: 5f/6f: 0-4 7f-8f: 0-3 9f-13f: 0-0 14f+: 0-0
Track : LH: 0-1 RH: 0-1 Tight: 0-1 Gall: 0-1
Aids: Bl: 0-0 Vi: 0-0 Tstrap: 0 0 Ckp: 0-0
Best Rating: 89 8/07 York 6f good

Useful half-brother to Safari Mischief and related to juvenile winners; stays 7f; acts on a sound surface.

Myraid

75 **33**

2-y-o b g Danbird (AUS)-My Desire (Grey Desire)

Ollie Pears J D Spensley & Mrs M A Spensley

Placings:0 **(6821)**

2009: 8^0GF,

	Starts	1st	2nd	3rd	Win & Pl
Career Total (Turf)	1	0	0	0	

Going (Turf): Sf: 0-0 GS: 0-0 Gd: 0-0 GF: 0-1 Fm: 0-0
Distance: 5f/6f: 0-0 7f-8f: 0-1 9f-13f: 0-0 14f+: 0-0
Track : LH: 0-0 RH: 0-0 Tight: 0-0 Gall: 0-0
Aids: Bl: 0-0 Vi: 0-0 Tstrap: 0-0 Ckp: 0-0
Best Rating: 33 10/09 Rdcr 1m gd-fm

Myriola

(95) (40)**49**

4-y-o ch f Captain Rio-Spaniola (IRE) (Desert King (IRE))

D Shaw L M Baker Racing Part 1

Placings:50636300/4000002000050-050 **(7839)**

2009: 5^0SD, 5^5SD, 5^0SS,

	Starts	1st	2nd	3rd	Win & Pl
Career Total (Turf)	12	0	1	1	1338
Career Total (AW)	12	0	0	1	433

Going (Turf): Sf: 0-3 GS: 0-2 Gd: 0-3 GF: 0-3 Fm: 0-1
Distance: 5f/6f: 0-20 7f-8f: 0-4 9f-13f: 0-0 14f+: 0-0
Track : LH: 0-12 RH: 0-0 Tight: 0-8 Gall: 0-0
Aids: Bl: 0-2 Vi: 0-0 Tstrap: 0-0 Ckp: 0-0
Best Rating: 62 6/07 Ayr 5f good

Moderate; effective over 5f-6f; acts on soft ground; also goes on Polytrack.

Myshkin

(96) (53)**51**

3-y-o b g Refuse To Bend (IRE)-Marmaga (IRE) (Shernazar)

R Curtis (I Semple 12/4) M J Tranter

Placings:00-54 **(1231)**

2009: 10^5SD, 12^4GF,

	Starts	1st	2nd	3rd	Win & Pl
Career Total (Turf)	3	0	0	0	192
Career Total (AW)	1	0	0	0	0

Going (Turf): Sf: 0-1 GS: 0-0 Gd: 0-1 GF: 0-1 Fm: 0-0
Distance: 5f/6f: 0-0 7f-8f: 0-1 9f-13f: 0-3 14f+: 0-0
Track : LH: 0-2 RH: 0-1 Tight: 0-2 Gall: 0-0
Aids: Bl: 0-2 Vi: 0-1 Tstrap: 0-0 Ckp: 0-0
Best Rating: 53 1/09 Ling 1m2f stand

Mystery Star (IRE)

107(104) (83)**104**

4-y-o ch g Kris Kin (USA)-Mystery Hill (USA) (Danehill (USA))

M H Tompkins John Brenchley

Placings:231/03300030-321525026230 **(6662)**

2009: 8^3G, 10^2G, 9^1G, 10^5GF, 10^2G, 10^5G, 11^0GF, 12^2G, 12^6GS, 13^2GF, 14^3GF, 12^0GS,

	Starts	1st	2nd	3rd	Win & Pl
Career Total (Turf)	20	1	5	5	35966
Career Total (AW)	3	1	0	1	4088

91 5/09 Gdwd 1m1f192y (0-90)H GD £9714
83 11/07 Wolv 1m141y STD £2968
Total win prize-money £12683

Going (Turf): Sf: 0-0 GS: 0-4 **Gd: 1-7** GF: 0-9 Fm: 0-0
Distance: 5f/6f: 0-0 7f-8f: 0-2 **9f-13f: 2-19** 14f+: 0-2
Track : LH: 1-11 RH: 1-9 **Tight: 2-11** Gall: 0-6
Aids: Bl: 0-0 Vi: 0-0 Tstrap: 0-2 Ckp: 0-2
Best Rating: 104 9/09 Yarm 1m6f17y gd-fm

Very useful; stays 1m6f; acts on most ground and on Polytrack.

Mystic Art (IRE)

93(104) (71)**68**

4-y-o b g Peintre Celebre (USA)-Mystic Lure (Green Desert (USA))

C R Egerton Longmoor Holdings Ltd

Placings:005/002563263-1320400 **(2708)**

2009: 10^1SD, 10^3SD, 10^2SD, 10^0G, 9^4F, 10^0G, 12^0SD,

	Starts	1st	2nd	3rd	Win & Pl
Career Total (Turf)	10	0	1	0	1233
Career Total (AW)	9	1	2	3	4163

62 2/09 Ling 1m2f STD £2047
Total win prize-money £2047

Going (Turf): Sf: 0-0 GS: 0-2 Gd: 0-4 GF: 0-3 Fm: 0-1
Distance: 5f/6f: 0-1 7f-8f: 0-3 **9f-13f: 1-15** 14f+: 0-0
Track : **LH: 1-11** RH: 0-4 **Tight: 1-10** Gall: 0-1
Aids: Bl: 0-1 Vi: 0-0 Tstrap: 0-3 Ckp: 0-3
Best Rating: 74 9/07 Ling 7f stand

Modest; effective at around 1m2f; acts on easy ground; goes on Polytrack; has worn cheekpieces.

Mystic Millie (IRE)

75 **46**

2-y-o ch f Bertolini (USA)-Present Imperfect (Cadeaux Genereux)

C G Cox Dennis Shaw

Placings:005 **(6416)**

2009: 6^0G, 6^0GF, 7^5GF,

	Starts	1st	2nd	3rd	Win & Pl
Career Total (Turf)	3	0	0	0	0

Going (Turf): Sf: 0-0 GS: 0-0 Gd: 0-1 GF: 0-2 Fm: 0-0
Distance: 5f/6f: 0-2 7f-8f: 0-1 9f-13f: 0-0 14f+: 0-0
Track : LH: 0-0 RH: 0-1 Tight: 0-0 Gall: 0-0
Aids: Bl: 0-0 Vi: 0-0 Tstrap: 0-0 Ckp: 0-0
Best Rating: 46 10/09 Gdwd 7f gd-fm

Mystic Prince

85 **65**

3-y-o b g Dubai Destination (USA)-Hazy Heights (Shirley Heights)

Miss Tor Sturgis Steven Astaire

Placings:00-000 **(3588)**

2009: 10^0S, 8^0GF, 10^0GF,

	Starts	1st	2nd	3rd	Win & Pl
Career Total (Turf)	5	0	0	0	

Going (Turf): Sf: 0-2 GS: 0-1 Gd: 0-0 GF: 0-2 Fm: 0-0
Distance: 5f/6f: 0-0 7f-8f: 0-3 9f-13f: 0-2 14f+: 0-0
Track : LH: 0-2 RH: 0-0 Tight: 0-0 Gall: 0-1
Aids: Bl: 0-0 Vi: 0-0 Tstrap: 0-0 Ckp: 0-0
Best Rating: 65 10/08 Newb 1m soft

Mystic Roll

92(99) (59)**48**

6-y-o br g Medicean-Pain Perdu (IRE) (Waajib)

Jane Chapple-Hyam Mrs B J Hirst

Placings:030/0000004/25004002-06 **(4005)**

2009: 6^0G, 7^6G,

	Starts	1st	2nd	3rd	Win & Pl
Career Total (Turf)	9	0	0	1	670
Career Total (AW)	11	0	2	0	1380

Going (Turf): Sf: 0-1 GS: 0-1 Gd: 0-5 GF: 0-1 Fm: 0-1
Distance: 5f/6f: 0-0 7f-8f: 0-13 9f-13f: 0-7 14f+: 0-0
Track : LH: 0-11 RH: 0-3 Tight: 0-10 Gall: 0-1
Aids: Bl: 0-1 Vi: 0-0 Tstrap: 0-0 Ckp: 0-0
Best Rating: 74 9/05 Sals 1m good

Moderate; suited by 7f and acts on Polytrack.

Mystic Touch

90(101) (60)**49**

3-y-o b g Systematic-Lycius Touch (Lycius (USA))

A B Haynes (Miss E C Lavelle 1/8) Caloona Racing

Placings:03004006100 **(7517)**

2009: 7^0SD, 8^3SD, 8^0SD, 9^0G, 8^4GF, 7^0F, 7^0GS, 10^6G, 9^1SD, 10^0SD, 7^0SD,

	Starts	1st	2nd	3rd	Win & Pl
Career Total (Turf)	5	0	0	0	226
Career Total (AW)	6	1	0	1	2450

59 10/09 Wolv 1m1f103y (0-55)H STD £2047
Total win prize-money £2047

Going (Turf): Sf: 0-0 GS: 0-1 Gd: 0-2 GF: 0-1 Fm: 0-1
Distance: 5f/6f: 0-0 7f-8f: 0-6 **9f-13f: 1-5** 14f+: 0-0
Track : **LH: 1-8** RH: 0-1 **Tight: 1-7** Gall: 0-1
Aids: Bl: 0-0 Vi: 0-0 Tstrap: 0-1 Ckp: 0-1
Best Rating: 60 3/09 Ling 1m stand

Modest; stays 1m and acts on Polytrack.

Mystical Ayr (IRE)

80(75) (17)**61**

7-y-o br m Namid-Scanno's Choice (IRE) (Pennine Walk)

Miss L A Perratt Ayrshire Racing

Placings:4062112/0220030/62034225254012232206/0406 0424450-060 **(4034)**

2009: 9^0G, 8^6G, 9^0G,

	Starts	1st	2nd	3rd	Win & Pl
Career Total (Turf)	47	3	13	3	28347
Career Total (AW)	1	0	0	0	

69 8/07 Ayr 1m1f20y (0-60)H SFT £2730
67 10/05 Ayr 1m (0-60)H SFT £3023
58 9/05 Ayr 1m (0-55)H SFT £3312
Total win prize-money £9065

Going (Turf): **Sf: 3-16** GS: 0-8 Gd: 0-16 GF: 0-7 Fm: 0-0
Distance: 5f/6f: 0-2 **7f-8f: 2-17** 9f-13f: 1-29 14f+: 0-0
Track : **LH: 3-25** RH: 0-19 Tight: 0-22 Gall: 0-2
Aids: Bl: 0-0 Vi: 0-0 Tstrap: 0-1 Ckp: 0-1
Best Rating: 72 9/07 Haml 1m1f36y gd-sft

Modest; effective at around 1m1f; acts on a sound surface, but suited by soft ground.

Mystical Spirit (IRE)

(82) (37)46

3-y-o b f Xaar-Samsung Spirit (Statoblest)

J R Weymes T A Scothern

Placings:34-P (1789)

2009: 11PGF,

	Starts	1st	2nd	3rd	Win & Pl
Career Total (Turf)	2	0	0	1	578
Career Total (AW)	1	0	0	0	289

Going (Turf): **Sf: 0-1 GS: 0-0 Gd: 0-0 GF: 0-1 Fm: 0-0**
Distance: 5f/6f: 0-0 7f-8f: 0-2 9f-13f: 0-1 14f+: 0-0
Track : LH: 0-2 RH: 0-1 Tight: 0-2 Gall: 0-0
Aids: Bl: 0-0 Vi: 0-0 Tstrap: 0-0 Ckp: 0-0
Best Rating: **46** 11/08 Muss 1m soft

Mystickhill (IRE)

(100) (65)60

4-y-o ch f Raise A Grand (IRE)-Lady Eberspacher (IRE) (Royal Abjar (USA))

J Balding Tickhill Racing Partnership

Placings:4330432/050624024-5 (0173)

2009: 55SD,

	Starts	1st	2nd	3rd	Win & Pl
Career Total (Turf)	6	0	1	2	2215
Career Total (AW)	11	0	2	1	1628

Going (Turf): **Sf: 0-0 GS: 0-0 Gd: 0-3 GF: 0-3 Fm: 0-0**
Distance: 5f/6f: 0-17 7f-8f: 0-0 9f-13f: 0-0 14f+: 0-0
Track : LH: 0-7 RH: 0-0 Tight: 0-5 Gall: 0-1
Aids: Bl: 0-0 Vi: 0-0 Tstrap: 0-0 Ckp: 0-0
Best Rating: **65** 10/07 Wolv 5f216y stand

Moderate; effective over 5f-6f; acts on good ground; also goes on Polytrack.

Mystified (IRE)

104(92) (37)61

6-y-o b g Raise A Grand (IRE)-Sunrise (IRE) (Sri Pekan (USA))

R F Fisher Des Johnston

Placings:3551003**002/1000055200**/42550100/06-122220430 (6558)

2009: 141GF, 142GF, 142GF, 162GF, 132G, 140GF, 164GS, 173GF, 150G,

	Starts	1st	2nd	3rd	Win & Pl
Career Total (Turf)	29	3	6	3	14482
Career Total (AW)	10	1	1	0	4103

54	6/09	Rdcr	1m6f19y		G-F	£2047
54	8/07	Catt	1m7f177y		FRM	£2730
62	2/06	Wolv	1m141y	(0-70)H	STD	£3238
58	8/05	Muss	7f30y		G-F	£3380

Total win prize-money £11396

Going (Turf): Sf: 0-2 GS: 0-3 Gd: 0-8 **GF: 2-15** Fm: 1-1
Distance: 5f/6f: 0-0 7f-8f: 1-9 9f-13f: 1-9 **14f+: 2-21**
Track : **LH: 3-23** RH: 1-13 **Tight: 4-32** Gall: 0-0
Aids: **Bl: 2-18** Vi: 0-0 Tstrap: 1-12 Ckp: 1-12
Best Rating: **64** 12/05 Wolv 1m141y stand

Moderate; acts on fast ground/Polytrack; stays 1m6f; has worn blinkers/cheekpieces.

Mythical Blue (IRE)

103(99) (64)83

3-y-o b g Acclamation-Proud Myth (IRE) (Mark Of Esteem (IRE))

J M Bradley Clifton Hunt

Placings:2501100-3211315110 (6647)

2009: 53G, 52F, 51GF, 51F, 53SD, 51G, 55G, 51G, 51GF, 50G,

	Starts	1st	2nd	3rd	Win & Pl
Career Total (Turf)	15	7	2	1	26139
Career Total (AW)	2	0	0	1	578

80	9/09	Gdwd	5f	(0-75)H	G-F	£3238
66	8/09	Wwck	5f		GD	£1942
83	7/09	Bath	5f11y	(0-70)H	GD	£2719
67	6/09	Bath	5f11y		FRM	£1942
61	5/09	Chep	5f16y		G-F	£1942
74	8/08	Sand	5f6y		G-F	£6476
74	8/08	NmkJ	5f		GD	£6476

Total win prize-money £24739

Going (Turf): Sf: 0-1 GS: 0-0 **Gd: 3-6 GF: 3-6** Fm: 1-2
Distance: **5f/6f: 7-15** 7f-8f: 0-2 9f-13f: 0-0 14f+: 0-0
Track : **LH: 3-7** RH: 0-1 Tight: 0-1 **Gall: 2-5**
Aids: Bl: 0-0 Vi: 0-0 Tstrap: 0-0 Ckp: 0-0
Best Rating: **83** 7/09 Bath 5f11y good

Fair; best over 5f; acts on good and faster ground; has worn a tongue tie; best when able to dominate.

Mythical Border (USA)

61 102

3-y-o ch f Johannesburg (USA)-Border Dispute (USA) (Boundary (USA))

J Noseda Sheikh Mohammed Bin Khalifa Al-Thani

Placings:130-0 (5233)

2009: 50GF,

	Starts	1st	2nd	3rd	Win & Pl
Career Total (Turf)	4	1	0	1	12178

82	5/08	Ling	5f	GD	£3561

Total win prize-money £3562

Going (Turf): Sf: 0-1 GS: 0-0 **Gd: 1-1** GF: 0-2 Fm: 0-0
Distance: **5f/6f: 1-4** 7f-8f: 0-0 9f-13f: 0-0 14f+: 0-0
Track : LH: 0-0 RH: 0-0 Tight: 0-0 Gall: 0-0
Aids: Bl: 0-0 Vi: 0-0 Tstrap: 0-0 Ckp: 0-0
Best Rating: **102** 9/08 Donc 5f soft

Smart; placed in Group 2 company; effective over 5f; acts on good and soft ground.

Mythical Charm

(99) (59)64

10-y-o b m Charnwood Forest (IRE)-Triple Tricks (IRE) (Royal Academy (USA))

J J Bridger Tommy Ware

Placings:6562/**021**0600006501/**6000633**00035002200/56464002116000030**120**/633000205**521610**/0060010100040403063/04000660000-0 (0043)

2009: 80SD,

	Starts	1st	2nd	3rd	Win & Pl
Career Total (Turf)	59	5	4	4	24196
Career Total (AW)	42	4	4	4	10995

64	7/07	Sals	6f212y	(0-75)H	SFT	£3123
63	7/07	Gdwd	1m	(0-65)H	G-S	£3123
62	12/06	Kemp	1m	(0-45)	STD	£1365
62	11/06	Kemp	1m	(0-45)	STD	£1365
59	12/05	Ling	1m2f	(0-45)	STD	£1450
68	8/05	Gdwd	1m	(0-55)H	G-F	£3870
59	8/05	Ling	7f140y	(0-55)H	G-S	£2772
61	9/03	Kemp	1m	D(0-80)H	GD	£3718
55	4/03	Ling	1m2f	G	STD	£2940

Total win prize-money £23727

Going (Turf): Sf: 1-5 **GS: 2-10**Gd: 1-19 GF: 1-22 Fm: 0-3
Distance: 5f/6f: 0-3 **7f-8f: 7-56** 9f-13f: 2-42 14f+: 0-0
Track : LH: 2-40 **RH: 5-49 Tight: 2-39** Gall: 1-11
Aids: Bl: 0-0 Vi: 0-0 Tstrap: 0-0 Ckp: 0-0
Best Rating: **68** 8/05 Gdwd 1m gd-fm

Moderate; effective at round 1m-1m2f; acts on a sound surface; also goes on Polytrack.

Mythical Flight (SAF)

104 112

6-y-o ch g Jet Master (SAF)-Mythical Bird (SAF) (Harry Hotspur (SAF))

S g Tarry C J H Van Niekerk & M J Jooste

Placings:1111/111231/200-600 (5233)

2009: 66G, 50GF, 50GF,

	Starts	1st	2nd	3rd	Win & Pl
Career Total (Turf)	16	8	2	1	102332

12/07	Turf	5f	H	GD	£6793
5/07	Turf	5f		GD	£27173
4/07	Vaal	5f		GD	£4528
1/07	Keni	5f		GD	£18115
12/06	Nmkt	5f	H	SFT	£8616
12/06	Turf	5f		GD	£4021
9/06	Turf	5f		GD	£10627
6/06	Claw	5f		GD	£3045

Total win prize-money £82923

Going (Turf): Sf: 1-2 GS: 0-0 **Gd: 7-12** GF: 0-2 Fm: 0-0
Distance: **5f/6f: 8-16** 7f-8f: 0-0 9f-13f: 0-0 14f+: 0-0
Track : LH: 0-0 RH: 0-0 Tight: 0-0 Gall: 0-0
Aids: Bl: 0-0 Vi: 0-0 Tstrap: 0-0 Ckp: 0-0
Best Rating: **112** 12/08 ShTn 6f good

Smart South African sprinter; best at 5f on good ground.

Mythical Thrill

43

3-y-o b g Alhaarth (IRE)-Mythical Girl (USA) (Gone West (USA))

J G Given The Thrill Seekers

Placings:00-00 (5010)

2009: 80HY, 80G,

	Starts	1st	2nd	3rd	Win & Pl
Career Total (Turf)	4	0	0	0	

Going (Turf): **Sf: 0-2 GS: 0-1 Gd: 0-1 GF: 0-0 Fm: 0-0**
Distance: 5f/6f: 0-0 7f-8f: 0-1 9f-13f: 0-3 14f+: 0-0
Track : LH: 0-3 RH: 0-0 Tight: 0-0 Gall: 0-0
Aids: Bl: 0-0 Vi: 0-0 Tstrap: 0-0 Ckp: 0-0

Mythicism

88 71

3-y-o b f Oasis Dream-Romantic Myth (Mind Games)

B Smart Crossfields Racing

Placings:610-00 (1736)

2009: 50GF, 60GS,

	Starts	1st	2nd	3rd	Win & Pl
Career Total (Turf)	5	1	0	0	3562

71	10/08	Rdcr	6f	GD	£3561

Total win prize-money £3562

Going (Turf): Sf: 0-2 GS: 0-1 **Gd: 1-1** GF: 0-1 Fm: 0-0
Distance: **5f/6f: 1-5** 7f-8f: 0-0 9f-13f: 0-0 14f+: 0-0
Track : LH: 0-0 RH: 0-0 Tight: 0-0 Gall: 0-0
Aids: Bl: 0-0 Vi: 0-0 Tstrap: 0-0 Ckp: 0-0
Best Rating: 71 10/08 Rdcr 6f good

Fair; stays 6f; acts on soft and on good; may do better.

Mytivil (IRE)

94(93) (64)69
3-y-o gr f Clodovil (IRE)-Mytilene (IRE) (Soviet Star (USA))
M Salaman (Tom Dascombe 12/1) W Fitzgerald O'Connor H Whittington

Placings:03-62000 **(2858)**
2009: 8^{6}SD, 8^{2}GF, 8^{0}G, 8^{0}SD, 10^{0}G,

	Starts	1st	2nd	3rd	Win & Pl
Career Total (Turf)	3	0	1	0	806
Career Total (AW)	4	0	0	1	403

Going (Turf): **Sf: 0-0 GS: 0-0 Gd: 0-2 GF: 0-1 Fm: 0-0**
Distance: 5f/6f: 0-0 7f-8f: 0-2 9f-13f: 0-5 14f+: 0-0
Track : LH: 0-5 RH: 0-1 Tight: 0-5 Gall: 0-0
Aids: Bl: 0-0 Vi: 0-0 Tstrap: 0-0 Ckp: 0-0
Best Rating: 69 5/09 Wind 1m67y gd-fm

Myttons Maid

90(76) (21)49
3-y-o b f Bertolini (USA)-The In-Laws (IRE) (Be My Guest (USA))
A Bailey A Bailey

Placings:040-02 **(4177)**
2009: 7^{0}GF, 10^{2}GS,

	Starts	1st	2nd	3rd	Win & Pl
Career Total (Turf)	4	0	1	0	963
Career Total (AW)	1	0	0	0	

Going (Turf): **Sf: 0-1 GS: 0-2 Gd: 0-0 GF: 0-1 Fm: 0-0**
Distance: 5f/6f: 0-1 7f-8f: 0-3 9f-13f: 0-1 14f+: 0-0
Track : LH: 0-3 RH: 0-0 Tight: 0-1 Gall: 0-1
Aids: Bl: 0-0 Vi: 0-0 Tstrap: 0-2 Ckp: 0-2
Best Rating: 49 7/09 Yarm 1m2f21y gd-sft

Very moderate; stays 1m2f and acts on easy ground; has worn cheekpieces.

Nabeeda

96(102) (63)59
4-y-o b g Namid-Lovellian (Machiavellian (USA))
M Brittain Mel Brittain

Placings:50515050-4335544 **(7710)**
2009: 7^{4}SS, 6^{3}SD, 6^{3}SD, 7^{5}SD, 7^{5}GF, 6^{4}SD, 5^{4}SD,

	Starts	1st	2nd	3rd	Win & Pl
Career Total (Turf)	7	1	0	0	3886
Career Total (AW)	8	0	0	2	605

58 8/08 Ripn 5f G-S £3885
Total win prize-money £3886

Going (Turf): Sf: 0-2 **GS: 1-3** Gd: 0-0 GF: 0-2 Fm: 0-0
Distance: **5f/6f: 1-10** 7f-8f: 0-5 9f-13f: 0-0 14f+: 0-0
Track : LH: 0-8 RH: 0-0 Tight: 0-3 Gall: 0-0
Aids: Bl: 0-0 Vi: 0-0 Tstrap: 0-0 Ckp: 0-0
Best Rating: 63 1/09 Sthl 7f std-slw

Moderate; effective at sprint trips; handles easy ground; goes on Fibresand.

Nabra

98(94) (50)56
5-y-o b m Kyllachy-Muja Farewell (Mujtahid (USA))
M Brittain Mel Brittain

Placings:300/60000/036000000-001000 **(6221)**
2009: 7^{0}SD, 6^{0}G, 5^{1}GF, 6^{0}GF, 5^{0}G, 6^{0}GF,

	Starts	1st	2nd	3rd	Win & Pl
Career Total (Turf)	15	1	0	1	5063
Career Total (AW)	8	0	0	1	262

56 8/09 Ripn 5f G-F £4533
Total win prize-money £4533

Going (Turf): Sf: 0-0 GS: 0-2 Gd: 0-5 **GF: 1-8** Fm: 0-0
Distance: **5f/6f: 1-18** 7f-8f: 0-5 9f-13f: 0-0 14f+: 0-0
Track : LH: 0-10 RH: 0-0 Tight: 0-7 Gall: 0-0
Aids: Bl: 0-1 Vi: 0-0 Tstrap: 0-0 Ckp: 0-0
Best Rating: 56 8/09 Ripn 5f gd-fm

Very moderate sprinter; acts on fast ground.

Nabrina (IRE)

90(87) (45)53
2-y-o ch f Namid-My Cadeaux (Cadeaux Genereux)
M Brittain Mel Brittain

Placings:56063064 **(7757)**
2009: 5^{5}G, 5^{6}S, 5^{0}G, 5^{6}GS, 5^{3}GF, 6^{0}GS, 6^{6}SD, 6^{4}SD,

	Starts	1st	2nd	3rd	Win & Pl
Career Total (Turf)	6	0	0	1	313
Career Total (AW)	2	0	0	0	0

Going (Turf): **Sf: 0-1 GS: 0-2 Gd: 0-2 GF: 0-1 Fm: 0-0**
Distance: 5f/6f: 0-7 7f-8f: 0-1 9f-13f: 0-0 14f+: 0-0
Track : LH: 0-2 RH: 0-0 Tight: 0-0 Gall: 0-0
Aids: Bl: 0-0 Vi: 0-0 Tstrap: 0-0 Ckp: 0-0
Best Rating: 53 7/09 Nott 5f13y good

Moderate; suited by 6f and acts on fast ground.

Nacho Libre

96(106) (67)77
4-y-o b g Kyllachy-Expectation (IRE) (Night Shift (USA))
M W Easterby Tri Nations Racing Syndicate

Placings:6125303/40000-0600404133 **(7735)**
2009: 5^{0}GF, 6^{6}G, 6^{0}GS, 7^{0}SD, 6^{4}GS, 5^{0}S, 7^{4}G, 5^{1}SD, 6^{3}SD, 5^{3}SD,

	Starts	1st	2nd	3rd	Win & Pl
Career Total (Turf)	18	1	1	2	15140
Career Total (AW)	4	1	0	2	2877

67 11/09 Wolv 5f216y (0-55)H STD £2047
78 6/07 Wind 6f GD £2914
Total win prize-money £4962

Going (Turf): Sf: 0-4 GS: 0-2 **Gd: 1-8** GF: 0-4 Fm: 0-0
Distance: **5f/6f: 2-14** 7f-8f: 0-8 9f-13f: 0-0 14f+: 0-0
Track : **LH: 1-9** RH: 0-0 Tight: 1-5 Gall: 1-1
Aids: **Bl: 1-4** Vi: 0-0 Tstrap: 0-0 Ckp: 0-0
Best Rating: 100 4/08 NmkR 7f good

Modest; stays 7f; acts on most ground; goes on Fibresand and Polytrack; has worn blinkers.

Naddwah

87 68
2-y-o ch f Pivotal-My Dubai (IRE) (Dubai Millennium)
M A Jarvis Sheikh Ahmed Al Maktoum

Placings:6 **(6730)**
2009: 6^{6}S,

	Starts	1st	2nd	3rd	Win & Pl
Career Total (Turf)	1	0	0	0	0

Going (Turf): **Sf: 0-1 GS: 0-0 Gd: 0-0 GF: 0-0 Fm: 0-0**
Distance: 5f/6f: 0-0 7f-8f: 0-1 9f-13f: 0-0 14f+: 0-0
Track : LH: 0-0 RH: 0-0 Tight: 0-0 Gall: 0-0
Aids: Bl: 0-0 Vi: 0-0 Tstrap: 0-0 Ckp: 0-0
Best Rating: 68 10/09 Sals 6f212y soft

Nadeen (IRE)

93 86
2-y-o b c Bahamian Bounty-Janayen (USA) (Zafonic (USA))
M R Channon Jaber Abdullah

Placings:13 **(2547)**
2009: 5^{1}GF, 5^{3}GF,

	Starts	1st	2nd	3rd	Win & Pl
Career Total (Turf)	2	1	0	1	4722

76 4/09 Brig 5f59y G-F £4144
Total win prize-money £4145

Going (Turf): Sf: 0-0 GS: 0-0 Gd: 0-0 **GF: 1-2** Fm: 0-0
Distance: **5f/6f: 1-2** 7f-8f: 0-0 9f-13f: 0-0 14f+: 0-0
Track : **LH: 1-1** RH: 0-0 Tight: 0-0 Gall: 0-1
Aids: Bl: 0-0 Vi: 0-0 Tstrap: 0-0 Ckp: 0-0
Best Rating: 86 6/09 Wind 5f10y gd-fm

Fair; effective at 5f; acts on fast ground.

Nafura

86(106) (86)62
2-y-o b f Dubawi (IRE)-Mysterial (USA) (Alleged (USA))
Saeed Bin Suroor Godolphin

Placings:50011 **(7359)**
2009: 7^{5}SD, 7^{0}GF, 7^{0}GF, 8^{1}SD, 8^{1}SD,

	Starts	1st	2nd	3rd	Win & Pl
Career Total (Turf)	2	0	0	0	
Career Total (AW)	3	2	0	0	7447

86 11/09 Wolv 1m141y (0-75)H STD £3238
76 10/09 Wolv 1m141y (0-80) STD £4209
Total win prize-money £7447

Going (Turf): **Sf: 0-0 GS: 0-0 Gd: 0-0 GF: 0-2 Fm: 0-0**
Distance: 5f/6f: 0-0 7f-8f: 0-3 **9f-13f: 2-2** 14f+: 0-0
Track : **LH: 2-2** RH: 0-2 **Tight: 2-2** Gall: 0-0
Aids: Bl: 0-0 Vi: 0-0 Tstrap: 2-2 Ckp: 2-2
Best Rating: 86 11/09 Wolv 1m141y stand

Useful; stays 1m and acts on Polytrack; has worn cheek-pieces and a tongue tie.

Naheell

90(100) (71)68
3-y-o ch c Lomitas-Seyooll (IRE) (Danehill (USA))
G Prodromou (M A Jarvis 29/6) P Hajipiery

Placings:523-6021000 **(7664)**
2009: 12^{6}SD, 10^{0}F, 9^{2}GF, 9^{1}SD, 10^{0}G, 10^{0}SD, 8^{0}SD,

	Starts	1st	2nd	3rd	Win & Pl
Career Total (Turf)	4	0	1	0	806
Career Total (AW)	6	1	1	1	3671

71 10/09 Wolv 1m1f103y (0-65)H STD £2388
Total win prize-money £2388

Going (Turf): **Sf: 0-0 GS: 0-0 Gd: 0-1 GF: 0-2 Fm: 0-1**
Distance: 5f/6f: 0-0 7f-8f: 0-2 **9f-13f: 1-8** 14f+: 0-0
Track : **LH: 1-8** RH: 0-2 **Tight: 1-8** Gall: 0-0
Aids: Bl: 0-0 Vi: 0-0 Tstrap: 0-0 Ckp: 0-0
Best Rating: 71 10/09 Wolv 1m1f103y stand

Fair; stays 1m1f; acts on Polytrack.

Naias (IRE)

(86) (7)45
4-y-o ch f Namid-Sovereign Grace (IRE) (Standaan (FR))
R A Fahey J J Staunton

Placings:205-0 (0153)
2009: 6^{0}SD,

	Starts	1st	2nd	3rd	Win & Pl
Career Total (Turf)	2	0	1	0	605
Career Total (AW)	2	0	0	0	0

Going (Turf): **Sf: 0-0 GS: 0-0 Gd: 0-0 GF: 0-2 Fm: 0-0**
Distance: 5f/6f: 0-3 7f-8f: 0-1 9f-13f: 0-0 14f+: 0-0
Track : LH: 0-3 RH: 0-1 Tight: 0-2 Gall: 0-0
Aids: Bl: 0-0 Vi: 0-0 Tstrap: 0-0 Ckp: 0-0
Best Rating: **45** 7/08 Catt 5f212y gd-fm

Moderate sprinter; stays 6f; acts on quick ground.

Nairana

(78) (34)
3-y-o b f Lend A Hand-Flukes (Distant Relative)
J G Given Mrs Carol Coe

Placings:00-6 (0298)
2009: 7^{8}SD,

	Starts	1st	2nd	3rd	Win & Pl
Career Total (Turf)	0	0	0	0	
Career Total (AW)	3	0	0	0	0

Going (Turf): **Sf: 0-0 GS: 0-0 Gd: 0-0 GF: 0-0 Fm: 0-0**
Distance: 5f/6f: 0-2 7f-8f: 0-1 9f-13f: 0-0 14f+: 0-0
Track : LH: 0-3 RH: 0-0 Tight: 0-3 Gall: 0-0
Aids: Bl: 0-0 Vi: 0-0 Tstrap: 0-0 Ckp: 0-0
Best Rating: **34** 11/08 Wolv 5f216y stand

Naizak

81(87) (56)72
3-y-o ch f Medicean-Sunny Davis (USA) (Alydar (USA))
J L Dunlop Hamdan Al Maktoum

Placings:0346-00 (1743)
2009: 8^{0}GF, 7^{0}GF,

	Starts	1st	2nd	3rd	Win & Pl
Career Total (Turf)	5	0	0	1	865
Career Total (AW)	1	0	0	0	0

Going (Turf): **Sf: 0-0 GS: 0-1 Gd: 0-2 GF: 0-2 Fm: 0-0**
Distance: 5f/6f: 0-0 7f-8f: 0-5 9f-13f: 0-1 14f+: 0-0
Track : LH: 0-4 RH: 0-0 Tight: 0-0 Gall: 0-1
Aids: Bl: 0-1 Vi: 0-0 Tstrap: 0-0 Ckp: 0-0
Best Rating: **72** 11/08 NmkR 7f gd-sft

Fair maiden form to date; effective over 7f.

Najd (USA)

97 83
2-y-o ch c Storm Cat (USA)-Miss Halory (USA) (Mr Prospector (USA))
Saeed Bin Suroor Godolphin

Placings:1 (4986)
2009: 7^{1}GF,

	Starts	1st	2nd	3rd	Win & Pl
Career Total (Turf)	1	1	0	0	4857

83 8/09 Newb 7f G-F £4857
Total win prize-money £4857

Going (Turf): Sf: 0-0 GS: 0-0 Gd: 0-0 **GF: 1-1** Fm: 0-0
Distance: 5f/6f: 0-0 **7f-8f: 1-1** 9f-13f: 0-0 14f+: 0-0
Track : LH: 0-0 RH: 0-0 Tight: 0-0 Gall: 0-0
Aids: Bl: 0-0 Vi: 0-0 Tstrap: 0-0 Ckp: 0-0
Best Rating: **83** 8/09 Newb 7f gd-fm

Nakoma (IRE)

92(99) (66)64
7-y-o b m Bahhare (USA)-Indian Imp (Indian Ridge)
B Ellison Racing Management & Training, K & BGM

Placings:6-4401**160** (7785)
2009: 9^{4}G, 12^{4}G, 14^{0}GS, 12^{1}GS, 13^{1}SD, 12^{6}SD, 13^{0}SD,

	Starts	1st	2nd	3rd	Win & Pl
Career Total (Turf)	5	1	0	0	2156
Career Total (AW)	3	1	0	0	3238

66 11/09 Wolv 1m5f194y (0-75)H STD £3238
64 10/09 Newc 1m4f93y (0-65)H G-S £1747
Total win prize-money £4985

Going (Turf): Sf: 0-0 **GS: 1-3** Gd: 0-2 GF: 0-0 Fm: 0-0
Distance: 5f/6f: 0-0 7f-8f: 0-0 9f-13f: 1-5 14f+: 1-3
Track : **LH: 2-5** RH: 0-3 Tight: 1-6 Gall: 1-1
Aids: Bl: 0-0 Vi: 0-0 Tstrap: 0-0 Ckp: 0-0
Best Rating: **66** 11/09 Wolv 1m5f194y stand

Modest; stays 1m6f; acts on Polytrack and easy ground on turf.

Naledi

89(91) (47)40
5-y-o b g Indian Ridge-Red Carnation (IRE) (Polar Falcon (USA))
J R Norton Mrs Janice Thompson

Placings:40**540**/00000-0**5**00 (3322)
2009: 7^{0}SD, 9^{5}SD, 10^{0}F, 8^{0}GF,

	Starts	1st	2nd	3rd	Win & Pl
Career Total (Turf)	8	0	0	0	216
Career Total (AW)	6	0	0	0	0

Going (Turf): **Sf: 0-3 GS: 0-0 Gd: 0-1 GF: 0-3 Fm: 0-1**
Distance: 5f/6f: 0-1 7f-8f: 0-7 9f-13f: 0-6 14f+: 0-0
Track : LH: 0-10 RH: 0-1 Tight: 0-3 Gall: 0-1
Aids: Bl: 0-5 Vi: 0-1 Tstrap: 0-0 Ckp: 0-0
Best Rating: **62** 10/07 Leic 7f9y soft

Namaskar

94 80
2-y-o b f Dansili-Namaste (Alzao (USA))
J H M Gosden K Abdulla

Placings:1 (5741)
2009: 8^{1}GF,

	Starts	1st	2nd	3rd	Win & Pl
Career Total (Turf)	1	1	0	0	3562

80 9/09 Gdwd 1m G-F £3561
Total win prize-money £3562

Going (Turf): Sf: 0-0 GS: 0-0 Gd: 0-0 **GF: 1-1** Fm: 0-0
Distance: 5f/6f: 0-0 **7f-8f: 1-1** 9f-13f: 0-0 14f+: 0-0
Track : LH: 0-0 **RH: 1-1** Tight: 0-0 Gall: 0-0
Aids: Bl: 0-0 Vi: 0-0 Tstrap: 0-0 Ckp: 0-0
Best Rating: **80** 9/09 Gdwd 1m gd-fm

Useful winner on debut over 1m on fast ground.

Namecheck (GER)

99 98
2-y-o ch c Shamardal (USA)-Nadia (Nashwan (USA))
Saeed Bin Suroor Godolphin

Placings:313 (6898)
2009: 6^{3}GS, 7^{1}GF, 8^{3}GF,

	Starts	1st	2nd	3rd	Win & Pl
Career Total (Turf)	3	1	0	2	8165

84 9/09 Bevl 7f100y G-F £3753
Total win prize-money £3753

Going (Turf): Sf: 0-0 GS: 0-1 Gd: 0-0 **GF: 1-2** Fm: 0-0
Distance: 5f/6f: 0-1 **7f-8f: 1-1** 9f-13f: 0-1 14f+: 0-0
Track : LH: 0-1 **RH: 1-1** Tight: 0-0 Gall: 0-0
Aids: Bl: 0-0 Vi: 0-0 Tstrap: 0-0 Ckp: 0-0
Best Rating: **98** 10/09 Pont 1m4y gd-fm

Very useful; stays 1m; acts on fast ground.

Named At Dinner

69 48
8-y-o ch g Halling (USA)-Salanka (IRE) (Persian Heights)
Miss Lucinda V Russell Dig In Racing

Placings:04224/00000000/0/640/0-0 (3444)
2009: 16^{0}GF,

	Starts	1st	2nd	3rd	Win & Pl
Career Total (Turf)	19	0	2	0	2537

Going (Turf): **Sf: 0-0 GS: 0-5 Gd: 0-2 GF: 0-11 Fm: 0-1**
Distance: 5f/6f: 0-0 7f-8f: 0-10 9f-13f: 0-4 14f+: 0-5
Track : LH: 0-8 RH: 0-6 Tight: 0-5 Gall: 0-2
Aids: Bl: 0-1 Vi: 0-3 Tstrap: 0-2 Ckp: 0-2
Best Rating: **71** 10/03 Brig 6f209y gd-fm

Namibian Orator (IRE)

106 92
3-y-o br c Cape Cross (IRE)-Drama Class (IRE) (Caerleon (USA))
Sir Michael Stoute Ballymacoll Stud

Placings:1634 (7035)
2009: 10^{1}GS, 10^{6}GF, 8^{3}GF, 10^{4}S,

	Starts	1st	2nd	3rd	Win & Pl
Career Total (Turf)	4	1	0	1	4876

86 4/09 Wind 1m2f7y G-S £2729
Total win prize-money £2730

Going (Turf): Sf: 0-1 **GS: 1-1** Gd: 0-0 GF: 0-2 Fm: 0-0
Distance: 5f/6f: 0-0 7f-8f: 0-1 **9f-13f: 1-3** 14f+: 0-0
Track : LH: 0-1 **RH: 1-1 Tight: 1-1** Gall: 0-1
Aids: Bl: 0-0 Vi: 0-0 Tstrap: 0-0 Ckp: 0-0
Best Rating: **92** 10/09 NmkR 1m gd-fm

Useful; stays 1m2f and acts on easy ground.

Namir (IRE)

102(97) (69)83
7-y-o b g Namid-Danalia (IRE) (Danehill (USA))
H J Evans (D Shaw 5/8) ownaracehorse.co.uk (Shakespeare)

Placings:2211300000**4060**/**503000**5614012405l000/516 1625020**600**/00260101405200150**6**-0020460062006266 (7329)

2009: 5⁰SD, 6⁰GF, 5²GF, 5⁰G, 5⁴GF, 5⁶GF, 5⁰G, 5⁰S, 5⁶GF, 5²G, 5⁰GS, 5⁰G, 5⁶GF, 5²GF, 5⁶G, 6⁶SD,

	Starts	1st	2nd	3rd	Win & Pl
Career Total (Turf)	65	10	10	1	63616
Career Total (AW)	17	0	0	1	353

83	9/08	NmkR	5f	(0-75)H	G-F	£3885
81	6/08	Pont	5f	(0-75)H	GD	£3238
78	5/08	Bevl	5f	(0-85)H	GD	£4209
81	5/07	Bevl	5f	(0-85)H	G-F	£6477
76	5/07	Nott	5f13y	(0-70)H	G-S	£3238
70	9/06	Pont	5f	(0-75)H	G-F	£4533
68	7/06	Nott	6f15y	(0-65)H	FRM	£2730
66	6/06	Pont	5f	(0-65)H	G-F	£3238
89	5/05	Haml	5f4y		G-S	£8882
84	4/05	Thsk	5f		SFT	£5629

Total win prize-money £46064

Going (Turf): Sf: 1-9 GS: 2-11 Gd: 2-21 **GF: 4-23** Fm: 1-1
Distance: **5f/6f: 9-77** 7f-8f: 1-4 9f-13f: 0-1 14f+: 0-0
Track : **LH: 3-35** RH: 0-3 Tight: 0-15 Gall: 0-3
Aids: Bl: 0-3 **Vi: 8-63** Tstrap: 0-1 Ckp: 0-1
Best Rating: **89** 5/05 Haml 5f4y gd-sft

Modest sprinter; acts on fast and soft ground; also goes on Polytrack; has worn a visor and a tongue tie.

Nampour (FR)

94 (78)87
4-y-o gr g Daylami (IRE)-Nadira (FR) (Green Desert (USA))
P J Hobbs Terry Warner

Placings:504513/1-4 **(5912)**
2009: 12⁴GF,

	Starts	1st	2nd	3rd	Win & Pl
Career Total (Turf)	7	2	0	0	15834
Career Total (AW)	1	0	0	1	2230

4/08	Nanc	1m1f165y		GD	£8455
11/07	Comp	7f		VS	£3378

Total win prize-money £11834

Going (Turf): Sf: 0-2 GS: 0-2 **Gd: 1-1** GF: 0-1 Fm: 0-0
Distance: 5f/6f: 0-0 7f-8f: 1-6 9f-13f: 1-2 14f+: 0-0
Track : **LH: 1-2** RH: 0-2 Tight: 0-1 Gall: 0-0
Aids: Bl: 0-0 Vi: 0-0 Tstrap: 0-0 Ckp: 0-0
Best Rating: **87** 9/09 Gdwd 1m4f gd-fm

Namu

97(106) (70)64
6-y-o b m Mujahid (USA)-Sheraton Heights (Deploy)
Miss T Spearing Advantage Chemicals Holdings Ltd

Placings:0262322/44161363150/03400554/003035040301004-1600002125600350 **(6933)**
2009: 6¹SD, 7⁶SD, 6⁰SD, 7⁰SD, 7⁰SD, 6⁰G, 5²F, 5¹F, 6²GF, 5⁵F, 6⁶GF, 6⁰SD, 5⁰GF, 5³GF, 6⁵SD, 5⁰G,

	Starts	1st	2nd	3rd	Win & Pl
Career Total (Turf)	43	4	6	8	31541
Career Total (AW)	14	2	0	0	3412

64	7/09	Brig	5f213y	(0-55)H	FRM	£2072
70	1/09	Kemp	6f	(0-60)H	STD	£1706
63	11/08	Kemp	6f	(0-60)H	STD	£1706
76	9/06	Pont	6f	(0-85)H	GD	£6477
76	7/06	Folk	6f	(0-70)H	G-F	£3886
75	7/06	Wwck	6f21y		FRM	£3238

Total win prize-money £19086

Going (Turf): Sf: 0-4 GS: 0-6 Gd: 1-12 GF: 1-15 **Fm: 2-5**
Distance: **5f/6f: 5-37** 7f-8f: 1-20 9f-13f: 0-0 14f+: 0-0
Track : **LH: 3-19** RH: 2-11 Tight: 0-3 Gall: 0-5
Aids: Bl: 0-0 Vi: 0-0 Tstrap: 3-19 Ckp: 3-19
Best Rating: **76** 4/07 Lonc 7f good

Moderate; ex-French; seems best suited by a strongly run 6f; handles most ground on turf; goes on Polytrack; has worn cheekpieces.

Nanny Doe (IRE)

(77) (23)
3-y-o b f Mujadil (USA)-Prima (Primo Dominie)
Lee Smyth Rodney Williamson

Placings:0000 **(7730)**
2009: 8⁰SD, 8⁰SD, 8⁰SD, 7⁰SD,

	Starts	1st	2nd	3rd	Win & Pl
Career Total (Turf)	0	0	0	0	
Career Total (AW)	4	0	0	0	

Going (Turf): **Sf: 0-0 GS: 0-0 Gd: 0-0 GF: 0-0 Fm: 0-0**
Distance: 5f/6f: 0-0 7f-8f: 0-3 9f-13f: 0-1 14f+: 0-0
Track : LH: 0-4 RH: 0-0 Tight: 0-2 Gall: 0-0
Aids: Bl: 0-1 Vi: 0-0 Tstrap: 0-2 Ckp: 0-2
Best Rating: **23** 11/09 Wolv 1m141y stand

Nanton (USA)

112(110) (94)109
7-y-o gr/ro g Spinning World (USA)-Grab The Green (USA) (Cozzene (USA))
J S Goldie J S Morrison

Placings:063311/5523113031O/5046231100/003455066/23100251-024002414304 **(7720)**
2009: 8⁰GF, 10²GF, 8⁴GF, 10⁰GF, 7⁰G, 10²G, 14⁴GF, 14¹GF, 10⁴G, 9³GF, 18⁰G, 12⁴SD,

	Starts	1st	2nd	3rd	Win & Pl
Career Total (Turf)	46	7	6	7	180301
Career Total (AW)	10	3	0	2	10088

109	9/09	Donc	1m6f132y	(0-110)H	G-F	£32380
94	8/08	Donc	1m2f60y	(0-100)H	GD	£12462
89	9/06	Rdcr	1m	H	GD	£18696
86	9/06	Rdcr	1m		FRM	£5505
87	9/05	Haml	1m1f36y		G-F	£6948
87	7/05	Nott	1m54y	(0-70)	G-F	£3484
83	7/05	Hayd	1m30y	(0-70)	G-F	£3464
79	12/04	Ling	1m		STD	£4121
71	12/04	Wolv	1m141y		STD	£4104

Total win prize-money £91167

Going (Turf): Sf: 0-0 GS: 0-6 Gd: 2-19 **GF: 4-20** Fm: 1-1
Distance: 5f/6f: 0-1 7f-8f: 3-14 **9f-13f: 6-38** 14f+: 1-3
Track : **LH: 7-29** RH: 1-13 **Tight: 4-23** Gall: 2-11
Aids: Bl: 0-0 Vi: 0-0 Tstrap: 0-0 Ckp: 0-0
Best Rating: **109** 9/09 Donc 1m6f132y gd-fm

Smart; stays 1m6f, but effective at much shorter; acts on good and faster ground; very useful on Polytrack; usually held up.

Naomh Geileis (USA)

95(100) (69)57
4-y-o ch f Grand Slam (USA)-St Aye (USA) (Nureyev (USA))
M Johnston Mrs Christine E Budden

Placings:21454/5-005040616350 **(7870)**
2009: 10⁰SD, 8⁰SD, 8⁵SD, 9⁰S, 10⁴GF, 11⁰G, 6⁶GF, 7¹SD, 6⁶SD, 8³SD, 7⁵SD, 6⁰SS,

	Starts	1st	2nd	3rd	Win & Pl
Career Total (Turf)	8	1	1	0	13566
Career Total (AW)	10	1	0	1	3004

69	11/09	Sthl	7f	(0-60)H	STD	£1706
74	8/07	Pont	6f		G-F	£3886

Total win prize-money £5592

Going (Turf): Sf: 0-1 GS: 0-2 Gd: 0-2 **GF: 1-3** Fm: 0-0
Distance: 5f/6f: 1-5 7f-8f: 1-8 9f-13f: 0-5 14f+: 0-0
Track : **LH: 2-11** RH: 0-5 Tight: 0-5 Gall: 0-1
Aids: **Bl: 1-7** Vi: 0-0 Tstrap: 0-0 Ckp: 0-0
Best Rating: **94** 10/07 Asct 1m gd-sft

Modest; formerly very useful; effective over 6f; acts on fast and easy ground and on sand; has worn blinkers.

Napa Starr (FR)

94(97) (78)71
5-y-o b g Marchand De Sable (USA)-Jade D'Eau (IRE) (Lion Cavern (USA))
C Byrnes Woodfield Syndicate

Placings:16/06000061/1020600-03120244 **(6780)**
2009: 7⁰HY, 7³GF, 8¹G, 9²GF, 8⁰S, 8²SD, 8⁴G, 8⁴SS,

	Starts	1st	2nd	3rd	Win & Pl
Career Total (Turf)	20	1	2	1	8052
Career Total (AW)	5	3	1	0	13790

69	7/09	Bell	1m	(47-65)H	GD	£5031
	1/08	Deau	7f110y	H	STD	£6250
	12/07	Deau	7f110y	H	STD	£5515
	11/06	Ghli	1m		STD	£1064

Total win prize-money £17861

Going (Turf): Sf: 0-4 GS: 0-3 **Gd: 1-4** GF: 0-4 Fm: 0-1
Distance: 5f/6f: 0-2 **7f-8f: 4-16** 9f-13f: 0-7 14f+: 0-0
Track : **LH: 1-11** RH: 0-5 Tight: 0-1 Gall: 0-0
Aids: Bl: 0-2 Vi: 0-0 Tstrap: 0-0 Ckp: 0-0
Best Rating: **78** 10/09 Ling 1m std-slw

Modest; effective at 1m; handles good ground.

Napoleons Mistress (IRE)

76 44
2-y-o ch f Peintre Celebre (USA)-State Crystal (IRE) (High Estate)
P F I Cole Mrs Christopher Hanbury

Placings:6 **(6389)**
2009: 8⁶GF,

	Starts	1st	2nd	3rd	Win & Pl
Career Total (Turf)	1	0	0	0	0

Going (Turf): **Sf: 0-0 GS: 0-0 Gd: 0-0 GF: 0-1 Fm: 0-0**
Distance: 5f/6f: 0-0 7f-8f: 0-0 9f-13f: 0-1 14f+: 0-0
Track : LH: 0-1 RH: 0-0 Tight: 0-0 Gall: 0-0
Aids: Bl: 0-0 Vi: 0-0 Tstrap: 0-0 Ckp: 0-0
Best Rating: **44** 9/09 Nott 1m75y gd-fm

Napoletano (GER)

100(105) (75)76
8-y-o b g Soviet Star (USA)-Noble House (GER) (Siberian Express (USA))
S Dow Miss Helen Chamberlain

Placings:33/11323/65601000/0000050533410002/2045461013452100030002 5-600245002365 **(6783)**
2009: 7⁶SD, 8⁰SD, 7⁰SD, 7²GF, 7⁴GF, 6⁵G, 7⁰GF, 6⁰GF, 7²G, 7³GF, 7⁶GF, 7⁵SS,

	Starts	1st	2nd	3rd	Win & Pl
Career Total (Turf)	39	6	4	8	45227
Career Total (AW)	27	1	3	1	4339

75	7/08	Brig	7f214y	(0-65)H	G-F	£2137
73	4/08	Brig	6f209y	(0-65)H	GD	£2331
61	3/08	Ling	7f	(0-55)H	STD	£2047

57 6/07 Ling 7f (0-65)H GD £2047
9/06 Hall 1m165y H FRM £1828
6/04 Lonc 1m G-S £10915
6/04 Hamb 7f GD £3309
Total win prize-money £24617

Going (Turf): Sf: 0-6 GS: 1-2 **Gd: 3-12** GF: 1-15 Fm: 1-3
Distance: 5f/6f: 0-1 **7f-8f: 6-61** 9f-13f: 1-4 14f+: 0-0
Track : **LH: 3-34** RH: 1-15 **Tight: 1-20** Gall: 0-0
Aids: Bl: 1-2 Vi: 0-0 Tstrap: 4-43 Ckp: 4-43
Best Rating: **101** 8/04 Deau 1m v soft

Modest; effective over 7f-1m; acts on fast ground and on Polytrack; has worn cheekpieces.

Napoletano (ITY)

82(65) **47**
3-y-o b g Kyllachy-Nationality (Nashwan (USA))
R Johnson A S Racing

Placings:0000 **(5342)**
2009: 7^{0}SD, 12^{0}GF, 10^{0}GS, 11^{0}GS,

	Starts	1st	2nd	3rd	Win & Pl
Career Total (Turf)	3	0	0	0	
Career Total (AW)	1	0	0	0	

Going (Turf): **Sf: 0-0 GS: 0-2 Gd: 0-0 GF: 0-1 Fm: 0-0**
Distance: 5f/6f: 0-0 7f-8f: 0-1 9f-13f: 0-3 14f+: 0-0
Track : LH: 0-4 RH: 0-0 Tight: 0-1 Gall: 0-2
Aids: Bl: 0-0 Vi: 0-0 Tstrap: 0-0 Ckp: 0-0
Best Rating: **47** 4/09 Newc 1m4f93y gd-fm

Napoletano (GER)

100(105) (75)**76**
8-y-o b g Soviet Star (USA)-Noble House (GER) (Siberian Express (USA))
S Dow Miss Helen Chamberlain

Placings:33/11323/65601000/0000050533410002/204546 1013452100030025-600245002365 **(6783)**
2009: 7^{6}SD, 8^{0}SD, 7^{0}SD, 7^{2}GF, 7^{4}GF, 6^{5}G, 7^{0}GF, 6^{0}GF, 7^{2}G, 7^{3}GF, 7^{6}GF, 7^{5}SS,

	Starts	1st	2nd	3rd	Win & Pl
Career Total (Turf)	39	6	4	8	45227
Career Total (AW)	27	1	3	1	4339

75 7/08 Brig 7f214y (0-65)H G-F £2137
73 4/08 Brig 6f209y (0-65)H GD £2331
61 3/08 Ling 7f (0-55)H STD £2047
57 6/07 Ling 7f (0-65)H GD £2047
9/06 Hall 1m165y H FRM £1828
6/04 Lonc 1m G-S £10915
6/04 Hamb 7f GD £3309
Total win prize-money £24617

Going (Turf): Sf: 0-6 GS: 1-2 **Gd: 3-12** GF: 1-15 Fm: 1-3
Distance: 5f/6f: 0-1 **7f-8f: 6-61** 9f-13f: 1-4 14f+: 0-0
Track : **LH: 3-34** RH: 1-15 **Tight: 1-20** Gall: 0-0
Aids: Bl: 1-2 Vi: 0-0 Tstrap: 4-43 Ckp: 4-43
Best Rating: **101** 8/04 Deau 1m v soft

Modest; effective over 7f-1m; acts on fast ground and on Polytrack; has worn cheekpieces.

Naseby (USA)

(83) (58)
2-y-o ch c Maria's Mon (USA)-Branchbury (USA) (Mt. Livermore (USA))
Miss S L Davison (R Charlton 24/9) Miss S L Davison

Placings:000 **(6774)**
2009: 7^{0}SD, 7^{0}SD, 6^{0}SD,

	Starts	1st	2nd	3rd	Win & Pl
Career Total (Turf)	0	0	0	0	
Career Total (AW)	3	0	0	0	

Going (Turf): **Sf: 0-0 GS: 0-0 Gd: 0-0 GF: 0-0 Fm: 0-0**
Distance: 5f/6f: 0-1 7f-8f: 0-2 9f-13f: 0-0 14f+: 0-0
Track : LH: 0-1 RH: 0-2 Tight: 0-1 Gall: 0-0
Aids: Bl: 0-0 Vi: 0-0 Tstrap: 0-0 Ckp: 0-0
Best Rating: **58** 10/09 Kemp 6f stand

Naseehah (USA)

(103) (90)
3-y-o ch c Rahy (USA)-Helwa (USA) (Silver Hawk (USA))
A bin Huzaim (Saeed Bin Suroor 12/11) Sheikh Hamdan Bin Mohammed Al Maktoum

Placings:122
2009: 9^{1}SD, 9^{2}SD, 8^{2}FT,

	Starts	1st	2nd	3rd	Win & Pl
Career Total (Turf)	0	0	0	0	
Career Total (AW)	3	1	2	0	8059

77 10/09 Wolv 1m1f103y STD £2729
Total win prize-money £2730

Going (Turf): **Sf: 0-0 GS: 0-0 Gd: 0-0 GF: 0-0 Fm: 0-0**
Distance: 5f/6f: 0-0 7f-8f: 0-1 **9f-13f: 1-2** 14f+: 0-0
Track : **LH: 1-2** RH: 0-0 **Tight: 1-2** Gall: 0-0
Aids: Bl: 0-0 Vi: 0-0 Tstrap: 0-0 Ckp: 0-0
Best Rating: **90** 11/09 Wolv 1m1f103y stand

Useful; stays 1m1f; acts on Polytrack.

Nashmiah (IRE)

108(107) (105)**110**
3-y-o b f Elusive City (USA)-Frond (Alzao (USA))
C E Brittain Saeed Manana

Placings:401453-10105031104 **(7046a)**
2009: 7^{1}SD, 8^{0}GF, 8^{1}GS, 8^{0}GF, 7^{5}GF, 9^{0}S, 8^{3}GF, 9^{1}GF, 10^{1}GF, 8^{0}GF, 10^{4}GS,

	Starts	1st	2nd	3rd	Win & Pl
Career Total (Turf)	15	4	0	2	109499
Career Total (AW)	2	1	0	0	34351

102 9/09 Yarm 1m2f21y G-F £22432
106 8/09 Gdwd 1m1f192y (0-110)H G-F £22708
100 5/09 York 1m G-S £22708
105 3/09 Ling 7f STD £34062
79 8/08 Ling 7f140y G-F £2047
Total win prize-money £103957

Going (Turf): Sf: 0-1 GS: 1-3 Gd: 0-1 **GF: 3-10** Fm: 0-0
Distance: 5f/6f: 0-0 **7f-8f: 3-12** 9f-13f: 2-5 14f+: 0-0
Track : **LH: 3-4** RH: 1-7 **Tight: 3-5** Gall: 1-2
Aids: Bl: 0-0 Vi: 0-0 Tstrap: 0-0 Ckp: 0-0
Best Rating: **110** 10/09 Capa 1m2f gd-sft

Smart; Listed winner and Group placed; stays 1m2f; acts on most ground and on Polytrack.

Nasri

105 **104**
3-y-o b c Kyllachy-Triple Sharp (Selkirk (USA))
B J Meehan Saleh Al Homaizi & Imad Al Sagar

Placings:021130-6230 **(3011)**
2009: 7^{6}S, 7^{2}GF, 7^{3}G, 7^{0}GF,

	Starts	1st	2nd	3rd	Win & Pl
Career Total (Turf)	10	2	2	2	132226

96 9/08 Newb 6f8y GD £12462
92 8/08 Newb 6f8y G-S £5828
Total win prize-money £18290

Going (Turf): Sf: 0-2 **GS: 1-1 Gd: 1-3** GF: 0-4 Fm: 0-0
Distance: 5f/6f: 0-2 **7f-8f: 2-8** 9f-13f: 0-0 14f+: 0-0
Track : LH: 0-1 RH: 0-0 Tight: 0-1 Gall: 0-1
Aids: Bl: 0-0 Vi: 0-0 Tstrap: 0-0 Ckp: 0-0
Best Rating: **104** 5/09 NmkR 7f gd-fm

Smart; suited by 6f-7f and acts on most ground.

Nassar (IRE)

100(103) (66)**67**
6-y-o b h Danehill (USA)-Regent Gold (USA) (Seeking The Gold (USA))
G Prodromou Faisal Al-Nassar

Placings:06000405660/2/5134-51334543046 **(7204)**
2009: 10^{5}SD, 9^{1}SD, 10^{3}SD, 11^{3}F, 9^{4}GF, 10^{5}GS, 11^{4}GF, 10^{3}F, 9^{0}GS, 9^{4}SD, 10^{6}SD,

	Starts	1st	2nd	3rd	Win & Pl
Career Total (Turf)	16	0	0	3	1922
Career Total (AW)	11	2	1	1	5599

66 4/09 Wolv 1m1f103y (0-55)H STD £2388
58 5/08 GrLe 1m (0-60)H STD £2266
Total win prize-money £4655

Going (Turf): **Sf: 0-0 GS: 0-3 Gd: 0-3 GF: 0-6 Fm: 0-4**
Distance: 5f/6f: 0-0 7f-8f: 1-5 9f-13f: 1-22 14f+: 0-0
Track : **LH: 2-19** RH: 0-5 Tight: 1-17 Gall: 1-2
Aids: Bl: 0-0 **Vi: 1-8** Tstrap: 0-4 Ckp: 0-4
Best Rating: **67** 5/09 Leic 1m1f218y gd-fm

Moderate; effective at around 1m-1m2f; acts on good ground and on Polytrack; has worn a visor.

Nassau Beach (IRE)

85 **44**
3-y-o b g Bahamian Bounty-Oh'Cecilia (IRE) (Scenic)
T D Easterby Mrs Jennifer E Pallister

Placings:00-5050 **(3125)**
2009: 5^{5}GF, 7^{0}GF, 8^{5}GF, 5^{0}GF,

	Starts	1st	2nd	3rd	Win & Pl
Career Total (Turf)	6	0	0	0	0

Going (Turf): **Sf: 0-0 GS: 0-0 Gd: 0-2 GF: 0-4 Fm: 0-0**
Distance: 5f/6f: 0-4 7f-8f: 0-2 9f-13f: 0-0 14f+: 0-0
Track : LH: 0-2 RH: 0-1 Tight: 0-3 Gall: 0-0
Aids: Bl: 0-0 Vi: 0-0 Tstrap: 0-0 Ckp: 0-0
Best Rating: **44** 6/09 Ripn 1m gd-fm

Natalie N G

66
2-y-o b f Zamindar (USA)-Tango Teaser (Shareef Dancer (USA))
J R Jenkins M Ng

Placings:0 **(7289)**
2009: 6^{0}S,

	Starts	1st	2nd	3rd	Win & Pl
Career Total (Turf)	1	0	0	0	

Going (Turf): **Sf: 0-1 GS: 0-0 Gd: 0-0 GF: 0-0 Fm: 0-0**
Distance: 5f/6f: 0-1 7f-8f: 0-0 9f-13f: 0-0 14f+: 0-0
Track : LH: 0-0 RH: 0-0 Tight: 0-0 Gall: 0-0
Aids: Bl: 0-0 Vi: 0-0 Tstrap: 0-0 Ckp: 0-0

Nathan Dee

(94) (41)**55**

4-y-o ch g Guys And Dolls-Blu Air Flow (ITY) (Entrepreneur)

M R Bosley David Cramm & Tom Campagne

Placings:064066/000-0 **(1568)**

2009: 11^{0}SD,

	Starts	1st	2nd	3rd	Win & Pl
Career Total (Turf)	5	0	0	0	0
Career Total (AW)	5	0	0	0	0

Going (Turf): **Sf: 0-1 GS: 0-2 Gd: 0-2 GF: 0-0 Fm: 0-0**
Distance: 5f/6f: 0-3 7f-8f: 0-3 9f-13f: 0-4 14f+: 0-0
Track : LH: 0-6 RH: 0-3 Tight: 0-4 Gall: 0-1
Aids: Bl: 0-1 Vi: 0-0 Tstrap: 0-1 Ckp: 0-1
Best Rating: **55** 5/07 Brig 5f213y soft

National Monument (IRE)

57(97) (69)

3-y-o b g Statue Of Liberty (USA)-Panpipes (USA) (Woodman (USA))

J A Osborne J Palmer-Brown

Placings:33400 **(6288)**

2009: 8^{3}SD, 8^{3}SD, 9^{4}SD, 11^{0}F, 10^{0}SD,

	Starts	1st	2nd	3rd	Win & Pl
Career Total (Turf)	1	0	0	0	
Career Total (AW)	4	0	0	2	981

Going (Turf): **Sf: 0-0 GS: 0-0 Gd: 0-0 GF: 0-0 Fm: 0-1**
Distance: 5f/6f: 0-0 7f-8f: 0-1 9f-13f: 0-4 14f+: 0-0
Track : LH: 0-3 RH: 0-2 Tight: 0-2 Gall: 0-0
Aids: Bl: 0-0 Vi: 0-0 Tstrap: 0-0 Ckp: 0-0
Best Rating: **69** 2/09 Wolv 1m141y stand

Native Dame (IRE)

96(81) (61)**52**

3-y-o b f Spartacus (IRE)-Wisecrack (IRE) (Lucky Guest)

Edgar Byrne (P D Deegan 17/4) Wisecrack Boys Partnership

Placings:000-**430026500** **(7703)**

2009: 8^{4}SD, 6^{3}SD, 12^{0}GF, 10^{0}SD, 7^{2}GF, 6^{6}G, 7^{5}F, 6^{0}SD, 6^{0}SD,

	Starts	1st	2nd	3rd	Win & Pl
Career Total (Turf)	6	0	1	0	674
Career Total (AW)	6	0	0	1	517

Going (Turf): **Sf: 0-0 GS: 0-0 Gd: 0-1 GF: 0-2 Fm: 0-1**
Distance: 5f/6f: 0-5 7f-8f: 0-5 9f-13f: 0-2 14f+: 0-0
Track : LH: 0-6 RH: 0-2 Tight: 0-3 Gall: 0-0
Aids: Bl: 0-7 Vi: 0-0 Tstrap: 0-0 Ckp: 0-0
Best Rating: **61** 4/09 Dund 1m stand

Native Ruler

109 **105**

3-y-o b c Cape Cross (IRE)-Love Divine (Diesis)

H R A Cecil Lordship Stud

Placings:21003 **(4760)**

2009: 10^{2}GF, 10^{1}G, 10^{0}G, 12^{0}GF, 10^{3}GS,

	Starts	1st	2nd	3rd	Win & Pl
Career Total (Turf)	5	1	1	1	6272
94	4/09	Pont	1m2f6y	GD	£3238

Total win prize-money £3238

Going (Turf): Sf: 0-0 GS: 0-1 **Gd: 1-2** GF: 0-2 Fm: 0-0
Distance: 5f/6f: 0-0 7f-8f: 0-0 **9f-13f: 1-5** 14f+: 0-0
Track : **LH: 1-2** RH: 0-2 Tight: 0-0 Gall: 0-3
Aids: Bl: 0-0 Vi: 0-0 Tstrap: 0-0 Ckp: 0-0
Best Rating: **105** 5/09 York 1m2f88y good

Very useful; effective over 1m2f; acts on good ground.

Nativity

97(105) (57)**63**

3-y-o ch f Kyllachy-Mistral's Dancer (Shareef Dancer (USA))

J L Spearing Robert Heathcote

Placings:54020-0602**025625** **(7835)**

2009: 5^{0}F, 5^{6}GF, 7^{0}GF, 6^{2}GF, 6^{0}GF, 6^{2}SD, 7^{5}SD, 7^{6}SD, 6^{2}SD, 6^{5}SD,

	Starts	1st	2nd	3rd	Win & Pl
Career Total (Turf)	10	0	2	0	2512
Career Total (AW)	5	0	2	0	1375

Going (Turf): **Sf: 0-1 GS: 0-1 Gd: 0-1 GF: 0-6 Fm: 0-1**
Distance: 5f/6f: 0-11 7f-8f: 0-4 9f-13f: 0-0 14f+: 0-0
Track : LH: 0-5 RH: 0-5 Tight: 0-0 Gall: 0-2
Aids: Bl: 0-0 Vi: 0-0 Tstrap: 0-0 Ckp: 0-0
Best Rating: **63** 5/08 Sand 5f6y gd-fm

Modest; best at 5f; acts on a sound surface.

Natural Flair (USA)

103 **85**

3-y-o ch f Giant's Causeway (USA)-Forest Lady (USA) (Woodman (USA))

P W Chapple-Hyam M Al-Qatami & K M Al-Mudhaf

Placings:02-106410 **(7302a)**

2009: 10^{1}GS, 10^{0}GF, 11^{6}G, 10^{4}GF, 10^{1}G, 10^{0}HY,

	Starts	1st	2nd	3rd	Win & Pl
Career Total (Turf)	8	2	1	0	11690
85	10/09 Newb	1m2f6y	(0-85)H	GD	£4857
85	4/09 Newb	1m2f6y		G-S	£5180

Total win prize-money £10038

Going (Turf): Sf: 0-1 **GS: 1-3 Gd: 1-2** GF: 0-2 Fm: 0-0
Distance: 5f/6f: 0-0 7f-8f: 0-0 **9f-13f: 2-8** 14f+: 0-0
Track : **LH: 2-4** RH: 0-1 Tight: 0-1 **Gall: 2-3**
Aids: Bl: 0-0 Vi: 0-0 Tstrap: 0-0 Ckp: 0-0
Best Rating: **85** 10/09 Newb 1m2f6y good

Useful; effective over 1m2f; acts on good and easy ground.

Natural Law (IRE)

92(95) (80)**80**

2-y-o b g Lomitas-Flying Squaw (Be My Chief (USA))

Saeed Bin Suroor Godolphin

Placings:0315 **(7184)**

2009: 8^{0}G, 8^{3}GF, 8^{1}SD, 10^{5}G,

	Starts	1st	2nd	3rd	Win & Pl
Career Total (Turf)	3	0	0	1	326
Career Total (AW)	1	1	0	0	2047
80	9/09	Kemp	1m	STD	£2047

Total win prize-money £2047

Going (Turf): **Sf: 0-0 GS: 0-0 Gd: 0-2 GF: 0-1 Fm: 0-0**
Distance: 5f/6f: 0-0 **7f-8f: 1-1** 9f-13f: 0-3 14f+: 0-0
Track : LH: 0-1 **RH: 1-1** Tight: 0-1 Gall: 0-0
Aids: Bl: 0-0 Vi: 0-1 Tstrap: 1-1 Ckp: 1-1
Best Rating: **80** 10/09 NmkR 1m2f good

Modest; stays 1m; acts on fast ground.

Natural Rhythm (IRE)

93(94) (50)**64**

4-y-o ch g Distant Music (USA)-Nationalartgallery (IRE) (Tate Gallery (USA))

Mrs R A Carr Michael Hill

Placings:530650136022063**5624/45**000300**35**0221100023 50-0000615000**4** **(7173)**

2009: 8^{0}GF, 8^{0}G, 8^{0}GS, 8^{0}G, 9^{6}G, 8^{1}G, 8^{5}HY, 8^{0}GS, 8^{0}GF, 8^{0}SD, 9^{4}S,

	Starts	1st	2nd	3rd	Win & Pl
Career Total (Turf)	42	4	5	4	17447
Career Total (AW)	10	0	1	2	1508
58	7/09 Bevl	1m100y	(0-75)H	GD	£2914
64	7/08 Hayd	1m30y	(0-70)H	HVY	£3238
58	7/08 Haml	1m65y	(0-60)H	G-S	£2388
53	8/07 Catt	7f		GD	£2730

Total win prize-money £11270

Going (Turf): Sf: 1-8 GS: 1-8 **Gd: 2-14** GF: 0-11 Fm: 0-1
Distance: 5f/6f: 0-6 7f-8f: 1-18 **9f-13f: 3-28** 14f+: 0-0
Track : LH: 2-29 RH: 2-14 **Tight: 2-19** Gall: 0-1
Aids: **Bl: 3-21** Vi: 0-3 Tstrap: 0-2 Ckp: 0-2
Best Rating: **67** 5/07 Pont 5f gd-fm

Modest; stays 1m; acts on good ground and Fibresand; has worn cheekpieces; often wears blinkers.

Naughty Girl (IRE)

(81) (28)**50**

9-y-o b m Dr Devious (IRE)-Mary Magdalene (Night Shift (USA))

John A Harris Mrs A E Harris

Placings:3226/04126560/000000054402010052/000001/0 6620/000030-00 **(0399)**

2009: 8^{0}SS, 8^{0}SD,

	Starts	1st	2nd	3rd	Win & Pl
Career Total (Turf)	30	3	4	2	17212
Career Total (AW)	19	0	2	0	851
54	5/05 Nott	1m54y	(0-45)	GD	£1512
54	9/04 Bath	1m5y	(0-55)H	FRM	£2623
57	7/03 Haml	6f5y	D	G-F	£5512

Total win prize-money £9648

Going (Turf): Sf: 0-2 GS: 0-1 **Gd: 1-8 GF: 1-15 Fm: 1-4**
Distance: 5f/6f: 0-16 7f-8f: 1-20 **9f-13f: 2-13** 14f+: 0-0
Track : **LH: 2-28** RH: 0-2 **Tight: 1-14** Gall: 0-5
Aids: Bl: 0-1 **Vi: 1-17** Tstrap: 0-0 Ckp: 0-0
Best Rating: **81** 4/02 Nott 5f13y good

Naughty Norris

75 **27**

2-y-o ch g Needwood Blade-Leave It To Lib (Tender King)

R Bastiman Scattered Friends Partnership

Placings:000 **(7244)**

2009: 6^{0}S, 7^{0}GF, 8^{0}S,

	Starts	1st	2nd	3rd	Win & Pl
Career Total (Turf)	3	0	0	0	

Going (Turf): **Sf: 0-2 GS: 0-0 Gd: 0-0 GF: 0-1 Fm: 0-0**

Distance: 5f/6f: 0-1 7f-8f: 0-1 9f-13f: 0-1 14f+: 0-0
Track : LH: 0-1 RH: 0-0 Tight: 0-0 Gall: 0-0
Aids: Bl: 0-0 Vi: 0-0 Tstrap: 0-0 Ckp: 0-0
Best Rating: **27** 11/09 Nott 1m75y soft

Nautical

(100) (64)**86**
11-y-o gr g Lion Cavern (USA)-Russian Royal (USA) (Nureyev (USA))
J R Holt P V Thomas

Placings:0203/441124310/0/004643020110 2/0222124000 6/052340132324200300/000053640624030/44421623000 0-2402010 **(0823)**
2009: 6^{2}SS, 7^{4}SD, 6^{0}SD, 8^{2}SD, 8^{0}SD, 9^{1}SD, 8^{0}SD,

	Starts	1st	2nd	3rd	Win & Pl
Career Total (Turf)	44	4	8	5	32315
Career Total (AW)	46	5	9	5	36388

55	2/09	Wolv	1m1f103y	(0-50)H	STD	£2047
64	2/08	Wolv	5f216y		STD	£1774
77	4/06	Wind	6f	(0-75)H	GD	£3238
72	10/04	Wolv	1m141y	(0-55)H	STD	£3038
62	9/04	Chep	7f16y	(0-55)H	GD	£2746
	4/02	Ndas	1m2f	(45-70)	FST	£6543
	2/02	Ghan	1m1f	(45-70)H	GD	£4672
	2/02	Jebl	1m	(30-60)H	FST	£6074

Total win prize-money £30137

Going (Turf): Sf: 0-4 GS: 0-6 **Gd: 4-17** GF: 0-16 Fm: 0-1
Distance: 5f/6f: 3-46 7f-8f: 2-24 **9f-13f: 4-20** 14f+: 0-0
Track : **LH: 3-34** RH: 0-12 **Tight: 3-21** Gall: 2-11
Aids: Bl: 0-0 Vi: 0-1 Tstrap: 0-1 Ckp: 0-1
Best Rating: **86** 6/06 Wind 6f gd-fm

Moderate; effective at up to 1m, but usually races over much shorter; acts on most ground and Polytrack; usually held up and can break slowly; has broken blood-vessels.

Navajo Chief

92 **82**
2-y-o b c King's Best (USA)-Navajo Rainbow (Rainbow Quest (USA))
A P Jarvis Geoffrey Bishop

Placings:1530 **(7030)**
2009: 5^{1}GF, 6^{5}G, 7^{3}G, 7^{0}S,

	Starts	1st	2nd	3rd	Win & Pl
Career Total (Turf)	4	1	0	1	7117

82	6/09	Wind	5f10y	G-F	£3885

Total win prize-money £3886

Going (Turf): Sf: 0-1 GS: 0-0 Gd: 0-2 **GF: 1-1** Fm: 0-0
Distance: **5f/6f: 1-2** 7f-8f: 0-2 9f-13f: 0-0 14f+: 0-0
Track : LH: 0-0 RH: 0-0 Tight: 0-0 **Gall: 1-1**
Aids: Bl: 0-0 Vi: 0-0 Tstrap: 0-0 Ckp: 0-0
Best Rating: **82** 7/09 Asct 7f good

Useful; Listed placed; stays 7f; acts on good and faster ground.

Navajo Joe (IRE)

101(103) (85)**86**
4-y-o ch g Indian Ridge-Maid Of Killeen (IRE) (Darshaan)
R Johnson A S Racing

Placings:0/210500-560300600 **(6383)**
2009: 12^{5}SD, 7^{6}SD, 7^{0}GS, 7^{3}GS, 7^{0}GF, 6^{0}G, 5^{6}GS, 6^{0}GF, 8^{0}GF,

	Starts	1st	2nd	3rd	Win & Pl
Career Total (Turf)	12	0	1	1	1252
Career Total (AW)	4	1	0	0	2736

85	6/08	Ling	1m	STD	£2456

Total win prize-money £2457

Going (Turf): **Sf: 0-1 GS: 0-3 Gd: 0-4 GF: 0-4 Fm: 0-0**
Distance: 5f/6f: 0-2 **7f-8f: 1-9** 9f-13f: 0-5 14f+: 0-0
Track : **LH: 1-8** RH: 0-2 **Tight: 1-3** Gall: 0-1
Aids: Bl: 0-2 Vi: 0-0 Tstrap: 0-0 Ckp: 0-0
Best Rating: **86** 5/08 Hayd 1m30y good

Useful; stays 1m; acts on good ground and on Polytrack; has worn blinkers.

Navajo Nation (IRE)

101(100) (68)**70**
3-y-o b g Indian Haven-Kathy Desert (Green Desert (USA))
W G M Turner (B J Meehan 5/10) R A Bracken

Placings:03-3020463 **(6549)**
2009: 7^{3}G, 11^{0}G, 10^{2}G, 10^{0}SD, 11^{4}GF, 9^{6}SD, 10^{3}G,

	Starts	1st	2nd	3rd	Win & Pl
Career Total (Turf)	7	0	1	3	2744
Career Total (AW)	2	0	0	0	0

Going (Turf): **Sf: 0-0 GS: 0-0 Gd: 0-6 GF: 0-1 Fm: 0-0**
Distance: 5f/6f: 0-0 7f-8f: 0-3 9f-13f: 0-6 14f+: 0-0
Track : LH: 0-3 RH: 0-3 Tight: 0-5 Gall: 0-0
Aids: Bl: 0-1 Vi: 0-0 Tstrap: 0-0 Ckp: 0-0
Best Rating: **70** 8/09 Yarm 1m2f21y good

Modest; stays 1m2f; acts on good ground and on Polytrack.

Nave (USA)

89(99) (73)**63**
2-y-o b c Pulpit (USA)-Lakabi (USA) (Nureyev (USA))
M Johnston Anthony Hogarth

Placings:03064122 **(7685)**
2009: 6^{0}S, 6^{3}GF, 6^{0}S, 6^{6}SD, 7^{4}SF, 8^{1}SD, 8^{2}SD, 8^{2}SD,

	Starts	1st	2nd	3rd	Win & Pl
Career Total (Turf)	3	0	0	1	482
Career Total (AW)	5	1	2	0	4472

66	11/09	Kemp	1m	(0-65)	STD	£1942

Total win prize-money £1943

Going (Turf): **Sf: 0-2 GS: 0-0 Gd: 0-0 GF: 0-1 Fm: 0-0**
Distance: 5f/6f: 0-4 **7f-8f: 1-4** 9f-13f: 0-0 14f+: 0-0
Track : LH: 0-3 **RH: 1-3** Tight: 0-2 Gall: 0-0
Aids: Bl: 0-0 Vi: 0-0 Tstrap: 0-0 Ckp: 0-0
Best Rating: **73** 12/09 Kemp 1m stand

Fair; stays 1m; acts on Polytrack; should improve further.

Navene (IRE)

43 (44)**70**
5-y-o b m Desert Style (IRE)-Majudel (IRE) (Revoque (IRE))
C F Wall Dr Philip Brown

Placings:06202/5162252-0 **(2166)**
2009: 8^{0}G,

	Starts	1st	2nd	3rd	Win & Pl
Career Total (Turf)	12	1	5	0	6166
Career Total (AW)	1	0	0	0	0

67	5/08	Yarm	1m3y	(0-65)H	GD	£1942

Total win prize-money £1943

Going (Turf): Sf: 0-1 GS: 0-2 **Gd: 1-6** GF: 0-3 Fm: 0-0
Distance: 5f/6f: 0-2 7f-8f: 0-6 **9f-13f: 1-5** 14f+: 0-0
Track : LH: 0-4 RH: 0-1 Tight: 0-1 Gall: 0-0
Aids: Bl: 0-0 Vi: 0-0 Tstrap: 0-0 Ckp: 0-0
Best Rating: **70** 9/08 Wwck 1m22y good

Modest; stays 1m; acts on good and easy ground.

Navy List (FR)

99(97) (80)**90**
2-y-o b c Nayef (USA)-Fasliyeva (FR) (Fasliyev (USA))
Saeed Bin Suroor Godolphin

Placings:02215 **(6993)**
2009: 7^{0}G, 8^{2}SD, 8^{2}SD, 9^{1}GF, 8^{5}GS,

	Starts	1st	2nd	3rd	Win & Pl
Career Total (Turf)	3	1	0	0	3562
Career Total (AW)	2	0	2	0	1866

85	9/09	Rdcr	1m1f	G-F	£3561

Total win prize-money £3562

Going (Turf): Sf: 0-0 GS: 0-1 Gd: 0-1 **GF: 1-1** Fm: 0-0
Distance: 5f/6f: 0-0 7f-8f: 0-4 **9f-13f: 1-1** 14f+: 0-0
Track : **LH: 1-3** RH: 0-1 **Tight: 1-2** Gall: 0-1
Aids: Bl: 0-0 Vi: 0-0 Tstrap: 0-0 Ckp: 0-0
Best Rating: **90** 10/09 Donc 1m gd-sft

Useful; stays 1m1f; acts on most ground.

Nawaadi (USA)

106(104) (78)**76**
3-y-o ch g El Corredor (USA)-Louise's Time (USA) (Gilded Time (USA))
J H M Gosden Hamdan Al Maktoum

Placings:1-6040256 **(6613)**
2009: 8^{6}SD, 10^{0}GF, 9^{4}GF, 12^{0}S, 10^{2}G, 10^{5}GF, 12^{6}SD,

	Starts	1st	2nd	3rd	Win & Pl
Career Total (Turf)	5	0	1	0	1902
Career Total (AW)	3	1	0	0	6616

78	9/08	GrLe	1m	STD	£6476

Total win prize-money £6476

Going (Turf): **Sf: 0-1 GS: 0-0 Gd: 0-1 GF: 0-3 Fm: 0-0**
Distance: 5f/6f: 0-0 **7f-8f: 1-2** 9f-13f: 0-6 14f+: 0-0
Track : **LH: 1-2** RH: 0-5 Tight: 0-1 **Gall: 1-2**
Aids: Bl: 0-0 Vi: 0-2 Tstrap: 0-0 Ckp: 0-0
Best Rating: **78** 9/08 GrLe 1m stand

Fair; stays 1m; acts on Polytrack; has worn a visor.

Nawaaff

96(100) (57)**65**
4-y-o ch g Compton Place-Amazed (Clantime)
M Quinn (M R Channon 6/7) A Newby

Placings:23221000/63000550403305033 0-410000005350 **(7771)**
2009: 6^{4}SD, 5^{1}SD, 5^{0}SD, 5^{0}SD, 6^{0}GF, 5^{0}GF, 5^{0}G, 6^{0}G, 5^{5}GF, 5^{3}F, 5^{5}SD, 6^{0}SD,

	Starts	1st	2nd	3rd	Win & Pl
Career Total (Turf)	21	1	3	2	9919
Career Total (AW)	17	1	0	5	4193

55	2/09	Wolv	5f20y	(0-50)H	STD	£2047
78	8/07	Thsk	5f		G-F	£4533

Total win prize-money £6581

Going (Turf): Sf: 0-0 GS: 0-5 Gd: 0-7 **GF: 1-7** Fm: 0-2
Distance: **5f/6f: 2-33** 7f-8f: 0-5 9f-13f: 0-0 14f+: 0-0
Track : **LH: 1-18** RH: 0-7 **Tight: 1-11** Gall: 0-3
Aids: Bl: 0-0 Vi: 0-9 Tstrap: 0-0 Ckp: 0-0
Best Rating: **82** 5/07 York 6f gd-sft

Moderate; suited by 5f-7f; acts on fast and easy ground; also goes on Polytrack.

Nawamees (IRE)

103(105) (79)**80**

11-y-o b g Darshaan-Truly Generous (IRE) (Generous (IRE))

P D Evans P D Evans

Placings:0213/564206/5236/42200/00022/3422460542/33 0350111/211012130305 3-4115420410532462444006046 **(7549)**

2009: 12^{4}SD, 12^{1}SD, 12^{1}SD, 12^{5}SD, 12^{4}SD, 12^{2}SD, 11^{0}GF, 12^{4}SD, 11^{1}G, 12^{0}GF, 12^{5}SD, 11^{3}GF, 11^{2}GF, 12^{4}S, 12^{6}SD, 11^{2}GF, 11^{4}GF, 12^{4}GF, 15^{4}GF, 11^{0}G, 13^{0}SS, 12^{6}S, 13^{0}SD,

	Starts	1st	2nd	3rd	Win & Pl
Career Total (Turf)	43	4	8	4	49867
Career Total (AW)	38	7	7	6	36340

70	5/09	Catt	1m3f214y	GD	£2047
70	2/09	Sthl	1m4f	STD	£2047
65	1/09	Sthl	1m4f	STD	£2047
72	9/08	Leic	1m1f218y	SFT	£3238
72	7/08	Leic	1m3f183y	GD	£3238
81	4/08	Ling	1m4f	STD	£1774
74	4/08	Wolv	1m4f50y	STD	£2047
81	12/07	Wolv	1m4f50y	STD	£2388
72	12/07	Ling	1m4f	STD	£2047
81	10/07	Wolv	1m4f50y	STD	£2047
	7/01	Leto	1m3f	GD	£2493

Total win prize-money £25416

Going (Turf): Sf: 1-6 GS: 0-5 **Gd: 3-14** GF: 0-17 Fm: 0-0
Distance: 5f/6f: 0-0 7f-8f: 0-0 **9f-13f: 11-70** 14f+: 0-11
Track : **LH: 8-52** RH: 2-20 **Tight: 6-44** Gall: 0-14
Aids: Bl: 0-1 Vi: 0-0 Tstrap: 10-60 Ckp: 10-60
Best Rating: **94** 5/06 Gdwd 1m4f gd-sft

Modest; effective over 1m2f-2m; acts on most ground on turf; goes on sand; usually wears cheekpieces and has worn a tongue tie; has a good record in claimers.

Nawojka (IRE)

78 **53**

3-y-o gr f Daylami (IRE)-Panna (Polish Precedent (USA))

J G Given Lord Halifax

Placings:3-06 **(4066)**

2009: 8^{0}G, 10^{6}HY,

	Starts	1st	2nd	3rd	Win & Pl
Career Total (Turf)	3	0	0	1	578

Going (Turf): **Sf: 0-2 GS: 0-0 Gd: 0-1 GF: 0-0 Fm: 0-0**
Distance: 5f/6f: 0-0 7f-8f: 0-1 9f-13f: 0-2 14f+: 0-0
Track : LH: 0-3 RH: 0-0 Tight: 0-0 Gall: 0-0
Aids: Bl: 0-0 Vi: 0-0 Tstrap: 0-0 Ckp: 0-0
Best Rating: **53** 9/08 Wwck 7f26y soft

Naxox (FR)

(90) (68)

8-y-o ch g Cupidon (FR)-Frou Frou Lou (FR) (Groom Dancer (USA))

George Baker (Miss Venetia Williams 30/4) Andrew Flintoff & Paul Beck

Placings:10/102/26 **(7724)**

2009: 13^{2}SF, 12^{6}SD,

	Starts	1st	2nd	3rd	Win & Pl
Career Total (Turf)	4	1	1	0	7141
Career Total (AW)	3	1	1	0	5832

1/05	Deau	1m4f	GD	£4965
6/04	Gran	1m4f110y	GD	£3169

Total win prize-money £8134

Going (Turf): Sf: 0-1 GS: 0-0 **Gd: 2-3** GF: 0-0 Fm: 0-0
Distance: 5f/6f: 0-0 7f-8f: 0-0 **9f-13f: 2-6** 14f+: 0-1
Track : LH: 0-4 RH: 0-0 Tight: 0-1 Gall: 0-0
Aids: Bl: 0-0 Vi: 0-0 Tstrap: 0-0 Ckp: 0-0
Best Rating: **68** 11/09 Wolv 1m5f194y std-fst

Modest; ex-French; better known as a hurdler/chaser; stays 1m6f; acts on Polytrack.

Nayef Star

95 **64**

4-y-o b g Nayef (USA)-Satin Bell (Midyan (USA))

J Noseda Mr And Mrs J D Cotton

Placings:6/3 **(2199)**

2009: 10^{3}S,

	Starts	1st	2nd	3rd	Win & Pl
Career Total (Turf)	2	0	0	1	482

Going (Turf): **Sf: 0-1 GS: 0-0 Gd: 0-1 GF: 0-0 Fm: 0-0**
Distance: 5f/6f: 0-0 7f-8f: 0-1 9f-13f: 0-1 14f+: 0-0
Track : LH: 0-1 RH: 0-0 Tight: 0-0 Gall: 0-0
Aids: Bl: 0-0 Vi: 0-0 Tstrap: 0-0 Ckp: 0-0
Best Rating: **70** 11/07 NmkR 7f good

Modest; stays 1m2f; acts on soft ground.

Nayessence

90 **56**

3-y-o ch g Nayef (USA)-Fragrant Oasis (USA) (Rahy (USA))

M W Easterby Steve Hull

Placings:00F0-46 **(7080)**

2009: 10^{4}GF, 11^{6}S,

	Starts	1st	2nd	3rd	Win & Pl
Career Total (Turf)	6	0	0	0	0

Going (Turf): **Sf: 0-2 GS: 0-1 Gd: 0-0 GF: 0-3 Fm: 0-0**
Distance: 5f/6f: 0-1 7f-8f: 0-3 9f-13f: 0-2 14f+: 0-0
Track : LH: 0-6 RH: 0-0 Tight: 0-4 Gall: 0-1
Aids: Bl: 0-0 Vi: 0-0 Tstrap: 0-0 Ckp: 0-0
Best Rating: **56** 10/09 Rdcr 1m2f gd-fm

Naywye

(76) (5)

3-y-o b f Nayef (USA)-Mount Hillaby (IRE) (Mujadil (USA))

M W Easterby D F Spence

Placings:00 **(1652)**

2009: 6^{0}SD, 6^{0}SD,

	Starts	1st	2nd	3rd	Win & Pl
Career Total (Turf)	0	0	0	0	
Career Total (AW)	2	0	0	0	

Going (Turf): **Sf: 0-0 GS: 0-0 Gd: 0-0 GF: 0-0 Fm: 0-0**
Distance: 5f/6f: 0-2 7f-8f: 0-0 9f-13f: 0-0 14f+: 0-0
Track : LH: 0-2 RH: 0-0 Tight: 0-0 Gall: 0-0
Aids: Bl: 0-0 Vi: 0-0 Tstrap: 0-0 Ckp: 0-0

Nazreef

(97) (75)

2-y-o b c Zafeen (FR)-Roofer (IRE) (Barathea (IRE))

H Morrison Deborah Collett & M J Watson

Placings:1 **(7502)**

2009: 8^{1}SD,

	Starts	1st	2nd	3rd	Win & Pl
Career Total (Turf)	0	0	0	0	
Career Total (AW)	1	1	0	0	2590

75	11/09	Sthl	1m	STD	£2590

Total win prize-money £2590

Going (Turf): **Sf: 0-0 GS: 0-0 Gd: 0-0 GF: 0-0 Fm: 0-0**
Distance: 5f/6f: 0-0 **7f-8f: 1-1** 9f-13f: 0-0 14f+: 0-0
Track : **LH: 1-1** RH: 0-0 Tight: 0-0 Gall: 0-0
Aids: Bl: 0-0 Vi: 0-0 Tstrap: 0-0 Ckp: 0-0
Best Rating: **75** 11/09 Sthl 1m stand

Related to winning milers; winner on debut at Southwell over 1m.

Nbhan (USA)

99(100) (80)**81**

3-y-o b c With Approval (CAN)-Crisp And Cool (USA) (Ogygian (USA))

L M Cumani Jaber Abdullah

Placings:055-32230 **(5834)**

2009: 10^{3}G, 10^{2}G, 9^{2}S, 8^{3}SD, 10^{0}GF,

	Starts	1st	2nd	3rd	Win & Pl
Career Total (Turf)	6	0	2	1	3921
Career Total (AW)	2	0	0	1	578

Going (Turf): **Sf: 0-1 GS: 0-1 Gd: 0-3 GF: 0-1 Fm: 0-0**
Distance: 5f/6f: 0-0 7f-8f: 0-3 9f-13f: 0-5 14f+: 0-0
Track : LH: 0-1 RH: 0-5 Tight: 0-1 Gall: 0-0
Aids: Bl: 0-0 Vi: 0-0 Tstrap: 0-0 Ckp: 0-0
Best Rating: **81** 7/09 Leic 1m1f218y soft

Fair; stays 1m2f; acts on good ground and Polytrack.

Nchike

97(91) (44)**67**

3-y-o b g Zaha (CAN)-Tinkerbird (Music Boy)

R C Guest (D Nicholls 14/7) S Hussey

Placings:060305202110-004205060 **(6001)**

2009: 7^{0}SD, 7^{0}GF, 7^{4}GF, 6^{2}GS, 8^{0}F, 8^{5}SD, 6^{0}S, 7^{6}S, 10^{0}GF,

	Starts	1st	2nd	3rd	Win & Pl
Career Total (Turf)	19	2	3	1	8715
Career Total (AW)	2	0	0	0	0

67	9/08	Muss	7f30y	SFT	£1942
67	9/08	Thsk	6f	SFT	£4274

Total win prize-money £6217

Going (Turf): **Sf: 2-4** GS: 0-5 Gd: 0-2 GF: 0-7 Fm: 0-1
Distance: 5f/6f: 1-9 7f-8f: 1-11 9f-13f: 0-1 14f+: 0-0
Track : LH: 0-8 **RH: 1-2 Tight: 1-8** Gall: 0-0
Aids: Bl: 0-2 **Vi: 2-10** Tstrap: 0-1 Ckp: 0-1
Best Rating: **67** 9/08 Muss 7f30y soft

Moderate; suited by 6f-7f; acts on good and soft ground; has worn a visor.

Ndola

(100) (46)**42**

10-y-o b g Emperor Jones (USA)-Lykoa (Shirley Heights)

P Butler Miss M Bryant

Placings:000/00/1/003/101/001604/16/23250000-40 **(0734)**

2009: 12^{4}SD, 13^{0}SD,

	Starts	1st	2nd	3rd	Win & Pl
Career Total (Turf)	7	1	0	0	1470
Career Total (AW)	23	4	2	2	8089

57	10/07	Wolv	1m4f50y	(0-45)	STD	£1911
50	5/06	Kemp	1m4f	(0-45)	STD	£1706
51	10/05	Yarm	1m2f21y	(0-45)	GD	£1470

54 2/05 Sthl 1m3f (0-40) STD £1470
51 1/04 Wolv 1m1f79y H(0-40) STD £1463
Total win prize-money £8020

Going (Turf): Sf: 0-2 GS: 0-1 **Gd: 1-3** GF: 0-1 Fm: 0-0
Distance: 5f/6f: 0-1 7f-8f: 0-1 **9f-13f: 5-26** 14f+: 0-2
Track : **LH: 4-22** RH: 1-8 **Tight: 3-14** Gall: 0-1
Aids: Bl: 0-1 **Vi: 2-13** Tstrap: 0-1 Ckp: 0-1
Best Rating: **57** 1/08 Kemp 1m3f stand

Near The Front

(99) (56)**57**
4-y-o b g Compton Place-Once In My Life (IRE) (Lomond (USA))
Miss Gay Kelleway Ballygriffin Gang, Gay Kelleway

Placings:52002043-2 **(0541)**
2009: 11^{2}SD,

	Starts	1st	2nd	3rd	Win & Pl
Career Total (Turf)	6	0	2	1	1612
Career Total (AW)	3	0	1	0	605

Going (Turf): Sf: 0-3 GS: 0-0 Gd: 0-2 GF: 0-1 Fm: 0-0
Distance: 5f/6f: 0-2 7f-8f: 0-2 9f-13f: 0-5 14f+: 0-0
Track : LH: 0-5 RH: 0-3 Tight: 0-3 Gall: 0-0
Aids: Bl: 0-0 Vi: 0-4 Tstrap: 0-0 Ckp: 0-0
Best Rating: **57** 9/08 Bevl 1m100y soft

Moderate; effective over 1m; acts on soft ground.

Neat 'n Tidy

78(84) (23)**25**
5-y-o b m Josr Algarhoud (IRE)-Raspberry Sauce (Niniski (USA))
A E Jones BPD Ltd

Placings:6000/0-00 **(7462)**
2009: 7^{0}S, 5^{0}SD,

	Starts	1st	2nd	3rd	Win & Pl
Career Total (Turf)	5	0	0	0	0
Career Total (AW)	2	0	0	0	

Going (Turf): Sf: 0-1 GS: 0-0 Gd: 0-0 GF: 0-4 Fm: 0-0
Distance: 5f/6f: 0-5 7f-8f: 0-2 9f-13f: 0-0 14f+: 0-0
Track : LH: 0-4 RH: 0-0 Tight: 0-2 Gall: 0-3
Aids: Bl: 0-0 Vi: 0-0 Tstrap: 0-0 Ckp: 0-0
Best Rating: **52** 9/06 Folk 6f gd-fm

Neboisha

93 (53)**44**
5-y-o ch m Ishiguru (USA)-Mariette (Blushing Scribe (USA))
M Wigham Steven Rees

Placings:20000/00P **(2806)**
2009: 10^{0}GF, 8^{0}GF, 6^{P}G,

	Starts	1st	2nd	3rd	Win & Pl
Career Total (Turf)	3	0	0	0	
Career Total (AW)	5	0	1	0	806

Going (Turf): Sf: 0-0 GS: 0-0 Gd: 0-1 GF: 0-2 Fm: 0-0
Distance: 5f/6f: 0-0 7f-8f: 0-5 9f-13f: 0-3 14f+: 0-0
Track : LH: 0-5 RH: 0-2 Tight: 0-5 Gall: 0-0
Aids: Bl: 0-3 Vi: 0-0 Tstrap: 0-0 Ckp: 0-0
Best Rating: **53** 6/07 Ling 7f stand

Ned Ludd (IRE)

106 **77**
6-y-o b g Montjeu (IRE)-Zanella (IRE) (Nordico (USA))
J G Portman Anthony Boswood

Placings:5205/6200/224400/36003-0360 **(6692)**
2009: 16^{0}S, 16^{3}G, 16^{6}G, 16^{0}GS,

	Starts	1st	2nd	3rd	Win & Pl
Career Total (Turf)	23	0	4	3	15380

Going (Turf): Sf: 0-5 GS: 0-5 Gd: 0-4 GF: 0-8 Fm: 0-1
Distance: 5f/6f: 0 0 7f 8f: 0 3 9f 13f: 0 5 14f+: 0 15
Track : LH: 0-6 RH: 0-15 Tight: 0-9 Gall: 0-6
Aids: Bl: 0-0 Vi: 0-0 Tstrap: 0-0 Ckp: 0-0
Best Rating: **92** 6/07 Asct 2m5f159y soft

Fair; winner over hurdles; stays 2m; acts on most ground.

Neduardo

(87) (49)
2-y-o ch c Monsieur Bond (IRE)-Bond Shakira (Daggers Drawn (USA))
P W Chapple-Hyam G Roeder & D Baldwin

Placings:5 **(7477)**
2009: 6^{5}SD,

	Starts	1st	2nd	3rd	Win & Pl
Career Total (Turf)	0	0	0	0	
Career Total (AW)	1	0	0	0	0

Going (Turf): Sf: 0-0 GS: 0-0 Gd: 0-0 GF: 0-0 Fm: 0-0
Distance: 5f/6f: 0-1 7f-8f: 0-0 9f-13f: 0-0 14f+: 0-0
Track : LH: 0-0 RH: 0-1 Tight: 0-0 Gall: 0-0
Aids: Bl: 0-0 Vi: 0-0 Tstrap: 0-0 Ckp: 0-0
Best Rating: **49** 11/09 Kemp 6f stand

Needs A Treat

74 **34**
2-y-o b f Needwood Blade-Goes A Treat (IRE) (Common Grounds)
N Tinkler Neville Spence & John Marshall

Placings:50 **(1624)**
2009: 5^{5}F, 5^{0}GF,

	Starts	1st	2nd	3rd	Win & Pl
Career Total (Turf)	2	0	0	0	0

Going (Turf): Sf: 0-0 GS: 0-0 Gd: 0-0 GF: 0-1 Fm: 0-1
Distance: 5f/6f: 0-2 7f-8f: 0-0 9f-13f: 0-0 14f+: 0-0
Track : LH: 0-0 RH: 0-0 Tight: 0-0 Gall: 0-0
Aids: Bl: 0-0 Vi: 0-0 Tstrap: 0-0 Ckp: 0-0
Best Rating: **34** 4/09 Thsk 5f firm

Needsamaite

75 **47**
2-y-o b c Needwood Blade-Dekelsmary (Komaite (USA))
D J S Ffrench Davis John Hughes

Placings:4 **(1249)**
2009: 5^{4}GF,

	Starts	1st	2nd	3rd	Win & Pl
Career Total (Turf)	1	0	0	0	0

Going (Turf): Sf: 0-0 GS: 0-0 Gd: 0-0 GF: 0-1 Fm: 0-0
Distance: 5f/6f: 0-1 7f-8f: 0-0 9f-13f: 0-0 14f+: 0-0
Track : LH: 0-1 RH: 0-0 Tight: 0-0 Gall: 0-0
Aids: Bl: 0-0 Vi: 0-0 Tstrap: 0-0 Ckp: 0-0
Best Rating: **47** 4/09 Wwck 5f gd-fm

Out of a dual winner at up to 7f; promise on debut over 5f on fast ground.

Needwood Dancer

76(70) (26)**26**
2-y-o br f Needwood Blade-Waterline Dancer (IRE) (Danehill Dancer (IRE))
Peter Grayson Mersey Racing

Placings:06045 **(2457)**
2009: 5^{0}SD, 5^{6}GF, 5^{0}GF, 5^{4}SD, 5^{5}GF,

	Starts	1st	2nd	3rd	Win & Pl
Career Total (Turf)	3	0	0	0	0
Career Total (AW)	2	0	0	0	0

Going (Turf): Sf: 0-0 GS: 0-0 Gd: 0-0 GF: 0-3 Fm: 0-0
Distance: 5f/6f: 0-5 7f-8f: 0-0 9f-13f: 0-0 14f+: 0-0
Track : LH: 0-2 RH: 0-1 Tight: 0-2 Gall: 0-0
Aids: Bl: 0-1 Vi: 0-0 Tstrap: 0-0 Ckp: 0-0
Best Rating: **26** 5/09 Yarm 5f43y gd-fm

Needy McCredie

92 **41**
3-y-o ch f Needwood Blade-Vocation (IRE) (Royal Academy (USA))
J R Turner J R Turner

Placings:0500 **(5948)**
2009: 7^{0}G, 7^{5}GS, 8^{0}GF, 7^{0}G,

	Starts	1st	2nd	3rd	Win & Pl
Career Total (Turf)	4	0	0	0	0

Going (Turf): Sf: 0-0 GS: 0-1 Gd: 0-2 GF: 0-1 Fm: 0-0
Distance: 5f/6f: 0-0 7f-8f: 0-3 9f-13f: 0-1 14f+: 0-0
Track : LH: 0-3 RH: 0-1 Tight: 0-3 Gall: 0-0
Aids: Bl: 0-0 Vi: 0-0 Tstrap: 0-0 Ckp: 0-0
Best Rating: **41** 8/09 Thsk 7f gd-sft

Nefyn

81(84) (31)**60**
2-y-o b f Tiger Hill (IRE)-Bread Of Heaven (Machiavellian (USA))
W R Muir Usk Valley Stud

Placings:600 **(7140)**
2009: 8^{6}GF, 8^{0}GF, 8^{0}SD,

	Starts	1st	2nd	3rd	Win & Pl
Career Total (Turf)	2	0	0	0	0
Career Total (AW)	1	0	0	0	

Going (Turf): Sf: 0-0 GS: 0-0 Gd: 0-0 GF: 0-2 Fm: 0-0
Distance: 5f/6f: 0-0 7f-8f: 0-1 9f-13f: 0-2 14f+: 0-0
Track : LH: 0-2 RH: 0-0 Tight: 0-1 Gall: 0-1
Aids: Bl: 0-0 Vi: 0-0 Tstrap: 0-0 Ckp: 0-0
Best Rating: **60** 10/09 Yarm 1m3y gd-fm

Negotiation (IRE)

102(98) (70)**90**
3-y-o b g Refuse To Bend (IRE)-Dona Royale (IRE) (Darshaan)

J H M Gosden H R H Princess Haya Of Jordan

Placings:31210 **(5475)**
2009: 7^{3}SD, 8^{1}G, 8^{2}G, 8^{1}GF, 9^{0}GF,

	Starts	1st	2nd	3rd	Win & Pl
Career Total (Turf)	4	2	1	0	11391
Career Total (AW)	1	0	0	1	385

90 8/09 NmkJ 1m (0-85)H G-F £6476
83 4/09 Yarm 1m3y GD £3469
Total win prize-money £9945

Going (Turf): Sf: 0-0 GS: 0-0 **Gd: 1-2 GF: 1-2** Fm: 0-0
Distance: 5f/6f: 0-0 7f-8f: 1-2 9f-13f: 1-3 14f+: 0-0
Track : LH: 0-0 RH: 0-3 Tight: 0-1 Gall: 0-0
Aids: Bl: 0-0 Vi: 0-0 Tstrap: 0-0 Ckp: 0-0
Best Rating: 90 8/09 NmkJ 1m gd-fm

Useful; suited by 1m; acts on good and faster ground.

Nehaam

113 **108**
3-y-o b g Nayef (USA)-Charm The Stars (Roi Danzig (USA))
J H M Gosden Hamdan Al Maktoum

Placings:1-10022 **(6854)**
2009: 10^{1}GF, 10^{0}G, 12^{0}GF, 14^{2}GF, 16^{2}G,

	Starts	1st	2nd	3rd	Win & Pl
Career Total (Turf)	6	2	2	0	245428

104 4/09 NmkR 1m2f G-F £216680
84 9/08 NmkR 7f G-F £6152
Total win prize-money £222832

Going (Turf): Sf: 0-0 GS: 0-0 Gd: 0-2 **GF: 2-4** Fm: 0-0
Distance: 5f/6f: 0-0 7f-8f: 1-1 9f-13f: 1-3 14f+: 0-2
Track : LH: 0-1 RH: 0-3 Tight: 0-0 Gall: 0-4
Aids: Bl: 0-0 Vi: 0-0 Tstrap: 0-0 Ckp: 0-0
Best Rating: 108 10/09 NmkR 1m6f gd-fm

Smart; stays 2m and acts on fast ground.

Nelsons Prospect (IRE)

(70) (2)
4-y-o b g Fayruz-Kiva (Indian Ridge)
R A Teal Chris Simpson

Placings:0 **(3384)**
2009: 10^{0}SD,

	Starts	1st	2nd	3rd	Win & Pl
Career Total (Turf)	0	0	0	0	
Career Total (AW)	1	0	0	0	

Going (Turf): Sf: 0-0 GS: 0-0 Gd: 0-0 GF: 0-0 Fm: 0-0
Distance: 5f/6f: 0-0 7f-8f: 0-0 9f-13f: 0-1 14f+: 0-0
Track : LH: 0-1 RH: 0-0 Tight: 0-1 Gall: 0-0
Aids: Bl: 0-0 Vi: 0-0 Tstrap: 0-0 Ckp: 0-0
Best Rating: 2 6/09 Ling 1m2f stand

Nemo Spirit (IRE)

105(112) (97)**98**
4-y-o gr g Daylami (IRE)-La Bayadere (Sadler's Wells (USA))
W R Muir Mrs Monique V Bruce Copp

Placings:32/2510016-401020 **(6851)**
2009: 16^{4}SD, 16^{0}G, 16^{1}GS, 16^{0}G, 14^{2}S, 18^{0}G,

	Starts	1st	2nd	3rd	Win & Pl
Career Total (Turf)	14	3	3	1	43790
Career Total (AW)	1	0	0	0	560

97 6/09 York 2m88y (0-90)H G-S £11009
98 11/08 Muss 2m (0-100)H SFT £12462
81 5/08 Chep 1m4f23y SFT £2590
Total win prize-money £26061

Going (Turf): Sf: 2-5 GS: 1-3 Gd: 0-5 GF: 0-1 Fm: 0-0
Distance: 5f/6f: 0-0 7f-8f: 0-2 9f-13f: 1-4 **14f+: 2-9**
Track : **LH: 2-10** RH: 1-3 Tight: 1-3 Gall: 1-4
Aids: Bl: 0-0 Vi: 0-0 Tstrap: 0-0 Ckp: 0-0
Best Rating: 98 11/08 Muss 2m soft

Useful; stays 2m; acts on soft ground.

Neo's Mate (IRE)

95(98) (53)**60**
3-y-o br f Modigliani (USA)-Gute (IRE) (Petardia)
Paul Green Derek A Howard

Placings:5060000-00161550002 **(7787)**
2009: 6^{0}SD, 5^{0}F, 5^{1}GF, 8^{6}S, 5^{1}S, 7^{5}GF, 5^{5}GS, 8^{0}SD, 8^{0}SD, 5^{0}SD, 7^{2}SD,

	Starts	1st	2nd	3rd	Win & Pl
Career Total (Turf)	12	2	0	0	4849
Career Total (AW)	6	0	1	0	504

60 7/09 Catt 5f212y (0-60)H SFT £2460
54 7/09 Catt 5f212y G-F £2388
Total win prize-money £4849

Going (Turf): Sf: 1-3 GS: 0-2 Gd: 0-1 **GF: 1-5** Fm: 0-1
Distance: **5f/6f: 2-13** 7f-8f: 0-2 9f-13f: 0-3 14f+: 0-0
Track : **LH: 2-12** RH: 0-2 **Tight: 2-10** Gall: 0-0
Aids: Bl: 0-0 Vi: 0-0 Tstrap: 0-0 Ckp: 0-0
Best Rating: 60 7/09 Catt 5f212y soft

Moderate; effective over 5-6f; acts on fast ground.

Neon Blue

94 (54)**63**
8-y-o b/br g Atraf-Desert Lynx (IRE) (Green Desert (USA))
R M Whitaker Country Lane Partnership

Placings:332204040/51033316000/0600011300/002136000/32403054160/00065500401-40004S0600 **(6818)**
2009: 10^{4}F, 10^{0}G, 9^{0}GF, 9^{0}GF, 9^{4}GF, 10^{S}GF, 10^{0}GF, 12^{6}G, 10^{0}GS, 10^{0}GF,

	Starts	1st	2nd	3rd	Win & Pl
Career Total (Turf)	68	7	4	9	58849
Career Total (AW)	3	0	0	0	

63 10/08 Rdcr 1m2f (0-60)H GD £2307
77 9/07 York 7f (0-75)H G-F £5181
79 7/06 York 7f G-F £6477
74 9/05 York 7f (0-75)H G-F £6401
72 9/05 Rdcr 6f (0-70)H G-F £3858
76 7/04 York 6f217y C(0-90)H G-F £11017
69 5/04 Donc 6f E G-F £3581
Total win prize-money £38826

Going (Turf): Sf: 0-7 GS: 0-10 Gd: 1-17 **GF: 6-30** Fm: 0-4
Distance: 5f/6f: 2-14 **7f-8f: 4-44** 9f-13f: 1-13 14f+: 0-0
Track : **LH: 5-30** RH: 0-5 Tight: 1-13 **Gall: 4-8**
Aids: Bl: 0-2 **Vi: 3-11** Tstrap: 1-12 Ckp: 1-12
Best Rating: 79 8/06 Newc 7f gd-fm

Moderate; stays 1m2f; acts on most ground, but prefers it fast; has worn a visor and cheekpieces.

Nepotism

93(80) (35)**74**
2-y-o b c Piccolo-Craic Sa Ceili (IRE) (Danehill Dancer (IRE))
M S Saunders Chris Scott

Placings:50216 **(5650)**
2009: 5^{5}F, 5^{0}F, 5^{2}GF, 5^{1}GF, 5^{6}SD,

	Starts	1st	2nd	3rd	Win & Pl
Career Total (Turf)	4	1	1	0	5283
Career Total (AW)	1	0	0	0	0

71 6/09 Ling 5f G-F £3885
Total win prize-money £3886

Going (Turf): Sf: 0-0 GS: 0-0 Gd: 0-0 **GF: 1-2** Fm: 0-2
Distance: **5f/6f: 1-5** 7f-8f: 0-0 9f-13f: 0-0 14f+: 0-0
Track : LH: 0-3 RH: 0-0 Tight: 0-1 Gall: 0-3
Aids: Bl: 0-0 Vi: 0-0 Tstrap: 0-0 Ckp: 0-0
Best Rating: 74 6/09 Wind 5f10y gd-fm

Fair; effective at 5f on fast ground.

Nero West (FR)

(96) (41)**78**
8-y-o ch g Pelder (IRE)-West River (USA) (Gone West (USA))
I Semple Mr & Mrs Charles Villiers

Placings:53/4132345/363000/421104450/216413204-0 **(0219)**
2009: 13^{0}SD,

	Starts	1st	2nd	3rd	Win & Pl
Career Total (Turf)	33	5	4	6	49139
Career Total (AW)	1	0	0	0	

78 7/08 Muss 1m6f (0-75)H GD £3885
77 5/08 Haml 1m5f9y (0-80)H G-S £6476
76 7/07 Ches 1m7f195y (0-85)H SFT £5829
74 6/07 Newc 2m19y (0-80)H SFT £5362
4/04 Mont 1m2f SFT £4225
Total win prize-money £25779

Going (Turf): Sf: 3-7 GS: 1-6 Gd: 1-15 GF: 0-3 Fm: 0-0
Distance: 5f/6f: 0-0 7f-8f: 0-1 9f-13f: 1-16 **14f+: 4-17**
Track : LH: 2-10 RH: 2-13 **Tight: 3-13** Gall: 1-3
Aids: **Bl: 4-16** Vi: 0-0 Tstrap: 0-3 Ckp: 0-3
Best Rating: 100 3/05 StCl 1m2f110y v soft

Fair; stays 2m; acts on soft ground; has worn blinkers and cheekpieces; winning hurdler.

Nesayem (IRE)

103(95) (67)**71**
3-y-o b f Diktat-Zibet (Kris)
D M Simcock Mohammed Al Nabouda

Placings:003-443524 **(6789)**
2009: 8^{4}GF, 7^{4}GF, 10^{3}SD, 10^{5}GF, 10^{2}GF, 11^{4}G,

	Starts	1st	2nd	3rd	Win & Pl
Career Total (Turf)	6	0	1	0	2370
Career Total (AW)	3	0	0	2	740

Going (Turf): Sf: 0-1 GS: 0-0 Gd: 0-1 GF: 0-4 Fm: 0-0
Distance: 5f/6f: 0-0 7f-8f: 0-4 9f-13f: 0-5 14f+: 0-0
Track : LH: 0-6 RH: 0-3 Tight: 0-4 Gall: 0-1
Aids: Bl: 0-0 Vi: 0-0 Tstrap: 0-0 Ckp: 0-0
Best Rating: 71 9/09 Ffos 1m2f gd-fm

Modest; stays 1m2f; acts on fast ground.

Nesno (USA)

99(107) (72)**71**
6-y-o ch g Royal Academy (USA)-Cognac Lady (USA) (Olympio (USA))
J D Bethell Elliott Brothers And Peacock

Placings:3430/023100/006000/3225100-000 **(6862)**
2009: 8^{0}GF, 9^{0}SD, 8^{0}SD,

	Starts	1st	2nd	3rd	Win & Pl
Career Total (Turf)	21	1	3	4	10456

	Starts	1st	2nd	3rd	Win & Pl
Career Total (AW)	**5**	**1**	**0**	**0**	**2388**

72	8/08	Wolv	1m141y	(0-65)H	STD	£2388
83	7/06	Pont	1m2f6y	(0-75)H	G-F	£4533

Total win prize-money £6922

Going (Turf): Sf: 0-2 GS: 0-4 Gd: 0-6 **GF: 1-9** Fm: 0-0
Distance: 5f/6f: 0-0 7f-8f: 0-5 **9f-13f: 2-20** 14f+: 0-1
Track : **LH: 2-22** RH: 0-2 **Tight: 1-9** Gall: 0-7
Aids: Bl: 1-1 Vi: 0-3 Tstrap: 1-6 Ckp: 1-6
Best Rating: 83 7/06 Pont 1m2f6y gd-fm

Modest; effective at around 1m2f and acts on fast ground; has worn blinkers.

Netta (IRE)

102 **85**

3-y-o b f Barathea (IRE)-Nishan (Nashwan (USA))
P J Makin Netta Racing

Placings:0-410 **(5996)**
2009: 8^4S, 6^1GF, 8^0GS,

	Starts	1st	2nd	3rd	Win & Pl
Career Total (Turf)	**4**	**1**	**0**	**0**	**4270**

85	8/09	Sals	6f212y		G-F	£3885

Total win prize-money £3886

Going (Turf): Sf: 0-1 GS: 0-1 Gd: 0-1 **GF: 1-1** Fm: 0-0
Distance: 5f/6f: 0-0 **7f-8f: 1-3** 9f-13f: 0-1 14f+: 0-0
Track : LH: 0-0 RH: 0-1 Tight: 0-0 Gall: 0-0
Aids: Bl: 0-0 Vi: 0-0 Tstrap: 0-0 Ckp: 0-0
Best Rating: 85 8/09 Sals 6f212y gd-fm

Useful; effective at around 7f; acts on fast ground.

Networker

106(102) (76)**71**

6-y-o ch g Danzig Connection (USA)-Trevorsninepoints (Jester)
P J McBride P J McBride

Placings:00/60056**314**/**00**41113**244**0/00**00530-03**0**4**243 **(7798)**
2009: 8^0SD, 7^3SD, 7^0G, 8^4SD, 8^2G, 7^4GF, 9^3SS,

	Starts	1st	2nd	3rd	Win & Pl
Career Total (Turf)	**20**	**3**	**1**	**1**	**11995**
Career Total (AW)	**15**	**1**	**1**	**4**	**6823**

70	6/07	Haml	1m65y	(0-70)H	G-F	£3886
77	5/07	Yarm	1m3y	(0-65)H	GD	£2137
65	5/07	Bevl	1m100y	(0-60)H	GD	£3241
62	12/06	Wolv	7f32y		STD	£3238

Total win prize-money £12504

Going (Turf): Sf: 0-0 GS: 0-3 **Gd: 2-6** GF: 1-9 Fm: 0-2
Distance: 5f/6f: 0-7 7f-8f: 1-21 **9f-13f: 3-7** 14f+: 0-0
Track : LH: 1-11 **RH: 2-9 Tight: 2-10** Gall: 0-1
Aids: Bl: 0-0 Vi: 0-0 Tstrap: 0-0 Ckp: 0-0
Best Rating: 81 7/07 Kemp 1m stand

Modest; effective at around 1m; acts on good ground; also goes on Polytrack.

Neuchatel (GER)

(101) (80)**79**

3-y-o b g Rahy (USA)-Nalani (IRE) (Sadler's Wells (USA))
Trainer Unknown (M Johnston 9/1) Unknown

Placings:414-411 **(0101)**
2009: 10^4SD, 11^1SD, 11^1SD,

	Starts	1st	2nd	3rd	Win & Pl
Career Total (Turf)	**1**	**1**	**0**	**0**	**3412**
Career Total (AW)	**5**	**2**	**0**	**0**	**5889**

	10/09	Ghli	1m3f110y		STD	£2912
	9/09	Ghli	1m3f110y		STD	£1941
79	10/08	Nott	1m75y		G-S	£3412

Total win prize-money £8267

Going (Turf): Sf: 0-0 **GS: 1-1** Gd: 0-0 GF: 0-0 Fm: 0-0
Distance: 5f/6f: 0-0 7f-8f: 0-2 **9f-13f: 3-4** 14f+: 0-0
Track : **LH: 1-4** RH: 0-0 Tight: 0-2 Gall: 0-1
Aids: Bl: 0-0 Vi: 0-0 Tstrap: 0-0 Ckp: 0-0
Best Rating: 80 1/09 Ling 1m2f stand

Fair on Polytrack; stays 1m2f.

Neva A Mull Moment (IRE)

99 **65**

3-y-o b g Mull Of Kintyre (USA)-Serious Contender (IRE) (Tenby)
D Nicholls Mike Browne

Placings:0-33320 **(5599)**
2009: 7^3F, 7^3G, 5^3GF, 5^2GS, 6^0GF,

	Starts	1st	2nd	3rd	Win & Pl
Career Total (Turf)	**6**	**0**	**1**	**3**	**2764**

Going (Turf): Sf: 0-0 GS: 0-1 Gd: 0-2 GF: 0-2 Fm: 0-1
Distance: 5f/6f: 0-3 7f-8f: 0-3 9f-13f: 0-0 14f+: 0-0
Track : LH: 0-3 RH: 0-0 Tight: 0-3 Gall: 0-0
Aids: Bl: 0-0 Vi: 0-0 Tstrap: 0-0 Ckp: 0-0
Best Rating: 65 8/09 Catt 5f212y gd-sft

Modest promise in maidens; stays 7f; acts on fast and easy ground.

Nevada Desert (IRE)

105(105) (84)**84**

9-y-o b g Desert King (IRE)-Kayanga (Green Desert (USA))
R M Whitaker J Barry Pemberton

Placings:655300/023133425/45201000**65342**/**0**15425653 44003**150**/0051042021204**13**/004**3**01124055300/0052305 61055432**-**0006660**0211**0 **(7194)**
2009: 8^0GF, 8^0HY, 9^0GS, 8^6S, 8^6GF, 8^6GS, 8^0G, 8^0GF, 9^0SD, 9^2SD, 9^1SD, 10^1GS, 9^0SD,

	Starts	1st	2nd	3rd	Win & Pl
Career Total (Turf)	**86**	**9**	**9**	**9**	**93954**
Career Total (AW)	**17**	**3**	**3**	**3**	**26486**

82	10/09	Donc	1m2f60y	(0-80)H	G-S	£4857
76	10/09	Wolv	1m1f103y	(0-65)H	STD	£2388
84	7/08	Bevl	1m100y	(0-85)H	G-F	£5180
92	7/07	Bevl	1m100y	(0-85)H	GD	£6477
78	7/07	York	1m		HVY	£6477
89	11/06	Sthl	1m	(0-90)H	STD	£7790
79	9/06	Hayd	1m30y	(0-85)H	HVY	£6477
75	6/06	Haml	1m65y	(0-70)H	G-F	£3886
87	10/05	Wolv	1m1f103y	(0-90)H	STD	£8518
79	4/05	Thsk	1m	(0-70)H	SFT	£4186
79	8/04	Haml	1m65y	C(0-90)H	G-S	£10409
73	6/03	Bevl	1m100y	D(0-80)H	G-F	£5622

Total win prize-money £72272

Going (Turf): Sf: 3-14 GS: 2-16 Gd: 1-21 **GF: 3-34** Fm: 0-1
Distance: 5f/6f: 0-1 7f-8f: 3-39 **9f-13f: 9-63** 14f+: 0-0
Track : **LH: 7-59** RH: 5-41 **Tight: 5-46** Gall: 2-8
Aids: Bl: 0-0 Vi: 0-0 Tstrap: 1-6 Ckp: 1-6
Best Rating: 92 9/07 Hayd 1m30y soft

Fair; stays 1m2f; acts on most types of ground and on sand.

Neve Lieve (IRE)

100(97) (56)**90**

4-y-o b/br f Dubai Destination (USA)-Love Of Silver (USA) (Arctic Tern (USA))
M Botti The Great Partnership

Placings:0304/531410134-65 **(2085)**
2009: 15^6G, 14^5GF,

	Starts	1st	2nd	3rd	Win & Pl
Career Total (Turf)	**13**	**3**	**0**	**3**	**20150**
Career Total (AW)	**2**	**0**	**0**	**0**	

76	10/08	Nott	2m9y	(0-85)H	G-S	£7123
78	8/08	Yarm	1m3f101y	(0-70)H	SFT	£2590
73	7/08	Ling	1m3f106y	(0-70)H	G-F	£2590

Total win prize-money £12304

Going (Turf): Sf: 1-2 GS: 1-1 Gd: 0-4 **GF: 1-5** Fm: 0-1
Distance: 5f/6f: 0-0 7f-8f: 0-3 **9f-13f: 2-7** 14f+: 1-5
Track : **LH: 3-10** RH: 0-5 **Tight: 2-5** Gall: 0-5
Aids: **Bl: 1-1** Vi: 0-1 Tstrap: 0-1 Ckp: 0-1
Best Rating: 90 11/08 StCl 1m4f110y heavy

Useful; stays 2m; acts on most ground; has worn blinkers, cheekpieces and a visor.

Never Ending Tale

105(100) (87)**89**

4-y-o ch g Singspiel (IRE)-Bright Finish (USA) (Zilzal (USA))
E F Vaughan Ali Saeed

Placings:510350-210 **(3154)**
2009: 8^2SD, 10^1GF, 8^0G,

	Starts	1st	2nd	3rd	Win & Pl
Career Total (Turf)	**7**	**1**	**0**	**1**	**7575**
Career Total (AW)	**2**	**1**	**1**	**0**	**3873**

89	6/09	Donc	1m2f60y	(0-85)H	G-F	£6476
76	5/08	Ling	1m2f		STD	£2331

Total win prize-money £8807

Going (Turf): Sf: 0-0 GS: 0-0 Gd: 0-2 **GF: 1-5** Fm: 0-0
Distance: 5f/6f: 0-0 7f-8f: 0-1 **9f-13f: 2-8** 14f+: 0-0
Track : **LH: 2-5** RH: 0-3 Tight: 1-4 Gall: 1-1
Aids: Bl: 0-0 Vi: 0-0 Tstrap: 1-2 Ckp: 1-2
Best Rating: 89 6/09 Donc 1m2f60y gd-fm

Useful; effective over 1m2f; acts on fast ground and on Polytrack; has worn cheekpieces.

Never Lose

104(102) (81)**93**

3-y-o br f Diktat-Enchanted Princess (Royal Applause)
C E Brittain Saeed Manana

Placings:2326-**1004**1340050 **(6814)**
2009: 6^1SD, 6^0SD, 7^0SD, 6^4SD, 7^1GS, 6^3HY, 5^4G, 7^0G, 8^0GS, 6^5G, 6^0G,

	Starts	1st	2nd	3rd	Win & Pl
Career Total (Turf)	**11**	**1**	**2**	**2**	**20118**
Career Total (AW)	**4**	**1**	**0**	**0**	**3307**

92	5/09	Newb	7f	(0-85)H	G-S	£6476
68	3/09	Sthl	6f		STD	£2729

Total win prize-money £9206

Going (Turf): Sf: 0-1 **GS: 1-3** Gd: 0-7 GF: 0-0 Fm: 0-0
Distance: 5f/6f: 1-7 7f-8f: 1-8 9f-13f: 0-0 14f+: 0-0
Track : **LH: 1-2** RH: 0-3 Tight: 0-1 Gall: 0-1
Aids: Bl: 0-2 Vi: 0-0 Tstrap: 0-0 Ckp: 0-0
Best Rating: 93 5/09 Hayd 6f heavy

Useful; Listed placed; effective over 6f-7f; acts on good and softer ground and on Fibresand; has worn blinkers.

Never On Sunday (FR)

122 **123**

4-y-o gr c Sunday Break (JPN)-Hexane (FR) (Kendor (FR))
J-C Rouget D-Y Treves

Placings:11/142111-51300 **(6850)**
2009: 10^{5}G, 9^{1}S, 10^{3}GF, 8^{0}G, 10^{0}G,

	Starts	1st	2nd	3rd	Win & Pl
Career Total (Turf)	**13**	**7**	**1**	**1**	**283233**

118 5/09 Lonc 1m1f55y SFT £138689
115 9/08 Lonc 1m2f GD £29412
102 7/08 Chan 1m2f GD £20221
101 6/08 Chan 1m GD £12500
3/08 Pari 1m G-S £9191
11/07 Pari 1m SFT £8445
10/07 Toul 1m G-S £4391
Total win prize-money £222851

Going (Turf): Sf: 2-3 GS: 2-2 **Gd: 3-7** GF: 0-1 Fm: 0-0
Distance: 5f/6f: 0-0 **7f-8f: 4-7** 9f-13f: 3-6 14f+: 0-0
Track : LH: 0-1 **RH: 5-8** Tight: 0-0 Gall: 0-1
Aids: **Bl: 3-3** Vi: 0-0 Tstrap: 0-0 Ckp: 0-0
Best Rating: **123** 6/09 Asct 1m2f gd-fm

High-class; won the Group 1 Prix d'Ispahan in 2009; effective at 1m-1m2f; acts on good ground or softer; has worn blinkers.

Never Sold Out (IRE)

100(93) (48)**58**

4-y-o ch g Captain Rio-Vicious Rosie (Dancing Spree (USA))
J G M O'Shea R D J East

Placings:0021000/55026-0403000 **(5211)**
2009: 7^{0}SD, 6^{4}GF, 8^{0}GF, 8^{3}F, 10^{0}F, 7^{0}F, 8^{0}G,

	Starts	1st	2nd	3rd	Win & Pl
Career Total (Turf)	**11**	**0**	**1**	**1**	**1175**
Career Total (AW)	**8**	**1**	**1**	**0**	**2652**

58 6/07 Wolv 7f32y SF £2047
Total win prize-money £2048

Going (Turf): **Sf: 0-0 GS: 0-2 Gd: 0-1 GF: 0-5 Fm: 0-3**
Distance: 5f/6f: 0-3 **7f-8f: 1-9** 9f-13f: 0-7 14f+: 0-0
Track : **LH: 1-13** RH: 0-2 **Tight: 1-9** Gall: 0-1
Aids: Bl: 0-2 Vi: 0-5 Tstrap: 0-0 Ckp: 0-0
Best Rating: **58** 5/09 Bath 1m5y firm

Moderate; stays 7f; acts on good to firm and Polytrack.

Never The Waiter

100(96) (86)**95**

2-y-o b c Kyllachy-Talighta (USA) (Barathea (IRE))
B J Meehan R P Foden

Placings:613 **(6677)**
2009: 7^{6}GF, 5^{1}SF, 6^{3}G,

	Starts	1st	2nd	3rd	Win & Pl
Career Total (Turf)	**2**	**0**	**0**	**1**	**3360**
Career Total (AW)	**1**	**1**	**0**	**0**	**3238**

86 10/09 Wolv 5f216y SF £3238
Total win prize-money £3238

Going (Turf): **Sf: 0-0 GS: 0-0 Gd: 0-1 GF: 0-1 Fm: 0-0**
Distance: **5f/6f: 1-2** 7f-8f: 0-1 9f-13f: 0-0 14f+: 0-0
Track : **LH: 1-1** RH: 0-0 **Tight: 1-1** Gall: 0-0
Aids: Bl: 0-0 Vi: 0-0 Tstrap: 0-0 Ckp: 0-0

Best Rating: **95** 10/09 York 6f good

Useful; Listed placed; acts on good ground and on Polytrack.

New Adventure

71 **44**

3-y-o b g Generous (IRE)-Sari (Faustus (USA))
P F I Cole R A Instone

Placings:000-0 **(2350)**
2009: 12^{0}GF,

	Starts	1st	2nd	3rd	Win & Pl
Career Total (Turf)	**4**	**0**	**0**	**0**	

Going (Turf): **Sf: 0-0 GS: 0-0 Gd: 0-2 GF: 0-2 Fm: 0-0**
Distance: 5f/6f: 0-0 7f-8f: 0-3 9f-13f: 0-1 14f+: 0-0
Track : LH: 0-3 RH: 0-0 Tight: 0-0 Gall: 0-0
Aids: Bl: 0-0 Vi: 0-0 Tstrap: 0-0 Ckp: 0-0
Best Rating: **44** 9/08 NmkR 1m gd-fm

New Beginning (FR)

79(92) (66)**47**

3-y-o b f Nayef (USA)-Chrysalu (Distant Relative)
H J L Dunlop H E Sheikh Sultan Bin Khalifa Al Nahyan

Placings:026-000 **(4196)**
2009: 10^{0}GF, 8^{0}SD, 8^{0}GS,

	Starts	1st	2nd	3rd	Win & Pl
Career Total (Turf)	**3**	**0**	**0**	**0**	
Career Total (AW)	**3**	**0**	**1**	**0**	**1156**

Going (Turf): **Sf: 0-1 GS: 0-1 Gd: 0-0 GF: 0-1 Fm: 0-0**
Distance: 5f/6f: 0-0 7f-8f: 0-2 9f-13f: 0-4 14f+: 0-0
Track : LH: 0-4 RH: 0-2 Tight: 0-3 Gall: 0-0
Aids: Bl: 0-1 Vi: 0-0 Tstrap: 0-0 Ckp: 0-0
Best Rating: **66** 10/08 Kemp 7f stand

Modest; effective over 7f; acts on Polytrack.

New Beginning (IRE)

97(104) (73)**84**

5-y-o b g Keltos (FR)-Goldthroat (IRE) (Zafonic (USA))
Mrs S Lamyman P Lamyman

Placings:0465**10**/**2451**303452/0062050004**5**-0**554**320 **(1615)**
2009: 8^{0}SS, 8^{5}SS, 9^{5}SD, 9^{4}SD, 10^{3}GF, 9^{2}GF, 10^{0}G,

	Starts	1st	2nd	3rd	Win & Pl
Career Total (Turf)	**22**	**1**	**3**	**3**	**10931**
Career Total (AW)	**12**	**1**	**1**	**0**	**5478**

75 11/06 Wolv 1m1f103y STD £3238
Total win prize-money £3239

Going (Turf): Sf: 0-2 GS: 0-4 Gd: 0-7 **GF: 1-9** Fm: 0-0
Distance: 5f/6f: 0-0 7f-8f: 0-5 **9f-13f: 2-28** 14f+: 0-1
Track : LH: 1-24 RH: 1-9 **Tight: 1-10** Gall: 0-10
Aids: Bl: 0-0 Vi: 0-0 Tstrap: 0-2 Ckp: 0-2
Best Rating: **103** 7/07 NmkJ 1m4f gd-fm

Modest; stays 1m4f; acts on fast ground; also goes on Polytrack.

New Christmas (USA)

81(98) (82)**69**

2-y-o gr/ro c Smoke Glacken (USA)-Occhi Verdi (IRE) (Mujtahid (USA))
B J Meehan Jaber Abdullah

Placings:4U0511 **(7804)**
2009: 6^{4}G, 6^{U}GF, 7^{0}G, 7^{5}SD, 8^{1}SD, 8^{1}SD,

	Starts	1st	2nd	3rd	Win & Pl
Career Total (Turf)	**3**	**0**	**0**	**0**	**385**
Career Total (AW)	**3**	**2**	**0**	**0**	**7263**

82 12/09 Wolv 1m141y (0-85) STD £4533
78 12/09 Ling 1m (0-75) STD £2729
Total win prize-money £7263

Going (Turf): **Sf: 0-0 GS: 0-0 Gd: 0-2 GF: 0-1 Fm: 0-0**
Distance: 5f/6f: 0-1 7f-8f: 1-4 9f-13f: 1-1 14f+: 0-0
Track : **LH: 2-4** RH: 0-0 **Tight: 2-3** Gall: 0-0
Aids: Bl: 0-0 Vi: 0-0 Tstrap: 0-0 Ckp: 0-0
Best Rating: **82** 12/09 Wolv 1m141y stand

Useful; stays 1m; acts on Polytrack.

New Couture (IRE)

(93) (54)

3-y-o b f Montjeu (IRE)-New Design (IRE) (Bluebird (USA))
P W Chapple-Hyam Sean P Burke

Placings:046 **(7882)**
2009: 10^{0}SD, 12^{4}SD, 10^{6}SD,

	Starts	1st	2nd	3rd	Win & Pl
Career Total (Turf)	**0**	**0**	**0**	**0**	
Career Total (AW)	**3**	**0**	**0**	**0**	**0**

Going (Turf): **Sf: 0-0 GS: 0-0 Gd: 0-0 GF: 0-0 Fm: 0-0**
Distance: 5f/6f: 0-0 7f-8f: 0-0 9f-13f: 0-3 14f+: 0-0
Track : LH: 0-3 RH: 0-0 Tight: 0-3 Gall: 0-0
Aids: Bl: 0-0 Vi: 0-0 Tstrap: 0-0 Ckp: 0-0
Best Rating: **54** 12/09 Wolv 1m4f50y stand

New Den

72(83) (55)**55**

2-y-o ch c Piccolo-Den's-Joy (Archway (IRE))
J R Boyle Joy Racing

Placings:0060 **(7865)**
2009: 6^{0}SD, 6^{0}GF, 8^{6}SD, 8^{0}SS,

	Starts	1st	2nd	3rd	Win & Pl
Career Total (Turf)	**1**	**0**	**0**	**0**	
Career Total (AW)	**3**	**0**	**0**	**0**	**0**

Going (Turf): **Sf: 0-0 GS: 0-0 Gd: 0-0 GF: 0-1 Fm: 0-0**
Distance: 5f/6f: 0-1 7f-8f: 0-3 9f-13f: 0-0 14f+: 0-0
Track : LH: 0-2 RH: 0-1 Tight: 0-1 Gall: 0-0
Aids: Bl: 0-0 Vi: 0-0 Tstrap: 0-0 Ckp: 0-0
Best Rating: **55** 12/09 Kemp 1m stand

New England

98(109) (65)**65**

7-y-o ch g Bachir (IRE)-West Escape (Gone West (USA))
F Sheridan (W M Brisbourne 21/8) Bould & Walker Racing

Placings:00600**0561**/**222123**0001**645**/P-**3312**002**653**10**60** **(6998)**

2009: 9^{3}SD, 11^{3}SD, 12^{1}SD, 12^{2}SD, 12^{0}GS, 11^{0}G, 10^{2}GF, 12^{6}GF, 10^{5}GF, 12^{3}SD, 12^{1}SD, 12^{0}SF, 12^{6}SD, 9^{0}SD,

	Starts	1st	2nd	3rd	Win & Pl
Career Total (Turf)	13	1	1	0	4531
Career Total (AW)	24	4	5	4	13028

63	8/09	Wolv	1m4f50y		STD	£2047
60	3/09	Wolv	1m4f50y		STD	£2047
69	9/06	Ches	1m2f75y	(0-70)H	G-F	£3562
67	2/06	Wolv	1m141y	(0-60)H	STD	£2388
55	12/05	Wolv	1m141y	(0-45)	SS	£1481

Total win prize-money £11526

Going (Turf): Sf: 0-1 GS: 0-3 Gd: 0-2 **GF: 1-6** Fm: 0-1
Distance: 5f/6f: 0-0 7f-8f: 0-4 **9f-13f: 5-33** 14f+: 0-0
Track : **LH: 5-33** RH: 0-4 **Tight: 5-24** Gall: 0-3
Aids: Bl: 0-0 Vi: 0-0 Tstrap: 0-0 Ckp: 0-0
Best Rating: **70** 3/06 Wolv 1m141y stand

Moderate; stays 1m4f; acts on fast ground and on Polytrack.

New Innocence

91(98) (72)74

2-y-o ch c Where Or When (IRE)-Scottendale (Zilzal (USA))

G A Butler Fawzi Abdulla Nass

Placings:644 **(7199)**

2009: 7^{6}G, 7^{4}GF, 8^{4}SD,

	Starts	1st	2nd	3rd	Win & Pl
Career Total (Turf)	2	0	0	0	289
Career Total (AW)	1	0	0	0	0

Going (Turf): **Sf: 0-0 GS: 0-0 Gd: 0-1 GF: 0-1 Fm: 0-0**
Distance: 5f/6f: 0-0 7f-8f: 0-3 9f-13f: 0-0 14f+: 0-0
Track : LH: 0-1 RH: 0-1 Tight: 0-1 Gall: 0-0
Aids: Bl: 0-0 Vi: 0-0 Tstrap: 0-0 Ckp: 0-0
Best Rating: **74** 7/09 NmkJ 7f good

New Leyf (IRE)

103(100) (81)77

3-y-o b/br g Kheleyf (USA)-Society Fair (FR) (Always Fair (USA))

J R Gask Horses First Racing Limited

Placings:6010352 **(7828)**

2009: 6^{6}GS, 6^{0}GF, 6^{1}GS, 6^{0}G, 7^{3}S, 6^{5}GF, 6^{2}SD,

	Starts	1st	2nd	3rd	Win & Pl
Career Total (Turf)	6	1	0	1	4105
Career Total (AW)	1	0	1	0	771

77	6/09	Ripn	6f	G-S	£3238

Total win prize-money £3238

Going (Turf): Sf: 0-1 **GS: 1-2** Gd: 0-1 GF: 0-2 Fm: 0-0
Distance: **5f/6f: 1-5** 7f-8f: 0-2 9f-13f: 0-0 14f+: 0-0
Track : LH: 0-1 RH: 0-1 Tight: 0-0 Gall: 0-0
Aids: Bl: 0-0 Vi: 0-0 Tstrap: 0-0 Ckp: 0-0
Best Rating: **81** 12/09 Kemp 6f stand

Fair; effective over 6f; acts on easy ground; goes on Polytrack.

New Star (UAE)

(109) (85)77

5-y-o b g Green Desert (USA)-Princess Haifa (USA) (Mr Prospector (USA))

W M Brisbourne Shropshire Wolves

Placings:0031050/5041620410**405-4121262** **(1133)**

2009: 9^{4}SD, 9^{1}SD, 9^{2}SD, 9^{1}SD, 8^{2}SD, 9^{6}SD, 9^{2}SD,

	Starts	1st	2nd	3rd	Win & Pl
Career Total (Turf)	15	2	1	1	15529
Career Total (AW)	12	3	3	0	15159

80	3/09	Wolv	1m1f103y		STD	£2729
80	2/09	Wolv	1m1f103y	(0-80)H	STD	£4857
85	10/08	Wolv	1m1f103y	(0-75)H	STD	£3238
75	5/08	Newb	1m2f6y	(0-70)H	SFT	£3123
80	8/07	Ches	1m2f75y	(0-90)H	G-F	£9348

Total win prize-money £23296

Going (Turf): **Sf: 1-3** GS: 0-1 Gd: 0-7 **GF: 1-4** Fm: 0-0
Distance: 5f/6f: 0-0 7f-8f: 0-1 **9f-13f: 5-26** 14f+: 0-0
Track : **LH: 5-26** RH: 0-1 **Tight: 4-19** Gall: 1-3
Aids: Bl: 0-0 Vi: 0-0 Tstrap: 0-0 Ckp: 0-0
Best Rating: **85** 10/08 Wolv 1m1f103y stand

Fair; effective at around 1m-1m2f; acts on fast ground; goes on Polytrack.

New Tricks

99 71

3-y-o b g Falbrav (IRE)-Numberonedance (USA) (Trempolino (USA))

P Monteith (I Semple 12/8) David McKenzie

Placings:505-20100 **(4898)**

2009: 12^{2}GS, 14^{0}GF, 11^{1}GF, 12^{0}GF, 12^{0}GS,

	Starts	1st	2nd	3rd	Win & Pl
Career Total (Turf)	8	1	1	0	3352

71	6/09	Haml	1m3f16y	(0-65)H	G-F	£2388

Total win prize-money £2388

Going (Turf): Sf: 0-2 GS: 0-2 Gd: 0-1 **GF: 1-3** Fm: 0-0
Distance: 5f/6f: 0-1 7f-8f: 0-1 **9f-13f: 1-5** 14f+: 0-1
Track : LH: 0-3 **RH: 1-4 Tight: 1-6** Gall: 0-0
Aids: **Bl: 1-3** Vi: 0-0 Tstrap: 0-1 Ckp: 0-1
Best Rating: **71** 6/09 Haml 1m3f16y gd-fm

Fair; stays 1m3f; acts on fast ground.

New World Order (IRE)

97(103) (68)53

5-y-o b g Night Shift (USA)-Kama Tashoof (Mtoto)

R Curtis (Edgar Byrne 14/11) R P Behan

Placings:300/3230040212023/0061002 **(7403)**

2009: 10^{0}SD, 11^{0}SD, 10^{6}G, 10^{1}SD, 8^{0}SD, 12^{0}SD, 8^{2}SD,

	Starts	1st	2nd	3rd	Win & Pl
Career Total (Turf)	9	0	1	1	3230
Career Total (AW)	14	2	4	3	9559

65	9/09	Kemp	1m2f	(0-55)H	STD	£1942
79	9/07	Wolv	1m141y		STD	£2388

Total win prize-money £4332

Going (Turf): **Sf: 0-1 GS: 0-0 Gd: 0-4 GF: 0-1 Fm: 0-0**
Distance: 5f/6f: 0-0 7f-8f: 0-7 **9f-13f: 2-16** 14f+: 0-0
Track : LH: 1-15 RH: 1-6 **Tight: 1-14** Gall: 0-1
Aids: Bl: 0-0 Vi: 0-0 Tstrap: 0-0 Ckp: 0-0
Best Rating: **84** 9/06 Curr 7f yld-sft

Moderate; effective at around 1m-1m1f; acts on good ground; also goes on Polytrack; has worn a tongue-tie.

New World Symphony (IRE)

75(61) (5)60

2-y-o b c War Chant (USA)-Bold Classic (USA) (Pembroke (USA))

J Howard Johnson Transcend Bloodstock LLP

Placings:66 **(5324)**

2009: 7^{6}GF, 8^{6}SD,

	Starts	1st	2nd	3rd	Win & Pl
Career Total (Turf)	1	0	0	0	0
Career Total (AW)	1	0	0	0	0

Going (Turf): **Sf: 0-0 GS: 0-0 Gd: 0-0 GF: 0-1 Fm: 0-0**
Distance: 5f/6f: 0-0 7f-8f: 0-2 9f-13f: 0-0 14f+: 0-0
Track : LH: 0-2 RH: 0-0 Tight: 0-1 Gall: 0-0
Aids: Bl: 0-0 Vi: 0-0 Tstrap: 0-0 Ckp: 0-0
Best Rating: **60** 6/09 Thsk 7f gd-fm

New York Lights (IRE)

84(87) (54)43

2-y-o b f Statue Of Liberty (USA)-Nautical Light (Slip Anchor)

M D I Usher R H Brookes

Placings:U00**52000000** **(7887)**

2009: 5^{U}GF, 5^{U}GF, 5^{U}GF, 7^{5}SD, 6^{2}SD, 6^{0}SD, 6^{0}SD, 8^{0}GF, 8^{0}GS, 7^{0}SD, 7^{0}SD,

	Starts	1st	2nd	3rd	Win & Pl
Career Total (Turf)	5	0	0	0	
Career Total (AW)	6	0	1	0	605

Going (Turf): **Sf: 0-0 GS: 0-1 Gd: 0-0 GF: 0-4 Fm: 0-0**
Distance: 5f/6f: 0-6 7f-8f: 0-3 9f-13f: 0-2 14f+: 0-0
Track : LH: 0-7 RH: 0-2 Tight: 0-6 Gall: 0-2
Aids: Bl: 0-1 Vi: 0-0 Tstrap: 0-0 Ckp: 0-0
Best Rating: **54** 8/09 Ling 6f stand

Moderate; effective over 6f; acts on Polytrack.

Newbury Street

97(93) (65)67

2-y-o b g Namid-Cautious Joe (First Trump)

R A Fahey J J Staunton

Placings:343213 **(6983)**

2009: 5^{3}GS, 5^{4}S, 5^{3}GF, 7^{2}GF, 5^{1}SD, 6^{3}G,

	Starts	1st	2nd	3rd	Win & Pl
Career Total (Turf)	5	0	1	3	3614
Career Total (AW)	1	1	0	0	2388

65	9/09	Wolv	5f216y	(0-65)H	STD	£2388

Total win prize-money £2388

Going (Turf): **Sf: 0-1 GS: 0-1 Gd: 0-1 GF: 0-2 Fm: 0-0**
Distance: **5f/6f: 1-5** 7f-8f: 0-1 9f-13f: 0-0 14f+: 0-0
Track : **LH: 1-3** RH: 0-0 **Tight: 1-2** Gall: 0-0
Aids: Bl: 0-0 Vi: 0-0 Tstrap: 0-0 Ckp: 0-0
Best Rating: **67** 10/09 Ayr 6f good

Modest; effective at 5-7f; acts on fast ground and Polytrack.

Newby Abbey (IRE)

(79) (12)

8-y-o b g Lord Of Appeal-Turramurra Girl (IRE) (Magical Wonder (USA))

D Flood Doug Ellis

Placings:00 **(2129)**

2009: 8^{0}SD, 12^{0}SD,

	Starts	1st	2nd	3rd	Win & Pl
Career Total (Turf)	0	0	0	0	
Career Total (AW)	2	0	0	0	

Going (Turf): **Sf: 0-0 GS: 0-0 Gd: 0-0 GF: 0-0 Fm: 0-0**

Distance: 5f/6f: 0-0 7f-8f: 0-0 9f-13f: 0-2 14f+: 0-0
Track : LH: 0-2 RH: 0-0 Tight: 0-1 Gall: 0-0
Aids: Bl: 0-0 Vi: 0-0 Tstrap: 0-1 Ckp: 0-1
Best Rating: 12 4/09 Wolv 1m141y stand

Newcastle Sam

66(70) (6)35
4-y-o b g Atraf-Ballyewry (Prince Tenderfoot (USA))
J J Bridger Gayler William Chambers

Placings:0000/000-6 **(5963)**
2009: 10^{6}G,

	Starts	1st	2nd	3rd	Win & Pl
Career Total (Turf)	5	0	0	0	0
Career Total (AW)	3	0	0	0	

Going (Turf): Sf: 0-1 GS: 0-1 Gd: 0-1 GF: 0-1 Fm: 0-1
Distance: 5f/6f: 0-3 7f-8f: 0-2 9f-13f: 0-3 14f+: 0-0
Track : LH: 0-2 RH: 0-3 Tight: 0-3 Gall: 0-0
Aids: Bl: 0-0 Vi: 0-0 Tstrap: 0-1 Ckp: 0-1
Best Rating: 35 7/08 Ling 7f firm

Newgate (UAE)

(102) (60)33
5-y-o b g Jade Robbery (USA)-Patruel (Rainbow Quest (USA))
Mrs R A Carr David W Chapman

Placings:0434001500000-0 **(0823)**
2009: 8^{0}SD,

	Starts	1st	2nd	3rd	Win & Pl
Career Total (Turf)	3	0	0	0	
Career Total (AW)	11	1	0	1	2410

60 4/08 Wolv 7f32y (0-65)H STD £2047
Total win prize-money £2047

Going (Turf): Sf: 0-0 GS: 0-1 Gd: 0-0 GF: 0-2 Fm: 0-0
Distance: 5f/6f: 0-0 **7f-8f: 1-10** 9f-13f: 0-4 14f+: 0-0
Track : **LH: 1-11** RH: 0-2 **Tight: 1-8** Gall: 0-0
Aids: **Bl: 1-6** Vi: 0-0 Tstrap: 0-1 Ckp: 0-1
Best Rating: 60 4/08 Wolv 7f32y stand

Modest; effective over 7f; acts on Polytrack; has won in blinkers.

Newmarket Story (IRE)

101 (38)56
7-y-o b m Desert Story (IRE)-Faramisa (IRE) (Doyoun)
W J Austin W J Austin

Placings:00/00/1000 **(5456a)**
2009: 11^{1}GF, 10^{0}S, 12^{0}S, 12^{0}SD,

	Starts	1st	2nd	3rd	Win & Pl
Career Total (Turf)	7	1	0	0	2047
Career Total (AW)	1	0	0	0	

56 6/09 Ling 1m3f106y (0-55)H G-F £2047
Total win prize-money £2047

Going (Turf): Sf: 0-3 GS: 0-0 Gd: 0-0 **GF: 1-2** Fm: 0-0
Distance: 5f/6f: 0-0 7f-8f: 0-1 **9f-13f: 1-6** 14f+: 0-1
Track : **LH: 1-3** RH: 0-5 **Tight: 1-1** Gall: 0-1
Aids: Bl: 0-0 Vi: 0-0 Tstrap: 0-0 Ckp: 0-0
Best Rating: 56 6/09 Ling 1m3f106y gd-fm

Plating-class; stays 1m4f; acts on fast ground.

Newton Circus

87(93) (67)69
2-y-o gr c Verglas (IRE)-Flying Finish (FR) (Priolo (USA))
Ollie Pears (R Hannon 10/9) Ian Bishop

Placings:3005132 **(6819)**
2009: 6^{3}GF, 7^{0}SD, 6^{0}S, 7^{5}SD, 7^{1}SD, 7^{3}SD, 7^{2}GF,

	Starts	1st	2nd	3rd	Win & Pl
Career Total (Turf)	3	0	1	1	1038
Career Total (AW)	4	1	0	1	2350

65 9/09 Kemp 7f STD £2047
Total win prize-money £2047

Going (Turf): Sf: 0-1 GS: 0-0 Gd: 0-0 GF: 0-2 Fm: 0-0
Distance: 5f/6f: 0-2 **7f-8f: 1-5** 9f-13f: 0-0 14f+: 0-0
Track : LH: 0-2 **RH: 1-2** Tight: 0-2 Gall: 0-0
Aids: Bl: 0-0 Vi: 0-0 Tstrap: 0-0 Ckp: 0-0
Best Rating: 69 6/09 Sals 6f gd-fm

Fair; stays 6f; acts on fast ground.

Newtons Cradle (IRE)

75 40
2-y-o b g Noverre (USA)-Lady Of Kildare (IRE) (Mujadil (USA))
J Howard Johnson Transcend Bloodstock LLP

Placings:00 **(4595)**
2009: 7^{0}G, 6^{0}G,

	Starts	1st	2nd	3rd	Win & Pl
Career Total (Turf)	2	0	0	0	

Going (Turf): Sf: 0-0 GS: 0-0 Gd: 0-2 GF: 0-0 Fm: 0-0
Distance: 5f/6f: 0-1 7f-8f: 0-1 9f-13f: 0-0 14f+: 0-0
Track : LH: 0-1 RH: 0-0 Tight: 0-0 Gall: 0-1
Aids: Bl: 0-0 Vi: 0-0 Tstrap: 0-0 Ckp: 0-0
Best Rating: 40 8/09 Ripn 6f good

Next Move (IRE)

(95) (79)
2-y-o b c Tiger Hill (IRE)-Cinnamon Rose (USA) (Trempolino (USA))
Saeed Bin Suroor Godolphin

Placings:1 **(7326)**
2009: 7^{1}SD,

	Starts	1st	2nd	3rd	Win & Pl
Career Total (Turf)	0	0	0	0	
Career Total (AW)	1	1	0	0	2267

79 11/09 Kemp 7f STD £2266
Total win prize-money £2267

Going (Turf): Sf: 0-0 GS: 0-0 Gd: 0-0 GF: 0-0 Fm: 0-0
Distance: 5f/6f: 0-0 **7f-8f: 1-1** 9f-13f: 0-0 14f+: 0-0
Track : LH: 0-0 **RH: 1-1** Tight: 0-0 Gall: 0-0
Aids: Bl: 0-0 Vi: 0-0 Tstrap: 0-0 Ckp: 0-0
Best Rating: 79 11/09 Kemp 7f stand

Useful; made winning debut over 7f on Polytrack.

Nezami (IRE)

107(106) (94)96
4-y-o b g Elnadim (USA)-Stands To Reason (USA) (Gulch (USA))
J Akehurst Only One Bid Partnership

Placings:02421/30041562-3420 **(7827)**
2009: 7^{3}SD, 7^{4}SD, 7^{2}GF, 8^{0}SD,

	Starts	1st	2nd	3rd	Win & Pl
Career Total (Turf)	12	2	3	1	39202
Career Total (AW)	5	0	1	1	5699

91 8/08 Leic 7f9y (0-100)H GD £11215
86 9/07 Haml 6f5y (0-95) GD £7772
Total win prize-money £18988

Going (Turf): Sf: 0-2 GS: 0-0 **Gd: 2-4** GF: 0-6 Fm: 0-0
Distance: 5f/6f: 0-1 **7f-8f: 2-16** 9f-13f: 0-0 14f+: 0-0
Track : LH: 0-5 RH: 0-5 Tight: 0-3 Gall: 0-1
Aids: Bl: 0-0 Vi: 0-0 Tstrap: 0-0 Ckp: 0-0
Best Rating: 96 5/09 Asct 7f gd-fm

Useful; effective at 7f; acts on fast ground; can take a hold.

Nibani (IRE)

98 74
2-y-o ch c Dalakhani (IRE)-Dance Of The Sea (IRE) (Sinndar (IRE))
Sir Michael Stoute Ballymacoll Stud

Placings:4 **(6810)**
2009: 8^{4}G,

	Starts	1st	2nd	3rd	Win & Pl
Career Total (Turf)	1	0	0	0	433

Going (Turf): Sf: 0-0 GS: 0-0 Gd: 0-1 GF: 0-0 Fm: 0-0
Distance: 5f/6f: 0-0 7f-8f: 0-1 9f-13f: 0-0 14f+: 0-0
Track : LH: 0-0 RH: 0-0 Tight: 0-0 Gall: 0-0
Aids: Bl: 0-0 Vi: 0-0 Tstrap: 0-0 Ckp: 0-0
Best Rating: 74 10/09 NmkR 1m good

Nicaldani

59(52)
2-y-o ch f Compton Place-Thamud (IRE) (Lahib (USA))
M Blanshard N Price & Partners

Placings:00 **(4839)**
2009: 6^{0}GF, 6^{0}SD,

	Starts	1st	2nd	3rd	Win & Pl
Career Total (Turf)	1	0	0	0	
Career Total (AW)	1	0	0	0	

Going (Turf): Sf: 0-0 GS: 0-0 Gd: 0-0 GF: 0-1 Fm: 0-0
Distance: 5f/6f: 0-1 7f-8f: 0-1 9f-13f: 0-0 14f+: 0-0
Track : LH: 0-1 RH: 0-0 Tight: 0-0 Gall: 0-0
Aids: Bl: 0-0 Vi: 0-0 Tstrap: 0-0 Ckp: 0-0

Nice Time (IRE)

102(94) (64)75
3-y-o ch f Tagula (IRE)-Nicea (IRE) (Dominion)
M H Tompkins Mrs Claudia Wiggins

Placings:001-6620044 **(6742)**
2009: 9^{6}G, 9^{6}G, 10^{2}GF, 12^{0}GF, 11^{0}SD, 10^{4}GF, 11^{4}GS,

	Starts	1st	2nd	3rd	Win & Pl
Career Total (Turf)	8	0	1	0	1204
Career Total (AW)	2	1	0	0	3926

64 11/08 GrLe 1m STD £3925
Total win prize-money £3926

Going (Turf): Sf: 0-0 GS: 0-3 Gd: 0-2 GF: 0-3 Fm: 0-0
Distance: 5f/6f: 0-0 **7f-8f: 1-2** 9f-13f: 0-8 14f+: 0-0
Track : **LH: 1-3** RH: 0-4 Tight: 0-3 **Gall: 1-3**
Aids: Bl: 0-0 Vi: 0-0 Tstrap: 0-0 Ckp: 0-0
Best Rating: 75 6/09 Donc 1m2f60y gd-fm

Modest; effective over 1m-1m2f; acts on Polytrack and fast turf.

Nice To Know (FR)

95(107) (89)79

5-y-o ch m Machiavellian (USA)-Entice (FR) (Selkirk (USA))

G L Moore C S C Hancock

Placings:5/4461164/2455060-00220 **(4259)**

2009: 8^{0}G, 7^{0}G, 8^{2}SD, 8^{2}SD, 8^{0}G,

	Starts	1st	2nd	3rd	Win & Pl
Career Total (Turf)	13	2	0	0	10541
Career Total (AW)	7	0	3	0	5760

78 8/07 Gdwd 7f (0-85)H GD £6477
74 8/07 Folk 7f (0-70)H G-F £2817
Total win prize-money £9294

Going (Turf): Sf: 0-1 GS: 0-1 **Gd: 1-5 GF: 1-6** Fm: 0-0
Distance: 5f/6f: 0-1 **7f-8f: 2-16** 9f-13f: 0-3 14f+: 0-0
Track : LH: 0-3 **RH: 1-11** Tight: 0-1 Gall: 0-1
Aids: Bl: 0-0 Vi: 0-0 Tstrap: 0-0 Ckp: 0-0
Best Rating: 89 4/08 Kemp 1m stand

Fair; effective at 7f-1m; acts on good and faster ground and on Polytrack.

Nicholas Pocock (IRE)

93 76

3-y-o b g King's Best (USA)-Sea Picture (IRE) (Royal Academy (USA))

Sir Michael Stoute Ballymacoll Stud

Placings:6 **(1295)**

2009: 7^{6}GF,

	Starts	1st	2nd	3rd	Win & Pl
Career Total (Turf)	1	0	0	0	0

Going (Turf): Sf: 0-0 GS: 0-0 Gd: 0-0 GF: 0-1 Fm: 0-0
Distance: 5f/6f: 0-0 7f-8f: 0-1 9f-13f: 0-0 14f+: 0-0
Track : LH: 0-0 RH: 0-0 Tight: 0-0 Gall: 0-0
Aids: Bl: 0-0 Vi: 0-0 Tstrap: 0-0 Ckp: 0-0
Best Rating: 76 4/09 NmkR 7f gd-fm

Nickel Silver

105(109) (94)85

4-y-o gr g Choisir (AUS)-Negligee (Night Shift (USA))

B Smart M Barber

Placings:2254/605420604-1113003535454121 **(7758)**

2009: 5^{1}SD, 5^{1}SD, 5^{1}SD, 5^{3}SD, 5^{0}GF, 5^{0}G, 5^{3}GF, 5^{5}GF, 5^{3}GF, 6^{4}GF, 5^{5}GF, 5^{4}SD, 5^{1}G, 5^{2}SD, 5^{1}SD,

	Starts	1st	2nd	3rd	Win & Pl
Career Total (Turf)	18	1	3	2	8659
Career Total (AW)	10	4	1	1	14409

94 12/09 Sthl 5f (0-85)H STD £4857
84 10/09 Nott 5f13y (0-75)H GD £2266
88 1/09 Ling 5f (0-75)H STD £2900
81 1/09 Ling 5f (0-65)H STD £1706
79 1/09 Wolv 5f20y (0-65)H STD £2047
Total win prize-money £13777

Going (Turf): Sf: 0-1 GS: 0-4 **Gd: 1-4** GF: 0-9 Fm: 0-0
Distance: 5f/6f: 5-27 7f-8f: 0-1 9f-13f: 0-0 14f+: 0-0
Track : LH: 3-10 RH: 0-0 **Tight: 3-9** Gall: 0-0
Aids: Bl: 3-11 Vi: 1-2 Tstrap: 1-2 Ckp: 1-2
Best Rating: 94 12/09 Sthl 5f stand

Useful; effective at 5f-6f; acts on most ground on turf; goes on both AW surfaces; usually wears headgear; likes to race prominently.

Nicky Nutjob (GER)

95(100) (62)60

3-y-o b c Fasliyev (USA)-Natalie Too (USA) (Irish River (FR))

J Pearce Macniler Racing Partnership

Placings:04052-500040000 **(4156)**

2009: 9^{5}SD, 10^{0}SD, 12^{0}SF, 12^{0}SD, 9^{4}GS, 10^{0}GF, 10^{0}GS, 10^{0}G, 11^{0}G,

	Starts	1st	2nd	3rd	Win & Pl
Career Total (Turf)	7	0	0	0	385
Career Total (AW)	7	0	1	0	771

Going (Turf): Sf: 0-0 GS: 0-2 Gd: 0-4 GF: 0-1 Fm: 0-0
Distance: 5f/6f: 0-0 7f-8f: 0-2 9f-13f: 0-12 14f+: 0-0
Track : LH: 0-11 RH: 0-2 Tight: 0-7 Gall: 0-2
Aids: Bl: 0-1 Vi: 0-1 Tstrap: 0-1 Ckp: 0-1
Best Rating: 62 12/08 GrLe 1m2f stand

Modest; stays 1m2f; acts on good ground and Polytrack.

Nicosia

71 8

2-y-o b f Imperial Dancer-Stride Home (Absalom)

M R Channon Capital

Placings:06 **(4101)**

2009: 6^{0}GF, 6^{6}S,

	Starts	1st	2nd	3rd	Win & Pl
Career Total (Turf)	2	0	0	0	0

Going (Turf): Sf: 0-1 GS: 0-0 Gd: 0-0 GF: 0-1 Fm: 0-0
Distance: 5f/6f: 0-2 7f-8f: 0-0 9f-13f: 0-0 14f+: 0-0
Track : LH: 0-0 RH: 0-0 Tight: 0-0 Gall: 0-1
Aids: Bl: 0-0 Vi: 0-0 Tstrap: 0-0 Ckp: 0-0
Best Rating: 8 6/09 Wind 6f gd-fm

Nidamar

63(68)

2-y-o b f Redoubtable (USA)-Marabar (Sri Pekan (USA))

Mrs R A Carr David W Chapman

Placings:0000050 **(7707)**

2009: 5^{0}GF, 5^{0}GF, 6^{0}F, 5^{0}SF, 5^{0}SD, 5^{5}SD, 6^{0}SD,

	Starts	1st	2nd	3rd	Win & Pl
Career Total (Turf)	3	0	0	0	
Career Total (AW)	4	0	0	0	0

Going (Turf): Sf: 0-0 GS: 0-0 Gd: 0-0 GF: 0-2 Fm: 0-1
Distance: 5f/6f: 0-7 7f-8f: 0-0 9f-13f: 0-0 14f+: 0-0
Track : LH: 0-2 RH: 0-0 Tight: 0-1 Gall: 0-0
Aids: Bl: 0-0 Vi: 0-0 Tstrap: 0-0 Ckp: 0-0

Nideeb

102 104

2-y-o ch c Exceed And Excel (AUS)-Mantesera (IRE) (In The Wings)

C E Brittain Saeed Manana

Placings:41125 **(6426)**

2009: 7^{4}G, 7^{1}S, 7^{1}G, 8^{2}S, 7^{5}GF,

	Starts	1st	2nd	3rd	Win & Pl
Career Total (Turf)	5	2	1	0	30347

104 7/09 Asct 7f GD £17031
88 7/09 Yarm 7f3y SFT £3784
Total win prize-money £20816

Going (Turf): Sf: 1-2 GS: 0-0 **Gd: 1-2** GF: 0-1 Fm: 0-0
Distance: 5f/6f: 0-0 **7f-8f: 2-4** 9f-13f: 0-1 14f+: 0-0
Track : LH: 0-1 RH: 0-0 Tight: 0-0 Gall: 0-0
Aids: Bl: 0-0 Vi: 0-0 Tstrap: 0-0 Ckp: 0-0
Best Rating: 104 9/09 Hayd 1m30y soft

Smart; Listed winner; effective over 7f; acts on good ground.

Night Affair

97(101) (79)79

3-y-o b f Bold Edge-Twilight Mistress (Bin Ajwaad (IRE))

D W P Arbuthnot Godfrey Wilson

Placings:1-42204 **(5877)**

2009: 6^{4}SD, 5^{2}SD, 5^{2}G, 5^{0}GF, 5^{4}GF,

	Starts	1st	2nd	3rd	Win & Pl
Career Total (Turf)	3	0	1	0	1204
Career Total (AW)	3	1	1	0	3741

76 12/08 Wolv 5f216y STD £2729
Total win prize-money £2730

Going (Turf): Sf: 0-0 GS: 0-0 Gd: 0-1 GF: 0-2 Fm: 0-0
Distance: 5f/6f: 1-6 7f-8f: 0-0 9f-13f: 0-0 14f+: 0-0
Track : LH: 1-2 RH: 0-1 **Tight: 1-2** Gall: 0-0
Aids: Bl: 0-0 Vi: 0-0 Tstrap: 0-0 Ckp: 0-0
Best Rating: 79 8/09 Sand 5f6y good

Fair; stays 6f; acts on good ground and on Polytrack.

Night Crescendo (USA)

111(106) (94)102

6-y-o b/br g Diesis-Night Fax (USA) (Known Fact (USA))

Mrs A J Perrett John Connolly

Placings:631/13/0300163/44000401100-500062030 **(6302)**

2009: 12^{5}GF, 14^{0}GF, 12^{0}GF, 12^{0}G, 12^{6}G, 12^{2}GS, 10^{0}GF, 12^{3}GF, 12^{0}GF,

	Starts	1st	2nd	3rd	Win & Pl
Career Total (Turf)	29	4	1	5	113500
Career Total (AW)	3	1	0	0	4343

97 10/08 Asct 1m4f (0-105)H G-S £46732
96 9/08 Asct 1m4f (0-105)H GD £17446
103 10/07 Asct 1m2f (0-105)H G-S £9971
98 4/06 Newb 1m (0-95)H GD £9971
85 10/05 Ling 1m STD £3783
Total win prize-money £87905

Going (Turf): Sf: 0-4 **GS: 2-4 Gd: 2-7** GF: 0-14 Fm: 0-0
Distance: 5f/6f: 0-0 7f-8f: 2-5 **9f-13f: 3-24** 14f+: 0-3
Track : LH: 1-9 **RH: 3-17** Tight: 1-5 **Gall: 3-16**
Aids: Bl: 0-0 Vi: 0-0 Tstrap: 2-10 Ckp: 2-10
Best Rating: 103 11/07 Donc 1m4f gd-fm

Very useful; effective at 1m4f; acts on good and easy ground; also goes on Polytrack; has worn cheekpieces.

Night Knight (IRE)

98(100) (64)69

3-y-o b g Bachelor Duke (USA)-Dark Albatross (USA) (Sheikh Albadou)

C Grant (M L W Bell 2/10) Panther Racing Ltd

Placings:000-0100014 **(6439)**

2009: 9^{0}GF, 8^{1}F, 8^{0}GF, 8^{0}G, 8^{0}G, 10^{1}GF, 10^{4}SS,

	Starts	1st	2nd	3rd	Win & Pl
Career Total (Turf)	9	2	0	0	3990
Career Total (AW)	1	0	0	0	0

63	9/09	Yarm	1m2f21y		G-F	£1942
69	5/09	Rdcr	1m	(0-60)H	FRM	£2047

Total win prize-money £3990

Going (Turf): Sf: 0-0 GS: 0-0 Gd: 0-5 **GF: 1-3 Fm: 1-1**
Distance: 5f/6f: 0-1 7f-8f: 1-4 9f-13f: 1-5 14f+: 0-0
Track : **LH: 1-4** RH: 0-1 **Tight: 1-2** Gall: 0-0
Aids: Bl: 0-0 **Vi: 2-6** Tstrap: 0-0 Ckp: 0-0
Best Rating: **69** 5/09 Rdcr 1m firm

Modest; stays 1m2f and acts on fast ground; has worn a visor.

Night Lily (IRE)

102(100) (68)74
3-y-o b f Night Shift (USA)-Kedross (IRE) (King Of Kings (IRE))
J Jay White & Mrs D Snell

Placings:43000420-304520521 **(6223)**
2009: 7^{3}SD, 7^{0}GF, 8^{4}GF, 12^{5}GF, 7^{2}GF, 10^{0}S, 10^{5}G, 7^{2}SD, 8^{1}SD,

	Starts	1st	2nd	3rd	Win & Pl
Career Total (Turf)	12	0	1	1	2648
Career Total (AW)	5	1	2	1	3461

67	9/09	Kemp	1m	STD	£2047

Total win prize-money £2047

Going (Turf): **Sf: 0-2 GS: 0-1 Gd: 0-3 GF: 0-6 Fm: 0-0**
Distance: 5f/6f: 0-1 **7f-8f: 1-12** 9f-13f: 0-4 14f+: 0-0
Track : LH: 0-7 **RH: 1-4** Tight: 0-3 Gall: 0-4
Aids: Bl: 0-0 Vi: 0-0 Tstrap: 0-1 Ckp: 0-1
Best Rating: **74** 8/08 NmkJ 7f soft

Modest; stays 1m4f but best at around 1m; acts on any ground and on Polytrack; has worn a tongue tie.

Night Orbit

84(99) (71)72
5-y-o b g Observatory (USA)-Dansara (Dancing Brave (USA))
Miss J Feilden Stowstowquickquickstow Partnership

Placings:0/540104200026433-14642 **(7124)**
2009: 12^{1}SD, 12^{4}SD, 13^{6}SD, 13^{4}SD, 16^{2}G,

	Starts	1st	2nd	3rd	Win & Pl
Career Total (Turf)	13	1	3	0	6358
Career Total (AW)	8	1	0	2	3709

71	1/09	Ling	1m4f	(0-70)H	STD	£2900
72	6/08	Newb	1m2f6y	(0-70)H	G-S	£3123

Total win prize-money £6023

Going (Turf): Sf: 0-3 **GS: 1-3** Gd: 0-5 GF: 0-2 Fm: 0-0
Distance: 5f/6f: 0-0 7f-8f: 0-0 **9f-13f: 2-19** 14f+: 0-2
Track : **LH: 2-17** RH: 0-3 Tight: 1-8 Gall: 1-5
Aids: Bl: 0-0 **Vi: 1-9** Tstrap: 0-0 Ckp: 0-0
Best Rating: **72** 10/08 Leic 1m1f218y good

Modest; stays 2m; acts on good and easy ground; has worn a visor.

Night Premiere (IRE)

(100) (59)61
4-y-o b f Night Shift (USA)-Star Studded (Cadeaux Genereux)
R Hannon Star Thoroughbreds

Placings:60/4466033640452-400 **(0710)**
2009: 5^{4}SD, 5^{0}SD, 5^{0}SD,

	Starts	1st	2nd	3rd	Win & Pl
Career Total (Turf)	5	0	0	1	818
Career Total (AW)	13	0	1	1	1403

Going (Turf): **Sf: 0-2 GS: 0-1 Gd: 0-0 GF: 0-2 Fm: 0-0**
Distance: 5f/6f: 0-14 7f-8f: 0-4 9f-13f: 0-0 14f+: 0-0
Track : LH: 0-8 RH: 0-5 Tight: 0-8 Gall: 0-0
Aids: Bl: 0-4 Vi: 0-0 Tstrap: 0-0 Ckp: 0-0
Best Rating: **61** 9/07 Gdwd 6f gd-fm

Moderate; stays 6f and acts on soft ground and Polytrack.

Night Prospector

(103) (62)68
9-y-o b g Night Shift (USA)-Pride Of My Heart (Lion Cavern (USA))
R A Harris C.C.C.4.C.

Placings:22/2125100/01000/03006000030/000200364004311160/0401030000000040/42305326352353143343606006460-0 **(0027)**
2009: 6^{0}SD,

	Starts	1st	2nd	3rd	Win & Pl
Career Total (Turf)	57	4	5	10	99123
Career Total (AW)	31	4	3	3	17688

58	8/08	Bath	5f161y		G-S	£3238
80	1/07	Ling	5f		STD	£2184
90	12/06	Wolv	5f20y	(0-80)H	STD	£5505
91	11/06	Sthl	6f	(0-75)H	STD	£3238
80	11/06	Wolv	5f216y	(0-75)H	STD	£3238
106	6/04	Epsm	5f	A	GD	£63800
98	8/03	Wind	5f10y	D(0-85)H	GD	£6909
85	5/03	Folk	5f	D	G-F	£3594

Total win prize-money £91710

Going (Turf): Sf: 0-4 GS: 1-14 **Gd: 2-17** GF: 1-18 Fm: 0-4
Distance: **5f/6f: 8-87** 7f-8f: 0-1 9f-13f: 0-0 14f+: 0-0
Track : **LH: 5-43** RH: 0-5 **Tight: 3-20** Gall: 2-9
Aids: Bl: 0-11 Vi: 0-0 Tstrap: 5-41 Ckp: 5-41
Best Rating: **106** 6/04 Epsm 5f good

Moderate; former winner of a Group 2, but nothing like as good now; effective from 5f-6f; acts on most ground and on sand; has worn blinkers and cheekpieces.

Night Sky

78 50
2-y-o b f Starcraft (NZ)-War Shanty (Warrshan (USA))
P J Makin Lady Whent

Placings:0 **(6730)**
2009: 6^{0}S,

	Starts	1st	2nd	3rd	Win & Pl
Career Total (Turf)	1	0	0	0	

Going (Turf): **Sf: 0-1 GS: 0-0 Gd: 0-0 GF: 0-0 Fm: 0-0**
Distance: 5f/6f: 0-0 7f-8f: 0-1 9f-13f: 0-0 14f+: 0-0
Track : LH: 0-0 RH: 0-0 Tight: 0-0 Gall: 0-0
Aids: Bl: 0-0 Vi: 0-0 Tstrap: 0-0 Ckp: 0-0
Best Rating: **50** 10/09 Sals 6f212y soft

Night Trade (IRE)

97(94) (72)75
2-y-o b f Trade Fair-Compton Girl (Compton Place)
Mrs D J Sanderson R J Budge

Placings:033134 **(7156)**
2009: 6^{0}G, 5^{3}SD, 5^{3}SD, 5^{1}GF, 5^{3}G, 5^{4}SD,

	Starts	1st	2nd	3rd	Win & Pl
Career Total (Turf)	3	1	0	1	2673
Career Total (AW)	3	0	0	2	1204

75	10/09	Catt	5f	(0-65)	G-F	£2047

Total win prize-money £2047

Going (Turf): Sf: 0-0 GS: 0-0 Gd: 0-2 **GF: 1-1** Fm: 0-0
Distance: **5f/6f: 1-5** 7f-8f: 0-1 9f-13f: 0-0 14f+: 0-0
Track : LH: 0-2 RH: 0-1 Tight: 0-2 Gall: 0-0
Aids: Bl: 0-0 Vi: 0-0 Tstrap: 0-0 Ckp: 0-0
Best Rating: **75** 10/09 Catt 5f gd-fm

Modest; effective at 5f on quick ground.

Nightboat To Cairo (IRE)

90 25
5-y-o b m Turtle Island (IRE)-Garryduff Breeze (IRE) (Strong Gale)
P A Kirby John Paul Edwards

Placings:4 **(2785)**
2009: 14^{4}GF,

	Starts	1st	2nd	3rd	Win & Pl
Career Total (Turf)	1	0	0	0	0

Going (Turf): **Sf: 0-0 GS: 0-0 Gd: 0-0 GF: 0-1 Fm: 0-0**
Distance: 5f/6f: 0-0 7f-8f: 0-0 9f-13f: 0-0 14f+: 0-1
Track : LH: 0-1 RH: 0-0 Tight: 0-1 Gall: 0-0
Aids: Bl: 0-0 Vi: 0-0 Tstrap: 0-0 Ckp: 0-0
Best Rating: **25** 6/09 Rdcr 1m6f19y gd-fm

Nightjar (USA)

109(111) (101)87
4-y-o b c Smoke Glacken (USA)-Night Risk (USA) (Wild Again (USA))
K A Ryan (M Johnston 21/10) Hambleton Racing Ltd XIV

Placings:06140222000012-151001000330004 23 **(7837)**
2009: 7^{1}SS, 7^{5}SD, 7^{1}SD, 5^{0}SD, 8^{0}SD, 6^{1}SD, 8^{0}GF, 7^{0}GF, 6^{0}F, 6^{3}GF, 6^{3}GS, 6^{0}GF, 7^{0}SD, 8^{0}GF, 8^{4}SD, 6^{2}SD, 7^{3}SS,

	Starts	1st	2nd	3rd	Win & Pl
Career Total (Turf)	15	1	3	2	13045
Career Total (AW)	16	4	2	1	37481

99	3/09	Sthl	6f	(0-95)H	STD	£9034
98	1/09	Sthl	7f	(0-100)H	STD	£11656
95	1/09	Sthl	7f	(0-85)H	SS	£4857
87	12/08	Sthl	7f	(0-85)H	STD	£4857
82	7/08	Wwck	7f26y		G-F	£3238

Total win prize-money £33644

Going (Turf): Sf: 0-0 GS: 0-2 Gd: 0-1 **GF: 1-11** Fm: 0-1
Distance: 5f/6f: 1-5 **7f-8f: 4-18** 9f-13f: 0-8 14f+: 0-0
Track : **LH: 5-21** RH: 0-3 Tight: 0-12 Gall: 0-0
Aids: Bl: 0-0 Vi: 0-0 Tstrap: 0-0 Ckp: 0-0
Best Rating: **101** 10/09 Sthl 6f stand

Very useful; effective from 6f-1m2f; acts on most ground and on sand; likes to race prominently.

Nightstrike (IRE)

(98) (45)67
6-y-o b m Night Shift (USA)-Come Together (Mtoto)
Luke Comer Brian Comer

Placings:063461500/00020/6500-00 **(7609)**
2009: 7^{0}SD, 8^{0}SD,

	Starts	1st	2nd	3rd	Win & Pl
Career Total (Turf)	8	1	0	0	3368
Career Total (AW)	12	0	1	1	1326

67	8/06	Chep	7f16y	G-F	£3368

Total win prize-money £3368

Going (Turf): Sf: 0-1 GS: 0-1 Gd: 0-4 **GF: 1-2** Fm: 0-0
Distance: 5f/6f: 0-7 **7f-8f: 1-13** 9f-13f: 0-0 14f+: 0-0
Track : LH: 0-8 RH: 0-5 Tight: 0-6 Gall: 0-1

Aids: Bl: 0-5 Vi: 0-0 Tstrap: 0-0 Ckp: 0-0
Best Rating: 67 8/06 Chep 7f16y gd-fm

Moderate filly; stays 7f; acts on good to firm and Polytrack; has worn headgear.

Nikki Bea (IRE)

(102) (66)64
6-y-o ch m Titus Livius (FR)-Strong Feeling (USA) (Devil's Bag (USA))
Jamie Poulton B Pearce

Placings:4/20420104P00/4003362151000035005/536003430-42260 (0706)
2009: 7^4SD, 8^2SD, 8^2SD, 8^6SD, 8^0SD,

	Starts	1st	2nd	3rd	Win & Pl
Career Total (Turf)	5	0	0	0	289
Career Total (AW)	40	3	5	6	14874

69 5/07 Ling 7f (0-60)H STD £3238
63 4/07 Ling 7f STD £2184
62 6/06 Ling 1m (0-60)H STD £3071
Total win prize-money £8494

Going (Turf): Sf: 0-0 GS: 0-1 Gd: 0-1 GF: 0-2 Fm: 0-1
Distance: 5f/6f: 0-2 7f-8f: 3-35 9f-13f: 0-8 14f+: 0-0
Track : LH: 3-39 RH: 0-5 Tight: 3-41 Gall: 0-1
Aids: Bl: 0-1 Vi: 0-0 Tstrap: 0-0 Ckp: 0-0
Best Rating: 69 5/07 Ling 7f stand

Moderate; effective over 7f-1m2f; acts on Polytrack.

Nimbelle (IRE)

(93) (56)50
4-y-o b/br f Namid-Bellissi (IRE) (Bluebird (USA))
J C Tuck J & D Syndicate

Placings:0/00400600-0 (0347)
2009: 6^0SD,

	Starts	1st	2nd	3rd	Win & Pl
Career Total (Turf)	4	0	0	0	
Career Total (AW)	6	0	0	0	317

Going (Turf): Sf: 0-0 GS: 0-0 Gd: 0-0 GF: 0-3 Fm: 0-0
Distance: 5f/6f: 0-8 7f-8f: 0-2 9f-13f: 0-0 14f+: 0-0
Track : LH: 0-5 RH: 0-0 Tight: 0-2 Gall: 0-0
Aids: Bl: 0-0 Vi: 0-0 Tstrap: 0-1 Ckp: 0-1
Best Rating: 56 10/08 Dund 6f stand

Nimmy's Special

95(92) (57)60
3-y-o ch f Monsieur Bond (IRE)-Mammas F-C (IRE) (Case Law)
M Mullineaux Noel Racing Partnership

Placings:064435-0460023 (5362)
2009: 9^0SD, 8^4SD, 7^6SD, 9^0GF, 8^0SD, 5^2GS, 6^3S,

	Starts	1st	2nd	3rd	Win & Pl
Career Total (Turf)	7	0	1	2	1533
Career Total (AW)	6	0	0	0	0

Going (Turf): Sf: 0-1 GS: 0-2 Gd: 0-0 GF: 0-4 Fm: 0-0
Distance: 5f/6f: 0-5 7f-8f: 0-4 9f-13f: 0-4 14f+: 0-0
Track : LH: 0-6 RH: 0-2 Tight: 0-5 Gall: 0-0
Aids: Bl: 0-2 Vi: 0-0 Tstrap: 0-0 Ckp: 0-0
Best Rating: 60 10/08 Leic 7f9y gd-sft

Moderate; stays 7f; acts on soft ground and on Polytrack; has worn blinkers.

Nimue (USA)

96(91) (51)84
2-y-o b/br f Speightstown (USA)-Flag Support (USA) (Personal Flag (USA))
P F I Cole Mrs Fitri Hay

Placings:200 (6582)
2009: 6^2G, 6^0GF, 5^0SD,

	Starts	1st	2nd	3rd	Win & Pl
Career Total (Turf)	2	0	1	0	3854
Career Total (AW)	1	0	0	0	

Going (Turf): Sf: 0-0 GS: 0-0 Gd: 0-1 GF: 0-1 Fm: 0-0
Distance: 5f/6f: 0-3 7f-8f: 0-0 9f-13f: 0-0 14f+: 0-0
Track : LH: 0-0 RH: 0-1 Tight: 0-0 Gall: 0-0
Aids: Bl: 0-0 Vi: 0-0 Tstrap: 0-0 Ckp: 0-0
Best Rating: 84 7/09 Gdwd 6f good

$310,000 filly; related to Pattern performers; useful form on debut but disappointing subsequently; has given problems in the stalls; stays 6f; acts on good ground.

Nina Rose

97 70
2-y-o ro f Pastoral Pursuits-Magnolia (Petong)
C G Cox Martin C Oliver

Placings:233404 (6793)
2009: 5^2F, 6^3GS, 6^3GF, 6^4GF, 7^0GF, 8^4S,

	Starts	1st	2nd	3rd	Win & Pl
Career Total (Turf)	6	0	1	2	2088

Going (Turf): Sf: 0-1 GS: 0-1 Gd: 0-0 GF: 0-3 Fm: 0-1
Distance: 5f/6f: 0-2 7f-8f: 0-3 9f-13f: 0-1 14f+: 0-0
Track : LH: 0-2 RH: 0-0 Tight: 0-0 Gall: 0-2
Aids: Bl: 0-0 Vi: 0-0 Tstrap: 0-0 Ckp: 0-0
Best Rating: 70 10/09 Nott 1m75y soft

Fair; stays 6f and acts on easy ground.

Nino Zachetti (IRE)

98 49
3-y-o ch g Daggers Drawn (USA)-Paganina (FR) (Galetto (FR))
G Verheye (E J Alston 1/10) G Verheye

Placings:006-06400060
2009: 7^0GF, 8^6G, 6^4S, 5^0G, 7^0GF, 6^0GF, 7^6GF, 7^0HY,

	Starts	1st	2nd	3rd	Win & Pl
Career Total (Turf)	11	0	0	0	289

Going (Turf): Sf: 0-2 GS: 0-1 Gd: 0-4 GF: 0-4 Fm: 0-0
Distance: 5f/6f: 0-5 7f-8f: 0-5 9f-13f: 0-1 14f+: 0-0
Track : LH: 0-1 RH: 0-4 Tight: 0-2 Gall: 0-1
Aids: Bl: 0-1 Vi: 0-0 Tstrap: 0-2 Ckp: 0-2
Best Rating: 49 7/09 Ripn 6f soft

Ninth House (USA)

105(107) (79)79
7-y-o b h Chester House (USA)-Ninette (USA) (Alleged (USA))
Mrs R A Carr Michael Hill

Placings:301/0100401006/2000042511/3321111045600000044-0003035124212521010000 (7633)
2009: 8^0SD, 8^0SD, 8^0SD, 8^3GF, 7^0G, 7^3F, 8^5GF, 7^1SD, 8^2SD, 7^4SD, 7^2SF, 8^1GF, 8^2GS, 8^5GF, 8^2GF, 7^1SD, 8^0GF, 8^1S, 8^0G, 7^0SD, 8^0G, 7^0S, 8^0SD,

	Starts	1st	2nd	3rd	Win & Pl
Career Total (Turf)	21	2	2	3	11063
Career Total (AW)	45	11	5	2	45810

79 9/09 Thsk 1m (0-75)H SFT £4274
79 8/09 Wolv 7f32y (0-80)H STD £5046
67 7/09 Rdcr 1m (0-65)H G-F £1942
72 6/09 Wolv 7f32y (0-60)H STD £2388
89 3/08 Wolv 7f32y (0-85)H STD £4533
84 3/08 Wolv 1m141y STD £2590
82 2/08 Wolv 1m141y STD £2914
81 2/08 Ling 7f STD £1774
79 12/07 Ling 1m STD £1943
71 12/07 Wolv 1m141y STD £2388
88 9/06 Wolv 7f32y STD £3238
91 8/06 Kemp 1m (0-90)H STD £7790
68 12/05 Wolv 1m141y STD £2998
Total win prize-money £43826

Going (Turf): Sf: 1-3 GS: 0-1 Gd: 0-3 GF: 1-12 Fm: 0-2
Distance: 5f/6f: 0-0 7f-8f: 9-44 9f-13f: 4-22 14f+: 0-0
Track : LH: 11-44 RH: 1-14 Tight: 11-41 Gall: 0-2
Aids: Bl: 6-27 Vi: 0-0 Tstrap: 0-1 Ckp: 0-1
Best Rating: 91 8/06 Kemp 1m stand

Modest; effective at around 7f-1m; acts on most ground; goes on Polytrack; has worn blinkers and a tongue tie.

Niqaab

(101) (63)70
5-y-o ch m Alhaarth (IRE)-Shanty (Selkirk (USA))
W J Musson Broughton Thermal Insulation

Placings:05/43005/3260006-60 (0169)
2009: 14^6SS, 13^0SD,

	Starts	1st	2nd	3rd	Win & Pl
Career Total (Turf)	4	0	0	1	1011
Career Total (AW)	12	0	1	1	1088

Going (Turf): Sf: 0-1 GS: 0-1 Gd: 0-1 GF: 0-1 Fm: 0-0
Distance: 5f/6f: 0-0 7f-8f: 0-2 9f-13f: 0-11 14f+: 0-3
Track : LH: 0-11 RH: 0-3 Tight: 0-7 Gall: 0-2
Aids: Bl: 0-0 Vi: 0-0 Tstrap: 0-0 Ckp: 0-0
Best Rating: 70 5/07 Sand 1m2f7y gd-sft

Modest; stays 1m4f; acts on Polytrack.

Niran (IRE)

87 81
2-y-o b c Captain Rio-Valley Lights (IRE) (Dance Of Life (USA))
C E Brittain Saeed Manana

Placings:110 (3779)
2009: 6^1GF, 6^1G, 6^0G,

	Starts	1st	2nd	3rd	Win & Pl
Career Total (Turf)	3	2	0	0	10513

81 5/09 Yarm 6f3y GD £4037
75 5/09 NmkR 6f G-F £6476
Total win prize-money £10513

Going (Turf): Sf: 0-0 GS: 0-0 Gd: 1-2 GF: 1-1 Fm: 0-0
Distance: 5f/6f: 1-2 7f-8f: 1-1 9f-13f: 0-0 14f+: 0-0
Track : LH: 0-0 RH: 0-0 Tight: 0-0 Gall: 0-0
Aids: Bl: 0-0 Vi: 0-0 Tstrap: 0-0 Ckp: 0-0
Best Rating: 81 5/09 Yarm 6f3y good

Useful; effective over 6f; acts on fast ground.

Nisaal (IRE)

96(97) (67)80

4-y-o b g Indian Ridge-Kahalah (IRE) (Darshaan)

J J Quinn Dark Horse Racing Partnership Three

Placings:062003-400246025 (6640)

2009: 7^{4}GF, 8^{0}G, 8^{0}HY, 8^{2}GF, 8^{4}S, 8^{6}GF, 10^{0}GF, 9^{2}G, 9^{5}SD,

	Starts	1st	2nd	3rd	Win & Pl
Career Total (Turf)	14	0	3	1	4672
Career Total (AW)	1	0	0	0	0

Going (Turf): Sf: 0-3 GS: 0-0 Gd: 0-6 GF: 0-5 Fm: 0-0
Distance: 5f/6f: 0-0 7f-8f: 0-2 9f-13f: 0-13 14f+: 0-0
Track : LH: 0-9 RH: 0-2 Tight: 0-3 Gall: 0-2
Aids: Bl: 0-0 Vi: 0-0 Tstrap: 0-3 Ckp: 0-3
Best Rating: 80 11/08 Donc 7f soft

Fair; stays 1m4f but proved effective at 7f; acts on most ground; has worn a tongue tie.

Nizaa (USA)

89(91) (69)66

2-y-o b/br c Dixieland Band (USA)-Star Queen (USA) (Kingmambo (USA))

B W Hills Hamdan Al Maktoum

Placings:435 (6943)

2009: 6^{4}G, 7^{3}G, 7^{5}SD,

	Starts	1st	2nd	3rd	Win & Pl
Career Total (Turf)	2	0	0	1	1059
Career Total (AW)	1	0	0	0	0

Going (Turf): Sf: 0-0 GS: 0-0 Gd: 0-2 GF: 0-0 Fm: 0-0
Distance: 5f/6f: 0-1 7f-8f: 0-2 9f-13f: 0-0 14f+: 0-0
Track : LH: 0-1 RH: 0-1 Tight: 0-0 Gall: 0-0
Aids: Bl: 0-0 Vi: 0-0 Tstrap: 0-0 Ckp: 0-0
Best Rating: 69 10/09 Kemp 7f stand

Modest ability at up to 7f on good ground and Polytrack.

Nizhoni (USA)

(96) (54)36

4-y-o ch f Mineshaft (USA)-Carinae (USA) (Nureyev (USA))

B Smart Crossfields Racing

Placings:03-03 (0758)

2009: 6^{0}SS, 5^{3}SF,

	Starts	1st	2nd	3rd	Win & Pl
Career Total (Turf)	1	0	0	0	
Career Total (AW)	3	0	0	2	806

Going (Turf): Sf: 0-0 GS: 0-0 Gd: 0-0 GF: 0-1 Fm: 0-0
Distance: 5f/6f: 0-4 7f-8f: 0-0 9f-13f: 0-0 14f+: 0-0
Track : LH: 0-3 RH: 0-0 Tight: 0-1 Gall: 0-0
Aids: Bl: 0-0 Vi: 0-0 Tstrap: 0-0 Ckp: 0-0
Best Rating: 54 12/08 Sthl 6f stand

Modest; stays 6f and acts on Fibresand.

Nizhoni Dancer

92(93) (58)78

3-y-o b f Bahamian Bounty-Hagwah (USA) (Dancing Brave (USA))

C F Wall Don Howlett

Placings:43412-0 (2890)

2009: 8^{0}G,

	Starts	1st	2nd	3rd	Win & Pl
Career Total (Turf)	5	1	1	1	5965
Career Total (AW)	1	0	0	0	0

76 9/08 Leic 7f9y (0-80) SFT £4371
Total win prize-money £4371

Going (Turf): Sf: 1-1 GS: 0-2 Gd: 0-2 GF: 0-0 Fm: 0-0
Distance: 5f/6f: 0-1 7f-8f: 1-3 9f-13f: 0-2 14f+: 0-0
Track : LH: 0-1 RH: 0-1 Tight: 0-1 Gall: 0-0
Aids: Bl: 0-0 Vi: 0-0 Tstrap: 0-0 Ckp: 0-0
Best Rating: 78 10/08 Yarm 1m3y gd-sft

Fair; stays 1m; acts on good and soft ground.

No Complaining (IRE)

69 38

2-y-o b f Alhaarth (IRE)-Rambler (Selkirk (USA))

B J Curley P Byrne

Placings:000 (7096)

2009: 6^{0}GF, 6^{0}G, 7^{0}G,

	Starts	1st	2nd	3rd	Win & Pl
Career Total (Turf)	3	0	0	0	

Going (Turf): Sf: 0-0 GS: 0-0 Gd: 0-2 GF: 0-1 Fm: 0-0
Distance: 5f/6f: 0-2 7f-8f: 0-1 9f-13f: 0-0 14f+: 0-0
Track : LH: 0-0 RH: 0-0 Tight: 0-0 Gall: 0-0
Aids: Bl: 0-0 Vi: 0-0 Tstrap: 0-0 Ckp: 0-0
Best Rating: 38 8/09 NmkJ 6f gd-fm

No Explaining (IRE)

101 76

2-y-o b f Azamour (IRE)-Claustra (FR) (Green Desert (USA))

B J Curley P Byrne

Placings:001 (6591)

2009: 6^{0}GF, 7^{0}GF, 6^{1}GS,

	Starts	1st	2nd	3rd	Win & Pl
Career Total (Turf)	3	1	0	0	5181

76 10/09 Nott 6f15y G-S £5180
Total win prize-money £5181

Going (Turf): Sf: 0-0 GS: 1-1 Gd: 0-0 GF: 0-2 Fm: 0-0
Distance: 5f/6f: 0-1 7f-8f: 1-2 9f-13f: 0-0 14f+: 0-0
Track : LH: 0-0 RH: 0-0 Tight: 0-0 Gall: 0-1
Aids: Bl: 0-0 Vi: 0-0 Tstrap: 0-0 Ckp: 0-0
Best Rating: 76 10/09 Nott 6f15y gd-sft

Fair; effective over 6f; acts on easy ground.

No Greater Love (FR)

(96) (68)81

7-y-o b g Take Risks (FR)-Desperate Virgin (BEL) (Chief Singer)

C E Longsdon The Ferandlin Peaches

Placings:3342/1/4 (1051)

2009: 11^{4}SD,

	Starts	1st	2nd	3rd	Win & Pl
Career Total (Turf)	4	0	1	2	10107
Career Total (AW)	2	1	0	0	3010

53 1/07 Sthl 1m3f SLW £2817
Total win prize-money £2817

Going (Turf): Sf: 0-0 GS: 0-0 Gd: 0-3 GF: 0-0 Fm: 0-0
Distance: 5f/6f: 0-0 7f-8f: 0-0 9f-13f: 1-5 14f+: 0-1
Track : LH: 1-2 RH: 0-3 Tight: 0-0 Gall: 0-0
Aids: Bl: 0-0 Vi: 0-0 Tstrap: 0-0 Ckp: 0-0
Best Rating: 81 7/05 Chan 1m4f good

No Grouse

103(96) (62)74

9-y-o b g Pursuit Of Love-Lady Joyce (FR) (Galetto (FR))

E J Alston The Grumpy Old Geezers

Placings:002/325110000/0500300000005054251/100130006 0500/545300400544/033500210000/0013122606-405020602005 (7179)

2009: 7^{4}GF, 7^{0}F, 6^{5}GF, 6^{0}GF, 6^{2}G, 6^{9}F, 7^{6}GF, 7^{0}GS, 7^{2}G, 7^{0}GF, 6^{0}G, 7^{5}SD,

	Starts	1st	2nd	3rd	Win & Pl
Career Total (Turf)	65	7	6	6	47027
Career Total (AW)	23	1	2	1	6013

69 7/08 Ayr 7f50y (0-65)H GD £2729
64 6/08 Haml 6f5y (0-75)H G-F £3238
64 9/07 Muss 7f30y (0-55)H G-F £2590
76 6/05 Thsk 6f (0-85)H G-F £6804
74 4/05 Sthl 7f (0-70)H G-F £4180
69 12/04 Wolv 7f32y (0-60) STD £3406
81 5/03 Ches 6f18y C(0-90)H G-F £12909
81 4/03 Catt 7f E(0-70)H G-F £3731
Total win prize-money £39590

Going (Turf): Sf: 0-2 GS: 0-9 Gd: 1-18 GF: 6-31 Fm: 0-5
Distance: 5f/6f: 1-18 7f-8f: 7-66 9f-13f: 0-4 14f+: 0-0
Track : LH: 5-51 RH: 1-12 Tight: 5-46 Gall: 0-5
Aids: Bl: 0-0 Vi: 0-0 Tstrap: 0-9 Ckp: 0-9
Best Rating: 81 5/03 Ches 6f18y gd-fm

Modest; effective at up to 7f; suited by fast ground and on Polytrack.

No Hubris (USA)

101 92

2-y-o b c Proud Citizen (USA)-Innateness (USA) (Flying Paster (USA))

P F I Cole Mrs Fitri Hay

Placings:16 (2993)

2009: 6^{1}G, 6^{6}GF,

	Starts	1st	2nd	3rd	Win & Pl
Career Total (Turf)	2	1	0	0	9186

91 5/09 York 6f GD £7835
Total win prize-money £7836

Going (Turf): Sf: 0-0 GS: 0-0 Gd: 1-1 GF: 0-1 Fm: 0-0
Distance: 5f/6f: 1-2 7f-8f: 0-0 9f-13f: 0-0 14f+: 0-0
Track : LH: 0-0 RH: 0-0 Tight: 0-0 Gall: 0-0
Aids: Bl: 0-0 Vi: 0-0 Tstrap: 0-0 Ckp: 0-0
Best Rating: 92 6/09 Asct 6f gd-fm

Very useful; suited by 6f and good ground.

No Mean Trick (USA)

(93) (68)

3-y-o b c Grand Slam (USA)-Ruby's Reception (USA) (Rubiano (USA))

C G Cox Mr And Mrs P Hargreaves

Placings:23 (7826)

2009: 8^{2}SD, 8^{3}SD,

	Starts	1st	2nd	3rd	Win & Pl
Career Total (Turf)	0	0	0	0	
Career Total (AW)	2	0	1	1	1156

Going (Turf): Sf: 0-0 GS: 0-0 Gd: 0-0 GF: 0-0 Fm: 0-0

Distance: 5f/6f: 0-0 7f-8f: 0-1 9f-13f: 0-1 14f+: 0-0
Track : LH: 0-1 RH: 0-1 Tight: 0-1 Gall: 0-0
Aids: Bl: 0-0 Vi: 0-0 Tstrap: 0-0 Ckp: 0-0
Best Rating: **68** 11/09 Wolv 1m141y stand

Modest; stays 1m; acts on Polytrack.

No Nightmare (USA)

90(85) (39)51
3-y-o b f Lion Heart (USA)-Attasliyah (IRE) (Marju (IRE))
A P Jarvis John A Duffy

Placings:60-050 (6414)
2009: 5^{0}SD, 5^{5}GS, 7^{0}GF,

	Starts	1st	2nd	3rd	Win & Pl
Career Total (Turf)	3	0	0	0	0
Career Total (AW)	2	0	0	0	

Going (Turf): **Sf: 0-0 GS: 0-1 Gd: 0-0 GF: 0-2 Fm: 0-0**
Distance: 5f/6f: 0-4 7f-8f: 0-1 9f-13f: 0-0 14f+: 0-0
Track : LH: 0-4 RH: 0-0 Tight: 0-2 Gall: 0-1
Aids: Bl: 0-0 Vi: 0-0 Tstrap: 0-0 Ckp: 0-0
Best Rating: **51** 7/08 Asct 6f gd-fm

No One Likes Us

25(94) (49)
2-y-o b g Lucky Owners (NZ)-Habibi (Alhijaz)
S Curran L M Power

Placings:600 (7482)
2009: 8^{6}SD, 8^{0}GF, 8^{0}SD,

	Starts	1st	2nd	3rd	Win & Pl
Career Total (Turf)	1	0	0	0	
Career Total (AW)	2	0	0	0	0

Going (Turf): **Sf: 0-0 GS: 0-0 Gd: 0-0 GF: 0-1 Fm: 0-0**
Distance: 5f/6f: 0-0 7f-8f: 0-2 9f-13f: 0-1 14f+: 0-0
Track : LH: 0-2 RH: 0-1 Tight: 0-1 Gall: 0-0
Aids: Bl: 0-0 Vi: 0-0 Tstrap: 0-0 Ckp: 0-0
Best Rating: **49** 10/09 Kemp 1m stand

No Quarter (IRE)

88 62
2-y-o b g Refuse To Bend (IRE)-Moonlight Wish (IRE) (Peintre Celebre (USA))
A Dickman The Marooned Crew

Placings:00400 (6096)
2009: 7^{0}GF, 7^{0}GS, 7^{4}G, 7^{0}GS, 5^{0}GF,

	Starts	1st	2nd	3rd	Win & Pl
Career Total (Turf)	5	0	0	0	317

Going (Turf): **Sf: 0-0 GS: 0-2 Gd: 0-1 GF: 0-2 Fm: 0-0**
Distance: 5f/6f: 0-1 7f-8f: 0-4 9f-13f: 0-0 14f+: 0-0
Track : LH: 0-3 RH: 0-1 Tight: 0-4 Gall: 0-0
Aids: Bl: 0-0 Vi: 0-0 Tstrap: 0-0 Ckp: 0-0
Best Rating: **62** 8/09 Thsk 7f good

No Rules

104(99) (60)75
4-y-o b g Fraam-Golden Daring (IRE) (Night Shift (USA))
M H Tompkins M P Bowring

Placings:05/0066454-516312051 (7084)
2009: 12^{5}SD, 16^{1}G, 16^{6}G, **16^{3}SD**, 16^{1}S, 16^{2}G, 17^{0}G, 16^{5}GS, 15^{1}S,

	Starts	1st	2nd	3rd	Win & Pl
Career Total (Turf)	15	3	1	0	10178
Career Total (AW)	3	0	0	1	302

75	10/09	Catt	1m7f177y	(0-70)H	SFT	£2914
64	7/09	Donc	2m110y	(0-65)H	SFT	£2729
58	4/09	Yarm	2m	(0-70)H	GD	£3238

Total win prize-money £8882

Going (Turf): **Sf: 2-5** GS: 0-2 Gd: 1-6 GF: 0-2 Fm: 0-0
Distance: 5f/6f: 0-0 7f-8f: 0-3 9f-13f: 0-3 **14f+: 3-12**
Track : **LH: 3-11** RH: 0-4 **Tight: 2-9** Gall: 1-3
Aids: Bl: 0-0 Vi: 0-0 Tstrap: 0-0 Ckp: 0-0
Best Rating: **75** 10/09 Catt 1m7f177y soft

Modest; stays 2m; acts on good and softer ground.

No Sting

97(89) (42)49
3-y-o b f Exit To Nowhere (USA)-Beacon Silver (Belmez (USA))
W S Kittow Mrs P A Cave, Dr S G F Cave & B Nettley

Placings:0-0503 (3205)
2009: 11^{0}SD, 12^{5}G, 14^{0}G, 12^{3}G,

	Starts	1st	2nd	3rd	Win & Pl
Career Total (Turf)	4	0	0	1	404
Career Total (AW)	1	0	0	0	

Going (Turf): **Sf: 0-1 GS: 0-0 Gd: 0-3 GF: 0-0 Fm: 0-0**
Distance: 5f/6f: 0-0 7f-8f: 0-1 9f-13f: 0-3 14f+: 0-1
Track : LH: 0-3 RH: 0-2 Tight: 0-1 Gall: 0-0
Aids: Bl: 0-0 Vi: 0-0 Tstrap: 0-0 Ckp: 0-0
Best Rating: **49** 6/09 Chep 1m4f23y good

No Supper (IRE)

90(84) (55)32
5-y-o ch g Inchinor-Be Thankfull (IRE) (Linamix (FR))
Tim Vaughan optimumracing.co.uk

Placings:5/5-00 (5790)
2009: 11^{0}GF, 10^{0}G,

	Starts	1st	2nd	3rd	Win & Pl
Career Total (Turf)	2	0	0	0	
Career Total (AW)	2	0	0	0	0

Going (Turf): **Sf: 0-0 GS: 0-0 Gd: 0-1 GF: 0-1 Fm: 0-0**
Distance: 5f/6f: 0-0 7f-8f: 0-0 9f-13f: 0-4 14f+: 0-0
Track : LH: 0-3 RH: 0-1 Tight: 0-2 Gall: 0-0
Aids: Bl: 0-0 Vi: 0-0 Tstrap: 0-0 Ckp: 0-0
Best Rating: **55** 12/06 Wolv 1m141y stand

No Wonga

97(101) (58)68
4-y-o b g Where Or When (IRE)-Fizzy Fiona (Efisio)
P D Evans B J Mould

Placings:00442-31024 (7222)
2009: 13^{3}S, 11^{1}GS, 13^{0}SD, 11^{2}S, 13^{4}S,

	Starts	1st	2nd	3rd	Win & Pl
Career Total (Turf)	9	1	2	1	5103
Career Total (AW)	1	0	0	0	

66	9/09	Hayd	1m3f200y	(0-70)H	G-S	£3123

Total win prize-money £3123

Going (Turf): Sf: 0-5 **GS: 1-2** Gd: 0-0 GF: 0-2 Fm: 0-0
Distance: 5f/6f: 0-0 7f-8f: 0-1 **9f-13f: 1-6** 14f+: 0-3
Track : **LH: 1-6** RH: 0-3 Tight: 0-6 Gall: 0-0
Aids: Bl: 0-0 Vi: 0-0 Tstrap: 0-0 Ckp: 0-0
Best Rating: **68** 10/09 Catt 1m3f214y soft

Moderate; stays 1m5f and acts on soft ground.

Noafal (IRE)

95 82
2-y-o ch c Bahamian Bounty-Miss Party Line (USA) (Phone Trick (USA))
M A Jarvis Hamdan Al Maktoum

Placings:31 (6616)
2009: 6^{3}G, 6^{1}G,

	Starts	1st	2nd	3rd	Win & Pl
Career Total (Turf)	2	1	0	1	5627

82	10/09	Newb	6f110y	GD	£4857

Total win prize-money £4857

Going (Turf): Sf: 0-0 GS: 0-0 **Gd: 1-2** GF: 0-0 Fm: 0-0
Distance: 5f/6f: 0-1 **7f-8f: 1-1** 9f-13f: 0-0 14f+: 0-0
Track : LH: 0-0 RH: 0-0 Tight: 0-0 Gall: 0-0
Aids: Bl: 0-0 Vi: 0-0 Tstrap: 0-0 Ckp: 0-0
Best Rating: **82** 10/09 Newb 6f110y good

Useful; suited by 6f and fast ground.

Noah Jameel

94(100) (61)61
7-y-o ch g Mark Of Esteem (IRE)-Subtle One (IRE) (Polish Patriot (USA))
A G Newcombe A G Newcombe

Placings:2/0/605310/16064203-2242602555 (7857)
2009: 10^{2}SD, 11^{2}SD, 9^{4}SD, 10^{2}GF, 10^{6}F, 10^{0}GF, 11^{2}SD, 10^{5}SD, 12^{5}SD, 9^{5}SD,

	Starts	1st	2nd	3rd	Win & Pl
Career Total (Turf)	9	0	3	0	2626
Career Total (AW)	17	2	3	2	4969

60	2/08	Kemp	1m3f	(0-55)H	STD	£2047

Total win prize-money £2048

Going (Turf): **Sf: 0-2 GS: 0-3 Gd: 0-1 GF: 0-2 Fm: 0-1**
Distance: 5f/6f: 0-0 7f-8f: 0-3 **9f-13f: 2-23** 14f+: 0-0
Track : LH: 0-13 **RH: 2-13** Tight: 0-8 Gall: 0-1
Aids: Bl: 0-0 Vi: 0-0 Tstrap: 0-0 Ckp: 0-0
Best Rating: **61** 4/09 Wwck 1m2f188y gd-fm

Moderate; effective at around 1m2f; acts on fast ground and on sand.

Nobelix (IRE)

84(101) (86)86
7-y-o gr g Linamix (FR)-Nataliana (Surumu (GER))
J R Gask Miss K M Dobb

Placings:4/4064423133/33100/010153/014-12 (3343)
2009: 14^{1}SD, 12^{2}G,

	Starts	1st	2nd	3rd	Win & Pl
Career Total (Turf)	17	4	2	3	28049
Career Total (AW)	10	2	0	3	13017

85	1/09	GrLe	1m6f	(0-85)H	STD	£5051
83	12/08	Wolv	1m4f50y	(0-75)H	STD	£3885
61	9/07	NmkR	1m4f		FRM	£6477
92	7/07	NmkJ	1m6f175y	(0-85)H	GD	£5181
89	7/06	Hayd	1m6f	(0-85)H	G-F	£6477
77	8/05	Ling	1m3f106y	(0-75)H	SFT	£3562

Total win prize-money £30635

Going (Turf): **Sf: 1-2** GS: 0-3 **Gd: 1-7 GF: 1-4 Fm: 1-1**
Distance: 5f/6f: 0-0 7f-8f: 0-2 9f-13f: 3-19 14f+: 3-6
Track : **LH: 4-15** RH: 2-11 Tight: 2-15 **Gall: 3-8**
Aids: Bl: 0-0 Vi: 0-0 Tstrap: 0-0 Ckp: 0-0
Best Rating: **92** 7/07 NmkJ 1m6f175y good

Useful; winning hurdler; effective over 1m4f-1m6f; acted on any ground; also went on Polytrack.(DEAD)

Nobilissima (IRE)

(91) (65)**88**

5-y-o b m Orpen (USA)-Shadow Smile (IRE) (Slip Anchor)

Miss Tor Sturgis Miss Tor Sturgis

Placings:6156/231015020/21001-0 (3272)

2009: 6^{0}SD,

	Starts	1st	2nd	3rd	Win & Pl
Career Total (Turf)	17	5	3	1	28275
Career Total (AW)	2	0	0	0	

88	9/08	Wwck	6f	(0-85)H	SFT	£6476
88	4/08	Leic	5f218y	(0-85)H	G-S	£4209
83	7/07	Wwck	6f	(0-95)H	SFT	£7124
80	5/07	Chep	6f16y	(0-70)H	G-S	£3044
68	7/06	Ling	5f		G-F	£3238

Total win prize-money £24093

Going (Turf): Sf: 2-4 GS: 2-3 Gd: 0-6 GF: 1-4 Fm: 0-0
Distance: 5f/6f: 4-16 7f-8f: 1-3 9f-13f: 0-0 14f+: 0-0
Track : LH: 2-5 RH: 0-2 Tight: 0-0 Gall: 0-4
Aids: Bl: 0-0 Vi: 0-0 Tstrap: 0-0 Ckp: 0-0
Best Rating: 88 9/08 Wwck 6f soft

Useful; suited by 6f; acts on fast and soft ground; likes to race prominently.

Noble Attitude

80 **59**

3-y-o b f Best Of The Bests (IRE)-Charming Lotte (Nicolotte)

N Tinkler Fishlake Commercial Motors Ltd

Placings:035 (4531)

2009: 6^{0}GF, 10^{3}HY, 6^{5}S,

	Starts	1st	2nd	3rd	Win & Pl
Career Total (Turf)	3	0	0	1	433

Going (Turf): Sf: 0-2 GS: 0-0 Gd: 0-0 GF: 0-1 Fm: 0-0
Distance: 5f/6f: 0-1 7f-8f: 0-1 9f-13f: 0-1 14f+: 0-0
Track : LH: 0-1 RH: 0-0 Tight: 0-0 Gall: 0-0
Aids: Bl: 0-0 Vi: 0-0 Tstrap: 0-0 Ckp: 0-0
Best Rating: 59 7/09 Nott 1m2f50y heavy

Moderate; stays 1m2f; acts on heavy ground.

Noble Citizen (USA)

106(107) (102)**97**

4-y-o b c Proud Citizen (USA)-Serene Nobility (USA) (His Majesty (USA))

D M Simcock Khalifa Dasmal

Placings:06215/653431103-022002020 (6270)

2009: 8^{0}G, 7^{2}FT, 7^{2}FT, 7^{0}GF, 7^{0}GF, 6^{2}GF, 7^{0}G, 7^{2}GF, 7^{0}G,

	Starts	1st	2nd	3rd	Win & Pl
Career Total (Turf)	16	2	2	2	23205
Career Total (AW)	7	1	3	1	40311

96	10/08	Kemp	7f	(0-85)H	STD	£6476
93	9/08	Ling	7f	(0-85)H	GD	£6308
82	9/07	NmkR	7f	(0-95)	G-F	£7772

Total win prize-money £20556

Going (Turf): Sf: 0-1 GS: 0-0 Gd: 1-6 GF: 1-8 Fm: 0-1
Distance: 5f/6f: 0-1 7f-8f: 3-21 9f-13f: 0-1 14f+: 0-0
Track : LH: 0-6 RH: 1-6 Tight: 0-3 Gall: 0-3
Aids: Bl: 0-6 Vi: 0-0 Tstrap: 0-0 Ckp: 0-0
Best Rating: 102 2/09 Ndas 7f110y fast

Very useful; effective over 7f-1m; acts on fast ground; also goes on dirt and Polytrack; has worn blinkers and an eye-shield.

Noble Dictator

96(104) (67)**65**

3-y-o b g Diktat-Noble Desert (FR) (Green Desert (USA))

E F Vaughan C J Murfitt

Placings:46051-000023 (6784)

2009: 8^{0}GF, 7^{0}GF, 8^{0}GF, 10^{0}F, 10^{2}SD, 10^{3}SS,

	Starts	1st	2nd	3rd	Win & Pl
Career Total (Turf)	6	0	0	0	164
Career Total (AW)	5	1	1	1	2793

64	11/08	Kemp	1m	(0-65)	STD	£1619

Total win prize-money £1619

Going (Turf): Sf: 0-0 GS: 0-0 Gd: 0-1 GF: 0-4 Fm: 0-1
Distance: 5f/6f: 0-0 7f-8f: 1-6 9f-13f: 0-5 14f+: 0-0
Track : LH: 0-4 RH: 1-4 Tight: 0-4 Gall: 0-0
Aids: Bl: 0-0 Vi: 0-0 Tstrap: 0-2 Ckp: 0-2
Best Rating: 67 9/09 Kemp 1m2f stand

Modest; stays 1m2f; acts on good ground and on Polytrack.

Noble Greek (USA)

96(96) (79)**79**

2-y-o b/br c Omega Code (USA)-Regal Beauty (USA) (Explosive Red (CAN))

J R Best Hucking Horses

Placings:2023 (6443)

2009: 6^{2}SD, 6^{0}G, 6^{2}GF, 5^{3}SS,

	Starts	1st	2nd	3rd	Win & Pl
Career Total (Turf)	2	0	1	0	4818
Career Total (AW)	2	0	1	1	1174

Going (Turf): Sf: 0-0 GS: 0-0 Gd: 0-1 GF: 0-1 Fm: 0-0
Distance: 5f/6f: 0-4 7f-8f: 0-0 9f-13f: 0-0 14f+: 0-0
Track : LH: 0-1 RH: 0-1 Tight: 0-1 Gall: 0-0
Aids: Bl: 0-0 Vi: 0-0 Tstrap: 0-0 Ckp: 0-0
Best Rating: 79 8/09 York 6f gd-fm

Useful; effective over 6f; acts on fast ground.

Noble Storm (USA)

110 **110**

3-y-o b c Yankee Gentleman (USA)-Changed Tune (USA) (Tunerup (USA))

E S McMahon R L Bedding

Placings:336114-221521142 (6427)

2009: 5^{2}GF, 5^{2}GF, 5^{1}GF, 5^{5}G, 5^{2}GF, 5^{1}G, 5^{1}GF, 5^{4}GF, 5^{2}GF,

	Starts	1st	2nd	3rd	Win & Pl
Career Total (Turf)	15	5	4	2	72481

109	8/09	York	5f	(0-100)H	G-F	£16190
103	7/09	Gdwd	5f	(0-95)H	GD	£12462
103	5/09	Bevl	5f		G-F	£7352
88	10/08	Wwck	6f	(0-95)	SFT	£7771
87	9/08	Wwck	5f110y	(0-75)	SFT	£3238

Total win prize-money £47014

Going (Turf): Sf: 2-3 GS: 0-1 Gd: 1-3 GF: 2-8 Fm: 0-0
Distance: 5f/6f: 5-13 7f-8f: 0-2 9f-13f: 0-0 14f+: 0-0
Track : LH: 2-4 RH: 0-0 Tight: 0-2 Gall: 0-0
Aids: Bl: 0-0 Vi: 0-0 Tstrap: 0-0 Ckp: 0-0
Best Rating: 110 10/09 NmkR 5f gd-fm

Smart; Listed placed; effective over 5f-6f; acts on any ground; likes to race prominently.

Noche De Reyes

97(97) (55)**60**

4-y-o b g Foxhound (USA)-Ashleigh Baker (IRE) (Don't Forget Me)

E J Alston The Melford Stud

Placings:0/5060-5660453 (7599)

2009: 8^{5}G, 10^{6}G, 10^{6}GS, 9^{0}SD, 8^{4}SD, 9^{5}S, 9^{3}SD,

	Starts	1st	2nd	3rd	Win & Pl
Career Total (Turf)	9	0	0	0	0
Career Total (AW)	3	0	0	1	302

Going (Turf): Sf: 0-1 GS: 0-2 Gd: 0-4 GF: 0-2 Fm: 0-0
Distance: 5f/6f: 0-3 7f-8f: 0-3 9f-13f: 0-6 14f+: 0-0
Track : LH: 0-7 RH: 0-1 Tight: 0-4 Gall: 0-0
Aids: Bl: 0-0 Vi: 0-0 Tstrap: 0-0 Ckp: 0-0
Best Rating: 60 6/09 Rdcr 1m good

Moderate; effective at around 1m1f; acts on Polytrack.

Nolecce

77 **38**

2-y-o ch g Reset (AUS)-Ghassanah (Pas De Seul)

R C Guest Red Lion Racing Limited

Placings:000 (6009)

2009: 6^{0}GF, 7^{0}S, 6^{0}GS,

	Starts	1st	2nd	3rd	Win & Pl
Career Total (Turf)	3	0	0	0	

Going (Turf): Sf: 0-1 GS: 0-1 Gd: 0-0 GF: 0-1 Fm: 0-0
Distance: 5f/6f: 0-2 7f-8f: 0-1 9f-13f: 0-0 14f+: 0-0
Track : LH: 0-1 RH: 0-0 Tight: 0-1 Gall: 0-0
Aids: Bl: 0-0 Vi: 0-0 Tstrap: 0-0 Ckp: 0-0
Best Rating: 38 5/09 Donc 6f gd-fm

Nom De La Rosa (IRE)

95 **66**

2-y-o b f Oratorio (IRE)-Cheal Rose (IRE) (Dr Devious (IRE))

G L Moore Findlay & Bloom

Placings:0400 (6305)

2009: 7^{0}GS, 6^{4}GF, 6^{0}F, 7^{0}GF,

	Starts	1st	2nd	3rd	Win & Pl
Career Total (Turf)	4	0	0	0	289

Going (Turf): Sf: 0-0 GS: 0-1 Gd: 0-0 GF: 0-2 Fm: 0-1
Distance: 5f/6f: 0-1 7f-8f: 0-3 9f-13f: 0-0 14f+: 0-0
Track : LH: 0-1 RH: 0-1 Tight: 0-0 Gall: 0-1
Aids: Bl: 0-0 Vi: 0-0 Tstrap: 0-0 Ckp: 0-0
Best Rating: 66 8/09 Wind 6f gd-fm

Nomadic Warrior

(93) (52)**40**

4-y-o b g Nomadic Way (USA)-Jesmund (Bishop Of Cashel)

J R Holt Ms Carol Lacey

Placings:0-00 (0779)

2009: 12^{0}SD, 12^{0}SD,

	Starts	1st	2nd	3rd	Win & Pl
Career Total (Turf)	1	0	0	0	

Career Total (AW)	**2**	**0**	**0**	**0**

Going (Turf): **Sf: 0-0 GS: 0-0 Gd: 0-1 GF: 0-0 Fm: 0-0**
Distance: 5f/6f: 0-0 7f-8f: 0-0 9f-13f: 0-2 14f+: 0-1
Track : LH: 0-3 RH: 0-0 Tight: 0-3 Gall: 0-0
Aids: Bl: 0-0 Vi: 0-0 Tstrap: 0-0 Ckp: 0-0
Best Rating: **52** 3/09 Wolv 1m4f50y stand

Nomoreblondes

101(104) (66)**76**
5-y-o ch m Ishiguru (USA)-Statuette (Statoblest)
P T Midgley Anthony D Copley

Placings:06/5342211/0420220-**5**10354U0**5**2100**60** **(7398)**
2009: 5^5SD, 5^1GF, 5^0GF, 5^3GF, 5^5GF, 5^4GF, 5^UGF, 5^0GF, 5^5GF, 5^2G, 5^1GF, 5^0GF, 5^0GF, 5^6SD, 5^0SD,

	Starts	1st	2nd	3rd	Win & Pl
Career Total (Turf)	**27**	**4**	**6**	**2**	**19842**
Career Total (AW)	**4**	**0**	**0**	**0**	**0**

76	8/09	Newc	5f	(0-65)H	G-F	£2838
76	4/09	Muss	5f	(0-70)H	G-F	£3238
70	8/07	Newc	5f	(0-75)H	GD	£3469
66	7/07	Muss	5f2y	(0-65)H	GD	£2590

Total win prize-money £12138

Going (Turf): Sf: 0-0 GS: 0-0 **Gd: 2-5 GF: 2-22** Fm: 0-0
Distance: **5f/6f: 4-31** 7f-8f: 0-0 9f-13f: 0-0 14f+: 0-0
Track : LH: 0-4 RH: 0-3 Tight: 0-2 Gall: 0-1
Aids: Bl: 0-0 Vi: 0-0 Tstrap: 4-26 Ckp: 4-26
Best Rating: **76** 8/09 Newc 5f gd-fm

Modest sprinter; effective over 5f; acts on good ground; has worn cheekpieces.

Nomoretaxes (BRZ)

81(85) (49)**32**
7-y-o b g First American (USA)-Raghida (BRZ) (Roi Normand (USA))
Miss D Mountain (Trainer Unknown 2/4) Al-Abdulmalik Hassan

Placings:563**1**020/30**1**06360/06405006/55010035263040 U600-06600 **(3736)**
2009: 6^0G, 7^6G, 6^6G, 9^0GF, 8^0SD,

	Starts	1st	2nd	3rd	Win & Pl
Career Total (Turf)	**33**	**1**	**2**	**2**	**2389**
Career Total (AW)	**13**	**2**	**0**	**3**	**16082**

	2/08	Dohr	7f	H	GD	£1333
100	2/06	Ndas	1m110y		SLP	£11337

Total win prize-money £14003

Going (Turf): Sf: 0-2 GS: 0-0 **Gd: 1-31** GF: 0-1 Fm: 0-0
Distance: 5f/6f: 0-10 **7f-8f: 2-25** 9f-13f: 1-11 14f+: 0-0
Track : LH: 0-4 RH: 0-1 Tight: 0-0 Gall: 0-4
Aids: Bl: 0-2 Vi: 0-0 Tstrap: 0-0 Ckp: 0-0
Best Rating: **100** 2/06 Ndas 1m110y sloppy

Non Dom (IRE)

103(84) (60)**85**
3-y-o br g Hawk Wing (USA)-Kafayef (USA) (Secreto (USA))
H Morrison Raymond Tooth

Placings:565-**1**2343243 **(6552)**
2009: 11^1GF, 11^2G, 12^3G, 14^4GF, 12^3G, 12^2G, 14^4G, 11^3G,

	Starts	1st	2nd	3rd	Win & Pl
Career Total (Turf)	**10**	**1**	**2**	**3**	**12271**
Career Total (AW)	**1**	**0**	**0**	**0**	**0**

74	5/09	Wind	1m3f135y	(0-75)H	G-F	£3070

Total win prize-money £3071

Going (Turf): Sf: 0-2 GS: 0-0 Gd: 0-6 **GF: 1-2** Fm: 0-0
Distance: 5f/6f: 0-0 7f-8f: 0-1 **9f-13f: 1-8** 14f+: 0-2
Track : LH: 0-3 RH: 0-5 **Tight: 1-6** Gall: 0-2
Aids: Bl: 0-0 Vi: 0-0 Tstrap: 0-0 Ckp: 0-0
Best Rating: **85** 9/09 Ffos 1m6f good

Fair; stays 1m6f; acts on fast ground.

Non Sucre (USA)

86(83) (47)**76**
4-y-o b/br g Minardi (USA)-Vieille Rose (IRE) (Dancing Spree (USA))
J Gallagher O Murphy

Placings:0223**1**0/3665-000 **(1248)**
2009: 7^0SD, 6^0SD, 6^0GF,

	Starts	1st	2nd	3rd	Win & Pl
Career Total (Turf)	**10**	**1**	**1**	**2**	**4514**
Career Total (AW)	**3**	**0**	**1**	**0**	**1156**

73	8/07	Chep	6f16y	GD	£2072

Total win prize-money £2073

Going (Turf): Sf: 0-1 GS: 0-1 **Gd: 1-4** GF: 0-4 Fm: 0-0
Distance: 5f/6f: 0-6 **7f-8f: 1-7** 9f-13f: 0-0 14f+: 0-0
Track : LH: 0-3 RH: 0-2 Tight: 0-2 Gall: 0-0
Aids: **Bl: 1-5** Vi: 0-0 Tstrap: 0-0 Ckp: 0-0
Best Rating: **76** 6/08 Sand 7f16y gd-sft

Fair; effective over6f-7f; acts on a sound surface and Polytrack; has won in blinkers.

Noodles Blue Boy

106(95) (76)**80**
3-y-o b g Makbul-Dee Dee Girl (IRE) (Primo Dominie)
Ollie Pears Ian Bishop

Placings:1240-460**1**32**1**5210024 **(7082)**
2009: 6^4SD, 7^6SD, 6^0GS, 5^1GF, 5^3GF, 5^2G, 5^1GS, 5^5GS, 5^2GF, 5^1GF, 5^0GF, 6^0GF, 6^7G, 5^4S,

	Starts	1st	2nd	3rd	Win & Pl
Career Total (Turf)	**15**	**4**	**3**	**1**	**17188**
Career Total (AW)	**3**	**0**	**1**	**0**	**1218**

78	8/09	Newc	5f	(0-75)H	G-F	£3784
79	6/09	Newc	5f	(0-75)H	G-S	£3885
71	5/09	Bevl	5f		G-F	£2428
70	7/08	Bevl	5f		GD	£3238

Total win prize-money £13337

Going (Turf): Sf: 0-2 GS: 1-3 Gd: 1-4 **GF: 2-6** Fm: 0-0
Distance: **5f/6f: 4-15** 7f-8f: 0-3 9f-13f: 0-0 14f+: 0-0
Track : LH: 0-7 RH: 0-1 Tight: 0-3 Gall: 0-2
Aids: Bl: 0-0 Vi: 0-0 Tstrap: 0-0 Ckp: 0-0
Best Rating: **80** 10/09 Newc 6f good

Fair; effective over 5f-6f; acts on most ground.

Noor Al Bahar (IRE)

72 **4**
3-y-o b f Bahri (USA)-Barbaresque (IRE) (Green Desert (USA))
M R Channon Ahmed Jaber

Placings:06 **(2738)**
2009: 10^0GS, 11^6G,

	Starts	1st	2nd	3rd	Win & Pl
Career Total (Turf)	**2**	**0**	**0**	**0**	**0**

Going (Turf): **Sf: 0-0 GS: 0-1 Gd: 0-1 GF: 0-0 Fm: 0-0**
Distance: 5f/6f: 0-0 7f-8f: 0-0 9f-13f: 0-2 14f+: 0-0
Track : LH: 0-2 RH: 0-0 Tight: 0-0 Gall: 0-1
Aids: Bl: 0-0 Vi: 0-0 Tstrap: 0-0 Ckp: 0-0
Best Rating: **4** 5/09 Newc 1m2f32y gd-sft

Noordhoek Kid

98(94) (71)**63**
3-y-o b g Dansili-Anqood (IRE) (Elmaamul (USA))
C R Egerton Lady Laidlaw Of Rothiemay

Placings:420-046 **(5381)**
2009: 10^0GS, 10^4G, 11^6G,

	Starts	1st	2nd	3rd	Win & Pl
Career Total (Turf)	**4**	**0**	**0**	**0**	**192**
Career Total (AW)	**2**	**0**	**1**	**0**	**1638**

Going (Turf): **Sf: 0-0 GS: 0-2 Gd: 0-2 GF: 0-0 Fm: 0-0**
Distance: 5f/6f: 0-0 7f-8f: 0-2 9f-13f: 0-4 14f+: 0-0
Track : LH: 0-5 RH: 0-1 Tight: 0-4 Gall: 0-1
Aids: Bl: 0-1 Vi: 0-0 Tstrap: 0-1 Ckp: 0-1
Best Rating: **71** 10/08 GrLe 1m stand

Modest; effective over 1m-1m2f; acts on Polytrack; has worn a tongue tie and cheekpieces and blinkers.

Nora Chrissie (IRE)

(90) (74)**52**
7-y-o b m Bahhare (USA)-Vino Veritas (USA) (Chief's Crown (USA))
Daniel Mark Loughnane (A M Hales 31/5) Leo Cox

Placings:U04/60**1**U2/0000/6064**1**543364052/5033066004 2-00 **(3666a)**
2009: 13^0SD, 11^0GF,

	Starts	1st	2nd	3rd	Win & Pl
Career Total (Turf)	**28**	**2**	**1**	**2**	**13882**
Career Total (AW)	**11**	**0**	**2**	**2**	**8642**

62	6/07	DRoy	1m4f190y	(42-60)H	GD	£3968
73	8/05	Slig	1m4f	(40-70)H	GD	£5390

Total win prize-money £9360

Going (Turf): Sf: 0-8 GS: 0-0 **Gd: 2-7** GF: 0-6 Fm: 0-1
Distance: 5f/6f: 0-0 7f-8f: 0-3 **9f-13f: 2-34** 14f+: 0-2
Track : LH: 0-17 **RH: 1-18** Tight: 0-3 Gall: 0-0
Aids: **Bl: 1-22** Vi: 0-3 Tstrap: 0-1 Ckp: 0-1
Best Rating: **75** 9/05 Rosc 1m2f gd-yld

Modest mare; stays 12f; acts on good ground on turf and handles Polytrack; has worn blinkers and a visor.

Nora Mae (IRE)

99(100) (80)**88**
3-y-o ch f Peintre Celebre (USA)-Wurfklinge (GER) (Acatenango (GER))
S Kirk Mrs Anne Gaffney

Placings:415-00600250 **(7741)**
2009: 7^0S, 6^0S, 8^6GS, 10^0G, 7^0SD, 8^2SD, 8^5SD, 7^0SD,

	Starts	1st	2nd	3rd	Win & Pl
Career Total (Turf)	**7**	**1**	**0**	**0**	**4628**
Career Total (AW)	**4**	**0**	**1**	**0**	**1407**

83	9/08	Wwck	7f26y	GD	£3412

Total win prize-money £3412

Going (Turf): Sf: 0-3 GS: 0-1 **Gd: 1-3** GF: 0-0 Fm: 0-0
Distance: 5f/6f: 0-0 **7f-8f: 1-9** 9f-13f: 0-2 14f+: 0-0
Track : **LH: 1-4** RH: 0-3 Tight: 0-2 Gall: 0-1
Aids: Bl: 0-0 Vi: 0-0 Tstrap: 0-0 Ckp: 0-0

Best Rating: 88 10/08 Newb 7f soft

Fair; stays 7f and acts on good ground and on Polytrack.

Norcroft

95(105) (73)56

7-y-o b g Fasliyev (USA)-Norcroft Joy (Rock Hopper)
Mrs C A Dunnett The Star Seekers

Placings:21600040030241300220021260020165006310 000610041005000/5434652353200106/004504030224363 5501-1506000302604000 (7348)

2009: 7^{1}SS, 7^{5}SD, 7^{0}SD, 7^{6}SD, 7^{0}SD, 7^{0}SD, 7^{0}SD, 7^{3}SD, 7^{0}G, 7^{2}GF, 7^{6}GF, 7^{0}GF, 7^{0}SD, 6^{4}GF, 7^{0}SF, 7^{0}SD, 7^{0}SD,

	Starts	1st	2nd	3rd	Win & Pl
Career Total (Turf)	46	3	5	2	21065
Career Total (AW)	59	7	7	8	31030

73	1/09	Sthl	7f	(0-60)H	SS	£2047
67	12/08	Sthl	7f	(0-60)H	STD	£1706
73	11/07	Wolv	5f216y	(0-70)H	STD	£2968
78	8/06	Yarm	6f3y	(0-75)H	G-F	£3691
76	7/06	Kemp	6f	(0-75)H	STD	£3238
75	4/06	Wolv	5f216y	(0-70)H	STD	£3886
74	11/05	Wolv	5f216y		STD	£2914
78	6/05	Pont	6f	(0-75)H	G-F	£5114
73	12/04	Wolv	5f216y	(0-75)	STD	£4498
71	4/04	Nott	5f13y	D	GD	£3682

Total win prize-money £33747

Going (Turf): Sf: 0-5 GS: 0-4 Gd: 1-15 **GF: 2-21** Fm: 0-1
Distance: **5f/6f: 7-60** 7f-8f: 3-44 9f-13f: 0-1 14f+: 0-0
Track : **LH: 7-52** RH: 1-15 **Tight: 4-36** Gall: 0-5
Aids: Bl: 0-4 Vi: 0-7 Tstrap: 9-74 Ckp: 9-74
Best Rating: 78 8/06 Yarm 6f3y gd-fm

Moderate; effective at around 6f; acts on good ground and on sand; has worn cheekpieces.

Nordic Light (USA)

87(102) (51)54

5-y-o b/br g Belong To Me (USA)-Midriff (USA) (Naevus (USA))
J M Bradley Philip Banfield

Placings:00/01154/00030000604400060-00403260040050000 (7689)

2009: 7^{0}SD, 7^{0}SD, 6^{4}SD, 6^{0}SD, 5^{3}SD, 5^{2}SD, 5^{6}SD, 5^{0}SD, 6^{0}SD, 5^{4}SD, 5^{0}GF, 5^{0}GF, 5^{5}G, 5^{0}G, 5^{0}G, 6^{0}G, 5^{0}SD,

	Starts	1st	2nd	3rd	Win & Pl
Career Total (Turf)	24	1	0	1	3966
Career Total (AW)	17	1	1	1	3575

81	4/07	Folk	6f	(0-70)H	G-F	£2914
73	3/07	Wolv	5f216y	(0-65)H	SF	£2730

Total win prize-money £5645

Going (Turf): Sf: 0-1 GS: 0-2 Gd: 0-7 **GF: 1-12** Fm: 0-2
Distance: **5f/6f: 2-34** 7f-8f: 0-7 9f-13f: 0-0 14f+: 0-0
Track : **LH: 1-23** RH: 0-5 **Tight: 1-10** Gall: 0-7
Aids: Bl: 0-28 Vi: 0-1 Tstrap: 0-0 Ckp: 0-0
Best Rating: 81 4/07 Folk 6f gd-fm

Moderate; effective at around 5f-6f; acts on fast ground; goes on Polytrack; has worn a tongue tie and blinkers.

Norman Beckett

(78) (64)74

6-y-o b g Beckett (IRE)-Classic Coral (USA) (Seattle Dancer (USA))
Jim Best (R T Phillips 10/5) Scott Sallis

Placings:30415300/404610266641/0 (1568)

2009: 11^{0}SD,

	Starts	1st	2nd	3rd	Win & Pl
Career Total (Turf)	16	3	1	2	18794
Career Total (AW)	5	0	0	0	722

71	10/06	Ayr	1m1f20y		HVY	£3238
74	5/06	Ayr	1m2f	(0-80)H	SFT	£8096
67	6/05	Rdcr	7f		FRM	£3558

Total win prize-money £14894

Going (Turf): **Sf: 2-4** GS: 0-3 Gd: 0-1 GF: 0-7 Fm: 1-1
Distance: 5f/6f: 0-3 7f-8f: 1-6 **9f-13f: 2-11** 14f+: 0-1
Track : **LH: 2-12** RH: 0-4 Tight: 0-9 Gall: 0-2
Aids: Bl: 0-1 **Vi: 1-1** Tstrap: 0-3 Ckp: 0-3
Best Rating: 74 5/06 Ayr 1m2f soft

Modest; stays 1m 2f; acts on quick and soft ground; has been successful in a visor.

Norman The Great

97(95) (74)82

5-y-o b g Night Shift (USA)-Encore Du Cristal (USA) (Quiet American (USA))
A King McNeill Family

Placings:00/223045214000/0-11166 (5649)

2009: 10^{1}GF, 13^{1}GF, 12^{1}G, 12^{6}GF, 12^{6}SD,

	Starts	1st	2nd	3rd	Win & Pl
Career Total (Turf)	12	3	1	1	13990
Career Total (AW)	8	1	2	0	4506

82	7/09	Epsm	1m4f10y	(0-80)H	GD	£5180
81	6/09	NmkJ	1m5f	(0-75)H	G-F	£3885
79	5/09	Newb	1m2f6y	(0-70)H	G-F	£3123
78	8/07	Kemp	1m3f	(0-75)H	STD	£2817

Total win prize-money £15007

Going (Turf): Sf: 0-0 GS: 0-2 Gd: 1-5 **GF: 2-5** Fm: 0-0
Distance: 5f/6f: 0-0 7f-8f: 0-2 **9f-13f: 4-18** 14f+: 0-0
Track : LH: 2-12 RH: 2-7 Tight: 1-9 **Gall: 2-4**
Aids: Bl: 0-0 Vi: 0-0 Tstrap: 0-0 Ckp: 0-0
Best Rating: 82 7/09 Epsm 1m4f10y good

Fair; stays 1m5f; acts on a sound surface.

Norse Warrior (USA)

93(102) (68)66

3-y-o ch g Newfoundland (USA)-Spicy Red (USA) (Tactical Advantage (USA))
Peter Grayson (David P Myerscough 4/12) Richard Teatum

Placings:620000010 (7872)

2009: 7^{6}GF, 6^{2}G, 6^{0}GF, 8^{0}Y, 7^{0}Y, 7^{0}S, 8^{0}SD, 5^{1}SD, 5^{0}SD,

	Starts	1st	2nd	3rd	Win & Pl
Career Total (Turf)	6	0	1	0	1954
Career Total (AW)	3	1	0	0	2730

68	12/09	Wolv	5f20y	STD	£2729

Total win prize-money £2730

Going (Turf): **Sf: 0-1 GS: 0-0 Gd: 0-1 GF: 0-2 Fm: 0-0**
Distance: **5f/6f: 1-3** 7f-8f: 0-6 9f-13f: 0-0 14f+: 0-0
Track : **LH: 1-2** RH: 0-5 **Tight: 1-1** Gall: 0-1
Aids: Bl: 0-0 **Vi: 1-2** Tstrap: 0-0 Ckp: 0-0
Best Rating: 68 12/09 Wolv 5f20y stand

Fair; suited by 5f and Polytrack; has worn a visor.

North Cape (USA)

100(104) (76)79

3-y-o b g Action This Day (USA)-Cape (USA) (Mr Prospector (USA))
H Candy Henry Candy

Placings:06-532143 (5315)

2009: 7^{5}GF, 8^{3}GS, 9^{2}GF, 10^{1}G, 10^{4}G, 12^{3}SD,

	Starts	1st	2nd	3rd	Win & Pl
Career Total (Turf)	7	1	1	1	5715
Career Total (AW)	1	0	0	1	1101

79	6/09	Sand	1m2f7y	(0-75)H	GD	£3885

Total win prize-money £3886

Going (Turf): Sf: 0-1 GS: 0-2 **Gd: 1-2** GF: 0-2 Fm: 0-0
Distance: 5f/6f: 0-0 7f-8f: 0-2 **9f-13f: 1-6** 14f+: 0-0
Track : LH: 0-3 **RH: 1-4** Tight: 0-3 Gall: 0-0
Aids: Bl: 0-0 Vi: 0-0 Tstrap: 0-0 Ckp: 0-0
Best Rating: 79 6/09 Sand 1m2f7y good

Fair; stays 1m2f; acts on good ground.

North Central (USA)

93 67

2-y-o b/br c Forest Camp (USA)-Brittan Lee (USA) (Forty Niner (USA))
J Howard Johnson Transcend Bloodstock LLP

Placings:664 (5253)

2009: 5^{6}G, 6^{6}GF, 6^{4}GF,

	Starts	1st	2nd	3rd	Win & Pl
Career Total (Turf)	3	0	0	0	581

Going (Turf): **Sf: 0-0 GS: 0-0 Gd: 0-1 GF: 0-2 Fm: 0-0**
Distance: 5f/6f: 0-3 7f-8f: 0-0 9f-13f: 0-0 14f+: 0-0
Track : LH: 0-0 RH: 0-0 Tight: 0-0 Gall: 0-0
Aids: Bl: 0-0 Vi: 0-0 Tstrap: 0-0 Ckp: 0-0
Best Rating: 67 6/09 Muss 5f good

Modest brother to South Central, a high-class dual 5f winner at two.

North East Corner (USA)

88 79

3-y-o b g Giant's Causeway (USA)-Saree (Barathea (IRE))
B W Hills Thomas Barr

Placings:10-0 (1987)

2009: 7^{0}GF,

	Starts	1st	2nd	3rd	Win & Pl
Career Total (Turf)	3	1	0	0	6152

79	9/08	NmkR	7f		G-F	£6152

Total win prize-money £6152

Going (Turf): Sf: 0-0 GS: 0-0 Gd: 0-0 **GF: 1-3** Fm: 0-0
Distance: 5f/6f: 0-0 **7f-8f: 1-3** 9f-13f: 0-0 14f+: 0-0
Track : LH: 0-1 RH: 0-0 Tight: 0-0 Gall: 0-1
Aids: Bl: 0-0 Vi: 0-0 Tstrap: 0-0 Ckp: 0-0
Best Rating: 79 9/08 NmkR 7f gd-fm

Useful; stays 7f and acts on fast ground.

North Parade

100(105) (78)85

4-y-o b g Nayef (USA)-Queen Sceptre (IRE) (Fairy King (USA))

A W Carroll R Buckland

Placings:62/5100206-**3152540** (2200)
2009: 10[3]SD, 8[1]SD, 9[5]SD, 11[2]SD, 8[5]G, 10[4]GF, 10[0]S,

	Starts	1st	2nd	3rd	Win & Pl
Career Total (Turf)	12	1	2	0	9528
Career Total (AW)	4	1	1	1	2954

78 2/09 Sthl 1m STD £2047
70 5/08 Hayd 1m3f200y GD £2590
Total win prize-money £4637

Going (Turf): Sf: 0-1 GS: 0-2 **Gd: 1-4** GF: 0-5 Fm: 0-0
Distance: 5f/6f: 0-0 7f-8f: 1-2 9f-13f: 1-13 14f+: 0-1
Track : **LH: 2-10** RH: 0-5 Tight: 0-6 Gall: 0-3
Aids: Bl: 0-1 Vi: 0-0 Tstrap: 0-0 Ckp: 0-0
Best Rating: **92** 9/07 Newb 1m gd-fm

Useful; effective at around 1m-1m4f; acts on good and faster ground and Fibresand; often wears a tongue tie.

North Shadow

101(97) (60)**62**
2-y-o ch g Motivator-Matoaka (USA) (A.P. Indy (USA))
A D Brown G Morrill

Placings:6601**560** (7597)
2009: 7[6]GF, 7[6]S, 9[0]GF, 6[1]GS, 7[5]SD, 6[6]SD, 8[0]SD,

	Starts	1st	2nd	3rd	Win & Pl
Career Total (Turf)	4	1	0	0	1706
Career Total (AW)	3	0	0	0	0

62 10/09 Nott 6f15y (0-60) G-S £1706
Total win prize-money £1706

Going (Turf): Sf: 0-1 **GS: 1-1** Gd: 0-0 GF: 0-2 Fm: 0-0
Distance: 5f/6f: 0-1 **7f-8f: 1-4** 9f-13f: 0-2 14f+: 0-0
Track : LH: 0-4 RH: 0-1 Tight: 0-3 Gall: 0-0
Aids: Bl: 0-0 Vi: 0-0 Tstrap: 0-1 Ckp: 0-1
Best Rating: **62** 10/09 Nott 6f15y gd-sft

Moderate; effective over 6f; acts on easy ground.

North South Divide (IRE)

83(100) (69)**85**
5-y-o b g Namid-Bush Rose (Rainbow Quest (USA))
K A Ryan (Peter Grayson 17/6) The Armchair Jockeys

Placings:U03/2320202006**3225**-000**56400** (7877)
2009: 5[0]SD, 5[0]SD, 5[0]SD, 6[5]GS, 5[6]G, 6[4]SD, 5[0]SD, 7[0]SD,

	Starts	1st	2nd	3rd	Win & Pl
Career Total (Turf)	10	0	3	1	4034
Career Total (AW)	15	0	3	2	2888

Going (Turf): **Sf: 0-2 GS: 0-3 Gd: 0-2 GF: 0-3 Fm: 0-0**
Distance: 5f/6f: 0-17 7f-8f: 0-8 9f-13f: 0-0 14f+: 0-0
Track : LH: 0-10 RH: 0-5 Tight: 0-8 Gall: 0-2
Aids: Bl: 0-1 Vi: 0-0 Tstrap: 0-14 Ckp: 0-14
Best Rating: **85** 6/08 Wind 6f gd-sft

Modest; effective at 6-7f; acts most ground and on Polytrack; has worn cheekpieces.

North Walk (IRE)

(95) (57)**84**
6-y-o b g Monashee Mountain (USA)-Celtic Link (IRE) (Toca Madera)
B N Pollock Ten Partnership

Placings:0441013/002243000**602**/3600/335-0 (3029)
2009: 16[0]SD,

	Starts	1st	2nd	3rd	Win & Pl
Career Total (Turf)	15	2	2	2	17242
Career Total (AW)	12	0	1	3	2370

81 10/05 Ayr 6f (0-75) SFT £4368
71 9/05 Rdcr 7f (0-75) G-F £4056
Total win prize-money £8424

Going (Turf): **Sf: 1-6** GS: 0-0 Gd: 0-3 **GF: 1-5** Fm: 0-1
Distance: 5f/6f: 1-5 7f-8f: 1-12 9f-13f: 0-8 14f+: 0-2
Track : LH: 0-17 RH: 0-3 Tight: 0-13 Gall: 0-2
Aids: Bl: 0-1 Vi: 0-0 Tstrap: 0-4 Ckp: 0-4
Best Rating: **84** 7/06 Thsk 1m firm

Moderate; stays 1m5f; acts on fast ground; goes on Polytrack.

Northern Acres

90 **70**
3-y-o b g Mtoto-Bunting (Shaadi (USA))
D Nicholls Jim Dale

Placings:6-400 (6052)
2009: 8[4]GF, 10[0]GF, 8[0]G,

	Starts	1st	2nd	3rd	Win & Pl
Career Total (Turf)	4	0	0	0	241

Going (Turf): **Sf: 0-0 GS: 0-1 Gd: 0-1 GF: 0-2 Fm: 0-0**
Distance: 5f/6f: 0-0 7f-8f: 0-2 9f-13f: 0-2 14f+: 0-0
Track : LH: 0-4 RH: 0-0 Tight: 0-2 Gall: 0-0
Aids: Bl: 0-0 Vi: 0-0 Tstrap: 0-0 Ckp: 0-0
Best Rating: **70** 4/09 Hayd 1m30y gd-fm

Northern Bolt

105(102) (68)**86**
4-y-o b g Cadeaux Genereux-Shafir (IRE) (Shaadi (USA))
D Nicholls Jim Dale

Placings:01/00602**30**-00**66643501** (7219)
2009: 5[0]SD, 5[0]G, **6[6]SD**, 5[6]GS, 5[6]GF, 5[4]GS, 5[3]S, 6[5]G, 5[0]G, 5[1]S,

	Starts	1st	2nd	3rd	Win & Pl
Career Total (Turf)	15	2	1	2	10633
Career Total (AW)	4	0	0	0	0

84 11/09 Catt 5f SFT £2388
85 9/07 Ayr 6f G-S £3886
Total win prize-money £6274

Going (Turf): **Sf: 1-3 GS: 1-4** Gd: 0-3 GF: 0-5 Fm: 0-0
Distance: **5f/6f: 2-18** 7f-8f: 0-1 9f-13f: 0-0 14f+: 0-0
Track : LH: 0-4 RH: 0-3 Tight: 0-3 Gall: 0-1
Aids: Bl: 0-0 **Vi: 1-4** Tstrap: 0-0 Ckp: 0-0
Best Rating: **86** 9/08 Donc 5f soft

Fair; effective over 5f-6f; seems best on easy ground; has worn a visor.

Northern Champ (IRE)

(91) (49)**41**
3-y-o b g Mull Of Kintyre (USA)-Comprehension (USA) (Diesis)
Patrick G Kelly J W Howley

Placings:000-0060 (5115a)
2009: 7[0]SD, 8[0]SD, 7[6]SH, 7[0]HY,

	Starts	1st	2nd	3rd	Win & Pl
Career Total (Turf)	5	0	0	0	
Career Total (AW)	2	0	0	0	

Going (Turf): **Sf: 0-3 GS: 0-0 Gd: 0-0 GF: 0-0 Fm: 0-0**
Distance: 5f/6f: 0-0 7f-8f: 0-7 9f-13f: 0-0 14f+: 0-0
Track : LH: 0-3 RH: 0-4 Tight: 0-2 Gall: 0-0

Aids: Bl: 0-0 Vi: 0-0 Tstrap: 0-0 Ckp: 0-0
Best Rating: **49** 3/09 Ling 1m stand

Northern Dare (IRE)

108(106) (92)**100**
5-y-o b g Fath (USA)-Farmers Swing (IRE) (River Falls)
D Nicholls Dr Marwan Koukash

Placings:0/0130131232/304250000-10441230000 (7015)
2009: 5[1]SF, 5[0]GF, 6[4]G, 5[4]G, 5[1]S, 6[2]G, 5[3]GF, 5[0]GS, 5[0]GF, 5[0]G, 5[0]GS,

	Starts	1st	2nd	3rd	Win & Pl
Career Total (Turf)	29	4	4	5	59170
Career Total (AW)	2	1	0	0	5181

96 7/09 Pont 5f (0-90)H SFT £9346
92 3/09 Wolv 5f20y (0-85)H SF £5180
88 7/07 York 6f (0-80)H HVY £6477
82 7/07 Ayr 5f (0-65)H G-S £2492
70 4/07 Thsk 6f G-F £3238
Total win prize-money £26737

Going (Turf): **Sf: 2-6** GS: 1-5 Gd: 0-9 GF: 1-8 Fm: 0-0
Distance: **5f/6f: 5-28** 7f-8f: 0-3 9f-13f: 0-0 14f+: 0-0
Track : **LH: 2-5** RH: 0-0 **Tight: 1-3** Gall: 0-0
Aids: Bl: 0-0 Vi: 0-0 Tstrap: 0-0 Ckp: 0-0
Best Rating: **100** 7/09 Gdwd 6f good

Useful; stays 6f; acts on most ground and on Polytrack; likes to race prominently.

Northern Desert (IRE)

100(106) (75)**56**
10-y-o b g Desert Style (IRE)-Rosie's Guest (IRE) (Be My Guest (USA))
S Curran L Power & Miss N Henton

Placings:22/1220054/0/000**30**/4153500005**32**/131555000 0000/331005042/2102104-124162022503 (6703)
2009: 7[1]SD, 8[2]SD, 7[4]SD, 7[1]SD, 8[6]SD, 7[2]SD, 7[0]G, 8[2]SD, 7[2]GS, 8[5]G, 7[0]GS, 8[3]SS,

	Starts	1st	2nd	3rd	Win & Pl
Career Total (Turf)	24	2	5	0	20205
Career Total (AW)	44	7	7	7	37799

75 2/09 Ling 7f STD £2047
68 1/09 Ling 7f STD £2047
68 2/08 Wolv 1m141y STD £1774
67 1/08 Wolv 7f32y STD £1774
61 4/07 Wwck 1m22y (0-70)H G-F £3886
91 2/06 Ling 1m (0-80)H STD £5297
86 1/06 Ling 1m (0-85)H STD £6477
84 1/05 Ling 1m (0-85)H STD £6905
81 3/02 Nott 1m54y D G-S £3705
Total win prize-money £33915

Going (Turf): Sf: 0-2 **GS: 1-6** Gd: 0-8 **GF: 1-8** Fm: 0-0
Distance: 5f/6f: 0-2 **7f-8f: 6-53** 9f-13f: 3-13 14f+: 0-0
Track : **LH: 9-47** RH: 0-12 **Tight: 7-42** Gall: 0-3
Aids: Bl: 0-0 Vi: 0-0 Tstrap: 4-18 Ckp: 4-18
Best Rating: **102** 8/02 York 6f214y gd-fm

Modest; effective over 7f; acts on Polytrack; often fitted with cheekpieces.

Northern Dune (IRE)

101(101) (56)**60**
5-y-o b g Dilshaan-Zoudie (Ezzoud (IRE))

B J Curley Curley Leisure

Placings:0/000/01-1 (1242)
2009: 16^{1}F,

	Starts	1st	2nd	3rd	Win & Pl
Career Total (Turf)	1	1	0	0	1943
Career Total (AW)	6	1	0	0	2590

60	4/09	Rdcr	2m4y	(0-65)H	FRM	£1942
56	12/08	GrLe	1m2f	(0-50)H	STD	£2590

Total win prize-money £4533

Going (Turf): Sf: 0-0 GS: 0-0 Gd: 0-0 GF: 0-0 **Fm: 1-1**
Distance: 5f/6f: 0-1 7f-8f: 0-1 9f-13f: 1-4 14f+: 1-1
Track : **LH: 2-6** RH: 0-1 Tight: 1-4 Gall: 1-1
Aids: Bl: 0-0 Vi: 0-0 Tstrap: 0-0 Ckp: 0-0
Best Rating: **60** 4/09 Rdcr 2m4y firm

Moderate; stays 2m; acts on Polytrack and fast turf.

Northern Empire (IRE)

103(109) (83)100
6-y-o ch g Namid-Bumble (Rainbow Quest (USA))
F Jordan (K A Ryan 29/6) Alan Spargo

Placings:2212/44/004000512/15224000000000213-5320021041522260430000 (7890)
2009: 5^{5}SS, 6^{3}SD, 5^{2}SD, 5^{0}SD, 5^{0}SD, 5^{2}SD, 6^{1}SD, 6^{0}SD, 5^{4}SD, 5^{1}F, 5^{5}GF, 5^{2}GF, 5^{2}G, 5^{2}SD, 5^{6}GF, 5^{0}HY, 5^{4}GS, 5^{3}GF, 5^{0}GS, 5^{0}SD, 5^{0}SD, 5^{0}SS, 6^{0}SD,

	Starts	1st	2nd	3rd	Win & Pl
Career Total (Turf)	29	2	5	1	34620
Career Total (AW)	27	4	7	2	33142

60	5/09	Rdcr	5f		FRM	£2047
61	3/09	Ling	6f		STD	£2047
81	12/08	Wolv	5f20y	(0-75)H	STD	£3885
93	1/08	Kemp	5f	(0-85)H	STD	£4210
90	12/07	Sthl	5f	(0-95)H	STD	£7772
97	6/05	Wind	5f10y		G-F	£4277

Total win prize-money £24239

Going (Turf): Sf: 0-3 GS: 0-7 Gd: 0-6 **GF: 1-12 Fm: 1-1**
Distance: **5f/6f: 6-55** 7f-8f: 0-1 9f-13f: 0-0 14f+: 0-0
Track : **LH: 2-18** RH: 1-3 **Tight: 2-13** Gall: 1-2
Aids: Bl: 0-1 Vi: 0-0 Tstrap: 1-16 Ckp: 1-16
Best Rating: **103** 7/05 NmkJ 6f gd-sft

Fair; effective over 5f-6f; acts on fast and easy ground; goes on sand.

Northern Fling

103(70) (17)104
5-y-o b g Mujadil (USA)-Donna Anna (Be My Chief (USA))
J S Goldie (D Nicholls 18/9) Paul Moulton

Placings:014310/30126010/140000300-040000000064 (7171)
2009: 6^{0}FT, 6^{4}GF, 6^{0}GF, 5^{0}GF, 5^{0}G, 7^{0}GF, 5^{0}G, 6^{0}G, 5^{0}GS, 5^{0}G, 5^{6}GF, 7^{4}S,

	Starts	1st	2nd	3rd	Win & Pl
Career Total (Turf)	33	5	1	2	64660
Career Total (AW)	2	0	0	1	674

109	4/08	Donc	5f	(0-100)H	SFT	£10904
102	8/07	York	5f	(0-100)H	GD	£16192
93	4/07	Ripn	6f	(0-95)H	G-F	£9348
88	8/06	Gdwd	6f	H	G-F	£10687
82	6/06	Ches	5f16y		GD	£5181

Total win prize-money £52314

Going (Turf): Sf: 1-5 GS: 0-1 **Gd: 2-11 GF: 2-16** Fm: 0-0
Distance: **5f/6f: 5-31** 7f-8f: 0-4 9f-13f: 0-0 14f+: 0-0
Track : **LH: 1-8** RH: 0-1 **Tight: 1-3** Gall: 0-2
Aids: Bl: 0-0 Vi: 0-0 Tstrap: 0-1 Ckp: 0-1
Best Rating: **109** 4/08 Donc 5f soft

Useful; suited by 5f-6f and acts on most ground.

Northern Flyer (GER)

103(86) (35)71
3-y-o b g Hawk Wing (USA)-Nachtigall (GER) (Danehill (USA))
J J Quinn N Chapman

Placings:00-56321223245 (6182)
2009: 6^{5}SD, 8^{6}SD, 8^{3}GS, 7^{2}G, 7^{1}GF, 7^{2}G, 7^{2}GF, 6^{3}G, 8^{2}S, 8^{4}S, 8^{5}GF,

	Starts	1st	2nd	3rd	Win & Pl
Career Total (Turf)	11	1	4	2	7291
Career Total (AW)	2	0	0	0	0

68	6/09	Muss	7f30y	(0-65)H	G-F	£2590

Total win prize-money £2590

Going (Turf): Sf: 0-3 GS: 0-2 Gd: 0-3 **GF: 1-3** Fm: 0-0
Distance: 5f/6f: 0-4 **7f-8f: 1-7** 9f-13f: 0-2 14f+: 0-0
Track : LH: 0-6 **RH: 1-5 Tight: 1-5** Gall: 0-0
Aids: Bl: 0-0 Vi: 0-0 Tstrap: 0-0 Ckp: 0-0
Best Rating: **71** 7/09 Bevl 7f100y gd-fm

Modest; effective over 7f-1m; acts on good and softer ground.

Northern Genes (AUS)

(92) (44)
3-y-o b g Refuse To Bend (IRE)-Cotswold Dancer (AUS) (Carnegie (IRE))
M R Bosley Colin Rogers

Placings:004 (7550)
2009: 10^{0}SD, 10^{0}SD, 10^{4}SD,

	Starts	1st	2nd	3rd	Win & Pl
Career Total (Turf)	0	0	0	0	
Career Total (AW)	3	0	0	0	0

Going (Turf): **Sf: 0-0 GS: 0-0 Gd: 0-0 GF: 0-0 Fm: 0-0**
Distance: 5f/6f: 0-0 7f-8f: 0-0 9f-13f: 0-3 14f+: 0-0
Track : LH: 0-2 RH: 0-1 Tight: 0-2 Gall: 0-0
Aids: Bl: 0-0 Vi: 0-0 Tstrap: 0-0 Ckp: 0-0
Best Rating: **44** 9/09 Kemp 1m2f stand

Northern Jem

103 82
5-y-o b g Mark Of Esteem (IRE)-Top Jem (Damister (USA))
D E Pipe (Jane Chapple-Hyam 24/10) Lady Clarke

Placings:36/3310200/3066-61003 (7014)
2009: 10^{6}GF, 8^{1}S, 8^{0}G, 10^{0}G, 10^{3}GS,

	Starts	1st	2nd	3rd	Win & Pl
Career Total (Turf)	18	2	1	5	12348

82	7/09	NmkJ	1m	(0-75)H	SFT	£3885
84	5/07	Ripn	1m1f		GD	£3562

Total win prize-money £7448

Going (Turf): **Sf: 1-1** GS: 0-4 **Gd: 1-6** GF: 0-7 Fm: 0-0
Distance: 5f/6f: 0-0 7f-8f: 1-4 9f-13f: 1-14 14f+: 0-0
Track : LH: 0-4 **RH: 1-6 Tight: 1-6** Gall: 0-3
Aids: Bl: 0-0 Vi: 0-0 Tstrap: 0-0 Ckp: 0-0
Best Rating: **87** 7/07 Folk 1m1f149y gd-sft

Fair; effective at around 1m1f; acts on good ground.

Northern Shore (IRE)

(89) (50)
3-y-o br g Clodovil (IRE)-Distant Shore (IRE) (Jareer (USA))
K A Ryan Sunpak Potatoes

Placings:00-0405 (0684)
2009: 7^{0}SD, 8^{4}SD, 7^{0}SD, 7^{5}SD,

	Starts	1st	2nd	3rd	Win & Pl
Career Total (Turf)	2	0	0	0	
Career Total (AW)	4	0	0	0	0

Going (Turf): **Sf: 0-0 GS: 0-0 Gd: 0-1 GF: 0-1 Fm: 0-0**
Distance: 5f/6f: 0-2 7f-8f: 0-4 9f-13f: 0-0 14f+: 0-0
Track : LH: 0-4 RH: 0-0 Tight: 0-1 Gall: 0-0
Aids: Bl: 0-4 Vi: 0-0 Tstrap: 0-0 Ckp: 0-0
Best Rating: **50** 2/09 Sthl 1m stand

Northern Spy (USA)

105(108) (78)78
5-y-o b g War Chant (USA)-Sunray Superstar (Nashwan (USA))
S Dow J R May

Placings:102/600206000-50014452000 (7662)
2009: 11^{5}GF, 10^{0}GF, 10^{0}SD, 8^{1}G, 8^{4}GF, 8^{4}GF, 8^{5}G, 8^{2}SD, 8^{0}GS, 10^{0}SD, 7^{0}SD,

	Starts	1st	2nd	3rd	Win & Pl
Career Total (Turf)	13	2	0	0	9654
Career Total (AW)	10	0	3	0	6258

78	7/09	Epsm	1m114y	(0-85)H	GD	£5180
81	10/07	Nott	1m54y		G-F	£3238

Total win prize-money £8420

Going (Turf): Sf: 0-2 GS: 0-1 **Gd: 1-5 GF: 1-5** Fm: 0-0
Distance: 5f/6f: 0-0 7f-8f: 0-8 **9f-13f: 2-15** 14f+: 0-0
Track : **LH: 2-9** RH: 0-12 **Tight: 1-8** Gall: 0-1
Aids: Bl: 0-0 Vi: 0-0 Tstrap: 0-0 Ckp: 0-0
Best Rating: **90** 12/07 Kemp 1m2f stand

Fair; stays 1m2f but probably best at around 1m; acts on fast ground and Polytrack.

Northern Tour

79(102) (79)80
3-y-o b g Tobougg (IRE)-Swift Spring (FR) (Bluebird (USA))
P F I Cole Hunter, Maynard, Ward

Placings:611336-5004 (7817)
2009: 8^{5}SD, 10^{0}G, 8^{0}SD, 9^{4}SD,

	Starts	1st	2nd	3rd	Win & Pl
Career Total (Turf)	5	2	0	1	8875
Career Total (AW)	5	0	0	1	1050

79	5/08	NmkR	6f	G-S	£5180
75	4/08	Folk	5f	G-S	£2388

Total win prize-money £7569

Going (Turf): Sf: 0-0 **GS: 2-3** Gd: 0-1 GF: 0-1 Fm: 0-0
Distance: **5f/6f: 2-4** 7f-8f: 0-3 9f-13f: 0-3 14f+: 0-0
Track : LH: 0-4 RH: 0-2 Tight: 0-4 Gall: 0-0
Aids: Bl: 0-0 Vi: 0-0 Tstrap: 0-0 Ckp: 0-0
Best Rating: **80** 6/08 Sals 6f gd-fm

Fair; stays 1m1f; acts on easy ground and on Polytrack.

Northerner (IRE)

(53)63
6-y-o b g Mark Of Esteem (IRE)-Ensorceleuse (FR)

(Fabulous Dancer (USA))
J O'Reilly Woodcock Electrical Limited

Placings:000/**66**23/0/0-00 **(7504)**
2009: 12^0G, 12^0SD,

	Starts	1st	2nd	3rd	Win & Pl
Career Total (Turf)	**7**	**0**	**1**	**1**	**2023**
Career Total (AW)	**4**	**0**	**0**	**0**	**0**

Going (Turf): **Sf: 0-1 GS: 0-1 Gd: 0-3 GF: 0-2 Fm: 0-0**
Distance: 5f/6f: 0-1 7f-8f: 0-1 9f-13f: 0-8 14f+: 0-1
Track : LH: 0-9 RH: 0-0 Tight: 0-2 Gall: 0-0
Aids: Bl: 0-0 Vi: 0-0 Tstrap: 0-0 Ckp: 0-0
Best Rating: **63** 4/06 Pont 1m4f8y good

Moderate; effective at around a mile and a half; acts on good ground.

Northgate Lodge (USA)

79(91) (45)**23**
4-y-o ch g Hold That Tiger (USA)-Sabaah Elfull (Kris)
M Brittain Mel Brittain

Placings:064000/0000-00 **(7718)**
2009: 6^0GF, 9^0SD,

	Starts	1st	2nd	3rd	Win & Pl
Career Total (Turf)	**9**	**0**	**0**	**0**	**385**
Career Total (AW)	**3**	**0**	**0**	**0**	

Going (Turf): **Sf: 0-0 GS: 0-1 Gd: 0-2 GF: 0-6 Fm: 0-0**
Distance: 5f/6f: 0-5 7f-8f: 0-4 9f-13f: 0-3 14f+: 0-0
Track : LH: 0-4 RH: 0-0 Tight: 0-3 Gall: 0-1
Aids: Bl: 0-4 Vi: 0-0 Tstrap: 0-0 Ckp: 0-0
Best Rating: **53** 4/07 Thsk 5f gd-fm

Modest Hold That Tiger colt; related to several speedy performers; effective at 5f; acts on a sound surface.

Northside Prince (IRE)

99 **70**
3-y-o b g Desert Prince (IRE)-Spartan Girl (IRE) (Ela-Mana-Mou)
G A Swinbank S S Anderson

Placings:00-344B223 **(5731)**
2009: 10^3G, 12^4GF, 12^4GF, 10^BGF, 10^2GF, 10^2S, 8^3GS,

	Starts	1st	2nd	3rd	Win & Pl
Career Total (Turf)	**9**	**0**	**2**	**2**	**3053**

Going (Turf): **Sf: 0-1 GS: 0-3 Gd: 0-1 GF: 0-4 Fm: 0-0**
Distance: 5f/6f: 0-0 7f-8f: 0-3 9f-13f: 0-6 14f+: 0-0
Track : LH: 0-6 RH: 0-2 Tight: 0-3 Gall: 0-2
Aids: Bl: 0-0 Vi: 0-0 Tstrap: 0-0 Ckp: 0-0
Best Rating: **70** 8/09 Ayr 1m2f soft

Modest; stays 1m4f; acts on fast and soft ground.

Norwegian

(99) (55)**57**
8-y-o b g Halling (USA)-Chicarica (USA) (The Minstrel (CAN))
Ian Williams Ian Williams

Placings:51430/54050550/000001/41313221126065000640**4**/444540-635 **(0368)**
2009: 11^6SD, 9^3SD, 12^5SD,

	Starts	1st	2nd	3rd	Win & Pl
Career Total (Turf)	**17**	**1**	**0**	**0**	**2915**
Career Total (AW)	**32**	**5**	**3**	**4**	**14971**

56	4/07	Folk	1m1f149y (0-60)H	G-F	£2914
66	3/07	Wolv	1m1f103y (0-58)H	STD	£2047
57	2/07	Wolv	1m1f103y	STD	£2047
59	1/07	Wolv	1m141y (0-58)H	STD	£3071
52	12/06	Wolv	1m1f103y (0-45)	STD	£1365
69	1/04	Sthl	1m E	SS	£3248

Total win prize-money £14695

Going (Turf): Sf: 0-0 GS: 0-1 Gd: 0-2 **GF: 1-14** Fm: 0-0
Distance: 5f/6f: 0-0 7f-8f: 1-5 **9f-13f: 5-44** 14f+: 0-0
Track : **LH: 5-42** RH: 1-6 **Tight: 5-33** Gall: 0-0
Aids: Bl: 0-3 Vi: 0-6 Tstrap: 5-31 Ckp: 5-31
Best Rating: **69** 4/07 Wolv 1m1f103y stand

Moderate gelding; effective over 1m-1m2f; acts on Polytrack, Fibresand and fast turf.

Norwegian Dancer (UAE)

112(99) (80)**92**
3-y-o b c Halling (USA)-Time Changes (USA) (Danzig (USA))
E S McMahon Philip Wilkins

Placings:53-501104050054 **(7373)**
2009: 10^5GF, 9^0GF, 10^1GF, 10^1GF, 12^0G, 10^4GF, 10^0SD, 10^5F, 10^0G, 10^0GS, 10^5GS, 12^4SD,

	Starts	1st	2nd	3rd	Win & Pl
Career Total (Turf)	**11**	**2**	**0**	**0**	**11996**
Career Total (AW)	**3**	**0**	**0**	**1**	**781**

89	7/09	Ches	1m2f75y (0-85)H	G-F	£5828
78	6/09	Ches	1m2f75y	G-F	£5180

Total win prize-money £11009

Going (Turf): Sf: 0-1 GS: 0-2 Gd: 0-2 **GF: 2-5** Fm: 0-1
Distance: 5f/6f: 0-0 7f-8f: 0-1 **9f-13f: 2-13** 14f+: 0-0
Track : **LH: 2-10** RH: 0-4 **Tight: 2-11** Gall: 0-2
Aids: Bl: 0-0 Vi: 0-0 Tstrap: 0-0 Ckp: 0-0
Best Rating: **92** 8/09 Ches 1m2f75y gd-fm

Useful; effective at 1m2f; acts on fast ground and on Polytrack.

Nosedive

103 **98**
2-y-o ch c Observatory (USA)-Resistance Heroine (Dr Fong (USA))
W J Haggas Duke/Roberts/Netherthorpe/Goddard

Placings:1406553 **(6486)**
2009: 5^1G, 5^4GF, 6^0G, 6^6G, 5^5GF, 5^5G, 6^3GF,

	Starts	1st	2nd	3rd	Win & Pl
Career Total (Turf)	**7**	**1**	**0**	**1**	**32941**

81	6/09	Sand	5f6y	GD	£5180

Total win prize-money £5181

Going (Turf): Sf: 0-0 GS: 0-0 **Gd: 1-4** GF: 0-3 Fm: 0-0
Distance: **5f/6f: 1-7** 7f-8f: 0-0 9f-13f: 0-0 14f+: 0-0
Track : LH: 0-0 RH: 0-0 Tight: 0-0 Gall: 0-0
Aids: Bl: 0-0 Vi: 0-0 Tstrap: 0-0 Ckp: 0-0
Best Rating: **98** 9/09 Chan 5f110y good

Very useful; effective from 5f-6f; acts on good ground.

Nosferatu (IRE)

105 **84**
6-y-o b g In The Wings-Gothic Dream (IRE) (Nashwan (USA))
J Howard Johnson Andrea & Graham Wylie

Placings:3/31/110000/10 **(3191)**
2009: 12^1GF, 17^0GF,

	Starts	1st	2nd	3rd	Win & Pl
Career Total (Turf)	**11**	**4**	**0**	**2**	**41614**

84	5/09	York	1m4f	G-F	£5828
97	6/07	Epsm	1m4f10y (0-100)H	GD	£24928
90	5/07	Wind	1m3f135y (0-85)H	GD	£4857
80	10/06	Wind	1m2f7y	SFT	£4533

Total win prize-money £40148

Going (Turf): Sf: 1-2 GS: 0-1 **Gd: 2-5** GF: 1-3 Fm: 0-0
Distance: 5f/6f: 0-0 7f-8f: 0-0 **9f-13f: 4-7** 14f+: 0-4
Track : **LH: 2-5** RH: 1-5 **Tight: 3-4** Gall: 1-4
Aids: **Bl: 1-2** Vi: 0-0 Tstrap: 0-0 Ckp: 0-0
Best Rating: **97** 6/07 Epsm 1m4f10y good

Useful; stays at least 1m4f, acts on good and softer ground; winning hurdler; has worn headgear.

Not In The Clock (USA)

(87) (58)
2-y-o b c Chapel Royal (USA)-Bavarian Girl (USA) (Unbridled (USA))
J R Best J R May

Placings:050 **(7886)**
2009: 6^0SD, 6^5SD, 7^0SD,

	Starts	1st	2nd	3rd	Win & Pl
Career Total (Turf)	**0**	**0**	**0**	**0**	
Career Total (AW)	**3**	**0**	**0**	**0**	**0**

Going (Turf): **Sf: 0-0 GS: 0-0 Gd: 0-0 GF: 0-0 Fm: 0-0**
Distance: 5f/6f: 0-2 7f-8f: 0-1 9f-13f: 0-0 14f+: 0-0
Track : LH: 0-2 RH: 0-1 Tight: 0-2 Gall: 0-0
Aids: Bl: 0-0 Vi: 0-0 Tstrap: 0-0 Ckp: 0-0
Best Rating: **58** 12/09 Ling 6f stand

Not My Choice (IRE)

102(102) (88)**89**
4-y-o ch g Choisir (AUS)-Northgate Raver (Absalom)
J Balding (S Parr 30/5) D Kilpatrick W McKay

Placings:4501606/01600643550-00004004 **(7555)**
2009: 5^0SD, 5^0SD, 5^0GF, 5^0GF, 5^4GF, 5^0SD, 7^0SD, 5^4SD,

	Starts	1st	2nd	3rd	Win & Pl
Career Total (Turf)	**16**	**2**	**0**	**0**	**20711**
Career Total (AW)	**10**	**0**	**0**	**1**	**1050**

89	5/08	Ches	6f18y	(0-90)H	G-F	£10361
83	9/07	Ches	5f16y	(0-85)	GD	£6477

Total win prize-money £16839

Going (Turf): Sf: 0-2 GS: 0-2 **Gd: 1-4 GF: 1-8** Fm: 0-0
Distance: 5f/6f: 1-23 7f-8f: 1-3 9f-13f: 0-0 14f+: 0-0
Track : **LH: 2-14** RH: 0-1 **Tight: 2-12** Gall: 0-2
Aids: Bl: 0-0 Vi: 0-0 Tstrap: 0-1 Ckp: 0-1
Best Rating: **89** 5/08 Bevl 5f gd-fm

Fair; effective at 5f; acts on good and softer ground; has worn a tongue tie.

Not Now Lewis (IRE)

99(102) (59)**61**
5-y-o b g Shinko Forest (IRE)-Pearl Egg (IRE) (Mukaddamah (USA))
F P Murtagh R & J Wharton

Placings:35334250/0113452400-536160600 **(6256)**

2009: 6^{5}GF, 8^{3}GF, 5^{6}GF, 8^{1}G, 8^{6}GS, 7^{0}G, 7^{6}GF, 8^{0}GS, 8^{0}SD,

	Starts	1st	2nd	3rd	Win & Pl
Career Total (Turf)	11	1	1	1	4324
Career Total (AW)	16	2	1	4	6115

61 6/09 Thsk 1m (0-55)H GD £3139
63 2/08 Kemp 1m (0-55)H STD £2047
58 1/08 Kemp 1m (0-50)H STD £2047
Total win prize-money £7235

Going (Turf): Sf: 0-1 GS: 0-2 **Gd: 1-3** GF: 0-5 Fm: 0-0
Distance: 5f/6f: 0-5 **7f-8f: 3-12** 9f-13f: 0-10 14f+: 0-0
Track : LH: 1-14 **RH: 2-11 Tight: 1-11** Gall: 0-3
Aids: Bl: 0-1 Vi: 0-0 Tstrap: 0-0 Ckp: 0-0
Best Rating: 66 3/07 Ling 7f stand

Moderate; stays 1m2f; acts on good ground and on Polytrack; has worn blinkers.

Nota Bene

107(111) (111)**106**
7-y-o b g Zafonic (USA)-Dodo (IRE) (Alzao (USA))
D R C Elsworth The Malzee Partnership

Placings:211/110/00/00/10605-0334001 **(4059)**
2009: 6^{0}GF, 6^{3}G, 6^{3}GF, 6^{4}SD, 6^{0}GF, 7^{0}GF, 5^{1}S,

	Starts	1st	2nd	3rd	Win & Pl
Career Total (Turf)	19	5	1	2	70179
Career Total (AW)	3	1	0	0	7813

106 7/09 NmkJ 5f SFT £9346
111 5/08 GrLe 6f STD £6799
113 5/05 Newb 6f8y G-F £16240
107 4/05 NmkR 6f (0-95)H G-F £9525
95 10/04 NmkR 6f SFT £12110
81 10/04 Wind 6f GD £5278
Total win prize-money £59300

Going (Turf): Sf: 2-3 GS: 0-1 Gd: 1-4 **GF: 2-11** Fm: 0-0
Distance: 5f/6f: 5-20 7f-8f: 1-2 9f-13f: 0-0 14f+: 0-0
Track : LH: 1-6 RH: 0-0 Tight: 0-1 **Gall: 2-7**
Aids: Bl: 0-0 Vi: 0-0 Tstrap: 0-0 Ckp: 0-0
Best Rating: 113 5/05 Newb 6f8y gd-fm

Very useful; winner in Listed company; suited by 6f; acts on any ground and on Polytrack; has worn a tongue-tie; likes to race prominently; has broken blood-vessels.

Nota Liberata

(88) (10)**69**
5-y-o b g Spinning World (USA)-Kyda (USA) (Gulch (USA))
Ollie Pears Brian Hughes

Placings:0250546232022/0023555150/**00-0** **(0571)**
2009: 9^{0}SD,

	Starts	1st	2nd	3rd	Win & Pl
Career Total (Turf)	22	1	6	1	11697
Career Total (AW)	4	0	0	1	770

66 7/07 Ayr 1m1f20y (0-65)H G-S £3238
Total win prize-money £3239

Going (Turf): Sf: 0-4 **GS: 1-4** Gd: 0-3 GF: 0-10 Fm: 0-1
Distance: 5f/6f: 0-7 7f-8f: 0-10 **9f-13f: 1-9** 14f+: 0-0
Track : LH: 1-14 RH: 0-4 Tight: 0-10 Gall: 0-0
Aids: Bl: 0-1 Vi: 0-0 Tstrap: 0-0 Ckp: 0-0
Best Rating: 69 10/06 Catt 7f soft

Note Perfect

77(98) (54)**55**
4-y-o b f Diktat-Better Still (IRE) (Glenstal (USA))
M W Easterby Mrs Jean Turpin

Placings:000/**214340000100-00** **(1781)**
2009: 5^{0}F, 6^{0}SD,

	Starts	1st	2nd	3rd	Win & Pl
Career Total (Turf)	9	1	0	0	2730
Career Total (AW)	8	1	1	1	2818

55 10/08 Ayr 5f (0-58)H HVY £2729
54 2/08 Sthl 6f (0-65)H STD £1911
Total win prize-money £4641

Going (Turf): Sf: 1-4 GS: 0-0 Gd: 0-3 GF: 0-1 Fm: 0-1
Distance: 5f/6f: 2-16 7f-8f: 0-1 9f-13f: 0-0 14f+: 0-0
Track : LH: 1-6 RH: 0-1 Tight: 0-0 Gall: 0-0
Aids: Bl: 2-13 Vi: 0-0 Tstrap: 0-0 Ckp: 0-0
Best Rating: 55 10/08 Ayr 5f heavy

Moderate; suited by 5f-6f; acts on testing ground; suited by Fibresand; has worn blinkers.

Nothing Is Forever (IRE)

(95) (56)**64**
5-y-o b g Daylami (IRE)-Bequeath (USA) (Lyphard (USA))
L Corcoran (D R Gandolfo 16/10) The Globe Partnership

Placings:450/0000/4P **(0449)**
2009: 16^{4}SD, 13^{P}SD,

	Starts	1st	2nd	3rd	Win & Pl
Career Total (Turf)	4	0	0	0	337
Career Total (AW)	5	0	0	0	192

Going (Turf): Sf: 0-1 GS: 0-0 Gd: 0-0 GF: 0-3 Fm: 0-0
Distance: 5f/6f: 0-0 7f-8f: 0-1 9f-13f: 0-5 14f+: 0-3
Track : LH: 0-5 RH: 0-4 Tight: 0-4 Gall: 0-0
Aids: Bl: 0-0 Vi: 0-0 Tstrap: 0-0 Ckp: 0-0
Best Rating: 64 8/06 Sand 1m14y gd-fm

Modest handicapper; stays quite well; handles Polytrack.

Notice Given

93 **70**
2-y-o b c Oasis Dream-Well Warned (Warning)
H R A Cecil K Abdulla

Placings:0026 **(7096)**
2009: 7^{0}S, 7^{0}G, 6^{2}GF, 7^{6}G,

	Starts	1st	2nd	3rd	Win & Pl
Career Total (Turf)	4	0	1	0	1208

Going (Turf): Sf: 0-1 GS: 0-0 Gd: 0-2 GF: 0-1 Fm: 0-0
Distance: 5f/6f: 0-0 7f-8f: 0-4 9f-13f: 0-0 14f+: 0-0
Track : LH: 0-0 RH: 0-0 Tight: 0-0 Gall: 0-0
Aids: Bl: 0-0 Vi: 0-0 Tstrap: 0-0 Ckp: 0-0
Best Rating: 70 9/09 Yarm 6f3y gd-fm

Fair; stays 6f; acts on fast ground.

Notorize

96 **88**
2-y-o ch c Hernando (FR)-Hypnotize (Machiavellian (USA))
R M Beckett R Roberts

Placings:12 **(6011)**
2009: 8^{1}G, 8^{2}GS,

	Starts	1st	2nd	3rd	Win & Pl
Career Total (Turf)	2	1	1	0	4972

76 8/09 Gdwd 1m GD £3238
Total win prize-money £3238

Going (Turf): Sf: 0-0 GS: 0-1 **Gd: 1-1** GF: 0-0 Fm: 0-0
Distance: 5f/6f: 0-0 **7f-8f: 1-2** 9f-13f: 0-0 14f+: 0-0
Track : LH: 0-1 **RH: 1-1** Tight: 0-0 Gall: 0-0
Aids: Bl: 0-0 Vi: 0-0 Tstrap: 0-0 Ckp: 0-0
Best Rating: 88 9/09 Ayr 1m gd-sft

33,000gns half-brother to Hypnotic and a couple of other winners; winner on debut over 1m on good ground and improved on that in defeat next time.

Notte Di Note (IRE)

90(88) (59)**53**
2-y-o b f Le Vie Dei Colori-Effetto Ottico (IRE) (Foxhound (USA))
L M Cumani Scuderia Archi Romani

Placings:555 **(7317)**
2009: 6^{5}GF, 5^{5}SF, 5^{5}SD,

	Starts	1st	2nd	3rd	Win & Pl
Career Total (Turf)	1	0	0	0	103
Career Total (AW)	2	0	0	0	0

Going (Turf): Sf: 0-0 GS: 0-0 Gd: 0-0 GF: 0-1 Fm: 0-0
Distance: 5f/6f: 0-2 7f-8f: 0-1 9f-13f: 0-0 14f+: 0-0
Track : LH: 0-3 RH: 0-0 Tight: 0-2 Gall: 0-0
Aids: Bl: 0-0 Vi: 0-0 Tstrap: 0-0 Ckp: 0-0
Best Rating: 59 11/09 Wolv 5f216y stand

Nouailhas

88(71) (20)**53**
3-y-o b g Mark Of Esteem (IRE)-Barachois Princess (USA) (Barachois (CAN))
R Hollinshead C W Wardle & Mrs J E Wardle

Placings:00036500 **(6788)**
2009: 8^{0}SD, 7^{0}F, 10^{0}GS, 9^{3}GF, 9^{6}G, 13^{5}GF, 9^{0}GF, 11^{0}G,

	Starts	1st	2nd	3rd	Win & Pl
Career Total (Turf)	7	0	0	1	289
Career Total (AW)	1	0	0	0	

Going (Turf): Sf: 0-0 GS: 0-1 Gd: 0-2 GF: 0-3 Fm: 0-1
Distance: 5f/6f: 0-0 7f-8f: 0-1 9f-13f: 0-6 14f+: 0-1
Track : LH: 0-5 RH: 0-3 Tight: 0-2 Gall: 0-0
Aids: Bl: 0-0 Vi: 0-0 Tstrap: 0-0 Ckp: 0-0
Best Rating: 53 6/09 Leic 1m1f218y gd-fm

Noubian (USA)

(102) (72)**74**
7-y-o ch g Diesis-Beraysim (Lion Cavern (USA))
C R Dore D C Cooper

Placings:13063/40/2016-**0600** **(0679)**
2009: 9^{0}SD, 12^{6}SD, 12^{0}SD, 13^{0}SF,

	Starts	1st	2nd	3rd	Win & Pl
Career Total (Turf)	9	1	1	2	9672
Career Total (AW)	6	1	0	0	3513

74 10/08 Limk 1m3f70y (50-70)H HVY £5080
69 4/05 Wolv 1m1f103y STD £3513
Total win prize-money £8594

Going (Turf): Sf: 1-2 GS: 0-0 Gd: 0-2 GF: 0-2 Fm: 0-0
Distance: 5f/6f: 0-0 7f-8f: 0-1 **9f-13f: 2-10** 14f+: 0-4
Track : LH: 1-7 RH: 1-7 **Tight: 1-7** Gall: 0-0
Aids: Bl: 0-0 Vi: 0-0 Tstrap: 0-0 Ckp: 0-0
Best Rating: 78 7/05 Sand 1m2f7y gd-fm

Fair performer; stays a mile; acts on a sound surface and Polytrack.

Nounou

(90) (63)60
8-y-o b g Starborough-Watheeqah (USA) (Topsider (USA))
Miss J E Foster The Smash Block Partnership

Placings:05001515/12165/05402-0 **(0449)**
2009: 13^{0}SD,

	Starts	1st	2nd	3rd	Win & Pl
Career Total (Turf)	13	3	1	0	17442
Career Total (AW)	6	1	1	0	4241

80 4/05 Muss 2m (0-75)H G-F £4095
73 2/05 Ling 1m5f (0-70)H STD £3435
73 10/04 Epsm 1m4f10y (0-70)H GD £6958
66 8/04 Folk 1m1f149yF(0-75)H G-S £4108
Total win prize-money £18596

Going (Turf): Sf: 0-1 **GS: 1-3 Gd: 1-3 GF: 1-6** Fm: 0-0
Distance: 5f/6f: 0-0 7f-8f: 0-3 **9f-13f: 3-6** 14f+: 1-10
Track : LH: 2-11 RH: 2-6 **Tight: 4-12** Gall: 0-2
Aids: Bl: 0-0 Vi: 0-1 Tstrap: 0-1 Ckp: 0-1
Best Rating: 80 4/05 Muss 2m gd-fm

Moderate; stays 2m; acts on most ground and on Polytrack; has worn cheekpieces and a tongue tie.

Nouriya

(97) (76)
2-y-o b f Danehill Dancer (IRE)-Majestic Sakeena (IRE) (King's Best (USA))
Sir Michael Stoute Saleh Al Homaizi & Imad Al Sagar

Placings:4 **(6628)**
2009: 8^{4}SS,

	Starts	1st	2nd	3rd	Win & Pl
Career Total (Turf)	0	0	0	0	
Career Total (AW)	1	0	0	0	289

Going (Turf): Sf: 0-0 GS: 0-0 Gd: 0-0 GF: 0-0 Fm: 0-0
Distance: 5f/6f: 0-0 7f-8f: 0-1 9f-13f: 0-0 14f+: 0-0
Track : LH: 0-1 RH: 0-0 Tight: 0-1 Gall: 0-0
Aids: Bl: 0-0 Vi: 0-0 Tstrap: 0-0 Ckp: 0-0
Best Rating: 76 10/09 Ling 1m std-slw

Novastasia (IRE)

86(92) (62)39
3-y-o b f Noverre (USA)-Pink Sovietstaia (FR) (Soviet Star (USA))
W R Swinburn The Happy Hoofers

Placings:60-6400000 **(6497)**
2009: 7^{6}SD, 7^{4}SD, 8^{0}GF, 8^{0}GF, 8^{0}GS, 8^{0}SF, 9^{0}SF,

	Starts	1st	2nd	3rd	Win & Pl
Career Total (Turf)	3	0	0	0	
Career Total (AW)	6	0	0	0	241

Going (Turf): Sf: 0-0 GS: 0-1 Gd: 0-0 GF: 0-2 Fm: 0-0
Distance: 5f/6f: 0-1 7f-8f: 0-4 9f-13f: 0-4 14f+: 0-0
Track : LH: 0-5 RH: 0-2 Tight: 0-5 Gall: 0-1
Aids: Bl: 0-0 Vi: 0-0 Tstrap: 0-3 Ckp: 0-3
Best Rating: 62 4/09 Ling 7f stand

Novay Essjay (IRE)

96(85) (54)72
2-y-o ch g Noverre (USA)-Arabian Hideway (IRE) (Desert Prince (IRE))
P C Haslam Middleham Park Racing XXXI

Placings:153656 **(6354)**
2009: 5^{1}GF, 6^{5}GS, 6^{3}G, 7^{6}GF, 7^{5}GF, 5^{6}SD,

	Starts	1st	2nd	3rd	Win & Pl
Career Total (Turf)	5	1	0	1	3912
Career Total (AW)	1	0	0	0	0

72 5/09 Ripn 5f G-F £3238
Total win prize-money £3238

Going (Turf): Sf: 0-0 GS: 0-1 Gd: 0-1 **GF: 1-3** Fm: 0-0
Distance: **5f/6f: 1-4** 7f-8f: 0-2 9f-13f: 0-0 14f+: 0-0
Track : LH: 0-1 RH: 0-0 Tight: 0-1 Gall: 0-0
Aids: Bl: 0-0 Vi: 0-0 Tstrap: 0-1 Ckp: 0-1
Best Rating: 72 5/09 Ripn 5f gd-fm

Fair; effective over 5f but stays further; acts on fast ground.

Novellen Lad (IRE)

107(80) (69)93
4-y-o b g Noverre (USA)-Lady Ellen (Horage)
E J Alston Con Harrington

Placings:6/5411460-3311055204 **(6282)**
2009: 7^{3}GF, 7^{3}GF, 5^{1}GF, 7^{1}GF, 6^{0}GS, 6^{5}GF, 7^{5}GF, 6^{2}GF, 6^{0}G, 6^{4}GF,

	Starts	1st	2nd	3rd	Win & Pl
Career Total (Turf)	17	4	1	2	30457
Career Total (AW)	1	0	0	0	0

93 6/09 Rdcr 7f (0-90)H G-F £7771
93 6/09 Catt 5f212y (0-85)H G-F £4857
82 6/08 Hayd 6f (0-95)H G-F £9714
77 5/08 Muss 7f30y (0-70)H G-F £2914
Total win prize-money £25256

Going (Turf): Sf: 0-0 GS: 0-2 Gd: 0-2 **GF: 4-13** Fm: 0-0
Distance: 5f/6f: 2-10 7f-8f: 2-8 9f-13f: 0-0 14f+: 0-0
Track : LH: 1-6 RH: 1-1 **Tight: 2-6** Gall: 0-0
Aids: Bl: 0-0 Vi: 0-0 Tstrap: 0-0 Ckp: 0-0
Best Rating: 93 6/09 Rdcr 7f gd-fm

Useful; effective at 6f-7f; goes well on fast ground.

Noverre Over There (IRE)

85(89) (58)58
2-y-o b g Noverre (USA)-Shirley Moon (IRE) (Montjeu (IRE))
M E Rimmer P Burban & D E Jenkins

Placings:000545 **(7139)**
2009: 7^{0}G, 7^{0}G, 7^{0}G, 8^{5}GF, 8^{4}SD, 9^{5}SD,

	Starts	1st	2nd	3rd	Win & Pl
Career Total (Turf)	4	0	0	0	0
Career Total (AW)	2	0	0	0	0

Going (Turf): Sf: 0-0 GS: 0-0 Gd: 0-3 GF: 0-1 Fm: 0-0
Distance: 5f/6f: 0-0 7f-8f: 0-3 9f-13f: 0-3 14f+: 0-0
Track : LH: 0-2 RH: 0-0 Tight: 0-2 Gall: 0-0
Aids: Bl: 0-0 Vi: 0-0 Tstrap: 0-0 Ckp: 0-0
Best Rating: 58 10/09 Wolv 1m141y stand

Noverre To Go (IRE)

109(100) (89)98
3-y-o ch c Noverre (USA)-Ukraine Venture (Slip Anchor)
Tom Dascombe Duddy Duffy Heeney McBride

Placings:23211-403100 **(6240)**
2009: 6^{4}SD, 7^{0}GS, 6^{3}GF, 6^{1}G, 6^{0}GF, 6^{0}G,

	Starts	1st	2nd	3rd	Win & Pl
Career Total (Turf)	8	1	2	2	20892
Career Total (AW)	3	2	0	0	9259

98 8/09 Asct 6f (0-100)H GD £17230
76 12/08 GrLe 6f STD £4533
86 12/08 Ling 6f (0-85) STD £3885
Total win prize-money £25650

Going (Turf): Sf: 0-0 GS: 0-2 **Gd: 1-3** GF: 0-3 Fm: 0-0
Distance: **5f/6f: 3-8** 7f-8f: 0-3 9f-13f: 0-0 14f+: 0-0
Track : **LH: 2-2** RH: 0-2 Tight: 1-1 Gall: 1-1
Aids: Bl: 0-0 Vi: 0-0 Tstrap: 0-0 Ckp: 0-0
Best Rating: 98 8/09 Asct 6f good

Very useful; effective over 6f; acts on good and softer ground and on Polytrack; has worn a tongue tie; likes to race prominently.

Noverre To Hide (USA)

93(90) (64)54
3-y-o b g Noverre (USA)-Zanoubia (USA) (Our Emblem (USA))
J R Best Kent Bloodstock

Placings:004-40050006 **(6206)**
2009: 6^{4}GF, 8^{0}GF, 6^{0}G, 6^{5}GF, 7^{0}GF, 8^{0}SD, 6^{0}GF, 5^{6}SD,

	Starts	1st	2nd	3rd	Win & Pl
Career Total (Turf)	8	0	0	0	168
Career Total (AW)	3	0	0	0	361

Going (Turf): Sf: 0-1 GS: 0-0 Gd: 0-2 GF: 0-5 Fm: 0-0
Distance: 5f/6f: 0-6 7f-8f: 0-4 9f-13f: 0-1 14f+: 0-0
Track : LH: 0-3 RH: 0-2 Tight: 0-2 Gall: 0-1
Aids: Bl: 0-1 Vi: 0-2 Tstrap: 0-0 Ckp: 0-0
Best Rating: 64 9/08 GrLe 6f stand

Moderate sprinter; handles fast ground and Polytrack.

Novikov

77(103) (87)93
5-y-o ch g Danehill Dancer (IRE)-Ardisia (USA) (Affirmed (USA))
P D Evans (G L Moore 10/12) Nick Shutts

Placings:053125/000311-00 **(6633)**
2009: 8^{0}G, 8^{0}SS,

	Starts	1st	2nd	3rd	Win & Pl
Career Total (Turf)	12	3	1	1	20853
Career Total (AW)	2	0	0	1	703

93 9/08 Yarm 1m2f21y (0-90)H GD £7477
90 8/08 Sand 1m2f7y (0-80)H G-S £5180
88 6/07 NmkJ 1m G-S £4533
Total win prize-money £17192

Going (Turf): Sf: 0-2 **GS: 2-5** Gd: 1-4 GF: 0-1 Fm: 0-0
Distance: 5f/6f: 0-0 7f-8f: 1-7 **9f-13f: 2-7** 14f+: 0-0
Track : LH: 1-4 RH: 1-6 **Tight: 1-3** Gall: 0-2
Aids: Bl: 0-1 Vi: 0-0 Tstrap: 2-4 Ckp: 2-4
Best Rating: 93 9/08 Yarm 1m2f21y good

Useful; stays 1m; acts on most ground.

Novillero

78(88) (41)42
2-y-o b c Noverre (USA)-Fairy Story (IRE) (Persian Bold)
J C Fox Lord Mutton Racing Partnership

Placings:0005 **(7513)**
2009: 6^{0}G, 7^{0}GF, 6^{0}G, 7^{5}SD,

	Starts	1st	2nd	3rd	Win & Pl
Career Total (Turf)	3	0	0	0	
Career Total (AW)	1	0	0	0	0

Going (Turf): **Sf: 0-0 GS: 0-0 Gd: 0-2 GF: 0-1 Fm: 0-0**
Distance: 5f/6f: 0-1 7f-8f: 0-3 9f-13f: 0-0 14f+: 0-0
Track : LH: 0-0 RH: 0-1 Tight: 0-0 Gall: 0-0
Aids: Bl: 0-0 Vi: 0-0 Tstrap: 0-0 Ckp: 0-0
Best Rating: **42** 9/09 Newb 7f gd-fm

Plating-class; stays 7f; acts on Polytrack.

Now

90 **58**

3-y-o br f Where Or When (IRE)-Tup Tim (Emperor Jones (USA))
P Winkworth Mrs Jenny Willment

Placings:600-00 **(3209)**
2009: 6^{0}GF, 8^{0}G,

	Starts	1st	2nd	3rd	Win & Pl
Career Total (Turf)	5	0	0	0	0

Going (Turf): **Sf: 0-1 GS: 0-1 Gd: 0-1 GF: 0-2 Fm: 0-0**
Distance: 5f/6f: 0-1 7f-8f: 0-2 9f-13f: 0-2 14f+: 0-0
Track : LH: 0-0 RH: 0-1 Tight: 0-1 Gall: 0-0
Aids: Bl: 0-0 Vi: 0-0 Tstrap: 0-0 Ckp: 0-0
Best Rating: **58** 6/08 Gdwd 6f gd-fm

Now Look Who'shere

50

2-y-o b g Kyllachy-Where's Carol (Anfield)
E S McMahon S L Edwards

Placings:0 **(4384)**
2009: 6^{0}G,

	Starts	1st	2nd	3rd	Win & Pl
Career Total (Turf)	1	0	0	0	

Going (Turf): **Sf: 0-0 GS: 0-0 Gd: 0-1 GF: 0-0 Fm: 0-0**
Distance: 5f/6f: 0-0 7f-8f: 0-1 9f-13f: 0-0 14f+: 0-0
Track : LH: 0-0 RH: 0-0 Tight: 0-0 Gall: 0-0
Aids: Bl: 0-0 Vi: 0-0 Tstrap: 0-0 Ckp: 0-0

Now You See Me

(102) (67)**27**

5-y-o b m Anabaa (USA)-Bright Vision (Indian Ridge)
D Flood S W Lang

Placings:50/634241510013-2000 **(0794)**
2009: 5^{2}SD, 5^{0}SD, 5^{0}SD, 5^{0}SD,

	Starts	1st	2nd	3rd	Win & Pl
Career Total (Turf)	2	0	0	0	
Career Total (AW)	16	3	2	2	7343
65	12/08	Sthl	5f	(0-60)H	STD £1706
64	4/08	Wolv	5f20y	(0-55)H	STD £2047
58	3/08	Wolv	5f20y	(0-50)H	STD £1774

Total win prize-money £5528

Going (Turf): **Sf: 0-0 GS: 0-1 Gd: 0-0 GF: 0-1 Fm: 0-0**
Distance: **5f/6f: 3-14** 7f-8f: 0-4 9f-13f: 0-0 14f+: 0-0
Track : **LH: 2-13** RH: 0-1 **Tight: 2-13** Gall: 0-0
Aids: Bl: 0-0 Vi: 0-0 Tstrap: 0-0 Ckp: 0-0
Best Rating: **67** 1/09 Ling 5f stand

Modest; best over 5f; acts on Polytrack.

Nufoudh (IRE)

102 **63**

5-y-o b g Key Of Luck (USA)-Limpopo (Green Desert (USA))
Miss Tracy Waggott H Conlon

Placings:4466/05400053346504/6006464000-033140122 **(6103)**
2009: 7^{0}GF, 7^{3}GF, 7^{3}G, 7^{1}GS, 7^{4}G, 6^{0}GF, 7^{1}GF, 7^{2}G, 7^{2}GF,

	Starts	1st	2nd	3rd	Win & Pl
Career Total (Turf)	37	2	2	4	9476
63	8/09	Catt	7f	(0-60)H	G-F £2388
55	7/09	Muss	7f30y	(0-60)H	G-S £2590

Total win prize-money £4978

Going (Turf): Sf: 0-4 **GS: 1-5** Gd: 0-10 **GF: 1-15** Fm: 0-3
Distance: 5f/6f: 0-16 **7f-8f: 2-21** 9f-13f: 0-0 14f+: 0-0
Track : LH: 1-10 RH: 1-13 **Tight: 2-17** Gall: 0-2
Aids: Bl: 0-0 Vi: 0-0 Tstrap: 0-0 Ckp: 0-0
Best Rating: **65** 5/06 Haml 5f4y gd-fm

Moderate; stays 7f and acts on any ground.

Nuit Sombre (IRE)

96(85) (25)**78**

9-y-o b g Night Shift (USA)-Belair Princess (USA) (Mr Prospector (USA))
G A Harker P I Harker

Placings:4115056/2460211200005405600/0546/1000/362106/1655011310/0050002043-00030600 **(7754)**
2009: 7^{0}GF, 7^{0}G, 7^{0}G, 7^{3}GF, 7^{0}GF, 7^{6}G, 8^{0}SF, 8^{0}SD,

	Starts	1st	2nd	3rd	Win & Pl
Career Total (Turf)	62	10	5	3	81302
Career Total (AW)	6	0	0	1	353
83	11/07	Catt	7f	(0-80)H	G-F £4857
82	10/07	Catt	7f	(0-75)H	GD £3238
78	9/07	Bevl	7f100y	(0-75)H	GD £3238
69	5/07	Chep	1m2f36y		G-F £2072
57	6/06	Brig	7f214y		FRM £2590
81	7/05	Hayd	1m2f120y	(0-75)H	G-F £3733
99	7/03	Sand	1m2f7y	B(0-105)H	GD £23200
94	6/03	Ripn	1m	C(0-90)H	G-F £9343
88	8/02	Newc	7f	E	GD £3584
86	7/02	Ayr	6f	E	G-S £3570

Total win prize-money £59432

Going (Turf): Sf: 0-7 GS: 1-7 **Gd: 4-21 GF: 4-24** Fm: 1-3
Distance: 5f/6f: 1-3 **7f-8f: 6-35** 9f-13f: 3-30 14f+: 0-0
Track : **LH: 5-36** RH: 3-18 **Tight: 3-27** Gall: 0-7
Aids: Bl: 0-2 Vi: 2-5 Tstrap: 3-21 Ckp: 3-21
Best Rating: **99** 7/03 York 7f205y gd-fm

Fair handicapper/claimer; effective over 7f-1m2f; acts on most types of ground; has worn cheekpieces.

Number One Guy

96 **72**

2-y-o br c Rock Of Gibraltar (IRE)-Dubious (Darshaan)
M H Tompkins GPD Ltd

Placings:65661 **(6923)**
2009: 6^{6}G, 7^{5}G, 7^{6}G, 9^{6}GF, 8^{1}GF,

	Starts	1st	2nd	3rd	Win & Pl
Career Total (Turf)	5	1	0	0	3886
72	10/09	Yarm	1m3y	(0-75)	G-F £3885

Total win prize-money £3886

Going (Turf): Sf: 0-0 GS: 0-0 Gd: 0-3 **GF: 1-2** Fm: 0-0
Distance: 5f/6f: 0-1 7f-8f: 0-2 **9f-13f: 1-2** 14f+: 0-0
Track : LH: 0-1 RH: 0-1 Tight: 0-1 Gall: 0-0
Aids: Bl: 0-0 Vi: 0-0 Tstrap: 0-0 Ckp: 0-0
Best Rating: **72** 10/09 Yarm 1m3y gd-fm

Fair; stays 1m and enjoys quick ground.

Numide (FR)

(88) (99)**105**

6-y-o b g Highest Honor (FR)-Numidie (FR) (Baillamont (USA))
G L Moore H R Hunt

Placings:061/121506/140/505-4 **(7237)**
2009: 12^{4}SD,

	Starts	1st	2nd	3rd	Win & Pl
Career Total (Turf)	15	4	1	0	113279
Career Total (AW)	1	0	0	0	2148
113	5/07	Lonc	1m2f110y		VS £7095
113	5/06	Lonc	1m3f		VS £51103
106	2/06	Toul	1m2f110y		GD £5172
	11/05	Toul	1m2f		G-S £4255

Total win prize-money £67625

Going (Turf): Sf: 0-1 **GS: 1-2 Gd: 1-9** GF: 0-0 Fm: 0-0
Distance: 5f/6f: 0-0 7f-8f: 0-2 **9f-13f: 4-13** 14f+: 0-1
Track : LH: 0-4 **RH: 3-10** Tight: 0-1 Gall: 0-2
Aids: Bl: 0-1 Vi: 0-0 Tstrap: 0-0 Ckp: 0-0
Best Rating: **115** 6/06 Chan 1m2f110y good

Smart; ex-French; winner in Group 2 company; stays 1m3f and acts on good and softer ground; winning hurdler.

Nun Today (USA)

85(95) (59)**54**

3-y-o b f Chapel Royal (USA)-Oldupai (USA) (Gulch (USA))
Karen George (J S Moore 30/1) Mrs Isabel Fraser

Placings:0000**1**3000064-045030500000 **(7051)**
2009: 7^{0}SD, 7^{4}SD, 7^{5}SD, 7^{0}F, 7^{3}SD, 8^{0}GF, 8^{5}SD, 7^{0}SD, 6^{0}GF, 8^{0}G, 7^{0}SD, 7^{0}SD,

	Starts	1st	2nd	3rd	Win & Pl
Career Total (Turf)	8	0	0	0	
Career Total (AW)	16	1	0	2	2882
59	7/08	Wolv	7f32y		STD £2047

Total win prize-money £2047

Going (Turf): **Sf: 0-1 GS: 0-0 Gd: 0-1 GF: 0-5 Fm: 0-1**
Distance: 5f/6f: 0-2 **7f-8f: 1-20** 9f-13f: 0-2 14f+: 0-0
Track : **LH: 1-14** RH: 0-4 **Tight: 1-13** Gall: 0-0
Aids: **Bl: 1-9** Vi: 0-6 Tstrap: 0-5 Ckp: 0-5
Best Rating: **59** 7/08 Wolv 7f32y stand

Moderate; effective over 7f and acts on Polytrack; has worn a visor.

Nurai

(69) (8)

2-y-o b f Danehill Dancer (IRE)-Lady High Havens (IRE) (Bluebird (USA))
P W D'Arcy K Snell

Placings:00 **(6254)**
2009: 8^{0}SD, 7^{0}SD,

	Starts	1st	2nd	3rd	Win & Pl
Career Total (Turf)	0	0	0	0	
Career Total (AW)	2	0	0	0	

Going (Turf): **Sf: 0-0 GS: 0-0 Gd: 0-0 GF: 0-0 Fm: 0-0**
Distance: 5f/6f: 0-0 7f-8f: 0-2 9f-13f: 0-0 14f+: 0-0
Track : LH: 0-1 RH: 0-1 Tight: 0-1 Gall: 0-0
Aids: Bl: 0-0 Vi: 0-0 Tstrap: 0-0 Ckp: 0-0
Best Rating: **8** 9/09 Wolv 7f32y stand

Nurture (IRE)

103(93) (72)**101**

2-y-o ch f Bachelor Duke (USA)-Sileslan (IRE) (Singspiel (IRE))

R Hannon Mrs C Hassett

Placings:5232 **(7187)**

2009: 6^{5}SD, 5^{2}SD, 8^{3}G, 8^{2}G,

	Starts	1st	2nd	3rd	Win & Pl
Career Total (Turf)	2	0	1	1	137524
Career Total (AW)	2	0	1	0	964

Going (Turf): **Sf: 0-0 GS: 0-0 Gd: 0-2 GF: 0-0 Fm: 0-0**
Distance: 5f/6f: 0-2 7f-8f: 0-2 9f-13f: 0-0 14f+: 0-0
Track : LH: 0-1 RH: 0-2 Tight: 0-1 Gall: 0-1
Aids: Bl: 0-0 Vi: 0-0 Tstrap: 0-0 Ckp: 0-0
Best Rating: **101** 10/09 NmkR 1m good

Useful; effective over 1m; acts on good ground and on Polytrack.

Nusoor (IRE)

92(92) (62)**76**

6-y-o b g Fasliyev (USA)-Zulfaa (USA) (Bahri (USA))

Peter Grayson R Teatum And Mrs S Grayson

Placings:1300400/0220302435540466341000000/5661232 1600-0000 **(2682)**

2009: 5^{0}G, 5^{0}GF, 5^{0}GF, 5^{0}SD,

	Starts	1st	2nd	3rd	Win & Pl
Career Total (Turf)	27	3	2	3	16065
Career Total (AW)	19	1	3	2	5066

76 7/08 Chep 5f16y (0-70)H G-F £2914
66 6/08 Ling 5f (0-75)H G-F £2331
72 9/07 Wolv 5f216y (0-65)H STD £2388
71 5/06 Thsk 6f GD £4533
Total win prize-money £12168

Going (Turf): Sf: 0-2 GS: 0-5 Gd: 1-6 **GF: 2-13** Fm: 0-1
Distance: **5f/6f: 4-44** 7f-8f: 0-2 9f-13f: 0-0 14f+: 0-0
Track : **LH: 1-17** RH: 0-1 **Tight: 1-17** Gall: 0-2
Aids: Bl: 1-17 **Vi: 2-13** Tstrap: 0-0 Ckp: 0-0
Best Rating: **81** 7/06 Hayd 6f gd-fm

Modest sprinter who likes to front-run; effective from 5f-6f; acts on most ground and both All-Weather surfaces; has worn blinkers and a visor.

Nut Hand (IRE)

103(79) (16)**57**

3-y-o b g Noverre (USA)-Walnut Lady (Forzando)

T D Easterby Habton Farms

Placings:005-003555 **(4822)**

2009: 7^{0}GF, 8^{0}F, 12^{3}F, 12^{5}GF, 14^{5}SD, 10^{5}GF,

	Starts	1st	2nd	3rd	Win & Pl
Career Total (Turf)	8	0	0	1	361
Career Total (AW)	1	0	0	0	93

Going (Turf): **Sf: 0-1 GS: 0-1 Gd: 0-0 GF: 0-4 Fm: 0-2**
Distance: 5f/6f: 0-0 7f-8f: 0-5 9f-13f: 0-3 14f+: 0-1
Track : LH: 0-4 RH: 0-3 Tight: 0-3 Gall: 0-0
Aids: Bl: 0-0 Vi: 0-0 Tstrap: 0-0 Ckp: 0-0
Best Rating: **57** 9/08 Rdcr 7f gd-sft

Moderate sort; stayed 1m4f; acted on fast ground; (DEAD).

Nuts About You (IRE)

45(59)

2-y-o b f Rakti-La Noisette (Rock Hopper)

A Berry Mr and Mrs Calderbank

Placings:0000 **(3572)**

2009: 5^{0}GF, 5^{0}SD, 7^{0}GF, 6^{0}G,

	Starts	1st	2nd	3rd	Win & Pl
Career Total (Turf)	3	0	0	0	
Career Total (AW)	1	0	0	0	

Going (Turf): **Sf: 0-0 GS: 0-0 Gd: 0-1 GF: 0-2 Fm: 0-0**
Distance: 5f/6f: 0-3 7f-8f: 0-1 9f-13f: 0-0 14f+: 0-0
Track : LH: 0-1 RH: 0-0 Tight: 0-1 Gall: 0-0
Aids: Bl: 0-0 Vi: 0-0 Tstrap: 0-0 Ckp: 0-0

Nyetimber (USA)

(88) (55)

3-y-o ch c Forest Wildcat (USA)-Once Around (CAN) (You And I (USA))

J A Osborne J A Osborne

Placings:6545 **(7712)**

2009: 9^{6}SD, 12^{5}SD, 13^{4}SD, 12^{5}SD,

	Starts	1st	2nd	3rd	Win & Pl
Career Total (Turf)	0	0	0	0	
Career Total (AW)	4	0	0	0	0

Going (Turf): **Sf: 0-0 GS: 0-0 Gd: 0-0 GF: 0-0 Fm: 0-0**
Distance: 5f/6f: 0-0 7f-8f: 0-0 9f-13f: 0-3 14f+: 0-1
Track : LH: 0-3 RH: 0-1 Tight: 0-2 Gall: 0-0
Aids: Bl: 0-0 Vi: 0-0 Tstrap: 0-0 Ckp: 0-0
Best Rating: **55** 11/09 Wolv 1m5f194y stand

Oak Leaves

87 **56**

2-y-o b f Mark Of Esteem (IRE)-Exotic Forest (Dominion)

J G Portman Mrs R Pease

Placings:000 **(7029)**

2009: 6^{0}GF, 6^{0}GF, 8^{0}S,

	Starts	1st	2nd	3rd	Win & Pl
Career Total (Turf)	3	0	0	0	

Going (Turf): **Sf: 0-1 GS: 0-0 Gd: 0-0 GF: 0-2 Fm: 0-0**
Distance: 5f/6f: 0-1 7f-8f: 0-2 9f-13f: 0-0 14f+: 0-0
Track : LH: 0-0 RH: 0-0 Tight: 0-0 Gall: 0-1
Aids: Bl: 0-0 Vi: 0-0 Tstrap: 0-0 Ckp: 0-0
Best Rating: **56** 8/09 Newb 6f8y gd-fm

Oakbridge (IRE)

(92) (40)**55**

7-y-o b g Indian Ridge-Chauncy Lane (IRE) (Sadler's Wells (USA))

R Brotherton Mrs Carol Newman

Placings:015000000/05/010/000-0 **(0117)**

2009: 11^{0}SD,

	Starts	1st	2nd	3rd	Win & Pl
Career Total (Turf)	7	1	0	0	5558
Career Total (AW)	11	1	0	0	2389

68 2/07 Wolv 1m1f103y (0-50)H SS £2388
75 7/05 Sals 6f G-F £5557
Total win prize-money £7947

Going (Turf): Sf: 0-0 GS: 0-1 Gd: 0-2 **GF: 1-4** Fm: 0-0
Distance: 5f/6f: 1-4 7f-8f: 0-7 9f-13f: 1-7 14f+: 0-0
Track : **LH: 1-11** RH: 0-2 **Tight: 1-7** Gall: 0-0
Aids: Bl: 0-1 Vi: 0-0 Tstrap: 0-0 Ckp: 0-0
Best Rating: **75** 7/05 Sals 6f gd-fm

Moderate sort; probably stays seven furlongs; acts on fast ground.

Oasis Dancer

104 **95**

2-y-o br/gr c Oasis Dream-Good Enough (FR) (Mukaddamah (USA))

R M Beckett Mrs M E Slade

Placings:021 **(6478)**

2009: 7^{0}GF, 7^{2}G, 7^{1}GF,

	Starts	1st	2nd	3rd	Win & Pl
Career Total (Turf)	3	1	1	0	542760

95 10/09 NmkR 7f G-F £541700
Total win prize-money £541700

Going (Turf): Sf: 0-0 GS: 0-0 Gd: 0-1 **GF: 1-2** Fm: 0-0
Distance: 5f/6f: 0-0 **7f-8f: 1-3** 9f-13f: 0-0 14f+: 0-0
Track : LH: 0-0 RH: 0-2 Tight: 0-0 Gall: 0-0
Aids: Bl: 0-0 Vi: 0-0 Tstrap: 0-0 Ckp: 0-0
Best Rating: **95** 10/09 NmkR 7f gd-fm

Very useful; stays 7f and acts on good and faster ground.

Oasis Jade

95(92) (64)**68**

2-y-o b f Oasis Dream-Royal Jade (Last Tycoon)

G L Moore D J Deer

Placings:5356040 **(6905)**

2009: 5^{5}GF, 5^{3}GF, 6^{5}GF, 5^{6}GF, 7^{0}GF, 6^{4}SD, 6^{0}G,

	Starts	1st	2nd	3rd	Win & Pl
Career Total (Turf)	6	0	0	1	530
Career Total (AW)	1	0	0	0	192

Going (Turf): **Sf: 0-0 GS: 0-0 Gd: 0-1 GF: 0-5 Fm: 0-0**
Distance: 5f/6f: 0-6 7f-8f: 0-1 9f-13f: 0-0 14f+: 0-0
Track : LH: 0-1 RH: 0-1 Tight: 0-0 Gall: 0-2
Aids: Bl: 0-0 Vi: 0-0 Tstrap: 0-0 Ckp: 0-0
Best Rating: **68** 7/09 Wind 6f gd-fm

Oasis Knight (IRE)

107 **104**

3-y-o b c Oasis Dream-Generous Lady (Generous (IRE))

M P Tregoning Lady Tennant

Placings:0031-01325 **(6854)**

2009: 10^{0}GF, 13^{1}GF, 14^{3}G, 16^{2}GF, 16^{5}G,

	Starts	1st	2nd	3rd	Win & Pl
Career Total (Turf)	9	2	1	2	29875

94 8/09 Newb 1m5f61y (0-90)H G-F £7771
84 9/08 NmkR 1m1f (0-85) G-F £6476
Total win prize-money £14247

Going (Turf): Sf: 0-0 GS: 0-0 Gd: 0-4 **GF: 2-5** Fm: 0-0
Distance: 5f/6f: 0-0 7f-8f: 0-3 9f-13f: 1-2 14f+: 1-4
Track : **LH: 1-1** RH: 0-4 Tight: 0-1 **Gall: 1-3**
Aids: Bl: 0-0 **Vi: 1-4** Tstrap: 0-0 Ckp: 0-0
Best Rating: **104** 10/09 NmkR 2m good

Very useful; stays 1m6f; handles quick ground; has worn a visor.

Obara D'Avril (FR)

95 **57**

7-y-o gr m April Night (FR)-Baraka De Thaix II (FR) (Olmeto)

S G West Miss Kate Milligan

Placings:50363 **(6769)**

2009: 11^{5}GF, 10^{0}GS, 10^{3}GF, 15^{6}G, 12^{3}GS,

	Starts	1st	2nd	3rd	Win & Pl
Career Total (Turf)	5	0	0	2	750

Going (Turf): Sf: 0-0 GS: 0-2 Gd: 0-1 GF: 0-2 Fm: 0-0
Distance: 5f/6f: 0-0 7f-8f: 0-0 9f-13f: 0-4 14f+: 0-1
Track : LH: 0-5 RH: 0-0 Tight: 0-2 Gall: 0-2
Aids: Bl: 0-0 Vi: 0-0 Tstrap: 0-0 Ckp: 0-0
Best Rating: **57** 5/09 Catt 1m3f214y gd-fm

Obe Brave

98(105) (65)**86**

6-y-o b g Agnes World (USA)-Pass The Rose (IRE) (Thatching)

Lee Smyth Mark Devlin

Placings:1/212400200/1002000/000000010104-000005130000003600 **(7860)**

2009: 8^{0}G, 6^{0}G, 7^{0}S, 7^{0}HY, 7^{0}G, 7^{5}GF, 7^{1}SD, 5^{3}SD, 6^{0}GF, 7^{0}SD, 8^{0}SD, 8^{0}SD, 7^{3}SD, 5^{6}SD, 7^{0}SD, 7^{0}SD,

	Starts	1st	2nd	3rd	Win & Pl
Career Total (Turf)	35	5	4	0	77292
Career Total (AW)	10	1	0	2	3694

65	9/09	Wolv	7f32y	(0-55)H	STD	£2729
73	9/08	Brig	6f209y		G-F	£1942
74	9/08	Haml	6f5y		G-S	£2388
107	1/07	Ndas	7f110y	(90-105)H	GD	£33673
107	4/06	Ripn	6f	(0-95)H	GD	£10906
87	10/05	York	6f		GD	£5668

Total win prize-money £57308

Going (Turf): Sf: 0-8 GS: 1-6 **Gd: 3-14** GF: 1-7 Fm: 0-0
Distance: 5f/6f: 2-20 **7f-8f: 4-24** 9f-13f: 0-1 14f+: 0-0
Track : **LH: 3-18** RH: 0-3 Tight: 1-9 Gall: 1-6
Aids: Bl: 0-4 Vi: 0-0 Tstrap: 1-6 Ckp: 1-6
Best Rating: **109** 8/07 Ripn 6f good

Moderate; effective over 6f-7f; acts on most ground; has worn cheekpieces.

Obe Gold

104(107) (93)**98**

7-y-o b g Namaqualand (USA)-Gagajulu (Al Hareb (USA))

P Howling (Miss D Mountain 15/8) Paul Howling

Placings:31424U331125/12400400000020/163160504000460/5400006426500165/06312060000-215306311335400032431 **(7879)**

2009: 5^{2}SD, 6^{1}SD, 5^{5}GF, 6^{3}F, 6^{0}GF, 5^{6}GF, 5^{3}GF, 5^{1}GF, 5^{1}S, 5^{3}G, 5^{3}GF, 6^{5}GF, 6^{4}G, 6^{0}SD, 7^{0}SD, 6^{3}SD, 7^{2}SD, 7^{4}SD, 7^{3}SD, 6^{1}SD,

	Starts	1st	2nd	3rd	Win & Pl
Career Total (Turf)	76	10	5	9	351050
Career Total (AW)	11	2	3	2	13061

	12/09	Ling	6f		STD	£1978
75	7/09	Catt	5f		SFT	£2388
87	7/09	Haml	5f4y		G-F	£2266
93	3/09	Ling	6f	(0-85)H	STD	£4857
98	5/08	Hayd	6f	(0-85)H	G-F	£5310
93	10/07	Gdwd	6f	(0-95)H	SFT	£7124
109	2/06	Ndas	6f	(95-110)H	G-S	£45348
107	1/06	Ndas	6f110y	(95-110)H	G-F	£45348
108	3/05	Kemp	6f		GD	£5945
97	10/04	Rdcr	6f		G-F	£128412
102	9/04	NmkR	6f	(0-95)H	GD	£13806
79	5/04	Sals	5f	D	GD	£4663

Total win prize-money £267451

Going (Turf): Sf: 2-14 GS: 1-4 Gd: 3-21 **GF: 4-31** Fm: 0-4
Distance: **5f/6f: 11-67** 7f-8f: 1-20 9f-13f: 0-0 14f+: 0-0
Track : **LH: 4-25** RH: 0-6 Tight: 2-9 Gall: 2-15
Aids: Bl: 0-2 **Vi: 8-50** Tstrap: 0-1 Ckp: 0-1
Best Rating: **109** 2/06 Ndas 6f gd-sft

Modest; effective over 5f-7f; acts on most ground; goes on Polytrack; has worn blinkers, cheekpieces and a visor.

Obe One

94(93) (48)**57**

9-y-o b g Puissance-Plum Bold (Be My Guest (USA))

A Berry Alan Berry

Placings:53132632044/034363010000/0006402306040445050/504000/46002200/000005003340000/5062534024320156030-0060000500300 **(6414)**

2009: 5^{0}SD, 5^{0}GF, 6^{6}GS, 5^{0}GF, 5^{0}GF, 6^{0}GF, 6^{0}GF, 6^{5}GF, 6^{0}GF, 6^{0}GS, 5^{3}GS, 7^{0}S, 7^{0}GF,

	Starts	1st	2nd	3rd	Win & Pl
Career Total (Turf)	95	3	8	12	38056
Career Total (AW)	7	0	0	1	282

57	9/08	Haml	5f4y	(0-65)H	SFT	£2266
84	8/03	Gdwd	5f	C(0-90)H	GD	£9175
70	5/02	Muss	5f	F	G-F	£3388

Total win prize-money £14831

Going (Turf): **Sf: 1-13** GS: 0-14 **Gd: 1-17** **GF: 1-45** Fm: 0-6
Distance: **5f/6f: 3-76** 7f-8f: 0-26 9f-13f: 0-0 14f+: 0-0
Track : LH: 0-19 RH: 0-10 Tight: 0-13 Gall: 0-2
Aids: Bl: 0-8 Vi: 0-0 Tstrap: 0-2 Ckp: 0-2
Best Rating: **84** 8/03 Gdwd 5f good

Moderate; effective over 5f-7f; acts on most ground and on Polytrack; has worn blinkers.

Obe Royal

98(111) (81)**76**

5-y-o b g Wizard King-Gagajulu (Al Hareb (USA))

P D Evans J E Abbey

Placings:560300/40232445021/4214353446252503026044000054-35652341121222014054000630000 **(6024)**

2009: 6^{3}SD, 6^{5}SD, 5^{6}SD, 6^{5}SD, 6^{2}SD, 6^{3}SD, 6^{4}SD, 7^{1}SS, 7^{1}SD, 7^{2}SD, 7^{1}SD, 7^{2}SD, 7^{2}SD, 7^{2}SD, 7^{0}SD, 7^{1}SD, 7^{4}SD, 7^{0}G, 7^{5}SD, 7^{4}SD, 8^{0}SD,

	Starts	1st	2nd	3rd	Win & Pl
Career Total (Turf)	26	0	4	3	5637
Career Total (AW)	47	6	8	5	25257

81	4/09	Kemp	7f	(0-80)H	STD	£4727
71	3/09	Sthl	7f		STD	£2047
76	2/09	Sthl	7f	(0-70)H	STD	£2729
69	2/09	Sthl	7f		SS	£2047
77	1/08	Wolv	5f216y	(0-70)H	STD	£2590
77	1/08	Wolv	7f32y		STD	£2047

Total win prize-money £16190

Going (Turf): **Sf: 0-8** **GS: 0-5** **Gd: 0-3** **GF: 0-10** **Fm: 0-0**
Distance: 5f/6f: 1-29 **7f-8f: 5-40** 9f-13f: 0-4 14f+: 0-0
Track : **LH: 5-49** RH: 1-11 **Tight: 2-32** Gall: 0-5
Aids: Bl: 3-48 Vi: 3-9 Tstrap: 0-8 Ckp: 0-8
Best Rating: **81** 4/09 Kemp 7f stand

Fair; effective over 5f-7f; acts on most ground on turf; goes on sand; has worn blinkers and a visor.

Oberlin (USA)

(106) (74)**63**

4-y-o ch g Gone West (USA)-Balanchine (USA) (Storm Bird (CAN))

M Wigham (T Keddy 19/3) Mrs Roxanne Simms

Placings:256/23100050260002-0000 **(0877)**

2009: 14^{0}SS, 16^{0}SD, 16^{0}SD, 12^{0}SD,

	Starts	1st	2nd	3rd	Win & Pl
Career Total (Turf)	7	0	0	0	0
Career Total (AW)	13	1	4	1	7540

58	2/08	Sthl	1m3f	SS	£2457

Total win prize-money £2457

Going (Turf): **Sf: 0-1** **GS: 0-1** **Gd: 0-2** **GF: 0-3** **Fm: 0-0**
Distance: 5f/6f: 0-0 7f-8f: 0-4 **9f-13f: 1-9** 14f+: 0-7
Track : **LH: 1-16** RH: 0-3 Tight: 0-6 Gall: 0-2
Aids: Bl: 0-1 Vi: 0-0 Tstrap: 0-1 Ckp: 0-1
Best Rating: **77** 9/07 Wolv 1m141y stand

Modest; stays 1m3f; acts on Polytrack and on Fibresand.

Obezyana (USA)

94(99) (79)**85**

7-y-o ch g Rahy (USA)-Polish Treaty (USA) (Danzig (USA))

A Bailey A Bailey

Placings:02/600011/60/000/0051205056305425245245660 **(3076)**

2009: 7^{5}SF, 8^{2}SD, 8^{4}SD, 8^{5}GF, 8^{6}SD, 7^{6}GF, 8^{0}G,

	Starts	1st	2nd	3rd	Win & Pl
Career Total (Turf)	23	2	1	1	14081
Career Total (AW)	15	1	4	0	10328

85	5/08	Hayd	1m30y	(0-80)H	G-F	£5180
90	11/05	Ling	1m	(0-80)H	STD	£5816
79	10/05	Pont	1m4y		GD	£4823

Total win prize-money £15820

Going (Turf): Sf: 0-2 GS: 0-3 **Gd: 1-8** **GF: 1-10** Fm: 0-0
Distance: 5f/6f: 0-0 7f-8f: 1-25 **9f-13f: 2-13** 14f+: 0-0
Track : **LH: 3-28** RH: 0-2 **Tight: 1-16** Gall: 0-6
Aids: **Bl: 2-5** Vi: 0-3 Tstrap: 0-4 Ckp: 0-4
Best Rating: **90** 11/05 Ling 1m stand

Fair; effective over 1m; acts on a sound surface on turf; goes on Polytrack; has worn a tongue tie, and most forms of headgear.

Observatory Star (IRE)

106 **88**

6-y-o br g Observatory (USA)-Pink Sovietstaia (FR) (Soviet Star (USA))

T D Easterby Mr And Mrs J D Cotton

Placings:51050/00000631/23621225/225015-524326330 **(7287)**

2009: 8^{5}GF, 8^{2}G, 7^{4}GF, 8^{3}GS, 8^{2}GF, 8^{6}GF, 7^{3}GS, 8^{3}G, 7^{0}S,

	Starts	1st	2nd	3rd	Win & Pl
Career Total (Turf)	36	4	8	5	46176

85	8/08	Thsk	1m	(0-90)H	GD	£8159
77	8/07	Rdcr	1m	(0-80)H	G-F	£5181
71	10/06	Catt	5f212y	(0-75)H	SFT	£3886
73	6/05	Ripn	6f		G-F	£4114

Total win prize-money £21343

Going (Turf): Sf: 1-9 GS: 0-5 Gd: 1-8 **GF: 2-12** Fm: 0-2
Distance: 5f/6f: 2-12 7f-8f: 2-18 9f-13f: 0-6 14f+: 0-0
Track : **LH: 2-11** RH: 0-8 **Tight: 2-7** Gall: 0-2
Aids: Bl: 1-10 Vi: 0-0 Tstrap: 2-15 Ckp: 2-15
Best Rating: **88** 10/09 Nott 1m75y good

Fair; stays 1m; acts on fast and soft ground; has worn blinkers, a tongue tie and cheekpieces.

Obvious

82(87) (57)26

3-y-o b f Falbrav (IRE)-Bright And Clear (Danehill (USA))

Miss J Feilden Geegeez.co.uk

Placings:0-000 (7796)

2009: 10^{0}G, 9^{0}GF, 7^{0}SS,

	Starts	1st	2nd	3rd	Win & Pl
Career Total (Turf)	2	0	0	0	
Career Total (AW)	2	0	0	0	

Going (Turf): **Sf: 0-0 GS: 0-0 Gd: 0-1 GF: 0-1 Fm: 0-0**
Distance: 5f/6f: 0-0 7f-8f: 0-2 9f-13f: 0-2 14f+: 0-0
Track : LH: 0-2 RH: 0-2 Tight: 0-1 Gall: 0-0
Aids: Bl: 0-0 Vi: 0-0 Tstrap: 0-0 Ckp: 0-0
Best Rating: **57** 9/08 Kemp 7f stand

Ocarito (GER)

(73) (4)

8-y-o b g Auenadler (GER)-Okkasion (Konigsstuhl (GER))

G F Bridgwater Mrs Gail Bridgwater

Placings:0/16/101214145/3/00 (0256)

2009: 10^{0}SD, 8^{0}SD,

	Starts	1st	2nd	3rd	Win & Pl
Career Total (Turf)	11	4	1	0	19986
Career Total (AW)	4	1	0	1	2154

	Date	Course	Dist		Going	Prize
	7/05	BDob	1m165y	H	GD	£7304
	6/05	Hamb	1m1f	H	SFT	£4965
	4/05	Duss	1m110y		GD	£2482
	3/05	Dort	1m110y		STD	£1843
	8/04	Mulh	1m		SFT	£2042

Total win prize-money £18638

Going (Turf): **Sf: 2-5** GS: 0-1 **Gd: 2-5** GF: 0-0 Fm: 0-0
Distance: 5f/6f: 0-0 7f-8f: 1-6 **9f-13f: 4-9** 14f+: 0-0
Track : LH: 0-3 RH: 0-2 Tight: 0-2 Gall: 0-0
Aids: Bl: 0-0 Vi: 0-0 Tstrap: 0-0 Ckp: 0-0
Best Rating: **4** 1/09 Wolv 1m141y stand

Occasion

85 32

4-y-o b f Zamindar (USA)-Set Fair (USA) (Alleged (USA))

G M Moore Mrs D N B Pearson

Placings:00-0 (4277)

2009: 7^{0}G,

	Starts	1st	2nd	3rd	Win & Pl
Career Total (Turf)	3	0	0	0	

Going (Turf): **Sf: 0-0 GS: 0-1 Gd: 0-2 GF: 0-0 Fm: 0-0**
Distance: 5f/6f: 0-0 7f-8f: 0-2 9f-13f: 0-1 14f+: 0-0
Track : LH: 0-3 RH: 0-0 Tight: 0-2 Gall: 0-0
Aids: Bl: 0-0 Vi: 0-0 Tstrap: 0-0 Ckp: 0-0
Best Rating: **32** 7/09 Thsk 7f good

Ocean Blaze

105(103) (83)88

5-y-o b m Polar Prince (IRE)-La Belle Vie (Indian King (USA))

B R Millman Gary Hancock (Staffs)

Placings:0503/0312240151/52302600-625053511662 (6972)

2009: 5^{6}G, 5^{2}GF, 5^{5}GF, 5^{0}G, 5^{5}GF, 5^{3}GF, 5^{5}GF, 5^{1}GF, 5^{1}GF, 5^{6}SD, 5^{6}G, 5^{2}SD,

	Starts	1st	2nd	3rd	Win & Pl
Career Total (Turf)	32	5	5	4	29269
Career Total (AW)	2	0	1	0	1407

	Date	Course	Dist		Going	Prize
87	9/09	NmkR	5f	(0-75)H	G-F	£3885
78	9/09	Gdwd	5f	(0-85)H	G-F	£5180
79	10/07	Rdcr	5f	(0-75)H	GD	£2817
76	9/07	Gdwd	5f	(0-75)H	G-F	£3238
66	6/07	Bath	5f11y	(0-70)H	GD	£2914

Total win prize-money £18038

Going (Turf): Sf: 0-2 GS: 0-2 Gd: 2-11 **GF: 3-15** Fm: 0-2
Distance: **5f/6f: 5-31** 7f-8f: 0-3 9f-13f: 0-0 14f+: 0-0
Track : **LH: 1-6** RH: 0-1 Tight: 0-0 **Gall: 1-8**
Aids: Bl: 0-0 Vi: 0-0 Tstrap: 0-0 Ckp: 0-0
Best Rating: **88** 7/08 NmkJ 5f gd-fm

Fair; effective at around 5f; acts on fast ground; goes on Polytrack.

Ocean Club

(76) (36)

2-y-o ch g Storming Home-Strictly Cool (USA) (Bering)

B W Hills H R Mould

Placings:0 (6943)

2009: 7^{0}SD,

	Starts	1st	2nd	3rd	Win & Pl
Career Total (Turf)	0	0	0	0	
Career Total (AW)	1	0	0	0	

Going (Turf): **Sf: 0-0 GS: 0-0 Gd: 0-0 GF: 0-0 Fm: 0-0**
Distance: 5f/6f: 0-0 7f-8f: 0-1 9f-13f: 0-0 14f+: 0-0
Track : LH: 0-0 RH: 0-1 Tight: 0-0 Gall: 0-0
Aids: Bl: 0-0 Vi: 0-0 Tstrap: 0-0 Ckp: 0-0
Best Rating: **36** 10/09 Kemp 7f stand

Ocean Countess (IRE)

101(91) (61)72

3-y-o b f Storming Home-Pennycairn (Last Tycoon)

Miss J Feilden Ocean Trailers Ltd

Placings:0-0010026011156 (7742)

2009: 8^{0}SD, 8^{0}G, 7^{1}GF, 8^{0}SD, 9^{0}GF, 6^{2}F, 8^{6}GF, 7^{0}GF, 6^{1}GF, 7^{1}G, 7^{1}G, 8^{5}SD, 8^{6}SD,

	Starts	1st	2nd	3rd	Win & Pl
Career Total (Turf)	10	4	1	0	11176
Career Total (AW)	4	0	0	0	0

	Date	Course	Dist		Going	Prize
72	10/09	Brig	7f214y	(0-63)H	GD	£2590
63	10/09	Brig	7f214y	(0-60)H	GD	£2590
63	9/09	Brig	6f209y	(0-60)H	G-F	£2460
55	5/09	Yarm	7f3y	(0-55)	G-F	£2590

Total win prize-money £10231

Going (Turf): Sf: 0-0 GS: 0-0 **Gd: 2-4 GF: 2-5** Fm: 0-1
Distance: 5f/6f: 0-0 **7f-8f: 4-10** 9f-13f: 0-4 14f+: 0-0
Track : **LH: 3-7** RH: 0-2 Tight: 0-3 Gall: 0-0
Aids: Bl: 0-0 Vi: 0-4 Tstrap: 0-0 Ckp: 0-0
Best Rating: **72** 10/09 Brig 7f214y good

Modest; stays 1m and acts on good and faster ground; likes Brighton.

Ocean Glory (IRE)

78(76) (46)16

4-y-o b g Redback-Finty (IRE) (Entrepreneur)

Patrick Morris Lloyd Partnership

Placings:1000006/6-0 (2801)

2009: 5^{0}F,

	Starts	1st	2nd	3rd	Win & Pl
Career Total (Turf)	3	1	0	0	3562
Career Total (AW)	6	0	0	0	0

	Date	Course	Dist	Going	Prize
63	9/07	Wwck	5f	G-F	£3562

Total win prize-money £3562

Going (Turf): Sf: 0-0 GS: 0-0 Gd: 0-1 **GF: 1-1** Fm: 0-1
Distance: **5f/6f: 1-8** 7f-8f: 0-1 9f-13f: 0-0 14f+: 0-0
Track : **LH: 1-4** RH: 0-3 Tight: 0-3 Gall: 0-0
Aids: Bl: 0-0 Vi: 0-0 Tstrap: 0-0 Ckp: 0-0
Best Rating: **63** 9/07 Wwck 5f gd-fm

Ocean Legend (IRE)

97(106) (84)78

4-y-o b g Night Shift (USA)-Rose Of Mooncoin (IRE) (Brief Truce (USA))

Miss J Feilden Ocean Trailers Ltd

Placings:03/321232305302354-25304506030001656 (7631)

2009: 8^{2}SD, 8^{5}SD, 8^{3}SD, 8^{0}SD, 8^{4}G, 8^{5}SD, 8^{0}G, 8^{6}SD, 8^{0}SD, 7^{3}G, 8^{0}SD, 7^{0}SD, 7^{0}SD, 8^{1}SS, 7^{6}GF, 8^{5}SD, 8^{6}SD,

	Starts	1st	2nd	3rd	Win & Pl
Career Total (Turf)	7	0	1	1	1921
Career Total (AW)	27	2	4	7	14139

	Date	Course	Dist	Going	Prize
73	10/09	Ling	1m	SS	£2047
74	3/08	Sthl	1m	STD	£2457

Total win prize-money £4504

Going (Turf): **Sf: 0-0 GS: 0-1 Gd: 0-4 GF: 0-2 Fm: 0-0**
Distance: 5f/6f: 0-1 **7f-8f: 2-27** 9f-13f: 0-6 14f+: 0-0
Track : **LH: 2-13** RH: 0-17 **Tight: 1-7** Gall: 0-2
Aids: Bl: 0-0 Vi: 0-3 Tstrap: 0-0 Ckp: 0-0
Best Rating: **84** 2/09 Kemp 1m stand

Modest; effective over 7f-1m2f; acts on good and easy ground; goes on sand; has worn a visor.

Ocean Of Peace (FR)

95(95) (54)53

6-y-o b g Volochine (IRE)-Sumatra (IRE) (Mukaddamah (USA))

M R Bosley Mrs Jean M O'Connor

Placings:0/04465124406024/00000420/061100003410P0-64306 (6966)

2009: 11^{6}S, 11^{4}GF, 11^{3}SD, 12^{0}SD, 9^{6}G,

	Starts	1st	2nd	3rd	Win & Pl
Career Total (Turf)	34	4	3	1	31848
Career Total (AW)	8	0	0	1	3750

	Date	Course	Dist		Going	Prize
	8/08	Vich	1m5f		HVY	£4779
54	4/08	Cros	2m	H	GD	£5882
56	4/08	Nanc	1m4f		GD	£4779
	2/06	Lyrh	1m1f110y		SFT	£4482

Total win prize-money £19923

Going (Turf): **Sf: 2-9** GS: 0-8 **Gd: 2-11** GF: 0-1 Fm: 0-0
Distance: 5f/6f: 0-0 7f-8f: 0-3 **9f-13f: 3-35** 14f+: 1-4
Track : LH: 0-5 RH: 0-6 Tight: 0-0 Gall: 0-1
Aids: Bl: 0-0 Vi: 0-0 Tstrap: 0-0 Ckp: 0-0
Best Rating: **78** 7/06 Deau 1m1f110y stand

Modest; stays 1m4f; acts on Polytrack.

Ocean Pride (IRE)

(96) (52)**82**
6-y-o b g Lend A Hand-Irish Understudy (ITY) (In The Wings)
L Wells R P Behan

Placings:3132416303/5**0044100000155/56/45630-0** **(0346)**
2009: 16^{0}SD,

	Starts	1st	2nd	3rd	Win & Pl
Career Total (Turf)	**18**	**3**	**0**	**4**	**20507**
Career Total (AW)	**14**	**1**	**1**	**1**	**4005**

58 12/06 Ling 1m4f STD £2388
82 6/06 Folk 7f (0-85)H GD £5505
83 8/05 Sand 7f16y SFT £5005
71 5/05 Chep 5f16y G-S £2926
Total win prize-money £15825

Going (Turf): **Sf: 1-4 GS: 1-5 Gd: 1-4** GF: 0-5 Fm: 0-0
Distance: 5f/6f: 1-5 **7f-8f: 2-14** 9f-13f: 1-12 14f+: 0-1
Track : LH: 1-16 RH: 1-8 **Tight: 1-11** Gall: 0-1
Aids: **Bl: 1-9** Vi: 0-0 Tstrap: 0-2 Ckp: 0-2
Best Rating: **87** 11/05 Donc 7f soft

Fair; stays 1m4f (in a moderately run race); acts on most ground and Polytrack, yet seems at his best with cut; has won in blinkers and a tongue tie.

Ocean Rosie (IRE)

(79) (40)
2-y-o b f One Cool Cat (USA)-Rose Of Mooncoin (IRE) (Brief Truce (USA))
Miss J Feilden Ocean Trailers Ltd

Placings:0 **(6164)**
2009: 7^{0}SD,

	Starts	1st	2nd	3rd	Win & Pl
Career Total (Turf)	**0**	**0**	**0**	**0**	
Career Total (AW)	**1**	**0**	**0**	**0**	

Going (Turf): **Sf: 0-0 GS: 0-0 Gd: 0-0 GF: 0-0 Fm: 0-0**
Distance: 5f/6f: 0-0 7f-8f: 0-1 9f-13f: 0-0 14f+: 0-0
Track : LH: 0-0 RH: 0-1 Tight: 0-0 Gall: 0-0
Aids: Bl: 0-0 Vi: 0-0 Tstrap: 0-0 Ckp: 0-0
Best Rating: **40** 9/09 Kemp 7f stand

Ocean Transit (IRE)

103(93) (74)**87**
4-y-o b f Trans Island-Wings Awarded (Shareef Dancer (USA))
R J Price Ocean's Five

Placings:00012U1624/6-2501220P0340 **(7287)**
2009: 7^{2}GF, 5^{5}GF, 8^{0}GF, 7^{1}GS, 7^{2}GF, 8^{2}GS, 9^{0}G, 8^{P}G, 10^{0}G, 7^{3}S, 8^{4}G, 7^{0}S,

	Starts	1st	2nd	3rd	Win & Pl
Career Total (Turf)	**21**	**3**	**5**	**1**	**24404**
Career Total (AW)	**2**	**0**	**0**	**0**	**0**

82 6/09 Wwck 7f26y (0-85)H G-S £6476
75 8/07 Wind 6f G-F £3886
56 5/07 Chep 6f16y G-S £2047
Total win prize-money £12410

Going (Turf): Sf: 0-2 **GS: 2-4** Gd: 0-5 GF: 1-9 Fm: 0-1
Distance: 5f/6f: 1-9 **7f-8f: 2-10** 9f-13f: 0-4 14f+: 0-0
Track : **LH: 1-7** RH: 0-2 Tight: 0-2 **Gall: 1-3**
Aids: Bl: 0-0 Vi: 0-0 Tstrap: 0-0 Ckp: 0-0
Best Rating: **87** 7/09 Newb 1m gd-sft

Useful; stays 1m; acts on fast and soft ground.

Ocean's Minstrel

106(105) (98)**101**
3-y-o b c Pivotal-Minstrel's Dance (CAN) (Pleasant Colony (USA))
J Ryan Ocean Trailers Ltd

Placings:5451-101040 **(4521)**
2009: 8^{1}SD, 8^{0}GF, 7^{1}G, 7^{0}GF, 7^{4}GF, 8^{0}S,

	Starts	1st	2nd	3rd	Win & Pl
Career Total (Turf)	**7**	**1**	**0**	**0**	**24856**
Career Total (AW)	**3**	**2**	**0**	**0**	**26235**

100 6/09 Epsm 7f GD £22708
98 4/09 Ling 1m STD £22708
74 12/08 Kemp 1m2f STD £3238
Total win prize-money £48654

Going (Turf): Sf: 0-2 GS: 0-0 **Gd: 1-1** GF: 0-3 Fm: 0-1
Distance: 5f/6f: 0-0 **7f-8f: 2-8** 9f-13f: 1-2 14f+: 0-0
Track : **LH: 2-3** RH: 1-3 **Tight: 2-3** Gall: 0-0
Aids: Bl: 0-0 Vi: 0-0 Tstrap: 0-0 Ckp: 0-0
Best Rating: **101** 5/09 NmkR 1m gd-fm

Very useful; winner in Listed company; effective from 7f-1m2f; acts on Polytrack and good ground.

Oceana Blue

106(100) (81)**88**
4-y-o b f Reel Buddy (USA)-Silken Dalliance (Rambo Dancer (CAN))
A M Balding The C H F Partnership

Placings:635655/0133140354**26-54**110000 **(6482)**
2009: 7^{5}SD, 6^{4}SD, 7^{1}GF, 7^{1}S, 7^{0}G, 7^{0}G, 7^{0}G, 7^{0}GF,

	Starts	1st	2nd	3rd	Win & Pl
Career Total (Turf)	**13**	**3**	**0**	**1**	**22429**
Career Total (AW)	**13**	**1**	**1**	**3**	**4981**

88 6/09 Donc 7f (0-90)H SFT £9714
85 5/09 NmkR 7f (0-80)H G-F £5180
75 5/08 Chep 6f16y (0-70)H SFT £2719
71 3/08 Kemp 7f (0-60)H STD £2047
Total win prize-money £19663

Going (Turf): **Sf: 2-3** GS: 0-0 Gd: 0-6 GF: 1-4 Fm: 0-0
Distance: 5f/6f: 0-2 **7f-8f: 4-22** 9f-13f: 0-2 14f+: 0-0
Track : LH: 0-7 **RH: 1-6** Tight: 0-6 Gall: 0-1
Aids: Bl: 0-0 Vi: 0-3 Tstrap: 0-0 Ckp: 0-0
Best Rating: **88** 6/09 Donc 7f soft

Useful; effective over 6f-7f; acts on most ground and on Polytrack; has worn a tongue tie and visor.

Oceanic Dancer (IRE)

89(70) (2)**47**
3-y-o b f Danetime (IRE)-Almasa (Faustus (USA))
Patrick Morris Rob Lloyd Racing Limited

Placings:04-P0000 **(5336)**
2009: 6^{P}SD, 5^{0}SD, 5^{0}GF, 5^{0}GF, 5^{0}S,

	Starts	1st	2nd	3rd	Win & Pl
Career Total (Turf)	**5**	**0**	**0**	**0**	**216**
Career Total (AW)	**2**	**0**	**0**	**0**	

Going (Turf): **Sf: 0-2 GS: 0-0 Gd: 0-1 GF: 0-2 Fm: 0-0**
Distance: 5f/6f: 0-7 7f-8f: 0-0 9f-13f: 0-0 14f+: 0-0
Track : LH: 0-1 RH: 0-1 Tight: 0-1 Gall: 0-0
Aids: Bl: 0-0 Vi: 0-0 Tstrap: 0-0 Ckp: 0-0
Best Rating: **47** 10/08 Nott 5f13y heavy

Ochilview Warrior (IRE)

98 **52**
2-y-o b c Trans Island-Lonely Brook (USA) (El Gran Senor (USA))
R Bastiman The McMaster Springford Partnership

Placings:0P50020 **(7168)**
2009: 5^{0}GF, 7^{P}G, 7^{5}S, 7^{0}GF, 6^{0}S, 6^{2}G, 7^{0}S,

	Starts	1st	2nd	3rd	Win & Pl
Career Total (Turf)	**7**	**0**	**1**	**0**	**964**

Going (Turf): **Sf: 0-3 GS: 0-0 Gd: 0-2 GF: 0-2 Fm: 0-0**
Distance: 5f/6f: 0-2 7f-8f: 0-5 9f-13f: 0-0 14f+: 0-0
Track : LH: 0-3 RH: 0-1 Tight: 0-1 Gall: 0-0
Aids: Bl: 0-2 Vi: 0-0 Tstrap: 0-0 Ckp: 0-0
Best Rating: **52** 10/09 Ayr 6f good

Moderate; suited by 6f and good ground.

Oddshoes (IRE)

(102) (62)**71**
7-y-o b g Mujadil (USA)-Another Baileys (Deploy)
P J Hobbs (K M Prendergast 9/5) Mrs Evelyn Madden

Placings:0640/041223450/2005500/00340425**0/3** **(0194)**
2009: 9^{3}SD,

	Starts	1st	2nd	3rd	Win & Pl
Career Total (Turf)	**28**	**1**	**4**	**2**	**18447**
Career Total (AW)	**2**	**0**	**0**	**1**	**353**

73 4/05 Leop 7f (60-90)H Y-S £7351
Total win prize-money £7351

Going (Turf): **Sf: 0-11 GS: 0-1 Gd: 0-1 GF: 0-2 Fm: 0-0**
Distance: 5f/6f: 0-3 **7f-8f: 1-21** 9f-13f: 0-6 14f+: 0-0
Track : **LH: 1-13** RH: 0-8 Tight: 0-1 Gall: 0-1
Aids: Bl: 0-2 Vi: 0-0 Tstrap: 0-1 Ckp: 0-1
Best Rating: **82** 5/05 Leop 1m sft-hvy

Moderate; stays 1m2f; acts on heavy ground and on Polytrack.

Oddsmaker (IRE)

103(91) (42)**71**
8-y-o b g Barathea (IRE)-Archipova (IRE) (Ela-Mana-Mou)
M A Barnes D Maloney

Placings:0300400015/325101530006/**0**00005400000/00 42033231010220/63611/300-000000151305**0**51 **(7118)**
2009: 8^{0}GF, 14^{0}GF, 13^{0}G, 12^{0}GF, 12^{0}GF, 7^{0}G, 12^{1}S, 12^{5}GS, 12^{1}G, 11^{3}G, **12**^{0}SF, 10^{5}G, 12^{1}GS,

	Starts	1st	2nd	3rd	Win & Pl
Career Total (Turf)	**71**	**10**	**5**	**9**	**88048**
Career Total (AW)	**2**	**0**	**0**	**0**	

71 10/09 Muss 1m4f100y G-S £1942
71 9/09 Muss 1m4f100y (0-65)H GD £2590
66 8/09 Muss 1m4f100y (0-65)H SFT £2590
84 6/07 Carl 1m3f107y (0-80)H G-S £19431
77 6/07 Muss 1m6f (0-85)H GD £6232
77 8/06 Hayd 1m3f200y (0-80)H G-F £6477
73 7/06 Hayd 1m6f (0-80)H G-F £6477
91 6/04 Donc 1m D(0-80) GD £5699
88 5/04 York 7f205y C(0-95)H G-S £10965
73 10/03 Yarm 1m3y E(0-85) G-F £2681
Total win prize-money £65086

Going (Turf): Sf: 1-8 **GS: 3-7 Gd: 3-22 GF: 3-31** Fm: 0-3

Distance: 5f/6f: 0-4 7f-8f: 2-18 **9f-13f: 6-40** 14f+: 2-11
Track : LH: 4-40 **RH: 5-21 Tight: 4-19** Gall: 2-13
Aids: Bl: 0-1 Vi: 0-1 Tstrap: 0-2 Ckp: 0-2
Best Rating: 92 7/04 NmkJ 1m good

Modest; stays 2m, but effective at shorter; acts on most types of ground; usually wears a tongue tie.

Off Chance

102 89

3-y-o b f Olden Times-La Notte (Factual (USA))
T D Easterby L B Holliday

Placings:310146113 (5670)
2009: 8³GF, 9¹GF, 12⁰S, 9¹GF, 9⁴GF, 10⁶G, 8¹GF, 8¹GF, 8³S,

	Starts	1st	2nd	3rd	Win & Pl
Career Total (Turf)	9	4	0	2	18509

87 8/09 Ripn 1m (0-80)H G-F £6308
84 8/09 Newc 1m3y (0-75)H G-F £2978
79 6/09 Carl 1m1f61y (0-70)H G-F £3238
65 4/09 Ripn 1m1f170y G-F £3885
Total win prize-money £16411

Going (Turf): Sf: 0-2 GS: 0-0 Gd: 0-1 **GF: 4-6** Fm: 0-0
Distance: 5f/6f: 0-0 7f-8f: 1-2 **9f-13f: 3-7** 14f+: 0-0
Track : LH: 0-3 **RH: 3-4 Tight: 2-3** Gall: 0-2
Aids: Bl: 0-0 Vi: 0-0 Tstrap: 0-0 Ckp: 0-0
Best Rating: 89 9/09 Thsk 1m soft

Useful; stays 1m1f and acts on most ground.

Off Hand

93(94) (23)42

3-y-o b f Lend A Hand-Off Camera (Efisio)
T D Easterby D B Lamplough

Placings:0-0004030 (4819)
2009: 6⁰GF, 6⁰GF, 7⁰GF, 6⁴GS, 8⁰SD, 7³GF, 8⁰GF,

	Starts	1st	2nd	3rd	Win & Pl
Career Total (Turf)	7	0	0	1	539
Career Total (AW)	1	0	0	0	

Going (Turf): **Sf: 0-0 GS: 0-1 Gd: 0-0 GF: 0-6 Fm: 0-0**
Distance: 5f/6f: 0-4 7f-8f: 0-4 9f-13f: 0-0 14f+: 0-0
Track : LH: 0-2 RH: 0-2 Tight: 0-0 Gall: 0-0
Aids: Bl: 0-3 Vi: 0-0 Tstrap: 0-0 Ckp: 0-0
Best Rating: 42 7/09 Bevl 7f100y gd-fm

Very moderate; stays 1m; acts on fast ground; has worn blinkers.

Officer In Command (USA)

96(100) (79)77

3-y-o b/br c Officer (USA)-Luv To Stay N Chat (USA) (Candi's Gold (USA))
J S Moore N Brunskill & J S Moore

Placings:3231-0064 (5366)
2009: 8⁰GF, 8⁰SD, 8⁶SD, 10⁴F,

	Starts	1st	2nd	3rd	Win & Pl
Career Total (Turf)	2	0	0	0	241
Career Total (AW)	6	1	1	2	5852

79 10/08 Kemp 1m STD £3885
Total win prize-money £3886

Going (Turf): **Sf: 0-0 GS: 0-0 Gd: 0-0 GF: 0-1 Fm: 0-1**
Distance: 5f/6f: 0-0 **7f-8f: 1-6** 9f-13f: 0-2 14f+: 0-0
Track : LH: 0-4 **RH: 1-4** Tight: 0-4 Gall: 0-1
Aids: Bl: 0-0 Vi: 0-0 Tstrap: 0-0 Ckp: 0-0
Best Rating: 79 10/08 Kemp 1m stand

Fair; effective over 1m; acts on Polytrack; has worn a tongue tie.

Officer Mor (USA)

85(94) (63)68

3-y-o ch g Officer (USA)-Hot August Nights (USA) (Summer Squall (USA))
A Berry (A P Jarvis 10/9) A B Parr

Placings:21044**5520034-4200**00 (7082)
2009: 6⁴SS, 5²SD, 6⁰G, 6⁰SD, 5⁰G, 5⁰S,

	Starts	1st	2nd	3rd	Win & Pl
Career Total (Turf)	9	1	1	0	5054
Career Total (AW)	9	0	2	1	2101

68 5/08 Bevl 5f G-F £3561
Total win prize-money £3562

Going (Turf): Sf: 0-1 GS: 0-1 Gd: 0-4 **GF: 1-3** Fm: 0-0
Distance: **5f/6f: 1-14** 7f-8f: 0-4 9f-13f: 0-0 14f+: 0-0
Track : LH: 0-11 RH: 0-1 Tight: 0-9 Gall: 0-1
Aids: Bl: 0-5 Vi: 0-0 Tstrap: 0-0 Ckp: 0-0
Best Rating: 68 5/08 Bevl 5f gd-fm

Modest; effective over 5f-6f; acts on fast ground; goes on Fibresand; has worn headgear.

Official Style

93 78

2-y-o b c Dansili-Reel Style (Rainbow Quest (USA))
Sir Michael Stoute K Abdulla

Placings:032 (6754)
2009: 7⁰GF, 7³GF, 7²G,

	Starts	1st	2nd	3rd	Win & Pl
Career Total (Turf)	3	0	1	1	2312

Going (Turf): **Sf: 0-0 GS: 0-0 Gd: 0-1 GF: 0-2 Fm: 0-0**
Distance: 5f/6f: 0-0 7f-8f: 0-3 9f-13f: 0-0 14f+: 0-0
Track : LH: 0-0 RH: 0-0 Tight: 0-0 Gall: 0-0
Aids: Bl: 0-0 Vi: 0-0 Tstrap: 0-0 Ckp: 0-0
Best Rating: 78 10/09 Leic 7f9y good

Fair; effective over 7f; acts on fast ground.

Ogre (USA)

105(100) (78)84

4-y-o b/br f Tale Of The Cat (USA)-Soverign Lady (USA) (Aloha Prospector (USA))
P D Evans Diamond Racing Ltd

Placings:000**421/3411110210-403110126** (6657a)
2009: 8⁴SD, 8⁰GF, 9³GF, 8¹GF, 7¹G, 8⁰GF, 10¹GS, 7²GF, 8⁶VS,

	Starts	1st	2nd	3rd	Win & Pl
Career Total (Turf)	17	7	1	1	24276
Career Total (AW)	8	2	2	1	6186

81 9/09 Epsm 1m2f18y (0-75)H G-S £3238
76 7/09 Epsm 7f GD £3238
71 7/09 Epsm 1m114y G-F £3412
81 10/08 Pont 1m4y GD £6476
73 8/08 Brig 7f214y (0-70)H G-F £2838
59 7/08 Chep 1m14y G-F £2072
73 6/08 Brig 1m1f209y FRM £1748
69 6/08 Wolv 1m1f103y STD £2047
67 12/07 Kemp 1m (0-65) STD £2047
Total win prize-money £27119

Going (Turf): Sf: 0-0 GS: 1-1 Gd: 2-3 **GF: 3-11** Fm: 1-1
Distance: 5f/6f: 0-2 7f-8f: 3-9 **9f-13f: 6-14** 14f+: 0-0
Track : **LH: 7-20** RH: 1-2 **Tight: 4-12** Gall: 0-1

Aids: Bl: 0-0 Vi: 0-0 Tstrap: 0-0 Ckp: 0-0
Best Rating: 84 10/09 StCl 1m v soft

Fair; effective from 1m-1m2f; acts on most ground and on Polytrack; has worn a tongue tie.

Oh Goodness Me

108 105

3-y-o b f Galileo (IRE)-Coyote (Indian Ridge)
J S Bolger Mrs June Judd

Placings:03122-1030520 (5487a)
2009: 8¹S, 8⁰G, 8³HY, 12⁰G, 12⁵HY, 8²Y, 9⁰HY,

	Starts	1st	2nd	3rd	Win & Pl
Career Total (Turf)	12	2	3	2	135118

96 3/09 Curr 1m SFT £56883
83 9/08 Gowr 1m GD £8637
Total win prize-money £65521

Going (Turf): **Sf: 1-6** GS: 0-0 **Gd: 1-3** GF: 0-0 Fm: 0-0
Distance: 5f/6f: 0-0 **7f-8f: 2-7** 9f-13f: 0-5 14f+: 0-0
Track : LH: 0-4 **RH: 2-7** Tight: 0-1 **Gall: 1-2**
Aids: Bl: 0-0 Vi: 0-0 Tstrap: 0-0 Ckp: 0-0
Best Rating: 105 5/09 Curr 1m heavy

Group class; Irish trained; winner in Group 3 company; third in the Irish 1000 Guineas; effective over 1m; acts on good and soft ground; likes to race prominently.

Oh Landino (GER)

90 46

4-y-o b g Lando (GER)-Oh La Belle (GER) (Dashing Blade)
P Monteith Ian G M Dalgleish

Placings:320160-04000 (4529)
2009: 13⁰G, 9⁴F, 10⁰G, 13⁰G, 11⁰GS,

	Starts	1st	2nd	3rd	Win & Pl
Career Total (Turf)	11	1	1	1	1727

6/08 Duin 1m2f110y GD £735
Total win prize money £735

Going (Turf): Sf: 0-0 GS: 0-1 **Gd: 1-9** GF: 0-0 Fm: 0-1
Distance: 5f/6f: 0-0 7f-8f: 0-0 **9f-13f: 1-9** 14f+: 0-2
Track : LH: 0-3 RH: 0-2 Tight: 0-2 Gall: 0-0
Aids: Bl: 0-0 Vi: 0-0 Tstrap: 0-0 Ckp: 0-0
Best Rating: 46 6/09 Ayr 1m1f20y firm

Oh So Saucy

95 (60)85

5-y-o b m Imperial Ballet (IRE)-Almasi (IRE) (Petorius)
C F Wall The Eight Of Diamonds

Placings:0530/353304/11221-0660 (5697)
2009: 7⁰GF, 7⁶G, 7⁶G, 7⁰GS,

	Starts	1st	2nd	3rd	Win & Pl
Career Total (Turf)	16	3	2	2	10720
Career Total (AW)	3	0	0	2	655

85 7/08 Yarm 7f3y (0-75)H G-F £2590
75 6/08 Leic 7f9y (0-70)H GD £3238
71 5/08 Yarm 7f3y (0-55) G-F £2266
Total win prize-money £8095

Going (Turf): Sf: 0-0 GS: 0-3 Gd: 1-5 **GF: 2-8** Fm: 0-0
Distance: 5f/6f: 0-6 **7f-8f: 3-13** 9f-13f: 0-0 14f+: 0-0
Track : LH: 0-5 RH: 0-1 Tight: 0-3 Gall: 0-3
Aids: Bl: 0-0 Vi: 0-0 Tstrap: 0-0 Ckp: 0-0
Best Rating: 85 7/08 Yarm 7f3y gd-fm

Fair; stays 7f; acts on good and fast ground.

Oil Strike

96(97) (79)76

2-y-o b g Lucky Story (USA)-Willisa (Polar Falcon (USA))

P Winkworth David Holden

Placings:210 (7290)

2009: 5²G, 6¹SD, 6⁰S,

	Starts	1st	2nd	3rd	Win & Pl
Career Total (Turf)	2	0	1	0	964
Career Total (AW)	1	1	0	0	2730

79 10/09 Ling 6f STD £2729

Total win prize-money £2730

Going (Turf): Sf: 0-1 GS: 0-0 Gd: 0-1 GF: 0-0 Fm: 0-0
Distance: 5f/6f: 1-3 7f-8f: 0-0 9f-13f: 0-0 14f+: 0-0
Track : LH: 1-1 RH: 0-0 Tight: 1-1 Gall: 0-0
Aids: Bl: 0-0 Vi: 0-0 Tstrap: 0-0 Ckp: 0-0
Best Rating: 79 10/09 Ling 6f stand

Fair; stays 6f; acts on good ground and on Polytrack.

Oisin's Boy

84(98) (59)60

3-y-o b g Catcher In The Rye (IRE)-Red Storm (Dancing Spree (USA))

J R Boyle Mcatavey Developments Ltd

Placings:006346-60 (1462)

2009: 6⁶G, 8⁰G,

	Starts	1st	2nd	3rd	Win & Pl
Career Total (Turf)	5	0	0	0	0
Career Total (AW)	3	0	0	1	554

Going (Turf): Sf: 0-0 GS: 0-0 Gd: 0-4 GF: 0-1 Fm: 0-0
Distance: 5f/6f: 0-4 7f-8f: 0-3 9f-13f: 0-1 14f+: 0-0
Track : LH: 0-4 RH: 0-0 Tight: 0-1 Gall: 0-2
Aids: Bl: 0-0 Vi: 0-0 Tstrap: 0-1 Ckp: 0-1
Best Rating: 60 10/08 Wind 6f good

Modest; effective over 6f; acts on Fibresand.

Ok Katie

(61) (6)

6-y-o b m Slip Anchor-Darling Splodge (Elegant Air)

R M Beckett The Foxons Fillies Partnership

Placings:00 (1286)

2009: 12⁰SD, 12⁰SD,

	Starts	1st	2nd	3rd	Win & Pl
Career Total (Turf)	0	0	0	0	
Career Total (AW)	2	0	0	0	

Going (Turf): Sf: 0-0 GS: 0-0 Gd: 0-0 GF: 0-0 Fm: 0-0
Distance: 5f/6f: 0-0 7f-8f: 0-0 9f-13f: 0-2 14f+: 0-0
Track : LH: 0-1 RH: 0-1 Tight: 0-1 Gall: 0-0
Aids: Bl: 0-0 Vi: 0-0 Tstrap: 0-0 Ckp: 0-0
Best Rating: 6 3/09 Ling 1m4f stand

Okafranca (IRE)

52(97) (63)75

4-y-o b g Okawango (USA)-Villafranca (IRE) (In The Wings)

J A B Old W E Sturt

Placings:000/4230001216-0 (6734)

2009: 14⁰S,

	Starts	1st	2nd	3rd	Win & Pl
Career Total (Turf)	11	2	2	0	10145
Career Total (AW)	3	0	0	1	302

75 9/08 Ches 1m7f195y (0-80)H G-S £5504
59 7/08 Folk 1m4f (0-70)H SFT £2590

Total win prize-money £8095

Going (Turf): Sf: 1-5 GS: 1-3 Gd: 0-1 GF: 0-2 Fm: 0-0
Distance: 5f/6f: 0-0 7f-8f: 0-3 9f-13f: 1-7 14f+: 1-4
Track : LH: 1-8 RH: 1-4 Tight: 2-6 Gall: 0-0
Aids: Bl: 0-0 Vi: 0-0 Tstrap: 0-1 Ckp: 0-1
Best Rating: 75 9/08 Ches 1m7f195y gd-sft

Moderate; stays at least 1m6f; likes soft ground; also goes on Polytrack; has worn cheekpieces and a tongue tie.

Oke Bay

93(95) (58)55

3-y-o b f Tobougg (IRE)-Barakat (Bustino)

R M Beckett D B Clark

Placings:00-03520 (7840)

2009: 10⁰G, 10³GS, 14⁵G, 14²SD, 12⁰SS,

	Starts	1st	2nd	3rd	Win & Pl
Career Total (Turf)	4	0	0	1	482
Career Total (AW)	3	0	1	0	746

Going (Turf): Sf: 0-0 GS: 0-1 Gd: 0-3 GF: 0-0 Fm: 0-0
Distance: 5f/6f: 0-0 7f-8f: 0-2 9f-13f: 0-3 14f+: 0-2
Track : LH: 0-5 RH: 0-1 Tight: 0-2 Gall: 0-1
Aids: Bl: 0-0 Vi: 0-4 Tstrap: 0-0 Ckp: 0-0
Best Rating: 58 7/09 Sthl 1m6f stand

Moderate; stays 1m6f; acts on easy ground and Fibresand; has worn a visor.

Old Devil Moon (IRE)

79(87) (52)42

2-y-o br g Johannesburg (USA)-Tencarola (IRE) (Night Shift (USA))

T G Mills J Humphreys, T G Mills, Mrs S Ecclestone

Placings:0004 (7089)

2009: 5⁰GF, 7⁰G, 7⁰SS, 6⁴SD,

	Starts	1st	2nd	3rd	Win & Pl
Career Total (Turf)	2	0	0	0	
Career Total (AW)	2	0	0	0	0

Going (Turf): Sf: 0-0 GS: 0-0 Gd: 0-1 GF: 0-1 Fm: 0-0
Distance: 5f/6f: 0-2 7f-8f: 0-2 9f-13f: 0-0 14f+: 0-0
Track : LH: 0-2 RH: 0-1 Tight: 0-1 Gall: 0-0
Aids: Bl: 0-0 Vi: 0-0 Tstrap: 0-0 Ckp: 0-0
Best Rating: 52 10/09 Ling 7f std-slw

Old Firm

63(89) (51)

3-y-o ch g Compton Place-Miriam (Forzando)

D A Nolan C McGaffin

Placings:005 (7459)

2009: 6⁰S, 5⁰GS, 7⁵SD,

	Starts	1st	2nd	3rd	Win & Pl
Career Total (Turf)	2	0	0	0	
Career Total (AW)	1	0	0	0	0

Going (Turf): Sf: 0-1 GS: 0-1 Gd: 0-0 GF: 0-0 Fm: 0-0
Distance: 5f/6f: 0-1 7f-8f: 0-2 9f-13f: 0-0 14f+: 0-0
Track : LH: 0-1 RH: 0-0 Tight: 0-1 Gall: 0-0
Aids: Bl: 0-0 Vi: 0-0 Tstrap: 0-0 Ckp: 0-0
Best Rating: 51 11/09 Wolv 7f32y stand

Old Money

101 77

2-y-o ch f Medicean-Nouveau Riche (IRE) (Entrepreneur)

H J L Dunlop Normandie Stud Ltd

Placings:032 (6561)

2009: 6⁰GF, 7³G, 7²G,

	Starts	1st	2nd	3rd	Win & Pl
Career Total (Turf)	3	0	1	1	1336

Going (Turf): Sf: 0-0 GS: 0-0 Gd: 0-2 GF: 0-1 Fm: 0-0
Distance: 5f/6f: 0-1 7f-8f: 0-2 9f-13f: 0-0 14f+: 0-0
Track : LH: 0-0 RH: 0-0 Tight: 0-0 Gall: 0-1
Aids: Bl: 0-0 Vi: 0-0 Tstrap: 0-0 Ckp: 0-0
Best Rating: 77 10/09 Folk 7f good

Useful; stays 7f and acts on good and easier ground.

Old Romney

93(110) (78)76

5-y-o br g Halling (USA)-Zaeema (Zafonic (USA))

P Howling (M Wigham 15/5) Andrew Baker

Placings:4116/0530025000/000004410225-12222400000 (7524)

2009: 10¹SD, 9²SD, 10²SD, 10²SD, 10²SD, 10⁴G, 10⁰GF, 10⁰GF, 10⁰GF, 10⁰GS, 10⁰SD,

	Starts	1st	2nd	3rd	Win & Pl
Career Total (Turf)	25	3	1	0	14621
Career Total (AW)	12	1	6	1	7555

71 1/09 Ling 1m2f (0-60)H STD £2047
67 8/08 Ling 1m1f GD £1978
89 8/06 Haml 1m65y G-F £5181
74 7/06 Sand 7f16y G-F £4533

Total win prize-money £13742

Going (Turf): Sf: 0-3 GS: 0-6 Gd: 1-4 GF: 2-12 Fm: 0-0
Distance: 5f/6f: 0-0 7f-8f: 1-4 9f-13f: 3-32 14f+: 0-1
Track : LH: 2-24 RH: 2-9 Tight: 3-16 Gall: 0-6
Aids: Bl: 1-5 Vi: 0-0 Tstrap: 0-0 Ckp: 0-0
Best Rating: 89 8/06 Haml 1m65y gd-fm

Modest; stays 1m2f; acts on fast ground and Polytrack; has worn blinkers.

Old Sarum (IRE)

(92) (59)28

3-y-o b g Elusive City (USA)-Quintellina (Robellino (USA))

P S McEntee (D R C Elsworth 21/1) Eventmaker Racehorses

Placings:0305-0 (0229)

2009: 6⁰SD,

	Starts	1st	2nd	3rd	Win & Pl
Career Total (Turf)	1	0	0	0	
Career Total (AW)	4	0	0	1	403

Going (Turf): Sf: 0-0 GS: 0-1 Gd: 0-0 GF: 0-0 Fm: 0-0
Distance: 5f/6f: 0-4 7f-8f: 0-1 9f-13f: 0-0 14f+: 0-0
Track : LH: 0-1 RH: 0-3 Tight: 0-1 Gall: 0-0
Aids: Bl: 0-0 Vi: 0-0 Tstrap: 0-0 Ckp: 0-0
Best Rating: 59 11/08 Ling 6f stand

Oldjoesaid

104(103) (108)113

5-y-o b g Royal Applause-Border Minstral (IRE) (Sri Pekan (USA))

H Candy J J Byrne

Placings:0211/2012/1505436-6040660 (6283)

2009: 5^{6}GS, 6^{0}GF, 5^{4}GF, 6^{0}GF, 5^{6}GF, 5^{6}GF, 5^{0}GF,

	Starts	1st	2nd	3rd	Win & Pl
Career Total (Turf)	20	4	3	1	57456
Career Total (AW)	2	0	0	0	419

113	4/08	Newb	5f34y	(0-110)H	G-S	£9969
107	9/07	Hayd	5f	(0-100)H	SFT	£19431
95	10/06	Wind	5f10y	(0-95)	SFT	£5181
79	9/06	Sand	5f6y		G-F	£3886

Total win prize-money £38469

Going (Turf): **Sf: 2-4** GS: 1-2 Gd: 0-3 GF: 1-11 Fm: 0-0
Distance: **5f/6f: 4-21** 7f-8f: 0-1 9f-13f: 0-0 14f+: 0-0
Track : LH: 0-2 RH: 0-1 Tight: 0-1 **Gall: 1-4**
Aids: Bl: 0-0 Vi: 0-0 Tstrap: 0-0 Ckp: 0-0
Best Rating: **113** 4/08 Newb 5f34y gd-sft

Very useful; effective over 5f-6f and acts on most ground; likes to race prominently.

Olive Green (USA)

96 **73**

3-y-o b f Diesis-Zaghruta (USA) (Gone West (USA))

Pat Eddery K Abdulla

Placings:44502 (6390)

2009: 8^{4}F, 8^{4}G, 8^{5}G, 8^{0}HY, 8^{2}GF,

	Starts	1st	2nd	3rd	Win & Pl
Career Total (Turf)	5	0	1	0	1180

Going (Turf): **Sf: 0-1 GS: 0-0 Gd: 0-2 GF: 0-1 Fm: 0-1**
Distance: 5f/6f: 0-0 7f-8f: 0-2 9f-13f: 0-3 14f+: 0-0
Track : LH: 0-3 RH: 0-2 Tight: 0-0 Gall: 0-0
Aids: Bl: 0-0 Vi: 0-0 Tstrap: 0-0 Ckp: 0-0
Best Rating: **73** 5/09 Gdwd 1m good

Fair; effective over 1m; acts on fast ground.

Olivino (GER)

(81) (20)**51**

8-y-o ch g Second Set (IRE)-Osdemona (GER) (Solarstern (FR))

B J Llewellyn Alex James

Placings:60101000/05251061**004**/300265/0 (0342)

2009: 12^{0}SD,

	Starts	1st	2nd	3rd	Win & Pl
Career Total (Turf)	17	4	1	0	10050
Career Total (AW)	9	0	1	1	808

8/05	Badn	1m2f	GD	£3830
7/05	Aabe	1m2f	FRM	£2270
8/04	BDob	1m2f	GD	£1655
5/04	Hanv	1m	GD	£1444

Total win prize-money £9199

Going (Turf): Sf: 0-5 GS: 0-0 **Gd: 3-9** GF: 0-0 Fm: 1-1
Distance: 5f/6f: 0-0 7f-8f: 1-5 **9f-13f: 3-18** 14f+: 0-3
Track : **LH: 1-9** RH: 0-2 Tight: 0-7 Gall: 0-0
Aids: Bl: 0-0 Vi: 0-0 Tstrap: 0-0 Ckp: 0-0
Best Rating: **61** 12/05 Ling 1m2f stand

Olney Lass

99(75) (45)**72**

2-y-o b f Lucky Story (USA)-Zalebe (Bahamian Bounty)

W J H Ratcliffe T H Rossiter

Placings:032 (7289)

2009: 7^{0}SD, 6^{3}GS, 6^{2}S,

	Starts	1st	2nd	3rd	Win & Pl
Career Total (Turf)	2	0	1	1	2601
Career Total (AW)	1	0	0	0	

Going (Turf): **Sf: 0-1 GS: 0-1 Gd: 0-0 GF: 0-0 Fm: 0-0**
Distance: 5f/6f: 0-1 7f-8f: 0-2 9f-13f: 0-0 14f+: 0-0
Track : LH: 0-0 RH: 0-1 Tight: 0-0 Gall: 0-0
Aids: Bl: 0-0 Vi: 0-0 Tstrap: 0-0 Ckp: 0-0
Best Rating: **72** 11/09 Donc 6f soft

Fair; suited by 6f and easy ground.

Olympic Ceremony

94(85) (63)**67**

2-y-o br g Kyllachy-Opening Ceremony (USA) (Quest For Fame)

R A Fahey H Hurst & P Sales

Placings:0303405324 (7636)

2009: 5^{0}GS, 5^{3}GF, 6^{0}GF, 6^{3}GS, 5^{4}GF, 6^{0}GF, 5^{5}GF, 6^{3}GF, 5^{2}S, 5^{4}SD,

	Starts	1st	2nd	3rd	Win & Pl
Career Total (Turf)	9	0	1	3	4270
Career Total (AW)	1	0	0	0	337

Going (Turf): **Sf: 0-1 GS: 0-2 Gd: 0-0 GF: 0-6 Fm: 0-0**
Distance: 5f/6f: 0-10 7f-8f: 0-0 9f-13f: 0-0 14f+: 0-0
Track : LH: 0-1 RH: 0-1 Tight: 0-1 Gall: 0-1
Aids: Bl: 0-0 Vi: 0-0 Tstrap: 0-0 Ckp: 0-0
Best Rating: **67** 5/09 Carl 5f gd-fm

Modest; suited by 6f and acts on most ground.

Olympic Dream

101 **79**

3-y-o b g Kyllachy-Opening Ceremony (USA) (Quest For Fame)

R A Fahey H Hurst

Placings:0023200-5461630 (5409)

2009: 7^{5}GF, 7^{4}GF, 8^{6}G, 7^{1}GF, 8^{6}GF, 7^{3}GF, 7^{0}G,

	Starts	1st	2nd	3rd	Win & Pl
Career Total (Turf)	14	1	2	2	7698

76	6/09	Newc	7f	(0-75)H	G-F	£3238

Total win prize-money £3238

Going (Turf): Sf: 0-2 GS: 0-1 Gd: 0-5 **GF: 1-6** Fm: 0-0
Distance: 5f/6f: 0-7 **7f-8f: 1-6** 9f-13f: 0-1 14f+: 0-0
Track : LH: 0-3 RH: 0-2 Tight: 0-2 Gall: 0-0
Aids: Bl: 0-0 Vi: 0-0 Tstrap: 0-0 Ckp: 0-0
Best Rating: **79** 7/08 Hayd 6f heavy

Fair; effective over 6f on most ground.

Olynard (IRE)

102(96) (86)**97**

3-y-o b g Exceed And Excel (AUS)-Reddening (Blushing Flame (USA))

R M Beckett R Roberts

Placings:0120-543110 (5263)

2009: 6^{5}F, 5^{4}GF, 5^{3}G, 6^{1}GF, 6^{1}GF, 5^{0}GF,

	Starts	1st	2nd	3rd	Win & Pl
Career Total (Turf)	8	2	0	1	14083
Career Total (AW)	2	1	1	0	5072

97	8/09	Wind	6f	(0-95)H	G-F	£7771
93	7/09	Wind	6f	(0-85)H	G-F	£5180
86	8/08	Ling	5f		STD	£3561

Total win prize-money £16514

Going (Turf): Sf: 0-0 GS: 0-0 Gd: 0-3 **GF: 2-4** Fm: 0-1
Distance: **5f/6f: 3-9** 7f-8f: 0-1 9f-13f: 0-0 14f+: 0-0
Track : **LH: 1-2** RH: 0-0 Tight: 1-2 **Gall: 2-4**
Aids: Bl: 0-0 Vi: 0-0 Tstrap: 0-0 Ckp: 0-0
Best Rating: **97** 8/09 Wind 6f gd-fm

Very useful; effective at 5f-6f; acts on fast ground; goes on Polytrack.

Omnium Duke (IRE)

92(100) (73)**68**

3-y-o ch c Indian Haven-Please Be Good (IRE) (Prince Of Birds (USA))

J W Hills Barnes/ Waterford Hall Stud

Placings:4050-31050200 (6861)

2009: 8^{3}SD, 8^{1}SD, 8^{0}GS, 8^{5}SD, 8^{0}SD, 8^{2}SD, 8^{0}SF, 8^{0}SD,

	Starts	1st	2nd	3rd	Win & Pl
Career Total (Turf)	4	0	0	0	313
Career Total (AW)	8	1	1	1	4681

73	7/09	Wolv	1m141y	STD	£3070

Total win prize-money £3071

Going (Turf): **Sf: 0-1 GS: 0-2 Gd: 0-0 GF: 0-1 Fm: 0-0**
Distance: 5f/6f: 0-0 7f-8f: 0-7 **9f-13f: 1-5** 14f+: 0-0
Track : **LH: 1-5** RH: 0-3 **Tight: 1-5** Gall: 0-0
Aids: Bl: 0-1 **Vi: 1-5** Tstrap: 0-0 Ckp: 0-0
Best Rating: **73** 7/09 Wolv 1m141y stand

Fair; stays 1m; acts on soft ground and on Polytrack; has worn a visor.

Omokoroa (IRE)

111(87) (62)**90**

3-y-o b g Hawkeye (IRE)-Alycus (USA) (Atticus (USA))

M H Tompkins Brendan Richardson

Placings:300-321222 (6734)

2009: 10^{3}GF, 12^{2}GS, 11^{1}GS, 12^{2}G, 14^{2}S, 14^{2}S,

	Starts	1st	2nd	3rd	Win & Pl
Career Total (Turf)	8	1	4	2	12256
Career Total (AW)	1	0	0	0	

80	7/09	Catt	1m3f214y	(0-70)H	G-S	£3238

Total win prize-money £3238

Going (Turf): Sf: 0-2 **GS: 1-2** Gd: 0-3 GF: 0-1 Fm: 0-0
Distance: 5f/6f: 0-0 7f-8f: 0-2 **9f-13f: 1-5** 14f+: 0-2
Track : **LH: 1-4** RH: 0-3 **Tight: 1-4** Gall: 0-1
Aids: Bl: 0-0 Vi: 0-0 Tstrap: 0-0 Ckp: 0-0
Best Rating: **90** 10/09 Sals 1m6f21y soft

Fair; effective at up to 1m4f; acts on good and easy ground.

On Cue (IRE)

89(101) (54)**49**

3-y-o ch f Indian Haven-On Time Arrival (USA) (Devil's Bag (USA))

J M P Eustace Peter Hillman

Placings:050-42002 (3383)

2009: 8^{4}SD, 10^{2}SD, 8^{0}SD, 10^{0}GF, 12^{2}SD,

	Starts	1st	2nd	3rd	Win & Pl
Career Total (Turf)	3	0	0	0	0
Career Total (AW)	5	0	2	0	1183

Going (Turf): **Sf: 0-1 GS: 0-1 Gd: 0-0 GF: 0-1 Fm: 0-0**
Distance: 5f/6f: 0-1 7f-8f: 0-3 9f-13f: 0-4 14f+: 0-0
Track : LH: 0-6 RH: 0-1 Tight: 0-4 Gall: 0-0
Aids: Bl: 0-0 Vi: 0-0 Tstrap: 0-0 Ckp: 0-0
Best Rating: **54** 6/09 Ling 1m4f stand

Moderate; stays 1m; acts on easy ground and on Polytrack.

On Her Way

63 20

2-y-o ch f Medicean-Singed (Zamindar (USA))
H R A Cecil Malih L Al Basti

Placings:0 (7183)
2009: 7⁰G,

	Starts	1st	2nd	3rd	Win & Pl
Career Total (Turf)	1	0	0	0	

Going (Turf): Sf: 0-0 GS: 0-0 Gd: 0-1 GF: 0-0 Fm: 0-0
Distance: 5f/6f: 0-0 7f-8f: 0-1 9f-13f: 0-0 14f+: 0-0
Track : LH: 0-0 RH: 0-0 Tight: 0-0 Gall: 0-0
Aids: Bl: 0-0 Vi: 0-0 Tstrap: 0-0 Ckp: 0-0
Best Rating: 20 10/09 NmkR 7f good

On Holiday

80 29

2-y-o b f Dubai Destination (USA)-Mount Hillaby (IRE) (Mujadil (USA))
M W Easterby D F Spence

Placings:050 (5417)
2009: 5⁰G, 6⁵S, 7⁰GF,

	Starts	1st	2nd	3rd	Win & Pl
Career Total (Turf)	3	0	0	0	0

Going (Turf): Sf: 0-1 GS: 0-0 Gd: 0-1 GF: 0-1 Fm: 0-0
Distance: 5f/6f: 0-1 7f-8f: 0-2 9f-13f: 0-0 14f+: 0-0
Track : LH: 0-0 RH: 0-1 Tight: 0-0 Gall: 0-0
Aids: Bl: 0-0 Vi: 0-0 Tstrap: 0-0 Ckp: 0-0
Best Rating: 29 8/09 Haml 6f5y soft

On Khee

78(86) (58)34

2-y-o b f Sakhee (USA)-Star Precision (Shavian)
H Morrison Miss B Swire

Placings:004 (7325)
2009: 8⁰G, 7⁰SD, 7⁴SD,

	Starts	1st	2nd	3rd	Win & Pl
Career Total (Turf)	1	0	0	0	
Career Total (AW)	2	0	0	0	168

Going (Turf): Sf: 0-0 GS: 0-0 Gd: 0-1 GF: 0-0 Fm: 0-0
Distance: 5f/6f: 0-0 7f-8f: 0-3 9f-13f: 0-0 14f+: 0-0
Track : LH: 0-1 RH: 0-1 Tight: 0-1 Gall: 0-0
Aids: Bl: 0-0 Vi: 0-0 Tstrap: 0-0 Ckp: 0-0
Best Rating: 58 11/09 Kemp 7f stand

Modest; should stay 1m; acts on Polytrack.

On Offer (IRE)

99 74

3-y-o b f Clodovil (IRE)-Camassina (IRE) (Taufan (USA))
T D Easterby Mrs Jennifer E Pallister

Placings:321-60355050 (5597)
2009: 8⁶GF, 7⁰GF, 6³HY, 6⁵GS, 6⁵GF, 6⁰GS, 6⁵S, 6⁰GF,

	Starts	1st	2nd	3rd	Win & Pl
Career Total (Turf)	11	1	1	2	7339
70 6/08 Newc 6f			G-S	£4209	
				Total win prize-money	£4209

Going (Turf): Sf: 0-2 GS: 1-3 Gd: 0-1 GF: 0-5 Fm: 0-0
Distance: 5f/6f: 1-9 7f-8f: 0-2 9f-13f: 0-0 14f+: 0-0
Track : LH: 0-2 RH: 0-1 Tight: 0-1 Gall: 0-0
Aids: Bl: 0-1 Vi: 0-0 Tstrap: 0-2 Ckp: 0-2
Best Rating: 74 6/08 Pont 6f good

Fair half-sister to a number of winners over various distances up to 1m2f; stays 6f; acts on good and softer ground; has worn cheekpieces and a tongue tie.

On Our Way

102 107

3-y-o b g Oasis Dream-Singed (Zamindar (USA))
H R A Cecil J R May

Placings:31231-40 (3050)
2009: 9⁴GF, 10⁰GF,

	Starts	1st	2nd	3rd	Win & Pl
Career Total (Turf)	7	2	1	2	40823
107 10/08 NmkR 1m			GD	£12462	
83 8/08 Sand 1m14y			G-S	£4533	
				Total win prize-money	£16995

Going (Turf): Sf: 0-0 GS: 1-1 Gd: 1-2 GF: 0-4 Fm: 0-0
Distance: 5f/6f: 0-0 7f-8f: 1-4 9f-13f: 1-3 14f+: 0-0
Track : LH: 0-0 RH: 1-3 Tight: 0-0 Gall: 0-2
Aids: Bl: 0-0 Vi: 0-0 Tstrap: 0-0 Ckp: 0-0
Best Rating: 107 10/08 NmkR 1m good

Smart; third in the 2008 Royal Lodge; effective over 1m; acts on fast and easy ground.

On Terms (USA)

(86) (54)

3-y-o b f Aptitude (USA)-Silver Yen (USA) (Silver Hawk (USA))
S Dow S Dow

Placings:4 (7694)
2009: 10⁴SD,

	Starts	1st	2nd	3rd	Win & Pl
Career Total (Turf)	0	0	0	0	
Career Total (AW)	1	0	0	0	0

Going (Turf): Sf: 0-0 GS: 0-0 Gd: 0-0 GF: 0-0 Fm: 0-0
Distance: 5f/6f: 0-0 7f-8f: 0-0 9f-13f: 0-1 14f+: 0-0
Track : LH: 0-1 RH: 0-0 Tight: 0-1 Gall: 0-0
Aids: Bl: 0-0 Vi: 0-0 Tstrap: 0-0 Ckp: 0-0
Best Rating: 54 12/09 Ling 1m2f stand

On The Bounty

92 73

2-y-o b c Bahamian Bounty-Dark Eyed Lady (IRE) (Exhibitioner)
R A Fahey S W Knowles

Placings:15360 (5795)
2009: 5¹GS, 5⁵GF, 5³GS, 6⁶GS, 6⁰GF,

	Starts	1st	2nd	3rd	Win & Pl
Career Total (Turf)	5	1	0	1	3816
73 5/09 Donc 5f			G-S	£3238	
				Total win prize-money	£3238

Going (Turf): Sf: 0-0 GS: 1-3 Gd: 0-0 GF: 0-2 Fm: 0-0
Distance: 5f/6f: 1-3 7f-8f: 0-2 9f-13f: 0-0 14f+: 0-0
Track : LH: 0-0 RH: 0-0 Tight: 0-0 Gall: 0-0
Aids: Bl: 0-0 Vi: 0-0 Tstrap: 0-0 Ckp: 0-0
Best Rating: 73 5/09 Donc 5f gd-sft

Useful; suited by 5f and easy ground.

On The Cusp (IRE)

85(86) (67)57

2-y-o b g Footstepsinthesand-Roman Love (IRE) (Perugino (USA))
M A Jarvis Stephen Dartnell

Placings:500 (6990)
2009: 7⁵SD, 8⁰G, 7⁰G,

	Starts	1st	2nd	3rd	Win & Pl
Career Total (Turf)	2	0	0	0	
Career Total (AW)	1	0	0	0	240

Going (Turf): Sf: 0-0 GS: 0-0 Gd: 0-2 GF: 0-0 Fm: 0-0
Distance: 5f/6f: 0-0 7f-8f: 0-3 9f-13f: 0-0 14f+: 0-0
Track : LH: 0-0 RH: 0-2 Tight: 0-0 Gall: 0-1
Aids: Bl: 0-0 Vi: 0-0 Tstrap: 0-0 Ckp: 0-0
Best Rating: 67 9/09 Kemp 7f stand

On The Loose (IRE)

92 (8)63

5-y-o gr g Great Palm (USA)-Marys Rival (IRE) (Soughaan (USA))
T G McCourt On The Loose Syndicate

Placings:60004410 (7342a)
2009: 10⁶S, 12⁰GF, 10⁰GF, 14⁰GF, 12⁴YS, 12⁴S, 9¹S, 12⁰SD,

	Starts	1st	2nd	3rd	Win & Pl
Career Total (Turf)	7	1	0	0	3202
Career Total (AW)	1	0	0	0	
63 10/09 Ayr 1m1f20y (0-60)H			SFT	£2266	
				Total win prize-money	£2267

Going (Turf): Sf: 1-3 GS: 0-0 Gd: 0-0 GF: 0-3 Fm: 0-0
Distance: 5f/6f: 0-0 7f-8f: 0-0 9f-13f: 1-7 14f+: 0-1
Track : LH: 1-6 RH: 0-2 Tight: 0-0 Gall: 0-0
Aids: Bl: 0-0 Vi: 0-0 Tstrap: 0-0 Ckp: 0-0
Best Rating: 63 10/09 Ayr 1m1f20y soft

On The Piste (IRE)

93(90) (50)64

2-y-o b f Distant Music (USA)-Lady Piste (IRE) (Ali-Royal (IRE))
L A Mullaney (P T Midgley 8/7) K Humphries & Sons Roofing Contractors

Placings:31510155 (7372)
2009: 5³GF, 5¹GF, 5⁵F, 5¹G, 5⁰SD, 5¹GF, 5⁵G, 5⁵SD,

	Starts	1st	2nd	3rd	Win & Pl
Career Total (Turf)	6	3	0	1	6730
Career Total (AW)	2	0	0	0	0
64 9/09 Rdcr 5f	(0-65)		G-F	£2104	
59 7/09 Catt 5f			GD	£2047	
57 5/09 Yarm 5f43y			G-F	£1942	
				Total win prize-money	£6095

Going (Turf): Sf: 0-0 GS: 0-0 Gd: 1-2 GF: 2-3 Fm: 0-1
Distance: 5f/6f: 3-8 7f-8f: 0-0 9f-13f: 0-0 14f+: 0-0
Track : LH: 0-1 RH: 0-0 Tight: 0-1 Gall: 0-0
Aids: Bl: 0-0 Vi: 0-0 Tstrap: 0-0 Ckp: 0-0
Best Rating: 64 9/09 Rdcr 5f gd-fm

Moderate; effective over 5f; acts on good ground.

Once More Dubai (USA)

108(93) (109)111

4-y-o b/br c E Dubai (USA)-Go Again Girl (USA) (Broad Brush (USA))

Saeed Bin Suroor Godolphin

Placings:331522/133643213-535611 **(7237)**

2009: 10⁵G, 10³GF, 9⁵GF, 10⁶G, 11¹GF, 12¹SD,

	Starts	1st	2nd	3rd	Win & Pl
Career Total (Turf)	20	4	3	7	114419
Career Total (AW)	1	1	0	0	22708

109	11/09	Kemp	1m4f	STD	£22708
110	10/09	Leic	1m3f183y	G-F	£7569
104	10/08	Capa	1m2f	HVY	£14705
96	1/08	Sira	1m110y	GD	£20588
	10/07	Capa	1m1f	GD	£6756

Total win prize-money £72329

Going (Turf): Sf: 1-6 GS: 0-0 **Gd: 2-9** GF: 1-4 Fm: 0-0
Distance: 5f/6f: 0-0 7f-8f: 0-4 **9f-13f: 5-17** 14f+: 0-0
Track : LH: 0-3 **RH: 3-8** Tight: 0-1 Gall: 0-3
Aids: **Bl: 3-8** Vi: 0-0 Tstrap: 0-0 Ckp: 0-0
Best Rating: **111** 11/08 Capa 1m2f heavy

Smart; effective over 1m2f-1m4f; acts on most ground and on Polytrack; has worn a tongue-tie/blinkers.

Onceaponatime (IRE)

102(105) (77)84

4-y-o b g Invincible Spirit (IRE)-Lake Nyasa (IRE) (Lake Coniston (IRE))

M D Squance M D Squance

Placings:0115000-64032330062641305342 **(7870)**

2009: 6⁶SD, 6⁴SD, 7⁰SD, 6³G, 6²SD, 6³GS, 6³GF, 6⁰SD, 5⁰GF, 6⁶SD, 5²SD, 6⁶SD, 6⁴SD, 5¹SD, 5³SD, 5⁰SD, 5⁵SD, 5³SD, 5⁴SD, 6²SS,

	Starts	1st	2nd	3rd	Win & Pl
Career Total (Turf)	8	1	0	3	4179
Career Total (AW)	19	2	3	2	11489

74	10/09	Wolv	5f216y	(0-75)H	STD	£3238
85	6/08	Kemp	6f	(0-80)H	STD	£4209
84	5/08	Leic	5f218y		G-F	£2590

Total win prize-money £10037

Going (Turf): Sf: 0-2 GS: 0-1 Gd: 0-1 **GF: 1-4** Fm: 0-0
Distance: **5f/6f: 3-22** 7f-8f: 0-5 9f-13f: 0-0 14f+: 0-0
Track : LH: 1-11 RH: 1-7 **Tight: 1-9** Gall: 0-3
Aids: Bl: 0-0 Vi: 0-0 Tstrap: 0-1 Ckp: 0-1
Best Rating: **85** 6/08 Kemp 6f stand

Modest; best over 6f; acts on fast ground and on both AW surfaces.

One Cat Diesel (IRE)

41

2-y-o b g One Cool Cat (USA)-Awaaser (USA) (Diesis)

N Wilson D & S L Tanker Transport Limited

Placings:0 **(6982)**

2009: 8⁰C,

	Starts	1st	2nd	3rd	Win & Pl
Career Total (Turf)	1	0	0	0	

Going (Turf): **Sf: 0-0 GS: 0-0 Gd: 0-1 GF: 0-0 Fm: 0-0**
Distance: 5f/6f: 0-0 7f-8f: 0-1 9f-13f: 0-0 14f+: 0-0
Track : LH: 0-1 RH: 0-0 Tight: 0-0 Gall: 0-0
Aids: Bl: 0-0 Vi: 0-0 Tstrap: 0-0 Ckp: 0-0

One Cool Buck (IRE)

83 65

2-y-o b g One Cool Cat (USA)-Simply Katie (Most Welcome)

R Hannon Morten Buck

Placings:05 **(2430)**

2009: 5⁰GS, 6⁵G,

	Starts	1st	2nd	3rd	Win & Pl
Career Total (Turf)	2	0	0	0	0

Going (Turf): **Sf: 0-0 GS: 0-1 Gd: 0-1 GF: 0-0 Fm: 0-0**
Distance: 5f/6f: 0-2 7f-8f: 0-0 9f-13f: 0-0 14f+: 0-0
Track : LH: 0-0 RH: 0-0 Tight: 0-0 Gall: 0-0
Aids: Bl: 0-0 Vi: 0-0 Tstrap: 0-0 Ckp: 0-0
Best Rating: **65** 5/09 Gdwd 6f good

One Cool Deal (IRE)

80(79) (50)52

2-y-o b g One Cool Cat (USA)-Acciacatura (USA) (Stravinsky (USA))

T D Easterby Trevor C Stewart

Placings:60500 **(5358)**

2009: 5⁶GF, 6⁰G, 5⁵SD, 7⁰S, 6⁰S,

	Starts	1st	2nd	3rd	Win & Pl
Career Total (Turf)	4	0	0	0	0
Career Total (AW)	1	0	0	0	0

Going (Turf): **Sf: 0-2 GS: 0-0 Gd: 0-1 GF: 0-1 Fm: 0-0**
Distance: 5f/6f: 0-4 7f-8f: 0-1 9f-13f: 0-0 14f+: 0-0
Track : LH: 0-2 RH: 0-1 Tight: 0-2 Gall: 0-0
Aids: Bl: 0-2 Vi: 0-0 Tstrap: 0-0 Ckp: 0-0
Best Rating: **52** 6/09 Thsk 6f good

One Cool Dream

96(93) (61)60

3-y-o b f One Cool Cat (USA)-Swift Baba (USA) (Deerhound (USA))

W R Swinburn Ships Cat Partnership

Placings:04430 **(6824)**

2009: 8⁰SD, 8⁴GF, 7⁴GF, 5³GF, 7⁰GF,

	Starts	1st	2nd	3rd	Win & Pl
Career Total (Turf)	4	0	0	1	482
Career Total (AW)	1	0	0	0	

Going (Turf): **Sf: 0-0 GS: 0-0 Gd: 0-0 GF: 0-4 Fm: 0-0**
Distance: 5f/6f: 0-1 7f-8f: 0-3 9f-13f: 0-1 14f+: 0-0
Track : LH: 0-0 RH: 0-2 Tight: 0-1 Gall: 0-0
Aids: Bl: 0-0 Vi: 0-0 Tstrap: 0-0 Ckp: 0-0
Best Rating: **61** 6/09 Kemp 1m stand

One Cool Kitty

82(95) (62)70

3-y-o b f One Cool Cat (USA)-Exultate Jubilate (USA) (With Approval (CAN))

M G Quinlan Roger Turner

Aids: Bl: 0-0 Vi: 0-0 Tstrap: 0-0 Ckp: 0-0

Placings:4036100-4560300 **(7432)**

2009: 7⁴SD, 6⁵GF, 7⁶SD, 8⁰GS, 6³SD, 5⁰SD, 7⁰SD,

	Starts	1st	2nd	3rd	Win & Pl
Career Total (Turf)	9	1	0	1	3327
Career Total (AW)	5	0	0	1	543

70	9/08	Rdcr	7f	(0-75)	G-S	£2590

Total win prize-money £2590

Going (Turf): Sf: 0-0 **GS: 1-3** Gd: 0-1 GF: 0-4 Fm: 0-1
Distance: 5f/6f: 0-4 **7f-8f: 1-7** 9f-13f: 0-3 14f+: 0-0
Track : LH: 0-2 RH: 0-4 Tight: 0-3 Gall: 0-0
Aids: Bl: 0-0 Vi: 0-0 Tstrap: 0-0 Ckp: 0-0
Best Rating: **70** 9/08 Rdcr 7f gd-sft

One Cool Mission (IRE)

78(94) (53)24

3-y-o b f One Cool Cat (USA)-San Luis Rey (Zieten (USA))

Tom Dascombe Daniel Perchard

Placings:50-360 **(4749)**

2009: 5³SD, 7⁶S, 7⁰SD,

	Starts	1st	2nd	3rd	Win & Pl
Career Total (Turf)	1	0	0	0	0
Career Total (AW)	4	0	0	1	403

Going (Turf): **Sf: 0-1 GS: 0-0 Gd: 0-0 GF: 0-0 Fm: 0-0**
Distance: 5f/6f: 0-2 7f-8f: 0-3 9f-13f: 0-0 14f+: 0-0
Track : LH: 0-4 RH: 0-0 Tight: 0-3 Gall: 0-1
Aids: Bl: 0-0 Vi: 0-0 Tstrap: 0-0 Ckp: 0-0
Best Rating: **53** 12/08 Ling 7f stand

One Cool Poppy (IRE)

90(84) (45)57

2-y-o b f One Cool Cat (USA)-Elusive Kitty (USA) (Elusive Quality (USA))

H J L Dunlop Star Pointe Ltd

Placings:406 **(6858)**

2009: 6⁴GF, 6⁰G, 8⁶SD,

	Starts	1st	2nd	3rd	Win & Pl
Career Total (Turf)	2	0	0	0	216
Career Total (AW)	1	0	0	0	0

Going (Turf): **Sf: 0-0 GS: 0-0 Gd: 0-1 GF: 0-1 Fm: 0-0**
Distance: 5f/6f: 0-0 7f-8f: 0-2 9f-13f: 0-1 14f+: 0-0
Track : LH: 0-1 RH: 0-0 Tight: 0-1 Gall: 0-0
Aids: Bl: 0-0 Vi: 0-0 Tstrap: 0-0 Ckp: 0-0
Best Rating: **57** 8/09 Sals 6f212y gd-fm

One Cool Slash (IRE)

(85) (40)

2-y-o b f One Cool Cat (USA)-Sun Slash (IRE) (Entrepreneur)

M J McGrath Michael O'Dea

Placings:06 **(7806)**

2009: 6⁰SD, 7⁶SD,

	Starts	1st	2nd	3rd	Win & Pl
Career Total (Turf)	0	0	0	0	
Career Total (AW)	2	0	0	0	0

Going (Turf): **Sf: 0-0 GS: 0-0 Gd: 0-0 GF: 0-0 Fm: 0-0**

Distance: 5f/6f: 0-1 7f-8f: 0-1 9f-13f: 0-0 14f+: 0-0
Track : LH: 0-2 RH: 0-0 Tight: 0-2 Gall: 0-0
Aids: Bl: 0-0 Vi: 0-0 Tstrap: 0-0 Ckp: 0-0
Best Rating: 40 12/09 Ling 7f stand

One For Joules (IRE)

86(68) (53)65
2-y-o b f Choisir (AUS)-Stuttgart (Groom Dancer (USA))
John Joseph Hanlon Glenview House Stud

Placings:50040 (7391)
2009: 7^{5}SH, 6^{0}SD, 7^{0}G, 7^{4}Y, 8^{0}SD,

	Starts	1st	2nd	3rd	Win & Pl
Career Total (Turf)	3	0	0	0	418
Career Total (AW)	2	0	0	0	

Going (Turf): Sf: 0-0 GS: 0-0 Gd: 0-1 GF: 0-0 Fm: 0-0
Distance: 5f/6f: 0-1 7f-8f: 0-4 9f-13f: 0-0 14f+: 0-0
Track : LH: 0-3 RH: 0-2 Tight: 0-1 Gall: 0-0
Aids: Bl: 0-0 Vi: 0-0 Tstrap: 0-0 Ckp: 0-0
Best Rating: 65 10/09 Leop 7f yield

One Good Emperor (IRE)

90(88) (77)58
2-y-o b c Antonius Pius (USA)-Break Of Day (USA) (Favorite Trick (USA))
J R Best S Malcolm M Winwright P Tindall

Placings:5330 (6826)
2009: 6^{5}G, 6^{3}SD, 7^{3}SD, 5^{0}SF,

	Starts	1st	2nd	3rd	Win & Pl
Career Total (Turf)	1	0	0	0	0
Career Total (AW)	3	0	0	2	688

Going (Turf): Sf: 0-0 GS: 0-0 Gd: 0-1 GF: 0-0 Fm: 0-0
Distance: 5f/6f: 0-3 7f-8f: 0-1 9f-13f: 0-0 14f+: 0-0
Track : LH: 0-2 RH: 0-1 Tight: 0-2 Gall: 0-0
Aids: Bl: 0-0 Vi: 0-0 Tstrap: 0-0 Ckp: 0-0
Best Rating: 77 8/09 Ling 6f stand

One Hit Wonder

(87) (56)
2-y-o b g Whipper (USA)-Swiftly (Cadeaux Genereux)
Mouse Hamilton-Fairley Mouse Hamilton-Fairley

Placings:56 (2825)
2009: 5^{5}SD, 6^{6}SD,

	Starts	1st	2nd	3rd	Win & Pl
Career Total (Turf)	0	0	0	0	
Career Total (AW)	2	0	0	0	0

Going (Turf): Sf: 0-0 GS: 0-0 Gd: 0-0 GF: 0-0 Fm: 0-0
Distance: 5f/6f: 0-2 7f-8f: 0-0 9f-13f: 0-0 14f+: 0-0
Track : LH: 0-0 RH: 0-2 Tight: 0-0 Gall: 0-0
Aids: Bl: 0-0 Vi: 0-0 Tstrap: 0-0 Ckp: 0-0
Best Rating: 56 6/09 Kemp 6f stand

One More Round (USA)

91(103) (79)76
11-y-o b g Ghazi (USA)-Life Of The Party (USA) (Pleasant Colony (USA))
P D Evans Mrs I M Folkes

Placings:6114/00102/20232524200/220062202/2660000/6035033000120004/5033000001000122/3362113031003-224140442005000 (7645)
2009: 6^{2}SD, 6^{2}SD, 6^{4}SD, 6^{1}SD, 5^{4}SD, 5^{0}SD, 6^{4}SD, 5^{4}GF, 6^{2}F, 5^{0}G, 7^{0}SD, 5^{5}SD, 5^{0}SD, 7^{0}SD, 6^{0}SD, 5^{0}SD,

	Starts	1st	2nd	3rd	Win & Pl
Career Total (Turf)	51	5	13	2	245854
Career Total (AW)	47	5	6	9	32189

70	1/09	Ling	6f		STD	£2047
79	11/08	Wolv	5f216y	(0-65)H	STD	£2047
69	6/08	Wolv	7f32y		STD	£2729
62	6/08	Ling	7f		STD	£1774
77	11/07	Ling	6f		STD	£2047
98	9/07	Hayd	6f	(0-90)	G-F	£9715
102	7/06	Wind	6f	(0-105)H	G-F	£31160
111	9/02	Leop	7f	H	GD	£27914
107	9/01	Curr	1m	(65-95)H	G-F	£15725
92	8/01	Gway	1m100y		G-Y	£6120

Total win prize-money £101283

Going (Turf): Sf: 0-6 GS: 0-3 Gd: 1-10 GF: 3-23 Fm: 0-1
Distance: 5f/6f: 5-50 7f-8f: 4-41 9f-13f: 1-7 14f+: 0-0
Track : LH: 6-57 RH: 1-7 Tight: 5-40 Gall: 2-13
Aids: Bl: 8-71 Vi: 0-0 Tstrap: 0-1 Ckp: 0-1
Best Rating: 115 9/03 Leop 7f gd-fm

Modest; stays 1m, but effective over shorter; acts on most ground and on Polytrack; wears blinkers and has worn cheekpieces; usually held up.

One Oi

(101) (63)
4-y-o b g Bertolini (USA)-Bogus Penny (IRE) (Pennekamp (USA))
D W P Arbuthnot Saxon Gate Partnership

Placings:06002-204 (4645)
2009: 8^{2}SD, 8^{0}SD, 8^{4}SD,

	Starts	1st	2nd	3rd	Win & Pl
Career Total (Turf)	0	0	0	0	
Career Total (AW)	8	0	2	0	1209

Going (Turf): Sf: 0-0 GS: 0-0 Gd: 0-0 GF: 0-0 Fm: 0-0
Distance: 5f/6f: 0-0 7f-8f: 0-6 9f-13f: 0-2 14f+: 0-0
Track : LH: 0-5 RH: 0-3 Tight: 0-5 Gall: 0-0
Aids: Bl: 0-0 Vi: 0-0 Tstrap: 0-0 Ckp: 0-0
Best Rating: 63 8/09 Kemp 1m stand

Moderate; acts on Polytrack; effective at 1m.

One Scoop Or Two

98(92) (55)56
3-y-o b g Needwood Blade-Rebel County (IRE) (Maelstrom Lake)
F Sheridan Showtime Ice Cream Concessionaire

Placings:65300050 (7105)
2009: 8^{6}SD, 7^{5}SD, 8^{3}SD, 10^{0}GF, 14^{0}G, 12^{0}SD, 9^{5}SF, 7^{0}SD,

	Starts	1st	2nd	3rd	Win & Pl
Career Total (Turf)	2	0	0	0	
Career Total (AW)	6	0	0	1	454

Going (Turf): Sf: 0-0 GS: 0-0 Gd: 0-1 GF: 0-1 Fm: 0-0
Distance: 5f/6f: 0-0 7f-8f: 0-2 9f-13f: 0-5 14f+: 0-1
Track : LH: 0-7 RH: 0-1 Tight: 0-6 Gall: 0-0
Aids: Bl: 0-0 Vi: 0-0 Tstrap: 0-0 Ckp: 0-0
Best Rating: 56 6/09 Ches 1m2f75y gd-fm

One Slick Chick (IRE)

(95) (70)
3-y-o b f One Cool Cat (USA)-Ms Mary C (IRE) (Dolphin Street (FR))
M Botti Miss Anita Farrell

Placings:2-1 (0556)
2009: 8^{1}SD,

	Starts	1st	2nd	3rd	Win & Pl
Career Total (Turf)	0	0	0	0	
Career Total (AW)	2	1	1	0	4079

70	2/09	Wolv	1m141y	STD	£2729

Total win prize-money £2730

Going (Turf): Sf: 0-0 GS: 0-0 Gd: 0-0 GF: 0-0 Fm: 0-0
Distance: 5f/6f: 0-0 7f-8f: 0-1 9f-13f: 1-1 14f+: 0-0
Track : LH: 1-2 RH: 0-0 Tight: 1-1 Gall: 0-1
Aids: Bl: 0-0 Vi: 0-0 Tstrap: 0-0 Ckp: 0-0
Best Rating: 70 2/09 Wolv 1m141y stand

Fair; effective over 1m; acts on Polytrack.

One Tou Many

93(71) 52
4-y-o b f Tobougg (IRE)-Reine De Thebes (FR) (Darshaan)
C W Fairhurst S Leggott

Placings:0/0-30000 (4617)
2009: 12^{3}GS, 16^{0}G, 14^{0}GF, 14^{0}SD, 15^{0}G,

	Starts	1st	2nd	3rd	Win & Pl
Career Total (Turf)	6	0	0	1	385
Career Total (AW)	1	0	0	0	

Going (Turf): Sf: 0-0 GS: 0-1 Gd: 0-3 GF: 0-2 Fm: 0-0
Distance: 5f/6f: 0-1 7f-8f: 0-0 9f-13f: 0-2 14f+: 0-4
Track : LH: 0-6 RH: 0-0 Tight: 0-2 Gall: 0-2
Aids: Bl: 0-0 Vi: 0-1 Tstrap: 0-0 Ckp: 0-0
Best Rating: 52 5/09 Newc 1m4f93y gd-sft

One Upmanship

(92) (35)
8-y-o ch g Bahamian Bounty-Magnolia (Petong)
M Salaman Mrs Victoria Keen

Placings:060502430/000632612300505/43552046655000 0/00 (0775)
2009: 8^{0}SD, 9^{0}SD,

	Starts	1st	2nd	3rd	Win & Pl
Career Total (Turf)	27	1	3	3	7532
Career Total (AW)	14	0	1	1	1674

63	8/04	Hayd	1m30y	F	GD	£3010

Total win prize-money £3010

Going (Turf): Sf: 0-0 GS: 0-4 Gd: 1-4 GF: 0-15 Fm: 0-4
Distance: 5f/6f: 0-9 7f-8f: 0-10 9f-13f: 1-22 14f+: 0-0
Track : LH: 1-26 RH: 0-2 Tight: 0-20 Gall: 0-0
Aids: Bl: 0-5 Vi: 0-0 Tstrap: 0-2 Ckp: 0-2
Best Rating: 71 9/03 NmkR 6f gd-fm

One Way Or Another (AUS)

107(103) (88)99
6-y-o b g Carnegie (IRE)-True Blonde (AUS) (Naturalism (NZ))
J R Gask Simon Rowlands

Placings:3253/32102222210/4416510630-01260204 **(7560)**

2009: 7^{0}S, 8^{1}G, 8^{2}G, 8^{6}G, 8^{0}G, 7^{2}GF, 7^{0}S, 8^{4}SD,

	Starts	1st	2nd	3rd	Win & Pl
Career Total (Turf)	**32**	**5**	**9**	**4**	**71920**
Career Total (AW)	**1**	**0**	**0**	**0**	**841**

94	6/09	Hayd	1m30y	(0-90)H	GD	£9066
	6/08	Sann	1m1f	H	HVY	£17181
	4/08	Sann	1m	H	GD	£6872
	10/07	Caul	1m2f	H	GD	£14677
	6/07	Morn	6f		HVY	£3145

Total win prize-money £50941

Going (Turf): Sf: 2-9 GS: 0-6 **Gd: 3-16** GF: 0-1 Fm: 0-0
Distance: 5f/6f: 1-7 7f-8f: 1-11 **9f-13f: 3-14** 14f+: 0-1
Track : **LH: 1-3** RH: 0-2 Tight: 0-2 Gall: 0-1
Aids: Bl: 0-0 Vi: 0-0 Tstrap: 0-1 Ckp: 0-1
Best Rating: **99** 10/09 NmkR 7f gd-fm

Useful; ex-Australian; effective at 7f-1m2f; acts on good ground.

One Way Ticket

91(100) (54)**65**

9-y-o ch g Pursuit Of Love-Prima Cominna (Unfuwain (USA))

J M Bradley Saracen Racing

Placings:530/22532341020/00032031000 4V502/2042301 1021002000/30106000000 22234/30232300053030/055200 00004-003300446660 **(5792)**

2009: 6^{0}SD, 6^{0}SD, 5^{3}SD, 5^{3}SD, 5^{0}GF, 5^{0}GF, 5^{4}G, 5^{4}G, 5^{6}F, 5^{6}G, 5^{6}GS, 5^{0}G,

	Starts	1st	2nd	3rd	Win & Pl
Career Total (Turf)	**76**	**6**	**12**	**10**	**55273**
Career Total (AW)	**23**	**0**	**3**	**5**	**3380**

89	7/06	Brig	5f59y	(0-80)H	FRM	£6309
89	7/05	Catt	5f	(0-85)H	FRM	£6831
82	6/05	Wwck	5f	(0-70)H	G-F	£3723
78	6/05	Ripn	5f	(0-75)H	G-F	£3468
76	6/04	Chep	6f16y	D(0-80)H	G-F	£5421
66	8/03	Wwck	7f26y	D	G-F	£3916

Total win prize-money £29669

Going (Turf): Sf: 0-3 GS: 0-5 Gd: 0-14**GF: 4-40** Fm: 2-14
Distance: **5f/6f: 4-82** 7f-8f: 2-16 9f-13f: 0-1 14f+: 0-0
Track : **LH: 3-43** RH: 0-7 Tight: 0-17 Gall: 0-6
Aids: Bl: 0-7 Vi: 0-0 Tstrap: 6-85 Ckp: 6-85
Best Rating: **89** 7/06 Brig 5f59y firm

Plating-class sprinter; acts on a sound surface.

One Zero (USA)

(95) (61)**62**

4-y-o ch f Theatrical-Binary (Rainbow Quest (USA))

M G Quinlan Mrs J Quinlan

Placings:36-54 **(0476)**

2009: 12^{5}SD, 12^{4}SD,

	Starts	1st	2nd	3rd	Win & Pl
Career Total (Turf)	**2**	**0**	**0**	**1**	**574**
Career Total (AW)	**2**	**0**	**0**	**0**	**0**

Going (Turf): **Sf: 0-0 GS: 0-0 Gd: 0-2 GF: 0-0 Fm: 0-0**
Distance: 5f/6f: 0-0 7f-8f: 0-0 9f-13f: 0-4 14f+: 0-0
Track : LH: 0-2 RH: 0-2 Tight: 0-2 Gall: 0-0
Aids: Bl: 0-0 Vi: 0-0 Tstrap: 0-0 Ckp: 0-0
Best Rating: **62** 7/08 Wxfd 1m6f good

Onebidkintymill (IRE)

105(75) (30)**71**

4-y-o b g Mull Of Kintyre (USA)-More Risk (IRE) (Fayruz)

R Hollinshead (B P J Baugh 1/7) Brian Hatton

Placings:306-15 **(4783)**

2009: 6^{1}GF, 6^{5}GF,

	Starts	1st	2nd	3rd	Win & Pl
Career Total (Turf)	**4**	**1**	**0**	**1**	**2594**
Career Total (AW)	**1**	**0**	**0**	**0**	

71	7/09	Chep	6f16y	(0-65)H	G-F	£2266

Total win prize-money £2267

Going (Turf): Sf: 0-1 GS: 0-0 Gd: 0-0 **GF: 1-3** Fm: 0-0
Distance: 5f/6f: 0-3 **7f-8f: 1-2** 9f-13f: 0-0 14f+: 0-0
Track : LH: 0-2 RH: 0-0 Tight: 0-2 Gall: 0-0
Aids: Bl: 0-0 Vi: 0-0 Tstrap: 0-0 Ckp: 0-0
Best Rating: **71** 7/09 Chep 6f16y gd-fm

Modest; effective 6f; handles fast ground.

Onemix

104(102) (76)**78**

3-y-o gr f Fair Mix (IRE)-One For Philip (Blushing Flame (USA))

B W Hills S W Group Logistics Limited

Placings:2-22143253 **(6671)**

2009: 8^{2}SD, 10^{2}SD, 10^{1}GF, 10^{4}G, 10^{3}GF, 11^{2}G, 10^{5}G, 13^{3}SD,

	Starts	1st	2nd	3rd	Win & Pl
Career Total (Turf)	**5**	**1**	**1**	**1**	**5393**
Career Total (AW)	**4**	**0**	**3**	**1**	**3357**

77	4/09	Bath	1m2f46y	G-F	£2590

Total win prize-money £2590

Going (Turf): Sf: 0-0 GS: 0-0 Gd: 0-3 **GF: 1-2** Fm: 0-0
Distance: 5f/6f: 0-0 7f-8f: 0-2 **9f-13f: 1-6** 14f+: 0-1
Track : **LH: 1-6** RH: 0-2 **Tight: 1-4** Gall: 0-2
Aids: Bl: 0-0 Vi: 0-0 Tstrap: 0-0 Ckp: 0-0
Best Rating: **78** 7/09 Wind 1m3f135y good

Fair; stays 1m2f; acts on fast ground and on Polytrack.

Onemoreandstay

100(103) (71)**73**

4-y-o ch f Dr Fong (USA)-Subito (Darshaan)

M D Squance (R W Price 8/1) Mrs Elizabeth Macdonald

Placings:3404-15035123 **(7779)**

2009: 11^{1}SD, 11^{5}SD, 10^{0}SD, 12^{3}GS, 10^{5}G, 12^{1}SD, 11^{2}SD, 12^{3}SD,

	Starts	1st	2nd	3rd	Win & Pl
Career Total (Turf)	**5**	**0**	**0**	**2**	**1354**
Career Total (AW)	**7**	**2**	**1**	**1**	**6974**

71	4/09	Sthl	1m4f	(0-75)H	STD	£3070
69	1/09	Sthl	1m3f		STD	£2729

Total win prize-money £5801

Going (Turf): **Sf: 0-1 GS: 0-3 Gd: 0-1 GF: 0-0 Fm: 0-0**
Distance: 5f/6f: 0-0 7f-8f: 0-3 **9f-13f: 2-9** 14f+: 0-0
Track : **LH: 2-7** RH: 0-3 Tight: 0-2 Gall: 0-0
Aids: Bl: 0-0 Vi: 0-0 Tstrap: 1-3 Ckp: 1-3
Best Rating: **73** 9/08 Pont 1m2f6y gd-sft

Modest; stays 1m3f but effective over shorter; acts on Fibresand.

Onenightinlisbon (IRE)

99(103) (76)**75**

5-y-o br m Bold Fact (USA)-Mickey Towbar (IRE) (Mujadil (USA))

J R Boyle Inside Track Racing Club

Placings:44055114362243/0043126/6432551420002200630-0000320060 **(6547)**

2009: 8^{0}SD, 8^{0}SD, 7^{0}SD, 7^{0}G, 9^{3}GF, 8^{2}G, 10^{0}SD, 8^{0}GF, 10^{6}SD, 8^{0}G,

	Starts	1st	2nd	3rd	Win & Pl
Career Total (Turf)	**19**	**2**	**2**	**2**	**12315**
Career Total (AW)	**31**	**2**	**6**	**4**	**15047**

70	6/08	Kemp	1m	(0-70)H	STD	£2590
63	11/07	Ling	7f		STD	£2047
80	8/06	Muss	5f		GD	£3886
78	7/06	Bevl	5f		G-F	£3412

Total win prize-money £11937

Going (Turf): Sf: 0-0 GS: 0-3 **Gd: 1-7 GF: 1-9** Fm: 0-0
Distance: 5f/6f: 2-14 7f-8f: 2-26 9f-13f: 0-10 14f+: 0-0
Track : LH: 1-22 RH: 1-18 **Tight: 1-26** Gall: 0-1
Aids: Bl: 0-0 Vi: 0-0 Tstrap: 0-0 Ckp: 0-0
Best Rating: **87** 11/06 Wolv 5f216y std-fst

Modest; stays 1m; acts on good and faster ground and on Polytrack.

Oneofapear (IRE)

100(97) (57)**80**

3-y-o b g Pyrus (USA)-Whitegate Way (Greensmith)

G A Swinbank Mrs I Gibson & Dr C Emmerson

Placings:5521 **(6158)**

2009: 8^{5}GF, 11^{5}SD, 8^{2}G, 9^{1}G,

	Starts	1st	2nd	3rd	Win & Pl
Career Total (Turf)	**3**	**1**	**1**	**0**	**3458**
Career Total (AW)	**1**	**0**	**0**	**0**	**0**

80	9/09	Haml	1m1f36y	GD	£2590

Total win prize-money £2590

Going (Turf): Sf: 0-0 GS: 0-0 **Gd: 1-2** GF: 0-1 Fm: 0-0
Distance: 5f/6f: 0-0 7f-8f: 0-1 **9f-13f: 1-3** 14f+: 0-0
Track : LH: 0-1 **RH: 1-3 Tight: 1-3** Gall: 0-0
Aids: Bl: 0-0 Vi: 0-0 Tstrap: 0-0 Ckp: 0-0
Best Rating: **80** 9/09 Haml 1m1f36y good

Fair; stays 1m1f; acts on good ground.

Oneofthesedayz (IRE)

84 **44**

3-y-o b f Acclamation-Thornby Park (Unfuwain (USA))

Mrs D J Sanderson Mrs Caren Walsh

Placings:000-000 **(3305)**

2009: 7^{0}GF, 8^{0}F, 7^{0}GF,

	Starts	1st	2nd	3rd	Win & Pl
Career Total (Turf)	**6**	**0**	**0**	**0**	

Going (Turf): **Sf: 0-1 GS: 0-0 Gd: 0-1 GF: 0-3 Fm: 0-1**
Distance: 5f/6f: 0-3 7f-8f: 0-3 9f-13f: 0-0 14f+: 0-0
Track : LH: 0-1 RH: 0-1 Tight: 0-0 Gall: 0-0
Aids: Bl: 0-0 Vi: 0-0 Tstrap: 0-2 Ckp: 0-2
Best Rating: **44** 9/08 Leic 5f218y soft

Ongoodform (IRE)

100(102) (92)90

2-y-o b c Invincible Spirit (IRE)-Elfin Queen (IRE) (Fairy King (USA))

P W D'Arcy Dr J S Kinnear

Placings:031222 (7251)

2009: 6^{0}G, 6^{3}SD, 6^{1}GF, 6^{2}GF, 6^{2}SD, 7^{2}SD,

	Starts	1st	2nd	3rd	Win & Pl
Career Total (Turf)	3	1	1	0	6446
Career Total (AW)	3	0	2	1	2698

85 9/09 Yarm 6f3y G-F £4037

Total win prize-money £4037

Going (Turf): Sf: 0-0 GS: 0-0 Gd: 0-1 GF: 1-2 Fm: 0-0
Distance: 5f/6f: 0-4 7f-8f: 1-2 9f-13f: 0-0 14f+: 0-0
Track : LH: 0-3 RH: 0-1 Tight: 0-2 Gall: 0-0
Aids: Bl: 0-0 Vi: 0-0 Tstrap: 0-0 Ckp: 0-0
Best Rating: 92 10/09 Ling 6f stand

Useful; effective at 6f; acts on fast ground and Polytrack.

Oniz Tiptoes (IRE)

105 47

8-y-o ch g Russian Revival (USA)-Edionda (IRE) (Magical Strike (USA))

J S Wainwright drawn2win.co.uk Partnership

Placings:00/06420/4660/0-6 (4806)

2009: 14^{6}GF,

	Starts	1st	2nd	3rd	Win & Pl
Career Total (Turf)	12	0	1	0	1388
Career Total (AW)	1	0	0	0	

Going (Turf): Sf: 0-0 GS: 0-2 Gd: 0-2 GF: 0-6 Fm: 0-2
Distance: 5f/6f: 0-1 7f-8f: 0-1 9f-13f: 0-8 14f+: 0-3
Track : LH: 0-7 RH: 0-5 Tight: 0-9 Gall: 0-0
Aids: Bl: 0-1 Vi: 0-7 Tstrap: 0-2 Ckp: 0-2
Best Rating: 66 7/07 Pont 1m4f8y good

Only A Game (IRE)

101(106) (61)67

4-y-o b g Foxhound (USA)-Compendium (Puissance)

I W McInnes (Miss M E Rowland 10/3) Hall Farm Racing

Placings:112022/1200-000005140000300421 (7771)

2009: 7^{0}SD, 7^{0}SD, 6^{0}SD, 7^{0}SD, 5^{0}SD, 5^{5}GF, 5^{1}F, 5^{4}GF, 5^{0}GF, 5^{0}GS, 5^{0}G, 7^{0}GF, 6^{3}GF, 7^{0}SD, 7^{0}G, 5^{4}SD, 6^{2}SD, 6^{1}SD,

	Starts	1st	2nd	3rd	Win & Pl
Career Total (Turf)	13	2	1	1	6086
Career Total (AW)	15	3	4	0	9836

61 12/09 Ling 6f (0-55)H STD £1637
67 6/09 Bevl 5f (0-65)H FRM £2428
78 1/08 Sthl 6f (0-75)H SS £2593
67 7/07 Yarm 6f3y G-F £1943
60 7/07 Ling 5f STD £2184

Total win prize-money £10787

Going (Turf): Sf: 0-0 GS: 0-2 Gd: 0-2 GF: 1-8 Fm: 1-1
Distance: 5f/6f: 4-17 7f-8f: 1-11 9f-13f: 0-0 14f+: 0-0
Track : LH: 3-18 RH: 0-2 Tight: 2-10 Gall: 0-0
Aids: Bl: 0-1 Vi: 0-0 Tstrap: 3-14 Ckp: 3-14
Best Rating: 78 1/08 Sthl 6f std-slw

Moderate; stays 7f but effective over shorter; acts on fast ground and sand; has worn cheekpieces.

Only A Grand

(98) (58)53

5-y-o b m Cloudings (IRE)-Magic Orb (Primo Dominie)

R Bastiman Robin Bastiman

Placings:060204154/000006023125/62326003500-0000 (0608)

2009: 8^{0}SS, 7^{0}SD, 8^{0}SD, 8^{0}SD,

	Starts	1st	2nd	3rd	Win & Pl
Career Total (Turf)	22	1	2	1	4779
Career Total (AW)	14	1	3	2	4303

58 12/07 Sthl 1m (0-58)H SS £2047
61 10/06 Muss 5f G-S £2047

Total win prize-money £4096

Going (Turf): Sf: 0-2 GS: 1-6 Gd: 0-5 GF: 0-7 Fm: 0-2
Distance: 5f/6f: 1-13 7f-8f: 1-20 9f-13f: 0-3 14f+: 0-0
Track : LH: 1-16 RH: 0-5 Tight: 0-5 Gall: 0-0
Aids: Bl: 2-29 Vi: 0-0 Tstrap: 0-0 Ckp: 0-0
Best Rating: 61 10/06 Muss 5f gd-sft

Very moderate; stays 1m; acts on most ground and Fibresand; has worn blinkers.

Only A Splash

101(86) (32)56

5-y-o b g Primo Valentino (IRE)-Water Well (Sadler's Wells (USA))

Mrs R A Carr David W Chapman

Placings:6502500600/000/6050005-600210005 (5332)

2009: 5^{6}G, 5^{0}GF, 5^{0}GF, 7^{2}GS, 6^{1}S, 7^{0}G, 5^{0}G, 6^{0}SD, 7^{5}S,

	Starts	1st	2nd	3rd	Win & Pl
Career Total (Turf)	22	1	2	0	5462
Career Total (AW)	7	0	0	0	0

56 7/09 Ripn 6f (0-70)H SFT £3885

Total win prize-money £3886

Going (Turf): Sf: 1-5 GS: 0-3 Gd: 0-5 GF: 0-9 Fm: 0-0
Distance: 5f/6f: 1-17 7f-8f: 0-10 9f-13f: 0-2 14f+: 0-0
Track : LH: 0-14 RH: 0-4 Tight: 0-11 Gall: 0-1
Aids: Bl: 0-0 Vi: 0-0 Tstrap: 0-1 Ckp: 0-1
Best Rating: 56 7/09 Ripn 6f soft

Moderate; stays 7f; acts on soft ground.

Only Hope

(99) (53)27

5-y-o b m Marju (IRE)-Sellette (IRE) (Selkirk (USA))

M Sheppard (P S McEntee 19/2) Team Fusion

Placings:05354030050/00040/06664000-40430 (0602)

2009: 6^{4}SD, 6^{0}SD, 6^{4}SD, 5^{3}SD, 5^{0}SD,

	Starts	1st	2nd	3rd	Win & Pl
Career Total (Turf)	11	0	0	2	1694
Career Total (AW)	18	0	0	1	548

Going (Turf): Sf: 0-2 GS: 0-2 Gd: 0-3 GF: 0-3 Fm: 0-1
Distance: 5f/6f: 0-7 7f-8f: 0-9 9f-13f: 0-12 14f+: 0-1
Track : LH: 0-12 RH: 0-8 Tight: 0-8 Gall: 0-2
Aids: Bl: 0-3 Vi: 0-6 Tstrap: 0-10 Ckp: 0-10
Best Rating: 64 10/06 NmkR 1m gd-sft

Plating-class filly; has worn headgear.

Onyx Of Arabia (IRE)

94 75

2-y-o b c Avonbridge-Fiamma Royale (IRE) (Fumo Di Londra (IRE))

B J Meehan Miss A Al-Hejailan

Placings:5240 (6842)

2009: 6^{5}G, 7^{2}GF, 7^{4}G, 7^{0}G,

	Starts	1st	2nd	3rd	Win & Pl
Career Total (Turf)	4	0	1	0	1071

Going (Turf): Sf: 0-0 GS: 0-0 Gd: 0-3 GF: 0-1 Fm: 0-0
Distance: 5f/6f: 0-1 7f-8f: 0-3 9f-13f: 0-0 14f+: 0-0
Track : LH: 0-1 RH: 0-0 Tight: 0-1 Gall: 0-1
Aids: Bl: 0-0 Vi: 0-0 Tstrap: 0-0 Ckp: 0-0
Best Rating: 75 8/09 Folk 7f gd-fm

Fair; stays 7f; acts on fast ground.

Oondiri (IRE)

95 69

2-y-o b f Trans Island-Nullarbor (Green Desert (USA))

T D Easterby C H Stevens

Placings:6313350545 (6554)

2009: 5^{6}GF, 5^{3}GF, 5^{1}GF, 5^{3}GF, 5^{3}F, 5^{5}G, 6^{0}GF, 5^{5}GF, 5^{4}GF, 5^{5}GF,

	Starts	1st	2nd	3rd	Win & Pl
Career Total (Turf)	10	1	0	3	4646

69 5/09 Rdcr 5f G-F £2729

Total win prize-money £2730

Going (Turf): Sf: 0-0 GS: 0-0 Gd: 0-1 GF: 1-8 Fm: 0-1
Distance: 5f/6f: 1-10 7f-8f: 0-0 9f-13f: 0-0 14f+: 0-0
Track : LH: 0-0 RH: 0-0 Tight: 0-0 Gall: 0-0
Aids: Bl: 0-1 Vi: 0-0 Tstrap: 0-0 Ckp: 0-0
Best Rating: 69 5/09 Rdcr 5f gd-fm

Modest; suited by 5f; acts on fast ground.

Oops Another Act

94(94) (59)42

4-y-o gr/ro f Act One-Oops Pettie (Machiavellian (USA))

A M Hales (W R Swinburn 19/5) Miss Sally Burnell

Placings:0550-00 (2171)

2009: 10^{0}SD, 10^{0}GF,

	Starts	1st	2nd	3rd	Win & Pl
Career Total (Turf)	2	0	0	0	0
Career Total (AW)	4	0	0	0	0

Going (Turf): Sf: 0-0 GS: 0-1 Gd: 0-0 GF: 0-1 Fm: 0-0
Distance: 5f/6f: 0-0 7f-8f: 0-0 9f-13f: 0-6 14f+: 0-0
Track : LH: 0-4 RH: 0-2 Tight: 0-4 Gall: 0-1
Aids: Bl: 0-0 Vi: 0-0 Tstrap: 0-1 Ckp: 0-1
Best Rating: 59 6/08 Kemp 1m2f stand

Oor Wee Miracle (GER)

52

3-y-o b f Tiger Hill (IRE)-Old Tradition (IRE) (Royal Academy (USA))

M Dods Gordon Coburn & Robert Reid Partnership

Placings:0 (3022)

2009: 9^{0}G,

	Starts	1st	2nd	3rd	Win & Pl
Career Total (Turf)	1	0	0	0	

Going (Turf): Sf: 0-0 GS: 0-0 Gd: 0-1 GF: 0-0 Fm: 0-0
Distance: 5f/6f: 0-0 7f-8f: 0-0 9f-13f: 0-1 14f+: 0-0

Track : LH: 0-0 RH: 0-1 Tight: 0-1 Gall: 0-0
Aids: Bl: 0-0 Vi: 0-0 Tstrap: 0-0 Ckp: 0-0

Open Glory (FR)

87(84) (57)62

2-y-o b f Lando (GER)-Lovigna (GER) (Komtur (USA))
Tom Dascombe Timeform Betfair Racing Club Partnership

Placings:00000 (5985)
2009: 7^0GF, 6^0GF, 6^0S, 7^0SD, 8^0SD,

	Starts	1st	2nd	3rd	Win & Pl
Career Total (Turf)	3	0	0	0	
Career Total (AW)	2	0	0	0	

Going (Turf): **Sf: 0-1 GS: 0-0 Gd: 0-0 GF: 0-2 Fm: 0-0**
Distance: 5f/6f: 0-0 7f-8f: 0-5 9f-13f: 0-0 14f+: 0-0
Track : LH: 0-1 RH: 0-1 Tight: 0-1 Gall: 0-0
Aids: Bl: 0-0 Vi: 0-0 Tstrap: 0-0 Ckp: 0-0
Best Rating: 62 7/09 Sals 6f212y gd-fm

Open Sesame (IRE)

109 (73)92

3-y-o b g Key Of Luck (USA)-Chiquita Linda (IRE) (Mujadil (USA))
P W Chapple-Hyam Joy And Valentine Feerick

Placings:111 (2230)
2009: 9^1SD, 8^1GF, 10^1HY,

	Starts	1st	2nd	3rd	Win & Pl
Career Total (Turf)	2	2	0	0	7124
Career Total (AW)	1	1	0	0	1943

84 5/09 Hayd 1m2f95y (0-75)H HVY £3238
92 5/09 NmkR 1m (0-75)H G-F £3885
73 1/09 GrLe 1m1f46y STD £1942
Total win prize-money £9067

Going (Turf): **Sf: 1-1** GS: 0-0 Gd: 0-0 **GF: 1-1** Fm: 0-0
Distance: 5f/6f: 0-0 7f-8f: **1-1 9f-13f: 2-2** 14f+: 0-0
Track : **LH: 2-2** RH: 0-0 Tight: 0-0 **Gall: 1-1**
Aids: Bl: 0-0 Vi: 0-0 Tstrap: 0-0 Ckp: 0-0
Best Rating: 92 5/09 NmkR 1m gd-fm

Useful; stays 1m2f; acts on fast and heavy ground; goes on Polytrack.

Openide

79(97) (42)37

8-y-o b g Key Of Luck (USA)-Eyelet (IRE) (Satco (FR))
B W Duke Brendan W Duke Racing

Placings:03044560/505/0-50 (2127)
2009: 16^5SD, 17^0GS,

	Starts	1st	2nd	3rd	Win & Pl
Career Total (Turf)	11	0	0	1	1395
Career Total (AW)	3	0	0	0	0

Going (Turf): **Sf: 0-2 GS: 0-2 Gd: 0-3 GF: 0-4 Fm: 0-0**
Distance: 5f/6f: 0-0 7f-8f: 0-0 9f-13f: 0-1 14f+: 0-13
Track : LH: 0-12 RH: 0-2 Tight: 0-6 Gall: 0-1
Aids: Bl: 0-0 Vi: 0-0 Tstrap: 0-1 Ckp: 0-1
Best Rating: 84 5/06 Ling 2m good

Opening Hand

(83) (38)58

4-y-o b g Observatory (USA)-Belle Ile (USA) (Diesis)
J Mackie (G J Smith 4/6) P Voce

Placings:60000-00 (1442)
2009: 8^0SD, 12^0SD,

	Starts	1st	2nd	3rd	Win & Pl
Career Total (Turf)	3	0	0	0	
Career Total (AW)	4	0	0	0	0

Going (Turf): **Sf: 0-0 GS: 0-0 Gd: 0-2 GF: 0-1 Fm: 0-0**
Distance: 5f/6f: 0-1 7f-8f: 0-2 9f-13f: 0-4 14f+: 0-0
Track : LH: 0-6 RH: 0-0 Tight: 0-2 Gall: 0-1
Aids: Bl: 0-0 Vi: 0-0 Tstrap: 0-3 Ckp: 0-3
Best Rating: 58 5/08 Newb 7f good

Moderate; stays qm; handles Polytrack; has worn cheek-pieces.

Opera Gal (IRE)

98 74

2-y-o b f Galileo (IRE)-Opera Glass (Barathea (IRE))
A M Balding J C Smith

Placings:542 (6729)
2009: 7^5GF, 8^4GS, 6^2S,

	Starts	1st	2nd	3rd	Win & Pl
Career Total (Turf)	3	0	1	0	1216

Going (Turf): **Sf: 0-1 GS: 0-1 Gd: 0-0 GF: 0-1 Fm: 0-0**
Distance: 5f/6f: 0-0 7f-8f: 0-3 9f-13f: 0-0 14f+: 0-0
Track : LH: 0-0 RH: 0-0 Tight: 0-0 Gall: 0-0
Aids: Bl: 0-0 Vi: 0-0 Tstrap: 0-0 Ckp: 0-0
Best Rating: 74 10/09 Sals 6f212y soft

Fair; stays 7f; acts on soft ground.

Opera Prince

104(106) (89)93

4-y-o b g Kyllachy-Optaria (Song)
S Kirk J C Smith

Placings:00/21344131-0000006 (6907)
2009: 11^0SD, 10^0G, 10^0G, 8^0G, 8^0G, 8^0GS, 10^6G,

	Starts	1st	2nd	3rd	Win & Pl
Career Total (Turf)	14	3	0	1	15691
Career Total (AW)	3	0	1	1	3058

93 10/08 Wind 1m2f7y (0-85)H GD £5375
89 9/08 Sand 1m14y (0-80)H SFT £5180
78 5/08 Wwck 7f26y (0-75)H G-F £3238
Total win prize-money £13794

Going (Turf): **Sf: 1-1** GS: 0-1 **Gd: 1-9 GF: 1-3** Fm: 0-0
Distance: 5f/6f: 0-3 7f-8f: 1-7 **9f-13f: 2-7** 14f+: 0-0
Track : LH: 1-5 **RH: 2-7 Tight: 1-5** Gall: 0-1
Aids: Bl: 0-0 Vi: 0-0 Tstrap: 0-0 Ckp: 0-0
Best Rating: 93 10/08 Wind 1m2f7y good

Useful; stays 1m2f; acts on most ground and on Polytrack.

Opera Wings

94(90) (60)65

3-y-o ch f Medicean-Wings Of Love (Groom Dancer (USA))
Sir Michael Stoute Patrick J Fahey

Placings:4-45 (5093)
2009: 10^4GF, 12^5SD,

	Starts	1st	2nd	3rd	Win & Pl
Career Total (Turf)	1	0	0	0	0
Career Total (AW)	2	0	0	0	241

Going (Turf): **Sf: 0-0 GS: 0-0 Gd: 0-0 GF: 0-1 Fm: 0-0**
Distance: 5f/6f: 0-0 7f-8f: 0-1 9f-13f: 0-2 14f+: 0-0
Track : LH: 0-1 RH: 0-2 Tight: 0-2 Gall: 0-0
Aids: Bl: 0-0 Vi: 0-0 Tstrap: 0-0 Ckp: 0-0
Best Rating: 65 8/09 Wind 1m2f7y gd-fm

Moderate; should stay 1m; acts on Poltrack; sure to improve.

Opera Writer (IRE)

(105) (71)74

6-y-o b g Rossini (USA)-Miss Flite (IRE) (Law Society (USA))
R Hollinshead John L Marriott

Placings:434/56445110500222/340603362/10320546163 0110254-0 (0324)
2009: 11^0SD,

	Starts	1st	2nd	3rd	Win & Pl
Career Total (Turf)	18	3	1	2	10774
Career Total (AW)	27	3	5	4	14402

71 10/08 Wwck 1m4f134y (0-65)H SFT £2729
70 9/08 Wwck 1m2f188y (0-60)H GD £1977
61 7/08 Wwck 1m4f134y (0-60)H G-F £2047
65 1/08 Wolv 1m5f194y (0-75)H STD £2590
74 7/06 Ling 1m STD £2388
71 7/06 Sthl 1m STD £3238
Total win prize-money £14974

Going (Turf): **Sf: 1-2** GS: 0-2 **Gd: 1-6 GF: 1-8** Fm: 0-0
Distance: 5f/6f: 0-6 7f-8f: 2-5 **9f-13f: 3-24** 14f+: 1-10
Track : **LH: 6-37** RH: 0-4 **Tight: 2-18** Gall: 0-3
Aids: Bl: 0-0 Vi: 0-2 Tstrap: 3-14 Ckp: 3-14
Best Rating: 74 11/08 Nott 1m2f50y heavy

Modest; effective over 1m2f-1m6f; acts on good and heavy ground; goes on sand; has worn cheekpieces and a visor.

Ophistrolie (IRE)

81 22

7-y-o b g Foxhound (USA)-Thoughtful Kate (Rock Hopper)
H J Manners Exors Of The Late H J Manners

Placings:0/0043040045005/0 (3533)
2009: 11^0GF,

	Starts	1st	2nd	3rd	Win & Pl
Career Total (Turf)	14	0	0	1	429
Career Total (AW)	1	0	0	0	

Going (Turf): **Sf: 0-2 GS: 0-2 Gd: 0-5 GF: 0-3 Fm: 0-2**
Distance: 5f/6f: 0-0 7f-8f: 0-2 9f-13f: 0-12 14f+: 0-1
Track : LH: 0-11 RH: 0-2 Tight: 0-7 Gall: 0-1
Aids: Bl: 0-1 Vi: 0-0 Tstrap: 0-0 Ckp: 0-0
Best Rating: 46 6/05 Yarm 1m3f101y firm

Opinion Poll (IRE)

111 109

3-y-o b c Halling (USA)-Ahead (Shirley Heights)
M A Jarvis Sheikh Ahmed Al Maktoum

Placings:01 3101 (6662)
2009: 10^3GF, 11^1HY, 12^0GF, 12^1GS,

	Starts	1st	2nd	3rd	Win & Pl
Career Total (Turf)	6	3	0	1	66241

109 10/09 Asct 1m4f (0-105)H G-S £46732
101 5/09 Hayd 1m3f200y (0-100)H HVY £12462
86 10/08 Leic 1m60y GD £5180
Total win prize-money £64376

Going (Turf): Sf: 1-1 GS: 1-1 Gd: 1-1 GF: 0-3 Fm: 0-0
Distance: 5f/6f: 0-0 7f-8f: 0-1 9f-13f: 3-5 14f+: 0-0
Track: LH: 1-1 RH: 2-3 Tight: 0-0 Gall: 1-2
Aids: Bl: 0-0 Vi: 0-0 Tstrap: 0-0 Ckp: 0-0
Best Rating: 109 10/09 Asct 1m4f gd-sft

Smart; stays 1m4f; suited by soft ground.

Optical Illusion (USA)

101(98) (61)67
5-y-o b g Theatrical-Paradise River (USA) (Irish River (FR))
R A Fahey James Gaffney

Placings:0/65035000/23160000200-430103405 (6925)
2009: 7^{4}G, 7^{3}GF, 5^{0}GF, 6^{1}GF, 6^{0}G, 7^{3}G, 7^{4}G, 5^{0}SD, 7^{5}GF,

	Starts	1st	2nd	3rd	Win & Pl
Career Total (Turf)	21	2	0	3	6539
Career Total (AW)	8	0	2	1	1511

63 6/09 Haml 6f5y (0-65)H G-F £2047
67 7/08 Haml 6f5y (0-65)H GD £2388
Total win prize-money £4435

Going (Turf): Sf: 0-2 GS: 0-3 Gd: 1-7 GF: 1-9 Fm: 0-0
Distance: 5f/6f: 0-3 7f-8f: 2-23 9f-13f: 0-3 14f+: 0-0
Track: LH: 0-10 RH: 0-8 Tight: 0-12 Gall: 0-1
Aids: Bl: 0-0 Vi: 0-0 Tstrap: 0-4 Ckp: 0-4
Best Rating: 74 10/06 Leic 7f9y gd-sft

Moderate; effective at 7f; acts on most types of ground and on Polytrack.

Optical Seclusion (IRE)

52(56) (56)16
6-y-o b g Second Empire (IRE)-Theda (Mummy's Pet)
K W Hogg (A Berry 17/2) K W Hogg

Placings:40040/3505050/35400/0-00 (2155)
2009: 5^{0}SD, 9^{0}GF,

	Starts	1st	2nd	3rd	Win & Pl
Career Total (Turf)	12	0	0	1	1003
Career Total (AW)	8	0	0	1	302

Going (Turf): Sf: 0-1 GS: 0-0 Gd: 0-4 GF: 0-6 Fm: 0-1
Distance: 5f/6f: 0-16 7f-8f: 0-3 9f-13f: 0-1 14f+: 0-0
Track: LH: 0-9 RH: 0-5 Tight: 0-10 Gall: 0-1
Aids: Bl: 0-8 Vi: 0-0 Tstrap: 0-0 Ckp: 0-0
Best Rating: 58 6/06 Carl 5f193y gd-fm

Optimistic Duke (IRE)

83(72) (19)53
2-y-o ch g Bachelor Duke (USA)-Gronchi Rosa (IRE) (Nashwan (USA))
W R Muir Linkslade Optimists

Placings:000 (7325)
2009: 7^{0}SS, 8^{0}S, 7^{0}SD,

	Starts	1st	2nd	3rd	Win & Pl
Career Total (Turf)	1	0	0	0	
Career Total (AW)	2	0	0	0	

Going (Turf): Sf: 0-1 GS: 0-0 Gd: 0-0 GF: 0-0 Fm: 0-0
Distance: 5f/6f: 0-0 7f-8f: 0-3 9f-13f: 0-0 14f+: 0-0
Track: LH: 0-1 RH: 0-1 Tight: 0-1 Gall: 0-0
Aids: Bl: 0-0 Vi: 0-0 Tstrap: 0-0 Ckp: 0-0
Best Rating: 53 10/09 Newb 1m soft

Optimum (IRE)

(93) (50)56
7-y-o br g King's Best (USA)-Colour Dance (Rainbow Quest (USA))
J T Stimpson J T Stimpson

Placings:050/0223/000100650/0/30-06 (0148)
2009: 16^{0}SS, 16^{6}SD,

	Starts	1st	2nd	3rd	Win & Pl
Career Total (Turf)	5	0	0	0	0
Career Total (AW)	16	1	2	2	5340

67 7/06 Sthl 1m6f (0-55)H STD £2730
Total win prize-money £2730

Going (Turf): Sf: 0-0 GS: 0-0 Gd: 0-2 GF: 0-2 Fm: 0-1
Distance: 5f/6f: 0-0 7f-8f: 0-2 9f-13f: 0-9 14f+: 1-10
Track: LH: 1-19 RH: 0-1 Tight: 0-8 Gall: 0-0
Aids: Bl: 0-0 Vi: 0-1 Tstrap: 0-0 Ckp: 0-0
Best Rating: 67 7/06 Sthl 1m6f stand

Opus Dei

95(99) (72)70
2-y-o b g Oasis Dream-Grail (USA) (Quest For Fame)
J A Glover (A J McCabe 19/6) Brian Morton

Placings:36020 (7494)
2009: 6^{3}G, 6^{6}GF, 6^{0}S, 7^{2}SD, 7^{0}SD,

	Starts	1st	2nd	3rd	Win & Pl
Career Total (Turf)	3	0	0	1	482
Career Total (AW)	2	0	1	0	1349

Going (Turf): Sf: 0-1 GS: 0-0 Gd: 0-1 GF: 0-1 Fm: 0-0
Distance: 5f/6f: 0-3 7f-8f: 0-2 9f-13f: 0-0 14f+: 0-0
Track: LH: 0-2 RH: 0-0 Tight: 0-2 Gall: 0-0
Aids: Bl: 0-1 Vi: 0-0 Tstrap: 0-0 Ckp: 0-0
Best Rating: 72 11/09 Wolv 7f32y stand

Fair; stays 7f; acts on good ground and on Polytrack.

Opus Maximus (IRE)

107(113) (87)96
4-y-o ch g Titus Livius (FR)-Law Review (IRE) (Case Law)
M Johnston Jim McGrath

Placings:2105104044106164-565001200500433025 (6485)
2009: 7^{5}SD, 8^{6}SD, 8^{5}SD, 8^{0}GF, 8^{0}SD, 7^{1}G, 7^{2}GF, 7^{0}GF, 8^{0}G, 7^{5}S, 6^{0}GS, 6^{0}G, 7^{4}G, 8^{3}G, 7^{3}GF, 8^{0}G, 8^{2}GF, 8^{5}GF,

	Starts	1st	2nd	3rd	Win & Pl
Career Total (Turf)	26	4	2	2	45825
Career Total (AW)	8	1	1	0	3703

94 5/09 Muss 7f30y (0-90)H GD £7477
90 9/08 Yarm 1m3y (0-85)H GD £4731
84 7/08 Nott 1m75y (0-85)H GD £6231
80 5/08 Haml 6f5y (0-80)H G-F £7123
74 3/08 Ling 6f STD £2331
Total win prize-money £27895

Going (Turf): Sf: 0-1 GS: 0-2 Gd: 3-13 GF: 1-9 Fm: 0-1
Distance: 5f/6f: 1-7 7f-8f: 2-22 9f-13f: 2-5 14f+: 0-0
Track: LH: 2-14 RH: 1-6 Tight: 2-10 Gall: 0-2
Aids: Bl: 0-0 Vi: 0-0 Tstrap: 0-0 Ckp: 0-0
Best Rating: 96 5/09 Ches 7f122y gd-fm

Useful; effective at 7f-1m; acts on good and faster ground; goes on Polytrack.

Orange Pip

100(99) (84)86
4-y-o ch f Bold Edge-Opopmil (IRE) (Pips Pride)
R Hannon Lady Whent

Placings:2/2210-025500 (5719)
2009: 6^{0}GS, 6^{2}SD, 6^{5}GF, 5^{5}GF, 6^{0}GS, 5^{0}G,

	Starts	1st	2nd	3rd	Win & Pl
Career Total (Turf)	10	1	3	0	6535
Career Total (AW)	1	0	1	0	1407

86 6/08 Wind 6f (0-70)H G-F £2729
Total win prize-money £2730

Going (Turf): Sf: 0-0 GS: 0-2 Gd: 0-2 GF: 1-6 Fm: 0-0
Distance: 5f/6f: 1-11 7f-8f: 0-0 9f-13f: 0-0 14f+: 0-0
Track: LH: 0-1 RH: 0-1 Tight: 0-0 Gall: 1-4
Aids: Bl: 0-0 Vi: 0-0 Tstrap: 0-0 Ckp: 0-0
Best Rating: 86 6/08 Wind 6f gd-fm

Useful; suited by 6f and acts on fast ground.

Orange Square (IRE)

(94) (65)48
4-y-o br g King Charlemagne (USA)-Unaria (Prince Tenderfoot (USA))
D W Barker D W Barker

Placings:0324/5332140000-40340 (1055)
2009: 6^{4}SD, 6^{0}SS, 6^{3}SD, 5^{4}SD, 5^{0}SD,

	Starts	1st	2nd	3rd	Win & Pl
Career Total (Turf)	4	0	0	0	
Career Total (AW)	15	1	2	4	4101

50 2/08 Wolv 5f20y STD £1774
Total win prize-money £1775

Going (Turf): Sf: 0-0 GS: 0-0 Gd: 0-3 GF: 0-1 Fm: 0-0
Distance: 5f/6f: 1-17 7f-8f: 0-2 9f-13f: 0-0 14f+: 0-0
Track: LH: 1-9 RH: 0-4 Tight: 1-6 Gall: 0-0
Aids: Bl: 0-0 Vi: 0-3 Tstrap: 0-1 Ckp: 0-1
Best Rating: 65 1/08 Kemp 5f stand

Moderate sprinter; acts on Fibresand and Polytrack.

Orangeleg

98(100) 55
3-y-o b g Intikhab (USA)-Red Shareef (Marju (IRE))
S C Williams K Harrison, J Allen

Placings:000-131 (7877)
2009: 6^{1}F, 7^{3}F, 7^{1}SD,

	Starts	1st	2nd	3rd	Win & Pl
Career Total (Turf)	5	1	0	1	2717
Career Total (AW)	1	1	0	0	1638

12/09 Ling 7f (0-52)H STD £1637
53 7/09 Brig 6f209y (0-65)H FRM £2331
Total win prize-money £3969

Going (Turf): Sf: 0-1 GS: 0-0 Gd: 0-0 GF: 0-1 Fm: 1-3
Distance: 5f/6f: 0-2 7f-8f: 2-4 9f-13f: 0-0 14f+: 0-0
Track: LH: 2-3 RH: 0-0 Tight: 1-1 Gall: 0-0
Aids: Bl: 0-0 Vi: 0-0 Tstrap: 0-0 Ckp: 0-0
Best Rating: 55 8/09 Brig 7f214y firm

Moderate; effective over 7f; acts on fast ground and on Polytrack.

Oratory (IRE)

96(98) (82)90
3-y-o b g Danehill Dancer (IRE)-Gentle Night (Zafonic (USA))

R Hannon Highclere Thoroughbred Racing (Munnings)

Placings:0120-00 (6702)
2009: 8⁰GS, 7⁰SS,

	Starts	1st	2nd	3rd	Win & Pl
Career Total (Turf)	5	1	1	0	6610
Career Total (AW)	1	0	0	0	

80 6/08 Sals 6f212y G-F £4371
Total win prize-money £4371

Going (Turf): Sf: 0-0 GS: 0-1 Gd: 0-2 **GF: 1-2** Fm: 0-0
Distance: 5f/6f: 0-1 **7f-8f: 1-5** 9f-13f: 0-0 14f+: 0-0
Track : LH: 0-1 RH: 0-1 Tight: 0-1 Gall: 0-0
Aids: Bl: 0-0 Vi: 0-0 Tstrap: 0-0 Ckp: 0-0
Best Rating: 90 8/08 Sand 7f16y good

Very useful; effective at 7f; acts fast ground.

Orbitor

103(99) (74)**78**
3-y-o b g Galileo (IRE)-Peacock Alley (IRE) (Salse (USA))
M L W Bell C Headfort and P Robinson

Placings:021-33 **(1512)**
2009: 10³G, 11³GF,

	Starts	1st	2nd	3rd	Win & Pl
Career Total (Turf)	4	0	1	2	3563
Career Total (AW)	1	1	0	0	3886

74 10/08 GrLe 1m2f STD £3885
Total win prize-money £3886

Going (Turf): Sf: 0-0 GS: 0-1 Gd: 0-1 GF: 0-2 Fm: 0-0
Distance: 5f/6f: 0-0 7f-8f: 0-1 **9f-13f: 1-4** 14f+: 0-0
Track : LH: 1-3 RH: 0-1 Tight: 0-0 **Gall: 1-2**
Aids: Bl: 0-0 Vi: 0-0 Tstrap: 0-0 Ckp: 0-0
Best Rating: 78 10/08 Nott 1m75y gd-sft

Fair; stays 1m; acts on Polytrack and easy ground on turf.

Orchard House (FR)

103(101) (54)**43**
6-y-o b g Medaaly-Louisa May (IRE) (Royal Abjar (USA))
Evan Williams R E R Williams

Placings:0006053/3100/00-30 **(1399)**
2009: 16³SD, 21⁰F,

	Starts	1st	2nd	3rd	Win & Pl
Career Total (Turf)	6	0	0	0	0
Career Total (AW)	9	1	0	3	3215

61 6/07 Sthl 1m6f (0-50)H STD £2388
Total win prize-money £2389

Going (Turf): Sf: 0-1 GS: 0-1 Gd: 0-3 GF: 0-0 Fm: 0-1
Distance: 5f/6f: 0-1 7f-8f: 0-1 9f-13f: 0-6 **14f+: 1-7**
Track : LH: 1-12 RH: 0-2 Tight: 0-5 Gall: 0-0
Aids: Bl: 1-8 Vi: 0-0 Tstrap: 0-0 Ckp: 0-0
Best Rating: 61 6/07 Sthl 1m6f stand

Moderate gelding; stays 1m6f and acts on Fibresand.

Orchard Supreme

103(112) (106)**96**
6-y-o ch g Titus Livius (FR)-Bogus Penny (IRE) (Pennekamp (USA))
R Hannon Brian C Oakley

Placings:0006102**221**/3115104063**62151**/444103051544**2**
52/26000100200461**005**-10450004006 **(7626)**
2009: 7¹SD, 8⁰SD, 8⁴SD, 7⁵SD, 7⁰GF, 8⁰G, 8⁰GF, 8⁴GF, 8⁰SS, 7⁰SD, 8⁶SD,

	Starts	1st	2nd	3rd	Win & Pl
Career Total (Turf)	28	3	1	0	28313
Career Total (AW)	40	9	7	3	120538

99 1/09 Wolv 7f32y STD £12462
106 11/08 GrLe 1m1f46y STD £8095
96 5/08 Gdwd 1m (0-85)H GD £4533
93 9/07 Asct 1m (0-100)H GD £15580
107 3/07 Wolv 1m141y (0-105)H STD £31160
103 12/06 Ling 1m (0-95)H STD £11092
100 11/06 Kemp 1m (0-95)H STD £7790
92 5/06 Ling 7f (0-95)H STD £11217
87 3/06 Ling 1m (0-75)H STD £3238
88 2/06 Ling 7f (0-75)H STD £3238
75 12/05 Ling 6f (0-85) STD £4663
72 11/05 Catt 7f SFT £3224
Total win prize-money £116297

Going (Turf): Sf: 1-6 GS: 0-2 **Gd: 2-8** GF: 0-11 Fm: 0-1
Distance: 5f/6f: 1-5 **7f-8f: 9-47** 9f-13f: 2-16 14f+: 0-0
Track : LH: 9-37 RH: 2-18 **Tight: 8-40** Gall: 1-1
Aids: Bl: 0-2 Vi: 0-1 Tstrap: 0-1 Ckp: 0-1
Best Rating: 107 3/08 Ling 1m2f stand

Smart on sand; useful on turf; effective over 7f-1m; acts well on soft ground; suited to Polytrack; has worn blinkers.

Orchestration (IRE)

(94) (49)**58**
8-y-o ch g Stravinsky (USA)-Mora (IRE) (Second Set (IRE))
Garry Moss Brooklands Racing

Placings:26/44000**6052**/03001**3260**06013**31115**/534020**2**
300004**3056021**/**4**00**1**06000266/04504400000**0-3**
(0475)
2009: 5³SD,

	Starts	1st	2nd	3rd	Win & Pl
Career Total (Turf)	11	0	1	0	1702
Career Total (AW)	65	7	6	8	17768

54 2/07 Wolv 5f20y (0-50)H STD £2388
55 12/06 Sthl 5f (0-45) STD £1365
62 12/05 Sthl 5f (0-45) STD £1409
57 11/05 Wolv 5f216y (0-45) STD £1521
61 11/05 Sthl 5f (0-45) STD £1416
55 10/05 Sthl 5f (0-45) STD £1487
51 3/05 Wolv 5f216y STD £1487
Total win prize-money £11077

Going (Turf): Sf: 0-0 GS: 0-0 Gd: 0-4 GF: 0-7 Fm: 0-0
Distance: 5f/6f: 7-64 7f-8f: 0-10 9f-13f: 0-2 14f+: 0-0
Track : LH: 3-45 RH: 0-6 **Tight: 3-28** Gall: 0-1
Aids: Bl: 0-3 **Vi: 7-51** Tstrap: 0-1 Ckp: 0-1
Best Rating: 65 7/03 Haml 5f4y gd-fm

Very moderate sprinter; effective over 5f-6f; acts on Fibresand and Polytrack; has worn a visor.

Orchestrion

47(67) **63**
4-y-o ch f Piccolo-Mindomica (Dominion)
Miss T Jackson H L Thompson

Placings:3/425500-0 **(4139)**
2009: 9⁰G,

	Starts	1st	2nd	3rd	Win & Pl
Career Total (Turf)	7	0	1	1	2620
Career Total (AW)	1	0	0	0	0

Going (Turf): Sf: 0-1 GS: 0-1 Gd: 0-3 GF: 0-2 Fm: 0-0
Distance: 5f/6f: 0-2 7f-8f: 0-4 9f-13f: 0-2 14f+: 0-0
Track : LH: 0-3 RH: 0-1 Tight: 0-2 Gall: 0-1
Aids: Bl: 0-0 Vi: 0-0 Tstrap: 0-0 Ckp: 0-0
Best Rating: 63 8/08 Thsk 7f good

Modest filly; stays 7f; acts on fast ground.

Orchid Wing

94(92) (68)**68**
2-y-o ch c Avonbridge-First Ace (First Trump)
R A Fahey Mrs D Jeromson

Placings:5002 **(7674)**
2009: 6⁵G, 5⁰GF, 6⁰S, 5²SD,

	Starts	1st	2nd	3rd	Win & Pl
Career Total (Turf)	3	0	0	0	0
Career Total (AW)	1	0	1	0	806

Going (Turf): Sf: 0-1 GS: 0-0 Gd: 0-1 GF: 0-1 Fm: 0-0
Distance: 5f/6f: 0-4 7f-8f: 0-0 9f-13f: 0-0 14f+: 0-0
Track : LH: 0-0 RH: 0-0 Tight: 0-0 Gall: 0-0
Aids: Bl: 0-0 Vi: 0-0 Tstrap: 0-0 Ckp: 0-0
Best Rating: 68 12/09 Sthl 5f stand

Modest; effective over 5f; acts on Fibresand.

Order Order

95(99) (64)**62**
3-y-o br f Diktat-Brocheta (Hector Protector (USA))
Tim Vaughan (H J L Dunlop 16/11) Notalotterry

Placings:60000-30400610 **(7413)**
2009: 7³SF, 8⁰GF, 8⁴SD, 6⁰GF, 7⁰SD, **10⁶SS, 12¹SD, 12⁰SD,**

	Starts	1st	2nd	3rd	Win & Pl
Career Total (Turf)	7	0	0	0	0
Career Total (AW)	6	1	0	1	2971

56 11/09 Wolv 1m4f50y STD £2388
Total win prize-money £2388

Going (Turf): Sf: 0-0 GS: 0-1 Gd: 0-2 GF: 0-4 Fm: 0-0
Distance: 5f/6f: 0-0 7f-8f: 0-7 **9f-13f: 1-6** 14f+: 0-0
Track : LH: 1-8 RH: 0-1 **Tight: 1-6** Gall: 0-0
Aids: Bl: 0-0 Vi: 0-2 Tstrap: 0-0 Ckp: 0-0
Best Rating: 64 3/09 Wolv 7f32y std-fst

Moderate; stays 1m4f and acts on Polytrack.

Ordnance Row

112 **117**
6-y-o b g Mark Of Esteem (IRE)-Language Of Love (Rock City)
R Hannon Mrs P Good

Placings:0221/0051/03353112525/51521330-
32164062100 **(6448)**
2009: 8³GF, 7²G, 8¹GF, 9⁶GF, 8⁴GF, 8⁰GF, 7⁶GF, 8²G, 7¹GF, 8⁰S, 8⁰GF,

	Starts	1st	2nd	3rd	Win & Pl
Career Total (Turf)	38	8	7	6	316129

116 8/09 Gdwd 7f G-F £36900
114 5/09 Wind 1m67y G-F £22708
116 8/08 Sals 1m G-S £36900
110 5/08 Wind 1m67y G-F £14760
111 7/07 Sand 1m14y H G-S £62320
108 6/07 Sals 1m (0-100)H G-S £11217
97 8/06 Ches 7f122y H GD £28044
93 11/05 Donc 7f (0-85) SFT £7506
Total win prize-money £220359

Going (Turf): Sf: 1-6 **GS: 3-7** Gd: 1-11 **GF: 3-14** Fm: 0-0
Distance: 5f/6f: 0-0 **7f-8f: 5-26** 9f-13f: 3-12 14f+: 0-0
Track : LH: 1-7 **RH: 4-14 Tight: 3-12** Gall: 0-1
Aids: Bl: 0-0 Vi: 0-0 Tstrap: 0-0 Ckp: 0-0
Best Rating: 117 10/08 NmkR 1m gd-fm

Group class; winner in Group 3 company; effective over 7f-1m; acts on fast and easy ground.

Ordoney (IRE)

106(104) (90)88

4-y-o b c Intikhab (USA)-Mitawa (IRE) (Alhaarth (IRE))

L M Cumani Sheikh Mohammed Obaid Al Maktoum

Placings:2131240 (7233)

2009: 7^{2}G, 7^{1}GF, 10^{3}GF, 9^{1}GF, 9^{2}SD, 10^{4}G, 10^{0}SD,

	Starts	1st	2nd	3rd	Win & Pl
Career Total (Turf)	5	2	1	1	12021
Career Total (AW)	2	0	1	0	1510

88 9/09 Folk 1m1f149y (0-85)H G-F £7123
79 8/09 Rdcr 7f G-F £2590
Total win prize-money £9714

Going (Turf): Sf: 0-0 GS: 0-0 Gd: 0-2 **GF: 2-3** Fm: 0-0
Distance: 5f/6f: 0-0 7f-8f: 1-2 9f-13f: 1-5 14f+: 0-0
Track : LH: 0-2 **RH: 1-4 Tight: 1-4** Gall: 0-0
Aids: Bl: 0-0 Vi: 0-0 Tstrap: 0-0 Ckp: 0-0
Best Rating: **90** 10/09 Wolv 1m1f103y stand

Useful; stays 1m2f; acts on fast ground and on Polytrack.

Oriental Cat

90 57

2-y-o b c Tiger Hill (IRE)-Sentimental Value (USA) (Diesis)

J H M Gosden H R H Princess Haya Of Jordan

Placings:6 (6990)

2009: 7^{6}G,

	Starts	1st	2nd	3rd	Win & Pl
Career Total (Turf)	1	0	0	0	0

Going (Turf): Sf: 0-0 GS: 0-0 Gd: 0-1 GF: 0-0 Fm: 0-0
Distance: 5f/6f: 0-0 7f-8f: 0-1 9f-13f: 0-0 14f+: 0-0
Track : LH: 0-0 RH: 0-0 Tight: 0-0 Gall: 0-0
Aids: Bl: 0-0 Vi: 0-0 Tstrap: 0-0 Ckp: 0-0
Best Rating: **57** 10/09 Donc 7f good

Oriental Cavalier

100(101) (76)73

3-y-o ch g Ishiguru (USA)-Gurleigh (IRE) (Pivotal)

R Hollinshead The Three R'S

Placings:0624-25334021244 (7847)

2009: 9^{2}GF, 10^{5}HY, 10^{3}GF, 10^{3}GF, 10^{4}GF, 12^{0}GF, 9^{2}SD, 9^{1}SD, 9^{2}SD, 9^{4}SD, 12^{4}SD,

	Starts	1st	2nd	3rd	Win & Pl
Career Total (Turf)	10	0	2	2	3635
Career Total (AW)	5	1	2	0	5277

63 11/09 Wolv 1m1f103y STD £2388
Total win prize-money £2388

Going (Turf): Sf: 0-4 GS: 0-1 Gd: 0-0 GF: 0-5 Fm: 0-0
Distance: 5f/6f: 0-0 7f-8f: 0-3 **9f-13f: 1-12** 14f+: 0-0
Track : **LH: 1-13** RH: 0-2 **Tight: 1-7** Gall: 0-0
Aids: Bl: 0-0 Vi: 0-0 Tstrap: 1-8 Ckp: 1-8
Best Rating: **76** 12/09 Wolv 1m4f50y stand

Fair; effective over 1m; acts on easy ground; goes on Polytrack; has worn cheekpieces.

Oriental Girl

102(95) (62)68

4-y-o b f Dr Fong (USA)-Zacchera (Zamindar (USA))

J A Geake Kimpton Down Partnership

Placings:000/5413100-64402020 (6733)

2009: 10^{6}SD, 8^{4}GF, 8^{4}F, 8^{0}GF, 9^{2}GF, 8^{0}G, 9^{2}GF, 9^{0}S,

	Starts	1st	2nd	3rd	Win & Pl
Career Total (Turf)	13	2	2	1	9632
Career Total (AW)	5	0	0	0	0

67 8/08 Bath 1m5y (0-75)H G-S £2914
68 6/08 Chep 1m14y (0-70)H G-F £3076
Total win prize-money £5990

Going (Turf): Sf: 0-2 **GS: 1-2** Gd: 0-1 **GF: 1-7** Fm: 0-1
Distance: 5f/6f: 0-0 7f-8f: 0-8 **9f-13f: 2-10** 14f+: 0-0
Track : **LH: 1-5** RH: 0-8 **Tight: 1-9** Gall: 0-0
Aids: Bl: 0-0 Vi: 0-4 Tstrap: 2-10 Ckp: 2-10
Best Rating: **68** 9/09 Gdwd 1m1f192y gd-fm

Moderate; effective at 1m; acts on fast ground; has worn cheekpieces.

Oriental Rose

96 76

3-y-o b f Dr Fong (USA)-Sahara Rose (Green Desert (USA))

G M Moore Ean Muller Associates

Placings:60160-02642440 (6233)

2009: 6^{0}GS, 6^{2}GF, 6^{6}GF, 5^{4}G, 6^{2}G, 6^{4}GF, 6^{4}GF, 5^{0}GF,

	Starts	1st	2nd	3rd	Win & Pl
Career Total (Turf)	13	1	2	0	2566

Going (Turf): Sf: 0-0 GS: 0-3 **Gd: 1-4** GF: 0-6 Fm: 0-0
Distance: **5f/6f: 1-10** 7f-8f: 0-3 9f-13f: 0-0 14f+: 0-0
Track : LH: 0-3 RH: 0-1 Tight: 0-1 Gall: 0-0
Aids: Bl: 0-0 Vi: 0-0 Tstrap: 0-0 Ckp: 0-0
Best Rating: **76** 7/08 Donc 6f good

Fair; effective at 6f; acts on good ground.

Oriental Scot

85(90) (69)64

2-y-o ch c Selkirk (USA)-Robe Chinoise (Robellino (USA))

W Jarvis Dr J Walker

Placings:525 (7721)

2009: 7^{5}G, 8^{2}SD, 8^{5}SD,

	Starts	1st	2nd	3rd	Win & Pl
Career Total (Turf)	1	0	0	0	0
Career Total (AW)	2	0	1	0	964

Going (Turf): Sf: 0-0 GS: 0-0 Gd: 0-1 GF: 0-0 Fm: 0-0
Distance: 5f/6f: 0-0 7f-8f: 0-2 9f-13f: 0-1 14f+: 0-0
Track : LH: 0-2 RH: 0-0 Tight: 0-1 Gall: 0-0
Aids: Bl: 0-0 Vi: 0-0 Tstrap: 0-0 Ckp: 0-0
Best Rating: **69** 11/09 Wolv 1m141y stand

Fair; stays 1m; acts on Polytrack.

Orientalist Art

98(108) (93)90

4-y-o b g Green Desert (USA)-Pink Cristal (Dilum (USA))

P W Chapple-Hyam Matthew Green

Placings:2/120-0 (5025)

2009: 7^{0}GF,

	Starts	1st	2nd	3rd	Win & Pl
Career Total (Turf)	3	0	1	0	1349
Career Total (AW)	2	1	1	0	7927

75 2/08 Ling 7f STD £2331
Total win prize-money £2332

Going (Turf): Sf: 0-0 GS: 0-0 Gd: 0-1 GF: 0-2 Fm: 0-0
Distance: 5f/6f: 0-1 **7f-8f: 1-4** 9f-13f: 0-0 14f+: 0-0
Track : **LH: 1-2** RH: 0-1 **Tight: 1-2** Gall: 0-0
Aids: Bl: 0-0 Vi: 0-0 Tstrap: 0-0 Ckp: 0-0
Best Rating: **93** 4/08 Ling 1m stand

Very useful; stays 1m; acts on fast ground and on Polytrack; likes to race prominently.

Original Dancer (IRE)

75 44

2-y-o b c Danehill Dancer (IRE)-Courtier (Saddlers' Hall (IRE))

M Johnston The Originals

Placings:00 (6047)

2009: 6^{0}G, 7^{0}G,

	Starts	1st	2nd	3rd	Win & Pl
Career Total (Turf)	2	0	0	0	

Going (Turf): Sf: 0-0 GS: 0-0 Gd: 0-2 GF: 0-0 Fm: 0-0
Distance: 5f/6f: 0-1 7f-8f: 0-1 9f-13f: 0-0 14f+: 0-0
Track : LH: 0-1 RH: 0-0 Tight: 0-0 Gall: 0-0
Aids: Bl: 0-0 Vi: 0-0 Tstrap: 0-0 Ckp: 0-0
Best Rating: **44** 5/09 York 6f good

Orizaba (IRE)

109 112

3-y-o b c Orpen (USA)-Jus'Chillin' (IRE) (Elbio)

Saeed Bin Suroor Godolphin

Placings:1514-3025 (4949)

2009: 8^{3}G, 8^{0}GF, 8^{2}G, 8^{5}GF,

	Starts	1st	2nd	3rd	Win & Pl
Career Total (Turf)	8	2	1	1	86562

112 7/08 Gdwd 7f G-F £48254
95 5/08 Newb 6f8y GD £5342
Total win prize-money £53598

Going (Turf): Sf: 0-0 GS: 0-0 **Gd: 1-4 GF: 1-4** Fm: 0-0
Distance: 5f/6f: 0-1 **7f-8f: 2-6** 9f-13f: 0-1 14f+: 0-0
Track : LH: 0-1 **RH: 1-4** Tight: 0-0 Gall: 0-2
Aids: Bl: 0-0 Vi: 0-0 Tstrap: 0-0 Ckp: 0-0
Best Rating: **112** 7/08 Gdwd 7f gd-fm

Smart; winner of the Group 2 Vintage Stakes at two; stays 1m; acts on good and fast ground.

Orkney (IRE)

96(100) (72)58

4-y-o b g Trans Island-Bitty Mary (Be My Chief (USA))

Miss J A Camacho Axom (XIII)

Placings:04/30311-060 (4737)

2009: 12^{0}SD, 13^{6}G, 11^{0}G,

	Starts	1st	2nd	3rd	Win & Pl
Career Total (Turf)	4	0	0	1	262
Career Total (AW)	6	2	0	1	6120

72 12/08 Sthl 1m4f (0-70)H STD £2729
71 12/08 Sthl 1m4f (0-70)H STD £2729
Total win prize-money £5460

Going (Turf): Sf: 0-0 GS: 0-0 Gd: 0-3 GF: 0-1 Fm: 0-0
Distance: 5f/6f: 0-0 7f-8f: 0-1 **9f-13f: 2-8** 14f+: 0-1
Track : **LH: 2-9** RH: 0-0 Tight: 0-4 Gall: 0-0
Aids: Bl: 0-0 Vi: 0-0 Tstrap: 0-1 Ckp: 0-1
Best Rating: **72** 12/08 Sthl 1m4f stand

Modest; stays 1m4f; acts on Fibresand.

Orlando's Tale (USA)

104(86) (45)83

4-y-o ch g Tale Of The Cat (USA)-Tell Seattle (USA) (A.P. Indy (USA))

J R Fanshawe Coriolan Partnership (I)

Placings:0-02201 (5747)

2009: 8^0G, 7^2GF, 7^2GF, 7^0G, 7^1GF,

	Starts	1st	2nd	3rd	Win & Pl
Career Total (Turf)	5	1	2	0	5042
Career Total (AW)	1	0	0	0	

83	9/09	Ling	7f	G-F	£2729

Total win prize-money £2730

Going (Turf): Sf: 0-0 GS: 0-0 Gd: 0-2 **GF: 1-3** Fm: 0-0
Distance: 5f/6f: 0-0 **7f-8f: 1-5** 9f-13f: 0-1 14f+: 0-0
Track : LH: 0-2 RH: 0-0 Tight: 0-1 Gall: 0-0
Aids: Bl: 0-0 Vi: 0-0 Tstrap: 0-0 Ckp: 0-0
Best Rating: 83 9/09 Ling 7f gd-fm

Fair; stays 7f; acts on fast ground.

Oronsay

95 (38)54

4-y-o ch f Elmaamul (USA)-Glenfinlass (Lomond (USA))

B R Millman Mrs Jenny Willment

Placings:0600/000234-062005530 (6966)

2009: 9^0GF, 10^6F, 12^2G, 10^0F, 11^0GF, 12^5HY, 9^5F, 9^3GS, 9^0G,

	Starts	1st	2nd	3rd	Win & Pl
Career Total (Turf)	19	0	2	2	2587
Career Total (AW)	1	0	0	0	

Going (Turf): Sf: 0-4 GS: 0-3 Gd: 0-4 GF: 0-4 Fm: 0-4
Distance: 5f/6f: 0-2 7f-8f: 0-6 9f-13f: 0-12 14f+: 0-0
Track : LH: 0-11 RH: 0-3 Tight: 0-3 Gall: 0-1
Aids: Bl: 0-0 Vi: 0-0 Tstrap: 0-0 Ckp: 0-0
Best Rating: 54 10/09 Folk 1m1f149y gd-sft

Moderate; stays 1m4f and best on soft ground; has worn a tongue tie.

Orpen All Hours (IRE)

80(80) (18)26

2-y-o b f Orpen (USA)-Devious Miss (IRE) (Dr Devious (IRE))

P C Haslam Middleham Park Racing XXIX

Placings:000F00 (6355)

2009: 6^0S, 6^0G, 5^0SF, 5^FS, 8^0GF, 5^0SD,

	Starts	1st	2nd	3rd	Win & Pl
Career Total (Turf)	4	0	0	0	
Career Total (AW)	2	0	0	0	

Going (Turf): Sf: 0-2 GS: 0-0 Gd: 0-1 GF: 0-1 Fm: 0-0
Distance: 5f/6f: 0-5 7f-8f: 0-0 9f-13f: 0-1 14f+: 0-0
Track : LH: 0-1 RH: 0-0 Tight: 0-1 Gall: 0-0
Aids: Bl: 0-0 Vi: 0-0 Tstrap: 0-2 Ckp: 0-2
Best Rating: 26 9/09 Yarm 1m3y gd-fm

Orpen Arms (IRE)

96 61

2-y-o b f Orpen (USA)-Lindas Delight (Batshoof)

R A Fahey Derwent Arms Racing Club Malton

Placings:23245026 (7055)

2009: 5^2F, 5^3G, 6^2GS, 6^4GF, 5^5G, 7^0GF, 7^2G, 7^6GF,

	Starts	1st	2nd	3rd	Win & Pl
Career Total (Turf)	8	0	3	1	3856

Going (Turf): Sf: 0-0 GS: 0-1 Gd: 0-3 GF: 0-3 Fm: 0-1
Distance: 5f/6f: 0-4 7f-8f: 0-4 9f-13f: 0-0 14f+: 0-0
Track : LH: 0-0 RH: 0-1 Tight: 0-1 Gall: 0-0
Aids: Bl: 0-0 Vi: 0-0 Tstrap: 0-0 Ckp: 0-0
Best Rating: 61 5/09 Rdcr 5f firm

Moderate; stays 7f and acts on most ground.

Orpen Bid (IRE)

74 51

4-y-o b f Orpen (USA)-Glorious Bid (IRE) (Horage)

A M Crow Good At It Too Partnership

Placings:56/050003550-00 (2816)

2009: 12^0GS, 8^0GF,

	Starts	1st	2nd	3rd	Win & Pl
Career Total (Turf)	13	0	0	1	403

Going (Turf): Sf: 0-4 GS: 0-3 Gd: 0-3 GF: 0-2 Fm: 0-1
Distance: 5f/6f: 0-1 7f-8f: 0-8 9f-13f: 0-4 14f+: 0-0
Track : LH: 0-6 RH: 0-5 Tight: 0-4 Gall: 0-1
Aids: Bl: 0-0 Vi: 0-0 Tstrap: 0-0 Ckp: 0-0
Best Rating: 51 8/08 Ayr 1m gd-sft

Moderate; effective over 1m; acts on easy ground.

Orpen Grey (IRE)

111 112

2-y-o gr g Orpen (USA)-Sky Red (Night Shift (USA))

Tom Dascombe The Folly Racers

Placings:51125 (5172)

2009: 6^5G, 5^1G, 6^1G, 6^2G, 6^5GF,

	Starts	1st	2nd	3rd	Win & Pl
Career Total (Turf)	5	2	1	0	28542

101	6/09	Sals	6f	GD	£8411
89	6/09	Wwck	5f	GD	£2914

Total win prize-money £11326

Going (Turf): Sf: 0-0 GS: 0-0 **Gd: 2-4** GF: 0-1 Fm: 0-0
Distance: 5f/6f: 2-5 7f-8f: 0-0 9f-13f: 0-0 14f+: 0-0
Track : LH: 1-1 RH: 0-0 Tight: 0-0 Gall: 0-0
Aids: Bl: 0-0 Vi: 0-0 Tstrap: 0-0 Ckp: 0-0
Best Rating: 112 7/09 NmkJ 6f good

Smart; effective over 5f-6f; acts on good ground.

Orpen Lady

51(64)

3-y-o b f Orpen (USA)-Gargren (IRE) (Mujtahid (USA))

J M Bradley J M Bradley

Placings:00 (4860)

2009: 6^0GF, 5^0SD,

	Starts	1st	2nd	3rd	Win & Pl
Career Total (Turf)	1	0	0	0	
Career Total (AW)	1	0	0	0	

Going (Turf): Sf: 0-0 GS: 0-0 Gd: 0-0 GF: 0-1 Fm: 0-0
Distance: 5f/6f: 0-1 7f-8f: 0-1 9f-13f: 0-0 14f+: 0-0
Track : LH: 0-1 RH: 0-0 Tight: 0-1 Gall: 0-0
Aids: Bl: 0-0 Vi: 0-0 Tstrap: 0-0 Ckp: 0-0

Orpen Wide (IRE)

105(104) (89)89

7-y-o b g Orpen (USA)-Melba (IRE) (Namaqualand (USA))

M C Chapman Andy & Bev Wright

Placings:03300251/110063000061453006601000/03000 0104211/0402023420254010425/0-30510040300 (6645)

2009: 8^3SD, 7^0SF, 6^5SD, 7^1GF, 8^0GF, 8^0GF, 8^4GF, 7^0GF, 8^3GS, 7^0G, 7^0G,

	Starts	1st	2nd	3rd	Win & Pl
Career Total (Turf)	54	6	6	5	43023
Career Total (AW)	22	4	1	3	18449

89	4/09	Leic	7f9y	(0-85)H	G-F	£4857
92	9/07	Hayd	1m30y	(0-85)H	G-F	£5505
84	12/06	Sthl	1m	(0-75)H	STD	£3238
81	9/06	Newc	1m3y	(0-70)H	GD	£3562
73	6/06	Bevl	7f100y	(0-70)H	G-F	£5181
73	10/05	Newc	1m	(0-65)H	G-F	£3597
74	6/05	NmkJ	5f	(0-70)H	G-F	£4145
81	1/05	Wolv	5f216y	(0-70)H	STD	£3392
79	1/05	Sthl	6f	(0-70)H	STD	£3370
75	12/04	Sthl	5f	(0-75)	STD	£4056

Total win prize-money £40907

Going (Turf): Sf: 0-6 GS: 0-8 Gd: 1-21 **GF: 5-17** Fm: 0-2
Distance: 5f/6f: 4-25 7f-8f: 4-36 9f-13f: 2-15 14f+: 0-0
Track : LH: 5-31 RH: 1-9 Tight: 1-14 Gall: 1-5
Aids: Bl: 4-30 Vi: 0-1 Tstrap: 0-0 Ckp: 0-0
Best Rating: 93 10/07 Leic 1m60y gd-sft

Useful handicapper; effective at around 7f-1m; acts on most ground on turf; handles Fibresand and Polytrack; very tough; usually blinkered.

Orpen Winger (IRE)

89 (54)58

4-y-o b g Orpen (USA)-Tahdid (Mtoto)

A J Martin IRS Syndicates Limited

Placings:40-0005 (6399)

2009: 10^0CF, 11^0YS, 8^0SD, 8^5GF,

	Starts	1st	2nd	3rd	Win & Pl
Career Total (Turf)	5	0	0	0	452
Career Total (AW)	1	0	0	0	

Going (Turf): Sf: 0-0 GS: 0-0 Gd: 0-0 GF: 0-2 Fm: 0-0
Distance: 5f/6f: 0-0 7f-8f: 0-4 9f-13f: 0-2 14f+: 0-0
Track : LH: 0-4 RH: 0-0 Tight: 0-0 Gall: 0-0
Aids: Bl: 0-0 Vi: 0-0 Tstrap: 0-0 Ckp: 0-0
Best Rating: 58 4/08 Limk 6f160y sft-hvy

Orpen's Art (IRE)

103(103) (77)75

4-y-o b c Invincible Spirit (IRE)-Bells Of Ireland (UAE) (Machiavellian (USA))

Ecurie Prince Rose (S A Callaghan 6/7) Ecurie Prince Rose

Placings:60050042000/123131602242000-063013560012550

2009: 7^0SD, 5^6SD, 5^3SD, 5^0GF, 5^1F, 5^3SD, 5^5GF, 5^6SD, 5^0GF, 5^0GF, 5^1F, 5^2F, 5^5G, 4^5VS, 5^0GS,

	Starts	1st	2nd	3rd	Win & Pl
Career Total (Turf)	23	2	2	0	11042
Career Total (AW)	19	3	4	4	11253

65	6/09	Brig	5f59y	(0-70)H	FRM	£3280
63	5/09	Brig	5f59y	(0-70)H	FRM	£3154
74	3/08	Ling	5f	(0-65)H	STD	£2590

66	2/08	Ling	5f	(0-55)H	STD	£2331
58	1/08	Sthl	5f	(0-60)H	STD	£1911

Total win prize-money £13268

Going (Turf): Sf: 0-2 GS: 0-1 Gd: 0-3 GF: 0-11 **Fm: 2-5**
Distance: **5f/6f: 5-38** 7f-8f: 0-3 9f-13f: 0-0 14f+: 0-0
Track : **LH: 4-18** RH: 0-4 **Tight: 2-8** Gall: 0-2
Aids: Bl: 0-2 Vi: 0-0 Tstrap: 0-0 Ckp: 0-0
Best Rating: **77** 5/08 GrLe 5f stand

Modest; effective at 5f; acts on fast ground; goes on Polytrack.

Orpenella

(102) (68)**32**

4-y-o b f Orpen (USA)-M N L Lady (Polar Falcon (USA))
K A Ryan Hambleton Racing Ltd IV

Placings:32030424-233 **(0323)**
2009: 11^{2}SS, 11^{3}SD, 8^{3}SD,

	Starts	1st	2nd	3rd	Win & Pl
Career Total (Turf)	2	0	0	0	
Career Total (AW)	9	0	3	4	3346

Going (Turf): **Sf: 0-0 GS: 0-1 Gd: 0-1 GF: 0-0 Fm: 0-0**
Distance: 5f/6f: 0-3 7f-8f: 0-6 9f-13f: 0-2 14f+: 0-0
Track : LH: 0-8 RH: 0-1 Tight: 0-0 Gall: 0-0
Aids: Bl: 0-5 Vi: 0-0 Tstrap: 0-0 Ckp: 0-0
Best Rating: **68** 12/08 Sthl 7f stand

Modest; probably stays 1m; acts on Fibresand; has worn blinkers.

Orpenindeed (IRE)

106(111) (96)**99**

6-y-o b/br g Orpen (USA)-Indian Goddess (IRE) (Indian Ridge)
M Botti Giuliano Manfredini

Placings:32/11043/21504636/2433626612-4326302314 **(7414)**
2009: 5^{4}SD, 7^{3}SD, 7^{2}SD, 7^{6}SD, 6^{3}GF, 6^{0}G, 7^{2}SD, 7^{3}SF, 5^{1}SD, 5^{4}SD,

	Starts	1st	2nd	3rd	Win & Pl
Career Total (Turf)	18	3	3	5	36084
Career Total (AW)	17	2	4	3	21498

96	10/09	Wolv	5f216y	(0-85)H	STD	£5046
89	11/08	GrLe	6f		STD	£3238
	7/07	Maia	1m		GD	£4882
	5/06	Siro	6f	H	G-F	£8793
	4/06	Pisa	6f		SFT	£3517

Total win prize-money £25476

Going (Turf): **Sf: 1-2** GS: 0-1 **Gd: 1-9 GF: 1-6** Fm: 0-0
Distance: **5f/6f: 4-21** 7f-8f: 1-14 9f-13f: 0-0 14f+: 0-0
Track : LH: 2-16 RH: 2-5 Tight: 1-12 Gall: 1-4
Aids: Bl: 0-0 Vi: 0-0 Tstrap: 2-8 Ckp: 2-8
Best Rating: **99** 4/08 Yarm 6f3y gd-fm

Useful; ex-Italian; effective over 6f-1m; acts on most ground and on Polytrack; has worn a tongue tie and cheekpieces.

Orphan Boy

(83) (14)

4-y-o b g Tipsy Creek (USA)-Miss Jingles (Muhtarram (USA))
H J Collingridge R J King

Placings:0/400-0 **(0166)**
2009: 6^{0}SD,

	Starts	1st	2nd	3rd	Win & Pl
Career Total (Turf)	0	0	0	0	
Career Total (AW)	5	0	0	0	0

Going (Turf): **Sf: 0-0 GS: 0-0 Gd: 0-0 GF: 0-0 Fm: 0-0**
Distance: 5f/6f: 0-4 7f-8f: 0-1 9f-13f: 0-0 14f+: 0-0
Track : LH: 0-3 RH: 0-0 Tight: 0-2 Gall: 0-0
Aids: Bl: 0-0 Vi: 0-0 Tstrap: 0-0 Ckp: 0-0
Best Rating: **14** 1/08 Sthl 7f stand

Orphaned Annie

96(88) (56)**57**

3-y-o b f Lend A Hand-Great Exception (Grundy)
B Ellison Black and White Diamond Partnership

Placings:0404330-46 **(1397)**
2009: 11^{4}GF, 12^{6}F,

	Starts	1st	2nd	3rd	Win & Pl
Career Total (Turf)	6	0	0	0	782
Career Total (AW)	3	0	0	2	877

Going (Turf): **Sf: 0-0 GS: 0-2 Gd: 0-0 GF: 0-3 Fm: 0-1**
Distance: 5f/6f: 0-3 7f-8f: 0-3 9f-13f: 0-3 14f+: 0-0
Track : LH: 0-7 RH: 0-0 Tight: 0-3 Gall: 0-0
Aids: Bl: 0-0 Vi: 0-0 Tstrap: 0-0 Ckp: 0-0
Best Rating: **57** 5/08 Newc 6f gd-fm

Moderate; dam won at up to 1m6f; acts on Fibresand.

Orpsie Boy (IRE)

108(112) (107)**104**

6-y-o b g Orpen (USA)-Nordicolini (IRE) (Nordico (USA))
N P Littmoden Miss Vanessa Church

Placings:0125013/204635000/11100453/41310500656-632454000000003 **(6540)**
2009: 5^{6}SD, 6^{3}SD, 5^{2}SD, 6^{4}SD, 6^{5}GF, 6^{4}GF, 6^{0}GF, 7^{0}GF, 7^{0}G, 6^{0}S, 5^{0}G, 5^{0}GF, 6^{0}GF, 6^{3}GF,

	Starts	1st	2nd	3rd	Win & Pl
Career Total (Turf)	34	3	2	2	45612
Career Total (AW)	16	4	1	4	44642

107	3/08	Wolv	5f216y	(0-100)H	STD	£10363
99	1/08	Kemp	6f	(0-100)H	STD	£10363
98	7/07	Asct	6f	(0-90)H	G-F	£9715
95	5/07	Sals	6f	(0-85)H	G-F	£6477
87	4/07	Ling	6f	(0-80)H	STD	£4857
85	9/05	Ling	6f	(0-85)	STD	£5005
65	7/05	Ches	5f16y		G-F	£4056

Total win prize-money £50838

Going (Turf): Sf: 0-3 GS: 0-0 Gd: 0-6 **GF: 3-25** Fm: 0-0
Distance: **5f/6f: 7-42** 7f-8f: 0-8 9f-13f: 0-0 14f+: 0-0
Track : **LH: 4-17** RH: 1-5 **Tight: 4-15** Gall: 0-2
Aids: Bl: 0-4 Vi: 0-2 Tstrap: 0-2 Ckp: 0-2
Best Rating: **107** 3/08 Wolv 5f216y stand

Useful; effective over 6f, but does get further; acts on fast ground and on Polytrack; has worn various headgear and a tongue tie; usually held up.

Orsett Lad (USA)

88(97) (68)**65**

2-y-o b g Essence Of Dubai (USA)-Sofisticada (USA) (Northern Jove (CAN))
J R Best Bob Malt

Placings:644300606 **(7887)**
2009: 7^{6}GF, 6^{4}SD, 7^{4}SD, 7^{3}GF, 7^{0}GF, 8^{0}SD, 7^{6}SD, 7^{0}SD, 7^{6}SD,

	Starts	1st	2nd	3rd	Win & Pl
Career Total (Turf)	3	0	0	1	403
Career Total (AW)	6	0	0	0	0

Going (Turf): **Sf: 0-0 GS: 0-0 Gd: 0-0 GF: 0-3 Fm: 0-0**
Distance: 5f/6f: 0-1 7f-8f: 0-8 9f-13f: 0-0 14f+: 0-0
Track : LH: 0-4 RH: 0-3 Tight: 0-4 Gall: 0-0
Aids: Bl: 0-0 Vi: 0-0 Tstrap: 0-0 Ckp: 0-0
Best Rating: **68** 7/09 Ling 6f stand

Orsippus (USA)

101(100) (78)**74**

3-y-o b/br g Sunday Break (JPN)-Mirror Dancing (USA) (Caveat (USA))
Michael Smith (M R Channon 16/6) Mrs Sandra Smith

Placings:013-5663040020 **(6767)**
2009: 10^{5}SD, 10^{6}SD, 10^{6}SD, 11^{3}GF, 12^{0}SD, 11^{4}GF, 12^{0}GF, 9^{0}G, 16^{2}GF, 16^{0}GS,

	Starts	1st	2nd	3rd	Win & Pl
Career Total (Turf)	7	1	1	1	4510
Career Total (AW)	6	0	0	1	403

74	8/08	Gdwd	1m	SFT	£3238

Total win prize-money £3238

Going (Turf): **Sf: 1-1** GS: 0-1 Gd: 0-1 GF: 0-4 Fm: 0-0
Distance: 5f/6f: 0-0 **7f-8f: 1-2** 9f-13f: 0-9 14f+: 0-2
Track : LH: 0-10 **RH: 1-2** Tight: 0-10 Gall: 0-2
Aids: Bl: 0-0 Vi: 0-3 Tstrap: 0-0 Ckp: 0-0
Best Rating: **78** 9/08 Wolv 1m141y stand

Moderate; stays 2m; acts on most ground and on Polytrack.

Orthology (IRE)

103(92) (56)**79**

3-y-o b g Kalanisi (IRE)-Al Shakoor (Barathea (IRE))
M H Tompkins M Winter

Placings:0525-5545551 **(7094)**
2009: 12^{5}GF, 12^{5}GS, 9^{4}GF, 8^{5}SD, 10^{5}G, 11^{5}G, 10^{1}G,

	Starts	1st	2nd	3rd	Win & Pl
Career Total (Turf)	9	1	1	0	3834
Career Total (AW)	2	0	0	0	0

60	10/09	Yarm	1m2f21y	GD	£1942

Total win prize-money £1943

Going (Turf): Sf: 0-0 GS: 0-2 **Gd: 1-4** GF: 0-3 Fm: 0-0
Distance: 5f/6f: 0-0 7f-8f: 0-3 **9f-13f: 1-8** 14f+: 0-0
Track : **LH: 1-4** RH: 0-5 **Tight: 1-4** Gall: 0-2
Aids: Bl: 0-4 Vi: 0-0 Tstrap: 1-1 Ckp: 1-1
Best Rating: **79** 5/09 NmkR 1m4f gd-fm

Useful; effective over 1m2f; acts on good ground.

Oscar Wild

91 **53**

7-y-o b g Tragic Role (USA)-Minster Lascar (Scallywag)
I Semple (James Moffatt 27/5) Alison Walker Sarah Cousins

Placings:040-4000 **(7173)**
2009: 7^{4}GF, 9^{0}GF, 7^{0}S, 9^{0}S,

	Starts	1st	2nd	3rd	Win & Pl
Career Total (Turf)	7	0	0	0	216

Going (Turf): **Sf: 0-2 GS: 0-3 Gd: 0-0 GF: 0-2 Fm: 0-0**
Distance: 5f/6f: 0-0 7f-8f: 0-2 9f-13f: 0-5 14f+: 0-0
Track : LH: 0-5 RH: 0-2 Tight: 0-3 Gall: 0-0
Aids: Bl: 0-0 Vi: 0-0 Tstrap: 0-1 Ckp: 0-1
Best Rating: **53** 9/08 Pont 1m2f6y gd-sft

Moderate; stays 7f; acts on fast ground.

Osiris Way

106 (89)**100**

7-y-o ch g Indian Ridge-Heady (Rousillon (USA))

P R Chamings Mrs Alexandra J Chandris

Placings:00/01113230/13542101-4000500 **(6694)**

2009: 6^4G, 6^0GF, 6^0GF, 6^0S, 6^5GF, 6^0G, 6^0GS,

	Starts	1st	2nd	3rd	Win & Pl
Career Total (Turf)	19	5	1	2	37388
Career Total (AW)	6	1	1	1	5776

99	10/08	Bath	5f11y	(0-95)H	GD	£7569
96	8/08	Gdwd	6f	(0-95)H	G-S	£7771
92	6/08	Sals	5f	(0-85)H	G-F	£4371
89	6/07	NmkJ	6f	(0-80)H	G-S	£6477
83	6/07	Gdwd	6f	(0-70)H	GD	£3238
71	5/07	Ling	6f	(0-60)H	STD	£3238

Total win prize-money £32667

Going (Turf): Sf: 0-3 **GS: 2-5 Gd: 2-4** GF: 1-7 Fm: 0-0
Distance: **5f/6f: 6-20** 7f-8f: 0-2 9f-13f: 0-3 14f+: 0-0
Track : **LH: 2-7** RH: 0-1 Tight: 1-7 Gall: 1-3
Aids: Bl: 0-0 Vi: 0-0 Tstrap: 0-0 Ckp: 0-0
Best Rating: **100** 5/09 Gdwd 6f good

Very useful; stays 6f; acts on fast and soft ground; also goes on Polytrack.

Oskari

97(99) (70)**54**

4-y-o b g Lear Spear (USA)-Cedar Jeneva (Muhtarram (USA))

P T Midgley The Howarting's Partnership

Placings:03-2200345 **(5329)**

2009: 7^2SD, 7^2SD, 8^0G, 7^0G, 8^3SD, 10^4GF, 8^5SD,

	Starts	1st	2nd	3rd	Win & Pl
Career Total (Turf)	4	0	0	0	192
Career Total (AW)	5	0	2	2	2114

Going (Turf): **Sf: 0-0 GS: 0-0 Gd: 0-3 GF: 0-1 Fm: 0-0**
Distance: 5f/6f: 0-0 7f-8f: 0-6 9f-13f: 0-3 14f+: 0-0
Track : LH: 0-7 RH: 0-1 Tight: 0-1 Gall: 0-0
Aids: Bl: 0-0 Vi: 0-0 Tstrap: 0-0 Ckp: 0-0
Best Rating: **70** 7/09 Sthl 1m stand

Modest; stays 1m; acts on Fibresand.

Osorios Trial

68 **25**

2-y-o ch c Osorio (GER)-Skytrial (USA) (Sky Classic (CAN))

M Johnston Mrs R J Jacobs

Placings:0 **(3750)**

2009: 7^0G,

	Starts	1st	2nd	3rd	Win & Pl
Career Total (Turf)	1	0	0	0	

Going (Turf): **Sf: 0-0 GS: 0-0 Gd: 0-1 GF: 0-0 Fm: 0-0**
Distance: 5f/6f: 0-0 7f-8f: 0-1 9f-13f: 0-0 14f+: 0-0
Track : LH: 0-0 RH: 0-0 Tight: 0-0 Gall: 0-0
Aids: Bl: 0-0 Vi: 0-0 Tstrap: 0-0 Ckp: 0-0
Best Rating: **25** 7/09 NmkJ 7f good

Ostaadi

86(102) (83)**66**

3-y-o b c Nayef (USA)-Blodwen (USA) (Mister Baileys)

M A Jarvis Sheikh Ahmed Al Maktoum

Placings:0122 **(3300)**

2009: 10^0GF, 11^1SD, 12^2SD, 16^2SD,

	Starts	1st	2nd	3rd	Win & Pl
Career Total (Turf)	1	0	0	0	
Career Total (AW)	3	1	2	0	7998

75	5/09	Sthl	1m3f	STD	£4857

Total win prize-money £4857

Going (Turf): **Sf: 0-0 GS: 0-0 Gd: 0-0 GF: 0-1 Fm: 0-0**
Distance: 5f/6f: 0-0 7f-8f: 0-0 **9f-13f: 1-3** 14f+: 0-1
Track : **LH: 1-1** RH: 0-2 Tight: 0-0 Gall: 0-0
Aids: Bl: 0-0 Vi: 0-0 Tstrap: 0-0 Ckp: 0-0
Best Rating: **83** 6/09 Kemp 1m4f stand

Useful; stays 2m and acts on sand.

Ostentation

85(88) (53)**60**

2-y-o ch g Dubawi (IRE)-Oshiponga (Barathea (IRE))

M Johnston Sheikh Hamdan Bin Mohammed Al Maktoum

Placings:5006 **(7551)**

2009: 7^5GF, 6^0GS, 8^0SD, 7^6SD,

	Starts	1st	2nd	3rd	Win & Pl
Career Total (Turf)	2	0	0	0	0
Career Total (AW)	2	0	0	0	0

Going (Turf): **Sf: 0-0 GS: 0-1 Gd: 0-0 GF: 0-1 Fm: 0-0**
Distance: 5f/6f: 0-0 7f-8f: 0-4 9f-13f: 0-0 14f+: 0-0
Track : LH: 0-2 RH: 0-1 Tight: 0-2 Gall: 0-0
Aids: Bl: 0-0 Vi: 0-0 Tstrap: 0-0 Ckp: 0-0
Best Rating: **60** 9/09 Bevl 7f100y gd-fm

Osteopathic Care (IRE)

(60) **57**

5-y-o b g Montjeu (IRE)-Super Gift (IRE) (Darshaan)

Miss Tracy Waggott Kevin Kirkup Jeff Redmayne

Placings:00000-0 **(1655)**

2009: 7^0SD,

	Starts	1st	2nd	3rd	Win & Pl
Career Total (Turf)	5	0	0	0	
Career Total (AW)	1	0	0	0	

Going (Turf): **Sf: 0-0 GS: 0-1 Gd: 0-3 GF: 0-1 Fm: 0-0**
Distance: 5f/6f: 0-0 7f-8f: 0-1 9f-13f: 0-4 14f+: 0-1
Track : LH: 0-6 RH: 0-0 Tight: 0-3 Gall: 0-1
Aids: Bl: 0-0 Vi: 0-0 Tstrap: 0-1 Ckp: 0-1
Best Rating: **57** 5/08 Thsk 1m4f good

Osteopathic Remedy (IRE)

106(99) (89)**100**

5-y-o ch g Inchinor-Dolce Vita (IRE) (Ela-Mana-Mou)

M Dods Kevin Kirkup

Placings:14/060025623404/0001113160-06003622053254 **(7169)**

2009: 8^0GF, 7^6GF, 7^0F, 8^0GF, 6^3G, 6^6GF, 7^2GF, 7^2S, 8^0GF, 7^5GS, 8^3G, 7^2G, 8^5SS, 8^4S,

	Starts	1st	2nd	3rd	Win & Pl
Career Total (Turf)	37	5	5	4	64859
Career Total (AW)	1	0	0	0	0

100	8/08	Ripn	1m	(0-100)H	G-S	£12462
90	6/08	Carl	7f200y	(0-80)H	SFT	£19428
88	5/08	Ayr	1m	(0-75)H	G-F	£3885
78	5/08	Thsk	1m	(0-75)H	G-F	£3885
79	9/06	Ayr	6f		GD	£3238

Total win prize-money £42901

Going (Turf): Sf: 1-10 GS: 1-6 Gd: 1-8 **GF: 2-11** Fm: 0-2
Distance: 5f/6f: 1-7 **7f-8f: 4-29** 9f-13f: 0-2 14f+: 0-0
Track : LH: 2-18 RH: 2-4 **Tight: 2-10** Gall: 0-2
Aids: Bl: 0-0 Vi: 0-0 Tstrap: 0-0 Ckp: 0-0
Best Rating: **100** 8/08 Ripn 1m gd-sft

Useful; effective from 6f-1m; acts on most ground.

Osterhase (IRE)

106 (78)**99**

10-y-o b g Flying Spur (AUS)-Ostrusa (AUT) (Rustan (HUN))

J E Mulhern Michael Rosenfeld

Placings:0433100/602231610/23261/061114340/1321606/0131120/4600/5-350000 **(5699a)**

2009: 5^3Y, 5^5G, 6^0GY, 5^0S, 6^0SD, 5^0SD,

	Starts	1st	2nd	3rd	Win & Pl
Career Total (Turf)	52	12	6	8	398211
Career Total (AW)	3	0	0	0	

112	7/06	Fair	6f		G-F	£24693
118	7/06	Curr	5f	H	G-F	£41448
115	6/06	Naas	5f		G-F	£22448
115	8/05	Curr	6f		GD	£34574
109	5/05	Fair	6f		YLD	£23085
110	7/04	Curr	5f	H	GD	£42323
119	6/04	Curr	5f		G-F	£45845
111	6/04	Naas	5f		G-F	£22922
112	7/03	Cork	5f	H	GD	£13717
108	10/02	Curr	5f	(0-105)H	GD	£10766
105	8/02	Curr	6f		G-Y	£23926
91	8/01	Fair	6f	(0-95)	GD	£7233

Total win prize-money £312985

Going (Turf): Sf: 0-6 GS: 0-1 **Gd: 5-20 GF: 5-14** Fm: 0-0
Distance: **5f/6f: 12-50** 7f-8f: 0-5 9f-13f: 0-0 14f+: 0-0
Track : LH: 2-19 RH: 2-3 Tight: 0-0 Gall: 0-0
Aids: **Bl: 11-42** Vi: 0-2 Tstrap: 0-0 Ckp: 0-0
Best Rating: **119** 7/04 Curr 5f good

Very useful; Irish trained; formerly successful in Group and Listed company; best over 5f; acts on good and faster ground; usually blinkered; suited by forcing tactics.

Othello (IRE)

76(80) (53)**40**

2-y-o b g Azamour (IRE)-Bonheur (IRE) (Royal Academy (USA))

E F Vaughan Hungerford Park Stud

Placings:000 **(7430)**

2009: 8^0S, 7^0SD, 7^0SD,

	Starts	1st	2nd	3rd	Win & Pl
Career Total (Turf)	1	0	0	0	
Career Total (AW)	2	0	0	0	

Going (Turf): **Sf: 0-1 GS: 0-0 Gd: 0-0 GF: 0-0 Fm: 0-0**
Distance: 5f/6f: 0-0 7f-8f: 0-2 9f-13f: 0-1 14f+: 0-0
Track : LH: 0-1 RH: 0-2 Tight: 0-0 Gall: 0-0
Aids: Bl: 0-0 Vi: 0-0 Tstrap: 0-0 Ckp: 0-0
Best Rating: **53** 11/09 Kemp 7f stand

Otterton

83 **39**

2-y-o b f Sampower Star-Parkside Prospect (Piccolo)

R Hollinshead J M Graham

Placings:60 **(4503)**

2009: 6^{6}G, 7^{0}G,

	Starts	1st	2nd	3rd	Win & Pl
Career Total (Turf)	2	0	0	0	0

Going (Turf): **Sf: 0-0 GS: 0-0 Gd: 0-2 GF: 0-0 Fm: 0-0**
Distance: 5f/6f: 0-1 7f-8f: 0-1 9f-13f: 0-0 14f+: 0-0
Track : LH: 0-1 RH: 0-0 Tight: 0-1 Gall: 0-0
Aids: Bl: 0-0 Vi: 0-0 Tstrap: 0-0 Ckp: 0-0
Best Rating: **39** 7/09 Hayd 6f good

Ottoman Empire (FR)

97(112) (99)87

3-y-o ch g Pivotal-Chesnut Bird (IRE) (Storm Bird (CAN))
D R Lanigan Plantation Stud

Placings:5251120 **(6795)**
2009: 8^{5}GF, 10^{2}G, 10^{5}GF, **11^{1}**SD, **12^{1}**SD, **12^{2}**SD, 10^{0}S,

	Starts	1st	2nd	3rd	Win & Pl
Career Total (Turf)	4	0	1	0	964
Career Total (AW)	3	2	1	0	11139

92	9/09	Kemp	1m4f	(0-85)H	STD	£4727
91	8/09	Sthl	1m3f		STD	£4209

Total win prize-money £8936

Going (Turf): **Sf: 0-1 GS: 0-0 Gd: 0-1 GF: 0-2 Fm: 0-0**
Distance: 5f/6f: 0-0 7f-8f: 0-1 **9f-13f: 2-6** 14f+: 0-0
Track : LH: 1-3 RH: 1-2 Tight: 0-0 Gall: 0-0
Aids: Bl: 0-0 Vi: 0-0 Tstrap: 0-0 Ckp: 0-0
Best Rating: **99** 9/09 Kemp 1m4f stand

Very useful; stays 1m4f; acts on good ground; goes on Fibresand and Polytrack.

Ouqba

110 116

3-y-o b c Red Ransom (USA)-Dancing Mirage (IRE) (Machiavellian (USA))
B W Hills Hamdan Al Maktoum

Placings:3210410-101642 **(6848)**
2009: 7^{1}GF, 8^{0}GF, 7^{1}GF, 7^{6}G, 7^{4}GF, 7^{2}G,

	Starts	1st	2nd	3rd	Win & Pl
Career Total (Turf)	13	4	2	1	140703

113	6/09	Asct	7f		G-F	£45416
112	4/09	NmkR	7f	H	G-F	£25546
102	10/08	Sals	6f		GD	£9034
92	7/08	NmkJ	6f		G-S	£9714

Total win prize-money £89712

Going (Turf): Sf: 0-1 GS: 1-1 Gd: 1-6 **GF: 2-5** Fm: 0-0
Distance: 5f/6f: 2-5 7f-8f: 2-8 9f-13f: 0-0 14f+: 0-0
Track : LH: 0-0 RH: 0-1 Tight: 0-0 Gall: 0-0
Aids: Bl: 0-0 Vi: 0-0 Tstrap: 0-0 Ckp: 0-0
Best Rating: **116** 10/09 NmkR 7f good

Group class; winner of the Free Handicap and Group 3 Jersey Stakes in 2009; stays 7f; acts on good and easier ground.

Our Acquaintance

84(99) (62)73

4-y-o ch g Bahamian Bounty-Lady Of Limerick (IRE) (Thatching)
W R Muir Quaintance Partnership

Placings:34320100/03654514550334-0000 **(2908)**
2009: 5^{0}SD, 5^{0}SD, 5^{0}GF, 5^{0}F,

	Starts	1st	2nd	3rd	Win & Pl
Career Total (Turf)	18	1	1	3	5805
Career Total (AW)	8	1	0	2	3703

68	8/08	Wind	5f10y	(0-75)H	G-S	£2729
73	9/07	Wolv	5f20y		SF	£2914

Total win prize-money £5645

Going (Turf): Sf: 0-4 **GS: 1-4** Gd: 0-5 GF: 0-3 Fm: 0-2
Distance: **5f/6f: 2-26** 7f-8f: 0-0 9f-13f: 0-0 14f+: 0-0
Track : **LH: 1-9** RH: 0-0 Tight: 1-5 Gall: 1-7
Aids: **Bl: 1-13** Vi: 0-0 Tstrap: 0-0 Ckp: 0-0
Best Rating: **75** 6/07 Ling 5f soft

Modest; effective over 5f-6f; acts on good and easier ground and on sand; has worn blinkers.

Our Apolonia (IRE)

90 49

3-y-o b f Intikhab (USA)-Algaira (USA) (Irish River (FR))
A Berry Pat Renoso

Placings:52060-000400 **(5549)**
2009: 6^{0}G, 7^{0}GF, 6^{0}S, 7^{4}G, 8^{0}HY, 9^{0}G,

	Starts	1st	2nd	3rd	Win & Pl
Career Total (Turf)	11	0	1	0	1156

Going (Turf): **Sf: 0-2 GS: 0-3 Gd: 0-5 GF: 0-1 Fm: 0-0**
Distance: 5f/6f: 0-3 7f-8f: 0-6 9f-13f: 0-2 14f+: 0-0
Track : LH: 0-4 RH: 0-5 Tight: 0-7 Gall: 0-0
Aids: Bl: 0-1 Vi: 0-0 Tstrap: 0-0 Ckp: 0-0
Best Rating: **49** 8/08 Ripn 6f gd-sft

Intikhab filly; effective at 6f; handles some ease in the ground.

Our Blessing (IRE)

99(107) (75)68

5-y-o b g Lujain (USA)-Berenice (ITY) (Marouble)
A P Jarvis Geoffrey Bishop

Placings:40401**525**/**1**4004030/**006**00434**320214**004-420 **(2088)**
2009: 6^{4}SD, 6^{2}GF, 6^{0}GF,

	Starts	1st	2nd	3rd	Win & Pl
Career Total (Turf)	17	1	1	2	6088
Career Total (AW)	19	2	3	1	8751

73	10/08	Kemp	6f	(0-65)H	STD	£1706
83	1/07	Kemp	5f	(0-75)H	STD	£2914
73	10/06	Pont	6f		G-S	£3238

Total win prize-money £7860

Going (Turf): Sf: 0-1 **GS: 1-1** Gd: 0-8 GF: 0-6 Fm: 0-1
Distance: **5f/6f: 3-23** 7f-8f: 0-10 9f-13f: 0-3 14f+: 0-0
Track : LH: 1-10 **RH: 2-13** Tight: 0-4 Gall: 0-5
Aids: Bl: 0-0 Vi: 0-2 Tstrap: 0-0 Ckp: 0-0
Best Rating: **84** 8/07 NmkJ 6f good

Modest; effective at around 6f; acts on good ground or softer ground and on Polytrack.

Our Boy Barrington (IRE)

84 62

2-y-o b c Catcher In The Rye (IRE)-Daily Double (FR) (Unfuwain (USA))
R Hannon Mrs J Wood

Placings:000 **(4908)**
2009: 6^{0}G, 7^{0}G, 7^{0}G,

	Starts	1st	2nd	3rd	Win & Pl
Career Total (Turf)	3	0	0	0	

Going (Turf): **Sf: 0-0 GS: 0-0 Gd: 0-3 GF: 0-0 Fm: 0-0**
Distance: 5f/6f: 0-0 7f-8f: 0-3 9f-13f: 0-0 14f+: 0-0
Track : LH: 0-0 RH: 0-1 Tight: 0-0 Gall: 0-0
Aids: Bl: 0-0 Vi: 0-0 Tstrap: 0-0 Ckp: 0-0
Best Rating: **62** 6/09 NmkJ 7f good

Our Day Will Come

88(93) (71)71

3-y-o b f Red Ransom (USA)-Dawnus (IRE) (Night Shift (USA))
R Hannon Derek And Jean Clee

Placings:042363440-500 **(2321)**
2009: 7^{5}G, 7^{0}F, 6^{0}G,

	Starts	1st	2nd	3rd	Win & Pl
Career Total (Turf)	8	0	1	1	1638
Career Total (AW)	4	0	0	1	842

Going (Turf): **Sf: 0-1 GS: 0-1 Gd: 0-3 GF: 0-2 Fm: 0-1**
Distance: 5f/6f: 0-1 7f-8f: 0-11 9f-13f: 0-0 14f+: 0-0
Track : LH: 0-5 RH: 0-1 Tight: 0-3 Gall: 0-0
Aids: Bl: 0-0 Vi: 0-0 Tstrap: 0-0 Ckp: 0-0
Best Rating: **71** 11/08 Kemp 1m stand

Fair; stays 7f; acts on fast ground but appears to handle cut.

Our Dream Queen

88 70

2-y-o b f Oasis Dream-Our Queen Of Kings (Arazi (USA))
B W Hills Lady Richard Wellesley

Placings:351300 **(7290)**
2009: 5^{3}GS, 6^{5}G, 6^{1}G, 6^{3}GF, 6^{0}G, 6^{0}S,

	Starts	1st	2nd	3rd	Win & Pl
Career Total (Turf)	6	1	0	2	6446

70	7/09	Ffos	6f	GD	£4857

Total win prize-money £4857

Going (Turf): Sf: 0-1 GS: 0-1 **Gd: 1-3** GF: 0-1 Fm: 0-0
Distance: **5f/6f: 1-5** 7f-8f: 0-1 9f-13f: 0-0 14f+: 0-0
Track : LH: 0-0 RH: 0-0 Tight: 0-0 Gall: 0-0
Aids: Bl: 0-0 Vi: 0-0 Tstrap: 0-0 Ckp: 0-0
Best Rating: **70** 7/09 Ffos 6f good

Fair; effective over 6f; acts on good and easy ground.

Our Fugitive (IRE)

(101) (68)71

7-y-o gr g Titus Livius (FR)-Mystical Jumbo (Mystiko (USA))
C Gordon Gordon Racing

Placings:403212/50006/22400/500210**5031**/03040020064 60-056 **(1055)**
2009: 5^{0}SD, 5^{5}SD, 5^{6}SD,

	Starts	1st	2nd	3rd	Win & Pl
Career Total (Turf)	31	2	5	2	18677
Career Total (AW)	11	1	1	1	2749

73	12/07	Wolv	5f20y	(0-65)H	STD	£1706
69	7/07	Chep	5f16y	(0-70)H	HVY	£3368
86	8/04	Chep	5f16y	D H	SFT	£4803

Total win prize-money £9878

Going (Turf): **Sf: 2-10** GS: 0-6 Gd: 0-5 GF: 0-10 Fm: 0-0
Distance: **5f/6f: 3-42** 7f-8f: 0-0 9f-13f: 0-0 14f+: 0-0
Track : **LH: 1-14** RH: 0-1 **Tight: 1-11** Gall: 0-5
Aids: **Bl: 1-4** Vi: 0-4 Tstrap: 0-6 Ckp: 0-6

Best Rating: 93 10/04 NmkR 6f soft

Moderate; suited by 5f-6f; acts on most ground on turf; goes on Polytrack; has worn headgear.

Our Georgie Girl

82 **34**

2-y-o ch f Zafeen (FR)-Rosina May (IRE) (Danehill Dancer (IRE))

G G Margarson M A J Daly

Placings:06060 **(2978)**

2009: 5^{0}GF, 5^{6}GF, 6^{0}G, 7^{6}S, 6^{0}GF,

	Starts	1st	2nd	3rd	Win & Pl
Career Total (Turf)	5	0	0	0	0

Going (Turf): **Sf: 0-1 GS: 0-0 Gd: 0-1 GF: 0-3 Fm: 0-0**
Distance: 5f/6f: 0-3 7f-8f: 0-2 9f-13f: 0-0 14f+: 0-0
Track : LH: 0-0 RH: 0-0 Tight: 0-0 Gall: 0-1
Aids: Bl: 0-1 Vi: 0-0 Tstrap: 0-0 Ckp: 0-0
Best Rating: **34** 6/09 Wind 6f gd-fm

Our Girl Ally (IRE)

66 **2**

3-y-o b f Captain Rio-Glenviews Big Bird (USA) (Danehill (USA))

A Berry Alan Berry

Placings:6064 **(5304)**

2009: 6^{6}GS, 5^{0}G, 6^{6}S, 6^{4}HY,

	Starts	1st	2nd	3rd	Win & Pl
Career Total (Turf)	4	0	0	0	356

Going (Turf): **Sf: 0-2 GS: 0-1 Gd: 0-1 GF: 0-0 Fm: 0-0**
Distance: 5f/6f: 0-1 7f-8f: 0-3 9f-13f: 0-0 14f+: 0-0
Track : LH: 0-0 RH: 0-0 Tight: 0-0 Gall: 0-0
Aids: Bl: 0-0 Vi: 0-0 Tstrap: 0-0 Ckp: 0-0

Our Glenard

(90) (40)**28**

10-y-o b g Royal Applause-Loucoum (FR) (Iron Duke (FR))

J E Long P Saxon

Placings:5500/0600P006/0411005005/220564064/03660 0/001042/00/006000-6 **(0838)**

2009: 12^{6}SD,

	Starts	1st	2nd	3rd	Win & Pl
Career Total (Turf)	23	2	0	1	6721
Career Total (AW)	29	1	3	0	4671
41 8/06 Brig	1m3f196y (0-55)H			FRM	£2590
57 5/03 Bevl	1m1f207yE(0-70)H			G-F	£3705
58 4/03 Ling	1m5f G			STD	£2947

Total win prize-money £9243

Going (Turf): Sf: 0-1 GS: 0-3 Gd: 0-7 **GF: 1-7 Fm: 1-5**
Distance: 5f/6f: 0-4 7f-8f: 0-4 **9f-13f: 3-42** 14f+: 0-2
Track : **LH: 2-39** RH: 1-9 **Tight: 1-25** Gall: 0-1
Aids: Bl: 0-0 Vi: 0-0 Tstrap: 0-0 Ckp: 0-0
Best Rating: **69** 8/01 Ling 5f gd-fm

Our Joe Mac (IRE)

99 **88**

2-y-o b g Celtic Swing-Vade Retro (IRE) (Desert Sun)

R A Fahey A Long

Placings:315 **(6088)**

2009: 7^{3}G, 7^{1}G, 8^{5}G,

	Starts	1st	2nd	3rd	Win & Pl
Career Total (Turf)	3	1	0	1	5511
86 8/09 Thsk 7f				GD	£4274

Total win prize-money £4274

Going (Turf): Sf: 0-0 GS: 0-0 **Gd: 1-3** GF: 0-0 Fm: 0-0
Distance: 5f/6f: 0-0 **7f-8f: 1-3** 9f-13f: 0-0 14f+: 0-0
Track : **LH: 1-3** RH: 0-0 **Tight: 1-1** Gall: 0-1
Aids: Bl: 0-0 Vi: 0-0 Tstrap: 0-0 Ckp: 0-0
Best Rating: **88** 9/09 Ayr 1m good

Stays 7f; handles good ground.

Our Jonathan

110 (103)**114**

2-y-o b c Invincible Spirit (IRE)-Sheik'n Swing (Celtic Swing)

K A Ryan (B Smart 3/7) Dr Marwan Koukash

Placings:311011 **(7231a)**

2009: 6^{3}G, 5^{1}GF, 5^{1}SD, 5^{0}GF, 5^{1}GS, 6^{1}HO,

	Starts	1st	2nd	3rd	Win & Pl
Career Total (Turf)	5	3	0	1	142679
Career Total (AW)	1	1	0	0	30022
114 11/09 MsnL 6f				HLD	£105146
110 10/09 Asct 5f				G-S	£31223
103 8/09 Dund 5f				STD	£30021
90 8/09 Pont 5f				G-F	£5828

Total win prize-money £172220

Going (Turf): Sf: 0-0 **GS: 1-1** Gd: 0-1 **GF: 1-2** Fm: 0-0
Distance: **5f/6f: 4-6** 7f-8f: 0-0 9f-13f: 0-0 14f+: 0-0
Track : **LH: 2-2** RH: 0-0 Tight: 0-0 Gall: 0-0
Aids: Bl: 0-0 Vi: 0-0 Tstrap: 0-0 Ckp: 0-0
Best Rating: **114** 11/09 MsnL 6f holding

Group class; Listed winner and landed the Group 3 Cornwallis in 2009; suited by 5f; acts on fast and easy ground; goes on Polytrack.

Our Kes (IRE)

90(108) (68)**67**

7-y-o gr m Revoque (IRE)-Gracious Gretclo (Common Grounds)

P Howling S J Hammond

Placings:00040011/10020/000365/00511443516062053154425/02353135312432000065-3000000241302665 **(7766)**

2009: 10^{3}SD, 9^{0}SD, 10^{0}SD, 12^{0}SD, 10^{0}G, 8^{0}SF, 10^{0}G, 10^{2}SD, 9^{4}SD, 12^{1}SD, 12^{3}SD, 9^{0}SD, 12^{2}SD, 8^{6}SD, 10^{6}SD, 11^{5}SD,

	Starts	1st	2nd	3rd	Win & Pl
Career Total (Turf)	18	1	1	2	4953
Career Total (AW)	61	9	7	8	32920
59 9/09 Wolv	1m4f50y (0-60)H			STD	£2388
74 5/08 Kemp	1m2f (0-65)H			STD	£2047
73 3/08 Wolv	1m1f103y (0-65)H			STD	£2047
73 10/07 Wolv	1m1f103y (0-70)H			STD	£2914
65 6/07 Bath	1m2f46y (0-70)H			GD	£2914
69 3/07 Ling	1m2f (0-60)H			STD	£1706
62 2/07 Wolv	1m141y (0-60)H			STD	£1706
79 1/05 Ling	7f (0-70)H			STD	£3382
74 12/04 Ling	7f (0-75)			STD	£3614
66 12/04 Wolv	7f32y			STD	£2548

Total win prize-money £25270

Going (Turf): Sf: 0-0 GS: 0-1 **Gd: 1-9** GF: 0-5 Fm: 0-3
Distance: 5f/6f: 0-3 7f-8f: 3-22 **9f-13f: 7-54** 14f+: 0-0
Track : **LH: 9-56** RH: 1-13 **Tight: 9-48** Gall: 0-7
Aids: Bl: 0-3 Vi: 0-0 Tstrap: 0-0 Ckp: 0-0
Best Rating: **79** 1/05 Ling 7f stand

Moderate; effective at around 1m2f-1m4f; acts on good ground and on Polytrack.

Our Last Call (IRE)

(85) (39)

3-y-o gr f Hernando (FR)-On Call (Alleged (USA))

Sir Mark Prescott Lady O'Reilly

Placings:0000 **(7154)**

2009: 10^{0}SD, 8^{0}SD, 11^{0}SD, 16^{0}SD,

	Starts	1st	2nd	3rd	Win & Pl
Career Total (Turf)	0	0	0	0	
Career Total (AW)	4	0	0	0	

Going (Turf): **Sf: 0-0 GS: 0-0 Gd: 0-0 GF: 0-0 Fm: 0-0**
Distance: 5f/6f: 0-0 7f-8f: 0-1 9f-13f: 0-2 14f+: 0-1
Track : LH: 0-1 RH: 0-3 Tight: 0-1 Gall: 0-0
Aids: Bl: 0-1 Vi: 0-0 Tstrap: 0-0 Ckp: 0-0
Best Rating: **39** 6/09 Kemp 1m2f stand

Moderate form so far; has worn blinkers.

Our Nations

(100) (70)**44**

4-y-o gr g Highest Honor (FR)-Lines Of Beauty (USA) (Line In The Sand (USA))

D Carroll Ninerus

Placings:00000-2P **(0249)**

2009: 12^{2}SS, 16^{P}SD,

	Starts	1st	2nd	3rd	Win & Pl
Career Total (Turf)	3	0	0	0	
Career Total (AW)	4	0	1	0	806

Going (Turf): **Sf: 0-0 GS: 0-0 Gd: 0-3 GF: 0-0 Fm: 0-0**
Distance: 5f/6f: 0-0 7f-8f: 0-0 9f-13f: 0-4 14f+: 0-3
Track : LH: 0-5 RH: 0-2 Tight: 0-2 Gall: 0-2
Aids: Bl: 0-0 Vi: 0-1 Tstrap: 0-0 Ckp: 0-0
Best Rating: **70** 1/09 Sthl 1m4f std-slw

Very moderate; stays 1m4f and acts on Fibresand.

Our Piccadilly (IRE)

105(100) (83)**84**

4-y-o b f Piccolo-Dilys (Efisio)

W S Kittow S Kittow, R Perry, B Hopkins

Placings:221/0056414-2310306420 **(6972)**

2009: 5^{2}G, 5^{3}G, 5^{1}GF, 5^{0}GF, 5^{3}GF, 5^{0}GS, 5^{6}G, 5^{4}GF, 5^{2}SS, 5^{0}SD,

	Starts	1st	2nd	3rd	Win & Pl
Career Total (Turf)	16	2	3	2	16239
Career Total (AW)	4	1	1	0	4316
83 5/09 Ling 5f	(0-85)H			G-F	£6476
75 9/08 Gdwd 5f	(0-75)H			SFT	£3238
70 9/07 Wolv 5f216y				STD	£2388

Total win prize-money £12103

Going (Turf): **Sf: 1-2** GS: 0-4 Gd: 0-5 **GF: 1-5** Fm: 0-0
Distance: **5f/6f: 3-19** 7f-8f: 0-1 9f-13f: 0-0 14f+: 0-0
Track : **LH: 1-3** RH: 0-2 **Tight: 1-2** Gall: 0-4
Aids: Bl: 0-0 Vi: 0-0 Tstrap: 0-0 Ckp: 0-0
Best Rating: **84** 7/09 Epsm 5f gd-fm

Fair; effective over 5f-6f; acts on most ground and on Polytrack.

Our Serendipity

(36) **1**

6-y-o ch m Presidium-Berl's Gift (Prince Sabo)
R C Guest Elevate Equestrian Ltd

Placings:000/00000/0-0 (1127)
2009: 10^{0}GF,

	Starts	1st	2nd	3rd	Win & Pl
Career Total (Turf)	9	0	0	0	
Career Total (AW)	1	0	0	0	

Going (Turf): Sf: 0-0 GS: 0-2 Gd: 0-1 GF: 0-5 Fm: 0-1
Distance: 5f/6f: 0-3 7f-8f: 0-3 9f-13f: 0-4 14f+: 0-0
Track : LH: 0-4 RH: 0-1 Tight: 0-0 Gall: 0-2
Aids: Bl: 0-0 Vi: 0-0 Tstrap: 0-0 Ckp: 0-0
Best Rating: 55 9/05 Hayd 6f gd-sft

Our Teddy (IRE)

(89) (46)**83**

9-y-o ch g Grand Lodge (USA)-Lady Windley (Baillamont (USA))
R Curtis The Beare Family

Placings:6142000/26100000/400544005/006350240450/051161040/003/0 (7393)
2009: 10^{0}SD,

	Starts	1st	2nd	3rd	Win & Pl
Career Total (Turf)	42	5	2	2	54373
Career Total (AW)	7	0	1	0	17127
91	8/06 NmkJ	1m4f	(0-85)H	G-F	£5505
84	7/06 Sals	1m4f	(0-75)H	G-F	£3562
81	7/06 Bevl	1m1f207y	(0-75)H	FRM	£5181
103	5/03 Donc	1m	C	GD	£9808
75	6/02 NmkJ	7f	D	G-F	£4823

Total win prize-money £28881

Going (Turf): Sf: 0-1 GS: 0-4 Gd: 1-10 GF: 3-23 Fm: 1-4
Distance: 5f/6f: 0-2 7f-8f: 2-16 9f-13f: 3-30 14f+: 0-1
Track : LH: 1-22 RH: 3-20 Tight: 1-16 Gall: 2-8
Aids: Bl: 0-6 Vi: 0-1 Tstrap: 0-2 Ckp: 0-2
Best Rating: 106 10/02 Lonc 7f good

Our Wee Girl (IRE)

69(94) (58)**77**

3-y-o b/br f Choisir (AUS)-Zwadi (IRE) (Dockside (USA))
Miss Tor Sturgis Miss Tor Sturgis

Placings:220342056-000 (6433)
2009: 5^{0}G, 5^{0}SD, 5^{0}SD,

	Starts	1st	2nd	3rd	Win & Pl
Career Total (Turf)	6	0	2	1	4056
Career Total (AW)	6	0	1	0	806

Going (Turf): Sf: 0-0 GS: 0-1 Gd: 0-2 GF: 0-3 Fm: 0-0
Distance: 5f/6f: 0-12 7f-8f: 0-0 9f-13f: 0-0 14f+: 0-0
Track : LH: 0-9 RH: 0-0 Tight: 0-7 Gall: 0-2
Aids: Bl: 0-0 Vi: 0-1 Tstrap: 0-1 Ckp: 0-1
Best Rating: 77 5/08 Leic 5f2y gd-fm

Fair; effective at 5f; acts on fast ground and on Polytrack.

Ourbelle

76 **10**

4-y-o b f Bertolini (USA)-Guardienne (Hector Protector (USA))
Miss Tracy Waggott H Conlon

Placings:00000-0 (5946)
2009: 5^{0}G,

	Starts	1st	2nd	3rd	Win & Pl
Career Total (Turf)	6	0	0	0	

Going (Turf): Sf: 0-0 GS: 0-2 Gd: 0-3 GF: 0-1 Fm: 0-0
Distance: 5f/6f: 0-5 7f-8f: 0-1 9f-13f: 0-0 14f+: 0-0
Track : LH: 0-0 RH: 0-0 Tight: 0-0 Gall: 0-0
Aids: Bl: 0-0 Vi: 0-0 Tstrap: 0-0 Ckp: 0-0
Best Rating: 10 8/08 Carl 5f153y good

Ours (IRE)

102(107) (85)**78**

6-y-o b g Mark Of Esteem (IRE)-Ellebanna (Tina's Pet)
John A Harris Peter Smith P C Coaches Limited

Placings:0250/026330421/0605002162323/52250152443136-32200352442325631 (7854)
2009: 9^{3}SD, 8^{2}SD, 8^{2}SD, 8^{0}GF, 8^{0}SD, 7^{3}SD, 8^{5}GF, 8^{2}S, 8^{4}G, 8^{4}HY, 8^{2}SD, 8^{3}GF, 8^{2}SD, 11^{5}SD, 8^{6}G, 8^{3}SD, 8^{1}SS,

	Starts	1st	2nd	3rd	Win & Pl
Career Total (Turf)	32	1	7	4	14509
Career Total (AW)	25	4	7	6	19401
85	12/09 Sthl	1m	(0-75)H	SS	£2729
74	11/08 Wolv	1m141y	(0-65)H	STD	£1706
71	7/08 Pont	1m4y	(0-70)H	GD	£3885
60	10/07 Kemp	1m	(0-55)	STD	£2047
63	11/06 Wolv	7f32y		SF	£2730

Total win prize-money £13100

Going (Turf): Sf: 0-5 GS: 0-2 Gd: 1-11 GF: 0-11 Fm: 0-3
Distance: 5f/6f: 0-3 7f-8f: 3-30 9f-13f: 2-24 14f+: 0-0
Track : LH: 4-39 RH: 1-11 Tight: 2-16 Gall: 0-1
Aids: Bl: 1-5 Vi: 0-0 Tstrap: 3-31 Ckp: 3-31
Best Rating: 85 12/09 Sthl 1m std-slw

Fair; suited by 7f-1m; acts on most ground and on sand; usually wears cheekpieces.

Ouste (FR)

(97) (44)**46**

7-y-o ch g Ragmar (FR)-Elbe (FR) (Royal Charter (FR))
Mrs A M Thorpe (Mrs S Leech 19/4) Centaur Global Partnership I

Placings:3/000/003/0300-6 (0541)
2009: 11^{6}SD,

	Starts	1st	2nd	3rd	Win & Pl
Career Total (Turf)	11	0	0	3	2179
Career Total (AW)	1	0	0	0	0

Going (Turf): Sf: 0-2 GS: 0-0 Gd: 0-5 GF: 0-1 Fm: 0-1
Distance: 5f/6f: 0-2 7f-8f: 0-3 9f-13f: 0-6 14f+: 0-1
Track : LH: 0-2 RH: 0-8 Tight: 0-0 Gall: 0-0
Aids: Bl: 0-0 Vi: 0-0 Tstrap: 0-1 Ckp: 0-1
Best Rating: 46 6/08 Baln 2m gd-fm

Ouster (GER)

101 **93**

3-y-o b c Lomitas-Odabella's Charm (Cadeaux Genereux)
D R C Elsworth Raymond Tooth

Placings:012-4 (1459)
2009: 10^{4}G,

	Starts	1st	2nd	3rd	Win & Pl
Career Total (Turf)	4	1	1	0	8104
93	10/08 Sals	1m	GD	£4371	

Total win prize-money £4371

Going (Turf): Sf: 0-1 GS: 0-1 Gd: 1-2 GF: 0-0 Fm: 0-0
Distance: 5f/6f: 0-0 7f-8f: 1-2 9f-13f: 0-2 14f+: 0-0
Track : LH: 0-1 RH: 0-0 Tight: 0-1 Gall: 0-0
Aids: Bl: 0-0 Vi: 0-0 Tstrap: 0-0 Ckp: 0-0
Best Rating: 93 10/08 Sals 1m good

Useful German-bred colt; keen type; stays 1m2f; handles good ground.

Out Of Eden

84 **55**

2-y-o b c Monsun (GER)-Eden (USA) (Holy Bull (USA))
H R A Cecil H E Sheikh Sultan Bin Khalifa Al Nahyan

Placings:0 (7034)
2009: 8^{0}S,

	Starts	1st	2nd	3rd	Win & Pl
Career Total (Turf)	1	0	0	0	

Going (Turf): Sf: 0-1 GS: 0-0 Gd: 0-0 GF: 0-0 Fm: 0-0
Distance: 5f/6f: 0-0 7f-8f: 0-1 9f-13f: 0-0 14f+: 0-0
Track : LH: 0-0 RH: 0-0 Tight: 0-0 Gall: 0-0
Aids: Bl: 0-0 Vi: 0-0 Tstrap: 0-0 Ckp: 0-0
Best Rating: 55 10/09 Newb 1m soft

Out Of India

(94) (51)**56**

7-y-o b m Marju (IRE)-Tide Of Fortune (Soviet Star (USA))
P T Dalton Mrs Julie Martin

Placings:0/6202660412/0005/503405066-00 (1655)
2009: 5^{0}SD, 7^{0}SD,

	Starts	1st	2nd	3rd	Win & Pl
Career Total (Turf)	12	1	1	1	6474
Career Total (AW)	14	0	2	0	2275
71	10/05 Rdcr	7f	(0-70)H	G-F	£4143

Total win prize-money £4144

Going (Turf): Sf: 0-2 GS: 0-3 Gd: 0-2 GF: 1-4 Fm: 0-1
Distance: 5f/6f: 0-6 7f-8f: 1-17 9f-13f: 0-3 14f+: 0-0
Track : LH: 0-17 RH: 0-2 Tight: 0-10 Gall: 0-1
Aids: Bl: 0-0 Vi: 0-0 Tstrap: 0-0 Ckp: 0-0
Best Rating: 73 1/06 Sthl 1m stand

Moderate; effective over 6f-1m; acts on quick surface; also goes on sand.

Out Of Nothing

81(99) (58)**66**

6-y-o br m Perryston View-Loves To Dare (IRE) (Desert King (IRE))
K M Prendergast R J Parsons

Placings:00462/4020600/04062015-0 (1775)
2009: 7^{0}GF,

	Starts	1st	2nd	3rd	Win & Pl
Career Total (Turf)	17	1	3	0	8753
Career Total (AW)	4	0	0	0	0
66	11/08 Ayr	7f50y	(0-75)H	HVY	£3885

Total win prize-money £3886

Going (Turf): Sf: 1-10 GS: 0-0 Gd: 0-0 GF: 0-3 Fm: 0-0
Distance: 5f/6f: 0-0 7f-8f: 1-13 9f-13f: 0-8 14f+: 0-0
Track : LH: 1-10 RH: 0-6 Tight: 0-1 Gall: 0-1
Aids: Bl: 0-0 Vi: 0-0 Tstrap: 0-0 Ckp: 0-0
Best Rating: 72 10/06 Navn 1m heavy

Out The Ring (IRE)

88(91) (66)**60**

2-y-o b g Acclamation-Residual (IRE) (Trempolino (USA))

Miss Gay Kelleway (K A Ryan 11/5) Eugene Woods, Gay Kelleway

Placings:232224060205 **(7748)**

2009: 5^{2}SD, 5^{3}GF, 5^{2}GF, 5^{2}SD, 5^{2}GF, 5^{4}F, 5^{0}SD, 6^{6}SD, 6^{0}SD, 5^{2}SD, 6^{0}SD, 5^{5}SD,

	Starts	1st	2nd	3rd	Win & Pl
Career Total (Turf)	4	0	2	1	3446
Career Total (AW)	8	0	3	0	3154

Going (Turf): **Sf: 0-0 GS: 0-0 Gd: 0-0 GF: 0-3 Fm: 0-1**
Distance: 5f/6f: 0-12 7f-8f: 0-0 9f-13f: 0-0 14f+: 0-0
Track : LH: 0-6 RH: 0-2 Tight: 0-5 Gall: 0-0
Aids: Bl: 0-0 Vi: 0-0 Tstrap: 0-2 Ckp: 0-2
Best Rating: **66** 5/09 Wolv 5f20y stand

Modest; suited by 5f; acts on fast ground and on Polytrack.

Outdroad

(78) (28)

3-y-o ch c Desert Sun-Loch Fyne (Ardkinglass)

P M Phelan Gleeson, Kennedy, Keely

Placings:000-0 **(0441)**

2009: 8^{6}SD,

	Starts	1st	2nd	3rd	Win & Pl
Career Total (Turf)	0	0	0	0	
Career Total (AW)	4	0	0	0	0

Going (Turf): **Sf: 0-0 GS: 0-0 Gd: 0-0 GF: 0-0 Fm: 0-0**
Distance: 5f/6f: 0-3 7f-8f: 0-1 9f-13f: 0-0 14f+: 0-0
Track : LH: 0-2 RH: 0-2 Tight: 0-1 Gall: 0-1
Aids: Bl: 0-0 Vi: 0-0 Tstrap: 0-0 Ckp: 0-0
Best Rating: **28** 11/08 Kemp 6f stand

Outer Hebrides

103(101) (62)**63**

8-y-o b g Efisio-Reuval (Sharpen Up)

J M Bradley Asterix Partnership

Placings:221/00422/**05041**012436615304/**026660323052 503423663**/55035000631000/000556032**50405330-44040**1022254061450**633303** **(7602)**

2009: 7^{4}SD, 7^{4}SD, 7^{0}SD, 7^{4}SD, 7^{0}SD, 6^{1}SD, 6^{0}GF, 6^{2}SD, 7^{2}GF, 6^{2}GF, 6^{5}GS, 5^{4}G, 8^{0}G, 7^{6}GF, 6^{1}G, 6^{4}GS, 6^{5}G, 6^{0}G, 5^{6}G, 7^{3}SD, 7^{3}SD, 6^{3}SD, 7^{0}SD, 6^{3}SD,

	Starts	1st	2nd	3rd	Win & Pl
Career Total (Turf)	60	4	7	7	33554
Career Total (AW)	42	3	6	9	27866

63 8/09 Chep 6f16y (0-55)H GD £2266
56 5/09 Sthl 6f (0-50)H STD £2183
77 8/07 Sals 6f212y (0-70)H G-S £3238
87 8/05 Sals 6f212y (0-80) G-S £8723
85 5/05 Donc 6f GD £3503
85 3/05 Wolv 7f32y (0-85)H STD £6763
71 8/03 Wolv 6f F STD £3150
Total win prize-money £29830

Going (Turf): Sf: 0-9 **GS: 2-8 Gd: 2-21** GF: 0-21 Fm: 0-1
Distance: 5f/6f: 3-22 **7f-8f: 4-69** 9f-13f: 0-11 14f+: 0-0
Track : **LH: 3-42** RH: 0-15 **Tight: 2-22** Gall: 0-7
Aids: Bl: 0-1 **Vi: 6-84** Tstrap: 0-1 Ckp: 0-1
Best Rating: **89** 6/06 Kemp 7f stand

Moderate; effective over 6f-1m; acts on most ground on turf; goes on sand; has worn a visor.

Outland (IRE)

105(94) (34)**63**

3-y-o br g Indian Haven-Sensuality (IRE) (Idris (IRE))

M H Tompkins Rob Douglas

Placings:000-0125220 **(7124)**

2009: 11^{0}SD, 11^{1}S, 12^{2}GF, 11^{5}G, 14^{2}GF, 16^{2}GS, 16^{0}G,

	Starts	1st	2nd	3rd	Win & Pl
Career Total (Turf)	9	1	3	0	4141
Career Total (AW)	1	0	0	0	

56 6/09 Yarm 1m3f101y (0-65)H SFT £2072
Total win prize-money £2072

Going (Turf): **Sf: 1-2** GS: 0-2 Gd: 0-2 GF: 0-3 Fm: 0-0
Distance: 5f/6f: 0-0 7f-8f: 0-3 **9f-13f: 1-4** 14f+: 0-3
Track : **LH: 1-6** RH: 0-1 **Tight: 1-4** Gall: 0-1
Aids: Bl: 0-0 Vi: 0-0 Tstrap: 0-0 Ckp: 0-0
Best Rating: **63** 10/09 Newc 2m19y gd-sft

Moderate; stays 1m6f; acts on soft ground.

Outlandish

104(104) (84)**81**

6-y-o b g Dr Fong (USA)-Velvet Lady (Nashwan (USA))

Miss E C Lavelle S Kimber

Placings:122062-2450 **(5321)**

2009: 12^{2}GF, 12^{4}G, 11^{5}F, 10^{0}GF,

	Starts	1st	2nd	3rd	Win & Pl
Career Total (Turf)	6	0	1	0	2270
Career Total (AW)	4	1	3	0	4984

67 1/08 Ling 1m4f STD £2331
Total win prize-money £2332

Going (Turf): **Sf: 0-1 GS: 0-1 Gd: 0-1 GF: 0-2 Fm: 0-1**
Distance: 5f/6f: 0-0 7f-8f: 0-0 **9f-13f: 1-10** 14f+: 0-0
Track : **LH: 1-5** RH: 0-5 **Tight: 1-5** Gall: 0-2
Aids: Bl: 0-0 Vi: 0-0 Tstrap: 0-0 Ckp: 0-0
Best Rating: **84** 12/08 Wolv 1m141y stand

Fair; dual bumper winner; effective over 1m4f; acts on Polytrack and fast ground.

Outofoil (IRE)

94 **79**

3-y-o b g King's Best (USA)-Simplicity (Polish Precedent (USA))

R M Beckett I J Heseltine

Placings:210-0 **(2329)**

2009: 8^{0}GF,

	Starts	1st	2nd	3rd	Win & Pl
Career Total (Turf)	4	1	1	0	5527

77 8/08 Sals 6f G-S £4371
Total win prize-money £4371

Going (Turf): Sf: 0-1 **GS: 1-1** Gd: 0-0 GF: 0-2 Fm: 0-0
Distance: **5f/6f: 1-3** 7f-8f: 0-1 9f-13f: 0-0 14f+: 0-0
Track : LH: 0-0 RH: 0-1 Tight: 0-0 Gall: 0-0
Aids: Bl: 0-0 Vi: 0-0 Tstrap: 0-0 Ckp: 0-0
Best Rating: **79** 7/08 Sals 6f gd-fm

32,000 half-brother to 6f and 1m winner Simplify; stays 6f; acts on a sound and easy surface.

Outrageous Request

98(100) (70)**85**

3-y-o ch g Rainbow Quest (USA)-La Sorrela (IRE) (Cadeaux Genereux)

Pat Eddery P J J Eddery

Placings:6624222 **(7867)**

2009: 10^{6}G, 10^{6}GF, 10^{2}GS, 10^{4}S, 11^{2}S, 11^{2}SD, 14^{2}SS,

	Starts	1st	2nd	3rd	Win & Pl
Career Total (Turf)	5	0	2	0	1914
Career Total (AW)	2	0	2	0	2299

Going (Turf): **Sf: 0-2 GS: 0-1 Gd: 0-1 GF: 0-1 Fm: 0-0**
Distance: 5f/6f: 0-0 7f-8f: 0-0 9f-13f: 0-6 14f+: 0-1
Track : LH: 0-5 RH: 0-2 Tight: 0-3 Gall: 0-2
Aids: Bl: 0-0 Vi: 0-0 Tstrap: 0-0 Ckp: 0-0
Best Rating: **85** 4/09 Wind 1m2f7y gd-sft

Fair; stays 1m6f; acts on most ground on turf and on Fibresand.

Outshine

92 **71**

2-y-o ch f Exceed And Excel (AUS)-Sunny Davis (USA) (Alydar (USA))

J H M Gosden H R H Princess Haya Of Jordan

Placings:330 **(5478)**

2009: 6^{3}GF, 6^{3}GF, 6^{0}GF,

	Starts	1st	2nd	3rd	Win & Pl
Career Total (Turf)	3	0	0	2	2273

Going (Turf): **Sf: 0-0 GS: 0-0 Gd: 0-0 GF: 0-3 Fm: 0-0**
Distance: 5f/6f: 0-2 7f-8f: 0-1 9f-13f: 0-0 14f+: 0-0
Track : LH: 0-0 RH: 0-0 Tight: 0-0 Gall: 0-1
Aids: Bl: 0-0 Vi: 0-0 Tstrap: 0-0 Ckp: 0-0
Best Rating: **71** 7/09 NmkJ 6f gd-fm

Fair; effective over 6f; acts on fast ground.

Over To You Bert

92(101) (66)**38**

10-y-o b g Overbury (IRE)-Silvers Era (Balidar)

R J Hodges R J Hodges

Placings:5040500/**0651**40003310406/106/**0/12224216**202 0026/**0124321**000**-010000**0 **(1535)**

2009: 7^{0}SD, 7^{1}SD, 7^{0}SD, 7^{0}SD, 7^{0}SD, 7^{0}SD, 6^{0}GF,

	Starts	1st	2nd	3rd	Win & Pl
Career Total (Turf)	24	3	2	2	10445
Career Total (AW)	34	5	7	1	12199

60 2/09 Wolv 7f32y (0-52)H STD £1706
5/08 Lanc 6f H G-F £1680
63 2/08 Kemp 7f (0-52)H STD £2047
57 3/07 Wolv 7f32y (0-50)H STD £1535
49 1/07 Kemp 1m (0-45) STD £1365
5/05 Lanc 1m H SFT £1500
48 7/04 Bath 1m5y E(0-75)H GD £4478
53 3/04 Ling 1m H STD £1326
Total win prize-money £15641

Going (Turf): **Sf: 1-1** GS: 0-4 **Gd: 1-4 GF: 1-13** Fm: 0-2
Distance: 5f/6f: 1-7 **7f-8f: 6-34** 9f-13f: 1-17 14f+: 0-0
Track : **LH: 4-33** RH: 2-12 **Tight: 4-26** Gall: 0-1
Aids: Bl: 0-0 Vi: 0-2 Tstrap: 0-1 Ckp: 0-1
Best Rating: **66** 4/08 Ling 7f stand

Moderate; effective at around 7f-1m; acts on fast ground; goes on Polytrack.

Overrule (USA)

107 **95**

5-y-o b g Diesis-Her Own Way (USA) (Danzig (USA))

B Ellison The Jury's Out Partnership

Placings:0/1560/6060000422-1403100 **(4769)**

2009: 13^{1}GF, 14^{4}G, 12^{0}GF, 10^{3}GF, 11^{1}GF, 12^{0}G, 16^{0}GS,

	Starts	1st	2nd	3rd	Win & Pl
Career Total (Turf)	**22**	**3**	**2**	**1**	**33681**

95	6/09	Carl	1m3f107y	(0-80)H	G-F	£19428
82	4/09	Catt	1m5f175y	(0-85)H	G-F	£4727
91	4/07	Wind	1m2f7y		G-F	£3238

Total win prize-money £27394

Going (Turf): Sf: 0-1 GS: 0-2 Gd: 0-9 **GF: 3-10** Fm: 0-0
Distance: 5f/6f: 0-0 7f-8f: 0-8 **9f-13f: 2-11** 14f+: 1-3
Track : LH: 1-12 **RH: 2-6 Tight: 2-8** Gall: 0-8
Aids: Bl: 0-0 Vi: 0-0 Tstrap: 0-0 Ckp: 0-0
Best Rating: **95** 6/09 Carl 1m3f107y gd-fm

Useful; effective at 1m2f-1m6f; acts on fast ground; usually held up.

Oversighted (GER)

(97) (72)**54**
8-y-o b g Selkirk (USA)-Obvious Appeal (IRE) (Danehill (USA))
Mrs Y Dunleavy P Dunleavy

Placings:1/260543/064420231000/0020504000/**0**/0000-**1014** **(7163a)**
2009: 8^{1}SD, 8^{0}SD, 8^{1}SD, 8^{4}SD,

	Starts	1st	2nd	3rd	Win & Pl
Career Total (Turf)	**33**	**2**	**4**	**2**	**31903**
Career Total (AW)	**5**	**2**	**0**	**0**	**9671**

72	10/09	Dund	1m	(47-65)H	STD	£4696
53	9/09	Dund	1m	(47-65)H	STD	£4696
92	7/05	Leop	7f		G-F	£6125
65	6/03	Leop	6f		Y-S	£8441

Total win prize-money £23960

Going (Turf): Sf: 0-7 GS: 0-0 Gd: 0-5 **GF: 1-10** Fm: 0-1
Distance: 5f/6f: 1-7 **7f-8f: 3-27** 9f-13f: 0-4 14f+: 0-0
Track : **LH: 4-20** RH: 0-9 Tight: 0-2 Gall: 0-2
Aids: **Bl: 2-17** Vi: 0-0 Tstrap: 0-1 Ckp: 0-1
Best Rating: **95** 6/05 Tipp 7f100y firm

Overturn (IRE)

107(109) (94)**101**
5-y-o b g Barathea (IRE)-Kristal Bridge (Kris)
D McCain Jnr (W R Swinburn 12/10) T G Leslie

Placings:514/40-030221 **(6734)**
2009: 8^{0}G, 10^{3}GF, 12^{0}G, 11^{2}SD, 14^{2}GF, 14^{1}S,

	Starts	1st	2nd	3rd	Win & Pl
Career Total (Turf)	**10**	**2**	**1**	**1**	**19665**
Career Total (AW)	**1**	**0**	**1**	**0**	**1407**

101	10/09	Sals	1m6f21y	(0-95)H	SFT	£7771
90	8/06	Sand	7f16y		G-F	£4533

Total win prize-money £12305

Going (Turf): **Sf: 1-2** GS: 0-1 Gd: 0-2 **GF: 1-5** Fm: 0-0
Distance: 5f/6f: 0-0 7f-8f: 1-5 9f-13f: 0-4 14f+: 1-2
Track : LH: 0-2 **RH: 2-7 Tight: 1-2** Gall: 0-2
Aids: Bl: 0-0 Vi: 0-0 Tstrap: 0-0 Ckp: 0-0
Best Rating: **101** 10/09 Sals 1m6f21y soft

Useful; stays 1m6f; acts on fast and soft ground; has worn a tongue tie.

Ovthenight (IRE)

101(97) (57)**74**
4-y-o b c Noverre (USA)-Night Beauty (King Of Kings (IRE))
Mrs P Sly D Bayliss, T Davies, G Libson & P Sly

Placings:0600**40**/113**00**-63205 **(5028)**

2009: 11^{6}GF, 12^{3}GF, 14^{2}G, 13^{0}GF, 12^{5}GF,

	Starts	1st	2nd	3rd	Win & Pl
Career Total (Turf)	**13**	**2**	**1**	**2**	**6558**
Career Total (AW)	**3**	**0**	**0**	**0**	

71	5/08	Leic	1m3f183y	(0-70)H	G-F	£2590
68	4/08	Sthl	1m3f	(0-60)H	G-F	£1774

Total win prize-money £4364

Going (Turf): Sf: 0-2 GS: 0-2 Gd: 0-2 **GF: 2-7** Fm: 0-0
Distance: 5f/6f: 0-0 7f-8f: 0-3 **9f-13f: 2-12** 14f+: 0-1
Track : LH: 1-8 RH: 1-7 **Tight: 1-4** Gall: 0-4
Aids: Bl: 0-0 Vi: 0-4 Tstrap: 0-0 Ckp: 0-0
Best Rating: **74** 6/08 Donc 1m4f gd-sft

Modest; effective over 1m4f; acts on fast ground; has worn a visor.

Owain James

90(87) (36)**39**
4-y-o ch g Dancing Spree (USA)-Jane Grey (Tragic Role (USA))
Miss A M Newton-Smith (M Salaman 22/7) S Hicks

Placings:0000-06 **(3675)**
2009: 17^{0}F, 9^{6}F,

	Starts	1st	2nd	3rd	Win & Pl
Career Total (Turf)	**5**	**0**	**0**	**0**	**0**
Career Total (AW)	**1**	**0**	**0**	**0**	

Going (Turf): **Sf: 0-0 GS: 0-0 Gd: 0-3 GF: 0-0 Fm: 0-2**
Distance: 5f/6f: 0-1 7f-8f: 0-1 9f-13f: 0-3 14f+: 0-1
Track : LH: 0-4 RH: 0-0 Tight: 0-2 Gall: 0-0
Aids: Bl: 0-1 Vi: 0-0 Tstrap: 0-3 Ckp: 0-3
Best Rating: **39** 8/08 Brig 1m1f209y good

Owed

86(101) (66)**28**
7-y-o b g Lujain (USA)-Nightingale (Night Shift (USA))
R Bastiman Robin Bastiman

Placings:004/**200023001002111**0/40000/1230214**0**/03043 3303251600**0**-**0003000** **(4372)**
2009: 6^{0}SD, 6^{0}SD, 6^{0}SD, 6^{3}SD, 6^{0}SD, 6^{0}G, 6^{0}SD,

	Starts	1st	2nd	3rd	Win & Pl
Career Total (Turf)	**8**	**0**	**0**	**0**	**0**
Career Total (AW)	**47**	**7**	**6**	**8**	**25708**

66	6/08	Sthl	6f	(0-60)H	STD	£1774
79	5/07	Sthl	6f	(0-70)H	STD	£3071
64	1/07	Sthl	6f		STD	£2184
79	1/06	Sthl	6f	(0-70)H	SF	£2914
64	12/05	Sthl	7f		STD	£2484
69	12/05	Sthl	7f		STD	£2566
63	10/05	Sthl	6f		STD	£1498

Total win prize-money £16492

Going (Turf): **Sf: 0-0 GS: 0-1 Gd: 0-7 GF: 0-0 Fm: 0-0**
Distance: **5f/6f: 5-39** 7f-8f: 2-15 9f-13f: 0-1 14f+: 0-0
Track : **LH: 7-46** RH: 0-0 Tight: 0-10 Gall: 0-0
Aids: Bl: 0-2 Vi: 0-1 Tstrap: 2-21 Ckp: 2-21
Best Rating: **79** 5/07 Sthl 6f stand

Moderate; suited by 6f-7f; acts on Fibresand.

Owen Jones (USA)

86 **61**
3-y-o b g Rahy (USA)-Batique (USA) (Storm Cat (USA))
P W Hiatt Clive Roberts

Placings:4 **(6741)**

2009: 8^{4}GS,

	Starts	1st	2nd	3rd	Win & Pl
Career Total (Turf)	**1**	**0**	**0**	**0**	**0**

Going (Turf): **Sf: 0-0 GS: 0-1 Gd: 0-0 GF: 0-0 Fm: 0-0**
Distance: 5f/6f: 0-0 7f-8f: 0-0 9f-13f: 0-1 14f+: 0-0
Track : LH: 0-0 RH: 0-1 Tight: 0-1 Gall: 0-0
Aids: Bl: 0-0 Vi: 0-0 Tstrap: 0-0 Ckp: 0-0
Best Rating: **61** 10/09 Wind 1m67y gd-sft

Owls FC (IRE)

81(58) **28**
3-y-o b f King's Best (USA)-Sadinga (IRE) (Sadler's Wells (USA))
M C Chapman Roy Gowans

Placings:500 **(7780)**
2009: 14^{5}GF, 11^{0}S, 11^{0}SD,

	Starts	1st	2nd	3rd	Win & Pl
Career Total (Turf)	**2**	**0**	**0**	**0**	**1076**
Career Total (AW)	**1**	**0**	**0**	**0**	

Going (Turf): **Sf: 0-1 GS: 0-0 Gd: 0-0 GF: 0-1 Fm: 0-0**
Distance: 5f/6f: 0-0 7f-8f: 0-0 9f-13f: 0-2 14f+: 0-1
Track : LH: 0-2 RH: 0-1 Tight: 0-1 Gall: 0-1
Aids: Bl: 0-0 Vi: 0-0 Tstrap: 0-0 Ckp: 0-0
Best Rating: **28** 10/09 NmkR 1m6f gd-fm

Owner Occupier

(73) (51)**54**
4-y-o ch g Foxhound (USA)-Miss Beverley (Beveled (USA))
Miss Susan A Finn Joseph C Murphy

Placings:56000 **(7753)**
2009: 8^{5}SH, 10^{6}HY, 8^{0}GY, 8^{0}SD, 8^{0}SD,

	Starts	1st	2nd	3rd	Win & Pl
Career Total (Turf)	**3**	**0**	**0**	**0**	
Career Total (AW)	**2**	**0**	**0**	**0**	

Going (Turf): **Sf: 0-1 GS: 0-0 Gd: 0-0 GF: 0-0 Fm: 0-0**
Distance: 5f/6f: 0-0 7f-8f: 0-2 9f-13f: 0-3 14f+: 0-0
Track : LH: 0-4 RH: 0-1 Tight: 0-1 Gall: 0-0
Aids: Bl: 0-0 Vi: 0-0 Tstrap: 0-0 Ckp: 0-0
Best Rating: **54** 8/09 Klny 1m100y sft-hvy

Oxbridge

90(92) (47)**53**
4-y-o ch g Tomba-Royal Passion (Ahonoora)
J M Bradley Mr & Mrs M B Carver

Placings:0640/660**00**-0000**4** **(7533)**
2009: 6^{0}G, 6^{0}GS, 7^{0}SD, 5^{0}SD, 6^{4}SD,

	Starts	1st	2nd	3rd	Win & Pl
Career Total (Turf)	**10**	**0**	**0**	**0**	**337**
Career Total (AW)	**4**	**0**	**0**	**0**	**0**

Going (Turf): **Sf: 0-1 GS: 0-2 Gd: 0-4 GF: 0-2 Fm: 0-1**
Distance: 5f/6f: 0-5 7f-8f: 0-7 9f-13f: 0-2 14f+: 0-0
Track : LH: 0-4 RH: 0-4 Tight: 0-1 Gall: 0-0
Aids: Bl: 0-0 Vi: 0-0 Tstrap: 0-1 Ckp: 0-1
Best Rating: **60** 9/07 Hayd 7f30y gd-fm

Very moderate; stays 6f; acts on Polytrack; has worn cheekpieces.

Oxford City (IRE)

94(98) (58)68

5-y-o ch g City On A Hill (USA)-Bold Nora (IRE) (Persian Bold)

P M Phelan (David Marnane 26/10) Mrs Norah Kennedy & Miss Alison Jones

Placings:00400/43100301**146**/060300 (7823)

2009: 10^{0}GF, 10^{6}GY, 10^{0}GY, 10^{3}GY, 8^{0}Y, 10^{0}SD,

	Starts	1st	2nd	3rd	Win & Pl
Career Total (Turf)	19	3	0	3	16664
Career Total (AW)	3	0	0	0	576

81	9/07	Clon	1m2f	(47-70)H	G-F	£4668
76	9/07	Rosc	1m4f	(50-75)H	G-F	£4668
71	5/07	Clon	1m2f	(47-70)H	G-F	£4668

Total win prize-money £14007

Going (Turf): Sf: 0-2 GS: 0-0 Gd: 0-2 **GF: 3-6** Fm: 0-1
Distance: 5f/6f: 0-3 7f-8f: 0-3 **9f-13f: 3-16** 14f+: 0-0
Track : LH: 0-10 **RH: 3-6** Tight: 0-0 Gall: 0-0
Aids: Bl: 0-0 Vi: 0-0 Tstrap: 0-0 Ckp: 0-0
Best Rating: 81 10/07 Dund 1m2f150y stand

Oxus (IRE)

(93) (52)

4-y-o ch g Sinndar (IRE)-River Dancer (Irish River (FR))

W Clay (B R Johnson 17/2) Mrs Lorna Clay

Placings:0-305 (0578)

2009: 10^{3}SD, 11^{0}SD, 9^{5}SD,

	Starts	1st	2nd	3rd	Win & Pl
Career Total (Turf)	0	0	0	0	
Career Total (AW)	4	0	0	1	403

Going (Turf): Sf: 0-0 GS: 0-0 Gd: 0-0 GF: 0-0 Fm: 0-0
Distance: 5f/6f: 0-0 7f-8f: 0-1 9f-13f: 0-3 14f+: 0-0
Track : LH: 0-3 RH: 0-1 Tight: 0-2 Gall: 0-1
Aids: Bl: 0-0 Vi: 0-0 Tstrap: 0-0 Ckp: 0-0
Best Rating: 52 1/09 Ling 1m2f stand

Ozone Trustee (NZ)

100(83) (36)82

5-y-o b g Montjeu (IRE)-Bold Faith (Warning)

G A Swinbank Panther Racing Ltd

Placings:05/100-**3**0066 (4344)

2009: 11^{3}GF, 12^{0}SD, 10^{0}GF, 7^{6}GS, 7^{6}G,

	Starts	1st	2nd	3rd	Win & Pl
Career Total (Turf)	9	1	0	1	3815
Career Total (AW)	1	0	0	0	

82	8/08	Haml	1m1f36y	G-S	£3412

Total win prize-money £3412

Going (Turf): Sf: 0-1 **GS: 1-2** Gd: 0-3 GF: 0-3 Fm: 0-0
Distance: 5f/6f: 0-0 7f-8f: 0-4 **9f-13f: 1-5** 14f+: 0-1
Track : LH: 0-4 **RH: 1-3 Tight: 1-3** Gall: 0-1
Aids: Bl: 0-0 Vi: 0-0 Tstrap: 0-0 Ckp: 0-0
Best Rating: 82 8/08 Haml 1m1f36y gd-sft

Useful; stays 1m1f and acts on easy ground.

Pab Special (IRE)

92(105) (72)64

6-y-o b g City On A Hill (USA)-Tinos Island (IRE) (Alzao (USA))

B R Johnson T Dempsey

Placings:025/**2436**563441**562**/**255**2340**52066**/**3263**43160 0041-212000 (2807)

2009: 8^{2}SD, 8^{1}SD, 8^{2}SD, 7^{0}GF, 10^{0}G, 7^{0}G,

	Starts	1st	2nd	3rd	Win & Pl
Career Total (Turf)	20	2	2	3	11379
Career Total (AW)	27	2	7	3	11433

71	2/09	Wolv	1m141y	(0-65)H	STD	£2388
66	12/08	Wolv	1m1f103y	(0-55)H	STD	£2047
62	5/08	Brig	1m1f209y		G-F	£1683
70	8/06	Ripn	1m		SFT	£3886

Total win prize-money £10005

Going (Turf): Sf: 1-2 GS: 0-0 Gd: 0-6 **GF: 1-11** Fm: 0-1
Distance: 5f/6f: 0-2 7f-8f: 1-22 **9f-13f: 3-23** 14f+: 0-0
Track : **LH: 3-37** RH: 1-6 **Tight: 3-24** Gall: 0-0
Aids: Bl: 0-0 Vi: 0-3 Tstrap: 0-3 Ckp: 0-3
Best Rating: 81 5/07 Hayd 1m30y good

Modest; effective at around 1m; acts on fast and soft ground; also goes on Polytrack; has worn cheekpieces.

Pachakutek (USA)

83(91) (62)71

3-y-o ch g Giant's Causeway (USA)-Charlotte Corday (Kris)

L M Cumani (E F Vaughan 26/5) El Catorce

Placings:5-004 (7803)

2009: 8^{0}S, 10^{0}GS, 9^{4}SD,

	Starts	1st	2nd	3rd	Win & Pl
Career Total (Turf)	3	0	0	0	0
Career Total (AW)	1	0	0	0	0

Going (Turf): Sf: 0-1 GS: 0-1 Gd: 0-1 GF: 0-0 Fm: 0-0
Distance: 5f/6f: 0-0 7f-8f: 0-2 9f-13f: 0-2 14f+: 0-0
Track : LH: 0-1 RH: 0-1 Tight: 0-2 Gall: 0-0
Aids: Bl: 0-0 Vi: 0-0 Tstrap: 0-0 Ckp: 0-0
Best Rating: 71 10/08 NmkR 1m good

Modest; stays 1m; acts on Polytrack.

Pachattack (USA)

108(110) (103)100

3-y-o ch f Pulpit (USA)-El Laoob (USA) (Red Ransom (USA))

G A Butler M V Deegan

Placings:4104-552**2**24 (7589)

2009: 10^{5}GF, 10^{5}GF, 10^{2}GF, 10^{2}G, **10^{2}SD**, 12^{4}SD,

	Starts	1st	2nd	3rd	Win & Pl
Career Total (Turf)	8	1	2	0	31577
Career Total (AW)	2	0	1	0	4350

84	7/08	Gdwd	7f	G-F	£12952

Total win prize-money £12952

Going (Turf): Sf: 0-0 GS: 0-1 Gd: 0-2 **GF: 1-5** Fm: 0-0
Distance: 5f/6f: 0-0 **7f-8f: 1-4** 9f-13f: 0-6 14f+: 0-0
Track : LH: 0-1 **RH: 1-5** Tight: 0-0 Gall: 0-1
Aids: Bl: 0-2 Vi: 0-0 Tstrap: 0-1 Ckp: 0-1
Best Rating: 103 11/09 Kemp 1m4f stand

Very useful; stays 1m2f; acts on fast ground and on Polytrack; has worn blinkers and cheekpieces.

Pacific Bay (IRE)

96(97) (63)64

3-y-o b f Diktat-Wild Clover (Lomitas)

D McCain Jnr (R A Fahey 11/10) Joe Royle & Brian Aughton

Placings:45602-5350165 (6701)

2009: 6^{5}G, 7^{3}GF, 6^{5}S, 7^{0}S, 8^{1}GF, 8^{6}F, 7^{5}SS,

	Starts	1st	2nd	3rd	Win & Pl
Career Total (Turf)	10	1	0	1	2514
Career Total (AW)	2	0	1	0	605

60	9/09	Bevl	1m100y (0-55)	G-F	£1876

Total win prize-money £1877

Going (Turf): Sf: 0-2 GS: 0-1 Gd: 0-1 **GF: 1-5** Fm: 0-1
Distance: 5f/6f: 0-5 7f-8f: 0-5 **9f-13f: 1-2** 14f+: 0-0
Track : LH: 0-5 **RH: 1-2** Tight: 0-4 Gall: 0-0
Aids: Bl: 0-0 Vi: 0-0 Tstrap: 0-0 Ckp: 0-0
Best Rating: 64 6/08 Pont 6f gd-fm

Modest; dam won over a mile at two in France; modest form to date.

Pacific Pride

103 79

6-y-o b g Compton Place-Only Yours (Aragon)

J J Quinn The New Century Partnership

Placings:321000/3502460/0000000/150002500-0010050660060 (6489)

2009: 6^{0}GF, 5^{0}GF, 5^{1}GF, 5^{0}GF, 6^{0}G, 5^{5}GF, 5^{0}G, 7^{6}G, 8^{6}GF, 6^{0}G, 6^{0}S, 5^{6}GF, 5^{0}GF,

	Starts	1st	2nd	3rd	Win & Pl
Career Total (Turf)	42	3	3	2	39451

78	5/09	Bevl	5f	(0-75)H	G-F	£3238
84	5/08	Ripn	6f	(0-85)H	GD	£5504
81	7/05	Ayr	6f		G-F	£4862

Total win prize-money £13605

Going (Turf): Sf: 0-6 GS: 0-5 Gd: 1-13 **GF: 2-18** Fm: 0-0
Distance: **5f/6f: 3-32** 7f-8f: 0-9 9f-13f: 0-1 14f+: 0-0
Track : LH: 0-6 RH: 0-0 Tight: 0-4 Gall: 0-0
Aids: Bl: 0-6 Vi: 0-4 Tstrap: 1-7 Ckp: 1-7
Best Rating: 106 8/06 York 6f gd-sft

Fair; suited by 5-6f and acts on most ground; has worn blinkers, cheekpieces and a visor.

Paco Boy (IRE)

115(103) (101)127

4-y-o b c Desert Style (IRE)-Tappen Zee (Sandhurst Prince)

R Hannon The Calvera Partnership No 2

Placings:311/1101101-014142 (4419)

2009: 8^{0}G, 8^{1}G, 8^{4}S, 8^{1}GF, 6^{4}GF, 8^{2}G,

	Starts	1st	2nd	3rd	Win & Pl
Career Total (Turf)	14	8	1	0	611627
Career Total (AW)	2	1	0	1	34471

125	6/09	Asct	1m	G-F	£167471
124	4/09	Sand	1m14y	GD	£56770
127	10/08	Lonc	7f	GD	£105037
121	8/08	Newb	7f	G-S	£56770
116	7/08	Gdwd	7f	GD	£87993
110	4/08	Newb	7f	SFT	£26681
101	3/08	Ling	7f	STD	£34068
94	11/07	NmkR	6f	GD	£5608
92	9/07	Newb	6f8y	G-F	£5829

Total win prize-money £546231

Going (Turf): Sf: 1-2 GS: 1-2 **Gd: 4-7** GF: 2-3 Fm: 0-0
Distance: 5f/6f: 1-3 **7f-8f: 7-11** 9f-13f: 1-2 14f+: 0-0
Track : LH: 1-2 **RH: 3-5 Tight: 1-1** Gall: 0-1
Aids: Bl: 0-0 Vi: 0-0 Tstrap: 0-0 Ckp: 0-0
Best Rating: 127 10/08 Lonc 7f good

High class; winner of the Greenham Stakes, Lennox Stakes, Hungerford Stakes and Group 1 Prix de la Foret in 2008; winner of Bet365 Mile and Group 1 Queen Anne

Stakes in 2009; effective over 7f-1m; acts on fast and easy ground and on Polytrack; possesses a smart turn of foot.

Paddy Bear

101 71

3-y-o b c Piccolo-Lily Of The Guild (IRE) (Lycius (USA))

R A Fahey J A & Kay Campbell

Placings:3244-106010 (4133)

2009: 6^{1}GF, 6^{0}GF, 6^{6}GF, 5^{0}GS, 5^{1}GS, 6^{0}G,

	Starts	1st	2nd	3rd	Win & Pl
Career Total (Turf)	10	2	1	1	7412

71	7/09	Catt	5f212y	G-S	£2047
69	4/09	Thsk	6f	G-F	£4274

Total win prize-money £6321

Going (Turf): Sf: 0-0 **GS: 1-3** Gd: 0-4 **GF: 1-3** Fm: 0-0
Distance: **5f/6f: 2-10** 7f-8f: 0-0 9f-13f: 0-0 14f+: 0-0
Track : **LH: 1-1** RH: 0-1 **Tight: 1-1** Gall: 0-1
Aids: Bl: 0-0 Vi: 0-0 Tstrap: 0-0 Ckp: 0-0
Best Rating: **71** 7/09 Catt 5f212y gd-sft

Fair; effective over 5f; acts on good and faster ground.

Paddy Jack

94(71) (2)61

4-y-o ch g Rambling Bear-Bayrami (Emarati (USA))

J R Weymes T W Batchelor

Placings:3633022/600442200020-50605306U0 (7629)

2009: 5^{5}GS, 5^{0}GF, 5^{6}GF, 5^{0}GF, 5^{5}GF, 5^{3}GF, 5^{0}GF, 5^{6}S, 5^{U}S, 5^{0}SD,

	Starts	1st	2nd	3rd	Win & Pl
Career Total (Turf)	27	0	5	4	7018
Career Total (AW)	2	0	0	0	

Going (Turf): **Sf: 0-3 GS: 0-5 Gd: 0-7 GF: 0-10 Fm: 0-2**
Distance: 5f/6f: 0-27 7f-8f: 0-2 9f-13f: 0-0 14f+: 0-0
Track : LH: 0-7 RH: 0-3 Tight: 0-4 Gall: 0-3
Aids: Bl: 0-6 Vi: 0-1 Tstrap: 0-9 Ckp: 0-9
Best Rating: **70** 10/07 Catt 5f good

Modest; effective at up to 6f; acts on a sound and soft surface.

Paddy Partridge

92 58

3-y-o b c Pivotal-Treble Heights (IRE) (Unfuwain (USA))

N J Vaughan Owen Promotions Limited

Placings:0000 (3336)

2009: 9^{0}GF, 10^{0}GF, 10^{0}S, 10^{0}GF,

	Starts	1st	2nd	3rd	Win & Pl
Career Total (Turf)	4	0	0	0	

Going (Turf): **Sf: 0-1 GS: 0-0 Gd: 0-0 GF: 0-3 Fm: 0-0**
Distance: 5f/6f: 0-0 7f-8f: 0-0 9f-13f: 0-4 14f+: 0-0
Track : LH: 0-3 RH: 0-1 Tight: 0-2 Gall: 0-0
Aids: Bl: 0-0 Vi: 0-0 Tstrap: 0-0 Ckp: 0-0
Best Rating: **58** 5/09 Ches 1m2f75y gd-fm

Moderate; stays 1m2f; best on fast ground.

Paddy Rielly (IRE)

102(101) (68)68

4-y-o b g Catcher In The Rye (IRE)-The Veil (IRE) (Barathea (IRE))

P D Evans M D Jones

Placings:050/0025306**136**044-25**1**3266 (4169)

2009: 12^{2}SD, 12^{5}SD, 12^{1}SD, 12^{3}SD, 12^{2}GF, 14^{6}F, 12^{6}G,

	Starts	1st	2nd	3rd	Win & Pl
Career Total (Turf)	13	0	2	1	2139
Career Total (AW)	10	2	1	2	6237

65	4/09	Sthl	1m4f	(0-60)H	STD	£2047
68	9/08	Sthl	1m4f	(0-60)H	STD	£2558

Total win prize-money £4606

Going (Turf): **Sf: 0-3 GS: 0-2 Gd: 0-2 GF: 0-5 Fm: 0-1**
Distance: 5f/6f: 0-1 7f-8f: 0-1 **9f-13f: 2-19** 14f+: 0-2
Track : **LH: 2-14** RH: 0-5 Tight: 0-10 Gall: 0-2
Aids: Bl: 0-0 Vi: 0-0 Tstrap: 2-10 Ckp: 2-10
Best Rating: **68** 6/09 Sals 1m4f gd-fm

Modest; stays 1m4f; acts on fast ground; goes on Fibresand; has worn cheekpieces.

Padlocked (IRE)

(100) (76)95

5-y-o b g Key Of Luck (USA)-Accelerating (USA) (Lear Fan (USA))

D M Simcock Saif Misfer

Placings:115120/0 (0910)

2009: 8^{0}SD,

	Starts	1st	2nd	3rd	Win & Pl
Career Total (Turf)	5	2	1	0	13898
Career Total (AW)	2	1	0	0	4081

91	8/07	Sals	1m	(0-85)H	G-S	£5181
92	5/07	Ling	1m1f	(0-85)H	G-F	£6477
77	5/07	Kemp	1m		STD	£4080

Total win prize-money £15740

Going (Turf): Sf: 0-0 **GS: 1-2** Gd: 0-0 **GF: 1-3** Fm: 0-0
Distance: 5f/6f: 0-0 **7f-8f: 2-3** 9f-13f: 1-4 14f+: 0-0
Track : LH: 1-2 RH: 1-4 **Tight: 1-3** Gall: 0-1
Aids: Bl: 0-0 Vi: 0-0 Tstrap: 0-0 Ckp: 0-0
Best Rating: **95** 9/07 Sand 1m14y gd-fm

Useful; stays 1m1f, acts on most ground and Polytrack.

Padmini

(94) (75)

2-y-o b f Tiger Hill (IRE)-Petrushka (IRE) (Unfuwain (USA))

Saeed Bin Suroor Godolphin

Placings:1 (7135)

2009: 7^{1}SD,

	Starts	1st	2nd	3rd	Win & Pl
Career Total (Turf)	0	0	0	0	
Career Total (AW)	1	1	0	0	4404

75	10/09	Ling	7f	STD	£4403

Total win prize-money £4404

Going (Turf): **Sf: 0-0 GS: 0-0 Gd: 0-0 GF: 0-0 Fm: 0-0**
Distance: 5f/6f: 0-0 **7f-8f: 1-1** 9f-13f: 0-0 14f+: 0-0
Track : **LH: 1-1** RH: 0-0 **Tight: 1-1** Gall: 0-0
Aids: Bl: 0-0 Vi: 0-0 Tstrap: 0-0 Ckp: 0-0
Best Rating: **75** 10/09 Ling 7f stand

Winner on debut over 7f; acts on Polytrack.

Pagan Flight (IRE)

90 51

3-y-o b g Hawk Wing (USA)-Regal Darcey (IRE) (Darshaan)

Mrs A J Perrett The Gap Partnership

Placings:00-0030 (4177)

2009: 8^{0}GF, 14^{0}G, 11^{3}G, 10^{0}GS,

	Starts	1st	2nd	3rd	Win & Pl
Career Total (Turf)	6	0	0	1	302

Going (Turf): **Sf: 0-0 GS: 0-2 Gd: 0-3 GF: 0-1 Fm: 0-0**
Distance: 5f/6f: 0-0 7f-8f: 0-3 9f-13f: 0-2 14f+: 0-1
Track : LH: 0-1 RH: 0-1 Tight: 0-3 Gall: 0-0
Aids: Bl: 0-0 Vi: 0-0 Tstrap: 0-0 Ckp: 0-0
Best Rating: **51** 5/09 NmkR 1m gd-fm

Pagan Force (IRE)

90(82) (39)64

3-y-o b c Green Desert (USA)-Brigitta (IRE) (Sadler's Wells (USA))

Mrs A J Perrett The Gap Partnership

Placings:04-0600 (6701)

2009: 7^{0}SD, 7^{6}GS, 8^{0}GF, 7^{0}SS,

	Starts	1st	2nd	3rd	Win & Pl
Career Total (Turf)	4	0	0	0	577
Career Total (AW)	2	0	0	0	

Going (Turf): **Sf: 0-0 GS: 0-2 Gd: 0-1 GF: 0-1 Fm: 0-0**
Distance: 5f/6f: 0-1 7f-8f: 0-5 9f-13f: 0-0 14f+: 0-0
Track : LH: 0-1 RH: 0-1 Tight: 0-1 Gall: 0-0
Aids: Bl: 0-2 Vi: 0-0 Tstrap: 0-0 Ckp: 0-0
Best Rating: **64** 7/08 Asct 6f gd-sft

Pagan Starprincess

104(100) (57)61

5-y-o b m Robertico-Pagan Star (Carlitin)

G M Moore Richard Phizacklea

Placings:4/0006301/4260 (6767)

2009: 16^{4}SD, 16^{2}G, 17^{6}G, 16^{0}GS,

	Starts	1st	2nd	3rd	Win & Pl
Career Total (Turf)	11	1	1	1	4656
Career Total (AW)	1	0	0	0	0

61	10/07	Catt	1m7f177y (0-60)H	GD	£2730

Total win prize-money £2730

Going (Turf): Sf: 0-1 GS: 0-2 **Gd: 1-5** GF: 0-3 Fm: 0-0
Distance: 5f/6f: 0-0 7f-8f: 0-2 9f-13f: 0-4 **14f+: 1-6**
Track : **LH: 1-6** RH: 0-6 **Tight: 1-7** Gall: 0-1
Aids: Bl: 0-0 Vi: 0-0 Tstrap: 1-2 Ckp: 1-2
Best Rating: **61** 5/09 Bevl 2m35y good

Modest; stays 2m; acts on soft ground; has worn cheekpieces and a tongue tie.

Pagan Sword

(90) (62)92

7-y-o ch g Selkirk (USA)-Vanessa Bell (IRE) (Lahib (USA))

D G Bridgwater Terry & Sarah Amos

Placings:00/**3116**13021/00650/3402062255003/0 (7005)

2009: 16^{0}SD,

	Starts	1st	2nd	3rd	Win & Pl
Career Total (Turf)	22	3	4	1	32085
Career Total (AW)	8	1	0	3	7564

93	9/05	NmkJ	1m2f	(0-85)H	G-F	£5986
85	5/05	Donc	1m2f60y	(0-85)H	G-F	£7072
81	5/05	Sals	1m1f198y	(0-85)H	G-S	£7269
72	4/05	Ling	1m2f	(0-75)H	STD	£3476

Total win prize-money £23805

Going (Turf): Sf: 0-0 GS: 1-4 Gd: 0-4 **GF: 2-12** Fm: 0-2
Distance: 5f/6f: 0-0 7f-8f: 0-3 **9f-13f: 4-26** 14f+: 0-1
Track : LH: 2-15 RH: 2-13 Tight: 2-15 Gall: 2-4
Aids: Bl: 0-0 **Vi: 1-3** Tstrap: 0-6 Ckp: 0-6
Best Rating: 95 8/06 Gdwd 1m1f192y good

Useful; stays 1m4f, but effective over shorter; acts with cut in the ground; has worn a cheekpieces and visor.

Painswick (USA)

85 63

2-y-o ch c Elusive Quality (USA)-Pleine Lune (IRE) (Alzao (USA))

J L Dunlop Robin F Scully

Placings:000 (6754)

2009: 7^0G, 7^0GF, 7^0G,

	Starts	1st	2nd	3rd	Win & Pl
Career Total (Turf)	3	0	0	0	

Going (Turf): Sf: 0-0 GS: 0-0 Gd: 0-2 GF: 0-1 Fm: 0-0
Distance: 5f/6f: 0-0 7f-8f: 0-3 9f-13f: 0-0 14f+: 0-0
Track : LH: 0-0 RH: 0-0 Tight: 0-0 Gall: 0-0
Aids: Bl: 0-0 Vi: 0-0 Tstrap: 0-0 Ckp: 0-0
Best Rating: 63 10/09 Leic 7f9y good

Paint By Numbers

(79) (38)

2-y-o b g Haafhd-Attention Seeker (USA) (Exbourne (USA))

J A Glover Brian Morton

Placings:00 (7825)

2009: 5^0SD, 8^0SD,

	Starts	1st	2nd	3rd	Win & Pl
Career Total (Turf)	0	0	0	0	
Career Total (AW)	2	0	0	0	

Going (Turf): Sf: 0-0 GS: 0-0 Gd: 0-0 GF: 0-0 Fm: 0-0
Distance: 5f/6f: 0-1 7f-8f: 0-1 9f-13f: 0-0 14f+: 0-0
Track : LH: 0-1 RH: 0-1 Tight: 0-1 Gall: 0-0
Aids: Bl: 0-0 Vi: 0-0 Tstrap: 0-0 Ckp: 0-0
Best Rating: 38 12/09 Wolv 5f216y stand

Paint Splash

97(98) (57)51

3-y-o ch f Beat Hollow-Questa Nova (Rainbow Quest (USA))

T D Barron Harrowgate Bloodstock Ltd

Placings:0641-633033234500 (6497)

2009: 8^6SD, 7^3SD, 7^3GF, 6^0SD, 8^3G, 8^3F, 7^2G, 8^3GF, 8^4G, 8^5GF, 8^0GF, 9^0SF,

	Starts	1st	2nd	3rd	Win & Pl
Career Total (Turf)	9	0	1	4	2153
Career Total (AW)	7	1	0	1	2281

55 12/08 Sthl 7f STD £1978
Total win prize-money £1979

Going (Turf): Sf: 0-0 GS: 0-1 Gd: 0-3 GF: 0-4 Fm: 0-1
Distance: 5f/6f: 0-1 **7f-8f: 1-11** 9f-13f: 0-4 14f+: 0-0
Track : **LH: 1-9** RH: 0-5 Tight: 0-6 Gall: 0-0
Aids: Bl: 0-1 Vi: 0-0 Tstrap: 0-0 Ckp: 0-0
Best Rating: 57 2/09 Sthl 7f stand

Moderate; stays 7f; acts on fast ground and on Fibresand.

Paint Stripper

96(74) 41

4-y-o b g Prince Sabo-Passing Fancy (Grand Lodge (USA))

W Storey Gremlin Racing

Placings:000621/0000000-04500500 (5254)

2009: 8^0GF, 7^4GS, 8^5GF, 7^0G, 6^0GS, 5^5G, 5^0GS, 6^0GF,

	Starts	1st	2nd	3rd	Win & Pl
Career Total (Turf)	20	1	1	0	4670
Career Total (AW)	1	0	0	0	

61 11/07 Ayr 6f (0-75) HVY £3562
Total win prize-money £3562

Going (Turf): **Sf: 1-7** GS: 0-7 Gd: 0-2 GF: 0-4 Fm: 0-0
Distance: **5f/6f: 1-11** 7f-8f: 0-8 9f-13f: 0-2 14f+: 0-0
Track : LH: 0-5 RH: 0-4 Tight: 0-4 Gall: 0-2
Aids: Bl: 0-0 Vi: 0-0 Tstrap: 0-3 Ckp: 0-3
Best Rating: 61 11/07 Ayr 6f heavy

Modest maiden; stays 7f; acts in soft ground.

Paint The Town (IRE)

86 (66)42

4-y-o b f Sadler's Wells (USA)-Minnie Habit (Habitat)

J G Given David Eiffe

Placings:003/00 (3188)

2009: 10^0S, 8^0GF,

	Starts	1st	2nd	3rd	Win & Pl
Career Total (Turf)	3	0	0	0	
Career Total (AW)	2	0	0	1	792

Going (Turf): Sf: 0-2 GS: 0-0 Gd: 0-0 GF: 0-1 Fm: 0-0
Distance: 5f/6f: 0-0 7f-8f: 0-3 9f-13f: 0-2 14f+: 0-0
Track : LH: 0-3 RH: 0-0 Tight: 0-0 Gall: 0-0
Aids: Bl: 0-0 Vi: 0-0 Tstrap: 0-0 Ckp: 0-0
Best Rating: 70 7/07 Leop 7f soft

Paint The Town Red

103(103) (79)79

4-y-o b g Mujahid (USA)-Onefortheditch (USA) (With Approval (CAN))

H J Collingridge Miss C Fordham

Placings:0/4166660-1050006004 (7461)

2009: 9^1GF, 10^0GF, 12^6G, 10^0GF, 8^0G, 10^0GS, 12^6SF, 9^0G, 13^0SD, 13^4SD,

	Starts	1st	2nd	3rd	Win & Pl
Career Total (Turf)	9	1	0	0	3238
Career Total (AW)	9	1	0	0	2700

79 4/09 Leic 1m1f218y (0-70)H G-F £3238
79 6/08 GrLe 1m STD £2266
Total win prize-money £5505

Going (Turf): Sf: 0-1 GS: 0-2 Gd: 0-3 **GF: 1-3** Fm: 0-0
Distance: 5f/6f: 0-0 7f-8f: 1-4 9f-13f: 1-12 14f+: 0-2
Track : LH: 1-12 RH: 1-4 Tight: 0-7 **Gall: 1-5**
Aids: Bl: 0-0 Vi: 0-0 Tstrap: 0-0 Ckp: 0-0
Best Rating: 79 4/09 Leic 1m1f218y gd-fm

Moderate; stays 1m5f; acts on fast ground and on Polytrack.

Paintball (IRE)

(84) (64)

2-y-o b c Le Vie Dei Colori-Camassina(IRE)(Taufan (USA))

W R Muir Mrs J M Muir

Placings:3 (7864)

2009: 6^3SS,

	Starts	1st	2nd	3rd	Win & Pl
Career Total (Turf)	0	0	0	0	
Career Total (AW)	1	0	0	1	385

Going (Turf): Sf: 0-0 GS: 0-0 Gd: 0-0 GF: 0-0 Fm: 0-0
Distance: 5f/6f: 0-1 7f-8f: 0-0 9f-13f: 0-0 14f+: 0-0
Track : LH: 0-1 RH: 0-0 Tight: 0-0 Gall: 0-0
Aids: Bl: 0-0 Vi: 0-0 Tstrap: 0-0 Ckp: 0-0
Best Rating: 64 12/09 Sthl 6f std-slw

Modest; stays 6f; handles Fibresand.

Painted Sky

(97) (66)66

6-y-o ch g Rainbow Quest (USA)-Emplane (USA) (Irish River (FR))

R A Fahey J P M Syndicate

Placings:4/260/01/00-46 (7817)

2009: 10^4SD, 9^6SD,

	Starts	1st	2nd	3rd	Win & Pl
Career Total (Turf)	7	0	1	0	3898
Career Total (AW)	3	1	0	0	3239

80 12/07 Wolv 7f32y (0-75)H STD £3238
Total win prize-money £3239

Going (Turf): Sf: 0-3 GS: 0-0 Gd: 0-1 GF: 0-1 Fm: 0-0
Distance: 5f/6f: 0-0 **7f-8f: 1-2** 9f-13f: 0-8 14f+: 0-0
Track : **LH: 1-8** RH: 0-2 **Tight: 1-3** Gall: 0-3
Aids: Bl: 0-0 Vi: 0-0 Tstrap: 0-0 Ckp: 0-0
Best Rating: 83 4/06 Lonc 1m4f v soft

Modest; effective over 7f; acts on Polytrack.

Pairumani Pat (IRE)

(93) (48)53

4-y-o ch g Pairumani Star (IRE)-Golden Skiis (IRE) (Hector Protector (USA))

J Pearce Mrs C P Robertson

Placings:620036-0 (1439)

2009: 16^0SD,

	Starts	1st	2nd	3rd	Win & Pl
Career Total (Turf)	4	0	1	0	605
Career Total (AW)	3	0	0	1	353

Going (Turf): Sf: 0-0 GS: 0-1 Gd: 0-1 GF: 0-2 Fm: 0-0
Distance: 5f/6f: 0-0 7f-8f: 0-0 9f-13f: 0-2 14f+: 0-5
Track : LH: 0-5 RH: 0-0 Tight: 0-6 Gall: 0-0
Aids: Bl: 0-0 Vi: 0-0 Tstrap: 0-0 Ckp: 0-0
Best Rating: 53 7/08 Wind 1m3f135y gd-fm

Plating class; stays 2m; acts on quick ground.

Palsley

98 77

3-y-o ch f Pivotal-Pongee (Barathea (IRE))

L M Cumani Fittocks Stud

Placings:514 (5910)

2009: 7^5G, 9^1G, 10^4GF,

	Starts	1st	2nd	3rd	Win & Pl
Career Total (Turf)	3	1	0	0	4263

77 8/09 Sals 1m1f198y GD £3885
Total win prize-money £3886

Going (Turf): Sf: 0-0 GS: 0-0 **Gd: 1-2** GF: 0-1 Fm: 0-0
Distance: 5f/6f: 0-0 7f-8f: 0-1 **9f-13f: 1-2** 14f+: 0-0
Track : LH: 0-1 **RH: 1-1 Tight: 1-1** Gall: 0-1
Aids: Bl: 0-0 Vi: 0-0 Tstrap: 0-0 Ckp: 0-0
Best Rating: 77 9/09 Ffos 1m2f gd-fm

Fair first foal of Pongee; stays 1m2f; acts on fast ground.

Pajada

(96) (48)**49**

5-y-o b m Bertolini (USA)-Last Ambition (IRE) (Cadeaux Genereux)
M D I Usher M D I Usher

Placings:000/**0004**40000**4**00**6**00/000**6**40004300**046-00** (0482)
2009: 10^{0}SD, 8^{0}SD,

	Starts	1st	2nd	3rd	Win & Pl
Career Total (Turf)	13	0	0	1	866
Career Total (AW)	24	0	0	0	0

Going (Turf): Sf: 0-4 GS: 0-3 Gd: 0-2 GF: 0-3 Fm: 0-1
Distance: 5f/6f: 0-5 7f-8f: 0-22 9f-13f: 0-10 14f+: 0-0
Track : LH: 0-20 RH: 0-9 Tight: 0-14 Gall: 0-2
Aids: Bl: 0-3 Vi: 0-15 Tstrap: 0-4 Ckp: 0-4
Best Rating: 52 11/06 Kemp 7f stand

Paktolos (FR)

97(110) (100)**95**

6-y-o b g Dansili-Pithara (GR) (Never So Bold)
John A Harris (A King 10/7) Martin Hignett

Placings:65044321/**21**300/**251401**-6000042 (7811)
2009: 12^{6}SD, 12^{0}G, 10^{0}SD, 12^{0}G, 12^{0}SD, 11^{4}SD, 12^{2}SD,

	Starts	1st	2nd	3rd	Win & Pl
Career Total (Turf)	16	2	1	1	23396
Career Total (AW)	10	2	3	1	19861
100 11/08 Kemp	1m4f	(0-90)H	STD	£7477	
91 6/08 Sals	1m4f	(0-85)H	G-F	£4371	
92 3/07 Ling	1m4f	(0-85)H	STD	£4210	
80 9/06 Lonc	1m	H	GD	£8966	

Total win prize-money £25024

Going (Turf): Sf: 0-1 GS: 0-5 **Gd: 1-5 GF: 1-4** Fm: 0-0
Distance: 5f/6f: 0-0 7f-8f: 1-5 **9f-13f: 3-19** 14f+: 0-2
Track : LH: 1-9 **RH: 2-9 Tight: 2-12** Gall: 0-3
Aids: **Bl: 2-9** Vi: 0-0 Tstrap: 0-1 Ckp: 0-1
Best Rating: 100 11/08 Kemp 1m4f stand

Useful; ex-French; stays 1m4f; acts on most surfaces; tried blinkered.

Palace Moon

111 **114**

4-y-o b g Fantastic Light (USA)-Palace Street (USA) (Secreto (USA))
H Morrison Miss B Swire

Placings:213-124100 (6661)
2009: 6^{1}GF, 6^{2}GF, 7^{4}GF, 6^{1}GF, 6^{0}GF, 6^{0}GS,

	Starts	1st	2nd	3rd	Win & Pl
Career Total (Turf)	9	3	2	1	55848
112 8/09 NmkJ	6f		G-F	£22708	
114 3/09 Donc	6f	(0-100)H	G-F	£12952	
89 7/08 Sals	6f		G-F	£3885	

Total win prize-money £39546

Going (Turf): Sf: 0-0 GS: 0-2 Gd: 0-1 **GF: 3-6** Fm: 0-0
Distance: **5f/6f: 3-8** 7f-8f: 0-1 9f-13f: 0-0 14f+: 0-0
Track : LH: 0-0 RH: 0-0 Tight: 0-0 Gall: 0-0
Aids: Bl: 0-0 Vi: 0-0 Tstrap: 0-0 Ckp: 0-0
Best Rating: 114 3/09 Donc 6f gd-fm

Smart; Listed winner; stays 7f; acts on most ground.

Palacefield (IRE)

103(101) (74)**81**

3-y-o b g Green Desert (USA)-Multaka (USA) (Gone West (USA))
P W Chapple-Hyam M J McStay

Placings:3-2215455 (6773)
2009: 8^{2}G, 7^{2}GF, 8^{1}G, 8^{5}G, 8^{4}GF, 8^{5}GF, 8^{5}SD,

	Starts	1st	2nd	3rd	Win & Pl
Career Total (Turf)	7	1	2	1	6054
Career Total (AW)	1	0	0	0	0
79 5/09 Chep	1m14y		GD	£2396	

Total win prize-money £2396

Going (Turf): Sf: 0-1 GS: 0-0 **Gd: 1-3** GF: 0-3 Fm: 0-0
Distance: 5f/6f: 0-0 7f-8f: 0-3 **9f-13f: 1-5** 14f+: 0-0
Track : LH: 0-2 RH: 0-3 Tight: 0-3 Gall: 0-0
Aids: Bl: 0-0 Vi: 0-0 Tstrap: 0-0 Ckp: 0-0
Best Rating: 81 8/09 Wind 1m67y gd-fm

Fair; effective over 1m; acts on good ground.

Palais Polaire

79(98) (62)**60**

7-y-o ch m Polar Falcon (USA)-Palace Street (USA) (Secreto (USA))
J A Geake Miss B Swire

Placings:0/54043430/00**2**50**2**645/**2**000**1**22**2**5-0000 (4266)
2009: 7^{0}SD, 7^{0}SD, 7^{0}SD, 7^{0}S,

	Starts	1st	2nd	3rd	Win & Pl
Career Total (Turf)	11	1	2	1	6038
Career Total (AW)	20	0	4	1	2907
57 8/08 Brig	6f209y	(0-70)H	GD	£3154	

Total win prize-money £3154

Going (Turf): Sf: 0-3 GS: 0-1 **Gd: 1-3** GF: 0-4 Fm: 0-0
Distance: 5f/6f: 0-3 **7f-8f: 1-26** 9f-13f: 0-2 14f+: 0-0
Track : **LH: 1-13** RH: 0-10 Tight: 0-7 Gall: 0-1
Aids: Bl: 0-0 Vi: 0-0 Tstrap: 1-17 Ckp: 1-17
Best Rating: 62 1/08 Sthl 7f std-slw

Moderate; effective over 7f; acts on fast and soft ground; goes on sand; may not be straightforward.

Palavicini (USA)

108 **112**

3-y-o b c Giant's Causeway (USA)-Cara Fantasy (IRE) (Sadler's Wells (USA))
J L Dunlop Windflower Overseas Holdings Inc

Placings:231-42101463 (6812)
2009: 10^{4}GS, 10^{2}GF, 10^{1}GF, 10^{0}GF, 8^{1}GF, 9^{4}GF, 12^{6}GF, 9^{3}G,

	Starts	1st	2nd	3rd	Win & Pl
Career Total (Turf)	11	3	2	2	110893
112 8/09 York	1m208y		G-F	£56770	
110 5/09 NmkR	1m2f		G-F	£22708	
86 10/08 Newb	1m		G-S	£5504	

Total win prize-money £84983

Going (Turf): Sf: 0-0 GS: 1-2 Gd: 0-3 **GF: 2-6** Fm: 0-0
Distance: 5f/6f: 0-0 7f-8f: 1-3 **9f-13f: 2-8** 14f+: 0-0
Track : **LH: 1-2** RH: 0-3 Tight: 0-1 **Gall: 1-4**
Aids: Bl: 0-0 Vi: 0-0 Tstrap: 0-0 Ckp: 0-0
Best Rating: 112 9/09 Asct 1m4f gd-fm

Smart; Group 3 and Listed winner; effective over 1m-1m2f; acts on fast and easy ground.

Palawi (IRE)

101 **72**

2-y-o ch c Dubawi (IRE)-Palwina (FR) (Unfuwain (USA))
J J Quinn Fergus J Grimes

Placings:33 (7116)
2009: 8^{3}GS, 8^{3}GS,

	Starts	1st	2nd	3rd	Win & Pl
Career Total (Turf)	2	0	0	2	1156

Going (Turf): Sf: 0-0 GS: 0-2 Gd: 0-0 GF: 0-0 Fm: 0-0
Distance: 5f/6f: 0-0 7f-8f: 0-2 9f-13f: 0-0 14f+: 0-0
Track : LH: 0-1 RH: 0-1 Tight: 0-1 Gall: 0-1
Aids: Bl: 0-0 Vi: 0-0 Tstrap: 0-0 Ckp: 0-0
Best Rating: 72 10/09 Newc 1m gd-sft

Paleo (IRE)

99 **82**

2-y-o ch f Indian Ridge-Crossbreeze (USA) (Red Ransom (USA))
R Hannon Knockainey Stud Ltd & Partners

Placings:001300 (6852)
2009: 6^{0}S, 7^{0}GS, 7^{1}G, 6^{3}GF, 7^{0}GF, 7^{0}G,

	Starts	1st	2nd	3rd	Win & Pl
Career Total (Turf)	6	1	0	1	8709
80 8/09 NmkJ	7f		GD	£4857	

Total win prize-money £4857

Going (Turf): Sf: 0-1 GS: 0-1 **Gd: 1-2** GF: 0-2 Fm: 0-0
Distance: 5f/6f: 0-0 **7f-8f: 1-6** 9f-13f: 0-0 14f+: 0-0
Track : LH: 0-0 RH: 0-1 Tight: 0-0 Gall: 0-0
Aids: Bl: 0-0 Vi: 0-0 Tstrap: 0-0 Ckp: 0-0
Best Rating: 82 9/09 Donc 6f110y gd-fm

Useful; stays 7f; acts on good and fast ground.

Palio Square (USA)

94 **82**

2-y-o b/br c Harlan's Holiday (USA)-Teewee's Hope (CAN) (Defrere (USA))
H R A Cecil (A P Jarvis 26/8) Mogeely Stud & Mrs Maura Gittins

Placings:044 (7121)
2009: 7^{0}G, 7^{4}G, 8^{4}GF,

	Starts	1st	2nd	3rd	Win & Pl
Career Total (Turf)	3	0	0	0	866

Going (Turf): Sf: 0-0 GS: 0-0 Gd: 0-2 GF: 0-1 Fm: 0-0
Distance: 5f/6f: 0-0 7f-8f: 0-2 9f-13f: 0-1 14f+: 0-0
Track : LH: 0-3 RH: 0-0 Tight: 0-0 Gall: 0-1
Aids: Bl: 0-0 Vi: 0-0 Tstrap: 0-0 Ckp: 0-0
Best Rating: 82 8/09 Wwck 7f26y good

Palisades Park

97 **78**

2-y-o b c Compton Place-Brooklyn's Sky (Septieme Ciel (USA))
R Hannon D Powell, R Dollar, Derek & Jean Clee

Placings:6215005 (5218)
2009: 5^{6}F, 5^{2}GF, 6^{1}GF, 5^{5}GF, 5^{0}GS, 6^{0}S, 5^{5}GF,

	Starts	1st	2nd	3rd	Win & Pl
Career Total (Turf)	7	1	1	0	3693
76 6/09 Wind	6f		G-F	£2729	

Total win prize-money £2730

Going (Turf): Sf: 0-1 GS: 0-1 Gd: 0-0 **GF: 1-4** Fm: 0-1
Distance: **5f/6f: 1-7** 7f-8f: 0-0 9f-13f: 0-0 14f+: 0-0
Track : LH: 0-0 RH: 0-0 Tight: 0-0 **Gall: 1-1**
Aids: Bl: 0-0 Vi: 0-0 Tstrap: 0-0 Ckp: 0-0
Best Rating: 78 6/09 Sand 5f6y gd-fm

Fair; out of a sprint winner from the family of Prospect Park; stays 6f; acts on fast ground.

Pallantes Cross

101(88) (95)95
2-y-o b c Cape Cross (IRE)-Palinisa (FR) (Night Shift (USA))
M Johnston Mrs R J Jacobs

Placings:012314 (6151a)
2009: 6^{0}S, 7^{1}GF, 7^{2}G, 7^{3}GF, 8^{1}SD, 8^{4}G,

	Starts	1st	2nd	3rd	Win & Pl
Career Total (Turf)	5	1	1	1	7285
Career Total (AW)	1	1	0	0	3412

95 9/09 Wolv 1m141y STD £3412
85 6/09 Muss 7f30y G-F £2266
Total win prize-money £5679

Going (Turf): Sf: 0-1 GS: 0-0 Gd: 0-2 **GF: 1-2** Fm: 0-0
Distance: 5f/6f: 0-1 7f-8f: 1-4 9f-13f: 1-1 14f+: 0-0
Track : LH: 1-1 RH: 1-2 **Tight: 2-2** Gall: 0-0
Aids: Bl: 0-0 Vi: 0-0 Tstrap: 0-0 Ckp: 0-0
Best Rating: 95 9/09 Wolv 1m141y stand

Very useful; stays 1m; acts on fast ground and Polytrack.

Pallaton

90(87) (43)59
3-y-o ch g Bertolini (USA)-Miss Honeypenny (IRE) (Old Vic)
R M Beckett D & J Newell

Placings:606 (2922)
2009: 10^{6}GF, 9^{0}G, 12^{6}SD,

	Starts	1st	2nd	3rd	Win & Pl
Career Total (Turf)	2	0	0	0	0
Career Total (AW)	1	0	0	0	0

Going (Turf): **Sf: 0-0 GS: 0-0 Gd: 0-1 GF: 0-1 Fm: 0-0**
Distance: 5f/6f: 0-0 7f-8f: 0-0 9f-13f: 0-3 14f+: 0-0
Track : LH: 0-2 RH: 0-1 Tight: 0-2 Gall: 0-0
Aids: Bl: 0-0 Vi: 0-0 Tstrap: 0-0 Ckp: 0-0
Best Rating: 59 5/09 Chep 1m2f36y gd-fm

Pan American

84(95) (74)73
2-y-o b g American Post-Pan Galactic (USA) (Lear Fan (USA))
P J Makin D R Tucker

Placings:42341 (7655)
2009: 5^{4}SF, 7^{2}GF, 7^{3}SD, 5^{4}SD, 6^{1}SD,

	Starts	1st	2nd	3rd	Win & Pl
Career Total (Turf)	1	0	1	0	964
Career Total (AW)	4	1	0	1	3082

73 12/09 Ling 6f STD £2729
Total win prize-money £2730

Going (Turf): **Sf: 0-0 GS: 0-0 Gd: 0-0 GF: 0-1 Fm: 0-0**
Distance: **5f/6f: 1-3** 7f-8f: 0-2 9f-13f: 0-0 14f+: 0-0
Track : **LH: 1-5** RH: 0-0 **Tight: 1-4** Gall: 0-0
Aids: Bl: 0-0 Vi: 0-0 Tstrap: 0-0 Ckp: 0-0
Best Rating: 74 10/09 Ling 7f stand

Fair; stays 7f; acts on fast ground and on Polytrack.

Panadin (IRE)

58 43
7-y-o b g Desert King (IRE)-Strident Note (The Minstrel (CAN))
Mrs L C Jewell Capt N M Davies

Placings:0000/0P/000-0 (3774)
2009: 16^{0}GF,

	Starts	1st	2nd	3rd	Win & Pl
Career Total (Turf)	7	0	0	0	
Career Total (AW)	3	0	0	0	

Going (Turf): **Sf: 0-0 GS: 0-0 Gd: 0-2 GF: 0-5 Fm: 0-0**
Distance: 5f/6f: 0-1 7f-8f: 0-0 9f-13f: 0-7 14f+: 0-2
Track : LH: 0-6 RH: 0-2 Tight: 0-7 Gall: 0-0
Aids: Bl: 0-0 Vi: 0-0 Tstrap: 0-6 Ckp: 0-6
Best Rating: 53 9/05 Nott 1m54y good

Panceltica

(80) (31)
4-y-o b g Makbul-Lady Kate (Bay Express)
Karen George Adam Richard Wilson

Placings:00 (3223)
2009: 7^{0}SD, 12^{0}SD,

	Starts	1st	2nd	3rd	Win & Pl
Career Total (Turf)	0	0	0	0	
Career Total (AW)	2	0	0	0	

Going (Turf): **Sf: 0-0 GS: 0-0 Gd: 0-0 GF: 0-0 Fm: 0-0**
Distance: 5f/6f: 0-0 7f-8f: 0-1 9f-13f: 0-1 14f+: 0-0
Track : LH: 0-2 RH: 0-0 Tight: 0-2 Gall: 0-0
Aids: Bl: 0-0 Vi: 0-0 Tstrap: 0-0 Ckp: 0-0
Best Rating: 31 5/09 Wolv 7f32y stand

Panpiper

91 66
2-y-o ch c Piccolo-Phi Beta Kappa (USA) (Diesis)
G L Moore Pillar To Post Racing (IV)

Placings:03 (3658)
2009: 6^{0}GF, 5^{3}F,

	Starts	1st	2nd	3rd	Win & Pl
Career Total (Turf)	2	0	0	1	566

Going (Turf): **Sf: 0-0 GS: 0-0 Gd: 0-0 GF: 0-1 Fm: 0-1**
Distance: 5f/6f: 0-2 7f-8f: 0-0 9f-13f: 0-0 14f+: 0-0
Track : LH: 0-1 RH: 0-0 Tight: 0-0 Gall: 0-1
Aids: Bl: 0-0 Vi: 0-0 Tstrap: 0-0 Ckp: 0-0
Best Rating: 66 7/09 Brig 5f213y firm

Pansy Potter

90(93) (59)56
3-y-o b f Auction House (USA)-Ellway Queen (USA) (Bahri (USA))
B J Meehan The Comic Strip Heroes

Placings:00546-0000 (3299)
2009: 6^{0}GF, 7^{0}GF, 6^{0}G, 6^{0}SD,

	Starts	1st	2nd	3rd	Win & Pl
Career Total (Turf)	6	0	0	0	1082
Career Total (AW)	3	0	0	0	0

Going (Turf): **Sf: 0-0 GS: 0-1 Gd: 0-1 GF: 0-4 Fm: 0-0**
Distance: 5f/6f: 0-3 7f-8f: 0-6 9f-13f: 0-0 14f+: 0-0
Track : LH: 0-0 RH: 0-3 Tight: 0-0 Gall: 0-1
Aids: Bl: 0-3 Vi: 0-0 Tstrap: 0-0 Ckp: 0-0
Best Rating: 59 12/08 Kemp 7f stand

Modest; effective at around 7f; acts on Polytrack.

Pantherii (USA)

98(91) (60)64
4-y-o ch f Forest Wildcat (USA)-Saraa Ree (USA) (Caro)
P F I Cole A H Robinson

Placings:4500/3603-2 (2590)
2009: 8^{2}GF,

	Starts	1st	2nd	3rd	Win & Pl
Career Total (Turf)	6	0	1	1	1814
Career Total (AW)	3	0	0	1	302

Going (Turf): **Sf: 0-0 GS: 0-1 Gd: 0-1 GF: 0-4 Fm: 0-0**
Distance: 5f/6f: 0-4 7f-8f: 0-4 9f-13f: 0-1 14f+: 0-0
Track : LH: 0-3 RH: 0-1 Tight: 0-1 Gall: 0-0
Aids: Bl: 0-0 Vi: 0-0 Tstrap: 0-0 Ckp: 0-0
Best Rating: 64 6/09 Ayr 1m gd-fm

Modest; effective at around 1m; acts on Polytrack.

Panto Princess

100 74
3-y-o b f Act One-Bob's Princess (Bob's Return (IRE))
H Candy Mrs J E L Wright

Placings:3254 (7101)
2009: 10^{3}GF, 9^{2}GF, 10^{5}S, 10^{4}G,

	Starts	1st	2nd	3rd	Win & Pl
Career Total (Turf)	4	0	1	1	1742

Going (Turf): **Sf: 0-1 GS: 0-0 Gd: 0-1 GF: 0-2 Fm: 0-0**
Distance: 5f/6f: 0-0 7f-8f: 0-0 9f-13f: 0-4 14f+: 0-0
Track : LH: 0-2 RH: 0-2 Tight: 0-3 Gall: 0-0
Aids: Bl: 0-0 Vi: 0-0 Tstrap: 0-0 Ckp: 0-0
Best Rating: 74 10/09 Yarm 1m2f21y good

Fair; stays 1m2f.; acts on good/fast ground.

Papa Power (IRE)

9
6-y-o b g Polish Precedent (USA)-Guignol (IRE) (Anita's Prince)
K M Prendergast Mrs L Skelly

Placings:0/000040000/0 (5911)
2009: 5^{0}GF,

	Starts	1st	2nd	3rd	Win & Pl
Career Total (Turf)	11	0	0	0	235

Going (Turf): **Sf: 0-2 GS: 0-0 Gd: 0-4 GF: 0-2 Fm: 0-1**
Distance: 5f/6f: 0-9 7f-8f: 0-1 9f-13f: 0-1 14f+: 0-0
Track : LH: 0-5 RH: 0-4 Tight: 0-0 Gall: 0-1
Aids: Bl: 0-0 Vi: 0-0 Tstrap: 0-0 Ckp: 0-0
Best Rating: 53 6/07 DRoy 5f good

Papa's Princess

96(81) (17)62
5-y-o b m Mujadil (USA)-Desert Flower (Green Desert (USA))
J S Goldie Sutherland Five

Placings:40450/0240241620-466654330005 (5944)
2009: 8^{4}G, 9^{6}GF, 8^{6}GF, 10^{6}G, 12^{5}GF, 10^{4}GF, 9^{3}G, 8^{3}GF, 8^{0}G, 8^{0}S, 8^{0}GS, 9^{5}G,

	Starts	1st	2nd	3rd	Win & Pl
Career Total (Turf)	26	1	3	2	7055
Career Total (AW)	1	0	0	0	

62 7/08 Ayr 1m1f20y (0-65)H G-S £2590
Total win prize-money £2590

Going (Turf): Sf: 0-1 **GS: 1-4** Gd: 0-12 GF: 0-9 Fm: 0-0
Distance: 5f/6f: 0-0 7f-8f: 0-12 **9f-13f: 1-15** 14f+: 0-0
Track : **LH: 1-10** RH: 0-17 Tight: 0-15 Gall: 0-2
Aids: Bl: 0-0 Vi: 0-0 Tstrap: 0-0 Ckp: 0-0
Best Rating: 62 5/09 Haml 1m65y good

Moderate; stays 1m; acts on a sound surface.

Papageno

89(94) (62)**62**
2-y-o b c Piccolo-Fresh Fruit Daily (Reprimand)
J R Jenkins The Papageno Partnership

Placings:05402400 (7365)
2009: 5^{0}GF, 5^{5}GF, 5^{4}GF, 5^{0}GF, 5^{2}SD, 5^{4}SD, 5^{0}G, 5^{0}SD,

	Starts	1st	2nd	3rd	Win & Pl
Career Total (Turf)	5	0	0	0	289
Career Total (AW)	3	0	1	0	797

Going (Turf): Sf: 0-0 GS: 0-0 Gd: 0-1 GF: 0-4 Fm: 0-0
Distance: 5f/6f: 0-8 7f-8f: 0-0 9f-13f: 0-0 14f+: 0-0
Track : LH: 0-1 RH: 0-2 Tight: 0-1 Gall: 0-1
Aids: Bl: 0-0 Vi: 0-0 Tstrap: 0-0 Ckp: 0-0
Best Rating: 62 9/09 Kemp 5f stand

Paparaazi (IRE)

93(81) (62)**62**
7-y-o b g Victory Note (USA)-Raazi (My Generation)
I W McInnes Mrs Jo Sharp

Placings:503413/44254100/06622632055/2343400100400/0106000-00 (3943)
2009: 10^{0}GF, 9^{0}GF,

	Starts	1st	2nd	3rd	Win & Pl
Career Total (Turf)	31	3	4	1	17983
Career Total (AW)	16	1	1	4	7676

62 7/08 Nott 1m2f50y (0-60)H G-F £1977
64 8/07 Catt 1m3f214y FRM £2730
78 8/05 Rdcr 1m2f (0-70)H GD £4446
71 11/04 Wolv 7f32y (0-75) STD £4212
Total win prize-money £13366

Going (Turf): Sf: 0-7 GS: 0-2 **Gd: 1-8 GF: 1-13 Fm: 1-1**
Distance: 5f/6f: 0-1 7f-8f: 1-9 **9f-13f: 3-37** 14f+: 0-0
Track : **LH: 4-32** RH: 0-14 **Tight: 3-23** Gall: 0-2
Aids: Bl: 0-2 Vi: 0-2 Tstrap: 1-13 Ckp: 1-13
Best Rating: 78 7/06 York 1m208y gd-fm

Moderate; effective at around 1m2f; acts on good and fast ground and Polytrack.

Papillio (IRE)

97(100) (77)**68**
4-y-o b g Marju (IRE)-Danish Gem (Danehill (USA))
J R Fanshawe Clipper Logistics

Placings:230/56-6030230 (3713)
2009: 7^{6}SD, 7^{0}SD, 7^{3}SD, 7^{0}GF, 6^{2}GF, 6^{3}G, 6^{0}SD,

	Starts	1st	2nd	3rd	Win & Pl
Career Total (Turf)	8	0	2	2	3398
Career Total (AW)	4	0	0	1	578

Going (Turf): Sf: 0-1 GS: 0-0 Gd: 0-3 GF: 0-4 Fm: 0-0
Distance: 5f/6f: 0-5 7f-8f: 0-7 9f-13f: 0-0 14f+: 0-0
Track : LH: 0-2 RH: 0-2 Tight: 0-1 Gall: 0-0
Aids: Bl: 0-0 Vi: 0-0 Tstrap: 0-0 Ckp: 0-0
Best Rating: 77 4/09 Wolv 7f32y stand

Modest; effective at 6f; acts on good, fast ground.

Pappoose

94(56) **49**
4-y-o b f Namid-Bryn (Saddlers' Hall (IRE))
H Candy Simon Broke And Partners

Placings:600-000 (4479)
2009: 6^{0}GF, 6^{0}SD, 5^{0}G,

	Starts	1st	2nd	3rd	Win & Pl
Career Total (Turf)	5	0	0	0	0
Career Total (AW)	1	0	0	0	

Going (Turf): Sf: 0-0 GS: 0-2 Gd: 0-2 GF: 0-1 Fm: 0-0
Distance: 5f/6f: 0-4 7f-8f: 0-2 9f-13f: 0-0 14f+: 0-0
Track : LH: 0-2 RH: 0-0 Tight: 0-1 Gall: 0-2
Aids: Bl: 0-0 Vi: 0-0 Tstrap: 0-0 Ckp: 0-0
Best Rating: 49 9/08 Yarm 6f3y good

Papradon

(103) (70)**70**
5-y-o b g Tobougg (IRE)-Salvezza (IRE) (Superpower)
N A Twiston-Davies N A Twiston-Davies

Placings:056/30416235/021002-0 (0342)
2009: 12^{0}SD,

	Starts	1st	2nd	3rd	Win & Pl
Career Total (Turf)	4	1	0	0	3886
Career Total (AW)	14	1	3	2	5157

70 7/08 NmkJ 1m2f (0-70)H G-F £3885
56 10/07 Kemp 1m2f (0-55) STD £2047
Total win prize-money £5934

Going (Turf): Sf: 0-0 GS: 0-1 Gd: 0-1 **GF: 1-2** Fm: 0-0
Distance: 5f/6f: 0-3 7f-8f: 0-0 **9f-13f: 2-13** 14f+: 0-2
Track : LH: 0-9 **RH: 2-8** Tight: 0-10 **Gall: 1-2**
Aids: Bl: 0-0 **Vi: 2-10** Tstrap: 0-0 Ckp: 0-0
Best Rating: 70 10/08 Kemp 1m4f stand

Moderate; stays 1m6f and acts on Polytrack; has worn a visor and blinkers.

Papyrian

101(98) (77)**82**
3-y-o b g Oasis Dream-La Papagena (Habitat)
W Jarvis Gillian, Lady Howard De Walden

Placings:0-3522443 (6977)
2009: 8^{3}GF, 8^{5}G, 7^{2}GF, 7^{2}GF, 8^{4}F, 8^{4}GF, 8^{3}SD,

	Starts	1st	2nd	3rd	Win & Pl
Career Total (Turf)	7	0	2	1	2789
Career Total (AW)	1	0	0	1	385

Going (Turf): Sf: 0-0 GS: 0-1 Gd: 0-1 GF: 0-4 Fm: 0-1
Distance: 5f/6f: 0-1 7f-8f: 0-3 9f-13f: 0-4 14f+: 0-0
Track : LH: 0-3 RH: 0-1 Tight: 0-1 Gall: 0-0
Aids: Bl: 0-3 Vi: 0-0 Tstrap: 0-0 Ckp: 0-0
Best Rating: 82 6/09 Newb 7f gd-fm

Fair; effective over 1m; acts on Polytrack.

Paquerettza (FR)

109 **87**
3-y-o ch f Dr Fong (USA)-Cover Look (SAF) (Fort Wood (USA))
D H Brown J B Smith & J M Smith

Placings:430-1142002 (6680)
2009: 8^{1}GF, 8^{1}GS, 8^{4}GF, 8^{2}GF, 8^{0}S, 8^{0}G, 10^{2}G,

	Starts	1st	2nd	3rd	Win & Pl
Career Total (Turf)	10	2	2	1	14761

80 7/09 NmkJ 1m (0-75)H G-S £3885
80 4/09 Rdcr 1m (0-75)H G-F £2590
Total win prize-money £6476

Going (Turf): Sf: 0-2 **GS: 1-2** Gd: 0-3 **GF: 1-3** Fm: 0-0
Distance: 5f/6f: 0-1 **7f-8f: 2-7** 9f-13f: 0-2 14f+: 0-0
Track : LH: 0-5 RH: 0-0 Tight: 0-2 Gall: 0-2
Aids: Bl: 0-0 Vi: 0-0 Tstrap: 0-0 Ckp: 0-0
Best Rating: 87 8/09 York 1m gd-fm

Fair; stays 1m and acts on fast ground.

Par Avion

92 **56**
4-y-o b f Efisio-Blow Me A Kiss (Kris)
Paul Murphy Guy Reed

Placings:5 (2030)
2009: 9^{5}G,

	Starts	1st	2nd	3rd	Win & Pl
Career Total (Turf)	1	0	0	0	0

Going (Turf): Sf: 0-0 GS: 0-0 Gd: 0-1 GF: 0-0 Fm: 0-0
Distance: 5f/6f: 0-0 7f-8f: 0-0 9f-13f: 0-1 14f+: 0-0
Track : LH: 0-0 RH: 0-1 Tight: 0-1 Gall: 0-0
Aids: Bl: 0-0 Vi: 0-0 Tstrap: 0-0 Ckp: 0-0
Best Rating: 56 5/09 Haml 1m1f36y good

Paradise Dancer (IRE)

(102) (80)**68**
5-y-o b m Danehill Dancer (IRE)-Pintada De Fresco (FR) (Marignan (USA))
J A R Toller The Perfect Partnership II

Placings:353230236/12534000-00 (0318)
2009: 10^{0}SD, 8^{0}SD,

	Starts	1st	2nd	3rd	Win & Pl
Career Total (Turf)	6	0	0	3	1751
Career Total (AW)	13	1	3	2	5759

77 2/08 Ling 1m (0-70)H STD £2331
Total win prize-money £2332

Going (Turf): Sf: 0-2 GS: 0-1 Gd: 0-2 GF: 0-1 Fm: 0-0
Distance: 5f/6f: 0-0 **7f-8f: 1-12** 9f-13f: 0-7 14f+: 0-0
Track : **LH: 1-16** RH: 0-1 **Tight: 1-14** Gall: 0-0
Aids: Bl: 0-0 Vi: 0-0 Tstrap: 0-0 Ckp: 0-0
Best Rating: 80 3/08 Ling 7f stand

Modest; stays 1m2f; acts on good and softer ground and on Polytrack.

Paradise Dream

86(75) (64)**59**
2-y-o b c Kyllachy-Wunders Dream (IRE) (Averti (IRE))
J Noseda Saeed Suhail

Placings:2304 (3682)
2009: 5^{2}SD, 5^{3}GF, 6^{0}G, 5^{4}GS,

	Starts	1st	2nd	3rd	Win & Pl
Career Total (Turf)	3	0	0	1	1637
Career Total (AW)	1	0	1	0	1493

Going (Turf): Sf: 0-0 GS: 0-1 Gd: 0-1 GF: 0-1 Fm: 0-0
Distance: 5f/6f: 0-3 7f-8f: 0-1 9f-13f: 0-0 14f+: 0-0
Track : LH: 0-0 RH: 0-1 Tight: 0-0 Gall: 0-0
Aids: Bl: 0-0 Vi: 0-0 Tstrap: 0-0 Ckp: 0-0
Best Rating: 64 5/09 Kemp 5f stand

Fair; suited by 5f and Polytrack.

Paradise Spectre

90 **79**

2-y-o b c Firebreak-Amber's Bluff (Mind Games)
K R Burke Findlay & Bloom

Placings:4202 (4306)
2009: 6^{4}GF, 6^{2}G, 6^{0}GF, 6^{2}GS,

	Starts	1st	2nd	3rd	Win & Pl
Career Total (Turf)	4	0	2	0	2492

Going (Turf): Sf: 0-0 GS: 0-1 Gd: 0-1 GF: 0-2 Fm: 0-0
Distance: 5f/6f: 0-3 7f-8f: 0-1 9f-13f: 0-0 14f+: 0-0
Track : LH: 0-0 RH: 0-0 Tight: 0-0 Gall: 0-0
Aids: Bl: 0-0 Vi: 0-1 Tstrap: 0-0 Ckp: 0-0
Best Rating: 79 7/09 Newc 6f gd-sft

Fair; effective over 6f; acts on good ground.

Paraguay (USA)

103(98) (78)**86**

6-y-o b g Pivotal-Grisonnante (FR) (Kaldoun (FR))
Mrs D J Sanderson R J Budge

Placings:5300121200040505/563500405000/511511204542-62166040 (4663)
2009: 8^{6}SD, 7^{2}GF, 7^{1}G, 8^{6}GF, 7^{6}GF, 8^{0}SD, 8^{4}GF, 8^{0}G,

	Starts	1st	2nd	3rd	Win & Pl
Career Total (Turf)	38	7	4	2	41516
Career Total (AW)	10	0	1	0	2797

82	5/09	Bevl	7f100y	(0-80)H	GD	£4727
78	6/08	Donc	1m	(0-80)H	G-F	£4857
73	6/08	Gdwd	1m	(0-70)H	G-F	£3412
75	5/08	Gdwd	1m1f	(0-70)H	SFT	£3238
67	5/08	Bevl	1m100y	(0-60)H	G-F	£2558
85	7/06	Epsm	1m114y	(0-85)H	GD	£6477
75	6/06	NmkJ	1m		G-F	£3886

Total win prize-money £29156

Going (Turf): Sf: 1-4 GS: 0-1 Gd: 2-11 **GF: 4-21** Fm: 0-1
Distance: 5f/6f: 0-0 **7f-8f: 4-30** 9f-13f: 3-18 14f+: 0-0
Track : LH: 2-16 **RH: 4-21 Tight: 2-13** Gall: 1-4
Aids: Bl: 0-0 Vi: 0-2 Tstrap: 0-0 Ckp: 0-0
Best Rating: 89 7/06 NmkJ 1m gd-fm

Fair; suited by 1m; acts on fast ground and on Fibresand.

Parallel (IRE)

88 **57**

3-y-o b f Refuse To Bend (IRE)-Iktidar (Green Desert (USA))
J H M Gosden H R H Princess Haya Of Jordan

Placings:36 (6741)
2009: 8^{3}G, 8^{6}GS,

	Starts	1st	2nd	3rd	Win & Pl
Career Total (Turf)	2	0	0	1	482

Going (Turf): Sf: 0-0 GS: 0-1 Gd: 0-1 GF: 0-0 Fm: 0-0
Distance: 5f/6f: 0-0 7f-8f: 0-0 9f-13f: 0-2 14f+: 0-0
Track : LH: 0-0 RH: 0-2 Tight: 0-1 Gall: 0-0
Aids: Bl: 0-0 Vi: 0-0 Tstrap: 0-0 Ckp: 0-0
Best Rating: 57 8/09 Sand 1m14y good

Parbold Hill

92 **69**

2-y-o br f Exceed And Excel (AUS)-Let Alone (Warning)
R A Fahey (T D Barron 2/7) David W Armstrong

Placings:52036 (3540)
2009: 5^{5}G, 5^{2}G, 5^{0}GF, 5^{3}GS, 5^{6}F,

	Starts	1st	2nd	3rd	Win & Pl
Career Total (Turf)	5	0	1	1	2688

Going (Turf): Sf: 0-0 GS: 0-1 Gd: 0-2 GF: 0-1 Fm: 0-1
Distance: 5f/6f: 0-5 7f-8f: 0-0 9f-13f: 0-0 14f+: 0-0
Track : LH: 0-1 RH: 0-0 Tight: 0-0 Gall: 0-0
Aids: Bl: 0-1 Vi: 0-0 Tstrap: 0-0 Ckp: 0-0
Best Rating: 69 5/09 Bevl 5f gd-fm

Fair; suited by 5f and good ground.

Parc Aux Boules

102(85) (67)**71**

8-y-o gr g Royal Applause-Aristocratique (Cadeaux Genereux)
Paul Stafford (Adrian McGuinness 5/8) Any News Syndicate

Placings:0/4/52202010/510006000-04250003065600 (7634)
2009: 6^{0}YS, 5^{4}Y, 5^{2}S, 5^{5}SD, 5^{0}HY, 6^{0}G, 6^{0}GF, 5^{3}S, 6^{0}Y, 5^{6}YS, 6^{5}S, 6^{8}S, 6^{0}SD, 5^{0}SD,

	Starts	1st	2nd	3rd	Win & Pl
Career Total (Turf)	19	1	1	1	10131
Career Total (AW)	14	1	3	0	4270

71	4/08	Naas	5f	(50-80)H	YLD	£6351
58	9/05	Ling	6f	(0-45)	STD	£1484

Total win prize-money £7835

Going (Turf): Sf: 0-9 GS: 0-1 Gd: 0-1 GF: 0-2 Fm: 0-1
Distance: **5f/6f: 2-26** 7f-8f: 0-7 9f-13f: 0-0 14f+: 0-0
Track : **LH: 2-22** RH: 0-2 **Tight: 1-5** Gall: 0-1
Aids: Bl: 0-4 Vi: 0-0 Tstrap: 0-0 Ckp: 0-0
Best Rating: 71 4/09 Navn 5f182y soft

Fair; stays 7f; acts on easy ground, Polytrack and Fibresand.

Parc Des Princes (USA)

99(102) (76)**66**

3-y-o b/br g Ten Most Wanted (USA)-Miss Orah (Unfuwain (USA))
A M Balding The James Gang

Placings:020-5043131 (4206)
2009: 10^{5}G, 11^{0}GF, 9^{4}GF, 11^{3}GF, 10^{1}GF, 12^{9}GF, 12^{1}SD,

	Starts	1st	2nd	3rd	Win & Pl
Career Total (Turf)	8	1	1	2	4995
Career Total (AW)	2	1	0	0	2730

76	7/09	Ling	1m4f	(0-75)H	STD	£2729
66	6/09	Wwck	1m2f188y	(0-75)H	G-F	£2914

Total win prize-money £5644

Going (Turf): Sf: 0-0 GS: 0-0 Gd: 0-2 **GF: 1-6** Fm: 0-0
Distance: 5f/6f: 0-0 7f-8f: 0-3 **9f-13f: 2-7** 14f+: 0-0
Track : **LH: 2-6** RH: 0-2 **Tight: 1-4** Gall: 0-1
Aids: Bl: 0-2 Vi: 0-0 Tstrap: 0-0 Ckp: 0-0
Best Rating: 76 7/09 Ling 1m4f stand

Modest; stays 1m4f; acts on fast ground and on Polytrack.

Paris In Mind

45

3-y-o b f Mind Games-Paris Babe (Teenoso (USA))
C N Kellett G C Chipman & R Charlesworth

Placings:0 (3071)
2009: 6^{0}G,

	Starts	1st	2nd	3rd	Win & Pl
Career Total (Turf)	1	0	0	0	

Going (Turf): Sf: 0-0 GS: 0-0 Gd: 0-1 GF: 0-0 Fm: 0-0
Distance: 5f/6f: 0-1 7f-8f: 0-0 9f-13f: 0-0 14f+: 0-0
Track : LH: 0-1 RH: 0-0 Tight: 0-0 Gall: 0-0
Aids: Bl: 0-0 Vi: 0-0 Tstrap: 0-0 Ckp: 0-0

Parisian Art (IRE)

90(88) (80)**86**

3-y-o b g Clodovil (IRE)-Cafe Creme (IRE) (Catrail (USA))
J Noseda Matthew Green

Placings:1055-0 (2821)
2009: 6^{0}GF,

	Starts	1st	2nd	3rd	Win & Pl
Career Total (Turf)	4	1	0	0	5589
Career Total (AW)	1	0	0	0	256

80	7/08	NmkJ	7f		G-F	£5180

Total win prize-money £5181

Going (Turf): Sf: 0-1 GS: 0-0 Gd: 0-1 **GF: 1-2** Fm: 0-0
Distance: 5f/6f: 0-2 **7f-8f: 1-3** 9f-13f: 0-0 14f+: 0-0
Track : LH: 0-0 RH: 0-2 Tight: 0-0 Gall: 0-0
Aids: **Bl: 1-4** Vi: 0-0 Tstrap: 0-0 Ckp: 0-0
Best Rating: 86 8/08 Sand 7f16y good

Very useful; effective over 6f-7f; acts on fast and soft ground; wears blinkers.

Parisian Dream

96(85) (46)**68**

5-y-o b g Sakhee (USA)-Boojum (Mujtahid (USA))
T J Pitt Ferrybank Properties Limited

Placings:0/312100/000000 (6998)
2009: 7^{0}GF, 7^{0}G, 10^{0}G, 9^{0}GF, 12^{0}SF, 9^{0}SD,

	Starts	1st	2nd	3rd	Win & Pl
Career Total (Turf)	11	2	1	1	15966
Career Total (AW)	2	0	0	0	

90	8/07	Pont	1m4y	(0-90)H	G-S	£9348
82	6/07	Sals	6f212y		G-F	£4210

Total win prize-money £13558

Going (Turf): Sf: 0-1 **GS: 1-2** Gd: 0-3 **GF: 1-5** Fm: 0-0
Distance: 5f/6f: 0-1 7f-8f: 1-5 9f-13f: 1-7 14f+: 0-0
Track : **LH: 1-7** RH: 0-1 Tight: 0-4 Gall: 0-1
Aids: Bl: 0-1 Vi: 0-0 Tstrap: 0-0 Ckp: 0-0
Best Rating: 90 8/07 Pont 1m4y gd-sft

Fair colt; stays 1m; acts on fast ground.

Parisian Gift (IRE)

93(100) (75)**84**

4-y-o b g Statue Of Liberty (USA)-My Micheline (Lion Cavern (USA))

J R Gask Horses First Racing Limited

Placings:01/626P-333 **(1628)**
2009: 6^{3}SD, 7^{3}SD, 6^{3}GF,

	Starts	1st	2nd	3rd	Win & Pl
Career Total (Turf)	4	0	1	1	1073
Career Total (AW)	5	1	0	2	3217

75 12/07 Ling 7f STD £2914
Total win prize-money £2915

Going (Turf): **Sf: 0-1 GS: 0-0 Gd: 0-0 GF: 0-3 Fm: 0-0**
Distance: 5f/6f: 0-3 **7f-8f: 1-6** 9f-13f: 0-0 14f+: 0-0
Track : **LH: 1-5** RH: 0-0 **Tight: 1-5** Gall: 0-0
Aids: Bl: 0-0 Vi: 0-0 Tstrap: 0-1 Ckp: 0-1
Best Rating: **84** 7/08 Yarm 7f3y gd-fm

Fair; stays 7f and acts on Polytrack.

Parisian Pyramid (IRE)

108 **98**
3-y-o gr g Verglas (IRE)-Sharadja (IRE) (Doyoun)
D Nicholls Dr Marwan Koukash

Placings:334123-300342500005 **(7015)**
2009: 6^{3}GF, 6^{0}GF, 5^{0}GF, 6^{3}GF, 7^{4}G, 6^{2}G, 6^{5}G, 6^{0}G, 7^{0}GF, 5^{0}GS, 6^{0}G, 5^{5}GS,

	Starts	1st	2nd	3rd	Win & Pl
Career Total (Turf)	18	1	2	5	48147

84 8/08 Gdwd 6f H GD £12952
Total win prize-money £12952

Going (Turf): Sf: 0-2 GS: 0-2 **Gd: 1-8** GF: 0-6 Fm: 0-0
Distance: **5f/6f: 1-14** 7f-8f: 0-4 9f-13f: 0-0 14f+: 0-0
Track : LH: 0-5 RH: 0-0 Tight: 0-5 Gall: 0-0
Aids: Bl: 0-0 Vi: 0-0 Tstrap: 0-0 Ckp: 0-0
Best Rating: **98** 6/09 York 6f good

Very useful; effective over 6f and acts on most types of ground.

Park Lane

101(106) (72)**81**
3-y-o b g Royal Applause-Kazeem (Darshaan)
B W Hills Raymond Tooth

Placings:420-2232150 **(5986)**
2009: 8^{2}SD, 8^{2}SD, 8^{3}G, 8^{2}S, 8^{1}GF, 10^{5}GF, 8^{0}SD,

	Starts	1st	2nd	3rd	Win & Pl
Career Total (Turf)	7	1	2	1	8633
Career Total (AW)	3	0	2	0	1577

81 8/09 Pont 1m4y G-F £4857
Total win prize-money £4857

Going (Turf): Sf: 0-2 GS: 0-1 Gd: 0-1 **GF: 1-3** Fm: 0-0
Distance: 5f/6f: 0-2 7f-8f: 0-5 **9f-13f: 1-3** 14f+: 0-0
Track : **LH: 1-3** RH: 0-2 Tight: 0-2 Gall: 0-1
Aids: Bl: 0-0 Vi: 0-0 Tstrap: 0-0 Ckp: 0-0
Best Rating: **81** 8/09 Pont 1m4y gd-fm

Fair; stays 1m; acts on soft ground and on Polytrack.

Park Melody (IRE)

85(74) (34)**59**
3-y-o b f Refuse To Bend (IRE)-Park Charger (Tirol)
B J Meehan Exors of the Late F C T Wilson

Placings:44000 **(6860)**
2009: 10^{4}GF, 12^{4}GF, 10^{0}GF, 12^{0}SD, 9^{0}SD,

	Starts	1st	2nd	3rd	Win & Pl
Career Total (Turf)	3	0	0	0	673
Career Total (AW)	2	0	0	0	

Going (Turf): **Sf: 0-0 GS: 0-0 Gd: 0-0 GF: 0-3 Fm: 0-0**
Distance: 5f/6f: 0-0 7f-8f: 0-0 9f-13f: 0-5 14f+: 0-0
Track : LH: 0-3 RH: 0-2 Tight: 0-2 Gall: 0-2
Aids: Bl: 0-1 Vi: 0-0 Tstrap: 0-0 Ckp: 0-0
Best Rating: **59** 6/09 Newb 1m4f5y gd-fm

Park View

78 **53**
2-y-o ch f With Approval (CAN)-Bayswater (Caerleon (USA))
B W Hills K Abdulla

Placings:0 **(7183)**
2009: 7^{0}G,

	Starts	1st	2nd	3rd	Win & Pl
Career Total (Turf)	1	0	0	0	

Going (Turf): **Sf: 0-0 GS: 0-0 Gd: 0-1 GF: 0-0 Fm: 0-0**
Distance: 5f/6f: 0-0 7f-8f: 0-1 9f-13f: 0-0 14f+: 0-0
Track : LH: 0-0 RH: 0-0 Tight: 0-0 Gall: 0-0
Aids: Bl: 0-0 Vi: 0-0 Tstrap: 0-0 Ckp: 0-0
Best Rating: **53** 10/09 NmkR 7f good

Park's Prodigy

101(94) (14)**63**
5-y-o b g Desert Prince (IRE)-Up And About (Barathea (IRE))
G A Harker (P C Haslam 30/6) John J Maguire

Placings:0064436/220-40042210 **(7154)**
2009: 6^{4}GF, 16^{0}G, 10^{0}GF, 12^{4}GS, 13^{2}GF, 15^{2}G, 11^{1}S, 16^{0}SD,

	Starts	1st	2nd	3rd	Win & Pl
Career Total (Turf)	13	1	3	1	4804
Career Total (AW)	5	0	1	0	564

63 10/09 Catt 1m3f214y (0-60)H SFT £2047
Total win prize-money £2047

Going (Turf): **Sf: 1-1** GS: 0-1 Gd: 0-5 GF: 0-6 Fm: 0-0
Distance: 5f/6f: 0-1 7f-8f: 0-2 **9f-13f: 1-6** 14f+: 0-9
Track : **LH: 1-15** RH: 0-2 **Tight: 1-10** Gall: 0-3
Aids: Bl: 0-0 Vi: 0-0 Tstrap: 0-2 Ckp: 0-2
Best Rating: **63** 10/09 Catt 1m3f214y soft

Modest; stays 1m6f; acts on easy ground and on Fibresand; has worn a tongue tie.

Parkview Love (USA)

(104) (61)**70**
8-y-o b/br g Mister Baileys-Jerre Jo Glanville (USA) (Skywalker (USA))
A G Newcombe (J G Given 12/9) Nigel Hardy

Placings:12165/030000045300060/000500354010021250/14043166000500/2553321513325200201053/032033005550062206-5000 **(7784)**
2009: 9^{5}SD, 9^{0}SD, 8^{0}SD, 8^{0}SD,

	Starts	1st	2nd	3rd	Win & Pl
Career Total (Turf)	32	2	3	4	45177
Career Total (AW)	65	7	8	8	31774

75 11/07 Wolv 7f32y (0-70)H STD £3071
76 3/07 Ling 1m (0-75)H STD £2914
71 3/07 Ling 1m (0-65)H STD £2047
77 4/06 Wolv 7f32y (0-75)H STD £3886
75 2/06 Wolv 1m1f103y (0-70)H STD £3238
71 12/05 Sthl 7f (0-65)H STD £2888
67 8/05 Ling 1m (0-60) STD £3484
98 6/03 Epsm 6f A GD £23200
60 5/03 Haml 5f4y E G-S £4576
Total win prize-money £49307

Going (Turf): Sf: 0-1 **GS: 1-7 Gd: 1-16** GF: 0-6 Fm: 0-2
Distance: 5f/6f: 2-10 **7f-8f: 6-59** 9f-13f: 1-27 14f+: 0-1
Track : **LH: 8-71** RH: 0-15 **Tight: 7-53** Gall: 0-3
Aids: Bl: 0-4 **Vi: 7-62** Tstrap: 0-6 Ckp: 0-6
Best Rating: **99** 4/04 NmkR 7f good

Moderate; effective over 7f-1m4f; acts on most types of ground, including sand.

Parnassian

78(102) (60)**60**
9-y-o ch g Sabrehill (USA)-Delphic Way (Warning)
J A Geake Miss B Swire

Placings:460030/44043342500/00331305115430310/30050020251/0000500150/430640/060325-50 **(4263)**
2009: 12^{5}SD, 12^{0}S,

	Starts	1st	2nd	3rd	Win & Pl
Career Total (Turf)	62	6	3	10	40347
Career Total (AW)	7	0	1	1	1108

76 10/06 Wind 1m67y (0-70)H SFT £3238
80 11/05 Nott 1m1f213y (0-75)H HVY £3517
81 10/04 Bath 1m5y (0-70)H G-S £4729
81 7/04 Donc 1m D(0-85)H G-S £5652
67 7/04 Hayd 1m30y E(0-70)H GD £4069
64 5/04 Nott 1m54y G(0-70)H GD £2856
Total win prize-money £24062

Going (Turf): **Sf: 2-14GS: 2-12 Gd: 2-21**GF: 0-14 Fm: 0-1
Distance: 5f/6f: 0-3 7f-8f: 1-22 **9f-13f: 5-44** 14f+: 0-0
Track : **LH: 4-27** RH: 1-22 **Tight: 2-17** Gall: 0-5
Aids: Bl: 0-0 Vi: 0-13 Tstrap: 0-0 Ckp: 0-0
Best Rating: **81** 10/04 Bath 1m5y gd-sft

Moderate; stays 1m4f; seems most effective on soft ground; goes on Fibresand; has worn a visor.

Parson's Punch

(102) (72)**70**
4-y-o b g Beat Hollow-Ordained (Mtoto)
Mrs L B Normile (P D Cundell 4/2) Thistle Bloodstock

Placings:3/04435-0 **(0392)**
2009: 10^{0}SD,

	Starts	1st	2nd	3rd	Win & Pl
Career Total (Turf)	1	0	0	0	202
Career Total (AW)	6	0	0	2	1161

Going (Turf): **Sf: 0-0 GS: 0-0 Gd: 0-0 GF: 0-1 Fm: 0-0**
Distance: 5f/6f: 0-0 7f-8f: 0-4 9f-13f: 0-3 14f+: 0-0
Track : LH: 0-2 RH: 0-5 Tight: 0-2 Gall: 0-0
Aids: Bl: 0-0 Vi: 0-0 Tstrap: 0-0 Ckp: 0-0
Best Rating: **72** 12/08 Kemp 1m2f stand

Modest; stays 1m3f; acts on a sound surface and on Polytrack.

Parthenon

107 **105**
3-y-o b g Dubai Destination (USA)-Grecian Slipper (Sadler's Wells (USA))
Saeed Bin Suroor (M Johnston 15/5) Godolphin

Placings:143-110 **(2756a)**
2009: 8^{1}G, 11^{1}GF, 10^{0}G,

	Starts	1st	2nd	3rd	Win & Pl
Career Total (Turf)	6	3	0	1	45525

105 5/09 Haml 1m3f16y G-F £30815

102 4/09 Sand 1m14y GD £7477
79 9/08 Leic 7f9y HVY £5180
Total win prize-money £43473

Going (Turf): Sf: 1-1 GS: 0-0 **Gd: 1-4 GF: 1-1** Fm: 0-0
Distance: 5f/6f: 0-0 7f-8f: 1-3 **9f-13f: 2-3** 14f+: 0-0
Track : LH: 0-1 **RH: 2-4 Tight: 1-1** Gall: 0-1
Aids: Bl: 0-0 Vi: 0-0 Tstrap: 0-0 Ckp: 0-0
Best Rating: 105 5/09 Haml 1m3f16y gd-fm

Smart; Listed winner; stays 1m3f; acts on good and softer ground; suited by forcing tactics.

Partner (IRE)

(100) (76)**61**
3-y-o b g Indian Ridge-Oregon Trail (USA) (Gone West (USA))
David Marnane Philip Lloyd/Mrs Melanie Marnane

Placings:000-30062131 **(7518)**
2009: 5^3GF, 6^0S, 6^0GY, 5^6S, 5^2GY, 5^1GY, 6^3SD, 6^1SD,

	Starts	1st	2nd	3rd	Win & Pl
Career Total (Turf)	9	1	1	1	6533
Career Total (AW)	2	1	0	1	2871

76 11/09 Ling 6f (0-70)H STD £2388
61 10/09 Cork 5f (47-65)H G-Y £4696
Total win prize-money £7084

Going (Turf): Sf: 0-2 GS: 0-0 Gd: 0-1 GF: 0-1 Fm: 0-0
Distance: 5f/6f: 2-9 7f-8f: 0-2 9f-13f: 0-0 14f+: 0-0
Track : LH: 1-5 RH: 0-3 **Tight: 1-1** Gall: 0-0
Aids: Bl: 2-5 Vi: 0-0 Tstrap: 0-0 Ckp: 0-0
Best Rating: 76 11/09 Ling 6f stand

Fair; stays 6f; acts on Polytrack; has worn blinkers.

Party Doctor

108 **104**
2-y-o ch c Dr Fong (USA)-Wedding Party (Groom Dancer (USA))
Tom Dascombe Sir Robert Ogden

Placings:23324 **(5133)**
2009: 5^2GF, 6^3GF, 7^3GF, 7^2G, 7^4GF,

	Starts	1st	2nd	3rd	Win & Pl
Career Total (Turf)	5	0	2	2	16568

Going (Turf): Sf: 0-0 GS: 0-0 Gd: 0-1 GF: 0-4 Fm: 0-0
Distance: 5f/6f: 0-1 7f-8f: 0-4 9f-13f: 0-0 14f+: 0-0
Track : LH: 0-1 RH: 0-0 Tight: 0-0 Gall: 0-1
Aids: Bl: 0-0 Vi: 0-0 Tstrap: 0-0 Ckp: 0-0
Best Rating: 104 8/09 York 7f gd-fm

Smart; Listed placed; stays 7f; acts on fast ground.

Party In The Park

100(103) (62)**68**
4-y-o b g Royal Applause-Halland Park Girl (IRE) (Primo Dominie)
J R Boyle (Miss J A Camacho 1/9) Elite Racing Club

Placings:323000/524120100-000052500622022 **(7754)**
2009: 7^0SD, 8^0SD, 6^0F, 7^0GF, 7^5GF, 7^4GF, 7^5G, 7^0GF, 7^0GF, 6^6GF, 8^6SD, 8^2SD, 8^2SD, 8^0SD, 8^2SD, 8^2SD,

	Starts	1st	2nd	3rd	Win & Pl
Career Total (Turf)	20	2	3	2	12673
Career Total (AW)	11	0	5	0	2891

68 7/08 Leic 7f9y G-F £3238
68 5/08 Sals 6f212y GD £3238
Total win prize-money £6476

Going (Turf): Sf: 0-0 GS: 0-2 **Gd: 1-5 GF: 1-12** Fm: 0-1
Distance: 5f/6f: 0-7 **7f-8f: 2-22** 9f-13f: 0-2 14f+: 0-0
Track : LH: 0-11 RH: 0-5 Tight: 0-9 Gall: 0-1
Aids: Bl: 0-5 Vi: 0-1 Tstrap: 0-1 Ckp: 0-1
Best Rating: 77 5/07 NmkR 5f gd-fm

Moderate; effective over 5f-1m; acts on fast and easy ground; also goes on Polytrack.

Party Palace

101(97) (52)**60**
5-y-o b m Auction House (USA)-Lady Love (Pursuit Of Love)
H S Howe Horses Away Racing Club

Placings:00310003434/5443054006226/05-3310443 **(3997)**
2009: 11^3GF, 11^3F, 12^1G, 11^0F, 12^4GF, 13^4GF, 17^3G,

	Starts	1st	2nd	3rd	Win & Pl
Career Total (Turf)	17	2	0	4	12728
Career Total (AW)	16	0	2	3	2217

57 5/09 Chep 1m4f23y (0-75)H GD £3885
52 6/06 York 6f G-F £6800
Total win prize-money £10687

Going (Turf): Sf: 0-1 GS: 0-0 **Gd: 1-5 GF: 1-6** Fm: 0-5
Distance: 5f/6f: 1-6 7f-8f: 0-2 9f-13f: 1-20 14f+: 0-5
Track : LH: 1-19 RH: 0-10 Tight: 0-18 Gall: 0-3
Aids: Bl: 0-0 Vi: 0-0 Tstrap: 0-1 Ckp: 0-1
Best Rating: 60 5/09 Bath 1m3f144y gd-fm

Moderate; stays 2m; acts on good and faster ground and on Polytrack.

Parvaaz (IRE)

90 **69**
2-y-o ch c Rahy (USA)-Saabga (USA) (Woodman (USA))
M A Jarvis Sheikh Ahmed Al Maktoum

Placings:3 **(7099)**
2009: 8^3G,

	Starts	1st	2nd	3rd	Win & Pl
Career Total (Turf)	1	0	0	1	519

Going (Turf): Sf: 0-0 GS: 0-0 Gd: 0-1 GF: 0-0 Fm: 0-0
Distance: 5f/6f: 0-0 7f-8f: 0-0 9f-13f: 0-1 14f+: 0-0
Track : LH: 0-0 RH: 0-0 Tight: 0-0 Gall: 0-0
Aids: Bl: 0-0 Vi: 0-0 Tstrap: 0-0 Ckp: 0-0
Best Rating: 69 10/09 Yarm 1m3y good

Fair debut over 1m on good ground.

Paschendale

94 **72**
2-y-o b c Refuse To Bend (IRE)-Fading Light (King's Best (USA))
Saeed Bin Suroor Godolphin

Placings:50 **(6821)**
2009: 8^5G, 8^0GF,

	Starts	1st	2nd	3rd	Win & Pl
Career Total (Turf)	2	0	0	0	0

Going (Turf): Sf: 0-0 GS: 0-0 Gd: 0-1 GF: 0-1 Fm: 0-0
Distance: 5f/6f: 0-0 7f-8f: 0-1 9f-13f: 0-1 14f+: 0-0
Track : LH: 0-0 RH: 0-1 Tight: 0-1 Gall: 0-0
Aids: Bl: 0-0 Vi: 0-0 Tstrap: 0-0 Ckp: 0-0
Best Rating: 72 10/09 Wind 1m67y good

Started slowly and well beaten on debut.

Pass The Port

(107) (88)**87**
8-y-o ch g Docksider (USA)-One Of The Family (Alzao (USA))
D Haydn Jones The Porters

Placings:51605/60061225320021**2**/01660542336/512422/55641413040453-2 **(0787)**
2009: 13^2SD,

	Starts	1st	2nd	3rd	Win & Pl
Career Total (Turf)	19	2	3	2	30766
Career Total (AW)	33	5	7	3	35500

85 5/08 Nott 1m6f15y (0-80)H GD £6476
84 3/08 Muss 1m6f (0-85)H GD £12464
81 2/07 Wolv 1m4f50y (0-75)H STD £3071
83 1/06 Sthl 1m4f (0-85)H STD £5505
82 12/05 Wolv 1m4f50y (0-85)H STD £5625
79 3/05 Sthl 1m4f (0-70)H STD £3427
78 6/04 Sthl 1m E STD £3454
Total win prize-money £40024

Going (Turf): Sf: 0-6 GS: 0-3 **Gd: 2-7** GF: 0-2 Fm: 0-1
Distance: 5f/6f: 0-0 7f-8f: 1-4 **9f-13f: 4-27** 14f+: 2-21
Track : LH: 6-42 RH: 1-10 **Tight: 3-27** Gall: 0-8
Aids: Bl: 0-0 Vi: 0-1 Tstrap: 1-2 Ckp: 1-2
Best Rating: 88 12/07 Wolv 1m4f50y stand

Fair; stays 1m6f; acts on soft ground; goes on Fibresand and Polytrack; has worn cheekpieces; usually held up.

Passage To India (IRE)

(95) (72)
3-y-o ch f Indian Ridge-Kathy College (IRE) (College Chapel)
Miss J R Tooth Raymond Tooth

Placings:64326-30 **(3274)**
2009: 7^3SD, 8^0SD,

	Starts	1st	2nd	3rd	Win & Pl
Career Total (Turf)	0	0	0	0	
Career Total (AW)	7	0	1	2	1879

Going (Turf): Sf: 0-0 GS: 0-0 Gd: 0-0 GF: 0-0 Fm: 0-0
Distance: 5f/6f: 0-0 7f-8f: 0-5 9f-13f: 0-2 14f+: 0-0
Track : LH: 0-6 RH: 0-1 Tight: 0-4 Gall: 0-0
Aids: Bl: 0-0 Vi: 0-0 Tstrap: 0-0 Ckp: 0-0
Best Rating: 72 12/08 Sthl 7f stand

Moderate; should stay 1m; acts on Polytrack and Fibresand.

Passion For Gold (USA)

112 **117**
2-y-o b c Medaglia D'Oro (USA)-C'Est L' Amour (USA) (Thunder Gulch (USA))
Saeed Bin Suroor Godolphin

Placings:131 **(7404a)**
2009: 8^1G, 8^3G, 10^1HY,

	Starts	1st	2nd	3rd	Win & Pl
Career Total (Turf)	3	2	0	1	154080

117 11/09 StCl 1m2f HVY £138689
87 8/09 Thsk 1m GD £5342
Total win prize-money £144032

Going (Turf): Sf: 1-1 GS: 0-0 **Gd: 1-2** GF: 0-0 Fm: 0-0
Distance: 5f/6f: 0-0 7f-8f: 1-2 9f-13f: 1-1 14f+: 0-0
Track : LH: 2-2 RH: 0-1 **Tight: 1-1** Gall: 0-1
Aids: Bl: 0-0 Vi: 0-0 Tstrap: 0-0 Ckp: 0-0

Best Rating: **117** 11/09 StCl 1m2f heavy

260,000gns two-year-old with a decent US pedigree; scored on debut over 1m on good/easy ground.

Passion Overflow (USA)

(98) (72)

2-y-o b f Hennessy (USA)-Polar Bird (Thatching)

J Noseda D Brennan

Placings:21 **(7736)**

2009: 6^{2}SD, 6^{1}SD,

	Starts	1st	2nd	3rd	Win & Pl
Career Total (Turf)	0	0	0	0	
Career Total (AW)	2	1	1	0	4202

67 12/09 Kemp 6f STD £3238

Total win prize-money £3238

Going (Turf): **Sf: 0-0 GS: 0-0 Gd: 0-0 GF: 0-0 Fm: 0-0**
Distance: **5f/6f: 1-2** 7f-8f: 0-0 9f-13f: 0-0 14f+: 0-0
Track : LH: 0-1 **RH: 1-1** Tight: 0-1 Gall: 0-0
Aids: Bl: 0-0 Vi: 0-0 Tstrap: 0-0 Ckp: 0-0
Best Rating: **72** 11/09 Ling 6f stand

Fair; suited by 6f and acts on Polytrack.

Passionate Cry (USA)

72(88) (52)**25**

2-y-o b/br c Street Cry (IRE)-Virtus (USA) (Silver Charm (USA))

W J Knight Bluehills Racing Limited

Placings:005 **(7050)**

2009: 7^{0}SD, 8^{0}G, 7^{5}SD,

	Starts	1st	2nd	3rd	Win & Pl
Career Total (Turf)	1	0	0	0	
Career Total (AW)	2	0	0	0	0

Going (Turf): **Sf: 0-0 GS: 0-0 Gd: 0-1 GF: 0-0 Fm: 0-0**
Distance: 5f/6f: 0-0 7f-8f: 0-3 9f-13f: 0-0 14f+: 0-0
Track : LH: 0-0 RH: 0-2 Tight: 0-0 Gall: 0-0
Aids: Bl: 0-0 Vi: 0-0 Tstrap: 0-0 Ckp: 0-0
Best Rating: **52** 10/09 Kemp 7f stand

Passkey

98(100) (80)**76**

3-y-o b f Medicean-Revival (Sadler's Wells (USA))

Sir Mark Prescott Cheveley Park Stud

Placings:32230 **(7730)**

2009: 8^{3}G, 7^{2}SD, 9^{2}G, 8^{3}SD, 7^{0}SD,

	Starts	1st	2nd	3rd	Win & Pl
Career Total (Turf)	2	0	1	1	1252
Career Total (AW)	3	0	1	1	1445

Going (Turf): **Sf: 0-0 GS: 0-0 Gd: 0-2 GF: 0-0 Fm: 0-0**
Distance: 5f/6f: 0-0 7f-8f: 0-3 9f-13f: 0-2 14f+: 0-0
Track : LH: 0-3 RH: 0-2 Tight: 0-4 Gall: 0-0
Aids: Bl: 0-1 Vi: 0-0 Tstrap: 0-0 Ckp: 0-0
Best Rating: **80** 8/09 Ling 7f stand

Fair; stays 1m; acts on good ground and on Polytrack.

Pasta Prayer

(96) (60)**55**

4-y-o br g Bertolini (USA)-Benedicite (Lomond (USA))

D E Cantillon Don Cantillon

Placings:0/05003200-0P **(1889)**

2009: 6^{0}SD, 7^{P}GF,

	Starts	1st	2nd	3rd	Win & Pl
Career Total (Turf)	4	0	0	1	302
Career Total (AW)	7	0	1	0	771

Going (Turf): **Sf: 0-0 GS: 0-1 Gd: 0-1 GF: 0-2 Fm: 0-0**
Distance: 5f/6f: 0-6 7f-8f: 0-5 9f-13f: 0-0 14f+: 0-0
Track : LH: 0-6 RH: 0-2 Tight: 0-5 Gall: 0-2
Aids: Bl: 0-4 Vi: 0-1 Tstrap: 0-0 Ckp: 0-0
Best Rating: **60** 8/08 GrLe 6f stand

Pastel Blue (IRE)

91(92) (68)**62**

2-y-o b f Shamardal (USA)-Painted Moon (USA) (Gone West (USA))

M L W Bell Sheikh Marwan Al Maktoum

Placings:4553 **(5369)**

2009: 6^{4}GF, 6^{5}SD, 6^{5}SD, 7^{3}SD,

	Starts	1st	2nd	3rd	Win & Pl
Career Total (Turf)	1	0	0	0	265
Career Total (AW)	3	0	0	1	403

Going (Turf): **Sf: 0-0 GS: 0-0 Gd: 0-0 GF: 0-1 Fm: 0-0**
Distance: 5f/6f: 0-3 7f-8f: 0-1 9f-13f: 0-0 14f+: 0-0
Track : LH: 0-2 RH: 0-1 Tight: 0-2 Gall: 0-0
Aids: Bl: 0-0 Vi: 0-0 Tstrap: 0-0 Ckp: 0-0
Best Rating: **68** 8/09 Ling 7f stand

Pastello

95(87) (59)**72**

2-y-o ch f Exceed And Excel (AUS)-Pastel (Lion Cavern (USA))

R Hannon Longview Stud & Bloodstock Ltd

Placings:02256000 **(7551)**

2009: 7^{0}S, 6^{2}F, 8^{2}GF, 8^{5}GF, 7^{6}GF, 8^{0}S, 8^{0}SD, 7^{0}SD,

	Starts	1st	2nd	3rd	Win & Pl
Career Total (Turf)	6	0	2	0	2740
Career Total (AW)	2	0	0	0	

Going (Turf): **Sf: 0-2 GS: 0-0 Gd: 0-0 GF: 0-3 Fm: 0-1**
Distance: 5f/6f: 0-0 7f-8f: 0-5 9f-13f: 0-3 14f+: 0-0
Track : LH: 0-4 RH: 0-1 Tight: 0-2 Gall: 0-0
Aids: Bl: 0-0 Vi: 0-0 Tstrap: 0-0 Ckp: 0-0
Best Rating: **72** 9/09 Leic 1m60y gd-fm

Fair; effective over 1m; acts on fast ground.

Pastoral Player

103 **92**

2-y-o b g Pastoral Pursuits-Copy-Cat (Lion Cavern (USA))

H Morrison The Pursuits Partnership

Placings:100 **(7150)**

2009: 6^{1}GF, 7^{0}S, 6^{0}G,

	Starts	1st	2nd	3rd	Win & Pl
Career Total (Turf)	3	1	0	0	5505

92 9/09 Newb 6f8y G-F £5504

Total win prize-money £5505

Going (Turf): Sf: 0-1 GS: 0-0 Gd: 0-1 **GF: 1-1** Fm: 0-0
Distance: 5f/6f: 0-1 **7f-8f: 1-2** 9f-13f: 0-0 14f+: 0-0
Track : LH: 0-0 RH: 0-0 Tight: 0-0 Gall: 0-0
Aids: Bl: 0-0 Vi: 0-0 Tstrap: 0-0 Ckp: 0-0
Best Rating: **92** 9/09 Newb 6f8y gd-fm

Very useful; suited by 6f and fast ground.

Pat Seamur

83(91) (67)**62**

2-y-o b g Compton Place-Superlove (IRE) (Hector Protector (USA))

E A L Dunlop Findlay & Bloom

Placings:06042 **(6829)**

2009: 6^{0}GF, 6^{6}G, 6^{0}GS, 7^{4}SD, 7^{2}SF,

	Starts	1st	2nd	3rd	Win & Pl
Career Total (Turf)	3	0	0	0	0
Career Total (AW)	2	0	1	0	1132

Going (Turf): **Sf: 0-0 GS: 0-1 Gd: 0-1 GF: 0-1 Fm: 0-0**
Distance: 5f/6f: 0-2 7f-8f: 0-3 9f-13f: 0-0 14f+: 0-0
Track : LH: 0-2 RH: 0-0 Tight: 0-2 Gall: 0-0
Aids: Bl: 0-0 Vi: 0-0 Tstrap: 0-0 Ckp: 0-0
Best Rating: **67** 10/09 Wolv 7f32y std-fst

Modest; stays 7f; handles Polytrack.

Pat Will (IRE)

(87) (9)**51**

5-y-o b m Danetime (IRE)-Northern Tara (IRE) (Fayruz)

M R Hoad P J Sharp

Placings:004301006**/4002250600**00**/0** **(0946)**

2009: 6^{0}SD,

	Starts	1st	2nd	3rd	Win & Pl
Career Total (Turf)	16	1	2	1	4854
Career Total (AW)	6	0	0	0	0

56 7/06 Leic 5f2y GD £2590

Total win prize-money £2591

Going (Turf): Sf: 0-1 GS: 0-2 **Gd: 1-7** GF: 0-5 Fm: 0-1
Distance: **5f/6f: 1-19** 7f-8f: 0-3 9f-13f: 0-0 14f+: 0-0
Track : LH: 0-11 RH: 0-0 Tight: 0-8 Gall: 0-6
Aids: Bl: 0-6 Vi: 0-2 Tstrap: 0-0 Ckp: 0-0
Best Rating: **57** 6/06 Ches 5f16y good

Patachou

87(82) (43)**49**

2-y-o b f Domedriver (IRE)-Pat Or Else (Alzao (USA))

R J Smith (Rae Guest 31/7) Tattenham Racing

Placings:430 **(7064)**

2009: 6^{4}S, 7^{3}G, 8^{0}SD,

	Starts	1st	2nd	3rd	Win & Pl
Career Total (Turf)	2	0	0	1	838
Career Total (AW)	1	0	0	0	

Going (Turf): **Sf: 0-1 GS: 0-0 Gd: 0-1 GF: 0-0 Fm: 0-0**
Distance: 5f/6f: 0-1 7f-8f: 0-2 9f-13f: 0-0 14f+: 0-0
Track : LH: 0-2 RH: 0-0 Tight: 0-2 Gall: 0-0
Aids: Bl: 0-0 Vi: 0-0 Tstrap: 0-0 Ckp: 0-0
Best Rating: **49** 7/09 Thsk 7f good

Patavian (IRE)

84 **42**

5-y-o b g Titus Livius (FR)-Five Of Wands (Caerleon (USA))

B Storey John Wade

Placings:65/6104030/40 **(3233)**

2009: 11^{4}GF, 12^{0}GF,

	Starts	1st	2nd	3rd	Win & Pl
Career Total (Turf)	11	1	0	1	3566

59	5/07	Haml	1m3f16y	G-F	£2730

Total win prize-money £2730

Going (Turf): Sf: 0-2 GS: 0-1 Gd: 0-4 **GF: 1-4** Fm: 0-0
Distance: 5f/6f: 0-0 7f-8f: 0-1 **9f-13f: 1-10** 14f+: 0-0
Track : LH: 0-0 **RH: 1-9 Tight: 1-9** Gall: 0-0
Aids: Bl: 0-1 Vi: 0-0 Tstrap: 0-5 Ckp: 0-5
Best Rating: **68** 8/06 Newb 7f gd-sft

Fair performer; stays 1m3f; acts on good to soft and firm ground.

Patavium (IRE)

105 (55)**66**

6-y-o b g Titus Livius (FR)-Arcevia (IRE) (Archway (IRE))
E W Tuer J A Nixon

Placings:2030/506504/3335030/P4151432 **(6769)**
2009: 14^{P}GF, 16^{4}G, 11^{1}S, 14^{5}GF, 9^{1}GF, 12^{4}G, 11^{3}G, 12^{2}GS,

	Starts	1st	2nd	3rd	Win & Pl
Career Total (Turf)	24	2	2	6	9984
Career Total (AW)	1	0	0	0	0

66	8/09	Bevl	1m1f207y (0-65)H	G-F	£2266
53	7/09	Catt	1m3f214y (0-65)H	SFT	£2729

Total win prize-money £4997

Going (Turf): **Sf: 1-4** GS: 0-2 Gd: 0-8 **GF: 1-10** Fm: 0-0
Distance: 5f/6f: 0-0 7f-8f: 0-4 **9f-13f: 2-13** 14f+: 0-8
Track : LH: 1-13 RH: 1-9 **Tight: 1-15** Gall: 0-3
Aids: Bl: 0-0 Vi: 0-0 Tstrap: 0-0 Ckp: 0-0
Best Rating: **72** 8/05 Yarm 1m3y gd-fm

Moderate; stays 1m4f; acts on easy and fast ground.

Patavium Prince (IRE)

103(101) (64)**81**

6-y-o ch g Titus Livius (FR)-Hoyland Common (IRE) (Common Grounds)
Miss Jo Crowley Mrs Liz Nelson

Placings:400/444013324454244250045 0/00000/2365302 21121000-3420212450 **(6964)**
2009: 7^{3}SD, 6^{4}SD, 6^{2}SD, 6^{0}G, 6^{2}G, 6^{1}GF, 6^{2}GF, 5^{4}GS, 6^{5}F, 5^{0}G,

	Starts	1st	2nd	3rd	Win & Pl
Career Total (Turf)	37	5	8	2	26980
Career Total (AW)	18	0	2	3	2959

81	6/09	Brig	6f209y	(0-75)H	G-F	£3280
81	8/08	Ling	6f	(0-70)H	G-S	£2590
73	7/08	Ling	6f	(0-65)H	G-F	£2047
67	7/08	Brig	6f209y	(0-75)H	FRM	£2775
71	5/06	Sals	6f	(0-70)H	G-S	£3562

Total win prize-money £14255

Going (Turf): Sf: 0-3 **GS: 2-7** Gd: 0-7 **GF: 2-17** Fm: 1-3
Distance: **5f/6f: 3-31** 7f-8f: 2-22 9f-13f: 0-2 14f+: 0-0
Track : **LH: 2-21** RH: 0-8 Tight: 0-13 Gall: 0-6
Aids: Bl: 0-0 Vi: 0-1 Tstrap: 0-0 Ckp: 0-0
Best Rating: **81** 6/09 Brig 6f209y gd-fm

Moderate; suited by 6f; acts on fast and easy ground; goes on Polytrack.

Patch Patch

87 **71**

2-y-o b g Avonbridge-Sandgate Cygnet (Fleetwood (IRE))
M Dods J M & Mrs E E Ranson

Placings:210 **(4875)**
2009: 6^{2}GF, 6^{1}C, 5^{0}C,

	Starts	1st	2nd	3rd	Win & Pl
Career Total (Turf)	3	1	1	0	3396

71	7/09	Carl	5f	GD	£2590

Total win prize-money £2590

Going (Turf): Sf: 0-0 GS: 0-0 **Gd: 1-2** GF: 0-1 Fm: 0-0
Distance: **5f/6f: 1-3** 7f-8f: 0-0 9f-13f: 0-0 14f+: 0-0
Track : LH: 0-0 **RH: 1-1** Tight: 0-0 **Gall: 1-1**
Aids: Bl: 0-0 Vi: 0-0 Tstrap: 0-0 Ckp: 0-0
Best Rating: **71** 7/09 Carl 5f good

Moderate; effective over 5f and should stay 6f; acts on fast ground; may do better.

Path Of Peace

86 **44**

2-y-o b f Rock Of Gibraltar (IRE)-Persian Song (Persian Bold)
J D Bethell Mrs R D Peacock

Placings:60 **(6990)**
2009: 6^{6}GF, 7^{0}G,

	Starts	1st	2nd	3rd	Win & Pl
Career Total (Turf)	2	0	0	0	0

Going (Turf): **Sf: 0-0 GS: 0-0 Gd: 0-1 GF: 0-1 Fm: 0-0**
Distance: 5f/6f: 0-1 7f-8f: 0-1 9f-13f: 0-0 14f+: 0-0
Track : LH: 0-0 RH: 0-0 Tight: 0-0 Gall: 0-0
Aids: Bl: 0-0 Vi: 0-0 Tstrap: 0-0 Ckp: 0-0
Best Rating: **44** 10/09 Donc 7f good

Path To Glory

(50)**33**

5-y-o b g Makbul-Just Glory (Glory Of Dancer)
Miss Z C Davison Shovelstrode Racing Club

Placings:550035/60200500/0-R **(3104)**
2009: 8^{R}G,

	Starts	1st	2nd	3rd	Win & Pl
Career Total (Turf)	9	0	1	0	1243
Career Total (AW)	7	0	0	1	353

Going (Turf): **Sf: 0-2 GS: 0-3 Gd: 0-3 GF: 0-0 Fm: 0-1**
Distance: 5f/6f: 0-6 7f-8f: 0-4 9f-13f: 0-6 14f+: 0-0
Track : LH: 0-4 RH: 0-10 Tight: 0-2 Gall: 0-1
Aids: Bl: 0-1 Vi: 0-0 Tstrap: 0-2 Ckp: 0-2
Best Rating: **58** 7/07 Nott 1m1f213y soft

Pathway To Heaven (IRE)

65 **47**

2-y-o ch f Indian Haven-Beckerson (IRE) (Alzao (USA))
J J Quinn Mrs D M Solomon

Placings:0 **(6762)**
2009: 8^{0}GS,

	Starts	1st	2nd	3rd	Win & Pl
Career Total (Turf)	1	0	0	0	

Going (Turf): **Sf: 0-0 GS: 0-1 Gd: 0-0 GF: 0-0 Fm: 0-0**
Distance: 5f/6f: 0-0 7f-8f: 0-1 9f-13f: 0-0 14f+: 0-0
Track : LH: 0-1 RH: 0-0 Tight: 0-0 Gall: 0-1
Aids: Bl: 0-0 Vi: 0-0 Tstrap: 0-0 Ckp: 0-0
Best Rating: **47** 10/09 Newc 1m gd-sft

Patience Rewarded

(74) (23)

3-y-o ch f Dr Fong (USA)-Breathing Space (USA) (Expelled (USA))
J S Moore Miss A Jones

Placings:00 **(0345)**
2009: 7^{0}SD, 7^{0}SD,

	Starts	1st	2nd	3rd	Win & Pl
Career Total (Turf)	0	0	0	0	
Career Total (AW)	2	0	0	0	

Going (Turf): **Sf: 0-0 GS: 0-0 Gd: 0-0 GF: 0-0 Fm: 0-0**
Distance: 5f/6f: 0-0 7f-8f: 0-2 9f-13f: 0-0 14f+: 0-0
Track : LH: 0-1 RH: 0-1 Tight: 0-1 Gall: 0-0
Aids: Bl: 0-0 Vi: 0-0 Tstrap: 0-0 Ckp: 0-0
Best Rating: **23** 1/09 Kemp 7f stand

Patkai (IRE)

116 **121**

4-y-o ch c Indian Ridge-Olympienne (IRE) (Sadler's Wells (USA))
Sir Michael Stoute Ballymacoll Stud

Placings:61/32114-122 **(3048)**
2009: 16^{1}GF, 16^{2}G, 20^{2}GF,

	Starts	1st	2nd	3rd	Win & Pl
Career Total (Turf)	10	4	3	1	170718

116	4/09	Asct	2m	G-F	£36900
103	6/08	Asct	2m	FRM	£34062
108	5/08	Hayd	1m3f200y (0-100)H	G-F	£12462
73	10/07	Nott	1m54y	G-S	£2590

Total win prize-money £86016

Going (Turf): Sf: 0-0 GS: 1-3 Gd: 0-2 **GF: 2-4** Fm: 1-1
Distance: 5f/6f: 0-0 7f-8f: 0-0 9f-13f: 2-6 14f+: 2-4
Track : LH: 2-4 RH: 2-6 Tight: 0-2 **Gall: 2-4**
Aids: Bl: 0-0 Vi: 0-0 Tstrap: 0-0 Ckp: 0-0
Best Rating: **121** 6/09 Asct 2m4f gd-fm

Group class; winner of the 2008 Queen's Vase and runner-up in 2009 Gold Cup; stays 2m4f; acts on firm and easy ground.

Patrician's Glory (USA)

103 **103**

3-y-o b c Proud Citizen (USA)-Landholder (USA) (Dixieland Band (USA))
T P Tate Mrs Fitri Hay

Placings:136-2650 **(5200)**
2009: 8^{2}GF, 7^{6}GF, 7^{5}GF, 8^{0}GF,

	Starts	1st	2nd	3rd	Win & Pl
Career Total (Turf)	7	1	1	1	16593

78	7/08	Newb	7f	GD	£5342

Total win prize-money £5343

Going (Turf): Sf: 0-0 GS: 0-0 **Gd: 1-3** GF: 0-4 Fm: 0-0
Distance: 5f/6f: 0-0 **7f-8f: 1-7** 9f-13f: 0-0 14f+: 0-0
Track : LH: 0-1 RH: 0-2 Tight: 0-0 Gall: 0-2
Aids: Bl: 0-0 Vi: 0-0 Tstrap: 0-0 Ckp: 0-0
Best Rating: **103** 8/08 Sand 7f16y good

Smart; Group 3 placed; effective at 7f-1m; acts on good and faster ground.

Patricks Lodge

72 **39**

2-y-o ch g Redoubtable (USA)-Duxford Lodge (Dara Monarch)

J D Bethell Graham Scruton

Placings:00 (5466)

2009: 6^{0}GF, 8^{0}F,

	Starts	1st	2nd	3rd	Win & Pl
Career Total (Turf)	2	0	0	0	

Going (Turf): Sf: 0-0 GS: 0-0 Gd: 0-0 GF: 0-1 Fm: 0-1
Distance: 5f/6f: 0-1 7f-8f: 0-0 9f-13f: 0-1 14f+: 0-0
Track : LH: 0-0 RH: 0-1 Tight: 0-0 Gall: 0-0
Aids: Bl: 0-0 Vi: 0-0 Tstrap: 0-0 Ckp: 0-0
Best Rating: 39 8/09 Bevl 1m100y firm

Patriot Jack (IRE)

(68) (50)**56**

4-y-o b g Desert Prince (IRE)-Summer Crush (USA) (Summer Squall (USA))

T G McCourt T Manley

Placings:00/0064000-000 (7732)

2009: 16^{0}GF, 14^{0}Y, 12^{0}SD,

	Starts	1st	2nd	3rd	Win & Pl
Career Total (Turf)	9	0	0	0	256
Career Total (AW)	3	0	0	0	

Going (Turf): Sf: 0-0 GS: 0-0 Gd: 0-3 GF: 0-2 Fm: 0-0
Distance: 5f/6f: 0-1 7f-8f: 0-1 9f-13f: 0-7 14f+: 0-3
Track : LH: 0-6 RH: 0-6 Tight: 0-1 Gall: 0-0
Aids: Bl: 0-1 Vi: 0-1 Tstrap: 0-0 Ckp: 0-0
Best Rating: 56 6/08 Fair 1m4f good

Patronne

(94) (56)

3-y-o b f Domedriver (IRE)-Pat Or Else (Alzao (USA))

Miss A Stokell (Sir Mark Prescott 1/2) Ms Caron Stokell

Placings:0-610 (0620)

2009: 8^{6}SD, 8^{1}SD, 8^{0}SD,

	Starts	1st	2nd	3rd	Win & Pl
Career Total (Turf)	0	0	0	0	
Career Total (AW)	4	1	0	0	2047
56 2/09 Sthl	1m		STD	£2047	

Total win prize-money £2047

Going (Turf): Sf: 0-0 GS: 0-0 Gd: 0-0 GF: 0-0 Fm: 0-0
Distance: 5f/6f: 0-1 **7f-8f: 1-2** 9f-13f: 0-1 14f+: 0-0
Track : **LH: 1-4** RH: 0-0 Tight: 0-2 Gall: 0-0
Aids: Bl: 0-0 Vi: 0-0 Tstrap: 0-0 Ckp: 0-0
Best Rating: 56 2/09 Sthl 1m stand

Moderate; stays 1m; acts on Fibresand.

Patteresa Girl

91(84) (46)**69**

2-y-o b f Auction House (USA)-Ellway Queen (USA) (Bahri (USA))

Mrs L Stubbs Cos We Can Partnership

Placings:0100 (3086)

2009: 5^{0}SD, 5^{1}GF, 5^{0}GF, 6^{0}GF,

	Starts	1st	2nd	3rd	Win & Pl
Career Total (Turf)	3	1	0	0	3886
Career Total (AW)	1	0	0	0	
69 4/09 Donc	5f		G-F	£3885	

Total win prize-money £3886

Going (Turf): Sf: 0-0 GS: 0-0 Gd: 0-0 **GF: 1-3** Fm: 0-0
Distance: **5f/6f: 1-4** 7f-8f: 0-0 9f-13f: 0-0 14f+: 0-0
Track : LH: 0-1 RH: 0-0 Tight: 0-1 Gall: 0-0
Aids: Bl: 0-0 Vi: 0-0 Tstrap: 0-0 Ckp: 0-0
Best Rating: 69 4/09 Donc 5f gd-fm

Modest winner over 5f on fast ground.

Pattern Mark

102 **54**

3-y-o b g Mark Of Esteem (IRE)-Latch Key Lady (USA) (Tejano (USA))

Ollie Pears David Scott and Co (Pattern Makers) Ltd

Placings:000-03660 (5442)

2009: 8^{0}F, 10^{3}G, 12^{6}GF, 14^{6}G, 14^{0}GF,

	Starts	1st	2nd	3rd	Win & Pl
Career Total (Turf)	8	0	0	1	302

Going (Turf): Sf: 0-1 GS: 0-1 Gd: 0-3 GF: 0-2 Fm: 0-1
Distance: 5f/6f: 0-0 7f-8f: 0-3 9f-13f: 0-3 14f+: 0-2
Track : LH: 0-5 RH: 0-0 Tight: 0-2 Gall: 0-0
Aids: Bl: 0-0 Vi: 0-0 Tstrap: 0-0 Ckp: 0-0
Best Rating: 54 6/09 Rdcr 1m2f good

Modest; stays 1m2f; capable of better.

Paul's Pet

91(90) (44)**58**

4-y-o b g Tobougg (IRE)-Cape Siren (Warning)

Karen George Mrs Isabel Fraser

Placings:000030000 (6255)

2009: 7^{0}SD, 7^{0}F, 8^{0}G, 10^{0}GS, 8^{3}GF, 8^{0}SD, 9^{0}GF, 9^{0}SD, 7^{0}SD,

	Starts	1st	2nd	3rd	Win & Pl
Career Total (Turf)	5	0	0	1	403
Career Total (AW)	4	0	0	0	

Going (Turf): Sf: 0-0 GS: 0-1 Gd: 0-1 GF: 0-2 Fm: 0-1
Distance: 5f/6f: 0-0 7f-8f: 0-4 9f-13f: 0-5 14f+: 0-0
Track : LH: 0-5 RH: 0-3 Tight: 0-5 Gall: 0-0
Aids: Bl: 0-0 Vi: 0-0 Tstrap: 0-0 Ckp: 0-0
Best Rating: 58 6/09 Wind 1m67y gd-fm

Pavement Games

92 **47**

2-y-o b f Mind Games-Pavement Gates (Bishop Of Cashel)

R C Guest S Hussey

Placings:505005 (7242)

2009: 5^{5}G, 6^{0}S, 6^{5}S, 6^{0}G, 6^{0}S, 5^{5}S,

	Starts	1st	2nd	3rd	Win & Pl
Career Total (Turf)	6	0	0	0	0

Going (Turf): Sf: 0-4 GS: 0-0 Gd: 0-2 GF: 0-0 Fm: 0-0
Distance: 5f/6f: 0-4 7f-8f: 0-2 9f-13f: 0-0 14f+: 0-0
Track : LH: 0-0 RH: 0-1 Tight: 0-0 Gall: 0-0
Aids: Bl: 0-0 Vi: 0-0 Tstrap: 0-0 Ckp: 0-0
Best Rating: 47 9/09 Thsk 6f soft

Promise at 6f on good and soft ground.

Pavershooz

109 **101**

4-y-o b g Bahamian Bounty-Stormswept (USA) (Storm Bird (CAN))

N Wilson Mrs Michael John Paver

Placings:54/52113503-200112100 (6843)

2009: 6^{2}GF, 6^{0}S, 6^{0}GF, 5^{1}G, 5^{1}G, 6^{2}GF, 5^{1}G, 5^{0}GF, 5^{0}G,

	Starts	1st	2nd	3rd	Win & Pl
Career Total (Turf)	19	5	3	2	79595
101 7/09 Ayr	5f	H	GD	£25904	
94 6/09 Newc	5f	(0-105)H	GD	£12462	
91 6/09 Muss	5f	(0-105)H	GD	£24924	
85 7/08 Catt	5f212y	(0-75)H	GD	£2590	
76 6/08 Ayr	6f	(0-80)H	G-F	£5828	

Total win prize-money £71708

Going (Turf): Sf: 0-2 GS: 0-1 **Gd: 4-8** GF: 1-8 Fm: 0-0
Distance: **5f/6f: 5-17** 7f-8f: 0-2 9f-13f: 0-0 14f+: 0-0
Track : **LH: 1-2** RH: 0-0 **Tight: 1-1** Gall: 0-0
Aids: Bl: 0-0 Vi: 0-0 Tstrap: 0-0 Ckp: 0-0
Best Rating: 101 7/09 Ayr 5f good

Very useful; effective from 5f-7f; acts on good and faster ground; has worn a tongue tie.

Pawan (IRE)

103(109) (99)**97**

9-y-o ch g Cadeaux Genereux-Born To Glamour (Ajdal (USA))

Miss A Stokell Ms Caron Stokell

Placings:4/202/52203530201663010500000010010/3653 2210505020000352044445/44455600500460252450150540 033/50365000523020233/0244202130225004526455034-1604020604552500500035 (7866)

2009: 5^{1}SS, 5^{6}SD, 5^{0}SD, 5^{4}SD, 5^{0}SD, 5^{2}GF, 5^{0}G, 6^{6}GF, 6^{0}G, 5^{4}SD, 5^{5}GS, 6^{5}G, 5^{2}GF, 5^{5}SD, 6^{0}SD, 7^{0}GS, 5^{5}SD, 8^{0}S, 6^{0}SD, 5^{0}SD, 5^{3}SD, 5^{5}SS,

	Starts	1st	2nd	3rd	Win & Pl
Career Total (Turf)	79	4	16	5	81511
Career Total (AW)	73	4	6	10	46572
99 1/09 Sthl	5f	H	SS	£11656	
95 7/08 Wwck	6f	(0-95)H	GD	£7771	
83 8/06 Bevl	5f	(0-85)H	GD	£7772	
77 2/05 Sthl	7f	(0-70)H	STD	£3396	
65 12/04 Ling	6f	(0-62)H	STD	£2927	
51 12/04 Sthl	6f	(0-45)	STD	£1477	
72 7/04 Rdcr	1m1f	E(0-70)	SFT	£3503	
72 6/04 Wwck	7f26y	D(0-80)	FRM	£5616	

Total win prize-money £44120

Going (Turf): Sf: 1-17 GS: 0-10 **Gd: 2-21** GF: 0-22 Fm: 1-9
Distance: **5f/6f: 5-98** 7f-8f: 2-42 9f-13f: 1-12 14f+: 0-0
Track : **LH: 6-66** RH: 0-8 **Tight: 2-33** Gall: 0-3
Aids: **Bl: 3-76** Vi: 0-0 Tstrap: 1-11 Ckp: 1-11
Best Rating: 104 9/06 Haml 6f5y gd-sft

Useful; effective over 5f-7f; acts on most types of ground and on sand; usually wears blinkers.

Paydaar

90 **72**

2-y-o ch c Sulamani (IRE)-Eternal Reve (USA) (Diesis)

B J Meehan (David Marnane 31/7) Habib Kozehli

Placings:004250 (6930)

2009: 6^{0}G, 6^{0}GF, 6^{4}G, 8^{2}YS, 7^{5}S, 8^{0}G,

	Starts	1st	2nd	3rd	Win & Pl
Career Total (Turf)	6	0	1	0	2335

Going (Turf): Sf: 0-1 GS: 0-0 Gd: 0-3 GF: 0-1 Fm: 0-0

Distance: 5f/6f: 0-3 7f-8f: 0-1 9f-13f: 0-2 14f+: 0-0
Track : LH: 0-3 RH: 0-3 Tight: 0-1 Gall: 0-0
Aids: Bl: 0-0 Vi: 0-0 Tstrap: 0-0 Ckp: 0-0
Best Rating: 72 7/09 Klny 1m100y yld-sft

Paymaster In Chief

92(93) (46)62
3-y-o b g Minardi (USA)-Allegedly (IRE) (Alhaarth (IRE))
M D I Usher The Goodracing Partnership

Placings:00634400-6653640043 (4065)
2009: 6^{6}SD, 7^{6}SD, 8^{5}SD, 7^{3}G, 10^{6}GF, 7^{4}SD, 8^{0}F, 8^{0}G, 11^{4}G, 10^{3}HY,

	Starts	1st	2nd	3rd	Win & Pl
Career Total (Turf)	14	0	0	3	1808
Career Total (AW)	5	0	0	0	0

Going (Turf): Sf: 0-4 GS: 0-2 Gd: 0-5 GF: 0-2 Fm: 0-1
Distance: 5f/6f: 0-5 7f-8f: 0-9 9f-13f: 0-5 14f+: 0-0
Track : LH: 0-7 RH: 0-4 Tight: 0-5 Gall: 0-1
Aids: Bl: 0-0 Vi: 0-4 Tstrap: 0-1 Ckp: 0-1
Best Rating: 62 7/08 Leic 5f218y good

Modest; effective over 1m2f-1m4f; acts on good or softer ground; has worn a visor and cheekpieces.

Peace And Glory (IRE)

26
2-y-o b f Antonius Pius (USA)-Rosy Lydgate (Last Tycoon)
J W Unett N B F Hubbard

Placings:0 (5852)
2009: 7^{0}GF,

	Starts	1st	2nd	3rd	Win & Pl
Career Total (Turf)	1	0	0	0	

Going (Turf): Sf: 0-0 GS: 0-0 Gd: 0-0 GF: 0-1 Fm: 0-0
Distance: 5f/6f: 0-0 7f-8f: 0-1 9f-13f: 0-0 14f+: 0-0
Track : LH: 0-1 RH: 0-0 Tight: 0-1 Gall: 0-0
Aids: Bl: 0-0 Vi: 0-0 Tstrap: 0-0 Ckp: 0-0

Peace Concluded

98(97) (65)68
3-y-o b f Bertolini (USA)-Effie (Royal Academy (USA))
B R Millman T E Pocock

Placings:025-004500 (5602)
2009: 9^{0}SD, 9^{0}GF, 6^{4}GF, 8^{5}SD, 8^{0}GF, 8^{0}GS,

	Starts	1st	2nd	3rd	Win & Pl
Career Total (Turf)	7	0	1	0	1300
Career Total (AW)	2	0	0	0	0

Going (Turf): Sf: 0-1 GS: 0-1 Gd: 0-1 GF: 0-4 Fm: 0-0
Distance: 5f/6f: 0-0 7f-8f: 0-7 9f-13f: 0-2 14f+: 0-0
Track : LH: 0-3 RH: 0-1 Tight: 0-2 Gall: 0-0
Aids: Bl: 0-1 Vi: 0-0 Tstrap: 0-1 Ckp: 0-1
Best Rating: 68 7/08 Folk 7f soft

Modest; effective over 7f; acts on soft ground.

Peace Corps

92(86) (59)74
3-y-o ch g Medicean-Tromond (Lomond (USA))
J R Fanshawe Elite Racing Club

Placings:06402 (3279)
2009: 8^{0}SD, 8^{6}G, 8^{4}GS, 10^{0}G, 9^{2}GF,

	Starts	1st	2nd	3rd	Win & Pl
Career Total (Turf)	4	0	1	0	1204
Career Total (AW)	1	0	0	0	

Going (Turf): Sf: 0-0 GS: 0-1 Gd: 0-2 GF: 0-1 Fm: 0-0
Distance: 5f/6f: 0-0 7f-8f: 0-1 9f-13f: 0-4 14f+: 0-0
Track : LH: 0-2 RH: 0-3 Tight: 0-1 Gall: 0-0
Aids: Bl: 0-0 Vi: 0-1 Tstrap: 0-0 Ckp: 0-0
Best Rating: 74 6/09 Sals 1m1f198y gd-fm

Fair ability in maidens at up to 1m; handles fast and easy ground.

Peace In Paradise (IRE)

85(85) (39)21
3-y-o b f Dubai Destination (USA)-Paola Maria (Daylami (IRE))
J A R Toller M E Wates

Placings:00-060 (3233)
2009: 8^{0}SD, 12^{6}SD, 12^{0}GF,

	Starts	1st	2nd	3rd	Win & Pl
Career Total (Turf)	2	0	0	0	
Career Total (AW)	3	0	0	0	0

Going (Turf): Sf: 0-0 GS: 0-1 Gd: 0-0 GF: 0-1 Fm: 0-0
Distance: 5f/6f: 0-0 7f-8f: 0-3 9f-13f: 0-2 14f+: 0-0
Track : LH: 0-2 RH: 0-2 Tight: 0-2 Gall: 0-1
Aids: Bl: 0-1 Vi: 0-0 Tstrap: 0-0 Ckp: 0-0
Best Rating: 39 12/08 GrLe 1m stand

Peace Offering (IRE)

106(98) (107)113
9-y-o b g Victory Note (USA)-Amnesty Bay (Thatching)
D Nicholls Lady O'Reilly

Placings:011/0500640/030404005/650425220/**434**200201 46010210/21244320/611414-305362 (5546)
2009: 5^{3}SD, 5^{0}G, 5^{5}G, 5^{3}S, 6^{8}S, 5^{2}GF,

	Starts	1st	2nd	3rd	Win & Pl
Career Total (Turf)	61	9	10	3	256081
Career Total (AW)	4	0	0	2	4808

105	10/08	NmkR	5f		G-F	£24978
113	8/08	Nott	5f13y		SFT	£7477
95	7/08	NmkJ	5f		G-F	£8723
113	5/07	Lonc	5f		GD	£27027
111	10/06	Tipp	5f		HVY	£22448
108	8/06	Nott	5f13y		GD	£6232
106	6/06	Newc	5f	(0-105)H	G-F	£18696
109	10/02	Asct	5f	A	G-F	£23200
82	9/02	Sand	5f6y	D	GD	£5278

Total win prize-money £144060

Going (Turf): Sf: 2-11GS: 0-4 Gd: 3-11 **GF: 4-29** Fm: 0-1
Distance: **5f/6f: 9-59** 7f-8f: 0-6 9f-13f: 0-0 14f+: 0-0
Track : **LH: 1-11** RH: 0-2 Tight: 0-4 Gall: 0-0
Aids: Bl: 0-1 Vi: 0-0 Tstrap: 0-3 Ckp: 0-3
Best Rating: 115 9/07 Donc 5f gd-fm

Smart; winner in Listed and Group 3 company; seems best at 5f; acts on any ground; suited by forcing tactics.

Peaceful Rule (USA)

101 75
3-y-o b g Peace Rules (USA)-La Cat (USA) (Mr Greeley (USA))
D Nicholls Eamon Maher

Placings:2-0202200 (5520)
2009: 8^{0}G, 10^{2}GF, 12^{0}G, 8^{2}G, 7^{2}GF, 8^{0}G, 8^{0}G,

	Starts	1st	2nd	3rd	Win & Pl
Career Total (Turf)	8	0	4	0	4634

Going (Turf): Sf: 0-1 GS: 0-0 Gd: 0-5 GF: 0-2 Fm: 0-0
Distance: 5f/6f: 0-0 7f-8f: 0-4 9f-13f: 0-4 14f+: 0-0
Track : LH: 0-4 RH: 0-3 Tight: 0-6 Gall: 0-0
Aids: Bl: 0-0 Vi: 0-0 Tstrap: 0-0 Ckp: 0-0
Best Rating: 75 7/09 Bevl 1m100y good

Modest; effective over 7f-1m2f; acts on most ground.

Peaceful Soul (USA)

82 61
2-y-o b f Dynaformer (USA)-Serenity Jane (USA) (Affirmed (USA))
D R Lanigan Saif Ali & Saeed H Altayer

Placings:0 (7182)
2009: 7^{0}G,

	Starts	1st	2nd	3rd	Win & Pl
Career Total (Turf)	1	0	0	0	

Going (Turf): Sf: 0-0 GS: 0-0 Gd: 0-1 GF: 0-0 Fm: 0-0
Distance: 5f/6f: 0-0 7f-8f: 0-1 9f-13f: 0-0 14f+: 0-0
Track : LH: 0-0 RH: 0-0 Tight: 0-0 Gall: 0-0
Aids: Bl: 0-0 Vi: 0-0 Tstrap: 0-0 Ckp: 0-0
Best Rating: 61 10/09 NmkR 7f good

Peachey Moment (USA)

(72) (20)
4-y-o b/br g Stormin Fever (USA)-Given Moment (USA) (Diesis)
H J Collingridge Tapas Partnership

Placings:0 (6880)
2009: 7^{0}SD,

	Starts	1st	2nd	3rd	Win & Pl
Career Total (Turf)	0	0	0	0	
Career Total (AW)	1	0	0	0	

Going (Turf): Sf: 0-0 GS: 0-0 Gd: 0-0 GF: 0-0 Fm: 0-0
Distance: 5f/6f: 0-0 7f-8f: 0-1 9f-13f: 0-0 14f+: 0-0
Track : LH: 0-1 RH: 0-0 Tight: 0-0 Gall: 0-0
Aids: Bl: 0-0 Vi: 0-0 Tstrap: 0-0 Ckp: 0-0
Best Rating: 20 10/09 Sthl 7f stand

Peak (IRE)

93(81) (41)56
3-y-o b c Exceed And Excel (AUS)-Glympse (IRE) (Spectrum (IRE))
H Morrison Bob Tullett & Michael Kerr-Dineen

Placings:0-05050 (3383)
2009: 7^{0}SD, 7^{5}GF, 8^{0}G, 9^{5}G, 12^{0}SD,

	Starts	1st	2nd	3rd	Win & Pl
Career Total (Turf)	3	0	0	0	94
Career Total (AW)	3	0	0	0	

Going (Turf): Sf: 0-0 GS: 0-0 Gd: 0-2 GF: 0-1 Fm: 0-0
Distance: 5f/6f: 0-0 7f-8f: 0-3 9f-13f: 0-3 14f+: 0-0
Track : LH: 0-4 RH: 0-0 Tight: 0-2 Gall: 0-1
Aids: Bl: 0-1 Vi: 0-0 Tstrap: 0-0 Ckp: 0-0
Best Rating: **56** 5/09 Ling 7f gd-fm

Peak District (IRE)

108(104) (97)**100**
5-y-o b g Danehill (USA)-Coralita (IRE) (Night Shift (USA))
K A Ryan (M W Easterby 27/4) Sunpak Potatoes

Placings:0001230/5404-**3221000000** **(7866)**
2009: 5^{3}SD, 5^{2}SD, 5^{2}GF, 5^{1}SD, 5^{0}G, 5^{0}GF, 5^{0}GF, 5^{0}GF, 5^{0}GF, 5^{0}SS,

	Starts	1st	2nd	3rd	Win & Pl
Career Total (Turf)	17	1	2	1	19755
Career Total (AW)	4	1	1	1	10506

97 6/09 Ling 5f (0-90)H STD £8418
83 5/07 Tipp 5f (60-90)H G-F £7003
Total win prize-money £15422

Going (Turf): Sf: 0-1 GS: 0-0 Gd: 0-4 **GF: 1-8** Fm: 0-1
Distance: **5f/6f: 2-20** 7f-8f: 0-1 9f-13f: 0-0 14f+: 0-0
Track : **LH: 2-8** RH: 0-0 **Tight: 1-2** Gall: 0-0
Aids: Bl: 0-0 Vi: 0-0 Tstrap: 0-0 Ckp: 0-0
Best Rating: **100** 5/09 York 5f gd-fm

Useful; effective over 5f-6f; acts on most ground on turf; goes on Polytrack; likes to race prominently.

Peal Park

95(86) (60)**38**
3-y-o b f Sulamani (IRE)-Cape Siren (Warning)
Karen George Mrs Isabel Fraser

Placings:05-505000 **(5750)**
2009: 8^{5}F, 8^{0}GF, 9^{5}GF, 8^{0}SD, 11^{0}G, 10^{0}SD,

	Starts	1st	2nd	3rd	Win & Pl
Career Total (Turf)	5	0	0	0	0
Career Total (AW)	3	0	0	0	0

Going (Turf): **Sf: 0-0 GS: 0-0 Gd: 0-1 GF: 0-3 Fm: 0-1**
Distance: 5f/6f: 0-0 7f-8f: 0-3 9f-13f: 0-5 14f+: 0-0
Track : LH: 0-6 RH: 0-0 Tight: 0-5 Gall: 0-1
Aids: Bl: 0-0 Vi: 0-0 Tstrap: 0-0 Ckp: 0-0
Best Rating: **60** 10/08 GrLe 1m stand

Peanut Girl (IRE)

96(92) (57)**56**
3-y-o b f Tillerman-Phintia (IRE) (Tagula (IRE))
B Palling Flying Eight Partnership

Placings:053230 **(2321)**
2009: 6^{0}SD, 5^{5}SD, 5^{3}GF, 7^{2}SD, 6^{3}GF, 6^{0}G,

	Starts	1st	2nd	3rd	Win & Pl
Career Total (Turf)	3	0	0	2	626
Career Total (AW)	3	0	1	0	605

Going (Turf): **Sf: 0-0 GS: 0-0 Gd: 0-1 GF: 0-2 Fm: 0-0**
Distance: 5f/6f: 0-3 7f-8f: 0-3 9f-13f: 0-0 14f+: 0-0
Track : LH: 0-3 RH: 0-0 Tight: 0-3 Gall: 0-0
Aids: Bl: 0-0 Vi: 0-0 Tstrap: 0-0 Ckp: 0-0

Best Rating: **57** 4/09 Wolv 7f32y stand

Moderate; stays 7f; acts on fast ground and Polytrack.

Pearl Dealer (IRE)

(104) (75)**69**
4-y-o b g Marju (IRE)-Anyaas (IRE) (Green Desert (USA))
R Lee (N J Vaughan 6/2) Mrs M A Boden

Placings:10/00604**504-05** **(0420)**
2009: 9^{0}SD, 8^{5}SD,

	Starts	1st	2nd	3rd	Win & Pl
Career Total (Turf)	6	0	0	0	322
Career Total (AW)	6	1	0	0	2969

75 9/07 Wolv 7f32y STD £2968
Total win prize-money £2969

Going (Turf): **Sf: 0-1 GS: 0-1 Gd: 0-3 GF: 0-1 Fm: 0-0**
Distance: 5f/6f: 0-3 **7f-8f: 1-6** 9f-13f: 0-3 14f+: 0-0
Track : **LH: 1-9** RH: 0-1 **Tight: 1-6** Gall: 0-0
Aids: Bl: 0-0 Vi: 0-0 Tstrap: 0-2 Ckp: 0-2
Best Rating: **75** 9/07 Wolv 7f32y stand

Fair; effective over 7f; acts on Polytrack.

Pearl Of Kent (IRE)

84 **50**
2-y-o ch f Pearl Of Love (IRE)-Kentmere (FR) (Galetto (FR))
P D Evans Bathwick Gold Partnership

Placings:040 **(7098)**
2009: 6^{0}G, 8^{4}G, 7^{0}G,

	Starts	1st	2nd	3rd	Win & Pl
Career Total (Turf)	3	0	0	0	241

Going (Turf): **Sf: 0-0 GS: 0-0 Gd: 0-3 GF: 0-0 Fm: 0-0**
Distance: 5f/6f: 0-0 7f-8f: 0-3 9f-13f: 0-0 14f+: 0-0
Track : LH: 0-1 RH: 0-0 Tight: 0-0 Gall: 0-1
Aids: Bl: 0-0 Vi: 0-0 Tstrap: 0-0 Ckp: 0-0
Best Rating: **50** 9/09 Ffos 1m good

Pearl Of Manacor (IRE)

77(99) (79)**76**
3-y-o b g Danehill Dancer (IRE)-Mountain Law (USA) (Mountain Cat (USA))
M R Channon Findlay Bloom & Channon

Placings:03-**13500** **(6695)**
2009: 5^{1}SD, 8^{3}SD, 8^{5}SD, 8^{0}GF, 8^{0}GS,

	Starts	1st	2nd	3rd	Win & Pl
Career Total (Turf)	4	0	0	1	867
Career Total (AW)	3	1	0	1	3433

78 1/09 Wolv 5f216y STD £2729
Total win prize-money £2730

Going (Turf): **Sf: 0-0 GS: 0-2 Gd: 0-1 GF: 0-1 Fm: 0-0**
Distance: **5f/6f: 1-1** 7f-8f: 0-5 9f-13f: 0-1 14f+: 0-0
Track : **LH: 1-1** RH: 0-3 **Tight: 1-1** Gall: 0-0
Aids: Bl: 0-0 Vi: 0-1 Tstrap: 0-0 Ckp: 0-0
Best Rating: **79** 3/09 Kemp 1m stand

Fair; effective over 6f-1m; acts on easy ground; goes on Polytrack.

Pearly Wey

105(101) (91)**104**
6-y-o b g Lujain (USA)-Dunkellin (USA) (Irish River (FR))
I W McInnes (C G Cox 3/10) I D Woolfitt

Placings:12200046/50103130/60160**6-0000565000** **(7702)**
2009: 6^{0}GF, 6^{0}GF, 6^{0}GF, 6^{0}GF, 6^{5}G, 6^{6}GF, 6^{5}GF, 7^{0}GF, 6^{0}SD, 6^{0}SD,

	Starts	1st	2nd	3rd	Win & Pl
Career Total (Turf)	29	4	2	2	67159
Career Total (AW)	3	0	0	0	468

104 8/08 Gdwd 6f H G-F £18693
100 8/07 Gdwd 6f H G-F £12464
95 6/07 Folk 6f (0-100)H GD £13710
86 4/06 NmkR 6f G-F £5181
Total win prize-money £50049

Going (Turf): Sf: 0-0 GS: 0-2 Gd: 1-7 **GF: 3-19** Fm: 0-1
Distance: **5f/6f: 4-26** 7f-8f: 0-6 9f-13f: 0-0 14f+: 0-0
Track : LH: 0-1 RH: 0-4 Tight: 0-1 Gall: 0-1
Aids: Bl: 0-0 Vi: 0-0 Tstrap: 0-0 Ckp: 0-0
Best Rating: **104** 8/08 Gdwd 6f gd-fm

Useful; effective over 6f and acts on good and faster ground; usually held up.

Peas 'n Beans (IRE)

(95) (49)**48**
6-y-o ch g Medicean-No Sugar Baby (FR) (Crystal Glitters (USA))
T Keddy Paddy Barrett

Placings:06**0**/036404620**2004/0000/**0065**000606-060** **(0385)**
2009: 16^{0}SD, 14^{6}SD, 12^{0}SD,

	Starts	1st	2nd	3rd	Win & Pl
Career Total (Turf)	15	0	1	1	1517
Career Total (AW)	18	0	1	0	806

Going (Turf): **Sf: 0-0 GS: 0-3 Gd: 0-6 GF: 0-5 Fm: 0-1**
Distance: 5f/6f: 0-0 7f-8f: 0-1 9f-13f: 0-17 14f+: 0-15
Track : LH: 0-25 RH: 0-7 Tight: 0-20 Gall: 0-5
Aids: Bl: 0-1 Vi: 0-0 Tstrap: 0-1 Ckp: 0-1
Best Rating: **64** 6/06 Yarm 1m3f101y gd-fm

Pebblesonthebeach

95 **67**
2-y-o b g Footstepsinthesand-Peep Show (In The Wings)
J W Hills Hammers & Woodies

Placings:6540 **(5715)**
2009: 6^{6}S, 7^{5}G, 6^{4}GF, 8^{0}G,

	Starts	1st	2nd	3rd	Win & Pl
Career Total (Turf)	4	0	0	0	216

Going (Turf): **Sf: 0-1 GS: 0-0 Gd: 0-2 GF: 0-1 Fm: 0-0**
Distance: 5f/6f: 0-0 7f-8f: 0-3 9f-13f: 0-1 14f+: 0-0
Track : LH: 0-1 RH: 0-1 Tight: 0-1 Gall: 0-0
Aids: Bl: 0-0 Vi: 0-0 Tstrap: 0-0 Ckp: 0-0
Best Rating: **67** 8/09 Sals 6f212y gd-fm

Peckforton Castle

(88) (50)
2-y-o b g Celtic Swing-Fleuve D'Or (IRE) (Last Tycoon)

Patrick Morris Chris Naylor

Placings:5 (7463)
2009: 7^{5}SD,

	Starts	1st	2nd	3rd	Win & Pl
Career Total (Turf)	0	0	0	0	
Career Total (AW)	1	0	0	0	0

Going (Turf): **Sf: 0-0 GS: 0-0 Gd: 0-0 GF: 0-0 Fm: 0-0**
Distance: 5f/6f: 0-0 7f-8f: 0-1 9f-13f: 0-0 14f+: 0-0
Track : LH: 0-1 RH: 0-0 Tight: 0-1 Gall: 0-0
Aids: Bl: 0-0 Vi: 0-0 Tstrap: 0-0 Ckp: 0-0
Best Rating: 50 11/09 Wolv 7f32y stand

Pedasus (USA)

91(94) (75)51
3-y-o b c Fusaichi Pegasus (USA)-Butterfly Cove (USA) (Storm Cat (USA))
T Keddy Andrew Duffield

Placings:2-000 (4930)
2009: 7^{0}SD, 7^{0}GF, 9^{0}G,

	Starts	1st	2nd	3rd	Win & Pl
Career Total (Turf)	2	0	0	0	
Career Total (AW)	2	0	1	0	1060

Going (Turf): **Sf: 0-0 GS: 0-0 Gd: 0-1 GF: 0-1 Fm: 0-0**
Distance: 5f/6f: 0-0 7f-8f: 0-3 9f-13f: 0-1 14f+: 0-0
Track : LH: 0-1 RH: 0-2 Tight: 0-1 Gall: 0-0
Aids: Bl: 0-0 Vi: 0-0 Tstrap: 0-0 Ckp: 0-0
Best Rating: 75 10/08 Ling 7f stand

Pedregal

101(94) (41)51
3-y-o b g Diktat-Bella Chica (IRE) (Bigstone (IRE))
J S Goldie (R A Fahey 1/5) Mrs Janis Macpherson

Placings:050-**0360**5364300 (4137)
2009: 5^{0}SD, 7^{3}SD, 7^{6}SD, 8^{0}SD, 5^{5}F, 5^{3}GF, 5^{6}GF, 6^{4}F, 5^{3}GF, 6^{0}G, 5^{0}G,

	Starts	1st	2nd	3rd	Win & Pl
Career Total (Turf)	10	0	0	2	828
Career Total (AW)	4	0	0	1	302

Going (Turf): **Sf: 0-0 GS: 0-0 Gd: 0-3 GF: 0-5 Fm: 0-2**
Distance: 5f/6f: 0-11 7f-8f: 0-3 9f-13f: 0-0 14f+: 0-0
Track : LH: 0-3 RH: 0-1 Tight: 0-2 Gall: 0-0
Aids: Bl: 0-0 Vi: 0-0 Tstrap: 0-0 Ckp: 0-0
Best Rating: 51 6/08 Rdcr 6f gd-fm

Plating-class; stays 7f; acts on Fibresand and fast ground.

Pegasus Again (USA)

107(106) (87)86
4-y-o b g Fusaichi Pegasus (USA)-Chit Chatter (USA) (Lost Soldier (USA))
T G Mills T G Mills

Placings:215/5600004-15222314021 (7883)
2009: 7^{1}SD, 7^{5}SD, 8^{2}SD, 8^{2}SD, 8^{2}SD, 8^{3}GF, 8^{1}GF, 7^{4}GF, 7^{0}G, 8^{2}SD, 8^{1}SD,

	Starts	1st	2nd	3rd	Win & Pl
Career Total (Turf)	10	1	1	1	19548
Career Total (AW)	11	3	4	0	16434

	12/09	Ling	1m	(0-85)H	STD	£4727
86	8/09	Wind	1m67y	(0-85)H	G-F	£5180
79	1/09	Ling	7f	(0-70)H	STD	£2900
79	8/07	Ling	1m		STD	£3141

Total win prize-money £15949

Going (Turf): Sf: 0-0 GS: 0-1 Gd: 0-4 **GF: 1-5** Fm: 0-0
Distance: 5f/6f: 0-0 **7f-8f: 3-15** 9f-13f: 1-6 14f+: 0-0
Track : **LH: 3-8** RH: 1-10 **Tight: 4-9** Gall: 0-1
Aids: Bl: 0-0 Vi: 0-0 Tstrap: 2-11 Ckp: 2-11
Best Rating: 95 6/07 Asct 7f good

Useful; stays 1m; acts on easy ground; goes on Polytrack; has worn cheekpieces.

Pegasus Dancer (FR)

88(105) (67)40
5-y-o b g Danehill Dancer (IRE)-Maruru (IRE) (Fairy King (USA))
R H York R H York

Placings:130/4563003030**321**/**3253041440-6**000 (2180)
2009: 5^{6}SD, 5^{0}SD, 5^{0}GF, 5^{0}G,

	Starts	1st	2nd	3rd	Win & Pl
Career Total (Turf)	16	1	0	4	9041
Career Total (AW)	14	2	2	3	7846

67	8/08	GrLe	5f		STD	£2590
74	12/07	Ling	5f	(0-70)H	STD	£2817
63	8/06	Pont	5f		GD	£5181

Total win prize-money £10589

Going (Turf): Sf: 0-2 GS: 0-0 **Gd: 1-6** GF: 0-7 Fm: 0-1
Distance: **5f/6f: 3-28** 7f-8f: 0-2 9f-13f: 0-0 14f+: 0-0
Track : **LH: 3-17** RH: 0-1 Tight: 1-10 Gall: 1-3
Aids: Bl: 0-4 Vi: 0-1 Tstrap: 2-15 Ckp: 2-15
Best Rating: 76 4/07 Thsk 5f firm

Modest sprinter; acts on fast ground; goes on Polytrack; has worn cheekpieces.

Pegasus Gold (USA)

80(92) (64)59
4-y-o ch g Fusaichi Pegasus (USA)-Little Treasure (FR) (Night Shift (USA))
W R Swinburn The Messengers

Placings:56 (2856)
2009: 7^{5}SD, 8^{6}G,

	Starts	1st	2nd	3rd	Win & Pl
Career Total (Turf)	1	0	0	0	0
Career Total (AW)	1	0	0	0	0

Going (Turf): **Sf: 0-0 GS: 0-0 Gd: 0-1 GF: 0-0 Fm: 0-0**
Distance: 5f/6f: 0-0 7f-8f: 0-1 9f-13f: 0-1 14f+: 0-0
Track : LH: 0-2 RH: 0-0 Tight: 0-1 Gall: 0-0
Aids: Bl: 0-0 Vi: 0-0 Tstrap: 0-0 Ckp: 0-0
Best Rating: 64 5/09 Ling 7f stand

Fair; caught eye on debut; should stay further than 7f; acts on Polytrack; sure to improve.

Pegasus Lad (USA)

98(103) (87)84
3-y-o b/br g Fusaichi Pegasus (USA)-Leo Girl (USA) (Seattle Slew (USA))
M Johnston A D Spence

Placings:30210-**23**0006023660 (6614)
2009: 8^{2}SD, 8^{3}SD, 8^{0}GS, 7^{0}G, 9^{0}G, 8^{6}GF, 9^{0}G, 8^{2}G, 8^{3}G, 8^{6}S, 8^{6}GF, 8^{0}SD,

	Starts	1st	2nd	3rd	Win & Pl
Career Total (Turf)	14	1	2	2	9468
Career Total (AW)	3	0	1	1	2177

84	7/08	Sand	7f16y	G-F	£5180

Total win prize-money £5181

Going (Turf): Sf: 0-1 GS: 0-2 Gd: 0-5 **GF: 1-6** Fm: 0-0
Distance: 5f/6f: 0-0 **7f-8f: 1-11** 9f-13f: 0-6 14f+: 0-0
Track : LH: 0-4 **RH: 1-9** Tight: 0-4 Gall: 0-1
Aids: Bl: 0-1 Vi: 0-0 Tstrap: 0-0 Ckp: 0-0
Best Rating: 87 4/09 Kemp 1m stand

Useful; effective at 7f-1m and acts on most ground; likes to race prominently.

Pegasus Prince (USA)

(108) (72)67
5-y-o b g Fusaichi Pegasus (USA)-Avian Eden (USA) (Storm Bird (CAN))
J Wade John Wade

Placings:06/03053/01101220-6 (7505)
2009: 12^{6}SD,

	Starts	1st	2nd	3rd	Win & Pl
Career Total (Turf)	9	0	2	1	2133
Career Total (AW)	7	3	0	1	6853

72	6/08	Sthl	1m4f	(0-60)H	STD	£1774
62	4/08	Sthl	1m3f	(0-60)H	STD	£2047
57	4/08	Sthl	1m3f	(0-52)H	STD	£2729

Total win prize-money £6551

Going (Turf): **Sf: 0-0 GS: 0-2 Gd: 0-2 GF: 0-4 Fm: 0-1**
Distance: 5f/6f: 0-1 7f-8f: 0-3 **9f-13f: 3-9** 14f+: 0-3
Track : **LH: 3-9** RH: 0-5 Tight: 0-8 Gall: 0-1
Aids: Bl: 0-0 Vi: 0-0 Tstrap: 0-0 Ckp: 0-0
Best Rating: 72 6/08 Sthl 1m4f stand

Modest; probably stays 2m but effective at shorter; acts on a sound surface and on sand.

Peintre D'Argent (IRE)

94(94) (59)60
3-y-o ch f Peintre Celebre (USA)-Petite-D-Argent (Noalto)
W J Knight (Tom Dascombe 29/10) The Pro-Claimers

Placings:003-355005 (7688)
2009: 10^{3}SD, 12^{5}GF, 12^{6}GF, 12^{0}SS, 9^{0}SD, 12^{5}SD,

	Starts	1st	2nd	3rd	Win & Pl
Career Total (Turf)	3	0	0	0	0
Career Total (AW)	6	0	0	2	756

Going (Turf): **Sf: 0-0 GS: 0-0 Gd: 0-1 GF: 0-2 Fm: 0-0**
Distance: 5f/6f: 0-0 7f-8f: 0-2 9f-13f: 0-7 14f+: 0-0
Track : LH: 0-7 RH: 0-2 Tight: 0-5 Gall: 0-2
Aids: Bl: 0-0 Vi: 0-0 Tstrap: 0-0 Ckp: 0-0
Best Rating: 60 5/09 Chep 1m4f23y gd-fm

Modest; stays 1m2f; handles Polytrack.

Pekan One

(90) (31)47
7-y-o ch g Grand Lodge (USA)-Ballet (Sharrood (USA))
John G Carr P J Lohan

Placings:0500/00/00600/04203000-0 (5885)
2009: 16^{0}SD,

	Starts	1st	2nd	3rd	Win & Pl
Career Total (Turf)	17	0	1	1	1840

Career Total (AW) 3 0 0 0

Going (Turf): Sf: 0-0 GS: 0-2 Gd: 0-7 GF: 0-2 Fm: 0-1
Distance: 5f/6f: 0-0 7f-8f: 0-0 9f-13f: 0-13 14f+: 0-7
Track : LH: 0-6 RH: 0-14 Tight: 0-2 Gall: 0-1
Aids: Bl: 0-8 Vi: 0-0 Tstrap: 0-2 Ckp: 0-2
Best Rating: 66 10/05 Nott 1m1f213y good

Pekan Star

87 63
2-y-o b c Montjeu (IRE)-Delicieuse Lady (Trempolino (USA))
M A Jarvis H R H Sultan Ahmad Shah

Placings:4 (5401)
2009: 7^{4}G,

	Starts	1st	2nd	3rd	Win & Pl
Career Total (Turf)	1	0	0	0	361

Going (Turf): Sf: 0-0 GS: 0-0 Gd: 0-1 GF: 0-0 Fm: 0-0
Distance: 5f/6f: 0-0 7f-8f: 0-1 9f-13f: 0-0 14f+: 0-0
Track : LH: 0-0 RH: 0-0 Tight: 0-0 Gall: 0-0
Aids: Bl: 0-0 Vi: 0-0 Tstrap: 0-0 Ckp: 0-0
Best Rating: 63 8/09 NmkJ 7f good

A half-brother to a French Derby winner Blue Canari and the smart Blue Ksar.

Pekan Three (IRE)

97 71
2-y-o b c Sadler's Wells (USA)-Frappe (IRE) (Inchinor)
P F I Cole H R H Sultan Ahmad Shah

Placings:6 (6810)
2009: 8^{6}G,

	Starts	1st	2nd	3rd	Win & Pl
Career Total (Turf)	1	0	0	0	0

Going (Turf): Sf: 0-0 GS: 0-0 Gd: 0-1 GF: 0-0 Fm: 0-0
Distance: 5f/6f: 0-0 7f-8f: 0-1 9f-13f: 0-0 14f+: 0-0
Track : LH: 0-0 RH: 0-0 Tight: 0-0 Gall: 0-0
Aids: Bl: 0-0 Vi: 0-0 Tstrap: 0-0 Ckp: 0-0
Best Rating: 71 10/09 NmkR 1m good

Peking Prince

107(90) (59)89
3-y-o b g Passing Glance-Brandon Princess (Waajib)
A M Balding Kingsclere Racing CLub

Placings:1-0451326 (4909)
2009: 7^{0}SD, 7^{4}GF, 8^{5}GF, 8^{1}GF, 8^{3}GF, 8^{2}G, 7^{6}G,

	Starts	1st	2nd	3rd	Win & Pl
Career Total (Turf)	7	2	1	1	16774
Career Total (AW)	1	0	0	0	

84	6/09	Newb	1m	(0-75)H	G-F	£3238
74	8/08	Bath	5f161y		G-S	£2590

Total win prize-money £5828

Going (Turf): Sf: 0-0 GS: 1-1 Gd: 0-2 GF: 1-4 Fm: 0-0
Distance: 5f/6f: 1-1 7f-8f: 1-6 9f-13f: 0-1 14f+: 0-0
Track : LH: 1-4 RH: 0-2 Tight: 0-1 Gall: 1-1
Aids: Bl: 0-0 Vi: 0-2 Tstrap: 0-0 Ckp: 0-0
Best Rating: 89 7/09 Asct 1m good

Useful; effective at 1m; acts on fast and easy ground; has worn a visor.

Pelham Crescent (IRE)

105(110) (70)85
6-y-o ch g Giant's Causeway (USA)-Sweet Times (Riverman (USA))
B Palling Wayne Devine

Placings:0421660026/600/40652031435135/365606300-4524221110355100 (6936)
2009: 9^{4}SD, 9^{5}SD, 9^{2}SD, 12^{4}SD, 12^{2}SD, 9^{2}SD, 10^{1}GF, 11^{1}GF, 10^{1}F, 10^{0}G, 10^{3}GF, 10^{5}G, 13^{5}SD, 12^{1}G, 9^{0}S, 11^{0}G,

	Starts	1st	2nd	3rd	Win & Pl
Career Total (Turf)	24	5	2	3	22596
Career Total (AW)	28	2	4	3	9409

85	9/09	Gdwd	1m4f	(0-80)H	GD	£4857
80	5/09	Bath	1m2f46y	(0-70)H	FRM	£2914
75	5/09	Bath	1m3f144y	(0-70)H	G-F	£2914
71	4/09	Bath	1m2f46y	(0-70)H	G-F	£2590
70	10/07	Wolv	1m141y	(0-60)H	STD	£2388
65	8/07	Wolv	1m1f103y	(0-60)H	STD	£2388
76	8/05	NmkJ	6f		G-S	£4793

Total win prize-money £22847

Going (Turf): Sf: 0-4 GS: 1-3 Gd: 1-10 GF: 2-6 Fm: 1-1
Distance: 5f/6f: 1-1 7f-8f: 0-13 9f-13f: 6-36 14f+: 0-2
Track : LH: 5-37 RH: 1-6 Tight: 6-37 Gall: 0-0
Aids: Bl: 0-5 Vi: 0-0 Tstrap: 0-5 Ckp: 0-5
Best Rating: 85 9/09 Gdwd 1m4f good

Fair; effective over 1m2f-1m4f; acts on fast and easy ground; goes on Polytrack.

Peligroso (FR)

108 107
3-y-o ch c Trempolino (USA)-Pitpit (IRE) (Rudimentary (USA))
Saeed Bin Suroor Godolphin

Placings:31-2631 (6644)
2009: 10^{2}G, 11^{6}G, 9^{3}GF, 10^{1}G,

	Starts	1st	2nd	3rd	Win & Pl
Career Total (Turf)	6	2	1	2	45028

103	10/09	York	1m2f88y	GD	£9714
107	11/08	Kref	1m110y	HVY	£22059

Total win prize-money £31773

Going (Turf): Sf: 1-1 GS: 0-1 Gd: 1-3 GF: 0-1 Fm: 0-0
Distance: 5f/6f: 0-0 7f-8f: 0-0 9f-13f: 2-6 14f+: 0-0
Track : LH: 1-3 RH: 1-3 Tight: 0-0 Gall: 1-2
Aids: Bl: 0-0 Vi: 0-0 Tstrap: 0-0 Ckp: 0-0
Best Rating: 107 11/08 Kref 1m110y heavy

Smart; effective over 1m2f; acts on good and soft ground.

Pellinore (USA)

83(81) (41)41
3-y-o b/br f Giant's Causeway (USA)-Glatisant (Rainbow Quest (USA))
E F Vaughan A E Oppenheimer

Placings:064 (5773)
2009: 8^{0}SD, 8^{6}G, 10^{4}GF,

	Starts	1st	2nd	3rd	Win & Pl
Career Total (Turf)	2	0	0	0	241
Career Total (AW)	1	0	0	0	

Going (Turf): Sf: 0-0 GS: 0-0 Gd: 0-1 GF: 0-1 Fm: 0-0
Distance: 5f/6f: 0-0 7f-8f: 0-1 9f-13f: 0-2 14f+: 0-0
Track : LH: 0-2 RH: 0-1 Tight: 0-2 Gall: 0-0
Aids: Bl: 0-0 Vi: 0-1 Tstrap: 0-0 Ckp: 0-0
Best Rating: 41 8/09 Sand 1m14y good

Plating-class; stays 1m2f; has worn a visor.

Pembo

(100) (52)52
4-y-o b g Choisir (AUS)-Focosa (ITY) (In The Wings)
S M Jacobs (R A Harris 22/2) S M Jacobs

Placings:00/16000-40505 (0608)
2009: 8^{4}SS, 12^{0}SD, 8^{5}SD, 9^{0}SD, 8^{5}SD,

	Starts	1st	2nd	3rd	Win & Pl
Career Total (Turf)	2	1	0	0	
Career Total (AW)	10	0	0	0	0

Going (Turf): Sf: 1-1 GS: 0-0 Gd: 0-0 GF: 0-1 Fm: 0-0
Distance: 5f/6f: 0-0 7f-8f: 0-7 9f-13f: 1-5 14f+: 0-0
Track : LH: 1-9 RH: 0-3 Tight: 1-4 Gall: 0-0
Aids: Bl: 0-1 Vi: 0-0 Tstrap: 0-1 Ckp: 0-1
Best Rating: 52 10/08 Kemp 1m stand

Pena Dorada (IRE)

92 72
2-y-o b c Key Of Luck (USA)-Uluwatu (IRE) (Unfuwain (USA))
A P Jarvis Mrs Elaine M Burke

Placings:525 (6533)
2009: 8^{5}G, 8^{2}G, 10^{5}GF,

	Starts	1st	2nd	3rd	Win & Pl
Career Total (Turf)	3	0	1	0	1156

Going (Turf): Sf: 0-0 GS: 0-0 Gd: 0-2 GF: 0-1 Fm: 0-0
Distance: 5f/6f: 0-0 7f-8f: 0-1 9f-13f: 0-2 14f+: 0-0
Track : LH: 0-2 RH: 0-1 Tight: 0-2 Gall: 0-0
Aids: Bl: 0-0 Vi: 0-0 Tstrap: 0-0 Ckp: 0-0
Best Rating: 72 9/09 Haml 1m65y good

Some promise in maidens at around 1m on good ground.

Penang Cinta

102(108) (68)72
6-y-o b g Halling (USA)-Penang Pearl (FR) (Bering)
P D Evans Trevor Gallienne

Placings:060/103025003/31521146020/044034332345-5635413501241106 (5594)
2009: 12^{5}SD, 9^{6}SD, 12^{3}SD, 9^{5}SD, 9^{4}GF, 12^{1}GF, 11^{3}G, 12^{5}GF, 12^{0}GF, 11^{1}GF, 11^{2}F, 10^{4}G, 11^{1}GF, 11^{1}GS, 12^{0}G, 10^{6}GS,

	Starts	1st	2nd	3rd	Win & Pl
Career Total (Turf)	31	5	4	5	21841
Career Total (AW)	20	3	1	4	9537

72	8/09	Brig	1m3f196y	(0-65)H	G-S	£2590
71	7/09	Brig	1m3f196y	(0-65)H	G-F	£2590
64	6/09	Brig	1m3f196y	(0-65)H	G-F	£2590
	5/09	Lanc	1m4f	H	G-F	£1680
80	5/07	Leic	1m3f183y	(0-70)H	G-F	£3886
71	4/07	Wolv	1m1f103y	(0-65)H	SF	£2388
64	2/07	Wolv	1m1f103y	(0-65)H	STD	£2388
57	1/06	Wolv	7f32y	(0-55)H	STD	£2388

Total win prize-money £20503

Going (Turf): Sf: 0-1 GS: 1-3 Gd: 0-8 GF: 4-16 Fm: 0-3
Distance: 5f/6f: 0-2 7f-8f: 1-4 9f-13f: 7-44 14f+: 0-1
Track : LH: 6-39 RH: 1-9 Tight: 3-31 Gall: 0-4
Aids: Bl: 0-1 Vi: 0-2 Tstrap: 0-14 Ckp: 0-14
Best Rating: 80 5/07 Leic 1m3f183y gd-fm

Moderate; stays 1m4f; acts on most ground and on Polytrack; has worn a visor and cheekpieces.

Penang Princess

104(99) (85)**88**

3-y-o gr f Act One-Pulau Pinang (IRE) (Dolphin Street (FR))

R M Beckett Mrs A K H Ooi

Placings:64-4421103 (6803)

2009: 8^{4}SD, 11^{4}GF, 14^{2}F, 14^{1}GF, 16^{1}SD, 14^{0}GF, 16^{3}SD,

	Starts	1st	2nd	3rd	Win & Pl
Career Total (Turf)	5	1	1	0	7011
Career Total (AW)	4	1	0	1	6776

85 6/09 Kemp 2m (0-80)H STD £5828
77 5/09 Sand 1m6f (0-85)H G-F £5180
Total win prize-money £11009

Going (Turf): Sf: 0-0 GS: 0-1 Gd: 0-0 **GF: 1-3** Fm: 0-1
Distance: 5f/6f: 0-0 7f-8f: 0-2 9f-13f: 0-2 **14f+: 2-5**
Track : LH: 0-4 **RH: 2-4** Tight: 0-4 Gall: 0-1
Aids: Bl: 0-0 Vi: 0-0 Tstrap: 0-0 Ckp: 0-0
Best Rating: 88 8/09 York 1m6f gd-fm

Useful; stays 2m; acts on fast ground; goes on Polytrack.

Penangdouble O One

(93) (72)

2-y-o ch c Starcraft (NZ)-Penang Pearl (FR) (Bering)

R M Beckett Mrs A K H Ooi

Placings:35 (7390)

2009: 8^{3}SD, 8^{5}SD,

	Starts	1st	2nd	3rd	Win & Pl
Career Total (Turf)	0	0	0	0	
Career Total (AW)	2	0	0	1	403

Going (Turf): Sf: 0-0 GS: 0-0 Gd: 0-0 GF: 0-0 Fm: 0-0
Distance: 5f/6f: 0-0 7f-8f: 0-2 9f-13f: 0-0 14f+: 0-0
Track : LH: 0-2 RH: 0-0 Tight: 0-2 Gall: 0-0
Aids: Bl: 0-0 Vi: 0-0 Tstrap: 0-0 Ckp: 0-0
Best Rating: 72 10/09 Ling 1m stand

Penchesco (IRE)

103(105) (76)**75**

4-y-o b g Orpen (USA)-Francesca (IRE) (Perugino (USA))

Pat Eddery Pat Eddery Racing (Sanglamore)

Placings:0552/0431400-4504 (6594)

2009: 8^{4}SD, 8^{5}SD, 9^{0}SD, 10^{4}GS,

	Starts	1st	2nd	3rd	Win & Pl
Career Total (Turf)	9	1	0	1	4221
Career Total (AW)	6	0	1	0	1031

74 7/08 Wind 1m67y (0-70)H SFT £2729
Total win prize-money £2730

Going (Turf): Sf: 1-3 GS: 0-2 Gd: 0-1 GF: 0-2 Fm: 0-1
Distance: 5f/6f: 0-1 7f-8f: 0-9 **9f-13f: 1-5** 14f+: 0-0
Track : LH: 0-9 **RH: 1-3 Tight: 1-5** Gall: 0-1
Aids: Bl: 0-0 Vi: 0-0 Tstrap: 0-0 Ckp: 0-0
Best Rating: 76 3/09 Sthl 1m stand

Fair; stays 1m; acts on soft ground.

Penderyn

82(82) (42)**48**

2-y-o b f Sakhee (USA)-Brecon (Unfuwain (USA))

C Smith (Mrs A J Perrett 14/11) Nicholas Baines

Placings:0666 (7792)

2009: 6^{0}S, 6^{6}G, 8^{6}SD, 8^{6}SS,

	Starts	1st	2nd	3rd	Win & Pl
Career Total (Turf)	2	0	0	0	0
Career Total (AW)	2	0	0	0	0

Going (Turf): Sf: 0-1 GS: 0-0 Gd: 0-1 GF: 0-0 Fm: 0-0
Distance: 5f/6f: 0-0 7f-8f: 0-4 9f-13f: 0-0 14f+: 0-0
Track : LH: 0-3 RH: 0-0 Tight: 0-1 Gall: 0-0
Aids: Bl: 0-0 Vi: 0-0 Tstrap: 0-0 Ckp: 0-0
Best Rating: 48 10/09 Sals 6f212y soft

Pendragon (USA)

(96) (56)**53**

6-y-o ch g Rahy (USA)-Turning Wheel (USA) (Seeking The Gold (USA))

B Ellison Mrs Claire Ellison

Placings:423-3 (7855)

2009: 8^{3}SS,

	Starts	1st	2nd	3rd	Win & Pl
Career Total (Turf)	3	0	1	1	957
Career Total (AW)	1	0	0	1	302

Going (Turf): Sf: 0-0 GS: 0-2 Gd: 0-1 GF: 0-0 Fm: 0-0
Distance: 5f/6f: 0-0 7f-8f: 0-1 9f-13f: 0-2 14f+: 0-1
Track : LH: 0-3 RH: 0-1 Tight: 0-3 Gall: 0-0
Aids: Bl: 0-0 Vi: 0-0 Tstrap: 0-0 Ckp: 0-0
Best Rating: 56 12/09 Sthl 1m std-slw

Moderate; stays 1m; acts on Fibresand and easy ground on turf.

Penel (IRE)

(94) (50)**61**

8-y-o b g Orpen (USA)-Jayess Elle (Sabrehill (USA))

P T Midgley Mrs K L Midgley

Placings:6540/60250431/32000406000/5045102015013/3032065332004630501 3/022304050-550 (0223)

2009: 8^{5}SS, 7^{5}SD, 7^{0}SD,

	Starts	1st	2nd	3rd	Win & Pl
Career Total (Turf)	32	1	4	4	8245
Career Total (AW)	36	4	3	6	10459

55 8/07 Newc 1m3y GD £1943
58 5/06 Sthl 7f (0-65)H STD £2590
51 2/06 Sthl 7f (0-45) STD £1365
56 12/04 Sthl 6f STD £2569
Total win prize-money £8468

Going (Turf): Sf: 0-3 GS: 0-7 **Gd: 1-9** GF: 0-11 Fm: 0-2
Distance: 5f/6f: 2-16 7f-8f: 2-34 9f-13f: 1-18 14f+: 0-0
Track : LH: 4-44 RH: 0-14 Tight: 0-8 Gall: 0-4
Aids: Bl: 1-10 Vi: 0-1 Tstrap: 4-44 Ckp: 4-44
Best Rating: 61 4/08 Bevl 1m100y gd-sft

Moderate; effective at up to 1m2f; acts on fast ground and on sand; wears cheekpieces.

Peninsula Girl (IRE)

90(96) (49)**69**

3-y-o b f Cape Cross (IRE)-Rio De Jumeirah (Seeking The Gold (USA))

M R Channon Jackie & George Smith

Placings:6206-4000660 (3859)

2009: 6^{4}SD, 6^{0}GF, 6^{0}G, 6^{0}GF, 6^{6}GS, 5^{6}G, 6^{0}GF,

	Starts	1st	2nd	3rd	Win & Pl
Career Total (Turf)	10	0	1	0	1542
Career Total (AW)	1	0	0	0	192

Going (Turf): Sf: 0-0 GS: 0-2 Gd: 0-5 GF: 0-3 Fm: 0-0
Distance: 5f/6f: 0-5 7f-8f: 0-6 9f-13f: 0-0 14f+: 0-0
Track : LH: 0-3 RH: 0-0 Tight: 0-1 Gall: 0-1
Aids: Bl: 0-0 Vi: 0-1 Tstrap: 0-0 Ckp: 0-0
Best Rating: 69 8/08 NmkJ 7f good

Modest; effective at 7f; acts on fast ground.

Peninsular War

104(96) (62)**80**

3-y-o b g Deportivo-Queens Jubilee (Cayman Kai (IRE))

R A Fahey (K R Burke 28/7) P Timmins & A Rhodes Haulage

Placings:323-4546204005 (7829)

2009: 6^{4}SD, 5^{5}G, 5^{4}GS, 5^{6}GS, 5^{2}GF, 5^{0}GF, 5^{4}GF, 5^{0}SD, 5^{0}GS, 7^{5}SD,

	Starts	1st	2nd	3rd	Win & Pl
Career Total (Turf)	10	0	2	2	4257
Career Total (AW)	3	0	0	0	351

Going (Turf): Sf: 0-0 GS: 0-4 Gd: 0-1 GF: 0-5 Fm: 0-0
Distance: 5f/6f: 0-12 7f-8f: 0-1 9f-13f: 0-0 14f+: 0-0
Track : LH: 0-2 RH: 0-2 Tight: 0-1 Gall: 0-0
Aids: Bl: 0-0 Vi: 0-0 Tstrap: 0-0 Ckp: 0-0
Best Rating: 80 7/09 Bevl 5f gd-fm

Fair; effective at 5f; acts on fast and easy ground.

Penitent

103(106) (107)**87**

3-y-o b g Kyllachy-Pious (Bishop Of Cashel)

W J Haggas Cheveley Park Stud

Placings:21212 (6876)

2009: 6^{2}S, 7^{1}G, 7^{2}SD, 8^{1}SD, 8^{2}SD,

	Starts	1st	2nd	3rd	Win & Pl
Career Total (Turf)	2	1	1	0	6188
Career Total (AW)	3	1	2	0	6983

87 7/09 NmkJ 7f GD £5180
Total win prize-money £5181

Going (Turf): Sf: 0-1 GS: 0-0 **Gd: 1-1** GF: 0-0 Fm: 0-0
Distance: 5f/6f: 0-1 **7f-8f: 2-4** 9f-13f: 0-0 14f+: 0-0
Track : LH: 0-1 **RH: 1-2** Tight: 0-0 Gall: 0-0
Aids: Bl: 0-0 Vi: 0-0 Tstrap: 0-0 Ckp: 0-0
Best Rating: 107 10/09 Sthl 1m stand

Very useful; stays 1m; acts on good and soft ground; goes om Fibresand.

Pennine Rose

73 **41**

3-y-o b f Reel Buddy (USA)-Adorable Cherub (USA) (Halo (USA))

A Berry Pennine Racing

Placings:000300-000 (2450)

2009: 5^{0}GF, 6^{0}GF, 7^{0}GF,

	Starts	1st	2nd	3rd	Win & Pl
Career Total (Turf)	9	0	0	1	578

Going (Turf): Sf: 0-2 GS: 0-1 Gd: 0-2 GF: 0-4 Fm: 0-0
Distance: 5f/6f: 0-8 7f-8f: 0-1 9f-13f: 0-0 14f+: 0-0
Track : LH: 0-2 RH: 0-2 Tight: 0-2 Gall: 0-1
Aids: Bl: 0-0 Vi: 0-0 Tstrap: 0-0 Ckp: 0-0
Best Rating: 41 7/08 Muss 5f gd-fm

Very moderate maiden; acts on fast ground.

Penny's Gift

111 **108**

3-y-o b f Tobougg (IRE)-Happy Lady (FR) (Cadeaux Genereux)

R Hannon Malcolm Brown & Mrs Penny Brown

Placings:311202161-361500 (6272)

2009: 7^{3}GF, 8^{6}GF, 8^{1}G, 8^{5}G, 7^{0}G, 7^{0}GF,

	Starts	1st	2nd	3rd	Win & Pl
Career Total (Turf)	15	5	2	2	281727

107 6/09 Duss 1m GD £73786
96 10/08 NmkR 6f G-S £17031
85 9/08 Asct 6f110y GD £136837
85 6/08 Chep 6f16y G-F £4630
77 5/08 Chep 5f16y SFT £2914
Total win prize-money £235199

Going (Turf): Sf: 1-1 GS: 1-1 **Gd: 2-7** GF: 1-5 Fm: 0-1
Distance: 5f/6f: 2-6 **7f-8f: 3-9** 9f-13f: 0-0 14f+: 0-0
Track : LH: 0-0 **RH: 1-2** Tight: 0-0 Gall: 0-0
Aids: Bl: 0-0 Vi: 0-0 Tstrap: 0-0 Ckp: 0-0
Best Rating: **108** 5/09 NmkR 1m gd-fm

Smart; winner of a German Group 2; effective over 1m; acts on most ground.

Pennybid (IRE)

75 **40**

7-y-o b g Benny The Dip (USA)-Stamatina (Warning)

C R Wilson Bill Martin

Placings:000-000 (3123)

2009: 7^{0}F, 13^{0}GF, 10^{0}GF,

	Starts	1st	2nd	3rd	Win & Pl
Career Total (Turf)	6	0	0	0	

Going (Turf): **Sf: 0-0 GS: 0-1 Gd: 0-1 GF: 0-2 Fm: 0-2**
Distance: 5f/6f: 0-0 7f-8f: 0-3 9f-13f: 0-2 14f+: 0-1
Track : LH: 0-3 RH: 0-1 Tight: 0-3 Gall: 0-0
Aids: Bl: 0-2 Vi: 0-0 Tstrap: 0-1 Ckp: 0-1
Best Rating: **40** 8/08 Rdcr 1m1f good

Penolva (IRE)

102(90) (58)**64**

3-y-o b f Galileo (IRE)-Jabali (FR) (Shirley Heights)

P D Deegan (A P Jarvis 17/8) Mark T Gittins

Placings:55243**564** (7336)

2009: 10^{5}GF, 11^{5}GF, 12^{2}GF, 11^{4}G, 14^{3}GF, **10**^{5}SD, **10**^{6}SD, **14**^{4}SD,

	Starts	1st	2nd	3rd	Win & Pl
Career Total (Turf)	5	0	1	1	1825
Career Total (AW)	3	0	0	0	0

Going (Turf): **Sf: 0-0 GS: 0-0 Gd: 0-1 GF: 0-4 Fm: 0-0**
Distance: 5f/6f: 0-0 7f-8f: 0-0 9f-13f: 0-6 14f+: 0-2
Track : LH: 0-6 RH: 0-2 Tight: 0-2 Gall: 0-1
Aids: Bl: 0-0 Vi: 0-0 Tstrap: 0-0 Ckp: 0-0
Best Rating: **64** 7/09 Newb 1m4f5y gd-fm

Moderate; stays 1m4f; acts on fast ground.

Penperth

79(93) (65)**37**

3-y-o b f Xaar-Penelewey (Groom Dancer (USA))

J M P Eustace Major M G Wyatt

Placings:32-0500 (4157)

2009: 8^{0}G, 7^{5}SD, 8^{0}SD, 10^{0}G,

	Starts	1st	2nd	3rd	Win & Pl
Career Total (Turf)	2	0	0	0	
Career Total (AW)	4	0	1	1	1753

Going (Turf): **Sf: 0-0 GS: 0-0 Gd: 0-2 GF: 0-0 Fm: 0-0**
Distance: 5f/6f: 0-0 7f-8f: 0-4 9f-13f: 0-2 14f+: 0-0
Track : LH: 0-3 RH: 0-2 Tight: 0-1 Gall: 0-2
Aids: Bl: 0-1 Vi: 0-0 Tstrap: 0-0 Ckp: 0-0
Best Rating: **65** 10/08 GrLe 1m stand

Modest; effective over 1m; acts on Polytrack.

Penrod Ballantyne (IRE)

83 **58**

2-y-o ch c Indian Ridge-Silvia Diletta (Mark Of Esteem (IRE))

B J Meehan B J Meehan

Placings:0 (6754)

2009: 7^{0}G,

	Starts	1st	2nd	3rd	Win & Pl
Career Total (Turf)	1	0	0	0	

Going (Turf): **Sf: 0-0 GS: 0-0 Gd: 0-1 GF: 0-0 Fm: 0-0**
Distance: 5f/6f: 0-0 7f-8f: 0-1 9f-13f: 0-0 14f+: 0-0
Track : LH: 0-0 RH: 0-0 Tight: 0-0 Gall: 0-0
Aids: Bl: 0-0 Vi: 0-0 Tstrap: 0-0 Ckp: 0-0
Best Rating: **58** 10/09 Leic 7f9y good

Brother to a minor Italian 5f-7f winner Sparkling Ridge; better than finishing position suggests on debut.

Pension Policy (USA)

86(103) (75)**68**

4-y-o b/br f Danzig (USA)-Domain (USA) (Kris S (USA))

J M P Eustace (R Charlton 13/1) Bridgewater Equine Ltd

Placings:4431003-3004 (2168)

2009: 8^{3}SD, 10^{0}G, 8^{0}SD, 7^{4}GF,

	Starts	1st	2nd	3rd	Win & Pl
Career Total (Turf)	4	0	0	0	779
Career Total (AW)	7	1	0	3	4462

75 10/08 GrLe 1m (0-75)H STD £3238
Total win prize-money £3238

Going (Turf): **Sf: 0-1 GS: 0-0 Gd: 0-1 GF: 0-2 Fm: 0-0**
Distance: 5f/6f: 0-0 **7f-8f: 1-10** 9f-13f: 0-1 14f+: 0-0
Track : **LH: 1-7** RH: 0-1 Tight: 0-3 **Gall: 1-3**
Aids: Bl: 0-1 Vi: 0-2 Tstrap: 0-0 Ckp: 0-0
Best Rating: **75** 10/08 GrLe 1m stand

Fair; stays 1m and acts on Polytrack; has worn a visor.

Pentominium

88 **71**

2-y-o b c Dubai Destination (USA)-Mouriyana (IRE) (Akarad (FR))

M Johnston Sheikh Hamdan Bin Mohammed Al Maktoum

Placings:3 (6382)

2009: 8^{3}GF,

	Starts	1st	2nd	3rd	Win & Pl
Career Total (Turf)	1	0	0	1	751

Going (Turf): **Sf: 0-0 GS: 0-0 Gd: 0-0 GF: 0-1 Fm: 0-0**
Distance: 5f/6f: 0-0 7f-8f: 0-1 9f-13f: 0-0 14f+: 0-0
Track : LH: 0-1 RH: 0-0 Tight: 0-0 Gall: 0-1
Aids: Bl: 0-0 Vi: 0-0 Tstrap: 0-0 Ckp: 0-0
Best Rating: **71** 9/09 Newc 1m gd-fm

Fair; stays 1m and acts on fast ground.

Penton Hook

(105) (82)**71**

3-y-o gr g Lucky Owners (NZ)-Cosmic Star (Siberian Express (USA))

P Winkworth Mrs Tessa Winkworth

Placings:632-12 (7134)

2009: 8^{1}SS, 10^{2}SD,

	Starts	1st	2nd	3rd	Win & Pl
Career Total (Turf)	2	0	1	0	771
Career Total (AW)	3	1	1	1	4195

82 10/09 Ling 1m (0-75)H SS £2729
Total win prize-money £2730

Going (Turf): **Sf: 0-1 GS: 0-1 Gd: 0-0 GF: 0-0 Fm: 0-0**
Distance: 5f/6f: 0-1 **7f-8f: 1-3** 9f-13f: 0-1 14f+: 0-0
Track : **LH: 1-3** RH: 0-0 **Tight: 1-3** Gall: 0-0
Aids: Bl: 0-0 Vi: 0-0 Tstrap: 0-0 Ckp: 0-0
Best Rating: **82** 10/09 Ling 1m2f stand

Fair; stays 1m; acts on Polytrack.

Penzena

99(105) (75)**70**

3-y-o ch f Tobougg (IRE)-Penmayne (Inchinor)

A M Balding (W J Knight 13/7) Spiers, Taylor, Taylor

Placings:0-402415 (7664)

2009: 8^{4}F, 8^{0}G, 8^{2}GF, 8^{4}G, 8^{1}SD, 8^{5}SD,

	Starts	1st	2nd	3rd	Win & Pl
Career Total (Turf)	5	0	1	0	2456
Career Total (AW)	2	1	0	0	2590

75 11/09 Kemp 1m STD £2590
Total win prize-money £2590

Going (Turf): **Sf: 0-1 GS: 0-0 Gd: 0-2 GF: 0-1 Fm: 0-1**
Distance: 5f/6f: 0-0 **7f-8f: 1-4** 9f-13f: 0-3 14f+: 0-0
Track : LH: 0-3 **RH: 1-3** Tight: 0-2 Gall: 0-0
Aids: Bl: 0-0 Vi: 0-0 Tstrap: 0-0 Ckp: 0-0
Best Rating: **75** 11/09 Kemp 1m stand

Modest; stays 1m; acts on fast ground and on Polytrack.

Peopleton Brook

100(102) (67)**67**

7-y-o b h Compton Place-Merch Rhyd-Y-Grug (Sabrehill (USA))

B G Powell G S Thompson & P Banfield

Placings:5**6**0000/113212223003**0**/011000600**5**/006135000 0**000**/000566000**6**3**4**0**60-2**0**0**661404340345**0260403** (7879)

2009: **6**^{2}SD, 6^{0}G, **6**^{0}SD, 6^{6}GF, 5^{6}F, 5^{1}G, 5^{4}GF, 5^{0}GF, 5^{4}GF, 5^{3}G, 5^{4}GF, 5^{0}GF, 6^{3}GF, 6^{4}G, 5^{5}GF, 5^{0}G, **6**^{2}SD, **7**^{6}SD, **6**^{0}SD, **6**^{4}SD, **5**^{0}SD, **6**^{3}SD,

	Starts	1st	2nd	3rd	Win & Pl
Career Total (Turf)	62	7	4	6	54121
Career Total (AW)	17	0	2	2	1887

67 5/09 Gdwd 5f (0-65)H GD £2590
87 5/07 Hayd 5f (0-75)H G-F £3238
93 5/06 Ling 5f (0-85)H GD £5505
89 5/06 Gdwd 5f (0-90)H GD £10201
84 7/05 Hayd 5f (0-80)H G-F £8160
77 6/05 Sand 5f6y (0-75)H G-F £4823
68 6/05 Chep 5f16y (0-70)H GD £3429
Total win prize-money £37948

Going (Turf): Sf: 0-1 GS: 0-8 **Gd: 4-24** GF: 3-26 Fm: 0-3
Distance: **5f/6f: 7-76** 7f-8f: 0-3 9f-13f: 0-0 14f+: 0-0
Track : LH: 0-21 RH: 0-8 Tight: 0-8 Gall: 0-9
Aids: Bl: 0-5 Vi: 0-0 Tstrap: 0-5 Ckp: 0-5
Best Rating: **93** 5/06 Ling 5f good

Moderate sprinter; effective over 5f-6f; acts on most ground on turf; goes on Polytrack; has worn a tongue tie.

Peper Harow (IRE)

100(104) (74)**79**

3-y-o b f Compton Place-Faraway Moon (Distant Relative)

M D I Usher Mr & Mrs Richard Hames & Friends 1

Placings:4402350-050016102100 (7000)

2009: 6^{0}GF, 5^{5}G, 5^{0}G, 5^{0}GF, 7^{1}GF, 7^{6}S, 6^{1}G, 6^{0}G, 7^{2}SD, 7^{1}SD, 7^{0}SD, 7^{0}SD,

	Starts	1st	2nd	3rd	Win & Pl
Career Total (Turf)	15	2	1	1	11355
Career Total (AW)	4	1	1	0	3194

74	10/09	Wolv	7f32y	(0-65)H	STD	£2388
68	8/09	Nott	6f15y	(0-80)H	GD	£5180
55	7/09	Newb	7f	(0-75)H	G-F	£3238

Total win prize-money £10807

Going (Turf): Sf: 0-2 GS: 0-0 **Gd: 1-5 GF: 1-7** Fm: 0-1
Distance: 5f/6f: 0-11 **7f-8f: 3-8** 9f-13f: 0-0 14f+: 0-0
Track: **LH: 1-5** RH: 0-0 **Tight: 1-4** Gall: 0-2
Aids: Bl: 0-0 Vi: 0-1 Tstrap: 0-0 Ckp: 0-0
Best Rating: **79** 6/08 NmkJ 6f firm

Modest; stays 7f and acts on fast ground.

Pepi Royal (IRE)

91(93) (68)**63**

2-y-o b f Royal Applause-Alenushka (Soviet Star (USA))

Pat Eddery Aitken & Phillips

Placings:4600031 (6775)

2009: 5^{4}GF, 6^{6}GF, 6^{0}GF, 6^{0}GS, 7^{0}GF, 5^{3}SF, 6^{1}SD,

	Starts	1st	2nd	3rd	Win & Pl
Career Total (Turf)	5	0	0	0	289
Career Total (AW)	2	1	0	1	2400

68	10/09	Kemp	6f	(0-65)	STD	£2047

Total win prize-money £2047

Going (Turf): **Sf: 0-0 GS: 0-1 Gd: 0-0 GF: 0-4 Fm: 0-0**
Distance: **5f/6f: 1-4** 7f-8f: 0-3 9f-13f: 0-0 14f+: 0-0
Track: LH: 0-2 **RH: 1-1** Tight: 0-1 Gall: 0-1
Aids: Bl: 0-0 Vi: 0-0 Tstrap: 0-0 Ckp: 0-0
Best Rating: **68** 10/09 Kemp 6f stand

Pepin (IRE)

81(101) (58)**21**

3-y-o ch g King Charlemagne (USA)-Consignia (IRE) (Definite Article)

D Haydn Jones Merry Llewelyn And Runeckles

Placings:000-0666434103640 (7002)

2009: 6^{0}SD, 6^{6}SD, 7^{6}SD, 5^{6}GF, 5^{4}SD, 6^{3}SD, 5^{4}SD, 6^{1}SD, 6^{0}GF, 6^{3}SD, 6^{6}SD, 6^{4}SD, 5^{0}SD,

	Starts	1st	2nd	3rd	Win & Pl
Career Total (Turf)	3	0	0	0	0
Career Total (AW)	13	1	0	2	2913

58	5/09	Sthl	6f	(0-60)H	STD	£2047

Total win prize-money £2047

Going (Turf): **Sf: 0-0 GS: 0-1 Gd: 0-0 GF: 0-2 Fm: 0-0**
Distance: **5f/6f: 1-14** 7f-8f: 0-2 9f-13f: 0-0 14f+: 0-0
Track: **LH: 1-10** RH: 0-4 Tight: 0-4 Gall: 0-0
Aids: Bl: 0-3 Vi: 0-0 Tstrap: 0-1 Ckp: 0-1
Best Rating: **58** 5/09 Sthl 6f stand

Moderate; effective over 6f; acts on Fibresand.

Peponi

(98) (68)

3-y-o ch c Kris Kin (USA)-Polmara (IRE) (Polish Precedent (USA))

P J Makin Raymond Gomersall

Placings:22 (7829)

2009: 8^{2}SD, 7^{2}SD,

	Starts	1st	2nd	3rd	Win & Pl
Career Total (Turf)	0	0	0	0	
Career Total (AW)	2	0	2	0	1375

Going (Turf): **Sf: 0-0 GS: 0-0 Gd: 0-0 GF: 0-0 Fm: 0-0**
Distance: 5f/6f: 0-0 7f-8f: 0-2 9f-13f: 0-0 14f+: 0-0
Track: LH: 0-1 RH: 0-1 Tight: 0-1 Gall: 0-0
Aids: Bl: 0-0 Vi: 0-0 Tstrap: 0-0 Ckp: 0-0
Best Rating: **68** 11/09 Ling 1m stand

Fair; stays 1m; acts on Polytrack.

Pepper Lane

94(91) (58)**68**

2-y-o ch f Exceed And Excel (AUS)-Maid To Matter (Pivotal)

J Hetherton (T D Barron 20/6) Mrs Lynne Lumley

Placings:24054355 (6819)

2009: 5^{2}GF, 5^{4}GF, 5^{0}G, 6^{5}GF, 5^{4}GS, 5^{3}SD, 7^{5}G, 7^{5}GF,

	Starts	1st	2nd	3rd	Win & Pl
Career Total (Turf)	7	0	1	0	1469
Career Total (AW)	1	0	0	1	353

Going (Turf): **Sf: 0-0 GS: 0-1 Gd: 0-2 GF: 0-4 Fm: 0-0**
Distance: 5f/6f: 0-6 7f-8f: 0-2 9f-13f: 0-0 14f+: 0-0
Track: LH: 0-2 RH: 0-0 Tight: 0-2 Gall: 0-0
Aids: Bl: 0-0 Vi: 0-0 Tstrap: 0-0 Ckp: 0-0
Best Rating: **68** 5/09 Ripn 5f gd-fm

Modest; effective over 5f; acts on fast ground.

Peppertree Lane (IRE)

75 **114**

6-y-o ch g Peintre Celebre (USA)-Salonrolle (IRE) (Tirol)

A P Boxhall (P Bowen 17/1) Walters Plant Hire Ltd

Placings:33/1150011310/01413165/2413302-6 (6306)

2009: 16^{6}GF,

	Starts	1st	2nd	3rd	Win & Pl
Career Total (Turf)	28	9	2	6	253854

114	6/08	Gdwd	1m4f		GD	£17778
111	6/07	Curr	1m6f		SFT	£31418
111	5/07	Newb	1m5f61y		G-S	£17034
95	4/07	Ripn	1m4f10y		G-F	£6855
112	10/06	Asct	1m4f	(0-105)H	SFT	£46740
106	9/06	Hayd	1m6f	(0-105)H	HVY	£51816
100	8/06	Ripn	1m4f10y	(0-90)H	HVY	£9348
99	5/06	York	1m	(0-100)H	SFT	£16516
88	4/06	Ripn	1m		SFT	£3562

Total win prize-money £201068

Going (Turf): **Sf: 6-12** GS: 1-6 Gd: 1-5 GF: 1-4 Fm: 0-0
Distance: 5f/6f: 0-0 7f-8f: 2-5 **9f-13f: 4-9** 14f+: 3-14
Track: LH: 3-11 **RH: 6-15 Tight: 4-6** Gall: 3-7
Aids: Bl: 0-0 Vi: 0-0 Tstrap: 0-0 Ckp: 0-0
Best Rating: **114** 6/08 Curr 1m6f yield

Smart; Group 3 winner; effective over 1m4f-2m; handles fast ground, but well suited by soft; likes to race prominently; very tough.

Perception (IRE)

100(98) (69)**69**

3-y-o b f Hawk Wing (USA)-Princesse Darsha (GER) (Darshaan)

A King (R Charlton 16/9) Incipe Partnership

Placings:435-06641 (5990)

2009: 10^{0}GS, 12^{6}GF, 13^{6}G, 15^{4}GF, 16^{1}SD,

	Starts	1st	2nd	3rd	Win & Pl
Career Total (Turf)	7	0	0	1	1043
Career Total (AW)	1	1	0	0	2047

69	9/09	Kemp	2m	(0-65)H	STD	£2047

Total win prize-money £2047

Going (Turf): **Sf: 0-0 GS: 0-2 Gd: 0-1 GF: 0-4 Fm: 0-0**
Distance: 5f/6f: 0-0 7f-8f: 0-2 9f-13f: 0-4 **14f+: 1-2**
Track: LH: 0-3 **RH: 1-3** Tight: 0-2 Gall: 0-2
Aids: Bl: 0-0 Vi: 0-1 Tstrap: 0-0 Ckp: 0-0
Best Rating: **69** 9/09 Kemp 2m stand

Modest; effective at 1m4f-2m; acts on fast ground and Polytrack; has worn a visor.

Perceptive

68(99) (69)**18**

2-y-o b f Carnival Dancer-Discerning (Darshaan)

J R Fanshawe Cheveley Park Stud

Placings:042 (7199)

2009: 7^{0}G, 8^{4}SD, 8^{2}SD,

	Starts	1st	2nd	3rd	Win & Pl
Career Total (Turf)	1	0	0	0	
Career Total (AW)	2	0	1	0	821

Going (Turf): **Sf: 0-0 GS: 0-0 Gd: 0-1 GF: 0-0 Fm: 0-0**
Distance: 5f/6f: 0-0 7f-8f: 0-2 9f-13f: 0-1 14f+: 0-0
Track: LH: 0-2 RH: 0-0 Tight: 0-2 Gall: 0-0
Aids: Bl: 0-0 Vi: 0-0 Tstrap: 0-0 Ckp: 0-0
Best Rating: **69** 11/09 Ling 1m stand

Fair; stays 1m; acts on Polytrack; should improve.

Percolator

92(86) (70)**106**

3-y-o b f Kheleyf (USA)-Coffee Cream (Common Grounds)

P F I Cole A H Robinson

Placings:2111120-000 (6180)

2009: 5^{0}G, 5^{0}GF, 5^{0}GF,

	Starts	1st	2nd	3rd	Win & Pl
Career Total (Turf)	9	3	2	0	84069
Career Total (AW)	1	1	0	0	2048

105	7/08	MsnL	5f	G-S	£29412
105	6/08	Lonc	5f	GD	£20221
102	5/08	Lonc	5f	G-S	£12500
70	3/08	Ling	5f	STD	£2047

Total win prize-money £64181

Going (Turf): Sf: 0-0 **GS: 2-3** Gd: 1-4 GF: 0-2 Fm: 0-0
Distance: **5f/6f: 4-10** 7f-8f: 0-0 9f-13f: 0-0 14f+: 0-0
Track: **LH: 1-2** RH: 0-0 **Tight: 1-1** Gall: 0-0
Aids: Bl: 0-0 Vi: 0-0 Tstrap: 0-0 Ckp: 0-0
Best Rating: **106** 7/08 MsnL 5f110y good

Smart; winner in Listed company and Group placed; effective over 5f; acts on good and easier ground and on Polytrack; suited by forcing tactics.

Percussionist (IRE)

80 53

8-y-o b g Sadler's Wells (USA)-Magnificient Style (USA) (Silver Hawk (USA))
J Howard Johnson J Howard Johnson

Placings:32/11402365/20/10/46/0 **(2056)**
2009: 14^{0}GS,

	Starts	1st	2nd	3rd	Win & Pl
Career Total (Turf)	17	3	3	2	253306

117 5/06 York 1m5f197y SFT £79492
116 5/04 Ling 1m3f106y A SFT £37200
93 4/04 NmkR 1m4f D G-S £5317
Total win prize-money £122009

Going (Turf): **Sf: 2-6** GS: 1-3 Gd: 0-6 GF: 0-2 Fm: 0-0
Distance: 5f/6f: 0-0 7f-8f: 0-0 **9f-13f: 2-8** 14f+: 1-9
Track : **LH: 2-9** RH: 1-7 Tight: 1-2 **Gall: 2-7**
Aids: Bl: 0-1 Vi: 0-0 Tstrap: 0-0 Ckp: 0-0
Best Rating: **121** 6/04 Epsm 1m4f10y good

Group class; winner of the Group 3 Lingfield Derby Trial in 2004 and the Group 2 Yorkshire Cup in in 2006; stays 1m6f and best on soft ground; winning hurdler and chaser.

Percys Corismatic

86 62

3-y-o b f Systematic-Corisa (IRE) (Be My Guest (USA))
J Gallagher Coombeshead Racing

Placings:000435-000 **(4640)**
2009: 8^{0}F, 7^{0}GF, 11^{0}GF,

	Starts	1st	2nd	3rd	Win & Pl
Career Total (Turf)	9	0	0	1	510

Going (Turf): **Sf: 0-0 GS: 0-1 Gd: 0-2 GF: 0-4 Fm: 0-2**
Distance: 5f/6f: 0-3 7f-8f: 0-4 9f-13f: 0-2 14f+: 0-0
Track : LH: 0-6 RH: 0-0 Tight: 0-1 Gall: 0-1
Aids: Bl: 0-0 Vi: 0-0 Tstrap: 0-0 Ckp: 0-0
Best Rating: **62** 7/08 Brig 6f209y firm

Plating class; effective at 7f; handles quick ground.

Perez Prado (USA)

83 63

4-y-o b g Kingmambo (USA)-Marisa (USA) (Swain (IRE))
W Jarvis Anthony Foster

Placings:0/0-500 **(4730)**
2009: 8^{5}G, 8^{0}GF, 6^{0}GS,

	Starts	1st	2nd	3rd	Win & Pl
Career Total (Turf)	5	0	0	0	0

Going (Turf): **Sf: 0-0 GS: 0-2 Gd: 0-2 GF: 0-1 Fm: 0-0**
Distance: 5f/6f: 0-0 7f-8f: 0-3 9f-13f: 0-2 14f+: 0-0
Track : LH: 0-3 RH: 0-0 Tight: 0-0 Gall: 0-0
Aids: Bl: 0-0 Vi: 0-0 Tstrap: 0-0 Ckp: 0-0
Best Rating: **63** 5/08 NmkR 1m gd-sft

First foal of an unraced half-sister to Russian Rhythm; signs of ability in maidens in good and easy ground.

Perfect Act

92(104) (84)69

4-y-o b f Act One-Markova's Dance (Mark Of Esteem (IRE))
C G Cox Dr Bridget Drew & E E Dedman

Placings:1254/00**3606-646**0331601 **(7828)**
2009: 8^{6}SD, 8^{4}SD, 7^{6}SD, 7^{0}G, 6^{3}SD, 6^{3}SD, 6^{1}SD, 6^{6}SD, 7^{0}SD, 6^{1}SD,

	Starts	1st	2nd	3rd	Win & Pl
Career Total (Turf)	7	1	1	0	22720
Career Total (AW)	13	2	0	3	7467

84 12/09 Kemp 6f (0-75)H STD £2590
78 10/09 Ling 6f (0-70)H STD £3070
80 8/07 Newb 7f GD £3562
Total win prize-money £9223

Going (Turf): Sf: 0-2 GS: 0-1 **Gd: 1-3** GF: 0-1 Fm: 0-0
Distance: **5f/6f: 2-6** 7f-8f: 1-13 9f-13f: 0-1 14f+: 0-0
Track : LH: 1-6 RH: 1-8 **Tight: 1-6** Gall: 0-0
Aids: Bl: 0-0 Vi: 0-0 Tstrap: 0-0 Ckp: 0-0
Best Rating: **87** 10/07 Newb 7f soft

Fair; effective over 6f-7f; acts on good and faster ground; goes on Polytrack.

Perfect Affair (USA)

100(93) (59)72

3-y-o b g Perfect Soul (IRE)-Caribbean Affair (USA) (Red Ransom (USA))
R M Beckett I J Heseltine

Placings:0-0030 **(2206)**
2009: 7^{0}SD, 7^{0}SD, 8^{3}F, 9^{0}GF,

	Starts	1st	2nd	3rd	Win & Pl
Career Total (Turf)	3	0	0	1	578
Career Total (AW)	2	0	0	0	

Going (Turf): **Sf: 0-0 GS: 0-0 Gd: 0-1 GF: 0-1 Fm: 0-1**
Distance: 5f/6f: 0-0 7f-8f: 0-3 9f-13f: 0-2 14f+: 0-0
Track : LH: 0-1 RH: 0-3 Tight: 0-1 Gall: 0-0
Aids: Bl: 0-0 Vi: 0-0 Tstrap: 0-0 Ckp: 0-0
Best Rating: **72** 10/08 Sals 1m good

Perfect Blossom

86 63

2-y-o b f One Cool Cat (USA)-Perfect Peach (Lycius (USA))
I W McInnes Mrs Ann Morris

Placings:4550 **(4928)**
2009: 6^{4}GF, 6^{5}G, 5^{5}GS, 5^{0}G,

	Starts	1st	2nd	3rd	Win & Pl
Career Total (Turf)	4	0	0	0	491

Going (Turf): **Sf: 0-0 GS: 0-1 Gd: 0-2 GF: 0-1 Fm: 0-0**
Distance: 5f/6f: 0-4 7f-8f: 0-0 9f-13f: 0-0 14f+: 0-0
Track : LH: 0-0 RH: 0-0 Tight: 0-0 Gall: 0-0
Aids: Bl: 0-0 Vi: 0-0 Tstrap: 0-0 Ckp: 0-0
Best Rating: **63** 5/09 York 6f gd-fm

Modest form at 6f on a sound surface.

Perfect Ch'l (IRE)

96(89) (73)81

2-y-o b f Choisir (AUS)-Agouti (Pennekamp (USA))
I A Wood Paddy Barrett

Placings:05121300**450** **(7320)**
2009: 5^{0}G, 5^{5}GF, 6^{1}G, 6^{2}G, 6^{1}GS, 6^{3}GF, 6^{0}GF, 6^{0}G, 6^{4}SD, 7^{5}G, 7^{0}SD,

	Starts	1st	2nd	3rd	Win & Pl
Career Total (Turf)	9	2	1	1	17378
Career Total (AW)	2	0	0	0	192

81 8/09 Nott 6f15y G-S £3885
72 6/09 Yarm 6f3y GD £2590
Total win prize-money £6476

Going (Turf): Sf: 0-0 **GS: 1-1 Gd: 1-5** GF: 0-3 Fm: 0-0
Distance: 5f/6f: 0-5 **7f-8f: 2-6** 9f-13f: 0-0 14f+: 0-0
Track : LH: 0-3 RH: 0-1 Tight: 0-2 Gall: 0-1
Aids: Bl: 0-0 Vi: 0-0 Tstrap: 0-0 Ckp: 0-0
Best Rating: **81** 8/09 Nott 6f15y gd-sft

Useful; stays 6f; acts on good ground; goes on Polytrack.

Perfect Citizen (USA)

104(99) (80)85

3-y-o ch g Proud Citizen (USA)-Near Mint (USA) (Dehere (USA))
W R Swinburn Clark, Cunnane, Godfrey & Rice

Placings:301206-006356 **(6462)**
2009: 8^{0}GF, 8^{0}SD, 7^{6}G, 7^{3}SD, 9^{5}GF, 8^{6}SD,

	Starts	1st	2nd	3rd	Win & Pl
Career Total (Turf)	8	0	1	1	4624
Career Total (AW)	4	1	0	1	3361

79 8/08 Kemp 7f STD £2590
Total win prize-money £2590

Going (Turf): **Sf: 0-0 GS: 0-1 Gd: 0-3 GF: 0-4 Fm: 0-0**
Distance: 5f/6f: 0-0 **7f-8f: 1-9** 9f-13f: 0-3 14f+: 0-0
Track : LH: 0-3 **RH: 1-6** Tight: 0-4 Gall: 0-0
Aids: Bl: 0-0 Vi: 0-0 Tstrap: 0-4 Ckp: 0-4
Best Rating: **85** 8/08 NmkJ 7f gd-fm

Fair $160,000 half-brother to two turf winners in the USA; effective over 7f; acts on good ground and on Polytrack.

Perfect Class

104(102) (71)73

3-y-o b f Cape Cross (IRE)-Liberty (Singspiel (IRE))
C G Cox The Perfect Partnership

Placings:650**0-125**03235**2**10 **(5099)**
2009: 6^{1}SD, 6^{2}SD, 7^{5}SD, 6^{0}GF, 7^{3}F, 7^{2}GF, 7^{3}GF, 6^{5}F, 8^{2}SD, 8^{1}G, 8^{0}GF,

	Starts	1st	2nd	3rd	Win & Pl
Career Total (Turf)	10	1	1	2	8352
Career Total (AW)	5	1	2	0	4602

73 7/09 Bath 1m5y (0-80)H GD £6308
64 1/09 Kemp 6f (0-70)H STD £2590
Total win prize-money £8898

Going (Turf): Sf: 0-1 GS: 0-2 **Gd: 1-1** GF: 0-4 Fm: 0-2
Distance: 5f/6f: 1-7 7f-8f: 0-6 9f-13f: 1-2 14f+: 0-0
Track : LH: 1-6 RH: 1-4 **Tight: 1-4** Gall: 0-1
Aids: Bl: 0-2 Vi: 0-1 Tstrap: 0-0 Ckp: 0-0
Best Rating: **73** 7/09 Bath 1m5y good

Fair; effective over 6f-1m; handles Polytrack and ggod/fast ground.

Perfect Flight

102 98

4-y-o b f Hawk Wing (USA)-Pretty Girl (IRE) (Polish Precedent (USA))
M Blanshard John Drew

Placings:54512302/600011100-4060 **(6694)**
2009: 6^{4}GS, 7^{0}G, 6^{6}S, 6^{0}GS,

	Starts	1st	2nd	3rd	Win & Pl
Career Total (Turf)	21	4	2	1	36416

98 9/08 Gdwd 6f (0-100)H SFT £11215
89 8/08 Gdwd 6f (0-95)H SFT £9714

78	8/08	Ling	6f	(0-85)H	SFT	£4604
76	8/07	Hayd	5f		G-F	£4857

Total win prize-money £30393

Going (Turf): **Sf: 3-5** GS: 0-5 Gd: 0-3 GF: 1-8 Fm: 0-0
Distance: **5f/6f: 4-16** 7f-8f: 0-5 9f-13f: 0-0 14f+: 0-0
Track : LH: 0-1 RH: 0-1 Tight: 0-0 Gall: 0-3
Aids: Bl: 0-0 Vi: 0-0 Tstrap: 0-0 Ckp: 0-0
Best Rating: **98** 9/08 Gdwd 6f soft

Useful; effective over 6f; acts on most ground, but well suited by soft.

Perfect Friend

100(97) (70)**83**
3-y-o b f Reel Buddy (USA)-Four Legs Good (IRE) (Be My Guest (USA))
S Kirk Lady Davis

Placings:5412**0**62-0212234120005 **(6621)**
2009: 9^{0}SD, 7^{2}SD, 7^{1}GF, 6^{2}G, 7^{2}GF, 7^{3}G, 7^{4}GF, 7^{1}GF, 8^{2}S, 6^{0}GF, 9^{0}G, 7^{0}SD, 8^{5}G,

	Starts	1st	2nd	3rd	Win & Pl
Career Total (Turf)	**15**	**3**	**4**	**1**	**17489**
Career Total (AW)	**5**	**0**	**2**	**0**	**1734**

83	7/09	Newb	7f	(0-80)H	G-F	£4857
70	5/09	Wwck	7f26y	(0-70)H	G-F	£3238
66	9/08	Bath	5f11y		SFT	£2266

Total win prize-money £10362

Going (Turf): Sf: 1-2 GS: 0-3 Gd: 0-5 **GF: 2-5** Fm: 0-0
Distance: 5f/6f: 1-2 **7f-8f: 2-14** 9f-13f: 0-4 14f+: 0-0
Track : **LH: 2-8** RH: 0-5 Tight: 0-4 **Gall: 1-3**
Aids: Bl: 0-0 Vi: 0-0 Tstrap: 0-0 Ckp: 0-0
Best Rating: **83** 7/09 Newb 7f gd-fm

Fair; stays 7f; acts on most ground and on Polytrack.

Perfect Honour (IRE)

(98) (58)
3-y-o ch f Exceed And Excel (AUS)-Porcelana (IRE) (Highest Honor (FR))
D Shaw Mrs Jackie Cornwell

Placings:00-446215 **(1529)**
2009: 6^{4}SD, 7^{4}SD, 5^{6}SD, 5^{2}SD, 5^{1}SD, 5^{5}SD,

	Starts	1st	2nd	3rd	Win & Pl
Career Total (Turf)	**1**	**0**	**0**	**0**	
Career Total (AW)	**7**	**1**	**1**	**0**	**2652**

58	4/09	Wolv	5f20y	(0-60)H	STD	£2047

Total win prize-money £2047

Going (Turf): **Sf: 0-0 GS: 0-1 Gd: 0-0 GF: 0-0 Fm: 0-0**
Distance: **5f/6f: 1-6** 7f-8f: 0-1 9f-13f: 0-1 14f+: 0-0
Track : **LH: 1-7** RH: 0-0 **Tight: 1-6** Gall: 0-0
Aids: Bl: 0-0 Vi: 0-0 Tstrap: 0-0 Ckp: 0-0
Best Rating: **58** 4/09 Wolv 5f20y stand

Moderate; effective over 5f; acts on Polytrack.

Perfect Note

85 **68**
2-y-o b f Shamardal (USA)-Mezzo Soprano (USA) (Darshaan)
Saeed Bin Suroor Godolphin

Placings:4 **(7183)**
2009: 7^{4}G,

	Starts	1st	2nd	3rd	Win & Pl
Career Total (Turf)	**1**	**0**	**0**	**0**	**361**

Going (Turf): **Sf: 0-0 GS: 0-0 Gd: 0-1 GF: 0-0 Fm: 0-0**
Distance: 5f/6f: 0-0 7f-8f: 0-1 9f-13f: 0-0 14f+: 0-0
Track : LH: 0-0 RH: 0-0 Tight: 0-0 Gall: 0-0
Aids: Bl: 0-0 Vi: 0-0 Tstrap: 0-0 Ckp: 0-0
Best Rating: **68** 10/09 NmkR 7f good

Perfect Pride (USA)

102 **89**
3-y-o b f Forest Wildcat (USA)-Kisses To Yall (USA) (Copelan (USA))
C G Cox Dr Bridget Drew & E E Dedman

Placings:0210-1045 **(5918)**
2009: 6^{1}G, 6^{0}GF, 6^{4}GF, 7^{5}GF,

	Starts	1st	2nd	3rd	Win & Pl
Career Total (Turf)	**8**	**2**	**1**	**0**	**10407**

89	6/09	Gdwd	6f	(0-85)H	GD	£4857
74	8/08	Sals	6f		G-F	£3238

Total win prize-money £8095

Going (Turf): Sf: 0-1 GS: 0-0 **Gd: 1-2 GF: 1-5** Fm: 0-0
Distance: **5f/6f: 2-4** 7f-8f: 0-4 9f-13f: 0-0 14f+: 0-0
Track : LH: 0-0 RH: 0-1 Tight: 0-0 Gall: 0-1
Aids: Bl: 0-0 Vi: 0-0 Tstrap: 0-0 Ckp: 0-0
Best Rating: **89** 6/09 Gdwd 6f good

Fair; effective over 6f on fast ground.

Perfect Secret

92(96) (55)**61**
3-y-o b f Spinning World (USA)-Sharp Secret (IRE) (College Chapel)
A M Balding John Drew and Dr Bridget Drew

Placings:43 **(7829)**
2009: 7^{4}G, 7^{3}SD,

	Starts	1st	2nd	3rd	Win & Pl
Career Total (Turf)	**1**	**0**	**0**	**0**	**241**
Career Total (AW)	**1**	**0**	**0**	**1**	**302**

Going (Turf): **Sf: 0-0 GS: 0-0 Gd: 0-1 GF: 0-0 Fm: 0-0**
Distance: 5f/6f: 0-0 7f-8f: 0-2 9f-13f: 0-0 14f+: 0-0
Track : LH: 0-0 RH: 0-2 Tight: 0-0 Gall: 0-0
Aids: Bl: 0-0 Vi: 0-0 Tstrap: 0-0 Ckp: 0-0
Best Rating: **61** 5/09 Gdwd 7f good

Modest; effective over 7f; acts on Polytrack.

Perfect Shot (IRE)

103 **89**
3-y-o b g High Chaparral (IRE)-Zoom Lens (IRE) (Caerleon (USA))
J L Dunlop Sir Philip Wroughton

Placings:4023-021214660 **(7151)**
2009: 10^{0}G, 11^{2}G, 12^{1}G, 14^{2}GF, 16^{1}G, 16^{4}GF, 16^{6}GF, 18^{6}G, 18^{0}G,

	Starts	1st	2nd	3rd	Win & Pl
Career Total (Turf)	**13**	**2**	**3**	**1**	**17784**

89	8/09	NmkJ	2m24y	(0-90)H	GD	£9066
66	6/09	Chep	1m4f23y		GD	£2719

Total win prize-money £11786

Going (Turf): Sf: 0-1 GS: 0-0 **Gd: 2-7** GF: 0-5 Fm: 0-0
Distance: 5f/6f: 0-0 7f-8f: 0-3 9f-13f: 1-4 14f+: 1-6
Track : LH: 1-5 RH: 1-5 Tight: 0-2 **Gall: 1-4**
Aids: Bl: 0-0 Vi: 0-0 Tstrap: 0-0 Ckp: 0-0
Best Rating: **89** 8/09 NmkJ 2m24y good

Fair; stays 2m; acts on fast and soft ground.

Perfect Silence

103(99) (83)**83**
4-y-o b f Dansili-Perfect Echo (Lycius (USA))
C G Cox Wild Beef Racing (Mr & Mrs R J Vines)

Placings:0/4311-3310**1**404 **(7189)**
2009: 5^{3}GF, 6^{3}G, 7^{1}GF, 7^{0}G, 7^{1}SD, 7^{4}SD, 7^{0}SD, 7^{4}G,

	Starts	1st	2nd	3rd	Win & Pl
Career Total (Turf)	**10**	**3**	**0**	**3**	**15976**
Career Total (AW)	**3**	**1**	**0**	**0**	**5079**

83	9/09	Kemp	7f	(0-80)H	STD	£4727
83	7/09	Wwck	7f26y	(0-80)H	G-F	£6799
81	10/08	Wind	6f	(0-70)H	GD	£2729
78	9/08	Folk	6f		G-S	£2914

Total win prize-money £17171

Going (Turf): Sf: 0-0 **GS: 1-2 Gd: 1-5 GF: 1-3** Fm: 0-0
Distance: 5f/6f: 2-4 7f-8f: 2-9 9f-13f: 0-0 14f+: 0-0
Track : LH: 1-1 RH: 1-3 Tight: 0-0 **Gall: 1-1**
Aids: **Bl: 1-4** Vi: 0-0 Tstrap: 0-0 Ckp: 0-0
Best Rating: **83** 10/09 NmkR 7f good

Fair; effective over 6f-7f; acts on most ground and Polytrack; has worn blinkers.

Perfect Star

109(108) (101)**105**
5-y-o b m Act One-Granted (FR) (Cadeaux Genereux)
C G Cox Dr Bridget Drew & E E Dedman

Placings:21/512211/013-2564205 **(7560)**
2009: 8^{2}SD, 8^{5}G, 8^{6}HY, 8^{4}G, 8^{2}G, 10^{0}S, 8^{5}SD,

	Starts	1st	2nd	3rd	Win & Pl
Career Total (Turf)	**16**	**5**	**4**	**1**	**80230**
Career Total (AW)	**2**	**0**	**1**	**0**	**9027**

105	8/08	Asct	1m	(0-100)H	G-S	£17230
104	9/07	Asct	1m	(0-110)H	SFT	£17034
94	9/07	Sals	6f212y	(0-100)H	G-F	£14956
86	7/07	Sals	1m	(0-95)H	G-F	£9348
77	10/06	NmkR	7f		G-S	£3886

Total win prize-money £62456

Going (Turf): Sf: 1-4 **GS: 2-3** Gd: 0-5 **GF: 2-4** Fm: 0-0
Distance: 5f/6f: 0-0 **7f-8f: 5-12** 9f-13f: 0-6 14f+: 0-0
Track : LH: 0-4 **RH: 2-11** Tight: 0-3 **Gall: 2-6**
Aids: Bl: 0-0 Vi: 0-0 Tstrap: 0-0 Ckp: 0-0
Best Rating: **105** 8/08 Asct 1m gd-sft

Very useful; winner in Listed company; stays 1m; acts on most ground on turf; goes on Polytrack.

Perfect Stride

111 **115**
4-y-o b c Oasis Dream-First (Highest Honor (FR))
Sir Michael Stoute Saeed Suhail

Placings:12/0160-161332 **(6202)**
2009: 8^{1}GF, 8^{6}G, 10^{1}GF, 8^{3}GF, 9^{3}GF, 9^{2}G,

	Starts	1st	2nd	3rd	Win & Pl
Career Total (Turf)	**12**	**4**	**2**	**2**	**113845**

115	6/09	Asct	1m2f	(0-110)H	G-F	£28385
112	4/09	Asct	1m		G-F	£23782
107	7/08	Asct	1m	H	G-F	£28039
89	8/07	Sand	7f16y		GD	£4533

Total win prize-money £84742

Going (Turf): Sf: 0-0 GS: 0-0 Gd: 1-5 **GF: 3-7** Fm: 0-0
Distance: 5f/6f: 0-0 **7f-8f: 3-8** 9f-13f: 1-4 14f+: 0-0
Track : LH: 0-1 **RH: 2-6** Tight: 0-2 **Gall: 1-2**
Aids: Bl: 0-0 Vi: 0-0 Tstrap: 0-0 Ckp: 0-0

Best Rating: **115** 6/09 Asct 1m2f gd-fm

Group-class; winner in Listed company and Group placed; effective at up to 1m2f; acts on good and faster ground.

Perfect Truth (IRE)

114 (97)**103**

3-y-o ch f Galileo (IRE)-Charroux (IRE) (Darshaan)

A P O'Brien Derrick Smith

Placings:00402-421020 (5796)

2009: 10^{4}GF, 10^{2}SD, 11^{1}GF, 12^{0}G, 12^{2}S, 14^{0}G,

	Starts	1st	2nd	3rd	Win & Pl
Career Total (Turf)	9	1	1	0	41774
Career Total (AW)	2	0	2	0	13829

103 5/09 Ches 1m3f79y G-F £22708

Total win prize-money £22708

Going (Turf): Sf: 0-2 GS: 0-0 Gd: 0-2 **GF: 1-3** Fm: 0-0
Distance: 5f/6f: 0-0 7f-8f: 0-5 **9f-13f: 1-5** 14f+: 0-1
Track : **LH: 1-7** RH: 0-3 **Tight: 1-2** Gall: 0-3
Aids: Bl: 0-0 Vi: 0-0 Tstrap: 0-0 Ckp: 0-0
Best Rating: **103** 8/09 Cork 1m4f soft

Smart; winner of the Cheshire Oaks; effective over 1m3f; acts on fast ground and on Polytrack.

Perfect Vision

85(94) (72)**57**

2-y-o b f Starcraft (NZ)-Auspicious (Shirley Heights)

C G Cox Mildmay Racing

Placings:001 (7106)

2009: 6^{0}GF, 8^{0}GF, 8^{1}SD,

	Starts	1st	2nd	3rd	Win & Pl
Career Total (Turf)	2	0	0	0	
Career Total (AW)	1	1	0	0	3886

72 10/09 Kemp 1m STD £3885

Total win prize-money £3886

Going (Turf): **Sf: 0-0 GS: 0-0 Gd: 0-0 GF: 0-2 Fm: 0-0**
Distance: 5f/6f: 0-0 **7f-8f: 1-3** 9f-13f: 0-0 14f+: 0-0
Track : LH: 0-0 **RH: 1-2** Tight: 0-0 Gall: 0-0
Aids: Bl: 0-0 Vi: 0-0 Tstrap: 0-0 Ckp: 0-0
Best Rating: **72** 10/09 Kemp 1m stand

Pergamon (IRE)

97(88) (39)**80**

3-y-o b g Dalakhani (IRE)-Pinaflore (FR) (Formidable (USA))

Miss C Dyson (J H M Gosden 5/5) Miss C Dyson

Placings:32-06 (1780)

2009: 10^{0}GF, 11^{6}SD,

	Starts	1st	2nd	3rd	Win & Pl
Career Total (Turf)	3	0	1	1	5847
Career Total (AW)	1	0	0	0	0

Going (Turf): **Sf: 0-1 GS: 0-0 Gd: 0-0 GF: 0-2 Fm: 0-0**
Distance: 5f/6f: 0-0 7f-8f: 0-1 9f-13f: 0-3 14f+: 0-0
Track : LH: 0-2 RH: 0-0 Tight: 0-0 Gall: 0-0
Aids: Bl: 0-2 Vi: 0-0 Tstrap: 0-0 Ckp: 0-0
Best Rating: **80** 8/08 Nott 1m75y soft

Fair; effective over 7f-1m; acts on fast and soft ground.

Perks (IRE)

109(97) (72)**112**

4-y-o b g Selkirk (USA)-Green Charter(GreenDesert (USA))

J L Dunlop Benny Andersson

Placings:004/1300113-5002305 (7188)

2009: 10^{5}HY, 10^{0}G, 10^{0}GF, 8^{2}GS, 8^{3}G, 10^{0}SD, 10^{5}G,

	Starts	1st	2nd	3rd	Win & Pl
Career Total (Turf)	16	3	1	3	84814
Career Total (AW)	1	0	0	0	

112 9/08 Donc 1m2f60y SFT £12462
109 8/08 Hayd 1m2f120y (0-105)H HVY £49848
91 4/08 Donc 1m (0-85)H G-S £4533

Total win prize-money £66843

Going (Turf): **Sf: 2-5** GS: 1-3 Gd: 0-5 GF: 0-3 Fm: 0-0
Distance: 5f/6f: 0-0 7f-8f: 1-8 **9f-13f: 2-9** 14f+: 0-0
Track : **LH: 2-4** RH: 0-4 Tight: 0-0 **Gall: 1-2**
Aids: Bl: 0-0 Vi: 0-0 Tstrap: 0-0 Ckp: 0-0
Best Rating: **112** 9/08 Donc 1m2f60y soft

Smart; suited by 1m2f; acts well on soft ground.

Perlachy

(107) (73)**50**

5-y-o b g Kyllachy-Perfect Dream (Emperor Jones (USA))

J R Holt (D Shaw 26/3) Mrs N Macauley

Placings:54323243**665**/3054504403**63242321**/335300604 1030431-2116002123 (7634)

2009: 5^{2}SD, 6^{1}SD, 5^{1}SD, 6^{6}SD, 5^{0}SD, 5^{0}SD, 5^{2}SD, 5^{1}SD, 5^{2}SD, 5^{3}SD,

	Starts	1st	2nd	3rd	Win & Pl
Career Total (Turf)	14	0	2	4	5831
Career Total (AW)	41	6	6	9	21683

73 11/09 Wolv 5f216y (0-75)H STD £3238
72 2/09 Wolv 5f20y (0-75)H STD £2729
66 2/09 Kemp 6f (0-65)H STD £1706
64 12/08 GrLe 6f (0-55)H STD £1942
60 4/08 Kemp 6f (0-55) STD £1683
65 12/07 Wolv 5f216y (0-60)H STD £2047

Total win prize-money £13349

Going (Turf): **Sf: 0-1 GS: 0-2 Gd: 0-2 GF: 0-7 Fm: 0-2**
Distance: **5f/6f: 6-53** 7f-8f: 0-2 9f-13f: 0-0 14f+: 0-0
Track : **LH: 4-30** RH: 2-8 **Tight: 3-26** Gall: 1-3
Aids: Bl: 0-0 **Vi: 6-39** Tstrap: 0-1 Ckp: 0-1
Best Rating: **73** 11/09 Wolv 5f216y stand

Modest; effective over 5f-7f; acts on fast ground; also goes on Polytrack; often wears a visor.

Perle D'Amour (IRE)

68 **9**

2-y-o b f Pearl Of Love (IRE)-Bella Vie (IRE) (Sadler's Wells (USA))

R Hannon Mrs Maeve Queally

Placings:4 (2514)

2009: 5^{4}F,

	Starts	1st	2nd	3rd	Win & Pl
Career Total (Turf)	1	0	0	0	168

Going (Turf): **Sf: 0-0 GS: 0-0 Gd: 0-0 GF: 0-0 Fm: 0-1**
Distance: 5f/6f: 0-1 7f-8f: 0-0 9f-13f: 0-0 14f+: 0-0
Track : LH: 0-1 RH: 0-0 Tight: 0-0 Gall: 0-1
Aids: Bl: 0-0 Vi: 0-0 Tstrap: 0-0 Ckp: 0-0
Best Rating: **9** 5/09 Bath 5f161y firm

Perpetually (IRE)

111 **95**

3-y-o b c Singspiel (IRE)-Set In Motion (USA) (Mr Prospector (USA))

M Johnston Sheikh Hamdan Bin Mohammed Al Maktoum

Placings:1-1 (1303)

2009: 10^{1}GF,

	Starts	1st	2nd	3rd	Win & Pl
Career Total (Turf)	2	2	0	0	16190

95 4/09 NmkR 1m2f (0-95)H G-F £9714
81 7/08 York 7f G-F £6476

Total win prize-money £16190

Going (Turf): Sf: 0-0 GS: 0-0 Gd: 0-0 **GF: 2-2** Fm: 0-0
Distance: 5f/6f: 0-0 7f-8f: 1-1 9f-13f: 1-1 14f+: 0-0
Track : **LH: 1-1** RH: 0-0 Tight: 0-0 **Gall: 1-1**
Aids: Bl: 0-0 Vi: 0-0 Tstrap: 0-0 Ckp: 0-0
Best Rating: **95** 4/09 NmkR 1m2f gd-fm

Useful; stays 1m2f and acts on fast ground.

Perse

73 **42**

2-y-o br f Rock Of Gibraltar (IRE)-La Persiana (Daylami (IRE))

W Jarvis Gillian, Lady Howard De Walden

Placings:0 (7183)

2009: 7^{0}G,

	Starts	1st	2nd	3rd	Win & Pl
Career Total (Turf)	1	0	0	0	

Going (Turf): **Sf: 0-0 GS: 0-0 Gd: 0-1 GF: 0-0 Fm: 0-0**
Distance: 5f/6f: 0-0 7f-8f: 0-1 9f-13f: 0-0 14f+: 0-0
Track : LH: 0-0 RH: 0-0 Tight: 0-0 Gall: 0-0
Aids: Bl: 0-0 Vi: 0-0 Tstrap: 0-0 Ckp: 0-0
Best Rating: **42** 10/09 NmkR 7f good

Persian Buddy

(90) (67)**46**

3-y-o b g Reel Buddy (USA)-Breeze Again (USA) (Favorite Trick (USA))

Jamie Poulton Ormonde Racing

Placings:050-6 (0397)

2009: 8^{6}SD,

	Starts	1st	2nd	3rd	Win & Pl
Career Total (Turf)	2	0	0	0	
Career Total (AW)	2	0	0	0	0

Going (Turf): **Sf: 0-0 GS: 0-0 Gd: 0-2 GF: 0-0 Fm: 0-0**
Distance: 5f/6f: 0-0 7f-8f: 0-3 9f-13f: 0-1 14f+: 0-0
Track : LH: 0-2 RH: 0-1 Tight: 0-2 Gall: 0-0
Aids: Bl: 0-0 Vi: 0-0 Tstrap: 0-0 Ckp: 0-0
Best Rating: **67** 2/09 Ling 1m stand

Persian Heroine (IRE)

78 **38**

2-y-o b f Intikhab (USA)-Persian Fantasy (Persian Bold)

J L Dunlop Windflower Overseas Holdings Inc

Placings:50 (6567)

2009: 6^{5}GF, 7^{0}GF,

	Starts	1st	2nd	3rd	Win & Pl
Career Total (Turf)	2	0	0	0	0

Going (Turf): **Sf: 0-0 GS: 0-0 Gd: 0-0 GF: 0-2 Fm: 0-0**
Distance: 5f/6f: 0-1 7f-8f: 0-1 9f-13f: 0-0 14f+: 0-0
Track : LH: 0-0 RH: 0-0 Tight: 0-0 Gall: 0-0

Aids: Bl: 0-0 Vi: 0-0 Tstrap: 0-0 Ckp: 0-0
Best Rating: 38 8/09 Folk 6f gd-fm

Persian Memories (IRE)

101(93) (67)72
3-y-o br f Indian Ridge-Persian Fantasy (Persian Bold)
J L Dunlop Windflower Overseas Holdings Inc

Placings:0344-0032235056 (7049)
2009: 11⁰GF, 10⁰SD, 11³GF, 11²GF, 12²GF, 11³GS, 13⁵G, 16⁰SD, 12⁵GF, 12⁶SD,

	Starts	1st	2nd	3rd	Win & Pl
Career Total (Turf)	10	0	2	3	4512
Career Total (AW)	4	0	0	0	433

Going (Turf): Sf: 0-0 GS: 0-1 Gd: 0-1 GF: 0-8 Fm: 0-0
Distance: 5f/6f: 0-0 7f-8f: 0-4 9f-13f: 0-8 14f+: 0-2
Track: LH: 0-6 RH: 0-5 Tight: 0-7 Gall: 0-1
Aids: Bl: 0-1 Vi: 0-0 Tstrap: 0-0 Ckp: 0-0
Best Rating: 72 7/08 Gdwd 7f gd-fm

Modest; stays 1m4f; acts on good ground.

Persian Peril

104(110) (87)92
5-y-o br g Erhaab (USA)-Brush Away (Ahonoora)
G A Swinbank Mrs J Porter

Placings:44221/4050/6010101322-013300230 (7375)
2009: 12⁰SD, 11¹SD, 10³G, 10³HY, 10⁰S, 12⁰S, 10²G, 11³SD, 8⁰SD,

	Starts	1st	2nd	3rd	Win & Pl
Career Total (Turf)	21	4	2	3	23360
Career Total (AW)	7	1	3	1	10195

87	5/09	Sthl	1m3f	(0-85)H	STD	£5828
79	8/08	Ayr	1m1f20y	(0-85)H	SFT	£6476
76	8/08	Hayd	1m2f120y		G-S	£3238
76	7/08	Hayd	1m2f120y		HVY	£3238
60	8/06	Muss	7f30y		GD	£3238

Total win prize-money £22019

Going (Turf): Sf: 2-6 GS: 1-3 Gd: 1-6 GF: 0-6 Fm: 0-0
Distance: 5f/6f: 0-3 7f-8f: 1-2 9f-13f: 4-23 14f+: 0-0
Track: LH: 4-21 RH: 1-4 Tight: 1-4 Gall: 0-5
Aids: Bl: 0-0 Vi: 0-0 Tstrap: 0-0 Ckp: 0-0
Best Rating: 92 10/09 York 1m2f88y good

Useful; stays 1m4f; acts on good and softer ground; goes on sand.

Persian Poet

80 44
2-y-o b g Dubai Destination (USA)-Salim Toto (Mtoto)
M Johnston Sheikh Hamdan Bin Mohammed Al Maktoum

Placings:000 (6821)
2009: 8⁰G, 8⁰GS, 8⁰GF,

	Starts	1st	2nd	3rd	Win & Pl
Career Total (Turf)	3	0	0	0	

Going (Turf): Sf: 0-0 GS: 0-1 Gd: 0-1 GF: 0-1 Fm: 0-0
Distance: 5f/6f: 0-0 7f-8f: 0-1 9f-13f: 0-2 14f+: 0-0
Track: LH: 0-1 RH: 0-0 Tight: 0-0 Gall: 0-0
Aids: Bl: 0-0 Vi: 0-0 Tstrap: 0-0 Ckp: 0-0
Best Rating: 44 10/09 Rdcr 1m gd-fm

Persian Storm (GER)

99(87) (62)103
5-y-o b g Monsun (GER)-Private Life (FR) (Bering)
G L Moore Graham Gillespie

Placings:14/61612/66-543 (4731)
2009: 10⁵SD, 8⁴G, 7³GS,

	Starts	1st	2nd	3rd	Win & Pl
Career Total (Turf)	11	3	1	1	60439
Career Total (AW)	1	0	0	0	1076

111	8/07	Badn	1m2f	GD	£20270
111	5/07	Muni	1m2f	GD	£21622
	9/06	Brem	7f	GD	£4138

Total win prize-money £46030

Going (Turf): Sf: 0-2 GS: 0-1 Gd: 3-7 GF: 0-0 Fm: 0-0
Distance: 5f/6f: 0-0 7f-8f: 1-4 9f-13f: 2-8 14f+: 0-0
Track: LH: 2-6 RH: 0-4 Tight: 0-1 Gall: 0-0
Aids: Bl: 0-0 Vi: 0-0 Tstrap: 0-0 Ckp: 0-0
Best Rating: 111 9/07 Frnk 1m2f good

Dual 1m2f Group 3 winner on the Flat in Germany.

Persian Tomcat (IRE)

95(100) (51)51
3-y-o gr g One Cool Cat (USA)-Persian Mistress (IRE) (Persian Bold)
Miss J Feilden Top Cat Partnership

Placings:0665-633203465035565 (7737)
2009: 8⁶SD, 8³SD, 10³SD, 11²GF, 11⁰S, 12³SD, 12⁴GF, 12⁶GF, 11⁵SD, 9⁰GF, 10³SS, 10⁵SS, 9⁵SD, 10⁶SD, 12⁵SD,

	Starts	1st	2nd	3rd	Win & Pl
Career Total (Turf)	9	0	1	0	605
Career Total (AW)	10	0	0	4	1159

Going (Turf): Sf: 0-1 GS: 0-1 Gd: 0-2 GF: 0-5 Fm: 0-0
Distance: 5f/6f: 0-2 7f-8f: 0-4 9f-13f: 0-13 14f+: 0-0
Track: LH: 0-9 RH: 0-7 Tight: 0-9 Gall: 0-0
Aids: Bl: 0-0 Vi: 0-2 Tstrap: 0-1 Ckp: 0-1
Best Rating: 51 10/09 Ling 1m2f std-slw

Plating-class; stays 1m4f; acts on Polytrack and fast ground.

Persistent (IRE)

93(97) (58)36
4-y-o b g Cape Cross (IRE)-Insistent (USA) (Diesis)
C T Pogson (D G Bridgwater 28/8) Wordingham Plant Hire

Placings:606/330402-0 (5381)
2009: 11⁰G,

	Starts	1st	2nd	3rd	Win & Pl
Career Total (Turf)	4	0	0	0	
Career Total (AW)	6	0	1	2	1214

Going (Turf): Sf: 0-0 GS: 0-0 Gd: 0-2 GF: 0-2 Fm: 0-0
Distance: 5f/6f: 0-1 7f-8f: 0-3 9f-13f: 0-6 14f+: 0-0
Track: LH: 0-8 RH: 0-0 Tight: 0-5 Gall: 0-0
Aids: Bl: 0-0 Vi: 0-0 Tstrap: 0-3 Ckp: 0-3
Best Rating: 58 7/08 Sthl 1m4f std-slw

Moderate; effective at around 1m2f-1m4f; acts on sand.

Persona Non Grata (IRE)

94(91) (65)71
2-y-o b g Azamour (IRE)-Private Life (FR) (Bering)
R Charlton B E Nielsen

Placings:460 (6721)
2009: 8⁴SD, 8⁶G, 8⁰SD,

	Starts	1st	2nd	3rd	Win & Pl
Career Total (Turf)	1	0	0	0	0
Career Total (AW)	2	0	0	0	397

Going (Turf): Sf: 0-0 GS: 0-0 Gd: 0-1 GF: 0-0 Fm: 0-0
Distance: 5f/6f: 0-0 7f-8f: 0-2 9f-13f: 0-1 14f+: 0-0
Track: LH: 0-0 RH: 0-3 Tight: 0-1 Gall: 0-0
Aids: Bl: 0-3 Vi: 0-0 Tstrap: 0-0 Ckp: 0-0
Best Rating: 71 10/09 Wind 1m67y good

Personify

96(100) (57)54
7-y-o ch g Zafonic (USA)-Dignify (IRE) (Rainbow Quest (USA))
J L Flint J L Flint

Placings:140/00012210/500300/4630035054304100-400 (3949)
2009: 10⁴GF, 12⁰GF, 9⁰GF,

	Starts	1st	2nd	3rd	Win & Pl
Career Total (Turf)	29	3	2	3	17736
Career Total (AW)	7	1	0	1	2852

57	9/08	GrLe	1m2f	(0-50)H	STD	£2590
80	9/06	Sand	1m14y	(0-80)H	G-F	£5505
75	6/06	Bath	1m5y	(0-70)H	G-F	£3886
76	6/04	Yarm	6f3y	D	FRM	£4735

Total win prize-money £16716

Going (Turf): Sf: 0-2 GS: 0-3 Gd: 0-6 GF: 2-14 Fm: 1-4
Distance: 5f/6f: 0-1 7f-8f: 1-4 9f-13f: 3-31 14f+: 0-0
Track: LH: 2-24 RH: 1-5 Tight: 1-16 Gall: 1-1
Aids: Bl: 0-3 Vi: 0-1 Tstrap: 3-25 Ckp: 3-25
Best Rating: 80 9/06 Sand 1m14y gd-fm

Moderate; stays 1m2f; acts on fast ground and Polytrack; often wears cheekpieces.

Pertemps Power

84(95) (58)55
5-y-o b g Zaha (CAN)-Peristyle (Tolomeo)
B G Powell Pertemps Group Limited

Placings:645044/0-32045345 (7154)
2009: 13³SD, 12²SD, 13⁰SD, 12⁴GF, 12⁵GS, 12³SD, 13⁴SD, 16⁵SD,

	Starts	1st	2nd	3rd	Win & Pl
Career Total (Turf)	6	0	0	0	0
Career Total (AW)	9	0	1	2	1264

Going (Turf): Sf: 0-1 GS: 0-1 Gd: 0-1 GF: 0-3 Fm: 0-0
Distance: 5f/6f: 0-0 7f-8f: 0-0 9f-13f: 0-7 14f+: 0-8
Track: LH: 0-13 RH: 0-2 Tight: 0-12 Gall: 0-0
Aids: Bl: 0-0 Vi: 0-0 Tstrap: 0-0 Ckp: 0-0
Best Rating: 58 6/09 Wolv 1m4f50y stand

Moderate; stays 1m6f; acts on Polytrack; has worn a tongue tie.

Pete's Passion

66 2
3-y-o b f Rock Of Gibraltar (IRE)-Three Days In May (Cadeaux Genereux)

R A Fahey P D Smith Holdings Ltd

Placings:0 **(3876)**
2009: 7^{0}GF,

	Starts	1st	2nd	3rd	Win & Pl
Career Total (Turf)	**1**	**0**	**0**	**0**	

Going (Turf): **Sf: 0-0 GS: 0-0 Gd: 0-0 GF: 0-1 Fm: 0-0**
Distance: 5f/6f: 0-0 7f-8f: 0-1 9f-13f: 0-0 14f+: 0-0
Track : LH: 0-1 RH: 0-0 Tight: 0-0 Gall: 0-1
Aids: Bl: 0-0 Vi: 0-0 Tstrap: 0-0 Ckp: 0-0
Best Rating: **2** 7/09 York 7f gd-fm

Petella

97 **63**
3-y-o b f Tamure (IRE)-Miss Petronella (Petoski)
C W Thornton A Crute & Partners

Placings:056-4550020 **(7124)**
2009: 8^{4}GF, 10^{5}G, 11^{5}G, 12^{0}G, 12^{0}GF, 16^{2}GF, 16^{0}G,

	Starts	1st	2nd	3rd	Win & Pl
Career Total (Turf)	**10**	**0**	**1**	**0**	**915**

Going (Turf): **Sf: 0-1 GS: 0-0 Gd: 0-5 GF: 0-4 Fm: 0-0**
Distance: 5f/6f: 0-3 7f-8f: 0-0 9f-13f: 0-5 14f+: 0-2
Track : LH: 0-5 RH: 0-2 Tight: 0-3 Gall: 0-0
Aids: Bl: 0-0 Vi: 0-0 Tstrap: 0-0 Ckp: 0-0
Best Rating: **63** 9/08 Hayd 6f gd-fm

Peter Grimes (IRE)

99(100) (63)**71**
3-y-o ch g Alhaarth (IRE)-Aldburgh (Bluebird (USA))
A King (H J L Dunlop 2/9) Let's Live Racing

Placings:0360-1405330 **(5570)**
2009: 9^{1}GS, 9^{4}G, 11^{0}GS, 11^{5}F, 10^{3}S, 10^{3}G, **10**^{0}SD,

	Starts	1st	2nd	3rd	Win & Pl
Career Total (Turf)	**10**	**1**	**0**	**3**	**4469**
Career Total (AW)	**1**	**0**	**0**	**0**	

69 3/09 Folk 1m1f149y (0-70)H G-S £3070
Total win prize-money £3071

Going (Turf): Sf: 0-2 **GS: 1-3** Gd: 0-3 GF: 0-1 Fm: 0-1
Distance: 5f/6f: 0-0 7f-8f: 0-4 **9f-13f: 1-7** 14f+: 0-0
Track : LH: 0-4 **RH: 1-6 Tight: 1-3** Gall: 0-3
Aids: Bl: 0-0 Vi: 0-0 Tstrap: 0-0 Ckp: 0-0
Best Rating: **71** 7/09 NmkJ 1m2f soft

Modest; effective at up to 1m2f; acts on good and softer ground.

Peter Island (FR)

105(108) (83)**94**
6-y-o b g Dansili-Catania (USA) (Aloma's Ruler (USA))
J Gallagher C R Marks (banbury)

Placings:005100/**054012**40545523**160**/403**0**0021**0540000**/
64132**2**01025-31604606030 **(6964)**
2009: 6^{3}SD, 5^{1}GF, 6^{6}G, 6^{0}G, 6^{4}GF, 5^{6}GF, 6^{0}G, 6^{6}GF, 6^{0}G, 6^{3}GF, 5^{0}G,

	Starts	1st	2nd	3rd	Win & Pl
Career Total (Turf)	**42**	**5**	**5**	**4**	**38728**
Career Total (AW)	**18**	**2**	**1**	**1**	**14331**

94 4/09 Leic 5f218y (0-85)H G-F £4857
84 9/08 Gdwd 6f (0-80)H G-F £4857
81 6/08 Wwck 6f (0-85)H G-F £6476
84 8/07 Brig 5f213y (0-80)H FRM £4731
82 8/06 Kemp 6f (0-80)H STD £7790
78 4/06 Kemp 6f (0-65)H STD £3238
78 8/05 Ches 7f2y G-F £4837
Total win prize-money £36788

Going (Turf): Sf: 0-1 GS: 0-2 Gd: 0-9 **GF: 4-28** Fm: 1-2
Distance: **5f/6f: 6-50** 7f-8f: 1-9 9f-13f: 0-1 14f+: 0-0
Track : **LH: 3-27** RH: 2-8 **Tight: 1-15** Gall: 0-6
Aids: Bl: 1-12 **Vi: 5-34** Tstrap: 0-0 Ckp: 0-0
Best Rating: **94** 4/09 Leic 5f218y gd-fm

Useful; effective over 5f-7f; acts on fast ground and on Polytrack; wears blinkers or a visor; suited by forcing tactics.

Peter's Follie

86 **57**
2-y-o gr f Highest Honor (FR)-Fabulous Speed (USA) (Silver Hawk (USA))
Tom Dascombe Northmore Stud

Placings:4300 **(6590)**
2009: 5^{4}G, 5^{3}G, 5^{0}G, 6^{0}GS,

	Starts	1st	2nd	3rd	Win & Pl
Career Total (Turf)	**4**	**0**	**0**	**1**	**722**

Going (Turf): **Sf: 0-0 GS: 0-1 Gd: 0-3 GF: 0-0 Fm: 0-0**
Distance: 5f/6f: 0-3 7f-8f: 0-1 9f-13f: 0-0 14f+: 0-0
Track : LH: 0-1 RH: 0-0 Tight: 0-0 Gall: 0-1
Aids: Bl: 0-0 Vi: 0-0 Tstrap: 0-0 Ckp: 0-0
Best Rating: **57** 8/09 Bevl 5f good

Peter's Gift (IRE)

102(101) (75)**74**
3-y-o b f Catcher In The Rye (IRE)-Eastern Blue (IRE) (Be My Guest (USA))
K A Ryan Mr & Mrs Julian And Rosie Richer

Placings:360412-25153500 **(6348)**
2009: 7^{2}GF, 7^{5}GF, 7^{1}SD, 8^{5}GF, 8^{3}G, 7^{5}SD, 8^{0}G, 7^{0}SD,

	Starts	1st	2nd	3rd	Win & Pl
Career Total (Turf)	**9**	**1**	**1**	**2**	**6005**
Career Total (AW)	**5**	**1**	**1**	**0**	**4901**

75 5/09 Sthl 7f (0-75)H STD £3070
59 11/08 Muss 7f30y SFT £3885
Total win prize-money £6957

Going (Turf): **Sf: 1-1** GS: 0-1 Gd: 0-4 GF: 0-3 Fm: 0-0
Distance: 5f/6f: 0-4 **7f-8f: 2-9** 9f-13f: 0-1 14f+: 0-0
Track : LH: 1-6 RH: 1-4 **Tight: 1-5** Gall: 0-2
Aids: Bl: 0-0 Vi: 0-0 Tstrap: 0-0 Ckp: 0-0
Best Rating: **75** 5/09 Sthl 7f stand

Fair; stays 7f; acts on most ground and on Fibresand.

Peter's Storm (USA)

(98) (78)**75**
4-y-o ch g Van Nistelrooy (USA)-Fairy Land Flyer (USA) (Lyphard's Wish (FR))
K A Ryan Peter & Richard Foden Racing Partnership

Placings:510/003250**026-33066040** **(0937)**
2009: 5^{3}SD, 5^{3}SD, 5^{0}SD, 7^{6}SD, 6^{6}SD, 5^{0}SD, 6^{4}SD, 5^{0}SD,

	Starts	1st	2nd	3rd	Win & Pl
Career Total (Turf)	**9**	**0**	**1**	**1**	**2312**
Career Total (AW)	**11**	**1**	**1**	**2**	**4628**

80 10/07 Wolv 5f20y STD £2047
Total win prize-money £2048

Going (Turf): **Sf: 0-4 GS: 0-1 Gd: 0-1 GF: 0-3 Fm: 0-0**
Distance: **5f/6f: 1-17** 7f-8f: 0-3 9f-13f: 0-0 14f+: 0-0
Track : **LH: 1-10** RH: 0-2 **Tight: 1-7** Gall: 0-0
Aids: Bl: 0-0 Vi: 0-0 Tstrap: 0-3 Ckp: 0-3
Best Rating: **80** 10/07 Wolv 5f20y stand

Fair; effective over 5f-6f; acts on soft ground; also goes on Polytrack.

Peters Pride

(64)
7-y-o b g Silver Patriarch (IRE)-Manzanilla (Mango Express)
M W Easterby T Bannister, M Hall & G Fawcett

Placings:0 **(1780)**
2009: 11^{0}SD,

	Starts	1st	2nd	3rd	Win & Pl
Career Total (Turf)	**0**	**0**	**0**	**0**	
Career Total (AW)	**1**	**0**	**0**	**0**	

Going (Turf): **Sf: 0-0 GS: 0-0 Gd: 0-0 GF: 0-0 Fm: 0-0**
Distance: 5f/6f: 0-0 7f-8f: 0-0 9f-13f: 0-1 14f+: 0-0
Track : LH: 0-1 RH: 0-0 Tight: 0-0 Gall: 0-0
Aids: Bl: 0-0 Vi: 0-0 Tstrap: 0-0 Ckp: 0-0

Pethers Dancer (IRE)

73(71) (5)
3-y-o b g Kyllachy-La Piaf (FR) (Fabulous Dancer (USA))
W R Muir Perspicacious Punters Racing Club

Placings:00-00 **(3305)**
2009: 8^{0}SD, 7^{0}GF,

	Starts	1st	2nd	3rd	Win & Pl
Career Total (Turf)	**1**	**0**	**0**	**0**	
Career Total (AW)	**3**	**0**	**0**	**0**	

Going (Turf): **Sf: 0-0 GS: 0-0 Gd: 0-0 GF: 0-1 Fm: 0-0**
Distance: 5f/6f: 0-2 7f-8f: 0-2 9f-13f: 0-0 14f+: 0-0
Track : LH: 0-1 RH: 0-2 Tight: 0-1 Gall: 0-0
Aids: Bl: 0-1 Vi: 0-0 Tstrap: 0-0 Ckp: 0-0
Best Rating: **5** 11/08 Kemp 6f stand

Petidium

(39) **40**
4-y-o b f Presidium-Efipetite (Efisio)
N Bycroft Hambleton Racing Partnership I

Placings:00/0 **(6880)**
2009: 7^{0}SD,

	Starts	1st	2nd	3rd	Win & Pl
Career Total (Turf)	**2**	**0**	**0**	**0**	
Career Total (AW)	**1**	**0**	**0**	**0**	

Going (Turf): **Sf: 0-0 GS: 0-0 Gd: 0-1 GF: 0-1 Fm: 0-0**
Distance: 5f/6f: 0-2 7f-8f: 0-1 9f-13f: 0-0 14f+: 0-0
Track : LH: 0-1 RH: 0-0 Tight: 0-0 Gall: 0-0
Aids: Bl: 0-0 Vi: 0-0 Tstrap: 0-0 Ckp: 0-0
Best Rating: **40** 10/07 Rdcr 6f good

Petit Belle

70(72) (18)
2-y-o b f Piccolo-Tallulah Belle (Crowning Honors (CAN))
N P Littmoden Mrs Emma Littmoden

Placings:000 (7556)
2009: 5^{0}G, 5^{0}SD, 5^{0}SD,

	Starts	1st	2nd	3rd	Win & Pl
Career Total (Turf)	1	0	0	0	
Career Total (AW)	2	0	0	0	

Going (Turf): Sf: 0-0 GS: 0-0 Gd: 0-1 GF: 0-0 Fm: 0-0
Distance: 5f/6f: 0-3 7f-8f: 0-0 9f-13f: 0-0 14f+: 0-0
Track : LH: 0-2 RH: 0-0 Tight: 0-2 Gall: 0-1
Aids: Bl: 0-0 Vi: 0-0 Tstrap: 0-0 Ckp: 0-0
Best Rating: 18 11/09 Wolv 5f216y stand

Petite Mambo

84(75) (51)**62**
2-y-o b g Miesque's Son (USA)-Chalet (Singspiel (IRE))
W De Best-Turner W De Best-Turner

Placings:006000 (7391)
2009: 6^{0}GF, 7^{0}GF, 7^{6}S, 8^{0}GS, 8^{0}G, 8^{0}SD,

	Starts	1st	2nd	3rd	Win & Pl
Career Total (Turf)	5	0	0	0	140
Career Total (AW)	1	0	0	0	

Going (Turf): Sf: 0-1 GS: 0-1 Gd: 0-1 GF: 0-2 Fm: 0-0
Distance: 5f/6f: 0-1 7f-8f: 0-3 9f-13f: 0-2 14f+: 0-0
Track : LH: 0-3 RH: 0-1 Tight: 0-3 Gall: 0-1
Aids: Bl: 0-0 Vi: 0-0 Tstrap: 0-0 Ckp: 0-0
Best Rating: 62 7/09 Newb 7f soft

Petite Rocket (IRE)

65
3-y-o b f Fayruz-Courtisane (Persepolis (FR))
J A McShane Lothian Recycling Limited

Placings:0-0 (2157)
2009: 5^{0}GF,

	Starts	1st	2nd	3rd	Win & Pl
Career Total (Turf)	2	0	0	0	

Going (Turf): Sf: 0-0 GS: 0-0 Gd: 0-1 GF: 0-1 Fm: 0-0
Distance: 5f/6f: 0-1 7f-8f: 0-1 9f-13f: 0-0 14f+: 0-0
Track : LH: 0-0 RH: 0-0 Tight: 0-0 Gall: 0-0
Aids: Bl: 0-0 Vi: 0-0 Tstrap: 0-0 Ckp: 0-0

Petomic (IRE)

103(100) (66)**68**
4-y-o ch g Dubai Destination (USA)-Petomi (Presidium)
M Hill (R M Beckett 1/7) EGHQ Partnership

Placings:0/0-036315450 (7236)
2009: 7^{0}SD, 8^{3}GF, 8^{6}G, 8^{3}G, 8^{1}G, 8^{5}GS, 10^{4}SD, 8^{5}SD, 8^{0}SD,

	Starts	1st	2nd	3rd	Win & Pl
Career Total (Turf)	6	1	0	2	5390
Career Total (AW)	5	0	0	0	0

68 8/09 Chep 1m14y (0-70)H GD £4533
Total win prize-money £4533

Going (Turf): Sf: 0-0 GS: 0-1 **Gd: 1-3** GF: 0-2 Fm: 0-0
Distance: 5f/6f: 0-1 7f-8f: 0-3 **9f-13f: 1-7** 14f+: 0-0
Track : LH: 0-3 RH: 0-3 Tight: 0-4 Gall: 0-0
Aids: Bl: 0-0 Vi: 0-0 Tstrap: 0-0 Ckp: 0-0
Best Rating: 68 8/09 Chep 1m14y good

Modest sort; effective at 1m; acts on good ground; has worn a tongue tie.

Petougg

94 **76**
2-y-o b g Tobougg (IRE)-Piroshka (Soviet Star (USA))
W Jarvis E Randall, N Rich & GB Turnbull Ltd

Placings:156 (6247)
2009: 6^{1}GS, 6^{5}GS, 6^{6}GF,

	Starts	1st	2nd	3rd	Win & Pl
Career Total (Turf)	3	1	0	0	3238

76 7/09 Hayd 6f G-S £3238
Total win prize-money £3238

Going (Turf): Sf: 0-0 **GS: 1-2** Gd: 0-0 GF: 0-1 Fm: 0-0
Distance: **5f/6f: 1-2** 7f-8f: 0-1 9f-13f: 0-0 14f+: 0-0
Track : LH: 0-0 RH: 0-0 Tight: 0-0 Gall: 0-0
Aids: Bl: 0-0 Vi: 0-0 Tstrap: 0-0 Ckp: 0-0
Best Rating: 76 7/09 Hayd 6f gd-sft

Fair; stays 7f; acts on easy ground.

Petrafied (FR)

94(84) (23)**66**
3-y-o ch f Gold Away (IRE)-Thai Rose (USA) (Gulch (USA))
P J Prendergast Mrs Patrick Prendergast

Placings:300-0600 (5016)
2009: 8^{0}HY, 8^{6}GF, 9^{0}Y, 8^{0}SD,

	Starts	1st	2nd	3rd	Win & Pl
Career Total (Turf)	6	0	0	1	574
Career Total (AW)	1	0	0	0	

Going (Turf): Sf: 0-1 GS: 0-0 Gd: 0-1 GF: 0-1 Fm: 0-0
Distance: 5f/6f: 0-0 7f-8f: 0-6 9f-13f: 0-1 14f+: 0-0
Track : LH: 0-3 RH: 0-4 Tight: 0-1 Gall: 0-2
Aids: Bl: 0-0 Vi: 0-0 Tstrap: 0-0 Ckp: 0-0
Best Rating: 66 9/08 Gowr 1m good

Petrenko

(76) (23)
3-y-o b g Efisio-Lambast (Relkino)
R A Fahey R Cowie

Placings:060 (0716)
2009: 5^{0}SD, 6^{6}SD, 8^{0}SD,

	Starts	1st	2nd	3rd	Win & Pl
Career Total (Turf)	0	0	0	0	
Career Total (AW)	3	0	0	0	0

Going (Turf): Sf: 0-0 GS: 0-0 Gd: 0-0 GF: 0-0 Fm: 0-0
Distance: 5f/6f: 0-2 7f-8f: 0-0 9f-13f: 0-1 14f+: 0-0
Track : LH: 0-3 RH: 0-0 Tight: 0-1 Gall: 0-1
Aids: Bl: 0-0 Vi: 0-0 Tstrap: 0-0 Ckp: 0-0
Best Rating: 23 1/09 GrLe 5f stand

Petrocelli

93(70) (28)**74**
2-y-o b g Piccolo-Sarcita (Primo Dominie)
A J McCabe Raymond Tooth

Placings:43530 (4858)
2009: 5^{4}GF, 5^{3}GF, 5^{5}GF, 6^{3}GF, 7^{0}SD,

	Starts	1st	2nd	3rd	Win & Pl
Career Total (Turf)	4	0	0	2	1083
Career Total (AW)	1	0	0	0	

Going (Turf): Sf: 0-0 GS: 0-0 Gd: 0-0 GF: 0-4 Fm: 0-0
Distance: 5f/6f: 0-4 7f-8f: 0-1 9f-13f: 0-0 14f+: 0-0
Track : LH: 0-1 RH: 0-0 Tight: 0-1 Gall: 0-0
Aids: Bl: 0-2 Vi: 0-0 Tstrap: 0-0 Ckp: 0-0
Best Rating: 74 5/09 Donc 6f gd-fm

Petroglyph

(86) (32)**64**
5-y-o ch g Indian Ridge-Madame Dubois (Legend Of France (USA))
M G Quinlan (P Bowen 20/1) Mrs J Quinlan

Placings:3/00-00 (6770)
2009: 8^{0}SD, 12^{0}SD,

	Starts	1st	2nd	3rd	Win & Pl
Career Total (Turf)	3	0	0	1	385
Career Total (AW)	2	0	0	0	

Going (Turf): Sf: 0-2 GS: 0-0 Gd: 0-0 GF: 0-1 Fm: 0-0
Distance: 5f/6f: 0-0 7f-8f: 0-2 9f-13f: 0-3 14f+: 0-0
Track : LH: 0-2 RH: 0-2 Tight: 0-0 Gall: 0-0
Aids: Bl: 0-0 Vi: 0-0 Tstrap: 0-1 Ckp: 0-1
Best Rating: 64 11/06 Nott 1m54y soft

Petrovsky

111(101) (87)**101**
3-y-o gr c Daylami (IRE)-Russian Society (Darshaan)
M Johnston Sheikh Hamdan Bin Mohammed Al Maktoum

Placings:351-11215 (6138)
2009: 8^{1}SD, 11^{1}SD, 12^{2}GF, 12^{1}GF, 13^{5}G,

	Starts	1st	2nd	3rd	Win & Pl
Career Total (Turf)	4	1	1	1	11338
Career Total (AW)	4	3	0	0	11182

100 9/09 Ffos 1m4f (0-95)H G-F £7569
87 2/09 Kemp 1m3f (0-80)H STD £4727
78 1/09 Wolv 1m141y (0-75)H STD £2729
77 12/08 Kemp 1m STD £3561
Total win prize-money £18589

Going (Turf): Sf: 0-1 GS: 0-0 Gd: 0-1 **GF: 1-2** Fm: 0-0
Distance: 5f/6f: 0-0 7f-8f: 1-2 **9f-13f: 3-5** 14f+: 0-1
Track : LH: 2-4 RH: 2-4 Tight: 1-2 Gall: 1-3
Aids: Bl: 0-0 Vi: 0-0 Tstrap: 0-0 Ckp: 0-0
Best Rating: 101 5/09 NmkR 1m4f gd-fm

Very useful; stays 1m4f; acts on fast ground; goes on Polytrack.

Petsas Pleasure

101(92) (66)**70**
3-y-o b g Observatory (USA)-Swynford Pleasure (Reprimand)
Ollie Pears PSB Holdings Ltd

Placings:302-0042100000 (7212)
2009: 9^{0}GF, 7^{0}SD, 8^{4}GF, 8^{2}GF, 8^{1}GF, 9^{0}S, 8^{0}GF, 8^{0}GF, 8^{0}SD, 12^{0}SD,

	Starts	1st	2nd	3rd	Win & Pl
Career Total (Turf)	9	1	1	1	5313
Career Total (AW)	4	0	1	0	947

70 7/09 Haml 1m65y (0-75)H G-F £3238
Total win prize-money £3238

Going (Turf): Sf: 0-1 GS: 0-0 Gd: 0-2 **GF: 1-6** Fm: 0-0
Distance: 5f/6f: 0-1 7f-8f: 0-5 **9f-13f: 1-7** 14f+: 0-0
Track : LH: 0-5 **RH: 1-5 Tight: 1-5** Gall: 0-1
Aids: Bl: 0-0 Vi: 0-0 Tstrap: 0-0 Ckp: 0-0
Best Rating: 70 7/09 Haml 1m65y gd-fm

Modest; effective over 1m; acts on fast ground; goes on Fibresand.

Pevensey (IRE)

107(109) (94)100

7-y-o b g Danehill (USA)-Champaka (IRE) (Caerleon (USA))

J J Quinn Dum Spiro Spero

Placings:6013/0020444105503/00400231444165/010050/02040442-40600140 **(7293)**

2009: 12^{4}SD, 9^{0}SD, 10^{6}GF, 12^{0}GF, 12^{0}G, 11^{1}GF, 12^{4}GS, 12^{0}S,

	Starts	1st	2nd	3rd	Win & Pl
Career Total (Turf)	49	6	4	3	170273
Career Total (AW)	4	0	0	0	866

98 9/09 Catt 1m3f214y (0-90)H G-F £7771
102 6/07 Asct 1m4f (0-105)H SFT £34276
96 9/06 Asct 1m4f H G-S £43624
92 7/06 Leic 1m3f183y (0-85)H G-F £5362
92 7/05 York 1m2f88y (0-100)H G-F £12597
89 9/04 NmkR 1m GD £8498

Total win prize-money £112131

Going (Turf): Sf: 1-7 GS: 1-10 Gd: 1-13 **GF: 3-19** Fm: 0-0
Distance: 5f/6f: 0-2 7f-8f: 1-4 **9f-13f: 5-45** 14f+: 0-2
Track : LH: 2-27 **RH: 3-21** Tight: 1-11 **Gall: 3-23**
Aids: Bl: 1-4 Vi: 0-1 Tstrap: 1-10 Ckp: 1-10
Best Rating: **102** 6/07 Asct 1m4f soft

Very useful; stays 1m4f, but effective at shorter; acts on most ground; usually held up and can start slowly; has worn a visor and cheekpieces; winning hurdler.

Pezula

88(88) (44)49

3-y-o b f Diktat-Mashmoum (Lycius (USA))

R T Phillips Mrs Claire Smith

Placings:0-6000 **(7025)**

2009: 10^{6}GF, 8^{0}G, 11^{0}SD, 16^{0}SD,

	Starts	1st	2nd	3rd	Win & Pl
Career Total (Turf)	3	0	0	0	0
Career Total (AW)	2	0	0	0	

Going (Turf): **Sf: 0-0 GS: 0-1 Gd: 0-1 GF: 0-1 Fm: 0-0**
Distance: 5f/6f: 0-0 7f-8f: 0-0 9f-13f: 0-4 14f+: 0-1
Track : LH: 0-1 RH: 0-4 Tight: 0-1 Gall: 0-0
Aids: Bl: 0-0 Vi: 0-0 Tstrap: 0-0 Ckp: 0-0
Best Rating: **49** 8/09 Wind 1m2f7y gd-fm

Pha Mai Blue

98(105) (75)66

4-y-o b g Acclamation-Queen Of Silk (IRE) (Brief Truce (USA))

J R Boyle Bluefriar Construction Ltd

Placings:305200/23100500000-033130610445000 **(7876)**

2009: 8^{0}SD, 8^{3}SD, 7^{3}GF, 8^{1}SD, 8^{3}SD, 8^{0}SD, 10^{6}G, 7^{1}SD, 8^{0}SD, 8^{4}G, 8^{4}SD, 8^{5}SD, 7^{0}SD, 8^{0}SD, 7^{0}SD,

	Starts	1st	2nd	3rd	Win & Pl
Career Total (Turf)	11	0	1	3	2649
Career Total (AW)	21	3	1	2	17554

73 8/09 Ling 7f (0-80)H STD £5828
71 5/09 Ling 1m (0-70)H STD £3070
79 5/08 Ling 6f (0-90)H STD £6938

Total win prize-money £15838

Going (Turf): **Sf: 0-0 GS: 0-3 Gd: 0-2 GF: 0-6 Fm: 0-0**
Distance: 5f/6f: 1-10 **7f-8f: 2-19** 9f-13f: 0-3 14f+: 0-0
Track : **LH: 3-17** RH: 0-10 **Tight: 3-16** Gall: 0-2
Aids: Bl: 0-0 **Vi: 1-4** Tstrap: 0-0 Ckp: 0-0
Best Rating: **79** 5/08 Ling 6f stand

Useful; stays 1m; acts on most ground and on Polytrack.

Phantasy Rock (IRE)

(85) (63)55

3-y-o b f Rock Of Gibraltar (IRE)-Phariseek (IRE) (Rainbow Quest (USA))

W P Mullins Ballylinch Stud

Placings:04046 **(7794)**

2009: 9^{0}G, 10^{4}GY, 8^{0}G, 10^{4}SD, 11^{6}SS,

	Starts	1st	2nd	3rd	Win & Pl
Career Total (Turf)	3	0	0	0	338
Career Total (AW)	2	0	0	0	338

Going (Turf): **Sf: 0-0 GS: 0-0 Gd: 0-2 GF: 0-0 Fm: 0-0**
Distance: 5f/6f: 0-0 7f-8f: 0-0 9f-13f: 0-5 14f+: 0-0
Track : LH: 0-3 RH: 0-2 Tight: 0-0 Gall: 0-0
Aids: Bl: 0-0 Vi: 0-0 Tstrap: 0-0 Ckp: 0-0
Best Rating: **63** 11/09 Dund 1m2f150y stand

Phantom Ridge (IRE)

95(93) (62)71

3-y-o b f Indian Ridge-Phantom Waters (Pharly (FR))

R Hannon Con Harrington

Placings:0636 **(4828)**

2009: 8^{0}G, 8^{6}SD, 10^{3}GF, 10^{6}G,

	Starts	1st	2nd	3rd	Win & Pl
Career Total (Turf)	3	0	0	1	403
Career Total (AW)	1	0	0	0	0

Going (Turf): **Sf: 0-0 GS: 0-0 Gd: 0-2 GF: 0-1 Fm: 0-0**
Distance: 5f/6f: 0-0 7f-8f: 0-2 9f-13f: 0-2 14f+: 0-0
Track : LH: 0-0 RH: 0-4 Tight: 0-2 Gall: 0-0
Aids: Bl: 0-0 Vi: 0-0 Tstrap: 0-0 Ckp: 0-0
Best Rating: **71** 7/09 Wind 1m2f7y gd-fm

Phantom Serenade (IRE)

99 65

4-y-o b g Orpen (USA)-Phantom Rain (Rainbow Quest (USA))

M Dods North Briton Racing

Placings:4006-61006100 **(6817)**

2009: 8^{6}G, 9^{1}G, 8^{0}GS, 7^{0}GF, 10^{6}GF, 10^{1}GF, 12^{0}GS, 10^{0}GF,

	Starts	1st	2nd	3rd	Win & Pl
Career Total (Turf)	12	2	0	0	4609

65 9/09 Rdcr 1m2f G-F £2047
58 7/09 Haml 1m1f36y (0-60)H GD £2388

Total win prize-money £4435

Going (Turf): Sf: 0-1 GS: 0-3 **Gd: 1-3 GF: 1-5** Fm: 0-0
Distance: 5f/6f: 0-0 7f-8f: 0-5 **9f-13f: 2-7** 14f+: 0-0
Track : LH: 1-7 RH: 1-1 **Tight: 2-5** Gall: 0-1
Aids: Bl: 0-0 Vi: 0-0 Tstrap: 0-0 Ckp: 0-0
Best Rating: **65** 9/09 Rdcr 1m2f gd-fm

Moderate; stays 1m2f and acts on fast ground.

Phantom Whisper

104(90) (66)99

6-y-o br g Makbul-La Belle Vie (Indian King (USA))

B R Millman Mrs T Dormer & C Dormer

Placings:1100004/36210030/03002230100/3021050010-005036000650 **(7026)**

2009: 5^{0}GS, 6^{0}GF, 6^{5}GS, 6^{0}G, 6^{3}GF, 6^{6}GF, 6^{0}G, 6^{0}GF, 7^{0}G, 6^{6}GF, 6^{5}GS, 6^{0}SD,

	Starts	1st	2nd	3rd	Win & Pl
Career Total (Turf)	43	5	4	4	68283
Career Total (AW)	6	1	0	2	13989

98 10/08 Gdwd 6f (0-95)H G-S £7771
99 7/08 Chep 6f16y (0-100)H SFT £11354
99 8/07 Wind 6f (0-95)H G-F £10094
93 6/06 Wind 5f10y (0-85)H G-F £7772
93 3/05 Donc 5f GD £7650
77 3/05 Ling 5f STD £12238

Total win prize-money £56879

Going (Turf): Sf: 1-8 GS: 1-7 Gd: 1-11 **GF: 2-17** Fm: 0-0
Distance: **5f/6f: 5-39** 7f-8f: 1-10 9f-13f: 0-0 14f+: 0-0
Track : **LH: 1-6** RH: 0-4 Tight: 1-3 **Gall: 2-5**
Aids: Bl: 0-3 Vi: 0-0 Tstrap: 0-1 Ckp: 0-1
Best Rating: **99** 7/08 Chep 6f16y soft

Useful; effective over 5f-6f; acts on most ground on turf; goes on Polytrack; has worn blinkers and cheekpieces.

Pharaohs Justice (USA)

78(97) (60)38

4-y-o br g Kafwain (USA)-Mary Linoa (USA) (L'Emigrant (USA))

N P Littmoden R D Hartshorn

Placings:051/0-6000000 **(2921)**

2009: 7^{6}SD, 7^{0}SD, 8^{0}SD, 8^{0}SD, 7^{0}SD, 8^{0}GF, 7^{0}GF,

	Starts	1st	2nd	3rd	Win & Pl
Career Total (Turf)	2	0	0	0	
Career Total (AW)	9	1	0	0	2969

80 12/07 Sthl 1m SS £2968

Total win prize-money £2969

Going (Turf): **Sf: 0-0 GS: 0-0 Gd: 0-0 GF: 0-2 Fm: 0-0**
Distance: 5f/6f: 0-0 **7f-8f: 1-9** 9f-13f: 0-2 14f+: 0-0
Track : **LH: 1-8** RH: 0-1 Tight: 0-5 Gall: 0-1
Aids: Bl: 0-4 Vi: 0-0 Tstrap: 0-0 Ckp: 0-0
Best Rating: **80** 12/07 Sthl 1m std-slw

Pherousa

101 66

2-y-o b f Dubawi (IRE)-Sea Nymph (IRE) (Spectrum (IRE))

M Blanshard Messrs Hall, Else & Murray

Placings:2004054160 **(6418)**

2009: 6^{2}GF, 6^{0}GF, 6^{0}G, 5^{4}G, 5^{0}G, 5^{5}GF, 5^{4}G, 5^{1}G, 5^{6}GF, 6^{0}GF,

	Starts	1st	2nd	3rd	Win & Pl
Career Total (Turf)	10	1	1	0	3156

66 9/09 Bath 5f11y GD £2072

Total win prize-money £2072

Going (Turf): Sf: 0-0 GS: 0-0 **Gd: 1-5** GF: 0-5 Fm: 0-0
Distance: **5f/6f: 1-9** 7f-8f: 0-1 9f-13f: 0-0 14f+: 0-0
Track : **LH: 1-4** RH: 0-0 Tight: 0-0 **Gall: 1-3**
Aids: Bl: 0-0 Vi: 0-0 Tstrap: 0-0 Ckp: 0-0
Best Rating: **66** 9/09 Bath 5f11y good

Modest; effective over 5f-6f; acts on good and fast ground.

Philander

100 80

2-y-o b c Red Ransom (USA)-Fidelio's Miracle (USA) (Mountain Cat (USA))

E J O'Neill Phil Cunningham & Dermot Hanafin

Placings:45325 **(7315a)**

2009: 8^{4}S, 8^{5}G, 8^{3}GF, 8^{2}VS, 9^{5}HY,

	Starts	1st	2nd	3rd	Win & Pl
Career Total (Turf)	5	0	1	1	10187

Going (Turf): Sf: 0-2 GS: 0-0 Gd: 0-1 GF: 0-1 Fm: 0-0
Distance: 5f/6f: 0-0 7f-8f: 0-3 9f-13f: 0-2 14f+: 0-0
Track : LH: 0-0 RH: 0-4 Tight: 0-0 Gall: 0-0
Aids: Bl: 0-0 Vi: 0-0 Tstrap: 0-0 Ckp: 0-0
Best Rating: 80 10/09 Chan 1m v soft

Useful; has raced mainly in France; stays 1m; acts on most ground.

Philario (IRE)

109(111) (104)**108**
4-y-o ch c Captain Rio-Salva (Grand Lodge (USA))
K R Burke Philip Richards

Placings:12014/030002-25602130 (3014)
2009: 8^{2}SD, 7^{5}SD, 8^{6}GF, 8^{0}GF, 8^{2}G, 8^{1}HY, 8^{3}G, 8^{0}GF,

	Starts	1st	2nd	3rd	Win & Pl
Career Total (Turf)	14	2	2	2	50633
Career Total (AW)	5	1	2	0	32966

108 5/09 Curr 1m H HVY £26861
104 9/07 Kemp 6f STD £21008
81 6/07 Carl 5f GD £1943
Total win prize-money £49814

Going (Turf): Sf: 1-3 GS: 0-0 Gd: 1-6 GF: 0-5 Fm: 0-0
Distance: 5f/6f: 2-8 7f-8f: 1-10 9f-13f: 0-1 14f+: 0-0
Track : LH: 0-6 RH: 3-4 Tight: 0-4 Gall: 2-4
Aids: Bl: 0-0 Vi: 0-0 Tstrap: 0-0 Ckp: 0-0
Best Rating: 108 6/09 Epsm 1m114y good

Smart; stays 1m; acts on any ground; also goes on Polytrack.

Philatelist (USA)

94(115) (112)**108**
5-y-o b h Rahy (USA)-Polent (Polish Precedent (USA))
M A Jarvis Gary A Tanaka

Placings:6312065/101305-4410005036 (7704a)
2009: 10^{4}SD, 10^{4}SD, 11^{1}SD, 10^{0}G, 10^{0}GF, 10^{0}SD, 10^{5}SD, 12^{0}G, 10^{3}SD, 9^{6}SD,

	Starts	1st	2nd	3rd	Win & Pl
Career Total (Turf)	10	0	1	2	11314
Career Total (AW)	13	4	0	1	47251

112 3/09 Kemp 1m3f (0-100)H STD £11215
107 3/08 Kemp 1m3f (0-105)H STD £21812
101 2/08 Ling 1m2f (0-95)H STD £6800
76 5/07 Ling 1m4f STD £3238
Total win prize-money £43068

Going (Turf): Sf: 0-0 GS: 0-1 Gd: 0-4 GF: 0-5 Fm: 0-0
Distance: 5f/6f: 0-0 7f-8f: 0-0 9f-13f: 4-23 14f+: 0-0
Track : LH: 2-10 RH: 2-12 Tight: 2-8 Gall: 0-3
Aids: Bl: 1-5 Vi: 0-2 Tstrap: 0-1 Ckp: 0-1
Best Rating: 112 3/09 Kemp 1m3f stand

Smart; effective at around 1m2f-1m4f; acts on fast and easy ground and on Polytrack; has worn blinkers; likes to race prominently.

Philippa Jane

(83) (45)
2-y-o ch f Muhtathir-Ante Futura (FR) (Suave Dancer (USA))
P Winkworth Dr J Safir

Placings:000 (7700)
2009: 8^{0}SD, 8^{0}SD, 7^{0}SD,

	Starts	1st	2nd	3rd	Win & Pl
Career Total (Turf)	0	0	0	0	
Career Total (AW)	3	0	0	0	

Going (Turf): Sf: 0-0 GS: 0-0 Gd: 0-0 GF: 0-0 Fm: 0-0
Distance: 5f/6f: 0-0 7f-8f: 0-3 9f-13f: 0-0 14f+: 0-0
Track : LH: 0-0 RH: 0-3 Tight: 0-0 Gall: 0-0
Aids: Bl: 0-0 Vi: 0-0 Tstrap: 0-0 Ckp: 0-0
Best Rating: 45 12/09 Kemp 7f stand

Phillipina

113 **103**
3-y-o b f Medicean-Discerning (Darshaan)
Sir Michael Stoute Cheveley Park Stud

Placings:0-526100 (6242)
2009: 10^{5}GS, 11^{2}GF, 12^{6}G, 10^{1}HY, 12^{0}G, 12^{0}G,

	Starts	1st	2nd	3rd	Win & Pl
Career Total (Turf)	7	1	1	0	16247

88 7/09 Nott 1m2f50y HVY £2914
Total win prize-money £2914

Going (Turf): Sf: 1-1 GS: 0-1 Gd: 0-4 GF: 0-1 Fm: 0-0
Distance: 5f/6f: 0-0 7f-8f: 0-1 9f-13f: 1-6 14f+: 0-0
Track : LH: 1-5 RH: 0-1 Tight: 0-2 Gall: 0-3
Aids: Bl: 0-0 Vi: 0-0 Tstrap: 0-0 Ckp: 0-0
Best Rating: 103 5/09 Ches 1m3f79y gd-fm

Smart; close second in the Cheshire Oaks; stays 1m3f; acts on any ground.

Philmack Dot Com

(100) (63)
3-y-o b g Traditionally (USA)-Lilli Marlane (Sri Pekan (USA))
D Donovan (Miss Amy Weaver 17/1) Philip Mclaughlin

Placings:06-60010 (7719)
2009: 8^{6}SD, 5^{0}SD, 7^{0}SD, 7^{1}SF, 9^{0}SD,

	Starts	1st	2nd	3rd	Win & Pl
Career Total (Turf)	0	0	0	0	
Career Total (AW)	7	1	0	0	2388

63 11/09 Wolv 7f32y (0-55)H SF £2388
Total win prize-money £2388

Going (Turf): Sf: 0-0 GS: 0-0 Gd: 0-0 GF: 0-0 Fm: 0-0
Distance: 5f/6f: 0-1 7f-8f: 1-5 9f-13f: 0-1 14f+: 0-0
Track : LH: 1-7 RH: 0-0 Tight: 1-5 Gall: 0-2
Aids: Bl: 0-0 Vi: 0-0 Tstrap: 0-0 Ckp: 0-0
Best Rating: 63 11/09 Wolv 7f32y std-fst

Moderate; stays 7f; acts on Polytrack; has worn a tongue tie.

Phinerine

(96) (50)**30**
6-y-o ch g Bahamian Bounty-Golden Panda (Music Boy)
A Berry P Grindrod

Placings:05250302425/45352536615000500306/3451445006050245/3200000-454 (0177)
2009: 6^{4}SS, 6^{5}SD, 5^{4}SD,

	Starts	1st	2nd	3rd	Win & Pl
Career Total (Turf)	15	1	1	0	3347
Career Total (AW)	42	1	5	6	8196

56 2/07 Wolv 5f216y STD £2047
66 5/06 Bath 5f161y G-S £2266
Total win prize-money £4315

Going (Turf): Sf: 0-1 GS: 1-3 Gd: 0-1 GF: 0-9 Fm: 0-1
Distance: 5f/6f: 2-51 7f-8f: 0-6 9f-13f: 0-0 14f+: 0-0
Track : LH: 2-42 RH: 0-1 Tight: 1-28 Gall: 1-3
Aids: Bl: 2-36 Vi: 0-0 Tstrap: 0-3 Ckp: 0-3
Best Rating: 70 3/06 Wolv 5f20y stand

Moderate gelding; effective at around 5f-6f; acts on easy ground and sand; has worn headgear.

Phluke

101(102) (82)**88**
8-y-o b g Most Welcome-Phlirty (Pharly (FR))
Eve Johnson Houghton Mrs R F Johnson Houghton

Placings:622432/530512040600/15225131200/015321414010060/311066000060/61036446030-6032605004600 (7250)
2009: 8^{6}SD, 8^{0}G, 7^{3}GF, 7^{2}G, 8^{6}SD, 7^{0}G, 8^{5}G, 8^{0}GF, 8^{0}G, 8^{4}SD, 6^{6}G, 8^{0}SD, 10^{0}SD,

	Starts	1st	2nd	3rd	Win & Pl
Career Total (Turf)	59	10	7	6	83803
Career Total (AW)	22	1	2	2	7310

88 5/08 Wwck 7f26y (0-85)H G-F £5180
95 5/07 Catt 7f (0-100)H G-F £11334
95 5/07 Wwck 7f26y (0-85)H G-S £6477
93 9/06 Ches 7f2y (0-95)H G-F £11658
88 7/06 Bevl 7f100y (0-80)H G-F £6477
88 7/06 Epsm 7f (0-85)H GD £6477
79 4/06 Sthl 7f (0-80)H GD £6477
79 8/05 Brig 6f209y (0-75)H FRM £4764
75 6/05 Wwck 7f26y (0-80)H G-F £7065
73 4/05 Ling 1m (0-70)H STD £3450
71 4/04 Bevl 7f100y E(0-75)H G-S £3718
Total win prize-money £73083

Going (Turf): Sf: 0-3 GS: 2-9 Gd: 2-20 GF: 5-25 Fm: 1-2
Distance: 5f/6f: 0-6 7f-8f: 11-58 9f-13f: 0-17 14f+: 0-0
Track : LH: 9-45 RH: 2-25 Tight: 5-29 Gall: 0-2
Aids: Bl: 0-0 Vi: 0-6 Tstrap: 0-0 Ckp: 0-0
Best Rating: 95 5/07 Catt 7f gd-fm

Useful; effective from 7f-1m; acts on most ground; likes to race prominently.

Phoenix Enforcer

98(81) (30)**72**
3-y-o b f Bahamian Bounty-Kythia (IRE) (Kahyasi)
George Baker Codrington, Crabtree, Jacovou

Placings:5030-04115 (5128)
2009: 9^{0}GF, 10^{4}GF, 10^{1}HY, 8^{1}GS, 10^{5}GF,

	Starts	1st	2nd	3rd	Win & Pl
Career Total (Turf)	8	2	0	1	4520
Career Total (AW)	1	0	0	0	

60 7/09 Leic 1m60y G-S £1942
59 7/09 Nott 1m2f50y HVY £2047
Total win prize-money £3990

Going (Turf): Sf: 1-1 GS: 1-3 Gd: 0-1 GF: 0-3 Fm: 0-0
Distance: 5f/6f: 0-2 7f-8f: 0-1 9f-13f: 2-6 14f+: 0-0
Track : LH: 1-6 RH: 1-3 Tight: 0-3 Gall: 0-1
Aids: Bl: 0-0 Vi: 0-0 Tstrap: 2-4 Ckp: 2-4
Best Rating: 72 10/08 Nott 1m75y gd-sft

Modest; stays 1m2f; acts on soft ground; has worn cheek-pieces.

Phoenix Flight (IRE)

102(104) (90)**88**
4-y-o b g Hawk Wing (USA)-Firecrest (IRE) (Darshaan)
H J Evans (Sir Mark Prescott 17/8) D Ross

Placings:31/041-60212124333250 (7151)
2009: 10^{6}SD, 10^{0}SD, 12^{2}SD, 12^{1}SD, 16^{2}SF, 12^{1}SD, 14^{2}GF,

16^{4}SD, 13^{3}G, 13^{3}G, 11^{3}GF, 12^{2}SD, 12^{5}SD, 16^{0}G,

	Starts	1st	2nd	3rd	Win & Pl
Career Total (Turf)	6	0	1	4	5994
Career Total (AW)	13	4	3	0	18719

85	3/09	Kemp	1m4f	(0-80)H	STD	£4727
69	3/09	Ling	1m4f		STD	£2047
88	10/08	GrLe	1m2f	(0-75)H	STD	£2914
74	7/07	Wolv	7f32y		STD	£3886

Total win prize-money £13574

Going (Turf): **Sf: 0-1 GS: 0-0 Gd: 0-3 GF: 0-2 Fm: 0-0**
Distance: 5f/6f: 0-0 7f-8f: 1-2 **9f-13f: 3-11** 14f+: 0-6
Track : **LH: 3-11** RH: 1-6 **Tight: 2-11** Gall: 1-3
Aids: Bl: 0-0 Vi: 0-0 Tstrap: 0-3 Ckp: 0-3
Best Rating: **90** 4/09 Kemp 2m stand

Useful; stays at least 1m6f; acts on fast ground; goes on sand.

Phoenix Hill (IRE)

100(98) (54)**49**

7-y-o b g Montjeu (IRE)-Cielo Vodkamartini (USA) (Conquistador Cielo (USA))

D R Gandolfo D R Gandolfo Ltd

Placings:300/**04**/6**05**0**50**/500-2024 **(3774)**

2009: 12^{2}SD, 12^{0}SD, 12^{2}GF, 16^{4}GF,

	Starts	1st	2nd	3rd	Win & Pl
Career Total (Turf)	6	0	1	1	1108
Career Total (AW)	12	0	1	0	674

Going (Turf): **Sf: 0-0 GS: 0-0 Gd: 0-1 GF: 0-3 Fm: 0-0**
Distance: 5f/6f: 0-0 7f-8f: 0-0 9f-13f: 0-8 14f+: 0-10
Track : LH: 0-7 RH: 0-11 Tight: 0-9 Gall: 0-0
Aids: Bl: 0-0 Vi: 0-0 Tstrap: 0-0 Ckp: 0-0
Best Rating: **71** 9/05 List 1m4f good

Plating-class; stays 1m4f; acts on Polytrack and fast turf.

Phoenix Nights (IRE)

80 **26**

9-y-o b g General Monash (USA)-Beauty Appeal (USA) (Shadeed (USA))

A Berry Alan Berry

Placings:00/**4**010**300**/**500**644606/000/6606/00-60 **(2656)**

2009: 15^{6}GF, 13^{0}GF,

	Starts	1st	2nd	3rd	Win & Pl
Career Total (Turf)	22	1	0	1	6142
Career Total (AW)	7	0	0	0	260

52	8/03	Newc	7f	D	G-F	£3818

Total win prize-money £3819

Going (Turf): Sf: 0-2 GS: 0-5 Gd: 0-4 **GF: 1-8** Fm: 0-3
Distance: 5f/6f: 0-3 **7f-8f: 1-6** 9f-13f: 0-17 14f+: 0-3
Track : LH: 0-19 RH: 0-6 Tight: 0-17 Gall: 0-2
Aids: Bl: 0-2 Vi: 0-0 Tstrap: 0-0 Ckp: 0-0
Best Rating: **52** 7/04 Ches 1m2f75y good

Phoenix Rising

86(69) (2)**34**

3-y-o b f Dr Fong (USA)-Dead Certain (Absalom)

H Morrison C E Trading & Crichel Farms Limited

Placings:000 **(2947)**

2009: 7^{0}SD, 6^{0}GF, 8^{0}GF,

	Starts	1st	2nd	3rd	Win & Pl
Career Total (Turf)	2	0	0	0	
Career Total (AW)	1	0	0	0	

Going (Turf): **Sf: 0-0 GS: 0-0 Gd: 0-0 GF: 0-2 Fm: 0-0**
Distance: 5f/6f: 0-1 7f-8f: 0-2 9f-13f: 0-0 14f+: 0-0
Track : LH: 0-1 RH: 0-0 Tight: 0-1 Gall: 0-0
Aids: Bl: 0-0 Vi: 0-0 Tstrap: 0-0 Ckp: 0-0
Best Rating: **34** 6/09 Sals 1m gd-fm

Phoenix Rose (IRE)

(89) (54)

2-y-o ch f Rakti-Fez (Mujtahid (USA))

J R Best Mrs Mary Boylan & Partners

Placings:405000 **(7514)**

2009: 6^{4}SD, 6^{0}SD, 6^{5}SD, 5^{0}SD, 7^{0}SD, 7^{0}SD,

	Starts	1st	2nd	3rd	Win & Pl
Career Total (Turf)	0	0	0	0	
Career Total (AW)	6	0	0	0	0

Going (Turf): **Sf: 0-0 GS: 0-0 Gd: 0-0 GF: 0-0 Fm: 0-0**
Distance: 5f/6f: 0-4 7f-8f: 0-2 9f-13f: 0-0 14f+: 0-0
Track : LH: 0-3 RH: 0-3 Tight: 0-2 Gall: 0-0
Aids: Bl: 0-0 Vi: 0-0 Tstrap: 0-0 Ckp: 0-0
Best Rating: **54** 9/09 Kemp 6f stand

Phonic (IRE)

94 **73**

2-y-o ch c Green Tune (USA)-Superfonic (FR) (Zafonic (USA))

J L Dunlop Gail Brown Racing (III)

Placings:030 **(6697)**

2009: 7^{0}GF, 8^{3}GF, 9^{0}GS,

	Starts	1st	2nd	3rd	Win & Pl
Career Total (Turf)	3	0	0	1	578

Going (Turf): **Sf: 0-0 GS: 0-1 Gd: 0-0 GF: 0-2 Fm: 0-0**
Distance: 5f/6f: 0-0 7f-8f: 0-2 9f-13f: 0-1 14f+: 0-0
Track : LH: 0-0 RH: 0-2 Tight: 0-1 Gall: 0-0
Aids: Bl: 0-0 Vi: 0-0 Tstrap: 0-0 Ckp: 0-0
Best Rating: **73** 9/09 NmkR 1m gd-fm

Photographic

106(104) (85)**99**

3-y-o b f Oasis Dream-Prophecy (IRE) (Warning)

B W Hills K Abdulla

Placings:112056 **(6815)**

2009: 8^{1}SD, 8^{1}GF, 7^{2}GF, 8^{0}GF, 7^{5}G, 7^{6}G,

	Starts	1st	2nd	3rd	Win & Pl
Career Total (Turf)	5	1	1	0	13884
Career Total (AW)	1	1	0	0	4727

91	5/09	NmkR	1m	(0-105)H	G-F	£12952
85	3/09	Kemp	1m		STD	£4727

Total win prize-money £17679

Going (Turf): Sf: 0-0 GS: 0-0 Gd: 0-2 **GF: 1-3** Fm: 0-0
Distance: 5f/6f: 0-0 **7f-8f: 2-6** 9f-13f: 0-0 14f+: 0-0
Track : LH: 0-1 **RH: 1-1** Tight: 0-0 Gall: 0-1
Aids: Bl: 0-0 Vi: 0-0 Tstrap: 0-0 Ckp: 0-0
Best Rating: **99** 5/09 York 7f gd-fm

Very useful; stays 1m; acts on fast ground; goes on Polytrack.

Pianoforte (USA)

98(102) (60)**68**

7-y-o b g Grand Slam (USA)-Far Too Loud (CAN) (No Louder (CAN))

E J Alston Nigel & Val Leadbeater

Placings:624/**61**200000/**00**0000120/00602603666300**0020**6/**3215**20324264140520-044300465**201005** **(7600)**

2009: 8^{0}GF, 9^{4}GF, 8^{4}GS, 7^{3}G, 8^{0}G, 7^{0}G, 9^{4}GF, 8^{6}GF, 8^{5}GS, 9^{2}SD, 8^{0}GF, 8^{1}SD, 8^{0}SD, 8^{0}SF, 9^{5}SD,

	Starts	1st	2nd	3rd	Win & Pl
Career Total (Turf)	53	2	6	4	16740
Career Total (AW)	19	3	5	1	12610

60	9/09	Wolv	1m141y	(0-55)H	STD	£2729
66	6/08	Haml	1m65y		G-F	£2914
65	1/08	Wolv	1m1f103y		STD	£1684
68	7/06	Ripn	1m	(0-70)H	G-F	£3886
74	1/05	Wolv	7f32y		STD	£3454

Total win prize-money £14669

Going (Turf): Sf: 0-5 GS: 0-5 Gd: 0-19 **GF: 2-22** Fm: 0-2
Distance: 5f/6f: 0-1 7f-8f: 2-34 **9f-13f: 3-37** 14f+: 0-0
Track : **LH: 3-35** RH: 2-24 **Tight: 5-34** Gall: 0-3
Aids: **Bl: 3-33** Vi: 1-3 Tstrap: 0-4 Ckp: 0-4
Best Rating: **83** 8/04 Leic 7f9y gd-fm

Moderate; stays 1m1f; acts on fast and easy ground; also goes on Polytrack; often wears headgear.

Piazza San Pietro

105(97) (59)**84**

3-y-o ch g Compton Place-Rainbow Spectrum (FR) (Spectrum (IRE))

A B Haynes (J R Gask 25/6) K Corke

Placings:534023-**2**0**22110033026** **(7534)**

2009: 5^{2}SD, 7^{0}SD, 5^{2}F, 7^{2}GF, 7^{1}GF, 5^{1}GF, 6^{0}SD, 6^{0}F, 5^{3}GF, 5^{3}G, 5^{0}GF, 7^{2}GF, 6^{6}SD,

	Starts	1st	2nd	3rd	Win & Pl
Career Total (Turf)	15	2	4	4	11005
Career Total (AW)	4	0	1	0	705

72	7/09	Bath	5f161y	G-F	£3561
60	7/09	Chep	7f16y	G-F	£1942

Total win prize-money £5505

Going (Turf): Sf: 0-1 GS: 0-2 Gd: 0-1 **GF: 2-8** Fm: 0-2
Distance: 5f/6f: 1-11 7f-8f: 1-8 9f-13f: 0-0 14f+: 0-0
Track : **LH: 1-7** RH: 0-1 Tight: 0-3 **Gall: 1-4**
Aids: Bl: 0-0 Vi: 0-0 Tstrap: 1-3 Ckp: 1-3
Best Rating: **84** 9/08 Curr 7f yield

Modest; effective over 5f-7f; acts on fast and easy ground.

Pic Up Sticks

101(100) (55)**70**

10-y-o gr g Piccolo-Between The Sticks (Pharly (FR))

B G Powell Mrs P Jubert

Placings:203213/3435032022204**3**/1000000P/3163600010 05/504000050014/2005**6**011030**004**/0306066004134**0**/005 5050262**00**-61350040500 **(7180)**

2009: 5^{6}G, 5^{1}GF, 5^{3}GF, 5^{5}F, 5^{0}F, 5^{0}GF, 5^{4}S, 5^{0}G, 5^{5}GF, 5^{0}S, 7^{0}SD,

	Starts	1st	2nd	3rd	Win & Pl
Career Total (Turf)	96	9	9	12	163086
Career Total (AW)	7	0	0	0	841

70	6/09	Folk	5f	(0-60)H	G-F	£2047
79	9/07	Sals	5f	(0-70)H	G-F	£3238
93	7/06	NmkJ	5f	(0-95)H	G-F	£8096
93	7/06	Sand	5f6y	(0-95)H	G-F	£8096
92	9/05	Gdwd	6f	(0-100)H	G-F	£15439
103	9/04	Ripn	6f	(0-100)H	G-F	£12255
92	2/04	Ndas	6f110y	(90-110)H	G-F	£36312

106 4/03 Bevl 5f C(0-90) FRM £9392
87 10/01 York 6f D SFT £7735
Total win prize-money £102614

Going (Turf): Sf: 1-8 GS: 0-2 Gd: 0-34 **GF: 7-44** Fm: 1-8
Distance: **5f/6f: 8-89** 7f-8f: 1-14 9f-13f: 0-0 14f+: 0-0
Track : **LH: 1-21** RH: 0-5 Tight: 0-6 **Gall: 1-13**
Aids: Bl: 0-0 Vi: 0-0 Tstrap: 0-1 Ckp: 0-1
Best Rating: **106** 4/03 Bevl 5f firm

Modest; formerly very useful; effective at up to 7f; seems best on fast ground; has worn cheekpieces.

Piccadilly Filly (IRE)

104(102) (93)96
2-y-o ch f Exceed And Excel (AUS)-Tortue (IRE) (Turtle Island (IRE))
E J Creighton The Ultimate Racing Fraternity

Placings:2021160 (6660)
2009: 6^{2}SD, 6^{0}SD, 6^{2}SD, 5^{1}SD, 5^{1}G, 5^{6}GF, 5^{0}GS,

	Starts	1st	2nd	3rd	Win & Pl
Career Total (Turf)	3	1	0	0	27779
Career Total (AW)	4	1	2	0	5551

96 8/09 Deau 5f GD £26699
93 8/09 Ling 5f STD £3335
Total win prize-money £30034

Going (Turf): Sf: 0-0 GS: 0-1 **Gd: 1-1** GF: 0-1 Fm: 0-0
Distance: **5f/6f: 2-7** 7f-8f: 0-0 9f-13f: 0-0 14f+: 0-0
Track : LH: 1-2 RH: 1-3 **Tight: 1-2** Gall: 0-0
Aids: Bl: 0-0 Vi: 0-0 Tstrap: 0-0 Ckp: 0-0
Best Rating: **96** 8/09 Deau 5f good

Very useful; Listed winner; suited by 5f; acts on good ground and Polytrack.

Piccaso's Sky

83(94) (49)38
3-y-o b c Piccolo-Skylark (Polar Falcon (USA))
A B Haynes K Corke

Placings:660-540050 (3926)
2009: 5^{5}SD, 5^{4}SD, 5^{0}F, 5^{0}F, 5^{5}F, 5^{0}SF,

	Starts	1st	2nd	3rd	Win & Pl
Career Total (Turf)	4	0	0	0	0
Career Total (AW)	5	0	0	0	0

Going (Turf): **Sf: 0-0 GS: 0-0 Gd: 0-1 GF: 0-0 Fm: 0-3**
Distance: 5f/6f: 0-9 7f-8f: 0-0 9f-13f: 0-0 14f+: 0-0
Track : LH: 0-7 RH: 0-1 Tight: 0-4 Gall: 0-2
Aids: Bl: 0-1 Vi: 0-1 Tstrap: 0-0 Ckp: 0-0
Best Rating: **49** 1/09 Ling 5f stand

Piccola Stella (IRE)

70 23
2-y-o b f Antonius Pius (USA)-Beeper's Lodge (IRE) (Grand Lodge (USA))
R M H Cowell D Moroni

Placings:0 (4546)
2009: 5^{0}GS,

	Starts	1st	2nd	3rd	Win & Pl
Career Total (Turf)	1	0	0	0	

Going (Turf): **Sf: 0-0 GS: 0-1 Gd: 0-0 GF: 0-0 Fm: 0-0**
Distance: 5f/6f: 0-1 7f-8f: 0-0 9f-13f: 0-0 14f+: 0-0
Track : LH: 0-0 RH: 0-0 Tight: 0-0 Gall: 0-0
Aids: Bl: 0-0 Vi: 0-0 Tstrap: 0-0 Ckp: 0-0
Best Rating: **23** 8/09 Thsk 5f gd-sft

Piccolinda

64(94) (64)47
3-y-o b f Piccolo-Belinda (Mizoram (USA))
W R Muir North Farm Stud

Placings:410-05004 (5316)
2009: 7^{0}SD, 5^{5}SD, 7^{0}SD, 7^{0}S, 7^{4}SD,

	Starts	1st	2nd	3rd	Win & Pl
Career Total (Turf)	2	0	0	0	
Career Total (AW)	6	1	0	0	4857

64 9/08 GrLe 6f STD £4857
Total win prize-money £4857

Going (Turf): **Sf: 0-1 GS: 0-0 Gd: 0-0 GF: 0-1 Fm: 0-0**
Distance: **5f/6f: 1-4** 7f-8f: 0-4 9f-13f: 0-0 14f+: 0-0
Track : **LH: 1-5** RH: 0-1 Tight: 0-4 **Gall: 1-2**
Aids: Bl: 0-1 Vi: 0-0 Tstrap: 0-0 Ckp: 0-0
Best Rating: **64** 9/08 GrLe 6f stand

Modest; effective over 6f; acts on Polytrack.

Piccolo Diamante (USA)

(100) (62)46
5-y-o b/br g Three Wonders (USA)-Bafooz (USA) (Clever Trick (USA))
S Parr Willie McKay

Placings:60/0644015363/0040120013000-600060 (0748)
2009: 5^{6}SD, 5^{0}SD, 8^{0}SD, 8^{0}SD, 5^{6}SD, 7^{0}SD,

	Starts	1st	2nd	3rd	Win & Pl
Career Total (Turf)	6	0	0	0	168
Career Total (AW)	25	3	1	3	7805

61 11/08 Kemp 7f (0-55)H STD £1706
59 9/08 GrLe 6f (0-50)H STD £2590
59 11/07 Kemp 6f (0-52)H STD £2047
Total win prize-money £6344

Going (Turf): **Sf: 0-0 GS: 0-0 Gd: 0-2 GF: 0-3 Fm: 0-1**
Distance: **5f/6f: 2-20** 7f-8f: 1-11 9f-13f: 0-0 14f+: 0-0
Track : LH: 1-17 **RH: 2-6** Tight: 0-12 **Gall: 1-1**
Aids: Bl: 0-0 Vi: 0-0 Tstrap: 0-0 Ckp: 0-0
Best Rating: **62** 11/08 Wolv 7f32y stand

Moderate; effective over 6f-7f; acts on Polytrack; has worn a tongue-tie and an eyeshield.

Piccolo Express

91(89) (50)54
3-y-o b g Piccolo-Ashfield (Zilzal (USA))
B P J Baugh G B Hignett

Placings:060-0543400 (4819)
2009: 8^{0}SD, 8^{5}SD, 7^{4}SD, 8^{3}F, 7^{4}GF, 8^{0}S, 8^{0}GF,

	Starts	1st	2nd	3rd	Win & Pl
Career Total (Turf)	7	0	0	1	638
Career Total (AW)	3	0	0	0	0

Going (Turf): **Sf: 0-1 GS: 0-0 Gd: 0-0 GF: 0-5 Fm: 0-1**
Distance: 5f/6f: 0-2 7f-8f: 0-4 9f-13f: 0-4 14f+: 0-0
Track : LH: 0-7 RH: 0-0 Tight: 0-6 Gall: 0-0
Aids: Bl: 0-0 Vi: 0-0 Tstrap: 0-0 Ckp: 0-0
Best Rating: **54** 6/09 Bath 1m5y firm

Modest; stays 1m.

Piccolo Mondo

102(98) (73)75
3-y-o b g Piccolo-Oriel Girl (Beveled (USA))
P Winkworth Dr Helen Parkhouse & Mrs F A Veasey

Placings:6022-3002253 (7452)
2009: 8^{3}SD, 8^{0}GF, 7^{0}GF, 7^{2}G, 8^{2}G, 8^{5}SD, 8^{3}SD,

	Starts	1st	2nd	3rd	Win & Pl
Career Total (Turf)	7	0	3	0	2794
Career Total (AW)	4	0	1	2	1367

Going (Turf): **Sf: 0-1 GS: 0-0 Gd: 0-2 GF: 0-4 Fm: 0-0**
Distance: 5f/6f: 0-3 7f-8f: 0-7 9f-13f: 0-1 14f+: 0-0
Track : LH: 0-3 RH: 0-2 Tight: 0-2 Gall: 0-2
Aids: Bl: 0-0 Vi: 0-0 Tstrap: 0-0 Ckp: 0-0
Best Rating: **75** 9/08 Wind 6f gd-fm

Fair; stays 1m; acts on fast ground and on Polytrack; has worn a tongue tie.

Piccolo Pete

80 61
4-y-o b g Piccolo-Goes A Treat (IRE) (Common Grounds)
R Johnson Miss S A Booth

Placings:00404/2000-000000 (4016)
2009: 10^{0}GF, 16^{0}F, 6^{0}GF, 7^{0}GS, 6^{0}G, 6^{0}G,

	Starts	1st	2nd	3rd	Win & Pl
Career Total (Turf)	15	0	1	0	861

Going (Turf): **Sf: 0-0 GS: 0-1 Gd: 0-6 GF: 0-5 Fm: 0-3**
Distance: 5f/6f: 0-8 7f-8f: 0-5 9f-13f: 0-1 14f+: 0-1
Track : LH: 0-4 RH: 0-2 Tight: 0-1 Gall: 0-2
Aids: Bl: 0-1 Vi: 0-1 Tstrap: 0-3 Ckp: 0-3
Best Rating: **61** 4/08 Sthl 6f good

Piccolo Pride

65(79) (12)
4-y-o ch g Piccolo-Jaycat (IRE) (Catrail (USA))
M A Barnes The Border Raiders

Placings:0/06-6 (3294)
2009: 9^{6}GF,

	Starts	1st	2nd	3rd	Win & Pl
Career Total (Turf)	1	0	0	0	0
Career Total (AW)	3	0	0	0	0

Going (Turf): **Sf: 0-0 GS: 0-0 Gd: 0-0 GF: 0-1 Fm: 0-0**
Distance: 5f/6f: 0-2 7f-8f: 0-1 9f-13f: 0-1 14f+: 0-0
Track : LH: 0-3 RH: 0-1 Tight: 0-4 Gall: 0-0
Aids: Bl: 0-0 Vi: 0-0 Tstrap: 0-0 Ckp: 0-0
Best Rating: **12** 1/08 Ling 1m stand

Pick Of The Day (IRE)

(91) (52)40
4-y-o ch g Choisir (AUS)-Reveuse De Jour (IRE) (Sadler's Wells (USA))
J G Given Tremousser Partnership

Placings:0505-460 (0790)
2009: 14^{4}SS, 12^{6}SD, 12^{0}SD,

	Starts	1st	2nd	3rd	Win & Pl
Career Total (Turf)	2	0	0	0	
Career Total (AW)	5	0	0	0	0

Going (Turf): **Sf: 0-1 GS: 0-0 Gd: 0-0 GF: 0-1 Fm: 0-0**
Distance: 5f/6f: 0-0 7f-8f: 0-2 9f-13f: 0-4 14f+: 0-1
Track : LH: 0-7 RH: 0-0 Tight: 0-1 Gall: 0-0
Aids: Bl: 0-0 Vi: 0-2 Tstrap: 0-0 Ckp: 0-0
Best Rating: **52** 12/08 Sthl 1m3f stand

Moderate; stays 1m 5f; effective on Fibresand.

Pickering

104 (65)**77**

5-y-o br g Prince Sabo-On The Wagon (Then Again)
E J Alston The Selebians

Placings:040/14040206/30000-133060 **(6413)**
2009: 6^{1}GF, 6^{3}GF, 6^{3}GF, 7^{0}G, 5^{6}GF, 6^{0}GF,

	Starts	1st	2nd	3rd	Win & Pl
Career Total (Turf)	20	2	1	3	10191
Career Total (AW)	2	0	0	0	289

77 4/09 Pont 6f (0-70)H G-F £3238
75 4/07 Nott 5f13y (0-70)H G-F £2914
Total win prize-money £6153

Going (Turf): Sf: 0-3 GS: 0-1 Gd: 0-6 **GF: 2-9** Fm: 0-1
Distance: **5f/6f: 2-18** 7f-8f: 0-4 9f-13f: 0-0 14f+: 0-0
Track : **LH: 1-9** RH: 0-0 Tight: 0-3 Gall: 0-0
Aids: Bl: 0-1 Vi: 0-0 Tstrap: 1-6 Ckp: 1-6
Best Rating: **80** 4/07 Ripn 6f gd-fm

Fair sprinter; stays 6f; acts on fast ground; has worn blinkers and cheekpieces.

Picky

82 (62)**29**

5-y-o b g Piccolo-Passerella (FR) (Brustolon)
C C Bealby Payplan Partnership

Placings:35630035101/4 **(3308)**
2009: 11^{4}GF,

	Starts	1st	2nd	3rd	Win & Pl
Career Total (Turf)	4	0	0	1	578
Career Total (AW)	8	2	0	2	5518

59 10/07 Ling 1m2f (0-60)H STD £2730
62 9/07 Ling 1m2f (0-55) STD £2047
Total win prize-money £4778

Going (Turf): **Sf: 0-0 GS: 0-0 Gd: 0-0 GF: 0-3 Fm: 0-1**
Distance: 5f/6f: 0-0 7f-8f: 0-1 **9f-13f: 2-11** 14f+: 0-0
Track : **LH: 2-9** RH: 0-3 **Tight: 2-8** Gall: 0-0
Aids: Bl: 0-1 **Vi: 2-5** Tstrap: 0-0 Ckp: 0-0
Best Rating: **62** 9/07 Ling 1m2f stand

Modest; stays 1m2f; acts on Polytrack; has worn a visor.

Picnic Party

94(96) (63)**62**

2-y-o ch f Indian Ridge-Antediluvian (Air Express (IRE))
J Noseda Lordship Stud

Placings:62 **(7436)**
2009: 6^{6}GS, 6^{2}SD,

	Starts	1st	2nd	3rd	Win & Pl
Career Total (Turf)	1	0	0	0	0
Career Total (AW)	1	0	1	0	1060

Going (Turf): **Sf: 0-0 GS: 0-1 Gd: 0-0 GF: 0-0 Fm: 0-0**
Distance: 5f/6f: 0-1 7f-8f: 0-1 9f-13f: 0-0 14f+: 0-0
Track : LH: 0-1 RH: 0-0 Tight: 0-1 Gall: 0-0
Aids: Bl: 0-0 Vi: 0-0 Tstrap: 0-0 Ckp: 0-0
Best Rating: **63** 11/09 Ling 6f stand

Modest; effective over 6f; acts on Polytrack.

Picot De Say

101 (13)**58**

7-y-o b g Largesse-Facsimile (Superlative)
C Roberts Irish Legend Racing Team

Placings:000325/0051/00/00/310 **(5790)**
2009: 12^{3}GF, 12^{1}HY, 10^{0}G,

	Starts	1st	2nd	3rd	Win & Pl
Career Total (Turf)	15	2	1	2	7491
Career Total (AW)	2	0	0	0	

58 8/09 Chep 1m4f23y (0-60)H HVY £2072
57 9/05 Yarm 1m3f101y GD £2933
Total win prize-money £5005

Going (Turf): **Sf: 1-3** GS: 0-0 **Gd: 1-7** GF: 0-5 Fm: 0-0
Distance: 5f/6f: 0-2 7f-8f: 0-2 **9f-13f: 2-12** 14f+: 0-1
Track : **LH: 2-12** RH: 0-2 **Tight: 1-4** Gall: 0-3
Aids: Bl: 0-0 Vi: 0-0 Tstrap: 0-0 Ckp: 0-0
Best Rating: **63** 11/04 Rdcr 1m soft

Moderate; stays a mile three; acts on good and soft ground.

Pictorial (USA)

99(76) (17)**83**

3-y-o b g Pivotal-Red Tulle (USA) (A.P. Indy (USA))
Sir Michael Stoute Highclere Thoroughbred Racing (Gimcrack)

Placings:6100 **(5315)**
2009: 10^{6}S, 10^{1}GF, 12^{0}GF, **12^{0}SD**,

	Starts	1st	2nd	3rd	Win & Pl
Career Total (Turf)	3	1	0	0	2730
Career Total (AW)	1	0	0	0	

83 6/09 Wind 1m2f7y G-F £2729
Total win prize-money £2730

Going (Turf): Sf: 0-1 GS: 0-0 Gd: 0-0 **GF: 1-2** Fm: 0-0
Distance: 5f/6f: 0-0 7f-8f: 0-0 **9f-13f: 1-4** 14f+: 0-0
Track : LH: 0-1 **RH: 1-3 Tight: 1-1** Gall: 0-2
Aids: Bl: 0-0 Vi: 0-0 Tstrap: 0-0 Ckp: 0-0
Best Rating: **83** 6/09 Wind 1m2f7y gd-fm

Useful; stays 10f; acts on quick ground.

Picture Frame

97(88) (43)**59**

5-y-o ch g Fraam-Floral Spark (Forzando)
J T Stimpson J T Stimpson

Placings:332310/640/050400 **(4845)**
2009: 7^{0}SD, 7^{5}GF, 7^{0}GF, 8^{4}GF, 10^{0}GF, 8^{0}G,

	Starts	1st	2nd	3rd	Win & Pl
Career Total (Turf)	14	1	1	3	6139
Career Total (AW)	1	0	0	0	

65 6/06 Hayd 5f G-F £3238
Total win prize-money £3239

Going (Turf): Sf: 0-0 GS: 0-2 Gd: 0-3 **GF: 1-9** Fm: 0-0
Distance: **5f/6f: 1-9** 7f-8f: 0-4 9f-13f: 0-2 14f+: 0-0
Track : LH: 0-4 RH: 0-0 Tight: 0-3 Gall: 0-0
Aids: Bl: 0-0 Vi: 0-0 Tstrap: 0-2 Ckp: 0-2
Best Rating: **66** 5/06 Haml 5f4y good

Pictures (IRE)

93(97) (73)**73**

2-y-o b f Le Vie Dei Colori-So Glam So Hip (IRE) (Spectrum (IRE))
L M Cumani Scuderia Archi Romani

Placings:23230 **(7363)**
2009: 6^{2}F, 5^{3}SD, 7^{2}SD, 7^{3}G, 7^{0}SD,

	Starts	1st	2nd	3rd	Win & Pl
Career Total (Turf)	2	0	1	1	1577
Career Total (AW)	3	0	1	1	1541

Going (Turf): **Sf: 0-0 GS: 0-0 Gd: 0-1 GF: 0-0 Fm: 0-1**
Distance: 5f/6f: 0-1 7f-8f: 0-4 9f-13f: 0-0 14f+: 0-0
Track : LH: 0-4 RH: 0-0 Tight: 0-3 Gall: 0-0
Aids: Bl: 0-0 Vi: 0-0 Tstrap: 0-0 Ckp: 0-0
Best Rating: **73** 10/09 Yarm 7f3y good

Picturethatmoment (USA)

78 **43**

3-y-o b/br f Mr Greeley (USA)-I'Maknightschoice (USA) (Knights Choice (USA))
K R Burke Mogeely Stud & Mrs Maura Gittins

Placings:0 **(2165)**
2009: 8^{0}G,

	Starts	1st	2nd	3rd	Win & Pl
Career Total (Turf)	1	0	0	0	

Going (Turf): **Sf: 0-0 GS: 0-0 Gd: 0-1 GF: 0-0 Fm: 0-0**
Distance: 5f/6f: 0-0 7f-8f: 0-0 9f-13f: 0-1 14f+: 0-0
Track : LH: 0-1 RH: 0-0 Tight: 0-0 Gall: 0-0
Aids: Bl: 0-0 Vi: 0-0 Tstrap: 0-0 Ckp: 0-0
Best Rating: **43** 5/09 Nott 1m75y good

Pie Poudre

81(91) (55)**49**

2-y-o ch g Zafeen (FR)-Eglantine (IRE) (Royal Academy (USA))
R Brotherton Bredon Hill Racing Club

Placings:06002 **(7788)**
2009: 6^{0}GF, 6^{6}GF, 6^{0}GS, 7^{0}SD, 8^{2}SD,

	Starts	1st	2nd	3rd	Win & Pl
Career Total (Turf)	3	0	0	0	0
Career Total (AW)	2	0	1	0	806

Going (Turf): **Sf: 0-0 GS: 0-1 Gd: 0-0 GF: 0-2 Fm: 0-0**
Distance: 5f/6f: 0-2 7f-8f: 0-2 9f-13f: 0-1 14f+: 0-0
Track : LH: 0-1 RH: 0-1 Tight: 0-1 Gall: 0-1
Aids: Bl: 0-0 Vi: 0-0 Tstrap: 0-0 Ckp: 0-0
Best Rating: **55** 12/09 Wolv 1m141y stand

Moderate; stays 1m; acts on fast and easy ground and Polytrack.

Piermarini

(99) (68)**76**

4-y-o b g Singspiel (IRE)-Allespagne (USA) (Trempolino (USA))
P T Midgley O R Dukes

Placings:540/4355-0040 **(0578)**
2009: 9^{0}SD, 10^{0}SD, 7^{4}SD, 9^{0}SD,

	Starts	1st	2nd	3rd	Win & Pl
Career Total (Turf)	3	0	0	0	481
Career Total (AW)	8	0	0	1	700

Going (Turf): **Sf: 0-0 GS: 0-0 Gd: 0-1 GF: 0-2 Fm: 0-0**
Distance: 5f/6f: 0-0 7f-8f: 0-2 9f-13f: 0-9 14f+: 0-0
Track : LH: 0-9 RH: 0-1 Tight: 0-5 Gall: 0-1
Aids: Bl: 0-0 Vi: 0-1 Tstrap: 0-0 Ckp: 0-0
Best Rating: **76** 9/07 Donc 1m gd-fm

Pilannski

75(73) (16)37

2-y-o b f Pilsudski (IRE)-Honey Mill (Milford)

R A Teal K W Anidjah

Placings:00 (7522)

2009: 8^{0}GF, 8^{0}SD,

	Starts	1st	2nd	3rd	Win & Pl
Career Total (Turf)	1	0	0	0	
Career Total (AW)	1	0	0	0	

Going (Turf): Sf: 0-0 GS: 0-0 Gd: 0-0 GF: 0-1 Fm: 0-0
Distance: 5f/6f: 0-0 7f-8f: 0-2 9f-13f: 0-0 14f+: 0-0
Track : LH: 0-1 RH: 0-1 Tight: 0-1 Gall: 0-0
Aids: Bl: 0-0 Vi: 0-0 Tstrap: 0-0 Ckp: 0-0
Best Rating: 37 9/09 Gdwd 1m gd-fm

Pilot Light

89 54

3-y-o b g Falbrav (IRE)-Bollin Jeannie (Royal Applause)

T D Easterby Habton Farms

Placings:400-000 (2370)

2009: 9^{0}GF, 12^{0}GF, 8^{0}GF,

	Starts	1st	2nd	3rd	Win & Pl
Career Total (Turf)	6	0	0	0	241

Going (Turf): Sf: 0-1 GS: 0-0 Gd: 0-1 GF: 0-4 Fm: 0-0
Distance: 5f/6f: 0-0 7f-8f: 0-3 9f-13f: 0-3 14f+: 0-0
Track : LH: 0-1 RH: 0-3 Tight: 0-1 Gall: 0-1
Aids: Bl: 0-0 Vi: 0-0 Tstrap: 0-2 Ckp: 0-2
Best Rating: 54 6/08 Donc 7f gd-fm

Pin Cushion

94 73

2-y-o ch f Pivotal-Frizzante (Efisio)

B J Meehan Lady Rothschild

Placings:034 (6737)

2009: 6^{0}GF, 6^{3}GF, 6^{4}GS,

	Starts	1st	2nd	3rd	Win & Pl
Career Total (Turf)	3	0	0	1	1011

Going (Turf): Sf: 0-0 GS: 0-1 Gd: 0-0 GF: 0-2 Fm: 0-0
Distance: 5f/6f: 0-2 7f-8f: 0-1 9f-13f: 0-0 14f+: 0-0
Track : LH: 0-0 RH: 0-0 Tight: 0-0 Gall: 0-2
Aids: Bl: 0-0 Vi: 0-0 Tstrap: 0-0 Ckp: 0-0
Best Rating: 73 8/09 Newb 6f8y gd-fm

Half-sister to 6f juvenile winner Greensward out of the high-class sprinter Frizzante; promise in 6f maidens on a sound surface.

Pinball (IRE)

99(100) (58)63

3-y-o b f Namid-Luceball (IRE) (Bluebird (USA))

Mrs L Williamson (Patrick Morris 29/5) D Goulding

Placings:0005-2434613U060504640 (7834)

2009: 5^{2}SD, 5^{4}SD, 5^{3}F, 5^{4}GF, 5^{6}SD, 5^{1}F, 5^{3}G, 5^{U}GF, 5^{0}G, 5^{6}GF, 6^{0}SD, 6^{5}GS, 5^{0}G, 5^{4}S, 6^{6}SD, 5^{4}SD, 6^{0}SD,

	Starts	1st	2nd	3rd	Win & Pl
Career Total (Turf)	12	1	0	2	3698
Career Total (AW)	9	0	1	0	964

63 5/09 Bath 5f161y (0-70)H FRM £2914

Total win prize-money £2914

Going (Turf): Sf: 0-2 GS: 0-1 Gd: 0-3 GF: 0-3 **Fm: 1-2**
Distance: **5f/6f: 1-21** 7f-8f: 0-0 9f-13f: 0-0 14f+: 0-0
Track : **LH: 1-9** RH: 0-2 Tight: 0-5 **Gall: 1-4**
Aids: Bl: 0-0 **Vi: 1-12** Tstrap: 0-0 Ckp: 0-0
Best Rating: 63 5/09 Bath 5f161y firm

Moderate; effective over 5f-6f; acts on fast and soft ground; goes on Polytrack; has worn a visor.

Pinch Of Salt (IRE)

103(109) (99)96

6-y-o b g Hussonet (USA)-Granita (CHI) (Roy (USA))

A M Balding The Hon Robert Hanson

Placings:502/62666/0511024/0232026-0000 (6724)

2009: 10^{0}G, 10^{0}GF, 11^{0}SD, 12^{0}SD,

	Starts	1st	2nd	3rd	Win & Pl
Career Total (Turf)	14	0	3	0	5625
Career Total (AW)	12	2	3	1	15265

91 10/07 Kemp 1m3f (0-75)H STD £2817
82 9/07 Kemp 1m4f (0-75)H STD £2914

Total win prize-money £5732

Going (Turf): Sf: 0-1 GS: 0-1 Gd: 0-6 GF: 0-6 Fm: 0-0
Distance: 5f/6f: 0-0 7f-8f: 0-3 **9f-13f: 2-23** 14f+: 0-0
Track : LH: 0-7 **RH: 2-17** Tight: 0-6 Gall: 0-4
Aids: Bl: 0-0 Vi: 0-1 Tstrap: 0-0 Ckp: 0-0
Best Rating: 99 6/08 Kemp 1m2f stand

Very useful; stays 1m4f but effective at shorter; acts on Polytrack and good ground; has worn a tongue tie; likes to race prominently.

Pinewood Legend (IRE)

83(100) (47)21

7-y-o br g Idris (IRE)-Blue Infanta (Chief Singer)

P D Niven The London Lads Syndicate

Placings:000/4/3-30 (4848)

2009: 16^{3}SD, 16^{0}G,

	Starts	1st	2nd	3rd	Win & Pl
Career Total (Turf)	5	0	0	0	429
Career Total (AW)	2	0	0	2	605

Going (Turf): Sf: 0-3 GS: 0-0 Gd: 0-1 GF: 0-0 Fm: 0-1
Distance: 5f/6f: 0-1 7f-8f: 0-1 9f-13f: 0-3 14f+: 0-2
Track : LH: 0-5 RH: 0-1 Tight: 0-1 Gall: 0-0
Aids: Bl: 0-3 Vi: 0-0 Tstrap: 0-0 Ckp: 0-0
Best Rating: 60 10/07 Navn 1m2f firm

Pinewood Lulu

68(67) (7)54

4-y-o br f Lujain (USA)-Lucy Glitters (USA) (Cryptoclearance (USA))

S A Harris (R C Guest 26/5) S A Harris

Placings:546/066-00000 (6029)

2009: 8^{0}G, 6^{0}GF, 7^{0}GF, 8^{0}GF, 8^{0}SD,

	Starts	1st	2nd	3rd	Win & Pl
Career Total (Turf)	9	0	0	0	289
Career Total (AW)	2	0	0	0	0

Going (Turf): Sf: 0-2 GS: 0-0 Gd: 0-3 GF: 0-4 Fm: 0-0
Distance: 5f/6f: 0-3 7f-8f: 0-4 9f-13f: 0-4 14f+: 0-0
Track : LH: 0-5 RH: 0-2 Tight: 0-3 Gall: 0-0
Aids: Bl: 0-2 Vi: 0-0 Tstrap: 0-0 Ckp: 0-0
Best Rating: 64 10/07 Leic 7f9y soft

Pinewood Polly

(58) (5)

2-y-o b f Lujain (USA)-Polmara (IRE) (Polish Precedent (USA))

S A Harris S & D Bloodstock

Placings:0 (7396)

2009: 7^{0}SD,

	Starts	1st	2nd	3rd	Win & Pl
Career Total (Turf)	0	0	0	0	
Career Total (AW)	1	0	0	0	

Going (Turf): Sf: 0-0 GS: 0-0 Gd: 0-0 GF: 0-0 Fm: 0-0
Distance: 5f/6f: 0-0 7f-8f: 0-1 9f-13f: 0-0 14f+: 0-0
Track : LH: 0-1 RH: 0-0 Tight: 0-1 Gall: 0-0
Aids: Bl: 0-0 Vi: 0-0 Tstrap: 0-0 Ckp: 0-0
Best Rating: 5 11/09 Wolv 7f32y stand

Pink Flames (IRE)

80 40

2-y-o ch f Redback-Flames (Blushing Flame (USA))

T P Tate Mrs Fitri Hay

Placings:6 (5674)

2009: 7^{6}S,

	Starts	1st	2nd	3rd	Win & Pl
Career Total (Turf)	1	0	0	0	0

Going (Turf): Sf: 0-1 GS: 0-0 Gd: 0-0 GF: 0-0 Fm: 0-0
Distance: 5f/6f: 0-0 7f-8f: 0-1 9f-13f: 0-0 14f+: 0-0
Track : LH: 0-1 RH: 0-0 Tight: 0-1 Gall: 0-0
Aids: Bl: 0-0 Vi: 0-0 Tstrap: 0-0 Ckp: 0-0
Best Rating: 40 9/09 Thsk 7f soft

210,000gns sister to Lahaleeb; showed ability on debut over 7f on soft ground.

Pink Lemonade (IRE)

89 62

2-y-o b f Shinko Forest (IRE)-Popular Tune (IRE) (Grand Lodge (USA))

John Joseph Murphy Mrs John J Murphy

Placings:00020 (4590)

2009: 6^{0}GY, 6^{0}G, 6^{0}G, 5^{2}G, 5^{0}G,

	Starts	1st	2nd	3rd	Win & Pl
Career Total (Turf)	5	0	1	0	1156

Going (Turf): Sf: 0-0 GS: 0-0 Gd: 0-4 GF: 0-0 Fm: 0-0
Distance: 5f/6f: 0-5 7f-8f: 0-0 9f-13f: 0-0 14f+: 0-0
Track : LH: 0-1 RH: 0-1 Tight: 0-0 Gall: 0-0
Aids: Bl: 0-0 Vi: 0-0 Tstrap: 0-0 Ckp: 0-0
Best Rating: 62 7/09 Muss 5f good

Pink Please (IRE)

72 12

2-y-o ch f Camacho-Inonder (Belfort (FR))

Tom Dascombe Manor House Stables LLP

Placings:0 (6591)

2009: 6^{0}GS,

	Starts	1st	2nd	3rd	Win & Pl
Career Total (Turf)	1	0	0	0	

Going (Turf): Sf: 0-0 GS: 0-1 Gd: 0-0 GF: 0-0 Fm: 0-0
Distance: 5f/6f: 0-0 7f-8f: 0-1 9f-13f: 0-0 14f+: 0-0
Track: LH: 0-0 RH: 0-0 Tight: 0-0 Gall: 0-0
Aids: Bl: 0-0 Vi: 0-0 Tstrap: 0-0 Ckp: 0-0
Best Rating: 12 10/09 Nott 6f15y gd-sft

Pink Symphony

99 84

2-y-o b f Montjeu (IRE)-Blue Symphony (Darshaan)
P F I Cole Mrs Fitri Hay

Placings:524 (6477)
2009: 7^5GS, 7^2G, 7^4GF,

	Starts	1st	2nd	3rd	Win & Pl
Career Total (Turf)	3	0	1	0	40805

Going (Turf): Sf: 0-0 GS: 0-1 Gd: 0-1 GF: 0-1 Fm: 0-0
Distance: 5f/6f: 0-0 7f-8f: 0-3 9f-13f: 0-0 14f+: 0-0
Track: LH: 0-0 RH: 0-1 Tight: 0-0 Gall: 0-0
Aids: Bl: 0-0 Vi: 0-0 Tstrap: 0-0 Ckp: 0-0
Best Rating: 84 10/09 NmkR 7f gd-fm

400,000gns Montjeu filly who is closely related to the high-class Fantasia; fair form to date; effective over 7f; acts on good ground.

Pinnacle Lad (IRE)

94(84) (43)68

2-y-o b g Titus Livius (FR)-Alyska (IRE) (Owington)
J L Spearing Moyden Partnership

Placings:63240400 (7242)
2009: 5^6G, 5^3GF, 5^2G, 5^4F, 5^0SD, 6^4S, 5^0G, 5^0S,

	Starts	1st	2nd	3rd	Win & Pl
Career Total (Turf)	7	0	1	1	1792
Career Total (AW)	1	0	0	0	

Going (Turf): Sf: 0-2 GS: 0-0 Gd: 0-3 GF: 0-1 Fm: 0-1
Distance: 5f/6f: 0-7 7f-8f: 0-1 9f-13f: 0-0 14f+: 0-0
Track: LH: 0-3 RH: 0-0 Tight: 0-1 Gall: 0-3
Aids: Bl: 0-1 Vi: 0-0 Tstrap: 0-0 Ckp: 0-0
Best Rating: 68 5/09 Bevl 5f good

Pinnacle Point

98(89) (52)64

4-y-o ch g Best Of The Bests (IRE)-Alessandra (Generous (IRE))
G L Moore Chegwidden Systems Ltd

Placings:000/0320666-455 (3675)
2009: 12^4SD, 12^5GF, 9^5F,

	Starts	1st	2nd	3rd	Win & Pl
Career Total (Turf)	11	0	1	1	1010
Career Total (AW)	2	0	0	0	0

Going (Turf): Sf: 0-2 GS: 0-1 Gd: 0-2 GF: 0-5 Fm: 0-1
Distance: 5f/6f: 0-0 7f-8f: 0-2 9f-13f: 0-11 14f+: 0-0
Track: LH: 0-6 RH: 0-7 Tight: 0-4 Gall: 0-0
Aids: Bl: 0-3 Vi: 0-0 Tstrap: 0-0 Ckp: 0-0
Best Rating: 64 7/08 Folk 1m4f gd-fm

Pinpoint (IRE)

103(105) (96)114

7-y-o b g Pivotal-Alessia (GER) (Warning)
W R Swinburn Full Circle

Placings:241251/46130/124003/4430264-200 (3089)
2009: 8^2GF, 9^0GF, 10^0GF,

	Starts	1st	2nd	3rd	Win & Pl
Career Total (Turf)	25	4	4	3	164574
Career Total (AW)	2	0	1	0	1851
112 4/07 Newb 1m	H			G-F	£24928
104 9/06 Newb 1m2f6y	(0-105)H			GD	£62320
101 10/05 Sals 1m	(0-85)H			GD	£8702
85 7/05 Donc 1m				GD	£5200

Total win prize-money £101150

Going (Turf): Sf: 0-1 GS: 0-4 Gd: 3-6 GF: 1-13 Fm: 0-1
Distance: 5f/6f: 0-0 7f-8f: 3-8 9f-13f: 1-19 14f+: 0-0
Track: LH: 1-4 RH: 0-13 Tight: 0-8 Gall: 1-4
Aids: Bl: 0-0 Vi: 0-0 Tstrap: 0-0 Ckp: 0-0
Best Rating: 116 5/07 NmkR 1m1f gd-fm

Smart; winner of the 2007 Newbury Spring Cup; stays 1m2f; acts on most types of ground.

Pintano

90(77) (23)63

4-y-o ch g Dr Fong (USA)-Heckle (In The Wings)
J M Bradley J M Bradley

Placings:350/303206-0000140600 (5628)
2009: 5^0SD, 6^0GF, 5^0GF, 6^0GF, 6^1G, 6^4F, 5^0GS, 6^6GF, 6^0G, 7^0GS,

	Starts	1st	2nd	3rd	Win & Pl
Career Total (Turf)	18	1	1	3	4176
Career Total (AW)	1	0	0	0	
51 7/09 Nott 6f15y				GD	£2047

Total win prize-money £2047

Going (Turf): Sf: 0-1 GS: 0-2 Gd: 1-6 GF: 0-8 Fm: 0-1
Distance: 5f/6f: 0-11 7f-8f: 1-8 9f-13f: 0-0 14f+: 0-0
Track: LH: 0-5 RH: 0-1 Tight: 0-4 Gall: 0-0
Aids: Bl: 0-5 Vi: 0-0 Tstrap: 0-2 Ckp: 0-2
Best Rating: 72 8/07 Hayd 6f gd-fm

Fair; stays 6f; acts on a sound surface; has worn a tongue tie.

Pintura

103 74

2-y-o ch g Efisio-Picolette (Piccolo)
M R Channon R Bastian

Placings:36031545510 (6693)
2009: 5^3GF, 5^6GS, 6^0G, 6^3S, 6^1GF, 6^5GF, 7^4GF, 6^5GS, 7^5GF, 7^1GF, 7^0GS,

	Starts	1st	2nd	3rd	Win & Pl
Career Total (Turf)	11	2	0	2	13588
73 9/09 Wwck 7f26y	(0-75)			G-F	£2590
72 8/09 Rdcr 6f				G-F	£7123

Total win prize-money £9714

Going (Turf): Sf: 0-1 GS: 0-3 Gd: 0-1 GF: 2-6 Fm: 0-0
Distance: 5f/6f: 1-7 7f-8f: 1-4 9f-13f: 0-0 14f+: 0-0
Track: LH: 1-1 RH: 0-2 Tight: 0-0 Gall: 0-1
Aids: Bl: 0-0 Vi: 0-0 Tstrap: 0-0 Ckp: 0-0
Best Rating: 74 8/09 York 6f gd-fm

Fair; stays 7f and acts on fast ground.

Pipedreamer

117 121

5-y-o b h Selkirk (USA)-Follow A Dream (USA) (Gone West (USA))
J H M Gosden Cheveley Park Stud

Placings:611411/3333140-2514 (6850)
2009: 10^2G, 10^5G, 9^1GS, 10^4G,

	Starts	1st	2nd	3rd	Win & Pl
Career Total (Turf)	17	6	1	4	457792
115 10/09 Lonc 1m1f165y				G-S	£71942
115 7/08 York 1m2f88y				G-F	£56770
116 10/07 NmkR 1m1f	H			G-F	£99712
108 8/07 Gdwd 1m1f192y	H			GD	£62320
101 6/07 Pont 1m2f6y	(0-85)H			G-F	£6477
85 5/07 Gdwd 1m				GD	£3238

Total win prize-money £300460

Going (Turf): Sf: 0-1 GS: 1-1 Gd: 2-7 GF: 3-8 Fm: 0-0
Distance: 5f/6f: 0-0 7f-8f: 1-2 9f-13f: 5-15 14f+: 0-0
Track: LH: 2-2 RH: 3-10 Tight: 1-1 Gall: 1-4
Aids: Bl: 0-0 Vi: 0-0 Tstrap: 0-0 Ckp: 0-0
Best Rating: 121 6/08 Asct 1m2f gd-fm

Group class; placed in the Prince Of Wales's Stakes and Eclipse before winning Group 2 Sky Bet York Stakes in 2008; won the Prix Dollar in 2009; effective from 1m1f-1m2f; acts on good and fast ground.

Piper's Song (IRE)

100(104) (67)84

6-y-o gr g Distant Music (USA)-Dane's Lane (IRE) (Danehill (USA))
Patrick Morris (Mrs L Williamson 28/1) D & D Coatings Ltd

Placings:04615/206630210/041460000-54622004254200 (7490)
2009: 9^5SD, 10^4SD, 12^6SD, 12^2GS, 11^2F, 16^0G, 12^0GF, 12^4GF, 14^2G, 12^5G, 14^4G, 11^2SD, 12^0G, 12^0SD,

	Starts	1st	2nd	3rd	Win & Pl
Career Total (Turf)	29	3	5	1	17804
Career Total (AW)	8	0	1	0	605
84 6/08 Bevl 1m1f207y	(0-80)H			G-F	£4209
84 9/07 Leic 7f9y	(0-70)H			GD	£3238
71 9/06 Sand 7f16y	(0-65)H			G-F	£3238

Total win prize-money £10687

Going (Turf): Sf: 0-2 GS: 0-3 Gd: 1-10 GF: 2-13 Fm: 0-1
Distance: 5f/6f: 0-0 7f-8f: 2-7 9f-13f: 1-27 14f+: 0-3
Track: LH: 0-20 RH: 2-12 Tight: 0-17 Gall: 0-3
Aids: Bl: 0-0 Vi: 1-4 Tstrap: 0-1 Ckp: 0-1
Best Rating: 84 6/08 Bevl 1m1f207y gd-fm

Moderate; effective at around 7f-1m2f; acts on fast ground.

Pipers Piping (IRE)

94(99) (68)58

3-y-o b c Noverre (USA)-Monarchy (IRE) (Common Grounds)
J A Osborne John Egan & 12 Day Partners

Placings:0312030356 (6587)
2009: 7^0SD, 5^3SD, 5^1SD, 6^2SD, 6^0F, 5^3G, 5^0SD, 5^3SD, 6^5SD, 7^6SD,

	Starts	1st	2nd	3rd	Win & Pl
Career Total (Turf)	2	0	0	1	520
Career Total (AW)	8	1	1	2	4395
65 4/09 Wolv 5f216y				STD	£2047

Total win prize-money £2047

Going (Turf): Sf: 0-0 GS: 0-0 Gd: 0-1 GF: 0-0 Fm: 0-1
Distance: 5f/6f: 1-8 7f-8f: 0-2 9f-13f: 0-0 14f+: 0-0
Track: LH: 1-8 RH: 0-2 Tight: 1-5 Gall: 0-0
Aids: Bl: 0-0 Vi: 0-0 Tstrap: 0-0 Ckp: 0-0
Best Rating: 68 4/09 Sthl 6f stand

Moderate; effective at 7f; acts on Polytrack.

Pipette

102 97

2-y-o b f Pivotal-Amaryllis (IRE) (Sadler's Wells (USA))
A M Balding George Strawbridge

Placings:13 **(7033)**
2009: 6^{1}S, 7^{3}S,

	Starts	1st	2nd	3rd	Win & Pl
Career Total (Turf)	2	1	0	1	9383

77 9/09 Sals 6f212y SFT £6152
Total win prize-money £6152

Going (Turf): **Sf: 1-2** GS: 0-0 Gd: 0-0 GF: 0-0 Fm: 0-0
Distance: 5f/6f: 0-0 **7f-8f: 1-2** 9f-13f: 0-0 14f+: 0-0
Track : LH: 0-0 RH: 0-0 Tight: 0-0 Gall: 0-0
Aids: Bl: 0-0 Vi: 0-0 Tstrap: 0-0 Ckp: 0-0
Best Rating: **97** 10/09 Newb 7f soft

Fair; stays 7f; acts on soft ground.

Pippbrook Gold

99(102) (78)78

4-y-o ch g Golden Snake (USA)-Chiaro (Safawan)
J R Boyle Prosser Family Partnership

Placings:5/210530-6440405053 **(7225)**
2009: 7^{6}SD, 7^{4}G, 7^{4}GF, 8^{0}G, 7^{4}GF, 8^{0}G, 7^{5}GF, 10^{0}F, 7^{5}G, 10^{3}SD,

	Starts	1st	2nd	3rd	Win & Pl
Career Total (Turf)	11	1	1	0	3518
Career Total (AW)	6	0	0	2	655

78 6/08 Bath 1m5y GD £1942
Total win prize-money £1943

Going (Turf): Sf: 0-0 GS: 0-1 **Gd: 1-6** GF: 0-3 Fm: 0-1
Distance: 5f/6f: 0-0 7f-8f: 0-11 **9f-13f: 1-6** 14f+: 0-0
Track : **LH: 1-8** RH: 0-7 **Tight: 1-9** Gall: 0-0
Aids: Bl: 0-0 Vi: 0-0 Tstrap: 0-0 Ckp: 0-0
Best Rating: **78** 11/08 Ling 1m stand

Modest; stays 1m; acts on good ground.

Piquante

106(101) (64)73

3-y-o b f Selkirk (USA)-China (Royal Academy (USA))
M L W Bell Highclere Thoroughbred Racing(Persimmon)

Placings:4-4644651 **(6967)**
2009: 10^{4}GS, 8^{6}G, 10^{4}G, 12^{4}GF, 9^{6}G, 10^{5}SD, 7^{1}G,

	Starts	1st	2nd	3rd	Win & Pl
Career Total (Turf)	7	1	0	0	4033
Career Total (AW)	1	0	0	0	0

73 10/09 Brig 7f214y (0-63)H GD £2590
Total win prize-money £2590

Going (Turf): Sf: 0-1 GS: 0-1 **Gd: 1-4** GF: 0-1 Fm: 0-0
Distance: 5f/6f: 0-0 **7f-8f: 1-2** 9f-13f: 0-6 14f+: 0-0
Track : **LH: 1-3** RH: 0-4 Tight: 0-3 Gall: 0-1
Aids: Bl: 0-0 Vi: 0-0 Tstrap: 0-0 Ckp: 0-0
Best Rating: **73** 10/09 Brig 7f214y good

Pirate's Song

90(90) (63)63

2-y-o b c Bahamian Bounty-Soviet Terms (Soviet Star (USA))
J A R Toller Saeed Manana

Placings:035 **(6443)**
2009: 6^{0}G, 6^{3}GF, 5^{5}SS,

	Starts	1st	2nd	3rd	Win & Pl
Career Total (Turf)	2	0	0	1	604
Career Total (AW)	1	0	0	0	0

Going (Turf): Sf: 0-0 GS: 0-0 Gd: 0-1 GF: 0-1 Fm: 0-0
Distance: 5f/6f: 0-2 7f-8f: 0-1 9f-13f: 0-0 14f+: 0-0
Track : LH: 0-1 RH: 0 0 Tight: 0-1 Gall: 0-0
Aids: Bl: 0-0 Vi: 0-0 Tstrap: 0-0 Ckp: 0-0
Best Rating: **63** 10/09 Ling 5f std-slw

Pires

105 (92)92

5-y-o br g Generous (IRE)-Kaydee Queen (IRE) (Bob's Return (IRE))
A J Martin Mrs E A Lawlor

Placings:2342125/0-5002 **(7567a)**
2009: 12^{5}GF, 8^{0}SH, 8^{0}HY, 12^{2}SD,

	Starts	1st	2nd	3rd	Win & Pl
Career Total (Turf)	10	1	3	1	16618
Career Total (AW)	2	0	1	0	3987

89 7/06 Rdcr 7f G-F £3886
Total win prize-money £3886

Going (Turf): Sf: 0-1 GS: 0-0 Gd: 0-1 **GF: 1-5** Fm: 0-2
Distance: 5f/6f: 0-2 **7f-8f: 1-7** 9f-13f: 0-3 14f+: 0-0
Track : LH: 0-5 RH: 0-3 Tight: 0-1 Gall: 0-2
Aids: Bl: 0-0 Vi: 0-0 Tstrap: 0-0 Ckp: 0-0
Best Rating: **97** 7/06 Asct 7f gd-fm

Very useful; stays 1m plus; acts on most ground; winning hurdler.

Piscean (USA)

105(104) (93)97

4-y-o b/br g Stravinsky (USA)-Navasha (USA) (Woodman (USA))
T Keddy Andrew Duffield

Placings:0430120**0**/2354610**0**00102-1000000500**0** **(6283)**
2009: 5^{1}GF, 6^{0}G, 6^{0}GF, 5^{0}G, 5^{0}GF, 5^{0}GS, 5^{0}GF, 5^{5}GF, 5^{0}G, 6^{0}GF, 5^{0}GF,

	Starts	1st	2nd	3rd	Win & Pl
Career Total (Turf)	27	3	0	2	31643
Career Total (AW)	5	1	3	0	10066

97 5/09 Gdwd 5f (0-105)H G-F £11656
86 10/08 Ling 5f (0-80)H STD £6308
84 8/08 Gdwd 5f (0-95)H G-F £12462
76 9/07 Gdwd 5f (0-75)H G-F £3238
Total win prize-money £33666

Going (Turf): Sf: 0-2 GS: 0-2 Gd: 0-9 **GF: 3-14** Fm: 0-0
Distance: **5f/6f: 4-31** 7f-8f: 0-1 9f-13f: 0-0 14f+: 0-0
Track : **LH: 1-6** RH: 0-1 **Tight: 1-4** Gall: 0-3
Aids: **Bl: 1-5** Vi: 0-0 Tstrap: 0-0 Ckp: 0-0
Best Rating: **97** 5/09 Gdwd 5f gd-fm

Useful; effective at 5f; acts on fast ground and on Polytrack; can break slowly; has worn blinkers.

Piste

99(98) (68)72

3-y-o b f Falbrav (IRE)-Arctic Char (Polar Falcon (USA))
Miss T Jackson (B J Meehan 28/6) H L Thompson

Placings:004045-344241600300 **(6413)**
2009: 5^{3}GF, 5^{4}G, 5^{4}SD, 5^{2}G, 5^{4}GF, 5^{1}GF, 5^{6}G, 5^{0}GF, 5^{0}G, 5^{3}GF, 5^{0}GF, 6^{0}GF,

	Starts	1st	2nd	3rd	Win & Pl
Career Total (Turf)	14	1	1	2	5486
Career Total (AW)	4	0	0	0	289

72 6/09 Wind 5f10y (0-70)H G-F £2729
Total win prize-money £2730

Going (Turf): Sf: 0-0 GS: 0-1 Gd: 0-4 **GF: 1-9** Fm: 0-0
Distance: **5f/6f: 1-17** 7f-8f: 0-1 9f-13f: 0-0 14f+: 0-0
Track : LH: 0-4 RH: 0-1 Tight: 0-2 **Gall: 1-4**
Aids: Bl: 0-1 Vi: 0-0 Tstrap: 0-0 Ckp: 0-0
Best Rating: **72** 6/09 Wind 5f10y gd-fm

Modest; effective over 5-6f; handles fast ground and Polytrack.

Pitbull

96(94) (63)68

6-y-o b g Makbul-Piccolo Cativo (Komaite (USA))
Mrs G S Rees Mrs G S Rees

Placings:65305/05020**6**/06635016616/6240562443620**4**-0032600 **(6761)**
2009: 9^{0}SD, 7^{0}G, 8^{3}S, 10^{2}G, 8^{6}HY, 10^{0}GS, 9^{0}G,

	Starts	1st	2nd	3rd	Win & Pl
Career Total (Turf)	33	2	5	4	14530
Career Total (AW)	10	0	0	0	241

65 10/07 Pont 1m2f6y (0-70)H GD £3886
61 8/07 Carl 6f192y (0-65)H GD £1943
Total win prize-money £5829

Going (Turf): Sf: 0-7 GS: 0-4 **Gd: 2-10** GF: 0-12 Fm: 0-0
Distance: 5f/6f: 0-7 7f-8f: 1-9 9f-13f: 1-27 14f+: 0-0
Track : LH: 1-34 RH: 1-6 Tight: 0-15 Gall: 0-0
Aids: Bl: 0-0 Vi: 0-0 Tstrap: 2-26 Ckp: 2-26
Best Rating: **68** 10/08 Wwck 1m22y soft

Moderate; stays 1m2f; acts on fast and soft ground; goes on Polytrack.

Pittodrie Star (IRE)

88(99) (76)59

2-y-o ch c Choisir (AUS)-Jupiter Inlet (IRE) (Jupiter Island)
A M Balding Evan M Sutherland

Placings:015 **(7611)**
2009: 7^{0}G, 6^{1}3D, 7^{5}3D,

	Starts	1st	2nd	3rd	Win & Pl
Career Total (Turf)	1	0	0	0	
Career Total (AW)	2	1	0	0	2590

76 11/09 Kemp 6f STD £2590
Total win prize-money £2590

Going (Turf): Sf: 0-0 GS: 0-0 Gd: 0-1 GF: 0-0 Fm: 0-0
Distance: **5f/6f: 1-1** 7f-8f: 0-2 9f-13f: 0-0 14f+: 0-0
Track : LH: 0-0 **RH: 1-2** Tight: 0-0 Gall: 0-0
Aids: Bl: 0-0 Vi: 0-0 Tstrap: 0-0 Ckp: 0-0
Best Rating: **76** 11/09 Kemp 6f stand

Fair; effective over 6f; acts on Polytrack.

Pitton Justice

52 (20)

7-y-o ch g Compton Place-Blind Justice (Mystiko (USA))
Dr J R J Naylor M Blandford

Placings:0/00 **(3577)**
2009: 5^{0}G, 6^{0}GF,

	Starts	1st	2nd	3rd	Win & Pl
Career Total (Turf)	2	0	0	0	
Career Total (AW)	1	0	0	0	

Going (Turf): Sf: 0-0 GS: 0-0 Gd: 0-1 GF: 0-1 Fm: 0-0
Distance: 5f/6f: 0-2 7f-8f: 0-1 9f-13f: 0-0 14f+: 0-0
Track : LH: 0-1 RH: 0-0 Tight: 0-1 Gall: 0-0
Aids: Bl: 0-0 Vi: 0-0 Tstrap: 0-0 Ckp: 0-0
Best Rating: **20** 2/06 Ling 5f stand

Piverina (IRE)

103(98) (55)**56**

4-y-o b f Pivotal-Alassio (USA) (Gulch (USA))

Miss J A Camacho Miss Julie Camacho

Placings:50/0005603304325-010504 **(5732)**

2009: 12^{0}GS, 12^{1}G, 14^{0}SD, 12^{5}GF, 12^{0}G, 12^{4}GS,

	Starts	1st	2nd	3rd	Win & Pl
Career Total (Turf)	15	1	0	2	3481
Career Total (AW)	6	0	1	1	907

56 6/09 Haml 1m4f17y (0-60)H GD £2388

Total win prize-money £2388

Going (Turf): Sf: 0-1 GS: 0-4 **Gd: 1-8** GF: 0-2 Fm: 0-0
Distance: 5f/6f: 0-4 7f-8f: 0-4 **9f-13f: 1-11** 14f+: 0-2
Track : LH: 0-9 **RH: 1-10 Tight: 1-4** Gall: 0-3
Aids: Bl: 0-0 Vi: 0-0 Tstrap: 0-0 Ckp: 0-0
Best Rating: **56** 6/09 Haml 1m4f17y good

Moderate; stays 1m4f; acts on easy ground and on Fibresand.

Pivotal Express (IRE)

71 **24**

3-y-o ch g Pivotal-Forest Express (AUS) (Kaaptive Edition (NZ))

J F Panvert The Greek Connection

Placings:0 **(6741)**

2009: 8^{0}GS,

	Starts	1st	2nd	3rd	Win & Pl
Career Total (Turf)	1	0	0	0	

Going (Turf): **Sf: 0-0 GS: 0-1 Gd: 0-0 GF: 0-0 Fm: 0-0**
Distance: 5f/6f: 0-0 7f-8f: 0-0 9f-13f: 0-1 14f+: 0-0
Track : LH: 0-0 RH: 0-1 Tight: 0-1 Gall: 0-0
Aids: Bl: 0-0 Vi: 0-0 Tstrap: 0-0 Ckp: 0-0
Best Rating: **24** 10/09 Wind 1m67y gd-sft

Place The Duchess

56(92) (52)**50**

3-y-o b f Compton Place-Barrantes (Distant Relative)

A J Lidderdale (Miss Sheena West 23/6) Mrs C Vanner & Lidderdale Racing LLP

Placings:66060-060230 **(7869)**

2009: 5^{0}GF, 5^{6}SD, 5^{0}SD, 6^{2}SD, 6^{3}SS, 6^{0}SS,

	Starts	1st	2nd	3rd	Win & Pl
Career Total (Turf)	6	0	0	0	0
Career Total (AW)	5	0	1	1	1008

Going (Turf): **Sf: 0-1 GS: 0-1 Gd: 0-1 GF: 0-3 Fm: 0-0**
Distance: 5f/6f: 0-11 7f-8f: 0-0 9f-13f: 0-0 14f+: 0-0
Track : LH: 0-6 RH: 0-1 Tight: 0-2 Gall: 0-1
Aids: Bl: 0-0 Vi: 0-0 Tstrap: 0-0 Ckp: 0-0
Best Rating: **52** 12/09 Kemp 6f stand

Moderate; effective over 6f; acts on Polytrack; handles Fibresand; has worn a tongue tie.

Placidity

(79) (25)

3-y-o ch f Compton Place-Wittily (Whittingham (IRE))

A J McCabe Paul J Dixon

Placings:00 **(0982)**

2009: 6^{0}SD, 5^{0}SD,

	Starts	1st	2nd	3rd	Win & Pl
Career Total (Turf)	0	0	0	0	
Career Total (AW)	2	0	0	0	

Going (Turf): **Sf: 0-0 GS: 0-0 Gd: 0-0 GF: 0-0 Fm: 0-0**
Distance: 5f/6f: 0-2 7f-8f: 0-0 9f-13f: 0-0 14f+: 0-0
Track : LH: 0-2 RH: 0-0 Tight: 0-1 Gall: 0-0
Aids: Bl: 0-0 Vi: 0-0 Tstrap: 0-0 Ckp: 0-0
Best Rating: **25** 3/09 Wolv 5f216y stand

Plaisterer

109(93) (58)**101**

4-y-o b f Best Of The Bests (IRE)-Lumiere D'Espoir (FR) (Saumarez)

C F Wall David Andrews Plastering

Placings:05225-35121260 **(7291)**

2009: 11^{3}GS, 10^{5}GF, 10^{1}G, 8^{2}GF, 10^{1}GS, 10^{2}GS, 10^{6}G, 10^{0}S,

	Starts	1st	2nd	3rd	Win & Pl
Career Total (Turf)	10	2	4	1	17314
Career Total (AW)	3	0	0	0	0

100 7/09 Donc 1m2f60y (0-85)H G-S £4857
89 6/09 Wind 1m2f7y (0-80)H GD £4857

Total win prize-money £9714

Going (Turf): Sf: 0-1 **GS: 1-4 Gd: 1-3** GF: 0-2 Fm: 0-0
Distance: 5f/6f: 0-0 7f-8f: 0-0 **9f-13f: 2-12** 14f+: 0-1
Track : LH: 1-5 RH: 1-4 Tight: 1-6 Gall: 1-3
Aids: Bl: 0-0 Vi: 0-0 Tstrap: 0-0 Ckp: 0-0
Best Rating: **101** 9/09 Ayr 1m2f gd-sft

Very useful; suited by 1m2f; acts on good, fast and easy ground.

Plaka (FR)

79(97) (56)**38**

4-y-o gr f Verglas (IRE)-Top Speed (IRE) (Wolfhound (USA))

W M Brisbourne M A Holmes

Placings:04000004/050-003000 **(2539)**

2009: 9^{0}SD, 8^{0}SD, 7^{3}SD, 8^{0}GF, 7^{0}F, 7^{0}GF,

	Starts	1st	2nd	3rd	Win & Pl
Career Total (Turf)	5	0	0	0	
Career Total (AW)	12	0	0	1	447

Going (Turf): **Sf: 0-0 GS: 0-0 Gd: 0-0 GF: 0-4 Fm: 0-1**
Distance: 5f/6f: 0-5 7f-8f: 0-6 9f-13f: 0-6 14f+: 0-0
Track : LH: 0-12 RH: 0-2 Tight: 0-9 Gall: 0-0
Aids: Bl: 0-0 Vi: 0-0 Tstrap: 0-0 Ckp: 0-0
Best Rating: **57** 9/07 Gdwd 6f gd-fm

Moderate filly; best at about a mile; handles Polytrack.

Plane Painter (IRE)

87 (77)**83**

5-y-o b g Orpen (USA)-Flight Sequence (Polar Falcon (USA))

B G Powell Favourites Racing XXIV

Placings:310/436505322541/04422-0 **(3143)**

2009: 21^{0}GF,

	Starts	1st	2nd	3rd	Win & Pl
Career Total (Turf)	17	2	4	3	20482
Career Total (AW)	4	0	0	0	361

78 10/07 Bath 2m1f34y (0-75)H G-S £2914
78 9/06 Ches 7f2y G-F £5505

Total win prize-money £8420

Going (Turf): Sf: 0-1 **GS: 1-3** Gd: 0-1 **GF: 1-10** Fm: 0-2
Distance: 5f/6f: 0-0 7f-8f: 1-4 9f-13f: 0-7 14f+: 1-10
Track : **LH: 2-13** RH: 0-8 **Tight: 2-10** Gall: 0-3
Aids: Bl: 0-0 Vi: 0-0 Tstrap: 0-0 Ckp: 0-0
Best Rating: **83** 5/08 Ayr 1m7f gd-fm

Modest; stays 2m1f; acts on fast and easy ground.

Planet Red (IRE)

102 **83**

2-y-o ch c Bahamian Bounty-Aries (GER) (Big Shuffle (USA))

R Hannon Jamie Perryman & Richard Morecombe

Placings:210 **(5133)**

2009: 5^{2}GS, 6^{1}G, 7^{0}GF,

	Starts	1st	2nd	3rd	Win & Pl
Career Total (Turf)	3	1	1	0	6399

83 7/09 Wind 6f GD £4857

Total win prize-money £4857

Going (Turf): Sf: 0-0 GS: 0-1 **Gd: 1-1** GF: 0-1 Fm: 0-0
Distance: **5f/6f: 1-2** 7f-8f: 0-1 9f-13f: 0-0 14f+: 0-0
Track : LH: 0-1 RH: 0-0 Tight: 0-0 **Gall: 1-2**
Aids: Bl: 0-0 Vi: 0-0 Tstrap: 0-0 Ckp: 0-0
Best Rating: **83** 7/09 Wind 6f good

Useful; effective over 5f-6f; acts on good and easy ground.

Planetary Motion (USA)

96(99) (85)**60**

4-y-o gr c Gone West (USA)-Gaviola (USA) (Cozzene (USA))

A bin Huzaim (M Johnston 21/4) Sheikh Hamdan Bin Mohammed Al Maktoum

Placings:001-104440

2009: 10^{1}SD, 10^{0}G, 12^{4}SD, 8^{4}FT, 7^{4}FT, 9^{0}FT,

	Starts	1st	2nd	3rd	Win & Pl
Career Total (Turf)	2	0	0	0	
Career Total (AW)	7	2	0	0	9229

85 2/09 Ling 1m2f (0-85)H STD £4727
76 12/08 Ling 1m2f STD £2729

Total win prize-money £7457

Going (Turf): **Sf: 0-1 GS: 0-0 Gd: 0-1 GF: 0-0 Fm: 0-0**
Distance: 5f/6f: 0-0 7f-8f: 0-3 **9f-13f: 2-6** 14f+: 0-0
Track : **LH: 2-5** RH: 0-1 **Tight: 2-3** Gall: 0-1
Aids: Bl: 0-0 Vi: 0-0 Tstrap: 0-0 Ckp: 0-0
Best Rating: **85** 2/09 Ling 1m2f stand

Fair; stays 1m2f; handles Polytrack.

Platinum Bounty

74 **33**

3-y-o ch f Bahamian Bounty-Maxizone (FR) (Linamix (FR))

J A Geake Mrs S A Geake

Placings:0 **(2433)**

2009: 8^{0}G,

	Starts	1st	2nd	3rd	Win & Pl
Career Total (Turf)	1	0	0	0	

Going (Turf): **Sf: 0-0 GS: 0-0 Gd: 0-1 GF: 0-0 Fm: 0-0**
Distance: 5f/6f: 0-0 7f-8f: 0-1 9f-13f: 0-0 14f+: 0-0
Track : LH: 0-0 RH: 0-1 Tight: 0-0 Gall: 0-0
Aids: Bl: 0-0 Vi: 0-0 Tstrap: 0-0 Ckp: 0-0

Best Rating: 33 5/09 Gdwd 1m good

Plato (JPN)

(93) (79)
2-y-o ch c Bago (FR)-Taygete (USA) (Miswaki (USA))
H R A Cecil Niarchos Family

Placings:52 **(6672)**
2009: 8^{5}SD, 8^{2}SD,

	Starts	1st	2nd	3rd	Win & Pl
Career Total (Turf)	0	0	0	0	
Career Total (AW)	2	0	1	0	806

Going (Turf): Sf: 0-0 GS: 0-0 Gd: 0-0 GF: 0-0 Fm: 0-0
Distance: 5f/6f: 0-0 7f-8f: 0-1 9f-13f: 0-1 14f+: 0-0
Track : LH: 0-1 RH: 0-1 Tight: 0-1 Gall: 0-0
Aids: Bl: 0-0 Vi: 0-0 Tstrap: 0-0 Ckp: 0-0
Best Rating: 79 10/09 Wolv 1m141y stand

Fair; stays 1m plus; acts on Polytrack.

Platoche (IRE)

82(107) (60)**60**
4-y-o b c Galileo (IRE)-Political Parody (USA) (Doonesbury (USA))
A W Carroll (G A Butler 1/8) Mrs Susan Keable

Placings:300-00030 **(4538)**
2009: 13^{0}SD, 11^{0}G, 11^{0}SD, 10^{3}SD, 10^{0}SD,

	Starts	1st	2nd	3rd	Win & Pl
Career Total (Turf)	4	0	0	1	347
Career Total (AW)	4	0	0	1	302

Going (Turf): Sf: 0-0 GS: 0-2 Gd: 0-1 GF: 0-1 Fm: 0-0
Distance: 5f/6f: 0-0 7f-8f: 0-0 9f-13f: 0-8 14f+: 0-0
Track : LH: 0-5 RH: 0-2 Tight: 0-6 Gall: 0-0
Aids: Bl: 0-1 Vi: 0-0 Tstrap: 0-1 Ckp: 0-1
Best Rating: 60 4/09 Ling 1m5f stand

Modest; stays 1m1f and acts on soft ground.

Play It Sam

102(96) (76)**78**
3-y-o b g Bahamian Bounty-Bombalarina (IRE) (Barathea (IRE))
W R Swinburn P W Harris

Placings:00-55412252 **(6421)**
2009: 7^{5}GF, 8^{5}GF, 8^{4}GF, 8^{1}S, 8^{2}G, 8^{2}G, 8^{5}SD, 8^{2}GF,

	Starts	1st	2nd	3rd	Win & Pl
Career Total (Turf)	9	1	3	0	6803
Career Total (AW)	1	0	0	0	0

74 7/09 Pont 1m4y (0-70)H SFT £3238
Total win prize-money £3238

Going (Turf): Sf: 1-1 GS: 0-0 Gd: 0-4 GF: 0-4 Fm: 0-0
Distance: 5f/6f: 0-0 7f-8f: 0-5 **9f-13f: 1-5** 14f+: 0-0
Track : **LH: 1-3** RH: 0-5 Tight: 0-2 Gall: 0-0
Aids: Bl: 0-0 Vi: 0-0 Tstrap: 0-0 Ckp: 0-0
Best Rating: 78 8/09 Sand 1m14y good

Fair; stays 1m; acts on good and soft ground; has worn a tongue tie.

Play Master (IRE)

(98) (62)**61**
8-y-o b g Second Empire (IRE)-Madam Waajib (IRE) (Waajib)
B J Llewellyn Dr Simon Clarke

Placings:212010305/0660/203105/044/00 **(0502)**
2009: 16^{0}SD, 16^{0}SD,

	Starts	1st	2nd	3rd	Win & Pl
Career Total (Turf)	8	1	0	0	5688
Career Total (AW)	16	2	3	2	9877

66 3/06 Wolv 1m1f103y STD £2730
76 4/04 Wind 1m67y D(0-85)H G-S £5687
76 1/04 Wolv 1m100y D STD £3386
Total win prize-money £11805

Going (Turf): Sf: 0-0 **GS: 1-3** Gd: 0-2 GF: 0-3 Fm: 0-0
Distance: 5f/6f: 0-0 7f-8f: 0-8 **9f-13f: 3-13** 14f+: 0-3
Track : **LH: 2-22** RH: 1-1 **Tight: 3-14** Gall: 0-2
Aids: Bl: 0-0 Vi: 0-1 Tstrap: 0-1 Ckp: 0-1
Best Rating: 76 9/04 Hayd 1m30y good

Modest sort on turf and Fibresand; stays a mile, but should get further; suited by soft ground.

Play To Win (IRE)

79(100) (61)**61**
3-y-o b c Singspiel (IRE)-Spot Prize (USA) (Seattle Dancer (USA))
D R C Elsworth J C Smith

Placings:00053-000 **(2635)**
2009: 12^{0}GF, 11^{0}GF, 11^{0}GF,

	Starts	1st	2nd	3rd	Win & Pl
Career Total (Turf)	6	0	0	0	
Career Total (AW)	2	0	0	1	385

Going (Turf): Sf: 0-1 GS: 0-0 Gd: 0-1 GF: 0-4 Fm: 0-0
Distance: 5f/6f: 0-0 7f-8f: 0-3 9f-13f: 0-5 14f+: 0-0
Track : LH: 0-3 RH: 0-1 Tight: 0-2 Gall: 0-1
Aids: Bl: 0-0 Vi: 0-0 Tstrap: 0-1 Ckp: 0-1
Best Rating: 61 12/08 GrLe 1m2f stand

Modest; stays 1m2f; acts on Polytrack.

Play Up Pompey

84(103) (59)**32**
7-y-o b g Dansili-Search For Love (FR) (Groom Dancer (USA))
J J Bridger double-r-racing.com

Placings:000000/050035636636540/050006000000145/3106000500004164/56633300004360304140-425050503060 **(5473)**
2009: 10^{4}SD, 10^{2}SD, 10^{5}SD, 11^{0}SD, 10^{5}SD, 12^{0}GF, 10^{5}SD, 10^{0}SD, 10^{3}G, 10^{0}SD, 8^{6}G, 9^{0}GF,

	Starts	1st	2nd	3rd	Win & Pl
Career Total (Turf)	35	0	0	4	2795
Career Total (AW)	50	4	1	6	10515

56 12/08 Ling 1m2f (0-52)H STD £1706
57 12/07 Ling 1m2f (0-52)H STD £1943
64 1/07 Ling 1m2f (0-58)H STD £1706
61 12/06 Kemp 1m2f STD £2388
Total win prize-money £7744

Going (Turf): Sf: 0-3 GS: 0-5 Gd: 0-14 GF: 0-10 Fm: 0-3
Distance: 5f/6f: 0-2 7f-8f: 0-14 **9f-13f: 4-68** 14f+: 0-1
Track : **LH: 3-39** RH: 1-38 **Tight: 3-39** Gall: 0-4
Aids: Bl: 0-0 Vi: 0-0 Tstrap: 0-0 Ckp: 0-0
Best Rating: 64 1/07 Ling 1m2f stand

Moderate; stays 1m4f; acts on fast ground and on Polytrack.

Playboy Blues (IRE)

(93) (75)
2-y-o b c Bertolini (USA)-Ingeburg (Hector Protector (USA))
P W Chapple-Hyam Playboy Kennels

Placings:41 **(7800)**
2009: 7^{4}SD, 7^{1}SD,

	Starts	1st	2nd	3rd	Win & Pl
Career Total (Turf)	0	0	0	0	
Career Total (AW)	2	1	0	0	3238

75 12/09 Wolv 7f32y STD £3238
Total win prize-money £3238

Going (Turf): Sf: 0-0 GS: 0-0 Gd: 0-0 GF: 0-0 Fm: 0-0
Distance: 5f/6f: 0-0 **7f-8f: 1-2** 9f-13f: 0-0 14f+: 0-0
Track : **LH: 1-2** RH: 0-0 **Tight: 1-2** Gall: 0-0
Aids: Bl: 0-0 Vi: 0-0 Tstrap: 0-0 Ckp: 0-0
Best Rating: 75 12/09 Wolv 7f32y stand

Fair; effective over 7f; acts on Polytrack.

Playful Asset (IRE)

98(98) (56)**62**
3-y-o ch f Johannesburg (USA)-Twickin (USA) (Two Punch (USA))
P Howling (R M Beckett 4/7) Joe Cole

Placings:00-4021306043 **(7888)**
2009: 7^{4}GF, 10^{0}G, 9^{2}G, 9^{1}G, 10^{3}G, 12^{0}GF, 12^{6}SD, 8^{0}SD, 12^{4}SD, 12^{3}SD,

	Starts	1st	2nd	3rd	Win & Pl
Career Total (Turf)	7	1	1	1	4201
Career Total (AW)	5	0	0	1	292

59 7/09 Leic 1m1f218y GD £3238
Total win prize-money £3238

Going (Turf): Sf: 0-0 GS: 0-0 **Gd: 1-5** GF: 0-2 Fm: 0-0
Distance: 5f/6f: 0-0 7f-8f: 0-4 **9f-13f: 1-8** 14f+: 0-0
Track : LH: 0-6 **RH: 1-5** Tight: 0-4 Gall: 0-0
Aids: Bl: 0-0 Vi: 0-0 Tstrap: 0-0 Ckp: 0-0
Best Rating: 62 4/09 Wwck 7f26y gd-fm

Modest; stays 1m2f; handles quick ground and Polytrack.

Pleasant Day (IRE)

106(95) (79)**102**
2-y-o b g Noverre (USA)-Sunblush (UAE) (Timber Country (USA))
B J Meehan Jaber Abdullah

Placings:001212 **(7030)**
2009: 7^{0}G, 7^{0}G, 7^{1}SD, 7^{2}GF, 7^{1}GF, 7^{2}S,

	Starts	1st	2nd	3rd	Win & Pl
Career Total (Turf)	5	1	2	0	20505
Career Total (AW)	1	1	0	0	3238

92 9/09 Asct 7f H G-F £6854
79 8/09 Ling 7f STD £3238
Total win prize-money £10092

Going (Turf): Sf: 0-1 GS: 0-0 Gd: 0-2 **GF: 1-2** Fm: 0-0
Distance: 5f/6f: 0-0 **7f-8f: 2-6** 9f-13f: 0-0 14f+: 0-0
Track : **LH: 1-2** RH: 0-0 **Tight: 1-2** Gall: 0-0
Aids: **Bl: 2-4** Vi: 0-0 Tstrap: 0-0 Ckp: 0-0
Best Rating: 102 10/09 Newb 7f soft

Useful; stays 7f; acts on fast ground and on Polytrack; has worn blinkers.

Pleasant Way (IRE)

81(83) (34)**61**

2-y-o ch f Barathea (IRE)-Eman's Joy (Lion Cavern (USA))
D R Lanigan Saif Ali & Saeed H Altayer

Placings:00 **(7199)**
2009: 8^{0}GF, 8^{0}SD,

	Starts	1st	2nd	3rd	Win & Pl
Career Total (Turf)	1	0	0	0	
Career Total (AW)	1	0	0	0	

Going (Turf): **Sf: 0-0 GS: 0-0 Gd: 0-0 GF: 0-1 Fm: 0-0**
Distance: 5f/6f: 0-0 7f-8f: 0-1 9f-13f: 0-1 14f+: 0-0
Track : LH: 0-1 RH: 0-0 Tight: 0-1 Gall: 0-0
Aids: Bl: 0-0 Vi: 0-0 Tstrap: 0-0 Ckp: 0-0
Best Rating: **61** 10/09 Yarm 1m3y gd-fm

Please Sing

108 **100**

3-y-o b f Royal Applause-Persian Song (Persian Bold)
M R Channon Mrs Ann C Black

Placings:10150-63332000 **(6272)**
2009: 7^{6}S, 7^{3}GF, 8^{3}GF, 7^{3}G, 8^{2}GF, 8^{0}GF, 7^{0}GF, 7^{0}GF,

	Starts	1st	2nd	3rd	Win & Pl
Career Total (Turf)	13	2	1	3	80435

96	7/08	NmkJ	6f	G-S	£45416
82	5/08	Leic	5f2y	G-F	£4533

Total win prize-money £49949

Going (Turf): Sf: 0-1 **GS: 1-2** Gd: 0-1 **GF: 1-8** Fm: 0-1
Distance: **5f/6f: 2-4** 7f-8f: 0-7 9f-13f: 0-2 14f+: 0-0
Track : LH: 0-1 RH: 0-2 Tight: 0-1 Gall: 0-0
Aids: Bl: 0-0 Vi: 0-0 Tstrap: 0-0 Ckp: 0-0
Best Rating: **100** 7/09 Gdwd 7f good

Smart; winner of the 2008 Cherry Hinton Stakes; effective at 7f-1m; acts on most ground.

Plenilune (IRE)

95(98) (53)**67**

4-y-o b g Fantastic Light (USA)-Kathleen's Dream (USA) (Last Tycoon)
M Brittain Mel Brittain

Placings:43050200-00005**06504** **(7784)**
2009: 12^{0}G, 8^{0}GF, 9^{0}GF, 8^{0}GS, 8^{5}GS, 10^{0}GS, 11^{0}SD, 9^{6}SD, 7^{5}SD, 8^{0}SD, 8^{4}SD,

	Starts	1st	2nd	3rd	Win & Pl
Career Total (Turf)	14	0	1	1	1601
Career Total (AW)	5	0	0	0	0

Going (Turf): **Sf: 0-1 GS: 0-8 Gd: 0-2 GF: 0-3 Fm: 0-0**
Distance: 5f/6f: 0-0 7f-8f: 0-4 9f-13f: 0-15 14f+: 0-0
Track : LH: 0-10 RH: 0-6 Tight: 0-10 Gall: 0-2
Aids: Bl: 0-1 Vi: 0-0 Tstrap: 0-0 Ckp: 0-0
Best Rating: **67** 8/08 Ripn 1m1f170y gd-sft

Modest; suited by 1m-1m2f; acts on soft ground; has worn blinkers.

Plenty O'Toole

(88) (69)

2-y-o ch g Monsieur Bond (IRE)-Marie La Rose (FR) (Night Shift (USA))
Mrs D J Sanderson R J Budge

Placings:042 **(7538)**
2009: 6^{0}SD, 7^{4}SD, 7^{2}SD,

	Starts	1st	2nd	3rd	Win & Pl
Career Total (Turf)	0	0	0	0	
Career Total (AW)	3	0	1	0	1132

Going (Turf): **Sf: 0-0 GS: 0-0 Gd: 0-0 GF: 0-0 Fm: 0-0**
Distance: 5f/6f: 0-1 7f-8f: 0-2 9f-13f: 0-0 14f+: 0-0
Track : LH: 0-1 RH: 0-2 Tight: 0-0 Gall: 0-0
Aids: Bl: 0-0 Vi: 0-0 Tstrap: 0-0 Ckp: 0-0
Best Rating: **69** 11/09 Kemp 7f stand

Modest; stays 7f; acts on Polytrack.

Plum Pudding (IRE)

110(114) (101)**113**

6-y-o b g Elnadim (USA)-Karayb (IRE) (Last Tycoon)
R Hannon Hyde Sporting Promotions Limited

Placings:0360/**2**210**2**01600/**5**010000000/**52**00301000110-1221352**505** **(7809)**
2009: 7^{1}GF, 8^{2}G, 7^{2}GF, 7^{1}GF, 7^{3}GF, 8^{5}G, 8^{2}S, 10^{5}SD, 8^{0}SD, 10^{5}SD,

	Starts	1st	2nd	3rd	Win & Pl
Career Total (Turf)	**39**	**8**	**5**	**2**	**154412**
Career Total (AW)	**8**	**0**	**2**	**1**	**13891**

113	7/09	NmkJ	7f	H	G-F	£62310
109	4/09	Wwck	7f26y		G-F	£7771
112	10/08	NmkR	7f	(0-100)H	GD	£12462
107	10/08	NmkR	7f	(0-100)H	G-F	£12462
109	5/08	NmkR	7f	(0-90)H	G-F	£7771
101	5/07	NmkR	1m	(0-95)H	GD	£9067
102	9/06	NmkR	1m	(0-95)H	GD	£8724
95	5/06	NmkR	1m	(0-75)H	GD	£3886

Total win prize-money £124455

Going (Turf): Sf: 0-6 GS: 0-6 **Gd: 4-13 GF: 4-14** Fm: 0-0
Distance: 5f/6f: 0-0 **7f-8f: 8-34** 9f-13f: 0-13 14f+: 0-0
Track : **LH: 1-13** RH: 0-5 Tight: 0-9 Gall: 0-3
Aids: Bl: 0-0 Vi: 0-0 Tstrap: 1-6 Ckp: 1-6
Best Rating: **113** 11/09 Nott 1m75y soft

Smart; winner of the 2009 Bunbury Cup and placed at Group 3 level; effective over 7f-1m; acts on most ground and on Polytrack; has worn cheekpieces; goes well at Newmarket; suited by forcing tactics.

Plumage

102(103) (64)**67**

4-y-o b f Royal Applause-Cask (Be My Chief (USA))
M Salaman Mrs N L Young

Placings:0/06532200-2250415 **(4051)**
2009: 5^{2}SD, 6^{2}G, 6^{5}G, 6^{0}GF, 6^{4}GF, 5^{1}GF, 5^{5}S,

	Starts	1st	2nd	3rd	Win & Pl
Career Total (Turf)	11	1	1	1	5441
Career Total (AW)	5	0	3	0	2015

67	7/09	Leic	5f218y	(0-70)H	G-F	£3885

Total win prize-money £3886

Going (Turf): Sf: 0-1 GS: 0-0 Gd: 0-3 **GF: 1-7** Fm: 0-0
Distance: **5f/6f: 1-3** 7f-8f: 0-12 9f-13f: 0-1 14f+: 0-0
Track : LH: 0-6 RH: 0-1 Tight: 0-5 Gall: 0-0
Aids: Bl: 0-0 Vi: 0-0 Tstrap: 0-0 Ckp: 0-0
Best Rating: **67** 7/09 Leic 5f218y gd-fm

Moderate; effective at 6f-1m; acts on good/fast ground; handles Polytrack.

Plume

99 **77**

2-y-o b f Pastoral Pursuits-Polar Storm (IRE) (Law Society (USA))
R Hannon Highclere Thoroughbred Racing Touchstone

Placings:01 **(6245)**
2009: 6^{0}S, 6^{1}GF,

	Starts	1st	2nd	3rd	Win & Pl
Career Total (Turf)	2	1	0	0	3238

77	9/09	Hayd	6f	G-F	£3238

Total win prize-money £3238

Going (Turf): Sf: 0-1 GS: 0-0 Gd: 0-0 **GF: 1-1** Fm: 0-0
Distance: **5f/6f: 1-1** 7f-8f: 0-1 9f-13f: 0-0 14f+: 0-0
Track : LH: 0-0 RH: 0-0 Tight: 0-0 Gall: 0-0
Aids: Bl: 0-0 Vi: 0-0 Tstrap: 0-0 Ckp: 0-0
Best Rating: **77** 9/09 Hayd 6f gd-fm

Useful; effective over 6f; acts on fast ground.

Plus Ultra (IRE)

78 **50**

2-y-o b g Rock Of Gibraltar (IRE)-Tafseer (IRE) (Grand Lodge (USA))
H R A Cecil Malih L Al Basti

Placings:0 **(4314)**
2009: 7^{0}G,

	Starts	1st	2nd	3rd	Win & Pl
Career Total (Turf)	1	0	0	0	

Going (Turf): **Sf: 0-0 GS: 0-0 Gd: 0-1 GF: 0-0 Fm: 0-0**
Distance: 5f/6f: 0-0 7f-8f: 0-1 9f-13f: 0-0 14f+: 0-0
Track : LH: 0-0 RH: 0-0 Tight: 0-0 Gall: 0-0
Aids: Bl: 0-1 Vi: 0-0 Tstrap: 0-0 Ckp: 0-0
Best Rating: **50** 7/09 NmkJ 7f good

Plush

(105) (87)**36**

6-y-o ch g Medicean-Glorious (Nashwan (USA))
Tom Dascombe John Reed

Placings:02300/0/**00411612-1415** **(7848)**
2009: 8^{1}SD, 8^{4}SD, 8^{1}SD, 9^{5}SD,

	Starts	1st	2nd	3rd	Win & Pl
Career Total (Turf)	3	0	0	0	
Career Total (AW)	**15**	**5**	**2**	**1**	**18584**

86	12/09	Wolv	1m141y	(0-85)H	STD	£5046
87	1/09	Wolv	1m141y	(0-75)H	STD	£2729
69	12/08	Wolv	1m1f103y	(0-60)H	STD	£2388
65	11/08	Wolv	1m141y	(0-60)H	STD	£2047
64	11/08	Wolv	1m141y	(0-55)H	STD	£2729

Total win prize-money £14941

Going (Turf): **Sf: 0-0 GS: 0-0 Gd: 0-1 GF: 0-2 Fm: 0-0**
Distance: 5f/6f: 0-1 7f-8f: 0-6 **9f-13f: 5-11** 14f+: 0-0
Track : **LH: 5-15** RH: 0-2 **Tight: 5-13** Gall: 0-0
Aids: Bl: 0-1 Vi: 0-0 Tstrap: 0-0 Ckp: 0-0
Best Rating: **87** 1/09 Wolv 1m141y stand

Useful; stays 1m and acts on sand.

Plutocraft

75(87) (68)**38**

2-y-o ch g Starcraft (NZ)-Angry Bark (USA) (Woodman (USA))
J R Fanshawe The Owl Society

Placings:43 **(7024)**

2009: 5^{4}GF, 7^{3}SD,

	Starts	1st	2nd	3rd	Win & Pl
Career Total (Turf)	1	0	0	0	241
Career Total (AW)	1	0	0	1	302

Going (Turf): Sf: 0-0 GS: 0-0 Gd: 0-0 GF: 0-1 Fm: 0-0
Distance: 5f/6f: 0-1 7f-8f: 0-1 9f-13f: 0-0 14f+: 0-0
Track : LH: 0-0 RH: 0-1 Tight: 0-0 Gall: 0-0
Aids: Bl: 0-0 Vi: 0-0 Tstrap: 0-0 Ckp: 0-0
Best Rating: 68 10/09 Kemp 7f stand

Modest; stays 7f and should stay 1m; acts on Polytrack.

Plymouth Rock (IRE)

105 **86**
3-y-o b c Sadler's Wells (USA)-Zarawa (IRE) (Kahyasi)
J Noseda M Tabor, Mrs J Magnier, D Smith, M Green

Placings:132 (6203)
2009: 10^{1}GF, 11^{3}G, 11^{2}G,

	Starts	1st	2nd	3rd	Win & Pl
Career Total (Turf)	3	1	1	1	4945

79	6/09	Wind	1m2f7y	G-F	£2729

Total win prize-money £2730

Going (Turf): Sf: 0-0 GS: 0-0 Gd: 0-2 **GF: 1-1** Fm: 0-0
Distance: 5f/6f: 0-0 7f-8f: 0-0 **9f-13f: 1-3** 14f+: 0-0
Track : LH: 0-0 **RH: 1-2 Tight: 1-3** Gall: 0-0
Aids: Bl: 0-0 Vi: 0-0 Tstrap: 0-0 Ckp: 0-0
Best Rating: 86 9/09 Gdwd 1m3f good

Useful; stays 1m2f; acts on fast ground.

Poaka Beck (IRE)

(76) (29)**33**
3-y-o b c Fath (USA)-Star Of The Future (USA) (El Gran Senor (USA))
R F Fisher Great Head House Estates Limited

Placings:0-6 (0429)
2009: 5^{6}SD,

	Starts	1st	2nd	3rd	Win & Pl
Career Total (Turf)	1	0	0	0	
Career Total (AW)	1	0	0	0	0

Going (Turf): Sf: 0-0 GS: 0-0 Gd: 0-0 GF: 0-1 Fm: 0-0
Distance: 5f/6f: 0-2 7f-8f: 0-0 9f-13f: 0-0 14f+: 0-0
Track : LH: 0-2 RH: 0-0 Tight: 0-2 Gall: 0-0
Aids: Bl: 0-0 Vi: 0-0 Tstrap: 0-0 Ckp: 0-0
Best Rating: 33 7/08 Catt 5f212y gd-fm

Pobs Trophy

(67) (15)
2-y-o b/br g Umistim-Admonish (Warning)
R C Guest Future Racing (Notts) Limited

Placings:0 (7420)
2009: 7^{0}SD,

	Starts	1st	2nd	3rd	Win & Pl
Career Total (Turf)	0	0	0	0	
Career Total (AW)	1	0	0	0	

Going (Turf): Sf: 0-0 GS: 0-0 Gd: 0-0 GF: 0-0 Fm: 0-0
Distance: 5f/6f: 0-0 7f-8f: 0-1 9f-13f: 0-0 14f+: 0-0
Track : LH: 0-1 RH: 0-0 Tight: 0-0 Gall: 0-0
Aids: Bl: 0-0 Vi: 0-0 Tstrap: 0-0 Ckp: 0-0

Best Rating: 15 11/09 Sthl 7f stand

Poca A Poca (IRE)

88(81) (40)**48**
5-y-o b m Namid-Cliveden Gail (IRE) (Law Society (USA))
G C Bravery Mrs Theresa Fitsall

Placings:0600056000 (5179)
2009: 7^{0}G, 8^{6}GF, 8^{0}SD, 6^{0}GS, 6^{0}SD, 8^{5}G, 8^{6}S, 6^{0}G, 10^{0}SD, 8^{0}G,

	Starts	1st	2nd	3rd	Win & Pl
Career Total (Turf)	7	0	0	0	0
Career Total (AW)	3	0	0	0	

Going (Turf): Sf: 0-1 GS: 0-1 Gd: 0-4 GF: 0-1 Fm: 0-0
Distance: 5f/6f: 0-2 7f-8f: 0-3 9f-13f: 0-5 14f+: 0-0
Track : LH: 0-6 RH: 0-0 Tight: 0-2 Gall: 0-0
Aids: Bl: 0-1 Vi: 0-0 Tstrap: 0-6 Ckp: 0-6
Best Rating: 48 6/09 Chep 1m14y good

Pocket Too

(106) (52)**76**
6-y-o b g Fleetwood (IRE)-Pocket Venus (IRE) (King's Theatre (IRE))
Matthew Salaman Oaktree Racing

Placings:006/00003/13020255/41110-0 (7785)
2009: 13^{0}SD,

	Starts	1st	2nd	3rd	Win & Pl
Career Total (Turf)	7	0	2	0	1782
Career Total (AW)	15	4	0	2	18894

82	4/08	GrLe	2m	(0-100)H	STD	£9969
74	1/08	Kemp	2m	(0-85)H	STD	£4210
71	1/08	Wolv	1m5f194y	(0-65)H	STD	£1774
63	1/07	Ling	2m		STD	£2184

Total win prize-money £18139

Going (Turf): Sf: 0-3 GS: 0-1 Gd: 0-2 GF: 0-0 Fm: 0-1
Distance: 5f/6f: 0-0 7f-8f: 0-2 9f-13f: 0-9 **14f+: 4-11**
Track : **LH: 3-15** RH: 1-5 **Tight: 2-12** Gall: 1-4
Aids: Bl: 0-2 Vi: 0-0 Tstrap: 4-11 Ckp: 4-11
Best Rating: 82 4/08 GrLe 2m stand

Fair; winning hurdler; stays 2m; acts on most ground on turf; also goes on Polytrack; has worn blinkers and often wears cheekpieces and a tongue tie.

Pocket's Pick (IRE)

92(103) (73)**83**
3-y-o ch g Exceed And Excel (AUS)-Swizzle (Efisio)
G L Moore David & Jane George

Placings:0320050-00**2**0**5**0**4**00**52410** (7890)
2009: 5^{0}GF, 6^{0}GF, 5^{2}SD, 6^{0}G, 5^{5}SD, 6^{0}SD, 5^{4}SD, 6^{0}SD, 6^{0}GS, 6^{5}SD, 6^{2}SD, 6^{4}SD, 5^{1}SS, 6^{0}SD,

	Starts	1st	2nd	3rd	Win & Pl
Career Total (Turf)	11	0	1	1	1864
Career Total (AW)	10	1	2	0	3577

72	12/09	Sthl	5f	(0-60)H	SS	£1706

Total win prize-money £1706

Going (Turf): Sf: 0-1 GS: 0-1 Gd: 0-5 GF: 0-3 Fm: 0-1
Distance: **5f/6f: 1-21** 7f-8f: 0-0 9f-13f: 0-0 14f+: 0-0
Track : LH: 0-9 RH: 0-1 Tight: 0-7 Gall: 0-1
Aids: Bl: 0-2 Vi: 0-0 Tstrap: 0-2 Ckp: 0-2
Best Rating: 83 7/08 Newb 5f34y good

Modest; effective at 5f; acts on firm and good ground and on both AW surfaces.

Poet's Place (USA)

(103) (76)
4-y-o b g Mutakddim (USA)-Legion Of Merit (USA) (Danzig (USA))
T D Barron Mrs Elaine Russell

Placings:1 (7853)
2009: 6^{1}SS,

	Starts	1st	2nd	3rd	Win & Pl
Career Total (Turf)	0	0	0	0	
Career Total (AW)	1	1	0	0	2730

76	12/09	Sthl	6f	SS	£2729

Total win prize-money £2730

Going (Turf): Sf: 0-0 GS: 0-0 Gd: 0-0 GF: 0-0 Fm: 0-0
Distance: **5f/6f: 1-1** 7f-8f: 0-0 9f-13f: 0-0 14f+: 0-0
Track : **LH: 1-1** RH: 0-0 Tight: 0-0 Gall: 0-0
Aids: Bl: 0-0 Vi: 0-0 Tstrap: 0-0 Ckp: 0-0
Best Rating: 76 12/09 Sthl 6f std-slw

Winner on belated debut over 6f on Fibresand.

Poet's Voice

110 **114**
2-y-o b c Dubawi (IRE)-Bright Tiara (USA) (Chief's Crown (USA))
Saeed Bin Suroor Godolphin

Placings:31314 (6450)
2009: 7^{3}G, 7^{1}G, 7^{3}GF, 7^{1}GF, 6^{4}GF,

	Starts	1st	2nd	3rd	Win & Pl
Career Total (Turf)	5	2	0	2	80139

114	9/09	Donc	7f	G-F	£56770
103	7/09	NmkJ	7f	GD	£6476

Total win prize-money £63246

Going (Turf): Sf: 0-0 GS: 0-0 **Gd: 1-2 GF: 1-3** Fm: 0-0
Distance: 5f/6f: 0-1 **7f-8f: 2-4** 9f-13f: 0-0 14f+: 0-0
Track : LH: 0-1 RH: 0-0 Tight: 0-0 Gall: 0-1
Aids: Bl: 0-0 Vi: 0 0 Tstrap: 0-0 Ckp: 0-0
Best Rating: 114 9/09 Donc 7f gd-fm

Group performer; effective over 7f; winner of the 2009 Champagne Stakes, acts on good and fast ground; has worn a tongue tie.

Point Of Light

109(86) (45)**90**
3-y-o b g Pivotal-Lighthouse (Warning)
Sir Mark Prescott Syndicate 2007

Placings:030-1111116 (6204)
2009: 10^{1}G, 10^{1}G, 11^{1}G, 11^{1}GF, 11^{1}G, 12^{1}GF, 12^{6}G,

	Starts	1st	2nd	3rd	Win & Pl
Career Total (Turf)	9	6	0	1	23982
Career Total (AW)	1	0	0	0	

90	9/09	Bevl	1m4f16y	(0-85)H	G-F	£5180
87	8/09	Yarm	1m3f101y	(0-70)H	GD	£2590
73	8/09	Wind	1m3f135y	(0-75)H	G-F	£2729
85	8/09	Bath	1m3f144y	(0-75)H	GD	£2590
72	7/09	Bath	1m2f46y	(0-80)H	GD	£6476
71	7/09	NmkJ	1m2f	(0-75)H	GD	£3885

Total win prize-money £23453

Going (Turf): Sf: 0-0 GS: 0-1 **Gd: 4-6** GF: 2-2 Fm: 0-0
Distance: 5f/6f: 0-3 7f-8f: 0-0 **9f-13f: 6-7** 14f+: 0-0
Track : **LH: 3-5** RH: 2-3 **Tight: 5-7** Gall: 1-3
Aids: Bl: 0-0 Vi: 0-0 Tstrap: 0-0 Ckp: 0-0
Best Rating: 90 9/09 Bevl 1m4f16y gd-fm

Fair; stays 1m4f; acts on good and easy ground.

Point Out (USA)

(90) (75)

2-y-o ch c Point Given (USA)-Dock Leaf (USA) (Woodman (USA))

J H M Gosden K Abdulla

Placings:2 **(7024)**

2009: 7^{2}SD,

	Starts	1st	2nd	3rd	Win & Pl
Career Total (Turf)	0	0	0	0	
Career Total (AW)	1	0	1	0	605

Going (Turf): Sf: 0-0 GS: 0-0 Gd: 0-0 GF: 0-0 Fm: 0-0
Distance: 5f/6f: 0-0 7f-8f: 0-1 9f-13f: 0-0 14f+: 0-0
Track : LH: 0-0 RH: 0-1 Tight: 0-0 Gall: 0-0
Aids: Bl: 0-0 Vi: 0-0 Tstrap: 0-0 Ckp: 0-0
Best Rating: 75 10/09 Kemp 7f stand

Fair; stays 7f; acts on Polytrack; sure to win a race.

Point To Prove

92(95) (69)69

2-y-o b c Refuse To Bend (IRE)-On Point (Kris)

Miss Amy Weaver Michael Bringloe

Placings:5526020640341 **(7636)**

2009: 5^{5}GF, 5^{5}GF, 5^{2}GF, 5^{6}GF, 5^{0}GF, 6^{2}SD, 6^{0}SD, 6^{8}SD, 5^{4}SD, 5^{0}S, 5^{3}SD, 5^{4}SD, 5^{1}SD,

	Starts	1st	2nd	3rd	Win & Pl
Career Total (Turf)	6	0	1	0	1156
Career Total (AW)	7	1	1	1	5992

64 12/09 Sthl 5f (0-85) STD £4533
Total win prize-money £4533

Going (Turf): Sf: 0-1 GS: 0-0 Gd: 0-0 GF: 0-5 Fm: 0-0
Distance: 5f/6f: 1-13 7f-8f: 0-0 9f-13f: 0-0 14f+: 0-0
Track : LH: 0-2 RH: 0-4 Tight: 0-1 Gall: 0-0
Aids: Bl: 0-0 Vi: 0-0 Tstrap: 0-0 Ckp: 0-0
Best Rating: 69 8/09 Kemp 6f stand

Modest; effective over 5f; acts on Fibresand; has worn an eyeshield.

Pointillist (IRE)

93 63

3-y-o b f Peintre Celebre (USA)-For Example (USA) (Northern Baby (CAN))

R M Beckett Mrs Sonia Rogers

Placings:5-5000 **(5121)**

2009: 10^{5}GF, 9^{0}G, 9^{0}GF, 7^{0}F,

	Starts	1st	2nd	3rd	Win & Pl
Career Total (Turf)	5	0	0	0	0

Going (Turf): Sf: 0-0 GS: 0-0 Gd: 0-2 GF: 0-2 Fm: 0-1
Distance: 5f/6f: 0-0 7f-8f: 0-2 9f-13f: 0-3 14f+: 0-0
Track : LH: 0-1 RH: 0-3 Tight: 0-3 Gall: 0-0
Aids: Bl: 0-0 Vi: 0-0 Tstrap: 0-1 Ckp: 0-1
Best Rating: 63 6/09 Wind 1m2f7y gd-fm

Pointing North (SAF)

111 104

5-y-o b g Joshua Dancer (USA)-Compass Point (SAF) (Model Man (SAF))

B Smart (S Seemar 19/2) H E Sheikh Rashid Bin Mohammed

Placings:111/1-0000 **(5434)**

2009: 7^{0}GF, 7^{0}G, 7^{0}GF, 6^{0}GF,

	Starts	1st	2nd	3rd	Win & Pl
Career Total (Turf)	8	4	0	0	57731

112 1/08 Keni 1m GD £45955
12/07 Turf 7f55y GD £5661
11/07 Turf 7f H GD £3170
10/07 Turf 6f GD £2943
Total win prize-money £57731

Going (Turf): Sf: 0-0 GS: 0-0 Gd: 4-5 GF: 0-3 Fm: 0-0
Distance: 5f/6f: 1-2 7f-8f: 3-6 9f-13f: 0-0 14f+: 0-0
Track : LH: 0-3 RH: 0-0 Tight: 0-0 Gall: 0-3
Aids: Bl: 0-0 Vi: 0-0 Tstrap: 0-0 Ckp: 0-0
Best Rating: 112 1/08 Keni 1m good

Smart; ex-South African and UAE performer; stays 1m; acts on a sound surface.

Pokfulham (IRE)

101(85) (51)67

3-y-o b g Mull Of Kintyre (USA)-Marjinal (Marju (IRE))

J S Goldie (A P Jarvis 5/7) Ambrose Turnbull

Placings:0062326-0445430100 **(6997)**

2009: 8^{0}G, 8^{4}F, 7^{4}GF, 6^{5}F, 8^{4}S, 6^{3}S, 6^{0}S, 8^{1}G, 8^{0}GF, 7^{0}G,

	Starts	1st	2nd	3rd	Win & Pl
Career Total (Turf)	16	1	2	2	8826
Career Total (AW)	1	0	0	0	0

64 9/09 Ayr 1m (0-70)H GD £4533
Total win prize-money £4533

Going (Turf): Sf: 0-4 GS: 0-2 Gd: 1-4 GF: 0-4 Fm: 0-2
Distance: 5f/6f: 0-4 7f-8f: 1-11 9f-13f: 0-2 14f+: 0-0
Track : LH: 1-7 RH: 0-1 Tight: 0-4 Gall: 0-0
Aids: Bl: 0-0 Vi: 1-12 Tstrap: 0-0 Ckp: 0-0
Best Rating: 67 9/08 Ayr 7f50y heavy

Moderate; stays 1m; acts on fast and easy ground; has worn a visor.

Polar Annie

98(82) (73)83

4-y-o b f Fraam-Willisa (Polar Falcon (USA))

M S Saunders Lockstone Business Services Ltd

Placings:54012/233130-6000040 **(5502)**

2009: 6^{6}SD, 5^{0}F, 6^{0}GF, 6^{0}G, 5^{0}S, 6^{4}GF, 7^{0}G,

	Starts	1st	2nd	3rd	Win & Pl
Career Total (Turf)	15	1	1	3	8882
Career Total (AW)	3	1	1	0	3257

83 8/08 Newb 6f8y (0-80)H G-S £4857
69 9/07 Kemp 7f (0-65) STD £2047
Total win prize-money £6905

Going (Turf): Sf: 0-2 GS: 1-2 Gd: 0-5 GF: 0-4 Fm: 0-2
Distance: 5f/6f: 0-11 7f-8f: 2-7 9f-13f: 0-0 14f+: 0-0
Track : LH: 0-5 RH: 1-2 Tight: 0-1 Gall: 0-6
Aids: Bl: 0-0 Vi: 0-0 Tstrap: 0-0 Ckp: 0-0
Best Rating: 83 8/08 Newb 6f8y gd-sft

Fair; probably best over 6f, though does stay further; acts on most ground and Polytrack.

Polar Gold

49(53)

7-y-o b m Lujain (USA)-Polar Fair (Polar Falcon (USA))

A J Chamberlain Jim White

Placings:000/0000245200/00 **(6800)**

2009: 7^{0}GF, 8^{0}SD,

	Starts	1st	2nd	3rd	Win & Pl
Career Total (Turf)	5	0	0	0	0
Career Total (AW)	10	0	2	0	1834

Going (Turf): Sf: 0-2 GS: 0-0 Gd: 0-2 GF: 0-1 Fm: 0-0
Distance: 5f/6f: 0-7 7f-8f: 0-4 9f-13f: 0-4 14f+: 0-0
Track : LH: 0-1 RH: 0-0 Tight: 0-1 Gall: 0-0
Aids: Bl: 0-0 Vi: 0-0 Tstrap: 0-0 Ckp: 0-0

Polebrook

73 38

2-y-o ch g Lomitas-Fifth Emerald (Formidable (USA))

J R Jenkins John White & David Tattersall

Placings:60000 **(6754)**

2009: 5^{6}GF, 6^{0}GF, 7^{0}G, 9^{0}G, 7^{0}G,

	Starts	1st	2nd	3rd	Win & Pl
Career Total (Turf)	5	0	0	0	0

Going (Turf): Sf: 0-0 GS: 0-0 Gd: 0-3 GF: 0-2 Fm: 0-0
Distance: 5f/6f: 0-2 7f-8f: 0-2 9f-13f: 0-1 14f+: 0-0
Track : LH: 0-0 RH: 0-1 Tight: 0-1 Gall: 0-1
Aids: Bl: 0-0 Vi: 0-1 Tstrap: 0-0 Ckp: 0-0
Best Rating: 38 10/09 Leic 7f9y good

Polemica (IRE)

95(89) (50)62

3-y-o b f Rock Of Gibraltar (IRE)-Lady Scarlett (Woodman (USA))

E A L Dunlop Thurloe Thoroughbreds XXIII

Placings:006040 **(4452)**

2009: 8^{0}SD, 8^{0}G, 8^{6}GF, 7^{0}GF, 8^{4}GS, 7^{0}G,

	Starts	1st	2nd	3rd	Win & Pl
Career Total (Turf)	5	0	0	0	212
Career Total (AW)	1	0	0	0	

Going (Turf): Sf: 0-0 GS: 0-1 Gd: 0-2 GF: 0-2 Fm: 0-0
Distance: 5f/6f: 0-0 7f-8f: 0-4 9f-13f: 0-2 14f+: 0-0
Track : LH: 0-1 RH: 0-3 Tight: 0-2 Gall: 0-0
Aids: Bl: 0-0 Vi: 0-0 Tstrap: 0-0 Ckp: 0-0
Best Rating: 62 5/09 Wind 1m67y good

Polish Power (GER)

100(110) (84)96

9-y-o br h Halling (USA)-Polish Queen (Polish Precedent (USA))

J S Moore J S Moore

Placings:13000/3300230040/4302000005/5212111421304 014/32163004455001322/26201100000 4-00151052060 **(6498)**

2009: 10^{0}SD, 10^{0}SD, 12^{1}SD, 10^{5}G, 10^{1}SD, 12^{0}SD, 10^{5}S, 10^{2}SD, 11^{0}SD, 11^{6}GF, 12^{0}SF,

	Starts	1st	2nd	3rd	Win & Pl
Career Total (Turf)	43	4	3	7	29998
Career Total (AW)	38	9	8	2	49622

71	5/09	Ling	1m2f		STD	£1942
72	4/09	Ling	1m4f		STD	£2047
96	5/08	Yarm	1m3f101y	(0-90)H	G-F	£6854
96	5/08	Donc	1m2f60y	(0-85)H	G-S	£4857
89	10/07	Ling	1m4f	(0-85)H	STD	£5362
93	3/07	Ling	1m4f	(0-85)H	STD	£4210
85	12/06	Ling	1m4f	(0-80)H	STD	£5505
82	5/06	Newc	1m4f93y	(0-75)H	G-S	£4210
76	4/06	Kemp	1m4f	(0-75)H	STD	£5505
78	3/06	Ling	1m2f	(0-70)H	STD	£3123
67	3/06	Ling	1m5f	(0-60)H	STD	£2388

57 2/06 Ling 1m4f (0-55)H STD £2307
4/03 Dort 1m165y SFT £1972
Total win prize-money £50286

Going (Turf): Sf: 1-12 **GS: 2-4** Gd: 0-20 GF: 1-6 Fm: 0-0
Distance: 5f/6f: 0-0 7f-8f: 0-0 **9f-13f: 13-79** 14f+: 0-2
Track : **LH: 11-53** RH: 2-19 **Tight: 9-39** Gall: 2-11
Aids: Bl: 0-5 Vi: 0-0 Tstrap: 0-2 Ckp: 0-2
Best Rating: **96** 5/08 Yarm 1m3f101y gd-fm

Useful; effective at around 1m4f; acts on good or softer ground and on Polytrack.

Polish Pride

90 **89**

3-y-o b f Polish Precedent (USA)-Purple Tiger (IRE) (Rainbow Quest (USA))
M Brittain Mel Brittain

Placings:12453103205-000 **(2270)**
2009: 6^{0}GF, 7^{0}GF, 7^{0}HY,

	Starts	1st	2nd	3rd	Win & Pl
Career Total (Turf)	14	2	2	2	20544

87 8/08 Hayd 6f (0-80) G-S £5504
67 4/08 Muss 5f SFT £3885
Total win prize-money £9391

Going (Turf): **Sf: 1-5 GS: 1-2** Gd: 0-3 GF: 0-4 Fm: 0-0
Distance: **5f/6f: 2-9** 7f-8f: 0-5 9f-13f: 0-0 14f+: 0-0
Track : LH: 0-3 RH: 0-0 Tight: 0-1 Gall: 0-1
Aids: Bl: 0-0 Vi: 0-0 Tstrap: 0-0 Ckp: 0-0
Best Rating: **89** 9/08 Ayr 6f heavy

Useful; effective from 5f-6f and acts on soft ground.

Polish Red

85(82) (30)**67**

5-y-o b g Polish Precedent (USA)-Norcroft Joy (Rock Hopper)
Jane Chapple-Hyam Norcroft Park Stud

Placings:565/60110/0000-0000 **(4156)**
2009: 12^{0}GS, 11^{0}GF, 14^{0}SD, 11^{0}G,

	Starts	1st	2nd	3rd	Win & Pl
Career Total (Turf)	15	2	0	0	9904
Career Total (AW)	1	0	0	0	

83 7/07 Wind 1m3f135y (0-80)H G-S £6477
81 6/07 Wind 1m3f135y(0-75)H SFT £3238
Total win prize-money £9716

Going (Turf): **Sf: 1-2 GS: 1-4** Gd: 0-5 GF: 0-4 Fm: 0-0
Distance: 5f/6f: 0-0 7f-8f: 0-1 **9f-13f: 2-13** 14f+: 0-2
Track : LH: 0-6 RH: 0-1 **Tight: 2-7** Gall: 0-4
Aids: Bl: 0-0 Vi: 0-0 Tstrap: 0-2 Ckp: 0-2
Best Rating: **83** 7/07 Wind 1m3f135y gd-sft

Fair; stays 1m4f; acts on good and easy ground.

Polish Steps (IRE)

78(80) (32)**47**

2-y-o b f Footstepsinthesand-Polish Spring (IRE) (Polish Precedent (USA))
J A Osborne D J P Turner

Placings:0000 **(7089)**
2009: 5^{0}GF, 6^{0}G, 8^{0}SD, 6^{0}SD,

	Starts	1st	2nd	3rd	Win & Pl
Career Total (Turf)	2	0	0	0	
Career Total (AW)	2	0	0	0	

Going (Turf): **Sf: 0-0 GS: 0-0 Gd: 0-1 GF: 0-1 Fm: 0-0**
Distance: 5f/6f: 0-4 7f-8f: 0-0 9f-13f: 0-0 14f+: 0-0
Track : LH: 0-2 RH: 0-1 Tight: 0-0 Gall: 0-2
Aids: Bl: 0-0 Vi: 0-0 Tstrap: 0-0 Ckp: 0-0
Best Rating: **47** 6/09 Wind 5f10y gd-fm

Polish World (USA)

88(95) (65)**26**

5-y-o b g Danzig (USA)-Welcometotheworld (USA) (Woodman (USA))
T J Etherington GEAR Racing Partners

Placings:06/612000/540-00 **(1924)**
2009: 5^{0}SD, 6^{0}F,

	Starts	1st	2nd	3rd	Win & Pl
Career Total (Turf)	4	0	1	0	806
Career Total (AW)	9	1	0	0	2389

73 4/07 Ling 6f (0-60)H STD £2388
Total win prize-money £2389

Going (Turf): **Sf: 0-1 GS: 0-0 Gd: 0-0 GF: 0-2 Fm: 0-1**
Distance: **5f/6f: 1-8** 7f-8f: 0-5 9f-13f: 0-0 14f+: 0-0
Track : **LH: 1-5** RH: 0-3 **Tight: 1-5** Gall: 0-0
Aids: Bl: 0-1 Vi: 0-0 Tstrap: 0-0 Ckp: 0-0
Best Rating: **73** 4/07 Ling 6f stand

Pollan Bay (IRE)

72(86) (53)**54**

2-y-o b g High Chaparral (IRE)-Rossa Di Rugiada (IRE) (College Chapel)
S Kirk Jim Horgan

Placings:00560 **(6639)**
2009: 6^{0}GF, 8^{0}GF, 8^{5}G, 8^{6}SD, 8^{0}SD,

	Starts	1st	2nd	3rd	Win & Pl
Career Total (Turf)	3	0	0	0	0
Career Total (AW)	2	0	0	0	0

Going (Turf): **Sf: 0-0 GS: 0-0 Gd: 0-1 GF: 0-2 Fm: 0-0**
Distance: 5f/6f: 0-0 7f-8f: 0-2 9f-13f: 0-3 14f+: 0-0
Track : LH: 0-3 RH: 0-1 Tight: 0-3 Gall: 0-1
Aids: Bl: 0-0 Vi: 0-0 Tstrap: 0-0 Ckp: 0-0
Best Rating: **54** 9/09 Ffos 1m good

Pollenator (IRE)

97 **107**

2-y-o ch f Motivator-Ceanothus (IRE) (Bluebird (USA))
R Hannon The Royal Ascot Racing Club

Placings:62211 **(5825)**
2009: 7^{6}GF, 7^{2}F, 7^{2}G, 7^{1}GF, 8^{1}GF,

	Starts	1st	2nd	3rd	Win & Pl
Career Total (Turf)	5	2	2	0	52971

107 9/09 Donc 1m G-F £45416
86 8/09 NmkJ 7f G-F £4857
Total win prize-money £50273

Going (Turf): Sf: 0-0 GS: 0-0 Gd: 0-1 **GF: 2-3** Fm: 0-1
Distance: 5f/6f: 0-0 **7f-8f: 2-5** 9f-13f: 0-0 14f+: 0-0
Track : LH: 0-0 RH: 0-0 Tight: 0-0 Gall: 0-0
Aids: Bl: 0-0 Vi: 0-0 Tstrap: 0-0 Ckp: 0-0
Best Rating: **107** 9/09 Donc 1m gd-fm

Very useful; winner of Group 2 May Hill Stakes; effective over 7f-1m; acts on fast ground.

Pollish

84(86) (39)**39**

3-y-o b f Polish Precedent (USA)-Fizzy Fiona (Efisio)
A Berry Alan Berry

Placings:600050-0505 **(3936)**
2009: 6^{0}G, 5^{5}GF, 5^{0}GF, 7^{5}GF,

	Starts	1st	2nd	3rd	Win & Pl
Career Total (Turf)	9	0	0	0	0
Career Total (AW)	1	0	0	0	0

Going (Turf): **Sf: 0-2 GS: 0-2 Gd: 0-1 GF: 0-4 Fm: 0-0**
Distance: 5f/6f: 0-9 7f-8f: 0-1 9f-13f: 0-0 14f+: 0-0
Track : LH: 0-3 RH: 0-1 Tight: 0-0 Gall: 0-0
Aids: Bl: 0-1 Vi: 0-0 Tstrap: 0-0 Ckp: 0-0
Best Rating: **39** 10/08 Sthl 6f stand

Polly Macho (IRE)

88 **62**

2-y-o b g Camacho-Polly Mills (Lugana Beach)
P D Evans M&R Refurbishments Ltd

Placings:60040 **(4384)**
2009: 5^{6}GF, 6^{0}G, 6^{0}GS, 5^{4}G, 6^{0}G,

	Starts	1st	2nd	3rd	Win & Pl
Career Total (Turf)	5	0	0	0	144

Going (Turf): **Sf: 0-0 GS: 0-1 Gd: 0-3 GF: 0-1 Fm: 0-0**
Distance: 5f/6f: 0-4 7f-8f: 0-1 9f-13f: 0-0 14f+: 0-0
Track : LH: 0-0 RH: 0-0 Tight: 0-0 Gall: 0-0
Aids: Bl: 0-0 Vi: 0-1 Tstrap: 0-0 Ckp: 0-0
Best Rating: **62** 4/09 Leic 5f2y gd-fm

Plating class; has worn a visor.

Polly's Mark (IRE)

108 **104**

3-y-o b f Mark Of Esteem (IRE)-Kotdiji (Mtoto)
C G Cox Wickham Stud

Placings:342-32103112 **(6242)**
2009: 9^{3}GF, 10^{2}G, 10^{1}G, 12^{0}GF, 10^{3}G, 12^{1}G, 12^{1}GS, 12^{2}G,

	Starts	1st	2nd	3rd	Win & Pl
Career Total (Turf)	11	3	3	3	61777

103 8/09 Asct 1m4f (0-100)H G-S £17230
104 8/09 Newb 1m4f5y GD £22708
90 5/09 Nott 1m2f50y (0-80)H GD £5828
Total win prize-money £45767

Going (Turf): Sf: 0-1 GS: 1-2 **Gd: 2-5** GF: 0-3 Fm: 0-0
Distance: 5f/6f: 0-0 7f-8f: 0-2 **9f-13f: 3-9** 14f+: 0-0
Track : **LH: 2-4** RH: 1-5 Tight: 0-1 **Gall: 2-5**
Aids: Bl: 0-0 Vi: 0-0 Tstrap: 0-0 Ckp: 0-0
Best Rating: **104** 9/09 Asct 1m4f good

Smart; Listed winner; stays 1m4f; seems to act on any ground.

Polmaily

85(88) (51)**75**

4-y-o b g Hawk Wing (USA)-Hampton Lucy (IRE) (Anabaa (USA))
J Akehurst Ok Partnership

Placings:23/540420-005 **(2630)**

2009: 6^{0}GF, 6^{0}F, 7^{5}SD,

	Starts	1st	2nd	3rd	Win & Pl
Career Total (Turf)	10	0	2	1	4442
Career Total (AW)	1	0	0	0	0

Going (Turf): Sf: 0-1 GS: 0-1 Gd: 0-2 GF: 0-5 Fm: 0-1
Distance: 5f/6f: 0-2 7f-8f: 0-6 9f-13f: 0-3 14f+: 0-0
Track : LH: 0-4 RH: 0-2 Tight: 0-3 Gall: 0-1
Aids: Bl: 0-2 Vi: 0-0 Tstrap: 0-0 Ckp: 0-0
Best Rating: 78 10/07 NmkR 1m soft

Modest; stays 1m2f; acts on fast ground but handles soft; has worn blinkers.

Polo Springs

65 31
2-y-o gr/b f Baryshnikov (AUS)-Cristal Springs (Dance Of Life (USA))
W G M Turner J C Boher

Placings:0 (5319)
2009: 8^{0}GF,

	Starts	1st	2nd	3rd	Win & Pl
Career Total (Turf)	1	0	0	0	

Going (Turf): Sf: 0-0 GS: 0-0 Gd: 0-0 GF: 0-1 Fm: 0-0
Distance: 5f/6f: 0-0 7f-8f: 0-0 9f-13f: 0-1 14f+: 0-0
Track : LH: 0-0 RH: 0-1 Tight: 0-1 Gall: 0-0
Aids: Bl: 0-0 Vi: 0-0 Tstrap: 0-0 Ckp: 0-0
Best Rating: 31 8/09 Wind 1m67y gd-fm

Poltergeist (IRE)

96 83
2-y-o b c Invincible Spirit (IRE)-Bayalika (IRE) (Selkirk (USA))
R Hannon Highclere Thoroughbred Racing (Diomed)

Placings:02 (4986)
2009: 7^{0}S, 7^{2}GF,

	Starts	1st	2nd	3rd	Win & Pl
Career Total (Turf)	2	0	1	0	1445

Going (Turf): Sf: 0-1 GS: 0-0 Gd: 0-0 GF: 0-1 Fm: 0-0
Distance: 5f/6f: 0-0 7f-8f: 0-2 9f-13f: 0-0 14f+: 0-0
Track : LH: 0-0 RH: 0-0 Tight: 0-0 Gall: 0-0
Aids: Bl: 0-0 Vi: 0-0 Tstrap: 0-0 Ckp: 0-0
Best Rating: 83 8/09 Newb 7f gd-fm

Useful; stays 7f; acts on fast ground.

Pomander (IRE)

(88) (20)46
6-y-o b m Bob's Return (IRE)-Pheisty (Faustus (USA))
C Gordon David O Moon

Placings:000/06/0 (0116)
2009: 11^{0}SD,

	Starts	1st	2nd	3rd	Win & Pl
Career Total (Turf)	5	0	0	0	
Career Total (AW)	1	0	0	0	

Going (Turf): Sf: 0-1 GS: 0-0 Gd: 0-1 GF: 0-1 Fm: 0-0
Distance: 5f/6f: 0-0 7f-8f: 0-4 9f-13f: 0-2 14f+: 0-0
Track : LH: 0-2 RH: 0-2 Tight: 0-0 Gall: 0-0
Aids: Bl: 0-0 Vi: 0-0 Tstrap: 0-0 Ckp: 0-0
Best Rating: 47 6/05 Gowr 7f good

Pomeroy

70(90) (67)46
2-y-o b c Green Desert (USA)-Ela Paparouna (Vettori (IRE))
Tom Dascombe South Wind Racing 2 & Partner

Placings:046 (7800)
2009: 7^{0}GF, 7^{4}SF, 7^{6}SD,

	Starts	1st	2nd	3rd	Win & Pl
Career Total (Turf)	1	0	0	0	
Career Total (AW)	2	0	0	0	241

Going (Turf): Sf: 0-0 GS: 0-0 Gd: 0-0 GF: 0-1 Fm: 0-0
Distance: 5f/6f: 0-0 7f-8f: 0-3 9f-13f: 0-0 14f+: 0-0
Track : LH: 0-2 RH: 0-0 Tight: 0-2 Gall: 0-0
Aids: Bl: 0-0 Vi: 0-0 Tstrap: 0-0 Ckp: 0-0
Best Rating: 67 12/09 Wolv 7f32y stand

Moderate; stays 7f; acts on Polytrack.

Pong Ping

76(63) (1)26
2-y-o ch f Dr Fong (USA)-Hoh Chi Min (Efisio)
T D Easterby www.realityracingsyndicate.co.uk III

Placings:055 (3119)
2009: 5^{0}SD, 5^{5}GF, 7^{5}GF,

	Starts	1st	2nd	3rd	Win & Pl
Career Total (Turf)	2	0	0	0	0
Career Total (AW)	1	0	0	0	

Going (Turf): Sf: 0-0 GS: 0-0 Gd: 0-0 GF: 0-2 Fm: 0-0
Distance: 5f/6f: 0-2 7f-8f: 0-1 9f-13f: 0-0 14f+: 0-0
Track : LH: 0-0 RH: 0-0 Tight: 0-0 Gall: 0-0
Aids: Bl: 0-0 Vi: 0-0 Tstrap: 0-0 Ckp: 0-0
Best Rating: 26 6/09 Rdcr 7f gd-fm

Pont D'Avignon

(93) (60)
2-y-o ch f Avonbridge-Ambonnay (Ashkalani (IRE))
F J Brennan (P Winkworth 24/9) Mrs L J Robins

Placings:0420 (7210)
2009: 6^{0}SD, 7^{4}SD, 7^{2}SD, 7^{0}SD,

	Starts	1st	2nd	3rd	Win & Pl
Career Total (Turf)	0	0	0	0	
Career Total (AW)	4	0	1	0	605

Going (Turf): Sf: 0-0 GS: 0-0 Gd: 0-0 GF: 0-0 Fm: 0-0
Distance: 5f/6f: 0-1 7f-8f: 0-3 9f-13f: 0-0 14f+: 0-0
Track : LH: 0-1 RH: 0-3 Tight: 0-1 Gall: 0-0
Aids: Bl: 0-0 Vi: 0-0 Tstrap: 0-0 Ckp: 0-0
Best Rating: 60 10/09 Kemp 7f stand

Modest; stays 7f; acts on Polytrack.

Pont De Nuit

85(92) (70)70
2-y-o b g Avonbridge-Belle De Nuit (IRE) (Statoblest)
R Hannon D J Deer

Placings:50030 (7333)
2009: 6^{5}SD, 7^{0}GF, 8^{0}G, 6^{3}S, 6^{0}SD,

	Starts	1st	2nd	3rd	Win & Pl
Career Total (Turf)	3	0	0	1	353
Career Total (AW)	2	0	0	0	0

Going (Turf): Sf: 0-1 GS: 0-0 Gd: 0-1 GF: 0-1 Fm: 0-0
Distance: 5f/6f: 0-2 7f-8f: 0-3 9f-13f: 0-0 14f+: 0-0
Track : LH: 0-1 RH: 0-1 Tight: 0-0 Gall: 0-0
Aids: Bl: 0-0 Vi: 0-0 Tstrap: 0-0 Ckp: 0-0
Best Rating: 70 10/09 Nott 6f15y soft

Modest; should stay further than 6f; acts on Polytrack; should improve.

Pontardawe

82 35
3-y-o ch f Noverre (USA)-Blaina (Compton Place)
T D Easterby Croft, Taylor & Hebdon Partnership

Placings:0 (1062)
2009: 5^{0}GF,

	Starts	1st	2nd	3rd	Win & Pl
Career Total (Turf)	1	0	0	0	

Going (Turf): Sf: 0-0 GS: 0-0 Gd: 0-0 GF: 0-1 Fm: 0-0
Distance: 5f/6f: 0-1 7f-8f: 0-0 9f-13f: 0-0 14f+: 0-0
Track : LH: 0-1 RH: 0-0 Tight: 0-1 Gall: 0-0
Aids: Bl: 0-0 Vi: 0-0 Tstrap: 0-0 Ckp: 0-0
Best Rating: 35 4/09 Catt 5f212y gd-fm

Ponting (IRE)

101(101) (69)72
3-y-o gr g Clodovil (IRE)-Polar Lady (Polar Falcon (USA))
P T Midgley (R M Beckett 27/11) A Taylor Jnr

Placings:55-500342101 (7795)
2009: 7^{5}SD, 8^{0}GS, 8^{0}GF, 6^{3}GF, 6^{4}SD, 6^{2}G, 6^{1}SD, 5^{0}SD, 6^{1}SS,

	Starts	1st	2nd	3rd	Win & Pl
Career Total (Turf)	5	0	1	1	1239
Career Total (AW)	6	2	0	0	5310
69	12/09 Sthl	6f		SS	£2047
63	11/09 Sthl	6f		STD	£3070

Total win prize-money £5118

Going (Turf): Sf: 0-0 GS: 0-1 Gd: 0-1 GF: 0-3 Fm: 0-0
Distance: 5f/6f: 2-8 7f-8f: 0-2 9f-13f: 0-1 14f+: 0-0
Track : LH: 2-7 RH: 0-0 Tight: 0-3 Gall: 0-2
Aids: Bl: 0-0 Vi: 0-0 Tstrap: 0-1 Ckp: 0-1
Best Rating: 72 10/09 Wind 6f good

Modest; suited by 6f; acts on good and fast ground; goes on Fibresand.

Ponty Rossa (IRE)

105 (78)92
5-y-o ch m Distant Music (USA)-Danish Gem (Danehill (USA))
T D Easterby The Lapin Blanc Racing Partnership

Placings:211105/6201/500-66140 (3389)
2009: 6^{6}GF, 7^{6}GF, 6^{1}GS, 7^{4}GF, 6^{0}S,

	Starts	1st	2nd	3rd	Win & Pl
Career Total (Turf)	17	4	2	0	49686
Career Total (AW)	1	1	0	0	4534
92	5/09 Ripn	6f	(0-95)H	G-S	£9462
96	6/07 Wwck	7f26y		SFT	£14762
88	8/06 NmkJ	6f		G-F	£12954
78	7/06 Wolv	5f216y		STD	£4533
65	6/06 Carl	5f		GD	£3886

Total win prize-money £45599

Going (Turf): Sf: 1-4 GS: 1-3 Gd: 1-3 GF: 1-7 Fm: 0-0
Distance: 5f/6f: 4-11 7f-8f: 1-6 9f-13f: 0-1 14f+: 0-0
Track : LH: 2-6 RH: 1-1 Tight: 1-3 Gall: 1-2
Aids: Bl: 0-0 Vi: 0-0 Tstrap: 0-0 Ckp: 0-0

Best Rating: 97 5/07 York 7f good

Useful; effective at up to 7f; acts on most ground and on Polytrack.

Poor Prince

93 **78**

2-y-o b g Royal Applause-Kahira (IRE) (King's Best (USA))
C G Cox The Bodkins

Placings:236 **(6754)**
2009: 7^{2}G, 7^{3}S, 7^{6}G,

	Starts	1st	2nd	3rd	Win & Pl
Career Total (Turf)	3	0	1	1	3853

Going (Turf): **Sf: 0-1 GS: 0-0 Gd: 0-2 GF: 0-0 Fm: 0-0**
Distance: 5f/6f: 0-0 7f-8f: 0-3 9f-13f: 0-0 14f+: 0-0
Track : LH: 0-0 RH: 0-2 Tight: 0-0 Gall: 0-0
Aids: Bl: 0-0 Vi: 0-0 Tstrap: 0-0 Ckp: 0-0
Best Rating: **78** 8/09 Gdwd 7f soft

Useful; stays 7f and acts on good ground.

Popcorn Rosie

(86) (52)

6-y-o b m Diktat-Real Popcorn (IRE) (Jareer (USA))
C J Down Mrs L M Edwards

Placings:0 **(0501)**
2009: 13^{0}SD,

	Starts	1st	2nd	3rd	Win & Pl
Career Total (Turf)	0	0	0	0	
Career Total (AW)	1	0	0	0	

Going (Turf): **Sf: 0-0 GS: 0-0 Gd: 0-0 GF: 0-0 Fm: 0-0**
Distance: 5f/6f: 0-0 7f-8f: 0-0 9f-13f: 0-1 14f+: 0-0
Track : LH: 0-1 RH: 0-0 Tight: 0-1 Gall: 0-0
Aids: Bl: 0-0 Vi: 0-0 Tstrap: 0-0 Ckp: 0-0
Best Rating: **52** 2/09 Ling 1m5f stand

Popmurphy

110 **101**

3-y-o b c Montjeu (IRE)-Lady Lahar (Fraam)
K R Burke Mogeely Stud & Mrs Maura Gittins

Placings:13450 **(3778)**
2009: 10^{1}G, 10^{3}G, 11^{4}GF, 16^{5}GF, 13^{0}G,

	Starts	1st	2nd	3rd	Win & Pl
Career Total (Turf)	5	1	0	1	9391

88 4/09 Wind 1m2f7y GD £2729
Total win prize-money £2730

Going (Turf): Sf: 0-0 GS: 0-0 **Gd: 1-3** GF: 0-2 Fm: 0-0
Distance: 5f/6f: 0-0 7f-8f: 0-0 **9f-13f: 1-4** 14f+: 0-1
Track : LH: 0-1 **RH: 1-4 Tight: 1-3** Gall: 0-2
Aids: Bl: 0-0 Vi: 0-2 Tstrap: 0-0 Ckp: 0-0
Best Rating: **101** 4/09 Epsm 1m2f18y good

Very useful; winner on debut; stays 2m; handles good ground; has worn a visor.

Poppanan (USA)

103(101) (75)**75**

3-y-o b g Mr Greeley (USA)-Tiny Decision (USA) (Ogygian (USA))
S Dow Joe Cole

Placings:012535 **(7891)**
2009: 6^{0}G, 5^{1}G, 6^{2}SS, 5^{5}SD, 6^{3}SD, 7^{5}SD,

	Starts	1st	2nd	3rd	Win & Pl
Career Total (Turf)	2	1	0	0	2590
Career Total (AW)	4	0	1	1	1778

75 9/09 Bath 5f161y GD £2590
Total win prize-money £2590

Going (Turf): Sf: 0-0 GS: 0-0 **Gd: 1-2** GF: 0-0 Fm: 0-0
Distance: **5f/6f: 1-5** 7f-8f: 0-1 9f-13f: 0-0 14f+: 0-0
Track : **LH: 1-5** RH: 0-0 Tight: 0-4 **Gall: 1-1**
Aids: Bl: 0-0 Vi: 0-0 Tstrap: 0-0 Ckp: 0-0
Best Rating: **75** 10/09 Ling 6f std-slw

Fair; effective over 6f; acts on fast ground.

Poppet's Lovein

101 **83**

3-y-o b f Lomitas-Our Poppet (IRE) (Warning)
A B Haynes Graham Robinson

Placings:201150 **(6731)**
2009: 8^{2}G, 8^{0}GF, 7^{1}G, 7^{1}GF, 8^{5}GF, 6^{0}S,

	Starts	1st	2nd	3rd	Win & Pl
Career Total (Turf)	6	2	1	0	8856

83 8/09 Newc 7f (0-75)H G-F £4415
76 8/09 Chep 7f16y GD £3238
Total win prize-money £7654

Going (Turf): Sf: 0-1 GS: 0-0 **Gd: 1-2 GF: 1-3** Fm: 0-0
Distance: 5f/6f: 0-0 **7f-8f: 2-5** 9f-13f: 0-1 14f+: 0-0
Track : LH: 0-0 RH: 0-2 Tight: 0-2 Gall: 0-0
Aids: Bl: 0-0 Vi: 0-0 Tstrap: 0-0 Ckp: 0-0
Best Rating: **83** 8/09 Newc 7f gd-fm

Fair filly; half-sister to Overdose; stays 7f; acts on good/fast ground.

Poppy Dean (IRE)

91(98) (58)**48**

4-y-o ch f Night Shift (USA)-Miss Devious (IRE) (Dr Devious (IRE))
J G Portman Prof C D Green

Placings:0446/006002-00650 **(4938)**
2009: 10^{0}SD, 8^{0}SD, 7^{6}SD, 8^{5}G, 8^{0}G,

	Starts	1st	2nd	3rd	Win & Pl
Career Total (Turf)	7	0	0	0	373
Career Total (AW)	8	0	1	0	645

Going (Turf): **Sf: 0-0 GS: 0-0 Gd: 0-5 GF: 0-1 Fm: 0-1**
Distance: 5f/6f: 0-2 7f-8f: 0-5 9f-13f: 0-8 14f+: 0-0
Track : LH: 0-6 RH: 0-6 Tight: 0-6 Gall: 0-1
Aids: Bl: 0-0 Vi: 0-0 Tstrap: 0-0 Ckp: 0-0
Best Rating: **58** 10/07 Wolv 1m141y stand

Poppy Morris (IRE)

60(84) (30)

4-y-o b f Namid-Coco Palm (Selkirk (USA))
A B Haynes P J Green

Placings:000 **(6458)**
2009: 5^{0}G, 5^{0}F, 5^{0}SD,

	Starts	1st	2nd	3rd	Win & Pl
Career Total (Turf)	2	0	0	0	
Career Total (AW)	1	0	0	0	

Going (Turf): **Sf: 0-0 GS: 0-0 Gd: 0-1 GF: 0-0 Fm: 0-1**
Distance: 5f/6f: 0-3 7f-8f: 0-0 9f-13f: 0-0 14f+: 0-0
Track : LH: 0-3 RH: 0-0 Tight: 0-1 Gall: 0-2
Aids: Bl: 0-0 Vi: 0-0 Tstrap: 0-0 Ckp: 0-0
Best Rating: **30** 10/09 Wolv 5f216y stand

Poppy N'Penny (IRE)

104(92) (69)**80**

2-y-o b f Redback-Lulu Island (Zafonic (USA))
W J Haggas M Scotney/ D Asplin/ A Symonds

Placings:3342601 **(6906)**
2009: 5^{3}G, 5^{3}G, 6^{4}G, 7^{2}SD, 7^{6}SD, 6^{0}G, 6^{1}G,

	Starts	1st	2nd	3rd	Win & Pl
Career Total (Turf)	5	1	0	2	3399
Career Total (AW)	2	0	1	0	771

80 10/09 Wind 6f (0-75) GD £2388
Total win prize-money £2388

Going (Turf): Sf: 0-0 GS: 0-0 **Gd: 1-5** GF: 0-0 Fm: 0-0
Distance: **5f/6f: 1-3** 7f-8f: 0-4 9f-13f: 0-0 14f+: 0-0
Track : LH: 0-1 RH: 0-1 Tight: 0-1 **Gall: 1-1**
Aids: Bl: 0-0 Vi: 0-0 Tstrap: 0-0 Ckp: 0-0
Best Rating: **80** 10/09 Wind 6f good

Modest; effective at 5f; acts on a sound surface.

Poppy Red

76(103) (53)**42**

4-y-o ch f Lear Spear (USA)-Pooka's Daughter (IRE) (Eagle Eyed (USA))
R G Hawker (C J Gray 5/5) Richard Hawker

Placings:0/2600050300002-20440 **(1770)**
2009: 12^{2}SD, 12^{0}SD, 12^{4}SD, 12^{4}SD, 10^{0}GF,

	Starts	1st	2nd	3rd	Win & Pl
Career Total (Turf)	7	0	0	1	289
Career Total (AW)	12	0	3	0	1713

Going (Turf): **Sf: 0-1 GS: 0-1 Gd: 0-0 GF: 0-3 Fm: 0-2**
Distance: 5f/6f: 0-0 7f-8f: 0-3 9f-13f: 0-16 14f+: 0-0
Track : LH: 0-15 RH: 0-2 Tight: 0-11 Gall: 0-1
Aids: Bl: 0-1 Vi: 0-0 Tstrap: 0-7 Ckp: 0-7
Best Rating: **53** 4/09 Ling 1m4f stand

Very moderate; stays 1m4f; acts on fast ground and on Polytrack; has worn cheekpieces.

Poppy Seed

92 **72**

2-y-o br f Bold Edge-Opopmil (IRE) (Pips Pride)
R Hannon Lady Whent

Placings:4 **(4047)**
2009: 6^{4}S,

	Starts	1st	2nd	3rd	Win & Pl
Career Total (Turf)	1	0	0	0	481

Going (Turf): **Sf: 0-1 GS: 0-0 Gd: 0-0 GF: 0-0 Fm: 0-0**
Distance: 5f/6f: 0-0 7f-8f: 0-1 9f-13f: 0-0 14f+: 0-0
Track : LH: 0-0 RH: 0-0 Tight: 0-0 Gall: 0-0
Aids: Bl: 0-0 Vi: 0-0 Tstrap: 0-0 Ckp: 0-0
Best Rating: **72** 7/09 Newb 6f8y soft

Poppy's Rose

99(102) (66)**72**

5-y-o b m Diktat-Perfect Peach (Lycius (USA))
I W McInnes Mrs Ann Morris

Placings:6106150526/40333535525-00023344 (5225)
2009: 7^0G, 7^0G, 6^0G, 7^2SD, 7^3SD, 6^3S, 6^4G, 5^4SD,

	Starts	1st	2nd	3rd	Win & Pl
Career Total (Turf)	25	2	2	5	10969
Career Total (AW)	4	0	1	1	1058

68 6/07 Rdcr 6f (0-70)H SFT £2817
64 4/07 Pont 6f GD £3238
Total win prize-money £6056

Going (Turf): **Sf: 1-4** GS: 0-4 **Gd: 1-10** GF: 0-6 Fm: 0-1
Distance: **5f/6f: 2-15** 7f-8f: 0-14 9f-13f: 0-0 14f+: 0-0
Track : **LH: 1-13** RH: 0-3 Tight: 0-7 Gall: 0-1
Aids: Bl: 0-0 Vi: 0-0 Tstrap: 0-3 Ckp: 0-3
Best Rating: 72 7/08 Pont 6f good

Modest filly; effective over 6f-7f acts on good and soft ground and on Polytrack.

Por Chablis (IRE)

37 22
10-y-o b g Key Of Luck (USA)-State Princess (IRE) (Flash Of Steel)
P J Lally P J Lally

Placings:00040/000/00 (4897)
2009: 12^0G, 8^0GS,

	Starts	1st	2nd	3rd	Win & Pl
Career Total (Turf)	10	0	0	0	233

Going (Turf): Sf: 0-0 GS: 0-1 Gd: 0-3 GF: 0-2 Fm: 0-1
Distance: 5f/6f: 0-0 7f-8f: 0-1 9f-13f: 0-7 14f+: 0-2
Track : LH: 0-2 RH: 0-8 Tight: 0-2 Gall: 0-0
Aids: Bl: 0-1 Vi: 0-0 Tstrap: 0-0 Ckp: 0-0
Best Rating: 53 7/05 Gway 1m6f gd-fm

Port Hill

75(70) (32)51
2-y-o ch g Deportivo-Hill Farm Dancer (Gunner B)
W M Brisbourne M Hughes Mark Brisbourne

Placings:600 (4557)
2009: 7^6SD, 7^0GS, 7^0G,

	Starts	1st	2nd	3rd	Win & Pl
Career Total (Turf)	2	0	0	0	
Career Total (AW)	1	0	0	0	0

Going (Turf): Sf: 0-0 GS: 0-1 Gd: 0-1 GF: 0-0 Fm: 0-0
Distance: 5f/6f: 0-0 7f-8f: 0-3 9f-13f: 0-0 14f+: 0-0
Track : LH: 0-3 RH: 0-0 Tight: 0-2 Gall: 0-0
Aids: Bl: 0-0 Vi: 0-0 Tstrap: 0-0 Ckp: 0-0
Best Rating: 51 7/09 Hayd 7f30y gd-sft

Port Ronan (USA)

96(73) (18)57
3-y-o gr/ro c Cozzene (USA)-Amber Token (USA) (Hennessy (USA))
J S Wainwright D R & E E Brown

Placings:004055-00005056356 (6101)
2009: 5^0SD, 6^0GS, 6^0GF, 5^0GF, 5^0GF, 5^5GF, 5^0GF, 5^5G, 5^6GF, 5^3GF, 7^5GF, 7^6GF,

	Starts	1st	2nd	3rd	Win & Pl
Career Total (Turf)	17	0	0	1	789
Career Total (AW)	1	0	0	0	

Going (Turf): Sf: 0-2 GS: 0-1 Gd: 0-2 GF: 0-12 Fm: 0-0
Distance: 5f/6f: 0-16 7f-8f: 0-2 9f-13f: 0-0 14f+: 0-0
Track : LH: 0-3 RH: 0-2 Tight: 0-2 Gall: 0-1
Aids: Bl: 0-0 Vi: 0-2 Tstrap: 0-7 Ckp: 0-7
Best Rating: 57 7/08 Pont 5f gd-fm

Portrush Storm

98(71) (8)70
4-y-o ch f Observatory (USA)-Overcast (IRE) (Caerleon (USA))
D Carroll M Symes G H & G J Briers S & A Franks

Placings:3/0641000-30600500 (4887)
2009: 9^3GF, 8^0GS, 8^6GF, 7^0G, 10^0GF, 7^5G, 8^0G, 7^0G,

	Starts	1st	2nd	3rd	Win & Pl
Career Total (Turf)	15	1	0	2	6146
Career Total (AW)	1	0	0	0	

64 6/08 Carl 1m1f61y (0-70)H GD £4533
Total win prize-money £4533

Going (Turf): Sf: 0-1 GS: 0-4 **Gd: 1-5** GF: 0-5 Fm: 0-0
Distance: 5f/6f: 0-3 7f-8f: 0-4 **9f-13f: 1-9** 14f+: 0-0
Track : LH: 0-6 **RH: 1-6** Tight: 0-3 Gall: 0-1
Aids: Bl: 0-4 Vi: 0-0 Tstrap: 0-0 Ckp: 0-0
Best Rating: 71 3/07 Newc 5f gd-sft

Modest Observatory filly; related to several multiple winners; should stay 1m2f acts fast and on soft ground.

Portugese Caddy

93(85) (47)80
3-y-o b g Great Palm (USA)-Paintbrush (IRE) (Groom Dancer (USA))
P Winkworth Mrs Tessa Winkworth

Placings:114-000640 (6170)
2009: 7^0G, 8^0SD, 10^0G, 8^6SD, 7^4GF, 7^0GF,

	Starts	1st	2nd	3rd	Win & Pl
Career Total (Turf)	7	2	0	0	7048
Career Total (AW)	2	0	0	0	0

80 9/08 Folk 6f SFT £3885
72 6/08 Wind 6f G-F £2729
Total win prize-money £6616

Going (Turf): **Sf: 1-2** GS: 0-0 Gd: 0-2 **GF: 1-3** Fm: 0-0
Distance: **5f/6f: 2-3** 7f-8f: 0-5 9f-13f: 0-1 14f+: 0-0
Track : LH: 0-0 RH: 0-4 Tight: 0-1 **Gall: 1-1**
Aids: Bl: 0-1 Vi: 0-0 Tstrap: 0-0 Ckp: 0-0
Best Rating: 80 9/08 Folk 6f soft

Pose (IRE)

99 82
2-y-o b f Acclamation-Lyca Ballerina (Marju (IRE))
R Hannon Highclere Thoroughbred Racing(Childers)1

Placings:042455 (6418)
2009: 5^0G, 6^4GF, 5^2G, 5^4S, 6^5G, 6^5GF,

	Starts	1st	2nd	3rd	Win & Pl
Career Total (Turf)	6	0	1	0	7623

Going (Turf): Sf: 0-1 GS: 0-0 Gd: 0-3 GF: 0-2 Fm: 0-0
Distance: 5f/6f: 0-5 7f-8f: 0-1 9f-13f: 0-0 14f+: 0-0
Track : LH: 0-0 RH: 0-0 Tight: 0-0 Gall: 0-2
Aids: Bl: 0-0 Vi: 0-0 Tstrap: 0-0 Ckp: 0-0
Best Rating: 82 9/09 Asct 6f110y good

Positivity

83(98) (54)67
3-y-o ch f Monsieur Bond (IRE)-Pretty Pollyanna (General Assembly (USA))
B Smart Mrs F Denniff

Placings:23064-05503302030 (7869)
2009: 5^0GS, 5^5G, 5^5GF, 7^0GF, 6^3SD, 6^3SD, 7^0GF, 7^2SD, 7^0SD, 7^3SD, 6^0SS,

	Starts	1st	2nd	3rd	Win & Pl
Career Total (Turf)	10	0	1	1	1589
Career Total (AW)	6	0	1	3	1695

Going (Turf): Sf: 0-1 GS: 0-2 Gd: 0-3 GF: 0-4 Fm: 0-0
Distance: 5f/6f: 0-10 7f-8f: 0-6 9f-13f: 0-0 14f+: 0-0
Track : LH: 0-7 RH: 0-2 Tight: 0-1 Gall: 0-1
Aids: Bl: 0-0 Vi: 0-0 Tstrap: 0-2 Ckp: 0-2
Best Rating: 67 7/08 Bevl 5f gd-fm

Moderate; effective over 5f; acts on good and fast ground; has worn cheekpieces.

Possibly A Ten (USA)

97 56
3-y-o b f Seeking The Gold (USA)-Possibly Perfect (USA) (Northern Baby (CAN))
J H M Gosden Robert Witt

Placings:06 (2051)
2009: 10^0G, 12^6GF,

	Starts	1st	2nd	3rd	Win & Pl
Career Total (Turf)	2	0	0	0	0

Going (Turf): Sf: 0-0 GS: 0-0 Gd: 0-1 GF: 0-1 Fm: 0-0
Distance: 5f/6f: 0-0 7f-8f: 0-0 9f-13f: 0-2 14f+: 0-0
Track : LH: 0-0 RH: 0-2 Tight: 0-0 Gall: 0-1
Aids: Bl: 0-0 Vi: 0-0 Tstrap: 0-0 Ckp: 0-0
Best Rating: 56 5/09 NmkR 1m4f gd-fm

Postage (USA)

93(101) (62)48
6-y-o b/br g Chester House (USA)-Nimble Mind (USA) (Lyphard (USA))
K A Morgan P Doughty

Placings:06300/6/10200 (2400)
2009: 10^1SD, 12^0SD, 9^2SD, 10^0GF, 8^0SD,

	Starts	1st	2nd	3rd	Win & Pl
Career Total (Turf)	2	0	0	0	
Career Total (AW)	9	1	1	1	2679

51 2/09 Ling 1m2f (0-45) STD £1619
Total win prize-money £1619

Going (Turf): Sf: 0-1 GS: 0-0 Gd: 0-0 GF: 0-1 Fm: 0-0
Distance: 5f/6f: 0-0 7f-8f: 0-7 **9f-13f: 1-4** 14f+: 0-0
Track : **LH: 1-10** RH: 0-1 **Tight: 1-9** Gall: 0-0
Aids: Bl: 0-0 Vi: 0-0 Tstrap: 0-3 Ckp: 0-3
Best Rating: 62 4/09 Wolv 1m1f103y stand

Modest form so far on Polytrack; stays 1m2f; has worn cheekpieces.

Postman

98(100) (75)75
3-y-o b g Dr Fong (USA)-Mail The Desert (IRE) (Desert Prince (IRE))
B Smart Crossfields Racing

Placings:4000-114435 (4741)
2009: 8^1SD, 8^1GS, 9^4F, 8^4S, 8^3G, 8^5G,

	Starts	1st	2nd	3rd	Win & Pl
Career Total (Turf)	9	1	0	1	4747

	Starts	1st	2nd	3rd	Win & Pl
Career Total (AW)	1	1	0	0	2047

75 4/09 Nott 1m75y (0-70)H G-S £3238
75 4/09 Sthl 1m (0-60)H STD £2047
Total win prize-money £5285

Going (Turf): Sf: 0-2 **GS: 1-2** Gd: 0-3 GF: 0-1 Fm: 0-1
Distance: 5f/6f: 0-1 7f-8f: 1-5 9f-13f: 1-4 14f+: 0-0
Track : **LH: 2-7** RH: 0-1 Tight: 0-1 Gall: 0-2
Aids: Bl: 0-0 Vi: 0-1 Tstrap: 0-0 Ckp: 0-0
Best Rating: 75 4/09 Nott 1m75y gd-sft

Modest; stays 7f; acts on easy ground; has worn a visor.

Posy Fossil (USA)

93(95) (60)63
2-y-o b/br f Malibu Moon (USA)-Fire And Shade (USA) (Shadeed (USA))
S C Williams J W Parry

Placings:0250 (7363)
2009: 7^{0}GF, 6^{2}GF, 5^{5}SD, 7^{0}SD,

	Starts	1st	2nd	3rd	Win & Pl
Career Total (Turf)	2	0	1	0	964
Career Total (AW)	2	0	0	0	0

Going (Turf): Sf: 0-0 GS: 0-0 Gd: 0-0 GF: 0-2 Fm: 0-0
Distance: 5f/6f: 0-2 7f-8f: 0-2 9f-13f: 0-0 14f+: 0-0
Track : LH: 0-1 RH: 0-1 Tight: 0-1 Gall: 0-0
Aids: Bl: 0-0 Vi: 0-0 Tstrap: 0-0 Ckp: 0-0
Best Rating: 63 9/09 Hayd 6f gd-fm

Moderate; effective over 6f; acts on fast ground and on Polytrack.

Potemkin (USA)

96(71) (6)59
4-y-o b/br g Van Nistelrooy (USA)-Bolshoia (USA) (Moscow Ballet (USA))
Ferdy Murphy (A King 20/8) Mr & Mrs David Thornhill

Placings:0000/03-00 (3303)
2009: 10^{0}G, 12^{0}SD,

	Starts	1st	2nd	3rd	Win & Pl
Career Total (Turf)	7	0	0	1	302
Career Total (AW)	1	0	0	0	

Going (Turf): Sf: 0-0 GS: 0-1 Gd: 0-2 GF: 0-3 Fm: 0-1
Distance: 5f/6f: 0-0 7f-8f: 0-4 9f-13f: 0-4 14f+: 0-0
Track : LH: 0-4 RH: 0-2 Tight: 0-1 Gall: 0-0
Aids: Bl: 0-0 Vi: 0-0 Tstrap: 0-0 Ckp: 0-0
Best Rating: 61 9/07 Hayd 7f30y gd-fm

Modest; stays 1m4f and acts on good ground.

Potentiale (IRE)

105(106) (80)87
5-y-o ch g Singspiel (IRE)-No Frills (IRE) (Darshaan)
J W Hills J W Hills

Placings:000/12222012/52303254245-23333110 (6470)
2009: 12^{2}SD, 12^{3}GF, 11^{3}GS, 9^{3}GF, 9^{3}GF, 9^{1}GF, 10^{1}GF, 10^{0}GF,

	Starts	1st	2nd	3rd	Win & Pl
Career Total (Turf)	20	3	5	6	21272
Career Total (AW)	10	1	4	0	5565

87 9/09 Epsm 1m2f18y (0-85)H G-F £5180
79 8/09 Gdwd 1m1f (0-75)H G-F £4684
66 9/07 Kemp 1m3f (0-65)H STD £2047
59 5/07 Bevl 1m1f207y (0-55) G-F £2730
Total win prize-money £14644

Going (Turf): Sf: 0-0 GS: 0-2 Gd: 0-8 **GF: 3-10** Fm: 0-0
Distance: 5f/6f: 0-0 7f-8f: 0-3 **9f-13f: 4-26** 14f+: 0-1
Track : LH: 1-17 **RH: 3-12 Tight: 2-15** Gall: 0-6
Aids: Bl: 0-0 Vi: 0-0 Tstrap: 3-16 Ckp: 3-16
Best Rating: 87 9/09 Epsm 1m2f18y gd-fm

Fair; effective over 1m1f-1m4f; seems best on a sound surface; goes on Polytrack; has worn cheekpieces.

Pounced (USA)

110 117
2-y-o ch c Rahy (USA)-Golden Cat (USA) (Storm Cat (USA))
J H M Gosden Lady Rothschild

Placings:2121 (7304a)
2009: 7^{2}G, 7^{1}GF, 7^{2}G, 8^{1}F,

	Starts	1st	2nd	3rd	Win & Pl
Career Total (Turf)	4	2	2	0	459849

117 11/09 SnAt 1m FRM £375000
85 8/09 Newb 7f G-F £4857
Total win prize-money £379857

Going (Turf): Sf: 0-0 GS: 0-0 Gd: 0-2 **GF: 1-1 Fm: 1-1**
Distance: 5f/6f: 0-0 **7f-8f: 2-4** 9f-13f: 0-0 14f+: 0-0
Track : **LH: 1-1** RH: 0-1 Tight: 0-0 Gall: 0-0
Aids: Bl: 0-0 Vi: 0-0 Tstrap: 0-0 Ckp: 0-0
Best Rating: 117 11/09 SnAt 1m firm

Group class; runner-up in the Group 1 Prix Jean-Luc Lagardere and winner of the Breeders' Cup Juvenile Turf; effective over 7f-1m; acts on good and fast ground.

Power Of Dreams (IRE)

91(88) (56)72
2-y-o b c Pearl Of Love (IRE)-Pussie Willow (IRE) (Catrail (USA))
M H Tompkins Miss Clare Hollest

Placings:50020 (7335)
2009: 6^{5}GF, 7^{0}G, 8^{0}G, 7^{2}GF, 8^{0}SD,

	Starts	1st	2nd	3rd	Win & Pl
Career Total (Turf)	4	0	1	0	674
Career Total (AW)	1	0	0	0	

Going (Turf): Sf: 0-0 GS: 0-0 Gd: 0-2 GF: 0-2 Fm: 0-0
Distance: 5f/6f: 0-0 7f-8f: 0-4 9f-13f: 0-1 14f+: 0-0
Track : LH: 0-1 RH: 0-1 Tight: 0-1 Gall: 0-0
Aids: Bl: 0-0 Vi: 0-0 Tstrap: 0-0 Ckp: 0-0
Best Rating: 72 10/09 Leic 7f9y gd-fm

Modest; stays 1m; acts on Fibresand.

Power Of Speech

(48)
4-y-o b g Advise (FR)-Marsara (Never So Bold)
J Gallagher Dave Stenning & Ken Miller

Placings:0-0 (0902)
2009: 12^{0}SF,

	Starts	1st	2nd	3rd	Win & Pl
Career Total (Turf)	1	0	0	0	
Career Total (AW)	1	0	0	0	

Going (Turf): Sf: 0-0 GS: 0-1 Gd: 0-0 GF: 0-0 Fm: 0-0
Distance: 5f/6f: 0-0 7f-8f: 0-0 9f-13f: 0-2 14f+: 0-0
Track : LH: 0-1 RH: 0-1 Tight: 0-2 Gall: 0-0
Aids: Bl: 0-0 Vi: 0-0 Tstrap: 0-0 Ckp: 0-0

Power Series (USA)

78 45
2-y-o gr/ro c Mizzen Mast (USA)-Diese (USA) (Diesis)
J H M Gosden K Abdulla

Placings:00 (5000)
2009: 7^{0}S, 7^{0}G,

	Starts	1st	2nd	3rd	Win & Pl
Career Total (Turf)	2	0	0	0	

Going (Turf): Sf: 0-1 GS: 0-0 Gd: 0-1 GF: 0-0 Fm: 0-0
Distance: 5f/6f: 0-0 7f-8f: 0-2 9f-13f: 0-0 14f+: 0-0
Track : LH: 0-0 RH: 0-0 Tight: 0-0 Gall: 0-0
Aids: Bl: 0-0 Vi: 0-0 Tstrap: 0-0 Ckp: 0-0
Best Rating: 45 8/09 NmkJ 7f good

Power Shared (IRE)

(95) (7)71
5-y-o gr g Kendor (FR)-Striking Pose (IRE) (Darshaan)
P G Murphy The Golden Anorak Partnership

Placings:0640/2-0 (7154)
2009: 16^{0}SD,

	Starts	1st	2nd	3rd	Win & Pl
Career Total (Turf)	3	0	0	0	
Career Total (AW)	3	0	1	0	1077

Going (Turf): Sf: 0-2 GS: 0-0 Gd: 0-0 GF: 0-0 Fm: 0-0
Distance: 5f/6f: 0-0 7f-8f: 0-0 9f-13f: 0-5 14f+: 0-1
Track : LH: 0-3 RH: 0-2 Tight: 0-3 Gall: 0-0
Aids: Bl: 0-0 Vi: 0-0 Tstrap: 0-0 Ckp: 0-0
Best Rating: 71 6/07 Curr 1m2f soft

Powerful Melody (USA)

(98) (74)
2-y-o b c Dynaformer (USA)-Song Track (USA) (Dixieland Band (USA))
Saeed Bin Suroor Godolphin

Placings:1 (7400)
2009: 9^{1}SD,

	Starts	1st	2nd	3rd	Win & Pl
Career Total (Turf)	0	0	0	0	
Career Total (AW)	1	1	0	0	3886

74 11/09 Wolv 1m1f103y STD £3885
Total win prize-money £3886

Going (Turf): Sf: 0-0 GS: 0-0 Gd: 0-0 GF: 0-0 Fm: 0-0
Distance: 5f/6f: 0-0 7f-8f: 0-0 **9f-13f: 1-1** 14f+: 0-0
Track : **LH: 1-1** RH: 0-0 **Tight: 1-1** Gall: 0-0
Aids: Bl: 0-0 Vi: 0-0 Tstrap: 0-0 Ckp: 0-0
Best Rating: 74 11/09 Wolv 1m1f103y stand

Created good impression on debut; potentially very useful; stays 1m1f; acts on Polytrack; sure to improve and win more races.

Powerful Pierre

97 68
2-y-o ch g Compton Place-Alzianah (Alzao (USA))
Jedd O'Keeffe Ken And Delia Shaw-KGS Consulting LLP

Placings:030060224 (6905)

2009: 6^{0}GS, 6^{3}GF, 5^{0}GF, 6^{0}GS, 6^{6}GF, 7^{0}GF, 5^{2}GF, 5^{2}GF, 6^{4}G,

	Starts	1st	2nd	3rd	Win & Pl
Career Total (Turf)	9	0	2	1	3385

Going (Turf): **Sf: 0-0 GS: 0-2 Gd: 0-1 GF: 0-6 Fm: 0-0**
Distance: 5f/6f: 0-8 7f-8f: 0-1 9f-13f: 0-0 14f+: 0-0
Track : LH: 0-0 RH: 0-0 Tight: 0-0 Gall: 0-1
Aids: Bl: 0-0 Vi: 0-3 Tstrap: 0-0 Ckp: 0-0
Best Rating: **68** 10/09 Wind 6f good

Modest; suited by 6f and fast ground; has worn a visor.

Poyle Meg

100(106) (89)80

3-y-o b f Dansili-Lost In Lucca (Inchinor)
R M Beckett Cecil Wiggins

Placings:234032-43212131 **(7684)**
2009: 6^{4}GF, 6^{3}GF, 8^{2}GF, 8^{1}G, 8^{2}GF, 10^{1}SD, 10^{3}SD, 10^{1}SD,

	Starts	1st	2nd	3rd	Win & Pl
Career Total (Turf)	9	1	3	2	13520
Career Total (AW)	5	2	1	2	12663

89	12/09	Kemp	1m2f	(0-85)H	STD	£4727
87	10/09	Kemp	1m2f	(0-80)H	STD	£4727
67	8/09	Nott	1m75y		GD	£2590

Total win prize-money £12044

Going (Turf): Sf: 0-0 GS: 0-0 **Gd: 1-3** GF: 0-6 Fm: 0-0
Distance: 5f/6f: 0-5 7f-8f: 0-3 **9f-13f: 3-6** 14f+: 0-0
Track : LH: 1-3 **RH: 2-5** Tight: 0-1 Gall: 0-2
Aids: Bl: 0-0 Vi: 0-0 Tstrap: 3-9 Ckp: 3-9
Best Rating: **89** 12/09 Kemp 1m2f stand

Useful; stays 1m2f; goes well on fast ground; acts on Polytrack; has worn cheekpieces.

Practitioner

101 88

2-y-o b g Dr Fong (USA)-Macina (IRE) (Platini (GER))
H J L Dunlop Here Come The Boys

Placings:13223 **(5827)**
2009: 6^{1}GF, 6^{3}G, 7^{2}S, 7^{2}GF, 7^{3}GF,

	Starts	1st	2nd	3rd	Win & Pl
Career Total (Turf)	5	1	2	2	14502

71	6/09	Sals	6f	G-F	£2914

Total win prize-money £2914

Going (Turf): Sf: 0-1 GS: 0-0 Gd: 0-1 **GF: 1-3** Fm: 0-0
Distance: **5f/6f: 1-2** 7f-8f: 0-3 9f-13f: 0-0 14f+: 0-0
Track : LH: 0-0 RH: 0-0 Tight: 0-0 Gall: 0-0
Aids: Bl: 0-2 Vi: 0-0 Tstrap: 0-0 Ckp: 0-0
Best Rating: **88** 8/09 Newb 7f gd-fm

Useful; Listed placed; effective over 6f-7f; acts on fast and soft ground; has worn blinkers.

Praesepe

(95) (69)

2-y-o b f Pivotal-Superstar Leo (IRE) (College Chapel)
W J Haggas Lael Stable

Placings:2 **(7843)**
2009: 5^{2}SD,

	Starts	1st	2nd	3rd	Win & Pl
Career Total (Turf)	0	0	0	0	
Career Total (AW)	1	0	1	0	1156

Going (Turf): **Sf: 0-0 GS: 0-0 Gd: 0-0 GF: 0-0 Fm: 0-0**
Distance: 5f/6f: 0-1 7f-8f: 0-0 9f-13f: 0-0 14f+: 0-0
Track : LH: 0-1 RH: 0-0 Tight: 0-1 Gall: 0-0
Aids: Bl: 0-0 Vi: 0-0 Tstrap: 0-0 Ckp: 0-0
Best Rating: **69** 12/09 Wolv 5f20y stand

Fair; suited by 5f and Polytrack.

Pragmatist

94(98) (68)68

5-y-o b m Piccolo-Shi Shi (Alnasr Alwasheek)
P Winkworth Mrs Jenny Willment

Placings:015150/01040-0 **(2381)**
2009: 6^{0}GS,

	Starts	1st	2nd	3rd	Win & Pl
Career Total (Turf)	10	3	0	0	8452
Career Total (AW)	2	0	0	0	0

68	5/08	Brig	6f209y	(0-65)H	G-S	£2396
67	8/07	Sals	6f	(0-70)H	G-S	£3238
58	6/07	Ling	6f		GD	£2817

Total win prize-money £8452

Going (Turf): Sf: 0-3 **GS: 2-4** Gd: 1-1 GF: 0-1 Fm: 0-1
Distance: **5f/6f: 2-5** 7f-8f: 1-7 9f-13f: 0-0 14f+: 0-0
Track : **LH: 1-5** RH: 0-1 Tight: 0-2 Gall: 0-0
Aids: Bl: 0-0 Vi: 0-0 Tstrap: 0-0 Ckp: 0-0
Best Rating: **68** 8/08 Ling 7f stand

Modest; effective over 6f-7f; acts on good and easy ground.

Prairie Hawk (USA)

95(105) (68)72

4-y-o b/br g Hawk Wing (USA)-Lady Carla (Caerleon (USA))
Tim Vaughan Chris Howell

Placings:0/0016-113 **(3346)**
2009: 13^{1}SD, 16^{1}SD, 16^{3}GF,

	Starts	1st	2nd	3rd	Win & Pl
Career Total (Turf)	2	0	0	1	963
Career Total (AW)	6	3	0	0	6142

68	2/09	Ling	2m	(0-60)H	STD	£2047
63	2/09	Wolv	1m5f194y	(0-60)H	STD	£1706
59	12/08	Wolv	1m5f194y	(0-55)H	STD	£2388

Total win prize-money £6141

Going (Turf): **Sf: 0-0 GS: 0-0 Gd: 0-1 GF: 0-1 Fm: 0-0**
Distance: 5f/6f: 0-1 7f-8f: 0-1 9f-13f: 0-2 **14f+: 3-4**
Track : **LH: 3-6** RH: 0-1 **Tight: 3-5** Gall: 0-1
Aids: Bl: 0-0 Vi: 0-0 Tstrap: 0-0 Ckp: 0-0
Best Rating: **72** 6/09 Folk 2m93y gd-fm

Modest; stays 2m; acts on Polytrack and fast turf; has worn a tongue-tie; said to dislike Southwell.

Prairie Spirit (FR)

(97) (67)93

5-y-o ch g Grape Tree Road-Prairie Runner (IRE) (Arazi (USA))
C E Longsdon Alan Halsall

Placings:01/02106/41110-**00** **(0585)**
2009: 10^{0}SD, 11^{0}SD,

	Starts	1st	2nd	3rd	Win & Pl
Career Total (Turf)	12	5	1	0	67035
Career Total (AW)	2	0	0	0	

93	7/08	MsnL	1m3f		G-S	£20588
93	5/08	Lonc	1m4f	H	G-S	£17647
	4/08	Nanc	1m4f		GD	£8455
	8/07	Claf	1m6f110y		VS	£7432
93	11/06	MsnL	1m		HVY	£6552

Total win prize-money £60675

Going (Turf): Sf: 1-4 **GS: 2-5** Gd: 1-2 GF: 0-0 Fm: 0-0
Distance: 5f/6f: 0-0 7f-8f: 1-2 **9f-13f: 3-11** 14f+: 1-1
Track : LH: 0-6 **RH: 1-3** Tight: 0-1 Gall: 0-0
Aids: Bl: 0-0 Vi: 0-0 Tstrap: 0-0 Ckp: 0-0
Best Rating: **93** 7/08 MsnL 1m3f gd-sft

Prairie Storm

99(101) (83)85

4-y-o b g Storming Home-Last Dream (IRE) (Alzao (USA))
A M Balding W V & Mrs E S Robins

Placings:55/65321-063 **(3024)**
2009: 10^{0}GS, 9^{6}G, 10^{3}SD,

	Starts	1st	2nd	3rd	Win & Pl
Career Total (Turf)	9	1	1	1	5142
Career Total (AW)	1	0	0	1	703

85	11/08	Nott	1m2f50y	(0-75)H	HVY	£3561

Total win prize-money £3562

Going (Turf): **Sf: 1-2** GS: 0-2 Gd: 0-4 GF: 0-1 Fm: 0-0
Distance: 5f/6f: 0-0 7f-8f: 0-0 **9f-13f: 1-10** 14f+: 0-0
Track : **LH: 1-6** RH: 0-4 Tight: 0-4 Gall: 0-1
Aids: Bl: 0-0 Vi: 0-0 Tstrap: 0-0 Ckp: 0-0
Best Rating: **85** 11/08 Nott 1m2f50y heavy

Fair; stays 1m3f; acts on good and soft ground.

Praise Of Folly

(92) (50)53

3-y-o b f Selkirk (USA)-Song Of Hope (Chief Singer)
A G Newcombe A G Newcombe

Placings:00-500 **(1183)**
2009: 7^{5}SD, 7^{0}SF, 10^{0}SD,

	Starts	1st	2nd	3rd	Win & Pl
Career Total (Turf)	1	0	0	0	
Career Total (AW)	4	0	0	0	0

Going (Turf): **Sf: 0-0 GS: 0-0 Gd: 0-0 GF: 0-1 Fm: 0-0**
Distance: 5f/6f: 0-0 7f-8f: 0-4 9f-13f: 0-1 14f+: 0-0
Track : LH: 0-2 RH: 0-2 Tight: 0-2 Gall: 0-0
Aids: Bl: 0-0 Vi: 0-0 Tstrap: 0-0 Ckp: 0-0
Best Rating: **53** 8/08 Folk 7f gd-fm

Pravda Street

106(98) (74)94

4-y-o ch g Soviet Star (USA)-Sari (Faustus (USA))
P F I Cole R A Instone

Placings:2/10-40410300 **(6482)**
2009: 7^{4}GF, 7^{0}SD, 5^{4}GF, 7^{1}GF, 7^{0}G, 7^{3}GF, 7^{0}G, 7^{0}GF,

	Starts	1st	2nd	3rd	Win & Pl
Career Total (Turf)	9	2	0	1	4756
Career Total (AW)	2	0	1	0	605

91	4/08	Folk	7f	SFT	£2590

Total win prize-money £2590

Going (Turf): **Sf: 1-1** GS: 0-1 Gd: 0-2 **GF: 1-5** Fm: 0-0
Distance: 5f/6f: 0-1 **7f-8f: 2-10** 9f-13f: 0-0 14f+: 0-0
Track : LH: 0-1 RH: 0-2 Tight: 0-1 Gall: 0-0
Aids: **Bl: 1-3** Vi: 0-0 Tstrap: 0-0 Ckp: 0-0
Best Rating: **94** 5/09 NmkR 7f gd-fm

Useful; effective over 7f; acts on fast and soft ground; goes on Polytrack; has worn blinkers.

Prayer Boat (IRE)

(99) (82)**82**

3-y-o b c Oasis Dream-Reasonably Devout (CAN) (St Jovite (USA))

John Joseph Murphy D Mac A'Bhaird

Placings:640025-0425500 **(5665)**

2009: 7^{0}G, 7^{4}GF, 8^{2}GF, 10^{5}GY, 8^{5}S, 10^{0}SD, 7^{0}SD,

	Starts	1st	2nd	3rd	Win & Pl
Career Total (Turf)	9	0	1	0	2984
Career Total (AW)	4	0	1	0	1413

Going (Turf): **Sf: 0-3 GS: 0-0 Gd: 0-2 GF: 0-3 Fm: 0-0**
Distance: 5f/6f: 0-3 7f-8f: 0-7 9f-13f: 0-3 14f+: 0-0
Track : LH: 0-6 RH: 0-5 Tight: 0-1 Gall: 0-1
Aids: Bl: 0-0 Vi: 0-0 Tstrap: 0-0 Ckp: 0-0
Best Rating: **82** 6/09 Naas 1m gd-fm

Useful; stays 7f and acts on Polytrack.

Precious Citizen (USA)

98(90) (49)**55**

4-y-o ch f Proud Citizen (USA)-Fasateen (USA) (Alysheba (USA))

J R Gask D Cox

Placings:000206-0354 **(5790)**

2009: 8^{0}SF, 10^{3}G, 13^{5}F, 10^{4}G,

	Starts	1st	2nd	3rd	Win & Pl
Career Total (Turf)	7	0	1	1	1463
Career Total (AW)	3	0	0	0	

Going (Turf): **Sf: 0-0 GS: 0-0 Gd: 0-4 GF: 0-2 Fm: 0-1**
Distance: 5f/6f: 0-1 7f-8f: 0-2 9f-13f: 0-6 14f+: 0-1
Track : LH: 0-8 RH: 0-2 Tight: 0-3 Gall: 0-0
Aids: Bl: 0-0 Vi: 0-0 Tstrap: 0-0 Ckp: 0-0
Best Rating: **55** 7/09 Ling 1m2f good

Precious Coral (IRE)

91(93) (68)**68**

2-y-o gr f Elusive City (USA)-Somaggia (IRE) (Desert King (IRE))

S A Callaghan Michael Tabor

Placings:0006230 **(6819)**

2009: 6^{0}GF, 6^{0}G, 7^{0}G, 5^{6}SD, 6^{2}SD, 7^{3}GF, 7^{0}GF,

	Starts	1st	2nd	3rd	Win & Pl
Career Total (Turf)	5	0	0	1	626
Career Total (AW)	2	0	1	0	674

Going (Turf): **Sf: 0-0 GS: 0-0 Gd: 0-2 GF: 0-3 Fm: 0-0**
Distance: 5f/6f: 0-4 7f-8f: 0-3 9f-13f: 0-0 14f+: 0-0
Track : LH: 0-0 RH: 0-2 Tight: 0-0 Gall: 0-0
Aids: Bl: 0-0 Vi: 0-0 Tstrap: 0-0 Ckp: 0-0
Best Rating: **68** 9/09 Leic 7f9y gd-fm

Fair; stays 6f; acts on Polytrack; should win a race.

Precious Secret (IRE)

94(78) (55)**62**

3-y-o b f Fusaichi Pegasus (USA)-Gharam (USA) (Green Dancer (USA))

C F Wall Stourbank Racing

Placings:00-405 **(4157)**

2009: 7^{4}G, 8^{0}GF, 10^{5}G,

	Starts	1st	2nd	3rd	Win & Pl
Career Total (Turf)	4	0	0	0	0
Career Total (AW)	1	0	0	0	

Going (Turf): **Sf: 0-0 GS: 0-1 Gd: 0-2 GF: 0-1 Fm: 0-0**
Distance: 5f/6f: 0-0 7f-8f: 0-3 9f-13f: 0-2 14f+: 0-0
Track : LH: 0-2 RH: 0-1 Tight: 0-2 Gall: 0-1
Aids: Bl: 0-0 Vi: 0-0 Tstrap: 0-0 Ckp: 0-0
Best Rating: **62** 11/08 NmkR 7f gd-sft

Precision Break (USA)

114(110) (93)**103**

4-y-o b g Silver Deputy (CAN)-Miss Kitty Cat (USA) (Tabasco Cat (USA))

P F I Cole Mrs Fitri Hay

Placings:561111051311-0201 **(5865)**

2009: 12^{0}GF, 14^{2}G, 14^{0}GF, 12^{1}GF,

	Starts	1st	2nd	3rd	Win & Pl
Career Total (Turf)	9	4	1	0	27369
Career Total (AW)	7	4	0	1	19097

103	9/09	Donc	1m4f	(0-105)H	G-F	£12952
93	11/08	Wolv	1m5f194y	(0-85)H	STD	£5180
91	10/08	GrLe	1m5f66y	(0-85)H	STD	£5180
84	9/08	Kemp	2m	(0-80)H	STD	£4727
84	6/08	Wolv	1m4f50y	(0-75)H	STD	£3238
74	6/08	Donc	1m4f	(0-70)H	G-S	£4857
66	5/08	Wwck	1m4f134y	(0-70)H	G-S	£3238
61	4/08	Folk	1m4f		G-S	£2590

Total win prize-money £41964

Going (Turf): Sf: 0-1 **GS: 3-3** Gd: 0-1 GF: 1-4 Fm: 0-0
Distance: 5f/6f: 0-0 7f-8f: 0-2 **9f-13f: 5-9** 14f+: 3-5
Track : **LH: 6-10** RH: 2-6 Tight: 3-8 Gall: 3-5
Aids: Bl: 0-0 Vi: 0-0 Tstrap: 0-0 Ckp: 0-0
Best Rating: **103** 9/09 Donc 1m4f gd-fm

Very useful; stays 2m; acts on good and easy ground; goes well on Polytrack.

Precocious Air (IRE)

(98) (61)

3-y-o b f Redback-Wee Merkin (IRE) (Thatching)

J A Osborne The Waney Racing Group Inc

Placings:034325-2634 **(0441)**

2009: 9^{2}SD, 8^{6}SD, 8^{3}SD, 8^{4}SD,

	Starts	1st	2nd	3rd	Win & Pl
Career Total (Turf)	0	0	0	0	
Career Total (AW)	10	0	2	3	2737

Going (Turf): **Sf: 0-0 GS: 0-0 Gd: 0-0 GF: 0-0 Fm: 0-0**
Distance: 5f/6f: 0-0 7f-8f: 0-5 9f-13f: 0-5 14f+: 0-0
Track : LH: 0-8 RH: 0-2 Tight: 0-7 Gall: 0-1
Aids: Bl: 0-0 Vi: 0-0 Tstrap: 0-0 Ckp: 0-0
Best Rating: **61** 1/09 Wolv 1m1f103y stand

Modest; stays 1m1f; acts on Polytrack.

Prelude

98 **77**

8-y-o b m Danzero (AUS)-Dancing Debut (Polar Falcon (USA))

W M Brisbourne A P Burgoyne

Placings:500666150/0300062322203/65010123154/0562 3126000-53000 **(5359)**

2009: 12^{5}GF, 11^{3}F, 12^{0}GF, 12^{0}G, 13^{0}S,

	Starts	1st	2nd	3rd	Win & Pl
Career Total (Turf)	48	5	7	6	36635
Career Total (AW)	1	0	0	0	

76	7/08	Ches	1m4f66y	(0-75)H	G-S	£4094
70	8/07	Ches	1m4f66y	(0-85)H	G-F	£5505
66	7/07	Ches	1m4f66y	(0-75)H	HVY	£3617
59	6/07	Ches	1m4f66y	(0-70)H	GD	£3435
63	8/04	Ripn	1m2f	E(0-70)H	G-S	£3863

Total win prize-money £20515

Going (Turf): Sf: 1-10 **GS: 2-8** Gd: 1-12GF: 1-17 Fm: 0-1
Distance: 5f/6f: 0-0 7f-8f: 0-2 **9f-13f: 5-43** 14f+: 0-4
Track : **LH: 4-34** RH: 1-14 **Tight: 5-30** Gall: 0-1
Aids: Bl: 0-0 Vi: 0-0 Tstrap: 0-0 Ckp: 0-0
Best Rating: **77** 7/08 Pont 1m4f8y good

Modest; stays 1m4f; acts on most ground; has a good record at Chester.

Premier Angel (USA)

74(95) (61)**18**

3-y-o b f Arch (USA)-Angel Song (USA) (Reign Road (USA))

Ollie Pears (Jane Chapple-Hyam 4/2) Ollie Pears

Placings:2-050 **(4846)**

2009: 8^{0}SD, 10^{5}SD, 8^{0}G,

	Starts	1st	2nd	3rd	Win & Pl
Career Total (Turf)	1	0	0	0	
Career Total (AW)	3	0	1	0	705

Going (Turf): **Sf: 0-0 GS: 0-0 Gd: 0-1 GF: 0-0 Fm: 0-0**
Distance: 5f/6f: 0-0 7f-8f: 0-3 9f-13f: 0-1 14f+: 0-0
Track : LH: 0-4 RH: 0-0 Tight: 0-4 Gall: 0-0
Aids: Bl: 0-0 Vi: 0-0 Tstrap: 0-0 Ckp: 0-0
Best Rating: **61** 12/08 Ling 7f stand

Fair; stays 7f and acts on Polytrack.

Premier Demon (IRE)

85(84) (22)**53**

3-y-o b f Tagula (IRE)-Luisa Demon (IRE) (Barathea (IRE))

P D Evans Mrs I M Folkes

Placings:000450-0005 **(3502)**

2009: 5^{0}SD, 7^{0}SD, 8^{0}F, 7^{5}GF,

	Starts	1st	2nd	3rd	Win & Pl
Career Total (Turf)	6	0	0	0	202
Career Total (AW)	4	0	0	0	

Going (Turf): **Sf: 0-1 GS: 0-0 Gd: 0-0 GF: 0-4 Fm: 0-1**
Distance: 5f/6f: 0-5 7f-8f: 0-4 9f-13f: 0-1 14f+: 0-0
Track : LH: 0-6 RH: 0-0 Tight: 0-6 Gall: 0-1
Aids: Bl: 0-0 Vi: 0-0 Tstrap: 0-0 Ckp: 0-0
Best Rating: **53** 7/08 Chep 6f16y gd-fm

Moderate; best around 6f; acts on good to firm.

Premier Krug (IRE)

95(91) (55)**62**

3-y-o b f Xaar-Perugia (IRE) (Perugino (USA))

P D Evans Mrs I M Folkes

Placings:5603044065404**6**-003464 **(3541)**
2009: 7^{0}F, 9^{0}GF, 7^{3}GF, 7^{4}GF, 8^{6}GF, 8^{4}F,

	Starts	1st	2nd	3rd	Win & Pl
Career Total (Turf)	12	0	0	2	1954
Career Total (AW)	8	0	0	0	0

Going (Turf): Sf: 0-1 GS: 0-1 Gd: 0-2 GF: 0-6 Fm: 0-2
Distance: 5f/6f: 0-10 7f-8f: 0-6 9f-13f: 0-4 14f+: 0-0
Track : LH: 0-9 RH: 0-3 Tight: 0-6 Gall: 0-0
Aids: Bl: 0-0 Vi: 0-3 Tstrap: 0-0 Ckp: 0-0
Best Rating: 62 5/08 York 6f good

Moderate filly; stays 7f; acts on a sound surface; handles Polytrack; has worn a visor.

Premier Lad

(103) (80)**65**
3-y-o b g Tobougg (IRE)-Al Joudha (FR) (Green Desert (USA))
T D Barron Harrowgate Bloodstock Ltd

Placings:43-**1**24000 **(7828)**
2009: 6^{1}SD, 6^{2}SD, 6^{4}SD, 6^{0}SD, 6^{0}SD, 6^{0}SD,

	Starts	1st	2nd	3rd	Win & Pl
Career Total (Turf)	2	0	0	1	554
Career Total (AW)	6	1	1	0	4560

75 2/09 Sthl 6f STD £2729
Total win prize-money £2730

Going (Turf): Sf: 0-1 GS: 0-0 Gd: 0-1 GF: 0-0 Fm: 0-0
Distance: 5f/6f: 1-8 7f-8f: 0-0 9f-13f: 0-0 14f+: 0-0
Track : LH: 1-5 RH: 0-1 Tight: 0-0 Gall: 0-0
Aids: Bl: 0-0 Vi: 0-0 Tstrap: 0-0 Ckp: 0-0
Best Rating: 80 2/09 Sthl 6f stand

Fair; suited by 5f-6f; acts on good ground; goes on Fibresand.

Premier Superstar

81 **53**
3-y-o ch f Bertolini (USA)-Absolve (USA) (Diesis)
M H Tompkins Robert M Jones

Placings:50-00 **(2635)**
2009: 10^{0}GF, 11^{0}GF,

	Starts	1st	2nd	3rd	Win & Pl
Career Total (Turf)	4	0	0	0	0

Going (Turf): Sf: 0-1 GS: 0-0 Gd: 0-0 GF: 0-3 Fm: 0-0
Distance: 5f/6f: 0-0 7f-8f: 0-2 9f-13f: 0-2 14f+: 0-0
Track : LH: 0-1 RH: 0-1 Tight: 0-2 Gall: 0-0
Aids: Bl: 0-0 Vi: 0-0 Tstrap: 0-0 Ckp: 0-0
Best Rating: 53 7/08 Folk 7f soft

Premio Loco (USA)

111(113) (114)**113**
5-y-o ch g Prized (USA)-Crazee Mental (Magic Ring (IRE))
C F Wall Bernard Westley

Placings:0/5**1**0**1**/0**11**6-**1121211** **(6323a)**
2009: 8^{1}SD, 8^{1}SD, 10^{2}SD, 8^{1}G, 8^{2}GF, 8^{1}G, 8^{1}G,

	Starts	1st	2nd	3rd	Win & Pl
Career Total (Turf)	9	4	1	0	115716
Career Total (AW)	7	5	1	0	93216

113 9/09 Colo 1m GD £38835
112 9/09 Badn 1m GD £38835
112 5/09 Gdwd 1m GD £22708
109 2/09 Kemp 1m STD £22708
94 1/09 Ling 1m STD £7771
114 9/08 Kemp 1m H STD £30825
106 7/08 Kemp 1m (0-95)H STD £7477
99 9/07 Newb 7f (0-85)H G-F £4857
91 4/07 Ling 1m STD £2914
Total win prize-money £176932

Going (Turf): Sf: 0-0 GS: 0-0 **Gd: 3-4** GF: 1-5 Fm: 0-0
Distance: 5f/6f: 0-1 **7f-8f: 9-11** 9f-13f: 0-4 14f+: 0-0
Track : LH: 3-5 **RH: 5-6 Tight: 2-5** Gall: 0-0
Aids: Bl: 0-0 Vi: 0-0 Tstrap: 0-0 Ckp: 0-0
Best Rating: 114 3/09 Ling 1m2f stand

Listed class; runner-up in the 2009 Winter Derby; effective at 7f-1m2f; acts on fast ground; goes on Polytrack.

Premium Charge

72(81) (47)**41**
2-y-o ch g Footstepsinthesand-Kallavesi (USA) (Woodman (USA))
C A Dwyer Mrs J A Chapman

Placings:40 **(7731)**
2009: 7^{4}G, 9^{0}SD,

	Starts	1st	2nd	3rd	Win & Pl
Career Total (Turf)	1	0	0	0	519
Career Total (AW)	1	0	0	0	

Going (Turf): Sf: 0-0 GS: 0-0 Gd: 0-1 GF: 0-0 Fm: 0-0
Distance: 5f/6f: 0-0 7f-8f: 0-1 9f-13f: 0-1 14f+: 0-0
Track : LH: 0-1 RH: 0-0 Tight: 0-1 Gall: 0-0
Aids: Bl: 0-1 Vi: 0-0 Tstrap: 0-0 Ckp: 0-0
Best Rating: 47 12/09 Wolv 1m1f103y stand

Presbyterian Nun (IRE)

106 **99**
4-y-o b f Daylami (IRE)-Conspiracy (Rudimentary (USA))
J L Dunlop The Earl Cadogan

Placings:0210/034635-36046204 **(7148)**
2009: 14^{3}GF, 14^{6}G, 14^{0}G, 12^{4}GF, 10^{6}GF, 10^{2}GF, 10^{0}G, 12^{4}G,

	Starts	1st	2nd	3rd	Win & Pl
Career Total (Turf)	18	1	2	3	44210

85 9/07 Folk 7f G-F £3465
Total win prize-money £3465

Going (Turf): Sf: 0-2 GS: 0-0 Gd: 0-7 **GF: 1-9** Fm: 0-0
Distance: 5f/6f: 0-0 **7f-8f: 1-4** 9f-13f: 0-10 14f+: 0-4
Track : LH: 0-8 RH: 0-5 Tight: 0-3 Gall: 0-7
Aids: Bl: 0-1 Vi: 0-0 Tstrap: 0-2 Ckp: 0-2
Best Rating: 99 8/08 Newb 1m4f5y good

Useful; Listed placed; stays 1m6f; acts on any ground; has worn cheekpieces.

Prescription

108(108) (102)**93**
4-y-o gr f Pivotal-Doctor's Glory (USA) (Elmaamul (USA))
Sir Mark Prescott Cheveley Park Stud

Placings:01113-612346 **(7488)**
2009: 7^{6}G, 6^{1}SD, 5^{2}SD, 7^{3}SS, 6^{4}S, 6^{6}SD,

	Starts	1st	2nd	3rd	Win & Pl
Career Total (Turf)	5	2	0	0	16725
Career Total (AW)	6	2	1	2	13161

101 8/09 Ling 6f (0-85)H STD £5828
84 9/08 Haml 6f5y (0-95)H SFT £11009
87 9/08 Ling 6f (0-75)H STD £2590
75 8/08 Yarm 6f3y G-S £2775
Total win prize-money £22203

Going (Turf): Sf: 1-3 GS: 1-1 Gd: 0-1 GF: 0-0 Fm: 0-0
Distance: 5f/6f: 2-6 7f-8f: 2-5 9f-13f: 0-0 14f+: 0-0
Track : LH: 2-6 RH: 0-0 **Tight: 2-5** Gall: 0-1
Aids: Bl: 0-0 Vi: 0-0 Tstrap: 0-0 Ckp: 0-0
Best Rating: 102 10/09 Ling 7f std-slw

Very useful; effective at 6f-7f; acts on soft ground and on Polytrack.

Present

85(72) (39)**45**
5-y-o ch m Generous (IRE)-Miss Picol (Exit To Nowhere (USA))
Miss Diana Weeden (M J Gingell 31/3) M Hole

Placings:000/0060**6**00**0**10/6-0040 **(7124)**
2009: 11^{0}SD, 11^{0}GF, 16^{4}GF, 16^{0}G,

	Starts	1st	2nd	3rd	Win & Pl
Career Total (Turf)	13	1	0	0	2184
Career Total (AW)	5	0	0	0	0

53 9/07 Yarm 1m2f21y GD £1943
Total win prize-money £1943

Going (Turf): Sf: 0-0 GS: 0-1 **Gd: 1-6** GF: 0-6 Fm: 0-0
Distance: 5f/6f: 0-0 7f-8f: 0-2 **9f-13f: 1-13** 14f+: 0-3
Track : LH: 1-11 RH: 0-4 **Tight: 1-8** Gall: 0-1
Aids: Bl: 0-0 Vi: 0-2 Tstrap: 0-2 Ckp: 0-2
Best Rating: 53 9/07 Yarm 1m2f21y good

Present Alchemy

111 **89**
3-y-o ch c Cadeaux Genereux-Desert Alchemy (IRE) (Green Desert (USA))
H Morrison Normandie Stud Ltd

Placings:65221 **(5422)**
2009: 8^{6}S, 8^{5}HY, 6^{2}GF, 6^{2}G, 5^{1}GF,

	Starts	1st	2nd	3rd	Win & Pl
Career Total (Turf)	5	1	2	0	4714

89 8/09 Bevl 5f G-F £2752
Total win prize-money £2752

Going (Turf): Sf: 0-2 GS: 0-0 Gd: 0-1 **GF: 1-2** Fm: 0-0
Distance: 5f/6f: 1-3 7f-8f: 0-1 9f-13f: 0-1 14f+: 0-0
Track : LH: 0-1 RH: 0-0 Tight: 0-0 Gall: 0-0
Aids: Bl: 0-0 Vi: 0-0 Tstrap: 0-0 Ckp: 0-0
Best Rating: 89 8/09 Bevl 5f gd-fm

Fair sprinter; effective at 5-f; acts on fast ground.

Presque Perdre

90 **53**
5-y-o ch g Desert Prince (IRE)-Kindle (Selkirk (USA))
G M Moore J W Andrews

Placings:00/005/4 **(2044)**
2009: 16^{4}GS,

	Starts	1st	2nd	3rd	Win & Pl
Career Total (Turf)	6	0	0	0	308

Going (Turf): Sf: 0-2 GS: 0-1 Gd: 0-1 GF: 0-2 Fm: 0-0
Distance: 5f/6f: 0-1 7f-8f: 0-1 9f-13f: 0-3 14f+: 0-1
Track : LH: 0-4 RH: 0-1 Tight: 0-1 Gall: 0-2
Aids: Bl: 0-0 Vi: 0-0 Tstrap: 0-0 Ckp: 0-0
Best Rating: 53 5/09 Newc 2m19y gd-sft

Press The Button (GER)

111(111) (102)98

6-y-o b g Dansili-Play Around (IRE) (Niniski (USA))

J R Boyle Brian McAtavey

Placings:053042124/00330142150/004114554613410502100 **(6106)**

2009: 10^{1}SD, 10^{0}G, 10^{5}GF, 12^{0}G, 10^{2}GF, 12^{1}GS, 13^{0}GF, 10^{0}GF,

	Starts	1st	2nd	3rd	Win & Pl
Career Total (Turf)	32	6	4	3	61033
Career Total (AW)	9	2	0	1	16682

98	8/09	Asct	1m4f	(0-100)H	G-S	£17230
102	4/09	Kemp	1m2f	(0-95)H	STD	£7771
91	11/08	Kemp	1m4f	(0-85)H	STD	£5180
88	7/08	Sals	1m1f198y	(0-85)H	G-F	£6799
86	6/08	Folk	1m1f149y	(0-75)H	G-F	£2590
92	9/07	Folk	1m1f149y	(0-90)H	FRM	£6855
88	8/07	Bath	1m2f46y	(0-80)H	GD	£4792
88	8/06	Epsm	1m114y	(0-80)H	GD	£7772

Total win prize-money £58993

Going (Turf): Sf: 0-5 GS: 1-5 **Gd: 2-11 GF: 2-10** Fm: 1-1
Distance: 5f/6f: 0-0 7f-8f: 0-9 **9f-13f: 8-31** 14f+: 0-1
Track: LH: 2-13 **RH: 6-25 Tight: 5-16** Gall: 1-7
Aids: Bl: 0-0 Vi: 0-0 Tstrap: 0-1 Ckp: 0-1
Best Rating: **102** 4/09 Kemp 1m2f stand

Very useful; effective over 1m2f-1m4f; acts on good and fast ground; goes on Polytrack; has worn cheekpieces.

Press To Reset

77(76) (18)53

2-y-o b g Reset (AUS)-Lady De Londres (Mtoto)

W G M Turner Lees & Cummings Bloodstock

Placings:0300 **(7139)**

2009: 7^{0}G, 8^{3}GF, 7^{0}GF, 9^{0}SD,

	Starts	1st	2nd	3rd	Win & Pl
Career Total (Turf)	3	0	0	1	302
Career Total (AW)	1	0	0	0	

Going (Turf): **Sf: 0-0 GS: 0-0 Gd: 0-1 GF: 0-2 Fm: 0-0**
Distance: 5f/6f: 0-0 7f-8f: 0-2 9f-13f: 0-2 14f+: 0-0
Track: LH: 0-1 RH: 0-1 Tight: 0-2 Gall: 0-0
Aids: Bl: 0-0 Vi: 0-0 Tstrap: 0-0 Ckp: 0-0
Best Rating: **53** 8/09 Wind 1m67y gd-fm

Pressed For Time (IRE)

94(99) (62)52

3-y-o b f Traditionally (USA)-Desert Palace (Green Desert (USA))

E J Creighton P Cafferty

Placings:450521130-0360600 **(4596)**

2009: 5^{0}SD, 5^{3}GF, 5^{6}F, 5^{0}G, 5^{6}SD, 5^{0}F, 5^{0}G,

	Starts	1st	2nd	3rd	Win & Pl
Career Total (Turf)	8	0	1	1	963
Career Total (AW)	8	2	0	1	6612

62	9/08	GrLe	5f	(0-70)	STD	£3885
61	8/08	Wolv	5f20y		STD	£2047

Total win prize-money £5933

Going (Turf): **Sf: 0-2 GS: 0-0 Gd: 0-2 GF: 0-1 Fm: 0-3**
Distance: **5f/6f: 2-16** 7f-8f: 0-0 9f-13f: 0-0 14f+: 0-0
Track: **LH: 2-10** RH: 0-2 Tight: 1-3 Gall: 1-2
Aids: Bl: 0-1 Vi: 0-0 Tstrap: 0-1 Ckp: 0-1
Best Rating: **62** 9/08 Kemp 6f stand

Modest; effective at 5f; acts on a sound surface and Polytrack; has worn a tongue tie.

Pressing (IRE)

100 118

6-y-o b/br h Soviet Star (USA)-Rafif (USA) (Riverman (USA))

M A Jarvis Gary A Tanaka

Placings:22220/2012032332/111250211/2442110-011130 **(7746a)**

2009: 8^{0}S, 8^{1}G, 10^{1}G, 8^{1}GF, 8^{3}HY, 8^{0}G,

	Starts	1st	2nd	3rd	Win & Pl
Career Total (Turf)	37	11	12	4	1428683

116	9/09	Veli	1m	G-F	£416667
118	7/09	Muni	1m2f	GD	£88350
113	5/09	Siro	1m	GD	£67962
114	11/08	Capa	1m	HVY	£42188
118	9/08	Veli	1m	GD	£301508
118	11/07	Capa	1m2f	SFT	£72973
114	9/07	Siro	1m3f	HVY	£24628
117	4/07	Siro	1m2f	G-F	£27365
	4/07	Siro	1m2f	GD	£8446
	3/07	Siro	1m2f	GD	£8446
	4/06	Siro	1m2f	SFT	£13793

Total win prize-money £1072326

Going (Turf): Sf: 4-12 GS: 0-1 **Gd: 5-20** GF: 2-4 Fm: 0-0
Distance: 5f/6f: 0-0 7f-8f: 4-15 **9f-13f: 7-22** 14f+: 0-0
Track: LH: 1-3 **RH: 7-19** Tight: 0-0 Gall: 0-3
Aids: Bl: 0-0 Vi: 0-0 Tstrap: 0-0 Ckp: 0-0
Best Rating: **118** 7/09 Muni 1m2f good

Group class; ex-Italian; effective at 1m-1m2f; acts well on most ground.

Pressing Matters (IRE)

98(91) (72)74

3-y-o br c Oasis Dream-Pasithea (IRE) (Celtic Swing)

M Botti Giuliano Manfredini

Placings:531-04100300 **(6924)**

2009: 8^{0}SD, 7^{4}GF, 7^{1}GF, 7^{0}SD, 7^{0}G, 7^{3}G, 8^{0}SD, 8^{0}GF,

	Starts	1st	2nd	3rd	Win & Pl
Career Total (Turf)	7	1	0	2	3827
Career Total (AW)	4	1	0	0	3238

74	7/09	Yarm	7f3y	(0-75)H	G-F	£2719
72	11/08	Wolv	7f32y		STD	£3238

Total win prize-money £5958

Going (Turf): Sf: 0-0 GS: 0-0 Gd: 0-3 **GF: 1-4** Fm: 0-0
Distance: 5f/6f: 0-2 **7f-8f: 2-8** 9f-13f: 0-1 14f+: 0-0
Track: **LH: 1-2** RH: 0-3 **Tight: 1-1** Gall: 0-2
Aids: Bl: 0-1 Vi: 0-0 Tstrap: 1-5 Ckp: 1-5
Best Rating: **74** 7/09 Yarm 7f3y gd-fm

Fair; stays 7f and acts on Polytrack; handles fast ground; has worn cheekpieces.

Presvis

114(109) (108)122

5-y-o b g Sakhee (USA)-Forest Fire (SWE) (Never So Bold)

L M Cumani L Marinopoulos

Placings:3551221-1121223 **(7747a)**

2009: 10^{1}G, 10^{1}GF, 8^{2}G, 10^{1}Y, 10^{2}G, 10^{2}SD, 10^{3}G,

	Starts	1st	2nd	3rd	Win & Pl
Career Total (Turf)	13	5	4	2	2082203
Career Total (AW)	1	0	1	0	8608

119	4/09	ShTn	1m2f		YLD	£718133
122	2/09	Ndas	1m2f	(100-116)H	G-F	£72916
115	1/09	Ndas	1m2f	(95-110)H	GD	£50000
113	9/08	Newb	1m2f6y	(0-105)H	GD	£62310
94	7/08	Sand	1m2f7y	(0-80)H	G-F	£5828

Total win prize-money £909188

Going (Turf): Sf: 0-0 GS: 0-1 **Gd: 2-6 GF: 2-5** Fm: 0-0
Distance: 5f/6f: 0-0 7f-8f: 0-1 **9f-13f: 5-13** 14f+: 0-0
Track: **LH: 3-9** RH: 2-5 Tight: 0-2 **Gall: 3-5**
Aids: Bl: 0-0 Vi: 0-0 Tstrap: 0-0 Ckp: 0-0
Best Rating: **122** 3/09 Ndas 1m194y good

Group-class globetrotter; winner of the QE II Cup at Sha Tin in 2009; highly effective over 1m2f; seems to act on most ground; has a fine turn of foot.

Prettiest Star (IRE)

90(85) (48)58

2-y-o ch f Footstepsinthesand-Alyousufeya (IRE) (Kingmambo (USA))

K A Ryan J Nattrass

Placings:646500520400 **(7352)**

2009: 5^{6}GF, 5^{4}GF, 5^{6}GF, 5^{5}F, 7^{0}S, 7^{0}G, 6^{5}GF, 5^{2}SF, 5^{0}GF, 5^{4}G, 7^{0}GF, 6^{0}SD,

	Starts	1st	2nd	3rd	Win & Pl
Career Total (Turf)	10	0	0	0	241
Career Total (AW)	2	0	1	0	806

Going (Turf): **Sf: 0-1 GS: 0-0 Gd: 0-2 GF: 0-6 Fm: 0-1**
Distance: 5f/6f: 0-9 7f-8f: 0-3 9f-13f: 0-0 14f+: 0-0
Track: LH: 0-4 RH: 0-0 Tight: 0-3 Gall: 0-0
Aids: Bl: 0-0 Vi: 0-0 Tstrap: 0-5 Ckp: 0-5
Best Rating: **58** 5/09 Leic 5f2y gd-fm

Modest; effective at 5f; acts on fast ground.

Pretty Bonnie

102(102) (90)93

4-y-o b f Kyllachy-Joonayh (Warning)

A E Price Mrs P Field

Placings:034006065/02214121150-013255350 **(6282)**

2009: 5^{0}G, 6^{1}SD, 6^{3}GS, 6^{2}GS, 6^{5}G, 6^{5}S, 6^{3}GF, 6^{5}S, 6^{0}GF,

	Starts	1st	2nd	3rd	Win & Pl
Career Total (Turf)	24	4	4	3	35087
Career Total (AW)	5	1	0	0	4727

90	5/09	Kemp	6f	(0-85)H	STD	£4727
86	9/08	Sand	5f6y	(0-85)H	SFT	£6476
87	8/08	Bath	5f161y	(0-85)H	GD	£6799
74	8/08	Bath	5f11y	(0-75)H	G-S	£3561
65	7/08	Wwck	5f110y	(0-70)H	G-F	£3885

Total win prize-money £25451

Going (Turf): **Sf: 1-5 GS: 1-4 Gd: 1-8 GF: 1-7** Fm: 0-0
Distance: **5f/6f: 5-26** 7f-8f: 0-3 9f-13f: 0-0 14f+: 0-0
Track: **LH: 3-12** RH: 1-1 Tight: 0-4 **Gall: 2-4**
Aids: Bl: 0-0 Vi: 0-0 Tstrap: 0-0 Ckp: 0-0
Best Rating: **93** 6/09 NmkJ 6f gd-sft

Useful; effective over 5f-6f; acts on most ground and on Polytrack.

Pretty Officer (USA)

101(91) (38)59

4-y-o b f Deputy Commander (USA)-La Samanna (USA) (Trempolino (USA))

Rae Guest ROA Racing Partnership VIII

Placings:000/652636-66234106 **(6184)**
2009: 11^{6}SD, 10^{6}G, 10^{2}GF, 10^{3}G, 8^{4}G, 10^{1}GF, 8^{0}GS, 9^{6}GF,

	Starts	1st	2nd	3rd	Win & Pl
Career Total (Turf)	13	1	2	2	4304
Career Total (AW)	4	0	0	0	0

59 8/09 Yarm 1m2f21y (0-60)H G-F £2331
Total win prize-money £2331

Going (Turf): Sf: 0-0 GS: 0-2 Gd: 0-5 **GF: 1-6** Fm: 0-0
Distance: 5f/6f: 0-2 7f-8f: 0-4 **9f-13f: 1-11** 14f+: 0-0
Track : **LH: 1-10** RH: 0-3 **Tight: 1-6** Gall: 0-1
Aids: Bl: 0-0 Vi: 0-0 Tstrap: 0-0 Ckp: 0-0
Best Rating: **59** 8/09 Yarm 1m2f21y gd-fm

Moderate; effective over 1m; acts on good ground.

Pretty Orchid

96(77) (43)**51**
4-y-o b f Forzando-Dunloe (IRE) (Shaadi (USA))
P T Midgley K L Man

Placings:0/0-003 **(5338)**
2009: 6^{0}G, 6^{0}S, 5^{3}GS,

	Starts	1st	2nd	3rd	Win & Pl
Career Total (Turf)	4	0	0	1	433
Career Total (AW)	1	0	0	0	

Going (Turf): **Sf: 0-2 GS: 0-1 Gd: 0-1 GF: 0-0 Fm: 0-0**
Distance: 5f/6f: 0-3 7f-8f: 0-2 9f-13f: 0-0 14f+: 0-0
Track : LH: 0-1 RH: 0-1 Tight: 0-1 Gall: 0-0
Aids: Bl: 0-0 Vi: 0-0 Tstrap: 0-1 Ckp: 0-1
Best Rating: **57** 10/07 Leic 7f9y soft

Pride Of Kings

107 **89**
3-y-o b c King's Best (USA)-Aunty Mary (Common Grounds)
M Johnston Jaber Abdullah

Placings:00313-41231060 **(5522)**
2009: 8^{4}G, 8^{1}F, 9^{2}GF, 8^{3}G, 8^{1}F, 8^{0}G, 8^{6}GF, 8^{0}G,

	Starts	1st	2nd	3rd	Win & Pl
Career Total (Turf)	13	3	1	3	19043

89 7/09 Hayd 1m30y (0-95)H FRM £9066
81 5/09 Nott 1m75y (0-75)H FRM £3885
74 7/08 Catt 7f G-F £2590
Total win prize-money £15542

Going (Turf): Sf: 0-0 GS: 0-1 Gd: 0-5 GF: 1-5 **Fm: 2-2**
Distance: 5f/6f: 0-2 7f-8f: 1-6 **9f-13f: 2-5** 14f+: 0-0
Track : **LH: 3-5** RH: 0-4 **Tight: 1-4** Gall: 0-0
Aids: Bl: 0-0 Vi: 0-0 Tstrap: 0-0 Ckp: 0-0
Best Rating: **89** 7/09 Hayd 1m30y firm

Useful; effective at 1m-1m2f and acts on fast ground; likes to race prominently.

Pride Of Nation (IRE)

86(103) (92)**81**
7-y-o b h Danehill Dancer (IRE)-Anita Via (IRE) (Anita's Prince)
A J McCabe (J W Hills 12/10) A J McCabe

Placings:221/1103/3641100/50000660-0000302453 **(7858)**
2009: 8^{0}SD, 8^{0}SD, 8^{0}S, 7^{0}SD, 7^{3}SD, 8^{0}SD, 8^{2}SF, 8^{4}SD, 8^{5}SD, 8^{3}SD,

	Starts	1st	2nd	3rd	Win & Pl
Career Total (Turf)	21	5	2	2	85947
Career Total (AW)	11	0	1	2	1902

116 8/07 Sals 1m G-S £36907
111 7/07 York 1m HVY £10363
107 5/06 Hayd 1m30y (0-90)H HVY £9715
102 4/06 Bath 1m5y (0-85)H GD £7886
82 9/05 Nott 1m54y GD £3951
Total win prize-money £68824

Going (Turf): **Sf: 2-6** GS: 1-6 **Gd: 2-5** GF: 0-4 Fm: 0-0
Distance: 5f/6f: 0-0 7f-8f: 2-22 **9f-13f: 3-10** 14f+: 0-0
Track : **LH: 4-17** RH: 0-6 Tight: 1-7 Gall: 1-5
Aids: Bl: 0-0 Vi: 0-0 Tstrap: 0-8 Ckp: 0-8
Best Rating: **116** 8/07 Sals 1m gd-sft

Modest; formerly smart when a winner in Group 3 company; stays 1m; acts on good and softer ground; handles Polytrack; has worn cheekpieces, earplugs and a tongue tie.

Pride Of Northcare (IRE)

(103) (77)**62**
5-y-o gr g Namid-Pride Of Pendle (Grey Desire)
D Shaw George Houghton

Placings:64450/60315126-0 **(0742)**
2009: 5^{0}SD,

	Starts	1st	2nd	3rd	Win & Pl
Career Total (Turf)	4	0	0	1	385
Career Total (AW)	10	2	1	0	6507

73 10/08 Wolv 5f20y (0-62)H SF £2388
63 9/08 Ling 5f STD £2729
Total win prize-money £5118

Going (Turf): **Sf: 0-1 GS: 0-1 Gd: 0-2 GF: 0-0 Fm: 0-0**
Distance: **5f/6f: 2-8** 7f-8f: 0-6 9f-13f: 0-0 14f+: 0-0
Track : **LH: 2-9** RH: 0-1 **Tight: 2-7** Gall: 0-1
Aids: Bl: 0-0 Vi: 0-1 Tstrap: 0-0 Ckp: 0-0
Best Rating: **77** 10/08 GrLe 5f stand

Modest; effective from 5f-7f; acts on good ground; goes on Polytrack; has worn cheekpieces.

Priestley (IRE)

77(73) (28)**26**
2-y-o b g Bahri (USA)-Siskin (IRE) (Royal Academy (USA))
J G Given Danethorpe Racing Partnership

Placings:000 **(7376)**
2009: 7^{0}G, 8^{0}S, 7^{0}SD,

	Starts	1st	2nd	3rd	Win & Pl
Career Total (Turf)	2	0	0	0	
Career Total (AW)	1	0	0	0	

Going (Turf): **Sf: 0-1 GS: 0-0 Gd: 0-1 GF: 0-0 Fm: 0-0**
Distance: 5f/6f: 0-0 7f-8f: 0-2 9f-13f: 0-1 14f+: 0-0
Track : LH: 0-2 RH: 0-0 Tight: 0-1 Gall: 0-0
Aids: Bl: 0-0 Vi: 0-0 Tstrap: 0-0 Ckp: 0-0
Best Rating: **28** 11/09 Wolv 7f32y stand

Prima Fonteyn

(87) (51)**34**
3-y-o ch f Imperial Dancer-Flying Wind (Forzando)
Miss Sheena West Heart Of The South Racing

Placings:00000-600 **(0647)**
2009: 10^{6}SD, 11^{0}SD, 10^{0}SD,

	Starts	1st	2nd	3rd	Win & Pl
Career Total (Turf)	3	0	0	0	
Career Total (AW)	5	0	0	0	0

Going (Turf): **Sf: 0-0 GS: 0-0 Gd: 0-2 GF: 0-1 Fm: 0-0**
Distance: 5f/6f: 0-2 7f-8f: 0-3 9f-13f: 0-3 14f+: 0-0
Track : LH: 0-3 RH: 0-2 Tight: 0-3 Gall: 0-1
Aids: Bl: 0-0 Vi: 0-0 Tstrap: 0-0 Ckp: 0-0
Best Rating: **51** 2/09 Kemp 1m3f stand

Primaeval

101 **82**
3-y-o ch c Pivotal-Langoustine (AUS) (Danehill (USA))
J R Fanshawe Lord Vestey

Placings:231 **(6823)**
2009: 7^{2}G, 6^{3}GF, 6^{1}GF,

	Starts	1st	2nd	3rd	Win & Pl
Career Total (Turf)	3	1	1	1	4613

77 10/09 Rdcr 6f G-F £2590
Total win prize-money £2590

Going (Turf): Sf: 0-0 GS: 0-0 Gd: 0-1 **GF: 1-2** Fm: 0-0
Distance: **5f/6f: 1-1** 7f-8f: 0-2 9f-13f: 0-0 14f+: 0-0
Track : LH: 0-0 RH: 0-0 Tight: 0-0 Gall: 0-0
Aids: Bl: 0-0 Vi: 0-0 Tstrap: 0-0 Ckp: 0-0
Best Rating: **82** 7/09 Donc 7f good

Fair; effective at 6-7f; acts on fast ground.

Primary Colors

88 **65**
2-y-o ch c Nayef (USA)-Red Yellow Blue (USA) (Sky Classic (CAN))
C G Cox H E Sheikh Sultan Bin Khalifa Al Nahyan

Placings:56 **(6617)**
2009: 7^{5}G, 8^{6}G,

	Starts	1st	2nd	3rd	Win & Pl
Career Total (Turf)	2	0	0	0	0

Going (Turf): **Sf: 0-0 GS: 0-0 Gd: 0-2 GF: 0-0 Fm: 0-0**
Distance: 5f/6f: 0-0 7f-8f: 0-2 9f-13f: 0-0 14f+: 0-0
Track : LH: 0-0 RH: 0-0 Tight: 0-0 Gall: 0-0
Aids: Bl: 0-0 Vi: 0-0 Tstrap: 0-0 Ckp: 0-0
Best Rating: **65** 8/09 NmkJ 7f good

Prime Aspiration (USA)

85 (77)**60**
4-y-o b/br c Tale Of The Cat (USA)-Bank On Her (USA) (Rahy (USA))
B Smart Prime Equestrian

Placings:00244/0 **(4346)**
2009: 6^{0}G,

	Starts	1st	2nd	3rd	Win & Pl
Career Total (Turf)	4	0	1	0	1173
Career Total (AW)	2	0	0	0	289

Going (Turf): **Sf: 0-1 GS: 0-2 Gd: 0-1 GF: 0-0 Fm: 0-0**
Distance: 5f/6f: 0-4 7f-8f: 0-2 9f-13f: 0-0 14f+: 0-0
Track : LH: 0-2 RH: 0-2 Tight: 0-1 Gall: 0-2
Aids: Bl: 0-0 Vi: 0-0 Tstrap: 0-0 Ckp: 0-0
Best Rating: **77** 10/07 Ling 6f stand

Modest; effective over 5f; acts on easy ground.

Prime Circle

98 **70**
3-y-o b g Green Desert (USA)-First Of Many (Darshaan)

M Johnston Sheikh Hamdan Bin Mohammed Al Maktoum

Placings:03 (3590)
2009: 6^{0}GS, 7^{3}GF,

	Starts	1st	2nd	3rd	Win & Pl
Career Total (Turf)	2	0	0	1	433

Going (Turf): **Sf: 0-0 GS: 0-1 Gd: 0-0 GF: 0-1 Fm: 0-0**
Distance: 5f/6f: 0-1 7f-8f: 0-1 9f-13f: 0-0 14f+: 0-0
Track : LH: 0-1 RH: 0-0 Tight: 0-0 Gall: 0-0
Aids: Bl: 0-0 Vi: 0-0 Tstrap: 0-0 Ckp: 0-0
Best Rating: **70** 7/09 Wwck 7f26y gd-fm

Prime Classique (USA)

83 45
3-y-o b f Elusive Quality (USA)-Via Borghese (USA) (Seattle Dancer (USA))
B Smart Prime Equestrian

Placings:6 (3703)
2009: 10^{6}GS,

	Starts	1st	2nd	3rd	Win & Pl
Career Total (Turf)	1	0	0	0	0

Going (Turf): **Sf: 0-0 GS: 0-1 Gd: 0-0 GF: 0-0 Fm: 0-0**
Distance: 5f/6f: 0-0 7f-8f: 0-0 9f-13f: 0-1 14f+: 0-0
Track : LH: 0-1 RH: 0-0 Tight: 0-0 Gall: 0-0
Aids: Bl: 0-0 Vi: 0-0 Tstrap: 0-0 Ckp: 0-0
Best Rating: **45** 7/09 Pont 1m2f6y gd-sft

Prime Defender

115 (105)115
5-y-o ch h Bertolini (USA)-Arian Da (Superlative)
B W Hills S Falle, M Franklin, J Sumsion

Placings:2130**1**/**2**10120530/400302000546-10020550 (6661)
2009: 6^{1}GF, 6^{0}G, 6^{0}GF, 6^{2}S, 7^{0}GF, 7^{5}GF, 6^{5}GF, 6^{0}GS,

	Starts	1st	2nd	3rd	Win & Pl
Career Total (Turf)	32	4	4	3	151344
Career Total (AW)	2	1	1	0	12450

112	3/09	Donc	6f		G-F	£22708
115	5/07	Hayd	6f		G-F	£14762
110	4/07	NmkR	7f	H	G-F	£17034
105	11/06	Wolv	5f216y		SF	£6855
89	7/06	Sand	5f6y		G-F	£3886

Total win prize-money £65246

Going (Turf): Sf: 0-3 GS: 0-5 Gd: 0-9 **GF: 4-15** Fm: 0-0
Distance: **5f/6f: 4-26** 7f-8f: 1-8 9f-13f: 0-0 14f+: 0-0
Track : **LH: 1-1** RH: 0-1 **Tight: 1-1** Gall: 0-1
Aids: Bl: 0-2 Vi: 0-0 Tstrap: 0-1 Ckp: 0-1
Best Rating: **115** 7/08 NmkJ 6f good

Smart; Listed winner and Group placed; best at 6f, acts on most ground and on Polytrack; has worn cheekpieces and blinkers.

Prime Exhibit

107 96
4-y-o b g Selkirk (USA)-First Exhibit (Machiavellian (USA))
R Charlton Beckhampton Stables Ltd

Placings:41/04-4132 (6732)
2009: 8^{4}HY, 7^{1}G, 7^{3}G, 8^{2}S,

	Starts	1st	2nd	3rd	Win & Pl
Career Total (Turf)	8	2	1	1	19151

94	8/09	Sand	7f16y	(0-90)H	GD	£7771
91	10/07	Leic	7f9y		G-S	£4210

Total win prize-money £11981

Going (Turf): Sf: 0-3 **GS: 1-1 Gd: 1-4** GF: 0-0 Fm: 0-0
Distance: 5f/6f: 0-0 **7f-8f: 2-5** 9f-13f: 0-3 14f+: 0-0
Track : LH: 0-3 **RH: 1-1** Tight: 0-0 Gall: 0-0
Aids: Bl: 0-0 Vi: 0-0 Tstrap: 0-0 Ckp: 0-0
Best Rating: **96** 10/09 Sals 1m soft

Useful; stays 1m; acts on good and softer ground.

Prime Mood (IRE)

100 92
3-y-o ch c Choisir (AUS)-There With Me (USA) (Distant View (USA))
X-Thomas Demeaulte (B Smart 13/6) Prime Equestrian

Placings:223010-600
2009: 6^{6}GF, 6^{0}G, 6^{0}G,

	Starts	1st	2nd	3rd	Win & Pl
Career Total (Turf)	9	1	2	1	15403

92	10/08	Newc	6f	HVY	£5180

Total win prize-money £5181

Going (Turf): **Sf: 1-3** GS: 0-0 Gd: 0-4 GF: 0-2 Fm: 0-0
Distance: **5f/6f: 1-8** 7f-8f: 0-1 9f-13f: 0-0 14f+: 0-0
Track : LH: 0-0 RH: 0-0 Tight: 0-0 Gall: 0-0
Aids: Bl: 0-0 Vi: 0-0 Tstrap: 0-0 Ckp: 0-0
Best Rating: **92** 10/08 Newc 6f heavy

Very useful; best over 6f and acts on any ground.

Prime Spirit (IRE)

102 95
3-y-o b c Invincible Spirit (IRE)-Turtulla (IRE) (Night Shift (USA))
X-Thomas Demeaulte (B Smart 30/7) Prime Equestrian

Placings:120-2041
2009: 7^{2}S, 7^{0}GS, 8^{4}G, 8^{1}VS,

	Starts	1st	2nd	3rd	Win & Pl
Career Total (Turf)	7	2	2	0	22845

90	10/09	StCl	1m	VS	£11650
72	5/08	Newc	6f	G-F	£4047

Total win prize-money £15697

Going (Turf): Sf: 0-1 GS: 0-1 Gd: 0-3 **GF: 1-1** Fm: 0-0
Distance: 5f/6f: 1-1 7f-8f: 1-6 9f-13f: 0-0 14f+: 0-0
Track : **LH: 1-2** RH: 0-1 Tight: 0-0 Gall: 0-0
Aids: Bl: 0-0 Vi: 0-0 Tstrap: 0-0 Ckp: 0-0
Best Rating: **95** 7/09 Hayd 7f30y soft

Very useful; stays 7f; acts on good and faster ground.

Primera Rossa

95(91) (39)52
3-y-o ch f Needwood Blade-Meandering Rose (USA) (Irish River (FR))
J S Moore Miss D L Wisbey & R J Viney

Placings:00006551250 (6446)
2009: 7^{0}SD, 8^{0}SD, 7^{0}GF, 8^{0}F, 11^{6}G, 10^{5}SD, 12^{5}GF, 12^{1}G, 13^{2}G, 16^{5}GF, 12^{0}SS,

	Starts	1st	2nd	3rd	Win & Pl
Career Total (Turf)	7	1	1	0	2733
Career Total (AW)	4	0	0	0	0

49	8/09	Chep	1m4f23y	GD	£1942

Total win prize-money £1943

Going (Turf): Sf: 0-0 GS: 0-0 **Gd: 1-3** GF: 0-3 Fm: 0-1
Distance: 5f/6f: 0-0 7f-8f: 0-3 **9f-13f: 1-6** 14f+: 0-2
Track : **LH: 1-8** RH: 0-1 Tight: 0-9 Gall: 0-0
Aids: Bl: 0-0 Vi: 0-0 Tstrap: 0-0 Ckp: 0-0
Best Rating: **52** 8/09 Bath 1m5f22y good

Plating-class; stays 1m5f; acts on good ground.

Primera Vista

93(98) (72)67
3-y-o b c Haafhd-Colorvista (Shirley Heights)
L M Cumani Castle Down Racing

Placings:0654 (5616)
2009: 8^{0}GF, 8^{6}S, 10^{5}S, 9^{4}SD,

	Starts	1st	2nd	3rd	Win & Pl
Career Total (Turf)	3	0	0	0	0
Career Total (AW)	1	0	0	0	0

Going (Turf): **Sf: 0-2 GS: 0-0 Gd: 0-0 GF: 0-1 Fm: 0-0**
Distance: 5f/6f: 0-0 7f-8f: 0-2 9f-13f: 0-2 14f+: 0-0
Track : LH: 0-2 RH: 0-0 Tight: 0-1 Gall: 0-1
Aids: Bl: 0-0 Vi: 0-0 Tstrap: 0-0 Ckp: 0-0
Best Rating: **72** 9/09 Wolv 1m1f103y stand

Modest form on turf and sand.

Primo De Vida (IRE)

88(92) (65)60
2-y-o b g Trade Fair-Rampage (Pivotal)
R M Beckett Prime Of Life

Placings:032 (6874)
2009: 5^{0}G, 5^{3}G, 7^{2}SD,

	Starts	1st	2nd	3rd	Win & Pl
Career Total (Turf)	2	0	0	1	578
Career Total (AW)	1	0	1	0	1156

Going (Turf): **Sf: 0-0 GS: 0-0 Gd: 0-2 GF: 0-0 Fm: 0-0**
Distance: 5f/6f: 0-2 7f-8f: 0-1 9f-13f: 0-0 14f+: 0-0
Track : LH: 0-3 RH: 0-0 Tight: 0-0 Gall: 0-2
Aids: Bl: 0-0 Vi: 0-0 Tstrap: 0-0 Ckp: 0-0
Best Rating: **65** 10/09 Sthl 7f stand

Modest; effective over 7f; acts on Fibresand.

Primo Dilettante

101(103) (66)65
3-y-o b g Primo Valentino (IRE)-Jezadil (IRE) (Mujadil (USA))
W J Knight O J Williams

Placings:06400-301035451052 (6966)
2009: 10^{3}GF, 10^{0}SD, 9^{1}GS, 10^{0}SD, 9^{3}G, 12^{5}SD, 9^{4}GF, 9^{5}GS, 10^{1}SD, 10^{0}G, 10^{5}SS, 9^{2}G,

	Starts	1st	2nd	3rd	Win & Pl
Career Total (Turf)	10	1	1	2	4332
Career Total (AW)	7	1	0	0	2047

66	9/09	Ling	1m2f		STD	£2047
61	5/09	Brig	1m1f209y	(0-65)H	G-S	£2590

Total win prize-money £4637

Going (Turf): Sf: 0-1 **GS: 1-3** Gd: 0-3 GF: 0-3 Fm: 0-0
Distance: 5f/6f: 0-0 7f-8f: 0-4 **9f-13f: 2-13** 14f+: 0-0
Track : **LH: 2-12** RH: 0-4 **Tight: 1-6** Gall: 0-1
Aids: Bl: 0-0 Vi: 0-0 Tstrap: 0-1 Ckp: 0-1
Best Rating: **66** 9/09 Ling 1m2f stand

Moderate; stays 1m2f; acts on most ground and on Polytrack; has worn cheekpieces.

Primo Way

98 (76)**65**

8-y-o b g Primo Dominie-Waypoint (Cadeaux Genereux)

D A Nolan Miss M McFadyen-Murray

Placings:435/13630300/010230060/04010300000532/464 1604001/5302203-0004343000 **(6157)**

2009: 8^{0}G, 7^{0}GS, 8^{0}G, 10^{4}G, 9^{3}G, 9^{4}G, 9^{3}S, 9^{0}S, 10^{0}G, 9^{0}G,

	Starts	1st	2nd	3rd	Win & Pl
Career Total (Turf)	54	5	3	10	42111
Career Total (AW)	7	0	1	1	1769
50	8/07	Haml	1m65y	G-S	£2388
76	5/07	Ayr	1m1f20y (0-85)H	G-S	£5181
87	7/06	Ayr	1m (0-80)H	GD	£6477
95	5/05	Ling	7f (0-80)H	GD	£7153
75	4/04	Sthl	6f D	G-S	£3523

Total win prize-money £24724

Going (Turf): Sf: 0-6 **GS: 3-14** Gd: 2-22 GF: 0-10 Fm: 0-2
Distance: 5f/6f: 1-7 7f-8f: 2-27 9f-13f: 2-26 14f+: 0-1
Track : **LH: 3-26** RH: 1-17 **Tight: 1-26** Gall: 0-4
Aids: **Bl: 2-22** Vi: 0-1 Tstrap: 0-4 Ckp: 0-4
Best Rating: **96** 8/05 Newb 7f gd-fm

Modest; effective up to 1m1f; acts on any ground; has worn blinkers and cheekpieces.

Primrose Bankes

(89) (68)

2-y-o b f Mark Of Esteem (IRE)-Lady Bankes (IRE) (Alzao (USA))

W G M Turner T Lightbowne

Placings:650 **(5984)**

2009: 8^{6}SD, 8^{5}SD, 8^{0}SD,

	Starts	1st	2nd	3rd	Win & Pl
Career Total (Turf)	0	0	0	0	
Career Total (AW)	3	0	0	0	0

Going (Turf): **Sf: 0-0 GS: 0-0 Gd: 0-0 GF: 0-0 Fm: 0-0**
Distance: 5f/6f: 0-0 7f-8f: 0-3 9f-13f: 0-0 14f+: 0-0
Track : LH: 0-2 RH: 0-1 Tight: 0-1 Gall: 0-0
Aids: Bl: 0-0 Vi: 0-0 Tstrap: 0-0 Ckp: 0-0
Best Rating: **68** 9/09 Ling 1m stand

Princability (IRE)

103(98) (72)**76**

3-y-o b g King's Best (USA)-Harmonic Sound (IRE) (Grand Lodge (USA))

M R Channon Jon and Julia Aisbitt

Placings:363-33600460 **(6975)**

2009: 8^{3}SD, 9^{3}GF, 9^{6}GF, 11^{0}GF, 11^{0}G, 10^{4}G, 12^{6}GS, 12^{0}SD,

	Starts	1st	2nd	3rd	Win & Pl
Career Total (Turf)	9	0	0	3	2484
Career Total (AW)	2	0	0	1	722

Going (Turf): **Sf: 0-1 GS: 0-2 Gd: 0-3 GF: 0-3 Fm: 0-0**
Distance: 5f/6f: 0-0 7f-8f: 0-3 9f-13f: 0-8 14f+: 0-0
Track : LH: 0-1 RH: 0-9 Tight: 0-6 Gall: 0-0
Aids: Bl: 0-0 Vi: 0-0 Tstrap: 0-0 Ckp: 0-0
Best Rating: **76** 5/09 Sals 1m1f198y gd-fm

Fair; effective at around 1m1f; acts on easy ground.

Prince Andjo (USA)

83(88) (58)**34**

3-y-o b g Van Nistelrooy (USA)-Magic Flare (USA) (Danzatore (CAN))

I W McInnes John Allan Milburn

Placings:00-200 **(6705)**

2009: 7^{2}SD, 7^{0}GF, 10^{0}SS,

	Starts	1st	2nd	3rd	Win & Pl
Career Total (Turf)	2	0	0	0	
Career Total (AW)	3	0	1	0	705

Going (Turf): **Sf: 0-0 GS: 0-0 Gd: 0-1 GF: 0-1 Fm: 0-0**
Distance: 5f/6f: 0-0 7f-8f: 0-4 9f-13f: 0-1 14f+: 0-0
Track : LH: 0-3 RH: 0-1 Tight: 0-3 Gall: 0-0
Aids: Bl: 0-0 Vi: 0-0 Tstrap: 0-0 Ckp: 0-0
Best Rating: **58** 4/09 Wolv 7f32y stand

Moderate; effective over 7f; acts on Polytrack.

Prince Charlemagne (IRE)

(110) (74)**79**

6-y-o br g King Charlemagne (USA)-Ciubanga (IRE) (Arazi (USA))

G L Moore A Grinter

Placings:0000/3111140106/5544655000/63425200000130 00000-51114323052140 **(7785)**

2009: 9^{5}SD, 12^{1}SD, 12^{1}SD, 12^{1}SD, 10^{4}SD, 12^{3}SD, 13^{2}SD, 16^{3}SD, 10^{0}SD, 12^{5}SD, 12^{2}SD, 13^{1}SD, 12^{4}SD, 13^{0}SD,

	Starts	1st	2nd	3rd	Win & Pl
Career Total (Turf)	16	1	0	0	7067
Career Total (AW)	41	9	4	5	31836
74	11/09	Wolv	1m5f194y (0-65)H	STD	£2307
66	3/09	Kemp	1m4f (0-60)H	STD	£1942
63	2/09	Kemp	1m4f (0-60)H	STD	£2047
54	2/09	Ling	1m4f (0-50)H	STD	£1706
66	6/08	Ling	1m2f (0-60)H	STD	£2047
87	5/06	Rdcr	1m3f (0-85)H	GD	£6477
80	2/06	Ling	1m2f (0-85)H	STD	£6477
78	2/06	Ling	1m2f (0-70)H	STD	£3238
69	1/06	Ling	1m2f (0-75)H	STD	£3238
67	1/06	Ling	1m (0-75)H	STD	£3238

Total win prize-money £32722

Going (Turf): Sf: 0-4 GS: 0-2 **Gd: 1-2** GF: 0-8 Fm: 0-0
Distance: 5f/6f: 0-2 7f-8f: 1-5 **9f-13f: 8-46** 14f+: 1-4
Track : **LH: 8-39** RH: 2-13 **Tight: 8-38** Gall: 0-3
Aids: **Bl: 1-6** Vi: 0-0 Tstrap: 0-10 Ckp: 0-10
Best Rating: **87** 5/06 Rdcr 1m3f good

Modest; stays 1m6f; acts on good ground; goes on Polytrack.

Prince De Fortune

76(92) (49)**51**

3-y-o b g Lend A Hand-Fortuitious (IRE) (Polish Patriot (USA))

Mrs C A Dunnett G K Hall

Placings:00000 **(7179)**

2009: 8^{0}SD, 7^{0}GS, 7^{0}GF, 7^{0}SD, 7^{0}SD,

	Starts	1st	2nd	3rd	Win & Pl
Career Total (Turf)	2	0	0	0	
Career Total (AW)	3	0	0	0	

Going (Turf): **Sf: 0-0 GS: 0-1 Gd: 0-0 GF: 0-1 Fm: 0-0**
Distance: 5f/6f: 0-0 7f-8f: 0-4 9f-13f: 0-1 14f+: 0-0
Track : LH: 0-1 RH: 0-2 Tight: 0-1 Gall: 0-0
Aids: Bl: 0-0 Vi: 0-0 Tstrap: 0-0 Ckp: 0-0
Best Rating: **51** 7/09 Yarm 7f3y gd-sft

Prince Evelith (GER)

105 **87**

6-y-o b g Dashing Blade-Peace Time (GER) (Surumu (GER))

J J Quinn Allan Stennett

Placings:2030/01131/53204/0-4431P **(3034)**

2009: 8^{4}GF, 9^{4}GS, 7^{3}GF, 8^{1}GS, 9^{P}GS,

	Starts	1st	2nd	3rd	Win & Pl
Career Total (Turf)	20	4	2	4	28822
87	6/09	York	1m208y (0-80)H	G-S	£5828
87	9/06	Bevl	1m100y (0-75)H	G-F	£3238
77	7/06	Newc	1m (0-80)H	G-F	£6232
74	6/06	Nott	1m54y (0-70)H	G-F	£3238

Total win prize-money £18538

Going (Turf): Sf: 0-2 GS: 1-4 Gd: 0-4 **GF: 3-10** Fm: 0-0
Distance: 5f/6f: 0-0 7f-8f: 1-7 **9f-13f: 3-13** 14f+: 0-0
Track : **LH: 3-10** RH: 1-7 Tight: 0-4 **Gall: 2-2**
Aids: Bl: 0-0 Vi: 0-0 Tstrap: 0-0 Ckp: 0-0
Best Rating: **87** 6/09 York 1m208y gd-sft

Fair sort; stays 1m; acts fast ground.

Prince Fortune

93 **66**

2-y-o b g Namid-Plumeria (Revoque (IRE))

Mrs L Stubbs D M Smith

Placings:561 **(4912)**

2009: 6^{5}GF, 5^{6}G, 5^{1}G,

	Starts	1st	2nd	3rd	Win & Pl
Career Total (Turf)	3	1	0	0	2084
66	8/09	Yarm	5f43y	GD	£1942

Total win prize-money £1943

Going (Turf): Sf: 0-0 GS: 0-0 **Gd: 1-2** GF: 0-1 Fm: 0-0
Distance: **5f/6f: 1-2** 7f-8f: 0-1 9f-13f: 0-0 14f+: 0-0
Track : LH: 0-0 RH: 0-1 Tight: 0-0 Gall: 0-1
Aids: Bl: 0-0 Vi: 0-0 Tstrap: 0-0 Ckp: 0-0
Best Rating: **66** 8/09 Yarm 5f43y good

Moderate; effective over 5f; acts on good ground.

Prince Golan (IRE)

88(102) (71)**74**

5-y-o b g Golan (IRE)-Mohican Princess (Shirley Heights)

R J Price (J W Unett 10/10) R J Price

Placings:41000/66060/02466001604213-50400503510 **(7668)**

2009: 12^{5}SS, 9^{0}SD, 9^{4}SD, 11^{0}SD, 8^{0}G, 10^{5}GS, 7^{0}SD, 8^{3}SD, 9^{5}SD, 8^{1}SD, 9^{0}SD,

	Starts	1st	2nd	3rd	Win & Pl
Career Total (Turf)	20	2	1	0	12256
Career Total (AW)	15	2	1	2	7008
64	11/09	Sthl	1m (0-60)H	STD	£1648
70	12/08	Wolv	1m1f103y (0-75)H	STD	£3238
66	9/08	Leic	7f9y (0-70)H	GD	£3238
85	5/06	Ripn	6f	HVY	£4533

Total win prize-money £12658

Going (Turf): **Sf: 1-7** GS: 0-5 **Gd: 1-7** GF: 0-1 Fm: 0-0
Distance: 5f/6f: 1-5 **7f-8f: 2-10** 9f-13f: 1-19 14f+: 0-1
Track : **LH: 2-24** RH: 0-1 **Tight: 1-12** Gall: 0-1
Aids: Bl: 0-0 Vi: 0-0 Tstrap: 1-13 Ckp: 1-13
Best Rating: **94** 6/06 Asct 6f gd-fm

Modest; effective over 7f-1m2f; acts on good, on easy ground; goes on Polytrack.

Prince Maggio

69 10

3-y-o b c Prince Sabo-Pieta (IRE) (Perugino (USA))

Pat Eddery Pat Eddery Racing (Grand Lodge)

Placings:00 **(4303)**

2009: 7⁰GS, 7⁰G,

	Starts	1st	2nd	3rd	Win & Pl
Career Total (Turf)	2	0	0	0	

Going (Turf): **Sf: 0-0 GS: 0-1 Gd: 0-1 GF: 0-0 Fm: 0-0**
Distance: 5f/6f: 0-0 7f-8f: 0-2 9f-13f: 0-0 14f+: 0-0
Track : LH: 0-1 RH: 0-0 Tight: 0-1 Gall: 0-0
Aids: Bl: 0-1 Vi: 0-0 Tstrap: 0-0 Ckp: 0-0
Best Rating: **10** 7/09 Catt 7f gd-sft

Prince Namid

103 (80)79

7-y-o b g Namid-Fen Princess (IRE) (Trojan Fen)

D Nicholls T Gould

Placings:431/3023420306/01512300650/0420604304005/052655630-001000 **(7119)**

2009: 6⁰HY, 6⁰S, 5¹G, 5⁰GF, 5⁰GF, 5⁰GS,

	Starts	1st	2nd	3rd	Win & Pl
Career Total (Turf)	50	4	5	7	65382
Career Total (AW)	2	0	0	0	
78	7/09	Bevl	5f	(0-75)H	GD £3238
94	5/06	Hayd	5f	(0-105)H	HVY £10431
90	5/06	Bevl	5f	(0-85)H	G-S £7772
66	5/04	Rdcr	5f	F	SFT £2934

Total win prize-money £33375

Going (Turf): **Sf: 2-15** GS: 1-12 Gd: 1-10 GF: 0-12 Fm: 0-1
Distance: **5f/6f: 4-47** 7f-8f: 0-5 9f-13f: 0-0 14f+: 0-0
Track : LH: 0-12 RH: 0-3 Tight: 0-8 Gall: 0-0
Aids: Bl: 0-0 Vi: 0-1 Tstrap: 0-3 Ckp: 0-3
Best Rating: **100** 6/06 Epsm 6f gd-fm

Fair; seems best at 5f-6f; best with cut in the ground but handles fast; consistent; has worn a visor and cheek-pieces.

Prince Noel

95(108) (80)70

5-y-o b g Dr Fong (USA)-Baileys On Line (Shareef Dancer (USA))

N Wilson Renaissance Racing

Placings:0400/0425606255113112/0642302205-04320306 **(1530)**

2009: 7⁰SD, 8⁴SD, 8³SD, 9²SD, 8⁰SD, 8³SD, 8⁰GF, 8⁶SD,

	Starts	1st	2nd	3rd	Win & Pl
Career Total (Turf)	22	1	3	1	5989
Career Total (AW)	16	3	4	3	12201
73	11/07	Wolv	1m1f103y (0-65)H		STD £2047
64	11/07	Wolv	1m141y (0-67)H		STD £2047
55	10/07	Wolv	1m1f103y	(0-55)	STD £2047
57	10/07	Muss	1m1f		GD £2590

Total win prize-money £8735

Going (Turf): Sf: 0-3 GS: 0-5 **Gd: 1-7** GF: 0-7 Fm: 0-0
Distance: 5f/6f: 0-2 7f-8f: 0-8 **9f-13f: 4-28** 14f+: 0-0
Track : **LH: 3-27** RH: 1-9 **Tight: 4-24** Gall: 0-1
Aids: Bl: 0-2 Vi: 0-2 Tstrap: 0-3 Ckp: 0-3
Best Rating: **80** 10/08 Wolv 1m141y stand

Modest; effective at around 1m-1m1f; acts on a sound surface; also goes on Polytrack; has worn cheekpieces and blinkers; goes well at Wolverhampton.

Prince Of Dance

103 112

3-y-o b c Danehill Dancer (IRE)-Princess Ellen (Tirol)

Tom Dascombe Five Horses Ltd

Placings:111 **(7186)**

2009: 7¹GS, 8¹S, 8¹G,

	Starts	1st	2nd	3rd	Win & Pl
Career Total (Turf)	3	3	0	0	40076
112	10/09	NmkR	1m		GD £22708
106	10/09	Sals	1m	(0-105)H	SFT £11215
97	5/09	Newb	7f		G-S £6152

Total win prize-money £40076

Going (Turf): **Sf: 1-1 GS: 1-1 Gd: 1-1** GF: 0-0 Fm: 0-0
Distance: 5f/6f: 0-0 **7f-8f: 3-3** 9f-13f: 0-0 14f+: 0-0
Track : LH: 0-0 RH: 0-0 Tight: 0-0 Gall: 0-0
Aids: Bl: 0-0 Vi: 0-0 Tstrap: 0-0 Ckp: 0-0
Best Rating: **112** 10/09 NmkR 1m good

Useful prospect; effective at 7f, but will get further; acts on easy ground.

Prince Of Delphi

90(103) (78)77

6-y-o b g Royal Applause-Princess Athena (Ahonoora)

Mrs A L M King All The Kings Horses

Placings:24/2022/2242624040-0346000 **(3246)**

2009: 6⁰SD, 6³SD, 6⁴SD, 6⁶SD, 5⁰GF, 6⁰GF, 5⁰GF,

	Starts	1st	2nd	3rd	Win & Pl
Career Total (Turf)	16	0	5	0	6662
Career Total (AW)	7	0	3	1	2894

Going (Turf): **Sf: 0-1 GS: 0-0 Gd: 0-3 GF: 0-12 Fm: 0-0**
Distance: 5f/6f: 0-18 7f-8f: 0-5 9f-13f: 0-0 14f+: 0-0
Track : LH: 0-10 RH: 0-3 Tight: 0-4 Gall: 0-4
Aids: Bl: 0-1 Vi: 0-1 Tstrap: 0-11 Ckp: 0-11
Best Rating: **78** 4/08 Wolv 5f216y stand

Modest; stays 7f; acts on fast ground; goes on Polytrack.

Prince Of Dreams

92 72

2-y-o b c Sadler's Wells (USA)-Questina (FR) (Rainbow Quest (USA))

W J Knight G Roddick

Placings:2 **(7034)**

2009: 8²S,

	Starts	1st	2nd	3rd	Win & Pl
Career Total (Turf)	1	0	1	0	1445

Going (Turf): **Sf: 0-1 GS: 0-0 Gd: 0-0 GF: 0-0 Fm: 0-0**
Distance: 5f/6f: 0-0 7f-8f: 0-1 9f-13f: 0-0 14f+: 0-0
Track : LH: 0-0 RH: 0-0 Tight: 0-0 Gall: 0-0
Aids: Bl: 0-0 Vi: 0-0 Tstrap: 0-0 Ckp: 0-0
Best Rating: **72** 10/09 Newb 1m soft

Prince Of Johanne (IRE)

104(84) (42)90

3-y-o gr c Johannesburg (USA)-Paiute Princess (FR) (Darshaan)

J Noseda M Tabor, Mrs Susan Roy, M Green

Placings:0411105 **(6114)**

2009: 7⁰SD, 8⁴GF, 7¹GS, 8¹GF, 10¹GF, 10⁰GF, 10⁵GF,

	Starts	1st	2nd	3rd	Win & Pl
Career Total (Turf)	6	3	0	0	16797
Career Total (AW)	1	0	0	0	
90	8/09	Sand	1m2f7y (0-80)H		G-F £5180
84	8/09	Wind	1m67y (0-85)H		G-F £5180
71	5/09	Newb	7f		G-S £6152

Total win prize-money £16514

Going (Turf): Sf: 0-0 GS: 1-1 Gd: 0-0 **GF: 2-5** Fm: 0-0
Distance: 5f/6f: 0-0 7f-8f: 1-2 **9f-13f: 2-5** 14f+: 0-0
Track : LH: 0-2 **RH: 2-2 Tight: 1-2** Gall: 0-1
Aids: Bl: 0-0 Vi: 0-0 Tstrap: 0-0 Ckp: 0-0
Best Rating: **90** 8/09 Sand 1m2f7y gd-fm

Useful; stays 1m; acts on fast and easy ground.

Prince Of Medina

(104) (53)57

6-y-o ch g Fraam-Medina De Rioseco (Puissance)

J R Best G G Racing

Placings:000/0230/03062004612/546126000300-230526404 **(0732)**

2009: 11²SD, 13³SD, 12⁰SD, 12⁵SD, 12²SD, 16⁶SD, 11⁴SD, 12⁰SD, 16⁴SD,

	Starts	1st	2nd	3rd	Win & Pl
Career Total (Turf)	12	0	1	2	2119
Career Total (AW)	27	2	5	2	7439
49	2/08	Ling	1m4f	(0-50)H	STD £1876
50	12/07	Wolv	1m5f194y		STD £2047

Total win prize-money £3925

Going (Turf): **Sf: 0-0 GS: 0-2 Gd: 0-1 GF: 0-8 Fm: 0-1**
Distance: 5f/6f: 0-3 7f-8f: 0-0 9f-13f: 1-15 14f+: 1-21
Track : **LH: 2-18** RH: 0-17 **Tight: 2-21** Gall: 0-3
Aids: Bl: 0-0 Vi: 0-0 Tstrap: 0-0 Ckp: 0-0
Best Rating: **65** 8/06 Ling 2m stand

Moderate; stays 2m; acts on good ground and on Polytrack; has worn a tongue tie.

Prince Of Sorrento

(95) (73)

2-y-o ch c Doyen (IRE)-Princess Galadriel (Magic Ring (IRE))

J Akehurst Mrs Pam Akhurst

Placings:31 **(7700)**

2009: 6³SD, 7¹SD,

	Starts	1st	2nd	3rd	Win & Pl
Career Total (Turf)	0	0	0	0	
Career Total (AW)	2	1	0	1	3444
73	12/09	Kemp	7f		STD £2914

Total win prize-money £2914

Going (Turf): **Sf: 0-0 GS: 0-0 Gd: 0-0 GF: 0-0 Fm: 0-0**
Distance: 5f/6f: 0-1 **7f-8f: 1-1** 9f-13f: 0-0 14f+: 0-0
Track : LH: 0-1 **RH: 1-1** Tight: 0-1 Gall: 0-0
Aids: Bl: 0-0 Vi: 0-0 Tstrap: 0-0 Ckp: 0-0
Best Rating: **73** 12/09 Kemp 7f stand

Fair; stays 7f; acts on Polytrack.

Prince Of Thebes (IRE)

100(109) (89)89

8-y-o b g Desert Prince (IRE)-Persian Walk (FR) (Persian Bold)

M J Attwater Canisbay Bloodstock

Placings:031/13/20400140/0230031300/03005000040204/62060204400611032-34000366000004030 (7823)

2009: 8^{3}SD, 7^{4}SD, 8^{0}GF, 8^{0}G, 8^{0}GF, 8^{3}SD, 7^{6}GF, 8^{6}G, 7^{0}G, 8^{0}SD, 8^{0}G, 8^{0}SD, 8^{0}GF, 8^{0}GF, 8^{4}SS, 8^{0}SD, 8^{3}SD, 10^{0}SD,

	Starts	1st	2nd	3rd	Win & Pl
Career Total (Turf)	53	4	4	6	86027
Career Total (AW)	19	2	2	4	15960

83	10/08	Kemp	1m	(0-80)H	STD	£5180
78	10/08	Ling	1m	(0-75)H	STD	£2590
103	8/06	Asct	1m	(0-100)H	G-F	£19696
98	8/05	Wwck	7f26y		G-F	£5915
97	7/04	Asct	1m	C(0-90)H	G-F	£9782
83	7/03	Epsm	7f	D	G-F	£5434

Total win prize-money £48599

Going (Turf): Sf: 0-3 GS: 0-8 Gd: 0-18 **GF: 4-23** Fm: 0-1
Distance: 5f/6f: 0-1 **7f-8f: 6-59** 9f-13f: 0-12 14f+: 0-0
Track : LH: 3-20 RH: 3-30 Tight: 2-14 Gall: 2-9
Aids: Bl: 0-0 Vi: 0-3 Tstrap: 0-0 Ckp: 0-0
Best Rating: **103** 9/06 Gdwd 7f good

Fair; effective at 7f-1m; acts on fast ground; goes on Polytrack.

Prince Of Vasa (IRE)

(87) (68)

2-y-o b c Kheleyf (USA)-Suzy Street (IRE) (Dancing Dissident (USA))
Saeed Bin Suroor Godolphin

Placings:3 (5325)

2009: 6^{3}SD,

	Starts	1st	2nd	3rd	Win & Pl
Career Total (Turf)	0	0	0	0	
Career Total (AW)	1	0	0	1	685

Going (Turf): **Sf: 0-0 GS: 0-0 Gd: 0-0 GF: 0-0 Fm: 0-0**
Distance: 5f/6f: 0-1 7f-8f: 0-0 9f-13f: 0-0 14f+: 0-0
Track : LH: 0-1 RH: 0-0 Tight: 0-0 Gall: 0-0
Aids: Bl: 0-0 Vi: 0-0 Tstrap: 0-0 Ckp: 0-0
Best Rating: **68** 8/09 Sthl 6f stand

Fair; stays 6f and acts on Fibresand.

Prince Picasso

104(102) (81)**82**

6-y-o b g Lomitas-Auspicious (Shirley Heights)
R A Fahey (E McNamara 13/6) Aidan J Ryan

Placings:000/151130/0-2336 (7775)

2009: 10^{2}GF, 8^{3}GF, 11^{3}SD, 10^{6}SD,

	Starts	1st	2nd	3rd	Win & Pl
Career Total (Turf)	12	3	1	2	13890
Career Total (AW)	2	0	0	1	1120

85	7/06	Carl	1m1f61y	(0-70)H	FRM	£3238
79	7/06	Brig	1m1f209y	(0-70)H	FRM	£3886
71	5/06	Yarm	1m3y	(0-65)H	G-F	£3238

Total win prize-money £10364

Going (Turf): Sf: 0-0 GS: 0-0 Gd: 0-2 GF: 1-7 **Fm: 2-2**
Distance: 5f/6f: 0-2 7f-8f: 0-2 **9f-13f: 3-10** 14f+: 0-0
Track : LH: 1-7 RH: 1-3 Tight: 0-5 Gall: 0-0
Aids: Bl: 0-0 Vi: 0-0 Tstrap: 0-0 Ckp: 0-0
Best Rating: **87** 7/06 Folk 1m1f149y gd-fm

Fair; stays 1m2f; acts on fast ground; likes to race prominently.

Prince Pippin (IRE)

(73) (17)

3-y-o b g King Charlemagne (USA)-Staploy (Deploy)
S Curran Ian M McGready

Placings:0 (5987)

2009: 12^{0}SD,

	Starts	1st	2nd	3rd	Win & Pl
Career Total (Turf)	0	0	0	0	
Career Total (AW)	1	0	0	0	

Going (Turf): **Sf: 0-0 GS: 0-0 Gd: 0-0 GF: 0-0 Fm: 0-0**
Distance: 5f/6f: 0-0 7f-8f: 0-0 9f-13f: 0-1 14f+: 0-0
Track : LH: 0-0 RH: 0-1 Tight: 0-0 Gall: 0-0
Aids: Bl: 0-0 Vi: 0-0 Tstrap: 0-0 Ckp: 0-0
Best Rating: **17** 9/09 Kemp 1m4f stand

Prince Rhyddarch

99(79) (18)**73**

4-y-o b g Josr Algarhoud (IRE)-Nova Zembla (Young Ern)
I Semple Mr & Mrs Charles Villiers

Placings:43001531-500000 (7354)

2009: 13^{5}G, 12^{0}GS, 13^{0}S, 16^{0}GS, 17^{0}G, 12^{0}SD,

	Starts	1st	2nd	3rd	Win & Pl
Career Total (Turf)	13	2	0	2	5367
Career Total (AW)	1	0	0	0	

73	10/08	Newc	1m4f93y	(0-65)H	HVY	£1977
69	8/08	Haml	1m4f17y	(0-60)	SFT	£2388

Total win prize-money £4366

Going (Turf): **Sf: 2-4** GS: 0-5 Gd: 0-2 GF: 0-2 Fm: 0-0
Distance: 5f/6f: 0-0 7f-8f: 0-0 **9f-13f: 2-10** 14f+: 0-4
Track : LH: 1-6 RH: 1-8 Tight: 1-8 Gall: 1-3
Aids: Bl: 0-0 Vi: 0-0 Tstrap: 0-2 Ckp: 0-2
Best Rating: **73** 10/08 Newc 1m4f93y heavy

Moderate gelding; stays 1m4f; acts on soft.

Prince Rossi (IRE)

105(100) (57)**67**

5-y-o b g Royal Applause-Miss Rossi (Artaius (USA))
A E Price Business Development Consultants Limited

Placings:210060/0005220503/000060-1151100 (3800)

2009: 8^{1}SD, 8^{1}SD, 9^{5}GF, 8^{1}GF, 8^{1}GF, 8^{0}GS, 8^{0}GF,

	Starts	1st	2nd	3rd	Win & Pl
Career Total (Turf)	23	3	3	0	12570
Career Total (AW)	6	2	0	1	4242

67	5/09	Chep	1m14y	(0-70)H	G-F	£3238
60	5/09	Chep	1m14y	(0-65)H	G-F	£2266
55	2/09	Kemp	1m	(0-50)H	STD	£1942
49	1/09	Kemp	1m	(0-45)	STD	£2047
75	6/06	Ripn	6f		G-F	£3886

Total win prize-money £13381

Going (Turf): Sf: 0-5 GS: 0-3 Gd: 0-4 **GF: 3-10** Fm: 0-1
Distance: 5f/6f: 1-8 7f-8f: 2-13 9f-13f: 2-8 14f+: 0-0
Track : LH: 0-10 **RH: 2-5** Tight: 0-10 Gall: 0-0
Aids: Bl: 0-0 **Vi: 4-7** Tstrap: 0-13 Ckp: 0-13
Best Rating: **78** 6/06 Newb 6f8y good

Moderate; effective at around 1m; acts on most surfaces.

Prince Samos (IRE)

94 (85)**76**

7-y-o b g Mujadil (USA)-Sabaniya (FR) (Lashkari)
C A Mulhall Keith Sivills & Mrs Martina Mulhall

Placings:40533/11606525560/051205/40040056202/030253-6600 (4434)

2009: 8^{6}G, 11^{6}GF, 11^{0}GS, 10^{0}GF,

	Starts	1st	2nd	3rd	Win & Pl
Career Total (Turf)	40	2	5	3	34862
Career Total (AW)	3	1	0	1	3521

92	4/06	Newb	1m2f6y	(0-85)H	GD	£6477
93	4/05	Sand	1m14y	(0-100)H	G-S	£12156
71	4/05	Ling	1m		STD	£2982

Total win prize-money £21616

Going (Turf): Sf: 0-5 **GS: 1-10 Gd: 1-18** GF: 0-7 Fm: 0-0
Distance: 5f/6f: 0-5 7f-8f: 1-11 **9f-13f: 2-27** 14f+: 0-0
Track : **LH: 2-22** RH: 1-12 Tight: 1-18 Gall: 1-6
Aids: Bl: 0-1 Vi: 0-7 Tstrap: 0-0 Ckp: 0-0
Best Rating: **94** 4/06 Hayd 1m2f120y good

Fair; stays 1m2f, but effective at shorter; suited by cut in the ground on turf, also acts on Polytrack; has worn blinkers and a visor.

Prince Siegfried (FR)

117(105) (89)**118**

3-y-o b g Royal Applause-Intrum Morshaan (IRE) (Darshaan)
Saeed Bin Suroor Godolphin

Placings:1602-33112 (7188)

2009: 8^{3}SD, 10^{3}GS, 10^{1}GS, 10^{1}G, 10^{2}G,

	Starts	1st	2nd	3rd	Win & Pl
Career Total (Turf)	8	3	2	1	150609
Career Total (AW)	1	0	0	1	1156

116	9/09	Ayr	1m2f	GD	£34062
111	8/09	NmkJ	1m2f	G-S	£9969
89	7/08	Sals	6f212y	G-S	£4695

Total win prize-money £48727

Going (Turf): Sf: 0-1 **GS: 2-3** Gd: 1-3 GF: 0-1 Fm: 0-0
Distance: 5f/6f: 0-0 7f-8f: 1-5 **9f-13f: 2-4** 14f+: 0-0
Track : LH: 1-2 RH: 1-3 Tight: 0-0 **Gall: 1-1**
Aids: Bl: 0-0 Vi: 0-0 Tstrap: 0-0 Ckp: 0-0
Best Rating: **118** 10/09 NmkR 1m2f good

Smart; Group 1 placed; stays 1m2f; acts on soft ground; goes on Polytrack.

Prince Valentine

98(102) (50)**58**

8-y-o b g My Best Valentine-Affaire De Coeur (Imperial Fling (USA))
G L Moore D R Hunnisett

Placings:00/0035404000/050403432/064622212100/060640423316/23500321640-0036430 (7880)

2009: 7^{0}GF, 5^{0}F, 7^{3}F, 7^{6}F, 9^{4}G, 8^{3}SD, 7^{0}SD,

	Starts	1st	2nd	3rd	Win & Pl
Career Total (Turf)	41	4	6	4	16951
Career Total (AW)	22	0	2	5	2062

58	7/08	Brig	7f214y	(0-60)H	G-F	£2396
59	9/07	Brig	7f214y	(0-60)H	GD	£2266
59	8/06	Brig	7f214y	(0-60)H	FRM	£3238
50	6/06	Brig	7f214y		FRM	£2266

Total win prize-money £10169

Going (Turf): Sf: 0-4 GS: 0-3 Gd: 1-9 GF: 1-12 **Fm: 2-13**

Distance: 5f/6f: 0-1 **7f-8f: 4-37** 9f-13f: 0-25 14f+: 0-0
Track : **LH: 4-55** RH: 0-7 Tight: 0-16 Gall: 0-1
Aids: Bl: 0-17 Vi: 0-0 Tstrap: 4-34 Ckp: 4-34
Best Rating: **62** 9/06 Brig 7f214y gd-fm

Moderate; effective over 7f-1m4f; acts on fast ground; also goes on Polytrack; goes quite well at Brighton.

Prince Yarraman (IRE)

(93) (68)
2-y-o b c Chineur (FR)-Church Mice (IRE) (Petardia)
J A Osborne J A Osborne

Placings:5223 **(7865)**
2009: 7^{5}SD, 7^{2}SD, 8^{2}SD, 8^{3}SS,

	Starts	1st	2nd	3rd	Win & Pl
Career Total (Turf)	0	0	0	0	
Career Total (AW)	4	0	2	1	2098

Going (Turf): **Sf: 0-0 GS: 0-0 Gd: 0-0 GF: 0-0 Fm: 0-0**
Distance: 5f/6f: 0-0 7f-8f: 0-4 9f-13f: 0-0 14f+: 0-0
Track : LH: 0-2 RH: 0-2 Tight: 0-0 Gall: 0-0
Aids: Bl: 0-0 Vi: 0-0 Tstrap: 0-0 Ckp: 0-0
Best Rating: **68** 12/09 Kemp 1m stand

Modest; effective over 1m; acts on Fibresand and Polytrack.

Prince Zafonic

99(103) (76)67
6-y-o ch g Zafonic (USA)-Kite Mark (Mark Of Esteem (IRE))
C A Dwyer (O Sherwood 17/6) Michael Cohen

Placings:0/0000/002422253/**446**-55 **(5545)**
2009: 14^{5}GF, 11^{5}GF,

	Starts	1st	2nd	3rd	Win & Pl
Career Total (Turf)	16	0	4	1	6464
Career Total (AW)	3	0	0	0	553

Going (Turf): **Sf: 0-4 GS: 0-2 Gd: 0-4 GF: 0-5 Fm: 0-1**
Distance: 5f/6f: 0-0 7f-8f: 0-3 9f-13f: 0-7 14f+: 0-9
Track : LH: 0-8 RH: 0-7 Tight: 0-8 Gall: 0-4
Aids: Bl: 0-0 Vi: 0-0 Tstrap: 0-0 Ckp: 0-0
Best Rating: **83** 9/07 Asct 2m soft

Modest; stays 2m but effective at shorter; acts on any ground; often wears a tongue tie and has worn blinkers.

Princely Hero (IRE)

99(107) (89)82
5-y-o b g Royal Applause-Dalu (IRE) (Dancing Brave (USA))
C Gordon (M Botti 9/5) L Gilbert

Placings:4/2212226/62**0000136-33260** **(6059)**
2009: 8^{3}SD, 8^{3}SD, 7^{2}SD, 7^{6}GF, 10^{0}GF,

	Starts	1st	2nd	3rd	Win & Pl
Career Total (Turf)	14	1	5	0	17245
Career Total (AW)	8	1	2	3	11110
88	11/08 Wolv	1m141y (0-80)H		STD	£5828
80	8/07 Gway	1m100y		G-Y	£8170

Total win prize-money £13999

Going (Turf): **Sf: 0-2 GS: 0-0 Gd: 0-4 GF: 0-3 Fm: 0-0**
Distance: 5f/6f: 0-1 7f-8f: 0-13 **9f-13f: 2-8** 14f+: 0-0
Track : LH: 1-11 RH: 1-7 **Tight: 1-2** Gall: 0-3
Aids: **Bl: 1-9** Vi: 0-0 Tstrap: 0-0 Ckp: 0-0
Best Rating: **89** 4/09 Kemp 7f stand

Useful; stays 1m; acts on easy ground; goes on Fibresand and Polytrack.

Princelywallywogan

99(85) (25)73
7-y-o b g Princely Heir (IRE)-Dublivia (Midyan (USA))
John A Harris Mrs A E Harris

Placings:6/34**001050310/000**3121134266-0022P **(4054)**
2009: 10^{0}GF, 9^{0}GF, 9^{2}GF, 10^{2}GF, 10^{P}S,

	Starts	1st	2nd	3rd	Win & Pl
Career Total (Turf)	22	5	4	2	21525
Career Total (AW)	8	0	0	2	1650
72	5/08 Leic	1m1f218y (0-70)H		GD	£2590
64	5/08 Nott	1m2f50y (0-60)H		GD	£2388
57	4/08 Folk	1m1f149y (0-60)H		G-S	£2047
76	10/05 Pont	1m2f6y (0-70)H		G-S	£4383
68	8/05 Brig	7f214y (0-70)H		G-F	£5831

Total win prize-money £17241

Going (Turf): Sf: 0-3 **GS: 2-5 Gd: 2-6** GF: 1-8 Fm: 0-0
Distance: 5f/6f: 0-0 7f-8f: 1-8 **9f-13f: 4-22** 14f+: 0-0
Track : **LH: 3-17** RH: 2-10 **Tight: 1-12** Gall: 0-1
Aids: Bl: 0-0 Vi: 0-0 Tstrap: 0-0 Ckp: 0-0
Best Rating: **76** 10/05 Pont 1m2f6y gd-sft

Modest; stays 1m2f; acts on most ground and on Polytrack.

Princeofthedesert

51
3-y-o b g Nayef (USA)-Twilight Sonnet (Exit To Nowhere (USA))
G Woodward Mr & Mrs Bloom

Placings:0 **(4519)**
2009: 10^{0}S,

	Starts	1st	2nd	3rd	Win & Pl
Career Total (Turf)	1	0	0	0	

Going (Turf): **Sf: 0-1 GS: 0-0 Gd: 0-0 GF: 0-0 Fm: 0-0**
Distance: 5f/6f: 0-0 7f-8f: 0-0 9f-13f: 0-1 14f+: 0-0
Track : LH: 0-1 RH: 0-0 Tight: 0-0 Gall: 0-1
Aids: Bl: 0-0 Vi: 0-0 Tstrap: 0-0 Ckp: 0-0

Princess Aliuska

90(68) 53
4-y-o b f Domedriver (IRE)-Aliuska (IRE) (Fijar Tango (FR))
Mrs S Lamyman R M Jeffs & J Potter

Placings:52U0 **(5093)**
2009: 9^{5}GF, 10^{2}GF, 12^{U}G, **12^{0}SD**,

	Starts	1st	2nd	3rd	Win & Pl
Career Total (Turf)	3	0	1	0	771
Career Total (AW)	1	0	0	0	

Going (Turf): **Sf: 0-0 GS: 0-0 Gd: 0-1 GF: 0-2 Fm: 0-0**
Distance: 5f/6f: 0-0 7f-8f: 0-0 9f-13f: 0-4 14f+: 0-0
Track : LH: 0-1 RH: 0-3 Tight: 0-2 Gall: 0-1
Aids: Bl: 0-0 Vi: 0-0 Tstrap: 0-0 Ckp: 0-0
Best Rating: **53** 6/09 Rdcr 1m2f gd-fm

Princess Cagliari

(107) (74)
3-y-o b f Efisio-Queenie (Indian Ridge)
R Hannon Richard Morecombe

Placings:544-222216 **(1068)**
2009: 6^{2}SD, 6^{2}SD, 6^{2}SD, 6^{2}SD, 6^{1}SD, 6^{6}SD,

	Starts	1st	2nd	3rd	Win & Pl
Career Total (Turf)	0	0	0	0	
Career Total (AW)	9	1	4	0	6084
74	3/09 Sthl	6f	(0-70)H	STD	£2729

Total win prize-money £2730

Going (Turf): **Sf: 0-0 GS: 0-0 Gd: 0-0 GF: 0-0 Fm: 0-0**
Distance: **5f/6f: 1-8** 7f-8f: 0-1 9f-13f: 0-0 14f+: 0-0
Track : **LH: 1-3** RH: 0-6 Tight: 0-2 Gall: 0-0
Aids: Bl: 0-0 Vi: 0-0 Tstrap: 0-0 Ckp: 0-0
Best Rating: **74** 3/09 Sthl 6f stand

Modest; effective over 6f and acts on sand.

Princess Charlmane (IRE)

103(103) (56)61
6-y-o b m King Charlemagne (USA)-Bint Alreeys (Polish Precedent (USA))
C J Teague M N Emmerson

Placings:0/005/**500**35020530-**2200**00104310000 **(6553)**
2009: 6^{2}SD, 6^{2}SD, 6^{0}SD, 6^{0}SD, 5^{0}GF, 5^{0}GF, 5^{1}G, 5^{0}GF, 5^{4}S, 5^{3}G, 5^{1}GF, 5^{0}G, 6^{0}GS, 5^{0}GF, 5^{0}GF,

	Starts	1st	2nd	3rd	Win & Pl
Career Total (Turf)	21	2	1	2	5737
Career Total (AW)	9	0	2	1	1809
61	8/09 Muss	5f	(0-65)H	G-F	£2590
60	7/09 Muss	5f		GD	£1942

Total win prize-money £4533

Going (Turf): Sf: 0-3 GS: 0-1 **Gd: 1-5 GF: 1-12** Fm: 0-0
Distance: **5f/6f: 2-29** 7f-8f: 0-1 9f-13f: 0-0 14f+: 0-0
Track : LH: 0-6 RH: 0-1 Tight: 0-1 Gall: 0-0
Aids: Bl: 0-0 Vi: 0-0 Tstrap: 2-9 Ckp: 2-9
Best Rating: **61** 8/09 Muss 5f gd-fm

Very moderate; stays 6f and acts on Fibresand; has a worn tongue tie.

Princess Cocoa (IRE)

(106) (82)78
6-y-o b m Desert Sun-Daily Double (FR) (Unfuwain (USA))
R A Fahey P Ashton

Placings:00/64312212/35323**152/43142**334265-**065** **(0477)**
2009: 10^{0}SD, 9^{6}SD, 9^{5}SD,

	Starts	1st	2nd	3rd	Win & Pl
Career Total (Turf)	21	2	5	5	24931
Career Total (AW)	11	2	2	2	12009
82	2/08 Wolv	1m1f103y (0-80)H		STD	£4533
78	10/07 Wolv	1m141y (0-70)H		STD	£2968
78	7/06 Bevl	1m1f207y (0-75)H		G-F	£4533
66	6/06 Ches	1m2f75y (0-70)H		GD	£3562

Total win prize-money £15599

Going (Turf): Sf: 0-2 GS: 0-1 **Gd: 1-8 GF: 1-8** Fm: 0-2
Distance: 5f/6f: 0-0 7f-8f: 0-3 **9f-13f: 4-29** 14f+: 0-0
Track : **LH: 3-17** RH: 1-15 **Tight: 3-19** Gall: 0-2
Aids: Bl: 0-0 Vi: 0-0 Tstrap: 0-0 Ckp: 0-0
Best Rating: **82** 2/08 Wolv 1m1f103y stand

Fair; stays 1m4f, but seems better suited to shorter distances; acts on most ground; also goes on Polytrack.

Princess Emma

80(79) (44)55

2-y-o b f Fantastic Light (USA)-Rosablanca (IRE) (Sinndar (IRE))

R A Fahey The G-Guck Group

Placings:30 **(6638)**

2009: 7^{3}GF, 7^{0}SD,

	Starts	1st	2nd	3rd	Win & Pl
Career Total (Turf)	1	0	0	1	554
Career Total (AW)	1	0	0	0	

Going (Turf): **Sf: 0-0 GS: 0-0 Gd: 0-0 GF: 0-1 Fm: 0-0**
Distance: 5f/6f: 0-0 7f-8f: 0-2 9f-13f: 0-0 14f+: 0-0
Track : LH: 0-1 RH: 0-1 Tight: 0-1 Gall: 0-0
Aids: Bl: 0-0 Vi: 0-0 Tstrap: 0-0 Ckp: 0-0
Best Rating: **55** 9/09 Bevl 7f100y gd-fm

Princess Flame (GER)

102(96) (64)76

7-y-o br m Tannenkonig (IRE)-Pacora (GER) (Lagunas)

B G Powell B G Powell

Placings:003041211-**05066024265** **(7036)**

2009: 13^{0}SD, 12^{5}GS, 10^{0}S, 10^{6}G, 12^{6}GS, 10^{0}GF, 12^{2}G, 11^{4}F, 11^{2}GF, 10^{6}GF, 12^{5}S,

	Starts	1st	2nd	3rd	Win & Pl
Career Total (Turf)	19	3	3	1	12741
Career Total (AW)	1	0	0	0	
74	9/08	Pont	1m2f6y (0-75)H	G-F	£3238
76	9/08	Pont	1m2f6y (0-70)H	G-S	£3238
63	6/08	Newb	1m3f5y (0-70)H	G-F	£2590

Total win prize-money £9066

Going (Turf): Sf: 0-3 GS: 1-4 Gd: 0-4 **GF: 2-7** Fm: 0-1
Distance: 5f/6f: 0-0 7f-8f: 0-0 **9f-13f: 3-20** 14f+: 0-0
Track : **LH: 3-15** RH: 0-5 Tight: 0-5 **Gall: 1-5**
Aids: Bl: 0-0 Vi: 0-0 Tstrap: 0-0 Ckp: 0-0
Best Rating: **76** 9/08 Pont 1m2f6y gd-sft

Modest; stays 1m3f; acts on most ground; winner of a bumper and also successful over hurdles.

Princess Gee

(94) (63)49

4-y-o b f Reel Buddy (USA)-Queen G (USA) (Matty G (USA))

B J McMath C L Sheen

Placings:00/4300-000 **(2746)**

2009: 8^{0}SD, 10^{0}SD, 8^{0}SD,

	Starts	1st	2nd	3rd	Win & Pl
Career Total (Turf)	3	0	0	0	
Career Total (AW)	6	0	0	1	497

Going (Turf): **Sf: 0-1 GS: 0-1 Gd: 0-0 GF: 0-1 Fm: 0-0**
Distance: 5f/6f: 0-0 7f-8f: 0-1 9f-13f: 0-8 14f+: 0-0
Track : LH: 0-5 RH: 0-2 Tight: 0-3 Gall: 0-2
Aids: Bl: 0-0 Vi: 0-1 Tstrap: 0-0 Ckp: 0-0
Best Rating: **63** 6/08 Wolv 1m141y stand

Modest; stays 1m2f and acts on Polytrack.

Princess Janet

76(73) (18)16

3-y-o ch f Deportivo-Idolize (Polish Precedent (USA))

A B Coogan A B Coogan

Placings:00-00 **(1270)**

2009: 7^{0}SD, 8^{0}G,

	Starts	1st	2nd	3rd	Win & Pl
Career Total (Turf)	3	0	0	0	
Career Total (AW)	1	0	0	0	

Going (Turf): **Sf: 0-0 GS: 0-0 Gd: 0-2 GF: 0-1 Fm: 0-0**
Distance: 5f/6f: 0-0 7f-8f: 0-3 9f-13f: 0-1 14f+: 0-0
Track : LH: 0-1 RH: 0-0 Tight: 0-1 Gall: 0-0
Aids: Bl: 0-0 Vi: 0-0 Tstrap: 0-0 Ckp: 0-0
Best Rating: **18** 4/09 Wolv 7f32y stand

Princess Lexi (IRE)

90 54

2-y-o ch f Rock Of Gibraltar (IRE)-Etaaq (IRE) (Sadler's Wells (USA))

K A Ryan Dr Marwan Koukash

Placings:50 **(6556)**

2009: 6^{5}GF, 5^{0}G,

	Starts	1st	2nd	3rd	Win & Pl
Career Total (Turf)	2	0	0	0	0

Going (Turf): **Sf: 0-0 GS: 0-0 Gd: 0-1 GF: 0-1 Fm: 0-0**
Distance: 5f/6f: 0-2 7f-8f: 0-0 9f-13f: 0-0 14f+: 0-0
Track : LH: 0-0 RH: 0-0 Tight: 0-0 Gall: 0-0
Aids: Bl: 0-0 Vi: 0-0 Tstrap: 0-0 Ckp: 0-0
Best Rating: **54** 9/09 Hayd 6f gd-fm

Princess Lomi (IRE)

104(101) (75)75

4-y-o b f Lomitas-Athlumney Lady (Lycius (USA))

Andrew Heffernan Mrs M Heffernan

Placings:3/32210-6050**2005** **(7724)**

2009: 10^{6}SW, 10^{0}GF, 12^{5}Y, 12^{0}GF, 12^{2}SD, 12^{0}SD, 10^{0}SD, 12^{5}SD,

	Starts	1st	2nd	3rd	Win & Pl
Career Total (Turf)	8	1	2	1	4693
Career Total (AW)	6	0	1	1	2115
75	5/08	Bevl	1m4f16y (0-70)H	G-F	£2914

Total win prize-money £2914

Going (Turf): Sf: 0-1 GS: 0-1 Gd: 0-0 **GF: 1-5** Fm: 0-0
Distance: 5f/6f: 0-0 7f-8f: 0-1 **9f-13f: 1-13** 14f+: 0-0
Track : LH: 0-8 **RH: 1-5 Tight: 1-3** Gall: 0-1
Aids: Bl: 0-0 Vi: 0-0 Tstrap: 0-0 Ckp: 0-0
Best Rating: **75** 7/09 Dund 1m4f stand

Fair Lomitas filly; stays 1m4f; acts on fast ground.

Princess Mandy (IRE)

89(91) (52)48

2-y-o gr f Desert Style (IRE)-Lady Fabiola (USA) (Open Forum (USA))

K A Ryan Dr Marwan Koukash

Placings:0463 **(7584)**

2009: 5^{0}SD, 5^{4}S, 7^{6}SD, 7^{3}SF,

	Starts	1st	2nd	3rd	Win & Pl
Career Total (Turf)	1	0	0	0	0
Career Total (AW)	3	0	0	1	353

Going (Turf): **Sf: 0-1 GS: 0-0 Gd: 0-0 GF: 0-0 Fm: 0-0**
Distance: 5f/6f: 0-2 7f-8f: 0-2 9f-13f: 0-0 14f+: 0-0
Track : LH: 0-4 RH: 0-0 Tight: 0-4 Gall: 0-0
Aids: Bl: 0-0 Vi: 0-0 Tstrap: 0-0 Ckp: 0-0
Best Rating: **52** 11/09 Wolv 7f32y std-fst

Moderate; stays 7f; acts on soft ground and on Polytrack.

Princess Neenee (IRE)

66 12

2-y-o b f King's Best (USA)-Precedence (IRE) (Polish Precedent (USA))

Paul Green Terry Cummins

Placings:000 **(6245)**

2009: 7^{0}G, 8^{0}G, 6^{0}GF,

	Starts	1st	2nd	3rd	Win & Pl
Career Total (Turf)	3	0	0	0	

Going (Turf): **Sf: 0-0 GS: 0-0 Gd: 0-2 GF: 0-1 Fm: 0-0**
Distance: 5f/6f: 0-1 7f-8f: 0-2 9f-13f: 0-0 14f+: 0-0
Track : LH: 0-2 RH: 0-0 Tight: 0-2 Gall: 0-0
Aids: Bl: 0-0 Vi: 0-0 Tstrap: 0-0 Ckp: 0-0
Best Rating: **12** 8/09 Thsk 1m good

Princess Of Aeneas (IRE)

87 (48)38

6-y-o b m Beckett (IRE)-Romangoddess (IRE) (Rhoman Rule (USA))

A G Foster D W Shaw

Placings:50/5603**001**/**00**/5-00 **(3499)**

2009: 10^{0}G, 11^{0}GF,

	Starts	1st	2nd	3rd	Win & Pl
Career Total (Turf)	11	1	0	1	2529
Career Total (AW)	3	0	0	0	
50	10/06	Muss	1m4f	G-S	£2047

Total win prize-money £2048

Going (Turf): Sf: 0-2 **GS: 1-2** Gd: 0-3 GF: 0-4 Fm: 0-0
Distance: 5f/6f: 0-0 7f-8f: 0-5 **9f-13f: 1-8** 14f+: 0-1
Track : LH: 0-8 **RH: 1-6 Tight: 1-8** Gall: 0-1
Aids: Bl: 0-0 Vi: 0-0 Tstrap: 1-6 Ckp: 1-6
Best Rating: **60** 8/06 Ayr 1m2f gd-sft

Princess Pivotal

(85) (47)

4-y-o gr f Pivotal-Santa Sophia (IRE) (Linamix (FR))

G A Butler Beetle N Wedge Partnership

Placings:0 **(7067)**

2009: 7^{0}SD,

	Starts	1st	2nd	3rd	Win & Pl
Career Total (Turf)	0	0	0	0	
Career Total (AW)	1	0	0	0	

Going (Turf): **Sf: 0-0 GS: 0-0 Gd: 0-0 GF: 0-0 Fm: 0-0**
Distance: 5f/6f: 0-0 7f-8f: 0-1 9f-13f: 0-0 14f+: 0-0
Track : LH: 0-1 RH: 0-0 Tight: 0-1 Gall: 0-0
Aids: Bl: 0-0 Vi: 0-0 Tstrap: 0-0 Ckp: 0-0
Best Rating: **47** 10/09 Ling 7f stand

Princess Podge

78 42

2-y-o b f Desert Sun-Medici Princess (Medicean)

M D I Usher Champagne And Shambles

Placings:0 (2175)
2009: 6^{0}G,

	Starts	1st	2nd	3rd	Win & Pl
Career Total (Turf)	1	0	0	0	

Going (Turf): Sf: 0-0 GS: 0-0 Gd: 0-1 GF: 0-0 Fm: 0-0
Distance: 5f/6f: 0-1 7f-8f: 0-0 9f-13f: 0-0 14f+: 0-0
Track : LH: 0-0 RH: 0-0 Tight: 0-0 Gall: 0-0
Aids: Bl: 0-0 Vi: 0-0 Tstrap: 0-0 Ckp: 0-0
Best Rating: 42 5/09 Gdwd 6f good

Princess Rainbow (FR)

100(101) (68)**76**
4-y-o b m Raintrap-Chausseneige (FR) (Mad Captain)
Jennie Candlish P and Mrs G A Clarke

Placings:622-0132362 (5625)
2009: 10^{0}G, 10^{1}S, 10^{3}G, 11^{2}F, 14^{3}S, 16^{6}G, 15^{2}S,

	Starts	1st	2nd	3rd	Win & Pl
Career Total (Turf)	9	1	4	2	8103
Career Total (AW)	1	0	0	0	0

73 5/09 Hayd 1m2f95y (0-75)H SFT £3238
Total win prize-money £3238

Going (Turf): Sf: 1-5 GS: 0-0 Gd: 0-3 GF: 0-0 Fm: 0-1
Distance: 5f/6f: 0-0 7f-8f: 0-0 **9f-13f: 1-7** 14f+: 0-3
Track : **LH: 1-8** RH: 0-2 Tight: 0-3 Gall: 0-1
Aids: Bl: 0-0 Vi: 0-0 Tstrap: 0-0 Ckp: 0-0
Best Rating: 76 9/09 Catt 1m7f177y soft

Fair; stays 1m4f and acts on soft ground.

Princess Rebecca

73(87) (47)**36**
3-y-o ch f Compton Place-Sunley Stars (Sallust)
H J Collingridge Peter Webb

Placings:606-00 (2132)
2009: 7^{0}GF, 6^{0}SD,

	Starts	1st	2nd	3rd	Win & Pl
Career Total (Turf)	2	0	0	0	0
Career Total (AW)	3	0	0	0	0

Going (Turf): Sf: 0-0 GS: 0-0 Gd: 0-0 GF: 0-2 Fm: 0-0
Distance: 5f/6f: 0-4 7f-8f: 0-1 9f-13f: 0-0 14f+: 0-0
Track : LH: 0-3 RH: 0-0 Tight: 0-0 Gall: 0-1
Aids: Bl: 0-0 Vi: 0-0 Tstrap: 0-0 Ckp: 0-0
Best Rating: 47 9/08 Sthl 6f stand

Princess Rose Anne (IRE)

105(102) (74)**81**
4-y-o ch f Danehill Dancer (IRE)-Hawksleys Jill (Mujtahid (USA))
M Ramadan (J R Best 27/6) Malaz Ibrahim Abdelmagid

Placings:60051/01500-5031411003561
2009: 7^{5}SD, 7^{0}SD, 4^{3}FZ, 4^{1}FZ, 6^{4}SD, 5^{1}GF, 5^{1}G, 5^{0}G, 5^{0}GF, 5^{3}GF, 5^{5}F, 5^{6}GF, 5^{1}FT,

	Starts	1st	2nd	3rd	Win & Pl
Career Total (Turf)	14	4	0	1	23501
Career Total (AW)	9	2	0	1	12360

72 12/09 Jebl 5f (60-85)H FST £7954
81 4/09 Folk 5f (0-80)H GD £5180
69 4/09 Bath 5f161y (0-75)H G-F £2590
66 2/09 StMz 4f FZ £9412
78 6/08 Ling 6f (0-75)H STD £2331
72 10/07 Leop 7f (52-70) G-F £5836
Total win prize-money £33305

Going (Turf): Sf: 0-2 GS: 0-0 Gd: 1-2 **GF: 2-7** Fm: 0-1
Distance: **5f/6f: 4-16** 7f-8f: 1-5 9f-13f: 0-0 14f+: 0-0
Track : **LH: 3-10** RH: 0-2 Tight: 1-5 Gall: 1-2
Aids: Bl: 0-0 Vi: 0-0 Tstrap: 0-1 Ckp: 0-1
Best Rating: 81 4/09 Folk 5f good

Fair; ex-Irish; stays 7f but effective at 5f; acts on fast ground and on Polytrack.

Princess Seren

60 **2**
2-y-o b f King's Best (USA)-Gold Field (IRE) (Unfuwain (USA))
B R Millman Lucky Generals Racing

Placings:0 (3101)
2009: 6^{0}G,

	Starts	1st	2nd	3rd	Win & Pl
Career Total (Turf)	1	0	0	0	

Going (Turf): Sf: 0-0 GS: 0-0 Gd: 0-1 GF: 0-0 Fm: 0-0
Distance: 5f/6f: 0-1 7f-8f: 0-0 9f-13f: 0-0 14f+: 0-0
Track : LH: 0-0 RH: 0-0 Tight: 0-0 Gall: 0-0
Aids: Bl: 0-0 Vi: 0-0 Tstrap: 0-0 Ckp: 0-0
Best Rating: 2 6/09 Gdwd 6f good

Princess Shamal

90(87) (56)**55**
2-y-o b f Kheleyf (USA)-Gentle Dame (Kris)
J R Jenkins The Papageno Partnership

Placings:0065505056 (7772)
2009: 5^{0}GF, 6^{0}G, 5^{6}SD, 5^{5}GF, 5^{5}G, 5^{0}SD, 5^{5}SD, 6^{0}G, 6^{5}SD, 7^{6}SD,

	Starts	1st	2nd	3rd	Win & Pl
Career Total (Turf)	5	0	0	0	0
Career Total (AW)	5	0	0	0	0

Going (Turf): Sf: 0-0 GS: 0-0 Gd: 0-3 GF: 0-2 Fm: 0-0
Distance: 5f/6f: 0-8 7f-8f: 0-2 9f-13f: 0-0 14f+: 0-0
Track : LH: 0-3 RH: 0-0 Tight: 0-2 Gall: 0-1
Aids: Bl: 0-0 Vi: 0-0 Tstrap: 0-0 Ckp: 0-0
Best Rating: 56 8/09 Sthl 5f stand

Very moderate; probably stays 7f; acts on fast ground and sand.

Princess Shirl

(51)
5-y-o b m Shahrastani (USA)-Shirl (Shirley Heights)
A D Brown The All For One Partnership

Placings:0 (7504)
2009: 12^{0}SD,

	Starts	1st	2nd	3rd	Win & Pl
Career Total (Turf)	0	0	0	0	
Career Total (AW)	1	0	0	0	

Going (Turf): Sf: 0-0 GS: 0-0 Gd: 0-0 GF: 0-0 Fm: 0-0
Distance: 5f/6f: 0-0 7f-8f: 0-0 9f-13f: 0-1 14f+: 0-0
Track : LH: 0-1 RH: 0-0 Tight: 0-0 Gall: 0-0
Aids: Bl: 0-0 Vi: 0-0 Tstrap: 0-0 Ckp: 0-0

Princess Soraya

74 **43**
3-y-o ch f Compton Place-Eurolink Cafe (Grand Lodge (USA))
B G Powell (George Baker 15/10) Hughes and Stewart

Placings:0-000 (2178)
2009: 8^{0}S, 6^{0}GF, 9^{0}G,

	Starts	1st	2nd	3rd	Win & Pl
Career Total (Turf)	4	0	0	0	

Going (Turf): Sf: 0-1 GS: 0-1 Gd: 0-1 GF: 0-1 Fm: 0-0
Distance: 5f/6f: 0-1 7f-8f: 0-2 9f-13f: 0-1 14f+: 0-0
Track : LH: 0-1 RH: 0-1 Tight: 0-1 Gall: 0-0
Aids: Bl: 0-0 Vi: 0-0 Tstrap: 0-0 Ckp: 0-0
Best Rating: 43 5/09 Gdwd 1m1f192y good

Princess Taylor

110(111) (94)**103**
5-y-o ch m Singspiel (IRE)-Tapas En Bal (FR) (Mille Balles (FR))
M Botti Rothmere Racing Limited

Placings:6344/322130/21406316-523522455440 (7589)
2009: 10^{5}GF, 10^{2}G, 10^{3}G, 11^{5}G, 10^{2}GS, 12^{2}G, 14^{4}G, 12^{5}GF, 14^{5}G, 12^{4}G, 13^{4}SD, 12^{0}SD,

	Starts	1st	2nd	3rd	Win & Pl
Career Total (Turf)	23	3	6	3	69217
Career Total (AW)	7	0	0	2	4613

93 9/08 Hayd 1m2f120y (0-90)H G-F £11656
90 6/08 Thsk 1m (0-90)H FRM £9714
79 9/07 Leic 1m60y (0-75)H FRM £3238
Total win prize-money £24610

Going (Turf): Sf: 0-2 GS: 0-1 Gd: 0-10 GF: 1-7 **Fm: 2-3**
Distance: 5f/6f: 0-0 7f-8f: 1-11 **9f-13f: 2-17** 14f+: 0-2
Track : **LH: 2-13** RH: 1-8 **Tight: 1-7** Gall: 0-6
Aids: Bl: 0-0 Vi: 0-0 Tstrap: 0-1 Ckp: 0-1
Best Rating: 103 7/09 NmkJ 1m4f good

Smart; Listed placed; effective at 1m2f-1m4f; acts on fast but handles soft ground; has worn a tongue tie.

Princess Teddy (IRE)

(96) (51)**51**
6-y-o b m Sayarshan (FR)-Bajan Girl (IRE) (Pips Pride)
Edgar Byrne Joseph Sullivan

Placings:040000/2606305-00 (0513)
2009: 7^{0}SD, 8^{0}SD,

	Starts	1st	2nd	3rd	Win & Pl
Career Total (Turf)	9	0	0	1	915
Career Total (AW)	6	0	1	0	1184

Going (Turf): Sf: 0-1 GS: 0-0 Gd: 0-1 GF: 0-4 Fm: 0-2
Distance: 5f/6f: 0-1 7f-8f: 0-13 9f-13f: 0-1 14f+: 0-0
Track : LH: 0-6 RH: 0-7 Tight: 0-1 Gall: 0-0
Aids: Bl: 0-5 Vi: 0-0 Tstrap: 0-0 Ckp: 0-0
Best Rating: 51 6/08 Rosc 7f gd-fm

Princess Valerina

100(107) (89)**87**
5-y-o ch m Beat Hollow-Heart So Blue (Dilum (USA))

D Haydn Jones G J Hicks

Placings:21/5003340000/6040123-145251000046006 (7875)
2009: 5^{1}SD, 5^{4}SD, 6^{5}SD, 5^{2}SD, 5^{5}SF, 5^{1}SD, 6^{0}F, 6^{0}HY, 6^{0}GF, 5^{0}SD, 6^{0}G, 6^{4}GF, 5^{6}SD, 6^{0}SD, 6^{0}SD, 6^{6}SD,

	Starts	1st	2nd	3rd	Win & Pl
Career Total (Turf)	17	2	1	2	12669
Career Total (AW)	18	2	2	1	14777

89 4/09 Wolv 5f216y (0-80)H STD £5180
83 1/09 Wolv 5f216y (0-80)H STD £5180
76 10/08 Folk 6f (0-80)H SFT £5046
86 10/06 NmkR 6f G-S £2590
Total win prize-money £17999

Going (Turf): **Sf: 1-6 GS: 1-2** Gd: 0-3 GF: 0-5 Fm: 0-1
Distance: **5f/6f: 4-20** 7f-8f: 0-14 9f-13f: 0-1 14f+: 0-0
Track : **LH: 2-15** RH: 0-7 **Tight: 2-13** Gall: 0-2
Aids: Bl: 0-0 Vi: 0-0 Tstrap: 0-0 Ckp: 0-0
Best Rating: **89** 4/09 Wolv 5f216y stand

Fair; effective at 6f-7f; acts on most ground on turf; goes on Polytrack.

Princess Zhukova (IRE)

(89) (41)
4-y-o b f Terroir (IRE)-Miss Bussell (Sabrehill (USA))
M Wellings (R J Price 17/2) Fox And Cub Partnership

Placings:6/0-50600 (7782)
2009: 8^{5}SD, 8^{0}SD, 6^{6}SD, 5^{0}SD, 8^{0}SD,

	Starts	1st	2nd	3rd	Win & Pl
Career Total (Turf)	0	0	0	0	
Career Total (AW)	7	0	0	0	0

Going (Turf): **Sf: 0-0 GS: 0-0 Gd: 0-0 GF: 0-0 Fm: 0-0**
Distance: 5f/6f: 0-3 7f-8f: 0-2 9f-13f: 0-2 14f+: 0-0
Track : LH: 0-6 RH: 0-1 Tight: 0-4 Gall: 0-0
Aids: Bl: 0-0 Vi: 0-0 Tstrap: 0-0 Ckp: 0-0
Best Rating: **41** 2/09 Sthl 6f stand

Princess Zohra

(98) (62)
3-y-o b f Royal Applause-Desert Royalty (IRE) (Alhaarth (IRE))
E A L Dunlop Quy, Dunlop & Gordon-Watson

Placings:62-160 (2632)
2009: 7^{1}SD, 8^{6}SD, 6^{0}SD,

	Starts	1st	2nd	3rd	Win & Pl
Career Total (Turf)	0	0	0	0	
Career Total (AW)	5	1	1	0	3361

62 2/09 Wolv 7f32y STD £2590
Total win prize-money £2590

Going (Turf): **Sf: 0-0 GS: 0-0 Gd: 0-0 GF: 0-0 Fm: 0-0**
Distance: 5f/6f: 0-2 **7f-8f: 1-3** 9f-13f: 0-0 14f+: 0-0
Track : **LH: 1-5** RH: 0-0 **Tight: 1-4** Gall: 0-1
Aids: Bl: 0-0 Vi: 0-0 Tstrap: 0-0 Ckp: 0-0
Best Rating: **62** 2/09 Wolv 7f32y stand

Modest; stays 7f; acts on Polytrack.

Principal Role (USA)

101 80
2-y-o b f Empire Maker (USA)-Interim (Sadler's Wells (USA))
H R A Cecil K Abdulla

Placings:1 (6921)
2009: 8^{1}GF,

	Starts	1st	2nd	3rd	Win & Pl
Career Total (Turf)	1	1	0	0	4100

80 10/09 Yarm 1m3y G-F £4100
Total win prize-money £4100

Going (Turf): Sf: 0-0 GS: 0-0 Gd: 0-0 **GF: 1-1** Fm: 0-0
Distance: 5f/6f: 0-0 7f-8f: 0-0 **9f-13f: 1-1** 14f+: 0-0
Track : LH: 0-0 RH: 0-0 Tight: 0-0 Gall: 0-0
Aids: Bl: 0-0 Vi: 0-0 Tstrap: 0-0 Ckp: 0-0
Best Rating: **80** 10/09 Yarm 1m3y gd-fm

Very promising filly; debut winner over 1m on quick ground at two; will stay further at three; acts on quick ground.

Print (IRE)

93 68
3-y-o b c Exceed And Excel (AUS)-Hariya (IRE) (Shernazar)
M R Channon Highclere Thoroughbred Racing (Ormonde)

Placings:04-00 (2160)
2009: 6^{0}GF, 6^{0}GF,

	Starts	1st	2nd	3rd	Win & Pl
Career Total (Turf)	4	0	0	0	241

Going (Turf): **Sf: 0-0 GS: 0-1 Gd: 0-1 GF: 0-2 Fm: 0-0**
Distance: 5f/6f: 0-1 7f-8f: 0-3 9f-13f: 0-0 14f+: 0-0
Track : LH: 0-0 RH: 0-0 Tight: 0-0 Gall: 0-0
Aids: Bl: 0-0 Vi: 0-0 Tstrap: 0-0 Ckp: 0-0
Best Rating: **68** 9/08 Yarm 6f3y good

Priti Fabulous (IRE)

103(105) (87)84
4-y-o b f Invincible Spirit (IRE)-Flying Diva (Chief Singer)
A J McCabe (W J Haggas 24/7) Kevin Murphy

Placings:04015214-0400066 (7872)
2009: 8^{0}GF, 8^{4}GF, 7^{0}SD, 5^{0}SD, 5^{0}SD, 5^{6}SD, 5^{6}SD,

	Starts	1st	2nd	3rd	Win & Pl
Career Total (Turf)	7	0	1	0	2178
Career Total (AW)	8	2	0	0	7703

87 9/08 Kemp 1m (0-85)H STD £4727
79 6/08 Kemp 7f (0-70)H STD £2590
Total win prize-money £7317

Going (Turf): **Sf: 0-2 GS: 0-1 Gd: 0-1 GF: 0-3 Fm: 0-0**
Distance: 5f/6f: 0-5 **7f-8f: 2-10** 9f-13f: 0-0 14f+: 0-0
Track : LH: 0-1 **RH: 2-6** Tight: 0-0 Gall: 0-1
Aids: Bl: 0-0 Vi: 0-0 Tstrap: 0-0 Ckp: 0-0
Best Rating: **87** 9/08 Kemp 1m stand

Useful; effective at 7f-1m; acts on Polytrack and fast ground.

Private Equity (IRE)

92(105) (63)46
3-y-o b f Haafhd-Profit Alert (IRE) (Alzao (USA))
W Jarvis Mrs Susan Davis

Placings:6-64115 (7740)
2009: 8^{6}GF, 9^{4}GF, 12^{1}SD, 13^{1}SD, 12^{5}SD,

	Starts	1st	2nd	3rd	Win & Pl
Career Total (Turf)	2	0	0	0	144
Career Total (AW)	4	2	0	0	5285

60 11/09 Wolv 1m5f194y (0-70)H STD £3238
63 11/09 Kemp 1m4f (0-50)H STD £2047
Total win prize-money £5285

Going (Turf): **Sf: 0-0 GS: 0-0 Gd: 0-0 GF: 0-2 Fm: 0-0**
Distance: 5f/6f: 0-1 7f-8f: 0-0 9f-13f: 1-4 14f+: 1-1
Track : LH: 1-2 RH: 1-3 **Tight: 1-1** Gall: 0-1
Aids: Bl: 0-0 Vi: 0-0 Tstrap: 0-0 Ckp: 0-0
Best Rating: **63** 11/09 Kemp 1m4f stand

Moderate; effective at 1m4f-1m6f; acts on Polytrack.

Private Olley

84(78) (43)44
2-y-o ch c Exceed And Excel (AUS)-My Daisychain (Hector Protector (USA))
J Akehurst David S M Caplin

Placings:000 (4568)
2009: 5^{0}GF, 6^{0}SD, 6^{0}G,

	Starts	1st	2nd	3rd	Win & Pl
Career Total (Turf)	2	0	0	0	
Career Total (AW)	1	0	0	0	

Going (Turf): **Sf: 0-0 GS: 0-0 Gd: 0-1 GF: 0-1 Fm: 0-0**
Distance: 5f/6f: 0-2 7f-8f: 0-1 9f-13f: 0-0 14f+: 0-0
Track : LH: 0-1 RH: 0-0 Tight: 0-1 Gall: 0-0
Aids: Bl: 0-0 Vi: 0-0 Tstrap: 0-0 Ckp: 0-0
Best Rating: **44** 8/09 Newb 6f8y good

Private Passion (IRE)

97(97) (57)55
3-y-o b g Captain Rio-Victoria's Secret (IRE) (Law Society (USA))
Pat Eddery Pat Eddery Racing (Lomond)

Placings:600-13430002060 (5287)
2009: 6^{1}SD, 7^{3}SD, 7^{4}SD, 5^{3}SD, 7^{0}SF, 7^{0}GF, 7^{0}SD, 5^{2}GF, 5^{0}F, 6^{6}GF, 7^{0}GF,

	Starts	1st	2nd	3rd	Win & Pl
Career Total (Turf)	7	0	1	0	771
Career Total (AW)	7	1	0	2	2677

57 2/09 Kemp 6f (0-55)H STD £2047
Total win prize-money £2047

Going (Turf): **Sf: 0-0 GS: 0-0 Gd: 0-1 GF: 0-5 Fm: 0-1**
Distance: **5f/6f: 1-7** 7f-8f: 0-7 9f-13f: 0-0 14f+: 0-0
Track : LH: 0-9 **RH: 1-1** Tight: 0-5 Gall: 0-2
Aids: Bl: 0-0 Vi: 0-0 Tstrap: 0-0 Ckp: 0-0
Best Rating: **57** 3/09 Wolv 5f216y stand

Moderate; effective at 6f-7f; handles Polytrack.

Private Soldier

81(104) (47)40
6-y-o gr g Dansili-Etienne Lady (IRE) (Imperial Frontier (USA))
Tom Dascombe (N J Vaughan 18/6) Owen Promotions Limited

Placings:004133/30-604 (6800)
2009: 8^{6}GF, 8^{0}G, 8^{4}SD,

	Starts	1st	2nd	3rd	Win & Pl
Career Total (Turf)	5	0	0	0	265
Career Total (AW)	6	1	0	3	2758

59 9/07 Wolv 1m1f103y (0-45) STD £1911
Total win prize-money £1911

Going (Turf): **Sf: 0-0 GS: 0-0 Gd: 0-2 GF: 0-3 Fm: 0-0**
Distance: 5f/6f: 0-0 7f-8f: 0-4 **9f-13f: 1-7** 14f+: 0-0

Track : LH: **1-7** RH: 0-2 **Tight: 1-6** Gall: 0-0
Aids: Bl: 0-0 Vi: 0-0 Tstrap: 0-0 Ckp: 0-0
Best Rating: 59 9/07 Wolv 1m1f103y stand

Moderate; effective at around 1m-1m2f; acts on Polytrack.

Private Story (USA)

105 **92**

2-y-o b c Yes It's True (USA)-Said Privately (USA) (Private Account (USA))
R Hannon Malih L Al Basti

Placings:1204 **(7184)**
2009: 7^{1}GF, 8^{2}GF, 8^{0}G, 10^{4}G,

	Starts	1st	2nd	3rd	Win & Pl
Career Total (Turf)	**4**	**1**	**1**	**0**	**9193**

80	8/09	Sand	7f16y	G-F	£5180

Total win prize-money £5181

Going (Turf): Sf: 0-0 GS: 0-0 Gd: 0-2 **GF: 1-2** Fm: 0-0
Distance: 5f/6f: 0-0 **7f-8f: 1-3** 9f-13f: 0-1 14f+: 0-0
Track : LH: 0-0 **RH: 1-2** Tight: 0-0 Gall: 0-1
Aids: Bl: 0-0 Vi: 0-0 Tstrap: 0-0 Ckp: 0-0
Best Rating: 92 10/09 NmkR 1m2f good

Useful; stays 1m2f; acts on a sound surface.

Privy Speech (IRE)

(92) (55)

2-y-o ch f El Corredor (USA)-Privileged Speech (USA) (General Assembly (USA))
Rae Guest J M Beever, Derek J Willis & Rae Guest

Placings:3 **(7792)**
2009: 8^{3}SS,

	Starts	1st	2nd	3rd	Win & Pl
Career Total (Turf)	**0**	**0**	**0**	**0**	
Career Total (AW)	**1**	**0**	**0**	**1**	**403**

Going (Turf): Sf: 0-0 GS: 0-0 Gd: 0-0 GF: 0-0 Fm: 0-0
Distance: 5f/6f: 0-0 7f-8f: 0-1 9f-13f: 0-0 14f+: 0-0
Track : LH: 0-1 RH: 0-0 Tight: 0-0 Gall: 0-0
Aids: Bl: 0-0 Vi: 0-0 Tstrap: 0-0 Ckp: 0-0
Best Rating: 55 12/09 Sthl 1m std-slw

Third on debut; effective over 1m; acts on Fibresand.

Prix Masque (IRE)

(97) (51)**33**

5-y-o b g Iron Mask (USA)-Prima Marta (Primo Dominie)
Christian Wroe Christian Wroe

Placings:04/0/000005066-000P **(0588)**
2009: 7^{0}SD, 8^{0}SD, 8^{0}SD, 10^{P}SD,

	Starts	1st	2nd	3rd	Win & Pl
Career Total (Turf)	**3**	**0**	**0**	**0**	**192**
Career Total (AW)	**13**	**0**	**0**	**0**	**0**

Going (Turf): Sf: 0-0 GS: 0-0 Gd: 0-1 GF: 0-2 Fm: 0-0
Distance: 5f/6f: 0-8 7f-8f: 0-7 9f-13f: 0-1 14f+: 0-0
Track : LH: 0-5 RH: 0-3 Tight: 0-5 Gall: 0-0
Aids: Bl: 0-0 Vi: 0-0 Tstrap: 0-0 Ckp: 0-0
Best Rating: 55 6/06 Hayd 6f gd-fm

Prize Fighter (IRE)

79(100) (74)**72**

7-y-o b g Desert Sun-Papal (Selkirk (USA))
Miss L C Siddall (A Berry 29/4) Pennine Racing Associates

Placings:212/33000/**0**00143526/0603404-0 **(1343)**
2009: 7^{0}GF,

	Starts	1st	2nd	3rd	Win & Pl
Career Total (Turf)	**18**	**1**	**2**	**3**	**15238**
Career Total (AW)	**7**	**1**	**1**	**1**	**5163**

86	6/07	Leic	1m1f218y	(0-75)H	SFT	£4533
79	7/04	Sthl	7f	E	STD	£3454

Total win prize-money £7989

Going (Turf): Sf: 1-5 GS: 0-3 Gd: 0-2 GF: 0-7 Fm: 0-0
Distance: 5f/6f: 0-0 7f-8f: 1-8 9f-13f: 1-17 14f+: 0-0
Track : LH: 1-12 RH: 1-7 Tight: 0-6 Gall: 0-3
Aids: Bl: 1-11 Vi: 0-0 Tstrap: 0-0 Ckp: 0-0
Best Rating: 96 6/05 Sand 1m1f gd-fm

Modest; stays 1m2f; acts on most surfaces and Fibresand.

Prize Point

97 **76**

3-y-o ch g Bahamian Bounty-Golden Symbol (Wolfhound (USA))
J R Boyle (K A Ryan 26/5) M Khan X2

Placings:15-34 **(2355)**
2009: 8^{3}GF, 5^{4}GF,

	Starts	1st	2nd	3rd	Win & Pl
Career Total (Turf)	**4**	**1**	**0**	**1**	**4848**

76	6/08	Ayr	6f	G-F	£3885

Total win prize-money £3886

Going (Turf): Sf: 0-0 GS: 0-0 Gd: 0-1 **GF: 1-3** Fm: 0-0
Distance: 5f/6f: 1-3 7f-8f: 0-0 9f-13f: 0-1 14f+: 0-0
Track : LH: 0-0 RH: 0-0 Tight: 0-0 Gall: 0-0
Aids: Bl: 0-0 Vi: 0-0 Tstrap: 0-0 Ckp: 0-0
Best Rating: 76 6/08 Ayr 6f gd-fm

Fair; effective over 6f; acts on fast ground.

Prizefighting (USA)

(101) (80)**102**

2-y-o ch c Smart Strike (CAN)-Allencat (USA) (Storm Cat (USA))
J H M Gosden H R H Princess Haya Of Jordan

Placings:15 **(7207a)**
2009: 7^{1}SD, 8^{5}VS,

	Starts	1st	2nd	3rd	Win & Pl
Career Total (Turf)	**1**	**0**	**0**	**0**	**6942**
Career Total (AW)	**1**	**1**	**0**	**0**	**3886**

80	10/09	Kemp	7f	STD	£3885

Total win prize-money £3886

Going (Turf): Sf: 0-0 GS: 0-0 Gd: 0-0 GF: 0-0 Fm: 0-0
Distance: 5f/6f: 0-0 **7f-8f: 1-2** 9f-13f: 0-0 14f+: 0-0
Track : LH: 0-1 **RH: 1-1** Tight: 0-0 Gall: 0-0
Aids: Bl: 0-0 Vi: 0-0 Tstrap: 0-0 Ckp: 0-0
Best Rating: 102 11/09 StCl 1m v soft

Very impressive winner on debut; effective over 7f; acts on Polytrack.

Proclaim

109(99) (82)**99**

3-y-o b c Noverre (USA)-Pescara (IRE) (Common Grounds)
M Johnston Sheikh Hamdan Bin Mohammed Al Maktoum

Placings:6103-**6**114100030033 **(6270)**
2009: 7^{6}SD, 6^{1}GF, 6^{1}GF, 6^{4}GF, 6^{1}GF, 6^{0}G, 6^{0}GF, 6^{0}G, 7^{3}G, 6^{0}G, 6^{0}GF, 6^{3}G, 7^{3}G,

	Starts	1st	2nd	3rd	Win & Pl
Career Total (Turf)	**16**	**4**	**0**	**4**	**41921**
Career Total (AW)	**1**	**0**	**0**	**0**	**0**

99	5/09	Donc	6f	(0-95)	G-F	£12952
97	4/09	Ripn	6f	(0-95)H	G-F	£9346
90	4/09	Donc	6f	(0-90)H	G-F	£7771
73	8/08	Ches	7f2y		GD	£5180

Total win prize-money £35251

Going (Turf): Sf: 0-0 GS: 0-1 Gd: 1-8 **GF: 3-7** Fm: 0-0
Distance: 5f/6f: 3-11 7f-8f: 1-5 9f-13f: 0-1 14f+: 0-0
Track : LH: 1-2 RH: 0-2 **Tight: 1-2** Gall: 0-0
Aids: Bl: 0-3 Vi: 0-2 Tstrap: 0-0 Ckp: 0-0
Best Rating: 99 9/09 Asct 7f good

Very useful; effective over 6f-7f; acts on good and faster ground; has worn blinkers and a visor; likes to race prominently.

Professor Bollini (IRE)

(81) (52)

2-y-o b c Bertolini (USA)-Nofa's Magic (IRE) (Rainbow Quest (USA))
H J L Dunlop Be Hopeful Partnership (2)

Placings:00 **(6781)**
2009: 6^{0}SD, 7^{0}SS,

	Starts	1st	2nd	3rd	Win & Pl
Career Total (Turf)	**0**	**0**	**0**	**0**	
Career Total (AW)	**2**	**0**	**0**	**0**	

Going (Turf): Sf: 0-0 GS: 0-0 Gd: 0-0 GF: 0-0 Fm: 0-0
Distance: 5f/6f: 0-1 7f-8f: 0-1 9f-13f: 0-0 14f+: 0-0
Track : LH: 0-1 RH: 0-1 Tight: 0-1 Gall: 0-0
Aids: Bl: 0-0 Vi: 0-0 Tstrap: 0-0 Ckp: 0-0
Best Rating: 52 10/09 Ling 7f std-slw

Professor John (IRE)

99(93) (77)**81**

2-y-o b g Haafhd-Dancing Flower (IRE) (Compton Place)
M L W Bell Paddy Barrett

Placings:61036600 **(7218)**
2009: 6^{6}GF, 5^{1}GF, 7^{0}GS, 7^{3}GF, 7^{6}SD, 8^{6}GF, 7^{0}GS, 7^{0}S,

	Starts	1st	2nd	3rd	Win & Pl
Career Total (Turf)	**7**	**1**	**0**	**1**	**4124**
Career Total (AW)	**1**	**0**	**0**	**0**	**0**

81	7/09	Brig	5f213y	G-F	£2775

Total win prize-money £2776

Going (Turf): Sf: 0-1 GS: 0-2 Gd: 0-0 **GF: 1-4** Fm: 0-0
Distance: 5f/6f: 1-1 7f-8f: 0-6 9f-13f: 0-1 14f+: 0-0
Track : LH: 1-4 RH: 0-1 Tight: 0-3 Gall: 0-0
Aids: Bl: 0-0 Vi: 0-0 Tstrap: 0-0 Ckp: 0-0
Best Rating: 81 8/09 Ches 7f2y gd-fm

Professor Malone

59(94) (48)29

4-y-o ch g Ishiguru (USA)-Molly Malone (Formidable (USA))

M S Tuck G S Tuck

Placings:000500-000 (6719)

2009: 5^{0}GF, 5^{0}SD, 8^{0}SD,

	Starts	1st	2nd	3rd	Win & Pl
Career Total (Turf)	3	0	0	0	0
Career Total (AW)	6	0	0	0	

Going (Turf): Sf: 0-1 GS: 0-0 Gd: 0-0 GF: 0-2 Fm: 0-0
Distance: 5f/6f: 0-8 7f-8f: 0-1 9f-13f: 0-0 14f+: 0-0
Track : LH: 0-6 RH: 0-2 Tight: 0-4 Gall: 0-3
Aids: Bl: 0-0 Vi: 0-0 Tstrap: 0-2 Ckp: 0-2
Best Rating: 48 11/08 Kemp 6f stand

Professor Twinkle

(88) (61)70

5-y-o ch h Dr Fong (USA)-Shining High (Shirley Heights)

I W McInnes The Pinkoes Partnership

Placings:005/412506264000/0-0 (0289)

2009: 7^{0}SD,

	Starts	1st	2nd	3rd	Win & Pl
Career Total (Turf)	9	0	1	0	1228
Career Total (AW)	8	1	1	0	4219

70 2/07 Ling 1m2f (0-70)H STD £3071

Total win prize-money £3071

Going (Turf): Sf: 0-1 GS: 0-4 Gd: 0-2 GF: 0-2 Fm: 0-0
Distance: 5f/6f: 0-0 7f-8f: 0-4 9f-13f: 1-13 14f+: 0-0
Track : LH: 1-9 RH: 0-7 Tight: 1-12 Gall: 0-0
Aids: Bl: 0-1 Vi: 0-6 Tstrap: 0-0 Ckp: 0-0
Best Rating: 76 3/07 Ling 1m stand

Fair; stays 1m2f; acts on Polytrack; has worn a visor.

Proficiency

98 64

4-y-o gr f El Prado (IRE)-Talent Quest (IRE) (Rainbow Quest (USA))

T D Walford G Mett Racing

Placings:4353-06310 (4498)

2009: 9^{0}G, 10^{6}G, 10^{3}GF, 10^{1}S, 12^{0}G,

	Starts	1st	2nd	3rd	Win & Pl
Career Total (Turf)	9	1	0	3	4652

64 7/09 Pont 1m2f6y (0-70)H SFT £3238

Total win prize-money £3238

Going (Turf): Sf: 1-3 GS: 0-1 Gd: 0-4 GF: 0-1 Fm: 0-0
Distance: 5f/6f: 0-0 7f-8f: 0-1 9f-13f: 1-8 14f+: 0-0
Track : LH: 1-5 RH: 0-4 Tight: 0-2 Gall: 0-1
Aids: Bl: 1-3 Vi: 0-0 Tstrap: 0-0 Ckp: 0-0
Best Rating: 64 7/09 Pont 1m2f6y soft

Modest; stays 1m2f and acts on fast ground; has worn blinkers.

Profit's Reality (IRE)

102(106) (91)96

7-y-o br g Key Of Luck (USA)-Teacher Preacher (IRE) (Taufan (USA))

M J Attwater Roger Milner & Charles Bamford

Placings:05543130/21014600/014330350/65610000604-30631004455612 (7841)

2009: 12^{3}SD, 12^{0}SD, 11^{6}SD, 12^{3}SD, 12^{1}SD, 16^{0}SD, 12^{0}G, 11^{4}SD, 12^{4}GF, 12^{5}G, 14^{5}G, 12^{6}G, 12^{1}SD, 11^{2}SS,

	Starts	1st	2nd	3rd	Win & Pl
Career Total (Turf)	36	5	1	5	64345
Career Total (AW)	14	2	1	2	10705

83 12/09 Sthl 1m4f (0-75)H STD £2729
91 2/09 Sthl 1m4f (0-85)H STD £4731
96 7/08 NmkJ 1m4f (0-90)H SFT £9714
106 4/06 Ripn 1m1f170y SFT £7790
101 6/05 Sand 1m2f7y (0-95)H G-F £9776
90 5/05 Chep 1m14y (0-85)H G-S £6929
81 9/04 Muss 7f30y GD £4075

Total win prize-money £45746

Going (Turf): Sf: 2-7 GS: 1-9 Gd: 1-14 GF: 1-6 Fm: 0-0
Distance: 5f/6f: 0-3 7f-8f: 1-5 9f-13f: 6-40 14f+: 0-2
Track : LH: 2-20 RH: 4-22 Tight: 2-12 Gall: 1-13
Aids: Bl: 0-1 Vi: 0-0 Tstrap: 0-2 Ckp: 0-2
Best Rating: 106 4/06 Ripn 1m1f170y soft

Useful; stays 1m4f, but effective at shorter; acts on most ground and sand; has worn a tongue tie.

Profligate (IRE)

67 28

2-y-o b f Soviet Star (USA)-Profit Alert (IRE) (Alzao (USA))

W Jarvis Mrs Susan Davis

Placings:0 (7182)

2009: 7^{0}G,

	Starts	1st	2nd	3rd	Win & Pl
Career Total (Turf)	1	0	0	0	

Going (Turf): Sf: 0-0 GS: 0-0 Gd: 0-1 GF: 0-0 Fm: 0-0
Distance: 5f/6f: 0-0 7f-8f: 0-1 9f-13f: 0-0 14f+: 0-0
Track : LH: 0-0 RH: 0-0 Tight: 0-0 Gall: 0-0
Aids: Bl: 0-0 Vi: 0-0 Tstrap: 0-0 Ckp: 0-0
Best Rating: 28 10/09 NmkR 7f good

Progress (IRE)

88 65

2-y-o br f Green Desert (USA)-Mille (Dubai Millennium)

J Noseda The Honorable Earle I Mack

Placings:5 (6809)

2009: 6^{5}G,

	Starts	1st	2nd	3rd	Win & Pl
Career Total (Turf)	1	0	0	0	0

Going (Turf): Sf: 0-0 GS: 0-0 Gd: 0-1 GF: 0-0 Fm: 0-0
Distance: 5f/6f: 0-1 7f-8f: 0-0 9f-13f: 0-0 14f+: 0-0
Track : LH: 0-0 RH: 0-0 Tight: 0-0 Gall: 0-0
Aids: Bl: 0-0 Vi: 0-0 Tstrap: 0-0 Ckp: 0-0
Best Rating: 65 10/09 NmkR 6f good

Prohibit

108(111) (108)107

4-y-o b g Oasis Dream-Well Warned (Warning)

J H M Gosden K Abdulla

Placings:261/1335010-60502 (6282)

2009: 6^{6}GF, 6^{0}GF, 6^{5}GF, 6^{0}S, 6^{2}GF,

	Starts	1st	2nd	3rd	Win & Pl
Career Total (Turf)	11	2	1	2	30105
Career Total (AW)	4	1	1	0	9637

108 10/08 GrLe 6f STD £7771
94 4/08 NmkR 6f (0-100)H GD £11656
83 10/07 Nott 6f15y G-F £3886

Total win prize-money £23314

Going (Turf): Sf: 0-1 GS: 0-1 Gd: 1-3 GF: 1-5 Fm: 0-1
Distance: 5f/6f: 2-12 7f-8f: 1-3 9f-13f: 0-0 14f+: 0-0
Track : LH: 1-3 RH: 0-1 Tight: 0-2 Gall: 1-1
Aids: Bl: 0-2 Vi: 0-0 Tstrap: 0-0 Ckp: 0-0
Best Rating: 108 10/08 GrLe 6f stand

Very useful; best at 6f; acts on good and faster ground; goes on Polytrack, but handles cut; has worn blinkers.

Prohibition (IRE)

(91) (66)82

3-y-o b c Danehill Dancer (IRE)-Crumpetsfortea (IRE) (Henbit (USA))

W J Haggas Ms Nicola Mahoney

Placings:041-0 (7620)

2009: 9^{0}SD,

	Starts	1st	2nd	3rd	Win & Pl
Career Total (Turf)	3	1	0	0	3599
Career Total (AW)	1	0	0	0	

82 11/08 Nott 1m75y HVY £3238

Total win prize-money £3238

Going (Turf): Sf: 1-1 GS: 0-0 Gd: 0-1 GF: 0-1 Fm: 0-0
Distance: 5f/6f: 0-0 7f-8f: 0-2 9f-13f: 1-2 14f+: 0-0
Track : LH: 1-2 RH: 0-0 Tight: 0-1 Gall: 0-0
Aids: Bl: 0-0 Vi: 0-0 Tstrap: 0-0 Ckp: 0-0
Best Rating: 82 11/08 Nott 1m75y heavy

Useful; effective over 1m; goes well on testing ground.

Prom

72 40

3-y-o b f Lujain (USA)-Ball Gown (Jalmood (USA))

M Brittain Mel Brittain

Placings:000-0 (3685)

2009: 9^{0}G,

	Starts	1st	2nd	3rd	Win & Pl
Career Total (Turf)	4	0	0	0	

Going (Turf): Sf: 0-0 GS: 0-2 Gd: 0-2 GF: 0-0 Fm: 0-0
Distance: 5f/6f: 0-0 7f-8f: 0-3 9f-13f: 0-1 14f+: 0-0
Track : LH: 0-1 RH: 0-1 Tight: 0-2 Gall: 0-0
Aids: Bl: 0-0 Vi: 0-0 Tstrap: 0-0 Ckp: 0-0
Best Rating: 40 7/08 Nott 6f15y good

Promise Maker (USA)

100(95) (48)71

4-y-o b g Empire Maker (USA)-Sunday Bazaar (USA) (Nureyev (USA))

T D Walford Walford, Hulme & Howarth

Placings:0000-10220215 (6021)

2009: 12^{1}GF, 12^{0}GS, 11^{2}GF, 11^{2}S, 12^{0}G, 15^{2}GS, 15^{1}S, 17^{5}GF,

	Starts	1st	2nd	3rd	Win & Pl
Career Total (Turf)	11	2	3	0	8246
Career Total (AW)	1	0	0	0	

70 9/09 Catt 1m7f177y (0-70)H SFT £3238
60 6/09 Ripn 1m4f10y (0-60)H G-F £2590

Total win prize-money £5828

Going (Turf): Sf: 1-2 GS: 0-3 Gd: 0-3 GF: 1-3 Fm: 0-0
Distance: 5f/6f: 0-0 7f-8f: 0-2 9f-13f: 1-7 14f+: 1-3
Track : LH: 1-8 RH: 1-3 Tight: 2-7 Gall: 0-0
Aids: Bl: 0-0 Vi: 0-0 Tstrap: 0-0 Ckp: 0-0

Best Rating: 71 8/09 Catt 1m7f177y gd-sft

Modest; stays 1m4f; handles quick ground.

Promised Gold

38(86) (31)36

4-y-o ch g Bahamian Bounty-Delphic Way (Warning)

J A Geake Miss B Swire

Placings:000/000-0 (2127)

2009: 17^{0}GS,

	Starts	1st	2nd	3rd	Win & Pl
Career Total (Turf)	6	0	0	0	
Career Total (AW)	1	0	0	0	

Going (Turf): **Sf: 0-1 GS: 0-3 Gd: 0-1 GF: 0-1 Fm: 0-0**
Distance: 5f/6f: 0-0 7f-8f: 0-1 9f-13f: 0-5 14f+: 0-1
Track : LH: 0-5 RH: 0-1 Tight: 0-3 Gall: 0-0
Aids: Bl: 0-0 Vi: 0-0 Tstrap: 0-1 Ckp: 0-1
Best Rating: 56 10/07 Bath 1m5y good

Prompter

101 108

2-y-o b c Motivator-Penny Cross (Efisio)

M L W Bell The Royal Ascot Racing Club

Placings:2162 (6664)

2009: 7^{2}G, 7^{1}G, 7^{6}GF, 8^{2}GS,

	Starts	1st	2nd	3rd	Win & Pl
Career Total (Turf)	4	1	2	0	18543

85	8/09	Ches	7f2y	GD	£5180

Total win prize-money £5181

Going (Turf): Sf: 0-0 GS: 0-1 **Gd: 1-2** GF: 0-1 Fm: 0-0
Distance: 5f/6f: 0-0 **7f-8f: 1-4** 9f-13f: 0-0 14f+: 0-0
Track : **LH: 1-1** RH: 0-2 **Tight: 1-1** Gall: 0-1
Aids: Bl: 0-0 Vi: 0-0 Tstrap: 0-0 Ckp: 0-0
Best Rating: 108 10/09 Asct 1m gd-sft

Smart; Group placed; stays 1m; acts on good and easy ground.

Proper Littlemadam

91(93) (58)68

2-y-o b f Statue Of Liberty (USA)-Aly McBe (USA) (Alydeed (CAN))

M Botti Dachel Stud

Placings:440**U60** (6721)

2009: 6^{4}GS, 6^{4}G, 7^{0}G, 8^{U}SD, 7^{6}SD, 8^{0}SD,

	Starts	1st	2nd	3rd	Win & Pl
Career Total (Turf)	3	0	0	0	625
Career Total (AW)	3	0	0	0	0

Going (Turf): **Sf: 0-0 GS: 0-1 Gd: 0-2 GF: 0-0 Fm: 0-0**
Distance: 5f/6f: 0-2 7f-8f: 0-4 9f-13f: 0-0 14f+: 0-0
Track : LH: 0-0 RH: 0-3 Tight: 0-0 Gall: 0-0
Aids: Bl: 0-0 Vi: 0-0 Tstrap: 0-0 Ckp: 0-0
Best Rating: 68 6/09 Donc 6f gd-sft

Ability in maidens; stays 6f; acts on a sound surface.

Proponent (IRE)

107 104

5-y-o b g Peintre Celebre (USA)-Pont Audemer (USA) (Chief's Crown (USA))

R Charlton B E Nielsen

Placings:11/5046/416050-00432061 (6429)

2009: 8^{0}S, 9^{0}GF, 8^{4}G, 10^{3}G, 10^{2}G, 10^{0}GF, 9^{6}GF, 8^{1}GF,

	Starts	1st	2nd	3rd	Win & Pl
Career Total (Turf)	20	4	1	1	69865

104	10/09	NmkR	1m	(0-95)H	G-F	£8723
104	5/08	NmkR	1m1f	H	G-F	£31155
91	10/06	NmkR	1m		G-S	£8101
84	9/06	Newb	7f		GD	£5829

Total win prize-money £53809

Going (Turf): Sf: 0-2 GS: 1-3 Gd: 1-8 **GF: 2-7** Fm: 0-0
Distance: 5f/6f: 0-0 **7f-8f: 3-6** 9f-13f: 1-14 14f+: 0-0
Track : LH: 0-4 RH: 0-9 Tight: 0-3 Gall: 0-6
Aids: Bl: 0-0 Vi: 0-0 Tstrap: 0-0 Ckp: 0-0
Best Rating: 104 10/09 NmkR 1m gd-fm

Very useful; suited by 1m-1m2f; acts on most ground; has worn a tongue tie.

Prospect Court

86(75) (37)69

7-y-o ch g Pivotal-Scierpan (USA) (Sharpen Up)

A C Whillans Mrs L M Whillans

Placings:0301000/0000**056**/003215001/00521111004/0006-000000 (5729)

2009: 6^{0}GF, 7^{0}G, 5^{0}S, 6^{0}G, 5^{0}HY, 6^{0}GS,

	Starts	1st	2nd	3rd	Win & Pl
Career Total (Turf)	40	7	2	2	39704
Career Total (AW)	5	0	0	0	0

83	7/07	York	5f89y	(0-80)H	HVY	£6477
78	7/07	York	6f	(0-95)H	HVY	£9715
80	7/07	Bevl	5f	(0-65)H	HVY	£3238
78	6/07	Newc	6f	(0-75)H	HVY	£3886
63	9/06	Newc	6f	(0-55)H	SFT	£3238
60	7/06	Newc	6f	(0-60)H	G-F	£2590
78	7/04	Pont	6f	D	G-F	£7241

Total win prize-money £36389

Going (Turf): **Sf: 5-10** GS: 0-4 Gd: 0-13 GF: 2-11Fm: 0-1
Distance: **5f/6f: 7-34** 7f-8f: 0-11 9f-13f: 0-0 14f+: 0-0
Track : **LH: 1-8** RH: 0-5 Tight: 0-6 Gall: 0-1
Aids: Bl: 0-2 Vi: 0-0 Tstrap: 0-0 Ckp: 0-0
Best Rating: 83 7/07 York 5f89y heavy

Fair; effective over 5f-7f; acts on any ground, but well suited by soft.

Protaras (USA)

88 74

2-y-o b/br c Lemon Drop Kid (USA)-Seven Moons (JPN) (Sunday Silence (USA))

H R A Cecil Niarchos Family

Placings:02 (6759)

2009: 8^{0}GF, 8^{2}G,

	Starts	1st	2nd	3rd	Win & Pl
Career Total (Turf)	2	0	1	0	1542

Going (Turf): **Sf: 0-0 GS: 0-0 Gd: 0-1 GF: 0-1 Fm: 0-0**
Distance: 5f/6f: 0-0 7f-8f: 0-1 9f-13f: 0-1 14f+: 0-0
Track : LH: 0-0 RH: 0-1 Tight: 0-0 Gall: 0-0
Aids: Bl: 0-0 Vi: 0-0 Tstrap: 0-0 Ckp: 0-0
Best Rating: 74 10/09 Leic 1m60y good

Fair; stays 1m; acts on good ground.

Protector (SAF)

103 (94)98

8-y-o b g Kilconnel (USA)-Mufski (SAF) (Al Mufti (USA))

A G Foster Joshua Snellings

Placings:21121/52250/340100**06**/100301200/0006040-00000 (7292)

2009: 6^{0}G, 7^{0}GS, 6^{0}G, 7^{0}GS, 6^{0}S,

	Starts	1st	2nd	3rd	Win & Pl
Career Total (Turf)	36	6	5	1	61661
Career Total (AW)	3	0	0	1	4868

108	6/07	Newc	6f	(0-100)H	HVY	£18696
93	1/07	Ndas	6f110y	(85-94)H	GD	£6675
91	7/06	Vich	5f		G-S	£6897
	11/04	Clai	5f		GD	£2405
	8/04	Clai	6f		GD	£2092
	7/04	Scot	5f		GD	£2092

Total win prize-money £38859

Going (Turf): Sf: 1-5 GS: 1-8 **Gd: 4-19** GF: 0-2 Fm: 0-1
Distance: **5f/6f: 5-24** 7f-8f: 1-13 9f-13f: 0-1 14f+: 0-0
Track : LH: 0-5 RH: 0-1 Tight: 0-0 Gall: 0-5
Aids: Bl: 0-1 Vi: 0-1 Tstrap: 0-1 Ckp: 0-1
Best Rating: 109 7/07 Haml 6f5y gd-sft

Very useful; formerly trained in Scandinavia and South Africa; effective from 5f-7f; acts on good and softer ground and on sand; has worn various headgear and a tongue tie.

Protiva

86(99) (62)62

3-y-o ch f Deportivo-Prowse (USA) (King Of Kings (IRE))

Karen George (A P Jarvis 16/6) Adrian Parr & Karen George

Placings:0600020400-530050 (5063)

2009: 7^{5}SD, 8^{3}SD, 10^{0}SD, 9^{0}G, 7^{5}S, 8^{0}GF,

	Starts	1st	2nd	3rd	Win & Pl
Career Total (Turf)	7	0	0	0	0
Career Total (AW)	9	0	1	1	1073

Going (Turf): **Sf: 0-1 GS: 0-2 Gd: 0-2 GF: 0-2 Fm: 0-0**
Distance: 5f/6f: 0-1 7f-8f: 0-10 9f-13f: 0-5 14f+: 0-0
Track : LH: 0-6 RH: 0-5 Tight: 0-6 Gall: 0-0
Aids: Bl: 0-0 Vi: 0-5 Tstrap: 0-0 Ckp: 0-0
Best Rating: 62 10/08 Kemp 1m stand

Modest; effective over 1m; acts on Polytrack.

Proud Junior (USA)

91 45

3-y-o b c Proud Citizen (USA)-Endless Reward (USA) (End Sweep (USA))

S A Callaghan Roldvale Limited

Placings:00640 (3985)

2009: 8^{0}G, 7^{0}GF, 6^{6}GF, 7^{4}F, 10^{0}GF,

	Starts	1st	2nd	3rd	Win & Pl
Career Total (Turf)	5	0	0	0	144

Going (Turf): **Sf: 0-0 GS: 0-0 Gd: 0-1 GF: 0-3 Fm: 0-1**
Distance: 5f/6f: 0-1 7f-8f: 0-2 9f-13f: 0-2 14f+: 0-0
Track : LH: 0-2 RH: 0-0 Tight: 0-1 Gall: 0-0
Aids: Bl: 0-0 Vi: 0-0 Tstrap: 0-0 Ckp: 0-0
Best Rating: 45 4/09 Yarm 1m3y good

Proud Killer

78(98) (69)67

6-y-o b g Killer Instinct-Thewaari (USA) (Eskimo (USA))

J R Jenkins Mrs Wendy Jenkins

Placings:00/3100/0020**104**/**4042650053-0** (4183)

2009: 6^{0}GS,

	Starts	1st	2nd	3rd	Win & Pl
Career Total (Turf)	18	2	2	2	8151
Career Total (AW)	6	0	0	0	351

72 10/07 Folk 6f (0-65)H HVY £2388
73 5/06 Chep 6f16y SFT £3238
Total win prize-money £5628

Going (Turf): **Sf: 2-8** GS: 0-6 Gd: 0-2 GF: 0-2 Fm: 0-0
Distance: 5f/6f: 1-12 7f-8f: 1-12 9f-13f: 0-0 14f+: 0-0
Track : LH: 0-4 RH: 0-2 Tight: 0-0 Gall: 0-3
Aids: Bl: 0-1 Vi: 0-4 Tstrap: 0-0 Ckp: 0-0
Best Rating: **73** 5/06 Chep 6f16y soft

Moderate; suited by 6f; acts on soft ground.

Proud Linus (USA)

(91) (37)**92**
4-y-o b g Proud Citizen (USA)-Radcliffe Yard (USA) (Boston Harbor (USA))
J Ryan We-Know Partnership

Placings:40/40-00 (7595)
2009: 7^{0}SD, 5^{0}SD,

	Starts	1st	2nd	3rd	Win & Pl
Career Total (Turf)	4	0	0	0	1872
Career Total (AW)	2	0	0	0	

Going (Turf): **Sf: 0-0 GS: 0-0 Gd: 0-2 GF: 0-2 Fm: 0-0**
Distance: 5f/6f: 0-4 7f-8f: 0-2 9f-13f: 0-0 14f+: 0-0
Track : LH: 0-2 RH: 0-0 Tight: 0-2 Gall: 0-0
Aids: Bl: 0-0 Vi: 0-0 Tstrap: 0-0 Ckp: 0-0
Best Rating: **92** 8/07 York 5f good

Proud Times (USA)

99 77
3-y-o b g Proud Citizen (USA)-Laura's Pistolette (USA) (Big Pistol (USA))
G A Swinbank J Townson

Placings:2-22625 (4280)
2009: 7^{2}GF, 8^{2}HY, 8^{6}G, 11^{2}GF, 12^{5}G,

	Starts	1st	2nd	3rd	Win & Pl
Career Total (Turf)	6	0	4	0	3565

Going (Turf): **Sf: 0-1 GS: 0-1 Gd: 0-2 GF: 0-2 Fm: 0-0**
Distance: 5f/6f: 0-1 7f-8f: 0-2 9f-13f: 0-3 14f+: 0-0
Track : LH: 0-3 RH: 0-1 Tight: 0-3 Gall: 0-0
Aids: Bl: 0-0 Vi: 0-0 Tstrap: 0-0 Ckp: 0-0
Best Rating: **77** 5/09 Hayd 1m30y heavy

Fair; stays 1m4f; best with cut.

Proviso

116 (114)**112**
4-y-o b f Dansili-Binche (USA) (Woodman (USA))
Robert Frankel (A Fabre 6/9) Juddmonte Farms

Placings:112/3343310-1503124 (7286a)
2009: 8^{1}GS, 9^{5}S, 8^{0}GF, 8^{3}S, 7^{1}GS, 9^{2}FT, 9^{4}FT,

	Starts	1st	2nd	3rd	Win & Pl
Career Total (Turf)	15	5	1	5	271928
Career Total (AW)	2	0	1	0	152777

112 9/09 Lonc 7f G-S £38835
102 4/09 Lonc 1m G-S £16019
103 9/08 Bord 1m1f110y VS £20220
113 8/07 Deau 7f GD £27027
92 7/07 Deau 7f SFT £7095
Total win prize-money £109197

Going (Turf): Sf: 1-6 **GS: 2-5** Gd: 1-2 GF: 0-1 Fm: 0-0
Distance: 5f/6f: 0-0 **7f-8f: 4-8** 9f-13f: 1-9 14f+: 0-0
Track : LH: 0-1 **RH: 4-12** Tight: 0-0 Gall: 0-1
Aids: Bl: 0-0 Vi: 0-0 Tstrap: 0-0 Ckp: 0-0
Best Rating: **114** 10/09 Keen 1m1f fast

Group-class filly; French trained; effective from 1m-1m2f; acts on good and softer ground.

Provost

(105) (74)**85**
5-y-o ch g Danehill Dancer (IRE)-Dixielake (IRE) (Lake Coniston (IRE))
M W Easterby A G Black

Placings:5/1/000000031043-130005 (7855)
2009: 8^{1}SD, 11^{3}SD, 8^{0}SD, 8^{0}SD, 7^{0}SD, 8^{5}SS,

	Starts	1st	2nd	3rd	Win & Pl
Career Total (Turf)	11	2	0	1	5932
Career Total (AW)	9	1	0	2	3708

74 3/09 Sthl 1m (0-60)H STD £3070
66 10/08 Ayr 7f50y (0-60)H HVY £2729
85 4/07 Yarm 1m3y G-F £2849
Total win prize-money £8651

Going (Turf): **Sf: 1-2** GS: 0-3 Gd: 0-3 **GF: 1-3** Fm: 0-0
Distance: 5f/6f: 0-0 **7f-8f: 2-14** 9f-13f: 1-6 14f+: 0-0
Track : **LH: 2-16** RH: 0-1 Tight: 0-5 Gall: 0-1
Aids: Bl: 0-0 Vi: 0-0 Tstrap: 0-0 Ckp: 0-0
Best Rating: **85** 4/07 Yarm 1m3y gd-fm

Modest; formerly useful; effective at around 7f-1m; acts on fast ground and Fibresand.

Prowl

94 55
3-y-o b f One Cool Cat (USA)-Go Supersonic (Zafonic (USA))
E A L Dunlop Highclere Thoroughbred Racing (St Simon)

Placings:30-56 (5717)
2009: 6^{5}G, 5^{6}G,

	Starts	1st	2nd	3rd	Win & Pl
Career Total (Turf)	4	0	0	1	674

Going (Turf): **Sf: 0-0 GS: 0-0 Gd: 0-3 GF: 0-1 Fm: 0-0**
Distance: 5f/6f: 0-2 7f-8f: 0-2 9f-13f: 0-0 14f+: 0-0
Track : LH: 0-1 RH: 0-0 Tight: 0-0 Gall: 0-1
Aids: Bl: 0-0 Vi: 0-0 Tstrap: 0-0 Ckp: 0-0
Best Rating: **76** 5/08 Leic 5f2y gd-fm

Fair; stays 6f plus; acts on a sound surface.

Pseudonym (IRE)

107(105) (73)**72**
7-y-o ch g Daylami (IRE)-Stage Struck (IRE) (Sadler's Wells (USA))
M F Harris (John Allen 12/6) Mrs D J Brown

Placings:60403/0/61240-2361165642P (5903)
2009: 16^{2}SD, 16^{3}SD, 16^{6}GF, 14^{1}GF, 16^{1}GF, 16^{6}G, 16^{5}G, 15^{6}GF, 14^{4}G, 14^{2}G, 17^{P}F,

	Starts	1st	2nd	3rd	Win & Pl
Career Total (Turf)	15	3	1	0	21221
Career Total (AW)	7	0	2	2	2356

72 7/09 Bevl 2m35y (0-85)H G-F £12952
69 7/09 Wwck 1m6f213y (0-70)H G-F £3238
72 9/08 Bath 2m1f34y (0-75)H G-F £3238
Total win prize-money £19428

Going (Turf): Sf: 0-0 GS: 0-2 Gd: 0-5 **GF: 3-7** Fm: 0-1
Distance: 5f/6f: 0-0 7f-8f: 0-0 9f-13f: 0-5 **14f+: 3-17**
Track : **LH: 2-17** RH: 1-4 **Tight: 2-14** Gall: 0-2
Aids: Bl: 0-0 Vi: 0-2 Tstrap: 0-0 Ckp: 0-0
Best Rating: **73** 11/08 Wolv 2m119y stand

Modest; stays 2m; acts on a sound surface and on Polytrack; has worn tongue tie and a visor.

Psychic Ability (USA)

98(89) (70)**85**
2-y-o b c Kingmambo (USA)-Speed Of Thought (USA) (Broad Brush (USA))
Saeed Bin Suroor Godolphin

Placings:61 (7121)
2009: 8^{6}SD, 8^{1}GF,

	Starts	1st	2nd	3rd	Win & Pl
Career Total (Turf)	1	1	0	0	3886
Career Total (AW)	1	0	0	0	0

85 10/09 Nott 1m75y G-F £3885
Total win prize-money £3886

Going (Turf): Sf: 0-0 GS: 0-0 Gd: 0-0 **GF: 1-1** Fm: 0-0
Distance: 5f/6f: 0-0 7f-8f: 0-0 **9f-13f: 1-2** 14f+: 0-0
Track : **LH: 1-2** RH: 0-0 Tight: 0-1 Gall: 0-0
Aids: Bl: 0-0 Vi: 0-0 Tstrap: 1-1 Ckp: 1-1
Best Rating: **85** 10/09 Nott 1m75y gd-fm

Useful; effective over 1m; acts on good ground.

Psychopathicsandra (IRE)

75 35
2-y-o ch f Reel Buddy (USA)-Waltzing Star (IRE) (Danehill (USA))
A Berry Alan Berry

Placings:05040 (7079)
2009: 5^{0}GF, 7^{5}GF, 5^{0}GF, 5^{4}GF, 5^{0}S,

	Starts	1st	2nd	3rd	Win & Pl
Career Total (Turf)	5	0	0	0	433

Going (Turf): **Sf: 0-1 GS: 0-0 Gd: 0-0 GF: 0-4 Fm: 0-0**
Distance: 5f/6f: 0-4 7f-8f: 0-1 9f-13f: 0-0 14f+: 0-0
Track : LH: 0-5 RH: 0-0 Tight: 0-4 Gall: 0-0
Aids: Bl: 0-0 Vi: 0-0 Tstrap: 0-0 Ckp: 0-0
Best Rating: **35** 7/09 Ches 5f16y gd-fm

Ptolomeos

79 (57)**65**
6-y-o b g Kayf Tara-Lucy Tufty (Vin St Benet)
Thomas McLaughlin Ace Partnership

Placings:01000-06 (3447)
2009: 10^{0}SD, 12^{6}GF,

	Starts	1st	2nd	3rd	Win & Pl
Career Total (Turf)	5	1	0	0	4319
Career Total (AW)	2	0	0	0	

65 7/08 Rosc 1m2f Y-S £4318
Total win prize-money £4319

Going (Turf): **Sf: 0-0 GS: 0-0 Gd: 0-2 GF: 0-1 Fm: 0-0**
Distance: 5f/6f: 0-0 7f-8f: 0-1 **9f-13f: 1-6** 14f+: 0-0
Track : LH: 0-3 **RH: 1-4** Tight: 0-1 Gall: 0-0
Aids: Bl: 0-0 Vi: 0-0 Tstrap: 0-0 Ckp: 0-0
Best Rating: **65** 7/08 Rosc 1m2f yld-sft

Public Image

83 **29**

3-y-o b f Bahamian Bounty-Shouting The Odds (IRE) (Victory Note (USA))

Jamie Poulton Oceana racing

Placings:00 **(4786)**

2009: 6^{0}GF, 6^{0}G,

	Starts	1st	2nd	3rd	Win & Pl
Career Total (Turf)	2	0	0	0	

Going (Turf): Sf: 0-0 GS: 0-0 Gd: 0-1 GF: 0-1 Fm: 0-0
Distance: 5f/6f: 0-1 7f-8f: 0-1 9f-13f: 0-0 14f+: 0-0
Track : LH: 0-0 RH: 0-0 Tight: 0-0 Gall: 0-0
Aids: Bl: 0-0 Vi: 0-0 Tstrap: 0-0 Ckp: 0-0
Best Rating: 29 6/09 Sals 6f212y gd-fm

Public Service (IRE)

86(89) (74)**72**

2-y-o ch g Danehill Dancer (IRE)-Sintra (IRE) (Kris)

B J Meehan The Honorable Earle I Mack

Placings:000206 **(6774)**

2009: 6^{0}GF, 6^{0}GF, 6^{0}S, 7^{2}GF, 7^{0}SD, 6^{6}SD,

	Starts	1st	2nd	3rd	Win & Pl
Career Total (Turf)	4	0	1	0	964
Career Total (AW)	2	0	0	0	0

Going (Turf): Sf: 0-1 GS: 0-0 Gd: 0-0 GF: 0-3 Fm: 0-0
Distance: 5f/6f: 0-4 7f-8f: 0-2 9f-13f: 0-0 14f+: 0-0
Track : LH: 0-1 RH: 0-1 Tight: 0-1 Gall: 0-0
Aids: Bl: 0-0 Vi: 0-0 Tstrap: 0-0 Ckp: 0-0
Best Rating: 74 10/09 Kemp 6f stand

Fair; stays 7f and acts on fast ground.

Puff (IRE)

103(95) (80)**106**

2-y-o b f Camacho-Kelsey Rose (Most Welcome)

R M Beckett Mrs David Aykroyd

Placings:14242 **(7147)**

2009: 6^{1}SD, 6^{4}GF, 5^{2}G, 6^{4}GF, 6^{2}G,

	Starts	1st	2nd	3rd	Win & Pl
Career Total (Turf)	4	0	2	0	28487
Career Total (AW)	1	1	0	0	3562
80	7/09 Ling	6f		STD	£3561

Total win prize-money £3562

Going (Turf): Sf: 0-0 GS: 0-0 Gd: 0-2 GF: 0-2 Fm: 0-0
Distance: 5f/6f: 1-5 7f-8f: 0-0 9f-13f: 0-0 14f+: 0-0
Track : LH: 1-1 RH: 0-0 Tight: 1-1 Gall: 0-0
Aids: Bl: 0-0 Vi: 0-0 Tstrap: 0-0 Ckp: 0-0
Best Rating: 106 10/09 NmkR 6f gd-fm

Smart; suited by 5f-6f; acts on fast ground; goes on Polytrack.

Puitin

(80) (37)

4-y-o b g Red Ransom (USA)-Pagoda (FR) (Sadler's Wells (USA))

M Madgwick M Madgwick

Placings:0 **(7826)**

2009: 8^{0}SD,

	Starts	1st	2nd	3rd	Win & Pl
Career Total (Turf)	0	0	0	0	
Career Total (AW)	1	0	0	0	

Going (Turf): Sf: 0-0 GS: 0-0 Gd: 0-0 GF: 0-0 Fm: 0-0
Distance: 5f/6f: 0-0 7f-8f: 0-1 9f-13f: 0-0 14f+: 0-0
Track : LH: 0-0 RH: 0-1 Tight: 0-0 Gall: 0-0
Aids: Bl: 0-0 Vi: 0-0 Tstrap: 0-0 Ckp: 0-0
Best Rating: 37 12/09 Kemp 1m stand

Pullyourfingerout (IRE)

99 **76**

2-y-o b c Indian Haven-Sandomierz (IRE) (Nordico (USA))

B G Powell K Rhatigan

Placings:0042456012 **(6793)**

2009: 5^{0}GF, 5^{0}GS, 5^{4}GF, 6^{2}GF, 5^{4}G, 6^{5}GF, 7^{6}GS, 6^{0}GF, 7^{1}GF, 8^{2}S,

	Starts	1st	2nd	3rd	Win & Pl
Career Total (Turf)	10	1	2	0	6145
71	9/09 Leic 7f9y	(0-70)		G-F	£4209

Total win prize-money £4209

Going (Turf): Sf: 0-1 GS: 0-2 Gd: 0-1 **GF: 1-6** Fm: 0-0
Distance: 5f/6f: 0-6 **7f-8f: 1-3** 9f-13f: 0-1 14f+: 0-0
Track : LH: 0-2 RH: 0-0 Tight: 0-0 Gall: 0-0
Aids: Bl: 0-0 Vi: 0-0 Tstrap: 0-0 Ckp: 0-0
Best Rating: 76 10/09 Nott 1m75y soft

Modest; effective over 7f; acts on fast ground.

Pumpkin

106(106) (88)**90**

3-y-o ch f Pivotal-Gallivant (Danehill (USA))

Sir Michael Stoute Cheveley Park Stud

Placings:0-21120 **(4500)**

2009: 7^{2}GF, 6^{1}S, 6^{1}SD, 6^{2}GS, 6^{0}G,

	Starts	1st	2nd	3rd	Win & Pl
Career Total (Turf)	4	1	2	0	7141
Career Total (AW)	2	1	0	0	4727
88	7/09 Kemp 6f	(0-80)H		STD	£4727
73	6/09 Yarm 6f3y			SFT	£2901

Total win prize-money £7629

Going (Turf): **Sf: 1-1** GS: 0-1 Gd: 0-1 GF: 0-1 Fm: 0-0
Distance: 5f/6f: 1-4 7f-8f: 1-2 9f-13f: 0-0 14f+: 0-0
Track : LH: 0-0 **RH: 1-2** Tight: 0-0 Gall: 0-0
Aids: Bl: 0-0 Vi: 0-0 Tstrap: 0-0 Ckp: 0-0
Best Rating: 90 7/09 NmkJ 6f gd-sft

Fair; effective at 6f-7f; acts on most ground.

Punch Drunk

102(97) (71)**76**

3-y-o b f Beat Hollow-Bebe De Cham (Tragic Role (USA))

J G Given Lovely Bubbly Racing

Placings:01603-03042226505 **(7014)**

2009: 9^{0}GF, 8^{3}SD, 8^{0}SD, 10^{4}GF, 10^{2}GS, 10^{2}HY, 10^{2}G, 11^{6}S, 10^{5}GF, 12^{0}GF, 10^{6}GS,

	Starts	1st	2nd	3rd	Win & Pl
Career Total (Turf)	14	1	3	1	8182
Career Total (AW)	2	0	0	1	560
70	8/08 Rdcr 7f		G-S	£3561	

Total win prize-money £3562

Going (Turf): Sf: 0-4 **GS: 1-3** Gd: 0-1 GF: 0-6 Fm: 0-0
Distance: 5f/6f: 0-0 **7f-8f: 1-5** 9f-13f: 0-11 14f+: 0-0
Track : LH: 0-10 RH: 0-1 Tight: 0-4 Gall: 0-3
Aids: Bl: 0-0 Vi: 0-0 Tstrap: 0-5 Ckp: 0-5
Best Rating: 76 8/09 Nott 1m2f50y good

Fair; effective over 7f-1m2f; acts on most ground; has worn cheekpieces.

Punching

97(105) (79)**74**

5-y-o b g Kyllachy-Candescent (Machiavellian (USA))

C R Dore Liam Breslin

Placings:0400043051565/26224113240400320403-04514330135000005013 **(7483)**

2009: 5^{0}SD, 5^{4}SD, 5^{5}SD, 6^{1}SD, 5^{4}SD, 6^{3}SD, 5^{3}SD, 7^{0}GF, 7^{1}SD, 7^{3}GF, 6^{5}GS, 6^{0}G, 6^{0}G, 5^{0}GF, 5^{0}SD, 5^{0}SD, 5^{5}SD, 5^{0}SD, 6^{1}SD, 6^{3}SD,

	Starts	1st	2nd	3rd	Win & Pl
Career Total (Turf)	21	2	0	4	7907
Career Total (AW)	32	4	5	4	13771
78	11/09 Sthl 6f	(0-60)H		STD	£1706
79	4/09 Sthl 7f	(0-70)H		STD	£2729
73	1/09 Sthl 6f	(0-65)H		STD	£2047
74	5/08 Wind 6f	(0-75)H		C-S	£2729
70	4/08 Brig 5f213y			GD	£1813
65	11/07 Wolv 5f216y	(0-55)H		STD	£2047

Total win prize-money £13074

Going (Turf): Sf: 0-1 **GS: 1-4 Gd: 1-4** GF: 0-10 Fm: 0-2
Distance: **5f/6f: 5-43** 7f-8f: 1-10 9f-13f: 0-0 14f+: 0-0
Track : **LH: 5-32** RH: 0-3 Tight: 1-20 Gall: 1-2
Aids: Bl: 0-7 Vi: 0-2 Tstrap: 0-0 Ckp: 0-0
Best Rating: 79 4/09 Sthl 7f stand

Modest; effective over 5f-6f; acts on fast ground; goes on Fibresand and Polytrack; has worn a visor.

Punta Galera (IRE)

86(105) (71)**66**

6-y-o br g Zafonic (USA)-Kobalt Sea (FR) (Akarad (FR))

Paul Green Derek A Howard

Placings:52615/60340100036/0000345002336/5445215530-00000 **(5150)**

2009: 12^{0}SD, 8^{0}SD, 12^{0}G, 11^{0}S, 5^{0}GS,

	Starts	1st	2nd	3rd	Win & Pl
Career Total (Turf)	26	2	1	2	19176
Career Total (AW)	18	1	2	4	7213
70	4/08 Kemp 1m4f	(0-65)H		STD	£2047
91	9/06 Sand 1m2f7y	(0-85)H		G-F	£8096
86	9/05 Gdwd 1m		G-F	£5668	

Total win prize-money £15811

Going (Turf): Sf: 0-7 GS: 0-4 Gd: 0-3 **GF: 2-12** Fm: 0-0
Distance: 5f/6f: 0-2 7f-8f: 1-7 **9f-13f: 2-35** 14f+: 0-0
Track : LH: 0-27 **RH: 3-13** Tight: 0-23 Gall: 0-4
Aids: Bl: 0-5 Vi: 0-2 Tstrap: 0-1 Ckp: 0-1
Best Rating: 93 9/05 Newb 1m gd-fm

Modest; stays 1m4f; acts on fast ground; also goes on Polytrack; has worn blinkers and a visor.

Pure Crystal

94(95) (53)**57**

3-y-o ch f Dubai Destination (USA)-Crystal Flute (Lycius (USA))

M G Quinlan T Manning

Placings:0000-0255035 **(7557)**

2009: 10^{0}SD, 12^{2}GF, 14^{5}GF, 14^{5}S, 16^{0}HY, 12^{3}SD, 13^{5}SD,

	Starts	1st	2nd	3rd	Win & Pl
Career Total (Turf)	4	0	1	0	594
Career Total (AW)	7	0	0	1	302

Going (Turf): Sf: 0-2 GS: 0-0 Gd: 0-0 GF: 0-2 Fm: 0-0
Distance: 5f/6f: 0-0 7f-8f: 0-4 9f-13f: 0-3 14f+: 0-4
Track : LH: 0-7 RH: 0-4 Tight: 0-4 Gall: 0-2
Aids: Bl: 0-4 Vi: 0-0 Tstrap: 0-0 Ckp: 0-0
Best Rating: 57 5/09 Rdcr 1m6f19y gd-fm

Moderate; effective at around 1m4f; acts on Polytrack.

Pure Heir (USA)

92 **51**

3-y-o b f Perfect Soul (IRE)-Regal Baby (USA) (Northern Baby (CAN))
T D Barron Clive Washbourn

Placings:4060 **(5972)**
2009: 7^{4}GS, 7^{0}GS, 7^{6}GF, 7^{0}GF,

	Starts	1st	2nd	3rd	Win & Pl
Career Total (Turf)	4	0	0	0	337

Going (Turf): Sf: 0-0 GS: 0-2 Gd: 0-0 GF: 0-2 Fm: 0-0
Distance: 5f/6f: 0-0 7f-8f: 0-4 9f-13f: 0-0 14f+: 0-0
Track : LH: 0-1 RH: 0-0 Tight: 0-1 Gall: 0-0
Aids: Bl: 0-0 Vi: 0-0 Tstrap: 0-0 Ckp: 0-0
Best Rating: 51 6/09 Newc 7f gd-sft

Plating-class; stays 7f; acts on easy ground.

Pure Nostalgia (IRE)

92 **66**

2-y-o ch f Choisir (AUS)-Montmartre (IRE) (Grand Lodge (USA))
J Howard Johnson Transcend Bloodstock LLP

Placings:420144 **(6557)**
2009: 6^{4}GF, 6^{2}GF, 6^{0}GF, 6^{1}S, 6^{4}HY, 7^{4}G,

	Starts	1st	2nd	3rd	Win & Pl
Career Total (Turf)	6	1	1	0	1516

Going (Turf): Sf: 1-2 GS: 0-0 Gd: 0-1 GF: 0-3 Fm: 0-0
Distance: 5f/6f: 1-4 7f-8f: 0-2 9f-13f: 0-0 14f+: 0-0
Track : LH: 0-2 RH: 0-0 Tight: 0-1 Gall: 0-0
Aids: Bl: 0-0 Vi: 0-0 Tstrap: 0-0 Ckp: 0-0
Best Rating: 66 5/09 Rdcr 6f gd-fm

Moderate; stays 6f and should stay 7f; acts on most ground.

Pure Poetry (IRE)

110(104) (102)**110**

3-y-o b g Tagula (IRE)-Express Logic (Air Express (IRE))
R Hannon Mrs J Wood

Placings:01010-13026305 **(5447)**
2009: 8^{1}SD, 8^{3}GF, 8^{0}GF, 8^{2}G, 8^{6}GF, 8^{3}S, 10^{0}G, 10^{5}GF,

	Starts	1st	2nd	3rd	Win & Pl
Career Total (Turf)	12	2	1	2	39410
Career Total (AW)	1	1	0	0	22708
102 4/09 Kemp 1m			STD	£22708	
96 7/08 NmkJ 6f			G-F	£9066	
86 7/08 Hayd 6f			GD	£3238	

Total win prize-money £35012

Going (Turf): Sf: 0-2 GS: 0-0 **Gd: 1-5 GF: 1-5** Fm: 0-0
Distance: 5f/6f: 2-3 7f-8f: 1-8 9f-13f: 0-2 14f+: 0-0
Track : LH: 0-0 **RH: 1-7** Tight: 0-1 Gall: 0-1
Aids: Bl: 0-0 Vi: 0-0 Tstrap: 0-0 Ckp: 0-0
Best Rating: 110 8/09 Gdwd 1m soft

Smart; Listed winner; effective over 6f-1m; acts on fast ground; goes on Polytrack.

Pure Rhythm

98(90) (48)**59**

3-y-o b f Oasis Dream-Degree (Warning)
S C Williams D A Shekells

Placings:060-31 **(2918)**
2009: 6^{3}GF, 5^{1}GF,

	Starts	1st	2nd	3rd	Win & Pl
Career Total (Turf)	4	1	0	1	2976
Career Total (AW)	1	0	0	0	0
59 6/09 Leic 5f218y (0-60)H			G-F	£2590	

Total win prize-money £2590

Going (Turf): Sf: 0-0 GS: 0-0 Gd: 0-0 **GF: 1-4** Fm: 0-0
Distance: 5f/6f: 1-3 7f-8f: 0-2 9f-13f: 0-0 14f+: 0-0
Track : LH: 0-1 RH: 0-0 Tight: 0-0 Gall: 0-2
Aids: Bl: 0-0 Vi: 0-0 Tstrap: 0-0 Ckp: 0-0
Best Rating: 59 6/09 Leic 5f218y gd-fm

Moderate; stays 6f; acts on fast ground.

Purely By Chance

(95) (55)**64**

4-y-o b f Galileo (IRE)-Sioux Chef (Be My Chief (USA))
J Pearce Lady Green

Placings:04454000-160 **(7750)**
2009: 16^{1}SD, 16^{8}SD, 13^{0}SD,

	Starts	1st	2nd	3rd	Win & Pl
Career Total (Turf)	6	0	0	0	722
Career Total (AW)	5	1	0	0	2047
55 11/09 Kemp 2m (0-65)H			STD	£2047	

Total win prize-money £2047

Going (Turf): Sf: 0-1 GS: 0-2 Gd: 0-1 GF: 0-2 Fm: 0-0
Distance: 5f/6f: 0-0 7f-8f: 0-0 9f-13f: 0-4 **14f+: 1-7**
Track : LH: 0-8 **RH: 1-3** Tight: 0-5 Gall: 0-1
Aids: Bl: 1-4 Vi: 0-3 Tstrap: 0-0 Ckp: 0-0
Best Rating: 64 6/08 Chep 1m4f23y gd-fm

Plating-class; staacts on most types of ground including Polytrack; has worn blinkers.

Purissima (USA)

100 **88**

3-y-o b f Fusaichi Pegasus (USA)-Willstar (USA) (Nureyev (USA))
Sir Michael Stoute K Abdulla

Placings:10-0 **(4423)**
2009: 7^{0}G,

	Starts	1st	2nd	3rd	Win & Pl
Career Total (Turf)	3	1	0	0	3886
82 10/08 Wwck 6f			G-S	£3885	

Total win prize-money £3886

Going (Turf): Sf: 0-0 **GS: 1-1** Gd: 0-2 GF: 0-0 Fm: 0-0
Distance: 5f/6f: 1-1 7f-8f: 0-2 9f-13f: 0-0 14f+: 0-0
Track : LH: 1-1 RH: 0-1 Tight: 0-0 Gall: 0-0
Aids: Bl: 0-0 Vi: 0-0 Tstrap: 0-0 Ckp: 0-0
Best Rating: 88 10/08 NmkR 7f good

Very useful; effective over 6f; acts on easy ground.

Purple Gallery (IRE)

(87) (56)

2-y-o b c Whipper (USA)-Daftara (IRE) (Caerleon (USA))
J S Moore The Chicken On A Chain Partnership

Placings:00 **(7773)**
2009: 6^{0}SD, 7^{0}SD,

	Starts	1st	2nd	3rd	Win & Pl
Career Total (Turf)	0	0	0	0	
Career Total (AW)	2	0	0	0	

Going (Turf): Sf: 0-0 GS: 0-0 Gd: 0-0 GF: 0-0 Fm: 0-0
Distance: 5f/6f: 0-1 7f-8f: 0-1 9f-13f: 0-0 14f+: 0-0
Track : LH: 0-2 RH: 0-0 Tight: 0-2 Gall: 0-0
Aids: Bl: 0-0 Vi: 0-0 Tstrap: 0-0 Ckp: 0-0
Best Rating: 56 12/09 Ling 7f stand

Pursestrings

(84) (57)

2-y-o b f Red Ransom (USA)-New Assembly (IRE) (Machiavellian (USA))
R Charlton The Queen

Placings:04 **(7624)**
2009: 8^{0}SD, 8^{4}SD,

	Starts	1st	2nd	3rd	Win & Pl
Career Total (Turf)	0	0	0	0	
Career Total (AW)	2	0	0	0	0

Going (Turf): Sf: 0-0 GS: 0-0 Gd: 0-0 GF: 0-0 Fm: 0-0
Distance: 5f/6f: 0-0 7f-8f: 0-2 9f-13f: 0-0 14f+: 0-0
Track : LH: 0-1 RH: 0-1 Tight: 0-1 Gall: 0-0
Aids: Bl: 0-0 Vi: 0-0 Tstrap: 0-0 Ckp: 0-0
Best Rating: 57 12/09 Ling 1m stand

Pursuit Of Glory (IRE)

104 (93)**106**

3-y-o b f Fusaichi Pegasus (USA)-Sophisticat (USA) (Storm Cat (USA))
David Wachman Michael Tabor

Placings:4130-00 **(2644a)**
2009: 8^{0}GF, 6^{0}GF,

	Starts	1st	2nd	3rd	Win & Pl
Career Total (Turf)	3	0	0	1	25606
Career Total (AW)	3	1	0	0	6459
93 9/08 Dund 6f			STD	£6097	

Total win prize-money £6097

Going (Turf): Sf: 0-0 GS: 0-0 Gd: 0-0 GF: 0-3 Fm: 0-0
Distance: 5f/6f: 1-4 7f-8f: 0-1 9f-13f: 0-1 14f+: 0-0
Track : LH: 1-4 RH: 0-0 Tight: 0-0 Gall: 0-0
Aids: Bl: 0-0 Vi: 0-0 Tstrap: 0-0 Ckp: 0-0
Best Rating: 106 10/08 NmkR 6f gd-fm

Very useful; Group 1 placed; effective at 6f; acts on fast ground and on Polytrack.

Pursuit Of Gold

96(85) (51)**62**

2-y-o b f Pastoral Pursuits-Sheer Gold (USA) (Cutlass (USA))
J R Best A Morris

Placings:0656060 **(7513)**
2009: 5^{0}GF, 5^{6}GF, 5^{5}G, 6^{6}SD, 6^{0}SD, 6^{6}G, 7^{0}SD,

	Starts	1st	2nd	3rd	Win & Pl
Career Total (Turf)	4	0	0	0	0
Career Total (AW)	3	0	0	0	0

Going (Turf): Sf: 0-0 GS: 0-0 Gd: 0-2 GF: 0-2 Fm: 0-0

Distance: 5f/6f: 0-6 7f-8f: 0-1 9f-13f: 0-0 14f+: 0-0
Track : LH: 0-0 RH: 0-3 Tight: 0-0 Gall: 0-2
Aids: Bl: 0-0 Vi: 0-0 Tstrap: 0-0 Ckp: 0-0
Best Rating: 62 5/09 Wind 5f10y good

Pursuit Of Purpose

89(93) (43)**39**
3-y-o b f Dansili-Sinead (USA) (Irish River (FR))
G L Moore G L Moore

Placings:0-00045 (6445)
2009: 8^{0}SD, 9^{0}GF, 10^{0}SD, 9^{4}F, 12^{5}SS,

	Starts	1st	2nd	3rd	Win & Pl
Career Total (Turf)	3	0	0	0	236
Career Total (AW)	3	0	0	0	0

Going (Turf): Sf: 0-0 GS: 0-0 Gd: 0-1 GF: 0-1 Fm: 0-1
Distance: 5f/6f: 0-0 7f-8f: 0-2 9f-13f: 0-4 14f+: 0-0
Track : LH: 0-4 RH: 0-1 Tight: 0-4 Gall: 0-0
Aids: Bl: 0-1 Vi: 0-0 Tstrap: 0-0 Ckp: 0-0
Best Rating: 43 10/09 Ling 1m4f std-slw

Purus (IRE)

103(106) (81)**88**
7-y-o b g Night Shift (USA)-Pariana (USA) (Bering)
R A Teal J Morton

Placings:3030/151/0055015000043/0050311303551/5004 0546650-242300060000 (7586)
2009: 7^{2}SD, 7^{4}SD, 7^{2}GF, 7^{3}GF, 7^{0}GS, 7^{0}GF, 7^{0}GF, 7^{6}GF, 7^{0}GF, 6^{0}G, 7^{0}SD, 8^{0}SD,

	Starts	1st	2nd	3rd	Win & Pl
Career Total (Turf)	34	5	1	5	30372
Career Total (AW)	22	1	1	2	9272

93 11/07 NmkR 7f (0-85)H GD £5181
89 6/07 Brig 6f209y (0-75)H G-S £2849
77 6/07 Brig 6f209y (0-70)H FRM £2775
89 6/06 Kemp 7f (0-85)H STD £5505
83 10/05 Chan 1m VS £7092
8/05 Duss 7f GD £1844
Total win prize-money £25249

Going (Turf): Sf: 0-6 GS: 1-3 Gd: 2-9 GF: 0-13 Fm: 1-2
Distance: 5f/6f: 0-6 7f-8f: 6-50 9f-13f: 0-0 14f+: 0-0
Track : LH: 2-19 RH: 3-19 Tight: 0-12 Gall: 0-0
Aids: Bl: 0-2 Vi: 0-0 Tstrap: 0-1 Ckp: 0-1
Best Rating: 93 11/07 NmkR 7f good

Fair; ex-German; stays 7f; acts on most ground on turf; goes on Polytrack; has worn cheekpieces.

Pusey Street Lady

114 (81)**105**
5-y-o b m Averti (IRE)-Pusey Street Girl (Gildoran)
J Gallagher C R Marks (banbury)

Placings:5/511360400/103030U-262350500 (6814)
2009: 6^{2}GF, 5^{6}G, 6^{2}HY, 6^{3}S, 6^{5}G, 6^{0}G, 6^{5}GF, 6^{0}G, 6^{0}G,

	Starts	1st	2nd	3rd	Win & Pl
Career Total (Turf)	24	3	2	4	51083
Career Total (AW)	2	0	0	0	0

98 3/08 Donc 6f (0-100)H SFT £10363
82 6/07 Nott 6f15y (0-75)H GD £3238
73 5/07 Wind 6f GD £3238
Total win prize-money £16841

Going (Turf): Sf: 1-5 GS: 0-4 Gd: 2-10 GF: 0-5 Fm: 0-0

Distance: 5f/6f: 2-24 7f-8f: 1-2 9f-13f: 0-0 14f+: 0-0
Track : LH: 0-7 RH: 0-0 Tight: 0-3 Gall: 1-2
Aids: Bl: 0-0 Vi: 0-0 Tstrap: 0-0 Ckp: 0-0
Best Rating: 105 5/09 Hayd 6f heavy

Very useful; Group and Listed placed; effective at 6f and acts on most ground; suited by forcing tactics.

Push Me (IRE)

77(91) (63)**45**
2-y-o gr f Verglas (IRE)-Gilda Lilly (USA) (War Chant (USA))
A J McCabe (John A Quinn 12/12) A J McCabe

Placings:16254 (7791)
2009: 7^{1}SD, 7^{6}GF, 7^{2}SD, 8^{5}SD, 7^{4}SS,

	Starts	1st	2nd	3rd	Win & Pl
Career Total (Turf)	1	0	0	0	0
Career Total (AW)	4	1	1	0	2752

58 9/09 Wolv 7f32y STD £2047
Total win prize-money £2047

Going (Turf): Sf: 0-0 GS: 0-0 Gd: 0-0 GF: 0-1 Fm: 0-0
Distance: 5f/6f: 0-0 7f-8f: 1-5 9f-13f: 0-0 14f+: 0-0
Track : LH: 1-4 RH: 0-0 Tight: 1-2 Gall: 0-0
Aids: Bl: 0-0 Vi: 0-0 Tstrap: 0-0 Ckp: 0-0
Best Rating: 63 12/09 Sthl 7f std-slw

Modest; effective over 7f; acts on Fibresand and Polytrack.

Puteri (IRE)

91(92) (64)**61**
2-y-o b f One Cool Cat (USA)-London Pride (USA) (Lear Fan (USA))
M A Jarvis H R H Sultan Ahmad Shah

Placings:0354 (7792)
2009: 7^{0}S, 7^{3}S, 8^{5}SD, 8^{4}SS,

	Starts	1st	2nd	3rd	Win & Pl
Career Total (Turf)	2	0	0	1	302
Career Total (AW)	2	0	0	0	0

Going (Turf): Sf: 0-2 GS: 0-0 Gd: 0-0 GF: 0-0 Fm: 0-0
Distance: 5f/6f: 0-0 7f-8f: 0-4 9f-13f: 0-0 14f+: 0-0
Track : LH: 0-1 RH: 0-1 Tight: 0-0 Gall: 0-0
Aids: Bl: 0-0 Vi: 0-0 Tstrap: 0-0 Ckp: 0-0
Best Rating: 64 8/09 Kemp 1m stand

Modest; stays 1m; acts on Polytrack.

Putra Laju (IRE)

(102) (73)**51**
5-y-o b h Trans Island-El Corazon (IRE) (Mujadil (USA))
J W Hills J W Hills

Placings:05531/0000002231**4**/6344300035040-36 (0216)
2009: 8^{3}SD, 8^{6}SD,

	Starts	1st	2nd	3rd	Win & Pl
Career Total (Turf)	7	0	0	0	
Career Total (AW)	24	2	2	6	11112

73 12/07 Wolv 1m141y (0-70)H STD £3238
68 12/06 Wolv 7f32y STD £3886
Total win prize-money £7125

Going (Turf): Sf: 0-0 GS: 0-1 Gd: 0-3 GF: 0-3 Fm: 0-0
Distance: 5f/6f: 0-1 7f-8f: 1-10 9f-13f: 1-20 14f+: 0-0
Track : LH: 2-25 RH: 0-6 Tight: 2-25 Gall: 0-0
Aids: Bl: 0-0 Vi: 0-2 Tstrap: 1-16 Ckp: 1-16
Best Rating: 73 12/07 Wolv 1m141y stand

Moderate; effective over 1m; acts on Polytrack.

Putra One (IRE)

103(102) (85)**83**
3-y-o b g Danehill Dancer (IRE)-Veronica Cooper (IRE) (Kahyasi)
M A Jarvis H R H Sultan Ahmad Shah

Placings:00-23143 (6583)
2009: 8^{2}G, 10^{3}GS, 12^{1}GF, 12^{4}SD, 10^{3}SD,

	Starts	1st	2nd	3rd	Win & Pl
Career Total (Turf)	5	1	1	1	5651
Career Total (AW)	2	0	0	1	1136

70 7/09 Newb 1m4f5y G-F £4209
Total win prize-money £4209

Going (Turf): Sf: 0-1 GS: 0-1 Gd: 0-2 GF: 1-1 Fm: 0-0
Distance: 5f/6f: 0-0 7f-8f: 0-1 9f-13f: 1-6 14f+: 0-0
Track : LH: 1-3 RH: 0-2 Tight: 0-2 Gall: 1-1
Aids: Bl: 0-0 Vi: 0-0 Tstrap: 0-0 Ckp: 0-0
Best Rating: 85 10/09 Kemp 1m2f stand

Useful; effective over 1m4f; acts on good/fast ground and on Polytrack.

Puy D'Arnac (FR)

106(103) (76)**83**
6-y-o b g Acteur Francais (USA)-Chaumeil (FR) (Mad Captain)
G A Swinbank Barrow Brook Racing

Placings:004/6114060/2110006166-4044445611363 (7170)
2009: 12^{4}SD, 14^{0}SD, 13^{4}G, 14^{4}S, 17^{4}G, 15^{4}G, 14^{5}S, 14^{6}G, 14^{1}GS, 11^{1}S, 16^{3}GS, 14^{6}GS, 15^{3}S,

	Starts	1st	2nd	3rd	Win & Pl
Career Total (Turf)	29	7	1	2	33127
Career Total (AW)	3	0	0	0	385

74 9/09 Catt 1m3f214y (0-75)H SFT £2914
68 8/09 Muss 1m6f (0-75)H G-S £3885
83 11/08 Ayr 1m7f (0-85)H HVY £7477
84 4/08 Donc 1m6f132y (0-80)H G-S £4533
77 4/08 Catt 1m5f175y (0-85)H G-S £4209
5/07 Libo 1m2f HVY £2027
4/07 Angl 1m3f GD £2364
Total win prize-money £27411

Going (Turf): Sf: 3-8 GS: 3-10 Gd: 1-9 GF: 0-1 Fm: 0-0
Distance: 5f/6f: 0-0 7f-8f: 0-0 9f-13f: 3-13 14f+: 4-19
Track : LH: 4-21 RH: 1-4 Tight: 3-8 Gall: 1-7
Aids: Bl: 0-0 Vi: 0-0 Tstrap: 0-0 Ckp: 0-0
Best Rating: 84 4/08 Donc 1m6f132y gd-sft

Fair; ex-French; effective at up to 1m7f; handles plenty of ease in the ground.

Puzzlemaster

104(97) (74)**89**
3-y-o ch g Lomitas-Norcroft Joy (Rock Hopper)
H Morrison (Jane Chapple-Hyam 23/10) Rory Sweet

Placings:66-1061650 (6996)
2009: 8^{1}SD, 10^{0}GF, 10^{6}GF, 10^{1}HY, 12^{6}SD, 12^{5}G, 10^{0}GS,

	Starts	1st	2nd	3rd	Win & Pl
Career Total (Turf)	7	1	0	0	7771
Career Total (AW)	2	1	0	0	2868

89 7/09 Nott 1m2f50y (0-85)H HVY £7771
74 4/09 Wolv 1m141y STD £2729
Total win prize-money £10501

Going (Turf): Sf: 1-2 GS: 0-1 Gd: 0-1 GF: 0-3 Fm: 0-0
Distance: 5f/6f: 0-1 7f-8f: 0-1 9f-13f: 2-7 14f+: 0-0
Track : LH: 2-7 RH: 0-1 Tight: 1-2 Gall: 0-3
Aids: Bl: 0-0 Vi: 0-0 Tstrap: 0-0 Ckp: 0-0
Best Rating: 89 7/09 Nott 1m2f50y heavy

Fair; stays 1m; acts on Polytrack.

Pycian

96 78

2-y-o b g Mark Of Esteem (IRE)-Beejay (Piccolo)
Mrs L Stubbs Tyme Partnership

Placings:130 (4086)
2009: 6[1]G, 7[3]G, 7[0]S,

	Starts	1st	2nd	3rd	Win & Pl
Career Total (Turf)	3	1	0	1	4070

75 5/09 Hayd 6f GD £2914
Total win prize-money £2914

Going (Turf): Sf: 0-1 GS: 0-0 **Gd: 1-2** GF: 0-0 Fm: 0-0
Distance: **5f/6f: 1-1** 7f-8f: 0-2 9f-13f: 0-0 14f+: 0-0
Track : LH: 0-0 RH: 0-0 Tight: 0-0 Gall: 0-0
Aids: Bl: 0-0 Vi: 0-0 Tstrap: 0-0 Ckp: 0-0
Best Rating: 78 6/09 Donc 7f good

Fair; stays 7f; acts on good ground

Pyrrha

109 107

3-y-o b f Pyrus (USA)-Demeter (USA) (Diesis)
C F Wall Lady Juliet Tadgell

Placings:2102-3411 (5005)
2009: 6[3]G, 7[4]G, 7[1]G, 7[1]G,

	Starts	1st	2nd	3rd	Win & Pl
Career Total (Turf)	8	3	2	1	91850

107 8/09 NmkJ 7f (0-95)H GD £9066
93 7/09 NmkJ 7f (0-100)H GD £16190
82 6/08 Newb 6f8y G-F £4533
Total win prize-money £29789

Going (Turf): Sf: 0-0 GS: 0-0 **Gd: 2-4** GF: 1-4 Fm: 0-0
Distance: 5f/6f: 0-3 **7f-8f: 3-5** 9f-13f: 0-0 14f+: 0-0
Track : LH: 0-0 RH: 0-0 Tight: 0-0 Gall: 0-0
Aids: Bl: 0-0 Vi: 0-0 Tstrap: 0-0 Ckp: 0-0
Best Rating: 107 8/09 NmkJ 7f good

Useful; effective over 6f and acts on fast ground.

Pyrus Time (IRE)

99(101) (76)72

3-y-o b g Pyrus (USA)-Spot In Time (Mtoto)
J S Moore J Wells & A Wright

Placings:00-53322223346251 (7694)
2009: 8[5]SD, 8[3]SD, 8[3]SD, 8[2]SD, 10[2]SD, 12[2]SD, 10[2]SD, 11[3]F, 10[3]SD, 12[4]SD, 10[6]F, 10[2]GF, 8[5]GF, 10[1]SD,

	Starts	1st	2nd	3rd	Win & Pl
Career Total (Turf)	5	0	1	1	2437
Career Total (AW)	11	1	4	3	6552

72 12/09 Ling 1m2f STD £1978
Total win prize-money £1979

Going (Turf): **Sf: 0-0 GS: 0-0 Gd: 0-1 GF: 0-2 Fm: 0-2**
Distance: 5f/6f: 0-1 7f-8f: 0-5 **9f-13f: 1-10** 14f+: 0-0
Track : **LH: 1-15** RH: 0-1 **Tight: 1-11** Gall: 0-1
Aids: Bl: 0-0 Vi: 0-0 Tstrap: 0-1 Ckp: 0-1
Best Rating: 76 5/09 Ling 1m2f stand

Fair; stays 1m2f; acts on fast ground; goes on Polytrack.

Pytheas (USA)

93(99) (80)79

2-y-o b g Seeking The Gold (USA)-Neptune's Bride (USA) (Bering)
M Johnston Sheikh Hamdan Bin Mohammed Al Maktoum

Placings:203223 (7121)
2009: 7[2]GF, 7[0]G, 7[3]GF, 8[2]SD, 8[2]GS, 8[3]GF,

	Starts	1st	2nd	3rd	Win & Pl
Career Total (Turf)	5	0	2	2	3083
Career Total (AW)	1	0	1	0	1510

Going (Turf): **Sf: 0-0 GS: 0-1 Gd: 0-1 GF: 0-3 Fm: 0-0**
Distance: 5f/6f: 0-0 7f-8f: 0-4 9f-13f: 0-2 14f+: 0-0
Track : LH: 0-3 RH: 0-2 Tight: 0-1 Gall: 0-1
Aids: Bl: 0-0 Vi: 0-0 Tstrap: 0-0 Ckp: 0-0
Best Rating: 80 9/09 Wolv 1m141y stand

Fair; stays 1m; acts on fast ground; goes on Polytrack.

Qadar (IRE)

92(114) (79)75

7-y-o b g Xaar-Iktidar (Green Desert (USA))
David Marnane (N P Littmoden 3/4) Mrs Linda Francis

Placings:231/430/**005214013060050333**2/**1412353202606 00335/30400604-5225443001345634** (7565a)
2009: 5[5]SD, 6[2]SD, 5[2]SD, 6[5]SD, 5[4]SD, 5[4]SD, 7[3]GF, 7[0]G, 7[0]GY, 6[1]SD, 8[3]SD, 6[4]GY, 8[5]SD, 6[6]SD, 8[3]SD, 7[4]SD,

	Starts	1st	2nd	3rd	Win & Pl
Career Total (Turf)	17	0	1	4	7245
Career Total (AW)	50	6	7	10	91287

71 9/09 Layt 6f (50-70)H STD £6037
109 1/07 Ling 6f (0-100)H STD £9971
106 1/07 Wolv 5f216y (0-100)H STD £11658
106 3/06 Ling 5f (0-100)H STD £11217
96 2/06 Ling 5f (0-85)H STD £6477
78 10/04 Ling 7f STD £4238
Total win prize-money £49601

Going (Turf): **Sf: 0-0 GS: 0-0 Gd: 0-5 GF: 0-10 Fm: 0-0**
Distance: **5f/6f: 5-49** 7f-8f: 1-17 9f-13f: 0-1 14f+: 0-0
Track : **LH: 6-51** RH: 0-6 **Tight: 5-37** Gall: 0-1
Aids: **Bl: 1-22** Vi: 0-1 Tstrap: 0-4 Ckp: 0-4
Best Rating: 109 1/07 Ling 6f stand

Fair; Listed placed; effective over 5f-7f; acts on good and faster ground and on Polytrack and on sand at Laytown; has worn various headgear and a tongue tie; likes to come late off a strong pace.

Qalahari (IRE)

99(99) (87)92

3-y-o b f Bahri (USA)-Daqtora (Dr Devious (IRE))
D J Coakley West Ilsley Racing

Placings:221022-0200 (4422)
2009: 7[0]SD, 7[2]GF, 8[0]GF, 9[0]G,

	Starts	1st	2nd	3rd	Win & Pl
Career Total (Turf)	9	1	5	0	17126
Career Total (AW)	1	0	0	0	

92 7/08 Bath 5f161y FRM £2266
Total win prize-money £2267

Going (Turf): Sf: 0-0 GS: 0-2 Gd: 0-3 GF: 0-3 **Fm: 1-1**
Distance: **5f/6f: 1-4** 7f-8f: 0-5 9f-13f: 0-1 14f+: 0-0
Track : **LH: 1-3** RH: 0-2 Tight: 0-2 **Gall: 1-2**
Aids: Bl: 0-0 Vi: 0-0 Tstrap: 0-0 Ckp: 0-0
Best Rating: 92 7/08 Bath 5f161y firm

Useful; stays 7f; acts on good and fast ground.

Qaraaba

91 82

2-y-o b f Shamardal (USA)-Mokaraba (Unfuwain (USA))
J L Dunlop Hamdan Al Maktoum

Placings:231 (6730)
2009: 7[2]S, 7[3]GF, 6[1]S,

	Starts	1st	2nd	3rd	Win & Pl
Career Total (Turf)	3	1	1	1	5178

76 10/09 Sals 6f212y SFT £2914
Total win prize-money £2914

Going (Turf): **Sf: 1-2** GS: 0-0 Gd: 0-0 GF: 0-1 Fm: 0-0
Distance: 5f/6f: 0-0 **7f-8f: 1-3** 9f-13f: 0-0 14f+: 0-0
Track : LH: 0-0 RH: 0-0 Tight: 0-0 Gall: 0-0
Aids: Bl: 0-0 Vi: 0-0 Tstrap: 0-0 Ckp: 0-0
Best Rating: 82 7/09 NmkJ 7f soft

Useful; stays 7f; acts on easy ground.

Qaraqum (USA)

(84) (53)

2-y-o b/br f Vindication (USA)-Code Of Ethics (USA) (Honour And Glory (USA))
D J Coakley Fairfax Racing

Placings:55 (7624)
2009: 8[5]SD, 8[5]SD,

	Starts	1st	2nd	3rd	Win & Pl
Career Total (Turf)	0	0	0	0	
Career Total (AW)	2	0	0	0	0

Going (Turf): **Sf: 0-0 GS: 0-0 Gd: 0-0 GF: 0-0 Fm: 0-0**
Distance: 5f/6f: 0-0 7f-8f: 0-2 9f-13f: 0-0 14f+: 0-0
Track : LH: 0-1 RH: 0-1 Tight: 0-1 Gall: 0-0
Aids: Bl: 0-0 Vi: 0-0 Tstrap: 0-0 Ckp: 0-0
Best Rating: 53 12/09 Ling 1m stand

Qedaam (IRE)

(78) (21)

3-y-o b f Daylami (IRE)-Zafzala (IRE) (Kahyasi)
Patrick Morris Haif Mohammed Al-Ghatani

Placings:0 (1286)
2009: 12[0]SD,

	Starts	1st	2nd	3rd	Win & Pl
Career Total (Turf)	0	0	0	0	
Career Total (AW)	1	0	0	0	

Going (Turf): **Sf: 0-0 GS: 0-0 Gd: 0-0 GF: 0-0 Fm: 0-0**
Distance: 5f/6f: 0-0 7f-8f: 0-0 9f-13f: 0-1 14f+: 0-0
Track : LH: 0-0 RH: 0-1 Tight: 0-0 Gall: 0-0
Aids: Bl: 0-0 Vi: 0-0 Tstrap: 0-0 Ckp: 0-0
Best Rating: 21 4/09 Kemp 1m4f stand

Qelaan (USA)

104(102) (68)92

3-y-o b f Dynaformer (USA)-Irtahal (USA) (Swain (IRE))
M P Tregoning Hamdan Al Maktoum

Placings:00-4261125 (7148)
2009: 9[4]GF, 9[2]GF, 11[6]SD, 12[1]GF, 11[1]GS, 12[2]GF, 12[5]G,

	Starts	1st	2nd	3rd	Win & Pl
Career Total (Turf)	7	2	2	0	10489
Career Total (AW)	2	0	0	0	0

92 9/09 Ling 1m3f106y (0-75)H G-S £3070
85 9/09 Folk 1m4f (0-70)H G-F £3238
Total win prize-money £6309

Going (Turf): Sf: 0-0 **GS: 1-1** Gd: 0-2 **GF: 1-4** Fm: 0-0
Distance: 5f/6f: 0-0 7f-8f: 0-2 **9f-13f: 2-7** 14f+: 0-0
Track : LH: 1-1 RH: 1-8 **Tight: 2-4** Gall: 0-1
Aids: Bl: 0-0 Vi: 0-0 Tstrap: 0-0 Ckp: 0-0
Best Rating: 92 10/09 Gdwd 1m4f gd-fm

Fair; stays 1m2f and acts on most ground.

Quadrifolio

81 31

3-y-o b g Key Of Luck (USA)-Berkeley Note (IRE) (Victory Note (USA))

Paul Green C J Dingwall

Placings:56000-0 (7126)

2009: 8^{0}G,

	Starts	1st	2nd	3rd	Win & Pl
Career Total (Turf)	6	0	0	0	0

Going (Turf): **Sf: 0-0 GS: 0-2 Gd: 0-3 GF: 0-1 Fm: 0-0**
Distance: 5f/6f: 0-4 7f-8f: 0-1 9f-13f: 0-1 14f+: 0-0
Track : LH: 0-1 RH: 0-0 Tight: 0-0 Gall: 0-0
Aids: Bl: 0-0 Vi: 0-2 Tstrap: 0-0 Ckp: 0-0
Best Rating: **31** 10/09 Nott 1m75y good

Quadrille

103(97) (95)102

2-y-o b c Danehill Dancer (IRE)-Fictitious (Machiavellian (USA))

R Hannon The Queen

Placings:112 (6663)

2009: 6^{1}G, 7^{1}SD, 7^{2}GS,

	Starts	1st	2nd	3rd	Win & Pl
Career Total (Turf)	2	1	1	0	7376
Career Total (AW)	1	1	0	0	6418

95 9/09 Kemp 7f STD £6417
89 8/09 Newb 6f8y GD £4857
Total win prize-money £11275

Going (Turf): Sf: 0-0 GS: 0-1 **Gd: 1-1** GF: 0-0 Fm: 0-0
Distance: 5f/6f: 0-0 **7f-8f: 2-3** 9f-13f: 0-0 14f+: 0-0
Track : LH: 0-0 **RH: 1-1** Tight: 0-0 Gall: 0-0
Aids: Bl: 0-0 Vi: 0-0 Tstrap: 0-0 Ckp: 0-0
Best Rating: **102** 10/09 Asct 7f gd-sft

Very useful; stays 7f; acts on easy ground; goes on Polytrack.

Quaestor (IRE)

92(91) (78)80

2-y-o b c Antonius Pius (USA)-Lucky Oakwood (USA) (Elmaamul (USA))

Tom Dascombe John Brown

Placings:6526020 (6104)

2009: 6^{6}SD, 6^{5}GF, 6^{2}SD, 6^{6}G, 6^{0}S, 6^{2}GF, 6^{0}GF,

	Starts	1st	2nd	3rd	Win & Pl
Career Total (Turf)	5	0	1	0	1534
Career Total (AW)	2	0	1	0	705

Going (Turf): **Sf: 0-1 GS: 0-0 Gd: 0-1 GF: 0-3 Fm: 0-0**
Distance: 5f/6f: 0-5 7f-8f: 0-2 9f-13f: 0-0 14f+: 0-0
Track : LH: 0-2 RH: 0-1 Tight: 0-2 Gall: 0-0
Aids: Bl: 0-0 Vi: 0-0 Tstrap: 0-0 Ckp: 0-0
Best Rating: **80** 9/09 Ling 6f gd-fm

Fair; stays 6f and acts on fast ground.

Quai D'Orsay

108 102

3-y-o ch c Sulamani (IRE)-Entente Cordiale (USA) (Affirmed (USA))

M Johnston Sheikh Hamdan Bin Mohammed Al Maktoum

Placings:10-20101505510 (6662)

2009: 12^{2}GF, 11^{0}HY, 12^{1}G, 12^{0}GF, 11^{1}GF, 14^{5}GF, 14^{0}G, 12^{5}GS, 12^{5}GF, 13^{1}GF, 12^{0}GS,

	Starts	1st	2nd	3rd	Win & Pl
Career Total (Turf)	13	4	1	0	60893

99 10/09 Ayr 1m5f13y (0-95)H G-F £7771
102 7/09 Hayd 1m3f200y (0-100)H G-F £19428
99 6/09 Muss 1m4f100y (0-90)H GD £24924
79 9/08 Haml 1m65y SFT £3885
Total win prize-money £56009

Going (Turf): Sf: 1-2 GS: 0-3 Gd: 1-2 **GF: 2-6** Fm: 0-0
Distance: 5f/6f: 0-0 7f-8f: 0-1 **9f-13f: 3-9** 14f+: 1-3
Track : LH: 2-6 RH: 2-7 **Tight: 2-4** Gall: 0-6
Aids: Bl: 0-0 Vi: 0-0 Tstrap: 0-0 Ckp: 0-0
Best Rating: **102** 7/09 Hayd 1m3f200y gd-fm

Very useful; stays 1m5f; acts on most ground.

Quaker Parrot

97(99) (80)83

2-y-o ch f Compton Place-Little Greenbird (Ardkinglass)

Tom Dascombe Deva Racing Kyllachy Partnership

Placings:010631022**420** (7846)

2009: 5^{0}G, 5^{1}GF, 5^{0}GF, 5^{6}GF, 5^{3}S, 5^{1}GF, 6^{0}G, 5^{2}F, 5^{2}GF, 5^{4}SD, 7^{2}SD, 7^{0}SD,

	Starts	1st	2nd	3rd	Win & Pl
Career Total (Turf)	9	2	2	1	11192
Career Total (AW)	3	0	1	0	1888

74 7/09 Bath 5f11y G-F £4209
71 5/09 Wwck 5f110y G-F £3885
Total win prize-money £8095

Going (Turf): Sf: 0-1 GS: 0-0 Gd: 0-2 **GF: 2-5** Fm: 0-1
Distance: **5f/6f: 2-10** 7f-8f: 0-2 9f-13f: 0-0 14f+: 0-0
Track : **LH: 2-7** RH: 0-0 Tight: 0-3 **Gall: 1-4**
Aids: Bl: 0-0 Vi: 0-0 Tstrap: 0-0 Ckp: 0-0
Best Rating: **83** 9/09 Bath 5f161y firm

Fair; effective over 5f-7f; acts on fast ground and Polytrack.

Qualitas

90(83) (41)57

3-y-o b g Orpen (USA)-Kiss Me Kate (Aragon)

M W Easterby Kevin McConnell

Placings:50005 (6831)

2009: 6^{5}GS, 6^{0}GS, 5^{0}SD, 6^{0}GS, 9^{5}SF,

	Starts	1st	2nd	3rd	Win & Pl
Career Total (Turf)	3	0	0	0	0
Career Total (AW)	2	0	0	0	0

Going (Turf): **Sf: 0-0 GS: 0-3 Gd: 0-0 GF: 0-0 Fm: 0-0**
Distance: 5f/6f: 0-4 7f-8f: 0-0 9f-13f: 0-1 14f+: 0-0
Track : LH: 0-1 RH: 0-0 Tight: 0-1 Gall: 0-0
Aids: Bl: 0-0 Vi: 0-0 Tstrap: 0-0 Ckp: 0-0
Best Rating: **57** 5/09 Donc 6f gd-sft

Quality Mover (USA)

74(85) (57)63

2-y-o b/br f Elusive Quality (USA)-Katherine Seymour (Green Desert (USA))

D M Simcock Dr Ali Ridha

Placings:60 (5165)

2009: 7^{6}G, 8^{0}SD,

	Starts	1st	2nd	3rd	Win & Pl
Career Total (Turf)	1	0	0	0	0
Career Total (AW)	1	0	0	0	0

Going (Turf): **Sf: 0-0 GS: 0-0 Gd: 0-1 GF: 0-0 Fm: 0-0**
Distance: 5f/6f: 0-0 7f-8f: 0-2 9f-13f: 0-0 14f+: 0-0
Track : LH: 0-0 RH: 0-1 Tight: 0-0 Gall: 0-0
Aids: Bl: 0-0 Vi: 0-0 Tstrap: 0-0 Ckp: 0-0
Best Rating: **63** 8/09 NmkJ 7f good

$140,000 filly; minor promise on debut over 7f on good.

Quality Street

(106) (72)67

7-y-o ch m Fraam-Pusey Street Girl (Gildoran)

P Butler E H Whatmough

Placings:12230/5253604003**0303**/**2206031146**00/**6646**00 5060-00 (0531)

2009: 8^{0}SD, 7^{0}SD,

	Starts	1st	2nd	3rd	Win & Pl
Career Total (Turf)	19	1	3	2	9233
Career Total (AW)	24	2	2	4	10058

79 7/07 Ling 6f (0-70)H STD £2817
74 7/07 Ling 6f (0-70)H STD £3071
65 5/05 Bath 5f11y G-F £2576
Total win prize-money £8464

Going (Turf): Sf: 0-1 GS: 0-0 Gd: 0-7 **GF: 1-9** Fm: 0-2
Distance: **5f/6f: 3-38** 7f-8f: 0-5 9f-13f: 0-0 14f+: 0-0
Track : **LH: 3-26** RH: 0-1 **Tight: 2-23** Gall: 1-4
Aids: Bl: 0-0 Vi: 0-1 Tstrap: 2-28 Ckp: 2-28
Best Rating: **83** 7/06 Sand 5f6y gd-fm

Modest mare; stays 6f and acts on fast ground and Polytrack.

Quam Celerrime

(86) (76)95

4-y-o b g Xaar-Divine Secret (Hernando (FR))

R Curtis Huw Downs & Joe McCarthy

Placings:5210/600-0 (0330)

2009: 12^{0}SD,

	Starts	1st	2nd	3rd	Win & Pl
Career Total (Turf)	5	1	0	0	2267
Career Total (AW)	3	0	1	0	1253

74 10/07 Folk 7f SFT £2266
Total win prize-money £2267

Going (Turf): **Sf: 1-4** GS: 0-0 Gd: 0-0 GF: 0-1 Fm: 0-0
Distance: 5f/6f: 0-1 **7f-8f: 1-3** 9f-13f: 0-4 14f+: 0-0
Track : LH: 0-2 RH: 0-4 Tight: 0-1 Gall: 0-0
Aids: Bl: 0-0 Vi: 0-0 Tstrap: 0-0 Ckp: 0-0
Best Rating: **95** 11/07 MsnL 6f soft

Useful; stays 1m; acts on Polytrack and soft ground.

Quanah Parker (IRE)

103 94

3-y-o b c Namid-Uncertain Affair (IRE) (Darshaan)

R M Whitaker Robert Macgregor

Placings:5210-3250 (3622)

2009: 7^{3}HY, 7^{2}GF, 6^{5}G, 6^{0}GF,

	Starts	1st	2nd	3rd	Win & Pl
Career Total (Turf)	8	1	2	1	8417

89 8/08 Ripn 6f GD £3561
Total win prize-money £3562

Going (Turf): Sf: 0-1 GS: 0-1 **Gd: 1-4** GF: 0-2 Fm: 0-0
Distance: **5f/6f: 1-5** 7f-8f: 0-3 9f-13f: 0-0 14f+: 0-0
Track : LH: 0-2 RH: 0-0 Tight: 0-0 Gall: 0-1
Aids: Bl: 0-0 Vi: 0-0 Tstrap: 0-0 Ckp: 0-0
Best Rating: **94** 5/09 York 7f gd-fm

Useful; effective over 6f-7f; acts on good and easier ground; likes to race prominently.

Quaroma

96(91) (69)97

4-y-o ch f Pivotal-Quiz Time (Efisio)

Jane Chapple-Hyam Miss C Roylance

Placings:31/5521135-40 **(1880)**

2009: 6^{4}F, 6^{0}F,

	Starts	1st	2nd	3rd	Win & Pl
Career Total (Turf)	10	3	1	2	20039
Career Total (AW)	1	0	0	0	0

96	8/08	Nott	6f15y	(0-80)H	GD	£5180
84	7/08	Yarm	6f3y	(0-75)H	G-F	£2719
69	11/07	Nott	5f13y		G-F	£3238

Total win prize-money £11140

Going (Turf): Sf: 0-1 GS: 0-1 Gd: **1-2 GF: 2-4** Fm: 0-2
Distance: 5f/6f: 1-7 **7f-8f: 2-4** 9f-13f: 0-0 14f+: 0-0
Track : LH: 0-1 RH: 0-0 Tight: 0-0 Gall: 0-2
Aids: Bl: 0-0 Vi: 0-0 Tstrap: 0-0 Ckp: 0-0
Best Rating: 97 10/08 Chan 5f110y soft

Useful; effective over 5f-6f; acts on most ground.

Quarrel (USA)

98 103

2-y-o gr/ro c Maria's Mon (USA)-Gender Dance (USA) (Miesque's Son (USA))

W J Haggas St Albans Bloodstock LLP

Placings:113 **(6105)**

2009: 6^{1}GF, 6^{1}GF, 6^{3}GF,

	Starts	1st	2nd	3rd	Win & Pl
Career Total (Turf)	3	2	0	1	24869

91	8/09	Ches	6f18y	G-F	£9777
87	7/09	Asct	6f	G-F	£6476

Total win prize-money £16253

Going (Turf): Sf: 0-0 GS: 0-0 Gd: 0-0 **GF: 2-3** Fm: 0-0
Distance: 5f/6f: 1-1 7f-8f: 1-2 9f-13f: 0-0 14f+: 0-0
Track : **LH: 1-1** RH: 0-0 **Tight: 1-1** Gall: 0-0
Aids: Bl: 0-0 Vi: 0-0 Tstrap: 0-0 Ckp: 0-0
Best Rating: 103 9/09 Newb 6f8y gd-fm

Smart; effective over 6f; acts on fast ground.

Quasi Congaree (GER)

101(100) (73)73

3-y-o ch g Congaree (USA)-Queens Wild (USA) (Spectacular Bid (USA))

I A Wood M I Forbes

Placings:622403056 **(7254)**

2009: 7^{6}GF, 6^{2}GF, 6^{2}GS, 6^{4}SD, 5^{0}SD, 6^{3}SD, 6^{0}SD, 5^{5}SD, 5^{6}SD,

	Starts	1st	2nd	3rd	Win & Pl
Career Total (Turf)	3	0	2	0	1734
Career Total (AW)	6	0	0	1	646

Going (Turf): **Sf: 0-0 GS: 0-1 Gd: 0-0 GF: 0-2 Fm: 0-0**
Distance: 5f/6f: 0-7 7f-8f: 0-2 9f-13f: 0-0 14f+: 0-0
Track : LH: 0-3 RH: 0-3 Tight: 0-3 Gall: 0-0
Aids: Bl: 0-0 Vi: 0-0 Tstrap: 0-0 Ckp: 0-0
Best Rating: 73 10/09 Ling 6f stand

Modest; suited by 6f; acts on most ground and on Polytrack.

Que Beauty (IRE)

(94) (46)26

4-y-o b f Val Royal (FR)-Ardbess (Balla Cove)

Kieran Purcell (R C Guest 5/2) T C Quinn

Placings:000/**000-3605** **(0402)**

2009: 16^{3}SS, 16^{6}SD, 14^{0}SD, 16^{5}SD,

	Starts	1st	2nd	3rd	Win & Pl
Career Total (Turf)	3	0	0	0	
Career Total (AW)	7	0	0	1	304

Going (Turf): **Sf: 0-1 GS: 0-0 Gd: 0-1 GF: 0-1 Fm: 0-0**
Distance: 5f/6f: 0-2 7f-8f: 0-1 9f-13f: 0-3 14f+: 0-4
Track : LH: 0-9 RH: 0-0 Tight: 0-1 Gall: 0-0
Aids: Bl: 0-1 Vi: 0-0 Tstrap: 0-4 Ckp: 0-4
Best Rating: 46 1/09 Wolv 2m119y stand

Moderate; stays 2m and acts on Fibresand; has worn cheekpieces.

Que Belle (IRE)

(81) (32)

2-y-o b f Hawk Wing (USA)-Enaya (Caerleon (USA))

Tom Dascombe Manor House Stables LLP

Placings:0 **(7792)**

2009: 8^{0}SS,

	Starts	1st	2nd	3rd	Win & Pl
Career Total (Turf)	0	0	0	0	
Career Total (AW)	1	0	0	0	

Going (Turf): **Sf: 0-0 GS: 0-0 Gd: 0-0 GF: 0-0 Fm: 0-0**
Distance: 5f/6f: 0-0 7f-8f: 0-1 9f-13f: 0-0 14f+: 0-0
Track : LH: 0-1 RH: 0-0 Tight: 0-0 Gall: 0-0
Aids: Bl: 0-0 Vi: 0-0 Tstrap: 0-0 Ckp: 0-0
Best Rating: 32 12/09 Sthl 1m std-slw

Que Calor La Vida (FR)

63

5-y-o b m Lavirco (GER)-Hasta Manana (FR) (Useful (FR))

N Wilson (G A Harker 20/1) A J Thomson & M Conley

Placings:00 **(1681)**

2009: 12^{0}GF, 12^{0}GF,

	Starts	1st	2nd	3rd	Win & Pl
Career Total (Turf)	2	0	0	0	

Going (Turf): **Sf: 0-0 GS: 0-0 Gd: 0-0 GF: 0-2 Fm: 0-0**
Distance: 5f/6f: 0-0 7f-8f: 0-0 9f-13f: 0-2 14f+: 0-0
Track : LH: 0-1 RH: 0-1 Tight: 0-2 Gall: 0-0
Aids: Bl: 0-0 Vi: 0-0 Tstrap: 0-0 Ckp: 0-0

Queen Eleanor

95(103) (81)75

3-y-o b f Cape Cross (IRE)-Rainbow Queen (Rainbow Quest (USA))

J H M Gosden Cheveley Park Stud

Placings:62-32310 **(5009)**

2009: 8^{3}SD, 9^{2}G, 10^{3}GF, 10^{1}SD, 10^{0}G,

	Starts	1st	2nd	3rd	Win & Pl
Career Total (Turf)	4	0	2	1	3372
Career Total (AW)	3	1	0	1	3115

81	7/09	Ling	1m2f	(0-75)H	STD	£2729

Total win prize-money £2730

Going (Turf): **Sf: 0-0 GS: 0-0 Gd: 0-3 GF: 0-1 Fm: 0-0**
Distance: 5f/6f: 0-0 7f-8f: 0-3 **9f-13f: 1-4** 14f+: 0-0
Track : **LH: 1-5** RH: 0-2 **Tight: 1-3** Gall: 0-1
Aids: Bl: 0-0 Vi: 0-0 Tstrap: 0-0 Ckp: 0-0
Best Rating: 81 7/09 Ling 1m2f stand

Fair; effective over 1m; acts on good ground.

Queen Excalibur

80 (21)61

10-y-o ch m Sabrehill (USA)-Blue Room (Gorytus (USA))

B J Llewellyn Dr Simon Clarke

Placings:64300/026000000400/**0000635/0/620000-0** **(4263)**

2009: 12^{0}S,

	Starts	1st	2nd	3rd	Win & Pl
Career Total (Turf)	26	0	2	2	3732
Career Total (AW)	7	0	0	0	0

Going (Turf): **Sf: 0-5 GS: 0-3 Gd: 0-5 GF: 0-13 Fm: 0-0**
Distance: 5f/6f: 0-0 7f-8f: 0-9 9f-13f: 0-22 14f+: 0-2
Track : LH: 0-22 RH: 0-2 Tight: 0-9 Gall: 0-2
Aids: Bl: 0-2 Vi: 0-0 Tstrap: 0-12 Ckp: 0-12
Best Rating: 66 8/02 Donc 1m4f soft

Queen Martha (USA)

99(93) (64)84

3-y-o b f Rahy (USA)-Cryptoqueen (USA) (Cryptoclearance (USA))

M A Magnusson Eastwind Racing Ltd and Martha Trussell

Placings:60116 **(3315)**

2009: 7^{6}SD, 8^{0}GF, 8^{1}F, 8^{1}GF, 10^{6}GF,

	Starts	1st	2nd	3rd	Win & Pl
Career Total (Turf)	4	2	0	0	7016
Career Total (AW)	1	0	0	0	0

77	6/09	Donc	1m	(0-75)H	G-F	£4209
74	5/09	Nott	1m75y		FRM	£2266

Total win prize-money £6476

Going (Turf): Sf: 0-0 GS: 0-0 Gd: 0-0 **GF: 1-3 Fm: 1-1**
Distance: 5f/6f: 0-0 7f-8f: 1-2 9f-13f: 1-3 14f+: 0-0
Track : **LH: 2-4** RH: 0-1 Tight: 0-2 **Gall: 1-2**
Aids: Bl: 0-0 Vi: 0-0 Tstrap: 0-0 Ckp: 0-0
Best Rating: 84 6/09 Newc 1m2f32y gd-fm

Fair; stays 1m; acts on fast ground.

Queen Of Dobbin (IRE)

(81) (52)28

3-y-o b f King Charlemagne (USA)-Tajikistan (IRE) (Among Men (USA))

Lee Smyth Rodney Williamson

Placings:000-000 **(7555)**

2009: 7^{0}GY, 5^{0}SD, 5^{0}SD,

	Starts	1st	2nd	3rd	Win & Pl
Career Total (Turf)	2	0	0	0	
Career Total (AW)	4	0	0	0	

Going (Turf): **Sf: 0-1 GS: 0-0 Gd: 0-0 GF: 0-0 Fm: 0-0**
Distance: 5f/6f: 0-4 7f-8f: 0-2 9f-13f: 0-0 14f+: 0-0
Track : LH: 0-6 RH: 0-0 Tight: 0-2 Gall: 0-0
Aids: Bl: 0-1 Vi: 0-0 Tstrap: 0-1 Ckp: 0-1
Best Rating: 52 9/08 Dund 7f stand

Queen Of Pentacles (IRE)

109(102) (81)**103**

3-y-o b f Selkirk (USA)-Maid To Perfection (Sadler's Wells (USA))

J Noseda Normandie Stud Ltd

Placings:414441 **(7291)**

2009: 10^{4}S, 10^{1}SD, 12^{4}G, 10^{4}GF, 10^{4}G, 10^{1}S,

	Starts	1st	2nd	3rd	Win & Pl
Career Total (Turf)	5	1	0	0	30617
Career Total (AW)	1	1	0	0	2590

103 11/09 Donc 1m2f60y SFT £23704
81 6/09 Kemp 1m2f STD £2590
Total win prize-money £26294

Going (Turf): **Sf: 1-2** GS: 0-0 Gd: 0-2 GF: 0-1 Fm: 0-0
Distance: 5f/6f: 0-0 7f-8f: 0-0 **9f-13f: 2-6** 14f+: 0-0
Track : LH: 1-4 RH: 1-1 Tight: 0-1 **Gall: 1-3**
Aids: Bl: 0-0 Vi: 0-0 Tstrap: 0-0 Ckp: 0-0
Best Rating: 103 11/09 Donc 1m2f60y soft

Listed class; effective over 1m2f-1m4f; acts on fast and soft ground and on Polytrack.

Queen Of Thebes (IRE)

94(96) (63)**79**

3-y-o b f Bahri (USA)-Sopran Marida (IRE) (Darshaan)

G L Moore The Horse Players

Placings:1000-0056600 **(6439)**

2009: 8^{0}GF, 5^{0}GF, 7^{5}GF, 8^{6}GF, 7^{6}SD, 7^{0}SD, 10^{0}SS,

	Starts	1st	2nd	3rd	Win & Pl
Career Total (Turf)	8	1	0	0	2730
Career Total (AW)	3	0	0	0	0

74 6/08 Wind 5f10y G-F £2729
Total win prize-money £2730

Going (Turf): Sf: 0-0 GS: 0-0 Gd: 0-2 **GF: 1-6** Fm: 0-0
Distance: **5f/6f: 1-5** 7f-8f: 0-3 9f-13f: 0-3 14f+: 0-0
Track : LH: 0-2 RH: 0-2 Tight: 0-2 **Gall: 1-1**
Aids: Bl: 0-0 Vi: 0-0 Tstrap: 0-0 Ckp: 0-0
Best Rating: 79 9/08 Sals 6f good

Modest; stays 6f; acts on fast ground; has worn a tongue tie.

Queen Of Wands

81 **54**

2-y-o b f Sakhee (USA)-Maid To Treasure (IRE) (Rainbow Quest (USA))

J L Dunlop Normandie Stud Ltd

Placings:00 **(5498)**

2009: 7^{0}G, 8^{0}G,

	Starts	1st	2nd	3rd	Win & Pl
Career Total (Turf)	2	0	0	0	

Going (Turf): Sf: 0-0 GS: 0-0 Gd: 0-2 GF: 0-0 Fm: 0-0
Distance: 5f/6f: 0-0 7f-8f: 0-1 9f-13f: 0-1 14f+: 0-0
Track : LH: 0-0 RH: 0-0 Tight: 0-0 Gall: 0-0
Aids: Bl: 0-0 Vi: 0-0 Tstrap: 0-0 Ckp: 0-0
Best Rating: 54 8/09 NmkJ 7f good

Queen Sally (IRE)

93(92) (56)**72**

3-y-o b f Key Of Luck(USA)-Crystal Blue(IRE)(Bluebird (USA))

Tom Dascombe David A Hunt

Placings:30300-3600 **(6799)**

2009: 7^{3}S, 6^{6}G, 7^{0}SD, 5^{0}S,

	Starts	1st	2nd	3rd	Win & Pl
Career Total (Turf)	8	0	0	3	1348
Career Total (AW)	1	0	0	0	

Going (Turf): Sf: 0-4 GS: 0-1 Gd: 0-3 GF: 0-0 Fm: 0-0
Distance: 5f/6f: 0-5 7f-8f: 0-4 9f-13f: 0-0 14f+: 0-0
Track : LH: 0-2 RH: 0-1 Tight: 0-0 Gall: 0-1
Aids: Bl: 0-0 Vi: 0-0 Tstrap: 0-0 Ckp: 0-0
Best Rating: 72 6/08 Hayd 5f good

Queen's Envoy

88(91) (69)**55**

2-y-o b f King's Best (USA)-Allied Cause (Giant's Causeway (USA))

L M Cumani Helena Springfield Ltd

Placings:63 **(7135)**

2009: 7^{6}GF, 7^{3}SD,

	Starts	1st	2nd	3rd	Win & Pl
Career Total (Turf)	1	0	0	0	0
Career Total (AW)	1	0	0	1	655

Going (Turf): Sf: 0-0 GS: 0-0 Gd: 0-0 GF: 0-1 Fm: 0-0
Distance: 5f/6f: 0-0 7f-8f: 0-2 9f-13f: 0-0 14f+: 0-0
Track : LH: 0-1 RH: 0-0 Tight: 0-1 Gall: 0-0
Aids: Bl: 0-0 Vi: 0-0 Tstrap: 0-0 Ckp: 0-0
Best Rating: 69 10/09 Ling 7f stand

Fair; effective over 7f; acts on Polytrack.

Queen's Grace

104 **102**

2-y-o ch f Bahamian Bounty-Palace Affair (Pursuit Of Love)

H Morrison Miss B Swire

Placings:0131 **(7147)**

2009: 6^{0}G, 6^{1}GF, 6^{3}S, 6^{1}G,

	Starts	1st	2nd	3rd	Win & Pl
Career Total (Turf)	4	2	0	1	25711

102 10/09 NmkR 6f GD £17031
81 8/09 Newb 6f8y G-F £4857
Total win prize-money £21888

Going (Turf): Sf: 0-1 GS: 0-0 **Gd: 1-2 GF: 1-1** Fm: 0-0
Distance: 5f/6f: 1-2 7f-8f: 1-2 9f-13f: 0-0 14f+: 0-0
Track : LH: 0-0 RH: 0-0 Tight: 0-0 Gall: 0-0
Aids: Bl: 0-0 Vi: 0-0 Tstrap: 0-0 Ckp: 0-0
Best Rating: 102 10/09 NmkR 6f good

Listed winner; half-sister to April Fool from family of Sakhee's Secret; suited by 6f on fast ground.

Queen's Hawk

95 **72**

2-y-o ch c Hawk Wing (USA)-Queen Of Africa (USA) (Peintre Celebre (USA))

D J Coakley Keeper's 12

Placings:010500666 **(6963)**

2009: 5^{0}G, 6^{1}GF, 7^{0}GF, 7^{5}G, 5^{0}GS, 7^{0}GS, 8^{6}G, 7^{6}GF, 6^{6}G,

	Starts	1st	2nd	3rd	Win & Pl
Career Total (Turf)	9	1	0	0	2914

70 5/09 Gdwd 6f G-F £2914
Total win prize-money £2914

Going (Turf): Sf: 0-0 GS: 0-2 Gd: 0-4 **GF: 1-3** Fm: 0-0
Distance: **5f/6f: 1-3** 7f-8f: 0-5 9f-13f: 0-1 14f+: 0-0
Track : LH: 0-4 RH: 0-0 Tight: 0-1 Gall: 0-1
Aids: Bl: 0-0 Vi: 0-1 Tstrap: 0-0 Ckp: 0-0
Best Rating: 72 7/09 Asct 7f good

Fair; effective at 6f; acts on fast ground.

Queens Flight

84(85) (57)**44**

3-y-o b f King's Best (USA)-Birdie (Alhaarth (IRE))

Tom Dascombe Lady Carolyn Warren

Placings:50-500 **(6340)**

2009: 8^{5}G, 7^{0}SD, 5^{0}GF,

	Starts	1st	2nd	3rd	Win & Pl
Career Total (Turf)	2	0	0	0	0
Career Total (AW)	3	0	0	0	0

Going (Turf): Sf: 0-0 GS: 0-0 Gd: 0-1 GF: 0-1 Fm: 0-0
Distance: 5f/6f: 0-1 7f-8f: 0-4 9f-13f: 0-0 14f+: 0-0
Track : LH: 0-4 RH: 0-1 Tight: 0-1 Gall: 0-1
Aids: Bl: 0-0 Vi: 0-0 Tstrap: 0-0 Ckp: 0-0
Best Rating: 57 12/08 GrLe 1m stand

Queens Forester

79 **35**

3-y-o b f Needwood Blade-Bonsai (IRE) (Woodman (USA))

P F I Cole W H Ponsonby

Placings:000-0 **(2652)**

2009: 8^{0}F,

	Starts	1st	2nd	3rd	Win & Pl
Career Total (Turf)	4	0	0	0	

Going (Turf): Sf: 0-1 GS: 0-1 Gd: 0-0 GF: 0-1 Fm: 0-1
Distance: 5f/6f: 0-1 7f-8f: 0-2 9f-13f: 0-1 14f+: 0-0
Track : LH: 0-1 RH: 0-1 Tight: 0-1 Gall: 0-1
Aids: Bl: 0-0 Vi: 0-0 Tstrap: 0-0 Ckp: 0-0
Best Rating: 35 8/08 Wind 6f gd-sft

Quella

88(81) (33)**39**

3-y-o ch f Falbrav (IRE)-Qirmazi (USA) (Riverman (USA))

J H M Gosden Dr Ornella Carlini Cozzi

Placings:00 **(1092)**

2009: 8^{0}SD, 10^{0}GF,

	Starts	1st	2nd	3rd	Win & Pl
Career Total (Turf)	1	0	0	0	
Career Total (AW)	1	0	0	0	

Going (Turf): Sf: 0-0 GS: 0-0 Gd: 0-0 GF: 0-1 Fm: 0-0
Distance: 5f/6f: 0-0 7f-8f: 0-1 9f-13f: 0-1 14f+: 0-0
Track : LH: 0-1 RH: 0-1 Tight: 0-1 Gall: 0-0
Aids: Bl: 0-0 Vi: 0-0 Tstrap: 0-0 Ckp: 0-0
Best Rating: 39 4/09 Bath 1m2f46y gd-fm

Querido (GER)

84 **57**

5-y-o b g Acatenango (GER)-Quest Of Fire (FR) (Rainbow Quest (USA))

M Bradstock Inglethorpe

Placings:34221/200-00 **(7174)**

2009: 7^{0}GF, 9^{0}S,

	Starts	1st	2nd	3rd	Win & Pl
Career Total (Turf)	**10**	**1**	**3**	**1**	**5240**
9/07 Hanv 1m			HVY	£2027	

Total win prize-money £2027

Going (Turf): **Sf: 1-5** GS: 0-0 Gd: 0-4 GF: 0-1 Fm: 0-0
Distance: 5f/6f: 0-0 **7f-8f: 1-2** 9f-13f: 0-8 14f+: 0-0
Track : LH: 0-1 RH: 0-2 Tight: 0-1 Gall: 0-0
Aids: Bl: 0-0 Vi: 0-0 Tstrap: 0-0 Ckp: 0-0
Best Rating: **57** 9/08 Leic 1m60y good

Quest For Success (IRE)

109(106) (85)**104**
4-y-o b g Noverre (USA)-Divine Pursuit (Kris)
R A Fahey Morebrooke Ltd

Placings:332001/3000**5**01**41**0-**5**100216**6**41 **(7015)**
2009: 7^{5}GF, 7^{1}F, 7^{0}GF, 6^{0}GF, 7^{2}G, 6^{1}G, 6^{6}G, 6^{6}G, **6**^{4}SD, 5^{1}GS,

	Starts	1st	2nd	3rd	Win & Pl
Career Total (Turf)	**23**	**6**	**2**	**3**	**85066**
Career Total (AW)	**3**	**0**	**0**	**0**	**701**

104 10/09 Donc 5f (0-100)H G-S £31155
100 7/09 Haml 6f5y (0-105)H GD £21808
97 4/09 Thsk 7f (0-90)H FRM £8159
94 11/08 Ayr 7f50y (0-80)H HVY £6231
83 10/08 Donc 7f (0-85)H GD £6476
86 10/07 Ayr 6f G-S £2914

Total win prize-money £76746

Going (Turf): Sf: 1-3 **GS: 2-5 Gd: 2-8** GF: 0-5 Fm: 1-2
Distance: 5f/6f: 2-15 **7f-8f: 4-11** 9f-13f: 0-0 14f+: 0-0
Track : **LH: 2-7** RH: 0-2 **Tight: 1-3** Gall: 0-1
Aids: Bl: 0-1 Vi: 0-0 Tstrap: 0-0 Ckp: 0-0
Best Rating: **104** 10/09 Donc 5f gd-sft

Very useful; effective at 5f-7f and acts on most ground; has worn blinkers; likes to race prominently.

Quick Gourmet

93 **61**
3-y-o b f Lend A Hand-Rhiann (Anshan)
G A Swinbank (J A McShane 19/8) Lothian Recycling Limited

Placings:64-6563340 **(6766)**
2009: 9^{6}G, 7^{5}G, 7^{6}GF, 6^{3}S, 6^{3}GS, 6^{4}S, 12^{0}GS,

	Starts	1st	2nd	3rd	Win & Pl
Career Total (Turf)	**9**	**0**	**0**	**2**	**1011**

Going (Turf): **Sf: 0-4 GS: 0-2 Gd: 0-2 GF: 0-1 Fm: 0-0**
Distance: 5f/6f: 0-0 7f-8f: 0-6 9f-13f: 0-3 14f+: 0-0
Track : LH: 0-1 RH: 0-5 Tight: 0-5 Gall: 0-1
Aids: Bl: 0-0 Vi: 0-0 Tstrap: 0-0 Ckp: 0-0
Best Rating: **61** 8/09 Haml 6f5y gd-sft

Modest sprinter; acts on easy ground.

Quick Off The Mark

93(102) (71)**53**
4-y-o b f Dr Fong (USA)-Equity Princess (Warning)
J G Given Peter Onslow & Ian Henderson

Placings:30/0**6351**-**2246**00**34**0**30** **(5103)**
2009: 8^{2}SD, 8^{2}SD, **11**^{4}SD, **9**^{6}SD, 10^{0}GS, 10^{0}G, **8**^{3}SD, 8^{4}GF, 8^{0}G, 9^{3}SD, **9**^{0}SD,

	Starts	1st	2nd	3rd	Win & Pl
Career Total (Turf)	**6**	**0**	**0**	**0**	**0**

	Starts	1st	2nd	3rd	Win & Pl
Career Total (AW)	**12**	**1**	**2**	**4**	**8492**

68 12/08 Wolv 1m1f103y (0-70)H STD £3885

Total win prize-money £3886

Going (Turf): **Sf: 0-1 GS: 0-1 Gd: 0-2 GF: 0-2 Fm: 0-0**
Distance: 5f/6f: 0-1 7f-8f: 0-3 **9f-13f: 1-14** 14f+: 0-0
Track : **LH: 1-16** RH: 0-0 **Tight: 1-10** Gall: 0-1
Aids: Bl: 0-0 Vi: 0-0 Tstrap: 0-0 Ckp: 0-0
Best Rating: **71** 1/09 Wolv 1m141y stand

Modest; stays 1m1f and acts on Polytrack.

Quick Reaction

93 **77**
2-y-o b g Elusive Quality (USA)-Arutua (USA) (Riverman (USA))
R Hannon The Queen

Placings:050 **(6393)**
2009: 7^{0}GF, 8^{5}GF, 8^{0}GF,

	Starts	1st	2nd	3rd	Win & Pl
Career Total (Turf)	**3**	**0**	**0**	**0**	**0**

Going (Turf): **Sf: 0-0 GS: 0-0 Gd: 0-0 GF: 0-3 Fm: 0-0**
Distance: 5f/6f: 0-0 7f-8f: 0-3 9f-13f: 0-0 14f+: 0-0
Track : LH: 0-0 RH: 0-0 Tight: 0-0 Gall: 0-0
Aids: Bl: 0-0 Vi: 0-0 Tstrap: 0-0 Ckp: 0-0
Best Rating: **77** 9/09 Donc 1m gd-fm

Quick Release (IRE)

(105) (79)**78**
4-y-o b c Red Ransom (USA)-Set The Mood (USA) (Dixie Brass (USA))
D M Simcock Tick Tock Partnership

Placings:21043/**6**-**504625441** **(7812)**
2009: **8**^{5}SD, **8**^{0}SD, **8**^{4}SD, **8**^{6}SD, **9**^{2}SD, **10**^{5}SD, **8**^{4}SD, **8**^{4}SD, **8**^{1}SD,

	Starts	1st	2nd	3rd	Win & Pl
Career Total (Turf)	**4**	**1**	**1**	**0**	**6619**
Career Total (AW)	**11**	**1**	**1**	**1**	**7986**

79 12/09 Wolv 1m141y (0-87)H STD £4731
76 8/07 Ches 7f2y G-F £5181

Total win prize-money £9913

Going (Turf): Sf: 0-0 GS: 0-0 Gd: 0-1 **GF: 1-3** Fm: 0-0
Distance: 5f/6f: 0-0 7f-8f: 1-12 9f-13f: 1-3 14f+: 0-0
Track : **LH: 2-5** RH: 0-7 **Tight: 2-5** Gall: 0-0
Aids: Bl: 0-0 Vi: 0-0 Tstrap: 0-0 Ckp: 0-0
Best Rating: **87** 11/07 Kemp 7f stand

Fair; effective over 1m; acts on fast ground; goes on Polytrack.

Quick Single (USA)

95(102) (69)**66**
3-y-o b/br g Doneraile Court (USA)-Summer Strike (USA) (Smart Strike (CAN))
P S McEntee (D R C Elsworth 23/1) Roberto Favarulo

Placings:6**5400**-**5343116**5060**4**000**400040** **(7588)**
2009: **6**^{5}SD, **6**^{3}SD, **5**^{4}SD, **6**^{3}SD, **6**^{1}SD, **6**^{1}SD, **6**^{6}SD, 5^{5}G, 7^{0}GF, 8^{6}GF, 7^{0}GF, 6^{4}GF, **6**^{4}SD, 8^{0}G, **6**^{0}SD, 5^{0}S, 6^{4}F, **7**^{0}SD, **7**^{0}SS, **10**^{0}SD, 10^{4}SD, 8^{0}SD,

	Starts	1st	2nd	3rd	Win & Pl
Career Total (Turf)	**10**	**0**	**0**	**0**	**625**
Career Total (AW)	**17**	**2**	**0**	**2**	**6577**

69 2/09 Ling 6f (0-70)H STD £2900
65 2/09 Ling 6f STD £2729

Total win prize-money £5630

Going (Turf): **Sf: 0-1 GS: 0-1 Gd: 0-2 GF: 0-5 Fm: 0-1**
Distance: **5f/6f: 2-15** 7f-8f: 0-10 9f-13f: 0-2 14f+: 0-0
Track : **LH: 2-15** RH: 0-4 **Tight: 2-12** Gall: 0-1
Aids: Bl: 0-4 **Vi: 2-14** Tstrap: 0-0 Ckp: 0-0
Best Rating: **69** 2/09 Ling 6f stand

Modest; effective over 6f-7f; acts on Polytrack.

Quick Wit

100(88) (70)**80**
2-y-o b c Oasis Dream-Roo (Rudimentary (USA))
Saeed Bin Suroor Godolphin

Placings:521 **(7146)**
2009: 7^{5}SS, 7^{2}G, 7^{1}G,

	Starts	1st	2nd	3rd	Win & Pl
Career Total (Turf)	**2**	**1**	**1**	**0**	**6530**
Career Total (AW)	**1**	**0**	**0**	**0**	**0**

80 10/09 NmkR 7f GD £5180

Total win prize-money £5181

Going (Turf): Sf: 0-0 GS: 0-0 **Gd: 1-2** GF: 0-0 Fm: 0-0
Distance: 5f/6f: 0-0 **7f-8f: 1-3** 9f-13f: 0-0 14f+: 0-0
Track : LH: 0-1 RH: 0-0 Tight: 0-1 Gall: 0-0
Aids: Bl: 0-0 Vi: 0-0 Tstrap: 0-0 Ckp: 0-0
Best Rating: **80** 10/09 NmkR 7f good

Useful; effective over 6f on good ground.

Quicks The Word

86 (28)**65**
9-y-o b g Sri Pekan (USA)-Fast Tempo (IRE) (Statoblest)
T A K Cuthbert W Hurst

Placings:0053023662/20205601600/0040002262**060**/03552/30310510/250350-0000 **(5443)**
2009: 5^{0}GF, 5^{0}GF, 6^{0}GF, 6^{0}GF,

	Starts	1st	2nd	3rd	Win & Pl
Career Total (Turf)	**54**	**3**	**9**	**6**	**25124**
Career Total (AW)	**3**	**0**	**0**	**0**	**0**

63 9/07 Newc 6f (0-55)H G-F £3238
57 7/07 Ayr 6f (0-70)H GD £3238
74 8/03 Nott 5f13y E(0-70) G-F £3711

Total win prize-money £10190

Going (Turf): Sf: 0-7 GS: 0-9 Gd: 1-15 **GF: 2-22** Fm: 0-1
Distance: **5f/6f: 3-39** 7f-8f: 0-15 9f-13f: 0-3 14f+: 0-0
Track : LH: 0-11 RH: 0-10 Tight: 0-6 Gall: 0-2
Aids: **Bl: 1-7** Vi: 0-0 Tstrap: 0-0 Ckp: 0-0
Best Rating: **81** 5/03 Hayd 6f soft

Moderate; effective over 5f-6f; acts well on good and easy ground.

Quiet

98 **94**
2-y-o ch f Observatory (USA)-Quandary (USA) (Blushing Groom (FR))
R Charlton K Abdulla

Placings:10 **(5825)**
2009: 8^{1}GF, 8^{0}GF,

	Starts	1st	2nd	3rd	Win & Pl
Career Total (Turf)	**2**	**1**	**0**	**0**	**4857**

80 9/09 Leic 1m60y G-F £4857

Total win prize-money £4857

Going (Turf): Sf: 0-0 GS: 0-0 Gd: 0-0 **GF: 1-2** Fm: 0-0
Distance: 5f/6f: 0-0 7f-8f: 0-1 **9f-13f: 1-1** 14f+: 0-0
Track : LH: 0-0 **RH: 1-1** Tight: 0-0 Gall: 0-0
Aids: Bl: 0-0 Vi: 0-0 Tstrap: 0-0 Ckp: 0-0
Best Rating: **94** 9/09 Donc 1m gd-fm

Winner on debut; effective over 1m; acts on fast ground.

Quiet Elegance

101 **92**

4-y-o b f Fantastic Light (USA)-Imperial Bailiwick (IRE) (Imperial Frontier (USA))

E J Alston Mr & Mrs G Middlebrook

Placings:1/100530-0000300 **(6050)**

2009: 6^{0}GF, 6^{0}F, 8^{0}S, 6^{0}GF, 6^{3}G, 6^{0}G, 6^{0}G,

	Starts	1st	2nd	3rd	Win & Pl
Career Total (Turf)	**14**	**2**	**0**	**2**	**15510**
96 4/08 Leic	5f218y		SFT	£6799	
75 10/07 Nott	5f13y		G-S	£3238	

Total win prize-money £10039

Going (Turf): **Sf: 1-2 GS: 1-3** Gd: 0-5 GF: 0-3 Fm: 0-1
Distance: **5f/6f: 2-10** 7f-8f: 0-3 9f-13f: 0-1 14f+: 0-0
Track : LH: 0-3 RH: 0-0 Tight: 0-1 Gall: 0-0
Aids: Bl: 0-0 Vi: 0-0 Tstrap: 0-0 Ckp: 0-0
Best Rating: **96** 4/08 Leic 5f218y soft

Fair; effective over 5f-6f; acts on easy ground.

Quiet Mountain (IRE)

(90) (58)

4-y-o ch g Monashee Mountain (USA)-Shalstayholy (IRE) (Shalford (IRE))

Ollie Pears O'Brien, Moll, Spencer, Vaux, Davies

Placings:065 **(7753)**

2009: 7^{0}SD, 7^{6}SD, 8^{5}SD,

	Starts	1st	2nd	3rd	Win & Pl
Career Total (Turf)	0	0	0	0	
Career Total (AW)	3	0	0	0	0

Going (Turf): **Sf: 0-0 GS: 0-0 Gd: 0-0 GF: 0-0 Fm: 0-0**
Distance: 5f/6f: 0-0 7f-8f: 0-2 9f-13f: 0-1 14f+: 0-0
Track : LH: 0-3 RH: 0-0 Tight: 0-2 Gall: 0-0
Aids: Bl: 0-0 Vi: 0-0 Tstrap: 0-0 Ckp: 0-0
Best Rating: **58** 12/09 Wolv 1m141y stand

Quince (IRE)

104(109) (86)**84**

6-y-o b g Fruits Of Love (USA)-Where's Charlotte (Sure Blade (USA))

J Pearce Mrs Jennifer Marsh

Placings:000111060/6252660142/22420046400/3000166 2020525-22421630030202250 **(7777)**

2009: 12^{2}SD, 13^{2}SD, 11^{4}SD, 12^{2}SD, 12^{1}SD, 12^{6}GF, 10^{3}G, 9^{0}G, 10^{0}GF, 10^{3}GF, 10^{0}GS, 9^{2}GF, 10^{0}GF, 12^{2}SD, 13^{2}SD, 13^{5}SF, 12^{0}SD,

	Starts	1st	2nd	3rd	Win & Pl
Career Total (Turf)	**37**	**4**	**4**	**3**	**28967**
Career Total (AW)	**24**	**2**	**11**	**0**	**24395**
62 2/09 Wolv	1m4f50y		STD	£2729	
84 6/08 Leic	1m1f218y (0-75)H		G-F	£3561	
86 11/06 Wolv	1m4f50y (0-85)H		STD	£5505	
83 9/05 Muss	1m	(0-85)	G-F	£6101	
78 9/05 Catt	7f	(0-80)	GD	£7241	
70 9/05 Leic	7f9y	(0-65)	G-F	£2860	

Total win prize-money £28000

Going (Turf): Sf: 0-4 GS: 0-3 Gd: 1-7 **GF: 3-23** Fm: 0-0
Distance: 5f/6f: 0-1 7f-8f: 3-8 9f-13f: 3-48 14f+: 0-4
Track : **LH: 3-34** RH: 2-17 **Tight: 4-24** Gall: 0-11
Aids: Bl: 0-0 **Vi: 3-45** Tstrap: 2-8 Ckp: 2-8

Best Rating: **93** 3/07 Ling 1m5f stand

Fair; stays 1m4f but effective at shorter; acts on a sound surface and Polytrack; usually wears a visor.

Quinmaster (USA)

110 (103)**99**

7-y-o gr g Linamix (FR)-Sherkiya (IRE) (Goldneyev (USA))

M Halford William Durkan

Placings:6/234123105/011140/44100/**55040212**-02004 **(5080a)**

2009: 8^{0}HY, 8^{2}GF, 8^{0}GF, 7^{0}G, 8^{4}SH,

	Starts	1st	2nd	3rd	Win & Pl
Career Total (Turf)	**27**	**6**	**3**	**2**	**177730**
Career Total (AW)	**7**	**1**	**2**	**0**	**18753**
100 11/08 Dund	1m	H	STD	£12445	
109 6/07 Leop	1m		GD	£21993	
114 8/06 Curr	1m	H	G-F	£41448	
105 8/06 Gway	1m100y	H	G-Y	£62620	
92 7/06 Curr	1m	(60-90)H	G-F	£8339	
8/05 Claf	1m3f		GD	£8865	
90 6/05 StCl	1m2f110y		G-S	£7092	

Total win prize-money £162805

Going (Turf): Sf: 0-6 GS: 1-1 **Gd: 2-8 GF: 2-6** Fm: 0-0
Distance: 5f/6f: 0-0 **7f-8f: 4-21** 9f-13f: 3-13 14f+: 0-0
Track : LH: 3-16 RH: 3-13 Tight: 0-0 **Gall: 2-6**
Aids: Bl: 0-0 Vi: 0-0 Tstrap: 2-11 Ckp: 2-11
Best Rating: **114** 8/06 Curr 1m gd-fm

Smart; Irish trained; best at 1m on a sound surface; has worn tongue tie and cheekpieces.

Quinner (IRE)

92(69) (17)**62**

2-y-o ch c Arakan (USA)-Quintellina (Robellino (USA))

P D Evans Bathwick Gold Partnership

Placings:63000 **(6343)**

2009: 6^{6}S, 6^{3}G, 6^{0}G, 6^{0}S, 5^{0}SD,

	Starts	1st	2nd	3rd	Win & Pl
Career Total (Turf)	4	0	0	1	722
Career Total (AW)	1	0	0	0	

Going (Turf): **Sf: 0-2 GS: 0-0 Gd: 0-2 GF: 0-0 Fm: 0-0**
Distance: 5f/6f: 0-3 7f-8f: 0-2 9f-13f: 0-0 14f+: 0-0
Track : LH: 0-1 RH: 0-0 Tight: 0-1 Gall: 0-1
Aids: Bl: 0-0 Vi: 0-0 Tstrap: 0-0 Ckp: 0-0
Best Rating: **62** 8/09 Newb 6f8y good

Quinsman

98(101) (72)**69**

3-y-o b c Singspiel (IRE)-Penny Cross (Efisio)

J S Moore Donald M Kerr

Placings:0456653131 **(7831)**

2009: 8^{0}S, 6^{4}GF, 6^{5}GF, 8^{0}GF, 8^{6}S, 8^{5}GS, 10^{3}GF, 10^{1}SS, 12^{3}SD, 12^{1}SD,

	Starts	1st	2nd	3rd	Win & Pl
Career Total (Turf)	7	0	0	1	1252
Career Total (AW)	3	2	0	1	5347
72 12/09 Kemp	1m4f	(0-75)H	STD	£3238	
67 10/09 Ling	1m2f	(0-65)H	SS	£1706	

Total win prize-money £4944

Going (Turf): **Sf: 0-2 GS: 0-1 Gd: 0-0 GF: 0-4 Fm: 0-0**
Distance: 5f/6f: 0-0 7f-8f: 0-4 **9f-13f: 2-6** 14f+: 0-0
Track : LH: 1-4 RH: 1-2 **Tight: 1-3** Gall: 0-0
Aids: Bl: 0-0 Vi: 0-0 Tstrap: 0-0 Ckp: 0-0
Best Rating: **72** 12/09 Kemp 1m4f stand

Modest; stays 1m4f; handles fast ground; goes on Polytrack.

Quiquillo (USA)

97(89) (62)**70**

3-y-o ch f Cape Canaveral (USA)-Only Seventeen (USA) (Exploit (USA))

P D Evans (H R A Cecil 16/7) Diamond Racing Ltd

Placings:56-445105 **(6798)**

2009: 8^{4}G, 10^{4}GF, 10^{5}GS, 6^{1}G, 7^{0}SD, 6^{5}S,

	Starts	1st	2nd	3rd	Win & Pl
Career Total (Turf)	**6**	**1**	**0**	**0**	**2507**
Career Total (AW)	**2**	**0**	**0**	**0**	**0**
70 8/09 Chep	6f16y	(0-65)H	GD	£2266	

Total win prize-money £2267

Going (Turf): Sf: 0-1 GS: 0-2 **Gd: 1-2** GF: 0-1 Fm: 0-0
Distance: 5f/6f: 0-0 **7f-8f: 1-5** 9f-13f: 0-3 14f+: 0-0
Track : LH: 0-3 RH: 0-1 Tight: 0-1 Gall: 0-1
Aids: Bl: 0-0 Vi: 0-0 Tstrap: 0-0 Ckp: 0-0
Best Rating: **70** 8/09 Chep 6f16y good

Modest; stays 6f; acts on good ground.

Quirina

101(100) (89)**92**

4-y-o b f Red Ransom (USA)-Qirmazi (USA) (Riverman (USA))

R M Beckett S Henderson R O'Donnell C Green & Partners

Placings:4/4011546-350 **(3509)**

2009: 10^{3}SD, 10^{5}G, 8^{0}SD,

	Starts	1st	2nd	3rd	Win & Pl
Career Total (Turf)	**9**	**2**	**0**	**0**	**13097**
Career Total (AW)	**2**	**0**	**0**	**1**	**867**
89 8/08 Nott	1m2f50y (0-85)H		GD	£6476	
83 7/08 Hayd	1m30y (0-75)H		GD	£3238	

Total win prize-money £9714

Going (Turf): Sf: 0-1 GS: 0-1 **Gd: 2-5** GF: 0-2 Fm: 0-0
Distance: 5f/6f: 0-0 7f-8f: 0-3 **9f-13f: 2-8** 14f+: 0-0
Track : **LH: 2-5** RH: 0-5 Tight: 0-4 Gall: 0-1
Aids: Bl: 0-0 Vi: 0-0 Tstrap: 0-0 Ckp: 0-0
Best Rating: **92** 9/08 Hayd 1m2f120y gd-fm

Useful; effective over 1m2f; acts on good ground and Polytrack.

Quite A Fella (USA)

(98) (69)

4-y-o b g Swain (IRE)-Magnificent Star (USA) (Silver Hawk (USA))

Andrew Turnell The Chosen Few

Placings:1P **(0726)**

2009: 12^{1}SD, 12^{P}SD,

	Starts	1st	2nd	3rd	Win & Pl
Career Total (Turf)	**0**	**0**	**0**	**0**	
Career Total (AW)	**2**	**1**	**0**	**0**	**2730**
69 1/09 Ling	1m4f		STD	£2729	

Total win prize-money £2730

Going (Turf): **Sf: 0-0 GS: 0-0 Gd: 0-0 GF: 0-0 Fm: 0-0**
Distance: 5f/6f: 0-0 7f-8f: 0-0 **9f-13f: 1-2** 14f+: 0-0
Track : **LH: 1-2** RH: 0-0 **Tight: 1-2** Gall: 0-0
Aids: Bl: 0-0 Vi: 0-0 Tstrap: 0-0 Ckp: 0-0

Best Rating: **69** 1/09 Ling 1m4f stand

Fair; effective at 1m4f on Polytrack.

Quite Something

90 **64**

2-y-o b f Footstepsinthesand-Quite Elusive (USA) (Elusive Quality (USA))

A M Balding Trebles Holford Thoroughbreds

Placings:4 **(6616)**

2009: 6^{4}G,

	Starts	1st	2nd	3rd	Win & Pl
Career Total (Turf)	1	0	0	0	361

Going (Turf): Sf: 0-0 GS: 0-0 Gd: 0-1 GF: 0-0 Fm: 0-0
Distance: 5f/6f: 0-0 7f-8f: 0-1 9f-13f: 0-0 14f+: 0-0
Track : LH: 0-0 RH: 0-0 Tight: 0-0 Gall: 0-0
Aids: Bl: 0-0 Vi: 0-0 Tstrap: 0-0 Ckp: 0-0
Best Rating: **64** 10/09 Newb 6f110y good

Quite Sparky

99 **72**

2-y-o b g Lucky Story (USA)-Imperialistic (IRE) (Imperial Ballet (IRE))

T P Tate A Crowther

Placings:62 **(5669)**

2009: 7^{6}G, 7^{2}S,

	Starts	1st	2nd	3rd	Win & Pl
Career Total (Turf)	2	0	1	0	1590

Going (Turf): **Sf: 0-1** GS: 0-0 Gd: 0-1 GF: 0-0 Fm: 0-0
Distance: 5f/6f: 0-0 7f-8f: 0-2 9f-13f: 0-0 14f+: 0-0
Track : LH: 0-2 RH: 0-0 Tight: 0-2 Gall: 0-0
Aids: Bl: 0-0 Vi: 0-0 Tstrap: 0-0 Ckp: 0-0
Best Rating: **72** 9/09 Thsk 7f soft

Fair first foal of multiple winner; built on debut when second over 7f on soft ground.

Quitit (IRE)

78 (61)**73**

4-y-o b g Kalanisi (IRE)-Wattrey (Royal Academy (USA))

Mrs S A Watt Lady Blackett Mrs G Handley Maj E J Watt

Placings:000/6602610-5 **(3609)**

2009: 16^{5}GF,

	Starts	1st	2nd	3rd	Win & Pl
Career Total (Turf)	10	1	1	0	4070
Career Total (AW)	1	0	0	0	

73	10/08	Catt	1m7f177y	(0-70)H	G-S	£2590

Total win prize-money £2590

Going (Turf): Sf: 0-1 **GS: 1-1** Gd: 0-2 GF: 0-2 Fm: 0-0
Distance: 5f/6f: 0-0 7f-8f: 0-4 9f-13f: 0-4 **14f+: 1-3**
Track : **LH: 1-4** RH: 0-6 **Tight: 1-3** Gall: 0-0
Aids: **Bl: 1-6** Vi: 0-0 Tstrap: 0-1 Ckp: 0-1
Best Rating: **73** 10/08 Catt 1m7f177y gd-sft

Modest; stays 2m; acts on soft ground.

R Woody

73(102) (72)**23**

2-y-o ch g Ishiguru (USA)-Yarrita (Tragic Role (USA))

Mrs L C Jewell Quintessential Thoroughbreds Solar Syn

Placings:00014 **(7871)**

2009: 6^{0}G, 6^{0}SD, 5^{0}SD, 5^{1}SD, 5^{4}SD,

	Starts	1st	2nd	3rd	Win & Pl
Career Total (Turf)	1	0	0	0	
Career Total (AW)	4	1	0	0	2135

72	12/09	Sthl	5f	STD	£1942

Total win prize-money £1943

Going (Turf): Sf: 0-0 GS: 0-0 Gd: 0-1 GF: 0-0 Fm: 0-0
Distance: **5f/6f: 1-5** 7f-8f: 0-0 9f-13f: 0-0 14f+: 0-0
Track : LH: 0-2 RH: 0-1 Tight: 0-2 Gall: 0-1
Aids: Bl: 0-0 Vi: 0-0 Tstrap: 0-0 Ckp: 0-0
Best Rating: **72** 12/09 Sthl 5f stand

Moderate; suited by 5f and Fibresand.

Ra Junior (USA)

104(92) (61)**99**

3-y-o b g Rahy (USA)-Fantasia Girl (IRE) (Caerleon (USA))

B J Meehan Roldvale Limited

Placings:4212-00000 **(6795)**

2009: 9^{0}FT, 10^{0}GF, 9^{0}G, 10^{0}GF, 10^{0}S,

	Starts	1st	2nd	3rd	Win & Pl
Career Total (Turf)	8	1	2	0	11787
Career Total (AW)	1	0	0	0	

91	10/08	NmkR	7f	G-F	£6152

Total win prize-money £6152

Going (Turf): Sf: 0-1 GS: 0-0 Gd: 0-4 **GF: 1-3** Fm: 0-0
Distance: 5f/6f: 0-0 **7f-8f: 1-3** 9f-13f: 0-6 14f+: 0-0
Track : LH: 0-4 RH: 0-3 Tight: 0-1 Gall: 0-3
Aids: Bl: 0-2 Vi: 0-0 Tstrap: 0-1 Ckp: 0-1
Best Rating: **99** 10/08 NmkR 1m good

Very useful; stays 1m; acts on good and faster ground; has worn blinkers.

Raaeidd (IRE)

99(91) (78)**86**

3-y-o b c King's Best (USA)-Bahr (Generous (IRE))

M A Jarvis Sheikh Ahmed Al Maktoum

Placings:61-35440 **(5511)**

2009: 10^{3}GF, 10^{5}G, 9^{4}S, 8^{4}G, 8^{0}G,

	Starts	1st	2nd	3rd	Win & Pl
Career Total (Turf)	6	0	0	1	1867
Career Total (AW)	1	1	0	0	4209

78	11/08	Kemp	7f	STD	£4209

Total win prize-money £4209

Going (Turf): **Sf: 0-1 GS: 0-1 Gd: 0-3 GF: 0-1 Fm: 0-0**
Distance: 5f/6f: 0-1 **7f-8f: 1-2** 9f-13f: 0-4 14f+: 0-0
Track : LH: 0-2 **RH: 1-3** Tight: 0-2 Gall: 0-1
Aids: Bl: 0-0 Vi: 0-0 Tstrap: 0-1 Ckp: 0-1
Best Rating: **86** 5/09 York 1m2f88y gd-fm

Useful; stays 1m2f; acts on fast ground and on Polytrack.

Rabbit Fighter (IRE)

91(101) (71)**78**

5-y-o ch g Observatory (USA)-Furnish (Green Desert (USA))

D Shaw Market Avenue Racing Club Ltd

Placings:6253/1050000232611/001642303600000-05100005 **(6825)**

2009: 7^{0}SS, 6^{5}SD, 5^{1}SD, 7^{0}GS, 7^{0}SD, 7^{0}SD, 6^{0}G, 5^{5}SD,

	Starts	1st	2nd	3rd	Win & Pl
Career Total (Turf)	17	0	2	2	5780
Career Total (AW)	24	5	2	2	14254

71	4/09	Wolv	5f216y	(0-60)H	STD	£1977
76	4/08	Wolv	5f216y	(0-70)H	STD	£2456
76	12/07	Kemp	6f	(0-65)H	STD	£2047
80	12/07	Kemp	6f	(0-65)H	STD	£2047
77	3/07	Wolv	1m141y		STD	£3238

Total win prize-money £11770

Going (Turf): **Sf: 0-8 GS: 0-3 Gd: 0-3 GF: 0-3 Fm: 0-0**
Distance: **5f/6f: 4-20** 7f-8f: 0-16 9f-13f: 1-5 14f+: 0-0
Track : **LH: 3-19** RH: 2-11 **Tight: 3-15** Gall: 0-1
Aids: Bl: 0-0 **Vi: 4-25** Tstrap: 0-0 Ckp: 0-0
Best Rating: **91** 8/06 Sand 7f16y good

Fair; effective over 6f-1m; acts on fast ground and on Polytrack; usually visored.

Rabeera

97 **59**

4-y-o b f Beat Hollow-Gai Bulga (Kris)

A M Balding John Dwyer & Crevan O'Grady

Placings:0/0040-0 **(1415)**

2009: 10^{0}GF,

	Starts	1st	2nd	3rd	Win & Pl
Career Total (Turf)	6	0	0	0	514

Going (Turf): **Sf: 0-0 GS: 0-1 Gd: 0-1 GF: 0-4 Fm: 0-0**
Distance: 5f/6f: 0-0 7f-8f: 0-1 9f-13f: 0-5 14f+: 0-0
Track : LH: 0-4 RH: 0-1 Tight: 0-3 Gall: 0-1
Aids: Bl: 0-0 Vi: 0-2 Tstrap: 0-0 Ckp: 0-0
Best Rating: **66** 9/07 NmkR 1m gd-fm

Raccoon (IRE)

105 **81**

9-y-o b g Raphane (USA)-Kunucu (IRE) (Bluebird (USA))

Mrs R A Carr P D Savill

Placings:02011/41100000/00000225/340356330006/1105 14055210030/34531025022-13313324221100 **(5767)**

2009: 5^{1}GF, 5^{3}GF, 5^{3}GF, 5^{1}GF, 5^{3}GF, 5^{3}GF, 5^{2}GF, 5^{4}G, 5^{2}GF, 5^{2}G, 5^{1}GF, 5^{1}G, 5^{0}S, 5^{0}GF,

	Starts	1st	2nd	3rd	Win & Pl
Career Total (Turf)	73	13	10	11	99487

69	8/09	Muss	5f		GD	£1942
81	8/09	Muss	5f	(0-85)H	G-F	£6476
78	6/09	Catt	5f	(0-70)H	G-F	£2914
74	4/09	Nott	5f13y	(0-65)H	G-F	£2047
71	6/08	Muss	5f	(0-65)H	G-F	£2590
71	8/07	Catt	5f		GD	£2730
86	6/07	Muss	5f	(0-85)H	GD	£6477
86	5/07	Catt	5f	(0-70)H	FRM	£3412
79	5/07	Nott	5f13y	(0-60)H	G-F	£2388
97	5/04	Muss	5f	B(0-105)H	G-F	£29000
97	5/04	Hayd	5f	B(0-105)H	G-F	£14092
85	9/03	Sand	5f6y	D(0-85)H	G-F	£4182
79	9/03	Thsk	5f	F(0-60)H	G-F	£3188

Total win prize-money £81443

Going (Turf): Sf: 0-3 GS: 0-7 Gd: 3-23 **GF: 9-36** Fm: 1-4
Distance: **5f/6f: 13-69** 7f-8f: 0-4 9f-13f: 0-0 14f+: 0-0
Track : LH: 0-3 RH: 0-0 Tight: 0-1 Gall: 0-0
Aids: Bl: 0-0 **Vi: 3-18** Tstrap: 0-0 Ckp: 0-0
Best Rating: **97** 5/04 Muss 5f gd-fm

Fair; has been tubed; best at 5f, but does stay 6f; effective on fast ground; has worn a visor and a tongue tie; suited by forcing tactics; consistent.

Racer Forever (USA)

106(105) (111)**112**

6-y-o b g Rahy (USA)-Ras Shaikh (USA) (Sheikh Albadou)

J H M Gosden Mohamed Obaida

Placings:62155/6106/30523046/41626010050-55500 **(5249)**
2009: 7^{5}GF, 7^{5}GF, 7^{5}GF, 7^{0}G, 7^{0}GF,

	Starts	1st	2nd	3rd	Win & Pl
Career Total (Turf)	30	4	2	1	139622
Career Total (AW)	3	0	1	1	5504

111 6/08 NmkJ 7f FRM £26681
116 2/08 Ndas 6f110y (95-110)H GD £36180
105 6/06 Epsm 7f GD £19873
88 8/05 Sals 6f G-F £4826
Total win prize-money £87562

Going (Turf): Sf: 0-1 GS: 0-2 **Gd: 2-15** GF: 1-10 Fm: 1-2
Distance: 5f/6f: 1-6 **7f-8f: 3-27** 9f-13f: 0-0 14f+: 0-0
Track : **LH: 2-11** RH: 0-3 Tight: 1-5 Gall: 1-5
Aids: **Bl: 2-22** Vi: 0-0 Tstrap: 0-0 Ckp: 0-0
Best Rating: **116** 2/08 Ndas 6f110y good

Smart; winner in Listed and Group 3 company; effective over 6f-7f; best on a quick surface; usually wears blinkers.

Racing Hero (IRE)

102(96) (69)**91**
3-y-o b g Montjeu (IRE)-Aim For The Top (USA) (Irish River (FR))
J Noseda Albert S N Hu

Placings:315012 **(7101)**
2009: 10^{3}GF, 12^{1}GF, 10^{5}GF, **10^{0}**SD, 10^{1}GS, 10^{2}G,

	Starts	1st	2nd	3rd	Win & Pl
Career Total (Turf)	5	2	1	1	10176
Career Total (AW)	1	0	0	0	

91 10/09 Donc 1m2f60y (0-80)H G-S £4857
80 6/09 Donc 1m4f G-F £3238
Total win prize-money £8095

Going (Turf): Sf: 0-0 **GS: 1-1** Gd: 0-1 **GF: 1-3** Fm: 0-0
Distance: 5f/6f: 0-0 7f-8f: 0-0 **9f-13f: 2-6** 14f+: 0-0
Track : **LH: 2-3** RH: 0-3 Tight: 0-2 **Gall: 2-2**
Aids: Bl: 0-0 Vi: 0-0 Tstrap: 0-0 Ckp: 0-0
Best Rating: **91** 10/09 Yarm 1m2f21y good

Fair; stays 1m4f and acts on most ground.

Racketeer (IRE)

105(98) (86)**102**
3-y-o b c Cape Cross (IRE)-Flirtation (Pursuit Of Love)
J H M Gosden Duke Of Roxburghe

Placings:21-15 **(2411)**
2009: 8^{1}G, 8^{5}G,

	Starts	1st	2nd	3rd	Win & Pl
Career Total (Turf)	2	1	0	0	16654
Career Total (AW)	2	1	1	0	3886

102 4/09 Sand 1m14y (0-100)H GD £15577
86 12/08 Sthl 1m STD £3885
Total win prize-money £19464

Going (Turf): Sf: 0-0 GS: 0-0 **Gd: 1-2** GF: 0-0 Fm: 0-0
Distance: 5f/6f: 0-0 7f-8f: 1-2 9f-13f: 1-2 14f+: 0-0
Track : LH: 1-2 RH: 1-2 Tight: 0-1 Gall: 0-0
Aids: Bl: 0-0 Vi: 0-0 Tstrap: 0-0 Ckp: 0-0
Best Rating: **102** 4/09 Sand 1m14y good

Fair; stays 7f and acts on Polytrack.

Racy

101(99) (85)**86**
2-y-o b c Medicean-Soar (Danzero (AUS))

Sir Michael Stoute Cheveley Park Stud

Placings:213 **(7063)**
2009: 5^{2}GF, 6^{1}GF, 6^{3}SD,

	Starts	1st	2nd	3rd	Win & Pl
Career Total (Turf)	2	1	1	0	6722
Career Total (AW)	1	0	0	1	578

86 9/09 Pont 6f G-F £5180
Total win prize-money £5181

Going (Turf): Sf: 0-0 GS: 0-0 Gd: 0-0 **GF: 1-2** Fm: 0-0
Distance: **5f/6f: 1-3** 7f-8f: 0-0 9f-13f: 0-0 14f+: 0-0
Track : **LH: 1-2** RH: 0-0 Tight: 0-1 Gall: 0-0
Aids: Bl: 0-0 Vi: 0-0 Tstrap: 0-0 Ckp: 0-0
Best Rating: **86** 9/09 Pont 6f gd-fm

Useful; effective over 5f-6f; acts on fast ground.

Raddy 'Ell Pauline (IRE)

99(99) (81)**85**
2-y-o ch f Dubawi (IRE)-Run For Me (IRE) (Danehill (USA))
K A Ryan Mike McGeever & Mrs Theresa Marnane

Placings:010200 **(5658)**
2009: 6^{0}GS, 6^{1}SD, 6^{0}G, 5^{2}GF, 6^{0}GF, 6^{0}GS,

	Starts	1st	2nd	3rd	Win & Pl
Career Total (Turf)	5	0	1	0	2312
Career Total (AW)	1	1	0	0	3886

81 6/09 Kemp 6f STD £3885
Total win prize-money £3886

Going (Turf): **Sf: 0-0 GS: 0-2 Gd: 0-1 GF: 0-2 Fm: 0-0**
Distance: **5f/6f: 1-6** 7f-8f: 0-0 9f-13f: 0-0 14f+: 0-0
Track : LH: 0-0 **RH: 1-1** Tight: 0-0 Gall: 0-0
Aids: Bl: 0-0 Vi: 0-0 Tstrap: 0-0 Ckp: 0-0
Best Rating: **85** 7/09 NmkJ 6f good

Useful filly; stays 6f; acts on Polytrack and fast turf.

Radiator Rooney (IRE)

95(108) (68)**60**
6-y-o br g Elnadim (USA)-Queen Of The May (IRE) (Nicolotte)
Patrick Morris Vincent Gleeson

Placings:06420**032/20162**030660400/**03006302050005**4/2141440310304**0**-6004530**U0033305** **(7889)**
2009: 6^{8}SD, 5^{0}GF, 5^{0}G, 6^{4}GF, 5^{5}SD, 5^{3}GF, 6^{0}GF, 6^{U}SD, 5^{0}SD, 6^{0}SD, 5^{3}SD, 5^{3}SD, 6^{3}SD, 6^{0}SD, 5^{5}SD,

	Starts	1st	2nd	3rd	Win & Pl
Career Total (Turf)	34	1	2	4	9789
Career Total (AW)	32	3	4	6	18651

60 6/08 DRoy 5f (45-60)H G-F £4318
70 3/08 Dund 5f (50-75)H STD £5334
67 2/08 Kemp 6f (0-70)H STD £2590
71 2/06 Ling 5f STD £3886
Total win prize-money £16131

Going (Turf): Sf: 0-2 GS: 0-1 Gd: 0-9 **GF: 1-11** Fm: 0-10
Distance: **5f/6f: 4-59** 7f-8f: 0-6 9f-13f: 0-1 14f+: 0-0
Track : LH: 2-40 RH: 2-17 **Tight: 1-17** Gall: 0-0
Aids: **Bl: 2-32** Vi: 1-11 Tstrap: 1-5 Ckp: 1-5
Best Rating: **73** 2/06 Ling 6f stand

Moderate; effective at around 6f; acts on good ground; also goes on Polytrack.

Radio City

95(97) (72)**78**
2-y-o b g Intikhab (USA)-Red Shareef (Marju (IRE))

R M Beckett Clipper Logistics

Placings:436316163 **(6541)**
2009: 5^{4}SD, 5^{3}GF, 6^{6}G, 5^{3}GF, 5^{1}GF, 5^{6}GF, 6^{1}GF, 5^{6}SD, 6^{3}GF,

	Starts	1st	2nd	3rd	Win & Pl
Career Total (Turf)	7	2	0	3	11097
Career Total (AW)	2	0	0	0	0

78 9/09 Epsm 6f (0-85) G-F £5180
71 8/09 Brig 5f59y G-F £3532
Total win prize-money £8713

Going (Turf): Sf: 0-0 GS: 0-0 Gd: 0-1 **GF: 2-6** Fm: 0-0
Distance: **5f/6f: 2-9** 7f-8f: 0-0 9f-13f: 0-0 14f+: 0-0
Track : **LH: 2-5** RH: 0-1 **Tight: 1-3** Gall: 0-0
Aids: Bl: 0-0 Vi: 0-0 Tstrap: 0-0 Ckp: 0-0
Best Rating: **78** 9/09 Epsm 6f gd-fm

Fair; effective at 5-6f; acts on fast ground.

Radio Wave

87 **78**
2-y-o ch f Dalakhani (IRE)-Tuning (Rainbow Quest (USA))
J H M Gosden K Abdulla

Placings:3 **(6920)**
2009: 8^{3}GF,

	Starts	1st	2nd	3rd	Win & Pl
Career Total (Turf)	1	0	0	1	614

Going (Turf): **Sf: 0-0 GS: 0-0 Gd: 0-0 GF: 0-1 Fm: 0-0**
Distance: 5f/6f: 0-0 7f-8f: 0-0 9f-13f: 0-1 14f+: 0-0
Track : LH: 0-0 RH: 0-0 Tight: 0-0 Gall: 0-0
Aids: Bl: 0-0 Vi: 0-0 Tstrap: 0-0 Ckp: 0-0
Best Rating: **78** 10/09 Yarm 1m3y gd-fm

Radiohead

114 (107)**117**
2-y-o ch c Johannesburg (USA)-Security Interest (USA) (Belong To Me (USA))
B J Meehan IEAH Stables, Pegasus Holding Group & Mrs Carmen Burrell & J

Placings:2113420 **(7307a)**
2009: 5^{2}GF, 5^{1}G, 5^{1}GF, 5^{3}GF, 6^{4}GF, 6^{2}GF, 8^{0}FT,

	Starts	1st	2nd	3rd	Win & Pl
Career Total (Turf)	6	2	2	1	127157
Career Total (AW)	1	0	0	0	0

106 6/09 Asct 5f G-F £51093
88 5/09 Bath 5f11y GD £3561
Total win prize-money £54655

Going (Turf): Sf: 0-0 GS: 0-0 **Gd: 1-1 GF: 1-5** Fm: 0-0
Distance: **5f/6f: 2-5** 7f-8f: 0-1 9f-13f: 0-1 14f+: 0-0
Track : **LH: 1-2** RH: 0-0 Tight: 0-0 **Gall: 1-1**
Aids: Bl: 0-0 Vi: 0-0 Tstrap: 0-0 Ckp: 0-0
Best Rating: **117** 10/09 NmkR 6f gd-fm

Group class; winner of the Norfolk Stakes, third in the same year's Nunthorpe and runner-up in the Middle Park in 2009; suited by 5-6f; acts on good/fast ground; has worn a tongue tie.

Radsky

74 **43**
2-y-o ch c Where Or When (IRE)-Radiant Sky (IRE) (Spectrum (IRE))
J G Portman Simon Skinner

Placings:000 **(6331)**
2009: 7^{0}GF, 8^{0}GF, 10^{0}F,

	Starts	1st	2nd	3rd	Win & Pl
Career Total (Turf)	3	0	0	0	

Going (Turf): **Sf: 0-0 GS: 0-0 Gd: 0-0 GF: 0-2 Fm: 0-1**
Distance: 5f/6f: 0-0 7f-8f: 0-1 9f-13f: 0-2 14f+: 0-0
Track : LH: 0-1 RH: 0-1 Tight: 0-2 Gall: 0-0
Aids: Bl: 0-0 Vi: 0-0 Tstrap: 0-0 Ckp: 0-0
Best Rating: **43** 8/09 Wind 1m67y gd-fm

Rafaan (USA)

93 **84**

3-y-o b/br g Gulch (USA)-Reem Al Barari (USA) (Storm Cat (USA))
M Johnston Hamdan Al Maktoum

Placings:23-100 **(2935)**
2009: 10¹GF, 10⁰G, 10⁰G,

	Starts	1st	2nd	3rd	Win & Pl
Career Total (Turf)	5	1	1	1	4424

84 4/09 Newc 1m2f32y G-F £2752
Total win prize-money £2752

Going (Turf): Sf: 0-0 GS: 0-0 Gd: 0-4 **GF: 1-1** Fm: 0-0
Distance: 5f/6f: 0-0 7f-8f: 0-2 **9f-13f: 1-3** 14f+: 0-0
Track : **LH: 1-2** RH: 0-1 Tight: 0-0 **Gall: 1-2**
Aids: Bl: 0-0 Vi: 0-0 Tstrap: 0-0 Ckp: 0-0
Best Rating: **84** 4/09 Newc 1m2f32y gd-fm

Useful; stays 1m2f and acts on fast ground; likes to race prominently.

Raffanetti (IRE)

75 **16**

3-y-o b g Raphane (USA)-Proud Boast (Komaite (USA))
T D Barron P D Savill

Placings:60 **(3003)**
2009: 6⁰GF, 5⁰GF,

	Starts	1st	2nd	3rd	Win & Pl
Career Total (Turf)	2	0	0	0	0

Going (Turf): **Sf: 0-0 GS: 0-0 Gd: 0-0 GF: 0-2 Fm: 0-0**
Distance: 5f/6f: 0-1 7f-8f: 0-1 9f-13f: 0-0 14f+: 0-0
Track : LH: 0-0 RH: 0-0 Tight: 0-0 Gall: 0-0
Aids: Bl: 0-0 Vi: 0-0 Tstrap: 0-0 Ckp: 0-0
Best Rating: **16** 6/09 Thsk 5f gd-fm

Rafiki (IRE)

(68) (17)

2-y-o b g Kheleyf (USA)-Jemalina (USA) (Trempolino (USA))
W R Swinburn Reddin & Harris

Placings:0 **(6802)**
2009: 5⁰SD,

	Starts	1st	2nd	3rd	Win & Pl
Career Total (Turf)	0	0	0	0	
Career Total (AW)	1	0	0	0	

Going (Turf): **Sf: 0-0 GS: 0-0 Gd: 0-0 GF: 0-0 Fm: 0-0**
Distance: 5f/6f: 0-1 7f-8f: 0-0 9f-13f: 0-0 14f+: 0-0
Track : LH: 0-1 RH: 0-0 Tight: 0-1 Gall: 0-0
Aids: Bl: 0-0 Vi: 0-0 Tstrap: 0-0 Ckp: 0-0
Best Rating: **17** 10/09 Wolv 5f216y stand

Rafiqa (IRE)

104 **96**

3-y-o b f Mujahid (USA)-Shamara (IRE) (Spectrum (IRE))
C F Wall The Equema Partnership

Placings:15014-3254 **(6239)**
2009: 7³GF, 8²S, 8⁵GF, 10⁴G,

	Starts	1st	2nd	3rd	Win & Pl
Career Total (Turf)	9	2	1	1	24925

89 9/08 Yarm 1m3y (0-85) GD £4415
75 7/08 Nott 6f15y G-S £3238
Total win prize-money £7654

Going (Turf): Sf: 0-2 **GS: 1-1 Gd: 1-4** GF: 0-2 Fm: 0-0
Distance: 5f/6f: 0-1 7f-8f: 1-5 9f-13f: 1-3 14f+: 0-0
Track : LH: 0-1 RH: 0-2 Tight: 0-0 Gall: 0-1
Aids: Bl: 0-0 Vi: 0-0 Tstrap: 0-0 Ckp: 0-0
Best Rating: **96** 7/09 Sals 1m soft

Useful; stays 1m but effective at 7f; acts on most ground.

Rafta (IRE)

105 **81**

3-y-o b f Atraf-First Kiss (GER) (Night Shift (USA))
T T Clement R L Gray

Placings:00-011112RR **(5471)**
2009: 7⁰GF, 6¹GF, 6¹S, 7¹S, 6¹G, 7²HY, 7ᴿSD, 6ᴿGF,

	Starts	1st	2nd	3rd	Win & Pl
Career Total (Turf)	9	4	1	0	20143
Career Total (AW)	1	0	0	0	

79 7/09 Thsk 6f (0-70)H GD £4274
74 7/09 Leic 7f9y (0-80)H SFT £6308
78 7/09 Nott 6f15y (0-70)H SFT £2590
65 6/09 Sals 6f (0-70)H G-F £3238
Total win prize-money £16410

Going (Turf): **Sf: 2-3** GS: 0-0 Gd: 1-3 GF: 1-3 Fm: 0-0
Distance: 5f/6f: 2-5 7f-8f: 2-5 9f-13f: 0-0 14f+: 0-0
Track : LH: 0-0 RH: 0-1 Tight: 0-0 Gall: 0-0
Aids: Bl: 0-0 Vi: 0-0 Tstrap: 0-0 Ckp: 0-0
Best Rating: **81** 8/09 Leic 7f9y heavy

Fair; effective at 6-7f; acts on any ground.

Ragamuffin Man (IRE)

107(100) (80)**83**

4-y-o gr g Dalakhani (IRE)-Chamela Bay (IRE) (Sadler's Wells (USA))
P J Hobbs (W J Knight 19/10) M Hutton & B Spiers

Placings:031/4043-4251 **(6899)**
2009: 16⁴G, 16²G, 18⁵GF, 17¹GF,

	Starts	1st	2nd	3rd	Win & Pl
Career Total (Turf)	10	2	1	1	9424
Career Total (AW)	1	0	0	1	433

83 10/09 Pont 2m1f216y (0-75)H G-F £3238
74 10/07 Bath 1m5y GD £2266
Total win prize-money £5505

Going (Turf): Sf: 0-0 GS: 0-2 **Gd: 1-5 GF: 1-3** Fm: 0-0
Distance: 5f/6f: 0-0 7f-8f: 0-1 9f-13f: 1-5 14f+: 1-5
Track : **LH: 2-5** RH: 0-4 **Tight: 1-3** Gall: 0-4
Aids: Bl: 0-0 Vi: 0-4 Tsrap: 1-1 Ckp: 1-1
Best Rating: **83** 10/09 Pont 2m1f216y gd-fm

Fair; stays 2m; acts on good and easy ground; has worn a visor.

Ragdollianna

92(94) (58)**87**

5-y-o b m Kayf Tara-Jupiters Princess (Jupiter Island)
Norma Twomey D M & Mrs M A Newland

Placings:20110-055 **(7201)**
2009: 14⁰G, 14⁵F, 13⁵SD,

	Starts	1st	2nd	3rd	Win & Pl
Career Total (Turf)	7	2	1	0	7382
Career Total (AW)	1	0	0	0	0

85 8/08 Wwck 1m4f134y (0-75)H SFT £3238
62 8/08 Bath 1m3f144y G-S £3335
Total win prize-money £6573

Going (Turf): **Sf: 1-1 GS: 1-1** Gd: 0-2 GF: 0-1 Fm: 0-2
Distance: 5f/6f: 0-0 7f-8f: 0-0 **9f-13f: 2-6** 14f+: 0-2
Track : **LH: 2-5** RH: 0-3 **Tight: 1-3** Gall: 0-2
Aids: Bl: 0-0 Vi: 0-0 Tstrap: 0-0 Ckp: 0-0
Best Rating: **87** 7/08 NmkJ 1m4f gd-fm

Fair mare; stays 1m4f; acts on most ground; progressive.

Ragetti (IRE)

91 **64**

2-y-o b f Hawk Wing (USA)-Renada (Sinndar (IRE))
J Howard Johnson Transcend Bloodstock LLP

Placings:4 **(5674)**
2009: 7⁴S,

	Starts	1st	2nd	3rd	Win & Pl
Career Total (Turf)	1	0	0	0	397

Going (Turf): **Sf: 0-1 GS: 0-0 Gd: 0-0 GF: 0-0 Fm: 0-0**
Distance: 5f/6f: 0-0 7f-8f: 0-1 9f-13f: 0-0 14f+: 0-0
Track : LH: 0-1 RH: 0-0 Tight: 0-1 Gall: 0-0
Aids: Bl: 0-0 Vi: 0-0 Tstrap: 0-0 Ckp: 0-0
Best Rating: **64** 9/09 Thsk 7f soft

First foal of a juvenile hurdle winner; promise on debut over 7f on soft.

Raggle Taggle (IRE)

101(101) (64)**97**

3-y-o b f Tagula (IRE)-Jesting (Muhtarram (USA))
R M Beckett Lady Marchwood

Placings:23214020-01000 **(6949)**
2009: 5⁰G, 6¹GS, 6⁰G, 5⁰F, 6⁰SD,

	Starts	1st	2nd	3rd	Win & Pl
Career Total (Turf)	11	2	2	1	24695
Career Total (AW)	2	0	1	0	1253

92 6/09 NmkJ 6f G-S £10361
81 6/08 Yarm 5f43y G-F £2266
Total win prize-money £12629

Going (Turf): Sf: 0-3 **GS: 1-2** Gd: 0-3 **GF: 1-2** Fm: 0-1
Distance: **5f/6f: 2-12** 7f-8f: 0-1 9f-13f: 0-0 14f+: 0-0
Track : LH: 0-4 RH: 0-1 Tight: 0-1 Gall: 0-2
Aids: Bl: 0-0 Vi: 0-0 Tstrap: 0-0 Ckp: 0-0
Best Rating: **97** 8/08 Deau 5f gd-sft

Useful; effective over 5f-6f; acts on most ground; also goes on Polytrack.

Ragsta (IRE)

98(87) (61)**68**

2-y-o b f Key Of Luck (USA)-Rag Top (IRE) (Barathea (IRE))
C A Dwyer (R Hannon 1/9) Miss Lilo Blum

Placings:24102060040 **(7098)**
2009: 5²G, 6⁴GF, 6¹GF, 7⁰SD, 7²GF, 7⁰GF, 7⁶SD, 8⁰SD, 7⁰SD, 8⁴GF, 7⁰G,

	Starts	1st	2nd	3rd	Win & Pl
Career Total (Turf)	7	1	2	0	3974

Career Total (AW)	4	0	0	0	0
65	6/09	Wind	6f	G-F	£2047

Total win prize-money £2047

Going (Turf): Sf: 0-0 GS: 0-0 Gd: 0-2 **GF: 1-5** Fm: 0-0
Distance: **5f/6f: 1-3** 7f-8f: 0-6 9f-13f: 0-2 14f+: 0-0
Track : LH: 0-2 RH: 0-3 Tight: 0-1 **Gall: 1-2**
Aids: Bl: 0-0 Vi: 0-0 Tstrap: 0-0 Ckp: 0-0
Best Rating: **68** 5/09 Ling 6f gd-fm

Modest; effective over 7f; acts on fast ground.

Rahaala (IRE)

(88) (65)
2-y-o b f Indian Ridge-Mythie (FR) (Octagonal (NZ))
Sir Michael Stoute Hamdan Al Maktoum

Placings:5 **(5752)**
2009: 7^5SD,

	Starts	1st	2nd	3rd	Win & Pl
Career Total (Turf)	0	0	0	0	
Career Total (AW)	1	0	0	0	0

Going (Turf): **Sf: 0-0 GS: 0-0 Gd: 0-0 GF: 0-0 Fm: 0-0**
Distance: 5f/6f: 0-0 7f-8f: 0-1 9f-13f: 0-0 14f+: 0-0
Track : LH: 0-1 RH: 0-0 Tight: 0-1 Gall: 0-0
Aids: Bl: 0-0 Vi: 0-0 Tstrap: 0-0 Ckp: 0-0
Best Rating: **65** 9/09 Ling 7f stand

Raimond Ridge (IRE)

101(103) (76)**78**
3-y-o b/br g Namid-Jinsiyah (USA) (Housebuster (USA))
J Jay (M R Channon 24/10) David Fremel

Placings:4265**566-41212132664434233203666**46 **(7808)**
2009: 5^4SD, 6^1SD, 6^2SD, 6^1SD, 6^2SD, 6^1SD, 5^3SD, 6^2GF, 6^6GF, 5^6GF, 5^4GF, 6^4GF, 5^3F, 6^4SD, 5^2F, 6^3GF, 5^3F, 5^2GS, 6^0G, 5^3GF, 6^6GS, 5^6GF, 5^6G, 6^4SD, 5^6SD,

	Starts	1st	2nd	3rd	Win & Pl
Career Total (Turf)	20	0	4	4	7470
Career Total (AW)	12	3	2	1	9961

74	3/09	Ling	6f	(0-75)H	STD	£2900
72	2/09	Kemp	6f	(0-75)H	STD	£2590
62	1/09	Ling	6f		STD	£2047

Total win prize-money £7537

Going (Turf): **Sf: 0-1 GS: 0-5 Gd: 0-3 GF: 0-8 Fm: 0-3**
Distance: **5f/6f: 3-30** 7f-8f: 0-2 9f-13f: 0-0 14f+: 0-0
Track : **LH: 2-16** RH: 1-3 **Tight: 2-9** Gall: 0-5
Aids: Bl: 0-0 Vi: 0-0 Tstrap: 0-0 Ckp: 0-0
Best Rating: **78** 5/09 Thsk 6f gd-fm

Fair; effective over 5-6f; acts on soft ground; goes well on Polytrack.

Rain And Shade

85 (76)**52**
5-y-o ch g Rainbow Quest (USA)-Coretta (IRE) (Caerleon (USA))
E W Tuer E Tuer

Placings:6/22000/6-000 **(2068)**
2009: 9^0GF, 11^0GF, 12^0GS,

	Starts	1st	2nd	3rd	Win & Pl
Career Total (Turf)	6	0	0	0	0
Career Total (AW)	4	0	2	0	1581

Going (Turf): **Sf: 0-0 GS: 0-1 Gd: 0-1 GF: 0-4 Fm: 0-0**
Distance: 5f/6f: 0-0 7f-8f: 0-0 9f-13f: 0-10 14f+: 0-0
Track : LH: 0-7 RH: 0-3 Tight: 0-5 Gall: 0-1
Aids: Bl: 0-0 Vi: 0-0 Tstrap: 0-0 Ckp: 0-0
Best Rating: **76** 1/07 Wolv 1m1f103y std-slw

Rain Delayed (IRE)

105 (99)**108**
3-y-o b g Oasis Dream-Forever Phoenix (Shareef Dancer (USA))
G M Lyons Anamoine Limited

Placings:06212-513122 **(7007a)**
2009: 6^5GY, 5^1Y, 5^3G, 5^1G, 5^2GF, 5^2SD,

	Starts	1st	2nd	3rd	Win & Pl
Career Total (Turf)	5	2	1	1	28245
Career Total (AW)	6	1	3	0	19920

93	6/09	Tipp	5f	GD	£11069
97	5/09	DRoy	5f	YLD	£8050
90	11/08	Dund	5f	STD	£6351

Total win prize-money £25470

Going (Turf): Sf: 0-0 GS: 0-0 **Gd: 1-2** GF: 0-1 Fm: 0-0
Distance: **5f/6f: 3-10** 7f-8f: 0-1 9f-13f: 0-0 14f+: 0-0
Track : **LH: 2-8** RH: 1-1 Tight: 0-0 Gall: 0-0
Aids: Bl: 0-0 Vi: 0-0 Tstrap: 0-0 Ckp: 0-0
Best Rating: **108** 8/09 York 5f gd-fm

Smart; best over 5f; acts on most ground and on Polytrack; has worn a tongue tie; likes to race prominently.

Rain In The Course

67 **13**
2-y-o b f Royal Applause-Numanthia (IRE) (Barathea (IRE))
M R Channon Ahmed Jaber

Placings:00 **(5980)**
2009: 8^0G, 7^0GF,

	Starts	1st	2nd	3rd	Win & Pl
Career Total (Turf)	2	0	0	0	

Going (Turf): **Sf: 0-0 GS: 0-0 Gd: 0-1 GF: 0-1 Fm: 0-0**
Distance: 5f/6f: 0-0 7f-8f: 0-1 9f-13f: 0-1 14f+: 0-0
Track : LH: 0-0 RH: 0-1 Tight: 0-0 Gall: 0-0
Aids: Bl: 0-0 Vi: 0-0 Tstrap: 0-0 Ckp: 0-0
Best Rating: **13** 8/09 Chep 1m14y good

Rain On The Wind (IRE)

(91) (63)
2-y-o b g Bahamian Bounty-Mix Me Up (FR) (Linamix (FR))
S C Williams Chris Watkins And David N Reynolds

Placings:004 **(6207)**
2009: 6^0SD, 6^0SD, 5^4SD,

	Starts	1st	2nd	3rd	Win & Pl
Career Total (Turf)	0	0	0	0	
Career Total (AW)	3	0	0	0	192

Going (Turf): **Sf: 0-0 GS: 0-0 Gd: 0-0 GF: 0-0 Fm: 0-0**
Distance: 5f/6f: 0-3 7f-8f: 0-0 9f-13f: 0-0 14f+: 0-0
Track : LH: 0-0 RH: 0-3 Tight: 0-0 Gall: 0-0
Aids: Bl: 0-0 Vi: 0-0 Tstrap: 0-0 Ckp: 0-0
Best Rating: **63** 9/09 Kemp 5f stand

Rain Stops Play (IRE)

100(93) (57)**58**
7-y-o b g Desert Prince (IRE)-Pinta (IRE) (Ahonoora)
N G Richards Paul Montgomery

Placings:3021/20544006100**6/000110000102130/005600 0206500**4/5600005000-5244400 **(6818)**
2009: 9^5SD, 9^2G, 8^4G, 7^4G, 10^4GF, 9^0GF, 10^0GF,

	Starts	1st	2nd	3rd	Win & Pl
Career Total (Turf)	56	6	5	2	53472
Career Total (AW)	6	0	0	0	0

96	10/06	NmkR	1m	(0-100)H	G-S	£11217
86	8/06	Epsm	1m114y	(0-80)H	G-S	£6477
89	6/06	Nott	1m54y	(0-75)H	GD	£5505
89	5/06	NmkR	1m	(0-75)H	SFT	£3886
83	9/05	Epsm	7f	(0-85)H	GD	£6844
76	10/04	Bath	1m5y		SFT	£4524

Total win prize-money £38455

Going (Turf): **Sf: 2-8 GS: 2-11 Gd: 2-22** GF: 0-15 Fm: 0-0
Distance: 5f/6f: 0-0 7f-8f: 3-35 9f-13f: 3-27 14f+: 0-0
Track : **LH: 4-28** RH: 0-10 **Tight: 3-15** Gall: 0-4
Aids: Bl: 0-0 Vi: 0-1 Tstrap: 0-1 Ckp: 0-1
Best Rating: **96** 10/06 NmkR 1m gd-sft

Fair; effective over 1m; acts on good or softer ground; suited by forcing tactics.

Rainbow Above You (IRE)

(85) (51)
3-y-o b f Mujadil (USA)-Kibarague (Barathea (IRE))
Noel Lawlor Ms Ciara Doyle

Placings:0-0040 **(7371)**
2009: 6^0SD, 5^0SD, 5^4SD, 5^0SD,

	Starts	1st	2nd	3rd	Win & Pl
Career Total (Turf)	1	0	0	0	
Career Total (AW)	4	0	0	0	0

Going (Turf): **Sf: 0-1 GS: 0-0 Gd: 0-0 GF: 0-0 Fm: 0-0**
Distance: 5f/6f: 0-4 7f-8f: 0-1 9f-13f: 0-0 14f+: 0-0
Track : LH: 0-4 RH: 0-1 Tight: 0-2 Gall: 0-1
Aids: Bl: 0-0 Vi: 0-0 Tstrap: 0-2 Ckp: 0-2
Best Rating: **51** 4/09 Dund 6f stand

Rainbow Bay

100(98) (70)**59**
6-y-o b g Komaite (USA)-Bollin Victoria (Jalmood (USA))
Miss Tracy Waggott Miss T Waggott

Placings:2424/41600440600**0**/4010**4115020605460020**/0 644443262403-000055046 **(6379)**
2009: 5^0SD, 6^0GF, 6^0F, 6^0GF, 5^5GS, 5^5S, 5^0G, 6^4GF, 5^6GF,

	Starts	1st	2nd	3rd	Win & Pl
Career Total (Turf)	49	4	5	1	29591
Career Total (AW)	9	0	1	1	957

74	6/07	Catt	5f212y	(0-85)H	G-F	£5181
70	6/07	Catt	5f212y	(0-80)H	G-F	£5181
59	5/07	Catt	5f212y		G-F	£2047
76	5/06	Ayr	5f	(0-85)H	GD	£8096

Total win prize-money £20508

Going (Turf): Sf: 0-6 GS: 0-4 Gd: 1-13 **GF: 3-23** Fm: 0-3
Distance: **5f/6f: 4-52** 7f-8f: 0-6 9f-13f: 0-0 14f+: 0-0
Track : **LH: 3-22** RH: 0-2 **Tight: 3-16** Gall: 0-4
Aids: Bl: 1-6 **Vi: 2-31** Tstrap: 0-11 Ckp: 0-11
Best Rating: **77** 7/06 Hayd 6f gd-fm

Moderate sprinter; acts on a sound surface; also goes on Polytrack; often wears headgear.

Rainbow Desert (USA)

101 90

3-y-o b/br f Dynaformer (USA)-Tuscoga (USA) (Theatrical)
Saeed Bin Suroor Godolphin

Placings:10 **(7291)**
2009: 8^{1}GS, 10^{0}S,

	Starts	1st	2nd	3rd	Win & Pl
Career Total (Turf)	2	1	0	0	2730

90 10/09 Wind 1m67y G-S £2729
Total win prize-money £2730

Going (Turf): Sf: 0-1 **GS: 1-1** Gd: 0-0 GF: 0-0 Fm: 0-0
Distance: 5f/6f: 0-0 7f-8f: 0-0 **9f-13f: 1-2** 14f+: 0-0
Track : LH: 0-1 **RH: 1-1 Tight: 1-1** Gall: 0-1
Aids: Bl: 0-0 Vi: 0-0 Tstrap: 0-0 Ckp: 0-0
Best Rating: 90 10/09 Wind 1m67y gd-sft

Potentially very useful filly; won 1m maiden on easy ground on debut.

Rainbow Mirage (IRE)

104(105) (92)92

5-y-o b g Spectrum (IRE)-Embers Of Fame (IRE) (Sadler's Wells (USA))
E S McMahon R L Bedding

Placings:511320/000302**362**/05031250136-243 **(5375)**
2009: 8^{2}SD, 8^{4}GF, 8^{3}SD,

	Starts	1st	2nd	3rd	Win & Pl
Career Total (Turf)	22	4	3	4	89765
Career Total (AW)	7	0	2	2	6399

92 9/08 Bevl 1m100y (0-95)H HVY £9714
88 7/08 Nott 1m75y (0-85)H G-S £6476
87 6/06 Sals 6f GD £14022
71 6/06 Chep 6f16y G-F £3368
Total win prize-money £33580

Going (Turf): Sf: 1-5 GS: 1-4 Gd: 1-6 GF: 1-7 Fm: 0-0
Distance: 5f/6f: 1-14 7f-8f: 1-8 **9f-13f: 2-7** 14f+: 0-0
Track : LH: 1-12 RH: 1-5 Tight: 0-5 Gall: 0-2
Aids: Bl: 0-1 Vi: 0-0 Tstrap: 0-0 Ckp: 0-0
Best Rating: 95 9/06 Rdcr 6f good

Useful; stays 1m; acts on most ground; has worn blinkers.

Rainbow Peak (IRE)

109(104) (92)110

3-y-o b g Hernando (FR)-Celtic Fling (Lion Cavern (USA))
M A Jarvis P D Savill

Placings:111 **(7035)**
2009: 8^{1}SD, 10^{1}G, 10^{1}S,

	Starts	1st	2nd	3rd	Win & Pl
Career Total (Turf)	2	2	0	0	22432
Career Total (AW)	1	1	0	0	4404

110 10/09 Newb 1m2f6y (0-100)H SFT £11215
99 9/09 Asct 1m2f (0-90) GD £11215
92 5/09 Kemp 1m STD £4403
Total win prize-money £26836

Going (Turf): Sf: 1-1 GS: 0-0 **Gd: 1-1** GF: 0-0 Fm: 0-0
Distance: 5f/6f: 0-0 7f-8f: 1-1 **9f-13f: 2-2** 14f+: 0-0
Track : LH: 1-1 **RH: 2-2** Tight: 0-0 **Gall: 2-2**
Aids: Bl: 0-0 Vi: 0-0 Tstrap: 0-0 Ckp: 0-0
Best Rating: 110 10/09 Newb 1m2f6y soft

Very useful; stays 1m2f; acts on fast ground; goes on Polytrack.

Rainbow Six

(83) (54)

2-y-o b g Tiger Hill (IRE)-Birthday Suit (IRE) (Daylami (IRE))
M Botti Op - Center

Placings:04 **(7491)**
2009: 8^{0}SD, 8^{4}SD,

	Starts	1st	2nd	3rd	Win & Pl
Career Total (Turf)	0	0	0	0	
Career Total (AW)	2	0	0	0	241

Going (Turf): Sf: 0-0 GS: 0-0 Gd: 0-0 GF: 0-0 Fm: 0-0
Distance: 5f/6f: 0-0 7f-8f: 0-0 9f-13f: 0-2 14f+: 0-0
Track : LH: 0-2 RH: 0-0 Tight: 0-2 Gall: 0-0
Aids: Bl: 0-0 Vi: 0-0 Tstrap: 0-0 Ckp: 0-0
Best Rating: 54 11/09 Wolv 1m141y stand

Modest; should stay 1m; acts on Polytrack.

Rainbow View (USA)

114 (105)117

3-y-o b f Dynaformer (USA)-No Matter What (USA) (Nureyev (USA))
J H M Gosden Augustin Stable

Placings:1111-54342125 **(7286a)**
2009: 8^{5}GF, 12^{4}G, 8^{3}GF, 8^{4}G, 9^{2}S, 8^{1}GY, 10^{2}F, 9^{5}FT,

	Starts	1st	2nd	3rd	Win & Pl
Career Total (Turf)	11	5	2	1	553879
Career Total (AW)	1	0	0	0	41667

116 9/09 Leop 1m G-Y £135679
117 9/08 Asct 1m GD £113540
112 9/08 Donc 1m SFT £45416
112 8/08 NmkJ 7f G-S £28385
90 7/08 NmkJ 7f G-F £5180
Total win prize-money £328202

Going (Turf): Sf: 1-2 GS: 1-1 Gd: 1-3 GF: 1-3 Fm: 0-1
Distance: 5f/6f: 0-0 **7f-8f: 5-8** 9f-13f: 0-4 14f+: 0-0
Track : LH: 1-4 RH: 1-3 Tight: 0-2 **Gall: 1-2**
Aids: Bl: 0-0 Vi: 0-0 Tstrap: 1-2 Ckp: 1-2
Best Rating: 117 9/08 Asct 1m good

Top class at two but not quite so good at three; unbeaten in four runs as a juvenile, including the Group 1 Fillies' Mile; winner of Group 1 Matron Stakes in 2009; effective over 1m-1m4f; acts on good and softer ground; has worn cheek-pieces.

Rainbow Zest

93 67

6-y-o b g Rainbow Quest (USA)-Original (Caerleon (USA))
W Storey H S Hutchinson

Placings:6535/610-000000 **(6817)**
2009: 12^{0}GF, 8^{0}F, 10^{0}G, 7^{0}G, 8^{0}GF, 10^{0}GF,

	Starts	1st	2nd	3rd	Win & Pl
Career Total (Turf)	13	1	0	1	2617

67 5/08 Carl 1m1f61y (0-65)H G-F £1942
Total win prize-money £1943

Going (Turf): Sf: 0-3 GS: 0-0 Gd: 0-2 **GF: 1-7** Fm: 0-1
Distance: 5f/6f: 0-0 7f-8f: 0-5 **9f-13f: 1-8** 14f+: 0-0
Track : LH: 0-6 **RH: 1-4** Tight: 0-3 Gall: 0-2
Aids: Bl: 0-0 Vi: 0-0 Tstrap: 0-0 Ckp: 0-0
Best Rating: 78 8/06 NmkJ 1m soft

Modest; should stay 1m2f; acts on fast ground.

Raine Supreme

86(86) (42)52

2-y-o b f Mind Games-Supreme Angel (Beveled (USA))
E S McMahon Least Moved Partners

Placings:60360 **(7749)**
2009: 5^{6}GF, 5^{0}G, 7^{3}GF, 7^{6}GF, 5^{0}SD,

	Starts	1st	2nd	3rd	Win & Pl
Career Total (Turf)	4	0	0	1	302
Career Total (AW)	1	0	0	0	

Going (Turf): Sf: 0-0 GS: 0-0 Gd: 0-1 GF: 0-3 Fm: 0-0
Distance: 5f/6f: 0-3 7f-8f: 0-2 9f-13f: 0-0 14f+: 0-0
Track : LH: 0-2 RH: 0-1 Tight: 0-2 Gall: 0-1
Aids: Bl: 0-0 Vi: 0-0 Tstrap: 0-0 Ckp: 0-0
Best Rating: 52 8/09 Catt 7f gd-fm

Raine's Cross

104 95

2-y-o b c Cape Cross (IRE)-Branston Jewel (IRE) (Prince Sabo)
P Winkworth David Holden

Placings:13043412 **(6472)**
2009: 5^{1}G, 5^{3}G, 6^{0}GF, 6^{4}G, 7^{3}G, 8^{4}G, 8^{1}GS, 8^{2}GF,

	Starts	1st	2nd	3rd	Win & Pl
Career Total (Turf)	8	2	1	2	16257

92 9/09 Sals 1m G-S £4695
91 4/09 Bath 5f11y GD £2266
Total win prize-money £6962

Going (Turf): Sf: 0-0 **GS: 1-1 Gd: 1-5** GF: 0-2 Fm: 0-0
Distance: 5f/6f: 1-4 7f-8f: 1-3 9f-13f: 0-1 14f+: 0-0
Track : LH: 1-2 RH: 0-1 Tight: 0-1 **Gall: 1-1**
Aids: Bl: 0-0 Vi: 0-0 Tstrap: 0-0 Ckp: 0-0
Best Rating: 95 10/09 Epsm 1m114y gd-fm

Very useful; stays 1m; acts on most ground.

Rainiers Girl

(90) (46)

3-y-o b f Tobougg (IRE)-Premier Night (Old Vic)
R A Teal Hanover Partnership

Placings:0055 **(7653)**
2009: 10^{0}SD, 12^{0}SD, 8^{5}SD, 8^{5}SD,

	Starts	1st	2nd	3rd	Win & Pl
Career Total (Turf)	0	0	0	0	
Career Total (AW)	4	0	0	0	0

Going (Turf): Sf: 0-0 GS: 0-0 Gd: 0-0 GF: 0-0 Fm: 0-0
Distance: 5f/6f: 0-0 7f-8f: 0-2 9f-13f: 0-2 14f+: 0-0
Track : LH: 0-2 RH: 0-2 Tight: 0-2 Gall: 0-0
Aids: Bl: 0-0 Vi: 0-0 Tstrap: 0-0 Ckp: 0-0
Best Rating: 46 12/09 Ling 1m stand

Rainsborough

91(92) (66)58

2-y-o b g Trans Island-Greeba (Fairy King (USA))
S Curran (M R Channon 10/9) Ian Hutchins

Placings:50100230002250 (7824)
2009: 6^{5}GF, 6^{0}G, 5^{1}G, 7^{0}GS, 8^{0}GF, 7^{2}SD, 7^{3}GF, 7^{0}SD, 8^{0}SD, 7^{0}GF, 8^{2}SD, 8^{2}SD, 8^{5}SD, 7^{0}SD,

	Starts	1st	2nd	3rd	Win & Pl
Career Total (Turf)	7	1	0	1	2713
Career Total (AW)	7	0	3	0	1793

58 7/09 Leic 5f218y GD £1942
Total win prize-money £1943

Going (Turf): Sf: 0-0 GS: 0-1 **Gd: 1-2** GF: 0-4 Fm: 0-0
Distance: **5f/6f: 1-2** 7f-8f: 0-11 9f-13f: 0-1 14f+: 0-0
Track : LH: 0-3 RH: 0-4 Tight: 0-1 Gall: 0-0
Aids: Bl: 0-1 Vi: 0-0 Tstrap: 0-3 Ckp: 0-3
Best Rating: 66 11/09 Ling 1m stand

Modest; stays 1m; acts on Fibresand, Polytrack and fast ground; has worn cheekpieces, blinkers and a tongue tie.

Rainy Night

98(98) (66)70
3-y-o b g Kyllachy-Rainy Day Song (Persian Bold)
R Hollinshead N Chapman

Placings:44-624502414 (6825)
2009: 6^{6}GF, 6^{2}GF, 6^{4}GF, 6^{5}G, 6^{0}GF, 5^{2}GF, 5^{4}G, 5^{1}SD, 5^{4}SD,

	Starts	1st	2nd	3rd	Win & Pl
Career Total (Turf)	8	0	2	0	2167
Career Total (AW)	3	1	0	0	2677

66 9/09 Wolv 5f20y (0-60)H STD £2388
Total win prize-money £2388

Going (Turf): Sf: 0-0 GS: 0-0 Gd: 0-3 GF: 0-5 Fm: 0-0
Distance: **5f/6f: 1-7** 7f-8f: 0-4 9f-13f: 0-0 14f+: 0-0
Track : **LH: 1-4** RH: 0-0 **Tight: 1-3** Gall: 0-1
Aids: Bl: 0-0 Vi: 0-0 Tstrap: 0-0 Ckp: 0-0
Best Rating: 70 5/09 Nott 6f15y gd-fm

Modest; effective over 5f-6f; acts on fast ground and on Polytrack.

Raise All In (IRE)

78(92) (64)65
3-y-o b f Exceed And Excel (AUS)-Inforapenny (Deploy)
N Wilson Renaissance Racing

Placings:233020000-00 (2361)
2009: 6^{0}GF, 7^{0}GF,

	Starts	1st	2nd	3rd	Win & Pl
Career Total (Turf)	7	0	1	1	1879
Career Total (AW)	4	0	1	1	1114

Going (Turf): Sf: 0-0 GS: 0-1 Gd: 0-2 GF: 0-4 Fm: 0-0
Distance: 5f/6f: 0-6 7f-8f: 0-4 9f-13f: 0-1 14f+: 0-0
Track : LH: 0-5 RH: 0-0 Tight: 0-4 Gall: 0-0
Aids: Bl: 0-0 Vi: 0-0 Tstrap: 0-0 Ckp: 0-0
Best Rating: 65 6/08 Newc 6f gd-sft

Fair; effective over 6f-7f; acts on easy and fast ground.

Rajamand (FR)

(100) (84)82
3-y-o gr g Linamix (FR)-Ridafa (IRE) (Darshaan)
Miss E C Lavelle (A De Royer-Dupre 10/10) Gdm Partnership

Placings:0454 (7612)
2009: 12^{0}GS, 13^{4}VS, 10^{5}SD, 12^{4}SD,

	Starts	1st	2nd	3rd	Win & Pl
Career Total (Turf)	2	0	0	0	2330
Career Total (AW)	2	0	0	0	626

Going (Turf): Sf: 0-0 GS: 0-1 Gd: 0-0 GF: 0-0 Fm: 0-0
Distance: 5f/6f: 0-0 7f-8f: 0-0 9f-13f: 0-4 14f+: 0-0
Track : LH: 0-0 RH: 0-3 Tight: 0-0 Gall: 0-0
Aids: Bl: 0-0 Vi: 0-0 Tstrap: 0-0 Ckp: 0-0
Best Rating: 84 11/09 Kemp 1m2f stand

Useful; ex-French; stays 1m4f.

Rajeh (IRE)

108 97
6-y-o b g Key Of Luck (USA)-Saramacca (IRE) (Kahyasi)
J L Spearing Miss C Ive

Placings:5/331300/3/66311330-33056 (4408)
2009: 12^{3}G, 14^{3}GF, 20^{0}GF, 12^{5}G, 14^{6}G,

	Starts	1st	2nd	3rd	Win & Pl
Career Total (Turf)	21	3	0	9	33046

92 7/08 Sand 1m6f (0-85)H G-F £6476
86 6/08 Donc 1m6f132y (0-85)H G-F £4857
84 8/06 Gway 1m4f G-F £8979
Total win prize-money £20312

Going (Turf): Sf: 0-1 GS: 0-0 Gd: 0-10 **GF: 3-8** Fm: 0-0
Distance: 5f/6f: 0-0 7f-8f: 0-1 9f-13f: 1-11 **14f+: 2-9**
Track : LH: 1-8 **RH: 2-13** Tight: 0-5 **Gall: 1-7**
Aids: Bl: 0-0 Vi: 0-0 Tstrap: 0-0 Ckp: 0-0
Best Rating: 97 4/09 Epsm 1m4f10y good

Very useful; ex-Irish; stays 1m6f and acts on fast ground; winning hurdler.

Rakaan (IRE)

104(89) (78)98
2-y-o ch g Bahamian Bounty-Petite Spectre (Spectrum (IRE))
B J Meehan Saleh Al Homaizi & Imad Al Sagar

Placings:22302201 (6328)
2009: 6^{2}G, 6^{2}G, 6^{3}GF, 6^{0}G, 6^{2}GF, 6^{2}SD, 6^{0}GF, 5^{1}F,

	Starts	1st	2nd	3rd	Win & Pl
Career Total (Turf)	7	1	3	1	18404
Career Total (AW)	1	0	1	0	605

82 9/09 Bath 5f161y FRM £2719
Total win prize-money £2720

Going (Turf): Sf: 0-0 GS: 0-0 Gd: 0-3 GF: 0-3 **Fm: 1-1**
Distance: **5f/6f: 1-6** 7f-8f: 0-2 9f-13f: 0-0 14f+: 0-0
Track : **LH: 1-2** RH: 0-0 Tight: 0-1 **Gall: 1-1**
Aids: Bl: 0-2 Vi: 0-0 Tstrap: 0-0 Ckp: 0-0
Best Rating: 98 6/09 Asct 6f gd-fm

Very useful; third in the 2009 Coventry Stakes; effective over 6f; acts on fast ground; goes on Polytrack; has worn blinkers.

Rakhapura (IRE)

80(90) (64)50
2-y-o b c Arakan (USA)-Indistinto (Groom Dancer (USA))
P R Webber The Bordeaux Bandits

Placings:056 (7064)
2009: 5^{0}GF, 8^{5}SD, 8^{6}SD,

	Starts	1st	2nd	3rd	Win & Pl
Career Total (Turf)	1	0	0	0	
Career Total (AW)	2	0	0	0	0

Going (Turf): Sf: 0-0 GS: 0-0 Gd: 0-0 GF: 0-1 Fm: 0-0
Distance: 5f/6f: 0-1 7f-8f: 0-2 9f-13f: 0-0 14f+: 0-0
Track : LH: 0-1 RH: 0-1 Tight: 0-1 Gall: 0-0
Aids: Bl: 0-0 Vi: 0-0 Tstrap: 0-0 Ckp: 0-0
Best Rating: 64 10/09 Kemp 1m stand

Rakhine (IRE)

89(88) (40)60
2-y-o b g Arakan (USA)-Amorous Pursuits (Pursuit Of Love)
P F I Cole Meyrick & Dunnington-Jefferson

Placings:540610 (6721)
2009: 6^{5}G, 5^{4}F, 6^{0}GS, 6^{6}GF, 8^{1}GF, 8^{0}SD,

	Starts	1st	2nd	3rd	Win & Pl
Career Total (Turf)	5	1	0	0	2231
Career Total (AW)	1	0	0	0	

60 9/09 Yarm 1m3y (0-65) G-F £1942
Total win prize-money £1943

Going (Turf): Sf: 0-0 GS: 0-1 Gd: 0-1 **GF: 1-2** Fm: 0-1
Distance: 5f/6f: 0-2 7f-8f: 0-3 **9f-13f: 1-1** 14f+: 0-0
Track : LH: 0-1 RH: 0-1 Tight: 0-0 Gall: 0-1
Aids: Bl: 0-1 Vi: 0-0 Tstrap: 0-0 Ckp: 0-0
Best Rating: 60 9/09 Yarm 1m3y gd-fm

Modest; stays 1m; acts on fast ground; has worn blinkers.

Raleigh Quay (IRE)

102 70
2-y-o b c Bachelor Duke (USA)-Speedbird (USA) (Sky Classic (CAN))
Micky Hammond S T Brankin

Placings:66210 (6895)
2009: 6^{6}GF, 5^{6}G, 6^{2}G, 7^{1}GS, 8^{0}GF,

	Starts	1st	2nd	3rd	Win & Pl
Career Total (Turf)	5	1	1	0	3616

70 8/09 Muss 7f30y G-S £2266
Total win prize-money £2267

Going (Turf): Sf: 0-0 **GS: 1-1** Gd: 0-2 GF: 0-2 Fm: 0-0
Distance: 5f/6f: 0-2 **7f-8f: 1-2** 9f-13f: 0-1 14f+: 0-0
Track : LH: 0-2 **RH: 1-2 Tight: 1-1** Gall: 0-0
Aids: Bl: 0-0 Vi: 0-0 Tstrap: 0-0 Ckp: 0-0
Best Rating: 70 8/09 Muss 7f30y gd-sft

Modest; stays 7f; acts on good and softer ground.

Ramamara (IRE)

98(100) (80)80
2-y-o ch f Trans Island-Kaskazi (Dancing Brave (USA))
P D Evans Raymond N R Auld

Placings:6121303063343240 (7824)
2009: 5^{6}GF, 6^{1}SD, 5^{2}F, 6^{1}GF, 7^{3}SD, 6^{0}GF, 5^{3}GF, 5^{0}G, 6^{6}SD, 5^{3}SD, 7^{3}SD, 7^{4}SD, 6^{3}SD, 5^{2}SD, 6^{4}SD, 7^{0}SD,

	Starts	1st	2nd	3rd	Win & Pl
Career Total (Turf)	6	1	1	1	5350
Career Total (AW)	10	1	1	4	5254

80 8/09 Wind 6f G-F £2729
66 8/09 Ling 6f STD £2047
Total win prize-money £4777

Going (Turf): Sf: 0-0 GS: 0-0 Gd: 0-1 **GF: 1-4** Fm: 0-1
Distance: **5f/6f: 2-11** 7f-8f: 0-5 9f-13f: 0-0 14f+: 0-0
Track : **LH: 1-12** RH: 0-1 Tight: 1-11 Gall: 1-2
Aids: Bl: 0-0 Vi: 0-0 Tstrap: 0-0 Ckp: 0-0
Best Rating: 80 9/09 Ling 7f stand

Fair; stays 6f; acts on fast ground; goes on Polytrack.

Ramayana (IRE)

77(88) (44)38
2-y-o b f Arakan (USA)-Dance Land (IRE) (Nordance (USA))

M R Channon M Channon

Placings:0000 (7391)
2009: 7^{0}GF, 6^{0}GF, 5^{0}SD, 8^{0}SD,

	Starts	1st	2nd	3rd	Win & Pl
Career Total (Turf)	2	0	0	0	
Career Total (AW)	2	0	0	0	

Going (Turf): **Sf: 0-0 GS: 0-0 Gd: 0-0 GF: 0-2 Fm: 0-0**
Distance: 5f/6f: 0-2 7f-8f: 0-2 9f-13f: 0-0 14f+: 0-0
Track : LH: 0-1 RH: 0-1 Tight: 0-1 Gall: 0-0
Aids: Bl: 0-0 Vi: 0-0 Tstrap: 0-0 Ckp: 0-0
Best Rating: **44** 10/09 Kemp 5f stand

Ramblin Bob

94(104) (54)**41**
4-y-o b g Piccolo-Bijan (IRE) (Mukaddamah (USA))
W J Musson The Roofing Guys

Placings:0410503**3300**/4000**0**60-**0**100060 (3401)
2009: 7^{0}SD, 5^{1}SD, 6^{0}SD, 6^{0}SD, 5^{0}G, 8^{6}SD, 7^{0}G,

	Starts	1st	2nd	3rd	Win & Pl
Career Total (Turf)	12	1	0	0	3575
Career Total (AW)	12	1	0	2	2662

54 3/09 Ling 5f (0-50)H STD £1878
68 6/07 Sals 6f G-F £3238
Total win prize-money £5117

Going (Turf): Sf: 0-0 GS: 0-1 Gd: 0-4 **GF: 1-7** Fm: 0-0
Distance: **5f/6f: 2-12** 7f-8f: 0-11 9f-13f: 0-1 14f+: 0-0
Track : **LH: 1-8** RH: 0-5 **Tight: 1-5** Gall: 0-3
Aids: **Bl: 1-3** Vi: 0-0 Tstrap: 0-0 Ckp: 0-0
Best Rating: **68** 6/07 Sals 6f gd-fm

Modest; effective over 6f; handles quick ground; also goes on Polytrack; has worn a tongue tie.

Rambling Dancer (IRE)

78(102) (65)**53**
5-y-o b g Imperial Ballet (IRE)-Wayfarer's Inn (IRE) (Lucky Guest)
Mrs Valerie Keatley Common Sense Partnership

Placings:0/006/20**421**-40**505**13 (7803)
2009: 9^{4}SD, 8^{0}GY, 12^{5}SD, 8^{0}SD, 8^{5}SD, 8^{1}SD, 9^{3}SD,

	Starts	1st	2nd	3rd	Win & Pl
Career Total (Turf)	7	0	1	0	1006
Career Total (AW)	9	2	1	1	8709

63 11/09 Dund 1m (47-65)H STD £4696
60 12/08 Wolv 1m1f103y SF £2388
Total win prize-money £7084

Going (Turf): **Sf: 0-1 GS: 0-0 Gd: 0-3 GF: 0-1 Fm: 0-0**
Distance: 5f/6f: 0-0 7f-8f: 1-7 9f-13f: 1-9 14f+: 0-0
Track : **LH: 2-12** RH: 0-2 **Tight: 1-3** Gall: 0-0
Aids: Bl: 0-0 Vi: 0-0 Tstrap: 0-0 Ckp: 0-0
Best Rating: **65** 12/09 Wolv 1m1f103y stand

Moderate; stays 1m1f; acts on Polytrack.

Rambling Light

98(107) (84)**79**
5-y-o b g Fantastic Light (USA)-Rambler (Selkirk (USA))
A M Balding Another Bottle Racing

Placings:0/314/604510032-40 (2883)
2009: 8^{4}GF, 7^{0}G,

	Starts	1st	2nd	3rd	Win & Pl
Career Total (Turf)	8	1	0	0	7821
Career Total (AW)	7	1	1	2	5956

79 6/08 Wind 1m67y (0-90)H G-F £7123
77 3/07 Wolv 1m141y STD £3412
Total win prize-money £10537

Going (Turf): Sf: 0-0 GS: 0-1 Gd: 0-3 **GF: 1-4** Fm: 0-0
Distance: 5f/6f: 0-0 7f-8f: 0-11 **9f-13f: 2-4** 14f+: 0-0
Track : LH: 1-4 RH: 1-9 **Tight: 2-6** Gall: 0-0
Aids: Bl: 0-0 Vi: 0-1 Tstrap: 1-6 Ckp: 1-6
Best Rating: **84** 11/08 Ling 1m stand

Fair; effective over 1m; acts on fast ground and on Polytrack; has worn a visor.

Rambling Rosie (IRE)

81(68) (1)**35**
3-y-o b f Rambling Bear-La Noisette (Rock Hopper)
C Drew C Drew

Placings:0004 (3632)
2009: 7^{0}GS, 8^{0}SD, 5^{0}SD, 6^{4}G,

	Starts	1st	2nd	3rd	Win & Pl
Career Total (Turf)	2	0	0	0	0
Career Total (AW)	2	0	0	0	

Going (Turf): **Sf: 0-0 GS: 0-1 Gd: 0-1 GF: 0-0 Fm: 0-0**
Distance: 5f/6f: 0-1 7f-8f: 0-3 9f-13f: 0-0 14f+: 0-0
Track : LH: 0-1 RH: 0-1 Tight: 0-1 Gall: 0-0
Aids: Bl: 0-0 Vi: 0-0 Tstrap: 0-0 Ckp: 0-0
Best Rating: **35** 7/09 Nott 6f15y good

Plating class; stays 6f; acts on a sound surface.

Ramona Chase

105(104) (98)**102**
4-y-o b g High Chaparral (IRE)-Audacieuse (Rainbow Quest (USA))
M J Attwater Bagden Wood Building Services Limited

Placings:2461U00/424200**6035**20-**40065030** (5915)
2009: 10^{4}SD, 10^{0}G, 9^{0}GF, 10^{6}G, 10^{5}G, 10^{0}GF, 10^{3}G, 9^{0}GF,

	Starts	1st	2nd	3rd	Win & Pl
Career Total (Turf)	24	1	4	1	32956
Career Total (AW)	3	0	0	1	2257

95 9/07 Sals 1m G-F £5181
Total win prize-money £5182

Going (Turf): Sf: 0-2 GS: 0-4 Gd: 0-9 **GF: 1-9** Fm: 0-0
Distance: 5f/6f: 0-1 **7f-8f: 1-7** 9f-13f: 0-19 14f+: 0-0
Track : LH: 0-8 RH: 0-10 Tight: 0-7 Gall: 0-8
Aids: Bl: 0-0 Vi: 0-0 Tstrap: 0-0 Ckp: 0-0
Best Rating: **102** 6/08 Epsm 1m2f18y good

Useful; stays 1m2f; acts on good and faster ground and on Polytrack; can take a hold.

Ramora (USA)

103(98) (71)**77**
3-y-o br f Monsun (GER)-Madame Cerito (USA) (Diesis)
H R A Cecil Plantation Stud

Placings:323220 (6975)
2009: 12^{3}GF, 12^{2}GF, 11^{3}GF, 10^{2}SD, 13^{2}SD, 12^{0}SD,

	Starts	1st	2nd	3rd	Win & Pl
Career Total (Turf)	3	0	1	2	2716
Career Total (AW)	3	0	2	0	2281

Going (Turf): **Sf: 0-0 GS: 0-0 Gd: 0-0 GF: 0-3 Fm: 0-0**
Distance: 5f/6f: 0-0 7f-8f: 0-0 9f-13f: 0-5 14f+: 0-1
Track : LH: 0-3 RH: 0-3 Tight: 0-2 Gall: 0-2
Aids: Bl: 0-0 Vi: 0-0 Tstrap: 0-0 Ckp: 0-0
Best Rating: **77** 6/09 Newb 1m4f5y gd-fm

Rampant Ronnie (USA)

88(98) (53)**60**
4-y-o b g Honor Glide (USA)-Jalfrezi (Jalmood (USA))
Mrs A M Thorpe (P W D'Arcy 15/2) Hanford's Chemist Ltd

Placings:05003/061050-**0040** (5179)
2009: 10^{0}SD, 9^{0}SD, 8^{4}SD, 8^{0}G,

	Starts	1st	2nd	3rd	Win & Pl
Career Total (Turf)	8	1	0	0	2047
Career Total (AW)	7	0	0	1	328

59 7/08 Wwck 1m2f188y G-F £2047
Total win prize-money £2047

Going (Turf): Sf: 0-0 GS: 0-1 Gd: 0-2 **GF: 1-4** Fm: 0-1
Distance: 5f/6f: 0-1 7f-8f: 0-4 **9f-13f: 1-9** 14f+: 0-1
Track : **LH: 1-10** RH: 0-3 Tight: 0-5 Gall: 0-1
Aids: Bl: 0-0 Vi: 0-0 Tstrap: 0-0 Ckp: 0-0
Best Rating: **65** 8/07 Kemp 1m stand

Modest; stays 1m2f; acts on a sound surface and on Polytrack.

Ramvaswani (IRE)

(98) (56)**41**
6-y-o b g Spectrum (IRE)-Caesarea (GER) (Generous (IRE))
N B King N J Catterwell, M Marris, N B King

Placings:00/4/0-**204** (0627)
2009: 11^{2}SD, 12^{0}SD, 16^{4}SD,

	Starts	1st	2nd	3rd	Win & Pl
Career Total (Turf)	2	0	0	0	
Career Total (AW)	5	0	1	0	507

Going (Turf): **Sf: 0-0 GS: 0-0 Gd: 0-1 GF: 0-1 Fm: 0-0**
Distance: 5f/6f: 0-0 7f-8f: 0-0 9f-13f: 0-6 14f+: 0-1
Track : LH: 0-3 RH: 0-4 Tight: 0-2 Gall: 0-0
Aids: Bl: 0-0 Vi: 0-0 Tstrap: 0-2 Ckp: 0-2
Best Rating: **56** 2/09 Sthl 1m3f stand

Moderate; stays 1m3f; acts on Fibresand and on Polytrack.

Randama Bay (IRE)

100(103) (81)**70**
4-y-o b/br g Frenchmans Bay (FR)-Randama (Akarad (FR))
I A Wood Neardown Stables

Placings:0025/04226166-**2436006426** (6288)
2009: 8^{2}SD, 8^{4}SD, 7^{3}SD, 8^{6}SD, 8^{0}SD, 8^{0}GF, 10^{6}G, 10^{4}G, 11^{2}GS, 10^{6}SD,

	Starts	1st	2nd	3rd	Win & Pl
Career Total (Turf)	8	0	3	0	2847
Career Total (AW)	14	1	2	1	6321

81 11/08 Kemp 1m (0-75)H STD £3238
Total win prize-money £3238

Going (Turf): **Sf: 0-0 GS: 0-2 Gd: 0-3 GF: 0-3 Fm: 0-0**
Distance: 5f/6f: 0-0 **7f-8f: 1-12** 9f-13f: 0-10 14f+: 0-0
Track : LH: 0-12 **RH: 1-7** Tight: 0-8 Gall: 0-2
Aids: Bl: 0-0 Vi: 0-0 Tstrap: 0-0 Ckp: 0-0
Best Rating: **81** 11/08 Kemp 1m stand

Modest; effective over 1m4f; acts on fast and easy ground and on Polytrack.

Rangefinder

104 95

5-y-o gr h Linamix (FR)-Risen Raven (USA) (Risen Star (USA))

Jane Chapple-Hyam (L M Cumani 10/10) Dr Marwan Koukash

Placings:0/31505210413/**0**033113-3032100 (7293)

2009: 9^{3}GF, 12^{0}GF, 10^{3}GS, 9^{2}HY, 12^{1}S, 12^{0}GS, 12^{0}S,

	Starts	1st	2nd	3rd	Win & Pl
Career Total (Turf)	25	6	2	7	43994
Career Total (AW)	1	0	0	0	0

95	9/09	Thsk	1m4f	(0-85)H	SFT	£6864
	7/08	Var	1m2f110y	H	GD	£5515
	6/08	Livo	1m1f165y	H	GD	£7353
	10/07	Gros	1m165y	H	GD	£3378
	9/07	Casc	7f110y	H	GD	£3378
	5/07	Casc	7f110y		HVY	£4054

Total win prize-money £30543

Going (Turf): Sf: 2-8 GS: 0-3 **Gd: 4-11** GF: 0-2 Fm: 0-0
Distance: 5f/6f: 0-0 7f-8f: 2-10 **9f-13f: 4-16** 14f+: 0-0
Track : **LH: 1-3** RH: 0-4 **Tight: 1-2** Gall: 0-4
Aids: Bl: 0-0 Vi: 0-0 Tstrap: 0-0 Ckp: 0-0
Best Rating: **95** 9/09 Thsk 1m4f soft

Useful; ex-Italian; effective over 1m2f-1m4f; acts on good and soft ground.

Rank Bajin

77 32

2-y-o b f Red Ransom (USA)-Sharp As A Tack (IRE) (Zafonic (USA))

E J Alston Les McLaughlin

Placings:0 (2819)

2009: 6^{0}GF,

	Starts	1st	2nd	3rd	Win & Pl
Career Total (Turf)	1	0	0	0	

Going (Turf): **Sf: 0-0 GS: 0-0 Gd: 0-0 GF: 0-1 Fm: 0-0**
Distance: 5f/6f: 0-1 7f-8f: 0-0 9f-13f: 0-0 14f+: 0-0
Track : LH: 0-0 RH: 0-0 Tight: 0-0 Gall: 0-0
Aids: Bl: 0-0 Vi: 0-0 Tstrap: 0-0 Ckp: 0-0
Best Rating: **32** 6/09 Hayd 6f gd-fm

Rann Na Cille (IRE)

(99) (67)66

5-y-o br m Agnes World (USA)-Omanah (USA) (Kayrawan (USA))

P T Midgley C Varley

Placings:04000**44/234**0033561066420**30/1**304502340-40 (1038)

2009: 5^{4}SD, 5^{0}SD,

	Starts	1st	2nd	3rd	Win & Pl
Career Total (Turf)	19	1	2	1	5013
Career Total (AW)	18	1	1	5	5198

54	2/08	Wolv	5f20y		STD	£1774
66	8/07	Ripn	5f	(0-65)H	G-F	£2590

Total win prize-money £4366

Going (Turf): Sf: 0-2 GS: 0-2 Gd: 0-6 **GF: 1-6** Fm: 0-0
Distance: **5f/6f: 2-27** 7f-8f: 0-9 9f-13f: 0-1 14f+: 0-0
Track : **LH: 1-19** RH: 0-5 **Tight: 1-11** Gall: 0-3
Aids: Bl: 0-6 Vi: 0-0 Tstrap: 1-5 Ckp: 1-5

Best Rating: **67** 10/07 Wolv 5f20y stand

Modest; stays 7f; acts on fast ground and on sand.

Rannoch Rose (IRE)

89(93) (47)44

3-y-o b f Court Cave (IRE)-Lady Semillon (IRE) (Semillon)

J L Spearing Leonard Kinsella

Placings:02050 (2635)

2009: 9^{0}SD, 11^{2}SD, 12^{0}SD, 9^{5}GF, 11^{0}GF,

	Starts	1st	2nd	3rd	Win & Pl
Career Total (Turf)	2	0	0	0	0
Career Total (AW)	3	0	1	0	605

Going (Turf): **Sf: 0-0 GS: 0-0 Gd: 0-0 GF: 0-2 Fm: 0-0**
Distance: 5f/6f: 0-0 7f-8f: 0-0 9f-13f: 0-5 14f+: 0-0
Track : LH: 0-3 RH: 0-2 Tight: 0-4 Gall: 0-0
Aids: Bl: 0-0 Vi: 0-0 Tstrap: 0-1 Ckp: 0-1
Best Rating: **47** 3/09 Wolv 1m4f50y stand

Moderate; effective over 1m3f; acts on Polytrack.

Ransom Note

102 77

2-y-o b c Red Ransom (USA)-Zacheta (Polish Precedent (USA))

B W Hills H R Mould

Placings:0101 (6693)

2009: 7^{0}G, 7^{1}GF, 7^{0}GF, 7^{1}GS,

	Starts	1st	2nd	3rd	Win & Pl
Career Total (Turf)	4	2	0	0	12822

77	10/09	Gdwd	7f	(0-85)	G-S	£5504
70	8/09	Ches	7f2y		G-F	£7317

Total win prize-money £12823

Going (Turf): Sf: 0-0 **GS: 1-1** Gd: 0-1 **GF: 1-2** Fm: 0-0
Distance: 5f/6f: 0-0 **7f-8f: 2-4** 9f-13f: 0-0 14f+: 0-0
Track : LH: 1-1 RH: 1-1 **Tight: 1-1** Gall: 0-0
Aids: Bl: 0-0 Vi: 0-0 Tstrap: 0-0 Ckp: 0-0
Best Rating: **77** 10/09 Gdwd 7f gd-sft

Fair; stays 7f; acts on fast and easy ground.

Rapanui Belle

93(96) (51)47

3-y-o b f Compton Place-Belle Ile (USA) (Diesis)

G L Moore C E Stedman

Placings:060660-**5**0200403003**4P** (6581)

2009: 7^{5}SD, 5^{0}SD, 5^{2}SD, 5^{0}SD, 5^{0}F, 5^{4}G, 5^{0}GF, 6^{3}G, 5^{0}F, 6^{0}GS, 5^{3}SD, 5^{4}SD, 5^{P}SD,

	Starts	1st	2nd	3rd	Win & Pl
Career Total (Turf)	11	0	0	1	759
Career Total (AW)	8	0	1	1	957

Going (Turf): **Sf: 0-1 GS: 0-2 Gd: 0-3 GF: 0-3 Fm: 0-2**
Distance: 5f/6f: 0-16 7f-8f: 0-3 9f-13f: 0-0 14f+: 0-0
Track : LH: 0-11 RH: 0-2 Tight: 0-6 Gall: 0-3
Aids: Bl: 0-3 Vi: 0-0 Tstrap: 0-0 Ckp: 0-0
Best Rating: **51** 4/09 Wolv 5f20y stand

Moderate; effective over 5f; acts on Polytrack; has worn blinkers.

Rapid City

93(108) (72)76

6-y-o b g Dansili-West Dakota (USA) (Gone West (USA))

G L Moore (Jim Best 4/6) The Bad Boys

Placings:026**11/2**12**4**0/534000045004**1**3-6**1**633**4**12105 (7776)

2009: 10^{6}SD, 12^{1}SD, 12^{6}SD, 10^{3}SD, 10^{3}SD, 12^{4}SD, 10^{1}SD, 9^{2}SD, 9^{1}GF, 10^{0}GF, 10^{5}SD,

	Starts	1st	2nd	3rd	Win & Pl
Career Total (Turf)	9	1	1	0	5220
Career Total (AW)	26	6	3	4	23430

71	4/09	Brig	1m1f209y	(0-65)H	G-F	£2590
70	3/09	Ling	1m2f		STD	£2047
63	1/09	Ling	1m4f		STD	£2047
70	12/08	Ling	1m2f		STD	£1978
86	1/07	Ling	1m2f	(0-80)H	STD	£4857
83	12/06	Ling	1m2f	(0-70)H	STD	£3238
73	12/06	Wolv	1m141y		STD	£3238

Total win prize-money £19999

Going (Turf): Sf: 0-2 GS: 0-0 Gd: 0-2 **GF: 1-4** Fm: 0-0
Distance: 5f/6f: 0-1 7f-8f: 0-4 **9f-13f: 7-30** 14f+: 0-0
Track : **LH: 7-24** RH: 0-6 **Tight: 6-19** Gall: 0-5
Aids: Bl: 0-0 Vi: 0-0 Tstrap: 3-15 Ckp: 3-15
Best Rating: **93** 2/07 Ling 1m2f stand

Modest; suited by 1m2f but stays further; acts on Polytrack; usually held up; has worn cheekpieces.

Rapid Desire (IRE)

98(68) 53

3-y-o b f Statue Of Liberty (USA)-Whistfilly (First Trump)

J R Weymes Ronald Lilley

Placings:300500 (7084)

2009: 10^{3}G, 10^{0}S, 11^{0}SD, 16^{5}GS, 16^{0}GS, 15^{0}S,

	Starts	1st	2nd	3rd	Win & Pl
Career Total (Turf)	5	0	0	1	482
Career Total (AW)	1	0	0	0	

Going (Turf): **Sf: 0-2 GS: 0-2 Gd: 0-1 GF: 0-0 Fm: 0-0**
Distance: 5f/6f: 0-0 7f-8f: 0-0 9f-13f: 0-3 14f+: 0-3
Track : LH: 0-5 RH: 0-1 Tight: 0-2 Gall: 0 3
Aids: Bl: 0-0 Vi: 0-0 Tstrap: 0-1 Ckp: 0-1
Best Rating: **53** 9/09 Ripn 2m gd-sft

Rapid Flow

73(94) (48)22

7-y-o b g Fasliyev (USA)-Fleet River (USA) (Riverman (USA))

J W Unett J E Price

Placings:00/0/0400500/**304**/04-050 (3304)

2009: 6^{0}SS, 5^{5}SD, 5^{0}GF,

	Starts	1st	2nd	3rd	Win & Pl
Career Total (Turf)	7	0	0	0	0
Career Total (AW)	11	0	0	1	691

Going (Turf): **Sf: 0-1 GS: 0-1 Gd: 0-2 GF: 0-2 Fm: 0-1**
Distance: 5f/6f: 0-12 7f-8f: 0-3 9f-13f: 0-3 14f+: 0-0
Track : LH: 0-13 RH: 0-0 Tight: 0-11 Gall: 0-0
Aids: Bl: 0-0 Vi: 0-0 Tstrap: 0-0 Ckp: 0-0
Best Rating: **64** 2/06 Wolv 5f216y stand

Plating-class gelding; probably at his best at 6f; handles Polytrack.

Rapid Light

(88) (66)

3-y-o ch f Tobougg (IRE)-La Coqueta (GER) (Kris)

E A L Dunlop Cheveley Park Stud

Placings:3-0 (2710)
2009: 8[0]SD,

	Starts	1st	2nd	3rd	Win & Pl
Career Total (Turf)	0	0	0	0	
Career Total (AW)	2	0	0	1	385

Going (Turf): Sf: 0-0 GS: 0-0 Gd: 0-0 GF: 0-0 Fm: 0-0
Distance: 5f/6f: 0-0 7f-8f: 0-2 9f-13f: 0-0 14f+: 0-0
Track : LH: 0-2 RH: 0-0 Tight: 0-1 Gall: 0-1
Aids: Bl: 0-0 Vi: 0-0 Tstrap: 0-0 Ckp: 0-0
Best Rating: 66 12/08 GrLe 1m stand

Rapid Water

104 86
3-y-o b g Anabaa (USA)-Lochsong (Song)
A M Balding J C Smith

Placings:0-15514 (4990)
2009: 6[1]GF, 5[5]G, 6[5]GF, 6[1]GF, 6[4]GF,

	Starts	1st	2nd	3rd	Win & Pl
Career Total (Turf)	6	2	0	0	11370

86 7/09 Asct 6f (0-85)H G-F £7123
75 5/09 Sals 6f G-F £3885
Total win prize-money £11010

Going (Turf): Sf: 0-0 GS: 0-0 Gd: 0-2 **GF: 2-4** Fm: 0-0
Distance: **5f/6f: 2-5** 7f-8f: 0-1 9f-13f: 0-0 14f+: 0-0
Track : LH: 0-0 RH: 0-0 Tight: 0-0 Gall: 0-1
Aids: Bl: 0-0 Vi: 0-0 Tstrap: 0-0 Ckp: 0-0
Best Rating: 86 7/09 Asct 6f gd-fm

Useful; effeftive at 6f; acts on fast ground.

Raptor (GER)

106(99) (106)106
6-y-o b g Auenadler (GER)-Royal Cat (Royal Academy (USA))
A P Jarvis (K R Burke 25/6) Mogeely Stud & Mark T Gittins

Placings:111445/40332/0214650000-003300 (5363)
2009: 8[0]SD, 8[0]GF, 8[3]S, 8[3]G, 8[0]GF, 7[0]S,

	Starts	1st	2nd	3rd	Win & Pl
Career Total (Turf)	24	4	1	3	44822
Career Total (AW)	3	0	1	1	4216

106 4/08 Yarm 1m3y GD £6542
5/06 Badn 6f GD £12414
5/06 Colo 7f H SFT £2759
4/06 Dort 7f HVY £2068
Total win prize-money £23785

Going (Turf): **Sf: 2-8** GS: 0-4 **Gd: 2-5** GF: 0-6 Fm: 0-0
Distance: 5f/6f: 1-3 **7f-8f: 2-17** 9f-13f: 1-7 14f+: 0-0
Track : **LH: 1-9** RH: 0-4 Tight: 0-3 Gall: 0-1
Aids: Bl: 0-1 Vi: 0-3 Tstrap: 0-0 Ckp: 0-0
Best Rating: 106 4/08 Yarm 1m3y good

Useful; winner in Listed company on the continent; effective at up to 1m; acts on good and softer ground and on Polytrack; has worn blinkers a visor and a tongue tie.

Raqeeb (USA)

(73) (38)
2-y-o b c Seeking The Gold (USA)-Sayedah (IRE) (Darshaan)
Sir Michael Stoute Hamdan Al Maktoum

Placings:0 (7390)
2009: 8[0]SD,

	Starts	1st	2nd	3rd	Win & Pl
Career Total (Turf)	0	0	0	0	
Career Total (AW)	1	0	0	0	

Going (Turf): Sf: 0-0 GS: 0-0 Gd: 0-0 GF: 0-0 Fm: 0-0
Distance: 5f/6f: 0-0 7f-8f: 0-1 9f-13f: 0-0 14f+: 0-0
Track : LH: 0-1 RH: 0-0 Tight: 0-1 Gall: 0-0
Aids: Bl: 0-0 Vi: 0-0 Tstrap: 0-0 Ckp: 0-0
Best Rating: 38 11/09 Ling 1m stand

Raquel White

(105) (70)64
5-y-o b m Robellino (USA)-Spinella (Teenoso (USA))
J L Flint N Poacher

Placings:644603/3440363513O2363/20000-16 (0368)
2009: 12[1]SS, 12[6]SD,

	Starts	1st	2nd	3rd	Win & Pl
Career Total (Turf)	8	1	0	2	3238
Career Total (AW)	20	1	2	5	6054

63 1/09 Sthl 1m4f (0-65)H SS £2047
63 6/07 Bevl 1m4f16y (0-60)H G-S £2590
Total win prize-money £4638

Going (Turf): Sf: 0-4 **GS: 1-1** Gd: 0-1 GF: 0-2 Fm: 0-0
Distance: 5f/6f: 0-1 7f-8f: 0-5 **9f-13f: 2-21** 14f+: 0-1
Track : LH: 1-22 RH: 1-4 **Tight: 1-19** Gall: 0-0
Aids: Bl: 0-1 Vi: 0-0 Tstrap: 0-0 Ckp: 0-0
Best Rating: 70 1/08 Wolv 1m4f50y stand

Modest; stays 1m4f; acts on soft ground; also goes on Polytrack.

Rare Art

100(97) (69)74
3-y-o b c Kyllachy-Succumb (Pursuit Of Love)
S A Callaghan Matthew Green

Placings:4301-350 (3738)
2009: 6[3]GF, 6[5]SD, 6[0]SD,

	Starts	1st	2nd	3rd	Win & Pl
Career Total (Turf)	3	1	0	2	4462
Career Total (AW)	4	0	0	0	289

70 11/08 Nott 5f13y HVY £3238
Total win prize-money £3238

Going (Turf): **Sf: 1-2** GS: 0-0 Gd: 0-0 GF: 0-1 Fm: 0-0
Distance: **5f/6f: 1-7** 7f-8f: 0-0 9f-13f: 0-0 14f+: 0-0
Track : LH: 0-3 RH: 0-1 Tight: 0-0 Gall: 0-2
Aids: Bl: 0-0 Vi: 0-0 Tstrap: 0-0 Ckp: 0-0
Best Rating: 74 4/09 Folk 6f gd-fm

Fair; stays 6f and acts on soft ground.

Rare Bet

83 40
3-y-o b f Bertolini (USA)-Rare Old Times (IRE) (Inzar (USA))
W G M Turner Graham Brown

Placings:050 (5716)
2009: 5[0]F, 7[5]G, 5[0]G,

	Starts	1st	2nd	3rd	Win & Pl
Career Total (Turf)	3	0	0	0	0

Going (Turf): Sf: 0-0 GS: 0-0 Gd: 0-2 GF: 0-0 Fm: 0-1
Distance: 5f/6f: 0-2 7f-8f: 0-1 9f-13f: 0-0 14f+: 0-0
Track : LH: 0-2 RH: 0-0 Tight: 0-0 Gall: 0-1
Aids: Bl: 0-0 Vi: 0-0 Tstrap: 0-0 Ckp: 0-0
Best Rating: 40 8/09 Chep 7f16y good

Rare Coincidence

99(103) (68)68
8-y-o ch g Atraf-Green Seed (IRE) (Lead On Time (USA))
R F Fisher Des Johnston

Placings:04006505320/11360444003400050/06261045505 001310225000/0323535415012500/311223013023/100 400643-130600500 (7751)
2009: 16[1]SD, 16[3]F, 16[0]SD, 13[6]GF, 16[0]SD, 16[0]GS, 12[5]SD, 13[0]SD, 13[0]SD,

	Starts	1st	2nd	3rd	Win & Pl
Career Total (Turf)	56	6	5	6	25843
Career Total (AW)	43	6	4	7	21418

68 4/09 Wolv 2m119y (0-65)H STD £2047
73 2/08 Wolv 1m5f194y (0-65)H STD £2047
75 9/07 Haml 1m5f9y (0-65)H G-F £2307
64 5/07 Nott 1m6f15y (0-60)H G-F £2047
71 4/07 Sthl 1m4f (0-70)H G-F £3071
62 8/06 Carl 1m6f32y (0-60)H GD £2730
61 6/06 Haml 1m5f9y (0-60)H G-S £2730
61 7/05 Catt 1m3f214y (0-55)H FRM £2990
67 6/05 Wolv 1m4f50y STD £3445
67 4/05 Wolv 1m1f103y (0-60)H STD £2609
71 2/04 Wolv 1m100yF(0-60)H STD £2954
63 1/04 Sthl 1m G(0-60)H STD £2541
Total win prize-money £31522

Going (Turf): Sf: 0-9 GS: 1-14 Gd: 1-8 **GF: 3-23** Fm: 1-2
Distance: 5f/6f: 0-4 7f-8f: 1-17 9f-13f: 5-41 **14f+: 6-37**
Track : **LH: 9-67** RH: 3-27 **Tight: 9-61** Gall: 0-3
Aids: Bl: 0-0 Vi: 0-0 Tstrap: 12-88 Ckp: 12-88
Best Rating: 75 9/07 Bevl 1m4f16y gd-fm

Modest; likes to front-run; stays 2m; acts on most ground; goes on sand; often wears cheekpieces.

Rare Malt (IRE)

76(95) (78)69
2-y-o b f Intikhab (USA)-A'Bunadh (USA) (Diesis)
Miss Amy Weaver Khalifa Dasmal

Placings:422 (5643)
2009: 7[4]G, 8[2]SD, 8[2]SD,

	Starts	1st	2nd	3rd	Win & Pl
Career Total (Turf)	1	0	0	0	385
Career Total (AW)	2	0	2	0	2155

Going (Turf): Sf: 0-0 GS: 0-0 Gd: 0-1 GF: 0-0 Fm: 0-0
Distance: 5f/6f: 0-0 7f-8f: 0-3 9f-13f: 0-0 14f+: 0-0
Track : LH: 0-1 RH: 0-1 Tight: 0-1 Gall: 0-0
Aids: Bl: 0-0 Vi: 0-0 Tstrap: 0-0 Ckp: 0-0
Best Rating: 78 8/09 Kemp 1m stand

Fair; stays 1m; acts on Polytrack and good ground on turf.

Rare Ruby (IRE)

104 73
5-y-o b m Dilshaan-Ruby Setting (Gorytus (USA))
Jennie Candlish Mrs Judith Ratcliff

Placings:0/545/0060-2115630 (7084)
2009: 16[2]G, 14[1]G, 14[1]GF, 17[5]GF, 14[6]G, 14[3]GS, 15[0]S,

	Starts	1st	2nd	3rd	Win & Pl
Career Total (Turf)	15	2	1	1	8370

70 7/09 Wwck 1m6f213y (0-75)H G-F £3885
67 6/09 Nott 1m6f15y (0-75)H GD £2590
Total win prize-money £6476

Going (Turf): Sf: 0-2 GS: 0-4 **Gd: 1-5 GF: 1-2** Fm: 0-0
Distance: 5f/6f: 0-0 7f-8f: 0-1 9f-13f: 0-3 **14f+: 2-11**

Track : LH: 2-10 RH: 0-4 Tight: 0-3 Gall: 0-1
Aids: Bl: 0-2 Vi: 0-0 Tstrap: 0-1 Ckp: 0-1
Best Rating: 73 9/09 Hayd 1m6f gd-sft

Modest; ex-Irish; stays 2m; acts on good ground; has worn blinkers.

Rare Virtue (USA)

75 30
3-y-o b f Empire Maker (USA)-Heat Haze (Green Desert (USA))
H R A Cecil K Abdulla

Placings:0 (1329)
2009: 10^0GS,

	Starts	1st	2nd	3rd	Win & Pl
Career Total (Turf)	1	0	0	0	

Going (Turf): Sf: 0-0 GS: 0-1 Gd: 0-0 GF: 0-0 Fm: 0-0
Distance: 5f/6f: 0-0 7f-8f: 0-0 9f-13f: 0-1 14f+: 0-0
Track : LH: 0-1 RH: 0-0 Tight: 0-0 Gall: 0-1
Aids: Bl: 0-0 Vi: 0-0 Tstrap: 0-0 Ckp: 0-0
Best Rating: 30 4/09 Newb 1m2f6y gd-sft

Rasaman (IRE)

104(102) (86)91
5-y-o b g Namid-Rasana (Royal Academy (USA))
J S Goldie (K A Ryan 4/8) Paul Moulton

Placings:04/11344030/00000211020020-216404031026010 (6647)
2009: 5^2GF, 5^1G, 5^6GF, 6^4GF, 6^0GF, 5^4GF, 6^0GF, 5^3S, 5^1G, 5^0GF, 5^2GF, 6^8GF, 6^0G, 6^1GF, 5^0G,

	Starts	1st	2nd	3rd	Win & Pl
Career Total (Turf)	33	5	4	2	35755
Career Total (AW)	6	2	1	1	12238

90	9/09	Ches	6f18y	(0-85)H	G-F	£7123
87	8/09	Catt	5f212y		GD	£2590
88	5/09	Thsk	5f	(0-85)H	GD	£5569
85	7/08	Bevl	5f	(0-75)H	G-F	£3238
83	7/08	Haml	5f4y	(0-80)H	G-S	£6476
83	5/07	Ling	6f	(0-85)H	STD	£6477
78	4/07	Ling	6f		STD	£2914

Total win prize-money £34389

Going (Turf): Sf: 0-2 GS: 1-4 Gd: 2-9 GF: 2-18 Fm: 0-0
Distance: 5f/6f: 6-36 7f-8f: 1-3 9f-13f: 0-0 14f+: 0-0
Track : LH: 4-9 RH: 0-2 Tight: 4-8 Gall: 0-0
Aids: Bl: 0-0 Vi: 2-7 Tstrap: 1-12 Ckp: 1-12
Best Rating: 91 9/09 Donc 5f gd-fm

Useful; suited by 5f-6f; handles most ground on turf; goes on sand; has worn cheekpieces, tongue tie and visor.

Rascal In The Mix (USA)

85(88) (56)50
3-y-o gr/ro f Tapit (USA)-Ready Cat (USA) (Storm Cat (USA))
R M Whitaker One-Six-One Partnership

Placings:5-360020 (7197)
2009: 6^3GF, 6^6GF, 8^0G, 8^0GF, 9^2SF, 8^0SD,

	Starts	1st	2nd	3rd	Win & Pl
Career Total (Turf)	4	0	0	1	385
Career Total (AW)	3	0	1	0	605

Going (Turf): Sf: 0-0 GS: 0-0 Gd: 0-1 GF: 0-3 Fm: 0-0
Distance: 5f/6f: 0-3 7f-8f: 0-1 9f-13f: 0-3 14f+: 0-0
Track : LH: 0-4 RH: 0-1 Tight: 0-2 Gall: 0-0
Aids: Bl: 0-0 Vi: 0-0 Tstrap: 0-0 Ckp: 0-0
Best Rating: 56 11/08 Sthl 6f stand

Modest; stays 1m1f; handles Polytrack.

Rascasse

76 46
4-y-o b g Where Or When (IRE)-Sure Flyer (IRE) (Sure Blade (USA))
Bruce Hellier J W Barrett

Placings:6/0500000-0000 (2969)
2009: 7^0GF, 11^0G, 7^0GF, 14^0GF,

	Starts	1st	2nd	3rd	Win & Pl
Career Total (Turf)	12	0	0	0	0

Going (Turf): Sf: 0-2 GS: 0-1 Gd: 0-6 GF: 0-3 Fm: 0-0
Distance: 5f/6f: 0-2 7f-8f: 0-5 9f-13f: 0-4 14f+: 0-1
Track : LH: 0-4 RH: 0-6 Tight: 0-6 Gall: 0-0
Aids: Bl: 0-2 Vi: 0-0 Tstrap: 0-0 Ckp: 0-0
Best Rating: 46 7/08 Haml 1m65y good

Rash Judgement

106 94
4-y-o b g Mark Of Esteem (IRE)-Let Alone (Warning)
W S Kittow Reg Gifford

Placings:32102/35640400-123000 (6694)
2009: 6^1GF, 6^2G, 6^3G, 6^0G, 6^0G, 6^0GS,

	Starts	1st	2nd	3rd	Win & Pl
Career Total (Turf)	19	2	3	3	19890

91	4/09	Folk	6f	(0-85)H	G-F	£5180
80	8/07	Wind	6f		GD	£4533

Total win prize-money £9715

Going (Turf): Sf: 0-1 GS: 0-3 Gd: 1-9 GF: 1-6 Fm: 0-0
Distance: 5f/6f: 2-18 7f-8f: 0-1 9f-13f: 0-0 14f+: 0-0
Track : LH: 0-0 RH: 0-0 Tight: 0-0 Gall: 1-2
Aids: Bl: 0-0 Vi: 0-0 Tstrap: 0-0 Ckp: 0-0
Best Rating: 94 5/09 Gdwd 6f good

Useful; effective from 5f-6f; acts on most ground on turf.

Rashaad (USA)

93 81
2-y-o b c Smart Strike (CAN)-Martinique (USA) (Pleasant Colony (USA))
B W Hills Hamdan Al Maktoum

Placings:1 (6991)
2009: 7^1G,

	Starts	1st	2nd	3rd	Win & Pl
Career Total (Turf)	1	1	0	0	4533

81	10/09	Donc	7f	GD	£4533

Total win prize-money £4533

Going (Turf): Sf: 0-0 GS: 0-0 Gd: 1-1 GF: 0-0 Fm: 0-0
Distance: 5f/6f: 0-0 7f-8f: 1-1 9f-13f: 0-0 14f+: 0-0
Track : LH: 0-0 RH: 0-0 Tight: 0-0 Gall: 0-0
Aids: Bl: 0-0 Vi: 0-0 Tstrap: 0-0 Ckp: 0-0
Best Rating: 81 10/09 Donc 7f good

Useful debut winner; stays 7f; acts on good ground.

Raslan

92 87
6-y-o b g Lomitas-Rosia (IRE) (Mr Prospector (USA))
D E Pipe D J Reid

Placings:0/264411/00/30 (6851)
2009: 17^3F, 18^0G,

	Starts	1st	2nd	3rd	Win & Pl
Career Total (Turf)	8	2	0	1	13623
Career Total (AW)	3	0	1	0	1806

91	7/06	Wwck	2m39y	(0-75)H	GD	£4533
87	7/06	Wwck	2m39y	(0-80)H	FRM	£6477

Total win prize-money £11011

Going (Turf): Sf: 0-1 GS: 0-2 Gd: 1-3 GF: 0-0 Fm: 1-2
Distance: 5f/6f: 0-0 7f-8f: 0-1 9f-13f: 0-4 14f+: 2-6
Track : LH: 2-6 RH: 0-4 Tight: 0-3 Gall: 0-3
Aids: Bl: 0-0 Vi: 0-3 Tstrap: 0-0 Ckp: 0-0
Best Rating: 91 7/06 Wwck 2m39y good

Useful; stays 2m; acts on good and faster ground and on Polytrack; winning hurdler.

Rasmy

104 85
2-y-o b c Red Ransom (USA)-Shadow Dancing (Unfuwain (USA))
M P Tregoning Hamdan Al Maktoum

Placings:51 (6930)
2009: 7^5GF, 8^1G,

	Starts	1st	2nd	3rd	Win & Pl
Career Total (Turf)	2	1	0	0	2267

85	10/09	Bath	1m5y	GD	£2266

Total win prize-money £2267

Going (Turf): Sf: 0-0 GS: 0-0 Gd: 1-1 GF: 0-1 Fm: 0-0
Distance: 5f/6f: 0-0 7f-8f: 0-1 9f-13f: 1-1 14f+: 0-0
Track : LH: 1-1 RH: 0-0 Tight: 1-1 Gall: 0-0
Aids: Bl: 0-0 Vi: 0-0 Tstrap: 0-0 Ckp: 0-0
Best Rating: 85 10/09 Bath 1m5y good

Fair; effective over 1m; acts on good ground.

Rasselas (IRE)

94 75
2-y-o b g Danehill Dancer (IRE)-Regal Darcey (IRE) (Darshaan)
B W Hills J Hanson,Cavendish InvLtd,Sir A Ferguson

Placings:5400 (6810)
2009: 7^5G, 7^4G, 7^0GF, 8^0G,

	Starts	1st	2nd	3rd	Win & Pl
Career Total (Turf)	4	0	0	0	10185

Going (Turf): Sf: 0-0 GS: 0-0 Gd: 0-3 GF: 0-1 Fm: 0-0
Distance: 5f/6f: 0-0 7f-8f: 0-4 9f-13f: 0-0 14f+: 0-0
Track : LH: 0-0 RH: 0-0 Tight: 0-0 Gall: 0-0
Aids: Bl: 0-0 Vi: 0-0 Tstrap: 0-0 Ckp: 0-0
Best Rating: 75 7/09 NmkJ 7f good

A son of Danehill Dancer who went for 120,000gns; fair maiden form to date.

Rathbawn Girl (IRE)

84(93) (58)43
2-y-o br f Alamshar (IRE)-Rathbawn Realm (Doulab (USA))
Miss J Feilden (M D Squance 6/10) J W Reynolds

Placings:045 (7864)
2009: 6^0GS, 6^4SD, 6^5SS,

	Starts	1st	2nd	3rd	Win & Pl
Career Total (Turf)	1	0	0	0	

Career Total (AW)	**2**	**0**	**0**	**0**	**241**

Going (Turf): **Sf: 0-0 GS: 0-1 Gd: 0-0 GF: 0-0 Fm: 0-0**
Distance: 5f/6f: 0-3 7f-8f: 0-0 9f-13f: 0-0 14f+: 0-0
Track : LH: 0-1 RH: 0-1 Tight: 0-0 Gall: 0-0
Aids: Bl: 0-0 Vi: 0-0 Tstrap: 0-0 Ckp: 0-0
Best Rating: **58** 12/09 Kemp 6f stand

Rathlin Light (USA)

101(97) (65)**70**

3-y-o b/br f Grand Slam (USA)-Baltic Sea (CAN) (Danzig (USA))
W R Swinburn Cricketers Club Racing Group

Placings:0-2210 **(3145)**
2009: 5^{2}SD, 5^{2}GF, 5^{1}GF, 5^{0}GF,

	Starts	1st	2nd	3rd	Win & Pl
Career Total (Turf)	**4**	**1**	**1**	**0**	**3877**
Career Total (AW)	**1**	**0**	**1**	**0**	**771**

70 5/09 Ling 5f (0-70)H G-F £3070
Total win prize-money £3071

Going (Turf): Sf: 0-0 GS: 0-1 Gd: 0-0 **GF: 1-3** Fm: 0-0
Distance: **5f/6f: 1-5** 7f-8f: 0-0 9f-13f: 0-0 14f+: 0-0
Track : LH: 0-1 RH: 0-1 Tight: 0-0 Gall: 0-1
Aids: Bl: 0-0 Vi: 0-0 Tstrap: 0-0 Ckp: 0-0
Best Rating: **70** 5/09 Ling 5f gd-fm

Fair; effective over 5f; acts on Polytrack and fast turf; has worn a tongue tie.

Rathmolyon

89(90) (58)**62**

4-y-o ch f Bahamian Bounty-Feather Circle (IRE) (Indian Ridge)
D Haydn Jones Miss Gillian Byrne

Placings:662230/2054400-00000 **(6329)**
2009: 5^{0}GF, 5^{0}F, 5^{0}G, 5^{0}GS, 5^{0}F,

	Starts	1st	2nd	3rd	Win & Pl
Career Total (Turf)	**13**	**0**	**3**	**0**	**2601**
Career Total (AW)	**5**	**0**	**0**	**1**	**433**

Going (Turf): **Sf: 0-0 GS: 0-2 Gd: 0-4 GF: 0-4 Fm: 0-3**
Distance: 5f/6f: 0-18 7f-8f: 0-0 9f-13f: 0-0 14f+: 0-0
Track : LH: 0-13 RH: 0-0 Tight: 0-4 Gall: 0-10
Aids: Bl: 0-2 Vi: 0-1 Tstrap: 0-0 Ckp: 0-0
Best Rating: **71** 8/07 Bath 5f11y gd-fm

Modest; effective over 5f-6f; acts on good and fast ground; also goes on Polytrack.

Rattan (USA)

106(103) (96)**93**

4-y-o ch c Royal Anthem (USA)-Rouwaki (USA) (Miswaki (USA))
Rae Guest J A Coleman & M S Head

Placings:222/1056-0220 **(5522)**
2009: 8^{0}GF, 8^{2}S, 10^{2}SD, 8^{0}G,

	Starts	1st	2nd	3rd	Win & Pl
Career Total (Turf)	**10**	**1**	**4**	**0**	**12567**
Career Total (AW)	**1**	**0**	**1**	**0**	**2202**

89 5/08 NmkR 1m G-S £5180
Total win prize-money £5181

Going (Turf): Sf: 0-2 **GS: 1-2** Gd: 0-4 GF: 0-2 Fm: 0-0
Distance: 5f/6f: 0-0 **7f-8f: 1-5** 9f-13f: 0-6 14f+: 0-0
Track : LH: 0-2 RH: 0-6 Tight: 0-2 Gall: 0-0
Aids: Bl: 0-0 Vi: 0-0 Tstrap: 0-0 Ckp: 0-0
Best Rating: **96** 6/09 Kemp 1m2f stand

Useful; stays 1m; acts on soft ground, but handles good.

Raucous (GER)

107(91) (73)**75**

6-y-o b g Zinaad-Roseola (GER) (Acatenango (GER))
Mrs R A Carr David W Chapman

Placings:44/21/160/41014 **(1765)**
2009: 12^{4}SD, 12^{1}GF, 14^{0}GF, 12^{1}GF, 11^{4}GF,

	Starts	1st	2nd	3rd	Win & Pl
Career Total (Turf)	**11**	**4**	**1**	**0**	**26413**
Career Total (AW)	**1**	**0**	**0**	**0**	**0**

75 4/09 Newc 1m4f93y (0-85)H G-F £5180
69 4/09 Muss 1m4f100y G-F £1942
87 4/07 Ripn 2m (0-100)H G-F £12464
82 8/06 Ripn 1m4f10y GD £4533
Total win prize-money £24122

Going (Turf): Sf: 0-0 GS: 0-1 Gd: 1-4 **GF: 3-5** Fm: 0-1
Distance: 5f/6f: 0-0 7f-8f: 0-0 **9f-13f: 3-8** 14f+: 1-4
Track : LH: 1-4 **RH: 3-8 Tight: 3-5** Gall: 1-3
Aids: Bl: 0-1 Vi: 0-0 Tstrap: 0-0 Ckp: 0-0
Best Rating: **87** 5/07 NmkR 1m6f good

Fair; stays 2m, effective at shorter, acts on fast and easy ground.

Ravenfield (IRE)

90 **59**

2-y-o b c Xaar-Rubyanne (IRE) (Fasliyev (USA))
D H Brown A K Smeaton

Placings:6 **(5977)**
2009: 5^{6}GF,

	Starts	1st	2nd	3rd	Win & Pl
Career Total (Turf)	**1**	**0**	**0**	**0**	**0**

Going (Turf): **Sf: 0-0 GS: 0-0 Gd: 0-0 GF: 0-1 Fm: 0-0**
Distance: 5f/6f: 0-1 7f-8f: 0-0 9f-13f: 0-0 14f+: 0-0
Track : LH: 0-0 RH: 0-0 Tight: 0-0 Gall: 0-0
Aids: Bl: 0-0 Vi: 0-0 Tstrap: 0-0 Ckp: 0-0
Best Rating: **59** 9/09 Bevl 5f gd-fm

Ravens Rose

67(80) (62)

2-y-o b f Bold Edge-Marjeune (Marju (IRE))
J G Portman Hydraulic Component Services Ltd

Placings:01 **(6441)**
2009: 6^{0}GF, 8^{1}SS,

	Starts	1st	2nd	3rd	Win & Pl
Career Total (Turf)	**1**	**0**	**0**	**0**	
Career Total (AW)	**1**	**1**	**0**	**0**	**2730**

62 10/09 Ling 1m SS £2729
Total win prize-money £2730

Going (Turf): **Sf: 0-0 GS: 0-0 Gd: 0-0 GF: 0-1 Fm: 0-0**
Distance: 5f/6f: 0-0 **7f-8f: 1-2** 9f-13f: 0-0 14f+: 0-0
Track : **LH: 1-1** RH: 0-0 **Tight: 1-1** Gall: 0-0
Aids: Bl: 0-0 Vi: 0-0 Tstrap: 0-0 Ckp: 0-0
Best Rating: **62** 10/09 Ling 1m std-slw

Modest; stays 1m; acts on Polytrack.

Ravi River (IRE)

(106) (85)**58**

5-y-o ch g Barathea (IRE)-Echo River (USA) (Irish River (FR))
P D Evans (J R Boyle 30/11) J L Guillambert

Placings:313/2006/0226-2110256150364 **(7883)**
2009: 7^{2}SD, 7^{1}SD, 7^{1}SD, 8^{0}SD, 7^{2}SD, 6^{5}SD, 7^{6}SD, 7^{1}SS, 7^{5}SD, 7^{0}SD, 7^{3}SD, 7^{6}SD, 8^{4}SD,

	Starts	1st	2nd	3rd	Win & Pl
Career Total (Turf)	**7**	**1**	**0**	**2**	**9178**
Career Total (AW)	**17**	**3**	**5**	**1**	**18816**

84 10/09 Ling 7f (0-80)H SS £6476
85 2/09 Kemp 7f STD £2047
84 2/09 Wolv 7f32y (0-80)H STD £5180
85 8/06 Ches 7f2y GD £6800
Total win prize-money £20505

Going (Turf): Sf: 0-0 GS: 0-1 **Gd: 1-4** GF: 0-2 Fm: 0-0
Distance: 5f/6f: 0-2 **7f-8f: 4-20** 9f-13f: 0-2 14f+: 0-0
Track : **LH: 3-16** RH: 1-7 **Tight: 3-18** Gall: 0-0
Aids: Bl: 0-0 Vi: 0-0 Tstrap: 0-0 Ckp: 0-0
Best Rating: **85** 2/09 Kemp 7f stand

Fair; effective over 7f-1m; acts on good ground; goes on Polytrack.

Rawaabet (IRE)

97(97) (48)**52**

7-y-o b g Bahhare (USA)-Haddeyah (USA) (Dayjur (USA))
R Hollinshead Phil Pye

Placings:00/016605202000/000000/004600/40630-400 **(4021)**
2009: 12^{4}GF, 11^{0}GS, 11^{0}GF,

	Starts	1st	2nd	3rd	Win & Pl
Career Total (Turf)	**21**	**0**	**2**	**0**	**2617**
Career Total (AW)	**13**	**1**	**0**	**1**	**3608**

73 1/05 Sthl 1m STD £3406
Total win prize-money £3406

Going (Turf): **Sf: 0-2 GS: 0-3 Gd: 0-6 GF: 0-10 Fm: 0-0**
Distance: 5f/6f: 0-0 **7f-8f: 1-8** 9f-13f: 0-26 14f+: 0-0
Track : **LH: 1-15** RH: 0-17 Tight: 0-16 Gall: 0-3
Aids: Bl: 0-0 Vi: 0-0 Tstrap: 0-0 Ckp: 0-0
Best Rating: **73** 5/05 Wind 1m67y gd-fm

Moderate performer; stays a mile; acts on easy ground.

Rawaaj

(88) (61)**62**

3-y-o ro g Linamix (FR)-Inaaq (Lammtarra (USA))
D McCain Jnr (Sir Michael Stoute 22/10) Tim & Miranda Johnson Partnership

Placings:064-0 **(6975)**
2009: 12^{0}SD,

	Starts	1st	2nd	3rd	Win & Pl
Career Total (Turf)	**2**	**0**	**0**	**0**	**0**
Career Total (AW)	**2**	**0**	**0**	**0**	**481**

Going (Turf): **Sf: 0-0 GS: 0-0 Gd: 0-2 GF: 0-0 Fm: 0-0**
Distance: 5f/6f: 0-1 7f-8f: 0-2 9f-13f: 0-1 14f+: 0-0
Track : LH: 0-1 RH: 0-1 Tight: 0-0 Gall: 0-1
Aids: Bl: 0-0 Vi: 0-0 Tstrap: 0-0 Ckp: 0-0
Best Rating: **62** 9/08 Ling 7f good

Modest; should stay 1m2f; acts on Polytrack.

Rawdon (IRE)

93(105) (81)**74**

8-y-o b g Singspiel (IRE)-Rebecca Sharp (Machiavellian (USA))
Miss Gay Kelleway (M L W Bell 27/1) Mrs Donna Joslyn

Placings:05/221103510/0006630200/05466331334/32-02120220203455 **(3244)**

2009: 10^{0}SD, 12^{2}SD, 12^{1}SD, 12^{2}SD, 12^{0}SD, 12^{2}SD, 13^{2}SD, 12^{0}GF, 12^{2}SD, 11^{0}GF, 12^{3}SD, 11^{4}GS, 12^{5}SD, 11^{5}GF,

	Starts	1st	2nd	3rd	Win & Pl
Career Total (Turf)	36	4	2	7	33412
Career Total (AW)	12	1	7	1	8000

68 2/09 Sthl 1m4f STD £2047
73 9/07 Hayd 1m2f120y (0-75)H G-F £2717
93 9/05 Hayd 1m2f120y (0-85)H G-S £7256
90 6/05 NmkJ 1m2f (0-85)H GD £6032
81 5/05 Hayd 1m2f120y G-F £7338
Total win prize-money £25392

Going (Turf): Sf: 0-7 GS: 1-5 Gd: 1-8 **GF: 2-16** Fm: 0-0
Distance: 5f/6f: 0-0 7f-8f: 0-1 **9f-13f: 5-47** 14f+: 0-0
Track : **LH: 4-31** RH: 1-14 Tight: 0-11 **Gall: 1-11**
Aids: Bl: 1-11 **Vi: 2-28** Tstrap: 0-1 Ckp: 0-1
Best Rating: **93** 9/05 Hayd 1m2f120y gd-sft

Fair; stays 1m4f but effective at shorter; acts on good and easier ground and on sand; has worn various headgear.

Rawnaq (IRE)

82 **61**

2-y-o b c Azamour (IRE)-Sharemata (IRE) (Doyoun)
M Johnston Hamdan Al Maktoum

Placings:4 **(5801)**
2009: 7^{4}GF,

	Starts	1st	2nd	3rd	Win & Pl
Career Total (Turf)	1	0	0	0	385

Going (Turf): **Sf: 0-0 GS: 0-0 Gd: 0-0 GF: 0-1 Fm: 0-0**
Distance: 5f/6f: 0-0 7f-8f: 0-1 9f-13f: 0-0 14f+: 0-0
Track : LH: 0-1 RH: 0-0 Tight: 0-1 Gall: 0-0
Aids: Bl: 0-0 Vi: 0-0 Tstrap: 0-0 Ckp: 0-0
Best Rating: **61** 9/09 Epsm 7f gd-fm

Ray Diamond

(94) (52)**52**

4-y-o ch g Medicean-Musical Twist (USA) (Woodman (USA))
M Madgwick Mrs L N Harmes

Placings:000/3300060-4 **(0120)**
2009: 10^{4}SD,

	Starts	1st	2nd	3rd	Win & Pl
Career Total (Turf)	7	0	0	0	
Career Total (AW)	4	0	0	2	564

Going (Turf): **Sf: 0-0 GS: 0-1 Gd: 0-1 GF: 0-5 Fm: 0-0**
Distance: 5f/6f: 0-0 7f-8f: 0-6 9f-13f: 0-5 14f+: 0-0
Track : LH: 0-1 RH: 0-6 Tight: 0-3 Gall: 0-0
Aids: Bl: 0-0 Vi: 0-0 Tstrap: 0-3 Ckp: 0-3
Best Rating: **52** 2/08 Kemp 1m stand

Moderate; stays 1m; acts on Polytrack.

Ray Of Joy

97(111) (88)**82**

3-y-o b f Tobougg (IRE)-Once Removed (Distant Relative)
J R Jenkins Robin Stevens

Placings:505313320-1036023400 **(7875)**
2009: 6^{1}SD, 6^{0}GF, 6^{3}SD, 6^{6}GF, 6^{0}SD, 6^{2}SD, 7^{3}SD, 6^{4}SD, 6^{0}SD, 6^{0}SD,

	Starts	1st	2nd	3rd	Win & Pl
Career Total (Turf)	6	0	0	1	385
Career Total (AW)	13	2	2	4	12287

84 4/09 Kemp 6f (0-80)H STD £4727
73 9/08 Kemp 6f (0-65) STD £2047
Total win prize-money £6774

Going (Turf): **Sf: 0-0 GS: 0-1 Gd: 0-1 GF: 0-4 Fm: 0-0**
Distance: **5f/6f: 2-15** 7f-8f: 0-4 9f-13f: 0-0 14f+: 0-0
Track : LH: 0-3 **RH: 2-10** Tight: 0-2 Gall: 0-4
Aids: Bl: 0-0 Vi: 0-0 Tstrap: 0-0 Ckp: 0-0
Best Rating: **88** 9/09 Kemp 6f stand

Useful; effective over 6f; acts on good ground and on Polytrack.

Rayhani (USA)

103(109) (96)**99**

6-y-o b g Theatrical-Bahr Alsalaam (USA) (Riverman (USA))
J A Nash (D Nicholls 6/10) I Murphy

Placings:510/02150/1054/34035400-00001 **(6560)**
2009: 10^{0}GF, 12^{0}SH, 12^{0}S, 13^{0}G, 11^{1}G,

	Starts	1st	2nd	3rd	Win & Pl
Career Total (Turf)	21	4	0	0	26220
Career Total (AW)	4	0	1	2	4411

84 10/09 Catt 1m3f214y (0-75)H GD £2914
105 5/07 NmkR 1m4f (0-90)H G-F £7772
99 7/06 Asct 1m4f (0-85)H G-F £6477
80 9/05 Gdwd 1m1f G-F £4849
Total win prize-money £22012

Going (Turf): Sf: 0-2 GS: 0-0 Gd: 1-8 **GF: 3-10** Fm: 0-0
Distance: 5f/6f: 0-0 7f-8f: 0-1 **9f-13f: 4-19** 14f+: 0-5
Track : LH: 1-9 **RH: 3-14** Tight: 2-7 Gall: 2-11
Aids: Bl: 0-1 Vi: 0-0 Tstrap: 0-0 Ckp: 0-0
Best Rating: **105** 5/07 NmkR 1m4f gd-fm

Useful; stays 1m4f, but effective at shorter; goes well on fast ground and handles Polytrack; has worn blinkers.

Re Barolo (IRE)

108(111) (112)**107**

6-y-o b h Cape Cross (IRE)-Dalaiya (USA) (Irish River (FR))
M Botti Effevi Snc Di Villa Felice & C

Placings:3131/6221611010/24101125/0410101052244-164340632 **(7588)**
2009: 10^{1}SD, 10^{6}SD, 10^{4}SD, 10^{3}GF, 10^{4}GF, 10^{0}GF, 10^{6}G, 10^{3}SD, 8^{2}SD,

	Starts	1st	2nd	3rd	Win & Pl
Career Total (Turf)	23	6	3	2	73865
Career Total (AW)	21	7	4	2	137097

110 2/09 Ling 1m2f STD £22708
106 6/08 York 1m208y (0-105)H GD £17485
111 4/08 GrLe 1m2f STD £6799
109 3/08 Wolv 1m141y (0-105)H STD £31160
9/07 Siro 1m HVY £6318
6/07 Siro 1m GD £6318
4/07 Capa 7f110y STD £6318
11/06 Capa 1m STD £7328
10/06 Casc 7f110y GD £4138
5/06 Capa 1m STD £10259
4/06 Capa 1m STD £10345
11/05 Capa 1m SFT £7535
11/05 Siro 1m SFT £6028
Total win prize-money £142740

Going (Turf): **Sf: 3-9** GS: 0-1 **Gd: 3-6** GF: 0-5 Fm: 0-0
Distance: 5f/6f: 0-0 **7f-8f: 9-26** 9f-13f: 4-18 14f+: 0-0
Track : **LH: 5-18** RH: 4-12 Tight: 2-9 Gall: 2-7
Aids: Bl: 0-0 Vi: 0-0 Tstrap: 0-0 Ckp: 0-0
Best Rating: **112** 11/08 Ling 1m2f stand

Smart; Listed winner; effective over 1m-1m4f; acts on good and easier ground and on Polytrack; often wears a tongue tie.

Reach For The Sky (IRE)

96(87) (61)**68**

2-y-o b f Elusive City (USA)-Zara Whetei (IRE) (Lomond (USA))
R Hannon B Bull

Placings:1004604 **(6906)**
2009: 6^{1}GF, 5^{0}GS, 6^{0}G, 6^{4}GF, 6^{6}SD, 6^{0}SD, 6^{4}G,

	Starts	1st	2nd	3rd	Win & Pl
Career Total (Turf)	5	1	0	0	2914
Career Total (AW)	2	0	0	0	0

68 5/09 Gdwd 6f G-F £2914
Total win prize-money £2914

Going (Turf): Sf: 0-0 GS: 0-1 Gd: 0-2 **GF: 1-2** Fm: 0-0
Distance: **5f/6f: 1-7** 7f-8f: 0-0 9f-13f: 0-0 14f+: 0-0
Track : LH: 0-0 RH: 0-2 Tight: 0-0 Gall: 0-2
Aids: Bl: 0-0 Vi: 0-0 Tstrap: 0-0 Ckp: 0-0
Best Rating: **68** 8/09 Wind 6f gd-fm

Fair; effective over 6f; acts on fast ground and on Polytrack.

Reaction

(87) (69)**79**

3-y-o ch g Alhaarth (IRE)-Hawas (Mujtahid (USA))
M R Channon Highclere Thoroughbred Racing (St Simon)

Placings:303551-40 **(6977)**
2009: 8^{4}G, 8^{0}SD,

	Starts	1st	2nd	3rd	Win & Pl
Career Total (Turf)	6	1	0	2	6770
Career Total (AW)	2	0	0	0	0

76 10/08 Gdwd 7f (0-85) G-S £5504
Total win prize-money £5505

Going (Turf): Sf: 0-0 **GS: 1-1** Gd: 0-1 GF: 0-3 Fm: 0-1
Distance: 5f/6f: 0-0 **7f-8f: 1-5** 9f-13f: 0-3 14f+: 0-0
Track : LH: 0-2 **RH: 1-3** Tight: 0-2 Gall: 0-1
Aids: Bl: 0-0 Vi: 0-0 Tstrap: 0-0 Ckp: 0-0
Best Rating: **79** 8/08 Ling 7f140y gd-fm

Fair; stays an extended 7f; acts on fast and easy ground.

Read The Script (IRE)

(95) (55)**46**

4-y-o b g King's Best (USA)-Grizel (Lion Cavern (USA))
Tom Dascombe Christopher McHale

Placings:000-30 **(6674)**
2009: 7^{3}SD, 7^{0}SD,

	Starts	1st	2nd	3rd	Win & Pl
Career Total (Turf)	2	0	0	0	
Career Total (AW)	3	0	0	1	323

Going (Turf): **Sf: 0-0 GS: 0-0 Gd: 0-0 GF: 0-0 Fm: 0-1**
Distance: 5f/6f: 0-1 7f-8f: 0-4 9f-13f: 0-0 14f+: 0-0
Track : LH: 0-3 RH: 0-0 Tight: 0-2 Gall: 0-0
Aids: Bl: 0-0 Vi: 0-0 Tstrap: 0-0 Ckp: 0-0
Best Rating: **55** 9/09 Wolv 7f32y stand

Moderate; stays 7f and acts on Polytrack.

Readily

(94) (58)**67**

3-y-o ch f Captain Rio-Presently (Cadeaux Genereux)
J G Portman Hockham Racing

Placings:4055251423-4040 (0955)

2009: 5^{4}SD, 6^{0}SD, 6^{4}SD, 5^{0}SD,

	Starts	1st	2nd	3rd	Win & Pl
Career Total (Turf)	6	0	1	0	617
Career Total (AW)	8	1	1	1	3847

58 11/08 Ling 6f STD £2729

Total win prize-money £2730

Going (Turf): Sf: 0-0 GS: 0-0 Gd: 0-2 GF: 0-3 Fm: 0-1
Distance: 5f/6f: 1-14 7f-8f: 0-0 9f-13f: 0-0 14f+: 0-0
Track : LH: 1-7 RH: 0-1 Tight: 1-5 Gall: 0-2
Aids: Bl: 0-0 Vi: 0-0 Tstrap: 0-0 Ckp: 0-0
Best Rating: 67 4/08 Wind 5f10y gd-fm

Moderate; effective over 6f; acts on fast ground; goes on Polytrack.

Ready For Battle (IRE)

74 **57**

3-y-o b g Namid-Enamoured (Groom Dancer (USA))
D W Thompson Opus Industrial Services Partnership

Placings:060-00000 (5621)

2009: 8^{0}G, 6^{0}S, 9^{0}G, 11^{0}GS, 7^{0}S,

	Starts	1st	2nd	3rd	Win & Pl
Career Total (Turf)	8	0	0	0	0

Going (Turf): Sf: 0-3 GS: 0-2 Gd: 0-3 GF: 0-0 Fm: 0-0
Distance: 5f/6f: 0-1 7f-8f: 0-5 9f-13f: 0-2 14f+: 0-0
Track : LH: 0-3 RH: 0-2 Tight: 0-3 Gall: 0-0
Aids: Bl: 0-0 Vi: 0-0 Tstrap: 0-3 Ckp: 0-3
Best Rating: 57 9/08 Newb 6f8y good

Ready To Crown (USA)

93(106) (60)**58**

5-y-o b m More Than Ready (USA)-Dili (USA) (Chief's Crown (USA))
J Mackie (Andrew Turnell 19/4) The Festival Dream Partnership

Placings:20/635330-024003 (5015)

2009: 12^{0}SD, 10^{2}SD, 10^{4}SD, 13^{0}SF, 11^{0}G, 10^{3}SD,

	Starts	1st	2nd	3rd	Win & Pl
Career Total (Turf)	3	0	0	1	289
Career Total (AW)	11	0	2	3	2489

Going (Turf): Sf: 0-0 GS: 0-0 Gd: 0-2 GF: 0-1 Fm: 0-0
Distance: 5f/6f: 0-0 7f-8f: 0-1 9f-13f: 0-12 14f+: 0-1
Track : LH: 0-12 RH: 0-2 Tight: 0-11 Gall: 0-1
Aids: Bl: 0-2 Vi: 0-0 Tstrap: 0-1 Ckp: 0-1
Best Rating: 60 1/09 Ling 1m2f stand

Moderate filly; acts on a sound surface and Polytrack; should stay well.

Ready To Prime

(81) (35)**24**

3-y-o ch f Primo Valentino (IRE)-Blue Topaz (IRE) (Bluebird (USA))
Mike Murphy Phil Woods

Placings:50000-00 (7426)

2009: 7^{0}SD, 10^{0}SD,

	Starts	1st	2nd	3rd	Win & Pl
Career Total (Turf)	2	0	0	0	
Career Total (AW)	5	0	0	0	0

Going (Turf): Sf: 0-0 GS: 0-0 Gd: 0-0 GF: 0-2 Fm: 0-0
Distance: 5f/6f: 0-3 7f-8f: 0-2 9f-13f: 0-2 14f+: 0-0
Track : LH: 0-3 RH: 0-2 Tight: 0-1 Gall: 0-3
Aids: Bl: 0-0 Vi: 0-0 Tstrap: 0-0 Ckp: 0-0
Best Rating: 35 11/08 Sthl 1m stand

Readymade (IRE)

91 **72**

2-y-o b g Dubai Destination (USA)-Onda Nova (USA) (Keos (USA))
Sir Michael Stoute Niarchos Family

Placings:62 (6792)

2009: 7^{6}GF, 8^{2}S,

	Starts	1st	2nd	3rd	Win & Pl
Career Total (Turf)	2	0	1	0	1108

Going (Turf): Sf: 0-1 GS: 0-0 Gd: 0-0 GF: 0-1 Fm: 0-0
Distance: 5f/6f: 0-0 7f-8f: 0-1 9f-13f: 0-1 14f+: 0-0
Track : LH: 0-1 RH: 0-0 Tight: 0-0 Gall: 0-0
Aids: Bl: 0-0 Vi: 0-0 Tstrap: 0-0 Ckp: 0-0
Best Rating: 72 10/09 Nott 1m75y soft

Fair; stays 1m; acts on soft ground.

Real Desire

95 **58**

3-y-o ch g Haafhd-Stop Press (USA) (Sharpen Up)
I Semple David McKenzie

Placings:0020000 (6385)

2009: 10^{0}G, 12^{0}GF, 9^{2}GF, 11^{0}G, 9^{0}G, 11^{0}G, 12^{0}GF,

	Starts	1st	2nd	3rd	Win & Pl
Career Total (Turf)	7	0	1	0	771

Going (Turf): Sf: 0-0 GS: 0-0 Gd: 0-4 GF: 0-3 Fm: 0-0
Distance: 5f/6f: 0-0 7f-8f: 0-0 9f-13f: 0-7 14f+: 0-0
Track : LH: 0-3 RH: 0-4 Tight: 0-4 Gall: 0-3
Aids: Bl: 0-2 Vi: 0-0 Tstrap: 0-1 Ckp: 0-1
Best Rating: 58 6/09 Haml 1m1f36y gd-fm

Real Diamond

98 **72**

3-y-o b f Bertolini (USA)-Miss Fit (IRE) (Hamas (IRE))
A Dickman John H Sissons

Placings:000231-0150002 (7082)

2009: 6^{0}GF, 5^{1}G, 5^{5}GS, 5^{0}G, 7^{0}GF, 6^{0}G, 5^{2}S,

	Starts	1st	2nd	3rd	Win & Pl
Career Total (Turf)	13	2	2	1	7644

72 7/09 Catt 5f212y (0-75)H GD £3043
69 10/08 Catt 5f212y G-S £2047

Total win prize-money £5091

Going (Turf): Sf: 0-2 GS: 1-3 Gd: 1-6 GF: 0-2 Fm: 0-0
Distance: 5f/6f: 2-12 7f-8f: 0-1 9f-13f: 0-0 14f+: 0-0
Track : LH: 2-5 RH: 0-0 Tight: 2-5 Gall: 0-0
Aids: Bl: 0-0 Vi: 0-0 Tstrap: 0-1 Ckp: 0-1
Best Rating: 72 7/09 Catt 5f212y good

Modest; effective over 6f; acts on good and easy ground; has worn cheekpieces; goes well at Catterick.

Realisation (USA)

97 **82**

2-y-o b g Alhaarth (IRE)-Live Your Dreams (USA) (Mt. Livermore (USA))
M Johnston Sheikh Hamdan Bin Mohammed Al Maktoum

Placings:3312 (6569)

2009: 7^{3}GS, 7^{3}G, 8^{1}GF, 9^{2}GF,

	Starts	1st	2nd	3rd	Win & Pl
Career Total (Turf)	4	1	1	2	8485

79 9/09 Epsm 1m114y G-F £5180

Total win prize-money £5181

Going (Turf): Sf: 0-0 GS: 0-1 Gd: 0-1 GF: 1-2 Fm: 0-0
Distance: 5f/6f: 0-0 7f-8f: 0-2 9f-13f: 1-2 14f+: 0-0
Track : LH: 1-3 RH: 0-1 Tight: 1-2 Gall: 0-0
Aids: Bl: 0-0 Vi: 0-0 Tstrap: 0-0 Ckp: 0-0
Best Rating: 82 10/09 Leic 1m1f218y gd-fm

Fair; stays 1m2f; acts on fast and easy ground.

Realism (FR)

99(104) (84)**66**

9-y-o b g Machiavellian (USA)-Kissing Cousin (IRE) (Danehill (USA))
M W Easterby S A Hollings

Placings:0350/44105036121101560/52530101/005200/01 5001200/0-201066060 (7776)

2009: 12^{2}SD, 12^{0}GF, 12^{1}SD, 12^{0}GS, 12^{6}G, 10^{6}GS, 12^{0}GS, 11^{6}SD, 10^{0}SD,

	Starts	1st	2nd	3rd	Win & Pl
Career Total (Turf)	41	8	4	2	106152
Career Total (AW)	13	2	1	1	6822

84 6/09 Sthl 1m4f STD £2729
86 9/07 York 1m2f88y G-F £5181
91 6/07 Ches 1m2f75y SFT £3432
104 10/05 York 1m2f88y (0-95)H GD £10264
104 8/05 York 1m2f88y (0-105)H GD £19957
87 7/04 Leic 1m1f218yD(0-80)H GD £6968
81 6/04 Pont 1m2f6yE(0-70)H G-F £4173
74 6/04 Chep 1m2f36yE(0-75)H G-F £3750
70 6/04 Nott 1m1f213yF(0-75)H G-F £3087
73 2/04 Sthl 1m F(0-60)H STD £2898

Total win prize-money £62445

Going (Turf): Sf: 1-3 GS: 0-7 Gd: 3-11 GF: 4-19 Fm: 0-1
Distance: 5f/6f: 0-0 7f-8f: 1-6 9f-13f: 9-48 14f+: 0-0
Track : LH: 9-44 RH: 1-8 Tight: 1-14 Gall: 3-19
Aids: Bl: 0-0 Vi: 0-1 Tstrap: 1-4 Ckp: 1-4
Best Rating: 104 10/05 York 1m2f88y good

Useful; seems best at around 1m2f-1m4f; acts well on a sound surface; goes on Fibresand; has worn a tongue tie.

Reallymissgreeley (USA)

90(98) (62)**60**

2-y-o b/br f Mr Greeley (USA)-Holiday Gold (USA) (Touch Gold (USA))
K A Ryan Mrs T Marnane

Placings:40002 (7140)

2009: 6^{4}GF, 5^{0}G, 6^{0}GF, 5^{0}SD, 8^{2}SD,

	Starts	1st	2nd	3rd	Win & Pl
Career Total (Turf)	3	0	0	0	241
Career Total (AW)	2	0	1	0	1060

Going (Turf): Sf: 0-0 GS: 0-0 Gd: 0-1 GF: 0-2 Fm: 0-0
Distance: 5f/6f: 0-4 7f-8f: 0-0 9f-13f: 0-1 14f+: 0-0
Track : LH: 0-2 RH: 0-1 Tight: 0-2 Gall: 0-0
Aids: Bl: 0-1 Vi: 0-0 Tstrap: 0-0 Ckp: 0-0
Best Rating: 62 10/09 Wolv 1m141y stand

Modest; stays 1m; acts on Polytrack.

Realt Na Mara (IRE)

99(107) (81)77

6-y-o b/br g Tagula (IRE)-Dwingeloo (IRE) (Dancing Dissident (USA))

H Morrison H Morrison

Placings:005131/1224602004-1400300251100010 (7287)

2009: 6^{1}SS, 6^{4}SD, 7^{0}SD, 6^{0}GF, 6^{3}SD, 6^{0}F, 5^{0}GF, 6^{2}GF, 6^{5}S, 6^{1}SD, 5^{1}GS, 5^{0}GS, 5^{0}G, 6^{0}GS, 7^{1}GF, 7^{0}S,

	Starts	1st	2nd	3rd	Win & Pl
Career Total (Turf)	17	2	1	0	5758
Career Total (AW)	15	5	3	2	17696

77 10/09 Leic 7f9y (0-70)H G-F £2637
77 8/09 Carl 5f193y (0-60)H G-S £1977
81 8/09 Sthl 6f (0-70)H STD £2590
79 1/09 Sthl 6f (0-70)H SS £2729
80 1/08 Sthl 6f (0-70)H STD £2593
73 12/07 Wolv 5f216y (0-75)H STD £2968
66 10/07 Kemp 6f STD £2047

Total win prize-money £17546

Going (Turf): Sf: 0-3 **GS: 1-3** Gd: 0-3 **GF: 1-6** Fm: 0-1
Distance: **5f/6f: 6-24** 7f-8f: 1-8 9f-13f: 0-0 14f+: 0-0
Track : **LH: 4-19** RH: 2-2 **Tight: 1-5** Gall: 0-4
Aids: Bl: 0-1 Vi: 0-0 Tstrap: 2-8 Ckp: 2-8
Best Rating: **82** 1/08 Sthl 7f stand

Fair; ex-Irish; suited by 6f but stays 7f; acts on Polytrack and Fibresand plus fast and easy ground on turf; has worn blinkers.

Rebecca De Winter

71(97) (75)83

3-y-o b f Kyllachy-Miss Adelaide (IRE) (Alzao (USA))

David Pinder Mrs Angela Pinder

Placings:21000-6605206 (7021)

2009: 5^{6}SD, 5^{8}SD, 5^{0}G, 5^{5}SF, 5^{2}SD, 6^{0}SD, 5^{6}SD,

	Starts	1st	2nd	3rd	Win & Pl
Career Total (Turf)	4	1	0	0	8419
Career Total (AW)	8	0	2	0	1927

83 5/08 Ches 5f16y G-F £8418

Total win prize-money £8419

Going (Turf): Sf: 0-0 GS: 0-0 Gd: 0-2 **GF: 1-2** Fm: 0-0
Distance: **5f/6f: 1-12** 7f-8f: 0-0 9f-13f: 0-0 14f+: 0-0
Track : **LH: 1-5** RH: 0-4 **Tight: 1-5** Gall: 0-0
Aids: Bl: 0-0 Vi: 0-0 Tstrap: 0-0 Ckp: 0-0
Best Rating: **83** 5/08 Ches 5f16y gd-fm

Useful; effective over 5f; acts on fast ground and on Polytrack.

Rebecca Romero

86(85) (46)49

2-y-o b f Exceed And Excel (AUS)-Cloud Dancer (Bishop Of Cashel)

D J Coakley Keepers Racing Ii

Placings:00600 (5589)

2009: 6^{0}GF, 6^{0}GF, 5^{6}SF, 7^{0}SD, 7^{0}GS,

	Starts	1st	2nd	3rd	Win & Pl
Career Total (Turf)	3	0	0	0	
Career Total (AW)	2	0	0	0	0

Going (Turf): **Sf: 0-0 GS: 0-1 Gd: 0-0 GF: 0-2 Fm: 0-0**
Distance: 5f/6f: 0-2 7f-8f: 0-3 9f-13f: 0-0 14f+: 0-0
Track : LH: 0-2 RH: 0-1 Tight: 0-2 Gall: 0-1
Aids: Bl: 0-0 Vi: 0-0 Tstrap: 0-0 Ckp: 0-0
Best Rating: **49** 5/09 Newb 6f8y gd-fm

Rebel Chieftain (IRE)

70 19

2-y-o b c Dansili-Desert Royalty (IRE) (Alhaarth (IRE))

Saeed Bin Suroor Godolphin

Placings:0 (6484)

2009: 7^{0}GF,

	Starts	1st	2nd	3rd	Win & Pl
Career Total (Turf)	1	0	0	0	

Going (Turf): **Sf: 0-0 GS: 0-0 Gd: 0-0 GF: 0-1 Fm: 0-0**
Distance: 5f/6f: 0-0 7f-8f: 0-1 9f-13f: 0-0 14f+: 0-0
Track : LH: 0-0 RH: 0-0 Tight: 0-0 Gall: 0-0
Aids: Bl: 0-0 Vi: 0-0 Tstrap: 0-0 Ckp: 0-0
Best Rating: **19** 10/09 Rdcr 7f gd-fm

Rebel City

94(100) (73)58

3-y-o b c Elusive City (USA)-Seguro (IRE) (Indian Ridge)

S A Callaghan Gallagher Equine Ltd

Placings:0633-22050 (3712)

2009: 7^{2}SD, 7^{2}SD, 7^{0}GF, 6^{5}GF, 6^{0}SD,

	Starts	1st	2nd	3rd	Win & Pl
Career Total (Turf)	3	0	0	0	122
Career Total (AW)	6	0	2	2	2470

Going (Turf): **Sf: 0-0 GS: 0-0 Gd: 0-0 GF: 0-3 Fm: 0-0**
Distance: 5f/6f: 0-4 7f-8f: 0-5 9f-13f: 0-0 14f+: 0-0
Track : LH: 0-7 RH: 0-1 Tight: 0-4 Gall: 0-1
Aids: Bl: 0-0 Vi: 0-0 Tstrap: 0-0 Ckp: 0-0
Best Rating: **73** 1/09 Ling 7f stand

Fair; suited by 6-7f and Polytrack.

Rebel Duke (IRE)

103(108) (94)94

5-y-o ch g Namid-Edwina (IRE) (Caerleon (USA))

Ollie Pears (D W Barker 22/4) Ian Bishop

Placings:341/512065335/115603-213243052 (7866)

2009: 5^{2}SS, 5^{1}SS, 5^{3}SD, 5^{2}SD, 5^{4}G, 5^{3}SD, 5^{0}SD, 5^{5}SD, 5^{2}SS,

	Starts	1st	2nd	3rd	Win & Pl
Career Total (Turf)	11	1	1	2	7364
Career Total (AW)	16	4	3	4	25999

92 1/09 Sthl 5f (0-85)H SS £4857
94 4/08 Muss 5f (0-70)H SFT £2914
84 4/08 Sthl 5f (0-70)H STD £2456
82 2/07 Sthl 5f (0-75)H SLW £3071
71 12/06 Wolv 5f20y STD £2730

Total win prize-money £16029

Going (Turf): **Sf: 1-2** GS: 0-2 Gd: 0-4 GF: 0-2 Fm: 0-1
Distance: **5f/6f: 5-27** 7f-8f: 0-0 9f-13f: 0-0 14f+: 0-0
Track : **LH: 1-7** RH: 0-0 **Tight: 1-6** Gall: 0-0
Aids: Bl: 0-1 Vi: 0-0 Tstrap: 0-1 Ckp: 0-1
Best Rating: **94** 3/09 Sthl 5f stand

Useful; probably best over 5f; acts on most ground on turf; goes on Fibresand; has worn a tongue tie and cheek-pieces; likes to race prominently.

Rebel Prince (IRE)

90(94) (45)56

3-y-o b g Barathea (IRE)-Rebel Clan (IRE) (Tagula (IRE))

M G Quinlan L Cashman

Placings:4-002604500 (6919)

2009: 10^{0}SD, 9^{0}SD, 10^{2}GS, 12^{6}GF, 12^{0}GF, 12^{4}SD, 14^{5}HY, 11^{0}SD, 11^{0}GF,

	Starts	1st	2nd	3rd	Win & Pl
Career Total (Turf)	6	0	1	0	989
Career Total (AW)	4	0	0	0	0

Going (Turf): **Sf: 0-1 GS: 0-1 Gd: 0-0 GF: 0-4 Fm: 0-0**
Distance: 5f/6f: 0-0 7f-8f: 0-0 9f-13f: 0-9 14f+: 0-1
Track : LH: 0-9 RH: 0-1 Tight: 0-4 Gall: 0-0
Aids: Bl: 0-1 Vi: 0-0 Tstrap: 0-0 Ckp: 0-0
Best Rating: **56** 4/09 Nott 1m2f50y gd-sft

Moderate; stays 1m2f; acts on easy ground.

Rebel Raider (IRE)

(99) (38)

10-y-o b g Mujadil (USA)-Emily's Pride (Shirley Heights)

B N Pollock Mrs Zoe Pruhs

Placings:00500/30300/**10220/400/3/6165-5** (0449)

2009: 13^{5}SD,

	Starts	1st	2nd	3rd	Win & Pl
Career Total (Turf)	10	0	0	2	1577
Career Total (AW)	14	2	2	1	6344

50 2/08 Wolv 2m119y (0-45) STD £1365
59 10/04 Wolv 1m141y (0-55)H STD £3015

Total win prize-money £4381

Going (Turf): **Sf: 0-4 GS: 0-0 Gd: 0-2 GF: 0-2 Fm: 0-0**
Distance: 5f/6f: 0-1 7f-8f: 0-9 9f-13f: 1-11 14f+: 1-3
Track : **LH: 2-16** RH: 0-3 **Tight: 2-11** Gall: 0-1
Aids: Bl: 0-1 **Vi: 1-3** Tstrap: 0-0 Ckp: 0-0
Best Rating: **69** 4/02 Curr 1m1f gd-yld

Moderate; ex-Irish; stays 1m4f; acts on Polytrack.

Rebel Swing

94(79) (36)63

3-y-o b g Robellino (USA)-Ninia (USA) (Affirmed (USA))

W R Muir Broadway Racing Club 15

Placings:050-56 (2350)

2009: 11^{5}GS, 12^{6}GF,

	Starts	1st	2nd	3rd	Win & Pl
Career Total (Turf)	4	0	0	0	0
Career Total (AW)	1	0	0	0	

Going (Turf): **Sf: 0-1 GS: 0-2 Gd: 0-0 GF: 0-1 Fm: 0-0**
Distance: 5f/6f: 0-0 7f-8f: 0-2 9f-13f: 0-3 14f+: 0-0
Track : LH: 0-3 RH: 0-0 Tight: 0-1 Gall: 0-1
Aids: Bl: 0-0 Vi: 0-0 Tstrap: 0-0 Ckp: 0-0
Best Rating: **63** 11/08 Nott 1m75y heavy

Rebel Woman

77(97) (58)52

3-y-o b f Royal Applause-Wild Woman (Polar Falcon (USA))

J A Osborne Mrs Judy Wilson

Placings:0062656 (7517)
2009: 7^{0}SD, 6^{0}G, 7^{6}G, 8^{2}SD, 8^{6}SD, 9^{5}SD, 7^{6}SD,

	Starts	1st	2nd	3rd	Win & Pl
Career Total (Turf)	2	0	0	0	0
Career Total (AW)	5	0	1	0	605

Going (Turf): **Sf: 0-0 GS: 0-0 Gd: 0-2 GF: 0-0 Fm: 0-0**
Distance: 5f/6f: 0-1 7f-8f: 0-5 9f-13f: 0-1 14f+: 0-0
Track : LH: 0-2 RH: 0-3 Tight: 0-2 Gall: 0-0
Aids: Bl: 0-0 Vi: 0-0 Tstrap: 0-0 Ckp: 0-0
Best Rating: **58** 10/09 Kemp 1m stand

Moderate; stays 1m1f; acts on Polytrack.

Rebellious Spirit

(105) (85)**81**
6-y-o b g Mark Of Esteem (IRE)-Robellino Miss (USA) (Robellino (USA))
S Curran Mrs Donna Hill

Placings:622/24502336031/2124205000061030/21221111504-0 (0079)
2009: 9^{0}SD,

	Starts	1st	2nd	3rd	Win & Pl
Career Total (Turf)	12	1	1	2	5104
Career Total (AW)	30	7	9	2	29067

81	3/08	Wwck	1m22y	(0-70)H	G-S	£3238
85	3/08	Wolv	1m1f103y	(0-65)H	STD	£1774
77	2/08	Kemp	1m2f	(0-65)H	STD	£2047
73	2/08	Wolv	1m141y	(0-65)H	STD	£2047
	1/08	Sthl	1m	(0-70)H	STD	£2593
67	11/07	Kemp	1m		STD	£2047
85	1/07	Kemp	1m	(0-75)H	STD	£4728
79	1/07	Sthl	1m	(0-70)H	STD	£2914

Total win prize-money £21395

Going (Turf): Sf: 0-3 **GS: 1-2** Gd: 0-3 GF: 0-3 Fm: 0-1
Distance: 5f/6f: 0-5 7f-8f: 4-21 9f-13f: 4-16 14f+: 0-0
Track : **LH: 5-26** RH: 3-14 **Tight: 2-14** Gall: 0-0
Aids: Bl: 0-0 Vi: 0-0 Tstrap: 0-0 Ckp: 0-0
Best Rating: **90** 2/07 Ling 1m stand

Fair; seems effective over 1m-1m1f; acts on fast ground and sand.

Rebelwithoutacause (IRE)

(84) (45)**45**
3-y-o b g Redback-Christmas Kiss (Taufan (USA))
George Baker James, Dean & Partners

Placings:0000-0 (0134)
2009: 9^{0}SD,

	Starts	1st	2nd	3rd	Win & Pl
Career Total (Turf)	2	0	0	0	
Career Total (AW)	3	0	0	0	

Going (Turf): **Sf: 0-1 GS: 0-0 Gd: 0-0 GF: 0-1 Fm: 0-0**
Distance: 5f/6f: 0-3 7f-8f: 0-1 9f-13f: 0-1 14f+: 0-0
Track : LH: 0-4 RH: 0-0 Tight: 0-1 Gall: 0-1
Aids: Bl: 0-0 Vi: 0-0 Tstrap: 0-1 Ckp: 0-1
Best Rating: **45** 7/08 GrLe 5f stand

Recalcitrant

102(97) (59)**64**
6-y-o b g Josr Algarhoud (IRE)-Lady Isabell (Rambo Dancer (CAN))
S Dow T Staplehurst

Placings:060/004662/304221003541530430260/53203600066-3612112 (6565)
2009: 9^{3}F, 12^{6}G, 7^{1}F, 9^{2}F, 10^{1}F, 10^{1}G, 9^{2}GS,

	Starts	1st	2nd	3rd	Win & Pl
Career Total (Turf)	30	5	5	3	17127
Career Total (AW)	18	0	2	4	2641

64	9/09	Chep	1m2f36y	(0-55)H	GD	£2072
55	8/09	Ling	1m2f	(0-65)H	FRM	£2047
55	8/09	Brig	7f214y	(0-60)H	FRM	£2590
61	8/07	Brig	1m1f209y	(0-70)H	FRM	£2839
61	5/07	Bath	1m3f144y	(0-65)H	GD	£2072

Total win prize-money £11621

Going (Turf): Sf: 0-1 GS: 0-4 Gd: 2-8 GF: 0-11 **Fm: 3-6**
Distance: 5f/6f: 0-0 7f-8f: 1-10 **9f-13f: 4-37** 14f+: 0-1
Track : **LH: 5-25** RH: 0-18 **Tight: 2-16** Gall: 0-3
Aids: Bl: 0-0 Vi: 0-0 Tstrap: 0-0 Ckp: 0-0
Best Rating: **64** 10/09 Folk 1m1f149y gd-sft

Modest; effective over 1m2f-1m4f; acts on most ground and on Polytrack.

Recession Proof (FR)

101(99) (80)**97**
3-y-o ch g Rock Of Gibraltar (IRE)-Elevate (Ela-Mana-Mou)
S A Callaghan Martin M Dempsey

Placings:005133-504211215 (5870)
2009: 11^{5}G, 8^{0}GF, 8^{4}GF, 10^{2}G, 10^{1}G, 10^{1}G, 10^{2}G, 14^{1}G, 14^{5}G,

	Starts	1st	2nd	3rd	Win & Pl
Career Total (Turf)	12	3	2	1	12133
Career Total (AW)	3	1	0	1	3536

95	8/09	Pont	1m2f6y	(0-75)H	GD	£3747
86	8/09	Newb	1m2f6y	(0-70)H	GD	£2498
79	10/08	Wolv	1m141y	(0-65)	STD	£2729

Total win prize-money £8976

Going (Turf): Sf: 0-1 GS: 0-1 **Gd: 3-8** GF: 0-2 Fm: 0-0
Distance: 5f/6f: 0-0 7f-8f: 0-2 **9f-13f: 3-11** 14f+: 1-2
Track : **LH: 3-7** RH: 1-5 Tight: 1-5 **Gall: 2-5**
Aids: Bl: 0-0 Vi: 0-0 Tstrap: 0-0 Ckp: 0-0
Best Rating: **97** 8/09 NmkJ 1m6f175y good

Useful; effective over 1m2f-1m6f; acts on good ground; goes on Polytrack.

Recette

80(70) (16)**49**
2-y-o b f Reset (AUS)-Sunny Times (IRE) (Raise A Grand (IRE))
R Ingram T H Barma

Placings:0460 (7389)
2009: 5^{0}GF, 5^{4}GF, 6^{6}GF, 7^{0}SD,

	Starts	1st	2nd	3rd	Win & Pl
Career Total (Turf)	3	0	0	0	0
Career Total (AW)	1	0	0	0	

Going (Turf): **Sf: 0-0 GS: 0-0 Gd: 0-0 GF: 0-3 Fm: 0-0**
Distance: 5f/6f: 0-3 7f-8f: 0-1 9f-13f: 0-0 14f+: 0-0
Track : LH: 0-2 RH: 0-0 Tight: 0-2 Gall: 0-0
Aids: Bl: 0-0 Vi: 0-0 Tstrap: 0-0 Ckp: 0-0
Best Rating: **49** 9/09 Epsm 6f gd-fm

Recoil (IRE)

87 **39**
4-y-o b g Red Ransom (USA)-Dazilyn Lady (USA) (Zilzal (USA))
R Johnson Robert Johnson

Placings:000U0/00-00005 (4995)
2009: 10^{0}G, 10^{0}GF, 7^{0}G, 6^{0}GF, 7^{5}GF,

	Starts	1st	2nd	3rd	Win & Pl
Career Total (Turf)	11	0	0	0	0
Career Total (AW)	1	0	0	0	

Going (Turf): **Sf: 0-1 GS: 0-0 Gd: 0-5 GF: 0-5 Fm: 0-0**
Distance: 5f/6f: 0-1 7f-8f: 0-7 9f-13f: 0-4 14f+: 0-0
Track : LH: 0-3 RH: 0-4 Tight: 0-2 Gall: 0-2
Aids: Bl: 0-4 Vi: 0-0 Tstrap: 0-1 Ckp: 0-1
Best Rating: **57** 7/07 NmkJ 7f gd-fm

Record Breaker (IRE)

109 **107**
5-y-o b g In The Wings-Overruled (IRE) (Last Tycoon)
M Johnston Triplin Racing

Placings:4/1165100/120020505-002412050415 (6662)
2009: 12^{0}G, 12^{0}GF, 14^{2}GF, 16^{4}G, 12^{1}GF, 12^{2}GF, 16^{0}S, 12^{5}G, 14^{0}GF, 14^{4}GF, 12^{1}GF, 12^{5}GS,

	Starts	1st	2nd	3rd	Win & Pl
Career Total (Turf)	29	6	4	0	96771

107	9/09	Asct	1m4f	(0-105)H	G-F	£11215
104	6/09	Haml	1m4f17y	(0-90)H	G-F	£21808
98	6/08	Muss	1m6f	(0-95)H	G-F	£9346
97	8/07	Pont	1m4f8y	(0-95)H	GD	£9348
84	5/07	Gdwd	1m3f	(0-85)H	GD	£7124
79	4/07	Muss	1m1f		G-F	£2914

Total win prize-money £61760

Going (Turf): Sf: 0-4 GS: 0-4 Gd: 2-7 **GF: 4-14** Fm: 0-0
Distance: 5f/6f: 0-0 7f-8f: 0-1 **9f-13f: 5-15** 14f+: 1-13
Track : LH: 1-12 **RH: 5-16 Tight: 4-8** Gall: 1-14
Aids: **Bl: 2-10** Vi: 0-0 Tstrap: 0-0 Ckp: 0-0
Best Rating: **107** 9/09 Asct 1m4f gd-fm

Smart; effective at 1m4f-2m; acts on good and faster ground; has worn blinkers.

Recurring Dream

88 **32**
3-y-o b f Beat All (USA)-Rewbell (Andy Rew)
P J Hobbs The Recurring Partnership

Placings:0 (4480)
2009: 11^{0}G,

	Starts	1st	2nd	3rd	Win & Pl
Career Total (Turf)	1	0	0	0	

Going (Turf): **Sf: 0-0 GS: 0-0 Gd: 0-1 GF: 0-0 Fm: 0-0**
Distance: 5f/6f: 0-0 7f-8f: 0-0 9f-13f: 0-1 14f+: 0-0
Track : LH: 0-1 RH: 0-0 Tight: 0-1 Gall: 0-0
Aids: Bl: 0-0 Vi: 0-0 Tstrap: 0-0 Ckp: 0-0
Best Rating: **32** 7/09 Bath 1m3f144y good

Red

(88) (24)**66**
5-y-o ch m Fraam-Great Tern (Simply Great (FR))
Mrs S J Humphrey (K C Bailey 13/4) Mrs S J Humphrey

Placings:005263/40204/0-0 (2580)
2009: 12^{0}SD,

	Starts	1st	2nd	3rd	Win & Pl
Career Total (Turf)	9	0	2	0	2572
Career Total (AW)	4	0	0	1	428

Going (Turf): Sf: 0-1 GS: 0-0 Gd: 0-3 GF: 0-5 Fm: 0-0
Distance: 5f/6f: 0-3 7f-8f: 0-0 9f-13f: 0-7 14f+: 0-3
Track: LH: 0-7 RH: 0-2 Tight: 0-5 Gall: 0-0
Aids: Bl: 0-0 Vi: 0-0 Tstrap: 0-0 Ckp: 0-0
Best Rating: 66 11/06 Wolv 1m1f103y stand

Red Amaryllis

95(88) (61)**63**
4-y-o ch f Piccolo-Passiflora (Night Shift (USA))
H J L Dunlop Barry Marsden & Shane Winslade

Placings:0530420/4450326-0000 **(2879)**
2009: 6^{0}GF, 6^{0}SD, 6^{0}GF, 6^{0}GF,

	Starts	1st	2nd	3rd	Win & Pl
Career Total (Turf)	12	0	1	2	2210
Career Total (AW)	6	0	1	0	877

Going (Turf): Sf: 0-0 GS: 0-3 Gd: 0-1 GF: 0-7 Fm: 0-1
Distance: 5f/6f: 0-14 7f-8f: 0-4 9f-13f: 0-0 14f+: 0-0
Track: LH: 0-8 RH: 0-3 Tight: 0-2 Gall: 0-1
Aids: Bl: 0-1 Vi: 0-0 Tstrap: 0-0 Ckp: 0-0
Best Rating: **70** 9/07 Wwck 6f gd-fm

Modest; effective at around 6f; acts on fast ground and on Polytrack.

Red Amy

83(83) (48)**54**
2-y-o b f Hawk Wing (USA)-Ballet Ballon (USA) (Rahy (USA))
M L W Bell Terry Neill

Placings:055 **(5192)**
2009: 7^{0}S, 7^{5}GF, 7^{5}SD,

	Starts	1st	2nd	3rd	Win & Pl
Career Total (Turf)	2	0	0	0	0
Career Total (AW)	1	0	0	0	0

Going (Turf): Sf: 0-1 GS: 0-0 Gd: 0-0 GF: 0-1 Fm: 0-0
Distance: 5f/6f: 0-0 7f-8f: 0-3 9f-13f: 0-0 14f+: 0-0
Track: LH: 0-1 RH: 0-0 Tight: 0-1 Gall: 0-0
Aids: Bl: 0-0 Vi: 0-0 Tstrap: 0-0 Ckp: 0-0
Best Rating: **54** 7/09 NmkJ 7f soft

Red Army Commander (IRE)

86(92) (49)**50**
4-y-o b g Soviet Star (USA)-Penny Fan (Nomination)
J A Geake Mrs S A Geake

Placings:0/46500 **(6969)**
2009: 12^{4}SD, 9^{6}G, 10^{5}GF, 16^{0}GF, 11^{0}G,

	Starts	1st	2nd	3rd	Win & Pl
Career Total (Turf)	5	0	0	0	0
Career Total (AW)	1	0	0	0	0

Going (Turf): Sf: 0-0 GS: 0-1 Gd: 0-2 GF: 0-2 Fm: 0-0
Distance: 5f/6f: 0-0 7f-8f: 0-1 9f-13f: 0-4 14f+: 0-1
Track: LH: 0-3 RH: 0-2 Tight: 0-4 Gall: 0-0
Aids: Bl: 0-0 Vi: 0-0 Tstrap: 0-0 Ckp: 0-0
Best Rating: **50** 8/09 Sals 1m1f198y good

Red Avalanche (IRE)

100(96) (99)**96**
2-y-o gr c Verglas (IRE)-Maura's Guest (IRE) (Be My Guest (USA))
P F I Cole P de Camaret

Placings:02123044350 **(6660)**
2009: 5^{0}SD, 5^{2}GF, 5^{1}GS, 5^{2}GF, 6^{3}G, 5^{0}GF, 5^{4}GF, 5^{4}GS, 5^{3}G, 6^{5}SD, 5^{0}GS,

	Starts	1st	2nd	3rd	Win & Pl
Career Total (Turf)	9	1	2	2	29622
Career Total (AW)	2	0	0	0	1345

85 4/09 Nott 5f13y G-S £3238
Total win prize-money £3238

Going (Turf): Sf: 0-0 **GS: 1-3** Gd: 0-2 GF: 0-4 Fm: 0-0
Distance: **5f/6f: 1-11** 7f-8f: 0-0 9f-13f: 0-0 14f+: 0-0
Track: LH: 0-1 RH: 0-3 Tight: 0-1 Gall: 0-1
Aids: Bl: 0-0 Vi: 0-0 Tstrap: 0-0 Ckp: 0-0
Best Rating: **99** 9/09 Kemp 6f stand

Useful; Listed placed; effective over 5f but stays 6f; acts on fast and easy ground; has worn a tongue tie.

Red Badge (IRE)

103 **92**
2-y-o ch c Captain Rio-Red Fuschia (Polish Precedent (USA))
R Hannon Michael Pescod

Placings:232610 **(7030)**
2009: 6^{2}GF, 6^{3}G, 6^{2}G, 6^{6}GF, 7^{1}GF, 7^{0}S,

	Starts	1st	2nd	3rd	Win & Pl
Career Total (Turf)	6	1	2	1	25649

92 8/09 NmkJ 7f G-F £12952
Total win prize-money £12952

Going (Turf): Sf: 0-1 GS: 0-0 Gd: 0-2 **GF: 1-3** Fm: 0-0
Distance: 5f/6f: 0-3 **7f-8f: 1-3** 9f-13f: 0-0 14f+: 0-0
Track: LH: 0-0 RH: 0-0 Tight: 0-0 Gall: 0-1
Aids: Bl: 0-0 Vi: 0-0 Tstrap: 0-0 Ckp: 0-0
Best Rating: **92** 8/09 NmkJ 7f gd-fm

Useful; suited by 7f and acts on good and faster ground.

Red Barcelona (IRE)

87 **60**
2-y-o ch c Indian Haven-Purepleasureseeker (IRE) (Grand Lodge (USA))
M H Tompkins Trevor Benton

Placings:000 **(6235)**
2009: 6^{0}G, 8^{0}G, 8^{0}GF,

	Starts	1st	2nd	3rd	Win & Pl
Career Total (Turf)	3	0	0	0	

Going (Turf): Sf: 0-0 GS: 0-0 Gd: 0-2 GF: 0-1 Fm: 0-0
Distance: 5f/6f: 0-0 7f-8f: 0-2 9f-13f: 0-1 14f+: 0-0
Track: LH: 0-1 RH: 0-1 Tight: 0-0 Gall: 0-0
Aids: Bl: 0-0 Vi: 0-0 Tstrap: 0-0 Ckp: 0-0
Best Rating: **60** 8/09 Cdwd 1m good

Red Birr (IRE)

102(97) (76)**82**
8-y-o b g Bahhare (USA)-Cappella (IRE) (College Chapel)
P R Webber John Nicholls (Trading) Ltd

Placings:043/04100/00006001/**2226524**/**050104315**/1030560-030 **(3635)**
2009: 8^{0}G, 10^{3}G, 10^{0}G,

	Starts	1st	2nd	3rd	Win & Pl
Career Total (Turf)	24	2	0	3	11934
Career Total (AW)	18	3	4	1	15320

82 6/08 Wwck 1m22y (0-75)H FRM £3238
82 9/07 Wolv 1m141y (0-75)H STD £3562
77 2/07 Wolv 1m141y (0-70)H STD £3238
70 12/05 Ling 1m2f (0-58)H STD £2886
82 6/04 Sals 1m1f198yD(0-75) GD £5707
Total win prize-money £18633

Going (Turf): Sf: 0-2 GS: 0-6 **Gd: 1-9** GF: 0-6 **Fm: 1-1**
Distance: 5f/6f: 0-2 7f-8f: 0-7 **9f-13f: 5-32** 14f+: 0-1
Track: **LH: 4-28** RH: 1-12 **Tight: 4-21** Gall: 0-2
Aids: Bl: 0-0 Vi: 0-0 Tstrap: 0-0 Ckp: 0-0
Best Rating: **83** 2/06 Ling 1m2f stand

Fair; stays 1m 2f; acts on a sound surface; goes on Polytrack; often front runs.

Red Cadeaux

108(104) (87)**94**
3-y-o ch g Cadeaux Genereux-Artisia (IRE) (Peintre Celebre (USA))
E A L Dunlop R J Arculli

Placings:6031215 **(5660)**
2009: 8^{6}G, 8^{0}SD, 9^{3}GS, 12^{1}SD, 12^{2}SD, 12^{1}S, 14^{5}S,

	Starts	1st	2nd	3rd	Win & Pl
Career Total (Turf)	4	1	0	1	5387
Career Total (AW)	3	1	1	0	6144

94 8/09 Donc 1m4f (0-85)H SFT £4857
84 6/09 Wolv 1m4f50y (0-80)H STD £5180
Total win prize-money £10038

Going (Turf): **Sf: 1-2** GS: 0-1 Gd: 0-1 GF: 0-0 Fm: 0-0
Distance: 5f/6f: 0-0 7f-8f: 0-1 **9f-13f: 2-5** 14f+: 0-1
Track: **LH: 2-4** RH: 0-2 Tight: 1-3 Gall: 1-1
Aids: Bl: 0-0 Vi: 0-0 Tstrap: 0-0 Ckp: 0-0
Best Rating: **94** 8/09 Donc 1m4f soft

Useful; stays 1m4f and acts on Polytrack and soft ground.

Red Cape (FR)

109(105) (86)**95**
6-y-o b g Cape Cross (IRE)-Muirfield (FR) (Crystal Glitters (USA))
Mrs R A Carr Middleham Park Racing LVI

Placings:612/010055**404**/**244014**/0066**0**530035**045**-**423300431014123021220030** **(6994)**
2009: 6^{4}SS, 7^{2}SD, 7^{3}SD, 5^{3}SF, 7^{0}GF, 6^{0}GF, 5^{4}SD, 7^{3}GF, 5^{1}G, 6^{0}G, 6^{1}GF, 6^{4}GS, 5^{1}GF, 6^{2}GS, 7^{3}G, 6^{0}G, 6^{2}G, 6^{1}G, 6^{2}GF, 6^{2}GF, 6^{0}GF, 6^{0}G, 6^{3}GF, 6^{0}G,

	Starts	1st	2nd	3rd	Win & Pl
Career Total (Turf)	35	5	4	5	45563
Career Total (AW)	21	2	3	2	30462

91 8/09 Ripn 6f (0-95)H GD £9346
91 7/09 Catt 5f212y (0-80)H G-F £5180
81 6/09 Thsk 6f (0-85)H G-F £5569
76 6/09 Catt 5f212y (0-65)H GD £2388
105 3/07 Ling 7f (0-100)H STD £15580
93 6/06 NmkJ 7f (0-95)H G-F £8096
84 12/05 Wolv 7f32y STD £3698
Total win prize-money £49859

Going (Turf): Sf: 0-1 GS: 0-2 Gd: 2-15 **GF: 3-17** Fm: 0-0
Distance: **5f/6f: 4-35** 7f-8f: 3-20 9f-13f: 0-1 14f+: 0-0
Track: **LH: 4-32** RH: 0-3 **Tight: 4-23** Gall: 0-1
Aids: Bl: 0-15 Vi: 0-0 Tstrap: 0-2 Ckp: 0-2
Best Rating: **105** 4/07 Ling 7f stand

Useful; effective over 6f-7f; acts on fast ground; goes on Polytrack; often wears blinkers.

Red Cell (IRE)

101(97) (68)59

3-y-o b g Kheleyf (USA)-Montana Lady (IRE) (Be My Guest (USA))

I W McInnes R E Hall & Son, I Woolfitt

Placings:215033226400-16500203000 **(6553)**

2009: 5^{1}SD, 5^{6}SD, 5^{5}GF, 5^{0}GF, 5^{0}GF, 5^{2}G, 5^{0}GF, 5^{3}S, 5^{0}SD, 5^{0}GF, 5^{0}GF,

	Starts	1st	2nd	3rd	Win & Pl
Career Total (Turf)	13	1	1	3	4542
Career Total (AW)	10	1	3	0	5172

61 1/09 Ling 5f STD £2047
61 5/08 Catt 5f GD £2047
Total win prize-money £4094

Going (Turf): Sf: 0-1 GS: 0-0 **Gd: 1-4** GF: 0-8 Fm: 0-0
Distance: **5f/6f: 2-23** 7f-8f: 0-0 9f-13f: 0-0 14f+: 0-0
Track : **LH: 1-11** RH: 0-0 **Tight: 1-5** Gall: 0-2
Aids: **Bl: 1-17** Vi: 0-0 Tstrap: 0-2 Ckp: 0-2
Best Rating: **68** 8/08 Ling 5f stand

Modest; effective over 5f; acts on good ground; also goes on Fibresand; has worn blinkers.

Red Century

(80) (12)

4-y-o ch f Captain Rio-Red Millennium (IRE) (Tagula (IRE))

Paul Mason P A Mason

Placings:0-0 **(1131)**

2009: 8^{0}SD,

	Starts	1st	2nd	3rd	Win & Pl
Career Total (Turf)	1	0	0	0	
Career Total (AW)	1	0	0	0	

Going (Turf): **Sf: 0-1 GS: 0-0 Gd: 0-0 GF: 0-0 Fm: 0-0**
Distance: 5f/6f: 0-0 7f-8f: 0-1 9f-13f: 0-1 14f+: 0-0
Track : LH: 0-1 RH: 0-0 Tight: 0-1 Gall: 0-0
Aids: Bl: 0-1 Vi: 0-0 Tstrap: 0-0 Ckp: 0-0
Best Rating: **12** 4/09 Wolv 1m141y stand

Red Chieftain (FR)

79(81) (50)34

4-y-o b g Red Ransom (USA)-Delimara (IRE) (In The Wings)

Mrs H S Main Wetumpka Racing

Placings:00 **(2229)**

2009: 7^{0}SD, 8^{0}HY,

	Starts	1st	2nd	3rd	Win & Pl
Career Total (Turf)	1	0	0	0	
Career Total (AW)	1	0	0	0	

Going (Turf): **Sf: 0-1 GS: 0-0 Gd: 0-0 GF: 0-0 Fm: 0-0**
Distance: 5f/6f: 0-0 7f-8f: 0-1 9f-13f: 0-1 14f+: 0-0
Track : LH: 0-2 RH: 0-0 Tight: 0-1 Gall: 0-0
Aids: Bl: 0-0 Vi: 0-0 Tstrap: 0-0 Ckp: 0-0
Best Rating: **50** 5/09 Ling 7f stand

Red China Blues (USA)

101 64

3-y-o ch g Royal Academy (USA)-Viewy (USA) (Majestic Light (USA))

R E Barr (J Howard Johnson 26/7) Brian Morton

Placings:6-0430250 **(5672)**

2009: 10^{0}G, 10^{4}GS, 7^{3}GF, 7^{0}GF, 7^{2}G, 9^{5}GF, 8^{0}S,

	Starts	1st	2nd	3rd	Win & Pl
Career Total (Turf)	8	0	1	1	1682

Going (Turf): **Sf: 0-1 GS: 0-1 Gd: 0-2 GF: 0-4 Fm: 0-0**
Distance: 5f/6f: 0-0 7f-8f: 0-5 9f-13f: 0-3 14f+: 0-0
Track : LH: 0-3 RH: 0-3 Tight: 0-3 Gall: 0-1
Aids: Bl: 0-0 Vi: 0-0 Tstrap: 0-0 Ckp: 0-0
Best Rating: **64** 5/09 Muss 7f30y gd-fm

Modest form in maidens; handles easy ground.

Red Courtier

87(102) (80)58

2-y-o b c Red Ransom (USA)-Lady In Waiting (Kylian (USA))

P F I Cole C Shiacolas

Placings:631 **(7683)**

2009: 7^{6}G, 8^{3}SD, 10^{1}SD,

	Starts	1st	2nd	3rd	Win & Pl
Career Total (Turf)	1	0	0	0	0
Career Total (AW)	2	1	0	1	3094

80 12/09 Kemp 1m2f STD £2590
Total win prize-money £2590

Going (Turf): **Sf: 0-0 GS: 0-0 Gd: 0-1 GF: 0-0 Fm: 0-0**
Distance: 5f/6f: 0-0 7f-8f: 0-1 **9f-13f: 1-2** 14f+: 0-0
Track : LH: 0-1 **RH: 1-1** Tight: 0-1 Gall: 0-0
Aids: Bl: 0-0 Vi: 0-0 Tstrap: 0-0 Ckp: 0-0
Best Rating: **80** 12/09 Kemp 1m2f stand

Useful; effective at 1m-1m2f; acts well on Polytrack.

Red Current

101(102) (58)68

5-y-o b m Soviet Star (USA)-Fleet Amour (USA) (Afleet (CAN))

R A Harris Ridge House Stables Ltd

Placings:30/43002100211302406/400032010600050-2435002066566001405463600 **(7787)**

2009: 8^{2}SD, 8^{4}SD, 8^{3}SD, 8^{5}SD, 7^{0}SD, 8^{0}SD, 8^{2}SD, 10^{0}GF, 8^{6}GF, 10^{6}G, 10^{5}GF, 7^{6}F, 9^{6}GF, 9^{0}GF, 10^{0}F, 8^{1}GF, 8^{4}SF, 8^{0}SD, 8^{5}G, 8^{4}G, 8^{6}SD, 8^{3}SD, 8^{6}SD, 10^{0}SD,

	Starts	1st	2nd	3rd	Win & Pl
Career Total (Turf)	30	4	3	4	14728
Career Total (AW)	29	1	3	2	5442

54 7/09 Chep 1m14y G-F £2072
67 9/08 Leic 1m1f218y GD £1942
70 9/07 Pont 1m2f6y (0-65)H G-F £3238
65 9/07 Chep 1m2f36y (0-65)H G-F £2590
57 7/07 Ling 1m STD £2968
Total win prize-money £12814

Going (Turf): Sf: 0-5 GS: 0-4 Gd: 1-7 **GF: 3-12** Fm: 0-2
Distance: 5f/6f: 0-0 7f-8f: 1-19 **9f-13f: 4-40** 14f+: 0-0
Track : **LH: 3-40** RH: 1-11 **Tight: 1-31** Gall: 0-2
Aids: Bl: 0-2 Vi: 0-0 Tstrap: 0-3 Ckp: 0-3
Best Rating: **70** 9/07 Pont 1m2f6y gd-fm

Moderate; effective over 1m-1m2f; acts on most ground on turf; goes on Polytrack; has worn cheekpieces.

Red Dagger (IRE)

95(90) (44)52

3-y-o b g Daggers Drawn (USA)-Dash Of Red (Red Sunset)

R J Price (T D McCarthy 22/6) Karl and Patricia Reece

Placings:0000-00050030 **(5998)**

2009: 8^{0}SD, 8^{0}G, 10^{0}SD, 9^{5}GF, 11^{0}GF, 9^{0}GF, 6^{3}GS, 7^{0}GF,

	Starts	1st	2nd	3rd	Win & Pl
Career Total (Turf)	7	0	0	1	318
Career Total (AW)	5	0	0	0	

Going (Turf): **Sf: 0-0 GS: 0-2 Gd: 0-1 GF: 0-4 Fm: 0-0**
Distance: 5f/6f: 0-1 7f-8f: 0-5 9f-13f: 0-6 14f+: 0-0
Track : LH: 0-9 RH: 0-1 Tight: 0-9 Gall: 0-0
Aids: Bl: 0-0 Vi: 0-0 Tstrap: 0-0 Ckp: 0-0
Best Rating: **52** 9/09 Chep 6f16y gd-sft

Red Dune (IRE)

106 103

4-y-o b f Red Ransom (USA)-Desert Beauty (IRE) (Green Desert (USA))

M A Jarvis Darley Stud Management Inc

Placings:4/211444-06404236 **(7621a)**

2009: 8^{0}G, 7^{6}GF, 7^{4}G, 6^{0}GF, 7^{4}GF, 7^{2}GF, 8^{3}S, 7^{6}SD,

	Starts	1st	2nd	3rd	Win & Pl
Career Total (Turf)	14	2	2	1	60950
Career Total (AW)	1	0	0	0	

100 7/08 NmkJ 7f (0-100)H GD £31155
85 6/08 Gdwd 1m GD £3238
Total win prize-money £34393

Going (Turf): Sf: 0-2 GS: 0-0 **Gd: 2-6** GF: 0-6 Fm: 0-0
Distance: 5f/6f: 0-2 **7f-8f: 2-11** 9f-13f: 0-2 14f+: 0-0
Track : LH: 0-4 **RH: 1-5** Tight: 0-3 Gall: 0-1
Aids: Bl: 0-0 Vi: 0-0 Tstrap: 0-0 Ckp: 0-0
Best Rating: **103** 9/09 Donc 7f gd-fm

Very useful; effective at 7f-1m; acts on good and faster ground; suited by forcing tactics.

Red Eddie

82 60

2-y-o b c Red Ransom (USA)-Sister Bluebird (Bluebird (USA))

B J Meehan Mrs Susanna O'Reilly Hyland

Placings:00600 **(6895)**

2009: 7^{0}GS, 7^{0}GF, 7^{6}G, 7^{0}GF, 8^{0}GF,

	Starts	1st	2nd	3rd	Win & Pl
Career Total (Turf)	5	0	0	0	0

Going (Turf): **Sf: 0-0 GS: 0-1 Gd: 0-1 GF: 0-3 Fm: 0-0**
Distance: 5f/6f: 0-0 7f-8f: 0-4 9f-13f: 0-1 14f+: 0-0
Track : LH: 0-2 RH: 0-1 Tight: 0-0 Gall: 0-0
Aids: Bl: 0-1 Vi: 0-0 Tstrap: 0-0 Ckp: 0-0
Best Rating: **60** 9/09 Chep 7f16y good

Red Eric

(77) (14)40

3-y-o ch g Reset (AUS)-Lady Soleas (Be My Guest (USA))

W M Brisbourne W M Clare

Placings:00000-0 **(0134)**

2009: 9^{0}SD,

	Starts	1st	2nd	3rd	Win & Pl
Career Total (Turf)	3	0	0	0	
Career Total (AW)	3	0	0	0	

Going (Turf): Sf: 0-1 GS: 0-1 Gd: 0-0 GF: 0-1 Fm: 0-0
Distance: 5f/6f: 0-0 7f-8f: 0-3 9f-13f: 0-3 14f+: 0-0
Track : LH: 0-6 RH: 0-0 Tight: 0-5 Gall: 0-0
Aids: Bl: 0-0 Vi: 0-0 Tstrap: 0-0 Ckp: 0-0
Best Rating: 40 7/08 Wwck 7f26y soft

Red Expresso (IRE)

(100) (68)**78**
4-y-o ch g Intikhab (USA)-Cafe Creme (IRE) (Catrail (USA))
Ollie Pears Reuben Glynn

Placings:30/303136-166 (7647)
2009: 12^{1}SD, 11^{6}SD, 12^{6}SD,

	Starts	1st	2nd	3rd	Win & Pl
Career Total (Turf)	2	0	0	1	482
Career Total (AW)	9	2	0	3	5444

65 9/09 Wolv 1m4f50y (0-65)H STD £2388
66 12/08 Sthl 1m3f STD £2047
Total win prize-money £4435

Going (Turf): Sf: 0-0 GS: 0-0 Gd: 0-1 GF: 0-1 Fm: 0-0
Distance: 5f/6f: 0-2 7f-8f: 0-3 **9f-13f: 2-5** 14f+: 0-1
Track : **LH: 2-9** RH: 0-0 **Tight: 1-3** Gall: 0-3
Aids: Bl: 0-0 Vi: 0-1 Tstrap: 0-0 Ckp: 0-0
Best Rating: 78 4/07 Wind 5f10y gd-fm

Modest; stays 1m4f; acts on sand; has worn a visor.

Red Fama

96(99) (65)**84**
5-y-o ch g Fraam-Carol Again (Kind Of Hush)
N Bycroft B F Rayner

Placings:0/2/45021112-600 (4332)
2009: 12^{6}SD, 10^{0}GS, 16^{0}G,

	Starts	1st	2nd	3rd	Win & Pl
Career Total (Turf)	9	3	2	0	9893
Career Total (AW)	4	0	1	0	564

79 9/08 Rdcr 1m6f19y (0-65)H G-S £2388
73 8/08 Bevl 1m4f16y (0-75)H SFT £3076
58 8/08 Bevl 1m4f16y (0-65)H G-S £2266
Total win prize-money £7731

Going (Turf): Sf: 1-3 **GS: 2-4** Gd: 0-2 GF: 0-0 Fm: 0-0
Distance: 5f/6f: 0-0 7f-8f: 0-1 **9f-13f: 2-9** 14f+: 1-3
Track : LH: 1-9 **RH: 2-3 Tight: 3-5** Gall: 0-2
Aids: Bl: 0-0 Vi: 0-0 Tstrap: 0-0 Ckp: 0-0
Best Rating: 84 9/08 Hayd 1m6f heavy

Fair; stays 1m6f; acts well on soft ground; also goes on Fibresand.

Red Fantasy (IRE)

94 **77**
2-y-o b f High Chaparral (IRE)-Petite Fantasy (Mansooj)
B W Hills R J Arculli

Placings:45 (6363)
2009: 7^{4}GF, 7^{5}GF,

	Starts	1st	2nd	3rd	Win & Pl
Career Total (Turf)	2	0	0	0	841

Going (Turf): Sf: 0-0 GS: 0-0 Gd: 0-0 GF: 0-2 Fm: 0-0
Distance: 5f/6f: 0-0 7f-8f: 0-2 9f-13f: 0-0 14f+: 0-0
Track : LH: 0-1 RH: 0-0 Tight: 0-0 Gall: 0-0
Aids: Bl: 0-0 Vi: 0-0 Tstrap: 0-0 Ckp: 0-0
Best Rating: 77 9/09 Newb 7f gd-fm

Red Farasi (IRE)

56(74) (27)
2-y-o ch g Redback-Boristova (IRE) (Royal Academy (USA))
B W Duke Brendan W Duke Racing

Placings:000 (7334)
2009: 6^{0}GF, 6^{0}SD, 8^{0}SD,

	Starts	1st	2nd	3rd	Win & Pl
Career Total (Turf)	1	0	0	0	
Career Total (AW)	2	0	0	0	

Going (Turf): Sf: 0-0 GS: 0-0 Gd: 0-0 GF: 0-1 Fm: 0-0
Distance: 5f/6f: 0-1 7f-8f: 0-2 9f-13f: 0-0 14f+: 0-0
Track : LH: 0-2 RH: 0-0 Tight: 0-1 Gall: 0-0
Aids: Bl: 0-0 Vi: 0-0 Tstrap: 0-1 Ckp: 0-1
Best Rating: 27 9/09 Ling 6f stand

Red Gulch

(87) (65)
2-y-o b c Kyllachy-Enrapture (USA) (Lear Fan (USA))
E A L Dunlop R J Arculli

Placings:3 (7537)
2009: 7^{3}SD,

	Starts	1st	2nd	3rd	Win & Pl
Career Total (Turf)	0	0	0	0	
Career Total (AW)	1	0	0	1	482

Going (Turf): Sf: 0-0 GS: 0-0 Gd: 0-0 GF: 0-0 Fm: 0-0
Distance: 5f/6f: 0-0 7f-8f: 0-1 9f-13f: 0-0 14f+: 0-0
Track : LH: 0-0 RH: 0-1 Tight: 0-0 Gall: 0-0
Aids: Bl: 0-0 Vi: 0-0 Tstrap: 0-0 Ckp: 0-0
Best Rating: 65 11/09 Kemp 7f stand

Fair; stays 7f; acts on Polytrack; should improve.

Red Horse (IRE)

96(96) (44)**52**
3-y-o ch g Bachelor Duke (USA)-Miss Childrey (IRE) (Dr Fong (USA))
M L W Bell Richard I Morris Jr

Placings:0000-0050 (7022)
2009: 7^{0}F, 7^{0}SD, 9^{5}GF, 10^{0}SD,

	Starts	1st	2nd	3rd	Win & Pl
Career Total (Turf)	6	0	0	0	0
Career Total (AW)	2	0	0	0	

Going (Turf): Sf: 0-1 GS: 0-0 Gd: 0-2 GF: 0-2 Fm: 0-1
Distance: 5f/6f: 0-3 7f-8f: 0-3 9f-13f: 0-2 14f+: 0-0
Track : LH: 0-2 RH: 0-2 Tight: 0-1 Gall: 0-0
Aids: Bl: 0-0 Vi: 0-0 Tstrap: 0-0 Ckp: 0-0
Best Rating: 52 8/09 Brig 7f214y firm

Red Hot Desert

(99) (67)
3-y-o b g Green Desert (USA)-Red Carnation (IRE) (Polar Falcon (USA))
W R Swinburn Mrs Doreen M Swinburn

Placings:00160 (7823)
2009: 9^{0}SD, 11^{0}SD, 12^{1}SD, 12^{6}SD, 10^{0}SD,

	Starts	1st	2nd	3rd	Win & Pl
Career Total (Turf)	0	0	0	0	
Career Total (AW)	5	1	0	0	2730

67 11/09 Ling 1m4f STD £2729
Total win prize-money £2730

Going (Turf): Sf: 0-0 GS: 0-0 Gd: 0-0 GF: 0-0 Fm: 0-0
Distance: 5f/6f: 0-0 7f-8f: 0-0 **9f-13f: 1-5** 14f+: 0-0
Track : **LH: 1-3** RH: 0-2 **Tight: 1-3** Gall: 0-0
Aids: Bl: 0-0 Vi: 0-0 Tstrap: 0-0 Ckp: 0-0
Best Rating: 67 11/09 Ling 1m4f stand

Modest; stays 1m4f and acts on Polytrack.

Red Intrigue (IRE)

95(95) (71)**62**
2-y-o b f Selkirk (USA)-Red Affair (IRE) (Generous (IRE))
Mrs A J Perrett Lady Clague

Placings:003 (6772)
2009: 6^{0}S, 7^{0}GF, 8^{3}SD,

	Starts	1st	2nd	3rd	Win & Pl
Career Total (Turf)	2	0	0	0	
Career Total (AW)	1	0	0	1	578

Going (Turf): Sf: 0-1 GS: 0-0 Gd: 0-0 GF: 0-1 Fm: 0-0
Distance: 5f/6f: 0-0 7f-8f: 0-3 9f-13f: 0-0 14f+: 0-0
Track : LH: 0-1 RH: 0-1 Tight: 0-0 Gall: 0-0
Aids: Bl: 0-0 Vi: 0-0 Tstrap: 0-0 Ckp: 0-0
Best Rating: 71 10/09 Kemp 1m stand

Fair; stays 1m; acts on Polytrack.

Red Jade

107 **89**
4-y-o ch g Dubai Destination (USA)-Red Slippers (USA) (Nureyev (USA))
R A Fahey (A P Jarvis 1/8) Keep Racing

Placings:31-200463363 (6648)
2009: 10^{2}GS, 10^{0}HY, 8^{0}G, 10^{4}GS, 10^{6}S, 10^{3}S, 10^{3}GF, 10^{6}GF, 10^{3}G,

	Starts	1st	2nd	3rd	Win & Pl
Career Total (Turf)	11	1	1	4	9103

79 10/08 Nott 1m2f50y SFT £2914
Total win prize-money £2914

Going (Turf): **Sf: 1-5** GS: 0-2 Gd: 0-2 GF: 0-2 Fm: 0-0
Distance: 5f/6f: 0-0 7f-8f: 0-0 **9f-13f: 1-11** 14f+: 0-0
Track : **LH: 1-10** RH: 0-1 Tight: 0-2 Gall: 0-3
Aids: Bl: 0-0 Vi: 0-0 Tstrap: 0-0 Ckp: 0-0
Best Rating: 89 4/09 Nott 1m2f50y gd-sft

Useful; stays 1m2f and acts on soft ground.

Red Jazz (USA)

107 **103**
2-y-o b c Johannesburg (USA)-Now That's Jazz (USA) (Sword Dance)
B W Hills R J Arculli

Placings:1103 (3779)
2009: 5^{1}G, 5^{1}GF, 6^{0}GF, 6^{3}G,

	Starts	1st	2nd	3rd	Win & Pl
Career Total (Turf)	4	2	0	1	17888

95 4/09 Asct 5f G-F £6542
91 4/09 Wind 5f10y GD £2729
Total win prize-money £9273

Going (Turf): Sf: 0-0 GS: 0-0 **Gd: 1-2 GF: 1-2** Fm: 0-0

Distance: 5f/6f: 2-4 7f-8f: 0-0 9f-13f: 0-0 14f+: 0-0
Track : LH: 0-0 RH: 0-0 Tight: 0-0 Gall: 1-1
Aids: Bl: 0-0 Vi: 0-0 Tstrap: 0-0 Ckp: 0-0
Best Rating: 103 7/09 NmkJ 6f good

Smart; 95,000gns half-brother to multiple winner in USA; effective at 5f on fast ground.

Red Kestrel (USA)

104(105) (93)89
4-y-o ch g Swain (IRE)-The Caretaker (Caerleon (USA))
K A Ryan Hambleton Racing Ltd XII

Placings:31-00646 (6281)
2009: 10^{0}GF, 12^{0}G, 12^{6}G, 14^{4}GS, 14^{6}GF,

	Starts	1st	2nd	3rd	Win & Pl
Career Total (Turf)	6	0	0	1	1269
Career Total (AW)	1	1	0	0	2590

93 8/08 Ling 1m4f STD £2590
Total win prize-money £2590

Going (Turf): Sf: 0-0 GS: 0-1 Gd: 0-3 GF: 0-2 Fm: 0-0
Distance: 5f/6f: 0-0 7f-8f: 0-0 9f-13f: 1-5 14f+: 0-2
Track : LH: 1-6 RH: 0-1 Tight: 1-2 Gall: 0-2
Aids: Bl: 0-0 Vi: 0-0 Tstrap: 0-0 Ckp: 0-0
Best Rating: 93 8/08 Ling 1m4f stand

Useful; stays 1m4f; acts on a sound surface and on Polytrack.

Red Kyte

97(92) (73)82
3-y-o br f Hawk Wing (USA)-Ruby Affair (IRE) (Night Shift (USA))
K A Ryan Malih L Al Basti

Placings:00104-00035014560 (5937)
2009: 7^{0}SD, 6^{0}GF, 6^{0}SD, 6^{3}GF, 7^{5}F, 6^{0}G, 5^{1}GS, 5^{4}S, 6^{5}G, 6^{6}G, 5^{0}GF,

	Starts	1st	2nd	3rd	Win & Pl
Career Total (Turf)	14	2	0	1	34859
Career Total (AW)	2	0	0	0	

76 7/09 Pont 5f (0-75)H G-S £3885
70 8/08 Bevl 5f SFT £5018
Total win prize-money £8905

Going (Turf): Sf: 1-2 GS: 1-2 Gd: 0-4 GF: 0-5 Fm: 0-1
Distance: 5f/6f: 2-11 7f-8f: 0-5 9f-13f: 0-0 14f+: 0-0
Track : LH: 1-5 RH: 0-0 Tight: 0-3 Gall: 0-0
Aids: Bl: 0-0 Vi: 0-0 Tstrap: 1-5 Ckp: 1-5
Best Rating: 82 10/08 NmkR 6f gd-fm

Fair; stays 6f and acts on soft ground; has worn cheek-pieces; likes to race prominently.

Red Margarita (IRE)

92(90) (37)53
3-y-o ch f Dalakhani (IRE)-Red Bartsia (Barathea (IRE))
D R C Elsworth McGrath, Huggins & Dunn

Placings:0-006000 (4142)
2009: 10^{0}SD, 8^{0}G, 11^{6}GS, 10^{0}GF, 12^{0}SD, 16^{0}G,

	Starts	1st	2nd	3rd	Win & Pl
Career Total (Turf)	5	0	0	0	0
Career Total (AW)	2	0	0	0	

Going (Turf): Sf: 0-0 GS: 0-2 Gd: 0-2 GF: 0-1 Fm: 0-0
Distance: 5f/6f: 0-0 7f-8f: 0-0 9f-13f: 0-6 14f+: 0-1
Track : LH: 0-3 RH: 0-2 Tight: 0-4 Gall: 0-0
Aids: Bl: 0-0 Vi: 0-0 Tstrap: 0-0 Ckp: 0-0
Best Rating: 53 4/09 Yarm 1m3y good

Red Max (IRE)

95 57
3-y-o b g Kheleyf (USA)-Set Trail (IRE) (Second Set (IRE))
T D Easterby C H Stevens

Placings:66560-00 (2162)
2009: 6^{0}GS, 5^{0}G,

	Starts	1st	2nd	3rd	Win & Pl
Career Total (Turf)	7	0	0	0	111

Going (Turf): Sf: 0-1 GS: 0-2 Gd: 0-3 GF: 0-1 Fm: 0-0
Distance: 5f/6f: 0-5 7f-8f: 0-2 9f-13f: 0-0 14f+: 0-0
Track : LH: 0-2 RH: 0-0 Tight: 0-2 Gall: 0-0
Aids: Bl: 0-1 Vi: 0-0 Tstrap: 0-1 Ckp: 0-1
Best Rating: 57 6/08 York 6f good

Red Merlin (IRE)

112(103) (83)107
4-y-o ch g Soviet Star (USA)-Truly Bewitched (USA) (Affirmed (USA))
C G Cox Reid's Allstars

Placings:050/024303121-321110 (5173)
2009: 12^{3}SD, 11^{2}GS, 12^{1}GF, 12^{1}G, 11^{1}GF, 14^{0}GF,

	Starts	1st	2nd	3rd	Win & Pl
Career Total (Turf)	17	5	3	2	73934
Career Total (AW)	1	0	0	1	703

107 7/09 Hayd 1m3f200y H G-F £52963
96 5/09 Gdwd 1m4f (0-90)H GD £9714
79 10/08 Gdwd 1m4f (0-75)H G-S £3238
74 9/08 Brig 1m3f196y SFT £2719
Total win prize-money £68636

Going (Turf): Sf: 1-2 GS: 1-5 Gd: 1-4 GF: 2-6 Fm: 0-0
Distance: 5f/6f: 0-0 7f-8f: 0-3 9f-13f: 5-14 14f+: 0-1
Track : LH: 3-6 RH: 2-9 Tight: 3-8 Gall: 0-3
Aids: Bl: 0-1 Vi: 5-9 Tstrap: 0-0 Ckp: 0-0
Best Rating: 107 7/09 Hayd 1m3f200y gd-fm

Very useful; winner of the 2009 Old Newton Cup; stays 1m4f and acts on most ground; has worn a visor.

Red Oriental

83 80
3-y-o ch f Zamindar (USA)-Pan Galactic (USA) (Lear Fan (USA))
N P Littmoden (A Fabre 2/7) Franconson Partners

Placings:443330 (4151)
2009: 6^{4}G, 7^{4}G, 10^{3}GS, 10^{3}GS, 10^{3}GS, 9^{0}GS,

	Starts	1st	2nd	3rd	Win & Pl
Career Total (Turf)	6	0	0	3	18543

Going (Turf): Sf: 0-0 GS: 0-4 Gd: 0-2 GF: 0-0 Fm: 0-0
Distance: 5f/6f: 0-1 7f-8f: 0-1 9f-13f: 0-4 14f+: 0-0
Track : LH: 0-3 RH: 0-1 Tight: 0-1 Gall: 0-0
Aids: Bl: 0-0 Vi: 0-0 Tstrap: 0-0 Ckp: 0-0
Best Rating: 80 6/09 Lonc 1m2f gd-sft

Fair; stays 1m2f; acts on easy ground.

Red Red Rascal

61(61) 25
3-y-o b f Red Ransom (USA)-Normandy (CHI) (Great Regent (CAN))
A M Balding Robert Hanson & Partners

Placings:00 (3297)
2009: 10^{0}GF, 8^{0}SD,

	Starts	1st	2nd	3rd	Win & Pl
Career Total (Turf)	1	0	0	0	
Career Total (AW)	1	0	0	0	

Going (Turf): Sf: 0-0 GS: 0-0 Gd: 0-0 GF: 0-1 Fm: 0-0
Distance: 5f/6f: 0-0 7f-8f: 0-1 9f-13f: 0-1 14f+: 0-0
Track : LH: 0-1 RH: 0-1 Tight: 0-0 Gall: 0-1
Aids: Bl: 0-0 Vi: 0-0 Tstrap: 0-0 Ckp: 0-0
Best Rating: 25 6/09 Newb 1m2f6y gd-fm

Red Reef

98(90) (55)68
3-y-o ch f King's Best (USA)-Rafiya (Halling (USA))
D J Coakley Scarlet Racing

Placings:0061-046200000 (6804)
2009: 9^{0}F, 11^{4}F, 10^{6}G, 10^{2}GS, 9^{0}F, 10^{0}F, 11^{0}SD, 12^{0}SD, 9^{0}SD,

	Starts	1st	2nd	3rd	Win & Pl
Career Total (Turf)	9	1	1	0	4045
Career Total (AW)	4	0	0	0	

64 8/08 Sals 1m (0-75) G-F £3238
Total win prize-money £3238

Going (Turf): Sf: 0-0 GS: 0-1 Gd: 0-1 GF: 1-3 Fm: 0-4
Distance: 5f/6f: 0-0 7f-8f: 1-4 9f-13f: 0-9 14f+: 0-0
Track : LH: 0-7 RH: 0-4 Tight: 0-6 Gall: 0-0
Aids: Bl: 0-0 Vi: 0-1 Tstrap: 0-0 Ckp: 0-0
Best Rating: 68 8/09 Ling 1m2f gd-sft

Modest; stays 1m2f; acts on fast and easy ground.

Red River Boy

97 53
4-y-o ch g Bahamian Bounty-Riviere Rouge (Forzando)
C W Fairhurst John Gibb

Placings:00/0010-556055 (3999)
2009: 6^{5}GF, 5^{5}GF, 5^{6}F, 5^{0}GF, 5^{5}G, 5^{5}GS,

	Starts	1st	2nd	3rd	Win & Pl
Career Total (Turf)	12	1	0	0	2730

53 6/08 Carl 5f (0-60)H GD £2729
Total win prize-money £2730

Going (Turf): Sf: 0-0 GS: 0-1 Gd: 1-4 GF: 0-6 Fm: 0-1
Distance: 5f/6f: 1-12 7f-8f: 0-0 9f-13f: 0-0 14f+: 0-0
Track : LH: 0-0 RH: 1-2 Tight: 0-0 Gall: 1-1
Aids: Bl: 0-0 Vi: 0-0 Tstrap: 0-0 Ckp: 0-0
Best Rating: 53 4/09 Rdcr 6f gd-fm

Modest sprinter; stays 6f; acts on easy ground.

Red River Rebel

(90) (50)59
11-y-o b g Inchinor-Bidweaya (USA) (Lear Fan (USA))
J R Norton Jeff Slaney

Placings:600/05350011135/U403221346/50654126340/040224/0056131500/4004266221210/001120/6-00 (1938)
2009: 12^{0}SD, 12^{0}SD,

	Starts	1st	2nd	3rd	Win & Pl
Career Total (Turf)	58	9	7	6	49354
Career Total (AW)	15	2	3	0	4503

59 7/07 Bevl 1m4f16y (0-70)H HVY £3886
54 5/07 Leic 1m3f183y (0-60)H SFT £2590
62 12/06 Sthl 1m6f (0-45) STD £1365
52 11/06 Sthl 1m6f (0-45) STD £1365
59 7/05 Bevl 1m4f16y (0-70)H GD £3962

59 5/05 Leic 1m3f183y (0-60)H GD £3620
66 7/03 Bevl 1m4f16yE(0-70)H G-F £3913
71 8/02 Bevl 1m4f16yE(0-75)H G-F £4605
72 9/01 Bevl 1m3f216yE(0-70)H GD £4810
62 8/01 Newc 1m4f93y(0-75)H G-F £3464
58 8/01 Newc 1m4f93yE(0-75)H GD £2975
Total win prize-money £36558

Going (Turf): Sf: 2-5 GS: 0-2 **Gd: 4-23** GF: 3-22 Fm: 0-6
Distance: 5f/6f: 0-1 7f-8f: 0-3 **9f-13f: 9-51** 14f+: 2-18
Track : LH: 4-41 **RH: 7-29 Tight: 5-33** Gall: 2-11
Aids: Bl: 0-0 Vi: 0-1 Tstrap: 0-0 Ckp: 0-0
Best Rating: 74 8/02 Ripn 1m4f60y gd-fm

Moderate; effective over 1m4f-2m acts on most ground, including Fibresand.

Red Rocks (IRE)

109 **118**
6-y-o b/br h Galileo (IRE)-Pharmacist (IRE) (Machiavellian (USA))
B J Meehan (Mark Hennig 28/3) J Paul Reddam

Placings:032/1122231/014430/1610-0045 **(7310a)**
2009: 9^{0}F, 12^{0}G, 12^{4}GF, 12^{5}F,

	Starts	1st	2nd	3rd	Win & Pl
Career Total (Turf)	24	6	4	3	1620424

118 7/08 Belm 1m3f FRM £150754
115 5/08 Ling 1m2f G-F £12462
125 4/07 Sand 1m2f7y GD £28390
125 11/06 Chur 1m4f FRM £941860
116 5/06 NmkR 1m2f SFT £15898
104 4/06 Wind 1m2f7y GD £3238
Total win prize-money £1152603

Going (Turf): Sf: 1-2 GS: 0-2 **Gd: 2-10** GF: 1-5 **Fm: 2-5**
Distance: 5f/6f: 0-0 7f-8f: 0-3 **9f-13f: 6-20** 14f+: 0-1
Track : **LH: 3-11** RH: 2-7 **Tight: 2-3** Gall: 0-7
Aids: **Bl: 1-4** Vi: 0-0 Tstrap: 0-0 Ckp: 0-0
Best Rating: 125 4/07 Sand 1m2f7y good

Group class; landed the 2006 Breeders' Cup Turf; winner of 2007 Brigadier Gerard; best at 1m4f, but effective at 1m2f, acts on most ground; has worn blinkers.

Red Rosanna

105 **82**
3-y-o b f Bertolini (USA)-Lamarita (Emarati (USA))
R Hollinshead Mrs Debbie Hodson

Placings:240210-404210155 **(4043)**
2009: 5^{4}GF, 5^{0}GF, 5^{4}F, 5^{2}GF, 5^{1}GF, 5^{0}G, 5^{1}G, 5^{5}GF, 5^{5}S,

	Starts	1st	2nd	3rd	Win & Pl
Career Total (Turf)	15	3	3	0	19201

82 7/09 Hayd 5f (0-80)H GD £6476
79 6/09 NmkJ 5f (0-75)H G-F £3885
72 9/08 Pont 5f G-S £3885
Total win prize-money £14248

Going (Turf): Sf: 0-2 **GS: 1-2 Gd: 1-2 GF: 1-6** Fm: 0-3
Distance: **5f/6f: 3-15** 7f-8f: 0-0 9f-13f: 0-0 14f+: 0-0
Track : **LH: 1-4** RH: 0-0 Tight: 0-2 Gall: 0-0
Aids: Bl: 0-0 Vi: 0-0 Tstrap: 0-0 Ckp: 0-0
Best Rating: 82 7/09 Hayd 5f good

Fair; effective over 5f and acts on most ground.

Red Rossini (IRE)

96(97) (73)**77**
3-y-o b g Rossini (USA)-La Scala (USA) (Theatrical)
R Hannon Terry Neill

Placings:2414404050-636505055 **(5716)**
2009: 6^{6}GF, 6^{3}F, 6^{6}GF, 6^{5}GF, 6^{0}G, 5^{5}F, 6^{0}GF, 5^{5}G, 5^{5}G,

	Starts	1st	2nd	3rd	Win & Pl
Career Total (Turf)	16	1	0	1	7555
Career Total (AW)	3	0	1	0	605

77 7/08 Wind 5f10y GD £4695
Total win prize-money £4695

Going (Turf): Sf: 0-1 GS: 0-1 **Gd: 1-6** GF: 0-6 Fm: 0-2
Distance: **5f/6f: 1-17** 7f-8f: 0-2 9f-13f: 0-0 14f+: 0-0
Track : LH: 0-7 RH: 0-2 Tight: 0-2 **Gall: 1-4**
Aids: Bl: 0-2 Vi: 0-1 Tstrap: 0-0 Ckp: 0-0
Best Rating: 77 8/08 Hayd 5f heavy

Fair; effective over 5f; acts on good ground and Polytrack.

Red Rudy

94(106) (75)**67**
7-y-o ch g Pivotal-Piroshka (Soviet Star (USA))
A W Carroll Winding Wheel Partnership

Placings:6300/06240405/2322150/05035120/342231520-040132300 **(1748)**
2009: 6^{0}SD, 6^{4}SD, 6^{0}SD, 7^{1}SD, 10^{3}SD, 8^{2}SD, 8^{3}SD, 8^{0}SD, 6^{0}GF,

	Starts	1st	2nd	3rd	Win & Pl
Career Total (Turf)	26	2	4	3	13157
Career Total (AW)	19	2	5	4	9822

68 2/09 Kemp 7f (0-65)H STD £2388
75 4/08 Kemp 6f STD £2047
73 8/07 Chep 7f16y (0-65)H G-F £2720
75 8/06 Chep 7f16y (0-65)H GD £3238
Total win prize-money £10394

Going (Turf): Sf: 0-2 GS: 0-6 **Gd: 1-7 GF: 1-10** Fm: 0-1
Distance: 5f/6f: 1-11 **7f-8f: 3-15** 9f-13f: 0-19 14f+: 0-0
Track : LH: 0-10 **RH: 2-21** Tight: 0-10 Gall: 0-3
Aids: Bl: 0-0 Vi: 0-0 Tstrap: 0-0 Ckp: 0-0
Best Rating: 75 4/08 Kemp 6f stand

Modest; effective over 6f-1m; acts on most ground and on Polytrack.

Red Scintilla

89 **55**
2-y-o b f Doyen (IRE)-Red To Violet (Spectrum (IRE))
N Tinkler Philip A Jarvis

Placings:0 **(7288)**
2009: 6^{0}S,

	Starts	1st	2nd	3rd	Win & Pl
Career Total (Turf)	1	0	0	0	

Going (Turf): **Sf: 0-1 GS: 0-0 Gd: 0-0 GF: 0-0 Fm: 0-0**
Distance: 5f/6f: 0-1 7f-8f: 0-0 9f-13f: 0-0 14f+: 0-0
Track : LH: 0-0 RH: 0-0 Tight: 0-0 Gall: 0-0
Aids: Bl: 0-0 Vi: 0-0 Tstrap: 0-0 Ckp: 0-0
Best Rating: 55 11/09 Donc 6f soft

Red Skipper (IRE)

101 **66**
4-y-o ch g Captain Rio-Speed To Lead (IRE) (Darshaan)
N Wilson The Sandburn Racing Partnership

Placings:0400002/0020155246-05252404404 **(7174)**
2009: 7^{0}G, 9^{5}G, 10^{2}GF, 9^{5}G, 9^{2}G, 10^{4}GS, 8^{0}GS, 8^{4}S, 10^{4}GS, 8^{0}GF, 9^{4}S,

	Starts	1st	2nd	3rd	Win & Pl
Career Total (Turf)	27	1	5	0	9213
Career Total (AW)	1	0	0	0	

66 8/08 Muss 7f30y (0-65)H SFT £2590
Total win prize-money £2590

Going (Turf): **Sf: 1-7** GS: 0-5 Gd: 0-9 GF: 0-6 Fm: 0-0
Distance: 5f/6f: 0-7 **7f-8f: 1-12** 9f-13f: 0-9 14f+: 0-0
Track : LH: 0-13 **RH: 1-7 Tight: 1-9** Gall: 0-0
Aids: Bl: 0-0 Vi: 0-2 Tstrap: 0-1 Ckp: 0-1
Best Rating: 66 8/08 Muss 7f30y soft

Modest; stays 1m2f; acts on any ground.

Red Somerset (USA)

90(113) (103)**93**
6-y-o b g Red Ransom (USA)-Bielska (USA) (Deposit Ticket (USA))
R J Hodges R J Hodges

Placings:314560/30004001221/563405211004121-21256236400002001 **(7845)**
2009: 8^{2}SD, 8^{1}SD, 8^{2}SD, 8^{5}SD, 8^{6}SD, 7^{2}SD, 8^{3}GF, 7^{6}SD, 8^{4}SD, 7^{0}GF, 8^{0}SS, 7^{0}SD, 8^{0}SD, 8^{2}SD, 8^{0}SD, 9^{0}SD, 7^{1}SD,

	Starts	1st	2nd	3rd	Win & Pl
Career Total (Turf)	30	4	3	4	31839
Career Total (AW)	19	5	5	0	43963

80 12/09 Wolv 7f32y STD £2729
97 1/09 Ling 1m (0-100)H STD £11656
94 12/08 GrLe 1m (0-95)H STD £7477
91 12/08 Wolv 1m141y STD £2729
93 8/08 Wind 1m67y (0-85)H G-S £5375
86 7/08 Asct 1m (0-85)H G-F £6476
86 10/07 Nott 1m54y (0-85)H G-F £6477
80 9/07 Leic 1m60y (0-75)H GD £3238
78 5/06 Kemp 1m STD £5181
Total win prize-money £51343

Going (Turf): Sf: 0-7 GS: 1-4 Gd: 1-11 **GF: 2-8** Fm: 0-0
Distance: 5f/6f: 0-0 **7f-8f: 5-25** 9f-13f: 4-24 14f+: 0-0
Track : **LH: 5-25** RH: 3-16 **Tight: 4-25** Gall: 1-6
Aids: Bl: 0-0 Vi: 0-0 Tstrap: 0-0 Ckp: 0-0
Best Rating: 103 3/09 Ling 7f stand

Useful; effective over 7f-1m; acts on most ground and on Polytrack.

Red Stiletto

72(72) (34)**36**
3-y-o b f Red Ransom (USA)-The Blade (GER) (Sure Blade (USA))
Rae Guest R Guest, L Vaessen & J Poulter

Placings:00-0 **(1423)**
2009: 7^{0}G,

	Starts	1st	2nd	3rd	Win & Pl
Career Total (Turf)	2	0	0	0	
Career Total (AW)	1	0	0	0	

Going (Turf): **Sf: 0-0 GS: 0-1 Gd: 0-1 GF: 0-0 Fm: 0-0**
Distance: 5f/6f: 0-0 7f-8f: 0-2 9f-13f: 0-1 14f+: 0-0
Track : LH: 0-0 RH: 0-1 Tight: 0-0 Gall: 0-0
Aids: Bl: 0-0 Vi: 0-0 Tstrap: 0-0 Ckp: 0-0
Best Rating: 36 10/08 Yarm 1m3y gd-sft

Red Suede Shoes

103(105) (82)**70**
3-y-o ch g Storming Home-Dipple (Komaite (USA))
B R Millman Essex Racing Club

Placings:0226444345123134 **(7769)**

2009: 8^{0}SD, 10^{2}SD, 12^{2}SD, 9^{6}G, 8^{4}GF, 8^{4}GF, 8^{4}G, 8^{3}SD, 10^{4}G, 8^{5}SD, 8^{1}SD, 8^{2}SD, 8^{3}SD, 8^{1}SD, 8^{3}SD, 8^{4}SD,

	Starts	1st	2nd	3rd	Win & Pl
Career Total (Turf)	5	0	0	0	1227
Career Total (AW)	11	2	3	3	8696

82 11/09 Kemp 1m (0-75)H STD £2590
75 10/09 Kemp 1m (0-65)H STD £1706
Total win prize-money £4296

Going (Turf): Sf: 0-0 GS: 0-0 Gd: 0-3 GF: 0-2 Fm: 0-0
Distance: 5f/6f: 0-0 **7f-8f: 2-8** 9f-13f: 0-8 14f+: 0-0
Track : LH: 0-6 **RH: 2-9** Tight: 0-7 Gall: 0-0
Aids: Bl: 0-0 Vi: 0-0 Tstrap: 2-6 Ckp: 2-6
Best Rating: 82 11/09 Kemp 1m stand

Fair; effective over 1m-1m4f; acts on fast ground; goes on Polytrack; has worn cheekpieces.

Red Tarn

(100) (64)**72**
4-y-o gr g Fraam-Cumbrian Melody (Petong)
B Smart Alan Zheng

Placings:450/2063**0352-10** **(0147)**
2009: 11^{1}SS, 12^{0}SD,

	Starts	1st	2nd	3rd	Win & Pl
Career Total (Turf)	6	0	1	0	1076
Career Total (AW)	7	1	1	2	3458

64 1/09 Sthl 1m3f SS £2047
Total win prize-money £2047

Going (Turf): Sf: 0-1 GS: 0-1 Gd: 0-1 GF: 0-3 Fm: 0-0
Distance: 5f/6f: 0-0 7f-8f: 0-8 **9f-13f: 1-5** 14f+: 0-0
Track : **LH: 1-8** RH: 0-1 Tight: 0-3 Gall: 0-0
Aids: Bl: 0-0 Vi: 0-1 Tstrap: 0-0 Ckp: 0-0
Best Rating: 72 5/08 Muss 7f30y gd-fm

Modest; stays 1m3f; acts on easy ground and on Fibresand.

Red Twist

91(95) (63)**57**
4-y-o b g Red Ransom (USA)-Spinning The Yarn (Barathea (IRE))
M Hill Fun In The Sun Partnership

Placings:605/0050-**4**000 **(2859)**
2009: 11^{4}SD, 14^{0}SD, 13^{0}GF, 10^{0}G,

	Starts	1st	2nd	3rd	Win & Pl
Career Total (Turf)	7	0	0	0	0
Career Total (AW)	4	0	0	0	192

Going (Turf): Sf: 0-2 GS: 0-2 Gd: 0-1 GF: 0-1 Fm: 0-1
Distance: 5f/6f: 0-0 7f-8f: 0-2 9f-13f: 0-7 14f+: 0-2
Track : LH: 0-5 RH: 0-4 Tight: 0-4 Gall: 0-1
Aids: Bl: 0-0 Vi: 0-0 Tstrap: 0-0 Ckp: 0-0
Best Rating: 71 10/07 Newb 1m gd-sft

Red Valerian Two (IRE)

(62)
2-y-o ch c Hawk Wing (USA)-La Turque (IRE) (Diesis)
P T Midgley Mrs Alurie O'Sullivan

Placings:00 **(7266)**
2009: 7^{0}SD, 8^{0}SD,

	Starts	1st	2nd	3rd	Win & Pl
Career Total (Turf)	0	0	0	0	
Career Total (AW)	2	0	0	0	

Going (Turf): Sf: 0-0 GS: 0-0 Gd: 0-0 GF: 0-0 Fm: 0-0
Distance: 5f/6f: 0-0 7f-8f: 0-2 9f-13f: 0-0 14f+: 0-0
Track : LH: 0-2 RH: 0-0 Tight: 0-0 Gall: 0-0
Aids: Bl: 0-0 Vi: 0-0 Tstrap: 0-0 Ckp: 0-0

Red Willow

80 **32**
3-y-o ch f Noverre (USA)-Chelsea Blue (ITY) (Barathea (IRE))
J E Long T H Bambridge

Placings:050 **(5747)**
2009: 6^{0}GF, 7^{5}G, 7^{0}GF,

	Starts	1st	2nd	3rd	Win & Pl
Career Total (Turf)	3	0	0	0	0

Going (Turf): Sf: 0-0 GS: 0-0 Gd: 0-1 GF: 0-2 Fm: 0-0
Distance: 5f/6f: 0-1 7f-8f: 0-2 9f-13f: 0-0 14f+: 0-0
Track : LH: 0-0 RH: 0-0 Tight: 0-0 Gall: 0-0
Aids: Bl: 0-0 Vi: 0-0 Tstrap: 0-0 Ckp: 0-0
Best Rating: 32 9/09 Ling 7f gd-fm

Red Wine

103(101) (68)**85**
10-y-o b g Hamas (IRE)-Red Bouquet (Reference Point)
J A Glover (A J McCabe 26/6) Paul J Dixon

Placings:42/140200104**32111**/53040/**50**/**666**00003**2**40/**034 4331**10641032056033006**3606-005**0**2**42104636**53540** **(7642)**
2009: 14^{0}SS, 12^{0}SD, 13^{5}SD, 13^{0}SD, 12^{2}G, 12^{4}GF, 14^{2}G, 12^{1}GS, 14^{0}GF, 12^{4}S, 11^{6}G, 16^{3}G, 15^{6}S, 16^{5}GS, 15^{3}S, 13^{5}S, 12^{4}SD, 14^{0}SD,

	Starts	1st	2nd	3rd	Win & Pl
Career Total (Turf)	51	7	5	9	78906
Career Total (AW)	29	2	2	3	11936

81 5/09 Donc 1m4f (0-70)H G-S £3238
82 5/08 Donc 1m6f132y (0-85)H G-S £4857
76 3/08 Pont 1m4f8y (0-75)H G-S £3238
75 3/08 Donc 1m4f (0-70)H GD £3412
102 11/02 Donc 1m4f B H HVY £29588
92 10/02 Donc 1m2f60yD(0-85)H G-S £5109
88 10/02 Bath 1m3f144yD(0-80)H GD £4836
90 8/02 Wolv 1m100yD(0-85)H STD £4516
77 1/02 Sthl 1m D SLW £3334
Total win prize-money £62132

Going (Turf): Sf: 1-11 **GS: 4-15** Gd: 2-16 GF: 0-8 Fm: 0-1
Distance: 5f/6f: 0-1 7f-8f: 1-4 **9f-13f: 7-48** 14f+: 1-27
Track : **LH: 9-61** RH: 0-17 Tight: 2-25 **Gall: 5-24**
Aids: Bl: 0-5 Vi: 0-0 Tstrap: 0-1 Ckp: 0-1
Best Rating: 102 11/02 Donc 1m4f heavy

Modest; stays 1m6f but effective at around 1m4f; acts on most ground; has worn blinkers and eyeshield.

Red Yarn

(98) (57)
2-y-o b f Lucky Story (USA)-Aunt Ruby (USA) (Rubiano (USA))
G L Moore Heart Of The South Racing

Placings:63 **(7885)**
2009: 7^{6}SD, 7^{3}SD,

	Starts	1st	2nd	3rd	Win & Pl
Career Total (Turf)	0	0	0	0	
Career Total (AW)	2	0	0	1	242

Going (Turf): Sf: 0-0 GS: 0-0 Gd: 0-0 GF: 0-0 Fm: 0-0
Distance: 5f/6f: 0-0 7f-8f: 0-2 9f-13f: 0-0 14f+: 0-0
Track : LH: 0-1 RH: 0-1 Tight: 0-1 Gall: 0-0
Aids: Bl: 0-0 Vi: 0-0 Tstrap: 0-0 Ckp: 0-0
Best Rating: 57 12/09 Kemp 7f stand

Red Zoe (USA)

87 **57**
3-y-o b f Danehill Dancer (IRE)-Starbourne (IRE) (Sadler's Wells (USA))
M L W Bell Terry Neill

Placings:00 **(2446)**
2009: 8^{0}G, 8^{0}GS,

	Starts	1st	2nd	3rd	Win & Pl
Career Total (Turf)	2	0	0	0	

Going (Turf): Sf: 0-0 GS: 0-1 Gd: 0-1 GF: 0-0 Fm: 0-0
Distance: 5f/6f: 0-0 7f-8f: 0-0 9f-13f: 0-2 14f+: 0-0
Track : LH: 0-1 RH: 0-1 Tight: 0-1 Gall: 0-0
Aids: Bl: 0-0 Vi: 0-0 Tstrap: 0-0 Ckp: 0-0
Best Rating: 57 5/09 Wind 1m67y good

Redarsene

(95) (71)**71**
4-y-o ch c Sakhee (USA)-Triple Zee (USA) (Zilzal (USA))
S Wynne Shropshire Wolves

Placings:600/05**1**00063-6 **(0215)**
2009: 8^{6}SD,

	Starts	1st	2nd	3rd	Win & Pl
Career Total (Turf)	6	0	0	0	0
Career Total (AW)	6	1	0	1	2741

71 6/08 Wolv 1m141y (0-65)H STD £2388
Total win prize-money £2388

Going (Turf): Sf: 0-2 GS: 0-1 Gd: 0-2 GF: 0-1 Fm: 0-0
Distance: 5f/6f: 0-0 7f-8f: 0-8 **9f-13f: 1-4** 14f+: 0-0
Track : **LH: 1-5** RH: 0-2 **Tight: 1-3** Gall: 0-0
Aids: Bl: 0-0 Vi: 0-0 Tstrap: 0-0 Ckp: 0-0
Best Rating: 71 11/08 Wolv 1m141y stand

Modest; stays at least 1m; acts on soft ground; goes on Polytrack.

Redden

94 **65**
2-y-o b g Pivotal-Coy (IRE) (Danehill (USA))
W J Haggas Cheveley Park Stud

Placings:604 **(7289)**
2009: 6^{6}GF, 7^{0}G, 6^{4}S,

	Starts	1st	2nd	3rd	Win & Pl
Career Total (Turf)	3	0	0	0	457

Going (Turf): Sf: 0-1 GS: 0-0 Gd: 0-1 GF: 0-1 Fm: 0-0
Distance: 5f/6f: 0-2 7f-8f: 0-1 9f-13f: 0-0 14f+: 0-0
Track : LH: 0-0 RH: 0-0 Tight: 0-0 Gall: 0-0
Aids: Bl: 0-0 Vi: 0-0 Tstrap: 0-0 Ckp: 0-0
Best Rating: 65 11/09 Donc 6f soft

Modest; seems best at 6f; acts on soft ground; played up in stalls on debut.

Reddy Ronnie (IRE)

92 (41)**55**
5-y-o b g Redback-Daffodil Dale (IRE) (Cyrano De Bergerac)

D W Thompson Mrs Dee Thompson

Placings:600/205-0000400 **(5983)**
2009: 8^{0}GF, 9^{0}GF, 8^{0}GF, 7^{0}G, 7^{4}GF, 8^{0}GF, 8^{0}GF,

	Starts	1st	2nd	3rd	Win & Pl
Career Total (Turf)	12	0	1	0	797
Career Total (AW)	1	0	0	0	

Going (Turf): Sf: 0-0 GS: 0-1 Gd: 0-2 GF: 0-9 Fm: 0-0
Distance: 5f/6f: 0-0 7f-8f: 0-9 9f-13f: 0-4 14f+: 0-0
Track : LH: 0-7 RH: 0-5 Tight: 0-6 Gall: 0-1
Aids: Bl: 0-0 Vi: 0-1 Tstrap: 0-1 Ckp: 0-1
Best Rating: 55 7/08 Thsk 1m gd-fm

Moderate maiden; stays 1m; acts on easy ground.

Reddy To Star (IRE)

94(91) (63)**76**
2-y-o b g Redback-Grade A Star (IRE) (Alzao (USA))
C G Cox Dennis Shaw

Placings:0222200403 **(6911)**
2009: 5^{0}G, 5^{2}GF, 5^{2}GF, 5^{2}GF, 5^{2}GF, 5^{0}GS, 5^{0}SD, 5^{4}F, 7^{0}GS, 7^{3}SD,

	Starts	1st	2nd	3rd	Win & Pl
Career Total (Turf)	8	0	4	0	4516
Career Total (AW)	2	0	0	1	353

Going (Turf): Sf: 0-0 GS: 0-2 Gd: 0-1 GF: 0-4 Fm: 0-1
Distance: 5f/6f: 0-8 7f-8f: 0-2 9f-13f: 0-0 14f+: 0-0
Track : LH: 0-6 RH: 0-1 Tight: 0-3 Gall: 0-1
Aids: Bl: 0-1 Vi: 0-0 Tstrap: 0-0 Ckp: 0-0
Best Rating: 76 6/09 Ches 5f16y gd-fm

Fair; stays 7f; acts on fast ground and on Polytrack.

Redeemed

(91) (44)**72**
4-y-o b f Red Ransom (USA)-Pastel (Lion Cavern (USA))
M Brittain S G Eaton

Placings:030/0006-00 **(0216)**
2009: 8^{0}SS, 8^{0}SD,

	Starts	1st	2nd	3rd	Win & Pl
Career Total (Turf)	4	0	0	1	674
Career Total (AW)	5	0	0	0	0

Going (Turf): Sf: 0-0 GS: 0-1 Gd: 0-1 GF: 0-1 Fm: 0-1
Distance: 5f/6f: 0-2 7f-8f: 0-5 9f-13f: 0-2 14f+: 0-0
Track : LH: 0-4 RH: 0-1 Tight: 0-2 Gall: 0-0
Aids: Bl: 0-0 Vi: 0-0 Tstrap: 0-0 Ckp: 0-0
Best Rating: 72 8/07 NmkJ 7f firm

Redesignation (IRE)

102 (80)**103**
4-y-o b g Key Of Luck (USA)-Disregard That (IRE) (Don't Forget Me)
R Pritchard-Gordon (R Hannon 15/5) Richard Morecombe

Placings:01F/2622142-1204325
2009: 10^{1}GF, 12^{2}GF, 12^{0}GS, **12^{4}SD**, 12^{3}GS, 12^{2}G, **12^{5}SD**,

	Starts	1st	2nd	3rd	Win & Pl
Career Total (Turf)	15	3	6	1	46681
Career Total (AW)	2	0	0	0	5000

103 4/09 Donc 1m2f60y (0-95)H G-F £7477
98 9/08 Sand 1m2f7y (0-90)H SFT £7771
85 8/07 NmkJ 7f GD £3886
Total win prize-money £19134

Going (Turf): Sf: 1-2 GS: 0-6 Gd: 1-3 GF: 1-4 Fm: 0-0
Distance: 5f/6f: 0-0 7f-8f: 1-4 9f-13f: 2-13 14f+: 0-0
Track : LH: 1-5 RH: 1-7 Tight: 0-0 Gall: 1-7
Aids: Bl: 0-0 Vi: 0-0 Tstrap: 0-0 Ckp: 0-0
Best Rating: 103 5/09 NmkR 1m4f gd-fm

Very useful; effective at 1m-1m4f and acts on most ground.

Redford (IRE)

109 **108**
4-y-o b g Bahri (USA)-Ida Lupino (IRE) (Statoblest)
M L W Bell Highclere T'bred Racing (Housemaster)

Placings:041/10164-436300 **(6270)**
2009: 6^{4}G, 7^{3}GF, 7^{6}GF, 7^{3}G, 6^{0}G, 7^{0}G,

	Starts	1st	2nd	3rd	Win & Pl
Career Total (Turf)	14	3	0	2	56100

108 6/08 Newc 7f (0-100)H SFT £12462
101 6/08 Donc 1m (0-100)H G-S £12952
85 10/07 Newc 1m GD £4339
Total win prize-money £29754

Going (Turf): Sf: 1-1 GS: 1-3 Gd: 1-5 GF: 0-5 Fm: 0-0
Distance: 5f/6f: 0-2 7f-8f: 3-12 9f-13f: 0-0 14f+: 0-0
Track : LH: 1-1 RH: 0-0 Tight: 0-0 Gall: 1-1
Aids: Bl: 0-0 Vi: 0-1 Tstrap: 0-0 Ckp: 0-0
Best Rating: 108 6/08 Newc 7f soft

Smart; effective at 7f but stays 1m; acts on good and easy ground.

Redlynch

43(69)
4-y-o b g Sinndar (IRE)-Red Azalea (Shirley Heights)
S Parr Willie McKay

Placings:P6-0000 **(3460)**
2009: 11^{0}SD, 12^{0}SD, 8^{0}SD, 6^{0}GF,

	Starts	1st	2nd	3rd	Win & Pl
Career Total (Turf)	2	0	0	0	
Career Total (AW)	4	0	0	0	0

Going (Turf): Sf: 0-0 GS: 0-0 Gd: 0-0 GF: 0-2 Fm: 0-0
Distance: 5f/6f: 0-2 7f-8f: 0-1 9f-13f: 0-3 14f+: 0-0
Track : LH: 0-5 RH: 0-0 Tight: 0-0 Gall: 0-1
Aids: Bl: 0-0 Vi: 0-1 Tstrap: 0-1 Ckp: 0-1

Redoubtable Grace

83(66) (7)**44**
2-y-o b g Redoubtable (USA)-Full Of Grace (Lucky Wednesday)
Mrs R A Carr David A Baird

Placings:0006 **(7674)**
2009: 5^{0}S, 5^{0}GF, 5^{0}SF, 5^{6}SD,

	Starts	1st	2nd	3rd	Win & Pl
Career Total (Turf)	2	0	0	0	
Career Total (AW)	2	0	0	0	0

Going (Turf): Sf: 0-1 GS: 0-0 Gd: 0-0 GF: 0-1 Fm: 0-0
Distance: 5f/6f: 0-4 7f-8f: 0-0 9f-13f: 0-0 14f+: 0-0
Track : LH: 0-1 RH: 0-0 Tight: 0-1 Gall: 0-0
Aids: Bl: 0-0 Vi: 0-0 Tstrap: 0-0 Ckp: 0-0
Best Rating: 44 9/09 Bevl 5f gd-fm

Redwater River

104(90) (65)**68**
5-y-o b g Kyllachy-Red Tulle (USA) (A.P. Indy (USA))
Mrs R A Carr David W Chapman

Placings:6/42450251-560000663351050 **(5601)**
2009: 8^{5}SD, 8^{6}SD, 9^{0}SD, 7^{0}SD, 7^{0}GS, 5^{0}GF, **6^{6}SD**, 6^{6}S, 5^{3}S, 6^{3}GF, 6^{5}G, 5^{1}G, 5^{0}GS, 6^{5}GF, 7^{0}GF,

	Starts	1st	2nd	3rd	Win & Pl
Career Total (Turf)	17	2	1	2	10447
Career Total (AW)	7	0	1	0	1367

61 8/09 Catt 5f212y (0-75)H GD £2914
68 10/08 Gowr 1m1f HVY £5080
Total win prize-money £7995

Going (Turf): Sf: 1-3 GS: 0-2 Gd: 1-3 GF: 0-4 Fm: 0-1
Distance: 5f/6f: 1-11 7f-8f: 0-9 9f-13f: 1-4 14f+: 0-0
Track : LH: 1-12 RH: 1-4 Tight: 1-4 Gall: 1-0
Aids: Bl: 1-11 Vi: 0-0 Tstrap: 0-0 Ckp: 0-0
Best Rating: 68 10/08 Gowr 1m1f heavy

Moderate; effective over 6f; acts on good ground.

Redwood

107 **108**
3-y-o b c High Chaparral (IRE)-Arum Lily (USA) (Woodman (USA))
B W Hills K Abdulla

Placings:1-10 **(2014)**
2009: 9^{1}GF, 10^{0}G,

	Starts	1st	2nd	3rd	Win & Pl
Career Total (Turf)	3	2	0	0	32023

108 4/09 NmkR 1m1f G-F £25546
88 10/08 NmkR 1m G-F £6476
Total win prize-money £32023

Going (Turf): Sf: 0-0 GS: 0-0 Gd: 0-1 GF: 2-2 Fm: 0-0
Distance: 5f/6f: 0-0 7f-8f: 1-1 9f-13f: 1-2 14f+: 0-0
Track : LH: 0-1 RH: 0-0 Tight: 0-0 Gall: 0-1
Aids: Bl: 0-0 Vi: 0-0 Tstrap: 0-0 Ckp: 0-0
Best Rating: 108 4/09 NmkR 1m1f gd-fm

Winner on debut; effective over 1m; acts on fast ground.

Reeds Bay (IRE)

99 **79**
2-y-o br c Monsieur Bond (IRE)-Paradise Blue (IRE) (Bluebird (USA))
E S McMahon J C Fretwell

Placings:35140433 **(6534)**
2009: 6^{3}G, 6^{5}GS, 6^{1}GF, 7^{4}G, 7^{0}GF, 7^{4}GS, 6^{3}G, 6^{3}GF,

	Starts	1st	2nd	3rd	Win & Pl
Career Total (Turf)	8	1	0	3	6126

78 6/09 Hayd 6f G-F £3238
Total win prize-money £3238

Going (Turf): Sf: 0-0 GS: 0-2 Gd: 0-3 GF: 1-3 Fm: 0-0
Distance: 5f/6f: 1-4 7f-8f: 0-4 9f-13f: 0-0 14f+: 0-0
Track : LH: 0-2 RH: 0-1 Tight: 0-0 Gall: 0-1
Aids: Bl: 0-4 Vi: 0-0 Tstrap: 0-0 Ckp: 0-0
Best Rating: 79 9/09 Haml 6f5y good

Fair; stays 7f; acts on fast ground.

Reel Bluff

89 **53**
3-y-o b g Reel Buddy (USA)-Amber's Bluff (Mind Games)
N Wilson (D W Barker 2/7) Fishing 4 Fun

Placings:6000-0000 **(6488)**

2009: 12^{0}GF, 7^{0}GF, 8^{0}F, 10^{0}GF,

	Starts	1st	2nd	3rd	Win & Pl
Career Total (Turf)	8	0	0	0	0

Going (Turf): **Sf: 0-1 GS: 0-2 Gd: 0-1 GF: 0-3 Fm: 0-1**
Distance: 5f/6f: 0-3 7f-8f: 0-3 9f-13f: 0-2 14f+: 0-0
Track : LH: 0-4 RH: 0-1 Tight: 0-4 Gall: 0-1
Aids: Bl: 0-0 Vi: 0-0 Tstrap: 0-0 Ckp: 0-0
Best Rating: **53** 9/08 Catt 5f212y gd-sft

Reel Buddy Star

105 **86**

4-y-o ch g Reel Buddy (USA)-So Discreet (Tragic Role (USA))
G M Moore J W Armstrong & M J Howarth

Placings:212/64423150-0562610340 **(6485)**
2009: 10^{0}GS, 8^{5}GF, 9^{6}GS, 8^{2}GF, 8^{6}GF, 8^{1}GF, 8^{0}GF, 8^{3}GF, 8^{4}GF, 8^{0}GF,

	Starts	1st	2nd	3rd	Win & Pl
Career Total (Turf)	21	3	4	2	24590

86	8/09	Newc	1m3y	(0-80)H	G-F	£6476
80	8/08	Ripn	1m	(0-80)H	GD	£6938
70	10/07	Newc	7f		GD	£1943

Total win prize-money £15358

Going (Turf): Sf: 0-4 GS: 0-3 **Gd: 2-6** GF: 1-8 Fm: 0-0
Distance: 5f/6f: 0-0 **7f-8f: 2-11** 9f-13f: 1-10 14f+: 0-0
Track : LH: 0-9 **RH: 1-4 Tight: 1-3** Gall: 0-3
Aids: Bl: 0-0 Vi: 0-0 Tstrap: 0-1 Ckp: 0-1
Best Rating: **86** 9/09 Hayd 1m30y gd-fm

Useful; stays 1m; acts on most ground.

Reel Credit Crunch

92(88) (64)**65**

2-y-o ch f Reel Buddy (USA)-Four Legs Good (IRE) (Be My Guest (USA))
I W McInnes (P D Evans 9/5) Wold Construction Company

Placings:3522465000 **(6586)**
2009: 5^{3}SD, 5^{5}GF, 5^{2}GF, 5^{2}GF, 5^{4}GF, 5^{6}F, 5^{5}SF, 5^{0}GF, 5^{0}GF, 7^{0}SD,

	Starts	1st	2nd	3rd	Win & Pl
Career Total (Turf)	7	0	2	0	4066
Career Total (AW)	3	0	0	1	433

Going (Turf): **Sf: 0-0 GS: 0-0 Gd: 0-0 GF: 0-6 Fm: 0-1**
Distance: 5f/6f: 0-9 7f-8f: 0-1 9f-13f: 0-0 14f+: 0-0
Track : LH: 0-3 RH: 0-1 Tight: 0-3 Gall: 0-0
Aids: Bl: 0-3 Vi: 0-0 Tstrap: 0-0 Ckp: 0-0
Best Rating: **65** 5/09 Ches 5f16y gd-fm

Modest; suited by 5f; acts on fast ground and on Polytrack.

Reel Easy

59(73) (27)**9**

2-y-o b c Reel Buddy (USA)-Easy Feeling (IRE) (Night Shift (USA))
J R Holt J R Holt

Placings:000 **(3709)**
2009: 5^{0}GF, 5^{0}GF, 5^{0}SD,

	Starts	1st	2nd	3rd	Win & Pl
Career Total (Turf)	2	0	0	0	
Career Total (AW)	1	0	0	0	

Going (Turf): **Sf: 0-0 GS: 0-0 Gd: 0-0 GF: 0-2 Fm: 0-0**
Distance: 5f/6f: 0-3 7f-8f: 0-0 9f-13f: 0-0 14f+: 0-0
Track : LH: 0-1 RH: 0-0 Tight: 0-0 Gall: 0-0
Aids: Bl: 0-0 Vi: 0-0 Tstrap: 0-0 Ckp: 0-0
Best Rating: **27** 7/09 Sthl 5f stand

Reel Hope

(80) (41)**46**

3-y-o b f Reel Buddy (USA)-Compton Amber (Puissance)
J R Best F J Perry

Placings:000-00 **(6166)**
2009: 7^{0}SD, 12^{0}SD,

	Starts	1st	2nd	3rd	Win & Pl
Career Total (Turf)	3	0	0	0	
Career Total (AW)	2	0	0	0	

Going (Turf): **Sf: 0-0 GS: 0-1 Gd: 0-0 GF: 0-2 Fm: 0-0**
Distance: 5f/6f: 0-0 7f-8f: 0-4 9f-13f: 0-1 14f+: 0-0
Track : LH: 0-1 RH: 0-1 Tight: 0-1 Gall: 0-0
Aids: Bl: 0-0 Vi: 0-0 Tstrap: 0-0 Ckp: 0-0
Best Rating: **46** 7/08 Folk 7f gd-fm

Reel Love

48(70) (31)

2-y-o b c Reel Buddy (USA)-Love Affair (IRE) (Tagula (IRE))
J R Holt Red Lion Racing Market Bosworth

Placings:00 **(3468)**
2009: 6^{0}GS, 7^{0}SD,

	Starts	1st	2nd	3rd	Win & Pl
Career Total (Turf)	1	0	0	0	
Career Total (AW)	1	0	0	0	

Going (Turf): **Sf: 0-0 GS: 0-1 Gd: 0-0 GF: 0-0 Fm: 0-0**
Distance: 5f/6f: 0-1 7f-8f: 0-1 9f-13f: 0-0 14f+: 0-0
Track : LH: 0-1 RH: 0-0 Tight: 0-1 Gall: 0-0
Aids: Bl: 0-0 Vi: 0-0 Tstrap: 0-0 Ckp: 0-0
Best Rating: **31** 6/09 Wolv 7f32y stand

Reel Man

(86) (49)**49**

4-y-o ch g Reel Buddy (USA)-Yanomami (USA) (Slew O'Gold (USA))
D K Ivory Radlett Racing

Placings:000/0300-000 **(6941)**
2009: 11^{0}SD, 12^{0}SD, 12^{0}SD,

	Starts	1st	2nd	3rd	Win & Pl
Career Total (Turf)	3	0	0	0	
Career Total (AW)	7	0	0	1	530

Going (Turf): **Sf: 0-0 GS: 0-0 Gd: 0-0 GF: 0-3 Fm: 0-0**
Distance: 5f/6f: 0-1 7f-8f: 0-5 9f-13f: 0-4 14f+: 0-0
Track : LH: 0-3 RH: 0-4 Tight: 0-2 Gall: 0-0
Aids: Bl: 0-0 Vi: 0-0 Tstrap: 0-0 Ckp: 0-0
Best Rating: **58** 10/07 Kemp 7f stand

Reflective Glory (IRE)

90(72) (27)**40**

5-y-o ch m City On A Hill (USA)-Sheznice (IRE) (Try My Best (USA))
J S Wainwright Tony Longbottom

Placings:6644400/406006/0-0 **(4804)**
2009: 9^{0}GF,

	Starts	1st	2nd	3rd	Win & Pl
Career Total (Turf)	11	0	0	0	931
Career Total (AW)	4	0	0	0	0

Going (Turf): **Sf: 0-0 GS: 0-2 Gd: 0-3 GF: 0-4 Fm: 0-2**
Distance: 5f/6f: 0-5 7f-8f: 0-5 9f-13f: 0-5 14f+: 0-0
Track : LH: 0-8 RH: 0-3 Tight: 0-4 Gall: 0-0
Aids: Bl: 0-0 Vi: 0-1 Tstrap: 0-5 Ckp: 0-5
Best Rating: **53** 6/06 Bevl 5f gd-fm

Refuse To Decline

(76) (32)**50**

3-y-o ch f Refuse To Bend (IRE)-Oulianovsk (IRE) (Peintre Celebre (USA))
D M Simcock Dr Ali Ridha

Placings:600-0 **(0196)**
2009: 8^{0}SD,

	Starts	1st	2nd	3rd	Win & Pl
Career Total (Turf)	2	0	0	0	0
Career Total (AW)	2	0	0	0	

Going (Turf): **Sf: 0-0 GS: 0-0 Gd: 0-0 GF: 0-2 Fm: 0-0**
Distance: 5f/6f: 0-1 7f-8f: 0-1 9f-13f: 0-2 14f+: 0-0
Track : LH: 0-2 RH: 0-0 Tight: 0-2 Gall: 0-0
Aids: Bl: 0-0 Vi: 0-0 Tstrap: 0-0 Ckp: 0-0
Best Rating: **50** 5/08 NmkR 6f gd-fm

Refuse To Sell (IRE)

(83) (67)**69**

4-y-o b g Brahms (USA)-Ruby Cairo (IRE) (Nashwan (USA))
F Costello F Costello

Placings:00/05000-441105100 **(7729)**
2009: 6^{4}SD, 7^{4}HY, 7^{1}SD, 7^{1}SD, 6^{0}SD, 7^{5}G, 6^{1}GF, 7^{0}GY, 7^{0}SD,

	Starts	1st	2nd	3rd	Win & Pl
Career Total (Turf)	7	1	0	0	6376
Career Total (AW)	9	2	0	0	11052

69	6/09	Limk	6f160y	(50-70)H	G-F	£6037
67	5/09	Dund	7f	(47-65)H	STD	£5366
58	4/09	Dund	7f	(47-65)H	STD	£5366

Total win prize-money £16772

Going (Turf): Sf: 0-1 GS: 0-0 Gd: 0-2 **GF: 1-2** Fm: 0-0
Distance: 5f/6f: 0-7 **7f-8f: 3-9** 9f-13f: 0-0 14f+: 0-0
Track : **LH: 2-10** RH: 0-2 Tight: 0-1 Gall: 0-0
Aids: Bl: 0-2 Vi: 0-0 Tstrap: 0-0 Ckp: 0-0
Best Rating: **69** 6/09 Limk 6f160y gd-fm

Refuse To Tell

81(76) (42)**40**

2-y-o b g Refuse To Bend (IRE)-Zibet (Kris)
C E Brittain Mohammed Al Nabouda

Placings:0060 **(6067)**
2009: 6^{0}GF, 7^{0}SD, 8^{6}GS, 9^{0}GF,

	Starts	1st	2nd	3rd	Win & Pl
Career Total (Turf)	3	0	0	0	0
Career Total (AW)	1	0	0	0	

Going (Turf): **Sf: 0-0 GS: 0-1 Gd: 0-0 GF: 0-2 Fm: 0-0**

Distance: 5f/6f: 0-0 7f-8f: 0-2 9f-13f: 0-2 14f+: 0-0
Track : LH: 0-1 RH: 0-1 Tight: 0-1 Gall: 0-0
Aids: Bl: 0-0 Vi: 0-0 Tstrap: 0-0 Ckp: 0-0
Best Rating: 42 8/09 Kemp 7f stand

Refuse To Wait (IRE)

98 **69**

2-y-o b f Refuse To Bend (IRE)-I'Ll Be Waiting (Vettori (IRE))
T D Easterby Ryedale Partners No 8

Placings:431004 (5550)
2009: 5^{4}GF, 6^{3}HY, 6^{1}G, 6^{0}G, 7^{0}GF, 6^{4}G,

	Starts	1st	2nd	3rd	Win & Pl
Career Total (Turf)	6	1	0	1	4393

69 6/09 Newc 6f GD £3238
Total win prize-money £3238

Going (Turf): Sf: 0-1 GS: 0-0 **Gd: 1-3** GF: 0-2 Fm: 0-0
Distance: **5f/6f: 1-5** 7f-8f: 0-1 9f-13f: 0-0 14f+: 0-0
Track : LH: 0-1 RH: 0-0 Tight: 0-1 Gall: 0-0
Aids: Bl: 0-1 Vi: 0-0 Tstrap: 0-0 Ckp: 0-0
Best Rating: 69 6/09 Newc 6f good

Fair; effective over 6f; acts on good ground.

Refuse Toulouse (IRE)

87(88) (46)**53**

3-y-o b c Refuse To Bend (IRE)-Continuous (IRE) (Darshaan)
C G Cox Lunchtime Legends

Placings:006000 (6758)
2009: 10^{0}G, 8^{0}S, 10^{6}GF, 11^{0}SD, 10^{0}SD, 11^{0}G,

	Starts	1st	2nd	3rd	Win & Pl
Career Total (Turf)	4	0	0	0	0
Career Total (AW)	2	0	0	0	

Going (Turf): Sf: 0-1 GS: 0-0 Gd: 0-2 GF: 0-1 Fm: 0-0
Distance: 5f/6f: 0-0 7f-8f: 0-1 9f-13f: 0-5 14f+: 0-0
Track : LH: 0-1 RH: 0-4 Tight: 0-0 Gall: 0-1
Aids: Bl: 0-1 Vi: 0-0 Tstrap: 0-0 Ckp: 0-0
Best Rating: 53 5/09 Sand 1m2f7y gd-fm

Regal Angel

79(97) (62)**55**

6-y-o ch m Roi De Rome (USA)-Dominion's Dream (Dominion)
Jean-Rene Auvray Nigel Kelly And Alison Auvray

Placings:323404 (5720)
2009: 12^{3}SD, 12^{2}SD, 13^{3}SD, 12^{4}G, 14^{0}G, 13^{4}G,

	Starts	1st	2nd	3rd	Win & Pl
Career Total (Turf)	3	0	0	0	883
Career Total (AW)	3	0	1	2	1612

Going (Turf): Sf: 0-0 GS: 0-0 Gd: 0-3 GF: 0-0 Fm: 0-0
Distance: 5f/6f: 0-0 7f-8f: 0-0 9f-13f: 0-4 14f+: 0-2
Track : LH: 0-4 RH: 0-1 Tight: 0-5 Gall: 0-0
Aids: Bl: 0-0 Vi: 0-0 Tstrap: 0-0 Ckp: 0-0
Best Rating: 62 1/09 Ling 1m4f stand

Modest; stays 1m4f; acts on good ground and Polytrack.

Regal Blush

98 **65**

3-y-o b f Bachelor Duke (USA)-Royale Rose (FR) (Bering)
A M Balding Horses for Causes

Placings:00020303 (6788)
2009: 7^{0}GS, 8^{0}GF, 10^{0}G, 10^{2}G, 9^{0}GF, 13^{3}G, 16^{0}SD, 11^{3}G,

	Starts	1st	2nd	3rd	Win & Pl
Career Total (Turf)	7	0	1	2	1466
Career Total (AW)	1	0	0	0	

Going (Turf): Sf: 0-0 GS: 0-1 Gd: 0-4 GF: 0-2 Fm: 0-0
Distance: 5f/6f: 0-0 7f-8f: 0-2 9f-13f: 0-4 14f+: 0-2
Track : LH: 0-3 RH: 0-3 Tight: 0-2 Gall: 0-2
Aids: Bl: 0-0 Vi: 0-0 Tstrap: 0-0 Ckp: 0-0
Best Rating: 65 8/09 Newb 1m2f6y good

Modest; stays 1m2f; acts on good ground.

Regal Dream (IRE)

77 (64)**44**

7-y-o b g Namid-Lovely Me (IRE) (Vision (USA))
J W Unett N B F Hubbard

Placings:0330/10446146126150 0/50345040560/00602004/00000-0 (2964)
2009: 5^{0}GF,

	Starts	1st	2nd	3rd	Win & Pl
Career Total (Turf)	29	2	2	3	19288
Career Total (AW)	15	2	0	0	7284

75 8/05 Wolv 7f32y (0-70) STD £3380
74 7/05 Epsm 7f (0-80)H G-F £8248
68 5/05 Brig 5f213y (0-70) FRM £3347
59 3/05 Ling 5f STD £3367
Total win prize-money £18344

Going (Turf): Sf: 0-2 GS: 0-2 Gd: 0-7 **GF: 1-14 Fm: 1-4**
Distance: 5f/6f: 2-14 7f-8f: 2-28 9f-13f: 0-2 14f+: 0-0
Track : **LH: 4-31** RH: 0-4 **Tight: 3-19** Gall: 0-4
Aids: Bl: 0-0 Vi: 0-1 Tstrap: 0-0 Ckp: 0-0
Best Rating: 79 6/06 Gdwd 7f gd-fm

Moderate; stays 7f; likes fast ground and Polytrack.

Regal Guest

96 **75**

2-y-o b c King's Best (USA)-Zuleika Dobson (Cadeaux Genereux)
M R Channon John Guest

Placings:022 (6697)
2009: 8^{0}G, 9^{2}G, 9^{2}GS,

	Starts	1st	2nd	3rd	Win & Pl
Career Total (Turf)	3	0	2	0	2939

Going (Turf): Sf: 0-0 GS: 0-1 Gd: 0-2 GF: 0-0 Fm: 0-0
Distance: 5f/6f: 0-0 7f-8f: 0-0 9f-13f: 0-3 14f+: 0-0
Track : LH: 0-0 RH: 0-2 Tight: 0-2 Gall: 0-0
Aids: Bl: 0-0 Vi: 0-0 Tstrap: 0-0 Ckp: 0-0
Best Rating: 75 10/09 Gdwd 1m1f gd-sft

Fair; stays 1m1f; acts on good and easy ground.

Regal Lyric (IRE)

100 **71**

3-y-o b g Royal Applause-Alignment (IRE) (Alzao (USA))
T P Tate Mrs Sylvia Clegg

Placings:100-40002423 (6538)
2009: 7^{4}GF, 7^{0}F, 8^{0}GF, 8^{0}G, 12^{2}G, 12^{4}F, 11^{2}G, 12^{3}GF,

	Starts	1st	2nd	3rd	Win & Pl
Career Total (Turf)	11	1	2	1	6644

71 9/08 Rdcr 7f G-S £3561
Total win prize-money £3562

Going (Turf): Sf: 0-1 **GS: 1-2** Gd: 0-3 GF: 0-3 Fm: 0-2
Distance: 5f/6f: 0-1 **7f-8f: 1-6** 9f-13f: 0-4 14f+: 0-0
Track : LH: 0-2 RH: 0-4 Tight: 0-5 Gall: 0-0
Aids: Bl: 0-0 Vi: 0-0 Tstrap: 0-0 Ckp: 0-0
Best Rating: 71 9/08 Rdcr 7f gd-sft

Fair; stays 7f and acts on easy ground.

Regal Parade

115(109) (97)**121**

5-y-o ch g Pivotal-Model Queen (USA) (Kingmambo (USA))
D Nicholls Dab Hand Racing

Placings:11100400640/5222613014-62101321 (5657)
2009: 6^{6}SD, 7^{2}GF, 7^{1}GF, 6^{0}GF, 7^{1}GF, 7^{3}G, 7^{2}GF, 6^{1}GS,

	Starts	1st	2nd	3rd	Win & Pl
Career Total (Turf)	25	6	4	2	405920
Career Total (AW)	4	2	1	0	11153

121 9/09 Hayd 6f G-S £163809
110 7/09 Ches 7f2y G-F £22708
110 5/09 York 7f G-F £8095
112 9/08 Ayr 6f H HVY £93465
104 6/08 Asct 7f (0-105)H FRM £37386
97 5/07 NmkR 7f (0-100)H G-F £12954
92 2/07 Sthl 7f (0-85)H STD £4857
73 1/07 Wolv 7f32y SS £3071
Total win prize-money £346347

Going (Turf): Sf: 1-2 GS: 1-3 Gd: 0-8 **GF: 3-11** Fm: 1-1
Distance: 5f/6f: 2-5 **7f-8f: 6-21** 9f-13f: 0-3 14f+: 0-0
Track : **LH: 4-9** RH: 0-8 **Tight: 2-8** Gall: 1-1
Aids: Bl: 0-0 Vi: 0-0 Tstrap: 0-0 Ckp: 0-0
Best Rating: 121 9/09 Hayd 6f gd-sft

Group class; winner of the 2008 Buckingham Palace Handicap at Royal Ascot and the Ayr Gold Cup; successful in Listed company and took the Group 1 Betfred Sprint Cup in 2009; effective over 6f-1m; acts on most ground and on sand.

Regal Park (IRE)

87 **60**

2-y-o b c Montjeu (IRE)-Classic Park (Robellino (USA))
J Noseda D Clark & Ms Frances Noseda

Placings:5 (6617)
2009: 8^{5}G,

	Starts	1st	2nd	3rd	Win & Pl
Career Total (Turf)	1	0	0	0	0

Going (Turf): Sf: 0-0 GS: 0-0 Gd: 0-1 GF: 0-0 Fm: 0-0
Distance: 5f/6f: 0-0 7f-8f: 0-1 9f-13f: 0-0 14f+: 0-0
Track : LH: 0-0 RH: 0-0 Tight: 0-0 Gall: 0-0
Aids: Bl: 0-0 Vi: 0-0 Tstrap: 0-0 Ckp: 0-0
Best Rating: 60 10/09 Newb 1m good

Regal Rave (USA)

84 **60**

2-y-o b c Wild Event (USA)-Golden Crown (USA) (Defensive Play (USA))
J R Best The Lurchers

Placings:0060 (7056)
2009: 6^{0}GF, 6^{0}GF, 6^{6}GF, 7^{0}GF,

	Starts	1st	2nd	3rd	Win & Pl
Career Total (Turf)	4	0	0	0	0

Going (Turf): Sf: 0-0 GS: 0-0 Gd: 0-0 GF: 0-4 Fm: 0-0
Distance: 5f/6f: 0-2 7f-8f: 0-2 9f-13f: 0-0 14f+: 0-0
Track: LH: 0-0 RH: 0-0 Tight: 0-0 Gall: 0-1
Aids: Bl: 0-0 Vi: 0-0 Tstrap: 0-0 Ckp: 0-0
Best Rating: 60 8/09 Nott 6f15y gd-fm

Regal Royale

99(103) (70)74
6-y-o b g Medicean-Regal Rose (Danehill (USA))
Peter Grayson S Kamis And Mrs S Grayson

Placings:10/020505**600**/**0606006**35400003300/**22103062 0200311021351004**-30**33**000413 (4870)
2009: 6^{3}SD, 6^{0}GF, 5^{3}SD, 5^{3}SD, 5^{0}G, 5^{0}GF, 6^{0}G, 6^{4}SD, 6^{1}S, 6^{3}SD,

	Starts	1st	2nd	3rd	Win & Pl
Career Total (Turf)	29	5	2	3	29811
Career Total (AW)	35	2	4	7	10855

70	8/09	Ling	6f	(0-65)H	SFT	£2388
74	9/08	Folk	5f	(0-85)H	SFT	£5361
74	8/08	Ling	6f	(0-75)H	SFT	£2590
69	7/08	Folk	5f	(0-70)H	SFT	£2590
65	6/08	Ling	6f	(0-60)H	STD	£2047
61	1/08	Kemp	6f	(0-55)H	STD	£2047
77	7/05	Newb	6f8y		G-F	£7085

Total win prize-money £24110

Going (Turf): Sf: 4-6 GS: 0-4 Gd: 0-6 GF: 1-13 Fm: 0-0
Distance: 5f/6f: 6-47 7f-8f: 1-14 9f-13f: 0-3 14f+: 0-0
Track: LH: 1-27 RH: 1-9 **Tight: 1-24** Gall: 0-4
Aids: Bl: 0-6 **Vi: 6-34** Tstrap: 0-0 Ckp: 0-0
Best Rating: 100 6/06 Asct 1m gd-fm

Modest; effective over 5f-6f; acts on most ground and on Polytrack; has worn blinkers and a visor; likes to race prominently.

Regal Tradition (IRE)

85(84) (29)73
4-y-o b g Traditionally (USA)-Dathuil (IRE) (Royal Academy (USA))
G J Smith Rod Sansom

Placings:033/0400 (2129)
2009: 9^{0}SD, 12^{4}GF, 9^{0}GF, 12^{0}SD,

	Starts	1st	2nd	3rd	Win & Pl
Career Total (Turf)	2	0	0	0	560
Career Total (AW)	5	0	0	2	605

Going (Turf): Sf: 0-0 GS: 0-0 Gd: 0-0 GF: 0-2 Fm: 0-0
Distance: 5f/6f: 0-1 7f-8f: 0-2 9f-13f: 0-4 14f+: 0-0
Track: LH: 0-5 RH: 0-2 Tight: 0-6 Gall: 0-0
Aids: Bl: 0-1 Vi: 0-0 Tstrap: 0-0 Ckp: 0-0
Best Rating: 73 4/09 Ripn 1m4f10y gd-fm

Regardless

93(85) (61)65
2-y-o ch f Reset (AUS)-Princess Of Garda (Komaite (USA))
Mrs G S Rees TBN Racing

Placings:0334220 (5658)
2009: 5^{0}GF, 5^{3}GF, 5^{3}SD, 6^{4}GF, 6^{2}GS, 6^{2}GF, 6^{0}GS,

	Starts	1st	2nd	3rd	Win & Pl
Career Total (Turf)	6	0	2	1	3438
Career Total (AW)	1	0	0	1	403

Going (Turf): Sf: 0-0 GS: 0-2 Gd: 0-0 GF: 0-4 Fm: 0-0
Distance: 5f/6f: 0-6 7f-8f: 0-1 9f-13f: 0-0 14f+: 0-0
Track: LH: 0-1 RH: 0-0 Tight: 0-1 Gall: 0-0
Aids: Bl: 0-0 Vi: 0-3 Tstrap: 0-0 Ckp: 0-0
Best Rating: 65 8/09 Hayd 6f gd-fm

Modest; stays 6f; acts on fast and easy ground and on Fibresand.

Regency Art (IRE)

88 72
2-y-o b c Titus Livius (FR)-Honey Storm (IRE) (Mujadil (USA))
D R C Elsworth Matthew Green

Placings:01 (6542)
2009: 5^{0}GS, 6^{1}GF,

	Starts	1st	2nd	3rd	Win & Pl
Career Total (Turf)	2	1	0	0	4209

72	10/09	Wwck	6f	G-F	£4209

Total win prize-money £4209

Going (Turf): Sf: 0-0 GS: 0-1 Gd: 0-0 **GF: 1-1** Fm: 0-0
Distance: 5f/6f: 1-2 7f-8f: 0-0 9f-13f: 0-0 14f+: 0-0
Track: LH: 1-1 RH: 0-0 Tight: 0-0 Gall: 0-0
Aids: Bl: 0-0 Vi: 0-0 Tstrap: 0-0 Ckp: 0-0
Best Rating: 72 10/09 Wwck 6f gd-fm

Fair; stays 6f; acts on fast ground.

Regeneration (IRE)

99(103) (80)77
3-y-o b g Chevalier (IRE)-Cappuchino (IRE) (Roi Danzig (USA))
M L W Bell (S A Callaghan 25/9) Tamdown Group Limited

Placings:6-41212160 (7189)
2009: 6^{4}S, 6^{1}SD, 7^{2}SD, 7^{1}SD, 7^{2}GF, 7^{1}SD, 8^{6}G, 7^{0}G,

	Starts	1st	2nd	3rd	Win & Pl
Career Total (Turf)	5	0	1	0	1065
Career Total (AW)	4	3	1	0	10614

80	9/09	Wolv	7f32y	(0-75)H	STD	£4209
72	8/09	Ling	7f	(0-70)H	STD	£3070
58	7/09	Ling	6f		STD	£2729

Total win prize-money £10010

Going (Turf): Sf: 0-1 GS: 0-1 Gd: 0-2 GF: 0-1 Fm: 0-0
Distance: 5f/6f: 1-1 **7f-8f: 2-8** 9f-13f: 0-0 14f+: 0-0
Track: LH: 3-4 RH: 0-0 **Tight: 3-3** Gall: 0-0
Aids: Bl: 0-0 Vi: 0-0 Tstrap: 0-0 Ckp: 0-0
Best Rating: 80 9/09 Wolv 7f32y stand

Fair; effective at 6-7f; acts on soft ground and Fibresand but well suited by Polytrack.

Regent's Secret (USA)

99 (85)67
9-y-o br g Cryptoclearance (USA)-Misty Regent (CAN) (Vice Regent (CAN))
J S Goldie Mrs M Craig

Placings:2263222/3030300040/4002403306033**153**/04440 11202122400**5**/050312660**2534**/000310020055/66006433 5-6443240 (5947)
2009: 12^{6}G, 9^{4}GF, 11^{4}GF, 9^{3}G, 12^{2}G, 12^{4}S, 12^{0}G,

	Starts	1st	2nd	3rd	Win & Pl
Career Total (Turf)	85	5	13	13	80290
Career Total (AW)	7	1	1	2	6097

82	6/07	Carl	7f200y	(0-70)H	G-S	£2817
86	6/06	Carl	7f200y	(0-80)H	GD	£19431
85	8/05	Haml	1m1f36y	(0-85)H	G-F	£7888
74	7/05	Haml	1m1f36y	(0-75)H	G-F	£4218
66	6/05	Haml	1m1f36y	(0-75)H	G-F	£4472
69	10/04	Wolv	1m1f103y	(0-62)H	STD	£3022

Total win prize-money £41850

Going (Turf): Sf: 0-5 GS: 1-14 Gd: 1-26 **GF: 3-38** Fm: 0-2
Distance: 5f/6f: 0-5 7f-8f: 2-25 **9f-13f: 4-62** 14f+: 0-0
Track: LH: 1-28 **RH: 5-54 Tight: 4-55** Gall: 0-6
Aids: Bl: 0-0 Vi: 0-2 Tstrap: 1-23 Ckp: 1-23
Best Rating: 88 7/06 Carl 7f200y gd-fm

Fair; stays 1m1f; acts on a sound surface and Polytrack; has worn cheekpieces; goes well at courses with stiff uphill finishes.

Reggane

107 115
3-y-o b f Red Ransom (USA)-Reine Zao (FR) (Alzao (USA))
A De Royer-Dupre Haras De La Perelle

Placings:12266 (6505a)
2009: 8^{1}G, 8^{2}G, 8^{2}GF, 8^{6}S, 8^{6}GS,

	Starts	1st	2nd	3rd	Win & Pl
Career Total (Turf)	5	1	2	0	98059

86	5/09	Chan	1m	GD	£11650

Total win prize-money £11650

Going (Turf): Sf: 0-1 GS: 0-1 **Gd: 1-2** GF: 0-1 Fm: 0-0
Distance: 5f/6f: 0-0 **7f-8f: 1-5** 9f-13f: 0-0 14f+: 0-0
Track: LH: 0-0 **RH: 1-4** Tight: 0-0 Gall: 0-1
Aids: Bl: 0-0 Vi: 0-0 Tstrap: 0-0 Ckp: 0-0
Best Rating: 115 6/09 Asct 1m gd-fm

Group-class French-trained filly; Group 1 placed; stays 1m; acts on good/fast ground; has worn a tongue tie.

Regional Counsel

96(110) (88)64
5-y-o b g Medicean-Regency Rose (Danehill (USA))
A M Hales A S Helaissi

Placings:2115/00000/**456**-6006 (5780)
2009: 10^{6}GF, 10^{0}G, 8^{0}GF, 8^{6}SD,

	Starts	1st	2nd	3rd	Win & Pl
Career Total (Turf)	11	2	1	0	47010
Career Total (AW)	5	0	0	0	1097

100	7/06	Curr	6f63y	G-F	£33672
83	6/06	Limk	7f	G-F	£8979

Total win prize-money £42651

Going (Turf): Sf: 0-1 GS: 0-0 Gd: 0-3 **GF: 2-7** Fm: 0-0
Distance: 5f/6f: 0-2 **7f-8f: 2-8** 9f-13f: 0-6 14f+: 0-0
Track: LH: 0-5 RH: 0-4 Tight: 0-3 Gall: 0-0
Aids: Bl: 0-3 Vi: 0-0 Tstrap: 0-0 Ckp: 0-0
Best Rating: 100 7/06 Curr 6f63y gd-fm

Useful; seems to stay 1m2f; acts on fast ground and on Polytrack.

Registrar

97(94) (60)68
7-y-o ch g Machiavellian (USA)-Confidante (USA) (Dayjur (USA))
Mrs C A Dunnett The Smart Syndicate

Placings:520/222310/**0**0430**4**00310/000310160050-

060201030 (6925)
2009: 7^{0}G, 7^{6}GF, 8^{0}G, 7^{2}GF, 6^{0}GS, 7^{1}G, 7^{0}GF, 7^{3}GF, 7^{0}GF,

	Starts	1st	2nd	3rd	Win & Pl
Career Total (Turf)	**36**	**5**	**5**	**5**	**25934**
Career Total (AW)	**6**	**0**	**0**	**0**	**0**

61 8/09 Yarm 7f3y (0-75)H GD £2590
68 7/08 Yarm 7f3y (0-80)H G-F £4667
60 7/08 Yarm 7f3y (0-75)H G-F £2719
58 11/07 Nott 5f13y (0-55)H G-F £2047
66 9/05 Ling 7f G-S £3916
Total win prize-money £15942

Going (Turf): Sf: 0-4 GS: 1-5 Gd: 1-9 **GF: 3-18** Fm: 0-0
Distance: 5f/6f: 1-11 **7f-8f: 4-26** 9f-13f: 0-5 14f+: 0-0
Track : LH: 0 7 RH: 0-6 Tight: 0-6 Gall: 0-1
Aids: Bl: 0-0 Vi: 0-0 Tstrap: 3-18 Ckp: 3-18
Best Rating: **78** 5/05 Sand 7f16y good

Modest; stays 7f; acts on fast ground; has worn cheek-pieces.

Rehabilitation

98(104) (76)**67**
4-y-o ch g Dr Fong (USA)-Lamees (USA) (Lomond (USA))
W R Swinburn Mrs Sue French

Placings:100060334-004400 (7212)
2009: 10^{0}G, 10^{0}GF, 10^{4}GS, 10^{4}F, 10^{0}GF, 12^{0}SD,

	Starts	1st	2nd	3rd	Win & Pl
Career Total (Turf)	**9**	**0**	**0**	**1**	**302**
Career Total (AW)	**6**	**1**	**0**	**1**	**2625**

72 4/08 Wolv 7f32y STD £2047
Total win prize-money £2047

Going (Turf): **Sf: 0-0 GS: 0-1 Gd: 0-3 GF: 0-4 Fm: 0-1**
Distance: 5f/6f: 0-0 **7f-8f: 1-4** 9f-13f: 0-11 14f+: 0-0
Track : **LH: 1-8** RH: 0-6 **Tight: 1-8** Gall: 0-2
Aids: Bl: 0-0 Vi: 0-2 Tstrap: 0-9 Ckp: 0-9
Best Rating: **76** 11/08 Kemp 1m2f stand

Modest; effective over 7f; acts on Polytrack; has worn cheekpieces.

Reignier

101 **98**
2-y-o b c Kheleyf (USA)-Komena (Komaite (USA))
A P Jarvis (K R Burke 28/7) Philip Richards

Placings:512246 (4407)
2009: 5^{5}GS, 5^{1}GF, 5^{2}G, 5^{2}GF, 6^{4}G, 5^{6}G,

	Starts	1st	2nd	3rd	Win & Pl
Career Total (Turf)	**6**	**1**	**2**	**0**	**33025**

80 5/09 Muss 5f G-F £3885
Total win prize-money £3886

Going (Turf): Sf: 0-0 GS: 0-1 Gd: 0-3 **GF: 1-2** Fm: 0-0
Distance: **5f/6f: 1-6** 7f-8f: 0-0 9f-13f: 0-0 14f+: 0-0
Track : LH: 0-0 RH: 0-0 Tight: 0-0 Gall: 0-0
Aids: Bl: 0-0 Vi: 0-0 Tstrap: 0-0 Ckp: 0-0
Best Rating: **98** 6/09 Asct 5f gd-fm

Very useful; Group 2 placed; effective over 5-6f; acts on good/fast ground.

Reigning In Rio (IRE)

(95) (51)**44**
3-y-o br f Captain Rio-Saibhreas (IRE) (Last Tycoon)
P T Midgley (P C Haslam 23/4) Mrs Alurie O'Sullivan

Placings:500-103 (1481)
2009: 8^{1}SD, 8^{0}SD, 8^{3}SD,

	Starts	1st	2nd	3rd	Win & Pl
Career Total (Turf)	**2**	**0**	**0**	**0**	**0**
Career Total (AW)	**4**	**1**	**0**	**1**	**2350**

51 2/09 Sthl 1m (0-55)H STD £2047
Total win prize-money £2047

Going (Turf): **Sf: 0-0 GS: 0-0 Gd: 0-1 GF: 0-1 Fm: 0-0**
Distance: 5f/6f: 0-1 **7f-8f: 1-5** 9f-13f: 0-0 14f+: 0-0
Track : **LH: 1-4** RH: 0-0 Tight: 0-0 Gall: 0-0
Aids: Bl: 0-0 Vi: 0-0 Tstrap: 0-0 Ckp: 0-0
Best Rating: **51** 2/09 Sthl 1m stand

Very moderate; stays 1m and acts on Fibresand.

Reigning Monarch (USA)

95(104) (56)**53**
6-y-o b g Fusaichi Pegasus (USA)-Torros Straits (USA) (Boundary (USA))
Miss Z C Davison Andy Irvine

Placings:0/0044100/**3166200400243666-0300305344** (7703)
2009: 6^{0}SD, 6^{3}SD, 6^{0}GF, 7^{0}GF, 5^{3}S, 6^{0}S, 5^{5}GF, 6^{3}SD, 6^{4}SD, 6^{4}SD,

	Starts	1st	2nd	3rd	Win & Pl
Career Total (Turf)	**19**	**1**	**1**	**1**	**3816**
Career Total (AW)	**15**	**1**	**1**	**4**	**3881**

60 1/08 Kemp 6f (0-55) STD £2047
61 8/07 Ling 6f (0-65)H G-F £2047
Total win prize-money £4096

Going (Turf): Sf: 0-4 GS: 0-2 Gd: 0-4 **GF: 1-8** Fm: 0-0
Distance: **5f/6f: 2-26** 7f-8f: 0-7 9f-13f: 0-1 14f+: 0-0
Track : LH: 0-2 **RH: 1-12** Tight: 0-0 Gall: 0-2
Aids: Bl: 0-4 Vi: 0-0 Tstrap: 0-4 Ckp: 0-4
Best Rating: **64** 1/08 Kemp 6f stand

Moderate; effective over 5f-1m; handles fast ground; also goes on Polytrack.

Reject

99 **78**
3-y-o b g Green Desert (USA)-Wardat Allayl (IRE) (Mtoto)
W J Haggas B Haggas

Placings:621406240 (6798)
2009: 6^{6}F, 6^{2}GF, 6^{1}GF, 7^{4}GF, 6^{0}GF, 7^{6}GF, 6^{2}GS, 6^{4}G, 6^{0}S,

	Starts	1st	2nd	3rd	Win & Pl
Career Total (Turf)	**9**	**1**	**2**	**0**	**5345**

78 5/09 Haml 6f5y G-F £2729
Total win prize-money £2730

Going (Turf): Sf: 0-1 GS: 0-1 Gd: 0-1 **GF: 1-5** Fm: 0-1
Distance: 5f/6f: 0-5 **7f-8f: 1-4** 9f-13f: 0-0 14f+: 0-0
Track : LH: 0-1 RH: 0-0 Tight: 0-0 Gall: 0-0
Aids: Bl: 0-0 Vi: 0-0 Tstrap: 0-0 Ckp: 0-0
Best Rating: **78** 5/09 Haml 6f5y gd-fm

Fair; effective over 6f; acts on most ground.

Relative Strength (IRE)

107(100) (82)**84**
4-y-o ch g Kris Kin (USA)-Monalee Lass (IRE) (Mujtahid (USA))
A M Balding D H Caslon

Placings:1/143-03320635 (6273)
2009: 11^{0}GS, 12^{3}GF, 14^{3}G, 12^{2}G, 21^{0}G, 16^{6}SD, 15^{3}GF, 16^{5}GF,

	Starts	1st	2nd	3rd	Win & Pl
Career Total (Turf)	**8**	**0**	**1**	**4**	**6736**
Career Total (AW)	**4**	**2**	**0**	**0**	**6570**

78 4/08 Kemp 1m3f (0-80)H STD £4209
70 12/07 Kemp 1m2f STD £2047
Total win prize-money £6257

Going (Turf): **Sf: 0-0 GS: 0-1 Gd: 0-4 GF: 0-3 Fm: 0-0**
Distance: 5f/6f: 0-0 7f-8f: 0-0 **9f-13f: 2-7** 14f+: 0-5
Track : LH: 0-2 **RH: 2-9** Tight: 0-5 Gall: 0-3
Aids: Bl: 0-0 Vi: 0-7 Tstrap: 0-0 Ckp: 0-0
Best Rating: **84** 7/09 Asct 1m4f good

Fair; stays 1m4f; acts on good ground and Polytrack; has worn a visor.

Remark (IRE)

85(94) (54)**31**
5-y-o b g Machiavellian (USA)-Remuria (USA) (Theatrical)
M W Easterby S A Hollings

Placings:4550/0000/060 (7500)
2009: 11^{0}C, 8^{6}SD, 8^{0}SD,

	Starts	1st	2nd	3rd	Win & Pl
Career Total (Turf)	**8**	**0**	**0**	**0**	**3424**
Career Total (AW)	**3**	**0**	**0**	**0**	**0**

Going (Turf): **Sf: 0-1 GS: 0-3 Gd: 0-2 GF: 0-1 Fm: 0-0**
Distance: 5f/6f: 0-3 7f-8f: 0-2 9f-13f: 0-6 14f+: 0-0
Track : LH: 0-4 RH: 0-4 Tight: 0-3 Gall: 0-1
Aids: Bl: 0-0 Vi: 0-0 Tstrap: 0-0 Ckp: 0-0
Best Rating: **71** 8/06 Deau 1m v soft

Remember Dougie (IRE)

68
2-y-o b f Namid-Proud Myth (IRE) (Mark Of Esteem (IRE))
A Berry Mr and Mrs Calderbank

Placings:000 (5977)
2009: 5^{0}GF, 5^{0}S, 5^{0}GF,

	Starts	1st	2nd	3rd	Win & Pl
Career Total (Turf)	**3**	**0**	**0**	**0**	

Going (Turf): **Sf: 0-1 GS: 0-0 Gd: 0-0 GF: 0-2 Fm: 0-0**
Distance: 5f/6f: 0-3 7f-8f: 0-0 9f-13f: 0-0 14f+: 0-0
Track : LH: 0-0 RH: 0-0 Tight: 0-0 Gall: 0-0
Aids: Bl: 0-0 Vi: 0-0 Tstrap: 0-0 Ckp: 0-0

Remember Ramon (USA)

107(109) (86)**88**
6-y-o ch g Diesis-Future Act (USA) (Known Fact (USA))
J R Gask Horses First Racing Limited

Placings:03/11654/**055156-414100** (6258)
2009: 12^{4}SD, 13^{1}SD, 12^{4}SD, 12^{1}GS, 12^{0}GS, 13^{0}SD,

	Starts	1st	2nd	3rd	Win & Pl
Career Total (Turf)	**8**	**3**	**0**	**0**	**19920**
Career Total (AW)	**11**	**2**	**0**	**1**	**7293**

88 7/09 NmkJ 1m4f (0-90)H G-S £9066
85 2/09 Wolv 1m5f194y (0-85)H STD £2590
80 11/08 Wolv 1m4f50y (0-75)H STD £3238
95 5/06 Wind 1m3f135y (0-85)H G-S £5505
71 4/06 Muss 1m4f G-F £3886
Total win prize-money £24285

Going (Turf): Sf: 0-0 **GS: 2-4** Gd: 0-1 GF: 1-3 Fm: 0-0
Distance: 5f/6f: 0-1 7f-8f: 0-1 **9f-13f: 4-14** 14f+: 1-3
Track : LH: 2-8 RH: 2-9 **Tight: 4-8** Gall: 1-5

Aids: Bl: 0-0 Vi: 0-0 Tstrap: 0-0 Ckp: 0-0
Best Rating: **95** 5/06 Wind 1m3f135y gd-sft

Useful; stays 1m6f; acts on fast and easy ground; goes on Polytrack.

Reminiscent (IRE)

(100) (50)**48**
10-y-o b g Kahyasi-Eliza Orzeszkowa (IRE) (Polish Patriot (USA))
B P J Baugh Miss S M Potts

Placings:0/50060326222314/200503453522/424500/1302 04060/50140600/213000400/6644404-0545 **(0735)**
2009: 16^{0}SS, 14^{5}SD, 11^{4}SD, 13^{5}SD,

	Starts	1st	2nd	3rd	Win & Pl
Career Total (Turf)	22	1	2	2	7629
Career Total (AW)	48	3	8	4	17071

59	1/07	Wolv	1m5f194y (0-65)H	STD	£2047
59	3/06	Wolv	1m5f194y (0-70)H	STD	£2810
49	7/05	Leic	1m3f183y	G-F	£4143
77	12/02	Wolv	1m6f166yF(0-65)H	STD	£3045

Total win prize-money £12048

Going (Turf): Sf: 0-1 GS: 0-0 Gd: 0-4 **GF: 1-16** Fm: 0-1
Distance: 5f/6f: 0-0 7f-8f: 0-1 9f-13f: 1-27 **14f+: 3-42**
Track : **LH: 3-61** RH: 1-8 **Tight: 3-44** Gall: 0-4
Aids: Bl: 0-5 Vi: 2-39 Tstrap: 2-17 Ckp: 2-17
Best Rating: **77** 2/03 Sthl 1m6f slow

Moderate; stays 2m, but effective at shorter; acts on fast ground and Polytrack; has worn blinkers and cheekpieces.

Rendezvous (IRE)

101 **90**
3-y-o b c Sadler's Wells (USA)-Gwynn (IRE) (Darshaan)
Sir Michael Stoute Mrs J Magnier, M Tabor & D Smith

Placings:12-400 **(6816)**
2009: 9^{4}GF, 10^{0}G, 12^{0}G,

	Starts	1st	2nd	3rd	Win & Pl
Career Total (Turf)	5	1	1	0	8654

89	10/08	Chan	1m	SFT	£8088

Total win prize-money £8088

Going (Turf): **Sf: 1-1** GS: 0-1 Gd: 0-2 GF: 0-1 Fm: 0-0
Distance: 5f/6f: 0-0 **7f-8f: 1-1** 9f-13f: 0-4 14f+: 0-0
Track : LH: 0-0 **RH: 1-5** Tight: 0-0 Gall: 0-2
Aids: Bl: 0-0 Vi: 0-1 Tstrap: 0-0 Ckp: 0-0
Best Rating: **90** 10/08 Lonc 1m1f gd-sft

Very useful; ex-French; stays 1m1f and acts on soft ground.

Renege The Joker

70(84) (35)
6-y-o b g Alflora (IRE)-Bunty (Presidium)
S Regan Sean Regan

Placings:000-00 **(5483)**
2009: 16^{0}G, 14^{0}GF,

	Starts	1st	2nd	3rd	Win & Pl
Career Total (Turf)	3	0	0	0	
Career Total (AW)	2	0	0	0	

Going (Turf): **Sf: 0-0 GS: 0-0 Gd: 0-1 GF: 0-2 Fm: 0-0**
Distance: 5f/6f: 0-0 7f-8f: 0-0 9f-13f: 0-3 14f+: 0-2
Track : LH: 0-5 RH: 0-0 Tight: 0-5 Gall: 0-0
Aids: Bl: 0-0 Vi: 0-0 Tstrap: 0-0 Ckp: 0-0
Best Rating: **35** 1/08 Ling 1m4f stand

Repealed

(95) (68)**65**
3-y-o b c Reset (AUS)-Great Verdict (AUS) (Christmas Tree (AUS))
H Morrison Mrs B Oppenheimer

Placings:5-2 **(1440)**
2009: 11^{2}SD,

	Starts	1st	2nd	3rd	Win & Pl
Career Total (Turf)	1	0	0	0	129
Career Total (AW)	1	0	1	0	605

Going (Turf): **Sf: 0-0 GS: 0-0 Gd: 0-1 GF: 0-0 Fm: 0-0**
Distance: 5f/6f: 0-0 7f-8f: 0-1 9f-13f: 0-1 14f+: 0-0
Track : LH: 0-2 RH: 0-0 Tight: 0-0 Gall: 0-0
Aids: Bl: 0-0 Vi: 0-0 Tstrap: 0-0 Ckp: 0-0
Best Rating: **68** 4/09 Sthl 1m3f stand

Repetischa (IRE)

92(96) (68)**71**
3-y-o ch f Peintre Celebre (USA)-Brief Escapade (IRE) (Brief Truce (USA))
E J O'Neill (E A L Dunlop 8/8) Ballygallon Stud Limited

Placings:63300 **(6753a)**
2009: 8^{6}GF, 9^{3}GF, 8^{3}SD, 8^{0}G, 11^{0}G,

	Starts	1st	2nd	3rd	Win & Pl
Career Total (Turf)	4	0	0	1	482
Career Total (AW)	1	0	0	1	722

Going (Turf): **Sf: 0-0 GS: 0-0 Gd: 0-2 GF: 0-2 Fm: 0-0**
Distance: 5f/6f: 0-0 7f-8f: 0-3 9f-13f: 0-2 14f+: 0-0
Track : LH: 0-0 RH: 0-2 Tight: 0-1 Gall: 0-0
Aids: Bl: 0-0 Vi: 0-0 Tstrap: 0-0 Ckp: 0-0
Best Rating: **71** 5/09 Gdwd 1m1f192y gd-fm

Fair; stays 1m2f; acts on fast ground and on Polytrack.

Replicator

79(99) (73)**65**
4-y-o b g Mujahid (USA)-Valldemosa (Music Boy)
Pat Eddery Pat Eddery Racing (Cadeaux Genereux)

Placings:04655241/0346563-40005F **(2686)**
2009: 6^{4}SS, 6^{0}SD, 5^{0}SD, 5^{0}SD, 6^{5}F, 7^{F}SD,

	Starts	1st	2nd	3rd	Win & Pl
Career Total (Turf)	6	1	0	0	2267
Career Total (AW)	15	0	1	2	2834

71	10/07	Brig	5f213y	G-S	£2266

Total win prize-money £2267

Going (Turf): Sf: 0-1 **GS: 1-1** Gd: 0-1 GF: 0-2 Fm: 0-1
Distance: **5f/6f: 1-19** 7f-8f: 0-2 9f-13f: 0-0 14f+: 0-0
Track : **LH: 1-10** RH: 0-5 Tight: 0-5 Gall: 0-3
Aids: Bl: 0-1 Vi: 0-4 Tstrap: 0-0 Ckp: 0-0
Best Rating: **73** 5/08 GrLe 5f stand

Fair; effective over 6f-7f; handles most ground, including Polytrack.

Reportage (USA)

97 **73**
3-y-o b g Elusive Quality (USA)-Journalist (IRE) (Night Shift (USA))
Robert Alan Hennessy (J H M Gosden 26/7) Mrs S Hennessy

Placings:63020 **(5538a)**
2009: 8^{6}S, 8^{3}G, 10^{0}G, 8^{2}G, 8^{0}HY,

	Starts	1st	2nd	3rd	Win & Pl
Career Total (Turf)	5	0	1	1	1320

Going (Turf): **Sf: 0-2 GS: 0-0 Gd: 0-3 GF: 0-0 Fm: 0-0**
Distance: 5f/6f: 0-0 7f-8f: 0-1 9f-13f: 0-4 14f+: 0-0
Track : LH: 0-1 RH: 0-2 Tight: 0-0 Gall: 0-1
Aids: Bl: 0-0 Vi: 0-0 Tstrap: 0-0 Ckp: 0-0
Best Rating: **73** 7/09 Pont 1m4y good

Fair; effective over 1m; acts on good ground.

Reprieved

(88) (58)**11**
4-y-o ch g Bertolini (USA)-Crystal Seas (Zamindar (USA))
Miss J A Camacho K H Benson & Kate Barrett

Placings:64306004-50 **(0972)**
2009: 11^{5}SD, 13^{0}SD,

	Starts	1st	2nd	3rd	Win & Pl
Career Total (Turf)	2	0	0	0	
Career Total (AW)	8	0	0	1	734

Going (Turf): **Sf: 0-0 GS: 0-0 Gd: 0-0 GF: 0-2 Fm: 0-0**
Distance: 5f/6f: 0-0 7f-8f: 0-4 9f-13f: 0-5 14f+: 0-1
Track : LH: 0-8 RH: 0-0 Tight: 0-1 Gall: 0-0
Aids: Bl: 0-0 Vi: 0-0 Tstrap: 0-0 Ckp: 0-0
Best Rating: **58** 5/08 Sthl 1m3f stand

Requisite

106(102) (73)**86**
4-y-o ch f Pivotal-Chicarica (USA) (The Minstrel (CAN))
I A Wood Paddy Barrett

Placings:52/113416220406660-503105320400000 **(7337)**
2009: 6^{5}SD, 5^{0}SD, 6^{3}S, 5^{1}GS, 5^{0}GF, 5^{5}GF, 5^{3}G, 5^{2}S, 5^{0}G, 5^{4}GS, 5^{0}GF, 5^{0}G, 6^{0}SD, 6^{0}SD, 6^{0}SD,

	Starts	1st	2nd	3rd	Win & Pl
Career Total (Turf)	20	2	3	3	16940
Career Total (AW)	12	2	1	0	3381

79	6/09	Ripn	5f	(0-75)H	G-S	£3238
82	6/08	Sand	5f6y	(0-75)H	GD	£4533
71	1/08	Ling	6f		STD	£2331

Total win prize-money £10103

Going (Turf): Sf: 0-3 **GS: 1-3 Gd: 1-8** GF: 0-6 Fm: 0-0
Distance: **5f/6f: 4-30** 7f-8f: 0-2 9f-13f: 0-0 14f+: 0-0
Track : **LH: 2-15** RH: 0-2 **Tight: 2-11** Gall: 0-3
Aids: Bl: 0-0 **Vi: 1-11** Tstrap: 0-0 Ckp: 0-0
Best Rating: **86** 7/08 Sand 5f6y gd-fm

Fair; effective over 5-6f; acts on good and easy ground and on Polytrack; has worn a visor.

Rescent

89(87) (54)**55**
2-y-o ch f Reset (AUS)-Bukhoor (IRE) (Danehill (USA))
Mrs R A Carr (Rae Guest 28/8) Ruth Carr Racing 2

Placings:2416000 **(7791)**
2009: 6^{2}G, 6^{4}SD, 7^{1}GF, 8^{6}GF, 7^{0}S, 8^{0}SD, 7^{0}SS,

	Starts	1st	2nd	3rd	Win & Pl
Career Total (Turf)	4	1	1	0	2780
Career Total (AW)	3	0	0	0	0

55	8/09	Newc	7f	G-F	£2201

Total win prize-money £2202

Going (Turf): Sf: 0-1 GS: 0-0 Gd: 0-1 **GF: 1-2** Fm: 0-0
Distance: 5f/6f: 0-1 **7f-8f: 1-5** 9f-13f: 0-1 14f+: 0-0
Track : LH: 0-5 RH: 0-0 Tight: 0-1 Gall: 0-0
Aids: Bl: 0-0 Vi: 0-0 Tstrap: 0-0 Ckp: 0-0

Best Rating: 55 8/09 Newc 7f gd-fm

Modest; stays 7f; acts on good and fast ground; handles Polytrack.

Resentful Angel

98(104) (74)**68**

4-y-o b f Danehill Dancer (IRE)-Leaping Flame (USA) (Trempolino (USA))

Pat Eddery P J J Eddery, Mrs John Magnier, M Tabor

Placings:0526-02433501312 (7699)

2009: 8^{0}F, 7^{2}GF, 8^{4}G, 7^{3}SD, 7^{3}GS, 10^{5}SD, 12^{0}GS, 10^{1}SD, 10^{3}SD, 9^{1}SD, 10^{2}SD,

	Starts	1st	2nd	3rd	Win & Pl
Career Total (Turf)	5	0	1	1	1266
Career Total (AW)	10	2	2	2	6632

74 12/09 Wolv 1m1f103y (0-65)H STD £2072

68 11/09 Ling 1m2f (0-65)H STD £2388

Total win prize-money £4460

Going (Turf): Sf: 0-0 GS: 0-2 Gd: 0-1 GF: 0-1 Fm: 0-1

Distance: 5f/6f: 0-0 7f-8f: 0-5 **9f-13f: 2-10** 14f+: 0-0

Track : **LH: 2-11** RH: 0-3 **Tight: 2-8** Gall: 0-1

Aids: Bl: 0-2 Vi: 0-0 Tstrap: 0-0 Ckp: 0-0

Best Rating: 74 12/09 Wolv 1m1f103y stand

Modest; stays 1m2f; acts on Polytrack.

Reset City

102 **67**

3-y-o ch f Reset (AUS)-City Of Angels (Woodman (USA))

A B Haynes R S Brookhouse

Placings:6250 (6698)

2009: 9^{6}GF, 11^{2}G, 11^{5}G, 12^{0}GS,

	Starts	1st	2nd	3rd	Win & Pl
Career Total (Turf)	4	0	1	0	1002

Going (Turf): Sf: 0-0 GS: 0-1 Gd: 0-2 GF: 0-1 Fm: 0-0

Distance: 5f/6f: 0-0 7f-8f: 0-0 9f-13f: 0-4 14f+: 0-0

Track : LH: 0-2 RH: 0-2 Tight: 0-3 Gall: 0-0

Aids: Bl: 0-0 Vi: 0-0 Tstrap: 0-0 Ckp: 0-0

Best Rating: 67 7/09 Bath 1m3f144y good

Modest; improved on debut when runner-up over an extended 1m3f on good ground.

Residency (IRE)

89(99) (68)**67**

3-y-o b g Danetime (IRE)-Muckross Park (Nomination)

B Smart B Smart

Placings:00-6202054 (7815)

2009: 5^{6}GF, 5^{2}SD, 5^{0}GF, 5^{2}S, 5^{0}GS, 6^{5}SD, 5^{4}SD,

	Starts	1st	2nd	3rd	Win & Pl
Career Total (Turf)	5	0	1	0	705
Career Total (AW)	4	0	1	0	1411

Going (Turf): Sf: 0-1 GS: 0-1 Gd: 0-0 GF: 0-3 Fm: 0-0

Distance: 5f/6f: 0-9 7f-8f: 0-0 9f-13f: 0-0 14f+: 0-0

Track : LH: 0-3 RH: 0-1 Tight: 0-1 Gall: 0-0

Aids: Bl: 0-0 Vi: 0-1 Tstrap: 0-1 Ckp: 0-1

Best Rating: 68 7/09 Sthl 5f stand

Modest; best effort over 5f on Fibresand; has worn a visor.

Resolute Defender (IRE)

63 **49**

4-y-o b g Namid-Snowspin (Carwhite)

R Johnson Robert Johnson

Placings:000/0006-00 (4656)

2009: 7^{0}GS, 8^{0}GF,

	Starts	1st	2nd	3rd	Win & Pl
Career Total (Turf)	9	0	0	0	0

Going (Turf): Sf: 0-2 GS: 0-2 Gd: 0-3 GF: 0-2 Fm: 0-0

Distance: 5f/6f: 0-5 7f-8f: 0-3 9f-13f: 0-1 14f+: 0-0

Track : LH: 0-1 RH: 0-1 Tight: 0-1 Gall: 0-0

Aids: Bl: 0-1 Vi: 0-0 Tstrap: 0-0 Ckp: 0-0

Best Rating: 57 8/07 Rdcr 6f good

Resort

103 **94**

3-y-o b f Oasis Dream-Gay Gallanta (USA) (Woodman (USA))

Sir Michael Stoute Cheveley Park Stud

Placings:5-1003120 (6267)

2009: 7^{1}GF, 7^{0}GF, 7^{0}G, 8^{3}G, 8^{1}GF, 9^{2}GF, 8^{0}G,

	Starts	1st	2nd	3rd	Win & Pl
Career Total (Turf)	8	2	1	1	15027

91 8/09 Wind 1m67y (0-85)H G-F £5180

82 4/09 NmkR 7f G-F £5180

Total win prize-money £10362

Going (Turf): Sf: 0-0 GS: 0-0 Gd: 0-3 **GF: 2-5** Fm: 0-0

Distance: 5f/6f: 0-1 7f-8f: 1-5 9f-13f: 1-2 14f+: 0-0

Track : LH: 0-1 **RH: 1-3 Tight: 1-3** Gall: 0-1

Aids: Bl: 0-0 Vi: 0-0 Tstrap: 0-0 Ckp: 0-0

Best Rating: 94 9/09 Gdwd 1m1f gd-fm

Useful; stays 1m1f; acts on fast ground.

Resounding Glory (USA)

67 **80**

4-y-o b g Honour And Glory (USA)-Resounding Grace (USA) (Thunder Gulch (USA))

R A Fahey M Wynne

Placings:0310/4504330-0 (4532)

2009: 9^{0}S,

	Starts	1st	2nd	3rd	Win & Pl
Career Total (Turf)	12	1	0	3	7491

82 10/07 Newc 6f GD £4533

Total win prize-money £4534

Going (Turf): Sf: 0-4 GS: 0-1 **Gd: 1-5** GF: 0-1 Fm: 0-1

Distance: **5f/6f: 1-3** 7f-8f: 0-3 9f-13f: 0-6 14f+: 0-0

Track : LH: 0-7 RH: 0-2 Tight: 0-2 Gall: 0-1

Aids: Bl: 0-0 Vi: 0-0 Tstrap: 0-0 Ckp: 0-0

Best Rating: 82 10/07 Newc 6f good

Fair; effective at around 1m-1m2f; acts on easy ground; useful hurdler.

Respite

92(102) (79)**72**

3-y-o ch f Pivotal-Truce (Nashwan (USA))

H-A Pantall (W J Haggas 10/10) Mme C Guitton

Placings:2-1502600

2009: 7^{1}SD, 7^{5}GS, 8^{0}G, 7^{2}SD, 8^{6}SD, 7^{0}SD, 6^{0}SD,

	Starts	1st	2nd	3rd	Win & Pl
Career Total (Turf)	3	0	1	0	2891
Career Total (AW)	5	1	1	0	3997

67 4/09 Kemp 7f STD £2590

Total win prize-money £2590

Going (Turf): Sf: 0-0 GS: 0-1 Gd: 0-2 GF: 0-0 Fm: 0-0

Distance: 5f/6f: 0-1 **7f-8f: 1-6** 9f-13f: 0-1 14f+: 0-0

Track : LH: 0-1 **RH: 1-4** Tight: 0-2 Gall: 0-0

Aids: Bl: 0-0 Vi: 0-0 Tstrap: 0-0 Ckp: 0-0

Best Rating: 79 8/09 Kemp 7f stand

Fair; suited by 7f; acts on good ground and Polytrack.

Resplendent Ace (IRE)

(106) (79)**70**

5-y-o b g Trans Island-Persian Polly (Persian Bold)

P Howling Paul Howling

Placings:2/521300006020005/10231640016336060-0046120263135236 (7851)

2009: 12^{0}SD, 12^{0}SD, 12^{4}SD, 10^{6}SD, 12^{1}SD, 9^{2}SD, 10^{0}SD, 12^{2}SD, 9^{6}SD, 10^{3}SD, 12^{1}SD, 13^{3}SD, 10^{5}SD, 9^{2}SD, 16^{3}SD, 11^{6}SS,

	Starts	1st	2nd	3rd	Win & Pl
Career Total (Turf)	7	0	0	1	688
Career Total (AW)	42	6	7	6	23002

76 11/09 Sthl 1m4f (0-75)H STD £3238

66 7/09 Wolv 1m4f50y (0-60) STD £2729

79 7/08 Kemp 1m4f (0-70)H STD £2590

73 4/08 Kemp 1m3f (0-70)H STD £2590

72 1/08 Kemp 1m4f (0-65)H STD £2047

79 3/07 Kemp 1m STD £2047

Total win prize-money £15244

Going (Turf): Sf: 0-0 GS: 0-2 Gd: 0-2 GF: 0-3 Fm: 0-0

Distance: 5f/6f: 0-0 7f-8f: 1-7 **9f-13f: 5-41** 14f+: 0-1

Track : LH: 2-29 **RH: 4-19 Tight: 1-24** Gall: 0-5

Aids: Bl: 0-0 Vi: 0-0 Tstrap: 0-0 Ckp: 0-0

Best Rating: 79 9/08 Ling 1m4f stand

Fair; stays 1m4f; acts well on Polytrack and on Fibresand; goes well at Kempton.

Resplendent Alpha

100(108) (85)**79**

5-y-o ch g Best Of The Bests (IRE)-Sunley Scent (Wolfhound (USA))

P Howling The Oh So Sharp Racing Partnership

Placings:12412/63060004600226/455046440024160521 43-614402605004006024 (7828)

2009: 6^{6}SD, 6^{1}SD, 6^{4}SD, 6^{4}SD, 6^{0}SD, 6^{2}SD, 6^{6}GF, 6^{0}GS, 6^{5}GF, 6^{0}GF, 6^{0}GF, 6^{4}F, 7^{0}SD, 6^{0}GF, 5^{6}SD, 6^{0}SD, 6^{2}SD, 6^{4}SD,

	Starts	1st	2nd	3rd	Win & Pl
Career Total (Turf)	24	1	3	0	18163
Career Total (AW)	33	4	5	2	30523

84 2/09 Ling 6f (0-80)H STD £4857

85 11/08 Kemp 6f (0-75)H STD £2590

79 8/08 NmkJ 6f (0-90)H G-F £9066

96 10/06 Ling 6f STD £4533

78 8/06 Ling 5f STD £3886

Total win prize-money £24933

Going (Turf): Sf: 0-0 GS: 0-3 Gd: 0-4 **GF: 1-16** Fm: 0-1

Distance: **5f/6f: 5-49** 7f-8f: 0-8 9f-13f: 0-0 14f+: 0-0

Track : **LH: 3-22** RH: 1-10 **Tight: 3-17** Gall: 0-4

Aids: Bl: 0-3 Vi: 0-0 Tstrap: 0-0 Ckp: 0-0

Best Rating: 98 10/06 Ling 6f stand

Fair; effective at around 6f; acts on good ground; goes on sand; has worn blinkers.

Resplendent Light

105(90) (69)96

4-y-o b g Fantastic Light (USA)-Bright Halo (IRE) (Bigstone (IRE))

W R Muir Middleham Park Racing XLIX & Partners

Placings:0461/0311444-650432032 (6483)

2009: 12^{6}GF, 10^{5}GF, 12^{0}G, 11^{4}GF, 12^{3}G, 12^{2}G, 12^{0}GF, 12^{3}GF, 12^{2}GF,

	Starts	1st	2nd	3rd	Win & Pl
Career Total (Turf)	18	3	2	3	48411
Career Total (AW)	2	0	0	0	168

94 6/08 Sals 1m4f (0-95)H G-F £7477
87 6/08 Muss 1m4f (0-85)H G-F £15577
81 10/07 Pont 1m4y (0-75) GD £3886

Total win prize-money £26941

Going (Turf): Sf: 0-0 GS: 0-0 Gd: 1-7 **GF: 2-10** Fm: 0-0
Distance: 5f/6f: 0-0 7f-8f: 0-3 **9f-13f: 3-16** 14f+: 0-1
Track : LH: 1-9 **RH: 2-9 Tight: 2-6** Gall: 0-7
Aids: Bl: 0-0 Vi: 0-0 Tstrap: 0-0 Ckp: 0-0
Best Rating: 96 9/08 Bord 1m4f v soft

Useful; stays at least 1m4f; acts on good and faster ground.

Resplendent Nova

81(110) (90)74

7-y-o b g Pivotal-Santiburi Girl (Casteddu)

P Howling The Oh So Sharp Racing Partnership

Placings:6210402050310/362001222/2200023021010/003335034006120-3150000000344 (7876)

2009: 7^{3}SS, 7^{1}SD, 8^{5}SD, 7^{0}G, 7^{0}GS, 7^{0}GF, 7^{0}SD, 8^{0}SD, 7^{0}SD, 7^{0}SD, 7^{3}SD, 7^{4}SD, 7^{4}SD,

	Starts	1st	2nd	3rd	Win & Pl
Career Total (Turf)	25	2	3	1	11213
Career Total (AW)	38	5	8	8	45691

90 1/09 Kemp 7f (0-85)H STD £4857
87 11/08 Kemp 7f (0-90)H STD £7477
93 8/07 Kemp 7f (0-85)H STD £4728
82 7/07 Yarm 7f3y (0-75)H G-S £2914
82 10/06 Brig 6f209y (0-70)H G-S £3368
87 8/05 Ling 7f (0-85)H STD £5898
70 3/05 Ling 7f STD £3513

Total win prize-money £32757

Going (Turf): Sf: 0-3 **GS: 2-9** Gd: 0-6 GF: 0-6 Fm: 0-1
Distance: 5f/6f: 0-3 **7f-8f: 7-52** 9f-13f: 0-8 14f+: 0-0
Track : LH: 3-25 RH: 3-23 **Tight: 2-17** Gall: 0-5
Aids: Bl: 0-0 Vi: 0-1 Tstrap: 0-0 Ckp: 0-0
Best Rating: 93 8/07 Kemp 7f stand

Fair; best over 7f; acts on soft ground and on Polytrack; likes to race prominently.

Rest By The River

80 52

3-y-o ch f Reset (AUS)-Palace Green (IRE) (Rudimentary (USA))

A G Newcombe Eagle Bevan & Newcombe

Placings:00-00 (3281)

2009: 6^{0}GF, 6^{0}GF,

	Starts	1st	2nd	3rd	Win & Pl
Career Total (Turf)	4	0	0	0	

Going (Turf): Sf: 0-0 GS: 0-1 Gd: 0-1 GF: 0-2 Fm: 0-0

Distance: 5f/6f: 0-3 7f-8f: 0-1 9f-13f: 0-0 14f+: 0-0
Track : LH: 0-0 RH: 0-0 Tight: 0-0 Gall: 0-0
Aids: Bl: 0-0 Vi: 0-0 Tstrap: 0-0 Ckp: 0-0
Best Rating: 52 9/08 Newb 6f8y good

Restart (IRE)

(99) (50)58

8-y-o b g Revoque (IRE)-Stargard (Polish Precedent (USA))

Lucinda Featherstone J Roundtree

Placings:6030/001020/345204/035000045-60 (0190)

2009: 16^{6}SS, 16^{0}SD,

	Starts	1st	2nd	3rd	Win & Pl
Career Total (Turf)	17	1	2	1	7887
Career Total (AW)	10	0	0	2	734

62 8/04 Rdcr 1m6f19yF(0-55)H G-S £3848

Total win prize-money £3848

Going (Turf): Sf: 0-1 **GS: 1-3** Gd: 0-7 GF: 0-6 Fm: 0-0
Distance: 5f/6f: 0-1 7f-8f: 0-3 9f-13f: 0-2 **14f+: 1-21**
Track : **LH: 1-23** RH: 0-2 **Tight: 1-10** Gall: 0-5
Aids: Bl: 0-0 Vi: 0-0 Tstrap: 0-4 Ckp: 0-4
Best Rating: 67 5/05 York 2m4f soft

Moderate; stays 2m4f, effective at shorter; acts on soft ground; also goes on Fibresand.

Restless Genius (IRE)

100(108) (73)78

4-y-o b g Captain Rio-Mainmise (USA) (Septieme Ciel (USA))

B Ellison Koo's Racing Club

Placings:0/10004340-2661445402506 (7870)

2009: 6^{2}SD, 5^{6}GF, 5^{6}GF, 5^{1}SD, 6^{4}GF, 5^{4}G, 5^{5}GF, 7^{4}SD, 7^{0}SD, 5^{2}SD, 5^{5}SD, 5^{0}SD, 6^{6}SS,

	Starts	1st	2nd	3rd	Win & Pl
Career Total (Turf)	11	1	0	0	4237
Career Total (AW)	11	1	2	1	5852

73 5/09 Wolv 5f216y (0-65)H STD £2388
78 4/08 Brig 5f213y G-S £2914

Total win prize-money £5302

Going (Turf): Sf: 0-1 **GS: 1-2** Gd: 0-3 GF: 0-5 Fm: 0-0
Distance: **5f/6f: 2-15** 7f-8f: 0-7 9f-13f: 0-0 14f+: 0-0
Track : **LH: 2-8** RH: 0-5 **Tight: 1-3** Gall: 0-2
Aids: Bl: 0-0 Vi: 0-0 Tstrap: 0-0 Ckp: 0-0
Best Rating: 78 4/08 Brig 5f213y gd-sft

Modest; effective over 6f; acts on easy ground and sand; has worn a tongue-tie.

Restless Swallow

84 20

4-y-o gr g Bandmaster (USA)-Pink Petal (Northern Game)

R A Harris (M J Scudamore 13/8) The Yes No Wait Sorries

Placings:0/000 (5720)

2009: 10^{0}GF, 12^{0}G, 13^{0}G,

	Starts	1st	2nd	3rd	Win & Pl
Career Total (Turf)	4	0	0	0	

Going (Turf): Sf: 0-0 GS: 0-0 Gd: 0-2 GF: 0-2 Fm: 0-0
Distance: 5f/6f: 0-0 7f-8f: 0-1 9f-13f: 0-2 14f+: 0-1
Track : LH: 0-2 RH: 0-1 Tight: 0-2 Gall: 0-0
Aids: Bl: 0-0 Vi: 0-0 Tstrap: 0-0 Ckp: 0-0
Best Rating: 20 6/09 Chep 1m4f23y good

Restyle

72 23

2-y-o b f Reset (AUS)-Surrealist (ITY) (Night Shift (USA))

D K Ivory K T Ivory

Placings:00000 (5811)

2009: 5^{0}G, 6^{0}GF, 7^{0}G, 6^{0}GF, 7^{0}SD,

	Starts	1st	2nd	3rd	Win & Pl
Career Total (Turf)	4	0	0	0	
Career Total (AW)	1	0	0	0	

Going (Turf): Sf: 0-0 GS: 0-0 Gd: 0-2 GF: 0-2 Fm: 0-0
Distance: 5f/6f: 0-3 7f-8f: 0-2 9f-13f: 0-0 14f+: 0-0
Track : LH: 0-0 RH: 0-1 Tight: 0-0 Gall: 0-2
Aids: Bl: 0-0 Vi: 0-0 Tstrap: 0-3 Ckp: 0-3
Best Rating: 23 8/09 Yarm 7f3y good

Resurge (IRE)

106(99) (92)94

4-y-o b g Danehill Dancer (IRE)-Resurgence (Polar Falcon (USA))

W S Kittow Chris & David Stam

Placings:0/2102-00541250056 (7066)

2009: 8^{0}G, 8^{0}GF, 8^{5}G, 8^{4}GF, 10^{1}GF, 10^{2}G, 10^{5}G, 8^{0}GF, 9^{0}GF, 9^{5}S, 12^{6}SD,

	Starts	1st	2nd	3rd	Win & Pl
Career Total (Turf)	14	2	2	0	14038
Career Total (AW)	2	0	1	0	1542

94 6/09 Wind 1m2f7y (0-85)H G-F £5180
82 5/08 NmkR 1m FRM £5180

Total win prize-money £10362

Going (Turf): Sf: 0-1 GS: 0-0 Gd: 0-5 **GF: 1-7 Fm: 1-1**
Distance: 5f/6f: 0-0 7f-8f: 1-7 9f-13f: 1-9 14f+: 0-0
Track : LH: 0-2 **RH: 1-10 Tight: 1-5** Gall: 0-2
Aids: Bl: 0-0 Vi: 0-0 Tstrap: 0-0 Ckp: 0-0
Best Rating: 94 6/09 Wind 1m2f7y gd-fm

Useful; half-brother to Arafaa; stays 1m2f; handles fast ground.

Resuscitator (USA)

(93) (75)

2-y-o b c Bernstein (USA)-Lac Du Printemps (USA) (Meadowlake (USA))

Mrs H S Main Wetumpka Racing

Placings:24 (5807)

2009: 7^{2}SD, 7^{4}SD,

	Starts	1st	2nd	3rd	Win & Pl
Career Total (Turf)	0	0	0	0	
Career Total (AW)	2	0	1	0	1156

Going (Turf): Sf: 0-0 GS: 0-0 Gd: 0-0 GF: 0-0 Fm: 0-0
Distance: 5f/6f: 0-0 7f-8f: 0-2 9f-13f: 0-0 14f+: 0-0
Track : LH: 0-1 RH: 0-1 Tight: 0-1 Gall: 0-0
Aids: Bl: 0-0 Vi: 0-0 Tstrap: 0-0 Ckp: 0-0
Best Rating: 75 8/09 Ling 7f stand

Fair; stays 7f and acts on Polytrack.

Retrato (USA)

88 65

2-y-o b/br f Fusaichi Pegasus (USA)-Painted Lady (USA) (Broad Brush (USA))

Rae Guest Triple R Racing

Placings:3 (6593)
2009: 8^{3}GS,

	Starts	1st	2nd	3rd	Win & Pl
Career Total (Turf)	1	0	0	1	433

Going (Turf): **Sf: 0-0 GS: 0-1 Gd: 0-0 GF: 0-0 Fm: 0-0**
Distance: 5f/6f: 0-0 7f-8f: 0-0 9f-13f: 0-1 14f+: 0-0
Track : LH: 0-1 RH: 0-0 Tight: 0-0 Gall: 0-0
Aids: Bl: 0-0 Vi: 0-0 Tstrap: 0-0 Ckp: 0-0
Best Rating: **65** 10/09 Nott 1m75y gd-sft

Promise on debut over 1m on easy ground.

Retro (IRE)

87(97) (75)73
3-y-o b c Tagula (IRE)-Cabcharge Princess (IRE) (Rambo Dancer (CAN))
R Hannon Mrs J Wood

Placings:5430413-00000 (6904)
2009: 9^{0}G, 7^{0}GF, 6^{0}SD, 7^{0}SD, 6^{0}G,

	Starts	1st	2nd	3rd	Win & Pl
Career Total (Turf)	7	0	0	0	577
Career Total (AW)	5	1	0	2	3567

74 10/08 Ling 6f STD £2266
Total win prize-money £2267

Going (Turf): **Sf: 0-0 GS: 0-1 Gd: 0-3 GF: 0-3 Fm: 0-0**
Distance: **5f/6f: 1-9** 7f-8f: 0-2 9f-13f: 0-1 14f+: 0-0
Track : **LH: 1-2** RH: 0-4 **Tight: 1-2** Gall: 0-3
Aids: Bl: 0-0 Vi: 0-0 Tstrap: 0-0 Ckp: 0-0
Best Rating: **75** 9/08 Kemp 6f stand

Fair; effective over 6f; acts on Polytrack.

Rettorical Lad

(101) (59)48
4-y-o gr/ro g Vettori (IRE)-Reciprocal (IRE) (Night Shift (USA))
Jamie Poulton J Wotherspoon

Placings:0/000005-500 (0816)
2009: 13^{b}SD, 16^{0}SD, 12^{0}SD,

	Starts	1st	2nd	3rd	Win & Pl
Career Total (Turf)	4	0	0	0	
Career Total (AW)	6	0	0	0	0

Going (Turf): **Sf: 0-1 GS: 0-2 Gd: 0-0 GF: 0-1 Fm: 0-0**
Distance: 5f/6f: 0-0 7f-8f: 0-5 9f-13f: 0-4 14f+: 0-1
Track : LH: 0-5 RH: 0-3 Tight: 0-5 Gall: 0-0
Aids: Bl: 0-0 Vi: 0-0 Tstrap: 0-0 Ckp: 0-0
Best Rating: **59** 2/09 Ling 1m5f stand

Reve De Mardi

63(71) (22)27
2-y-o b g Cyrano De Bergerac-Dreams Forgotten (IRE) (Victory Note (USA))
George Baker Bob And Diana Whitney

Placings:00 (6727)
2009: 8^{0}SD, 8^{0}S,

	Starts	1st	2nd	3rd	Win & Pl
Career Total (Turf)	1	0	0	0	
Career Total (AW)	1	0	0	0	

Going (Turf): **Sf: 0-1 GS: 0-0 Gd: 0-0 GF: 0-0 Fm: 0-0**
Distance: 5f/6f: 0-0 7f-8f: 0-1 9f-13f: 0-1 14f+: 0-0
Track : LH: 0-1 RH: 0-0 Tight: 0-1 Gall: 0-0
Aids: Bl: 0-0 Vi: 0-0 Tstrap: 0-0 Ckp: 0-0
Best Rating: **27** 10/09 Sals 1m soft

Reve Vert (FR)

92(93) (56)49
4-y-o b c Oasis Dream-Comme D'Habitude (USA) (Caro)
Tim Vaughan C J Wheeler

Placings:000/045263026-000 (2746)
2009: 8^{0}GF, 8^{0}GF, 8^{0}SD,

	Starts	1st	2nd	3rd	Win & Pl
Career Total (Turf)	11	0	1	1	1565
Career Total (AW)	4	0	1	0	578

Going (Turf): **Sf: 0-2 GS: 0-2 Gd: 0-0 GF: 0-6 Fm: 0-1**
Distance: 5f/6f: 0-1 7f-8f: 0-9 9f-13f: 0-5 14f+: 0-0
Track : LH: 0-6 RH: 0-2 Tight: 0-1 Gall: 0-2
Aids: Bl: 0-0 Vi: 0-0 Tstrap: 0-0 Ckp: 0-0
Best Rating: **56** 9/08 GrLe 1m stand

Moderate; stays 1m; acts on easy ground.

Revelator (IRE)

98 74
2-y-o b c One Cool Cat (USA)-Capades Band (FR) (Chimes Band (USA))
A P Jarvis Cyril Wall

Placings:41 (7079)
2009: 6^{4}GF, 5^{1}S,

	Starts	1st	2nd	3rd	Win & Pl
Career Total (Turf)	2	1	0	0	2677

74 10/09 Catt 5f212y SFT £2388
Total win prize-money £2388

Going (Turf): **Sf: 1-1** GS: 0-0 Gd: 0-0 GF: 0-1 Fm: 0-0
Distance: **5f/6f: 1-2** 7f-8f: 0-0 9f-13f: 0-0 14f+: 0-0
Track : **LH: 1-1** RH: 0-0 **Tight: 1-1** Gall: 0-0
Aids: Bl: 0-0 Vi: 0-0 Tstrap: 0-0 Ckp: 0-0
Best Rating: **74** 10/09 Catt 5f212y soft

Fair; stays 6f; acts on soft.

Revered

96 79
2-y-o b f Oasis Dream-Arrive (Kahyasi)
Sir Michael Stoute K Abdulla

Placings:31 (7182)
2009: 6^{3}S, 7^{1}G,

	Starts	1st	2nd	3rd	Win & Pl
Career Total (Turf)	2	1	0	1	5290

79 10/09 NmkR 7f GD £4857
Total win prize-money £4857

Going (Turf): Sf: 0-1 GS: 0-0 **Gd: 1-1** GF: 0-0 Fm: 0-0
Distance: 5f/6f: 0-0 **7f-8f: 1-2** 9f-13f: 0-0 14f+: 0-0
Track : LH: 0-0 RH: 0-0 Tight: 0-0 Gall: 0-0
Aids: Bl: 0-0 Vi: 0-0 Tstrap: 0-0 Ckp: 0-0
Best Rating: **79** 10/09 NmkR 7f good

Fair; stays 7f; acts on good ground.

Reverence

112(104) (103)108
8-y-o ch g Mark Of Esteem (IRE)-Imperial Bailiwick (IRE) (Imperial Frontier (USA))
E J Alston Mr & Mrs G Middlebrook

Placings:210111/314105112/560/530105030050-2044010 (6522a)
2009: 5^{2}Y, 5^{0}HY, 5^{4}G, 5^{4}G, 5^{0}G, 5^{1}HY, 5^{0}G,

	Starts	1st	2nd	3rd	Win & Pl
Career Total (Turf)	36	10	3	3	528793
Career Total (AW)	1	0	0	0	932

108 8/09 Curr 5f HVY £39126
108 5/08 Hayd 6f GD £10904
120 9/06 Hayd 6f HVY £170340
121 8/06 York 5f SFT £147400
117 5/06 Sand 5f6y SFT £51102
114 4/06 Nott 5f13y SFT £6477
107 10/05 Donc 5f (0-100)H HVY £12240
93 10/05 Pont 5f (0-80)H G-S £7020
86 9/05 Donc 5f (0-85)H G-S £6500
86 8/05 Ripn 5f G-S £5470
Total win prize-money £456580

Going (Turf): **Sf: 6-13** GS: 3-6 Gd: 1-11 GF: 0-4 Fm: 0-0
Distance: **5f/6f: 10-36** 7f-8f: 0-1 9f-13f: 0-0 14f+: 0-0
Track : **LH: 1-4** RH: 0-1 Tight: 0-1 Gall: 0-0
Aids: Bl: 0-0 Vi: 0-0 Tstrap: 0-0 Ckp: 0-0
Best Rating: **121** 8/06 York 5f soft

Smart; formerly Group class; winner of the Group 2 Temple Stakes at Sandown in May 2006 and then completed a Group 1 double in the Nunthorpe at York and the Betfred Sprint Cup at Haydock; effective over 5f-6f; very effective in soft ground.

Revoltinthedesert

84 53
2-y-o b f Dubai Destination (USA)-Cloud Hill (Danehill (USA))
E S McMahon J C Fretwell

Placings:64 (4194)
2009: 6^{6}GF, 7^{4}GS,

	Starts	1st	2nd	3rd	Win & Pl
Career Total (Turf)	2	0	0	0	216

Going (Turf): **Sf: 0-0 GS: 0-1 Gd: 0-0 GF: 0-1 Fm: 0-0**
Distance: 5f/6f: 0-1 7f-8f: 0-1 9f-13f: 0-0 14f+: 0-0
Track : LH: 0-0 RH: 0-0 Tight: 0-0 Gall: 0-0
Aids: Bl: 0-0 Vi: 0-0 Tstrap: 0-0 Ckp: 0-0
Best Rating: **53** 7/09 Leic 7f9y gd-sft

Revolving World (IRE)

68(71) (39)40
6-y-o b g Spinning World (USA)-Mannakea (USA) (Fairy King (USA))
L R James L R James Limited

Placings:0/000000/150/400-00 (6818)
2009: 16^{0}GF, 10^{0}GF,

	Starts	1st	2nd	3rd	Win & Pl
Career Total (Turf)	12	1	0	0	2591
Career Total (AW)	3	0	0	0	0

56 6/07 Ripn 1m4f10y (0-60)H G-F £2590
Total win prize-money £2591

Going (Turf): Sf: 0-1 GS: 0-1 Gd: 0-3 **GF: 1-7** Fm: 0-0
Distance: 5f/6f: 0-0 7f-8f: 0-1 **9f-13f: 1-11** 14f+: 0-3
Track : LH: 0-8 **RH: 1-6 Tight: 1-11** Gall: 0-2
Aids: Bl: 0-2 Vi: 0-0 Tstrap: 0-1 Ckp: 0-1
Best Rating: **56** 6/07 Ripn 1m4f10y gd-fm

Plater; suited by a mile and a half; acts on fast ground.

Revue Princess (IRE)

103(98) (61)72

4-y-o b f Mull Of Kintyre (USA)-Blues Queen (Lahib (USA))
T D Easterby S A Heley

Placings:5321/001000-010060315500 (7269)
2009: 5⁰F, 5¹GS, 5⁰F, 5⁰GS, 5⁶G, 5⁰G, 5³G, 5¹GF, 6⁵G, 5⁵SD, 5⁰S, 5⁰SD,

	Starts	1st	2nd	3rd	Win & Pl
Career Total (Turf)	20	4	1	2	14457
Career Total (AW)	2	0	0	0	188

70	9/09	Newc	5f	(0-60)H	G-F	£1748
72	5/09	Newc	5f	(0-70)H	G-S	£3561
71	5/08	Newc	5f	(0-70)H	G-F	£3885
68	7/07	Bevl	5f		GD	£3238

Total win prize-money £12436

Going (Turf): Sf: 0-4 GS: 1-5 Gd: 1-6 **GF: 2-3** Fm: 0-2
Distance: **5f/6f: 4-22** 7f-8f: 0-0 9f-13f: 0-0 14f+: 0-0
Track : LH: 0-2 RH: 0-0 Tight: 0-1 Gall: 0-0
Aids: **Bl: 2-13** Vi: 0-0 Tstrap: 0-0 Ckp: 0-0
Best Rating: 72 5/09 Newc 5f gd-sft

Modest; effective at 5f and acts on most ground; has worn blinkers.

Rezwaan

105(90) (58)75

2-y-o b g Alhaarth (IRE)-Nasij (USA) (Elusive Quality (USA))
M J McGrath (E A L Dunlop 15/10) Gallagher Equine Ltd

Placings:0562310 (7654)
2009: 7⁰SD, 7⁵S, 6⁶GF, 8²G, 9³GF, 8¹S, 7⁰SD,

	Starts	1st	2nd	3rd	Win & Pl
Career Total (Turf)	5	1	1	1	5043
Career Total (AW)	2	0	0	0	

75	10/09	Nott	1m75y	(0-70)	SFT	£2590

Total win prize-money £2590

Going (Turf): **Sf: 1-2** GS: 0-0 Gd: 0-1 GF: 0-2 Fm: 0-0
Distance: 5f/6f: 0-0 7f-8f: 0-5 **9f-13f: 1-2** 14f+: 0-0
Track : **LH: 1-3** RH: 0-1 Tight: 0-1 Gall: 0-0
Aids: Bl: 0-0 Vi: 0-0 Tstrap: 0-0 Ckp: 0-0
Best Rating: 75 10/09 Nott 1m75y soft

Fair; stays 1m; acts on most ground.

Rhapsilian

97(111) (66)63

5-y-o br m Dansili-Rivers Rhapsody (Dominion)
J R Jenkins (J A Geake 27/6) David Mead

Placings:04060501462/62006422335-524054004 (6581)
2009: 6⁵GF, 6²GF, 6⁴GF, 6⁰GF, 6⁵GF, 5⁴G, 5⁰GF, 6⁰GF, 5⁴SD,

	Starts	1st	2nd	3rd	Win & Pl
Career Total (Turf)	17	0	1	1	1614
Career Total (AW)	14	1	4	1	4884

61	10/07	Ling	6f	(0-53)H	STD	£2047

Total win prize-money £2048

Going (Turf): **Sf: 0-0 GS: 0-4 Gd: 0-1 GF: 0-12 Fm: 0-0**
Distance: **5f/6f: 1-26** 7f-8f: 0-5 9f-13f: 0-0 14f+: 0-0
Track : **LH: 1-8** RH: 0-9 **Tight: 1-5** Gall: 0-3
Aids: Bl: 0-2 Vi: 0-4 Tstrap: 0-1 Ckp: 0-1
Best Rating: 66 9/08 Kemp 6f stand

Moderate; effective over 6f; acts on a sound surface; also goes on Polytrack.

Rhythmic Star

74 38

2-y-o ch c Starcraft (NZ)-Markova's Dance (Mark Of Esteem (IRE))
W J Haggas D J Fish

Placings:0 (5000)
2009: 7⁰G,

	Starts	1st	2nd	3rd	Win & Pl
Career Total (Turf)	1	0	0	0	

Going (Turf): **Sf: 0-0 GS: 0-0 Gd: 0-1 GF: 0-0 Fm: 0-0**
Distance: 5f/6f: 0-0 7f-8f: 0-1 9f-13f: 0-0 14f+: 0-0
Track : LH: 0-0 RH: 0-0 Tight: 0-0 Gall: 0-0
Aids: Bl: 0-0 Vi: 0-0 Tstrap: 0-0 Ckp: 0-0
Best Rating: 38 8/09 NmkJ 7f good

Ricci De Mare

(98) (58)58

4-y-o b f Cadeaux Genereux-Procession (Zafonic (USA))
G J Smith Graham Smith

Placings:500/0100022105-50 (0254)
2009: 12⁵SS, 9⁰SD,

	Starts	1st	2nd	3rd	Win & Pl
Career Total (Turf)	4	1	2	0	3099
Career Total (AW)	11	1	0	0	1775

58	10/08	Yarm	1m2f21y		SFT	£1942
58	3/08	Sthl	1m	(0-60)H	STD	£1774

Total win prize-money £3718

Going (Turf): **Sf: 1-2** GS: 0-1 Gd: 0-1 GF: 0-0 Fm: 0-0
Distance: 5f/6f: 0-3 7f-8f: 1-3 9f-13f: 1-8 14f+: 0-1
Track : **LH: 2-12** RH: 0-2 **Tight: 1-7** Gall: 0-1
Aids: Bl: 0-1 Vi: 0-0 Tstrap: 1-2 Ckp: 1-2
Best Rating: 58 10/08 Yarm 1m2f21y soft

Moderate; stays 1m2f; acts on good ground and on Polytrack.

Riccoche (IRE)

(62)

2-y-o b f Oasis Dream-Ammo (IRE) (Sadler's Wells (USA))
J H M Gosden Mrs Emily Oppenheimer Turner

Placings:0 (7491)
2009: 8⁰SD,

	Starts	1st	2nd	3rd	Win & Pl
Career Total (Turf)	0	0	0	0	
Career Total (AW)	1	0	0	0	

Going (Turf): **Sf: 0-0 GS: 0-0 Gd: 0-0 GF: 0-0 Fm: 0-0**
Distance: 5f/6f: 0-0 7f-8f: 0-0 9f-13f: 0-1 14f+: 0-0
Track : LH: 0-1 RH: 0-0 Tight: 0-1 Gall: 0-0
Aids: Bl: 0-0 Vi: 0-0 Tstrap: 0-0 Ckp: 0-0

Rich Red (IRE)

(82) (28)61

3-y-o ch g Redback-Pink N Prosperous (IRE) (Grand Lodge (USA))
R Hannon Mrs John Lee

Placings:00430-0 (0162)
2009: 6⁰SD,

	Starts	1st	2nd	3rd	Win & Pl
Career Total (Turf)	5	0	0	1	1300
Career Total (AW)	1	0	0	0	

Going (Turf): **Sf: 0-0 GS: 0-4 Gd: 0-0 GF: 0-1 Fm: 0-0**
Distance: 5f/6f: 0-5 7f-8f: 0-1 9f-13f: 0-0 14f+: 0-0
Track : LH: 0-1 RH: 0-0 Tight: 0-1 Gall: 0-1
Aids: Bl: 0-0 Vi: 0-0 Tstrap: 0-0 Ckp: 0-0
Best Rating: 61 7/08 Asct 6f gd-sft

Modest; effective from 5f-6f; acts on most ground.

Richardlionheart (USA)

90(83) (24)39

3-y-o ch g Lion Heart (USA)-Cleito (USA) (Unbridled's Song (USA))
M Madgwick (B Gubby 29/6) R G Gianfriglia

Placings:0-0600 (6966)
2009: 7⁰GF, 6⁶GF, 8⁰SD, 9⁰G,

	Starts	1st	2nd	3rd	Win & Pl
Career Total (Turf)	4	0	0	0	0
Career Total (AW)	1	0	0	0	

Going (Turf): **Sf: 0-0 GS: 0-0 Gd: 0-1 GF: 0-3 Fm: 0-0**
Distance: 5f/6f: 0-2 7f-8f: 0-2 9f-13f: 0-1 14f+: 0-0
Track : LH: 0-1 RH: 0-1 Tight: 0-0 Gall: 0-2
Aids: Bl: 0-0 Vi: 0-0 Tstrap: 0-0 Ckp: 0-0
Best Rating: 39 7/08 Wind 6f gd-fm

Richardthesecond (IRE)

87(94) (57)48

4-y-o b g Acclamation-Tahlil (Cadeaux Genereux)
W M Brisbourne W M Clare

Placings:03652642/6450-000 (1360)
2009: 5⁰SD, 5⁰SD, 5⁰GF,

	Starts	1st	2nd	3rd	Win & Pl
Career Total (Turf)	7	0	1	1	1493
Career Total (AW)	8	0	1	0	605

Going (Turf): **Sf: 0-1 GS: 0-0 Gd: 0-2 GF: 0-4 Fm: 0-0**
Distance: 5f/6f: 0-14 7f-8f: 0-1 9f-13f: 0-0 14f+: 0-0
Track : LH: 0-7 RH: 0-2 Tight: 0-7 Gall: 0-0
Aids: Bl: 0-1 Vi: 0-0 Tstrap: 0-0 Ckp: 0-0
Best Rating: 65 9/07 Ling 6f gd-fm

Modest maiden sprinter; effective over 5f and 6f; acts on fast ground and Polytrack; has worn blinkers.

Richboy

74(95) (65)34

2-y-o ch c Bahamian Bounty-West Humble (Pharly (FR))
Mrs L J Mongan Mrs P J Sheen

Placings:644 (7538)
2009: 6⁶GF, 6⁴SD, 7⁴SD,

	Starts	1st	2nd	3rd	Win & Pl
Career Total (Turf)	1	0	0	0	0
Career Total (AW)	2	0	0	0	505

Going (Turf): **Sf: 0-0 GS: 0-0 Gd: 0-0 GF: 0-1 Fm: 0-0**
Distance: 5f/6f: 0-2 7f-8f: 0-1 9f-13f: 0-0 14f+: 0-0
Track : LH: 0-1 RH: 0-1 Tight: 0-1 Gall: 0-1
Aids: Bl: 0-0 Vi: 0-0 Tstrap: 0-0 Ckp: 0-0
Best Rating: 65 11/09 Kemp 7f stand

Modest; stays 7f; acts on Polytrack.

Richelieu

103(104) (79)**74**

7-y-o b g Machiavellian (USA)-Darling Flame (USA) (Capote (USA))

J J Lambe Orchard County Syndicate

Placings:3260000/00014220036/00000210215-5032520100300 **(7527a)**

2009: 6^{5}YS, 5^{0}S, 8^{3}SD, 6^{2}G, 5^{5}GF, 5^{2}GF, 6^{0}GY, 7^{1}SD, 7^{0}SD, 8^{0}SD, 6^{3}SD, 7^{0}SD, 8^{0}SD,

	Starts	1st	2nd	3rd	Win & Pl
Career Total (Turf)	25	1	6	1	12149
Career Total (AW)	17	3	1	3	19639

76 9/09 Layt 7f (50-80)H STD £7379
76 12/08 Wolv 5f216y (0-70)H STD £3885
66 9/08 Layt 6f (45-60)H STD £4572
70 4/07 Navn 5f182y (42-60)H FRM £3968
Total win prize-money £19808

Going (Turf): Sf: 0-7 GS: 0-1 Gd: 0-4 GF: 0-3 **Fm: 1-5**
Distance: **5f/6f: 3-21** 7f-8f: 1-17 9f-13f: 0-4 14f+: 0-0
Track : **LH: 4-24** RH: 0-8 **Tight: 1-10** Gall: 0-0
Aids: Bl: 0-0 Vi: 0-0 Tstrap: 0-0 Ckp: 0-0
Best Rating: **80** 6/07 Curr 6f good

Fair Irish-trained gelding; effective over 6f-7f; acts on fast ground; goes on Polytrack.

Richo

97(98) (78)**79**

3-y-o ch g Bertolini (USA)-Noble Water (FR) (Noblequest (FR))

S A Harris (D H Brown 14/8) Ron Hull

Placings:04510304-20300040460 **(7246)**

2009: 7^{2}GF, 7^{0}F, 7^{3}GF, 7^{0}GF, 7^{0}GF, 7^{0}GS, 7^{4}GF, 7^{0}GF, 8^{4}G, 8^{6}G, 8^{0}S,

	Starts	1st	2nd	3rd	Win & Pl
Career Total (Turf)	18	1	1	2	9357
Career Total (AW)	1	0	0	0	409

79 7/08 Newc 7f G-F £5504
Total win prize-money £5505

Going (Turf): Sf: 0-1 GS: 0-3 Gd: 0-4 **GF: 1-9** Fm: 0-1
Distance: 5f/6f: 0-3 **7f-8f: 1-15** 9f-13f: 0-1 14f+: 0-0
Track : LH: 0-9 RH: 0-0 Tight: 0-4 Gall: 0-2
Aids: Bl: 0-4 Vi: 0-0 Tstrap: 0-1 Ckp: 0-1
Best Rating: **79** 6/09 Hayd 7f30y gd-fm

Fair; stays 7f, acts on a sound surface and Polytrack; has worn blinkers.

Ride A White Swan

96(93) (63)**64**

4-y-o gr g Baryshnikov (AUS)-The Manx Touch (IRE) (Petardia)

D Shaw N Morgan

Placings:000/563626320-0000655430 **(7727)**

2009: 7^{0}SD, 7^{0}SD, 8^{0}SD, 6^{0}GF, 8^{6}GF, 6^{5}GF, 6^{5}GF, 5^{4}SD, 6^{3}SD, 7^{0}SD,

	Starts	1st	2nd	3rd	Win & Pl
Career Total (Turf)	13	0	1	2	1638
Career Total (AW)	9	0	1	1	881

Going (Turf): **Sf: 0-0 GS: 0-1 Gd: 0-6 GF: 0-6 Fm: 0-0**
Distance: 5f/6f: 0-3 7f-8f: 0-19 9f-13f: 0-0 14f+: 0-0
Track : LH: 0-10 RH: 0-6 Tight: 0-5 Gall: 0-3
Aids: Bl: 0-0 Vi: 0-0 Tstrap: 0-1 Ckp: 0-1
Best Rating: **66** 8/07 Sand 7f16y good

Very moderate; stays 1m; acts on good ground and on Polytrack.

Ridgetime Anna (IRE)

92 (43)**43**

4-y-o b f Chevalier (IRE)-Annaduff (IRE) (Indian Ridge)

Daniel Mark Loughnane Leo Cox

Placings:060000 **(6519a)**

2009: 10^{0}Y, 8^{6}SD, 8^{0}YS, 11^{0}GF, 16^{0}GY, 10^{0}SD,

	Starts	1st	2nd	3rd	Win & Pl
Career Total (Turf)	4	0	0	0	
Career Total (AW)	2	0	0	0	

Going (Turf): **Sf: 0-0 GS: 0-0 Gd: 0-0 GF: 0-1 Fm: 0-0**
Distance: 5f/6f: 0-0 7f-8f: 0-1 9f-13f: 0-4 14f+: 0-1
Track : LH: 0-3 RH: 0-2 Tight: 0-1 Gall: 0-0
Aids: Bl: 0-0 Vi: 0-0 Tstrap: 0-0 Ckp: 0-0
Best Rating: **43** 5/09 Wxfd 1m110y yld-sft

Ridgeway Jazz

(105) (69)

4-y-o b f Kalanisi (IRE)-Billie Holiday (Fairy King (USA))

M D I Usher M D I Usher

Placings:4000313/00-451341210 **(0981)**

2009: 8^{4}SD, 8^{5}SD, 9^{1}SD, 9^{3}SD, 12^{4}SD, 9^{1}SD, 9^{2}SD, 9^{1}SD, 9^{0}SD,

	Starts	1st	2nd	3rd	Win & Pl
Career Total (Turf)	0	0	0	0	
Career Total (AW)	18	4	1	3	11076

69 3/09 Wolv 1m1f103y (0-70)H STD £2729
67 2/09 Wolv 1m1f103y (0-55)H STD £2388
60 1/09 Wolv 1m1f103y (0-52)H STD £2047
47 12/07 Sthl 1m (0-65) SS £2047
Total win prize-money £9213

Going (Turf): **Sf: 0-0 GS: 0-0 Gd: 0-0 GF: 0-0 Fm: 0-0**
Distance: 5f/6f: 0-2 7f-8f: 1-4 **9f-13f: 3-12** 14f+: 0-0
Track : **LH: 4-15** RH: 0-2 **Tight: 3-12** Gall: 0-0
Aids: Bl: 0-0 Vi: 0-0 Tstrap: 0-0 Ckp: 0-0
Best Rating: **69** 3/09 Wolv 1m1f103y stand

Moderate; stays 1m and acts on Fibresand.

Ridgeway Sapphire

87(80) (26)**54**

2-y-o b f Zafeen (FR)-Barefooted Flyer (USA) (Fly So Free (USA))

M D I Usher The Ridgeway Bloodstock Company Ltd

Placings:0500 **(6355)**

2009: 6^{0}S, 6^{5}G, 7^{0}SD, 5^{0}SD,

	Starts	1st	2nd	3rd	Win & Pl
Career Total (Turf)	2	0	0	0	0
Career Total (AW)	2	0	0	0	

Going (Turf): **Sf: 0-1 GS: 0-0 Gd: 0-1 GF: 0-0 Fm: 0-0**
Distance: 5f/6f: 0-1 7f-8f: 0-3 9f-13f: 0-0 14f+: 0-0
Track : LH: 0-0 RH: 0-1 Tight: 0-0 Gall: 0-0
Aids: Bl: 0-0 Vi: 0-0 Tstrap: 0-0 Ckp: 0-0
Best Rating: **54** 7/09 Newb 6f8y soft

Ridgeway Silver

91(96) (65)**65**

3-y-o b f Lujain (USA)-Barefooted Flyer (USA) (Fly So Free (USA))

M D I Usher I Sheward

Placings:46516330010-54404000450 **(6442)**

2009: 6^{5}SS, 5^{4}SD, 7^{4}SD, 6^{0}GF, 7^{4}SD, 5^{0}SD, 6^{0}F, 7^{0}SD, 6^{4}SD, 7^{5}SD, 7^{0}SS,

	Starts	1st	2nd	3rd	Win & Pl
Career Total (Turf)	7	1	0	0	4155
Career Total (AW)	15	1	0	2	3640

65 11/08 Wolv 5f216y (0-65) STD £2388
65 7/08 Sals 6f G-F £3885
Total win prize-money £6274

Going (Turf): Sf: 0-1 GS: 0-2 Gd: 0-0 **GF: 1-3** Fm: 0-1
Distance: **5f/6f: 2-14** 7f-8f: 0-8 9f-13f: 0-0 14f+: 0-0
Track : **LH: 1-13** RH: 0-2 **Tight: 1-9** Gall: 0-3
Aids: Bl: 0-0 Vi: 0-0 Tstrap: 0-1 Ckp: 0-1
Best Rating: **65** 11/08 Wolv 5f216y stand

Modest; effective up to 7f; acts on most ground and on Polytrack.

Ridley Didley (IRE)

95(100) (60)**60**

4-y-o b g Tagula (IRE)-Dioscorea (IRE) (Pharly (FR))

N Wilson Feenan Tobin Wilson

Placings:0/402-2205206 **(3111)**

2009: 5^{2}SD, 5^{2}SD, 5^{0}SD, 5^{5}GF, 5^{2}GF, 5^{0}GF, 5^{6}GF,

	Starts	1st	2nd	3rd	Win & Pl
Career Total (Turf)	6	0	1	0	843
Career Total (AW)	5	0	3	0	1814

Going (Turf): **Sf: 0-0 GS: 0-2 Gd: 0-0 GF: 0-4 Fm: 0-0**
Distance: 5f/6f: 0-11 7f-8f: 0-0 9f-13f: 0-0 14f+: 0-0
Track : LH: 0-3 RH: 0-0 Tight: 0-3 Gall: 0-0
Aids: Bl: 0-1 Vi: 0-0 Tstrap: 0-0 Ckp: 0-0
Best Rating: **60** 5/09 Muss 5f gd-fm

Moderate; effective over 5f; acts on fast ground and sand; has worn a tongue tie.

Rievaulx World

106 **102**

3-y-o b g Compton Place-Adhaaba (USA) (Dayjur (USA))

K A Ryan Rievaulx Racing Syndicate

Placings:522114-052080 **(4456)**

2009: 5^{6}GF, 5^{5}GF, 5^{2}G, 5^{0}GF, 5^{6}GF, 5^{0}G,

	Starts	1st	2nd	3rd	Win & Pl
Career Total (Turf)	12	2	3	0	18091

100 7/08 Rdcr 5f G-F £3885
90 6/08 Ripn 5f G-F £2914
Total win prize-money £6800

Going (Turf): Sf: 0-0 GS: 0-0 Gd: 0-4 **GF: 2-8** Fm: 0-0
Distance: **5f/6f: 2-12** 7f-8f: 0-0 9f-13f: 0-0 14f+: 0-0
Track : LH: 0-2 RH: 0-0 Tight: 0-2 Gall: 0-0
Aids: Bl: 0-0 Vi: 0-0 Tstrap: 0-0 Ckp: 0-0
Best Rating: **102** 5/09 NmkR 5f gd-fm

Smart; effective at 5f and acts on fast ground; likes to race prominently.

Riffelalp (IRE)

87(69) (33)**52**

2-y-o ch f Bachelor Duke (USA)-Alpenrot (IRE) (Barathea (IRE))

Eve Johnson Houghton Mrs Virginia Neale

Placings:60560 (5543)

2009: 5^{6}G, 5^{0}G, 7^{5}SD, 7^{6}GF, 7^{0}GF,

	Starts	1st	2nd	3rd	Win & Pl
Career Total (Turf)	4	0	0	0	0
Career Total (AW)	1	0	0	0	0

Going (Turf): Sf: 0-0 GS: 0-0 Gd: 0-2 GF: 0-2 Fm: 0-0
Distance: 5f/6f: 0-2 7f-8f: 0-3 9f-13f: 0-0 14f+: 0-0
Track : LH: 0-0 RH: 0-1 Tight: 0-0 Gall: 0-1
Aids: Bl: 0-0 Vi: 0-0 Tstrap: 0-0 Ckp: 0-0
Best Rating: 52 5/09 Gdwd 5f good

Riflessione

99(103) (74)**76**

3-y-o ch c Captain Rio-Hilites (IRE) (Desert King (IRE))

R A Harris Paul Moulton

Placings:5236030150-433201433034400 (7861)

2009: 6^{4}SD, 5^{3}SD, 6^{3}SD, 5^{2}SD, 6^{0}GF, 5^{1}G, 6^{4}F, 5^{3}GF, 6^{3}GF, 7^{0}G, 6^{3}SD, 5^{4}G, 5^{4}GS, 6^{0}GS, 7^{0}SD,

	Starts	1st	2nd	3rd	Win & Pl
Career Total (Turf)	15	1	1	3	3393
Career Total (AW)	10	1	1	4	4833

71 10/08 Kemp 6f STD £2047
Total win prize-money £2047

Going (Turf): Sf: 0-2 GS: 0-5 Gd: 1-4 GF: 0-3 Fm: 0-1
Distance: 5f/6f: 2-23 7f-8f: 0-2 9f-13f: 0-0 14f+: 0-0
Track : LH: 1-13 RH: 1-2 Tight: 0-6 Gall: 1-6
Aids: Bl: 1-10 Vi: 0-0 Tstrap: 1-11 Ckp: 1-11
Best Rating: 76 4/08 Folk 5f soft

Fair; effective at 5f-6f; acts on good and soft ground; goes on Polytrack; has worn cheekpieces and blinkers.

Rigat

(107) (68)**72**

6-y-o b g Dansili-Fudge (Polar Falcon (USA))

J S Goldie The Vital Sparks

Placings:04105/30000005532210/555-03 (0898)

2009: 9^{0}SD, 8^{3}SD,

	Starts	1st	2nd	3rd	Win & Pl
Career Total (Turf)	16	1	1	2	7348
Career Total (AW)	8	1	1	1	2954

68 12/07 Wolv 1m1f103y (0-55)H STD £2047
54 7/06 Thsk 7f FRM £5181
Total win prize-money £7230

Going (Turf): Sf: 0-2 GS: 0-2 Gd: 0-5 GF: 0-5 Fm: 1-2
Distance: 5f/6f: 0-3 7f-8f: 1-11 9f-13f: 1-10 14f+: 0-0
Track : LH: 2-15 RH: 0-3 Tight: 2-14 Gall: 0-1
Aids: Bl: 0-0 Vi: 0-0 Tstrap: 0-0 Ckp: 0-0
Best Rating: 72 8/06 Rdcr 1m gd-fm

Modest; stays 1m4f; acts on fast ground and Polytrack.

Rigged

(91) (49)**42**

3-y-o b g Desert Sun-Emma Peel (Emarati (USA))

J A Osborne J A Osborne

Placings:P400-364 (0383)

2009: 8^{3}SD, 8^{6}SD, 8^{4}SD,

	Starts	1st	2nd	3rd	Win & Pl
Career Total (Turf)	4	0	0	0	269
Career Total (AW)	3	0	0	1	353

Going (Turf): Sf: 0-1 GS: 0-0 Gd: 0-1 GF: 0-2 Fm: 0-0
Distance: 5f/6f: 0-3 7f-8f: 0-2 9f-13f: 0-2 14f+: 0-0
Track : LH: 0-6 RH: 0-0 Tight: 0-2 Gall: 0-0
Aids: Bl: 0-1 Vi: 0-0 Tstrap: 0-0 Ckp: 0-0
Best Rating: 49 1/09 Wolv 1m141y stand

Moderate; stays 1m; acts on Polytrack.

Riggins (IRE)

111(101) (92)**104**

5-y-o b g Cape Cross (IRE)-Rentless (Zafonic (USA))

L M Cumani Scuderia Rencati Srl

Placings:1/1-010 (3873)

2009: 8^{0}GF, 8^{1}G, 10^{0}GF,

	Starts	1st	2nd	3rd	Win & Pl
Career Total (Turf)	3	1	0	0	7477
Career Total (AW)	2	2	0	0	9744

104 5/09 Gdwd 1m (0-90)H GD £7477
92 8/08 GrLe 1m (0-90)H STD £7477
92 4/07 Wolv 7f32y STD £2266
Total win prize-money £17221

Going (Turf): Sf: 0-0 GS: 0-0 Gd: 1-1 GF: 0-2 Fm: 0-0
Distance: 5f/6f: 0-0 7f-8f: 3-4 9f-13f: 0-1 14f+: 0-0
Track : LH: 2-3 RH: 1-1 Tight: 1-1 Gall: 1-2
Aids: Bl: 0-0 Vi: 0-0 Tstrap: 0-0 Ckp: 0-0
Best Rating: 104 5/09 Gdwd 1m good

Very useful; off for 16 months after a successful debut due to several problems including a split pastern; stays 1m; acts on Polytrack and good ground.

Riggs (IRE)

(72)

3-y-o b c Daggers Drawn (USA)-Jay And-A (IRE) (Elbio)

Peter Grayson Haldane Racing & D L Rhodes

Placings:00 (7254)

2009: 5^{0}SD, 5^{0}SD,

	Starts	1st	2nd	3rd	Win & Pl
Career Total (Turf)	0	0	0	0	
Career Total (AW)	2	0	0	0	

Going (Turf): Sf: 0-0 GS: 0-0 Gd: 0-0 GF: 0-0 Fm: 0-0
Distance: 5f/6f: 0-2 7f-8f: 0-0 9f-13f: 0-0 14f+: 0-0
Track : LH: 0-2 RH: 0-0 Tight: 0-2 Gall: 0-0
Aids: Bl: 0-1 Vi: 0-0 Tstrap: 0-0 Ckp: 0-0

Right Grand

(95) (77)

2-y-o b c Exceed And Excel (AUS)-Baileys Dancer (Groom Dancer (USA))

W J Haggas Clipper Logistics

Placings:01 (7705)

2009: 7^{0}SF, 7^{1}SD,

	Starts	1st	2nd	3rd	Win & Pl
Career Total (Turf)	0	0	0	0	
Career Total (AW)	2	1	0	0	3753

77 12/09 Sthl 7f STD £3753
Total win prize-money £3753

Going (Turf): Sf: 0-0 GS: 0-0 Gd: 0-0 GF: 0-0 Fm: 0-0
Distance: 5f/6f: 0-0 7f-8f: 1-2 9f-13f: 0-0 14f+: 0-0
Track : LH: 1-2 RH: 0-0 Tight: 0-1 Gall: 0-0
Aids: Bl: 0-0 Vi: 0-0 Tstrap: 0-0 Ckp: 0-0
Best Rating: 77 12/09 Sthl 7f stand

Fair; out of a 1m4f winner; stays 7f; acts on Fibresand.

Right Of Veto

(76) (11)**39**

3-y-o b c Lucky Owners (NZ)-Lana Turrel (USA) (Trempolino (USA))

P J Rothwell Adelaide Racing Syndicate

Placings:0000 (7002)

2009: 7^{0}Y, 9^{0}G, 10^{0}GY, 5^{0}SD,

	Starts	1st	2nd	3rd	Win & Pl
Career Total (Turf)	3	0	0	0	
Career Total (AW)	1	0	0	0	

Going (Turf): Sf: 0-0 GS: 0-0 Gd: 0-1 GF: 0-0 Fm: 0-0
Distance: 5f/6f: 0-1 7f-8f: 0-1 9f-13f: 0-2 14f+: 0-0
Track : LH: 0-3 RH: 0-1 Tight: 0-1 Gall: 0-0
Aids: Bl: 0-0 Vi: 0-0 Tstrap: 0-0 Ckp: 0-0
Best Rating: 39 9/09 List 1m1f180y good

Right Option (IRE)

95(106) (83)**79**

5-y-o b g Daylami (IRE)-Option (IRE) (Red Ransom (USA))

J L Flint Roy Mathias

Placings:50053023342/26310630221522155546/22344510-1405 (5903)

2009: 16^{1}SD, 16^{4}SD, 16^{0}S, 17^{5}F,

	Starts	1st	2nd	3rd	Win & Pl
Career Total (Turf)	16	1	3	2	6106
Career Total (AW)	26	4	6	4	20756

83 2/09 Kemp 2m (0-85)H STD £4727
74 9/08 Wolv 1m5f194y (0-75)H SF £3238
72 10/07 Wolv 1m4f50y (0-70)H STD £2914
61 9/07 Ling 2m (0-65)H G-F £2047
57 6/07 Ling 1m4f STD £2047
Total win prize-money £14976

Going (Turf): Sf: 0-4 GS: 0-2 Gd: 0-2 GF: 1-6 Fm: 0-2
Distance: 5f/6f: 0-1 7f-8f: 0-4 9f-13f: 2-19 14f+: 3-18
Track : LH: 4-29 RH: 1-8 Tight: 4-21 Gall: 0-2
Aids: Bl: 0-1 Vi: 0-0 Tstrap: 0-2 Ckp: 0-2
Best Rating: 83 2/09 Kemp 2m stand

Fair; effective at around 1m5f-2m; acts on most ground and on Polytrack.

Right Rave (IRE)

96(93) (69)**68**

2-y-o b f Soviet Star (USA)-Genuinely (IRE) (Entrepreneur)

P J McBride Jason Anderson

Placings:016523 (6215)

2009: 6^{0}GF, 5^{1}G, 6^{6}GF, 7^{5}GF, 8^{2}SD, 8^{3}GF,

	Starts	1st	2nd	3rd	Win & Pl
Career Total (Turf)	5	1	0	1	2879
Career Total (AW)	1	0	1	0	605

66 7/09 Yarm 5f43y GD £2590
Total win prize-money £2590

Going (Turf): Sf: 0-0 GS: 0-0 Gd: 1-1 GF: 0-4 Fm: 0-0
Distance: 5f/6f: 1-3 7f-8f: 0-3 9f-13f: 0-0 14f+: 0-0
Track : LH: 0-0 RH: 0-1 Tight: 0-0 Gall: 0-1
Aids: Bl: 0-0 Vi: 0-0 Tstrap: 0-0 Ckp: 0-0
Best Rating: 69 9/09 Kemp 1m stand

Modest; effective at 5f on good ground.

Right Step

98 84

2-y-o b c Xaar-Maid To Dance (Pyramus (USA))

A P Jarvis Allen B Pope

Placings:315 (6011)

2009: 6^{3}GF, 7^{1}GF, 8^{5}GS,

	Starts	1st	2nd	3rd	Win & Pl
Career Total (Turf)	3	1	0	1	4201

84 8/09 Newc 7f G-F £3238

Total win prize-money £3238

Going (Turf): Sf: 0-0 GS: 0-1 Gd: 0-0 **GF: 1-2** Fm: 0-0
Distance: 5f/6f: 0-1 **7f-8f: 1-2** 9f-13f: 0-0 14f+: 0-0
Track : LH: 0-1 RH: 0-0 Tight: 0-0 Gall: 0-0
Aids: Bl: 0-0 Vi: 0-0 Tstrap: 0-0 Ckp: 0-0
Best Rating: **84** 8/09 Newc 7f gd-fm

Useful; effective at 7f; acts on fast ground.

Right Stuff (FR)

105(106) (85)90

6-y-o b/br g Dansili-Specificity (USA) (Alleged (USA))

G L Moore The Ashden Partnership & Partners

Placings:060041/4020561/00115-212 (4988)

2009: 12^{2}SD, 12^{1}SD, 13^{2}GF,

	Starts	1st	2nd	3rd	Win & Pl
Career Total (Turf)	15	2	2	0	12896
Career Total (AW)	6	3	1	0	19692

85 4/09 Kemp 1m4f (0-85)H STD £4727
78 8/08 Folk 1m4f (0-70)H G-S £2590
78 8/08 Wind 1m3f135y (0-70)H G-S £2729
69 12/07 Deau 1m1f110y H STD £6418
12/06 Deau 1m1f110y H STD £5517

Total win prize-money £21983

Going (Turf): Sf: 0-3 **GS: 2-5** Gd: 0-2 GF: 0-2 Fm: 0-0
Distance: 5f/6f: 0-0 7f-8f: 0-0 **9f-13f: 5-18** 14f+: 0-3
Track : LH: 0-2 **RH: 2-8 Tight: 2-3** Gall: 0-1
Aids: Bl: 0-0 Vi: 0-0 Tstrap: 0-0 Ckp: 0-0
Best Rating: **90** 8/09 Newb 1m5f61y gd-fm

Fair; ex-French; effective over 1m4f; acts on easy ground; also goes on Polytrack.

Right You Are (IRE)

63(93) (52)52

9-y-o ch g Right Win (IRE)-Ancadia (Hønbit (USA))

Paul Green Paul Green (Oaklea)

Placings:440030600-0 (3450)

2009: 10^{0}GF,

	Starts	1st	2nd	3rd	Win & Pl
Career Total (Turf)	5	0	0	1	578
Career Total (AW)	5	0	0	0	0

Going (Turf): **Sf: 0-1 GS: 0-1 Gd: 0-1 GF: 0-2 Fm: 0-0**
Distance: 5f/6f: 0-0 7f-8f: 0-1 9f-13f: 0-8 14f+: 0-1
Track : LH: 0-8 RH: 0-2 Tight: 0-6 Gall: 0-0
Aids: Bl: 0-0 Vi: 0-1 Tstrap: 0-0 Ckp: 0-0
Best Rating: **52** 7/08 Pont 1m2f6y good

Rightcar

82(92) (54)51

2-y-o b c Bertolini (USA)-Loblolly Bay (Halling (USA))

Peter Grayson S Kamis & PGRC Ltd

Placings:6664400065064052 (7884)

2009: 5^{6}GF, 5^{6}GF, 7^{6}GF, 5^{4}SD, 5^{4}SD, 5^{0}SD, 5^{0}SD, 5^{0}SD, 5^{6}SS, 5^{5}SD, 5^{0}S, 5^{6}SD, 5^{4}SD, 6^{0}SD, 6^{5}SS, 7^{2}SD,

	Starts	1st	2nd	3rd	Win & Pl
Career Total (Turf)	4	0	0	0	0
Career Total (AW)	12	0	1	0	724

Going (Turf): **Sf: 0-1 GS: 0-0 Gd: 0-0 GF: 0-3 Fm: 0-0**
Distance: 5f/6f: 0-14 7f-8f: 0-2 9f-13f: 0-0 14f+: 0-0
Track : LH: 0-9 RH: 0-2 Tight: 0-8 Gall: 0-0
Aids: Bl: 0-4 Vi: 0-0 Tstrap: 0-0 Ckp: 0-0
Best Rating: **54** 10/09 Ling 5f std-slw

Moderate; effective at 5f; acts on sand; has worn blinkers.

Rightcar Dominic

(90) (49)

4-y-o b c Kyllachy-Vallauris (Faustus (USA))

Peter Grayson S Kamis And Mrs S Grayson

Placings:3006-000060 (7869)

2009: 6^{0}SD, 5^{0}SD, 5^{0}SD, 7^{0}SD, 5^{6}SD, 6^{0}SS,

	Starts	1st	2nd	3rd	Win & Pl
Career Total (Turf)	0	0	0	0	
Career Total (AW)	10	0	0	1	347

Going (Turf): **Sf: 0-0 GS: 0-0 Gd: 0-0 GF: 0-0 Fm: 0-0**
Distance: 5f/6f: 0-8 7f-8f: 0-2 9f-13f: 0-0 14f+: 0-0
Track : LH: 0-8 RH: 0-2 Tight: 0-7 Gall: 0-0
Aids: Bl: 0-3 Vi: 0-0 Tstrap: 0-0 Ckp: 0-0
Best Rating: **54** 2/08 Ling 5f stand

Modest; suited by 5f and Polytrack.

Rightcar Lewis

95(94) (53)49

4-y-o ch f Noverre (USA)-Abeyr (Unfuwain (USA))

Peter Grayson S Kamis And Mrs S Grayson

Placings:00/550066-30505060040344 (5629)

2009: 5^{3}SD, 5^{0}SD, 5^{5}SD, 5^{0}SD, 5^{5}GF, 6^{0}GS, 6^{6}GF, 5^{0}GF, 5^{0}GF, 5^{4}GF, 5^{0}GF, 5^{3}S, 5^{4}GF, 5^{4}GS,

	Starts	1st	2nd	3rd	Win & Pl
Career Total (Turf)	10	0	0	1	740
Career Total (AW)	12	0	0	1	292

Going (Turf): **Sf: 0-1 GS: 0-2 Gd: 0-0 GF: 0-7 Fm: 0-0**
Distance: 5f/6f: 0-21 7f-8f: 0-1 9f-13f: 0-0 14f+: 0-0
Track : LH: 0-9 RH: 0-2 Tight: 0-9 Gall: 0-0
Aids: Bl: 0-16 Vi: 0-0 Tstrap: 0-0 Ckp: 0-0
Best Rating: **53** 11/08 Wolv 5f20y stand

Moderate form to date; best at 5f; acts on Polytrack; has worn blinkers.

Rightcar Marian

(82) (30)

2-y-o b f Oasis Dream-Top Flight Queen (Mark Of Esteem (IRE))

Peter Grayson S A Kamis

Placings:00000 (7843)

2009: 5^{0}SD, 5^{0}SD, 5^{0}SD, 5^{0}SD, 5^{0}SD,

	Starts	1st	2nd	3rd	Win & Pl
Career Total (Turf)	0	0	0	0	
Career Total (AW)	5	0	0	0	

Going (Turf): **Sf: 0-0 GS: 0-0 Gd: 0-0 GF: 0-0 Fm: 0-0**
Distance: 5f/6f: 0-5 7f-8f: 0-0 9f-13f: 0-0 14f+: 0-0
Track : LH: 0-2 RH: 0-2 Tight: 0-2 Gall: 0-0
Aids: Bl: 0-0 Vi: 0-0 Tstrap: 0-0 Ckp: 0-0
Best Rating: **30** 10/09 Kemp 5f stand

Rightful Ruler

(47) (59)53

7-y-o b g Montjoy (USA)-Lady Of The Realm (Prince Daniel (USA))

N Wilson The Centaur Group Partnership II

Placings:440/42336006/6650/20-0 (1938)

2009: 12^{0}SD,

	Starts	1st	2nd	3rd	Win & Pl
Career Total (Turf)	12	0	1	1	1837
Career Total (AW)	6	0	1	1	2032

Going (Turf): **Sf: 0-2 GS: 0-3 Gd: 0-2 GF: 0-3 Fm: 0-2**
Distance: 5f/6f: 0-0 7f-8f: 0-2 9f-13f: 0-10 14f+: 0-6
Track : LH: 0-11 RH: 0-5 Tight: 0-15 Gall: 0-0
Aids: Bl: 0-0 Vi: 0-0 Tstrap: 0-1 Ckp: 0-1
Best Rating: **75** 9/04 Bath 1m5y good

Moderate; stays 2m; acts on a sound surface; has worn headgear.

Rigid

91(83) (52)69

2-y-o ch g Refuse To Bend (IRE)-Supersonic (Shirley Heights)

J G Given C G Rowles Nicholson

Placings:4040 (6829)

2009: 6^{4}GF, 7^{0}GF, 7^{4}GS, 7^{0}SF,

	Starts	1st	2nd	3rd	Win & Pl
Career Total (Turf)	3	0	0	0	601
Career Total (AW)	1	0	0	0	

Going (Turf): **Sf: 0-0 GS: 0-1 Gd: 0-0 GF: 0-2 Fm: 0-0**
Distance: 5f/6f: 0-1 7f-8f: 0-3 9f-13f: 0-0 14f+: 0-0
Track : LH: 0-1 RH: 0-0 Tight: 0-1 Gall: 0-0
Aids: Bl: 0-0 Vi: 0-0 Tstrap: 0-0 Ckp: 0-0
Best Rating: **69** 5/09 Donc 6f gd-fm

Modest half-brother to a middle-distance winner and a hurdler; stays 6f; acts on fast ground.

Rigidity

96 81

2-y-o b c Indian Ridge-Alakananda (Hernando (FR))

H R A Cecil Thomas Barr

Placings:21 (6033)

2009: 8^{2}G, 8^{1}GF,

	Starts	1st	2nd	3rd	Win & Pl
Career Total (Turf)	2	1	1	0	6588

81 9/09 Yarm 1m3y G-F £5046

Total win prize-money £5046

Going (Turf): Sf: 0-0 GS: 0-0 Gd: 0-1 **GF: 1-1** Fm: 0-0
Distance: 5f/6f: 0-0 7f-8f: 0-1 **9f-13f: 1-1** 14f+: 0-0
Track : LH: 0-0 RH: 0-0 Tight: 0-0 Gall: 0-0
Aids: Bl: 0-0 Vi: 0-0 Tstrap: 0-0 Ckp: 0-0
Best Rating: **81** 9/09 Yarm 1m3y gd-fm

Useful; effective at 1m; acts on fast ground.

Riguez Dancer

73(111) (97)78

5-y-o b g Dansili-Tricoteuse (Kris)

Ferdy Murphy (P C Haslam 13/6) The DPRP Second Dance Partnership

Placings:6/440613/2000-**111**0 **(2932)**
2009: 13^{1}SD, 16^{1}SD, 11^{1}SD, 12^{0}G,

	Starts	1st	2nd	3rd	Win & Pl
Career Total (Turf)	10	1	1	1	5309
Career Total (AW)	5	3	0	0	8050

97	2/09	Sthl	1m3f (0-75)H	STD	£2729
94	1/09	Wolv	2m119y (0-75)H	STD	£2590
76	1/09	Wolv	1m5f194y (0-70)H	STD	£2729
76	8/07	Ripn	1m4f10y (0-70)H	G-F	£3238

Total win prize-money £11289

Going (Turf): Sf: 0-1 GS: 0-4 Gd: 0-3 **GF: 1-2** Fm: 0-0
Distance: 5f/6f: 0-0 7f-8f: 0-2 9f-13f: 2-10 14f+: 2-3
Track : **LH: 3-14** RH: 1-1 **Tight: 3-4** Gall: 0-3
Aids: Bl: 0-0 Vi: 0-0 Tstrap: 0-0 Ckp: 0-0
Best Rating: **97** 2/09 Sthl 1m3f stand

Useful; effective at around 1m3f-1m6f; acts on easy ground and on sand; has worn a tongue tie.

Riley Boys (IRE)

90 (70)**81**
8-y-o ch g Most Welcome-Scarlett Holly (Red Sunset)
J G Given Paul Riley

Placings:033000/1212122226/464360201000/00112240/0260000/514316-005 **(3035)**
2009: 8^{0}GF, 9^{0}GF, 12^{5}GS,

	Starts	1st	2nd	3rd	Win & Pl
Career Total (Turf)	50	7	10	3	64494
Career Total (AW)	4	1	0	1	1864

81	7/08	Bevl	1m1f207y (0-75)H	G-S	£3561
76	6/08	Bevl	1m1f207y (0-70)H	G-F	£4533
83	6/06	Bevl	1m1f207y (0-85)H	G-F	£6477
82	6/06	Bevl	1m1f207y (0-80)H	G-F	£8096
87	7/05	Bevl	1m100y (0-85)H	GD	£6869
74	6/04	Bevl	1m100yE(0-75)H	G-F	£4728
69	4/04	Nott	1m54y E(0-70)H	SFT	£3926
58	3/04	Wolv	7f H	SS	£1431

Total win prize-money £39624

Going (Turf): Sf: 1-7 GS: 1-11 Gd: 1-10 **GF: 4-20** Fm: 0-2
Distance: 5f/6f: 0-3 7f-8f: 1-16 **9f-13f: 7-35** 14f+: 0-0
Track : LH: 2-16 **RH: 6-29 Tight: 1-9** Gall: 0-2
Aids: Bl: 0-0 Vi: 0-1 Tstrap: 0-1 Ckp: 0-1
Best Rating: **94** 7/06 Bevl 1m100y firm

Fair; effective over 1m-1m2f; acts on any ground; reserves his best for Beverley; has been tried in a visor.

Riley Queen Bee (USA)

90 **57**
3-y-o b f Mr Greeley (USA)-Quarrel Over Halo (USA) (Halo (USA))
K R Burke Mogeely Stud & Mrs Maura Gittins

Placings:000 **(3352)**
2009: 7^{0}GF, 7^{0}G, 7^{0}GS,

	Starts	1st	2nd	3rd	Win & Pl
Career Total (Turf)	3	0	0	0	

Going (Turf): **Sf: 0-0 GS: 0-1 Gd: 0-1 GF: 0-1 Fm: 0-0**
Distance: 5f/6f: 0-0 7f-8f: 0-3 9f-13f: 0-0 14f+: 0-0
Track : LH: 0-2 RH: 0-0 Tight: 0-1 Gall: 0-0
Aids: Bl: 0-0 Vi: 0-0 Tstrap: 0-0 Ckp: 0-0
Best Rating: **57** 5/09 Ches 7f2y gd-fm

Rimsky Korsakov (IRE)

107 **53**
5-y-o b g Sadler's Wells (USA)-Tedarshana (Darshaan)
Micky Hammond Parklane Textiles Ltd

Placings:0/00-3 **(1399)**
2009: 21^{3}F,

	Starts	1st	2nd	3rd	Win & Pl
Career Total (Turf)	4	0	0	1	578

Going (Turf): **Sf: 0-0 GS: 0-1 Gd: 0-1 GF: 0-0 Fm: 0-1**
Distance: 5f/6f: 0-0 7f-8f: 0-0 9f-13f: 0-3 14f+: 0-1
Track : LH: 0-2 RH: 0-2 Tight: 0-1 Gall: 0-0
Aids: Bl: 0-0 Vi: 0-1 Tstrap: 0-0 Ckp: 0-0
Best Rating: **53** 4/09 Pont 2m5f122y firm

Moderate; stays 2m5f; acts on fast ground.

Rindless

82(85) (35)**26**
4-y-o b f Bertolini (USA)-Streaky (IRE) (Danetime (IRE))
J F Panvert Graham Brown

Placings:00-000 **(5963)**
2009: 6^{0}SD, 6^{0}F, 10^{0}G,

	Starts	1st	2nd	3rd	Win & Pl
Career Total (Turf)	2	0	0	0	
Career Total (AW)	3	0	0	0	

Going (Turf): **Sf: 0-0 GS: 0-0 Gd: 0-1 GF: 0-0 Fm: 0-1**
Distance: 5f/6f: 0-3 7f-8f: 0-1 9f-13f: 0-1 14f+: 0-0
Track : LH: 0-5 RH: 0-0 Tight: 0-4 Gall: 0-0
Aids: Bl: 0-0 Vi: 0-0 Tstrap: 0-0 Ckp: 0-0
Best Rating: **35** 11/08 Ling 5f stand

Ring Of Fire

(77) (49)
2-y-o b c Firebreak-Sweet Patoopie (Indian Ridge)
J L Spearing Advantage Chemicals Holdings Ltd

Placings:00 **(7764)**
2009: 7^{0}SD, 8^{0}SD,

	Starts	1st	2nd	3rd	Win & Pl
Career Total (Turf)	0	0	0	0	
Career Total (AW)	2	0	0	0	

Going (Turf): **Sf: 0-0 GS: 0-0 Gd: 0-0 GF: 0-0 Fm: 0-0**
Distance: 5f/6f: 0-0 7f-8f: 0-2 9f-13f: 0-0 14f+: 0-0
Track : LH: 0-0 RH: 0-2 Tight: 0-0 Gall: 0-0
Aids: Bl: 0-0 Vi: 0-0 Tstrap: 0-0 Ckp: 0-0
Best Rating: **49** 11/09 Kemp 7f stand

Ringo Zaar

(89) (55)**16**
3-y-o b g Xaar-Tomanivi (Caerleon (USA))
A B Haynes Sills Racing

Placings:004-00 **(0520)**
2009: 10^{0}SD, 8^{0}SD,

	Starts	1st	2nd	3rd	Win & Pl
Career Total (Turf)	1	0	0	0	
Career Total (AW)	4	0	0	0	0

Going (Turf): **Sf: 0-0 GS: 0-1 Gd: 0-0 GF: 0-0 Fm: 0-0**
Distance: 5f/6f: 0-0 7f-8f: 0-3 9f-13f: 0-2 14f+: 0-0
Track : LH: 0-5 RH: 0-0 Tight: 0-3 Gall: 0-1
Aids: Bl: 0-3 Vi: 0-0 Tstrap: 0-0 Ckp: 0-0
Best Rating: **55** 11/08 Ling 1m stand

Ringsider (IRE)

(93) (51)**2**
8-y-o ch g Docksider (USA)-Red Comes Up (USA) (Blushing Groom (FR))
R J Osborne William Hitchen

Placings:01/002101/4003300/0000/6000/00 **(5015)**
2009: 10^{0}Y, 10^{0}SD,

	Starts	1st	2nd	3rd	Win & Pl
Career Total (Turf)	18	3	1	1	32035
Career Total (AW)	7	0	0	1	2252

93	9/04	Wind	1m3f135y (0-85)H	G-F	£7100
89	7/04	Gdwd	1m1f D(0-80)H	G-F	£10692
78	8/03	Ches	7f2y D	G-F	£6938

Total win prize-money £24733

Going (Turf): Sf: 0-1 GS: 0-3 Gd: 0-4 **GF: 3-7** Fm: 0-1
Distance: 5f/6f: 0-1 7f-8f: 1-3 **9f-13f: 2-21** 14f+: 0-0
Track : LH: 1-12 RH: 1-11 **Tight: 3-11** Gall: 0-6
Aids: Bl: 0-0 Vi: 0-0 Tstrap: 0-2 Ckp: 0-2
Best Rating: **95** 5/05 NmkR 1m4f gd-fm

Rinky Dink Lady (IRE)

87 **40**
3-y-o b f Tiger Hill (IRE)-Glady Starlet (GER) (Big Shuffle (USA))
W R Swinburn London Market Racing Club

Placings:5 **(4381)**
2009: 8^{5}G,

	Starts	1st	2nd	3rd	Win & Pl
Career Total (Turf)	1	0	0	0	0

Going (Turf): **Sf: 0-0 GS: 0-0 Gd: 0-1 GF: 0-0 Fm: 0-0**
Distance: 5f/6f: 0-0 7f-8f: 0-0 9f-13f: 0-1 14f+: 0-0
Track : LH: 0-0 RH: 0-1 Tight: 0-1 Gall: 0-0
Aids: Bl: 0-0 Vi: 0-0 Tstrap: 0-0 Ckp: 0-0
Best Rating: **40** 7/09 Wind 1m67y good

Rio Caribe (IRE)

91 **71**
2-y-o b g Captain Rio-Kadja Chenee (Spectrum (IRE))
T D Walford Pedro Rosas

Placings:5250 **(4515)**
2009: 5^{5}GF, 5^{2}GS, 5^{5}G, 6^{0}S,

	Starts	1st	2nd	3rd	Win & Pl
Career Total (Turf)	4	0	1	0	964

Going (Turf): **Sf: 0-1 GS: 0-1 Gd: 0-1 GF: 0-1 Fm: 0-0**
Distance: 5f/6f: 0-4 7f-8f: 0-0 9f-13f: 0-0 14f+: 0-0
Track : LH: 0-0 RH: 0-0 Tight: 0-0 Gall: 0-0
Aids: Bl: 0-0 Vi: 0-0 Tstrap: 0-0 Ckp: 0-0
Best Rating: **71** 5/09 Donc 5f gd-sft

Fair; suited by 5f and easy ground.

Rio Carnival (USA)

69(75) (47)**20**
3-y-o b f Storm Cat (USA)-Zenda (Zamindar (USA))

J H M Gosden K Abdulla

Placings:0-0 (1128)
2009: 8^{0}GF,

	Starts	1st	2nd	3rd	Win & Pl
Career Total (Turf)	1	0	0	0	
Career Total (AW)	1	0	0	0	

Going (Turf): **Sf: 0-0 GS: 0-0 Gd: 0-0 GF: 0-1 Fm: 0-0**
Distance: 5f/6f: 0-0 7f-8f: 0-1 9f-13f: 0-1 14f+: 0-0
Track : LH: 0-0 RH: 0-1 Tight: 0-0 Gall: 0-0
Aids: Bl: 0-0 Vi: 0-0 Tstrap: 0-0 Ckp: 0-0
Best Rating: **47** 9/08 Kemp 1m stand

Rio Cobolo (IRE)

105(99) (78)79

3-y-o b c Captain Rio-Sofistication (IRE) (Dayjur (USA))
Paul Green The Keely Gang

Placings:460463122130-500233132023104100520 (7506)
2009: 6^{5}SD, 5^{0}GF, 6^{0}GF, 5^{2}GF, 5^{3}GF, 5^{3}GF, 7^{1}GF, 6^{3}G, 7^{2}GF, 7^{0}S, 6^{2}GF, 7^{3}GS, 5^{1}S, 5^{0}GF, 6^{4}GF, 7^{1}GF, 5^{0}SD, 6^{0}S, 8^{5}SD, 6^{2}SD, 6^{0}SD,

	Starts	1st	2nd	3rd	Win & Pl
Career Total (Turf)	23	4	3	5	23759
Career Total (AW)	10	1	3	1	4653

79	9/09	Bevl	7f100y	(0-75)H	G-F	£3238
74	9/09	Catt	5f212y	(0-80)H	SFT	£5180
66	6/09	Ches	7f122y	(0-70)H	G-F	£4047
67	12/08	Sthl	5f	(0-75)	STD	£2047
64	11/08	Nott	5f13y	(0-70)	HVY	£3238

Total win prize-money £17751

Going (Turf): **Sf: 2-6** GS: 0-1 Gd: 0-1 **GF: 2-15** Fm: 0-0
Distance: **5f/6f: 3-23** 7f-8f: 2-9 9f-13f: 0-1 14f+: 0-0
Track : **LH: 2-15** RH: 1-4 **Tight: 2-7** Gall: 0-1
Aids: Bl: 0-1 **Vi: 5-27** Tstrap: 0-0 Ckp: 0-0
Best Rating: **79** 9/09 Bevl 7f100y gd-fm

Modest; effective over 5f-7f; acts on fast and soft ground and Fibresand; has worn a visor.

Rio Command (IRE)

96 79

2-y-o b g Captain Rio-Happy To Chat (IRE) (Alzao (USA))
Daniel Mark Loughnane Raymond Yeung

Placings:04235 (6082a)
2009: 7^{0}S, 7^{4}S, 7^{2}G, 8^{3}G, 8^{5}S,

	Starts	1st	2nd	3rd	Win & Pl
Career Total (Turf)	5	0	1	1	4089

Going (Turf): **Sf: 0-3 GS: 0-0 Gd: 0-2 GF: 0-0 Fm: 0-0**
Distance: 5f/6f: 0-0 7f-8f: 0-4 9f-13f: 0-1 14f+: 0-0
Track : LH: 0-2 RH: 0-1 Tight: 0-0 Gall: 0-0
Aids: Bl: 0-0 Vi: 0-0 Tstrap: 0-0 Ckp: 0-0
Best Rating: **79** 7/09 Gway 7f soft

Rio De La Plata (USA)

107 118

4-y-o ch c Rahy (USA)-Express Way (ARG) (Ahmad (ARG))
Saeed Bin Suroor Godolphin

Placings:311214/203-025 (6812)
2009: 8^{0}S, 8^{2}GF, 9^{5}G,

	Starts	1st	2nd	3rd	Win & Pl
Career Total (Turf)	12	3	3	2	355070

118	10/07	Lonc	7f	G-S	£135128
115	8/07	Gdwd	7f	GD	£39746
99	7/07	NmkJ	7f	GD	£9715

Total win prize-money £184590

Going (Turf): Sf: 0-1 GS: 1-2 **Gd: 2-7** GF: 0-2 Fm: 0-0
Distance: 5f/6f: 0-1 **7f-8f: 3-8** 9f-13f: 0-3 14f+: 0-0
Track : LH: 0-2 **RH: 2-3** Tight: 0-1 Gall: 0-0
Aids: Bl: 0-0 Vi: 0-0 Tstrap: 0-0 Ckp: 0-0
Best Rating: **118** 7/08 Chan 1m good

Group class; winner of the Group 2 Veuve Clicquot Vintage Stakes at Goodwood and Group 1 Grand Criterium in 2007; runner-up in French 2000 Guineas in 2008; stays 1m2f; acts on good and easier ground; usually held up.

Rio Guru (IRE)

106(107) (83)83

4-y-o b f Spartacus (IRE)-Montessori (Akarad (FR))
M R Channon Norman Court Stud

Placings:3043210240412-4054520453520 (7684)
2009: 10^{4}GF, 10^{0}G, 10^{5}G, 9^{4}GF, 8^{5}G, 10^{2}GF, 9^{0}G, 10^{4}G, 10^{5}HY, 10^{3}GF, 10^{5}GF, 10^{2}HY, 10^{0}SD,

	Starts	1st	2nd	3rd	Win & Pl
Career Total (Turf)	19	0	2	3	9905
Career Total (AW)	7	2	3	0	14051

83	11/08	GrLe	1m2f	(0-80)H	STD	£5180
77	8/08	Wolv	1m4f50y		STD	£3238

Total win prize-money £8419

Going (Turf): **Sf: 0-4 GS: 0-1 Gd: 0-6 GF: 0-8 Fm: 0-0**
Distance: 5f/6f: 0-0 7f-8f: 0-2 **9f-13f: 2-24** 14f+: 0-0
Track : **LH: 2-18** RH: 0-7 Tight: 1-10 Gall: 1-8
Aids: Bl: 0-0 Vi: 0-0 Tstrap: 0-0 Ckp: 0-0
Best Rating: **83** 11/08 Ling 1m2f stand

Fair; effective at 1m2f-1m4f; acts on fast and soft ground; goes on Polytrack.

Rio L'Oren (IRE)

87(98) (62)39

4-y-o ch f Captain Rio-Princess Sofie (Efisio)
N J Vaughan Super Saturday Syndicate

Placings:0/316660-00200006 (3479)
2009: 7^{0}SD, 7^{0}SD, 7^{2}SD, 7^{0}SD, 7^{0}SD, 5^{0}GF, 7^{0}SD, 5^{6}GF,

	Starts	1st	2nd	3rd	Win & Pl
Career Total (Turf)	4	0	0	0	0
Career Total (AW)	11	1	1	1	3457

62	2/08	Wolv	7f32y	STD	£2590

Total win prize-money £2591

Going (Turf): **Sf: 0-1 GS: 0-0 Gd: 0-0 GF: 0-3 Fm: 0-0**
Distance: 5f/6f: 0-3 **7f-8f: 1-12** 9f-13f: 0-0 14f+: 0-0
Track : **LH: 1-8** RH: 0-5 **Tight: 1-8** Gall: 0-1
Aids: Bl: 0-6 Vi: 0-0 Tstrap: 0-2 Ckp: 0-2
Best Rating: **62** 2/08 Wolv 7f32y stand

Moderate; effective over 7f; acts on Polytrack.

Rio Mist

88(89) (59)54

2-y-o b f Captain Rio-Welsh Mist (Damister (USA))
R Hannon The Early Bath Partnership

Placings:60 (3271)
2009: 5^{6}GF, 6^{0}SD,

	Starts	1st	2nd	3rd	Win & Pl
Career Total (Turf)	1	0	0	0	0
Career Total (AW)	1	0	0	0	

Going (Turf): **Sf: 0-0 GS: 0-0 Gd: 0-0 GF: 0-1 Fm: 0-0**
Distance: 5f/6f: 0-2 7f-8f: 0-0 9f-13f: 0-0 14f+: 0-0
Track : LH: 0-0 RH: 0-1 Tight: 0-0 Gall: 0-0
Aids: Bl: 0-0 Vi: 0-0 Tstrap: 0-0 Ckp: 0-0
Best Rating: **59** 6/09 Kemp 6f stand

Rio Pomba (IRE)

80 55

3-y-o b f Captain Rio-Lyrebird (USA) (Storm Bird (CAN))
D Carroll B R Tregurtha

Placings:550-000 (3239)
2009: 5^{0}G, 5^{0}GF, 5^{0}GF,

	Starts	1st	2nd	3rd	Win & Pl
Career Total (Turf)	6	0	0	0	0

Going (Turf): **Sf: 0-1 GS: 0-0 Gd: 0-2 GF: 0-3 Fm: 0-0**
Distance: 5f/6f: 0-6 7f-8f: 0-0 9f-13f: 0-0 14f+: 0-0
Track : LH: 0-0 RH: 0-1 Tight: 0-0 Gall: 0-2
Aids: Bl: 0-1 Vi: 0-0 Tstrap: 0-0 Ckp: 0-0
Best Rating: **55** 7/08 Carl 5f good

Rio Royale (IRE)

99(100) (76)78

3-y-o b g Captain Rio-Lady Nasrana (FR) (Al Nasr (FR))
Mrs A J Perrett Mrs Amanda Perrett

Placings:254210325-3051024045000 (7329)
2009: 8^{3}SD, 7^{0}SD, 8^{5}SD, 6^{1}F, 6^{0}HY, 6^{2}GF, 6^{4}G, 6^{0}GF, 5^{4}F, 7^{5}G, 6^{0}GS, 5^{0}SD, 6^{0}SD,

	Starts	1st	2nd	3rd	Win & Pl
Career Total (Turf)	14	2	3	0	10332
Career Total (AW)	8	0	1	2	1808

78	5/09	Sals	6f	(0-75)H	FRM	£3238
77	6/08	Folk	7f		G-F	£2817

Total win prize-money £6055

Going (Turf): Sf: 0-1 GS: 0-4 Gd: 0-2 **GF: 1-5 Fm: 1-2**
Distance: 5f/6f: 1-15 7f-8f: 1-7 9f-13f: 0-0 14f+: 0-0
Track : LH: 0-8 RH: 0-3 Tight: 0-4 Gall: 0-1
Aids: Bl: 0-0 Vi: 0-0 Tstrap: 0-2 Ckp: 0-2
Best Rating: **78** 5/09 Sals 6f firm

Modest; effective at 7f; acts on fast ground; has worn cheekpieces.

Rio Sands

96(86) (34)76

4-y-o b g Captain Rio-Sally Traffic (River Falls)
R M Whitaker Barry & The Barflys

Placings:50500/62212523350-0603050530100 (6765)
2009: 6^{0}GF, 5^{6}GF, 5^{0}GF, 5^{3}GF, 5^{0}F, 5^{5}GF, 6^{0}SD, 5^{5}G, 6^{3}GF, 5^{0}GF, 5^{1}GF, 5^{0}SD, 6^{0}G,

	Starts	1st	2nd	3rd	Win & Pl
Career Total (Turf)	27	2	4	4	11144
Career Total (AW)	2	0	0	0	

66	9/09	Newc	5f	(0-60)H	G-F	£1748
72	5/08	Muss	5f		G-F	£2590

Total win prize-money £4339

Going (Turf): Sf: 0-5 GS: 0-2 Gd: 0-6 **GF: 2-13** Fm: 0-1
Distance: **5f/6f: 2-29** 7f-8f: 0-0 9f-13f: 0-0 14f+: 0-0
Track : LH: 0-8 RH: 0-1 Tight: 0-2 Gall: 0-1
Aids: Bl: 0-0 Vi: 0-0 Tstrap: 0-0 Ckp: 0-0
Best Rating: **76** 6/08 Newc 5f soft

Moderate; effective over 5f-6f; acts on fast ground.

Rio's Girl

63 7

2-y-o b f Captain Rio-African Breeze (Atraf)

R M Whitaker Tracey Gaunt & David Gibbons

Placings:0 (3032)

2009: 5^{0}G,

	Starts	1st	2nd	3rd	Win & Pl
Career Total (Turf)	1	0	0	0	

Going (Turf): **Sf: 0-0 GS: 0-0 Gd: 0-1 GF: 0-0 Fm: 0-0**
Distance: 5f/6f: 0-1 7f-8f: 0-0 9f-13f: 0-0 14f+: 0-0
Track : LH: 0-0 RH: 0-0 Tight: 0-0 Gall: 0-0
Aids: Bl: 0-0 Vi: 0-0 Tstrap: 0-0 Ckp: 0-0
Best Rating: **7** 6/09 Ripn 5f good

Rioja Ruby (IRE)

78 43

3-y-o b f Redback-Bacchanalia (IRE) (Blues Traveller (IRE))

S G West David Ryan

Placings:3445000-00 (2790)

2009: 8^{0}F, 10^{0}G,

	Starts	1st	2nd	3rd	Win & Pl
Career Total (Turf)	9	0	0	1	938

Going (Turf): **Sf: 0-1 GS: 0-2 Gd: 0-2 GF: 0-3 Fm: 0-1**
Distance: 5f/6f: 0-7 7f-8f: 0-1 9f-13f: 0-1 14f+: 0-0
Track : LH: 0-1 RH: 0-0 Tight: 0-1 Gall: 0-0
Aids: Bl: 0-1 Vi: 0-1 Tstrap: 0-1 Ckp: 0-1
Best Rating: **43** 5/08 Thsk 5f gd-fm

Rioliina (IRE)

103(98) (65)82

3-y-o b f Captain Rio-Anneliina (Cadeaux Genereux)

J G Portman Exors of the late A S B Portman

Placings:515-600130 (7662)

2009: 6^{6}SD, 7^{0}GS, 6^{0}GF, 7^{1}GF, 7^{3}SD, 7^{0}SD,

	Starts	1st	2nd	3rd	Win & Pl
Career Total (Turf)	6	2	0	0	4857
Career Total (AW)	3	0	0	1	292

74 10/09 Leic 7f9y G-F £2590
82 8/08 Bath 5f161y G-S £2266
Total win prize-money £4857

Going (Turf): Sf: 0-0 **GS: 1-2** Gd: 0-1 **GF: 1-3** Fm: 0-0
Distance: 5f/6f: 1-3 7f-8f: 1-6 9f-13f: 0-0 14f+: 0-0
Track : **LH: 1-4** RH: 0-0 Tight: 0-3 **Gall: 1-1**
Aids: Bl: 0-0 Vi: 0-0 Tstrap: 0-0 Ckp: 0-0
Best Rating: **82** 8/08 Bath 5f161y gd-sft

Fair; effective over 7f; acts on easy ground and on Polytrack.

Rip Van Winkle (IRE)

121 (95)132

3-y-o b c Galileo (IRE)-Looking Back (IRE) (Stravinsky (USA))

A P O'Brien Mrs John Magnier, M Tabor & D Smith

Placings:110-442110 (7311a)

2009: 8^{4}GF, 12^{4}G, 10^{2}G, 8^{1}G, 8^{1}GF, 10^{0}FT,

	Starts	1st	2nd	3rd	Win & Pl
Career Total (Turf)	8	4	1	0	552917
Career Total (AW)	1	0	0	0	

128 9/09 Asct 1m G-F £141925
131 7/09 Gdwd 1m GD £170310
108 7/08 Leop 7f G-F £33507
90 6/08 Curr 7f G-Y £9573
Total win prize-money £355316

Going (Turf): Sf: 0-0 GS: 0-0 Gd: 1-4 **GF: 2-3** Fm: 0-0
Distance: 5f/6f: 0-0 **7f-8f: 4-6** 9f-13f: 0-3 14f+: 0-0
Track : LH: 1-3 **RH: 2-3** Tight: 0-1 **Gall: 1-1**
Aids: Bl: 0-0 Vi: 0-0 Tstrap: 0-0 Ckp: 0-0
Best Rating: **132** 7/09 Sand 1m2f7y good

Group class; runner-up to Sea The Stars in the 2009 Eclipse before winning the Sussex Stakes and Queen Elizabeth II Stakes; effective over 1m, probably stays 1m2f; acts on most ground.

Riptide

91 63

3-y-o b g Val Royal (FR)-Glittering Image (IRE) (Sadler's Wells (USA))

D McCain Jnr (C F Wall 21/7) Gone To The Bar Racing

Placings:0-040 (4178)

2009: 10^{0}S, 12^{4}GF, 11^{0}GS,

	Starts	1st	2nd	3rd	Win & Pl
Career Total (Turf)	4	0	0	0	241

Going (Turf): **Sf: 0-1 GS: 0-1 Gd: 0-1 GF: 0-1 Fm: 0-0**
Distance: 5f/6f: 0-0 7f-8f: 0-1 9f-13f: 0-3 14f+: 0-0
Track : LH: 0-3 RH: 0-0 Tight: 0-1 Gall: 0-0
Aids: Bl: 0-0 Vi: 0-0 Tstrap: 0-0 Ckp: 0-0
Best Rating: **63** 6/09 Pont 1m4f8y gd-fm

Riqaab (IRE)

99(100) (70)77

4-y-o b g Peintre Celebre (USA)-Jeed (IRE) (Mujtahid (USA))

E A L Dunlop Hamdan Al Maktoum

Placings:0/26512-26 (1581)

2009: 9^{2}G, 11^{6}G,

	Starts	1st	2nd	3rd	Win & Pl
Career Total (Turf)	6	1	2	0	5668
Career Total (AW)	2	0	1	0	694

74 7/08 Yarm 1m1f (0-70)H G-F £2719
Total win prize-money £2720

Going (Turf): Sf: 0-0 GS: 0-1 Gd: 0-4 **GF: 1-1** Fm: 0-0
Distance: 5f/6f: 0-0 7f-8f: 0-2 **9f-13f: 1-6** 14f+: 0-0
Track : **LH: 1-5** RH: 0-2 **Tight: 1-5** Gall: 0-0
Aids: Bl: 0-0 Vi: 0-0 Tstrap: 0-0 Ckp: 0-0
Best Rating: **77** 4/09 Brig 1m1f209y good

Fair; stays 1m 1f; acts on quick ground.

Rising Force (IRE)

86(94) (67)71

6-y-o b g Selkirk (USA)-Singing Diva (IRE) (Royal Academy (USA))

J L Spearing Masonaires

Placings:000210/42006/31455340-600 (7670)

2009: 11^{6}G, 11^{0}SD, 12^{0}SD,

	Starts	1st	2nd	3rd	Win & Pl
Career Total (Turf)	13	1	2	1	7147
Career Total (AW)	9	1	0	1	3361

70 2/08 Kemp 1m3f (0-70)H STD £2590
69 9/06 Clon 1m2f (40-60)H FRM £3812
Total win prize-money £6403

Going (Turf): Sf: 0-1 GS: 0-0 Gd: 0-2 GF: 0-3 **Fm: 1-3**
Distance: 5f/6f: 0-3 7f-8f: 0-5 **9f-13f: 2-14** 14f+: 0-0
Track : LH: 0-10 **RH: 2-9** Tight: 0-5 Gall: 0-4
Aids: **Bl: 2-16** Vi: 0-0 Tstrap: 0-0 Ckp: 0-0
Best Rating: **76** 8/07 Gway 1m100y gd-yld

Modest; stays 1m3f and acts on Polytrack; has worn blinkers.

Rising Kheleyf (IRE)

104 77

3-y-o ch g Kheleyf (USA)-Rising Spirits (Cure The Blues (USA))

G A Swinbank D Bamlet

Placings:0054-12451450 (6015)

2009: 7^{1}GF, 8^{2}GF, 7^{4}GS, 7^{5}GF, 6^{1}G, 7^{4}G, 6^{5}G, 7^{0}G,

	Starts	1st	2nd	3rd	Win & Pl
Career Total (Turf)	12	2	1	0	5712

77 7/09 Carl 6f192y (0-70)H GD £2590
70 4/09 Catt 7f (0-65)H G-F £2183
Total win prize-money £4774

Going (Turf): Sf: 0-0 GS: 0-3 **Gd: 1-6 GF: 1-3** Fm: 0-0
Distance: 5f/6f: 0-3 **7f-8f: 2-9** 9f-13f: 0-0 14f+: 0-0
Track : LH: 1-6 RH: 1-4 **Tight: 1-4** Gall: 0-0
Aids: Bl: 0-0 Vi: 0-0 Tstrap: 0-0 Ckp: 0-0
Best Rating: **77** 7/09 Carl 6f192y good

Fair; stays 1m; acts on fast and easy ground.

Rising Prospect

(99) (76)82

3-y-o ch c Traditionally (USA)-La Sylphide (Rudimentary (USA))

L M Cumani Geoff & Sandra Turnbull

Placings:13010-0P (7141)

2009: 8^{0}SF, 8^{P}SD,

	Starts	1st	2nd	3rd	Win & Pl
Career Total (Turf)	5	2	0	1	24987
Career Total (AW)	2	0	0	0	

82 9/08 Ayr 1m HVY £16574
74 7/08 York 7f HVY £7641
Total win prize-money £24216

Going (Turf): **Sf: 2-4** GS: 0-0 Gd: 0-1 GF: 0-0 Fm: 0-0
Distance: 5f/6f: 0-0 **7f-8f: 2-4** 9f-13f: 0-3 14f+: 0-0
Track : **LH: 2-4** RH: 0-1 Tight: 0-3 **Gall: 1-1**
Aids: Bl: 0-0 Vi: 0-0 Tstrap: 0-0 Ckp: 0-0
Best Rating: **82** 9/08 Ayr 1m heavy

Useful; stays 1m; effective on heavy ground.

Rising Shadow (IRE)

103 (81)101

8-y-o b g Efisio-Jouet (Reprimand)

A D Brown (C W Thornton 14/7) G Morrill

Placings:0135/624600/2661332005350/00220061043411/1404060006/0000145000000-00003500 (7287)

2009: 6^{0}S, 6^{0}G, 6^{0}GF, 8^{0}GF, 7^{3}G, 6^{5}G, 7^{0}G, 7^{0}S,

	Starts	1st	2nd	3rd	Win & Pl
Career Total (Turf)	67	7	5	5	132164
Career Total (AW)	1	0	0	1	440

101 6/08 Ripn 6f (0-95)H HVY £8200
113 3/07 Newc 6f G-S £17034
109 11/06 Wind 6f G-S £16595
108 10/06 York 6f (0-105)H SFT £22669

98	8/06	Ripn	6f	(0-95)H	GD	£11217
92	6/05	Newc	6f	(0-85)H	GD	£6996
75	10/03	Newc	6f	D	GD	£2506

Total win prize-money £85221

Going (Turf): Sf: 2-18 GS: 2-14 **Gd: 3-21** GF: 0-14 Fm: 0-0
Distance: **5f/6f: 7-53** 7f-8f: 0-14 9f-13f: 0-1 14f+: 0-0
Track : LH: 0-11 RH: 0-1 Tight: 0-6 **Gall: 1-2**
Aids: Bl: 0-1 Vi: 0-0 Tstrap: 0-0 Ckp: 0-0
Best Rating: **113** 3/07 Newc 6f gd-sft

Very useful; winner in Listed company; seems best at 6f; suited by good or softer ground; has worn blinkers; can miss the break.

Risk Runner (IRE)

91 **71**
6-y-o b g Mull Of Kintyre (USA)-Fizzygig (Efisio)
James Moffatt V R Vyner-Brooks

Placings:42501/0425020/000-0 **(2725)**
2009: 16^{0}G,

	Starts	1st	2nd	3rd	Win & Pl
Career Total (Turf)	16	1	3	0	8763

73	11/05	Yarm	1m3y	(0-75)	HVY	£4728

Total win prize-money £4728

Going (Turf): **Sf: 1-4** GS: 0-2 Gd: 0-6 GF: 0-4 Fm: 0-0
Distance: 5f/6f: 0-0 7f-8f: 0-1 **9f-13f: 1-13** 14f+: 0-2
Track : LH: 0-8 RH: 0-2 Tight: 0-8 Gall: 0-2
Aids: Bl: 0-3 **Vi: 1-8** Tstrap: 0-0 Ckp: 0-0
Best Rating: **83** 9/06 Nott 1m1f213y good

Risky Lady (IRE)

84(72) (28)**35**
3-y-o b f Tamarisk (IRE)-My Croft (Crofter (USA))
J Ryan John Ryan Racing Partnership

Placings:000-00000 **(2633)**
2009: 7^{0}SD, 7^{0}GF, 6^{0}SD, 8^{0}GF, 10^{0}GF,

	Starts	1st	2nd	3rd	Win & Pl
Career Total (Turf)	3	0	0	0	
Career Total (AW)	5	0	0	0	

Going (Turf): **Sf: 0-0 GS: 0-0 Gd: 0-0 GF: 0-3 Fm: 0-0**
Distance: 5f/6f: 0-4 7f-8f: 0-2 9f-13f: 0-2 14f+: 0-0
Track : LH: 0-6 RH: 0-1 Tight: 0-4 Gall: 0-1
Aids: Bl: 0-0 Vi: 0-1 Tstrap: 0-0 Ckp: 0-0
Best Rating: **35** 6/09 Ling 1m2f gd-fm

Risque Belle

(48)
3-y-o b f Fantastic Light (USA)-Risque Lady (Kenmare (FR))
E J Creighton Travel Spot LLP

Placings:0-0 **(0272)**
2009: 10^{0}SD,

	Starts	1st	2nd	3rd	Win & Pl
Career Total (Turf)	0	0	0	0	
Career Total (AW)	2	0	0	0	

Going (Turf): **Sf: 0-0 GS: 0-0 Gd: 0-0 GF: 0-0 Fm: 0-0**
Distance: 5f/6f: 0-0 7f-8f: 0-1 9f-13f: 0-1 14f+: 0-0
Track : LH: 0-2 RH: 0-0 Tight: 0-2 Gall: 0-0
Aids: Bl: 0-0 Vi: 0-0 Tstrap: 0-0 Ckp: 0-0

Risque Heights

101(104) (83)**74**
5-y-o b g Mark Of Esteem (IRE)-Risque Lady (Kenmare (FR))
J R Boyle Serendipity Syndicate 2006

Placings:0223/65202143134000/500006524411-600400 **(5035)**
2009: 10^{6}SD, 10^{0}SD, 10^{0}SD, 12^{4}G, 12^{0}GF, 10^{0}GF,

	Starts	1st	2nd	3rd	Win & Pl
Career Total (Turf)	14	0	2	1	3949
Career Total (AW)	22	4	3	2	18090

81	12/08	Ling	1m2f	(0-70)H	STD	£2729
72	12/08	Kemp	1m2f	(0-65)H	STD	£2047
90	10/07	Ling	1m2f	(0-80)H	STD	£5362
78	8/07	Ling	1m2f		STD	£2730

Total win prize-money £12870

Going (Turf): **Sf: 0-1 GS: 0-4 Gd: 0-4 GF: 0-5 Fm: 0-0**
Distance: 5f/6f: 0-0 7f-8f: 0-9 **9f-13f: 4-27** 14f+: 0-0
Track : **LH: 3-16** RH: 1-18 **Tight: 3-18** Gall: 0-3
Aids: Bl: 0-4 Vi: 0-0 Tstrap: 0-1 Ckp: 0-1
Best Rating: **90** 10/07 Ling 1m2f stand

Modest; stays 1m3f; acts on easy ground; also goes on Polytrack.

River Ardeche

102(109) (84)**85**
4-y-o b g Elnadim (USA)-Overcome (Belmez (USA))
P C Haslam Mark James & Mrs C Barclay

Placings:1/500-312336 **(7640)**
2009: 12^{3}SD, 12^{1}SD, 13^{2}GF, 12^{3}SD, 12^{3}GF, 11^{6}SD,

	Starts	1st	2nd	3rd	Win & Pl
Career Total (Turf)	6	1	1	1	9103
Career Total (AW)	4	1	0	2	6427

83	1/09	Sthl	1m4f	(0-85)H	STD	£5180
78	7/07	York	6f		HVY	£6541

Total win prize-money £11723

Going (Turf): **Sf: 1-1** GS: 0-0 Gd: 0-2 GF: 0-3 Fm: 0-0
Distance: 5f/6f: 1-1 7f-8f: 0-2 9f-13f: 1-6 14f+: 0-1
Track : **LH: 1-6** RH: 0-2 Tight: 0-3 Gall: 0-0
Aids: Bl: 0-0 Vi: 0-0 Tstrap: 0-0 Ckp: 0-0
Best Rating: **85** 4/09 Catt 1m5f175y gd-fm

Fair; stays 1m6f; acts on fast ground and on sand.

River Captain (IRE)

110(101) (82)**101**
3-y-o ch c Captain Rio-Pardoned (IRE) (Mujadil (USA))
S Kirk S J McCay & Mrs Liam Duddy

Placings:5001100-316154 **(4455)**
2009: 9^{3}SD, 8^{1}G, 10^{6}S, 10^{1}G, 8^{5}GF, 9^{4}G,

	Starts	1st	2nd	3rd	Win & Pl
Career Total (Turf)	11	4	0	0	47764
Career Total (AW)	2	0	0	1	770

99	6/09	Epsm	1m2f18y	(0-105)H	GD	£31155
87	4/09	Epsm	1m114y	(0-75)H	GD	£4857
74	9/08	Bath	1m5y	(0-75)	SFT	£2914
70	8/08	Sals	6f212y		G-S	£3238

Total win prize-money £42164

Going (Turf): Sf: 1-3 GS: 1-1 **Gd: 2-3** GF: 0-3 Fm: 0-0
Distance: 5f/6f: 0-3 7f-8f: 1-4 **9f-13f: 3-6** 14f+: 0-0
Track : **LH: 3-5** RH: 0-3 **Tight: 3-5** Gall: 0-2
Aids: Bl: 0-0 Vi: 0-0 Tstrap: 0-0 Ckp: 0-0
Best Rating: **101** 7/09 Gdwd 1m1f192y good

Very useful; stays 1m2f; acts on most ground and on Polytrack.

River Danube

88(82) (65)**68**
6-y-o b g Dansili-Campaspe (Dominion)
T J Fitzgerald A Huddlestone

Placings:0034033-0000566 **(7635)**
2009: 16^{0}SD, 16^{0}GS, 16^{0}GS, 15^{0}S, 15^{5}S, 13^{6}S, 14^{6}SD,

	Starts	1st	2nd	3rd	Win & Pl
Career Total (Turf)	11	0	0	2	1179
Career Total (AW)	3	0	0	1	403

Going (Turf): **Sf: 0-3 GS: 0-5 Gd: 0-3 GF: 0-0 Fm: 0-0**
Distance: 5f/6f: 0-0 7f-8f: 0-0 9f-13f: 0-3 14f+: 0-11
Track : LH: 0-14 RH: 0-0 Tight: 0-9 Gall: 0-1
Aids: Bl: 0-0 Vi: 0-0 Tstrap: 0-0 Ckp: 0-0
Best Rating: **68** 8/08 Catt 1m3f214y gd-sft

Modest; stays 2m; acts on easy ground; goes on Fibresand; has worn a tongue tie.

River Dee (IRE)

96(73) (6)**76**
3-y-o b g Almutawakel-Fiaba (Precocious)
D Donovan Philip Mclaughlin

Placings:01322540-0354300 **(5326)**
2009: 8^{0}GF, 5^{3}G, 6^{5}GF, 8^{4}G, 7^{3}GF, 5^{0}S, 6^{0}SD,

	Starts	1st	2nd	3rd	Win & Pl
Career Total (Turf)	14	1	2	3	7927
Career Total (AW)	1	0	0	0	

63	7/08	Yarm	6f3y		G-F	£1942

Total win prize-money £1943

Going (Turf): Sf: 0-1 GS: 0-3 Gd: 0-4 **GF: 1-6** Fm: 0-0
Distance: 5f/6f: 0-4 **7f-8f: 1-10** 9f-13f: 0-1 14f+: 0-0
Track : LH: 0-6 RH: 0-2 Tight: 0-2 Gall: 0-0
Aids: Bl: 0-1 Vi: 0-0 Tstrap: 0-0 Ckp: 0-0
Best Rating: **76** 8/08 Ches 7f2y gd-fm

Fair; effective over 6f-7f; acts on fast and easy ground.

River Falcon

107 (93)**102**
9-y-o b g Pivotal-Pearly River (Elegant Air)
J S Goldie F Brady, E Bruce & S Bruce

Placings:03000/64301420000/50100301004500/5115503000/260440/22204600106640/03200562054-05532030000000 **(7015)**
2009: 6^{0}GF, 5^{3}G, 6^{5}S, 5^{3}GF, 5^{2}G, 5^{0}G, 5^{3}G, 6^{0}G, 5^{0}GF, 5^{0}GF, 6^{0}G, 5^{0}GF, 6^{0}G, 5^{0}GS,

	Starts	1st	2nd	3rd	Win & Pl
Career Total (Turf)	84	6	8	7	160863
Career Total (AW)	1	0	0	0	

104	8/07	York	5f	(0-100)H	GD	£16192
102	5/05	York	5f	(0-100)H	SFT	£16153
89	4/05	Thsk	5f	(0-80)	SFT	£6773
94	8/04	Hayd	6f	C(0-85)	GD	£9236
88	5/04	York	5f3y	B(0-110)H	G-S	£14820
85	5/03	Rdcr	5f	C(0-90)H	G-F	£10871

Total win prize-money £74047

Going (Turf): **Sf: 2-21** GS: 1-16 **Gd: 2-23** GF: 1-23 Fm: 0-1
Distance: **5f/6f: 6-79** 7f-8f: 0-6 9f-13f: 0-0 14f+: 0-0
Track : LH: 0-2 RH: 0-0 Tight: 0-2 Gall: 0-0
Aids: Bl: 0-0 Vi: 0-0 Tstrap: 0-1 Ckp: 0-1
Best Rating: **104** 8/07 York 5f good

Useful; effective over 5f-6f; handles most ground, but best on soft; has worn cheekpieces; usually held up.

River Kirov (IRE)

108(112) (86)85

6-y-o b g Soviet Star (USA)-Night Shifter (IRE) (Night Shift (USA))

M Wigham A Darke T Matthews M Wigham

Placings:2514146/420000**066**/006**041213241**-110**0132500120000** **(7662)**

2009: 6^{1}SD, 5^{1}SD, 6^{0}SD, 6^{0}G, 6^{1}GF, 6^{3}GS, 6^{2}G, 6^{5}G, 6^{0}SD, 6^{0}G, 5^{1}SD, 6^{2}SD, 6^{0}SD, 6^{0}SD, 6^{0}SD, 7^{0}SD,

	Starts	1st	2nd	3rd	Win & Pl
Career Total (Turf)	24	3	3	1	19868
Career Total (AW)	20	6	3	1	19108

85	10/09	Wolv	5f216y		STD	£2729
82	6/09	NmkJ	6f	(0-80)H	G-F	£6476
83	1/09	Wolv	5f216y	(0-75)H	STD	£2729
86	1/09	Kemp	6f	(0-85)H	STD	£4857
79	12/08	Ling	6f	(0-65)H	STD	£2047
69	11/08	Ling	6f	(0-60)H	STD	£1706
62	11/08	Kemp	6f	(0-52)H	STD	£1706
85	7/06	Nott	6f15y	(0-75)H	G-F	£3238
68	5/06	Rdcr	6f		GD	£3238

Total win prize-money £28730

Going (Turf): Sf: 0-0 GS: 0-6 Gd: 1-10 **GF: 2-7** Fm: 0-1
Distance: **5f/6f: 8-35** 7f-8f: 1-9 9f-13f: 0-0 14f+: 0-0
Track : **LH: 4-16** RH: 2-7 **Tight: 4-12** Gall: 0-2
Aids: Bl: 0-1 Vi: 0-0 Tstrap: 0-0 Ckp: 0-0
Best Rating: **88** 4/07 Wind 6f gd-fm

Fair; effective over 6f-7f; acts on good/fast ground and on Polytrack.

River Landing

76 34

2-y-o b c Lucky Story (USA)-Beechnut (IRE) (Mujadil (USA))

R M Beckett Thurloe Thoroughbreds XXV

Placings:00 **(6727)**

2009: 7^{0}G, 8^{0}S,

	Starts	1st	2nd	3rd	Win & Pl
Career Total (Turf)	2	0	0	0	

Going (Turf): **Sf: 0-1 GS: 0-0 Gd: 0-1 GF: 0-0 Fm: 0-0**
Distance: 5f/6f: 0-0 7f-8f: 0-2 9f-13f: 0-0 14f+: 0-0
Track : LH: 0-0 RH: 0-1 Tight: 0-0 Gall: 0-0
Aids: Bl: 0-0 Vi: 0-0 Tstrap: 0-0 Ckp: 0-0
Best Rating: **34** 9/09 Gdwd 7f good

River Rye (IRE)

89(97) (71)76

3-y-o b f Acclamation-Rye (IRE) (Charnwood Forest (IRE))

J S Moore Roger Ambrose Richard Moore Ken Duncan

Placings:51343**520404**-**6442200** **(2321)**

2009: 5^{6}SD, 7^{4}SD, 6^{4}SD, 7^{2}SD, 7^{2}G, 7^{0}SD, 6^{0}G,

	Starts	1st	2nd	3rd	Win & Pl
Career Total (Turf)	9	1	1	2	7203
Career Total (AW)	9	0	2	0	1761

76	5/08	Wind	5f10y		G-F	£3885

Total win prize-money £3886

Going (Turf): Sf: 0-1 GS: 0-1 Gd: 0-4 **GF: 1-3** Fm: 0-0
Distance: **5f/6f: 1-12** 7f-8f: 0-6 9f-13f: 0-0 14f+: 0-0
Track : LH: 0-10 RH: 0-1 Tight: 0-7 **Gall: 1-3**
Aids: Bl: 0-0 Vi: 0-0 Tstrap: 0-6 Ckp: 0-6
Best Rating: **76** 5/08 Wind 5f10y gd-fm

Moderate; effective over 7f; acts on fast ground; goes on Polytrack; has worn cheekpieces.

River Thames

(103) (73)85

6-y-o b g Efisio-Dashing Water (Dashing Blade)

J S Goldie (K A Ryan 2/1) Whitestonecliffe Racing Partnership

Placings:31130/000**600**/4006614020**6**/636230304500164-0 **(0013)**

2009: 6^{0}SS,

	Starts	1st	2nd	3rd	Win & Pl
Career Total (Turf)	30	3	2	5	31326
Career Total (AW)	8	1	0	0	2067

73	11/08	Ling	6f	(0-60)H	STD	£1706
88	7/07	Ayr	6f	(0-80)H	G-S	£6477
88	8/05	NmkJ	6f		GD	£5616
87	8/05	Yarm	6f3y		G-F	£4104

Total win prize-money £17904

Going (Turf): Sf: 0-4 **GS: 1-8 Gd: 1-11 GF: 1-6** Fm: 0-1
Distance: **5f/6f: 3-31** 7f-8f: 1-7 9f-13f: 0-0 14f+: 0-0
Track : **LH: 1-13** RH: 0-0 **Tight: 1-8** Gall: 0-0
Aids: Bl: 0-1 Vi: 0-0 Tstrap: 0-2 Ckp: 0-2
Best Rating: **95** 9/05 Newb 6f8y gd-fm

Fair; seems best at 6f; acts on good and easier ground; goes on Polytrack; has worn blinkers and cheekpieces.

River Till (IRE)

95 65

3-y-o b f Bachelor Duke (USA)-The Poachers Lady (IRE) (Salmon Leap (USA))

W Jarvis A Reed

Placings:30 **(3338)**

2009: 6^{3}S, 6^{0}G,

	Starts	1st	2nd	3rd	Win & Pl
Career Total (Turf)	2	0	0	1	434

Going (Turf): **Sf: 0-1 GS: 0-0 Gd: 0-1 GF: 0-0 Fm: 0-0**
Distance: 5f/6f: 0-1 7f-8f: 0-1 9f-13f: 0-0 14f+: 0-0
Track : LH: 0-0 RH: 0-0 Tight: 0-0 Gall: 0-0
Aids: Bl: 0-0 Vi: 0-0 Tstrap: 0-0 Ckp: 0-0
Best Rating: **65** 6/09 Yarm 6f3y soft

Fair; suited by 6f and soft ground.

Riverside

85(87) (16)27

4-y-o b f Kyllachy-My Cadeaux (Cadeaux Genereux)

M Brittain Mel Brittain

Placings:0/600-00 **(7678)**

2009: 8^{0}GF, 7^{0}SD,

	Starts	1st	2nd	3rd	Win & Pl
Career Total (Turf)	5	0	0	0	0
Career Total (AW)	1	0	0	0	

Going (Turf): **Sf: 0-1 GS: 0-2 Gd: 0-0 GF: 0-2 Fm: 0-0**
Distance: 5f/6f: 0-1 7f-8f: 0-4 9f-13f: 0-1 14f+: 0-0
Track : LH: 0-1 RH: 0-1 Tight: 0-0 Gall: 0-0
Aids: Bl: 0-0 Vi: 0-0 Tstrap: 0-0 Ckp: 0-0
Best Rating: **38** 4/08 Donc 7f gd-sft

Riviera Chic (USA)

(92) (63)

2-y-o b f Medaglia D'Oro (USA)-Hurricane Warning (USA) (Thunder Gulch (USA))

R M Beckett Trevor C Stewart

Placings:33 **(7816)**

2009: 7^{3}SF, 8^{3}SD,

	Starts	1st	2nd	3rd	Win & Pl
Career Total (Turf)	0	0	0	0	
Career Total (AW)	2	0	0	2	867

Going (Turf): **Sf: 0-0 GS: 0-0 Gd: 0-0 GF: 0-0 Fm: 0-0**
Distance: 5f/6f: 0-0 7f-8f: 0-1 9f-13f: 0-1 14f+: 0-0
Track : LH: 0-2 RH: 0-0 Tight: 0-2 Gall: 0-0
Aids: Bl: 0-0 Vi: 0-0 Tstrap: 0-0 Ckp: 0-0
Best Rating: **63** 12/09 Wolv 1m141y stand

Modest $60,000 yearling; effective over 7f-1m; acts on Polytrack.

Riviera Red (IRE)

(99) (51)

9-y-o b g Rainbow Quest (USA)-Banquise (IRE) (Last Tycoon)

L Montague Hall Michael S Green & Partners

Placings:0006/0001/000/6404/30-0410 **(7197)**

2009: 8^{0}SD, 8^{4}SD, 8^{1}SD, 8^{0}SD,

	Starts	1st	2nd	3rd	Win & Pl
Career Total (Turf)	1	0	0	0	
Career Total (AW)	20	2	0	1	3464

51	2/09	Ling	1m	(0-45)	STD	£1619
51	12/05	Ling	1m	(0-45)	STD	£1423

Total win prize-money £3042

Going (Turf): **Sf: 0-0 GS: 0-0 Gd: 0-0 GF: 0-1 Fm: 0-0**
Distance: 5f/6f: 0-0 **7f-8f: 2-12** 9f-13f: 0-8 14f+: 0-1
Track : **LH: 2-15** RH: 0-6 **Tight: 2-13** Gall: 0-2
Aids: Bl: 0-2 **Vi: 2-9** Tstrap: 0-0 Ckp: 0-0
Best Rating: **51** 2/09 Ling 1m stand

Plating-class performer; stays a mile but has been tried over further; acts on Polytrack; has worn a visor.

Rivitivo

57(74) (31)

2-y-o b f Deportivo-River Ensign (River God (USA))

W M Brisbourne Mrs Mary Brisbourne

Placings:000 **(4188)**

2009: 5^{0}GF, 5^{0}SD, 7^{0}S,

	Starts	1st	2nd	3rd	Win & Pl
Career Total (Turf)	2	0	0	0	
Career Total (AW)	1	0	0	0	

Going (Turf): **Sf: 0-1 GS: 0-0 Gd: 0-0 GF: 0-1 Fm: 0-0**
Distance: 5f/6f: 0-2 7f-8f: 0-1 9f-13f: 0-0 14f+: 0-0
Track : LH: 0-2 RH: 0-0 Tight: 0-2 Gall: 0-0
Aids: Bl: 0-0 Vi: 0-0 Tstrap: 0-0 Ckp: 0-0
Best Rating: **31** 7/09 Wolv 5f216y stand

Rjeef (IRE)

94 69

2-y-o b c Red Ransom (USA)-Sun Chaser (IRE) (King's Best (USA))

C E Brittain Saeed Manana

Placings:225 (5542)
2009: 6^{2}S, 6^{2}GF, 7^{5}GF,

	Starts	1st	2nd	3rd	Win & Pl
Career Total (Turf)	3	0	2	0	1831

Going (Turf): Sf: 0-1 GS: 0-0 Gd: 0-0 GF: 0-2 Fm: 0-0
Distance: 5f/6f: 0-2 7f-8f: 0-1 9f-13f: 0-0 14f+: 0-0
Track : LH: 0-0 RH: 0-0 Tight: 0-0 Gall: 0-0
Aids: Bl: 0-0 Vi: 0-0 Tstrap: 0-0 Ckp: 0-0
Best Rating: 69 6/09 Ripn 6f gd-fm

Modest; runner-up in 6f maidens; handles fast ground.

Road To Love (IRE)

103(96) (94)**88**
6-y-o ch g Fruits Of Love (USA)-Alpine Flair (IRE) (Tirol)
M Johnston Grant Mercer

Placings:0013/62010116333/004520/**3**-000004 **(4716)**
2009: 9^{0}GF, 10^{0}GF, 12^{0}GF, 10^{0}G, 10^{0}GF, 10^{4}GS,

	Starts	1st	2nd	3rd	Win & Pl
Career Total (Turf)	27	4	2	4	122732
Career Total (AW)	1	0	0	1	1011

115	8/06	Gdwd	1m1f192y	H	G-F	£62320
113	7/06	Asct	1m2f	(0-105)H	G-F	£18696
103	7/06	Sand	1m2f7y	(0-85)H	G-F	£7772
88	8/05	Bevl	1m100y		G-S	£4966

Total win prize-money £93754

Going (Turf): Sf: 0-1 GS: 1-5 Gd: 0-5 **GF: 3-15** Fm: 0-1
Distance: 5f/6f: 0-1 7f-8f: 0-4 **9f-13f: 4-23** 14f+: 0-0
Track : LH: 0-9 **RH: 4-14** Tight: 1-5 Gall: 1-11
Aids: Bl: 0-0 Vi: 0-0 Tstrap: 0-0 Ckp: 0-0
Best Rating: 115 9/06 Gdwd 1m1f192y gd-fm

Very useful; stays 1m2f; seems best on fast, but handles easy ground; likes to race prominently.

Roar Of Applause

103(102) (85)**91**
3-y-o b g Royal Applause-Les Hurlants (IRE) (Barathea (IRE))
B J Meehan Raymond Tooth

Placings:006**1**-1513406**2**3**0**3312 **(6537)**
2009: 8^{1}GF, 8^{5}F, 8^{1}GF, 8^{3}GF, 8^{4}G, 8^{0}S, 8^{6}G, 8^{2}SD, 8^{3}GF, 8^{0}SD, 8^{3}GF, 8^{3}G, 8^{1}GF, 8^{2}GF,

	Starts	1st	2nd	3rd	Win & Pl
Career Total (Turf)	15	3	1	4	20892
Career Total (AW)	3	1	1	0	3113

91	10/09	Epsm	1m114y	(0-90)H	G-F	£7771
79	5/09	Wind	1m67y	(0-70)H	G-F	£2729
74	5/09	Chep	1m14y	(0-80)H	G-F	£4857
64	11/08	Kemp	1m	(0-60)	STD	£1706

Total win prize-money £17064

Going (Turf): Sf: 0-1 GS: 0-0 Gd: 0-6 **GF: 3-7** Fm: 0-1
Distance: 5f/6f: 0-0 7f-8f: 1-9 **9f-13f: 3-9** 14f+: 0-0
Track : LH: 1-4 **RH: 2-6 Tight: 2-3** Gall: 0-0
Aids: **Bl: 1-7** Vi: 0-0 Tstrap: 0-0 Ckp: 0-0
Best Rating: 91 10/09 Epsm 1m114y gd-fm

Fair; stays 1m; acts on fast ground; goes on Polytrack; has worn blinkers.

Roar Of The King (USA)

90(87) (60)**58**
3-y-o b c Lion Heart (USA)-V V S Flawless (USA) (Deputy Minister (CAN))
J Noseda Sir Robert Ogden

Placings:06 **(2282)**
2009: 7^{0}SD, 8^{6}GF,

	Starts	1st	2nd	3rd	Win & Pl
Career Total (Turf)	1	0	0	0	0
Career Total (AW)	1	0	0	0	

Going (Turf): Sf: 0-0 GS: 0-0 Gd: 0-0 GF: 0-1 Fm: 0-0
Distance: 5f/6f: 0-0 7f-8f: 0-2 9f-13f: 0-0 14f+: 0-0
Track : LH: 0-1 RH: 0-0 Tight: 0-1 Gall: 0-0
Aids: Bl: 0-0 Vi: 0-0 Tstrap: 0-0 Ckp: 0-0
Best Rating: 60 5/09 Ling 7f stand

Roar Talent (USA)

(67) (19)
2-y-o ch c Roar Of The Tiger (USA)-Laurie's Folly (USA) (Kris S (USA))
J R Best Miss Sara Furnival

Placings:0P **(6913)**
2009: 8^{0}SD, 6^{P}SD,

	Starts	1st	2nd	3rd	Win & Pl
Career Total (Turf)	0	0	0	0	
Career Total (AW)	2	0	0	0	

Going (Turf): Sf: 0-0 GS: 0-0 Gd: 0-0 GF: 0-0 Fm: 0-0
Distance: 5f/6f: 0-1 7f-8f: 0-1 9f-13f: 0-0 14f+: 0-0
Track : LH: 0-1 RH: 0-1 Tight: 0-1 Gall: 0-0
Aids: Bl: 0-0 Vi: 0-0 Tstrap: 0-0 Ckp: 0-0
Best Rating: 19 9/09 Kemp 1m stand

Roaring Forte (IRE)

117(109) (108)**111**
4-y-o b c Cape Cross (IRE)-Descant (USA) (Nureyev (USA))
W J Haggas Flying Tiger Partnership

Placings:41/3221-101 **(5200)**
2009: 7^{1}GF, 7^{0}G, 8^{1}GF,

	Starts	1st	2nd	3rd	Win & Pl
Career Total (Turf)	7	2	2	1	47948
Career Total (AW)	2	2	0	0	18168

111	8/09	York	1m	H	G-F	£32380
107	5/09	NmkR	7f	(0-95)H	G-F	£9066
108	9/08	GrLe	1m	(0-100)H	STD	£15577
85	11/07	Ling	7f		STD	£2590

Total win prize-money £59615

Going (Turf): Sf: 0-1 GS: 0-1 Gd: 0-2 **GF: 2-3** Fm: 0-0
Distance: 5f/6f: 0-0 **7f-8f: 4-8** 9f-13f: 0-1 14f+: 0-0
Track : **LH: 3-3** RH: 0-1 Tight: 1-2 **Gall: 2-2**
Aids: Bl: 0-0 Vi: 0-0 Tstrap: 0-0 Ckp: 0-0
Best Rating: 111 8/09 York 1m gd-fm

Smart; effective over 7f-1m; acts on most ground and on Polytrack.

Robbmaa (FR)

86 (30)**49**
4-y-o bl g Cape Cross (IRE)-Native Twine (Be My Native (USA))
A W Carroll Group 1 Racing (1994) Ltd

Placings:06/00006-405 **(3259)**
2009: 11^{4}F, 10^{0}GF, 10^{5}F,

	Starts	1st	2nd	3rd	Win & Pl
Career Total (Turf)	9	0	0	0	236
Career Total (AW)	1	0	0	0	

Going (Turf): Sf: 0-1 GS: 0-1 Gd: 0-1 GF: 0-3 Fm: 0-3
Distance: 5f/6f: 0-1 7f-8f: 0-2 9f-13f: 0-7 14f+: 0-0
Track : LH: 0-5 RH: 0-1 Tight: 0-2 Gall: 0-0
Aids: Bl: 0-0 Vi: 0-0 Tstrap: 0-0 Ckp: 0-0
Best Rating: 57 10/07 Wwck 7f26y gd-fm

Robby Bobby

106(107) (102)**90**
4-y-o ch g Selkirk (USA)-Dancing Mirage (IRE) (Machiavellian (USA))
M Johnston C M , B J & R F Batterham li

Placings:21/40**6013-12040**030065064 **(4840)**
2009: **12**^{1}SD, **11**^{2}SD, **11**^{0}SD, **11**^{4}SD, **11**^{0}SD, 12^{0}G, 10^{3}GF, 12^{0}GS, 10^{0}G, 12^{6}GF, 12^{5}G, 12^{0}G, 12^{6}G, **12**^{4}SD,

	Starts	1st	2nd	3rd	Win & Pl
Career Total (Turf)	12	1	1	1	10863
Career Total (AW)	10	2	1	1	24404

96	1/09	Ling	1m4f	(0-100)H	STD	£11656
95	12/08	Sthl	1m3f	(0-80)H	STD	£6476
84	10/07	Newb	1m		G-S	£5829

Total win prize-money £23962

Going (Turf): Sf: 0-0 **GS: 1-3** Gd: 0-6 GF: 0-3 Fm: 0-0
Distance: 5f/6f: 0-0 7f-8f: 1-4 **9f-13f: 2-18** 14f+: 0-0
Track : **LH: 2-11** RH: 0-8 **Tight: 1-7** Gall: 0-4
Aids: Bl: 0-0 Vi: 0-0 Tstrap: 0-0 Ckp: 0-0
Best Rating: 102 2/09 Sthl 1m3f stand

Useful; stays 1m4f; acts on easy ground and on sand; likes to race prominently.

Robens Rock (IRE)

95(97) (67)**61**
2-y-o b g Rock Of Gibraltar (IRE)-Qhazeenah (Marju (IRE))
A B Haynes R S Brookhouse

Placings:06**2**5 **(6932)**
2009: 7^{0}G, 6^{6}G, **5**^{2}SS, 5^{5}G,

	Starts	1st	2nd	3rd	Win & Pl
Career Total (Turf)	3	0	0	0	0
Career Total (AW)	1	0	1	0	964

Going (Turf): Sf: 0-0 GS: 0-0 Gd: 0-3 GF: 0-0 Fm: 0-0
Distance: 5f/6f: 0-3 7f-8f: 0-1 9f-13f: 0-0 14f+: 0-0
Track : LH: 0-2 RH: 0-1 Tight: 0-1 Gall: 0-1
Aids: Bl: 0-0 Vi: 0-0 Tstrap: 0-0 Ckp: 0-0
Best Rating: 67 10/09 Ling 5f std-slw

Modest; effective over 5f; acts on Polytrack.

Robert Burns (IRE)

(69) (1)**71**
4-y-o b g Invincible Spirit (IRE)-Double Red (IRE)

(Thatching)
Miss D Mountain Miss Debbie Mountain

Placings:6/303300-0 **(1606)**
2009: 8^{0}SD,

	Starts	1st	2nd	3rd	Win & Pl
Career Total (Turf)	7	0	0	3	1175
Career Total (AW)	1	0	0	0	

Going (Turf): Sf: 0-0 GS: 0-2 Gd: 0-1 GF: 0-4 Fm: 0-0
Distance: 5f/6f: 0-0 7f-8f: 0-5 9f-13f: 0-3 14f+: 0-0
Track : LH: 0-3 RH: 0-1 Tight: 0-0 Gall: 0-0
Aids: Bl: 0-0 Vi: 0-0 Tstrap: 0-0 Ckp: 0-0
Best Rating: 71 7/08 Hayd 1m30y good

Robert The Brave

81 (82)68
5-y-o b g Primo Valentino (IRE)-Sandicliffe (USA) (Imp Society (USA))
P R Webber T R Pearson

Placings:3024/501116/0000-4 **(4053)**
2009: 11^{4}S,

	Starts	1st	2nd	3rd	Win & Pl
Career Total (Turf)	7	0	0	0	192
Career Total (AW)	8	3	1	1	8894
82 11/07 Wolv	1m4f50y (0-75)H			STD	£2968
79 10/07 Wolv	1m1f103y (0-65)H			STD	£2047
71 10/07 Wolv	1m141y (0-65)H			STD	£2047

Total win prize-money £7065

Going (Turf): Sf: 0-2 GS: 0-0 Gd: 0-3 GF: 0-2 Fm: 0-0
Distance: 5f/6f: 0-0 7f-8f: 0-1 **9f-13f: 3-14** 14f+: 0-0
Track : **LH: 3-11** RH: 0-2 **Tight: 3-9** Gall: 0-1
Aids: Bl: 0-0 Vi: 0-0 Tstrap: 0-0 Ckp: 0-0
Best Rating: 82 11/07 Wolv 1m4f50y stand

Fair; stays 1m4f and acts on Polytrack.

Robin The Till

97(96) (67)62
3-y-o ch g Bold Edge-My Dancer (IRE) (Alhaarth (IRE))
R Hannon The Fifth Pheasant Inn Partnership

Placings:6052-320405005 **(5500)**
2009: 6^{3}SD, 6^{2}SD, 6^{0}GF, 6^{4}GF, 5^{0}G, 5^{5}GF, 6^{0}G, 5^{0}GF, 5^{5}G,

	Starts	1st	2nd	3rd	Win & Pl
Career Total (Turf)	11	0	1	0	1301
Career Total (AW)	2	0	1	1	1184

Going (Turf): Sf: 0-0 GS: 0-1 Gd: 0-5 GF: 0-5 Fm: 0-0
Distance: 5f/6f: 0-10 7f-8f: 0-3 9f-13f: 0-0 14f+: 0-0
Track : LH: 0-4 RH: 0-0 Tight: 0-3 Gall: 0-3
Aids: Bl: 0-0 Vi: 0-0 Tstrap: 0-0 Ckp: 0-0
Best Rating: 67 3/09 Ling 6f stand

Modest; stays 6f; acts on most ground; goes on Polytrack.

Robinson Cruso

100 82
2-y-o b c Footstepsinthesand-Miss Hawai (FR) (Peintre Celebre (USA))
M A Jarvis P D Smith

Placings:262 **(6991)**
2009: 6^{2}GF, 6^{6}GF, 7^{2}G,

	Starts	1st	2nd	3rd	Win & Pl
Career Total (Turf)	3	0	2	0	4859

Going (Turf): Sf: 0-0 GS: 0-0 Gd: 0-1 GF: 0-2 Fm: 0-0
Distance: 5f/6f: 0-2 7f-8f: 0-1 9f-13f: 0-0 14f+: 0-0
Track : LH: 0-0 RH: 0-0 Tight: 0-0 Gall: 0-1
Aids: Bl: 0-0 Vi: 0-0 Tstrap: 0-0 Ckp: 0-0
Best Rating: 82 8/09 Wind 6f gd-fm

Useful; effective over 6f; acts on fast ground.

Robust Wish (USA)

(100) (78)
2-y-o b g Strong Hope (USA)-Copper Rose (USA) (Unbridled (USA))
B J Meehan Thomas Conway

Placings:0221 **(7580)**
2009: 7^{0}SD, 7^{2}SD, 8^{2}SD, 7^{1}SF,

	Starts	1st	2nd	3rd	Win & Pl
Career Total (Turf)	0	0	0	0	
Career Total (AW)	4	1	2	0	5550
78 11/09 Wolv	7f32y			SF	£3238

Total win prize-money £3238

Going (Turf): Sf: 0-0 GS: 0-0 Gd: 0-0 GF: 0-0 Fm: 0-0
Distance: 5f/6f: 0-0 **7f-8f: 1-4** 9f-13f: 0-0 14f+: 0-0
Track : **LH: 1-2** RH: 0-2 **Tight: 1-2** Gall: 0-0
Aids: **Bl: 1-1** Vi: 0-0 Tstrap: 0-0 Ckp: 0-0
Best Rating: 78 11/09 Wolv 7f32y std-fst

Fair; stays 7f; acts on Polytrack; has worn blinkers.

Rock 'N' Royal

95 79
2-y-o b c Royal Applause-Grande Terre (IRE) (Grand Lodge (USA))
R A Fahey Mr & Mrs G Calder

Placings:1 **(6896)**
2009: 6^{1}GF,

	Starts	1st	2nd	3rd	Win & Pl
Career Total (Turf)	1	1	0	0	3238
79 10/09 Pont	6f		G-F		£3238

Total win prize-money £3238

Going (Turf): Sf: 0-0 GS: 0-0 Gd: 0-0 **GF: 1-1** Fm: 0-0
Distance: **5f/6f: 1-1** 7f-8f: 0-0 9f-13f: 0-0 14f+: 0-0
Track : **LH: 1-1** RH: 0-0 Tight: 0-0 Gall: 0-0
Aids: Bl: 0-0 Vi: 0-0 Tstrap: 0-0 Ckp: 0-0
Best Rating: 79 10/09 Pont 6f gd-fm

Fair; effective at 6f; acts on quick ground.

Rock A Doodle Doo (IRE)

80 51
2-y-o b c Oratorio (IRE)-Nousaiyra (IRE) (Be My Guest (USA))
W Jarvis The Doodle Doo Partnership

Placings:000 **(6737)**
2009: 5^{0}GF, 6^{0}GF, 6^{0}GS,

	Starts	1st	2nd	3rd	Win & Pl
Career Total (Turf)	3	0	0	0	

Going (Turf): Sf: 0-0 GS: 0-1 Gd: 0-0 GF: 0-2 Fm: 0-0
Distance: 5f/6f: 0-3 7f-8f: 0-0 9f-13f: 0-0 14f+: 0-0
Track : LH: 0-0 RH: 0-0 Tight: 0-0 Gall: 0-1
Aids: Bl: 0-0 Vi: 0-0 Tstrap: 0-0 Ckp: 0-0
Best Rating: 51 10/09 NmkR 6f gd-fm

Rock And Roll Kid (IRE)

110 105
4-y-o b g Danehill Dancer (IRE)-Milly's Song (Millfontaine)
Anthony Mullins Barry Connell

Placings:0002101-422155 **(7259a)**
2009: 8^{4}S, 8^{2}HY, 8^{2}GY, 8^{1}SH, 8^{5}S, 7^{5}HY,

	Starts	1st	2nd	3rd	Win & Pl
Career Total (Turf)	13	3	3	0	119918
105 7/09 Gway	1m100y	H		SH	£81689
86 9/08 Curr	7f	(50-80)H		HVY	£7367
70 8/08 Curr	7f	(50-80)H		HVY	£6351

Total win prize-money £95407

Going (Turf): Sf: 2-6 GS: 0-0 Gd: 0-1 GF: 0-2 Fm: 0-1
Distance: 5f/6f: 0-0 **7f-8f: 2-7** 9f-13f: 1-6 14f+: 0-0
Track : LH: 0-5 **RH: 1-6** Tight: 0-0 Gall: 0-3
Aids: Bl: 0-0 Vi: 0-0 Tstrap: 0-0 Ckp: 0-0
Best Rating: 105 7/09 Gway 1m100y sft-hvy

Smart; Irish trained; effective from 7f-1m1f; acts on good ground, but best on soft.

Rock Anthem (IRE)

104(104) (75)81
5-y-o ch g Rock Of Gibraltar (IRE)-Regal Portrait (IRE) (Royal Academy (USA))
Mike Murphy Ronald Bright

Placings:040/0216460/**6510060002-2265**240345110135 **(7229)**
2009: 8^{2}SS, 8^{2}SD, 8^{6}SD, 8^{5}SD, 8^{2}GS, 10^{4}GF, 8^{0}SD, 8^{3}G, 8^{4}GF, 8^{5}G, 7^{1}GF, 8^{1}G, 8^{0}SD, 8^{1}GF, 8^{3}GF, 8^{5}SD,

	Starts	1st	2nd	3rd	Win & Pl
Career Total (Turf)	24	4	2	2	23050
Career Total (AW)	12	1	3	0	4976
79 9/09 Sand	1m14y	(0-80)H		G-F	£4857
77 8/09 Sals	1m	(0-70)H		GD	£3123
72 8/09 Ling	7f140y	(0-65)H		G-F	£2047
77 3/08 Sthl	1m	(0-75)H		STD	£2593
79 6/07 Gdwd	1m1f192y	(0-85)H		G-F	£7124

Total win prize-money £19746

Going (Turf): Sf: 0-2 GS: 0-5 Gd: 1-8 **GF: 3-8** Fm: 0-1
Distance: 5f/6f: 0-0 **7f-8f: 3-16** 9f-13f: 2-20 14f+: 0-0
Track : LH: 1-13 **RH: 2-16 Tight: 1-10** Gall: 0-1
Aids: Bl: 0-0 Vi: 0-0 Tstrap: 0-0 Ckp: 0-0
Best Rating: 81 10/09 Leic 1m60y gd-fm

Modest; stays 1m2f; acts on easy ground and Fibresand.

Rock Art (IRE)

95(84) (51)59
3-y-o ch f Rock Of Gibraltar (IRE)-Lindesberg (Doyoun)
Karen George (B J Meehan 4/9) Mrs Isabel Fraser

Placings:0-02600000 **(7677)**
2009: 8^{0}GF, 7^{2}G, 8^{6}GS, 9^{0}GF, 9^{0}F, 7^{0}GS, 8^{0}SD, 11^{0}SD,

	Starts	1st	2nd	3rd	Win & Pl
Career Total (Turf)	7	0	1	0	1445
Career Total (AW)	2	0	0	0	

Going (Turf): Sf: 0-0 GS: 0-2 Gd: 0-2 GF: 0-2 Fm: 0-1
Distance: 5f/6f: 0-0 7f-8f: 0-5 9f-13f: 0-4 14f+: 0-0
Track : LH: 0-2 RH: 0-2 Tight: 0-2 Gall: 0-0
Aids: Bl: 0-2 Vi: 0-0 Tstrap: 0-2 Ckp: 0-2
Best Rating: 59 8/09 Folk 1m1f149y gd-fm

sModerate; stays 1m1f; acts on fast ground; has worn various headgear.

Rock Ascot (URU)

88(104) (100)87

5-y-o gr h Mantle Rock (USA)-Maria Fumadora (URU) (Sportin' Gold (USA))

G L Moore (H J Brown 22/1) Ramzan Kadyrov

Placings:01/1-000016 (7226)

2009: 8^{0}FT, 10^{0}GS, 14^{0}G, 10^{0}SD, 8^{1}SS, 10^{6}SD,

	Starts	1st	2nd	3rd	Win & Pl
Career Total (Turf)	2	0	0	0	
Career Total (AW)	7	3	0	0	47035

100 10/09 Ling 1m (0-95)H SS £9066
1/08 Maro 1m4f FST £33416
12/07 Maro 7f110y FST £4344
Total win prize-money £46826

Going (Turf): **Sf: 0-0 GS: 0-1 Gd: 0-1 GF: 0-0 Fm: 0-0**
Distance: 5f/6f: 0-0 **7f-8f: 2-2** 9f-13f: 1-6 14f+: 0-1
Track : **LH: 1-3** RH: 0-3 **Tight: 1-2** Gall: 0-2
Aids: **Bl: 1-2** Vi: 0-0 Tstrap: 0-0 Ckp: 0-0
Best Rating: **100** 10/09 Ling 1m std-slw

Very useful; formerly Uruguaian-trained; stays 1m4f; acts on fast ground and on Polytrack; has worn blikers and a tongue tie.

Rock Exhibition

93(87) (30)70

4-y-o ch f Rock Of Gibraltar (IRE)-Finity (USA) (Diesis)

B W Duke Mrs J S Bolger

Placings:5130-060 (7225)

2009: 8^{0}GF, 8^{6}SD, 10^{0}SD,

	Starts	1st	2nd	3rd	Win & Pl
Career Total (Turf)	5	1	0	1	8431
Career Total (AW)	2	0	0	0	0

70 8/08 Curr 1m HVY £7621
Total win prize-money £7621

Going (Turf): **Sf: 1-2** GS: 0-0 Gd: 0-0 GF: 0-1 Fm: 0-0
Distance: 5f/6f: 0-0 **7f-8f: 1-4** 9f-13f: 0-3 14f+: 0-0
Track : LH: 0-3 **RH: 1-4** Tight: 0-1 **Gall: 1-2**
Aids: Bl: 0-0 Vi: 0-0 Tstrap: 0-0 Ckp: 0-0
Best Rating: **70** 8/08 Klny 1m100y gd-yld

Rock Me (IRE)

(85) (34)41

4-y-o ch g Rock Of Gibraltar (IRE)-Final Farewell (USA) (Proud Truth (USA))

Mrs Lawney Hill (D E Cantillon 6/9) For Fun Partnership

Placings:000605/04-5 (7881)

2009: 10^{5}SD,

	Starts	1st	2nd	3rd	Win & Pl
Career Total (Turf)	5	0	0	0	144
Career Total (AW)	4	0	0	0	0

Going (Turf): **Sf: 0-1 GS: 0-2 Gd: 0-1 GF: 0-1 Fm: 0-0**
Distance: 5f/6f: 0-0 7f-8f: 0-5 9f-13f: 0-4 14f+: 0-0
Track : LH: 0-5 RH: 0-2 Tight: 0-2 Gall: 0-0
Aids: Bl: 0-3 Vi: 0-0 Tstrap: 0-2 Ckp: 0-2
Best Rating: **41** 10/07 Yarm 7f3y gd-sft

Rock My World (IRE)

(97) (70)

2-y-o b f Rock Of Gibraltar (IRE)-Arctic Hunt (IRE) (Bering)

M A Jarvis Stephen Dartnell

Placings:2 (7522)

2009: 8^{2}SD,

	Starts	1st	2nd	3rd	Win & Pl
Career Total (Turf)	0	0	0	0	
Career Total (AW)	1	0	1	0	1060

Going (Turf): **Sf: 0-0 GS: 0-0 Gd: 0-0 GF: 0-0 Fm: 0-0**
Distance: 5f/6f: 0-0 7f-8f: 0-1 9f-13f: 0-0 14f+: 0-0
Track : LH: 0-1 RH: 0-0 Tight: 0-1 Gall: 0-0
Aids: Bl: 0-0 Vi: 0-0 Tstrap: 0-0 Ckp: 0-0
Best Rating: **70** 11/09 Ling 1m stand

Fair; effective over 1m; acts on Polytrack; sure to improve.

Rock Of Behistun (IRE)

69(59) (8)11

2-y-o b g Antonius Pius (USA)-Persian Flower (Persian Heights)

P L Gilligan Treasure Seekers

Placings:0P00 (7120)

2009: 7^{0}SD, 7^{P}SD, 7^{0}SD, 8^{0}GF,

	Starts	1st	2nd	3rd	Win & Pl
Career Total (Turf)	1	0	0	0	
Career Total (AW)	3	0	0	0	

Going (Turf): **Sf: 0-0 GS: 0-0 Gd: 0-0 GF: 0-1 Fm: 0-0**
Distance: 5f/6f: 0-0 7f-8f: 0-3 9f-13f: 0-1 14f+: 0-0
Track : LH: 0-3 RH: 0-1 Tight: 0-2 Gall: 0-0
Aids: Bl: 0-0 Vi: 0-0 Tstrap: 0-0 Ckp: 0-0
Best Rating: **11** 10/09 Nott 1m75y gd-fm

Rock Of Eire

74(83) (49)55

2-y-o b g Rock Of Gibraltar (IRE)-Graceful Lass (Sadler's Wells (USA))

E J Creighton Level Par Racing

Placings:3065 (7502)

2009: 6^{3}G, 8^{0}SD, 7^{6}GF, 8^{5}SD,

	Starts	1st	2nd	3rd	Win & Pl
Career Total (Turf)	2	0	0	1	623
Career Total (AW)	2	0	0	0	0

Going (Turf): **Sf: 0-0 GS: 0-0 Gd: 0-1 GF: 0-1 Fm: 0-0**
Distance: 5f/6f: 0-0 7f-8f: 0-4 9f-13f: 0-0 14f+: 0-0
Track : LH: 0-1 RH: 0-1 Tight: 0-0 Gall: 0-0
Aids: Bl: 0-0 Vi: 0-0 Tstrap: 0-0 Ckp: 0-0
Best Rating: **55** 9/09 NmkR 7f gd-fm

Rock Of Love (IRE)

97 89

2-y-o b c Rock Of Gibraltar (IRE)-Ridotto (Salse (USA))

M Johnston Crone Stud Farms Ltd

Placings:4423140 (4488)

2009: 5^{4}G, 5^{4}GS, 6^{2}GF, 6^{3}GF, 7^{1}GF, 7^{4}GF, 7^{0}G,

	Starts	1st	2nd	3rd	Win & Pl
Career Total (Turf)	7	1	1	1	5389

87 6/09 Bevl 7f100y G-F £2331
Total win prize-money £2331

Going (Turf): Sf: 0-0 GS: 0-1 Gd: 0-2 **GF: 1-4** Fm: 0-0
Distance: 5f/6f: 0-2 **7f-8f: 1-5** 9f-13f: 0-0 14f+: 0-0
Track : LH: 0-1 **RH: 1-2** Tight: 0-0 Gall: 0-0
Aids: Bl: 0-0 Vi: 0-0 Tstrap: 0-0 Ckp: 0-0
Best Rating: **89** 7/09 NmkJ 7f gd-fm

Fair; stays an extended 7f; acts on fast ground.

Rock Of Rochelle (USA)

110 (89)111

4-y-o br c Rock Of Gibraltar (IRE)-Recoleta (USA) (Wild Again (USA))

A Kinsella Her Diamond Necklace Limited

Placings:2110/600142-503663 (7044a)

2009: 6^{5}GF, 7^{0}G, 6^{3}GF, 7^{6}S, 8^{6}GF, 7^{3}S,

	Starts	1st	2nd	3rd	Win & Pl
Career Total (Turf)	15	3	2	2	99425
Career Total (AW)	1	0	0	0	

108 9/08 Curr 6f SH £35845
98 9/07 Curr 6f G-F £24192
82 9/07 Curr 6f GD £8797
Total win prize-money £68836

Going (Turf): Sf: 0-6 GS: 0-0 **Gd: 1-3 GF: 1-5** Fm: 0-0
Distance: **5f/6f: 3-8** 7f-8f: 0-8 9f-13f: 0-0 14f+: 0-0
Track : LH: 0-6 RH: 0-1 Tight: 0-0 Gall: 0-0
Aids: Bl: 0-0 Vi: 0-0 Tstrap: 0-0 Ckp: 0-0
Best Rating: **111** 6/09 Asct 6f gd-fm

Smart; Irish trained; winner in Group 3 company; suited by 6f and acts on most ground; has worn a tongue tie.

Rock Peak (IRE)

(100) (67)76

4-y-o b g Dalakhani (IRE)-Convenience (IRE) (Ela-Mana-Mou)

B J Llewellyn B J Llewellyn

Placings:4/45633000-604 (0502)

2009: 12^{6}SD, 12^{0}SD, 16^{4}SD,

	Starts	1st	2nd	3rd	Win & Pl
Career Total (Turf)	7	0	0	2	1850
Career Total (AW)	5	0	0	0	173

Going (Turf): **Sf: 0-1 GS: 0-2 Gd: 0-1 GF: 0-3 Fm: 0-0**
Distance: 5f/6f: 0-0 7f-8f: 0-0 9f-13f: 0-8 14f+: 0-4
Track : LH: 0-4 RH: 0-7 Tight: 0-8 Gall: 0-0
Aids: Bl: 0-0 Vi: 0-0 Tstrap: 0-2 Ckp: 0-2
Best Rating: **76** 7/08 Sand 1m6f gd-fm

Fair; stays 1m6f; suited by fast ground; has worn cheek-pieces.

Rock Relief (IRE)

(94) (59)66

3-y-o gr g Daylami (IRE)-Sheer Bliss (IRE) (Sadler's Wells (USA))

Sir Mark Prescott S Munir

Placings:002-50 (4650)

2009: 12^{5}SD, 11^{0}SD,

	Starts	1st	2nd	3rd	Win & Pl
Career Total (Turf)	2	0	1	0	925
Career Total (AW)	3	0	0	0	0

Going (Turf): **Sf: 0-1 GS: 0-1 Gd: 0-0 GF: 0-0 Fm: 0-0**
Distance: 5f/6f: 0-1 7f-8f: 0-2 9f-13f: 0-2 14f+: 0-0
Track : LH: 0-3 RH: 0-2 Tight: 0-2 Gall: 0-0
Aids: Bl: 0-0 Vi: 0-0 Tstrap: 0-0 Ckp: 0-0

Best Rating: **66** 10/08 Brig 6f209y gd-sft

Fair; effective over 7f; acts on easy ground.

Rock Tech

81(98) (52)34
4-y-o b c High Estate-Mrs Fire Cracker (Rock City)
J R Jenkins Miss P Casey

Placings:060004 (7767)
2009: 7^{0}SD, 7^{6}GF, 6^{0}GF, 8^{0}G, 8^{0}SD, 11^{4}SD,

	Starts	1st	2nd	3rd	Win & Pl
Career Total (Turf)	3	0	0	0	0
Career Total (AW)	3	0	0	0	0

Going (Turf): Sf: 0-0 GS: 0-0 Gd: 0-1 GF: 0-2 Fm: 0-0
Distance: 5f/6f: 0-1 7f-8f: 0-3 9f-13f: 0-2 14f+: 0-0
Track : LH: 0-1 RH: 0-3 Tight: 0-0 Gall: 0-1
Aids: Bl: 0-0 Vi: 0-0 Tstrap: 0-0 Ckp: 0-0
Best Rating: **52** 12/09 Kemp 1m3f stand

Rock The Stars (IRE)

87(85) (52)47
2-y-o ch g Rock Of Gibraltar (IRE)-Crimphill (IRE) (Sadler's Wells (USA))
M G Quinlan David Cohen

Placings:00 (7773)
2009: 8^{0}S, 7^{0}SD,

	Starts	1st	2nd	3rd	Win & Pl
Career Total (Turf)	1	0	0	0	
Career Total (AW)	1	0	0	0	

Going (Turf): Sf: 0-1 GS: 0-0 Gd: 0-0 GF: 0-0 Fm: 0-0
Distance: 5f/6f: 0-0 7f-8f: 0-1 9f-13f: 0-1 14f+: 0-0
Track : LH: 0-2 RH: 0-0 Tight: 0-1 Gall: 0-0
Aids: Bl: 0-0 Vi: 0-0 Tstrap: 0-0 Ckp: 0-0
Best Rating: **52** 12/09 Ling 7f stand

Rockabilly Rebel

95 64
2-y-o b c Kyllachy-Its All Relative (Distant Relative)
B W Hills P Cunningham R Crothers Phil Cunningham

Placings:05356 (5526)
2009: 6^{0}GF, 6^{5}G, 5^{3}GF, 5^{5}GF, 5^{6}G,

	Starts	1st	2nd	3rd	Win & Pl
Career Total (Turf)	5	0	0	1	770

Going (Turf): Sf: 0-0 GS: 0-0 Gd: 0-2 GF: 0-3 Fm: 0-0
Distance: 5f/6f: 0-5 7f-8f: 0-0 9f-13f: 0-0 14f+: 0-0
Track : LH: 0-1 RH: 0-0 Tight: 0-0 Gall: 0-2
Aids: Bl: 0-0 Vi: 0-0 Tstrap: 0-0 Ckp: 0-0
Best Rating: **64** 8/09 NmkJ 5f gd-fm

Modest; suited by 5f and acts on fast ground.

Rockabout (IRE)

95(95) (50)61
3-y-o b f Rock Of Gibraltar (IRE)-Capades Dancer (USA) (Gate Dancer (USA))
B J Meehan Lady Rothschild

Placings:604000040 (7143)
2009: 8^{6}F, 8^{0}G, 8^{4}GF, 8^{0}GF, 8^{0}SD, 8^{0}GS, 10^{0}G, 10^{4}SS, 9^{0}SD,

	Starts	1st	2nd	3rd	Win & Pl
Career Total (Turf)	6	0	0	0	0
Career Total (AW)	3	0	0	0	0

Going (Turf): Sf: 0-0 GS: 0-1 Gd: 0-2 GF: 0-2 Fm: 0-1
Distance: 5f/6f: 0-0 7f-8f: 0-2 9f-13f: 0-7 14f+: 0-0
Track : LH: 0-6 RH: 0-2 Tight: 0-5 Gall: 0-0
Aids: Bl: 0-2 Vi: 0-0 Tstrap: 0-0 Ckp: 0-0
Best Rating: **61** 5/09 Nott 1m75y firm

Rocker

105(94) (74)85
5-y-o b g Rock Of Gibraltar (IRE)-Jessica's Dream (IRE) (Desert Style (IRE))
G L Moore Sir Eric Parker

Placings:03341/2155533003200**0**/20322**2**010062112-33024104405 (6964)
2009: 5^{3}G, 5^{3}HY, 5^{0}GF, 5^{2}GF, 5^{4}G, 5^{1}GF, 5^{0}GS, 5^{4}GF, 6^{4}GS, 5^{0}GS, 5^{5}G,

	Starts	1st	2nd	3rd	Win & Pl
Career Total (Turf)	35	4	7	7	29163
Career Total (AW)	10	2	2	1	9910

84	7/09	Epsm	5f	(0-85)H	G-F	£5180
82	10/08	Brig	5f59y	(0-75)H	GD	£3027
77	10/08	Nott	5f13y	(0-75)H	G-S	£2590
73	7/08	Sand	5f6y	(0-75)H	G-F	£4533
74	3/07	Ling	5f	(0-85)H	STD	£4857
68	12/06	Kemp	5f		STD	£3238

Total win prize-money £23429

Going (Turf): Sf: 0-2 GS: 1-8 Gd: 1-9 **GF: 2-14** Fm: 0-2
Distance: **5f/6f: 6-44** 7f-8f: 0-1 9f-13f: 0-0 14f+: 0-0
Track : **LH: 2-15** RH: 1-4 **Tight: 1-7** Gall: 0-4
Aids: **Bl: 1-6** Vi: 0-11 Tstrap: 0-0 Ckp: 0-0
Best Rating: **85** 10/08 Brig 5f213y gd-sft

Fair; seems best at 5f-6f; acts on most ground and on Polytrack; has worn blinkers and a visor.

Rocket (IRE)

25 (12)27
8-y-o ch g Cadeaux Genereux-Prends Ca (IRE) (Reprimand)
H J Manners Exors Of The Late H J Manners

Placings:04303/06060/000/0 (5028)
2009: 12^{0}GF,

	Starts	1st	2nd	3rd	Win & Pl
Career Total (Turf)	11	0	0	2	1289
Career Total (AW)	3	0	0	0	0

Going (Turf): Sf: 0-1 GS: 0-3 Gd: 0-2 GF: 0-4 Fm: 0-1
Distance: 5f/6f: 0-5 7f-8f: 0-5 9f-13f: 0-4 14f+: 0-0
Track : LH: 0-7 RH: 0-2 Tight: 0-4 Gall: 0-6
Aids: Bl: 0-0 Vi: 0-0 Tstrap: 0-0 Ckp: 0-0
Best Rating: **57** 8/04 Wind 6f good

Rocket Rob (IRE)

103(100) (69)88
3-y-o b g Danetime (IRE)-Queen Of Fibres (IRE) (Scenic)
S A Callaghan Bill Hinge, J Searchfield & N Callaghan

Placings:01102152-550131412140 (5871)
2009: 5^{5}SD, 5^{5}GF, 5^{0}G, 6^{1}G, 6^{3}F, 5^{1}GF, 6^{4}G, 5^{1}G, 5^{2}GF, 5^{1}GF, 5^{4}GF, 5^{0}G,

	Starts	1st	2nd	3rd	Win & Pl
Career Total (Turf)	15	5	2	1	21104
Career Total (AW)	5	2	1	0	7370

88	8/09	Sand	5f6y	(0-80)H	G-F	£5180
80	8/09	Sand	5f6y	(0-75)H	GD	£3238
75	7/09	Epsm	5f	(0-80)H	G-F	£4857
72	6/09	Yarm	6f3y	(0-65)H	GD	£2331
68	9/08	Kemp	6f	(0-70)	STD	£2590
60	8/08	Wolv	7f32y		STD	£3238
58	7/08	Yarm	6f3y		G-F	£1942

Total win prize-money £23378

Going (Turf): Sf: 0-1 GS: 0-0 Gd: 2-7 **GF: 3-6** Fm: 0-1
Distance: **5f/6f: 4-14** 7f-8f: 3-6 9f-13f: 0-0 14f+: 0-0
Track : LH: 1-6 RH: 1-1 **Tight: 1-4** Gall: 0-2
Aids: Bl: 0-0 Vi: 0-0 Tstrap: 0-0 Ckp: 0-0
Best Rating: **88** 8/09 Sand 5f6y gd-fm

Useful; effective at 5f-7f; acts on fast ground and on Polytrack.

Rocket Ruby

96(101) (61)58
3-y-o br f Piccolo-Kitty Kitty Cancan (Warrshan (USA))
D Shaw Mrs Lyndsey Shaw

Placings:000503-524020220230 (7889)
2009: 5^{5}SD, 6^{2}SD, 5^{4}SD, 5^{0}SD, 5^{2}G, 5^{0}SD, 5^{2}GS, 5^{2}G, 5^{0}SD, 5^{2}SD, 5^{3}SD, 5^{0}SD,

	Starts	1st	2nd	3rd	Win & Pl
Career Total (Turf)	4	0	3	0	2020
Career Total (AW)	14	0	2	2	2116

Going (Turf): Sf: 0-0 GS: 0-1 Gd: 0-3 GF: 0-0 Fm: 0-0
Distance: 5f/6f: 0-18 7f-8f: 0-0 9f-13f: 0-0 14f+: 0-0
Track : LH: 0-8 RH: 0-1 Tight: 0-8 Gall: 0-0
Aids: Bl: 0-0 Vi: 0-1 Tstrap: 0-0 Ckp: 0-0
Best Rating: **61** 12/09 Wolv 5f20y stand

Moderate; suited by 5f; acts on good ground and on sand.

Rocketball (IRE)

101(101) (62)69
4-y-o b g Namid-Luceball (IRE) (Bluebird (USA))
Mrs L Williamson (Patrick Morris 15/5) J Levenson

Placings:0/5330003-046210411440664 (6314)
2009: 5^{0}SD, 5^{4}SD, 5^{6}SD, 5^{2}GS, 5^{1}G, 5^{0}G, 5^{4}GF, 5^{1}GF, 5^{1}GF, 5^{4}G, 5^{4}G, 5^{0}G, 5^{6}GF, 5^{6}GF, 5^{4}GF,

	Starts	1st	2nd	3rd	Win & Pl
Career Total (Turf)	17	3	1	2	10317
Career Total (AW)	6	0	0	1	302

69	6/09	Muss	5f	(0-65)H	G-F	£2590
66	6/09	Muss	5f	(0-65)H	G-F	£2590
64	5/09	Haml	5f4y	(0-60)H	GD	£2729

Total win prize-money £7910

Going (Turf): Sf: 0-1 GS: 0-2 Gd: 1-8 **GF: 2-6** Fm: 0-0
Distance: **5f/6f: 3-23** 7f-8f: 0-0 9f-13f: 0-0 14f+: 0-0
Track : LH: 0-3 RH: 0-1 Tight: 0-0 Gall: 0-0
Aids: Bl: 0-0 Vi: 0-4 Tstrap: 0-0 Ckp: 0-0
Best Rating: **69** 9/09 Gdwd 5f gd-fm

Moderate; stays 6f; acts on good ground and Fibresand.

Rockfella

105(94) (59)82
3-y-o ch g Rock Of Gibraltar (IRE)-Afreeta (USA) (Afleet (CAN))
D J Coakley L M A Hurley

Placings:040305-35511516 (7373)
2009: 10^{3}GS, 10^{5}G, 9^{5}F, 10^{1}GF, 12^{1}GF, 11^{5}GF, 11^{1}G, 12^{6}SD,

	Starts	1st	2nd	3rd	Win & Pl
Career Total (Turf)	11	3	0	2	14608

Career Total (AW)	3	0	0	0	0

82 10/09 Bath 1m3f144y (0-80)H GD £4727
74 9/09 Gdwd 1m4f (0-80)H G-F £5180
70 7/09 Wind 1m2f7y (0-70)H G-F £2729
Total win prize-money £12638

Going (Turf): Sf: 0-1 GS: 0-3 Gd: 1-2 **GF: 2-4** Fm: 0-1
Distance: 5f/6f: 0-1 7f-8f: 0-4 **9f-13f: 3-9** 14f+: 0-0
Track : LH: 1-7 **RH: 2-6 Tight: 3-6** Gall: 0-1
Aids: Bl: 0-0 Vi: 0-0 Tstrap: 0-0 Ckp: 0-0
Best Rating: 82 10/09 Bath 1m3f144y good

Fair; stays 1m4f; acts on fast ground.

Rockfield Lodge (IRE)

99(99) (75)81
4-y-o b g Stravinsky (USA)-La Belle Simone (IRE) (Grand Lodge (USA))
Ian Williams (R A Harris 31/7) M Ioannou

Placings:42216/3602261436262000-666643635 (7726)
2009: 6^6SD, 5^6GF, 5^6GF, 5^6GF, 5^4S, 5^3G, 7^6SD, 7^3SD, 7^5SD,

	Starts	1st	2nd	3rd	Win & Pl
Career Total (Turf)	16	1	3	1	7136
Career Total (AW)	14	1	3	3	5885

58 6/08 Leic 7f9y G-F £1942
71 8/07 Ling 6f STD £1943
Total win prize-money £3886

Going (Turf): Sf: 0-1 GS: 0-1 Gd: 0-4 **GF: 1-9** Fm: 0-1
Distance: 5f/6f: 1-17 7f-8f: 1-12 9f-13f: 0-1 14f+: 0-0
Track : **LH: 1-13** RH: 0-6 **Tight: 1-6** Gall: 0-2
Aids: Bl: 0-6 Vi: 0-1 Tstrap: 0-1 Ckp: 0-1
Best Rating: 81 8/08 NmkJ 6f good

Modest; stays 7f; acts on fast ground and Polytrack; has worn cheekpieces and a visor.

Rockhampton (IRE)

111 (95)99
3-y-o b c Galileo (IRE)-Green Rosy (USA) (Green Dancer (USA))
A P O'Brien Mrs John Magnier

Placings:24-13100400 (5688a)
2009: 10^1GF, 10^3GF, 12^1SD, 8^0GF, 12^0GY, 9^4S, 12^0G, 10^0GY,

	Starts	1st	2nd	3rd	Win & Pl
Career Total (Turf)	9	1	1	1	56378
Career Total (AW)	1	1	0	0	12076

95 5/09 Dund 1m4f STD £12075
90 3/09 Leop 1m2f G-F £8721
Total win prize-money £20797

Going (Turf): Sf: 0-3 GS: 0-0 Gd: 0-1 **GF: 1-3** Fm: 0-0
Distance: 5f/6f: 0-0 7f-8f: 0-3 **9f-13f: 2-7** 14f+: 0-0
Track : **LH: 2-5** RH: 0-3 Tight: 0-0 Gall: 0-1
Aids: Bl: 0-0 Vi: 0-0 Tstrap: 0-0 Ckp: 0-0
Best Rating: 99 4/09 NmkR 1m2f gd-fm

Very useful: Irish trained: stays 1m2f; acts on fast ground.

Rockinit (IRE)

(79) (32)67
3-y-o b f Rock Of Gibraltar (IRE)-Tidal Reach (USA) (Kris S (USA))
R A Harris Peter A Price

Placings:42002-00 (0741)
2009: 8^0SD, 8^0SD,

	Starts	1st	2nd	3rd	Win & Pl
Career Total (Turf)	4	0	2	0	1946
Career Total (AW)	3	0	0	0	

Going (Turf): Sf: 0-0 GS: 0-0 Gd: 0-2 GF: 0-1 Fm: 0-1
Distance: 5f/6f: 0-2 7f-8f: 0-3 9f-13f: 0-2 14f+: 0-0
Track : LH: 0-5 RH: 0-1 Tight: 0-1 Gall: 0-1
Aids: Bl: 0-0 Vi: 0-0 Tstrap: 0-0 Ckp: 0-0
Best Rating: 67 9/08 Yarm 1m3y good

Modest; stays 1m; acts on a sound surface.

Rockjumper

(102) (54)57
4-y-o br g Cape Cross (IRE)-Bronzewing (Beldale Flutter (USA))
Mrs Lawney Hill Wacky Racers

Placings:00/0000260-40 (1442)
2009: 11^4SD, 12^0SD,

	Starts	1st	2nd	3rd	Win & Pl
Career Total (Turf)	7	0	1	0	617
Career Total (AW)	4	0	0	0	0

Going (Turf): Sf: 0-0 GS: 0-1 Gd: 0-3 GF: 0-3 Fm: 0-0
Distance: 5f/6f: 0-2 7f-8f: 0-2 9f-13f: 0-7 14f+: 0-0
Track : LH: 0-7 RH: 0-3 Tight: 0-2 Gall: 0-2
Aids: Bl: 0-1 Vi: 0-0 Tstrap: 0-0 Ckp: 0-0
Best Rating: 57 8/08 Brig 7f214y good

Rocknest Island (IRE)

91 (59)58
6-y-o b m Bahhare (USA)-Margin Call (IRE) (Tirol)
P D Niven Mrs Kate Young

Placings:0/0202/0151342265/053540500-0600 (4848)
2009: 14^0GF, 14^6GF, 16^0GF, 16^0G,

	Starts	1st	2nd	3rd	Win & Pl
Career Total (Turf)	26	1	4	2	9058
Career Total (AW)	2	1	0	0	2048

61 5/07 Newc 2m19y (0-70)H G-S £3562
59 4/07 Wolv 2m119y (0-50)H STD £2047
Total win prize-money £5610

Going (Turf): Sf: 0-2 **GS: 1-8** Gd: 0-3 GF: 0-9 Fm: 0-2
Distance: 5f/6f: 0-0 7f-8f: 0-2 9f-13f: 0-3 **14f+: 2-23**
Track : **LH: 2-18** RH: 0-9 Tight: 1-13 Gall: 1-3
Aids: Bl: 0-0 Vi: 0-3 Tstrap: 2-18 Ckp: 2-18
Best Rating: 66 7/07 Bevl 2m35y heavy

Moderate; ex-Irish; stays 2m; acts on fast ground and on Polytrack.

Rockson (IRE)

94(95) (53)53
3-y-o b/br f Rock Of Gibraltar (IRE)-Opera Star (IRE) (Sadler's Wells (USA))
Ian Williams (B W Hills 22/7) Clive Buckle

Placings:0-00602000006 (7818)
2009: 10^0SD, 9^0SD, 8^6SD, 8^0SD, 8^2GS, 7^0SD, 7^0GF, 8^0SD, 7^0SD, 8^0SD, 9^6SD,

	Starts	1st	2nd	3rd	Win & Pl
Career Total (Turf)	2	0	1	0	578
Career Total (AW)	10	0	0	0	0

Going (Turf): Sf: 0-0 GS: 0-1 Gd: 0-0 GF: 0-1 Fm: 0-0
Distance: 5f/6f: 0-0 7f-8f: 0-0 9f-13f: 0-4 14f+: 0-0
Track : LH: 0-6 RH: 0-5 Tight: 0-3 Gall: 0-0
Aids: Bl: 0-0 Vi: 0-1 Tstrap: 0-0 Ckp: 0-0
Best Rating: 53 7/09 Leic 1m60y gd-sft

Rocksy

72(74) (38)62
3-y-o b f Kyllachy-Sea Music (Inchinor)
D J Coakley Count Calypso Racing

Placings:003-0 (1253)
2009: 7^0GF,

	Starts	1st	2nd	3rd	Win & Pl
Career Total (Turf)	3	0	0	1	433
Career Total (AW)	1	0	0	0	

Going (Turf): Sf: 0-1 GS: 0-0 Gd: 0-0 GF: 0-2 Fm: 0-0
Distance: 5f/6f: 0-2 7f-8f: 0-2 9f-13f: 0-0 14f+: 0-0
Track : LH: 0-3 RH: 0-0 Tight: 0-1 Gall: 0-0
Aids: Bl: 0-0 Vi: 0-0 Tstrap: 0-0 Ckp: 0-0
Best Rating: 62 8/08 Wwck 7f26y soft

Modest; stays 7f acts on soft ground; handles Polytrack.

Rockweiller

90(72) (26)69
2-y-o b c Rock Of Gibraltar (IRE)-Ballerina Suprema (IRE) (Sadler's Wells (USA))
C R Egerton Longmoor Holdings Ltd

Placings:0300 (6829)
2009: 6^0GF, 6^3GF, 5^0SD, 7^0SF,

	Starts	1st	2nd	3rd	Win & Pl
Career Total (Turf)	2	0	0	1	530
Career Total (AW)	2	0	0	0	

Going (Turf): Sf: 0-0 GS: 0-0 Gd: 0-0 GF: 0-2 Fm: 0-0
Distance: 5f/6f: 0-3 7f-8f: 0-1 9f-13f: 0-0 14f+: 0-0
Track : LH: 0-2 RH: 0-0 Tight: 0-2 Gall: 0-1
Aids: Bl: 0-1 Vi: 0-0 Tstrap: 0-0 Ckp: 0-0
Best Rating: 69 8/09 Wind 6f gd-fm

Rocky Heights (IRE)

105 57
3-y-o b f Rock Of Gibraltar (IRE)-Height Of Fantasy (IRE) (Shirley Heights)
J L Dunlop Windflower Overseas Holdings Inc

Placings:0-0032 (3454)
2009: 10^0GF, 9^0F, 11^3GF, 12^2GF,

	Starts	1st	2nd	3rd	Win & Pl
Career Total (Turf)	5	0	1	1	1266

Going (Turf): Sf: 0-0 GS: 0-1 Gd: 0-0 GF: 0-3 Fm: 0-1
Distance: 5f/6f: 0-0 7f 8f: 0-1 9f-13f: 0-4 14f+: 0-0
Track : LH: 0-2 RH: 0-2 Tight: 0-3 Gall: 0-0
Aids: Bl: 0-0 Vi: 0-0 Tstrap: 0-0 Ckp: 0-0
Best Rating: 57 6/09 Pont 1m4f8y gd-fm

Moderate; stays at least 1m3f; acts on fast ground.

Rocky's Pride (IRE)

99(97) (79)78
3-y-o b g Rock Of Gibraltar (IRE)-L'Animee (Green Tune (USA))

G L Moore (T R George 11/9) Mrs M Findlay

Placings:221031 (7881)
2009: 8^{2}G, 8^{2}GF, 9^{1}F, 10^{0}G, 12^{3}SD, 10^{1}SD,

	Starts	1st	2nd	3rd	Win & Pl
Career Total (Turf)	4	1	2	0	5176
Career Total (AW)	2	1	0	1	2682

12/09 Ling 1m2f STD £1978
78 6/09 Brig 1m1f209y FRM £3406
Total win prize-money £5385

Going (Turf): Sf: 0-0 GS: 0-0 Gd: 0-2 GF: 0-1 **Fm: 1-1**
Distance: 5f/6f: 0-0 7f-8f: 0-1 **9f-13f: 2-5** 14f+: 0-0
Track : **LH: 2-2** RH: 0-4 **Tight: 1-3** Gall: 0-0
Aids: Bl: 0-0 Vi: 0-0 Tstrap: 0-0 Ckp: 0-0
Best Rating: **79** 12/09 Kemp 1m4f stand

Fair; stays 1m2f; acts on fast ground and on Polytrack.

Rocoppelia (USA)

(92) (63)**59**
3-y-o ch c Hennessy (USA)-Eternally (USA) (Timeless Moment (USA))
Mrs A J Perrett John Connolly

Placings:404606-613 (0593)
2009: 8^{6}SD, 6^{1}SD, 6^{3}SD,

	Starts	1st	2nd	3rd	Win & Pl
Career Total (Turf)	3	0	0	0	192
Career Total (AW)	6	1	0	1	2476

63 1/09 Ling 6f (0-65)H STD £2047
Total win prize-money £2047

Going (Turf): **Sf: 0-0 GS: 0-0 Gd: 0-2 GF: 0-1 Fm: 0-0**
Distance: **5f/6f: 1-5** 7f-8f: 0-4 9f-13f: 0-0 14f+: 0-0
Track : **LH: 1-4** RH: 0-2 **Tight: 1-4** Gall: 0-1
Aids: **Bl: 1-2** Vi: 0-0 Tstrap: 0-0 Ckp: 0-0
Best Rating: **63** 1/09 Ling 6f stand

Modest; effective at around 6f; acts on fast ground; goes on Polytrack.

Rodrigo De Freitas (IRE)

90(89) (60)**60**
2-y-o b g Captain Rio-Brazilian Sun (IRE) (Barathea (IRE))
J R Boyle The Rodrigo De Freitas Partnership

Placings:0062540 (6793)
2009: 6^{0}SD, 7^{0}G, 7^{6}S, 8^{2}SD, 8^{5}SD, 8^{4}GS, 8^{0}S,

	Starts	1st	2nd	3rd	Win & Pl
Career Total (Turf)	4	0	0	0	0
Career Total (AW)	3	0	1	0	605

Going (Turf): **Sf: 0-2 GS: 0-1 Gd: 0-1 GF: 0-0 Fm: 0-0**
Distance: 5f/6f: 0-1 7f-8f: 0-4 9f-13f: 0-2 14f+: 0-0
Track : LH: 0-3 RH: 0-3 Tight: 0-3 Gall: 0-0
Aids: Bl: 0-0 Vi: 0-0 Tstrap: 0-0 Ckp: 0-0
Best Rating: **60** 10/09 Wind 1m67y gd-sft

Modest; stays 1m; acts on Polytrack.

Rodrigo De Torres

95 **89**
2-y-o ch c Bahamian Bounty-Leonica (Lion Cavern (USA))
H R A Cecil (A P Jarvis 20/8) Mogeely Stud & Mrs Maura Gittins

Placings:1U04 (6811)
2009: 6^{1}G, 6^{U}GF, 6^{0}GF, 8^{4}G,

	Starts	1st	2nd	3rd	Win & Pl
Career Total (Turf)	4	1	0	0	7371

89 7/09 York 6f GD £6670
Total win prize-money £6670

Going (Turf): Sf: 0-0 GS: 0-0 **Gd: 1-2** GF: 0-2 Fm: 0-0
Distance: **5f/6f: 1-3** 7f-8f: 0-1 9f-13f: 0-0 14f+: 0-0
Track : LH: 0-0 RH: 0-0 Tight: 0-0 Gall: 0-0
Aids: Bl: 0-0 Vi: 0-0 Tstrap: 0-0 Ckp: 0-0
Best Rating: **89** 10/09 NmkR 1m good

Useful; effective at 6f; acts on good ground.

Rogalt (IRE)

92 **67**
3-y-o b c Rock Of Gibraltar (IRE)-Rills (USA) (Clever Trick (USA))
B Smart Prime Equestrian

Placings:0-03255 (3856)
2009: 10^{0}GS, 6^{3}G, 6^{2}GF, 5^{5}GS, 6^{5}GF,

	Starts	1st	2nd	3rd	Win & Pl
Career Total (Turf)	6	0	1	1	1288

Going (Turf): **Sf: 0-0 GS: 0-3 Gd: 0-1 GF: 0-2 Fm: 0-0**
Distance: 5f/6f: 0-2 7f-8f: 0-2 9f-13f: 0-2 14f+: 0-0
Track : LH: 0-3 RH: 0-0 Tight: 0-0 Gall: 0-1
Aids: Bl: 0-0 Vi: 0-0 Tstrap: 0-0 Ckp: 0-0
Best Rating: **67** 5/09 Pont 6f good

Modest; effective over 6f; acts on fast ground.

Roi De Vitesse (IRE)

102 **102**
2-y-o ch c Chineur (FR)-Face The Storm (IRE) (Barathea (IRE))
B R Millman Mustajed Partnership

Placings:011325440 (6524a)
2009: 5^{0}G, 5^{1}GF, 6^{1}G, 6^{3}G, 7^{2}GF, 7^{5}G, 7^{4}G, 7^{4}GF, 7^{0}G,

	Starts	1st	2nd	3rd	Win & Pl
Career Total (Turf)	9	2	1	1	46212

93 5/09 Pont 6f GD £9346
77 4/09 Nott 5f13y G-F £2590
Total win prize-money £11937

Going (Turf): Sf: 0-0 GS: 0-0 **Gd: 1-6 GF: 1-3** Fm: 0-0
Distance: **5f/6f: 2-4** 7f-8f: 0-5 9f-13f: 0-0 14f+: 0-0
Track : **LH: 1-1** RH: 0-3 Tight: 0-0 Gall: 0-0
Aids: Bl: 0-0 Vi: 0-0 Tstrap: 0-0 Ckp: 0-0
Best Rating: **102** 7/09 NmkJ 7f gd-fm

Smart; Group 2 placed; stays 7f; acts on good and fast ground.

Roisin's Prince (IRE)

86(97) (56)**28**
7-y-o br g Bold Fact (USA)-Rosie Jaques (Doyoun)
M Sheppard The Aftertimers

Placings:5/230000400/3060/00/0-200 (3617)
2009: 16^{2}SD, 17^{0}F, 17^{0}G,

	Starts	1st	2nd	3rd	Win & Pl
Career Total (Turf)	19	0	1	2	2763
Career Total (AW)	1	0	1	0	605

Going (Turf): **Sf: 0-7 GS: 0-0 Gd: 0-4 GF: 0-3 Fm: 0-1**
Distance: 5f/6f: 0-3 7f-8f: 0-13 9f-13f: 0-1 14f+: 0-3
Track : LH: 0-8 RH: 0-4 Tight: 0-1 Gall: 0-1
Aids: Bl: 0-1 Vi: 0-0 Tstrap: 0-0 Ckp: 0-0
Best Rating: **73** 4/05 Gowr 7f soft

Roker Park (IRE)

111 **103**
4-y-o b g Choisir (AUS)-Joyful (IRE) (Green Desert (USA))
K A Ryan T Alderson

Placings:1000/001-001130300 (6270)
2009: 6^{0}S, 5^{0}G, 6^{1}GF, 6^{1}S, 6^{3}G, 6^{0}G, 5^{3}GF, 6^{0}G, 7^{0}G,

	Starts	1st	2nd	3rd	Win & Pl
Career Total (Turf)	16	4	0	2	41108

103 6/09 Newc 6f (0-100)H SFT £16200
96 6/09 Donc 6f (0-95)H G-F £7771
91 11/08 Muss 5f (0-85)H SFT £5180
89 6/07 Ripn 5f G-F £4210
Total win prize-money £33363

Going (Turf): **Sf: 2-4** GS: 0-1 Gd: 0-6 **GF: 2-5** Fm: 0-0
Distance: **5f/6f: 4-14** 7f-8f: 0-2 9f-13f: 0-0 14f+: 0-0
Track : LH: 0-0 RH: 0-0 Tight: 0-0 Gall: 0-0
Aids: Bl: 0-1 Vi: 0-0 Tstrap: 2-7 Ckp: 2-7
Best Rating: **103** 8/09 Bevl 5f gd-fm

Very useful; effective over 5f-6f; acts on most ground on turf; has worn blinkers and cheekpieces.

Roleplay (IRE)

88(101) (61)**50**
4-y-o b f Singspiel (IRE)-In Your Dreams (IRE) (Suave Dancer (USA))
J M P Eustace Hockham Lodge Stud

Placings:030-0200306 (7374)
2009: 7^{0}G, 5^{2}SD, 7^{0}SD, 8^{0}GF, 12^{3}SD, 12^{0}SD, 9^{6}SD,

	Starts	1st	2nd	3rd	Win & Pl
Career Total (Turf)	3	0	0	0	
Career Total (AW)	7	0	1	2	1443

Going (Turf): **Sf: 0-0 GS: 0-0 Gd: 0-2 GF: 0-1 Fm: 0-0**
Distance: 5f/6f: 0-1 7f-8f: 0-3 9f-13f: 0-6 14f+: 0-0
Track : LH: 0-7 RH: 0-1 Tight: 0-7 Gall: 0-1
Aids: Bl: 0-9 Vi: 0-0 Tstrap: 0-0 Ckp: 0-0
Best Rating: **61** 7/09 Wolv 5f216y stand

Moderate; effective over 1m2f; acts on Polytrack; has worn blinkers.

Rolling Hills (IRE)

97 **75**
2-y-o b g Celtic Swing-Silk Suivante (IRE) (Danehill (USA))
H Candy Six Too Many

Placings:02 (7058)
2009: 6^{0}GS, 5^{2}GF,

	Starts	1st	2nd	3rd	Win & Pl
Career Total (Turf)	2	0	1	0	1542

Going (Turf): **Sf: 0-0 GS: 0-1 Gd: 0-0 GF: 0-1 Fm: 0-0**
Distance: 5f/6f: 0-2 7f-8f: 0-0 9f-13f: 0-0 14f+: 0-0
Track : LH: 0-0 RH: 0-0 Tight: 0-0 Gall: 0-0
Aids: Bl: 0-0 Vi: 0-0 Tstrap: 0-0 Ckp: 0-0
Best Rating: **75** 10/09 Leic 5f218y gd-fm

Fair; effective at 6f; acts on fast ground.

Roly Boy

102(98) (83)89
3-y-o b g Dansili-Night At Sea (Night Shift (USA))
R Hannon The Calvera Partnership No 2

Placings:44154230-40606440 (5403)
2009: 8⁴SD, 8⁰GF, 8⁶F, 9⁰G, 10⁶GF, 8⁴GF, 7⁴G, 7⁰G,

	Starts	1st	2nd	3rd	Win & Pl
Career Total (Turf)	14	0	1	1	6494
Career Total (AW)	2	1	0	0	4237
74 6/08 Kemp 7f			STD	£3885	

Total win prize-money £3886

Going (Turf): **Sf: 0-1 GS: 0-1 Gd: 0-6 GF: 0-5 Fm: 0-1**
Distance: 5f/6f: 0-3 **7f-8f: 1-8** 9f-13f: 0-5 14f+: 0-0
Track : LH: 0-4 **RH: 1-6** Tight: 0-6 Gall: 0-0
Aids: Bl: 0-3 Vi: 0-0 Tstrap: 0-0 Ckp: 0-0
Best Rating: **89** 9/08 Donc 1m soft

Useful; stays 1m; acts on good ground and Polytrack.

Roman Empress (IRE)

112 115
3-y-o b f Sadler's Wells (USA)-Ionian Sea (Slip Anchor)
A P O'Brien Mrs John Magnier

Placings:3-01665232004 (6884a)
2009: 10⁰GF, 11¹GF, 10⁶Y, 12⁶HY, 12⁵S, 9²G, 12³GF, 10²S, 9⁰GF, 12⁰S, 8⁴GY,

	Starts	1st	2nd	3rd	Win & Pl
Career Total (Turf)	12	1	2	2	81213
76 6/09 Limk 1m3f70y			G-F	£8385	

Total win prize-money £8386

Going (Turf): Sf: 0-4 GS: 0-0 Gd: 0-1 **GF: 1-4** Fm: 0-0
Distance: 5f/6f: 0-0 7f-8f: 0-2 **9f-13f: 1-10** 14f+: 0-0
Track : LH: 0-4 **RH: 1-8** Tight: 0-0 Gall: 0-1
Aids: Bl: 0-0 Vi: 0-0 Tstrap: 0-0 Ckp: 0-0
Best Rating: **115** 8/09 York 1m4f gd-fm

Very useful; stays 1m3f; acts on fast but handles soft ground.

Roman Glory (IRE)

91 94
3-y-o b g Soviet Star (USA)-Putout (Dowsing (USA))
B J Meehan Martin Doran

Placings:02326-400 (2674)
2009: 7⁴F, 8⁰HY, 7⁰G,

	Starts	1st	2nd	3rd	Win & Pl
Career Total (Turf)	8	0	2	1	5785

Going (Turf): **Sf: 0-1 GS: 0-0 Gd: 0-4 GF: 0-2 Fm: 0-1**
Distance: 5f/6f: 0-0 7f-8f: 0-7 9f-13f: 0-1 14f+: 0-0
Track : LH: 0-4 RH: 0-2 Tight: 0-1 Gall: 0-0
Aids: Bl: 0-0 Vi: 0-0 Tstrap: 0-0 Ckp: 0-0
Best Rating: **94** 10/08 Donc 1m good

Very useful; stays 1m; acts on good and faster ground; likes to race prominently.

Roman History (IRE)

96(100) (58)59
6-y-o b g Titus Livius (FR)-Tetradonna (IRE) (Teenoso (USA))
N Waggott (Miss Tracy Waggott 25/8) Mrs J Waggott

Placings:06320002406**0**/00562061641/000204400/00040 3060300-630 (4944)
2009: 10⁶GF, 9³GF, 10⁰GF,

	Starts	1st	2nd	3rd	Win & Pl
Career Total (Turf)	42	2	4	2	11458
Career Total (AW)	5	0	0	2	723
58 9/06 Rdcr 1m2f (0-55)H			G-F	£2730	
54 8/06 Ayr 7f50y			G-F	£3238	

Total win prize-money £5969

Going (Turf): Sf: 0-2 GS: 0-4 Gd: 0-11 **GF: 2-23** Fm: 0-2
Distance: 5f/6f: 0-2 7f-8f: 1-19 9f-13f: 1-26 14f+: 0-0
Track : **LH: 2-29** RH: 0-13 **Tight: 1-23** Gall: 0-8
Aids: Bl: 0-0 Vi: 0-1 Tstrap: 2-36 Ckp: 2-36
Best Rating: **61** 9/05 Newc 1m gd-fm

Moderate; effective at around 1m2f; acts on most surfaces.

Roman Maze

(94) (59)95
9-y-o ch g Lycius (USA)-Maze Garden (USA) (Riverman (USA))
W M Brisbourne The Jenko and Thomo Partnership

Placings:05**5**1**4**/0500042420**315461**/**432130**3126120500/544063300000/1401522000**540500**/00000-00000 (7462)
2009: 7⁰SD, 7⁰SD, 8⁰SD, 7⁰SD, 5⁰SD,

	Starts	1st	2nd	3rd	Win & Pl
Career Total (Turf)	44	4	6	3	73396
Career Total (AW)	31	4	1	3	22182
91 6/07 Bath 5f161y (0-85)H			FRM	£4857	
89 4/07 Wind 6f (0-80)H			G-F	£6477	
95 8/05 Ches 7f122y H			G-F	£29000	
88 8/05 Rdcr 7f (0-80)H			G-F	£6315	
89 2/05 Wolv 5f216y (0-85)H			STD	£6815	
85 12/04 Wolv 5f216y (0-77)H			STD	£3389	
77 11/04 Wolv 5f216y (0-65)			STD	£3497	
73 11/03 Wolv 7f D			STD	£2415	

Total win prize-money £62766

Going (Turf): Sf: 0-5 GS: 0-5 Gd: 0-9 **GF: 3-23** Fm: 1-1
Distance: **5f/6f: 5-25** 7f-8f: 3-45 9f-13f: 0-5 14f+: 0-0
Track : **LH: 6-55** RH: 0-3 **Tight: 5-44** Gall: 2-6
Aids: Bl: 0-0 Vi: 0-0 Tstrap: 0-0 Ckp: 0-0
Best Rating: **102** 9/05 Ayr 6f good

Useful; effective at around 6f-7f; acts on fast ground and Polytrack; likes to come late.

Roman Republic (FR)

109 105
3-y-o b c Cape Cross (IRE)-Mare Nostrum (Caerleon (USA))
M Johnston Sheikh Hamdan Bin Mohammed Al Maktoum

Placings:01-10621 (4455)
2009: 8¹S, 8⁰GF, 8⁶G, 10²G, 9¹G,

	Starts	1st	2nd	3rd	Win & Pl
Career Total (Turf)	7	3	1	0	74531
105 7/09 Gdwd 1m1f192y H			GD	£37386	
93 6/09 Donc 1m (0-100)H			SFT	£16190	
82 10/08 Donc 7f			GD	£4857	

Total win prize-money £58433

Going (Turf): Sf: 1-1 GS: 0-1 **Gd: 2-4** GF: 0-1 Fm: 0-0
Distance: 5f/6f: 0-0 **7f-8f: 2-4** 9f-13f: 1-3 14f+: 0-0
Track : LH: 0-0 **RH: 1-3 Tight: 1-1** Gall: 0-1
Aids: Bl: 0-0 Vi: 0-0 Tstrap: 0-0 Ckp: 0-0
Best Rating: **105** 7/09 Gdwd 1m1f192y good

Very useful; stays 1m2f; acts on most ground.

Roman Sioux (IRE)

57
2-y-o b c Antonius Pius (USA)-Blue Sioux (Indian Ridge)
R Bastiman Ms M Austerfield

Placings:0 (6679)
2009: 7⁰G,

	Starts	1st	2nd	3rd	Win & Pl
Career Total (Turf)	1	0	0	0	

Going (Turf): **Sf: 0-0 GS: 0-0 Gd: 0-1 GF: 0-0 Fm: 0-0**
Distance: 5f/6f: 0-0 7f-8f: 0-1 9f-13f: 0-0 14f+: 0-0
Track : LH: 0-1 RH: 0-0 Tight: 0-0 Gall: 0-1
Aids: Bl: 0-0 Vi: 0-0 Tstrap: 0-0 Ckp: 0-0
Best Rating:

Dam comes from a good sprinting family.

Roman The Emperor (IRE)

83 35
3-y-o ch g Spartacus (IRE)-Honey Bee (Alnasr Alwasheek)
S W Hall Claydon Hall Stud Partnership No 1

Placings:050 (2181)
2009: 10⁰G, 9⁵GF, 11⁰G,

	Starts	1st	2nd	3rd	Win & Pl
Career Total (Turf)	3	0	0	0	0

Going (Turf): **Sf: 0-0 GS: 0-0 Gd: 0-2 GF: 0-1 Fm: 0-0**
Distance: 5f/6f: 0-0 7f-8f: 0-0 9f-13f: 0-3 14f+: 0-0
Track : LH: 0-2 RH: 0-1 Tight: 0-3 Gall: 0-0
Aids: Bl: 0-0 Vi: 0-0 Tstrap: 0-0 Ckp: 0-0
Best Rating: **35** 5/09 Ling 1m3f106y good

Romancea (USA)

72 51
2-y-o ch f Mr Greeley (USA)-Two Halos (USA) (Saint Ballado (CAN))
E F Vaughan Ali Saeed

Placings:0 (4055)
2009: 7⁰S,

	Starts	1st	2nd	3rd	Win & Pl
Career Total (Turf)	1	0	0	0	

Going (Turf): **Sf: 0-1 GS: 0-0 Gd: 0-0 GF: 0-0 Fm: 0-0**
Distance: 5f/6f: 0-0 7f-8f: 0-1 9f-13f: 0-0 14f+: 0-0
Track : LH: 0-0 RH: 0-0 Tight: 0-0 Gall: 0-0
Aids: Bl: 0-0 Vi: 0-0 Tstrap: 0-0 Ckp: 0-0
Best Rating: **51** 7/09 NmkJ 7f soft

Romantic Bond

81 18
3-y-o ch f Monsieur Bond (IRE)-Romantic Drama (IRE) (Primo Dominie)
T D Easterby Reality Partnerships III

Placings:00 (5422)
2009: 7⁰G, 5⁰GF,

	Starts	1st	2nd	3rd	Win & Pl
Career Total (Turf)	2	0	0	0	

Going (Turf): **Sf: 0-0 GS: 0-0 Gd: 0-1 GF: 0-1 Fm: 0-0**

Distance: 5f/6f: 0-1 7f-8f: 0-1 9f-13f: 0-0 14f+: 0-0
Track : LH: 0-1 RH: 0-0 Tight: 0-1 Gall: 0-0
Aids: Bl: 0-1 Vi: 0-0 Tstrap: 0-0 Ckp: 0-0
Best Rating: **18** 8/09 Bevl 5f gd-fm

Romantic Interlude (IRE)

78(89) (56)**48**

3-y-o b f Hawk Wing (USA)-Kissin A Lot (USA) (Kissin Kris (USA))
A P Jarvis Philip Milburn

Placings:040-000000 **(4995)**
2009: 12^{0}SD, 10^{0}GF, 11^{0}SD, 10^{0}GF, 10^{0}SD, 7^{0}GF,

	Starts	1st	2nd	3rd	Win & Pl
Career Total (Turf)	**4**	**0**	**0**	**0**	**433**
Career Total (AW)	**5**	**0**	**0**	**0**	

Going (Turf): **Sf: 0-1 GS: 0-0 Gd: 0-0 GF: 0-3 Fm: 0-0**
Distance: 5f/6f: 0-0 7f-8f: 0-4 9f-13f: 0-5 14f+: 0-0
Track : LH: 0-6 RH: 0-2 Tight: 0-2 Gall: 0-1
Aids: Bl: 0-0 Vi: 0-3 Tstrap: 0-0 Ckp: 0-0
Best Rating: **56** 10/08 GrLe 1m stand

Romantic Queen

80(98) (69)**52**

3-y-o b f Medicean-Bandit Queen (Desert Prince (IRE))
George Baker (E A L Dunlop 23/3) The Betfair Radioheads

Placings:065222-14436F10030650 **(7602)**
2009: 5^{1}SD, 6^{4}SD, 6^{4}SD, 7^{3}SD, 5^{6}SD, 5^{F}GF, 5^{1}SD, 5^{0}GF, 7^{0}SS, 6^{3}SD, 5^{0}SD, 5^{6}SD, 6^{5}SD, 6^{0}SD,

	Starts	1st	2nd	3rd	Win & Pl
Career Total (Turf)	**3**	**0**	**0**	**0**	
Career Total (AW)	**17**	**2**	**3**	**2**	**8932**

67 9/09 Wolv 5f216y STD £2047
68 1/09 Wolv 5f216y STD £3070
Total win prize-money £5118

Going (Turf): **Sf: 0-0 GS: 0-0 Gd: 0-0 GF: 0-3 Fm: 0-0**
Distance: **5f/6f: 2-18** 7f-8f: 0-2 9f-13f: 0-0 14f+: 0-0
Track : **LH: 2-17** RH: 0-0 **Tight: 2-13** Gall: 0-5
Aids: Bl: 0-0 Vi: 0-0 Tstrap: 0-0 Ckp: 0-0
Best Rating: **69** 3/09 Ling 7f stand

Modest; effective over 6f; acts on Polytrack; has worn a tongue-tie.

Romantic Retreat

(88) (54)**62**

4-y-o ch f Rainbow Quest (USA)-Magical Retreat (USA) (Sir Ivor (USA))
G L Moore Mrs Charles Cyzer

Placings:050-560 **(0972)**
2009: 12^{5}SD, 13^{6}SD, 13^{0}SD,

	Starts	1st	2nd	3rd	Win & Pl
Career Total (Turf)	**2**	**0**	**0**	**0**	**0**
Career Total (AW)	**4**	**0**	**0**	**0**	**0**

Going (Turf): **Sf: 0-0 GS: 0-0 Gd: 0-0 GF: 0-2 Fm: 0-0**
Distance: 5f/6f: 0-0 7f-8f: 0-0 9f-13f: 0-5 14f+: 0-1
Track : LH: 0-5 RH: 0-1 Tight: 0-5 Gall: 0-0
Aids: Bl: 0-0 Vi: 0-0 Tstrap: 0-0 Ckp: 0-0
Best Rating: **62** 5/08 Gdwd 1m1f gd-fm

Romantic Verse

92(107) (71)**62**

4-y-o b f Kyllachy-Romancing (Dr Devious (IRE))
S Curran (E S McMahon 23/3) David Greenwood

Placings:61/6326106-020100000500 **(7815)**
2009: 7^{0}SD, 7^{2}SD, 7^{0}SD, 5^{1}SD, 6^{0}SD, 7^{0}SD, 8^{0}GF, 7^{0}SD, 8^{0}SD, 7^{5}SF, 6^{0}SD, 5^{0}SD,

	Starts	1st	2nd	3rd	Win & Pl
Career Total (Turf)	**5**	**0**	**0**	**1**	**403**
Career Total (AW)	**16**	**3**	**2**	**0**	**8916**

69 3/09 Wolv 5f216y STD £2047
69 9/08 Wolv 7f32y (0-65)H STD £2388
58 11/07 Wolv 7f32y STD £2968
Total win prize-money £7404

Going (Turf): **Sf: 0-1 GS: 0-0 Gd: 0-2 GF: 0-2 Fm: 0-0**
Distance: 5f/6f: 1-6 **7f-8f: 2-14** 9f-13f: 0-1 14f+: 0-0
Track : **LH: 3-15** RH: 0-4 **Tight: 3-13** Gall: 0-0
Aids: **Bl: 2-10** Vi: 0-0 Tstrap: 0-0 Ckp: 0-0
Best Rating: **71** 2/09 Wolv 7f32y stand

Modest; looks ideally suited by 6f; acts on Polytrack; has worn blinkers.

Romanticize

100 **77**

3-y-o b f Kyllachy-Romancing (Dr Devious (IRE))
Dr J D Scargill Mrs Susan Scargill

Placings:120 **(3163)**
2009: 6^{1}GF, 6^{2}GF, 7^{0}GF,

	Starts	1st	2nd	3rd	Win & Pl
Career Total (Turf)	**3**	**1**	**1**	**0**	**5620**

69 5/09 Sals 6f G-F £3885
Total win prize-money £3886

Going (Turf): Sf: 0-0 GS: 0-0 Gd: 0-0 **GF: 1-3** Fm: 0-0
Distance: **5f/6f: 1-2** 7f-8f: 0-1 9f-13f: 0-0 14f+: 0-0
Track : LH: 0-0 RH: 0-0 Tight: 0-0 Gall: 0-0
Aids: Bl: 0-0 Vi: 0-0 Tstrap: 0-0 Ckp: 0-0
Best Rating: **77** 5/09 NmkR 6f gd-fm

Fair filly; suited by 6f; acts on fast ground.

Romany Princess (IRE)

105(108) (88)**95**

4-y-o b f Viking Ruler (AUS)-Fag End (IRE) (Treasure Kay)
R Hannon Con Harrington

Placings:0323010/34031-3050116546 **(6307)**
2009: 6^{3}SD, 7^{0}GF, 7^{5}SD, 8^{0}SD, 8^{1}G, 8^{1}GF, 9^{6}G, 8^{5}GF, 6^{4}S, 8^{6}GF,

	Starts	1st	2nd	3rd	Win & Pl
Career Total (Turf)	**16**	**2**	**1**	**3**	**17251**
Career Total (AW)	**6**	**2**	**0**	**2**	**9680**

93 7/09 Sand 1m14y (0-80)H G-F £4857
85 7/09 Wind 1m67y (0-80)H GD £4857
88 11/08 Ling 1m (0-85)H STD £4857
74 9/07 Ling 7f STD £3465
Total win prize-money £18036

Going (Turf): Sf: 0-3 GS: 0-0 **Gd: 1-5 GF: 1-8** Fm: 0-0
Distance: 5f/6f: 0-6 7f-8f: 2-12 9f-13f: 2-4 14f+: 0-0
Track : LH: 2-4 RH: 2-7 **Tight: 3-5** Gall: 0-0
Aids: Bl: 0-0 Vi: 0-0 Tstrap: 0-0 Ckp: 0-0
Best Rating: **95** 7/09 Gdwd 1m1f good

Fair; effective over 7f-1m; acts on most ground and on Polytrack.

Romeos Girl

85 **55**

2-y-o b f Statue Of Liberty (USA)-Fadaki Hawaki (USA) (Vice Regent (CAN))
Jennie Candlish P and Mrs G A Clarke

Placings:405 **(5934)**
2009: 6^{4}S, 8^{0}GF, 5^{5}GF,

	Starts	1st	2nd	3rd	Win & Pl
Career Total (Turf)	**3**	**0**	**0**	**0**	**289**

Going (Turf): **Sf: 0-1 GS: 0-0 Gd: 0-0 GF: 0-2 Fm: 0-0**
Distance: 5f/6f: 0-2 7f-8f: 0-0 9f-13f: 0-1 14f+: 0-0
Track : LH: 0-0 RH: 0-1 Tight: 0-0 Gall: 0-0
Aids: Bl: 0-0 Vi: 0-0 Tstrap: 0-0 Ckp: 0-0
Best Rating: **55** 7/09 Hayd 6f soft

Ron The Don

67(-11) **21**

2-y-o ch g Paris House-Hillside Heather (IRE) (Tagula (IRE))
A Berry Hillside Racing

Placings:0000000 **(7419)**
2009: 5^{0}GS, 5^{0}G, 5^{0}GF, 6^{0}S, 7^{0}G, 7^{0}GF, 7^{0}SD,

	Starts	1st	2nd	3rd	Win & Pl
Career Total (Turf)	**6**	**0**	**0**	**0**	
Career Total (AW)	**1**	**0**	**0**	**0**	

Going (Turf): **Sf: 0-1 GS: 0-1 Gd: 0-2 GF: 0-2 Fm: 0-0**
Distance: 5f/6f: 0-4 7f-8f: 0-3 9f-13f: 0-0 14f+: 0-0
Track : LH: 0-2 RH: 0-0 Tight: 0-1 Gall: 0-0
Aids: Bl: 0-2 Vi: 0-0 Tstrap: 0-1 Ckp: 0-1
Best Rating: **21** 6/09 Haml 5f4y gd-fm

Rondeau (GR)

104(108) (82)**76**

4-y-o ch g Harmonic Way-Areti (GR) (Wadood (USA))
P R Chamings The Foxford House Partnership

Placings:500/62444014-55106001420 **(7830)**
2009: 6^{5}G, 6^{5}GF, 6^{1}SD, 5^{0}GF, 6^{6}SD, 5^{0}G, 6^{0}SD, 6^{1}G, 7^{4}SD, 7^{2}SD, 7^{0}SD,

	Starts	1st	2nd	3rd	Win & Pl
Career Total (Turf)	**10**	**1**	**1**	**0**	**4454**
Career Total (AW)	**12**	**2**	**1**	**0**	**5775**

76 10/09 Brig 6f209y (0-70)H GD £3154
82 7/09 Ling 6f (0-70)H STD £2729
77 9/08 Kemp 6f (0-65)H STD £2047
Total win prize-money £7931

Going (Turf): Sf: 0-1 GS: 0-0 **Gd: 1-4** GF: 0-4 Fm: 0-1
Distance: **5f/6f: 2-8** 7f-8f: 1-13 9f-13f: 0-1 14f+: 0-0
Track : **LH: 2-8** RH: 1-8 **Tight: 1-6** Gall: 0-4
Aids: Bl: 0-0 Vi: 0-0 Tstrap: 0-0 Ckp: 0-0
Best Rating: **82** 7/09 Ling 6f stand

Fair; effective over 6f-1m; acts on fast ground and on Polytrack.

Ronnie Howe

101(100) (59)**72**

5-y-o b g Hunting Lion (IRE)-Arasong (Aragon)
S R Bowring The High Five Partnership

Placings:0244033/21456200/002106050-043050340000000 **(7838)**
2009: 7^{0}SS, 5^{4}SD, 6^{3}SD, 5^{0}SD, 5^{5}SD, 6^{0}SD, 5^{3}GF, 5^{4}GS, 5^{0}F, 5^{0}F, 5^{0}GF, 5^{0}S, 5^{0}GS, 6^{0}GF, 5^{0}SS,

	Starts	1st	2nd	3rd	Win & Pl
Career Total (Turf)	26	1	3	3	6857
Career Total (AW)	13	1	1	1	4077

72 6/08 Haml 5f4y (0-65)H G-F £2047
55 2/07 Sthl 5f SS £2968
Total win prize-money £5016

Going (Turf): Sf: 0-2 GS: 0-5 Gd: 0-6 **GF: 1-11** Fm: 0-2
Distance: **5f/6f: 2-38** 7f-8f: 0-1 9f-13f: 0-0 14f+: 0-0
Track : LH: 0-6 RH: 0-0 Tight: 0-2 Gall: 0-0
Aids: Bl: 0-11 Vi: 0-1 Tstrap: 0-1 Ckp: 0-1
Best Rating: **72** 6/08 Haml 5f4y gd-fm

Modest sprinter; acts on a sound surface and Fibresand; has worn a visor and tongue-tie.

Ronnies Girl

(34)
5-y-o b m Tobougg (IRE)-Tryptonic (FR) (Baryshnikov (AUS))
C J Teague Roland Bowman

Placings:00/0000-**00** **(0963)**
2009: 7^{0}SD, 7^{0}SD,

	Starts	1st	2nd	3rd	Win & Pl
Career Total (Turf)	6	0	0	0	
Career Total (AW)	2	0	0	0	

Going (Turf): **Sf: 0-2 GS: 0-1 Gd: 0-2 GF: 0-0 Fm: 0-1**
Distance: 5f/6f: 0-2 7f-8f: 0-5 9f-13f: 0-1 14f+: 0-0
Track : LH: 0-4 RH: 0-2 Tight: 0-3 Gall: 0-0
Aids: Bl: 0-0 Vi: 0-1 Tstrap: 0-0 Ckp: 0-0

Rony Dony (IRE)

90(80) (27)**39**
5-y-o b g Revoque (IRE)-Farrans Guest (IRE) (Tagula (IRE))
M E Rimmer Ady Boughen

Placings:000000 **(5124)**
2009: 7^{0}SD, 8^{0}G, 8^{0}SD, 15^{0}GF, 8^{0}G, 6^{0}F,

	Starts	1st	2nd	3rd	Win & Pl
Career Total (Turf)	4	0	0	0	
Career Total (AW)	2	0	0	0	

Going (Turf): **Sf: 0-0 GS: 0-0 Gd: 0-2 GF: 0-1 Fm: 0-1**
Distance: 5f/6f: 0-0 7f-8f: 0-3 9f-13f: 0-2 14f+: 0-1
Track : LH: 0-3 RH: 0-1 Tight: 0-3 Gall: 0-0
Aids: Bl: 0-1 Vi: 0-0 Tstrap: 0-0 Ckp: 0-0
Best Rating: **39** 8/09 Yarm 1m3y good

Roodee King

91(90) (40)**55**
3-y-o b g Auction House (USA)-Antithesis (IRE) (Fairy King (USA))
Patrick Morris Chester Racing Club Ltd

Placings:62450 **(7052)**
2009: 5^{6}GS, 5^{2}GF, 5^{4}SD, 5^{5}SD, 7^{0}SD,

	Starts	1st	2nd	3rd	Win & Pl
Career Total (Turf)	2	0	1	0	705
Career Total (AW)	3	0	0	0	0

Going (Turf): **Sf: 0-0 GS: 0-1 Gd: 0-0 GF: 0-1 Fm: 0-0**
Distance: 5f/6f: 0-4 7f-8f: 0-1 9f-13f: 0-0 14f+: 0-0
Track : LH: 0-2 RH: 0-2 Tight: 0-2 Gall: 0-0
Aids: Bl: 0-0 Vi: 0-0 Tstrap: 0-0 Ckp: 0-0
Best Rating: **55** 6/09 Donc 5f gd-sft

Moderate; effective at 5f on fast and easy ground.

Roodle

100 **89**
2-y-o b f Xaar-Roodeye (Inchinor)
Eve Johnson Houghton Mrs R F Johnson Houghton

Placings:2165206 **(7147)**
2009: 5^{2}GF, 5^{1}GF, 6^{6}G, 5^{5}GF, 6^{2}GF, 6^{0}GF, 6^{6}G,

	Starts	1st	2nd	3rd	Win & Pl
Career Total (Turf)	7	1	2	0	11798

77 7/09 Chep 5f16y G-F £5180
Total win prize-money £5181

Going (Turf): Sf: 0-0 GS: 0-0 Gd: 0-2 **GF: 1-5** Fm: 0-0
Distance: **5f/6f: 1-7** 7f-8f: 0-0 9f-13f: 0-0 14f+: 0-0
Track : LH: 0-0 RH: 0-0 Tight: 0-0 Gall: 0-0
Aids: Bl: 0-0 Vi: 0-0 Tstrap: 0-0 Ckp: 0-0
Best Rating: **89** 10/09 NmkR 6f good

Useful; suited by 5f-6f and acts on fast ground.

Rookwith (IRE)

98 (65)**63**
9-y-o b g Revoque (IRE)-Resume (IRE) (Lahib (USA))
T G McCourt James Gogarty

Placings:0665606**200**/**2**500441546/156405/3530053/0341 35600200/00000403**06**/**51**00300510**02**0-**0**00000410 **(5355a)**
2009: 7^{0}GF, 8^{0}SD, 8^{0}Y, 10^{0}GF, 8^{0}GF, 8^{0}G, 9^{4}GF, 8^{1}GF, 8^{0}HY,

	Starts	1st	2nd	3rd	Win & Pl
Career Total (Turf)	63	4	1	7	28985
Career Total (AW)	14	2	3	0	12869

62 8/09 Muss 1m (0-75)H G-F £3885
65 7/08 Dund 1m (45-60)H STD £4826
62 4/08 Dund 1m (45-60)H STD £4572
67 5/06 Leop 1m (40-70)H GD £4765
71 7/04 Bell 1m (50-80)H GD £6812
71 7/03 Ripn 1m1f F G-F £4186
Total win prize-money £29051

Going (Turf): Sf: 0-8 GS: 0-4 **Gd: 2-13 GF: 2-25** Fm: 0-5
Distance: 5f/6f: 0-3 **7f-8f: 5-42** 9f-13f: 1-32 14f+: 0-0
Track : **LH: 4-43** RH: 2-25 **Tight: 2-12** Gall: 0-2
Aids: Bl: 2-26 Vi: 2-5 Tstrap: 0-3 Ckp: 0-3
Best Rating: **71** 8/06 Gowr 1m gd-yld

Modest; stays 1m; acts on a sound surface on turf and Polytrack; has worn various headgear.

Ros Cuire (IRE)

95(88) (60)**51**
4-y-o br c Expelled (USA)-Haven Island (IRE) (Revoque (IRE))
W A Murphy John A Murphy

Placings:056/660606-00300 **(6984)**
2009: 7^{0}SD, 8^{0}G, 7^{3}GF, 7^{0}SF, 7^{0}G,

	Starts	1st	2nd	3rd	Win & Pl
Career Total (Turf)	6	0	0	1	353
Career Total (AW)	8	0	0	0	0

Going (Turf): **Sf: 0-0 GS: 0-2 Gd: 0-2 GF: 0-1 Fm: 0-0**
Distance: 5f/6f: 0-2 7f-8f: 0-11 9f-13f: 0-1 14f+: 0-0
Track : LH: 0-11 RH: 0-0 Tight: 0-5 Gall: 0-1
Aids: Bl: 0-0 Vi: 0-0 Tstrap: 0-0 Ckp: 0-0
Best Rating: **68** 3/08 Dund 7f stand

Moderate Irish-trained colt, stays 7f; acts on fast ground.

Rosa Gurney (IRE)

90 **56**
2-y-o b f Antonius Pius (USA)-Nonsense (IRE) (Soviet Star (USA))
J R Best John Mayne

Placings:005 **(6563)**
2009: 6^{0}GF, 7^{0}GS, 6^{5}GS,

	Starts	1st	2nd	3rd	Win & Pl
Career Total (Turf)	3	0	0	0	0

Going (Turf): **Sf: 0-0 GS: 0-2 Gd: 0-0 GF: 0-1 Fm: 0-0**
Distance: 5f/6f: 0-2 7f-8f: 0-1 9f-13f: 0-0 14f+: 0-0
Track : LH: 0-0 RH: 0-1 Tight: 0-0 Gall: 0-0
Aids: Bl: 0-0 Vi: 0-0 Tstrap: 0-0 Ckp: 0-0
Best Rating: **56** 10/09 Folk 6f gd-sft

Rosabee (IRE)

97 **97**
3-y-o ch f No Excuse Needed-Tilbrook (IRE) (Don't Forget Me)
Mrs D J Sanderson R J Budge

Placings:535111200-000 **(4352)**
2009: 6^{0}GF, 7^{0}G, 8^{0}G,

	Starts	1st	2nd	3rd	Win & Pl
Career Total (Turf)	12	3	1	1	25678

82 7/08 Leic 5f218y GD £3885
86 7/08 Donc 5f GD £4209
79 7/08 Pont 6f GD £6476
Total win prize-money £14571

Going (Turf): Sf: 0-1 GS: 0-1 **Gd: 3-6** GF: 0-4 Fm: 0-0
Distance: **5f/6f: 3-9** 7f-8f: 0-2 9f-13f: 0-1 14f+: 0-0
Track : **LH: 1-3** RH: 0-0 Tight: 0-0 Gall: 0-0
Aids: Bl: 0-0 Vi: 0-0 Tstrap: 0-0 Ckp: 0-0
Best Rating: **97** 7/08 Asct 6f gd-fm

Smart; placed in Group company; effective at 5f-6f; acts on good and faster ground.

Rosaleen (IRE)

105(102) (96)**99**
4-y-o b f Cadeaux Genereux-Dark Rosaleen (IRE) (Darshaan)
B J Meehan Exors of the Late F C T Wilson

Placings:4140/4105100-105305 **(7132)**
2009: 8^{1}G, 8^{0}GF, 8^{5}G, 12^{3}G, 8^{0}GF, 8^{5}SD,

	Starts	1st	2nd	3rd	Win & Pl
Career Total (Turf)	15	4	0	1	71838
Career Total (AW)	2	0	0	0	1365

92 6/09 Pont 1m4y GD £25236
98 7/08 Sand 1m14y G-F £22708
95 4/08 Asct 1m SFT £6854
85 7/07 Thsk 7f GD £5181
Total win prize-money £59980

Going (Turf): Sf: 1-1 GS: 0-0 **Gd: 2-9** GF: 1-5 Fm: 0-0
Distance: 5f/6f: 0-0 7f-8f: 2-11 9f-13f: 2-6 14f+: 0-0
Track : LH: 2-4 RH: 2-9 Tight: 1-3 Gall: 1-4
Aids: Bl: 0-0 Vi: 0-0 Tstrap: 0-0 Ckp: 0-0
Best Rating: **99** 7/09 Asct 1m good

Very useful; Listed winner; stays 1m4f but effective at 1m; acts on most ground; handles Polytrack.

Rosbay (IRE)

106 92

5-y-o b g Desert Prince (IRE)-Dark Rosaleen (IRE) (Darshaan)

T D Easterby Croft, Taylor & Hebdon Partnership

Placings:64512140/43102500/432053335-203420554004 **(6648)**

2009: 12^{2}GF, 12^{0}GF, 9^{3}GF, 10^{4}GF, 9^{2}GS, 12^{0}G, 10^{5}HY, 9^{5}G, 9^{4}G, 10^{0}S, 12^{0}S, 10^{4}G,

	Starts	1st	2nd	3rd	Win & Pl
Career Total (Turf)	37	3	5	6	37927

89	7/07	Ches	1m2f75y (0-85)H	HVY	£5829
84	8/06	Newc	1m3y H	G-S	£11217
76	7/06	Thsk	7f	FRM	£3562

Total win prize-money £20609

Going (Turf): **Sf: 1-9 GS: 1-6** Gd: 0-13 GF: 0-7 **Fm: 1-2**
Distance: 5f/6f: 0-3 7f-8f: 1-5 **9f-13f: 2-28** 14f+: 0-1
Track : **LH: 2-23** RH: 0-10 **Tight: 2-14** Gall: 0-10
Aids: Bl: 0-1 Vi: 0-0 Tstrap: 0-0 Ckp: 0-0
Best Rating: 92 8/08 Pont 1m4f8y good

Fair; stays 1m4f and acts on most ground; has worn blinkers.

Rosco Flyer (IRE)

93(97) (71)57

3-y-o b g Val Royal (FR)-Palace Soy (IRE) (Tagula (IRE))

J R Boyle Chris Simpson, Miss Elizabeth Ross

Placings:066-6265 **(6698)**

2009: 8^{6}SD, 8^{2}SD, 10^{6}SS, 12^{5}GS,

	Starts	1st	2nd	3rd	Win & Pl
Career Total (Turf)	3	0	0	0	0
Career Total (AW)	4	0	1	0	605

Going (Turf): Sf: 0-1 GS: 0-1 Gd: 0-1 GF: 0-0 Fm: 0-0
Distance: 5f/6f: 0-0 7f-8f: 0-5 9f-13f: 0-2 14f+: 0-0
Track : LH: 0-2 RH: 0-3 Tight: 0-3 Gall: 0-0
Aids: Bl: 0-0 Vi: 0-0 Tstrap: 0-0 Ckp: 0-0
Best Rating: 71 9/09 Kemp 1m stand

Modest form to date.

Rose Alba (IRE)

91 66

2-y-o gr f Verglas (IRE)-Green Rosy (USA) (Green Dancer (USA))

J L Dunlop Mrs Dan Abbott (susan Abbott Racing)

Placings:0020 **(6067)**

2009: 7^{0}GF, 7^{0}S, 8^{2}G, 9^{0}GF,

	Starts	1st	2nd	3rd	Win & Pl
Career Total (Turf)	4	0	1	0	1156

Going (Turf): Sf: 0-1 GS: 0-0 Gd: 0-1 GF: 0-2 Fm: 0-0
Distance: 5f/6f: 0-0 7f-8f: 0-2 9f-13f: 0-2 14f+: 0-0
Track : LH: 0-0 RH: 0-0 Tight: 0-0 Gall: 0-0
Aids: Bl: 0-0 Vi: 0-0 Tstrap: 0-0 Ckp: 0-0
Best Rating: 66 8/09 Chep 1m14y good

Modest; stays 1m; acts on good ground.

Rose Aurora

72(79) (27)39

2-y-o gr f Pastoral Pursuits-Khaladja (IRE) (Akarad (FR))

M P Tregoning Shoreham Stud

Placings:50 **(7234)**

2009: 6^{5}GF, 6^{0}SD,

	Starts	1st	2nd	3rd	Win & Pl
Career Total (Turf)	1	0	0	0	0
Career Total (AW)	1	0	0	0	

Going (Turf): Sf: 0-0 GS: 0-0 Gd: 0-0 GF: 0-1 Fm: 0-0
Distance: 5f/6f: 0-2 7f-8f: 0-0 9f-13f: 0-0 14f+: 0-0
Track : LH: 0-0 RH: 0-1 Tight: 0-0 Gall: 0-0
Aids: Bl: 0-0 Vi: 0-0 Tstrap: 0-0 Ckp: 0-0
Best Rating: 39 9/09 Ling 6f gd-fm

Rose Avelina

84 25

3-y-o b f Xaar-B'Elanna Torres (Entrepreneur)

I W McInnes D & S L Tanker Transport Limited

Placings:500000 **(6098)**

2009: 7^{5}GF, 8^{0}G, 8^{0}G, 8^{0}GF, 9^{0}F, 13^{0}GF,

	Starts	1st	2nd	3rd	Win & Pl
Career Total (Turf)	6	0	0	0	0

Going (Turf): Sf: 0-0 GS: 0-0 Gd: 0-2 GF: 0-3 Fm: 0-1
Distance: 5f/6f: 0-0 7f-8f: 0-2 9f-13f: 0-3 14f+: 0-1
Track : LH: 0-2 RH: 0-3 Tight: 0-2 Gall: 0-0
Aids: Bl: 0-1 Vi: 0-0 Tstrap: 0-0 Ckp: 0-0
Best Rating: 25 6/09 Bevl 7f100y gd-fm

Rose Bed (IRE)

79(85) (52)41

2-y-o ch f Namid-Daqtora (Dr Devious (IRE))

M G Quinlan Liam Mulryan

Placings:00 **(6228)**

2009: 5^{0}GF, 7^{0}SD,

	Starts	1st	2nd	3rd	Win & Pl
Career Total (Turf)	1	0	0	0	
Career Total (AW)	1	0	0	0	

Going (Turf): Sf: 0-0 GS: 0-0 Gd: 0-0 GF: 0-1 Fm: 0-0
Distance: 5f/6f: 0-1 7f-8f: 0-1 9f-13f: 0-0 14f+: 0-0
Track : LH: 0-0 RH: 0-1 Tight: 0-0 Gall: 0-0
Aids: Bl: 0-0 Vi: 0-0 Tstrap: 0-0 Ckp: 0-0
Best Rating: 52 9/09 Kemp 7f stand

Rose Bien

104(102) (61)67

7-y-o b/br m Bien Bien (USA)-Madame Bovary (Ile De Bourbon (USA))

P J McBride PMRacing

Placings:0/56235/**00521411152520/50454/03452320-3602531** **(5068)**

2009: 16^{3}SD, 16^{6}G, **16^{0}SD**, 18^{2}G, 14^{5}GF, 16^{3}G, 17^{1}GF,

	Starts	1st	2nd	3rd	Win & Pl
Career Total (Turf)	26	4	5	3	24539
Career Total (AW)	14	1	2	2	3924

65	8/09	Pont	2m1f22y (0-70)H	G-F	£3885
68	7/06	Rdcr	1m6f19y (0-70)H	G-F	£3238
65	7/06	Bevl	2m35y (0-70)H	FRM	£5181
61	6/06	Folk	1m4f (0-60)H	G-F	£2730
61	5/06	Wolv	1m5f194y (0-45)	STD	£1876

Total win prize-money £16914

Going (Turf): Sf: 0-0 GS: 0-3 Gd: 0-6 **GF: 3-16** Fm: 1-1
Distance: 5f/6f: 0-0 7f-8f: 0-1 9f-13f: 1-10 **14f+: 4-29**
Track : **LH: 3-27** RH: 2-11 **Tight: 4-20** Gall: 0-8
Aids: Bl: 0-1 Vi: 0-0 Tstrap: 5-30 Ckp: 5-30
Best Rating: 69 9/06 Yarm 2m good

Modest; stays 2m1f; acts on fast ground and on Polytrack; has worn cheekpieces.

Rose Blossom

106 97

2-y-o b f Pastoral Pursuits-Lamarita (Emarati (USA))

R A Fahey Highclere Thoroughbred Racing (Blossom)

Placings:10104 **(5822)**

2009: 5^{1}GF, 5^{0}GF, 6^{1}F, 6^{0}GF, 5^{4}GF,

	Starts	1st	2nd	3rd	Win & Pl
Career Total (Turf)	5	2	0	0	13502

90	7/09	Hayd	6f	FRM	£6476
87	5/09	Haml	5f4y	G-F	£2729

Total win prize-money £9206

Going (Turf): Sf: 0-0 GS: 0-0 Gd: 0-0 **GF: 1-4 Fm: 1-1**
Distance: **5f/6f: 2-5** 7f-8f: 0-0 9f-13f: 0-0 14f+: 0-0
Track : LH: 0-0 RH: 0-0 Tight: 0-0 Gall: 0-0
Aids: Bl: 0-0 Vi: 0-0 Tstrap: 0-0 Ckp: 0-0
Best Rating: 97 9/09 Donc 5f gd-fm

Very useful; suited by 5-6f and fast ground.

Rose Cheval (USA)

97(87) (60)72

3-y-o ro f Johannesburg (USA)-La Samanna (USA) (Trempolino (USA))

M R Channon Capital

Placings:626-30003320 **(6219)**

2009: 8^{3}SD, 9^{0}SD, 8^{0}GF, 8^{0}S, 8^{3}G, 9^{3}F, 8^{2}F, 10^{0}GF,

	Starts	1st	2nd	3rd	Win & Pl
Career Total (Turf)	8	0	2	2	3000
Career Total (AW)	3	0	0	1	403

Going (Turf): Sf: 0-1 GS: 0-1 Gd: 0-1 GF: 0-3 Fm: 0-2
Distance: 5f/6f: 0-1 7f-8f: 0-2 9f-13f: 0-8 14f+: 0-0
Track : LH: 0-6 RH: 0-1 Tight: 0-5 Gall: 0-0
Aids: Bl: 0-0 Vi: 0-0 Tstrap: 0-0 Ckp: 0-0
Best Rating: 72 6/08 Newb 7f gd-fm

Moderate; stays 1m1f and acts on fast ground.

Rose De Rita

68(84) (26)36

4-y-o br f Superior Premium-Rita's Rock Ape (Mon Tresor)

L P Grassick L P Grassick

Placings:000/300066-0 **(3204)**

2009: 5^{0}G,

	Starts	1st	2nd	3rd	Win & Pl
Career Total (Turf)	7	0	0	1	260
Career Total (AW)	3	0	0	0	0

Going (Turf): Sf: 0-2 GS: 0-1 Gd: 0-2 GF: 0-1 Fm: 0-1
Distance: 5f/6f: 0-10 7f-8f: 0-0 9f-13f: 0-0 14f+: 0-0
Track : LH: 0-6 RH: 0-0 Tight: 0-2 Gall: 0-4
Aids: Bl: 0-0 Vi: 0-0 Tstrap: 0-0 Ckp: 0-0
Best Rating: 36 6/08 Bath 5f11y good

-

Rose Diamond (IRE)

99 (102)101

3-y-o gr f Daylami (IRE)-Tante Rose (IRE) (Barathea (IRE))

Patrick L Biancone (R Charlton 17/6) B E Nielsen

Placings:415240-4304 (3016)
2009: 7[4]GF, 8[3]GF, 8[0]GF, 7[4]FT,

	Starts	1st	2nd	3rd	Win & Pl
Career Total (Turf)	9	1	1	1	26531
Career Total (AW)	1	0	0	0	12500

78 6/08 NmkJ 6f G-F £5180
Total win prize-money £5181

Going (Turf): Sf: 0-1 GS: 0-3 Gd: 0-0 **GF: 1-5** Fm: 0-0
Distance: **5f/6f: 1-3** 7f-8f: 0-7 9f-13f: 0-0 14f+: 0-0
Track : LH: 0-0 RH: 0-2 Tight: 0-0 Gall: 0-1
Aids: Bl: 0-0 Vi: 0-0 Tstrap: 0-0 Ckp: 0-0
Best Rating: **102** 12/09 SnAt 7f fast

Very useful; stays 7f; acts on fast and easy ground.

Rose Of Coma (IRE)

95(89) (47)**59**
3-y-o br f Kheleyf (USA)-Rosalia (USA) (Red Ransom (USA))
A G Juckes (Miss Gay Kelleway 30/8) Whispering Winds

Placings:3242113260050-00315342205646 (7094)
2009: 8[0]G, 7[0]GF, 9[3]GF, 9[1]GF, 10[5]SD, 9[3]G, 9[4]G, 10[2]GF, 9[2]F, 9[0]GS, 11[5]F, 9[6]F, 11[4]GF, 10[6]G,

	Starts	1st	2nd	3rd	Win & Pl
Career Total (Turf)	22	3	5	4	12897
Career Total (AW)	5	0	0	0	0

54 5/09 Leic 1m1f218y G-F £1942
55 7/08 Yarm 7f3y G-F £1942
56 6/08 Yarm 7f3y G-F £1683
Total win prize-money £5570

Going (Turf): Sf: 0-2 GS: 0-2 Gd: 0-5 **GF: 3-10** Fm: 0-3
Distance: 5f/6f: 0-4 **7f-8f: 2-9** 9f-13f: 1-14 14f+: 0-0
Track : LH: 0-13 **RH: 1-5** Tight: 0-8 Gall: 0-1
Aids: Bl: 0-0 Vi: 0-1 Tstrap: 0-4 Ckp: 0-4
Best Rating: **59** 6/09 Newc 1m2f32y gd-fm

Moderate, effective at 7f-1m2f: acts on fast ground; has worn cheekpieces and a visor.

Rose Row

103(107) (85)**72**
5-y-o gr m Act One-D'Azy (Persian Bold)
Mrs Mary Hambro Mrs Richard Hambro

Placings:L05/325131-44001124 (6636)
2009: 12[4]SD, 11[4]GF, 10[0]G, 12[0]G, 12[1]SF, 16[1]SD, 13[2]SD, 13[4]SD,

	Starts	1st	2nd	3rd	Win & Pl
Career Total (Turf)	7	2	0	1	6370
Career Total (AW)	10	2	2	1	9628

76 9/09 Kemp 2m (0-70)H STD £2590
71 8/09 Wolv 1m4f50y (0-70)H SF £3885
72 6/08 Wind 1m3f135y (0-75)H G-S £3070
72 4/08 Bath 1m3f144y (0-75)H SFT £2914
Total win prize-money £12461

Going (Turf): **Sf: 1-1 GS: 1-1** Gd: 0-2 GF: 0-3 Fm: 0-0
Distance: 5f/6f: 0-0 7f-8f: 0-1 **9f-13f: 3-12** 14f+: 1-4
Track : **LH: 2-9** RH: 1-5 **Tight: 3-12** Gall: 0-1
Aids: Bl: 0-0 Vi: 0-0 Tstrap: 0-0 Ckp: 0-0
Best Rating: **85** 10/09 Wolv 1m5f194y stand

Fair; effective from 1m4f-2m; acts on soft ground and Polytrack.

Rose Street (IRE)

106(107) (94)**101**
5-y-o b m Noverre (USA)-Archipova (IRE) (Ela-Mana-Mou)
Miss P Robson (M A Jarvis 13/5) Mr & Mrs Raymond Anderson Green

Placings:12/212-5 (1986)
2009: 10[5]GF,

	Starts	1st	2nd	3rd	Win & Pl
Career Total (Turf)	4	1	2	0	28829
Career Total (AW)	2	1	1	0	5154

101 8/08 Ripn 1m1f170y (0-90)H G-S £8723
81 6/07 Kemp 1m2f STD £2914
Total win prize-money £11638

Going (Turf): Sf: 0-0 **GS: 1-2** Gd: 0-1 GF: 0-1 Fm: 0-0
Distance: 5f/6f: 0-0 7f-8f: 0-1 **9f-13f: 2-5** 14f+: 0-0
Track : LH: 0-3 **RH: 2-3 Tight: 1-2** Gall: 0-2
Aids: Bl: 0-0 Vi: 0-0 Tstrap: 0-0 Ckp: 0-0
Best Rating: **101** 8/08 Ripn 1m1f170y gd-sft

Very useful; stays 1m2f; acts on easy ground and on Polytrack; likes to race prominently.

Rosedale

93(88) (53)**57**
2-y-o b f Pastoral Pursuits-Wyoming (Inchinor)
J A R Toller Alan Gibson

Placings:05410634 (7097)
2009: 5[0]G, 5[5]GF, 6[4]SD, 5[1]GS, 6[0]GS, 6[6]SD, 5[3]GF, 7[4]G,

	Starts	1st	2nd	3rd	Win & Pl
Career Total (Turf)	6	1	0	1	4608
Career Total (AW)	2	0	0	0	0

57 7/09 Leic 5f218y G-S £3885
Total win prize-money £3886

Going (Turf): Sf: 0-0 **GS: 1-2** Gd: 0-2 GF: 0-2 Fm: 0-0
Distance: **5f/6f: 1-6** 7f-8f: 0-2 9f-13f: 0-0 14f+: 0-0
Track : LH: 0-1 RH: 0-1 Tight: 0 1 Gall: 0-1
Aids: Bl: 0-0 Vi: 0-0 Tstrap: 0-0 Ckp: 0-0
Best Rating: **57** 7/09 Leic 5f218y gd-sft

Moderate; stays 6f; handles Polytrack and fast and easy turf.

Rosemarkie

84(68) (1)**25**
5-y-o br m Diktat-Sparkling Isle (Inchinor)
J M Bradley J Hinch

Placings:0/0-000 (5120)
2009: 8[0]SD, 10[0]G, 6[0]F,

	Starts	1st	2nd	3rd	Win & Pl
Career Total (Turf)	3	0	0	0	
Career Total (AW)	2	0	0	0	

Going (Turf): **Sf: 0-0 GS: 0-1 Gd: 0-1 GF: 0-0 Fm: 0-1**
Distance: 5f/6f: 0-0 7f-8f: 0-2 9f-13f: 0-3 14f+: 0-0
Track : LH: 0-4 RH: 0-1 Tight: 0-3 Gall: 0-0
Aids: Bl: 0-0 Vi: 0-0 Tstrap: 0-2 Ckp: 0-2
Best Rating: **25** 8/09 Brig 6f209y firm

Roses

94 **47**
4-y-o b f Muhtarram (USA)-Sublime (Conquering Hero (USA))
G A Swinbank Guy Reed

Placings:5 (3731)
2009: 13[5]G,

	Starts	1st	2nd	3rd	Win & Pl
Career Total (Turf)	1	0	0	0	0

Going (Turf): **Sf: 0-0 GS: 0-0 Gd: 0-1 GF: 0-0 Fm: 0-0**
Distance: 5f/6f: 0-0 7f-8f: 0-0 9f-13f: 0-0 14f+: 0-1
Track : LH: 0-1 RH: 0-0 Tight: 0-1 Gall: 0-0
Aids: Bl: 0-0 Vi: 0-0 Tstrap: 0-0 Ckp: 0-0
Best Rating: **47** 7/09 Catt 1m5f175y good

Roses For The Lady (IRE)

113 **112**
3-y-o b f Sadler's Wells (USA)-Head In The Clouds (IRE) (Rainbow Quest (USA))
John M Oxx Neil Jones

Placings:05-1352 (3896a)
2009: 10[1]GF, 11[3]GF, 12[5]G, 12[2]HY,

	Starts	1st	2nd	3rd	Win & Pl
Career Total (Turf)	6	1	1	1	108431

91 3/09 Leop 1m2f G-F £11404
Total win prize-money £11405

Going (Turf): Sf: 0-2 GS: 0-0 Gd: 0-1 **GF: 1-2** Fm: 0-0
Distance: 5f/6f: 0-0 7f-8f: 0-2 **9f-13f: 1-4** 14f+: 0-0
Track : **LH: 1-3** RH: 0-2 Tight: 0-1 Gall: 0-0
Aids: Bl: 0-0 Vi: 0-0 Tstrap: 0-0 Ckp: 0-0
Best Rating: **112** 7/09 Curr 1m4f heavy

Very useful; stays 1m2f and acts on fast ground.

Rosetta Hill

83 **48**
2-y-o ch f Compton Place-Fruit Of Glory (Glory Of Dancer)
J R Jenkins R B Hill

Placings:000 (6903)
2009: 5[0]GF, 6[0]GF, 5[0]G,

	Starts	1st	2nd	3rd	Win & Pl
Career Total (Turf)	3	0	0	0	

Going (Turf): **Sf: 0-0 GS: 0-0 Gd: 0-1 GF: 0-2 Fm: 0-0**
Distance: 5f/6f: 0-2 7f-8f: 0-1 9f-13f: 0-0 14f+: 0-0
Track : LH: 0-0 RH: 0-0 Tight: 0-0 Gall: 0-2
Aids: Bl: 0-0 Vi: 0-0 Tstrap: 0-0 Ckp: 0-0
Best Rating: **48** 6/09 Wind 5f10y gd-fm

Rosewin (IRE)

102 (20)**72**
3-y-o b f Hawkeye (IRE)-African Scene (IRE) (Scenic)
A Dickman (O Brennan 15/7) Major P H K Steveney

Placings:0-00315301126 (6560)
2009: 8[0]GF, 10[0]G, 10[3]GF, 12[1]F, 12[5]GF, 11[3]GS, 14[0]GF, 11[1]GS, 12[1]GS, 12[2]GF, 11[6]G,

	Starts	1st	2nd	3rd	Win & Pl
Career Total (Turf)	11	3	1	2	9670
Career Total (AW)	1	0	0	0	

72 9/09 Newc 1m4f93y (0-65)H G-S £2525
60 8/09 Catt 1m3f214y (0-60)H G-S £2388
56 6/09 Bevl 1m4f16y (0-55)H FRM £2428
Total win prize-money £7342

Going (Turf): Sf: 0-0 **GS: 2-3** Gd: 0-2 GF: 0-5 Fm: 1-1
Distance: 5f/6f: 0-0 7f-8f: 0-1 **9f-13f: 3-10** 14f+: 0-1
Track : **LH: 2-8** RH: 1-4 **Tight: 2-7** Gall: 1-1

Aids: Bl: 0-0 Vi: 0-0 Tstrap: 0-0 Ckp: 0-0
Best Rating: **72** 9/09 Bevl 1m4f16y gd-fm

Modest; stays 1m4f; handles fast and easy ground.

Rosie Cross (IRE)

(96) (61)**64**

5-y-o b m Cape Cross (IRE)-Professional Mom (USA) (Spinning World (USA))
Eve Johnson Houghton Eden Racing (II)

Placings:46000/303610233106050/5000546024-0540 **(0802)**
2009: 7^{0}SD, 6^{5}SD, 7^{4}SD, 8^{0}SD,

	Starts	1st	2nd	3rd	Win & Pl
Career Total (Turf)	9	0	1	2	1542
Career Total (AW)	26	2	1	2	5870

67 9/07 Kemp 5f (0-60)H STD £2047
59 7/07 Wolv 5f20y (0-65)H STD £2388
Total win prize-money £4437

Going (Turf): **Sf: 0-0 GS: 0-2 Gd: 0-3 GF: 0-3 Fm: 0-1**
Distance: **5f/6f: 2-23** 7f-8f: 0-12 9f-13f: 0-0 14f+: 0-0
Track : LH: 1-18 RH: 1-13 **Tight: 1-13** Gall: 0-2
Aids: Bl: 0-1 Vi: 0-0 Tstrap: 0-6 Ckp: 0-6
Best Rating: **67** 9/07 Kemp 5f stand

Plater; effective over 6f; acts on fast ground; also goes on Polytrack.

Rosie Says No

99(102) (70)**68**

4-y-o b m Catcher In The Rye (IRE)-Curlew Calling (IRE) (Pennine Walk)
A J McCabe (R M H Cowell 27/10) A J McCabe

Placings:040/123556523-403240150430 **(7852)**
2009: 5^{4}SD, 6^{0}SD, 6^{3}G, 6^{2}SD, 6^{4}SD, 5^{0}S, 5^{1}G, 5^{5}SD, 7^{0}SD, 5^{4}SD, 5^{3}SS, 5^{0}SS,

	Starts	1st	2nd	3rd	Win & Pl
Career Total (Turf)	8	1	2	1	4057
Career Total (AW)	16	1	1	3	3722

68 10/09 Yarm 5f43y (0-60)H GD £2072
65 5/08 GrLe 6f (0-65)H STD £2266
Total win prize-money £4339

Going (Turf): Sf: 0-3 GS: 0-2 **Gd: 1-2** GF: 0-1 Fm: 0-0
Distance: **5f/6f: 2-18** 7f-8f: 0-6 9f-13f: 0-0 14f+: 0-0
Track : **LH: 1-11** RH: 0-3 Tight: 0-6 **Gall: 1-3**
Aids: Bl: 0-0 Vi: 0-0 Tstrap: 1-13 Ckp: 1-13
Best Rating: **70** 11/08 Sthl 7f stand

Modest; effective over 6-7f; acts on soft ground and on Polytrack; has worn cheekpieces.

Rosie Two

85(87) (50)**37**

3-y-o b f Acclamation-Just A Glimmer (Bishop Of Cashel)
W S Kittow P A & M J Reditt

Placings:0056060 **(6170)**
2009: 6^{0}GF, 6^{0}G, 6^{5}GF, 5^{6}G, 6^{0}G, 7^{6}SD, 7^{0}GF,

	Starts	1st	2nd	3rd	Win & Pl
Career Total (Turf)	6	0	0	0	0
Career Total (AW)	1	0	0	0	0

Going (Turf): **Sf: 0-0 GS: 0-0 Gd: 0-3 GF: 0-3 Fm: 0-0**
Distance: 5f/6f: 0-4 7f-8f: 0-3 9f-13f: 0-0 14f+: 0-0
Track : LH: 0-2 RH: 0-1 Tight: 0-0 Gall: 0-2
Aids: Bl: 0-0 Vi: 0-0 Tstrap: 0-0 Ckp: 0-0
Best Rating: **50** 8/09 Kemp 7f stand

Rosie's Magic

76 **36**

2-y-o b f Auction House (USA)-Sachiko (Celtic Swing)
W De Best-Turner W De Best-Turner

Placings:05 **(6756)**
2009: 7^{0}GF, 7^{5}G,

	Starts	1st	2nd	3rd	Win & Pl
Career Total (Turf)	2	0	0	0	259

Going (Turf): **Sf: 0-0 GS: 0-0 Gd: 0-1 GF: 0-1 Fm: 0-0**
Distance: 5f/6f: 0-0 7f-8f: 0-2 9f-13f: 0-0 14f+: 0-0
Track : LH: 0-0 RH: 0-0 Tight: 0-0 Gall: 0-0
Aids: Bl: 0-0 Vi: 0-0 Tstrap: 0-0 Ckp: 0-0
Best Rating: **36** 9/09 Newb 7f gd-fm

Rosika

104(113) (100)**99**

3-y-o b f Sakhee (USA)-Blush Rambler (IRE) (Blushing Groom (FR))
Sir Michael Stoute Sir Evelyn De Rothschild

Placings:3-110212 **(7131)**
2009: 10^{1}G, 9^{1}F, 11^{0}GF, 10^{2}F, 12^{1}GF, 13^{2}SD,

	Starts	1st	2nd	3rd	Win & Pl
Career Total (Turf)	5	3	1	0	22364
Career Total (AW)	2	0	1	1	9011

99 10/09 Gdwd 1m4f (0-95)H G-F £9714
85 5/09 Sals 1m1f198y (0-85)H FRM £7447
72 4/09 Bath 1m2f46y GD £2590
Total win prize-money £19751

Going (Turf): Sf: 0-0 GS: 0-0 **Gd: 1-1 GF: 1-2 Fm: 1-2**
Distance: 5f/6f: 0-0 7f-8f: 0-1 **9f-13f: 3-6** 14f+: 0-0
Track : LH: 1-5 **RH: 2-2 Tight: 3-6** Gall: 0-0
Aids: Bl: 0-0 Vi: 0-0 Tstrap: 0-0 Ckp: 0-0
Best Rating: **100** 10/09 Ling 1m5f stand

Useful; stays at least 1m2f; acts on good ground and on Polytrack.

Rosiliant (IRE)

84(85) (48)**59**

2-y-o ch f Refuse To Bend (IRE)-Rosy Dudley (IRE) (Grand Lodge (USA))
C G Cox The Roseate Partnership

Placings:000005 **(7056)**
2009: 6^{0}GF, 6^{0}SD, 5^{0}GF, 7^{0}GF, 7^{0}SF, 7^{5}GF,

	Starts	1st	2nd	3rd	Win & Pl
Career Total (Turf)	4	0	0	0	0
Career Total (AW)	2	0	0	0	

Going (Turf): **Sf: 0-0 GS: 0-0 Gd: 0-0 GF: 0-4 Fm: 0-0**
Distance: 5f/6f: 0-3 7f-8f: 0-3 9f-13f: 0-0 14f+: 0-0
Track : LH: 0-2 RH: 0-1 Tight: 0-1 Gall: 0-1
Aids: Bl: 0-2 Vi: 0-0 Tstrap: 0-0 Ckp: 0-0
Best Rating: **59** 9/09 Leic 5f218y gd-fm

Rosko

103(99) (66)**76**

5-y-o b g Selkirk (USA)-Desert Alchemy (IRE) (Green Desert (USA))
B Ellison Racing Management & Training Ltd

Placings:033652641340 **(5160)**
2009: 12^{0}SD, 9^{3}SD, 9^{3}SD, 9^{6}F, 10^{5}F, 8^{2}G, 9^{6}GF, 8^{4}GF, 8^{1}GS, 8^{3}GS, 8^{4}GF, 9^{0}S,

	Starts	1st	2nd	3rd	Win & Pl
Career Total (Turf)	9	1	1	1	7319
Career Total (AW)	3	0	0	2	788

71 6/09 Newc 1m3y (0-85)H G-S £5046
Total win prize-money £5046

Going (Turf): Sf: 0-1 **GS: 1-2** Gd: 0-1 GF: 0-3 Fm: 0-2
Distance: 5f/6f: 0-0 7f-8f: 0-2 **9f-13f: 1-10** 14f+: 0-0
Track : LH: 0-7 RH: 0-2 Tight: 0-8 Gall: 0-0
Aids: Bl: 0-0 Vi: 0-0 Tstrap: 0-0 Ckp: 0-0
Best Rating: **76** 8/09 Thsk 1m gd-sft

Modest; effective over 1m1f; acts on Polytrack.

Ross Moor

102(101) (64)**70**

7-y-o b g Dansili-Snipe Hall (Crofthall)
Mike Murphy M Murphy

Placings:0/40520/1/4022624002306/44410300-5002301300P **(7776)**
2009: 13^{5}SD, 10^{0}GF, 10^{0}SD, 10^{2}G, 10^{3}GS, 12^{0}G, 10^{1}GF, 10^{3}G, 10^{0}G, 12^{0}SD, 10^{P}SD,

	Starts	1st	2nd	3rd	Win & Pl
Career Total (Turf)	22	2	3	3	14027
Career Total (AW)	17	1	3	1	9321

68 7/09 Sand 1m2f7y (0-75)H G-F £3238
73 6/08 Sand 1m2f7y (0-80)H G-S £4533
71 12/06 Ling 1m5f STD £4533
Total win prize-money £12305

Going (Turf): Sf: 0-0 **GS: 1-3** Gd: 0-9 **GF: 1-10** Fm: 0-0
Distance: 5f/6f: 0-1 7f-8f: 0-3 **9f-13f: 3-31** 14f+: 0-4
Track : LH: 1-23 **RH: 2-12 Tight: 1-18** Gall: 0-5
Aids: Bl: 0-4 Vi: 0-0 Tstrap: 0-1 Ckp: 0-1
Best Rating: **77** 2/07 Wolv 1m5f194y stand

Modest; effective at 1m2f to 1m5f; acted on easy ground and on Polytrack; sometimes blinkered. (DEAD)

Rossatron

82(90) (48)**53**

3-y-o b c Primo Valentino (IRE)-Sunday Night (GER) (Bakharoff (USA))
T T Clement Steve Sun

Placings:4640 **(2004)**
2009: 11^{4}SD, 12^{6}SF, 10^{4}GF, 8^{0}GF,

	Starts	1st	2nd	3rd	Win & Pl
Career Total (Turf)	2	0	0	0	0
Career Total (AW)	2	0	0	0	0

Going (Turf): **Sf: 0-0 GS: 0-0 Gd: 0-0 GF: 0-2 Fm: 0-0**
Distance: 5f/6f: 0-0 7f-8f: 0-1 9f-13f: 0-3 14f+: 0-0
Track : LH: 0-2 RH: 0-1 Tight: 0-1 Gall: 0-0
Aids: Bl: 0-0 Vi: 0-0 Tstrap: 0-0 Ckp: 0-0
Best Rating: **53** 4/09 Nott 1m2f50y gd-fm

Rossett Rose (IRE)

93(76) (37)**66**

3-y-o ch f Rossini (USA)-Sabaah Elfull (Kris)
M Brittain Mel Brittain

Placings:034440200-460005 **(5254)**
2009: 5^{4}G, 5^{6}GF, 5^{0}G, 6^{0}S, 8^{0}G, 6^{5}GF,

	Starts	1st	2nd	3rd	Win & Pl
Career Total (Turf)	14	0	1	1	2596
Career Total (AW)	1	0	0	0	

Going (Turf): **Sf: 0-2 GS: 0-3 Gd: 0-5 GF: 0-4 Fm: 0-0**
Distance: 5f/6f: 0-11 7f-8f: 0-4 9f-13f: 0-0 14f+: 0-0
Track : LH: 0-4 RH: 0-0 Tight: 0-3 Gall: 0-1
Aids: Bl: 0-0 Vi: 0-0 Tstrap: 0-0 Ckp: 0-0
Best Rating: **66** 7/08 Ripn 6f heavy

Moderate; suited by 6f and good ground.

Rossini's Dancer

103(93) (63)**73**
4-y-o b g Rossini (USA)-Bint Alhabib (Nashwan (USA))
Mrs S C Bradburne (R A Fahey 13/10) H W Turcan

Placings:06/46205500333316-14600206151 **(6769)**
2009: 8^{1}SD, 7^{4}GF, 8^{6}GF, 8^{0}G, 8^{0}GS, 9^{2}G, 9^{0}GF, 8^{6}G, 9^{1}G, 10^{5}GS, 12^{1}GS,

	Starts	1st	2nd	3rd	Win & Pl
Career Total (Turf)	24	3	2	4	10182
Career Total (AW)	3	1	0	0	1978

73 10/09 Newc 1m4f93y (0-65)H G-S £1747
69 9/09 Ripn 1m1f170y GD £2590
63 4/09 Wolv 1m141y (0-60)H STD £1977
58 9/08 Bevl 1m100y (0-55) SFT £2217
Total win prize-money £8533

Going (Turf): **Sf: 1-6 GS: 1-4 Gd: 1-8** GF: 0-6 Fm: 0-0
Distance: 5f/6f: 0-4 7f-8f: 0-8 **9f-13f: 4-15** 14f+: 0-0
Track : LH: 2-8 RH: 2-16 **Tight: 2-10** Gall: 1-1
Aids: Bl: 0-0 Vi: 0-0 Tstrap: 1-5 Ckp: 1-5
Best Rating: **73** 10/09 Newc 1m4f93y gd-sft

Moderate; stays 1m1f; acts on soft ground and on Polytrack; has worn cheekpieces.

Rosy Alexander

77 (56)**72**
4-y-o ch f Spartacus (IRE)-Sweet Angeline (Deploy)
G G Margarson Mrs T A Foreman

Placings:061/560-0 **(2052)**
2009: 10^{0}GF,

	Starts	1st	2nd	3rd	Win & Pl
Career Total (Turf)	6	1	0	0	1943
Career Total (AW)	1	0	0	0	

69 7/07 Yarm 7f3y G-F £1943
Total win prize-money £1943

Going (Turf): Sf: 0-0 GS: 0-2 Gd: 0-2 **GF: 1-2** Fm: 0-0
Distance: 5f/6f: 0-0 **7f-8f: 1-4** 9f-13f: 0-3 14f+: 0-0
Track : LH: 0-1 RH: 0-2 Tight: 0-1 Gall: 0-0
Aids: Bl: 0-0 Vi: 0-0 Tstrap: 0-0 Ckp: 0-0
Best Rating: **72** 8/08 Sand 1m14y gd-sft

Rosy Dawn

100(99) (55)**56**
4-y-o ch f Bertolini (USA)-Blushing Sunrise (USA) (Cox's Ridge (USA))
J J Bridger Gayler William Chambers

Placings:040**006102/001**0000000060030**2550600-0002024**P52041000**6**00 **(7250)**
2009: 12^{0}SD, 10^{0}SD, 10^{0}SD, 9^{2}F, 11^{0}GF, 12^{2}SD, 10^{4}SD, 10^{P}G, 11^{5}GF, 9^{2}GF, 12^{0}GF, 10^{4}G, 9^{1}GF, 9^{0}F, 10^{0}F, 11^{0}SD, 9^{6}GS, 12^{0}SD, 10^{0}SD,

	Starts	1st	2nd	3rd	Win & Pl
Career Total (Turf)	25	1	2	1	4917
Career Total (AW)	25	2	3	0	5775

56 8/09 Folk 1m1f149y (0-70)H G-F £2729
52 4/08 Ling 1m2f STD £1774
51 10/07 Ling 1m2f STD £2047
Total win prize-money £6552

Going (Turf): Sf: 0-0 GS: 0-3 Gd: 0-5 **GF: 1-13** Fm: 0-4
Distance: 5f/6f: 0-1 7f-8f: 0-8 **9f-13f: 3-41** 14f+: 0-0
Track : **LH: 2-25** RH: 1-19 **Tight: 3-22** Gall: 0-3
Aids: Bl: 1-11 Vi: 1-7 Tstrap: 0-0 Ckp: 0-0
Best Rating: **56** 8/09 Folk 1m1f149y gd-fm

Moderate; stays 1m2f; acts on fast ground; goes on Polytrack; has worn a visor, eyeshield and blinkers.

Rotative

106(106) (82)**96**
4-y-o ch f Spinning World (USA)-Kristal Bridge (Kris)
W R Swinburn Pendley Farm

Placings:14-10211 **(5917)**
2009: 12^{1}SD, 12^{0}SD, 11^{2}GS, 14^{1}GS, 16^{1}GF,

	Starts	1st	2nd	3rd	Win & Pl
Career Total (Turf)	3	2	1	0	14397
Career Total (AW)	4	2	0	0	6173

96 9/09 Gdwd 2m (0-85)H G-F £5180
89 8/09 Nott 1m6f15y (0-90)H G-S £7771
82 6/09 Wolv 1m4f50y (0-75)H STD £3885
70 9/08 Kemp 1m2f STD £2047
Total win prize-money £18885

Going (Turf): Sf: 0-0 **GS: 1-2** Gd: 0-0 **GF: 1-1** Fm: 0-0
Distance: 5f/6f: 0-0 7f-8f: 0-0 9f-13f: 2-5 14f+: 2-2
Track : LH: 2-2 RH: 2-5 **Tight: 2-2** Gall: 0-0
Aids: Bl: 0-0 Vi: 0-0 Tstrap: 0-1 Ckp: 0-1
Best Rating: **96** 9/09 Gdwd 2m gd-fm

Fair; should stay further than 1m2f; acts on Polytrack.

Rothesay Dancer

108(105) (77)**88**
6-y-o b m Lujain (USA)-Rhinefield Beauty (IRE) (Shalford (IRE))
J S Goldie Highland Racing

Placings:035303232021/00305321240000002**0**/40336063220123015600020**00**/0361255052221035100**4**5-**2**42361031006010005**0** **(6902)**
2009: 5^{2}SF, 5^{4}GF, 5^{2}GF, 5^{3}G, 5^{6}HY, 5^{1}GF, 5^{0}G, 5^{3}GF, 5^{1}GF, 5^{0}G, 5^{0}G, 5^{8}S, 5^{0}GF, 5^{1}GS, 5^{0}S, 5^{0}GF, 5^{0}G, 6^{5}G, 5^{0}GF,

	Starts	1st	2nd	3rd	Win & Pl
Career Total (Turf)	91	10	14	14	81141
Career Total (AW)	4	0	2	0	2632

88 8/09 Carl 5f (0-80)H G-S £4856
84 6/09 Haml 5f4y (0-80)H G-F £5180
81 6/09 Ayr 5f (0-90)H G-F £7641
77 8/08 Haml 5f4y (0-70)H SFT £3885
74 7/08 Ayr 6f (0-85)H GD £5607
72 5/08 Haml 5f4y (0-60)H G-S £2047
71 8/07 Haml 5f4y (0-85)H G-F £6477
66 7/07 Muss 5f (0-80)H GD £5181
71 7/06 Ayr 5f (0-65)H FRM £2866
71 10/05 Catt 5f G-F £3640
Total win prize-money £47387

Going (Turf): Sf: 1-14GS: 2-16Gd: 2-28**GF: 4-28** Fm: 1-5
Distance: **5f/6f: 10-94** 7f-8f: 0-1 9f-13f: 0-0 14f+: 0-0
Track : LH: 0-5 **RH: 1-1** Tight: 0-4 **Gall: 1-1**
Aids: Bl: 0-1 Vi: 0-0 Tstrap: 1-15 Ckp: 1-15
Best Rating: **88** 8/09 Carl 5f gd-sft

Useful; Listed placed; effective over 5f-6f and acts on most ground; goes well at Hamilton.

Rough Rock (IRE)

96(92) (35)**67**
4-y-o ch g Rock Of Gibraltar (IRE)-Amitie Fatale (IRE) (Night Shift (USA))
C A Dwyer M M Foulger

Placings:0450**0**1600/030066**P**006**00**-**0**404501050442 **(7100)**
2009: 7^{0}SD, 6^{4}G, 6^{0}GF, 6^{4}S, 7^{5}G, 7^{0}G, 5^{1}GS, 5^{0}HY, 6^{5}G, 5^{0}G, 7^{4}GF, 6^{4}GS, 5^{2}G,

	Starts	1st	2nd	3rd	Win & Pl
Career Total (Turf)	29	2	1	1	6989
Career Total (AW)	5	0	0	0	

57 7/09 Yarm 5f43y (0-60)H G-S £2183
70 7/07 Yarm 6f3y G-F £1943
Total win prize-money £4127

Going (Turf): Sf: 0-5 **GS: 1-6** Gd: 0-7 **GF: 1-10** Fm: 0-1
Distance: 5f/6f: 1-18 7f-8f: 1-16 9f-13f: 0-0 14f+: 0-0
Track : LH: 0-6 RH: 0-2 Tight: 0-1 Gall: 0-4
Aids: **Bl: 1-11** Vi: 0-0 Tstrap: 0-0 Ckp: 0-0
Best Rating: **70** 7/07 Yarm 6f3y gd-fm

Fair; effective over 5f-6f; acts on most ground; often wears blinkers.

Rough Sketch (USA)

95(103) (64)**61**
4-y-o b g Peintre Celebre (USA)-Drama Club (IRE) (Sadler's Wells (USA))
Sir Mark Prescott Edward S A Belcher

Placings:0**00/50144**001500 **(6566)**
2009: 10^{5}SD, 10^{0}SD, 13^{1}SF, 13^{4}SD, 16^{4}SD, 16^{0}G, 12^{0}GF, 11^{1}F, 14^{5}GF, 11^{0}GF, 12^{0}GS,

	Starts	1st	2nd	3rd	Win & Pl
Career Total (Turf)	7	1	0	0	3406
Career Total (AW)	7	1	0	0	2047

61 6/09 Brig 1m3f196y (0-70)H FRM £3406
63 2/09 Wolv 1m5f194y (0-65)H SF £2047
Total win prize-money £5453

Going (Turf): Sf: 0-1 GS: 0-1 Gd: 0-1 GF: 0-3 **Fm: 1-1**
Distance: 5f/6f: 0-1 7f-8f: 0-2 9f-13f: 1-7 14f+: 1-4
Track : **LH: 2-10** RH: 0-3 **Tight: 1-8** Gall: 0-2
Aids: **Bl: 1-3** Vi: 0-1 Tstrap: 0-0 Ckp: 0-0
Best Rating: **64** 3/09 Ling 1m5f stand

Moderate; stays 1m5f; acts on fast ground and on Polytrack; has worn blinkers and a visor.

Rougham

99(92) (63)**75**
3-y-o b g Red Ransom (USA)-Louella (USA) (El Gran Senor (USA))
P J Hobbs (A M Balding 24/9) Mr & Mrs James Wigan

Placings:424 **(6225)**
2009: 12^{4}G, 11^{2}GF, 12^{4}SD,

	Starts	1st	2nd	3rd	Win & Pl
Career Total (Turf)	2	0	1	0	1194
Career Total (AW)	1	0	0	0	192

Going (Turf): **Sf: 0-0 GS: 0-0 Gd: 0-1 GF: 0-1 Fm: 0-0**
Distance: 5f/6f: 0-0 7f-8f: 0-0 9f-13f: 0-3 14f+: 0-0
Track : LH: 0-1 RH: 0-2 Tight: 0-1 Gall: 0-1
Aids: Bl: 0-0 Vi: 0-0 Tstrap: 0-0 Ckp: 0-0
Best Rating: **75** 7/09 NmkJ 1m4f good

Fair; stays 1m4f; acts on good/fast ground.

Round Won (USA)

69(92) (71)**61**
2-y-o ch c Two Punch (USA)-Indy Go Go (USA) (A.P. Indy (USA))
W J Knight Bluehills Racing Limited

Placings:003 **(6629)**
2009: 7^0G, 8^0GF, 7^3SS,

	Starts	1st	2nd	3rd	Win & Pl
Career Total (Turf)	2	0	0	0	
Career Total (AW)	1	0	0	1	530

Going (Turf): **Sf: 0-0 GS: 0-0 Gd: 0-1 GF: 0-1 Fm: 0-0**
Distance: 5f/6f: 0-0 7f-8f: 0-3 9f-13f: 0-0 14f+: 0-0
Track : LH: 0-2 RH: 0-0 Tight: 0-1 Gall: 0-1
Aids: Bl: 0-0 Vi: 0-0 Tstrap: 0-0 Ckp: 0-0
Best Rating: **71** 10/09 Ling 7f std-slw

Roundthetwist (IRE)

(97) (71)**63**
4-y-o b g Okawango (USA)-Delta Town (USA) (Sanglamore (USA))
K R Burke Mrs Elaine M Burke

Placings:2/2556503640005-55 **(0872)**
2009: 12^5SD, 10^5SD,

	Starts	1st	2nd	3rd	Win & Pl
Career Total (Turf)	6	0	0	1	433
Career Total (AW)	10	0	2	0	1602

Going (Turf): **Sf: 0-1 GS: 0-1 Gd: 0-2 GF: 0-2 Fm: 0-0**
Distance: 5f/6f: 0-1 7f-8f: 0-4 9f-13f: 0-11 14f+: 0-0
Track : LH: 0-10 RH: 0-6 Tight: 0-12 Gall: 0-0
Aids: Bl: 0-0 Vi: 0-1 Tstrap: 0-1 Ckp: 0-1
Best Rating: **71** 1/08 Wolv 1m141y stand

Modest sort; probably stays a mile; has worn cheekpieces, a visor and a tongue tie.

Rowaad

99 (69)**72**
4-y-o ch g Compton Place-Level Pegging (IRE) (Common Grounds)
A E Price Business Development Consultants Limited

Placings:04/036000000-0003300 **(5549)**
2009: 7^0GF, 7^0GF, 6^0G, 8^3F, 8^3GF, 8^0GF, 9^0G,

	Starts	1st	2nd	3rd	Win & Pl
Career Total (Turf)	16	0	0	3	1414
Career Total (AW)	2	0	0	0	241

Going (Turf): **Sf: 0-1 GS: 0-2 Gd: 0-6 GF: 0-6 Fm: 0-1**
Distance: 5f/6f: 0-2 7f-8f: 0-14 9f-13f: 0-2 14f+: 0-0
Track : LH: 0-3 RH: 0-3 Tight: 0-2 Gall: 0-0
Aids: Bl: 0-0 Vi: 0-5 Tstrap: 0-0 Ckp: 0-0
Best Rating: **72** 5/08 Leic 7f9y gd-fm

Modest; stays 1m and acts on fast ground; has worn a visor.

Rowan Light

86 **54**
3-y-o b f Fantastic Light (USA)-Filippa (GER) (Dashing Blade)
J R Boyle Rowan Stud Partnership 1

Placings:0 **(1269)**
2009: 8^0G,

	Starts	1st	2nd	3rd	Win & Pl
Career Total (Turf)	1	0	0	0	

Going (Turf): **Sf: 0-0 GS: 0-0 Gd: 0-1 GF: 0-0 Fm: 0-0**
Distance: 5f/6f: 0-0 7f-8f: 0-0 9f-13f: 0-1 14f+: 0-0
Track : LH: 0-0 RH: 0-0 Tight: 0-0 Gall: 0-0
Aids: Bl: 0-0 Vi: 0-0 Tstrap: 0-0 Ckp: 0-0
Best Rating: **54** 4/09 Yarm 1m3y good

Rowan Lodge (IRE)

101(99) (65)**69**
7-y-o ch g Indian Lodge (IRE)-Tirol Hope (IRE) (Tirol)
Ollie Pears K C West & Venture Racing

Placings:031210204/5303505/**3**4035036010/**3**5434241206 0/01034261**1**20203-3012115**3**034000 **(7755)**
2009: 8^3SD, 9^0SD, 8^1GF, 9^2GF, 7^1GF, 9^1GF, 10^5GF, 7^3G, 9^0SD, 8^3GF, 8^4SD, 9^0G, 9^0SD, 8^0SD,

	Starts	1st	2nd	3rd	Win & Pl
Career Total (Turf)	50	10	6	10	41769
Career Total (AW)	17	0	2	3	2860

69	6/09	Carl	1m1f61y	G-F	£2047
66	6/09	Carl	7f200y	G-F	£2047
59	4/09	Bevl	1m100y	G-F	£2590
69	8/08	Rdcr	1m1f	GD	£2388
67	7/08	Carl	7f200y	FRM	£2047
62	4/08	Bevl	1m100y	G-S	£2331
62	9/07	Chep	1m2f36y	G-F	£1943
71	10/06	Yarm	1m3y	SFT	£2364
83	8/04	Catt	5f212y D	SFT	£4823
74	7/04	Brig	5f213y E	G-F	£3359

Total win prize-money £25939

Going (Turf): Sf: 2-14 GS: 1-7 Gd: 1-14 **GF: 5-13** Fm: 1-2
Distance: 5f/6f: 2-9 7f-8f: 2-21 **9f-13f: 6-37** 14f+: 0-0
Track : LH: 4-36 **RH: 5-15 Tight: 2-22** Gall: 0-3
Aids: **Bl: 6-33** Vi: 1-5 Tstrap: 0-0 Ckp: 0-0
Best Rating: **84** 9/04 Ches 7f2y good

Moderate; effective over 1m-1m2f; acts on any ground; has worn blinkers.

Rowan Rio

97(98) (71)**90**
4-y-o ch g Lomitas-Lemon Tree (USA) (Zilzal (USA))
W J Haggas Rowan Stud Partnership 1

Placings:101165-0000000 **(4544)**
2009: 12^0G, 14^0G, **12^0SD**, 10^0G, 10^0GF, 10^0G, 12^0G,

	Starts	1st	2nd	3rd	Win & Pl
Career Total (Turf)	10	2	0	0	9714
Career Total (AW)	3	1	0	0	1943

90	8/08	Wwck	1m2f188y	(0-80)H	SFT	£4857
82	7/08	Ripn	1m4f10y	(0-75)H	HVY	£4857
74	2/08	Ling	1m2f		STD	£1943

Total win prize-money £11657

Going (Turf): **Sf: 2-3** GS: 0-0 Gd: 0-5 GF: 0-2 Fm: 0-0
Distance: 5f/6f: 0-0 7f-8f: 0-0 **9f-13f: 3-12** 14f+: 0-1
Track : **LH: 2-3** RH: 1-9 **Tight: 2-5** Gall: 0-3
Aids: Bl: 0-0 Vi: 0-0 Tstrap: 0-0 Ckp: 0-0
Best Rating: **90** 8/08 Wwck 1m2f188y soft

Useful; stays 1m4f but effective at shorter; acts on soft ground on turf and on Polytrack.

Rowan River

84(94) (64)**74**
5-y-o b m Invincible Spirit (IRE)-Lemon Tree (USA) (Zilzal (USA))
Mrs A M Thorpe (A Middleton 10/6) W A Thomas

Placings:650/4433100/30400-0 **(2808)**
2009: 9^0G,

	Starts	1st	2nd	3rd	Win & Pl
Career Total (Turf)	13	1	0	2	5282
Career Total (AW)	3	0	0	1	602

77	8/07	NmkJ	1m2f	(0-70)H	GD	£3886

Total win prize-money £3886

Going (Turf): Sf: 0-0 GS: 0-4 **Gd: 1-4** GF: 0-5 Fm: 0-0
Distance: 5f/6f: 0-1 7f-8f: 0-3 **9f-13f: 1-12** 14f+: 0-0
Track : LH: 0-6 **RH: 1-8** Tight: 0-4 **Gall: 1-3**
Aids: Bl: 0-0 Vi: 0-0 Tstrap: 0-1 Ckp: 0-1
Best Rating: **77** 8/07 NmkJ 1m2f good

Modest; effective over 1m2f; acts on fast ground; also goes on Polytrack.

Rowan Tiger

93(106) (79)**59**
3-y-o b g Tiger Hill (IRE)-Lemon Tree (USA) (Zilzal (USA))
J R Boyle Rowan Stud Partnership 1

Placings:00-056111 **(6634)**
2009: 8^0G, 10^5SD, 11^6S, **12^1SD**, **12^1SD**, **12^1SS**,

	Starts	1st	2nd	3rd	Win & Pl
Career Total (Turf)	4	0	0	0	0
Career Total (AW)	4	3	0	0	11114

79	10/09	Ling	1m4f	(0-80)H	SS	£6476
74	9/09	Kemp	1m4f	(0-70)H	STD	£2590
68	9/09	Kemp	1m4f	(0-60)H	STD	£2047

Total win prize-money £11113

Going (Turf): **Sf: 0-2 GS: 0-1 Gd: 0-1 GF: 0-0 Fm: 0-0**
Distance: 5f/6f: 0-0 7f-8f: 0-2 **9f-13f: 3-6** 14f+: 0-0
Track : LH: 1-4 **RH: 2-2 Tight: 1-4** Gall: 0-0
Aids: Bl: 0-0 Vi: 0-0 Tstrap: 0-0 Ckp: 0-0
Best Rating: **79** 10/09 Ling 1m4f std-slw

Fair; effective at 1m4f; goes well on Polytrack.

Rowayton

104(106) (86)**85**
3-y-o br/gr f Lujain (USA)-Bandanna (Bandmaster (USA))
J D Bethell Mrs J E Vickers

Placings:10324-04546 **(4601)**
2009: 6^0GF, 6^4G, 5^5GF, 6^4G, 5^6G,

	Starts	1st	2nd	3rd	Win & Pl
Career Total (Turf)	7	1	0	0	12403
Career Total (AW)	3	0	1	1	3146

78	5/08	Rdcr	5f	G-F	£2456

Total win prize-money £2457

Going (Turf): Sf: 0-0 GS: 0-0 Gd: 0-4 **GF: 1-3** Fm: 0-0
Distance: **5f/6f: 1-10** 7f-8f: 0-0 9f-13f: 0-0 14f+: 0-0
Track : LH: 0-1 RH: 0-2 Tight: 0-0 Gall: 0-1
Aids: Bl: 0-0 Vi: 0-0 Tstrap: 0-0 Ckp: 0-0
Best Rating: **86** 10/08 Kemp 6f stand

Useful; effective at 5f-6f; acts on fast ground; goes on Polytrack.

Rowe Park

106(107) (109)**109**
6-y-o b g Dancing Spree (USA)-Magic Legs (Reprimand)
Mrs L C Jewell Mrs Sue Ashdown

Placings:0060111/2126113312/00006460-616660010 (7488)

2009: 5^{6}SD, 5^{1}SD, 5^{6}GF, 5^{6}G, 6^{0}GF, 6^{0}GS, 5^{1}SD, 6^{0}SD,

	Starts	1st	2nd	3rd	Win & Pl
Career Total (Turf)	20	3	1	1	54188
Career Total (AW)	14	6	2	1	32882

108	10/09	Sthl	5f		STD	£9714
109	4/09	Ling	5f		STD	£7352
115	9/07	Newb	5f34y		G-F	£26686
95	5/07	Gdwd	5f	(0-100)H	GD	£10363
93	5/07	Ling	5f	(0-85)H	GD	£4857
89	2/07	Sthl	5f	(0-75)H	SS	£3241
76	12/06	Wolv	5f20y	(0-60)H	STD	£2730
66	12/06	Ling	5f	(0-60)H	STD	£1706
60	11/06	Ling	5f		STD	£2388

Total win prize-money £69042

Going (Turf): Sf: 0-1 GS: 0-1 **Gd: 2-7** GF: 1-11 Fm: 0-0
Distance: **5f/6f: 9-30** 7f-8f: 0-3 9f-13f: 0-1 14f+: 0-0
Track : **LH: 4-10** RH: 0-2 **Tight: 4-11** Gall: 0-0
Aids: Bl: 0-0 Vi: 0-0 Tstrap: 0-2 Ckp: 0-2
Best Rating: **116** 10/07 NmkR 5f good

Smart; winner in Group 3 company; suited by 5f-6f; acts good ground and on sand; likes to race prominently; has worn cheekpieces.

Roxy Flyer (IRE)

95(88) (62)**67**

2-y-o b f Rock Of Gibraltar (IRE)-Dyna Flyer (USA) (Marquetry (USA))

Mrs A J Perrett Mr & Mrs F Cotton Mrs S Conway

Placings:46 (7135)

2009: 6^{4}S, 7^{6}SD,

	Starts	1st	2nd	3rd	Win & Pl
Career Total (Turf)	1	0	0	0	216
Career Total (AW)	1	0	0	0	0

Going (Turf): **Sf: 0-1 GS: 0-0 Gd: 0-0 GF: 0-0 Fm: 0-0**
Distance: 5f/6f: 0-0 7f-8f: 0-2 9f-13f: 0-0 14f+: 0-0
Track : LH: 0-1 RH: 0-0 Tight: 0-1 Gall: 0-0
Aids: Bl: 0-0 Vi: 0-0 Tstrap: 0-0 Ckp: 0-0
Best Rating: **67** 10/09 Sals 6f212y soft

Royaaty (IRE)

(101) (84)

3-y-o b c Singspiel (IRE)-Whisper To Dream (USA) (Gone West (USA))

Saeed Bin Suroor Godolphin

Placings:1 (7439)

2009: 10^{1}SD,

	Starts	1st	2nd	3rd	Win & Pl
Career Total (Turf)	0	0	0	0	
Career Total (AW)	1	1	0	0	2730

84	11/09	Ling	1m2f	STD	£2729

Total win prize-money £2730

Going (Turf): **Sf: 0-0 GS: 0-0 Gd: 0-0 GF: 0-0 Fm: 0-0**
Distance: 5f/6f: 0-0 7f-8f: 0-0 **9f-13f: 1-1** 14f+: 0-0
Track : **LH: 1-1** RH: 0-0 **Tight: 1-1** Gall: 0-0
Aids: Bl: 0-0 Vi: 0-0 Tstrap: 0-0 Ckp: 0-0
Best Rating: **84** 11/09 Ling 1m2f stand

Very useful prospect; effective over 1m2f; acts on Polytrack.

Royal Acclamation (IRE)

97(90) (48)**71**

4-y-o b g Acclamation-Lady Abigail (IRE) (Royal Academy (USA))

H J Evans (G A Harker 25/6) Mrs J Evans

Placings:054/00001240000500-000244 (3296)

2009: 5^{0}SD, 5^{0}GF, 6^{0}G, 5^{2}G, 5^{4}GF, 6^{4}GF,

	Starts	1st	2nd	3rd	Win & Pl
Career Total (Turf)	21	1	2	0	3999
Career Total (AW)	3	0	0	0	

71	6/08	Catt	5f212y	(0-65)H	G-S	£2047

Total win prize-money £2047

Going (Turf): Sf: 0-2 **GS: 1-6** Gd: 0-6 GF: 0-7 Fm: 0-0
Distance: **5f/6f: 1-16** 7f-8f: 0-7 9f-13f: 0-1 14f+: 0-0
Track : **LH: 1-12** RH: 0-3 **Tight: 1-9** Gall: 0-0
Aids: Bl: 0-0 Vi: 0-3 Tstrap: 0-0 Ckp: 0-0
Best Rating: **71** 6/08 Rdcr 6f gd-fm

Modest sort; effective at 6f and acts on fast ground.

Royal Adelaide (IRE)

95(84) (37)**40**

3-y-o ch f Redback-Ball Cat (FR) (Cricket Ball (USA))

J A Osborne Mrs F Walwyn

Placings:000500 (7105)

2009: 7^{0}GF, 6^{0}SD, 7^{0}GF, 7^{5}GF, 7^{0}G, 7^{0}SD,

	Starts	1st	2nd	3rd	Win & Pl
Career Total (Turf)	4	0	0	0	0
Career Total (AW)	2	0	0	0	

Going (Turf): **Sf: 0-0 GS: 0-0 Gd: 0-1 GF: 0-3 Fm: 0-0**
Distance: 5f/6f: 0-1 7f-8f: 0-5 9f-13f: 0-0 14f+: 0-0
Track : LH: 0-3 RH: 0-1 Tight: 0-0 Gall: 0-0
Aids: Bl: 0-0 Vi: 0-0 Tstrap: 0-0 Ckp: 0-0
Best Rating: **40** 9/09 Leic 7f9y gd-fm

Royal Amnesty

109(108) (84)**88**

6-y-o br g Desert Prince (IRE)-Regal Peace (Known Fact (USA))

I Semple Mrs Francesca Mitchell

Placings:000/1111010064345З/0560005000455/4121311 63216-05120034 (5915)

2009: 9^{0}SD, 9^{5}SD, 10^{1}SD, 9^{2}G, 10^{0}GF, 12^{0}GF, 10^{3}GF, 9^{4}GF,

	Starts	1st	2nd	3rd	Win & Pl
Career Total (Turf)	15	2	1	1	11064
Career Total (AW)	35	9	2	4	42666

84	3/09	Ling	1m2f	(0-85)H	STD	£4857
82	10/08	Wolv	1m1f103y	(0-85)H	STD	£5180
75	5/08	Muss	1m4f	(0-80)H	G-F	£5504
71	5/08	Haml	1m1f36y	(0-70)H	G-F	£2590
78	3/08	Wolv	1m1f103y	(0-75)H	STD	£2730
66	2/08	Wolv	1m1f103y	(0-60)H	STD	£2047
80	6/06	Kemp	1m	(0-80)H	STD	£5699
74	5/06	Kemp	1m2f	(0-80)H	STD	£7790
68	4/06	Wolv	1m1f103y	(0-75)H	STD	£3238
66	3/06	Wolv	1m141y	(0-75)H	STD	£3238
59	3/06	Wolv	1m141y		STD	£2388

Total win prize-money £45268

Going (Turf): Sf: 0-1 GS: 0-0 Gd: 0-2 **GF: 2-12** Fm: 0-0
Distance: 5f/6f: 0-3 7f 8f: 1-11 **9f-13f: 10-35** 14f+: 0-1
Track : **LH: 7-29** RH: 4-17 **Tight: 9-32** Gall: 0-2
Aids: **Bl: 6-22** Vi: 0-0 Tstrap: 0-0 Ckp: 0-0
Best Rating: **88** 5/09 Muss 1m1f good

Useful; stays 1m4f; acts on fast ground and on Polytrack; has worn blinkers; can be slowly away.

Royal And Regal (IRE)

106 **119**

5-y-o b g Sadler's Wells (USA)-Smart 'n Noble (USA) (Smarten (USA))

Luke Comer (M A Jarvis 19/8) Brian Comer

Placings:21/210331/12303-403 (5171)

2009: 12^{4}S, 14^{0}GS, 16^{3}GF,

	Starts	1st	2nd	3rd	Win & Pl
Career Total (Turf)	16	4	3	5	189062

119	4/08	Newb	1m4f5y	SFT	£26681
115	10/07	NmkR	2m	G-S	£28390
102	5/07	Lonc	1m4f	HVY	£17568
89	10/06	StCl	1m	G-S	£6552

Total win prize-money £79192

Going (Turf): **Sf: 2-8 GS: 2-5** Gd: 0-0 GF: 0-2 Fm: 0-0
Distance: 5f/6f: 0-0 7f-8f: 1-2 **9f-13f: 2-5** 14f+: 1-9
Track : LH: 2-7 RH: 2-9 Tight: 0-0 **Gall: 2-7**
Aids: Bl: 0-0 Vi: 0-0 Tstrap: 0-0 Ckp: 0-0
Best Rating: **119** 5/08 York 1m6f gd-fm

Group class; ex-French; winner in Group 3 company; effective over 1m4f-2m2f; acts best on soft ground.

Royal Applord

88(98) (74)**67**

4-y-o b g Royal Applause-Known Class (USA) (Known Fact (USA))

P T Midgley Bull & Bell Partnership

Placings:35204/13300164503460-0006 (3174)

2009: 8^{0}G, 8^{0}GF, 8^{0}GF, 7^{6}GF,

	Starts	1st	2nd	3rd	Win & Pl
Career Total (Turf)	18	1	1	2	5624
Career Total (AW)	5	1	0	2	4030

66	7/08	Bevl	7f100y	GD	£2590
65	1/08	Sthl	7f	STD	£2730

Total win prize-money £5320

Going (Turf): Sf: 0-2 GS: 0-4 **Gd: 1-5** GF: 0-5 Fm: 0-2
Distance: 5f/6f: 0-1 **7f-8f: 2-18** 9f-13f: 0-4 14f+: 0-0
Track : LH: 1-11 RH: 1-7 Tight: 0-7 Gall: 0-1
Aids: Bl: 0-0 Vi: 0-0 Tstrap: 0-7 Ckp: 0-7
Best Rating: **74** 2/08 Ling 1m stand

Modest; stays at least 7f; acts on good ground; also goes on Polytrack; has worn cheekpieces.

Royal Arthur

87(87) (28)**35**

3-y-o ch g Imperial Dancer-Scenic Lady (IRE) (Scenic)

L A Dace L P Dace

Placings:00-00060000 (5579)

2009: 8^{0}SD, 9^{0}G, 9^{0}GS, 11^{6}G, 12^{0}GF, 11^{0}GF, 16^{0}GF, 16^{0}GF,

	Starts	1st	2nd	3rd	Win & Pl
Career Total (Turf)	9	0	0	0	0
Career Total (AW)	1	0	0	0	

Going (Turf): **Sf: 0-1 GS: 0-1 Gd: 0-3 GF: 0-4 Fm: 0-0**
Distance: 5f/6f: 0-0 7f-8f: 0-3 9f-13f: 0-5 14f+: 0-2
Track : LH: 0-6 RH: 0-2 Tight: 0-5 Gall: 0-0

Aids: Bl: 0-2 Vi: 0-1 Tstrap: 0-3 Ckp: 0-3
Best Rating: 35 8/09 Nott 2m9y gd-fm

Royal Bet (IRE)

99(94) (57)61
3-y-o b g Montjeu (IRE)-Queen Of Norway (USA) (Woodman (USA))
M L W Bell Tsega Horses

Placings:0-00245 (6371)
2009: 9^{0}GF, 9^{0}GS, 11^{2}G, 14^{4}GF, 11^{5}SD,

	Starts	1st	2nd	3rd	Win & Pl
Career Total (Turf)	5	0	1	0	973
Career Total (AW)	1	0	0	0	0

Going (Turf): **Sf: 0-0 GS: 0-2 Gd: 0-1 GF: 0-2 Fm: 0-0**
Distance: 5f/6f: 0-0 7f-8f: 0-1 9f-13f: 0-4 14f+: 0-1
Track : LH: 0-2 RH: 0-3 Tight: 0-3 Gall: 0-0
Aids: Bl: 0-0 Vi: 0-0 Tstrap: 0-0 Ckp: 0-0
Best Rating: 61 8/09 Yarm 1m3f101y good

Moderate; looks best at 1m4f on a sound surface.

Royal Blade (IRE)

97(75) (22)71
2-y-o ch g Needwood Blade-Royal Dream (Ardkinglass)
A P Jarvis Christopher Shankland

Placings:06100 (5650)
2009: 6^{0}S, 5^{6}GF, 5^{1}G, 5^{0}GF, 5^{0}SD,

	Starts	1st	2nd	3rd	Win & Pl
Career Total (Turf)	4	1	0	0	3886
Career Total (AW)	1	0	0	0	

71 7/09 Wind 5f10y GD £3885
Total win prize-money £3886

Going (Turf): Sf: 0-1 GS: 0-0 **Gd: 1-1** GF: 0-2 Fm: 0-0
Distance: **5f/6f: 1-5** 7f-8f: 0-0 9f-13f: 0-0 14f+: 0-0
Track : LH: 0-1 RH: 0-0 Tight: 0-1 **Gall: 1-1**
Aids: Bl: 0-0 Vi: 0-0 Tstrap: 0-0 Ckp: 0-0
Best Rating: 71 7/09 Wind 5f10y good

Royal Bloom (IRE)

86 48
4-y-o b f Royal Applause-Bethesda (Distant Relative)
J R Fanshawe Mrs V Shelton

Placings:0-00026 (4238)
2009: 8^{0}G, 8^{0}G, 9^{0}GF, 6^{2}G, 6^{6}F,

	Starts	1st	2nd	3rd	Win & Pl
Career Total (Turf)	6	0	1	0	605

Going (Turf): **Sf: 0-0 GS: 0-1 Gd: 0-3 GF: 0-1 Fm: 0-1**
Distance: 5f/6f: 0-1 7f-8f: 0-2 9f-13f: 0-3 14f+: 0-0
Track : LH: 0-2 RH: 0-1 Tight: 0-2 Gall: 0-0
Aids: Bl: 0-0 Vi: 0-0 Tstrap: 0-1 Ckp: 0-1
Best Rating: 48 6/09 Nott 1m75y good

Plating class; effective at 6f; acts on good ground.

Royal Box

98(97) (72)74
2-y-o b c Royal Applause-Diamond Lodge (Grand Lodge (USA))
A J McCabe (R Hannon 18/11) T R Pearson

Placings:014650 (7669)
2009: 6^{0}GF, 5^{1}S, 6^{4}SD, 7^{6}GF, 7^{5}SD, 8^{0}SD,

	Starts	1st	2nd	3rd	Win & Pl
Career Total (Turf)	3	1	0	0	4857
Career Total (AW)	3	0	0	0	289

74 7/09 Leic 5f218y SFT £4857
Total win prize-money £4857

Going (Turf): **Sf: 1-1** GS: 0-0 Gd: 0-0 GF: 0-2 Fm: 0-0
Distance: **5f/6f: 1-3** 7f-8f: 0-2 9f-13f: 0-1 14f+: 0-0
Track : LH: 0-3 RH: 0-1 Tight: 0-3 Gall: 0-1
Aids: Bl: 0-1 Vi: 0-0 Tstrap: 0-0 Ckp: 0-0
Best Rating: 74 7/09 Leic 5f218y soft

Fair; stays 6f; acts on soft ground.

Royal Challenge

97(104) (79)72
8-y-o b g Royal Applause-Anotheranniversary (Emarati (USA))
I W McInnes Truck Export

Placings:0/2116320/050610040/03551021/000006600045 362150/44300600404615461122O-026600000010200 (7275)
2009: 6^{0}SD, 7^{2}SD, 7^{6}SD, 5^{6}SD, 7^{0}SD, 7^{0}GF, 6^{0}G, 6^{0}S, 7^{0}SD, 7^{0}GF, 7^{1}SD, 7^{0}SD, 6^{2}GF, 7^{0}SS, 7^{0}SD,

	Starts	1st	2nd	3rd	Win & Pl
Career Total (Turf)	51	6	4	2	43468
Career Total (AW)	28	4	4	2	17252

66	9/09	Wolv	7f32y		STD	£3238
79	9/08	Wolv	5f216y	(0-70)H	STD	£4209
74	9/08	Wolv	5f216y	(0-65)H	STD	£2388
72	7/08	Pont	6f	(0-75)H	GD	£3885
74	12/07	Wolv	5f216y	(0-70)H	STD	£2968
91	7/06	York	5f89y	(0-90)H	G-F	£8096
88	6/06	Wind	6f	(0-80)H	G-F	£6477
85	8/05	Yarm	6f3y	(0-75)H	GD	£4061
86	7/04	Sand	5f6y	D(0-85)H	G-F	£6971
82	7/04	Bevl	5f	D	G-S	£3435

Total win prize-money £45730

Going (Turf): Sf: 0-5 GS: 1-4 Gd: 2-17 **GF: 3-25** Fm: 0-0
Distance: **5f/6f: 8-60** 7f-8f: 2-19 9f-13f: 0-0 14f+: 0-0
Track : **LH: 5-37** RH: 0-8 **Tight: 4-29** Gall: 1-3
Aids: Bl: 0-1 Vi: 0-0 Tstrap: 0-0 Ckp: 0-0
Best Rating: 91 7/06 York 5f89y gd-fm

Modest; effective at 6-7f; acts on fast ground; suited by Polytrack; goes well at Wolverhampton.

Royal Cheer

70 6
2-y-o b f Royal Applause-Rise 'n Shine (Night Shift (USA))
Mrs A Duffield Mrs D G Garrity

Placings:06 (5957)
2009: 6^{0}GF, 5^{6}GF,

	Starts	1st	2nd	3rd	Win & Pl
Career Total (Turf)	2	0	0	0	0

Going (Turf): **Sf: 0-0 GS: 0-0 Gd: 0-0 GF: 0-2 Fm: 0-0**
Distance: 5f/6f: 0-2 7f-8f: 0-0 9f-13f: 0-0 14f+: 0-0
Track : LH: 0-0 RH: 0-0 Tight: 0-0 Gall: 0-0
Aids: Bl: 0-0 Vi: 0-0 Tstrap: 0-0 Ckp: 0-0
Best Rating: 6 9/09 Hayd 5f gd-fm

£36,000 half-sister to winning sprinters; finished last on debut over 6f on fast ground.

Royal Choir

75(103) (56)39
5-y-o ch m King's Best (USA)-Harmonic Sound (IRE) (Grand Lodge (USA))
H E Haynes The Reddown High Explosive Partnership

Placings:4/600/000600531-0000 (1589)
2009: 10^{0}SD, 9^{0}SD, 10^{0}GF, 10^{0}SD,

	Starts	1st	2nd	3rd	Win & Pl
Career Total (Turf)	8	0	0	0	0
Career Total (AW)	9	1	0	1	2658

56 12/08 Ling 1m2f (0-65)H STD £2047
Total win prize-money £2047

Going (Turf): **Sf: 0-1 GS: 0-1 Gd: 0-4 GF: 0-1 Fm: 0-1**
Distance: 5f/6f: 0-1 7f-8f: 0-7 **9f-13f: 1-9** 14f+: 0-0
Track : **LH: 1-12** RH: 0-1 **Tight: 1-10** Gall: 0-0
Aids: Bl: 0-0 Vi: 0-0 Tstrap: 0-0 Ckp: 0-0
Best Rating: 72 10/06 Ling 7f stand

Royal Collection (IRE)

(103) (82)72
3-y-o b c Val Royal (FR)-Rachel Green (IRE) (Case Law)
J Pearce Matthew Green

Placings:003-11 (0312)
2009: 7^{1}SD, 8^{1}SD,

	Starts	1st	2nd	3rd	Win & Pl
Career Total (Turf)	3	0	0	1	770
Career Total (AW)	2	2	0	0	6775

82 1/09 Kemp 1m (0-85)H STD £4727
78 1/09 Ling 7f STD £2047
Total win prize-money £6774

Going (Turf): **Sf: 0-0 GS: 0-1 Gd: 0-1 GF: 0-1 Fm: 0-0**
Distance: 5f/6f: 0-2 **7f-8f: 2-2** 9f-13f: 0-1 14f+: 0-0
Track : LH: 1-1 RH: 1-2 **Tight: 1-1** Gall: 0-1
Aids: Bl: 0-0 Vi: 0-0 Tstrap: 0-0 Ckp: 0-0
Best Rating: 82 1/09 Kemp 1m stand

Fair; effective at up to 1m; acts on Polytrack and easy ground.

Royal Composer (IRE)

98 67
6-y-o b g Mozart (IRE)-Susun Kelapa (USA) (St Jovite (USA))
T D Easterby Mrs B Oughtred

Placings:30/62453000/020123/420056-40040300 (6174)
2009: 6^{4}F, 5^{0}GF, 5^{0}GF, 7^{4}G, 7^{0}G, 7^{3}GF, 6^{0}GF, 8^{0}GF,

	Starts	1st	2nd	3rd	Win & Pl
Career Total (Turf)	30	1	4	4	10435

59 8/07 Bevl 5f G-F £2590
Total win prize-money £2591

Going (Turf): Sf: 0-1 GS: 0-2 Gd: 0-7 **GF: 1-17** Fm: 0-3
Distance: **5f/6f: 1-18** 7f-8f: 0-7 9f-13f: 0-5 14f+: 0-0
Track : LH: 0-7 RH: 0-7 Tight: 0-3 Gall: 0-0
Aids: **Bl: 1-9** Vi: 0-1 Tstrap: 0-1 Ckp: 0-1
Best Rating: 73 7/05 York 6f gd-fm

Moderate; effective over 5f-6f; acts on good and faster ground.

Royal Confidence

114 107
4-y-o b f Royal Applause-Never A Doubt (Night Shift (USA))
B W Hills D M James

Placings:2521143/3000510-46003564 (6487)
2009: 7^{4}GF, 7^{6}G, 8^{0}GF, 7^{0}G, 7^{3}GF, 7^{5}GF, 7^{6}GF, 7^{4}GF,

	Starts	1st	2nd	3rd	Win & Pl
Career Total (Turf)	22	3	2	3	87298

103 9/08 Donc 7f SFT £26667
90 9/07 Donc 6f110y G-F £25908
75 8/07 Sand 5f6y GD £3886
Total win prize-money £56461

Going (Turf): **Sf: 1-1** GS: 0-3 **Gd: 1-7 GF: 1-11** Fm: 0-0
Distance: 5f/6f: 1-4 **7f-8f: 2-18** 9f-13f: 0-0 14f+: 0-0
Track : LH: 0-4 RH: 0-2 Tight: 0-0 Gall: 0-2
Aids: Bl: 0-0 Vi: 0-0 Tstrap: 0-1 Ckp: 0-1
Best Rating: **107** 5/08 NmkR 1m gd-fm

Smart; Listed winner and Group placed; stays 7f; acts on most ground.

Royal Crest

96(98) (63)**59**

3-y-o b g Royal Applause-Noble Lady (Primo Dominie)
J A Osborne J A Osborne

Placings:31000**50** (6804)
2009: 7^{3}SD, **6^{1}SD**, 7^{0}GF, 6^{0}GF, 7^{0}G, **8^{5}SD**, **9^{0}SD**,

	Starts	1st	2nd	3rd	Win & Pl
Career Total (Turf)	3	0	0	0	
Career Total (AW)	4	1	0	1	3133

62 3/09 Sthl 6f STD £2729
Total win prize-money £2730

Going (Turf): **Sf: 0-0 GS: 0-0 Gd: 0-1 GF: 0-2 Fm: 0-0**
Distance: **5f/6f: 1-1** 7f-8f: 0-4 9f-13f: 0-2 14f+: 0-0
Track : **LH: 1-4** RH: 0-0 Tight: 0-2 Gall: 0-0
Aids: Bl: 0-0 Vi: 0-0 Tstrap: 0-0 Ckp: 0-0
Best Rating: **63** 2/09 Sthl 7f stand

Modest; stays 7f and acts on Fibresand.

Royal Defence (IRE)

100 **85**

3-y-o b g Refuse To Bend (IRE)-Alessia (GER) (Warning)
D Nicholls Mrs C C Regalado-Gonzalez

Placings:2-440114 (5670)
2009: 7^{4}GF, 8^{4}G, 9^{0}GF, 8^{1}G, 9^{1}GF, 8^{4}S,

	Starts	1st	2nd	3rd	Win & Pl
Career Total (Turf)	7	2	1	0	14792

85 8/09 Ripn 1m1f170y (0-80)H G-F £6308
76 7/09 Thsk 1m GD £5634
Total win prize-money £11942

Going (Turf): Sf: 0-1 GS: 0-1 **Gd: 1-2 GF: 1-3** Fm: 0-0
Distance: 5f/6f: 0-0 7f-8f: 1-4 9f-13f: 1-3 14f+: 0-0
Track : LH: 1-5 RH: 1-2 **Tight: 2-6** Gall: 0-0
Aids: Bl: 0-0 Vi: 0-0 Tstrap: 0-0 Ckp: 0-0
Best Rating: **85** 8/09 Ripn 1m1f170y gd-fm

Useful; effective at around 1m; handles easy ground.

Royal Desert

93 **86**

2-y-o b c Pastoral Pursuits-Overcome (Belmez (USA))
M R Channon Jaber Abdullah

Placings:631025 (4049)
2009: 5^{6}GF, 5^{3}GF, 5^{1}GF, 6^{0}G, 6^{2}G, 6^{5}S,

	Starts	1st	2nd	3rd	Win & Pl
Career Total (Turf)	6	1	1	1	6479

86 5/09 Bath 5f11y G-F £2719
Total win prize-money £2720

Going (Turf): Sf: 0-1 GS: 0-0 Gd: 0-2 **GF: 1-3** Fm: 0-0
Distance: **5f/6f: 1-5** 7f-8f: 0-1 9f-13f: 0-0 14f+: 0-0
Track : **LH: 1-2** RH: 0-0 Tight: 0-1 **Gall: 1-1**
Aids: Bl: 0-0 Vi: 0-0 Tstrap: 0-0 Ckp: 0-0
Best Rating: **86** 5/09 Bath 5f11y gd-fm

Useful; effective over 5f; acts on fast ground.

Royal Destination (IRE)

109 **105**

4-y-o b g Dubai Destination (USA)-Royale (IRE) (Royal Academy (USA))
J Noseda Vimal Khosla

Placings:40-113100 (6480)
2009: 8^{1}G, 8^{1}G, 9^{3}G, 10^{1}GF, 10^{0}GF, 9^{0}GF,

	Starts	1st	2nd	3rd	Win & Pl
Career Total (Turf)	8	3	0	1	30810

105 8/09 York 1m2f88y (0-105)H G-F £16190
99 7/09 Ayr 1m (0-85)H GD £6476
85 6/09 Hayd 1m30y GD £3238
Total win prize-money £25904

Going (Turf): Sf: 0-0 GS: 0-0 **Gd: 2-3** GF: 1-5 Fm: 0-0
Distance: 5f/6f: 0-0 7f-8f: 1-2 **9f-13f: 2-6** 14f+: 0-0
Track : **LH: 3-4** RH: 0-1 Tight: 0-1 **Gall: 1-2**
Aids: Bl: 0-0 Vi: 0-0 Tstrap: 0-0 Ckp: 0-0
Best Rating: **105** 8/09 York 1m2f88y gd-fm

Very useful; effective at 1m-1m2f; goes well on good and fast ground.

Royal Diamond (IRE)

107(104) (101)**90**

3-y-o b g King's Best (USA)-Irresistible Jewel (IRE) (Danehill (USA))
Sir Mark Prescott E B Rimmer-Osborne House

Placings:460-021111 (6671)
2009: 12^{0}GS, 14^{2}S, 14^{1}G, 14^{1}G, 14^{1}G, **13^{1}SD**,

	Starts	1st	2nd	3rd	Win & Pl
Career Total (Turf)	7	3	1	0	25405
Career Total (AW)	2	1	0	0	5046

101 10/09 Wolv 1m5f194y (0-85)H STD £5046
90 9/09 Ffos 1m6f (0-100)H GD £15577
84 8/09 Yarm 1m6f17y (0-75)H GD £2978
75 7/09 Sand 1m6f (0-80)H GD £4857
Total win prize-money £28460

Going (Turf): Sf: 0-1 GS: 0-1 **Gd: 3-5** GF: 0-0 Fm: 0-0
Distance: 5f/6f: 0-0 7f-8f: 0-3 9f-13f: 0-1 **14f+: 4-5**
Track : **LH: 3-6** RH: 1-2 **Tight: 2-4** Gall: 1-1
Aids: Bl: 0-0 Vi: 0-0 Tstrap: 0-0 Ckp: 0-0
Best Rating: **101** 10/09 Wolv 1m5f194y stand

Fair; effective over 1m6f; acts on good ground.

Royal Dignitary (USA)

94(103) (90)**85**

9-y-o br g Saint Ballado (CAN)-Star Actress (USA) (Star De Naskra (USA))
D Nicholls Middleham Park Racing XXXVI

Placings:14/134500/**3650**/0065003310/00101630610/**526**30130040/0**21**12111-**10**1251**4**0 (6217)
2009: **7^{1}SD**, **8^{0}SD**, 8^{1}SD, 7^{2}GF, 8^{5}G, 7^{1}GF, **8^{4}SD**, 8^{0}GF,

	Starts	1st	2nd	3rd	Win & Pl
Career Total (Turf)	49	12	2	6	115153
Career Total (AW)	11	3	2	1	16781

72 8/09 Bevl 7f100y G-F £2590
87 5/09 Sthl 1m STD £2729
90 3/09 Sthl 7f (0-85)H STD £4857
78 7/08 Muss 1m G-F £1942
85 7/08 Rdcr 7f G-F £3561
80 6/08 Rdcr 7f G-F £2331
64 5/08 Muss 1m G-F £1942
82 5/08 Sthl 1m STD £2047
93 6/07 Ripn 1m (0-95)H G-F £9348
91 8/06 Muss 1m (0-85)H GD £7772
91 6/06 Muss 7f30y (0-85)H G-F £6477
85 5/06 Muss 1m (0-75)H FRM £4533
82 8/05 Haml 1m65y (0-85)H G-F £6941
108 4/03 Thsk 1m A FRM £19040
80 7/02 Sand 7f16y D G-F £5050
Total win prize-money £81166

Going (Turf): Sf: 0-3 GS: 0-7 Gd: 1-12 **GF: 9-24** Fm: 2-3
Distance: 5f/6f: 0-0 **7f-8f: 14-53** 9f-13f: 1-7 14f+: 0-0
Track : LH: 4-23 **RH: 9-25 Tight: 8-23** Gall: 0-6
Aids: Bl: 0-1 **Vi: 1-9** Tstrap: 0-0 Ckp: 0-0
Best Rating: **108** 5/03 Kemp 1m gd-fm

Useful; effective at around 7f-1m; acts on fast ground and on sand; has worn a visor.

Royal Encore

(103) (65)**58**

5-y-o b m Royal Applause-Footlight Fantasy (USA) (Nureyev (USA))
J R Fanshawe Helena Springfield Ltd

Placings:4/530002522-3 (0217)
2009: 9^{3}SD,

	Starts	1st	2nd	3rd	Win & Pl
Career Total (Turf)	5	0	0	1	843
Career Total (AW)	6	0	3	1	2217

Going (Turf): **Sf: 0-0 GS: 0-0 Gd: 0-3 GF: 0-2 Fm: 0-0**
Distance: 5f/6f: 0-4 7f-8f: 0-4 9f-13f: 0-3 14f+: 0-0
Track : LH: 0-5 RH: 0-2 Tight: 0-3 Gall: 0-1
Aids: Bl: 0-0 Vi: 0-0 Tstrap: 0-0 Ckp: 0-0
Best Rating: **65** 12/08 Wolv 1m1f103y stand

Moderate; effective at 6f-1m; acts on good ground.

Royal Entourage

102 (82)**86**

4-y-o b g Royal Applause-Trempkate (USA) (Trempolino (USA))
C A Mulhall (G M Lyons 6/9) Keith Sivills

Placings:0/030**46-2212**00**1160** (6676)
2009: 8^{2}SD, 7^{2}SD, **10^{1}SD**, 8^{2}SD, **8^{0}SD**, 9^{0}G, **7^{1}SD**, **16^{1}SD**, 11^{6}GF, 18^{0}G,

	Starts	1st	2nd	3rd	Win & Pl
Career Total (Turf)	6	0	0	1	626
Career Total (AW)	10	3	3	0	21606

82 9/09 Dund 2m (50-75)H STD £6037
78 9/09 Layt 7f STD £5031
73 4/09 Dund 1m2f150y (47-65)H STD £5702
Total win prize-money £16772

Going (Turf): **Sf: 0-1 GS: 0-0 Gd: 0-2 GF: 0-1 Fm: 0-0**
Distance: 5f/6f: 0-1 7f-8f: 1-7 9f-13f: 1-6 14f+: 1-2
Track : **LH: 2-12** RH: 0-2 Tight: 0-1 Gall: 0-1
Aids: Bl: 0-0 Vi: 0-0 Tstrap: 0-0 Ckp: 0-0
Best Rating: **86** 9/09 Catt 1m3f214y gd-fm

Useful; has won at Laytown and on the Polytrack at Dundalk; has won over 7f but stays up to 2m.

Royal Envoy (IRE)

101(112) (78)86

6-y-o b g Royal Applause-Seven Notes (Zafonic (USA))

P Howling The Circle Bloodstock I Limited

Placings:05/21000/004300300022162/2136101431500003 056-014340566206000 (7506)

2009: 7^{0}SD, 6^{1}SD, 8^{4}SD, 8^{3}SD, 6^{4}G, 6^{0}HY, 8^{5}SD, 6^{6}SD, 7^{6}SF, 5^{2}SD, 7^{0}SD, 7^{6}SS, 6^{0}SD, 7^{0}SD, 6^{0}SD,

	Starts	1st	2nd	3rd	Win & Pl
Career Total (Turf)	14	2	1	0	11808
Career Total (AW)	42	5	5	6	17725

75 2/09 Kemp 6f (0-65)H STD £1706
86 5/08 Thsk 5f (0-80)H GD £5180
82 4/08 Wolv 5f216y (0-70)H STD £2456
72 3/08 Kemp 6f (0-70)H STD £2590
65 1/08 Kemp 6f (0-70)H STD £2331
63 10/07 Kemp 7f (0-55) STD £2047
75 5/06 Thsk 7f FRM £5181

Total win prize-money £21497

Going (Turf): Sf: 0-2 GS: 0-2 **Gd: 1-6** GF: 0-3 **Fm: 1-1**
Distance: **5f/6f: 5-29** 7f-8f: 2-26 9f-13f: 0-1 14f+: 0-0
Track : LH: 2-28 **RH: 4-18 Tight: 2-22** Gall: 0-3
Aids: Bl: 0-0 Vi: 0-0 Tstrap: 0-0 Ckp: 0-0
Best Rating: **86** 5/08 Thsk 5f good

Modest; effective over 5f-1m; suited by fast ground; also goes on Polytrack.

Royal Etiquette (IRE)

94(96) (72)75

2-y-o b g Royal Applause-Alpine Gold (IRE) (Montjeu (IRE))

H J L Dunlop Anamoine Ltd

Placings:3523 (7400)

2009: 6^{3}S, 5^{5}S, 8^{2}GF, 9^{3}SD,

	Starts	1st	2nd	3rd	Win & Pl
Career Total (Turf)	3	0	1	1	2240
Career Total (AW)	1	0	0	1	578

Going (Turf): **Sf: 0-2 GS: 0-0 Gd: 0-0 GF: 0-1 Fm: 0-0**
Distance: 5f/6f: 0-1 7f-8f: 0-2 9f-13f: 0-1 14f+: 0-0
Track : LH: 0-2 RH: 0-0 Tight: 0-1 Gall: 0-1
Aids: Bl: 0-0 Vi: 0-0 Tstrap: 0-0 Ckp: 0-0
Best Rating: **75** 9/09 Ffos 1m gd-fm

Fair; stays 1m1f; acts on fast ground and on Polytrack.

Royal Executioner (USA)

110(105) (84)89

3-y-o b c Royal Academy (USA)-Guillotine (USA) (Proud Truth (USA))

D M Simcock DXB Bloodstock Ltd

Placings:0233-1231 (3156)

2009: 8^{1}SD, 8^{2}SD, 8^{3}SD, 8^{1}G,

	Starts	1st	2nd	3rd	Win & Pl
Career Total (Turf)	5	1	1	2	9213
Career Total (AW)	3	1	1	1	5836

89 6/09 Hayd 1m30y (0-80)H GD £5504
78 2/09 Ling 1m STD £2729

Total win prize-money £8235

Going (Turf): Sf: 0-0 GS: 0-0 **Gd: 1-1** GF: 0-4 Fm: 0-0
Distance: 5f/6f: 0-1 7f-8f: 1-6 9f-13f: 1-1 14f+: 0-0
Track : **LH: 2-3** RH: 0-1 **Tight: 1-2** Gall: 0-0
Aids: Bl: 0-0 Vi: 0-0 Tstrap: 0-0 Ckp: 0-0
Best Rating: **89** 6/09 Hayd 1m30y good

Useful; effective at 7f-1m and acts on fast ground and Polytrack.

Royal Fantasy (IRE)

95(100) (84)85

6-y-o b/br m King's Best (USA)-Dreams (Rainbow Quest (USA))

N Tinkler James Marshall & Mrs Susan Marshall

Placings:0/52/1056235/23324600-06045060 (6184)

2009: 8^{0}GS, 10^{6}G, 10^{0}F, 10^{4}G, 9^{5}GF, 10^{0}GF, 10^{6}GF, 9^{0}GF,

	Starts	1st	2nd	3rd	Win & Pl
Career Total (Turf)	22	1	3	1	13450
Career Total (AW)	4	0	1	2	1898

82 4/07 Yarm 1m3y (0-85)H G-F £4731

Total win prize-money £4732

Going (Turf): Sf: 0-0 GS: 0-3 Gd: 0-5 **GF: 1-12** Fm: 0-2
Distance: 5f/6f: 0-0 7f-8f: 0-5 **9f-13f: 1-21** 14f+: 0-0
Track : LH: 0-15 RH: 0-4 Tight: 0-6 Gall: 0-5
Aids: Bl: 0-0 Vi: 0-1 Tstrap: 0-4 Ckp: 0-4
Best Rating: **85** 6/08 Wwck 1m2f188y gd-fm

Fair; stays 1m2f; acts on fast ground; also goes on Polytrack.

Royal Flynn

101 64

7-y-o b g Royal Applause-Shamriyna (IRE) (Darshaan)

Mrs K Walton Mr and Mrs Paul Chapman

Placings:64065/1203000554/65403240341014/310513110 5/26-00544000 (6822)

2009: 10^{0}G, 10^{0}G, 12^{5}GS, 12^{4}G, 12^{4}G, 13^{0}HY, 12^{0}GS, 14^{0}GF,

	Starts	1st	2nd	3rd	Win & Pl
Career Total (Turf)	49	7	3	5	30647

82 7/07 Hayd 1m2f120y (0-75)H HVY £3886
76 7/07 Bevl 1m1f207y (0-75)H HVY £3886
74 6/07 Hayd 1m2f120y (0-75)H HVY £2817
67 5/07 Newc 1m2f32y (0-65)H GD £2914
67 10/06 Wwck 1m2f188y (0-60)H SFT £2388
64 9/06 Wwck 1m2f188y (0-57)H G-S £2388
68 4/05 Catt 1m3f214y (0-70)H GD £3497

Total win prize-money £21780

Going (Turf): **Sf: 4-9** GS: 1-10 Gd: 2-15 GF: 0-14 Fm: 0-1
Distance: 5f/6f: 0-2 7f-8f: 0-3 **9f-13f: 7-41** 14f+: 0-3
Track : **LH: 6-33** RH: 1-15 Tight: 1-10 Gall: 1-16
Aids: Bl: 0-2 Vi: 0-0 Tstrap: 0-8 Ckp: 0-8
Best Rating: **82** 7/07 Hayd 1m2f120y heavy

Fair; stays 1m4f and acts on good or softer ground.

Royal God (USA)

88 104

4-y-o b g Royal Academy (USA)-Gold Splash (USA) (Blushing Groom (FR))

Saeed Bin Suroor Godolphin

Placings:12/216205-6 (2606)

2009: 8^{6}GF,

	Starts	1st	2nd	3rd	Win & Pl
Career Total (Turf)	9	2	3	0	48173

102 4/08 Toul 1m SFT £20220
79 10/07 Chan 7f VS £7095

Total win prize-money £27316

Going (Turf): **Sf: 1-5** GS: 0-1 Gd: 0-1 GF: 0-1 Fm: 0-0
Distance: 5f/6f: 0-0 **7f-8f: 2-8** 9f-13f: 0-1 14f+: 0-0
Track : LH: 0-3 **RH: 2-5** Tight: 0-0 Gall: 0-0
Aids: Bl: 0-0 Vi: 0-0 Tstrap: 0-0 Ckp: 0-0
Best Rating: **104** 11/08 StCl 1m heavy

Smart; ex-French; stays 1m; acts on soft ground.

Royal Holiday (IRE)

80(90) (69)50

2-y-o ch g Captain Rio-Sunny Slope (Mujtahid (USA))

B Ellison Dorothy & William Gibson

Placings:010 (6829)

2009: 6^{0}G, 6^{1}SD, 7^{0}SF,

	Starts	1st	2nd	3rd	Win & Pl
Career Total (Turf)	1	0	0	0	
Career Total (AW)	2	1	0	0	3886

69 8/09 Sthl 6f STD £3885

Total win prize-money £3886

Going (Turf): **Sf: 0-0 GS: 0-0 Gd: 0-1 GF: 0-0 Fm: 0-0**
Distance: **5f/6f: 1-2** 7f-8f: 0-1 9f-13f: 0-0 14f+: 0-0
Track : **LH: 1-2** RH: 0-0 Tight: 0-1 Gall: 0-0
Aids: Bl: 0-0 Vi: 0-0 Tstrap: 0-0 Ckp: 0-0
Best Rating: **69** 8/09 Sthl 6f stand

Modest; effective over 6f; acts on Fibresand.

Royal Intruder

105(106) (92)98

4-y-o b g Royal Applause-Surprise Visitor (IRE) (Be My Guest (USA))

S Donohoe Mrs Anna McDwyer

Placings:014/62450200000-0000041015311 (6972)

2009: 5^{0}Y, 5^{0}S, 5^{0}HY, 6^{0}HY, 7^{0}Y, 6^{4}GF, 5^{1}G, 7^{0}SH, 5^{1}G, 6^{5}G, 5^{3}GF, 6^{1}GF, 5^{1}SD,

	Starts	1st	2nd	3rd	Win & Pl
Career Total (Turf)	22	4	1	1	29872
Career Total (AW)	5	1	1	0	6710

92 10/09 Kemp 5f (0-85)H STD £4727
86 9/09 Sals 6f (0-85)H G-F £4857
81 8/09 Sand 5f6y (0-80)H GD £4857
80 6/09 Sand 5f6y (0-80)H GD £5180
78 7/07 Sand 5f6y GD £4533

Total win prize-money £24156

Going (Turf): Sf: 0-4 GS: 0-2 **Gd: 3-7** GF: 1-6 Fm: 0-0
Distance: **5f/6f: 5-21** 7f-8f: 0-6 9f-13f: 0-0 14f+: 0-0
Track : LH: 0-6 **RH: 1-5** Tight: 0-0 Gall: 0-2
Aids: Bl: 0-0 Vi: 0-0 Tstrap: 0-1 Ckp: 0-1
Best Rating: **98** 8/08 NmkJ 6f good

Useful; effective over 5f-6f; acts on good ground; goes on Polytrack; has a good record at Sandown.

Royal Island (IRE)

90(102) (82)86

7-y-o b g Trans Island-Royal House (FR) (Royal Academy (USA))

M G Quinlan M T Neville

Placings:112000/01254124/3402000000/40633/40645050 1640006051-000000002 (6256)

2009: 7^{0}SD, 10^{0}SD, 7^{0}SD, 9^{0}SD, 10^{0}GF, 7^{0}G, 8^{0}SD, 6^{0}GF, 8^{2}SD,

	Starts	1st	2nd	3rd	Win & Pl
Career Total (Turf)	34	5	4	0	75966
Career Total (AW)	22	1	1	3	8798

74 12/08 Wolv 1m141y (0-58)H STD £2047

74 8/08 Chep 1m14y SFT £1942
99 8/05 Hayd 1m30y (0-100)H G-F £14129
72 4/05 Diel 1m HVY £4404
85 5/04 Newc 5f D G-F £3536
87 5/04 Bevl 5f E HVY £4472
Total win prize-money £30532

Going (Turf): Sf: 3-12 GS: 0-4 Gd: 0-8 GF: 2-8 Fm: 0-0
Distance: 5f/6f: 2-9 7f-8f: 1-25 9f-13f: 3-22 14f+: 0-0
Track : LH: 3-26 RH: 0-10 Tight: 1-16 Gall: 0-7
Aids: Bl: 0-1 Vi: 0-0 Tstrap: 0-0 Ckp: 0-0
Best Rating: 109 3/06 Rdcr 1m soft

Moderate; stays 1m2f but better around 1m; acts on most ground.

Royal Jasra

(96) (66)77
5-y-o b g Royal Applause-Lake Pleasant (IRE) (Elegant Air)
Mrs S Leech C J Leech

Placings:21/60400-0 (0497)
2009: 12⁰SD,

	Starts	1st	2nd	3rd	Win & Pl
Career Total (Turf)	5	1	1	0	4122
Career Total (AW)	3	0	0	0	0

78 9/07 Hayd 1m2f120y G-F £2817
Total win prize-money £2817

Going (Turf): Sf: 0-0 GS: 0-0 Gd: 0-2 GF: 1-3 Fm: 0-0
Distance: 5f/6f: 0-0 7f-8f: 0-0 9f-13f: 1-8 14f+: 0-0
Track : LH: 1-3 RH: 0-5 Tight: 0-2 Gall: 0-3
Aids: Bl: 0-1 Vi: 0-0 Tstrap: 0-0 Ckp: 0-0
Best Rating: 78 9/07 Hayd 1m2f120y gd-fm

Royal Jet

99(110) (98)92
7-y-o b g Royal Applause-Red Bouquet (Reference Point)
Mrs S Leech (M R Channon 28/4) C J Leech

Placings:3625/01064222104232/05202233/130/005030-300 (3382)
2009: 12³SD, 16⁰GF, 12⁰SD,

	Starts	1st	2nd	3rd	Win & Pl
Career Total (Turf)	27	2	7	2	42379
Career Total (AW)	11	1	2	5	22637

102 2/07 Ling 1m4f (0-100)H STD £11217
82 8/05 Leic 1m3f183y (0-75) GD £6662
Total win prize-money £17881

Going (Turf): Sf: 0-1 GS: 0-0 Gd: 1-10 GF: 0-15 Fm: 1-1
Distance: 5f/6f: 0-0 7f-8f: 0-2 9f-13f: 3-35 14f+: 0-1
Track : LH: 2-17 RH: 1-19 Tight: 2-13 Gall: 0-8
Aids: Bl: 0-0 Vi: 0-3 Tstrap: 0-0 Ckp: 0-0
Best Rating: 102 2/07 Ling 1m4f stand

Useful; stays 1m4f; suited by good or faster ground and Polytrack.

Royal Keva (IRE)

92(98) (65)46
3-y-o b g Medecis-Karmafair (IRE) (Always Fair (USA))
A D Brown Frank Halkett

Placings:6443-050606004432 (7727)
2009: 8⁰GS, 10⁵G, 8⁰G, 7⁶GF, 9⁰G, 13⁶GF, 12⁰SF, 12⁰SD, 9⁴SD, 9⁴SD, 8³SD, 7²SD,

	Starts	1st	2nd	3rd	Win & Pl
Career Total (Turf)	6	0	0	0	0
Career Total (AW)	10	0	1	2	1060

Going (Turf): Sf: 0-0 GS: 0-1 Gd: 0-3 GF: 0-2 Fm: 0-0
Distance: 5f/6f: 0-0 7f-8f: 0-7 9f-13f: 0-8 14f+: 0-1
Track : LH: 0-12 RH: 0-3 Tight: 0-7 Gall: 0-1
Aids: Bl: 0-3 Vi: 0-0 Tstrap: 0-0 Ckp: 0-0
Best Rating: 65 11/08 Sthl 1m stand

Moderate; stays 1m; acts on Fibresand and on Polytrack; has worn blinkers.

Royal Manor

87(106) (70)57
4-y-o b f King's Best (USA)-She's Classy (USA) (Boundary (USA))
Tom Dascombe (N J Vaughan 2/1) Lower Soughton Stud

Placings:0/45063106-66626 (7650)
2009: 5⁶SD, 6⁶GF, 7⁶SD, 8²SD, 8⁶SD,

	Starts	1st	2nd	3rd	Win & Pl
Career Total (Turf)	4	0	0	0	0
Career Total (AW)	10	1	1	1	2801

70 11/08 Ling 7f (0-58)H STD £1706
Total win prize-money £1706

Going (Turf): Sf: 0-0 GS: 0-1 Gd: 0-0 GF: 0-3 Fm: 0-0
Distance: 5f/6f: 0-3 7f-8f: 1-6 9f-13f: 0-5 14f+: 0-0
Track : LH: 1-9 RH: 0-4 Tight: 1-8 Gall: 0-1
Aids: Bl: 0-0 Vi: 0-0 Tstrap: 0-0 Ckp: 0-0
Best Rating: 70 11/08 Ling 7f stand

Modest; stays 1m and acts on Polytrack.

Royal Max (IRE)

96(97) (54)54
3-y-o b g Hawkeye (IRE)-Baccara (IRE) (Sri Pekan (USA))
M C Chapman (Evan Williams 13/8) R S Brookhouse

Placings:050400-53 (3511)
2009: 9⁵G, 12³SD,

	Starts	1st	2nd	3rd	Win & Pl
Career Total (Turf)	5	0	0	0	366
Career Total (AW)	3	0	0	1	302

Going (Turf): Sf: 0-2 GS: 0-1 Gd: 0-1 GF: 0-1 Fm: 0-0
Distance: 5f/6f: 0-3 7f-8f: 0-3 9f-13f: 0-2 14f+: 0-0
Track : LH: 0-0 RH: 0-4 Tight: 0-1 Gall: 0-0
Aids: Bl: 0-1 Vi: 0-1 Tstrap: 0-0 Ckp: 0-0
Best Rating: 54 7/09 Kemp 1m4f stand

Royal Mischief (IRE)

(83) (34)32
3-y-o b f Val Royal (FR)-Anearlybird (USA) (Sheikh Albadou)
P D Evans Ms Geraldine Smith

Placings:0000-5000 (0403)
2009: 6⁵SD, 5⁰SD, 8⁰SD, 7⁰SD,

	Starts	1st	2nd	3rd	Win & Pl
Career Total (Turf)	3	0	0	0	
Career Total (AW)	5	0	0	0	0

Going (Turf): Sf: 0-0 GS: 0-0 Gd: 0-1 GF: 0-0 Fm: 0-0
Distance: 5f/6f: 0-4 7f-8f: 0-3 9f-13f: 0-1 14f+: 0-0
Track : LH: 0-6 RH: 0-2 Tight: 0-2 Gall: 0-0
Aids: Bl: 0-0 Vi: 0-0 Tstrap: 0-0 Ckp: 0-0
Best Rating: 34 1/09 Wolv 1m141y stand

Royal Orissa

(91) (48)69
7-y-o b g Royal Applause-Ling Lane (Slip Anchor)
D Haydn Jones Llewelyn, Runeckles

Placings:4530252/1350000/0000000/330601030600000 040/00-000 (0598)
2009: 6⁰SD, 7⁰SD, 8⁰SD,

	Starts	1st	2nd	3rd	Win & Pl
Career Total (Turf)	23	1	2	2	24139
Career Total (AW)	22	1	0	3	3530

59 6/07 Wolv 7f32y (0-60)H STD £2388
91 3/05 Kemp 6f (0-85)H G-S £6139
Total win prize-money £8528

Going (Turf): Sf: 0-3 GS: 1-5 Gd: 0-5 GF: 0-10 Fm: 0-0
Distance: 5f/6f: 1-26 7f-8f: 1-18 9f-13f: 0-1 14f+: 0-0
Track : LH: 1-16 RH: 0-8 Tight: 1-10 Gall: 0-7
Aids: Bl: 0-1 Vi: 0-0 Tstrap: 0-5 Ckp: 0-5
Best Rating: 95 4/05 Ling 6f soft

Royal Patriot (IRE)

78 43
2-y-o b c King's Best (USA)-Lady Ragazza (IRE) (Bering)
W J Haggas Ms Nicola Mahoney

Placings:0 (5401)
2009: 7⁰G,

	Starts	1st	2nd	3rd	Win & Pl
Career Total (Turf)	1	0	0	0	

Going (Turf): Sf: 0-0 GS: 0-0 Gd: 0-1 GF: 0-0 Fm: 0-0
Distance: 5f/6f: 0-0 7f-8f: 0-1 9f-13f: 0-0 14f+: 0-0
Track : LH: 0-0 RH: 0-0 Tight: 0-0 Gall: 0-0
Aids: Bl: 0-0 Vi: 0-0 Tstrap: 0-0 Ckp: 0-0
Best Rating: 43 8/09 NmkJ 7f good

Royal Power (IRE)

107(101) (107)103
6-y-o b g Xaar-Magic Touch (Fairy King (USA))
D Nicholls Leavy,McManus,Flood,Devaney & Reynolds

Placings:3521322/2210050/00300000/3630001-00400400063 (6312)
2009: 8⁰G, 8⁰GF, 7⁴FT, 7⁰FT, 8⁰GF, 8⁴G, 8⁰GF, 8⁰SH, 8⁰G, 8⁶G, 9³GF,

	Starts	1st	2nd	3rd	Win & Pl
Career Total (Turf)	36	2	4	6	173260
Career Total (AW)	4	1	1	0	17762

107 8/08 GrLe 1m STD £7569
106 5/06 Colo 1m GD £68966
79 6/05 Thsk 7f GD £3750
Total win prize-money £80287

Going (Turf): Sf: 0-5 GS: 0-5 Gd: 2-15 GF: 0-9 Fm: 0-0
Distance: 5f/6f: 0-3 7f-8f: 3-31 9f-13f: 0-6 14f+: 0-0
Track : LH: 2-17 RH: 1-12 Tight: 1-5 Gall: 1-12
Aids: Bl: 0-0 Vi: 0-0 Tstrap: 0-0 Ckp: 0-0
Best Rating: 107 8/08 GrLe 1m stand

Very useful; Listed-placed domestically and won German 2000 Guineas in 2006; stays 1m; acts on most ground; also goes on Polytrack.

Royal Premier (IRE)

98(92) (63)**65**

6-y-o b g King's Theatre (IRE)-Mystic Shadow (IRE) (Mtoto)
H J Collingridge Maynard Durrant Partnership I

Placings:6050/00610**002**/**6**11**00540001**/**0**16104**000**-6644020**600** **(7767)**
2009: 12^{6}GF, 14^{6}GS, 14^{4}G, 16^{4}S, 16^{0}G, 14^{2}G, 14^{0}GF, 11^{6}GF, 12^{0}SD, 11^{0}SD,

	Starts	1st	2nd	3rd	Win & Pl
Career Total (Turf)	**28**	**5**	**1**	**0**	**15847**
Career Total (AW)	**14**	**1**	**1**	**0**	**2854**

73	5/08	Leic	1m3f183y	(0-70)H	GD	£2590
72	4/08	Yarm	1m3f101y	(0-60)H	G-F	£1942
61	12/07	Kemp	1m4f	(0-55)H	STD	£2047
73	5/07	Gdwd	1m3f	(0-70)H	GD	£4857
70	4/07	Yarm	1m3f101y	(0-65)H	G-F	£2137
61	9/06	Chep	1m2f36y	(0-65)H	GD	£2590

Total win prize-money £16167

Going (Turf): Sf: 0-5 GS: 0-3 **Gd: 3-11** GF: 2-9 Fm: 0-0
Distance: 5f/6f: 0-0 7f-8f: 0-3 **9f-13f: 6-29** 14f+: 0-10
Track : LH: 3-25 RH: 3-14 **Tight: 3-19** Gall: 0-4
Aids: Bl: 0-0 **Vi: 6-35** Tstrap: 0-1 Ckp: 0-1
Best Rating: 73 5/08 Leic 1m3f183y good

Moderate; stays 1m6f; acts on fast ground; has worn headgear.

Royal Premium

97(77) (14)**62**

3-y-o b c Superior Premium-Royal Shepley (Royal Applause)
James Moffatt (Mrs G S Rees 1/10) P B J Racing

Placings:005404250-6223514500 **(6411)**
2009: 6^{6}SD, 8^{2}F, 8^{2}G, 7^{3}GF, 6^{5}G, 8^{1}HY, 8^{4}GF, 8^{5}S, 7^{0}GF, 8^{0}GF,

	Starts	1st	2nd	3rd	Win & Pl
Career Total (Turf)	**17**	**1**	**3**	**1**	**5986**
Career Total (AW)	**2**	**0**	**0**	**0**	**0**

62	7/09	Hayd	1m30y	(0-70)H	HVY	£3238

Total win prize-money £3238

Going (Turf): Sf: 1-4 GS: 0-2 Gd: 0-3 GF: 0-7 Fm: 0-1
Distance: 5f/6f: 0-6 7f-8f: 0-11 **9f-13f: 1-2** 14f+: 0-0
Track : LH: 1-7 RH: 0-4 Tight: 0-5 Gall: 0-1
Aids: Bl: 0-0 **Vi: 1-8** Tstrap: 0-6 Ckp: 0-6
Best Rating: 62 7/09 Hayd 1m30y heavy

Moderate; stays 1m; acts on most ground; has worn cheekpieces and a visor.

Royal Prodigy (USA)

98 **48**

10-y-o ch g Royal Academy (USA)-Prospector's Queen (USA) (Mr Prospector (USA))
R J Hodges The Gardens Entertainments Ltd

Placings:30/1**0**0**00**/**5**13**01311**/**0420**/1/1/4-16 **(2519)**
2009: 17^{1}GF, 17^{6}F,

	Starts	1st	2nd	3rd	Win & Pl
Career Total (Turf)	**12**	**3**	**0**	**1**	**7955**
Career Total (AW)	**12**	**5**	**1**	**2**	**14703**

	5/09	Lanc	2m1f	(0-60)H	G-F	£3100
	5/06	Lanc	1m7f	H	FRM	£2220
	5/05	Lanc	1m7f	H	SFT	£1500
69	12/03	Ling	1m5f	F(0-65)H	STD	£2058
63	11/03	Wolv	1m4f	G	STD	£2093
65	6/03	Wolv	1m4f	G	SLW	£3010
66	2/03	Sthl	1m4f	G	SLW	£2982
79	2/02	Ling	1m	D	STD	£2758

Total win prize-money £19721

Going (Turf): Sf: 1-1 GS: 0-4 Gd: 0-1 **GF: 1-4 Fm: 1-2**
Distance: 5f/6f: 0-0 7f-8f: 1-4 **9f-13f: 4-14** 14f+: 3-6
Track : LH: 5-16 RH: 0-2 **Tight: 4-15** Gall: 0-2
Aids: Bl: 0-0 Vi: 0-1 Tstrap: 0-0 Ckp: 0-0
Best Rating: 79 2/02 Ling 1m stand

Royal Rainbow

91(97) (52)**45**

5-y-o ch g Rainbow Quest (USA)-Royal Future (IRE) (Royal Academy (USA))
P W Hiatt Clive Roberts

Placings:00/000-06**063** **(7750)**
2009: 9^{0}GF, 11^{6}GF, 13^{0}SD, 12^{6}SD, 13^{3}SD,

	Starts	1st	2nd	3rd	Win & Pl
Career Total (Turf)	**6**	**0**	**0**	**0**	**0**
Career Total (AW)	**4**	**0**	**0**	**1**	**302**

Going (Turf): Sf: 0-1 GS: 0-2 Gd: 0-1 GF: 0-2 Fm: 0-0
Distance: 5f/6f: 0-0 7f-8f: 0-0 9f-13f: 0-8 14f+: 0-2
Track : LH: 0-6 RH: 0-4 Tight: 0-5 Gall: 0-1
Aids: Bl: 0-0 Vi: 0-0 Tstrap: 0-0 Ckp: 0-0
Best Rating: 52 12/09 Wolv 1m5f194y stand

Moderate; stays 1m6f; acts on Polytrack.

Royal Rationale (IRE)

98 (76)**92**

5-y-o b g Desert Prince (IRE)-Logic (Slip Anchor)
D E Pipe Pond House Racing

Placings:50**62**/**2**1**2**/**3**0 **(6851)**
2009: 20^{3}GF, 18^{0}G,

	Starts	1st	2nd	3rd	Win & Pl
Career Total (Turf)	**6**	**1**	**1**	**1**	**10086**
Career Total (AW)	**3**	**0**	**2**	**0**	**1445**

77	5/07	Ling	1m1f	G-F	£3108

Total win prize-money £3109

Going (Turf): Sf: 0-1 GS: 0-1 Gd: 0-1 **GF: 1-3** Fm: 0-0
Distance: 5f/6f: 0-2 7f-8f: 0-2 **9f-13f: 1-3** 14f+: 0-2
Track : LH: 1-4 RH: 0-3 **Tight: 1-4** Gall: 0-2
Aids: Bl: 0-2 Vi: 0-0 Tstrap: 0-0 Ckp: 0-0
Best Rating: 92 6/09 Asct 2m4f gd-fm

Useful; stays 2m4f and acts on most ground and on Polytrack; has worn blinkers; winning hurdler.

Royal Record

94 **67**

2-y-o b f Royal Applause-First Musical (First Trump)
M Brittain Mel Brittain

Placings:6642300 **(6820)**
2009: 6^{6}G, 7^{6}G, 6^{4}S, 6^{2}GF, 6^{3}S, 6^{0}G, 6^{0}GF,

	Starts	1st	2nd	3rd	Win & Pl
Career Total (Turf)	**7**	**0**	**1**	**1**	**2345**

Going (Turf): Sf: 0-2 GS: 0-0 Gd: 0-3 GF: 0-2 Fm: 0-0
Distance: 5f/6f: 0-5 7f-8f: 0-2 9f-13f: 0-0 14f+: 0-0
Track : LH: 0-0 RH: 0-0 Tight: 0-0 Gall: 0-0
Aids: Bl: 0-0 Vi: 0-0 Tstrap: 0-0 Ckp: 0-0
Best Rating: 67 8/09 Ripn 6f gd-fm

Moderate; effective over 6-7f; acts on a sound surface but handles soft.

Royal Rock

113 (89)**115**

5-y-o b g Sakhee (USA)-Vanishing Point (USA) (Caller I.D. (USA))
C F Wall Ms Aida Fustoq

Placings:0312116/13-16410 **(7232a)**
2009: 6^{1}G, 5^{6}G, 6^{4}S, 6^{1}GS, 6^{0}HO,

	Starts	1st	2nd	3rd	Win & Pl
Career Total (Turf)	**12**	**5**	**1**	**1**	**74100**
Career Total (AW)	**2**	**1**	**0**	**1**	**5065**

115	10/09	Asct	6f		G-S	£36900
113	5/09	Hayd	6f		GD	£12462
107	4/08	Yarm	6f3y	(0-100)H	G-F	£9969
104	7/07	Wind	6f	(0-85)H	SFT	£6477
89	6/07	Kemp	6f	(0-80)H	STD	£4728
81	5/07	Ling	7f		GD	£2590

Total win prize-money £73129

Going (Turf): Sf: 1-2 GS: 1-1 **Gd: 2-6** GF: 1-2 Fm: 0-0
Distance: 5f/6f: 4-8 7f-8f: 2-5 9f-13f: 0-1 14f+: 0-0
Track : LH: 0-1 **RH: 1-1** Tight: 0-1 **Gall: 1-1**
Aids: Bl: 0-0 Vi: 0-0 Tstrap: 0-1 Ckp: 0-1
Best Rating: 115 10/09 Asct 6f gd-sft

Group class; Group 3 winner; effective over 6f-7f; acts on fast and soft ground, also goes on Polytrack.

Royal Salsa (IRE)

(82) (46)**52**

3-y-o b f Royal Applause-Lady Salsa (IRE) (Gone West (USA))
R A Fahey Minster Commercial Leasing

Placings:5000-**3**00 **(0383)**
2009: 8^{3}SD, 8^{0}SD, 8^{0}SD,

	Starts	1st	2nd	3rd	Win & Pl
Career Total (Turf)	**4**	**0**	**0**	**0**	**0**
Career Total (AW)	**3**	**0**	**0**	**1**	**302**

Going (Turf): Sf: 0-0 GS: 0-2 Gd: 0-2 GF: 0-0 Fm: 0-0
Distance: 5f/6f: 0-3 7f-8f: 0-2 9f-13f: 0-2 14f+: 0-0
Track : LH: 0-3 RH: 0-0 Tight: 0-2 Gall: 0-0
Aids: Bl: 0-0 Vi: 0-0 Tstrap: 0-1 Ckp: 0-1
Best Rating: 52 8/08 Donc 6f good

Moderate; effective over 1m; acts on Polytrack.

Royal Society

37(98) (63)**54**

3-y-o b g King's Best (USA)-Nawaiet (USA) (Zilzal (USA))
R A Farrant (Miss L A Perratt 23/10) M Sawers

Placings:50-**32**000**01**00 **(7856)**
2009: 8^{3}SD, 12^{2}SD, 14^{0}GF, 8^{0}G, 10^{0}S, 9^{0}G, 9^{1}SD, 12^{0}SD, 9^{0}SD,

	Starts	1st	2nd	3rd	Win & Pl
Career Total (Turf)	**6**	**0**	**0**	**0**	**0**
Career Total (AW)	**5**	**1**	**1**	**1**	**3203**

61	11/09	Wolv	1m1f103y	(0-55)H	STD	£2047

Total win prize-money £2047

Going (Turf): Sf: 0-2 GS: 0-0 Gd: 0-2 GF: 0-2 Fm: 0-0
Distance: 5f/6f: 0-0 7f-8f: 0-2 **9f-13f: 1-8** 14f+: 0-1
Track : LH: 1-7 RH: 0-4 **Tight: 1-5** Gall: 0-0
Aids: Bl: 0-0 Vi: 0-0 Tstrap: 0-0 Ckp: 0-0
Best Rating: 63 3/09 Kemp 1m4f stand

Moderate; stays 1m4f; acts on Polytrack.

Royal Straight

(102) (74)63

4-y-o ch g Halling (USA)-High Straits (Bering)

B N Pollock McAndrew Utilities Limited

Placings:05/4003015000-460 (0500)

2009: 10^{4}SD, 8^{6}SD, 10^{0}SD,

	Starts	1st	2nd	3rd	Win & Pl
Career Total (Turf)	3	0	0	0	0
Career Total (AW)	12	1	0	1	2548

74 9/08 Ling 1m2f STD £1978

Total win prize-money £1979

Going (Turf): Sf: 0-0 GS: 0-1 Gd: 0-2 GF: 0-0 Fm: 0-0
Distance: 5f/6f: 0-0 7f-8f: 0-5 9f-13f: 1-10 14f+: 0-0
Track : LH: 1-11 RH: 0-3 Tight: 1-11 Gall: 0-0
Aids: Bl: 0-1 Vi: 0-1 Tstrap: 0-0 Ckp: 0-0
Best Rating: 74 9/08 Ling 1m2f stand

Modest; stays 1m2f; handles Polytrack.

Royal Superlative

97(94) (56)79

3-y-o b f King's Best (USA)-Supereva (IRE) (Sadler's Wells (USA))

R M Beckett Prince Of Wales And Duchess Of Cornwall

Placings:0-412040 (6346)

2009: 8^{4}G, 8^{1}G, 8^{2}GF, 10^{0}G, 8^{4}GF, 9^{0}SD,

	Starts	1st	2nd	3rd	Win & Pl
Career Total (Turf)	6	1	1	0	4246
Career Total (AW)	1	0	0	0	

63 6/09 Chep 1m14y GD £2719

Total win prize-money £2720

Going (Turf): Sf: 0-0 GS: 0-1 Gd: 1-3 GF: 0-2 Fm: 0-0
Distance: 5f/6f: 0-0 7f-8f: 0-1 9f-13f: 1-6 14f+: 0-0
Track : LH: 0-3 RH: 0-0 Tight: 0-2 Gall: 0-1
Aids: Bl: 0-0 Vi: 0-0 Tstrap: 0-0 Ckp: 0-0
Best Rating: 79 7/09 Chep 1m14y gd-fm

Fair; effective at 1m; acts on good ground.

Royal Torbo (ISR)

(81) (53)

2-y-o b c Tabari (GER)-Royal Dutch (GER) (Monsun (GER))

George Baker Arik & Betty Rayzner

Placings:0 (7800)

2009: 7^{0}SD,

	Starts	1st	2nd	3rd	Win & Pl
Career Total (Turf)	0	0	0	0	
Career Total (AW)	1	0	0	0	

Going (Turf): Sf: 0-0 GS: 0-0 Gd: 0-0 GF: 0-0 Fm: 0-0
Distance: 5f/6f: 0-0 7f-8f: 0-1 9f-13f: 0-0 14f+: 0-0
Track : LH: 0-1 RH: 0-0 Tight: 0-1 Gall: 0-0
Aids: Bl: 0-0 Vi: 0-0 Tstrap: 0-0 Ckp: 0-0
Best Rating: 53 12/09 Wolv 7f32y stand

Royal Treasure (IRE)

(84) (44)

2-y-o b c Arakan (USA)-Isticanna (USA) (Far North (CAN))

J A Osborne H R H Prince of Saxe-Weimar

Placings:00 (7391)

2009: 8^{0}SD, 8^{0}SD,

	Starts	1st	2nd	3rd	Win & Pl
Career Total (Turf)	0	0	0	0	
Career Total (AW)	2	0	0	0	

Going (Turf): Sf: 0-0 GS: 0-0 Gd: 0-0 GF: 0-0 Fm: 0-0
Distance: 5f/6f: 0-0 7f-8f: 0-1 9f-13f: 0-1 14f+: 0-0
Track : LH: 0-2 RH: 0-0 Tight: 0-2 Gall: 0-0
Aids: Bl: 0-0 Vi: 0-0 Tstrap: 0-0 Ckp: 0-0
Best Rating: 44 11/09 Ling 1m stand

Royal Trooper (IRE)

102(103) (75)78

3-y-o b g Hawk Wing (USA)-Strawberry Roan (IRE) (Sadler's Wells (USA))

J G Given J Barson

Placings:064-334315004451 (7222)

2009: 9^{3}GF, 12^{3}GF, 12^{4}GS, 12^{3}G, 12^{1}G, 11^{5}GS, 14^{0}GF, 14^{0}G, 12^{4}SD, 12^{4}SD, 14^{5}GS, 13^{1}S,

	Starts	1st	2nd	3rd	Win & Pl
Career Total (Turf)	13	2	0	3	10987
Career Total (AW)	2	0	0	0	697

78 11/09 Catt 1m5f175y (0-75)H SFT £2914
78 7/09 Thsk 1m4f (0-80)H GD £5569

Total win prize-money £8483

Going (Turf): Sf: 1-3 GS: 0-3 Gd: 1-4 GF: 0-3 Fm: 0-0
Distance: 5f/6f: 0-0 7f-8f: 0-3 9f-13f: 1-8 14f+: 1-4
Track : LH: 2-9 RH: 0-4 Tight: 2-4 Gall: 0-6
Aids: Bl: 0-0 Vi: 0-0 Tstrap: 0-0 Ckp: 0-0
Best Rating: 78 11/09 Catt 1m5f175y soft

Fair; stays 1m5f; acts on fast and soft ground.

Royal Wedding

(100) (62)

7-y-o b g King's Best (USA)-Liaison (USA) (Blushing Groom (FR))

N J Gifford D G Trangmar

Placings:000/1620040/050 (0631)

2009: 10^{0}SD, 13^{5}SD, 13^{0}SD,

	Starts	1st	2nd	3rd	Win & Pl
Career Total (Turf)	7	0	0	0	394
Career Total (AW)	6	1	1	0	5554

71 1/05 Sthl 1m STD £3484

Total win prize-money £3484

Going (Turf): Sf: 0-1 GS: 0-1 Gd: 0-3 GF: 0-1 Fm: 0-1
Distance: 5f/6f: 0-1 7f-8f: 1-3 9f-13f: 0-9 14f+: 0-0
Track : LH: 1-8 RH: 0-2 Tight: 0-7 Gall: 0-1
Aids: Bl: 0-0 Vi: 0-0 Tstrap: 0-0 Ckp: 0-0
Best Rating: 74 2/05 Wolv 1m141y stand

Royal Willy (IRE)

96(97) (74)71

3-y-o b g Val Royal (FR)-Neat Dish (CAN) (Stalwart (USA))

W Jarvis The Stand At Ease Partnership

Placings:002-0340060 (7211)

2009: 8^{0}GF, 8^{3}SD, 9^{4}GF, 12^{0}GS, 14^{0}GF, 10^{6}SS, 8^{0}SD,

	Starts	1st	2nd	3rd	Win & Pl
Career Total (Turf)	7	0	1	0	1647
Career Total (AW)	3	0	0	1	578

Going (Turf): Sf: 0-1 GS: 0-2 Gd: 0-0 GF: 0-4 Fm: 0-0
Distance: 5f/6f: 0-0 7f-8f: 0-4 9f-13f: 0-5 14f+: 0-1
Track : LH: 0-5 RH: 0-1 Tight: 0-6 Gall: 0-0
Aids: Bl: 0-0 Vi: 0-0 Tstrap: 0-0 Ckp: 0-0
Best Rating: 74 6/09 Wolv 1m141y stand

Fair maiden form to date; stays 7f; acts on easy ground.

Roybuoy

71(92) (57)48

2-y-o b c Royal Applause-Wavy Up (IRE) (Brustolon)

H J L Dunlop Barnet, Charnwood Boy & Star pointe Ltd

Placings:000660 (7887)

2009: 7^{0}G, 8^{0}S, 7^{0}SD, 8^{6}SD, 7^{6}SD, 7^{0}SD,

	Starts	1st	2nd	3rd	Win & Pl
Career Total (Turf)	2	0	0	0	
Career Total (AW)	4	0	0	0	0

Going (Turf): Sf: 0-1 GS: 0-0 Gd: 0-1 GF: 0-0 Fm: 0-0
Distance: 5f/6f: 0-0 7f-8f: 0-6 9f-13f: 0-0 14f+: 0-0
Track : LH: 0-3 RH: 0-2 Tight: 0-3 Gall: 0-0
Aids: Bl: 0-3 Vi: 0-0 Tstrap: 0-0 Ckp: 0-0
Best Rating: 57 12/09 Ling 7f stand

Rub Of The Relic (IRE)

(104) (63)75

4-y-o b g Chevalier (IRE)-Bayletta (IRE) (Woodborough (USA))

P T Midgley O R Dukes

Placings:023232240333/360050152-4030020 (0979)

2009: 8^{4}SS, 8^{0}SD, 8^{3}SD, 12^{0}SD, 9^{0}SD, 8^{2}SD, 8^{0}SD,

	Starts	1st	2nd	3rd	Win & Pl
Career Total (Turf)	12	0	3	3	4443
Career Total (AW)	16	1	3	4	5500

62 12/08 Sthl 1m (0-65)H STD £2047

Total win prize-money £2047

Going (Turf): Sf: 0-7 GS: 0-1 Gd: 0-3 GF: 0-1 Fm: 0-0
Distance: 5f/6f: 0-8 7f-8f: 1-16 9f-13f: 0-4 14f+: 0-0
Track : LH: 1-20 RH: 0-0 Tight: 0-3 Gall: 0-0
Aids: Bl: 0-1 Vi: 1-9 Tstrap: 0-1 Ckp: 0-1
Best Rating: 75 7/07 Nott 6f15y heavy

Modest; suited by 5f-7f; acts on good and softer ground and on Fibresand; has worn a visor.

Rubbinghousedotcom (IRE)

86(87) (48)51

3-y-o b g Desert Style (IRE)-Marain (IRE) (Marju (IRE))

P M Phelan The Rubbing House (on Epsom racecourse)

Placings:00-0400 (1967)

2009: 7^{0}SD, 8^{4}GF, 10^{0}GF, 10^{0}SD,

	Starts	1st	2nd	3rd	Win & Pl
Career Total (Turf)	2	0	0	0	0
Career Total (AW)	4	0	0	0	

Going (Turf): Sf: 0-0 GS: 0-0 Gd: 0-0 GF: 0-2 Fm: 0-0
Distance: 5f/6f: 0-0 7f-8f: 0-3 9f-13f: 0-3 14f+: 0-0
Track : LH: 0-4 RH: 0-2 Tight: 0-5 Gall: 0-0
Aids: Bl: 0-1 Vi: 0-0 Tstrap: 0-0 Ckp: 0-0
Best Rating: 51 4/09 Bath 1m5y gd-fm

Rubenstar (IRE)

99(103) (75)72

6-y-o b g Soviet Star (USA)-Ansariya (USA) (Shahrastani (USA))

Patrick Morris L Walsh

Placings:0652101/0632550651/0530066260/40-033102 **(7860)**

2009: 7^0SD, 7^3SD, 7^3G, 7^1SD, 7^0SD, 7^2SD,

	Starts	1st	2nd	3rd	Win & Pl
Career Total (Turf)	25	2	3	3	16225
Career Total (AW)	10	2	1	1	10133

71	4/09	Ling	7f	(0-70)H	STD	£2900
84	10/06	Ling	7f	(0-85)H	STD	£6477
81	10/05	Gdwd	7f	(0-75)H	GD	£3698
73	9/05	Folk	6f	(0-75)	G-F	£4381

Total win prize-money £17457

Going (Turf): Sf: 0-2 GS: 0-1 **Gd: 1-13 GF: 1-9** Fm: 0-0
Distance: 5f/6f: 1-5 **7f-8f: 3-27** 9f-13f: 0-3 14f+: 0-0
Track : **LH: 2-11** RH: 1-12 **Tight: 2-8** Gall: 0-1
Aids: Bl: 0-0 Vi: 0-0 Tstrap: 0-0 Ckp: 0-0
Best Rating: 85 6/06 Sand 1m14y gd-fm

Modest; effective over 1m; acts on fast ground and on Polytrack.

Rubicon Bay (IRE)

85 38

2-y-o b f One Cool Cat (USA)-Mrs Moonlight (Ajdal (USA))

C J Teague Collins Chauffeur Driven Executive Cars

Placings:06 **(7114)**

2009: 6^0G, 7^6GS,

	Starts	1st	2nd	3rd	Win & Pl
Career Total (Turf)	2	0	0	0	0

Going (Turf): Sf: 0-0 GS: 0-1 Gd: 0-1 GF: 0-0 Fm: 0-0
Distance: 5f/6f: 0-1 7f-8f: 0-1 9f-13f: 0-0 14f+: 0-0
Track : LH: 0-0 RH: 0-1 Tight: 0-1 Gall: 0-0
Aids: Bl: 0-0 Vi: 0-0 Tstrap: 0-0 Ckp: 0-0
Best Rating: 38 10/09 Muss 7f30y gd-sft

Rublevka Star (USA)

90(96) (67)63

3-y-o b f Elusive Quality (USA)-Al Desima (Emperor Jones (USA))

James M Ryan (J Noseda 27/5) Mrs J M Ryan

Placings:61-050 **(4570a)**

2009: 5^0GF, 5^5SD, 5^0Y,

	Starts	1st	2nd	3rd	Win & Pl
Career Total (Turf)	3	0	0	0	0
Career Total (AW)	2	1	0	0	3886

67	10/08	GrLe	5f	STD	£3885

Total win prize-money £3886

Going (Turf): Sf: 0-0 GS: 0-0 Gd: 0-1 GF: 0-1 Fm: 0-0
Distance: 5f/6f: 1-4 7f-8f: 0-1 9f-13f: 0-0 14f+: 0-0
Track : LH: 1-2 RH: 0-0 Tight: 0-1 **Gall: 1-1**
Aids: Bl: 0-0 Vi: 0-0 Tstrap: 0-0 Ckp: 0-0
Best Rating: 67 10/08 GrLe 5f stand

Modest; effective at 5f; acts on Polytrack.

Ruby Best

(90) (43)43

3-y-o b f Best Of The Bests (IRE)-Ice Bird (Polar Falcon (USA))

D K Ivory P Willis & Dean Ivory

Placings:000-0 **(0159)**

2009: 7^0SD,

	Starts	1st	2nd	3rd	Win & Pl
Career Total (Turf)	2	0	0	0	
Career Total (AW)	2	0	0	0	

Going (Turf): Sf: 0-1 GS: 0-0 Gd: 0-0 GF: 0-1 Fm: 0-0
Distance: 5f/6f: 0-3 7f-8f: 0-1 9f-13f: 0-0 14f+: 0-0
Track : LH: 0-1 RH: 0-1 Tight: 0-1 Gall: 0-1
Aids: Bl: 0-0 Vi: 0-0 Tstrap: 0-0 Ckp: 0-0
Best Rating: 43 1/09 Ling 7f stand

Ruby Delta

(94) (56)45

4-y-o b g Delta Dancer-Picolette (Piccolo)

A G Juckes A G Juckes

Placings:04242460/0000001-0 **(0448)**

2009: 13^0SD,

	Starts	1st	2nd	3rd	Win & Pl
Career Total (Turf)	11	0	2	0	2726
Career Total (AW)	5	1	0	0	1979

56	9/08	Wolv	1m4f50y	STD	£1978

Total win prize-money £1979

Going (Turf): Sf: 0-2 GS: 0-0 Gd: 0-4 GF: 0-5 Fm: 0-0
Distance: 5f/6f: 0-3 7f-8f: 0-9 **9f-13f: 1-3** 14f+: 0-1
Track : LH: 1-6 RH: 0-1 **Tight: 1-7** Gall: 0-0
Aids: Bl: 0-2 **Vi: 1-2** Tstrap: 0-0 Ckp: 0-0
Best Rating: 69 7/07 Leic 7f9y soft

Moderate; stays 1m4f acts on good ground and on Polytrack.

Ruby Tallulah

(98) (73)75

3-y-o b f Piccolo-Tallulah Belle (Crowning Honors (CAN))

C R Dore Mrs A N Durkan

Placings:424134000-44555660 **(0955)**

2009: 5^4SD, 5^4SD, 5^5SD, 5^5SD, 6^5SD, 5^6SD, 5^6SD, 5^0SD,

	Starts	1st	2nd	3rd	Win & Pl
Career Total (Turf)	5	0	1	1	1957
Career Total (AW)	12	1	0	0	4343

73	8/08	Ling	5f	STD	£3885

Total win prize-money £3886

Going (Turf): Sf: 0-1 GS: 0-0 Gd: 0-1 GF: 0-2 Fm: 0-1
Distance: 5f/6f: 1-17 7f-8f: 0-0 9f-13f: 0-0 14f+: 0-0
Track : LH: 1-10 RH: 0-2 **Tight: 1-7** Gall: 0-4
Aids: Bl: 0-0 Vi: 0-0 Tstrap: 0-0 Ckp: 0-0
Best Rating: 75 8/08 NmkJ 5f good

Modest; stays 6f; acts on fast ground and on Polytrack.

Rudolph Schmidt (IRE)

74(99) (79)81

3-y-o br f Catcher In The Rye (IRE)-Enaya (Caerleon (USA))

David P Myerscough Fergus Jones

Placings:0412-003001 **(6442)**

2009: 8^0HY, 7^0HY, 8^3S, 8^0GY, 7^0GF, 7^1SS,

	Starts	1st	2nd	3rd	Win & Pl
Career Total (Turf)	9	1	1	1	16799
Career Total (AW)	1	1	0	0	2047

79	10/09	Ling	7f	SS	£2047
75	10/08	Navn	5f162y	HVY	£8637

Total win prize-money £10685

Going (Turf): Sf: 1-7 GS: 0-0 Gd: 0-0 GF: 0-1 Fm: 0-0
Distance: 5f/6f: 1-2 7f-8f: 1-7 9f-13f: 0-1 14f+: 0-0
Track : LH: 2-5 RH: 0-4 **Tight: 1-1** Gall: 0-1
Aids: Bl: 1-1 Vi: 0-0 Tstrap: 0-2 Ckp: 0-2
Best Rating: 81 11/08 Leop 7f soft

Fair; stays 7f; acts on Polytrack and soft ground on turf.

Rudry World (IRE)

88(91) (53)68

6-y-o ch g Spinning World (USA)-Fancy Boots (IRE) (Salt Dome (USA))

M Mullineaux Noel Racing Partnership

Placings:0040/3431522104311244/20003500-204200 **(7440)**

2009: 12^2GS, 12^0S, 13^4HY, 12^2GS, 12^0S, 12^0SD,

	Starts	1st	2nd	3rd	Win & Pl
Career Total (Turf)	21	2	5	3	12501
Career Total (AW)	13	2	1	1	6127

76	8/07	Haml	1m4f17y	(0-70)H	G-S	£3238
69	8/07	Haml	1m4f17y	(0-70)H	G-S	£3238
61	7/07	Ling	1m4f	(0-65)H	STD	£2388
59	4/07	Wolv	1m4f50y		STD	£2184

Total win prize-money £11051

Going (Turf): Sf: 0-8 **GS: 2-5** Gd: 0-4 GF: 0-4 Fm: 0-0
Distance: 5f/6f: 0-1 7f-8f: 0-3 **9f-13f: 4-24** 14f+: 0-6
Track : LH: 2-25 RH: 2-9 **Tight: 4-19** Gall: 0-3
Aids: Bl: 0-0 Vi: 0-0 Tstrap: 0-0 Ckp: 0-0
Best Rating: 78 9/07 Hayd 1m3f200y soft

Modest; stays 1m4f; acts on easy ground and on Polytrack; usually held up.

Rue De Cabestan (IRE)

88 (21)57

4-y-o b f Orpen (USA)-Beaufort Lady (IRE) (Alhaarth (IRE))

T G McCourt Elm Court Developments Ltd

Placings:0/050203130-52365003030 **(7383a)**

2009: 10^5GY, 9^2S, 10^3Y, 10^6GF, 8^5YS, 9^0YS, 12^0S, 9^3HY, 8^0S, 9^3S, 10^0SD,

	Starts	1st	2nd	3rd	Win & Pl
Career Total (Turf)	18	1	2	5	9017
Career Total (AW)	3	0	0	0	

53	9/08	Cork	1m	(45-65)H	Y-S	£4318

Total win prize-money £4319

Going (Turf): Sf: 0-8 GS: 0-0 Gd: 0-2 GF: 0-1 Fm: 0-0
Distance: 5f/6f: 0-0 **7f-8f: 1-7** 9f-13f: 0-14 14f+: 0-0
Track : LH: 0-7 **RH: 1-13** Tight: 0-1 Gall: 0-1
Aids: Bl: 0-1 Vi: 0-0 Tstrap: 0-3 Ckp: 0-3
Best Rating: 57 9/09 Tipp 1m1f heavy

Moderate; effective at 1m; handles heavy.

Rue Soleil

78(67) (29)53

5-y-o ch m Zaha (CAN)-Maria Cappuccini (Siberian Express (USA))

J R Weymes Ray Burton

Placings:0004306430/020303416520/0040000-00 (5309)

2009: 5^{0}S, 5^{0}HY,

	Starts	1st	2nd	3rd	Win & Pl
Career Total (Turf)	29	1	2	4	7174
Career Total (AW)	2	0	0	0	

59 7/07 Haml 5f4y SFT £2914

Total win prize-money £2915

Going (Turf): **Sf: 1-7** GS: 0-7 Gd: 0-8 GF: 0-7 Fm: 0-0
Distance: **5f/6f: 1-29** 7f-8f: 0-2 9f-13f: 0-0 14f+: 0-0
Track : LH: 0-8 RH: 0-2 Tight: 0-3 Gall: 0-2
Aids: Bl: 0-2 Vi: 0-0 Tstrap: 0-0 Ckp: 0-0
Best Rating: **62** 9/06 Haml 6f5y gd-sft

Ruff Diamond (USA)

92(102) (82)81

4-y-o b/br g Stormin Fever (USA)-Whalah (USA) (Dixieland Band (USA))

M F Harris (J S Moore 20/6) A J Duffield

Placings:4104/0000000-334400 (3143)

2009: 10^{3}SD, 10^{3}SD, 12^{4}SD, 14^{4}GF, 13^{0}SD, 21^{0}GF,

	Starts	1st	2nd	3rd	Win & Pl
Career Total (Turf)	12	1	0	0	5204
Career Total (AW)	5	0	0	2	1776

85 6/07 Folk 6f GD £3886

Total win prize-money £3886

Going (Turf): Sf: 0-1 GS: 0-1 **Gd: 1-4** GF: 0-6 Fm: 0-0
Distance: **5f/6f: 1-3** 7f-8f: 0-2 9f-13f: 0-9 14f+: 0-3
Track : LH: 0-7 RH: 0-6 Tight: 0-7 Gall: 0-4
Aids: Bl: 0-1 Vi: 0-2 Tstrap: 0-1 Ckp: 0-1
Best Rating: **85** 6/07 Folk 6f good

Modest; stays 1m2f and acts on good ground; likes to race prominently; has worn various headgear; winning hurdler.

Rufus Roughcut

82 34

2-y-o b c Auction House (USA)-Shining Oasis (IRE) (Mujtahid (USA))

S C Williams Thomo & Me

Placings:00000 (7098)

2009: 5^{0}GF, 7^{0}GF, 7^{0}S, 6^{0}GF, 7^{0}G,

	Starts	1st	2nd	3rd	Win & Pl
Career Total (Turf)	5	0	0	0	

Going (Turf): **Sf: 0-1 GS: 0-0 Gd: 0-1 GF: 0-3 Fm: 0-0**
Distance: 5f/6f: 0-1 7f-8f: 0-4 9f-13f: 0-0 14f+: 0-0
Track : LH: 0-0 RH: 0-0 Tight: 0-0 Gall: 0-0
Aids: Bl: 0-0 Vi: 0-0 Tstrap: 0-0 Ckp: 0-0
Best Rating: **34** 10/09 Yarm 7f3y good

Rugell (ARG)

103 89

4-y-o b c Interprete (ARG)-Realize (ARG) (Confidental Talk (USA))

H R A Cecil H E Sheikh Sultan Bin Khalifa Al Nahyan

Placings:052212610-4536 (6036)

2009: 10^{4}G, 10^{5}G, 14^{3}G, 14^{6}GF,

	Starts	1st	2nd	3rd	Win & Pl
Career Total (Turf)	13	2	3	1	32583

11/08 Sani 1m4f FRM £19962
6/08 Sani 1m FRM £5342

Total win prize-money £25305

Going (Turf): Sf: 0-1 GS: 0-0 Gd: 0-3 GF: 0-1 **Fm: 2-8**
Distance: 5f/6f: 0-1 7f-8f: 1-4 9f-13f: 1-6 14f+: 0-2
Track : LH: 0-2 RH: 0-2 Tight: 0-2 Gall: 0-2
Aids: Bl: 0-0 Vi: 0-0 Tstrap: 0-0 Ckp: 0-0
Best Rating: **89** 8/09 NmkJ 1m6f175y good

Useful; Grade 2 winner in Argentina; stays 1m4f; handles very quick ground.

Rule Of Nature

104 77

2-y-o b f Oasis Dream-Jolie Etoile (USA) (Diesis)

Sir Michael Stoute K Abdulla

Placings:21 (6922)

2009: 7^{2}GF, 6^{1}GF,

	Starts	1st	2nd	3rd	Win & Pl
Career Total (Turf)	2	1	1	0	4994

77 10/09 Yarm 6f3y G-F £3784

Total win prize-money £3785

Going (Turf): Sf: 0-0 GS: 0-0 Gd: 0-0 **GF: 1-2** Fm: 0-0
Distance: 5f/6f: 0-0 **7f-8f: 1-2** 9f-13f: 0-0 14f+: 0-0
Track : LH: 0-1 RH: 0-0 Tight: 0-0 Gall: 0-0
Aids: Bl: 0-0 Vi: 0-0 Tstrap: 0-0 Ckp: 0-0
Best Rating: **77** 10/09 Yarm 6f3y gd-fm

Useful prospect; stays 7f; acts on quick ground.

Ruler Of All (IRE)

101 79

3-y-o b g Sadler's Wells (USA)-Shabby Chic (USA) (Red Ransom (USA))

H Candy (B W Hills 14/6) Thomas Barr

Placings:0-2000 (6936)

2009: 10^{2}GF, 11^{0}GS, 14^{0}S, 11^{0}G,

	Starts	1st	2nd	3rd	Win & Pl
Career Total (Turf)	5	0	1	0	819

Going (Turf): **Sf: 0-1 GS: 0-1 Gd: 0-1 GF: 0-2 Fm: 0-0**
Distance: 5f/6f: 0-0 7f-8f: 0-1 9f-13f: 0-3 14f+: 0-1
Track : LH: 0-3 RH: 0-1 Tight: 0-2 Gall: 0-2
Aids: Bl: 0-0 Vi: 0-0 Tstrap: 0-0 Ckp: 0-0
Best Rating: **79** 4/09 Newc 1m2f32y gd-fm

Fair; stays 1m2f and acts on fast ground.

Ruler Of My Heart (IRE)

87 101

2-y-o br f Green Tune (USA)-Dirigeante (FR) (Lead On Time (USA))

F Rossi (Tom Dascombe 17/9) J-C Seroul

Placings:5105 (7407a)

2009: 7^{5}G, 8^{1}G, 8^{0}G, 9^{5}GS,

	Starts	1st	2nd	3rd	Win & Pl
Career Total (Turf)	4	1	0	0	61893

101 8/09 Deau 1m GD £59223

Total win prize-money £59223

Going (Turf): Sf: 0-0 GS: 0-1 **Gd: 1-3** GF: 0-0 Fm: 0-0
Distance: 5f/6f: 0-0 **7f-8f: 1-3** 9f-13f: 0-1 14f+: 0-0
Track : LH: 0-0 **RH: 1-2** Tight: 0-0 Gall: 0-0
Aids: Bl: 0-0 Vi: 0-0 Tstrap: 0-0 Ckp: 0-0
Best Rating: **101** 8/09 Deau 1m good

Ruler's Honour (IRE)

(78) (33)

2-y-o b g Antonius Pius (USA)-Naughty Reputation (IRE) (Shalford (IRE))

T J Etherington Tim Etherington

Placings:6 (7485)

2009: 5^{6}SD,

	Starts	1st	2nd	3rd	Win & Pl
Career Total (Turf)	0	0	0	0	
Career Total (AW)	1	0	0	0	0

Going (Turf): **Sf: 0-0 GS: 0-0 Gd: 0-0 GF: 0-0 Fm: 0-0**
Distance: 5f/6f: 0-1 7f-8f: 0-0 9f-13f: 0-0 14f+: 0-0
Track : LH: 0-1 RH: 0-0 Tight: 0-1 Gall: 0-0
Aids: Bl: 0-0 Vi: 0-0 Tstrap: 0-0 Ckp: 0-0
Best Rating: **33** 11/09 Ling 5f stand

Rulesn'regulations

107(104) (91)96

3-y-o b c Forzando-Al Awaalah (Mukaddamah (USA))

Matthew Salaman M Salaman & J H Widdows

Placings:011-100 (7227)

2009: 6^{1}G, 5^{0}GS, 6^{0}SD,

	Starts	1st	2nd	3rd	Win & Pl
Career Total (Turf)	3	1	0	0	12462
Career Total (AW)	3	2	0	0	7980

96 9/09 Asct 6f (0-100)H GD £12462
91 12/08 Ling 6f STD £3885
88 11/08 Wolv 5f20y STD £4094

Total win prize-money £20442

Going (Turf): Sf: 0-0 GS: 0-1 **Gd: 1-2** GF: 0-0 Fm: 0-0
Distance: **5f/6f: 3-5** 7f-8f: 0-1 9f-13f: 0-0 14f+: 0-0
Track : **LH: 2-2** RH: 0-1 **Tight: 2-2** Gall: 0-0
Aids: Bl: 0-0 Vi: 0-0 Tstrap: 0-0 Ckp: 0-0
Best Rating: **96** 9/09 Asct 6f good

Very useful; effective over 5f-6f; acts on fast ground and on Polytrack.

Ruling Reef

(100) (54)51

7-y-o b m Diktat-Horseshoe Reef (Mill Reef (USA))

M R Bosley Mrs Jean M O'Connor

Placings:0/065001040210**0**0/400054230/22300-0 (0566)

2009: 12^{0}SD,

	Starts	1st	2nd	3rd	Win & Pl
Career Total (Turf)	21	2	2	2	10028
Career Total (AW)	9	0	2	0	1048

57 8/05 Bevl 1m1f207y (0-75)H G-S £4322
44 6/05 Bath 1m5y (0-55)H FRM £2598

Total win prize-money £6921

Going (Turf): Sf: 0-1 **GS: 1-2** Gd: 0-7 GF: 0-3 **Fm: 1-8**
Distance: 5f/6f: 0-0 7f-8f: 0-3 **9f-13f: 2-26** 14f+: 0-1
Track : LH: 1-25 RH: 1-5 **Tight: 1-17** Gall: 0-1
Aids: Bl: 0-0 Vi: 0-0 Tstrap: 0-0 Ckp: 0-0
Best Rating: **57** 8/05 Bevl 1m1f207y gd-sft

Moderate; stays 1m4f; acts on most ground, including sand.

Rum Jungle

99(95) (73)87

5-y-o b g Robellino (USA)-Anna Karietta (Precocious)

H Candy The Earl Cadogan

Placings:4/0321231-006 (4501)
2009: 7[0]G, 7[0]GF, 7[6]G,

	Starts	1st	2nd	3rd	Win & Pl
Career Total (Turf)	10	2	2	1	15499
Career Total (AW)	1	0	0	1	337

87 9/08 Folk 7f (0-85)H SFT £5046
86 8/08 NmkJ 7f (0-85)H G-F £6476
Total win prize-money £11522

Going (Turf): **Sf: 1-3** GS: 0-1 Gd: 0-3 **GF: 1-3** Fm: 0-0
Distance: 5f/6f: 0-0 **7f-8f: 2-9** 9f-13f: 0-2 14f+: 0-0
Track : LH: 0-1 RH: 0-5 Tight: 0-2 Gall: 0-1
Aids: Bl: 0-0 Vi: 0-0 Tstrap: 0-0 Ckp: 0-0
Best Rating: **87** 9/08 Folk 7f soft

Useful; effective at 7f-1m; acts on fast and easy ground; also goes on Polytrack.

Rum King (USA)

100 **92**
2-y-o b/br c Montbrook (USA)-Cut Class Leanne (USA) (Cutlass (USA))
R Hannon Sir David Seale

Placings:0311 (7150)
2009: 7[0]GS, 6[3]GF, 6[1]GF, 6[1]G,

	Starts	1st	2nd	3rd	Win & Pl
Career Total (Turf)	4	2	0	1	13061

92 10/09 NmkR 6f (0-126) GD £7477
82 10/09 NmkR 6f G-F £5180
Total win prize-money £12658

Going (Turf): Sf: 0-0 GS: 0-1 **Gd: 1-1 GF: 1-2** Fm: 0-0
Distance: **5f/6f: 2-3** 7f-8f: 0-1 9f-13f: 0-0 14f+: 0-0
Track : LH: 0-0 RH: 0-0 Tight: 0-0 Gall: 0-0
Aids: Bl: 0-0 Vi: 0-0 Tstrap: 0-0 Ckp: 0-0
Best Rating: **92** 10/09 NmkR 6f good

Useful; effective at 6f and acts on fast ground.

Rum Raisin

96(82) (63)**65**
3-y-o b f Invincible Spirit (IRE)-Femme Femme (USA) (Lyphard (USA))
John Joseph Murphy Mrs John J Murphy

Placings:00053-060006502 (6847)
2009: 7[0]HY, 8[6]G, 6[0]G, 8[0]SD, 8[0]GY, 6[6]S, 8[5]G, 9[0]G, 7[2]G,

	Starts	1st	2nd	3rd	Win & Pl
Career Total (Turf)	12	0	1	0	867
Career Total (AW)	2	0	0	1	588

Going (Turf): **Sf: 0-4 GS: 0-0 Gd: 0-7 GF: 0-0 Fm: 0-0**
Distance: 5f/6f: 0-3 7f-8f: 0-8 9f-13f: 0-3 14f+: 0-0
Track : LH: 0-10 RH: 0-1 Tight: 0-1 Gall: 0-1
Aids: Bl: 0-1 Vi: 0-0 Tstrap: 0-0 Ckp: 0-0
Best Rating: **65** 10/09 Catt 7f good

Modest; effective over 1m; acts on Polytrack.

Rumble Of Thunder (IRE)

108(101) (77)**89**
3-y-o b g Fath (USA)-Honey Storm (IRE) (Mujadil (USA))
D W P Arbuthnot Francis Ward and Anthony Ward

Placings:345223-3010222 (6453)
2009: 11[3]SD, 12[0]GF, 10[1]GS, 9[0]G, 10[2]G, 10[2]GF, 10[2]GF,

	Starts	1st	2nd	3rd	Win & Pl
Career Total (Turf)	10	1	4	1	11840
Career Total (AW)	3	0	1	2	2671

81 5/09 Bath 1m2f46y (0-75)H G-S £2914
Total win prize-money £2914

Going (Turf): Sf: 0-0 **GS: 1-2** Gd: 0-3 GF: 0-5 Fm: 0-0
Distance: 5f/6f: 0-3 7f-8f: 0-1 **9f-13f: 1-9** 14f+: 0-0
Track : **LH: 1-5** RH: 0-3 **Tight: 1-6** Gall: 0-2
Aids: Bl: 0-0 Vi: 0-0 Tstrap: 0-0 Ckp: 0-0
Best Rating: **89** 8/09 Sand 1m2f7y gd-fm

Useful front runner; stays 1m2f and acts on most ground and on Polytrack.

Rumool

83(94) (85)**66**
2-y-o b c Exceed And Excel (AUS)-Silent Heir (AUS) (Sunday Silence (USA))
C E Brittain Saeed Manana

Placings:51 (2599)
2009: 6[5]GF, 6[1]SD,

	Starts	1st	2nd	3rd	Win & Pl
Career Total (Turf)	1	0	0	0	0
Career Total (AW)	1	1	0	0	5019

85 6/09 Kemp 6f STD £5018
Total win prize-money £5019

Going (Turf): **Sf: 0-0 GS: 0-0 Gd: 0-0 GF: 0-1 Fm: 0-0**
Distance: **5f/6f: 1-2** 7f-8f: 0-0 9f-13f: 0-0 14f+: 0-0
Track : LH: 0-0 **RH: 1-1** Tight: 0-0 Gall: 0-0
Aids: Bl: 0-0 Vi: 0-0 Tstrap: 0-0 Ckp: 0-0
Best Rating: **85** 6/09 Kemp 6f stand

Useful; stays 6f and acts on Polytrack.

Rumoush (USA)

(94) (76)
2-y-o b f Rahy (USA)-Sarayir (USA) (Mr Prospector (USA))
M P Tregoning Hamdan Al Maktoum

Placings:1 (7388)
2009: 8[1]SD,

	Starts	1st	2nd	3rd	Win & Pl
Career Total (Turf)	0	0	0	0	
Career Total (AW)	1	1	0	0	3412

76 11/09 Ling 1m STD £3412
Total win prize-money £3412

Going (Turf): **Sf: 0-0 GS: 0-0 Gd: 0-0 GF: 0-0 Fm: 0-0**
Distance: 5f/6f: 0-0 **7f-8f: 1-1** 9f-13f: 0-0 14f+: 0-0
Track : **LH: 1-1** RH: 0-0 **Tight: 1-1** Gall: 0-0
Aids: Bl: 0-0 Vi: 0-0 Tstrap: 0-0 Ckp: 0-0
Best Rating: **76** 11/09 Ling 1m stand

Very useful prospect; effective over 1m; acts on Polytrack.

Rumramah (USA)

81(79) (32)**56**
3-y-o b f Mr Greeley (USA)-She's Vested (USA) (Boundary (USA))
D M Simcock Abdullah Saeed Belhab

Placings:0-050 (6497)
2009: 7[0]SD, 7[5]G, 9[0]SF,

	Starts	1st	2nd	3rd	Win & Pl
Career Total (Turf)	2	0	0	0	0
Career Total (AW)	2	0	0	0	

Going (Turf): **Sf: 0-0 GS: 0-0 Gd: 0-2 GF: 0-0 Fm: 0-0**
Distance: 5f/6f: 0-0 7f-8f: 0-3 9f-13f: 0-1 14f+: 0-0
Track : LH: 0-2 RH: 0-0 Tight: 0-2 Gall: 0-0
Aids: Bl: 0-0 Vi: 0-0 Tstrap: 0-0 Ckp: 0-0
Best Rating: **56** 9/08 Yarm 6f3y good

Run For Ede's

106(100) (71)**84**
5-y-o b m Peintre Celebre (USA)-Raincloud (Rainbow Quest (USA))
P M Phelan Ede's (uk) Ltd

Placings:5/306562020/052103640-14311420 (6936)
2009: 11[1]GS, 10[4]G, 10[3]G, 12[1]G, 12[1]G, 12[4]G, 12[2]G, 11[0]G,

	Starts	1st	2nd	3rd	Win & Pl
Career Total (Turf)	18	4	1	3	27085
Career Total (AW)	9	0	3	0	2214

77 7/09 Epsm 1m4f10y (0-80)H GD £5180
79 7/09 Asct 1m4f (0-85)H GD £7123
73 4/09 Wind 1m3f135y (0-80)H G-S £4857
72 7/08 Wind 1m67y (0-80)H GD £4857
Total win prize-money £22019

Going (Turf): Sf: 0-0 GS: 1-5 **Gd: 3-12** GF: 0-1 Fm: 0-0
Distance: 5f/6f: 0-0 7f-8f: 0-10 **9f-13f: 4-17** 14f+: 0-0
Track : LH: 1-13 **RH: 2-11 Tight: 3-19** Gall: 1-3
Aids: Bl: 0-0 Vi: 0-0 Tstrap: 1-13 Ckp: 1-13
Best Rating: **84** 7/09 Asct 1m4f good

Fair; effective over 1m4f; acts on good ground and on Polytrack; has worn headgear.

Run For The Hills

104 **105**
3-y-o b c Oasis Dream-Maid For The Hills (Indian Ridge)
J H M Gosden Normandie Stud Ltd

Placings:321-0063 (6427)
2009: 6[0]G, 6[0]G, 6[6]G, 5[3]GF,

	Starts	1st	2nd	3rd	Win & Pl
Career Total (Turf)	7	1	1	2	16787

96 10/08 NmkR 6f GD £6476
Total win prize-money £6476

Going (Turf): Sf: 0-0 GS: 0-0 **Gd: 1-5** GF: 0-2 Fm: 0-0
Distance: **5f/6f: 1-6** 7f-8f: 0-1 9f-13f: 0-0 14f+: 0-0
Track : LH: 0-0 RH: 0-0 Tight: 0-0 Gall: 0-0
Aids: Bl: 0-0 Vi: 0-0 Tstrap: 0-0 Ckp: 0-0
Best Rating: **105** 10/09 NmkR 5f gd-fm

Useful; Listed palced; effective at 6f; acts on good ground.

Run Free

95(109) (63)**53**
5-y-o b g Agnes World (USA)-Ellie Ardensky (Slip Anchor)
N Wilson The Run Free Partnership

Placings:024/62060003463/50053211-60300006300 (5953)
2009: 8[6]SS, 7[0]SD, 7[3]SD, 7[0]SD, 8[0]SD, 10[0]GF, 9[0]GF, 7[6]SD, 12[3]G, 12[0]S, 10[0]GF,

	Starts	1st	2nd	3rd	Win & Pl
Career Total (Turf)	18	0	3	1	3873
Career Total (AW)	15	2	0	4	4984

63 12/08 Sthl 7f (0-60)H STD £1706
63 12/08 Sthl 7f (0-55)H STD £1706
Total win prize-money £3412

Going (Turf): **Sf: 0-4 GS: 0-2 Gd: 0-6 GF: 0-6 Fm: 0-0**
Distance: 5f/6f: 0-2 **7f-8f: 2-15** 9f-13f: 0-16 14f+: 0-0
Track : **LH: 2-26** RH: 0-6 Tight: 0-14 Gall: 0-1
Aids: Bl: 0-0 Vi: 0-1 Tstrap: 0-4 Ckp: 0-4
Best Rating: **71** 5/07 Thsk 1m good

Moderate; stays 1m4f and acts on sand; has worn a visor and cheekpieces.

Runaway Pegasus (USA)

84 48

4-y-o b f Fusaichi Pegasus (USA)-Runaway Venus (USA) (Runaway Groom (CAN))

H R A Cecil H E Sheikh Sultan Bin Khalifa Al Nahyan

Placings:00-5 (1427)

2009: 12^5G,

	Starts	1st	2nd	3rd	Win & Pl
Career Total (Turf)	3	0	0	0	0

Going (Turf): Sf: 0-0 GS: 0-0 Gd: 0-3 GF: 0-0 Fm: 0-0
Distance: 5f/6f: 0-0 7f-8f: 0-1 9f-13f: 0-2 14f+: 0-0
Track: LH: 0-0 RH: 0-3 Tight: 0-1 Gall: 0-0
Aids: Bl: 0-1 Vi: 0-0 Tstrap: 0-0 Ckp: 0-0
Best Rating: 48 4/09 Folk 1m4f good

Running Buck (USA)

(96) (49)54

4-y-o b c Running Stag (USA)-Dinghy (USA) (Fortunate Prospect (USA))

A Bailey Allan McNamee

Placings:00006/06-040 (0775)

2009: 6^0SD, 7^4SD, 9^0SD,

	Starts	1st	2nd	3rd	Win & Pl
Career Total (Turf)	4	0	0	0	0
Career Total (AW)	6	0	0	0	0

Going (Turf): Sf: 0-0 GS: 0-0 Gd: 0-1 GF: 0-3 Fm: 0-0
Distance: 5f/6f: 0-6 7f-8f: 0-3 9f-13f: 0-1 14f+: 0-0
Track: LH: 0-6 RH: 0-1 Tight: 0-3 Gall: 0-2
Aids: Bl: 0-2 Vi: 0-3 Tstrap: 0-0 Ckp: 0-0
Best Rating: 54 7/07 Sand 5f6y good

Running Flush (USA)

93(96) (59)50

3-y-o ch g Grand Slam (USA)-Holiday Gold (USA) (Touch Gold (USA))

J R Gask Horses First Racing Limited

Placings:003666030 (7796)

2009: 6^0G, 6^0GF, 5^3SD, 6^6GS, 5^6SD, 6^6SD, 7^0SD, 7^3SD, 7^0SS,

	Starts	1st	2nd	3rd	Win & Pl
Career Total (Turf)	3	0	0	0	0
Career Total (AW)	6	0	0	2	784

Going (Turf): Sf: 0-0 GS: 0-1 Gd: 0-1 GF: 0-1 Fm: 0-0
Distance: 5f/6f: 0-4 7f-8f: 0-5 9f-13f: 0-0 14f+: 0-0
Track: LH: 0-4 RH: 0-2 Tight: 0-3 Gall: 0-0
Aids: Bl: 0-2 Vi: 0-0 Tstrap: 0-0 Ckp: 0-0
Best Rating: 59 10/09 Wolv 5f216y stand

Modest; suited by 5f and Polytrack.

Running Mate (IRE)

93 75

2-y-o b c Acclamation-It Takes Two (IRE) (Alzao (USA))

J H M Gosden H R H Princess Haya Of Jordan

Placings:44010 (4525)

2009: 6^4G, 6^4GF, 5^0GF, 6^1HY, 6^0S,

	Starts	1st	2nd	3rd	Win & Pl
Career Total (Turf)	5	1	0	0	4487
75 7/09 Nott 6f15y			HVY	£3885	

Total win prize-money £3886

Going (Turf): Sf: 1-2 GS: 0-0 Gd: 0-1 GF: 0-2 Fm: 0-0
Distance: 5f/6f: 0-4 **7f-8f: 1-1** 9f-13f: 0-0 14f+: 0-0
Track: LH: 0-0 RH: 0-0 Tight: 0-0 Gall: 0-0
Aids: Bl: 0-0 Vi: 0-1 Tstrap: 0-0 Ckp: 0-0
Best Rating: 75 7/09 Nott 6f15y heavy

Fair; speedily-bred; stays 6f; acts on most ground.

Runswick Bay

80 27

4-y-o b g Intikhab (USA)-Upend (Main Reef)

G M Moore John Lishman

Placings:5333114 0/P-0000 (3974)

2009: 8^0GS, 12^0GS, 10^0GS, 11^0GS,

	Starts	1st	2nd	3rd	Win & Pl
Career Total (Turf)	13	2	0	3	10943
84 7/07 Pont 6f			GD	£6477	
78 6/07 Rdcr 7f			SFT	£2169	

Total win prize-money £8647

Going (Turf): Sf: 1-2 GS: 0-7 **Gd: 1-2** GF: 0-2 Fm: 0-0
Distance: 5f/6f: 1-5 7f-8f: 1-5 9f-13f: 0-3 14f+: 0-0
Track: LH: 1-4 RH: 0-2 Tight: 0-3 Gall: 0-1
Aids: Bl: 0-0 Vi: 0-0 Tstrap: 0-0 Ckp: 0-0
Best Rating: 84 7/07 Pont 6f good

Useful; suited by 6f; acts on most ground; suited by forcing tactics.

Rupestrian

92(90) (70)73

3-y-o b g Fantastic Light (USA)-Upper Strata (Shirley Heights)

Tim Vaughan (M Johnston 29/3) The Select Racing Club Limited

Placings:044-16 (1019)

2009: 12^1SD, 10^6G,

	Starts	1st	2nd	3rd	Win & Pl
Career Total (Turf)	3	0	0	0	409
Career Total (AW)	2	1	0	0	3018
70 3/09 Ling 1m4f			STD	£2729	

Total win prize-money £2730

Going (Turf): Sf: 0-0 GS: 0-2 Gd: 0-1 GF: 0-0 Fm: 0-0
Distance: 5f/6f: 0-0 7f-8f: 0-2 **9f-13f: 1-3** 14f+: 0-0
Track: LH: 1-4 RH: 0-0 **Tight: 1-3** Gall: 0-1
Aids: Bl: 0-0 Vi: 0-0 Tstrap: 0-0 Ckp: 0-0
Best Rating: 73 10/08 Newb 1m gd-sft

Fair; stays 1m and acts on Polytrack.

Russian Angel

98(102) (54)54

5-y-o gr m Baryshnikov (AUS)-Eventuality (Petoski)

Jean-Rene Auvray Nigel Kelly And Alison Auvray

Placings:43-4033455320 (7802)

2009: 11^4SD, 10^0G, 8^3GF, 8^3GF, 9^4G, 8^5G, 7^5SD, 8^3SD, 9^2SD, 8^0SD,

	Starts	1st	2nd	3rd	Win & Pl
Career Total (Turf)	5	0	0	2	2422
Career Total (AW)	7	0	1	2	1399

Going (Turf): Sf: 0-0 GS: 0-0 Gd: 0-3 GF: 0-2 Fm: 0-0
Distance: 5f/6f: 0-0 7f-8f: 0-3 9f-13f: 0-9 14f+: 0-0
Track: LH: 0-4 RH: 0-4 Tight: 0-3 Gall: 0-0
Aids: Bl: 0-0 Vi: 0-0 Tstrap: 0-0 Ckp: 0-0
Best Rating: 54 11/09 Wolv 1m1f103y stand

Moderate; stays 1m3f; acts on fast ground; goes on Polytrack.

Russian Brigadier

81 38

2-y-o b g Xaar-Brigadiers Bird (IRE) (Mujadil (USA))

M Brittain Northgate Yellow

Placings:0 (6990)

2009: 7^0G,

	Starts	1st	2nd	3rd	Win & Pl
Career Total (Turf)	1	0	0	0	

Going (Turf): Sf: 0-0 GS: 0-0 Gd: 0-1 GF: 0-0 Fm: 0-0
Distance: 5f/6f: 0-0 7f-8f: 0-1 9f-13f: 0-0 14f+: 0-0
Track: LH: 0-0 RH: 0-0 Tight: 0-0 Gall: 0-0
Aids: Bl: 0-0 Vi: 0-0 Tstrap: 0-0 Ckp: 0-0
Best Rating: 38 10/09 Donc 7f good

Russian Davis (IRE)

94(93) (68)62

2-y-o b c Mull Of Kintyre (USA)-Sunny Isles Beauty (USA) (Tale Of The Cat (USA))

R M H Cowell Stennett/Morley/Warner

Placings:0461365 (6983)

2009: 5^0G, 5^4G, 5^6SD, 7^1SD, 7^3SD, 7^6SF, 6^5G,

	Starts	1st	2nd	3rd	Win & Pl
Career Total (Turf)	3	0	0	0	0
Career Total (AW)	4	1	0	1	3346
67 8/09 Kemp 7f	(0-70)		STD	£2590	

Total win prize-money £2590

Going (Turf): Sf: 0-0 GS: 0-0 Gd: 0-3 GF: 0-0 Fm: 0-0
Distance: 5f/6f: 0-4 **7f-8f: 1-3** 9f-13f: 0-0 14f+: 0-0
Track: LH: 0-2 **RH: 1-1** Tight: 0-2 Gall: 0-0
Aids: Bl: 0-0 Vi: 0-0 Tstrap: 0-0 Ckp: 0-0
Best Rating: 68 9/09 Wolv 7f32y stand

Modest; effective at 7f; acts on good ground and Polytrack.

Russian Empress (IRE)

106(102) (95)95

5-y-o b m Trans Island-Russian Countess (USA) (Nureyev (USA))

David P Myerscough Mrs P Myerscough

Placings:53213/1235506-40000056320 (7566a)

2009: 8^4S, 7^0HY, 8^0HY, 8^0GY, 7^0GY, 6^0G, 6^5S, 8^6SD, 8^3SD, 6^2SD, 6^0SD,

	Starts	1st	2nd	3rd	Win & Pl
Career Total (Turf)	17	1	2	2	31611
Career Total (AW)	6	1	1	2	13666
94 4/08 Naas 7f	(60-100)H		YLD	£11966	
78 10/07 Dund 6f			STD	£6069	

Total win prize-money £18037

Going (Turf): Sf: 0-7 GS: 0-0 Gd: 0-4 GF: 0-1 Fm: 0-1
Distance: 5f/6f: 1-6 7f-8f: 1-16 9f-13f: 0-1 14f+: 0-0
Track: LH: 1-11 RH: 0-6 Tight: 0-1 Gall: 0-2
Aids: Bl: 0-0 Vi: 0-0 Tstrap: 0-0 Ckp: 0-0

Best Rating: 95 11/09 Dund 1m stand

Very useful; effective at around 1m; suited by easy ground.

Russian Epic

88(94) (58)84

5-y-o b g Diktat-Russian Rhapsody (Cosmonaut)
Andrew Turnell Cromhall Stud

Placings:021345/045010-5 **(1753)**
2009: 11^{5}GF,

	Starts	1st	2nd	3rd	Win & Pl
Career Total (Turf)	12	2	1	1	10615
Career Total (AW)	1	0	0	0	

84 8/08 Leic 1m60y (0-75)H GD £3885
79 5/07 Leic 7f9y SFT £3238
Total win prize-money £7125

Going (Turf): **Sf: 1-3** GS: 0-2 **Gd: 1-4** GF: 0-3 Fm: 0-0
Distance: 5f/6f: 0-0 7f-8f: 1-4 9f-13f: 1-9 14f+: 0-0
Track : LH: 0-2 **RH: 1-7** Tight: 0-3 Gall: 0-1
Aids: Bl: 0-0 Vi: 0-0 Tstrap: 0-0 Ckp: 0-0
Best Rating: 84 8/08 Leic 1m60y good

Fair; effective at around 7f; acts in soft ground.

Russian George (IRE)

98(96) (76)81

3-y-o ch g Sendawar (IRE)-Mannsara (IRE) (Royal Academy (USA))
S Gollings (T P Tate 4/7) P J Martin

Placings:3442-1204200 **(6680)**
2009: 8^{1}GF, 8^{2}GF, 7^{0}G, 8^{4}GF, 9^{2}GF, 10^{0}GF, 10^{0}G,

	Starts	1st	2nd	3rd	Win & Pl
Career Total (Turf)	10	1	3	0	12664
Career Total (AW)	1	0	0	1	578

61 5/09 Thsk 1m G-F £4274
Total win prize-money £4274

Going (Turf): Sf: 0-1 GS: 0-0 Gd: 0-2 **GF: 1-7** Fm: 0-0
Distance: 5f/6f: 0-0 **7f-8f: 1-6** 9f-13f: 0-5 14f+: 0-0
Track : **LH: 1-5** RH: 0-4 **Tight: 1-3** Gall: 0-2
Aids: Bl: 0-0 Vi: 0-0 Tstrap: 0-0 Ckp: 0-0
Best Rating: 81 8/09 Ripn 1m1f170y gd-fm

Useful; stays 1m and acts on fast ground.

Russian Invader (IRE)

92(100) (66)68

5-y-o ch g Acatenango (GER)-Ukraine Venture (Slip Anchor)
R C Guest Future Racing (Notts) Limited

Placings:2031/0-**42035005** **(7840)**
2009: 12^{4}SD, 12^{2}SD, 16^{0}SD, 16^{3}G, 16^{5}SD, 16^{0}G, 14^{0}SD, 12^{5}SS,

	Starts	1st	2nd	3rd	Win & Pl
Career Total (Turf)	6	1	1	2	6467
Career Total (AW)	7	0	1	0	605

84 10/07 Wind 1m3f135y (0-85)H GD £4728
Total win prize-money £4728

Going (Turf): Sf: 0-1 GS: 0-0 **Gd: 1-3** GF: 0-2 Fm: 0-0
Distance: 5f/6f: 0-0 7f-8f: 0-0 **9f-13f: 1-8** 14f+: 0-5
Track : LH: 0-11 RH: 0-1 **Tight: 1-3** Gall: 0-0
Aids: Bl: 0-3 Vi: 0-0 Tstrap: 0-0 Ckp: 0-0
Best Rating: 84 10/07 Wind 1m3f135y good

Fair; stays 1m4f; acts on fast and easy ground; has worn an eyeshield and blinkers.

Russian Jar (IRE)

101 90

3-y-o b g Xaar-Lady Windermere (IRE) (Lake Coniston (IRE))
M A Jarvis J A R Partnership

Placings:12250 **(6732)**
2009: 8^{1}GF, 8^{2}GF, 7^{2}GF, 7^{5}GF, 8^{0}S,

	Starts	1st	2nd	3rd	Win & Pl
Career Total (Turf)	5	1	2	0	8329

81 5/09 Leic 1m60y G-F £3238
Total win prize-money £3238

Going (Turf): Sf: 0-1 GS: 0-0 Gd: 0-0 **GF: 1-4** Fm: 0-0
Distance: 5f/6f: 0-0 7f-8f: 0-4 **9f-13f: 1-1** 14f+: 0-0
Track : LH: 0-0 **RH: 1-1** Tight: 0-0 Gall: 0-0
Aids: Bl: 0-0 Vi: 0-0 Tstrap: 0-0 Ckp: 0-0
Best Rating: 90 8/09 NmkJ 7f gd-fm

Useful; stays 1m; acts on fast ground.

Russian Music (USA)

91(105) (60)51

4-y-o b g Stravinsky (USA)-Private Seductress (USA) (Private Account (USA))
Ian Williams (M W Easterby 16/9) R J Turton

Placings:00020521 **(7751)**
2009: 5^{0}GF, 6^{0}F, 5^{0}GS, 8^{2}SD, 7^{0}S, 8^{5}GF, 12^{2}SD, 13^{1}SD,

	Starts	1st	2nd	3rd	Win & Pl
Career Total (Turf)	5	0	0	0	0
Career Total (AW)	3	1	2	0	3256

60 12/09 Wolv 1m5f194y (0-55)H STD £2047
Total win prize-money £2047

Going (Turf): **Sf: 0-1 GS: 0-1 Gd: 0-0 GF: 0-2 Fm: 0-1**
Distance: 5f/6f: 0-3 7f-8f: 0-2 9f-13f: 0-2 **14f+: 1-1**
Track : **LH: 1-6** RH: 0-1 **Tight: 1-3** Gall: 0-0
Aids: Bl: 0-4 Vi: 0-0 Tstrap: 0-0 Ckp: 0-0
Best Rating: 60 12/09 Wolv 1m5f194y stand

Moderate; stays 1m6f; acts on Polytrack and Fibresand.

Russian Rave

95(100) (76)68

3-y-o ch f Danehill Dancer (IRE)-Russian Ruby (FR) (Vettori (IRE))
J G Portman The Traditionalists

Placings:4400-35614500 **(6699)**
2009: 7^{3}SD, 7^{5}F, 7^{6}GF, 7^{1}SD, 8^{4}SD, 7^{5}SD, 8^{0}GF, 7^{0}SS,

	Starts	1st	2nd	3rd	Win & Pl
Career Total (Turf)	7	0	0	0	722
Career Total (AW)	5	1	0	1	3423

76 6/09 Kemp 7f (0-70)H STD £2590
Total win prize-money £2590

Going (Turf): **Sf: 0-0 GS: 0-0 Gd: 0-1 GF: 0-5 Fm: 0-1**
Distance: 5f/6f: 0-1 **7f-8f: 1-10** 9f-13f: 0-1 14f+: 0-0
Track : LH: 0-3 **RH: 1-5** Tight: 0-3 Gall: 0-0
Aids: Bl: 0-0 Vi: 0-0 Tstrap: 0-0 Ckp: 0-0
Best Rating: 76 6/09 Kemp 7f stand

Modest; stays 7f and acts on Polytrack.

Russian Rock (IRE)

88 78

2-y-o b c Rock Of Gibraltar (IRE)- Mala Mala (IRE) (Brief Truce (USA))
R A Teal M Vickers

Placings:510 **(2995)**
2009: 5^{5}G, 5^{1}F, 5^{0}GF,

	Starts	1st	2nd	3rd	Win & Pl
Career Total (Turf)	3	1	0	0	6476

78 5/09 Sals 5f FRM £6476
Total win prize-money £6476

Going (Turf): Sf: 0-0 GS: 0-0 Gd: 0-1 GF: 0-1 **Fm: 1-1**
Distance: **5f/6f: 1-3** 7f-8f: 0-0 9f-13f: 0-0 14f+: 0-0
Track : LH: 0-0 RH: 0-0 Tight: 0-0 Gall: 0-0
Aids: Bl: 0-0 Vi: 0-0 Tstrap: 0-0 Ckp: 0-0
Best Rating: 78 5/09 Sals 5f firm

Fair half-brother to sprinter Contest out of a half-sister to Irish 1000 Guineas winner Tarascon; effective at 5f on fast ground.

Russian Rocket (IRE)

103(101) (72)74

7-y-o b g Indian Rocket-Soviet Girl (IRE) (Soviet Star (USA))
Mrs C A Dunnett Mrs Christine Dunnett

Placings:052125010/000/**05**0645210150**040**/**40560000520**/**10035120**-**46451360003** **(7100)**
2009: 5^{4}SD, 6^{8}G, 5^{4}SD, 5^{5}SD, 5^{1}GF, 5^{3}SD, 5^{6}GS, 5^{0}SD, 5^{0}GF, 5^{0}S, 5^{3}G,

	Starts	1st	2nd	3rd	Win & Pl
Career Total (Turf)	32	4	4	2	17900
Career Total (AW)	25	3	1	1	10153

70 7/09 Nott 5f13y (0-70)H G-F £2729
59 3/08 Sthl 5f STD £1774
74 7/06 Ling 6f (0-70)H STD £3238
69 6/06 Nott 6f15y (0-65)H G-F £2730
82 10/04 Yarm 5f43y (0-85) SFT £6708
73 6/04 Ling 5f E STD £3406
Total win prize-money £20588

Going (Turf): Sf: 1-5 GS: 1-5 Gd: 0-8 **GF: 2-13** Fm: 0-1
Distance: **5f/6f: 6-50** 7f-8f: 1-7 9f-13f: 0-0 14f+: 0-0
Track : **LH: 2-17** RH: 0-3 **Tight: 2-14** Gall: 0-2
Aids: Bl: 0-0 Vi: 0-0 Tstrap: 0-0 Ckp: 0-0
Best Rating: 83 7/04 Ling 5f good

Modest; acts over 5f-6f; acts on most ground and on sand.

Russian Sage (SAF)

113(102) (94)122

5-y-o b h Jallad (USA)-Sage Blue (SAF) (Badger Land (USA))
M F De Kock Team Valor Intl, L Nestadt & G Barber

Placings:321320111/21210-220004 **(7323)**
2009: 8^{2}GF, 8^{2}GF, 12^{0}G, 8^{0}GF, 9^{0}G, 10^{4}SD,

	Starts	1st	2nd	3rd	Win & Pl
Career Total (Turf)	19	6	6	2	129372
Career Total (AW)	1	0	0	0	551

6/08 Grey 1m2f GD £45955
1/08 Keni 1m2f GD £22977
12/07 Keni 1m GD £11322
11/07 Keni 1m GD £2807
11/07 Keni 7f GD £2717
6/07 Keni 5f SFT £2491
Total win prize-money £88273

Going (Turf): Sf: 1-6 GS: 0-0 **Gd: 5-10** GF: 0-3 Fm: 0-0
Distance: 5f/6f: 1-5 **7f-8f: 3-7** 9f-13f: 2-8 14f+: 0-0
Track : LH: 0-4 RH: 0-1 Tight: 0-0 Gall: 0-4

Aids: Bl: 0-0 Vi: 0-0 Tstrap: 0-0 Ckp: 0-0

Best Rating: **122** 3/09 Ndas 1m194y gd-fm

Smart; stays 1m2f; acts on fast and soft ground and Polytrack.

Russian Saint

(25) **32**

3-y-o b f Red Ransom (USA)-Tessara (GER) (Big Shuffle (USA))

D Shaw Derek Shaw

Placings:0-0 **(1605)**

2009: 8^{0}SD,

	Starts	1st	2nd	3rd	Win & Pl
Career Total (Turf)	1	0	0	0	
Career Total (AW)	1	0	0	0	

Going (Turf): **Sf: 0-1 GS: 0-0 Gd: 0-0 GF: 0-0 Fm: 0-0**

Distance: 5f/6f: 0-0 7f-8f: 0-2 9f-13f: 0-0 14f+: 0-0

Track : LH: 0-1 RH: 0-1 Tight: 0-0 Gall: 0-0

Aids: Bl: 0-0 Vi: 0-0 Tstrap: 0-0 Ckp: 0-0

Best Rating: **32** 8/08 Wwck 7f26y soft

Russian Spirit

105 **91**

3-y-o b f Falbrav (IRE)-Russian Rhapsody (Cosmonaut)

M A Jarvis Cromhall Stud

Placings:5-212310 **(6994)**

2009: 6^{2}GF, 6^{1}S, 6^{2}G, 6^{3}GF, 5^{1}G, 6^{0}G,

	Starts	1st	2nd	3rd	Win & Pl
Career Total (Turf)	7	2	2	1	13604

91	10/09	York	5f	(0-85)H	GD	£6540
84	7/09	Donc	6f		SFT	£3412

Total win prize-money £9953

Going (Turf): **Sf: 1-1** GS: 0-1 **Gd: 1-3** GF: 0-2 Fm: 0-0

Distance: **5f/6f: 2-6** 7f-8f: 0-1 9f-13f: 0-0 14f+: 0-0

Track : LH: 0-1 RH: 0-0 Tight: 0-0 Gall: 0-1

Aids: Bl: 0-0 Vi: 0-0 Tstrap: 0-0 Ckp: 0-0

Best Rating: **91** 10/09 York 5f good

Useful; effective at 6f; acts on fast and soft ground.

Russian Symphony (USA)

(104) (82)**81**

8-y-o ch g Stravinsky (USA)-Backwoods Teacher (USA) (Woodman (USA))

C R Egerton Longmoor Holdings Ltd

Placings:05/060021614/2123304620200/000/004002054/0020202-462 **(0891)**

2009: 5^{4}SD, 5^{6}SF, 6^{2}SD,

	Starts	1st	2nd	3rd	Win & Pl
Career Total (Turf)	20	0	1	1	7547
Career Total (AW)	26	3	9	1	31340

95	2/05	Ling	6f	(0-85)H	STD	£5987
88	12/04	Wolv	7f32y	(0-77)H	STD	£4079
71	11/04	Wolv	7f32y		STD	£3523

Total win prize-money £13590

Going (Turf): **Sf: 0-1 GS: 0-4 Gd: 0-6 GF: 0-9 Fm: 0-0**

Distance: 5f/6f: 1-31 **7f-8f: 2-15** 9f-13f: 0-0 14f+: 0-0

Track : **LH: 3-25** RH: 0-3 **Tight: 3-22** Gall: 0-6

Aids: **Bl: 3-32** Vi: 0-0 Tstrap: 0-2 Ckp: 0-2

Best Rating: **95** 10/05 Ling 6f stand

Fair; effective over 5f-7f; acts on fast ground, but all wins to date have come on Polytrack; often wears blinkers.

Rusty Pelican

2-y-o ch g Tobougg (IRE)-Opalite (Opening Verse (USA))

P J Makin Mrs P J Makin

Placings:0 **(7024)**

2009: 7^{0}SD,

	Starts	1st	2nd	3rd	Win & Pl
Career Total (Turf)	0	0	0	0	
Career Total (AW)	1	0	0	0	

Going (Turf): **Sf: 0-0 GS: 0-0 Gd: 0-0 GF: 0-0 Fm: 0-0**

Distance: 5f/6f: 0-0 7f-8f: 0-1 9f-13f: 0-0 14f+: 0-0

Track : LH: 0-0 RH: 0-1 Tight: 0-0 Gall: 0-0

Aids: Bl: 0-0 Vi: 0-0 Tstrap: 0-0 Ckp: 0-0

Rutba

93(95) (70)**63**

4-y-o b f Act One-Elhilmeya (IRE) (Unfuwain (USA))

M P Tregoning William Lea Screed Mac's Plaster & Home

Placings:00/0501113-06 **(1732)**

2009: 15^{0}G, 16^{6}SD,

	Starts	1st	2nd	3rd	Win & Pl
Career Total (Turf)	7	3	0	0	7228
Career Total (AW)	4	0	0	1	482

63	10/08	Bath	2m1f34y	(0-75)H	G-S	£2914
62	9/08	Ling	2m	(0-65)H	SFT	£2047
60	8/08	Yarm	1m6f17y	(0-65)H	G-S	£2266

Total win prize-money £7228

Going (Turf): Sf: 1-1 **GS: 2-2** Gd: 0-2 GF: 0-2 Fm: 0-0

Distance: 5f/6f: 0-0 7f-8f: 0-1 9f-13f: 0-2 **14f+: 3-8**

Track : **LH: 3-6** RH: 0-5 **Tight: 3-8** Gall: 0-0

Aids: Bl: 0-0 **Vi: 3-6** Tstrap: 0-0 Ckp: 0-0

Best Rating: **70** 11/08 Ling 2m stand

Modest; stays beyond 2m; acts on soft ground; has worn a visor.

Ruthle Babe

95(96) (66)**67**

2-y-o b f Exceed And Excel (AUS)-Lady Oriande (Makbul)

W J Haggas Exors of the Late F C T Wilson

Placings:654134 **(6827)**

2009: 5^{6}GF, 6^{5}GF, 5^{4}SD, 5^{1}GF, 5^{3}GF, 5^{4}SF,

	Starts	1st	2nd	3rd	Win & Pl
Career Total (Turf)	4	1	0	1	6490
Career Total (AW)	2	0	0	0	577

67	9/09	Ffos	5f	(0-85)	G-F	£4857

Total win prize-money £4857

Going (Turf): Sf: 0-0 GS: 0-0 Gd: 0-0 **GF: 1-4** Fm: 0-0

Distance: **5f/6f: 1-6** 7f-8f: 0-0 9f-13f: 0-0 14f+: 0-0

Track : LH: 0-2 RH: 0-0 Tight: 0-2 Gall: 0-0

Aids: Bl: 0-0 Vi: 0-0 Tstrap: 0-0 Ckp: 0-0

Best Rating: **67** 9/09 Ffos 5f gd-fm

Modest; effective over 5f; acts on fast ground.

Ruud Revenge (USA)

102 **76**

3-y-o b g Van Nistelrooy (USA)-Savannah's Revenge (USA) (West By West (USA))

Mrs D J Sanderson R J Budge

Placings:60-3240 **(2932)**

2009: 12^{3}GF, 12^{2}G, 12^{4}F, 12^{0}G,

	Starts	1st	2nd	3rd	Win & Pl
Career Total (Turf)	6	0	1	1	2321

Going (Turf): **Sf: 0-1 GS: 0-0 Gd: 0-2 GF: 0-2 Fm: 0-1**

Distance: 5f/6f: 0-0 7f-8f: 0-2 9f-13f: 0-4 14f+: 0-0

Track : LH: 0-5 RH: 0-0 Tight: 0-3 Gall: 0-1

Aids: Bl: 0-0 Vi: 0-0 Tstrap: 0-0 Ckp: 0-0

Best Rating: **76** 5/09 Thsk 1m4f good

Fair; stays 1m4f; handles fast ground.

Ruwain

95(102) (56)**48**

5-y-o b g Lujain (USA)-Ruwaya (USA) (Red Ransom (USA))

P J McBride P J McBride

Placings:0050/5000031604-100464600 **(7466)**

2009: 10^{1}SD, 12^{0}SD, 9^{0}SD, 10^{4}SD, 9^{6}SD, 10^{4}GF, 8^{6}SD, 9^{0}GF, 9^{0}SD,

	Starts	1st	2nd	3rd	Win & Pl
Career Total (Turf)	7	0	0	1	443
Career Total (AW)	16	2	0	0	4533

54	1/09	GrLe	1m2f	(0-50)H	STD	£1942
56	7/08	GrLe	1m2f	(0-65)H	STD	£2590

Total win prize-money £4533

Going (Turf): **Sf: 0-0 GS: 0-1 Gd: 0-0 GF: 0-6 Fm: 0-0**

Distance: 5f/6f: 0-0 7f-8f: 0-3 **9f-13f: 2-20** 14f+: 0-0

Track : **LH: 2-18** RH: 0-4 Tight: 0-12 **Gall: 2-4**

Aids: Bl: 0-1 Vi: 0-0 Tstrap: 0-0 Ckp: 0-0

Best Rating: **56** 7/08 GrLe 1m2f stand

Moderate; stays 1m2f and acts on Polytrack.

Ryan's Rock

11(91) (48)**33**

4-y-o b g Lujain (USA)-Diamond Jayne (IRE) (Royal Abjar (USA))

R J Price R J Price

Placings:0500/004-0 **(1741)**

2009: 8^{0}GF,

	Starts	1st	2nd	3rd	Win & Pl
Career Total (Turf)	5	0	0	0	
Career Total (AW)	3	0	0	0	0

Going (Turf): **Sf: 0-1 GS: 0-1 Gd: 0-1 GF: 0-2 Fm: 0-0**

Distance: 5f/6f: 0-0 7f-8f: 0-5 9f-13f: 0-3 14f+: 0-0

Track : LH: 0-3 RH: 0-4 Tight: 0-4 Gall: 0-0

Aids: Bl: 0-0 Vi: 0-0 Tstrap: 0-0 Ckp: 0-0

Best Rating: **48** 8/08 Ling 1m stand

Rydal (USA)

86(97) (61)**52**

8-y-o ch g Gilded Time (USA)-Tennis Partner (USA) (Northern Dancer (CAN))

Miss Jo Crowley Mrs Liz Nelson

Placings:42221/0406240145003/2023500002020/064/224 0202/50045-56500 **(6251)**

2009: 7^{5}SD, 7^{6}SD, 7^{5}SD, 7^{0}GF, 5^{0}SD,

	Starts	1st	2nd	3rd	Win & Pl
Career Total (Turf)	30	2	5	0	23576
Career Total (AW)	21	0	7	2	23018

89	8/04	Sand	5f6y	D(0-85)H	G-S	£6841
87	11/03	Muss	1m	D	G-F	£5671

Total win prize-money £12512

Going (Turf): Sf: 0-3 **GS: 1-6** Gd: 0-6 **GF: 1-12** Fm: 0-2
Distance: 5f/6f: 1-33 7f-8f: 1-16 9f-13f: 0-2 14f+: 0-0
Track : LH: 0-17 **RH: 1-7 Tight: 1-17** Gall: 0-1
Aids: Bl: 1-15 Vi: 1-10 Tstrap: 0-1 Ckp: 0-1
Best Rating: 94 1/05 Wolv 5f216y stand

Moderate; stays 1m but fully effective over as short as 5f; acts on varying ground; also goes on sand.

Ryedale Ovation (IRE)

96(106) (76)**73**

6-y-o b g Royal Applause-Passe Passe (USA) (Lear Fan (USA))

G L Moore (M Hill 1/4) G L Moore

Placings:5130/33400435/4500601/102005200125-04001256 **(1876)**

2009: 11^{0}SD, 12^{4}SD, 12^{0}SD, 6^{0}SD, 7^{1}SD, 8^{2}SD, 7^{5}GF, 7^{6}GF,

	Starts	1st	2nd	3rd	Win & Pl
Career Total (Turf)	**25**	**1**	**2**	**4**	**16586**
Career Total (AW)	**14**	**4**	**2**	**0**	**11299**

76 4/09 Kemp 7f STD £2047
69 10/08 Kemp 1m2f (0-75)H STD £3238
72 2/08 Kemp 1m3f (0-75)H STD £2590
68 11/07 Kemp 1m3f (0-60)H STD £2047
71 4/05 Rdcr 5f GD £3721
Total win prize-money £13645

Going (Turf): Sf: 0-5 GS: 0-1 **Gd: 1-8** GF: 0-11 Fm: 0-0
Distance: 5f/6f: 1-13 7f-8f: 1-11 **9f-13f: 3-15** 14f+: 0-0
Track : LH: 0-10 **RH: 4-14** Tight: 0-5 Gall: 0-2
Aids: Bl: 0-2 Vi: 0-0 Tstrap: 0-2 Ckp: 0-2
Best Rating: 83 4/06 Ripn 6f soft

Modest; stays 1m3f; acts on good and soft ground as well as Polytrack.

Ryedane (IRE)

100(102) (71)**66**

7-y-o b g Danetime (IRE)-Miss Valediction (IRE) (Petardia)

T D Easterby Ryedale Partners No 5

Placings:0305300251101000001/00006001103600445/0454323321130/0004004152061263-5061330535000 **(6216)**

2009: 5^{5}SD, 5^{0}GS, 5^{6}F, 5^{1}GF, 5^{3}F, 5^{3}GF, 5^{0}GF, 5^{5}G, 6^{3}GF, 5^{5}G, 5^{0}SD, 5^{0}GF, 6^{0}GF,

	Starts	1st	2nd	3rd	Win & Pl
Career Total (Turf)	**57**	**6**	**2**	**8**	**32586**
Career Total (AW)	**21**	**5**	**3**	**3**	**22184**

62 5/09 Carl 5f (0-60)H G-F £2047
67 11/08 Wolv 5f20y (0-60)H STD £3070
66 8/08 Thsk 6f (0-55)H GD £2873
75 9/07 Wolv 5f216y (0-70)H STD £3071
67 8/07 Catt 5f212y (0-75)H G-F £3238
77 7/06 Newc 5f (0-80)H G-F £5505
74 7/06 Catt 5f (0-70)H FRM £5181
81 12/05 Wolv 5f216y (0-75)H STD £2910
84 7/05 Catt 5f (0-85)H G-F £6741
84 12/04 Wolv 5f20y (0-85) STD £5356
71 12/04 Wolv 5f216y (0-75) STD £4163
Total win prize-money £44160

Going (Turf): Sf: 0-2 GS: 0-11Gd: 1-10**GF: 4-24** Fm: 1-10
Distance: **5f/6f: 11-77** 7f-8f: 0-1 9f-13f: 0-1 14f+: 0-0
Track : **LH: 6-33** RH: 1-5 **Tight: 6-28** Gall: 1-4
Aids: **Bl: 5-35** Vi: 0-0 Tstrap: 0-0 Ckp: 0-0
Best Rating: 84 7/05 Catt 5f gd-fm

Modest sprinter; stays 6f; acts on Polytrack and fast turf; has worn blinkers and an eyeshield.

Ryedon Bye

80 **48**

3-y-o ch g Distant Music (USA)-Payphone (Anabaa (USA))

T D Easterby Rapcalone

Placings:6-000 **(1926)**

2009: 6^{0}GF, 7^{0}GF, 8^{0}F,

	Starts	1st	2nd	3rd	Win & Pl
Career Total (Turf)	**4**	**0**	**0**	**0**	**0**

Going (Turf): Sf: 0-1 GS: 0-0 Gd: 0-0 GF: 0-2 Fm: 0-1
Distance: 5f/6f: 0-2 7f-8f: 0-2 9f-13f: 0-0 14f+: 0-0
Track : LH: 0-0 RH: 0-1 Tight: 0-0 Gall: 0-0
Aids: Bl: 0-0 Vi: 0-0 Tstrap: 0-0 Ckp: 0-0
Best Rating: 48 6/08 Carl 5f193y soft

Ryker (IRE)

85(94) (62)**57**

3-y-o ch g Halling (USA)-Charlock (IRE) (Nureyev (USA))

J W Hills R J Tufft

Placings:000043 **(7765)**

2009: 7^{0}GS, 7^{0}GF, 8^{0}SD, 8^{0}SD, 9^{4}SD, 11^{3}SD,

	Starts	1st	2nd	3rd	Win & Pl
Career Total (Turf)	**2**	**0**	**0**	**0**	
Career Total (AW)	**4**	**0**	**0**	**1**	**302**

Going (Turf): Sf: 0-0 GS: 0-1 Gd: 0-0 GF: 0-1 Fm: 0-0
Distance: 5f/6f: 0-0 7f-8f: 0-4 9f-13f: 0-2 14f+: 0-0
Track : LH: 0-2 RH: 0-2 Tight: 0-2 Gall: 0-0
Aids: Bl: 0-0 Vi: 0-0 Tstrap: 0-0 Ckp: 0-0
Best Rating: 62 12/09 Wolv 1m1f103y stand

Moderate; stays 1m1f; acts on Polytrack.

Sa Nau

(92) (46)**62**

6-y-o b g Generous (IRE)-Trellis Bay (Sadler's Wells (USA))

T Keddy Howard Fielding

Placings:00050121/563442440/00 **(6785)**

2009: 16^{0}SD, 16^{0}SS,

	Starts	1st	2nd	3rd	Win & Pl
Career Total (Turf)	**15**	**2**	**2**	**1**	**9244**
Career Total (AW)	**5**	**0**	**0**	**0**	**0**

64 9/06 Newc 2m19y (0-70)H GD £3238
55 8/06 Rdcr 1m6f19y (0-55)H GD £2590
Total win prize-money £5830

Going (Turf): Sf: 0-1 GS: 0-3 **Gd: 2-3** GF: 0-8 Fm: 0-0
Distance: 5f/6f: 0-0 7f-8f: 0-2 9f-13f: 0-3 **14f+: 2-15**
Track : **LH: 2-16** RH: 0-2 Tight: 1-12 Gall: 1-2
Aids: Bl: 0-0 Vi: 0-0 Tstrap: 0-0 Ckp: 0-0
Best Rating: 64 9/06 Newc 2m19y good

Saa'Ida (IRE)

105 **81**

3-y-o ch f Diesis-Westernize (USA) (Gone West (USA))

C E Brittain Saeed Manana

Placings:00100046 **(6420)**

2009: 9^{0}GF, 10^{0}GF, 9^{1}GF, 10^{0}G, 10^{0}S, 8^{0}GS, 8^{4}GF, 11^{6}GF,

	Starts	1st	2nd	3rd	Win & Pl
Career Total (Turf)	**8**	**1**	**0**	**0**	**7447**

74 5/09 Gdwd 1m1f192y G-F £3238
Total win prize-money £3238

Going (Turf): Sf: 0-1 GS: 0-1 Gd: 0-1 **GF: 1-5** Fm: 0-0
Distance: 5f/6f: 0-0 7f-8f: 0-0 **9f-13f: 1-8** 14f+: 0-0
Track : LH: 0-3 **RH: 1-4 Tight: 1-4** Gall: 0-1
Aids: Bl: 0-2 Vi: 0-0 Tstrap: 0-0 Ckp: 0-0
Best Rating: 81 4/09 NmkR 1m2f gd-fm

Fair; stays 1m2f and acts on fast ground; has worn blinkers.

Saachi's Vision (IRE)

85(80) (38)**41**

2-y-o ch f Compton Place-Ash Moon (IRE) (General Monash (USA))

D K Ivory Rahul Bajaj & John F Connolly

Placings:060600P0 **(6610)**

2009: 5^{0}GF, 5^{6}SD, 5^{0}SD, 6^{6}G, 6^{0}GF, 5^{0}SD, 5^{P}GF, 6^{0}SD,

	Starts	1st	2nd	3rd	Win & Pl
Career Total (Turf)	**4**	**0**	**0**	**0**	**0**
Career Total (AW)	**4**	**0**	**0**	**0**	**0**

Going (Turf): Sf: 0-0 GS: 0-0 Gd: 0-1 GF: 0-3 Fm: 0-0
Distance: 5f/6f: 0-7 7f-8f: 0-1 9f-13f: 0-0 14f+: 0-0
Track : LH: 0-2 RH: 0-1 Tight: 0-2 Gall: 0-1
Aids: Bl: 0-5 Vi: 0-0 Tstrap: 0-0 Ckp: 0-0
Best Rating: 41 6/09 Wind 6f gd-fm

Saafia (USA)

88 **77**

2-y-o b/br f Swain (IRE)-Reem Al Barari (USA) (Storm Cat (USA))

M Johnston Hamdan Al Maktoum

Placings:561 **(5417)**

2009: 7^{5}GS, 7^{6}GS, 7^{1}GF,

	Starts	1st	2nd	3rd	Win & Pl
Career Total (Turf)	**3**	**1**	**0**	**0**	**5019**

77 8/09 Bevl 7f100y G-F £5018
Total win prize-money £5019

Going (Turf): Sf: 0-0 GS: 0-2 Gd: 0-0 **GF: 1-1** Fm: 0-0
Distance: 5f/6f: 0-0 **7f-8f: 1-3** 9f-13f: 0-0 14f+: 0-0
Track : LH: 0-0 **RH: 1-2** Tight: 0-0 Gall: 0-0
Aids: Bl: 0-0 Vi: 0-0 Tstrap: 0-0 Ckp: 0-0
Best Rating: 77 8/09 Bevl 7f100y gd-fm

Fair; stays 7f; acts on fast ground.

Saameq (IRE)

(89) (61)**52**

8-y-o b g Bahhare (USA)-Tajawuz (Kris)

D W Thompson Mrs L Irving

Placings:0/600344/100000551/04001/053/1-0 **(3223)**

2009: 12^{0}SD,

	Starts	1st	2nd	3rd	Win & Pl
Career Total (Turf)	**11**	**0**	**0**	**1**	**1025**
Career Total (AW)	**15**	**4**	**0**	**1**	**9139**

61 8/08 Wolv 1m4f50y STD £1978
59 12/06 Wolv 1m4f50y SS £2388
56 11/05 Wolv 1m4f50y (0-45) STD £1535
59 1/05 Wolv 1m4f50y (0-55)H STD £2933
Total win prize-money £8837

Going (Turf): Sf: 0-2 GS: 0-1 Gd: 0-5 GF: 0-3 Fm: 0-0
Distance: 5f/6f: 0-0 7f-8f: 0-0 **9f-13f: 4-22** 14f+: 0-4
Track : **LH: 4-23** RH: 0-2 **Tight: 4-15** Gall: 0-4
Aids: Bl: 0-0 Vi: 0-0 Tstrap: 0-2 Ckp: 0-2
Best Rating: 61 8/08 Wolv 1m4f50y stand

Moderate; stays 1m4f; acts on a sound surface and on Polytrack; likes to be held up; goes well fresh.

Sabancaya

(99) (73)**65**

4-y-o b f Nayef (USA)-Serra Negra (Kris)

Mrs P Sly David L Bayliss

Placings:0/00304434**446**-141363 **(0734)**

2009: 14^{1}SS, 16^{4}SD, 14^{1}SD, 16^{3}SD, 14^{6}SD, 13^{3}SD,

	Starts	1st	2nd	3rd	Win & Pl
Career Total (Turf)	8	0	0	2	819
Career Total (AW)	10	2	0	2	4521

73 1/09 Sthl 1m6f (0-65)H STD £1648
66 1/09 Sthl 1m6f (0-60)H SS £2047
Total win prize-money £3695

Going (Turf): **Sf: 0-0 GS: 0-2 Gd: 0-3 GF: 0-3 Fm: 0-0**
Distance: 5f/6f: 0-0 7f-8f: 0-2 9f-13f: 0-9 **14f+: 2-7**
Track : **LH: 2-12** RH: 0-3 Tight: 0-6 Gall: 0-3
Aids: Bl: 0-0 Vi: 0-0 Tstrap: 0-0 Ckp: 0-0
Best Rating: **73** 1/09 Sthl 1m6f stand

Moderate; effective at around 1m4f; acts on fast and easy ground, plus Fibresand.

Sabander Bleue (IRE)

92 **73**

2-y-o b c Peintre Celebre (USA)-Sabander Bay (USA) (Lear Fan (USA))

M R Channon Box 41

Placings:652336 **(6382)**

2009: 7^{6}GS, 7^{5}GF, 8^{2}F, 8^{3}GF, 8^{3}G, 8^{6}GF,

	Starts	1st	2nd	3rd	Win & Pl
Career Total (Turf)	6	0	1	2	2541

Going (Turf): **Sf: 0-0 GS: 0-1 Gd: 0-1 GF: 0-3 Fm: 0-1**
Distance: 5f/6f: 0-0 7f-8f: 0-3 9f-13f: 0-3 14f+: 0-0
Track : LH: 0-2 RH: 0-2 Tight: 0-2 Gall: 0-1
Aids: Bl: 0-0 Vi: 0-0 Tstrap: 0-0 Ckp: 0-0
Best Rating: **73** 8/09 Bevl 1m100y firm

Fair; stays 1m and acts on fast ground.

Sabatini (IRE)

89(104) (79)**65**

2-y-o b f One Cool Cat (USA)-Two Sets To Love (IRE) (Cadeaux Genereux)

J Pearce (R Hannon 16/11) A Watford

Placings:044112 **(7786)**

2009: 6^{0}GF, 8^{4}S, 6^{4}GF, **5^{1}SD**, 6^{1}SD, 5^{2}SD,

	Starts	1st	2nd	3rd	Win & Pl
Career Total (Turf)	3	0	0	0	457
Career Total (AW)	3	2	1	0	8473

79 12/09 Ling 6f (0-85) STD £3885
77 11/09 Wolv 5f216y STD £3238
Total win prize-money £7124

Going (Turf): **Sf: 0-1 GS: 0-0 Gd: 0-0 GF: 0-2 Fm: 0-0**
Distance: **5f/6f: 2-4** 7f-8f: 0-2 9f-13f: 0-0 14f+: 0-0
Track : **LH: 2-4** RH: 0-0 **Tight: 2-3** Gall: 0-0
Aids: Bl: 0-0 Vi: 0-0 Tstrap: 0-0 Ckp: 0-0
Best Rating: **79** 12/09 Wolv 5f216y stand

Fair; effective over 6f; acts on Polytrack.

Sabi Star

97 **76**

3-y-o b c Green Desert (USA)-Balisada (Kris)

J H M Gosden A E Oppenheimer

Placings:5-5336 **(4381)**

2009: 8^{5}G, 8^{3}G, 8^{3}S, 8^{6}G,

	Starts	1st	2nd	3rd	Win & Pl
Career Total (Turf)	5	0	0	2	1156

Going (Turf): **Sf: 0-1 GS: 0-0 Gd: 0-3 GF: 0-1 Fm: 0-0**
Distance: 5f/6f: 0-0 7f-8f: 0-2 9f-13f: 0-3 14f+: 0-0
Track : LH: 0-1 RH: 0-2 Tight: 0-1 Gall: 0-0
Aids: Bl: 0-0 Vi: 0-0 Tstrap: 0-0 Ckp: 0-0
Best Rating: **76** 6/09 Nott 1m75y good

Fair; dam-class top class at a mile.stays 1m; acts on good and soft ground.

Sabii Sands (IRE)

93 **80**

2-y-o b c Invincible Spirit (IRE)-Miriana (IRE) (Bluebird (USA))

R Hannon Andrew Russell

Placings:134 **(4086)**

2009: 6^{1}GF, 6^{3}G, 7^{4}S,

	Starts	1st	2nd	3rd	Win & Pl
Career Total (Turf)	3	1	0	1	6372

80 6/09 Gdwd 6f G-F £3885
Total win prize-money £3886

Going (Turf): Sf: 0-1 GS: 0-0 Gd: 0-1 **GF: 1-1** Fm: 0-0
Distance: **5f/6f: 1-2** 7f-8f: 0-1 9f-13f: 0-0 14f+: 0-0
Track : LH: 0-0 RH: 0-0 Tight: 0-0 Gall: 0-0
Aids: Bl: 0-0 Vi: 0-0 Tstrap: 0-0 Ckp: 0-0
Best Rating: **80** 7/09 Newb 7f soft

Useful; effective at 6f; acts on fast ground.

Saborido (USA)

106(70) (33)**72**

3-y-o gr g Dixie Union (USA)-Alexine (ARG) (Runaway Groom (CAN))

Mrs A J Perrett Tracey, Cotton, James, Slade

Placings:000-3240341121 **(6935)**

2009: 10^{3}GF, 12^{2}GF, 11^{4}G, 14^{0}G, 10^{3}S, 12^{4}GF, 14^{1}GF, 14^{1}G, 16^{2}GF, 17^{1}G,

	Starts	1st	2nd	3rd	Win & Pl
Career Total (Turf)	12	3	2	2	11956
Career Total (AW)	1	0	0	0	

71 10/09 Bath 2m1f34y (0-75)H GD £2590
72 8/09 Wwck 1m6f213y (0-70)H GD £3238
72 8/09 Sals 1m6f21y (0-70)H G-F £3238
Total win prize-money £9066

Going (Turf): Sf: 0-1 GS: 0-1 **Gd: 2-5** GF: 1-5 Fm: 0-0
Distance: 5f/6f: 0-0 7f-8f: 0-3 9f-13f: 0-5 **14f+: 3-5**
Track : **LH: 2-7** RH: 1-4 **Tight: 2-7** Gall: 0-0
Aids: Bl: 0-1 Vi: 0-0 Tstrap: 0-1 Ckp: 0-1
Best Rating: **72** 8/09 Wwck 1m6f213y good

Fair; stays 2m; acts on good and fast ground; has worn blinkers/chekpieces.

Sabotage (UAE)

108 **103**

3-y-o b g Halling (USA)-Cunas (USA) (Irish River (FR))

M Johnston Sheikh Hamdan Bin Mohammed Al Maktoum

Placings:21023033 **(5248)**

2009: 9^{2}G, 11^{1}GF, 16^{0}GF, 14^{2}G, 12^{3}G, 12^{0}G, 12^{3}GS, 13^{3}GF,

	Starts	1st	2nd	3rd	Win & Pl
Career Total (Turf)	8	1	2	3	17022

88 6/09 Leic 1m3f183y G-F £2986
Total win prize-money £2986

Going (Turf): Sf: 0-0 GS: 0-1 Gd: 0-4 **GF: 1-3** Fm: 0-0
Distance: 5f/6f: 0-0 7f-8f: 0-0 **9f-13f: 1-5** 14f+: 0-3
Track : LH: 0-2 **RH: 1-6** Tight: 0-3 Gall: 0-4
Aids: Bl: 0-0 Vi: 0-0 Tstrap: 0-0 Ckp: 0-0
Best Rating: **103** 8/09 Asct 1m4f gd-sft

Very useful; effective at 1m4f-1m6f; acts on good and faster ground.

Saboteur

98(97) (79)**89**

2-y-o b c Shamardal (USA)-Croeso Cariad (Most Welcome)

Saeed Bin Suroor Godolphin

Placings:434010 **(6993)**

2009: 6^{4}G, 7^{3}SD, 6^{4}GF, 7^{0}GF, 8^{1}S, 8^{0}GS,

	Starts	1st	2nd	3rd	Win & Pl
Career Total (Turf)	5	1	0	0	16438
Career Total (AW)	1	0	0	1	385

89 10/09 Nott 1m75y SFT £3753
Total win prize-money £3753

Going (Turf): **Sf: 1-1** GS: 0-1 Gd: 0-1 GF: 0-2 Fm: 0-0
Distance: 5f/6f: 0-2 7f-8f: 0-3 **9f-13f: 1-1** 14f+: 0-0
Track : **LH: 1-2** RH: 0-1 Tight: 0-0 Gall: 0-1
Aids: Bl: 0-0 Vi: 0-0 Tstrap: 0-0 Ckp: 0-0
Best Rating: **89** 10/09 Nott 1m75y soft

Useful 130,000gns half-brother to the 1m2f winner Monmouthshire; effective over 7f-1m; acts on most ground and on Polytrack.

Sabre Light

(109) (85)**69**

4-y-o b g Fantastic Light (USA)-Good Grounds (USA) (Alleged (USA))

J Pearce Jeff Pearce

Placings:00500/0001515210420151115-1132 **(0825)**

2009: 10^{1}SD, 10^{1}SD, 9^{3}SD, 10^{2}SD,

	Starts	1st	2nd	3rd	Win & Pl
Career Total (Turf)	15	3	1	0	6437
Career Total (AW)	13	6	2	1	16432

83 1/09 Kemp 1m2f STD £3561
85 1/09 Ling 1m2f STD £2047
82 12/08 Ling 1m2f STD £1978
78 11/08 Kemp 1m3f STD £2047
74 11/08 Kemp 1m3f STD £2047
66 10/08 GrLe 1m2f STD £2266
69 7/08 Yarm 1m3y (0-65)H G-F £1998
68 6/08 Yarm 1m1f G-F £1813
56 5/08 Rdcr 1m2f G-F £2047
Total win prize-money £19808

Going (Turf): Sf: 0-0 GS: 0-4 Gd: 0-4 **GF: 3-7** Fm: 0-0
Distance: 5f/6f: 0-0 7f-8f: 0-5 **9f-13f: 9-23** 14f+: 0-0
Track : **LH: 5-19** RH: 3-6 **Tight: 4-13** Gall: 1-4
Aids: Bl: 0-1 Vi: 2-4 Tstrap: 7-13 Ckp: 7-13
Best Rating: **85** 1/09 Ling 1m2f stand

Useful; stays 1m3f; acts on fast ground; goes on Polytrack; has worn blinkers and a visor.

Sacco D'Oro

(85)

3-y-o b f Rainbow High-Speedy Native (IRE) (Be My Native (USA))

M Mullineaux Paul D'Amato

Placings:0 (7882)
2009: 10^0SD,

	Starts	1st	2nd	3rd	Win & Pl
Career Total (Turf)	0	0	0	0	
Career Total (AW)	1	0	0	0	

Going (Turf): Sf: 0-0 GS: 0-0 Gd: 0-0 GF: 0-0 Fm: 0-0
Distance: 5f/6f: 0-0 7f-8f: 0-0 9f-13f: 0-1 14f+: 0-0
Track : LH: 0-1 RH: 0-0 Tight: 0-1 Gall: 0-0
Aids: Bl: 0-1 Vi: 0-0 Tstrap: 0-0 Ckp: 0-0

Sacred Kingdom (AUS)

104 125
6-y-o b g Encosta De Lago (AUS)-Courtroom Sweetie (AUS) (Zeditave (AUS))
P F Yiu Sin Kang Yuk

Placings:11/1114111/2121-43611521 (7745a)
2009: 5^4G, 6^3G, 7^6G, 6^1GF, 6^1G, 6^5GF, 6^2G, 6^1G,

	Starts	1st	2nd	3rd	Win & Pl
Career Total (Turf)	21	13	3	1	2451708
118	12/09	ShTn	6f	GD	£614004
125	5/09	Kran	6f	GD	£275362
115	5/09	ShTn	6f	G-F	£153500
124	5/08	ShTn	6f	G-F	£110180
126	2/08	ShTn	6f	GD	£165270
129	12/07	ShTn	6f	GD	£449409
125	11/07	ShTn	6f	G-F	£112352
114	10/07	ShTn	5f H	G-F	£86136
	5/07	ShTn	6f H	G-F	£59921
	3/07	ShTn	5f H	G-F	£59921
	1/07	ShTn	5f	GD	£28088
	12/06	ShTn	5f H	G-F	£32118
	12/06	ShTn	5f H	G-F	£24410

Total win prize-money £2170675

Going (Turf): Sf: 0-0 GS: 0-0 Gd: 5-11 **GF: 8-9** Fm: 0-0
Distance: **5f/6f: 13-19** 7f-8f: 0-2 9f-13f: 0-0 14f+: 0-0
Track : LH: 0-0 **RH: 1-5** Tight: 0-0 Gall: 0-0
Aids: Bl: 0-0 Vi: 0-0 Tstrap: 0-0 Ckp: 0-0
Best Rating: 129 12/07 ShTn 6f good

High-class Hong Kong-trained sprinter; effective at 5f-7f; acts on good ground or faster; often wears a tongue tie.

Sacred Star (IRE)

84 40
2-y-o b f Xaar-Mono Star (IRE) (Soviet Star (USA))
M Brittain Mel Brittain

Placings:5006 (3726)
2009: 5^5GF, 5^0G, 5^0G, 5^6G,

	Starts	1st	2nd	3rd	Win & Pl
Career Total (Turf)	4	0	0	0	0

Going (Turf): Sf: 0-0 GS: 0-0 Gd: 0-3 GF: 0-1 Fm: 0-0
Distance: 5f/6f: 0-4 7f-8f: 0-0 9f-13f: 0-0 14f+: 0-0
Track : LH: 0-0 RH: 0-0 Tight: 0-0 Gall: 0-0
Aids: Bl: 0-1 Vi: 0-0 Tstrap: 0-0 Ckp: 0-0
Best Rating: 40 5/09 Ripn 5f gd-fm

Sadaska

100(86) (52)47
3-y-o ch f Fantastic Light (USA)-Sadaka (USA) (Kingmambo (USA))
S C Williams P Lee

Placings:3060300 (6375)
2009: 7^3SD, 7^0SD, 10^6GF, 12^0GF, 14^3S, 16^0GF, 12^0SD,

	Starts	1st	2nd	3rd	Win & Pl
Career Total (Turf)	4	0	0	1	404
Career Total (AW)	3	0	0	1	403

Going (Turf): Sf: 0-1 GS: 0-0 Gd: 0-0 GF: 0-3 Fm: 0-0
Distance: 5f/6f: 0-0 7f-8f: 0-2 9f-13f: 0-3 14f+: 0-2
Track : LH: 0-5 RH: 0-2 Tight: 0-3 Gall: 0-0
Aids: Bl: 0-0 Vi: 0-0 Tstrap: 0-0 Ckp: 0-0
Best Rating: 52 1/09 Wolv 7f32y stand

Plating class; has been tried over different distances.

Saddlers Lodge

97 75
2-y-o b g Motivator-Grandalea (Grand Lodge (USA))
G A Swinbank G H Bell

Placings:22 (5006)
2009: 5^2G, 6^2G,

	Starts	1st	2nd	3rd	Win & Pl
Career Total (Turf)	2	0	2	0	2457

Going (Turf): Sf: 0-0 GS: 0-0 Gd: 0-2 GF: 0-0 Fm: 0-0
Distance: 5f/6f: 0-1 7f-8f: 0-1 9f-13f: 0-0 14f+: 0-0
Track : LH: 0-1 RH: 0-0 Tight: 0-0 Gall: 0-0
Aids: Bl: 0-0 Vi: 0-0 Tstrap: 0-0 Ckp: 0-0
Best Rating: 75 8/09 Nott 6f15y good

Fair; effective over 5f; acts on fast ground.

Sadeek

95(101) (67)83
5-y-o ch g Kyllachy-Miss Mercy (IRE) (Law Society (USA))
B Smart Mrs Patricia Brown

Placings:110200/000/05310-000040 (7830)
2009: 7^0GF, 7^0G, 7^0GS, 7^0G, 7^4SD, 7^0SD,

	Starts	1st	2nd	3rd	Win & Pl
Career Total (Turf)	18	3	1	1	40330
Career Total (AW)	2	0	0	0	241
83	6/08	Donc	7f (0-85)H	GD	£4857
87	6/06	Epsm	6f	G-F	£17034
87	5/06	York	6f	SFT	£7837

Total win prize-money £29728

Going (Turf): **Sf: 1-5** GS: 0-2 **Gd: 1-5 GF: 1-6** Fm: 0-0
Distance: **5f/6f: 2-8** 7f-8f: 1-12 9f-13f: 0-0 14f+: 0-0
Track : **LH: 1-5** RH: 0-1 **Tight: 1-4** Gall: 0-1
Aids: Bl: 0-0 Vi: 0-0 Tstrap: 0-0 Ckp: 0-0
Best Rating: 99 7/06 Curr 6f63y gd-fm

Modest; winner of theWoodcote Stakes and runner-up in Group 3 company at two; stays 7f; acts on soft and fast ground.

Sadler's Kingdom (IRE)

85 (54)81
5-y-o b g Sadler's Wells (USA)-Artful Pleasure (USA) (Nasty And Bold (USA))
R A Fahey J J Staunton

Placings:5006142114210/0660-0 (2249)
2009: 12^0G,

	Starts	1st	2nd	3rd	Win & Pl
Career Total (Turf)	15	4	2	0	29882
Career Total (AW)	3	0	0	0	0
96	9/07	Haml	1m5f9y (0-95)H	G-S	£11217
82	7/07	Gway	1m4f (60-90)H	SFT	£8170
67	7/07	Nott	1m1f213y (0-70)H	SFT	£3238
62	5/07	Bevl	1m4f16y (0-60)H	GD	£3076

Total win prize-money £25705

Going (Turf): **Sf: 2-5** GS: 1-1 Gd: 1-5 GF: 0-3 Fm: 0-0
Distance: 5f/6f: 0-0 7f-8f: 0-0 **9f-13f: 3-13** 14f+: 1-5
Track : LH: 1-10 **RH: 3-8 Tight: 2-8** Gall: 0-1
Aids: Bl: 0-0 Vi: 0-0 Tstrap: 0-0 Ckp: 0-0
Best Rating: 96 9/07 Haml 1m5f9y gd-sft

Fair stayer; stays 1m5f and acts on soft ground.

Sadler's Mark

83 55
2-y-o b c Sadler's Wells (USA)-Waldmark (GER) (Mark Of Esteem (IRE))
T P Tate Mrs Fitri Hay

Placings:05 (7244)
2009: 8^0S, 8^5S,

	Starts	1st	2nd	3rd	Win & Pl
Career Total (Turf)	2	0	0	0	0

Going (Turf): Sf: 0-2 GS: 0-0 Gd: 0-0 GF: 0-0 Fm: 0-0
Distance: 5f/6f: 0-0 7f-8f: 0-0 9f-13f: 0-2 14f+: 0-0
Track : LH: 0-2 RH: 0-0 Tight: 0-0 Gall: 0-0
Aids: Bl: 0-0 Vi: 0-0 Tstrap: 0-0 Ckp: 0-0
Best Rating: 55 11/09 Nott 1m75y soft

Sadler's Star (GER)

97(96) (64)56
6-y-o b g Alwuhush (USA)-Sadlerella (IRE) (King's Theatre (IRE))
A King Jonny & Richard Kirkham

Placings:212405/0/0-5 (4815)
2009: 9^5HY,

	Starts	1st	2nd	3rd	Win & Pl
Career Total (Turf)	7	1	2	0	7586
Career Total (AW)	2	0	0	0	
	4/06	Dres	1m2f	SFT	£1793

Total win prize-money £1793

Going (Turf): **Sf: 1-3** GS: 0-0 Gd: 0-4 GF: 0-0 Fm: 0-0
Distance: 5f/6f: 0-0 7f-8f: 0-0 **9f-13f: 1-9** 14f+: 0-0
Track : LH: 0-2 RH: 0-2 Tight: 0-2 Gall: 0-0
Aids: Bl: 0-0 Vi: 0-0 Tstrap: 0-0 Ckp: 0-0
Best Rating: 90 7/06 Dres 1m3f good

Safari

85 (25)35
6-y-o b m Namaqualand (USA)-Breakfast Creek (Hallgate)
S Curran Miss H P J Scheffers

Placings:0006/2050/0000/056 (4146)
2009: 8^0G, 10^5GF, 11^6GF,

	Starts	1st	2nd	3rd	Win & Pl
Career Total (Turf)	13	0	1	0	806
Career Total (AW)	2	0	0	0	

Going (Turf): Sf: 0-2 GS: 0-2 Gd: 0-3 GF: 0-5 Fm: 0-1
Distance: 5f/6f: 0-6 7f-8f: 0-3 9f-13f: 0-6 14f+: 0-0
Track : LH: 0-9 RH: 0-0 Tight: 0-4 Gall: 0-4
Aids: Bl: 0-3 Vi: 0-0 Tstrap: 0-0 Ckp: 0-0
Best Rating: 50 6/05 Sals 5f gd-fm

Safari Camp (IRE)

90(80) (28)57

2-y-o b c Camacho-Consensus (IRE) (Common Grounds)

A Berry (P Winkworth 5/8) A B Parr

Placings:566330003**006** (7637)

2009: 5^{5}GF, 5^{6}GF, 5^{6}GF, 5^{3}GF, 5^{3}G, 5^{0}GF, 5^{0}S, 5^{0}GF, 5^{3}G, 5^{0}GS, 5^{0}SD, 5^{6}SD,

	Starts	1st	2nd	3rd	Win & Pl
Career Total (Turf)	10	0	0	3	1878
Career Total (AW)	2	0	0	0	0

Going (Turf): Sf: 0-1 GS: 0-1 Gd: 0-2 GF: 0-6 Fm: 0-0
Distance: 5f/6f: 0-12 7f-8f: 0-0 9f-13f: 0-0 14f+: 0-0
Track : LH: 0-4 RH: 0-0 Tight: 0-1 Gall: 0-1
Aids: Bl: 0-0 Vi: 0-0 Tstrap: 0-0 Ckp: 0-0
Best Rating: 57 4/09 Brig 5f59y gd-fm

Safari Guide

100(94) (57)74

3-y-o b g Primo Valentino (IRE)-Sabalara (IRE) (Mujadil (USA))

P Winkworth P Winkworth

Placings:30-22603460 (7246)

2009: 7^{2}G, 7^{2}GF, 5^{6}G, 6^{0}SD, 7^{3}G, 7^{4}GF, 7^{6}SS, 8^{0}S,

	Starts	1st	2nd	3rd	Win & Pl
Career Total (Turf)	8	0	2	2	2856
Career Total (AW)	2	0	0	0	0

Going (Turf): Sf: 0-1 GS: 0-2 Gd: 0-3 GF: 0-2 Fm: 0-0
Distance: 5f/6f: 0-4 7f-8f: 0-5 9f-13f: 0-1 14f+: 0-0
Track : LH: 0-5 RH: 0-0 Tight: 0-2 Gall: 0-2
Aids: Bl: 0-0 Vi: 0-0 Tstrap: 0-0 Ckp: 0-0
Best Rating: 74 5/09 Ling 7f gd-fm

Fair; stays 7f and acts on fast ground.

Safari Journey (USA)

92 (64)72

5-y-o ch h Johannesburg (USA)-Alvernia (USA) (Alydar (USA))

P J Hobbs Hill, Trembath, Bryan & Outhart

Placings:03/**2043360100000/120016-54** (3247)

2009: 10^{5}GF, 11^{4}GF,

	Starts	1st	2nd	3rd	Win & Pl
Career Total (Turf)	20	3	1	3	33726
Career Total (AW)	3	0	1	0	2838

71	6/08	Chan	1m2f	H	SFT	£8824
	3/08	Fntb	1m2f	H	VS	£6985
69	7/07	Lonc	1m4f		G-S	£6757

Total win prize-money £22566

Going (Turf): Sf: 1-7 GS: 1-5 Gd: 0-3 GF: 0-2 Fm: 0-0
Distance: 5f/6f: 0-0 7f-8f: 0-2 9f-13f: 3-21 14f+: 0-0
Track : LH: 0-9 RH: 2-6 Tight: 0-1 Gall: 0-1
Aids: Bl: 0-0 Vi: 0-0 Tstrap: 0-0 Ckp: 0-0
Best Rating: 78 4/07 Lonc 1m4f good

Safari Mischief

98(108) (96)97

6-y-o b g Primo Valentino (IRE)-Night Gypsy (Mind Games)

P Winkworth Betfair Club ROA

Placings:43506/1302216/31616534/1232431-4000 (4341)

2009: 5^{4}GF, 5^{0}GF, 5^{0}G, 5^{0}GF,

	Starts	1st	2nd	3rd	Win & Pl
Career Total (Turf)	27	4	3	6	38212
Career Total (AW)	4	2	1	0	13812

96	10/08	Ling	6f	(0-90)H	STD	£8100
94	5/08	Gdwd	5f	(0-90)H	G-S	£7771
85	7/07	Ling	5f	(0-75)H	STD	£3071
81	6/07	Brig	5f59y	(0-80)H	FRM	£4605
76	9/06	Gdwd	5f	(0-75)H	GD	£3238
63	6/06	Folk	5f		G-F	£3886

Total win prize-money £30673

Going (Turf): Sf: 0-1 GS: 1-2 Gd: 1-9 GF: 1-13 Fm: 1-2
Distance: 5f/6f: 6-29 7f-8f: 0-2 9f-13f: 0-0 14f+: 0-0
Track : LH: 3-11 RH: 0-1 Tight: 2-4 Gall: 0-6
Aids: Bl: 0-0 Vi: 0-0 Tstrap: 0-0 Ckp: 0-0
Best Rating: 97 6/08 Epsm 5f good

Useful; best at 5f; acts on fast ground; also goes on Polytrack; goes well on an undulating track.

Safari Song (IRE)

101 72

3-y-o b c War Chant (USA)-Leopard Hunt (USA) (Diesis)

B Smart Pinnacle War Chant Partnership

Placings:00-206 (5954)

2009: 7^{2}G, 8^{0}G, 7^{6}GF,

	Starts	1st	2nd	3rd	Win & Pl
Career Total (Turf)	5	0	1	0	1175

Going (Turf): Sf: 0-0 GS: 0-1 Gd: 0-3 GF: 0-1 Fm: 0-0
Distance: 5f/6f: 0-0 7f-8f: 0-5 9f-13f: 0-0 14f+: 0-0
Track : LH: 0-2 RH: 0-1 Tight: 0-3 Gall: 0-0
Aids: Bl: 0-0 Vi: 0-0 Tstrap: 0-0 Ckp: 0-0
Best Rating: 72 7/09 Thsk 7f good

Modest form in maidens; stays 7f; acts on easy ground.

Safari Special

88(92) (67)68

2-y-o ch g Pastoral Pursuits-Quiz Time (Efisio)

P Winkworth P Winkworth

Placings:3551 (6774)

2009: 5^{3}GF, 5^{5}GF, 6^{5}SD, 6^{1}SD,

	Starts	1st	2nd	3rd	Win & Pl
Career Total (Turf)	2	0	0	1	403
Career Total (AW)	2	1	0	0	2047

67	10/09	Kemp	6f	STD	£2047

Total win prize-money £2047

Going (Turf): Sf: 0-0 GS: 0-0 Gd: 0-0 GF: 0-2 Fm: 0-0
Distance: 5f/6f: 1-4 7f-8f: 0-0 9f-13f: 0-0 14f+: 0-0
Track : LH: 0-1 RH: 1-1 Tight: 0-1 Gall: 0-0
Aids: Bl: 0-0 Vi: 0-0 Tstrap: 0-0 Ckp: 0-0
Best Rating: 68 4/09 Folk 5f gd-fm

Modest; stays 6f; acts on fast ground and Polytrack.

Safari Sunup (IRE)

107(113) (100)103

4-y-o b g Catcher In The Rye (IRE)-Nuit Des Temps (Sadler's Wells (USA))

P Winkworth P Winkworth

Placings:51210/60031-0233230 (7293)

2009: 10^{0}G, 10^{2}SD, 10^{3}GS, 10^{3}S, 11^{2}SD, 12^{3}GS, 12^{0}S,

	Starts	1st	2nd	3rd	Win & Pl
Career Total (Turf)	13	3	1	4	27011
Career Total (AW)	4	0	2	0	6056

95	10/08	Bath	1m2f46y (0-90)H	GD	£7771
89	10/07	Wind	1m67y (0-85)	G-S	£3886
75	7/07	Ling	7f	SFT	£3562

Total win prize-money £15219

Going (Turf): Sf: 1-3 GS: 1-5 Gd: 1-3 GF: 0-2 Fm: 0-0
Distance: 5f/6f: 0-0 7f-8f: 1-4 9f-13f: 2-13 14f+: 0-0
Track : LH: 1-8 RH: 1-7 Tight: 2-5 Gall: 0-5
Aids: Bl: 0-0 Vi: 0-0 Tstrap: 0-0 Ckp: 0-0
Best Rating: 103 10/09 Asct 1m4f gd-sft

Very useful; stays 1m4f; acts on good and softer ground; handles Polytrack.

Safaseef (IRE)

75(96) (51)55

4-y-o b f Cadeaux Genereux-Asaafeer (USA) (Dayjur (USA))

K A Morgan P Doughty

Placings:20600-0000 (7770)

2009: 6^{0}G, 8^{0}SD, 7^{0}SD, 6^{0}SD,

	Starts	1st	2nd	3rd	Win & Pl
Career Total (Turf)	5	0	1	0	1204
Career Total (AW)	4	0	0	0	

Going (Turf): Sf: 0-2 GS: 0-1 Gd: 0-1 GF: 0-1 Fm: 0-0
Distance: 5f/6f: 0-4 7f-8f: 0-5 9f-13f: 0-0 14f+: 0-0
Track : LH: 0-2 RH: 0-2 Tight: 0-1 Gall: 0-0
Aids: Bl: 0-0 Vi: 0-2 Tstrap: 0-0 Ckp: 0-0
Best Rating: 55 6/08 Donc 5f gd-sft

Safe Investment (USA)

(98) (63)89

5-y-o b g Gone West (USA)-Fully Invested (USA) (Irish River (FR))

B N Pollock R Catton

Placings:212/50000/5650-0 (0749)

2009: 8^{0}SD,

	Starts	1st	2nd	3rd	Win & Pl
Career Total (Turf)	6	1	2	0	8195
Career Total (AW)	7	0	0	0	326

81	7/06	NmkJ	7f	G-F	£4533

Total win prize-money £4534

Going (Turf): Sf: 0-0 GS: 0-0 Gd: 0-2 GF: 1-4 Fm: 0-0
Distance: 5f/6f: 0-0 7f-8f: 1-9 9f-13f: 0-4 14f+: 0-0
Track : LH: 0-3 RH: 0-5 Tight: 0-3 Gall: 0-0
Aids: Bl: 0-0 Vi: 0-1 Tstrap: 0-0 Ckp: 0-0
Best Rating: 89 8/06 Ling 7f good

Safebreaker

102(106) (74)76

4-y-o b g Key Of Luck (USA)-Insijaam (USA) (Secretariat (USA))

K A Ryan Hambleton Racing Ltd X

Placings:32231/203506560-1123122332123 (6900)

2009: 8^{1}SD, 8^{1}SD, 8^{2}SD, 8^{3}SD, 10^{1}F, 11^{2}SD, 12^{2}GS, 10^{3}GS, 10^{3}G, 12^{2}GF, 12^{1}GF, 12^{2}G, 10^{3}GF,

	Starts	1st	2nd	3rd	Win & Pl
Career Total (Turf)	14	2	4	4	14384

Career Total (AW)	13	3	4	3	10693

71 8/09 Ches 1m4f66y (0-75)H G-F £3903
65 4/09 Pont 1m2f6y (0-70)H FRM £3238
63 2/09 Sthl 1m (0-50)H STD £1706
56 1/09 GrLe 1m (0-52)H STD £2047
75 12/07 Sthl 7f SS £2968
Total win prize-money £13864

Going (Turf): Sf: 0-1 GS: 0-5 Gd: 0-3 **GF: 1-4 Fm: 1-1**
Distance: 5f/6f: 0-1 **7f-8f: 3-10** 9f-13f: 2-16 14f+: 0-0
Track : **LH: 5-21** RH: 0-4 Tight: 1-8 Gall: 1-6
Aids: Bl: 0-0 Vi: 0-0 Tstrap: 3-13 Ckp: 3-13
Best Rating: **80** 1/08 Sthl 1m stand

Modest; effective at around 1m-1m4f; acts on fast and easy ground on turf, and on sand; has worn cheekpieces.

Saffron's Son (IRE)

96(84) (49)56

3-y-o b c Saffron Walden (FR)-Try My Rosie (Try My Best (USA))
R Ducasteele (P T Midgley 22/9) R Ducasteele

Placings:030-0060333434410 **(7302a)**
2009: 12^0SF, 12^0GF, 12^6GF, 12^0GF, 14^3GF, 14^3GF, 16^4G, 12^3GF, 12^4G, 11^4GS, 13^1GF, 10^0HY,

	Starts	1st	2nd	3rd	Win & Pl
Career Total (Turf)	14	1	0	4	4215
Career Total (AW)	1	0	0	0	

56 9/09 Catt 1m5f175y G-F £2047
Total win prize-money £2047

Going (Turf): Sf: 0-2 GS: 0-1 Gd: 0-3 **GF: 1-8** Fm: 0-0
Distance: 5f/6f: 0-0 7f-8f: 0-1 9f-13f: 0-10 **14f+: 1-4**
Track : **LH: 1-9** RH: 0-5 **Tight: 1-10** Gall: 0-1
Aids: **Bl: 1-5** Vi: 0-3 Tstrap: 0-0 Ckp: 0-0
Best Rating: **56** 9/09 Catt 1m5f175y gd-fm

Moderate; effective over 1m6f; acts on fast ground.

Safin (GER)

(105) (64)

9-y-o b g Pennekamp (USA)-Sankt Johanna (GER) (High Game)
Mrs S C Bradburne (R Curtis 31/8) Cornelius Lysaght, Quandt & Cochrane

Placings:561/4250011/0120/33003551/56034/**0000/12020 10340** **(1568)**
2009: 12^1SD, 12^2SD, 16^0SD, 14^2SD, 16^0SD, 12^1SD, 13^0SF, 12^3SD, 13^4SD, 11^0SD,

	Starts	1st	2nd	3rd	Win & Pl
Career Total (Turf)	25	5	1	4	28076
Career Total (AW)	16	2	3	1	6691

64 2/09 Sthl 1m4f (0-60)H STD £2047
55 1/09 Wolv 1m4f50y (0-55)H STD £2388
8/05 Diel 1m2f GD £1541
4/04 Fehr 1m2f GD £2715
10/03 Muni 1m3f SFT £2078
9/03 Maia 1m1f110y GD £2597
12/02 MsnL 1m HVY £5521
Total win prize-money £18887

Going (Turf): Sf: 2-5 GS: 0-0 **Gd: 3-17** GF: 0-0 Fm: 0-0
Distance: 5f/6f: 0-0 7f-8f: 1-5 **9f-13f: 6-31** 14f+: 0-5
Track : **LH: 2-13** RH: 0-6 **Tight: 1-7** Gall: 0-0
Aids: Bl: 0-0 Vi: 0-0 Tstrap: 0-0 Ckp: 0-0
Best Rating: **81** 2/05 StMz 1m2f good

Moderate; ex-German; stays 1m4f; acts on Polytrack and Fibresand.

Safina

86 70

2-y-o ch f Pivotal-Russian Rhythm (USA) (Kingmambo (USA))
Sir Michael Stoute Cheveley Park Stud

Placings:3 **(7183)**
2009: 7^3G,

	Starts	1st	2nd	3rd	Win & Pl
Career Total (Turf)	1	0	0	1	722

Going (Turf): **Sf: 0-0 GS: 0-0 Gd: 0-1 GF: 0-0 Fm: 0-0**
Distance: 5f/6f: 0-0 7f-8f: 0-1 9f-13f: 0-0 14f+: 0-0
Track : LH: 0-0 RH: 0-0 Tight: 0-0 Gall: 0-0
Aids: Bl: 0-0 Vi: 0-0 Tstrap: 0-0 Ckp: 0-0
Best Rating: **70** 10/09 NmkR 7f good

Daughter of 1000 Guineas winner; fair debut over 7f on good.

Safranine (IRE)

(87) (40)61

12-y-o b m Dolphin Street (FR)-Webbiana (African Sky)
Miss A Stokell Ms Caron Stokell

Placings:0120/**00000/0000000500/0130**330105405/**0003** 5602006315100100060000/**000000000006000622/2452000** 000003**6600/0636**00312350604060/565**044660000**/006000 **0-0** **(0367)**
2009: 5^0SD,

	Starts	1st	2nd	3rd	Win & Pl
Career Total (Turf)	89	6	3	6	38268
Career Total (AW)	42	1	4	3	5777

61 7/06 Wwck 5f110y (0-70)H GD £3238
84 9/03 Rdcr 6f D(0-85)H G-F £4810
77 7/03 Wwck 5f110y D(0-85)H FRM £7522
58 7/03 Wwck 5f110y E(0-70)H G-F £3851
59 6/02 Haml 5f4y E(0-75)H SFT £4858
59 3/02 Sthl 5f E(0-70)H STD £2380
88 7/99 Rdcr 6f E FRM £2994
Total win prize-money £29656

Going (Turf): Sf: 1-3 GS: 0-8 Gd: 1-19 **GF: 2-46 Fm: 2-13**
Distance: **5f/6f: 7-107** 7f-8f: 0-21 9f-13f: 0-3 14f+: 0-0
Track : **LH: 3-51** RH: 0-3 Tight: 0-24 Gall: 0-3
Aids: Bl: 0-1 Vi: 0-4 Tstrap: 3-52 Ckp: 3-52
Best Rating: **88** 7/99 Rdcr 6f firm

Modest mare; may be best over 6f these days; acts on fast ground and on sand.

Saga De Tercey (FR)

107 92

4-y-o b g Sagacity (FR)-Fanciulla Del West (USA) (Manila (USA))
G A Swinbank Andrew Dick, Brian Dunn & Philip Holden

Placings:121210 **(6115)**
2009: 12^1GF, 11^2G, 13^1G, 16^2GF, 16^1G, 18^0GF,

	Starts	1st	2nd	3rd	Win & Pl
Career Total (Turf)	6	3	2	0	20095

89 8/09 Thsk 2m (0-85)H GD £5569
85 8/09 Catt 1m5f175y (0-85)H GD £5180
74 4/09 Muss 1m4f100y G-F £2590
Total win prize-money £13340

Going (Turf): Sf: 0-0 GS: 0-0 **Gd: 2-3** GF: 1-3 Fm: 0-0
Distance: 5f/6f: 0-0 7f-8f: 0-0 9f-13f: 1-2 **14f+: 2-4**
Track : **LH: 2-3** RH: 1-3 **Tight: 3-3** Gall: 0-2
Aids: Bl: 0-0 Vi: 0-0 Tstrap: 0-0 Ckp: 0-0
Best Rating: **92** 8/09 York 2m88y gd-fm

Useful; bumper winner; stays 2m; acts on fast and good/easy ground.

Sagara (USA)

106 113

5-y-o b g Sadler's Wells (USA)-Rangoon Ruby (USA) (Kingmambo (USA))
Saeed Bin Suroor Godolphin

Placings:2/1203523/0553632-54 **(3048)**
2009: 12^5GF, 20^4GF,

	Starts	1st	2nd	3rd	Win & Pl
Career Total (Turf)	17	1	4	4	307640

83 4/07 MsnL 1m2f110y SFT £7095
Total win prize-money £7095

Going (Turf): **Sf: 1-3** GS: 0-5 Gd: 0-4 GF: 0-4 Fm: 0-0
Distance: 5f/6f: 0-0 7f-8f: 0-0 **9f-13f: 1-11** 14f+: 0-6
Track : LH: 0-2 RH: 0-13 Tight: 0-3 Gall: 0-6
Aids: Bl: 0-0 Vi: 0-4 Tstrap: 0-1 Ckp: 0-1
Best Rating: **123** 10/07 Lonc 1m4f gd-sft

Group class; third in the 2007 Arc de Triomphe; effective from 1m4f-2m4f; acts on good and softer ground; has worn cheekpieces.

Sagarich (FR)

94 68

5-y-o gr m Sagamix (FR)-Baranciaga (USA) (Bering)
M G Quinlan Liam Mulryan

Placings:4044020/504100030-0300 **(6244)**
2009: 10^0G, 10^3G, 12^0G, 12^0G,

	Starts	1st	2nd	3rd	Win & Pl
Career Total (Turf)	20	1	1	2	9122

68 6/08 Wxfd 1m4f50y G-Y £4826
Total win prize-money £4827

Going (Turf): **Sf: 0-3 GS: 0-0 Gd: 0-9 GF: 0-5 Fm: 0-0**
Distance: 5f/6f: 0-0 7f-8f: 0-0 **9f-13f: 1-19** 14f+: 0-1
Track : LH: 0-7 RH: 0-11 Tight: 0-2 Gall: 0-2
Aids: Bl: 0-0 Vi: 0-0 Tstrap: 0-0 Ckp: 0-0
Best Rating: **72** 6/07 Curr 1m2f soft

Saggiatore

81 53

2-y-o b f Galileo (IRE)-Madame Dubois (Legend Of France (USA))
E A L Dunlop Cliveden Stud

Placings:0 **(6062)**
2009: 8^0GF,

	Starts	1st	2nd	3rd	Win & Pl
Career Total (Turf)	1	0	0	0	

Going (Turf): **Sf: 0-0 GS: 0-0 Gd: 0-0 GF: 0-1 Fm: 0-0**
Distance: 5f/6f: 0-0 7f-8f: 0-1 9f-13f: 0-0 14f+: 0-0
Track : LH: 0-0 RH: 0-0 Tight: 0-0 Gall: 0-0
Aids: Bl: 0-0 Vi: 0-0 Tstrap: 0-0 Ckp: 0-0
Best Rating: **53** 9/09 NmkR 1m gd-fm

Sagredo (USA)

93(96) (76)70

5-y-o b g Diesis-Eternity (Suave Dancer (USA))
Jonjo O'Neill John P McManus

Placings:4212/63113006/0054 (7413)
2009: 16⁰GF, 14⁰S, 14⁵SD, 12⁴SD,

	Starts	1st	2nd	3rd	Win & Pl
Career Total (Turf)	11	3	1	2	19656
Career Total (AW)	5	0	1	0	1558

108 8/07 Nott 1m1f213y (0-85)H GD £5181
97 7/07 Pont 1m2f6y (0-85)H G-S £6477
86 11/06 Nott 1m54y SFT £2590
Total win prize-money £14250

Going (Turf): Sf: 1-4 GS: 1-2 Gd: 1-2 GF: 0-3 Fm: 0-0
Distance: 5f/6f: 0-0 7f-8f: 0-2 9f-13f: 3-8 14f+: 0-6
Track : LH: 3-11 RH: 0-5 Tight: 0-6 Gall: 0-2
Aids: Bl: 0-0 Vi: 0-0 Tstrap: 0-0 Ckp: 0-0
Best Rating: 108 8/07 Nott 1m1f213y good

Very useful; seems to get 1m5f; acts on any ground and Polytrack; usually held up.

Sagunt (GER)

95(99) (59)72
6-y-o ch g Tertullian (USA)-Suva (GER) (Arazi (USA))
S Curran L M Power

Placings:10/00/0006100/060003210-011215 (6566)
2009: 12⁰SD, 10¹GF, 12¹GF, 11²GF, 12¹S, 12⁵GS,

	Starts	1st	2nd	3rd	Win & Pl
Career Total (Turf)	17	5	2	0	12434
Career Total (AW)	9	1	0	1	3115

72 7/09 Chep 1m4f23y (0-65)H SFT £2186
63 6/09 Folk 1m4f (0-60)H G-F £2047
58 4/09 Wwck 1m2f188y (0-60)H G-F £2047
59 12/08 Ling 1m4f (0-50)H STD £2729
67 10/07 Brig 7f214y (0-63)H GD £2483
9/05 Brem 7f GD £2127
Total win prize-money £13622

Going (Turf): Sf: 1-1 GS: 0-2 Gd: 2-8 GF: 2-6 Fm: 0-0
Distance: 5f/6f: 0-1 7f-8f: 2-9 9f-13f: 4-16 14f+: 0-0
Track : LH: 4-16 RH: 1-7 Tight: 2-6 Gall: 0-3
Aids: Bl: 0-0 Vi: 0-0 Tstrap: 0-1 Ckp: 0-1
Best Rating: 72 7/09 Chep 1m4f23y soft

Moderate; effective at 1m2f-1m4f; acts on good and fast ground; goes on Polytrack.

Sahaal (USA)

99(99) (74)80
3-y-o b c Rahy (USA)-Thaminah (USA) (Danzig (USA))
M P Tregoning Hamdan Al Maktoum

Placings:03063150 (6973)
2009: 8⁰G, 8³G, 9⁰G, 7⁶G, 7³G, 8¹F, 8⁵GF, 10⁰SD,

	Starts	1st	2nd	3rd	Win & Pl
Career Total (Turf)	7	1	0	2	3554
Career Total (AW)	1	0	0	0	

80 8/09 Bath 1m5y FRM £2687
Total win prize-money £2688

Going (Turf): Sf: 0-0 GS: 0-0 Gd: 0-5 GF: 0-1 Fm: 1-1
Distance: 5f/6f: 0-0 7f-8f: 0-3 9f-13f: 1-5 14f+: 0-0
Track : LH: 1-3 RH: 0-3 Tight: 1-3 Gall: 0-0
Aids: Bl: 0-0 Vi: 0-0 Tstrap: 0-1 Ckp: 0-1
Best Rating: 80 8/09 Bath 1m5y firm

Fair; effective over 1m; acts on firm ground.

Sahara Kingdom (IRE)

(97) (93)
2-y-o gr c Cozzene (USA)-Rose Indien (FR) (Crystal Glitters (USA))
Saeed Bin Suroor Godolphin

Placings:11 (7251)
2009: 7¹SS, 7¹SD,

	Starts	1st	2nd	3rd	Win & Pl
Career Total (Turf)	0	0	0	0	
Career Total (AW)	2	2	0	0	7447

93 11/09 Ling 7f STD £3885
80 10/09 Ling 7f SS £3561
Total win prize-money £7448

Going (Turf): Sf: 0-0 GS: 0-0 Gd: 0-0 GF: 0-0 Fm: 0-0
Distance: 5f/6f: 0-0 7f-8f: 2-2 9f-13f: 0-0 14f+: 0-0
Track : LH: 2-2 RH: 0-0 Tight: 2-2 Gall: 0-0
Aids: Bl: 0-0 Vi: 0-0 Tstrap: 0-0 Ckp: 0-0
Best Rating: 93 11/09 Ling 7f stand

Very useful; stays 7f and acts on Polytrack.

Sahara Prince (IRE)

(90) (44)49
9-y-o b g Desert King (IRE)-Chehana (Posse (USA))
K A Morgan D S Cooper

Placings:060/004026/02052321205/001003000005/50000/2020035/00-0 (0131)
2009: 8⁰SD,

	Starts	1st	2nd	3rd	Win & Pl
Career Total (Turf)	32	2	5	3	28417
Career Total (AW)	15	0	2	0	907

88 5/05 Leop 7f (60-90)H G-F £7351
88 8/04 Hayd 6f C(0-90)H HVY £9854
Total win prize-money £17205

Going (Turf): Sf: 1-4 GS: 0-0 Gd: 0-10 GF: 1-11 Fm: 0-2
Distance: 5f/6f: 1-4 7f-8f: 1-34 9f-13f: 0-9 14f+: 0-0
Track : LH: 1-24 RH: 0-10 Tight: 0-12 Gall: 0-6
Aids: Bl: 0-1 Vi: 0-2 Tstrap: 1-23 Ckp: 1-23
Best Rating: 89 7/05 Leop 7f good

Sahara Sunshine

98(80) (39)75
4-y-o b f Hernando (FR)-Sahara Sunrise (USA) (Houston (USA))
Mrs L J Mongan Mrs P J Sheen

Placings:03232232-00300 (4744)
2009: 16⁰SD, 11⁰GF, 11³GF, 10⁰GF, 11⁰GS,

	Starts	1st	2nd	3rd	Win & Pl
Career Total (Turf)	12	0	4	4	17144
Career Total (AW)	1	0	0	0	

Going (Turf): Sf: 0-3 GS: 0-5 Gd: 0-1 GF: 0-3 Fm: 0-0
Distance: 5f/6f: 0-0 7f-8f: 0-0 9f-13f: 0-12 14f+: 0-1
Track : LH: 0-2 RH: 0-3 Tight: 0-3 Gall: 0-0
Aids: Bl: 0-0 Vi: 0-0 Tstrap: 0-0 Ckp: 0-0
Best Rating: 75 10/08 MsnL 1m2f110y heavy

Modest; stays 1m3f and acts on fast ground.

Saharan Royal

76(96) (48)65
3-y-o b f Val Royal (FR)-Saharan Song (IRE) (Singspiel (IRE))
Matthew Salaman (M Salaman 3/7) Mrs P G Lewin & D Grieve

Placings:022-000 (7776)
2009: 8⁰GF, 10⁰SD, 10⁰GD,

	Starts	1st	2nd	3rd	Win & Pl
Career Total (Turf)	4	0	2	0	3060
Career Total (AW)	2	0	0	0	

Going (Turf): Sf: 0-0 GS: 0-0 Gd: 0-2 GF: 0-2 Fm: 0-0
Distance: 5f/6f: 0-1 7f-8f: 0-3 9f-13f: 0-2 14f+: 0-0
Track : LH: 0-4 RH: 0-1 Tight: 0-1 Gall: 0-1
Aids: Bl: 0-0 Vi: 0-0 Tstrap: 0-0 Ckp: 0-0
Best Rating: 65 8/08 Brig 6f209y gd-fm

Modest; stays 7f; acts on good ground.

Saharia (IRE)

(95) (80)
2-y-o b c Oratorio (IRE)-Inchiri (Sadler's Wells (USA))
J Noseda Timeform Betfair Racing Club Ltd

Placings:01 (7644)
2009: 6⁰SD, 7¹SD,

	Starts	1st	2nd	3rd	Win & Pl
Career Total (Turf)	0	0	0	0	
Career Total (AW)	2	1	0	0	3238

80 12/09 Wolv 7f32y STD £3238
Total win prize-money £3238

Going (Turf): Sf: 0-0 GS: 0-0 Gd: 0-0 GF: 0-0 Fm: 0-0
Distance: 5f/6f: 0-1 7f-8f: 1-1 9f-13f: 0-0 14f+: 0-0
Track : LH: 1-2 RH: 0-0 Tight: 1-2 Gall: 0-0
Aids: Bl: 0-0 Vi: 0-0 Tstrap: 0-0 Ckp: 0-0
Best Rating: 80 12/09 Wolv 7f32y stand

Fair; stays 7f; acts on Polytrack.

Sahpresa (USA)

114 119
4-y-o b f Sahm (USA)-Sorpresa (USA) (Pleasant Tap (USA))
Rod Collet D O McIntyre

Placings:1314-124213 (7498a)
2009: 8¹G, 8²GS, 8⁴S, 8²G, 8¹GF, 8³F,

	Starts	1st	2nd	3rd	Win & Pl
Career Total (Turf)	10	4	2	2	415087

119 10/09 NmkR 1m G-F £113540
114 5/09 Lonc 1m GD £25243
113 9/08 StCl 1m GD £20221
7/08 MsnL 1m G-S £8088
Total win prize-money £167092

Going (Turf): Sf: 0-1 GS: 1-3 Gd: 2-4 GF: 1-1 Fm: 0-1
Distance: 5f/6f: 0-0 7f-8f: 4-8 9f-13f: 0-2 14f+: 0-0
Track : LH: 1-1 RH: 0-4 Tight: 0-0 Gall: 0-0
Aids: Bl: 0-0 Vi: 0-0 Tstrap: 0-0 Ckp: 0-0
Best Rating: 119 10/09 NmkR 1m gd-fm

Group-class; Group 1 Sun Chariot winner; stays 1m; acts on fast and easy ground.

Sahrati

106(104) (83)98
5-y-o ch g In The Wings-Shimna (Mr Prospector (USA))
A King (D R C Elsworth 19/8) Raymond Tooth

Placings:26014/64341021003/0561650000-226550 (5170)
2009: 12²SD, 12²GS, 12⁶SD, 12⁵GF, 10⁵S, 12⁰GF,

	Starts	1st	2nd	3rd	Win & Pl
Career Total (Turf)	24	4	3	2	50050
Career Total (AW)	8	0	1	0	1888

98 6/08 Wind 1m3f135y (0-100)H G-F £10092
96 7/07 NmkJ 1m2f (0-95)H G-F £8724
88 5/07 Sand 1m2f7y (0-90)H G-S £7772

78	10/06	Nott	1m54y	SFT	£4404

Total win prize-money £30994

Going (Turf): Sf: 1-2 GS: 1-4 Gd: 0-5 **GF: 2-12** Fm: 0-1
Distance: 5f/6f: 0-0 7f-8f: 0-6 **9f-13f: 4-23** 14f+: 0-3
Track : LH: 1-13 **RH: 2-15** Tight: 1-6 Gall: 1-11
Aids: **Bl: 1-6** Vi: 0-1 Tstrap: 0-6 Ckp: 0-6
Best Rating: 98 6/08 Wind 1m3f135y gd-fm

Useful; effective from 1m2f-1m4f; acts on most ground; has worn blinkers/visor/cheekpieces.

Saif Al Fahad (IRE)

102(100) (77)**70**

3-y-o ch c Shinko Forest (IRE)-Golden Ciel (USA) (Septieme Ciel (USA))
E J O'Neill Sheikh Naser Fahad Al Sabah

Placings:245241-40 **(2148)**
2009: 5^{4}GF, 5^{0}G,

	Starts	1st	2nd	3rd	Win & Pl
Career Total (Turf)	4	0	1	0	2459
Career Total (AW)	4	1	1	0	5788

77	12/08	Wolv	5f20y	STD	£3070

Total win prize-money £3071

Going (Turf): Sf: 0-0 GS: 0-1 Gd: 0-1 GF: 0-2 Fm: 0-0
Distance: **5f/6f: 1-6** 7f-8f: 0-2 9f-13f: 0-0 14f+: 0-0
Track : **LH: 1-5** RH: 0-0 **Tight: 1-2** Gall: 0-2
Aids: Bl: 0-0 Vi: 0-0 Tstrap: 0-0 Ckp: 0-0
Best Rating: 77 12/08 Wolv 5f20y stand

Fair; suited by 6f; acts on fast ground; goes on Polytrack.

Sainglend

102(84) (40)**76**

4-y-o b g Galileo (IRE)-Verbal Intrigue (USA) (Dahar (USA))
S Curran W J M Byrne

Placings:4364/00001-5 **(2552)**
2009: 11^{5}GF,

	Starts	1st	2nd	3rd	Win & Pl
Career Total (Turf)	9	1	0	1	3933
Career Total (AW)	1	0	0	0	

76	10/08	Wind	1m2f7y	(0-65)H	G-S	£2729

Total win prize-money £2730

Going (Turf): Sf: 0-0 **GS: 1-3** Gd: 0-3 GF: 0-3 Fm: 0-0
Distance: 5f/6f: 0-0 7f-8f: 0-3 **9f-13f: 1-7** 14f+: 0-0
Track : LH: 0-1 **RH: 1-5 Tight: 1-4** Gall: 0-0
Aids: Bl: 0-0 Vi: 0-0 Tstrap: 0-0 Ckp: 0-0
Best Rating: 77 7/07 Sand 7f16y good

Modest; effective at around 1m2f; goes well on easy ground.

Saint Arch (CAN)

100(108) (101)**91**

3-y-o b g Arch (USA)-Halo Silver (USA) (Silver Buck (USA))
M Johnston Sheikh Hamdan Bin Mohammed Al Maktoum

Placings:11-165 **(1459)**
2009: 8^{1}SD, 8^{6}SD, 10^{5}G,

	Starts	1st	2nd	3rd	Win & Pl
Career Total (Turf)	2	1	0	0	3056
Career Total (AW)	3	2	0	0	11903

101	3/09	Kemp	1m	(0-90)H	STD	£7477
89	11/08	Ling	7f		STD	£3885
91	10/08	Folk	7f		SFT	£2590

Total win prize-money £13953

Going (Turf): Sf: 1-1 GS: 0-0 Gd: 0-1 GF: 0-0 Fm: 0-0
Distance: 5f/6f: 0-0 **7f-8f: 3-4** 9f-13f: 0-1 14f+: 0-0
Track : LH: 1-2 RH: 1-2 **Tight: 1-2** Gall: 0-0
Aids: Bl: 0-0 Vi: 0-0 Tstrap: 0-0 Ckp: 0-0
Best Rating: 101 3/09 Kemp 1m stand

Very useful; stays 1m; acts on soft ground and on Polytrack.

Saint Chapelle (IRE)

63(73) (11)**51**

3-y-o b f Noverre (USA)-Chartres (IRE) (Danehill (USA))
Mrs A J Perrett Lady Clague

Placings:0-06 **(6332)**
2009: 12^{0}SD, 10^{6}F,

	Starts	1st	2nd	3rd	Win & Pl
Career Total (Turf)	2	0	0	0	0
Career Total (AW)	1	0	0	0	

Going (Turf): Sf: 0-1 GS: 0-0 Gd: 0-0 GF: 0-0 Fm: 0-1
Distance: 5f/6f: 0-0 7f-8f: 0-1 9f-13f: 0-2 14f+: 0-0
Track : LH: 0-1 RH: 0-1 Tight: 0-1 Gall: 0-0
Aids: Bl: 0-0 Vi: 0-0 Tstrap: 0-0 Ckp: 0-0
Best Rating: 51 10/08 Newb 1m soft

Saint Sebastian (IRE)

97(79) (31)**66**

2-y-o ch c Captain Rio-Paris Song (IRE) (Peintre Celebre (USA))
E S McMahon Allan McWilliam/Christopher McWilliam

Placings:42643052 **(6590)**
2009: 6^{4}G, 5^{2}GF, 5^{6}GF, 5^{4}G, 6^{3}HY, 7^{0}SD, 5^{5}GF, 6^{2}GS,

	Starts	1st	2nd	3rd	Win & Pl
Career Total (Turf)	7	0	2	1	2237
Career Total (AW)	1	0	0	0	

Going (Turf): Sf: 0-1 GS: 0-1 Gd: 0-2 GF: 0-3 Fm: 0-0
Distance: 5f/6f: 0-5 7f-8f: 0-3 9f-13f: 0-0 14f+: 0-0
Track : LH: 0-1 RH: 0-1 Tight: 0-1 Gall: 0-0
Aids: Bl: 0-0 Vi: 0-0 Tstrap: 0-2 Ckp: 0-2
Best Rating: 66 6/09 Leic 5f218y gd-fm

Moderate; stays 6f; acts on fast ground and soft ground; has worn cheekpieces.

Saint Thomas (IRE)

91(89) (59)**74**

2-y-o b g Alhaarth (IRE)-Aguilas Perla (IRE) (Indian Ridge)
J A Osborne Mrs F Walwyn & Anthony Taylor

Placings:304022 **(7474)**
2009: 6^{3}F, 7^{0}G, 8^{4}SD, 8^{0}GS, 8^{2}SD, 10^{2}SD,

	Starts	1st	2nd	3rd	Win & Pl
Career Total (Turf)	3	0	0	1	472
Career Total (AW)	3	0	2	0	1471

Going (Turf): Sf: 0-0 GS: 0-1 Gd: 0-1 GF: 0-0 Fm: 0-1
Distance: 5f/6f: 0-0 7f-8f: 0-3 9f-13f: 0-3 14f+: 0-0
Track : LH: 0-3 RH: 0-2 Tight: 0-3 Gall: 0-0
Aids: Bl: 0-1 Vi: 0-0 Tstrap: 0-0 Ckp: 0-0
Best Rating: 74 8/09 Brig 6f209y firm

Modest; effective over 1m-1m2f; acts on Polytrack.

Saints Bay (IRE)

73(98) (56)**2**

3-y-o b f Redback-Alexander Eliott (IRE) (Night Shift (USA))
R Hannon N A Woodcock & A C Pickford

Placings:32300 **(1536)**
2009: 7^{3}SD, 6^{2}SD, 6^{3}SD, 7^{0}SD, 5^{0}GF,

	Starts	1st	2nd	3rd	Win & Pl
Career Total (Turf)	1	0	0	0	
Career Total (AW)	4	0	1	2	1594

Going (Turf): Sf: 0-0 GS: 0-0 Gd: 0-0 GF: 0-1 Fm: 0-0
Distance: 5f/6f: 0-3 7f-8f: 0-2 9f-13f: 0-0 14f+: 0-0
Track : LH: 0-4 RH: 0-1 Tight: 0-3 Gall: 0-0
Aids: Bl: 0-0 Vi: 0-0 Tstrap: 0-0 Ckp: 0-0
Best Rating: 56 1/09 Kemp 7f stand

Moderate; effective at 7f; acts on Polytrack.

Sairaam (IRE)

99(95) (55)**63**

3-y-o b/br f Marju (IRE)-Sayedati Eljamilah (USA) (Mr Prospector (USA))
C Smith (J L Dunlop 29/6) Phil Martin & Trev Sleath

Placings:050-050000134304400 **(7856)**
2009: 8^{0}G, 9^{5}GF, 8^{0}GF, 16^{0}G, 8^{0}G, 10^{0}GF, 7^{1}GF, 7^{3}GF, 7^{4}GF, 7^{3}GF, 8^{0}S, 7^{4}SD, 9^{4}SD, 7^{0}SD, 9^{0}SD,

	Starts	1st	2nd	3rd	Win & Pl
Career Total (Turf)	14	1	0	2	2926
Career Total (AW)	4	0	0	0	0

56	9/09	Yarm	7f3y	G-F	£1942

Total win prize-money £1943

Going (Turf): Sf: 0-2 GS: 0-1 Gd: 0-3 **GF: 1-8** Fm: 0-0
Distance: 5f/6f: 0-0 **7f-8f: 1-9** 9f-13f: 0-8 14f+: 0-1
Track : LH: 0-9 RH: 0-3 Tight: 0-5 Gall: 0-0
Aids: Bl: 0-0 Vi: 0-0 Tstrap: 0-0 Ckp: 0-0
Best Rating: 63 9/08 Gdwd 7f gd-fm

Modest; stays 7f; acts on fast ground.

Sakhee's Pearl

98(98) (82)**86**

3-y-o gr f Sakhee (USA)-Grey Pearl (Ali-Royal (IRE))
Miss Gay Kelleway The Peregrina Partnership

Placings:2-14640 **(7032)**
2009: 7^{1}G, 7^{4}G, 6^{6}G, 7^{4}SD, 7^{0}S,

	Starts	1st	2nd	3rd	Win & Pl
Career Total (Turf)	5	1	1	0	7055
Career Total (AW)	1	0	0	0	378

75	7/09	Donc	7f	GD	£4857

Total win prize-money £4857

Going (Turf): Sf: 0-1 GS: 0-1 **Gd: 1-3** GF: 0-0 Fm: 0-0
Distance: 5f/6f: 0-0 **7f-8f: 1-6** 9f-13f: 0-0 14f+: 0-0
Track : LH: 0-1 RH: 0-0 Tight: 0-1 Gall: 0-0
Aids: Bl: 0-0 Vi: 0-0 Tstrap: 0-0 Ckp: 0-0
Best Rating: 86 7/09 Donc 7f good

Smart; stays 7f; acts on good and easy ground; handles Polytrack.

Sakile

84(107) (77)**57**

2-y-o ch f Johannesburg (USA)-Crooked Wood (USA) (Woodman (USA))
P W Chapple-Hyam C G P Wyatt

Placings:5631 **(7485)**

2009: 6^{5}GF, 5^{6}GF, 5^{3}SD, 5^{1}SD,

	Starts	1st	2nd	3rd	Win & Pl
Career Total (Turf)	2	0	0	0	0
Career Total (AW)	2	1	0	1	4415

77 11/09 Ling 5f STD £3885
Total win prize-money £3886

Going (Turf): **Sf: 0-0 GS: 0-0 Gd: 0-0 GF: 0-2 Fm: 0-0**
Distance: **5f/6f: 1-4** 7f-8f: 0-0 9f-13f: 0-0 14f+: 0-0
Track : **LH: 1-3** RH: 0-0 **Tight: 1-2** Gall: 0-0
Aids: Bl: 0-0 Vi: 0-0 Tstrap: 0-0 Ckp: 0-0
Best Rating: **77** 11/09 Ling 5f stand

Fair; suited by 5f and Polytrack.

Saladin's Vow (USA)

66(79) (54)36
2-y-o ch c Broken Vow (USA)-Morena Park (Pivotal)
G A Butler Miss R Al-Attiya

Placings:00 (6372)
2009: 6^{0}GF, 7^{0}SD,

	Starts	1st	2nd	3rd	Win & Pl
Career Total (Turf)	1	0	0	0	
Career Total (AW)	1	0	0	0	

Going (Turf): **Sf: 0-0 GS: 0-0 Gd: 0-0 GF: 0-1 Fm: 0-0**
Distance: 5f/6f: 0-1 7f-8f: 0-1 9f-13f: 0-0 14f+: 0-0
Track : LH: 0-0 RH: 0-1 Tight: 0-0 Gall: 0-0
Aids: Bl: 0-1 Vi: 0-0 Tstrap: 0-0 Ckp: 0-0
Best Rating: **54** 9/09 Kemp 7f stand

Salamon

90(82) (42)56
3-y-o gr f Montjeu (IRE)-Farfala (FR) (Linamix (FR))
P F I Cole Ben & Sir Martyn Arbib

Placings:0-0455 (5470)
2009: 8^{0}G, 10^{4}HY, 6^{5}GS, 9^{5}F,

	Starts	1st	2nd	3rd	Win & Pl
Career Total (Turf)	4	0	0	0	325
Career Total (AW)	1	0	0	0	

Going (Turf): **Sf: 0-1 GS: 0-1 Gd: 0-1 GF: 0-0 Fm: 0-1**
Distance: 5f/6f: 0-0 7f-8f: 0-2 9f-13f: 0-3 14f+: 0-0
Track : LH: 0-3 RH: 0-2 Tight: 0-1 Gall: 0-1
Aids: Bl: 0-0 Vi: 0-0 Tstrap: 0-0 Ckp: 0-0
Best Rating: **56** 7/09 Nott 1m2f50y heavy

Moderate; stays 1m2f; acts on heavy ground.

Salden Licht

107(97) (78)102
5-y-o b g Fantastic Light (USA)-Salde (GER) (Alkalde (GER))
A King (J M P Eustace 7/11) Dai Griffiths

Placings:22/11/5213-0035 (7293)
2009: 8^{0}SD, 8^{0}S, 10^{3}S, 12^{5}S,

	Starts	1st	2nd	3rd	Win & Pl
Career Total (Turf)	11	3	3	2	58855
Career Total (AW)	1	0	0	0	

8/08 Vich 1m1f SFT £9926
111 10/07 Chan 1m1f SFT £17568
90 9/07 Lonc 1m1f55y G-S £9459
Total win prize-money £36953

Going (Turf): **Sf: 2-6** GS: 1-2 Gd: 0-3 GF: 0-0 Fm: 0-0
Distance: 5f/6f: 0-0 7f-8f: 0-4 **9f-13f: 3-8** 14f+: 0-0
Track : LH: 0-4 **RH: 2-4** Tight: 0-1 Gall: 0-2
Aids: Bl: 0-0 Vi: 0-0 Tstrap: 0-0 Ckp: 0-0
Best Rating: **111** 10/07 Chan 1m1f soft

Very useful; effective over 1m2f-1m4f; acts on soft ground.

Salerosa (IRE)

107(105) (86)69
4-y-o b f Monashee Mountain (USA)-Sainte Gig (FR) (Saint Cyrien (FR))
Mrs A Duffield David K Barker & Phil White

Placings:4/450114-621413030315211 (7711)
2009: 9^{6}GF, 7^{2}GF, 8^{1}G, 8^{4}GF, 8^{1}GF, 9^{3}G, 8^{0}S, 7^{3}GF, 8^{0}G, 7^{3}GF, 7^{1}SD, 7^{5}G, 8^{2}SD, 8^{1}SD, 8^{1}SD,

	Starts	1st	2nd	3rd	Win & Pl
Career Total (Turf)	15	2	1	3	9715
Career Total (AW)	7	5	1	0	19369

86 12/09 Sthl 1m (0-75)H STD £2729
82 11/09 Sthl 1m (0-85)H STD £6152
78 9/09 Sthl 7f (0-75)H STD £3753
68 6/09 Ayr 1m (0-70)H G-F £3238
69 5/09 Bevl 1m100y (0-70)H GD £2914
65 11/08 Sthl 1m (0-60)H STD £1648
67 11/08 Sthl 1m STD £3070
Total win prize-money £23506

Going (Turf): Sf: 0-1 GS: 0-2 **Gd: 1-5 GF: 1-7** Fm: 0-0
Distance: 5f/6f: 0-0 **7f-8f: 6-17** 9f-13f: 1-5 14f+: 0-0
Track : **LH: 6-11** RH: 1-10 Tight: 0-7 Gall: 0-1
Aids: Bl: 0-0 Vi: 0-0 Tstrap: 0-0 Ckp: 0-0
Best Rating: **86** 12/09 Sthl 1m stand

Fair; effective at around 1m; handles fast ground and Fibresand.

Salgrev (IRE)

102(74) (25)55
3-y-o gr f Verglas (IRE)-Leverick Bay (Octagonal (NZ))
Paul W Flynn (Irene J Monaghan 12/6) J J Keogh

Placings:0004-0062012 (4834a)
2009: 7^{0}SF, 7^{0}Y, 10^{6}S, 6^{2}F, 8^{0}GF, 6^{1}S, 7^{2}S,

	Starts	1st	2nd	3rd	Win & Pl
Career Total (Turf)	10	1	2	0	6919
Career Total (AW)	1	0	0	0	

55 8/09 Naas 6f (47-65)H SFT £4696
Total win prize-money £4696

Going (Turf): **Sf: 1-3** GS: 0-1 Gd: 0-2 GF: 0-1 Fm: 0-1
Distance: **5f/6f: 1-4** 7f-8f: 0-6 9f-13f: 0-1 14f+: 0-0
Track : **LH: 1-7** RH: 0-0 Tight: 0-1 Gall: 0-0
Aids: Bl: 0-0 Vi: 0-0 Tstrap: 0-0 Ckp: 0-0
Best Rating: **55** 8/09 Tipp 7f100y soft

Moderate; stays 7f plus but effective at 6f; acts on soft ground.

Salient

106(106) (91)92
5-y-o b g Fasliyev (USA)-Savannah Belle (Green Desert (USA))
M J Attwater Canisbay Bloodstock

Placings:601134/033520321002523/30104004032000-440300646430000 (7271)
2009: 8^{4}GF, 7^{4}GF, 7^{0}GF, 8^{3}SD, 7^{0}GS, 8^{0}SD, 8^{6}GF, 8^{4}G, 7^{4}SD, 8^{6}GF, 7^{4}GF, 7^{3}GF, 8^{0}GF, 8^{0}GS, 7^{0}SD, 8^{0}SD,

	Starts	1st	2nd	3rd	Win & Pl
Career Total (Turf)	32	2	3	5	32976
Career Total (AW)	19	2	2	4	19789

92 5/08 Gdwd 1m (0-100)H SFT £9969
93 9/07 Sand 7f16y (0-80)H GD £5181
81 11/06 Ling 7f (0-85) STD £4533
79 9/06 Ling 7f STD £3238
Total win prize-money £22925

Going (Turf): **Sf: 1-5** GS: 0-7 **Gd: 1-5** GF: 0-14 Fm: 0-1
Distance: 5f/6f: 0-1 **7f-8f: 4-46** 9f-13f: 0-4 14f+: 0-0
Track : LH: 2-20 RH: 2-21 **Tight: 2-18** Gall: 0-1
Aids: Bl: 0-0 Vi: 0-0 Tstrap: 0-0 Ckp: 0-0
Best Rating: **95** 5/08 Ling 7f stand

Useful; effective at around 7f-1m; acts on most ground; also goes on Polytrack.

Sally Bawn (IRE)

(100) (65)54
4-y-o b f Rossini (USA)-Finnegans Dilemma (IRE) (Marktingo)
Gordon Elliott (Ms Caroline Hutchinson 23/10) S Class BMW Syndicate

Placings:0000-3421054 (7785)
2009: 6^{3}S, 6^{4}SD, 9^{2}YS, 10^{1}SD, 8^{0}SD, 9^{5}SD, 13^{4}SD,

	Starts	1st	2nd	3rd	Win & Pl
Career Total (Turf)	6	0	1	1	1655
Career Total (AW)	5	1	0	0	5235

60 10/09 Dund 1m2f150y (47-65)H STD £4696
Total win prize-money £4696

Going (Turf): **Sf: 0-1 GS: 0-0 Gd: 0-3 GF: 0-0 Fm: 0-0**
Distance: 5f/6f: 0-2 7f-8f: 0-1 **9f-13f: 1-7** 14f+: 0-1
Track : **LH: 1-8** RH: 0-3 Tight: 0-2 Gall: 0-0
Aids: Bl: 0-0 Vi: 0-0 Tstrap: 0-0 Ckp: 0-0
Best Rating: **65** 12/09 Wolv 1m5f194y stand

Sally Forth

93(109) (83)71
3-y-o b f Dubai Destination (USA)-Daralbayda (IRE) (Doyoun)
R Charlton The Queen

Placings:63315 (6388)
2009: 12^{6}GF, 12^{3}GF, 12^{3}G, 16^{1}SD, 16^{5}GF,

	Starts	1st	2nd	3rd	Win & Pl
Career Total (Turf)	4	0	0	2	1204
Career Total (AW)	1	1	0	0	6476

83 8/09 Sthl 2m (0-80)H STD £6476
Total win prize-money £6476

Going (Turf): **Sf: 0-0 GS: 0-0 Gd: 0-1 GF: 0-3 Fm: 0-0**
Distance: 5f/6f: 0-0 7f-8f: 0-0 9f-13f: 0-3 **14f+: 1-2**
Track : **LH: 1-4** RH: 0-1 Tight: 0-0 Gall: 0-2
Aids: Bl: 0-0 Vi: 0-0 Tstrap: 0-0 Ckp: 0-0
Best Rating: **83** 8/09 Sthl 2m stand

Fair; stays 2m; acts on fast ground and on Fibresand.

Sally O'Riley

39
3-y-o ch f Vettori (IRE)-Swallow Breeze (Salse (USA))
F Watson Barry Emery

Placings:00 (4347)
2009: 10^{0}GF, 9^{0}G,

	Starts	1st	2nd	3rd	Win & Pl
Career Total (Turf)	2	0	0	0	

Going (Turf): **Sf: 0-0 GS: 0-0 Gd: 0-1 GF: 0-1 Fm: 0-0**
Distance: 5f/6f: 0-0 7f-8f: 0-0 9f-13f: 0-2 14f+: 0-0
Track : LH: 0-1 RH: 0-1 Tight: 0-1 Gall: 0-0

Aids:	Bl: 0-0 Vi: 0-0 Tstrap: 0-1 Ckp: 0-1			

Sally's Dilemma

(94) (55)79

3-y-o b f Primo Valentino (IRE)-Lake Mistassiu (Tina's Pet)

W G M Turner E A Brook

Placings:125426**030-54** (0064)

2009: 6^{5}SS, 7^{4}SS,

	Starts	1st	2nd	3rd	Win & Pl
Career Total (Turf)	5	1	2	0	12586
Career Total (AW)	6	0	0	1	302

79	3/08	Donc	5f	G-S	£9715

Total win prize-money £9716

Going (Turf):	Sf: 0-1 **GS: 1-1** Gd: 0-2 GF: 0-1 Fm: 0-0
Distance:	**5f/6f: 1-9** 7f-8f: 0-2 9f-13f: 0-0 14f+: 0-0
Track :	LH: 0-5 RH: 0-2 Tight: 0-0 Gall: 0-2
Aids:	Bl: 0-0 Vi: 0-0 Tstrap: 0-1 Ckp: 0-1
Best Rating:	**79** 3/08 Donc 5f gd-sft

Fair juvenile; winner of the 2008 Brocklesby; held since; effective at 5f; acts on good to soft ground.

Sally's Swansong

81(80) (33)34

3-y-o b f Mind Games-Sister Sal (Bairn (USA))

M Wellings Miss F Fenley

Placings:0-000050 (4281)

2009: 6^{0}GF, 7^{0}SD, 7^{0}SD, 6^{0}G, 6^{5}G, 6^{0}G,

	Starts	1st	2nd	3rd	Win & Pl
Career Total (Turf)	4	0	0	0	0
Career Total (AW)	3	0	0	0	

Going (Turf):	**Sf: 0-0 GS: 0-0 Gd: 0-3 GF: 0-1 Fm: 0-0**
Distance:	5f/6f: 0-3 7f-8f: 0-4 9f-13f: 0-0 14f+: 0-0
Track :	LH: 0-4 RH: 0-0 Tight: 0-2 Gall: 0-0
Aids:	Bl: 0-0 Vi: 0-0 Tstrap: 0-4 Ckp: 0-4
Best Rating:	**34** 7/09 Nott 6f15y good

Salontiger (GER)

57 91

7-y-o b g Tiger Hill (IRE)-She's His Guest (IRE) (Be My Guest (USA))

P J Hobbs Brian Barry-Murphy

Placings:0/120000/262412405/26340/0 (2351)

2009: 10^{0}GF,

	Starts	1st	2nd	3rd	Win & Pl
Career Total (Turf)	22	2	5	1	20292

7/06	Muni	1m	H	GD	£3448
5/05	Muni	1m		GD	£1808

Total win prize-money £5257

Going (Turf):	Sf: 0-6 GS: 0-0 **Gd: 2-14** GF: 0-2 Fm: 0-0
Distance:	5f/6f: 0-5 **7f-8f: 2-14** 9f-13f: 0-3 14f+: 0-0
Track :	**LH: 1-4** RH: 0-4 Tight: 0-0 Gall: 0-0
Aids:	Bl: 0-0 Vi: 0-0 Tstrap: 0-0 Ckp: 0-0
Best Rating:	**91** 4/07 Colo 6f good

Saloon (USA)

103(110) (79)80

5-y-o b g Sadler's Wells (USA)-Fire The Groom (USA) (Blushing Groom (FR))

Jane Chapple-Hyam (P Bowen 13/2) Mrs Jane Chapple-Hyam

Placings:0/2/0**606P5323-121232402042** (7675)

2009: 12^{1}SD, 13^{2}SD, 12^{1}GF, 11^{2}GF, 12^{3}GF, 14^{2}GF, 14^{4}G, 12^{0}GF, 11^{2}G, 14^{0}GS, 12^{4}SD, 14^{2}SD,

	Starts	1st	2nd	3rd	Win & Pl
Career Total (Turf)	15	1	5	3	9833
Career Total (AW)	8	1	2	0	4010

74	5/09	Gdwd	1m4f	(0-70)H	G-F	£3238
65	4/09	Kemp	1m4f	(0-55)H	STD	£2047

Total win prize-money £5285

Going (Turf):	Sf: 0-2 GS: 0-3 Gd: 0-5 **GF: 1-5** Fm: 0-0
Distance:	5f/6f: 0-0 7f-8f: 0-1 **9f-13f: 2-14** 14f+: 0-8
Track :	LH: 0-13 **RH: 2-9 Tight: 1-7** Gall: 0-5
Aids:	Bl: 0-0 Vi: 0-0 Tstrap: 2-12 Ckp: 2-12
Best Rating:	**80** 10/09 Catt 1m3f214y good

Fair; stays 1m6f; acts on fast and easy ground; goes on Polytrack and on Fibresand; has worn cheekpieces/tongue tie.

Salt Lake (GER)

(78) 62

7-y-o b g Monsun (GER)-Shine (GER) (Sanglamore (USA))

John Joseph Murphy (E J O'Grady 11/4) Pacmen Syndicate

Placings:600/321611400/0/6/0-0050 (5642)

2009: 16^{0}GF, 16^{0}SH, 16^{5}GF, 16^{0}SD,

	Starts	1st	2nd	3rd	Win & Pl
Career Total (Turf)	18	3	1	1	10281
Career Total (AW)	1	0	0	0	

8/05	Duss	1m	H	SFT	£3333
7/05	Duss	1m110y	H	GD	£2907
6/05	Dres	1m2f		GD	£1843

Total win prize-money £8085

Going (Turf):	Sf: 1-6 GS: 0-0 **Gd: 2-6** GF: 0-3 Fm: 0-0
Distance:	5f/6f: 0-0 7f-8f: 1-7 **9f-13f: 2-7** 14f+: 0-5
Track :	LH: 0-2 RH: 0-7 Tight: 0-0 Gall: 0-0
Aids:	Bl: 0-0 Vi: 0-0 Tstrap: 0-0 Ckp: 0-0
Best Rating:	**79** 4/07 Curr 1m4f gd-fm

Salt Of The Earth (IRE)

84(105) (73)62

4-y-o b g Invincible Spirit (IRE)-Get The Accountant (Vettori (IRE))

T G Mills Mrs Yvonne Russell

Placings:3/222400002103-53043000 (2598)

2009: 8^{5}SD, 7^{3}SD, 8^{0}SD, 7^{4}SD, 8^{3}SD, 6^{0}F, 8^{0}GF, 7^{0}SD,

	Starts	1st	2nd	3rd	Win & Pl
Career Total (Turf)	4	0	0	0	
Career Total (AW)	17	1	4	4	6304

71	11/08	Kemp	7f	(0-65)H	STD	£1706

Total win prize-money £1706

Going (Turf):	**Sf: 0-0 GS: 0-1 Gd: 0-0 GF: 0-2 Fm: 0-1**
Distance:	5f/6f: 0-6 **7f-8f: 1-15** 9f-13f: 0-0 14f+: 0-0
Track :	LH: 0-10 **RH: 1-9** Tight: 0-8 Gall: 0-1
Aids:	Bl: 0-1 Vi: 0-0 Tstrap: 0-0 Ckp: 0-0
Best Rating:	**76** 2/08 Ling 1m stand

Fair; stays 1m and acts on Polytrack.

Saltagioo (ITY)

102(109) (92)91

5-y-o b g Dr Devious (IRE)-Sces (Kris)

A King (I A Wood 9/9) Richard Abbott & Mario Stavrou

Placings:3152165236/01100120**542-421**0300**10** (5725)

2009: 8^{4}SD, 8^{2}SD, 8^{1}SD, 8^{0}SD, 8^{3}GF, 10^{0}GF, 8^{0}G, 8^{1}G, 9^{0}GF,

	Starts	1st	2nd	3rd	Win & Pl
Career Total (Turf)	22	6	3	3	47036
Career Total (AW)	8	1	2	0	11431

70	7/09	Sand	1m14y		GD	£3238
92	3/09	Kemp	1m	(0-95)H	STD	£7771
	7/08	Livo	1m1f165y		GD	£3125
	3/08	Siro	1m		GD	£9375
	2/08	Gros	1m165y		GD	£9375
	6/07	Siro	1m2f		GD	£3445
	3/07	Siro	1m1f		SFT	£5743

Total win prize-money £42072

Going (Turf):	Sf: 1-5 GS: 0-0 **Gd: 5-14** GF: 0-3 Fm: 0-0
Distance:	5f/6f: 0-0 7f-8f: 2-8 **9f-13f: 5-22** 14f+: 0-0
Track :	LH: 0-6 **RH: 2-5** Tight: 0-5 Gall: 0-2
Aids:	Bl: 0-0 Vi: 0-0 Tstrap: 0-0 Ckp: 0-0
Best Rating:	**92** 3/09 Kemp 1m stand

Useful; stays 1m2f ; handles a sound surface on turf and acts on Polytrack; has worn a tongue tie; likes to race prominently.

Saluscraggie

90 64

7-y-o b m Most Welcome-Upper Caen (High Top)

R E Barr Brian Morton

Placings:000/03003051/14450/01560204000-2P (1692)

2009: 11^{2}GF, 13^{P}G,

	Starts	1st	2nd	3rd	Win & Pl
Career Total (Turf)	29	3	2	2	10986

66	4/08	Catt	1m3f214y	(0-70)H	G-S	£2331
61	6/07	Nott	1m1f213y	(0-60)H	GD	£2388
58	10/06	Catt	1m5f175y	(0-60)H	SFT	£3238

Total win prize-money £7959

Going (Turf):	**Sf: 1-6 GS: 1-7 Gd: 1-9** GF: 0-7 Fm: 0-0
Distance:	5f/6f: 0-1 7f-8f: 0-1 **9f-13f: 2-21** 14f+: 1-6
Track :	**LH: 3-20** RH: 0-7 **Tight: 2-11** Gall: 0-3
Aids:	Bl: 0-0 Vi: 0-0 Tstrap: 0-2 Ckp: 0-2
Best Rating:	**66** 4/08 Catt 1m3f214y gd-sft

Moderate; suited by 1m6f; acts on fast and easy ground.

Salut Saint Cloud

99(112) (58)58

8-y-o b g Primo Dominie-Tiriana (Common Grounds)

G L Moore A Grinter

Placings:64600600004**5**/60513331410/00/**12014**/0451260 000/004222-000 (2429)

2009: 13^{0}SD, 16^{0}SD, 16^{0}G,

	Starts	1st	2nd	3rd	Win & Pl
Career Total (Turf)	20	2	1	2	8286
Career Total (AW)	29	4	4	1	15099

71	3/07	Kemp	2m	(0-65)H	STD	£2047
71	12/06	Sthl	2m	(0-75)H	STD	£3238
63	3/06	Wolv	2m119y	(0-65)H	STD	£2388
71	8/04	Chep	2m49y	F(0-55)H	SFT	£3241
66	8/04	Sthl	1m6f	G(0-55)H	STD	£2996
57	6/04	Rdcr	1m2f	F	GD	£2968

Total win prize-money £16881

Going (Turf):	**Sf: 1-2** GS: 0-2 **Gd: 1-6** GF: 0-8 Fm: 0-2
Distance:	5f/6f: 0-5 7f-8f: 0-9 9f-13f: 1-13 **14f+: 5-22**
Track :	**LH: 5-32** RH: 1-8 **Tight: 2-17** Gall: 0-1
Aids:	Bl: 0-1 Vi: 0-5 Tstrap: 5-24 Ckp: 5-24
Best Rating:	**79** 3/07 Kemp 2m stand

Moderate handicapper; stays 2m; acts on good and soft ground and both All-Weather surfaces; useful hurdler.

Salute (IRE)

(108) (83)**89**

10-y-o b g Muhtarram (USA)-Alasib (Siberian Express (USA))

P G Murphy The Golden Anorak Partnership

Placings:142150/020205/326060/03/4402100000/003035 10503420311/12054431024 1/263551040424-261400560 (5837)

2009: 16^{2}SD, 16^{6}SD, 13^{1}SD, 16^{4}SD, 16^{0}SD, 12^{0}SD, 16^{5}SD, 16^{6}SD, 13^{0}SD,

	Starts	1st	2nd	3rd	Win & Pl
Career Total (Turf)	41	5	5	3	87837
Career Total (AW)	39	6	6	5	45470

83	3/09	Wolv	1m5f194y	(0-85)H	STD	£4857
82	7/08	Kemp	2m	(0-90)H	STD	£7352
81	12/07	Wolv	1m5f194y		STD	£2047
59	9/07	Wwck	1m4f134y		G-F	£3562
87	3/07	Wolv	1m5f194y	(0-85)H	STD	£5505
78	12/06	Kemp	2m	(0-75)H	STD	£4533
76	12/06	Wolv	2m119y	(0-75)H	STD	£3886
85	6/06	Sand	1m6f	(0-85)H	GD	£5505
93	6/05	Wind	1m3f135y	(0-100)H	GD	£12098
89	8/01	Newc	1m3y	B H	G-F	£29250
71	6/01	Wind	6f	E	G-F	£4165

Total win prize-money £82764

Going (Turf): Sf: 0-4 GS: 0-8 Gd: 2-8 **GF: 3-19** Fm: 0-2
Distance: 5f/6f: 1-3 7f-8f: 0-2 9f-13f: 3-30 **14f+: 7-45**
Track : **LH: 5-39** RH: 3-32 **Tight: 5-33** Gall: 1-15
Aids: Bl: 0-1 Vi: 0-2 Tstrap: 0-1 Ckp: 0-1
Best Rating: 100 5/03 York 1m2f88y gd-fm

Fair; stays 2m; acts on good ground; goes on Polytrack.

Salute Him (IRE)

110 **106**

6-y-o b g Mull Of Kintyre (USA)-Living Legend (ITY) (Archway (IRE))

A J Martin Byrne Bros (Formwork) Limited

Placings:136120/060120012/0/200-0130 (6480)

2009: 10^{0}GF, 10^{1}GF, 10^{3}GF, 9^{0}GF,

	Starts	1st	2nd	3rd	Win & Pl
Career Total (Turf)	23	5	4	2	64286

95	6/09	Navn	1m2f	(60-90)H	G-F	£9056
97	8/06	Sand	1m2f7y	(0-90)H	GD	£9715
91	6/06	Sand	1m2f7y	(0-90)H	GD	£8096
81	7/05	Newb	7f		G-S	£4277
69	3/05	Folk	5f		SFT	£4108

Total win prize-money £35254

Going (Turf): Sf: 1-3 GS: 1-2 **Gd: 2-4** GF: 1-12 Fm: 0-0
Distance: 5f/6f: 1-2 7f-8f: 1-7 **9f-13f: 3-13** 14f+: 0-1
Track : LH: 1-5 **RH: 2-9** Tight: 0-3 Gall: 0-4
Aids: Bl: 0-0 Vi: 0-0 Tstrap: 0-0 Ckp: 0-0
Best Rating: 106 6/09 Asct 1m2f gd-fm

Useful; stays 1m4f but effective at shorter; acts on most ground; effective with forcing tactics.

Salvation

69 **4**

2-y-o b f Montjeu (IRE)-Birdie (Alhaarth (IRE))

M L W Bell Highclere Thoroughbred Racing (Birdie) I

Placings:0 (7243)

2009: 8^{0}S,

	Starts	1st	2nd	3rd	Win & Pl
Career Total (Turf)	1	0	0	0	

Going (Turf): Sf: 0-1 GS: 0-0 Gd: 0-0 GF: 0-0 Fm: 0-0
Distance: 5f/6f: 0-0 7f-8f: 0-0 9f-13f: 0-1 14f+: 0-0
Track : LH: 0-1 RH: 0-0 Tight: 0-0 Gall: 0-0
Aids: Bl: 0-0 Vi: 0-0 Tstrap: 0-0 Ckp: 0-0
Best Rating: 4 11/09 Nott 1m75y soft

Salybia Bay

101(101) (67)**70**

3-y-o b f Fraam-Down The Valley (Kampala)

R Hannon J R Shannon

Placings:0050-002223040242333 (7392)

2009: 8^{0}GF, 10^{0}GF, 10^{2}G, 11^{2}GF, 12^{2}GF, 12^{3}GF, 11^{0}GF, 12^{4}SD, 10^{0}G, 12^{2}GF, 12^{4}SD, 12^{2}SD, 9^{3}GF, 10^{3}G, 10^{3}SD,

	Starts	1st	2nd	3rd	Win & Pl
Career Total (Turf)	11	0	4	3	4650
Career Total (AW)	8	0	1	1	907

Going (Turf): Sf: 0-0 GS: 0-0 Gd: 0-3 GF: 0-8 Fm: 0-0
Distance: 5f/6f: 0-0 7f-8f: 0-4 9f-13f: 0-15 14f+: 0-0
Track : LH: 0-8 RH: 0-9 Tight: 0-11 Gall: 0-2
Aids: Bl: 0-0 Vi: 0-0 Tstrap: 0-0 Ckp: 0-0
Best Rating: 70 5/09 Wind 1m3f135y gd-fm

Modest; stays 1m3f; acts on a sound surface and Polytrack.

Sam Jicaro

78 **42**

2-y-o b g Mind Games-Claradotnet (Sri Pekan (USA))

Mrs L Williamson G D Kendrick

Placings:00 (4557)

2009: 6^{0}GS, 7^{0}G,

	Starts	1st	2nd	3rd	Win & Pl
Career Total (Turf)	2	0	0	0	

Going (Turf): Sf: 0-0 GS: 0-1 Gd: 0-1 GF: 0-0 Fm: 0-0
Distance: 5f/6f: 0-1 7f-8f: 0-1 9f-13f: 0-0 14f+: 0-0
Track : LH: 0-1 RH: 0-0 Tight: 0-1 Gall: 0-0
Aids: Bl: 0-0 Vi: 0-0 Tstrap: 0-0 Ckp: 0-0
Best Rating: 42 8/09 Ches 7f2y good

Sam Lord

99(103) (86)**90**

5-y-o ch g Observatory (USA)-My Mariam (Salse (USA))

James Moffatt (A King 18/7) Coachmans Cottagers

Placings:561/004/1654-05015 (4098)

2009: 12^{0}SD, 12^{5}G, 14^{0}G, 14^{1}G, 14^{5}G,

	Starts	1st	2nd	3rd	Win & Pl
Career Total (Turf)	11	3	0	0	16061
Career Total (AW)	4	0	0	0	351

88	6/09	Sals	1m6f21y	(0-85)H	GD	£4857
87	7/08	Wind	1m2f7y	(0-85)H	SFT	£5504
80	10/06	NmkR	1m		G-S	£5181

Total win prize-money £15544

Going (Turf): Sf: 1-1 GS: 1-1 Gd: 1-5 GF: 0-4 Fm: 0-0
Distance: 5f/6f: 0-1 7f-8f: 1-2 9f-13f: 1-9 14f+: 1-3
Track : LH: 0-3 **RH: 2-10 Tight: 2-8** Gall: 0-2
Aids: Bl: 0-0 Vi: 0-0 Tstrap: 0-0 Ckp: 0-0
Best Rating: 90 7/08 Newb 1m2f6y good

Fair; stays 1m6f; acts on good and soft ground.

Sam Sharp (USA)

111(99) (80)**83**

3-y-o b/br g Johannesburg (USA)- Caffe (USA) (Mr Prospector (USA))

H R A Cecil N Martin

Placings:0-210606524 (6680)

2009: 8^{2}SD, 10^{1}S, 10^{0}G, 10^{6}S, 8^{0}SD, 10^{6}GF, 12^{5}GF, 11^{2}GF, 10^{4}G,

	Starts	1st	2nd	3rd	Win & Pl
Career Total (Turf)	8	1	1	0	9060
Career Total (AW)	2	0	1	0	1310

83	5/09	Newb	1m2f6y	SFT	£6476

Total win prize-money £6476

Going (Turf): Sf: 1-2 GS: 0-0 Gd: 0-3 GF: 0-3 Fm: 0-0
Distance: 5f/6f: 0-0 7f-8f: 0-3 **9f-13f: 1-7** 14f+: 0-0
Track : **LH: 1-4** RH: 0-6 Tight: 0-4 **Gall: 1-3**
Aids: Bl: 0-0 Vi: 0-0 Tstrap: 0-0 Ckp: 0-0
Best Rating: 83 5/09 Newb 1m2f6y soft

Useful; stays 1m2f; acts on Polytrack and easy ground.

Sam's Cross (IRE)

101(102) (78)**74**

4-y-o b g Cape Cross (IRE)-Fancy Lady (Cadeaux Genereux)

J J Bridger (Pat Eddery 6/7) J J Bridger

Placings:2130/04000420-04434010050600 1006 (7879)

2009: 8^{0}SD, 7^{4}SD, 6^{4}GF, 6^{3}GF, 6^{4}G, 6^{0}GF, 5^{1}F, 7^{0}GF, 5^{0}GS, 6^{5}GF, 7^{0}G, 6^{6}GF, 7^{0}SD, 7^{0}GF, 6^{1}SD, 6^{0}SD, 6^{0}SD, 6^{6}SD,

	Starts	1st	2nd	3rd	Win & Pl
Career Total (Turf)	20	2	1	2	10640
Career Total (AW)	10	1	1	0	2945

67	9/09	Kemp	6f	(0-60)H	STD	£2047
66	7/09	Brig	5f213y		FRM	£1942
86	9/07	Gdwd	6f		G-F	£4857

Total win prize-money £8848

Going (Turf): Sf: 0-0 GS: 0-2 Gd: 0-5 **GF: 1-12 Fm: 1-1**
Distance: **5f/6f: 3-18** 7f-8f: 0-11 9f-13f: 0-1 14f+: 0-0
Track : LH: 1-11 RH: 1-7 Tight: 0-7 Gall: 0-2
Aids: **Bl: 1-3** Vi: 0-1 Tstrap: 0-1 Ckp: 0-1
Best Rating: 86 10/07 Asct 7f gd-sft

Modest; effective over 6f-7f; acts on fast ground; goes on Polytrack.

Sam's Secret

96 (69)**87**

7-y-o b m Josr Algarhoud (IRE)-Twilight Time (Aragon)

G A Swinbank Copskam Partnership

Placings:232030/0320022160/400000/114111626/435222 -03045 (3174)

2009: 7^{0}GF, 7^{3}F, 7^{0}GF, 8^{4}GF, 7^{5}GF,

	Starts	1st	2nd	3rd	Win & Pl
Career Total (Turf)	40	6	9	4	39157
Career Total (AW)	2	0	0	1	641

82	8/07	Muss	7f30y	(0-75)H	G-F	£3886
75	8/07	Rdcr	1m	(0-65)H	GD	£2817
78	7/07	Muss	1m	(0-70)H	GD	£3238
68	5/07	Rdcr	7f		G-F	£2047
53	5/07	Muss	1m		G-F	£1943
74	9/05	Newc	7f	(0-70)	G-F	£4186

Total win prize-money £18119

Going (Turf): Sf: 0-2 GS: 0-1 Gd: 2-8 **GF: 4-26** Fm: 0-3
Distance: 5f/6f: 0-3 **7f-8f: 6-35** 9f-13f: 0-4 14f+: 0-0
Track : LH: 0-13 **RH: 3-7 Tight: 3-12** Gall: 0-4
Aids: Bl: 0-0 Vi: 0-1 Tstrap: 0-4 Ckp: 0-4
Best Rating: 87 6/08 Haml 1m65y good

Fair; effective over 7f-1m; acts on good and fast ground; has worn cheekpieces.

Samaaha

102(94) (82)76
3-y-o b f Singspiel (IRE)-Genovefa (USA) (Woodman (USA))
Saeed Bin Suroor Godolphin

Placings:232125 (7402)
2009: 10²HY, 10³G, 11²GF, 12¹SD, 16²SD, 16⁵SD,

	Starts	1st	2nd	3rd	Win & Pl
Career Total (Turf)	3	0	2	1	2076
Career Total (AW)	3	1	1	0	6322

75 9/09 Kemp 1m4f STD £4727
Total win prize-money £4727

Going (Turf): Sf: 0-1 GS: 0-0 Gd: 0-1 GF: 0-1 Fm: 0-0
Distance: 5f/6f: 0-0 7f-8f: 0-0 **9f-13f: 1-4** 14f+: 0-2
Track : LH: 0-3 **RH: 1-3** Tight: 0-3 Gall: 0-0
Aids: Bl: 0-0 Vi: 0-0 Tstrap: 0-0 Ckp: 0-0
Best Rating: 82 10/09 Kemp 2m stand

Fair; effective at 1m2f-1m4f; acts on heavy ground and Polytrack.

Samarinda (USA)

99(107) (101)77
6-y-o ch g Rahy (USA)-Munnaya (USA) (Nijinsky (CAN))
Mrs P Sly D Bayliss, T Davies, G Libson & P Sly

Placings:004561/2410111330/410040000163-36046000 (7626)
2009: 8³SD, 8⁶SD, 8⁰SD, 8⁴SD, 8⁶SD, 8⁰GF, 8⁰GF, 8⁰SD,

	Starts	1st	2nd	3rd	Win & Pl
Career Total (Turf)	9	0	0	1	2333
Career Total (AW)	27	7	1	3	62690

99 10/08 Kemp 1m (0-100)H STD £11215
99 2/08 Ling 1m2f (0-100)H STD £9971
97 7/07 Ling 1m (0-90) STD £9348
93 7/07 Kemp 1m (0-80)H STD £4728
85 6/07 Kemp 1m (0-80)H STD £4728
81 3/07 Wolv 1m141y (0-75)H STD £3238
66 12/06 Ling 1m2f STD £3886
Total win prize-money £47116

Going (Turf): Sf: 0-1 GS: 0-2 Gd: 0-1 GF: 0-5 Fm: 0-0
Distance: 5f/6f: 0-0 **7f-8f: 4-23** 9f-13f: 3-13 14f+: 0-0
Track : LH: 4-17 RH: 3-13 **Tight: 4-15** Gall: 0-1
Aids: Bl: 0-0 Vi: 0-0 Tstrap: 0-0 Ckp: 0-0
Best Rating: 101 12/08 GrLe 1m stand

Very useful; effective from 1m-1m2f; acts well on Polytrack; can break slowly.

Samba Mirander

(90) (53)
3-y-o b f Zaha (CAN)-Silent Scream (IRE) (Lahib (USA))
C Drew C Drew

Placings:0-30 (3508)
2009: 10³SD, 11⁰SD,

	Starts	1st	2nd	3rd	Win & Pl
Career Total (Turf)	0	0	0	0	
Career Total (AW)	3	0	0	1	385

Going (Turf): Sf: 0-0 GS: 0-0 Gd: 0-0 GF: 0-0 Fm: 0-0
Distance: 5f/6f: 0-0 7f-8f: 0-1 9f-13f: 0-2 14f+: 0-0
Track : LH: 0-1 RH: 0-2 Tight: 0-0 Gall: 0-1
Aids: Bl: 0-0 Vi: 0-0 Tstrap: 0-1 Ckp: 0-1
Best Rating: 53 6/09 Kemp 1m2f stand

Sambulando (FR)

(100) (71)79
6-y-o gr g Kouroun (FR)-Somnambula (IRE) (Petoski)
T R George Oliver Pawle & Tim Syder

Placings:3523/2 (0621)
2009: 11²SD,

	Starts	1st	2nd	3rd	Win & Pl
Career Total (Turf)	4	0	1	2	7449
Career Total (AW)	1	0	1	0	806

Going (Turf): Sf: 0-3 GS: 0-1 Gd: 0-0 GF: 0-0 Fm: 0-0
Distance: 5f/6f: 0-0 7f-8f: 0-1 9f-13f: 0-3 14f+: 0-1
Track : LH: 0-2 RH: 0-1 Tight: 0-0 Gall: 0-0
Aids: Bl: 0-0 Vi: 0-0 Tstrap: 0-0 Ckp: 0-0
Best Rating: 79 4/06 Chan 1m2f soft

Modest; ex-French; stays 1m3f; acts on Fibresand.

Samizdat (FR)

96 59
6-y-o b g Soviet Star (USA)-Secret Account (FR) (Bering)
Mrs Dianne Sayer (James Moffatt 25/6) Mrs Freda Rayson

Placings:15023250/00/5550 (6769)
2009: 11⁵GF, 12⁵GS, 10⁵GF, 12⁰GS,

	Starts	1st	2nd	3rd	Win & Pl
Career Total (Turf)	13	1	2	1	9346
Career Total (AW)	1	0	0	0	0

4/06 Saum 1m4f GD £2758
Total win prize-money £2759

Going (Turf): Sf: 0-2 GS: 0-4 **Gd: 1-3** GF: 0-4 Fm: 0-0
Distance: 5f/6f: 0-0 7f-8f: 0-0 **9f-13f: 1-10** 14f+: 0-4
Track : LH: 0-7 RH: 0-2 Tight: 0-2 Gall: 0-3
Aids: Bl: 0-6 Vi: 0-3 Tstrap: 0-1 Ckp: 0-1
Best Rating: 72 8/06 Deau 1m7f soft

Sammy The Snake (IRE)

92(97) (86)58
4-y-o b g Diktat-Love Emerald (USA) (Mister Baileys)
B W Duke B W Duke

Placings:1/500000 (6909)
2009: 6⁵SD, 7⁰G, 6⁰GF, 8⁰SD, 7⁰SD, 8⁰G,

	Starts	1st	2nd	3rd	Win & Pl
Career Total (Turf)	4	1	0	0	8797
Career Total (AW)	3	0	0	0	0

86 3/07 Curr 5f HVY £8797
Total win prize-money £8797

Going (Turf): Sf: 1-1 GS: 0-0 Gd: 0-2 GF: 0-1 Fm: 0-0
Distance: 5f/6f: 1-3 7f-8f: 0-3 9f-13f: 0-1 14f+: 0-0
Track : LH: 0-2 RH: 0-3 Tight: 0-2 Gall: 0-0
Aids: Bl: 0-1 Vi: 0-0 Tstrap: 0-1 Ckp: 0-1
Best Rating: 86 4/09 Kemp 6f stand

Useful; effective over 5f; acts on heavy ground; has worn blinkers.

Sampi

89(90) (66)82
3-y-o ch f Beat Hollow-Delta (Zafonic (USA))
Mrs A J Perrett K Abdulla

Placings:51-00 (5475)
2009: 9⁰GF, 9⁰GF,

	Starts	1st	2nd	3rd	Win & Pl
Career Total (Turf)	3	1	0	0	3562
Career Total (AW)	1	0	0	0	0

82 10/08 Nott 1m75y SFT £3561
Total win prize-money £3562

Going (Turf): Sf: 1-1 GS: 0-0 Gd: 0-0 GF: 0-2 Fm: 0-0
Distance: 5f/6f: 0-0 7f-8f: 0-1 **9f-13f: 1-3** 14f+: 0-0
Track : LH: 1-1 RH: 0-3 Tight: 0-2 Gall: 0-0
Aids: Bl: 0-0 Vi: 0-0 Tstrap: 0-0 Ckp: 0-0
Best Rating: 82 10/08 Nott 1m75y soft

Fair; stays 1m; acts on soft ground.

Sampower Quin (IRE)

94(84) (61)66
3-y-o b g Sampower Star-Quinolina (Shareef Dancer (USA))
D Carroll David Watts

Placings:0003-00000 (6919)
2009: 12⁰GF, 10⁰GF, 9⁰F, 12⁰SD, 11⁰GF,

	Starts	1st	2nd	3rd	Win & Pl
Career Total (Turf)	5	0	0	1	578
Career Total (AW)	4	0	0	0	

Going (Turf): Sf: 0-0 GS: 0-1 Gd: 0-0 GF: 0-3 Fm: 0-1
Distance: 5f/6f: 0-0 7f-8f: 0-2 9f-13f: 0-7 14f+: 0-0
Track : LH: 0-8 RH: 0-1 Tight: 0-6 Gall: 0-1
Aids: Bl: 0-1 Vi: 0-0 Tstrap: 0-0 Ckp: 0-0
Best Rating: 66 10/08 Pont 1m4y gd-sft

Modest; stays 1m; acts on easy ground.

Sampower Rose (IRE)

98(75) (10)65
3-y-o b f Sampower Star-Rosebank (USA) (El Prado (IRE))
D Carroll D Wallis

Placings:0561-00202000 (6924)
2009: 8⁰G, 8⁰GF, 8²G, 10⁰S, 8²S, 8⁰GF, 7⁰SD, 8⁰GF,

	Starts	1st	2nd	3rd	Win & Pl
Career Total (Turf)	11	1	2	0	6121
Career Total (AW)	1	0	0	0	

63 9/08 Catt 7f (0-85) G-S £3885
Total win prize-money £3886

Going (Turf): Sf: 0-2 **GS: 1-1** Gd: 0-4 GF: 0-4 Fm: 0-0
Distance: 5f/6f: 0-3 **7f-8f: 1-4** 9f-13f: 0-5 14f+: 0-0
Track : LH: 1-8 RH: 0-2 **Tight: 1-5** Gall: 0-0
Aids: Bl: 0-1 Vi: 0-0 Tstrap: 0-0 Ckp: 0-0
Best Rating: 65 9/09 Thsk 1m soft

Modest; stays 1m; acts on good or softer ground.

Sampower Sarge (IRE)

(67) (4)
3-y-o b f Sampower Star-Desert Skimmer (USA) (Shadeed (USA))
D Carroll J F O'Sullivan

Placings:0 (0251)
2009: 7⁰SD,

	Starts	1st	2nd	3rd	Win & Pl
Career Total (Turf)	0	0	0	0	
Career Total (AW)	1	0	0	0	

Going (Turf): Sf: 0-0 GS: 0-0 Gd: 0-0 GF: 0-0 Fm: 0-0
Distance: 5f/6f: 0-0 7f-8f: 0-1 9f-13f: 0-0 14f+: 0-0
Track : LH: 0-1 RH: 0-0 Tight: 0-1 Gall: 0-0
Aids: Bl: 0-0 Vi: 0-0 Tstrap: 0-0 Ckp: 0-0
Best Rating: 4 1/09 Wolv 7f32y stand

Sampower Shamrock (IRE)

(76) (35)
3-y-o b f Sampower Star-Sans Escale (USA) (Diesis)
D Carroll J F O'Sullivan

Placings:06 **(0364)**
2009: 7^{0}SD, 6^{6}SD,

	Starts	1st	2nd	3rd	Win & Pl
Career Total (Turf)	0	0	0	0	
Career Total (AW)	2	0	0	0	0

Going (Turf): Sf: 0-0 GS: 0-0 Gd: 0-0 GF: 0-0 Fm: 0-0
Distance: 5f/6f: 0-1 7f-8f: 0-1 9f-13f: 0-0 14f+: 0-0
Track : LH: 0-2 RH: 0-0 Tight: 0-1 Gall: 0-0
Aids: Bl: 0-0 Vi: 0-0 Tstrap: 0-0 Ckp: 0-0
Best Rating: 35 2/09 Sthl 6f stand

Sams Lass

38 79
3-y-o b f Refuse To Bend (IRE)-Dina Line (USA) (Diesis)
D Nicholls Robert Reid

Placings:4-U01 **(4164)**
2009: 6^{U}GF, 7^{0}G, 6^{1}G,

	Starts	1st	2nd	3rd	Win & Pl
Career Total (Turf)	4	1	0	0	3503

79 7/09 Ffos 6f GD £3238
Total win prize-money £3238

Going (Turf): Sf: 0-0 GS: 0-0 Gd: 1-3 GF: 0-1 Fm: 0-0
Distance: 5f/6f: 1-3 7f-8f: 0-1 9f-13f: 0-0 14f+: 0-0
Track : LH: 0-0 RH: 0-0 Tight: 0-0 Gall: 0-0
Aids: Bl: 0-0 Vi: 0-0 Tstrap: 0-0 Ckp: 0-0
Best Rating: 79 7/09 Ffos 6f good

Moderate; should stay 7f; may improve.

Sams Spirit

80(81) (59)13
3-y-o br g Diktat-Winning Girl (Green Desert (USA))
P J McBride Robert Reid

Placings:0-600 **(1281)**
2009: 8^{6}SD, 7^{0}G, 7^{0}GF,

	Starts	1st	2nd	3rd	Win & Pl
Career Total (Turf)	2	0	0	0	
Career Total (AW)	2	0	0	0	0

Going (Turf): Sf: 0-0 GS: 0-0 Gd: 0-1 GF: 0-1 Fm: 0-0
Distance: 5f/6f: 0-0 7f-8f: 0-4 9f-13f: 0-0 14f+: 0-0
Track : LH: 0-1 RH: 0-2 Tight: 0-0 Gall: 0-1
Aids: Bl: 0-0 Vi: 0-0 Tstrap: 0-0 Ckp: 0-0
Best Rating: 59 10/08 GrLe 1m stand

Samson Quest

(103) (53)
7-y-o b g Cyrano De Bergerac-Zenita (IRE) (Zieten (USA))
B Smart John McMahon

Placings:50/42003041005/2245140000460/006-14 **(0131)**
2009: 8^{1}SD, 8^{4}SD,

	Starts	1st	2nd	3rd	Win & Pl
Career Total (Turf)	9	0	1	1	2235
Career Total (AW)	22	3	2	0	8044

53 1/09 Ling 1m STD £1706
56 2/06 Ling 1m STD £2388
62 9/05 Ling 1m STD £2639
Total win prize-money £6734

Going (Turf): Sf: 0-1 GS: 0-1 Gd: 0-3 GF: 0-4 Fm: 0-0
Distance: 5f/6f: 0-4 7f-8f: 3-19 9f-13f: 0-8 14f+: 0-0
Track : LH: 3-23 RH: 0-2 Tight: 3-18 Gall: 0-3
Aids: Bl: 0-1 Vi: 2-17 Tstrap: 0-1 Ckp: 0-1
Best Rating: 65 2/06 Ling 1m stand

Plating class; stays a mile, acts on quick ground and Polytrack; has worn headgear.

Samurai Warrior

104(108) (68)73
4-y-o br g Beat All (USA)-Ma Vie (Salse (USA))
Jamie Snowden (P D Evans 23/7) J E Snowden

Placings:020/54036010003-12326011003330220 **(4951)**
2009: 10^{1}SD, 10^{2}SD, 9^{3}SD, 8^{2}SD, 8^{6}SD, 8^{0}GF, 10^{1}G, 10^{1}F, 10^{0}SD, 11^{0}GF, 8^{3}F, 10^{3}GF, 10^{0}GF, 10^{2}S, 10^{2}G, 14^{0}GF,

	Starts	1st	2nd	3rd	Win & Pl
Career Total (Turf)	15	2	2	3	7985
Career Total (AW)	15	2	3	2	6605

73 5/09 Bath 1m2f46y (0-65)H FRM £2266
67 5/09 Ling 1m2f (0-70)H GD £3238
63 1/09 GrLe 1m2f (0-60)H STD £1942
68 11/08 Wolv 7f32y STD £2047
Total win prize-money £9495

Going (Turf): Sf: 0-1 GS: 0-0 Gd: 1-5 GF: 0-7 Fm: 1-2
Distance: 5f/6f: 0-0 7f-8f: 1-11 9f-13f: 3-18 14f+: 0-1
Track : LH: 4-23 RH: 0-1 Tight: 3-22 Gall: 1-1
Aids: Bl: 0-3 Vi: 0-0 Tstrap: 1-5 Ckp: 1-5
Best Rating: 73 6/09 Ches 1m2f75y gd-fm

Modest; effective over 1m-1m2f; acts on fast ground and on Polytrack; has worn cheekpieces.

San Antonio

102 (96)81
9-y-o b g Efisio-Winnebago (Kris)
Mrs P Sly R Brazier

Placings:001122000/060/0111425353024/24466000/00306/061214-2 **(3076)**
2009: 8^{2}G,

	Starts	1st	2nd	3rd	Win & Pl
Career Total (Turf)	37	7	5	3	64530
Career Total (AW)	8	0	2	0	3862

81 7/08 Ripn 1m (0-70)H HVY £2914
75 6/08 Ripn 1m (0-65)H SFT £2590
90 5/05 Kemp 1m (0-80)H GD £9323
84 4/05 Pont 1m4y (0-70)H GD £4196
83 4/05 Pont 1m4y (0-65) SFT £4153
91 5/03 Pont 1m4y D(0-85)H GD £8541
86 5/03 Donc 7f D GD £5761
Total win prize-money £37481

Going (Turf): Sf: 3-9 GS: 0-5 Gd: 4-13 GF: 0-10 Fm: 0-0
Distance: 5f/6f: 0-2 7f-8f: 4-23 9f-13f: 3-20 14f+: 0-0
Track : LH: 3-21 RH: 3-16 Tight: 2-17 Gall: 1-1
Aids: Bl: 5-28 Vi: 0-0 Tstrap: 0-1 Ckp: 0-1
Best Rating: 96 1/06 Ling 7f stand

Fair; effective over 7f-1m; acts on good and soft ground; very effective from the front; usually blinkered.

San Cassiano (IRE)

95(97) (75)88
2-y-o b g Bertolini (USA)-Celtic Silhouette (FR) (Celtic Swing)
R M Beckett P D Savill

Placings:13 **(6398)**
2009: 6^{1}SD, 6^{3}GF,

	Starts	1st	2nd	3rd	Win & Pl
Career Total (Turf)	1	0	0	1	1260
Career Total (AW)	1	1	0	0	2590

75 9/09 Kemp 6f STD £2590
Total win prize-money £2590

Going (Turf): Sf: 0-0 GS: 0-0 Gd: 0-0 GF: 0-1 Fm: 0-0
Distance: 5f/6f: 1-2 7f-8f: 0-0 9f-13f: 0-0 14f+: 0-0
Track : LH: 0-0 RH: 1-1 Tight: 0-0 Gall: 0-0
Aids: Bl: 0-0 Vi: 0-0 Tstrap: 0-0 Ckp: 0-0
Best Rating: 88 9/09 Sals 6f gd-fm

Fair half-brother to Celtic Silence; made a winning debut over 6f on Polytrack.

San Deng

99 (68)59
7-y-o gr g Averti (IRE)-Miss Mirror (Magic Mirror)
Micky Hammond Oakwood Racing Partnership

Placings:03000/2140543266/60232504/4/6055-54 **(1242)**
2009: 15^{5}GF, 16^{4}F,

	Starts	1st	2nd	3rd	Win & Pl
Career Total (Turf)	28	1	4	3	13183
Career Total (AW)	2	0	0	0	0

66 6/05 Sals 1m (0-55)H G-F £3731
Total win prize-money £3731

Going (Turf): Sf: 0-0 GS: 0-3 Gd: 0-7 GF: 1-17 Fm: 0-1
Distance: 5f/6f: 0-4 7f-8f: 1-4 9f-13f: 0-19 14f+: 0-3
Track : LH: 0-18 RH: 0-5 Tight: 0-16 Gall: 0-3
Aids: Bl: 0-0 Vi: 0-0 Tstrap: 0-0 Ckp: 0-0
Best Rating: 69 9/05 Folk 1m4f gd-fm

Moderate; effective at up to 2m; acts on fast ground.

San Diego Prince

97 55
5-y-o b/br g Primo Valentino (IRE)-Lalique (IRE) (Lahib (USA))
Muredach Kelly D Grealish

Placings:43000/00-04040 **(6410)**
2009: 5^{0}GF, 7^{4}GF, 7^{0}S, 5^{4}G, 5^{0}GF,

	Starts	1st	2nd	3rd	Win & Pl
Career Total (Turf)	12	0	0	1	1331

Going (Turf): Sf: 0-2 GS: 0-0 Gd: 0-3 GF: 0-4 Fm: 0-1
Distance: 5f/6f: 0-9 7f-8f: 0-3 9f-13f: 0-0 14f+: 0-0
Track : LH: 0-4 RH: 0-4 Tight: 0-0 Gall: 0-0
Aids: Bl: 0-4 Vi: 0-0 Tstrap: 0-2 Ckp: 0-2
Best Rating: 61 8/07 Cork 6f sft-hvy

San Giustino (IRE)

(77) (8)63
7-y-o b g Night Shift (USA)-Nambucca (Shirley Heights)
B P Galvin Mrs Audrey O'Connor

Placings:130600/050040/00 (7754)
2009: 12^0SD, 8^0SD,

	Starts	1st	2nd	3rd	Win & Pl
Career Total (Turf)	12	1	0	1	7063
Career Total (AW)	2	0	0	0	

73 6/05 Rosc 7f FRM £5390
Total win prize-money £5391

Going (Turf): Sf: 0-0 GS: 0-0 Gd: 0-4 GF: 0-6 **Fm: 1-1**
Distance: 5f/6f: 0-1 **7f-8f: 1-4** 9f-13f: 0-9 14f+: 0-0
Track : LH: 0-4 **RH: 1-8** Tight: 0-1 Gall: 0-0
Aids: Bl: 0-1 Vi: 0-0 Tstrap: 0-0 Ckp: 0-0
Best Rating: **76** 7/05 Gowr 7f good

San Jemeniano (IRE)

89(91) (75)**80**
2-y-o b c Bertolini (USA)-Kafayef (USA) (Secreto (USA))
P W Chapple-Hyam Ziad A Galadari

Placings:3334 (6809)
2009: 6^3GF, 6^3G, 5^3SF, 6^4G,

	Starts	1st	2nd	3rd	Win & Pl
Career Total (Turf)	3	0	0	2	1460
Career Total (AW)	1	0	0	1	482

Going (Turf): **Sf: 0-0 GS: 0-0 Gd: 0-2 GF: 0-1 Fm: 0-0**
Distance: 5f/6f: 0-4 7f-8f: 0-0 9f-13f: 0-0 14f+: 0-0
Track : LH: 0-1 RH: 0-0 Tight: 0-1 Gall: 0-1
Aids: Bl: 0-0 Vi: 0-0 Tstrap: 0-0 Ckp: 0-0
Best Rating: **80** 7/09 NmkJ 6f good

Fair half-brother to five winners; effective atr 6f on fast ground.

San Marco (GER)

(92) (58)
7-y-o b g Military (USA)-Stormin' Sun (USA) (Buddy (USA))
P Butler (Gerard Cully 16/9) Miss M Bryant

Placings:2111622/00 (7524)
2009: 10^0HY, **10^0SD**,

	Starts	1st	2nd	3rd	Win & Pl
Career Total (Turf)	8	3	3	0	8174
Career Total (AW)	1	0	0	0	

7/06 Hopp 1m H GD £2414
7/06 Colo 1m H GD £2069
6/06 Brem 1m GD £1414
Total win prize-money £5897

Going (Turf): Sf: 0-2 GS: 0-0 **Gd: 3-6** GF: 0-0 Fm: 0-0
Distance: 5f/6f: 0-0 **7f-8f: 3-6** 9f-13f: 0-3 14f+: 0-0
Track : LH: 0-1 **RH: 2-5** Tight: 0-1 Gall: 0-0
Aids: Bl: 0-0 Vi: 0-0 Tstrap: 0-0 Ckp: 0-0
Best Rating: **58** 11/09 Ling 1m2f stand

San Sicharia (IRE)

110 (105)**105**
4-y-o ch f Daggers Drawn (USA)-Spinamix (Spinning World (USA))
Ms Joanna Morgan P Twomey

Placings:41/331345-1266652 (7380a)
2009: 7^1GF, 6^2GF, 7^6G, 8^6G, 7^6G, 8^5GY, 8^2SD,

	Starts	1st	2nd	3rd	Win & Pl
Career Total (Turf)	13	2	1	3	86152
Career Total (AW)	2	1	1	0	14976

103 5/09 Ling 7f G-F £36900
85 5/08 Chan 7f GD £8456
85 11/07 Deau 7f110y STD £7095
Total win prize-money £52452

Going (Turf): Sf: 0-4 GS: 0-0 **Gd: 1-5 GF: 1-2** Fm: 0-0
Distance: 5f/6f: 0-2 **7f-8f: 3-13** 9f-13f: 0-0 14f+: 0-0
Track : LH: 0-4 **RH: 1-4** Tight: 0-0 Gall: 0-0
Aids: Bl: 0-0 Vi: 0-0 Tstrap: 0-2 Ckp: 0-2
Best Rating: **105** 11/09 Dund 1m stand

Usefu; effective over 7f; acts on most types of ground.

San Silvestro (IRE)

100(95) (59)**68**
4-y-o b g Fayruz-Skehana (IRE) (Mukaddamah (USA))
Mrs A Duffield Middleham Park Racing Xiv

Placings:1/365000-002101424 (4876)
2009: 8^0GF, 8^0G, 8^2GF, 9^1G, 10^0G, 8^1GF, 8^4G, 8^2GS, 8^4G,

	Starts	1st	2nd	3rd	Win & Pl
Career Total (Turf)	15	3	2	1	10636
Career Total (AW)	1	0	0	0	

67 6/09 Muss 1m (0-65)H G-F £2590
61 6/09 Muss 1m1f GD £3238
68 11/07 Catt 7f G-F £2730
Total win prize-money £8558

Going (Turf): Sf: 0-1 GS: 0-3 Gd: 1-6 **GF: 2-5** Fm: 0-0
Distance: 5f/6f: 0-0 **7f-8f: 2-7** 9f-13f: 1-9 14f+: 0-0
Track : LH: 1-9 **RH: 2-7 Tight: 3-8** Gall: 0-1
Aids: Bl: 0-0 Vi: 0-0 Tstrap: 2-8 Ckp: 2-8
Best Rating: **68** 8/08 Bevl 7f100y soft

Modest; stays 1m1f and handles quick ground.

Sana Abel (IRE)

101(102) (79)**73**
3-y-o b f Alhaarth (IRE)-Midway Lady (USA) (Alleged (USA))
M A Jarvis Hamdan Al Maktoum

Placings:4654201 (6417)
2009: 8^4G, 10^6GS, 10^5GF, 11^4G, 12^2SD, 11^0G, 14^1GF,

	Starts	1st	2nd	3rd	Win & Pl
Career Total (Turf)	6	1	0	0	3825
Career Total (AW)	1	0	1	0	771

73 10/09 Gdwd 1m6f G-F £3238
Total win prize-money £3238

Going (Turf): Sf: 0-0 GS: 0-1 Gd: 0-3 **GF: 1-2** Fm: 0-0
Distance: 5f/6f: 0-0 7f-8f: 0-0 9f-13f: 0-6 **14f+: 1-1**
Track : LH: 0-4 **RH: 1-2 Tight: 1-4** Gall: 0-1
Aids: Bl: 0-0 Vi: 0-0 Tstrap: 1-3 Ckp: 1-3
Best Rating: **79** 8/09 Kemp 1m4f stand

Fair half-sister to the Oaks winner Eswarah; stayed on well when fourth on debut in a 1m Yarmouth maiden; beaten on easy ground next time; has worn cheekpieces.

Sancho Panza

74(81) (43)**38**
2-y-o b g Zafeen (FR)-Malvadilla (IRE) (Doyoun)
Miss J Feilden Carol Bushnell & Partners

Placings:000 (4839)
2009: 6^0SD, 7^0G, 6^0SD,

	Starts	1st	2nd	3rd	Win & Pl
Career Total (Turf)	1	0	0	0	
Career Total (AW)	2	0	0	0	

Going (Turf): **Sf: 0-0 GS: 0-0 Gd: 0-1 GF: 0-0 Fm: 0-0**
Distance: 5f/6f: 0-2 7f-8f: 0-1 9f-13f: 0-0 14f+: 0-0
Track : LH: 0-1 RH: 0-1 Tight: 0-0 Gall: 0-0
Aids: Bl: 0-0 Vi: 0-0 Tstrap: 0-0 Ckp: 0-0
Best Rating: **43** 6/09 Kemp 6f stand

Sanctuary

100 **87**
3-y-o ch g Dr Fong (USA)-Wondrous Maid (GER) (Mondrian I (GER))
B Smart Mrs Julie Martin

Placings:321420 (6138)
2009: 10^3GS, 10^2GS, 10^1GF, 9^4GF, 12^2S, 13^0G,

	Starts	1st	2nd	3rd	Win & Pl
Career Total (Turf)	6	1	2	1	7159

69 6/09 Hayd 1m2f95y G-F £3238
Total win prize-money £3238

Going (Turf): Sf: 0-1 GS: 0-2 Gd: 0-1 **GF: 1-2** Fm: 0-0
Distance: 5f/6f: 0-0 7f-8f: 0-0 **9f-13f: 1-5** 14f+: 0-1
Track : **LH: 1-4** RH: 0-2 Tight: 0-2 Gall: 0-1
Aids: Bl: 0-0 Vi: 0-0 Tstrap: 0-0 Ckp: 0-0
Best Rating: **87** 9/09 Thsk 1m4f soft

Fair; stays 1m4f; acts on most ground.

Sanctum

91(86) (37)**58**
3-y-o b f Medicean-Auspicious (Shirley Heights)
Dr J D Scargill J P T Partnership

Placings:005 (4828)
2009: 10^0SD, 10^0SD, 10^5G,

	Starts	1st	2nd	3rd	Win & Pl
Career Total (Turf)	1	0	0	0	0
Career Total (AW)	2	0	0	0	

Going (Turf): **Sf: 0-0 GS: 0-0 Gd: 0-1 GF: 0-0 Fm: 0-0**
Distance: 5f/6f: 0-0 7f-8f: 0-0 9f-13f: 0-3 14f+: 0-0
Track : LH: 0-1 RH: 0-2 Tight: 0-2 Gall: 0-0
Aids: Bl: 0-0 Vi: 0-0 Tstrap: 0-0 Ckp: 0-0
Best Rating: **58** 8/09 Wind 1m2f7y good

Sand Repeal (IRE)

101(98) (58)**68**
7-y-o b g Revoque (IRE)-Columbian Sand (IRE) (Salmon Leap (USA))
Miss J Feilden The Sultans of Speed

Placings:032/330502/11200152000 5/3336214404543/230 44455231150-50034312032660 (6969)
2009: 11^5SD, 13^0SD, 13^0SD, 12^3GF, 17^4GS, 12^3GS, 12^1GF, 16^2GF, 12^0GF, 11^3GF, 11^2GF, 15^6GF, 12^6G, 11^0G,

	Starts	1st	2nd	3rd	Win & Pl
Career Total (Turf)	39	4	5	7	20009
Career Total (AW)	23	3	4	5	12973

64 6/09 Folk 1m4f (0-60)H G-F £2047
68 8/08 Ches 1m4f66y (0-75)H G-F £3435
65 8/08 Wind 1m3f135y (0-75)H G-S £2637
71 6/07 Folk 1m7f92y (0-70)H GD £3238
76 4/06 Sthl 1m6f (0-65)H STD £2730
69 1/06 Wolv 1m4f50y (0-60)H STD £2047
63 1/06 Sthl 1m3f STD £3238
Total win prize-money £19375

Going (Turf): Sf: 0-12 GS: 1-4 Gd: 1-9 **GF: 2-14** Fm: 0-0
Distance: 5f/6f: 0-0 7f-8f: 0-1 **9f-13f: 5-32** 14f+: 2-29

Track : LH: **4-40** RH: 2-18 **Tight: 5-30** Gall: 0-4
Aids: Bl: 0-0 **Vi: 1-22** Tstrap: 0-1 Ckp: 0-1
Best Rating: 76 5/06 Sthl 1m3f stand

Modest; effective at 1m4f-2m; acts on good and soft ground; also goes on Fibresand; has worn headgear.

Sand Skier

101 **87**
2-y-o b c Shamardal (USA)-Dubai Surprise (IRE) (King's Best (USA))
M Johnston Sheikh Hamdan Bin Mohammed Al Maktoum

Placings:4213 **(7013)**
2009: 6^{4}G, 7^{2}GF, 6^{1}G, 7^{3}GS,

	Starts	1st	2nd	3rd	Win & Pl
Career Total (Turf)	**4**	**1**	**1**	**1**	**7052**

85	9/09	Haml	6f5y	GD	£3885

Total win prize-money £3886

Going (Turf): Sf: 0-0 GS: 0-1 **Gd: 1-2** GF: 0-1 Fm: 0-0
Distance: 5f/6f: 0-0 **7f-8f: 1-4** 9f-13f: 0-0 14f+: 0-0
Track : LH: 0-0 RH: 0-0 Tight: 0-0 Gall: 0-0
Aids: Bl: 0-0 Vi: 0-0 Tstrap: 0-0 Ckp: 0-0
Best Rating: 87 10/09 Donc 7f gd-sft

Useful; effective over 6f-7f; acts on most ground.

Sand Vixen

110(97) (83)**108**
2-y-o b f Dubawi (IRE)-Fur Will Fly (Petong)
Saeed Bin Suroor Godolphin

Placings:513110 **(6449)**
2009: 6^{5}GF, 6^{1}SD, 6^{3}G, 5^{1}GF, 5^{1}GF, 6^{0}GF,

	Starts	1st	2nd	3rd	Win & Pl
Career Total (Turf)	**5**	**2**	**0**	**1**	**68371**
Career Total (AW)	**1**	**1**	**0**	**0**	**3886**

108	9/09	Donc	5f	G-F	£45416
100	8/09	Newb	5f34y	G-F	£17031
83	7/09	Kemp	6f	STD	£3885

Total win prize-money £66333

Going (Turf): Sf: 0-0 GS: 0-0 Gd: 0-1 **GF: 2-4** Fm: 0-0
Distance: 5f/6f: 3-6 7f-8f: 0-0 9f-13f: 0-0 14f+: 0-0
Track : LH: 0-0 **RH: 1-1** Tight: 0-0 Gall: 0-0
Aids: Bl: 0-0 Vi: 0-0 Tstrap: 0-0 Ckp: 0-0
Best Rating: 108 9/09 Donc 5f gd-fm

Smart; Group 2 Flying Childers winner; effective at 5-6f; acts on Polytrack and fast turf.

Sandfairyann

(70) (24)
2-y-o b f Dubai Destination (USA)-Alhufoof (USA) (Dayjur (USA))
B R Johnson Peter Crate

Placings:000 **(7106)**
2009: 7^{0}SD, 6^{0}SD, 8^{0}SD,

	Starts	1st	2nd	3rd	Win & Pl
Career Total (Turf)	**0**	**0**	**0**	**0**	
Career Total (AW)	**3**	**0**	**0**	**0**	

Going (Turf): Sf: 0-0 GS: 0-0 Gd: 0-0 GF: 0-0 Fm: 0-0
Distance: 5f/6f: 0-1 7f-8f: 0-2 9f-13f: 0-0 14f+: 0-0
Track : LH: 0-0 RH: 0-3 Tight: 0-0 Gall: 0-0
Aids: Bl: 0-0 Vi: 0-0 Tstrap: 0-0 Ckp: 0-0
Best Rating: 24 10/09 Kemp 6f stand

Sandor

107(102) (90)**95**
3-y-o ch g Fantastic Light (USA)-Crystal Star (Mark Of Esteem (IRE))
P J Makin Keith And Brian Brackpool

Placings:03223-123150 **(5209)**
2009: 8^{1}SD, 9^{2}G, 10^{3}SD, 10^{1}G, 9^{5}G, 10^{0}GF,

	Starts	1st	2nd	3rd	Win & Pl
Career Total (Turf)	**5**	**1**	**2**	**0**	**10574**
Career Total (AW)	**6**	**1**	**1**	**3**	**5454**

94	7/09	Sand	1m2f7y	(0-85)H	GD	£6476
77	4/09	Ling	1m		STD	£2729

Total win prize-money £9206

Going (Turf): Sf: 0-0 GS: 0-0 **Gd: 1-4** GF: 0-1 Fm: 0-0
Distance: 5f/6f: 0-0 7f-8f: 1-6 9f-13f: 1-5 14f+: 0-0
Track : LH: 1-5 RH: 1-5 **Tight: 1-7** Gall: 0-0
Aids: Bl: 0-0 Vi: 0-0 Tstrap: 0-0 Ckp: 0-0
Best Rating: 95 7/09 Gdwd 1m1f192y good

Useful; stays 1m2f; acts on good ground and on Polytrack.

Sands Crooner (IRE)

103(109) (84)**85**
6-y-o b g Imperial Ballet (IRE)-Kurfuffle (Bluebird (USA))
J G Given Danethorpe Racing Partnership

Placings:6455560**654033/1431**100**005/540000465**016001 5/22136551140035034201520-01R21406060050 **(7398)**
2009: 5^{0}SS, 5^{1}F, 5^{R}G, 5^{2}GF, 5^{1}GF, 5^{4}CF, 5^{0}G, 5^{6}G, 5^{0}GF, 5^{6}GF, 5^{0}GS, 5^{0}GF, 5^{5}G, 5^{0}SD,

	Starts	1st	2nd	3rd	Win & Pl
Career Total (Turf)	**34**	**3**	**2**	**2**	**14018**
Career Total (AW)	**42**	**8**	**3**	**4**	**33500**

85	6/09	Ling	5f	(0-75)H	G-F	£3238
79	5/09	Wwck	5f	(0-70)H	FRM	£3070
83	11/08	Wolv	5f20y	(0-75)H	STD	£3885
81	3/08	Ling	5f	(0-75)H	STD	£2590
81	3/08	Wolv	5f20y	(0-75)H	STD	£2457
77	1/08	Ling	5f	(0-75)H	STD	£2590
66	12/07	Ling	5f	(0-60)H	STD	£2137
66	7/07	Bath	5f11y	(0-65)H	G-S	£2072
78	3/06	Ling	5f	(0-85)H	STD	£6477
75	2/06	Ling	5f	(0-70)H	STD	£3238
63	1/06	Wolv	5f20y		STD	£3238

Total win prize-money £34999

Going (Turf): Sf: 0-1 **GS: 1-10** Gd: 0-9 **GF: 1-12 Fm: 1-2**
Distance: 5f/6f: 11-75 7f-8f: 0-1 9f-13f: 0-0 14f+: 0-0
Track : LH: 10-41 RH: 0-4 **Tight: 8-35** Gall: 1-6
Aids: Bl: 0-0 **Vi: 10-60** Tstrap: 0-0 Ckp: 0-0
Best Rating: 85 6/09 Ling 5f gd-fm

Fair; effective at 5f; acts with cut in the ground; also acts on Polytrack; has worn tongue tie, often visored.

Sands Of Barra (IRE)

101(95) (61)**73**
6-y-o gr g Marju (IRE)-Purple Risks (FR) (Take Risks (FR))
I W McInnes Wold Construction Company

Placings:6004016**061/544**1000500**050000**/005200000121 650/0350020005605330**0-600**0540503 **(4845)**
2009: 7^{6}SD, 7^{0}SD, 7^{0}G, 7^{0}GF, 7^{5}GF, 7^{4}GS, 7^{0}GF, 7^{5}G, 6^{0}GS, 8^{3}G,

	Starts	1st	2nd	3rd	Win & Pl
Career Total (Turf)	**52**	**4**	**3**	**4**	**23835**
Career Total (AW)	**16**	**1**	**0**	**0**	**4801**

75	9/07	Ayr	7f50y	(0-70)H	SFT	£4533
67	8/07	Ches	7f122y	(0-65)H	G-F	£2730
78	5/06	Yarm	7f3y	(0-85)H	G-F	£7790
75	12/05	Ling	7f	(0-85)	STD	£4320
73	10/05	Brig	6f209y	(0-75)	G-S	£3749

Total win prize-money £23123

Going (Turf): Sf: 1-9 GS: 1-6 Gd: 0-16 **GF: 2-16** Fm: 0-5
Distance: 5f/6f: 0-4 **7f-8f: 5-59** 9f-13f: 0-5 14f+: 0-0
Track : LH: 4-40 RH: 0-16 **Tight: 2-39** Gall: 0-0
Aids: Bl: 0-2 Vi: 0-0 Tstrap: 0-7 Ckp: 0-7
Best Rating: 78 5/06 Yarm 7f3y gd-fm

Moderate; stays 1m; acts on most ground on turf; goes on Polytrack.

Sands Of Dee (USA)

100(44) **66**
2-y-o b g Dixieland Band (USA)-Diamond Bracelet (USA) (Metfield (USA))
J A Glover (R A Fahey 24/8) Paul J Dixon & Brian Morton

Placings:040210 **(6071)**
2009: 5^{0}GF, 6^{4}GF, 6^{0}G, 5^{2}GF, 6^{1}HY, 7^{0}SD,

	Starts	1st	2nd	3rd	Win & Pl
Career Total (Turf)	**5**	**1**	**1**	**0**	**3064**
Career Total (AW)	**1**	**0**	**0**	**0**	

66	8/09	Haml	6f5y	HVY	£2266

Total win prize-money £2267

Going (Turf): Sf: 1-1 GS: 0-0 Gd: 0-1 GF: 0-3 Fm: 0-0
Distance: 5f/6f: 0-3 **7f-8f: 1-3** 9f-13f: 0-0 14f+: 0-0
Track : LH: 0-1 RH: 0-0 Tight: 0-1 Gall: 0-0
Aids: Bl: 0-0 Vi: 0-2 Tstrap: 0-0 Ckp: 0-0
Best Rating: 66 8/09 Haml 6f5y heavy

Modest; suited by 5-6f and most ground.

Sandwith

104(101) (70)**81**
6-y-o ch g Perryston View-Bodfari Times (Clantime)
A G Foster A G Foster

Placings:05200**500/16/40**0056011**545**/10031043400-022020200005 **(7119)**
2009: 5^{0}SD, 5^{2}GF, 5^{2}GF, 5^{0}GF, 5^{2}G, 5^{0}G, 5^{2}G, 5^{0}GS, 5^{0}G, 5^{0}G, 6^{0}G, 5^{5}GS,

	Starts	1st	2nd	3rd	Win & Pl
Career Total (Turf)	**36**	**4**	**5**	**2**	**24811**
Career Total (AW)	**9**	**1**	**0**	**0**	**2048**

78	7/08	Muss	5f	(0-80)H	G-S	£6476
76	4/08	Ripn	5f	(0-75)H	GD	£2914
66	10/07	Wolv	5f20y	(0-62)H	STD	£2047
67	9/07	Muss	5f	(0-65)H	GD	£2590
72	4/06	Muss	5f	(0-75)H	GD	£3886

Total win prize-money £17915

Going (Turf): Sf: 0-2 GS: 1-4 **Gd: 3-18** GF: 0-12 Fm: 0-0
Distance: 5f/6f: 5-44 7f-8f: 0-1 9f-13f: 0-0 14f+: 0-0
Track : LH: 1-9 RH: 0-2 **Tight: 1-9** Gall: 0-1
Aids: Bl: 0-0 Vi: 0-0 Tstrap: 3-14 Ckp: 3-14
Best Rating: 81 7/09 Muss 5f good

Fair sprinter; seems best at 5f; acts on most surfaces; likes Musselburgh.

Sandy Par

95(91) (53)**55**
4-y-o ch g No Excuse Needed-Nesting (Thatching)
J M Bradley J M Bradley

Placings:33000/06050-0046400030004005**4** **(7714)**
2009: 5^{0}SD, 5^{0}SD, 5^{4}GF, 5^{6}GS, 5^{4}GF, 5^{0}GF, 5^{0}GF, 5^{0}G, 5^{3}G, 6^{0}G, 5^{0}GS, 5^{0}G, 5^{4}GF, 6^{0}SD, 5^{0}SD, 5^{5}SD, 5^{4}SD,

	Starts	1st	2nd	3rd	Win & Pl
Career Total (Turf)	20	0	0	3	1724
Career Total (AW)	7	0	0	0	0

Going (Turf): **Sf: 0-2 GS: 0-3 Gd: 0-8 GF: 0-7 Fm: 0-0**
Distance: 5f/6f: 0-26 7f-8f: 0-1 9f-13f: 0-0 14f+: 0-0
Track : LH: 0-10 RH: 0-4 Tight: 0-3 Gall: 0-3
Aids: Bl: 0-13 Vi: 0-0 Tstrap: 0-6 Ckp: 0-6
Best Rating: **62** 6/07 Folk 6f good

Plating-class gelding; effective over 6f; acts on good ground; has been tried in cheekpieces and blinkers.

Sandy Shaw

85(82) (58)**69**
2-y-o ch f Footstepsinthesand-Susi Wong (IRE) (Selkirk (USA))
J W Hills Burton Agnes Bloodstock & Partners

Placings:003 **(5906)**
2009: 7^{0}SD, 8^{0}G, 8^{3}GF,

	Starts	1st	2nd	3rd	Win & Pl
Career Total (Turf)	2	0	0	1	770
Career Total (AW)	1	0	0	0	

Going (Turf): **Sf: 0-0 GS: 0-0 Gd: 0-1 GF: 0-1 Fm: 0-0**
Distance: 5f/6f: 0-0 7f-8f: 0-3 9f-13f: 0-0 14f+: 0-0
Track : LH: 0-1 RH: 0-2 Tight: 0-0 Gall: 0-1
Aids: Bl: 0-0 Vi: 0-0 Tstrap: 0-0 Ckp: 0-0
Best Rating: **69** 9/09 Ffos 1m gd-fm

Sandy Toes

76 **36**
2-y-o b g Footstepsinthesand-Scrooby Baby (Mind Games)
J A Glover (A J McCabe 30/5) Sexy Six Partnership

Placings:005 **(4738)**
2009: 5^{0}G, 6^{0}GF, 6^{5}GF,

	Starts	1st	2nd	3rd	Win & Pl
Career Total (Turf)	3	0	0	0	0

Going (Turf): **Sf: 0-0 GS: 0-0 Gd: 0-1 GF: 0-2 Fm: 0-0**
Distance: 5f/6f: 0-3 7f-8f: 0-0 9f-13f: 0-0 14f+: 0-0
Track : LH: 0-0 RH: 0-0 Tight: 0-0 Gall: 0-0
Aids: Bl: 0-0 Vi: 0-0 Tstrap: 0-0 Ckp: 0-0
Best Rating: **36** 5/09 Donc 6f gd-fm

Sanjay's Choice (IRE)

75(104) (74)**17**
3-y-o br g Trans Island-Livy Park (IRE) (Titus Livius (FR))
T G McCourt Sean Foran

Placings:034-000030330 **(7528a)**
2009: 10^{0}G, 8^{0}G, 7^{0}SD, 6^{0}S, 7^{3}SD, 5^{0}SD, 5^{3}SD, 5^{3}SD, 8^{0}SD,

	Starts	1st	2nd	3rd	Win & Pl
Career Total (Turf)	3	0	0	0	
Career Total (AW)	9	0	0	4	2654

Going (Turf): **Sf: 0-1 GS: 0-0 Gd: 0-2 GF: 0-0 Fm: 0-0**
Distance: 5f/6f: 0-4 7f-8f: 0-7 9f-13f: 0-1 14f+: 0-0
Track : LH: 0-11 RH: 0-0 Tight: 0-3 Gall: 0-0
Aids: Bl: 0-0 Vi: 0-0 Tstrap: 0-1 Ckp: 0-1

Best Rating: **74** 11/09 Wolv 5f216y stand

Modest; effective over 6f; acts on Polytrack.

Sans Frontieres (IRE)

112 **111**
3-y-o ch c Galileo (IRE)-Llia (Shirley Heights)
J Noseda Sir Robert Ogden

Placings:1-23 **(2014)**
2009: 8^{2}GF, 10^{3}G,

	Starts	1st	2nd	3rd	Win & Pl
Career Total (Turf)	3	1	1	1	33381

72 9/08 Ling 7f GD £3238
Total win prize-money £3238

Going (Turf): Sf: 0-0 GS: 0-0 **Gd: 1-2** GF: 0-1 Fm: 0-0
Distance: 5f/6f: 0-0 **7f-8f: 1-2** 9f-13f: 0-1 14f+: 0-0
Track : LH: 0-1 RH: 0-0 Tight: 0-0 Gall: 0-1
Aids: Bl: 0-0 Vi: 0-0 Tstrap: 0-0 Ckp: 0-0
Best Rating: **111** 5/09 York 1m2f88y good

Smart; winner on debut; runner-up in the Craven Stakes; stays 1m; acts on good/fast ground.

Sansili

71(85) (62)**24**
2-y-o gr c Dansili-Salinova (FR) (Linamix (FR))
Pat Eddery Baron F C Oppenheim

Placings:06 **(7388)**
2009: 8^{0}GF, 8^{6}SD,

	Starts	1st	2nd	3rd	Win & Pl
Career Total (Turf)	1	0	0	0	
Career Total (AW)	1	0	0	0	0

Going (Turf): **Sf: 0-0 GS: 0-0 Gd: 0-0 GF: 0-1 Fm: 0-0**
Distance: 5f/6f: 0-0 7f-8f: 0-1 9f-13f: 0-1 14f+: 0-0
Track : LH: 0-2 RH: 0-0 Tight: 0-1 Gall: 0-0
Aids: Bl: 0-0 Vi: 0-0 Tstrap: 0-0 Ckp: 0-0
Best Rating: **62** 11/09 Ling 1m stand

Santa Margherita

90 **64**
2-y-o b f Titus Livius (FR)-A Simple Path (IRE) (Imperial Ballet (IRE))
H J L Dunlop B H Simpson

Placings:444 **(6786)**
2009: 7^{4}GS, 7^{4}GF, 7^{4}G,

	Starts	1st	2nd	3rd	Win & Pl
Career Total (Turf)	3	0	0	0	769

Going (Turf): **Sf: 0-0 GS: 0-1 Gd: 0-1 GF: 0-1 Fm: 0-0**
Distance: 5f/6f: 0-0 7f-8f: 0-3 9f-13f: 0-0 14f+: 0-0
Track : LH: 0-1 RH: 0-1 Tight: 0-0 Gall: 0-0
Aids: Bl: 0-0 Vi: 0-0 Tstrap: 0-0 Ckp: 0-0
Best Rating: **64** 10/09 Brig 7f214y good

Santas Pal

68(77) (30)**14**
2-y-o b f Chineur (FR)-Khafayif (USA) (Swain (IRE))
C J Teague Michael Marsh Racing

Placings:0000 **(3709)**
2009: 5^{0}GF, 5^{0}G, 5^{0}SD, 5^{0}SD,

	Starts	1st	2nd	3rd	Win & Pl
Career Total (Turf)	2	0	0	0	
Career Total (AW)	2	0	0	0	

Going (Turf): **Sf: 0-0 GS: 0-0 Gd: 0-1 GF: 0-1 Fm: 0-0**
Distance: 5f/6f: 0-4 7f-8f: 0-0 9f-13f: 0-0 14f+: 0-0
Track : LH: 0-0 RH: 0-0 Tight: 0-0 Gall: 0-0
Aids: Bl: 0-0 Vi: 0-0 Tstrap: 0-0 Ckp: 0-0
Best Rating: **30** 7/09 Sthl 5f stand

Santefisio

102(105) (86)**85**
3-y-o b g Efisio-Impulsive Decision (IRE) (Nomination)
P J Makin Weldspec Glasgow Limited

Placings:0123311 **(6111)**
2009: 6^{0}GF, 6^{1}GF, 7^{2}GF, 7^{3}G, 6^{3}GF, 7^{1}SD, 7^{1}GF,

	Starts	1st	2nd	3rd	Win & Pl
Career Total (Turf)	6	2	1	2	12511
Career Total (AW)	1	1	0	0	5181

85 9/09 Newb 7f (0-80)H G-F £4857
86 9/09 Ling 7f (0-80)H STD £5180
77 5/09 Newb 6f8y G-F £3885
Total win prize-money £13924

Going (Turf): Sf: 0-0 GS: 0-0 Gd: 0-1 **GF: 2-5** Fm: 0-0
Distance: 5f/6f: 0-1 **7f-8f: 3-6** 9f-13f: 0-0 14f+: 0-0
Track : **LH: 1-1** RH: 0-1 **Tight: 1-1** Gall: 0-0
Aids: Bl: 0-0 Vi: 0-0 Tstrap: 0-0 Ckp: 0-0
Best Rating: **86** 9/09 Ling 7f stand

Useful; effective over 6f-7f; acts on fast ground; goes on Polytrack.

Santiago Atitlan

98 (95)**81**
7-y-o b g Stravinsky (USA)-Sylvette (USA) (Silver Hawk (USA))
P Monteith (A Wohler 6/2) Dennis J Coppola

Placings:4210604/31121313/0456255/330-00000000 **(7171)**
2009: 6^{0}G, 6^{0}GF, 6^{0}G, 7^{0}GS, 8^{0}GF, 8^{0}S, 14^{0}G, 7^{0}S,

	Starts	1st	2nd	3rd	Win & Pl
Career Total (Turf)	32	5	3	4	51379
Career Total (AW)	1	0	0	1	4484

9/06 Colo 6f110y GD £8965
8/06 Brem 6f GD £3448
7/06 BDob 1m1f H GD £3448
6/06 Colo 6f H GD £2758
5/05 Mulh 7f GD £2127
Total win prize-money £20749

Going (Turf): Sf: 0-9 GS: 0-1 **Gd: 5-18** GF: 0-3 Fm: 0-1
Distance: 5f/6f: 2-12 7f-8f: 2-18 9f-13f: 1-2 14f+: 0-1
Track : LH: 0-8 RH: 0-5 Tight: 0-1 Gall: 0-3
Aids: Bl: 0-3 Vi: 0-1 Tstrap: 0-0 Ckp: 0-0
Best Rating: **103** 8/07 Badn 6f good

Useful; winner between 6f and 1m1f in Germany; acts on good ground.

Santo Padre (IRE)

109 (98)**107**
5-y-o b g Elnadim (USA)-Tshusick (Dancing Brave (USA))
David Marnane Victor Partnership

Placings:010-4651114 **(7007a)**
2009: 5^{4}GF, 5^{6}S, 5^{5}HY, 5^{1}S, 5^{1}S, 5^{1}GF, 5^{4}SD,

	Starts	1st	2nd	3rd	Win & Pl
Career Total (Turf)	7	3	0	0	71860
Career Total (AW)	3	1	0	0	7630

107 9/09 Donc 5f140y H G-F £46732
98 8/09 DRoy 5f (60-95)H SFT £9056
89 8/09 Tipp 5f (60-100)H SFT £13588
86 10/08 Dund 5f STD £6351
Total win prize-money £75730

Going (Turf): **Sf: 2-4** GS: 0-0 Gd: 0-0 GF: 1-2 Fm: 0-1
Distance: **5f/6f: 4-9** 7f-8f: 0-1 9f-13f: 0-0 14f+: 0-0
Track : **LH: 2-6** RH: 1-1 Tight: 0-0 Gall: 0-0
Aids: Bl: 0-0 Vi: 0-0 Tstrap: 0-0 Ckp: 0-0
Best Rating: **107** 9/09 Donc 5f140y gd-fm

Very useful; Irish trained; winner of the 2009 Portland; best over 5f; acts on soft ground and on Polytrack.

Sanvean (IRE)

100(92) (67)**91**
3-y-o b f Danehill Dancer (IRE)-Russian Muse (FR) (Machiavellian (USA))
M R Channon Findlay & Bloom

Placings:3650-100060523 **(5514)**
2009: 8^{1}SD, 8^{0}GF, 11^{0}GF, 11^{0}HY, 8^{6}GF, 8^{0}S, 7^{5}S, 7^{2}GF, 7^{3}GF,

	Starts	1st	2nd	3rd	Win & Pl
Career Total (Turf)	12	0	1	2	3922
Career Total (AW)	1	1	0	0	2590

67 3/09 Kemp 1m STD £2590
Total win prize-money £2590

Going (Turf): **Sf: 0-3 GS: 0-1 Gd: 0-2 GF: 0-6 Fm: 0-0**
Distance: 5f/6f: 0-1 **7f-8f: 1-9** 9f-13f: 0-3 14f+: 0-0
Track : LH: 0-2 **RH: 1-4** Tight: 0-1 Gall: 0-1
Aids: Bl: 0-0 Vi: 0-0 Tstrap: 0-0 Ckp: 0-0
Best Rating: **91** 7/08 NmkJ 7f good

Useful; stays 1m; acts on good ground.

Saorocain (IRE)

52 (43)**39**
3-y-o b f Kheleyf (USA)-Compradore (Mujtahid (USA))
John Joseph Hanlon (Mrs John Harrington 9/8)
Kennelwood Racing Partnership

Placings:00-00000 **(6653a)**
2009: 8^{0}GY, 10^{0}GF, 8^{0}GF, 5^{0}GY, 8^{0}SD,

	Starts	1st	2nd	3rd	Win & Pl
Career Total (Turf)	4	0	0	0	
Career Total (AW)	3	0	0	0	

Going (Turf): **Sf: 0-0 GS: 0-0 Gd: 0-0 GF: 0-2 Fm: 0-0**
Distance: 5f/6f: 0-3 7f-8f: 0-3 9f-13f: 0-1 14f+: 0-0
Track : LH: 0-5 RH: 0-1 Tight: 0-0 Gall: 0-0
Aids: Bl: 0-2 Vi: 0-1 Tstrap: 0-0 Ckp: 0-0
Best Rating: **43** 9/08 Dund 6f stand

Saphira's Fire (IRE)

106(111) (105)**111**
4-y-o b f Cape Cross (IRE)-All Our Hope (USA) (Gulch (USA))
W R Muir M J Caddy

Placings:1103-5063334 **(7809)**
2009: 11^{5}GF, 9^{0}S, 12^{6}GF, 12^{3}G, 10^{3}G, 12^{3}SD, 10^{4}SD,

	Starts	1st	2nd	3rd	Win & Pl
Career Total (Turf)	8	1	0	3	50524
Career Total (AW)	3	1	0	1	8913

92 5/08 NmkR 1m2f G-F £17031
79 4/08 Wolv 1m141y STD £2456
Total win prize-money £19488

Going (Turf): Sf: 0-1 GS: 0-0 Gd: 0-4 **GF: 1-3** Fm: 0-0
Distance: 5f/6f: 0-0 7f-8f: 0-0 **9f-13f: 2-11** 14f+: 0-0
Track : **LH: 1-5** RH: 0-4 **Tight: 1-4** Gall: 0-3
Aids: Bl: 0-0 Vi: 0-0 Tstrap: 0-0 Ckp: 0-0
Best Rating: **111** 10/09 NmkR 1m4f good

Smart; winner of the Listed Pretty Polly Stakes in 2008; stays 1m4f; acts on fast ground; goes on Polytrack.

Sapphire Prince (USA)

100(99) (78)**74**
3-y-o b c Read The Footnotes (USA)-Anna Jackson (USA) (Houston (USA))
J R Best Ian Beach & John Fletcher

Placings:5100-005000104600 **(7742)**
2009: 8^{0}GF, 8^{0}SD, 8^{5}GF, 8^{0}S, 7^{0}GS, 7^{0}SD, 8^{1}G, 8^{0}G, 10^{4}SD, 12^{6}SD, 8^{0}SD, 8^{0}SD,

	Starts	1st	2nd	3rd	Win & Pl
Career Total (Turf)	8	1	0	0	2730
Career Total (AW)	8	1	0	0	2135

74 10/09 Wind 1m67y (0-70)H GD £2729
78 6/08 GrLe 6f STD £1942
Total win prize-money £4673

Going (Turf): Sf: 0-1 GS: 0-1 **Gd: 1-4** GF: 0-2 Fm: 0-0
Distance: 5f/6f: 1-2 7f-8f: 0-10 9f-13f: 1-4 14f+: 0-0
Track : LH: 1-3 RH: 1-8 Tight: 1-4 Gall: 1-1
Aids: Bl: 0-0 Vi: 0-0 Tstrap: 0-0 Ckp: 0-0
Best Rating: **78** 6/08 GrLe 6f stand

Fair; stays 1m2f; acts on Polytrack.

Sapphire Rose

96(92) (54)**63**
3-y-o b f Tobougg (IRE)-Pearly River (Elegant Air)
J G Portman P A & M J Reditt

Placings:0006-013000 **(6370)**
2009: 10^{0}GS, 8^{1}F, 8^{3}F, 8^{0}GF, 10^{0}G, 8^{0}SD,

	Starts	1st	2nd	3rd	Win & Pl
Career Total (Turf)	8	1	0	1	2477
Career Total (AW)	2	0	0	0	0

63 5/09 Bath 1m5y (0-60)H FRM £2072
Total win prize-money £2072

Going (Turf): Sf: 0-2 GS: 0-1 Gd: 0-1 GF: 0-2 **Fm: 1-2**
Distance: 5f/6f: 0-2 7f-8f: 0-4 **9f-13f: 1-4** 14f+: 0-0
Track : **LH: 1-4** RH: 0-2 **Tight: 1-3** Gall: 0-0
Aids: Bl: 0-0 Vi: 0-0 Tstrap: 0-0 Ckp: 0-0
Best Rating: **63** 5/09 Bath 1m5y firm

Modest; effective over 1m; acts on fast ground.

Sapphire Spirit (USA)

77(61) (5)**43**
2-y-o gr/ro g Unbridled Time (USA)-Mimi's Tizzy (USA) (Cee's Tizzy (USA))
J R Best Ian Beach & John Fletcher

Placings:000 **(6903)**
2009: 5^{0}SD, 6^{0}GS, 5^{0}G,

	Starts	1st	2nd	3rd	Win & Pl
Career Total (Turf)	2	0	0	0	
Career Total (AW)	1	0	0	0	

Going (Turf): **Sf: 0-0 GS: 0-1 Gd: 0-1 GF: 0-0 Fm: 0-0**
Distance: 5f/6f: 0-3 7f-8f: 0-0 9f-13f: 0-0 14f+: 0-0
Track : LH: 0-0 RH: 0-1 Tight: 0-0 Gall: 0-1
Aids: Bl: 0-0 Vi: 0-0 Tstrap: 0-0 Ckp: 0-0
Best Rating: **43** 10/09 Gdwd 6f gd-sft

Saptapadi (IRE)

110(89) (70)**108**
3-y-o ch g Indian Ridge-Olympienne (IRE) (Sadler's Wells (USA))
Sir Michael Stoute Ballymacoll Stud

Placings:2-45 **(1800)**
2009: 10^{4}G, 12^{5}GF,

	Starts	1st	2nd	3rd	Win & Pl
Career Total (Turf)	2	0	0	0	5374
Career Total (AW)	1	0	1	0	

Going (Turf): **Sf: 0-0 GS: 0-0 Gd: 0-1 GF: 0-1 Fm: 0-0**
Distance: 5f/6f: 0-0 7f-8f: 0-1 9f-13f: 0-2 14f+: 0-0
Track : LH: 0-2 RH: 0-1 Tight: 0-2 Gall: 0-0
Aids: Bl: 0-0 Vi: 0-0 Tstrap: 0-0 Ckp: 0-0
Best Rating: **108** 5/09 Ches 1m4f66y gd-fm

Fair; should stays at least 1m2f; and acts on Polytrack.

Sarah Park (IRE)

106(102) (98)**90**
4-y-o ch f Redback-Brillano (FR) (Desert King (IRE))
B J Meehan Mrs J & D E Cash

Placings:5000/21551-01336114205 **(7588)**
2009: 8^{0}SD, 8^{1}G, 8^{3}SD, 8^{3}G, 8^{6}G, 8^{1}GF, 8^{1}GF, 8^{4}G, 8^{2}SS, 8^{0}SD, 8^{5}SD,

	Starts	1st	2nd	3rd	Win & Pl
Career Total (Turf)	13	5	1	1	20799
Career Total (AW)	7	0	1	1	4623

87 9/09 Gdwd 1m (0-80)H G-F £4857
84 8/09 Epsm 1m114y (0-75)H G-F £3885
81 6/09 Wind 1m67y (0-75)H GD £3070
76 10/08 Yarm 7f3y (0-65)H G-S £2719
69 7/08 Nott 1m75y (0-60)H GD £2047
Total win prize-money £16581

Going (Turf): Sf: 0-0 GS: 1-2 **Gd: 2-6 GF: 2-5** Fm: 0-0
Distance: 5f/6f: 0-2 7f-8f: 2-13 **9f-13f: 3-5** 14f+: 0-0
Track : LH: 2-6 RH: 2-8 **Tight: 2-6** Gall: 0-2
Aids: Bl: 0-0 Vi: 0-0 Tstrap: 0-0 Ckp: 0-0
Best Rating: **98** 10/09 Ling 1m std-slw

Fair; effective at 7f-1m; acts on fast and easy ground; goes on Polytrack.

Sarah's Art (IRE)

103(107) (80)**77**
6-y-o gr g City On A Hill (USA)-Treasure Bleue (IRE) (Treasure Kay)
Stef Liddiard ownaracehorse.co.uk (Shefford)

Placings:0000/5621132120200/00010/025302-3114465210101 **(7735)**
2009: 7^{3}SD, 5^{1}SD, 5^{1}SD, 5^{4}SD, 5^{4}SD, 6^{6}SD, 5^{5}SD, 6^{2}G, 6^{1}GF, 6^{0}GF, 6^{1}GF, 6^{0}G, 5^{1}SD,

	Starts	1st	2nd	3rd	Win & Pl
Career Total (Turf)	18	4	4	0	26495
Career Total (AW)	23	5	3	3	15386

80 12/09 Wolv 5f216y (0-75)H STD £3885
77 8/09 NmkJ 6f (0-85)H G-F £12462
71 4/09 Wwck 6f (0-75)H G-F £2729
75 1/09 Wolv 5f216y (0-55)H STD £2388
67 1/09 Wolv 5f216y (0-55)H STD £2388

61	9/07	Kemp	7f	(0-50)H	STD	£2047
66	6/06	Brig	5f213y	(0-70)H	FRM	£3886
62	5/06	Haml	5f4y	(0-60)H	G-F	£3238
52	5/06	Wolv	5f20y	(0-45)	STD	£1382

Total win prize-money £34409

Going (Turf): Sf: 0-1 GS: 0-2 Gd: 0-4 **GF: 3-7** Fm: 1-4
Distance: **5f/6f: 8-36** 7f-8f: 1-5 9f-13f: 0-0 14f+: 0-0
Track : **LH: 6-20** RH: 1-8 **Tight: 4-14** Gall: 0-4
Aids: **Bl: 3-14** Vi: 0-0 Tstrap: 0-0 Ckp: 0-0
Best Rating: **80** 12/09 Wolv 5f216y stand

Modest; stays 6f; acts on fast ground and on Polytrack; has worn blinkers and a tongue tie.

Sarahthecarer (IRE)

83 (59)**61**

2-y-o b f Littletown Boy (USA)-Peaceful Sarah (Sharpo)
P M Mooney Mrs Oliver Sheils

Placings:6U34 **(3902a)**
2009: 6^{6}GF, 7^{U}GF, 7^{3}GF, 5^{4}SD,

	Starts	1st	2nd	3rd	Win & Pl
Career Total (Turf)	3	0	0	1	602
Career Total (AW)	1	0	0	0	677

Going (Turf): **Sf: 0-0 GS: 0-0 Gd: 0-0 GF: 0-3 Fm: 0-0**
Distance: 5f/6f: 0-2 7f-8f: 0-2 9f-13f: 0-0 14f+: 0-0
Track : LH: 0-2 RH: 0-0 Tight: 0-1 Gall: 0-0
Aids: Bl: 0-0 Vi: 0-0 Tstrap: 0-0 Ckp: 0-0
Best Rating: **61** 6/09 Ches 7f2y gd-fm

Moderate; stays 7f; acts on fast ground.

Sarando

(96) (65)**62**

4-y-o b g Hernando (FR)-Dansara (Dancing Brave (USA))
P R Webber (R Charlton 11/1) Eight Men & A Hoss

Placings:044-6 **(0126)**
2009: 13^{6}SD,

	Starts	1st	2nd	3rd	Win & Pl
Career Total (Turf)	1	0	0	0	
Career Total (AW)	3	0	0	0	0

Going (Turf): **Sf: 0-0 GS: 0-0 Gd: 0-1 GF: 0-0 Fm: 0-0**
Distance: 5f/6f: 0-0 7f-8f: 0-0 9f-13f: 0-3 14f+: 0-1
Track : LH: 0-3 RH: 0-1 Tight: 0-2 Gall: 0-1
Aids: Bl: 0-0 Vi: 0-0 Tstrap: 0-0 Ckp: 0-0
Best Rating: **65** 1/09 GrLe 1m5f66y stand

Modest; stays 1m4f; acts on Polytrack.

Sarasota Sunshine

104(103) (80)**75**

3-y-o b f Oasis Dream-Never Explain (IRE) (Fairy King (USA))
N P Littmoden Franconson Partners

Placings:003-132113110 **(5432)**
2009: 7^{1}SD, 7^{3}SD, 6^{2}G, 6^{1}GS, 5^{1}SD, 6^{3}S, 6^{1}GF, 7^{1}SD, 7^{0}GF,

	Starts	1st	2nd	3rd	Win & Pl
Career Total (Turf)	8	2	1	2	6958
Career Total (AW)	4	3	0	1	9907

80	8/09	Kemp	7f	(0-80)H	STD	£4727
75	8/09	Hayd	6f	(0-70)H	G-F	£3238
69	6/09	Wolv	5f216y	(0-65)H	STD	£2729
68	6/09	Wwck	6f	(0-65)H	G-S	£2047
63	2/09	Ling	7f	(0-60)H	STD	£2047

Total win prize-money £14789

Going (Turf): Sf: 0-3 **GS: 1-2** Gd: 0-1 **GF: 1-2** Fm: 0-0
Distance: **5f/6f: 3-7** 7f-8f: 2-5 9f-13f: 0-0 14f+: 0-0
Track : **LH: 3-4** RH: 1-1 **Tight: 2-3** Gall: 0-1
Aids: **Bl: 4-6** Vi: 0-0 Tstrap: 0-0 Ckp: 0-0
Best Rating: **80** 8/09 Kemp 7f stand

Fair; effective over 6f-7f; acts on fast and soft ground; goes on Polytrack; has worn blinkers.

Sard

86 **51**

2-y-o b f Bahamian Bounty-Clincher Club (Polish Patriot (USA))
M A Jarvis Tony Bloom

Placings:00 **(6563)**
2009: 6^{0}G, 6^{0}GS,

	Starts	1st	2nd	3rd	Win & Pl
Career Total (Turf)	2	0	0	0	

Going (Turf): **Sf: 0-0 GS: 0-1 Gd: 0-1 GF: 0-0 Fm: 0-0**
Distance: 5f/6f: 0-2 7f-8f: 0-0 9f-13f: 0-0 14f+: 0-0
Track : LH: 0-0 RH: 0-0 Tight: 0-0 Gall: 0-0
Aids: Bl: 0-0 Vi: 0-0 Tstrap: 0-0 Ckp: 0-0
Best Rating: **51** 8/09 NmkJ 6f good

Sardan Dansar (IRE)

99(94) (28)**53**

3-y-o b f Alhaarth (IRE)-Peruvian Witch (IRE) (Perugino (USA))
Mrs A Duffield Stewart Dalziel

Placings:0400-50056300 **(5621)**
2009: 7^{5}GF, 8^{0}SD, 7^{0}GF, 5^{5}G, 5^{6}GS, 6^{3}G, 6^{0}GF, 7^{0}S,

	Starts	1st	2nd	3rd	Win & Pl
Career Total (Turf)	11	0	0	1	828
Career Total (AW)	1	0	0	0	

Going (Turf): **Sf: 0-2 GS: 0-2 Gd: 0-2 GF: 0-5 Fm: 0-0**
Distance: 5f/6f: 0-5 7f-8f: 0-6 9f-13f: 0-1 14f+: 0-0
Track : LH: 0-6 RH: 0-3 Tight: 0-7 Gall: 0-0
Aids: Bl: 0-0 Vi: 0-0 Tstrap: 0-0 Ckp: 0-0
Best Rating: **53** 7/08 Catt 7f gd-fm

Modest-looking sort; stays 7f; acts on fast and easy ground.

Sariska

117 **123**

3-y-o b f Pivotal-Maycocks Bay (Muhtarram (USA))
M L W Bell Lady Bamford

Placings:1-411123 **(6850)**
2009: 7^{4}S, 10^{1}GF, 12^{1}G, 12^{1}HY, 12^{2}GF, 10^{3}G,

	Starts	1st	2nd	3rd	Win & Pl
Career Total (Turf)	7	4	1	1	623534

123	7/09	Curr	1m4f	HVY	£272330
120	6/09	Epsm	1m4f10y	GD	£198695
117	5/09	York	1m2f88y	G-F	£36900
88	11/08	NmkR	7f	G-S	£4857

Total win prize-money £512783

Going (Turf): **Sf: 1-2 GS: 1-1 Gd: 1-2 GF: 1-2** Fm: 0-0
Distance: 5f/6f: 0-0 7f-8f: 1-2 **9f-13f: 3-5** 14f+: 0-0
Track : **LH: 2-3** RH: 1-1 Tight: 1-1 Gall: 1-2
Aids: Bl: 0-0 Vi: 0-0 Tstrap: 0-0 Ckp: 0-0
Best Rating: **123** 7/09 Curr 1m4f heavy

High-class; winner of the Group 3 Musidora Stakes before landing the Epsom Oaks; impressive in the Irish Oaks; beaten at short odds into second in the 2009 Yorkshire Oaks; good third in the Champion Stakes; effective from 1m2f-1m4f; acts on fast and soft ground.

Sarmad (USA)

87 **55**

2-y-o b/br f Dynaformer (USA)-Performing Arts (IRE) (The Minstrel (CAN))
C E Brittain Saeed Manana

Placings:000 **(5547)**
2009: 6^{0}GF, 7^{0}GF, 8^{0}GF,

	Starts	1st	2nd	3rd	Win & Pl
Career Total (Turf)	3	0	0	0	

Going (Turf): **Sf: 0-0 GS: 0-0 Gd: 0-0 GF: 0-3 Fm: 0-0**
Distance: 5f/6f: 0-1 7f-8f: 0-1 9f-13f: 0-1 14f+: 0-0
Track : LH: 0-0 RH: 0-2 Tight: 0-0 Gall: 0-0
Aids: Bl: 0-0 Vi: 0-0 Tstrap: 0-0 Ckp: 0-0
Best Rating: **55** 5/09 NmkR 6f gd-fm

Sarraaf (IRE)

97(95) (60)**59**

13-y-o ch g Perugino (USA)-Blue Vista (IRE) (Pennine Walk)
I Semple Gordon McDowall

Placings:04/5501521600/006404402301040/65322543006 3050/2350042030013400l0561**P0004/431**0040343010300 320031042/**4232**0533505203460400**60**/4125042303130 46**143/344**/44024000**4230/5**014604303-064 **(2440)**
2009: 8^{0}SD, 10^{6}GF, 9^{4}GF,

	Starts	1st	2nd	3rd	Win & Pl
Career Total (Turf)	139	11	14	21	100312
Career Total (AW)	24	2	1	5	9573

58	7/08	Haml	1m1f36y	(0-65)H	GD	£2388
65	11/05	Wolv	7f32y	(0-55)H	STD	£2888
57	8/05	Haml	1m65y		G-F	£2754
65	5/05	Muss	7f30y	(0-70)H	G-F	£4052
74	9/03	Hayd	1m30y	D(0-85)H	SFT	£3822
71	6/03	Muss	1m1f	E	G-F	£4085
78	2/03	Wolv	7f	E(0-70)	STD	£3227
91	10/02	Leic	7f9y	C	SFT	£7426
60	10/02	Catt	5f212y	F(0-85)	FRM	£2968
69	8/02	Epsm	1m114y	E	G-F	£3721
87	9/00	Curr	1m	(0-85)H	Y-S	£5520
84	8/99	Tral	1m	(0-85)H	YLD	£3573
81	6/99	Bell	1m		G-F	£2915

Total win prize-money £49342

Going (Turf): Sf: 2-19 GS: 0-10Gd: 1-33**GF: 5-49** Fm: 1-9
Distance: 5f/6f: 1-7 **7f-8f: 7-94** 9f-13f: 5-61 14f+: 0-0
Track : **LH: 7-83** RH: 4-55 **Tight: 7-74** Gall: 1-16
Aids: Bl: 0-1 Vi: 0-2 Tstrap: 0-0 Ckp: 0-0
Best Rating: **91** 10/02 Leic 7f9y soft

Moderate; effective at up to 1m1f; acts on any ground on turf; also goes on Fibresand and Polytrack.

Sarrsar

93 **74**

2-y-o b g Shamardal (USA)-Bahr (Generous (IRE))
M A Jarvis Sheikh Ahmed Al Maktoum

Placings:3 **(7095)**
2009: 8^{3}G,

	Starts	1st	2nd	3rd	Win & Pl
Career Total (Turf)	1	0	0	1	519

Going (Turf): **Sf: 0-0 GS: 0-0 Gd: 0-1 GF: 0-0 Fm: 0-0**
Distance: 5f/6f: 0-0 7f-8f: 0-0 9f-13f: 0-1 14f+: 0-0
Track : LH: 0-0 RH: 0-0 Tight: 0-0 Gall: 0-0
Aids: Bl: 0-0 Vi: 0-0 Tstrap: 0-0 Ckp: 0-0
Best Rating: **74** 10/09 Yarm 1m3y good

Fair debut over 1m on good ground.

Sarwin (USA)

103(102) (67)**71**
6-y-o gr/ro g Holy Bull (USA)-Olive The Twist (USA) (Theatrical)
G A Swinbank S Rudolf

Placings:000/031605**325/21/00-001**13160650 **(6900)**
2009: 7^{0}SD, 7^{0}SD, **8**^{1}SD, 8^{1}GF, 9^{3}GF, 9^{1}GF, 7^{6}GF, 8^{0}GF, 8^{6}S, 8^{5}GF, 10^{0}GF,

	Starts	1st	2nd	3rd	Win & Pl
Career Total (Turf)	**15**	**2**	**0**	**2**	**7612**
Career Total (AW)	**12**	**3**	**2**	**1**	**10479**

71 5/09 Haml 1m1f36y (0-70)H G-F £4094
68 5/09 Bevl 1m100y (0-60)H G-F £2729
67 4/09 Wolv 1m141y (0-65)H STD £2388
75 2/07 Wolv 1m1f103y (0-70)H STD £3238
65 6/06 Wolv 1m1f103y (0-60)H SS £2730
Total win prize-money £15181

Going (Turf): Sf: 0-4 GS: 0-0 Gd: 0-2 **GF: 2-9** Fm: 0-0
Distance: 5f/6f: 0-2 7f-8f: 0-6 **9f-13f: 5-19** 14f+: 0-0
Track : **LH: 3-14** RH: 2-9 **Tight: 4-11** Gall: 0-1
Aids: Bl: 0-0 Vi: 0-0 Tstrap: 0-0 Ckp: 0-0
Best Rating: **75** 2/07 Wolv 1m1f103y stand

Modest; effective over 1m-1m4f; acts on fast ground; goes on Polytrack.

Sasheen

(98) (72)
2-y-o b f Zafeen (FR)-Sashay (Bishop Of Cashel)
J R Boyle Sashay Partnership

Placings:035 **(7763)**
2009: 8^{0}SD, 8^{3}SD, 8^{5}SD,

	Starts	1st	2nd	3rd	Win & Pl
Career Total (Turf)	**0**	**0**	**0**	**0**	
Career Total (AW)	**3**	**0**	**0**	**1**	**353**

Going (Turf): **Sf: 0-0 GS: 0-0 Gd: 0-0 GF: 0-0 Fm: 0-0**
Distance: 5f/6f: 0-0 7f-8f: 0-3 9f-13f: 0-0 14f+: 0-0
Track : LH: 0-2 RH: 0-1 Tight: 0-2 Gall: 0-0
Aids: Bl: 0-0 Vi: 0-0 Tstrap: 0-0 Ckp: 0-0
Best Rating: **72** 12/09 Ling 1m stand

Fair; stays 1m; acts on Polytrack.

Sassanian (IRE)

85(89) (55)**62**
2-y-o b g Clodovil (IRE)-Persian Sally (IRE) (Persian Bold)
Jane Chapple-Hyam (J Howard Johnson 22/7) Mrs Jane Chapple-Hyam

Placings:0450**44** **(7731)**
2009: 6^{0}G, 7^{4}S, 7^{5}GF, 6^{0}GF, **8**^{4}SD, **9**^{4}SD,

	Starts	1st	2nd	3rd	Win & Pl
Career Total (Turf)	**4**	**0**	**0**	**0**	**0**
Career Total (AW)	**2**	**0**	**0**	**0**	**289**

Going (Turf): **Sf: 0-1 GS: 0-0 Gd: 0-1 GF: 0-2 Fm: 0-0**
Distance: 5f/6f: 0-2 7f-8f: 0-3 9f-13f: 0-1 14f+: 0-0
Track : LH: 0-3 RH: 0-0 Tight: 0-2 Gall: 0-0

Aids: Bl: 0-0 Vi: 0-0 Tstrap: 0-0 Ckp: 0-0
Best Rating: **62** 9/09 NmkR 7f gd-fm

Modest; stays 1m; acts on Fibresand.

Satin Princess (IRE)

79(86) (26)**48**
2-y-o b f Royal Applause-College Of Arms (Lujain (USA))
A M Hales (Paul Mason 25/7) J H And N J Foxon

Placings:0004**00** **(7453)**
2009: 5^{0}GS, 5^{0}G, 5^{0}GF, 5^{4}GF, **5**^{0}SD, **6**^{0}SD,

	Starts	1st	2nd	3rd	Win & Pl
Career Total (Turf)	**4**	**0**	**0**	**0**	**0**
Career Total (AW)	**2**	**0**	**0**	**0**	

Going (Turf): **Sf: 0-0 GS: 0-1 Gd: 0-1 GF: 0-2 Fm: 0-0**
Distance: 5f/6f: 0-6 7f-8f: 0-0 9f-13f: 0-0 14f+: 0-0
Track : LH: 0-2 RH: 0-1 Tight: 0-1 Gall: 0-0
Aids: Bl: 0-0 Vi: 0-0 Tstrap: 0-0 Ckp: 0-0
Best Rating: **48** 7/09 Ling 5f good

Satindra (IRE)

(102) (65)**53**
5-y-o b g Lil's Boy (USA)-Voronova (IRE) (Sadler's Wells (USA))
C R Dore D C Cooper & G D J Linder

Placings:0000/00**633315/200020000-404** **(0385)**
2009: 11^{4}SD, **12**^{0}SD, **12**^{4}SD,

	Starts	1st	2nd	3rd	Win & Pl
Career Total (Turf)	**7**	**0**	**0**	**1**	**289**
Career Total (AW)	**17**	**1**	**2**	**2**	**4239**

65 12/07 Sthl 1m3f SS £2968
Total win prize-money £2969

Going (Turf): **Sf: 0-1 GS: 0-1 Gd: 0-0 GF: 0-2 Fm: 0-0**
Distance: 5f/6f: 0-2 7f-8f: 0-3 **9f-13f: 1-17** 14f+: 0-2
Track : **LH: 1-13** RH: 0-9 Tight: 0-5 Gall: 0-1
Aids: Bl: 0-0 Vi: 0-0 Tstrap: 1-19 Ckp: 1-19
Best Rating: **65** 3/08 Sthl 1m3f stand

Moderate; stays 1m3f; acts on easy ground; also goes on sand; has worn cheekpieces and a tongue tie.

Satisfaction Life (IRE)

(97) (72)**69**
3-y-o b f Acclamation-Etica (IRE) (Barathea (IRE))
M Botti (Giuseppe Chianese 24/5) Giuseppe Piccinni

Placings:1-644020**06** **(5616)**
2009: 7^{6}HY, 8^{4}S, 8^{4}G, 9^{0}G, 10^{2}G, 11^{0}GF, **11**^{0}SD, **9**^{6}SD,

	Starts	1st	2nd	3rd	Win & Pl
Career Total (Turf)	**7**	**1**	**1**	**0**	**12771**
Career Total (AW)	**2**	**0**	**0**	**0**	**0**

12/08 Agno 7f110y SFT £4411
Total win prize-money £4412

Going (Turf): **Sf: 1-3** GS: 0-0 Gd: 0-3 GF: 0-1 Fm: 0-0
Distance: 5f/6f: 0-0 **7f-8f: 1-4** 9f-13f: 0-5 14f+: 0-0
Track : LH: 0-1 RH: 0-3 Tight: 0-1 Gall: 0-0
Aids: Bl: 0-0 Vi: 0-0 Tstrap: 0-0 Ckp: 0-0
Best Rating: **72** 9/09 Wolv 1m1f103y stand

Saturn Girl (IRE)

92 **71**
3-y-o ch f Danehill Dancer (IRE)-Lilissa (IRE) (Doyoun)
S A Callaghan Michael Tabor

Placings:4100 **(6174)**
2009: 8^{4}GF, 8^{1}GF, 8^{0}S, 8^{0}GF,

	Starts	1st	2nd	3rd	Win & Pl
Career Total (Turf)	**4**	**1**	**0**	**0**	**2730**

71 6/09 Wind 1m67y G-F £2729
Total win prize-money £2730

Going (Turf): Sf: 0-1 GS: 0-0 Gd: 0-0 **GF: 1-3** Fm: 0-0
Distance: 5f/6f: 0-0 7f-8f: 0-1 **9f-13f: 1-3** 14f+: 0-0
Track : LH: 0-1 **RH: 1-3 Tight: 1-3** Gall: 0-0
Aids: Bl: 0-0 Vi: 0-0 Tstrap: 0-0 Ckp: 0-0
Best Rating: **71** 6/09 Wind 1m67y gd-fm

Fair; effective over 1m; acts on fast ground.

Saturn Way (GR)

97(81) (53)**72**
3-y-o b g Bachelor Duke (USA)-Senseansensibility (USA) (Capote (USA))
P R Chamings Mrs Alexandra J Chandris

Placings:01-62004 **(4956)**
2009: 7^{6}GF, 8^{2}G, 8^{0}GF, 8^{0}G, 8^{4}G,

	Starts	1st	2nd	3rd	Win & Pl
Career Total (Turf)	**6**	**1**	**1**	**0**	**3915**
Career Total (AW)	**1**	**0**	**0**	**0**	

71 10/08 Folk 7f SFT £2590
Total win prize-money £2590

Going (Turf): **Sf: 1-1** GS: 0-0 Gd: 0-3 GF: 0-2 Fm: 0-0
Distance: 5f/6f: 0-0 **7f-8f: 1-4** 9f-13f: 0-3 14f+: 0-0
Track : LH: 0-1 RH: 0-4 Tight: 0-2 Gall: 0-0
Aids: Bl: 0-0 Vi: 0-0 Tstrap: 0-0 Ckp: 0-0
Best Rating: **72** 5/09 Gdwd 1m good

Satwa Crown

70(78) (29)**24**
2-y-o b c Dubai Destination (USA)-Crown Of Spring (USA) (Chief's Crown (USA))
E A L Dunlop The Lamprell Partnership

Placings:000 **(4200)**
2009: 5^{0}SD, 6^{0}GF, 7^{0}SD,

	Starts	1st	2nd	3rd	Win & Pl
Career Total (Turf)	**1**	**0**	**0**	**0**	
Career Total (AW)	**2**	**0**	**0**	**0**	

Going (Turf): **Sf: 0-0 GS: 0-0 Gd: 0-0 GF: 0-1 Fm: 0-0**
Distance: 5f/6f: 0-2 7f-8f: 0-1 9f-13f: 0-0 14f+: 0-0
Track : LH: 0-2 RH: 0-0 Tight: 0-2 Gall: 0-1
Aids: Bl: 0-0 Vi: 0-0 Tstrap: 0-0 Ckp: 0-0
Best Rating: **29** 6/09 Wolv 5f216y stand

Satwa Excel

56 **24**
2-y-o b f Exceed And Excel (AUS)-Pericardia (Petong)
E A L Dunlop The Lamprell Partnership

Placings:0 **(4542)**
2009: 7^{0}G,

	Starts	1st	2nd	3rd	Win & Pl
Career Total (Turf)	**1**	**0**	**0**	**0**	

Going (Turf): **Sf: 0-0 GS: 0-0 Gd: 0-1 GF: 0-0 Fm: 0-0**

Distance: 5f/6f: 0-0 7f-8f: 0-1 9f-13f: 0-0 14f+: 0-0
Track : LH: 0-0 RH: 0-0 Tight: 0-0 Gall: 0-0
Aids: Bl: 0-0 Vi: 0-0 Tstrap: 0-0 Ckp: 0-0
Best Rating: **24** 8/09 NmkJ 7f good

Satwa Gold (USA)

91(103) (88)**57**
3-y-o ch c Rahy (USA)-No More Ironing (USA) (Slew O'Gold (USA))
E A L Dunlop The Lamprell Partnership

Placings:0-120001315 **(7612)**
2009: 8^{1}SD, 8^{2}SD, 8^{0}SD, 10^{0}SD, 10^{0}GS, 10^{1}SD, 10^{3}SD, 12^{1}SD, 12^{5}SD,

	Starts	1st	2nd	3rd	Win & Pl
Career Total (Turf)	2	0	0	0	
Career Total (AW)	8	3	1	1	8668

74 11/09 Kemp 1m4f STD £2047
73 10/09 Kemp 1m2f STD £2047
81 3/09 Wolv 1m141y STD £2729
Total win prize-money £6824

Going (Turf): **Sf: 0-0 GS: 0-1 Gd: 0-1 GF: 0-0 Fm: 0-0**
Distance: 5f/6f: 0-0 7f-8f: 0-3 **9f-13f: 3-7** 14f+: 0-0
Track : LH: 1-4 **RH: 2-5 Tight: 1-3** Gall: 0-0
Aids: Bl: 0-0 Vi: 0-0 Tstrap: 0-0 Ckp: 0-0
Best Rating: **88** 4/09 Kemp 1m stand

Useful; stays 1m4f and acts on Polytrack.

Satwa Laird

103(103) (86)**92**
3-y-o b c Johannesburg (USA)-Policy Setter (USA) (Deputy Minister (CAN))
E A L Dunlop The Lamprell Partnership

Placings:31402-40004220 **(6702)**
2009: 7^{4}GF, 7^{0}G, 8^{0}GF, 7^{0}GF, 6^{4}GF, 7^{2}GF, 8^{2}G, 7^{0}SS,

	Starts	1st	2nd	3rd	Win & Pl
Career Total (Turf)	12	1	3	1	12604
Career Total (AW)	1	0	0	0	

82 8/08 Nott 6f15y GD £3238
Total win prize-money £3238

Going (Turf): Sf: 0-1 GS: 0-0 **Gd: 1-4** GF: 0-7 Fm: 0-0
Distance: 5f/6f: 0-1 **7f-8f: 1-12** 9f-13f: 0-0 14f+: 0-0
Track : LH: 0-3 RH: 0-1 Tight: 0-2 Gall: 0-2
Aids: Bl: 0-0 Vi: 0-0 Tstrap: 0-0 Ckp: 0-0
Best Rating: **92** 9/09 Asct 1m good

Useful; stays 1m; acts on most ground on turf.

Satwa Moon (USA)

(96) (77)
3-y-o ch c Horse Chestnut (SAF)-Double Schott (USA) (Demons Begone (USA))
E A L Dunlop The Lamprell Partnership

Placings:636 **(5614)**
2009: 10^{6}SD, 8^{3}SF, 8^{6}SD,

	Starts	1st	2nd	3rd	Win & Pl
Career Total (Turf)	0	0	0	0	
Career Total (AW)	3	0	0	1	302

Going (Turf): **Sf: 0-0 GS: 0-0 Gd: 0-0 GF: 0-0 Fm: 0-0**
Distance: 5f/6f: 0-0 7f-8f: 0-0 9f-13f: 0-3 14f+: 0-0
Track : LH: 0-3 RH: 0-0 Tight: 0-3 Gall: 0-0
Aids: Bl: 0-0 Vi: 0-0 Tstrap: 0-0 Ckp: 0-0
Best Rating: **77** 8/09 Wolv 1m141y std-fst

Satwa Ruby (FR)

87 (73)**95**
3-y-o gr f Verglas (IRE)-Vezina (FR) (Bering)
J De Roualle Steven & Gillian Lamprell

Placings:53-411500 **(4334a)**
2009: 9^{4}SD, 10^{1}GS, 10^{1}S, 11^{5}S, 10^{0}GF, 10^{0}S,

	Starts	1st	2nd	3rd	Win & Pl
Career Total (Turf)	7	2	0	1	28838
Career Total (AW)	1	0	0	0	2330

86 5/09 Le L 1m2f SFT £13106
4/09 Cros 1m2f110y G-S £10194
Total win prize-money £23301

Going (Turf): **Sf: 1-4 GS: 1-2** Gd: 0-0 GF: 0-1 Fm: 0-0
Distance: 5f/6f: 0-0 7f-8f: 0-0 **9f-13f: 2-8** 14f+: 0-0
Track : LH: 0-0 RH: 0-2 Tight: 0-0 Gall: 0-1
Aids: Bl: 0-0 Vi: 0-0 Tstrap: 0-0 Ckp: 0-0
Best Rating: **95** 7/09 Vich 1m2f soft

Useful; stays 1m2f; acts on soft ground.

Satwa Son (IRE)

69(85) (58)**31**
2-y-o gr c Oasis Dream-Cozy Maria (USA) (Cozzene (USA))
E A L Dunlop The Lamprell Partnership

Placings:00 **(5191)**
2009: 6^{0}G, 7^{0}SD,

	Starts	1st	2nd	3rd	Win & Pl
Career Total (Turf)	1	0	0	0	
Career Total (AW)	1	0	0	0	

Going (Turf): **Sf: 0-0 GS: 0-0 Gd: 0-1 GF: 0-0 Fm: 0-0**
Distance: 5f/6f: 0-1 7f-8f: 0-1 9f-13f: 0-0 14f+: 0-0
Track : LH: 0-1 RH: 0-0 Tight: 0-1 Gall: 0-0
Aids: Bl: 0-0 Vi: 0-0 Tstrap: 0-0 Ckp: 0-0
Best Rating: **58** 8/09 Ling 7f stand

Satwa Star (IRE)

91(99) (70)**56**
3-y-o b g King's Best (USA)-Sheppard's Watch (Night Shift (USA))
E A L Dunlop The Lamprell Partnership

Placings:5505400 **(6701)**
2009: 7^{5}SD, 8^{5}G, 5^{0}S, 7^{5}SD, 7^{4}SD, 7^{0}SD, 7^{0}SS,

	Starts	1st	2nd	3rd	Win & Pl
Career Total (Turf)	2	0	0	0	0
Career Total (AW)	5	0	0	0	313

Going (Turf): **Sf: 0-1 GS: 0-0 Gd: 0-1 GF: 0-0 Fm: 0-0**
Distance: 5f/6f: 0-1 7f-8f: 0-5 9f-13f: 0-1 14f+: 0-0
Track : LH: 0-5 RH: 0-1 Tight: 0-4 Gall: 0-0
Aids: Bl: 0-0 Vi: 0-0 Tstrap: 0-0 Ckp: 0-0
Best Rating: **70** 9/09 Kemp 7f stand

Modest; stays 7f and should stay 1m; acts on Polytrack.

Satwa Street (IRE)

103(102) (89)**86**
3-y-o br c Elusive City (USA)-Black Tribal (IRE) (Mukaddamah (USA))
D M Simcock Khalifa Dasmal

Placings:032212-432305551230 **(5032)**
2009: 5^{4}SD, 6^{3}SD, 6^{2}SD, 6^{3}SD, 5^{0}GF, 5^{5}G, 5^{5}F, 6^{5}SD, 5^{1}F, 5^{2}GF, 6^{3}GF, 6^{0}GF,

	Starts	1st	2nd	3rd	Win & Pl
Career Total (Turf)	7	1	1	1	5195
Career Total (AW)	11	1	4	3	11555

84 7/09 Brig 5f213y (0-75)H FRM £3154
86 11/08 Ling 5f STD £3561
Total win prize-money £6716

Going (Turf): Sf: 0-0 GS: 0-0 Gd: 0-1 GF: 0-4 **Fm: 1-2**
Distance: **5f/6f: 2-18** 7f-8f: 0-0 9f-13f: 0-0 14f+: 0-0
Track : **LH: 2-13** RH: 0-2 **Tight: 1-9** Gall: 0-3
Aids: Bl: 0-0 Vi: 0-0 Tstrap: 0-0 Ckp: 0-0
Best Rating: **89** 1/09 Ling 6f stand

Useful; effective over 5f-6f; acts on fast ground; goes on Polytrack.

Saucy

(105) (71)**52**
8-y-o b m Muhtarram (USA)-So Saucy (Teenoso (USA))
Tom Dascombe Mrs Bernadette Quinn

Placings:0/66053500/6141155/0006031/120305006030/25205024031012-35 **(0651)**
2009: 10^{3}SD, 8^{5}SD,

	Starts	1st	2nd	3rd	Win & Pl
Career Total (Turf)	27	1	3	2	6555
Career Total (AW)	24	6	2	4	12990

61 12/08 Ling 1m2f (0-60)H STD £1706
58 11/08 Ling 1m2f (0-60)H STD £2729
56 1/07 Kemp 1m (0-50)H STD £2047
51 12/06 Ling 1m2f (0-45) STD £1433
61 4/05 Ling 1m2f (0-45) STD £1487
53 4/05 Brig 1m1f209y (0-45) GD £1687
54 3/05 Ling 1m2f (0-45) STD £1494
Total win prize-money £12587

Going (Turf): Sf: 0-2 GS: 0-2 **Gd: 1-8** GF: 0-10 Fm: 0-2
Distance: 5f/6f: 0-1 7f-8f: 1-5 **9f-13f: 6-45** 14f+: 0-0
Track : **LH: 6-32** RH: 1-15 **Tight: 5-23** Gall: 0-1
Aids: Bl: 0-5 Vi: 0-0 Tstrap: 0-0 Ckp: 0-0
Best Rating: **71** 12/08 Ling 1m2f stand

Modest; stays 1m2f; acts on good ground and on Polytrack.

Saucy Brown (IRE)

107 **95**
3-y-o b g Fasliyev (USA)-Danseuse Du Bois (USA) (Woodman (USA))
R Hannon The Heffer Syndicate

Placings:152006-30130505 **(5025)**
2009: 5^{3}GF, 7^{0}GS, 7^{1}G, 6^{3}GF, 7^{0}GF, 7^{5}G, 7^{0}G, 7^{5}GF,

	Starts	1st	2nd	3rd	Win & Pl
Career Total (Turf)	14	2	1	2	24107

93 5/09 Donc 7f GD £7477
74 5/08 NmkR 5f GD £4533
Total win prize-money £12010

Going (Turf): Sf: 0-1 GS: 0-1 **Gd: 2-5** GF: 0-7 Fm: 0-0
Distance: 5f/6f: 1-6 7f-8f: 1-8 9f-13f: 0-0 14f+: 0-0
Track : LH: 0-0 RH: 0-1 Tight: 0-0 Gall: 0-0
Aids: Bl: 0-0 Vi: 0-0 Tstrap: 0-0 Ckp: 0-0
Best Rating: **95** 5/09 Donc 6f gd-fm

Very useful; Listed placed; effective at 6-7f; acts on good and faster ground.

Saucy Girl (IRE)

90(83) (42)69

2-y-o b f Footstepsinthesand-Leenane (IRE) (Grand Lodge (USA))

T D Easterby Peter C Bourke

Placings:230000 **(6345)**

2009: 5^{2}GF, 5^{3}G, 6^{0}GS, 6^{0}GF, 5^{0}S, 5^{0}SD,

	Starts	1st	2nd	3rd	Win & Pl
Career Total (Turf)	5	0	1	1	2119
Career Total (AW)	1	0	0	0	

Going (Turf): Sf: 0-1 GS: 0-1 Gd: 0-1 GF: 0-2 Fm: 0-0
Distance: 5f/6f: 0-6 7f-8f: 0-0 9f-13f: 0-0 14f+: 0-0
Track : LH: 0-1 RH: 0-0 Tight: 0-1 Gall: 0-0
Aids: Bl: 0-0 Vi: 0-0 Tstrap: 0-0 Ckp: 0-0
Best Rating: 69 4/09 Ripn 5f gd-fm

Modest; placed in 5f maidens on fast ground.

Saunton Sands

63 33

3-y-o ch g Best Of The Bests (IRE)-Victoriet (Hamas (IRE))

A G Newcombe David Bramhill

Placings:000-0 **(2950)**

2009: 8^{0}GF,

	Starts	1st	2nd	3rd	Win & Pl
Career Total (Turf)	4	0	0	0	

Going (Turf): Sf: 0-0 GS: 0-0 Gd: 0-1 GF: 0-3 Fm: 0-0
Distance: 5f/6f: 0-2 7f-8f: 0-2 9f-13f: 0-0 14f+: 0-0
Track : LH: 0-2 RH: 0-1 Tight: 0-0 Gall: 0-2
Aids: Bl: 0-0 Vi: 0-0 Tstrap: 0-0 Ckp: 0-0
Best Rating: 33 5/08 Bath 5f11y gd-fm

Saute

80(102) (72)38

3-y-o br g Hawk Wing (USA)-Lifting (IRE) (Nordance (USA))

W R Swinburn The Lucky Few

Placings:0-00030121 **(7642)**

2009: 8^{0}GF, 8^{0}SD, 8^{0}SD, 12^{3}SD, 12^{0}SS, 12^{1}SD, 14^{2}SD, 14^{1}SD,

	Starts	1st	2nd	3rd	Win & Pl
Career Total (Turf)	1	0	0	0	
Career Total (AW)	8	2	1	1	4674

72	12/09	Sthl	1m6f	(0-60)H	STD	£1619
60	10/09	Kemp	1m4f	(0-60)H	STD	£2047

Total win prize-money £3666

Going (Turf): Sf: 0-0 GS: 0-0 Gd: 0-0 GF: 0-1 Fm: 0-0
Distance: 5f/6f: 0-0 7f-8f: 0-4 9f-13f: 1-3 14f+: 1-2
Track : LH: 1-6 RH: 1-3 Tight: 0-4 Gall: 0-0
Aids: Bl: 0-0 Vi: 0-0 Tstrap: 0-0 Ckp: 0-0
Best Rating: 72 12/09 Sthl 1m6f stand

Moderate; stays 1m6f; acts on Polytrack and Fibresand.

Savaronola (USA)

(99) (73)79

4-y-o ch g Pulpit (USA)-Running Debate (USA) (Open Forum (USA))

B J Curley (A P Stringer 4/1) Curley Leisure

Placings:5/2034-50 **(1568)**

2009: 12^{5}SS, 11^{0}SD,

	Starts	1st	2nd	3rd	Win & Pl
Career Total (Turf)	3	0	1	0	1539
Career Total (AW)	4	0	0	1	653

Going (Turf): Sf: 0-0 GS: 0-0 Gd: 0-0 GF: 0-1 Fm: 0-1
Distance: 5f/6f: 0-0 7f-8f: 0-1 9f-13f: 0-6 14f+: 0-0
Track : LH: 0-5 RH: 0-1 Tight: 0-0 Gall: 0-0
Aids: Bl: 0-0 Vi: 0-0 Tstrap: 0-0 Ckp: 0-0
Best Rating: 79 6/08 Navn 1m2f firm

Saveiro (FR)

74 13

5-y-o b g Raintrap-Branceilles (FR) (Satin Wood)

G A Swinbank Andrew Dick & Brian Dunn

Placings:0 **(1681)**

2009: 12^{0}GF,

	Starts	1st	2nd	3rd	Win & Pl
Career Total (Turf)	1	0	0	0	

Going (Turf): Sf: 0-0 GS: 0-0 Gd: 0-0 GF: 0-1 Fm: 0-0
Distance: 5f/6f: 0-0 7f-8f: 0-0 9f-13f: 0-1 14f+: 0-0
Track : LH: 0-1 RH: 0-0 Tight: 0-1 Gall: 0-0
Aids: Bl: 0-0 Vi: 0-0 Tstrap: 0-0 Ckp: 0-0
Best Rating: 13 5/09 Thsk 1m4f gd-fm

Savile's Delight (IRE)

(103) (78)83

10-y-o b g Cadeaux Genereux-Across The Ice (USA) (General Holme (USA))

Tom Dascombe ONEWAY Partners

Placings:541/460062360/00041020302004/32431201143 0404/00215305100550030/30304050/000040406/122151 3223212233-05000 **(0739)**

2009: 5^{0}SD, 5^{5}SD, 6^{0}SD, 6^{0}SD, 5^{0}SD,

	Starts	1st	2nd	3rd	Win & Pl
Career Total (Turf)	49	7	7	7	52363
Career Total (AW)	48	4	6	7	17452

78	4/08	Wind	6f	(0-75)H	GD	£3070
76	2/08	Sthl	5f	(0-70)H	STD	£2593
70	2/08	Sthl	5f	(0-65)H	STD	£2047
53	1/08	Sthl	5f	(0-52)H	STD	£1714
83	6/05	Wind	5f10y	(0-80)H	G-F	£7026
75	2/05	Wolv	5f20y	(0-70)H	STD	£3361
84	7/04	Hayd	7f30y	E(0-70)H	G-S	£5720
78	7/04	Hayd	6f	D(0-80)H	GD	£6223
74	5/04	Wwck	6f21y	E(0-70)H	HVY	£3916
65	7/03	Catt	5f212y G		FRM	£3136
89	7/01	Tipp	5f		GD	£7790

Total win prize-money £46602

Going (Turf): Sf: 1-9 GS: 1-7 **Gd: 3-16** GF: 1-14 Fm: 1-3
Distance: **5f/6f: 9-71** 7f-8f: 2-26 9f-13f: 0-0 14f+: 0-0
Track : **LH: 4-48** RH: 0-2 Tight: 2-29 Gall: 2-8
Aids: **Bl: 2-32** Vi: 0-4 Tstrap: 1-4 Ckp: 1-4
Best Rating: 95 5/02 Navn 5f soft

Fair; effective at sprint trips, but stays further; acts on good ground; also goes on Fibresand.

Saving Grace

(97) (47)42

3-y-o br f Lend A Hand-Damalis (IRE) (Mukaddamah (USA))

E J Alston Liam & Tony Ferguson

Placings:000-00 **(7754)**

2009: 7^{0}SD, 8^{0}SD,

	Starts	1st	2nd	3rd	Win & Pl
Career Total (Turf)	3	0	0	0	
Career Total (AW)	2	0	0	0	

Going (Turf): Sf: 0-1 GS: 0-0 Gd: 0-1 GF: 0-1 Fm: 0-0
Distance: 5f/6f: 0-1 7f-8f: 0-2 9f-13f: 0-2 14f+: 0-0
Track : LH: 0-3 RH: 0-1 Tight: 0-2 Gall: 0-0
Aids: Bl: 0-0 Vi: 0-0 Tstrap: 0-0 Ckp: 0-0
Best Rating: 47 12/09 Wolv 1m141y stand

Saviour Sand (IRE)

(104) (77)76

5-y-o b g Desert Sun-Teacher Preacher (IRE) (Taufan (USA))

T Keddy (M E Rimmer 8/4) A C Maylam

Placings:26/625043/426100610-540 **(1833)**

2009: 8^{5}SD, 9^{4}SD, 8^{0}SD,

	Starts	1st	2nd	3rd	Win & Pl
Career Total (Turf)	5	1	1	0	3484
Career Total (AW)	15	1	2	1	5101

76	7/08	Yarm	1m2f21y	G-F	£1942
77	3/08	Wolv	1m1f103y (0-75)H	STD	£2590

Total win prize-money £4534

Going (Turf): Sf: 0-0 GS: 0-2 Gd: 0-0 **GF: 1-3** Fm: 0-0
Distance: 5f/6f: 0-1 7f-8f: 0-9 **9f-13f: 2-10** 14f+: 0-0
Track : **LH: 2-16** RH: 0-2 **Tight: 2-15** Gall: 0-0
Aids: **Bl: 1-3** Vi: 0-0 Tstrap: 0-0 Ckp: 0-0
Best Rating: 77 3/08 Wolv 1m1f103y stand

Fair; stays 1m2f; acts on fast ground and Polytrack; has worn blinkers.

Sawab

95(105) (68)69

3-y-o b f Tobougg (IRE)-Skew (Niniski (USA))

C E Brittain Saeed Manana

Placings:230045 **(3550)**

2009: 8^{2}SD, 8^{3}SD, 8^{0}G, 9^{0}GF, 8^{4}GF, 10^{5}GF,

	Starts	1st	2nd	3rd	Win & Pl
Career Total (Turf)	4	0	0	0	241
Career Total (AW)	2	0	1	1	1191

Going (Turf): Sf: 0-0 GS: 0-0 Gd: 0-1 GF: 0-3 Fm: 0-0
Distance: 5f/6f: 0-0 7f-8f: 0-2 9f-13f: 0-4 14f+: 0-0
Track : LH: 0-4 RH: 0-2 Tight: 0-3 Gall: 0-0
Aids: Bl: 0-2 Vi: 0-0 Tstrap: 0-0 Ckp: 0-0
Best Rating: 69 7/09 Yarm 1m2f21y gd-fm

Fair maiden; acts on Polytrack.

Sawpit Sunshine (IRE)

83(76) (19)60

4-y-o b f Mujadil (USA)-Curie Express (IRE) (Fayruz)

J L Spearing David A Hunt

Placings:40310/06-0000 **(6596)**

2009: 7^{0}GF, 7^{0}SD, 7^{0}GF, 6^{0}GS,

	Starts	1st	2nd	3rd	Win & Pl
Career Total (Turf)	10	1	0	1	4368
Career Total (AW)	1	0	0	0	

65	7/07	Leic	5f218y	SFT	£3886

Total win prize-money £3886

Going (Turf): **Sf: 1-4** GS: 0-1 Gd: 0-1 GF: 0-4 Fm: 0-0
Distance: **5f/6f: 1-4** 7f-8f: 0-6 9f-13f: 0-1 14f+: 0-0
Track : LH: 0-2 RH: 0-1 Tight: 0-0 Gall: 0-1
Aids: Bl: 0-2 Vi: 0-0 Tstrap: 0-0 Ckp: 0-0
Best Rating: **65** 7/07 Leic 5f218y soft

Saxby (IRE)

96(97) (70)**70**
2-y-o ch c Pastoral Pursuits-Madam Waajib (IRE) (Waajib)
G A Harker (M R Channon 26/9) John J Maguire

Placings:66136652210 **(6557)**
2009: 5^{6}GF, 6^{6}GF, 6^{1}GF, 6^{3}F, 6^{6}GF, 5^{6}GS, 7^{5}SD, 7^{2}GF, 7^{2}SD, 6^{1}SD, 7^{0}G,

	Starts	1st	2nd	3rd	Win & Pl
Career Total (Turf)	**8**	**1**	**1**	**1**	**6169**
Career Total (AW)	**3**	**1**	**1**	**0**	**3558**

70 9/09 Kemp 6f STD £2047
70 6/09 Thsk 6f G-F £4274
Total win prize-money £6321

Going (Turf): Sf: 0-0 GS: 0-1 Gd: 0-1 **GF: 1-5** Fm: 0-1
Distance: **5f/6f: 2-7** 7f-8f: 0-4 9f-13f: 0-0 14f+: 0-0
Track : LH: 0-4 **RH: 1-1** Tight: 0-4 Gall: 0-0
Aids: Bl: 0-0 Vi: 0-0 Tstrap: 0-0 Ckp: 0-0
Best Rating: **70** 9/09 Kemp 6f stand

Modest; stays 7f; acts on fast ground and on Polytrack.

Saxford

90 **104**
3-y-o b g Reset (AUS)-Bint Makbul (Makbul)
Mrs L Stubbs D Arundale

Placings:016211442-00 **(2035)**
2009: 7^{0}GF, 6^{0}G,

	Starts	1st	2nd	3rd	Win & Pl
Career Total (Turf)	**11**	**3**	**2**	**0**	**47164**

95 7/08 Newb 6f8y G-F £17031
93 6/08 Newc 6f G-S £4209
67 4/08 Newc 5f G-S £4630
Total win prize-money £25870

Going (Turf): Sf: 0-0 **GS: 2-6** Gd: 0-1 GF: 1-4 Fm: 0-0
Distance: **5f/6f: 2-7** 7f-8f: 1-4 9f-13f: 0-0 14f+: 0-0
Track : LH: 0-0 RH: 0-0 Tight: 0-0 Gall: 0-0
Aids: Bl: 0-0 Vi: 0-0 Tstrap: 0-0 Ckp: 0-0
Best Rating: **104** 10/08 Chan 6f gd-sft

Smart; Listed winner; effective at 6f; acts on quick and easy ground.

Saxona (IRE)

100 **61**
5-y-o b m Jade Robbery (USA)-Saxon Maid (Sadler's Wells (USA))
Ian Williams Mr & Mrs G Middlebrook

Placings:002150 **(5068)**
2009: 10^{0}GS, 12^{0}GF, 12^{2}G, 17^{1}G, 15^{5}GF, 17^{0}GF,

	Starts	1st	2nd	3rd	Win & Pl
Career Total (Turf)	**6**	**1**	**1**	**0**	**2857**

61 7/09 Carl 2m1f52y (0-65)H GD £2047
Total win prize-money £2047

Going (Turf): Sf: 0-0 GS: 0-1 **Gd: 1-2** GF: 0-3 Fm: 0-0
Distance: 5f/6f: 0-0 7f-8f: 0-0 9f-13f: 0-3 **14f+: 1-3**
Track : LH: 0-4 **RH: 1-2** Tight: 0-1 **Gall: 1-1**
Aids: Bl: 0-0 Vi: 0-0 Tstrap: 0-0 Ckp: 0-0
Best Rating: **61** 7/09 Carl 2m1f52y good

Moderate; bumper winner; stays 2m1f; acts on good ground.

Say Anything (IRE)

(95) (53)**48**
8-y-o b m Perugino (USA)-Dama De Noche (Rusticaro (FR))
Patrick Allen His N Hers Syndicate

Placings:606/0/01164660/0000/4000/5-40 **(3178a)**
2009: 7^{4}SD, 7^{0}GF,

	Starts	1st	2nd	3rd	Win & Pl
Career Total (Turf)	**21**	**2**	**0**	**0**	**9390**
Career Total (AW)	**2**	**0**	**0**	**0**	**0**

59 7/05 Gowr 1m (40-70)H GD £4900
51 6/05 DRoy 7f (36-60)H GD £3920
Total win prize-money £8822

Going (Turf): Sf: 0-2 GS: 0-0 **Gd: 2-8** GF: 0-5 Fm: 0-3
Distance: 5f/6f: 0-0 **7f-8f: 2-18** 9f-13f: 0-5 14f+: 0-0
Track : LH: 0-6 **RH: 2-12** Tight: 0-2 Gall: 0-1
Aids: Bl: 0-0 Vi: 0-0 Tstrap: 0-1 Ckp: 0-1
Best Rating: **60** 8/05 Baln 1m1f good

Say No Now (IRE)

105(97) (84)**104**
3-y-o b f Refuse To Bend (IRE)-Star Studded (Cadeaux Genereux)
D R Lanigan Saif Ali & Saeed H Altayer

Placings:22-1302534 **(6605a)**
2009: 8^{1}F, 9^{3}GF, 8^{0}GF, 8^{2}G, 8^{5}GF, 7^{3}GF, 7^{4}G,

	Starts	1st	2nd	3rd	Win & Pl
Career Total (Turf)	**7**	**1**	**1**	**2**	**22076**
Career Total (AW)	**2**	**0**	**2**	**0**	**3636**

83 5/09 Nott 1m75y FRM £2266
Total win prize-money £2267

Going (Turf): Sf: 0-0 GS: 0-0 Gd: 0-2 GF: 0-4 **Fm: 1-1**
Distance: 5f/6f: 0-0 7f-8f: 0-5 **9f-13f: 1-4** 14f+: 0-0
Track : **LH: 1-1** RH: 0-5 Tight: 0-1 Gall: 0-0
Aids: Bl: 0-0 Vi: 0-0 Tstrap: 0-0 Ckp: 0-0
Best Rating: **104** 9/09 Donc 7f gd-fm

Very useful; Listed placed; effective over 7f-1m; acts on fast ground and on Polytrack; likes to race prominently.

Say You Say Me

91 **63**
3-y-o b f Acclamation-Mindfulness (Primo Dominie)
N J Vaughan R Kent

Placings:3-02 **(2820)**
2009: 6^{0}GS, 6^{2}GF,

	Starts	1st	2nd	3rd	Win & Pl
Career Total (Turf)	**3**	**0**	**1**	**1**	**1589**

Going (Turf): **Sf: 0-0 GS: 0-1 Gd: 0-1 GF: 0-1 Fm: 0-0**
Distance: 5f/6f: 0-3 7f-8f: 0-0 9f-13f: 0-0 14f+: 0-0
Track : LH: 0-1 RH: 0-0 Tight: 0-1 Gall: 0-0
Aids: Bl: 0-0 Vi: 0-0 Tstrap: 0-0 Ckp: 0-0
Best Rating: **63** 7/08 Ches 5f16y good

Modest; suited by 5f and acts on good ground.

Sayif (IRE)

115 **119**
3-y-o b c Kheleyf (USA)-Sewards Folly (Rudimentary (USA))
P W Chapple-Hyam Saleh Al Homaizi & Imad Al Sagar

Placings:223320-14541 **(6304)**
2009: 5^{1}GF, 6^{4}G, 6^{5}GS, 6^{4}GS, 6^{1}GF,

	Starts	1st	2nd	3rd	Win & Pl
Career Total (Turf)	**11**	**2**	**3**	**2**	**169726**

119 9/09 Asct 6f G-F £56770
97 4/09 Leic 5f218y G-F £7569
Total win prize-money £64340

Going (Turf): Sf: 0-0 GS: 0-3 Gd: 0-3 **GF: 2-5** Fm: 0-0
Distance: **5f/6f: 2-8** 7f-8f: 0-3 9f-13f: 0-0 14f+: 0-0
Track : LH: 0-0 RH: 0-2 Tight: 0-0 Gall: 0-1
Aids: Bl: 0-0 Vi: 0-0 Tstrap: 0-0 Ckp: 0-0
Best Rating: **119** 9/09 Asct 6f gd-fm

Group class; runner-up in the 2008 Middle Park; winner of the 2009 Diadem Stakes; effective over 5f-7f and acts on most ground.

Scamperdale

97(115) (98)**62**
7-y-o br g Compton Place-Miss Up N Go (Gorytus (USA))
B P J Baugh Saddle Up Racing

Placings:6402/540120321/4612152345551/111336000-50253001001 **(7848)**
2009: 9^{5}SD, 10^{0}SD, 9^{2}SD, 8^{5}SD, 9^{3}SD, 10^{0}G, 10^{0}GF, 11^{1}SD, 12^{0}SD, 10^{0}SD, 9^{1}SD,

	Starts	1st	2nd	3rd	Win & Pl
Career Total (Turf)	**7**	**0**	**0**	**0**	**0**
Career Total (AW)	**39**	**10**	**6**	**5**	**46792**

92 12/09 Wolv 1m1f103y (0-85)H STD £6308
93 7/09 Kemp 1m3f (0-80)H STD £4727
92 2/08 Kemp 1m2f (0-85)H STD £4210
85 1/08 Wolv 1m1f103y (0-85)H STD £4533
83 1/08 Wolv 1m141y (0-85)H STD £4210
81 12/07 Wolv 1m1f103y (0-75)H SS £2968
71 4/07 Wolv 1m141y (0-65)H STD £2388
68 3/07 Wolv 1m1f103y (0-65)H STD £2388
66 12/06 Wolv 1m141y (0-60)H STD £2590
55 5/06 Wolv 1m1f103y STD £1365
Total win prize-money £35692

Going (Turf): **Sf: 0-0 GS: 0-0 Gd: 0-4 GF: 0-2 Fm: 0-1**
Distance: 5f/6f: 0-0 7f-8f: 0-0 **9f-13f: 10-46** 14f+: 0-0
Track : **LH: 8-38** RH: 2-8 **Tight: 8-34** Gall: 0-1
Aids: Bl: 0-0 Vi: 0-0 Tstrap: 1-10 Ckp: 1-10
Best Rating: **98** 11/08 Ling 1m2f stand

Useful; effective at around 1m-1m2f; acts on Polytrack; goes well at Wolverhampton.

Scandal

(98) (65)
4-y-o b g Reel Buddy (USA)-Milliscent (Primo Dominie)
Andrew Turnell John Hatherell

Placings:43 **(0704)**
2009: 13^{4}SD, 12^{3}SD,

	Starts	1st	2nd	3rd	Win & Pl
Career Total (Turf)	**0**	**0**	**0**	**0**	
Career Total (AW)	**2**	**0**	**0**	**1**	**403**

Going (Turf): **Sf: 0-0 GS: 0-0 Gd: 0-0 GF: 0-0 Fm: 0-0**
Distance: 5f/6f: 0-0 7f-8f: 0-0 9f-13f: 0-2 14f+: 0-0
Track : LH: 0-2 RH: 0-0 Tight: 0-2 Gall: 0-0
Aids: Bl: 0-0 Vi: 0-0 Tstrap: 0-0 Ckp: 0-0

Best Rating: 65 2/09 Ling 1m4f stand

Scar Tissue

82(91) (53)31
5-y-o ch m Medicean-Possessive Lady (Dara Monarch)
E J Creighton The Vixens

Placings:3/5200/0005-60 **(2519)**
2009: 9^{6}GF, 17^{0}F,

	Starts	1st	2nd	3rd	Win & Pl
Career Total (Turf)	5	0	0	0	0
Career Total (AW)	6	0	1	1	957

Going (Turf): Sf: 0-0 GS: 0-1 Gd: 0-1 GF: 0-2 Fm: 0-1
Distance: 5f/6f: 0-0 7f-8f: 0-3 9f-13f: 0-7 14f+: 0-1
Track : LH: 0-7 RH: 0-4 Tight: 0-5 Gall: 0-2
Aids: Bl: 0-1 Vi: 0-0 Tstrap: 0-0 Ckp: 0-0
Best Rating: 58 5/07 Wind 1m67y good

Scarab (IRE)

88(107) (87)83
4-y-o br g Machiavellian (USA)-Russian Society (Darshaan)
T D Walford (M Johnston 14/2) G Mett Racing

Placings:521232-1500 **(6681)**
2009: 12^{1}SD, 12^{5}SD, 14^{0}GS, 12^{0}G,

	Starts	1st	2nd	3rd	Win & Pl
Career Total (Turf)	4	1	1	0	3458
Career Total (AW)	6	1	2	1	9558

85 1/09 Kemp 1m4f (0-85)H STD £4727
83 11/08 Catt 1m3f214y HVY £2590
Total win prize-money £7317

Going (Turf): Sf: 1-2 GS: 0-1 Gd: 0-1 GF: 0-0 Fm: 0-0
Distance: 5f/6f: 0-0 7f-8f: 0-0 **9f-13f: 2-9** 14f+: 0-1
Track : LH: 1-8 RH: 1-2 **Tight: 1-4** Gall: 0-2
Aids: Bl: 0-0 Vi: 0-0 Tstrap: 0-0 Ckp: 0-0
Best Rating: 87 2/09 Ling 1m4f stand

Fair; effective over 1m2f 1m4f; acts on soft ground; goes on Polytrack.

Scarboro Warning (IRE)

93(77) (30)74
2-y-o ch g Footstepsinthesand-Spring Easy (IRE) (Alzao (USA))
J G Given Richard Walker

Placings:300 **(7146)**
2009: 7^{3}S, 7^{0}SD, 7^{0}G,

	Starts	1st	2nd	3rd	Win & Pl
Career Total (Turf)	2	0	0	1	794
Career Total (AW)	1	0	0	0	

Going (Turf): Sf: 0-1 GS: 0-0 Gd: 0-1 GF: 0-0 Fm: 0-0
Distance: 5f/6f: 0-0 7f-8f: 0-3 9f-13f: 0-0 14f+: 0-0
Track : LH: 0-2 RH: 0-0 Tight: 0-2 Gall: 0-0
Aids: Bl: 0-0 Vi: 0-0 Tstrap: 0-0 Ckp: 0-0
Best Rating: 74 9/09 Thsk 7f soft

£12,000 two-year-old from a mainly middle-distance family; promising debut over 7f on soft ground.

Scarcity (IRE)

89 55
2-y-o b f Invincible Spirit (IRE)-Sanpa Fan (ITY) (Sikeston (USA))
E A L Dunlop Highclere Thoroughbred Racing (Buchan)

Placings:00 **(6729)**
2009: 6^{0}GF, 6^{0}S,

	Starts	1st	2nd	3rd	Win & Pl
Career Total (Turf)	2	0	0	0	

Going (Turf): Sf: 0-1 GS: 0-0 Gd: 0-0 GF: 0-1 Fm: 0-0
Distance: 5f/6f: 0-0 7f-8f: 0-2 9f-13f: 0-0 14f+: 0-0
Track : LH: 0-0 RH: 0-0 Tight: 0-0 Gall: 0-0
Aids: Bl: 0-0 Vi: 0-0 Tstrap: 0-0 Ckp: 0-0
Best Rating: 55 10/09 Sals 6f212y soft

Scarlet Oak

(104) (63)70
5-y-o b m Zamindar (USA)-Flamenco Red (Warning)
A M Hales Gary P Martin

Placings:601205300100/0650146006020-55202 **(1134)**
2009: 5^{5}SD, 6^{5}SD, 5^{2}SD, 5^{0}SD, 5^{2}SD,

	Starts	1st	2nd	3rd	Win & Pl
Career Total (Turf)	14	2	0	1	11286
Career Total (AW)	16	1	4	0	5792

70 7/08 Nott 6f15y (0-80)H G-S £7447
71 10/07 Leic 5f218y (0-70)H SFT £2914
60 2/07 Ling 5f STD £3071
Total win prize-money £13433

Going (Turf): Sf: 1-4 GS: 1-3 Gd: 0-3 GF: 0-4 Fm: 0-0
Distance: **5f/6f: 2-19** 7f-8f: 1-9 9f-13f: 0-2 14f+: 0-0
Track : **LH: 1-17** RH: 0-3 **Tight: 1-15** Gall: 0-6
Aids: Bl: 0-0 Vi: 0-0 Tstrap: 1-11 Ckp: 1-11
Best Rating: 71 10/07 Leic 5f218y soft

Modest sprinter; acts on soft ground and on Polytrack; has worn cheekpieces.

Scarlet Ridge

(58) (38)
2-y-o ch f Tumbleweed Ridge-Kayartis (Kaytu)
D K Ivory Mrs J Cornwell & Alan Pryer

Placings:00 **(7663)**
2009: 8^{0}SD, 8^{0}SD,

	Starts	1st	2nd	3rd	Win & Pl
Career Total (Turf)	0	0	0	0	
Career Total (AW)	2	0	0	0	

Going (Turf): Sf: 0-0 GS: 0-0 Gd: 0-0 GF: 0-0 Fm: 0-0
Distance: 5f/6f: 0-0 7f-8f: 0-2 9f-13f: 0-0 14f+: 0-0
Track : LH: 0-1 RH: 0-1 Tight: 0-1 Gall: 0-0
Aids: Bl: 0-0 Vi: 0-0 Tstrap: 0-0 Ckp: 0-0
Best Rating: 38 12/09 Ling 1m stand

Scarlett Angel (IRE)

78(61) 34
3-y-o b f Xaar-Mildred (IRE) (Peintre Celebre (USA))
W J Knight Lower Coombe Racing

Placings:000 **(2487)**
2009: 8^{0}GF, 9^{0}G, 12^{0}SD,

	Starts	1st	2nd	3rd	Win & Pl
Career Total (Turf)	2	0	0	0	
Career Total (AW)	1	0	0	0	

Going (Turf): Sf: 0-0 GS: 0-0 Gd: 0-1 GF: 0-1 Fm: 0-0
Distance: 5f/6f: 0-0 7f-8f: 0-0 9f-13f: 0-3 14f+: 0-0
Track : LH: 0-1 RH: 0-2 Tight: 0-3 Gall: 0-0
Aids: Bl: 0-0 Vi: 0-0 Tstrap: 0-0 Ckp: 0-0
Best Rating: 34 5/09 Wind 1m67y gd-fm

Scarth Hill (IRE)

81(67) (22)53
3-y-o ch g Selkirk (USA)-Louve Sereine (FR) (Sadler's Wells (USA))
G M Moore M R Johnson

Placings:40-00 **(1926)**
2009: 8^{0}GF, 8^{0}F,

	Starts	1st	2nd	3rd	Win & Pl
Career Total (Turf)	3	0	0	0	216
Career Total (AW)	1	0	0	0	

Going (Turf): Sf: 0-1 GS: 0-0 Gd: 0-0 GF: 0-1 Fm: 0-1
Distance: 5f/6f: 0-1 7f-8f: 0-3 9f-13f: 0-0 14f+: 0-0
Track : LH: 0-1 RH: 0-1 Tight: 0-2 Gall: 0-0
Aids: Bl: 0-0 Vi: 0-0 Tstrap: 0-0 Ckp: 0-0
Best Rating: 53 6/08 Ripn 6f soft

Scartozz

(103) (92)99
7-y-o b g Barathea (IRE)-Amazing Bay (Mazilier (USA))
M Botti Dioscuri Srl

Placings:11/10/36221/121335211/3620506400-010 **(6030)**
2009: 8^{0}SD, 8^{1}SD, 8^{0}SD,

	Starts	1st	2nd	3rd	Win & Pl
Career Total (Turf)	18	7	3	1	84025
Career Total (AW)	13	2	2	3	26060

81 4/09 Kemp 1m STD £2047
11/07 Capa 1m STD £7432
9/07 Siro 7f SFT £6317
3/07 Capa 1m110y HVY £8446
1/07 Pisa 7f110y SFT £4054
10/06 Capa 7f110y HVY £8621
4/05 Siro 1m HVY £22340
11/04 Siro 1m SFT £12324
10/04 Siro 7f SFT £7042
Total win prize-money £78623

Going (Turf): **Sf: 7-10** GS: 0-2 Gd: 0-4 GF: 0-2 Fm: 0-0
Distance: 5f/6f: 0-0 **7f-8f: 8-23** 9f-13f: 1-8 14f+: 0-0
Track : LH: 0-5 **RH: 1-7** Tight: 0-3 Gall: 0-2
Aids: Bl: 0-9 Vi: 0-0 Tstrap: 0-2 Ckp: 0-2
Best Rating: 99 6/08 Rdcr 1m gd-fm

Useful; ex-Italian-trained; stays 1m; acts on soft ground on turf; also goes on dirt; has worn blinkers and a tongue tie.

Sceilin (IRE)

103(98) (52)66
5-y-o b m Lil's Boy (USA)-Sharifa (IRE) (Cryptoclearance (USA))
J Mackie W I Bloomfield

Placings:000/500/022122500040-0512116 **(6760)**
2009: 12^{0}SD, 9^{5}GF, 10^{1}F, 10^{2}G, 9^{1}F, 10^{1}GF, 9^{6}G,

	Starts	1st	2nd	3rd	Win & Pl
Career Total (Turf)	19	4	5	0	13693
Career Total (AW)	6	0	0	0	0

66 9/09 Wwck 1m2f188y (0-60)H G-F £1873
65 8/09 Brig 1m1f209y (0-70)H FRM £3027
56 6/09 Bath 1m2f46y (0-65)H FRM £2183
62 6/08 Bath 1m2f46y (0-65)H FRM £2388
Total win prize-money £9474

Going (Turf): Sf: 0-0 GS: 0-1 Gd: 0-4 GF: 1-8 **Fm: 3-3**
Distance: 5f/6f: 0-0 7f-8f: 0-5 **9f-13f: 4-20** 14f+: 0-0
Track : **LH: 4-19** RH: 0-4 **Tight: 2-9** Gall: 0-1
Aids: Bl: 0-0 Vi: 0-0 Tstrap: 0-0 Ckp: 0-0
Best Rating: **66** 9/09 Wwck 1m2f188y gd-fm

Moderate filly; stays 1m2f and acts on fast ground; has worn a tongue tie; likes to race prominently.

Scene Two

102(104) (75)78
3-y-o gr g Act One-Gleaming Water (Kalaglow)
L M Cumani Team Spirit 2

Placings:01-5601 **(6698)**
2009: 12^{5}SD, 12^{6}G, 11^{0}SD, 12^{1}GS,

	Starts	1st	2nd	3rd	Win & Pl
Career Total (Turf)	2	1	0	0	3238
Career Total (AW)	4	1	0	0	2730

78 10/09 Gdwd 1m4f (0-75)H G-S £3238
75 12/08 Wolv 7f32y STD £2729
Total win prize-money £5968

Going (Turf): Sf: 0-0 **GS: 1-1** Gd: 0-1 GF: 0-0 Fm: 0-0
Distance: 5f/6f: 0-0 7f-8f: 1-2 9f-13f: 1-4 14f+: 0-0
Track : LH: 1-4 RH: 1-2 **Tight: 2-4** Gall: 0-1
Aids: Bl: 0-0 Vi: 0-1 Tstrap: 0-0 Ckp: 0-0
Best Rating: **78** 10/09 Gdwd 1m4f gd-sft

Fair; stays 7f and should stay at least 1m; acts on Polytrack; sure to improve.

Scenic Blast (AUS)

115 127
5-y-o b/br g Scenic-Daughter's Charm (AUS) (Delgado (USA))
Daniel Morton Elio Anthony Galante & Partners

Placings:122112623/3110-21511000 **(7745a)**
2009: 5^{2}G, 5^{1}G, 5^{5}G, 6^{1}G, 5^{1}GF, 6^{0}GF, 6^{0}F, 6^{0}G,

	Starts	1st	2nd	3rd	Win & Pl
Career Total (Turf)	21	8	5	2	870569

127 6/09 Asct 5f G-F £170310
123 3/09 Flem 6f H GD £293689
120 1/09 Flem 5f GD £146845
8/08 Caul 6f H SFT £16123
4/08 Asco 6f H GD £14317
9/07 Caul 6f GD £30544
8/07 BlmP 5f H GD £11794
2/07 Asco 5f110y GD £15847
Total win prize-money £699470

Going (Turf): Sf: 1-1 GS: 0-1 **Gd: 6-16** GF: 1-2 Fm: 0-1
Distance: **5f/6f: 8-17** 7f-8f: 0-4 9f-13f: 0-0 14f+: 0-0
Track : **LH: 1-2** RH: 0-1 Tight: 0-0 Gall: 0-0
Aids: Bl: 0-0 Vi: 0-0 Tstrap: 0-0 Ckp: 0-0
Best Rating: **127** 6/09 Asct 5f gd-fm

High-class; Group 1 winner in Australia and won King's Stand Stakes in 2009; effective at 5f-6f and acts on most ground.

Schiaparelli (GER)

120 121
6-y-o ch h Monsun (GER)-Sacarina (Old Vic)
Saeed Bin Suroor Godolphin

Placings:1112161/031111/20-311312 **(7047a)**
2009: 12^{3}G, 16^{1}G, 15^{1}G, 14^{3}S, 12^{1}G, 15^{2}S,

	Starts	1st	2nd	3rd	Win & Pl
Career Total (Turf)	21	12	3	3	881952

117 10/09 Siro 1m4f GD £155709
111 8/09 Deau 1m7f GD £71942
119 7/09 Gdwd 2m GD £56770
119 10/07 Siro 1m4f GD £72973
116 9/07 Colo 1m4f GD £67568
119 7/07 Duss 1m4f GD £60811
119 6/07 Hamb 1m3f HVY £40541
102 10/06 Dort 1m6f GD £27586
115 7/06 Hamb 1m4f GD £165517
6/06 Hanv 1m3f GD £8275
5/06 Hanv 1m3f H GD £3241
4/06 Colo 1m3f HVY £2068
Total win prize-money £733003

Going (Turf): Sf: 2-5 GS: 0-2 **Gd: 10-14** GF: 0-0 Fm: 0-0
Distance: 5f/6f: 0-0 7f-8f: 0-0 **9f-13f: 9-16** 14f+: 3-5
Track : LH: 0-2 **RH: 9-16 Tight: 1-1** Gall: 0-1
Aids: Bl: 0-0 Vi: 0-0 Tstrap: 0-0 Ckp: 0-0
Best Rating: **121** 10/09 Lonc 1m7f110y soft

Group class; ex-German trained; Group 1 winner in Germany and Italy in 2007; lightly raced since but winner of the Goodwood Cup, Prix Kergorlay and Gran Premio del Jockey Club in 2009; effective from 1m4f-2m; acts on good or softer ground.

Schinken Otto (IRE)

(97) (55)36
8-y-o ch g Shinko Forest (IRE)-Athassel Rose (IRE) (Reasonable (FR))
J M Jefferson John Donald

Placings:060/06050/5/4406/113006-045 **(0734)**
2009: 12^{0}SD, 12^{4}SD, 13^{5}SD,

	Starts	1st	2nd	3rd	Win & Pl
Career Total (Turf)	11	0	0	0	0
Career Total (AW)	11	2	0	1	3707

61 1/08 Kemp 1m3f (0-60)H STD £1977
57 1/08 Wolv 1m1f103y (0-55)H STD £1249
Total win prize-money £3227

Going (Turf): **Sf: 0-0 GS: 0-4 Gd: 0-4 GF: 0-3 Fm: 0-0**
Distance: 5f/6f: 0-4 7f-8f: 0-2 **9f-13f: 2-15** 14f+: 0-1
Track : LH: 1-12 RH: 1-7 **Tight: 1-10** Gall: 0-1
Aids: Bl: 0-0 Vi: 0-0 Tstrap: 0-0 Ckp: 0-0
Best Rating: **61** 1/08 Kemp 1m3f stand

Moderate; stays 1m3f; acts on Polytrack.

Scholars Lass (IRE)

(101) (47)26
4-y-o b f Spartacus (IRE)-Blanche Neige (USA) (Lit De Justice (USA))
J Balding John Balding

Placings:0000-0400 **(1563)**
2009: 7^{0}SD, 6^{4}SD, 6^{0}SD, 6^{0}SD,

	Starts	1st	2nd	3rd	Win & Pl
Career Total (Turf)	3	0	0	0	
Career Total (AW)	5	0	0	0	0

Going (Turf): **Sf: 0-0 GS: 0-0 Gd: 0-3 GF: 0-0 Fm: 0-0**
Distance: 5f/6f: 0-3 7f-8f: 0-4 9f-13f: 0-1 14f+: 0-0
Track : LH: 0-6 RH: 0-2 Tight: 0-2 Gall: 0-0
Aids: Bl: 0-0 Vi: 0-0 Tstrap: 0-0 Ckp: 0-0
Best Rating: **47** 3/09 Sthl 6f stand

Schoolboy Champ

99(86) (69)74
2-y-o ch g Trade Fair-Aswhatilldois (IRE) (Blues Traveller (IRE))
Patrick Morris Chester Racing Club & Rob Lloyd Racing

Placings:150020 **(6983)**
2009: 5^{1}G, 5^{5}SD, 6^{0}GF, 6^{0}GF, 6^{2}G, 6^{0}G,

	Starts	1st	2nd	3rd	Win & Pl
Career Total (Turf)	5	1	1	0	3943
Career Total (AW)	1	0	0	0	0

74 6/09 Hayd 5f GD £3238
Total win prize-money £3238

Going (Turf): Sf: 0-0 GS: 0-0 **Gd: 1-3** GF: 0-2 Fm: 0-0
Distance: **5f/6f: 1-6** 7f-8f: 0-0 9f-13f: 0-0 14f+: 0-0
Track : LH: 0-1 RH: 0-0 Tight: 0-1 Gall: 0-1
Aids: Bl: 0-0 Vi: 0-0 Tstrap: 0-0 Ckp: 0-0
Best Rating: **74** 6/09 Hayd 5f good

Fair; effective at 5f on good ground.

Scilly Breeze

87 58
2-y-o gr g Linamix (FR)-Mitraillette (USA) (Miswaki (USA))
A M Hales (Rae Guest 11/6) Gary P Martin

Placings:4242 **(3958)**
2009: 6^{4}G, 7^{2}S, 7^{4}GF, 7^{2}S,

	Starts	1st	2nd	3rd	Win & Pl
Career Total (Turf)	4	0	2	0	1474

Going (Turf): **Sf: 0-2 GS: 0-0 Gd: 0-1 GF: 0-1 Fm: 0-0**
Distance: 5f/6f: 0-0 7f-8f: 0-4 9f-13f: 0-0 14f+: 0-0
Track : LH: 0-0 RH: 0-1 Tight: 0-0 Gall: 0-0
Aids: Bl: 0-0 Vi: 0-0 Tstrap: 0-0 Ckp: 0-0
Best Rating: **58** 7/09 Yarm 7f3y soft

Modest; stays 7f and acts on soft ground.

Scintillating (IRE)

81(88) (47)33
2-y-o b f Cape Cross (IRE)-Announcing Peace (Danehill (USA))
R Hollinshead John P Evitt

Placings:0PP000046 **(7706)**
2009: 5^{0}GF, 5^{P}GF, 7^{P}SD, 7^{0}SD, 8^{0}GS, 8^{0}GF, 7^{0}SD, 7^{4}SD, 8^{6}SD,

	Starts	1st	2nd	3rd	Win & Pl
Career Total (Turf)	4	0	0	0	
Career Total (AW)	5	0	0	0	0

Going (Turf): **Sf: 0-0 GS: 0-1 Gd: 0-0 GF: 0-3 Fm: 0-0**
Distance: 5f/6f: 0-2 7f-8f: 0-6 9f-13f: 0-1 14f+: 0-0
Track : LH: 0-7 RH: 0-0 Tight: 0-3 Gall: 0-1
Aids: Bl: 0-0 Vi: 0-0 Tstrap: 0-1 Ckp: 0-1
Best Rating: **47** 11/09 Wolv 7f32y stand

Scintillo

104(112) (114)115
4-y-o ch c Fantastic Light (USA)-Danseuse Du Soir (IRE) (Thatching)
R Hannon Leonard Lucas

Placings:50143231/002534305-3110210060 **(7593a)**

2009: 10^{3}SD, 12^{1}SD, 10^{1}SD, 12^{0}S, 13^{2}GF, 12^{1}G, 12^{0}S, 12^{0}G, 12^{6}GS, 12^{0}F,

	Starts	1st	2nd	3rd	Win & Pl
Career Total (Turf)	21	3	3	3	214511
Career Total (AW)	6	2	0	2	89170

115 5/09 Chan 1m4f GD £71942
114 3/09 Ling 1m2f STD £56770
108 3/09 Kemp 1m4f STD £22708
110 10/07 Siro 1m GD £72973
92 7/07 Sand 7f16y G-S £6477
Total win prize-money £230870

Going (Turf): Sf: 0-4 GS: 1-3 **Gd: 2-11** GF: 0-2 Fm: 0-1
Distance: 5f/6f: 0-1 7f-8f: 2-9 **9f-13f: 3-16** 14f+: 0-1
Track : LH: 1-8 **RH: 4-13 Tight: 1-7** Gall: 0-4
Aids: Bl: 0-4 Vi: 0-0 Tstrap: 0-0 Ckp: 0-0
Best Rating: 115 5/09 Chan 1m4f good

Group class; winner of the Group 1 Grand Criterium at San Siro as a juvenile and the Group 2 Grand Prix de Chantilly in 2009; successful in the 2009 Winter Derby; effective over 1m2f-1m4f; acts on good and easier ground; handles Polytrack; has worn blinkers.

Scooby Dee

87 49

2-y-o b f Captain Rio-Scooby Dooby Do (Atraf)
R M Whitaker Paul Davies (H'gte)

Placings:0500 **(6895)**
2009: 6^{0}G, 5^{5}G, 6^{0}GF, 8^{0}GF,

	Starts	1st	2nd	3rd	Win & Pl
Career Total (Turf)	4	0	0	0	0

Going (Turf): Sf: 0-0 GS: 0-0 Gd: 0-2 GF: 0-2 Fm: 0-0
Distance: 5f/6f: 0-3 7f-8f: 0-0 9f-13f: 0-1 14f+: 0-0
Track : LH: 0-2 RH: 0-0 Tight: 0-0 Gall: 0-0
Aids: Bl: 0-0 Vi: 0-0 Tstrap: 0-0 Ckp: 0-0
Best Rating: 49 8/09 Bevl 5f good

Scopey

99(102) (65)72

4-y-o b g Bertolini (USA)-Red Symphony (Merdon Melody)
Gerard Keane (Ms Joanna Morgan 26/8) Mrs E Keane

Placings:5534046/32000-000246600**460** **(7716)**
2009: 7^{0}GF, 5^{0}S, 7^{0}HY, 7^{2}Y, 7^{4}GF, 7^{6}S, 6^{6}GF, 8^{0}Y, 7^{0}Y, 7^{4}SD, 7^{6}SD, 7^{0}SD,

	Starts	1st	2nd	3rd	Win & Pl
Career Total (Turf)	21	0	2	2	4768
Career Total (AW)	3	0	0	0	0

Going (Turf): Sf: 0-5 GS: 0-0 Gd: 0-2 GF: 0-7 Fm: 0-1
Distance: 5f/6f: 0-6 7f-8f: 0-18 9f-13f: 0-0 14f+: 0-0
Track : LH: 0-9 RH: 0-9 Tight: 0-2 Gall: 0-0
Aids: Bl: 0-5 Vi: 0-0 Tstrap: 0-4 Ckp: 0-4
Best Rating: 72 6/08 Fair 7f gd-yld

Scorn (USA)

88 74

2-y-o b f Seeking The Gold (USA)-Sulk (IRE) (Selkirk (USA))
J H M Gosden James Wigan

Placings:42 **(7183)**
2009: 6^{4}S, 7^{2}G,

	Starts	1st	2nd	3rd	Win & Pl
Career Total (Turf)	2	0	1	0	1662

Going (Turf): Sf: 0-1 GS: 0-0 Gd: 0-1 GF: 0-0 Fm: 0-0
Distance: 5f/6f: 0-0 7f-8f: 0-2 9f-13f: 0-0 14f+: 0-0
Track : LH: 0-0 RH: 0-0 Tight: 0-0 Gall: 0-0
Aids: Bl: 0-0 Vi: 0-0 Tstrap: 0-0 Ckp: 0-0
Best Rating: 74 10/09 NmkR 7f good

Scotch And Soda (IRE)

88(73) (17)50

3-y-o b f Mull Of Kintyre (USA)-Buddy And Soda (IRE) (Imperial Frontier (USA))
Jedd O'Keeffe Three Coins Racing

Placings:5650000 **(6880)**
2009: 6^{5}GF, 7^{6}GF, 6^{5}F, 8^{0}S, 5^{0}G, 7^{0}S, 7^{0}SD,

	Starts	1st	2nd	3rd	Win & Pl
Career Total (Turf)	6	0	0	0	0
Career Total (AW)	1	0	0	0	

Going (Turf): Sf: 0-2 GS: 0-0 Gd: 0-1 GF: 0-2 Fm: 0-1
Distance: 5f/6f: 0-3 7f-8f: 0-3 9f-13f: 0-1 14f+: 0-0
Track : LH: 0-4 RH: 0-1 Tight: 0-1 Gall: 0-0
Aids: Bl: 0-0 Vi: 0-0 Tstrap: 0-0 Ckp: 0-0
Best Rating: 50 4/09 Pont 6f gd-fm

Scottish Affair

90(101) (66)52

3-y-o b g Selkirk (USA)-Southern Queen (Anabaa (USA))
E A L Dunlop E A L Dunlop

Placings:560-51060 **(3511)**
2009: 8^{5}SD, 9^{1}SD, 10^{0}G, 11^{6}G, 12^{0}SD,

	Starts	1st	2nd	3rd	Win & Pl
Career Total (Turf)	3	0	0	0	0
Career Total (AW)	5	1	0	0	2047

66 3/09 Wolv 1m1f103y (0-65)H STD £2047
Total win prize-money £2047

Going (Turf): Sf: 0-0 GS: 0-0 Gd: 0-3 GF: 0-0 Fm: 0-0
Distance: 5f/6f: 0-2 7f-8f: 0-2 **9f-13f: 1-4** 14f+: 0-0
Track : **LH: 1-4** RH: 0-3 **Tight: 1-3** Gall: 0-1
Aids: Bl: 0-0 Vi: 0-0 Tstrap: 0-0 Ckp: 0-0
Best Rating: 66 3/09 Wolv 1m1f103y stand

Modest; stays an extended 1m1f; acts on Polytrack.

Scottish Boogie (IRE)

95 77

2-y-o b c Tobougg (IRE)-Scottish Spice (Selkirk (USA))
S Kirk J C Smith

Placings:0031 **(7097)**
2009: 6^{0}GF, 6^{0}GF, 6^{3}G, 7^{1}G,

	Starts	1st	2nd	3rd	Win & Pl
Career Total (Turf)	4	1	0	1	3960

77 10/09 Yarm 7f3y (0-75) GD £3238
Total win prize-money £3238

Going (Turf): Sf: 0-0 GS: 0-0 **Gd: 1-2** GF: 0-2 Fm: 0-0
Distance: 5f/6f: 0-0 **7f-8f: 1-4** 9f-13f: 0-0 14f+: 0-0
Track : LH: 0-1 RH: 0-0 Tight: 0-0 Gall: 0-0
Aids: Bl: 0-0 Vi: 0-0 Tstrap: 0-0 Ckp: 0-0
Best Rating: 77 10/09 Yarm 7f3y good

Fair; stays 7f; acts on good ground.

Scottish Glen

71 40

3-y-o ch g Kyllachy-Dance For Fun (Anabaa (USA))
P R Chamings The Foxford House Partnership

Placings:5 **(3319)**
2009: 7^{5}GF,

	Starts	1st	2nd	3rd	Win & Pl
Career Total (Turf)	1	0	0	0	0

Going (Turf): Sf: 0-0 GS: 0-0 Gd: 0-0 GF: 0-1 Fm: 0-0
Distance: 5f/6f: 0-0 7f-8f: 0-1 9f-13f: 0-0 14f+: 0-0
Track : LH: 0-1 RH: 0-0 Tight: 0-0 Gall: 0-0
Aids: Bl: 0-0 Vi: 0-0 Tstrap: 0-0 Ckp: 0-0
Best Rating: 40 6/09 Wwck 7f26y gd-fm

Scotty's Future (IRE)

76(91) (39)58

11-y-o b g Namaqualand (USA)-Persian Empress (IRE) (Persian Bold)
A Berry Alan Berry

Placings:000/2221134/50106000000/00050000/**01010**654 0/3254063/**650633**54154100340650036**0**0/**0**01503000500 05/0045006360534U0**60**-0000 **(6817)**
2009: 9^{0}G, 9^{0}GF, 7^{0}G, 10^{0}GF,

	Starts	1st	2nd	3rd	Win & Pl
Career Total (Turf)	89	6	4	8	69851
Career Total (AW)	16	2	0	2	4757

54 7/07 Bevl 7f100y HVY £2914
69 5/06 Bevl 1m1f207y (0-70)H G-S £3435
63 4/06 Bevl 1m100y G-S £3400
58 2/04 Ling 1m2f G STD £2583
45 2/04 Ling 1m2f H STD £1519
104 5/02 Asct 7f B(0-110)H G-S £20300
87 8/01 Donc 1m2f60yD(0-85)H G-F £18408
86 7/01 Ripn 1m2f D(0-80)H G-F £4875
Total win prize-money £57435

Going (Turf): Sf: 1-16**GS: 3-13**Gd: 0-29GF: 2-27 Fm: 0-4
Distance: 5f/6f: 0-2 7f-8f: 2-36 **9f-13f: 6-66** 14f+: 0-1
Track : LH: 3-50 RH: 3-40 **Tight: 2-34** Gall: 1-10
Aids: Bl: 0-0 Vi: 0-1 Tstrap: 0-0 Ckp: 0-0
Best Rating: 104 5/02 Asct 7f gd-sft

Moderate these days; winner of the 2002 Victoria Cup; effective over 7f-1m3f; acts on most ground on turf; also goes on Polytrack.

Scrapper Smith (IRE)

100(88) (65)68

3-y-o b g Choisir (AUS)-Lady Ounavarra (IRE) (Simply Great (FR))
A C Whillans A C Whillans

Placings:03650 36416163 **(7172)**
2009: 5^{3}G, 6^{6}G, 6^{4}G, 5^{1}G, 6^{6}GS, 5^{1}S, 5^{6}G, 7^{3}S,

	Starts	1st	2nd	3rd	Win & Pl
Career Total (Turf)	12	2	0	2	6158
Career Total (AW)	1	0	0	1	302

68 8/09 Ayr 5f (0-65)H SFT £2388
65 7/09 Carl 5f (0-70)H GD £2590
Total win prize-money £4978

Going (Turf): Sf: 1-2 GS: 0-1 **Gd: 1-6** GF: 0-2 Fm: 0-1
Distance: 5f/6f: 2-11 7f-8f: 0-2 9f-13f: 0-0 14f+: 0-0
Track : LH: 0 2 **RH: 1-2** Tight: 0-0 **Gall: 1-1**
Aids: Bl: 0-0 Vi: 0-1 Tstrap: 0-0 Ckp: 0-0

Best Rating: 68 8/09 Ayr 5f soft

Modest; effective at 5f; acts on soft ground and Polytrack.

Screaming Brave

104(95) (55)**65**

3-y-o br g Hunting Lion (IRE)-Hana Dee (Cadeaux Genereux)

Miss Sheena West (M R Channon 12/9) Tracey Walsom & Alex Woodger

Placings:06-04054321135646262 (5872)

2009: 8^{0}SD, 8^{4}SD, 12^{0}SF, 12^{5}SD, 12^{4}SD, 12^{3}GF, 14^{2}GF, 10^{1}GF, 11^{1}GF, 12^{3}GF, 12^{5}S, 11^{6}GS, 11^{4}G, 11^{6}F, 9^{2}F, 12^{6}SD, 10^{2}G,

	Starts	1st	2nd	3rd	Win & Pl
Career Total (Turf)	12	2	3	2	7238
Career Total (AW)	7	0	0	0	0

63	6/09	Ling	1m3f106y (0-60)H	G-F	£2047
59	5/09	Yarm	1m2f21y (0-55)H	G-F	£2072

Total win prize-money £4119

Going (Turf): Sf: 0-1 GS: 0-2 Gd: 0-2 **GF: 2-5** Fm: 0-2
Distance: 5f/6f: 0-0 7f-8f: 0-3 **9f-13f: 2-15** 14f+: 0-1
Track: **LH: 2-12** RH: 0-6 **Tight: 2-11** Gall: 0-1
Aids: Bl: 0-0 Vi: 0-3 Tstrap: 0-0 Ckp: 0-0
Best Rating: 65 6/09 Pont 1m4f8y gd-fm

Modest; effective from 1m2f-1m6f; acts on fast ground.

Scruffy Skip (IRE)

96(97) (58)**56**

4-y-o b g Diktat-Capoeira (USA) (Nureyev (USA))

Mrs C A Dunnett C Dunnett, D Cooper, R Clarke & J Power

Placings:04500/30056020613000-60500052060100000 (6926)

2009: 6^{6}SD, 6^{0}SD, 5^{5}GF, 7^{0}GF, 6^{0}GF, 7^{0}G, 5^{5}F, 5^{2}F, 6^{0}G, 6^{6}GS, 5^{0}GS, 5^{1}F, 6^{0}GF, 5^{0}GF, 5^{0}SD, 6^{0}SD, 6^{0}GF,

	Starts	1st	2nd	3rd	Win & Pl
Career Total (Turf)	23	1	1	0	2910
Career Total (AW)	14	1	1	2	3497

56	9/09	Brig	5f213y	FRM	£1942
58	10/08	GrLe	6f (0-55)H	STD	£2388

Total win prize-money £4331

Going (Turf): Sf: 0-0 GS: 0-4 Gd: 0-6 GF: 0-10 **Fm: 1-3**
Distance: **5f/6f: 2-19** 7f-8f: 0-16 9f-13f: 0-2 14f+: 0-0
Track: **LH: 2-20** RH: 0-4 Tight: 0-8 **Gall: 1-1**
Aids: Bl: 0-5 Vi: 0-4 Tstrap: 0-4 Ckp: 0-4
Best Rating: 64 8/07 Newc 6f good

Modest gelding; stays 7f; acts on sand.

Scrupulous

91(92) (60)**65**

3-y-o gr f Dansili-Mrs Gray (Red Sunset)

Tom Dascombe (David Wachman 18/8) M V Magnier

Placings:00-0003106 (7620)

2009: 8^{0}S, 10^{0}G, 8^{0}G, 10^{3}G, 9^{1}YS, 8^{0}GY, 9^{6}SD,

	Starts	1st	2nd	3rd	Win & Pl
Career Total (Turf)	8	1	0	1	5179
Career Total (AW)	1	0	0	0	0

65	8/09	Baln	1m1f	Y-S	£4696

Total win prize-money £4696

Going (Turf): **Sf: 0-2 GS: 0-0 Gd: 0-3 GF: 0-0 Fm: 0-0**
Distance: 5f/6f: 0-1 7f-8f: 0-3 **9f-13f: 1-5** 14f+: 0-0
Track: LH: 0-5 **RH: 1-3** Tight: 0-1 Gall: 0-1
Aids: Bl: 0-0 Vi: 0-0 Tstrap: 0-0 Ckp: 0-0
Best Rating: 65 8/09 Baln 1m1f yld-sft

Scuffle

110(108) (100)**103**

4-y-o gr f Daylami (IRE)-Tantina (USA) (Distant View (USA))

R Charlton K Abdulla

Placings:3/1110-36455 (6094)

2009: 8^{3}SD, 8^{6}G, 10^{4}G, 8^{5}GF, 8^{5}G,

	Starts	1st	2nd	3rd	Win & Pl
Career Total (Turf)	9	3	0	1	22547
Career Total (AW)	1	0	0	1	4308

103	7/08	Sals	1m (0-95)H	G-S	£9969
94	6/08	Nott	1m75y (0-95)H	G-F	£6799
82	5/08	Nott	1m75y	GD	£2428

Total win prize-money £19198

Going (Turf): Sf: 0-1 **GS: 1-1 Gd: 1-5 GF: 1-2** Fm: 0-0
Distance: 5f/6f: 0-0 7f-8f: 1-7 **9f-13f: 2-3** 14f+: 0-0
Track: **LH: 2-4** RH: 0-3 Tight: 0-0 Gall: 0-2
Aids: Bl: 0-0 Vi: 0-0 Tstrap: 0-0 Ckp: 0-0
Best Rating: 103 8/09 NmkJ 1m2f good

Smart; effective at 1m-1m2f; acts on most ground.

Scutch Mill (IRE)

(104) (63)**65**

7-y-o ch g Alhaarth (IRE)-Bumble (Rainbow Quest (USA))

W B Stone (P C Haslam 13/1) Miss Caroline Scott

Placings:44346102540/020630400011/3060/60000-24 (0145)

2009: 9^{2}SD, 10^{4}SD,

	Starts	1st	2nd	3rd	Win & Pl
Career Total (Turf)	13	0	1	2	2502
Career Total (AW)	21	3	2	1	11586

68	12/06	Wolv	1m1f103y (0-58)H	STD	£2730
70	12/06	Kemp	1m (0-58)H	STD	£2590
59	4/05	Ling	1m	STD	£2870

Total win prize-money £8191

Going (Turf): **Sf: 0-0 GS: 0-3 Gd: 0-3 GF: 0-6 Fm: 0-1**
Distance: 5f/6f: 0-1 **7f-8f: 2-9** 9f-13f: 1-23 14f+: 0-1
Track: **LH: 2-21** RH: 1-11 **Tight: 2-23** Gall: 0-1
Aids: Bl: 0-0 Vi: 0-0 Tstrap: 0-0 Ckp: 0-0
Best Rating: 73 5/06 Ling 1m2f stand

Modest; stays 1m2f; acts on good ground and Polytrack; winner over hurdles; has worn a tongue tie.

Sea Cliff (IRE)

(102) (67)**36**

5-y-o b g Golan (IRE)-Prosaic Star (IRE) (Common Grounds)

Jonjo O'Neill John P McManus

Placings:0005/00046-152334 (1609)

2009: 16^{1}SD, 16^{5}SD, 14^{2}SD, 13^{3}SD, 14^{3}SD, 16^{4}SD,

	Starts	1st	2nd	3rd	Win & Pl
Career Total (Turf)	5	0	0	0	
Career Total (AW)	10	1	1	2	3354

56	1/09	Sthl	2m (0-60)H	STD	£2047

Total win prize-money £2047

Going (Turf): **Sf: 0-0 GS: 0-0 Gd: 0-1 GF: 0-2 Fm: 0-0**
Distance: 5f/6f: 0-1 7f-8f: 0-3 9f-13f: 0-5 **14f+: 1-6**
Track: **LH: 1-10** RH: 0-4 Tight: 0-4 Gall: 0-0
Aids: Bl: 0-0 Vi: 0-0 Tstrap: 0-3 Ckp: 0-3
Best Rating: 67 1/09 Sthl 1m6f stand

Modest; stays 2m; handles Fibresand.

Sea Cove

94 (33)**40**

9-y-o b m Terimon-Regal Pursuit (IRE) (Roi Danzig (USA))

Mrs Dianne Sayer (Mrs E Slack 13/6) Mrs Freda Rayson

Placings:6500/45554/5/500 (4848)

2009: 17^{5}G, 13^{0}G, 16^{0}G,

	Starts	1st	2nd	3rd	Win & Pl
Career Total (Turf)	9	0	0	0	0
Career Total (AW)	4	0	0	0	0

Going (Turf): **Sf: 0-0 GS: 0-2 Gd: 0-3 GF: 0-4 Fm: 0-0**
Distance: 5f/6f: 0-0 7f-8f: 0-0 9f-13f: 0-8 14f+: 0-5
Track: LH: 0-8 RH: 0-5 Tight: 0-5 Gall: 0-2
Aids: Bl: 0-0 Vi: 0-0 Tstrap: 0-0 Ckp: 0-0
Best Rating: 49 4/04 Sthl 1m4f stand

Sea Crest

101(85) (30)**65**

3-y-o b f Xaar-Talah (Danehill (USA))

M Brittain Mel Brittain

Placings:5245200-0232600 (6988)

2009: 5^{0}GF, 5^{2}S, 6^{3}GF, 5^{2}GF, 6^{6}SD, 5^{0}GF, 5^{0}G,

	Starts	1st	2nd	3rd	Win & Pl
Career Total (Turf)	13	0	4	1	5125
Career Total (AW)	1	0	0	0	0

Going (Turf): **Sf: 0-1 GS: 0-3 Gd: 0-1 GF: 0-8 Fm: 0-0**
Distance: 5f/6f: 0-14 7f-8f: 0-0 9f-13f: 0-0 14f+: 0-0
Track: LH: 0-1 RH: 0-0 Tight: 0-0 Gall: 0-1
Aids: Bl: 0-0 Vi: 0-0 Tstrap: 0-0 Ckp: 0-0
Best Rating: 65 7/08 Thsk 5f gd-fm

Modest; effective at sprint trips; acts on easy ground.

Sea Dubai

90(90) (72)**65**

2-y-o b c Mark Of Esteem (IRE)-Royal Flame (IRE) (Royal Academy (USA))

R Hannon Malih L Al Basti

Placings:620 (5528)

2009: 6^{6}G, 7^{2}SD, 7^{0}G,

	Starts	1st	2nd	3rd	Win & Pl
Career Total (Turf)	2	0	0	0	0
Career Total (AW)	1	0	1	0	771

Going (Turf): **Sf: 0-0 GS: 0-0 Gd: 0-2 GF: 0-0 Fm: 0-0**
Distance: 5f/6f: 0-0 7f-8f: 0-3 9f-13f: 0-0 14f+: 0-0
Track: LH: 0-1 RH: 0-1 Tight: 0-0 Gall: 0-0
Aids: Bl: 0-0 Vi: 0-0 Tstrap: 0-0 Ckp: 0-0
Best Rating: 72 8/09 Kemp 7f stand

Fair; stays 7f; acts on Polytrack.

Sea Land (FR)

82(99) (67)**48**

5-y-o ch g King's Best (USA)-Green Bonnet (IRE) (Green Desert (USA))

B Ellison Brian Ellison

Placings:2/10005/00000-104050200 (6861)

2009: 5^{1}SD, 7^{0}SD, 6^{4}GS, 5^{0}GS, 7^{5}SD, 7^{0}SD, 7^{2}SD, 7^{0}SD, 8^{0}SD,

	Starts	1st	2nd	3rd	Win & Pl
Career Total (Turf)	10	0	0	0	223
Career Total (AW)	10	2	2	0	7357

66	7/09	Wolv	5f216y (0-60)H	STD	£2388

75 2/07 Ling 7f STD £2914

Total win prize-money £5303

Going (Turf): Sf: 0-3 GS: 0-3 Gd: 0-1 GF: 0-3 Fm: 0-0
Distance: 5f/6f: 1-9 7f-8f: 1-9 9f-13f: 0-2 14f+: 0-0
Track : **LH: 2-9** RH: 0-5 **Tight: 2-10** Gall: 0-1
Aids: Bl: 0-0 Vi: 0-2 Tstrap: 0-0 Ckp: 0-0
Best Rating: 76 10/06 Ling 7f stand

Fair; effective at around 7f; acts on Polytrack.

Sea Lavender

99(80) (29)75

3-y-o b f Diktat-Satin Bell (Midyan (USA))

R Charlton Nicholas Jones

Placings:005200 **(6975)**

2009: 7^{0}GS, 8^{0}SD, 10^{5}GF, 9^{2}GF, 11^{0}GS, 12^{0}SD,

	Starts	1st	2nd	3rd	Win & Pl
Career Total (Turf)	4	0	1	0	964
Career Total (AW)	2	0	0	0	

Going (Turf): Sf: 0-0 GS: 0-2 Gd: 0-0 GF: 0-2 Fm: 0-0
Distance: 5f/6f: 0-0 7f-8f: 0-2 9f-13f: 0-4 14f+: 0-0
Track : LH: 0-0 RH: 0-4 Tight: 0-2 Gall: 0-0
Aids: Bl: 0 1 Vi: 0-0 Tstrap: 0-0 Ckp: 0-0
Best Rating: 75 9/09 Leic 1m1f218y gd-fm

Modest; stays 1m2f; acts on fast ground.

Sea Lord (IRE)

99 87

2-y-o b c Cape Cross (IRE)-First Fleet (USA) (Woodman (USA))

M Johnston Sheikh Hamdan Bin Mohammed Al Maktoum

Placings:210020 **(7013)**

2009: 7^{2}G, 7^{1}G, 7^{0}GF, 6^{0}GS, 7^{2}GF, 7^{0}GS,

	Starts	1st	2nd	3rd	Win & Pl
Career Total (Turf)	6	1	2	0	11625

84 7/09 Asct 7f GD £7771

Total win prize-money £7771

Going (Turf): Sf: 0-0 GS: 0-2 **Gd: 1-2** GF: 0-2 Fm: 0-0
Distance: 5f/6f: 0-1 **7f-8f: 1-5** 9f-13f: 0-0 14f+: 0-0
Track : LH: 0-2 RH: 0-0 Tight: 0-1 Gall: 0-1
Aids: Bl: 0-0 Vi: 0-0 Tstrap: 0-0 Ckp: 0-0
Best Rating: 87 9/09 NmkR 7f gd-fm

Useful; effective over 7f on fast ground.

Sea Of Heartbreak (IRE)

81(90) (69)37

2-y-o b f Rock Of Gibraltar (IRE)-Top Forty (Rainbow Quest (USA))

R Charlton D G Hardisty Bloodstock

Placings:01 **(7276)**

2009: 8^{0}S, 7^{1}SD,

	Starts	1st	2nd	3rd	Win & Pl
Career Total (Turf)	1	0	0	0	
Career Total (AW)	1	1	0	0	3238

69 11/09 Wolv 7f32y STD £3238

Total win prize-money £3238

Going (Turf): Sf: 0-1 GS: 0-0 Gd: 0-0 GF: 0-0 Fm: 0-0
Distance: 5f/6f: 0-0 **7f-8f: 1-2** 9f-13f: 0-0 14f+: 0-0
Track : **LH: 1-1** RH: 0-0 **Tight: 1-1** Gall: 0-0
Aids: Bl: 0-0 Vi: 0-0 Tstrap: 0-0 Ckp: 0-0
Best Rating: 69 11/09 Wolv 7f32y stand

Modest; stays 7f; acts on Polytrack.

Sea Of Leaves (USA)

108 99

3-y-o b f Stormy Atlantic (USA)-Dock Leaf (USA) (Woodman (USA))

J S Goldie Frank & Annette Brady

Placings:5160-0520014 **(6814)**

2009: 7^{0}G, 5^{5}G, 6^{2}GF, 6^{0}GS, 6^{0}G, 6^{1}GF, 6^{4}G,

	Starts	1st	2nd	3rd	Win & Pl
Career Total (Turf)	11	2	1	0	27525

99 10/09 NmkR 6f (0-100)H G-F £12462
78 6/08 Sals 5f G-F £4371

Total win prize-money £16833

Going (Turf): Sf: 0-0 GS: 0-2 Gd: 0-5 **GF: 2-4** Fm: 0-0
Distance: **5f/6f: 2-10** 7f-8f: 0-1 9f-13f: 0-0 14f+: 0-0
Track : LH: 0-0 RH: 0-0 Tight: 0-0 Gall: 0-0
Aids: Bl: 0-0 Vi: 0-0 Tstrap: 0-0 Ckp: 0-0
Best Rating: 99 10/09 NmkR 6f gd-fm

Useful; stays 6f; acts on fast ground; has worn tongue tie.

Sea Rover (IRE)

106(103) (73)76

5-y-o b h Jade Robbery (USA)-Talah (Danehill (USA))

M Brittain Mel Brittain

Placings:1255/000-25000100000020 **(7595)**

2009: 6^{2}GF, 5^{5}GF, 5^{0}GF, 5^{0}G, 7^{0}GF, 6^{1}F, 5^{0}G, 6^{0}GF, 6^{0}G, 6^{0}GF, 6^{0}GF, 6^{0}G, 5^{2}SD, 5^{0}SD,

	Starts	1st	2nd	3rd	Win & Pl
Career Total (Turf)	19	2	2	0	11075
Career Total (AW)	2	0	1	0	605

76 7/09 Hayd 6f (0-80)H FRM £5504
76 4/07 Thsk 6f G-F £3238

Total win prize-money £8744

Going (Turf): Sf: 0-0 GS: 0-1 Gd: 0-6 **GF: 1-11 Fm: 1-1**
Distance: **5f/6f: 2-19** 7f 8f: 0-2 9f-13f: 0-0 14f+: 0-0
Track : LH: 0-5 RH: 0-1 Tight: 0-3 Gall: 0-0
Aids: Bl: 0-0 Vi: 0-0 Tstrap: 0-0 Ckp: 0-0
Best Rating: 76 7/09 Hayd 6f firm

Modest; effective over 6f; acts on fast ground.

Sea Salt

103(63) (59)87

6-y-o b g Titus Livius (FR)-Carati (Selkirk (USA))

R E Barr (A J McCabe 11/5) Brian Morton

Placings:054/21601004/4500060/112000-0354120014206 **(7083)**

2009: 6^{0}F, 5^{3}GS, 7^{5}GS, 7^{4}G, 6^{1}GF, 7^{2}GF, 5^{0}GS, 6^{0}GF, 6^{1}S, 6^{4}G, 7^{2}GF, 6^{0}G, 7^{6}S,

	Starts	1st	2nd	3rd	Win & Pl
Career Total (Turf)	34	6	4	1	26621
Career Total (AW)	3	0	0	0	0

77 9/09 Thsk 6f (0-70)H SFT £4274
62 8/09 Newc 6f G-F £1942
52 8/08 Ayr 7f50y G-S £3238
73 5/08 Rdcr 7f SFT £1774
80 8/06 Newc 5f (0-75)H G-S £3886
70 5/06 Muss 5f G-F £4095

Total win prize-money £19210

Going (Turf): Sf: 2-7 GS: 2-10 Gd: 0-9 **GF: 2-7** Fm: 0-1
Distance: **5f/6f: 4-26** 7f-8f: 2-11 9f-13f: 0-0 14f+: 0-0
Track : **LH: 1-11** RH: 0-1 Tight: 0-8 Gall: 0-0
Aids: Bl: 0-0 Vi: 0-0 Tstrap: 0-0 Ckp: 0-0
Best Rating: 87 9/09 Haml 6f5y good

Fair; has only one eye; suited by 7f but effective at 6f; acts on most ground; wears an eyeshield; effective with forcing tactics.

Sea Storm (IRE)

85 (67)52

11-y-o b g Dolphin Street (FR)-Prime Interest (IRE) (Kings Lake (USA))

James Moffatt Maurice Chapman

Placings:00/4161126/006506533232151/003501401600205/050301006564302105/040033310000660/000/500/0-6 **(6769)**

2009: 12^{6}GS,

	Starts	1st	2nd	3rd	Win & Pl
Career Total (Turf)	73	8	5	9	89622
Career Total (AW)	7	2	0	0	12660

89 6/05 Ayr 1m (0-85)H G-S £6847
87 9/04 Muss 7f30y (0-85)H G-F £6780
87 5/04 Muss 1m D(0-75) G-F £5421
94 7/03 Wwck 7f26y C(0-90) FRM £8201
94 6/03 Newc 7f C(0-100)H G-S £13877
101 12/02 Ling 7f C(0-95)H STD £7447
94 11/02 Ling 7f D(0-80) STD £5213
88 7/01 Bevl 7f100y D(0-85)H G-F £8853
79 7/01 Sthl 7f E(0-75)H G-F £3710
74 5/01 Sthl 7f F G-F £2401

Total win prize-money £68753

Going (Turf): Sf: 0-4 GS: 2-10 Gd: 0-19**GF: 5-34** Fm: 1-6
Distance: 5f/6f: 0-2 **7f-8f: 10-66** 9f-13f: 0-12 14f+: 0-0
Track : **LH: 6-46** RH: 3-18 **Tight: 6-38** Gall: 0-4
Aids: Bl: 0-1 Vi: 0-0 Tstrap: 3-26 Ckp: 3-26
Best Rating: 101 12/02 Ling 7f stand

Useful handicapper; stays a mile, but effective over seven; acts on most ground and Polytrack; has worn cheekpieces.

Sea The Stars (IRE)

125 138

3-y-o b c Cape Cross (IRE)-Urban Sea (USA) (Miswaki (USA))

John M Oxx Christopher Tsui

Placings:411-111111 **(6526a)**

2009: 8^{1}GF, 12^{1}G, 10^{1}G, 10^{1}GF, 10^{1}GY, 12^{1}G,

	Starts	1st	2nd	3rd	Win & Pl
Career Total (Turf)	9	8	0	0	4417163

132 10/09 Lonc 1m4f GD £2219029
138 9/09 Leop 1m2f G-Y £552427
131 8/09 York 1m2f88y G-F £340620
135 7/09 Sand 1m2f7y GD £283850
124 6/09 Epsm 1m4f10y GD £709625
124 5/09 NmkR 1m G-F £241840
112 9/08 Curr 1m YLD £59742
94 8/08 Leop 7f SH £9573

Total win prize-money £4416708

Going (Turf): Sf: 0-0 GS: 0-0 **Gd: 3-4** GF: 2-2 Fm: 0-0
Distance: 5f/6f: 0-0 7f-8f: 3-4 **9f-13f: 5-5** 14f+: 0-0
Track : **LH: 4-4** RH: 3-3 Tight: 1-1 **Gall: 2-2**
Aids: Bl: 0-0 Vi: 0-0 Tstrap: 0-0 Ckp: 0-0
Best Rating: 138 9/09 Leop 1m2f gd-yld

Top-class Irish-trained colt; winner of the 2000 Guineas, Derby, Eclipse, Juddmonte International, Irish Champion and Arc in 2009; first horse ever to complete the Guineas/Derby/Arc treble; effective from 1m-1m4f and acts on most ground, though best when it's quick; boasts a high cruising speed and a terrific turn of foot.

Seader (USA)

99(97) (66)56

4-y-o b/br g Mr Greeley (USA)-Evangel (USA) (Danzig (USA))

Tim Vaughan (M Halford 28/5) John Wholey

Placings:46/4-50005 (5103)

2009: 8^5SD, 8^0Y, 8^0G, 12^0HY, 9^5SD,

	Starts	1st	2nd	3rd	Win & Pl
Career Total (Turf)	5	0	0	0	833
Career Total (AW)	3	0	0	0	0

Going (Turf): **Sf: 0-1 GS: 0-0 Gd: 0-1 GF: 0-0 Fm: 0-1**
Distance: 5f/6f: 0-0 7f-8f: 0-5 9f-13f: 0-3 14f+: 0-0
Track : LH: 0-4 RH: 0-2 Tight: 0-1 Gall: 0-0
Aids: Bl: 0-0 Vi: 0-0 Tstrap: 0-1 Ckp: 0-1
Best Rating: **69** 9/07 Tipp 7f100y firm

Moderate; stays 1m1f; acts on Polytrack.

Seafield Towers

88 57

9-y-o ch g Compton Place-Midnight Spell (Night Shift (USA))

D A Nolan Miss M McFadyen-Murray

Placings:55240043/0000203221316 0/0030000000/60134/000000060050000/000400455 0000-000600 (3148)

2009: 5^0GF, 5^0G, 6^0F, 6^6G, 5^0GF, 6^0GF,

	Starts	1st	2nd	3rd	Win & Pl
Career Total (Turf)	71	3	4	5	51343
69 7/05 Ayr	5f	(0-60)H		GD	£3550
82 8/03 York	5f3y	C(0-100)H		G-F	£19893
78 7/03 Ripn	6f	D(0-80)H		GD	£10296

Total win prize-money £33739

Going (Turf): Sf: 0-6 GS: 0-11 **Gd: 2-19** GF: 1-31 Fm: 0-4
Distance: **5f/6f: 3-61** 7f-8f: 0-9 9f-13f: 0-1 14f+: 0-0
Track : LH: 0-1 RH: 0-5 Tight: 0-2 Gall: 0-4
Aids: Bl: 0-4 Vi: 0-0 Tstrap: 2-41 Ckp: 2-41
Best Rating: **82** 8/03 York 5f3y gd-fm

Plating class; best at 5f but stays 6f; acts best on fast ground; often wears cheekpieces; has worn blinkers.

Seamster

78(94) (66)46

2-y-o ch g Pivotal-Needles And Pins (IRE) (Fasliyev (USA))

M Johnston (Saeed Bin Suroor 14/7) Sheikh Hamdan Bin Mohammed Al Maktoum

Placings:002 (7580)

2009: 6^0GF, 7^0S, 7^2SF,

	Starts	1st	2nd	3rd	Win & Pl
Career Total (Turf)	2	0	0	0	
Career Total (AW)	1	0	1	0	964

Going (Turf): **Sf: 0-1 GS: 0-0 Gd: 0-0 GF: 0-1 Fm: 0-0**
Distance: 5f/6f: 0-0 7f-8f: 0-3 9f-13f: 0-0 14f+: 0-0
Track : LH: 0-1 RH: 0-0 Tight: 0-1 Gall: 0-0
Aids: Bl: 0-0 Vi: 0-0 Tstrap: 0-0 Ckp: 0-0
Best Rating: **66** 11/09 Wolv 7f32y std-fst

Modest; stays 7f; acts on Polytrack.

Seamus Shindig

106(93) (59)94

7-y-o b g Aragon-Sheesha (USA) (Shadeed (USA))

H Candy Henry Candy

Placings:14/5634460/442545/5115013-50041040 (6994)

2009: 6^5GF, 6^0G, 6^0GF, 6^4G, 6^1G, 6^0GF, 6^4GS, 6^0G,

	Starts	1st	2nd	3rd	Win & Pl
Career Total (Turf)	26	5	1	1	32259
Career Total (AW)	4	0	0	1	1540
94 8/09 NmkJ	6f	(0-85)H		GD	£5180
91 8/08 NmkJ	6f	(0-85)H		G-S	£6476
88 5/08 Sals	6f	(0-85)H		G-F	£4209
85 5/08 Gdwd	6f	(0-80)H		GD	£4533
87 9/04 Pont	5f			FRM	£4124

Total win prize-money £24523

Going (Turf): Sf: 0-3 GS: 1-5 **Gd: 2-7** GF: 1-10 Fm: 1-1
Distance: **5f/6f: 5-29** 7f-8f: 0-1 9f-13f: 0-0 14f+: 0-0
Track : **LH: 1-5** RH: 0-3 Tight: 0-1 Gall: 0-1
Aids: Bl: 0-0 Vi: 0-0 Tstrap: 0-1 Ckp: 0-1
Best Rating: **94** 8/09 NmkJ 6f good

Useful sprinter; effective at around 6f; acts on fast and easy ground; also goes on Polytrack; goes well for Amy Scott.

Seaquel

94(89) (54)58

3-y-o b f Kyllachy-Broughton Singer (IRE) (Common Grounds)

A B Haynes P Cook

Placings:406-4602 (7740)

2009: 7^4G, 9^6S, 10^0SD, 12^2SD,

	Starts	1st	2nd	3rd	Win & Pl
Career Total (Turf)	5	0	0	0	409
Career Total (AW)	2	0	1	0	605

Going (Turf): **Sf: 0-4 GS: 0-0 Gd: 0-1 GF: 0-0 Fm: 0-0**
Distance: 5f/6f: 0-0 7f-8f: 0-4 9f-13f: 0-3 14f+: 0-0
Track : LH: 0-5 RH: 0-2 Tight: 0-1 Gall: 0-0
Aids: Bl: 0-0 Vi: 0-0 Tstrap: 0-0 Ckp: 0-0
Best Rating: **58** 9/08 Gdwd 1m soft

Moderate; effective at 1m2f-1m4f; acts on Polytrack and soft ground.

Search For The Key (USA)

86(90) (66)64

2-y-o b/br c El Corredor (USA)-Lo Cal Bread (USA) (Native Prospector (USA))

P F I Cole D S Lee

Placings:36 (5778)

2009: 6^3GS, 6^6SD,

	Starts	1st	2nd	3rd	Win & Pl
Career Total (Turf)	1	0	0	1	482
Career Total (AW)	1	0	0	0	0

Going (Turf): **Sf: 0-0 GS: 0-1 Gd: 0-0 GF: 0-0 Fm: 0-0**
Distance: 5f/6f: 0-2 7f-8f: 0-0 9f-13f: 0-0 14f+: 0-0
Track : LH: 0-0 RH: 0-1 Tight: 0-0 Gall: 0-0
Aids: Bl: 0-0 Vi: 0-0 Tstrap: 0-0 Ckp: 0-0
Best Rating: **66** 9/09 Kemp 6f stand

$135,000 yearling from a good sprinting family in the USA; moderate form on debut; should improve.

Seaside Sizzler

87 73

2-y-o ch g Rahy (USA)-Via Borghese (USA) (Seattle Dancer (USA))

R M Beckett I J Heseltine

Placings:054 (6393)

2009: 7^0G, 7^5G, 8^4GF,

	Starts	1st	2nd	3rd	Win & Pl
Career Total (Turf)	3	0	0	0	349

Going (Turf): **Sf: 0-0 GS: 0-0 Gd: 0-2 GF: 0-1 Fm: 0-0**
Distance: 5f/6f: 0-0 7f-8f: 0-3 9f-13f: 0-0 14f+: 0-0
Track : LH: 0-0 RH: 0-0 Tight: 0-0 Gall: 0-0
Aids: Bl: 0-0 Vi: 0-0 Tstrap: 0-0 Ckp: 0-0
Best Rating: **73** 9/09 Sals 1m gd-fm

Seasider

85 (90)79

4-y-o b g Zamindar (USA)-Esplanade (Danehill (USA))

Sir Michael Stoute K Abdulla

Placings:12/0-0 (3091)

2009: 7^0GF,

	Starts	1st	2nd	3rd	Win & Pl
Career Total (Turf)	3	1	0	0	2817
Career Total (AW)	1	0	1	0	1866
76 10/07 Wind	6f		G-S	£2817	

Total win prize-money £2817

Going (Turf): Sf: 0-0 **GS: 1-1** Gd: 0-0 GF: 0-2 Fm: 0-0
Distance: **5f/6f: 1-1** 7f-8f: 0-3 9f-13f: 0-0 14f+: 0-0
Track : LH: 0-1 RH: 0-1 Tight: 0-0 **Gall: 1-2**
Aids: Bl: 0-0 Vi: 0-0 Tstrap: 0-0 Ckp: 0-0
Best Rating: **90** 11/07 Kemp 7f stand

Seasonal Cross

105(98) (60)74

4-y-o b f Cape Cross (IRE)-Seasonal Blossom (IRE) (Fairy King (USA))

S Dow Mrs Alicia Aldis

Placings:360500-03243320115 (6790)

2009: 7^0SD, 8^3GF, 8^2GF, 8^4GF, 8^3GF, 9^3G, 8^2G, 7^0G, 8^1F, 8^1GF, 6^5G,

	Starts	1st	2nd	3rd	Win & Pl
Career Total (Turf)	12	2	2	3	8706
Career Total (AW)	5	0	0	1	363
74 9/09 Sals	1m	(0-65)H		G-F	£2719
67 9/09 Bath	1m5y	(0-60)H		FRM	£2266

Total win prize-money £4987

Going (Turf): Sf: 0-0 GS: 0-0 Gd: 0-6 **GF: 1-5 Fm: 1-1**
Distance: 5f/6f: 0-1 7f-8f: 1-12 9f-13f: 1-4 14f+: 0-0
Track : **LH: 1-8** RH: 0-5 **Tight: 1-6** Gall: 0-0
Aids: Bl: 0-0 Vi: 0-0 Tstrap: 0-0 Ckp: 0-0
Best Rating: **74** 9/09 Sals 1m gd-fm

Modest; stays 1m and acts on fast ground.

Seasons Estates

65 9

7-y-o b m Mark Of Esteem (IRE)-La Fazenda (Warning)

F J Brennan Seasons Holidays

Placings:40431/020161500/0 (3322)

2009: 8^0GF,

	Starts	1st	2nd	3rd	Win & Pl
Career Total (Turf)	14	3	1	1	13405
Career Total (AW)	1	0	0	0	
80 7/05 Wind	1m67y	(0-75)H		G-F	£3534
83 6/05 Chep	1m14y	(0-70)H		G-S	£3495
66 10/04 Ling	7f	(0-75)		G-F	£3776

Total win prize-money £10808

Going (Turf): Sf: 0-1 GS: 1-3 Gd: 0-3 **GF: 2-6** Fm: 0-1

Distance: 5f/6f: 0-2 7f-8f: 1-6 **9f-13f: 2-7** 14f+: 0-0
Track : LH: 0-6 **RH: 1-3 Tight: 1-4** Gall: 0-2
Aids: Bl: 0-0 Vi: 0-0 Tstrap: 0-0 Ckp: 0-0
Best Rating: **83** 6/05 Chep 1m14y gd-sft

Seattle Speight (USA)

69(64) (12)**23**
2-y-o b f Speightstown (USA)-Gal From Seattle (USA) (A.P. Indy (USA))
W J Knight Bluehills Racing Limited

Placings:00 **(5752)**
2009: 6^{0}S, 7^{0}SD,

	Starts	1st	2nd	3rd	Win & Pl
Career Total (Turf)	1	0	0	0	
Career Total (AW)	1	0	0	0	

Going (Turf): Sf: 0-1 GS: 0-0 Gd: 0-0 GF: 0-0 Fm: 0-0
Distance: 5f/6f: 0-0 7f-8f: 0-2 9f-13f: 0-0 14f+: 0-0
Track : LH: 0-1 RH: 0-0 Tight: 0-1 Gall: 0-0
Aids: Bl: 0-0 Vi: 0-0 Tstrap: 0-0 Ckp: 0-0
Best Rating: **23** 9/09 Sals 6f212y soft

Seaway

96 **94**
3-y-o b c Dr Fong (USA)-Atlantic Destiny (IRE) (Royal Academy (USA))
Saeed Bin Suroor Godolphin

Placings:222-231 **(4022)**
2009: 8^{2}GF, 8^{3}G, 9^{1}GF,

	Starts	1st	2nd	3rd	Win & Pl
Career Total (Turf)	6	1	4	1	20495
66 7/09 Leic 1m1f218y				G-F	£3238

Total win prize-money £3238

Going (Turf): Sf: 0-0 GS: 0-0 Gd: 0-3 **GF: 1-3** Fm: 0-0
Distance: 5f/6f: 0-2 7f-8f: 0-3 **9f-13f: 1-1** 14f+: 0-0
Track : LH: 0-1 **RH: 1-1** Tight: 0-0 Gall: 0-1
Aids: Bl: 0-0 Vi: 0-0 Tstrap: 0-0 Ckp: 0-0
Best Rating: **94** 6/08 Asct 7f gd-fm

Useful; Listed placed at two; effective at up to 1m2f; acts on good and faster ground; has worn a tongue tie.

Sebastian Flyte

104 **103**
2-y-o ch c Observatory (USA)-Aravonian (Night Shift (USA))
Francis Ennis Plantation Stud

Placings:0132 **(6426)**
2009: 5^{0}S, 7^{1}G, 6^{3}HY, 7^{2}GF,

	Starts	1st	2nd	3rd	Win & Pl
Career Total (Turf)	4	1	1	1	29937
85 8/09 Gowr 7f				GD	£10398

Total win prize-money £10399

Going (Turf): Sf: 0-2 GS: 0-0 **Gd: 1-1** GF: 0-1 Fm: 0-0
Distance: 5f/6f: 0-2 **7f-8f: 1-2** 9f-13f: 0-0 14f+: 0-0
Track : LH: 0-0 **RH: 1-1** Tight: 0-0 Gall: 0-0
Aids: Bl: 0-0 Vi: 0-0 Tstrap: 0-0 Ckp: 0-0
Best Rating: **103** 10/09 NmkR 7f gd-fm

Second Brook (IRE)

83(91) (52)**52**
2-y-o b g Celtic Swing-Mur Taasha (USA) (Riverman (USA))
R Hollinshead John L Marriott

Placings:40004 **(7722)**
2009: 7^{4}GF, 7^{0}G, 5^{0}SD, 8^{0}SD, 8^{4}SD,

	Starts	1st	2nd	3rd	Win & Pl
Career Total (Turf)	2	0	0	0	337
Career Total (AW)	3	0	0	0	0

Going (Turf): Sf: 0-0 GS: 0-0 Gd: 0-1 GF: 0-1 Fm: 0-0
Distance: 5f/6f: 0-1 7f-8f: 0-3 9f-13f: 0-1 14f+: 0-0
Track : LH: 0-3 RH: 0-0 Tight: 0-2 Gall: 0-0
Aids: Bl: 0-0 Vi: 0-0 Tstrap: 0-0 Ckp: 0-0
Best Rating: **52** 11/09 Wolv 5f216y stand

Second Reef

86 (64)**42**
7-y-o b g Second Empire (IRE)-Vax Lady (Millfontaine)
T A K Cuthbert Mrs Joyce Cuthbert

Placings:30/16605**30/30006042300421002242/5300004** 060/0000-06000 **(6817)**
2009: 6^{0}GF, 7^{6}G, 5^{0}GS, 8^{0}GF, 10^{0}GF,

	Starts	1st	2nd	3rd	Win & Pl
Career Total (Turf)	30	2	1	1	8116
Career Total (AW)	19	0	4	4	4775
57 9/06 Rdcr 1m2f				FRM	£2730
69 4/05 Rdcr 7f				GD	£3851

Total win prize-money £6581

Going (Turf): Sf: 0-2 GS: 0-3 **Gd: 1-8** GF: 0-13 **Fm: 1-4**
Distance: 5f/6f: 0-7 7f-8f: 1-20 9f-13f: 1-22 14f+: 0-0
Track : **LH: 1-32** RH: 0-9 **Tight: 1-27** Gall: 0-1
Aids: Bl: 0-1 Vi: 0-3 Tstrap: 0-4 Ckp: 0-4
Best Rating: **69** 4/05 Rdcr 7f good

Second To Nun (IRE)

94(82) (48)**62**
3-y-o b f Bishop Of Cashel-One For Me (Tragic Role (USA))
Jean-Rene Auvray The Dragon Partnership No 2

Placings:400-13050050 **(7587)**
2009: 8^{1}GF, 8^{3}F, 8^{0}GF, 8^{5}GF, 9^{0}GS, 8^{0}GS, 8^{5}F, 8^{0}SD,

	Starts	1st	2nd	3rd	Win & Pl
Career Total (Turf)	9	1	0	1	2552
Career Total (AW)	2	0	0	0	
62 4/09 Bath 1m5y (0-55)				G-F	£1978

Total win prize-money £1979

Going (Turf): Sf: 0-1 GS: 0-2 Gd: 0-1 **GF: 1-3** Fm: 0-2
Distance: 5f/6f: 0-0 7f-8f: 0-5 **9f-13f: 1-6** 14f+: 0-0
Track : **LH: 1-6** RH: 0-2 **Tight: 1-4** Gall: 0-0
Aids: Bl: 0-0 Vi: 0-0 Tstrap: 0-0 Ckp: 0-0
Best Rating: **62** 5/09 Bath 1m5y firm

Moderate; stays 1m; acts on fast ground.

Secrecy

109 **116**
3-y-o b g King's Best (USA)-Wink (Salse (USA))
Saeed Bin Suroor Godolphin

Placings:12-331 **(7185)**
2009: 8^{3}GF, 8^{3}S, 8^{1}G,

	Starts	1st	2nd	3rd	Win & Pl
Career Total (Turf)	5	2	1	2	26702
116 10/09 NmkR 1m (0-105)H				GD	£11215
100 9/08 Donc 7f				SFT	£9346

Total win prize-money £20563

Going (Turf): **Sf: 1-2** GS: 0-0 **Gd: 1-2** GF: 0-1 Fm: 0-0
Distance: 5f/6f: 0-0 **7f-8f: 2-5** 9f-13f: 0-0 14f+: 0-0
Track : LH: 0-0 RH: 0-0 Tight: 0-0 Gall: 0-0
Aids: Bl: 0-0 Vi: 0-0 Tstrap: 0-0 Ckp: 0-0
Best Rating: **116** 10/09 NmkR 1m good

Very useful; effective over 7f; acts on good and softer ground.

Secret City (IRE)

98 **59**
3-y-o b g City On A Hill (USA)-Secret Combe (IRE) (Mujadil (USA))
R Bastiman Ms M Austerfield

Placings:305450-051050 **(6926)**
2009: 7^{0}GF, 7^{5}GF, 6^{1}G, 6^{0}G, 7^{5}GF, 6^{0}GF,

	Starts	1st	2nd	3rd	Win & Pl
Career Total (Turf)	12	1	0	1	3831
59 7/09 Ayr 6f (0-60)H				GD	£2266

Total win prize-money £2267

Going (Turf): Sf: 0-1 GS: 0-1 **Gd: 1-5** GF: 0-5 Fm: 0-0
Distance: **5f/6f: 1-8** 7f-8f: 0-4 9f-13f: 0-0 14f+: 0-0
Track : LH: 0-4 RH: 0-0 Tight: 0-3 Gall: 0-0
Aids: **Bl: 1-8** Vi: 0-0 Tstrap: 0-0 Ckp: 0-0
Best Rating: **59** 9/09 Catt 7f gd-fm

Moderate; effective at 5f-6f; acts on good ground; has worn blinkers.

Secret Desert

99(90) (50)**60**
3-y-o b g Dubai Destination (USA)-Lady Bankes (IRE) (Alzao (USA))
D M Simcock Tick Tock Partnership

Placings:064042 **(6919)**
2009: 8^{0}G, 10^{6}SD, 11^{4}GF, 10^{0}G, 11^{4}G, 11^{2}GF,

	Starts	1st	2nd	3rd	Win & Pl
Career Total (Turf)	5	0	1	0	722
Career Total (AW)	1	0	0	0	0

Going (Turf): Sf: 0-0 GS: 0-0 Gd: 0-3 GF: 0-2 Fm: 0-0
Distance: 5f/6f: 0-0 7f-8f: 0-0 9f-13f: 0-6 14f+: 0-0
Track : LH: 0-3 RH: 0-3 Tight: 0-4 Gall: 0-0
Aids: Bl: 0-0 Vi: 0-0 Tstrap: 0-0 Ckp: 0-0
Best Rating: **60** 9/09 Ling 1m3f106y gd-fm

Moderate; stays 1m4f; acts on quick ground.

Secret Dubai (IRE)

101(102) (75)**79**
4-y-o b c Dubai Destination (USA)-Secret Pride (Green Desert (USA))
Mrs L Stubbs (M Botti 13/4) D Arundale

Placings:21214/1052003**355-654250046000** **(5443)**
2009: 7^{6}SD, 7^{5}SD, 7^{4}SD, 6^{2}G, 6^{5}G, 6^{0}GF, 5^{0}GF, 6^{4}GF, 5^{6}SD, 6^{0}GS, 6^{0}GF, 6^{0}GF,

	Starts	1st	2nd	3rd	Win & Pl
Career Total (Turf)	21	3	4	2	37976

Career Total (AW)	6	0	0	0	0
3/08	Siro	6f		GD	£8088
10/07	Siro	7f		GD	£8446
9/07	Siro	7f		GD	£6757

Total win prize-money £23291

Going (Turf): Sf: 0-1 GS: 0-3 **Gd: 3-10** GF: 0-5 Fm: 0-0
Distance: 5f/6f: 1-10 **7f-8f: 2-16** 9f-13f: 0-1 14f+: 0-0
Track : LH: 0-5 RH: 0-2 Tight: 0-3 Gall: 0-1
Aids: Bl: 0-2 Vi: 0-0 Tstrap: 0-0 Ckp: 0-0
Best Rating: **86** 12/07 Pisa 7f110y good

Modest; effective over 6fl acts on good ground.

Secret Hero

102(89) (48)**76**
3-y-o b c Cadeaux Genereux-Valiantly (Anabaa (USA))
Lee Smyth (R Hannon 19/10) Mark Devlin

Placings:0061521060 **(7672)**
2009: 7^{0}SD, 8^{0}S, 7^{6}GS, 6^{1}GF, 7^{5}GF, 7^{2}S, 7^{1}S, 7^{0}GF, 8^{6}G, 8^{0}SD,

	Starts	1st	2nd	3rd	Win & Pl
Career Total (Turf)	8	2	1	0	7245
Career Total (AW)	2	0	0	0	

76	8/09	Ling	7f	(0-75)H	SFT	£3238
71	6/09	Sals	6f212y	(0-65)H	G-F	£3043

Total win prize-money £6282

Going (Turf): **Sf: 1-3** GS: 0-1 Gd: 0-1 **GF: 1-3** Fm: 0-0
Distance: 5f/6f: 0-0 **7f-8f: 2-8** 9f-13f: 0-2 14f+: 0-0
Track : LH: 0-2 RH: 0-2 Tight: 0-2 Gall: 0-0
Aids: **Bl: 1-3** Vi: 0-0 Tstrap: 0-0 Ckp: 0-0
Best Rating: **76** 8/09 Ling 7f soft

Modest; effective over 7f; acts on fast ground.

Secret Life

98(101) (81)**76**
3-y-o b c Montjeu (IRE)-Bright Halo (IRE) (Bigstone (IRE))
J Noseda Mrs Susan Roy

Placings:04342 **(6855)**
2009: 8^{0}GF, 10^{4}SD, 10^{3}G, 10^{4}SD, 12^{2}SD,

	Starts	1st	2nd	3rd	Win & Pl
Career Total (Turf)	2	0	0	1	482
Career Total (AW)	3	0	1	0	1862

Going (Turf): **Sf: 0-0 GS: 0-0 Gd: 0-1 GF: 0-1 Fm: 0-0**
Distance: 5f/6f: 0-0 7f-8f: 0-1 9f-13f: 0-4 14f+: 0-0
Track : LH: 0-2 RH: 0-2 Tight: 0-2 Gall: 0-0
Aids: Bl: 0-0 Vi: 0-0 Tstrap: 0-0 Ckp: 0-0
Best Rating: **81** 10/09 Wolv 1m4f50y stand

Fair; stays 1m4f; acts on good ground and Polytrack.

Secret Millionaire (IRE)

100(99) (84)**86**
2-y-o b g Kyllachy-Mithl Al Hawa (Salse (USA))
Patrick Morris Rob Lloyd Racing Limited

Placings:2314120 **(6486)**
2009: 5^{2}GF, 5^{3}G, 5^{1}G, 5^{4}GF, 5^{1}SD, 5^{2}GF, 6^{0}GF,

	Starts	1st	2nd	3rd	Win & Pl
Career Total (Turf)	6	1	2	1	6085
Career Total (AW)	1	1	0	0	5181

84	9/09	Ling	5f	(0-85)	STD	£5180
81	8/09	Chep	5f16y		GD	£2752

Total win prize-money £7933

Going (Turf): Sf: 0-0 GS: 0-0 **Gd: 1-2** GF: 0-4 Fm: 0-0
Distance: **5f/6f: 2-7** 7f-8f: 0-0 9f-13f: 0-0 14f+: 0-0
Track : **LH: 1-1** RH: 0-0 **Tight: 1-1** Gall: 0-0
Aids: Bl: 0-0 Vi: 0-0 Tstrap: 0-0 Ckp: 0-0
Best Rating: **86** 10/09 Rdcr 6f gd-fm

Useful; effective at 5f; acts on fast ground.

Secret Night

105(107) (90)**88**
6-y-o gr m Dansili-Night Haven (Night Shift (USA))
C G Cox Hants and Herts

Placings:03421035**102/24435**2355**302/03200**0**50/0**153522 00342-13235 **(4293)**
2009: 7^{1}SD, 7^{3}GF, 8^{2}GF, 7^{3}GF, 7^{5}G,

	Starts	1st	2nd	3rd	Win & Pl
Career Total (Turf)	23	1	5	6	31166
Career Total (AW)	25	3	5	4	42416

90	4/09	Ling	7f	(0-90)H	STD	£7771
85	2/08	Ling	7f	(0-85)H	STD	£4100
85	11/05	Ling	6f	(0-85)	STD	£4818
72	7/05	Nott	5f13y		GD	£2667

Total win prize-money £19358

Going (Turf): Sf: 0-1 GS: 0-0 **Gd: 1-7** GF: 0-15 Fm: 0-0
Distance: 5f/6f: 2-19 7f-8f: 2-29 9f-13f: 0-0 14f+: 0-0
Track : **LH: 3-26** RH: 0-5 **Tight: 3-21** Gall: 0-2
Aids: **Bl: 1-2** Vi: 0-3 Tstrap: 0-7 Ckp: 0-7
Best Rating: **93** 12/06 Ling 1m stand

Useful; effective over 7f-1m; acts on a sound surface and on Polytrack; has worn blinkers, cheekpieces and a visor.

Secret Ploy

95 **71**
9-y-o b g Deploy-By Line (High Line)
H Morrison A M Carding

Placings:164130/0506 **(6021)**
2009: 14^{0}GF, 16^{5}GS, 17^{0}GF, 17^{6}GF,

	Starts	1st	2nd	3rd	Win & Pl
Career Total (Turf)	10	2	0	1	37681

80	8/07	Gdwd	2m5f	(0-95)H	GD	£31160
73	5/07	Thsk	1m4f		G-F	£3886

Total win prize-money £35046

Going (Turf): Sf: 0-2 GS: 0-2 **Gd: 1-1 GF: 1-4** Fm: 0-1
Distance: 5f/6f: 0-0 7f-8f: 0-0 9f-13f: 1-1 14f+: 1-9
Track : LH: 1-7 RH: 1-3 **Tight: 2-4** Gall: 0-2
Aids: Bl: 0-0 Vi: 0-0 Tstrap: 0-1 Ckp: 0-1
Best Rating: **80** 8/07 Gdwd 2m5f good

Secret Queen

101(89) (66)**85**
2-y-o b f Zafeen (FR)-Gold Queen (Grand Lodge (USA))
B J Meehan Jaber Abdullah

Placings:322416 **(6486)**
2009: 5^{3}F, 7^{2}GF, 7^{2}GF, 8^{4}SD, 6^{1}GF, 6^{6}GF,

	Starts	1st	2nd	3rd	Win & Pl
Career Total (Turf)	5	1	2	1	9234
Career Total (AW)	1	0	0	0	337

85	9/09	Rdcr	6f	G-F	£3561

Total win prize-money £3562

Going (Turf): Sf: 0-0 GS: 0-0 Gd: 0-0 **GF: 1-4** Fm: 0-1
Distance: **5f/6f: 1-3** 7f-8f: 0-3 9f-13f: 0-0 14f+: 0-0
Track : LH: 0-1 RH: 0-1 Tight: 0-0 Gall: 0-1
Aids: Bl: 0-0 Vi: 0-0 Tstrap: 0-0 Ckp: 0-0
Best Rating: **85** 9/09 Rdcr 6f gd-fm

Useful; stays 7f and acts on fast ground and Polytrack.

Secret Rose

51(71) (11)
2-y-o b f Deportivo-Kingston Rose (GER) (Robellino (USA))
W G M Turner Sparsholt Stud

Placings:00 **(1249)**
2009: 5^{0}SD, 5^{0}GF,

	Starts	1st	2nd	3rd	Win & Pl
Career Total (Turf)	1	0	0	0	
Career Total (AW)	1	0	0	0	

Going (Turf): **Sf: 0-0 GS: 0-0 Gd: 0-0 GF: 0-1 Fm: 0-0**
Distance: 5f/6f: 0-2 7f-8f: 0-0 9f-13f: 0-0 14f+: 0-0
Track : LH: 0-2 RH: 0-0 Tight: 0-1 Gall: 0-0
Aids: Bl: 0-0 Vi: 0-0 Tstrap: 0-0 Ckp: 0-0
Best Rating: **11** 3/09 Ling 5f stand

Secret Society

114(101) (85)**109**
3-y-o b c Exceed And Excel (AUS)-Shady Point (IRE) (Unfuwain (USA))
M L W Bell Sheikh Marwan Al Maktoum

Placings:62-14121246 **(5709a)**
2009: 7^{1}SD, 8^{4}GF, 7^{1}F, 8^{2}GF, 7^{1}GF, 7^{2}G, 7^{4}GF, 7^{6}GS,

	Starts	1st	2nd	3rd	Win & Pl
Career Total (Turf)	9	2	3	0	87059
Career Total (AW)	1	1	0	0	2730

109	7/09	Asct	7f	H	G-F	£31155
98	6/09	Thsk	7f	(0-85)H	FRM	£5569
85	4/09	Ling	7f		STD	£2729

Total win prize-money £39454

Going (Turf): Sf: 0-0 GS: 0-1 Gd: 0-2 **GF: 1-5 Fm: 1-1**
Distance: 5f/6f: 0-1 **7f-8f: 3-9** 9f-13f: 0-0 14f+: 0-0
Track : **LH: 2-3** RH: 0-1 **Tight: 2-2** Gall: 0-1
Aids: Bl: 0-1 Vi: 0-0 Tstrap: 0-0 Ckp: 0-0
Best Rating: **109** 8/09 York 7f gd-fm

Smart; effective at 7f-1m; acts on fast ground; goes on Polytrack.

Secret Venue

105 **77**
3-y-o ch g Where Or When (IRE)-Sheila's Secret (IRE) (Bluebird (USA))
Jedd O'Keeffe Ken And Delia Shaw-KGS Consulting LLP

Placings:22310604-011120001 **(6387)**
2009: 5^{0}GF, 5^{1}GF, 5^{1}GF, 5^{1}G, 5^{2}G, 5^{0}G, 5^{0}GF, 5^{0}GF, 5^{1}GF,

	Starts	1st	2nd	3rd	Win & Pl
Career Total (Turf)	17	5	3	1	23309

77	9/09	Nott	5f13y	(0-75)H	G-F	£2590
73	7/09	Muss	5f	(0-80)H	GD	£6476
69	6/09	Muss	5f	(0-65)H	G-F	£2266
64	5/09	Muss	5f	(0-65)H	G-F	£2590
71	7/08	Thsk	5f		G-F	£4274

Total win prize-money £18197

Going (Turf): Sf: 0-2 GS: 0-1 Gd: 1-4 **GF: 4-10** Fm: 0-0
Distance: **5f/6f: 5-17** 7f-8f: 0-0 9f-13f: 0-0 14f+: 0-0
Track : LH: 0-2 RH: 0-0 Tight: 0-2 Gall: 0-0
Aids: Bl: 0-0 Vi: 0-0 Tstrap: 0-0 Ckp: 0-0
Best Rating: **77** 9/09 Nott 5f13y gd-fm

Fair; effective over 5f-6f; suited by fast ground.

Secret Witness

79(104) (81)**52**
3-y-o ch g Pivotal-It's A Secret (Polish Precedent (USA))

R A Harris (J Noseda 14/10) Ridge House Stables Ltd

Placings:10020065 (7795)
2009: 7^1SD, 7^0S, 7^0G, 7^2SD, 7^0SD, 7^0SD, 7^6SD, 6^5SS,

	Starts	1st	2nd	3rd	Win & Pl
Career Total (Turf)	2	0	0	0	
Career Total (AW)	6	1	1	0	5103

74 5/09 Ling 7f STD £3561
Total win prize-money £3562

Going (Turf): **Sf:** 0-1 **GS:** 0-0 **Gd:** 0-1 **GF:** 0-0 **Fm:** 0-0
Distance: 5f/6f: 0-1 **7f-8f: 1-7** 9f-13f: 0-0 14f+: 0-0
Track : **LH: 1-5** RH: 0-2 **Tight: 1-3** Gall: 0-0
Aids: Bl: 0-2 Vi: 0-1 Tstrap: 0-0 Ckp: 0-0
Best Rating: **81** 9/09 Ling 7f stand

Fair; stays 7f and acts on Polytrack.

Secretive

(89) (77)
2-y-o b c Shamardal (USA)-Samsung Spirit (Statoblest)
M Johnston Sheikh Hamdan Bin Mohammed Al Maktoum

Placings:1 (7836)
2009: 7^1SS,

	Starts	1st	2nd	3rd	Win & Pl
Career Total (Turf)	0	0	0	0	
Career Total (AW)	1	1	0	0	3753

77 12/09 Sthl 7f SS £3753
Total win prize-money £3753

Going (Turf): **Sf:** 0-0 **GS:** 0-0 **Gd:** 0-0 **GF:** 0-0 **Fm:** 0-0
Distance: 5f/6f: 0-0 **7f-8f: 1-1** 9f-13f: 0-0 14f+: 0-0
Track : **LH: 1-1** RH: 0-0 Tight: 0-0 Gall: 0-0
Aids: Bl: 0-0 Vi: 0-0 Tstrap: 0-0 Ckp: 0-0
Best Rating: **77** 12/09 Sthl 7f std-slw

60,000gns half-brother to, among others, smart sprinter Mystical Land; effective over 7f; acts on Fibresand.

Securitisation (IRE)

69 26
2-y-o ch c Rock Of Gibraltar (IRE)-Maria Delfina (IRE) (Giant's Causeway (USA))
B J Curley Curley Leisure

Placings:0000 (6991)
2009: 6^0GF, 5^0GF, 8^0GS, 7^0G,

	Starts	1st	2nd	3rd	Win & Pl
Career Total (Turf)	4	0	0	0	

Going (Turf): **Sf:** 0-0 **GS:** 0-1 **Gd:** 0-1 **GF:** 0-2 **Fm:** 0-0
Distance: 5f/6f: 0-1 7f-8f: 0-2 9f-13f: 0-1 14f+: 0-0
Track : LH: 0-1 RH: 0-0 Tight: 0-0 Gall: 0-0
Aids: Bl: 0-0 Vi: 0-0 Tstrap: 0-0 Ckp: 0-0
Best Rating: **26** 10/09 Donc 7f good

Sedge (USA)

(95) (59)70
9-y-o b g Lure (USA)-First Flyer (USA) (Riverman (USA))
P T Midgley Colin Alton

Placings:100004/3106545/5203222320/02150105002013/000033005046-0 (1153)
2009: 8^0SD,

	Starts	1st	2nd	3rd	Win & Pl
Career Total (Turf)	26	2	4	4	12569
Career Total (AW)	24	3	3	2	10323

77 10/07 Wolv 7f32y (0-65)H STD £2047
73 7/07 Wolv 7f32y (0-65)H STD £2388
68 5/07 Thsk 7f (0-60)H G-F £2590
61 2/05 Wolv 7f32y (0-55)H STD £2930
62 5/04 Rdcr 7f F G-F £2989
Total win prize-money £12947

Going (Turf): Sf: 0-2 GS: 0-1 Gd: 0-2 **GF: 2-19** Fm: 0-2
Distance: 5f/6f: 0-1 **7f-8f: 5-42** 9f-13f: 0-7 14f+: 0-0
Track : **LH: 4-31** RH: 0-14 **Tight: 4-24** Gall: 0-3
Aids: **Bl: 2-14** Vi: 0-0 Tstrap: 1-16 Ckp: 1-16
Best Rating: **77** 10/07 Wolv 7f32y stand

Modest; suited by 7f; acts on fast ground; also goes on sand; has gone well in blinkers.

Seductive Witch

(103) (61)45
4-y-o ch f Zamindar (USA)-Thicket (Wolfhound (USA))
J Balding John Howard Wilson

Placings:0055/**655112250000-50** (1182)
2009: 6^0SD, 5^0SD,

	Starts	1st	2nd	3rd	Win & Pl
Career Total (Turf)	3	0	0	0	
Career Total (AW)	15	2	2	0	3239

57 2/08 Wolv 5f216y (0-60)H STD £1774
Total win prize-money £1775

Going (Turf): **Sf:** 0-1 **GS:** 0-1 **Gd:** 0-1 **GF:** 0-0 **Fm:** 0-0
Distance: **5f/6f: 2-15** 7f-8f: 0-3 9f-13f: 0-0 14f+: 0-0
Track : **LH: 2-12** RH: 0-3 **Tight: 2-11** Gall: 0-3
Aids: Bl: 0-0 Vi: 0-0 Tstrap: 0-0 Ckp: 0-0
Best Rating: **61** 3/08 Ling 6f stand

Moderate; suited by 6f and Polytrack; suited by forcing tactics.

See Elsie Play

88 48
3-y-o b f King O' The Mana (IRE)-Liebside Lass (IRE) (Be My Guest (USA))
Miss Z C Davison Mrs D L Smith-Hooper

Placings:00 (3161)
2009: 6^0S, 6^0GF,

	Starts	1st	2nd	3rd	Win & Pl
Career Total (Turf)	2	0	0	0	

Going (Turf): **Sf:** 0-1 **GS:** 0-0 **Gd:** 0-0 **GF:** 0-1 **Fm:** 0-0
Distance: 5f/6f: 0-1 7f-8f: 0-1 9f-13f: 0-0 14f+: 0-0
Track : LH: 0-0 RH: 0-0 Tight: 0-0 Gall: 0-0
Aids: Bl: 0-0 Vi: 0-0 Tstrap: 0-0 Ckp: 0-0
Best Rating: **48** 6/09 Yarm 6f3y soft

See That Girl

90(74) (3)44
3-y-o b f Hawk Wing (USA)-Hampton Lucy (IRE) (Anabaa (USA))
B Smart Dr Philip Brown

Placings:0-040 (7176)
2009: 7^0GS, 7^4GF, 6^0SD,

	Starts	1st	2nd	3rd	Win & Pl
Career Total (Turf)	3	0	0	0	204
Career Total (AW)	1	0	0	0	

Going (Turf): **Sf:** 0-0 **GS:** 0-2 **Gd:** 0-0 **GF:** 0-1 **Fm:** 0-0
Distance: 5f/6f: 0-1 7f-8f: 0-3 9f-13f: 0-0 14f+: 0-0
Track : LH: 0-0 RH: 0-1 Tight: 0-0 Gall: 0-0
Aids: Bl: 0-0 Vi: 0-0 Tstrap: 0-0 Ckp: 0-0
Best Rating: **44** 9/09 Rdcr 7f gd-fm

Seedless

83(94) (58)64
4-y-o br m Mtoto-Unseeded (Unfuwain (USA))
D McCain Jnr (A M Balding 30/5) R Kent

Placings:0046-50 (2497)
2009: 13^5GS, 13^0GF,

	Starts	1st	2nd	3rd	Win & Pl
Career Total (Turf)	4	0	0	0	0
Career Total (AW)	2	0	0	0	168

Going (Turf): **Sf:** 0-1 **GS:** 0-2 **Gd:** 0-0 **GF:** 0-1 **Fm:** 0-0
Distance: 5f/6f: 0-0 7f-8f: 0-0 9f-13f: 0-3 14f+: 0-3
Track : LH: 0-5 RH: 0-1 Tight: 0-2 Gall: 0-2
Aids: Bl: 0-0 Vi: 0-0 Tstrap: 0-0 Ckp: 0-0
Best Rating: **64** 4/08 Sand 1m2f7y gd-sft

Seek N' Destroy (IRE)

103(102) (84)96
3-y-o b c Exceed And Excel (AUS)-Very Nice (Daylami (IRE))
B W Hills R J Arculli

Placings:50-1214310 (6270)
2009: 7^1SD, 7^2SD, 7^1GF, 7^4GF, 7^3GF, 7^1GF, 7^0G,

	Starts	1st	2nd	3rd	Win & Pl
Career Total (Turf)	7	2	0	1	20679
Career Total (AW)	2	1	1	0	3997

96 8/09 NmkJ 7f (0-90)H G-F £9066
86 5/09 Ling 7f (0-90)H G-F £9714
74 3/09 Kemp 7f STD £2590
Total win prize-money £21370

Going (Turf): Sf: 0-1 GS: 0-0 Gd: 0-1 **GF: 2-5** Fm: 0-0
Distance: 5f/6f: 0-2 **7f-8f: 3-7** 9f-13f: 0-0 14f+: 0-0
Track : LH: 0-2 **RH: 1-2** Tight: 0-1 Gall: 0-1
Aids: Bl: 0-0 Vi: 0-0 Tstrap: 0-0 Ckp: 0-0
Best Rating: **96** 8/09 NmkJ 7f gd-fm

Very useful; effective at 7f; acts on fast ground and on Polytrack.

Seek The Cash (USA)

(85) (52)
2-y-o ch c Mr Greeley (USA)-Cash Deal (USA) (Danzig (USA))
M Quinn Miss K Davies

Placings:0 (7773)
2009: 7^0SD,

	Starts	1st	2nd	3rd	Win & Pl
Career Total (Turf)	0	0	0	0	
Career Total (AW)	1	0	0	0	

Going (Turf): **Sf:** 0-0 **GS:** 0-0 **Gd:** 0-0 **GF:** 0-0 **Fm:** 0-0
Distance: 5f/6f: 0-0 7f-8f: 0-1 9f-13f: 0-0 14f+: 0-0
Track : LH: 0-1 RH: 0-0 Tight: 0-1 Gall: 0-0
Aids: Bl: 0-0 Vi: 0-0 Tstrap: 0-0 Ckp: 0-0
Best Rating: **52** 12/09 Ling 7f stand

Seek The Fair Land

100(112) (91)76

3-y-o b g Noverre (USA)-Duchcov (Caerleon (USA))
J R Boyle Chris Watkins And David N Reynolds

Placings:504-115404044112 **(7833)**
2009: 7^{1}SD, 7^{1}SD, 7^{5}GF, 6^{4}SD, 6^{0}SD, 7^{4}SD, 7^{0}G, 7^{4}SD, 8^{4}SD, 7^{1}SD, 7^{1}SD, 7^{2}SD,

	Starts	1st	2nd	3rd	Win & Pl
Career Total (Turf)	3	0	0	0	0
Career Total (AW)	12	4	1	0	17394

91 12/09 Kemp 7f (0-80)H STD £4727
83 12/09 Ling 7f (0-75)H STD £2729
78 4/09 Kemp 7f (0-80)H STD £4727
72 4/09 Wolv 7f32y STD £2388
Total win prize-money £14572

Going (Turf): Sf: 0-0 GS: 0-0 Gd: 0-2 GF: 0-1 Fm: 0-0
Distance: 5f/6f: 0-3 **7f-8f: 4-12** 9f-13f: 0-0 14f+: 0-0
Track : LH: 2-3 RH: 2-9 **Tight: 2-3** Gall: 0-0
Aids: Bl: 0-0 Vi: 0-0 Tstrap: 0-0 Ckp: 0-0
Best Rating: 91 12/09 Kemp 7f stand

Useful; effective over 7f; acts on Polytrack.

Seeker Rainbow

74(61) (8)40

2-y-o ch f Mark Of Esteem (IRE)-Seeker (Rainbow Quest (USA))
Mrs L C Jewell E A Condon

Placings:00 **(4200)**
2009: 7^{0}GF, 7^{0}SD,

	Starts	1st	2nd	3rd	Win & Pl
Career Total (Turf)	1	0	0	0	
Career Total (AW)	1	0	0	0	

Going (Turf): Sf: 0-0 GS: 0-0 Gd: 0-0 GF: 0-1 Fm: 0-0
Distance: 5f/6f: 0-0 7f-8f: 0-2 9f-13f: 0-0 14f+: 0-0
Track : LH: 0-1 RH: 0-0 Tight: 0-1 Gall: 0-0
Aids: Bl: 0-0 Vi: 0-0 Tstrap: 0-0 Ckp: 0-0
Best Rating: 40 6/09 Ling 7f gd-fm

Seeking Dubai

98(96) (82)91

2-y-o b f Dubawi (IRE)-Placement (Kris)
E F Vaughan Nabil Mourad

Placings:321140 **(7147)**
2009: 6^{3}G, 6^{2}G, 6^{1}GF, 6^{1}SD, 6^{4}G, 6^{0}G,

	Starts	1st	2nd	3rd	Win & Pl
Career Total (Turf)	5	1	1	1	13559
Career Total (AW)	1	1	0	0	3886

82 8/09 Kemp 6f (0-85) STD £3885
79 8/09 Wind 6f G-F £5569
Total win prize-money £9455

Going (Turf): Sf: 0-0 GS: 0-0 Gd: 0-4 **GF: 1-1** Fm: 0-0
Distance: **5f/6f: 2-5** 7f-8f: 0-1 9f-13f: 0-0 14f+: 0-0
Track : LH: 0-0 **RH: 1-1** Tight: 0-0 **Gall: 1-1**
Aids: Bl: 0-0 Vi: 0-0 Tstrap: 0-0 Ckp: 0-0
Best Rating: 91 9/09 MsnL 6f110y good

Half-sister to the smart Presto Vento; promising debut over 6f on fast ground.

Seeking Faith (USA)

80(78) (42)50

3-y-o b/br f Chapel Royal (USA)-Padrao Global (USA) (Storm Bird (CAN))
C G Cox S R Hope And S W Barrow

Placings:0-00 **(4145)**
2009: 8^{0}G, 10^{0}GF,

	Starts	1st	2nd	3rd	Win & Pl
Career Total (Turf)	2	0	0	0	
Career Total (AW)	1	0	0	0	

Going (Turf): Sf: 0-0 GS: 0-0 Gd: 0-1 GF: 0-1 Fm: 0-0
Distance: 5f/6f: 0-0 7f-8f: 0-1 9f-13f: 0-2 14f+: 0-0
Track : LH: 0-0 RH: 0-3 Tight: 0-2 Gall: 0-0
Aids: Bl: 0-0 Vi: 0-0 Tstrap: 0-0 Ckp: 0-0
Best Rating: 50 7/09 Wind 1m67y good

Seeking Rio

(85) (39)

2-y-o b f Captain Rio-True Seeker (Lujain (USA))
R J Hodges Miss R Dobson

Placings:000 **(7859)**
2009: 7^{0}SD, 5^{0}SD, 7^{0}SD,

	Starts	1st	2nd	3rd	Win & Pl
Career Total (Turf)	0	0	0	0	
Career Total (AW)	3	0	0	0	

Going (Turf): Sf: 0-0 GS: 0-0 Gd: 0-0 GF: 0-0 Fm: 0-0
Distance: 5f/6f: 0-1 7f-8f: 0-2 9f-13f: 0-0 14f+: 0-0
Track : LH: 0-3 RH: 0-0 Tight: 0-3 Gall: 0-0
Aids: Bl: 0-0 Vi: 0-0 Tstrap: 0-0 Ckp: 0-0
Best Rating: 39 12/09 Wolv 5f216y stand

Seeking Rose

78(80) (36)35

2-y-o b f Where Or When (IRE)-Selkirk Rose (IRE) (Pips Pride)
E A L Dunlop The Serendipity Partnership

Placings:000 **(6728)**
2009: 8^{0}GF, 8^{0}SD, 8^{0}S,

	Starts	1st	2nd	3rd	Win & Pl
Career Total (Turf)	2	0	0	0	
Career Total (AW)	1	0	0	0	

Going (Turf): Sf: 0-1 GS: 0-0 Gd: 0-0 GF: 0-1 Fm: 0-0
Distance: 5f/6f: 0-0 7f-8f: 0-2 9f-13f: 0-1 14f+: 0-0
Track : LH: 0-0 RH: 0-2 Tight: 0-0 Gall: 0-0
Aids: Bl: 0-0 Vi: 0-0 Tstrap: 0-0 Ckp: 0-0
Best Rating: 36 9/09 Kemp 1m stand

Seeking Stardom

87 58

2-y-o ch g Starcraft (NZ)-Lunar Goddess (Royal Applause)
P M Phelan Highgrange Syndicate

Placings:000 **(6054)**
2009: 6^{0}G, 6^{0}GF, 6^{0}GF,

	Starts	1st	2nd	3rd	Win & Pl
Career Total (Turf)	3	0	0	0	

Going (Turf): Sf: 0-0 GS: 0-0 Gd: 0-1 GF: 0-2 Fm: 0-0
Distance: 5f/6f: 0-2 7f-8f: 0-1 9f-13f: 0-0 14f+: 0-0
Track : LH: 0-0 RH: 0-0 Tight: 0-0 Gall: 0-1
Aids: Bl: 0-0 Vi: 0-0 Tstrap: 0-0 Ckp: 0-0
Best Rating: 58 9/09 Newb 6f8y gd-fm

Seeking The Buck (USA)

110 97

5-y-o b g Seeking The Gold (USA)-Cuanto Es (USA) (Exbourne (USA))
R M Beckett Malcolm C Denmark

Placings:0/651223210/11245 **(5170)**
2009: 10^{1}GF, 10^{1}G, 10^{2}GF, 10^{4}GF, 12^{5}GF,

	Starts	1st	2nd	3rd	Win & Pl
Career Total (Turf)	15	4	4	1	59801

96 6/09 Epsm 1m2f18y H GD £24924
95 5/09 NmkR 1m2f (0-90)H G-F £7771
93 9/07 Hayd 1m2f120y (0-85)H G-F £6477
74 6/07 Brig 1m1f209y (0-70)H FRM £2849
Total win prize-money £42022

Going (Turf): Sf: 0-0 GS: 0-0 Gd: 1-6 **GF: 2-8** Fm: 1-1
Distance: 5f/6f: 0-0 7f-8f: 0-3 **9f-13f: 4-12** 14f+: 0-0
Track : **LH: 3-9** RH: 0-4 **Tight: 1-4** Gall: 0-4
Aids: **Bl: 1-3** Vi: 0-0 Tstrap: 0-0 Ckp: 0-0
Best Rating: 97 8/09 York 1m4f gd-fm

Very useful; effective over 1m2f-1m4f; acts on good and faster ground; has worn blinkers and a tongue tie.

Seeu Central (IRE)

87(97) (61)38

5-y-o br g Lahib (USA)-Mottaret (IRE) (Forest Wind (USA))
P J Rothwell Eugene/Sean Kenny Partnership

Placings:4000000400 **(5142a)**
2009: 8^{4}SD, 12^{0}SW, 10^{0}Y, 8^{0}HY, 8^{0}G, 12^{0}GF, 9^{0}GF, 8^{4}S, 7^{0}HY, 8^{0}GY,

	Starts	1st	2nd	3rd	Win & Pl
Career Total (Turf)	8	0	0	0	318
Career Total (AW)	2	0	0	0	0

Going (Turf): Sf: 0-3 GS: 0-0 Gd: 0-1 GF: 0-2 Fm: 0-0
Distance: 5f/6f: 0-0 7f-8f: 0-3 9f-13f: 0-7 14f+: 0-0
Track : LH: 0-6 RH: 0-4 Tight: 0-1 Gall: 0-0
Aids: Bl: 0-0 Vi: 0-0 Tstrap: 0-1 Ckp: 0-1
Best Rating: 61 1/09 Wolv 1m141y stand

Sefton Park

78(84) (51)51

2-y-o b g Dansili-Optimistic (Reprimand)
C R Egerton Brent Thomas & Partners

Placings:000 **(6772)**
2009: 7^{0}G, 7^{0}GS, 8^{0}SD,

	Starts	1st	2nd	3rd	Win & Pl
Career Total (Turf)	2	0	0	0	
Career Total (AW)	1	0	0	0	

Going (Turf): Sf: 0-0 GS: 0-1 Gd: 0-1 GF: 0-0 Fm: 0-0
Distance: 5f/6f: 0-0 7f-8f: 0-3 9f-13f: 0-0 14f+: 0-0
Track : LH: 0-1 RH: 0-1 Tight: 0-0 Gall: 0-0
Aids: Bl: 0-0 Vi: 0-0 Tstrap: 0-0 Ckp: 0-0
Best Rating: 51 10/09 Kemp 1m stand

Segal (IRE)

94(97) (82)**76**

4-y-o b g Cadeaux Genereux-Camcorder (Nashwan (USA))

A M Hales Andrew L Cohen

Placings:032/212446-6 (2566)

2009: 12^{6}GF,

	Starts	1st	2nd	3rd	Win & Pl
Career Total (Turf)	4	0	0	0	496
Career Total (AW)	6	1	3	1	7192

76 2/08 Ling 1m STD £2331

Total win prize-money £2332

Going (Turf): Sf: 0-1 GS: 0-1 Gd: 0-1 GF: 0-1 Fm: 0-0
Distance: 5f/6f: 0-0 **7f-8f: 1-5** 9f-13f: 0-5 14f+: 0-0
Track : **LH: 1-6** RH: 0-3 **Tight: 1-7** Gall: 0-0
Aids: Bl: 0-0 Vi: 0-0 Tstrap: 0-0 Ckp: 0-0
Best Rating: **82** 3/08 Wolv 1m1f103y stand

Fair; stays 1m; acts on Polytrack.

Sehoy (USA)

101(110) (91)**90**

3-y-o b/br c Menifee (USA)-Another Storm (USA) (Gone West (USA))

J H M Gosden George Strawbridge

Placings:0-1204420 (6724)

2009: 12^{1}SD, 12^{2}SD, 10^{0}S, 10^{4}GS, 12^{4}G, 12^{2}GF, 12^{0}SD,

	Starts	1st	2nd	3rd	Win & Pl
Career Total (Turf)	5	0	1	0	3204
Career Total (AW)	3	1	1	0	4271

77 3/09 Ling 1m4f STD £2729

Total win prize-money £2730

Going (Turf): Sf: 0-1 GS: 0-1 Gd: 0-1 GF: 0-2 Fm: 0-0
Distance: 5f/6f: 0-0 7f-8f: 0-1 **9f-13f: 1-7** 14f+: 0-0
Track : **LH: 1-4** RH: 0-4 **Tight: 1-3** Gall: 0-2
Aids: Bl: 0-0 Vi: 0-0 Tstrap: 0-0 Ckp: 0-0
Best Rating: **91** 5/09 Ling 1m4f stand

Useful; stays 1m4f; acts on Polytrack.

Sejanus

88(96) (81)**67**

2-y-o b g Dubai Destination (USA)-Agrippina (Timeless Times (USA))

K A Ryan Mrs Margaret Forsyth

Placings:65420120 (6805)

2009: 6^{6}S, 6^{5}GF, 6^{4}S, 7^{2}SD, 7^{0}G, 8^{1}SD, 8^{2}SD, 8^{0}SD,

	Starts	1st	2nd	3rd	Win & Pl
Career Total (Turf)	4	0	0	0	337
Career Total (AW)	4	1	2	0	5231

74 9/09 Wolv 1m141y STD £2914

Total win prize-money £2914

Going (Turf): Sf: 0-2 GS: 0-0 Gd: 0-1 GF: 0-1 Fm: 0-0
Distance: 5f/6f: 0-3 7f-8f: 0-2 **9f-13f: 1-3** 14f+: 0-0
Track : **LH: 1-5** RH: 0-1 **Tight: 1-3** Gall: 0-0
Aids: Bl: 0-0 Vi: 0-0 Tstrap: 0-0 Ckp: 0-0
Best Rating: **81** 10/09 Wolv 1m141y stand

Fair; effective over 7f-1m; acts on Fibresand and on Polytrack.

Seldom (IRE)

97(100) (68)**70**

3-y-o b g Sesaro (USA)-Daisy Dancer (IRE) (Distinctly North (USA))

M Brittain Mel Brittain

Placings:21030000F2 (7716)

2009: 6^{2}GF, 7^{1}GF, 5^{0}GS, 6^{3}GF, 7^{0}F, 7^{0}GF, 7^{0}GF, 7^{0}GF, 7^{F}GF, 7^{2}SD,

	Starts	1st	2nd	3rd	Win & Pl
Career Total (Turf)	9	1	1	1	4247
Career Total (AW)	1	0	1	0	705

68 4/09 Rdcr 7f G-F £2590

Total win prize-money £2590

Going (Turf): Sf: 0-0 GS: 0-1 Gd: 0-0 **GF: 1-7** Fm: 0-1
Distance: 5f/6f: 0-3 **7f-8f: 1-7** 9f-13f: 0-0 14f+: 0-0
Track : LH: 0-2 RH: 0-0 Tight: 0-2 Gall: 0-0
Aids: Bl: 0-0 Vi: 0-0 Tstrap: 0-0 Ckp: 0-0
Best Rating: **70** 5/09 Rdcr 6f gd-fm

Modest; stays 7f and acts on fast ground and on Polytrack.

Seldom Seen Kid (IRE)

85(77) (41)**45**

2-y-o ch c Captain Rio-North Cider Rose (IRE) (Goldmark (USA))

T D Easterby April Fools

Placings:00000 (4800)

2009: 6^{0}GS, 7^{0}SD, 6^{0}S, 7^{0}G, 6^{0}GF,

	Starts	1st	2nd	3rd	Win & Pl
Career Total (Turf)	4	0	0	0	
Career Total (AW)	1	0	0	0	

Going (Turf): Sf: 0-1 GS: 0-1 Gd: 0-1 GF: 0-1 Fm: 0-0
Distance: 5f/6f: 0-3 7f-8f: 0-2 9f-13f: 0-0 14f+: 0-0
Track : LH: 0-3 RH: 0-0 Tight: 0-2 Gall: 0-0
Aids: Bl: 0-1 Vi: 0-0 Tstrap: 0-0 Ckp: 0-0
Best Rating: **45** 7/09 Pont 6f soft

Select (IRE)

105 **101**

3-y-o ch f Choisir (AUS)-Intercession (Bluebird (USA))

P W Chapple-Hyam De La Warr Racing

Placings:620-10342 (4489)

2009: 6^{1}GF, 7^{0}GF, 7^{3}GF, 7^{4}G, 7^{2}G,

	Starts	1st	2nd	3rd	Win & Pl
Career Total (Turf)	8	1	2	1	31285

77 4/09 Pont 6f G-F £2914

Total win prize-money £2914

Going (Turf): Sf: 0-0 GS: 0-1 Gd: 0-2 **GF: 1-4** Fm: 0-1
Distance: **5f/6f: 1-3** 7f-8f: 0-5 9f-13f: 0-0 14f+: 0-0
Track : **LH: 1-2** RH: 0-2 Tight: 0-0 Gall: 0-0
Aids: Bl: 0-0 Vi: 0-0 Tstrap: 0-0 Ckp: 0-0
Best Rating: **101** 7/09 Gdwd 7f good

Very useful; runner-up in Listed company; effective over 6f; acts on fast ground.

Select Committee

107 **75**

4-y-o b g Fayruz-Demolition Jo (Petong)

J J Quinn Which Bits Mine Syndicate

Placings:32300/4000154322353-5432201051020 1 (6489)

2009: 5^{5}G, 5^{4}GS, 5^{3}GF, 5^{2}S, 5^{2}G, 5^{0}G, 5^{1}GF, 5^{0}GS, 5^{5}GS, 5^{1}GF, 5^{0}GF, 5^{2}G, 5^{0}GF, 5^{1}GF,

	Starts	1st	2nd	3rd	Win & Pl
Career Total (Turf)	32	4	6	6	22879

75 10/09 Rdcr 5f (0-75)H G-F £3238
72 8/09 Bevl 5f (0-75)H G-F £2849
68 7/09 Bevl 5f (0-75)H G-F £3238
63 6/08 Newc 5f (0-75)H SFT £4209

Total win prize-money £13534

Going (Turf): Sf: 1-9 GS: 0-8 Gd: 0-6 **GF: 3-9** Fm: 0-0
Distance: **5f/6f: 4-32** 7f-8f: 0-0 9f-13f: 0-0 14f+: 0-0
Track : LH: 0-4 RH: 0-0 Tight: 0-1 Gall: 0-0
Aids: Bl: 0-0 **Vi: 4-18** Tstrap: 0-5 Ckp: 0-5
Best Rating: **75** 10/09 Rdcr 5f gd-fm

Modest; effective over 5f; acts on fast and soft ground; has worn cheekpieces and a visor.

Selina Rio

75(78) (29)**21**

2-y-o ch f Captain Rio-Encanto (IRE) (Bahhare (USA))

L A Mullaney Bavill & White

Placings:0606060 (7501)

2009: 5^{0}GF, 5^{6}GF, 5^{0}G, 5^{6}GF, 5^{0}S, 6^{6}SD, 7^{0}SD,

	Starts	1st	2nd	3rd	Win & Pl
Career Total (Turf)	5	0	0	0	0
Career Total (AW)	2	0	0	0	0

Going (Turf): Sf: 0-1 GS: 0-0 Gd: 0-1 GF: 0-3 Fm: 0-0
Distance: 5f/6f: 0-6 7f-8f: 0-1 9f-13f: 0-0 14f+: 0-0
Track : LH: 0-3 RH: 0-0 Tight: 0-1 Gall: 0-0
Aids: Bl: 0-0 Vi: 0-0 Tstrap: 0-1 Ckp: 0-1
Best Rating: **29** 11/09 Sthl 6f stand

Semah Harold

(98) (68)**63**

4-y-o b g Beat All (USA)-Semah's Dream (Gunner B)

J R Holt (E S McMahon 23/1) J P Hames

Placings:13306/000460040660-56 (0277)

2009: 9^{5}SD, 7^{6}SD,

	Starts	1st	2nd	3rd	Win & Pl
Career Total (Turf)	9	0	0	1	1020
Career Total (AW)	10	1	0	1	3553

76 7/07 Wolv 7f32y STD £3071

Total win prize-money £3071

Going (Turf): Sf: 0-1 GS: 0-3 Gd: 0-2 GF: 0-3 Fm: 0-0
Distance: 5f/6f: 0-0 **7f-8f: 1-12** 9f-13f: 0-7 14f+: 0-0
Track : **LH: 1-12** RH: 0-3 **Tight: 1-8** Gall: 0-0
Aids: Bl: 0-3 Vi: 0-6 Tstrap: 0-0 Ckp: 0-0
Best Rating: **77** 8/07 Nott 1m54y good

Moderate; best at around 7f; acts on fast ground and Polytrack; has worn blinkers.

Semi Detached (IRE)

(96) (59)**63**

6-y-o b g Distant Music (USA)-Relankina (IRE) (Broken Hearted)

J W Unett Allen B Pope

Placings:320/65065/604550/465665-6 (0107)

2009: 12^{8}SD,

	Starts	1st	2nd	3rd	Win & Pl
Career Total (Turf)	9	0	1	1	2292
Career Total (AW)	12	0	0	0	0

Going (Turf): Sf: 0-1 GS: 0-3 Gd: 0-1 GF: 0-4 Fm: 0-0
Distance: 5f/6f: 0-0 7f-8f: 0-6 9f-13f: 0-15 14f+: 0-0

Track : LH: 0-15 RH: 0-4 Tight: 0-12 Gall: 0-0
Aids: Bl: 0-0 Vi: 0-0 Tstrap: 0-0 Ckp: 0-0
Best Rating: 75 10/05 NmkR 1m gd-sft

Seminal Moment

95(101) (60)49
3-y-o b f Sakhee (USA)-Thracian (Green Desert (USA))
J G Given Moonfleet Racing

Placings:00-04150600 (7642)
2009: 8[0]G, 13[4]G, 14[1]SD, 16[5]HY, 14[0]G, 16[6]SD, 12[0]SD, 14[0]SD,

	Starts	1st	2nd	3rd	Win & Pl
Career Total (Turf)	4	0	0	0	241
Career Total (AW)	6	1	0	0	3238

60 7/09 Sthl 1m6f (0-70)H STD £3238
Total win prize-money £3238

Going (Turf): Sf: 0-1 GS: 0-0 Gd: 0-3 GF: 0-0 Fm: 0-0
Distance: 5f/6f: 0-0 7f-8f: 0-2 9f-13f: 0-2 14f+: 1-6
Track : LH: 1-9 RH: 0-1 Tight: 0-2 Gall: 0-1
Aids: Bl: 0-0 Vi: 0-0 Tstrap: 0-0 Ckp: 0-0
Best Rating: 60 7/09 Sthl 1m6f stand

Moderate; stays 1m6f and should stay 2m; acts on good ground and on Fibresand.

Senate

(78) (42)
2-y-o ch c Pivotal-Sauterne (Rainbow Quest (USA))
J H M Gosden H R H Princess Haya Of Jordan

Placings:0 (7491)
2009: 8[0]SD,

	Starts	1st	2nd	3rd	Win & Pl
Career Total (Turf)	0	0	0	0	
Career Total (AW)	1	0	0	0	

Going (Turf): Sf: 0-0 GS: 0-0 Gd: 0-0 GF: 0-0 Fm: 0-0
Distance: 5f/6f: 0-0 7f-8f: 0-0 9f-13f: 0-1 14f+: 0-0
Track : LH: 0-1 RH: 0-0 Tight: 0-1 Gall: 0-0
Aids: Bl: 0-0 Vi: 0-0 Tstrap: 0-0 Ckp: 0-0
Best Rating: 42 11/09 Wolv 1m141y stand

Senate Majority

93(96) (53)59
2-y-o ch g Avonbridge-Benjarong (Sharpo)
T D Easterby The Senators

Placings:644500 (6068)
2009: 5[6]GF, 5[4]G, 5[4]G, 5[5]GS, 6[0]GS, 5[0]SD,

	Starts	1st	2nd	3rd	Win & Pl
Career Total (Turf)	5	0	0	0	529
Career Total (AW)	1	0	0	0	

Going (Turf): Sf: 0-0 GS: 0-2 Gd: 0-2 GF: 0-1 Fm: 0-0
Distance: 5f/6f: 0-5 7f-8f: 0-1 9f-13f: 0-0 14f+: 0-0
Track : LH: 0-1 RH: 0-0 Tight: 0-1 Gall: 0-0
Aids: Bl: 0-1 Vi: 0-0 Tstrap: 0-0 Ckp: 0-0
Best Rating: 59 8/09 Thsk 5f gd-sft

Sendali (FR)

97 57
5-y-o b g Daliapour (IRE)-Lady Senk (FR) (Pink (FR))
J D Bethell Elliott Brothers And Peacock

Placings:546/655060/0106265-1 (5734)
2009: 16[1]GS,

	Starts	1st	2nd	3rd	Win & Pl
Career Total (Turf)	17	2	1	0	7019

54 9/09 Newc 2m19y (0-65)H G-S £2849
57 6/08 Newc 2m19y (0-65)H G-S £2590
Total win prize-money £5439

Going (Turf): Sf: 0-3 GS: 2-5 Gd: 0-3 GF: 0-6 Fm: 0-0
Distance: 5f/6f: 0-0 7f-8f: 0-3 9f-13f: 0-4 14f+: 2-10
Track : LH: 2-12 RH: 0-4 Tight: 0-9 Gall: 2-5
Aids: Bl: 0-0 Vi: 0-0 Tstrap: 0-1 Ckp: 0-1
Best Rating: 69 8/06 Ches 7f2y good

Moderate; stays 2m; acts well in soft ground.

Sendreni (FR)

101(101) (79)76
5-y-o b g Night Shift (USA)-Sendana (FR) (Darshaan)
M Wigham G Swan

Placings:2/040/50012122-031000000 (7596)
2009: 7[0]SD, 6[3]SD, 7[1]G, 7[0]GS, 7[0]SD, 7[0]SD, 7[0]SD, 7[0]SD, 7[0]SD,

	Starts	1st	2nd	3rd	Win & Pl
Career Total (Turf)	7	2	1	0	9476
Career Total (AW)	14	1	3	1	5406

76 3/09 Folk 7f (0-75)H GD £3070
72 10/08 Brig 6f209y (0-70)H GD £3108
70 9/08 Wolv 7f32y (0-55)H STD £2388
Total win prize-money £8567

Going (Turf): Sf: 0-1 GS: 0-2 Gd: 2-2 GF: 0-0 Fm: 0-0
Distance: 5f/6f: 0-1 7f-8f: 3-16 9f-13f: 0-4 14f+: 0-0
Track : LH: 2-12 RH: 0-3 Tight: 1-10 Gall: 0-1
Aids: Bl: 0-0 Vi: 0-0 Tstrap: 0-0 Ckp: 0-0
Best Rating: 79 12/08 Wolv 7f32y stand

Modest; effective over 7f; acts on good ground and on Polytrack; has worn a tongue tie.

Seneschal

102(106) (74)81
8-y-o b g Polar Falcon (USA)-Broughton Singer (IRE) (Common Grounds)
A B Haynes P Cook

Placings:21/00000516261/020000600363/66520560002 40/001030302106000511600/4104525003410540-62101146302606 (5566)
2009: 8[6]SD, 7[2]SD, 7[1]G, 7[0]GF, 6[1]F, 6[1]F, 7[4]G, 7[6]G, 7[3]F, 7[0]G, 7[2]GS, 6[6]F, 7[0]G, 5[6]F,

	Starts	1st	2nd	3rd	Win & Pl
Career Total (Turf)	55	9	4	1	38223
Career Total (AW)	36	3	5	5	13516

81 5/09 Sals 6f212y (0-70)H FRM £3238
78 5/09 Brig 6f209y FRM £1942
72 4/09 Yarm 7f3y (0-65)H GD £2201
71 8/08 Brig 6f209y G-S £1942
74 1/08 Kemp 1m (0-65)H STD £2047
71 10/07 Yarm 7f3y (0-65)H SFT £3238
68 10/07 Ling 1m (0-65)H STD £3071
71 5/07 Chep 1m14y (0-65)H G-F £2266
73 2/07 Ling 7f STD £2184
89 10/04 Donc 7f (0-92)H SFT £6839
79 10/04 Newc 7f (0-70)H GD £5426
93 4/03 Wind 5f10y D G-F £4108
Total win prize-money £38508

Going (Turf): Sf: 2-10GS: 1-12Gd: 2-14GF: 2-14 Fm: 2-5
Distance: 5f/6f: 1-18 7f-8f:10-61 9f-13f: 1-12 14f+: 0-0
Track : LH: 4-46 RH: 1-21 Tight: 2-32 Gall: 1-4
Aids: Bl: 0-0 Vi: 0-0 Tstrap: 0-1 Ckp: 0-1
Best Rating: 93 4/03 Wind 5f10y gd-fm

Modest; effective at around 7f-1m; acts on most ground and on Polytrack.

Senor Berti

81 73
3-y-o b g Bertolini (USA)-Pewter Lass (Dowsing (USA))
B Smart A Turton & S Brown

Placings:5631-6 (2917)
2009: 7[6]GF,

	Starts	1st	2nd	3rd	Win & Pl
Career Total (Turf)	5	1	0	1	2871

73 10/08 Catt 7f G-S £2047
Total win prize-money £2047

Going (Turf): Sf: 0-0 GS: 1-2 Gd: 0-1 GF: 0-2 Fm: 0-0
Distance: 5f/6f: 0-2 7f-8f: 1-3 9f-13f: 0-0 14f+: 0-0
Track : LH: 1-1 RH: 0-0 Tight: 1-1 Gall: 0-0
Aids: Bl: 0-0 Vi: 0-0 Tstrap: 0-0 Ckp: 0-0
Best Rating: 73 10/08 Catt 7f gd-sft

Fair; effective over 6f-7f; acts on fast and easy ground.

Senora Verde

65(77) (35)37
3-y-o ch f Bahamian Bounty-Spain (Polar Falcon (USA))
P T Midgley C R Green

Placings:000630-000 (1084)
2009: 6[0]SS, 5[0]SD, 5[0]GF,

	Starts	1st	2nd	3rd	Win & Pl
Career Total (Turf)	5	0	0	1	302
Career Total (AW)	4	0	0	0	

Going (Turf): Sf: 0-0 GS: 0-0 Gd: 0-1 GF: 0-4 Fm: 0-0
Distance: 5f/6f: 0-8 7f-8f: 0-1 9f-13f: 0-0 14f+: 0-0
Track : LH: 0-5 RH: 0-0 Tight: 0-1 Gall: 0-0
Aids: Bl: 0-0 Vi: 0-0 Tstrap: 0-2 Ckp: 0-2
Best Rating: 37 8/08 Rdcr 6f good

Sensacion Sensual

23(85) (43)58
3-y-o b f Josr Algarhoud (IRE)-Charlie Girl (Puissance)
J G Given Danethorpe Racing Partnership

Placings:300-0 (1173)
2009: 6[0]GF,

	Starts	1st	2nd	3rd	Win & Pl
Career Total (Turf)	3	0	0	1	482
Career Total (AW)	1	0	0	0	

Going (Turf): Sf: 0-0 GS: 0-1 Gd: 0-1 GF: 0-1 Fm: 0-0
Distance: 5f/6f: 0-3 7f-8f: 0-1 9f-13f: 0-0 14f+: 0-0
Track : LH: 0-2 RH: 0-0 Tight: 0-0 Gall: 0-1
Aids: Bl: 0-0 Vi: 0-0 Tstrap: 0-0 Ckp: 0-0
Best Rating: 58 8/08 Nott 6f15y good

Senses (USA)

103(92) (73)82
3-y-o ch c Rahy (USA)-Sweet And Steady (USA) (Steady Growth (CAN))
J Noseda Sir Robert Ogden

Placings:6214513 (6483)
2009: 8[6]SD, 10[2]GF, 10[1]GF, 10[4]G, 12[5]G, 10[1]GF, 12[3]GF,

	Starts	1st	2nd	3rd	Win & Pl
Career Total (Turf)	6	2	1	1	11424
Career Total (AW)	1	0	0	0	0

82 9/09 Sand 1m2f7y (0-85)H G-F £4857

79 6/09 Sand 1m2f7y G-F £3238
Total win prize-money £8095

Going (Turf): Sf: 0-0 GS: 0-0 Gd: 0-2 **GF: 2-4** Fm: 0-0
Distance: 5f/6f: 0-0 7f-8f: 0-1 **9f-13f: 2-6** 14f+: 0-0
Track : LH: 0-0 **RH: 2-6** Tight: 0-0 Gall: 0-2
Aids: Bl: 0-0 Vi: 0-1 Tstrap: 0-0 Ckp: 0-0
Best Rating: 82 10/09 NmkR 1m4f gd-fm

Useful; stays 1m2f; acts on fast ground and on Polytrack.

Sent From Heaven (IRE)

105(96) (80)**105**
2-y-o b f Footstepsinthesand-Crystal Valkyrie (IRE) (Danehill (USA))
B W Hills Triermore Stud

Placings:1314 **(6269)**
2009: 7^{1}SD, 7^{3}G, 7^{1}G, 8^{4}G,

	Starts	1st	2nd	3rd	Win & Pl
Career Total (Turf)	**3**	**1**	**0**	**1**	**45477**
Career Total (AW)	**1**	**1**	**0**	**0**	**5019**

103 8/09 Gdwd 7f GD £28385
80 7/09 Kemp 7f STD £5018
Total win prize-money £33404

Going (Turf): Sf: 0-0 GS: 0-0 **Gd: 1-3** GF: 0-0 Fm: 0-0
Distance: 5f/6f: 0-0 **7f-8f: 2-4** 9f-13f: 0-0 14f+: 0-0
Track : LH: 0-0 **RH: 2-3** Tight: 0-0 Gall: 0-1
Aids: Bl: 0-0 Vi: 0-0 Tstrap: 0-0 Ckp: 0-0
Best Rating: 105 9/09 Asct 1m good

Smart; won the Group 3 Prestige Stakes in 2009; stays 7f; acts on good ground; goes on Polytrack.

Septemberintherain

69(88) (72)**52**
2-y-o gr c Verglas (IRE)-Gwyneth (Zafonic (USA))
T G Mills J Humphreys, T G Mills, Mrs S Ecclestone

Placings:04 **(7390)**
2009: 7^{0}G, 8^{4}SD,

	Starts	1st	2nd	3rd	Win & Pl
Career Total (Turf)	**1**	**0**	**0**	**0**	
Career Total (AW)	**1**	**0**	**0**	**0**	**0**

Going (Turf): Sf: 0-0 GS: 0-0 Gd: 0-1 GF: 0-0 Fm: 0-0
Distance: 5f/6f: 0-0 7f-8f: 0-2 9f-13f: 0-0 14f+: 0-0
Track : LH: 0-1 RH: 0-1 Tight: 0-1 Gall: 0-0
Aids: Bl: 0-0 Vi: 0-0 Tstrap: 0-0 Ckp: 0-0
Best Rating: 72 11/09 Ling 1m stand

Sequillo

105(104) (85)**85**
3-y-o b g Lucky Story (USA)-Tranquillity (Night Shift (USA))
R Hannon White Beech Farm

Placings:00410-0411223430 **(6996)**
2009: 8^{0}SD, 9^{4}G, 10^{1}GF, 9^{1}GF, 10^{2}GS, 10^{2}G, 8^{3}SD, 10^{4}GF, 10^{3}GF, 10^{0}GS,

	Starts	1st	2nd	3rd	Win & Pl
Career Total (Turf)	**12**	**3**	**2**	**1**	**17608**
Career Total (AW)	**3**	**0**	**0**	**1**	**2799**

79 7/09 Folk 1m1f149y (0-85)H G-F £4727
77 6/09 Wind 1m2f7y (0-75)H G-F £3070
72 9/08 Wind 1m67y (0-85) G-F £3885
Total win prize-money £11684

Going (Turf): Sf: 0-1 GS: 0-3 Gd: 0-3 **GF: 3-5** Fm: 0-0
Distance: 5f/6f: 0-0 7f-8f: 0-6 **9f-13f: 3-9** 14f+: 0-0
Track : LH: 0-4 **RH: 3-10 Tight: 3-5** Gall: 0-2
Aids: Bl: 0-0 Vi: 0-0 Tstrap: 0-0 Ckp: 0-0
Best Rating: 85 9/09 Kemp 1m stand

Useful; stays 1m2f; acts on fast ground and on Polytrack.

Seradim

104 (97)**95**
3-y-o ch f Elnadim (USA)-Seren Devious (Dr Devious (IRE))
P F I Cole The Fairy Story Partnership

Placings:410341-035464 **(5175)**
2009: 8^{0}GF, 8^{3}GS, 8^{5}S, 7^{4}GF, 8^{6}G, 8^{4}GF,

	Starts	1st	2nd	3rd	Win & Pl
Career Total (Turf)	**11**	**1**	**0**	**2**	**20881**
Career Total (AW)	**1**	**1**	**0**	**0**	**12500**

97 12/08 Deau 7f110y STD £12500
73 8/08 Rdcr 7f G-S £3561
Total win prize-money £16062

Going (Turf): Sf: 0-2 **GS: 1-3** Gd: 0-2 GF: 0-4 Fm: 0-0
Distance: 5f/6f: 0-2 **7f-8f: 2-9** 9f-13f: 0-1 14f+: 0-0
Track : LH: 0-4 RH: 0-2 Tight: 0-0 Gall: 0-2
Aids: Bl: 0-1 Vi: 0-0 Tstrap: 0-0 Ckp: 0-0
Best Rating: 97 12/08 Deau 7f110y stand

Very useful; Listed placed; effective over 6f-1m; acts on good and easier ground; handles Polytrack; has worn blinkers.

Serafina's Flight

89(95) (72)**67**
2-y-o b f Fantastic Light (USA)-Seven Of Nine (IRE) (Alzao (USA))
W R Muir M J Caddy

Placings:432 **(6638)**
2009: 6^{4}S, 8^{3}SD, 7^{2}SD,

	Starts	1st	2nd	3rd	Win & Pl
Career Total (Turf)	**1**	**0**	**0**	**0**	**457**
Career Total (AW)	**2**	**0**	**1**	**1**	**907**

Going (Turf): Sf: 0-1 GS: 0-0 Gd: 0-0 GF: 0-0 Fm: 0-0
Distance: 5f/6f: 0-0 7f-8f: 0-3 9f-13f: 0-0 14f+: 0-0
Track : LH: 0-1 RH: 0-1 Tight: 0-1 Gall: 0-0
Aids: Bl: 0-0 Vi: 0-0 Tstrap: 0-0 Ckp: 0-0
Best Rating: 72 10/09 Wolv 7f32y stand

Fair; stays 7f and acts on Polytrack.

Seren Arian

75(70) (8)**2**
3-y-o r f Dreams End-Westfield Mist (Scallywag)
B Palling Bryn Palling

Placings:000 **(7596)**
2009: 10^{0}G, 9^{0}SD, 7^{0}SD,

	Starts	1st	2nd	3rd	Win & Pl
Career Total (Turf)	**1**	**0**	**0**	**0**	
Career Total (AW)	**2**	**0**	**0**	**0**	

Going (Turf): Sf: 0-0 GS: 0-0 Gd: 0-1 GF: 0-0 Fm: 0-0
Distance: 5f/6f: 0-0 7f-8f: 0-1 9f-13f: 0-2 14f+: 0-0
Track : LH: 0-3 RH: 0-0 Tight: 0-3 Gall: 0-0
Aids: Bl: 0-0 Vi: 0-0 Tstrap: 0-0 Ckp: 0-0
Best Rating: 8 11/09 Wolv 1m1f103y stand

Sereth (IRE)

109 **103**
6-y-o b g Monsun (GER)-Saderlina (IRE) (Sadler's Wells (USA))
B J Curley P Byrne

Placings:021/3411/5151-000053 **(6851)**
2009: 12^{0}S, 12^{0}GF, 14^{0}GF, 12^{0}GF, 12^{5}GS, 18^{3}G,

	Starts	1st	2nd	3rd	Win & Pl
Career Total (Turf)	**17**	**5**	**1**	**2**	**60124**

103 6/08 Muni 1m6f GD £8824
5/08 Dort 1m6f GD £11029
10/07 Muni 1m3f SFT £18243
9/07 Colo 1m4f H GD £2702
10/06 Badn 1m3f SFT £2896
Total win prize-money £43696

Going (Turf): Sf: 2-6 GS: 0-1 **Gd: 3-7** GF: 0-3 Fm: 0-0
Distance: 5f/6f: 0-0 7f-8f: 0-0 **9f-13f: 3-12** 14f+: 2-5
Track : LH: 0-2 **RH: 1-7** Tight: 0-0 Gall: 0-6
Aids: Bl: 0-0 Vi: 0-0 Tstrap: 0-0 Ckp: 0-0
Best Rating: 103 6/08 Muni 1m6f good

Useful; ex-German-trained; Listed winner; stays 2m2f; acts on good or softer ground.

Sergeant Pink (IRE)

95(88) (57)**70**
3-y-o b c Fasliyev (USA)-Ring Pink (USA) (Bering)
S Gollings P J Martin

Placings:51000-346 **(7084)**
2009: 10^{3}HY, 11^{4}GS, 15^{6}S,

	Starts	1st	2nd	3rd	Win & Pl
Career Total (Turf)	**7**	**1**	**0**	**1**	**4391**
Career Total (AW)	**1**	**0**	**0**	**0**	**0**

70 8/08 Bevl 1m100y SFT £3668
Total win prize-money £3669

Going (Turf): Sf: 1-5 GS: 0-2 Gd: 0-0 GF: 0-0 Fm: 0-0
Distance: 5f/6f: 0-0 7f-8f: 0-2 **9f-13f: 1-5** 14f+: 0-1
Track : LH: 0-6 **RH: 1-1** Tight: 0-3 Gall: 0-0
Aids: Bl: 0-0 Vi: 0-0 Tstrap: 0-0 Ckp: 0-0
Best Rating: 70 8/08 Bevl 1m100y soft

Fair; effective over 1m; acts on soft ground.

Sergeant Sharpe

(93) (64)**65**
4-y-o ch g Cadeaux Genereux-Halcyon Daze (Halling (USA))
H J Evans Battlefield Brook Racing

Placings:046/63340-**50** **(0918)**
2009: 12^{5}SD, 11^{0}SD,

	Starts	1st	2nd	3rd	Win & Pl
Career Total (Turf)	**7**	**0**	**0**	**1**	**927**
Career Total (AW)	**3**	**0**	**0**	**1**	**353**

Going (Turf): Sf: 0-1 GS: 0-1 Gd: 0-1 GF: 0-4 Fm: 0-0
Distance: 5f/6f: 0-0 7f-8f: 0-3 9f-13f: 0-7 14f+: 0-0
Track : LH: 0-5 RH: 0-2 Tight: 0-5 Gall: 0-1
Aids: Bl: 0-1 Vi: 0-0 Tstrap: 0-0 Ckp: 0-0
Best Rating: 65 9/07 Ches 7f2y gd-fm

Modest; effective at around 1m4f; acts on fast ground.

Serhaal (IRE)

82(87) (65)68

2-y-o b c Green Desert (USA)-Lucky For Me (USA) (King Of Kings (IRE))

Sir Michael Stoute Hamdan Al Maktoum

Placings:20 (6781)

2009: 6^{2}G, 7^{0}SS,

	Starts	1st	2nd	3rd	Win & Pl
Career Total (Turf)	1	0	1	0	1246
Career Total (AW)	1	0	0	0	

Going (Turf): Sf: 0-0 GS: 0-0 Gd: 0-1 GF: 0-0 Fm: 0-0
Distance: 5f/6f: 0-0 7f-8f: 0-2 9f-13f: 0-0 14f+: 0-0
Track : LH: 0-1 RH: 0-0 Tight: 0-1 Gall: 0-0
Aids: Bl: 0-0 Vi: 0-0 Tstrap: 0-0 Ckp: 0-0
Best Rating: 68 8/09 Yarm 6f3y good

Serious Attitude (IRE)

113 113

3-y-o b f Mtoto-Zameyla (IRE) (Cape Cross (IRE))

Rae Guest Derek J Willis & Rae Guest

Placings:111-010 (4837a)

2009: 8^{0}GF, 6^{1}G, 6^{0}GS,

	Starts	1st	2nd	3rd	Win & Pl
Career Total (Turf)	6	4	0	0	196315

113 7/09 York 6f GD £38519
110 10/08 NmkR 6f G-F £134970
105 9/08 Sals 6f GD £20437
80 8/08 Wind 6f G-S £2388
Total win prize-money £196315

Going (Turf): Sf: 0-0 GS: 1-2 **Gd: 2-2** GF: 1-2 Fm: 0-0
Distance: **5f/6f: 4-4** 7f-8f: 0-2 9f-13f: 0-0 14f+: 0-0
Track : LH: 0-0 RH: 0-1 Tight: 0-0 **Gall: 1-1**
Aids: Bl: 0-0 Vi: 0-0 Tstrap: 0-0 Ckp: 0-0
Best Rating: 113 7/09 York 6f good

High class; winner of the Group 1 Cheveley Park Stakes at two and successful at Group 3 level at three; best over 6f and acts on most ground.

Serious Choice (IRE)

105(94) (59)83

4-y-o b g Choisir (AUS)-Printaniere (USA) (Sovereign Dancer (USA))

P J Hobbs (J R Boyle 8/7) The Serious Choice Partnership

Placings:000/010025-1000 (3734)

2009: 10^{1}G, 10^{0}GF, 14^{0}G, 11^{0}SD,

	Starts	1st	2nd	3rd	Win & Pl
Career Total (Turf)	10	2	1	0	8453
Career Total (AW)	3	0	0	0	

83 4/09 Yarm 1m2f21y (0-85)H GD £5828
73 6/08 Yarm 1m3y (0-65)H G-F £1813
Total win prize-money £7641

Going (Turf): Sf: 0-4 GS: 0-1 **Gd: 1-2 GF: 1-3** Fm: 0-0
Distance: 5f/6f: 0-1 7f-8f: 0-3 **9f-13f: 2-8** 14f+: 0-1
Track : **LH: 1-4** RH: 0-5 **Tight: 1-2** Gall: 0-2
Aids: Bl: 0-0 Vi: 0-0 Tstrap: 0-0 Ckp: 0-0
Best Rating: 83 4/09 Yarm 1m2f21y good

Fair; effective at around 1m2f and acts on most ground.

Serious Drinking (USA)

90(92) (62)66

3-y-o b f Successful Appeal (USA)-Cup Match (USA) (Kingmambo (USA))

W R Swinburn Andrew Gemmell

Placings:43 (6741)

2009: 7^{4}SD, 8^{3}GS,

	Starts	1st	2nd	3rd	Win & Pl
Career Total (Turf)	1	0	0	1	403
Career Total (AW)	1	0	0	0	241

Going (Turf): Sf: 0-0 GS: 0-1 Gd: 0-0 GF: 0-0 Fm: 0-0
Distance: 5f/6f: 0-0 7f-8f: 0-1 9f-13f: 0-1 14f+: 0-0
Track : LH: 0-1 RH: 0-1 Tight: 0-2 Gall: 0-0
Aids: Bl: 0-0 Vi: 0-0 Tstrap: 0-0 Ckp: 0-0
Best Rating: 66 10/09 Wind 1m67y gd-sft

Modest; stays 1m; acts on easy ground.

Serious Impact (USA)

104 89

4-y-o b g Empire Maker (USA)-Diese (USA) (Diesis)

J H M Gosden K Abdulla

Placings:0-136 (5321)

2009: 9^{1}GF, 12^{3}GF, 10^{6}GF,

	Starts	1st	2nd	3rd	Win & Pl
Career Total (Turf)	4	1	0	1	4297

79 4/09 Leic 1m1f218y G-F £3238
Total win prize-money £3238

Going (Turf): Sf: 0-0 GS: 0-0 Gd: 0-0 **GF: 1-4** Fm: 0-0
Distance: 5f/6f: 0-0 7f-8f: 0-0 **9f-13f: 1-4** 14f+: 0-0
Track : LH: 0-1 **RH: 1-3** Tight: 0-1 Gall: 0-1
Aids: Bl: 0-0 Vi: 0-0 Tstrap: 0-0 Ckp: 0-0
Best Rating: 89 5/09 York 1m4f gd-fm

Useful; stays 1m4f; acts on fast ground.

Serious Spirit

57

2-y-o b f Pastoral Pursuits-Motto (FR) (Mtoto)

Rae Guest Derek J Willis, Tom Murray & Rae Guest

Placings:0 (6620)

2009: 8^{0}G,

	Starts	1st	2nd	3rd	Win & Pl
Career Total (Turf)	1	0	0	0	

Going (Turf): Sf: 0-0 GS: 0-0 Gd: 0-1 GF: 0-0 Fm: 0-0
Distance: 5f/6f: 0-0 7f-8f: 0-1 9f-13f: 0-0 14f+: 0-0
Track : LH: 0-0 RH: 0-0 Tight: 0-0 Gall: 0-0
Aids: Bl: 0-0 Vi: 0-0 Tstrap: 0-0 Ckp: 0-0

Sermons Mount (USA)

96(98) (66)56

3-y-o b/br g Vicar (USA)-Ginny Auxier (USA) (Racing Star (USA))

Mouse Hamilton-Fairley Fairley Risky

Placings:00-4000252052222 (7052)

2009: 8^{4}SD, 10^{0}G, 7^{0}GF, 8^{0}SD, 6^{2}F, 6^{5}G, 7^{2}F, 6^{0}GS, 6^{5}GF, 7^{2}SD, 7^{2}SD, 7^{2}SD, 7^{2}SD,

	Starts	1st	2nd	3rd	Win & Pl
Career Total (Turf)	8	0	2	0	1298
Career Total (AW)	7	0	4	0	2777

Going (Turf): Sf: 0-0 GS: 0-2 Gd: 0-2 GF: 0-2 Fm: 0-2
Distance: 5f/6f: 0-1 7f-8f: 0-12 9f-13f: 0-2 14f+: 0-0
Track : LH: 0-5 RH: 0-5 Tight: 0-3 Gall: 0-0
Aids: Bl: 0-0 Vi: 0-0 Tstrap: 0-3 Ckp: 0-3
Best Rating: 66 10/09 Kemp 7f stand

Moderate; effective over 7f; acts on fast ground; goes on Polytrack; has worn cheekpieces.

Serva Jugum (USA)

111(94) (86)110

3-y-o b/br c Fusaichi Pegasus (USA)-Shake The Yoke (Caerleon (USA))

P F I Cole Mrs Fitri Hay

Placings:10-420 (6198a)

2009: 10^{4}GF, 10^{2}G, 12^{0}G,

	Starts	1st	2nd	3rd	Win & Pl
Career Total (Turf)	4	0	1	0	8424
Career Total (AW)	1	1	0	0	6854

86 10/08 Kemp 1m STD £6854
Total win prize-money £6854

Going (Turf): Sf: 0-1 GS: 0-0 Gd: 0-2 GF: 0-1 Fm: 0-0
Distance: 5f/6f: 0-0 **7f-8f: 1-2** 9f-13f: 0-3 14f+: 0-0
Track : LH: 0-2 **RH: 1-3** Tight: 0-1 Gall: 0-1
Aids: Bl: 0-0 Vi: 0-0 Tstrap: 0-0 Ckp: 0-0
Best Rating: 110 8/09 Wind 1m2f7y gd-fm

Smart; stays 1m2f; acts on Polytrack and fast turf.

Servetius (USA)

(79) (52)

2-y-o b c Eurosilver (USA)-Golden Envoy (USA) (Dayjur (USA))

G A Butler Miss R Al-Attiya

Placings:40 (6493)

2009: 5^{4}SD, 5^{0}SF,

	Starts	1st	2nd	3rd	Win & Pl
Career Total (Turf)	0	0	0	0	
Career Total (AW)	2	0	0	0	265

Going (Turf): Sf: 0-0 GS: 0-0 Gd: 0-0 GF: 0-0 Fm: 0-0
Distance: 5f/6f: 0-2 7f-8f: 0-0 9f-13f: 0-0 14f+: 0-0
Track : LH: 0-2 RH: 0-0 Tight: 0-2 Gall: 0-0
Aids: Bl: 0-0 Vi: 0-0 Tstrap: 0-0 Ckp: 0-0
Best Rating: 52 9/09 Wolv 5f216y stand

Servoca (CAN)

109(108) (99)98

3-y-o gr c El Prado (IRE)-Cinderellaslipper (USA) (Touch Gold (USA))

Mike Murphy (B W Hills 23/10) Nick & Shona McLeod-Clarke & M Murphy

Placings:2203222-132020056212 (7227)

2009: 5^{1}SD, 6^{3}GF, 6^{2}F, 5^{0}GS, 6^{2}GF, 7^{0}GS, 6^{0}G, 6^{5}GF, 6^{6}G, 5^{2}GS, 6^{1}G, 6^{2}SD,

	Starts	1st	2nd	3rd	Win & Pl
Career Total (Turf)	16	1	7	2	29027
Career Total (AW)	3	1	2	0	6334

98 10/09 Donc 6f (0-105)H GD £11656
90 3/09 Wolv 5f216y STD £2590
Total win prize-money £14247

Going (Turf): Sf: 0-0 GS: 0-4 **Gd: 1-5** GF: 0-6 Fm: 0-1
Distance: **5f/6f: 2-16** 7f-8f: 0-3 9f-13f: 0-0 14f+: 0-0
Track : **LH: 1-2** RH: 0-2 **Tight: 1-1** Gall: 0-1
Aids: Bl: 0-0 Vi: 0-0 Tstrap: 0-0 Ckp: 0-0
Best Rating: **99** 11/09 Kemp 6f stand

Useful; effective over 5f-7f; acts on most ground and on Polytrack; has worn a tongue tie.

Sesenta (IRE)

109 **102**
5-y-o b m King's Theatre (IRE)-Cincuenta (IRE) (Bob Back (USA))
W P Mullins M Carroll

Placings:0552150/213-12016 **(5796)**
2009: 12^{1}HY, 20^{2}GF, 12^{0}SH, 14^{1}GF, 14^{6}G,

	Starts	1st	2nd	3rd	Win & Pl
Career Total (Turf)	15	4	3	1	200212

102	8/09	York	1m6f	H	G-F £130851
89	5/09	Curr	1m4f	H	HVY £41082
82	8/08	Baln	2m	(50-80)H	Y-S £6605
72	10/07	Tram	1m4f		GD £3968

Total win prize-money £182508

Going (Turf): **Sf: 1-3** GS: 0-0 **Gd: 1-5 GF: 1-4** Fm: 0-0
Distance: 5f/6f: 0-0 7f-8f: 0-0 9f-13f: 2-9 14f+: 2-6
Track : LH: 1-6 **RH: 3-9** Tight: 0-0 **Gall: 1-3**
Aids: Bl: 0-0 Vi: 0-0 Tstrap: 0-0 Ckp: 0-0
Best Rating: **102** 8/09 York 1m6f gd-fm

Very useful; winner of 2009 Ebor; effective from 1m6f-2m4f; acts on most ground; winning hurdler.

Sestet

(97) (54)**46**
4-y-o b f Golden Snake (USA)-Sestina (FR) (Bering)
S Dow S Dow

Placings:02-50354 **(7666)**
2009: 11^{5}SD, 10^{0}SD, 10^{3}SD, 10^{5}SD, 10^{4}SD,

	Starts	1st	2nd	3rd	Win & Pl
Career Total (Turf)	1	0	0	0	
Career Total (AW)	6	0	1	1	1266

Going (Turf): **Sf: 0-0 GS: 0-0 Gd: 0-1 GF: 0-0 Fm: 0-0**
Distance: 5f/6f: 0-0 7f-8f: 0-0 9f-13f: 0-7 14f+: 0-0
Track : LH: 0-1 RH: 0-6 Tight: 0-2 Gall: 0-0
Aids: Bl: 0-0 Vi: 0-0 Tstrap: 0-0 Ckp: 0-0
Best Rating: **54** 9/09 Kemp 1m2f stand

Moderate; stays 1m2f; acts on Polytrack.

Set Back

90 **53**
2-y-o b g Reset (AUS)-No Comebacks (Last Tycoon)
D Nicholls D W Barker

Placings:400 **(7289)**
2009: 5^{4}G, 6^{0}GF, 6^{0}S,

	Starts	1st	2nd	3rd	Win & Pl
Career Total (Turf)	3	0	0	0	313

Going (Turf): **Sf: 0-1 GS: 0-0 Gd: 0-1 GF: 0-1 Fm: 0-0**
Distance: 5f/6f: 0-3 7f-8f: 0-0 9f-13f: 0-0 14f+: 0-0
Track : LH: 0-1 RH: 0-0 Tight: 0-0 Gall: 0-0
Aids: Bl: 0-0 Vi: 0-0 Tstrap: 0-0 Ckp: 0-0
Best Rating: **53** 11/09 Donc 6f soft

Set Em Up Mo

(89) (54)
3-y-o b f Reset (AUS)-Mo Stopher (Sharpo)
M J Attwater Canisbay Bloodstock

Placings:00-0000050 **(7882)**
2009: 7^{0}SD, 7^{0}SD, 7^{0}SD, 8^{0}SD, 12^{0}SD, 10^{5}SD, 10^{0}SD,

	Starts	1st	2nd	3rd	Win & Pl
Career Total (Turf)	0	0	0	0	
Career Total (AW)	9	0	0	0	0

Going (Turf): **Sf: 0-0 GS: 0-0 Gd: 0-0 GF: 0-0 Fm: 0-0**
Distance: 5f/6f: 0-1 7f-8f: 0-5 9f-13f: 0-3 14f+: 0-0
Track : LH: 0-5 RH: 0-4 Tight: 0-5 Gall: 0-0
Aids: Bl: 0-0 Vi: 0-3 Tstrap: 0-1 Ckp: 0-1
Best Rating: **54** 12/08 Ling 7f stand

Set In Ice

80(75) (37)**41**
2-y-o b g Reset (AUS)-Masrora (USA) (Woodman (USA))
Mark Gillard Miss Kay Russell

Placings:060000 **(7644)**
2009: 5^{0}G, 8^{6}GF, 8^{0}GF, 8^{0}G, 8^{0}SD, 7^{0}SD,

	Starts	1st	2nd	3rd	Win & Pl
Career Total (Turf)	4	0	0	0	0
Career Total (AW)	2	0	0	0	

Going (Turf): **Sf: 0-0 GS: 0-0 Gd: 0-2 GF: 0-2 Fm: 0-0**
Distance: 5f/6f: 0-1 7f-8f: 0-2 9f-13f: 0-3 14f+: 0-0
Track : LH: 0-4 RH: 0-2 Tight: 0-4 Gall: 0-1
Aids: Bl: 0-0 Vi: 0-0 Tstrap: 0-0 Ckp: 0-0
Best Rating: **41** 10/09 Bath 1m5y good

Set Sail (IRE)

110 **108**
3-y-o ch c Danehill Dancer (IRE)-Ahdaab (USA) (Rahy (USA))
A P O'Brien D Smith, Mrs J Magnier, M Tabor

Placings:6104-400023000 **(6850)**
2009: 8^{4}GS, 10^{0}G, 8^{0}GF, 10^{0}G, 10^{2}S, 10^{3}GF, 10^{0}GY, 12^{0}G, 10^{0}G,

	Starts	1st	2nd	3rd	Win & Pl
Career Total (Turf)	13	1	1	1	95203

81 5/08 Gowr 7f G-F £8637
Total win prize-money £8638

Going (Turf): Sf: 0-2 GS: 0-1 Gd: 0-5 **GF: 1-4** Fm: 0-0
Distance: 5f/6f: 0-0 **7f-8f: 1-6** 9f-13f: 0-7 14f+: 0-0
Track : LH: 0-2 **RH: 1-8** Tight: 0-0 Gall: 0-2
Aids: Bl: 0-0 Vi: 0-0 Tstrap: 0-0 Ckp: 0-0
Best Rating: **108** 4/09 Lonc 1m gd-sft

Smart; stays 1m2f; acts on good and faster ground; sometimes used as a pacemaker.

Set The Trend

104(110) (100)**96**
3-y-o b/br c Reset (AUS)-Masrora (USA) (Woodman (USA))
A M Balding Favourites Racing XXII

Placings:1312200 **(5663)**
2009: 7^{1}SD, 7^{3}SD, 8^{1}SD, 8^{2}HY, 8^{2}SD, 9^{0}G, 8^{0}SD,

	Starts	1st	2nd	3rd	Win & Pl
Career Total (Turf)	2	0	1	0	15861
Career Total (AW)	5	2	1	1	10492

94	4/09	Kemp	1m	(0-80)H	STD £4727
77	2/09	Ling	7f		STD £2729

Total win prize-money £7457

Going (Turf): **Sf: 0-1 GS: 0-0 Gd: 0-1 GF: 0-0 Fm: 0-0**
Distance: 5f/6f: 0-0 **7f-8f: 2-5** 9f-13f: 0-2 14f+: 0-0
Track : LH: 1-3 RH: 1-4 **Tight: 1-3** Gall: 0-0
Aids: Bl: 0-0 Vi: 0-0 Tstrap: 0-0 Ckp: 0-0
Best Rating: **100** 9/09 Kemp 1m stand

Very useful; effective over 1m; acts on heavy ground and on Polytrack.

Set To Go

74(83) (59)**36**
2-y-o b g Reset (AUS)-Golubitsa (IRE) (Bluebird (USA))
H J L Dunlop Hart Royal Partnership

Placings:0000 **(7235)**
2009: 8^{0}SD, 8^{0}S, 7^{0}SD, 8^{0}SD,

	Starts	1st	2nd	3rd	Win & Pl
Career Total (Turf)	1	0	0	0	
Career Total (AW)	3	0	0	0	

Going (Turf): **Sf: 0-1 GS: 0-0 Gd: 0-0 GF: 0-0 Fm: 0-0**
Distance: 5f/6f: 0-0 7f-8f: 0-4 9f-13f: 0-0 14f+: 0-0
Track : LH: 0-0 RH: 0-3 Tight: 0-0 Gall: 0-0
Aids: Bl: 0-0 Vi: 0-0 Tstrap: 0-0 Ckp: 0-0
Best Rating: **59** 10/09 Kemp 7f stand

Set To Rock

63(72) (32)**14**
2-y-o ch g Reset (AUS)-Crocolat (Croco Rouge (IRE))
J G Portman Mrs S Clifford

Placings:000 **(7120)**
2009: 8^{0}SD, 8^{0}S, 8^{0}GF,

	Starts	1st	2nd	3rd	Win & Pl
Career Total (Turf)	2	0	0	0	
Career Total (AW)	1	0	0	0	

Going (Turf): **Sf: 0-1 GS: 0-0 Gd: 0-0 GF: 0-1 Fm: 0-0**
Distance: 5f/6f: 0-0 7f-8f: 0-1 9f-13f: 0-2 14f+: 0-0
Track : LH: 0-3 RH: 0-0 Tight: 0-0 Gall: 0-0
Aids: Bl: 0-0 Vi: 0-0 Tstrap: 0-0 Ckp: 0-0
Best Rating: **32** 8/09 Sthl 1m stand

Seta

95 **104**
2-y-o ch f Pivotal-Bombazine (IRE) (Generous (IRE))
L M Cumani Miss Sarah J Leigh

Placings:13 **(5825)**
2009: 7^{1}G, 8^{3}GF,

	Starts	1st	2nd	3rd	Win & Pl
Career Total (Turf)	2	1	0	1	13797

95 8/09 NmkJ 7f GD £5180
Total win prize-money £5181

Going (Turf): Sf: 0-0 GS: 0-0 **Gd: 1-1** GF: 0-1 Fm: 0-0
Distance: 5f/6f: 0-0 **7f-8f: 1-2** 9f-13f: 0-0 14f+: 0-0
Track : LH: 0-0 RH: 0-0 Tight: 0-0 Gall: 0-0
Aids: Bl: 0-0 Vi: 0-0 Tstrap: 0-0 Ckp: 0-0
Best Rating: **104** 9/09 Donc 1m gd-fm

Useful half-sister to five winners, including the useful Gravitas, from the family of Gossamer and Barathea; runaway winner of a maiden; beaten favourite in Group 2 next time; stays 7f; acts on a sound surface.

Settigano (IRE)

(110) (104)**104**

6-y-o b g Sadler's Wells (USA)-Bonita Francita (CAN) (Devil's Bag (USA))

Michael Joseph Fitzgerald Andrew Farnan

Placings:3235/0131225261/1441655-013 (7809)

2009: 8^{0}SH, 8^{1}SD, 10^{3}SD,

	Starts	1st	2nd	3rd	Win & Pl
Career Total (Turf)	22	5	4	3	114823
Career Total (AW)	2	1	0	1	15377

90	11/09	Dund	1m		STD	£11069
104	6/08	Curr	1m	H	G-Y	£47867
96	4/08	Gowr	1m	(60-100)H	GD	£11966
97	9/07	List	1m1f	(60-100)H	SFT	£13195
88	6/07	Gowr	1m	(50-80)H	Y-S	£6303
70	5/07	Baln	1m1f		G-F	£4902

Total win prize-money £95305

Going (Turf): Sf: 1-5 GS: 0-0 Gd: 1-3 GF: 1-3 Fm: 0-1
Distance: 5f/6f: 0-0 7f-8f: 4-9 9f-13f: 2-15 14f+: 0-0
Track : LH: 1-3 RH: 4-18 Tight: 0-1 Gall: 1-5
Aids: Bl: 0-0 Vi: 0-0 Tstrap: 3-10 Ckp: 3-10
Best Rating: 104 12/09 Ling 1m2f stand

Smart; effective at around 1m-1m2f; acts on good and soft ground; goes on Polytrack.

Seven Of Diamonds (IRE)

90 **62**

2-y-o gr f Clodovil (IRE)-Tres Sage (Reprimand)

T D Easterby Mrs Jennifer E Pallister

Placings:4444 (6820)

2009: 6^{4}GF, 6^{4}GF, 7^{4}G, 6^{4}GF,

	Starts	1st	2nd	3rd	Win & Pl
Career Total (Turf)	4	0	0	0	1570

Going (Turf): Sf: 0-0 GS: 0-0 Gd: 0-1 GF: 0-3 Fm: 0-0
Distance: 5f/6f: 0-3 7f-8f: 0-1 9f-13f: 0-0 14f+: 0-0
Track : LH: 0-1 RH: 0-0 Tight: 0-1 Gall: 0-0
Aids: Bl: 0-0 Vi: 0-0 Tstrap: 0-0 Ckp: 0-0
Best Rating: 62 7/09 York 6f gd-fm

Modest form in maidens on fast and easy ground; has worn a tongue tie.

Seven Royals (IRE)

(82) (29)**62**

4-y-o b g Val Royal (FR)-Seven Notes (Zafonic (USA))

Miss A M Newton-Smith Miss Sally Harler

Placings:004500-0 (7105)

2009: 7^{0}SD,

	Starts	1st	2nd	3rd	Win & Pl
Career Total (Turf)	6	0	0	0	433
Career Total (AW)	1	0	0	0	

Going (Turf): Sf: 0-3 GS: 0-0 Gd: 0-1 GF: 0-2 Fm: 0-0
Distance: 5f/6f: 0-1 7f-8f: 0-6 9f-13f: 0-0 14f+: 0-0
Track : LH: 0-0 RH: 0-1 Tight: 0-0 Gall: 0-0
Aids: Bl: 0-0 Vi: 0-0 Tstrap: 0-0 Ckp: 0-0
Best Rating: 62 7/08 Newb 6f8y soft

Modest; effective over 6-7f; handles fast ground.

Seven Sky (FR)

(62)

6-y-o b g Septieme Ciel (USA)-Nuit De Crystal (FR) (Crystal Glitters (USA))

P F I Cole The Cristal Racing Partnership

Placings:050/0001022060**0/00** (0872)

2009: 12^{0}SD, 10^{0}SD,

	Starts	1st	2nd	3rd	Win & Pl
Career Total (Turf)	14	1	2	0	7564
Career Total (AW)	2	0	0	0	

5/06	Evre	1m2f110y		GD	£2413

Total win prize-money £2414

Going (Turf): Sf: 0-5 GS: 0-2 Gd: 1-3 GF: 0-0 Fm: 0-0
Distance: 5f/6f: 0-0 7f-8f: 0-1 9f-13f: 1-13 14f+: 0-2
Track : LH: 0-5 RH: 0-1 Tight: 0-1 Gall: 0-0
Aids: Bl: 1-3 Vi: 0-0 Tstrap: 0-0 Ckp: 0-0
Best Rating: 57 4/06 StCl 1m4f gd-sft

Sevenna (FR)

110(112) (93)**102**

4-y-o b f Galileo (IRE)-Silvassa (IRE) (Darshaan)

H R A Cecil Gestut Ammerland

Placings:0145**2-5**6210 (7047a)

2009: 16^{5}SD, 12^{6}GF, 14^{2}G, 14^{1}G, 15^{0}S,

	Starts	1st	2nd	3rd	Win & Pl
Career Total (Turf)	8	2	1	0	47543
Career Total (AW)	2	0	1	0	3638

102	7/09	Gdwd	1m6f	GD	£39739
85	6/08	Newb	1m2f6y	GD	£3723

Total win prize-money £43463

Going (Turf): Sf: 0-2 GS: 0-0 Gd: 2-3 GF: 0-3 Fm: 0-0
Distance: 5f/6f: 0-0 7f-8f: 0-0 9f-13f: 1-3 14f+: 1-7
Track : LH: 1-5 RH: 1-5 Tight: 1-4 Gall: 1-3
Aids: Bl: 0-0 Vi: 0-0 Tstrap: 0-0 Ckp: 0-0
Best Rating: 102 7/09 Gdwd 1m6f good

Smart; Group 3 winner; stays 1m6f; acts on good ground and on Polytrack.

Seventh Cavalry (IRE)

102(96) (67)**79**

4-y-o gr g No Excuse Needed-Mixwayda (FR) (Linamix (FR))

A King W H Ponsonby

Placings:34332333244-6023242 (5802)

2009: 10^{6}GS, 10^{0}GF, 9^{2}G, 12^{3}S, 10^{2}GS, 10^{4}GF, 12^{2}GF,

	Starts	1st	2nd	3rd	Win & Pl
Career Total (Turf)	13	0	5	4	8752
Career Total (AW)	5	0	0	3	1204

Going (Turf): Sf: 0-3 GS: 0-4 Gd: 0-1 GF: 0-5 Fm: 0-0
Distance: 5f/6f: 0-0 7f-8f: 0-4 9f-13f: 0-14 14f+: 0-0
Track : LH: 0-12 RH: 0-5 Tight: 0-9 Gall: 0-4
Aids: Bl: 0-3 Vi: 0-3 Tstrap: 0-0 Ckp: 0-0
Best Rating: 79 7/08 Wwck 1m2f188y soft

Modest; stays 1m2f; acts on fast ground; goes on Polytrack; has worn blinkers.

Seventh Hill

101(104) (69)**70**

4-y-o ch g Compton Place-Dream Baby (Master Willie)

M Blanshard Stanley Hinton

Placings:060/040400205-330536**020024** (7524)

2009: 10^{3}SD, 11^{3}G, 10^{0}GS, 13^{5}GF, 10^{3}GF, 9^{6}G, 10^{0}G, 12^{2}SD, 12^{0}SF, 12^{0}SD, 10^{2}SD, 10^{4}SD,

	Starts	1st	2nd	3rd	Win & Pl
Career Total (Turf)	18	0	1	2	2398
Career Total (AW)	6	0	2	1	1612

Going (Turf): Sf: 0-2 GS: 0-4 Gd: 0-4 GF: 0-8 Fm: 0-0
Distance: 5f/6f: 0-0 7f-8f: 0-5 9f-13f: 0-18 14f+: 0-1
Track : LH: 0-12 RH: 0-8 Tight: 0-8 Gall: 0-2
Aids: Bl: 0-0 Vi: 0-0 Tstrap: 0-0 Ckp: 0-0
Best Rating: 72 9/07 Newb 7f gd-fm

Modest; stays 1m4f; acts on most ground and on Polytrack.

Severio (IRE)

96(34) **59**

3-y-o b f Captain Rio-Good Forecast (Unfuwain (USA))

A P Jarvis (K R Burke 24/7) Clipper Logistics

Placings:05500 (7173)

2009: 7^{0}G, 7^{5}GF, 8^{5}GS, 8^{0}SD, 9^{0}S,

	Starts	1st	2nd	3rd	Win & Pl
Career Total (Turf)	4	0	0	0	141
Career Total (AW)	1	0	0	0	

Going (Turf): Sf: 0-1 GS: 0-1 Gd: 0-1 GF: 0-1 Fm: 0-0
Distance: 5f/6f: 0-0 7f-8f: 0-4 9f-13f: 0-1 14f+: 0-0
Track : LH: 0-4 RH: 0-0 Tight: 0-1 Gall: 0-1
Aids: Bl: 0-0 Vi: 0-0 Tstrap: 0-0 Ckp: 0-0
Best Rating: 59 9/09 Newc 1m gd-sft

Sew'N'So Character (IRE)

(102) (75)**93**

8-y-o b g Imperial Ballet (IRE)-Hope And Glory (USA) (Well Decorated (USA))

M Blanshard Aykroyd And Sons Ltd

Placings:421326225/40344046024/351003303000340/2066 4514604605**5/5**00/**602355600050** (6208)

2009: 8^{6}SD, 8^{0}SD, 7^{2}SD, 7^{3}SD, 7^{5}SD, 8^{5}SD, 8^{6}SD, 7^{0}SD, 8^{0}SD, 11^{0}SD, 11^{5}SD, 10^{0}SD,

	Starts	1st	2nd	3rd	Win & Pl
Career Total (Turf)	46	3	5	6	64952
Career Total (AW)	18	0	2	2	3581

92	6/06	Sals	1m	(0-100)H	GD	£13398
96	5/05	Ches	7f122y	(0-100)H	G-S	£12374
87	7/03	Hayd	6f	E	GD	£3900

Total win prize-money £29674

Going (Turf): Sf: 0-6 GS: 1-8 Gd: 2-16 GF: 0-16 Fm: 0-0
Distance: 5f/6f: 1-3 7f-8f: 2-30 9f-13f: 0-31 14f+: 0-0
Track : LH: 1-34 RH: 0-16 Tight: 1-23 Gall: 0-4
Aids: Bl: 0-2 Vi: 0-0 Tstrap: 0-0 Ckp: 0-0
Best Rating: 98 7/05 Ling 1m stand

Modest; best over 1m; acts on any ground on turf and Polytrack.

Sgt Roberts (IRE)

92(99) (73)**73**

3-y-o b g Diktat-Ann's Annie (IRE) (Alzao (USA))

J S Moore J Barnes & N J Clifford

Placings:420-46500 (2126)

2009: 10^{4}SD, 12^{6}SD, 10^{5}SD, 11^{0}GF, 10^{0}GS,

	Starts	1st	2nd	3rd	Win & Pl
Career Total (Turf)	5	0	1	0	1011

	Starts	1st	2nd	3rd	Win & Pl
Career Total (AW)	3	0	0	0	361

Going (Turf): **Sf: 0-1 GS: 0-2 Gd: 0-1 GF: 0-1 Fm: 0-0**
Distance: 5f/6f: 0-0 7f-8f: 0-2 9f-13f: 0-6 14f+: 0-0
Track : LH: 0-4 RH: 0-2 Tight: 0-6 Gall: 0-0
Aids: Bl: 0-0 Vi: 0-0 Tstrap: 0-0 Ckp: 0-0
Best Rating: **73** 3/09 Ling 1m2f stand

Fair; stays 1m2f; acts on soft ground and on Polytrack.

Sgt Schultz (IRE)

105(114) (102)**85**

6-y-o b g In The Wings-Ann's Annie (IRE) (Alzao (USA))
J S Moore Jim Barnes

Placings:0503540/**663023263243/11644134406301/2334100601-300100245050** **(7720)**
2009: 10^3SD, 10^0FT, 8^0FT, 12^1SD, 12^0SD, 11^0GS, 11^2GF, 12^4GF, 12^5GF, 12^0G, 10^5SD, 12^0SD,

	Starts	1st	2nd	3rd	Win & Pl
Career Total (Turf)	25	0	3	5	10552
Career Total (AW)	30	7	2	5	53907

100	3/09	Ling	1m4f	(0-95)H	STD	£9714
102	12/08	GrLe	1m2f	(0-95)H	STD	£7477
97	3/08	Ling	1m4f	(0-95)H	STD	£9348
87	12/07	Ling	1m4f	(0-85)H	STD	£4605
87	3/07	Ling	1m4f	(0-85)H	STD	£4857
83	2/07	Ling	1m4f	(0-85)H	STD	£4857
75	1/07	Ling	1m4f		STD	£2817

Total win prize-money £43678

Going (Turf): **Sf: 0-0 GS: 0-4 Gd: 0-7 GF: 0-13 Fm: 0-1**
Distance: 5f/6f: 0-0 7f-8f: 0-11 **9f-13f: 7-43** 14f+: 0-1
Track : **LH: 7-41** RH: 0-9 **Tight: 6-33** Gall: 1-11
Aids: Bl: 0-0 Vi: 0-0 Tstrap: 0-0 Ckp: 0-0
Best Rating: **102** 1/09 Ling 1m2f stand

Fair; effective over 1m2f-1m4f; acts on fast ground; also goes on Polytrack; usually held up; can take a hold.

Shaaridh (USA)

96 **73**

3-y-o b/br f Dixieland Band (USA)-Boston Lady (USA) (Boston Harbor (USA))
M Johnston Hamdan Al Maktoum

Placings:0-34 **(4955)**
2009: 10^3GF, 8^4G,

	Starts	1st	2nd	3rd	Win & Pl
Career Total (Turf)	3	0	0	1	1011

Going (Turf): **Sf: 0-0 GS: 0-0 Gd: 0-2 GF: 0-1 Fm: 0-0**
Distance: 5f/6f: 0-0 7f-8f: 0-0 9f-13f: 0-3 14f+: 0-0
Track : LH: 0-1 RH: 0-1 Tight: 0-0 Gall: 0-0
Aids: Bl: 0-0 Vi: 0-0 Tstrap: 0-0 Ckp: 0-0
Best Rating: **73** 8/09 Sand 1m14y good

Modest; stays 1m2f; acts on fast ground.

Shaayeq (IRE)

103(92) (72)**82**

2-y-o b/br c Dubawi (IRE)-Shohrah (IRE) (Giant's Causeway (USA))
M P Tregoning Hamdan Al Maktoum

Placings:3143 **(6569)**
2009: 7^3SD, 8^1GS, 8^4GF, 9^3GF,

	Starts	1st	2nd	3rd	Win & Pl
Career Total (Turf)	3	1	0	1	7048
Career Total (AW)	1	0	0	1	482

76	9/09	Epsm	1m114y	G-S	£5180

Total win prize-money £5181

Going (Turf): Sf: 0-0 **GS: 1-1** Gd: 0-0 GF: 0-2 Fm: 0-0
Distance: 5f/6f: 0-0 7f-8f: 0-2 **9f-13f: 1-2** 14f+: 0-0
Track : **LH: 1-2** RH: 0-1 **Tight: 1-2** Gall: 0-0
Aids: Bl: 0-0 Vi: 0-2 Tstrap: 0-0 Ckp: 0-0
Best Rating: **82** 9/09 Newb 1m gd-fm

Fair; stays 1m; acts on easy ground and on Polytrack; has worn a visor.

Shabak Hom (IRE)

93(86) (60)**70**

2-y-o b c Exceed And Excel (AUS)-Shbakni (USA) (Mr Prospector (USA))
D M Simcock Ahmed Ali

Placings:025 **(6125)**
2009: 7^0SD, 8^2GS, 8^5SD,

	Starts	1st	2nd	3rd	Win & Pl
Career Total (Turf)	1	0	1	0	1542
Career Total (AW)	2	0	0	0	0

Going (Turf): **Sf: 0-0 GS: 0-1 Gd: 0-0 GF: 0-0 Fm: 0-0**
Distance: 5f/6f: 0-0 7f-8f: 0-1 9f-13f: 0-2 14f+: 0-0
Track : LH: 0-3 RH: 0-0 Tight: 0-3 Gall: 0-0
Aids: Bl: 0-0 Vi: 0-0 Tstrap: 0-0 Ckp: 0-0
Best Rating: **70** 9/09 Epsm 1m114y gd-sft

Fair; stays 1m and acts on easy ground.

Shabib (USA)

99(100) (84)**94**

3-y-o b c Intidab (USA)-Muklah (IRE) (Singspiel (IRE))
B W Hills Hamdan Al Maktoum

Placings:33-2110 **(4954)**
2009: 7^2SD, 7^1G, 7^1S, 7^0G,

	Starts	1st	2nd	3rd	Win & Pl
Career Total (Turf)	5	2	0	2	9806
Career Total (AW)	1	0	1	0	806

94	7/09	NmkJ	7f	(0-85)H	SFT	£5828
84	4/09	Folk	7f		GD	£2388

Total win prize-money £8216

Going (Turf): **Sf: 1-1** GS: 0-1 **Gd: 1-2** GF: 0-1 Fm: 0-0
Distance: 5f/6f: 0-1 **7f-8f: 2-5** 9f-13f: 0-0 14f+: 0-0
Track : LH: 0-1 RH: 0-1 Tight: 0-1 Gall: 0-0
Aids: Bl: 0-0 Vi: 0-0 Tstrap: 0-0 Ckp: 0-0
Best Rating: **94** 7/09 NmkJ 7f soft

Fair; effective over 6f-7f; acts on fast and soft ground; goes on Polytrack.

Shaded Edge

99(107) (77)**76**

5-y-o b g Bold Edge-Twilight Mistress (Bin Ajwaad (IRE))
D W P Arbuthnot P M Claydon

Placings:00/41214/34004503142-02314115020026202 **(7891)**
2009: 7^0SD, 7^2SD, 7^3SD, 7^1SD, 7^4SD, 6^1GF, 7^1GF, 7^5GF, 7^0G, 7^2SD, 7^0G, 7^0SD, 7^2SD, 7^6SD, 8^2SD, 7^0SD, 7^2SD,

	Starts	1st	2nd	3rd	Win & Pl
Career Total (Turf)	9	2	0	1	6736
Career Total (AW)	26	4	7	2	16290

75	5/09	Ling	7f	(0-75)H	G-F	£3123
76	5/09	Sals	6f212y	(0-65)H	G-F	£2935
66	3/09	Ling	7f	(0-65)H	STD	£2047
59	12/08	Ling	6f	(0-60)H	STD	£1706
63	9/07	Ling	7f	(0-65)H	STD	£2817
63	7/07	Ling	6f		STD	£2730

Total win prize-money £15359

Going (Turf): Sf: 0-0 GS: 0-0 Gd: 0-3 **GF: 2-5** Fm: 0-1
Distance: 5f/6f: 2-9 **7f-8f: 4-26** 9f-13f: 0-0 14f+: 0-0
Track : **LH: 4-22** RH: 0-5 **Tight: 4-21** Gall: 0-0
Aids: Bl: 0-0 Vi: 0-1 Tstrap: 1-5 Ckp: 1-5
Best Rating: **77** 8/09 Ling 7f stand

Modest; effective over 6f-1m; handles Polytrack well.

Shadow Bay (IRE)

98(94) (68)**75**

3-y-o b g Deportivo-Champion Tipster (Pursuit Of Love)
Miss Z C Davison David J Bearman

Placings:05401103021-01560500 **(7053)**
2009: 6^0GF, 5^1G, 7^5GF, 5^6GF, 6^0SD, 6^5SD, 7^0SS, 6^0SD,

	Starts	1st	2nd	3rd	Win & Pl
Career Total (Turf)	11	3	0	0	8188
Career Total (AW)	8	1	1	1	3497

73	4/09	Folk	5f		GD	£2047
68	12/08	GrLe	1m		STD	£2590
75	8/08	Nott	6f15y	(0-75)	SFT	£3238
72	7/08	Ripn	6f		GD	£2590

Total win prize-money £10465

Going (Turf): Sf: 1-1 GS: 0-3 **Gd: 2-3** GF: 0-4 Fm: 0-0
Distance: 5f/6f: 2-11 7f-8f: 2-8 9f-13f: 0-0 14f+: 0-0
Track : **LH: 1-5** RH: 0-4 Tight: 0-2 **Gall: 1-1**
Aids: Bl: 0-0 Vi: 0-0 Tstrap: 0-0 Ckp: 0-0
Best Rating: **75** 8/08 Nott 6f15y soft

Modest; stays 1m; acts on soft ground and on Polytrack.

Shadow Jumper (IRE)

(93) (36)**47**

8-y-o b g Dayjur (USA)-Specifically (USA) (Sky Classic (CAN))
J T Stimpson J T Stimpson

Placings:400/0033600/**0020005301200146332/11425000 0/000052040205000406020/000000-00050** **(0744)**
2009: 8^0SS, 8^0SD, 7^0SS, 12^5SD, 11^0SD,

	Starts	1st	2nd	3rd	Win & Pl
Career Total (Turf)	17	0	1	2	2856
Career Total (AW)	53	4	6	3	12833

67	1/06	Sthl	6f	(0-55)H	STD	£2388
58	1/06	Wolv	5f216y		STD	£2388
58	10/05	Sthl	6f	(0-45)	STD	£1473
54	5/05	Sthl	5f	(0-45)	STD	£1456

Total win prize-money £7708

Going (Turf): **Sf: 0-3 GS: 0-3 Gd: 0-4** GF: 0-1 **Fm: 0-2**
Distance: **5f/6f: 4-37** 7f-8f: 0-20 9f-13f: 0-13 14f+: 0-0
Track : **LH: 3-55** RH: 0-7 **Tight: 1-17** Gall: 0-0
Aids: Bl: 0-7 **Vi: 4-45** Tstrap: 0-5 Ckp: 0-5
Best Rating: **70** 6/04 Cork 5f firm

Shadows Lengthen

85(108) (86)**56**

3-y-o b g Dansili-Bay Shade (USA) (Sharpen Up)
M W Easterby T A F Frost

Placings:0660-50360011111 **(7712)**
2009: 11^5SD, 11^0SD, 10^3GF, 10^6S, 12^0SD, 12^0GS, 12^1SD, 12^1SD, 11^1SD, 11^1SD, 12^1SD,

	Starts	1st	2nd	3rd	Win & Pl
Career Total (Turf)	6	0	0	1	347
Career Total (AW)	9	5	0	0	10779

84 12/09 Sthl 1m4f (0-65)H STD £2047
86 12/09 Sthl 1m3f (0-65)H STD £2047
84 12/09 Sthl 1m3f (0-75)H STD £2590
69 11/09 Wolv 1m4f50y (0-65)H STD £2047
71 11/09 Sthl 1m4f (0-60)H STD £2047
Total win prize-money £10778

Going (Turf): **Sf: 0-1 GS: 0-3 Gd: 0-1 GF: 0-1 Fm: 0-0**
Distance: 5f/6f: 0-3 7f-8f: 0-1 **9f-13f: 5-11** 14f+: 0-0
Track : **LH: 5-11** RH: 0-0 **Tight: 1-2** Gall: 0-2
Aids: **Bl: 5-7** Vi: 0-0 Tstrap: 0-0 Ckp: 0-0
Best Rating: **86** 12/09 Sthl 1m3f stand

Fair; stays 1m4f; acts on Fibresand and on Polytrack; has worn blinkers; progressive.

Shadowtime

105(96) (73)73
4-y-o b g Singspiel (IRE)-Massomah (USA) (Seeking The Gold (USA))
Miss Tracy Waggott H Conlon

Placings:3435153000-040232026305404 **(6383)**
2009: 7^{0}F, 8^{4}F, 8^{0}G, 8^{2}GF, 8^{3}G, 7^{2}GF, 7^{0}G, 8^{2}GF, 7^{6}GF, 8^{3}GF, 9^{0}S, 8^{5}GF, 8^{4}GF, 9^{0}G, 8^{4}GF,

	Starts	1st	2nd	3rd	Win & Pl
Career Total (Turf)	22	1	3	4	8810
Career Total (AW)	3	0	0	1	448

73 5/08 Bevl 1m100y (0-70)H G-F £2914
Total win prize-money £2914

Going (Turf): Sf: 0-3 GS: 0-2 Gd: 0-5 **GF: 1-10** Fm: 0-2
Distance: 5f/6f: 0-0 7f-8f: 0-13 **9f-13f: 1-12** 14f+: 0-0
Track : LH: 0-9 **RH: 1-15** Tight: 0-8 Gall: 0-3
Aids: Bl: 0-0 Vi: 0-0 Tstrap: 0-0 Ckp: 0-0
Best Rating: **73** 7/09 Bevl 1m100y gd-fm

Modest; stays 1m; acts on fast and easy ground; goes on Polytrack.

Shady Gloom (IRE)

104(104) (71)85
4-y-o b g Traditionally (USA)-Last Drama (IRE) (Last Tycoon)
K A Ryan Mrs J Ryan

Placings:0/32126-0024550302 **(6832)**
2009: 10^{0}G, 12^{0}SD, 10^{2}GF, 12^{4}G, 9^{5}GF, 10^{5}G, 9^{0}S, 11^{3}HY, 11^{0}GS, 12^{2}SF,

	Starts	1st	2nd	3rd	Win & Pl
Career Total (Turf)	14	1	3	2	8603
Career Total (AW)	2	0	1	0	867

78 6/08 Haml 1m1f36y G-F £2047
Total win prize-money £2047

Going (Turf): Sf: 0-2 GS: 0-3 Gd: 0-4 **GF: 1-5** Fm: 0-0
Distance: 5f/6f: 0-0 7f-8f: 0-0 **9f-13f: 1-16** 14f+: 0-0
Track : LH: 0-10 **RH: 1-6 Tight: 1-6** Gall: 0-4
Aids: Bl: 0-0 Vi: 0-1 Tstrap: 0-0 Ckp: 0-0
Best Rating: **85** 8/08 Donc 1m4f good

Fair; stays 1m4f; acts on good and fast ground; likes to race prominently; has worn headgear.

Shady Lady (IRE)

(82) (36)78
3-y-o b f Celtic Swing-Viola Royale (IRE) (Royal Academy (USA))
M Johnston Ascot In Mind

Placings:016-0 **(7066)**
2009: 12^{0}SD,

	Starts	1st	2nd	3rd	Win & Pl
Career Total (Turf)	3	1	0	0	2388
Career Total (AW)	1	0	0	0	

73 10/08 Rdcr 1m GD £2388
Total win prize-money £2388

Going (Turf): Sf: 0-2 GS: 0-0 **Gd: 1-1** GF: 0-0 Fm: 0-0
Distance: 5f/6f: 0-0 **7f-8f: 1-1** 9f-13f: 0-3 14f+: 0-0
Track : LH: 0-3 RH: 0-0 Tight: 0-1 Gall: 0-0
Aids: Bl: 0-0 Vi: 0-0 Tstrap: 0-0 Ckp: 0-0
Best Rating: **78** 11/08 Leop 1m1f soft

Fair; stays 1m1f; acts on good and soft ground.

Shafrons Canyon (IRE)

(92) (47)74
6-y-o b m Lend A Hand-Carroll's Canyon (IRE) (Hatim (USA))
P J Lally Mrs Christine Kiernan

Placings:00/000/0/50-0 **(1496)**
2009: 9^{0}SD,

	Starts	1st	2nd	3rd	Win & Pl
Career Total (Turf)	6	0	0	0	532
Career Total (AW)	3	0	0	0	0

Going (Turf): **Sf: 0-1 GS: 0-0 Gd: 0-1 GF: 0-1 Fm: 0-1**
Distance: 5f/6f: 0-2 7f-8f: 0-3 9f-13f: 0-4 14f+: 0-0
Track : LH: 0-4 RH: 0-4 Tight: 0-3 Gall: 0-0
Aids: Bl: 0-0 Vi: 0-0 Tstrap: 0-0 Ckp: 0-0
Best Rating: **74** 8/05 Curr 6f good

Shakalaka (IRE)

103(110) (81)81
3-y-o b g Montjeu (IRE)-Sweet Times (Riverman (USA))
G L Moore Graham Gillespie

Placings:4356-2244321 **(7882)**
2009: 10^{2}GF, 9^{2}GF, 8^{4}SD, 10^{4}SD, 10^{3}SD, 12^{2}SD, 10^{1}SD,

	Starts	1st	2nd	3rd	Win & Pl
Career Total (Turf)	6	0	2	1	2713
Career Total (AW)	5	1	1	1	4440

12/09 Ling 1m2f STD £2729
Total win prize-money £2730

Going (Turf): **Sf: 0-2 GS: 0-0 Gd: 0-0 GF: 0-3 Fm: 0-0**
Distance: 5f/6f: 0-0 7f-8f: 0-5 **9f-13f: 1-6** 14f+: 0-0
Track : **LH: 1-5** RH: 0-6 **Tight: 1-4** Gall: 0-0
Aids: **Bl: 1-2** Vi: 0-0 Tstrap: 0-1 Ckp: 0-1
Best Rating: **81** 9/09 Kemp 1m2f stand

Fair; ex-Irish; stays 1m4f and acts on fast and soft ground and Polytrack; has worn cheekpieces/blinkers.

Shake On It

97(106) (72)88
5-y-o b g Lomitas-Decision Maid (USA) (Diesis)
M R Hoad (M J Gingell 25/3) Mrs L Bangs

Placings:022/105453105/255000000000-32040000040630340041 **(7802)**
2009: 8^{3}SD, 8^{2}SD, 8^{0}SD, 8^{4}SD, 8^{0}SD, 8^{0}SD, 7^{0}SD, 9^{0}G, 8^{0}GF, 7^{0}F, 8^{4}SD, 7^{0}G, 8^{6}SD, 7^{3}SD, 7^{0}SD, 8^{3}SD, 8^{4}SD, 8^{0}SD, 7^{0}SD, 8^{4}SD, 8^{1}SD,

	Starts	1st	2nd	3rd	Win & Pl
Career Total (Turf)	22	2	3	1	11705
Career Total (AW)	23	1	1	3	3419

59 12/09 Wolv 1m141y (0-50)H STD £1706
82 8/07 Ling 1m2f (0-75)H G-F £2817
71 4/07 Bath 1m5y FRM £2914
Total win prize-money £7438

Going (Turf): Sf: 0-0 GS: 0-0 Gd: 0-7 **GF: 1-11 Fm: 1-4**
Distance: 5f/6f: 0-0 7f-8f: 0-28 **9f-13f: 3-17** 14f+: 0-0
Track : **LH: 3-28** RH: 0-11 **Tight: 3-23** Gall: 0-5
Aids: Bl: 0-0 Vi: 0-2 Tstrap: 0-2 Ckp: 0-2
Best Rating: **88** 4/08 Wind 1m2f7y gd-fm

Moderate; stays 1m2f; acts on a sound surface; wears a tongue tie.

Shaker Style (USA)

96(95) (64)64
3-y-o ch g Gulch (USA)-Carr Shaker (USA) (Carr De Naskra (USA))
M Todhunter (J D Bethell 1/4) K Fitzsimons

Placings:6040040-4145 **(1063)**
2009: 9^{4}SD, 9^{1}SD, 12^{4}SD, 11^{5}GF,

	Starts	1st	2nd	3rd	Win & Pl
Career Total (Turf)	5	0	0	0	265
Career Total (AW)	6	1	0	0	2388

64 2/09 Wolv 1m1f103y (0-65)H STD £2388
Total win prize-money £2388

Going (Turf): **Sf: 0-0 GS: 0-1 Gd: 0-2 GF: 0-2 Fm: 0-0**
Distance: 5f/6f: 0-2 7f-8f: 0-2 **9f-13f: 1-7** 14f+: 0-0
Track : **LH: 1-8** RH: 0-0 **Tight: 1-7** Gall: 0-1
Aids: **Bl: 1-7** Vi: 0-2 Tstrap: 0-0 Ckp: 0-0
Best Rating: **64** 2/09 Wolv 1m1f103y stand

Fair; stays 1m1f; effective on good ground; has worn blinkers.

Shakespeare's Son

98(102) (75)74
4-y-o b g Mind Games-Eastern Blue (IRE) (Be My Guest (USA))
H J Evans ownaracehorse.co.uk (Shakespeare)

Placings:044054/325221225330-0005320045200063 **(7889)**
2009: 7^{0}SD, 5^{0}GF, 7^{0}GF, 6^{5}GF, 6^{3}GF, 5^{2}GF, 6^{0}GS, 5^{0}SD, 5^{4}G, 6^{5}GF, 5^{2}SD, 7^{0}SD, 6^{0}SD, 5^{0}SD, 5^{6}SD, 6^{3}SD, 5^{3}SD,

	Starts	1st	2nd	3rd	Win & Pl
Career Total (Turf)	16	0	5	2	5675
Career Total (AW)	19	1	2	4	6986

68 9/08 Sthl 5f (0-70)H STD £3753
Total win prize-money £3753

Going (Turf): **Sf: 0-0 GS: 0-1 Gd: 0-5 GF: 0-10 Fm: 0-0**
Distance: **5f/6f: 1-27** 7f-8f: 0-8 9f-13f: 0-0 14f+: 0-0
Track : LH: 0-8 RH: 0-7 Tight: 0-8 Gall: 0-3
Aids: Bl: 0-3 Vi: 0-4 Tstrap: 0-0 Ckp: 0-0
Best Rating: **75** 11/08 Sthl 5f stand

Modest; effective over 5f-6f; acts on good/fast ground; also goes on both All-Weather surfaces; has worn blinkers.

Shakespearean (IRE)

102 107
2-y-o b c Shamardal (USA)-Paimpolaise (IRE) (Priolo (USA))
M Johnston Sheikh Hamdan Bin Mohammed Al Maktoum

Placings:153116 (7017)
2009: 6^{1}GS, 7^{5}GF, 7^{3}GF, 7^{1}GF, 8^{1}G, 8^{6}GS,

	Starts	1st	2nd	3rd	Win & Pl
Career Total (Turf)	6	3	0	1	1001242

99 9/09 Curr 1m GD £956310
107 8/09 Sand 7f16y G-F £28385
82 5/09 Hayd 6f G-S £3885
Total win prize-money £988582

Going (Turf): Sf: 0-0 **GS: 1-2 Gd: 1-1 GF: 1-3** Fm: 0-0
Distance: 5f/6f: 1-1 **7f-8f: 2-5** 9f-13f: 0-0 14f+: 0-0
Track : LH: 0-0 **RH: 2-2** Tight: 0-0 **Gall: 1-1**
Aids: Bl: 0-0 Vi: 0-0 Tstrap: 0-0 Ckp: 0-0
Best Rating: 107 8/09 Sand 7f16y gd-fm

Smart; won Group 3 Solario Stakes and Goffs Million Mile at two; stays 1m and acts on most ground.

Shakin John

70(66) 52
3-y-o b g Refuse To Bend (IRE)-Qudrah (IRE) (Darshaan)
E J O'Neill Red Army Partnership

Placings:000-00 (1594)
2009: 11^{0}SD, 10^{0}GS,

	Starts	1st	2nd	3rd	Win & Pl
Career Total (Turf)	4	0	0	0	
Career Total (AW)	1	0	0	0	

Going (Turf): **Sf: 0-1 GS: 0-2 Gd: 0-1 GF: 0-0 Fm: 0-0**
Distance: 5f/6f: 0-0 7f-8f: 0-0 9f-13f: 0-5 14f+: 0-0
Track : LH: 0-4 RH: 0-0 Tight: 0-0 Gall: 0-0
Aids: Bl: 0-1 Vi: 0-0 Tstrap: 0-0 Ckp: 0-0
Best Rating: 52 10/08 Nott 1m75y gd-sft

Shallal

106 101
4-y-o b c Cape Cross (IRE)-First Waltz (FR) (Green Dancer (USA))
P W Chapple-Hyam Ziad A Galadari

Placings:31/40-5400 (6815)
2009: 7^{5}G, 6^{4}S, 6^{0}S, 7^{0}G,

	Starts	1st	2nd	3rd	Win & Pl
Career Total (Turf)	8	1	0	1	17823

89 7/07 Gdwd 6f GD £9715
Total win prize-money £9716

Going (Turf): Sf: 0-3 GS: 0-0 **Gd: 1-4** GF: 0-1 Fm: 0-0
Distance: **5f/6f: 1-3** 7f-8f: 0-5 9f-13f: 0-0 14f+: 0-0
Track : LH: 0-1 RH: 0-0 Tight: 0-0 Gall: 0-0
Aids: Bl: 0-0 Vi: 0-0 Tstrap: 0-0 Ckp: 0-0
Best Rating: 101 6/09 Newc 6f soft

Very useful; effective over 6f; acts on good ground.

Shaloo Diamond

105 91
4-y-o b g Captain Rio-Alacrity (Alzao (USA))
R M Whitaker G B Bedford

Placings:634/431445412-00441225200 (6681)
2009: 9^{0}GF, 8^{0}S, 10^{4}GF, 11^{4}GF, 12^{1}S, 10^{2}GS, 10^{2}S, 12^{5}G, 10^{2}S, 12^{0}S, 12^{0}G,

	Starts	1st	2nd	3rd	Win & Pl
Career Total (Turf)	23	3	4	2	26629

89 7/09 Donc 1m4f (0-80)H SFT £4857
83 9/08 Bevl 1m100y (0-75)H SFT £3238
81 6/08 Ripn 1m1f170y (0-80)H HVY £4533
Total win prize-money £12628

Going (Turf): **Sf: 3-10** GS: 0-1 Gd: 0-4 GF: 0-8 Fm: 0-0
Distance: 5f/6f: 0-1 7f-8f: 0-3 **9f-13f: 3-19** 14f+: 0-0
Track : LH: 1-14 **RH: 2-7** Tight: 1-5 Gall: 1-7
Aids: Bl: 0-0 Vi: 0-0 Tstrap: 0-0 Ckp: 0-0
Best Rating: 91 8/09 Ayr 1m2f soft

Useful; effective at around 1m2f-1m4f; acts on fast ground but may be best suited by a soft surface.

Shaluca

88(91) (47)69
2-y-o b/br f Shamardal (USA)-Noushkey (Polish Precedent (USA))
E S McMahon Martin W Crane

Placings:34 (7140)
2009: 8^{3}GF, 8^{4}SD,

	Starts	1st	2nd	3rd	Win & Pl
Career Total (Turf)	1	0	0	1	578
Career Total (AW)	1	0	0	0	265

Going (Turf): **Sf: 0-0 GS: 0-0 Gd: 0-0 GF: 0-1 Fm: 0-0**
Distance: 5f/6f: 0-0 7f-8f: 0-0 9f-13f: 0-2 14f+: 0-0
Track : LH: 0-2 RH: 0-0 Tight: 0-1 Gall: 0-0
Aids: Bl: 0-0 Vi: 0-0 Tstrap: 0-0 Ckp: 0-0
Best Rating: 69 9/09 Nott 1m75y gd-fm

Modest; stays 1m; handles fast ground and Polytrack.

Sham Sheer

100(102) (82)76
3-y-o br g Cape Cross (IRE)-Viola Da Braccio (IRE) (Vettori (IRE))
L M Cumani Sheikh Mohammed Obaid Al Maktoum

Placings:00-40661121 (6977)
2009: 7^{4}SD, 8^{0}GF, 12^{6}GF, 10^{6}G, 7^{1}F, 8^{1}SD, 8^{2}GF, 8^{1}SD,

	Starts	1st	2nd	3rd	Win & Pl
Career Total (Turf)	5	1	1	0	4394
Career Total (AW)	5	2	0	0	6717

82 10/09 Kemp 1m (0-75)H STD £2590
76 9/09 Wolv 1m141y (0-70)H STD £3885
69 9/09 Folk 7f (0-70)H FRM £3238
Total win prize-money £9714

Going (Turf): Sf: 0-0 GS: 0-0 Gd: 0-1 GF: 0-3 **Fm: 1-1**
Distance: 5f/6f: 0-0 **7f-8f: 2-6** 9f-13f: 1-4 14f+: 0-0
Track : LH: 1-7 RH: 1-1 **Tight: 1-3** Gall: 0-3
Aids: Bl: 0-0 Vi: 0-1 Tstrap: 0-0 Ckp: 0-0
Best Rating: 82 10/09 Kemp 1m stand

Fair; effective over 7f-1m; acts on fast ground; goes on Polytrack.

Shamali

109(98) (92)107
4-y-o ch c Selkirk (USA)-Shamaiel (IRE) (Lycius (USA))
W J Haggas Abdulla Al Khalifa

Placings:631-0311 (4339)
2009: 8^{0}G, 10^{3}G, 10^{1}GF, 10^{1}G,

	Starts	1st	2nd	3rd	Win & Pl
Career Total (Turf)	6	2	0	2	20588
Career Total (AW)	1	1	0	0	2730

107 7/09 Asct 1m2f (0-95) GD £11215
102 7/09 Asct 1m2f (0-90)H G-F £7771
92 11/08 Wolv 1m141y STD £2729
Total win prize-money £21717

Going (Turf): Sf: 0-1 GS: 0-0 **Gd: 1-4 GF: 1-1** Fm: 0-0
Distance: 5f/6f: 0-0 7f-8f: 0-1 **9f-13f: 3-6** 14f+: 0-0
Track : LH: 1-2 **RH: 2-4** Tight: 1-1 **Gall: 2-2**
Aids: Bl: 0-0 Vi: 0-0 Tstrap: 0-0 Ckp: 0-0
Best Rating: 107 7/09 Asct 1m2f good

Smart; stays 1m2f; acts on good and faster ground and on Polytrack.

Shamandar (FR)

105 100
2-y-o ch f Exceed And Excel (AUS)-Sensational Mover (USA) (Theatrical)
W J Haggas Mr & Mrs R Scott

Placings:122115 (6449)
2009: 6^{1}G, 5^{2}GS, 5^{2}GF, 6^{1}S, 6^{1}G, 6^{5}GF,

	Starts	1st	2nd	3rd	Win & Pl
Career Total (Turf)	6	3	2	0	199057

87 9/09 Asct 6f110y GD £123100
99 9/09 Sals 6f SFT £20153
78 7/09 Ripn 6f GD £2914
Total win prize-money £146167

Going (Turf): Sf: 1-1 GS: 0-1 **Gd: 2-2** GF: 0-2 Fm: 0-0
Distance: **5f/6f: 2-5** 7f-8f: 1-1 9f-13f: 0-0 14f+: 0-0
Track : LH: 0-0 RH: 0-0 Tight: 0-0 Gall: 0-0
Aids: Bl: 0-0 Vi: 0-0 Tstrap: 0-0 Ckp: 0-0
Best Rating: 100 8/09 Newb 5f34y gd-fm

Smart; Listed winner; won the Watership Down Stud Sales race in 2009; effective over 5f-6f plus; acts on fast and easy ground.

Shame The Devil (IRE)

75 23
4-y-o b g Danehill Dancer (IRE)-Iles Piece (Shirley Heights)
Jonjo O'Neill The Escaped Goats

Placings:0 (2229)
2009: 8^{0}HY,

	Starts	1st	2nd	3rd	Win & Pl
Career Total (Turf)	1	0	0	0	

Going (Turf): **Sf: 0-1 GS: 0-0 Gd: 0-0 GF: 0-0 Fm: 0-0**
Distance: 5f/6f: 0-0 7f-8f: 0-0 9f-13f: 0-1 14f+: 0-0
Track : LH: 0-1 RH: 0-0 Tight: 0-0 Gall: 0-0
Aids: Bl: 0-0 Vi: 0-0 Tstrap: 0-0 Ckp: 0-0
Best Rating: 23 5/09 Hayd 1m30y heavy

Shamir

80(100) (78)66
2-y-o b c Dubai Destination (USA)-Lake Nyasa (IRE) (Lake Coniston (IRE))
Miss Jo Crowley Kilstone Limited

Placings:0223 (7388)
2009: 7^{0}GF, 7^{2}SS, 7^{2}SD, 8^{3}SD,

	Starts	1st	2nd	3rd	Win & Pl
Career Total (Turf)	1	0	0	0	
Career Total (AW)	3	0	2	1	2874

Going (Turf): **Sf: 0-0 GS: 0-0 Gd: 0-0 GF: 0-1 Fm: 0-0**
Distance: 5f/6f: 0-0 7f-8f: 0-4 9f-13f: 0-0 14f+: 0-0
Track : LH: 0-3 RH: 0-0 Tight: 0-3 Gall: 0-0
Aids: Bl: 0-0 Vi: 0-0 Tstrap: 0-0 Ckp: 0-0
Best Rating: 78 10/09 Ling 7f stand

Fair; effective over 7f; acts on Polytrack.

Shampagne

105(104) (101)**106**

3-y-o b c Orpen (USA)-Arndilly (Robellino (USA))

P F I Cole Sisters Syndicate

Placings:2110001010-622305234 (7588)

2009: 9^{6}SD, 8^{2}SD, 8^{2}GF, 8^{3}GF, 8^{0}GF, 8^{5}G, 8^{2}S, 8^{3}G, 8^{4}SD,

	Starts	1st	2nd	3rd	Win & Pl
Career Total (Turf)	13	1	3	2	24249
Career Total (AW)	6	3	1	0	44203

100 9/08 GrLe 1m STD £24924
100 7/08 Sthl 7f STD £2729
93 5/08 Pont 6f G-F £9346
81 5/08 Kemp 5f STD £4857
Total win prize-money £41858

Going (Turf): Sf: 0-3 GS: 0-0 Gd: 0-4 **GF: 1-6** Fm: 0-0
Distance: 5f/6f: 2-6 7f-8f: 2-12 9f-13f: 0-1 14f+: 0-0
Track : **LH: 3-3** RH: 1-5 Tight: 0-0 **Gall: 1-1**
Aids: Bl: 0-0 Vi: 0-0 Tstrap: 0-0 Ckp: 0-0
Best Rating: **106** 5/09 NmkR 1m gd-fm

Very useful; effective over 6f-1m; acts on fast ground; also goes on Fibresand and Polytrack.

Shamrock Lady (IRE)

98(102) (81)**76**

4-y-o b f Orpen (USA)-Shashi (IRE) (Shaadi (USA))

J Gallagher Mrs Irene Clifford

Placings:32510000/505001061-60600 (6630)

2009: 7^{6}G, 5^{0}GS, 8^{6}GF, 7^{0}GF, 7^{0}SS,

	Starts	1st	2nd	3rd	Win & Pl
Career Total (Turf)	20	2	1	1	11335
Career Total (AW)	2	1	0	0	6308

81 10/08 Ling 7f (0-80)H STD £6308
76 8/08 Brig 6f209y (0-70)H G-S £2978
74 7/07 Gdwd 6f G-S £6477
Total win prize-money £15764

Going (Turf): Sf: 0-2 **GS: 2-5** Gd: 0-8 GF: 0-5 Fm: 0-0
Distance: 5f/6f: 1-8 **7f-8f: 2-11** 9f-13f: 0-3 14f+: 0-0
Track : **LH: 2-8** RH: 0-6 **Tight: 1-6** Gall: 0-1
Aids: Bl: 0-0 Vi: 0-0 Tstrap: 0-0 Ckp: 0-0
Best Rating: **81** 10/08 Ling 7f stand

Fair; effective over 5f-7f; acts on good and soft ground.

Shamwari Lodge (IRE)

111 **107**

3-y-o b f Hawk Wing (USA)-Ripalong (IRE) (Revoque (IRE))

R Hannon Andrew Russell

Placings:01-12021250 (6505a)

2009: 6^{1}GF, 7^{2}G, 6^{0}G, 7^{2}GS, 8^{1}GF, 7^{2}GF, 8^{5}G, 8^{0}GS,

	Starts	1st	2nd	3rd	Win & Pl
Career Total (Turf)	10	3	3	0	50054

107 8/09 York 1m (0-100)H G-F £16190
95 5/09 NmkR 6f (0-95)H G-F £9714
82 9/08 Hayd 6f G-F £2914
Total win prize-money £28818

Going (Turf): Sf: 0-0 GS: 0-3 Gd: 0-3 **GF: 3-4** Fm: 0-0
Distance: **5f/6f: 2-3** 7f-8f: 1-7 9f-13f: 0-0 14f+: 0-0
Track : **LH: 1-2** RH: 0-2 Tight: 0-1 **Gall: 1-2**
Aids: Bl: 0-0 Vi: 0-0 Tstrap: 0-0 Ckp: 0-0
Best Rating: **107** 8/09 York 1m gd-fm

Smart; effective at 7f-1m; acts on fast ground.

Shanafarahan (IRE)

91(100) (68)**64**

4-y-o b g Marju (IRE)-Sedna (FR) (Bering)

K A Morgan J D M Stables

Placings:505/000664-01110005 (7732)

2009: 13^{0}SD, 13^{1}SD, 12^{1}SD, 12^{1}SD, 12^{0}GF, 12^{0}SD, 13^{0}SD, 12^{5}SD,

	Starts	1st	2nd	3rd	Win & Pl
Career Total (Turf)	10	0	0	0	192
Career Total (AW)	7	3	0	0	7433

68 4/09 Kemp 1m4f (0-70)H STD £2590
63 3/09 Kemp 1m4f (0-65)H STD £1942
59 3/09 Ling 1m5f (0-70)H STD £2900
Total win prize-money £7433

Going (Turf): **Sf: 0-1 GS: 0-3 Gd: 0-3 GF: 0-3 Fm: 0-0**
Distance: 5f/6f: 0-0 7f-8f: 0-5 **9f-13f: 3-10** 14f+: 0-2
Track : LH: 1-8 **RH: 2-5 Tight: 1-6** Gall: 0-2
Aids: Bl: 0-0 Vi: 0-0 Tstrap: 0-0 Ckp: 0-0
Best Rating: **68** 4/09 Kemp 1m4f stand

Modest; stays 1m5f and acts on Polytrack.

Shanavaz

98(100) (58)**63**

3-y-o gr f Golden Snake (USA)-Safinaz (Environment Friend)

C J Teague (Mrs G S Rees 6/8) Richard Underwood

Placings:500-005445000544006 (7557)

2009: 8^{0}GS, 10^{0}HY, 10^{5}GF, 10^{4}GF, 12^{4}SD, 11^{5}GS, 10^{0}GS, 9^{0}F, 12^{0}GS, 13^{5}GF, 16^{4}GF, 15^{4}G, 15^{0}S, 12^{0}SD, 13^{6}SD,

	Starts	1st	2nd	3rd	Win & Pl
Career Total (Turf)	15	0	0	0	438
Career Total (AW)	3	0	0	0	241

Going (Turf): **Sf: 0-3 GS: 0-5 Gd: 0-1 GF: 0-5 Fm: 0-1**
Distance: 5f/6f: 0-2 7f-8f: 0-0 9f-13f: 0-11 14f+: 0-5
Track : LH: 0-15 RH: 0-1 Tight: 0-7 Gall: 0-2
Aids: Bl: 0-0 Vi: 0-0 Tstrap: 0-6 Ckp: 0-6
Best Rating: **63** 9/08 Hayd 1m30y gd-fm

Moderate; stays 1m4f; acts on Polytrack; has worn cheek-pieces.

Shandelight (IRE)

(104) (55)**63**

5-y-o b m Dilshaan-By Candlelight (IRE) (Roi Danzig (USA))

Miss J A Camacho Bolingbroke, Andrew, Jordan, Thompson

Placings:006/4102042/5035516600-2 (7670)

2009: 12^{2}SD,

	Starts	1st	2nd	3rd	Win & Pl
Career Total (Turf)	12	1	2	0	4288
Career Total (AW)	9	1	1	1	2941

63 6/08 Bath 1m3f144y (0-65)H GD £2072
52 5/07 Sthl 1m (0-45) STD £2047
Total win prize-money £4120

Going (Turf): Sf: 0-2 GS: 0-1 **Gd: 1-4** GF: 0-3 Fm: 0-2
Distance: 5f/6f: 0-2 7f-8f: 1-2 9f-13f: 1-16 14f+: 0-1
Track : **LH: 2-14** RH: 0-4 **Tight: 1-11** Gall: 0-0
Aids: Bl: 0-0 Vi: 0-0 Tstrap: 2-13 Ckp: 2-13
Best Rating: **63** 6/08 Bath 1m3f144y good

Moderate filly; stays 1m4f; acts on good ground and both All-Weather surfaces; has worn cheekpieces.

Shangani

104(89) (70)**85**

3-y-o b f Ishiguru (USA)-Sheesha (USA) (Shadeed (USA))

H Candy Henry Candy

Placings:2-1516345 (7032)

2009: 6^{1}GF, 7^{5}GF, 6^{1}G, 6^{6}GF, 6^{3}GF, 6^{4}S, 7^{5}S,

	Starts	1st	2nd	3rd	Win & Pl
Career Total (Turf)	7	2	0	1	9850
Career Total (AW)	1	0	1	0	705

85 7/09 Wind 6f (0-80)H GD £4857
74 6/09 Sals 6f212y G-F £3885
Total win prize-money £8743

Going (Turf): Sf: 0-2 GS: 0-0 **Gd: 1-1 GF: 1-4** Fm: 0-0
Distance: 5f/6f: 1-3 7f-8f: 1-5 9f-13f: 0-0 14f+: 0-0
Track : LH: 0-1 RH: 0-0 Tight: 0-1 **Gall: 1-1**
Aids: Bl: 0-0 Vi: 0-0 Tstrap: 0-0 Ckp: 0-0
Best Rating: **85** 7/09 Wind 6f good

Useful; effective over 6f-7f; acts on good/fast ground; goes on Polytrack.

Shanghai Star (IRE)

84(88) (41)**76**

5-y-o b g Soviet Star (USA)-Sweet Surrender (IRE) (Pennekamp (USA))

Patrick Allen (Irene J Monaghan 11/8) Michael Gavigan

Placings:0/620100-0010500 (7043a)

2009: 16^{0}YS, 10^{0}GF, 10^{1}G, 10^{0}G, 10^{5}GF, 12^{0}SD, 12^{0}HY,

	Starts	1st	2nd	3rd	Win & Pl
Career Total (Turf)	13	2	1	0	11020
Career Total (AW)	1	0	0	0	

64 6/09 Slig 1m2f GD £4696
76 9/08 Rosc 1m4f YLD £5080
Total win prize-money £9777

Going (Turf): Sf: 0-2 GS: 0-0 **Gd: 1-5** GF: 0-2 Fm: 0-0
Distance: 5f/6f: 0-0 7f-8f: 0-0 **9f-13f: 2-12** 14f+: 0-2
Track : LH: 0-6 **RH: 2-7** Tight: 0-2 Gall: 0-0
Aids: Bl: 0-1 Vi: 0-0 Tstrap: 0-0 Ckp: 0-0
Best Rating: **76** 9/08 Rosc 1m4f yield

Shannersburg (IRE)

92(102) (69)**70**

4-y-o b/br g Johannesburg (USA)-Shahoune (USA) (Blushing Groom (FR))

D E Pipe (A B Haynes 21/10) Mrs S J Brookhouse

Placings:052214/06-60001 (7888)

2009: 9^{6}GF, 8^{0}SS, 8^{0}G, 10^{0}SD, 12^{1}SD,

	Starts	1st	2nd	3rd	Win & Pl
Career Total (Turf)	10	1	2	0	6990
Career Total (AW)	3	1	0	0	1979

12/09 Ling 1m4f STD £1978
80 8/07 Nott 1m54y GD £4533
Total win prize-money £6513

Going (Turf): Sf: 0-1 GS: 0-2 **Gd: 1-5** GF: 0-2 Fm: 0-0
Distance: 5f/6f: 0-1 7f-8f: 0-5 **9f-13f: 2-7** 14f+: 0-0
Track : **LH: 2-6** RH: 0-5 **Tight: 1-7** Gall: 0-0
Aids: **Bl: 1-3** Vi: 0-0 Tstrap: 0-0 Ckp: 0-0
Best Rating: **80** 8/07 Nott 1m54y good

Fair sort; stays 1m4f; acts on polytrack and good ground.

Shannon Golden

91(97) (61)44
3-y-o b g Tumbleweed Ridge-Cledeschamps (Doc Marten)
S R Bowring P O'Boyle

Placings:40500105 (7615)
2009: 7[4]SD, 6[0]S, 5[5]SD, 5[0]G, 6[0]SD, 5[1]SD, 5[0]S, 8[5]SD,

	Starts	1st	2nd	3rd	Win & Pl
Career Total (Turf)	3	0	0	0	
Career Total (AW)	5	1	0	0	2047

61 10/09 Wolv 5f216y (0-55) STD £2047
Total win prize-money £2047

Going (Turf): Sf: 0-2 GS: 0-0 Gd: 0-1 GF: 0-0 Fm: 0-0
Distance: 5f/6f: 1-6 7f-8f: 0-1 9f-13f: 0-1 14f+: 0-0
Track : LH: 1-4 RH: 0-0 Tight: 1-2 Gall: 0-0
Aids: Bl: 0-0 Vi: 0-0 Tstrap: 0-0 Ckp: 0-0
Best Rating: 61 10/09 Wolv 5f216y stand

Moderate; effective over 5f-6f and acts on sand; has worn a tongue-tie.

Shannon Weir (IRE)

20
7-y-o br g Norwich-Go Meekly (IRE) (Bulldozer)
E J Creighton Four Provinces Partnership

Placings:0 (2738)
2009: 11[0]G,

	Starts	1st	2nd	3rd	Win & Pl
Career Total (Turf)	1	0	0	0	

Going (Turf): Sf: 0-0 GS: 0-0 Gd: 0-1 GF: 0-0 Fm: 0-0
Distance: 5f/6f: 0-0 7f-8f: 0-0 9f-13f: 0-1 14f+: 0-0
Track : LH: 0-1 RH: 0-0 Tight: 0-0 Gall: 0-0
Aids: Bl: 0-0 Vi: 0-0 Tstrap: 0-0 Ckp: 0-0

Shanzu

97(88) (65)81
4-y-o b f Kyllachy-Limuru (Salse (USA))
G L Moore Baraka Partnership

Placings:625/415010-00000 (4262)
2009: 8[0]G, 8[0]G, 9[0]GF, 8[0]SD, 8[0]G,

	Starts	1st	2nd	3rd	Win & Pl
Career Total (Turf)	12	2	1	0	7920
Career Total (AW)	2	0	0	0	192

81 9/08 Leic 1m60y (0-75)H SFT £3885
74 6/08 Wind 1m67y (0-75)H G-F £3070
Total win prize-money £6957

Going (Turf): Sf: 1-2 GS: 0-2 Gd: 0-3 GF: 1-5 Fm: 0-0
Distance: 5f/6f: 0-1 7f-8f: 0-6 9f-13f: 2-7 14f+: 0-0
Track : LH: 0-0 RH: 2-10 Tight: 1-4 Gall: 0-0
Aids: Bl: 0-3 Vi: 0-0 Tstrap: 0-0 Ckp: 0-0
Best Rating: 81 9/08 Leic 1m60y soft

Fair; stays 1m and acts on most ground.

Shape Shifter (USA)

83 40
3-y-o ch g Performing Magic (USA)-Shot Gun Frances (USA) (Commemorate (USA))
J R Best Kent Bloodstock

Placings:000-0000 (6758)
2009: 9[0]F, 14[0]GF, 15[0]GF, 11[0]G,

	Starts	1st	2nd	3rd	Win & Pl
Career Total (Turf)	7	0	0	0	

Going (Turf): Sf: 0-0 GS: 0-0 Gd: 0-2 GF: 0-4 Fm: 0-1
Distance: 5f/6f: 0-0 7f-8f: 0-3 9f-13f: 0-2 14f+: 0-2
Track : LH: 0-2 RH: 0-3 Tight: 0-2 Gall: 0-0
Aids: Bl: 0-0 Vi: 0-0 Tstrap: 0-0 Ckp: 0-0
Best Rating: 40 7/08 Yarm 7f3y gd-fm

Sharaayeen

86(87) (67)77
2-y-o br c Singspiel (IRE)-Corinium (IRE) (Turtle Island (IRE))
B W Hills Hamdan Al Maktoum

Placings:510 (6993)
2009: 8[5]SD, 8[1]GF, 8[0]GS,

	Starts	1st	2nd	3rd	Win & Pl
Career Total (Turf)	2	1	0	0	5181
Career Total (AW)	1	0	0	0	0

77 9/09 Ffos 1m G-F £5180
Total win prize-money £5181

Going (Turf): Sf: 0-0 GS: 0-1 Gd: 0-0 GF: 1-1 Fm: 0-0
Distance: 5f/6f: 0-0 7f-8f: 1-3 9f-13f: 0-0 14f+: 0-0
Track : LH: 1-2 RH: 0-1 Tight: 0-0 Gall: 1-2
Aids: Bl: 0-0 Vi: 0-0 Tstrap: 0-0 Ckp: 0-0
Best Rating: 77 9/09 Ffos 1m gd-fm

Fair; effective over 1m; acts on fast ground; handles Polytrack.

Sharakti (IRE)

(64) (16)
2-y-o b g Rakti-Easter Parade (Entrepreneur)
A J McCabe Mrs D E Sharp

Placings:0 (6125)
2009: 8[0]SD,

	Starts	1st	2nd	3rd	Win & Pl
Career Total (Turf)	0	0	0	0	
Career Total (AW)	1	0	0	0	

Going (Turf): Sf: 0-0 GS: 0-0 Gd: 0-0 GF: 0-0 Fm: 0-0
Distance: 5f/6f: 0-0 7f-8f: 0-0 9f-13f: 0-1 14f+: 0-0
Track : LH: 0-1 RH: 0-0 Tight: 0-1 Gall: 0-0
Aids: Bl: 0-0 Vi: 0-0 Tstrap: 0-0 Ckp: 0-0
Best Rating: 16 9/09 Wolv 1m141y stand

Share Option

(89) (45)55
7-y-o b g Polish Precedent (USA)-Quota (Rainbow Quest (USA))
A W Carroll Last Day Racing Partnership

Placings:231/500/000/0 (1609)
2009: 16[0]SD,

	Starts	1st	2nd	3rd	Win & Pl
Career Total (Turf)	9	1	1	1	10851
Career Total (AW)	1	0	0	0	

8/05 Claf 1m4f SFT £6383
Total win prize-money £6383

Going (Turf): Sf: 1-2 GS: 0-1 Gd: 0-3 GF: 0-1 Fm: 0-0
Distance: 5f/6f: 0-0 7f-8f: 0-0 9f-13f: 1-3 14f+: 0-7
Track : LH: 0-5 RH: 1-4 Tight: 0-0 Gall: 0-0
Aids: Bl: 0-0 Vi: 0-0 Tstrap: 0-0 Ckp: 0-0
Best Rating: 88 5/05 StCl 1m2f110y gd-sft

Shared Moment (IRE)

100 65
3-y-o ch f Tagula (IRE)-Good Thought (IRE) (Mukaddamah (USA))
J Gallagher (Ollie Pears 24/7) Mark Benton

Placings:3215364200 (6394)
2009: 8[3]G, 9[2]G, 8[1]GF, 8[5]G, 7[3]GF, 10[6]GF, 8[4]G, 8[2]GF, 8[0]GF, 8[0]GF,

	Starts	1st	2nd	3rd	Win & Pl
Career Total (Turf)	10	1	2	2	4898

64 7/09 Nott 1m75y G-F £2047
Total win prize-money £2047

Going (Turf): Sf: 0-0 GS: 0-0 Gd: 0-4 GF: 1-6 Fm: 0-0
Distance: 5f/6f: 0-0 7f-8f: 0-3 9f-13f: 1-7 14f+: 0-0
Track : LH: 1-4 RH: 0-3 Tight: 0-3 Gall: 0-0
Aids: Bl: 0-0 Vi: 0-0 Tstrap: 1-9 Ckp: 1-9
Best Rating: 65 8/09 Brig 7f214y gd-fm

Modest; suited by 1m; acts on good and faster ground; has worn cheekpieces.

Shark Man (IRE)

89(95) (78)78
2-y-o b g Arakan (USA)-Sharklyah (IRE) (Polish Precedent (USA))
P J McBride J Burns

Placings:521200500121 (7319)
2009: 5[5]GF, 5[2]SD, 5[1]SD, 6[2]GF, 6[0]G, 6[0]G, 7[5]SD, 7[0]GF, 8[0]GF, 7[1]SD, 6[2]SD, 7[1]SD,

	Starts	1st	2nd	3rd	Win & Pl
Career Total (Turf)	6	0	1	0	1927
Career Total (AW)	6	3	2	0	9102

68 11/09 Wolv 7f32y STD £2729
69 10/09 Kemp 7f STD £2047
78 4/09 Wolv 5f20y STD £2914
Total win prize-money £7691

Going (Turf): Sf: 0-0 GS: 0-0 Gd: 0-2 GF: 0-4 Fm: 0-0
Distance: 5f/6f: 1-7 7f-8f: 2-4 9f-13f: 0-1 14f+: 0-0
Track : LH: 2-4 RH: 1-4 Tight: 2-3 Gall: 0-0
Aids: Bl: 0-0 Vi: 0-0 Tstrap: 1-1 Ckp: 1-1
Best Rating: 78 5/09 NmkR 6f gd-fm

Fair; effective at 5f-7f; acts on fast ground and on Polytrack; has worn cheekpieces.

Sharp And Chic

67(72) (47)16
2-y-o b f Needwood Blade-Moreover (IRE) (Caerleon (USA))
M L W Bell Thurloe Thoroughbreds XXV

Placings:00 (6728)
2009: 8[0]SS, 8[0]S,

	Starts	1st	2nd	3rd	Win & Pl
Career Total (Turf)	1	0	0	0	
Career Total (AW)	1	0	0	0	

Going (Turf): Sf: 0-1 GS: 0-0 Gd: 0-0 GF: 0-0 Fm: 0-0
Distance: 5f/6f: 0-0 7f-8f: 0-2 9f-13f: 0-0 14f+: 0-0
Track : LH: 0-1 RH: 0-0 Tight: 0-1 Gall: 0-0
Aids: Bl: 0-0 Vi: 0-0 Tstrap: 0-0 Ckp: 0-0
Best Rating: 47 10/09 Ling 1m std-slw

Sharp Bullet (IRE)

92(100) (74)76

3-y-o b g Royal Applause-Anna Frid (GER) (Big Shuffle (USA))

W R Swinburn P W Harris

Placings:1-4050 (6434)

2009: 5[4]GF, 5[0]GF, 5[5]SD, 5[0]SD,

	Starts	1st	2nd	3rd	Win & Pl
Career Total (Turf)	3	1	0	0	4270
Career Total (AW)	2	0	0	0	0

76 8/08 Sand 5f6y SFT £3885

Total win prize-money £3886

Going (Turf): Sf: 1-1 GS: 0-0 Gd: 0-1 GF: 0-1 Fm: 0-0
Distance: 5f/6f: 1-5 7f-8f: 0-0 9f-13f: 0-0 14f+: 0-0
Track : LH: 0-1 RH: 0-1 Tight: 0-1 Gall: 0-2
Aids: Bl: 0-0 Vi: 0-0 Tstrap: 0-0 Ckp: 0-0
Best Rating: 76 8/08 Sand 5f6y soft

Fairl 105,000euros first foal of a smart dual 5-6f juvenile winner; effective at 5f on soft ground.

Sharp Discovery

81(13) 26

3-y-o b f Needwood Blade-You Found Me (Robellino (USA))

J M Bradley racingshares.co.uk

Placings:000000-000 (2744)

2009: 6[0]GF, 8[0]F, 7[0]SD,

	Starts	1st	2nd	3rd	Win & Pl
Career Total (Turf)	8	0	0	0	
Career Total (AW)	1	0	0	0	

Going (Turf): Sf: 0-0 GS: 0-1 Gd: 0-3 GF: 0-2 Fm: 0-2
Distance: 5f/6f: 0-6 7f-8f: 0-2 9f-13f: 0-1 14f+: 0-0
Track : LH: 0-6 RH: 0-0 Tight: 0-0 Gall: 0-3
Aids: Bl: 0-1 Vi: 0-0 Tstrap: 0-2 Ckp: 0-2
Best Rating: 26 5/08 Wwck 5f gd-sft

Sharp Eclipse

90 65

2-y-o ch g Exceed And Excel (AUS)-Helen Sharp (Pivotal)

K A Ryan Hambleton Racing Ltd XI

Placings:530 (2099)

2009: 5[5]GF, 5[3]GS, 6[0]GS,

	Starts	1st	2nd	3rd	Win & Pl
Career Total (Turf)	3	0	0	1	482

Going (Turf): Sf: 0-0 GS: 0-2 Gd: 0-0 GF: 0-1 Fm: 0-0
Distance: 5f/6f: 0-3 7f-8f: 0-0 9f-13f: 0-0 14f+: 0-0
Track : LH: 0-0 RH: 0-0 Tight: 0-0 Gall: 0-0
Aids: Bl: 0-0 Vi: 0-0 Tstrap: 0-0 Ckp: 0-0
Best Rating: 65 5/09 Newc 5f gd-sft

Modest; effective over 5f; acts on easy ground.

Sharp Shoes

87 57

2-y-o br g Needwood Blade-Mary Jane (Tina's Pet)

Mrs A Duffield T P McMahon and D McMahon

Placings:0523 (6542)

2009: 5[0]GS, 5[5]GF, 6[2]GF, 6[3]GF,

	Starts	1st	2nd	3rd	Win & Pl
Career Total (Turf)	4	0	1	1	1589

Going (Turf): Sf: 0-0 GS: 0-1 Gd: 0-0 GF: 0-3 Fm: 0-0
Distance: 5f/6f: 0-4 7f-8f: 0-0 9f-13f: 0-0 14f+: 0-0
Track : LH: 0-2 RH: 0-0 Tight: 0-0 Gall: 0-0
Aids: Bl: 0-0 Vi: 0-0 Tstrap: 0-0 Ckp: 0-0
Best Rating: 57 10/09 Wwck 6f gd-fm

Moderate; stays 6f; acts on fast ground.

Sharp Sovereign (USA)

96 67

3-y-o b g Cactus Ridge (USA)-Queen Of Humor (USA) (Distorted Humor (USA))

Miss L A Perratt (I Semple 21/9) Raymond Miquel

Placings:6010-640500050040 (6987)

2009: 8[6]GF, 12[4]GS, 12[0]GF, 12[5]GS, 12[0]GF, 9[0]G, 11[0]GS, 10[5]GF, 12[0]S, 12[0]GS, 11[4]G, 9[0]G,

	Starts	1st	2nd	3rd	Win & Pl
Career Total (Turf)	16	1	0	0	2999

67 9/08 Bevl 7f100y SFT £2590

Total win prize-money £2590

Going (Turf): Sf: 1-2 GS: 0-6 Gd: 0-3 GF: 0-5 Fm: 0-0
Distance: 5f/6f: 0-1 **7f-8f: 1-2** 9f-13f: 0-13 14f+: 0-0
Track : LH: 0-5 **RH: 1-9** Tight: 0-7 Gall: 0-2
Aids: Bl: 0-1 Vi: 0-0 Tstrap: 0-1 Ckp: 0-1
Best Rating: 67 5/09 Haml 1m4f17y gd-sft

Modest; stays 1m4f; acts on easy or soft ground; has worn blinkers, cheekpieces and a tongue tie.

Sharpazmax (IRE)

101(108) (84)79

5-y-o b g Daggers Drawn (USA)-Amour Toujours (IRE) (Law Society (USA))

P J Makin Weldspec Glasgow Limited

Placings:5111/60/5643620 (7775)

2009: 10[5]SD, 10[6]G, 12[4]GF, 11[3]SD, 12[6]GF, 10[2]SD, 10[0]SD,

	Starts	1st	2nd	3rd	Win & Pl
Career Total (Turf)	6	0	0	0	361
Career Total (AW)	7	3	1	1	11421

83 12/06 Ling 7f (0-85) STD £4533
72 11/06 Ling 7f STD £2388
74 11/06 Ling 7f STD £2388

Total win prize-money £9312

Going (Turf): Sf: 0-0 GS: 0-0 Gd: 0-2 GF: 0-4 Fm: 0-0
Distance: 5f/6f: 0-1 **7f-8f: 3-5** 9f-13f: 0-7 14f+: 0-0
Track : LH: 3-6 RH: 0-5 **Tight: 3-6** Gall: 0-1
Aids: Bl: 0-0 Vi: 0-0 Tstrap: 0-0 Ckp: 0-0
Best Rating: 84 9/09 Kemp 1m3f stand

Fair; stays 1m4f; acts on Polytrack.

Sharpened Edge

105 87

3-y-o b f Exceed And Excel (AUS)-Beveled Edge (Beveled (USA))

B Palling Christopher J Mason

Placings:3-031363430 (6666)

2009: 7[0]S, 6[3]GF, 5[1]G, 5[3]G, 5[6]GF, 5[3]GF, 5[4]GF, 5[3]G, 5[0]GS,

	Starts	1st	2nd	3rd	Win & Pl
Career Total (Turf)	10	1	0	5	8989

85 6/09 Sand 5f6y (0-75)H GD £3885

Total win prize-money £3886

Going (Turf): Sf: 0-1 GS: 0-1 **Gd: 1-4** GF: 0-4 Fm: 0-0
Distance: 5f/6f: 1-8 7f-8f: 0-2 9f-13f: 0-0 14f+: 0-0
Track : LH: 0-0 RH: 0-0 Tight: 0-0 Gall: 0-0
Aids: Bl: 0-0 Vi: 0-0 Tstrap: 0-0 Ckp: 0-0
Best Rating: 87 7/09 Sand 5f6y good

Useful; effective at 5f-6f; acts on good ground.

Sharpener (IRE)

(94) (69)71

3-y-o b f Invincible Spirit (IRE)-Daily Double (FR) (Unfuwain (USA))

R Hannon Mrs J Wood

Placings:30542014-5 (0203)

2009: 6[5]SD,

	Starts	1st	2nd	3rd	Win & Pl
Career Total (Turf)	4	0	1	1	2721
Career Total (AW)	5	1	0	0	4198

69 11/08 Ling 5f STD £3885

Total win prize-money £3886

Going (Turf): Sf: 0-1 GS: 0-1 Gd: 0-2 GF: 0-0 Fm: 0-0
Distance: 5f/6f: 1-8 7f-8f: 0-1 9f-13f: 0-0 14f+: 0-0
Track : LH: 1-5 RH: 0-1 **Tight: 1-3** Gall: 0-2
Aids: Bl: 0-0 Vi: 0-0 Tstrap: 0-0 Ckp: 0-0
Best Rating: 71 7/08 NmkJ 6f good

Fair; suited by 5f-6f; acts on good ground; goes on Polytrack.

Sharps Gold

(99) (56)40

4-y-o ch f Twice As Sharp-Toking N' Joken (IRE) (Mukaddamah (USA))

D Morris R Nunn

Placings:556160003/62000-001600 (2924)

2009: 7[0]SD, 8[0]SD, 7[1]SD, 8[6]SD, 7[0]SD, 8[0]SD,

	Starts	1st	2nd	3rd	Win & Pl
Career Total (Turf)	5	0	0	0	0
Career Total (AW)	15	2	1	1	4319

52 2/09 Kemp 7f (0-45) STD £1364
47 9/07 Ling 6f STD £2047

Total win prize-money £3413

Going (Turf): Sf: 0-2 GS: 0-1 Gd: 0-1 GF: 0-1 Fm: 0-0
Distance: 5f/6f: 1-6 7f-8f: 1-10 9f-13f: 0-4 14f+: 0-0
Track : LH: 1-12 RH: 1-4 **Tight: 1-10** Gall: 0-0
Aids: Bl: 0-4 Vi: 0-1 Tstrap: 0-0 Ckp: 0-0
Best Rating: 56 2/08 Kemp 1m stand

Moderate; stays 1m; acts on Polytrack.

Shava

(100) (56)48

9-y-o b g Atraf-Anita Marie (IRE) (Anita's Prince)

H J Evans Mrs J Evans

Placings:600/10605/5/3031/1542650503/3010005-066 (0661)

2009: 7[0]SS, 7[6]SD, 7[6]SD,

	Starts	1st	2nd	3rd	Win & Pl
Career Total (Turf)	8	1	0	0	4407
Career Total (AW)	26	3	1	4	6465

56 2/08 Kemp 7f (0-45) STD £1365
58 1/07 Wolv 7f32y (0-50)H STD £2149
56 12/06 Ling 6f (0-45) STD £1433
56 5/03 Newc 7f E(0-70)H G-F £4407

Total win prize-money £9355

Going (Turf): Sf: 0-0 GS: 0-1 Gd: 0-2 **GF: 1-5** Fm: 0-0
Distance: 5f/6f: 1-14 **7f-8f: 3-19** 9f-13f: 0-1 14f+: 0-0
Track : LH: 2-20 RH: 1-8 **Tight: 2-11** Gall: 0-2

Aids: Bl: 0-2 Vi: 0-0 Tstrap: 0-1 Ckp: 0-1
Best Rating: 59 2/07 Sthl 6f stand

Moderate; effective over 6f-7f; acts on Polytrack.

Shavansky

108(103) (88)**90**
5-y-o b g Rock Of Gibraltar (IRE)-Limelighting (USA) (Alleged (USA))
B R Millman John Southway & Andrew Hughes

Placings:026/010-1140550 (7194)
2009: 10^{1}GF, 10^{1}GF, 10^{4}GF, 9^{0}S, 10^{5}GF, 9^{5}GF, 9^{0}SD,

	Starts	1st	2nd	3rd	Win & Pl
Career Total (Turf)	10	2	1	0	14763
Career Total (AW)	3	1	0	0	2730

90 6/09 Ling 1m2f (0-95)H G-F £9066
81 11/08 Ling 1m2f STD £2729
Total win prize-money £11796

Going (Turf): Sf: 0-1 GS: 0-0 Gd: 0-2 **GF: 2-7** Fm: 0-0
Distance: 5f/6f: 0-0 7f-8f: 0-1 **9f-13f: 3-12** 14f+: 0-0
Track : **LH: 2-7** RH: 1-5 **Tight: 2-6** Gall: 0-2
Aids: Bl: 0-0 Vi: 0-0 Tstrap: 0-0 Ckp: 0-0
Best Rating: 90 7/09 Asct 1m2f gd-fm

Useful; stays 1m2f; acts on fast ground; goes on Polytrack.

Shavoulin (USA)

99(85) (31)**58**
5-y-o b/br g Johannesburg (USA)-Hello Josephine (USA) (Take Me Out (USA))
P W Hiatt H3

Placings:04/**3603**0000/00-2304500 (4916)
2009: 9^{2}GF, 9^{3}GF, 11^{0}SD, 9^{4}F, 10^{5}S, 7^{0}F, 8^{0}G,

	Starts	1st	2nd	3rd	Win & Pl
Career Total (Turf)	13	0	1	2	3021
Career Total (AW)	6	0	0	1	1836

Going (Turf): **Sf: 0-3 GS: 0-2 Gd: 0-3 GF: 0-3 Fm: 0-2**
Distance: 5f/6f: 0-4 7f-8f: 0-8 9f-13f: 0-7 14f+: 0-0
Track : LH: 0-8 RH: 0-4 Tight: 0-2 Gall: 0-3
Aids: Bl: 0-2 Vi: 0-1 Tstrap: 0-1 Ckp: 0-1
Best Rating: 77 3/07 Ndas 1m good

Moderate; stays 1m2f and acts on fast ground; has worn various headgear.

Shaweel

106 **117**
3-y-o b c Dansili-Cooden Beach (IRE) (Peintre Celebre (USA))
Saeed Bin Suroor Godolphin

Placings:31035124-502 (7186)
2009: 7^{5}S, 8^{0}G, 8^{2}G,

	Starts	1st	2nd	3rd	Win & Pl
Career Total (Turf)	11	2	2	2	124678

114 8/08 Newb 6f8y G-S £39739
85 5/08 Ayr 6f G-F £4857
Total win prize-money £44596

Going (Turf): Sf: 0-2 **GS: 1-1** Gd: 0-4 **GF: 1-4** Fm: 0-0
Distance: 5f/6f: 1-3 7f-8f: 1-8 9f-13f: 0-0 14f+: 0-0
Track : LH: 0-0 RH: 0-1 Tight: 0-0 Gall: 0-0
Aids: Bl: 0-0 Vi: 0-0 Tstrap: 0-0 Ckp: 0-0
Best Rating: 117 9/08 Curr 7f heavy

Group class; winner of the 2008 Group 2 Gimcrack Stakes; effective at 6f-7f; acts on any ground.

Shaws Diamond (USA)

101(98) (81)**81**
3-y-o ch f Ecton Park (USA)-Dear Abigail (USA) (Dehere (USA))
D Shaw Mrs Lyndsey Shaw

Placings:62003-222604104 (5005)
2009: 7^{2}SD, 8^{2}SD, 7^{2}SD, 6^{6}GF, 7^{0}G, 6^{4}GS, 7^{1}GF, 7^{0}G, 7^{4}G,

	Starts	1st	2nd	3rd	Win & Pl
Career Total (Turf)	8	1	0	0	8452
Career Total (AW)	6	0	4	1	5174

78 7/09 York 7f G-F £6540
Total win prize-money £6541

Going (Turf): Sf: 0-0 GS: 0-2 Gd: 0-3 **GF: 1-3** Fm: 0-0
Distance: 5f/6f: 0-3 **7f-8f: 1-10** 9f-13f: 0-1 14f+: 0-0
Track : **LH: 1-8** RH: 0-2 Tight: 0-6 **Gall: 1-1**
Aids: Bl: 0-0 Vi: 0-0 Tstrap: 0-0 Ckp: 0-0
Best Rating: 81 3/09 Wolv 7f32y stand

Fair; effective over 7f-1m; acts on Polytrack.

Shayera

(96) (56)**66**
4-y-o b f Hawk Wing (USA)-Trick (IRE) (Shirley Heights)
B R Johnson C Lefevre

Placings:0340**40-40** (0346)
2009: 12^{4}SD, 16^{0}SD,

	Starts	1st	2nd	3rd	Win & Pl
Career Total (Turf)	4	0	0	1	644
Career Total (AW)	4	0	0	0	0

Going (Turf): **Sf: 0-1 GS: 0-1 Gd: 0-2 GF: 0-0 Fm: 0-0**
Distance: 5f/6f: 0-0 7f-8f: 0-0 9f-13f: 0-7 14f+: 0-1
Track : LH: 0-2 RH: 0-5 Tight: 0-6 Gall: 0-0
Aids: Bl: 0-0 Vi: 0-0 Tstrap: 0-1 Ckp: 0-1
Best Rating: 66 8/08 Wind 1m2f7y gd-sft

Shayla

85 **59**
2-y-o ch f Pastoral Pursuits-Honours Even (Highest Honor (FR))
G A Swinbank Panther Racing Ltd

Placings:50 (6762)
2009: 6^{5}G, 8^{0}GS,

	Starts	1st	2nd	3rd	Win & Pl
Career Total (Turf)	2	0	0	0	0

Going (Turf): **Sf: 0-0 GS: 0-1 Gd: 0-1 GF: 0-0 Fm: 0-0**
Distance: 5f/6f: 0-0 7f-8f: 0-2 9f-13f: 0-0 14f+: 0-0
Track : LH: 0-1 RH: 0-0 Tight: 0-0 Gall: 0-1
Aids: Bl: 0-0 Vi: 0-0 Tstrap: 0-0 Ckp: 0-0
Best Rating: 59 10/09 Newc 1m gd-sft

Shaylee

101 **61**
4-y-o b f Muhtarram (USA)-Fairywings (Kris)
T D Walford L C And A E Sigsworth

Placings:0621606-6341 (3561)
2009: 10^{6}GS, 7^{3}GF, 9^{4}F, 12^{1}GF,

	Starts	1st	2nd	3rd	Win & Pl
Career Total (Turf)	11	2	1	1	6400

61 7/09 Bevl 1m4f16y (0-60)H G-F £2266
57 8/08 Ripn 1m1f170y (0-70)H G-S £2914
Total win prize-money £5181

Going (Turf): Sf: 0-1 **GS: 1-3** Gd: 0-3 **GF: 1-3** Fm: 0-1
Distance: 5f/6f: 0-0 7f-8f: 0-1 **9f-13f: 2-10** 14f+: 0-0
Track : LH: 0-5 **RH: 2-6 Tight: 2-4** Gall: 0-1
Aids: Bl: 0-0 Vi: 0-0 Tstrap: 0-0 Ckp: 0-0
Best Rating: 61 7/09 Bevl 1m4f16y gd-fm

Moderate; stays 1m4f and acts on most ground; has shown signs of temperament.

She Goes Nowhere (IRE)

(86) (46)
3-y-o br f Pyrus (USA)-Peking Dancer (USA) (King Of Kings (IRE))
M S Tuck J & D Syndicate

Placings:06 (6344)
2009: 7^{0}SD, 5^{6}SD,

	Starts	1st	2nd	3rd	Win & Pl
Career Total (Turf)	0	0	0	0	
Career Total (AW)	2	0	0	0	

Going (Turf): **Sf: 0-0 GS: 0-0 Gd: 0-0 GF: 0-0 Fm: 0-0**
Distance: 5f/6f: 0-1 7f-8f: 0-1 9f-13f: 0-0 14f+: 0-0
Track : LH: 0-1 RH: 0-1 Tight: 0-1 Gall: 0-0
Aids: Bl: 0-0 Vi: 0-0 Tstrap: 0-0 Ckp: 0-0
Best Rating: 46 9/09 Wolv 5f216y stand

She Knows It All (IRE)

83 **57**
2-y-o gr f Verglas (IRE)-Tatamagouche (IRE) (Sadler's Wells (USA))
G A Swinbank John P Jones

Placings:01 (3605)
2009: 5^{0}GF, 7^{1}GF,

	Starts	1st	2nd	3rd	Win & Pl
Career Total (Turf)	2	1	0	0	2590

57 7/09 Bevl 7f100y G-F £2590
Total win prize-money £2590

Going (Turf): Sf: 0-0 GS: 0-0 Gd: 0-0 **GF: 1-2** Fm: 0-0
Distance: 5f/6f: 0-1 **7f-8f: 1-1** 9f-13f: 0-0 14f+: 0-0
Track : LH: 0-0 **RH: 1-1** Tight: 0-0 Gall: 0-0
Aids: Bl: 0-0 Vi: 0-0 Tstrap: 0-0 Ckp: 0-0
Best Rating: 57 7/09 Bevl 7f100y gd-fm

Moderate, stays 7f plus; acts on fast ground.

She Who Dares Wins

(92) (41)**48**
9-y-o b m Atraf-Mirani (IRE) (Danehill (USA))
L R James L R James Limited

Placings:53/4000/**2200**/00/0500-4 (1055)
2009: 5^{4}SD,

	Starts	1st	2nd	3rd	Win & Pl
Career Total (Turf)	10	0	0	1	1081
Career Total (AW)	7	0	2	0	1388

Going (Turf): **Sf: 0-0 GS: 0-1 Gd: 0-1 GF: 0-4 Fm: 0-4**
Distance: 5f/6f: 0-17 7f-8f: 0-0 9f-13f: 0-0 14f+: 0-0
Track : LH: 0-3 RH: 0-0 Tight: 0-1 Gall: 0-0

Aids: Bl: 0-0 Vi: 0-0 Tstrap: 0-0 Ckp: 0-0
Best Rating: 57 5/02 Thsk 5f firm

She's A Character

99 94

2-y-o b f Invincible Spirit (IRE)-Cavernista (Lion Cavern (USA))
R A Fahey Aykroyd And Sons Ltd

Placings:14600 (6090)
2009: 6^{1}GS, 6^{4}GF, 7^{6}G, 6^{0}S, 6^{0}G,

	Starts	1st	2nd	3rd	Win & Pl
Career Total (Turf)	5	1	0	0	9696

85 6/09 Donc 6f G-S £4857
Total win prize-money £4857

Going (Turf): Sf: 0-1 **GS: 1-1** Gd: 0-2 GF: 0-1 Fm: 0-0
Distance: **5f/6f: 1-4** 7f-8f: 0-1 9f-13f: 0-0 14f+: 0-0
Track : LH: 0-0 RH: 0-1 Tight: 0-0 Gall: 0-0
Aids: Bl: 0-0 Vi: 0-0 Tstrap: 0-0 Ckp: 0-0
Best Rating: 94 7/09 Gdwd 7f good

Very useful; stays 6f; acts on good/fast ground.

She's A Model

76(92) (26)17

3-y-o b f Erhaab (USA)-Bedtime Model (Double Bed (FR))
R Ingram Royal Flush Partnership

Placings:00 (3382)
2009: 10^{0}GF, 12^{0}SD,

	Starts	1st	2nd	3rd	Win & Pl
Career Total (Turf)	1	0	0	0	
Career Total (AW)	1	0	0	0	

Going (Turf): Sf: 0-0 GS: 0-0 Gd: 0-0 GF: 0-1 Fm: 0-0
Distance: 5f/6f: 0-0 7f-8f: 0-0 9f-13f: 0-2 14f+: 0-0
Track : LH: 0-2 RH: 0-0 Tight: 0-2 Gall: 0-0
Aids: Bl: 0-0 Vi: 0-0 Tstrap: 0-0 Ckp: 0-0
Best Rating: 26 6/09 Ling 1m4f stand

She's In The Money

105 84

3-y-o b f High Chaparral (IRE)-Luminda (IRE) (Danehill (USA))
R A Fahey (J G Given 26/6) Cavan Pickering & Stewart Whitehead

Placings:2026512512 (6311)
2009: 6^{2}GF, 7^{0}GF, 5^{2}GS, 6^{6}G, 8^{5}G, 7^{1}GF, 7^{2}GS, 7^{5}GF, 7^{1}G, 8^{2}GF,

	Starts	1st	2nd	3rd	Win & Pl
Career Total (Turf)	10	2	4	0	15058

84 9/09 Ayr 7f50y (0-75)H GD £4533
73 8/09 Newc 7f (0-75)H G-F £3238
Total win prize-money £7771

Going (Turf): Sf: 0-0 GS: 0-2 **Gd: 1-3 GF: 1-5** Fm: 0-0
Distance: 5f/6f: 0-3 **7f-8f: 2-7** 9f-13f: 0-0 14f+: 0-0
Track : **LH: 1-4** RH: 0-1 Tight: 0-2 Gall: 0-1
Aids: Bl: 0-0 Vi: 0-0 Tstrap: 0-0 Ckp: 0-0
Best Rating: 84 9/09 Muss 1m gd-fm

Modest; stays 6f and acts on good ground.

She's My Rock (IRE)

(91) (56)

2-y-o b f Rock Of Gibraltar (IRE)-Love And Affection (USA) (Exclusive Era (USA))
S Kirk Miss A Jones

Placings:006304 (7887)
2009: 7^{0}SD, 6^{0}SD, 6^{6}SD, 8^{3}SD, 8^{0}SD, 7^{4}SD,

	Starts	1st	2nd	3rd	Win & Pl
Career Total (Turf)	0	0	0	0	
Career Total (AW)	6	0	0	1	433

Going (Turf): Sf: 0-0 GS: 0-0 Gd: 0-0 GF: 0-0 Fm: 0-0
Distance: 5f/6f: 0-2 7f-8f: 0-3 9f-13f: 0-1 14f+: 0-0
Track : LH: 0-4 RH: 0-2 Tight: 0-3 Gall: 0-0
Aids: Bl: 0-0 Vi: 0-0 Tstrap: 0-0 Ckp: 0-0
Best Rating: 56 8/09 Kemp 7f stand

Moderate; stays 1m; acts on Polytrack.

She's Ok (IRE)

100 79

2-y-o b f Xaar-Silvertine (IRE) (Alzao (USA))
C E Brittain Saeed Manana

Placings:62221004 (6241)
2009: 5^{6}GF, 6^{2}G, 5^{2}GF, 7^{2}G, 6^{1}G, 6^{0}GF, 6^{0}GS, 6^{4}G,

	Starts	1st	2nd	3rd	Win & Pl
Career Total (Turf)	8	1	3	0	28769

79 8/09 NmkJ 6f GD £12952
Total win prize-money £12952

Going (Turf): Sf: 0-0 GS: 0-1 **Gd: 1-4** GF: 0-3 Fm: 0-0
Distance: **5f/6f: 1-6** 7f-8f: 0-2 9f-13f: 0-0 14f+: 0-0
Track : LH: 0-1 RH: 0-0 Tight: 0-1 Gall: 0-0
Aids: Bl: 0-0 Vi: 0-0 Tstrap: 0-0 Ckp: 0-0
Best Rating: 79 8/09 NmkJ 6f good

Fair; effective over 6-7f; acts on good ground.

She's Our Beauty (IRE)

(103) (51)56

6-y-o b m Imperial Ballet (IRE)-Eleonora D'Arborea (Prince Sabo)
S T Mason The Mason Racing Partnership I

Placings:01455/50000535000100/504025331050/0006030 100-6405 (0919)
2009: 5^{6}SD, 5^{4}SD, 5^{0}SD, 5^{5}SD,

	Starts	1st	2nd	3rd	Win & Pl
Career Total (Turf)	27	2	1	4	7896
Career Total (AW)	18	2	0	0	3412

51 12/08 Sthl 5f STD £2047
56 7/07 Catt 5f G-S £2730
51 11/06 Sthl 5f (0-45) STD £1365
67 5/05 Catt 5f G-S £2951
Total win prize-money £9093

Going (Turf): Sf: 0-5 **GS: 2-8** Gd: 0-7 GF: 0-7 Fm: 0-0
Distance: **5f/6f: 4-45** 7f-8f: 0-0 9f-13f: 0-0 14f+: 0-0
Track : LH: 0-7 RH: 0-1 Tight: 0-6 Gall: 0-1
Aids: Bl: 0-2 Vi: 1-19 Tstrap: 2-15 Ckp: 2-15
Best Rating: 67 5/05 Catt 5f gd-sft

Moderate sprinter; best over 5f; acts on soft ground and Fibresand; has worn a visor.

She's Our Dream

82(86) (39)20

4-y-o b f Statue Of Liberty (USA)-Mainly Sunset (Red Sunset)
R C Guest You Trotters Trois

Placings:50306000/0-00000 (1689)
2009: 5^{0}SD, 7^{0}SD, 7^{0}F, 6^{0}GF, 6^{0}G,

	Starts	1st	2nd	3rd	Win & Pl
Career Total (Turf)	11	0	0	1	482
Career Total (AW)	3	0	0	0	

Going (Turf): Sf: 0-0 GS: 0-0 Gd: 0-5 GF: 0-3 Fm: 0-3
Distance: 5f/6f: 0-9 7f-8f: 0-5 9f-13f: 0-0 14f+: 0-0
Track : LH: 0-3 RH: 0-0 Tight: 0-3 Gall: 0-0
Aids: Bl: 0-0 Vi: 0-2 Tstrap: 0-0 Ckp: 0-0
Best Rating: 60 7/07 Bevl 5f good

She's Our Mark

114 (101)109

5-y-o ch m Ishiguru (USA)-Markskeepingfaith (IRE) (Ajraas (USA))
Patrick J Flynn B & M Syndicate

Placings:060422/1122221405/355022023-01251133024 (7077a)
2009: 10^{0}Y, 9^{1}HY, 10^{2}G, 8^{5}GF, 9^{1}S, 10^{1}YS, 9^{3}G, 10^{3}S, 9^{0}GF, 8^{2}GY, 10^{4}Y,

	Starts	1st	2nd	3rd	Win & Pl
Career Total (Turf)	35	6	11	3	284523
Career Total (AW)	1	0	0	1	1673

109 7/09 Leop 1m2f Y-S £39126
104 7/09 Curr 1m1f SFT £30021
106 5/09 Gowr 1m1f100y HVY £41082
106 8/07 Leop 1m YLD £30743
97 5/07 Curr 1m (60-90)H G-F £7003
79 5/07 Limk 6f160y GD £8404
Total win prize-money £156381

Going (Turf): **Sf: 2-6** GS: 0-0 Gd: 1-8 GF: 1-5 Fm: 0-1
Distance: 5f/6f: 0-1 7f-8f: 3-18 9f-13f: 3-17 14f+: 0-0
Track : LH: 2-12 **RH: 3-19** Tight: 0-0 **Gall: 1-2**
Aids: Bl: 0-0 Vi: 0-0 Tstrap: 0-0 Ckp: 0-0
Best Rating: 109 9/09 Curr 1m2f soft

Smart Irish-trained mare; effective from 1m-1m2f; handles fast and soft ground.

She's Pivotal (IRE)

83(78) (28)40

3-y-o ch f Pivotal-Born Beautiful (USA) (Silver Deputy (CAN))
J A Osborne Ben Arbib & Partners

Placings:0060 (7374)
2009: 8^{0}G, 7^{0}SD, 7^{6}GF, 9^{0}SD,

	Starts	1st	2nd	3rd	Win & Pl
Career Total (Turf)	2	0	0	0	0
Career Total (AW)	2	0	0	0	

Going (Turf): Sf: 0-0 GS: 0-0 Gd: 0-1 GF: 0-1 Fm: 0-0
Distance: 5f/6f: 0-0 7f-8f: 0-2 9f-13f: 0-2 14f+: 0-0
Track : LH: 0-2 RH: 0-1 Tight: 0-3 Gall: 0-0
Aids: Bl: 0-0 Vi: 0-0 Tstrap: 0-0 Ckp: 0-0
Best Rating: 40 10/09 Leic 7f9y gd-fm

She's So Pretty (IRE)

(102) (75)**68**

5-y-o ch m Grand Lodge (USA)-Plymsole (USA) (Diesis)

G L Moore Miss S Bowles

Placings:000/0350400330/0226011-5 **(0341)**

2009: 12^{5}SD,

	Starts	1st	2nd	3rd	Win & Pl
Career Total (Turf)	16	1	2	1	4485
Career Total (AW)	5	1	0	2	2652

75 11/08 Kemp 1m3f (0-65)H STD £2047
68 10/08 Brig 1m3f196y (0-55)H G-S £2590
Total win prize-money £4637

Going (Turf): Sf: 0-2 **GS: 1-3** Gd: 0-4 GF: 0-6 Fm: 0-1
Distance: 5f/6f: 0-0 7f-8f: 0-3 **9f-13f: 2-17** 14f+: 0-1
Track : LH: 1-10 RH: 1-7 Tight: 0-7 Gall: 0-1
Aids: **Bl: 2-7** Vi: 0-2 Tstrap: 0-3 Ckp: 0-3
Best Rating: **75** 11/08 Kemp 1m3f stand

Modest; stays 1m4f; acts on most ground on turf; goes on Polytrack.

Sheer Fantastic

(108) (72)**70**

4-y-o b g Fantastic Light (USA)-Sheer Bliss (USA) (Relaunch (USA))

P C Haslam Middleham Park Racing Xviii

Placings:041/1530-451 **(0428)**

2009: 10^{4}SD, 13^{5}SD, 12^{1}SD,

	Starts	1st	2nd	3rd	Win & Pl
Career Total (Turf)	4	0	0	1	385
Career Total (AW)	6	3	0	0	7031

72 2/09 Wolv 1m4f50y (0-75)H STD £2914
70 1/08 Ling 1m2f (0-65)H STD £1876
64 11/07 Kemp 1m2f STD £2047
Total win prize-money £6839

Going (Turf): **Sf: 0-0 GS: 0-2 Gd: 0-1 GF: 0-1 Fm: 0-0**
Distance: 5f/6f: 0-0 7f-8f: 0-1 **9f-13f: 3-8** 14f+: 0-1
Track : **LH: 2-8** RH: 1-2 **Tight: 2-7** Gall: 0-1
Aids: **Bl: 2-4** Vi: 1-4 Tstrap: 0-1 Ckp: 0-1
Best Rating: **72** 2/09 Wolv 1m4f50y stand

Moderate; stays 1m4f; acts on Polytrack; has worn a visor.

Sheer Force (IRE)

96(97) (74)**70**

2-y-o b g Invincible Spirit (IRE)-Imperial Graf (USA) (Blushing John (USA))

W J Knight Bluehills Racing Limited

Placings:030433 **(6627)**

2009: 6^{0}GF, 6^{3}G, 6^{0}G, 7^{4}SD, 7^{3}GF, 7^{3}SS,

	Starts	1st	2nd	3rd	Win & Pl
Career Total (Turf)	4	0	0	2	1878
Career Total (AW)	2	0	0	1	770

Going (Turf): **Sf: 0-0 GS: 0-0 Gd: 0-2 GF: 0-2 Fm: 0-0**
Distance: 5f/6f: 0-2 7f-8f: 0-4 9f-13f: 0-0 14f+: 0-0
Track : LH: 0-2 RH: 0-1 Tight: 0-2 Gall: 0-0
Aids: Bl: 0-0 Vi: 0-0 Tstrap: 0-0 Ckp: 0-0
Best Rating: **74** 10/09 Ling 7f std-slw

Fair; stays 7f; acts on polytrack and fast turf.

Shegarrdi

75 **16**

2-y-o b c Efisio-Elleray (IRE) (Docksider (USA))

K A Ryan Tariq Al Nisf

Placings:00 **(5360)**

2009: 5^{0}G, 6^{0}S,

	Starts	1st	2nd	3rd	Win & Pl
Career Total (Turf)	2	0	0	0	

Going (Turf): **Sf: 0-1 GS: 0-0 Gd: 0-1 GF: 0-0 Fm: 0-0**
Distance: 5f/6f: 0-2 7f-8f: 0-0 9f-13f: 0-0 14f+: 0-0
Track : LH: 0-0 RH: 0-0 Tight: 0-0 Gall: 0-0
Aids: Bl: 0-0 Vi: 0-0 Tstrap: 0-0 Ckp: 0-0
Best Rating: **16** 8/09 Thsk 5f good

Sheik'N'Knotsterd

100(85) (42)**57**

4-y-o ch g Zaha (CAN)-Royal Ivy (Mujtahid (USA))

J F Coupland J F Coupland

Placings:363660/606060-04600434600 **(5254)**

2009: 8^{0}GF, 6^{4}SD, 6^{6}F, 6^{0}GF, 6^{0}SD, 6^{4}G, 6^{3}GF, 7^{4}F, 6^{6}GF, 6^{0}GF, 6^{0}GF,

	Starts	1st	2nd	3rd	Win & Pl
Career Total (Turf)	17	0	0	3	1637
Career Total (AW)	6	0	0	0	0

Going (Turf): **Sf: 0-2 GS: 0-0 Gd: 0-3 GF: 0-10 Fm: 0-2**
Distance: 5f/6f: 0-14 7f-8f: 0-7 9f-13f: 0-2 14f+: 0-0
Track : LH: 0-8 RH: 0-3 Tight: 0-3 Gall: 0-0
Aids: Bl: 0-1 Vi: 0-0 Tstrap: 0-0 Ckp: 0-0
Best Rating: **60** 6/07 Gdwd 6f good

Moderate; stays 6f; acts on fast ground.

Sheila Toss (IRE)

(92) (68)

2-y-o b f Galileo (IRE)-Palacoona (FR) (Last Tycoon)

R Hannon P Byrne

Placings:5 **(6164)**

2009: 7^{5}SD,

	Starts	1st	2nd	3rd	Win & Pl
Career Total (Turf)	0	0	0	0	
Career Total (AW)	1	0	0	0	0

Going (Turf): **Sf: 0-0 GS: 0-0 Gd: 0-0 GF: 0-0 Fm: 0-0**
Distance: 5f/6f: 0-0 7f-8f: 0-1 9f-13f: 0-0 14f+: 0-0
Track : LH: 0-0 RH: 0-1 Tight: 0-0 Gall: 0-0
Aids: Bl: 0-0 Vi: 0-0 Tstrap: 0-0 Ckp: 0-0
Best Rating: **68** 9/09 Kemp 7f stand

Sheila's Castle

101(101) (63)**71**

5-y-o b m Karinga Bay-Candarela (Damister (USA))

S Regan N Trevithick

Placings:13600 **(7785)**

2009: 12^{1}SD, 11^{3}GF, 13^{6}SS, 13^{0}SD, 13^{0}SD,

	Starts	1st	2nd	3rd	Win & Pl
Career Total (Turf)	1	0	0	1	433
Career Total (AW)	4	1	0	0	2730

63 8/09 Ling 1m4f STD £2729
Total win prize-money £2730

Going (Turf): **Sf: 0-0 GS: 0-0 Gd: 0-0 GF: 0-1 Fm: 0-0**

Distance: 5f/6f: 0-0 7f-8f: 0-0 **9f-13f: 1-3** 14f+: 0-2
Track : **LH: 1-4** RH: 0-1 **Tight: 1-4** Gall: 0-0
Aids: Bl: 0-0 Vi: 0-0 Tstrap: 0-0 Ckp: 0-0
Best Rating: **71** 9/09 Leic 1m3f183y gd-fm

Modest; stays 1m4f; acts on Polytrack.

Sheka

94 **74**

2-y-o b f Ishiguru (USA)-Maid For Running (Namaqualand (USA))

I W McInnes T Elsey, S A Elsey, R Mustill

Placings:4164 **(3559)**

2009: 5^{4}GF, 5^{1}GF, 5^{6}GF, 5^{4}GF,

	Starts	1st	2nd	3rd	Win & Pl
Career Total (Turf)	4	1	0	0	4988

74 4/09 Ripn 5f G-F £3885
Total win prize-money £3886

Going (Turf): Sf: 0-0 GS: 0-0 Gd: 0-0 **GF: 1-4** Fm: 0-0
Distance: **5f/6f: 1-4** 7f-8f: 0-0 9f-13f: 0-0 14f+: 0-0
Track : LH: 0-0 RH: 0-0 Tight: 0-0 Gall: 0-0
Aids: Bl: 0-0 Vi: 0-0 Tstrap: 0-0 Ckp: 0-0
Best Rating: **74** 4/09 Ripn 5f gd-fm

Shekan Star

100 (53)**59**

7-y-o b m Sri Pekan (USA)-Celestial Welcome (Most Welcome)

K G Reveley D Young

Placings:0000/0526606421243/1200315222360/000/040-134025423625 **(6310)**

2009: 9^{1}GF, 10^{3}G, 13^{4}GF, 10^{0}GF, 12^{2}GF, 12^{6}GF, 9^{4}GF, 11^{2}G, 12^{3}G, 12^{6}F, 12^{2}GS, 12^{5}GF,

	Starts	1st	2nd	3rd	Win & Pl
Career Total (Turf)	42	3	8	4	18524
Career Total (AW)	6	1	2	1	3466

59 4/09 Bevl 1m1f207y (0-70)H G-F £2590
56 6/06 Haml 1m5f9y (0-70)H G-F £3886
51 4/06 Kemp 1m4f (0-45) STD £2388
54 10/05 Wwck 1m2f188y (0-45) GD £1505
Total win prize-money £10370

Going (Turf): Sf: 0-3 GS: 0-8 Gd: 1-15 **GF: 2-14** Fm: 0-2
Distance: 5f/6f: 0-4 7f-8f: 0-0 **9f-13f: 3-39** 14f+: 1-5
Track : LH: 1-16 **RH: 3-26 Tight: 1-20** Gall: 0-4
Aids: Bl: 0-0 Vi: 0-0 Tstrap: 0-0 Ckp: 0-0
Best Rating: **62** 8/06 Leic 1m3f183y good

Moderate; stays 1m5f; acts on fast ground and Polytrack.

Shelfah (IRE)

91 **58**

2-y-o b f Selkirk (USA)-Pass The Peace (Alzao (USA))

M A Jarvis Sheikh Ahmed Al Maktoum

Placings:045 **(6792)**

2009: 6^{0}S, 6^{4}GF, 8^{5}S,

	Starts	1st	2nd	3rd	Win & Pl
Career Total (Turf)	3	0	0	0	241

Going (Turf): **Sf: 0-2 GS: 0-0 Gd: 0-0 GF: 0-1 Fm: 0-0**
Distance: 5f/6f: 0-1 7f-8f: 0-1 9f-13f: 0-1 14f+: 0-0
Track : LH: 0-1 RH: 0-0 Tight: 0-0 Gall: 0-0
Aids: Bl: 0-0 Vi: 0-0 Tstrap: 0-0 Ckp: 0-0
Best Rating: **58** 9/09 Hayd 6f gd-fm

Shemima

96 110

4-y-o gr f Dalakhani (IRE)-Shemaka (IRE) (Nishapour (FR))
A De Royer-Dupre H H Aga Khan

Placings:012212-14324 (5796)
2009: 10^{1}S, 10^{4}GS, 14^{3}GS, 12^{2}G, 14^{4}G,

	Starts	1st	2nd	3rd	Win & Pl
Career Total (Turf)	11	3	4	1	175015

110	4/09	Chan	1m2f	SFT	£38835
106	9/08	Lonc	1m7f	G-S	£29412
77	6/08	Chan	1m4f	GD	£10662

Total win prize-money £78909

Going (Turf): **Sf: 1-1 GS: 1-4 Gd: 1-6** GF: 0-0 Fm: 0-0
Distance: 5f/6f: 0-0 7f-8f: 0-0 **9f-13f: 2-7** 14f+: 1-4
Track : LH: 0-2 **RH: 3-8** Tight: 0-0 Gall: 0-1
Aids: Bl: 0-0 Vi: 0-0 Tstrap: 0-0 Ckp: 0-0
Best Rating: **110** 7/09 Lonc 1m6f gd-sft

Smart filly; effective at between 1m2f-1m6f; acts well on easy ground.

Shemoli

99 81

3-y-o ch g Singspiel (IRE)-Felawnah (USA) (Mr Prospector (USA))
M A Jarvis Sheikh Ahmed Al Maktoum

Placings:0-223140 (5216)
2009: 11^{2}GF, 12^{2}GF, 12^{3}G, 12^{1}GF, 14^{4}GF, 12^{0}G,

	Starts	1st	2nd	3rd	Win & Pl
Career Total (Turf)	7	1	2	1	6763

81	6/09	Pont	1m4f8y	G-F	£3238

Total win prize-money £3238

Going (Turf): Sf: 0-0 GS: 0-0 Gd: 0-2 **GF: 1-5** Fm: 0-0
Distance: 5f/6f: 0-0 7f-8f: 0-1 **9f-13f: 1-5** 14f+: 0-1
Track : **LH: 1-4** RH: 0-2 Tight: 0-2 Gall: 0-1
Aids: Bl: 0-0 Vi: 0-0 Tstrap: 0-0 Ckp: 0-0
Best Rating: **81** 6/09 Pont 1m4f8y gd-fm

Fair; stays 1m4f and acts on fast ground.

Shenandoah Girl

(103) (57)62

6-y-o b m Almushtarak (IRE)-Thundering Papoose (Be My Chief (USA))
Miss A M Newton-Smith (Miss Gay Kelleway 19/2) David O Moon

Placings:000100310343010000**30-015** (0601)
2009: 11^{0}SD, 12^{1}SD, 12^{5}SD,

	Starts	1st	2nd	3rd	Win & Pl
Career Total (Turf)	13	3	0	3	7253
Career Total (AW)	10	1	0	1	2091

56	2/09	Ling	1m4f	(0-50)H	STD	£1706
62	8/08	Bevl	1m4f16y	(0-60)H	SFT	£2266
56	6/08	Folk	1m4f	(0-55)	G-S	£2047
57	4/08	Sthl	1m4f		GD	£1714

Total win prize-money £7734

Going (Turf): **Sf: 1-3 GS: 1-3 Gd: 1-3** GF: 0-3 Fm: 0-1
Distance: 5f/6f: 0-0 7f-8f: 0-3 **9f-13f: 4-17** 14f+: 0-3
Track : LH: 2-13 RH: 2-10 **Tight: 4-13** Gall: 0-2
Aids: Bl: 0-2 Vi: 0-0 Tstrap: 3-13 Ckp: 3-13
Best Rating: **62** 8/08 Bevl 1m4f16y soft

Moderate; stays 1m4f; acts on good ground and on Polytrack; has worn cheekpieces.

Shercon (IRE)

77 30

2-y-o ch g Redback-Snow Eagle (IRE) (Polar Falcon (USA))
N Tinkler P Beecroft & D Bloy

Placings:000 (6819)
2009: 7^{0}GF, 6^{0}S, 7^{0}GF,

	Starts	1st	2nd	3rd	Win & Pl
Career Total (Turf)	3	0	0	0	

Going (Turf): **Sf: 0-1 GS: 0-0 Gd: 0-0 GF: 0-2 Fm: 0-0**
Distance: 5f/6f: 0-1 7f-8f: 0-2 9f-13f: 0-0 14f+: 0-0
Track : LH: 0-0 RH: 0-0 Tight: 0-0 Gall: 0-0
Aids: Bl: 0-0 Vi: 0-0 Tstrap: 0-0 Ckp: 0-0
Best Rating: **30** 10/09 Rdcr 7f gd-fm

Sheriff's Silk

92(101) (70)46

5-y-o b g Forzando-Sylhall (Sharpo)
B N Pollock (Paul Mason 5/8) Mrs Linda Pestell

Placings:03510/132250/40343656-060 (5479)
2009: 8^{0}SD, 6^{6}G, 8^{0}GF,

	Starts	1st	2nd	3rd	Win & Pl
Career Total (Turf)	5	0	0	0	0
Career Total (AW)	17	2	2	4	8746

67	1/07	Sthl	7f	SLW	£2184
59	11/06	Sthl	7f	STD	£2388

Total win prize-money £4573

Going (Turf): **Sf: 0-0 GS: 0-1 Gd: 0-2 GF: 0-1 Fm: 0-1**
Distance: 5f/6f: 0-6 **7f-8f: 2-15** 9f-13f: 0-1 14f+: 0-0
Track : **LH: 2-15** RH: 0-2 Tight: 0-1 Gall: 0-0
Aids: **Bl: 1-16** Vi: 0-1 Tstrap: 0-0 Ckp: 0-0
Best Rating: **77** 3/07 Sthl 6f stand

Modest; effective at around 7f; acts on Fibresand.

Sherjawy (IRE)

104(105) (62)62

5-y-o b g Diktat-Arruhan (IRE) (Mujtahid (USA))
Miss Z C Davison Charlie's Starrs

Placings:66040/406045R044/2114060000603-61430102545010000003**21** (7835)
2009: 6^{6}SD, 6^{1}SD, 6^{4}SD, 6^{3}SD, 5^{0}SD, 6^{1}SD, 5^{0}SD, 5^{2}SD, 5^{5}SD, 6^{4}GF, 5^{5}F, 5^{0}GF, 6^{1}GF, 6^{0}S, 5^{0}GF, 6^{0}GF, 5^{0}GF, 6^{0}GF, 5^{0}GF, 5^{3}SD, 5^{2}SD, 6^{1}SD,

	Starts	1st	2nd	3rd	Win & Pl
Career Total (Turf)	25	1	0	0	4526
Career Total (AW)	25	5	3	3	11278

62	12/09	Kemp	6f	(0-55)H	STD	£1706
62	6/09	Gdwd	6f	(0-70)H	G-F	£3885
57	3/09	Kemp	6f	(0-55)H	STD	£1706
50	1/09	Kemp	6f		STD	£1706
63	2/08	Kemp	6f	(0-50)H	STD	£1943
56	2/08	Sthl	5f		STD	£1774

Total win prize-money £12722

Going (Turf): Sf: 0-3 GS: 0-4 Gd: 0-5 **GF: 1-12** Fm: 0-1
Distance: **5f/6f: 6-43** 7f-8f: 0-7 9f-13f: 0-0 14f+: 0-0
Track : LH: 0-11 **RH: 4-13** Tight: 0-3 Gall: 0-5
Aids: **Bl: 5-42** Vi: 0-0 Tstrap: 1-3 Ckp: 1-3
Best Rating: **63** 2/08 Kemp 6f stand

Moderate; effective over 5f-6f; acts on fast ground; goes on Fibresand and Polytrack; has worn blinkers and cheekpieces.

Sherman McCoy

111 86

3-y-o ch g Reset (AUS)-Naomi Wildman (USA) (Kingmambo (USA))
B R Millman Mustajed Partnership

Placings:056-23121434 (6388)
2009: 10^{2}GF, 11^{3}GF, 11^{1}G, 11^{2}GF, 13^{1}G, 14^{4}G, 14^{3}S, 16^{4}GF,

	Starts	1st	2nd	3rd	Win & Pl
Career Total (Turf)	11	2	2	2	12836

85	7/09	NmkJ	1m5f	(0-80)H	GD	£5180
75	5/09	Gdwd	1m3f	(0-70)H	GD	£3238

Total win prize-money £8419

Going (Turf): Sf: 0-2 GS: 0-0 **Gd: 2-3** GF: 0-6 Fm: 0-0
Distance: 5f/6f: 0-0 7f-8f: 0-2 **9f-13f: 2-6** 14f+: 0-3
Track : LH: 0-4 **RH: 2-4** Tight: 1-5 Gall: 1-1
Aids: Bl: 0-0 Vi: 0-0 Tstrap: 0-0 Ckp: 0-0
Best Rating: **86** 9/09 Hayd 1m6f soft

Fair; stays 1m4f; acts on fast ground.

Shernando

95 67

2-y-o b c Hernando (FR)-Shimmering Sea (Slip Anchor)
M Johnston The Originals

Placings:5 (6592)
2009: 8^{5}GS,

	Starts	1st	2nd	3rd	Win & Pl
Career Total (Turf)	1	0	0	0	0

Going (Turf): **Sf: 0-0 GS: 0-1 Gd: 0-0 GF: 0-0 Fm: 0-0**
Distance: 5f/6f: 0-0 7f-8f: 0-0 9f-13f: 0-1 14f+: 0-0
Track : LH: 0-1 RH: 0-0 Tight: 0-0 Gall: 0-0
Aids: Bl: 0-0 Vi: 0-0 Tstrap: 0-0 Ckp: 0-0
Best Rating: **67** 10/09 Nott 1m75y gd-sft

Shesha Bear

103(89) (65)76

4-y-o b f Tobougg (IRE)-Sunny Davis (USA) (Alydar (USA))
W R Muir Joe Bear Racing

Placings:40/550612400-50231 (4744)
2009: 9^{5}GF, 10^{0}GF, 10^{2}G, 10^{3}GF, 11^{1}GS,

	Starts	1st	2nd	3rd	Win & Pl
Career Total (Turf)	12	2	2	1	8566
Career Total (AW)	4	0	0	0	0

69	8/09	Ling	1m3f106y	(0-70)H	G-S	£3070
75	8/08	Brig	1m1f209y	(0-70)H	G-S	£2978

Total win prize-money £6050

Going (Turf): Sf: 0-1 **GS: 2-3** Gd: 0-2 GF: 0-5 Fm: 0-1
Distance: 5f/6f: 0-0 7f-8f: 0-2 **9f-13f: 2-14** 14f+: 0-0
Track : **LH: 2-9** RH: 0-7 **Tight: 1-10** Gall: 0-2
Aids: **Bl: 1-3** Vi: 0-0 Tstrap: 0-0 Ckp: 0-0
Best Rating: **76** 9/08 Brig 1m1f209y good

Modest; stays 1m3f; acts on easy ground.

Sheshali (IRE)

103 74

5-y-o b g Kalanisi (IRE)-Sheshara (IRE) (Kahyasi)
Evan Williams Edwards, Swinnerton, Babb, Howell

Placings:60/1 (4480)
2009: 11^{1}G,

	Starts	1st	2nd	3rd	Win & Pl
Career Total (Turf)	3	1	0	0	3368

74	7/09	Bath	1m3f144y	GD	£3367

Total win prize-money £3368

Going (Turf): Sf: 0-1 GS: 0-0 **Gd: 1-2** GF: 0-0 Fm: 0-0
Distance: 5f/6f: 0-0 7f-8f: 0-2 **9f-13f: 1-1** 14f+: 0-0
Track : **LH: 1-2** RH: 0-0 **Tight: 1-1** Gall: 0-0
Aids: Bl: 0-0 Vi: 0-0 Tstrap: 0-0 Ckp: 0-0
Best Rating: **74** 7/09 Bath 1m3f144y good

Moderate; winning staying hurdler; stays 1m3f plus; acts on good ground.

Shi Shan

92 **65**
2-y-o b c Sampower Star-Nanna (IRE) (Danetime (IRE))
T D Barron R G Toes

Placings:64 **(5439)**
2009: 5^{6}G, 6^{4}GF,

	Starts	1st	2nd	3rd	Win & Pl
Career Total (Turf)	2	0	0	0	241

Going (Turf): **Sf: 0-0 GS: 0-0 Gd: 0-1 GF: 0-1 Fm: 0-0**
Distance: 5f/6f: 0-2 7f-8f: 0-0 9f-13f: 0-0 14f+: 0-0
Track : LH: 0-0 RH: 0-0 Tight: 0-0 Gall: 0-0
Aids: Bl: 0-0 Vi: 0-0 Tstrap: 0-0 Ckp: 0-0
Best Rating: **65** 8/09 Rdcr 6f gd-fm

Speedily bred; promising debut over 5f on good/easy ground.

Shianda

76 **47**
2-y-o b f Kyllachy-Limuru (Salse (USA))
G L Moore Baraka 2 Partnership

Placings:0 **(7183)**
2009: 7^{0}G,

	Starts	1st	2nd	3rd	Win & Pl
Career Total (Turf)	1	0	0	0	

Going (Turf): **Sf: 0-0 GS: 0-0 Gd: 0-1 GF: 0-0 Fm: 0-0**
Distance: 5f/6f: 0-0 7f-8f: 0-1 9f-13f: 0-0 14f+: 0-0
Track : LH: 0-0 RH: 0-0 Tight: 0-0 Gall: 0-0
Aids: Bl: 0-0 Vi: 0-0 Tstrap: 0-0 Ckp: 0-0
Best Rating: **47** 10/09 NmkR 7f good

Shibhan

100 **73**
2-y-o ch f Compton Place-Untold Riches (USA) (Red Ransom (USA))
C E Brittain Saeed Manana

Placings:335003142 **(6534)**
2009: 5^{3}GF, 6^{3}G, 6^{5}GF, 6^{0}GF, 5^{0}G, 5^{3}GF, 7^{1}GF, 7^{4}GF, 6^{2}GF,

	Starts	1st	2nd	3rd	Win & Pl
Career Total (Turf)	9	1	1	3	13004

70 8/09 Ches 7f2y G-F £9066
Total win prize-money £9066

Going (Turf): Sf: 0-0 GS: 0-0 Gd: 0-2 **GF: 1-7** Fm: 0-0
Distance: 5f/6f: 0-5 **7f-8f: 1-4** 9f-13f: 0-0 14f+: 0-0
Track : **LH: 1-3** RH: 0-0 **Tight: 1-1** Gall: 0-2
Aids: Bl: 0-0 Vi: 0-0 Tstrap: 0-2 Ckp: 0-2
Best Rating: **73** 10/09 Pont 6f gd-fm

Fair; stays 7f; acts on a sound surface; has worn cheek-pieces.

Shifting Gold (IRE)

98(97) (67)**72**
3-y-o b g Night Shift (USA)-Gold Bust (Nashwan (USA))
K A Ryan Hambleton Racing Ltd VIII

Placings:56020**0**1**6-10**03**0**1421 **(5733)**
2009: 8^{1}SD, **8**^{0}SD, 11^{0}GF, 11^{3}G, **12**^{0}SD, 11^{1}GS, 12^{4}GS, 12^{2}S, 12^{1}GS,

	Starts	1st	2nd	3rd	Win & Pl
Career Total (Turf)	12	3	2	1	9689
Career Total (AW)	5	1	0	0	2047

72 9/09 Newc 1m4f93y (0-65)H G-S £2525
67 8/09 Haml 1m3f16y (0-60)H G-S £2266
67 1/09 Sthl 1m (0-60)H STD £2047
60 10/08 Nott 1m75y HVY £2729
Total win prize-money £9570

Going (Turf): Sf: 1-5 **GS: 2-4** Gd: 0-2 GF: 0-1 Fm: 0-0
Distance: 5f/6f: 0-2 7f-8f: 1-6 **9f-13f: 3-9** 14f+: 0-0
Track : **LH: 3-9** RH: 1-5 Tight: 1-6 Gall: 1-1
Aids: **Bl: 4-11** Vi: 0-0 Tstrap: 0-1 Ckp: 0-1
Best Rating: **72** 9/09 Newc 1m4f93y gd-sft

Modest; stays 1m4f; acts on easy ground and Fibresand; often blinkered.

Shifting Star (IRE)

103(103) (103)**103**
4-y-o ch g Night Shift (USA)-Ahshado (Bin Ajwaad (IRE))
W R Swinburn Night Shadow Syndicate

Placings:31260/**3**111**4**03-00003 **(7454)**
2009: 6^{0}GF, 6^{0}G, 7^{0}GF, 7^{0}GF, **6**^{3}SD,

	Starts	1st	2nd	3rd	Win & Pl
Career Total (Turf)	15	4	1	2	42748
Career Total (AW)	3	0	0	2	2980

101 8/08 Asct 6f (0-100)H G-S £17230
96 7/08 Asct 6f (0-90)H G-S £9066
98 6/08 Gdwd 6f (0-85)H GD £4533
79 6/07 NmkJ 6f GD £6477
Total win prize-money £37307

Going (Turf): Sf: 0-1 **GS: 2-3 Gd: 2-6** GF: 0-5 Fm: 0-0
Distance: **5f/6f: 4-15** 7f-8f: 0-3 9f-13f: 0-0 14f+: 0-0
Track : LH: 0-1 RH: 0-3 Tight: 0-1 Gall: 0-1
Aids: Bl: 0-0 Vi: 0-0 Tstrap: 0-0 Ckp: 0-0
Best Rating: **103** 10/08 Donc 6f good

Very useful; effective over 6-7f; handles most ground; goes on Polytrack; has worn a tongue tie.

Shimah (USA)

97 **109**
3-y-o ch f Storm Cat (USA)-Sayedat Alhadh (USA) (Mr Prospector (USA))
Kevin Prendergast Hamdan Al Maktoum

Placings:112-0 **(1698)**
2009: 8^{0}GF,

	Starts	1st	2nd	3rd	Win & Pl
Career Total (Turf)	4	2	1	0	78254

109 6/08 Curr 6f G-Y £26327
99 6/08 Curr 6f FRM £9573
Total win prize-money £35901

Going (Turf): Sf: 0-1 GS: 0-0 Gd: 0-0 GF: 0-1 **Fm: 1-1**
Distance: **5f/6f: 2-2** 7f-8f: 0-2 9f-13f: 0-0 14f+: 0-0
Track : LH: 0-0 RH: 0-0 Tight: 0-0 Gall: 0-0
Aids: Bl: 0-0 Vi: 0-0 Tstrap: 0-0 Ckp: 0-0
Best Rating: **109** 8/08 Curr 7f soft

Group class; Irish trained; Group 1 placed; stays 7f; acts on fast and easy ground.

Shimmering Moment (USA)

94(87) (66)**64**
2-y-o ch f Afleet Alex (USA)-Vassar (USA) (Royal Academy (USA))
H R A Cecil (A P Jarvis 11/8) Mogeely Stud & Mrs Maura Gittins

Placings:30 **(6729)**
2009: 6^{3}SD, 6^{0}S,

	Starts	1st	2nd	3rd	Win & Pl
Career Total (Turf)	1	0	0	0	
Career Total (AW)	1	0	0	1	403

Going (Turf): **Sf: 0-1 GS: 0-0 Gd: 0-0 GF: 0-0 Fm: 0-0**
Distance: 5f/6f: 0-1 7f-8f: 0-1 9f-13f: 0-0 14f+: 0-0
Track : LH: 0-1 RH: 0-0 Tight: 0-1 Gall: 0-0
Aids: Bl: 0-0 Vi: 0-0 Tstrap: 0-0 Ckp: 0-0
Best Rating: **66** 8/09 Ling 6f stand

Shimmering Surf (IRE)

(99) (76)
2-y-o b f Danehill Dancer (IRE)-Sun On The Sea (IRE) (Bering)
P Winkworth Butterfield, Strong & Williams

Placings:42 **(6628)**
2009: 7^{4}SD, 8^{2}SS,

	Starts	1st	2nd	3rd	Win & Pl
Career Total (Turf)	0	0	0	0	
Career Total (AW)	2	0	1	0	1445

Going (Turf): **Sf: 0-0 GS: 0-0 Gd: 0-0 GF: 0-0 Fm: 0-0**
Distance: 5f/6f: 0-0 7f-8f: 0-2 9f-13f: 0-0 14f+: 0-0
Track : LH: 0-2 RH: 0-0 Tight: 0-2 Gall: 0-0
Aids: Bl: 0-0 Vi: 0-0 Tstrap: 0-0 Ckp: 0-0
Best Rating: **76** 10/09 Ling 1m std-slw

Fair; stays 1m; acts on Polytrack.

Shimoni

94(104) (85)**88**
5-y-o b m Mark Of Esteem (IRE)-Limuru (Salse (USA))
G L Moore The Welldiggers Partnership

Placings:01/46000**5**0**2**0**6**/**1**46610-1 **(1753)**
2009: 11^{1}GF,

	Starts	1st	2nd	3rd	Win & Pl
Career Total (Turf)	14	3	1	0	17960
Career Total (AW)	5	1	0	0	5124

88 5/09 Wind 1m3f135y (0-85)H G-F £5180
87 9/08 Gdwd 1m4f (0-80)H G-F £4857
85 8/08 Kemp 1m3f (0-85)H STD £4727
75 10/06 Yarm 1m2f21y SFT £3238
Total win prize-money £18004

Going (Turf): Sf: 1-3 GS: 0-3 Gd: 0-3 **GF: 2-5** Fm: 0-0
Distance: 5f/6f: 0-0 7f-8f: 0-1 **9f-13f: 4-15** 14f+: 0-3
Track : LH: 1-6 **RH: 2-11 Tight: 3-11** Gall: 0-4
Aids: Bl: 0-0 **Vi: 1-7** Tstrap: 0-0 Ckp: 0-0
Best Rating: **88** 5/09 Wind 1m3f135y gd-fm

Useful; stays 1m4f; acts on fast and soft ground; has worn a visor.

Shining Times (IRE)

79(77) (25)48

3-y-o br f Danetime (IRE)-Shining Desert (IRE) (Green Desert (USA))

P T Midgley W R Arblaster

Placings:006-00006 **(7270)**

2009: 5^{0}GS, 5^{0}GS, 5^{0}GF, 5^{0}GF, 6^{6}SD,

	Starts	1st	2nd	3rd	Win & Pl
Career Total (Turf)	7	0	0	0	0
Career Total (AW)	1	0	0	0	0

Going (Turf): Sf: 0-0 GS: 0-3 Gd: 0-2 GF: 0-2 Fm: 0-0
Distance: 5f/6f: 0-8 7f-8f: 0-0 9f-13f: 0-0 14f+: 0-0
Track : LH: 0-1 RH: 0-1 Tight: 0-0 Gall: 0-0
Aids: Bl: 0-1 Vi: 0-0 Tstrap: 0-0 Ckp: 0-0
Best Rating: 48 10/08 Rdcr 6f good

Ship's Biscuit

(89) (70)

2-y-o b f Tiger Hill (IRE)-Threefold (USA) (Gulch (USA))

Sir Michael Stoute Philip Newton

Placings:5 **(7450)**

2009: 8^{5}SD,

	Starts	1st	2nd	3rd	Win & Pl
Career Total (Turf)	0	0	0	0	
Career Total (AW)	1	0	0	0	0

Going (Turf): Sf: 0-0 GS: 0-0 Gd: 0-0 GF: 0-0 Fm: 0-0
Distance: 5f/6f: 0-0 7f-8f: 0-1 9f-13f: 0-0 14f+: 0-0
Track : LH: 0-0 RH: 0-1 Tight: 0-0 Gall: 0-0
Aids: Bl: 0-0 Vi: 0-0 Tstrap: 0-0 Ckp: 0-0
Best Rating: 70 11/09 Kemp 1m stand

Shirley High

69(93) (51)

3-y-o b f Forzando-Ripple Effect (Elmaamul (USA))

P Howling Charles Castle

Placings:0650-00520450 **(7714)**

2009: 6^{0}SD, 6^{0}GF, 5^{5}SD, 5^{2}SD, 5^{0}SD, 5^{4}SD, 5^{5}SD, 5^{0}SD,

	Starts	1st	2nd	3rd	Win & Pl
Career Total (Turf)	1	0	0	0	
Career Total (AW)	11	0	1	0	806

Going (Turf): Sf: 0-0 GS: 0-0 Gd: 0-0 GF: 0-1 Fm: 0-0
Distance: 5f/6f: 0-11 7f-8f: 0-1 9f-13f: 0-0 14f+: 0-0
Track : LH: 0-9 RH: 0-2 Tight: 0-8 Gall: 0-1
Aids: Bl: 0-0 Vi: 0-0 Tstrap: 0-0 Ckp: 0-0
Best Rating: 51 10/09 Wolv 5f20y stand

Moderate efforts so far; stays 6f; acts on Polytrack.

Shoot The Pot (IRE)

73(94) (69)33

2-y-o b g Intikhab (USA)-Kerasana (IRE) (Kahyasi)

R M Beckett Des Anderson & Richard Morecombe

Placings:01 **(7825)**

2009: 8^{0}S, 8^{1}SD,

	Starts	1st	2nd	3rd	Win & Pl
Career Total (Turf)	1	0	0	0	
Career Total (AW)	1	1	0	0	2047
69 12/09 Kemp 1m			STD		£2047

Total win prize-money £2047

Going (Turf): Sf: 0-1 GS: 0-0 Gd: 0-0 GF: 0-0 Fm: 0-0
Distance: 5f/6f: 0-0 **7f-8f: 1-2** 9f-13f: 0-0 14f+: 0-0
Track : LH: 0-0 **RH: 1-1** Tight: 0-0 Gall: 0-0
Aids: Bl: 0-0 Vi: 0-0 Tstrap: 0-0 Ckp: 0-0
Best Rating: 69 12/09 Kemp 1m stand

Modest; effective over 1m; acts on Polytrack.

Shooting Party (IRE)

92(99) (76)77

3-y-o b g Noverre (USA)-L-Way First (IRE) (Vision (USA))

R Hannon Mrs R Ablett

Placings:6401-6000 **(6733)**

2009: 8^{6}G, 8^{0}SD, 10^{0}GS, 9^{0}S,

	Starts	1st	2nd	3rd	Win & Pl
Career Total (Turf)	6	1	0	0	2730
Career Total (AW)	2	0	0	0	289
77 10/08 Wind 1m67y (0-75)			GD		£2729

Total win prize-money £2730

Going (Turf): Sf: 0-1 GS: 0-1 **Gd: 1-3** GF: 0-1 Fm: 0-0
Distance: 5f/6f: 0-0 7f-8f: 0-4 **9f-13f: 1-4** 14f+: 0-0
Track : LH: 0-0 **RH: 1-6 Tight: 1-2** Gall: 0-0
Aids: Bl: 0-0 Vi: 0-0 Tstrap: 0-0 Ckp: 0-0
Best Rating: 77 10/08 Wind 1m67y good

Fair; acts on good ground and Polytrack; stays 1m.

Shore Thing (IRE)

105 73

6-y-o b g Docksider (USA)-Spicebird (IRE) (Ela-Mana-Mou)

C R Egerton Vineste

Placings:00/60123320/20/04 **(5530)**

2009: 21^{0}G, 14^{4}G,

	Starts	1st	2nd	3rd	Win & Pl
Career Total (Turf)	14	1	3	2	9267
69 6/06 Yarm 1m6f17y (0-70)H			G-F		£3400

Total win prize-money £3400

Going (Turf): Sf: 0-2 GS: 0-1 Gd: 0-4 **GF: 1-6** Fm: 0-1
Distance: 5f/6f: 0-0 7f-8f: 0-3 9f-13f: 0-3 **14f+: 1-8**
Track : **LH: 1-6** RH: 0-4 **Tight: 1-5** Gall: 0-3
Aids: Bl: 0-0 Vi: 0-0 Tstrap: 0-0 Ckp: 0-0
Best Rating: 81 7/06 Hayd 1m6f gd-fm

Fair; stays 1m6f; acts on fast ground; has worn a tongue tie; winning hurdler/chaser.

Short Affair

101 99

4-y-o b f Singspiel (IRE)-L'Affaire Monique (Machiavellian (USA))

L M Cumani Aston House Stud

Placings:122/340033-1500 **(7291)**

2009: 10^{1}GS, 10^{5}G, 9^{0}GF, 10^{0}S,

	Starts	1st	2nd	3rd	Win & Pl
Career Total (Turf)	13	2	2	3	53230
99 6/09 Donc 1m2f60y (0-100)H			G-S		£16190
8/07 Maia 7f110y			SFT		£4054

Total win prize-money £20244

Going (Turf): Sf: 1-5 GS: 1-1 Gd: 0-6 GF: 0-1 Fm: 0-0
Distance: 5f/6f: 0-0 7f-8f: 1-7 9f-13f: 1-6 14f+: 0-0
Track : **LH: 1-3** RH: 0-8 Tight: 0-1 **Gall: 1-3**
Aids: Bl: 0-0 Vi: 0-0 Tstrap: 0-0 Ckp: 0-0
Best Rating: 99 6/09 Donc 1m2f60y gd-sft

Useful filly; ex-Italian; stays 1m2f and acts on good and soft ground.

Short Cut

99(96) (52)55

3-y-o b g Compton Place-Rush Hour (IRE) (Night Shift (USA))

Ian Williams (S Kirk 28/9) Philip Holden

Placings:00000-0324434 **(7787)**

2009: 5^{0}GF, 5^{3}GF, 6^{2}GS, 6^{4}G, 7^{4}SD, 6^{3}GF, 7^{4}SD,

	Starts	1st	2nd	3rd	Win & Pl
Career Total (Turf)	9	0	1	2	1721
Career Total (AW)	3	0	0	0	0

Going (Turf): Sf: 0-2 GS: 0-1 Gd: 0-1 GF: 0-5 Fm: 0-0
Distance: 5f/6f: 0-7 7f-8f: 0-5 9f-13f: 0-0 14f+: 0-0
Track : LH: 0-4 RH: 0-1 Tight: 0-2 Gall: 0-0
Aids: Bl: 0-0 Vi: 0-0 Tstrap: 0-0 Ckp: 0-0
Best Rating: 55 9/09 Yarm 6f3y gd-fm

Short Sharp Shock

76(85) (59)39

3-y-o b c Mujahid (USA)-Possibility (Robellino (USA))

J Mackie The Boulder Brothers

Placings:006-000 **(4845)**

2009: 10^{0}HY, 8^{0}SD, 8^{0}G,

	Starts	1st	2nd	3rd	Win & Pl
Career Total (Turf)	4	0	0	0	
Career Total (AW)	2	0	0	0	0

Going (Turf): Sf: 0-1 GS: 0-0 Gd: 0-2 GF: 0-1 Fm: 0-0
Distance: 5f/6f: 0-1 7f-8f: 0-4 9f-13f: 0-1 14f+: 0-0
Track : LH: 0-4 RH: 0-0 Tight: 0-2 Gall: 0-0
Aids: Bl: 0-0 Vi: 0-0 Tstrap: 0-0 Ckp: 0-0
Best Rating: 59 11/08 Wolv 7f32y stand

Short Supply (USA)

91(82) (22)48

3-y-o b f Point Given (USA)-Introducing (USA) (Deputy Minister (CAN))

T D Walford B Selective Partnership

Placings:600 **(7353)**

2009: 8^{6}G, 8^{0}GS, 7^{0}SD,

	Starts	1st	2nd	3rd	Win & Pl
Career Total (Turf)	2	0	0	0	0
Career Total (AW)	1	0	0	0	

Going (Turf): Sf: 0-0 GS: 0-1 Gd: 0-1 GF: 0-0 Fm: 0-0
Distance: 5f/6f: 0-0 7f-8f: 0-3 9f-13f: 0-0 14f+: 0-0
Track : LH: 0-2 RH: 0-1 Tight: 0-1 Gall: 0-1
Aids: Bl: 0-0 Vi: 0-0 Tstrap: 0-0 Ckp: 0-0
Best Rating: 48 9/09 Newc 1m gd-sft

Shortwall Lady (IRE)

(88) (29)

4-y-o b f Court Cave (IRE)-Vanished (IRE) (Fayruz)

J L Spearing The Real North Siders

Placings:04-50 (0210)
2009: 8[5]SS, 8[0]SD,

	Starts	1st	2nd	3rd	Win & Pl
Career Total (Turf)	0	0	0	0	
Career Total (AW)	4	0	0	0	289

Going (Turf): Sf: 0-0 GS: 0-0 Gd: 0-0 GF: 0-0 Fm: 0-0
Distance: 5f/6f: 0-0 7f-8f: 0-3 9f-13f: 0-1 14f+: 0-0
Track : LH: 0-2 RH: 0-2 Tight: 0-1 Gall: 0-0
Aids: Bl: 0-2 Vi: 0-0 Tstrap: 0-0 Ckp: 0-0
Best Rating: 29 12/08 Kemp 7f stand

Shosolosa (IRE)

84(95) (55)60
7-y-o b m Dansili-Hajat (Mujtahid (USA))
S A Harris (R C Guest 30/5) S A Harris

Placings:0223050/04302000/063024425103040-000000 (5872)
2009: 8[0]GF, 10[0]G, 8[0]GF, 9[0]GF, 10[0]GF, 10[0]G,

	Starts	1st	2nd	3rd	Win & Pl
Career Total (Turf)	26	1	3	3	15945
Career Total (AW)	10	0	2	1	1431

60 5/08 Donc 1m (0-60)H GD £2914
Total win prize-money £2914

Going (Turf): Sf: 0-0 GS: 0-3 Gd: 1-12 GF: 0-10 Fm: 0-1
Distance: 5f/6f: 0-2 7f-8f: 1-14 9f-13f: 0-20 14f+: 0-0
Track : LH: 0-21 RH: 0-5 Tight: 0-13 Gall: 0-5
Aids: Bl: 0-0 Vi: 0-0 Tstrap: 0-2 Ckp: 0-2
Best Rating: 71 9/04 Newb 6f110y good

Moderate; stays 1m and acts on good ground; usually held up.

Shotley Mac

102 88
5-y-o ch g Abou Zouz (USA)-Julie's Gift (Presidium)
N Bycroft J A Swinburne

Placings:400/00002232025422/21440331106211O-00140 (4310)
2009: 7[0]GF, 6[0]G, 7[1]G, 7[4]G, 7[0]GS,

	Starts	1st	2nd	3rd	Win & Pl
Career Total (Turf)	37	6	8	3	35757

87 6/09 Donc 7f (0-80)H GD £4857
85 11/08 Catt 7f (0-80)H HVY £4857
78 10/08 Catt 7f (0-85)H G-S £4857
76 9/08 Rdcr 7f (0-70)H G-S £2590
75 8/08 Rdcr 1m G-S £2388
74 6/08 Bevl 7f100y (0-70)H G-F £4533
Total win prize-money £24082

Going (Turf): Sf: 1-6 GS: 3-7 Gd: 1-13 GF: 1-10 Fm: 0-1
Distance: 5f/6f: 0-6 7f-8f: 6-20 9f-13f: 0-11 14f+: 0-0
Track : LH: 2-12 RH: 1-12 Tight: 2-9 Gall: 0-4
Aids: Bl: 5-24 Vi: 0-0 Tstrap: 0-0 Ckp: 0-0
Best Rating: 88 7/09 York 7f good

Useful; stays 1m; acts on most ground; has worn blinkers.

Shouldntbethere (IRE)

(100) (68)56
5-y-o ch g Soviet Star (USA)-Octomone (USA) (Hennessy (USA))
Mrs P N Dutfield Mrs Linda Salter

Placings:000312/006002005020/305003620504-66 (0528)
2009: 12[6]SD, 12[6]SD,

	Starts	1st	2nd	3rd	Win & Pl
Career Total (Turf)	7	0	0	0	
Career Total (AW)	25	1	4	3	6233

70 11/06 Sthl 1m STD £2730
Total win prize-money £2730

Going (Turf): Sf: 0-0 GS: 0-2 Gd: 0-3 GF: 0-2 Fm: 0-0
Distance: 5f/6f: 0-1 7f-8f: 1-15 9f-13f: 0-16 14f+: 0-0
Track : LH: 1-13 RH: 0-15 Tight: 0-11 Gall: 0-0
Aids: Bl: 0-0 Vi: 0-0 Tstrap: 0-0 Ckp: 0-0
Best Rating: 70 11/06 Sthl 1m stand

Moderate; stays 1m4f and acts a sound surface.

Show Willing (IRE)

80(88) (60)25
2-y-o b f Elusive City (USA)-Showboat (USA) (Theatrical)
A P Jarvis Christopher Shankland

Placings:00055 (7177)
2009: 6[0]GS, 6[0]SD, 5[0]G, 7[5]SD, 7[5]SD,

	Starts	1st	2nd	3rd	Win & Pl
Career Total (Turf)	2	0	0	0	
Career Total (AW)	3	0	0	0	0

Going (Turf): Sf: 0-0 GS: 0-1 Gd: 0-1 GF: 0-0 Fm: 0-0
Distance: 5f/6f: 0-3 7f-8f: 0-2 9f-13f: 0-0 14f+: 0-0
Track : LH: 0-1 RH: 0-2 Tight: 0-1 Gall: 0-0
Aids: Bl: 0-0 Vi: 0-0 Tstrap: 0-0 Ckp: 0-0
Best Rating: 60 10/09 Ling 7f stand

Showcasing

107 116
2-y-o b c Oasis Dream-Arabesque (Zafonic (USA))
J H M Gosden K Abdulla

Placings:2113 (6450)
2009: 6[2]GF, 6[1]GF, 6[1]GF, 6[3]GF,

	Starts	1st	2nd	3rd	Win & Pl
Career Total (Turf)	4	2	1	1	108043

116 8/09 York 6f G-F £82964
89 7/09 Yarm 6f3y G-F £3784
Total win prize-money £86749

Going (Turf): Sf: 0-0 GS: 0-0 Gd: 0-0 GF: 2-4 Fm: 0-0
Distance: 5f/6f: 1-2 7f-8f: 1-2 9f-13f: 0-0 14f+: 0-0
Track : LH: 0-0 RH: 0-0 Tight: 0-0 Gall: 0-0
Aids: Bl: 0-0 Vi: 0-0 Tstrap: 0-0 Ckp: 0-0
Best Rating: 116 10/09 NmkR 6f gd-fm

Group class; winner of Gimcrack in 2009; effective over 6f; acts on fast ground.

Shubbaan (USA)

(91) (72)
4-y-o b/br c Kingmambo (USA)-Sayedah (IRE) (Darshaan)
M P Tregoning Hamdan Al Maktoum

Placings:2 (6974)
2009: 11[2]SD,

	Starts	1st	2nd	3rd	Win & Pl
Career Total (Turf)	0	0	0	0	
Career Total (AW)	1	0	1	0	771

Going (Turf): Sf: 0-0 GS: 0-0 Gd: 0-0 GF: 0-0 Fm: 0-0
Distance: 5f/6f: 0-0 7f-8f: 0-0 9f-13f: 0-1 14f+: 0-0
Track : LH: 0-0 RH: 0-1 Tight: 0-0 Gall: 0-0
Aids: Bl: 0-0 Vi: 0-0 Tstrap: 0-0 Ckp: 0-0
Best Rating: 72 10/09 Kemp 1m3f stand

Runner-up on belated debut; stays 1m3f; acts on Polytrack.

Shunkawakhan (IRE)

100(101) (70)65
6-y-o b g Indian Danehill (IRE)-Special Park (USA) (Trempolino (USA))
Miss L A Perratt Partick Thistle Racing Club

Placings:2200/5300365662450/63202444333050/324114036131-000060320 (6637)
2009: 8[0]GF, 8[0]GF, 7[0]G, 7[0]G, 7[6]G, 8[0]GS, 7[3]G, 7[2]GF, 7[0]SD,

	Starts	1st	2nd	3rd	Win & Pl
Career Total (Turf)	18	1	2	2	5708
Career Total (AW)	34	3	5	8	13614

70 11/08 Wolv 7f32y (0-62)H STD £2729
65 8/08 Muss 1m (0-60)H GD £2590
62 4/08 Wolv 1m141y (0-65)H STD £2047
60 3/08 Wolv 1m141y (0-55)H STD £2047
Total win prize-money £9415

Going (Turf): Sf: 0-1 GS: 0-3 Gd: 1-5 GF: 0-8 Fm: 0-1
Distance: 5f/6f: 0-14 7f-8f: 2-33 9f-13f: 2-5 14f+: 0-0
Track : LH: 3-25 RH: 1-22 Tight: 4-27 Gall: 0-0
Aids: Bl: 0-7 Vi: 0-0 Tstrap: 4-32 Ckp: 4-32
Best Rating: 70 11/08 Wolv 7f32y stand

Modest; effective at around 1m; acts on sand; wears cheekpieces, has worn blinkers.

Shy

95(101) (75)80
4-y-o ch f Erhaab (USA)-Shi Shi (Alnasr Alwasheek)
P Winkworth Mrs Jenny Willment

Placings:3/23225423-200 (4301)
2009: 13[2]GS, 14[0]G, 16[0]G,

	Starts	1st	2nd	3rd	Win & Pl
Career Total (Turf)	8	0	5	1	4464
Career Total (AW)	4	0	0	2	784

Going (Turf): Sf: 0-1 GS: 0-2 Gd: 0-2 GF: 0-3 Fm: 0-0
Distance: 5f/6f: 0-0 7f-8f: 0-1 9f-13f: 0-7 14f+: 0-4
Track : LH: 0-6 RH: 0-5 Tight: 0-6 Gall: 0-1
Aids: Bl: 0-0 Vi: 0-0 Tstrap: 0-0 Ckp: 0-0
Best Rating: 80 6/08 Wind 1m3f135y gd-fm

Fair; stays 1m4f; acts on easy ground; also goes on Polytrack.

Shy Glance (USA)

103 (76)77
7-y-o b g Red Ransom (USA)-Royal Shyness (Royal Academy (USA))
P Monteith Walcal Property Development Ltd

Placings:0/454536301/15526024640/0630161060-533100010 (6648)
2009: 8[5]G, 10[3]GS, 10[3]G, 10[1]GF, 9[0]S, 9[0]S, 10[0]S, 9[1]G, 10[0]G,

	Starts	1st	2nd	3rd	Win & Pl
Career Total (Turf)	37	5	2	4	23983
Career Total (AW)	3	1	0	1	3212

77 9/09 Haml 1m1f36y (0-70)H GD £3238
74 6/09 Ayr 1m2f (0-75)H G-F £3238

74	7/08	Ayr	1m2f	(0-70)H	GD	£3561
71	6/08	Ayr	1m2f	(0-65)H	G-F	£3070
79	4/07	Thsk	1m	(0-70)H	G-F	£3886
71	11/06	Wolv	7f32y	(0-63)H	SF	£2730

Total win prize-money £19725

Going (Turf): Sf: 0-6 GS: 0-6 Gd: 2-13 **GF: 3-11** Fm: 0-1
Distance: 5f/6f: 0-0 7f-8f: 2-9 **9f-13f: 4-31** 14f+: 0-0
Track : **LH: 5-25** RH: 1-13 **Tight: 3-17** Gall: 0-4
Aids: Bl: 0-0 Vi: 0-0 Tstrap: 0-0 Ckp: 0-0
Best Rating: **79** 6/07 Ayr 1m1f20y good

Modest; stays 1m2f; acts on Polytrack and on fast ground.

Shybutwilling (IRE)

90(71) (28)**49**
4-y-o ch f Best Of The Bests (IRE)-Reticent Bride (IRE) (Shy Groom (USA))
Mrs P N Dutfield Mrs Caren Walsh

Placings:0/00-00560 **(3994)**
2009: 6^{0}GF, 6^{0}GF, 5^{5}GF, 6^{6}GF, 5^{0}GF,

	Starts	1st	2nd	3rd	Win & Pl
Career Total (Turf)	6	0	0	0	0
Career Total (AW)	2	0	0	0	

Going (Turf): **Sf: 0-0 GS: 0-0 Gd: 0-1 GF: 0-5 Fm: 0-0**
Distance: 5f/6f: 0-5 7f-8f: 0-2 9f-13f: 0-1 14f+: 0-0
Track : LH: 0-2 RH: 0-2 Tight: 0-1 Gall: 0-1
Aids: Bl: 0-0 Vi: 0-0 Tstrap: 0-0 Ckp: 0-0
Best Rating: **49** 5/09 Sals 6f gd-fm

Si Belle (IRE)

104(100) (78)**91**
4-y-o gr f Dalakhani (IRE)-Stunning (USA) (Nureyev (USA))
Rae Guest Miss K Rausing

Placings:4/502351125-6000 **(5248)**
2009: 14^{6}GF, 16^{0}G, 12^{0}G, 13^{0}GF,

	Starts	1st	2nd	3rd	Win & Pl
Career Total (Turf)	8	1	1	0	5909
Career Total (AW)	6	1	1	1	2865
76	6/08	Yarm	1m6f17y (0-70)H	G-F	£2428
78	6/08	Sthl	1m4f (0-65)H	STD	£1774

Total win prize-money £4202

Going (Turf): Sf: 0-2 GS: 0-0 Gd: 0-2 **GF: 1-4** Fm: 0-0
Distance: 5f/6f: 0-0 7f-8f: 0-3 9f-13f: 1-5 14f+: 1-6
Track : **LH: 2-8** RH: 0-4 **Tight: 1-5** Gall: 0-2
Aids: Bl: 0-0 Vi: 0-0 Tstrap: 0-0 Ckp: 0-0
Best Rating: **91** 8/09 Ches 1m5f89y gd-fm

Very useful; Listed placed on the continent; stays 1m6f; acts on fast ground and on sand.

Siberian Tiger (IRE)

105(91) (87)**107**
4-y-o b g Xaar-Flying Millie (IRE) (Flying Spur (AUS))
A J Martin G Swan

Placings:4531101 5/044540021004-0060 **(7293)**
2009: 12^{0}GF, 14^{0}GF, 12^{6}GS, 12^{0}S,

	Starts	1st	2nd	3rd	Win & Pl
Career Total (Turf)	21	4	1	1	54860
Career Total (AW)	3	0	0	0	1203

107	9/08	Gdwd	1m1f	(0-100)H	SFT	£11215
101	10/07	Pont	1m4y		GD	£19873
90	8/07	Sals	1m		G-F	£3238
78	8/07	NmkJ	7f		G-F	£6477

Total win prize-money £40805

Going (Turf): Sf: 1-2 GS: 0-3 Gd: 1-5 **GF: 2-10** Fm: 0-0
Distance: 5f/6f: 0-2 7f-8f: 2-6 9f-13f: 2-15 14f+: 0-1
Track : LH: 1-8 RH: 1-8 **Tight: 1-5** Gall: 0-8
Aids: Bl: 0-2 Vi: 0-0 Tstrap: 0-1 Ckp: 0-1
Best Rating: **107** 9/08 Gdwd 1m1f soft

Very useful; Listed winner; stays 1m2f and acts on most ground, but suited by soft.

Sicilian Warrior (USA)

(92) (66)
3-y-o b c War Chant (USA)-Gravina (CAN) (Sir Ivor (USA))
P F I Cole C Shiacolas

Placings:000-41 **(0134)**
2009: 8^{4}SD, 9^{1}SD,

	Starts	1st	2nd	3rd	Win & Pl
Career Total (Turf)	0	0	0	0	
Career Total (AW)	5	1	0	0	2047
66	1/09	Wolv	1m1f103y (0-60)H	STD	£2047

Total win prize-money £2047

Going (Turf): **Sf: 0-0 GS: 0-0 Gd: 0-0 GF: 0-0 Fm: 0-0**
Distance: 5f/6f: 0-1 7f-8f: 0-2 **9f-13f: 1-2** 14f+: 0-0
Track : **LH: 1-3** RH: 0-2 **Tight: 1-2** Gall: 0-1
Aids: Bl: 0-0 Vi: 0-0 Tstrap: 0-0 Ckp: 0-0
Best Rating: **66** 1/09 Wolv 1m1f103y stand

Modest; effective over an extended 1m1f; acts on Polytrack.

Side Glance

97 **90**
2-y-o br g Passing Glance-Averami (Averti (IRE))
A M Balding Kingsclere Racing CLub

Placings:12 **(6397)**
2009: 6^{1}GF, 6^{2}GF,

	Starts	1st	2nd	3rd	Win & Pl
Career Total (Turf)	2	1	1	0	5813
83	9/09	NmkR	6f	G-F	£3885

Total win prize-money £3886

Going (Turf): Sf: 0-0 GS: 0-0 Gd: 0-0 **GF: 1-2** Fm: 0-0
Distance: **5f/6f: 1-1** 7f-8f: 0-1 9f-13f: 0-0 14f+: 0-0
Track : LH: 0-0 RH: 0-0 Tight: 0-0 Gall: 0-0
Aids: Bl: 0-0 Vi: 0-0 Tstrap: 0-0 Ckp: 0-0
Best Rating: **90** 9/09 Sals 6f212y gd-fm

Useful; stays 6f; acts on fast ground.

Sidney Melbourne (USA)

87(96) (67)**65**
2-y-o ch c Lemon Drop Kid (USA)-Tolltally Light (USA) (Majestic Light (USA))
J R Best Mrs A M Riney

Placings:401 **(7463)**
2009: 5^{4}GF, 7^{0}GF, 7^{1}SD,

	Starts	1st	2nd	3rd	Win & Pl
Career Total (Turf)	2	0	0	0	253
Career Total (AW)	1	1	0	0	2730
67	11/09	Wolv	7f32y	STD	£2729

Total win prize-money £2730

Going (Turf): **Sf: 0-0 GS: 0-0 Gd: 0-0 GF: 0-2 Fm: 0-0**
Distance: 5f/6f: 0-1 **7f-8f: 1-2** 9f-13f: 0-0 14f+: 0-0
Track : **LH: 1-2** RH: 0-0 **Tight: 1-1** Gall: 0-0
Aids: Bl: 0-0 Vi: 0-0 Tstrap: 0-0 Ckp: 0-0
Best Rating: **67** 11/09 Wolv 7f32y stand

Modest; effective over 7f; acts on Polytrack.

Siegfrieds Night (IRE)

(86) (24)**54**
8-y-o ch g Night Shift (USA)-Shelbiana (USA) (Chieftain)
M C Chapman K D Blanch

Placings:0406554000035/14323336213355300250/600/506/600/0-600 **(0252)**
2009: 12^{6}SS, 16^{0}SD, 16^{0}SD,

	Starts	1st	2nd	3rd	Win & Pl
Career Total (Turf)	32	1	2	5	13419
Career Total (AW)	14	1	1	3	5435
66	5/04	Ripn	1m4f60yE(0-75)H	GD	£6271
52	1/04	Sthl	6f E(0-70)H	STD	£3290

Total win prize-money £9561

Going (Turf): Sf: 0-4 GS: 0-5 **Gd: 1-5** GF: 0-15 Fm: 0-3
Distance: 5f/6f: 1-11 7f-8f: 0-6 9f-13f: 1-19 14f+: 0-10
Track : LH: 1-25 RH: 1-8 **Tight: 1-17** Gall: 0-6
Aids: Bl: 0-0 Vi: 0-0 Tstrap: 0-0 Ckp: 0-0
Best Rating: **68** 8/04 Yarm 1m6f17y gd-fm

Siena

(92) (56)**30**
4-y-o b f Lomitas-Sea Lane (Zafonic (USA))
Mrs C A Dunnett Mrs Christine Dunnett

Placings:0/000000-0060 **(0813)**
2009: 8^{0}SD, 7^{0}SD, 7^{6}SD, 10^{0}SD,

	Starts	1st	2nd	3rd	Win & Pl
Career Total (Turf)	3	0	0	0	
Career Total (AW)	8	0	0	0	0

Going (Turf): **Sf: 0-0 GS: 0-1 Gd: 0-2 GF: 0-0 Fm: 0-0**
Distance: 5f/6f: 0-0 7f-8f: 0-5 9f-13f: 0-6 14f+: 0-0
Track : LH: 0-4 RH: 0-4 Tight: 0-2 Gall: 0-0
Aids: Bl: 0-0 Vi: 0-5 Tstrap: 0-0 Ckp: 0-0
Best Rating: **56** 7/08 Kemp 1m3f stand

Siena Star (IRE)

102(106) (69)**69**
11-y-o b g Brief Truce (USA)-Gooseberry Pie (Green Desert (USA))
Stef Liddiard ownaracehorse.co.uk (Shefford)

Placings:0044322104/5664564143252 1/212314163/224023561025 0/2/0/004646103620452251 0/601010506026404450 0/53251200005132 5-60123606 **(7699)**
2009: 10^{6}SD, 10^{0}SD, 9^{1}GF, 10^{2}GF, 10^{3}F, 10^{6}F, 10^{0}SD, 10^{6}SD,

	Starts	1st	2nd	3rd	Win & Pl
Career Total (Turf)	56	8	9	6	42928
Career Total (AW)	53	6	10	3	29079

68	4/09	Folk	1m1f149y (0-60)H	G-F	£2047
62	10/08	Brig	1m1f209y (0-60)H	G-S	£2320
64	4/08	Ling	1m2f (0-60)H	STD	£2047
72	6/07	Bath	1m2f46y (0-65)H	FRM	£2202
68	2/07	Ling	1m2f (0-65)H	STD	£3071
67	12/06	Ling	1m2f (0-62)H	STD	£2730
66	6/06	Wwck	1m2f188y (0-65)H	G-F	£2730
86	8/03	Leic	1m1f218yD(0-85)H	G-F	£5603
82	12/02	Ling	1m E(0-75)H	STD	£3497
80	6/02	Ches	1m2f75yD(0-80)H	G-S	£4329
76	2/02	Ling	1m2f E(0-75)H	STD	£3705
68	12/01	Ling	1m2f F(0-60)H	STD	£1806

66 8/01 Muss 1m1f E G-F £3066
76 8/00 NmkJ 1m C G-F £6240
Total win prize-money £45393

Going (Turf): Sf: 0-2 GS: 2-5 Gd: 0-7 **GF: 5-30** Fm: 1-12
Distance: 5f/6f: 0-3 7f-8f: 2-15 **9f-13f: 12-91** 14f+: 0-0
Track : **LH: 10-77** RH: 2-27 **Tight: 9-61** Gall: 0-10
Aids: Bl: 0-1 Vi: 0-0 Tstrap: 0-0 Ckp: 0-0
Best Rating: 86 8/03 Leic 1m1f218y gd-fm

Moderate; stays 1m2f; acts on fast and easy ground; goes on Polytrack.

Sienna Lake (IRE)

(86) (60)**63**
3-y-o b f Fasliyev (USA)-Lolita's Gold (USA) (Royal Academy (USA))
T D McCarthy Philip Chakko

Placings:0002104**0-0** (6699)
2009: 7^{0}SS,

	Starts	1st	2nd	3rd	Win & Pl
Career Total (Turf)	5	1	0	0	3886
Career Total (AW)	4	0	1	0	605

63 8/08 NmkJ 7f G-S £3885
Total win prize-money £3886

Going (Turf): Sf: 0-0 **GS: 1-1** Gd: 0-1 GF: 0-3 Fm: 0-0
Distance: 5f/6f: 0-4 **7f-8f: 1-5** 9f-13f: 0-0 14f+: 0-0
Track : LH: 0-2 RH: 0-2 Tight: 0-2 Gall: 0-1
Aids: Bl: 0-0 Vi: 0-0 Tstrap: 0-0 Ckp: 0-0
Best Rating: 63 8/08 NmkJ 7f gd-sft

Modest; effective over 7f; acts on easy ground; goes on Polytrack.

Sierra Alpha

91 **78**
2-y-o b c Dansili-Sound Asleep (USA) (Woodman (USA))
Mrs A J Perrett K Abdulla

Placings:1 (5528)
2009: 7^{1}G,

	Starts	1st	2nd	3rd	Win & Pl
Career Total (Turf)	1	1	0	0	3562

78 8/09 Wwck 7f26y GD £3561
Total win prize-money £3562

Going (Turf): Sf: 0-0 GS: 0-0 **Gd: 1-1** GF: 0-0 Fm: 0-0
Distance: 5f/6f: 0-0 **7f-8f: 1-1** 9f-13f: 0-0 14f+: 0-0
Track : LH: 1-1 RH: 0-0 Tight: 0-0 Gall: 0-0
Aids: Bl: 0-0 Vi: 0-0 Tstrap: 0-0 Ckp: 0-0
Best Rating: 78 8/09 Wwck 7f26y good

Winner on debut over 7f on good ground.

Sight Unseen

110 **105**
3-y-o b c Sadler's Wells (USA)-High Praise (USA) (Quest For Fame)
H R A Cecil K Abdulla

Placings:143 (2176)
2009: 11^{1}GS, 12^{4}GF, 11^{3}G,

	Starts	1st	2nd	3rd	Win & Pl
Career Total (Turf)	3	1	0	1	13248

98 4/09 Newb 1m3f5y G-S £5180
Total win prize-money £5181

Going (Turf): Sf: 0-0 **GS: 1-1** Gd: 0-1 GF: 0-1 Fm: 0-0
Distance: 5f/6f: 0-0 7f-8f: 0-0 **9f-13f: 1-3** 14f+: 0-0
Track : **LH: 1-2** RH: 0-1 Tight: 0-2 **Gall: 1-1**
Aids: Bl: 0-0 Vi: 0-0 Tstrap: 0-0 Ckp: 0-0
Best Rating: 105 5/09 Ches 1m4f66y gd-fm

Very useful: stays 1m3f and acts on easy ground; has worn a tongue tie.

Sign Of Approval

100(102) (79)**81**
3-y-o b c Refuse To Bend (IRE)-Scarlet Plume (Warning)
K R Burke Cyril Wall

Placings:200**233-3510222** (3543)
2009: 7^{3}SD, 11^{5}SD, 9^{1}SD, 10^{0}GF, 9^{2}GF, 10^{2}SD, 10^{2}F,

	Starts	1st	2nd	3rd	Win & Pl
Career Total (Turf)	6	0	3	0	4432
Career Total (AW)	7	1	2	3	7672

73 2/09 Wolv 1m1f103y STD £2729
Total win prize-money £2730

Going (Turf): **Sf: 0-1 GS: 0-0 Gd: 0-1 GF: 0-3 Fm: 0-1**
Distance: 5f/6f: 0-1 7f-8f: 0-5 **9f-13f: 1-7** 14f+: 0-0
Track : **LH: 1-6** RH: 0-3 **Tight: 1-7** Gall: 0-0
Aids: Bl: 0-0 Vi: 0-1 Tstrap: 0-2 Ckp: 0-2
Best Rating: 81 10/08 NmkR 7f gd-fm

Fair; stays 1m2f; acts on fast and soft ground; goes on Polytrack.

Sign Of Life

93(87) (62)**63**
2-y-o b f Haafhd-Three Piece (Jaazeiro (USA))
W R Swinburn Mrs Doreen M Swinburn

Placings:04 (6567)
2009: 7^{0}SD, 7^{4}GF,

	Starts	1st	2nd	3rd	Win & Pl
Career Total (Turf)	1	0	0	0	385
Career Total (AW)	1	0	0	0	

Going (Turf): **Sf: 0-0 GS: 0-0 Gd: 0-0 GF: 0-1 Fm: 0-0**
Distance: 5f/6f: 0-0 7f-8f: 0-2 9f-13f: 0-0 14f+: 0-0
Track : LH: 0-1 RH: 0-0 Tight: 0-1 Gall: 0-0
Aids: Bl: 0-0 Vi: 0-0 Tstrap: 0-0 Ckp: 0-0
Best Rating: 63 10/09 Leic 7f9y gd-fm

Sign Of The Cross

101(108) (78)**80**
5-y-o b g Mark Of Esteem (IRE)-Thea (USA) (Marju (IRE))
C R Dore (G L Moore 19/5) Mrs Louise Marsh

Placings:2/4140024/53000154-601100050000030 (7239)
2009: 10^{6}SD, 10^{0}SD, 8^{1}SD, 8^{1}G, 8^{0}G, 7^{0}GF, 8^{0}SD, 8^{5}G, 8^{0}SD, 8^{0}SD, 7^{0}SD, 8^{0}SD, 8^{0}SD, 7^{3}SD, 7^{0}SD,

	Starts	1st	2nd	3rd	Win & Pl
Career Total (Turf)	11	2	0	0	5268
Career Total (AW)	20	2	2	2	8107

72 5/09 Leic 1m60y GD £1942
69 4/09 Wolv 1m141y STD £2047
74 11/08 Kemp 1m2f STD £2047
84 6/07 Nott 1m54y G-F £2266
Total win prize-money £8304

Going (Turf): Sf: 0-1 GS: 0-0 **Gd: 1-8 GF: 1-2** Fm: 0-0
Distance: 5f/6f: 0-0 7f-8f: 0-13 **9f-13f: 4-18** 14f+: 0-0
Track : LH: 2-15 RH: 2-14 **Tight: 1-11** Gall: 0-3
Aids: Bl: 0-0 Vi: 0-0 Tstrap: 0-0 Ckp: 0-0
Best Rating: 86 10/07 Ling 1m2f stand

Moderate; stays 1m2f; acts on fast ground; goes on Polytrack.

Signaller (USA)

96 **75**
3-y-o ch g Rahy (USA)-Tango Charlie (USA) (Cure The Blues (USA))
M Johnston Sheikh Hamdan Bin Mohammed Al Maktoum

Placings:326 (1874)
2009: 8^{3}GF, 9^{2}GF, 10^{6}GF,

	Starts	1st	2nd	3rd	Win & Pl
Career Total (Turf)	3	0	1	1	1638

Going (Turf): **Sf: 0-0 GS: 0-0 Gd: 0-0 GF: 0-3 Fm: 0-0**
Distance: 5f/6f: 0-0 7f-8f: 0-1 9f-13f: 0-2 14f+: 0-0
Track : LH: 0-1 RH: 0-2 Tight: 0-3 Gall: 0-0
Aids: Bl: 0-0 Vi: 0-0 Tstrap: 0-0 Ckp: 0-0
Best Rating: 75 4/09 Ripn 1m gd-fm

Signalman

102 **61**
5-y-o gr g Silver Patriarch (IRE)-Kairine (IRE) (Kahyasi)
P Monteith Mrs Margaret Coppola

Placings:04543554010/000F162232-0 (1692)
2009: 13^{0}G,

	Starts	1st	2nd	3rd	Win & Pl
Career Total (Turf)	19	2	3	2	12157
Career Total (AW)	3	0	0	0	0

57 7/08 Ayr 1m5f13y (0-70)H GD £3885
12/07 Gros 1m4f H G-S £2703
Total win prize-money £6589

Going (Turf): Sf: 0-7 **GS: 1-3 Gd: 1-6** GF: 0-3 Fm: 0-0
Distance: 5f/6f: 0-0 7f-8f: 0-0 9f-13f: 1-15 14f+: 1-7
Track : **LH: 1-5** RH: 0-3 Tight: 0-2 Gall: 0-1
Aids: Bl: 0-0 Vi: 0-0 Tstrap: 0-0 Ckp: 0-0
Best Rating: 61 10/08 Newc 1m4f93y heavy

Ex-Italian; moderate performer; stays 1m7f; acts on easy ground.

Signella

94(89) (66)**62**
3-y-o ch f Selkirk (USA)-Sarah Georgina (Persian Bold)
P W Chapple-Hyam Woodcote Stud Ltd

Placings:0-16 (1050)
2009: 10^{1}SD, 9^{6}GS,

	Starts	1st	2nd	3rd	Win & Pl
Career Total (Turf)	1	0	0	0	0
Career Total (AW)	2	1	0	0	2730

66 1/09 Ling 1m2f STD £2729
Total win prize-money £2730

Going (Turf): **Sf: 0-0 GS: 0-1 Gd: 0-0 GF: 0-0 Fm: 0-0**
Distance: 5f/6f: 0-0 7f-8f: 0-1 **9f-13f: 1-2** 14f+: 0-0
Track : **LH: 1-2** RH: 0-1 **Tight: 1-3** Gall: 0-0
Aids: Bl: 0-0 Vi: 0-0 Tstrap: 0-0 Ckp: 0-0
Best Rating: 66 1/09 Ling 1m2f stand

Signor Peltro

108 (86)**108**
6-y-o b g Bertolini (USA)-Pewter Lass (Dowsing (USA))
H Candy First Of Many Partnership

Placings:100/32316/601/3403421302-410522006 (6732)
2009: 7^{4}GF, 7^{1}GF, 7^{0}GF, 7^{5}G, 7^{2}G, 7^{2}GF, 6^{0}G, 7^{0}G, 8^{6}S,

	Starts	1st	2nd	3rd	Win & Pl
Career Total (Turf)	29	5	5	4	88732
Career Total (AW)	1	0	0	1	819

102 5/09 Donc 7f (0-100)H G-F £15577
96 8/08 Gdwd 7f (0-105)H SFT £12462
93 7/07 NmkJ 6f (0-90)H G-F £7772
95 8/06 Sand 7f16y (0-90)H G-F £8096
76 9/05 Hayd 6f G-S £3591
Total win prize-money £47499

Going (Turf): Sf: 1-6 GS: 1-5 Gd: 0-9 **GF: 3-9** Fm: 0-0
Distance: 5f/6f: 2-9 **7f-8f: 3-21** 9f-13f: 0-0 14f+: 0-0
Track : LH: 0-2 **RH: 2-6** Tight: 0-1 Gall: 0-0
Aids: **Bl: 1-1** Vi: 0-2 Tstrap: 0-0 Ckp: 0-0
Best Rating: **108** 8/09 NmkJ 7f good

Smart; suited by 7f; handles most ground on turf; goes on Polytrack; has worn blinkers and visor.

Signor Verdi

85 **45**
2-y-o b c Green Tune (USA)-Calling Card (Bering)
B J Meehan Mrs Sheila Tucker

Placings:0 (6990)
2009: 7^{0}G,

	Starts	1st	2nd	3rd	Win & Pl
Career Total (Turf)	1	0	0	0	

Going (Turf): **Sf: 0-0 GS: 0-0 Gd: 0-1 GF: 0-0 Fm: 0-0**
Distance: 5f/6f: 0-0 7f-8f: 0-1 9f-13f: 0-0 14f+: 0-0
Track : LH: 0-0 RH: 0-0 Tight: 0-0 Gall: 0-0
Aids: Bl: 0-0 Vi: 0-0 Tstrap: 0-0 Ckp: 0-0
Best Rating: **45** 10/09 Donc 7f good

Signora Frasi (IRE)

95 (103) (62) **74**
4-y-o b f Indian Ridge-Sheba (IRE) (Lycius (USA))
A G Newcombe A G Newcombe

Placings:434050-3031 (6945)
2009: 5^{3}SD, 6^{0}G, 8^{3}G, 8^{1}SD,

	Starts	1st	2nd	3rd	Win & Pl
Career Total (Turf)	6	0	0	2	2037
Career Total (AW)	4	1	0	1	2340

62 10/09 Kemp 1m (0-52)H STD £2047
Total win prize-money £2047

Going (Turf): **Sf: 0-1 GS: 0-0 Gd: 0-4 GF: 0-1 Fm: 0-0**
Distance: 5f/6f: 0-3 **7f-8f: 1-6** 9f-13f: 0-1 14f+: 0-0
Track : LH: 0-5 **RH: 1-3** Tight: 0-1 Gall: 0-2
Aids: Bl: 0-0 Vi: 0-0 Tstrap: 0-0 Ckp: 0-0
Best Rating: **74** 5/08 Leop 7f gd-fm

Moderate; effective at around 7f-1m; acts on good ground; goes on Polytrack.

Silaah

105 (106) (91) **99**
5-y-o b g Mind Games-Ocean Grove (IRE) (Fairy King (USA))
D Nicholls (E A L Dunlop 10/6) Mrs Jackie Love & David Nicholls

Placings:0/412-35621226 (6050)
2009: 7^{3}SD, 6^{5}G, 7^{6}GF, 6^{2}SD, 7^{1}SD, 6^{2}G, 6^{2}GF, 6^{6}G,

	Starts	1st	2nd	3rd	Win & Pl
Career Total (Turf)	6	0	2	0	4976
Career Total (AW)	6	2	2	1	11297

91 6/09 Kemp 7f (0-85)H STD £4727
83 10/08 Kemp 6f STD £2590
Total win prize-money £7317

Going (Turf): **Sf: 0-0 GS: 0-0 Gd: 0-3 GF: 0-3 Fm: 0-0**
Distance: 5f/6f: 1-8 7f-8f: 1-4 9f-13f: 0-0 14f+: 0-0
Track : LH: 0-1 **RH: 2-5** Tight: 0-1 Gall: 0-0
Aids: Bl: 0-0 Vi: 0-0 Tstrap: 0-0 Ckp: 0-0
Best Rating: **99** 9/09 Hayd 6f gd-fm

Useful; effective over 6f-7f; acts on decent ground; goes on Polytrack.

Silca Meydan

89 (95) (65) **44**
3-y-o b g Diktat-Golden Silca (Inchinor)
R J Price (M R Channon 10/9) My Left Foot Racing Syndicate

Placings:644205000 (7755)
2009: 8^{6}SD, 7^{4}SD, 6^{4}SD, 5^{2}SF, 6^{0}G, 5^{5}SD, 8^{0}G, 7^{0}SF, 8^{0}SD,

	Starts	1st	2nd	3rd	Win & Pl
Career Total (Turf)	2	0	0	0	
Career Total (AW)	7	0	1	0	806

Going (Turf): **Sf: 0-0 GS: 0-0 Gd: 0-2 GF: 0-0 Fm: 0-0**
Distance: 5f/6f: 0-3 7f-8f: 0-4 9f-13f: 0-2 14f+: 0-0
Track : LH: 0-7 RH: 0-0 Tight: 0-7 Gall: 0-0
Aids: Bl: 0-0 Vi: 0-0 Tstrap: 0-0 Ckp: 0-0
Best Rating: **65** 1/09 Ling 1m stand

Modest sprinter; handles Polytrack.

Silenceofthewind (USA)

99 **95**
2-y-o b c Eddington (USA)-Betty's Solutions (USA) (Eltish (USA))
K R Burke Mogeely Stud & Mrs Maura Gittins

Placings:610 (3817)
2009: 6^{6}G, 6^{1}GF, 7^{0}GF,

	Starts	1st	2nd	3rd	Win & Pl
Career Total (Turf)	3	1	0	0	3414

87 6/09 Newc 6f G-F £3238
Total win prize-money £3238

Going (Turf): Sf: 0-0 GS: 0-0 Gd: 0-1 **GF: 1-2** Fm: 0-0
Distance: **5f/6f: 1-2** 7f-8f: 0-1 9f-13f: 0-0 14f+: 0-0
Track : LH: 0-1 RH: 0-0 Tight: 0-0 Gall: 0-0
Aids: Bl: 0-0 Vi: 0-0 Tstrap: 0-0 Ckp: 0-0
Best Rating: **95** 7/09 NmkJ 7f gd-fm

Useful; $310,000 purchase; effective over 6f; acts on fast ground.

Silent Act (USA)

100 (103) (73) **66**
3-y-o b f Theatrical-Vinista (USA) (Jade Hunter (USA))
Mrs A J Perrett Mr & Mrs R Scott

Placings:0-52043212 (7238)
2009: 10^{5}G, 10^{2}GF, 11^{0}G, 9^{4}GF, 12^{3}SD, 12^{2}GF, 12^{1}SD, 12^{2}SD,

	Starts	1st	2nd	3rd	Win & Pl
Career Total (Turf)	6	0	2	0	2264
Career Total (AW)	3	1	1	1	3120

69 10/09 Kemp 1m4f (0-65)H STD £2047
Total win prize-money £2047

Going (Turf): **Sf: 0-0 GS: 0-1 Gd: 0-2 GF: 0-3 Fm: 0-0**
Distance: 5f/6f: 0-0 7f-8f: 0-1 **9f-13f: 1-8** 14f+: 0-0
Track : LH: 0-3 **RH: 1-5** Tight: 0-2 Gall: 0-0
Aids: Bl: 0-0 Vi: 0-0 Tstrap: 0-0 Ckp: 0-0
Best Rating: **73** 11/09 Kemp 1m4f stand

Fair; stays 1m4f; acts on Polytrack.

Silent Applause

86 (91) (53) **71**
6-y-o b g Royal Applause-Billie Blue (Ballad Rock)
Dr J D Scargill J P T Partnership

Placings:623030/26340/05023440-1 (3114)
2009: 12^{1}GF,

	Starts	1st	2nd	3rd	Win & Pl
Career Total (Turf)	18	1	3	4	11264
Career Total (AW)	2	0	0	0	

70 6/09 NmkJ 1m4f (0-75)H G-F £3885
Total win prize-money £3886

Going (Turf): Sf: 0-1 GS: 0-0 Gd: 0-5 **GF: 1-10** Fm: 0-2
Distance: 5f/6f: 0-0 7f-8f: 0-10 **9f-13f: 1-10** 14f+: 0-0
Track : LH: 0-3 **RH: 1-9** Tight: 0-3 **Gall: 1-3**
Aids: Bl: 0-0 Vi: 0-2 Tstrap: 0-0 Ckp: 0-0
Best Rating: **76** 8/07 NmkJ 1m gd-fm

Modest; stays 1m4f; acts on good and faster ground.

Silent Dancer (IRE)

70 (85) (46) **64**
2-y-o b g Danehill Dancer (IRE)-Silent Crystal (USA) (Diesis)
S Donohoe Star Contractors Limited

Placings:0000300 (7050)
2009: 5^{0}Y, 7^{0}S, 7^{0}S, 5^{0}HY, 7^{3}Y, 7^{0}G, 7^{0}SD,

	Starts	1st	2nd	3rd	Win & Pl
Career Total (Turf)	6	0	0	1	1241
Career Total (AW)	1	0	0	0	

Going (Turf): **Sf: 0-3 GS: 0-0 Gd: 0-1 GF: 0-0 Fm: 0-0**
Distance: 5f/6f: 0-2 7f-8f: 0-5 9f-13f: 0-0 14f+: 0-0
Track : LH: 0-3 RH: 0-2 Tight: 0-0 Gall: 0-0
Aids: Bl: 0-0 Vi: 0-0 Tstrap: 0-0 Ckp: 0-0
Best Rating: **64** 9/09 List 7f yield

Silent Hero

99 (102) (86) **78**
3-y-o b g Oasis Dream-Royal Passion (Ahonoora)
M A Jarvis Mrs P Good

Placings:004401215-50150336 (6946)
2009: 7^{5}SD, 7^{0}GF, 7^{1}SD, 8^{5}GF, 6^{0}SD, 7^{3}GS, 7^{3}SD, 8^{6}SD,

	Starts	1st	2nd	3rd	Win & Pl
Career Total (Turf)	10	1	0	1	5197
Career Total (AW)	7	2	1	1	9173

85 6/09 Sthl 7f (0-75)H STD £3412
78 9/08 Wwck 7f26y (0-75) GD £3753
68 9/08 Sthl 7f (0-70) STD £3753
Total win prize-money £10918

Going (Turf): Sf: 0-1 GS: 0-2 **Gd: 1-3** GF: 0-3 Fm: 0-1
Distance: 5f/6f: 0-3 **7f-8f: 3-13** 9f-13f: 0-1 14f+: 0-0
Track : **LH: 3-8** RH: 0-2 Tight: 0-4 Gall: 0-0
Aids: Bl: 0-0 Vi: 0-0 Tstrap: 0-2 Ckp: 0-2
Best Rating: **86** 9/09 Wolv 7f32y stand

Useful; stays 7f; acts on most ground and on Fibresand; handles Polytrack; has worn cheekpieces.

Silent Lucidity (IRE)

92(98) (51)40

5-y-o ch g Ashkalani (IRE)-Mimansa (USA) (El Gran Senor (USA))

P D Niven P D Niven

Placings:00/13/0006 **(7733)**

2009: 11^{0}GF, 13^{0}SD, 13^{0}G, 12^{6}SD,

	Starts	1st	2nd	3rd	Win & Pl
Career Total (Turf)	6	1	0	1	2296
Career Total (AW)	2	0	0	0	0

64 5/07 Haml 1m65y G-F £1943

Total win prize-money £1943

Going (Turf): Sf: 0-1 GS: 0-0 Gd: 0-2 **GF: 1-3** Fm: 0-0
Distance: 5f/6f: 0-0 7f-8f: 0-2 **9f-13f: 1-4** 14f+: 0-2
Track : LH: 0-4 **RH: 1-3 Tight: 1-6** Gall: 0-0
Aids: Bl: 0-0 Vi: 0-0 Tstrap: 0-0 Ckp: 0-0
Best Rating: 64 6/07 Haml 1m3f16y gd-fm

Silent Majority (IRE)

90(80) (42)58

2-y-o b c Refuse To Bend (IRE)-Queen Shy (Marju (IRE))

E A L Dunlop St Albans Bloodstock LLP

Placings:50 **(7376)**

2009: 7^{5}G, 7^{0}SD,

	Starts	1st	2nd	3rd	Win & Pl
Career Total (Turf)	1	0	0	0	0
Career Total (AW)	1	0	0	0	

Going (Turf): Sf: 0-0 GS: 0-0 Gd: 0-1 GF: 0-0 Fm: 0-0
Distance: 5f/6f: 0-0 7f-8f: 0-2 9f-13f: 0-0 14f+: 0-0
Track : LH: 0-1 RH: 0-0 Tight: 0-1 Gall: 0-0
Aids: Bl: 0-0 Vi: 0-0 Tstrap: 0-0 Ckp: 0-0
Best Rating: 58 10/09 Donc 7f good

Silent Oasis

99 72

3-y-o b f Oasis Dream-Silence Is Golden (Danehill Dancer (IRE))

B J Meehan Miss J Semple

Placings:42340 **(6621)**

2009: 8^{4}G, 8^{2}GF, 9^{3}G, 8^{4}G, 8^{0}G,

	Starts	1st	2nd	3rd	Win & Pl
Career Total (Turf)	5	0	1	1	2071

Going (Turf): Sf: 0-0 GS: 0-0 Gd: 0-4 GF: 0-1 Fm: 0-0
Distance: 5f/6f: 0-0 7f-8f: 0-1 9f-13f: 0-4 14f+: 0-0
Track : LH: 0-2 RH: 0-3 Tight: 0-2 Gall: 0-1
Aids: Bl: 0-0 Vi: 0-0 Tstrap: 0-0 Ckp: 0-0
Best Rating: 72 6/09 Gdwd 1m1f good

In the frame in 1m maidens; acts on fast ground.

Silent Secret (IRE)

99 77

2-y-o ch f Dubai Destination (USA)-Charita (IRE) (Lycius (USA))

R Hannon Noel O'Callaghan

Placings:043210 **(7033)**

2009: 6^{0}GF, 6^{4}GF, 6^{3}G, 8^{2}GF, 7^{1}GF, 7^{0}S,

	Starts	1st	2nd	3rd	Win & Pl
Career Total (Turf)	6	1	1	1	5788

72 9/09 Bevl 7f100y G-F £3885

Total win prize-money £3886

Going (Turf): Sf: 0-1 GS: 0-0 Gd: 0-1 **GF: 1-4** Fm: 0-0
Distance: 5f/6f: 0-2 **7f-8f: 1-4** 9f-13f: 0-0 14f+: 0-0
Track : LH: 0-0 **RH: 1-2** Tight: 0-0 Gall: 0-0
Aids: Bl: 0-0 Vi: 0-0 Tstrap: 0-0 Ckp: 0-0
Best Rating: 77 9/09 Gdwd 1m gd-fm

Useful; stays 1m; acts on fast ground.

Silent Treatment (IRE)

81(95) (58)62

3-y-o ch f Captain Rio-Without Words (Lion Cavern (USA))

Miss Gay Kelleway Countrywide Classics Limited

Placings:051313530-0400 **(4279)**

2009: 7^{0}G, 8^{4}SD, 8^{0}SD, 8^{0}C,

	Starts	1st	2nd	3rd	Win & Pl
Career Total (Turf)	7	1	0	2	2752
Career Total (AW)	6	1	0	1	2416

62 8/08 Yarm 5f43y SFT £1942
54 7/08 Sthl 5f STD £1978

Total win prize-money £3922

Going (Turf): Sf: 1-3 GS: 0-1 Gd: 0-2 GF: 0-1 Fm: 0-0
Distance: 5f/6f: 2-8 7f-8f: 0-5 9f-13f: 0-0 14f+: 0-0
Track : LH: 0-4 RH: 0-2 Tight: 0-2 Gall: 0-1
Aids: Bl: 0-0 Vi: 0-0 Tstrap: 0-2 Ckp: 0-2
Best Rating: 62 8/08 Yarm 5f43y soft

Modest; effective at 5f; acts on easy ground; also goes on Polytrack.

Silidan

(99) (57)55

6-y-o b g Dansili-In Love Again (IRE) (Prince Rupert (FR))

Miss M E Rowland (G L Moore 1/4) Miss M E Rowland

Placings:14012/6500/0000/**02450010000-01050** **(7349)**

2009: 7^{0}SD, 7^{1}SD, 7^{0}SD, 7^{5}SD, 7^{0}SD,

	Starts	1st	2nd	3rd	Win & Pl
Career Total (Turf)	16	2	1	0	13921
Career Total (AW)	13	2	1	0	6973

57 2/09 Ling 7f (0-55)H STD £1706
55 9/08 Layt 7f STD £4572
88 9/05 York 7f (0-85) G-F £6344
76 6/05 Newc 6f G-F £5102

Total win prize-money £17726

Going (Turf): Sf: 0-0 GS: 0-1 Gd: 0-3 **GF: 2-11** Fm: 0-1
Distance: 5f/6f: 1-6 **7f-8f: 3-20** 9f-13f: 0-3 14f+: 0-0
Track : LH: 3-15 RH: 0-4 Tight: 1-10 Gall: 1-1
Aids: Bl: 0-1 Vi: 0-0 Tstrap: 0-0 Ckp: 0-0
Best Rating: 90 10/05 Leic 7f9y gd-fm

Moderate; effective over 7f; acts on fast ground; goes on Polytrack.

Silk Affair (IRE)

98 94

4-y-o b f Barathea (IRE)-Uncertain Affair (IRE) (Darshaan)

M G Quinlan L Mulryan & M C Fahy

Placings:615/265605P0-0 **(6851)**

2009: 18^{0}G,

	Starts	1st	2nd	3rd	Win & Pl
Career Total (Turf)	11	1	1	0	10673
Career Total (AW)	1	0	0	0	

73 10/07 Ayr 1m SFT £4533

Total win prize-money £4534

Going (Turf): Sf: 1-5 GS: 0-1 Gd: 0-4 GF: 0-1 Fm: 0-0
Distance: 5f/6f: 0-0 **7f-8f: 1-2** 9f-13f: 0-8 14f+: 0-2
Track : LH: 1-8 RH: 0-4 Tight: 0-3 Gall: 0-3
Aids: Bl: 0-0 Vi: 0-0 Tstrap: 0-0 Ckp: 0-0
Best Rating: 94 6/08 Newb 1m2f6y good

Useful; stays 1m4f; best on soft ground.

Silk And Satin (USA)

98 55

3-y-o b/br f Storm Cat (USA)-Rafina (USA) (Mr Prospector (USA))

H R A Cecil Michael Tabor

Placings:0403 **(6189)**

2009: 10^{0}G, 10^{4}GF, 11^{0}G, 9^{3}GF,

	Starts	1st	2nd	3rd	Win & Pl
Career Total (Turf)	4	0	0	1	704

Going (Turf): Sf: 0-0 GS: 0-0 Gd: 0-2 GF: 0-2 Fm: 0-0
Distance: 5f/6f: 0-0 7f-8f: 0-0 9f-13f: 0-4 14f+: 0-0
Track : LH: 0-2 RH: 0-2 Tight: 0-4 Gall: 0-0
Aids: Bl: 0-0 Vi: 0-0 Tstrap: 0-0 Ckp: 0-0
Best Rating: 55 8/09 Ches 1m2f75y gd-fm

Silk Cotton (USA)

82(85) (70)64

3-y-o b f Giant's Causeway (USA)-Calico Moon (USA) (Seeking The Gold (USA))

E A L Dunlop Rick Barnes

Placings:045-00 **(2685)**

2009: 10^{0}GF, 8^{0}SD,

	Starts	1st	2nd	3rd	Win & Pl
Career Total (Turf)	3	0	0	0	265
Career Total (AW)	2	0	0	0	0

Going (Turf): Sf: 0-0 GS: 0-1 Gd: 0-0 GF: 0-2 Fm: 0-0
Distance: 5f/6f: 0-0 7f-8f: 0-3 9f-13f: 0-2 14f+: 0-0
Track : LH: 0-1 RH: 0-2 Tight: 0-2 Gall: 0-0
Aids: Bl: 0-1 Vi: 0-0 Tstrap: 0-0 Ckp: 0-0
Best Rating: 70 9/08 Kemp 1m stand

Modest maiden; acts on easy ground and on Polytrack.

Silk Gallery (USA)

104(101) (60)64

4-y-o b f Kingmambo (USA)-Moon Flower (IRE) (Sadler's Wells (USA))

E J Alston Mr & Mrs G Middlebrook

Placings:0/03-**224350522401300** **(7503)**

2009: 6^{2}SS, 6^{2}SD, 5^{4}SD, 5^{3}SD, 6^{5}SD, 5^{0}F, 8^{5}S, 7^{2}GS, 6^{2}S, 7^{4}S, 5^{0}SD, 5^{1}S, 5^{3}S, 5^{0}SD, 5^{0}SD,

	Starts	1st	2nd	3rd	Win & Pl
Career Total (Turf)	9	1	2	1	4813
Career Total (AW)	9	0	2	2	2368

63 10/09 Catt 5f (0-65)H SFT £2047

Total win prize-money £2047

Going (Turf): Sf: 1-5 GS: 0-1 Gd: 0-1 GF: 0-1 Fm: 0-1

Distance: **5f/6f: 1-14** 7f-8f: 0-3 9f-13f: 0-1 14f+: 0-0
Track : LH: 0-9 RH: 0-0 Tight: 0-5 Gall: 0-0
Aids: Bl: 0-0 Vi: 0-0 Tstrap: 0-0 Ckp: 0-0
Best Rating: **64** 11/09 Nott 5f13y soft

Modest; effective over 5f-6f; acts on soft ground; goes on Fibresand and Polytrack; has worn a tongue tie.

Silk Hall (UAE)

102(104) (87)**90**
4-y-o b g Halling (USA)-Velour (Mtoto)
A King Thurloe 50

Placings:540/053423411-26 **(2283)**
2009: 14^{2}F, 14^{6}GF,

	Starts	1st	2nd	3rd	Win & Pl
Career Total (Turf)	9	0	2	2	5580
Career Total (AW)	5	2	0	0	6465

87 10/08 GrLe 1m6f (0-75)H STD £2914
82 10/08 Wolv 1m5f194y (0-70)H SF £3238
Total win prize-money £6152

Going (Turf): **Sf: 0-0 GS: 0-2 Gd: 0-3 GF: 0-3 Fm: 0-1**
Distance: 5f/6f: 0-0 7f-8f: 0-3 9f-13f: 0-2 **14f+: 2-9**
Track : **LH: 2-6** RH: 0-8 Tight: 1-7 Gall: 1-2
Aids: Bl: 0-0 Vi: 0-0 Tstrap: 0-0 Ckp: 0-0
Best Rating: **90** 5/09 Nott 1m6f15y firm

Fair; stays 1m6f; acts on good ground; goes on Polytrack.

Silk Runner (IRE)

68(80) (35)**51**
2-y-o ch f Barathea (IRE)-Sao Gabriel (IRE) (Persian Bold)
J W Hills Tony Waspe Partnership

Placings:00 **(5984)**
2009: 7^{0}G, 8^{0}SD,

	Starts	1st	2nd	3rd	Win & Pl
Career Total (Turf)	1	0	0	0	
Career Total (AW)	1	0	0	0	

Going (Turf): **Sf: 0-0 GS: 0-0 Gd: 0-1 GF: 0-0 Fm: 0-0**
Distance: 5f/6f: 0-0 7f-8f: 0-2 9f-13f: 0-0 14f+: 0-0
Track : LH: 0-0 RH: 0-1 Tight: 0-0 Gall: 0-0
Aids: Bl: 0-0 Vi: 0-0 Tstrap: 0-0 Ckp: 0-0
Best Rating: **51** 8/09 NmkJ 7f good

Silk Slippers

70(86) (61)**31**
2-y-o b f Oasis Dream-Interpose (Indian Ridge)
John Joseph Murphy Shanakiel Racing Syndicate

Placings:40 **(6317a)**
2009: 6^{4}SD, 6^{0}G,

	Starts	1st	2nd	3rd	Win & Pl
Career Total (Turf)	1	0	0	0	
Career Total (AW)	1	0	0	0	385

Going (Turf): **Sf: 0-0 GS: 0-0 Gd: 0-1 GF: 0-0 Fm: 0-0**
Distance: 5f/6f: 0-2 7f-8f: 0-0 9f-13f: 0-0 14f+: 0-0
Track : LH: 0-0 RH: 0-1 Tight: 0-0 Gall: 0-0
Aids: Bl: 0-0 Vi: 0-0 Tstrap: 0-0 Ckp: 0-0
Best Rating: **61** 9/09 Kemp 6f stand

Moderate; acts on Polytrack.

Silk Star (IRE)

82(82) (36)**34**
3-y-o b f Pyrus (USA)-Silk Feather (USA) (Silver Hawk (USA))

Patrick Morris Rob Lloyd Racing Limited

Placings:0-006 **(7500)**
2009: 8^{0}G, 8^{0}SD, 8^{6}SD,

	Starts	1st	2nd	3rd	Win & Pl
Career Total (Turf)	1	0	0	0	
Career Total (AW)	3	0	0	0	0

Going (Turf): **Sf: 0-0 GS: 0-0 Gd: 0-1 GF: 0-0 Fm: 0-0**
Distance: 5f/6f: 0-0 7f-8f: 0-1 9f-13f: 0-3 14f+: 0-0
Track : LH: 0-3 RH: 0-0 Tight: 0-2 Gall: 0-0
Aids: Bl: 0-0 Vi: 0-0 Tstrap: 0-0 Ckp: 0-0
Best Rating: **36** 11/09 Sthl 1m stand

Silk Street (USA)

96(100) (78)**76**
2-y-o b c Street Cry (IRE)-High Potential (USA) (Pleasant Colony (USA))
R A Fahey R A Fahey

Placings:22 **(7050)**
2009: 6^{2}S, 7^{2}SD,

	Starts	1st	2nd	3rd	Win & Pl
Career Total (Turf)	1	0	1	0	705
Career Total (AW)	1	0	1	0	1156

Going (Turf): **Sf: 0-1 GS: 0-0 Gd: 0-0 GF: 0-0 Fm: 0-0**
Distance: 5f/6f: 0-0 7f-8f: 0-2 9f-13f: 0-0 14f+: 0-0
Track : LH: 0-0 RH: 0-1 Tight: 0-0 Gall: 0-0
Aids: Bl: 0-0 Vi: 0-0 Tstrap: 0-0 Ckp: 0-0
Best Rating: **78** 10/09 Kemp 7f stand

Fair; effective over 7f; acts on Polytrack.

Silk Trail

103(94) (70)**72**
3-y-o b f Dubai Destination (USA)-Satin Flower (USA) (Shadeed (USA))
H-A Pantall (Saeed Bin Suroor 27/10) Sheikh Mohammed

Placings:2-332120 **(7509a)**
2009: 8^{3}G, 8^{3}GF, 7^{2}GS, 7^{1}GF, 8^{2}VS, 7^{0}HY,

	Starts	1st	2nd	3rd	Win & Pl
Career Total (Turf)	6	1	2	2	5060
Career Total (AW)	1	0	1	0	1214

66 7/09 Folk 7f G-F £2729
Total win prize-money £2730

Going (Turf): Sf: 0-1 GS: 0-1 Gd: 0-1 **GF: 1-2** Fm: 0-0
Distance: 5f/6f: 0-0 **7f-8f: 1-6** 9f-13f: 0-1 14f+: 0-0
Track : LH: 0-2 RH: 0-1 Tight: 0-2 Gall: 0-0
Aids: Bl: 0-0 Vi: 0-0 Tstrap: 0-0 Ckp: 0-0
Best Rating: **72** 6/09 Sals 1m gd-fm

Fair; stays 7f and acts on Polytrack.

Silken Aunt

(88) (56)
2-y-o b f Barathea (IRE)-Aunt Susan (Distant Relative)
J A R Toller P C J Dalby & R Schuster

Placings:44 **(7630)**
2009: 7^{4}SD, 7^{4}SD,

	Starts	1st	2nd	3rd	Win & Pl
Career Total (Turf)	0	0	0	0	
Career Total (AW)	2	0	0	0	529

Going (Turf): **Sf: 0-0 GS: 0-0 Gd: 0-0 GF: 0-0 Fm: 0-0**
Distance: 5f/6f: 0-0 7f-8f: 0-2 9f-13f: 0-0 14f+: 0-0
Track : LH: 0-2 RH: 0-0 Tight: 0-2 Gall: 0-0
Aids: Bl: 0-0 Vi: 0-0 Tstrap: 0-0 Ckp: 0-0
Best Rating: **56** 11/09 Wolv 7f32y stand

Silken Promise (USA)

104(97) (66)**68**
3-y-o b/br f Pulpit (USA)-Banksia (Marju (IRE))
W R Swinburn The Pulpit Congregation

Placings:0-45650022 **(7766)**
2009: 10^{4}G, 9^{5}F, 11^{6}GF, 12^{5}SD, 12^{0}SD, 10^{0}SD, 12^{2}SD, 11^{2}SD,

	Starts	1st	2nd	3rd	Win & Pl
Career Total (Turf)	4	0	0	0	385
Career Total (AW)	5	0	2	0	1008

Going (Turf): **Sf: 0-0 GS: 0-0 Gd: 0-2 GF: 0-1 Fm: 0-1**
Distance: 5f/6f: 0-0 7f-8f: 0-1 9f-13f: 0-8 14f+: 0-0
Track : LH: 0-2 RH: 0-6 Tight: 0-3 Gall: 0-1
Aids: Bl: 0-0 Vi: 0-0 Tstrap: 0-2 Ckp: 0-2
Best Rating: **68** 5/09 Sals 1m1f198y firm

Modest; stays 1m4f; acts on Polytrack; has worn cheek-pieces.

Silken Sands (IRE)

86(88) (54)**55**
3-y-o b f Green Desert (USA)-Arctic Silk (Selkirk (USA))
C G Cox John And Anne Soul

Placings:55 **(7826)**
2009: 8^{5}GS, 8^{5}SD,

	Starts	1st	2nd	3rd	Win & Pl
Career Total (Turf)	1	0	0	0	0
Career Total (AW)	1	0	0	0	0

Going (Turf): **Sf: 0-0 GS: 0-1 Gd: 0-0 GF: 0-0 Fm: 0-0**
Distance: 5f/6f: 0-0 7f-8f: 0-1 9f-13f: 0-1 14f+: 0-0
Track : LH: 0-0 RH: 0-2 Tight: 0-1 Gall: 0-0
Aids: Bl: 0-0 Vi: 0-0 Tstrap: 0-0 Ckp: 0-0
Best Rating: **55** 10/09 Wind 1m67y gd-sft

Silkenveil (IRE)

(78) (38)
2-y-o b f Indian Ridge-Line Ahead (IRE) (Sadler's Wells (USA))
R A Fahey Mrs H Steel

Placings:0 **(7816)**
2009: 8^{0}SD,

	Starts	1st	2nd	3rd	Win & Pl
Career Total (Turf)	0	0	0	0	
Career Total (AW)	1	0	0	0	

Going (Turf): **Sf: 0-0 GS: 0-0 Gd: 0-0 GF: 0-0 Fm: 0-0**
Distance: 5f/6f: 0-0 7f-8f: 0-0 9f-13f: 0-1 14f+: 0-0
Track : LH: 0-1 RH: 0-0 Tight: 0-1 Gall: 0-0
Aids: Bl: 0-0 Vi: 0-0 Tstrap: 0-0 Ckp: 0-0
Best Rating: **38** 12/09 Wolv 1m141y stand

Silky Way (GR)

98(93) (60)**70**
3-y-o b f Harmonic Way-Flourishing Way (Sadler's Wells (USA))

P R Chamings Mrs Alexandra J Chandris

Placings:505-1650 **(5877)**
2009: 5^{1}G, 5^{6}SD, 5^{5}G, 5^{0}GF,

	Starts	1st	2nd	3rd	Win & Pl
Career Total (Turf)	5	1	0	0	3238
Career Total (AW)	2	0	0	0	0

70	5/09	Gdwd	5f	(0-70)H	GD	£3238

Total win prize-money £3238

Going (Turf): Sf: 0-0 GS: 0-0 **Gd: 1-2** GF: 0-2 Fm: 0-1
Distance: **5f/6f: 1-7** 7f-8f: 0-0 9f-13f: 0-0 14f+: 0-0
Track : LH: 0-5 RH: 0-0 Tight: 0-1 Gall: 0-4
Aids: Bl: 0-0 Vi: 0-0 Tstrap: 0-0 Ckp: 0-0
Best Rating: **70** 5/09 Gdwd 5f good

Sills Vincero

84(102) (61)**68**

3-y-o b f Piccolo-Aegean Magic (Wolfhound (USA))
D Shaw Simon Mapletoft Racing & R G Botham

Placings:32460**4-554312303060** **(1529)**
2009: 5^{5}SD, 5^{5}SD, 6^{4}SD, 6^{3}SD, 5^{1}SD, 5^{2}SD, 5^{3}SD, 5^{0}SD, 5^{3}SD, 5^{0}GF, 5^{6}SD, 5^{0}SD,

	Starts	1st	2nd	3rd	Win & Pl
Career Total (Turf)	6	0	1	1	1618
Career Total (AW)	12	1	1	3	5023

60	2/09	Wolv	5f20y	(0-70)H	STD	£2729

Total win prize-money £2730

Going (Turf): **Sf: 0-1 GS: 0-0 Gd: 0-0 GF: 0-4 Fm: 0-1**
Distance: **5f/6f: 1-18** 7f-8f: 0-0 9f-13f: 0-0 14f+: 0-0
Track : **LH: 1-9** RH: 0-2 **Tight: 1-8** Gall: 0-1
Aids: Bl: 0-0 Vi: 0-0 Tstrap: 0-0 Ckp: 0-0
Best Rating: **68** 7/08 Wind 6f gd-fm

Modest; effective over 5f; acts on fast ground; goes on Polytrack.

Silly Gilly (IRE)

102(98) (40)**65**

5-y-o b m Mull Of Kintyre (USA)-Richly Deserved (IRE) (Kings Lake (USA))
R E Barr R E Barr

Placings:000500405**54/50**0002213**2**3455/**360**4**0331425-0133203043300 **(7500)**
2009: 8^{0}F, 7^{1}GF, 8^{3}GF, 8^{3}GF, 7^{2}G, 7^{0}G, 7^{3}G, 8^{0}G, 8^{4}GS, 8^{3}GF, 7^{3}GF, 9^{0}GF, 8^{0}SD,

	Starts	1st	2nd	3rd	Win & Pl
Career Total (Turf)	42	3	5	8	17181
Career Total (AW)	7	0	0	2	744

64	5/09	Thsk	7f	(0-55)H	G-F	£2978
61	7/08	Rdcr	1m	(0-65)H	G-F	£2266
58	7/07	Rdcr	5f	(0-70)H	G-S	£2817

Total win prize-money £8063

Going (Turf): Sf: 0-5 GS: 1-7 Gd: 0-13 **GF: 2-15** Fm: 0-2
Distance: 5f/6f: 1-25 **7f-8f: 2-21** 9f-13f: 0-3 14f+: 0-0
Track : **LH: 1-19** RH: 0-9 **Tight: 1-12** Gall: 0-2
Aids: Bl: 0-0 Vi: 0-0 Tstrap: 0-4 Ckp: 0-4
Best Rating: **65** 7/09 Catt 7f good

Moderate; effective at around 1m; acts on most ground; also goes on Fibresand.

Silvador

98 **70**

3-y-o gr g Selkirk (USA)-Dali's Grey (Linamix (FR))
W R Muir C Edginton, K Jeffery & P Wheatley

Placings:03-2 **(2181)**
2009: 11^{2}G,

	Starts	1st	2nd	3rd	Win & Pl
Career Total (Turf)	3	0	1	1	1528

Going (Turf): **Sf: 0-0 GS: 0-0 Gd: 0-3 GF: 0-0 Fm: 0-0**
Distance: 5f/6f: 0-0 7f-8f: 0-2 9f-13f: 0-1 14f+: 0-0
Track : LH: 0-1 RH: 0-0 Tight: 0-1 Gall: 0-0
Aids: Bl: 0-0 Vi: 0-0 Tstrap: 0-0 Ckp: 0-0
Best Rating: **70** 5/09 Ling 1m3f106y good

Fair; half brother to the useful middle-distance performers Boz and Bauer; promise in maidens at up to 1m3f; acts on good.

Silvanus (IRE)

103(102) (81)**80**

4-y-o b g Danehill Dancer (IRE)-Mala Mala (IRE) (Brief Truce (USA))
P T Midgley (I Semple 14/8) Colin Alton

Placings:50/23**10342-230**6540631435104**50** **(6877)**
2009: 5^{2}SD, 5^{3}SD, 5^{0}SF, 5^{6}GF, 5^{5}GF, 6^{4}G, 5^{0}G, 5^{6}GF, 5^{3}G, 5^{1}GF, 5^{4}GF, 5^{3}GF, 5^{5}G, 5^{1}GF, 5^{0}GF, 5^{4}SD, 5^{5}GF, 5^{0}SD,

	Starts	1st	2nd	3rd	Win & Pl
Career Total (Turf)	17	2	1	3	7543
Career Total (AW)	10	1	2	2	7827

62	8/09	Catt	5f	G-F	£2388
62	6/09	Muss	5f	G-F	£1942
70	7/08	Kemp	5f	STD	£4727

Total win prize-money £9058

Going (Turf): Sf: 0-0 GS: 0-0 Gd: 0-6 **GF: 2-11** Fm: 0-0
Distance: **5f/6f: 3-25** 7f-8f: 0-2 9f-13f: 0-0 14f+: 0-0
Track : LH: 0-8 **RH: 1-1** Tight: 0-6 Gall: 0-2
Aids: Bl: 0-3 Vi: 0-0 Tstrap: 1-6 Ckp: 1-6
Best Rating: **81** 1/09 GrLe 5f stand

Modest sprinter; seems best at 5f; acts on good going; suited by Polytrack.

Silvee

90(81) (23)**52**

2-y-o gr f Avonbridge-Silver Louie (IRE) (Titus Livius (FR))
J J Bridger Mr & Mrs K Finch

Placings:0060000005 **(5967)**
2009: 5^{0}G, 5^{0}GF, 6^{8}G, 5^{0}GF, 5^{0}GF, 6^{0}GF, 5^{0}GF, 8^{0}G, 6^{0}SD, 6^{5}GS,

	Starts	1st	2nd	3rd	Win & Pl
Career Total (Turf)	9	0	0	0	0
Career Total (AW)	1	0	0	0	

Going (Turf): **Sf: 0-0 GS: 0-1 Gd: 0-3 GF: 0-5 Fm: 0-0**
Distance: 5f/6f: 0-9 7f-8f: 0-1 9f-13f: 0-0 14f+: 0-0
Track : LH: 0-1 RH: 0-1 Tight: 0-0 Gall: 0-3
Aids: Bl: 0-0 Vi: 0-0 Tstrap: 0-0 Ckp: 0-0
Best Rating: **52** 6/09 Wind 5f10y gd-fm

Silver Blue (IRE)

81(103) (64)**74**

6-y-o ch g Indian Lodge (IRE)-Silver Echo (Caerleon (USA))
W K Goldsworthy D Hughes M Edwards G Miller & Partners

Placings:6313140/346000000005/0045540/0532005021315130055**00**-5606 **(5444)**
2009: 11^{5}GS, 8^{6}GF, 9^{0}F, 11^{6}GF,

	Starts	1st	2nd	3rd	Win & Pl
Career Total (Turf)	35	4	0	5	22058
Career Total (AW)	16	1	2	1	4638

74	6/08	Chep	1m2f36y	(0-75)H	G-F	£2719
61	5/08	Brig	1m1f209y	(0-60)H	G-F	£1942
56	5/08	Brig	7f214y	(0-60)H	G-F	£2266
92	9/05	Sals	1m		G-F	£5284
88	7/05	Ling	7f		STD	£3129

Total win prize-money £15345

Going (Turf): Sf: 0-3 GS: 0-4 Gd: 0-10 **GF: 4-17** Fm: 0-1
Distance: 5f/6f: 0-2 **7f-8f: 3-19** 9f-13f: 2-29 14f+: 0-1
Track : **LH: 4-21** RH: 0-18 **Tight: 1-13** Gall: 0-6
Aids: Bl: 0-13 Vi: 0-1 Tstrap: 0-0 Ckp: 0-0
Best Rating: **99** 4/06 NmkR 1m1f gd-fm

Modest; stays 1m2f; acts on fast ground and Polytrack; has worn blinkers.

Silver Deal

(81) (42)**42**

4-y-o b f Lujain (USA)-Deal In Facts (So Factual (USA))
J A Pickering S Kitching

Placings:4000**5/440-0** **(0328)**
2009: 5^{0}SD,

	Starts	1st	2nd	3rd	Win & Pl
Career Total (Turf)	3	0	0	0	192
Career Total (AW)	6	0	0	0	0

Going (Turf): **Sf: 0-1 GS: 0-1 Gd: 0-1 GF: 0-0 Fm: 0-0**
Distance: 5f/6f: 0-8 7f-8f: 0-1 9f-13f: 0-0 14f+: 0-0
Track : LH: 0-4 RH: 0-0 Tight: 0-4 Gall: 0-0
Aids: Bl: 0-0 Vi: 0-0 Tstrap: 0-0 Ckp: 0-0
Best Rating: **42** 1/08 Sthl 5f stand

Silver Games (IRE)

108(96) (81)**91**

3-y-o gr f Verglas (IRE)-Mise (IRE) (Indian Ridge)
M R Channon The Hon Mrs J M Corbett & Mr & Mrs C Wright

Placings:0150-**0**04314235330 **(6267)**
2009: 7^{0}SD, 7^{0}GS, 8^{4}GF, 9^{3}G, 8^{1}GF, 8^{4}GF, 8^{2}GF, 8^{3}GF, 8^{5}GS, 8^{3}GF, 6^{3}S, 8^{0}G,

	Starts	1st	2nd	3rd	Win & Pl
Career Total (Turf)	15	2	1	4	24761
Career Total (AW)	1	0	0	0	

90	5/09	Newc	1m3y	(0-85)H	G-F	£5180
82	8/08	Folk	7f		G-F	£5204

Total win prize-money £10385

Going (Turf): Sf: 0-1 GS: 0-3 Gd: 0-4 **GF: 2-7** Fm: 0-0
Distance: 5f/6f: 0-0 7f-8f: 1-13 9f-13f: 1-3 14f+: 0-0
Track : LH: 0-2 RH: 0-5 Tight: 0-3 Gall: 0-3
Aids: Bl: 0-0 Vi: 0-0 Tstrap: 0-0 Ckp: 0-0
Best Rating: **91** 9/09 Sals 6f212y soft

Useful; stays 1m and acts on fast ground.

Silver Grecian

105 **114**

2-y-o gr c Haafhd-Regrette Rien (USA) (Unbridled's Song (USA))
J Ryan Ocean Trailers Ltd

Placings:11130 **(6849)**
2009: 7^{1}GF, 7^{1}GF, 7^{1}GF, 7^{3}GF, 7^{0}G,

	Starts	1st	2nd	3rd	Win & Pl
Career Total (Turf)	5	3	0	1	64605

104	7/09	NmkJ	7f	G-F	£45416

91 7/09 Wwck 7f26y G-F £3238

85 6/09 NmkJ 7f G-F £5180

Total win prize-money £53835

Going (Turf): Sf: 0-0 GS: 0-0 Gd: 0-1 **GF: 3-4** Fm: 0-0

Distance: 5f/6f: 0-0 **7f-8f: 3-5** 9f-13f: 0-0 14f+: 0-0

Track : **LH: 1-1** RH: 0-0 Tight: 0-0 Gall: 0-0

Aids: Bl: 0-0 Vi: 0-0 Tstrap: 0-0 Ckp: 0-0

Best Rating: **114** 9/09 Donc 7f gd-fm

Smart; won the 2009 Group 2 Superlative Stakes; stays 7f; acts on fast ground.

Silver Grey (IRE)

99 **98**

2-y-o gr f Chineur (FR)-Operissimo (Singspiel (IRE))

R Ingram Z Malik

Placings:2102352 **(6656a)**

2009: 5^{2}GF, 6^{1}G, 6^{0}G, 6^{2}GF, 7^{3}GF, 7^{5}GF, 8^{2}VS,

	Starts	1st	2nd	3rd	Win & Pl
Career Total (Turf)	**7**	**1**	**3**	**1**	**21965**

69 7/09 Epsm 6f GD £3238

Total win prize-money £3238

Going (Turf): Sf: 0-0 GS: 0-0 **Gd: 1-2** GF: 0-4 Fm: 0-0

Distance: **5f/6f: 1-4** 7f-8f: 0-3 9f-13f: 0-0 14f+: 0-0

Track : **LH: 1-2** RH: 0-2 **Tight: 1-1** Gall: 0-1

Aids: Bl: 0-0 Vi: 0-0 Tstrap: 0-0 Ckp: 0-0

Best Rating: **98** 10/09 StCl 1m v soft

Fair; effective over 6f; acts on good ground.

Silver Guest

99(108) (84)**73**

4-y-o br g Lujain (USA)-Ajig Dancer (Niniski (USA))

M R Channon John Guest

Placings:223244/14-000040**11433** **(7627)**

2009: 5^{0}GF, 7^{0}GF, 6^{0}GF, 7^{0}GF, 6^{0}G, 6^{4}GF, 6^{0}G, 7^{1}SD, 5^{1}SD, 7^{4}SD, 8^{3}SD, 7^{3}SD,

	Starts	1st	2nd	3rd	Win & Pl
Career Total (Turf)	**13**	**0**	**3**	**1**	**11427**
Career Total (AW)	**7**	**3**	**0**	**2**	**11497**

79 10/09 Wolv 5f216y (0-65)H STD £2388

76 10/09 Wolv 7f32y (0-65)H STD £2388

76 2/08 Ling 6f STD £2331

Total win prize-money £7108

Going (Turf): **Sf: 0-1 GS: 0-0 Gd: 0-5 GF: 0-7 Fm: 0-0**

Distance: **5f/6f: 2-13** 7f-8f: 1-7 9f-13f: 0-0 14f+: 0-0

Track : **LH: 3-8** RH: 0-0 **Tight: 3-8** Gall: 0-0

Aids: Bl: 0-0 Vi: 0-0 Tstrap: 0-0 Ckp: 0-0

Best Rating: **97** 6/07 Asct 5f gd-fm

Very useful; Listed placed at two; effective over 5f-7f; acts on good ground and on Polytrack.

Silver Hotspur

94(111) (88)**75**

5-y-o b g Royal Applause-Noble View (USA) (Distant View (USA))

C R Dore Patrick Wilmott

Placings:032400/0305400616/31135121311000500005441-05526600005000060 **(7854)**

2009: 9^{0}SD, 8^{5}SD, 8^{5}SD, 8^{2}SD, 8^{6}SD, 10^{6}SD, 7^{0}SF, 7^{0}GF, 8^{0}GS, 8^{0}GS, 8^{5}GF, 7^{0}F, 7^{0}SD, 7^{0}SD, 8^{0}SD, 7^{0}SD, 8^{6}SD, 8^{0}SS,

	Starts	1st	2nd	3rd	Win & Pl
Career Total (Turf)	**16**	**0**	**1**	**1**	**2215**
Career Total (AW)	**41**	**8**	**2**	**4**	**25158**

86 12/08 Sthl 1m (0-75)H STD £2729

94 3/08 Sthl 7f (0-75)H STD £2593

90 3/08 Sthl 1m (0-85)H STD £4210

81 2/08 Sthl 7f (0-85)H SS £4210

79 2/08 Sthl 7f (0-70)H STD £2457

69 1/08 Sthl 7f (0-52)H SS £1911

67 1/08 Sthl 6f (0-52)H STD £1399

57 11/07 Wolv 7f32y (0-45) STD £1911

Total win prize-money £21422

Going (Turf): **Sf: 0-2 GS: 0-2 Gd: 0-3 GF: 0-8 Fm: 0-1**

Distance: 5f/6f: 1-14 **7f-8f: 7-34** 9f-13f: 0-9 14f+: 0-0

Track : **LH: 8-39** RH: 0-7 **Tight: 1-16** Gall: 0-4

Aids: Bl: 0-1 Vi: 0-0 Tstrap: 0-1 Ckp: 0-1

Best Rating: **94** 3/08 Sthl 7f stand

Fair; stays 1m; acts on Polytrack, but very effective on Fibresand.

Silver In The Sand

94 **61**

2-y-o b f Fasliyev (USA)-Dances With Dreams (Be My Chief (USA))

J D Bethell Dr Anne J F Gillespie

Placings:634000 **(6215)**

2009: 5^{6}G, 5^{3}GF, 5^{4}G, 5^{0}GF, 6^{0}G, 8^{0}GF,

	Starts	1st	2nd	3rd	Win & Pl
Career Total (Turf)	**6**	**0**	**0**	**1**	**799**

Going (Turf): **Sf: 0-0 GS: 0-0 Gd: 0-3 GF: 0-3 Fm: 0-0**

Distance: 5f/6f: 0-5 7f-8f: 0-1 9f-13f: 0-0 14f+: 0-0

Track : LH: 0-1 RH: 0-1 Tight: 0-1 Gall: 0-1

Aids: Bl: 0-0 Vi: 0-0 Tstrap: 0-0 Ckp: 0-0

Best Rating: **61** 7/09 Thsk 5f good

Modest efforts in 5f maidens on fast and easy ground.

Silver Linnet (IRE)

97(72) (30)**68**

2-y-o gr f Acclamation-Nadeema (FR) (Linamix (FR))

M G Quinlan (T D Easterby 6/10) Donal Flynn

Placings:03520316 **(7849)**

2009: 5^{0}G, 5^{3}GF, 5^{5}GF, 5^{2}GS, 6^{0}GF, 5^{3}GF, 5^{1}G, 6^{6}SS,

	Starts	1st	2nd	3rd	Win & Pl
Career Total (Turf)	**7**	**1**	**1**	**2**	**3974**
Career Total (AW)	**1**	**0**	**0**	**0**	**0**

68 10/09 Catt 5f (0-65) GD £2047

Total win prize-money £2047

Going (Turf): Sf: 0-0 GS: 0-1 **Gd: 1-2** GF: 0-4 Fm: 0-0

Distance: **5f/6f: 1-7** 7f-8f: 0-1 9f-13f: 0-0 14f+: 0-0

Track : LH: 0-1 RH: 0-0 Tight: 0-0 Gall: 0-0

Aids: **Bl: 1-1** Vi: 0-0 Tstrap: 0-0 Ckp: 0-0

Best Rating: **68** 10/09 Catt 5f good

Modest; effective over 5f; acts on fast ground but possibly best with cut.

Silver Prelude

103(106) (73)**68**

8-y-o gr g Prince Sabo-Silver Blessings (Statoblest)

S C Williams Mrs A Shone

Placings:02215250/00031000000/000060/0002021050221020511/2360660606-605502101203404 **(7682)**

2009: 5^{6}SD, 6^{0}SD, 6^{5}SD, 6^{5}G, 5^{0}F, 5^{2}SD, 5^{1}S, 5^{0}GS, 5^{1}SD, 5^{2}GF, 5^{0}GF, 5^{3}SD, 5^{4}SD, 5^{0}SD, 5^{4}SD,

	Starts	1st	2nd	3rd	Win & Pl
Career Total (Turf)	**42**	**4**	**4**	**1**	**30259**
Career Total (AW)	**27**	**4**	**7**	**2**	**19939**

73 8/09 Kemp 5f (0-75)H STD £2590

66 7/09 Yarm 5f43y (0-70)H SFT £2719

87 12/07 Wolv 5f20y (0-75)H STD £2914

75 11/07 Ling 5f (0-70)H STD £2817

71 9/07 Wolv 5f20y (0-65)H STD £2218

67 7/07 Yarm 5f43y (0-70)H G-F £3238

88 7/04 NmkJ 5f D(0-85)H G-F £10249

85 7/03 Wind 5f10y E G-F £3672

Total win prize-money £30421

Going (Turf): Sf: 1-1 GS: 0-5 Gd: 0-11 **GF: 3-20** Fm: 0-5

Distance: **5f/6f: 8-68** 7f-8f: 0-1 9f-13f: 0-0 14f+: 0-0

Track : **LH: 3-21** RH: 1-8 **Tight: 3-17** Gall: 1-9

Aids: Bl: 0-0 Vi: 0-0 Tstrap: 0-0 Ckp: 0-0

Best Rating: **96** 1/08 Ling 6f stand

Modest; best over 5f; acts on fast ground and on Polytrack; suited by forcing tactics; has worn a tongue tie.

Silver Print (USA)

101(100) (76)**76**

3-y-o gr/ro g Maria's Mon (USA)-Shutterbug (USA) (Deputy Minister (CAN))

W R Swinburn P W Harris

Placings:43220-50635 **(6376)**

2009: 8^{5}SD, 8^{0}GS, 10^{6}G, 9^{3}SD, 12^{5}SD,

	Starts	1st	2nd	3rd	Win & Pl
Career Total (Turf)	**6**	**0**	**1**	**1**	**2420**
Career Total (AW)	**4**	**0**	**1**	**1**	**1559**

Going (Turf): **Sf: 0-1 GS: 0-2 Gd: 0-2** GF: 0-1 **Fm: 0-0**

Distance: 5f/6f: 0-0 7f-8f: 0-7 9f-13f: 0-3 14f+: 0-0

Track : LH: 0-2 RH: 0-6 Tight: 0-1 Gall: 0-1

Aids: Bl: 0-0 Vi: 0-0 Tstrap: 0-0 Ckp: 0-0

Best Rating: **76** 10/08 Kemp 1m stand

Fair; effective over 1m; acts on Polytrack.

Silver Rime (FR)

101 **91**

4-y-o gr c Verglas (IRE)-Severina (Darshaan)

Miss L A Perratt Ken McGarrity

Placings:041/2103535-00306 **(7169)**

2009: 8^{0}G, 7^{0}S, 8^{3}G, 7^{0}G, 8^{6}S,

	Starts	1st	2nd	3rd	Win & Pl
Career Total (Turf)	**15**	**2**	**1**	**3**	**14945**

89 4/08 Wind 1m67y (0-85)H GD £5180

77 9/07 Gdwd 7f G-S £3238

Total win prize-money £8420

Going (Turf): Sf: 0-4 **GS: 1-2 Gd: 1-6** GF: 0-3 Fm: 0-0

Distance: 5f/6f: 0-0 7f-8f: 1-9 9f-13f: 1-6 14f+: 0-0

Track : LH: 0-8 **RH: 2-3 Tight: 1-1** Gall: 0-2

Aids: Bl: 0-0 Vi: 0-0 Tstrap: 0-0 Ckp: 0-0

Best Rating: **91** 9/08 Sand 1m14y soft

Useful; stays 1m; acts on most ground.

Silver Rock (IRE)

99 **84**

2-y-o ch f Rock Of Gibraltar (IRE)-Ribblesdale (Northern Park (USA))

M A Magnusson Eastwind Racing Ltd and Martha Trussell

Placings:10 **(6852)**

2009: 7^{1}GF, 7^{0}G,

	Starts	1st	2nd	3rd	Win & Pl
Career Total (Turf)	**2**	**1**	**0**	**0**	**11216**

84 9/09 Newb 7f G-F £11215
Total win prize-money £11216

Going (Turf): Sf: 0-0 GS: 0-0 Gd: 0-1 **GF: 1-1** Fm: 0-0
Distance: 5f/6f: 0-0 **7f-8f: 1-2** 9f-13f: 0-0 14f+: 0-0
Track : LH: 0-0 RH: 0-0 Tight: 0-0 Gall: 0-0
Aids: Bl: 0-0 Vi: 0-0 Tstrap: 0-0 Ckp: 0-0
Best Rating: 84 9/09 Newb 7f gd-fm

Useful; effective over 7f; acts on fast ground.

Silver Salsa

75(89) (49)50
3-y-o b f Lujain (USA)-Tango Teaser (Shareef Dancer (USA))
J R Jenkins D Bryans

Placings:0004504-50060 (3459)
2009: 6^{5}SD, 6^{0}G, 8^{0}G, 5^{6}G, 6^{0}GF,

	Starts	1st	2nd	3rd	Win & Pl
Career Total (Turf)	9	0	0	0	0
Career Total (AW)	3	0	0	0	202

Going (Turf): **Sf: 0-1 GS: 0-1 Gd: 0-4 GF: 0-3 Fm: 0-0**
Distance: 5f/6f: 0-10 7f-8f: 0-2 9f-13f: 0-0 14f+: 0-0
Track : LH: 0-2 RH: 0-3 Tight: 0-0 Gall: 0-4
Aids: Bl: 0-0 Vi: 0-1 Tstrap: 0-0 Ckp: 0-0
Best Rating: 50 8/08 Folk 5f gd-fm

Moderate filly; best at 5f on fast ground.

Silver Sceptre (IRE)

(89) (35)39
3-y-o b g Intikhab (USA)-Silver Pursuit (Rainbow Quest (USA))
W J Musson Lord Rowallan & W J Musson

Placings:000-4 (5328)
2009: 11^{4}SD,

	Starts	1st	2nd	3rd	Win & Pl
Career Total (Turf)	3	0	0	0	
Career Total (AW)	1	0	0	0	154

Going (Turf): **Sf: 0-1 GS: 0-0 Gd: 0-2 GF: 0-0 Fm: 0-0**
Distance: 5f/6f: 0-3 7f-8f: 0-0 9f-13f: 0-1 14f+: 0-0
Track : LH: 0-1 RH: 0-0 Tight: 0-0 Gall: 0-2
Aids: Bl: 0-0 Vi: 0-0 Tstrap: 0-0 Ckp: 0-0
Best Rating: 39 7/08 Wind 6f soft

Silver Socks

87 58
2-y-o br c Captain Rio-Silver Blessings (Statoblest)
Miss L A Perratt (I Semple 1/10) Raymond Miquel

Placings:5500 (6983)
2009: 6^{5}GS, 7^{5}G, 6^{0}GF, 6^{0}G,

	Starts	1st	2nd	3rd	Win & Pl
Career Total (Turf)	4	0	0	0	160

Going (Turf): **Sf: 0-0 GS: 0-1 Gd: 0-2 GF: 0-1 Fm: 0-0**
Distance: 5f/6f: 0-3 7f-8f: 0-1 9f-13f: 0-0 14f+: 0-0
Track : LH: 0-1 RH: 0-0 Tight: 0-0 Gall: 0-0
Aids: Bl: 0-0 Vi: 0-0 Tstrap: 0-0 Ckp: 0-0
Best Rating: 58 9/09 Ayr 7f50y good

Silver Spruce

(96) (47)65
4-y-o gr g First Trump-Red Typhoon (Belfort (FR))
D Flood Miss E A Smith

Placings:1505066-0050 (0247)
2009: 10^{0}SD, 10^{0}SD, 10^{5}SD, 8^{0}SD,

	Starts	1st	2nd	3rd	Win & Pl
Career Total (Turf)	4	1	0	0	2593
Career Total (AW)	7	0	0	0	0

65 4/08 Wind 1m2f7y G-S £2593
Total win prize-money £2593

Going (Turf): Sf: 0-1 **GS: 1-1** Gd: 0-0 GF: 0-2 Fm: 0-0
Distance: 5f/6f: 0-0 7f-8f: 0-2 **9f-13f: 1-9** 14f+: 0-0
Track : LH: 0-8 **RH: 1-3 Tight: 1-6** Gall: 0-2
Aids: Bl: 0-6 Vi: 0-0 Tstrap: 0-1 Ckp: 0-1
Best Rating: 65 4/08 Wind 1m2f7y gd-sft

Moderate; effective over 1m2f; acts on easy ground.

Silver Surprise

93(95) (57)52
5-y-o gr m Orpen (USA)-Dim Ofan (Petong)
J J Bridger Mr & Mrs K Finch

Placings:U00000000500060/0005060024606-0360000 (5579)
2009: 11^{0}GF, 16^{3}GF, 16^{6}G, 11^{0}GS, 12^{0}GF, 14^{0}G, 16^{0}GF,

	Starts	1st	2nd	3rd	Win & Pl
Career Total (Turf)	22	0	0	1	302
Career Total (AW)	13	0	1	0	771

Going (Turf): **Sf: 0-0 GS: 0-5 Gd: 0-5 GF: 0-12 Fm: 0-0**
Distance: 5f/6f: 0-0 7f-8f: 0-4 9f-13f: 0-24 14f+: 0-7
Track : LH: 0-10 RH: 0-23 Tight: 0-16 Gall: 0-3
Aids: Bl: 0-3 Vi: 0-0 Tstrap: 0-0 Ckp: 0-0
Best Rating: 57 10/08 Kemp 1m4f stand

Plating class; effective over 1m4f; acts on Polytrack.

Silver Symphony (IRE)

99(92) (82)79
2-y-o b/br f Pastoral Pursuits-Streak Of Silver (USA) (Dynaformer (USA))
P F I Cole Manley, Meyrick & Sullivan

Placings:042130 (5797)
2009: 5^{0}GF, 6^{4}GF, 6^{2}GF, 7^{1}SD, 7^{3}SD, 6^{0}GF,

	Starts	1st	2nd	3rd	Win & Pl
Career Total (Turf)	4	0	1	0	1541
Career Total (AW)	2	1	0	1	4560

82 6/09 Kemp 7f STD £3885
Total win prize-money £3886

Going (Turf): **Sf: 0-0 GS: 0-0 Gd: 0-0 GF: 0-4 Fm: 0-0**
Distance: 5f/6f: 0-2 **7f-8f: 1-4** 9f-13f: 0-0 14f+: 0-0
Track : LH: 0-1 **RH: 1-1** Tight: 0-1 Gall: 0-0
Aids: Bl: 0-0 Vi: 0-0 Tstrap: 0-0 Ckp: 0-0
Best Rating: 82 6/09 Kemp 7f stand

Fair; effective over 6f-7f; acts on fast ground and on Polytrack.

Silver Waters

85(97) (68)65
4-y-o gr g Fantastic Light (USA)-Silent Waters (Polish Precedent (USA))
Tim Vaughan T Vaughan

Placings:3/0523133000-05 (3308)
2009: 11^{0}GF, 11^{5}GF,

	Starts	1st	2nd	3rd	Win & Pl
Career Total (Turf)	7	1	0	2	5068
Career Total (AW)	6	0	1	2	1470

79 4/08 Pont 1m4f8y (0-70)H G-S £3238
Total win prize-money £3238

Going (Turf): Sf: 0-2 **GS: 1-3** Gd: 0-0 GF: 0-2 Fm: 0-0
Distance: 5f/6f: 0-1 7f-8f: 0-1 **9f-13f: 1-11** 14f+: 0-0
Track : **LH: 1-7** RH: 0-4 Tight: 0-4 Gall: 0-2
Aids: Bl: 0-0 Vi: 0-0 Tstrap: 0-0 Ckp: 0-0
Best Rating: 79 4/08 Pont 1m4f8y gd-sft

Fair colt; stays 1m4f; acts on soft ground on turf and Polytrack.

Silver Wind

107(108) (83)89
4-y-o b g Ishiguru (USA)-My Bonus (Cyrano De Bergerac)
P D Evans Silver Wind Partnership

Placings:0023100225/3050612000454-41562050210451000 (6994)
2009: 7^{4}SD, 7^{1}SD, 7^{5}SD, 6^{6}GF, 6^{2}G, 6^{0}GF, 6^{5}GF, 7^{0}GF, 6^{2}G, 6^{1}GS, 6^{0}GF, 6^{4}G, 6^{5}GS, 6^{1}GF, 6^{0}G, 6^{0}GF, 6^{0}G,

	Starts	1st	2nd	3rd	Win & Pl
Career Total (Turf)	33	4	6	2	42066
Career Total (AW)	7	1	0	0	4019

89 9/09 Donc 6f (0-90)H G-F £9714
88 8/09 NmkJ 6f (0-85)H G-S £5828
75 1/09 Wolv 7f32y STD £2047
87 7/08 Asct 6f (0-85)H G-F £7123
82 7/07 Folk 6f G-F £3886
Total win prize-money £28599

Going (Turf): Sf: 0-5 GS: 1-4 Gd: 0-9 **GF: 3-15** Fm: 0-0
Distance: **5f/6f: 4-27** 7f-8f: 1-13 9f-13f: 0-0 14f+: 0-0
Track : **LH: 1-10** RH: 0-2 **Tight: 1-5** Gall: 0-4
Aids: Bl: 0-7 **Vi: 5-31** Tstrap: 0-0 Ckp: 0-0
Best Rating: 89 9/09 Donc 6f gd-fm

Useful; effective over 6f-7f; acts on most ground on turf; goes on Polytrack; has worn blinkers and a visor.

Silverglas (IRE)

107(98) (70)79
3-y-o gr g Verglas (IRE)-Yellow Trumpet (Petong)
M P Tregoning Mrs B Sumner

Placings:0-35210 (6740)
2009: 7^{3}SD, 8^{5}SD, 9^{2}GF, 9^{1}GF, 10^{0}GS,

	Starts	1st	2nd	3rd	Win & Pl
Career Total (Turf)	4	1	1	0	6722
Career Total (AW)	2	0	0	1	530

79 9/09 Folk 1m1f149y (0-80)H G-F £5180
Total win prize-money £5181

Going (Turf): Sf: 0-0 GS: 0-1 Gd: 0-1 **GF: 1-2** Fm: 0-0
Distance: 5f/6f: 0-0 7f-8f: 0-3 **9f-13f: 1-3** 14f+: 0-0
Track : LH: 0-1 **RH: 1-4 Tight: 1-4** Gall: 0-0
Aids: Bl: 0-0 Vi: 0-0 Tstrap: 0-0 Ckp: 0-0
Best Rating: 79 9/09 Folk 1m1f149y gd-fm

Fair; stays 1m1f; acts on fast ground; goes on Polytrack.

Silvermine Bay (IRE)

83(73) (48)37
2-y-o br f Act One-Quittance (USA) (Riverman (USA))
A P Jarvis Ambrose Turnbull

Placings:000 (6441)
2009: 6^{0}S, 6^{0}GS, 8^{0}SS,

	Starts	1st	2nd	3rd	Win & Pl
Career Total (Turf)	2	0	0	0	
Career Total (AW)	1	0	0	0	

Going (Turf): Sf: 0-1 GS: 0-1 Gd: 0-0 GF: 0-0 Fm: 0-0
Distance: 5f/6f: 0-2 7f-8f: 0-1 9f-13f: 0-0 14f+: 0-0
Track : LH: 0-1 RH: 0-0 Tight: 0-1 Gall: 0-0
Aids: Bl: 0-0 Vi: 0-0 Tstrap: 0-0 Ckp: 0-0
Best Rating: 48 10/09 Ling 1m std-slw

Silvertown Boy

46(86) (35)
3-y-o gr g Cape Town (IRE)-Optimistic Dreamer (IRE) (Topanoora)
H A McWilliams Ron Holford

Placings:50000 (7464)
2009: 10^{5}GF, 8^{0}SF, 8^{0}GS, 9^{0}SD, 7^{0}SD,

	Starts	1st	2nd	3rd	Win & Pl
Career Total (Turf)	2	0	0	0	0
Career Total (AW)	3	0	0	0	

Going (Turf): Sf: 0-0 GS: 0-1 Gd: 0-0 GF: 0-1 Fm: 0-0
Distance: 5f/6f: 0-0 7f-8f: 0-2 9f-13f: 0-3 14f+: 0-0
Track : LH: 0-5 RH: 0-0 Tight: 0-4 Gall: 0-1
Aids: Bl: 0-0 Vi: 0-0 Tstrap: 0-2 Ckp: 0-2
Best Rating: 35 11/09 Wolv 7f32y stand

Silvester

76(83) (40)21
3-y-o gr g Silver Patriarch (IRE)-Raintree Venture (Good Times (ITY))
R M H Cowell Miss Diana Birkbeck

Placings:00000 (7694)
2009: 8^{0}SD, 8^{0}SD, 10^{0}S, 12^{0}SD, 10^{0}SD,

	Starts	1st	2nd	3rd	Win & Pl
Career Total (Turf)	1	0	0	0	
Career Total (AW)	4	0	0	0	

Going (Turf): Sf: 0-1 GS: 0-0 Gd: 0-0 GF: 0-0 Fm: 0-0
Distance: 5f/6f: 0-0 7f-8f: 0-2 9f-13f: 0-3 14f+: 0-0
Track : LH: 0-4 RH: 0-1 Tight: 0-3 Gall: 0-0
Aids: Bl: 0-0 Vi: 0-0 Tstrap: 0-1 Ckp: 0-1
Best Rating: 40 12/09 Ling 1m2f stand

Simenon (IRE)

98 99
2-y-o b c Marju (IRE)-Epistoliere (IRE) (Alzao (USA))
A M Balding Mr Greenwood, Ms James & Mr Cockburn

Placings:31513 (6664)
2009: 7^{3}G, 7^{1}G, 7^{5}GF, 8^{1}GS, 8^{3}GS,

	Starts	1st	2nd	3rd	Win & Pl
Career Total (Turf)	5	2	0	2	18510
95 9/09 Ayr	1m		G-S		£5828
88 7/09 NmkJ	7f		GD		£5180

Total win prize-money £11009

Going (Turf): Sf: 0-0 GS: 1-2 Gd: 1-2 GF: 0-1 Fm: 0-0
Distance: 5f/6f: 0-0 7f-8f: 2-5 9f-13f: 0-0 14f+: 0-0
Track : LH: 1-1 RH: 0-2 Tight: 0-0 Gall: 0-1
Aids: Bl: 0-0 Vi: 0-0 Tstrap: 0-0 Ckp: 0-0
Best Rating: 99 8/09 Sand 7f16y gd-fm

Smart; effective at 7f-1m; acts on good and easy ground.

Simla Sunset (IRE)

56(102) (72)72
3-y-o b f One Cool Cat (USA)-Simla Bibi (Indian Ridge)
J R Gask (David P Myerscough 16/8) The Simla Sunset Partnership

Placings:5-3430210 (7830)
2009: 8^{3}GY, 7^{4}GY, 6^{3}S, 7^{0}GF, 7^{2}SD, 7^{1}SD, 7^{0}SD,

	Starts	1st	2nd	3rd	Win & Pl
Career Total (Turf)	5	0	0	2	2255
Career Total (AW)	3	1	1	0	3352
71 11/09 Wolv	7f32y		STD		£2388

Total win prize-money £2388

Going (Turf): Sf: 0-1 GS: 0-0 Gd: 0-0 GF: 0-1 Fm: 0-0
Distance: 5f/6f: 0-1 7f-8f: 1-7 9f-13f: 0-0 14f+: 0-0
Track : LH: 1-5 RH: 0-2 Tight: 1-2 Gall: 0-0
Aids: Bl: 0-0 Vi: 0-0 Tstrap: 0-0 Ckp: 0-0
Best Rating: 72 12/09 Kemp 7f stand

Modest; stays 1m; acts on soft ground and on Polytrack; has worn a tongue-tie.

Simola

89 42
3-y-o ch f Bold Edge-Amused (Prince Sabo)
R A Fahey D R Brotherton

Placings:65 (4276)
2009: 5^{6}GF, 7^{5}G,

	Starts	1st	2nd	3rd	Win & Pl
Career Total (Turf)	2	0	0	0	0

Going (Turf): Sf: 0-0 GS: 0-0 Gd: 0-1 GF: 0-1 Fm: 0-0
Distance: 5f/6f: 0-1 7f-8f: 0-1 9f-13f: 0-0 14f+: 0-0
Track : LH: 0-1 RH: 0-0 Tight: 0-1 Gall: 0-0
Aids: Bl: 0-0 Vi: 0-0 Tstrap: 0-0 Ckp: 0-0
Best Rating: 42 6/09 Thsk 5f gd-fm

From a good sprinting family; moderate form in maidens at up to 7f.

Simon Gray

90(103) (89)87
3-y-o b c Act One-Shardette (IRE) (Darshaan)
R Hannon Mrs James Wigan

Placings:565-111 (3026)
2009: 8^{1}GF, 11^{1}GS, 10^{1}SD,

	Starts	1st	2nd	3rd	Win & Pl
Career Total (Turf)	4	2	0	0	8419
Career Total (AW)	2	1	0	0	4727
89 6/09 Kemp	1m2f	(0-85)H		STD	£4727
87 5/09 Newb	1m3f5y	(0-80)H		G-S	£5180
81 4/09 Hayd	1m30y	(0-75)H		G-F	£3238

Total win prize-money £13146

Going (Turf): Sf: 0-1 GS: 1-1 Gd: 0-1 GF: 1-1 Fm: 0-0
Distance: 5f/6f: 0-0 7f-8f: 0-3 9f-13f: 3-3 14f+: 0-0
Track : LH: 2-3 RH: 1-1 Tight: 0-1 Gall: 1-1
Aids: Bl: 0-0 Vi: 0-0 Tstrap: 0-0 Ckp: 0-0
Best Rating: 89 6/09 Kemp 1m2f stand

Useful; stays 1m3f; acts on most ground and on Polytrack.

Simonside

107(97) (75)78
6-y-o b g Shahrastani (USA)-Only So Far (Teenoso (USA))
B Ellison Racing Management & Training Ltd

Placings:0143003316334 (6767)
2009: 9^{0}SD, 12^{1}SD, 13^{4}SD, 12^{3}GF, 16^{0}GF, 11^{0}GF, 12^{3}GS, 16^{3}GF, 11^{1}G, 12^{6}GF, 16^{3}GS, 17^{3}G, 16^{4}GS,

	Starts	1st	2nd	3rd	Win & Pl
Career Total (Turf)	10	1	0	5	9969
Career Total (AW)	3	1	0	0	2730
75 7/09 Carl	1m3f107y (0-80)H			GD	£6246
60 3/09 Wolv	1m4f50y			STD	£2729

Total win prize-money £8976

Going (Turf): Sf: 0-0 GS: 0-3 Gd: 1-2 GF: 0-5 Fm: 0-0
Distance: 5f/6f: 0-0 7f-8f: 0-0 9f-13f: 2-7 14f+: 0-6
Track : LH: 1-9 RH: 1-4 Tight: 1-5 Gall: 0-4
Aids: Bl: 0-0 Vi: 0-0 Tstrap: 0-0 Ckp: 0-0
Best Rating: 78 9/09 York 2m88y gd-sft

Fair; bumper winner; stays 1m4f; acts on easy ground; goes on Polytrack.

Simple Jim (FR)

104(99) (66)59
5-y-o b g Jimble (FR)-Stop The Wedding (USA) (Stop The Music (USA))
J Hetherton (A D Brown 21/5) R G Fell

Placings:301514026/062050414-054611414 (7080)
2009: 13^{0}GF, 16^{5}G, 12^{4}GF, 16^{6}G, 14^{1}GF, 13^{1}GF, 15^{4}G, 13^{1}G, 11^{4}S,

	Starts	1st	2nd	3rd	Win & Pl
Career Total (Turf)	18	5	0	1	13398
Career Total (AW)	9	1	2	0	5551
59 10/09 Catt	1m5f175y (0-60)H			GD	£2590
56 9/09 Catt	1m5f175y (0-65)H			G-F	£2047
55 9/09 Rdcr	1m6f19y (0-65)H			G-F	£2047
62 12/08 Sthl	1m6f (0-75)H			STD	£2729
8/07 Rcft	1m4f			GD	£2364
7/07 Erbr	1m2f110y			GD	£2364

Total win prize-money £14144

Going (Turf): Sf: 0-2 GS: 0-2 Gd: 3-10 GF: 2-4 Fm: 0-0
Distance: 5f/6f: 0-0 7f-8f: 0-0 9f-13f: 2-14 14f+: 4-13
Track : LH: 4-17 RH: 0-2 Tight: 3-14 Gall: 0-0
Aids: Bl: 0-0 Vi: 0-0 Tstrap: 0-1 Ckp: 0-1
Best Rating: 66 2/08 Sthl 1m4f stand

Moderate; ex-French; stays 1m6f; acts on fast ground; goes on sand.

Simple Rhythm

103(97) (68)87
3-y-o b f Piccolo-Easy Beat (IRE) (Orpen (USA))
J Ryan (J G Given 22/8) J Ryan

Placings:61201260-302024144324101140 (6877)
2009: 5^{3}SD, 6^{0}SD, 5^{2}SD, 5^{0}F, 5^{2}GF, 5^{4}G, 5^{1}SD, 5^{4}GF, 5^{4}SD, 5^{3}G, 6^{2}GF, 5^{4}F, 6^{1}GS, 6^{0}SD, 5^{1}GF, 6^{1}GS, 5^{4}G, 5^{0}SD,

	Starts	1st	2nd	3rd	Win & Pl
Career Total (Turf)	16	5	3	1	15874
Career Total (AW)	11	1	2	1	4014
87 10/09 Nott	6f15y	(0-70)H		G-S	£2590
74 9/09 Brig	5f59y	(0-65)H		G-F	£2590
70 9/09 Ling	6f	(0-75)H		G-S	£3070
68 6/09 Sthl	5f	(0-60)H		STD	£2047
64 8/08 Yarm	6f3y			G-S	£2201
68 5/08 Yarm	5f43y			G-F	£1683

Total win prize-money £14184

Going (Turf): Sf: 0-0 GS: 3-4 Gd: 0-3 GF: 2-7 Fm: 0-2

Distance: **5f/6f: 4-25** 7f-8f: 2-2 9f-13f: 0-0 14f+: 0-0
Track : **LH: 1-7** RH: 0-4 Tight: 0-5 Gall: 0-0
Aids: Bl: 0-0 Vi: 0-0 Tstrap: 0-0 Ckp: 0-0
Best Rating: 87 10/09 Nott 6f15y gd-sft

Fair; effective over 5f-6f; acts on most ground and on sand.

Simple Solution (USA)

106(101) (81)**83**
3-y-o b f Dynaformer (USA)-Super Staff (USA) (Secretariat (USA))
B W Hills K Abdulla

Placings:51-5055 **(6165)**
2009: 11^5GF, 11^0HY, 12^5GF, 12^5SD,

	Starts	1st	2nd	3rd	Win & Pl
Career Total (Turf)	4	0	0	0	1356
Career Total (AW)	2	1	0	0	3837

81 9/08 Kemp 1m STD £3561
Total win prize-money £3562

Going (Turf): **Sf: 0-1 GS: 0-0 Gd: 0-1 GF: 0-2 Fm: 0-0**
Distance: 5f/6f: 0-0 **7f-8f: 1-2** 9f-13f: 0-4 14f+: 0-0
Track : LH: 0-2 **RH: 1-3** Tight: 0-2 Gall: 0-0
Aids: Bl: 0-0 Vi: 0-0 Tstrap: 0-0 Ckp: 0-0
Best Rating: 83 5/09 Ches 1m3f79y gd-fm

Useful; stays 1m; acts on a sound surface and on Polytrack.

Simplification

106(99) (78)**78**
3-y-o gr f Daylami (IRE)-Bella Cantata (Singspiel (IRE))
R Hannon J N Reus

Placings:550-23365 **(3751)**
2009: 7^2SD, 8^3SD, 10^3GF, 9^6G, 10^5G,

	Starts	1st	2nd	3rd	Win & Pl
Career Total (Turf)	5	0	0	1	1573
Career Total (AW)	3	0	1	1	1509

Going (Turf): **Sf: 0-0 GS: 0-0 Gd: 0-3 GF: 0-2 Fm: 0-0**
Distance: 5f/6f: 0-0 7f-8f: 0-5 9f-13f: 0-3 14f+: 0-0
Track : LH: 0-3 RH: 0-4 Tight: 0-3 Gall: 0-1
Aids: Bl: 0-0 Vi: 0-0 Tstrap: 0-0 Ckp: 0-0
Best Rating: 78 4/09 Kemp 1m stand

Fair; stays 1m2f; acts on Polytrack; handles fast turf.

Simplified

(89) (47)**43**
6-y-o b m Lend A Hand-Houston Heiress (USA) (Houston (USA))
M C Chapman R A Gadd

Placings:5040005023534002/641000/00-6 **(0129)**
2009: 8^6SD,

	Starts	1st	2nd	3rd	Win & Pl
Career Total (Turf)	9	0	1	2	1553
Career Total (AW)	16	1	1	0	2009

49 2/07 Kemp 1m3f (0-45) STD £1365
Total win prize-money £1365

Going (Turf): **Sf: 0-1 GS: 0-0 Gd: 0-4 GF: 0-3 Fm: 0-1**
Distance: 5f/6f: 0-1 7f-8f: 0-7 **9f-13f: 1-17** 14f+: 0-0
Track : LH: 0-14 **RH: 1-8** Tight: 0-11 Gall: 0-1
Aids: Bl: 0-0 Vi: 0-0 Tstrap: 0-0 Ckp: 0-0
Best Rating: 53 3/06 Ling 7f stand

Simply Sensational (IRE)

73 **16**
3-y-o ch g Tendulkar (USA)-Grange Clare (IRE) (Bijou D'Inde)
Patrick Morris Rob Lloyd Racing Limited

Placings:06 **(3936)**
2009: 7^0F, 7^6GF,

	Starts	1st	2nd	3rd	Win & Pl
Career Total (Turf)	2	0	0	0	0

Going (Turf): **Sf: 0-0 GS: 0-0 Gd: 0-0 GF: 0-1 Fm: 0-1**
Distance: 5f/6f: 0-0 7f-8f: 0-2 9f-13f: 0-0 14f+: 0-0
Track : LH: 0-1 RH: 0-1 Tight: 0-1 Gall: 0-0
Aids: Bl: 0-0 Vi: 0-0 Tstrap: 0-0 Ckp: 0-0
Best Rating: 16 6/09 Thsk 7f firm

Simpsons Gamble (IRE)

101(105) (66)**61**
6-y-o b g Tagula (IRE)-Kiva (Indian Ridge)
R A Teal Mrs Sue Teal

Placings:00O0/000554/050433005522/3416301304-4303040400140 **(7109)**
2009: 6^4SD, 6^3SD, 5^0SD, 6^3SD, 6^0SD, 7^4F, 8^0SD, 8^4SD, 7^0SD, 8^0SD, 9^1F, 10^4G, 8^0SD,

	Starts	1st	2nd	3rd	Win & Pl
Career Total (Turf)	8	1	0	0	2230
Career Total (AW)	37	2	2	7	7471

61 8/09 Ling 1m1f FRM £2047
63 4/08 Ling 6f (0-55)H STD £2047
63 1/08 Kemp 6f STD £2047
Total win prize-money £6142

Going (Turf): Sf: 0-0 GS: 0-1 Gd: 0-5 GF: 0-0 **Fm: 1-2**
Distance: **5f/6f: 2-18** 7f-8f: 0-22 9f-13f: 1-5 14f+: 0-0
Track : **LH: 2-20** RH: 1-22 **Tight: 2-21** Gall: 0-1
Aids: Bl. 0-3 Vi: 0-0 Tstrap: 3-23 Ckp: 3-23
Best Rating: 66 4/09 Ling 6f stand

Moderate; effective at around 6f-1m1f; acts on fast ground; goes on Polytrack; has worn cheekpieces.

Simulate

84 **41**
3-y-o b c Dansili-Orford Ness (Selkirk (USA))
Sir Michael Stoute K Abdulla

Placings:0 **(6794)**
2009: 10^0S,

	Starts	1st	2nd	3rd	Win & Pl
Career Total (Turf)	1	0	0	0	

Going (Turf): **Sf: 0-1 GS: 0-0 Gd: 0-0 GF: 0-0 Fm: 0-0**
Distance: 5f/6f: 0-0 7f-8f: 0-0 9f-13f: 0-1 14f+: 0-0
Track : LH: 0-1 RH: 0-0 Tight: 0-0 Gall: 0-0
Aids: Bl: 0-0 Vi: 0-0 Tstrap: 0-0 Ckp: 0-0
Best Rating: 41 10/09 Nott 1m2f50y soft

Sinbad The Sailor

102(98) (58)**75**
4-y-o b g Cape Cross (IRE)-Sinead (USA) (Irish River (FR))
J W Hills Wauchope Cottam Sir S Dunning Mrs Caroe

Placings:050/23015000-600154463432 **(6969)**
2009: 10^6G, 10^0GS, 10^0GF, 9^1G, 11^5GF, 12^4GF, 14^4GF, 14^6GF, 11^3GF, 10^4SD, 12^3SD, 11^2G,

	Starts	1st	2nd	3rd	Win & Pl
Career Total (Turf)	21	2	2	2	9394
Career Total (AW)	2	0	0	1	447

66 6/09 Brig 1m1f209y (0-65)H GD £2460
75 7/08 Donc 1m2f60y (0-70)H G-F £3238
Total win prize-money £5699

Going (Turf): Sf: 0-0 GS: 0-1 **Gd: 1-7 GF: 1-12** Fm: 0-1
Distance: 5f/6f: 0-0 7f-8f: 0-2 **9f-13f: 2-19** 14f+: 0-2
Track : **LH: 2-11** RH: 0-11 Tight: 0-8 **Gall: 1-6**
Aids: Bl: 0-0 **Vi: 1-9** Tstrap: 0-0 Ckp: 0-0
Best Rating: 75 8/08 Gdwd 1m3f gd-fm

Modest; stays 1m2f; acts on good and fast ground; has worn a visor.

Sinchiroka (FR)

(75) (30)**58**
3-y-o b c Della Francesca (USA)-Great Care (USA) (El Gran Senor (USA))
R J Smith Alastair Elliott & Kevin Old

Placings:0-0 **(7694)**
2009: 10^0SD,

	Starts	1st	2nd	3rd	Win & Pl
Career Total (Turf)	1	0	0	0	
Career Total (AW)	1	0	0	0	

Going (Turf): **Sf: 0-0 GS: 0-0 Gd: 0-1 GF: 0-0 Fm: 0-0**
Distance: 5f/6f: 0-0 7f-8f: 0-1 9f-13f: 0-1 14f+: 0-0
Track : LH: 0-1 RH: 0-0 Tight: 0-1 Gall: 0-0
Aids: Bl: 0-0 Vi: 0-0 Tstrap: 0-0 Ckp: 0-0
Best Rating: 58 10/08 Rdcr 1m good

Sing Of Run

60
2-y-o bl c Singspiel (IRE)-Crimson Rosella (Polar Falcon (USA))
J F Panvert Sport Of Gentleman Ltd

Placings:0 **(5499)**
2009: 8^0G,

	Starts	1st	2nd	3rd	Win & Pl
Career Total (Turf)	1	0	0	0	

Going (Turf): **Sf: 0-0 GS: 0-0 Gd: 0-1 GF: 0-0 Fm: 0-0**
Distance: 5f/6f: 0-0 7f-8f: 0-0 9f-13f: 0-1 14f+: 0-0
Track : LH: 0-0 RH: 0-0 Tight: 0-0 Gall: 0-0
Aids: Bl: 0-0 Vi: 0-0 Tstrap: 0-0 Ckp: 0-0

Sing Sweetly

89(89) (77)**62**
2-y-o b f Singspiel (IRE)-Sweetness Herself (Unfuwain (USA))
G A Butler The Distaff 2 Partnership

Placings:20 **(6477)**
2009: 7^2SD, 7^0GF,

	Starts	1st	2nd	3rd	Win & Pl
Career Total (Turf)	1	0	0	0	
Career Total (AW)	1	0	1	0	1397

Going (Turf): **Sf: 0-0 GS: 0-0 Gd: 0-0 GF: 0-1 Fm: 0-0**
Distance: 5f/6f: 0-0 7f-8f: 0-2 9f-13f: 0-0 14f+: 0-0

Track : LH: 0-0 RH: 0-1 Tight: 0-0 Gall: 0-0
Aids: Bl: 0-0 Vi: 0-0 Tstrap: 0-0 Ckp: 0-0
Best Rating: **77** 9/09 Kemp 7f stand

By Singspiel out of Sweetness Herself, who was good from 1m3f to nearly 2m; promise in maiden company; effective over 7f; acts on Polytrack.

Singapore Girl

80(86) (48)**24**

3-y-o b f Danehill Dancer (IRE)-Musical Refrain (IRE) (Dancing Dissident (USA))
G R Oldroyd R C Bond

Placings:450066000 **(7709)**
2009: 6^{4}SS, 7^{5}SD, 6^{0}SD, 5^{0}GF, 5^{6}G, 7^{6}GF, 5^{0}GF, 5^{0}SD, 5^{0}SD,

	Starts	1st	2nd	3rd	Win & Pl
Career Total (Turf)	4	0	0	0	0
Career Total (AW)	5	0	0	0	0

Going (Turf): **Sf: 0-0 GS: 0-0 Gd: 0-1 GF: 0-3 Fm: 0-0**
Distance: 5f/6f: 0-7 7f-8f: 0-2 9f-13f: 0-0 14f+: 0-0
Track : LH: 0-4 RH: 0-0 Tight: 0-2 Gall: 0-0
Aids: Bl: 0-0 Vi: 0-3 Tstrap: 0-0 Ckp: 0-0
Best Rating: **48** 1/09 Wolv 7f32y stand

Moderate; seems best on sand; has worn a visor.

Singbella

95 **63**

3-y-o b f Singspiel (IRE)-B Beautiful (IRE) (Be My Guest (USA))
C G Cox A Parker (London)

Placings:000 **(2947)**
2009: 8^{0}GF, 8^{0}G, 8^{0}GF,

	Starts	1st	2nd	3rd	Win & Pl
Career Total (Turf)	3	0	0	0	

Going (Turf): **Sf: 0-0 GS: 0-0 Gd: 0-1 GF: 0-2 Fm: 0-0**
Distance: 5f/6f: 0-0 7f-8f: 0-1 9f-13f: 0-2 14f+: 0-0
Track : LH: 0-1 RH: 0-1 Tight: 0-1 Gall: 0-0
Aids: Bl: 0-0 Vi: 0-0 Tstrap: 0-0 Ckp: 0-0
Best Rating: **63** 4/09 Wind 1m67y gd-fm

Singeur (IRE)

102(92) (70)**101**

2-y-o b c Chineur (FR)-Singitta (Singspiel (IRE))
R Bastiman Ms M Austerfield

Placings:211114042 **(7016)**
2009: 5^{2}SD, 5^{1}SD, 5^{1}F, 5^{1}G, 5^{1}GF, 5^{4}GF, 6^{0}GF, 6^{4}G, 6^{2}GS,

	Starts	1st	2nd	3rd	Win & Pl
Career Total (Turf)	7	3	1	0	30955
Career Total (AW)	2	1	1	0	3536

89	8/09	Muss	5f		G-F	£7771
86	7/09	York	5f		GD	£6799
77	7/09	Rdcr	5f		FRM	£5180
70	6/09	Sthl	5f		STD	£2729

Total win prize-money £22482

Going (Turf): Sf: 0-0 GS: 0-1 **Gd: 1-2 GF: 1-3 Fm: 1-1**
Distance: **5f/6f: 4-9** 7f-8f: 0-0 9f-13f: 0-0 14f+: 0-0
Track : LH: 0-0 RH: 0-0 Tight: 0-0 Gall: 0-0
Aids: Bl: 0-0 Vi: 0-0 Tstrap: 0-0 Ckp: 0-0
Best Rating: **101** 10/09 Donc 6f gd-sft

Very useful; Listed placed; suited by 5f; acts on fast ground and on Fibresand.

Singin' The Blues

90(82) (54)**63**

2-y-o b g Superior Premium-Not So Generous (IRE) (Fayruz)
J M P Eustace Blue Peter Racing 9

Placings:050 **(7288)**
2009: 5^{0}SF, 6^{5}S, 6^{0}S,

	Starts	1st	2nd	3rd	Win & Pl
Career Total (Turf)	2	0	0	0	0
Career Total (AW)	1	0	0	0	

Going (Turf): **Sf: 0-2 GS: 0-0 Gd: 0-0 GF: 0-0 Fm: 0-0**
Distance: 5f/6f: 0-2 7f-8f: 0-1 9f-13f: 0-0 14f+: 0-0
Track : LH: 0-1 RH: 0-0 Tight: 0-1 Gall: 0-0
Aids: Bl: 0-0 Vi: 0-0 Tstrap: 0-0 Ckp: 0-0
Best Rating: **63** 11/09 Donc 6f soft

Singing Scott (IRE)

74 **34**

2-y-o b g Royal Applause-Ciel Bleu (Septieme Ciel (USA))
R Bastiman Robin Bastiman

Placings:00 **(7288)**
2009: 6^{0}GF, 6^{0}S,

	Starts	1st	2nd	3rd	Win & Pl
Career Total (Turf)	2	0	0	0	

Going (Turf): **Sf: 0-1 GS: 0-0 Gd: 0-0 GF: 0-1 Fm: 0-0**
Distance: 5f/6f: 0-2 7f-8f: 0-0 9f-13f: 0-0 14f+: 0-0
Track : LH: 0-1 RH: 0-0 Tight: 0-0 Gall: 0-0
Aids: Bl: 0-0 Vi: 0-0 Tstrap: 0-0 Ckp: 0-0
Best Rating: **34** 10/09 Pont 6f gd-fm

Singingintherain (IRE)

(88) (58)

2-y-o ch f Kyllachy-Comeraincomeshine (IRE) (Night Shift (USA))
T G Mills T G Mills & J Humphreys

Placings:04 **(7772)**
2009: 6^{0}SD, 7^{4}SD,

	Starts	1st	2nd	3rd	Win & Pl
Career Total (Turf)	0	0	0	0	
Career Total (AW)	2	0	0	0	265

Going (Turf): **Sf: 0-0 GS: 0-0 Gd: 0-0 GF: 0-0 Fm: 0-0**
Distance: 5f/6f: 0-1 7f-8f: 0-1 9f-13f: 0-0 14f+: 0-0
Track : LH: 0-1 RH: 0-1 Tight: 0-1 Gall: 0-0
Aids: Bl: 0-0 Vi: 0-0 Tstrap: 0-0 Ckp: 0-0
Best Rating: **58** 11/09 Kemp 6f stand

Singleb (IRE)

96(108) (79)**75**

5-y-o b g Intikhab (USA)-Bubble N Squeak (IRE) (Catrail (USA))
Miss Gay Kelleway Mrs Donna Joslyn

Placings:360150/0211410313-111466030 **(3980)**
2009: 8^{1}SD, 8^{1}SD, 7^{1}SD, 7^{4}SD, 7^{6}SD, 8^{6}G, 7^{0}SD, 8^{3}G, 8^{0}SD,

	Starts	1st	2nd	3rd	Win & Pl
Career Total (Turf)	12	4	1	2	11359
Career Total (AW)	13	4	0	2	9882

76	2/09	Wolv	7f32y	(0-70)H	STD	£2590
71	1/09	Wolv	1m141y		STD	£2047
70	1/09	GrLe	1m		STD	£2590
71	12/08	Wolv	7f32y		STD	£1978
72	10/08	Leic	7f9y		GD	£1942
65	8/08	Folk	7f		G-F	£2047
61	8/08	Leic	7f9y		GD	£2590
66	9/07	Catt	7f		GD	£3238

Total win prize-money £19025

Going (Turf): Sf: 0-0 GS: 0-2 **Gd: 3-7** GF: 1-3 Fm: 0-0
Distance: 5f/6f: 0-1 **7f-8f: 7-19** 9f-13f: 1-5 14f+: 0-0
Track : **LH: 5-16** RH: 0-2 **Tight: 4-10** Gall: 1-1
Aids: Bl: 0-0 Vi: 0-0 Tstrap: 4-11 Ckp: 4-11
Best Rating: **79** 2/09 Ling 7f stand

Modest; effective at 7f-1m; acts on good, fast and easy ground; goes on Polytrack.

Singora Lady (IRE)

99(98) (53)**64**

4-y-o ch f Intikhab (USA)-Unicamp (Royal Academy (USA))
P T Midgley M McGinn

Placings:44610/00-054042313130 **(5035)**
2009: 8^{0}SD, 8^{5}SD, 8^{4}SD, 9^{0}SD, 8^{4}G, 8^{2}GF, 8^{3}GF, 8^{1}GF, 8^{3}GF, 10^{1}GF, 9^{3}G, 10^{0}GF,

	Starts	1st	2nd	3rd	Win & Pl
Career Total (Turf)	15	3	1	3	13459
Career Total (AW)	4	0	0	0	0

63	7/09	Rdcr	1m2f	(0-70)H	G-F	£2590
58	6/09	Pont	1m4y	(0-70)H	G-F	£3238
60	8/07	DRoy	7f		GD	£4668

Total win prize-money £10497

Going (Turf): Sf: 0-0 GS: 0-0 Gd: 1-5 **GF: 2-7** Fm: 0-0
Distance: 5f/6f: 0-0 7f-8f: 1-6 **9f-13f: 2-13** 14f+: 0-0
Track : **LH: 2-13** RH: 1-6 **Tight: 1-5** Gall: 0-1
Aids: Bl: 0-0 Vi: 0-0 Tstrap: 1-4 Ckp: 1-4
Best Rating: **64** 8/09 Yarm 1m1f good

Moderate; stays 1m2f; acts on fast ground; goes on Fibresand.

Sion Hill (IRE)

101(104) (61)**70**

8-y-o b g Desert Prince (IRE)-Mobilia (Last Tycoon)
John A Harris Peter Taylor

Placings:202/00000000/000050322340300040005/30662 62500/60030214022204/1206212031100005003503-620003222360650 **(7755)**
2009: 7^{6}SS, 8^{2}SD, 8^{0}SD, 6^{0}F, 8^{0}GF, 8^{3}GF, 8^{2}SD, 8^{2}G, 8^{2}GF, 8^{3}G, 8^{6}G, 8^{0}GF, 7^{6}GF, 8^{5}SD, 8^{0}SD,

	Starts	1st	2nd	3rd	Win & Pl
Career Total (Turf)	35	1	5	6	8714
Career Total (AW)	59	4	12	4	13906

70	5/08	Sthl	7f	(0-60)H	GD	£1774
69	4/08	Wolv	7f32y	(0-55)H	STD	£2047
59	2/08	Kemp	1m	(0-50)H	STD	£2047
53	1/08	Kemp	7f	(0-45)	STD	£1365
51	9/07	Wolv	1m141y	(0-45)	STD	£1706

Total win prize-money £8940

Going (Turf): Sf: 0-1 GS: 0-0 **Gd: 1-14** GF: 0-17 Fm: 0-3
Distance: 5f/6f: 0-18 **7f-8f: 4-51** 9f-13f: 1-25 14f+: 0-0
Track : **LH: 3-64** RH: 2-13 **Tight: 3-30** Gall: 0-2
Aids: Bl: 0-3 Vi: 0-1 Tstrap: 5-67 Ckp: 5-67
Best Rating: **74** 10/03 Wind 6f gd-fm

Moderate; effective over 7f-1m2f; acts on fast ground and on Polytrack; has worn cheekpieces.

Sioux City Sue

75 12

3-y-o b f Noverre (USA)-Sartiglia (Efisio)

J R Boyle Sean C Gollogly

Placings:0 (5322)

2009: 10^{0}GF,

	Starts	1st	2nd	3rd	Win & Pl
Career Total (Turf)	1	0	0	0	

Going (Turf): **Sf: 0-0 GS: 0-0 Gd: 0-0 GF: 0-1 Fm: 0-0**
Distance: 5f/6f: 0-0 7f-8f: 0-0 9f-13f: 0-1 14f+: 0-0
Track : LH: 0-0 RH: 0-1 Tight: 0-1 Gall: 0-0
Aids: Bl: 0-0 Vi: 0-0 Tstrap: 0-0 Ckp: 0-0
Best Rating: **12** 8/09 Wind 1m2f7y gd-fm

Sioux Rising (IRE)

101 84

3-y-o b f Danetime (IRE)-Arvika (FR) (Baillamont (USA))

R A Fahey Mrs Una Towell

Placings:0-1160 (5032)

2009: 8^{1}G, 6^{1}GF, 7^{6}GF, 6^{0}GF,

	Starts	1st	2nd	3rd	Win & Pl
Career Total (Turf)	5	2	0	0	13170

84 6/09 Pont 6f (0-90)H G-F £9346
83 5/09 Pont 6f GD £3238
Total win prize-money £12585

Going (Turf): Sf: 0-0 GS: 0-0 **Gd: 1-1 GF: 1-4** Fm: 0-0
Distance: **5f/6f: 2-4** 7f-8f: 0-1 9f-13f: 0-0 14f+: 0-0
Track : **LH: 2-2** RH: 0-0 Tight: 0-0 Gall: 0-0
Aids: Bl: 0-0 Vi: 0-0 Tstrap: 0-0 Ckp: 0-0
Best Rating: **84** 6/09 Pont 6f gd-fm

Useful; effective at 6f; goes well on fast ground.

Sir Billy Nick

(98) (67)70

4-y-o b c Bortolini (USA)-Follow Flanders (Pursuit Of Love)

S Wynne M W Harris

Placings:316000404003-000 (6999)

2009: 8^{0}SS, 12^{0}SD, 8^{0}SD,

	Starts	1st	2nd	3rd	Win & Pl
Career Total (Turf)	2	0	0	0	0
Career Total (AW)	13	1	0	2	3605

70 4/08 Ling 1m STD £2388
Total win prize-money £2388

Going (Turf): **Sf: 0-0 GS: 0-1 Gd: 0-0 GF: 0-1 Fm: 0-0**
Distance: 5f/6f: 0-1 **7f-8f: 1-7** 9f-13f: 0-7 14f+: 0-0
Track : **LH: 1-10** RH: 0-3 **Tight: 1-7** Gall: 0-1
Aids: Bl: 0-1 Vi: 0-1 Tstrap: 0-1 Ckp: 0-1
Best Rating: **70** 4/08 Yarm 1m3y gd-fm

Modest; stays 1m; acts on Polytrack.

Sir Boss (IRE)

103(103) (75)86

4-y-o b g Tagula (IRE)-Good Thought (IRE) (Mukaddamah (USA))

D E Cantillon Don Cantillon Racing

Placings:510663-3621160006 (6473)

2009: 10^{3}GF, 10^{6}GF, 10^{2}GF, 12^{1}GF, 12^{1}G, 12^{6}G, 12^{0}GF, 11^{0}SD, 10^{0}GF, 12^{6}GF,

	Starts	1st	2nd	3rd	Win & Pl
Career Total (Turf)	14	3	1	2	11165
Career Total (AW)	2	0	0	0	0

86 7/09 Ffos 1m4f (0-75)H GD £2590
78 7/09 Chep 1m4f23y (0-70)H G-F £2590
72 6/08 Donc 5f G-S £4047
Total win prize-money £9227

Going (Turf): Sf: 0-0 **GS: 1-1 Gd: 1-4 GF: 1-9** Fm: 0-0
Distance: 5f/6f: 1-2 7f-8f: 0-3 **9f-13f: 2-11** 14f+: 0-0
Track : **LH: 2-7** RH: 0-4 Tight: 0-1 **Gall: 1-5**
Aids: Bl: 0-0 Vi: 0-0 Tstrap: 0-0 Ckp: 0-0
Best Rating: **86** 8/09 NmkJ 1m4f good

Useful; effective over 1m4f; acts on easy and fast ground.

Sir Bruno (FR)

95 73

2-y-o ch g Hernando (FR)-Moon Tree (FR) (Groom Dancer (USA))

B Palling G Deren

Placings:02343 (6366)

2009: 7^{0}GF, 7^{2}GF, 6^{3}F, 8^{4}G, 7^{3}GF,

	Starts	1st	2nd	3rd	Win & Pl
Career Total (Turf)	5	0	1	2	2233

Going (Turf): **Sf: 0-0 GS: 0-0 Gd: 0-1 GF: 0-3 Fm: 0-1**
Distance: 5f/6f: 0-0 7f-8f: 0-4 9f-13f: 0-1 14f+: 0-0
Track : LH: 0-3 RH: 0-0 Tight: 0-0 Gall: 0-0
Aids: Bl: 0-0 Vi: 0-0 Tstrap: 0-0 Ckp: 0-0
Best Rating: **73** 8/09 Brig 6f209y firm

Modest; effective over 7f; acts on fast ground.

Sir Christie

84 60

2-y-o b g Auction House (USA)-Dazzling Quintet (Superlative)

N Tinkler Mrs Janis Macpherson

Placings:06046 (3446)

2009: 5^{0}GF, 5^{6}G, 6^{0}G, 5^{4}GF, 5^{6}GF,

	Starts	1st	2nd	3rd	Win & Pl
Career Total (Turf)	5	0	0	0	0

Going (Turf): **Sf: 0-0 GS: 0-0 Gd: 0-2 GF: 0-3 Fm: 0-0**
Distance: 5f/6f: 0-5 7f-8f: 0-0 9f-13f: 0-0 14f+: 0-0
Track : LH: 0-0 RH: 0-0 Tight: 0-0 Gall: 0-0
Aids: Bl: 0-0 Vi: 0-0 Tstrap: 0-0 Ckp: 0-0
Best Rating: **60** 6/09 Muss 5f gd-fm

Moderate; effective over 5f; acts on fast ground.

Sir Don (IRE)

82(103) (45)25

10-y-o b g Lake Coniston (IRE)-New Sensitive (Wattlefield)

E S McMahon Mrs Dian Plant

Placings:322/50040/**505**413000202153**0**/0000103500000 0/000000/026520**140**/**01**/**01**-000 (5610)

2009: 5^{0}SD, 5^{0}F, 5^{0}SD,

	Starts	1st	2nd	3rd	Win & Pl
Career Total (Turf)	47	3	6	4	33191
Career Total (AW)	13	3	0	0	6016

63 1/08 Wolv 5f20y (0-55)H STD £1684
59 12/07 Ling 6f (0-55)H STD £1943
59 11/06 Wolv 5f20y (0-60)H STD £2388
71 6/04 Haml 6f5y D(0-80)H G-F £6357
73 7/03 York 6f3y C(0-90)H G-F £11943
68 4/03 Thsk 1m F(0-65)H FRM £3934
Total win prize-money £28251

Going (Turf): Sf: 0-2 GS: 0-5 Gd: 0-7 **GF: 2-25** Fm: 1-8
Distance: 5f/6f: 3-37 7f-8f: 3-22 9f-13f: 0-1 14f+: 0-0
Track : **LH: 4-31** RH: 0-3 **Tight: 4-25** Gall: 0-1
Aids: Bl: 0-1 Vi: 3-31 Tstrap: 3-12 Ckp: 3-12
Best Rating: **74** 8/03 Gdwd 6f good

Moderate handicapper; lightly-raced of late; effective from 5f-6f; acts on fast ground and Polytrack.

Sir Edwin Landseer (USA)

67(108) (93)83

9-y-o gr g Lit De Justice (USA)-Wildcat Blue (USA) (Cure The Blues (USA))

G L Moore EERC

Placings:21013251/403555600/00000**616**/**620**01622634 401/5100054/53660/025060-200535 (7879)

2009: 5^{2}SD, 6^{0}GF, 6^{0}SD, 5^{5}SD, 5^{3}SD, 6^{5}SD,

	Starts	1st	2nd	3rd	Win & Pl
Career Total (Turf)	42	5	4	3	116525
Career Total (AW)	22	2	3	2	35364

100 2/06 Ndas 6f (90-105)H FRM £41569
85 12/05 Ndas 5f (75-100)H FST £5531
82 12/04 Ndas 6f (55-85) FST £4148
103 9/02 Kemp 6f A G-F £15730
100 6/02 Donc 5f C G-F £6922
79 5/02 Newb 5f34y D G-S £5005
Total win prize-money £78909

Going (Turf): Sf: 0-2 GS: 1-5 Gd: 1-19 **GF: 2-14** Fm: 1-3
Distance: **5f/6f: 7-50** 7f-8f: 0-14 9f-13f: 0-0 14f+: 0-0
Track : **LH: 2-20** RH: 0-2 Tight: 0-6 **Gall: 3-14**
Aids: Bl: 0-2 Vi: 0-3 Tstrap: 3-26 Ckp: 3-26
Best Rating: **104** 4/03 NmkR 7f gd-fm

Fair; effective at up to 7f, but looks better over shorter; acts on most types of ground; goes on sand; has worn various headgear.

Sir Frank Wappat

89 62

2-y-o b c Oasis Dream-Trevillari (USA) (Riverman (USA))

M Johnston Paul Dean

Placings:45 (6386)

2009: 6^{4}GF, 6^{5}GF,

	Starts	1st	2nd	3rd	Win & Pl
Career Total (Turf)	2	0	0	0	302

Going (Turf): **Sf: 0-0 GS: 0-0 Gd: 0-0 GF: 0-2 Fm: 0-0**
Distance: 5f/6f: 0-0 7f-8f: 0-2 9f-13f: 0-0 14f+: 0-0
Track : LH: 0-0 RH: 0-0 Tight: 0-0 Gall: 0-0
Aids: Bl: 0-0 Vi: 0-0 Tstrap: 0-0 Ckp: 0-0
Best Rating: **62** 9/09 Yarm 6f3y gd-fm

Sir Freddie

104(86) (57)72

3-y-o b g Fraam-Height Of Folly (Shirley Heights)

Lady Herries Lady Herries and Friends

Placings:00-404 (4442)

2009: 10^{4}G, 10^{0}GS, 14^{4}G,

	Starts	1st	2nd	3rd	Win & Pl
Career Total (Turf)	4	0	0	0	553
Career Total (AW)	1	0	0	0	

Going (Turf): **Sf: 0-1 GS: 0-1 Gd: 0-2 GF: 0-0 Fm: 0-0**
Distance: 5f/6f: 0-0 7f-8f: 0-1 9f-13f: 0-3 14f+: 0-1

Track : LH: 0-3 RH: 0-1 Tight: 0-2 Gall: 0-1
Aids: Bl: 0-0 Vi: 0-0 Tstrap: 0-0 Ckp: 0-0
Best Rating: **72** 7/09 Sand 1m6f good

Sir Geoffrey (IRE)

100(102) (83)**79**

3-y-o b g Captain Rio-Disarm (IRE) (Bahamian Bounty)
J A Glover (A J McCabe 10/6) Dixon, Howlett & The Chrystal Maze Ptn

Placings:3243151-60503630000 **(6765)**
2009: 5^{6}SD, 6^{0}SD, 6^{5}SD, 5^{0}SD, 5^{3}F, 5^{6}GS, 5^{3}GF, 6^{0}SD, 5^{0}GF, 5^{0}SD, 6^{0}G,

	Starts	1st	2nd	3rd	Win & Pl
Career Total (Turf)	8	1	0	3	5512
Career Total (AW)	10	1	1	1	5282

83 10/08 Kemp 5f (0-85) STD £3885
74 9/08 Rdcr 5f G-S £2388
Total win prize-money £6274

Going (Turf): Sf: 0-1 **GS: 1-3** Gd: 0-1 GF: 0-2 Fm: 0-1
Distance: **5f/6f: 2-18** 7f-8f: 0-0 9f-13f: 0-0 14f+: 0-0
Track : LH: 0-7 **RH: 1-4** Tight: 0-5 Gall: 0-2
Aids: Bl: 0-2 Vi: 0-0 Tstrap: 0-0 Ckp: 0-0
Best Rating: **83** 10/08 Kemp 5f stand

Modest; suited by 6f and Polytrack.

Sir George (IRE)

84(103) (69)**51**

4-y-o b g Mujadil (USA)-Torrmana (IRE) (Ela-Mana-Mou)
P D Evans Diamond Racing Ltd

Placings:20/1-65142 **(7861)**
2009: 7^{6}G, 7^{5}SD, 7^{1}SD, 7^{4}SD, 7^{2}SD,

	Starts	1st	2nd	3rd	Win & Pl
Career Total (Turf)	3	0	1	0	605
Career Total (AW)	5	2	1	0	5171

65 11/09 Wolv 7f32y STD £2047
75 4/08 Ling 6f STD £2331
Total win prize-money £4378

Going (Turf): **Sf: 0-2 GS: 0-0 Gd: 0-1 GF: 0-0 Fm: 0-0**
Distance: 5f/6f: 1-2 7f-8f: 1-6 9f-13f: 0-0 14f+: 0-0
Track : **LH: 2-5** RH: 0-0 **Tight: 2-5** Gall: 0-0
Aids: Bl: 0-0 Vi: 0-0 Tstrap: 0-0 Ckp: 0-0
Best Rating: **75** 4/08 Ling 6f stand

Modest; stays 7f; acts on Polytrack.

Sir Gerry (USA)

99(107) (97)**116**

4-y-o ch c Carson City (USA)-Incredulous (FR) (Indian Ridge)
J R Best (J R Fanshawe 13/5) Mrs Gerry Galligan

Placings:1410/0133033-0000 **(7768)**
2009: 6^{0}GF, 6^{0}S, 6^{0}SD, 7^{0}SD,

	Starts	1st	2nd	3rd	Win & Pl
Career Total (Turf)	13	3	0	4	165695
Career Total (AW)	2	0	0	0	

116 4/08 Asct 6f G-S £17031
112 8/07 York 6f GD £76653
90 7/07 Thsk 6f SFT £3238
Total win prize-money £96923

Going (Turf): **Sf: 1-4 GS: 1-2 Gd: 1-4** GF: 0-3 Fm: 0-0
Distance: **5f/6f: 3-13** 7f-8f: 0-2 9f-13f: 0-0 14f+: 0-0
Track : LH: 0-1 RH: 0-1 Tight: 0-1 Gall: 0-0
Aids: Bl: 0-0 Vi: 0-0 Tstrap: 0-0 Ckp: 0-0
Best Rating: **116** 6/08 Asct 6f gd-fm

Smart; effective over 6f; suited by fast and soft ground.

Sir Haydn

92(100) (59)**49**

9-y-o ch g Definite Article-Snowscape (Niniski (USA))
J R Jenkins R.M.G.R. Syndicate

Placings:61/406033/360605300002/21211060600005 2/1/0000454203651/66003050-033326100504504 **(7766)**
2009: 12^{0}SD, 12^{3}SD, 11^{3}SD, 10^{3}SD, 12^{2}SD, 12^{6}GF, 11^{1}SD, 10^{0}G, 11^{0}SD, 11^{5}SD, 11^{0}SD, 10^{4}SD, 12^{5}SD, 12^{0}SD, 11^{4}SD,

	Starts	1st	2nd	3rd	Win & Pl
Career Total (Turf)	29	1	0	4	8331
Career Total (AW)	43	6	6	5	24017

56 5/09 Sthl 1m3f (0-55)H STD £2388
81 1/06 Ling 1m2f (0-75)H STD £3238
83 4/05 Wolv 1m141y (0-70)H STD £4110
75 4/05 Ling 1m2f (0-75)H STD £3473
70 2/05 Ling 1m2f (0-65) STD £3454
73 10/02 Rdcr 1m E GD £4143
Total win prize-money £20811

Going (Turf): Sf: 0-3 GS: 0-4 **Gd: 1-5** GF: 0-16 Fm: 0-1
Distance: 5f/6f: 0-0 7f-8f: 1-4 **9f-13f: 6-67** 14f+: 0-1
Track : **LH: 5-35** RH: 1-31 **Tight: 4-30** Gall: 0-5
Aids: Bl: 0-6 **Vi: 6-47** Tstrap: 0-1 Ckp: 0-1
Best Rating: **83** 4/05 Wolv 1m141y stand

Moderate; stays 1m3f; acts on a decent surface and on Polytrack; has been tried in blinkers and a visor; likes to be held up.

Sir Ike (IRE)

95(104) (67)**71**

4-y-o b g Xaar-Iktidar (Green Desert (USA))
W S Kittow Mrs Susan Arnesen

Placings:40/636433036-625314100 **(6755)**
2009: 7^{6}SD, 8^{2}SD, 8^{5}SD, 8^{3}SD, 8^{1}GF, 8^{4}GF, 7^{1}GF, 7^{0}SD, 7^{0}G,

	Starts	1st	2nd	3rd	Win & Pl
Career Total (Turf)	10	2	0	2	6875
Career Total (AW)	10	0	1	3	1966

60 8/09 Folk 7f G-F £2047
71 7/09 Chep 1m14y (0-70)H G-F £3238
Total win prize-money £5285

Going (Turf): Sf: 0-1 GS: 0-0 Gd: 0-2 **GF: 2-6** Fm: 0-1
Distance: 5f/6f: 0-4 7f-8f: 1-12 9f-13f: 1-4 14f+: 0-0
Track : LH: 0-8 RH: 0-3 Tight: 0-7 Gall: 0-2
Aids: Bl: 0-0 Vi: 0-1 Tstrap: 1-6 Ckp: 1-6
Best Rating: **71** 7/09 Chep 1m14y gd-fm

Modest; stays 1m; acts on fast ground; goes on Polytrack; has worn a tongue tie.

Sir Isaac

101 **87**

3-y-o b g Key Of Luck (USA)-Rainbow Queen (FR) (Spectrum (IRE))
W J Haggas Mr & Mrs R Scott

Placings:0-142231 **(4909)**
2009: 7^{1}G, 7^{4}GF, 8^{2}G, 8^{2}GF, 7^{3}G, 7^{1}G,

	Starts	1st	2nd	3rd	Win & Pl
Career Total (Turf)	7	2	2	1	16018

87 8/09 Sand 7f16y (0-90)H GD £7771
75 5/09 Gdwd 7f GD £3238
Total win prize-money £11009

Going (Turf): Sf: 0-0 GS: 0-0 **Gd: 2-4** GF: 0-3 Fm: 0-0
Distance: 5f/6f: 0-1 **7f-8f: 2-5** 9f-13f: 0-1 14f+: 0-0
Track : LH: 0-0 **RH: 2-5** Tight: 0-1 Gall: 0-0
Aids: Bl: 0-0 Vi: 0-0 Tstrap: 0-0 Ckp: 0-0
Best Rating: **87** 8/09 Sand 7f16y good

Useful; effective at 7f; acts on good and fast ground.

Sir Jake

45(95) (53)**34**

5-y-o b h Killer Instinct-Waikiki Dancer (IRE) (General Monash (USA))
T T Clement Miss Sophie Atkins

Placings:00/0000-600 **(7336)**
2009: 14^{6}G, 16^{0}SD, 14^{0}SD,

	Starts	1st	2nd	3rd	Win & Pl
Career Total (Turf)	4	0	0	0	0
Career Total (AW)	5	0	0	0	

Going (Turf): **Sf: 0-0 GS: 0-0 Gd: 0-3 GF: 0-1 Fm: 0-0**
Distance: 5f/6f: 0-0 7f-8f: 0-0 9f-13f: 0-5 14f+: 0-4
Track : LH: 0-5 RH: 0-4 Tight: 0-3 Gall: 0-0
Aids: Bl: 0-0 Vi: 0-0 Tstrap: 0-0 Ckp: 0-0
Best Rating: **53** 3/08 Kemp 1m4f stand

Sir Joey

(81) (51)**51**

4-y-o ch g Forzando-Estabella (IRE) (Mujtahid (USA))
B D Leavy S H Riley

Placings:50000460/U60-00 **(0302)**
2009: 13^{0}SD, 12^{0}SD,

	Starts	1st	2nd	3rd	Win & Pl
Career Total (Turf)	2	0	0	0	
Career Total (AW)	11	0	0	0	0

Going (Turf): **Sf: 0-1 GS: 0-0 Gd: 0-0 GF: 0-1 Fm: 0-0**
Distance: 5f/6f: 0-5 7f-8f: 0-3 9f-13f: 0-4 14f+: 0-1
Track : LH: 0-11 RH: 0-0 Tight: 0-6 Gall: 0-1
Aids: Bl: 0-1 Vi: 0-1 Tstrap: 0-2 Ckp: 0-2
Best Rating: **51** 11/07 Nott 5f13y gd-fm

Sir Kyffin's Folly

80(94) (37)**71**

4-y-o b f Dansili-Persia (IRE) (Persian Bold)
J A Geake Dr & Mrs Peter Leftley

Placings:500200-000 **(7840)**
2009: 8^{0}G, 12^{0}SD, 12^{0}SS,

	Starts	1st	2nd	3rd	Win & Pl
Career Total (Turf)	7	0	1	0	1060
Career Total (AW)	2	0	0	0	

Going (Turf): **Sf: 0-2 GS: 0-1 Gd: 0-3 GF: 0-1 Fm: 0-0**
Distance: 5f/6f: 0-0 7f-8f: 0-4 9f-13f: 0-5 14f+: 0-0
Track : LH: 0-3 RH: 0-2 Tight: 0-0 Gall: 0-0
Aids: Bl: 0-0 Vi: 0-0 Tstrap: 0-0 Ckp: 0-0
Best Rating: **71** 7/08 Newb 7f soft

Modest; effective over 7f; acts on soft ground.

Sir Liam (USA)

(107) (70)**69**

5-y-o b g Monarchos (USA)-Tears (USA) (Red Ransom (USA))
Tim Vaughan (Tom Dascombe 20/3) M Khan X2

Placings:020/15005600/606506464452-031235 **(0871)**
2009: 12^{0}SD, 12^{3}SD, 16^{1}SD, 16^{2}SD, 13^{3}SD, 12^{5}SD,

	Starts	1st	2nd	3rd	Win & Pl
Career Total (Turf)	**12**	**0**	**1**	**0**	**1315**
Career Total (AW)	**17**	**2**	**2**	**2**	**6437**

60 1/09 Ling 2m (0-60)H STD £2047
60 3/07 Kemp 1m2f STD £2047
Total win prize-money £4095

Going (Turf): **Sf: 0-1 GS: 0-0 Gd: 0-3 GF: 0-5 Fm: 0-3**
Distance: 5f/6f: 0-0 7f-8f: 0-7 9f-13f: 1-20 14f+: 1-2
Track : LH: 1-15 RH: 1-10 **Tight: 1-12** Gall: 0-0
Aids: Bl: 0-1 Vi: 0-0 Tstrap: 0-2 Ckp: 0-2
Best Rating: **77** 4/07 Ling 1m2f stand

Moderate; stays 2m; acts on Polytrack.

Sir Loin

77(107) (43)**2**
8-y-o ch g Compton Place-Charnwood Queen (Cadeaux Genereux)
P Burgoyne L Tomlin

Placings:20600/005260222/0100030050/50**3**0104140/**460**
0001003044600320044/1410-005065 **(7460)**
2009: 5^{0}SD, 5^{0}SD, 5^{5}SD, 5^{0}GF, 5^{6}SD, 5^{5}SD,

	Starts	1st	2nd	3rd	Win & Pl
Career Total (Turf)	**40**	**2**	**5**	**2**	**15267**
Career Total (AW)	**26**	**4**	**1**	**2**	**11103**

61 2/08 Kemp 5f (0-60)H STD £2047
56 1/08 Kemp 5f (0-58)H STD £2047
62 6/07 Wolv 5f20y (0-55)H STD £2388
64 8/06 Pont 5f (0-70)H GD £4533
59 7/06 Wolv 5f20y (0-60)H STD £3071
64 5/05 Newc 5f GD £2933
Total win prize-money £17023

Going (Turf): Sf: 0-5 GS: 0-4 **Gd: 2-11** GF: 0-19 Fm: 0-1
Distance: **5f/6f: 6-63** 7f-8f: 0-3 9f-13f: 0-0 14f+: 0-0
Track : **LH: 3-20** RH: 2-11 **Tight: 2-16** Gall: 0-2
Aids: Bl: 1-4 **Vi: 5-41** Tstrap: 0-1 Ckp: 0-1
Best Rating: **68** 10/04 Ayr 5f soft

Moderate sprinter; suited by 5f; acts on most surfaces, including Polytrack; best in a visor or blinkers.

Sir Louis

83 **62**
2-y-o b g Compton Place-Heuston Station (IRE) (Fairy King (USA))
R A Fahey P Ashton

Placings:500 **(6646)**
2009: 6^{5}S, 6^{0}GF, 6^{0}G,

	Starts	1st	2nd	3rd	Win & Pl
Career Total (Turf)	**3**	**0**	**0**	**0**	**0**

Going (Turf): **Sf: 0-1 GS: 0-0 Gd: 0-1 GF: 0-1 Fm: 0-0**
Distance: 5f/6f: 0-3 7f-8f: 0-0 9f-13f: 0-0 14f+: 0-0
Track : LH: 0-1 RH: 0-0 Tight: 0-0 Gall: 0-0
Aids: Bl: 0-0 Vi: 0-0 Tstrap: 0-0 Ckp: 0-0
Best Rating: **62** 7/09 Pont 6f soft

Sir Nod

105(105) (80)**80**
7-y-o b g Tagula (IRE)-Nordan Raider (Domynsky)
Miss J A Camacho Brian Nordan

Placings:41/60**0**210**2**/5300210**2**/02204**20**/5000-
1600144640 **(5768)**
2009: **5**^{1}SD, **5**^{6}SD, 6^{0}GS, 6^{0}G, 5^{1}GF, 5^{4}GF, 5^{4}G, 5^{6}G, 5^{4}GF, 5^{0}GF,

	Starts	1st	2nd	3rd	Win & Pl
Career Total (Turf)	**29**	**3**	**4**	**1**	**27102**
Career Total (AW)	**9**	**2**	**3**	**0**	**13672**

80 6/09 Carl 5f (0-85)H G-F £5504
80 1/09 Wolv 5f216y (0-85)H STD £5180
84 9/06 Bevl 5f (0-75)H G-F £5181
79 8/05 York 6f (0-80)H GD £8001
71 12/04 Wolv 7f32y STD £4095
Total win prize-money £27965

Going (Turf): Sf: 0-1 GS: 0-6 Gd: 1-10 **GF: 2-12** Fm: 0-0
Distance: **5f/6f: 4-32** 7f-8f: 1-6 9f-13f: 0-0 14f+: 0-0
Track : **LH: 2-17** RH: 1-3 **Tight: 2-11** Gall: 1-2
Aids: Bl: 0-0 Vi: 0-2 Tstrap: 0-0 Ckp: 0-0
Best Rating: **87** 8/07 Thsk 6f gd-fm

Modest; effective at 5f-6f; acts on fast ground and on Polytrack; has worn a visor; likes to race prominently.

Sir Orpen (IRE)

83(83) (36)**50**
6-y-o gr g Orpen (USA)-Yalciyna (Nishapour (FR))
J F Panvert J P Allen

Placings:022200/15554443400/150600000/060 **(7197)**
2009: 8^{0}G, 7^{6}GF, 8^{0}SD,

	Starts	1st	2nd	3rd	Win & Pl
Career Total (Turf)	**27**	**2**	**3**	**1**	**25204**
Career Total (AW)	**2**	**0**	**0**	**0**	**0**

76 4/07 Catt 7f (0-75)H G-F £3238
71 5/06 Catt 7f G-F £3886
Total win prize-money £7125

Going (Turf): Sf: 0-4 GS: 0-5 Gd: 0-4 **GF: 2-11** Fm: 0-3
Distance: 5f/6f: 0-13 **7f-8f: 2-16** 9f-13f: 0-0 14f+: 0-0
Track : **LH: 2-11** RH: 0-1 **Tight: 2-9** Gall: 0-2
Aids: Bl: 0-2 Vi: 0-0 Tstrap: 0-1 Ckp: 0-1
Best Rating: **79** 5/06 Thsk 1m heavy

Fair gelding; both his wins have been at Catterick; stays seven furlongs; acts on most ground; has worn blinkers; likes to race prominently.

Sir Parky (IRE)

105 **104**
2-y-o b c Choisir (AUS)-Jorghinia (FR) (Seattle Slew (USA))
R Hannon Sir David Seale

Placings:01131061 **(6426)**
2009: 6^{0}G, 5^{1}GF, 6^{1}GF, 7^{3}GF, 7^{1}S, 6^{0}GF, 7^{6}GF, 7^{1}GF,

	Starts	1st	2nd	3rd	Win & Pl
Career Total (Turf)	**8**	**4**	**0**	**1**	**61126**

104 10/09 NmkR 7f G-F £34062
91 7/09 Newb 7f SFT £7477
88 6/09 Chep 6f16y G-F £5180
84 5/09 Sals 5f G-F £4695
Total win prize-money £51415

Going (Turf): Sf: 1-1 GS: 0-0 Gd: 0-1 **GF: 3-6** Fm: 0-0
Distance: 5f/6f: 1-3 **7f-8f: 3-5** 9f-13f: 0-0 14f+: 0-0
Track : LH: 0-0 RH: 0-1 Tight: 0-0 Gall: 0-0
Aids: Bl: 0-0 Vi: 0-0 Tstrap: 0-0 Ckp: 0-0
Best Rating: **104** 10/09 NmkR 7f gd-fm

Very useful; stays 7f; acts on most ground.

Sir Pitt

84 **75**
2-y-o b c Tiger Hill (IRE)-Rebecca Sharp (Machiavellian (USA))
J H M Gosden A E Oppenheimer

Placings:50 **(7029)**
2009: 8^{5}GS, 8^{0}S,

	Starts	1st	2nd	3rd	Win & Pl
Career Total (Turf)	**2**	**0**	**0**	**0**	**0**

Going (Turf): **Sf: 0-1 GS: 0-1 Gd: 0-0 GF: 0-0 Fm: 0-0**
Distance: 5f/6f: 0-0 7f-8f: 0-2 9f-13f: 0-0 14f+: 0-0
Track : LH: 0-1 RH: 0-0 Tight: 0-0 Gall: 0-1
Aids: Bl: 0-0 Vi: 0-0 Tstrap: 0-0 Ckp: 0-0
Best Rating: **75** 10/09 Newc 1m gd-sft

Sir Royal (USA)

105 **80**
4-y-o b g Diesis-Only Royale (IRE) (Caerleon (USA))
G A Swinbank Lennox Ferdinand

Placings:5/32-56220 **(3265)**
2009: 12^{5}GF, 12^{6}GF, 8^{2}G, 8^{2}G, 7^{0}GF,

	Starts	1st	2nd	3rd	Win & Pl
Career Total (Turf)	**8**	**0**	**3**	**1**	**3203**

Going (Turf): **Sf: 0-3 GS: 0-0 Gd: 0-2 GF: 0-3 Fm: 0-0**
Distance: 5f/6f: 0-0 7f-8f: 0-4 9f-13f: 0-4 14f+: 0-0
Track : LH: 0-5 RH: 0-2 Tight: 0-2 Gall: 0-0
Aids: Bl: 0-0 Vi: 0-0 Tstrap: 0-0 Ckp: 0-0
Best Rating: **80** 4/08 Pont 1m2f6y soft

Useful; stays 1m2f; acts on soft ground.

Sir Sandicliffe (IRE)

102(99) (70)**69**
5-y-o b g Distant Music (USA)-Desert Rose (Green Desert (USA))
W M Brisbourne The Blacktoffee Partnership

Placings:354/**0200**63**46000**2**012**/05233**5**3203153**0**-
2360350**2443**0000 **(7751)**
2009: 14^{2}GF, 14^{3}S, 14^{6}GF, 14^{0}G, 16^{3}GF, 15^{5}CF, 16^{0}GS, **16**^{2}SD, 15^{4}GS, 15^{4}S, 13^{3}GF, **16**^{0}SD, **16**^{U}SD, **16**^{0}SD, **13**^{0}SD,

	Starts	1st	2nd	3rd	Win & Pl
Career Total (Turf)	**27**	**1**	**3**	**9**	**11063**
Career Total (AW)	**20**	**1**	**4**	**1**	**5362**

69 10/08 Catt 1m5f175y (0-60)H G-S £2266
63 12/07 Wolv 1m4f50y (0-55)H STD £2218
Total win prize-money £4485

Going (Turf): Sf: 0-3 **GS: 1-9** Gd: 0-3 GF: 0-12 Fm: 0-0
Distance: 5f/6f: 0-2 7f-8f: 0-2 9f-13f: 1-17 14f+: 1-26
Track : **LH: 2-37** RH: 0-7 **Tight: 2-35** Gall: 0-2
Aids: Bl: 0-1 Vi: 0-1 Tstrap: 0-1 Ckp: 0-1
Best Rating: **71** 8/06 Hayd 6f gd-fm

Modest; stays 1m7f; acts on a sound and easy surface; also goes on Polytrack.

Sir Tom

(86) (44)
4-y-o b g Medicean-Shasta (Shareef Dancer (USA))
J J Bridger Mrs W Miller

Placings:00 **(7826)**
2009: 7^{0}SD, 8^{0}SD,

	Starts	1st	2nd	3rd	Win & Pl
Career Total (Turf)	**0**	**0**	**0**	**0**	
Career Total (AW)	**2**	**0**	**0**	**0**	

Going (Turf): **Sf: 0-0 GS: 0-0 Gd: 0-0 GF: 0-0 Fm: 0-0**

Distance: 5f/6f: 0-0 7f-8f: 0-2 9f-13f: 0-0 14f+: 0-0
Track : LH: 0-0 RH: 0-2 Tight: 0-0 Gall: 0-0
Aids: Bl: 0-0 Vi: 0-0 Tstrap: 0-0 Ckp: 0-0
Best Rating: **44** 12/09 Kemp 7f stand

Sir Walter Raleigh

82 **53**

2-y-o b g Galileo (IRE)-Elizabethan Age (FR) (King's Best (USA))
Sir Michael Stoute Highclere Thoroughbred Racing Churchill

Placings:0 **(7244)**
2009: 8^{0}S,

	Starts	1st	2nd	3rd	Win & Pl
Career Total (Turf)	**1**	**0**	**0**	**0**	

Going (Turf): **Sf: 0-1 GS: 0-0 Gd: 0-0 GF: 0-0 Fm: 0-0**
Distance: 5f/6f: 0-0 7f-8f: 0-0 9f-13f: 0-1 14f+: 0-0
Track : LH: 0-1 RH: 0-0 Tight: 0-0 Gall: 0-0
Aids: Bl: 0-0 Vi: 0-0 Tstrap: 0-0 Ckp: 0-0
Best Rating: **53** 11/09 Nott 1m75y soft

Sir William Orpen

84(86) (63)**66**

2-y-o b g Orpen (USA)-Ashover Amber (Green Desert (USA))
P M Phelan Tony Smith

Placings:036 **(6372)**
2009: 6^{0}SD, 7^{3}GF, 7^{6}SD,

	Starts	1st	2nd	3rd	Win & Pl
Career Total (Turf)	**1**	**0**	**0**	**1**	**770**
Career Total (AW)	**2**	**0**	**0**	**0**	**0**

Going (Turf): **Sf: 0-0 GS: 0-0 Gd: 0-0 GF: 0-1 Fm: 0-0**
Distance: 5f/6f: 0-1 7f-8f: 0-2 9f-13f: 0-0 14f+: 0-0
Track : LH: 0-1 RH: 0-2 Tight: 0-1 Gall: 0-0
Aids: Bl: 0-0 Vi: 0-0 Tstrap: 0-0 Ckp: 0-0
Best Rating: **66** 9/09 Epsm 7f gd-fm

Sir Xaar (IRE)

91 (58)**94**

6-y-o b/br g Xaar-Cradle Brief (IRE) (Brief Truce (USA))
B Smart Pinnacle Smart Partnership

Placings:11465251**2**/025040/00200020/06001000-40000 **(5697)**
2009: 7^{4}GF, 7^{0}G, 7^{0}GS, 8^{0}GF, 7^{0}GS,

	Starts	1st	2nd	3rd	Win & Pl
Career Total (Turf)	**35**	**4**	**5**	**0**	**87187**
Career Total (AW)	**1**	**0**	**0**	**0**	

94	7/08	Newc	7f	(0-95)H	G-F	£9969
103	8/05	Ripn	6f		G-F	£15660
88	5/05	Pont	6f		G-F	£9140
78	5/05	Donc	6f		G-F	£4387

Total win prize-money £39159

Going (Turf): Sf: 0-3 GS: 0-4 Gd: 0-9 **GF: 4-17** Fm: 0-1
Distance: **5f/6f: 3-8** 7f-8f: 1-26 9f-13f: 0-2 14f+: 0-0
Track : **LH: 1-9** RH: 0-1 Tight: 0-4 Gall: 0-2
Aids: Bl: 0-3 **Vi: 1-11** Tstrap: 0-0 Ckp: 0-0
Best Rating: **107** 5/06 Curr 7f gd-yld

Useful; effective at 7f; acts on fast ground; has worn blinkers/visor/tongue tie.

Siraj

(87) (58)**59**

10-y-o b g Piccolo-Masuri Kabisa (USA) (Ascot Knight (CAN))
J Ryan Only Foals & Horses

Placings:0/3031**6**/0410**025**/0100**040506**/21520350**00**/6000 44035**511141**/64**60044**/000 **(0854)**
2009: 7^{0}SD, 6^{0}SD, 6^{0}SD,

	Starts	1st	2nd	3rd	Win & Pl
Career Total (Turf)	**22**	**1**	**1**	**4**	**8841**
Career Total (AW)	**37**	**7**	**2**	**0**	**17908**

68	12/06	Kemp	6f	(0-60)H	STD	£2388
69	12/06	Kemp	6f	(0-65)H	STD	£2388
64	11/06	Kemp	6f	(0-45)	STD	£1365
59	11/06	Wolv	5f216y	(0-45)	STD	£1365
71	2/05	Sthl	6f	(0-55)H	STD	£2905
57	8/04	Sthl	6f	G	STD	£2618
71	7/03	Pont	6f	E(0-65)	G-F	£4901
67	11/02	Ling	6f	D	STD	£3435

Total win prize-money £21367

Going (Turf): Sf: 0-6 GS: 0-1 Gd: 0-5 **GF: 1-9** Fm: 0-1
Distance: **5f/6f: 8-42** 7f-8f: 0-17 9f-13f: 0-0 14f+: 0-0
Track : **LH: 5-32** RH: 3-11 **Tight: 2-21** Gall: 0-2
Aids: Bl: 2-7 Vi: 2-3 Tstrap: 1-24 Ckp: 1-24
Best Rating: **73** 7/02 Hayd 7f30y gd-fm

Modest; effective at 5f and 6f; suited by fast ground or Polytrack; usually wears headgear.

Sircozy (IRE)

93(103) (72)**50**

3-y-o b g Celtic Swing-Furnish (Green Desert (USA))
S C Williams R Friends Electric

Placings:00-000**2201112** **(7831)**
2009: 5^{0}GF, 8^{0}G, 12^{0}G, 10^{2}SD, 11^{2}SD, 12^{0}SD, 9^{1}SD, 12^{1}SD, 12^{1}SD, 12^{2}SD,

	Starts	1st	2nd	3rd	Win & Pl
Career Total (Turf)	**5**	**0**	**0**	**0**	
Career Total (AW)	**7**	**3**	**3**	**0**	**8374**

72	12/09	Ling	1m4f	(0-75)H	STD	£2729
62	12/09	Ling	1m4f	(0-70)H	STD	£2729
67	11/09	Wolv	1m1f103y	(0-55)	STD	£1706

Total win prize-money £7166

Going (Turf): **Sf: 0-2 GS: 0-0 Gd: 0-2 GF: 0-1 Fm: 0-0**
Distance: 5f/6f: 0-2 7f-8f: 0-1 **9f-13f: 3-9** 14f+: 0-0
Track : **LH: 3-3** RH: 0-6 **Tight: 3-4** Gall: 0-1
Aids: Bl: 0-0 Vi: 0-0 Tstrap: 0-0 Ckp: 0-0
Best Rating: **72** 12/09 Ling 1m4f stand

Modest; stays 1m4f; goes well on Polytrack.

Siren's Gift

109 (100)**102**

5-y-o ch m Cadeaux Genereux-Blue Siren (Bluebird (USA))
A M Balding J C Smith

Placings:621444/2454164/53300320-30640100 **(6427)**
2009: 5^{3}G, 5^{0}GF, 5^{6}GF, 5^{4}GF, 5^{0}G, 5^{1}G, 5^{0}GF, 5^{0}GF,

	Starts	1st	2nd	3rd	Win & Pl
Career Total (Turf)	**28**	**3**	**3**	**4**	**74984**
Career Total (AW)	**1**	**0**	**0**	**0**	**1868**

98	8/09	Epsm	5f	(0-105)H	GD	£12462
102	9/07	Leic	5f2y		G-F	£6232
84	7/06	Bevl	5f		FRM	£5311

Total win prize-money £24005

Going (Turf): Sf: 0-2 GS: 0-3 **Gd: 1-11 GF: 1-11 Fm: 1-1**
Distance: **5f/6f: 3-29** 7f-8f: 0-0 9f-13f: 0-0 14f+: 0-0
Track : LH: 0-1 RH: 0-1 Tight: 0-0 Gall: 0-3
Aids: **Bl: 1-11** Vi: 0-0 Tstrap: 0-0 Ckp: 0-0
Best Rating: **102** 9/08 Donc 5f140y soft

Very useful; Listed placed; effective from 5f-6f; acts on most ground on turf; goes on Polytrack; has worn blinkers.

Sirenuse (IRE)

101(90) (62)**85**

3-y-o b f Exceed And Excel (AUS)-Cefira (USA) (Distant View (USA))
B Smart M Barber

Placings:412-220 **(6253)**
2009: 5^{2}G, 5^{2}GS, 5^{0}SD,

	Starts	1st	2nd	3rd	Win & Pl
Career Total (Turf)	**5**	**1**	**3**	**0**	**11029**
Career Total (AW)	**1**	**0**	**0**	**0**	

77	7/08	Ripn	5f	GD	£5180

Total win prize-money £5181

Going (Turf): Sf: 0-0 GS: 0-1 **Gd: 1-3** GF: 0-1 Fm: 0-0
Distance: **5f/6f: 1-6** 7f-8f: 0-0 9f-13f: 0-0 14f+: 0-0
Track : LH: 0-1 RH: 0-1 Tight: 0-1 Gall: 0-1
Aids: Bl: 0-0 Vi: 0-0 Tstrap: 0-0 Ckp: 0-0
Best Rating: **85** 8/09 Carl 5f gd-sft

Fair form in maidens; better effort when winning at Ripon on second start; stays 6f; acts on a sound surface; should improve further.

Sirjosh

95(92) (55)**60**

3-y-o b g Josr Algarhoud (IRE)-Special Gesture (IRE) (Brief Truce (USA))
D Donovan River Racing

Placings:50P603500 **(5549)**
2009: 8^{5}GF, 10^{0}SD, 12^{P}GF, 8^{6}SD, 7^{0}SD, 7^{3}S, 7^{5}SD, 8^{0}GF, 9^{0}G,

	Starts	1st	2nd	3rd	Win & Pl
Career Total (Turf)	**5**	**0**	**0**	**1**	**526**
Career Total (AW)	**4**	**0**	**0**	**0**	**0**

Going (Turf): **Sf: 0-1 GS: 0-0 Gd: 0-1 GF: 0-3 Fm: 0-0**
Distance: 5f/6f: 0-0 7f-8f: 0-3 9f-13f: 0-6 14f+: 0-0
Track : LH: 0-4 RH: 0-2 Tight: 0-4 Gall: 0-0
Aids: Bl: 0-0 Vi: 0-2 Tstrap: 0-0 Ckp: 0-0
Best Rating: **60** 5/09 Yarm 1m3y gd-fm

Sirocco Breeze

(108) (111)**94**

4-y-o b c Green Desert (USA)-Baldemosa (FR) (Lead On Time (USA))
Saeed Bin Suroor Godolphin

Placings:10-1 **(7133)**
2009: 7^{1}SD,

	Starts	1st	2nd	3rd	Win & Pl
Career Total (Turf)	**2**	**1**	**0**	**0**	**2590**
Career Total (AW)	**1**	**1**	**0**	**0**	**7771**

111	10/09	Ling	7f	(0-95)H	STD	£7771
94	10/08	Leic	7f9y		SFT	£2590

Total win prize-money £10361

Going (Turf): **Sf: 1-1** GS: 0-0 Gd: 0-1 GF: 0-0 Fm: 0-0
Distance: 5f/6f: 0-0 **7f-8f: 2-3** 9f-13f: 0-0 14f+: 0-0
Track : **LH: 1-1** RH: 0-0 **Tight: 1-1** Gall: 0-0
Aids: Bl: 0-0 Vi: 0-0 Tstrap: 0-0 Ckp: 0-0
Best Rating: **111** 10/09 Ling 7f stand

Smart; stays 7f; acts on soft ground; well suited by Polytrack.

Sirri

85(78) (39)40
2-y-o b f Ishiguru (USA)-Sumitra (Tragic Role (USA))
C E Brittain Saeed Manana

Placings:00 (5605)
2009: 6⁰SD, 6⁰S,

	Starts	1st	2nd	3rd	Win & Pl
Career Total (Turf)	1	0	0	0	
Career Total (AW)	1	0	0	0	

Going (Turf): Sf: 0-1 GS: 0-0 Gd: 0-0 GF: 0-0 Fm: 0-0
Distance: 5f/6f: 0-1 7f-8f: 0-1 9f-13f: 0-0 14f+: 0-0
Track : LH: 0-1 RH: 0-0 Tight: 0-1 Gall: 0-0
Aids: Bl: 0-0 Vi: 0-0 Tstrap: 0-0 Ckp: 0-0
Best Rating: 40 9/09 Sals 6f212y soft

Sirvino

115 105
4-y-o b g Vettori (IRE)-Zenita (IRE) (Zieten (USA))
T D Barron Theo Williams and Charles Mocatta

Placings:4452-111110 (6480)
2009: 9¹GF, 9¹G, 9¹GS, 10¹G, 10¹GF, 9⁰GF,

	Starts	1st	2nd	3rd	Win & Pl
Career Total (Turf)	10	5	1	0	117281

105	7/09	York	1m2f88y	H	G-F	£97140
96	5/09	Ayr	1m2f	(0-80)H	GD	£5828
96	5/09	Ripn	1m1f170y	(0-85)H	G-S	£5180
82	5/09	Muss	1m1f	(0-80)H	GD	£5180
74	4/09	Bevl	1m1f207y	(0-70)H	G-F	£2590

Total win prize-money £115920

Going (Turf): Sf: 0-2 GS: 1-2 **Gd: 2-3 GF: 2-3** Fm: 0-0
Distance: 5f/6f: 0-0 7f-8f: 0-1 **9f-13f: 5-9** 14f+: 0-0
Track : LH: 2-3 **RH: 3-6 Tight: 2-4** Gall: 1-1
Aids: Bl: 0-0 Vi: 0-0 Tstrap: 0-0 Ckp: 0-0
Best Rating: 105 7/09 York 1m2f88y gd-fm

Very useful; effective over 1m2f; acts on fast and soft ground.

Siryena

71(95) (57)55
4-y-o b f Oasis Dream-Ard Na Sighe (IRE) (Kenmare (FR))
B I Case Mrs A D Bourne

Placings:0660/6050160-6060 (1538)
2009: 8⁶SD, 10⁰SD, 9⁶SD, 9⁰GF,

	Starts	1st	2nd	3rd	Win & Pl
Career Total (Turf)	9	1	0	0	1943
Career Total (AW)	6	0	0	0	0

55	9/08	Brig	1m1f209y	GD	£1942

Total win prize-money £1943

Going (Turf): Sf: 0-3 GS: 0-1 **Gd: 1-1** GF: 0-4 Fm: 0-0
Distance: 5f/6f: 0-1 7f-8f: 0-4 **9f-13f: 1-10** 14f+: 0-0
Track : LH: 1-7 RH: 0-4 Tight: 0-6 Gall: 0-0
Aids: Bl: 0-0 Vi: 0-1 Tstrap: 1-7 Ckp: 1-7
Best Rating: 57 9/07 Ling 7f stand

Plating-class; stays 9f; acts on easy ground; has worn tongue tie and cheekpieces.

Sister Clement (IRE)

103(104) (85)75
3-y-o b f Oasis Dream-Miss Party Line (USA) (Phone Trick (USA))
R Hannon (C R Egerton 28/5) P Byrne

Placings:0605-02125021 (7203)
2009: 7⁰G, 6²GF, 5¹S, 6²G, 5⁰GF, 6⁰G, 6²SD, 6¹SD,

	Starts	1st	2nd	3rd	Win & Pl
Career Total (Turf)	9	1	2	0	4903
Career Total (AW)	3	1	1	0	3636

85	11/09	Ling	6f	(0-70)H	STD	£2729
73	7/09	Newb	5f34y	(0-70)H	SFT	£2590

Total win prize-money £5320

Going (Turf): Sf: 1-1 GS: 0-2 Gd: 0-3 GF: 0-3 Fm: 0-0
Distance: 5f/6f: 2-10 7f-8f: 0-2 9f-13f: 0-0 14f+: 0-0
Track : LH: 1-3 RH: 0-0 **Tight: 1-2** Gall: 0-4
Aids: Bl: 0-0 Vi: 0-0 Tstrap: 1-1 Ckp: 1-1
Best Rating: 85 11/09 Ling 6f stand

Fair; suited by 5f-6f; acts on most ground; goes on Polytrack.

Sister Earth (IRE)

(92) (49)
2-y-o ch f Galileo (IRE)-Time Ahead (Spectrum (IRE))
J H M Gosden Lady Bamford

Placings:3 (7140)
2009: 8³SD,

	Starts	1st	2nd	3rd	Win & Pl
Career Total (Turf)	0	0	0	0	
Career Total (AW)	1	0	0	1	530

Going (Turf): Sf: 0-0 GS: 0-0 Gd: 0-0 GF: 0-0 Fm: 0-0
Distance: 5f/6f: 0-0 7f-8f: 0-0 9f-13f: 0-1 14f+: 0-0
Track : LH: 0-1 RH: 0-0 Tight: 0-1 Gall: 0-0
Aids: Bl: 0-0 Vi: 0-0 Tstrap: 0-0 Ckp: 0-0
Best Rating: 49 10/09 Wolv 1m141y stand

Sister Moonshine

76(87) (46)61
4-y-o b f Averti (IRE)-Cal Norma's Lady (IRE) (Lyphard's Special (USA))
W R Muir M J Caddy

Placings:50/3660-30 (1890)
2009: 6³SD, 6⁰GF,

	Starts	1st	2nd	3rd	Win & Pl
Career Total (Turf)	6	0	0	1	385
Career Total (AW)	2	0	0	1	302

Going (Turf): Sf: 0-0 GS: 0-1 Gd: 0-2 GF: 0-3 Fm: 0-0
Distance: 5f/6f: 0-5 7f-8f: 0-3 9f-13f: 0-0 14f+: 0-0
Track : LH: 0-3 RH: 0-1 Tight: 0-1 Gall: 0-2
Aids: Bl: 0-0 Vi: 0-0 Tstrap: 0-0 Ckp: 0-0
Best Rating: 64 10/07 Bath 5f161y gd-sft

Moderate; stays 6f; acts on Polytrack and easy ground.

Sisters Warning

67(78) (23)31
2-y-o b f Bishop Of Cashel-Slite (Mind Games)
J Ryan G Wilson

Placings:00000 (7683)
2009: 5⁰SD, 6⁰GS, 8⁰SD, 7⁰SD, 10⁰SD,

	Starts	1st	2nd	3rd	Win & Pl
Career Total (Turf)	1	0	0	0	
Career Total (AW)	4	0	0	0	

Going (Turf): Sf: 0-0 GS: 0-1 Gd: 0-0 GF: 0-0 Fm: 0-0
Distance: 5f/6f: 0-2 7f-8f: 0-2 9f-13f: 0-1 14f+: 0-0
Track : LH: 0-1 RH: 0-2 Tight: 0-1 Gall: 0-0
Aids: Bl: 0-0 Vi: 0-0 Tstrap: 0-0 Ckp: 0-0
Best Rating: 31 6/09 NmkJ 6f gd-sft

Sitwell

100(90) (64)67
3-y-o b g Dr Fong (USA)-First Fantasy (Be My Chief (USA))
J R Fanshawe Rupert Hambro & Nigel & Carolyn Elwes

Placings:0-00601651 (6758)
2009: 9⁰G, 10⁰GF, 10⁶S, 9⁰G, 12¹GF, 11⁶GF, 13⁵SD, 11¹G,

	Starts	1st	2nd	3rd	Win & Pl
Career Total (Turf)	7	2	0	0	5661
Career Total (AW)	2	0	0	0	0

66	10/09	Leic	1m3f183y	(0-70)	GD	£2590
67	8/09	Folk	1m4f	(0-70)H	G-F	£3070

Total win prize-money £5661

Going (Turf): Sf: 0-1 GS: 0-0 **Gd: 1-3 GF: 1-3** Fm: 0-0
Distance: 5f/6f: 0-0 7f-8f: 0-1 **9f-13f: 2-7** 14f+: 0-1
Track : LH: 0-2 **RH: 2-7 Tight: 1-5** Gall: 0-1
Aids: Bl: 0-0 **Vi: 1-2** Tstrap: 0-0 Ckp: 0-0
Best Rating: 67 8/09 Folk 1m4f gd-fm

Modest; best at around 1m4f; suited by fast ground; has worn a visor.

Six Diamonds

99(100) (81)75
2-y-o b f Exceed And Excel (AUS)-Daltak (Night Shift (USA))
H Morrison A J Struthers Mrs J Scott Mrs F Woodd

Placings:02102134 (5945)
2009: 5⁰G, 5²F, 5¹F, 6⁰G, 5²GF, 5¹SD, 5³SD, 5⁴G,

	Starts	1st	2nd	3rd	Win & Pl
Career Total (Turf)	6	1	2	0	5331
Career Total (AW)	2	1	0	1	5951

81	8/09	Ling	5f	(0-85)	STD	£5180
73	6/09	Bath	5f11y		FRM	£2072

Total win prize-money £7253

Going (Turf): Sf: 0-0 GS: 0-0 Gd: 0-3 GF: 0-1 **Fm: 1-2**
Distance: 5f/6f: 2-8 7f-8f: 0-0 9f-13f: 0-0 14f+: 0-0
Track : LH: 2-4 RH: 0-0 Tight: 1-2 Gall: 1-3
Aids: Bl: 0-0 Vi: 0-0 Tstrap: 0-0 Ckp: 0-0
Best Rating: 81 8/09 Ling 5f stand

Fair; effective at 5f; handles fast ground and Polytrack.

Six Of Clubs

(80) (33)
3-y-o ch g Bertolini (USA)-Windmill Princess (Gorytus (USA))
W G M Turner Gongolfin

Placings:0-0 (5987)
2009: 12⁰SD,

	Starts	1st	2nd	3rd	Win & Pl
Career Total (Turf)	1	0	0	0	
Career Total (AW)	1	0	0	0	

Going (Turf): Sf: 0-0 GS: 0-0 Gd: 0-0 GF: 0-1 Fm: 0-0
Distance: 5f/6f: 0-0 7f-8f: 0-0 9f-13f: 0-2 14f+: 0-0
Track : LH: 0-0 RH: 0-2 Tight: 0-1 Gall: 0-0
Aids: Bl: 0-0 Vi: 0-0 Tstrap: 0-1 Ckp: 0-1
Best Rating: 33 9/09 Kemp 1m4f stand

Six Of Hearts

108 (93)**98**

5-y-o b g Pivotal-Additive (USA) (Devil's Bag (USA))
Cecil Ross Round Tower Syndicate

Placings:253005330/025341343313226**0**-0011000430363062**1** **(7565a)**
2009: 7^{0}SH, 5^{0}S, 7^{1}YS, 7^{1}GF, 7^{0}GF, 8^{0}SH, 8^{0}G, 5^{4}S, 5^{3}SH, 6^{0}G, 7^{3}G, 6^{6}S, 8^{3}G, 7^{0}HY, **6**^{6}SD, **8**^{2}SD, **7**^{1}SD,

	Starts	1st	2nd	3rd	Win & Pl
Career Total (Turf)	**31**	**4**	**3**	**9**	**64220**
Career Total (AW)	**11**	**1**	**2**	**2**	**14928**

85	11/09	Dund	7f		STD	£11069
94	6/09	Naas	7f	(60-90)H	G-F	£9056
83	5/09	Gowr	7f	(60-100)H	Y-S	£14220
76	8/08	Slig	6f110y	(60-90)H	YLD	£8129
67	6/08	Limk	6f160y	(50-70)H	G-F	£5588

Total win prize-money £48065

Going (Turf): Sf: 0-7 GS: 0-0 Gd: 0-8 **GF: 2-4** Fm: 0-2
Distance: 5f/6f: 0-12 **7f-8f: 5-25** 9f-13f: 0-5 14f+: 0-0
Track : LH: 2-15 RH: 2-16 Tight: 0-4 Gall: 0-0
Aids: Bl: 1-3 Vi: 0-0 Tstrap: 4-27 Ckp: 4-27
Best Rating: **98** 10/09 Cork 1m100y good

Very useful; suited by 7f; acts on fast and easy ground; goes on Polytrack.

Six Wives

90(100) (78)**68**

2-y-o b f Kingsalsa (USA)-Regina (Green Desert (USA))
J A Glover (A J McCabe 3/6) Sexy Six Partnership

Placings:63**1**0**33**60**126532303**20 **(7871)**
2009: 5^{6}GF, 5^{3}GF, **5**^{1}SD, 5^{0}GF, **6**^{3}SD, **5**^{3}SD, 5^{6}GF, 5^{0}G, **5**^{1}SD, **5**^{2}SD, 5^{6}GF, **5**^{5}SD, **6**^{3}SD, **5**^{2}SF, **5**^{3}SD, **6**^{0}SD, **5**^{3}SD, **5**^{2}SS, **5**^{0}SD,

	Starts	1st	2nd	3rd	Win & Pl
Career Total (Turf)	**6**	**0**	**0**	**1**	**578**
Career Total (AW)	**13**	**2**	**3**	**5**	**14103**

75	8/09	Ling	5f	STD	£3885
66	5/09	Wolv	5f20y	STD	£2729

Total win prize-money £6616

Going (Turf): **Sf: 0-0 GS: 0-0 Gd: 0-1 GF: 0-5 Fm: 0-0**
Distance: **5f/6f: 2-19** 7f-8f: 0-0 9f-13f: 0-0 14f+: 0-0
Track : **LH: 2-8** RH: 0-4 **Tight: 2-7** Gall: 0-0
Aids: Bl: 0-0 Vi: 0-0 Tstrap: 0-0 Ckp: 0-0
Best Rating: **78** 8/09 Ling 5f stand

Fair; suited by 5f; acts on fast ground; goes on Polytrack.

Sixbox

57(65)

2-y-o br f Kyllachy-Lady's Walk (IRE) (Charnwood Forest (IRE))
D Shaw Market Avenue Racing Club Ltd

Placings:000 **(5611)**
2009: 6^{0}GF, 5^{0}SD, 5^{0}SD,

	Starts	1st	2nd	3rd	Win & Pl
Career Total (Turf)	**1**	**0**	**0**	**0**	
Career Total (AW)	**2**	**0**	**0**	**0**	

Going (Turf): **Sf: 0-0 GS: 0-0 Gd: 0-0 GF: 0-1 Fm: 0-0**
Distance: 5f/6f: 0-3 7f-8f: 0-0 9f-13f: 0-0 14f+: 0-0
Track : LH: 0-2 RH: 0-0 Tight: 0-2 Gall: 0-0
Aids: Bl: 0-0 Vi: 0-0 Tstrap: 0-0 Ckp: 0-0
Best Rating:

Sixpenny Moon (USA)

89(92) (60)**60**

2-y-o b f Johannesburg (USA)-Shirazi (USA) (Stephen Got Even (USA))
R Hannon B Bull

Placings:000360050 **(6721)**
2009: 5^{0}G, 6^{0}GF, 7^{0}GF, 7^{3}SD, 8^{6}G, **8**^{0}SD, 10^{0}GF, 7^{5}SD, 8^{0}SD,

	Starts	1st	2nd	3rd	Win & Pl
Career Total (Turf)	**5**	**0**	**0**	**0**	**0**
Career Total (AW)	**4**	**0**	**0**	**1**	**385**

Going (Turf): **Sf: 0-0 GS: 0-0 Gd: 0-2 GF: 0-3 Fm: 0-0**
Distance: 5f/6f: 0-2 7f-8f: 0-6 9f-13f: 0-1 14f+: 0-0
Track : LH: 0-1 RH: 0-4 Tight: 0-0 Gall: 0-1
Aids: Bl: 0-2 Vi: 0-0 Tstrap: 0-0 Ckp: 0-0
Best Rating: **60** 7/09 Kemp 7f stand

Modest; stays 7f; acts on Polytrack.

Sixth Zak

62(92) (53)

4-y-o br g Fantastic Light (USA)-Zakuska (Zafonic (USA))
M W Easterby (S R Bowring 6/2) Clark Industrial Services Partnership

Placings:45-50050 **(3068)**
2009: 7^{5}SD, 8^{0}SD, 16^{0}SD, 12^{5}SD, 12^{0}GS,

	Starts	1st	2nd	3rd	Win & Pl
Career Total (Turf)	**1**	**0**	**0**	**0**	
Career Total (AW)	**6**	**0**	**0**	**0**	**0**

Going (Turf): **Sf: 0-0 GS: 0-1 Gd: 0-0 GF: 0-0 Fm: 0-0**
Distance: 5f/6f: 0-0 7f-8f: 0-2 9f-13f: 0-4 14f+: 0-1
Track : LH: 0-6 RH: 0-1 Tight: 0-4 Gall: 0-0
Aids: Bl: 0-2 Vi: 0-0 Tstrap: 0-0 Ckp: 0-0
Best Rating: **53** 2/09 Sthl 7f stand

Sixties Gift (UAE)

89(88) (56)**37**

3-y-o b/br f Singspiel (IRE)-Sicily (USA) (Kris S (USA))
Rae Guest C J Murfitt

Placings:4-005 **(6788)**
2009: 7^{0}SD, 10^{0}GF, 11^{5}G,

	Starts	1st	2nd	3rd	Win & Pl
Career Total (Turf)	**2**	**0**	**0**	**0**	**0**
Career Total (AW)	**2**	**0**	**0**	**0**	**0**

Going (Turf): **Sf: 0-0 GS: 0-0 Gd: 0-1 GF: 0-1 Fm: 0-0**
Distance: 5f/6f: 0-0 7f-8f: 0-2 9f-13f: 0-2 14f+: 0-0
Track : LH: 0-3 RH: 0-1 Tight: 0-1 Gall: 0-1
Aids: Bl: 0-0 Vi: 0-0 Tstrap: 0-0 Ckp: 0-0
Best Rating: **56** 12/08 Sthl 7f stand

Sixties Rock

90(89) (52)**51**

2-y-o ch g Rock Of Gibraltar (IRE)-Scene (IRE) (Scenic)
J A Glover Sexy Six Partnership

Placings:02006 **(7791)**
2009: 7^{0}G, 6^{2}GF, 7^{0}G, 5^{0}SD, 7^{6}SS,

	Starts	1st	2nd	3rd	Win & Pl
Career Total (Turf)	**3**	**0**	**1**	**0**	**1503**

Career Total (AW) **2** **0** **0** **0** **0**

Going (Turf): **Sf: 0-0 GS: 0-0 Gd: 0-2 GF: 0-1 Fm: 0-0**
Distance: 5f/6f: 0-2 7f-8f: 0-3 9f-13f: 0-0 14f+: 0-0
Track : LH: 0-3 RH: 0-0 Tight: 0-1 Gall: 0-0
Aids: Bl: 0-0 Vi: 0-0 Tstrap: 0-0 Ckp: 0-0
Best Rating: **52** 12/09 Sthl 7f std-slw

Moderate; suited by 6f and fast ground.

Sixties Swinger (USA)

100(97) (71)**74**

3-y-o b g Refuse To Bend (IRE)-Kardashina (FR) (Darshaan)
M A Jarvis A D Spence

Placings:304-**0**0250220 **(6940)**
2009: 12^{0}SD, 11^{0}GS, 11^{2}G, 11^{5}F, 9^{0}GF, 10^{2}GF, 9^{2}GF, **10**^{0}SD,

	Starts	1st	2nd	3rd	Win & Pl
Career Total (Turf)	**9**	**0**	**3**	**1**	**4065**
Career Total (AW)	**2**	**0**	**0**	**0**	

Going (Turf): **Sf: 0-1 GS: 0-3 Gd: 0-1 GF: 0-3 Fm: 0-1**
Distance: 5f/6f: 0-0 7f-8f: 0-1 9f-13f: 0-10 14f+: 0-0
Track : LH: 0-5 RH: 0-5 Tight: 0-4 Gall: 0-1
Aids: Bl: 0-1 Vi: 0-0 Tstrap: 0-1 Ckp: 0-1
Best Rating: **74** 10/08 Nott 1m75y heavy

Fair; effective at 7f; acts on most ground.

Siyaadah

99 **82**

2-y-o b f Shamardal (USA)-River Belle (Lahib (USA))
Saeed Bin Suroor Godolphin

Placings:106 **(6477)**
2009: 7^{1}GF, 7^{0}G, 7^{6}GF,

	Starts	1st	2nd	3rd	Win & Pl
Career Total (Turf)	**3**	**1**	**0**	**0**	**11726**

82	8/09	Rdcr	7f	G-F	£3885

Total win prize-money £3886

Going (Turf): Sf: 0-0 GS: 0-0 Gd: 0-1 **GF: 1-2** Fm: 0-0
Distance: 5f/6f: 0-0 **7f-8f: 1-3** 9f-13f: 0-0 14f+: 0-0
Track : LH: 0-0 RH: 0-1 Tight: 0-0 Gall: 0-0
Aids: Bl: 0-0 Vi: 0-0 Tstrap: 0-0 Ckp: 0-0
Best Rating: **82** 8/09 Rdcr 7f gd-fm

Useful; made winning debut over 7f on fast ground.

Skhilling Spirit

103 **103**

6-y-o b g Most Welcome-Calcavella (Pursuit Of Love)
T D Barron I Hill

Placings:50351031021/5210020/30203R006/604105010-6 **(2059)**

2009: 6^{6}S,

	Starts	1st	2nd	3rd	Win & Pl
Career Total (Turf)	**37**	**6**	**4**	**4**	**110487**

103	10/08	Donc	6f	(0-100)H	GD	£16190
100	5/08	Muss	7f30y	(0-90)H	G-S	£7477
100	5/06	Hayd	6f		HVY	£15898
93	10/05	Donc	6f		SFT	£21055
80	8/05	Catt	5f212y		G-F	£7007
79	7/05	Carl	5f		G-F	£3484

Total win prize-money £71111

Going (Turf): **Sf: 2-10** GS: 1-8 Gd: 1-10 **GF: 2-9** Fm: 0-0
Distance: **5f/6f: 5-23** 7f-8f: 1-14 9f-13f: 0-0 14f+: 0-0

Track : LH: 1-5 **RH: 2-4 Tight: 2-3** Gall: 1-6
Aids: Bl: 0-3 Vi: 0-1 Tstrap: 0-0 Ckp: 0-0
Best Rating: **103** 10/08 Donc 6f good

Very useful; winner in Listed company; effective over 6f-7f; acts on any ground; has worn blinkers and a visor; usually held up; can start very slowly.

Sky Crusader

(108) (105)**91**
7-y-o b g Mujahid (USA)-Red Cloud (IRE) (Taufan (USA))
M Nigge Franklin Finance S.A.

Placings:1653/5146200305/000000/114111/611114211-4161311416 (7809)
2009: 7^{4}SD, 10^{1}SD, 10^{6}SD, 9^{1}SD, 12^{3}SD, 9^{1}SD, 9^{1}SD, 12^{4}SD, 9^{1}SD, 10^{6}SD,

	Starts	1st	2nd	3rd	Win & Pl
Career Total (Turf)	**25**	**7**	**1**	**2**	**46359**
Career Total (AW)	**20**	**11**	**1**	**1**	**156617**

105	12/09	Deau	1m1f110y		STD	£26699
103	8/09	Deau	1m1f110y		STD	£16990
99	7/09	Deau	1m1f110y		STD	£10680
104	3/09	Deau	1m1f110y		STD	£16019
	1/09	Cagn	1m2f	H	STD	£10679
	12/08	Deau	7f110y		STD	£5147
	12/08	Deau	1m1f110y		STD	£5882
79	8/08	Deau	7f110y		STD	£6618
	5/08	Badn	1m1f	H	GD	£4779
	2/08	Mija	1m3f		STD	£37500
	2/08	Dort	1m1f	H	STD	£2794
	8/07	Aikn	1m1f110y		GD	£1047
	7/07	BDob	1m1f110y		GD	£1351
	7/07	Aabe	7f165y		GD	£912
	4/07	Frnk	1m2f		GD	£1385
	1/07	Dort	1m1f		STD	£1351
92	6/05	Epsm	7f	(0-100)H	GD	£20300
76	6/04	Folk	7f	F	G-F	£3024

Total win prize-money £173158

Going (Turf): Sf: 0-1 GS: 0-1 **Gd: 6-14** GF: 1-8 Fm: 0-1
Distance: 5f/6f: 0-0 7f-8f: 5-24 **9f-13f: 13-21** 14f+: 0-0
Track : **LH: 2-10** RH: 0-7 **Tight: 1-9** Gall: 0-2
Aids: Bl: 0-0 Vi: 0-1 Tstrap: 0-0 Ckp: 0-0
Best Rating: **105** 12/09 Deau 1m1f110y stand

Smart; French-trained; stays 1m2f, but effective at shorter; acts on a sound surface and well suited by Polytrack.

Sky Gate (USA)

90(99) (79)**63**
3-y-o b c Arch (USA)-Mista Mayberry (USA) (Touch Gold (USA))
B J Meehan J Paul Reddam & Andrew Rosen

Placings:0061-60 **(3051)**
2009: 10^{6}G, 12^{0}GF,

	Starts	1st	2nd	3rd	Win & Pl
Career Total (Turf)	**3**	**0**	**0**	**0**	**0**
Career Total (AW)	**3**	**1**	**0**	**0**	**3753**

79	12/08	Sthl	1m	STD	£3753

Total win prize-money £3753

Going (Turf): **Sf: 0-0 GS: 0-0 Gd: 0-2 GF: 0-1 Fm: 0-0**
Distance: 5f/6f: 0-0 **7f-8f: 1-4** 9f-13f: 0-2 14f+: 0-0
Track : **LH: 1-4** RH: 0-1 Tight: 0-1 Gall: 0-2
Aids: **Bl: 1-3** Vi: 0-0 Tstrap: 0-0 Ckp: 0-0
Best Rating: **79** 12/08 Sthl 1m stand

Sky High Kid (IRE)

94(90) (64)**57**
3-y-o b g One Cool Cat (USA)-Market Hill (IRE) (Danehill (USA))
M R Channon Box 41

Placings:61-00020000 **(6442)**
2009: 8^{0}S, 5^{0}G, 5^{0}G, 6^{2}GF, 5^{0}GF, 5^{0}G, 6^{0}SD, 7^{0}SS,

	Starts	1st	2nd	3rd	Win & Pl
Career Total (Turf)	**6**	**0**	**1**	**0**	**605**
Career Total (AW)	**4**	**1**	**0**	**0**	**2590**

64	12/08	GrLe	6f	STD	£2590

Total win prize-money £2590

Going (Turf): **Sf: 0-1 GS: 0-0 Gd: 0-3 GF: 0-2 Fm: 0-0**
Distance: **5f/6f: 1-7** 7f-8f: 0-3 9f-13f: 0-0 14f+: 0-0
Track : **LH: 1-6** RH: 0-1 Tight: 0-2 **Gall: 1-4**
Aids: Bl: 0-0 Vi: 0-1 Tstrap: 0-0 Ckp: 0-0
Best Rating: **64** 12/08 GrLe 6f stand

Moderate; stays 7f; acts on Polytrack.

Sky Quest (IRE)

93(103) (69)**71**
11-y-o b g Spectrum (IRE)-Rose Vibert (Caerleon (USA))
J R Boyle M C Cook

Placings:2/250310045/3252021226P21/11055/0000005/05454550/34502153006/4000000441-1000145145 **(6244)**
2009: 11^{1}SD, 10^{0}SD, 10^{0}SD, 12^{0}SD, 11^{1}S, 10^{4}G, 12^{5}GF, 11^{1}GF, 11^{4}GF, 12^{5}G,

	Starts	1st	2nd	3rd	Win & Pl
Career Total (Turf)	**53**	**8**	**8**	**2**	**58621**
Career Total (AW)	**21**	**2**	**1**	**2**	**8508**

71	8/09	Wind	1m3f135y (0-70)H	G-F	£2637
71	7/09	Newb	1m3f5y (0-75)H	SFT	£2590
68	1/09	Kemp	1m3f (0-75)H	STD	£2590
69	12/08	Kemp	1m3f (0-60)H	STD	£2047
76	8/07	Sand	1m2f7y (0-70)H	GD	£3886
93	8/04	Gdwd	1m1f192yC(0-90)H	GD	£10192
92	7/04	Sand	1m2f7yC(0-90)H	G-F	£10192
89	10/03	Yarm	1m2f21yD(0-85)H	G-F	£3510
82	6/03	Bath	1m2f46yE(0-70)H	FRM	£4280
77	7/02	Yarm	1m3f101yE(0-70)H	G-F	£3703

Total win prize-money £45627

Going (Turf): Sf: 1-2 GS: 0-3 Gd: 2-14 **GF: 4-32** Fm: 1-2
Distance: 5f/6f: 0-0 7f-8f: 0-6 **9f-13f: 10-68** 14f+: 0-0
Track : LH: 4-35 **RH: 5-36 Tight: 5-32** Gall: 1-12
Aids: Bl: 0-0 Vi: 0-0 Tstrap: 4-28 Ckp: 4-28
Best Rating: **93** 8/04 Gdwd 1m1f192y good

Modest; formerly useful; stays 1m4f; acts on fast and soft ground; goes on Polytrack.

Skybob

78 **14**
3-y-o b g Tobougg (IRE)-Heavens Above (FR) (Pistolet Bleu (IRE))
D W Thompson A Suddes

Placings:0000P **(6098)**
2009: 7^{0}GS, 8^{0}G, 11^{0}GF, 16^{0}GS, 13^{P}GF,

	Starts	1st	2nd	3rd	Win & Pl
Career Total (Turf)	**5**	**0**	**0**	**0**	

Going (Turf): **Sf: 0-0 GS: 0-2 Gd: 0-1 GF: 0-2 Fm: 0-0**
Distance: 5f/6f: 0-0 7f-8f: 0-1 9f-13f: 0-2 14f+: 0-2
Track : LH: 0-4 RH: 0-1 Tight: 0-4 Gall: 0-0
Aids: Bl: 0-0 Vi: 0-1 Tstrap: 0-0 Ckp: 0-0
Best Rating: **14** 8/09 Catt 1m3f214y gd-fm

Skyflight

83(90) (63)**68**
2-y-o ch f Observatory (USA)-Flight Soundly (IRE) (Caerleon (USA))
Eve Johnson Houghton Mrs P Robeson

Placings:001 **(6386)**
2009: 6^{0}GF, 7^{0}SD, 6^{1}GF,

	Starts	1st	2nd	3rd	Win & Pl
Career Total (Turf)	**2**	**1**	**0**	**0**	**3886**
Career Total (AW)	**1**	**0**	**0**	**0**	

68	9/09	Nott	6f15y	G-F	£3885

Total win prize-money £3886

Going (Turf): Sf: 0-0 GS: 0-0 Gd: 0-0 **GF: 1-2** Fm: 0-0
Distance: 5f/6f: 0-1 **7f-8f: 1-2** 9f-13f: 0-0 14f+: 0-0
Track : LH: 0-1 RH: 0-0 Tight: 0-1 Gall: 0-0
Aids: Bl: 0-0 Vi: 0-0 Tstrap: 0-0 Ckp: 0-0
Best Rating: **68** 9/09 Nott 6f15y gd-fm

Fair; effective over 6f; acts on fast ground.

Skylarker (USA)

70 19
11-y-o b g Sky Classic (CAN)-O My Darling (USA) (Mr Prospector (USA))
T A K Cuthbert Mrs Joyce Cuthbert

Placings:0136/0654563/623604304/2330004415512/520300304/0/000-00 **(6769)**
2009: 10^{0}GS, 12^{0}GS,

	Starts	1st	2nd	3rd	Win & Pl
Career Total (Turf)	**41**	**3**	**2**	**6**	**29608**
Career Total (AW)	**7**	**0**	**2**	**2**	**4031**

86	9/04	Asct	1m4f	(0-85)H	G-F	£7033
79	7/04	Wwck	1m4f134yF(0-70)H		G-F	£3542
83	6/01	NmkJ	1m2f	D	G-F	£4212

Total win prize-money £14788

Going (Turf): Sf: 0-5 GS: 0-7 Gd: 0-7 **GF: 3-20** Fm: 0-2
Distance: 5f/6f: 0-0 7f-8f: 0-2 **9f-13f: 3-44** 14f+: 0-2
Track : LH: 1-22 **RH: 2-21** Tight: 0-22 **Gall: 2-13**
Aids: Bl: 0-0 Vi: 0-1 Tstrap: 0-2 Ckp: 0-2
Best Rating: **90** 8/02 NmkJ 1m2f good

Fair; stays 1m4f; suited by fast ground; acts on Fibresand; has worn cheekpieces and visor.

Skylla

104 93
2-y-o b f Kyllachy-Day Star (Dayjur (USA))
J R Holt Facts & Figures

Placings:121260 **(7147)**
2009: 5^{1}G, 6^{2}GS, 5^{1}GF, 6^{2}G, 5^{6}G, 6^{0}G,

	Starts	1st	2nd	3rd	Win & Pl
Career Total (Turf)	**6**	**2**	**2**	**0**	**22008**

90	8/09	Hayd	5f	G-F	£11333
81	7/09	Nott	5f13y	GD	£2590

Total win prize-money £13923

Going (Turf): Sf: 0-0 GS: 0-1 **Gd: 1-4 GF: 1-1** Fm: 0-0
Distance: **5f/6f: 2-6** 7f-8f: 0-0 9f-13f: 0-0 14f+: 0-0
Track : LH: 0-0 RH: 0-0 Tight: 0-0 Gall: 0-0
Aids: Bl: 0-0 Vi: 0-0 Tstrap: 0-0 Ckp: 0-0
Best Rating: **93** 8/09 Ripn 6f good

Very useful half-sister to three sprint winners; stays 6f; acts on good/fast ground.

Skyrider (IRE)

98 75

2-y-o gr f Dalakhani (IRE)-Future Flight (Polar Falcon (USA))

R Charlton B E Nielsen

Placings:2 **(6591)**

2009: 6^{2}GS,

	Starts	1st	2nd	3rd	Win & Pl
Career Total (Turf)	1	0	1	0	1542

Going (Turf): **Sf: 0-0 GS: 0-1 Gd: 0-0 GF: 0-0 Fm: 0-0**
Distance: 5f/6f: 0-0 7f-8f: 0-1 9f-13f: 0-0 14f+: 0-0
Track : LH: 0-0 RH: 0-0 Tight: 0-0 Gall: 0-0
Aids: Bl: 0-0 Vi: 0-0 Tstrap: 0-0 Ckp: 0-0
Best Rating: **75** 10/09 Nott 6f15y gd-sft

Fair; effective over 6f; acts on easy ground.

Skysurfers

(100) (92)

3-y-o b c E Dubai (USA)-Fortune (IRE) (Night Shift (USA))

Saeed Bin Suroor Godolphin

Placings:1 **(6880)**

2009: 7^{1}SD,

	Starts	1st	2nd	3rd	Win & Pl
Career Total (Turf)	0	0	0	0	
Career Total (AW)	1	1	0	0	2047

92 10/09 Sthl 7f STD £2047

Total win prize-money £2047

Going (Turf): **Sf: 0-0 GS: 0-0 Gd: 0-0 GF: 0-0 Fm: 0-0**
Distance: 5f/6f: 0-0 **7f-8f: 1-1** 9f-13f: 0-0 14f+: 0-0
Track : **LH: 1-1** RH: 0-0 Tight: 0-0 Gall: 0-0
Aids: Bl: 0-0 Vi: 0-0 Tstrap: 0-0 Ckp: 0-0
Best Rating: **92** 10/09 Sthl 7f stand

Impressive winner of a terrible maiden on debut; effective over 7f; acts on Fibresand.

Slam

106(106) (100)91

4-y-o b g Beat Hollow-House Hunting (Zafonic (USA))

B W Hills K Abdulla

Placings:5223/1301**3**0-20 **(1986)**

2009: 9^{2}GF, 10^{0}GF,

	Starts	1st	2nd	3rd	Win & Pl
Career Total (Turf)	9	0	3	2	9341
Career Total (AW)	3	2	0	1	11747

100 8/08 GrLe 1m (0-95)H STD £7477
89 5/08 GrLe 1m STD £2590

Total win prize-money £10067

Going (Turf): **Sf: 0-0 GS: 0-1 Gd: 0-3 GF: 0-5 Fm: 0-0**
Distance: 5f/6f: 0-0 **7f-8f: 2-8** 9f-13f: 0-4 14f+: 0-0
Track : **LH: 2-5** RH: 0-2 Tight: 0-1 **Gall: 2-5**
Aids: Bl: 0-0 Vi: 0-0 Tstrap: 0-0 Ckp: 0-0
Best Rating: **100** 9/08 GrLe 1m stand

Very useful; stays 1m1f; acts on fast ground and on Polytrack.

Slant (IRE)

(84) (52)78

3-y-o b/br f Spinning World (USA)-Sweet Honesty (IRE) (Charnwood Forest (IRE))

Eve Johnson Houghton R F Johnson Houghton

Placings:36452-0P **(2001)**

2009: 7^{0}SD, 8^{P}GF,

	Starts	1st	2nd	3rd	Win & Pl
Career Total (Turf)	6	0	1	1	15976
Career Total (AW)	1	0	0	0	

Going (Turf): **Sf: 0-1 GS: 0-1 Gd: 0-2 GF: 0-2 Fm: 0-0**
Distance: 5f/6f: 0-3 7f-8f: 0-4 9f-13f: 0-0 14f+: 0-0
Track : LH: 0-0 RH: 0-1 Tight: 0-0 Gall: 0-0
Aids: Bl: 0-0 Vi: 0-0 Tstrap: 0-0 Ckp: 0-0
Best Rating: **78** 10/08 Leic 5f218y gd-sft

Fair; suited by 6f; acts on good and easy ground.

Slasl

84(85) (54)32

2-y-o b f Dubawi (IRE)-Mazuna (IRE) (Cape Cross (IRE))

C E Brittain Saeed Manana

Placings:0040 **(6590)**

2009: 6^{0}SD, 6^{0}SD, 8^{4}SD, 6^{0}GS,

	Starts	1st	2nd	3rd	Win & Pl
Career Total (Turf)	1	0	0	0	
Career Total (AW)	3	0	0	0	385

Going (Turf): **Sf: 0-0 GS: 0-1 Gd: 0-0 GF: 0-0 Fm: 0-0**
Distance: 5f/6f: 0-2 7f-8f: 0-2 9f-13f: 0-0 14f+: 0-0
Track : LH: 0-1 RH: 0-2 Tight: 0-1 Gall: 0-0
Aids: Bl: 0-0 Vi: 0-0 Tstrap: 0-0 Ckp: 0-0
Best Rating: **54** 9/09 Kemp 1m stand

Moderate; should stay 1m; acts on Polytrack.

Sleepy Blue Ocean

92(77) (18)68

3-y-o b c Oasis Dream-Esteemed Lady (IRE) (Mark Of Esteem (IRE))

J Balding (J Noseda 10/6) Tykes And Terriers Racing Club

Placings:01000 **(7418)**

2009: 8^{0}G, 6^{1}GF, 6^{0}G, 7^{0}GF, 6^{0}SD,

	Starts	1st	2nd	3rd	Win & Pl
Career Total (Turf)	4	1	0	0	3238
Career Total (AW)	1	0	0	0	

68 6/09 Hayd 6f G-F £3238

Total win prize-money £3238

Going (Turf): Sf: 0-0 GS: 0-0 Gd: 0-2 **GF: 1-2** Fm: 0-0
Distance: **5f/6f: 1-2** 7f-8f: 0-2 9f-13f: 0-1 14f+: 0-0
Track : LH: 0-1 RH: 0-0 Tight: 0-0 Gall: 0-0
Aids: Bl: 0-0 Vi: 0-0 Tstrap: 0-0 Ckp: 0-0
Best Rating: **68** 6/09 Hayd 6f gd-fm

Modest; stays 6f; acts on fast ground.

Sleepy Dove

76(70) (1)13

4-y-o b f Muhtarram (USA)-Robins Meg (Skyliner)

M E Sowersby Mrs Jean W Robinson

Placings:50 **(7361)**

2009: 8^{5}GF, 9^{0}SD,

	Starts	1st	2nd	3rd	Win & Pl
Career Total (Turf)	1	0	0	0	0
Career Total (AW)	1	0	0	0	

Going (Turf): **Sf: 0-0 GS: 0-0 Gd: 0-0 GF: 0-1 Fm: 0-0**
Distance: 5f/6f: 0-0 7f-8f: 0-0 9f-13f: 0-2 14f+: 0-0
Track : LH: 0-2 RH: 0-0 Tight: 0-1 Gall: 0-0
Aids: Bl: 0-0 Vi: 0-0 Tstrap: 0-0 Ckp: 0-0
Best Rating: **13** 8/09 Pont 1m4y gd-fm

Sleepy Hollow

105(96) (69)93

4-y-o b g Beat Hollow-Crackling (Electric)

H Morrison Lady Blyth

Placings:001/1022024-203 **(6734)**

2009: 12^{2}G, 12^{0}SD, 14^{3}S,

	Starts	1st	2nd	3rd	Win & Pl
Career Total (Turf)	12	2	4	1	15265
Career Total (AW)	1	0	0	0	

83 5/08 Wind 1m3f135y (0-75)H G-F £3070
74 10/07 Nott 1m54y SFT £3071

Total win prize-money £6142

Going (Turf): **Sf: 1-2** GS: 0-2 Gd: 0-5 **GF: 1-3** Fm: 0-0
Distance: 5f/6f: 0-0 7f-8f: 0-1 **9f-13f: 2-10** 14f+: 0-2
Track : **LH: 1-4** RH: 0-6 **Tight: 1-5** Gall: 0-4
Aids: Bl: 0-0 Vi: 0-0 Tstrap: 0-0 Ckp: 0-0
Best Rating: **93** 10/09 Sals 1m6f21y soft

Useful; stays 1m6f; acts on most ground.

Sleepy Mountain

(103) (61)63

5-y-o ch g Beat Hollow-La Sorrela (IRE) (Cadeaux Genereux)

A Middleton Mrs C Middleton

Placings:00546023-00 **(7549)**

2009: 12^{0}SD, 12^{0}SD,

	Starts	1st	2nd	3rd	Win & Pl
Career Total (Turf)	3	0	0	0	0
Career Total (AW)	7	0	1	1	887

Going (Turf): **Sf: 0-2 GS: 0-0 Gd: 0-1 GF: 0-0 Fm: 0-0**
Distance: 5f/6f: 0-0 7f-8f: 0-0 9f-13f: 0-8 14f+: 0-2
Track : LH: 0-10 RH: 0-0 Tight: 0-8 Gall: 0-0
Aids: Bl: 0-0 Vi: 0-0 Tstrap: 0-0 Ckp: 0-0
Best Rating: **63** 8/08 Ling 1m6f good

Sleepy Silver

47

4-y-o gr f Silver Patriarch (IRE)-Hustle An Bustle (USA) (Lomond (USA))

J Mackie D Forrester D Forrester R Egan A Wood

Placings:0 **(2447)**

2009: 10^{0}GS,

	Starts	1st	2nd	3rd	Win & Pl
Career Total (Turf)	1	0	0	0	

Going (Turf): **Sf: 0-0 GS: 0-1 Gd: 0-0 GF: 0-0 Fm: 0-0**
Distance: 5f/6f: 0-0 7f-8f: 0-0 9f-13f: 0-1 14f+: 0-0
Track : LH: 0-1 RH: 0-0 Tight: 0-0 Gall: 0-0
Aids: Bl: 0-0 Vi: 0-0 Tstrap: 0-0 Ckp: 0-0

Sleepy Valley (IRE)

92 57

3-y-o b f Clodovil (IRE)-Kilkee Bay (IRE) (Case Law)

A Dickman Allan Dickman

Placings:46-0020000 (6823)
2009: 6^{0}GF, 6^{0}G, 5^{2}G, 5^{0}GS, 5^{0}S, 5^{0}GF, 6^{0}GF,

	Starts	1st	2nd	3rd	Win & Pl
Career Total (Turf)	9	0	1	0	1023

Going (Turf): Sf: 0-2 GS: 0-1 Gd: 0-2 GF: 0-4 Fm: 0-0
Distance: 5f/6f: 0-8 7f-8f: 0-1 9f-13f: 0-0 14f+: 0-0
Track : LH: 0-3 RH: 0-0 Tight: 0-2 Gall: 0-0
Aids: Bl: 0-0 Vi: 0-0 Tstrap: 0-5 Ckp: 0-5
Best Rating: 57 5/09 Catt 5f212y good

Slew Charm (FR)

(104) (62)
7-y-o b g Marathon (USA)-Slew Bay (FR) (Beaudelaire (USA))
Noel T Chance Premier Chance Racing

Placings:020342400/40/24 (0493)
2009: 12^{2}SD, 12^{4}SD,

	Starts	1st	2nd	3rd	Win & Pl
Career Total (Turf)	7	0	2	1	6631
Career Total (AW)	6	0	1	0	922

Going (Turf): Sf: 0-2 GS: 0-1 Gd: 0-4 GF: 0-0 Fm: 0-0
Distance: 5f/6f: 0-0 7f-8f: 0-1 9f-13f: 0-12 14f+: 0-0
Track : LH: 0-6 RH: 0-2 Tight: 0-3 Gall: 0-0
Aids: Bl: 0-0 Vi: 0-0 Tstrap: 0-0 Ckp: 0-0
Best Rating: 66 3/05 StCl 1m2f110y soft

Moderate; stays 1m4f; acts on Polytrack.

Sley (FR)

91(86) (54)65
3-y-o ch f Lomitas-Samara (IRE) (Polish Patriot (USA))
B J Meehan Nigel & Carolyn Elwes

Placings:5600-000 (3387)
2009: 8^{0}SD, 8^{0}F, 7^{0}GF,

	Starts	1st	2nd	3rd	Win & Pl
Career Total (Turf)	4	0	0	0	188
Career Total (AW)	3	0	0	0	

Going (Turf): Sf: 0-1 GS: 0-0 Gd: 0-1 GF: 0-1 Fm: 0-1
Distance: 5f/6f: 0-1 7f-8f: 0-4 9f-13f: 0-2 14f+: 0-0
Track : LH: 0-3 RH: 0-1 Tight: 0-3 Gall: 0-0
Aids: Bl: 0-2 Vi: 0-0 Tstrap: 0-0 Ckp: 0-0
Best Rating: 65 9/08 Yarm 6f3y good

Slice (IRE)

98(86) (56)75
2-y-o b c Daggers Drawn (USA)-Windomen (IRE) (Forest Wind (USA))
Eve Johnson Houghton Eden Racing (III)

Placings:510000 (6211)
2009: 5^{5}G, 6^{1}GF, 6^{0}S, 6^{0}S, 6^{0}GF, 8^{0}SD,

	Starts	1st	2nd	3rd	Win & Pl
Career Total (Turf)	5	1	0	0	3562
Career Total (AW)	1	0	0	0	

75 7/09 Chep 6f16y G-F £3561
Total win prize-money £3562

Going (Turf): Sf: 0-2 GS: 0-0 Gd: 0-1 **GF: 1-2** Fm: 0-0
Distance: 5f/6f: 0-4 **7f-8f: 1-2** 9f-13f: 0-0 14f+: 0-0
Track : LH: 0-2 RH: 0-2 Tight: 0-1 Gall: 0-1
Aids: Bl: 0-1 Vi: 0-0 Tstrap: 0-0 Ckp: 0-0
Best Rating: 75 7/09 Chep 6f16y gd-fm

Fair; effective at 6f; handles firm ground; has worn blinkers.

Slick Mover (IRE)

84(101) (57)33
4-y-o gr m Slickly (FR)-Agnessa (FR) (Niniski (USA))
B G Powell R Stanley

Placings:6405 (7112)
2009: 12^{6}SD, 14^{4}GF, 8^{0}GS, 12^{5}SD,

	Starts	1st	2nd	3rd	Win & Pl
Career Total (Turf)	2	0	0	0	241
Career Total (AW)	2	0	0	0	0

Going (Turf): Sf: 0-0 GS: 0-1 Gd: 0-0 GF: 0-1 Fm: 0-0
Distance: 5f/6f: 0-0 7f-8f: 0-0 9f-13f: 0-3 14f+: 0-1
Track : LH: 0-0 RH: 0-4 Tight: 0-2 Gall: 0-0
Aids: Bl: 0-0 Vi: 0-0 Tstrap: 0-0 Ckp: 0-0
Best Rating: 57 10/09 Kemp 1m4f stand

Slicker (IRE)

91(86) (39)49
3-y-o b g Marju (IRE)-Farthingale (IRE) (Nashwan (USA))
David P Myerscough Richard Barnes

Placings:0000 (6445)
2009: 12^{0}GF, 12^{0}G, 12^{0}G, 12^{0}SS,

	Starts	1st	2nd	3rd	Win & Pl
Career Total (Turf)	3	0	0	0	
Career Total (AW)	1	0	0	0	

Going (Turf): Sf: 0-0 GS: 0-0 Gd: 0-2 GF: 0-1 Fm: 0-0
Distance: 5f/6f: 0-0 7f-8f: 0-0 9f-13f: 0-4 14f+: 0-0
Track : LH: 0-2 RH: 0-2 Tight: 0-1 Gall: 0-0
Aids: Bl: 0-0 Vi: 0-0 Tstrap: 0-1 Ckp: 0-1
Best Rating: 49 6/09 Leop 1m4f good

Sligo

83 (75)59
4-y-o b c Sadler's Wells (USA)-Arabesque (Zafonic (USA))
A J McCabe Chris Howell

Placings:55/46-00 (7293)
2009: 11^{0}S, 12^{0}S,

	Starts	1st	2nd	3rd	Win & Pl
Career Total (Turf)	5	0	0	0	6760
Career Total (AW)	1	0	0	0	

Going (Turf): Sf: 0-3 GS: 0-0 Gd: 0-1 GF: 0-1 Fm: 0-0
Distance: 5f/6f: 0-0 7f-8f: 0-2 9f-13f: 0-4 14f+: 0-0
Track : LH: 0-3 RH: 0-1 Tight: 0-2 Gall: 0-1
Aids: Bl: 0-1 Vi: 0-0 Tstrap: 0-0 Ckp: 0-0
Best Rating: 87 4/08 Lonc 1m2f heavy

Slip

93(109) (89)90
4-y-o b g Fraam-Niggle (Night Shift (USA))
Tim Vaughan (J R Boyle 30/7) M Khan X2

Placings:004/1412535425-15145 (7628)
2009: 10^{1}SD, 10^{5}SD, 10^{1}GF, 10^{4}G, 12^{5}SD,

	Starts	1st	2nd	3rd	Win & Pl
Career Total (Turf)	9	3	1	1	15683
Career Total (AW)	9	1	1	0	6248

60 7/09 Ling 1m2f G-F £2047
75 1/09 Ling 1m2f STD £2047
79 7/08 Sand 1m2f7y (0-85)H G-F £7447
78 6/08 Sals 1m (0-65)H GD £2914
Total win prize-money £14455

Going (Turf): Sf: 0-0 GS: 0-2 Gd: 1-4 **GF: 2-3** Fm: 0-0
Distance: 5f/6f: 0-0 7f-8f: 1-4 **9f-13f: 3-13** 14f+: 0-1
Track : **LH: 2-10** RH: 1-6 **Tight: 2-9** Gall: 0-2
Aids: Bl: 0-1 Vi: 0-0 Tstrap: 0-1 Ckp: 0-1
Best Rating: 90 8/08 Sand 1m2f7y gd-sft

Useful; effective over 1m4f; acts on good and faster ground and on Polytrack; has worn blinkers.

Slip Silver

68(75) (20)41
5-y-o gr m Slip Anchor-New Wind (GER) (Windwurf (GER))
R C Guest Camela Racing Limited

Placings:00060060/000 (1533)
2009: 16^{0}F, 12^{0}SD, 12^{0}SD,

	Starts	1st	2nd	3rd	Win & Pl
Career Total (Turf)	3	0	0	0	
Career Total (AW)	8	0	0	0	0

Going (Turf): Sf: 0-0 GS: 0-0 Gd: 0-2 GF: 0-0 Fm: 0-1
Distance: 5f/6f: 0-0 7f-8f: 0-0 9f-13f: 0-8 14f+: 0-3
Track : LH: 0-9 RH: 0-2 Tight: 0-8 Gall: 0-1
Aids: Bl: 0-0 Vi: 0-0 Tstrap: 0-5 Ckp: 0-5
Best Rating: 45 9/07 Wolv 1m4f50y stand

Slip Sliding Away (IRE)

(98) (66)
2-y-o b c Whipper (USA)-Sandy Lady (IRE) (Desert King (IRE))
J R Best Bernard Keay & Partners

Placings:304344 (7846)
2009: 7^{3}SD, 7^{0}SD, 5^{4}SD, 5^{3}SD, 6^{4}SD, 7^{4}SD,

	Starts	1st	2nd	3rd	Win & Pl
Career Total (Turf)	0	0	0	0	
Career Total (AW)	6	0	0	2	1933

Going (Turf): Sf: 0-0 GS: 0-0 Gd: 0-0 GF: 0-0 Fm: 0-0
Distance: 5f/6f: 0-3 7f-8f: 0-3 9f-13f: 0-0 14f+: 0-0
Track : LH: 0-5 RH: 0-1 Tight: 0-5 Gall: 0-0
Aids: Bl: 0-0 Vi: 0-0 Tstrap: 0-0 Ckp: 0-0
Best Rating: 66 11/09 Ling 7f stand

Modest; promise on debut; acts on Polytrack.

Slip Star

92(81) (18)56
6-y-o b m Slip Anchor-Shiny Kay (Star Appeal)
T J Etherington Russell Bradley

Placings:00/600330420/00160-060500060 (6218)
2009: 7^{0}F, 8^{6}GF, 8^{0}GF, 9^{5}G, 7^{0}GF, 6^{0}G, 7^{0}GF, 7^{6}G, 10^{0}GF,

	Starts	1st	2nd	3rd	Win & Pl
Career Total (Turf)	21	1	1	2	5646
Career Total (AW)	4	0	0	0	0

56 6/08 Donc 7f (0-70)H G-F £3238
Total win prize-money £3238

Going (Turf): Sf: 0-0 GS: 0-0 Gd: 0-7 **GF: 1-12** Fm: 0-2
Distance: 5f/6f: 0-5 **7f-8f: 1-15** 9f-13f: 0-4 14f+: 0-1
Track : LH: 0-12 RH: 0-4 Tight: 0-13 Gall: 0-1
Aids: Bl: 0-0 Vi: 0-0 Tstrap: 0-0 Ckp: 0-0
Best Rating: 56 6/08 Donc 7f gd-fm

Moderate; stays 7f and acts on fast ground.

Sloop Johnb

107 89

3-y-o b g Bahamian Bounty-Soundwave (Prince Sabo)
R A Fahey Jonathan Gill

Placings:262100-2110040 **(4490)**
2009: 5²GF, 5¹GF, 5¹GS, 6⁰G, 6⁰G, 5⁴GS, 5⁰G,

	Starts	1st	2nd	3rd	Win & Pl
Career Total (Turf)	13	3	3	0	16099

89	5/09	York	5f	(0-80)H	G-S	£6476
81	5/09	Bevl	5f	(0-75)H	G-F	£2752
74	7/08	Carl	5f		FRM	£2590

Total win prize-money £11818

Going (Turf): Sf: 0-2 **GS: 1-2** Gd: 0-4 **GF: 1-4 Fm: 1-1**
Distance: **5f/6f: 3-13** 7f-8f: 0-0 9f-13f: 0-0 14f+: 0-0
Track : LH: 0-0 **RH: 1-2** Tight: 0-0 **Gall: 1-2**
Aids: Bl: 0-0 Vi: 0-0 Tstrap: 0-0 Ckp: 0-0
Best Rating: **89** 5/09 York 5f gd-sft

Useful; effective at 5f; acts on most ground.

Slugger O'Toole

91(89) (89)100

4-y-o br g Intikhab (USA)-Haddeyah (USA) (Dayjur (USA))
S C Williams M Hargreaves, G Edwards, P Kendall

Placings:0/4113000103-00000 **(7287)**
2009: 8⁰GF, 8⁰S, 7⁰GF, 7⁰GF, 7⁰S,

	Starts	1st	2nd	3rd	Win & Pl
Career Total (Turf)	15	2	0	2	29531
Career Total (AW)	1	1	0	0	3071

100	9/08	Donc	7f	(0-100)H	SFT	£12462
89	5/08	NmkR	7f	(0-100)H	G-F	£12952
89	4/08	Wolv	7f32y		STD	£3070

Total win prize-money £28485

Going (Turf): **Sf: 1-3** GS: 0-0 Gd: 0-4 **GF: 1-8** Fm: 0-0
Distance: 5f/6f: 0-0 **7f-8f: 3-16** 9f-13f: 0-0 14f+: 0-0
Track : **LH: 1-2** RH: 0-0 **Tight: 1-2** Gall: 0-0
Aids: Bl: 0-0 Vi: 0-0 Tstrap: 0-0 Ckp: 0-0
Best Rating: **100** 10/08 NmkR 7f good

Useful; stays 7f; acts on most ground and on Polytrack.

Slumdog (IRE)

50

4-y-o b c Alzao (USA)-Chardania (IRE) (Rainbows For Life (CAN))
Garry Moss Brooklands Racing

Placings:00 **(4812)**
2009: 8⁰G, 7⁰HY,

	Starts	1st	2nd	3rd	Win & Pl
Career Total (Turf)	2	0	0	0	

Going (Turf): **Sf: 0-1 GS: 0-0 Gd: 0-1 GF: 0-0 Fm: 0-0**
Distance: 5f/6f: 0-0 7f-8f: 0-1 9f-13f: 0-1 14f+: 0-0
Track : LH: 0-1 RH: 0-0 Tight: 0-0 Gall: 0-0
Aids: Bl: 0-0 Vi: 0-0 Tstrap: 0-0 Ckp: 0-0

Smalljohn

91(101) (73)76

3-y-o ch g Needwood Blade-My Bonus (Cyrano De Bergerac)
B Smart B Smart

Placings:366461262101231-3000042 **(7691)**
2009: 7³SS, 7⁰GF, 7⁰G, 7⁰GF, 7⁰SD, 7⁴SD, 7²SD,

	Starts	1st	2nd	3rd	Win & Pl
Career Total (Turf)	12	2	2	0	13499
Career Total (AW)	10	2	2	3	7210

71	12/08	Wolv	7f32y	STD	£2729
73	11/08	Wolv	7f32y	STD	£2047
75	8/08	Thsk	7f	G-S	£4338
75	6/08	York	6f	G-F	£6476

Total win prize-money £15592

Going (Turf): Sf: 0-2 **GS: 1-1** Gd: 0-4 **GF: 1-5** Fm: 0-0
Distance: **5f/6f: 1-9 7f-8f: 3-13** 9f-13f: 0-0 14f+: 0-0
Track : **LH: 3-13** RH: 0-1 **Tight: 3-10** Gall: 0-1
Aids: Bl: 0-0 **Vi: 4-16** Tstrap: 0-0 Ckp: 0-0
Best Rating: **76** 7/08 Bevl 5f gd-fm

Modest; effective over 5f-7f; acts on good and fast ground; goes on Polytrack.

Smart Endeavour (USA)

91(99) (88)83

3-y-o ch g Smart Strike (CAN)-Luminance (USA) (Deputy Minister (CAN))
W R Swinburn The Lamplighters

Placings:0-1640 **(4715)**
2009: 7¹SD, 7⁶GF, 8⁴GF, 10⁰GS,

	Starts	1st	2nd	3rd	Win & Pl
Career Total (Turf)	4	0	0	0	385
Career Total (AW)	1	1	0	0	3238

88	4/09	Wolv	7f32y	STD	£3238

Total win prize-money £3238

Going (Turf): **Sf: 0-0 GS: 0-1 Gd: 0-1 GF: 0-2 Fm: 0-0**
Distance: 5f/6f: 0-0 **7f-8f: 1-3** 9f-13f: 0-2 14f+: 0-0
Track : **LH: 1-2** RH: 0-2 **Tight: 1-2** Gall: 0-1
Aids: Bl: 0-0 Vi: 0-0 Tstrap: 0-0 Ckp: 0-0
Best Rating: **88** 4/09 Wolv 7f32y stand

Useful; stays 7f and acts on Polytrack.

Smart John

84 13

9-y-o b g Bin Ajwaad (IRE)-Katy-Q (IRE) (Taufan (USA))
S T Lewis (H J Evans 12/6) Mr & Mrs D J Smart

Placings:006/03050/414213541306/564413254226/004/00 0/0 **(5530)**
2009: 14⁰G,

	Starts	1st	2nd	3rd	Win & Pl
Career Total (Turf)	39	4	4	4	27153

74	6/05	Wwck	1m4f134y	(0-70)H	G-F	£3779
76	8/04	Wwck	1m4f134yE	(0-75)H	G-S	£4046
76	7/04	Hayd	1m3f200yE	(0-85)H	GD	£3471
65	5/04	Hayd	1m2f120yE	(0-75)H	G-F	£3770

Total win prize-money £15067

Going (Turf): Sf: 0-7 GS: 1-5 Gd: 1-10 **GF: 2-16** Fm: 0-1
Distance: 5f/6f: 0-0 7f-8f: 0-4 **9f-13f: 4-32** 14f+: 0-3
Track : **LH: 4-32** RH: 0-3 Tight: 0-4 Gall: 0-6
Aids: Bl: 0-0 Vi: 0-0 Tstrap: 0-0 Ckp: 0-0
Best Rating: **77** 9/05 Hayd 1m3f200y gd-sft

Smart Pick

81 (48)47

6-y-o ch m Piccolo-Nevita (Never So Bold)
Mrs L Williamson Mrs Lisa Williamson

Placings:62604/**606**000550244550**3060**/50006-00 **(6183)**
2009: 9⁰G, 9⁰GF,

	Starts	1st	2nd	3rd	Win & Pl
Career Total (Turf)	23	0	2	0	2402
Career Total (AW)	8	0	0	1	302

Going (Turf): **Sf: 0-2 GS: 0-3 Gd: 0-7 GF: 0-9 Fm: 0-2**
Distance: 5f/6f: 0-7 7f-8f: 0-14 9f-13f: 0-10 14f+: 0-0
Track : LH: 0-18 RH: 0-10 Tight: 0-21 Gall: 0-0
Aids: Bl: 0-1 Vi: 0-1 Tstrap: 0-2 Ckp: 0-2
Best Rating: **57** 4/05 Hayd 5f soft

Moderate; stays 1m; acts on most ground.

Smart Tazz

84(83) (36)26

4-y-o b g Mujahid (USA)-Katy-Q (IRE) (Taufan (USA))
S T Lewis (H J Evans 5/6) Mr & Mrs D J Smart

Placings:00-00040 **(5614)**
2009: 10⁰GF, 9⁰GF, 12⁰SD, 8⁴SD, 8⁰SD,

	Starts	1st	2nd	3rd	Win & Pl
Career Total (Turf)	4	0	0	0	
Career Total (AW)	3	0	0	0	289

Going (Turf): **Sf: 0-2 GS: 0-0 Gd: 0-0 GF: 0-2 Fm: 0-0**
Distance: 5f/6f: 0-0 7f-8f: 0-1 9f-13f: 0-6 14f+: 0-0
Track : LH: 0-7 RH: 0-0 Tight: 0-3 Gall: 0-0
Aids: Bl: 0-1 Vi: 0-0 Tstrap: 0-0 Ckp: 0-0
Best Rating: **36** 8/09 Wolv 1m141y stand

Smarten Die (IRE)

(110) (101)89

6-y-o ch h Diesis-Highest Dream (IRE) (Highest Honor (FR))
Frau E Mader Stall Capricorn

Placings:3/**1211**56**2**/**502**3305**52**-11**6**0
2009: 6¹SD, 6¹SD, 6⁶SD, 6⁰G,

	Starts	1st	2nd	3rd	Win & Pl
Career Total (Turf)	9	1	1	3	4431
Career Total (AW)	12	4	3	0	12479

2/09	Dort	6f	H	STD	£2524
1/09	Dort	6f	H	STD	£2912
4/07	Brem	6f		GD	£2027
3/07	Dort	6f		STD	£1351
1/07	Neus	5f110y		STD	£1283

Total win prize-money £10099

Going (Turf): Sf: 0-3 GS: 0-0 **Gd: 1-6** GF: 0-0 Fm: 0-0
Distance: **5f/6f: 5-19** 7f-8f: 0-2 9f-13f: 0-0 14f+: 0-0
Track : LH: 0-3 RH: 0-2 Tight: 0-2 Gall: 0-0
Aids: Bl: 0-0 Vi: 0-0 Tstrap: 0-0 Ckp: 0-0
Best Rating: **101** 11/08 Ling 6f stand

Useful German-trained sprinter; best over 6f; acts on good ground and on sand.

Smarterthanuthink (USA)

88(97) (73)71

4-y-o b g Smart Strike (CAN)-Dance Gaily (USA) (Nureyev (USA))
R A Fahey David And Jackie Knaggs

Placings:600/6120020-06 **(3235)**
2009: 12⁰GF, 9⁶GF,

	Starts	1st	2nd	3rd	Win & Pl
Career Total (Turf)	10	1	1	0	3492
Career Total (AW)	2	0	1	0	771

71	6/08	Haml	1m3f16y	(0-65)H	G-F	£2047

Total win prize-money £2047

Going (Turf): Sf: 0-1 GS: 0-0 Gd: 0-2 **GF: 1-7** Fm: 0-0

Distance: 5f/6f: 0-3 7f-8f: 0-1 **9f-13f: 1-8** 14f+: 0-0
Track : LH: 0-6 **RH: 1-3 Tight: 1-4** Gall: 0-3
Aids: Bl: 0-0 Vi: 0-1 Tstrap: 1-4 Ckp: 1-4
Best Rating: **73** 10/08 Ling 1m2f stand

Modest; stays 1m4f; acts on most ground and on Polytrack.

Smarties Party

83(90) (55)**53**
6-y-o b m Tamure (IRE)-Maries Party (The Parson)
C W Thornton Team 30 & Partner

Placings:463 **(7557)**
2009: 10^{4}GF, 11^{6}S, 13^{3}SD,

	Starts	1st	2nd	3rd	Win & Pl
Career Total (Turf)	2	0	0	0	241
Career Total (AW)	1	0	0	1	403

Going (Turf): **Sf: 0-1 GS: 0-0 Gd: 0-0 GF: 0-1 Fm: 0-0**
Distance: 5f/6f: 0-0 7f-8f: 0-0 9f-13f: 0-2 14f+: 0-1
Track : LH: 0-3 RH: 0-0 Tight: 0-2 Gall: 0-1
Aids: Bl: 0-0 Vi: 0-0 Tstrap: 0-0 Ckp: 0-0
Best Rating: **55** 11/09 Wolv 1m5f194y stand

Moderate; stays 1m6f; acts on Polytrack.

Smarty Socks (IRE)

105(111) (80)**90**
5-y-o ch g Elnadim (USA)-Unicamp (Royal Academy (USA))
P T Midgley R G Fell

Placings:231/6204**060**/**0000**1161-1**4**016501430 **(5375)**
2009: 7^{1}SD, 7^{4}SD, 7^{0}GF, 7^{1}GF, 7^{6}GF, 8^{5}G, 7^{0}GF, 7^{1}G, 7^{4}GS, 6^{3}G, 8^{0}SD,

	Starts	1st	2nd	3rd	Win & Pl
Career Total (Turf)	20	4	2	2	37864
Career Total (AW)	9	3	0	0	11701

90	7/09	York	7f	(0-85)H	GD	£6476
86	4/09	Donc	7f	(0-80)H	G-F	£4684
79	2/09	Sthl	7f	(0-80)H	STD	£4857
80	11/08	Sthl	1m	(0-70)H	STD	£2729
80	11/08	Sthl	7f	(0-70)H	STD	£3753
76	10/08	Leic	7f9y	(0-70)H	G-S	£2590
90	10/06	Thur	1m		Y-S	£6671

Total win prize-money £31763

Going (Turf): Sf: 0-2 **GS: 1-4 Gd: 1-5 GF: 1-5** Fm: 0-0
Distance: 5f/6f: 0-0 **7f-8f: 7-25** 9f-13f: 0-4 14f+: 0-0
Track : **LH: 4-13** RH: 0-3 Tight: 0-0 **Gall: 1-2**
Aids: Bl: 0-0 Vi: 0-0 Tstrap: 0-1 Ckp: 0-1
Best Rating: **92** 5/07 Baln 1m1f good

Useful; ex-Irish; effective over 7f-1m; handles fast going, but well suited by soft ground and Fibresand.

Smayal (USA)

79 **34**
2-y-o b f Kingmambo (USA)-Cloud Castle (In The Wings)
C E Brittain Saeed Manana

Placings:6 **(6484)**
2009: 7^{6}GF,

	Starts	1st	2nd	3rd	Win & Pl
Career Total (Turf)	1	0	0	0	0

Going (Turf): **Sf: 0-0 GS: 0-0 Gd: 0-0 GF: 0-1 Fm: 0-0**
Distance: 5f/6f: 0-0 7f-8f: 0-1 9f-13f: 0-0 14f+: 0-0
Track : LH: 0-0 RH: 0-0 Tight: 0-0 Gall: 0-0
Aids: Bl: 0-0 Vi: 0-0 Tstrap: 0-0 Ckp: 0-0
Best Rating: **34** 10/09 Rdcr 7f gd-fm

Smelly Cat

91 **47**
3-y-o b f One Cool Cat (USA)-Grecian Halo (USA) (Southern Halo (USA))
D W Thompson (T D Easterby 1/5) J Greenbank

Placings:00-55600 **(3852)**
2009: 5^{5}GF, 5^{5}GF, 6^{6}GF, 7^{0}G, 6^{0}GF,

	Starts	1st	2nd	3rd	Win & Pl
Career Total (Turf)	7	0	0	0	0

Going (Turf): **Sf: 0-1 GS: 0-0 Gd: 0-2 GF: 0-4 Fm: 0-0**
Distance: 5f/6f: 0-4 7f-8f: 0-3 9f-13f: 0-0 14f+: 0-0
Track : LH: 0-1 RH: 0-1 Tight: 0-1 Gall: 0-0
Aids: Bl: 0-0 Vi: 0-0 Tstrap: 0-0 Ckp: 0-0
Best Rating: **47** 4/09 Catt 5f212y gd-fm

Smetana

(94) (57)**56**
4-y-o b g Kylian (USA)-Shimmer (Bustino)
E J Creighton Miss Alicia Murray

Placings:000/542060-660 **(2580)**
2009: 16^{6}SD, 11^{6}SD, 12^{0}SD,

	Starts	1st	2nd	3rd	Win & Pl
Career Total (Turf)	5	0	0	0	173
Career Total (AW)	7	0	1	0	524

Going (Turf): **Sf: 0-1 GS: 0-1 Gd: 0-2 GF: 0-1 Fm: 0-0**
Distance: 5f/6f: 0-0 7f-8f: 0-2 9f-13f: 0-6 14f+: 0-4
Track : LH: 0-11 RH: 0-1 Tight: 0-1 Gall: 0-1
Aids: Bl: 0-0 Vi: 0-1 Tstrap: 0-0 Ckp: 0-0
Best Rating: **58** 11/07 Kemp 1m stand

Smicker Smacker

84(81) (56)**58**
2-y-o gr f Verglas (IRE)-Vallee Blanche (IRE) (Zafonic (USA))
George Baker Jerry Jamgotchian

Placings:0060 **(5498)**
2009: 6^{0}GF, 6^{0}G, 7^{6}SD, 8^{0}G,

	Starts	1st	2nd	3rd	Win & Pl
Career Total (Turf)	3	0	0	0	
Career Total (AW)	1	0	0	0	0

Going (Turf): **Sf: 0-0 GS: 0-0 Gd: 0-2 GF: 0-1 Fm: 0-0**
Distance: 5f/6f: 0-2 7f-8f: 0-1 9f-13f: 0-1 14f+: 0-0
Track : LH: 0-1 RH: 0-1 Tight: 0-0 Gall: 0-0
Aids: Bl: 0-0 Vi: 0-0 Tstrap: 0-0 Ckp: 0-0
Best Rating: **58** 6/09 Pont 6f good

Smirfy's Silver

70 (31)**71**
5-y-o b g Desert Prince (IRE)-Goodwood Blizzard (Inchinor)
E S McMahon Mrs Dian Plant

Placings:450000/0123/10305-0 **(5438)**
2009: 10^{0}GF,

	Starts	1st	2nd	3rd	Win & Pl
Career Total (Turf)	15	2	1	2	6941
Career Total (AW)	1	0	0	0	

69	4/08	Leic	1m1f218y (0-70)H	G-S	£2590
60	7/07	Yarm	1m2f21y (0-65)H	G-F	£2137

Total win prize-money £4727

Going (Turf): Sf: 0-1 **GS: 1-4** Gd: 0-1 **GF: 1-9** Fm: 0-0
Distance: 5f/6f: 0-6 7f-8f: 0-1 **9f-13f: 2-9** 14f+: 0-0
Track : LH: 1-8 RH: 1-3 **Tight: 1-7** Gall: 0-1
Aids: Bl: 0-0 Vi: 0-0 Tstrap: 0-0 Ckp: 0-0
Best Rating: **71** 6/08 Leic 1m1f218y gd-fm

Modest; stays 1m2f; acts on fast and easy ground.

Smirfys Copper (IRE)

35
2-y-o ch f Choisir (AUS)-Fer De Lance (IRE) (Diesis)
D Nicholls Mrs Dian Plant

Placings:0 **(4187)**
2009: 5^{0}S,

	Starts	1st	2nd	3rd	Win & Pl
Career Total (Turf)	1	0	0	0	

Going (Turf): **Sf: 0-1 GS: 0-0 Gd: 0-0 GF: 0-0 Fm: 0-0**
Distance: 5f/6f: 0-1 7f-8f: 0-0 9f-13f: 0-0 14f+: 0-0
Track : LH: 0-1 RH: 0-0 Tight: 0-1 Gall: 0-0
Aids: Bl: 0-0 Vi: 0-0 Tstrap: 0-0 Ckp: 0-0

Smirfys Systems

(103) (71)**53**
10-y-o b g Safawan-Saint Systems (Uncle Pokey)
E S McMahon Mrs Dian Plant

Placings:4100/50012/005002**00**/**0**0060/**50**/3141-215540 **(7860)**
2009: 5^{2}SD, 5^{1}SD, 5^{5}SF, 7^{5}SD, 5^{4}SD, 7^{0}SD,

	Starts	1st	2nd	3rd	Win & Pl
Career Total (Turf)	20	2	2	0	18075
Career Total (AW)	15	3	1	1	7220

71	2/09	Wolv	5f216y	(0-60)H	STD	£2047
64	12/08	Wolv	7f32y		STD	£2388
59	2/08	Wolv	5f216y	(0-50)H	STD	£1774
86	8/03	Thsk	6f	D(0-80)H	G-F	£6087
75	9/02	Catt	7f	D	FRM	£3997

Total win prize-money £16295

Going (Turf): Sf: 0-3 GS: 0-3 Gd: 0-3 **GF: 1-10 Fm: 1-1**
Distance: **5f/6f: 3-21** 7f-8f: 2-14 9f-13f: 0-0 14f+: 0-0
Track : **LH: 4-21** RH: 0-1 **Tight: 4-17** Gall: 0-1
Aids: Bl: 0-1 Vi: 0-0 Tstrap: 1-2 Ckp: 1-2
Best Rating: **92** 8/03 York 6f3y gd-fm

Modest; effective at 6f-7f; suited by fast ground; goes on Polytrack.

Smitain

72(57) **32**
3-y-o b g Lujain (USA)-Mitsuki (Puissance)
Mrs S Lamyman S Nicholson

Placings:60-06 **(3238)**
2009: 7^{0}GF, 8^{6}GF,

	Starts	1st	2nd	3rd	Win & Pl
Career Total (Turf)	3	0	0	0	0
Career Total (AW)	1	0	0	0	0

Going (Turf): Sf: 0-0 GS: 0-0 Gd: 0-1 GF: 0-2 Fm: 0-0
Distance: 5f/6f: 0-2 7f-8f: 0-1 9f-13f: 0-1 14f+: 0-0
Track : LH: 0-1 RH: 0-1 Tight: 0-1 Gall: 0-0
Aids: Bl: 0-0 Vi: 0-0 Tstrap: 0-0 Ckp: 0-0
Best Rating: 32 8/08 Catt 5f good

Smog (IRE)

85(78) (25)**41**
2-y-o gr c Verglas (IRE)-Dollysister (FR) (Alydar (USA))
B J Meehan Stephen Dartnell

Placings:0400 (5613)
2009: 6^{0}G, 6^{4}S, 8^{0}GS, 7^{0}SD,

	Starts	1st	2nd	3rd	Win & Pl
Career Total (Turf)	3	0	0	0	202
Career Total (AW)	1	0	0	0	

Going (Turf): Sf: 0-1 GS: 0-1 Gd: 0-1 GF: 0-0 Fm: 0-0
Distance: 5f/6f: 0-1 7f-8f: 0-2 9f-13f: 0-1 14f+: 0-0
Track : LH: 0-2 RH: 0-0 Tight: 0-1 Gall: 0-0
Aids: Bl: 0-1 Vi: 0-0 Tstrap: 0-0 Ckp: 0-0
Best Rating: 41 7/09 Chep 6f16y soft

Smokey Oakey (IRE)

108 (76)**113**
5-y-o b g Tendulkar (USA)-Veronica (Persian Bold)
M H Tompkins Judi Dench and Bryan Agar

Placings:3230100/01063451/161660-00506005 (7245)
2009: 10^{0}G, 8^{0}G, 10^{5}GS, 10^{0}G, 8^{6}G, 8^{0}S, 9^{0}GF, 8^{5}S,

	Starts	1st	2nd	3rd	Win & Pl
Career Total (Turf)	27	5	0	3	147665
Career Total (AW)	2	0	1	0	771

113	5/08	Sand	1m2f7y		SFT	£26681
105	3/08	Donc	1m	H	G-S	£77900
98	11/07	Ayr	1m	(0-90)H	HVY	£7772
88	5/07	NmkR	1m2f	(0-100)H	G-S	£11658
85	9/06	Ayr	1m	(0-95)	G-S	£12464

Total win prize-money £136477

Going (Turf): Sf: 2-6 GS: 3-8 Gd: 0-10 GF: 0-3 Fm: 0-0
Distance: 5f/6f: 0-4 7f-8f: 3-8 9f-13f: 2-17 14f+: 0-0
Track : LH: 2-14 RH: 1-5 Tight: 0-5 Gall: 0-5
Aids: Bl: 0-0 Vi: 0-0 Tstrap: 0-0 Ckp: 0-0
Best Rating: 113 5/08 Sand 1m2f7y soft

Smart; winner of the 2008 Lincoln and Group 3 Brigadier Gerard Stakes; effective from 1m-1m2f; likes soft ground.

Smokey Ryder

97(104) (96)**91**
3-y-o ch f Bertolini (USA)-Another Secret (Efisio)
R A Harris The Govin Partnership

Placings:031000111-141130064000 (7862)
2009: 5^{1}SD, 6^{4}SD, 5^{1}SD, 6^{1}SD, 7^{3}SD, 6^{0}SD, 7^{0}GF, 6^{6}GF, 6^{4}F, 6^{0}GS, 6^{0}G, 5^{0}SD,

	Starts	1st	2nd	3rd	Win & Pl
Career Total (Turf)	10	1	0	1	4304
Career Total (AW)	11	6	0	1	28924

89	2/09	Ling	6f	(0-85)H	STD	£4857
90	2/09	Sthl	5f	(0-85)H	STD	£4731
82	1/09	Wolv	5f216y	(0-85)H	STD	£5180
80	12/08	Ling	5f		STD	£2047
77	12/08	Kemp	6f		STD	£2047
76	10/08	GrLe	6f		STD	£3238
69	8/08	Folk	5f		G-F	£2388

Total win prize-money £24489

Going (Turf): Sf: 0-0 GS: 0-3 Gd: 0-3 GF: 1-3 Fm: 0-1
Distance: 5f/6f: 7-17 7f-8f: 0-4 9f-13f: 0-0 14f+: 0-0
Track : LH: 4-9 RH: 1-3 Tight: 3-6 Gall: 1-3
Aids: Bl: 0-0 Vi: 0-0 Tstrap: 0-0 Ckp: 0-0
Best Rating: 96 3/09 Ling 7f stand

Very useful; Listed placed; effective at 5f-7f; acts on fast, but handles easy ground; also goes on Polytrack; likes to race prominently.

Smokey Rye

95(105) (83)**78**
4-y-o b f Bertolini (USA)-Another Secret (Efisio)
George Baker Mrs Beverley Paterson

Placings:002003122/2260543101-41013103 (1256)
2009: 8^{4}SD, 8^{1}SD, 8^{0}SD, 7^{1}SD, 8^{3}SD, 8^{1}SD, 8^{0}SD, 8^{3}G,

	Starts	1st	2nd	3rd	Win & Pl
Career Total (Turf)	8	0	1	1	1677
Career Total (AW)	19	6	4	3	19206

64	3/09	Wolv	1m141y		STD	£2047
74	3/09	Ling	7f	(0-70)H	STD	£2729
69	2/09	Ling	1m		STD	£2047
60	12/08	Ling	1m		STD	£2047
66	10/08	Kemp	1m		STD	£2047
72	11/07	Kemp	6f		STD	£2388

Total win prize-money £13307

Going (Turf): Sf: 0-1 GS: 0-1 Gd: 0-3 GF: 0-2 Fm: 0-1
Distance: 5f/6f: 1-5 7f-8f: 4-20 9f-13f: 1-2 14f+: 0-0
Track : LH: 4-13 RH: 2-10 Tight: 4-11 Gall: 0-1
Aids: Bl: 1-8 Vi: 0-0 Tstrap: 0-1 Ckp: 0-1
Best Rating: 83 4/09 Kemp 1m stand

Fair; effective over 6f-1m; acts on fast ground and on Polytrack; has been blinkered; can look moody and often swishes her tail.

Smokin Beau

(104) (72)**46**
12-y-o b g Cigar-Beau Dada (IRE) (Pine Circle (USA))
N P Littmoden Miss Vanessa Church

Placings:043315/3200200036110000/10024010012132/12160201221/3030605400/62000400111/4022001000000030 00/45000232100340/000300004011/40500-0 (0956)
2009: 5^{0}SD,

	Starts	1st	2nd	3rd	Win & Pl
Career Total (Turf)	94	13	13	9	327591
Career Total (AW)	24	5	1	2	28517

74	12/07	Kemp	5f	(0-75)H	STD	£2817
71	11/07	Kemp	5f	(0-65)H	STD	£2047
92	8/06	Muss	5f	(0-80)H	G-F	£6232
108	7/05	Ling	5f	(0-105)H	STD	£11934
116	8/04	Sand	5f6y	B(0-100)H	SFT	£15314
116	8/04	Ripn	6f	B(0-105)H	SFT	£29000
104	8/04	Hayd	5f	C(0-100)H	GD	£17862
116	10/02	Newb	6f8y	B(0-110)H	G-S	£11774
114	9/02	Gdwd	6f	A	GD	£17014
98	5/02	Gdwd	6f	B	GD	£10155
87	4/02	Nott	5f13y	C	G-F	£6206
108	9/01	Donc	5f140y	B(0-110)H	G-F	£30290
101	8/01	Gdwd	6f	C(0-95)H	GD	£23107
98	7/01	Asct	5f	B H	G-F	£46400
90	3/01	Wolv	5f	D(0-85)H	STD	£3796
90	8/00	Newb	5f34y	C(0-95)H	G-F	£6604
83	8/00	Gdwd	5f	C(0-90)H	GD	£9262
69	11/99	Sthl	5f	D	STD	£2822

Total win prize-money £252640

Going (Turf): Sf: 2-15GS: 1-13Gd: 5-33 GF: 5-31 Fm: 0-2
Distance: 5f/6f: 17-113 7f-8f: 1-5 9f-13f: 0-0 14f+: 0-0
Track : LH: 2-23 RH: 2-6 Tight: 2-17 Gall: 0-10
Aids: Bl: 0-3 Vi: 0-2 Tstrap: 0-4 Ckp: 0-4
Best Rating: 116 8/04 Sand 5f6y soft

Modest once useful sprinter; effective over 5f-6f; acts on most types of ground, including sand; sometimes wears headgear.

Smokin Joe

(106) (82)**6**
8-y-o b g Cigar-Beau Dada (IRE) (Pine Circle (USA))
J R Best G G Racing

Placings:0662216/4050000053211120/4406000/3000430 4430/00002516533122/50060600006-00 (1589)
2009: 7^{0}SD, 10^{0}SD,

	Starts	1st	2nd	3rd	Win & Pl
Career Total (Turf)	9	0	0	0	0
Career Total (AW)	60	6	7	6	31108

82	12/07	Kemp	7f	(0-70)H	STD	£2817
71	11/07	Kemp	1m	(0-65)H	STD	£2047
83	12/04	Ling	6f	(0-77)H	STD	£3493
84	12/04	Ling	7f	(0-77)H	STD	£3485
69	11/04	Ling	6f	(0-60)	STD	£3396
65	12/03	Ling	6f	D	STD	£2982

Total win prize-money £18223

Going (Turf): Sf: 0-1 GS: 0-1 Gd: 0-2 GF: 0-5 Fm: 0-0
Distance: 5f/6f: 3-20 7f-8f: 3-39 9f-13f: 0-10 14f+: 0-0
Track : LH: 4-49 RH: 2-12 Tight: 4-47 Gall: 0-0
Aids: Bl: 5-49 Vi: 0-4 Tstrap: 0-0 Ckp: 0-0
Best Rating: 87 1/05 Ling 7f stand

Modest; effective from 6f-1m2f; acts on Polytrack; likes to come late off a strong pace.

Smooth As Silk (IRE)

88(102) (70)**70**
4-y-o b f Danehill Dancer (IRE)-Doula (USA) (Gone West (USA))
C R Egerton Longmoor Holdings Ltd

Placings:05/5200-30404430 (7440)
2009: 12^{3}SD, 11^{0}GF, 13^{4}SF, 12^{0}SD, 12^{4}SF, 12^{4}SD, 12^{3}SD, 12^{0}SD,

	Starts	1st	2nd	3rd	Win & Pl
Career Total (Turf)	6	0	1	0	867
Career Total (AW)	8	0	0	2	893

Going (Turf): Sf: 0-0 GS: 0-0 Gd: 0-1 GF: 0-5 Fm: 0-0
Distance: 5f/6f: 0-2 7f-8f: 0-1 9f-13f: 0-10 14f+: 0-1
Track : LH: 0-7 RH: 0-4 Tight: 0-5 Gall: 0-2
Aids: Bl: 0-2 Vi: 0-0 Tstrap: 0-2 Ckp: 0-2
Best Rating: 70 6/09 Kemp 1m4f stand

Moderate; stays 1m4f; acts on Polytrack; has worn cheek-pieces and blinkers.

Smooth Sovereign (IRE)

101(96) (60)**67**
4-y-o ch g King's Best (USA)-Mellow Park (IRE) (In The Wings)
M Johnston Mark Johnston Racing Ltd

Placings:2-5002 (1125)
2009: 9^{5}SD, 8^{0}SD, 8^{0}SD, 12^{2}GF,

	Starts	1st	2nd	3rd	Win & Pl
Career Total (Turf)	1	0	1	0	867
Career Total (AW)	4	0	1	0	694

Going (Turf): Sf: 0-0 GS: 0-0 Gd: 0-0 GF: 0-1 Fm: 0-0

Distance: 5f/6f: 0-0 7f-8f: 0-1 9f-13f: 0-4 14f+: 0-0
Track : LH: 0-5 RH: 0-0 Tight: 0-3 Gall: 0-1
Aids: Bl: 0-0 Vi: 0-0 Tstrap: 0-0 Ckp: 0-0
Best Rating: 67 4/09 Newc 1m4f93y gd-fm

Modest; stays 1m4f; acts on fast ground and on Polytrack.

Smoothly Does It

(89) (43)58
8-y-o b g Efisio-Exotic Forest (Dominion)
Jim Best Chrisco Syndicate

Placings:55530020/020604012600/043240/5000/0433-0 (1463)
2009: 12⁰SD,

	Starts	1st	2nd	3rd	Win & Pl
Career Total (Turf)	28	1	4	4	11409
Career Total (AW)	7	0	0	0	0

73 8/04 Chep 1m14y E(0-70)H SFT £4052
Total win prize-money £4053

Going (Turf): Sf: 1-7 GS: 0-4 Gd: 0-7 GF: 0-10 Fm: 0-0
Distance: 5f/6f: 0-3 7f-8f: 0-4 9f-13f: 1-28 14f+: 0-0
Track : LH: 0-16 RH: 0-8 Tight: 0-17 Gall: 0-2
Aids: Bl: 0-1 Vi: 0-0 Tstrap: 0-0 Ckp: 0-0
Best Rating: 76 9/04 Chep 1m14y heavy

Modest performer; stays 1m4f; handles quick ground but goes well in soft; winning hurdler.

Smugglers Bay (IRE)

88 77
5-y-o b g Celtic Swing-Princess Mood (GER) (Muhtarram (USA))
T D Easterby C H Stevens

Placings:030/0051222443/460-500 (2315)
2009: 9⁵GF, 16⁰GS, 11⁰GF,

	Starts	1st	2nd	3rd	Win & Pl
Career Total (Turf)	19	1	3	2	10996

70 6/07 Bevl 1m100y (0-60)H G-S £2590
Total win prize-money £2591

Going (Turf): Sf: 0-4 GS: 1-3 Gd: 0-5 GF: 0-7 Fm: 0-0
Distance: 5f/6f: 0-0 7f-8f: 0-4 9f-13f: 1-12 14f+: 0-3
Track : LH: 0-6 RH: 1-11 Tight: 0-8 Gall: 0-3
Aids: Bl: 1-7 Vi: 0-0 Tstrap: 0-0 Ckp: 0-0
Best Rating: 78 9/07 Bevl 1m1f207y gd-fm

Fair sort; stays a mile plus; acts on fast and heavy ground; has worn blinkers.

Snake Skin

(93) (44)66
6-y-o ch m Golden Snake (USA)-Silken Dalliance (Rambo Dancer (CAN))
J Gallagher Adweb Ltd

Placings:0401200233O/66440300/031240350/1202400-00 (0623)
2009: 10⁰SD, 12⁰SD,

	Starts	1st	2nd	3rd	Win & Pl
Career Total (Turf)	22	3	5	2	13314
Career Total (AW)	15	0	0	3	1600

66 3/08 Wwck 1m2f188y (0-60)H SFT £2047
64 5/07 Brig 1m3f196y (0-65)H SFT £2137
52 7/05 Bevl 7f100y GD £3415
Total win prize-money £7601

Going (Turf): Sf: 2-6 GS: 0-1 Gd: 1-4 GF: 0-7 Fm: 0-4
Distance: 5f/6f: 0-3 7f-8f: 1-8 9f-13f: 2-26 14f+: 0-0
Track : LH: 2-20 RH: 1-12 Tight: 0-11 Gall: 0-1
Aids: Bl: 0-1 Vi: 0-0 Tstrap: 0-1 Ckp: 0-1
Best Rating: 66 5/08 Brig 1m3f196y gd-fm

Moderate; effective at around 1m2f-1m5f; acts on any ground.

Sneak Preview

105 98
3-y-o ch f Monsieur Bond (IRE)-Harryana (Efisio)
E S McMahon J C Fretwell

Placings:31222-2 (1085)
2009: 5²GF,

	Starts	1st	2nd	3rd	Win & Pl
Career Total (Turf)	6	1	4	1	33619

86 7/08 Nott 6f15y G-S £3885
Total win prize-money £3886

Going (Turf): Sf: 0-2 GS: 1-1 Gd: 0-1 GF: 0-2 Fm: 0-0
Distance: 5f/6f: 0-5 7f-8f: 1-1 9f-13f: 0-0 14f+: 0-0
Track : LH: 0-0 RH: 0-0 Tight: 0-0 Gall: 0-0
Aids: Bl: 0-0 Vi: 0-0 Tstrap: 0-0 Ckp: 0-0
Best Rating: 98 9/08 Ayr 6f heavy

Smart; Group 3 placed; effective over 6f; acts on fast and soft ground.

Sneem's Rock

(80) (10)
8-y-o b g Daylami (IRE)-Urchin (IRE) (Fairy King (USA))
P R Hedger P C F Racing Ltd

Placings:00/063300/0 (5015)
2009: 10⁰SD,

	Starts	1st	2nd	3rd	Win & Pl
Career Total (Turf)	1	0	0	0	
Career Total (AW)	8	0	0	2	838

Going (Turf): Sf: 0-0 GS: 0-1 Gd: 0-0 GF: 0-0 Fm: 0-0
Distance: 5f/6f: 0-0 7f-8f: 0-1 9f-13f: 0-8 14f+: 0-0
Track : LH: 0-9 RH: 0-0 Tight: 0-8 Gall: 0-0
Aids: Bl: 0-1 Vi: 0-0 Tstrap: 0-3 Ckp: 0-3
Best Rating: 59 3/05 Ling 1m2f stand

Snoozing

65(72) (18)
3-y-o b f Where Or When (IRE)-Tenpence (Bob Back (USA))
Mrs L C Jewell (M H Tompkins 1/2) Valence Racing

Placings:5000 (1046)
2009: 7⁵SD, 8⁰SD, 8⁰SD, 7⁰G,

	Starts	1st	2nd	3rd	Win & Pl
Career Total (Turf)	1	0	0	0	
Career Total (AW)	3	0	0	0	0

Going (Turf): Sf: 0-0 GS: 0-0 Gd: 0-1 GF: 0-0 Fm: 0-0
Distance: 5f/6f: 0-0 7f-8f: 0-4 9f-13f: 0-0 14f+: 0-0
Track : LH: 0-2 RH: 0-1 Tight: 0-0 Gall: 0-0
Aids: Bl: 0-0 Vi: 0-0 Tstrap: 0-1 Ckp: 0-1
Best Rating: 18 1/09 Sthl 7f stand

Snoqualmie Boy

108(98) (97)99
6-y-o b g Montjeu (IRE)-Seattle Ribbon (USA) (Seattle Dancer (USA))
T P Tate Mrs Fitri Hay

Placings:44/3130160035/544200/5064660-406204200 (7018)
2009: 9⁴GF, 10⁰GF, 10⁶GF, 12²GS, 16⁰GF, 12⁴GF, 12²G, 11⁰SD, 12⁰GS,

	Starts	1st	2nd	3rd	Win & Pl
Career Total (Turf)	30	2	3	3	82431
Career Total (AW)	4	0	0	0	1409

109 6/06 Asct 1m2f G-F £31229
88 5/06 Sals 1m1f198y (0-85)H FRM £7124
Total win prize-money £38354

Going (Turf): Sf: 0-2 GS: 0-4 Gd: 0-8 GF: 1-15 Fm: 1-1
Distance: 5f/6f: 0-0 7f-8f: 0-3 9f-13f: 2-30 14f+: 0-1
Track : LH: 0-20 RH: 2-10 Tight: 1-8 Gall: 1-17
Aids: Bl: 0-0 Vi: 0-0 Tstrap: 0-0 Ckp: 0-0
Best Rating: 111 7/06 Sand 1m2f7y gd-fm

Useful; winner in Listed company in 2006; effective at 1m2f-1m4f and acts on fast ground.

Snoqualmie Girl (IRE)

111(99) (68)103
3-y-o b f Montjeu (IRE)-Seattle Ribbon (USA) (Seattle Dancer (USA))
D R C Elsworth J C Smith

Placings:4031120-60541600 (7131)
2009: 7⁶GF, 10⁰GF, 10⁵GF, 12⁴GF, 12¹GF, 12⁶G, 12⁰G, 13⁰SD,

	Starts	1st	2nd	3rd	Win & Pl
Career Total (Turf)	14	3	1	1	68760
Career Total (AW)	1	0	0	0	

103 9/09 Ches 1m4f66y G-F £23704
97 8/08 Sals 1m G-F £17031
86 8/08 NmkJ 7f SFT £5180
Total win prize-money £45916

Going (Turf): Sf: 1-2 GS: 0-0 Gd: 0-2 GF: 2-10 Fm: 0-0
Distance: 5f/6f: 0-1 7f-8f: 2-7 9f-13f: 1-7 14f+: 0-0
Track : LH: 1-4 RH: 0-2 Tight: 1-2 Gall: 0-5
Aids: Bl: 0-0 Vi: 0-0 Tstrap: 0-0 Ckp: 0-0
Best Rating: 103 9/09 Ches 1m4f66y gd-fm

Smart; stays 1m4f and acts on most ground.

Snoqualmie Star

92 67
2-y-o ch f Galileo (IRE)-Seattle Ribbon (USA) (Seattle Dancer (USA))
D R C Elsworth J C Smith

Placings:550 (7099)
2009: 7⁵GS, 7⁵G, 8⁰G,

	Starts	1st	2nd	3rd	Win & Pl
Career Total (Turf)	3	0	0	0	0

Going (Turf): Sf: 0-0 GS: 0-1 Gd: 0-2 GF: 0-0 Fm: 0-0
Distance: 5f/6f: 0-0 7f-8f: 0-2 9f-13f: 0-1 14f+: 0-0
Track : LH: 0-0 RH: 0-0 Tight: 0-0 Gall: 0-0
Aids: Bl: 0-0 Vi: 0-0 Tstrap: 0-0 Ckp: 0-0
Best Rating: 67 8/09 NmkJ 7f good

Snow Bay

104(106) (88)82
3-y-o ch c Bahamian Bounty-Goodwood Blizzard (Inchinor)
B Smart Pinnacle Bahamian Bounty Partnership

Placings:421-410653010 (7837)

2009: 7^{4}F, 7^{1}G, 8^{0}G, 7^{6}GS, 7^{5}SD, 7^{3}SD, 7^{0}SD, 8^{1}SD, 7^{0}SS,

	Starts	1st	2nd	3rd	Win & Pl
Career Total (Turf)	7	2	1	0	8140
Career Total (AW)	5	1	0	1	5748

88 12/09 Sthl 1m (0-85)H STD £4857
82 7/09 Catt 7f (0-75)H GD £3043
70 7/08 Ayr 6f GD £3238
Total win prize-money £11139

Going (Turf): Sf: 0-0 GS: 0-2 **Gd: 2-3** GF: 0-1 Fm: 0-1
Distance: 5f/6f: 1-3 **7f-8f: 2-9** 9f-13f: 0-0 14f+: 0-0
Track : **LH: 2-6** RH: 0-2 **Tight: 1-4** Gall: 0-0
Aids: Bl: 0-0 Vi: 0-1 Tstrap: 0-0 Ckp: 0-0
Best Rating: **88** 12/09 Sthl 1m stand

Fair; effective over 7f-1m; acts on good ground and on Fibresand.

Snow Dancer (IRE)

104(104) (78)72
5-y-o b m Desert Style (IRE)-Bella Vie (IRE) (Sadler's Wells (USA))
H A McWilliams Mrs L Wohlers

Placings:323**622/434**013400201/00056325**004-**
6122030022220**3023156** **(7848)**
2009: 12^{6}SD, 9^{1}SD, 9^{2}SD, 9^{2}SD, 9^{0}GF, 9^{3}GF, 10^{0}GS, 9^{0}GF, 10^{2}GF, 9^{2}GF, 9^{2}GF, 10^{2}G, 9^{0}G, 8^{3}GF, 8^{0}GF, 9^{2}SD, 9^{3}SD, 9^{1}SD, 9^{5}SF, 9^{6}SD,

	Starts	1st	2nd	3rd	Win & Pl
Career Total (Turf)	32	2	7	6	22152
Career Total (AW)	17	2	5	2	11978

76 11/09 Wolv 1m1f103y (0-85)H STD £5180
67 1/09 Wolv 1m1f103y (0-55)H STD £2047
72 10/07 Pont 1m4y GD £5181
71 5/07 Bevl 1m100y (0-70)H GD £3562
Total win prize-money £15972

Going (Turf): Sf: 0-4 GS: 0-4 **Gd: 2-11** GF: 0-13 Fm: 0-0
Distance: 5f/6f: 0-2 7f-8f: 0-3 **9f-13f: 4-44** 14f+: 0-0
Track : **LH: 3-35** RH: 1-12 **Tight: 2-25** Gall: 0-2
Aids: Bl: 0-2 Vi: 0-0 Tstrap: 1-19 Ckp: 1-19
Best Rating: **78** 12/09 Wolv 1m1f103y stand

Modest; stays 1m2f; acts on fast and soft ground; also goes on Polytrack; has worn cheekpieces.

Snow Fairy (IRE)

103(100) (84)103
2-y-o b f Intikhab (USA)-Woodland Dream (IRE) (Charnwood Forest (IRE))
E A L Dunlop Anamoine Ltd

Placings:312430 **(7033)**
2009: 6^{3}GF, 6^{1}SD, 6^{2}G, 7^{4}G, 7^{3}G, 7^{0}S,

	Starts	1st	2nd	3rd	Win & Pl
Career Total (Turf)	5	0	1	2	12694
Career Total (AW)	1	1	0	0	2388

84 7/09 Ling 6f STD £2388
Total win prize-money £2388

Going (Turf): **Sf: 0-1 GS: 0-0 Gd: 0-3 GF: 0-1 Fm: 0-0**
Distance: **5f/6f: 1-2** 7f-8f: 0-4 9f-13f: 0-0 14f+: 0-0
Track : **LH: 1-1** RH: 0-1 **Tight: 1-1** Gall: 0-0
Aids: Bl: 0-0 Vi: 0-0 Tstrap: 0-0 Ckp: 0-0
Best Rating: **103** 8/09 Gdwd 7f good

Very useful; Group 3 placed; stays 7f; acts on Polytrack and good ground.

Snowberry Hill (USA)

98(105) (64)63
6-y-o b g Woodman (USA)-Class Skipper (USA) (Skip Trial (USA))
Lucinda Featherstone J Roundtree

Placings:0550/00**006/6141/402016-206**200066314 **(6025)**
2009: 16^{2}SD, 14^{0}SD, 13^{6}SD, 17^{2}GF, 16^{0}G, 17^{0}G, 16^{0}S, 16^{6}SD, 15^{6}GS, 16^{3}GF, 16^{1}SD, 13^{4}SD,

	Starts	1st	2nd	3rd	Win & Pl
Career Total (Turf)	13	0	1	1	1266
Career Total (AW)	18	4	2	0	9767

58 9/09 Wolv 2m119y (0-60)H STD £2388
62 12/08 Wolv 1m5f194y (0-65)H STD £2307
63 1/08 Kemp 2m (0-65)H STD £2047
57 11/07 Wolv 1m5f194y (0-65)H STD £1648
Total win prize-money £8392

Going (Turf): **Sf: 0-2 GS: 0-2 Gd: 0-3 GF: 0-6 Fm: 0-0**
Distance: 5f/6f: 0-1 7f-8f: 0-3 9f-13f: 0-6 **14f+: 4-21**
Track : **LH: 3-21** RH: 1-6 **Tight: 3-18** Gall: 0-1
Aids: Bl: 0-1 Vi: 0-0 Tstrap: 0-2 Ckp: 0-2
Best Rating: **68** 8/05 Ches 7f2y gd-fm

Moderate; stays 2m and acts on Polytrack; has worn blinkers and cheekpieces.

Snowed Under

95 (79)86
8-y-o gr g Most Welcome-Snowy Mantle (Siberian Express (USA))
J D Bethell Mrs G Fane

Placings:0/555001630/0211321500/230154600/60310440/
41300100-1030 **(4426)**
2009: 9^{1}GF, 9^{0}G, 9^{3}GF, 9^{0}S,

	Starts	1st	2nd	3rd	Win & Pl
Career Total (Turf)	48	9	3	5	58154
Career Total (AW)	1	0	0	1	1166

83 5/09 Bevl 1m1f207y (0-80)H G-F £4759
86 7/08 Leic 1m1f218y (0-80)H G-F £4731
81 5/08 Bevl 1m1f207y (0-80)H GD £4209
81 8/07 Leic 1m1f218y (0-80)H G-S £6309
88 6/06 Leic 1m1f218y (0-75)H G-F £5362
81 8/05 Leic 1m1f218y (0-85)H GD £6913
75 6/05 Leic 1m1f218y (0-75)H G-F £5652
69 5/05 Leic 1m1f218y (0-70)H G-F £4807
64 8/04 Bevl 1m1f207yF(0-55)H G-S £3412
Total win prize-money £46157

Going (Turf): Sf: 0-6 GS: 2-9 Gd: 2-11 **GF: 5-20** Fm: 0-2
Distance: 5f/6f: 0-0 7f-8f: 0-1 **9f-13f: 9-48** 14f+: 0-0
Track : LH: 0-14 **RH: 9-34** Tight: 0-7 Gall: 0-5
Aids: Bl: 0-0 Vi: 0-0 Tstrap: 0-0 Ckp: 0-0
Best Rating: **88** 6/06 Leic 1m1f218y gd-fm

Fair; effective over 1m2f-1m4f; acts on most types of ground; has a very good record at Leicester.

Snowy Indian

(94) (65)74
4-y-o b f Indian Ridge-Snow Princess (IRE) (Ela-Mana-Mou)
M Botti Mrs R J Jacobs

Placings:363/0530-06 **(0512)**
2009: 8^{0}SD, 8^{6}SD,

	Starts	1st	2nd	3rd	Win & Pl
Career Total (Turf)	6	0	0	2	1541
Career Total (AW)	3	0	0	1	482

Going (Turf): **Sf: 0-1 GS: 0-2 Gd: 0-1 GF: 0-2 Fm: 0-0**
Distance: 5f/6f: 0-0 7f-8f: 0-2 9f-13f: 0-7 14f+: 0-0
Track : LH: 0-7 RH: 0-1 Tight: 0-3 Gall: 0-3
Aids: Bl: 0-0 Vi: 0-0 Tstrap: 0-1 Ckp: 0-1
Best Rating: **74** 9/07 Sals 6f212y gd-fm

Modest; stays 1m2f; acts on fast ground.

So Bazaar (IRE)

93 65
2-y-o b g Xaar-Nature Girl (USA) (Green Dancer (USA))
G A Swinbank Chris Tremewan

Placings:3555 **(6096)**
2009: 6^{3}GF, 7^{5}GS, 5^{5}G, 5^{5}GF,

	Starts	1st	2nd	3rd	Win & Pl
Career Total (Turf)	4	0	0	1	433

Going (Turf): **Sf: 0-0 GS: 0-1 Gd: 0-1 GF: 0-2 Fm: 0-0**
Distance: 5f/6f: 0-3 7f-8f: 0-1 9f-13f: 0-0 14f+: 0-0
Track : LH: 0-1 RH: 0-0 Tight: 0-1 Gall: 0-0
Aids: Bl: 0-0 Vi: 0-0 Tstrap: 0-0 Ckp: 0-0
Best Rating: **65** 7/09 Ayr 6f gd-fm

Modest; stays 6f; acts on fast ground.

So Blissful (IRE)

100(88) (60)78
3-y-o b f Cape Cross (IRE)-Royal Devotion (IRE) (Sadler's Wells (USA))
Mrs L Wadham (T G Mills 8/8) Mrs Johnny Eddis

Placings:610064 **(6761)**
2009: 8^{6}SD, 7^{1}G, 7^{0}GF, 8^{0}G, 8^{6}G, 9^{4}G,

	Starts	1st	2nd	3rd	Win & Pl
Career Total (Turf)	5	1	0	0	3332
Career Total (AW)	1	0	0	0	0

74 5/09 Gdwd 7f GD £3115
Total win prize-money £3116

Going (Turf): Sf: 0-0 GS: 0-0 **Gd: 1-4** GF: 0-1 Fm: 0-0
Distance: 5f/6f: 0-0 **7f-8f: 1-4** 9f-13f: 0-2 14f+: 0-0
Track : LH: 0-3 **RH: 1-2** Tight: 0-2 Gall: 0-0
Aids: Bl: 0-0 Vi: 0-0 Tstrap: 0-0 Ckp: 0-0
Best Rating: **78** 7/09 Bath 1m5y good

Fair; stays 7f and acts on good ground.

So Glamorous

93 53
4-y-o b f Diktat-Gena Ivor (USA) (Sir Ivor (USA))
C F Wall Mervyn Ayers

Placings:0/0600 **(6926)**
2009: 7^{0}GS, 6^{6}G, 7^{0}GF, 6^{0}GF,

	Starts	1st	2nd	3rd	Win & Pl
Career Total (Turf)	5	0	0	0	0

Going (Turf): **Sf: 0-0 GS: 0-2 Gd: 0-1 GF: 0-2 Fm: 0-0**
Distance: 5f/6f: 0-2 7f-8f: 0-3 9f-13f: 0-0 14f+: 0-0
Track : LH: 0-0 RH: 0-0 Tight: 0-0 Gall: 0-1
Aids: Bl: 0-0 Vi: 0-0 Tstrap: 0-0 Ckp: 0-0
Best Rating: **53** 8/09 Ling 6f good

So Sublime

71(96) (69)45
4-y-o b g Bertolini (USA)-Petalite (Petong)
M C Chapman Fools Who Dream

Placings:10000000600-00042000000 (2456)

2009: 7^{0}SD, 7^{0}SD, 7^{0}SD, 5^{4}SD, 5^{2}SD, 6^{0}SS, 5^{0}SD, 9^{0}SD, 7^{0}SD, 9^{0}GF, 6^{0}GF,

	Starts	1st	2nd	3rd	Win & Pl
Career Total (Turf)	8	0	0	0	
Career Total (AW)	15	1	1	0	2256

69 1/08 Sthl 7f STD £1774

Total win prize-money £1775

Going (Turf): Sf: 0-0 GS: 0-4 Gd: 0-1 GF: 0-3 Fm: 0-0
Distance: 5f/6f: 0-5 7f-8f: 1-13 9f-13f: 0-5 14f+: 0-0
Track : LH: 1-20 RH: 0-1 Tight: 0-9 Gall: 0-0
Aids: Bl: 0-11 Vi: 0-1 Tstrap: 0-0 Ckp: 0-0
Best Rating: 69 1/08 Sthl 7f stand

Plating-class; effective at 5f; acts on POlytrack; has worn blinkers.

So Surreal (IRE)

95(94) (73)68

2-y-o b f Avonbridge-Secret Circle (Magic Ring (IRE))
G L Moore R Henderson & B Cunningham

Placings:63000105 (7551)

2009: 5^{6}GF, 6^{3}SD, 6^{0}G, 6^{0}GF, 6^{0}G, 5^{1}SF, 6^{0}SD, 7^{5}SD,

	Starts	1st	2nd	3rd	Win & Pl
Career Total (Turf)	4	0	0	0	0
Career Total (AW)	4	1	0	1	2918

73 10/09 Wolv 5f216y SF £2388

Total win prize-money £2388

Going (Turf): Sf: 0-0 GS: 0-0 Gd: 0-2 GF: 0-2 Fm: 0-0
Distance: 5f/6f: 1-6 7f-8f: 0-2 9f-13f: 0-0 14f+: 0-0
Track : LH: 1-3 RH: 0-1 Tight: 1-3 Gall: 0-2
Aids: Bl: 1-4 Vi: 0-0 Tstrap: 0-0 Ckp: 0-0
Best Rating: 73 10/09 Wolv 5f216y std-fst

Fair; suited by 6f and Polytrack.

Soap Wars

97 (95)80

4-y-o b g Acclamation-Gooseberry Pie (Green Desert (USA))
M Halford William Durkan

Placings:043335/100203216-10200405 (7566a)

2009: 6^{1}SD, 6^{0}GF, 6^{2}SD, 6^{0}SD, 6^{0}G, 6^{4}SD, 6^{0}SD, 6^{5}SD,

	Starts	1st	2nd	3rd	Win & Pl
Career Total (Turf)	11	0	1	2	5537
Career Total (AW)	12	3	2	2	42967

94 4/09 Dund 6f (60-100)H STD £14220
87 11/08 Dund 6f STD £6351
89 4/08 Dund 6f STD £6351

Total win prize-money £26923

Going (Turf): Sf: 0-2 GS: 0-0 Gd: 0-4 GF: 0-3 Fm: 0-0
Distance: 5f/6f: 3-23 7f-8f: 0-0 9f-13f: 0-0 14f+: 0-0
Track : LH: 3-16 RH: 0-0 Tight: 0-0 Gall: 0-0
Aids: Bl: 0-0 Vi: 0-0 Tstrap: 0-4 Ckp: 0-4
Best Rating: 95 10/09 Dund 6f stand

Very useful; effective over 6f; acts on fast ground and on Polytrack.

Soba Jones

(102) (64)41

12-y-o b g Emperor Jones (USA)-Soba (Most Secret)
J Balding R L Crowe

Placings:3/66023431533350/100250150020/00110000030/01544005000052/124325654250506/24056234040300041/02511434554/2424110540/463511100-60060 (0746)

2009: 6^{6}SS, 6^{0}SD, 6^{0}SS, 6^{6}SD, 6^{0}SD,

	Starts	1st	2nd	3rd	Win & Pl
Career Total (Turf)	60	5	5	7	37606
Career Total (AW)	58	10	7	4	35542

64 2/08 Sthl 6f SS £1774
63 2/08 Sthl 6f (0-60) SS £1774
64 2/08 Sthl 6f (0-55)H STD £1911
61 3/07 Sthl 6f STD £2184
61 2/07 Sthl 6f (0-55)H STD £1706
71 3/06 Sthl 6f STD £2388
69 2/06 Sthl 6f (0-55)H STD £2047
62 1/06 Sthl 6f STD £2388
81 1/04 Wolv 6f E(0-75)H SLW £3386
83 2/03 Sthl 6f E(0-75)H SLW £3341
85 6/02 Haml 6f5y D(0-80)H HVY £4368
77 6/02 Haml 6f5y E(0-70) HVY £3737
77 8/01 Catt 5f212y E(0-70) G-F £3332
73 6/01 Hayd 5f D(0-80)H GD £4394
61 7/00 Newc 5f D GD £3328

Total win prize-money £42065

Going (Turf): Sf: 2-8 GS: 0-8 Gd: 1-18 GF: 1-21 Fm: 0-4
Distance: 5f/6f: 12-108 7f-8f: 2-9 9f-13f: 0-0 14f+: 0-0
Track : LH: 11-64 RH: 0-3 Tight: 2-13 Gall: 0-1
Aids: Bl: 1-14 Vi: 0-0 Tstrap: 0-2 Ckp: 0-2
Best Rating: 85 6/02 Haml 6f5y heavy

Moderate handicapper/claimer; best over 6f; three-time winner on the All Weather in 2006; has not won on turf since 2002; acts on Fibresand and most ground on turf.

Soccer (USA)

97(94) (92)87

2-y-o ch c Van Nistelrooy (USA)-Bonita Gail (USA) (Geiger Counter (USA))
Tom Dascombe Findlay & Bloom

Placings:1242030 (6550)

2009: 5^{1}SD, 5^{2}GF, 5^{4}G, 5^{2}SD, 5^{0}G, 5^{3}F, 5^{0}G,

	Starts	1st	2nd	3rd	Win & Pl
Career Total (Turf)	5	0	1	1	4896
Career Total (AW)	2	1	1	0	3693

84 4/09 Ling 5f STD £2729

Total win prize-money £2730

Going (Turf): Sf: 0-0 GS: 0-0 Gd: 0-3 GF: 0-1 Fm: 0-1
Distance: 5f/6f: 1-7 7f-8f: 0-0 9f-13f: 0-0 14f+: 0-0
Track : LH: 1-3 RH: 0-0 Tight: 1-2 Gall: 0-2
Aids: Bl: 0-0 Vi: 0-0 Tstrap: 0-0 Ckp: 0-0
Best Rating: 92 7/09 Ling 5f stand

Very useful; suited by 5f; acts on fast ground and Polytrack; has worn a tongue tie.

Soccerjackpot (USA)

95(109) (100)82

5-y-o b g Mizzen Mast (USA)-Rahbaby (USA) (Rahy (USA))
C G Cox sportaracing.com & George Houghton

Placings:221354/00-110435 (7431)

2009: 8^{1}SD, 8^{1}SD, 8^{0}GF, 7^{4}G, 8^{3}SD, 7^{5}SD,

	Starts	1st	2nd	3rd	Win & Pl
Career Total (Turf)	9	1	2	1	9587
Career Total (AW)	5	2	0	1	11608

100 3/09 Wolv 1m141y (0-85)H STD £5504
99 3/09 Kemp 1m (0-85)H STD £4727
85 5/07 Bevl 7f100y GD £3238

Total win prize-money £13471

Going (Turf): Sf: 0-0 GS: 0-0 Gd: 1-4 GF: 0-5 Fm: 0-0
Distance: 5f/6f: 0-2 7f-8f: 2-11 9f-13f: 1-1 14f+: 0-0
Track : LH: 1-3 RH: 2-4 Tight: 1-3 Gall: 0-0
Aids: Bl: 0-0 Vi: 0-0 Tstrap: 0-0 Ckp: 0-0
Best Rating: 100 3/09 Wolv 1m141y stand

Very useful; effective over 7f-1m; acts on a sound surface and on Polytrack.

Social Grace

91 73

2-y-o gr f Pastoral Pursuits-Zilkha (Petong)
D H Brown Norton Common Farm Racing

Placings:24210000060 (6819)

2009: 5^{2}GF, 5^{4}GF, 5^{2}G, 5^{1}GF, 5^{0}GS, 5^{0}GS, 5^{0}GF, 5^{0}GF, 5^{0}GF, 5^{6}G, 7^{0}GF,

	Starts	1st	2nd	3rd	Win & Pl
Career Total (Turf)	11	1	2	0	5974

73 7/09 Ches 5f16y G-F £4047

Total win prize-money £4047

Going (Turf): Sf: 0-0 GS: 0-2 Gd: 0-2 GF: 1-7 Fm: 0-0
Distance: 5f/6f: 1-10 7f-8f: 0-1 9f-13f: 0-0 14f+: 0-0
Track : LH: 1-2 RH: 0-0 Tight: 1-2 Gall: 0-0
Aids: Bl: 0-0 Vi: 0-0 Tstrap: 0-2 Ckp: 0-2
Best Rating: 73 7/09 Ches 5f16y gd-fm

Modest; effective at 5f; acts on good/fast ground.

Social Rhythm

106(103) (71)65

5-y-o b m Beat All (USA)-Highly Sociable (Puissance)
A C Whillans Mrs L M Whillans

Placings:13322/6105030/3650000604-16513 (7173)

2009: 8^{1}G, 8^{6}GS, 9^{5}G, 8^{1}GF, 9^{3}S,

	Starts	1st	2nd	3rd	Win & Pl
Career Total (Turf)	15	3	0	2	9672
Career Total (AW)	13	1	2	3	7092

65 10/09 Ayr 1m (0-65)H G-F £2729
59 8/09 Muss 1m (0-65)H GD £2590
81 4/07 Sthl 6f (0-70)H G-F £3071
70 8/06 Wolv 5f216y STD £3238

Total win prize-money £11630

Going (Turf): Sf: 0-2 GS: 0-3 Gd: 1-6 GF: 2-4 Fm: 0-0
Distance: 5f/6f: 2-11 7f-8f: 2-12 9f-13f: 0-5 14f+: 0-0
Track : LH: 3-16 RH: 1-11 Tight: 2-15 Gall: 0-1
Aids: Bl: 0-0 Vi: 0-0 Tstrap: 0-1 Ckp: 0-1
Best Rating: 81 4/07 Sthl 6f gd-fm

Moderate; stays 1m; acts on fast ground; also goes on Polytrack.

Society Music (IRE)

101 74

7-y-o b m Almutawakel-Society Fair (FR) (Always Fair (USA))
M Dods Mrs C M Hewitson

Placings:131360500/026112006/000335040/51042022214/000410032650-200300 (6383)

2009: 8^{2}F, 8^{0}GF, 8^{0}G, 8^{3}GF, 8^{0}GS, 8^{0}GF,

	Starts	1st	2nd	3rd	Win & Pl
Career Total (Turf)	56	7	8	6	50638

73 6/08 Haml 1m65y (0-80)H G-F £5180
79 9/07 Thsk 1m (0-85)H G-F £5181
74 5/07 Pont 1m4y (0-65)H GD £3238
83 7/05 Hayd 1m30y (0-75)H G-F £3680
81 6/05 Ayr 1m (0-80)H G-S £7013
79 6/04 Muss 7f30y E G-F £3987
79 4/04 Pont 5f E SFT £5447

Total win prize-money £33732

Going (Turf): Sf: 1-6 GS: 1-14 Gd: 1-15 **GF: 4-20** Fm: 0-1
Distance: 5f/6f: 1-5 7f-8f: 3-26 9f-13f: 3-25 14f+: 0-0
Track : **LH: 5-36** RH: 2-10 **Tight: 3-10** Gall: 0-4
Aids: Bl: 0-2 Vi: 0-0 Tstrap: 3-25 Ckp: 3-25
Best Rating: **84** 7/05 Donc 1m gd-sft

Fair sort; stays 1m; handles fast ground, but probably better suited by an easy surface; has worn cheekpieces.

Society Rock (IRE)

102 **94**
2-y-o b c Rock Of Gibraltar (IRE)-High Society (IRE) (Key Of Luck (USA))
J R Fanshawe Simon Gibson

Placings:5110 **(6478)**
2009: 7^{5}G, 6^{1}G, 6^{1}GF, 7^{0}GF,

	Starts	1st	2nd	3rd	Win & Pl
Career Total (Turf)	**4**	**2**	**0**	**0**	**148949**

94 9/09 NmkR 6f G-F £135425
79 8/09 Nott 6f15y GD £3723
Total win prize-money £139149

Going (Turf): Sf: 0-0 GS: 0-0 **Gd: 1-2 GF: 1-2** Fm: 0-0
Distance: 5f/6f: 1-1 7f-8f: 1-3 9f-13f: 0-0 14f+: 0-0
Track : LH: 0-0 RH: 0-0 Tight: 0-0 Gall: 0-0
Aids: Bl: 0-0 Vi: 0-0 Tstrap: 0-0 Ckp: 0-0
Best Rating: **94** 9/09 NmkR 6f gd-fm

Very useful; effective at 6f; acts on good and fast ground.

Society Venue

102 **80**
4-y-o b g Where Or When (IRE)-Society Rose (Saddlers' Hall (IRE))
M J Scudamore (Jedd O'Keeffe 13/10) Mr And Mrs T P Winnell

Placings:3065/32050-3321266033 **(6760)**
2009: 8^{3}F, 9^{3}GF, 10^{2}GS, 9^{1}GF, 10^{2}G, 12^{6}G, 9^{6}G, 9^{0}GS, 9^{3}G, 9^{3}G,

	Starts	1st	2nd	3rd	Win & Pl
Career Total (Turf)	**19**	**1**	**3**	**6**	**7670**

75 5/09 Carl 1m1f61y (0-65)H G-F £1942
Total win prize-money £1943

Going (Turf): Sf: 0-0 GS: 0-3 Gd: 0-8 **GF: 1-7** Fm: 0-1
Distance: 5f/6f: 0-2 7f-8f: 0-3 **9f-13f: 1-14** 14f+: 0-0
Track : LH: 0-8 **RH: 1-8** Tight: 0-6 Gall: 0-3
Aids: Bl: 0-0 Vi: 0-0 Tstrap: 0-0 Ckp: 0-0
Best Rating: **80** 6/09 Newc 1m2f32y good

Fair; stays 1m 1f; acts on fast and easy ground.

Sofia's Star

102(102) (81)**75**
4-y-o b/br g Lend A Hand-Charolles (Ajdal (USA))
S Dow P Jacobs, N Scandrett, W J Taylor

Placings:415004/**600053401512-350502** **(2807)**
2009: 7^{3}SD, 8^{5}SD, 8^{0}SD, 8^{5}GF, 8^{0}GF, 7^{2}G,

	Starts	1st	2nd	3rd	Win & Pl
Career Total (Turf)	**14**	**2**	**1**	**1**	**7827**
Career Total (AW)	**10**	**1**	**1**	**1**	**4429**

80 11/08 Kemp 7f (0-70)H STD £3238
72 10/08 Wind 1m67y (0-70)H G-S £2729
82 6/07 Gdwd 6f GD £2752
Total win prize-money £8721

Going (Turf): Sf: 0-1 **GS: 1-4 Gd: 1-3** GF: 0-6 Fm: 0-0
Distance: 5f/6f: 1-5 7f-8f: 1-15 9f-13f: 1-4 14f+: 0-0
Track : LH: 0-3 **RH: 2-16 Tight: 1-4** Gall: 0-0
Aids: Bl: 0-2 Vi: 0-0 Tstrap: 0-2 Ckp: 0-2
Best Rating: **82** 6/07 Gdwd 6f good

Fair; effective over 6f-7f; acts on good ground, on Polytrack and on Fibresand.

Sofinella (IRE)

94(96) (59)**63**
6-y-o gr m Titus Livius (FR)-Mystical Jumbo (Mystiko (USA))
A W Carroll Serafino Agodino

Placings:3150/00046**000/0066021105**/030400-24600505005 **(7100)**
2009: 5^{2}SD, 5^{4}SD, 5^{6}GF, 5^{0}G, 5^{0}HY, 5^{5}G, 5^{0}GS, 5^{5}GS, 5^{0}G, 5^{0}GS, 5^{5}G,

	Starts	1st	2nd	3rd	Win & Pl
Career Total (Turf)	**25**	**2**	**0**	**2**	**7518**
Career Total (AW)	**14**	**1**	**2**	**0**	**3418**

66 10/07 Brig 5f59y (0-65)H G-S £2266
61 9/07 Wolv 5f20y (0-50)H STD £2047
71 9/05 Ripn 5f GD £3399
Total win prize-money £7715

Going (Turf): Sf: 0-3 **GS: 1-6 Gd: 1-8** GF: 0-8 Fm: 0-0
Distance: **5f/6f: 3-39** 7f-8f: 0-0 9f-13f: 0-0 14f+: 0-0
Track : **LH: 2-15** RH: 0-4 **Tight: 1-11** Gall: 0-3
Aids: Bl: 0-0 Vi: 0-0 Tstrap: 0-1 Ckp: 0-1
Best Rating: **71** 9/05 Ripn 5f good

Moderate; effective over 5f; acts on Polytrack; likes to dominate.

Sofonisba

(80) (31)**54**
3-y-o b f Rock Of Gibraltar (IRE)-Lothlorien (USA) (Woodman (USA))
M L W Bell Marco & Sara Moretti

Placings:060-00 **(2143)**
2009: 8^{0}SD, 8^{0}SD,

	Starts	1st	2nd	3rd	Win & Pl
Career Total (Turf)	**2**	**0**	**0**	**0**	**0**
Career Total (AW)	**3**	**0**	**0**	**0**	

Going (Turf): **Sf: 0-1 GS: 0-0 Gd: 0-1 GF: 0-0 Fm: 0-0**
Distance: 5f/6f: 0-1 7f-8f: 0-3 9f-13f: 0-1 14f+: 0-0
Track : LH: 0-3 RH: 0-0 Tight: 0-1 Gall: 0-1
Aids: Bl: 0-0 Vi: 0-0 Tstrap: 0-0 Ckp: 0-0
Best Rating: **54** 10/08 Yarm 7f3y soft

Softly Killing Me

(91) (52)**56**
4-y-o b f Umistim-Slims Lady (Theatrical Charmer)
B Forsey Mrs P Bosley

Placings:034006/00 **(0874)**
2009: 8^{0}SD, 7^{0}SD,

	Starts	1st	2nd	3rd	Win & Pl
Career Total (Turf)	**5**	**0**	**0**	**1**	**1035**
Career Total (AW)	**3**	**0**	**0**	**0**	

Going (Turf): **Sf: 0-2 GS: 0-2 Gd: 0-0 GF: 0-1 Fm: 0-0**
Distance: 5f/6f: 0-0 7f-8f: 0-6 9f-13f: 0-2 14f+: 0-0
Track : LH: 0-4 RH: 0-2 Tight: 0-2 Gall: 0-0
Aids: Bl: 0-0 Vi: 0-1 Tstrap: 0-0 Ckp: 0-0
Best Rating: **56** 7/07 Wwck 7f26y soft

Softly Spoken

87 **49**
2-y-o b f Forzando-Star Of Flanders (Puissance)
A W Carroll D Lowe

Placings:5600 **(5992)**
2009: 5^{5}GF, 5^{6}G, 5^{0}G, 5^{0}S,

	Starts	1st	2nd	3rd	Win & Pl
Career Total (Turf)	**4**	**0**	**0**	**0**	**0**

Going (Turf): **Sf: 0-1 GS: 0-0 Gd: 0-2 GF: 0-1 Fm: 0-0**
Distance: 5f/6f: 0-4 7f-8f: 0-0 9f-13f: 0-0 14f+: 0-0
Track : LH: 0-0 RH: 0-0 Tight: 0-0 Gall: 0-1
Aids: Bl: 0-0 Vi: 0-0 Tstrap: 0-0 Ckp: 0-0
Best Rating: **49** 7/09 Wind 5f10y good

Sohcahtoa (IRE)

102(103) (100)**96**
3-y-o b g Val Royal (FR)-Stroke Of Six (IRE) (Woodborough (USA))
R Hannon Mrs Sue Brendish

Placings:511440-**305545005** **(7226)**
2009: 9^{3}SD, 8^{0}SD, 8^{5}G, 8^{5}GF, 7^{4}GF, 8^{5}G, 8^{0}S, 10^{0}S, 10^{5}SD,

	Starts	1st	2nd	3rd	Win & Pl
Career Total (Turf)	**12**	**2**	**0**	**0**	**30696**
Career Total (AW)	**3**	**0**	**0**	**1**	**7879**

92 8/08 Gdwd 7f G-F £12952
84 6/08 Gdwd 6f GD £3561
Total win prize-money £16514

Going (Turf): Sf: 0-3 GS: 0-0 **Gd: 1-4 GF: 1-5** Fm: 0-0
Distance: 5f/6f: 1-1 7f-8f: 1-10 9f-13f: 0-4 14f+: 0-0
Track : LH: 0-1 **RH: 1-8** Tight: 0-0 Gall: 0-1
Aids: Bl: 0-0 Vi: 0-0 Tstrap: 0-0 Ckp: 0-0
Best Rating: **100** 3/09 Kemp 1m1f stand

Very useful; effective up to 1m1f; acts on good, fast ground; goes on Polytrack.

Soho Secrets

82(81) (24)**62**
3-y-o b f Lucky Owners (NZ)-Meritxell (IRE) (Thatching)
M Johnston Triplin Racing

Placings:055 **(3061)**
2009: 7^{0}SD, 8^{5}F, 8^{5}GF,

	Starts	1st	2nd	3rd	Win & Pl
Career Total (Turf)	**2**	**0**	**0**	**0**	**0**
Career Total (AW)	**1**	**0**	**0**	**0**	

Going (Turf): **Sf: 0-0 GS: 0-0 Gd: 0-0 GF: 0-1 Fm: 0-1**
Distance: 5f/6f: 0-0 7f-8f: 0-2 9f-13f: 0-1 14f+: 0-0
Track : LH: 0-2 RH: 0-1 Tight: 0-2 Gall: 0-0
Aids: Bl: 0-0 Vi: 0-0 Tstrap: 0-0 Ckp: 0-0
Best Rating: **62** 5/09 Nott 1m75y firm

Soho Theatre

85(90) (72)**69**
2-y-o b c Indian Ridge-Costa Brava (IRE) (Sadler's Wells (USA))
D R C Elsworth G B Partnership

Placings:0530 **(7095)**
2009: 7^{0}G, 7^{5}GF, 7^{3}SS, 8^{0}G,

	Starts	1st	2nd	3rd	Win & Pl
Career Total (Turf)	**3**	**0**	**0**	**0**	**0**
Career Total (AW)	**1**	**0**	**0**	**1**	**578**

Going (Turf): **Sf: 0-0 GS: 0-0 Gd: 0-2 GF: 0-1 Fm: 0-0**
Distance: 5f/6f: 0-0 7f-8f: 0-3 9f-13f: 0-1 14f+: 0-0
Track : LH: 0-2 RH: 0-0 Tight: 0-1 Gall: 0-0
Aids: Bl: 0-0 Vi: 0-0 Tstrap: 0-0 Ckp: 0-0
Best Rating: **72** 10/09 Ling 7f std-slw

Fair; stays 7f and acts on Polytrack.

Sohraab

111 (77)**108**

5-y-o b g Erhaab (USA)-Riverine (Risk Me (FR))
H Morrison Pangfield Racing

Placings:6/**611222**22222020/101000-214042200 **(6522a)**
2009: 5^{2}GS, 5^{1}GF, 6^{4}GF, 6^{0}GF, 5^{4}GF, 6^{2}G, 5^{2}GF, 5^{0}GF, 5^{0}G,

	Starts	1st	2nd	3rd	Win & Pl
Career Total (Turf)	**23**	**3**	**8**	**0**	**69288**
Career Total (AW)	**5**	**2**	**2**	**0**	**7877**

106	5/09	Ches	5f16y	(0-105)H	G-F	£13877
102	7/08	NmkJ	5f	(0-95)H	G-F	£9066
101	6/08	York	5f	(0-95)H	G-F	£8289
75	3/07	Sthl	6f	(0-70)H	STD	£3071
61	2/07	Ling	5f		STD	£3071

Total win prize-money £37375

Going (Turf): Sf: 0-2 GS: 0-2 Gd: 0-6 **GF: 3-13** Fm: 0-0
Distance: **5f/6f: 5-26** 7f-8f: 0-2 9f-13f: 0-0 14f+: 0-0
Track : **LH: 3-7** RH: 0-1 **Tight: 2-6** Gall: 0-3
Aids: Bl: 0-0 Vi: 0-0 Tstrap: 0-0 Ckp: 0-0
Best Rating: **108** 8/09 Ches 6f18y good

Smart; suited by 5f-6f; acts on most ground on turf; goes on sand.

Sokoke

84 (2)**25**

8-y-o ch g Compton Place-Sally Green (IRE) (Common Grounds)
D A Nolan Miss M McFadyen-Murray

Placings:2300**00**/0000/5600/000000/0000000-00 **(3853)**
2009: 5^{0}GF, 5^{0}GF,

	Starts	1st	2nd	3rd	Win & Pl
Career Total (Turf)	**27**	**0**	**1**	**1**	**1348**
Career Total (AW)	**2**	**0**	**0**	**0**	

Going (Turf): **Sf: 0-4 GS: 0-3 Gd: 0-7 GF: 0-12 Fm: 0-1**
Distance: 5f/6f: 0-27 7f-8f: 0-2 9f-13f: 0-0 14f+: 0-0
Track : LH: 0-3 RH: 0-0 Tight: 0-1 Gall: 0-1
Aids: Bl: 0-0 Vi: 0-0 Tstrap: 0-2 Ckp: 0-2
Best Rating: **73** 5/07 Muss 5f gd-fm

Solar Graphite (IRE)

105 **81**

3-y-o b g Rock Of Gibraltar (IRE)-Solar Crystal (IRE) (Alzao (USA))
Robert Alan Hennessy (J L Dunlop 21/10) David Eiffe

Placings:606-132456 **(6936)**
2009: 9^{1}G, 11^{3}GF, 12^{2}GS, 12^{4}G, 12^{5}G, 11^{6}G,

	Starts	1st	2nd	3rd	Win & Pl
Career Total (Turf)	**9**	**1**	**1**	**1**	**6249**

71	4/09	Folk	1m1f149y	(0-75)H	GD	£3070

Total win prize-money £3071

Going (Turf): Sf: 0-0 GS: 0-2 **Gd: 1-4** GF: 0-3 Fm: 0-0
Distance: 5f/6f: 0-0 7f-8f: 0-3 **9f-13f: 1-6** 14f+: 0-0
Track : LH: 0-1 **RH: 1-5 Tight: 1-4** Gall: 0-2
Aids: Bl: 0-0 Vi: 0-0 Tstrap: 0-0 Ckp: 0-0
Best Rating: **81** 5/09 Gdwd 1m3f gd-fm

Fair; stays 1m3f; acts on good and faster ground.

Solar Spirit (IRE)

107(97) (76)**90**

4-y-o b g Invincible Spirit (IRE)-Misaayef (USA) (Swain (IRE))
J J Quinn Christopher James Allan

Placings:2/1430303-233053506**5** **(6776)**
2009: 6^{2}G, 6^{3}GF, 6^{3}GF, 5^{0}GS, 6^{5}GS, 5^{3}S, 6^{5}G, 6^{0}G, 6^{6}GF, 7^{5}SD,

	Starts	1st	2nd	3rd	Win & Pl
Career Total (Turf)	**17**	**1**	**2**	**6**	**13609**
Career Total (AW)	**1**	**0**	**0**	**0**	**0**

85	4/08	Pont	6f	G-S	£3238

Total win prize-money £3238

Going (Turf): Sf: 0-2 **GS: 1-5** Gd: 0-3 GF: 0-6 Fm: 0-1
Distance: **5f/6f: 1-13** 7f-8f: 0-5 9f-13f: 0-0 14f+: 0-0
Track : **LH: 1-4** RH: 0-1 Tight: 0-1 Gall: 0-0
Aids: Bl: 0-0 Vi: 0-1 Tstrap: 0-2 Ckp: 0-2
Best Rating: **90** 5/09 Donc 6f good

Useful, effective at 6f-7f; acts on fast and easy ground.

Solas Alainn (IRE)

104 **77**

4-y-o b g Fantastic Light (USA)-Littlepacepaddocks (IRE) (Accordion)
M Johnston Mrs Joan Keaney

Placings:550**P**-330463330 **(4742)**
2009: 12^{3}F, 14^{3}GF, 12^{0}GS, 16^{4}G, 12^{6}GF, 12^{3}GF, 13^{3}G, 14^{3}G, 14^{0}G,

	Starts	1st	2nd	3rd	Win & Pl
Career Total (Turf)	**12**	**0**	**0**	**5**	**4006**
Career Total (AW)	**1**	**0**	**0**	**0**	

Going (Turf): **Sf: 0-1 GS: 0-1 Gd: 0-5 GF: 0-4 Fm: 0-1**
Distance: 5f/6f: 0-0 7f-8f: 0-0 9f-13f: 0-7 14f+: 0-6
Track : LH: 0-7 RH: 0-6 Tight: 0-6 Gall: 0-3
Aids: Bl: 0-4 Vi: 0-1 Tstrap: 0-0 Ckp: 0-0
Best Rating: **77** 4/09 Hayd 1m6f gd-fm

Modest; stays 1m6f; acts on good/fast ground; has worn blinkers.

Soldier Soldier

73 **5**

3-y-o ch g Tobougg (IRE)-Bijan (IRE) (Mukaddamah (USA))
J R Jenkins The Soldier Trio

Placings:0-0050 **(5972)**
2009: 7^{0}G, 8^{0}GF, 7^{5}GF, 7^{0}GF,

	Starts	1st	2nd	3rd	Win & Pl
Career Total (Turf)	**5**	**0**	**0**	**0**	**0**

Going (Turf): **Sf: 0-0 GS: 0-1 Gd: 0-1 GF: 0-3 Fm: 0-0**
Distance: 5f/6f: 0-0 7f-8f: 0-4 9f-13f: 0-1 14f+: 0-0
Track : LH: 0-0 RH: 0-0 Tight: 0-0 Gall: 0-0
Aids: Bl: 0-0 Vi: 0-1 Tstrap: 0-0 Ckp: 0-0
Best Rating: **5** 9/09 Yarm 7f3y gd-fm

Sole Power

102 (92)**92**

2-y-o b g Kyllachy-Demerger (USA) (Distant View (USA))
Edward Lynam Mrs S Power

Placings:3230**14** **(7446a)**
2009: 6^{3}Y, 5^{2}HY, 6^{3}GF, 5^{0}GS, **5**^{1}SD, **6**^{4}SD,

	Starts	1st	2nd	3rd	Win & Pl
Career Total (Turf)	**4**	**0**	**1**	**2**	**39239**
Career Total (AW)	**2**	**1**	**0**	**0**	**9714**

92	11/09	Dund	5f	STD	£9056

Total win prize-money £9057

Going (Turf): **Sf: 0-1 GS: 0-1 Gd: 0-0 GF: 0-1 Fm: 0-0**
Distance: **5f/6f: 1-6** 7f-8f: 0-0 9f-13f: 0-0 14f+: 0-0
Track : **LH: 1-2** RH: 0-0 Tight: 0-0 Gall: 0-0
Aids: Bl: 0-0 Vi: 0-0 Tstrap: 0-0 Ckp: 0-0
Best Rating: **92** 11/09 Dund 5f stand

Useful; Listed placed; stays 6f; acts on any ground.

Solemn

103(102) (81)**76**

4-y-o b g Pivotal-Pious (Bishop Of Cashel)
J M Bradley E A Hayward

Placings:03/04000000006-011211345212 **(7269)**
2009: 5^{0}G, 5^{1}G, 5^{1}GF, 5^{2}GF, 5^{1}S, 5^{1}GF, 5^{3}GF, 5^{4}G, 6^{5}G, 6^{2}GS, 5^{1}S, **5**^{2}SD,

	Starts	1st	2nd	3rd	Win & Pl
Career Total (Turf)	**16**	**5**	**2**	**1**	**14608**
Career Total (AW)	**8**	**0**	**1**	**1**	**2168**

76	10/09	Nott	5f13y	(0-65)H	SFT	£2047
74	8/09	Wind	5f10y	(0-70)H	G-F	£2729
69	7/09	Chep	5f16y	(0-70)H	SFT	£2914
67	7/09	Bevl	5f	(0-65)H	G-F	£2590
58	6/09	Chep	5f16y		GD	£2047

Total win prize-money £12328

Going (Turf): **Sf: 2-3** GS: 0-3 Gd: 1-5 **GF: 2-5** Fm: 0-0
Distance: **5f/6f: 5-21** 7f-8f: 0-3 9f-13f: 0-0 14f+: 0-0
Track : LH: 0-8 RH: 0-0 Tight: 0-3 **Gall: 1-5**
Aids: **Bl: 5-13** Vi: 0-0 Tstrap: 0-2 Ckp: 0-2
Best Rating: **81** 11/09 Sthl 5f stand

Fair; suited by 5f and acts on most types of ground; has worn blinkers and cheekpieces.

Solent Ridge (IRE)

91(105) (80)**80**

4-y-o b g Namid-Carrozzina (Vettori (IRE))
J S Moore Chris P Dineen

Placings:60**2311566/6**00060**0-4341**0**0**0600 **(6370)**
2009: 8^{4}SD, 8^{3}SD, 8^{4}SD, 8^{1}SD, 8^{0}GF, 8^{0}SD, 8^{0}GF, 9^{6}F, 8^{0}G, 8^{0}SD,

	Starts	1st	2nd	3rd	Win & Pl
Career Total (Turf)	**13**	**1**	**0**	**0**	**3194**
Career Total (AW)	**13**	**2**	**1**	**2**	**8267**

80	3/09	Ling	1m	(0-75)H	STD	£2900
87	8/07	Ling	7f		STD	£2388
80	8/07	Chep	6f16y		G-F	£2914

Total win prize-money £8204

Going (Turf): Sf: 0-1 GS: 0-1 Gd: 0-4 **GF: 1-6** Fm: 0-1
Distance: 5f/6f: 0-2 **7f-8f: 3-20** 9f-13f: 0-4 14f+: 0-0
Track : **LH: 2-12** RH: 0-4 **Tight: 2-10** Gall: 0-1
Aids: Bl: 0-1 Vi: 0-0 Tstrap: 1-6 Ckp: 1-6
Best Rating: **92** 5/08 Colo 1m good

Fair; effective over 6f-1m; acts on fast ground; goes on

Polytrack; has wornblinkers, cheekpieces and a tongue tie; likes to race prominently.

Solicitor

92(97) (83)**72**

2-y-o ch c Halling (USA)-Tolzey (USA) (Rahy (USA))

M Johnston Sheikh Hamdan Bin Mohammed Al Maktoum

Placings:41 (7420)

2009: 8^{4}G, 7^{1}SD,

	Starts	1st	2nd	3rd	Win & Pl
Career Total (Turf)	1	0	0	0	260
Career Total (AW)	1	1	0	0	2590

83 11/09 Sthl 7f STD £2590

Total win prize-money £2590

Going (Turf): **Sf: 0-0 GS: 0-0 Gd: 0-1 GF: 0-0 Fm: 0-0**
Distance: 5f/6f: 0-0 **7f-8f: 1-1** 9f-13f: 0-1 14f+: 0-0
Track : **LH: 1-1** RH: 0-0 Tight: 0-0 Gall: 0-0
Aids: Bl: 0-0 Vi: 0-0 Tstrap: 0-0 Ckp: 0-0
Best Rating: **83** 11/09 Sthl 7f stand

Useful; effective over 7f; acts on Fibresand.

Solicitude

(104) (65)**9**

6-y-o ch m Bertolini (USA)-Sibilant (Selkirk (USA))

D Haydn Jones D Llewelyn

Placings:013/00032033/530301026/23140000323-630 (0155)

2009: 7^{6}SS, 7^{3}SD, 7^{0}SD,

	Starts	1st	2nd	3rd	Win & Pl
Career Total (Turf)	5	0	0	0	
Career Total (AW)	30	3	4	10	13246

65 1/08 Wolv 7f32y (0-60)H STD £1684
58 9/07 Kemp 7f (0-50)H STD £2047
69 11/05 Sthl 7f STD £3426

Total win prize-money £7158

Going (Turf): **Sf: 0-0 GS: 0-0 Gd: 0-2 GF: 0-3 Fm: 0-0**
Distance: 5f/6f: 0-3 **7f-8f: 3-26** 9f-13f: 0-6 14f+: 0-0
Track : **LH: 2-25** RH: 1-6 **Tight: 1-15** Gall: 0-1
Aids: Bl: 0-3 Vi: 0-0 Tstrap: 1-18 Ckp: 1-18
Best Rating: **69** 12/05 Sthl 7f stand

Moderate; effective over 7f-1m; acts on Polytrack and Fibresand; has worn cheekpieces.

Solis (GER)

91 **71**

6-y-o ch g In The Wings-Seringa (GER) (Acatenango (GER))

P Monteith Dennis J Coppola

Placings:31/00123/0152/50630-000 (6156)

2009: 12^{0}GS, 10^{0}GS, 11^{0}G,

	Starts	1st	2nd	3rd	Win & Pl
Career Total (Turf)	18	3	2	3	13160
Career Total (AW)	1	0	0	0	0

5/07 Frnk 1m H GD £3378
7/06 Hopp 1m2f H GD £2413
10/05 Hall 1m165y GD £1985

Total win prize-money £7778

Going (Turf): Sf: 0-7 GS: 0-2 **Gd: 3-9** GF: 0-0 Fm: 0-0
Distance: 5f/6f: 0-0 7f-8f: 1-4 **9f-13f: 2-15** 14f+: 0-0
Track : LH: 0-3 RH: 0-6 Tight: 0-4 Gall: 0-1
Aids: Bl: 0-0 Vi: 0-1 Tstrap: 0-0 Ckp: 0-0
Best Rating: **71** 9/08 Haml 1m1f36y soft

Solis

103(88) (40)**68**

3-y-o b g Josr Algarhoud (IRE)-Passiflora (Night Shift (USA))

J J Quinn Ross Harmon

Placings:06-6123 (2154)

2009: 6^{6}SD, 7^{1}GF, 6^{2}GS, 7^{3}GF,

	Starts	1st	2nd	3rd	Win & Pl
Career Total (Turf)	5	1	1	1	3232
Career Total (AW)	1	0	0	0	0

64 4/09 Wwck 7f26y (0-60)H G-F £2047

Total win prize-money £2047

Going (Turf): Sf: 0-1 GS: 0-1 Gd: 0-0 **GF: 1-3** Fm: 0-0
Distance: 5f/6f: 0-4 **7f-8f: 1-2** 9f-13f: 0-0 14f+: 0-0
Track : **LH: 1-3** RH: 0-1 Tight: 0-1 Gall: 0-0
Aids: Bl: 0-0 Vi: 0-0 Tstrap: 0-0 Ckp: 0-0
Best Rating: **68** 5/09 Muss 7f30y gd-fm

Modest half-brother to several sprint winners; winner over 7f on fast ground.

Solitary

96(89) (51)**72**

3-y-o b f Lahib (USA)-Bond Solitaire (Atraf)

H Candy Major M G Wyatt

Placings:452-600 (6120)

2009: 7^{6}S, 6^{0}G, 5^{0}SD,

	Starts	1st	2nd	3rd	Win & Pl
Career Total (Turf)	5	0	1	0	1493
Career Total (AW)	1	0	0	0	

Going (Turf): **Sf: 0-1 GS: 0-1 Gd: 0-2 GF: 0-1 Fm: 0-0**
Distance: 5f/6f: 0-2 7f-8f: 0-4 9f-13f: 0-0 14f+: 0-0
Track : LH: 0-1 RH: 0-0 Tight: 0-1 Gall: 0-1
Aids: Bl: 0-0 Vi: 0-0 Tstrap: 0-0 Ckp: 0-0
Best Rating: **72** 8/08 Wind 6f gd-sft

Solo Attempt

(100) (87)**82**

3-y-o b f Anabaa (USA)-Sonja's Faith (IRE) (Sharp Victor (USA))

M Botti Mrs R J Jacobs

Placings:21155-3 (3509)

2009: 8^{3}SD,

	Starts	1st	2nd	3rd	Win & Pl
Career Total (Turf)	2	1	0	0	3397
Career Total (AW)	4	1	1	1	4257

78 7/08 Catt 7f G-F £2590
73 6/08 Kemp 6f STD £2590

Total win prize-money £5180

Going (Turf): Sf: 0-0 GS: 0-0 Gd: 0-0 **GF: 1-2** Fm: 0-0
Distance: 5f/6f: 1-2 7f-8f: 1-3 9f-13f: 0-1 14f+: 0-0
Track : LH: 1-3 RH: 1-3 **Tight: 1-2** Gall: 0-1
Aids: Bl: 0-0 Vi: 0-0 Tstrap: 0-0 Ckp: 0-0
Best Rating: **87** 7/09 Kemp 1m stand

Useful sort, 19,000gns daughter of a high-class 1m2f performer in the USA; effective at 6f and 7f; handles fast ground on Polytrack.

Solo Choice

97(94) (65)**68**

3-y-o b g Needwood Blade-Top Of The Class (IRE) (Rudimentary (USA))

I W McInnes (D Flood 15/6) Barrie Kirby

Placings:53-222040600000 (7425)

2009: 9^{2}SD, 8^{2}SD, 11^{2}SD, 10^{0}SD, 11^{4}GS, 12^{0}GF, 12^{6}SD, 10^{0}GF, 10^{0}SS, 10^{0}GF, 9^{0}SD, 12^{0}SD,

	Starts	1st	2nd	3rd	Win & Pl
Career Total (Turf)	4	0	0	0	0
Career Total (AW)	10	0	3	1	2543

Going (Turf): **Sf: 0-0 GS: 0-1 Gd: 0-0 GF: 0-3 Fm: 0-0**
Distance: 5f/6f: 0-0 7f-8f: 0-3 9f-13f: 0-11 14f+: 0-0
Track : LH: 0-11 RH: 0-2 Tight: 0-7 Gall: 0-1
Aids: Bl: 0-6 Vi: 0-0 Tstrap: 0-0 Ckp: 0-0
Best Rating: **68** 4/09 Wind 1m3f135y gd-sft

Modest; effective over 1m3f; acts on Polytrack.

Solo River

102(106) (68)**72**

4-y-o b f Averti (IRE)-Surakarta (Bin Ajwaad (IRE))

P J Makin Ten Of Hearts II

Placings:3440/663463210-42042144326 (7524)

2009: 10^{4}SD, 10^{2}SD, 9^{0}GF, 10^{4}SD, 9^{2}GF, 9^{1}GF, 10^{4}F, 10^{4}GF, 7^{3}F, 8^{2}GF, 10^{6}SD,

	Starts	1st	2nd	3rd	Win & Pl
Career Total (Turf)	13	2	3	3	8543
Career Total (AW)	11	0	1	1	1116

67 6/09 Leic 1m1f218y G-F £2590
67 8/08 Brig 1m1f209y (0-60)H GD £2331

Total win prize-money £4921

Going (Turf): Sf: 0-0 GS: 0-0 **Gd: 1-2 GF: 1-6** Fm: 0-5
Distance: 5f/6f: 0-5 7f-8f: 0-4 **9f-13f: 2-15** 14f+: 0-0
Track : LH: 1-18 RH: 1-4 Tight: 0-11 Gall: 0-1
Aids: Bl: 0-0 Vi: 0-0 Tstrap: 0-0 Ckp: 0-0
Best Rating: **72** 9/09 Sals 1m gd-fm

Modest; effective over 1m2f; acts on Polytrack and Polytrack.

Som Tala

105(88) (94)**101**

6-y-o ch g Fantastic Light (USA)-One Of The Family (Alzao (USA))

M R Channon Sheikh Ahmed Al Maktoum

Placings:3424144116/535030/3250-05100006 (7117)

2009: 18^{0}GF, 20^{5}GF, 16^{1}S, 21^{0}G, 14^{0}GF, 14^{0}S, 18^{0}G, 16^{6}GS,

	Starts	1st	2nd	3rd	Win & Pl
Career Total (Turf)	27	4	2	3	170031
Career Total (AW)	1	0	0	1	1493

99 6/09 Newc 2m19y H SFT £110970
91 9/06 Pont 2m1f216y G-S £8101
90 8/06 Bevl 2m35y (0-85)H GD £5505
87 6/06 Sals 1m6f15y (0-85)H G-F £5505

Total win prize-money £130082

Going (Turf): **Sf: 1-3 GS: 1-5 Gd: 1-8 GF: 1-10** Fm: 0-1
Distance: 5f/6f: 0-0 7f-8f: 0-0 9f-13f: 0-3 **14f+: 4-25**
Track : LH: 2-13 RH: 2-15 **Tight: 2-10** Gall: 1-12
Aids: Bl: 0-0 Vi: 0-0 Tstrap: 0-0 Ckp: 0-0
Best Rating: **101** 6/08 Asct 2m4f gd-fm

Very useful; won the 2009 Northumberland Plate; stays 2m4f; acts on most ground.

Some Sunny Day

105(99) (79)**79**

3-y-o ch f Where Or When (IRE)-Palace Street (USA) (Secreto (USA))

H Morrison Miss B Swire

Placings:5622421153 (7134)

2009: 8^{5}SD, 8^{6}SD, 8^{2}GF, 8^{2}GF, 8^{4}GF, **10**^{2}SD, **10**^{1}SD, 10^{1}GF, 10^{5}G, **10**^{3}SD,

	Starts	1st	2nd	3rd	Win & Pl
Career Total (Turf)	5	1	2	0	7647
Career Total (AW)	5	1	1	1	5196

79 9/09 Ffos 1m2f (0-80)H G-F £5046
74 8/09 Ling 1m2f (0-70)H STD £3885
Total win prize-money £8932

Going (Turf): Sf: 0-0 GS: 0-0 Gd: 0-1 **GF: 1-4** Fm: 0-0
Distance: 5f/6f: 0-0 7f-8f: 0-3 **9f-13f: 2-7** 14f+: 0-0
Track : **LH: 2-7** RH: 0-1 Tight: 1-5 Gall: 1-2
Aids: Bl: 0-0 Vi: 0-0 Tstrap: 0-0 Ckp: 0-0
Best Rating: **79** 10/09 Ling 1m2f stand

Fair; stays 1m2f; acts on fast ground; goes on Polytrack.

Some Time Good (IRE)

92(85) (69)**69**

3-y-o br/gr g Clodovil (IRE)-El Alma (IRE) (Goldmark (USA))

Miss J S Davis (M R Channon 27/5) V R Bedley & C James

Placings:05-4060 (2380)

2009: 12^{4}SD, 11^{0}GF, 12^{6}GS, 9^{0}GS,

	Starts	1st	2nd	3rd	Win & Pl
Career Total (Turf)	5	0	0	0	0
Career Total (AW)	1	0	0	0	0

Going (Turf): **Sf: 0-0 GS: 0-2 Gd: 0-1 GF: 0-2 Fm: 0-0**
Distance: 5f/6f: 0-0 7f-8f: 0-1 9f-13f: 0-5 14f+: 0-0
Track : LH: 0-2 RH: 0-2 Tight: 0-4 Gall: 0-0
Aids: Bl: 0-0 Vi: 0-0 Tstrap: 0-0 Ckp: 0-0
Best Rating: **69** 3/09 Ling 1m4f stand

Something (IRE)

109(109) (99)**103**

7-y-o b g Trans Island-Persian Polly (Persian Bold)

D Nicholls Middleham Park Racing LIII

Placings:26/4100/**1**160/34303/03000004-13050500356 (6675)

2009: 7^{1}SD, 6^{3}G, 7^{0}GF, 6^{5}GY, 6^{0}G, 7^{5}G, **5**^{0}SD, 7^{0}G, 7^{3}G, 7^{5}GF, 7^{6}G,

	Starts	1st	2nd	3rd	Win & Pl
Career Total (Turf)	30	1	1	6	30839
Career Total (AW)	4	3	0	0	39135

99 4/09 Kemp 7f (0-100)H STD £11091
111 3/06 Ling 7f (0-100)H STD £15580
103 2/06 Ling 7f (0-100)H STD £12464
95 5/05 NmkR 7f G-F £4871
Total win prize-money £44007

Going (Turf): Sf: 0-1 GS: 0-5 Gd: 0-12 **GF: 1-11** Fm: 0-0
Distance: 5f/6f: 0-15 **7f-8f: 4-18** 9f-13f: 0-1 14f+: 0-0
Track : **LH: 2-9** RH: 1-3 **Tight: 2-4** Gall: 0-6
Aids: Bl: 0-0 Vi: 0-0 Tstrap: 0-3 Ckp: 0-3
Best Rating: **112** 7/07 NmkJ 7f gd-fm

Very useful; Listed placed; effective at around 6f-7f; acts on most ground on turf; goes well on Polytrack; likes to race prominently; has worn a tongue tie.

Something Perfect (USA)

102(99) (81)**85**

3-y-o b f Perfect Soul (IRE)-Lady Angharad (IRE) (Tenby)

H R A Cecil The Sticky Wicket Syndicate III

Placings:130-333200 (6773)

2009: 8^{3}SD, 8^{3}GF, 8^{3}GF, 10^{2}GF, 8^{0}GS, 8^{0}SD,

	Starts	1st	2nd	3rd	Win & Pl
Career Total (Turf)	5	0	1	2	4913
Career Total (AW)	4	1	0	2	3829

76 9/08 Kemp 1m STD £2047
Total win prize-money £2047

Going (Turf): **Sf: 0-0 GS: 0-1 Gd: 0-1 GF: 0-3 Fm: 0-0**
Distance: 5f/6f: 0-0 **7f-8f: 1-7** 9f-13f: 0-2 14f+: 0-0
Track : LH: 0-2 **RH: 1-5** Tight: 0-2 Gall: 0-1
Aids: Bl: 0-0 Vi: 0-1 Tstrap: 0-0 Ckp: 0-0
Best Rating: **85** 6/09 Wind 1m2f7y gd-fm

Useful; effective over 1m; acts on fast ground and on Polytrack.

Sometsuke

102(93) (68)**74**

3-y-o br g Efisio-Peyto Princess (Bold Arrangement)

P J Makin M H Holland R P Marchant T W Wellard

Placings:0230 (6798)

2009: 7^{0}SD, 5^{2}G, 7^{3}SD, 6^{0}S,

	Starts	1st	2nd	3rd	Win & Pl
Career Total (Turf)	2	0	1	0	771
Career Total (AW)	2	0	0	1	482

Going (Turf): **Sf: 0-1 GS: 0-0 Gd: 0-1 GF: 0-0 Fm: 0-0**
Distance: 5f/6f: 0-1 7f-8f: 0-3 9f-13f: 0-0 14f+: 0-0
Track : LH: 0-2 RH: 0-1 Tight: 0-1 Gall: 0-1
Aids: Bl: 0-0 Vi: 0-0 Tstrap: 0-0 Ckp: 0-0
Best Rating: **74** 9/09 Bath 5f161y good

Fair; effective over 5f; acts on fast ground.

Somewhere Else

67(73) (4)**16**

2-y-o b f Firebreak-Royal Future (IRE) (Royal Academy (USA))

A Berry Alan Berry

Placings:0050 (6355)

2009: 5^{0}GF, 7^{0}GS, 5^{5}GF, **5**^{0}SD,

	Starts	1st	2nd	3rd	Win & Pl
Career Total (Turf)	3	0	0	0	0
Career Total (AW)	1	0	0	0	

Going (Turf): **Sf: 0-0 GS: 0-1 Gd: 0-0 GF: 0-2 Fm: 0-0**
Distance: 5f/6f: 0-3 7f-8f: 0-1 9f-13f: 0-0 14f+: 0-0
Track : LH: 0-0 RH: 0-0 Tight: 0-0 Gall: 0-0
Aids: Bl: 0-0 Vi: 0-0 Tstrap: 0-0 Ckp: 0-0
Best Rating: **16** 8/09 Ayr 5f gd-fm

Sommersturm (GER)

(97) (77)**103**

5-y-o b g Tiger Hill (IRE)-Sommernacht (GER) (Monsun (GER))

B J Curley (A P Stringer 20/1) Curley Leisure

Placings:11400U3/066-**00500** (4373)

2009: 12^{0}SD, 12^{0}SD, 12^{5}SD, 12^{0}SD, 12^{0}SD,

	Starts	1st	2nd	3rd	Win & Pl
Career Total (Turf)	9	2	0	1	7871
Career Total (AW)	6	0	0	0	0

5/07 Kref 1m2f55y GD £1790
5/07 Frnk 1m2f GD £2027
Total win prize-money £3818

Going (Turf): Sf: 0-2 GS: 0-0 **Gd: 2-7** GF: 0-0 Fm: 0-0
Distance: 5f/6f: 0-0 7f-8f: 0-0 **9f-13f: 2-15** 14f+: 0-0
Track : LH: 0-5 RH: 0-6 Tight: 0-1 Gall: 0-0
Aids: Bl: 0-0 Vi: 0-0 Tstrap: 0-0 Ckp: 0-0
Best Rating: **103** 6/07 Colo 1m3f good

Son Of Monsieur

83(94) (49)**46**

3-y-o ch g Monsieur Bond (IRE)-Triple Tricks (IRE) (Royal Academy (USA))

G R Oldroyd R C Bond

Placings:64000**040** (7818)

2009: 8^{6}GF, 7^{4}F, 10^{0}GF, 11^{0}GS, 10^{0}GF, **7**^{0}SD, **8**^{4}SD, **9**^{0}SD,

	Starts	1st	2nd	3rd	Win & Pl
Career Total (Turf)	5	0	0	0	317
Career Total (AW)	3	0	0	0	192

Going (Turf): **Sf: 0-0 GS: 0-1 Gd: 0-0 GF: 0-3 Fm: 0-1**
Distance: 5f/6f: 0-0 7f-8f: 0-3 9f-13f: 0-5 14f+: 0-0
Track : LH: 0-8 RH: 0-0 Tight: 0-8 Gall: 0-0
Aids: Bl: 0-0 Vi: 0-0 Tstrap: 0-0 Ckp: 0-0
Best Rating: **49** 12/09 Wolv 1m141y stand

Moderate; stays 1m plus; acts on Polytrack.

Son Of My Heart (USA)

98(99) (65)**63**

4-y-o b/br g Dynaformer (USA)-Sophie My Love (USA) (Danzig (USA))

P F I Cole Mrs Ramona Seeligson Bass

Placings:U3-0033 (3158)

2009: 10^{0}GF, **11**^{0}SD, 9^{3}GF, **10**^{3}SD,

	Starts	1st	2nd	3rd	Win & Pl
Career Total (Turf)	2	0	0	1	366
Career Total (AW)	4	0	0	2	706

Going (Turf): **Sf: 0-0 GS: 0-0 Gd: 0-0 GF: 0-2 Fm: 0-0**
Distance: 5f/6f: 0-0 7f-8f: 0-0 9f-13f: 0-6 14f+: 0-0
Track : LH: 0-5 RH: 0-1 Tight: 0-3 Gall: 0-0
Aids: Bl: 0-1 Vi: 0-0 Tstrap: 0-0 Ckp: 0-0
Best Rating: **65** 12/08 Sthl 1m3f stand

Modest; stays 1m3f; acts on fast ground and on both sand surfaces.

Son Of The Cat (USA)

106(110) (101)**100**

3-y-o b g Tale Of The Cat (USA)-Dixieland Gal (USA) (Dixieland Band (USA))

B Gubby Brian Gubby

Placings:4122-0564153224 (7488)

2009: 7^{0}SD, 5^{5}GF, 6^{6}SD, 6^{4}SD, 6^{1}G, 7^{5}SD, 6^{3}G, 6^{2}GS, 6^{2}SD, 6^{4}SD,

	Starts	1st	2nd	3rd	Win & Pl
Career Total (Turf)	5	2	1	1	12555
Career Total (AW)	9	0	3	0	8676

94 8/09 Ling 6f (0-85)H GD £4857
84 10/08 Gdwd 6f G-S £3238
Total win prize-money £8095

Going (Turf): Sf: 0-0 **GS: 1-2 Gd: 1-2** GF: 0-1 Fm: 0-0

Distance: 5f/6f: **2-11** 7f-8f: 0-3 9f-13f: 0-0 14f+: 0-0
Track : LH: 0-7 RH: 0-2 Tight: 0-6 Gall: 0-1
Aids: Bl: 0-0 Vi: 0-0 Tstrap: 0-0 Ckp: 0-0
Best Rating: 101 11/09 Ling 6f stand

Very useful; effective over 6f; acts on easy ground; goes on Polytrack; has worn a tongue tie.

Sonara (IRE)

105 **74**

5-y-o b g Peintre Celebre (USA)-Fay (IRE) (Polish Precedent (USA))
J Howard Johnson Andrea & Graham Wylie

Placings:000/314200013420/252 **(3313)**
2009: 15^{2}GF, 14^{5}GF, 16^{2}GF,

	Starts	1st	2nd	3rd	Win & Pl
Career Total (Turf)	18	2	4	2	13504

71 8/07 Rdcr 1m6f19y (0-65)H G-F £1943
68 5/07 Pont 1m4f8y (0-75)H G-F £4533
Total win prize-money £6477

Going (Turf): Sf: 0-1 GS: 0-2 Gd: 0-6 **GF: 2-9** Fm: 0-0
Distance: 5f/6f: 0-0 7f-8f: 0-3 9f-13f: 1-7 14f+: 1-8
Track : **LH: 2-9** RH: 0-7 **Tight: 1-10** Gall: 0-2
Aids: Bl: 0-0 Vi: 0-0 Tstrap: 0-0 Ckp: 0-0
Best Rating: 74 6/09 Newc 2m19y gd-fm

Modest; stays 2m and acts on quick ground.

Sonate De La Tour (FR)

78 **39**

4-y-o b f Timboroa-Damanka (IRE) (Slip Anchor)
J L Flint David Brace

Placings:1605413000/4400-0 **(4263)**
2009: 12^{0}S,

	Starts	1st	2nd	3rd	Win & Pl
Career Total (Turf)	14	2	0	1	13732
Career Total (AW)	1	0	0	0	0

70 10/07 StCl 1m VS £5743
3/07 Bord 5f HVY £3378
Total win prize-money £9121

Going (Turf): **Sf: 1-7** GS: 0-3 Gd: 0-0 GF: 0-0 Fm: 0-0
Distance: 5f/6f: 1-3 7f-8f: 1-7 9f-13f: 0-4 14f+: 0-1
Track : **LH: 1-3** RH: 0-1 Tight: 0-0 Gall: 0-0
Aids: Bl: 0-0 Vi: 0-0 Tstrap: 0-0 Ckp: 0-0
Best Rating: 70 10/07 StCl 1m v soft

Song Of My Heart (IRE)

100 **102**

2-y-o ch f Footstepsinthesand-Catch The Moon (IRE) (Peintre Celebre (USA))
David Wachman Sir Robert Ogden

Placings:6116 **(6449)**
2009: 6^{6}G, 6^{1}SH, 6^{1}SH, 6^{6}GF,

	Starts	1st	2nd	3rd	Win & Pl
Career Total (Turf)	4	2	0	0	42871

102 9/09 Curr 6f SH £27493
82 8/09 Curr 6f SH £13082
Total win prize-money £40576

Going (Turf): **Sf: 0-0 GS: 0-0 Gd: 0-1 GF: 0-1 Fm: 0-0**
Distance: **5f/6f: 2-4** 7f-8f: 0-0 9f-13f: 0-0 14f+: 0-0
Track : LH: 0-1 RH: 0-0 Tight: 0-0 Gall: 0-0
Aids: Bl: 0-0 Vi: 0-0 Tstrap: 0-0 Ckp: 0-0
Best Rating: 102 9/09 Curr 6f sft-hvy

Smart; Listed winner; stays 6f; handles soft ground.

Song Of Parkes

76 **35**

2-y-o b f Fantastic Light (USA)-My Melody Parkes (Teenoso (USA))
E J Alston Joseph Heler

Placings:4 **(7167)**
2009: 7^{4}S,

	Starts	1st	2nd	3rd	Win & Pl
Career Total (Turf)	1	0	0	0	289

Going (Turf): **Sf: 0-1 GS: 0-0 Gd: 0-0 GF: 0-0 Fm: 0-0**
Distance: 5f/6f: 0-0 7f-8f: 0-1 9f-13f: 0-0 14f+: 0-0
Track : LH: 0-1 RH: 0-0 Tight: 0-0 Gall: 0-0
Aids: Bl: 0-0 Vi: 0-0 Tstrap: 0-0 Ckp: 0-0
Best Rating: 35 10/09 Ayr 7f50y soft

Song Of Praise

92(103) (78)**63**

3-y-o b f Compton Place-Greensand (Green Desert (USA))
M Blanshard Tom Wellman

Placings:00440260012-411202006050 **(6915)**
2009: 7^{4}SD, 6^{1}SD, 5^{1}SD, 6^{2}SD, 6^{0}F, 6^{2}SD, 5^{0}G, 5^{0}G, 6^{6}SD, 7^{0}SD, 6^{5}SD, 6^{0}SD,

	Starts	1st	2nd	3rd	Win & Pl
Career Total (Turf)	11	0	1	0	867
Career Total (AW)	12	3	3	0	9929

71 3/09 Wolv 5f216y (0-70)H STD £2729
67 2/09 Kemp 6f (0-65)H STD £2047
59 11/08 Ling 7f (0-75) STD £2914
Total win prize-money £7691

Going (Turf): **Sf: 0-2 GS: 0-1 Gd: 0-5 GF: 0-2 Fm: 0-1**
Distance: **5f/6f: 2-18** 7f-8f: 1-5 9f-13f: 0-0 14f+: 0-0
Track : **LH: 2-10** RH: 1-5 **Tight: 2-7** Gall: 0-2
Aids: Bl: 0-0 Vi: 0-0 Tstrap: 0-0 Ckp: 0-0
Best Rating: 78 6/09 Ling 6f stand

Modest; effective over 6f-7f; acts on fast ground; goes on Polytrack.

Song To The Moon (IRE)

90 **65**

2-y-o b f Oratorio (IRE)-Jojeema (Barathea (IRE))
A M Balding John K Gale

Placings:00 **(6992)**
2009: 7^{0}GF, 8^{0}GS,

	Starts	1st	2nd	3rd	Win & Pl
Career Total (Turf)	2	0	0	0	

Going (Turf): **Sf: 0-0 GS: 0-1 Gd: 0-0 GF: 0-1 Fm: 0-0**
Distance: 5f/6f: 0-0 7f-8f: 0-2 9f-13f: 0-0 14f+: 0-0
Track : LH: 0-1 RH: 0-0 Tight: 0-0 Gall: 0-1
Aids: Bl: 0-0 Vi: 0-0 Tstrap: 0-0 Ckp: 0-0
Best Rating: 65 10/09 Donc 1m gd-sft

Songful (IRE)

85(90) (57)**45**

3-y-o b/br f Captain Rio-Trillie (Never So Bold)
Pat Eddery Pat Eddery Racing (One So Wonderful)

Placings:56060000 **(5574)**
2009: 8^{5}SD, 8^{6}SD, 7^{0}SD, 8^{6}GF, 6^{0}G, 7^{0}HY, 6^{0}GF, 8^{0}SD,

	Starts	1st	2nd	3rd	Win & Pl
Career Total (Turf)	4	0	0	0	0
Career Total (AW)	4	0	0	0	0

Going (Turf): **Sf: 0-1 GS: 0-0 Gd: 0-1 GF: 0-2 Fm: 0-0**
Distance: 5f/6f: 0-1 7f-8f: 0-6 9f-13f: 0-1 14f+: 0-0
Track : LH: 0-1 RH: 0-4 Tight: 0-1 Gall: 0-0
Aids: Bl: 0-0 Vi: 0-0 Tstrap: 0-1 Ckp: 0-1
Best Rating: 57 3/09 Kemp 1m stand

Sonhador

94(99) (68)**68**

3-y-o b g Compton Place-Fayre Holly (IRE) (Fayruz)
G Prodromou George Prodromou

Placings:36230040220-6**000021066** **(7889)**
2009: 5^{6}GF, 6^{0}GF, 5^{0}SD, 5^{0}SF, 6^{0}G, 5^{2}SD, 6^{1}SD, 5^{0}SD, 6^{6}SD, 5^{6}SD,

	Starts	1st	2nd	3rd	Win & Pl
Career Total (Turf)	10	0	1	2	1763
Career Total (AW)	11	1	3	0	4316

57 10/09 Kemp 6f (0-50)H STD £2047
Total win prize-money £2047

Going (Turf): **Sf: 0-0 GS: 0-1 Gd: 0-5 GF: 0-3 Fm: 0-1**
Distance: **5f/6f: 1-19** 7f-8f: 0-2 9f-13f: 0-0 14f+: 0-0
Track : LH: 0-10 **RH: 1-5** Tight: 0-5 Gall: 0-3
Aids: Bl: 0-2 Vi: 0-0 Tstrap: 0-0 Ckp: 0-0
Best Rating: 68 12/08 Kemp 6f stand

Moderate; stays 6f; acts on fast ground and on Polytrack; has worn blinkers.

Sonic Anthem (USA)

95(88) (39)**46**

7-y-o b g Royal Anthem (USA)-Whisperifyoudare (USA) (Red Ransom (USA))
B D Leavy Shearstud Ltd

Placings:0/3020631/**500**/**100**/00 **(7354)**
2009: 12^{0}G, 12^{0}SD,

	Starts	1st	2nd	3rd	Win & Pl
Career Total (Turf)	9	0	1	2	1920
Career Total (AW)	7	2	0	0	3890

65 3/07 Sthl 1m (0-55) STD £1501
70 1/06 Sthl 1m3f SF £2388
Total win prize-money £3891

Going (Turf): **Sf: 0-0 GS: 0-2 Gd: 0-2 GF: 0-3 Fm: 0-2**
Distance: 5f/6f: 0-1 7f-8f: 1-9 9f-13f: 1-6 14f+: 0-0
Track : **LH: 2-9** RH: 0-6 Tight: 0-7 Gall: 0-0
Aids: Bl: 0-0 Vi: 0-0 Tstrap: 0-0 Ckp: 0-0
Best Rating: 70 1/06 Sthl 1m3f std-fst

Sonnengold (GER)

70 **59**

8-y-o b/br m Java Gold (USA)-Standing Ovation (ITY) (Law Society (USA))
B J Llewellyn B J Llewellyn

Placings:465116/56014/53410-5 **(4264)**
2009: 16^{5}S,

	Starts	1st	2nd	3rd	Win & Pl
Career Total (Turf)	17	4	0	1	9529

59 7/08 Chep 2m49y G-F £2266

7/05 Muni 1m4f H SFT £2269
11/04 Muni 1m3f H SFT £2112
10/04 Muni 1m3f SFT £1795
Total win prize-money £8446

Going (Turf): **Sf: 3-9** GS: 0-1 Gd: 0-5 GF: 1-2 Fm: 0-0
Distance: 5f/6f: 0-0 7f-8f: 0-0 **9f-13f: 3-13** 14f+: 1-4
Track : **LH: 1-7** RH: 0-0 Tight: 0-2 Gall: 0-0
Aids: Bl: 0-0 Vi: 0-0 Tstrap: 0-0 Ckp: 0-0
Best Rating: **59** 7/08 Chep 2m49y gd-fm

Modest handicapper; successful three times on soft ground in Germany in 2004/5; stays 2m; acts on soft ground and good to firm.

Sonning Gate

97(94) (87)**92**
3-y-o b g Desert Sun-Sunley Scent (Wolfhound (USA))
D R C Elsworth A Heaney

Placings:511-340 **(2273)**
2009: 8^{3}G, 8^{4}GF, 8^{0}HY,

	Starts	1st	2nd	3rd	Win & Pl
Career Total (Turf)	4	0	0	1	1721
Career Total (AW)	2	2	0	0	7124

87 12/08 Ling 7f STD £3885
77 11/08 Ling 1m STD £3238
Total win prize-money £7124

Going (Turf): **Sf: 0-1 GS: 0-1 Gd: 0-1 GF: 0-1 Fm: 0-0**
Distance: 5f/6f: 0-0 **7f-8f: 2-3** 9f-13f: 0-3 14f+: 0-0
Track : **LH: 2-3** RH: 0-2 **Tight: 2-3** Gall: 0-0
Aids: Bl: 0-0 Vi: 0-0 Tstrap: 0-0 Ckp: 0-0
Best Rating: **92** 4/09 Sand 1m14y good

Useful; stays 1m; acts good and faster ground and on Polytrack.

Sonny G (IRE)

74(90) (50)**40**
2-y-o ch c Desert Sun-Broughton Zest (Colonel Collins (USA))
J R Best G G Racing

Placings:0605 **(7884)**
2009: 7^{0}GF, 6^{6}GF, 7^{0}SS, 7^{5}SD,

	Starts	1st	2nd	3rd	Win & Pl
Career Total (Turf)	2	0	0	0	0
Career Total (AW)	2	0	0	0	0

Going (Turf): **Sf: 0-0 GS: 0-0 Gd: 0-0 GF: 0-2 Fm: 0-0**
Distance: 5f/6f: 0-1 7f-8f: 0-3 9f-13f: 0-0 14f+: 0-0
Track : LH: 0-3 RH: 0-1 Tight: 0-2 Gall: 0-0
Aids: Bl: 0-0 Vi: 0-0 Tstrap: 0-0 Ckp: 0-0
Best Rating: **50** 10/09 Ling 7f std-slw

Sonny Parkin

103(93) (56)**81**
7-y-o b g Spinning World (USA)-No Miss Kris (USA) (Capote (USA))
J Pearce S & M Supplies (Aylsham) Ltd

Placings:5230143300636/063146200/5340003433100/56 43104454004-61P600600 **(7512)**
2009: 8^{6}GF, 8^{1}GF, 8^{P}GS, 8^{6}G, 10^{0}GS, 8^{0}G, 8^{6}GF, 8^{0}SD, 10^{0}SD,

	Starts	1st	2nd	3rd	Win & Pl
Career Total (Turf)	43	5	1	8	31879
Career Total (AW)	14	0	1	2	2922

74 6/09 NmkJ 1m (0-70)H G-F £3885
80 6/08 NmkJ 1m (0-75)H G-F £3885
83 8/07 NmkJ 1m (0-75)H G-F £3886
83 8/06 NmkJ 1m (0-80)H G-F £5505
80 6/05 NmkJ 1m (0-75)H G-F £4323
Total win prize-money £21486

Going (Turf): Sf: 0-3 GS: 0-5 Gd: 0-11 **GF: 5-24** Fm: 0-0
Distance: 5f/6f: 0-0 **7f-8f: 5-32** 9f-13f: 0-25 14f+: 0-0
Track : LH: 0-14 RH: 0-13 Tight: 0-14 Gall: 0-9
Aids: Bl: 0-3 **Vi: 5-44** Tstrap: 0-4 Ckp: 0-4
Best Rating: **85** 8/06 NmkJ 1m2f soft

Fair; suited by 1m; acts on fast ground; also goes on Polytrack; has a good record on the Newmarket July Course; sometimes does not find as much off the bridle as seems likely; usually visored.

Sonny Red (IRE)

109 **106**
5-y-o b g Redback-Magic Melody (Petong)
D Nicholls Alex Nicholls E Maher & J E Greaves

Placings:114/2063400/21400060-40106050 **(6270)**
2009: 5^{4}GS, 5^{0}G, 5^{1}GF, 6^{0}S, 5^{6}GF, 5^{0}GS, 6^{5}G, 7^{0}G,

	Starts	1st	2nd	3rd	Win & Pl
Career Total (Turf)	26	4	2	1	74849

106 7/09 Asct 5f (0-105)H G-F £11215
109 4/08 Nott 5f13y SFT £6799
97 5/06 Gdwd 5f SFT £14195
89 5/06 NmkR 5f SFT £7772
Total win prize-money £39983

Going (Turf): **Sf: 3-5** GS: 0-6 Gd: 0-7 GF: 1-8 Fm: 0-0
Distance: **5f/6f: 4-21** 7f-8f: 0-5 9f-13f: 0-0 14f+: 0-0
Track : LH: 0-1 RH: 0-0 Tight: 0-0 Gall: 0-1
Aids: Bl: 0-0 Vi: 0-0 Tstrap: 0-4 Ckp: 0-4
Best Rating: **112** 4/08 NmkR 6f good

Smart; winner in Listed company and Group placed; stays 1m, but effective at sprint trips; acts on most ground; has worn cheekpieces.

Sonny Sam (IRE)

100(93) (58)**64**
4-y-o b g Black Sam Bellamy (IRE)-Purple Risks (FR) (Take Risks (FR))
R A Fahey (M H Tompkins 22/3) Mike Browne

Placings:00/03600-230 **(2018)**
2009: 16^{2}F, 14^{3}G, 18^{0}G,

	Starts	1st	2nd	3rd	Win & Pl
Career Total (Turf)	8	0	1	2	1458
Career Total (AW)	2	0	0	0	

Going (Turf): **Sf: 0-0 GS: 0-0 Gd: 0-3 GF: 0-4 Fm: 0-1**
Distance: 5f/6f: 0-0 7f-8f: 0-2 9f-13f: 0-1 14f+: 0-7
Track : LH: 0-6 RH: 0-2 Tight: 0-6 Gall: 0-2
Aids: Bl: 0-0 Vi: 0-0 Tstrap: 0-0 Ckp: 0-0
Best Rating: **64** 5/08 Rdcr 1m6f19y gd-fm

Moderate; stays 2m; acts on fast ground.

Sonofdon

67 **10**
2-y-o ch g Stage Pass-Moore Appeal (Homo Sapien)
C W Moore Cant Do More

Placings:0 **(5253)**
2009: 6^{0}GF,

	Starts	1st	2nd	3rd	Win & Pl
Career Total (Turf)	1	0	0	0	

Going (Turf): **Sf: 0-0 GS: 0-0 Gd: 0-0 GF: 0-1 Fm: 0-0**
Distance: 5f/6f: 0-1 7f-8f: 0-0 9f-13f: 0-0 14f+: 0-0
Track : LH: 0-0 RH: 0-0 Tight: 0-0 Gall: 0-0
Aids: Bl: 0-0 Vi: 0-0 Tstrap: 0-0 Ckp: 0-0
Best Rating: **10** 8/09 Ripn 6f gd-fm

Soopacal (IRE)

(108) (92)**82**
4-y-o b g Captain Rio-Fiddes (IRE) (Alzao (USA))
B Smart Brian Grieve & Jeff Evans

Placings:135050/120405-30604 **(0965)**
2009: 6^{3}SD, 5^{0}SD, 5^{6}SD, 5^{0}SF, 5^{4}SD,

	Starts	1st	2nd	3rd	Win & Pl
Career Total (Turf)	7	1	0	0	5463
Career Total (AW)	10	1	1	2	8971

89 2/08 Wolv 5f20y (0-85)H STD £4210
72 7/07 Bevl 5f HVY £3886
Total win prize-money £8096

Going (Turf): **Sf: 1-1** GS: 0-2 Gd: 0-2 GF: 0-2 Fm: 0-0
Distance: **5f/6f: 2-14** 7f-8f: 0-3 9f-13f: 0-0 14f+: 0-0
Track : **LH: 1-8** RH: 0-1 **Tight: 1-7** Gall: 0-1
Aids: Bl: 0-1 Vi: 0-1 Tstrap: 0-0 Ckp: 0-0
Best Rating: **92** 3/08 Kemp 6f stand

Useful; effective at 5f-6f; handles easy ground and Polytrack.

Sophie's Beau (USA)

96(93) (64)**79**
2-y-o b g Stormy Atlantic (USA)-Lady Buttercup (USA) (Meadowlake (USA))
B J Meehan Iraj Parvizi

Placings:524 **(7001)**
2009: 7^{5}G, 6^{2}GF, 5^{4}SD,

	Starts	1st	2nd	3rd	Win & Pl
Career Total (Turf)	2	0	1	0	1156
Career Total (AW)	1	0	0	0	241

Going (Turf): **Sf: 0-0 GS: 0-0 Gd: 0-1 GF: 0-1 Fm: 0-0**
Distance: 5f/6f: 0-2 7f-8f: 0-1 9f-13f: 0-0 14f+: 0-0
Track : LH: 0-1 RH: 0-0 Tight: 0-1 Gall: 0-0
Aids: Bl: 0-0 Vi: 0-0 Tstrap: 0-0 Ckp: 0-0
Best Rating: **79** 9/09 NmkR 6f gd-fm

Fair; effective over 6f; acts on fast ground.

Sophist (IRE)

(91) (60)**59**
6-y-o b g Montjeu (IRE)-Cordon Bleu (USA) (D'Accord (USA))
Evan Williams Mrs D E Cheshire

Placings:05/00/046000-3 **(0603)**
2009: 12^{3}SD,

	Starts	1st	2nd	3rd	Win & Pl
Career Total (Turf)	9	0	0	0	0
Career Total (AW)	2	0	0	1	574

Going (Turf): **Sf: 0-1 GS: 0-2 Gd: 0-1 GF: 0-2 Fm: 0-0**
Distance: 5f/6f: 0-0 7f-8f: 0-4 9f-13f: 0-7 14f+: 0-0
Track : LH: 0-4 RH: 0-5 Tight: 0-0 Gall: 0-0
Aids: Bl: 0-4 Vi: 0-0 Tstrap: 0-4 Ckp: 0-4
Best Rating: **73** 9/05 NmkR 7f gd-sft

Sopranist

108 **108**

3-y-o b c Singspiel (IRE)-Trefoil (Kris)

J H M Gosden H R H Princess Haya Of Jordan

Placings:1022 **(4455)**

2009: 10^{1}GF, 10^{0}GF, 10^{2}S, 9^{2}G,

	Starts	1st	2nd	3rd	Win & Pl
Career Total (Turf)	4	1	2	0	19176
88 4/09 NmkR 1m2f			G-F		£5180

Total win prize-money £5181

Going (Turf): Sf: 0-1 GS: 0-0 Gd: 0-1 **GF: 1-2** Fm: 0-0
Distance: 5f/6f: 0-0 7f-8f: 0-0 **9f-13f: 1-4** 14f+: 0-0
Track : LH: 0-0 RH: 0-2 Tight: 0-1 Gall: 0-1
Aids: Bl: 0-0 Vi: 0-0 Tstrap: 0-0 Ckp: 0-0
Best Rating: **108** 7/09 Gdwd 1m1f192y good

Very useful; effective over 1m2f; acts on fast and soft ground.

Sorrel Point

95(98) (58)**44**

6-y-o b h Bertolini (USA)-Lightning Princess (Puissance)

H J Collingridge Mrs Doreen Carter

Placings:0/040053/00/0000-00065303 **(7371)**

2009: 8^{0}G, 7^{0}GF, 6^{0}GS, 6^{6}G, 6^{5}GF, 5^{3}SD, 5^{0}G, 5^{3}SD,

	Starts	1st	2nd	3rd	Win & Pl
Career Total (Turf)	11	0	0	1	657
Career Total (AW)	10	0	0	2	946

Going (Turf): Sf: 0-2 GS: 0-1 Gd: 0-4 GF: 0-4 Fm: 0-0
Distance: 5f/6f: 0-7 7f-8f: 0-12 9f-13f: 0-2 14f+: 0-0
Track : LH: 0-9 RH: 0-3 Tight: 0-6 Gall: 0-1
Aids: Bl: 0-0 Vi: 0-3 Tstrap: 0-0 Ckp: 0-0
Best Rating: **61** 8/06 Yarm 7f3y soft

Modest sort; stays 7f; acts on soft; has worn a visor.

Sorrel Ridge (IRE)

83(96) (57)**43**

3-y-o ch g Namid-She Legged It (IRE) (Cape Cross (IRE))

M G Quinlan Swan Inn Racing

Placings:3003005-52200450 **(1958)**

2009: 5^{5}SD, 6^{2}SD, 5^{2}SD, 5^{0}SD, 5^{0}SD, 5^{4}GF, 5^{5}G, 6^{0}F,

	Starts	1st	2nd	3rd	Win & Pl
Career Total (Turf)	7	0	0	2	930
Career Total (AW)	8	0	2	0	1712

Going (Turf): Sf: 0-1 GS: 0-2 Gd: 0-1 GF: 0-2 Fm: 0-1
Distance: 5f/6f: 0-14 7f-8f: 0-1 9f-13f: 0-0 14f+: 0-0
Track : LH: 0-8 RH: 0-1 Tight: 0-4 Gall: 0-2
Aids: Bl: 0-2 Vi: 0-0 Tstrap: 0-6 Ckp: 0-6
Best Rating: **57** 1/09 Wolv 5f20y stand

Moderate; effective over 5f; acts on easy ground.

Sorrento Moon (IRE)

95 (28)**52**

5-y-o b m Tagula (IRE)-Honey For Money (IRE) (Alzao (USA))

G A Harker Mrs J A Smith

Placings:00/0635/00315-000 **(3171)**

2009: 12^{0}GS, 12^{0}GF, 14^{0}GF,

	Starts	1st	2nd	3rd	Win & Pl
Career Total (Turf)	13	1	0	2	3399
Career Total (AW)	1	0	0	0	
52 8/08 Ripn 1m1f170y				G-S	£2590

Total win prize-money £2590

Going (Turf): Sf: 0-3 **GS: 1-3** Gd: 0-0 GF: 0-4 Fm: 0-0
Distance: 5f/6f: 0-0 7f-8f: 0-7 **9f-13f: 1-6** 14f+: 0-1
Track : LH: 0-6 **RH: 1-7 Tight: 1-4** Gall: 0-2
Aids: Bl: 0-0 Vi: 0-0 Tstrap: 0-0 Ckp: 0-0
Best Rating: **56** 4/07 Curr 1m gd-fm

Moderate; ex-Irish; effective at around 1m-1m2f; acts on easy ground.

Sory

69 **20**

2-y-o b g Sakhee (USA)-Rule Britannia (Night Shift (USA))

L M Cumani Sheikh Mohammed Obaid Al Maktoum

Placings:0 **(7099)**

2009: 8^{0}G,

	Starts	1st	2nd	3rd	Win & Pl
Career Total (Turf)	1	0	0	0	

Going (Turf): Sf: 0-0 GS: 0-0 Gd: 0-1 GF: 0-0 Fm: 0-0
Distance: 5f/6f: 0-0 7f-8f: 0-0 9f-13f: 0-1 14f+: 0-0
Track : LH: 0-0 RH: 0-0 Tight: 0-0 Gall: 0-0
Aids: Bl: 0-0 Vi: 0-0 Tstrap: 0-0 Ckp: 0-0
Best Rating: **20** 10/09 Yarm 1m3y good

Sostenuto

71 **26**

2-y-o ch f Compton Place-Hufflepuff (IRE) (Desert King (IRE))

T H Caldwell Thorn Cross

Placings:0 **(7061)**

2009: 5^{0}GF,

	Starts	1st	2nd	3rd	Win & Pl
Career Total (Turf)	1	0	0	0	

Going (Turf): Sf: 0-0 GS: 0-0 Gd: 0-0 GF: 0-1 Fm: 0-0
Distance: 5f/6f: 0-1 7f-8f: 0-0 9f-13f: 0-0 14f+: 0-0
Track : LH: 0-0 RH: 0-0 Tight: 0-0 Gall: 0-0
Aids: Bl: 0-0 Vi: 0-0 Tstrap: 0-0 Ckp: 0-0
Best Rating: **26** 10/09 Leic 5f218y gd-fm

Sotelo

67(90) (66)**10**

7-y-o ch h Monsun (GER)-Seringa (GER) (Acatenango (GER))

S Gollings Rupert Webb

Placings:1/3/325154/50 **(6668)**

2009: 11^{5}GS, 9^{0}SD,

	Starts	1st	2nd	3rd	Win & Pl
Career Total (Turf)	9	2	1	2	11320
Career Total (AW)	1	0	0	0	
6/06 Colo 1m3f H				GD	£3448
9/04 Hopp 1m				GD	£2183

Total win prize-money £5631

Going (Turf): Sf: 0-2 GS: 0-1 **Gd: 2-6** GF: 0-0 Fm: 0-0
Distance: 5f/6f: 0-0 7f-8f: 1-1 9f-13f: 1-9 14f+: 0-0
Track : LH: 0-1 **RH: 1-3** Tight: 0-1 Gall: 0-0
Aids: **Bl: 1-3** Vi: 0-0 Tstrap: 0-0 Ckp: 0-0
Best Rating: **66** 10/09 Wolv 1m1f103y stand

Sotik Star (IRE)

96(101) (75)**79**

6-y-o b g Elnadim (USA)-Crystal Springs (IRE) (Kahyasi)

K A Morgan J D M Stables

Placings:032/4110/500/62625106-200421 **(5229)**

2009: 8^{2}SD, 8^{0}SD, 8^{0}SD, 8^{4}SD, 8^{2}G, 8^{1}SF,

	Starts	1st	2nd	3rd	Win & Pl
Career Total (Turf)	14	1	4	1	9260
Career Total (AW)	10	3	1	0	11255
67 8/09 Wolv 1m141y (0-60)H				SF	£2388
79 8/08 Bath 1m5y (0-75)H				GD	£4533
85 11/06 Ling 1m (0-80)H				STD	£5505
84 9/06 Ling 1m				STD	£2590

Total win prize-money £15017

Going (Turf): Sf: 0-1 GS: 0-3 **Gd: 1-6** GF: 0-4 Fm: 0-0
Distance: 5f/6f: 0-3 7f-8f: 2-12 9f-13f: 2-9 14f+: 0-0
Track : **LH: 4-13** RH: 0-3 **Tight: 4-10** Gall: 0-2
Aids: Bl: 0-0 Vi: 0-0 Tstrap: 0-2 Ckp: 0-2
Best Rating: **85** 12/06 Ling 1m stand

Modest; stays 1m; acts on a sound surface; goes on Polytrack.

Soto

103(88) (34)**70**

6-y-o b g Averti (IRE)-Belle Of The Blues (IRE) (Blues Traveller (IRE))

M W Easterby W H & Mrs J A Tinning

Placings:21255425065O/00320033144/05001050020455/0 2030262255-0632224435420 **(6847)**

2009: 6^{0}SD, 6^{6}F, 6^{3}F, 6^{2}G, 5^{2}F, 6^{2}GS, 5^{4}G, 6^{4}GF, 6^{3}GF, 5^{5}GS, 7^{4}GF, 7^{2}GF, 7^{0}G,

	Starts	1st	2nd	3rd	Win & Pl
Career Total (Turf)	58	2	13	6	38360
Career Total (AW)	3	1	0	0	1442
72 6/07 Yarm 6f3y (0-75)H				SFT	£2914
78 7/06 Newc 6f H				G-F	£12464
59 4/05 Sthl 5f				STD	£1442

Total win prize-money £16821

Going (Turf): **Sf: 1-8** GS: 0-10 Gd: 0-15 **GF: 1-20** Fm: 0-5
Distance: **5f/6f: 2-50** 7f-8f: 1-11 9f-13f: 0-0 14f+: 0-0
Track : LH: 0-13 RH: 0-3 Tight: 0-5 Gall: 0-1
Aids: Bl: 0-12 Vi: 0-1 Tstrap: 0-0 Ckp: 0-0
Best Rating: **78** 7/06 Newc 6f gd-fm

Modest; stays 7f; acts on fast and easy ground; has worn heagear.

Soul City (IRE)

104 **112**

3-y-o b c Elusive City (USA)-Savage (IRE) (Polish Patriot (USA))

R Hannon Patrick J Fahey

Placings:4141110-30 **(2992)**

2009: 8^{3}HY, 8^{0}GF,

	Starts	1st	2nd	3rd	Win & Pl
Career Total (Turf)	9	4	0	1	823858
102 9/08 Curr 7f				YLD	£724264
112 9/08 Lonc 7f				G-S	£29412
104 8/08 Deau 7f				G-S	£20221
80 7/08 NmkJ 7f				SFT	£9714

Total win prize-money £783612

Going (Turf): Sf: 1-2 **GS: 2-2** Gd: 0-1 GF: 0-3 Fm: 0-0
Distance: 5f/6f: 0-1 **7f-8f: 4-8** 9f-13f: 0-0 14f+: 0-0
Track : LH: 0-0 **RH: 2-5** Tight: 0-0 Gall: 0-3
Aids: Bl: 0-0 Vi: 0-0 Tstrap: 0-0 Ckp: 0-0
Best Rating: **112** 9/08 Lonc 7f gd-sft

Smart; Group 3 and sales race winner in 2008; effective at around 7f-1m; handles fast but best on soft ground.

Soul Heaven

98(93) (75)77

2-y-o b g Oratorio (IRE)-Pilgrim Spirit (USA) (Saint Ballado (CAN))

M L W Bell Lady Bamford

Placings:411 **(3842)**

2009: 5^{4}GF, 6^{1}SD, 6^{1}GF,

	Starts	1st	2nd	3rd	Win & Pl
Career Total (Turf)	2	1	0	0	6476
Career Total (AW)	1	1	0	0	3071

77 7/09 Asct 6f G-F £6476
75 5/09 Ling 6f STD £3070
Total win prize-money £9547

Going (Turf): Sf: 0-0 GS: 0-0 Gd: 0-0 **GF: 1-2** Fm: 0-0
Distance: **5f/6f: 2-3** 7f-8f: 0-0 9f-13f: 0-0 14f+: 0-0
Track : **LH: 1-2** RH: 0-0 **Tight: 1-1** Gall: 0-0
Aids: Bl: 0-0 Vi: 0-0 Tstrap: 0-0 Ckp: 0-0
Best Rating: **77** 7/09 Asct 6f gd-fm

Fair; stays 6f; acts on fast ground and on Polytrack.

Soul Murmur (IRE)

62(79) (61)79

4-y-o br g Indian Ridge-My Potters (USA) (Irish River (FR))

F Sheridan Dr Franco Moretti

Placings:30/5322046-00 **(6755)**

2009: 7^{0}SD, 7^{0}G,

	Starts	1st	2nd	3rd	Win & Pl
Career Total (Turf)	9	0	2	2	4800
Career Total (AW)	2	0	0	0	

Going (Turf): **Sf: 0-0 GS: 0-0 Gd: 0-4 GF: 0-1 Fm: 0-1**
Distance: 5f/6f: 0-1 7f-8f: 0-9 9f-13f: 0-1 14f+: 0-0
Track : LH: 0-6 RH: 0-4 Tight: 0-1 Gall: 0-0
Aids: Bl: 0-2 Vi: 0-0 Tstrap: 0-0 Ckp: 0-0
Best Rating: **80** 10/07 Naas 6f good

Fair; stays 1m and acts on most ground; has worn blinkers and a tongue tie.

Soul Singer

99(94) (53)52

3-y-o br f Where Or When (IRE)-Tancholo (So Factual (USA))

J G Portman Hockham Racing

Placings:61000333400 **(7324)**

2009: 11^{6}SD, 11^{1}SD, 12^{0}SD, 12^{0}SD, 11^{0}GF, 11^{3}GF, 12^{3}G, 11^{3}G, 16^{4}SD, 13^{0}SD, 12^{0}SD,

	Starts	1st	2nd	3rd	Win & Pl
Career Total (Turf)	4	0	0	3	870
Career Total (AW)	7	1	0	0	2047

51 2/09 Kemp 1m3f STD £2047
Total win prize-money £2047

Going (Turf): **Sf: 0-0 GS: 0-0 Gd: 0-2 GF: 0-2 Fm: 0-0**
Distance: 5f/6f: 0-0 7f-8f: 0-0 **9f-13f: 1-9** 14f+: 0-2
Track : LH: 0-4 **RH: 1-6** Tight: 0-4 Gall: 0-0
Aids: Bl: 0-0 Vi: 0-0 Tstrap: 0-0 Ckp: 0-0
Best Rating: **53** 3/09 Kemp 1m4f stand

Moderate; effective over 1m3f; acts on Polytrack and good ground on turf.

Soul Sista (IRE)

99(92) (49)77

3-y-o b f City On A Hill (USA)-Fraamtastic (Fraam)

J L Spearing Living In The Saddle Syndicate

Placings:2145135-0500460 **(7587)**

2009: 6^{0}GF, 6^{5}HY, 6^{0}S, 6^{0}G, 7^{4}GF, 8^{6}S, 8^{0}SD,

	Starts	1st	2nd	3rd	Win & Pl
Career Total (Turf)	13	2	1	1	7914
Career Total (AW)	1	0	0	0	

77 7/08 Sals 6f G-S £3885
70 4/08 Bevl 5f G-S £2428
Total win prize-money £6314

Going (Turf): Sf: 0-4 **GS: 2-4** Gd: 0-2 GF: 0-3 Fm: 0-0
Distance: **5f/6f: 2-9** 7f-8f: 0-4 9f-13f: 0-1 14f+: 0-0
Track : LH: 0-1 RH: 0-1 Tight: 0-0 Gall: 0-1
Aids: Bl: 0-1 Vi: 0-0 Tstrap: 0-0 Ckp: 0-0
Best Rating: **77** 7/08 Sals 6f gd-sft

Useful; effective over 5f-6f; acts on easy ground.

Soul Station (FR)

96(87) (65)84

2-y-o b g Starcraft (NZ)-Allumette (Rainbow Quest (USA))

R Charlton Michael Pescod

Placings:51 **(6728)**

2009: 7^{5}SD, 8^{1}S,

	Starts	1st	2nd	3rd	Win & Pl
Career Total (Turf)	1	1	0	0	2914
Career Total (AW)	1	0	0	0	0

84 10/09 Sals 1m SFT £2914
Total win prize-money £2914

Going (Turf): **Sf: 1-1** GS: 0-0 Gd: 0-0 GF: 0-0 Fm: 0-0
Distance: 5f/6f: 0-0 **7f-8f: 1-2** 9f-13f: 0-0 14f+: 0-0
Track : LH: 0-0 RH: 0-1 Tight: 0-0 Gall: 0-0
Aids: Bl: 0-0 Vi: 0-0 Tstrap: 0-0 Ckp: 0-0
Best Rating: **84** 10/09 Sals 1m soft

Fair; stays 1m, will get further; acts on easy ground.

Soundbyte

100(102) (79)79

4-y-o b g Beat All (USA)-Gloaming (Celtic Swing)

J Gallagher Oliver Parsons

Placings:0/03201122-333055015642 **(7222)**

2009: 12^{3}SD, 14^{3}GF, 14^{3}GF, 18^{0}G, 14^{5}G, 12^{5}G, 11^{0}F, 11^{1}GF, 11^{5}GS, 12^{6}SS, 14^{4}GS, 13^{2}S,

	Starts	1st	2nd	3rd	Win & Pl
Career Total (Turf)	15	3	2	2	14287
Career Total (AW)	6	0	2	2	2452

71 9/09 Gdwd 1m3f (0-70)H G-F £3123
73 8/08 Brig 1m3f196y (0-70)H G-S £2978
66 8/08 Brig 1m3f196y (0-65)H GD £2331
Total win prize-money £8433

Going (Turf): Sf: 0-1 **GS: 1-3 Gd: 1-5 GF: 1-5** Fm: 0-1
Distance: 5f/6f: 0-0 7f-8f: 0-0 **9f-13f: 3-14** 14f+: 0-7
Track : **LH: 2-17** RH: 1-4 **Tight: 1-10** Gall: 0-3
Aids: Bl: 0-0 Vi: 0-1 Tstrap: 0-0 Ckp: 0-0
Best Rating: **79** 3/09 Kemp 1m4f stand

Modest; stays 1m6f; acts on good and easy ground; goes on Polytrack.

Sounds Of Jupiter (IRE)

105(102) (71)82

3-y-o ch g Galileo (IRE)-Sena Desert (Green Desert (USA))

C Byrnes (D M Simcock 5/10) Gigginstown House Stud

Placings:03-124003110 **(5641)**

2009: 11^{1}SD, 12^{2}SD, 12^{4}F, 14^{0}F, 12^{0}GF, 11^{3}G, 11^{1}F, 12^{1}GF, 11^{0}SD,

	Starts	1st	2nd	3rd	Win & Pl
Career Total (Turf)	6	2	0	1	6168
Career Total (AW)	5	1	1	1	3782

82 8/09 Folk 1m4f (0-65)H G-F £2388
78 8/09 Brig 1m3f196y (0-70)H FRM £3154
64 1/09 Kemp 1m3f STD £2590
Total win prize-money £8132

Going (Turf): Sf: 0-0 GS: 0-0 Gd: 0-1 **GF: 1-2 Fm: 1-3**
Distance: 5f/6f: 0-0 7f-8f: 0-2 **9f-13f: 3-8** 14f+: 0-1
Track : LH: 1-7 **RH: 2-4 Tight: 1-5** Gall: 0-1
Aids: Bl: 0-0 Vi: 0-0 Tstrap: 0-0 Ckp: 0-0
Best Rating: **82** 8/09 Folk 1m4f gd-fm

Useful; stays 1m4f; acts on fast ground; goes on Polytrack.

Sounds Of Thunder

90(101) (70)66

2-y-o b f Tobougg (IRE)-Distant Music (Darshaan)

H J L Dunlop Lady Mary Manton & Dr Fred Mosselmans

Placings:6545041 **(7597)**

2009: 6^{6}GF, 7^{5}F, 7^{4}G, 7^{5}GF, 8^{0}S, 8^{4}SD, 8^{1}SD,

	Starts	1st	2nd	3rd	Win & Pl
Career Total (Turf)	5	0	0	0	265
Career Total (AW)	2	1	0	0	3155

70 11/09 Wolv 1m141y (0-65) STD £2914
Total win prize-money £2914

Going (Turf): **Sf: 0-1 GS: 0-0 Gd: 0-1 GF: 0-2 Fm: 0-1**
Distance: 5f/6f: 0-0 7f-8f: 0-4 **9f-13f: 1-3** 14f+: 0-0
Track : **LH: 1-4** RH: 0-0 **Tight: 1-2** Gall: 0-0
Aids: Bl: 0-0 Vi: 0-0 Tstrap: 0-0 Ckp: 0-0
Best Rating: **70** 11/09 Wolv 1m141y stand

Modest; stays 1m; acts on Polytrack.

Sour Mash (IRE)

87 48

2-y-o b c Danehill Dancer (IRE)-Landmark (USA) (Arch (USA))

L M Cumani The Honorable Earle I Mack

Placings:0 **(6810)**

2009: 8^{0}G,

	Starts	1st	2nd	3rd	Win & Pl
Career Total (Turf)	1	0	0	0	

Going (Turf): **Sf: 0-0 GS: 0-0 Gd: 0-1 GF: 0-0 Fm: 0-0**
Distance: 5f/6f: 0-0 7f-8f: 0-1 9f-13f: 0-0 14f+: 0-0
Track : LH: 0-0 RH: 0-0 Tight: 0-0 Gall: 0-0
Aids: Bl: 0-0 Vi: 0-0 Tstrap: 0-0 Ckp: 0-0
Best Rating: **48** 10/09 NmkR 1m good

Souter Point (USA)

104(103) (72)89

3-y-o b/br g Giant's Causeway (USA)-Wires Crossed

(USA) (Caller I.D. (USA))
R Charlton Michael Pescod

Placings:25-2432132322 **(6571)**
2009: 10^{2}G, 10^{4}GF, 9^{3}G, 12^{2}GF, **12^{1}SD**, 10^{3}GF, 10^{2}G, 10^{3}F, 11^{2}G, 11^{2}GF,

	Starts	1st	2nd	3rd	Win & Pl
Career Total (Turf)	11	0	6	3	12490
Career Total (AW)	1	1	0	0	2730

72 7/09 Ling 1m4f STD £2729
Total win prize-money £2730

Going (Turf): **Sf: 0-0 GS: 0-0 Gd: 0-6 GF: 0-4 Fm: 0-1**
Distance: 5f/6f: 0-0 7f-8f: 0-2 **9f-13f: 1-10** 14f+: 0-0
Track : **LH: 1-5** RH: 0-5 **Tight: 1-7** Gall: 0-0
Aids: Bl: 0-0 Vi: 0-0 Tstrap: 0-0 Ckp: 0-0
Best Rating: 89 10/09 Leic 1m3f183y gd-fm

Useful; stays 1m4f; acts on fast ground; goes on Polytrack.

South African (USA)

(94) (65)
3-y-o gr/ro f Johannesburg (USA)-River Cache (USA) (Unbridled (USA))
M A Magnusson Eastwind Racing Ltd and Martha Trussell

Placings:22 **(5882)**
2009: 5^{2}SD, 5^{2}SD,

	Starts	1st	2nd	3rd	Win & Pl
Career Total (Turf)	0	0	0	0	
Career Total (AW)	2	0	2	0	1770

Going (Turf): **Sf: 0-0 GS: 0-0 Gd: 0-0 GF: 0-0 Fm: 0-0**
Distance: 5f/6f: 0-2 7f-8f: 0-0 9f-13f: 0-0 14f+: 0-0
Track : LH: 0-2 RH: 0-0 Tight: 0-2 Gall: 0-0
Aids: Bl: 0-0 Vi: 0-0 Tstrap: 0-0 Ckp: 0-0
Best Rating: 65 9/09 Wolv 5f216y stand

Modest; suited by 5f-6f and acts on Polytrack.

South African Gold (USA)

74(94) (69)24
2-y-o ch c Johannesburg (USA)-Coesse Gold (USA) (Seeking The Gold (USA))
J M P Eustace William Mocatta

Placings:004 **(7859)**
2009: 6^{0}G, 6^{0}SD, 7^{4}SD,

	Starts	1st	2nd	3rd	Win & Pl
Career Total (Turf)	1	0	0	0	
Career Total (AW)	2	0	0	0	241

Going (Turf): **Sf: 0-0 GS: 0-0 Gd: 0-1 GF: 0-0 Fm: 0-0**
Distance: 5f/6f: 0-2 7f-8f: 0-1 9f-13f: 0-0 14f+: 0-0
Track : LH: 0-2 RH: 0-0 Tight: 0-2 Gall: 0-1
Aids: Bl: 0-0 Vi: 0-0 Tstrap: 0-0 Ckp: 0-0
Best Rating: 69 12/09 Wolv 7f32y stand

Modest; best effort over 7f; acts on Polytrack.

South Cape

105(105) (94)95
6-y-o b g Cape Cross (IRE)-Aunt Ruby (USA) (Rubiano (USA))
G L Moore Heart Of The South Racing

Placings:135/105043302200/0015004512100/006452051056-006U03001 **(7125)**
2009: 8^{0}G, 7^{0}GF, 7^{6}G, 8^{U}G, 7^{0}G, 7^{3}GF, 8^{0}GF, 7^{0}G, 8^{1}G,

	Starts	1st	2nd	3rd	Win & Pl
Career Total (Turf)	47	7	4	3	91321
Career Total (AW)	3	0	0	1	1866

88 10/09 Nott 1m75y (0-85)H GD £6476
95 9/08 Gdwd 7f (0-100)H SFT £11215
97 9/07 Ches 7f2y (0-95)H GD £9715
95 9/07 Gdwd 7f (0-100)H G-F £11217
90 6/07 Folk 7f (0-90)H GD £9067
80 3/06 Sthl 7f HVY £9067
78 9/05 Newb 6f8y G-F £6532
Total win prize-money £63295

Going (Turf): Sf: 2-6 GS: 0-8 **Gd: 3-16** GF: 2-15 Fm: 0-2
Distance: 5f/6f: 0-2 **7f-8f: 6-42** 9f-13f: 1-6 14f+: 0-0
Track : **LH: 3-10** RH: 2-12 **Tight: 2-7** Gall: 0-4
Aids: Bl: 0-0 Vi: 0-0 Tstrap: 0-6 Ckp: 0-6
Best Rating: 99 9/06 Sand 1m14y gd-fm

Useful; effective over 7f-1m; acts on any ground on turf; has worn cheekpieces.

South Easter (IRE)

109 105
3-y-o ch c Galileo (IRE)-Dance Treat (USA) (Nureyev (USA))
W J Haggas Markus Jooste & Bernard Kantor

Placings:216 **(3087)**
2009: 8^{2}S, 10^{1}GF, 12^{6}GF,

	Starts	1st	2nd	3rd	Win & Pl
Career Total (Turf)	3	1	1	0	43395

105 5/09 Ches 1m2f75y G-F £39739
Total win prize-money £39739

Going (Turf): Sf: 0-1 GS: 0-0 Gd: 0-0 **GF: 1-2** Fm: 0-0
Distance: 5f/6f: 0-0 7f-8f: 0-1 **9f-13f: 1-2** 14f+: 0-0
Track : **LH: 1-1** RH: 0-1 **Tight: 1-1** Gall: 0-1
Aids: Bl: 0-0 Vi: 0-0 Tstrap: 0-0 Ckp: 0-0
Best Rating: 105 5/09 Ches 1m2f75y gd-fm

Smart; stays 1m2f and acts on fast and soft ground.

South Wing (IRE)

108 (86)86
5-y-o ch g In The Wings-Desert Grouse (USA) (Gulch (USA))
Ms Caroline Hutchinson (Eoin Griffin 21/9) Up The Yard Syndicate

Placings:306/30431**1**065/00-3205000 **(7261a)**
2009: 10^{3}GF, 12^{2}G, 16^{0}G, 12^{5}SH, 12^{0}GF, 10^{0}S, 16^{0}HY,

	Starts	1st	2nd	3rd	Win & Pl
Career Total (Turf)	16	1	1	4	15480
Career Total (AW)	5	1	0	0	12096

86 9/07 Dund 1m2f150y H STD £12096
80 9/07 Curr 1m2f (50-80)H G-F £6769
Total win prize-money £18866

Going (Turf): Sf: 0-5 GS: 0-0 Gd: 0-4 **GF: 1-5** Fm: 0-0
Distance: 5f/6f: 0-0 7f-8f: 0-3 **9f-13f: 2-16** 14f+: 0-2
Track : LH: 0-9 **RH: 1-7** Tight: 0-0 Gall: 0-1
Aids: Bl: 0-2 Vi: 0-0 Tstrap: 0-0 Ckp: 0-0
Best Rating: 86 5/09 Leop 1m4f good

Southandwest (IRE)

101(112) (94)91
5-y-o ch g Titus Livius (FR)-Cheviot Indian (IRE) (Indian Ridge)
J S Moore Wall To Wall Partnership

Placings:215120/2026054/0616006060**4231**-1302300000062353 **(7883)**
2009: 7^{1}SD, 7^{3}SD, 7^{0}SD, 7^{2}SD, 7^{3}SD, 8^{0}SD, 7^{0}SD, 7^{0}SD, 8^{0}SD, 7^{0}SD, 7^{0}G, 8^{0}GF, 8^{6}GF, 7^{2}SD, 7^{3}SD, 8^{5}SD, 8^{3}SD,

	Starts	1st	2nd	3rd	Win & Pl
Career Total (Turf)	26	3	4	0	61896
Career Total (AW)	18	2	3	5	21275

94 1/09 Wolv 7f32y (0-85)H STD £5180
88 12/08 Ling 7f (0-85)H STD £4727
91 5/08 Newc 7f (0-90)H G-F £6938
86 7/06 Bath 5f11y FRM £3562
86 6/06 Bath 5f11y FRM £2590
Total win prize-money £23000

Going (Turf): Sf: 0-0 GS: 0-6 Gd: 0-4 GF: 1-14 **Fm: 2-2**
Distance: 5f/6f: 2-13 **7f-8f: 3-25** 9f-13f: 0-6 14f+: 0-0
Track : **LH: 4-14** RH: 0-12 Tight: 2-13 Gall: 2-3
Aids: Bl: 0-0 Vi: 0-0 Tstrap: 0-1 Ckp: 0-1
Best Rating: 94 2/09 Wolv 7f32y stand

Useful; stays 7f; suited by fast ground; goes on Polytrack; has worn cheekpieces.

Southern Breeze

(64) (14)
2-y-o b c Dansili-Michelle Ma Belle (IRE) (Shareef Dancer (USA))
S Kirk Mrs Michelle Cousins

Placings:0 **(7537)**
2009: 7^{0}SD,

	Starts	1st	2nd	3rd	Win & Pl
Career Total (Turf)	0	0	0	0	
Career Total (AW)	1	0	0	0	

Going (Turf): **Sf: 0-0 GS: 0-0 Gd: 0-0 GF: 0-0 Fm: 0-0**
Distance: 5f/6f: 0-0 7f-8f: 0-1 9f-13f: 0-0 14f+: 0-0
Track : LH: 0-0 RH: 0-1 Tight: 0-0 Gall: 0-0
Aids: Bl: 0-0 Vi: 0-0 Tstrap: 0-0 Ckp: 0-0
Best Rating: 14 11/09 Kemp 7f stand

Southern Goddess (IRE)

81 38
2-y-o b f Avonbridge-Northern Secret (Sinndar (IRE))
P D Evans Raymond N R Auld

Placings:00 **(2319)**
2009: 5^{0}GF, 6^{0}G,

	Starts	1st	2nd	3rd	Win & Pl
Career Total (Turf)	2	0	0	0	

Going (Turf): **Sf: 0-0 GS: 0-0 Gd: 0-1 GF: 0-1 Fm: 0-0**
Distance: 5f/6f: 0-1 7f-8f: 0-1 9f-13f: 0-0 14f+: 0-0
Track : LH: 0-1 RH: 0-0 Tight: 0-0 Gall: 0-1
Aids: Bl: 0-0 Vi: 0-0 Tstrap: 0-0 Ckp: 0-0
Best Rating: 38 5/09 Bath 5f11y gd-fm

Southern Mistral

94(99) (62)61
4-y-o b g Desert Prince (IRE)-Hyperspectra (Rainbow Quest (USA))
Miss Gay Kelleway Eugene Woods

Placings:0435/0030005-0150 **(1881)**
2009: 9^{0}GF, 9^{1}GF, **10^{5}SD**, 10^{0}F,

	Starts	1st	2nd	3rd	Win & Pl
Career Total (Turf)	6	1	0	0	2590
Career Total (AW)	9	0	0	2	736

61 4/09 Ripn 1m1f170y G-F £2590
Total win prize-money £2590

Going (Turf): Sf: 0-0 GS: 0-2 Gd: 0-0 **GF: 1-3** Fm: 0-1
Distance: 5f/6f: 0-2 7f-8f: 0-3 **9f-13f: 1-10** 14f+: 0-0
Track : LH: 0-5 **RH: 1-9 Tight: 1-3** Gall: 0-3
Aids: Bl: 0-0 Vi: 0-0 Tstrap: 1-4 Ckp: 1-4
Best Rating: 69 9/07 Kemp 7f stand

Moderate; stays 1m3f; acts on Polytrack.

Southern Waters (FR)

46

5-y-o br g Sinndar (IRE)-Due South (Darshaan)
G A Swinbank D C Mitchell & R H Hall

Placings:0 (1099)
2009: 12^0GF,

	Starts	1st	2nd	3rd	Win & Pl
Career Total (Turf)	1	0	0	0	

Going (Turf): **Sf: 0-0 GS: 0-0 Gd: 0-0 GF: 0-1 Fm: 0-0**
Distance: 5f/6f: 0-0 7f-8f: 0-0 9f-13f: 0-1 14f+: 0-0
Track : LH: 0-0 RH: 0-1 Tight: 0-1 Gall: 0-0
Aids: Bl: 0-0 Vi: 0-0 Tstrap: 0-0 Ckp: 0-0
Best Rating: 46 4/09 Muss 1m4f100y gd-fm

Southoffrance (IRE)

33(79) (42)26

3-y-o b f Dr Fong (USA)-Mystery Solved (USA) (Royal Academy (USA))
W G M Turner Marbary Partnership

Placings:06-00 (7369)
2009: 11^0G, 9^0SD,

	Starts	1st	2nd	3rd	Win & Pl
Career Total (Turf)	2	0	0	0	
Career Total (AW)	2	0	0	0	0

Going (Turf): **Sf: 0-0 GS: 0-0 Gd: 0-1 GF: 0-1 Fm: 0-0**
Distance: 5f/6f: 0-1 7f-8f: 0-1 9f-13f: 0-2 14f+: 0-0
Track : LH: 0-3 RH: 0-0 Tight: 0-2 Gall: 0-1
Aids: Bl: 0-1 Vi: 0-0 Tstrap: 0-1 Ckp: 0-1
Best Rating: 42 7/08 Wolv 7f32y stand

Southwark Newshawk

80(90) (52)55

2-y-o ch f Piccolo-Be Bop Aloha (Most Welcome)
Mrs C A Dunnett Southwark News Racing Club

Placings:003003430504 (7331)
2009: 5^0GF, 5^0GF, 5^3SD, 6^0SD, 5^0G, 5^3SD, 6^4SD, 5^3G, 5^0G, 5^5SD, 5^0GF, 5^4SD,

	Starts	1st	2nd	3rd	Win & Pl
Career Total (Turf)	6	0	0	1	385
Career Total (AW)	6	0	0	2	706

Going (Turf): **Sf: 0-0 GS: 0-0 Gd: 0-3 GF: 0-3 Fm: 0-0**
Distance: 5f/6f: 0-12 7f-8f: 0-0 9f-13f: 0-0 14f+: 0-0
Track : LH: 0-2 RH: 0-0 Tight: 0-1 Gall: 0-0
Aids: Bl: 0-0 Vi: 0-0 Tstrap: 0-0 Ckp: 0-0
Best Rating: 55 7/09 Yarm 5f43y good

Moderate; effective at 5f; acts on Fibresand and good ground.

Sovento (GER)

91(96) (59)63

5-y-o ch g Kornado-Second Game (GER) (Second Set (IRE))
Shaun Harley Lough Derg Syndicate

Placings:31531402-00652 (7687)
2009: 12^0HY, 12^0G, 12^6S, 13^5G, 12^2SD,

	Starts	1st	2nd	3rd	Win & Pl
Career Total (Turf)	12	2	1	2	7721
Career Total (AW)	1	0	1	0	504

7/08 Muni 1m3f GD £2205
5/08 Colo 1m4f GD £1470
Total win prize-money £3677

Going (Turf): Sf: 0-4 GS: 0-0 **Gd: 2-8** GF: 0-0 Fm: 0-0
Distance: 5f/6f: 0-0 7f-8f: 0-0 **9f-13f: 2-12** 14f+: 0-1
Track : LH: 0-1 RH: 0-5 Tight: 0-1 Gall: 0-0
Aids: Bl: 0-0 Vi: 0-0 Tstrap: 0-0 Ckp: 0-0
Best Rating: 63 10/08 MsnL 1m4f soft

Moderate; ex-Irish; best at around 1m4f; acts on soft ground and Polytrack.

Sovereign Remedy (USA)

106(109) (111)97

3-y-o ch c Elusive Quality (USA)-Lailani (Unfuwain (USA))
Saeed Bin Suroor Godolphin

Placings:21632216 (7060)
2009: 8^2SD, 8^1G, 10^6G, 8^3GF, 8^2G, 8^2GF, 8^1SD, 8^6GF,

	Starts	1st	2nd	3rd	Win & Pl
Career Total (Turf)	6	1	2	1	11393
Career Total (AW)	2	1	1	0	13615

111 10/09 Sthl 1m (0-100)H STD £12304
78 5/09 Nott 1m75y GD £2590
Total win prize-money £14894

Going (Turf): Sf: 0-0 GS: 0-0 **Gd: 1-3** GF: 0-3 Fm: 0-0
Distance: 5f/6f: 0-0 7f-8f: 1-4 9f-13f: 1-4 14f+: 0-0
Track : **LH: 2-4** RH: 0-2 Tight: 0-1 Gall: 0-1
Aids: Bl: 0-0 Vi: 0-0 Tstrap: 0-0 Ckp: 0-0
Best Rating: 111 10/09 Sthl 1m stand

Very useful; stays 1m; acts on good ground; goes on Fibresand and Polytrack.

Sovereign Secure (IRE)

91(91) (62)68

2-y-o ch f Kyllachy-Affaire Royale (IRE) (Royal Academy (USA))
Lee Smyth Mrs M A McNiece

Placings:00300654 (7372)
2009: 7^0G, 5^0SD, 6^3GF, 6^0G, 6^0GY, 5^6SD, 5^5SD, 5^4SD,

	Starts	1st	2nd	3rd	Win & Pl
Career Total (Turf)	4	0	0	1	4925
Career Total (AW)	4	0	0	0	241

Going (Turf): **Sf: 0-0 GS: 0-0 Gd: 0-2 GF: 0-1 Fm: 0-0**
Distance: 5f/6f: 0-7 7f-8f: 0-1 9f-13f: 0-0 14f+: 0-0
Track : LH: 0-6 RH: 0-0 Tight: 0-3 Gall: 0-1
Aids: Bl: 0-0 Vi: 0-0 Tstrap: 0-3 Ckp: 0-3
Best Rating: 68 8/09 Ripn 6f gd-fm

Very moderate form at 6-7f on good ground and Polytrack.

Sovereign Spirit (IRE)

(97) (25)30

7-y-o b g Desert Prince (IRE)-Sheer Spirit (IRE) (Caerleon (USA))
C Gordon (Mme L Braem 3/10) Mrs C M Grant

Placings:006/5306512/11440236/00264235/00-02000 (7608)
2009: 15^0GS, 11^2SD, 11^0SD, 11^0SD, 16^0SD,

	Starts	1st	2nd	3rd	Win & Pl
Career Total (Turf)	11	0	1	1	1220
Career Total (AW)	22	3	4	2	11621

72 2/06 Wolv 1m5f194y (0-65)H STD £2388
69 1/06 Sthl 1m4f (0-65)H STD £2388
63 12/05 Wolv 1m5f194y (0-55)H STD £2878
Total win prize-money £7657

Going (Turf): **Sf: 0-0 GS: 0-2 Gd: 0-3 GF: 0-5 Fm: 0-1**
Distance: 5f/6f: 0-0 7f-8f: 0-2 9f-13f: 1-15 **14f+: 2-16**
Track : **LH: 3-21** RH: 0-8 **Tight: 2-16** Gall: 0-1
Aids: Bl: 0-0 Vi: 0-0 Tstrap: 0-1 Ckp: 0-1
Best Rating: 74 10/06 Wolv 1m5f194y std-fst

Modest gelding; suited by 14f; acts on both All-Weather surfaces; has worn a tongue tie.

Sovereignty (JPN)

94(102) (73)73

7-y-o b g King's Best (USA)-Calando (USA) (Storm Cat (USA))
D K Ivory Three Cool Cats

Placings:24/23434104062/000410426146303516/000005640/511063332042014006000 0050115053006406 (7834)
2009: 6^0CF, 6^0CF, 5^5SD, 6^0SD, 8^1SD, 8^1SD, 8^5SD, 8^0SD, 7^5SD, 8^3SD, 8^0SD, 6^0G, 8^6SD, 7^4SD, 7^0SD, 6^6SD,

	Starts	1st	2nd	3rd	Win & Pl
Career Total (Turf)	21	1	3	1	9714
Career Total (AW)	56	8	3	7	24512

67 7/09 Kemp 1m (0-58)H STD £2047
65 6/09 Kemp 1m (0-60)H STD £2047
73 7/08 Kemp 7f (0-65)H STD £2047
66 1/08 Kemp 7f (0-55)H STD £2047
63 1/08 Wolv 7f32y (0-50)H STD £1774
73 12/06 Wolv 7f32y (0-65)H STD £3238
70 9/06 Wolv 7f32y (0-65)H STD £2730
64 7/06 Wolv 5f20y STD £2388
54 7/05 Ayr 7f50y (0-70) G-F £3334
Total win prize-money £21657

Going (Turf): Sf: 0-0 GS: 0-4 Gd: 0-5 **GF: 1-10** Fm: 0-2
Distance: 5f/6f: 1-20 **7f-8f: 8-53** 9f-13f: 0-4 14f+: 0-0
Track : **LH: 5-42** RH: 4-24 **Tight: 4-31** Gall: 0-6
Aids: Bl: 0-0 Vi: 0-1 Tstrap: 0-1 Ckp: 0-1
Best Rating: 77 7/04 Wind 6f gd-sft

Moderate; effective over 6f-1m; acts well on sand.

Soviet Rhythm

92 65

3-y-o b f Soviet Star (USA)-Aldevonie (Green Desert (USA))
M Dods (G M Moore 9/6) Geoff & Sandra Turnbull

Placings:55040-0004 (5145)

2009: 8^{0}GF, 7^{0}GF, 5^{0}GF, 5^{4}GS,

	Starts	1st	2nd	3rd	Win & Pl
Career Total (Turf)	9	0	0	0	505

Going (Turf): Sf: 0-1 GS: 0-1 Gd: 0-3 GF: 0-4 Fm: 0-0
Distance: 5f/6f: 0-7 7f-8f: 0-2 9f-13f: 0-0 14f+: 0-0
Track : LH: 0-3 RH: 0-1 Tight: 0-2 Gall: 0-0
Aids: Bl: 0-0 Vi: 0-0 Tstrap: 0-0 Ckp: 0-0
Best Rating: 65 7/08 Donc 5f good

Soviet Sceptre (IRE)

82(95) (54)**62**

8-y-o ch g Soviet Star (USA)-Princess Sceptre (Cadeaux Genereux)
Tim Vaughan Welsh Valleys Syndicate No. 2

Placings:56/304600150/00066001/20456/240/10300-6 **(2337)**
2009: 11^{6}GF,

	Starts	1st	2nd	3rd	Win & Pl
Career Total (Turf)	22	3	1	2	10849
Career Total (AW)	11	0	1	0	964

62 7/08 Chep 1m4f23y(0-65)H G-F £2428
60 6/05 Chep 1m4f23y (0-55)H GD £3161
62 9/04 Wind 1m2f7y G-F £3532
Total win prize-money £9122

Going (Turf): Sf: 0-4 GS: 0-3 Gd: 1-7 GF: 2-8 Fm: 0-0
Distance: 5f/6f: 0-1 7f-8f: 0-5 9f-13f: 3-23 14f+: 0-4
Track : LH: 2-22 RH: 1-7 Tight: 1-18 Gall: 0-0
Aids: Bl: 0-0 Vi: 0-0 Tstrap: 1-6 Ckp: 1-6
Best Rating: 76 8/03 Gdwd 7f good

Moderate gelding; stays a 1m4f; acts on ground either side of good and Polytrack; has worn a tongue tie and cheek-pieces.

Sovietta (IRE)

(101) (56)**60**

8-y-o b m Soviet Star (USA)-La Riveraine (USA) (Riverman (USA))
Ian Williams Ian Williams

Placings:4301/006100/430210/0352406/0341300-0000 **(2601)**
2009: 16^{0}SS, 12^{0}SD, 13^{0}SD, 12^{0}SD,

	Starts	1st	2nd	3rd	Win & Pl
Career Total (Turf)	20	3	2	3	12880
Career Total (AW)	14	1	0	2	2050

54 3/08 Kemp 1m4f (0-45) STD £1365
60 5/06 Leic 1m3f183y (0-60)H G-S £3154
65 5/05 Bath 1m3f144y (0-60)H HVY £3388
60 10/04 Leic 1m3f183y GD £3542
Total win prize-money £11451

Going (Turf): Sf: 1-9 GS: 1-2 Gd: 1-3 GF: 0-5 Fm: 0-1
Distance: 5f/6f: 0-0 7f-8f: 0-0 9f-13f: 4-24 14f+: 0-10
Track : LH: 1-23 RH: 3-10 Tight: 1-15 Gall: 0-1
Aids: Bl: 0-0 Vi: 0-0 Tstrap: 0-1 Ckp: 0-1
Best Rating: 65 5/05 Bath 1m3f144y heavy

Moderate mare who has shown a tendency to go right-handed; probably stays 2m; acts on easy ground and Fibresand.

Sowaylm

(102) (82)

2-y-o b c Tobougg (IRE)-Ameerat (Mark Of Esteem (IRE))
Saeed Bin Suroor Godolphin

Placings:1 **(7199)**
2009: 8^{1}SD,

	Starts	1st	2nd	3rd	Win & Pl
Career Total (Turf)	0	0	0	0	
Career Total (AW)	1	1	0	0	2047

82 11/09 Ling 1m STD £2047
Total win prize-money £2047

Going (Turf): Sf: 0-0 GS: 0-0 Gd: 0-0 GF: 0-0 Fm: 0-0
Distance: 5f/6f: 0-0 7f-8f: 1-1 9f-13f: 0-0 14f+: 0-0
Track : LH: 1-1 RH: 0-0 Tight: 1-1 Gall: 0-0
Aids: Bl: 0-0 Vi: 0-0 Tstrap: 0-0 Ckp: 0-0
Best Rating: 82 11/09 Ling 1m stand

Winner on debut; effective over 1m; acts on Polytrack.

Spa's Dancer (IRE)

93 **85**

2-y-o b c Danehill Dancer (IRE)-Spa (Sadler's Wells (USA))
J W Hills The Seventh Pheasant Inn Partnership

Placings:4023 **(6931)**
2009: 7^{4}GF, 7^{0}GF, 7^{2}GS, 8^{3}G,

	Starts	1st	2nd	3rd	Win & Pl
Career Total (Turf)	4	0	1	1	2774

Going (Turf): Sf: 0-0 GS: 0-1 Gd: 0-1 GF: 0-2 Fm: 0-0
Distance: 5f/6f: 0-0 7f-8f: 0-3 9f-13f: 0-1 14f+: 0-0
Track : LH: 0-1 RH: 0-2 Tight: 0-1 Gall: 0-0
Aids: Bl: 0-0 Vi: 0-0 Tstrap: 0-0 Ckp: 0-0
Best Rating: 85 9/09 Sand 7f16y gd-sft

Fair; effective over 1m; acts on good ground.

Space Pirate

91(101) (52)**58**

4-y-o b g Bahamian Bounty-Science Fiction (Starborough)
J Pearce Oceana racing

Placings:0065230/40030106000-000000 **(4667)**
2009: 10^{0}SD, 10^{0}SD, 9^{0}GF, 10^{0}SD, 9^{0}GF, 8^{0}G,

	Starts	1st	2nd	3rd	Win & Pl
Career Total (Turf)	15	1	1	2	4531
Career Total (AW)	9	0	0	0	0

58 8/08 Brig 7f214y (0-65)H G-S £2201
Total win prize-money £2202

Going (Turf): Sf: 0-2 GS: 1-1 Gd: 0-5 GF: 0-6 Fm: 0-1
Distance: 5f/6f: 0-1 7f-8f: 1-5 9f-13f: 0-17 14f+: 0-1
Track : LH: 1-16 RH: 0-1 Tight: 0-7 Gall: 0-2
Aids: Bl: 0-1 Vi: 0-5 Tstrap: 1-9 Ckp: 1-9
Best Rating: 62 8/07 NmkJ 7f good

Moderate; effective over 7f-1m; handles quick and soft ground.

Space Station

96(104) (76)**74**

3-y-o b g Anabaa (USA)-Spacecraft (USA) (Distant View (USA))
S Dow (P Bary 1/6) Mr & Mrs Chua, Moore & Jurd

Placings:460245425 **(7876)**
2009: 8^{4}G, 8^{6}GS, 7^{0}SD, 7^{2}GS, 7^{4}GF, 6^{5}SD, 7^{4}SD, 6^{2}SD, 7^{5}SD,

	Starts	1st	2nd	3rd	Win & Pl
Career Total (Turf)	4	0	1	0	3617
Career Total (AW)	5	0	1	0	1026

Going (Turf): Sf: 0-0 GS: 0-2 Gd: 0-1 GF: 0-1 Fm: 0-0
Distance: 5f/6f: 0-2 7f-8f: 0-7 9f-13f: 0-0 14f+: 0-0
Track : LH: 0-3 RH: 0-5 Tight: 0-2 Gall: 0-0
Aids: Bl: 0-0 Vi: 0-0 Tstrap: 0-0 Ckp: 0-0
Best Rating: 76 12/09 Kemp 6f stand

Modest; stays 7f and acts on fast and easy ground; handles Polytrack.

Spacious

111 **115**

4-y-o b f Nayef (USA)-Palatial (Green Desert (USA))
J R Fanshawe Cheveley Park Stud

Placings:11/24144-31303 **(6479)**
2009: 8^{3}G, 8^{1}GF, 8^{3}G, 9^{0}S, 8^{3}GF,

	Starts	1st	2nd	3rd	Win & Pl
Career Total (Turf)	12	4	1	3	292874

115 6/09 Asct 1m G-F £70962
99 9/08 Donc 1m SFT £15577
107 9/07 Donc 1m G-F £42585
92 8/07 Leic 7f9y G-S £4533
Total win prize-money £133660

Going (Turf): Sf: 1-2 GS: 1-1 Gd: 0-3 GF: 2-5 Fm: 0-1
Distance: 5f/6f: 0-0 7f-8f: 4-9 9f-13f: 0-3 14f+: 0-0
Track : LH: 0-1 RH: 0-2 Tight: 0-2 Gall: 0-1
Aids: Bl: 0-0 Vi: 0-0 Tstrap: 0-0 Ckp: 0-0
Best Rating: 115 6/09 Asct 1m gd-fm

Group class; runner-up in the 1000 Guineas in 2008; winner of a Group 2 in 2009; effective at 1m; acts on most ground.

Spanish Acclaim

85 **76**

2-y-o b g Acclamation-Spanish Gold (Vettori (IRE))
J G Portman The Farleigh Court Racing Partnership

Placings:02U0 **(5318)**
2009: 5^{0}GS, 5^{2}F, 5^{U}F, 6^{0}GF,

	Starts	1st	2nd	3rd	Win & Pl
Career Total (Turf)	4	0	1	0	1927

Going (Turf): Sf: 0-0 GS: 0-1 Gd: 0-0 GF: 0-1 Fm: 0-2
Distance: 5f/6f: 0-4 7f-8f: 0-0 9f-13f: 0-0 14f+: 0-0
Track : LH: 0-1 RH: 0-0 Tight: 0-0 Gall: 0-2
Aids: Bl: 0-0 Vi: 0-0 Tstrap: 0-0 Ckp: 0-0
Best Rating: 76 5/09 Sals 5f firm

Fair 90,000 half-brother to Spanish Bounty; has looked a difficult ride and has been gelded.

Spanish Ace

85(95) (47)**55**

8-y-o b g First Trump-Spanish Heart (King Of Spain)
J M Bradley racingshares.co.uk

Placings:216260/0000550410/0004000/1102006000/11604240000000/005000000-6044563600 **(3204)**
2009: 7^{6}SD, 6^{0}SD, 5^{4}SD, 5^{4}SD, 5^{5}SD, 5^{6}SD, 5^{3}SD, 5^{6}SD, 5^{0}GF, 5^{0}G,

	Starts	1st	2nd	3rd	Win & Pl
Career Total (Turf)	56	6	4	0	57102
Career Total (AW)	12	0	0	1	493

90 4/07 Wwck 5f (0-75)H G-F £3071
84 4/07 Bath 5f11y (0-75)H FRM £3238
89 4/06 Folk 5f (0-75)H G-F £3886
86 4/06 Wwck 5f (0-75)H GD £3238
97 8/04 Bath 5f11y D(0-80) G-S £5811
88 4/03 Asct 5f B GD £11005
Total win prize-money £30251

Going (Turf): Sf: 0-1 GS: 1-8 Gd: 2-15 GF: 2-30 Fm: 1-2

Distance: **5f/6f: 6-59** 7f-8f: 0-8 9f-13f: 0-1 14f+: 0-0
Track : **LH: 4-22** RH: 0-5 Tight: 0-10 **Gall: 2-8**
Aids: **Bl: 1-13** Vi: 0-6 Tstrap: 0-8 Ckp: 0-8
Best Rating: **98** 6/03 Curr 6f good

Moderate; effective over 5f; best on a sound surface, but handles cut; goes on Polytrack; has been tried in various headgear.

Spanish Bounty

108(100) (87)98
4-y-o b g Bahamian Bounty-Spanish Gold (Vettori (IRE))
J G Portman The Farleigh Court Racing Partnership

Placings:0121600/023140-606304000 (6482)
2009: 6^{6}SD, 6^{0}GF, 6^{6}GS, 6^{3}GF, 7^{0}GF, 7^{4}G, 7^{0}GF, 6^{0}GF, 7^{0}GF,

	Starts	1st	2nd	3rd	Win & Pl
Career Total (Turf)	20	3	2	2	89005
Career Total (AW)	2	0	0	0	138

98 7/08 NmkJ 6f (0-105)H G-S £62310
91 7/07 NmkJ 6f G-F £9715
82 6/07 Bath 5f161y GD £3562
Total win prize-money £75588

Going (Turf): Sf: 0-0 **GS: 1-6 Gd: 1-5 GF: 1-9** Fm: 0-0
Distance: **5f/6f: 3-15** 7f-8f: 0-7 9f-13f: 0-0 14f+: 0-0
Track : **LH: 1-2** RH: 0-4 Tight: 0-0 **Gall: 1-2**
Aids: Bl: 0-0 Vi: 0-0 Tstrap: 0-1 Ckp: 0-1
Best Rating: **98** 7/09 Gdwd 7f good

Very useful; effective at 6-7f and acts on most ground; likes to race prominently.

Spanish Conquest

86(100) (75)76
5-y-o b g Hernando (FR)-Sirena (GER) (Tejano (USA))
P J Hobbs Michael H Watt & J A McGrath

Placings:000/2126/30124-2 (6368)
2009: 14^{2}GF,

	Starts	1st	2nd	3rd	Win & Pl
Career Total (Turf)	3	0	1	1	1927
Career Total (AW)	10	2	3	0	6422

65 7/08 Sthl 1m6f (0-65)H STD £1978
62 10/07 Ling 1m4f (0-60)H STD £2047
Total win prize-money £4027

Going (Turf): **Sf: 0-0 GS: 0-1 Gd: 0-0 GF: 0-2 Fm: 0-0**
Distance: 5f/6f: 0-0 7f-8f: 0-3 9f-13f: 1-3 14f+: 1-7
Track : **LH: 2-9** RH: 0-4 **Tight: 1-5** Gall: 0-0
Aids: Bl: 0-0 Vi: 0-0 Tstrap: 0-0 Ckp: 0-0
Best Rating: **76** 9/09 Wwck 1m6f213y gd-fm

Modest; effective over 1m4f-2m; acts on Polytrack.

Spanish Cross (IRE)

99(100) (51)64
4-y-o gr f Cape Cross (IRE)-Espana (Hernando (FR))
G Prodromou George Prodromou

Placings:602660-00534 (7466)
2009: 12^{0}SD, 8^{0}GF, 9^{5}G, 10^{3}G, 9^{4}SD,

	Starts	1st	2nd	3rd	Win & Pl
Career Total (Turf)	9	0	1	1	1828
Career Total (AW)	2	0	0	0	0

Going (Turf): **Sf: 0-2 GS: 0-0 Gd: 0-3 GF: 0-1 Fm: 0-0**
Distance: 5f/6f: 0-0 7f-8f: 0-1 9f-13f: 0-10 14f+: 0-0
Track : LH: 0-5 RH: 0-5 Tight: 0-3 Gall: 0-1

Aids: Bl: 0-1 Vi: 0-0 Tstrap: 0-0 Ckp: 0-0
Best Rating: **64** 5/08 Clon 1m2f good

Moderate; effective at around 1m2f; acts on good ground.

Spanish Cygnet (USA)

84(94) (90)84
3-y-o b f El Corredor (USA)-Dixie Dos (USA) (Dixieland Band (USA))
Mrs A J Perrett Slade, Cotton, James, Tracey

Placings:2143-00 (5005)
2009: 7^{0}G, 7^{0}G,

	Starts	1st	2nd	3rd	Win & Pl
Career Total (Turf)	4	0	1	0	2767
Career Total (AW)	2	1	0	1	5339

81 7/08 Kemp 7f STD £4857
Total win prize-money £4857

Going (Turf): **Sf: 0-0 GS: 0-0 Gd: 0-2 GF: 0-2 Fm: 0-0**
Distance: 5f/6f: 0-1 **7f-8f: 1-5** 9f-13f: 0-0 14f+: 0-0
Track : LH: 0-1 **RH: 1-2** Tight: 0-1 Gall: 0-0
Aids: Bl: 0-0 Vi: 0-0 Tstrap: 0-0 Ckp: 0-0
Best Rating: **90** 9/08 Ling 7f stand

Useful; effective over 7f; acts on Polytrack and on fast ground.

Spanish Duke (IRE)

98(99) (82)77
2-y-o b g Big Bad Bob (IRE)-Spanish Lady (IRE) (Bering)
J L Dunlop Windflower Overseas Holdings Inc

Placings:054211 (6805)
2009: 7^{0}GF, 7^{5}G, 7^{4}GF, 8^{2}G, 6^{1}GF, 8^{1}SD,

	Starts	1st	2nd	3rd	Win & Pl
Career Total (Turf)	5	1	1	0	3585
Career Total (AW)	1	1	0	0	4533

82 10/09 Wolv 1m141y (0-85) STD £4533
77 9/09 Brig 6f209y G-F £2775
Total win prize-money £7309

Going (Turf): Sf: 0-0 GS: 0-0 Gd: 0-2 **GF: 1-3** Fm: 0-0
Distance: 5f/6f: 0-0 7f-8f: 1-4 9f-13f: 1-2 14f+: 0-0
Track : **LH: 2-3** RH: 0-0 **Tight: 1-2** Gall: 0-0
Aids: Bl: 0-0 Vi: 0-0 Tstrap: 0-0 Ckp: 0-0
Best Rating: **82** 10/09 Wolv 1m141y stand

Fair; effective over 1m; acts on fast ground.

Spanish Hidalgo (IRE)

88 107
5-y-o b g Night Shift (USA)-Spanish Lady (IRE) (Bering)
J L Dunlop Windflower Overseas Holdings Inc

Placings:23110/3156210/33320-3P (2075)
2009: 12^{3}GF, 13^{P}S,

	Starts	1st	2nd	3rd	Win & Pl
Career Total (Turf)	19	4	3	6	64030

104 10/07 Siro 1m6f SFT £18919
102 7/07 Ripn 1m4f10y (0-90)H HVY £11217
91 8/06 NmkJ 1m SFT £4533
79 8/06 Ling 7f140y G-F £3238
Total win prize-money £37910

Going (Turf): **Sf: 3-8** GS: 0-2 Gd: 0-5 GF: 1-3 Fm: 0-1
Distance: 5f/6f: 0-0 **7f-8f: 2-5** 9f-13f: 1-5 14f+: 1-9
Track : LH: 0-6 **RH: 1-9 Tight: 1-3** Gall: 0-5

Aids: Bl: 0-0 Vi: 0-0 Tstrap: 0-0 Ckp: 0-0
Best Rating: **111** 10/07 NmkR 1m6f good

Smart; Listed winner in Italy; stays 1m6f; acts on any ground; has worn a tongue tie.

Spares And Repairs

101(99) (67)51
6-y-o b g Robellino (USA)-Lady Blackfoot (Prince Tenderfoot (USA))
Mrs S Lamyman P Lamyman

Placings:3344/30-62500000 (2746)
2009: 9^{6}SD, 11^{2}SD, 12^{5}SD, 10^{0}F, 10^{0}F, 10^{0}GF, 8^{0}GF, 8^{0}SD,

	Starts	1st	2nd	3rd	Win & Pl
Career Total (Turf)	5	0	0	1	433
Career Total (AW)	9	0	1	2	1379

Going (Turf): **Sf: 0-0 GS: 0-0 Gd: 0-0 GF: 0-3 Fm: 0-2**
Distance: 5f/6f: 0-0 7f-8f: 0-1 9f-13f: 0-12 14f+: 0-1
Track : LH: 0-13 RH: 0-0 Tight: 0-4 Gall: 0-0
Aids: Bl: 0-0 Vi: 0-0 Tstrap: 0-0 Ckp: 0-0
Best Rating: **67** 12/07 Sthl 1m4f std-slw

Moderate; stays at least 1m4f; acts on Fibresand.

Sparkaway

108(95) (49)65
3-y-o ch g Gold Away (IRE)-West River (USA) (Gone West (USA))
W J Musson KCS Partnership

Placings:0000-511620 (7214)
2009: 12^{5}SD, 12^{1}GF, 14^{1}S, 13^{6}SD, 11^{2}GS, 13^{0}SD,

	Starts	1st	2nd	3rd	Win & Pl
Career Total (Turf)	6	2	1	0	6764
Career Total (AW)	4	0	0	0	0

65 7/09 Yarm 1m6f17y(0-70)H SFT £2719
56 6/09 Pont 1m4f8y (0-70)H G-F £3238
Total win prize money £5958

Going (Turf): **Sf: 1-1** GS: 0-1 Gd: 0-2 **GF: 1-2** Fm: 0-0
Distance: 5f/6f: 0-0 7f-8f: 0-4 9f-13f: 1-3 14f+: 1-3
Track : **LH: 2-4** RH: 0-2 **Tight: 1-4** Gall: 0-0
Aids: Bl: 0-0 Vi: 0-0 Tstrap: 0-0 Ckp: 0-0
Best Rating: **65** 7/09 Yarm 1m6f17y soft

Modest; stays well; handles ease.

Sparkbridge (IRE)

(94) (42)56
6-y-o b g Mull Of Kintyre (USA)-Persian Velvet (IRE) (Distinctly North (USA))
S C Burrough H J W Davies

Placings:26040/04000000/0000/3-6 (3275)
2009: 16^{6}SD,

	Starts	1st	2nd	3rd	Win & Pl
Career Total (Turf)	15	0	1	0	2000
Career Total (AW)	4	0	0	1	202

Going (Turf): **Sf: 0-4 GS: 0-1 Gd: 0-3 GF: 0-6 Fm: 0-1**
Distance: 5f/6f: 0-2 7f-8f: 0-7 9f-13f: 0-8 14f+: 0-2
Track : LH: 0-7 RH: 0-8 Tight: 0-8 Gall: 0-0
Aids: Bl: 0-3 Vi: 0-0 Tstrap: 0-2 Ckp: 0-2
Best Rating: **60** 7/05 Ayr 6f gd-fm

Sparking

70(89) (56)**8**

2-y-o ch f Exceed And Excel (AUS)-Twilight Time (Aragon)

Mrs G S Rees P Bamford

Placings:03 **(7618)**

2009: 5^{0}G, 5^{3}SD,

	Starts	1st	2nd	3rd	Win & Pl
Career Total (Turf)	1	0	0	0	
Career Total (AW)	1	0	0	1	385

Going (Turf): Sf: 0-0 GS: 0-0 Gd: 0-1 GF: 0-0 Fm: 0-0
Distance: 5f/6f: 0-2 7f-8f: 0-0 9f-13f: 0-0 14f+: 0-0
Track : LH: 0-1 RH: 0-0 Tight: 0-1 Gall: 0-0
Aids: Bl: 0-0 Vi: 0-0 Tstrap: 0-0 Ckp: 0-0
Best Rating: 56 12/09 Wolv 5f216y stand

Half-sister to six winners; promise on second start over 6f on Polytrack.

Sparkle Park

(53)

2-y-o b f Kyllachy-Petonellajill (Petong)

B J Meehan Mrs J & D E Cash

Placings:0 **(7886)**

2009: 7^{0}SD,

	Starts	1st	2nd	3rd	Win & Pl
Career Total (Turf)	0	0	0	0	
Career Total (AW)	1	0	0	0	

Going (Turf): Sf: 0-0 GS: 0-0 Gd: 0-0 GF: 0-0 Fm: 0-0
Distance: 5f/6f: 0-0 7f-8f: 0-1 9f-13f: 0-0 14f+: 0-0
Track : LH: 0-1 RH: 0-0 Tight: 0-1 Gall: 0-0
Aids: Bl: 0-0 Vi: 0-0 Tstrap: 0-0 Ckp: 0-0

Sparkling Crown

83(82) (50)**49**

2-y-o br f Xaar-Crown Water (USA) (Chief's Crown (USA))

J Ryan John Ryan Racing Partnership

Placings:0000 **(7683)**

2009: 7^{0}G, 7^{0}G, 8^{0}SD, 10^{0}SD,

	Starts	1st	2nd	3rd	Win & Pl
Career Total (Turf)	2	0	0	0	
Career Total (AW)	2	0	0	0	

Going (Turf): Sf: 0-0 GS: 0-0 Gd: 0-2 GF: 0-0 Fm: 0-0
Distance: 5f/6f: 0-0 7f-8f: 0-3 9f-13f: 0-1 14f+: 0-0
Track : LH: 0-0 RH: 0-2 Tight: 0-0 Gall: 0-0
Aids: Bl: 0-0 Vi: 0-0 Tstrap: 0-0 Ckp: 0-0
Best Rating: 50 11/09 Kemp 1m stand

Sparkling Crystal (IRE)

101(95) (71)**78**

3-y-o ch f Danehill Dancer (IRE)-Crystal Curling (IRE) (Peintre Celebre (USA))

B W Hills Triermore Stud

Placings:2434625-32155300 **(6975)**

2009: 7^{3}GF, 8^{2}GF, 8^{1}GF, 8^{5}S, 8^{5}G, 9^{3}GF, 10^{0}GF, 12^{0}SD,

	Starts	1st	2nd	3rd	Win & Pl
Career Total (Turf)	11	1	2	3	10512
Career Total (AW)	4	0	1	0	1059

78 6/09 Wind 1m67y (0-85)H G-F £5180

Total win prize-money £5181

Going (Turf): Sf: 0-1 GS: 0-0 Gd: 0-5 **GF: 1-5** Fm: 0-0
Distance: 5f/6f: 0-4 7f-8f: 0-6 **9f-13f: 1-5** 14f+: 0-0
Track : LH: 0-6 **RH: 1-5 Tight: 1-4** Gall: 0-3
Aids: Bl: 0-0 Vi: 0-0 Tstrap: 0-0 Ckp: 0-0
Best Rating: 78 6/09 Wind 1m67y gd-fm

Fair; effective at around 6f-1m; acts on good and on fast ground.

Sparkling Smile (IRE)

91(93) (63)**60**

2-y-o b/br f Cape Cross (IRE)-Starlight Smile (USA) (Green Dancer (USA))

D R Lanigan Saif Ali & Saeed H Altayer

Placings:040 **(6628)**

2009: 6^{0}GF, 7^{4}GF, 8^{0}SS,

	Starts	1st	2nd	3rd	Win & Pl
Career Total (Turf)	2	0	0	0	385
Career Total (AW)	1	0	0	0	

Going (Turf): Sf: 0-0 GS: 0-0 Gd: 0-0 GF: 0-2 Fm: 0-0
Distance: 5f/6f: 0-0 7f-8f: 0-3 9f-13f: 0-0 14f+: 0-0
Track : LH: 0-2 RH: 0-0 Tight: 0-2 Gall: 0-0
Aids: Bl: 0-0 Vi: 0-0 Tstrap: 0-0 Ckp: 0-0
Best Rating: 63 10/09 Ling 1m std-slw

Sparkling Suzie

81(89) (61)**35**

3-y-o b f Deportivo-Sparkling Jewel (Bijou D'Inde)

J S Moore G Bosley, G Mulford & D Sinclair

Placings:05-05000 **(6445)**

2009: 6^{0}GF, 6^{5}F, 7^{0}SD, 7^{0}SD, 12^{0}SS,

	Starts	1st	2nd	3rd	Win & Pl
Career Total (Turf)	3	0	0	0	118
Career Total (AW)	4	0	0	0	0

Going (Turf): Sf: 0-0 GS: 0-0 Gd: 0-0 GF: 0-2 Fm: 0-1
Distance: 5f/6f: 0-3 7f-8f: 0-3 9f-13f: 0-1 14f+: 0-0
Track : LH: 0-4 RH: 0-2 Tight: 0-2 Gall: 0-0
Aids: Bl: 0-1 Vi: 0-0 Tstrap: 0-0 Ckp: 0-0
Best Rating: 61 7/08 Kemp 6f stand

Sparky Vixen

87(102) (51)**56**

5-y-o b m Mujahid (USA)-Lucy Glitters (USA) (Cryptoclearance (USA))

C J Teague Collins Chauffeur Driven Executive Cars

Placings:000/345003/310446343500-45000 **(7500)**

2009: 8^{4}SD, 9^{5}GF, 8^{0}SD, 9^{0}GF, 8^{0}SD,

	Starts	1st	2nd	3rd	Win & Pl
Career Total (Turf)	15	0	0	3	1080
Career Total (AW)	11	1	0	2	2460

56 2/08 Sthl 1m (0-58)H STD £1774

Total win prize-money £1775

Going (Turf): Sf: 0-2 GS: 0-1 Gd: 0-6 GF: 0-6 Fm: 0-0
Distance: 5f/6f: 0-3 **7f-8f: 1-13** 9f-13f: 0-10 14f+: 0-0
Track : **LH: 1-17** RH: 0-6 Tight: 0-11 Gall: 0-0
Aids: Bl: 0-0 Vi: 0-0 Tstrap: 0-0 Ckp: 0-0
Best Rating: 56 4/08 Wolv 1m1f103y stand

Spartan Dance

93(66) (65)**33**

5-y-o ch g Groom Dancer (USA)-Delphic Way (Warning)

J A Geake Miss B Swire

Placings:0533/000/0-065 **(5122)**

2009: 11^{0}GF, 11^{6}GS, 9^{5}F,

	Starts	1st	2nd	3rd	Win & Pl
Career Total (Turf)	8	0	0	0	113
Career Total (AW)	3	0	0	2	1396

Going (Turf): Sf: 0-3 GS: 0-3 Gd: 0-0 GF: 0-1 Fm: 0-1
Distance: 5f/6f: 0-0 7f-8f: 0-2 9f-13f: 0-9 14f+: 0-0
Track : LH: 0-10 RH: 0-0 Tight: 0-5 Gall: 0-0
Aids: Bl: 0-0 Vi: 0-2 Tstrap: 0-0 Ckp: 0-0
Best Rating: 65 11/06 Sthl 1m stand

Spartan Prince (USA)

95(99) (67)**69**

3-y-o b c Mr Greeley (USA)-Yalta (USA) (Private Terms (USA))

T D Barron Harrowgate Bloodstock Ltd

Placings:5-410204 **(4431)**

2009: 9^{4}SD, 9^{1}SD, 9^{0}GF, 10^{2}GF, 12^{0}GF, 10^{4}GF,

	Starts	1st	2nd	3rd	Win & Pl
Career Total (Turf)	4	0	1	0	963
Career Total (AW)	3	1	0	0	2730

67 2/09 Wolv 1m1f103y STD £2729

Total win prize-money £2730

Going (Turf): Sf: 0-0 GS: 0-0 Gd: 0-0 GF: 0-4 Fm: 0-0
Distance: 5f/6f: 0-0 7f-8f: 0-1 **9f-13f: 1-6** 14f+: 0-0
Track : **LH: 1-6** RH: 0-1 **Tight: 1-4** Gall: 0-1
Aids: Bl: 0-0 Vi: 0-0 Tstrap: 0-0 Ckp: 0-0
Best Rating: 69 4/09 Rdcr 1m2f gd-fm

Fair; effective over 1m1f; acts on Polytrack.

Spartan Princess (IRE)

81 **15**

3-y-o ch f Spartacus (IRE)-Stormchaser (IRE) (Titus Livius (FR))

M Brittain Mel Brittain

Placings:0 **(4550)**

2009: 7^{0}GS,

	Starts	1st	2nd	3rd	Win & Pl
Career Total (Turf)	1	0	0	0	

Going (Turf): Sf: 0-0 GS: 0-1 Gd: 0-0 GF: 0-0 Fm: 0-0
Distance: 5f/6f: 0-0 7f-8f: 0-1 9f-13f: 0-0 14f+: 0-0
Track : LH: 0-1 RH: 0-0 Tight: 0-1 Gall: 0-0
Aids: Bl: 0-0 Vi: 0-0 Tstrap: 0-0 Ckp: 0-0
Best Rating: 15 8/09 Thsk 7f gd-sft

Spartan Storm (IRE)

78 **18**

3-y-o b c Spartacus (IRE)-Sylvan Princess (Sylvan Express)

M Brittain Mel Brittain

Placings:00 **(4805)**

2009: 6[0]S, 7[0]GF,

	Starts	1st	2nd	3rd	Win & Pl
Career Total (Turf)	2	0	0	0	

Going (Turf): Sf: 0-1 GS: 0-0 Gd: 0-0 GF: 0-1 Fm: 0-0
Distance: 5f/6f: 0-1 7f-8f: 0-1 9f-13f: 0-0 14f+: 0-0
Track : LH: 0-0 RH: 0-0 Tight: 0-0 Gall: 0-0
Aids: Bl: 0-0 Vi: 0-0 Tstrap: 0-0 Ckp: 0-0
Best Rating: 18 7/09 Donc 6f soft

Sparton Duke (IRE)

98(105) (83)**84**
4-y-o b g Xaar-Blueberry Walk (Green Desert (USA))
K A Ryan I Campbell J C Fretwell & C Evans

Placings:00/13244442300-506400 (3615)
2009: 5[5]GF, 6[0]GS, 7[6]GF, 8[4]SD, 8[0]SD, 7[0]G,

	Starts	1st	2nd	3rd	Win & Pl
Career Total (Turf)	11	0	1	0	3135
Career Total (AW)	8	1	1	2	6436

74 1/08 Kemp 6f STD £2590
Total win prize-money £2591

Going (Turf): Sf: 0-0 GS: 0-2 Gd: 0-3 GF: 0-6 Fm: 0-0
Distance: **5f/6f: 1-11** 7f-8f: 0-8 9f-13f: 0-0 14f+: 0-0
Track : LH: 0-5 **RH: 1-6** Tight: 0-4 Gall: 0-2
Aids: Bl: 0-0 Vi: 0-0 Tstrap: 0-15 Ckp: 0-15
Best Rating: 84 8/08 Rdcr 6f gd-sft

Fair; effective over 6f-7f; acts on easy ground and on Polytrack; often wears cheekpieces.

Spate River

102(105) (93)**85**
4-y-o b g Zaha (CAN)-Rion River (IRE) (Taufan (USA))
Jonjo O'Neill (C F Wall 2/10) John P McManus

Placings:0/031210-501 (6462)
2009: 7[5]G, 8[0]SD, 8[1]SD,

	Starts	1st	2nd	3rd	Win & Pl
Career Total (Turf)	5	1	1	0	4009
Career Total (AW)	5	2	0	1	9234

93 10/09 Wolv 1m141y (0-80)H STD £5046
85 10/08 Gdwd 1m (0-75)H G-F £3238
79 9/08 Wolv 7f32y (0-75)H STD £3885
Total win prize-money £12170

Going (Turf): Sf: 0-1 GS: 0-0 Gd: 0-2 **GF: 1-2** Fm: 0-0
Distance: 5f/6f: 0-1 **7f-8f: 2-5** 9f-13f: 1-4 14f+: 0-0
Track : **LH: 2-3** RH: 1-5 **Tight: 2-3** Gall: 0-1
Aids: Bl: 0-0 Vi: 0-0 Tstrap: 0-0 Ckp: 0-0
Best Rating: 93 10/09 Wolv 1m141y stand

Useful; effective over 7f-1m; acts on good ground; goes on Poltrack.

Speagle (IRE)

98(103) (37)**53**
7-y-o ch g Desert Sun-Pohutakawa (FR) (Affirmed (USA))
A J Chamberlain (D Shaw 25/2) Miss J M Foran

Placings:0560/100/0110111/005000452062055/052160-000004406600 (3997)
2009: 12[0]SD, 12[0]SD, 8[0]SF, 11[0]SD, 11[0]GF, 11[4]F, 11[4]G, 12[0]SD, 12[6]GF, 11[6]GF, 12[0]GF, 17[0]G,

	Starts	1st	2nd	3rd	Win & Pl
Career Total (Turf)	22	1	1	0	5109
Career Total (AW)	25	6	2	0	19593

65 2/08 Wolv 1m4f50y (0-60)H STD £2047
85 12/06 Sthl 1m4f (0-70)H STD £3238
75 12/06 Wolv 1m1f103y (0-65)H STD £2590
64 11/06 Wolv 1m141y STD £2388
66 9/06 Layt 7f STD £4050
71 6/06 Slig 1m2f GD £3812
68 2/05 Ling 1m4f STD £4108
Total win prize-money £22238

Going (Turf): Sf: 0-0 GS: 0-2 **Gd: 1-8** GF: 0-8 Fm: 0-4
Distance: 5f/6f: 0-1 7f-8f: 1-4 **9f-13f: 6-40** 14f+: 0-2
Track : **LH: 6-34** RH: 0-9 **Tight: 4-23** Gall: 0-1
Aids: Bl: 0-0 Vi: 0-1 Tstrap: 0-0 Ckp: 0-0
Best Rating: 85 12/06 Sthl 1m4f stand

Plating class; stays 1m 4f; acts on both All-Weather surfaces and a sound surface on turf; has worn a tongue tie and a visor.

Speak Freely

69(65) **17**
3-y-o b f Domedriver (IRE)-Miss Tolerance (USA) (Mt. Livermore (USA))
C Smith John Martin-Hoyes

Placings:0-00 (1362)
2009: 6[0]SD, 10[0]GF,

	Starts	1st	2nd	3rd	Win & Pl
Career Total (Turf)	1	0	0	0	
Career Total (AW)	2	0	0	0	

Going (Turf): Sf: 0-0 GS: 0-0 Gd: 0-0 GF: 0-1 Fm: 0-0
Distance: 5f/6f: 0-1 7f-8f: 0-1 9f-13f: 0-1 14f+: 0-0
Track : LH: 0-3 RH: 0-0 Tight: 0-0 Gall: 0-0
Aids: Bl: 0-0 Vi: 0-0 Tstrap: 0-0 Ckp: 0-0
Best Rating: 17 4/09 Nott 1m2f50y gd-fm

Speak The Truth (IRE)

100(102) (74)**73**
3-y-o br g Statue Of Liberty (USA)-Brave Truth (IRE) (Brief Truce (USA))
J R Boyle Inside Track Racing Club

Placings:004550-2120113156120460105 (7739)
2009: 5[2]SD, 5[1]SD, 5[2]SD, 5[0]SD, 5[1]SD, 6[1]SD, 5[3]SD, 5[1]G, 5[5]GF, 5[6]SD, 5[1]G, 5[2]G, 5[0]SD, 6[4]SS, 6[6]S, 6[0]SD, 6[1]SD, 5[0]SD, 6[5]SD,

	Starts	1st	2nd	3rd	Win & Pl
Career Total (Turf)	7	2	1	0	4692
Career Total (AW)	18	4	2	1	10475

74 11/09 Kemp 6f (0-65)H STD £1706
71 7/09 Bath 5f11y (0-75)H GD £3885
57 4/09 Ling 6f STD £2047
64 3/09 Ling 5f STD £2047
69 2/09 Wolv 5f20y STD £2590
Total win prize-money £12276

Going (Turf): Sf: 0-1 GS: 0-0 **Gd: 2-4** GF: 0-2 Fm: 0-0
Distance: **5f/6f: 6-24** 7f-8f: 0-1 9f-13f: 0-0 14f+: 0-0
Track : **LH: 5-17** RH: 1-4 **Tight: 3-12** Gall: 2-6
Aids: Bl: 0-0 Vi: 0-0 Tstrap: 5-17 Ckp: 5-17
Best Rating: 74 11/09 Kemp 6f stand

Modest; effective over 5f-6f; acts on good ground; goes on Polytrack; has worn cheekpieces.

Spear Thistle

99 (87)**68**
7-y-o ch g Selkirk (USA)-Ardisia (USA) (Affirmed (USA))
C J Mann Tony Hayward & Sue Head

Placings:441/054242/30030/0-3 (7248)
2009: 10[3]HY,

	Starts	1st	2nd	3rd	Win & Pl
Career Total (Turf)	14	1	2	2	15050
Career Total (AW)	2	0	0	1	1166

81 10/04 Newb 1m HVY £6734
Total win prize-money £6734

Going (Turf): Sf: 1-4 GS: 0-4 Gd: 0-3 GF: 0-3 Fm: 0-0
Distance: 5f/6f: 0-0 **7f-8f: 1-3** 9f-13f: 0-8 14f+: 0-5
Track : LH: 0-5 RH: 0-9 Tight: 0-1 Gall: 0-8
Aids: Bl: 0-0 Vi: 0-0 Tstrap: 0-1 Ckp: 0-1
Best Rating: 91 9/05 Newb 1m3f5y gd-fm

Modest; winning hurdler; stays 2m; acts well on soft ground; has worn cheekpieces.

Special Adviser

74(81) (52)**19**
3-y-o b g Dr Fong (USA)-Dimakya (USA) (Dayjur (USA))
T J Etherington KevinHart AndyHunter MiriamGreenwood

Placings:0-60 (3120)
2009: 7[6]F, 10[0]GF,

	Starts	1st	2nd	3rd	Win & Pl
Career Total (Turf)	2	0	0	0	0
Career Total (AW)	1	0	0	0	

Going (Turf): Sf: 0-0 GS: 0-0 Gd: 0-0 GF: 0-1 Fm: 0-1
Distance: 5f/6f: 0-0 7f-8f: 0-2 9f-13f: 0-1 14f+: 0-0
Track : LH: 0-3 RH: 0-0 Tight: 0-3 Gall: 0-0
Aids: Bl: 0-0 Vi: 0-0 Tstrap: 0-0 Ckp: 0-0
Best Rating: 52 11/08 Wolv 7f32y stand

Special Betty

(87) (52)
2-y-o b f Tamayaz (CAN)-Natural Key (Safawan)
D Haydn Jones Mrs T P James

Placings:00400 (7871)
2009: 5[0]SD, 5[0]SD, 5[4]SD, 5[0]SD, 5[0]SD,

	Starts	1st	2nd	3rd	Win & Pl
Career Total (Turf)	0	0	0	0	
Career Total (AW)	5	0	0	0	192

Going (Turf): Sf: 0-0 GS: 0-0 Gd: 0-0 GF: 0-0 Fm: 0-0
Distance: 5f/6f: 0-5 7f-8f: 0-0 9f-13f: 0-0 14f+: 0-0
Track : LH: 0-4 RH: 0-1 Tight: 0-4 Gall: 0-0
Aids: Bl: 0-0 Vi: 0-0 Tstrap: 0-0 Ckp: 0-0
Best Rating: 52 12/09 Wolv 5f216y stand

Best effort over 6f on Polytrack.

Special Bond

(103) (66)**57**
3-y-o b f Monsieur Bond (IRE)-Fizzy Treat (Efisio)
J A Osborne Finian O'Sullivan & Christian Marner

Placings:40436-3035 (0441)
2009: 10[3]SD, 8[0]SD, 8[3]SD, 8[5]SD,

	Starts	1st	2nd	3rd	Win & Pl
Career Total (Turf)	1	0	0	0	
Career Total (AW)	8	0	0	3	1501

Going (Turf): Sf: 0-0 GS: 0-0 Gd: 0-1 GF: 0-0 Fm: 0-0
Distance: 5f/6f: 0-0 7f-8f: 0-6 9f-13f: 0-3 14f+: 0-0
Track : LH: 0-7 RH: 0-2 Tight: 0-4 Gall: 0-1
Aids: Bl: 0-3 Vi: 0-0 Tstrap: 0-0 Ckp: 0-0

Best Rating: **66** 12/08 Kemp 1m2f stand

Modest; stays 1m2f and acts on sand; has worn blinkers.

Special Chapter (IRE)

96(91) (39)**47**

4-y-o b f Acclamation-Literary (Woodman (USA))
A B Haynes WCR V - The Conkwell Connection

Placings:0-645053000 **(7761)**
2009: 8^{6}SD, 12^{4}SD, 12^{5}SD, 9^{0}GF, 11^{5}GF, 11^{3}GF, 11^{0}G, 14^{0}SD, 11^{0}SD,

	Starts	1st	2nd	3rd	Win & Pl
Career Total (Turf)	4	0	0	1	289
Career Total (AW)	6	0	0	0	0

Going (Turf): **Sf: 0-0 GS: 0-0 Gd: 0-1 GF: 0-3 Fm: 0-0**
Distance: 5f/6f: 0-0 7f-8f: 0-2 9f-13f: 0-7 14f+: 0-1
Track : LH: 0-8 RH: 0-2 Tight: 0-5 Gall: 0-0
Aids: Bl: 0-0 Vi: 0-0 Tstrap: 0-0 Ckp: 0-0
Best Rating: **47** 8/09 Brig 1m3f196y gd-fm

Special Cuvee

94(99) (78)**67**

3-y-o b g Diktat-Iris May (Brief Truce (USA))
A B Haynes The Villains

Placings:5216-0541106060430 **(7818)**
2009: 5^{0}SD, 6^{5}SD, 7^{4}SD, 7^{1}G, 8^{1}G, 8^{0}GS, 7^{6}GF, 8^{0}G, 8^{6}G, 9^{0}S, 7^{4}SD, 8^{3}SD, 9^{0}SD,

	Starts	1st	2nd	3rd	Win & Pl
Career Total (Turf)	8	2	0	0	3990
Career Total (AW)	9	1	1	1	2859
67 4/09 Yarm 1m3y			GD		£1942
58 3/09 Folk 7f			GD		£2047
78 7/08 Sthl 6f			SS		£1978

Total win prize-money £5969

Going (Turf): Sf: 0-1 GS: 0-1 **Gd: 2-5** GF: 0-1 Fm: 0-0
Distance: 5f/6f: 1-6 7f-8f: 1-6 9f-13f: 1-5 14f+: 0-0
Track : **LH: 1-11** RH: 0-1 Tight: 0-2 Gall: 0-1
Aids: Bl: 0-0 Vi: 0-4 Tstrap: 0-0 Ckp: 0-0
Best Rating: **78** 7/08 Sthl 6f std-slw

Moderate; stays 1m; acts on good ground and on sand; has worn a visor.

Special Duty

108 **117**

2-y-o ch f Hennessy (USA)-Quest To Peak (USA) (Distant View (USA))
Mme C Head-Maarek K Abdulla

Placings:2121 **(6449)**
2009: 5^{2}GS, 5^{1}GS, 6^{2}G, 6^{1}GF,

	Starts	1st	2nd	3rd	Win & Pl
Career Total (Turf)	4	2	2	0	256811
117 10/09 NmkR 6f			G-F		£96509
113 7/09 MsnL 5f110y			G-S		£71942

Total win prize-money £168451

Going (Turf): Sf: 0-0 **GS: 1-2** Gd: 0-1 **GF: 1-1** Fm: 0-0
Distance: **5f/6f: 2-4** 7f-8f: 0-0 9f-13f: 0-0 14f+: 0-0
Track : LH: 0-0 RH: 0-2 Tight: 0-0 Gall: 0-0
Aids: Bl: 0-0 Vi: 0-0 Tstrap: 0-0 Ckp: 0-0
Best Rating: **117** 10/09 NmkR 6f gd-fm

Group-class; Prix Robert Papin winner and narrowly beaten in the Prix Morny; stays 6f; acts on good and easy ground.

Special Reserve (IRE)

105(105) (74)**89**

4-y-o b c Sadler's Wells (USA)-Ionian Sea (Slip Anchor)
R Hannon Mrs J Wood

Placings:0/322202324244-213664103 **(6907)**
2009: 9^{2}GF, 10^{1}GF, 10^{3}GF, 12^{6}G, 10^{6}G, 10^{4}G, 10^{1}GF, 10^{0}GS, 10^{3}G,

	Starts	1st	2nd	3rd	Win & Pl
Career Total (Turf)	20	2	7	3	22790
Career Total (AW)	2	0	0	1	363
87 8/09 Wind 1m2f7y (0-85)H			G-F		£5180
87 5/09 Wind 1m2f7y (0-80)H			G-F		£5180

Total win prize-money £10362

Going (Turf): Sf: 0-3 GS: 0-1 Gd: 0-8 **GF: 2-8** Fm: 0-0
Distance: 5f/6f: 0-0 7f-8f: 0-2 **9f-13f: 2-20** 14f+: 0-0
Track : LH: 0-7 **RH: 2-12 Tight: 2-14** Gall: 0-4
Aids: Bl: 0-0 Vi: 0-0 Tstrap: 0-2 Ckp: 0-2
Best Rating: **89** 10/09 Wind 1m2f7y good

Useful; effective at 1m2f-1m4f; acts on any ground on turf; also goes on Polytrack; has worn cheekpieces.

Specialising

89 **57**

2-y-o ch f Nayef (USA)-Spry (Suave Dancer (USA))
M R Channon Mrs Ann C Black

Placings:60 **(6930)**
2009: 6^{6}G, 8^{0}G,

	Starts	1st	2nd	3rd	Win & Pl
Career Total (Turf)	2	0	0	0	0

Going (Turf): **Sf: 0-0 GS: 0-0 Gd: 0-2 GF: 0-0 Fm: 0-0**
Distance: 5f/6f: 0-1 7f-8f: 0-0 9f-13f: 0-1 14f+: 0-0
Track : LH: 0-1 RH: 0-0 Tight: 0-1 Gall: 0-0
Aids: Bl: 0-0 Vi: 0-0 Tstrap: 0-0 Ckp: 0-0
Best Rating: **57** 7/09 Gdwd 6f good

Spectait

108(111) (100)**100**

7-y-o b g Spectrum (IRE)-Shanghai Girl (Distant Relative)
Jonjo O'Neill John P McManus

Placings:203/1114/12510/00045-111L402 **(4486)**
2009: 9^{1}SD, 8^{1}SD, 9^{1}SD, 8^{L}GF, 8^{4}S, 7^{0}G, 8^{2}G,

	Starts	1st	2nd	3rd	Win & Pl
Career Total (Turf)	13	2	3	0	135887
Career Total (AW)	11	6	0	1	36574
100 3/09 Wolv 1m1f103y (0-100)H			STD		£7352
95 1/09 Wolv 1m141y (0-85)H			STD		£5180
88 1/09 Wolv 1m1f103y (0-85)H			STD		£4857
107 8/06 Gdwd 1m H			G-F		£93480
109 5/06 Kemp 7f (0-85)H			STD		£7790
94 7/05 Sand 7f16y (0-85)H			G-S		£8106
85 7/05 Wolv 1m141y (0-75)H			STD		£4165
84 7/05 Ling 7f (0-70)H			STD		£3554

Total win prize-money £134487

Going (Turf): Sf: 0-4 **GS: 1-3** Gd: 0-4 **GF: 1-2** Fm: 0-0
Distance: 5f/6f: 0-1 7f-8f: 4-12 9f-13f: 4-11 14f+: 0-0
Track : **LH: 5-13** RH: 3-6 **Tight: 5-9** Gall: 0-1
Aids: Bl: 0-0 Vi: 0-0 Tstrap: 0-0 Ckp: 0-0
Best Rating: **109** 7/06 Ling 1m stand

Very useful; formerly smart; effective at 1m; acts on most ground and on Polytrack; usually held up.

Speed Dating

102(84) (53)**72**

3-y-o ch g Pivotal-Courting (Pursuit Of Love)
Sir Mark Prescott Cheveley Park Stud

Placings:000-32142 **(5524)**
2009: 8^{3}GS, 8^{2}S, 9^{1}G, 10^{4}GF, 9^{2}G,

	Starts	1st	2nd	3rd	Win & Pl
Career Total (Turf)	7	1	2	1	5512
Career Total (AW)	1	0	0	0	
72 7/09 Carl 1m1f61y (0-70)H			GD		£3238

Total win prize-money £3238

Going (Turf): Sf: 0-2 GS: 0-2 **Gd: 1-2** GF: 0-1 Fm: 0-0
Distance: 5f/6f: 0-1 7f-8f: 0-3 **9f-13f: 1-4** 14f+: 0-0
Track : LH: 0-3 **RH: 1-3** Tight: 0-3 Gall: 0-1
Aids: Bl: 0-0 Vi: 0-0 Tstrap: 0-0 Ckp: 0-0
Best Rating: **72** 7/09 Carl 1m1f61y good

Fair; stays 1m; acts on good and soft ground.

Speed Song

104 **90**

4-y-o b f Fasliyev (USA)-Superstar Leo (IRE) (College Chapel)
W J Haggas Lael Stable

Placings:3140/12-003 **(2653)**
2009: 5^{0}G, 6^{0}G, 5^{3}F,

	Starts	1st	2nd	3rd	Win & Pl
Career Total (Turf)	9	2	1	2	12545
90 7/08 Sand 5f6y (0-80)H			G-F		£5828
78 7/07 Yarm 5f43y			GD		£3562

Total win prize-money £9390

Going (Turf): Sf: 0-0 GS: 0-0 **Gd: 1-4 GF: 1-4** Fm: 0-1
Distance: **5f/6f: 2-9** 7f-8f: 0-0 9f-13f: 0-0 14f+: 0-0
Track : LH: 0-2 RH: 0-0 Tight: 0-0 Gall: 0-2
Aids: Bl: 0-1 Vi: 0-0 Tstrap: 0-0 Ckp: 0-0
Best Rating: **90** 7/08 Sand 5f6y gd-fm

Useful; effective at 5f; acts on fast and good ground; has worn blinkers.

Speedy Guru

100(98) (70)**75**

3-y-o b f Ishiguru (USA)-Gowon (Aragon)
H Candy Henry Candy

Placings:031-051000 **(7738)**
2009: 7^{0}GF, 6^{5}S, 5^{1}GF, 7^{0}G, 5^{0}SD, 6^{0}SD,

	Starts	1st	2nd	3rd	Win & Pl
Career Total (Turf)	7	2	0	1	6958
Career Total (AW)	2	0	0	0	
75 10/09 Leic 5f218y (0-70)H			G-F		£3238
71 10/08 Pont 6f			G-S		£3238

Total win prize-money £6476

Going (Turf): Sf: 0-2 **GS: 1-1** Gd: 0-1 **GF: 1-3** Fm: 0-0
Distance: **5f/6f: 2-6** 7f-8f: 0-3 9f-13f: 0-0 14f+: 0-0
Track : **LH: 1-2** RH: 0-1 Tight: 0-1 Gall: 0-0
Aids: Bl: 0-0 Vi: 0-0 Tstrap: 0-0 Ckp: 0-0
Best Rating: **75** 10/09 Leic 5f218y gd-fm

Fair; effective over 6f; acts on fast and soft ground.

Speedy Senorita (IRE)

103 (64)**79**

4-y-o b f Fayruz-Sinora Wood (IRE) (Shinko Forest (IRE))
J J Quinn F D C Racing Club

Placings:22254310155/506211120400-433025510000 (7122)

2009: 5^{4}GF, 5^{3}GS, 5^{3}F, 5^{0}GF, 5^{2}GF, 5^{5}G, 5^{5}GF, 5^{1}G, 5^{0}GF, 5^{0}GF, 5^{0}GF, 5^{0}G,

	Starts	1st	2nd	3rd	Win & Pl
Career Total (Turf)	32	6	5	3	23655
Career Total (AW)	3	0	1	0	867

76	8/09	Bevl	5f	(0-70)H	GD	£2914
76	6/08	Muss	5f	(0-65)H	G-F	£2266
68	6/08	Brig	5f59y	(0-70)H	G-F	£2590
73	5/08	Ayr	5f	(0-70)H	G-F	£2914
65	9/07	Brig	5f59y		GD	£2072
65	8/07	Haml	5f4y		G-S	£2388

Total win prize-money £15147

Going (Turf): Sf: 0-1 GS: 1-5 Gd: 2-9 **GF: 3-15** Fm: 0-2
Distance: **5f/6f: 6-34** 7f-8f: 0-1 9f-13f: 0-0 14f+: 0-0
Track : **LH: 2-7** RH: 0-1 Tight: 0-3 Gall: 0-1
Aids: Bl: 0-0 Vi: 0-0 Tstrap: 0-1 Ckp: 0-1
Best Rating: 79 6/08 NmkJ 5f gd-fm

Fair; suited by 5f; acts on fast and easy ground.

Speedyfix

88(93) (47)**43**

2-y-o b g Chineur (FR)-Zonnebeke (Orpen (USA))
Mrs C A Dunnett Mark Riley

Placings:0600042000 (7453)

2009: 5^{0}G, 6^{6}SD, 6^{0}G, 5^{0}SD, 5^{0}GF, 5^{4}SD, 6^{2}SD, 6^{0}SD, 6^{0}SD, 6^{0}SD,

	Starts	1st	2nd	3rd	Win & Pl
Career Total (Turf)	3	0	0	0	
Career Total (AW)	7	0	1	0	605

Going (Turf): **Sf: 0-0 GS: 0-0 Gd: 0-2 GF: 0-1 Fm: 0-0**
Distance: 5f/6f: 0-9 7f-8f: 0-1 9f-13f: 0-0 14f+: 0-0
Track : LH: 0-4 RH: 0-3 Tight: 0-2 Gall: 0-0
Aids: Bl: 0-0 Vi: 0-0 Tstrap: 0-6 Ckp: 0-6
Best Rating: 47 10/09 Kemp 6f stand

Plating-class; stays 6f; acts on Polytrack; has worn a tongue tie and cheekpieces.

Spell Caster

101 (82)**91**

4-y-o ch f Bertolini (USA)-Princess Claudia (IRE) (Kahyasi)
R M Beckett D P Barrie & M J Rees

Placings:166/655215-4250 (7035)

2009: 10^{4}GF, 9^{2}GF, 10^{5}GF, 10^{0}S,

	Starts	1st	2nd	3rd	Win & Pl
Career Total (Turf)	12	2	2	0	26037
Career Total (AW)	1	0	0	0	0

89	7/08	Gdwd	1m1f	(0-100)H	G-F	£12462
82	8/07	Chep	1m14y		G-F	£3562

Total win prize-money £16024

Going (Turf): Sf: 0-1 GS: 0-0 Gd: 0-2 **GF: 2-9** Fm: 0-0
Distance: 5f/6f: 0-0 7f-8f: 0-2 **9f-13f: 2-11** 14f+: 0-0
Track : LH: 0-2 **RH: 1-7 Tight: 1-3** Gall: 0-4
Aids: Bl: 0-0 Vi: 0-0 Tstrap: 0-0 Ckp: 0-0
Best Rating: 91 6/09 Sals 1m1f198y gd-fm

Useful; stays 1m2f; acts on a sound surface.

Spensley (IRE)

103(85) (50)79

3-y-o ch g Dr Fong (USA)-Genoa (Zafonic (USA))
J R Fanshawe Axom (XV)

Placings:005061 (6760)

2009: 8^{0}SD, 10^{0}G, 10^{5}GF, 12^{0}S, 10^{6}GS, 9^{1}G,

	Starts	1st	2nd	3rd	Win & Pl
Career Total (Turf)	5	1	0	0	2914
Career Total (AW)	1	0	0	0	

79	10/09	Leic	1m1f218y (0-75)H	GD	£2914

Total win prize-money £2914

Going (Turf): Sf: 0-1 GS: 0-1 **Gd: 1-2** GF: 0-1 Fm: 0-0
Distance: 5f/6f: 0-0 7f-8f: 0-1 **9f-13f: 1-5** 14f+: 0-0
Track : LH: 0-1 **RH: 1-5** Tight: 0-0 Gall: 0-3
Aids: Bl: 0-0 Vi: 0-0 Tstrap: 0-0 Ckp: 0-0
Best Rating: 79 10/09 Leic 1m1f218y good

Modest; effective at 1m2f; acts on a sound surface.

Spent

82(93) (58)**64**

4-y-o b g Averti (IRE)-Top (Shirley Heights)
Mrs A M Thorpe (Mouse Hamilton-Fairley 10/6) Tristar

Placings:06456/060514060-060 (2807)

2009: 7^{0}SD, 8^{6}SD, 7^{0}G,

	Starts	1st	2nd	3rd	Win & Pl
Career Total (Turf)	13	1	0	0	3131
Career Total (AW)	4	0	0	0	0

64	8/08	Brig	6f209y	(0-65)H	GD	£2396

Total win prize-money £2396

Going (Turf): Sf: 0-3 GS: 0-3 **Gd: 1-3** GF: 0-4 Fm: 0-0
Distance: 5f/6f: 0-3 **7f-8f: 1-8** 9f-13f: 0-6 14f+: 0-0
Track : **LH: 1-8** RH: 0-4 Tight: 0-6 Gall: 0-1
Aids: Bl: 0-1 Vi: 0-0 Tstrap: 0-0 Ckp: 0-0
Best Rating: 68 8/07 Sals 6f gd-sft

Modest sort; stays at least a mile; has worn blinkers.

Sphere (IRE)

104(99) (56)**76**

4-y-o b f Daylami (IRE)-Apple Town (Warning)
J Mackie (P T Midgley 22/9) Derbyshire Racing II

Placings:3062236-44664043106 (7357)

2009: 12^{4}GS, 14^{4}GF, 16^{6}GF, 14^{6}G, 12^{4}G, 10^{0}SD, 12^{4}SD, 12^{3}G, 12^{1}GF, 13^{0}G, 13^{6}SD,

	Starts	1st	2nd	3rd	Win & Pl
Career Total (Turf)	14	1	2	3	5585
Career Total (AW)	4	0	0	0	0

59	9/09	Bevl	1m4f16y	G-F	£2590

Total win prize-money £2590

Going (Turf): Sf: 0-1 GS: 0-2 Gd: 0-8 **GF: 1-3** Fm: 0-0
Distance: 5f/6f: 0-0 7f-8f: 0-0 **9f-13f: 1-10** 14f+: 0-8
Track : LH: 0-13 **RH: 1-5 Tight: 1-12** Gall: 0-2
Aids: Bl: 0-0 Vi: 0-0 Tstrap: 1-5 Ckp: 1-5
Best Rating: 76 8/08 Yarm 1m6f17y good

Fair; stays 1m6f; acts on good ground; handles Polytrack.

Sphinx (FR)

95 (59)**86**

11-y-o b g Snurge-Egyptale (Crystal Glitters (USA))
E W Tuer E Tuer

Placings:03/211006221/21010/000043/004/0015114P/23 01235/30004242104-0001 (7170)

2009: 16^{0}G, 17^{0}G, 18^{0}G, 15^{1}S,

	Starts	1st	2nd	3rd	Win & Pl
Career Total (Turf)	46	10	8	5	98538
Career Total (AW)	9	1	0	0	8489

77	10/09	Ayr	1m7f (0-85)H	SFT	£7352
86	9/08	Ayr	2m1f105y (0-80)H	HVY	£6476
93	8/07	Nott	1m6f15y (0-90)H	GD	£7124
88	5/06	Nott	1m6f15y (0-80)H	SFT	£6477
84	5/06	York	1m5f197y (0-85)H	SFT	£8096
73	4/06	Nott	1m6f15y (0-70)H	SFT	£5181
89	11/02	Ling	1m4f C(0-95)H	STD	£8229
	4/02	Lonc	1m1f165y	G-F	£4908
	12/01	Pari	1m3f H	G-S	£7669
	4/01	Pari	1m3f	SFT	£8244
	3/01	Pari	1m3f	HVY	£4850

Total win prize-money £74609

Going (Turf): **Sf: 7-14** GS: 1-12 Gd: 1-11GF: 1-4 Fm: 0-0
Distance: 5f/6f: 0-1 7f-8f: 0-0 9f-13f: 5-22 **14f+: 6-32**
Track : **LH: 7-36** RH: 1-13 Tight: 1-16 Gall: 1-11
Aids: **Bl: 6-23** Vi: 0-0 Tstrap: 0-2 Ckp: 0-2
Best Rating: 96 9/07 Haml 1m5f9y gd-sft

Fair; stays 2m; acts on most types of ground but prefers ease; usually wears blinkers/cheekpieces.

Spic 'n Span

99(103) (72)**66**

4-y-o b g Piccolo-Sally Slade (Dowsing (USA))
R A Harris Mrs Ruth M Serrell

Placings:030520/U462665300460326362105-160551222004134300 (6669)

2009: 5^{1}SD, 5^{6}SD, 5^{0}SD, 5^{5}SD, 5^{5}SD, 5^{1}SD, 5^{2}SD, 5^{2}SD, 5^{2}SD, 5^{0}G, 5^{0}G, 5^{4}SD, 5^{1}SF, 5^{3}G, 5^{4}SD, 5^{3}G, 5^{0}F, 5^{0}SD,

	Starts	1st	2nd	3rd	Win & Pl
Career Total (Turf)	18	0	1	4	2245
Career Total (AW)	28	4	6	2	15106

69	7/09	Wolv	5f20y		SF	£2047
68	3/09	Sthl	5f	(0-65)H	STD	£2047
69	1/09	Sthl	5f	(0-60)H	STD	£2729
69	12/08	Sthl	5f		STD	£2388

Total win prize-money £9212

Going (Turf): **Sf: 0-1 GS: 0-1 Gd: 0-6 GF: 0-7 Fm: 0-3**
Distance: **5f/6f: 4-41** 7f-8f: 0-5 9f-13f: 0-0 14f+: 0-0
Track : **LH: 1-23** RH: 0-3 **Tight: 1-11** Gall: 0-6
Aids: **Bl: 4-28** Vi: 0-0 Tstrap: 0-2 Ckp: 0-2
Best Rating: 72 3/09 Sthl 5f stand

Modest; effective over 5f-6f; acts on fast ground; goes on Fibresand; has worn blinkers.

Spice Fair

(93) (67)

2-y-o ch g Trade Fair-Focosa (ITY) (In The Wings)
M D I Usher M D I Usher

Placings:26 (7885)

2009: 8^{2}SD, 7^{6}SD,

	Starts	1st	2nd	3rd	Win & Pl
Career Total (Turf)	0	0	0	0	
Career Total (AW)	2	0	1	0	584

Going (Turf): **Sf: 0-0 GS: 0-0 Gd: 0-0 GF: 0-0 Fm: 0-0**
Distance: 5f/6f: 0-0 7f-8f: 0-2 9f-13f: 0-0 14f+: 0-0
Track : LH: 0-2 RH: 0-0 Tight: 0-2 Gall: 0-0
Aids: Bl: 0-0 Vi: 0-0 Tstrap: 0-0 Ckp: 0-0
Best Rating: 67 12/09 Ling 1m stand

Modest; stays 1m and acts on Polytrack.

Spice Run

(99) (74)**29**

6-y-o b g Zafonic (USA)-Palatial (Green Desert (USA))
Stef Liddiard Mrs Sally Doyle

Placings:00-61 (7411)

2009: 7^{6}SD, 5^{1}SD,

	Starts	1st	2nd	3rd	Win & Pl
Career Total (Turf)	1	0	0	0	
Career Total (AW)	3	1	0	0	2730

74 11/09 Wolv 5f216y STD £2729
Total win prize-money £2730

Going (Turf): Sf: 0-0 GS: 0-0 Gd: 0-0 GF: 0-1 Fm: 0-0
Distance: **5f/6f: 1-1** 7f-8f: 0-3 9f-13f: 0-0 14f+: 0-0
Track : **LH: 1-2** RH: 0-1 **Tight: 1-2** Gall: 0-0
Aids: Bl: 0-0 Vi: 0-0 Tstrap: 0-0 Ckp: 0-0
Best Rating: 74 11/09 Wolv 5f216y stand

Modest; effective over 6f; acts on Polytrack.

Spiders Star

103 **69**
6-y-o br m Cayman Kai (IRE)-Kiss In The Dark (Starry Night (USA))
S G West Miss Kate Milligan

Placings:1060-4113210 **(5696)**
2009: 16^{4}GF, 16^{1}G, 16^{1}GF, 16^{3}G, 17^{2}GF, 15^{1}GS, 16^{0}GS,

	Starts	1st	2nd	3rd	Win & Pl
Career Total (Turf)	11	4	1	1	13986

69 8/09 Catt 1m7f177y (0-70)H G-S £3070
66 7/09 Bevl 2m35y (0-70)H G-F £3561
59 6/09 Thsk 2m (0-60)H GD £3139
47 8/08 Catt 1m7f177y G-F £2047
Total win prize-money £11819

Going (Turf): Sf: 0-0 GS: 1-3 Gd: 1-4 **GF: 2-4** Fm: 0-0
Distance: 5f/6f: 0-0 7f-8f: 0-0 9f-13f: 0-1 **14f+: 4-10**
Track : **LH: 3-6** RH: 1-5 **Tight: 4-9** Gall: 0-1
Aids: Bl: 0-0 Vi: 0-0 Tstrap: 0-0 Ckp: 0-0
Best Rating: 69 8/09 Catt 1m7f177y gd-sft

Moderate; stays 2m; acts on good and faster ground.

Spiders Tern

41(76) (19)
4-y-o b g Sooty Tern-Miss Money Spider (IRE) (Statoblest)
J M Bradley J M Bradley

Placings:000 **(7596)**
2009: 9^{0}GF, 9^{0}SD, 7^{0}SD,

	Starts	1st	2nd	3rd	Win & Pl
Career Total (Turf)	1	0	0	0	
Career Total (AW)	2	0	0	0	

Going (Turf): Sf: 0-0 GS: 0-0 Gd: 0-0 GF: 0-1 Fm: 0-0
Distance: 5f/6f: 0-0 7f-8f: 0-1 9f-13f: 0-2 14f+: 0-0
Track : LH: 0-2 RH: 0-1 Tight: 0-2 Gall: 0-0
Aids: Bl: 0-0 Vi: 0-0 Tstrap: 0-0 Ckp: 0-0
Best Rating: 19 11/09 Wolv 1m1f103y stand

Spiekeroog

101(74) (22)**84**
3-y-o ch c Lomitas-Special (Polar Falcon (USA))
H R A Cecil G Schoeningh

Placings:22144 **(6803)**
2009: 10^{2}GF, 12^{2}GF, 13^{1}G, 14^{4}G, **16^{4}SD**,

	Starts	1st	2nd	3rd	Win & Pl
Career Total (Turf)	4	1	2	0	6214
Career Total (AW)	1	0	0	0	378

68 7/09 Catt 1m5f175y GD £3238
Total win prize-money £3238

Going (Turf): Sf: 0-0 GS: 0-0 **Gd: 1-2** GF: 0-2 Fm: 0-0
Distance: 5f/6f: 0-0 7f-8f: 0-0 9f-13f: 0-2 **14f+: 1-3**
Track : **LH: 1-4** RH: 0-1 **Tight: 1-2** Gall: 0-0
Aids: Bl: 0-1 Vi: 0-0 Tstrap: 0-0 Ckp: 0-0
Best Rating: 84 8/09 Hayd 1m6f good

Useful; stays 1m6f; acts on good and fast ground.

Spin Again (IRE)

98(99) (73)**78**
4-y-o b g Intikhab (USA)-Queen Of The May (IRE) (Nicolotte)
D Nicholls Nice To See You Euro-Racing & Partner

Placings:4/21603212-6050000255 **(4845)**
2009: 7^{6}SD, 7^{0}GF, 8^{5}F, 8^{0}GF, 8^{0}GF, 7^{0}G, 6^{0}GS, 7^{2}GF, 7^{5}SF, 8^{5}G,

	Starts	1st	2nd	3rd	Win & Pl
Career Total (Turf)	14	1	3	0	5625
Career Total (AW)	5	1	1	1	3632

77 8/08 Ling 7f (0-75)H G-F £2590
70 4/08 Wolv 5f216y STD £2456
Total win prize-money £5047

Going (Turf): Sf: 0-1 GS: 0-1 Gd: 0-4 **GF: 1-7** Fm: 0-1
Distance: 5f/6f: 1-3 7f-8f: 1-15 9f-13f: 0-1 14f+: 0-0
Track : **LH: 1-9** RH: 0-4 **Tight: 1-7** Gall: 0-0
Aids: Bl: 0-0 Vi: 0-1 Tstrap: 0-0 Ckp: 0-0
Best Rating: 78 8/08 NmkJ 7f good

Fair; effective over 6f-7f; acts on Polytrack and a sound surface on turf.

Spin Cycle (IRE)

109 **111**
3-y-o b c Exceed And Excel (AUS)-Spinamix (Spinning World (USA))
B Smart H E Sheikh Rashid Bin Mohammed

Placings:5112500-1005261 **(6427)**
2009: 5^{1}G, 5^{0}GF, 5^{0}G, 5^{5}GF, 5^{2}GF, 5^{6}GF, 5^{1}GF,

	Starts	1st	2nd	3rd	Win & Pl
Career Total (Turf)	14	4	2	0	80189

111 10/09 NmkR 5f G-F £22708
109 5/09 Muss 5f GD £12462
86 6/08 Muss 5f G-F £12462
89 5/08 Haml 5f4y G-F £3885
Total win prize-money £51518

Going (Turf): Sf: 0-0 GS: 0-2 Gd: 1-4 **GF: 3-8** Fm: 0-0
Distance: **5f/6f: 4-13** 7f-8f: 0-1 9f-13f: 0-0 14f+: 0-0
Track : LH: 0-0 RH: 0-0 Tight: 0-0 Gall: 0-0
Aids: Bl: 0-0 Vi: 0-1 Tstrap: 0-0 Ckp: 0-0
Best Rating: 111 10/09 NmkR 5f gd-fm

Smart; Listed winner and Group placed; effective at 5f and acts on fast ground.

Spin Sister

72(86) (36)**6**
3-y-o b f Umistim-Gloaming (Celtic Swing)
J Gallagher J Gallagher

Placings:00-0000 **(6788)**
2009: 10^{0}SD, 7^{0}GS, 8^{0}SD, 11^{0}G,

	Starts	1st	2nd	3rd	Win & Pl
Career Total (Turf)	2	0	0	0	
Career Total (AW)	4	0	0	0	

Going (Turf): Sf: 0-0 GS: 0-1 Gd: 0-1 GF: 0-0 Fm: 0-0
Distance: 5f/6f: 0-0 7f-8f: 0-3 9f-13f: 0-3 14f+: 0-0
Track : LH: 0-4 RH: 0-1 Tight: 0-3 Gall: 0-0
Aids: Bl: 0-0 Vi: 0-0 Tstrap: 0-0 Ckp: 0-0
Best Rating: 36 9/09 Wolv 1m141y stand

Spinight (IRE)

96(99) (64)**60**
3-y-o b c Spinning World (USA)-Adjtiya (IRE) (Green Desert (USA))
M Botti Giuliano Manfredini

Placings:40540-352430 **(3632)**
2009: 7^{3}SD, 7^{5}SD, 7^{2}SD, 7^{4}SD, 7^{3}GF, 6^{0}G,

	Starts	1st	2nd	3rd	Win & Pl
Career Total (Turf)	4	0	0	1	572
Career Total (AW)	7	0	1	1	1109

Going (Turf): Sf: 0-1 GS: 0-1 Gd: 0-1 GF: 0-1 Fm: 0-0
Distance: 5f/6f: 0-3 7f-8f: 0-8 9f-13f: 0-0 14f+: 0-0
Track : LH: 0-7 RH: 0-0 Tight: 0-4 Gall: 0-2
Aids: Bl: 0-1 Vi: 0-0 Tstrap: 0-5 Ckp: 0-5
Best Rating: 64 3/09 Ling 7f stand

Modest; stays 7f and acts on Polytrack and fast turf; has worn blinkers and cheekpieces.

Spinners End (IRE)

102 **88**
3-y-o b c Royal Applause-Needwood Epic (Midyan (USA))
A P Jarvis (K R Burke 25/7) Mogeely Stud & Mrs Maura Gittins

Placings:0420-31310014 **(4591)**
2009: 8^{3}GF, 8^{1}G, 8^{3}GF, 8^{1}GF, 8^{0}GF, 8^{0}GF, 6^{1}GF, 6^{4}G,

	Starts	1st	2nd	3rd	Win & Pl
Career Total (Turf)	12	3	1	2	18538

88 7/09 Sals 6f212y (0-85)H G-F £4857
83 6/09 Muss 1m (0-80)H G-F £5828
76 5/09 Pont 1m4y (0-85)H GD £5180
Total win prize-money £15866

Going (Turf): Sf: 0-0 GS: 0-1 Gd: 1-4 **GF: 2-7** Fm: 0-0
Distance: 5f/6f: 0-2 **7f-8f: 2-8** 9f-13f: 1-2 14f+: 0-0
Track : LH: 1-3 RH: 1-2 **Tight: 1-1** Gall: 0-0
Aids: Bl: 0-0 Vi: 0-0 Tstrap: 0-0 Ckp: 0-0
Best Rating: 88 7/09 Sals 6f212y gd-fm

Useful; stays 1m; acts on most ground.

Spinning

102(109) (103)**87**
6-y-o ch g Pivotal-Starring (FR) (Ashkalani (IRE))
T D Barron Mrs J Hazell

Placings:352432401/534200045520011**41**/211005003113-615050000244113 **(7827)**
2009: 8^{6}SS, 8^{1}SD, 7^{5}GF, 8^{0}GF, 8^{5}S, 8^{0}GS, 8^{0}GF, 8^{0}GF, 8^{0}SD, 8^{2}SD, 8^{4}SF, 9^{4}SD, 8^{1}SD, 8^{1}SD, 8^{3}SD,

	Starts	1st	2nd	3rd	Win & Pl
Career Total (Turf)	37	5	5	2	27499
Career Total (AW)	16	6	1	4	41058

98 11/09 Wolv 1m141y (0-100)H STD £11215
95 11/09 Wolv 1m141y (0-80)H STD £5046
88 2/09 Wolv 1m141y (0-85)H STD £5180
84 12/08 Wolv 1m141y (0-85)H STD £5677
82 11/08 Wolv 1m141y (0-80)H STD £5180
87 6/08 Newc 1m3y (0-85)H SFT £6231
84 4/08 Thsk 7f (0-75)H G-S £3885
77 11/07 Wolv 1m141y (0-70)H STD £2968
74 10/07 Ayr 7f50y (0-70)H SFT £3238
65 10/07 Muss 7f30y (0-65)H GD £2590
65 9/06 Rdcr 7f G-F £2590
Total win prize-money £53808

Going (Turf): Sf: 2-8 GS: 1-7 Gd: 1-9 GF: 1-12 Fm: 0-1

Distance: 5f/6f: 0-6 7f-8f: 4-31 **9f-13f: 7-16** 14f+: 0-0
Track : **LH: 8-29** RH: 1-9 **Tight: 8-20** Gall: 0-2
Aids: **Bl: 10-37** Vi: 0-0 Tstrap: 0-0 Ckp: 0-0
Best Rating: **103** 12/09 Kemp 1m stand

Very useful; stays 1m1f; acts on most ground; goes on sand; often wears blinkers.

Spinning Bailiwick

(101) (79)
3-y-o b f Spinning World (USA)-Zietunzeen (IRE) (Zieten (USA))
G L Moore (Ms V S Lucas 31/8) Dr Ian R Shenkin

Placings:046541113 (7828)
2009: 7^{0}G, 6^{4}GF, 5^{6}G, 5^{5}F, 5^{4}SD, 5^{1}SD, 6^{1}SD, 5^{1}SD, 6^{3}SD,

	Starts	1st	2nd	3rd	Win & Pl
Career Total (Turf)	4	0	0	0	
Career Total (AW)	5	3	0	1	6527

76 12/09 Ling 5f (0-60)H STD £2047
74 11/09 Ling 6f (0-50)H STD £2047
71 11/09 Kemp 5f STD £2047
Total win prize-money £6141

Going (Turf): **Sf: 0-0 GS: 0-0 Gd: 0-2 GF: 0-1 Fm: 0-1**
Distance: **5f/6f: 3-8** 7f-8f: 0-1 9f-13f: 0-0 14f+: 0-0
Track : **LH: 2-4** RH: 1-2 **Tight: 2-3** Gall: 0-0
Aids: Bl: 0-1 Vi: 0-0 Tstrap: 0-0 Ckp: 0-0
Best Rating: **79** 12/09 Kemp 6f stand

Fair; formerly trained in Jersey; effective over 5f-6f; acts on Polytrack.

Spinning Joy

71(76) (54)28
3-y-o b f Josr Algarhoud (IRE)-Den's-Joy (Archway (IRE))
J R Boyle Joy Racing

Placings:00-000 (2431)
2009: 8^{0}SD, 10^{0}SD, 8^{0}G,

	Starts	1st	2nd	3rd	Win & Pl
Career Total (Turf)	2	0	0	0	
Career Total (AW)	3	0	0	0	

Going (Turf): **Sf: 0-0 GS: 0-1 Gd: 0-1 GF: 0-0 Fm: 0-0**
Distance: 5f/6f: 0-0 7f-8f: 0-4 9f-13f: 0-1 14f+: 0-0
Track : LH: 0-1 RH: 0-3 Tight: 0-1 Gall: 0-0
Aids: Bl: 0-0 Vi: 0-0 Tstrap: 0-0 Ckp: 0-0
Best Rating: **54** 3/09 Kemp 1m stand

Spinning Ridge (IRE)

(100) (64)61
4-y-o ch g Spinning World (USA)-Summer Style (IRE) (Indian Ridge)
R A Harris Robert & Nina Bailey

Placings:00630015/0305-0000122305 (7856)
2009: 8^{0}SD, 9^{0}SD, 8^{0}SD, 8^{0}SD, 8^{1}SD, 8^{2}SD, 7^{2}SF, 7^{3}SD, 8^{0}SD, 9^{5}SD,

	Starts	1st	2nd	3rd	Win & Pl
Career Total (Turf)	4	0	0	1	506
Career Total (AW)	18	2	2	2	6416

59 11/09 Ling 1m (0-55)H STD £1706
68 10/07 Wolv 5f216y STD £2730
Total win prize-money £4436

Going (Turf): **Sf: 0-2 GS: 0-1 Gd: 0-1 GF: 0-0 Fm: 0-0**
Distance: 5f/6f: 1-5 7f-8f: 1-11 9f-13f: 0-6 14f+: 0-0
Track : **LH: 2-19** RH: 0-3 **Tight: 2-15** Gall: 0-0
Aids: Bl: 0-0 Vi: 0-0 Tstrap: 0-2 Ckp: 0-2
Best Rating: **68** 10/07 Wolv 5f216y stand

Modest; effective at around 7f-1m2f; acts on a sound surface; goes on Polytrack; has worn cheekpieces.

Spinning Spirit (IRE)

89(90) (63)66
2-y-o b g Invincible Spirit (IRE)-Vencera (FR) (Green Tune (USA))
J G Given R Jones & Patrick B Doyle Construction

Placings:035030 (7514)
2009: 6^{0}GF, 7^{3}G, 7^{5}GF, 8^{0}S, 6^{3}SD, 7^{0}SD,

	Starts	1st	2nd	3rd	Win & Pl
Career Total (Turf)	4	0	0	1	530
Career Total (AW)	2	0	0	1	373

Going (Turf): **Sf: 0-1 GS: 0-0 Gd: 0-1 GF: 0-2 Fm: 0-0**
Distance: 5f/6f: 0-1 7f-8f: 0-4 9f-13f: 0-1 14f+: 0-0
Track : LH: 0-4 RH: 0-1 Tight: 0-1 Gall: 0-0
Aids: Bl: 0-0 Vi: 0-0 Tstrap: 0-0 Ckp: 0-0
Best Rating: **66** 8/09 Wwck 7f26y good

Moderate; stays 7f; acts on good ground.

Spinning Waters

103(92) (57)67
3-y-o b g Vettori (IRE)-Secret Waters (Pharly (FR))
Eve Johnson Houghton R Crutchley

Placings:300-16023564 (6330)
2009: 12^{1}F, 12^{6}GF, 11^{0}G, 11^{2}F, 11^{3}F, 12^{5}GF, 16^{6}SD, 17^{4}F,

	Starts	1st	2nd	3rd	Win & Pl
Career Total (Turf)	10	1	1	2	5096
Career Total (AW)	1	0	0	0	0

66 4/09 Pont 1m4f8y (0-70)H FRM £3238
Total win prize-money £3238

Going (Turf): Sf: 0-0 GS: 0-0 Gd: 0-2 GF: 0-4 **Fm: 1-4**
Distance: 5f/6f: 0-0 7f-8f: 0-3 **9f-13f: 1-6** 14f+: 0-2
Track : **LH: 1-5** RH: 0-5 Tight: 0-4 Gall: 0-0
Aids: Bl: 0-0 Vi: 0-0 Tstrap: 0-2 Ckp: 0-2
Best Rating: **67** 6/09 Brig 1m3f196y firm

Modest; effective over 1m4f; acts on fast ground.

Spinning Well (IRE)

100(89) (64)75
3-y-o ch f Pivotal-Kiltubber (IRE) (Sadler's Wells (USA))
R M Beckett (D K Weld 21/6) Ballylinch Stud

Placings:30244 (7439)
2009: 7^{3}SD, 8^{0}G, 8^{2}S, 9^{4}GF, 10^{4}SD,

	Starts	1st	2nd	3rd	Win & Pl
Career Total (Turf)	3	0	1	0	2531
Career Total (AW)	2	0	0	1	758

Going (Turf): **Sf: 0-1 GS: 0-0 Gd: 0-1 GF: 0-1 Fm: 0-0**
Distance: 5f/6f: 0-0 7f-8f: 0-3 9f-13f: 0-2 14f+: 0-0
Track : LH: 0-3 RH: 0-2 Tight: 0-1 Gall: 0-1
Aids: Bl: 0-0 Vi: 0-0 Tstrap: 0-0 Ckp: 0-0
Best Rating: **75** 6/09 Curr 1m soft

Spiosra (USA)

83 29
3-y-o ch f Mr Greeley (USA)-Laptop (USA) (Phone Trick (USA))
C J Teague Mrs David Hodgkinson

Placings:000 (6823)
2009: 8^{0}GS, 7^{0}GF, 6^{0}GF,

	Starts	1st	2nd	3rd	Win & Pl
Career Total (Turf)	3	0	0	0	

Going (Turf): **Sf: 0-0 GS: 0-1 Gd: 0-0 GF: 0-2 Fm: 0-0**
Distance: 5f/6f: 0-1 7f-8f: 0-2 9f-13f: 0-0 14f+: 0-0
Track : LH: 0-1 RH: 0-0 Tight: 0-0 Gall: 0-1
Aids: Bl: 0-0 Vi: 0-0 Tstrap: 0-0 Ckp: 0-0
Best Rating: **29** 9/09 Rdcr 7f gd-fm

Spirit Child (USA)

69(69) 7
3-y-o b/br f Hennessy (USA)-Babeinthewoods (USA) (Woodman (USA))
J A Osborne T Busher & A Taylor

Placings:00 (6573)
2009: 7^{0}SD, 7^{0}GF,

	Starts	1st	2nd	3rd	Win & Pl
Career Total (Turf)	1	0	0	0	
Career Total (AW)	1	0	0	0	

Going (Turf): **Sf: 0-0 GS: 0-0 Gd: 0-0 GF: 0-1 Fm: 0-0**
Distance: 5f/6f: 0-0 7f-8f: 0-2 9f-13f: 0-0 14f+: 0-0
Track : LH: 0-1 RH: 0-0 Tight: 0-1 Gall: 0-0
Aids: Bl: 0-0 Vi: 0-0 Tstrap: 0-0 Ckp: 0-0
Best Rating: **7** 10/09 Leic 7f9y gd-fm

Spirit Is Needed (IRE)

101 88
3-y-o b g No Excuse Needed-The Spirit Of Pace (IRE) (In The Wings)
M Johnston Mrs Joan Keaney

Placings:P12 (6313)
2009: 11^{P}GF, 11^{1}GF, 14^{2}GF,

	Starts	1st	2nd	3rd	Win & Pl
Career Total (Turf)	3	1	1	0	5165

74 9/09 Leic 1m3f183y G-F £3238
Total win prize-money £3238

Going (Turf): Sf: 0-0 GS: 0-0 Gd: 0-0 **GF: 1-3** Fm: 0-0
Distance: 5f/6f: 0-0 7f-8f: 0-0 **9f-13f: 1-2** 14f+: 0-1
Track : LH: 0-0 **RH: 1-3** Tight: 0-1 Gall: 0-0
Aids: Bl: 0-0 Vi: 0-0 Tstrap: 0-0 Ckp: 0-0
Best Rating: **88** 9/09 Muss 1m6f gd-fm

Useful; stays 1m4f; acts on fast ground.

Spirit Land (IRE)

81(87) (50)52
2-y-o ch c Indian Haven-Reborn (IRE) (Idris (IRE))
M H Tompkins Miss Clare Hollest

Placings:05046 (7482)
2009: 7^{0}GF, 8^{5}GF, 7^{0}GF, 8^{4}SD, 8^{6}SD,

	Starts	1st	2nd	3rd	Win & Pl
Career Total (Turf)	3	0	0	0	0

Career Total (AW)	2	0	0	0	0

Going (Turf): **Sf: 0-0 GS: 0-0 Gd: 0-0 GF: 0-3 Fm: 0-0**
Distance: 5f/6f: 0-0 7f-8f: 0-4 9f-13f: 0-1 14f+: 0-0
Track : LH: 0-4 RH: 0-0 Tight: 0-1 Gall: 0-0
Aids: Bl: 0-0 Vi: 0-0 Tstrap: 0-0 Ckp: 0-0
Best Rating: **52** 10/09 Wwck 7f26y gd-fm

Moderate; stays 1m; acts on Fibresand.

Spirit Of A Nation (IRE)

102(106) (89)**92**

4-y-o b c Invincible Spirit (IRE)-Fabulous Pet (Somethingfabulous (USA))
D H Brown Bezwell Fixings Limited

Placings:0/5511-32 **(6014)**
2009: 8^3SD, 8^2G,

	Starts	1st	2nd	3rd	Win & Pl
Career Total (Turf)	6	2	1	0	9019
Career Total (AW)	1	0	0	1	746

89	6/08	Donc	7f	(0-80)H	GD	£4857
83	5/08	Rdcr	1m	(0-75)H	SFT	£2331

Total win prize-money £7188

Going (Turf): **Sf: 1-2** GS: 0-1 **Gd: 1-3** GF: 0-0 Fm: 0-0
Distance: 5f/6f: 0-1 **7f-8f: 2-6** 9f-13f: 0-0 14f+: 0-0
Track : LH: 0-1 RH: 0-1 Tight: 0-0 Gall: 0-0
Aids: Bl: 0-0 Vi: 0-0 Tstrap: 0-0 Ckp: 0-0
Best Rating: **92** 9/09 Ayr 1m good

Useful; effective at 7f-1m; acts on good and soft ground and on Polytrack.

Spirit Of Adjisa (IRE)

106(105) (84)**90**

5-y-o br g Invincible Spirit (IRE)-Adjisa (IRE) (Doyoun)
A King (Pat Eddery 30/10) Darr, Johnson, Weston & Whitaker

Placings:64/4**5**061**13**/356234301-**24**02464116 **(7151)**
2009: 12^{2}SD, **12**^{4}SD, 14^0S, 11^2GF, 12^4GS, 12^6G, 12^4G, 12^1GS, 13^1GF, 16^6G,

	Starts	1st	2nd	3rd	Win & Pl
Career Total (Turf)	21	4	2	3	24158
Career Total (AW)	7	1	1	1	4444

90	9/09	Ches	1m5f89y	(0-80)H	G-F	£7123
84	9/09	Epsm	1m4f10y	(0-75)H	G-S	£3885
83	10/08	Bath	1m3f144y	(0-80)H	G-S	£4857
77	10/07	Kemp	1m4f	(0-65)H	STD	£2047
81	10/07	Brig	1m1f209y	(0-65)H	G-S	£2266

Total win prize-money £20182

Going (Turf): Sf: 0-4 **GS: 3-5** Gd: 0-5 GF: 1-7 Fm: 0-0
Distance: 5f/6f: 0-0 7f-8f: 0-2 **9f-13f: 4-23** 14f+: 1-3
Track : **LH: 4-18** RH: 1-7 **Tight: 3-13** Gall: 0-4
Aids: **Bl: 3-12** Vi: 0-1 Tstrap: 0-0 Ckp: 0-0
Best Rating: **90** 9/09 Ches 1m5f89y gd-fm

Useful; stays 1m5f; acts on fast ans easy ground; goes on Polytrack; has worn blinkers.

Spirit Of Coniston

108(98) (59)**73**

6-y-o b g Lake Coniston (IRE)-Kigema (IRE) (Case Law)
P T Midgley P O'Gara & N Kelly

Placings:0050542520**200/0306631**33214360**00041/12501 46123**5050**0**02112/60**4**0**4**00600123**46-5033**30043501561**0** **(7398)**
2009: 5^{5}SD, **5**^{0}SD, **5**^{3}SD, **5**^{3}SD, 5^3GF, **5**^{0}SD, 5^0GF, 5^4F, 5^3GF, 5^5GF, 5^0G, 5^1GS, 5^5GS, 5^6G, 5^1S, **5**^{0}SD,

	Starts	1st	2nd	3rd	Win & Pl
Career Total (Turf)	45	5	5	5	21398
Career Total (AW)	39	6	4	6	19999

73	10/09	Catt	5f	(0-65)H	SFT	£2047
67	8/09	Catt	5f	(0-65)H	G-S	£2388
63	9/08	Muss	5f	(0-65)H	GD	£2590
73	10/07	Catt	5f	(0-65)H	GD	£2730
68	10/07	Kemp	5f	(0-55)H	STD	£2047
57	5/07	Wolv	5f20y	(0-50)H	STD	£2388
56	2/07	Sthl	5f		STD	£2184
55	1/07	Sthl	5f		SLW	£2184
57	12/06	Sthl	5f		STD	£2730
64	6/06	Kemp	5f	(0-75)H	STD	£3238
61	4/06	Folk	5f		G-F	£2730

Total win prize-money £27259

Going (Turf): Sf: 1-4 GS: 1-6 **Gd: 2-13** GF: 1-16 Fm: 0-6
Distance: **5f/6f: 11-84** 7f-8f: 0-0 9f-13f: 0-0 14f+: 0-0
Track : LH: 1-35 **RH: 2-6 Tight: 1-29** Gall: 0-3
Aids: **Bl: 5-26** Vi: 1-3 Tstrap: 0-2 Ckp: 0-2
Best Rating: **73** 10/09 Catt 5f soft

Moderate; effective over 5f-6f; acts on good ground; also goes on Fibresand and Polytrack.

Spirit Of Dubai (IRE)

109 **101**

3-y-o b f Cape Cross (IRE)-Questina (FR) (Rainbow Quest (USA))
D M Simcock Ahmad Al Shaikh

Placings:00-402411 **(6242)**
2009: 11^4GF, 11^0GF, 10^2GF, 10^4GF, 11^1GF, 12^1G,

	Starts	1st	2nd	3rd	Win & Pl
Career Total (Turf)	8	2	1	0	32743

101	9/09	Asct	1m4f		GD	£25546
78	9/09	Ling	1m3f106y		G-F	£2729

Total win prize-money £28277

Going (Turf): Sf: 0-1 GS: 0-0 **Gd: 1-2 GF: 1-5** Fm: 0-0
Distance: 5f/6f: 0-0 7f-8f: 0-0 **9f-13f: 2-8** 14f+: 0-0
Track : LH: 1-5 RH: 1-2 Tight: 1-3 Gall: 1-2
Aids: Bl: 0-0 Vi: 0-0 Tstrap: 0-0 Ckp: 0-0
Best Rating: **101** 9/09 Asct 1m4f good

Very useful; Listed winner; effective over 1m4f; acts on good ground.

Spirit Of France (IRE)

99 **74**

7-y-o b g Anabaa (USA)-Les Planches (Tropular)
D Carroll D Hardy

Placings:221256/0446402103050130/23500/0/00-00023455 **(3121)**
2009: 6^0GF, 7^0GF, 8^0G, 9^2GF, 9^3GF, 7^4F, 8^5GS, 10^5GF,

	Starts	1st	2nd	3rd	Win & Pl
Career Total (Turf)	38	3	6	4	83889

95	9/05	Muss	1m	(0-100)H	GD	£14828
94	7/05	Haml	6f5y	(0-105)H	G-F	£18339
82	6/04	Ripn	6f	D	G-F	£5538

Total win prize-money £38707

Going (Turf): Sf: 0-3 GS: 0-7 Gd: 1-9 **GF: 2-17** Fm: 0-2
Distance: 5f/6f: 1-12 **7f-8f: 2-20** 9f-13f: 0-6 14f+: 0-0
Track : LH: 0-14 **RH: 1-6 Tight: 1-6** Gall: 0-6
Aids: Bl: 0-0 Vi: 0-0 Tstrap: 0-0 Ckp: 0-0
Best Rating: **98** 2/06 Ndas 1m gd-fm

Fair; effective at around 1m1f; acts on most ground.

Spirit Of Love (IRE)

(92) (66)

2-y-o b g Pearl Of Love (IRE)-Sesleria (IRE) (Mark Of Esteem (IRE))
M Wigham D Hassan, R Kibble

Placings:4 **(7556)**
2009: 5^4SD,

	Starts	1st	2nd	3rd	Win & Pl
Career Total (Turf)	0	0	0	0	
Career Total (AW)	1	0	0	0	0

Going (Turf): **Sf: 0-0 GS: 0-0 Gd: 0-0 GF: 0-0 Fm: 0-0**
Distance: 5f/6f: 0-1 7f-8f: 0-0 9f-13f: 0-0 14f+: 0-0
Track : LH: 0-1 RH: 0-0 Tight: 0-1 Gall: 0-0
Aids: Bl: 0-0 Vi: 0-0 Tstrap: 0-0 Ckp: 0-0
Best Rating: **66** 11/09 Wolv 5f216y stand

Spirit Of Normandy

(68) (22)

2-y-o ch f Auction House (USA)-Charlottevalentina (IRE) (Perugino (USA))
R Ingram Ellangowan Racing Partners

Placings:0 **(7430)**
2009: 7^0SD,

	Starts	1st	2nd	3rd	Win & Pl
Career Total (Turf)	0	0	0	0	
Career Total (AW)	1	0	0	0	

Going (Turf): **Sf: 0-0 GS: 0-0 Gd: 0-0 GF: 0-0 Fm: 0-0**
Distance: 5f/6f: 0-0 7f-8f: 0-1 9f-13f: 0-0 14f+: 0-0
Track : LH: 0-0 RH: 0-1 Tight: 0-0 Gall: 0-0
Aids: Bl: 0-0 Vi: 0-0 Tstrap: 0-0 Ckp: 0-0
Best Rating: **22** 11/09 Kemp 7f stand

Spirit Of Sharjah (IRE)

105(106) (95)**100**

4-y-o b g Invincible Spirit (IRE)-Rathbawn Realm (Doulab (USA))
Miss J Feilden A Dee

Placings:1130620/00000-0666436103046**24** **(7133)**
2009: 6^0GF, 5^6G, 5^6G, 6^6GF, 6^4GF, 6^3GF, 7^6G, 7^1GF, 6^0G, 7^3G, 8^0GF, 8^4GF, 7^6GF, **7**^{2}SS, **7**^{4}SD,

	Starts	1st	2nd	3rd	Win & Pl
Career Total (Turf)	25	3	1	3	53377
Career Total (AW)	2	0	1	0	3197

92	7/09	Epsm	7f	(0-85)H	G-F	£5180
92	5/07	Gdwd	5f		GD	£12491
92	4/07	NmkR	5f		G-F	£6477

Total win prize-money £24150

Going (Turf): Sf: 0-0 GS: 0-1 Gd: 1-11 **GF: 2-13** Fm: 0-0
Distance: **5f/6f: 2-18** 7f-8f: 1-8 9f-13f: 0-1 14f+: 0-0
Track : **LH: 1-4** RH: 0-2 **Tight: 1-3** Gall: 0-1
Aids: Bl: 0-0 Vi: 0-1 Tstrap: 0-0 Ckp: 0-0
Best Rating: **107** 9/07 Donc 5f gd-fm

Useful; Listed winner and Group placed; effective over 5-7f; acts on good and faster ground; has worn a visor.

Spirit Of The Glen

81(83) (50)28

3-y-o b f Catcher In The Rye (IRE)-Sentiment (Dancing Brave (USA))

Jamie Poulton Gleneagles Racing Partnership

Placings:5400 **(4569)**

2009: 10^{5}SD, 12^{4}SD, 10^{0}GF, 10^{0}G,

	Starts	1st	2nd	3rd	Win & Pl
Career Total (Turf)	2	0	0	0	
Career Total (AW)	2	0	0	0	0

Going (Turf): **Sf: 0-0 GS: 0-0 Gd: 0-1 GF: 0-1 Fm: 0-0**
Distance: 5f/6f: 0-0 7f-8f: 0-0 9f-13f: 0-4 14f+: 0-0
Track : LH: 0-4 RH: 0-0 Tight: 0-2 Gall: 0-2
Aids: Bl: 0-0 Vi: 0-0 Tstrap: 0-0 Ckp: 0-0
Best Rating: **50** 2/09 Ling 1m4f stand

Modest; stays 1m4f; acts on Polytrack.

Spiritofthewest (IRE)

98(100) (74)82

3-y-o b g Invincible Spirit (IRE)-Rosie's Guest (IRE) (Be My Guest (USA))

D H Brown (S Parr 18/4) J P Hardiman

Placings:01000-643000055040 **(7759)**

2009: 6^{6}GF, 5^{4}GS, 6^{3}GF, 5^{0}GF, 5^{0}GF, 6^{0}G, 5^{0}GF, 5^{5}GF, 5^{5}SD, 6^{0}S, 8^{4}SD, 8^{0}SD,

	Starts	1st	2nd	3rd	Win & Pl
Career Total (Turf)	14	1	0	1	4671
Career Total (AW)	3	0	0	0	192

82 9/08 Bevl 5f SFT £2914

Total win prize-money £2914

Going (Turf): **Sf: 1-3** GS: 0-2 Gd: 0-3 GF: 0-6 Fm: 0-0
Distance: **5f/6f: 1-14** 7f-8f: 0-3 9f-13f: 0-0 14f+: 0-0
Track : LH: 0-3 RH: 0-1 Tight: 0-1 Gall: 0-0
Aids: Bl: 0-0 Vi: 0-1 Tstrap: 0-0 Ckp: 0-0
Best Rating: **82** 9/08 Bevl 5f soft

Fair; effective over 1m; acts on soft ground and on Polytrack.

Spiritonthemount (USA)

74(103) (70)77

4-y-o b/br g Pulpit (USA)-Stirling Bridge (USA) (Prized (USA))

P W Hiatt Bob Coles

Placings:56/2542000-0005462003 **(7873)**

2009: 16^{0}SS, 13^{0}SD, 13^{0}SD, 14^{5}SD, 14^{4}SD, 16^{6}SD, 16^{2}SD, 15^{0}GF, 14^{0}SD, 16^{3}SD,

	Starts	1st	2nd	3rd	Win & Pl
Career Total (Turf)	8	0	2	0	1975
Career Total (AW)	11	0	1	1	1182

Going (Turf): **Sf: 0-2 GS: 0-1 Gd: 0-2 GF: 0-3 Fm: 0-0**
Distance: 5f/6f: 0-0 7f-8f: 0-1 9f-13f: 0-5 14f+: 0-13
Track : LH: 0-15 RH: 0-3 Tight: 0-6 Gall: 0-1
Aids: Bl: 0-11 Vi: 0-0 Tstrap: 0-0 Ckp: 0-0
Best Rating: **77** 7/08 Hayd 1m6f good

Moderate; probably stays 2m; acts on soft ground; sometimes blinkered.

Spiritual Art

97(105) (79)69

3-y-o b f Invincible Spirit (IRE)-Oatey (Master Willie)

L A Dace (S A Callaghan 29/6) Gerry Boyer & Mike Tokarski

Placings:400211-6050622146 **(7883)**

2009: 6^{6}GF, 7^{0}SD, 6^{5}GF, 7^{0}GF, 7^{6}SS, 7^{2}SS, 8^{2}SD, 8^{1}SD, 8^{4}SD, 8^{6}SD,

	Starts	1st	2nd	3rd	Win & Pl
Career Total (Turf)	6	0	1	0	1191
Career Total (AW)	10	3	2	0	9963

79 11/09 Ling 1m (0-75)H STD £2388
75 12/08 Sthl 6f (0-70) SS £2729
71 12/08 GrLe 6f (0-65) STD £2719

Total win prize-money £7838

Going (Turf): **Sf: 0-1 GS: 0-0 Gd: 0-2 GF: 0-3 Fm: 0-0**
Distance: **5f/6f: 2-7** 7f-8f: 1-9 9f-13f: 0-0 14f+: 0-0
Track : **LH: 3-9** RH: 0-2 Tight: 1-6 Gall: 1-1
Aids: Bl: 0-0 Vi: 0-0 Tstrap: 1-8 Ckp: 1-8
Best Rating: **79** 11/09 Ling 1m stand

Fair; stays 1m; acts on good and softer ground and on Polytrack; has worn cheekpieces.

Spiritual Bond

(81) (48)18

3-y-o b f Monsieur Bond (IRE)-Country Spirit (Sayf El Arab (USA))

R A Harris Ridge House Stables Ltd

Placings:00050-0 **(0267)**

2009: 7^{0}SD,

	Starts	1st	2nd	3rd	Win & Pl
Career Total (Turf)	2	0	0	0	
Career Total (AW)	4	0	0	0	0

Going (Turf): **Sf: 0-0 GS: 0-0 Gd: 0-0 GF: 0-0 Fm: 0-2**
Distance: 5f/6f: 0-2 7f-8f: 0-4 9f-13f: 0-0 14f+: 0-0
Track : LH: 0-5 RH: 0-1 Tight: 0-2 Gall: 0-2
Aids: Bl: 0-0 Vi: 0-0 Tstrap: 0-0 Ckp: 0-0
Best Rating: **48** 10/08 Wolv 7f32y std-fst

Spiritual Healing (IRE)

(93) (65)

3-y-o b f Invincible Spirit (IRE)-Tarbela (IRE) (Grand Lodge (USA))

J A Osborne Mountgrange Stud

Placings:51 **(0381)**

2009: 6^{5}SD, 6^{1}SD,

	Starts	1st	2nd	3rd	Win & Pl
Career Total (Turf)	0	0	0	0	
Career Total (AW)	2	1	0	0	2730

65 2/09 Sthl 6f STD £2729

Total win prize-money £2730

Going (Turf): **Sf: 0-0 GS: 0-0 Gd: 0-0 GF: 0-0 Fm: 0-0**
Distance: **5f/6f: 1-2** 7f-8f: 0-0 9f-13f: 0-0 14f+: 0-0
Track : **LH: 1-2** RH: 0-0 Tight: 0-1 Gall: 0-0
Aids: Bl: 0-0 Vi: 0-0 Tstrap: 0-0 Ckp: 0-0
Best Rating: **65** 2/09 Sthl 6f stand

Modest; stays 6f and acts on Fibresand.

Spiritual Treasure (USA)

81(93) (74)14

3-y-o b/br g Perfect Soul (IRE)-Storm Runner (USA) (Miswaki (USA))

M A Magnusson Eastwind Racing Ltd and Martha Trussell

Placings:01-0500 **(6832)**

2009: 10^{0}SD, 12^{5}SD, 10^{0}G, 12^{0}SF,

	Starts	1st	2nd	3rd	Win & Pl
Career Total (Turf)	1	0	0	0	
Career Total (AW)	5	1	0	0	2388

74 10/08 Ling 1m STD £2388

Total win prize-money £2388

Going (Turf): **Sf: 0-0 GS: 0-0 Gd: 0-1 GF: 0-0 Fm: 0-0**
Distance: 5f/6f: 0-0 **7f-8f: 1-2** 9f-13f: 0-4 14f+: 0-0
Track : **LH: 1-4** RH: 0-2 **Tight: 1-4** Gall: 0-0
Aids: Bl: 0-0 Vi: 0-0 Tstrap: 0-0 Ckp: 0-0
Best Rating: **74** 10/08 Ling 1m stand

Fair; stays at least 1m; acts on Polytrack.

Spit And Polish

94(96) (63)67

3-y-o b g Pulish Precedent (USA)-Brooklyn's Sky (Septieme Ciel (USA))

C A Dwyer (J L Dunlop 12/5) S B Components Ltd & Mrs Shelley Dwyer

Placings:635505-62206006 **(3225)**

2009: 7^{6}SD, 7^{2}SD, 6^{2}F, 5^{0}G, 5^{6}SD, 5^{0}SD, 5^{0}GF, 5^{6}SD,

	Starts	1st	2nd	3rd	Win & Pl
Career Total (Turf)	8	0	1	1	1022
Career Total (AW)	6	0	1	0	605

Going (Turf): **Sf: 0-1 GS: 0-1 Gd: 0-2 GF: 0-3 Fm: 0-1**
Distance: 5f/6f: 0-8 7f-8f: 0-6 9f-13f: 0-0 14f+: 0-0
Track : LH: 0-7 RH: 0-1 Tight: 0-5 Gall: 0-0
Aids: Bl: 0-7 Vi: 0-2 Tstrap: 0-0 Ckp: 0-0
Best Rating: **67** 8/08 Folk 7f gd-sft

Modest; stays 7f; acts on soft ground and on Polytrack; has worn blinkers and a visor.

Spitfire

100(105) (97)101

4-y-o b g Mujahid (USA)-Fresh Fruit Daily (Reprimand)

J R Jenkins The Spitfire Partnership

Placings:1104104/2052506-4003663440 **(7626)**

2009: 7^{4}SD, 7^{0}GF, 7^{0}GF, 6^{3}G, 6^{6}G, 7^{6}GF, 8^{3}SS, 7^{4}SD, 10^{4}SD, 8^{0}SD,

	Starts	1st	2nd	3rd	Win & Pl
Career Total (Turf)	18	3	2	1	45714
Career Total (AW)	6	0	0	1	3934

98 9/07 Donc 6f G-F £11217
87 5/07 Yarm 6f3y GD £3469
74 5/07 Wwck 5f110y G-S £3412

Total win prize-money £18101

Going (Turf): Sf: 0-1 **GS: 1-3 Gd: 1-8 GF: 1-6** Fm: 0-0
Distance: **5f/6f: 2-12** 7f-8f: 1-11 9f-13f: 0-1 14f+: 0-0
Track : **LH: 1-7** RH: 0-1 Tight: 0-5 Gall: 0-0
Aids: Bl: 0-0 Vi: 0-1 Tstrap: 0-0 Ckp: 0-0
Best Rating: **101** 7/08 NmkJ 6f gd-sft

Useful; effective over 6f-7f; acts on most ground; usually held up.

Splash The Cash

104(101) (65)**78**

4-y-o b g Lomitas-Bandit Queen (Desert Prince (IRE))
K A Ryan The Armchair Jockeys

Placings:6420063203/64334321020-055010014P **(2998)**
2009: 6^{0}SD, 7^{5}SD, 5^{5}SD, 7^{0}SD, 7^{1}GF, 6^{0}G, 7^{0}GF, 7^{1}G, 5^{4}GF, 7^{P}GF,

	Starts	1st	2nd	3rd	Win & Pl
Career Total (Turf)	16	3	1	2	10277
Career Total (AW)	15	0	3	3	4057

78	5/09	Catt	7f	(0-75)H	GD	£3412
78	4/09	Catt	7f		G-F	£2047
70	7/08	Haml	6f5y	(0-60)H	GD	£2266

Total win prize-money £7726

Going (Turf): Sf: 0-2 GS: 0-1 **Gd: 2-4** GF: 1-9 Fm: 0-0
Distance: 5f/6f: 0-19 **7f-8f: 3-12** 9f-13f: 0-0 14f+: 0-0
Track : **LH: 2-23** RH: 0-2 **Tight: 2-19** Gall: 0-3
Aids: Bl: 0-0 Vi: 0-0 Tstrap: 1-5 Ckp: 1-5
Best Rating: **78** 5/09 Catt 7f good

Fair; effective over 6f-7f; acts on most ground; goes on Polytrack.

Splashdown

108(95) (75)**105**

3-y-o ch f Falbrav (IRE)-Space Time (FR) (Bering)
L M Cumani Fittocks Stud

Placings:13-415233 **(6813)**
2009: 9^{4}GF, 10^{1}GF, 12^{5}G, 9^{2}GF, 10^{3}GF, 10^{3}G,

	Starts	1st	2nd	3rd	Win & Pl
Career Total (Turf)	7	1	1	3	48599
Career Total (AW)	1	1	0	0	4695

105	6/09	Newb	1m2f6y	G-F	£22708
75	9/08	Kemp	7f	STD	£4695

Total win prize-money £27403

Going (Turf): Sf: 0-0 GS: 0-1 Gd: 0-2 **GF: 1-4** Fm: 0-0
Distance: 5f/6f: 0-0 7f-8f: 1-2 9f-13f: 1-6 14f+: 0-0
Track : LH: 1-2 RH: 1-4 Tight: 0-3 **Gall: 1-2**
Aids: Bl: 0-0 Vi: 0-0 Tstrap: 0-0 Ckp: 0-0
Best Rating: **105** 6/09 Newb 1m2f6y gd-fm

Smart; Listed winner; stays 1m2f; acts on good and faster ground; goes on Polytrack.

Splendorinthegrass (IRE)

106 **99**

3-y-o ch c Selkirk (USA)-Portelet (Night Shift (USA))
R Charlton B E Nielsen

Placings:05-2130 **(6675)**
2009: 7^{2}F, 8^{1}S, 7^{3}G, 7^{0}G,

	Starts	1st	2nd	3rd	Win & Pl
Career Total (Turf)	6	1	1	1	11530

93	7/09	NmkJ	1m	SFT	£5180

Total win prize-money £5181

Going (Turf): **Sf: 1-2** GS: 0-0 Gd: 0-3 GF: 0-0 Fm: 0-1
Distance: 5f/6f: 0-0 **7f-8f: 1-6** 9f-13f: 0-0 14f+: 0-0
Track : LH: 0-2 RH: 0-0 Tight: 0-1 Gall: 0-1
Aids: Bl: 0-0 Vi: 0-0 Tstrap: 0-0 Ckp: 0-0
Best Rating: **99** 8/09 NmkJ 7f good

Very useful; lightly raced; stays 1m; acts on most ground.

Splinter Cell (USA)

104(108) (99)**96**

3-y-o b/br c Johannesburg (USA)-Rock Salt (Selkirk (USA))
M Botti Op - Center

Placings:31-2053151401 **(7789)**
2009: 8^{2}SD, 9^{0}GF, 11^{5}HY, 10^{3}G, 8^{1}G, 8^{5}S, 10^{1}GS, 10^{4}GS, 10^{0}SD, 9^{1}SD,

	Starts	1st	2nd	3rd	Win & Pl
Career Total (Turf)	9	3	0	2	15118
Career Total (AW)	3	1	1	0	12709

99	12/09	Wolv	1m1f103y (0-100)H	STD	£11215
91	10/09	Wind	1m2f7y (0-85)H	G-S	£4857
87	7/09	Bevl	1m100y (0-85)H	GD	£4727
84	8/08	Hayd	1m30y	SFT	£3238

Total win prize-money £24038

Going (Turf): **Sf: 1-3 GS: 1-2 Gd: 1-2** GF: 0-2 Fm: 0-0
Distance: 5f/6f: 0-0 7f-8f: 0-2 **9f-13f: 4-10** 14f+: 0-0
Track : LH: 2-8 RH: 2-3 **Tight: 2-5** Gall: 0-1
Aids: Bl: 0-0 Vi: 0-0 Tstrap: 0-0 Ckp: 0-0
Best Rating: **99** 12/09 Wolv 1m1f103y stand

Useful; stays 1m2f; acts on fast and soft ground, also Polytrack; has worn a tongue-tie.

Split The Pot (IRE)

87(73) (21)**57**

2-y-o b g Chevalier (IRE)-Autumn Fall (USA) (Sanglamore (USA))
P R Chamings Inhurst Players

Placings:65400 **(6610)**
2009: 5^{6}GF, 5^{5}GF, 5^{4}F, 8^{0}SD, 6^{0}SD,

	Starts	1st	2nd	3rd	Win & Pl
Career Total (Turf)	3	0	0	0	283
Career Total (AW)	2	0	0	0	

Going (Turf): **Sf: 0-0 GS: 0-0 Gd: 0-0 GF: 0-2 Fm: 0-1**
Distance: 5f/6f: 0-4 7f-8f: 0-1 9f-13f: 0-0 14f+: 0-0
Track : LH: 0-2 RH: 0-2 Tight: 0-0 Gall: 0-1
Aids: Bl: 0-0 Vi: 0-0 Tstrap: 0-0 Ckp: 0-0
Best Rating: **57** 7/09 Brig 5f213y firm

Spoken

100 **76**

2-y-o ch c Medicean-Spout (Salse (USA))
R Charlton Lady Rothschild

Placings:41 **(6393)**
2009: 8^{4}GF, 8^{1}GF,

	Starts	1st	2nd	3rd	Win & Pl
Career Total (Turf)	2	1	0	0	5080

76	9/09	Sals	1m	G-F	£4695

Total win prize-money £4695

Going (Turf): Sf: 0-0 GS: 0-0 Gd: 0-0 **GF: 1-2** Fm: 0-0
Distance: 5f/6f: 0-0 **7f-8f: 1-1** 9f-13f: 0-1 14f+: 0-0
Track : LH: 0-0 RH: 0-1 Tight: 0-0 Gall: 0-0
Aids: Bl: 0-0 Vi: 0-0 Tstrap: 0-0 Ckp: 0-0
Best Rating: **76** 9/09 Sals 1m gd-fm

Fair; stays 1m; acts on fast ground.

Sponge

87(92) (38)**53**

4-y-o b g Zaha (CAN)-Glensara (Petoski)
P R Chamings Basingstoke Commercials

Placings:045-000 **(4263)**
2009: 10^{0}SD, 11^{0}G, 12^{0}S,

	Starts	1st	2nd	3rd	Win & Pl
Career Total (Turf)	3	0	0	0	0
Career Total (AW)	3	0	0	0	265

Going (Turf): **Sf: 0-1 GS: 0-1 Gd: 0-1 GF: 0-0 Fm: 0-0**
Distance: 5f/6f: 0-0 7f-8f: 0-0 9f-13f: 0-5 14f+: 0-1
Track : LH: 0-4 RH: 0-1 Tight: 0-4 Gall: 0-1
Aids: Bl: 0-0 Vi: 0-0 Tstrap: 0-0 Ckp: 0-0
Best Rating: **53** 8/08 Wind 1m67y gd-sft

Spoof Master (IRE)

(104) (73)**81**

5-y-o b g Invincible Spirit (IRE)-Talbiya (IRE) (Mujtahid (USA))
C R Dore Mrs Jennifer Marsh

Placings:21233042/505000/22242236000012000665-5364556160 **(7839)**
2009: 5^{5}SD, 5^{3}SD, 6^{6}SD, 6^{4}SD, 6^{5}SD, 8^{5}SD, 8^{6}SD, 5^{1}SD, 5^{6}SD, 5^{0}SS,

	Starts	1st	2nd	3rd	Win & Pl
Career Total (Turf)	13	1	4	2	14235
Career Total (AW)	30	2	5	2	13008

60	10/09	Kemp	5f	(0-55)H	STD	£2047
73	8/08	GrLe	5f	(0-70)H	STD	£2590
84	3/06	Rdcr	5f		SFT	£6855

Total win prize-money £11492

Going (Turf): **Sf: 1-5** GS: 0-2 Gd: 0-4 GF: 0-2 Fm: 0-0
Distance: **5f/6f: 3-40** 7f-8f: 0-3 9f-13f: 0-0 14f+: 0-0
Track : LH: 1-17 RH: 1-8 Tight: 0-11 **Gall: 1-6**
Aids: Bl: 0-0 Vi: 0-0 Tstrap: 1-12 Ckp: 1-12
Best Rating: **84** 7/06 Ches 5f16y gd-fm

Modest; effective over 5f; acts on soft ground and on sand; likes to race prominently.

Sporting Gesture

110(80) (32)**77**

12-y-o ch g Safawan-Polly Packer (Reform)
M W Easterby Steve Hull

Placings:0566010/000161000/0000011143005/000650663/41422412061200/0544436U25/00021005120144/03005604303603/03322251203/346253200-600051504 **(5962)**
2009: 12^{6}F, 12^{0}SD, 12^{0}GS, 12^{0}GF, 12^{5}G, 12^{1}G, 12^{5}GF, 12^{0}GS, 11^{4}GS,

	Starts	1st	2nd	3rd	Win & Pl
Career Total (Turf)	119	14	13	12	144819
Career Total (AW)	1	0	0	0	

64	7/09	Pont	1m4f8y	(0-70)H	GD	£3885
75	9/07	York	1m4f	(0-80)H	G-F	£6246
89	9/05	Thsk	1m4f	(0-80)H	G-F	£8772
82	7/05	York	1m4f	(0-80)H	G-F	£7052
82	5/05	Donc	1m4f	(0-85)H	G-F	£6987
81	9/03	York	1m3f198yD	(0-85)H	G-F	£6480
78	6/03	York	1m3f198yC	(0-95)H	G-F	£13455
71	4/03	Pont	1m2f6yE	(0-75)H	G-F	£4299
70	8/01	Pont	1m4f8yC	(0-100)H	G-F	£7117
65	8/01	Thsk	1m4f D	(0-80)H	FRM	£4264
64	7/01	Nott	1m1f213yE	(0-70)H	G-F	£3682
78	8/00	Ches	1m2f75yC	(0-90)H	GD	£7085
76	7/00	York	7f202y D	(0-85)H	GD	£11017
76	9/99	Catt	7f E	(0-75)H	G-F	£3072

Total win prize-money £93421

Going (Turf): Sf: 0-11GS: 0-15Gd: 3-31**GF: 10-52**Fm: 1-10

Distance:	5f/6f: 0-4 7f-8f: 2-7 **9f-13f: 12-100** 14f+: 0-9
Track :	**LH: 14-95** RH: 0-22 Tight: 4-44 **Gall: 6-47**
Aids:	Bl: 0-1 Vi: 0-0 Tstrap: 0-0 Ckp: 0-0
Best Rating:	**89** 9/05 Thsk 1m4f gd-fm

Moderate; stays 1m4f; suited by fast ground; likes York.

Spotty Muldoon (IRE)

92(87) (41)**77**

4-y-o b g Mull Of Kintyre (USA)-Fashion Guide (IRE) (Bluebird (USA))

R M Beckett Axis Partnership

Placings:421-000 **(2977)**

2009: 8^{0}G, 8^{0}SD, 8^{0}GF,

	Starts	1st	2nd	3rd	Win & Pl
Career Total (Turf)	5	1	1	0	4127
Career Total (AW)	1	0	0	0	
77 9/08 Wwck 1m22y			SFT	£2729	

Total win prize-money £2730

Going (Turf):	**Sf: 1-2** GS: 0-0 Gd: 0-1 GF: 0-2 Fm: 0-0
Distance:	5f/6f: 0-0 7f-8f: 0-3 **9f-13f: 1-3** 14f+: 0-0
Track :	**LH: 1-3** RH: 0-2 Tight: 0-2 Gall: 0-0
Aids:	Bl: 0-0 Vi: 0-1 Tstrap: 0-0 Ckp: 0-0
Best Rating:	**77** 9/08 Wwck 1m22y soft

Fair; stays 1m; acts on fast and soft ground.

Spouk

108(108) (79)**85**

4-y-o b f Pivotal-Souk (IRE) (Ahonoora)

L M Cumani Fittocks Stud

Placings:021-2 **(4328)**

2009: 10^{2}G,

	Starts	1st	2nd	3rd	Win & Pl
Career Total (Turf)	2	0	1	0	2891
Career Total (AW)	2	1	1	0	3536
66 11/08 Ling 1m2f			STD	£2729	

Total win prize-money £2730

Going (Turf):	**Sf: 0-0 GS: 0-0 Gd: 0-1 GF: 0-0 Fm: 0-1**
Distance:	5f/6f: 0-0 7f-8f: 0-1 **9f-13f: 1-3** 14f+: 0-0
Track :	**LH: 1-3** RH: 0-0 **Tight: 1-2** Gall: 0-1
Aids:	Bl: 0-0 Vi: 0-0 Tstrap: 0-0 Ckp: 0-0
Best Rating:	**85** 7/09 York 1m2f88y good

Fair; stays 1m; acts on firm ground and on Polytrack.

Spring Adventure

102(98) (77)**78**

3-y-o b f Dr Fong (USA)-Yavari (IRE) (Alzao (USA))

E A L Dunlop Mrs Susan Roy

Placings:3-31043300 **(6977)**

2009: 7^{3}GF, 8^{1}SD, 8^{0}SD, 8^{4}G, 8^{3}G, 8^{3}G, 8^{0}GF, 8^{0}SD,

	Starts	1st	2nd	3rd	Win & Pl
Career Total (Turf)	6	0	0	4	3611
Career Total (AW)	3	1	0	0	2590
74 5/09 Ling 1m			STD	£2590	

Total win prize-money £2590

Going (Turf):	**Sf: 0-1 GS: 0-0 Gd: 0-3 GF: 0-2 Fm: 0-0**
Distance:	5f/6f: 0-0 **7f-8f: 1-7** 9f-13f: 0-2 14f+: 0-0
Track :	**LH: 1-2** RH: 0-4 **Tight: 1-3** Gall: 0-0
Aids:	Bl: 0-0 Vi: 0-3 Tstrap: 0-0 Ckp: 0-0
Best Rating:	**78** 7/09 Sand 1m14y good

Fair; stays 1m; acts on fast ground and on Polytrack; has worn a visor.

Spring Breeze

88 **62**

8-y-o ch g Dr Fong (USA)-Trading Aces (Be My Chief (USA))

J J Quinn J N Blackburn

Placings:04030/602325216322/1335201/460-3 **(3760)**

2009: 16^{3}S,

	Starts	1st	2nd	3rd	Win & Pl
Career Total (Turf)	26	3	4	6	16628
Career Total (AW)	2	0	2	0	1682
77 8/05 Catt 1m7f177y (0-65)H			G-F	£3003	
67 4/05 Catt 1m7f177y (0-65)H			GD	£2998	
62 9/04 Catt 1m7f177y (0-55)H			FRM	£3091	

Total win prize-money £9094

Going (Turf):	Sf: 0-3 GS: 0-3 **Gd: 1-5 GF: 1-11 Fm: 1-4**
Distance:	5f/6f: 0-0 7f-8f: 0-4 9f-13f: 0-3 **14f+: 3-21**
Track :	**LH: 3-21** RH: 0-5 **Tight: 3-16** Gall: 0-5
Aids:	Bl: 0-2 **Vi: 3-15** Tstrap: 0-4 Ckp: 0-4
Best Rating:	**77** 8/05 Catt 1m7f177y gd-fm

Moderate staying handicapper; likes to front-run; stays 2m; acts on fast ground; wears a visor.

Spring Bridge (IRE)

83(90) (43)**33**

3-y-o b g Tagula (IRE)-Miss Lainey (IRE) (Woodborough (USA))

Mrs L C Jewell Ms Vanessa Jane Sparkes

Placings:4000300 **(6206)**

2009: 7^{4}GF, 7^{0}G, 6^{0}G, 7^{0}GF, 5^{3}SD, 5^{0}SD, 5^{0}SD,

	Starts	1st	2nd	3rd	Win & Pl
Career Total (Turf)	4	0	0	0	0
Career Total (AW)	3	0	0	1	403

Going (Turf):	**Sf: 0-0 GS: 0-0 Gd: 0-2 GF: 0-2 Fm: 0-0**
Distance:	5f/6f: 0-4 7f-8f: 0-3 9f-13f: 0-0 14f+: 0-0
Track :	LH: 0-2 RH: 0-1 Tight: 0-2 Gall: 0-0
Aids:	Bl: 0-0 Vi: 0-0 Tstrap: 0-3 Ckp: 0-3
Best Rating:	**43** 9/09 Ling 5f stand

Spring Fashion (IRE)

94(87) (51)**48**

3-y-o b f Galileo (IRE)-Darina (IRE) (Danehill (USA))

M Botti Can Artam

Placings:6400 **(7687)**

2009: 10^{6}G, 9^{4}SD, 13^{0}SD, 12^{0}SD,

	Starts	1st	2nd	3rd	Win & Pl
Career Total (Turf)	1	0	0	0	0
Career Total (AW)	3	0	0	0	192

Going (Turf):	**Sf: 0-0 GS: 0-0 Gd: 0-1 GF: 0-0 Fm: 0-0**
Distance:	5f/6f: 0-0 7f-8f: 0-0 9f-13f: 0-3 14f+: 0-1
Track :	LH: 0-3 RH: 0-1 Tight: 0-3 Gall: 0-0
Aids:	Bl: 0-0 Vi: 0-0 Tstrap: 0-0 Ckp: 0-0
Best Rating:	**51** 11/09 Wolv 1m1f103y stand

Spring Goddess (IRE)

101(105) (83)**83**

8-y-o b m Daggers Drawn (USA)-Easter Girl (Efisio)

A P Jarvis Grant & Bowman Limited

Placings:03160/30433/1000002/**2223**5600**050**/**631**205500 1/4530126-10660610 **(7475)**

2009: 8^{1}GF, 10^{0}GF, 8^{6}G, 8^{6}G, 12^{0}S, 10^{6}GS, 8^{1}GF, 10^{0}SD,

	Starts	1st	2nd	3rd	Win & Pl
Career Total (Turf)	31	4	2	5	26501
Career Total (AW)	22	3	4	2	24261
62 10/09 Yarm 1m3y				G-F	£2266
83 3/09 Donc 1m (0-85)H				G-F	£5180
83 10/08 Donc 1m2f60y (0-80)H				GD	£4996
83 12/07 Kemp 1m (0-75)H				STD	£2590
81 4/07 Ling 1m (0-80)H				STD	£4857
90 5/05 Ling 1m (0-85)H				STD	£6917
77 9/03 Bevl 7f100y D				G-F	£3779

Total win prize-money £30591

Going (Turf):	Sf: 0-2 GS: 0-3 Gd: 1-10 **GF: 3-15** Fm: 0-1
Distance:	5f/6f: 0-1 **7f-8f: 5-31** 9f-13f: 2-21 14f+: 0-0
Track :	**LH: 3-25** RH: 2-17 **Tight: 2-19** Gall: 1-8
Aids:	Bl: 0-0 Vi: 0-0 Tstrap: 0-0 Ckp: 0-0
Best Rating:	**90** 5/05 Ling 1m stand

Fair; stays 1m2f, but effective at shorter; acts on fast ground; goes on Polytrack.

Spring Green

101(102) (81)**81**

3-y-o b f Bahamian Bounty-Star Tulip (Night Shift (USA))

H Morrison Nicholas Jones

Placings:0-013106440 **(6647)**

2009: 6^{0}GF, 5^{1}GS, 6^{3}SD, 5^{1}SD, 6^{0}G, 6^{6}G, 6^{4}SD, 5^{4}G, 5^{0}G,

	Starts	1st	2nd	3rd	Win & Pl
Career Total (Turf)	7	1	0	0	2748
Career Total (AW)	3	1	0	1	3457
81 7/09 Kemp 5f (0-75)H				STD	£2590
65 5/09 Bath 5f11y				G-S	£2266

Total win prize-money £4857

Going (Turf):	Sf: 0-0 **GS: 1-1** Gd: 0-4 GF: 0-2 Fm: 0-0
Distance:	**5f/6f: 2-10** 7f-8f: 0-0 9f-13f: 0-0 14f+: 0-0
Track :	LH: 1-3 RH: 1-1 Tight: 0-2 **Gall: 1-3**
Aids:	Bl: 0-0 Vi: 0-0 Tstrap: 0-0 Ckp: 0-0
Best Rating:	**81** 9/09 Ayr 5f good

Fair; suited by 5-6f; acts on easy ground and Polytrack.

Spring Hawk (IRE)

(101) (58)**58**

3-y-o ch f Hawk Wing (USA)-Spring Easy (IRE) (Alzao (USA))

T G McCourt (Patrick Martin 20/11) John P McGovern

Placings:000-00234 **(7798)**

2009: 6^{0}SD, 8^{0}G, 8^{2}SD, 8^{3}SD, 9^{4}SS,

	Starts	1st	2nd	3rd	Win & Pl
Career Total (Turf)	4	0	0	0	
Career Total (AW)	4	0	1	1	1577

Going (Turf):	**Sf: 0-1 GS: 0-0 Gd: 0-1 GF: 0-1 Fm: 0-0**
Distance:	5f/6f: 0-3 7f-8f: 0-4 9f-13f: 0-1 14f+: 0-0
Track :	LH: 0-6 RH: 0-1 Tight: 0-1 Gall: 0-0
Aids:	Bl: 0-0 Vi: 0-0 Tstrap: 0-0 Ckp: 0-0
Best Rating:	**58** 11/09 Dund 1m stand

Moderate; stays 1m1f; acts on Polytrack.

Spring Heather (IRE)

83 **48**

2-y-o b f Montjeu (IRE)-Spotlight (Dr Fong (USA))
J L Dunlop Bluehills Racing Limited

Placings:00 **(6363)**
2009: 7^{0}GS, 7^{0}GF,

	Starts	1st	2nd	3rd	Win & Pl
Career Total (Turf)	2	0	0	0	

Going (Turf): Sf: 0-0 GS: 0-1 Gd: 0-0 GF: 0-1 Fm: 0-0
Distance: 5f/6f: 0-0 7f-8f: 0-2 9f-13f: 0-0 14f+: 0-0
Track : LH: 0-1 RH: 0-0 Tight: 0-0 Gall: 0-0
Aids: Bl: 0-0 Vi: 0-0 Tstrap: 0-0 Ckp: 0-0
Best Rating: **48** 9/09 Ling 7f gd-sft

Spring Jim

108 **94**

8-y-o b g First Trump-Spring Sixpence (Dowsing (USA))
J R Fanshawe Andrew & Julia Turner

Placings:450/41242/16320/16140620 **(7018)**
2009: 10^{1}G, 10^{6}GF, 12^{1}GF, 11^{4}GF, 12^{0}G, 14^{6}S, 14^{2}GF, 12^{0}GS,

	Starts	1st	2nd	3rd	Win & Pl
Career Total (Turf)	21	4	4	1	52348

93	5/09	York	1m4f	(0-85)H	G-F	£7123
86	3/09	Donc	1m2f60y	(0-85)H	GD	£6476
91	5/05	Donc	1m2f60y	(0-90)H	G-S	£10706
83	6/04	Nott	1m54y E	(0-75)H	G-F	£3997

Total win prize-money £28305

Going (Turf): Sf: 0-1 GS: 1-2 Gd: 1-6 **GF: 2-12** Fm: 0-0
Distance: 5f/6f: 0-2 7f-8f: 0-2 **9f-13f: 4-15** 14f+: 0-2
Track : **LH: 4-13** RH: 0-5 Tight: 0-1 **Gall: 3-8**
Aids: Bl: 0-0 Vi: 0-0 Tstrap: 0-0 Ckp: 0-0
Best Rating: **97** 7/05 Sand 1m2f7y good

Useful; effective at 1m2f-1m4f; acts on most ground.

Spring Of Fame (USA)

106(103) (102)**111**

3-y-o b c Grand Slam (USA)-Bloomy (USA) (Polish Numbers (USA))
Saeed Bin Suroor (M A Magnusson 18/3) Godolphin

Placings:51-123301140 **(6505a)**
2009: 8^{1}SD, 9^{2}SD, 10^{3}GF, 8^{3}G, 10^{0}GF, 8^{1}G, 8^{1}G, 8^{4}GF, 8^{0}GS,

	Starts	1st	2nd	3rd	Win & Pl
Career Total (Turf)	8	2	0	2	54224
Career Total (AW)	3	2	1	0	22893

111	8/09	Deau	1m		GD	£26699
107	7/09	NmkJ	1m		GD	£12462
90	3/09	Wolv	1m141y	(0-85)H	STD	£4727
82	9/08	Ling	7f		STD	£3238

Total win prize-money £47126

Going (Turf): Sf: 0-0 GS: 0-1 **Gd: 2-4** GF: 0-3 Fm: 0-0
Distance: 5f/6f: 0-0 **7f-8f: 3-5** 9f-13f: 1-6 14f+: 0-0
Track : **LH: 2-3** RH: 1-5 **Tight: 2-2** Gall: 0-2
Aids: Bl: 0-0 Vi: 0-0 Tstrap: 0-0 Ckp: 0-0
Best Rating: **111** 8/09 Deau 1m good

Smart; Listed placed; stays 1m2f; acts on fast ground; goes on Polytrack.

Spring Quartet

86(102) (56)**57**

3-y-o b g Captain Rio-Alice Blackthorn (Forzando)
Pat Eddery Anderson,Devenish,McCullough & Slogrove

Placings:005005-053303002 **(5328)**
2009: 8^{0}SD, 10^{5}SD, 12^{3}SF, 12^{3}SD, 12^{0}SD, 11^{3}SD, 12^{0}GF, 11^{0}GF, 11^{2}SD,

	Starts	1st	2nd	3rd	Win & Pl
Career Total (Turf)	6	0	0	0	0
Career Total (AW)	9	0	1	3	1524

Going (Turf): Sf: 0-0 GS: 0-3 Gd: 0-0 GF: 0-3 Fm: 0-0
Distance: 5f/6f: 0-3 7f-8f: 0-3 9f-13f: 0-9 14f+: 0-0
Track : LH: 0-9 RH: 0-3 Tight: 0-3 Gall: 0-3
Aids: Bl: 0-1 Vi: 0-8 Tstrap: 0-0 Ckp: 0-0
Best Rating: **57** 8/08 Wind 6f gd-sft

Moderate; stays 1m4f; handles soft ground and sand; has worn a visor.

Spring Secret

100 **72**

3-y-o b g Reset (AUS)-Miss Brooks (Bishop Of Cashel)
B Palling Flying Eight Partnership

Placings:606-000434512120 **(7247)**
2009: 8^{0}GF, 12^{0}GF, 9^{0}GF, 7^{4}GF, 7^{3}GF, 7^{4}S, 7^{5}F, 8^{1}GS, 8^{2}G, 8^{1}GS, 8^{2}G, 10^{0}S,

	Starts	1st	2nd	3rd	Win & Pl
Career Total (Turf)	15	2	2	1	6897

66	9/09	Chep	1m14y	(0-65)H	G-S	£2266
61	8/09	Bath	1m5y	(0-65)H	G-S	£1942

Total win prize-money £4210

Going (Turf): Sf: 0-2 **GS: 2-2** Gd: 0-4 GF: 0-6 Fm: 0-1
Distance: 5f/6f: 0-0 7f-8f: 0-7 **9f-13f: 2-8** 14f+: 0-0
Track : **LH: 1-7** RH: 0-1 **Tight: 1-1** Gall: 0-0
Aids: Bl: 0-0 Vi: 0-0 Tstrap: 0-0 Ckp: 0-0
Best Rating: **72** 9/09 Chep 1m14y good

Modest; stays 1m; acts on most ground.

Springwell Giant (IRE)

90(90) (65)**49**

2-y-o ch g Choisir (AUS)-Glasnas Giant (Giant's Causeway (USA))
A J McCabe Michael O'Mahony

Placings:3340 **(7003)**
2009: 7^{3}GF, 7^{3}SD, 8^{4}SD, 8^{0}SD,

	Starts	1st	2nd	3rd	Win & Pl
Career Total (Turf)	1	0	0	1	289
Career Total (AW)	3	0	0	1	302

Going (Turf): Sf: 0-0 GS: 0-0 Gd: 0-0 GF: 0-1 Fm: 0-0
Distance: 5f/6f: 0-0 7f-8f: 0-2 9f-13f: 0-2 14f+: 0-0
Track : LH: 0-3 RH: 0-0 Tight: 0-3 Gall: 0-0
Aids: Bl: 0-0 Vi: 0-0 Tstrap: 0-0 Ckp: 0-0
Best Rating: **65** 10/09 Wolv 1m141y stand

Modest; stays 1m plus; acts on Polytrack.

Sprinkler

89 **21**

6-y-o b m Emperor Fountain-Ryewater Dream (Touching Wood (USA))
C W Thornton Queens Own Hussars Racing Partnership

Placings:5 **(2785)**
2009: 14^{5}GF,

	Starts	1st	2nd	3rd	Win & Pl
Career Total (Turf)	1	0	0	0	0

Going (Turf): Sf: 0-0 GS: 0-0 Gd: 0-0 GF: 0-1 Fm: 0-0
Distance: 5f/6f: 0-0 7f-8f: 0-0 9f-13f: 0-0 14f+: 0-1
Track : LH: 0-1 RH: 0-0 Tight: 0-1 Gall: 0-0
Aids: Bl: 0-0 Vi: 0-0 Tstrap: 0-0 Ckp: 0-0
Best Rating: **21** 6/09 Rdcr 1m6f19y gd-fm

Spruzzo

70(85) (46)**36**

3-y-o b g Emperor Fountain-Ryewater Dream (Touching Wood (USA))
C W Thornton 980 Racing

Placings:00-0000 **(7750)**
2009: 9^{0}SD, 11^{0}SD, 10^{0}GF, 13^{0}SD,

	Starts	1st	2nd	3rd	Win & Pl
Career Total (Turf)	3	0	0	0	
Career Total (AW)	3	0	0	0	

Going (Turf): Sf: 0-1 GS: 0-1 Gd: 0-0 GF: 0-1 Fm: 0-0
Distance: 5f/6f: 0-1 7f-8f: 0-1 9f-13f: 0-3 14f+: 0-1
Track : LH: 0-6 RH: 0-0 Tight: 0-3 Gall: 0-0
Aids: Bl: 0-0 Vi: 0-0 Tstrap: 0-0 Ckp: 0-0
Best Rating: **46** 1/09 Wolv 1m1f103y stand

Spume (IRE)

(99) (60)**67**

5-y-o b g Alhaarth (IRE)-Sea Spray (IRE) (Royal Academy (USA))
S Parr Willie McKay

Placings:001/603610000005/0034**0550060013-03450600** **(0790)**
2009: 13^{0}SD, 12^{3}SD, 14^{4}SD, 16^{5}SD, 13^{0}SD, 13^{6}SD, 8^{0}SD, 12^{0}SD,

	Starts	1st	2nd	3rd	Win & Pl
Career Total (Turf)	18	2	0	2	9311
Career Total (AW)	19	1	0	2	3365

57	12/08	GrLe	1m5f66y	(0-60)H	STD	£2590
80	8/07	Thsk	1m	(0-75)H	GD	£3886
77	9/06	Sals	1m		GD	£4210

Total win prize-money £10686

Going (Turf): Sf: 0-2 GS: 0-2 **Gd: 2-10** GF: 0-4 Fm: 0-0
Distance: 5f/6f: 0-0 **7f-8f: 2-11** 9f-13f: 0-17 14f+: 1-9
Track : **LH: 2-23** RH: 0-9 Tight: 1-13 Gall: 1-4
Aids: Bl: 0-2 Vi: 0-0 Tstrap: 0-2 Ckp: 0-2
Best Rating: **80** 8/07 Thsk 1m good

Moderate; stays 1m5f; acts on easy ground and Polytrack; has worn blinkers and cheekpieces; wears a tongue tie.

Sputnik One (IRE)

62

2-y-o b c Soviet Star (USA)-Walnut Lady (Forzando)
J S Moore The Moore The Merrier

Placings:000 **(5543)**
2009: 5^{0}G, 7^{0}G, 7^{0}GF,

	Starts	1st	2nd	3rd	Win & Pl
Career Total (Turf)	3	0	0	0	

Going (Turf): Sf: 0-0 GS: 0-0 Gd: 0-2 GF: 0-1 Fm: 0-0

Distance: 5f/6f: 0-1 7f-8f: 0-2 9f-13f: 0-0 14f+: 0-0
Track : LH: 0-1 RH: 0-0 Tight: 0-0 Gall: 0-1
Aids: Bl: 0-1 Vi: 0-0 Tstrap: 0-1 Ckp: 0-1

Spy Gun (USA)

(97) (53)**51**
9-y-o ch g Mt. Livermore (USA)-Takeover Target (USA) (Nodouble (USA))
T Wall Derek & Mrs Marie Dean

Placings:0/00014/35005040620000/06255045400500521 00/4024524400/64304005503050004050/54500-002000 **(0578)**
2009: 7^{0}SD, 7^{0}SD, 9^{2}SD, 9^{0}SD, 9^{0}SD, 9^{0}SD,

	Starts	1st	2nd	3rd	Win & Pl
Career Total (Turf)	15	0	0	0	0
Career Total (AW)	65	2	6	3	8060

56 11/05 Sthl 7f (0-40) STD £1457
65 12/03 Sthl 1m F(0-60)H STD £2072
Total win prize-money £3529

Going (Turf): **Sf: 0-4 GS: 0-1 Gd: 0-2 GF: 0-8 Fm: 0-0**
Distance: 5f/6f: 0-12 **7f-8f: 2-42** 9f-13f: 0-26 14f+: 0-0
Track : **LH: 2-69** RH: 0-2 Tight: 0-40 Gall: 0-1
Aids: Bl: 0-2 Vi: 0-1 Tstrap: 0-14 Ckp: 0-14
Best Rating: **74** 8/02 NmkJ 7f gd-fm

Banded class; stays a mile but effective over shorter; acts on Fibresand; has worn cheekpieces.

Spying

97 **91**
2-y-o ch g Observatory (USA)-Mint Royale (IRE) (Cadeaux Genereux)
Mrs A Duffield Evelyn Duchess Of Sutherland

Placings:110 **(5795)**
2009: 7^{1}GF, 7^{1}GF, 6^{0}GF,

	Starts	1st	2nd	3rd	Win & Pl
Career Total (Turf)	3	2	0	0	8419

91 8/09 Newc 7f G-F £4533
82 7/09 Bevl 7f100y G-F £3885
Total win prize-money £8419

Going (Turf): Sf: 0-0 GS: 0-0 Gd: 0-0 **GF: 2-3** Fm: 0-0
Distance: 5f/6f: 0-0 **7f-8f: 2-3** 9f-13f: 0-0 14f+: 0-0
Track : LH: 0-0 **RH: 1-1** Tight: 0-0 Gall: 0-0
Aids: Bl: 0-0 Vi: 0-0 Tstrap: 0-0 Ckp: 0-0
Best Rating: **91** 8/09 Newc 7f gd-fm

Useful; stays 7f; handles quick ground.

Squad

102(96) (70)**74**
3-y-o ch g Choisir (AUS)-Widescreen (USA) (Distant View (USA))
S Dow Classics P'ship, Devine, Snell & Chua

Placings:040-044306353122130 **(7699)**
2009: 8^{0}SD, 10^{4}SD, 10^{4}SD, 10^{3}G, 12^{0}GF, 9^{6}G, 8^{3}GF, 9^{5}GF, 8^{3}G, 9^{1}GS, 10^{2}F, 11^{2}GS, 9^{1}GF, 12^{3}GS, 10^{0}SD,

	Starts	1st	2nd	3rd	Win & Pl
Career Total (Turf)	14	2	2	4	9061
Career Total (AW)	4	0	0	0	0

72 9/09 Brig 1m1f209y (0-65)H G-F £2590
64 8/09 Brig 1m1f209y (0-60)H G-S £2590
Total win prize-money £5180

Going (Turf): Sf: 0-1 **GS: 1-3** Gd: 0-4 **GF: 1-5** Fm: 0-1
Distance: 5f/6f: 0-0 7f-8f: 0-4 **9f-13f: 2-14** 14f+: 0-0
Track : **LH: 2-12** RH: 0-5 Tight: 0-11 Gall: 0-0
Aids: Bl: 0-0 Vi: 0-1 Tstrap: 0-0 Ckp: 0-0

Best Rating: **74** 9/09 Ling 1m3f106y gd-sft

Modest; stays 1m2f; acts on fast ground and on Polytrack.

Squadron

101 (64)**70**
5-y-o b g Sakhee (USA)-Machaera (Machiavellian (USA))
A King Tony Fisher & Mrs Jeni Fisher

Placings:035/5211043/5 **(1356)**
2009: 16^{5}S,

	Starts	1st	2nd	3rd	Win & Pl
Career Total (Turf)	9	2	1	1	9498
Career Total (AW)	2	0	0	1	578

79 7/07 Sals 1m6f21y (0-75)H SFT £3238
73 6/07 Gdwd 1m6f (0-75)H G-F £3562
Total win prize-money £6801

Going (Turf): **Sf: 1-3** GS: 0-4 Gd: 0-1 **GF: 1-1** Fm: 0-0
Distance: 5f/6f: 0-0 7f-8f: 0-0 9f-13f: 0-4 **14f+: 2-7**
Track : LH: 0-5 **RH: 2-5 Tight: 2-6** Gall: 0-0
Aids: Bl: 0-0 Vi: 0-0 Tstrap: 0-0 Ckp: 0-0
Best Rating: **79** 10/07 Sals 1m6f21y gd-sft

Modest sort; gets 1m6f; acts on easy ground.

Squander

72 **36**
3-y-o b f Dr Fong (USA)-Ghariba (Final Straw)
Sir Michael Stoute J Wigan & G Strawbridge

Placings:0 **(4180)**
2009: 7^{0}GS,

	Starts	1st	2nd	3rd	Win & Pl
Career Total (Turf)	1	0	0	0	

Going (Turf): **Sf: 0-0 GS: 0-1 Gd: 0-0 GF: 0-0 Fm: 0-0**
Distance: 5f/6f: 0-0 7f-8f: 0-1 9f-13f: 0-0 14f+: 0-0
Track : LH: 0-0 RH: 0-0 Tight: 0-0 Gall: 0-0
Aids: Bl: 0-0 Vi: 0-0 Tstrap: 0-0 Ckp: 0-0
Best Rating: **36** 7/09 Yarm 7f3y gd-sft

Square Of Gold (FR)

86 **37**
3-y-o ch g Gold Away (IRE)-All Square (FR) (Holst (USA))
A W Carroll R D Willis & Maureen Willis

Placings:6000 **(5632)**
2009: 8^{6}G, 7^{0}GF, 5^{0}S, 6^{0}GS,

	Starts	1st	2nd	3rd	Win & Pl
Career Total (Turf)	4	0	0	0	0

Going (Turf): **Sf: 0-1 GS: 0-1 Gd: 0-1 GF: 0-1 Fm: 0-0**
Distance: 5f/6f: 0-1 7f-8f: 0-2 9f-13f: 0-1 14f+: 0-0
Track : LH: 0-1 RH: 0-0 Tight: 0-0 Gall: 0-0
Aids: Bl: 0-0 Vi: 0-0 Tstrap: 0-0 Ckp: 0-0
Best Rating: **37** 7/09 Leic 5f218y soft

Square Pants (IRE)

(82) (46)
2-y-o b g Kheleyf (USA)-Bron Hilda (IRE) (Namaqualand (USA))
J A Osborne J A Osborne

Placings:0 **(6431)**
2009: 8^{0}SD,

	Starts	1st	2nd	3rd	Win & Pl
Career Total (Turf)	0	0	0	0	
Career Total (AW)	1	0	0	0	

Going (Turf): **Sf: 0-0 GS: 0-0 Gd: 0-0 GF: 0-0 Fm: 0-0**
Distance: 5f/6f: 0-0 7f-8f: 0-0 9f-13f: 0-1 14f+: 0-0
Track : LH: 0-1 RH: 0-0 Tight: 0-1 Gall: 0-0
Aids: Bl: 0-0 Vi: 0-0 Tstrap: 0-0 Ckp: 0-0
Best Rating: **46** 10/09 Wolv 1m141y stand

Squirtle (IRE)

101(103) (69)**69**
6-y-o ch m In The Wings-Manilia (FR) (Kris)
W M Brisbourne J Jones Racing Ltd

Placings:00300/522021350230/554460332060344234/31 16210465633502-5510604433341 **(7750)**
2009: 16^{5}SD, 16^{5}SD, 14^{1}G, 16^{0}G, 16^{6}GS, 16^{0}G, 16^{4}SD, 16^{4}SD, 16^{3}SD, 13^{3}SD, 16^{3}SD, 16^{4}SD, 13^{1}SD,

	Starts	1st	2nd	3rd	Win & Pl
Career Total (Turf)	37	4	6	4	21883
Career Total (AW)	27	2	2	9	9160

57 12/09 Wolv 1m5f194y (0-55)H STD £2047
63 6/09 Wwck 1m6f213y (0-75)H GD £3238
65 8/08 Thsk 2m (0-65)H SFT £2978
57 7/08 Wolv 1m5f194y (0-65)H STD £2388
62 7/08 Thsk 2m (0-60)H G-F £3139
74 8/06 Hayd 1m6f (0-70)H G-F £3238
Total win prize-money £17030

Going (Turf): Sf: 1-6 GS: 0-8 Gd: 1-10 **GF: 2-12** Fm: 0-1
Distance: 5f/6f: 0-3 7f-8f: 0-2 9f-13f: 0-9 **14f+: 6-50**
Track : **LH: 6-54** RH: 0-6 **Tight: 4-45** Gall: 0-1
Aids: Bl: 0-0 Vi: 0-3 Tstrap: 0-0 Ckp: 0-0
Best Rating: **74** 8/06 Hayd 1m6f gd-fm

Moderate; stays 2m; acts on fast and soft ground; also goes on Polytrack.

Sri Kandi

90(92) (73)**74**
3-y-o ch f Pivotal-Aunt Pearl (USA) (Seattle Slew (USA))
P F I Cole Mrs Fitri Hay

Placings:021-06 **(2384)**
2009: 9^{0}F, 10^{6}SD,

	Starts	1st	2nd	3rd	Win & Pl
Career Total (Turf)	3	1	0	0	3886
Career Total (AW)	2	0	1	0	1060

74 9/08 Bevl 7f100y SFT £3885
Total win prize-money £3886

Going (Turf): **Sf: 1-1** GS: 0-0 Gd: 0-1 GF: 0-0 Fm: 0-1
Distance: 5f/6f: 0-0 **7f-8f: 1-3** 9f-13f: 0-2 14f+: 0-0
Track : LH: 0-1 **RH: 1-3** Tight: 0-2 Gall: 0-0
Aids: Bl: 0-0 Vi: 0-0 Tstrap: 0-0 Ckp: 0-0
Best Rating: **74** 9/08 Bevl 7f100y soft

Fair; stays 1m; acts on Polytrack and soft turf.

Sri Kuantan (IRE)

98(102) (80)**82**
5-y-o ch g Spinning World (USA)-Miss Asia Quest (Rainbow Quest (USA))
R C Guest S Hussey

Placings:263/2112600-04224163200000 **(6648)**

2009: 8^0SD, 11^4SD, 10^2SD, 10^2G, 10^4G, 14^1GF, 14^6F, 11^3GF, 9^2GF, 10^0G, 12^0GF, 12^0GF, 10^0GF, 10^0G,

	Starts	1st	2nd	3rd	Win & Pl
Career Total (Turf)	12	1	2	1	8638
Career Total (AW)	12	2	4	1	8744

79 4/09 Yarm 1m6f17y (0-85)H G-F £4792
79 1/08 Ling 1m2f (0-70)H STD £2331
75 1/08 Ling 1m2f STD £2331
Total win prize-money £9456

Going (Turf): Sf: 0-0 GS: 0-1 Gd: 0-4 **GF: 1-6** Fm: 0-1
Distance: 5f/6f: 0-0 7f-8f: 0-2 **9f-13f: 2-20** 14f+: 1-2
Track : **LH: 3-18** RH: 0-5 **Tight: 3-13** Gall: 0-2
Aids: Bl: 0-1 Vi: 0-0 Tstrap: 0-0 Ckp: 0-0
Best Rating: 82 5/09 Bevl 1m1f207y gd-fm

Fair; effective at around 1m2f-1m6f; acts on fast ground and Polytrack; often wears a tongue tie.

Sri Putra

112 **113**
3-y-o b c Oasis Dream-Wendylina (IRE) (In The Wings)
M A Jarvis H R H Sultan Ahmad Shah

Placings:1100-451150 **(7313a)**
2009: 7^4S, 8^5S, 8^1G, 10^1G, 10^5G, 10^0HY,

	Starts	1st	2nd	3rd	Win & Pl
Career Total (Turf)	10	4	0	0	151368

112 8/09 Deau 1m2f GD £71942
113 7/09 Asct 1m H GD £28039
105 8/08 Sand 7f16y GD £28385
87 6/08 Newb 6f8y GD £5828
Total win prize-money £134195

Going (Turf): Sf: 0-3 GS: 0-0 **Gd: 4-6** GF: 0-1 Fm: 0-0
Distance: 5f/6f: 0-0 **7f-8f: 3-7** 9f-13f: 1-3 14f+: 0-0
Track : LH: 0-0 **RH: 2-5** Tight: 0-0 Gall: 0-0
Aids: Bl: 0-0 Vi: 0-0 Tstrap: 0-0 Ckp: 0-0
Best Rating: 113 7/09 Asct 1m good

Smart; winner of the Group 3 Solario Stakes at two; suited by 7f-1m; acts on good and fast ground.

St Ignatius

(89) (65)
2-y-o b g Ishiguru (USA)-Branston Berry (IRE) (Mukaddamah (USA))
R M Beckett A W A Partnership

Placings:045 **(7700)**
2009: 7^0SD, 7^4SD, 7^5SD,

	Starts	1st	2nd	3rd	Win & Pl
Career Total (Turf)	0	0	0	0	
Career Total (AW)	3	0	0	0	0

Going (Turf): **Sf: 0-0 GS: 0-0 Gd: 0-0 GF: 0-0 Fm: 0-0**
Distance: 5f/6f: 0-0 7f-8f: 0-3 9f-13f: 0-0 14f+: 0-0
Track : LH: 0-0 RH: 0-3 Tight: 0-0 Gall: 0-0
Aids: Bl: 0-0 Vi: 0-0 Tstrap: 0-0 Ckp: 0-0
Best Rating: 65 10/09 Kemp 7f stand

Modest; stays 7f; acts on Polytrack.

St Jean Cap Ferrat

105(105) (76)**93**
4-y-o b/br g Domedriver (IRE)-Miss Cap Ferrat (Darshaan)
S Jensen (P J Hobbs 3/7) Beatrice Marsing

Placings:0402/2312402253-0016 **(4585a)**
2009: 10^0GS, 10^0GF, 9^1GF, 12^6GF,

	Starts	1st	2nd	3rd	Win & Pl
Career Total (Turf)	17	2	5	1	18764
Career Total (AW)	1	0	0	1	385

92 7/09 Sals 1m1f198y (0-85)H G-F £6476
77 4/08 Nott 1m1f213y SFT £2047
Total win prize-money £8523

Going (Turf): **Sf: 1-2** GS: 0-2 Gd: 0-4 **GF: 1-9** Fm: 0-0
Distance: 5f/6f: 0-1 7f-8f: 0-2 **9f-13f: 2-15** 14f+: 0-0
Track : LH: 1-8 RH: 1-7 **Tight: 1-5** Gall: 0-2
Aids: Bl: 0-1 **Vi: 2-8** Tstrap: 0-0 Ckp: 0-0
Best Rating: 93 8/09 Klam 1m4f gd-fm

Useful; stays 1m2f; acts on easy ground; has worn a visor.

St Moritz (IRE)

(98) (95)**97**
3-y-o b g Medicean-Statua (IRE) (Statoblest)
M Johnston Mrs R J Jacobs

Placings:115 **(1395a)**
2009: 7^1SD, 7^1SD, 8^5S,

	Starts	1st	2nd	3rd	Win & Pl
Career Total (Turf)	1	0	0	0	
Career Total (AW)	2	2	0	0	7910

95 2/09 Wolv 7f32y (0-85)H STD £5180
80 1/09 Ling 7f STD £2729
Total win prize-money £7911

Going (Turf): **Sf: 0-1 GS: 0-0 Gd: 0-0 GF: 0-0 Fm: 0-0**
Distance: 5f/6f: 0-0 **7f-8f: 2-2** 9f-13f: 0-1 14f+: 0-0
Track : **LH: 2-2** RH: 0-1 **Tight: 2-2** Gall: 0-0
Aids: Bl: 0-0 Vi: 0-0 Tstrap: 0-0 Ckp: 0-0
Best Rating: 97 4/09 Kref 1m110y soft

Very useful; effective over 7f; acts on Polytrack; sure to win more races.

St Nicholas Abbey (IRE)

101 **123**
2-y-o b c Montjeu (IRE)-Leaping Water (Sure Blade (USA))
A P O'Brien D Smith, Mrs J Magnier, M Tabor

Placings:111 **(7017)**
2009: 8^1SH, 8^1G, 8^1GS,

	Starts	1st	2nd	3rd	Win & Pl
Career Total (Turf)	3	3	0	0	197853

123 10/09 Donc 1m G-S £113540
112 9/09 Curr 1m GD £72572
92 8/09 Curr 1m SH £11740
Total win prize-money £197853

Going (Turf): Sf: 0-0 **GS: 1-1 Gd: 1-1** GF: 0-0 Fm: 0-0
Distance: 5f/6f: 0-0 **7f-8f: 3-3** 9f-13f: 0-0 14f+: 0-0
Track : LH: 0-0 **RH: 2-2** Tight: 0-0 **Gall: 2-2**
Aids: Bl: 0-0 Vi: 0-0 Tstrap: 0-0 Ckp: 0-0
Best Rating: 123 10/09 Donc 1m gd-sft

High-class; winner of the Group 2 Beresford Stakes and the Group 1 Racing Post Trophy at two; stays 1m and acts on good and softer ground; usually held up and possesses a potent turn of foot.

St Savarin (FR)

(102) (64)**101**
8-y-o ch g Highest Honor (FR)-Sacara (GER) (Monsagem (USA))
M S Tuck (B R Johnson 23/2) J & D Syndicate

Placings:5000026**1051**/**2531**0033**1000**525/15/**0432**312020 13/661261/54556-2000 **(7677)**
2009: 12^2SS, 12^0SD, 12^0SD, 11^0SD,

	Starts	1st	2nd	3rd	Win & Pl
Career Total (Turf)	27	5	4	3	68190
Career Total (AW)	28	4	4	3	32996

83 12/07 Sthl 1m3f SS £2047
94 10/07 Ayr 1m5f13y (0-90)H G-S £7124
89 11/06 Sthl 1m3f (0-100)H STD £11217
95 9/06 Hayd 1m3f200y (0-85)H HVY £6477
82 4/05 Hayd 1m2f120y (0-85)H SFT £7223
79 7/04 Muss 7f30y D(0-80)H G-F £6773
76 2/04 Ling 7f E(0-75)H STD £3412
72 12/03 Ling 7f D(0-85) STD £3066
70 11/03 Catt 7f E G-S £2261
Total win prize-money £49604

Going (Turf): **Sf: 2-3 GS: 2-10** Gd: 0-5 GF: 1-9 Fm: 0-0
Distance: 5f/6f: 0-8 7f-8f: 4-17 9f-13f: 4-25 14f+: 1-5
Track : **LH: 8-35** RH: 1-14 **Tight: 4-20** Gall: 0-4
Aids: Bl: 0-0 Vi: 0-0 Tstrap: 0-1 Ckp: 0-1
Best Rating: 101 10/07 Asct 1m4f gd-sft

Very useful; stays 1m4f; acts on most ground and on sand.

Stadium Of Light (IRE)

79 **36**
2-y-o b g Fantastic Light (USA)-Treble Seven (USA) (Fusaichi Pegasus (USA))
H Morrison Dr John Wilson (beaconsfield)

Placings:000 **(6965)**
2009: 7^0GF, 8^0G, 7^0G,

	Starts	1st	2nd	3rd	Win & Pl
Career Total (Turf)	3	0	0	0	

Going (Turf): **Sf: 0-0 GS: 0-0 Gd: 0-2 GF: 0-1 Fm: 0-0**
Distance: 5f/6f: 0-0 7f-8f: 0-3 9f-13f: 0-0 14f+: 0-0
Track : LH: 0-1 RH: 0-0 Tight: 0-0 Gall: 0-0
Aids: Bl: 0-0 Vi: 0-0 Tstrap: 0-0 Ckp: 0-0
Best Rating: 36 6/09 Ling 7f gd-fm

Staff Sergeant

(82) (51)
2-y-o b c Dubawi (IRE)-Miss Particular (IRE) (Sadler's Wells (USA))
M Johnston Sheikh Hamdan Bin Mohammed Al Maktoum

Placings:0 **(7429)**
2009: 7^0SD,

	Starts	1st	2nd	3rd	Win & Pl
Career Total (Turf)	0	0	0	0	
Career Total (AW)	1	0	0	0	

Going (Turf): **Sf: 0-0 GS: 0-0 Gd: 0-0 GF: 0-0 Fm: 0-0**
Distance: 5f/6f: 0-0 7f-8f: 0-1 9f-13f: 0-0 14f+: 0-0
Track : LH: 0-0 RH: 0-1 Tight: 0-0 Gall: 0-0
Aids: Bl: 0-0 Vi: 0-0 Tstrap: 0-0 Ckp: 0-0
Best Rating: 51 11/09 Kemp 7f stand

Stafford Charlie

58(77) (29)**28**
3-y-o ch g Silver Patriarch (IRE)-Miss Roberto (IRE) (Don Roberto (USA))
J G M O'Shea N G H Ayliffe

Placings:00-60 **(1580)**
2009: 9^6SD, 10^0G,

	Starts	1st	2nd	3rd	Win & Pl
Career Total (Turf)	2	0	0	0	

Career Total (AW) 2 0 0 0 0

Going (Turf): **Sf: 0-0 GS: 0-1 Gd: 0-1 GF: 0-0 Fm: 0-0**
Distance: 5f/6f: 0-0 7f-8f: 0-1 9f-13f: 0-3 14f+: 0-0
Track : LH: 0-3 RH: 0-1 Tight: 0-3 Gall: 0-0
Aids: Bl: 0-0 Vi: 0-0 Tstrap: 0-0 Ckp: 0-0
Best Rating: 29 12/08 Kemp 1m stand

Stage Acclaim (IRE)

(94) (46)**72**
4-y-o b g Acclamation-Open Stage (IRE) (Sadler's Wells (USA))
C J Down G Carstairs

Placings:616000650/00144005-6 (7212)
2009: 12⁶SD,

	Starts	1st	2nd	3rd	Win & Pl
Career Total (Turf)	16	2	0	0	7899
Career Total (AW)	2	0	0	0	0

70 7/08 Ling 1m1f (0-65)H SFT £2047
76 5/07 Sals 5f G-F £4533
Total win prize-money £6581

Going (Turf): **Sf: 1-3** GS: 0-2 Gd: 0-4 **GF: 1-6** Fm: 0-1
Distance: 5f/6f: 1-6 7f-8f: 0-3 9f-13f: 1-9 14f+: 0-0
Track : **LH: 1-8** RH: 0-4 **Tight: 1-7** Gall: 0-3
Aids: Bl: 0-1 Vi: 0-0 Tstrap: 1-5 Ckp: 1-5
Best Rating: 76 7/07 Pont 6f good

Fair; probably stays 1m2f but effective over shorter; acts on fast and soft ground; has worn cheekpieces/blinkers.

Stage Dream (IRE)

81(79) (44)**66**
4-y-o b f Golan (IRE)-Bernhardt (IRE) (Alzao (USA))
Lee Smyth Mrs M A McNeice/F McNeice

Placings:05640-0600 (7719)
2009: 8⁰SD, 8⁶S, 9⁰SD, 9⁰SD,

	Starts	1st	2nd	3rd	Win & Pl
Career Total (Turf)	6	0	0	0	271
Career Total (AW)	3	0	0	0	

Going (Turf): **Sf: 0-1 GS: 0-0 Gd: 0-0 GF: 0-2 Fm: 0-0**
Distance: 5f/6f: 0-0 7f-8f: 0-4 9f-13f: 0-5 14f+: 0-0
Track : LH: 0-5 RH: 0-3 Tight: 0-2 Gall: 0-1
Aids: Bl: 0-0 Vi: 0-0 Tstrap: 0-1 Ckp: 0-1
Best Rating: 66 6/08 Naas 1m2f gd-fm

Stage Performance (IRE)

84 **31**
3-y-o ch f Danehill Dancer (IRE)-Stage Presence (IRE) (Selkirk (USA))
J H M Gosden Lady Bamford

Placings:00 (6934)
2009: 10⁰GF, 10⁰C,

	Starts	1st	2nd	3rd	Win & Pl
Career Total (Turf)	2	0	0	0	

Going (Turf): **Sf: 0-0 GS: 0-0 Gd: 0-1 GF: 0-1 Fm: 0-0**
Distance: 5f/6f: 0-0 7f-8f: 0-0 9f-13f: 0-2 14f+: 0-0
Track : LH: 0-2 RH: 0-0 Tight: 0-1 Gall: 0-1
Aids: Bl: 0-0 Vi: 0-0 Tstrap: 0-0 Ckp: 0-0
Best Rating: 31 8/09 Newb 1m2f6y gd-fm

Stagecoach Emerald

84(98) (62)**46**
7-y-o ch g Spectrum (IRE)-Musician (Shirley Heights)
R W Price Future Electrical Services Ltd

Placings:060/40022/220156/00-000014 (7635)
2009: 13⁰SD, 11⁰G, 14⁰SD, 16⁰SS, 14¹SD, 14⁴SD,

	Starts	1st	2nd	3rd	Win & Pl
Career Total (Turf)	4	0	0	0	0
Career Total (AW)	18	2	4	0	9046

62 11/09 Sthl 1m6f (0-60)H STD £2047
70 10/07 Wolv 1m4f50y (0-65)H STD £2900
Total win prize-money £4948

Going (Turf): **Sf: 0-0 GS: 0-1 Gd: 0-2 GF: 0-1 Fm: 0-0**
Distance: 5f/6f: 0-0 7f-8f: 0-1 9f-13f: 1-9 14f+: 1-12
Track : **LH: 2-20** RH: 0-1 **Tight: 1-12** Gall: 0-1
Aids: Bl: 1-2 Vi: 0-1 Tstrap: 1-6 Ckp: 1-6
Best Rating: 70 10/07 Wolv 1m4f50y stand

Modest; stays 2m; acts on Polytrack and Fibresand; has worn cheekpieces and blinkers.

Stagecoach Jade (IRE)

98(96) (73)**76**
3-y-o ch f Peintre Celebre (USA)-Starring Role (IRE) (Glenstal (USA))
M Johnston Mrs Jacqueline Conroy

Placings:1124 (3393)
2009: 9¹SD, 9¹SD, 10²GF, 10⁴S,

	Starts	1st	2nd	3rd	Win & Pl
Career Total (Turf)	2	0	1	0	2301
Career Total (AW)	2	2	0	0	5828

73 4/09 Wolv 1m1f103y (0-75)H STD £2914
64 3/09 Wolv 1m1f103y STD £2914
Total win prize-money £5828

Going (Turf): **Sf: 0-1 GS: 0-0 Gd: 0-0 GF: 0-1 Fm: 0-0**
Distance: 5f/6f: 0-0 7f-8f: 0-0 **9f-13f: 2-4** 14f+: 0-0
Track : **LH: 2-4** RH: 0-0 **Tight: 2-3** Gall: 0-1
Aids: Bl: 0-0 Vi: 0-0 Tstrap: 0-0 Ckp: 0-0
Best Rating: 76 5/09 Rdcr 1m2f gd-fm

Fair; stays 1m2f; acts on fast ground; goes on Polytrack.

Stags Leap (IRE)

96 **87**
2-y-o b c Refuse To Bend (IRE)-Swingsky (IRE) (Indian Ridge)
R Hannon Mrs J Wood

Placings:5110 (6664)
2009: 7⁵GF, 7¹S, 7¹G, 8⁰GS,

	Starts	1st	2nd	3rd	Win & Pl
Career Total (Turf)	4	2	0	0	20723

85 8/09 Wwck 7f26y GD £7771
81 8/09 Gdwd 7f SFT £12952
Total win prize-money £20723

Going (Turf): **Sf: 1-1** GS: 0-1 **Gd: 1-1** GF: 0-1 Fm: 0-0
Distance: 5f/6f: 0-0 **7f-8f: 2-4** 9f-13f: 0-0 14f+: 0-0
Track : LH: 1-1 RH: 1-3 Tight: 0-0 Gall: 0-1
Aids: Bl: 0-0 Vi: 0-0 Tstrap: 0-0 Ckp: 0-0
Best Rating: 87 10/09 Asct 1m gd-sft

Fair; effective over 7f; acts on soft ground.

Stalingrad (IRE)

(88) (68)**63**
4-y-o ch g King's Best (USA)-Bold Bold (IRE) (Sadler's Wells (USA))
Thomas Cleary (J E Hammond 9/4) Thomas Cleary

Placings:005-0440600 (7785)
2009: 9⁰G, 14⁴G, 12⁴GF, 14⁰S, 12⁶SD, 12⁰SD, 13⁰SD,

	Starts	1st	2nd	3rd	Win & Pl
Career Total (Turf)	7	0	0	0	1853
Career Total (AW)	3	0	0	0	

Going (Turf): **Sf: 0-3 GS: 0-0 Gd: 0-3 GF: 0-1 Fm: 0-0**
Distance: 5f/6f: 0-0 7f-8f: 0-0 9f-13f: 0-7 14f+: 0-3
Track : LH: 0-4 RH: 0-3 Tight: 0-1 Gall: 0-0
Aids: Bl: 0-0 Vi: 0-0 Tstrap: 0-1 Ckp: 0-1
Best Rating: 68 11/09 Dund 1m4f stand

Stalking Shadow (USA)

101(97) (92)**98**
4-y-o b c Storm Cat (USA)-Strategic Maneuver (USA) (Cryptoclearance (USA))
Saeed Bin Suroor (M bin Shafya 15/3) Godolphin

Placings:3110-051140 (3116)
2009: 8⁰G, 5⁵SD, 8¹SD, 6¹GF, 8⁴GF, 7⁰GF,

	Starts	1st	2nd	3rd	Win & Pl
Career Total (Turf)	7	3	0	1	17918
Career Total (AW)	3	1	0	0	10142

98 3/09 AbuD 6f110y (65-95)H G-F £7954
92 2/09 Jebl 1m (75-95)H STD £9659
91 8/08 Sals 1m (0-85)H G-S £5180
86 7/08 Thsk 7f G-F £3788
Total win prize-money £26583

Going (Turf): Sf: 0-1 GS: 1-1 Gd: 0-1 **GF: 2-4** Fm: 0-0
Distance: 5f/6f: 0-1 **7f-8f: 4-8** 9f-13f: 0-1 14f+: 0-0
Track : **LH: 1-1** RH: 0-2 **Tight: 1-2** Gall: 0-0
Aids: Bl: 0-0 Vi: 0-0 Tstrap: 0-0 Ckp: 0-0
Best Rating: 98 3/09 AbuD 6f110y gd-fm

Very useful; suited by 1m and acts on most ground; has looked wayward; sometimes tongue tied.

Stamford Blue

102(87) (46)**86**
8-y-o b g Bluegrass Prince (IRE)-Fayre Holly (IRE) (Fayruz)
R A Harris Brian Hicks

Placings:610000035/246206012005/0000U01011500662/ 00061034103343100/0011161104500/00022304060-6600034136000 (5719)
2009: 6⁶GF, 5⁶GF, 6⁰GF, 6⁰GF, 6⁰GF, 6³GF, 6⁴GS, 6¹G, 5³S, 6⁶S, 5⁰G, 7⁰G, 5⁰G,

	Starts	1st	2nd	3rd	Win & Pl
Career Total (Turf)	70	14	4	7	51764
Career Total (AW)	22	0	2	1	1849

69 7/09 Ling 6f (0-65)H GD £2047
92 7/07 Wwck 6f (0-85)H GD £6232
85 6/07 Bath 5f161y (0-75)H GD £2914
81 5/07 Chep 6f16y (0-65)H GD £2072
69 5/07 Sals 6f (0-70)H G-F £3123
71 9/06 Chep 5f16y (0-65)H GD £2461
69 6/06 Chep 6f16y (0-70)H G-S £3886
66 5/06 Chep 6f16y (0-65)H SFT £2590

66	6/05	Thsk	1m	G-F	£4231
62	6/05	Sals	6f212y	G-F	£3835
66	5/05	Leic	5f218y	SFT	£3031
60	4/04	Leic	5f218y G	G-S	£2618
58	8/03	Wind	5f10y F	G-F	£3045

Total win prize-money £42089

Going (Turf): Sf: 2-11GS: 3-11**Gd: 5-17** GF: 4-27 Fm: 0-4
Distance: **5f/6f: 8-60** 7f-8f: 6-28 9f-13f: 0-4 14f+: 0-0
Track : **LH: 3-41** RH: 0-3 Tight: 1-23 **Gall: 2-13**
Aids: **Bl: 13-82** Vi: 0-0 Tstrap: 0-2 Ckp: 0-2
Best Rating: **92** 7/07 Wwck 6f good

Fair; effective between 5f-7f and acts on most ground; wears blinkers.

Stan's Cool Cat (IRE)

106(103) (81)**89**
3-y-o b f One Cool Cat (USA)-Beautiful France (IRE) (Sadler's Wells (USA))
P F I Cole Stan James Syndicate 1

Placings:242130-03130446 **(7540)**
2009: 7^{0}F, 8^{3}G, 10^{1}S, 10^{3}G, **10^{0}SD**, 10^{4}GF, **10^{4}SD**, 8^{6}SD,

	Starts	1st	2nd	3rd	Win & Pl
Career Total (Turf)	10	2	2	2	13499
Career Total (AW)	4	0	0	1	1145

87	7/09	Newb	1m2f6y (0-80)H	SFT	£4857
79	7/08	Chep	6f16y	G-F	£2719

Total win prize-money £7577

Going (Turf): **Sf: 1-1** GS: 0-0 Gd: 0-3 **GF: 1-4** Fm: 0-1
Distance: 5f/6f: 0-4 7f-8f: 1-5 9f-13f: 1-5 14f+: 0-0
Track : **LH: 1-8** RH: 0-1 Tight: 0-3 **Gall: 1-3**
Aids: Bl: 0-2 Vi: 0-0 Tstrap: 0-0 Ckp: 0-0
Best Rating: **89** 8/09 Nott 1m2f50y good

Useful; stays 1m2f; acts on fast and soft ground; has worn blinkers.

Stand And Fight (IRE)

85 (83)**89**
2-y-o b g Invincible Spirit (IRE)-Up On Points (Royal Academy (USA))
Kevin Prendergast Mrs K Prendergast

Placings:042310 **(2995)**
2009: 5^{0}YS, 5^{4}Y, **5^{2}SD**, **5^{3}SD**, 5^{1}Y, 5^{0}GF,

	Starts	1st	2nd	3rd	Win & Pl
Career Total (Turf)	4	1	0	0	8352
Career Total (AW)	2	0	1	1	4965

89	5/09	DRoy	5f	YLD	£7715

Total win prize-money £7715

Going (Turf): **Sf: 0-0 GS: 0-0 Gd: 0-0 GF: 0-1 Fm: 0-0**
Distance: **5f/6f: 1-6** 7f-8f: 0-0 9f-13f: 0-0 14f+: 0-0
Track : LH: 0-3 **RH: 1-1** Tight: 0-0 Gall: 0-0
Aids: Bl: 0-0 Vi: 0-0 Tstrap: 0-0 Ckp: 0-0
Best Rating: **89** 5/09 DRoy 5f yield

Stand Guard

96(110) (96)**70**
5-y-o b g Danehill (USA)-Protectress (Hector Protector (USA))
P Howling The Circle Bloodstock I Limited

Placings:0/5504311143-2441100042031**00** **(7827)**
2009: 9^{2}SD, 10^{4}SD, 9^{4}SD, 9^{1}SD, 10^{1}SD, 11^{0}SD, 10^{0}G, 12^{0}GF, 11^{4}SD, 8^{2}SD, 9^{0}SD, 9^{3}SD, 8^{1}SD, 10^{0}SD, 8^{0}SD,

	Starts	1st	2nd	3rd	Win & Pl
Career Total (Turf)	3	0	0	0	
Career Total (AW)	23	6	2	3	34537

96	11/09	Wolv	1m141y (0-100)H	STD	£11215
93	3/09	Kemp	1m2f (0-85)H	STD	£4727
89	2/09	Wolv	1m1f103y (0-80)H	STD	£5180
84	11/08	Kemp	1m2f (0-70)H	STD	£2590
78	11/08	Kemp	1m2f (0-60)H	STD	£2047
66	10/08	Kemp	1m2f (0-55)	STD	£2047

Total win prize-money £27808

Going (Turf): **Sf: 0-0 GS: 0-0 Gd: 0-1 GF: 0-2 Fm: 0-0**
Distance: 5f/6f: 0-2 7f-8f: 0-4 **9f-13f: 6-20** 14f+: 0-0
Track : LH: 2-14 **RH: 4-11 Tight: 2-10** Gall: 0-3
Aids: Bl: 0-0 Vi: 0-0 Tstrap: 0-0 Ckp: 0-0
Best Rating: **96** 11/09 Wolv 1m141y stand

Useful; stays 1m3f; acts on Polytrack.

Stand In Flames

101(92) (42)**84**
4-y-o b f Celtic Swing-Maid Of Arc (USA) (Patton (USA))
George Baker (Pat Eddery 9/8) Mrs C E S Baker

Placings:003030/224311060126-000010330600 **(7416)**
2009: 6^{0}GF, 7^{0}GF, 7^{0}GF, 8^{0}HY, 7^{1}HY, 7^{0}G, 7^{3}GS, 7^{3}G, 9^{0}G, 7^{6}GF, 7^{0}SD, 8^{0}SD,

	Starts	1st	2nd	3rd	Win & Pl
Career Total (Turf)	26	4	3	5	13398
Career Total (AW)	4	0	0	0	0

63	8/09	Leic	7f9y	HVY	£2590
76	10/08	Wind	6f	G-F	£2388
84	8/08	Ling	7f140y (0-65)H	G-S	£2047
83	8/08	Ling	7f140y (0-65)H	SFT	£2047

Total win prize-money £9072

Going (Turf): **Sf: 2-6** GS: 1-3 Gd: 0-5 GF: 1-11 Fm: 0-1
Distance: 5f/6f: 1-6 **7f-8f: 3-18** 9f-13f: 0-6 14f+: 0-0
Track : LH: 0-11 RH: 0-4 Tight: 0-5 **Gall: 1-3**
Aids: Bl: 0-0 Vi: 0-0 Tstrap: 0-0 Ckp: 0-0
Best Rating: **84** 8/08 Ling 7f140y gd-sft

Fair; effective at around 6-7f; acts on most ground; handles Polytrack.

Standpoint

99(93) (75)**79**
3-y-o b g Oasis Dream-Waki Music (USA) (Miswaki (USA))
Sir Michael Stoute K Abdulla

Placings:442-2160 **(3643)**
2009: 6^{2}F, 7^{1}F, 8^{6}S, 7^{0}G,

	Starts	1st	2nd	3rd	Win & Pl
Career Total (Turf)	5	1	2	0	5094
Career Total (AW)	2	0	0	0	514

71	5/09	Wwck	7f26y	FRM	£3070

Total win prize-money £3071

Going (Turf): Sf: 0-1 GS: 0-0 Gd: 0-2 GF: 0-0 **Fm: 1-2**
Distance: 5f/6f: 0-2 **7f-8f: 1-5** 9f-13f: 0-0 14f+: 0-0
Track : **LH: 1-3** RH: 0-2 Tight: 0-1 Gall: 0-1
Aids: Bl: 0-0 Vi: 0-0 Tstrap: 0-0 Ckp: 0-0
Best Rating: **79** 7/09 Sand 7f16y good

Fair; effective over 7f; acts on Polytrack.

Stanley Bridge

74 **25**
2-y-o b g Avonbridge-Antonia's Folly (Music Boy)
A Berry The Early Doors Partnership

Placings:000600 **(7168)**
2009: 5^{0}GF, 5^{0}GF, 5^{0}G, 6^{6}GS, 8^{0}G, 7^{0}S,

	Starts	1st	2nd	3rd	Win & Pl
Career Total (Turf)	6	0	0	0	0

Going (Turf): **Sf: 0-1 GS: 0-1 Gd: 0-2 GF: 0-2 Fm: 0-0**
Distance: 5f/6f: 0-4 7f-8f: 0-2 9f-13f: 0-0 14f+: 0-0
Track : LH: 0-2 RH: 0-2 Tight: 0-0 Gall: 0-2
Aids: Bl: 0-0 Vi: 0-0 Tstrap: 0-0 Ckp: 0-0
Best Rating: **25** 5/09 Muss 5f gd-fm

Stanley Goodspeed

103(106) (83)**76**
6-y-o ch g Inchinor-Flying Carpet (Barathea (IRE))
J W Hills R J Tufft

Placings:014604121/04-40660645523260300 **(7870)**
2009: 6^{4}SD, 7^{0}SD, 6^{6}GS, 6^{6}HY, 7^{0}G, 7^{6}SD, 7^{4}G, 7^{5}GF, 8^{5}HY, 7^{2}G, 7^{3}SD, 7^{2}SD, 7^{6}SD, 7^{0}SD, 7^{3}SD, 7^{0}SD, 6^{0}SS,

	Starts	1st	2nd	3rd	Win & Pl
Career Total (Turf)	14	3	2	0	25776
Career Total (AW)	14	0	1	2	2178

93	9/06	Hayd	6f (0-100)H	GD	£12954
82	8/06	Newb	6f8y (0-80)H	GD	£6477
77	5/06	Nott	6f15y	G-F	£3238

Total win prize-money £22670

Going (Turf): Sf: 0-4 GS: 0-1 **Gd: 2-6** GF: 1-3 Fm: 0-0
Distance: 5f/6f: 1-7 **7f-8f: 2-18** 9f-13f: 0-3 14f+: 0-0
Track : LH: 0-10 RH: 0-11 Tight: 0-9 Gall: 0-0
Aids: Bl: 0-2 Vi: 0-2 Tstrap: 0-6 Ckp: 0-6
Best Rating: **93** 9/06 Hayd 6f good

Modest; effective over 6f, but stays further; acts on good and faster ground and on Polytrack; has worn a tongue tie/cheekpieces/blinkers.

Stanley Rigby

85 **41**
3-y-o b g Dr Fong (USA)-Crystal (IRE) (Danehill (USA))
C F Wall Dean Hardman and Stella Kelsall

Placings:0-06 **(5322)**
2009: 10^{0}S, 10^{6}GF,

	Starts	1st	2nd	3rd	Win & Pl
Career Total (Turf)	3	0	0	0	0

Going (Turf): **Sf: 0-1 GS: 0-0 Gd: 0-1 GF: 0-1 Fm: 0-0**
Distance: 5f/6f: 0-0 7f-8f: 0-1 9f-13f: 0-2 14f+: 0-0
Track : LH: 0-1 RH: 0-1 Tight: 0-1 Gall: 0-0
Aids: Bl: 0-0 Vi: 0-0 Tstrap: 0-0 Ckp: 0-0
Best Rating: **41** 8/09 Wind 1m2f7y gd-fm

Stanstill (IRE)

102 **94**
3-y-o b g Statue Of Liberty (USA)-Fervent Wish (Rainbow Quest (USA))
G A Swinbank The Twopin Partnership

Placings:04-2221116 **(6095)**
2009: 11^{2}G, 10^{2}GS, 10^{2}G, 12^{1}GF, 12^{1}G, 14^{1}G, 13^{6}G,

	Starts	1st	2nd	3rd	Win & Pl
Career Total (Turf)	9	3	3	0	27192

94	8/09	Hayd	1m6f (0-95)H	GD	£11527
89	7/09	Asct	1m4f (0-85)H	GD	£6476
83	6/09	Ches	1m4f66y (0-85)H	G-F	£5504

Total win prize-money £23508

Going (Turf): Sf: 0-1 GS: 0-1 **Gd: 2-6** GF: 1-1 Fm: 0-0

Distance: 5f/6f: 0-0 7f-8f: 0-2 **9f-13f: 2-5** 14f+: 1-2
Track : **LH: 2-5** RH: 1-2 Tight: 1-2 Gall: 1-2
Aids: Bl: 0-0 Vi: 0-0 Tstrap: 0-0 Ckp: 0-0
Best Rating: 94 8/09 Hayd 1m6f good

Useful; stays 1m6f; acts on fast and easy ground.

Star Acclaim

45(92) (48)67
4-y-o b f Acclamation-Tropical Lass (IRE) (Ballad Rock)
E V Stanford CK Too

Placings:0050-00005 (5883)
2009: 6^{0}G, 6^{0}SD, 8^{0}SD, 8^{0}SD, 7^{5}SD,

	Starts	1st	2nd	3rd	Win & Pl
Career Total (Turf)	4	0	0	0	0
Career Total (AW)	5	0	0	0	0

Going (Turf): Sf: 0-1 GS: 0-1 Gd: 0-2 GF: 0-0 Fm: 0-0
Distance: 5f/6f: 0-1 7f-8f: 0-8 9f-13f: 0-0 14f+: 0-0
Track : LH: 0-4 RH: 0-1 Tight: 0-1 Gall: 0-0
Aids: Bl: 0-0 Vi: 0-0 Tstrap: 0-0 Ckp: 0-0
Best Rating: 67 4/08 NmkR 7f good

Moderate; stays 6f; seems to act on soft ground.

Star Addition

97 61
3-y-o ch g Medicean-Star Cast (IRE) (In The Wings)
E J Alston John & Maria Thompson, John Jackson

Placings:60003025 (6988)
2009: 6^{6}GF, 5^{0}GF, 6^{0}S, 5^{0}GF, 5^{3}GF, 5^{0}GF, 6^{2}GF, 5^{5}G,

	Starts	1st	2nd	3rd	Win & Pl
Career Total (Turf)	8	0	1	1	1031

Going (Turf): Sf: 0-1 GS: 0-0 Gd: 0-1 GF: 0-6 Fm: 0-0
Distance: 5f/6f: 0-7 7f-8f: 0-1 9f-13f: 0-0 14f+: 0-0
Track : LH: 0-0 RH: 0-0 Tight: 0-0 Gall: 0-0
Aids: Bl: 0-0 Vi: 0-0 Tstrap: 0-0 Ckp: 0-0
Best Rating: 61 10/09 Rdcr 6f gd-fm

Very moderate; suited by 5f and acts on fast ground.

Star Choice

98(111) (72)72
4-y-o ch g Choisir (AUS)-Bay Queen (Damister (USA))
J Pearce Macniler Racing Partnership

Placings:4001320-24251425204050 (7695)
2009: 12^{2}SD, 13^{4}SD, 12^{2}SD, 16^{5}SD, 12^{1}SD, 12^{4}SD, 11^{2}G, 12^{5}SD, 11^{2}F, 12^{0}GF, 10^{4}GS, 11^{0}GF, 12^{5}G, 12^{0}SD,

	Starts	1st	2nd	3rd	Win & Pl
Career Total (Turf)	9	0	2	0	2015
Career Total (AW)	12	2	3	1	7451

72 3/09 Wolv 1m4f50y (0-65)H STD £2217
64 10/08 Wolv 1m1f103y (0-55)H STD £2388
Total win prize-money £4606

Going (Turf): Sf: 0-1 GS: 0-3 Gd: 0-2 GF: 0-2 Fm: 0-1
Distance: 5f/6f: 0-0 7f-8f: 0-3 **9f-13f: 2-17** 14f+: 0-1
Track : **LH: 2-14** RH: 0-4 **Tight: 2-9** Gall: 0-2
Aids: Bl: 0-0 **Vi: 1-7** Tstrap: 0-1 Ckp: 0-1
Best Rating: 72 4/09 Brig 1m3f196y good

Modest; stays 1m4f; acts on good ground; goes on Polytrack.

Star Cruiser (USA)

89 49
2-y-o b g Golden Missile (USA)-Beautiful Star (USA) (War Chant (USA))
T D Easterby The Senators

Placings:00 (4430)
2009: 7^{0}GF, 6^{0}GF,

	Starts	1st	2nd	3rd	Win & Pl
Career Total (Turf)	2	0	0	0	

Going (Turf): Sf: 0-0 GS: 0-0 Gd: 0-0 GF: 0-2 Fm: 0-0
Distance: 5f/6f: 0-1 7f-8f: 0-1 9f-13f: 0-0 14f+: 0-0
Track : LH: 0-1 RH: 0-0 Tight: 0-1 Gall: 0-0
Aids: Bl: 0-0 Vi: 0-0 Tstrap: 0-0 Ckp: 0-0
Best Rating: 49 7/09 Rdcr 6f gd-fm

Star Links (USA)

102(99) (85)87
3-y-o b c Bernstein (USA)-Startarette (USA) (Dixieland Band (USA))
R Hannon Coriolan Partnership V

Placings:4421-4233264006 (6537)
2009: 9^{4}G, 8^{2}GF, 7^{3}SD, 8^{3}S, 7^{2}GF, 7^{6}G, 8^{4}GF, 8^{0}GF, 8^{0}G, 8^{6}GF,

	Starts	1st	2nd	3rd	Win & Pl
Career Total (Turf)	12	0	3	1	7141
Career Total (AW)	2	1	0	1	5107

85 10/08 Ling 7f STD £4403
Total win prize-money £4404

Going (Turf): Sf: 0-2 GS: 0-0 Gd: 0-5 GF: 0-5 Fm: 0-0
Distance: 5f/6f: 0-0 **7f-8f: 1-10** 9f-13f: 0-4 14f+: 0-0
Track : **LH: 1-3** RH: 0-5 **Tight: 1-3** Gall: 0-0
Aids: Bl: 0-0 Vi: 0-0 Tstrap: 0-0 Ckp: 0-0
Best Rating: 87 7/09 Sand 7f16y gd-fm

Useful; stays 1m but effective at 7f; acts on fast ground and on Polytrack; handles soft going.

Star Of Kalani (IRE)

76 38
2-y-o b g Ashkalani (IRE)-La Bekkah (FR) (Nononito (FR))
G M Moore J Pickavance

Placings:000 (7120)
2009: 8^{0}F, 8^{0}S, 8^{0}GF,

	Starts	1st	2nd	3rd	Win & Pl
Career Total (Turf)	3	0	0	0	

Going (Turf): Sf: 0-1 GS: 0-0 Gd: 0-0 GF: 0-1 Fm: 0-1
Distance: 5f/6f: 0-0 7f-8f: 0-0 9f-13f: 0-3 14f+: 0-0
Track : LH: 0-2 RH: 0-1 Tight: 0-0 Gall: 0-0
Aids: Bl: 0-0 Vi: 0-0 Tstrap: 0-0 Ckp: 0-0
Best Rating: 38 8/09 Bevl 1m100y firm

Star Of Memory (FR)

79 36
5-y-o b g Starborough-Desert Memory (FR) (Desert King (IRE))
D G Bridgwater Terry & Sarah Amos

Placings:32/00 (6392)
2009: 11^{0}GF, 10^{0}GF,

	Starts	1st	2nd	3rd	Win & Pl
Career Total (Turf)	4	0	1	1	4156

Going (Turf): Sf: 0-0 GS: 0-2 Gd: 0-0 GF: 0-2 Fm: 0-0
Distance: 5f/6f: 0-0 7f-8f: 0-1 9f-13f: 0-3 14f+: 0-0
Track : LH: 0-3 RH: 0-0 Tight: 0-1 Gall: 0-0
Aids: Bl: 0-0 Vi: 0-0 Tstrap: 0-0 Ckp: 0-0
Best Rating: 80 6/07 StCl 1m gd-sft

Star Of Pompey

97(95) (62)63
5-y-o b m Hernando (FR)-Discerning (Darshaan)
A B Haynes double-r-racing.com

Placings:062/003-0125060 (6785)
2009: 12^{0}SD, 16^{1}SD, 17^{2}G, 16^{5}G, 14^{0}G, 16^{6}G, 16^{0}SS,

	Starts	1st	2nd	3rd	Win & Pl
Career Total (Turf)	8	0	1	1	1926
Career Total (AW)	5	1	1	0	2652

62 6/09 Kemp 2m (0-65)H STD £2047
Total win prize-money £2047

Going (Turf): Sf: 0-1 GS: 0-1 Gd: 0-6 GF: 0-0 Fm: 0-0
Distance: 5f/6f: 0-0 7f-8f: 0-0 9f-13f: 0-7 **14f+: 1-6**
Track : LH: 0-6 **RH: 1-7** Tight: 0-7 Gall: 0-0
Aids: Bl: 0-0 Vi: 0-0 Tstrap: 0-0 Ckp: 0-0
Best Rating: 63 7/09 Bath 2m1f34y good

Moderate; stays 2m; acts on Polytrack.

Star Of Soho (IRE)

71 36
2-y-o b f Starcraft (NZ)-Trois Graces (USA) (Alysheba (USA))
E J Creighton The Vixens

Placings:0 (7182)
2009: 7^{0}G,

	Starts	1st	2nd	3rd	Win & Pl
Career Total (Turf)	1	0	0	0	

Going (Turf): Sf: 0-0 GS: 0-0 Gd: 0-1 GF: 0-0 Fm: 0-0
Distance: 5f/6f: 0-0 7f-8f: 0-1 9f-13f: 0-0 14f+: 0-0
Track : LH: 0-0 RH: 0-0 Tight: 0-0 Gall: 0-0
Aids: Bl: 0-0 Vi: 0-0 Tstrap: 0-0 Ckp: 0-0
Best Rating: 36 10/09 NmkR 7f good

Star Of Sophia (IRE)

(83) (39)7
3-y-o b f Hawk Wing (USA)-Sofia Aurora (USA) (Chief Honcho (USA))
Mrs A Duffield Middleham Park Racing XVII

Placings:0040-0 (1183)
2009: 10^{0}SD,

	Starts	1st	2nd	3rd	Win & Pl
Career Total (Turf)	1	0	0	0	
Career Total (AW)	4	0	0	0	0

Going (Turf): Sf: 0-1 GS: 0-0 Gd: 0-0 GF: 0-0 Fm: 0-0
Distance: 5f/6f: 0-0 7f-8f: 0-3 9f-13f: 0-2 14f+: 0-0
Track : LH: 0-3 RH: 0-2 Tight: 0-1 Gall: 0-0
Aids: Bl: 0-0 Vi: 0-2 Tstrap: 0-0 Ckp: 0-0
Best Rating: 39 9/08 Wolv 7f32y stand

Star Promise

94(94) (76)**76**

2-y-o b f Mujahid (USA)-Diamond Promise (IRE) (Fayruz)

T D Barron Coney Farms

Placings:01202 (7850)

2009: 5^{0}G, 5^{1}SD, 5^{2}G, 5^{0}SF, 5^{2}SS,

	Starts	1st	2nd	3rd	Win & Pl
Career Total (Turf)	2	0	1	0	1156
Career Total (AW)	3	1	1	0	4490

76 7/09 Sthl 5f STD £3885

Total win prize-money £3886

Going (Turf): Sf: 0-0 GS: 0-0 Gd: 0-2 GF: 0-0 Fm: 0-0
Distance: 5f/6f: 1-5 7f-8f: 0-0 9f-13f: 0-0 14f+: 0-0
Track : LH: 0-1 RH: 0-0 Tight: 0-1 Gall: 0-0
Aids: Bl: 0-0 Vi: 0-0 Tstrap: 0-0 Ckp: 0-0
Best Rating: 76 8/09 Muss 5f good

Modest; effective over 5f; acts on Fibresand.

Star Rover (IRE)

104(97) (82)**102**

2-y-o ch c Camacho-Charlene Lacy (IRE) (Pips Pride)

P D Evans Christy Leo

Placings:11113260641000 (6660)

2009: 5^{1}SD, 5^{1}GF, 5^{1}GF, 5^{1}GF, 5^{3}GF, 5^{2}G, 5^{6}GF, 5^{0}GF, 5^{6}GS, 5^{4}G, 5^{1}GF, 5^{0}GF, 6^{0}GF, 5^{0}GS,

	Starts	1st	2nd	3rd	Win & Pl
Career Total (Turf)	13	4	1	1	59011
Career Total (AW)	1	1	0	0	5181

102 8/09 York 5f G-F £17778
95 5/09 Ches 5f16y G-F £13085
86 4/09 Thsk 5f G-F £5569
90 4/09 Nott 5f13y G-F £5018
82 3/09 Kemp 5f STD £5180

Total win prize-money £46632

Going (Turf): Sf: 0-0 GS: 0-2 Gd: 0-2 GF: 4-9 Fm: 0-0
Distance: 5f/6f: 5-14 7f-8f: 0-0 9f-13f: 0-0 14f+: 0-0
Track : LH: 1-1 RH: 1-1 Tight: 1-1 Gall: 0-0
Aids: Bl: 0-0 Vi: 0-0 Tstrap: 0-0 Ckp: 0-0
Best Rating: 102 8/09 York 5f gd-fm

Very useful; Listed winner; suited by 5f; acts on fast ground and on Polytrack; suited by forcing tactics.

Star Ruby (IRE)

106 **109**

3-y-o b f Rock Of Gibraltar (IRE)-Purple Spirit (IRE) (Sadler's Wells (USA))

P W Chapple-Hyam Michael Tabor

Placings:12 (1988)

2009: 10^{1}G, 10^{2}GF,

	Starts	1st	2nd	3rd	Win & Pl
Career Total (Turf)	2	1	1	0	19169

96 4/09 Sand 1m2f7y GD £5180

Total win prize-money £5181

Going (Turf): Sf: 0-0 GS: 0-0 Gd: 1-1 GF: 0-1 Fm: 0-0
Distance: 5f/6f: 0-0 7f-8f: 0-0 9f-13f: 1-2 14f+: 0-0
Track : LH: 0-1 RH: 1-1 Tight: 0-0 Gall: 0-1
Aids: Bl: 0-0 Vi: 0-0 Tstrap: 0-0 Ckp: 0-0
Best Rating: 109 5/09 York 1m2f88y gd-fm

Smart; runner-up in the 2009 Group 3 Musidora Stakes; stays 1m2f; acts on fast ground.

Star Strider

98(106) (80)**67**

5-y-o gr g Royal Applause-Onefortheditch (USA) (With Approval (CAN))

T Keddy (Miss Gay Kelleway 15/8) A C Maylam

Placings:043030663/36065301/430565403230012O-2456004503OO56100 (7861)

2009: 8^{2}SD, 8^{4}SD, 8^{5}SD, 9^{6}G, 8^{0}F, 8^{0}GF, 7^{4}GF, 7^{5}G, 7^{0}G, 5^{3}GS, 6^{0}GF, 6^{0}GF, 8^{5}SD, 7^{6}SD, 7^{1}SD, 9^{0}SS, 7^{0}SD,

	Starts	1st	2nd	3rd	Win & Pl
Career Total (Turf)	32	0	1	8	9426
Career Total (AW)	18	3	2	1	8817

67 11/09 Kemp 7f (0-60)H STD £1619
70 12/08 Ling 1m (0-60)H STD £2047
74 1/08 Wolv 5f20y STD £2457

Total win prize-money £6123

Going (Turf): Sf: 0-0 GS: 0-3 Gd: 0-14 GF: 0-10 Fm: 0-5
Distance: 5f/6f: 1-23 7f-8f: 2-22 9f-13f: 0-5 14f+: 0-0
Track : LH: 2-26 RH: 1-7 Tight: 2-13 Gall: 0-7
Aids: Bl: 0-3 Vi: 0-1 Tstrap: 0-4 Ckp: 0-4
Best Rating: 80 1/09 Wolv 1m141y stand

Modest; stays 1m; acts on good ground and on Polytrack; has worn blinkers and cheekpieces.

Star Twilight

86(79) (45)**58**

2-y-o b f King's Best (USA)-Star Express (Sadler's Wells (USA))

D R Lanigan Dr Ali Ridha

Placings:0400 (7619)

2009: 6^{0}GF, 7^{4}F, 7^{0}SD, 5^{0}SD,

	Starts	1st	2nd	3rd	Win & Pl
Career Total (Turf)	2	0	0	0	313
Career Total (AW)	2	0	0	0	

Going (Turf): Sf: 0-0 GS: 0-0 Gd: 0-0 GF: 0-1 Fm: 0-1
Distance: 5f/6f: 0-2 7f-8f: 0-2 9f-13f: 0-0 14f+: 0-0
Track : LH: 0-1 RH: 0-1 Tight: 0-1 Gall: 0-0
Aids: Bl: 0-0 Vi: 0-0 Tstrap: 0-0 Ckp: 0-0
Best Rating: 58 7/09 NmkJ 6f gd-fm

Starbougg

78 **27**

5-y-o b m Tobougg (IRE)-Celestial Welcome (Most Welcome)

K G Reveley Star Alliance (II) & Reveley Farms

Placings:20/5000/05-0 (7084)

2009: 15^{0}S,

	Starts	1st	2nd	3rd	Win & Pl
Career Total (Turf)	9	0	1	0	1156

Going (Turf): Sf: 0-2 GS: 0-2 Gd: 0-2 GF: 0-1 Fm: 0-2
Distance: 5f/6f: 0-0 7f-8f: 0-2 9f-13f: 0-3 14f+: 0-4
Track : LH: 0-8 RH: 0-0 Tight: 0-4 Gall: 0-3
Aids: Bl: 0-0 Vi: 0-0 Tstrap: 0-0 Ckp: 0-0
Best Rating: 70 8/06 Rdcr 7f gd-fm

Starburst

94(101) (67)**61**

4-y-o b f Fantastic Light (USA)-Rasmalai (Sadler's Wells (USA))

A M Balding Holistic Racing Ltd

Placings:403-05221 (7790)

2009: 12^{0}SD, 9^{5}G, 12^{2}SD, 12^{2}SD, 12^{1}SD,

	Starts	1st	2nd	3rd	Win & Pl
Career Total (Turf)	2	0	0	0	0
Career Total (AW)	6	1	2	1	4027

67 12/09 Wolv 1m4f50y STD £2047

Total win prize-money £2047

Going (Turf): Sf: 0-0 GS: 0-0 Gd: 0-1 GF: 0-1 Fm: 0-0
Distance: 5f/6f: 0-0 7f-8f: 0-0 9f-13f: 1-8 14f+: 0-0
Track : LH: 1-4 RH: 0-3 Tight: 1-5 Gall: 0-0
Aids: Bl: 0-0 Vi: 0-0 Tstrap: 0-0 Ckp: 0-0
Best Rating: 67 12/09 Wolv 1m4f50y stand

Modest; stays 1m4f; acts on Polytrack.

Starburst Excel

88(84) (46)**70**

2-y-o b f Exceed And Excel (AUS)-Homeward (IRE) (Kris)

M G Quinlan J W Haydon

Placings:45000 (6970)

2009: 5^{4}GF, 5^{5}GF, 5^{0}GF, 5^{0}SF, 5^{0}SD,

	Starts	1st	2nd	3rd	Win & Pl
Career Total (Turf)	3	0	0	0	385
Career Total (AW)	2	0	0	0	

Going (Turf): Sf: 0-0 GS: 0-0 Gd: 0-0 GF: 0-3 Fm: 0-0
Distance: 5f/6f: 0-5 7f-8f: 0-0 9f-13f: 0-0 14f+: 0-0
Track : LH: 0-1 RH: 0-1 Tight: 0-1 Gall: 0-0
Aids: Bl: 0-0 Vi: 0-0 Tstrap: 0-0 Ckp: 0-0
Best Rating: 70 4/09 NmkR 5f gd-fm

Starclass

87 **68**

2-y-o b f Starcraft (NZ)-Classic Millennium (Midyan (USA))

W R Swinburn Borgatti & Moir

Placings:0 (6730)

2009: 6^{0}S,

	Starts	1st	2nd	3rd	Win & Pl
Career Total (Turf)	1	0	0	0	

Going (Turf): Sf: 0-1 GS: 0-0 Gd: 0-0 GF: 0-0 Fm: 0-0
Distance: 5f/6f: 0-0 7f-8f: 0-1 9f-13f: 0-0 14f+: 0-0
Track : LH: 0-0 RH: 0-0 Tight: 0-0 Gall: 0-0
Aids: Bl: 0-0 Vi: 0-0 Tstrap: 0-0 Ckp: 0-0
Best Rating: 68 10/09 Sals 6f212y soft

Starcross Maid

(100) (59)**61**

7-y-o ch m Zaha (CAN)-Maculatus (USA) (Sharpen Up)

A G Juckes Whispering Winds

Placings:03/0650344030200/3056554162031/2250123006 65/134320304460-632 (1651)

2009: 12^{6}SD, 11^{3}SD, 11^{2}SD,

	Starts	1st	2nd	3rd	Win & Pl
Career Total (Turf)	16	0	1	2	2113
Career Total (AW)	39	4	6	8	17361

61 1/08 Sthl 1m3f (0-58)H STD £1774
61 5/07 Sthl 1m3f (0-65)H STD £3238
53 7/06 Sthl 1m4f STD £2730
56 5/06 Sthl 1m4f STD £2730

Total win prize-money £10474

Going (Turf): Sf: 0-1 GS: 0-0 Gd: 0-7 GF: 0-8 Fm: 0-0
Distance: 5f/6f: 0-0 7f-8f: 0-9 9f-13f: 4-46 14f+: 0-0
Track : LH: 4-47 RH: 0-7 Tight: 0-15 Gall: 0-1

Aids: Bl: 0-1 Vi: 0-0 Tstrap: 0-0 Ckp: 0-0
Best Rating: **61** 1/08 Sthl 1m4f std-slw

Very moderate; stays 1m4f; acts on a sound surface, Fibresand and Polytrack.

Stardust Memories (UAE)

74(83) (35)

3-y-o b f Halling (USA)-Clarinda (IRE) (Lomond (USA))
John Berry Huelin-Jakobsen

Placings:000 **(7367)**
2009: 8^{0}SD, 10^{0}S, 12^{0}SD,

	Starts	1st	2nd	3rd	Win & Pl
Career Total (Turf)	1	0	0	0	
Career Total (AW)	2	0	0	0	

Going (Turf): **Sf: 0-1 GS: 0-0 Gd: 0-0 GF: 0-0 Fm: 0-0**
Distance: 5f/6f: 0-0 7f-8f: 0-1 9f-13f: 0-2 14f+: 0-0
Track : LH: 0-3 RH: 0-0 Tight: 0-2 Gall: 0-0
Aids: Bl: 0-0 Vi: 0-0 Tstrap: 0-0 Ckp: 0-0
Best Rating: **35** 11/09 Ling 1m4f stand

Starfala

108(112) (89)106

4-y-o gr f Galileo (IRE)-Farfala (FR) (Linamix (FR))
P F I Cole Ben & Sir Martyn Arbib

Placings:003/211520-2430026 **(6854)**
2009: 12^{2}GF, 11^{4}G, 11^{3}GF, 14^{0}G, 12^{0}GF, 14^{2}G, 16^{6}G,

	Starts	1st	2nd	3rd	Win & Pl
Career Total (Turf)	12	0	3	2	37792
Career Total (AW)	4	2	1	0	13011

89 9/08 Kemp 1m4f (0-95)H STD £7477
78 7/08 Kemp 1m4f STD £4727
Total win prize-money £12204

Going (Turf): **Sf: 0-0 GS: 0-2 Gd: 0-4 GF: 0-6 Fm: 0-0**
Distance: 5f/6f: 0-0 7f-8f: 0-3 **9f-13f: 2-10** 14f+: 0-3
Track : LH: 0-5 **RH: 2-10** Tight: 0-2 Gall: 0-6
Aids: Bl: 0-0 Vi: 0-0 Tstrap: 0-0 Ckp: 0-0
Best Rating: **106** 9/09 Donc 1m6f132y good

Smart; Group 2 placed; stays 1m6f; acts on fast ground and on Polytrack.

Stargaze (IRE)

99(97) (88)98

2-y-o b c Oasis Dream-Dafariyna (IRE) (Nashwan (USA))
A Bailey (A M Balding 19/9) John Stocker

Placings:0411352 **(7806)**
2009: 5^{0}GS, 5^{4}G, 5^{1}GF, 5^{1}G, 6^{3}G, 6^{5}GF, 7^{2}SD,

	Starts	1st	2nd	3rd	Win & Pl
Career Total (Turf)	6	2	0	1	19355
Career Total (AW)	1	0	1	0	1156

93 7/09 Bath 5f11y GD £4857
80 5/09 Ling 5f G-F £3561
Total win prize-money £8419

Going (Turf): Sf: 0-0 GS: 0-1 **Gd: 1-3 GF: 1-2** Fm: 0-0
Distance: **5f/6f: 2-5** 7f-8f: 0-2 9f-13f: 0-0 14f+: 0-0
Track : **LH: 1-3** RH: 0-0 Tight: 0-1 **Gall: 1-2**
Aids: Bl: 0-0 Vi: 0-0 Tstrap: 0-0 Ckp: 0-0
Best Rating: **98** 9/09 Newb 6f8y gd-fm

Very useful; suited by 5-6f; acts on good and faster ground; acts on Polytrack.

Stargazing (IRE)

84 37

3-y-o b f Galileo (IRE)-Autumnal (IRE) (Indian Ridge)
B J Meehan Paul & Jenny Green

Placings:0 **(6390)**
2009: 8^{0}GF,

	Starts	1st	2nd	3rd	Win & Pl
Career Total (Turf)	1	0	0	0	

Going (Turf): **Sf: 0-0 GS: 0-0 Gd: 0-0 GF: 0-1 Fm: 0-0**
Distance: 5f/6f: 0-0 7f-8f: 0-0 9f-13f: 0-1 14f+: 0-0
Track : LH: 0-1 RH: 0-0 Tight: 0-0 Gall: 0-0
Aids: Bl: 0-0 Vi: 0-0 Tstrap: 0-0 Ckp: 0-0
Best Rating: **37** 9/09 Nott 1m75y gd-fm

Stargazy

(99) (56)51

5-y-o b g Observatory (USA)-Romantic Myth (Mind Games)
A J Lidderdale (W G M Turner 9/2) C S J Beek

Placings:00220004/00000/52154030050-0163000 **(7768)**
2009: 7^{0}SD, 7^{1}SD, 7^{6}SD, 7^{3}SD, 7^{0}SD, 8^{0}SD, 7^{0}SD,

	Starts	1st	2nd	3rd	Win & Pl
Career Total (Turf)	8	0	2	0	2409
Career Total (AW)	23	2	1	2	4061

55 1/09 Wolv 7f32y (0-45) STD £1364
53 1/08 Wolv 7f32y (0-45) STD £1365
Total win prize-money £2730

Going (Turf): **Sf: 0-0 GS: 0-1 Gd: 0-1 GF: 0-4 Fm: 0-2**
Distance: 5f/6f: 0-13 **7f-8f: 2-17** 9f-13f: 0-1 14f+: 0-0
Track : **LH: 2-18** RH: 0-7 **Tight: 2-16** Gall: 0-2
Aids: Bl: 0-2 Vi: 0-0 Tstrap: 0-1 Ckp: 0-1
Best Rating: **70** 7/06 Wind 5f10y gd-fm

Moderate; effective at around 6f-7f; acts on fast ground; also goes on Polytrack.

Stark Contrast (USA)

96(100) (68)49

5-y-o ch g Gulch (USA)-A Stark Is Born (USA) (Graustark)
M D I Usher R H Brookes

Placings:44/22000340105/643020001060-065040060306360 **(7856)**
2009: 10^{0}SD, 8^{6}SD, 8^{5}SD, 8^{0}SD, 8^{4}SD, 9^{0}SD, 9^{0}SD, 8^{6}SD, 6^{0}F, 10^{3}F, 9^{0}G, 8^{6}F, 8^{3}SD, 8^{6}SD, 9^{0}SD,

	Starts	1st	2nd	3rd	Win & Pl
Career Total (Turf)	15	0	2	2	3611
Career Total (AW)	25	2	1	2	6801

66 11/08 Wolv 1m141y (0-75)H STD £3238
70 11/07 Ling 1m2f (0-62)H STD £2047
Total win prize-money £5286

Going (Turf): **Sf: 0-2 GS: 0-1 Gd: 0-3 GF: 0-6 Fm: 0-3**
Distance: 5f/6f: 0-0 7f-8f: 0-5 **9f-13f: 2-35** 14f+: 0-0
Track : **LH: 2-32** RH: 0-5 **Tight: 2-30** Gall: 0-1
Aids: Bl: 0-2 Vi: 0-0 Tstrap: 0-2 Ckp: 0-2
Best Rating: **78** 7/06 York 7f gd-fm

Modest; effective over 1m-1m2f; acts on fast ground; goes on Polytrack.

Starkat

100(79) (36)74

3-y-o b f Diktat-Star Of Normandie (USA) (Gulch (USA))
Jane Chapple-Hyam (J A R Toller 20/7) Norcroft Park Stud

Placings:024 **(6794)**
2009: 8^{0}SD, 9^{2}GS, 10^{4}S,

	Starts	1st	2nd	3rd	Win & Pl
Career Total (Turf)	2	0	1	0	1011
Career Total (AW)	1	0	0	0	

Going (Turf): **Sf: 0-1 GS: 0-1 Gd: 0-0 GF: 0-0 Fm: 0-0**
Distance: 5f/6f: 0-0 7f-8f: 0-1 9f-13f: 0-2 14f+: 0-0
Track : LH: 0-3 RH: 0-0 Tight: 0-2 Gall: 0-0
Aids: Bl: 0-0 Vi: 0-0 Tstrap: 0-0 Ckp: 0-0
Best Rating: **74** 10/09 Nott 1m2f50y soft

Fair; effective at 1m2f; acts on easy ground.

Starla Dancer (GER)

111(96) (74)84

3-y-o b f Danehill Dancer (IRE)-Starla (GER) (Lando (GER))
R A Fahey Aricabeau Racing Limited

Placings:30-324224412 **(7014)**
2009: 8^{3}GF, 7^{2}GF, 8^{4}GF, 9^{2}G, 8^{2}GF, 9^{4}GF, 9^{4}SD, 10^{1}G, 10^{2}GS,

	Starts	1st	2nd	3rd	Win & Pl
Career Total (Turf)	10	1	4	2	12294
Career Total (AW)	1	0	0	0	289

82 10/09 York 1m2f88y (0-80)H GD £6476
Total win prize-money £6476

Going (Turf): Sf: 0-1 GS: 0-2 **Gd: 1-2** GF: 0-5 Fm: 0-0
Distance: 5f/6f: 0-2 7f-8f: 0-2 **9f-13f: 1-7** 14f+: 0-0
Track : **LH: 1-5** RH: 0-4 Tight: 0-3 **Gall: 1-2**
Aids: Bl: 0-0 Vi: 0-0 Tstrap: 0-0 Ckp: 0-0
Best Rating: **84** 10/09 Donc 1m2f60y gd-sft

Fair; stays 1m2f; acts on most ground and on Polytrack.

Starlight Boy

2-y-o b c Firebreak-Dispol Verity (Averti (IRE))
S Wynne L R Owen

Placings:0 **(5958)**
2009: 6^{0}GF,

	Starts	1st	2nd	3rd	Win & Pl
Career Total (Turf)	1	0	0	0	

Going (Turf): **Sf: 0-0 GS: 0-0 Gd: 0-0 GF: 0-1 Fm: 0-0**
Distance: 5f/6f: 0-1 7f-8f: 0-0 9f-13f: 0-0 14f+: 0-0
Track : LH: 0-0 RH: 0-0 Tight: 0-0 Gall: 0-0
Aids: Bl: 0-0 Vi: 0-0 Tstrap: 0-0 Ckp: 0-0

Starlight Gazer

(90) (62)87

6-y-o b g Observatory (USA)-Dancing Fire (USA) (Dayjur (USA))
J A Geake The Burning Stars

Placings:3/515450/0121060/066450415-05 **(7728)**
2009: 7^{0}SD, 8^{5}SD,

	Starts	1st	2nd	3rd	Win & Pl
Career Total (Turf)	22	4	1	1	22950
Career Total (AW)	3	0	0	0	0

73 10/08 Wwck 1m22y (0-75)H SFT £3885
87 7/07 Leic 7f9y (0-80)H SFT £6309

81 7/07 Newb 7f (0-80)H HVY £4857
73 5/06 Wind 6f G-S £3238
Total win prize-money £18292

Going (Turf): **Sf: 3-11** GS: 1-4 Gd: 0-3 GF: 0-4 Fm: 0-0
Distance: 5f/6f: 1-6 **7f-8f: 2-18** 9f-13f: 1-1 14f+: 0-0
Track : **LH: 1-3** RH: 0-3 Tight: 0-1 **Gall: 1-1**
Aids: Bl: 0-0 **Vi: 1-4** Tstrap: 0-0 Ckp: 0-0
Best Rating: 87 7/07 Leic 7f9y soft

Modest; stays 7f; needs soft ground; has worn a tongue tie and visor.

Starlit Sands

96(109) (103)**105**
4-y-o b f Oasis Dream-Shimmering Sea (Slip Anchor)
Sir Mark Prescott Miss K Rausing

Placings:112461/343P-00 **(5507)**
2009: 5^{0}G, 5^{0}G,

	Starts	1st	2nd	3rd	Win & Pl
Career Total (Turf)	11	3	1	1	62716
Career Total (AW)	1	0	0	1	1166

106 9/07 Chan 5f110y GD £27027
87 6/07 Catt 5f G-F £3562
79 5/07 Thsk 5f GD £5181
Total win prize-money £35771

Going (Turf): Sf: 0-0 GS: 0-0 **Gd: 2-7** GF: 1-4 Fm: 0-0
Distance: **5f/6f: 3-12** 7f-8f: 0-0 9f-13f: 0-0 14f+: 0-0
Track : LH: 0-3 RH: 0-0 Tight: 0-0 Gall: 0-2
Aids: Bl: 0-1 Vi: 0-0 Tstrap: 0-0 Ckp: 0-0
Best Rating: 106 9/07 Chan 5f110y good

Formerly smart; runner-up in Queen Mary in 2007; effective over 5f but appears to get 6f; acts on fast ground; handles Polytrack.

Starmaamul

55
2-y-o b g Elmaamul (USA)-Catwalk Girl (Skyliner)
K A Ryan Mr & Mrs Julian And Rosie Richer

Placings:0 **(5407)**
2009: 8^{0}G,

	Starts	1st	2nd	3rd	Win & Pl
Career Total (Turf)	1	0	0	0	

Going (Turf): **Sf: 0-0 GS: 0-0 Gd: 0-1 GF: 0-0 Fm: 0-0**
Distance: 5f/6f: 0-0 7f-8f: 0-1 9f-13f: 0-0 14f+: 0-0
Track : LH: 0-1 RH: 0-0 Tight: 0-1 Gall: 0-0
Aids: Bl: 0-0 Vi: 0-0 Tstrap: 0-0 Ckp: 0-0

Starry Mount

96 **73**
2-y-o ch c Observatory (USA)-Lady Lindsay (IRE) (Danehill Dancer (IRE))
A B Haynes Graham Robinson

Placings:0451 **(7168)**
2009: 6^{0}G, 7^{4}GF, 8^{5}G, 7^{1}S,

	Starts	1st	2nd	3rd	Win & Pl
Career Total (Turf)	4	1	0	0	4353

73 10/09 Ayr 7f50y (0-75) SFT £3885
Total win prize-money £3886

Going (Turf): **Sf: 1-1** GS: 0-0 Gd: 0-2 GF: 0-1 Fm: 0-0
Distance: 5f/6f: 0-0 **7f-8f: 1-3** 9f-13f: 0-1 14f+: 0-0
Track : **LH: 1-1** RH: 0-1 Tight: 0-1 Gall: 0-0
Aids: Bl: 0-0 Vi: 0-0 Tstrap: 0-0 Ckp: 0-0
Best Rating: 73 10/09 Ayr 7f50y soft

Fair; stays 7f; acts on soft ground.

Starstreamer (IRE)

75 **31**
2-y-o ch f Captain Rio-Petra Nova (First Trump)
M P Tregoning R C C Villers

Placings:0 **(5026)**
2009: 6^{0}GF,

	Starts	1st	2nd	3rd	Win & Pl
Career Total (Turf)	1	0	0	0	

Going (Turf): **Sf: 0-0 GS: 0-0 Gd: 0-0 GF: 0-1 Fm: 0-0**
Distance: 5f/6f: 0-0 7f-8f: 0-1 9f-13f: 0-0 14f+: 0-0
Track : LH: 0-0 RH: 0-0 Tight: 0-0 Gall: 0-0
Aids: Bl: 0-0 Vi: 0-0 Tstrap: 0-0 Ckp: 0-0
Best Rating: 31 8/09 Newb 6f8y gd-fm

Starstruck Peter (IRE)

100(108) (58)**64**
5-y-o b g Iron Mask (USA)-Daraliya (IRE) (Kahyasi)
Jim Best (S Curran 26/3) W P K Racing

Placings:0/0050/410343-00110 **(3927)**
2009: 16^{0}SD, 12^{0}SD, 12^{1}GF, 16^{1}GF, 13^{0}SF,

	Starts	1st	2nd	3rd	Win & Pl
Career Total (Turf)	6	2	0	0	4314
Career Total (AW)	10	1	0	2	2486

64 7/09 Folk 2m93y (0-60)H G-F £2047
59 7/09 Chep 1m4f23y (0-60)H G-F £2266
59 1/08 Wolv 2m119y (0-55)H STD £1684
Total win prize-money £5998

Going (Turf): Sf: 0-1 GS: 0-0 Gd: 0-2 **GF: 2-2** Fm: 0-1
Distance: 5f/6f: 0-0 7f-8f: 0-3 9f-13f: 1-5 **14f+: 2-8**
Track : **LH: 2-10** RH: 1-3 **Tight: 2-8** Gall: 0-1
Aids: **Bl: 2-5** Vi: 0-0 Tstrap: 0-0 Ckp: 0-0
Best Rating: 64 7/09 Folk 2m93y gd-fm

Moderate ex-Irish gelding; stays 2m; acts on Polytrack; has worn blinkers.

Start Right

102(95) (82)**83**
2-y-o b c Footstepsinthesand-Time Crystal (IRE) (Sadler's Wells (USA))
L M Cumani L Marinopoulos

Placings:062321 **(6672)**
2009: 6^{0}GF, 7^{6}G, 7^{2}G, 8^{3}GF, 8^{2}GF, 8^{1}SD,

	Starts	1st	2nd	3rd	Win & Pl
Career Total (Turf)	5	0	2	1	4142
Career Total (AW)	1	1	0	0	2730

82 10/09 Wolv 1m141y STD £2729
Total win prize-money £2730

Going (Turf): **Sf: 0-0 GS: 0-0 Gd: 0-2 GF: 0-3 Fm: 0-0**
Distance: 5f/6f: 0-1 7f-8f: 0-3 **9f-13f: 1-2** 14f+: 0-0
Track : **LH: 1-4** RH: 0-0 **Tight: 1-1** Gall: 0-2
Aids: Bl: 0-0 Vi: 0-0 Tstrap: 0-0 Ckp: 0-0
Best Rating: 83 9/09 Donc 1m gd-fm

Useful; stays 7f; acts on good ground.

Starwatch

92(92) (59)**82**
2-y-o b g Observatory (USA)-Trinity Reef (Bustino)
J J Bridger J J Bridger

Placings:02660444 **(7824)**
2009: 6^{0}GF, 6^{2}G, 7^{6}GS, 8^{6}GF, 6^{0}GS, 8^{4}SD, 7^{4}SD, 7^{4}SD,

	Starts	1st	2nd	3rd	Win & Pl
Career Total (Turf)	5	0	1	0	2575
Career Total (AW)	3	0	0	0	337

Going (Turf): **Sf: 0-0 GS: 0-2 Gd: 0-1 GF: 0-2 Fm: 0-0**
Distance: 5f/6f: 0-3 7f-8f: 0-5 9f-13f: 0-0 14f+: 0-0
Track : LH: 0-0 RH: 0-4 Tight: 0-0 Gall: 0-2
Aids: Bl: 0-0 Vi: 0-0 Tstrap: 0-0 Ckp: 0-0
Best Rating: 82 8/09 Wind 6f good

Modest; stays 1m; acts on fast ground; goes on Polytrack.

Stash

77(106) (81)**42**
3-y-o b g Bold Edge-Gemtastic (Tagula (IRE))
R Hollinshead Edenbrook Partnership

Placings:1-3360050 **(7673)**
2009: 5^{3}SD, 5^{3}SD, 5^{6}SD, 5^{0}G, 5^{0}G, 5^{5}SD, 5^{0}SD,

	Starts	1st	2nd	3rd	Win & Pl
Career Total (Turf)	2	0	0	0	
Career Total (AW)	6	1	0	2	4311

81 11/08 Wolv 5f20y STD £3238
Total win prize-money £3238

Going (Turf): **Sf: 0-0 GS: 0-0 Gd: 0-2 GF: 0-0 Fm: 0-0**
Distance: **5f/6f: 1-8** 7f-8f: 0-0 9f-13f: 0-0 14f+: 0-0
Track : **LH: 1-6** RH: 0-0 **Tight: 1-5** Gall: 0-0
Aids: Bl: 0-0 Vi: 0-0 Tstrap: 0-0 Ckp: 0-0
Best Rating: 81 11/08 Wolv 5f20y stand

Fair; suited by 5f; acts on Polytrack.

State Banquet (USA)

109(102) (82)**90**
3-y-o br g Fusaichi Pegasus (USA)-Gracie Lady (IRE) (Generous (IRE))
H Morrison De La Warr Racing

Placings:1-23256 **(6203)**
2009: 10^{2}GF, 10^{3}G, 12^{2}G, 12^{5}SD, 11^{6}G,

	Starts	1st	2nd	3rd	Win & Pl
Career Total (Turf)	5	1	2	1	17879
Career Total (AW)	1	0	0	0	275

82 10/08 Sals 1m GD £4371
Total win prize-money £4371

Going (Turf): Sf: 0-0 GS: 0-0 **Gd: 1-4** GF: 0-1 Fm: 0-0
Distance: 5f/6f: 0-0 **7f-8f: 1-1** 9f-13f: 0-5 14f+: 0-0
Track : LH: 0-0 RH: 0-5 Tight: 0-3 Gall: 0-0
Aids: Bl: 0-0 Vi: 0-0 Tstrap: 0-2 Ckp: 0-2
Best Rating: 90 7/09 Gdwd 1m4f good

Useful; stays 1m2f; handles quick ground.

State Fair

92(84) (31)**75**
2-y-o b g Marju (IRE)-Baralinka (IRE) (Barathea (IRE))
P F I Cole Elite Racing Club

Placings:523300 **(7209)**
2009: 5^{5}GS, 5^{2}G, 6^{3}G, 7^{3}G, 8^{0}S, 7^{0}SD,

	Starts	1st	2nd	3rd	Win & Pl
Career Total (Turf)	5	0	1	2	3179
Career Total (AW)	1	0	0	0	

Going (Turf): **Sf: 0-1 GS: 0-1 Gd: 0-3 GF: 0-0 Fm: 0-0**
Distance: 5f/6f: 0-3 7f-8f: 0-3 9f-13f: 0-0 14f+: 0-0
Track : LH: 0-1 RH: 0-0 Tight: 0-1 Gall: 0-0
Aids: Bl: 0-0 Vi: 0-0 Tstrap: 0-0 Ckp: 0-0
Best Rating: **75** 5/09 Gdwd 6f good

Modest; should stay 6f; acts on easy ground and on a sound surface.

State Function (IRE)

89(83) (20)**60**
4-y-o b g Grand Slam (USA)-Well Designed (IRE) (Sadler's Wells (USA))
G Prodromou George H Brown

Placings:50-60 **(6256)**
2009: 5^{6}F, 8^{0}SD,

	Starts	1st	2nd	3rd	Win & Pl
Career Total (Turf)	3	0	0	0	0
Career Total (AW)	1	0	0	0	

Going (Turf): **Sf: 0-0 GS: 0-1 Gd: 0-0 GF: 0-1 Fm: 0-1**
Distance: 5f/6f: 0-1 7f-8f: 0-2 9f-13f: 0-1 14f+: 0-0
Track : LH: 0-2 RH: 0-0 Tight: 0-1 Gall: 0-0
Aids: Bl: 0-0 Vi: 0-0 Tstrap: 0-0 Ckp: 0-0
Best Rating: **60** 6/08 Yarm 6f3y gd-fm

State Gathering

91 **55**
2-y-o b c Royal Applause-Flag (Selkirk (USA))
H Candy Six Too Many

Placings:00 **(7145)**
2009: 6^{0}G, 6^{0}G,

	Starts	1st	2nd	3rd	Win & Pl
Career Total (Turf)	2	0	0	0	

Going (Turf): **Sf: 0-0 GS: 0-0 Gd: 0-2 GF: 0-0 Fm: 0-0**
Distance: 5f/6f: 0-1 7f-8f: 0-1 9f-13f: 0-0 14f+: 0-0
Track : LH: 0-0 RH: 0-0 Tight: 0-0 Gall: 0-0
Aids: Bl: 0-0 Vi: 0-0 Tstrap: 0-0 Ckp: 0-0
Best Rating: **55** 10/09 NmkR 6f good

State General (IRE)

99(104) (81)**64**
3-y-o b g Statue Of Liberty (USA)-Nisibis (In The Wings)
Miss J Feilden Ocean Trailers & Partners

Placings:600226-1000P **(6680)**
2009: 10^{1}SD, 10^{0}GF, 12^{0}SD, 11^{0}GF, 10^{P}G,

	Starts	1st	2nd	3rd	Win & Pl
Career Total (Turf)	6	0	0	0	0
Career Total (AW)	5	1	2	0	7222

81 1/09 Ling 1m2f (0-85)H STD £4857
Total win prize-money £4857

Going (Turf): **Sf: 0-0 GS: 0-0 Gd: 0-3 GF: 0-3 Fm: 0-0**
Distance: 5f/6f: 0-0 7f-8f: 0-3 **9f-13f: 1-8** 14f+: 0-0
Track : **LH: 1-5** RH: 0-2 **Tight: 1-2** Gall: 0-3
Aids: Bl: 0-0 Vi: 0-0 Tstrap: 0-0 Ckp: 0-0
Best Rating: **81** 1/09 Ling 1m2f stand

Fair; stays 1m2f; acts on Polytrack.

State Visit

84(85) (64)**59**
2-y-o b c Dr Fong (USA)-Saint Ann (USA) (Geiger Counter (USA))
W R Muir The Stately Partnership

Placings:005 **(7024)**
2009: 8^{0}GF, 8^{0}GF, 7^{5}SD,

	Starts	1st	2nd	3rd	Win & Pl
Career Total (Turf)	2	0	0	0	
Career Total (AW)	1	0	0	0	0

Going (Turf): **Sf: 0-0 GS: 0-0 Gd: 0-0 GF: 0-2 Fm: 0-0**
Distance: 5f/6f: 0-0 7f-8f: 0-2 9f-13f: 0-1 14f+: 0-0
Track : LH: 0-2 RH: 0-1 Tight: 0-0 Gall: 0-1
Aids: Bl: 0-1 Vi: 0-0 Tstrap: 0-0 Ckp: 0-0
Best Rating: **64** 10/09 Kemp 7f stand

Modest; stays 7f; acts on Polytrack.

Stately Home (IRE)

110 **100**
3-y-o b c Montjeu (IRE)-Pescia (IRE) (Darshaan)
A P O'Brien Mrs John Magnier

Placings:1266 **(4962a)**
2009: 10^{1}GY, 11^{2}GF, 16^{6}GF, 12^{6}G,

	Starts	1st	2nd	3rd	Win & Pl
Career Total (Turf)	4	1	1	0	24003

94 4/09 Leop 1m2f G-Y £11404
Total win prize-money £11405

Going (Turf): **Sf: 0-0 GS: 0-0 Gd: 0-1 GF: 0-2 Fm: 0-0**
Distance: 5f/6f: 0-0 7f-8f: 0-0 **9f-13f: 1-3** 14f+: 0-1
Track : **LH: 1-2** RH: 0-2 Tight: 0-1 Gall: 0-1
Aids: Bl: 0-0 Vi: 0-0 Tstrap: 0-0 Ckp: 0-0
Best Rating: **100** 5/09 Haml 1m3f16y gd-fm

Very useful; stays 1m2f; acts on easy ground.

Stateside (CAN)

105(85) (12)**68**
4-y-o b f El Corredor (USA)-Double Trick (USA) (Phone Trick (USA))
R A Fahey P Timmins

Placings:060/00-2112530 **(5698)**
2009: 10^{2}F, 9^{1}G, 9^{1}GF, 10^{2}F, 12^{5}S, 9^{3}S, 12^{0}GS,

	Starts	1st	2nd	3rd	Win & Pl
Career Total (Turf)	11	2	2	1	9812
Career Total (AW)	1	0	0	0	

66 6/09 Haml 1m1f36y (0-75)H G-F £3885
59 5/09 Ayr 1m1f20y (0-60)H GD £2914
Total win prize-money £6800

Going (Turf): Sf: 0-3 GS: 0-1 **Gd: 1-2 GF: 1-3** Fm: 0-2
Distance: 5f/6f: 0-0 7f-8f: 0-3 **9f-13f: 2-9** 14f+: 0-0
Track : LH: 1-8 RH: 1-3 **Tight: 1-4** Gall: 0-2
Aids: Bl: 0-0 Vi: 0-0 Tstrap: 0-0 Ckp: 0-0
Best Rating: **68** 8/09 Haml 1m1f36y soft

Modest; stays 1m1f; acts on any ground.

Station Place

87(89) (39)**55**
4-y-o b f Bahamian Bounty-Twin Time (Syrtos)
A B Haynes Dajam Ltd

Placings:0/0210-0050 **(7068)**
2009: 7^{0}GF, 7^{0}G, 7^{5}GF, 6^{0}SD,

	Starts	1st	2nd	3rd	Win & Pl
Career Total (Turf)	5	1	1	0	3094
Career Total (AW)	4	0	0	0	

55 7/08 Ling 7f FRM £2388
Total win prize-money £2388

Going (Turf): Sf: 0-0 GS: 0-0 Gd: 0-1 GF: 0-3 **Fm: 1-1**
Distance: 5f/6f: 0-1 **7f-8f: 1-8** 9f-13f: 0-0 14f+: 0-0
Track : LH: 0-4 RH: 0-0 Tight: 0-4 Gall: 0-0
Aids: Bl: 0-0 Vi: 0-0 Tstrap: 0-0 Ckp: 0-0
Best Rating: **55** 7/08 Ling 7f firm

Moderate; effective at 7f; acts on fast ground.

Statute Book (IRE)

99(100) (76)**72**
3-y-o br c Statue Of Liberty (USA)-Velvet Slipper (Muhtafal (USA))
S Kirk R J Brennan and D Boocock

Placings:042-1113040333060 **(6370)**
2009: 8^{1}SD, 8^{1}SD, 8^{1}SD, 8^{3}SD, 8^{0}SD, 8^{4}GS, 10^{0}G, 8^{3}SD, 8^{3}GF, 8^{3}SD, 8^{0}SD, 7^{6}SD, 8^{0}SD,

	Starts	1st	2nd	3rd	Win & Pl
Career Total (Turf)	3	0	0	1	770
Career Total (AW)	13	3	1	3	10836

76 3/09 Kemp 1m (0-85)H STD £4727
76 2/09 Ling 1m (0-60)H STD £2047
68 2/09 Sthl 1m (0-60)H STD £2047
Total win prize-money £8821

Going (Turf): **Sf: 0-0 GS: 0-1 Gd: 0-1 GF: 0-1 Fm: 0-0**
Distance: 5f/6f: 0-0 **7f-8f: 3-15** 9f-13f: 0-1 14f+: 0-0
Track : **LH: 2-7** RH: 1-7 **Tight: 1-5** Gall: 0-0
Aids: Bl: 0-0 Vi: 0-0 Tstrap: 0-0 Ckp: 0-0
Best Rating: **76** 8/09 Kemp 1m stand

Fair; effective over 7f-1m; acts on both All-Weather surfaces.

Stay On Track (IRE)

65 **7**
2-y-o b c Refuse To Bend (IRE)-Blue Lightning (Machiavellian (USA))
E F Vaughan Mohamed Obaida

Placings:0 **(2771)**
2009: 6^{0}GS,

	Starts	1st	2nd	3rd	Win & Pl
Career Total (Turf)	1	0	0	0	

Going (Turf): **Sf: 0-0 GS: 0-1 Gd: 0-0 GF: 0-0 Fm: 0-0**
Distance: 5f/6f: 0-1 7f-8f: 0-0 9f-13f: 0-0 14f+: 0-0
Track : LH: 0-0 RH: 0-0 Tight: 0-0 Gall: 0-1
Aids: Bl: 0-0 Vi: 0-0 Tstrap: 0-0 Ckp: 0-0
Best Rating: **7** 6/09 Wind 6f gd-sft

Staying On (IRE)

113 (84)**110**
4-y-o b g Invincible Spirit (IRE)-Lakatoi (Saddlers' Hall (IRE))
W R Swinburn M H Dixon

Placings:1/4112600-126256 **(5447)**

2009: 8^{1}GF, 10^{2}GF, 10^{6}G, 9^{2}S, 10^{5}G, 10^{6}GF,

	Starts	1st	2nd	3rd	Win & Pl
Career Total (Turf)	13	3	3	0	138560
Career Total (AW)	1	1	0	0	3465

109	4/09	Donc	1m		G-F	£23704
103	5/08	Hayd	1m30y	H	G-F	£62310
102	5/08	Wind	1m67y	(0-90)H	GD	£7771
84	10/07	Wolv	7f32y		STD	£3465

Total win prize-money £97250

Going (Turf): Sf: 0-1 GS: 0-1 Gd: 1-5 **GF: 2-6** Fm: 0-0
Distance: 5f/6f: 0-0 7f-8f: 2-3 9f-13f: 2-11 14f+: 0-0
Track : **LH: 3-7** RH: 1-5 **Tight: 2-4** Gall: 1-4
Aids: Bl: 0-0 Vi: 0-1 Tstrap: 0-0 Ckp: 0-0
Best Rating: **110** 7/09 Curr 1m1f soft

Smart; Listed winner; stays 1m2f but effective at shorter; acts on fast ground and Polytrack; has worn a tongue tie; suited by forcing tactics.

Steady Gaze

(91) (40)**28**

4-y-o b g Zamindar (USA)-Krisia (Kris)
M A Allen Miss Sarah Anne Phillips

Placings:000-000 **(1081)**
2009: 12^{0}SD, 9^{0}SD, 12^{0}SD,

	Starts	1st	2nd	3rd	Win & Pl
Career Total (Turf)	2	0	0	0	
Career Total (AW)	4	0	0	0	

Going (Turf): **Sf: 0-1 GS: 0-0 Gd: 0-0 GF: 0-1 Fm: 0-0**
Distance: 5f/6f: 0-0 7f-8f: 0-1 9f-13f: 0-5 14f+: 0-0
Track : LH: 0-5 RH: 0-1 Tight: 0-3 Gall: 0-1
Aids: Bl: 0-0 Vi: 0-0 Tstrap: 0-0 Ckp: 0-0
Best Rating: **40** 2/09 Wolv 1m1f103y stand

Steamer (IRE)

87 **32**

3-y-o b g Xaar-Antigone (IRE) (Cape Cross (IRE))
P Winkworth P Winkworth

Placings:000 **(3501)**
2009: 6^{0}F, 5^{0}GF, 8^{0}GF,

	Starts	1st	2nd	3rd	Win & Pl
Career Total (Turf)	3	0	0	0	

Going (Turf): **Sf: 0-0 GS: 0-0 Gd: 0-0 GF: 0-2 Fm: 0-1**
Distance: 5f/6f: 0-1 7f-8f: 0-1 9f-13f: 0-1 14f+: 0-0
Track : LH: 0-0 RH: 0-0 Tight: 0-0 Gall: 0-0
Aids: Bl: 0-0 Vi: 0-0 Tstrap: 0-0 Ckp: 0-0
Best Rating: **32** 5/09 Sals 6f212y firm

Steel Blue

97(99) (52)**75**

9-y-o b g Atraf-Something Blue (Petong)
R M Whitaker Country Lane Partnership

Placings:020210011/560405002200/1001253/0030000400 4010300/050641025000004/04000021000230/060062646 1104004-000060061245000 **(7418)**
2009: 6^{0}GF, 6^{0}HY, 6^{0}GS, 6^{0}GS, 6^{6}GF, 6^{0}G, 5^{0}GF, 6^{6}GF, 5^{1}S, 6^{2}G, 6^{4}S, 7^{5}GF, 6^{0}GF, 5^{0}SD, 6^{0}SD,

	Starts	1st	2nd	3rd	Win & Pl
Career Total (Turf)	94	10	10	4	98796
Career Total (AW)	12	1	0	0	10223

58	8/09	Haml	5f4y		SFT	£2388
75	8/08	Thsk	6f	(0-85)H	G-S	£5634
74	7/08	Donc	6f	(0-70)H	G-F	£3412
79	8/07	Thsk	6f	(0-85)H	G-F	£5181
87	7/06	Epsm	6f	(0-95)H	GD	£8096
91	10/05	Epsm	7f	(0-80)	SFT	£6890
94	5/04	Ripn	6f	C(0-95)H	G-F	£9100
89	3/04	Donc	6f	C(0-90)H	GD	£9946
	12/02	Ndas	6f		FST	£9346
93	10/02	NmkR	6f	C(0-95)	G-S	£7871
88	8/02	NmkJ	5f	B	G-F	£10894

Total win prize-money £78760

Going (Turf): Sf: 2-16GS: 2-20Gd: 2-27 **GF: 4-30** Fm: 0-1
Distance: **5f/6f: 10-91** 7f-8f: 1-15 9f-13f: 0-0 14f+: 0-0
Track : **LH: 2-19** RH: 0-1 **Tight: 2-10** Gall: 0-0
Aids: Bl: 0-0 Vi: 0-2 Tstrap: 3-23 Ckp: 3-23
Best Rating: **99** 6/04 Newc 5f soft

Moderate; effective at up to 7f; suited by a sound surface, but acts on softer; has worn cheekpieces; likes to race prominently.

Steel City Boy (IRE)

86(105) (76)**75**

6-y-o b g Bold Fact (USA)-Balgren (IRE) (Ballad Rock)
D Shaw J Medley

Placings:0/05135/1006002500/30433000501260040340602450-445150000000 **(7807)**
2009: 5^{4}SD, 5^{4}SD, 5^{5}SD, 5^{1}SD, 5^{5}SD, 5^{0}SD, 5^{0}SD, 5^{0}SD, 5^{0}G, 6^{0}SD, 5^{0}SD, 5^{0}SD,

	Starts	1st	2nd	3rd	Win & Pl
Career Total (Turf)	28	1	2	3	8940
Career Total (AW)	26	3	1	2	13207

76	2/09	Kemp	5f	(0-70)H	STD	£2590
72	7/08	Wwck	6f	(0-85)H	SFT	£4984
82	5/07	Sthl	5f	(0-75)H	STD	£3562
73	6/06	Wolv	5f20y	(0-70)H	STD	£3238

Total win prize-money £14376

Going (Turf): **Sf: 1-9** GS: 0-1 Gd: 0-11 GF: 0-7 Fm: 0-0
Distance: **5f/6f: 4-51** 7f-8f: 0-3 9f-13f: 0-0 14f+: 0-0
Track : **LH: 2-22** RH: 1-4 **Tight: 1-13** Gall: 0-2
Aids: Bl: 0-0 Vi: 0-0 Tstrap: 0-1 Ckp: 0-1
Best Rating: **82** 5/07 Sthl 5f stand

Modest; suited by 5f-6f; goes on soft going and on sand.

Steel Free (IRE)

103(95) (67)**76**

3-y-o b f Danehill Dancer (IRE)-Candelabra (Grand Lodge (USA))
M L W Bell Recycled Products Limited

Placings:23106645 **(6997)**
2009: 7^{2}GS, 5^{3}G, 7^{1}GF, 7^{0}G, 7^{6}SD, 7^{6}GS, 7^{4}G, 7^{5}G,

	Starts	1st	2nd	3rd	Win & Pl
Career Total (Turf)	7	1	1	1	5178
Career Total (AW)	1	0	0	0	0

76	7/09	Wwck	7f26y	G-F	£2914

Total win prize-money £2914

Going (Turf): Sf: 0-0 GS: 0-2 Gd: 0-4 **GF: 1-1** Fm: 0-0
Distance: 5f/6f: 0-1 **7f-8f: 1-7** 9f-13f: 0-0 14f+: 0-0
Track : **LH: 1-3** RH: 0-1 Tight: 0-1 Gall: 0-0
Aids: Bl: 0-0 Vi: 0-0 Tstrap: 0-0 Ckp: 0-0
Best Rating: **76** 7/09 Wwck 7f26y gd-fm

Fair; stays 7f; acts on easy ground.

Steel Giant (USA)

79 **44**

4-y-o b g Giant's Causeway (USA)-Ride The Wind (USA) (Meadowlake (USA))
J J Lambe Mrs Rita Lee/Ian L Davies

Placings:000 **(4599)**
2009: 10^{0}GF, 12^{0}G, 12^{0}G,

	Starts	1st	2nd	3rd	Win & Pl
Career Total (Turf)	3	0	0	0	

Going (Turf): **Sf: 0-0 GS: 0-0 Gd: 0-2 GF: 0-1 Fm: 0-0**
Distance: 5f/6f: 0-0 7f-8f: 0-0 9f-13f: 0-3 14f+: 0-0
Track : LH: 0-1 RH: 0-2 Tight: 0-1 Gall: 0-0
Aids: Bl: 0-0 Vi: 0-0 Tstrap: 0-0 Ckp: 0-0
Best Rating: **44** 7/09 Fair 1m4f good

Steel Mask (IRE)

(88) (37)**47**

4-y-o b c Iron Mask (USA)-Thorn Tree (Zafonic (USA))
M Brittain Mel Brittain

Placings:3000-0 **(7709)**
2009: 5^{0}SD,

	Starts	1st	2nd	3rd	Win & Pl
Career Total (Turf)	3	0	0	1	385
Career Total (AW)	2	0	0	0	

Going (Turf): **Sf: 0-0 GS: 0-0 Gd: 0-2 GF: 0-1 Fm: 0-0**
Distance: 5f/6f: 0-5 7f-8f: 0-0 9f-13f: 0-0 14f+: 0-0
Track : LH: 0-0 RH: 0-0 Tight: 0-0 Gall: 0-0
Aids: Bl: 0-0 Vi: 0-0 Tstrap: 0-0 Ckp: 0-0
Best Rating: **47** 4/08 Yarm 5f43y good

Steel My Heart (IRE)

89(84) (44)**45**

2-y-o b f Clodovil (IRE)-Antigonel (IRE) (Fairy King (USA))
Miss D Mountain Miss Debbie Mountain

Placings:04650 **(5583)**
2009: 6^{0}GF, 6^{4}G, 7^{6}GS, 7^{5}GF, 6^{0}SD,

	Starts	1st	2nd	3rd	Win & Pl
Career Total (Turf)	4	0	0	0	144
Career Total (AW)	1	0	0	0	

Going (Turf): **Sf: 0-0 GS: 0-1 Gd: 0-1 GF: 0-2 Fm: 0-0**
Distance: 5f/6f: 0-1 7f-8f: 0-4 9f-13f: 0-0 14f+: 0-0
Track : LH: 0-2 RH: 0-0 Tight: 0-2 Gall: 0-0
Aids: Bl: 0-0 Vi: 0-1 Tstrap: 0-0 Ckp: 0-0
Best Rating: **45** 8/09 NmkJ 7f gd-sft

Steel Stockholder

100(96) (52)**70**

3-y-o b c Mark Of Esteem (IRE)-Pompey Blue (Abou Zouz (USA))
M Brittain Mel Brittain

Placings:4544-366405440422210 **(7729)**
2009: 6^{3}GF, 7^{6}GF, 6^{6}GS, 8^{4}G, 8^{0}GF, 6^{5}G, 7^{4}G, 8^{4}G, 8^{0}GS, 8^{4}G, 8^{2}GF, 7^{2}S, 7^{2}GF, 7^{1}G, 7^{0}SD,

	Starts	1st	2nd	3rd	Win & Pl
Career Total (Turf)	18	1	3	1	11523
Career Total (AW)	1	0	0	0	

70	10/09	Donc	7f	(0-75)H	GD	£5180

Total win prize-money £5181

Going (Turf): Sf: 0-1 GS: 0-3 **Gd: 1-8** GF: 0-6 Fm: 0-0
Distance: 5f/6f: 0-7 **7f-8f: 1-12** 9f-13f: 0-0 14f+: 0-0

Track : LH: 0-9 RH: 0-1 Tight: 0-8 Gall: 0-2
Aids: Bl: 0-0 Vi: 0-0 Tstrap: 0-0 Ckp: 0-0
Best Rating: 70 10/09 Donc 7f good

Modest; stays 6f and acts on fast ground.

Steel Trade

102 **75**

3-y-o b g Sakhee (USA)-Hammiya (IRE) (Darshaan)
M Brittain Mel Brittain

Placings:65203403634 **(6182)**
2009: 8^{6}GF, 7^{5}GF, 7^{2}GF, 8^{0}G, 8^{3}GF, 8^{4}G, 10^{0}C, 8^{3}CF, 9^{6}C, 9^{3}GF, 8^{4}GF,

	Starts	1st	2nd	3rd	Win & Pl
Career Total (Turf)	11	0	1	3	2687

Going (Turf): Sf: 0-0 GS: 0-0 Gd: 0-4 GF: 0-7 Fm: 0-0
Distance: 5f/6f: 0-0 7f-8f: 0-5 9f-13f: 0-6 14f+: 0-0
Track : LH: 0-3 RH: 0-7 Tight: 0-4 Gall: 0-2
Aids: Bl: 0-0 Vi: 0-0 Tstrap: 0-0 Ckp: 0-0
Best Rating: 75 5/09 Bevl 7f100y gd-fm

Modest; stays 1m; acts on a sound surface.

Steelcut

105(103) (74)**85**

5-y-o b g Iron Mask (USA)-Apple Sauce (Prince Sabo)
M J Scudamore (Andrew Reid 24/10) A S Reid

Placings:313/30005003/00610002263-315305404042031**300** **(7758)**
2009: 5^{3}GF, 5^{1}GF, 5^{5}G, 5^{3}G, 5^{0}G, 5^{5}GS, 5^{4}GF, 5^{0}GF, 5^{4}S, 5^{0}GS, 5^{4}GS, 5^{2}GS, 5^{0}GF, 5^{3}G, 6^{1}SD, 6^{3}GF, 5^{0}SS, 5^{0}SD,

	Starts	1st	2nd	3rd	Win & Pl
Career Total (Turf)	38	3	3	9	24301
Career Total (AW)	3	1	0	0	2590

74	9/09	Kemp	6f	(0-70)	STD	£2590
85	4/09	Thsk	5f	(0-80)H	G-F	£5569
82	5/08	Haml	5f4y	(0-75)H	G-F	£3238
84	5/06	Rdcr	5f		GD	£3238

Total win prize-money £14636

Going (Turf): Sf: 0-2 GS: 0-6 Gd: 1-14 **GF: 2-15** Fm: 0-1
Distance: **5f/6f: 4-41** 7f-8f: 0-0 9f-13f: 0-0 14f+: 0-0
Track : LH: 0-3 **RH: 1-3** Tight: 0-2 Gall: 0-1
Aids: Bl: 0-1 Vi: 0-1 Tstrap: 0-1 Ckp: 0-1
Best Rating: 90 4/07 Thsk 5f firm

Fair; effective over 5f-6f and acts on a sound surface and Polytrack; has worn cheekpieces.

Steele Tango (USA)

112(94) (78)**113**

4-y-o ch c Okawango (USA)-Waltzing Around (IRE) (Ela-Mana-Mou)
R A Teal The Thirty Acre Racing Partnership

Placings:46/121252-24300501 **(6812)**
2009: 9^{2}GF, 10^{4}G, 12^{3}GF, 10^{0}G, 12^{0}GF, 10^{5}G, 12^{0}G, 9^{1}G,

	Starts	1st	2nd	3rd	Win & Pl
Career Total (Turf)	13	2	4	1	104752
Career Total (AW)	3	1	0	0	2824

113	10/09	NmkR	1m1f		GD	£36900
93	6/08	Sand	1m1f	(0-90)H	GD	£7771
78	1/08	Kemp	7f		STD	£2590

Total win prize-money £47263

Going (Turf): Sf: 0-0 GS: 0-3 **Gd: 2-6** GF: 0-4 Fm: 0-0
Distance: 5f/6f: 0-1 7f-8f: 1-2 **9f-13f: 2-13** 14f+: 0-0
Track : LH: 0-2 **RH: 2-12** Tight: 0-3 Gall: 0-4
Aids: Bl: 0-0 Vi: 0-0 Tstrap: 0-0 Ckp: 0-0
Best Rating: 113 10/09 NmkR 1m1f good

Group class; Group 3 winner; effective at 1m-1m2f; acts on fast and easy ground; goes on Polytrack.

Steeley Flyer

82(71) (18)**42**

2-y-o b f Needwood Blade-Gymcrak Flyer (Aragon)
P D Evans D Maloney

Placings:00250 **(4747)**
2009: 5^{0}GF, 6^{0}GF, 6^{2}GF, 7^{5}S, 6^{0}SD,

	Starts	1st	2nd	3rd	Win & Pl
Career Total (Turf)	4	0	1	0	578
Career Total (AW)	1	0	0	0	

Going (Turf): Sf: 0-1 GS: 0-0 Gd: 0-0 GF: 0-3 Fm: 0-0
Distance: 5f/6f: 0-3 7f-8f: 0-2 9f-13f: 0-0 14f+: 0-0
Track : LH: 0-1 RH: 0-1 Tight: 0-1 Gall: 0-1
Aids: Bl: 0-0 Vi: 0-0 Tstrap: 0-0 Ckp: 0-0
Best Rating: 42 7/09 Yarm 7f3y soft

Steely Bird

81 **60**

2-y-o gr g Needwood Blade-La Cygne Blanche (IRE) (Saddlers' Hall (IRE))
Miss Jo Crowley Mrs Liz Nelson

Placings:00 **(6931)**
2009: 8^{0}GF, 8^{0}G,

	Starts	1st	2nd	3rd	Win & Pl
Career Total (Turf)	2	0	0	0	

Going (Turf): Sf: 0-0 GS: 0-0 Gd: 0-1 GF: 0-1 Fm: 0-0
Distance: 5f/6f: 0-0 7f-8f: 0-1 9f-13f: 0-1 14f+: 0-0
Track : LH: 0-1 RH: 0-0 Tight: 0-1 Gall: 0-0
Aids: Bl: 0-0 Vi: 0-0 Tstrap: 0-0 Ckp: 0-0
Best Rating: 60 9/09 Sals 1m gd-fm

Steeple Caster

66

3-y-o ch g Compton Place-Antonia's Double (Primo Dominie)
J M Bradley J M Bradley

Placings:00 **(2122)**
2009: 5^{0}GF, 5^{0}GS,

	Starts	1st	2nd	3rd	Win & Pl
Career Total (Turf)	2	0	0	0	

Going (Turf): Sf: 0-0 GS: 0-1 Gd: 0-0 GF: 0-1 Fm: 0-0
Distance: 5f/6f: 0-2 7f-8f: 0-0 9f-13f: 0-0 14f+: 0-0
Track : LH: 0-2 RH: 0-0 Tight: 0-0 Gall: 0-2
Aids: Bl: 0-0 Vi: 0-0 Tstrap: 0-0 Ckp: 0-0

Stef And Stelio

77(93) (74)**42**

2-y-o ch g Bertolini (USA)-Cashmere (Barathea (IRE))
G A Butler Stef Stefanou

Placings:0030120 **(7320)**
2009: 6^{0}GF, 5^{0}G, 6^{3}SD, 6^{0}GF, 7^{1}SD, 7^{2}SD, 7^{0}SD,

	Starts	1st	2nd	3rd	Win & Pl
Career Total (Turf)	3	0	0	0	1230
Career Total (AW)	4	1	1	1	4945

74	9/09	Wolv	7f32y	STD	£2729

Total win prize-money £2730

Going (Turf): Sf: 0-0 GS: 0-0 Gd: 0-1 GF: 0-2 Fm: 0-0
Distance: 5f/6f: 0-4 **7f-8f: 1-3** 9f-13f: 0-0 14f+: 0-0
Track : **LH: 1-4** RH: 0-1 **Tight: 1-2** Gall: 0-0
Aids: **Bl: 1-3** Vi: 0-0 Tstrap: 0-0 Ckp: 0-0
Best Rating: 74 9/09 Wolv 7f32y stand

Fair; suited by 7f and acts on Polytrack; has worn blinkers.

Stefanki (IRE)

80(87) (54)**75**

2-y-o b g Danehill Dancer (IRE)-Ghana (IRE) (Lahib (USA))
R Curtis Mrs Joanna Hughes

Placings:200 **(7580)**
2009: 6^{2}G, 7^{0}G, 7^{0}SF,

	Starts	1st	2nd	3rd	Win & Pl
Career Total (Turf)	2	0	1	0	1542
Career Total (AW)	1	0	0	0	

Going (Turf): Sf: 0-0 GS: 0-0 Gd: 0-2 GF: 0-0 Fm: 0-0
Distance: 5f/6f: 0-1 7f-8f: 0-2 9f-13f: 0-0 14f+: 0-0
Track : LH: 0-1 RH: 0-0 Tight: 0-1 Gall: 0-0
Aids: Bl: 0-0 Vi: 0-0 Tstrap: 0-0 Ckp: 0-0
Best Rating: 75 9/09 Ffos 6f good

Fair; stays 6f and acts on good ground.

Steig (IRE)

98(107) (74)**88**

6-y-o b g Xaar-Ring Of Kerry (IRE) (Kenmare (FR))
C Moore (George Baker 23/6) D J Dolan

Placings:52/32/**2**/**13234256**103210-2633122113000 **(6468a)**
2009: 8^{2}SD, 8^{6}G, 8^{3}GF, 7^{3}G, 7^{1}G, 9^{2}GF, 8^{2}YS, 9^{1}YS, 8^{1}S, 8^{3}SH, 8^{0}HY, 8^{0}S, 10^{0}SD,

	Starts	1st	2nd	3rd	Win & Pl
Career Total (Turf)	20	5	4	5	29290
Career Total (AW)	12	1	5	2	6881

88	7/09	Gway	1m100y	(50-70)H	SFT	£8385
77	7/09	Baln	1m1f	(50-70)H	Y-S	£6037
67	6/09	Brig	7f214y		GD	£1942
63	8/08	Brig	7f214y		GD	£2072
74	4/08	Brig	7f214y	(0-70)H	G-S	£2590
60	1/08	Wolv	1m4f50y		STD	£2457

Total win prize-money £23486

Going (Turf): Sf: 1-3 GS: 1-2 **Gd: 2-6** GF: 0-4 Fm: 0-1
Distance: 5f/6f: 0-2 7f-8f: 3-12 9f-13f: 3-18 14f+: 0-0
Track : **LH: 4-21** RH: 2-10 **Tight: 1-9** Gall: 0-2
Aids: Bl: 0-0 Vi: 0-0 Tstrap: 0-0 Ckp: 0-0
Best Rating: 88 7/09 Gway 1m100y soft

Modest; effective at around 1m-1m4f; acts on easy ground; also goes on Polytrack.

Steinbeck (IRE)

111 **116**

2-y-o b c Footstepsinthesand-Castara Beach (IRE) (Danehill (USA))
A P O'Brien M Tabor, D Smith & Mrs John Magnier

Placings:14 **(6849)**
2009: 6^{1}GY, 7^{4}G,

	Starts	1st	2nd	3rd	Win & Pl
Career Total (Turf)	2	1	0	0	28782

99	5/09	Naas	6f	G-Y	£11740

Total win prize-money £11740

Going (Turf): Sf: 0-0 GS: 0-0 Gd: 0-1 GF: 0-0 Fm: 0-0
Distance: 5f/6f: 1-1 7f-8f: 0-1 9f-13f: 0-0 14f+: 0-0
Track : LH: 1-1 RH: 0-0 Tight: 0-0 Gall: 0-0
Aids: Bl: 0-0 Vi: 0-0 Tstrap: 0-0 Ckp: 0-0
Best Rating: 116 10/09 NmkR 7f good

Group-class colt; winning debut over 6f on easy ground; fourth in the Dewhurst following an absence.

Stellar Cause (USA)

97 71

3-y-o ch g Giant's Causeway (USA)-Stellar (USA) (Grand Slam (USA))
R Curtis (P F I Cole 25/9) R P Behan

Placings:50406 **(6248)**
2009: 10^{5}S, 10^{0}GF, 8^{4}G, 8^{0}GF, 10^{6}GF,

	Starts	1st	2nd	3rd	Win & Pl
Career Total (Turf)	5	0	0	0	202

Going (Turf): Sf: 0-1 GS: 0-0 Gd: 0-1 GF: 0-3 Fm: 0-0
Distance: 5f/6f: 0-0 7f-8f: 0-0 9f-13f: 0-5 14f+: 0-0
Track : LH: 0-2 RH: 0-2 Tight: 0-1 Gall: 0-1
Aids: Bl: 0-0 Vi: 0-0 Tstrap: 0-0 Ckp: 0-0
Best Rating: 71 5/09 Newb 1m2f6y soft

Stellarina (IRE)

95(93) (68)65

3-y-o b f Night Shift (USA)-Accelerating (USA) (Lear Fan (USA))
G A Swinbank S Rudolf

Placings:053-030 **(2769)**
2009: 6^{0}GF, 7^{3}GF, 6^{0}G,

	Starts	1st	2nd	3rd	Win & Pl
Career Total (Turf)	5	0	0	1	482
Career Total (AW)	1	0	0	1	607

Going (Turf): Sf: 0-0 GS: 0-1 Gd: 0-1 GF: 0-3 Fm: 0-0
Distance: 5f/6f: 0-3 7f-8f: 0-3 9f-13f: 0-0 14f+: 0-0
Track : LH: 0-5 RH: 0-0 Tight: 0-2 Gall: 0-0
Aids: Bl: 0-0 Vi: 0-0 Tstrap: 0-0 Ckp: 0-0
Best Rating: 68 10/08 Ling 7f stand

Fair; stays 7f and acts on Polytrack.

Stellino (GER)

102 79

6-y-o b g Monashee Mountain (USA)-Sweet Tern (GER) (Arctic Tern (USA))
James Moffatt (N J Henderson 18/5) V R Vyner-Brooks

Placings:51522012/6640421/0-0 **(6100)**
2009: 11^{0}GF,

	Starts	1st	2nd	3rd	Win & Pl
Career Total (Turf)	17	3	4	0	24426

9/07	Frnk	1m2f	H	GD	£3378
9/06	Dres	1m2f		GD	£4068
5/06	Frnk	1m2f		GD	£2068

Total win prize-money £9516

Going (Turf): Sf: 0-4 GS: 0-0 Gd: 3-12 GF: 0-1 Fm: 0-0
Distance: 5f/6f: 0-0 7f-8f: 0-2 9f-13f: 3-15 14f+: 0-0
Track : LH: 0-5 RH: 0-0 Tight: 0-2 Gall: 0-0
Aids: Bl: 0-0 Vi: 0-0 Tstrap: 0-0 Ckp: 0-0
Best Rating: 82 8/06 Hanv 1m2f good

Stellite

105 (71)77

9-y-o ch g Pivotal-Donation (Generous (IRE))
J S Goldie M Mackay, S Bruce, J S Goldie

Placings:0050/01000210/23244350212/134264210460/000350000/11256-6101624220423 **(7171)**
2009: 7^{6}GS, 7^{1}GF, 7^{0}GF, 7^{1}G, 8^{6}G, 6^{2}G, 6^{4}GF, 7^{2}G, 8^{2}S, 7^{0}G, 7^{4}GF, 7^{2}G, 7^{3}S,

	Starts	1st	2nd	3rd	Win & Pl
Career Total (Turf)	52	8	9	4	45018
Career Total (AW)	10	1	3	1	3677

74	6/09	Ayr	7f50y	(0-85)H	GD	£7123
70	5/09	Muss	7f30y	(0-70)H	G-F	£3238
73	5/08	Muss	7f30y	(0-70)H	G-F	£2914
68	5/08	Muss	7f30y	(0-65)H	G-S	£2266
81	8/06	Newc	7f	(0-80)H	SFT	£5505
75	4/06	Thsk	7f	(0-70)H	G-S	£3886
69	9/05	Ayr	7f50y	(0-55)H	SFT	£3388
56	12/04	Sthl	7f	(0-45)	STD	£1470
49	4/04	Ayr	7f50y	H(0-45)	GD	£1624

Total win prize-money £31416

Going (Turf): Sf: 2-12 GS: 2-11 Gd: 2-16 GF: 2-13 Fm: 0-0
Distance: 5f/6f: 0-14 7f-8f: 9-41 9f-13f: 0-7 14f+: 0-0
Track : LH: 5-30 RH: 3-15 Tight: 4-22 Gall: 0-2
Aids: Bl: 0-0 Vi: 0-0 Tstrap: 0-0 Ckp: 0-0
Best Rating: 81 9/06 Muss 7f30y soft

Fair; effective over 7f-1m; acts on most ground and on Fibresand.

Step At A Time (IRE)

67 4

3-y-o ch f Danehill Dancer (IRE)-Zing Ping (IRE) (Thatching)
M Johnston S R Counsell

Placings:0 **(3703)**
2009: 10^{0}GS,

	Starts	1st	2nd	3rd	Win & Pl
Career Total (Turf)	1	0	0	0	

Going (Turf): Sf: 0-0 GS: 0-1 Gd: 0-0 GF: 0-0 Fm: 0-0
Distance: 5f/6f: 0-0 7f-8f: 0-0 9f-13f: 0-1 14f+: 0-0
Track : LH: 0-1 RH: 0-0 Tight: 0-0 Gall: 0-0
Aids: Bl: 0-0 Vi: 0-0 Tstrap: 0-0 Ckp: 0-0
Best Rating: 4 7/09 Pont 1m2f6y gd-sft

Danehill Dancer half-sister to three winners including Fear And Greed.

Step Fast (USA)

89(77) (37)44

3-y-o ch f Giant's Causeway (USA)-Nannerl (USA) (Valid Appeal (USA))
M Johnston S R Counsell

Placings:000-040 **(3482)**
2009: 12^{0}GF, 11^{4}GF, 12^{0}GF,

	Starts	1st	2nd	3rd	Win & Pl
Career Total (Turf)	4	0	0	0	0
Career Total (AW)	2	0	0	0	

Going (Turf): Sf: 0-0 GS: 0-0 Gd: 0-0 GF: 0-4 Fm: 0-0
Distance: 5f/6f: 0-0 7f-8f: 0-1 9f-13f: 0-5 14f+: 0-0
Track : LH: 0-2 RH: 0-4 Tight: 0-4 Gall: 0-0
Aids: Bl: 0-1 Vi: 0-0 Tstrap: 0-0 Ckp: 0-0
Best Rating: 44 9/08 Hayd 1m30y gd-fm

Step In Time (IRE)

97 83

2-y-o b c Giant's Causeway (USA)-Cash Run (USA) (Seeking The Gold (USA))
M Johnston S R Counsell

Placings:2102000 **(6317a)**
2009: 6^{2}G, 6^{1}GF, 7^{0}GF, 6^{2}GF, 6^{0}GF, 6^{0}GF, 6^{0}G,

	Starts	1st	2nd	3rd	Win & Pl
Career Total (Turf)	7	1	2	0	7975

75	5/09	NmkR	6f	G-F	£5180

Total win prize-money £5181

Going (Turf): Sf: 0-0 GS: 0-0 Gd: 0-2 GF: 1-5 Fm: 0-0
Distance: 5f/6f: 1-5 7f-8f: 0-2 9f-13f: 0-0 14f+: 0-0
Track : LH: 0-0 RH: 0-0 Tight: 0-0 Gall: 0-0
Aids: Bl: 0-0 Vi: 0-0 Tstrap: 0-0 Ckp: 0-0
Best Rating: 83 7/09 Asct 6f gd-fm

Useful; stays 6f; acts on fast ground.

Step Into Sunshine (USA)

80 34

3-y-o b f The Cliff's Edge (USA)-Iridescence (USA) (Mt. Livermore (USA))
M Johnston Jim McGrath

Placings:006 **(5348)**
2009: 8^{0}G, 8^{0}GF, 8^{6}G,

	Starts	1st	2nd	3rd	Win & Pl
Career Total (Turf)	3	0	0	0	0

Going (Turf): Sf: 0-0 GS: 0-0 Gd: 0-2 GF: 0-1 Fm: 0-0
Distance: 5f/6f: 0-0 7f-8f: 0-1 9f-13f: 0-2 14f+: 0-0
Track : LH: 0-3 RH: 0-0 Tight: 0-1 Gall: 0-0
Aids: Bl: 0-0 Vi: 0-0 Tstrap: 0-0 Ckp: 0-0
Best Rating: 34 7/09 Thsk 1m good

Step It Up (IRE)

104(105) (83)77

5-y-o ch g Daggers Drawn (USA)-Leitrim Lodge (IRE) (Classic Music (USA))
J R Boyle The Vine Associates

Placings:05/200/001020006450160-422233636021102413 **(6972)**
2009: 6^{4}SD, 6^{2}SD, 5^{2}SD, 5^{2}SD, 5^{3}SD, 5^{3}G, 6^{6}GF, 5^{3}GF, 5^{6}G, 5^{0}GF, 5^{2}G, 5^{1}GF, 5^{1}GF, 6^{0}GF, 5^{2}GF, 5^{4}GS, 5^{1}SD, 5^{3}SD,

	Starts	1st	2nd	3rd	Win & Pl
Career Total (Turf)	21	2	3	2	12082
Career Total (AW)	17	3	4	2	15925

83	10/09	Ling	5f	(0-75)H	STD	£3412
76	8/09	Sand	5f6y	(0-75)H	G-F	£3238
67	8/09	Folk	5f	(0-75)H	G-F	£3070
73	11/08	Ling	5f	(0-70)H	STD	£2729
68	4/08	Dund	5f	(50-75)H	STD	£5334

Total win prize-money £17786

Going (Turf): Sf: 0-1 GS: 0-1 Gd: 0-5 GF: 2-8 Fm: 0-4
Distance: 5f/6f: 5-37 7f-8f: 0-1 9f-13f: 0-0 14f+: 0-0
Track : LH: 3-18 RH: 0-6 Tight: 2-5 Gall: 0-3
Aids: Bl: 0-0 Vi: 0-0 Tstrap: 0-0 Ckp: 0-0
Best Rating: 83 10/09 Ling 5f stand

Fair; suited by 5f; acts on fast ground; goes on Polytrack.

Step This Way (USA)

104 (83)**92**

4-y-o ch f Giant's Causeway (USA)-Lady In Waiting (USA) (Woodman (USA))

M Johnston S R Counsell

Placings:0512/061050-4435220300 **(5235)**

2009: 13^{4}GF, 14^{4}GF, 12^{3}GF, 14^{5}F, 14^{2}GF, 14^{2}GF, 16^{0}GS, 11^{3}F, 12^{0}GF, 16^{0}GF,

	Starts	1st	2nd	3rd	Win & Pl
Career Total (Turf)	18	1	2	2	20231
Career Total (AW)	2	1	1	0	4896

92	6/08	York	1m4f	(0-95)H	GD	£12492
79	9/07	Wolv	1m141y		STD	£2968

Total win prize-money £15461

Going (Turf): Sf: 0-1 GS: 0-2 **Gd: 1-2** GF: 0-11 Fm: 0-2
Distance: 5f/6f: 0-0 7f-8f: 0-2 **9f-13f: 2-10** 14f+: 0-8
Track : **LH: 2-11** RH: 0-6 Tight: 1-9 Gall: 1-6
Aids: Bl: 0-0 Vi: 0-0 Tstrap: 0-0 Ckp: 0-0
Best Rating: **92** 6/08 York 1m4f good

Useful; effective at 1m4f-1m6f; acts on good ground and on Polytrack; likes to race prominently.

Step To It (IRE)

70 **23**

2-y-o b g Footstepsinthesand-Lilly Gee (IRE) (Ashkalani (IRE))

K A Ryan D W Barker

Placings:000 **(5942)**

2009: 6^{0}GS, 6^{0}G, 7^{0}G,

	Starts	1st	2nd	3rd	Win & Pl
Career Total (Turf)	3	0	0	0	

Going (Turf): **Sf: 0-0 GS: 0-1 Gd: 0-2 GF: 0-0 Fm: 0-0**
Distance: 5f/6f: 0-2 7f-8f: 0-1 9f-13f: 0-0 14f+: 0-0
Track : LH: 0-0 RH: 0-1 Tight: 0-1 Gall: 0-0
Aids: Bl: 0-0 Vi: 0-0 Tstrap: 0-0 Ckp: 0-0
Best Rating: **23** 8/09 Ripn 6f good

Sterling Moll

88 (37)**46**

6-y-o gr m Lord Of Men-Princess Maud (USA) (Irish River (FR))

W De Best-Turner De Best racing

Placings:060/**0000500**/0 **(3143)**

2009: 21^{0}GF,

	Starts	1st	2nd	3rd	Win & Pl
Career Total (Turf)	7	0	0	0	0
Career Total (AW)	4	0	0	0	0

Going (Turf): **Sf: 0-1 GS: 0-1 Gd: 0-1 GF: 0-4 Fm: 0-0**
Distance: 5f/6f: 0-0 7f-8f: 0-0 9f-13f: 0-7 14f+: 0-4
Track : LH: 0-7 RH: 0-4 Tight: 0-5 Gall: 0-4
Aids: Bl: 0-0 Vi: 0-0 Tstrap: 0-0 Ckp: 0-0
Best Rating: **50** 8/06 Newb 1m4f5y gd-fm

Sterling Sound (USA)

106(93) (66)**94**

3-y-o b f Street Cry (IRE)-Lady In Silver (USA) (Silver Hawk (USA))

M P Tregoning Miss K Rausing

Placings:24234-33130 **(5472)**

2009: 8^{3}GF, 8^{3}GF, 8^{1}GF, 9^{3}GF, 9^{0}GF,

	Starts	1st	2nd	3rd	Win & Pl
Career Total (Turf)	9	1	1	4	17339
Career Total (AW)	1	0	1	0	1060

87	7/09	Asct	1m	G-F	£7123

Total win prize-money £7124

Going (Turf): Sf: 0-0 GS: 0-1 Gd: 0-0 **GF: 1-8** Fm: 0-0
Distance: 5f/6f: 0-4 **7f-8f: 1-3** 9f-13f: 0-3 14f+: 0-0
Track : LH: 0-2 RH: 0-4 Tight: 0-4 Gall: 0-1
Aids: Bl: 0-0 Vi: 0-0 Tstrap: 0-0 Ckp: 0-0
Best Rating: **94** 8/09 Sals 1m1f198y gd-fm

Fair; effective over 1m-1m2f; acts on fast ground; also goes on Polytrack.

Sternian

(76) (26)

2-y-o ch f Where Or When (IRE)-Fly In Style (Hernando (FR))

M E Rimmer Clive Dennett

Placings:6 **(7865)**

2009: 8^{6}SS,

	Starts	1st	2nd	3rd	Win & Pl
Career Total (Turf)	0	0	0	0	
Career Total (AW)	1	0	0	0	0

Going (Turf): **Sf: 0-0 GS: 0-0 Gd: 0-0 GF: 0-0 Fm: 0-0**
Distance: 5f/6f: 0-0 7f-8f: 0-1 9f-13f: 0-0 14f+: 0-0
Track : LH: 0-1 RH: 0-0 Tight: 0-0 Gall: 0-0
Aids: Bl: 0-0 Vi: 0-0 Tstrap: 0-0 Ckp: 0-0
Best Rating: **26** 12/09 Sthl 1m std-slw

Sternlight (IRE)

88 **70**

2-y-o b c Kheleyf (USA)-Sail By Night (USA) (Nureyev (USA))

E S McMahon J C Fretwell

Placings:043 **(6364)**

2009: 6^{0}GF, 7^{4}GF, 7^{3}GF,

	Starts	1st	2nd	3rd	Win & Pl
Career Total (Turf)	3	0	0	1	907

Going (Turf): **Sf: 0-0 GS: 0-0 Gd: 0-0 GF: 0-3 Fm: 0-0**
Distance: 5f/6f: 0-1 7f-8f: 0-2 9f-13f: 0-0 14f+: 0-0
Track : LH: 0-1 RH: 0-0 Tight: 0-0 Gall: 0-1
Aids: Bl: 0-0 Vi: 0-0 Tstrap: 0-0 Ckp: 0-0
Best Rating: **70** 9/09 Yarm 7f3y gd-fm

Fair; stays 7f; acts on fast ground.

Stevie Gee (IRE)

106(102) (77)**96**

5-y-o b g Invincible Spirit (IRE)-Margaree Mary (CAN) (Seeking The Gold (USA))

Ian Williams (G A Swinbank 3/8) Steve Gray

Placings:051110/06/**65**013523605000-000201500000 **(7252)**

2009: 7^{0}SD, 6^{0}GF, 7^{0}G, 7^{2}GF, 6^{0}GF, 7^{1}GF, 7^{5}G, 7^{0}GS, 9^{0}G, 8^{0}S, 8^{0}GF, 7^{0}SD,

	Starts	1st	2nd	3rd	Win & Pl
Career Total (Turf)	27	4	2	2	61617
Career Total (AW)	7	1	0	0	3886

92	6/09	Carl	7f200y	(0-80)H	G-F	£19428
93	4/08	Donc	7f	(0-80)H	SFT	£5180
100	8/06	Ripn	6f		SFT	£17115
92	8/06	Rdcr	6f		G-F	£9715
80	7/06	Sthl	5f		STD	£3886

Total win prize-money £55326

Going (Turf): **Sf: 2-7** GS: 0-3 Gd: 0-7 **GF: 2-10** Fm: 0-0
Distance: **5f/6f: 3-14** 7f-8f: 2-17 9f-13f: 0-3 14f+: 0-0
Track : LH: 0-8 **RH: 1-7** Tight: 0-8 Gall: 0-0
Aids: Bl: 0-2 Vi: 0-0 Tstrap: 0-0 Ckp: 0-0
Best Rating: **100** 8/06 Ripn 6f soft

Useful; effective at around 7f-1m; acts on most ground; goes on Fibresand; has worn blinkers.

Stevie Thunder

107 (64)**94**

4-y-o ch g Storming Home-Social Storm (USA) (Future Storm (USA))

Ian Williams Steve Gray

Placings:13/212411445-34402560 **(6665)**

2009: 8^{3}G, 8^{4}GS, 8^{4}G, 7^{0}G, 10^{2}GF, 10^{5}GS, 9^{6}GF, 10^{0}GS,

	Starts	1st	2nd	3rd	Win & Pl
Career Total (Turf)	18	4	3	1	34905
Career Total (AW)	1	0	0	1	353

94	6/08	Newc	1m	(0-85)H	SFT	£6231
86	6/08	Sand	7f16y	(0-90)H	GD	£7771
80	4/08	Muss	7f30y	(0-70)H	SFT	£2914
61	9/07	Muss	7f30y		G-S	£3238

Total win prize-money £20155

Going (Turf): **Sf: 2-5** GS: 1-5 Gd: 1-5 GF: 0-3 Fm: 0-0
Distance: 5f/6f: 0-0 **7f-8f: 4-12** 9f-13f: 0-7 14f+: 0-0
Track : LH: 1-8 **RH: 3-7 Tight: 2-5** Gall: 1-4
Aids: Bl: 0-0 Vi: 0-2 Tstrap: 0-0 Ckp: 0-0
Best Rating: **94** 8/09 York 1m2f88y gd-fm

Useful; effective over 7f-1m2f; acts on good and softer ground and on Polytrack; has worn a tongue tie.

Still Dreaming

82(103) (61)**54**

5-y-o ch m Singspiel (IRE)-Three Green Leaves (IRE) (Environment Friend)

R J Price The Net Partnership

Placings:03300063/**312243033000**-0650 **(5962)**

2009: 12^{0}SD, 11^{6}GF, 11^{5}GF, 11^{0}GS,

	Starts	1st	2nd	3rd	Win & Pl
Career Total (Turf)	15	0	0	5	1992
Career Total (AW)	9	1	2	2	3548

51	1/08	Wolv	1m4f50y	(0-55)H	STD	£1774

Total win prize-money £1775

Going (Turf): **Sf: 0-1 GS: 0-3 Gd: 0-5 GF: 0-6 Fm: 0-0**
Distance: 5f/6f: 0-0 7f-8f: 0-0 **9f-13f: 1-19** 14f+: 0-5
Track : **LH: 1-21** RH: 0-1 **Tight: 1-18** Gall: 0-1
Aids: **Bl: 1-15** Vi: 0-0 Tstrap: 0-0 Ckp: 0-0
Best Rating: **61** 2/08 Wolv 1m4f50y stand

Moderate;stays 1m4f; acts on most ground and Polytrack; has worn blinkers.

Stimulation (IRE)

106 **118**

4-y-o b c Choisir (AUS)-Damiana (IRE) (Thatching)

H Morrison Michael Kerr-Dineen

Placings:122/1024231-54 **(6058)**

2009: 7^{5}GF, 7^{4}GF,

	Starts	1st	2nd	3rd	Win & Pl
Career Total (Turf)	12	3	4	1	200157

118	10/08	NmkR	7f		GD	£56770
111	4/08	NmkR	7f	H	GD	£17031
89	9/07	Newb	6f8y		G-F	£5829

Total win prize-money £79630

Going (Turf): Sf: 0-1 GS: 0-1 **Gd: 2-5** GF: 1-4 Fm: 0-1
Distance: 5f/6f: 0-0 **7f-8f: 3-12** 9f-13f: 0-0 14f+: 0-0
Track : LH: 0-0 RH: 0-2 Tight: 0-0 Gall: 0-0
Aids: Bl: 0-0 Vi: 0-0 Tstrap: 0-0 Ckp: 0-0
Best Rating: **118** 10/08 NmkR 7f good

Group class; winner of the Free Handicap and Group 2 Challenge Stakes in 2008; effective over 6f-7f; acts on most ground; can break slowly and take a hold.

Stockman

(91) (44)
5-y-o b g Kylian (USA)-Fabriana (Northern State (USA))
H Morrison H Morrison

Placings:0-0500 **(1586)**
2009: 12⁰SS, 11⁵SD, 11⁰SD, 12⁰SD,

	Starts	1st	2nd	3rd	Win & Pl
Career Total (Turf)	0	0	0	0	
Career Total (AW)	5	0	0	0	0

Going (Turf): **Sf: 0-0 GS: 0-0 Gd: 0-0 GF: 0-0 Fm: 0-0**
Distance: 5f/6f: 0-0 7f-8f: 0-0 9f-13f: 0-5 14f+: 0-0
Track : LH: 0-5 RH: 0-0 Tight: 0-1 Gall: 0-0
Aids: Bl: 0-0 Vi: 0-0 Tstrap: 0-0 Ckp: 0-0
Best Rating: **44** 3/09 Sthl 1m3f stand

Stoic (IRE)

111(105) (103)99
3-y-o b g Green Desert (USA)-Silver Bracelet (Machiavellian (USA))
J Noseda Highclere Thoroughbred Racing (Gimcrack)

Placings:5-2111 **(6229)**
2009: 8²GF, 8¹GF, 8¹GF, 8¹SD,

	Starts	1st	2nd	3rd	Win & Pl
Career Total (Turf)	4	2	1	0	13758
Career Total (AW)	1	1	0	0	

98	9/09	Sand	1m14y	(0-90)H	G-F	£7771
99	8/09	NmkJ	1m		G-F	£5180

Total win prize-money £12952

Going (Turf): Sf: 0-0 GS: 0-0 Gd: 0-0 **GF: 2-4** Fm: 0-0
Distance: 5f/6f: 0-0 **7f-8f: 2-3** 9f-13f: 1-2 14f+: 0-0
Track : LH: 0-0 **RH: 2-3** Tight: 0-1 Gall: 0-0
Aids: Bl: 0-0 Vi: 0-0 Tstrap: 0-0 Ckp: 0-0
Best Rating: **103** 9/09 Kemp 1m stand

Useful; stays 1m and acts on fast ground.

Stoic Leader (IRE)

99(97) (65)78
9-y-o b g Danehill Dancer (IRE)-Starlust (Sallust)
R F Fisher Alan Willoughby

Placings:0561444660/5331124040600042000/401140111002426525640440**60104**/**50546**1115534050300450**56000**
5/102540023**4644**00641300**0360/3406**1000034425050000
0/02403155400-**4020**400464**6000** **(7754)**
2009: 9⁴SD, 7⁰SD, 8²SF, 8⁰SD, 8⁴F, 8⁰F, 8⁰GF, 7⁴GF, 8⁶GF, 7⁴G, 9⁶SD, 9⁰SD, 9⁰SD, 8⁰SD,

	Starts	1st	2nd	3rd	Win & Pl
Career Total (Turf)	107	12	8	8	104784
Career Total (AW)	50	4	2	2	18454

78	5/08	Carl	7f200y	(0-80)H	G-F	£4533
85	4/07	Muss	7f30y	(0-85)H	G-F	£5505
85	8/06	Muss	7f30y	(0-80)H	GD	£6477
76	1/06	Ling	7f	(0-70)H	STD	£3238
94	5/05	Catt	7f	(0-90)H	FRM	£13795
90	5/05	Rdcr	1m	(0-85)H	G-F	£7368
84	4/05	Muss	1m	(0-75)H	GD	£4048
82	12/04	Wolv	7f32y	(0-77)H	STD	£3447
84	5/04	Haml	6f5y	F(0-65)	G-S	£3024
84	5/04	Muss	7f30y	E(0-70)H	GD	£4134
85	5/04	Hayd	1m30y	E(0-70)H	GD	£6987
74	3/04	Ling	7f	F(0-55)H	STD	£3010
73	3/04	Wolv	7f	E(0-70)H	SS	£4046
76	5/03	Haml	5f4y	F(0-60)H	G-S	£3607
73	5/03	Sthl	6f	F(0-60)H	G-F	£3115
60	6/02	Muss	5f	E	G-F	£5473

Total win prize-money £81812

Going (Turf): Sf: 0-5 GS: 2-16Gd: 4-27**GF: 5-47** Fm: 1-12
Distance: 5f/6f: 3-35 **7f-8f:12-98** 9f-13f: 1-24 14f+: 0-0
Track : **LH: 7-86** RH: 5-27 **Tight: 9-86** Gall: 0-1
Aids: Bl: 0-0 Vi: 0-0 Tstrap: 0-2 Ckp: 0-2
Best Rating: **96** 6/05 Newc 7f good

Moderate; effective over 7f-1m; acts on most ground and on Polytrack.

Stolen Affection

35
2-y-o b g Pursuit Of Love-Thieves Welcome (Most Welcome)
J R Weymes Mrs R L Heaton

Placings:0 **(5942)**
2009: 7⁰G,

	Starts	1st	2nd	3rd	Win & Pl
Career Total (Turf)	1	0	0	0	

Going (Turf): **Sf: 0-0 GS: 0-0 Gd: 0-1 GF: 0-0 Fm: 0-0**
Distance: 5f/6f: 0-0 7f-8f: 0-1 9f-13f: 0-0 14f+: 0-0
Track : LH: 0-0 RH: 0-1 Tight: 0-1 Gall: 0-0
Aids: Bl: 0-0 Vi: 0-0 Tstrap: 0-0 Ckp: 0-0

Stolt (IRE)

105(105) (84)93
5-y-o b g Tagula (IRE)-Cabcharge Princess (IRE) (Rambo Dancer (CAN))
N Wilson Darron McIntyre Frank Tobin

Placings:140032/**000041/50262**1001525-0005066100**604** **(7758)**
2009: 5⁰G, 5⁰GF, 5⁰G, 5⁵GF, 5⁰G, 5⁶S, 5⁶GF, 5¹GF, 5⁰G, 5⁰G, 5⁶SD, 5⁰SD, 5⁴SD,

	Starts	1st	2nd	3rd	Win & Pl
Career Total (Turf)	25	4	2	1	26758
Career Total (AW)	12	1	2	0	5839

93	9/09	Ches	5f16y	(0-85)H	G-F	£5504
93	5/08	York	5f	(0-80)H	GD	£7123
84	4/08	Thsk	5f	(0-80)H	G-S	£5180
83	12/07	Wolv	5f20y	(0-75)H	STD	£3238
73	4/06	Muss	5f		GD	£3886

Total win prize-money £24935

Going (Turf): Sf: 0-2 GS: 1-2 **Gd: 2-12** GF: 1-8 Fm: 0-1
Distance: **5f/6f: 5-37** 7f-8f: 0-0 9f-13f: 0-0 14f+: 0-0
Track : **LH: 2-13** RH: 0-1 **Tight: 2-12** Gall: 0-0
Aids: Bl: 0-0 Vi: 0-0 Tstrap: 0-1 Ckp: 0-1
Best Rating: **93** 9/09 Ches 5f16y gd-fm

Useful; effective over 5f; acts on good ground and on Polytrack; likes to race prominently.

Stone Of Scone

109(103) (89)103
4-y-o b g Pivotal-Independence (Selkirk (USA))
E A L Dunlop Cliveden Stud

Placings:61-130 **(3089)**
2009: 10¹GS, 10³GF, 10⁰GF,

	Starts	1st	2nd	3rd	Win & Pl
Career Total (Turf)	4	1	0	1	9496
Career Total (AW)	1	1	0	0	2590

98	4/09	Nott	1m2f50y	(0-90)H	G-S	£7569
89	5/08	GrLe	1m		STD	£2590

Total win prize-money £10160

Going (Turf): Sf: 0-0 **GS: 1-1** Gd: 0-1 GF: 0-2 Fm: 0-0
Distance: 5f/6f: 0-0 7f-8f: 1-2 9f-13f: 1-3 14f+: 0-0
Track : **LH: 2-3** RH: 0-1 Tight: 0-0 **Gall: 1-3**
Aids: Bl: 0-0 Vi: 0-0 Tstrap: 0-0 Ckp: 0-0
Best Rating: **103** 5/09 York 1m2f88y gd-fm

Very useful; stays 1m2f; acts on easy ground; goes on Polytrack.

Stoneacre Baby (USA)

83(92) (36)35
4-y-o ch f Stravinsky (USA)-Katiba (USA) (Gulch (USA))
Peter Grayson Richard Teatum

Placings:006/0-00000 **(2625)**
2009: 5⁰SD, 5⁰SF, 5⁰SD, 5⁰GF, 5⁰GF,

	Starts	1st	2nd	3rd	Win & Pl
Career Total (Turf)	2	0	0	0	
Career Total (AW)	7	0	0	0	0

Going (Turf): **Sf: 0-0 GS: 0-0 Gd: 0-0 GF: 0-2 Fm: 0-0**
Distance: 5f/6f: 0-9 7f-8f: 0-0 9f-13f: 0-0 14f+: 0-0
Track : LH: 0-5 RH: 0-1 Tight: 0-5 Gall: 0-0
Aids: Bl: 0-0 Vi: 0-0 Tstrap: 0-0 Ckp: 0-0
Best Rating: **36** 2/09 Wolv 5f20y std-fst

Stoneacre Donny (IRE)

85(96) (54)22
5-y-o br h Lend A Hand-Election Special (Chief Singer)
Peter Grayson Richard Teatum

Placings:000000064/1600000-5000 **(2473)**
2009: 6⁵SD, 6⁰SD, 5⁰G, 8⁰GF,

	Starts	1st	2nd	3rd	Win & Pl
Career Total (Turf)	3	0	0	0	
Career Total (AW)	17	1	0	0	1365

54	1/08	Kemp	6f	(0-45)	STD	£1365

Total win prize-money £1365

Going (Turf): **Sf: 0-0 GS: 0-1 Gd: 0-1 GF: 0-1 Fm: 0-0**
Distance: **5f/6f: 1-18** 7f-8f: 0-2 9f-13f: 0-0 14f+: 0-0
Track : LH: 0-10 **RH: 1-5** Tight: 0-8 Gall: 0-1
Aids: Bl: 0-1 Vi: 0-0 Tstrap: 0-0 Ckp: 0-0
Best Rating: **54** 1/08 Kemp 6f stand

Moderate; effective over 6f; acts on Polytrack.

Stoneacre Joe (IRE)

(50)
2-y-o b c Iron Mask (USA)-Jarmar Moon (Unfuwain (USA))
Peter Grayson Richard Teatum

Placings:004 (7850)
2009: 5^{0}SS, 5^{0}SD, 5^{4}SS,

	Starts	1st	2nd	3rd	Win & Pl
Career Total (Turf)	0	0	0	0	
Career Total (AW)	3	0	0	0	0

Going (Turf): Sf: 0-0 GS: 0-0 Gd: 0-0 GF: 0-0 Fm: 0-0
Distance: 5f/6f: 0-3 7f-8f: 0-0 9f-13f: 0-0 14f+: 0-0
Track : LH: 0-2 RH: 0-0 Tight: 0-2 Gall: 0-0
Aids: Bl: 0-0 Vi: 0-0 Tstrap: 0-0 Ckp: 0-0

Stoneacre Lad (IRE)

102(109) (106)82
6-y-o b h Bluebird (USA)-Jay And-A (IRE) (Elbio)
Peter Grayson Richard Teatum

Placings:6001015/1330201000361/4330010/301000-006504040065 (5293)
2009: 5^{0}SD, 5^{0}SD, 5^{6}SD, 5^{5}SD, 5^{0}G, 5^{4}G, 5^{0}GF, 5^{4}GS, 5^{0}SD, 5^{0}G, 5^{6}SD, 5^{5}S,

	Starts	1st	2nd	3rd	Win & Pl
Career Total (Turf)	23	2	1	1	65883
Career Total (AW)	22	5	0	5	46982

106 6/08 Kemp 5f STD £14760
104 7/07 Ascl 5f H G-S £43624
92 12/06 Sthl 5f (0-90)H STD £8096
93 6/06 Leic 5f2y (0-95)H G-F £11217
83 2/06 Sthl 5f (0-75)H STD £3238
75 12/05 Sthl 5f (0-85) STD £6719
71 11/05 Wolv 5f20y (0-75) STD £3746
Total win prize-money £91404

Going (Turf): Sf: 0-4 **GS: 1-6** Gd: 0-6 **GF: 1-7** Fm: 0-0
Distance: **5f/6f: 7-44** 7f-8f: 0-1 9f-13f: 0-0 14f+: 0-0
Track : LH: 1-16 RH: 1-3 **Tight: 1-15** Gall: 0-0
Aids: **Bl: 5-38** Vi: 0-0 Tstrap: 0-0 Ckp: 0-0
Best Rating: **106** 6/08 Kemp 5f stand

Useful; Listed winner; suited by 5f-6f; acts on most ground and on sand; usually wears blinkers.

Stoneacre Pat (IRE)

(98) (56)51
4-y-o b c Iron Mask (USA)-Sans Ceriph (IRE) (Thatching)
Peter Grayson R Teatum And Mrs S Grayson

Placings:05/15650016544204-0000600 (7657)
2009: 6^{0}SD, 5^{0}SD, 5^{0}SF, 5^{0}SD, 5^{6}SD, 5^{0}SD, 5^{0}SD,

	Starts	1st	2nd	3rd	Win & Pl
Career Total (Turf)	2	0	0	0	0
Career Total (AW)	21	2	1	0	6223

57 6/08 Wolv 5f20y (0-70)H STD £3070
63 2/08 Ling 5f STD £2331
Total win prize-money £5403

Going (Turf): **Sf: 0-1 GS: 0-1 Gd: 0-0 GF: 0-0 Fm: 0-0**
Distance: **5f/6f: 2-23** 7f-8f: 0-0 9f-13f: 0-0 14f+: 0-0
Track : **LH: 2-18** RH: 0-3 **Tight: 2-17** Gall: 0-1
Aids: Bl: 0-7 Vi: 0-0 Tstrap: 0-0 Ckp: 0-0
Best Rating: 63 2/08 Ling 5f stand

Moderate; effective over 5f; acts on easy ground; also goes on Polytrack; can start very slowly.

Stonecrabstomorrow (IRE)

106(106) (80)78
6-y-o b g Fasliyev (USA)-Tordasia (IRE) (Dr Devious (IRE))
R A Fahey Miss S Bowles

Placings:22/21213042/00003234060/3211223110 (2402)
2009: 6^{3}SD, 6^{2}SD, 5^{1}SD, 5^{1}SF, 6^{2}SD, 5^{2}SD, 7^{3}GF, 6^{1}G, 6^{1}F, 7^{0}GF,

	Starts	1st	2nd	3rd	Win & Pl
Career Total (Turf)	14	2	1	4	11578
Career Total (AW)	17	4	8	1	23859

73 5/09 Rdcr 6f FRM £2047
78 5/09 Haml 6f5y GD £2729
73 3/09 Wolv 5f216y (0-75)H SF £3070
67 2/09 Wolv 5f216y STD £2047
84 8/06 Ling 6f (0-80)H STD £5505
63 2/06 Ling 7f STD £2914
Total win prize-money £18315

Going (Turf): Sf: 0-3 GS: 0-1 **Gd: 1-5** GF: 0-4 **Fm: 1-1**
Distance: **5f/6f: 4-21** 7f-8f: 2-10 9f-13f: 0-0 14f+: 0-0
Track : **LH: 4-18** RH: 0-4 **Tight: 4-15** Gall: 0-1
Aids: **Bl: 3-7** Vi: 0-0 Tstrap: 1-4 Ckp: 1-4
Best Rating: 88 10/06 Wolv 7f32y std-fst

Fair; effective over 6f-7f; acts on soft ground; goes on Polytrack; has worn blinkers and cheekpieces.

Stonehaugh (IRE)

104 81
6-y-o b g King Charlemagne (USA)-Canary Bird (IRE) (Catrail (USA))
J Howard Johnson J Howard Johnson

Placings:636/16310/260/2004-0510 (4621)
2009: 7^{0}GF, 7^{5}GF, 6^{1}GF, 5^{0}G,

	Starts	1st	2nd	3rd	Win & Pl
Career Total (Turf)	19	3	2	2	19821

81 6/09 Carl 6f192y (0-70)H G-F £2590
81 7/06 Bevl 7f100y (0-85)H G-F £7772
74 4/06 Catt 7f FRM £3886
Total win prize-money £14248

Going (Turf): Sf: 0-0 GS: 0-3 Gd: 0-2 **GF: 2-13** Fm: 1-1
Distance: 5f/6f: 0-2 **7f-8f: 3-16** 9f-13f: 0-1 14f+: 0-0
Track : LH: 1-7 **RH: 2-9 Tight: 1-8** Gall: 0-1
Aids: Bl: 0-0 Vi: 0-0 Tstrap: 0-0 Ckp: 0-0
Best Rating: 85 5/07 Muss 7f30y gd-fm

Fair performer; stays a mile; acts on fast ground; has worn tongue tie.

Stoop To Conquer

101(96) (77)72
9-y-o b g Polar Falcon (USA)-Princess Genista (Ile De Bourbon (USA))
A W Carroll B Ward

Placings:05356/0014101/4/300166/006/403006224-640 (7124)
2009: 13^{6}SD, 14^{4}GF, 16^{0}G,

	Starts	1st	2nd	3rd	Win & Pl
Career Total (Turf)	30	4	2	2	32924
Career Total (AW)	4	0	0	1	939

91 8/06 Newb 1m5f61y (0-90)H GD £8096
84 10/04 Newb 2m (0-92)H SFT £7559
83 8/04 Gdwd 1m6f E(0-75)H G-S £4309
78 6/04 Pont 2m1f22yE(0-70)H G-F £6971
Total win prize-money £26937

Going (Turf): **Sf: 1-7 GS: 1-6 Gd: 1-9 GF: 1-8** Fm: 0-0
Distance: 5f/6f: 0-0 7f-8f: 0-0 9f-13f: 0-5 **14f+: 4-29**
Track : **LH: 3-21** RH: 1-13 Tight: 1-11 Gall: 1-8
Aids: Bl: 0-0 Vi: 0-0 Tstrap: 0-0 Ckp: 0-0
Best Rating: 91 8/06 Newb 1m5f61y good

Modest; winning hurdler; stays 2m; acts on most types of ground.

Storey Hill (USA)

(100) (81)53
4-y-o b/br g Richter Scale (USA)-Crafty Nan (USA) (Crafty Prospector (USA))
D Shaw Jim Goose & Richard Hall

Placings:401/00104-0400 (0757)
2009: 5^{0}SD, 6^{4}SD, 6^{0}SD, 5^{0}SF,

	Starts	1st	2nd	3rd	Win & Pl
Career Total (Turf)	1	0	0	0	337
Career Total (AW)	11	2	0	0	7283

81 4/08 Kemp 5f (0-85)H STD £4533
69 11/07 Ling 6f STD £2388
Total win prize-money £6922

Going (Turf): **Sf: 0-1 GS: 0-0 Gd: 0-0 GF: 0-0 Fm: 0-0**
Distance: **5f/6f: 2-12** 7f-8f: 0-0 9f-13f: 0-0 14f+: 0-0
Track : LH: 1-8 RH: 1-3 **Tight: 1-7** Gall: 0-1
Aids: Bl: 0-0 Vi: 0-0 Tstrap: 0-0 Ckp: 0-0
Best Rating: 81 4/08 Kemp 5f stand

Fair; effective over 5f-6f; acts on Polytrack; suited by forcing tactics.

Storm Command (IRE)

87 59
2-y-o ch g Halling (USA)-Clarinda (IRE) (Lomond (USA))
B Smart Clipper Logistics

Placings:05420 (6391)
2009: 7^{0}GF, 8^{5}GS, 8^{4}F, 9^{2}GF, 10^{0}GF,

	Starts	1st	2nd	3rd	Win & Pl
Career Total (Turf)	5	0	1	0	1348

Going (Turf): **Sf: 0-0 GS: 0-1 Gd: 0-0 GF: 0-3 Fm: 0-1**
Distance: 5f/6f: 0-0 7f-8f: 0-1 9f-13f: 0-4 14f+: 0-0
Track : LH: 0-3 RH: 0-2 Tight: 0-1 Gall: 0-0
Aids: Bl: 0-0 Vi: 0-0 Tstrap: 0-0 Ckp: 0-0
Best Rating: 59 9/09 Rdcr 1m1f gd-fm

Storm Hawk (IRE)

94 70
2-y-o b g Hawk Wing (USA)-Stormy Larissa (IRE) (Royal Applause)
Pat Eddery Pat Eddery Racing (Bigstone)

Placings:55320004 (6901)
2009: 5^{5}GF, 6^{5}GS, 5^{3}GF, 7^{2}S, 7^{0}G, 7^{0}GF, 8^{0}GS, 8^{4}GF,

	Starts	1st	2nd	3rd	Win & Pl
Career Total (Turf)	8	0	1	1	1661

Going (Turf): **Sf: 0-1 GS: 0-2 Gd: 0-1 GF: 0-4 Fm: 0-0**
Distance: 5f/6f: 0-3 7f-8f: 0-3 9f-13f: 0-2 14f+: 0-0
Track : LH: 0-2 RH: 0-2 Tight: 0-2 Gall: 0-0

Aids: Bl: 0-0 Vi: 0-2 Tstrap: 0-0 Ckp: 0-0
Best Rating: 70 7/09 Catt 7f soft

Moderate form so far; stays 6f; handles fast and easy ground.

Stormbeam (USA)

(86) (59)64
4-y-o b g Tale Of The Cat (USA)-Broad Smile (USA) (Broad Brush (USA))
G A Butler Mr And Mrs P Hargreaves

Placings:55/0362-0 (2601)
2009: 12⁰SD,

	Starts	1st	2nd	3rd	Win & Pl
Career Total (Turf)	4	0	1	1	981
Career Total (AW)	3	0	0	0	0

Going (Turf): Sf: 0-1 GS: 0-0 Gd: 0-0 GF: 0-3 Fm: 0-0
Distance: 5f/6f: 0-0 7f-8f: 0-4 9f-13f: 0-3 14f+: 0-0
Track : LH: 0-3 RH: 0-2 Tight: 0-4 Gall: 0-0
Aids: Bl: 0-0 Vi: 0-0 Tstrap: 0-0 Ckp: 0-0
Best Rating: 64 8/08 Yarm 1m1f soft

Stormburst (IRE)

87(100) (51)49
5-y-o b m Mujadil (USA)-Isca (Caerleon (USA))
A J Chamberlain N F B P L Racing

Placings:50/560035165422/530600230066-0060040036 (7869)
2009: 7⁰SD, 6⁰SD, 6⁶SD, 7⁰SD, 6⁰SD, 5⁴GF, 5⁰SD, 6⁰SD, 6³SD, 6⁶SS,

	Starts	1st	2nd	3rd	Win & Pl
Career Total (Turf)	14	0	0	2	1011
Career Total (AW)	22	1	3	2	4655

61 10/07 Kemp 6f (0-52)H STD £2047
Total win prize-money £2048

Going (Turf): Sf: 0-2 GS: 0-0 Gd: 0-5 GF: 0-5 Fm: 0-2
Distance: 5f/6f: 1-29 7f-8f: 0-7 9f-13f: 0-0 14f+: 0-0
Track : LH: 0-19 RH: 1-8 Tight: 0-14 Gall: 0-0
Aids: Bl: 0-1 Vi: 0-2 Tstrap: 0-0 Ckp: 0-0
Best Rating: 64 12/07 Ling 6f stand

Moderate;effective over 6f; acts on good ground; also goes on Polytrack.

Stormglass

70 50
2-y-o ch c Galileo (IRE)-Aberdovey (Mister Baileys)
W R Muir C Edginton, M Graham & K Mercer

Placings:60 (6478)
2009: 9⁶G, 7⁰GF,

	Starts	1st	2nd	3rd	Win & Pl
Career Total (Turf)	2	0	0	0	0

Going (Turf): Sf: 0-0 GS: 0-0 Gd: 0-1 GF: 0-1 Fm: 0-0
Distance: 5f/6f: 0-0 7f-8f: 0-1 9f-13f: 0-1 14f+: 0-0
Track : LH: 0-0 RH: 0-1 Tight: 0-1 Gall: 0-0
Aids: Bl: 0-0 Vi: 0-0 Tstrap: 0-0 Ckp: 0-0
Best Rating: 50 9/09 Gdwd 1m1f good

110,000gns son of Galileo out of a mare who was a dual 6f-1m winner at two and three; modest promise in maiden company.

Storming Sioux

101(97) (64)68
3-y-o b f Storming Home-Sueboog (IRE) (Darshaan)
W J Haggas Mohamed Obaida

Placings:24-22034 (6941)
2009: 8²GF, 8²GF, 8⁰GF, 12³SD, 12⁴SD,

	Starts	1st	2nd	3rd	Win & Pl
Career Total (Turf)	4	0	3	0	2247
Career Total (AW)	3	0	0	1	578

Going (Turf): Sf: 0-0 GS: 0-0 Gd: 0-1 GF: 0-3 Fm: 0-0
Distance: 5f/6f: 0-0 7f-8f: 0-3 9f-13f: 0-4 14f+: 0-0
Track : LH: 0-2 RH: 0-3 Tight: 0-2 Gall: 0-0
Aids: Bl: 0-0 Vi: 0-0 Tstrap: 0-0 Ckp: 0-0
Best Rating: 68 5/09 Wwck 1m22y gd-fm

Fair; stays 1m; acts on good ground and on Polytrack.

Stormy Morning

91(90) (63)65
3-y-o ch g Nayef (USA)-Sokoa (USA) (Peintre Celebre (USA))
Mrs Lawney Hill (W R Swinburn 2/10) McClenaghan & Reddin

Placings:0040100 (6457)
2009: 10⁰GF, 10⁰GS, 9⁴GF, 12⁰G, 13¹G, 16⁰SD, 13⁰SD,

	Starts	1st	2nd	3rd	Win & Pl
Career Total (Turf)	5	1	0	0	2896
Career Total (AW)	2	0	0	0	

65 8/09 Bath 1m5f22y (0-70)H GD £2655
Total win prize-money £2655

Going (Turf): Sf: 0-0 GS: 0-1 Gd: 1-2 GF: 0-2 Fm: 0-0
Distance: 5f/6f: 0-0 7f-8f: 0-0 9f-13f: 0-4 14f+: 1-3
Track : LH: 1-2 RH: 0-5 Tight: 1-4 Gall: 0-1
Aids: Bl: 0-0 Vi: 0-0 Tstrap: 0-0 Ckp: 0-0
Best Rating: 65 8/09 Bath 1m5f22y good

Modest; stays 1m5f; acts on good ground.

Stormy Summer

91(98) (66)61
4-y-o b g Observatory (USA)-Khambani (IRE) (Royal Academy (USA))
R W Price Michael C Whatley

Placings:60-000602020 (7842)
2009: 10⁰G, 10⁰GF, 10⁰SD, 14⁶SD, 10⁰G, 12²SD, 12⁰SD, 12²SD, 14⁰SS,

	Starts	1st	2nd	3rd	Win & Pl
Career Total (Turf)	4	0	0	0	
Career Total (AW)	7	0	2	0	1568

Going (Turf): Sf: 0-1 GS: 0-0 Gd: 0-2 GF: 0-1 Fm: 0-0
Distance: 5f/6f: 0-0 7f-8f: 0-0 9f-13f: 0-9 14f+: 0-2
Track : LH: 0-9 RH: 0-1 Tight: 0-2 Gall: 0-2
Aids: Bl: 0-4 Vi: 0-0 Tstrap: 0-1 Ckp: 0-1
Best Rating: 66 12/09 Sthl 1m4f stand

Modest; effective over 1m4f; acts on Fibresand; has worn blinkers.

Stormy Weather (FR)

102 102
3-y-o gr g Highest Honor (FR)-Stormy Moud (USA) (Storm Bird (CAN))
J Howard Johnson Andrea & Graham Wylie

Placings:162-30 (7293)
2009: 11³HY, 12⁰S,

	Starts	1st	2nd	3rd	Win & Pl
Career Total (Turf)	5	1	1	1	18042

85 9/08 Lonc 1m G-S £8088
Total win prize-money £8088

Going (Turf): Sf: 0-3 GS: 1-2 Gd: 0-0 GF: 0-0 Fm: 0-0
Distance: 5f/6f: 0-0 7f-8f: 1-3 9f-13f: 0-2 14f+: 0-0
Track : LH: 0-4 RH: 0-0 Tight: 0-0 Gall: 0-1
Aids: Bl: 0-0 Vi: 0-0 Tstrap: 0-0 Ckp: 0-0
Best Rating: 102 5/09 Hayd 1m3f200y heavy

Very useful; ex-French; Listed placed; stays 1m4f; acts on heavy ground.

Stormy's Prelude

89(100) (60)61
3-y-o ch f Alhaarth (IRE)-Far Reaching (USA) (Distant View (USA))
P Winkworth Mrs I Russell

Placings:35P (2051)
2009: 10³SD, 9⁵GF, 12ᴾGF,

	Starts	1st	2nd	3rd	Win & Pl
Career Total (Turf)	2	0	0	0	0
Career Total (AW)	1	0	0	1	403

Going (Turf): Sf: 0-0 GS: 0-0 Gd: 0-0 GF: 0-2 Fm: 0-0
Distance: 5f/6f: 0-0 7f-8f: 0-0 9f-13f: 0-3 14f+: 0-0
Track : LH: 0-1 RH: 0-2 Tight: 0-2 Gall: 0-1
Aids: Bl: 0-0 Vi: 0-0 Tstrap: 0-0 Ckp: 0-0
Best Rating: 61 4/09 Folk 1m1f149y gd-fm

Modest; stays 1m and acts on Polytrack.

Storyland (USA)

105(111) (96)95
4-y-o b f Menifee (USA)-Auspice (USA) (Robellino (USA))
W J Haggas Mr & Mrs R Scott

Placings:0/11335116-04560253 (7131)
2009: 12⁰GF, 12⁴G, 14⁵G, 12⁶G, 12⁰GF, 12²GF, 12⁵GF, 13³SD,

	Starts	1st	2nd	3rd	Win & Pl
Career Total (Turf)	15	4	1	2	34011
Career Total (AW)	2	0	0	1	4848

93 10/08 Gdwd 1m4f (0-95)H G-F £9714
89 9/08 NmkR 1m4f (0-95)H G-F £9714
75 5/08 Donc 1m (0-85)H G-F £4857
73 5/08 Rdcr 7f SFT £2331
Total win prize-money £26616

Going (Turf): Sf: 1-1 GS: 0-0 Gd: 0-6 GF: 3-8 Fm: 0-0
Distance: 5f/6f: 0-1 7f-8f: 2-2 9f-13f: 2-13 14f+: 0-1
Track : LH: 1-6 RH: 2-9 Tight: 1-7 Gall: 2-7
Aids: Bl: 0-0 Vi: 0-0 Tstrap: 0-0 Ckp: 0-0
Best Rating: 96 10/09 Ling 1m5f stand

Useful; stays at least 1m4f; acts on fast and soft ground.

Stotsfold

114 (95)119
6-y-o b g Barathea (IRE)-Eliza Acton (Shirley Heights)
W R Swinburn P W Harris

Placings:065113110/2031/556601-4313246 (6812)
2009: 8⁴G, 10³G, 10¹GS, 10³G, 9²GF, 9⁴GS, 9⁶G,

	Starts	1st	2nd	3rd	Win & Pl
Career Total (Turf)	24	5	2	4	260482
Career Total (AW)	2	2	0	0	14249

113	6/09	Lonc	1m2f	G-S	£38835
119	8/08	Wind	1m2f7y	G-F	£39739
113	9/07	Gdwd	1m1f192y	G-F	£28390
105	9/06	Ches	1m2f75y (0-100)H	G-F	£20565
95	9/06	Kemp	1m2f (0-85)H	STD	£6477
84	7/06	Ches	1m2f75y (0-85)H	G-F	£5829
78	6/06	Ling	1m2f (0-85)H	STD	£7772

Total win prize-money £147608

Going (Turf): Sf: 0-1 GS: 1-4 Gd: 0-6 **GF: 4-13** Fm: 0-0
Distance: 5f/6f: 0-0 7f-8f: 0-1 **9f-13f: 7-25** 14f+: 0-0
Track : LH: 3-9 **RH: 4-15 Tight: 5-12** Gall: 0-4
Aids: Bl: 0-0 Vi: 0-0 Tstrap: 0-0 Ckp: 0-0
Best Rating: 119 8/09 Arlt 1m2f good

Group class; effective at around 1m2f; acts on easy and fast ground and on Polytrack.

Strabinios King

90(108) (84)73

5-y-o b g King's Best (USA)-Strawberry Morn (CAN) (Travelling Victor (CAN))

A Berry (K J Burke 7/2) Sam Thompson

Placings:4/40100201342/1013003-31230000060 (5147)

2009: 7^{3}SD, 7^{1}SD, 7^{2}SD, 7^{3}SD, 7^{0}G, 7^{0}GS, 6^{0}G, 5^{0}GF, 7^{0}SD, 6^{6}G, 5^{0}GS,

	Starts	1st	2nd	3rd	Win & Pl
Career Total (Turf)	13	1	1	1	3215
Career Total (AW)	17	4	2	4	14832

84	1/09	Wolv	7f32y	(0-80)H	STD	£4857
73	6/08	Ling	7f	(0-65)H	STD	£2047
74	3/08	Wolv	5f216y	(0-60)H	STD	£1774
63	12/07	Wolv	5f216y		STD	£2047
57	6/07	Catt	7f	(0-60)	G-F	£2047

Total win prize-money £12775

Going (Turf): Sf: 0-0 GS: 0-4 Gd: 0-4 **GF: 1-4** Fm: 0-1
Distance: 5f/6f: 2-11 **7f-8f: 3-19** 9f-13f: 0-0 14f+: 0-0
Track : **LH: 5-19** RH: 0-6 **Tight: 5-19** Gall: 0-0
Aids: Bl: 0-1 Vi: 0-0 Tstrap: 0-0 Ckp: 0-0
Best Rating: 84 1/09 Wolv 7f32y stand

Fair; effective over 6f-7f; acts on fast ground and Polytrack.

Straboe (USA)

101(98) (53)53

3-y-o b g Green Desert (USA)-Staff Nurse (USA) (Arch (USA))

S C Williams Brigid & Damian Hennessy-Bourke

Placings:0-00015 (7834)

2009: 7^{0}G, 7^{0}G, 8^{0}G, 6^{1}G, 6^{5}SD,

	Starts	1st	2nd	3rd	Win & Pl
Career Total (Turf)	5	1	0	0	2202
Career Total (AW)	1	0	0	0	0

53	8/09	Yarm	6f3y	(0-65)H	GD	£2201

Total win prize-money £2202

Going (Turf): Sf: 0-1 GS: 0-0 **Gd: 1-4** GF: 0-0 Fm: 0-0
Distance: 5f/6f: 0-1 **7f-8f: 1-4** 9f-13f: 0-1 14f+: 0-0
Track : LH: 0-1 RH: 0-1 Tight: 0-0 Gall: 0-0
Aids: Bl: 0-0 Vi: 0-0 Tstrap: 0-0 Ckp: 0-0
Best Rating: 53 12/09 Kemp 6f stand

Straight And Level (CAN)

(100) (72)63

4-y-o gr g Buddha (USA)-Azusa (USA) (Flying Paster (USA))

Miss Jo Crowley Mrs Liz Nelson

Placings:405324301/40000464-0000 (7586)

2009: 8^{0}SD, 10^{0}SD, 8^{0}SD, 8^{0}SD,

	Starts	1st	2nd	3rd	Win & Pl
Career Total (Turf)	5	0	1	0	578
Career Total (AW)	16	1	0	2	5238

74	12/07	Ling	1m	STD	£3886

Total win prize-money £3886

Going (Turf): Sf: 0-0 GS: 0-2 Gd: 0-1 GF: 0-1 Fm: 0-1
Distance: 5f/6f: 0-5 **7f-8f: 1-11** 9f-13f: 0-5 14f+: 0-0
Track : **LH: 1-16** RH: 0-4 **Tight: 1-12** Gall: 0-2
Aids: Bl: 0-0 Vi: 0-3 Tstrap: 0-1 Ckp: 0-1
Best Rating: 76 3/08 Ling 1m2f stand

Fair; stays 1m; acts on Polytrack; has worn a visor.

Straight Face (IRE)

102(109) (61)61

5-y-o b g Princely Heir (IRE)-Dakota Sioux (IRE) (College Chapel)

Miss Gay Kelleway J L Guillambert

Placings:0263044220/62000000/00211120305200-05321661006033510104 (7726)

2009: 7^{0}SD, 6^{5}SD, 6^{3}SD, 6^{2}SD, 7^{1}SD, 8^{6}SD, 6^{6}GF, 7^{1}GS, 7^{0}GF, 7^{0}GF, 8^{6}SD, 6^{0}GF, 7^{3}GS, 7^{3}G, 8^{5}GS, 8^{0}GS, 7^{1}SD, 7^{0}SD, 7^{1}SS, 7^{0}SD, 7^{4}SD,

	Starts	1st	2nd	3rd	Win & Pl
Career Total (Turf)	22	1	4	3	6961
Career Total (AW)	31	6	4	2	13753

60	10/09	Ling	7f	(0-70)	SS	£1706
61	9/09	Kemp	7f	(0-55)H	STD	£2047
61	5/09	Newc	7f		G-S	£1942
57	3/09	Sthl	7f	(0-50)H	STD	£2047
60	4/08	Kemp	7f	(0-52)H	STD	£2047
58	3/08	Kemp	7f	(0-45)	STD	£1365
57	3/08	Kemp	7f	(0-45)	STD	£1365

Total win prize-money £12520

Going (Turf): Sf: 0-0 **GS: 1-5** Gd: 0-9 GF: 0-7 Fm: 0-1
Distance: 5f/6f: 0-10 **7f-8f: 7-39** 9f-13f: 0-4 14f+: 0-0
Track : LH: 2-22 **RH: 4-17 Tight: 1-11** Gall: 0-1
Aids: **Bl: 3-15** Vi: 1-10 Tstrap: 1-2 Ckp: 1-2
Best Rating: 74 6/06 Kemp 7f stand

Moderate; effective over 7f-1m; acts on fast ground and on sand; has worn various headgear.

Straight Laced

93 55

3-y-o b f Refuse To Bend (IRE)-Gaelic Swan (IRE) (Nashwan (USA))

W J Knight Mrs P A Cooke

Placings:660 (2877)

2009: 10^{6}GF, 11^{6}G, 12^{0}GF,

	Starts	1st	2nd	3rd	Win & Pl
Career Total (Turf)	3	0	0	0	0

Going (Turf): Sf: 0-0 GS: 0-0 Gd: 0-1 GF: 0-2 Fm: 0-0
Distance: 5f/6f: 0-0 7f-8f: 0-0 9f-13f: 0-3 14f+: 0-0
Track : LH: 0-3 RH: 0-0 Tight: 0-1 Gall: 0-0
Aids: Bl: 0-0 Vi: 0-0 Tstrap: 0-0 Ckp: 0-0
Best Rating: 55 5/09 Ling 1m3f106y good

Strait Street (IRE)

(72) (29)

2-y-o gr f Verglas (IRE)-Savoy Street (Vettori (IRE))

P Winkworth D B Clark

Placings:0 (7135)

2009: 7^{0}SD,

	Starts	1st	2nd	3rd	Win & Pl
Career Total (Turf)	0	0	0	0	
Career Total (AW)	1	0	0	0	

Going (Turf): Sf: 0-0 GS: 0-0 Gd: 0-0 GF: 0-0 Fm: 0-0
Distance: 5f/6f: 0-0 7f-8f: 0-1 9f-13f: 0-0 14f+: 0-0
Track : LH: 0-1 RH: 0-0 Tight: 0-1 Gall: 0-0
Aids: Bl: 0-0 Vi: 0-0 Tstrap: 0-0 Ckp: 0-0
Best Rating: 29 10/09 Ling 7f stand

Straitjacket

87(95) (57)70

3-y-o b f Refuse To Bend (IRE)-Thara'A (IRE) (Desert Prince (IRE))

Miss J R Tooth Raymond Tooth

Placings:256050-3016000 (4202)

2009: 6^{3}SD, 6^{0}G, 7^{1}SD, 5^{6}SD, 8^{0}SD, 6^{0}GF, 7^{0}SD,

	Starts	1st	2nd	3rd	Win & Pl
Career Total (Turf)	7	0	1	0	1060
Career Total (AW)	6	1	0	1	2432

57	6/09	Ling	7f	STD	£2047

Total win prize-money £2047

Going (Turf): Sf: 0-0 GS: 0-0 Gd: 0-3 GF: 0-4 Fm: 0-0
Distance: 5f/6f: 0-6 **7f-8f: 1-6** 9f-13f: 0-1 14f+: 0-0
Track : **LH: 1-6** RH: 0-2 **Tight: 1-4** Gall: 0-0
Aids: Bl: 0-2 Vi: 0-0 Tstrap: 1-4 Ckp: 1-4
Best Rating: 70 5/08 Gdwd 6f good

Modest; effective at 6f-7f but should stay further; handles a sound surface and Polytrack; has worn cheekpieces/blinkers.

Straits Of Hormuz (USA)

105(93) (66)84

3-y-o gr/ro f War Chant (USA)-Tjinouska (USA) (Cozzene (USA))

M Johnston R S Brookhouse

Placings:0-13365 (6671)

2009: 10^{1}GF, 10^{3}S, 12^{3}GS, 12^{6}GF, 13^{5}SD,

	Starts	1st	2nd	3rd	Win & Pl
Career Total (Turf)	5	1	0	2	3960
Career Total (AW)	1	0	0	0	188

75	6/09	Pont	1m2f6y	G-F	£3238

Total win prize-money £3238

Going (Turf): Sf: 0-1 GS: 0-2 Gd: 0-0 **GF: 1-2** Fm: 0-0
Distance: 5f/6f: 0-0 7f-8f: 0-1 **9f-13f: 1-4** 14f+: 0-1
Track : **LH: 1-4** RH: 0-1 Tight: 0-2 Gall: 0-2
Aids: Bl: 0-0 Vi: 0-0 Tstrap: 0-0 Ckp: 0-0
Best Rating: 84 7/09 Newb 1m2f6y soft

Fair; effective over 1m4f; acts on fast ground.

Strange Fiction

59

2-y-o ch c Avonbridge-Science Fiction (Starborough)

R A Fahey Percy/Green Racing

Placings:00 (1624)
2009: 5[0]GF, 5[0]GF,

	Starts	1st	2nd	3rd	Win & Pl
Career Total (Turf)	2	0	0	0	

Going (Turf): Sf: 0-0 GS: 0-0 Gd: 0-0 GF: 0-2 Fm: 0-0
Distance: 5f/6f: 0-2 7f-8f: 0-0 9f-13f: 0-0 14f+: 0-0
Track : LH: 0-0 RH: 0-0 Tight: 0-0 Gall: 0-0
Aids: Bl: 0-1 Vi: 0-0 Tstrap: 0-0 Ckp: 0-0

Strategic Knight (USA)

98(99) (62)61
4-y-o b g Johannesburg (USA)-Western Friend (USA) (Gone West (USA))
R C Guest Shaun Taylor

Placings:33/000004000000 (3717)
2009: 8[0]SD, 8[0]SD, 9[0]SD, 7[0]SD, 7[0]G, 8[4]F, 9[0]GF, 8[0]G, 9[0]GF, 10[0]G, 8[0]G, 8[0]SD,

	Starts	1st	2nd	3rd	Win & Pl
Career Total (Turf)	7	0	0	0	241
Career Total (AW)	7	0	0	2	949

Going (Turf): Sf: 0-0 GS: 0-0 Gd: 0-4 GF: 0-2 Fm: 0-1
Distance: 5f/6f: 0-0 7f-8f: 0-7 9f-13f: 0-7 14f+: 0-0
Track : LH: 0-11 RH: 0-2 Tight: 0-7 Gall: 0-0
Aids: Bl: 0-0 Vi: 0-0 Tstrap: 0-0 Ckp: 0-0
Best Rating: 69 12/07 Sthl 1m std-slw

Strategic Mount

100 (63)106
6-y-o b g Montjeu (IRE)-Danlu (USA) (Danzig (USA))
P F I Cole Ben & Sir Martyn Arbib

Placings:56/34241110/61000/001230-000 (5170)
2009: 12[0]GF, 12[0]G, 12[0]GF,

	Starts	1st	2nd	3rd	Win & Pl
Career Total (Turf)	23	5	2	2	114066
Career Total (AW)	1	0	0	0	

103	8/08	Asct	1m4f	(0-100)H	G-S	£17230
102	8/07	Asct	1m4f	(0-100)H	G-F	£17234
98	8/06	Gdwd	1m4f	(0-105)H	G-F	£52972
90	7/06	Nott	1m6f15y	(0-85)H	G-F	£6477
84	6/06	Bath	1m3f144y		G-F	£3238

Total win prize-money £97153

Going (Turf): Sf: 0-2 GS: 1-4 Gd: 0-7 GF: 4-10 Fm: 0-0
Distance: 5f/6f: 0-0 7f-8f: 0-2 9f-13f: 4-17 14f+: 1-5
Track : LH: 2-9 RH: 3-11 Tight: 2-7 Gall: 2-10
Aids: Bl: 0-2 Vi: 0-0 Tstrap: 0-0 Ckp: 0-0
Best Rating: 106 8/08 Ches 1m5f89y gd-fm

Very useful; effective at up to 1m6f; best on fast ground; has worn blinkers and a tongue tie.

Strategic Mover (USA)

97(100) (71)77
4-y-o ch g Grand Slam (USA)-Efficient Frontier (USA) (Mt. Livermore (USA))
P Butler (P F I Cole 26/10) Miss M Bryant

Placings:344/244-56300004 (7834)
2009: 7[5]SD, 5[6]SD, 7[3]GF, 10[0]SD, 12[0]SD, 8[0]SD, 9[0]SD, 6[4]SD,

	Starts	1st	2nd	3rd	Win & Pl
Career Total (Turf)	7	0	1	2	4311
Career Total (AW)	7	0	0	0	0

Going (Turf): Sf: 0-0 GS: 0-1 Gd: 0-1 GF: 0-4 Fm: 0-1
Distance: 5f/6f: 0-2 7f-8f: 0-9 9f-13f: 0-3 14f+: 0-0
Track : LH: 0-3 RH: 0-6 Tight: 0-3 Gall: 0-0
Aids: Bl: 0-1 Vi: 0-3 Tstrap: 0-0 Ckp: 0-0
Best Rating: 92 8/07 Sals 1m gd-fm

Moderate; stays 7f; acts on most ground and Polytrack; has worn a tongue tie and a visor.

Strategic Princess (IRE)

96(91) (57)57
3-y-o b f Hawk Wing (USA)-Puteri Wentworth (Sadler's Wells (USA))
P F I Cole H R H Sultan Ahmad Shah

Placings:054540 (5990)
2009: 12[0]GF, 12[5]GF, 12[4]SD, 18[5]G, 16[4]G, 16[0]SD,

	Starts	1st	2nd	3rd	Win & Pl
Career Total (Turf)	4	0	0	0	241
Career Total (AW)	2	0	0	0	289

Going (Turf): Sf: 0-0 GS: 0-0 Gd: 0-2 GF: 0-2 Fm: 0-0
Distance: 5f/6f: 0-0 7f-8f: 0-0 9f-13f: 0-3 14f+: 0-3
Track : LH: 0-4 RH: 0-2 Tight: 0-1 Gall: 0-1
Aids: Bl: 0-0 Vi: 0-0 Tstrap: 0-0 Ckp: 0-0
Best Rating: 57 8/09 Gdwd 2m good

Moderate form at up to 2m2f on fast ground and Fibresand.

Stratford Bridge

76 12
6-y-o b g Fraam-Moorland Stroll (IRE) (Inzar (USA))
J L Spearing R D Tudor

Placings:0 (6551)
2009: 6[0]G,

	Starts	1st	2nd	3rd	Win & Pl
Career Total (Turf)	1	0	0	0	

Going (Turf): Sf: 0-0 GS: 0-0 Gd: 0-1 GF: 0-0 Fm: 0-0
Distance: 5f/6f: 0-1 7f-8f: 0-0 9f-13f: 0-0 14f+: 0-0
Track : LH: 0-0 RH: 0-0 Tight: 0-0 Gall: 0-1
Aids: Bl: 0-0 Vi: 0-0 Tstrap: 0-0 Ckp: 0-0
Best Rating: 12 10/09 Wind 6f good

Strathcal

105(99) (79)82
3-y-o b g Beat Hollow-Shall We Run (Hotfoot)
H Morrison The Caledonian Racing Society

Placings:6650-41123633 (7476)
2009: 12[4]GF, 12[1]GF, 12[1]GF, 14[2]G, 14[3]G, 13[6]GF, 16[3]SD, 12[3]SD,

	Starts	1st	2nd	3rd	Win & Pl
Career Total (Turf)	7	2	1	1	9147
Career Total (AW)	5	0	0	2	1088

79	6/09	Newb	1m4f5y	(0-75)H	G-F	£3238
73	5/09	Sals	1m4f	(0-65)H	G-F	£3043

Total win prize-money £6282

Going (Turf): Sf: 0-1 GS: 0-0 Gd: 0-2 GF: 2-4 Fm: 0-0
Distance: 5f/6f: 0-0 7f-8f: 0-4 9f-13f: 2-4 14f+: 0-4
Track : LH: 1-5 RH: 1-7 Tight: 1-2 Gall: 1-2
Aids: Bl: 0-0 Vi: 0-0 Tstrap: 0-0 Ckp: 0-0
Best Rating: 82 7/09 Sand 1m6f good

Fair; stays 1m6f; acts on fast ground and on Polytrack.

Strathmore (IRE)

99(106) (73)68
5-y-o gr g Fath (USA)-In The Highlands (Petong)
R A Fahey Jonathan Gill

Placings:003/54415000332636 3/122620404-330220602404044400 (6220)
2009: 5[3]SD, 5[3]SD, 5[0]SD, 5[2]SD, 5[2]GF, 5[0]GF, 5[6]G, 5[0]GF, 5[2]GF, 6[4]GF, 5[0]GF, 5[4]GF, 5[0]G, 6[4]GS, 5[4]S, 5[4]GF, 6[0]GS, 5[0]GF,

	Starts	1st	2nd	3rd	Win & Pl
Career Total (Turf)	27	1	2	1	5486
Career Total (AW)	18	1	5	6	7056

71	1/08	Sthl	6f	(0-65)H	STD	£2047
73	5/07	Rdcr	6f	(0-70)H	GD	£2817

Total win prize-money £4865

Going (Turf): Sf: 0-4 GS: 0-4 Gd: 1-6 GF: 0-13 Fm: 0-0
Distance: 5f/6f: 2-38 7f-8f: 0-7 9f-13f: 0-0 14f+: 0-0
Track : LH: 1-17 RH: 0-3 Tight: 0-15 Gall: 0-1
Aids: Bl: 0-1 Vi: 0-0 Tstrap: 0-6 Ckp: 0-6
Best Rating: 73 4/08 Sthl 5f stand

Modest; effective over 6f; acts on fast and easy ground; also goes on Fibresand and Polytrack;has worn cheek-pieces.

Stratton Banker (IRE)

82 51
2-y-o b g One Cool Cat (USA)-Birthday (IRE) (Singspiel (IRE))
S C Williams James & Sarah

Placings:00 (5722)
2009: 7[0]GF, 7[0]F,

	Starts	1st	2nd	3rd	Win & Pl
Career Total (Turf)	2	0	0	0	

Going (Turf): Sf: 0-0 GS: 0-0 Gd: 0-0 GF: 0-1 Fm: 0-1
Distance: 5f/6f: 0-0 7f-8f: 0-2 9f-13f: 0-0 14f+: 0-0
Track : LH: 0-0 RH: 0-0 Tight: 0-0 Gall: 0-0
Aids: Bl: 0-0 Vi: 0-0 Tstrap: 0-0 Ckp: 0-0
Best Rating: 51 9/09 Folk 7f firm

Stravella (IRE)

101 80
4-y-o b f Stravinsky (USA)-Princess Ellen (Tirol)
R M Beckett Five Horses Ltd

Placings:51530 (4526)
2009: 8[5]GF, 8[1]G, 8[5]G, 9[3]G, 9[0]S,

	Starts	1st	2nd	3rd	Win & Pl
Career Total (Turf)	5	1	0	1	3422

77	5/09	Chep	1m14y	GD	£2396

Total win prize-money £2396

Going (Turf): Sf: 0-1 GS: 0-0 Gd: 1-3 GF: 0-1 Fm: 0-0
Distance: 5f/6f: 0-0 7f-8f: 0-1 9f-13f: 1-4 14f+: 0-0
Track : LH: 0-0 RH: 0-4 Tight: 0-2 Gall: 0-0
Aids: Bl: 0-0 Vi: 0-0 Tstrap: 0-0 Ckp: 0-0
Best Rating: 80 7/09 Leic 1m1f218y good

Fair; stays 1m and acts on good ground.

Straversjoy

88(76) (25)44
2-y-o b f Kayf Tara-Stravsea (Handsome Sailor)
R Hollinshead E Bennion

Placings:000 (7638)
2009: 8^0GS, 8^0S, 8^0SD,

	Starts	1st	2nd	3rd	Win & Pl
Career Total (Turf)	2	0	0	0	
Career Total (AW)	1	0	0	0	

Going (Turf): **Sf: 0-1 GS: 0-1 Gd: 0-0 GF: 0-0 Fm: 0-0**
Distance: 5f/6f: 0-0 7f-8f: 0-2 9f-13f: 0-1 14f+: 0-0
Track : LH: 0-3 RH: 0-0 Tight: 0-0 Gall: 0-1
Aids: Bl: 0-0 Vi: 0-0 Tstrap: 0-0 Ckp: 0-0
Best Rating: 44 11/09 Nott 1m75y soft

Stravita

(105) (68)**63**
5-y-o b m Weet-A-Minute (IRE)-Stravsea (Handsome Sailor)
R Hollinshead E Bennion

Placings:1/5F050/64020135501-530566 (7840)
2009: 16^5SS, 14^3SD, 12^0SD, 14^5SD, 13^6SD, 12^6SS,

	Starts	1st	2nd	3rd	Win & Pl
Career Total (Turf)	6	1	1	1	3576
Career Total (AW)	17	2	0	1	5945
68	12/08 Sthl	1m4f	(0-60)H	STD	£2047
60	10/08 Leic	1m3f183y		GD	£2498
70	11/06 Wolv	1m141y		SF	£3469

Total win prize-money £8015

Going (Turf): Sf: 0-3 GS: 0-1 **Gd: 1-1** GF: 0-1 Fm: 0-0
Distance: 5f/6f: 0-0 7f-8f: 0-0 **9f-13f: 3-16** 14f+: 0-7
Track : **LH: 2-21** RH: 1-2 **Tight: 1-11** Gall: 0-0
Aids: Bl: 0-0 Vi: 0-0 Tstrap: 2-13 Ckp: 2-13
Best Rating: 70 11/06 Wolv 1m141y std-fst

Moderate; acts on Polytrack and good ground; stays 1m4f; has worn cheekpieces.

Stravonian

75 **47**
9-y-o b g Luso-In The Evening (IRE) (Distinctly North (USA))
D A Nolan Miss M McFadyen-Murray

Placings:00560/00/005/6004004460-0 (1102)
2009: 16^0GF,

	Starts	1st	2nd	3rd	Win & Pl
Career Total (Turf)	20	0	0	0	722
Career Total (AW)	1	0	0	0	

Going (Turf): **Sf: 0-4 GS: 0-4 Gd: 0-4 GF: 0-8 Fm: 0-0**
Distance: 5f/6f: 0-0 7f-8f: 0-0 9f-13f: 0-13 14f+: 0-8
Track : LH: 0-4 RH: 0-15 Tight: 0-15 Gall: 0-1
Aids: Bl: 0-0 Vi: 0-0 Tstrap: 0-1 Ckp: 0-1
Best Rating: 47 8/08 Muss 1m6f soft

Strawberry Moon (IRE)

96 **79**
4-y-o b f Alhaarth (IRE)-Dancing Drop (Green Desert (USA))
B Smart Mrs Julie Martin

Placings:223333131-14 (2313)
2009: 7^1F, 7^4GF,

	Starts	1st	2nd	3rd	Win & Pl
Career Total (Turf)	11	3	2	5	14956
79	5/09 Rdcr	7f	(0-85)H	FRM	£4857
74	10/08 Rdcr	7f	(0-70)H	GD	£2914
68	9/08 Rdcr	6f		G-S	£2590

Total win prize-money £10361

Going (Turf): Sf: 0-2 **GS: 1-3 Gd: 1-1** GF: 0-4 **Fm: 1-1**
Distance: 5f/6f: 1-6 **7f-8f: 2-5** 9f-13f: 0-0 14f+: 0-0
Track : LH: 0-2 RH: 0-1 Tight: 0-1 Gall: 0-0
Aids: Bl: 0-0 Vi: 0-0 Tstrap: 0-0 Ckp: 0-0
Best Rating: 79 5/09 Carl 7f200y gd-fm

Modest; effective over 6f-7f; acts on fast and easy ground.

Strawberrydaiquiri

110 **116**
3-y-o gr f Dansili-Strawberry Morn (CAN) (Travelling Victor (CAN))
Sir Michael Stoute Mrs R J Jacobs

Placings:211114 (6479)
2009: 8^2GF, 8^1G, 8^1G, 8^1G, 8^1GF, 8^4GF,

	Starts	1st	2nd	3rd	Win & Pl
Career Total (Turf)	6	4	1	0	85238
116	8/09 Sand	1m14y		G-F	£22708
106	7/09 Asct	1m		GD	£25546
106	7/09 Sand	1m14y		GD	£22708
87	5/09 Wind	1m67y		GD	£2729

Total win prize-money £73693

Going (Turf): Sf: 0-0 GS: 0-0 **Gd: 3-3** GF: 1-3 Fm: 0-0
Distance: 5f/6f: 0-0 7f-8f: 1-2 **9f-13f: 3-4** 14f+: 0-0
Track : LH: 0-0 **RH: 4-5** Tight: 1-2 Gall: 1-1
Aids: Bl: 0-0 Vi: 0-0 Tstrap: 0-0 Ckp: 0-0
Best Rating: 116 8/09 Sand 1m14y gd-fm

Group class; triple Listed winner; stays 1m; acts on good and faster ground.

Street Crime

(88) (66)**65**
4-y-o b g Tagula (IRE)-Brandon Princess (Waajib)
R Lee Richard Lee

Placings:03320-0 (3223)
2009: 12^0SD,

	Starts	1st	2nd	3rd	Win & Pl
Career Total (Turf)	3	0	0	1	496
Career Total (AW)	3	0	1	1	990

Going (Turf): **Sf: 0-1 GS: 0-1 Gd: 0-1 GF: 0-0 Fm: 0-0**
Distance: 5f/6f: 0-0 7f-8f: 0-0 9f-13f: 0-6 14f+: 0-0
Track : LH: 0-5 RH: 0-1 Tight: 0-5 Gall: 0-0
Aids: Bl: 0-0 Vi: 0-0 Tstrap: 0-0 Ckp: 0-0
Best Rating: 66 8/08 Wolv 1m1f103y stand

Modest; stays 1m 4f; acts on good to soft and Polytrack.

Street Devil (USA)

101(100) (80)**73**
4-y-o gr g Street Cry (IRE)-Math (USA) (Devil's Bag (USA))
R Curtis John Wardle

Placings:3/036020-1436 (2263)
2009: 8^1SD, 10^4GF, 8^3SD, 9^6G,

	Starts	1st	2nd	3rd	Win & Pl
Career Total (Turf)	9	0	1	2	2283
Career Total (AW)	2	1	0	1	2994
80	3/09 Sthl	1m	STD	£2590	

Total win prize-money £2590

Going (Turf): **Sf: 0-4 GS: 0-1 Gd: 0-2 GF: 0-2 Fm: 0-0**
Distance: 5f/6f: 0-0 **7f-8f: 1-7** 9f-13f: 0-4 14f+: 0-0
Track : **LH: 1-5** RH: 0-1 Tight: 0-2 Gall: 0-0
Aids: Bl: 0-0 Vi: 0-0 Tstrap: 0-0 Ckp: 0-0
Best Rating: 80 3/09 Sthl 1m stand

Fair; stays 1m; acts on easy ground; suited by Fibresand.

Street Diva (USA)

95(96) (64)**42**
4-y-o ch f Street Cry (IRE)-Arctic Valley (USA) (Arctic Tern (USA))
A B Haynes (R Curtis 6/8) Joe McCarthy

Placings:6504/00000-00050 (5632)
2009: 8^0GF, 7^0F, 5^0G, 6^5G, 6^0GS,

	Starts	1st	2nd	3rd	Win & Pl
Career Total (Turf)	6	0	0	0	0
Career Total (AW)	8	0	0	0	142

Going (Turf): **Sf: 0-0 GS: 0-1 Gd: 0-3 GF: 0-1 Fm: 0-1**
Distance: 5f/6f: 0-5 7f-8f: 0-7 9f-13f: 0-2 14f+: 0-0
Track : LH: 0-8 RH: 0-3 Tight: 0-5 Gall: 0-2
Aids: Bl: 0-0 Vi: 0-0 Tstrap: 0-0 Ckp: 0-0
Best Rating: 64 9/07 Kemp 7f stand

Street Entertainer (IRE)

80(94) (80)**50**
2-y-o br c Danehill Dancer (IRE)-Opera Ridge (FR) (Indian Ridge)
Mrs A J Perrett George Materna

Placings:024 (7522)
2009: 8^0G, 8^2SD, 8^4SD,

	Starts	1st	2nd	3rd	Win & Pl
Career Total (Turf)	1	0	0	0	
Career Total (AW)	2	0	1	0	1272

Going (Turf): **Sf: 0-0 GS: 0-0 Gd: 0-1 GF: 0-0 Fm: 0-0**
Distance: 5f/6f: 0-0 7f-8f: 0-3 9f-13f: 0-0 14f+: 0-0
Track : LH: 0-2 RH: 0-0 Tight: 0-2 Gall: 0-0
Aids: Bl: 0-0 Vi: 0-0 Tstrap: 0-0 Ckp: 0-0
Best Rating: 80 11/09 Ling 1m stand

Fair; effective over 1m; acts on Polytrack.

Street Power (USA)

104(107) (96)**84**
4-y-o b/br g Street Cry (IRE)-Javana (USA) (Sandpit (BRZ))
J R Gask Horses First Racing Limited

Placings:0/00-110123411120 (7558)
2009: 7^1SD, 7^1SD, 7^0SD, 6^1SD, 5^2SF, 6^3GF, 6^4HY, 7^1SD, 6^1G, 6^1SD, 6^2SD, 7^0SD,

	Starts	1st	2nd	3rd	Win & Pl
Career Total (Turf)	4	1	0	1	9023
Career Total (AW)	11	5	2	0	18816
96	8/09 Kemp	6f	(0-80)H	STD	£4727
84	7/09 Asct	6f	(0-90)H	GD	£7771
88	6/09 Kemp	7f	(0-85)H	STD	£4727
78	2/09 Ling	6f	(0-65)H	STD	£2047
71	1/09 Kemp	7f	(0-60)H	STD	£2047
63	1/09 Kemp	7f	(0-55)H	STD	£2047

Total win prize-money £23366

Going (Turf): Sf: 0-1 GS: 0-0 **Gd: 1-1** GF: 0-2 Fm: 0-0

Distance: 5f/6f: 3-7 7f-8f: 3-8 9f-13f: 0-0 14f+: 0-0
Track : LH: 1-6 **RH: 4-5 Tight: 1-5** Gall: 0-1
Aids: Bl: 0-0 Vi: 0-0 Tstrap: 0-0 Ckp: 0-0
Best Rating: 96 8/09 Kemp 6f stand

Very useful; effective over 6f-7f; well suited to Polytrack and a sound surface on turf.

Street Spirit (USA)

92(92) (53)**51**
3-y-o b/br f Street Cry (IRE)-Be Good Or Be Gone (USA) (Gulch (USA))
T D Easterby Ann & Dale Wilsdon

Placings:200300 (3449)
2009: 5^{2}GF, 6^{0}F, 5^{0}GS, 7^{3}SD, 8^{0}G, 7^{0}GF,

	Starts	1st	2nd	3rd	Win & Pl
Career Total (Turf)	5	0	1	0	674
Career Total (AW)	1	0	0	1	302

Going (Turf): Sf: 0-0 GS: 0-1 Gd: 0-1 GF: 0-2 Fm: 0-1
Distance: 5f/6f: 0-3 7f-8f: 0-2 9f-13f: 0-1 14f+: 0-0
Track : LH: 0-3 RH: 0-2 Tight: 0-3 Gall: 0-0
Aids: Bl: 0-0 Vi: 0-0 Tstrap: 0-0 Ckp: 0-0
Best Rating: 53 6/09 Sthl 7f stand

Moderate; stays 7f; acts on fast ground and on Fibresand.

Street Warrior (IRE)

83 (83)**55**
6-y-o b g Royal Applause-Anne Bonny (Ajdal (USA))
H J Evans Battlefield Brook Racing

Placings:024/523014000/54144005/0 (1014)
2009: 10^{0}G,

	Starts	1st	2nd	3rd	Win & Pl
Career Total (Turf)	17	2	2	1	12961
Career Total (AW)	4	0	0	0	481

78 4/07 Bath 1m5y (0-80)H FRM £5181
85 9/06 Leic 1m60y (0-75)H G-F £3238
Total win prize-money £8421

Going (Turf): Sf: 0-1 GS: 0-1 Gd: 0-7 **GF: 1-7 Fm: 1-1**
Distance: 5f/6f: 0-1 7f-8f: 0-6 **9f-13f: 2-14** 14f+: 0-0
Track : LH: 1-16 RH: 1-2 **Tight: 1-10** Gall: 0-1
Aids: Bl: 0-0 Vi: 0-0 Tstrap: 0-0 Ckp: 0-0
Best Rating: 85 9/06 Leic 1m60y gd-fm

Fair; half-brother to several winners; effective at around 1m; acts on fast ground.

Streets Apart (USA)

99(102) (75)**68**
4-y-o b f Street Cry (IRE)-Saintly Speaking (USA) (Dahar (USA))
W R Swinburn P W Harris

Placings:623-430234 (6074)
2009: 10^{4}GF, 12^{3}GF, 12^{0}GS, 10^{2}S, 9^{3}GF, 9^{4}SD,

	Starts	1st	2nd	3rd	Win & Pl
Career Total (Turf)	7	0	1	3	2841
Career Total (AW)	2	0	1	0	1927

Going (Turf): Sf: 0-1 GS: 0-2 Gd: 0-0 GF: 0-4 Fm: 0-0
Distance: 5f/6f: 0-0 7f-8f: 0-0 9f-13f: 0-9 14f+: 0-0
Track : LH: 0-4 RH: 0-5 Tight: 0-6 Gall: 0-2
Aids: Bl: 0-0 Vi: 0-2 Tstrap: 0-3 Ckp: 0-3
Best Rating: 75 9/08 GrLe 1m2f stand

Fair maiden; stays 1m2f; acts on Polytrack.

Streets Of War (USA)

85 **57**
2-y-o b/br c Street Cry (IRE)-Saint Boom (USA) (Saint Ballado (CAN))
P W Chapple-Hyam Mrs Violet Mercer

Placings:6 (7034)
2009: 8^{6}S,

	Starts	1st	2nd	3rd	Win & Pl
Career Total (Turf)	1	0	0	0	0

Going (Turf): Sf: 0-1 GS: 0-0 Gd: 0-0 GF: 0-0 Fm: 0-0
Distance: 5f/6f: 0-0 7f-8f: 0-1 9f-13f: 0-0 14f+: 0-0
Track : LH: 0-0 RH: 0-0 Tight: 0-0 Gall: 0-0
Aids: Bl: 0-0 Vi: 0-0 Tstrap: 0-0 Ckp: 0-0
Best Rating: 57 10/09 Newb 1m soft

Strensall

100 (32)**56**
12-y-o b g Beveled (USA)-Payvashooz (Ballacashtal (CAN))
R E Barr R E Barr

Placings:00/0/0345060205020066**3/152006**003101160420/**60**22040333203031206001**420**/020034050552000/**0**5500 10033060306/026365160430/02001052500**0**/0000660-030642620 (7081)
2009: 5^{0}F, 5^{3}GF, 5^{0}GF, 5^{6}G, 5^{4}GF, 5^{2}GF, 5^{6}GF, 5^{2}GF, 5^{0}S,

	Starts	1st	2nd	3rd	Win & Pl
Career Total (Turf)	121	8	14	14	76997
Career Total (AW)	14	1	2	1	4827

76	8/07	Muss	5f	(0-70)H	GD	£3886
76	7/06	Catt	5f	(0-85)H	FRM	£6477
78	6/05	Thsk	5f	(0-70)H	G-F	£5447
84	10/03	Catt	5f	D(0-80)H	G-F	£3571
83	7/03	Newc	5f	C(0-90)H	GD	£10227
68	8/02	Catt	5f	F(0-65)H	G-F	£3290
68	7/02	Catt	5f	D(0-85)H	G-F	£4875
59	7/02	Muss	5f	F(0-60)H	G-F	£3241
54	1/02	Wolv	5f	D	STD	£2989

Total win prize-money £44006

Going (Turf): Sf: 0-6 GS: 0-13Gd: 2-31**GF: 5-56** Fm: 1-15
Distance: 5f/6f: 9-133 7f-8f: 0-1 9f-13f: 0-1 14f+: 0-0
Track : LH: 1-14 RH: 0-3 **Tight: 1-12** Gall: 0-2
Aids: Bl: 0-0 Vi: 0-0 Tstrap: 0-0 Ckp: 0-0
Best Rating: 86 8/03 Ches 5f16y gd-fm

Modest handicapper; suited by 5f; has won on easy ground, but is best on a fast surface; goes well at Catterick.

Strevelyn

81(59) **47**
3-y-o br g Namid-Kali (Linamix (FR))
Mrs A Duffield Les Stirling

Placings:006-000 (3711)
2009: 8^{0}GS, 11^{0}GF, 8^{0}SD,

	Starts	1st	2nd	3rd	Win & Pl
Career Total (Turf)	5	0	0	0	0
Career Total (AW)	1	0	0	0	

Going (Turf): Sf: 0-0 GS: 0-2 Gd: 0-2 GF: 0-1 Fm: 0-0
Distance: 5f/6f: 0-1 7f-8f: 0-3 9f-13f: 0-2 14f+: 0-0
Track : LH: 0-2 RH: 0-1 Tight: 0-2 Gall: 0-0
Aids: Bl: 0-0 Vi: 0-0 Tstrap: 0-0 Ckp: 0-0
Best Rating: 47 10/08 Rdcr 7f good

Strictly

105(97) (68)**87**
3-y-o b f Falbrav (IRE)-Dance On (Caerleon (USA))
Sir Michael Stoute Cheveley Park Stud

Placings:2-2132023**0** (6167)
2009: 5^{2}GS, 6^{1}GS, 5^{3}GF, 5^{2}GF, 5^{0}G, 5^{2}GF, 5^{3}F, **6**^{0}SD,

	Starts	1st	2nd	3rd	Win & Pl
Career Total (Turf)	7	1	3	2	10203
Career Total (AW)	2	0	1	0	1445

75 5/09 Donc 6f G-S £3238
Total win prize-money £3238

Going (Turf): Sf: 0-0 **GS: 1-2** Gd: 0-1 GF: 0-3 Fm: 0-1
Distance: 5f/6f: 1-9 7f-8f: 0-0 9f-13f: 0-0 14f+: 0-0
Track : LH: 0-2 RH: 0-1 Tight: 0-0 Gall: 0-2
Aids: Bl: 0-0 Vi: 0-0 Tstrap: 0-0 Ckp: 0-0
Best Rating: 87 8/09 Sand 5f6y gd-fm

Fair; stays 6f; acts on easy ground but handles fast.

Strictly Dancing (IRE)

93 **70**
2-y-o b f Danehill Dancer (IRE)-Lochangel (Night Shift (USA))
A M Balding J C Smith

Placings:52 (6615)
2009: 6^{5}GF, 6^{2}G,

	Starts	1st	2nd	3rd	Win & Pl
Career Total (Turf)	2	0	1	0	1445

Going (Turf): Sf: 0-0 GS: 0-0 Gd: 0-1 GF: 0-1 Fm: 0-0
Distance: 5f/6f: 0-0 7f-8f: 0-2 9f-13f: 0-0 14f+: 0-0
Track : LH: 0-0 RH: 0-0 Tight: 0-0 Gall: 0-0
Aids: Bl: 0-0 Vi: 0-0 Tstrap: 0-0 Ckp: 0-0
Best Rating: 70 10/09 Newb 6f110y good

Strictly Lambada

86 **71**
2-y-o b f Red Ransom (USA)-Bella Lambada (Lammtarra (USA))
J H M Gosden Helena Springfield Ltd

Placings:5 (6920)
2009: 8^{5}GF,

	Starts	1st	2nd	3rd	Win & Pl
Career Total (Turf)	1	0	0	0	153

Going (Turf): Sf: 0-0 GS: 0-0 Gd: 0-0 GF: 0-1 Fm: 0-0
Distance: 5f/6f: 0-0 7f-8f: 0-0 9f-13f: 0-1 14f+: 0-0
Track : LH: 0-0 RH: 0-0 Tight: 0-0 Gall: 0-0
Aids: Bl: 0-0 Vi: 0-0 Tstrap: 0-0 Ckp: 0-0
Best Rating: 71 10/09 Yarm 1m3y gd-fm

Strictly Royal

76(88) (27)**21**
3-y-o ch g Imperial Dancer-Royal Logic (Royal Applause)
M R Channon Miss Bridget Coyle

Placings:4600-00 (1270)
2009: 12^{0}SD, 8^{0}G,

	Starts	1st	2nd	3rd	Win & Pl
Career Total (Turf)	5	0	0	0	0
Career Total (AW)	1	0	0	0	

Going (Turf): **Sf: 0-1 GS: 0-1 Gd: 0-2 GF: 0-1 Fm: 0-0**
Distance: 5f/6f: 0-2 7f-8f: 0-2 9f-13f: 0-2 14f+: 0-0
Track : LH: 0-0 RH: 0-2 Tight: 0-0 Gall: 0-0
Aids: Bl: 0-0 Vi: 0-1 Tstrap: 0-0 Ckp: 0-0
Best Rating: **27** 4/09 Kemp 1m4f stand

Strident (USA)

(88) (40)**57**
8-y-o ch g Deputy Commander (USA)-Regrets Only (USA) (Black Tie Affair)
N P Moore Miss M A Smith

Placings:6/5400/**00**/200150-0 (0169)
2009: 13^{0}SD,

	Starts	1st	2nd	3rd	Win & Pl
Career Total (Turf)	10	1	1	0	2503
Career Total (AW)	4	0	0	0	0

10/08 Mulh 1m6f165y GD £1176
Total win prize-money £1176

Going (Turf): Sf: 0-1 GS: 0-0 **Gd: 1-3** GF: 0-2 Fm: 0-1
Distance: 5f/6f: 0-1 7f-8f: 0-0 9f-13f: 0-10 **14f+: 1-3**
Track : LH: 0-3 RH: 0-6 Tight: 0-2 Gall: 0-1
Aids: Bl: 0-0 Vi: 0-1 Tstrap: 0-1 Ckp: 0-1
Best Rating: **71** 7/05 Curr 1m2f gd-fm

Striding Edge (IRE)

103(100) (82)**72**
3-y-o b/br g Rock Of Gibraltar (IRE)-For Criquette (IRE) (Barathea (IRE))
W R Muir Linkslade Racing

Placings:05132423-002351264 (6496)
2009: 7^{0}SD, 8^{0}GF, 8^{2}G, 8^{3}GF, 8^{5}GF, 8^{1}SD, 8^{2}SD, 8^{6}SD, 8^{4}SF,

	Starts	1st	2nd	3rd	Win & Pl
Career Total (Turf)	8	0	2	2	2593
Career Total (AW)	9	2	2	1	8095

75 8/09 Kemp 1m (0-75)H STD £2590
66 6/08 GrLe 6f STD £2388
Total win prize-money £4978

Going (Turf): **Sf: 0-0 GS: 0-1 Gd: 0-4 GF: 0-3 Fm: 0-0**
Distance: 5f/6f: 1-4 7f-8f: 1-8 9f-13f: 0-5 14f+: 0-0
Track : LH: 1-4 RH: 1-9 Tight: 0-7 **Gall: 1-2**
Aids: Bl: 0-0 Vi: 0-0 Tstrap: 0-0 Ckp: 0-0
Best Rating: **82** 9/09 Kemp 1m stand

Fair; effective over 7f-1m; acts on Polytrack and fast ground.

Strike A Deal (IRE)

90 **62**
2-y-o b f Chineur (FR)-Bishop's Lake (Lake Coniston (IRE))
C F Wall Racingeight Partners

Placings:065 (7095)
2009: 6^{0}G, 8^{6}S, 8^{5}G,

	Starts	1st	2nd	3rd	Win & Pl
Career Total (Turf)	3	0	0	0	129

Going (Turf): **Sf: 0-1 GS: 0-0 Gd: 0-2 GF: 0-0 Fm: 0-0**
Distance: 5f/6f: 0-0 7f-8f: 0-2 9f-13f: 0-1 14f+: 0-0
Track : LH: 0-0 RH: 0-0 Tight: 0-0 Gall: 0-0
Aids: Bl: 0-0 Vi: 0-0 Tstrap: 0-0 Ckp: 0-0
Best Rating: **62** 10/09 Yarm 1m3y good

Strike Force

101(104) (70)**67**
5-y-o b g Dansili-Miswaki Belle (USA) (Miswaki (USA))
Miss J Feilden Miss A L Hutchinson

Placings:0155/**4424154344230210**6**V3**/**000300621**10452 0-**0606**20235353504300 (7495)
2009: 12^{0}SD, 9^{6}SD, 9^{0}SD, 10^{6}F, 12^{2}GF, 10^{0}GF, 11^{2}GF, 10^{3}GF, 11^{5}GF, 9^{3}F, 11^{5}GF, 9^{3}SD, 12^{5}SD, 10^{0}GF, 12^{4}SF, 9^{3}SD, 9^{0}SD, 12^{0}SD,

	Starts	1st	2nd	3rd	Win & Pl
Career Total (Turf)	24	2	3	4	10783
Career Total (AW)	32	3	4	4	12835

70 9/08 Wolv 1m1f103y (0-65)H STD £2388
69 9/08 Wolv 1m141y (0-60)H STD £2388
65 7/07 Catt 5f212y GD £2730
60 3/07 Wolv 5f216y STD £2388
69 6/06 Ling 6f G-F £3886
Total win prize-money £13781

Going (Turf): Sf: 0-1 GS: 0-1 **Gd: 1-5 GF: 1-14** Fm: 0-3
Distance: **5f/6f: 3-12** 7f-8f: 0-9 9f-13f: 2-35 14f+: 0-0
Track : **LH: 4-44** RH: 0-2 **Tight: 4-33** Gall: 0-5
Aids: Bl: 0-1 Vi: 0-0 Tstrap: 2-22 Ckp: 2-22
Best Rating: **70** 9/08 Wolv 1m1f103y stand

Modest; stays 1m3f; acts on fast ground; goes on Polytrack; has worn cheekpieces.

Strike Shot

94(87) (56)**75**
2-y-o b g Avonbridge-Final Shot (Dalsaan)
W R Muir The Strike Partnership

Placings:615056 (5194)
2009: 5^{6}GF, 5^{1}G, 6^{5}GF, 5^{0}GS, 6^{5}GS, 5^{6}SD,

	Starts	1st	2nd	3rd	Win & Pl
Career Total (Turf)	5	1	0	0	3886
Career Total (AW)	1	0	0	0	0

75 5/09 Hayd 5f GD £3885
Total win prize-money £3886

Going (Turf): Sf: 0-0 GS: 0-2 **Gd: 1-1** GF: 0-2 Fm: 0-0
Distance: **5f/6f: 1-5** 7f-8f: 0-1 9f-13f: 0-0 14f+: 0-0
Track : LH: 0-1 RH: 0-0 Tight: 0-1 Gall: 0-0
Aids: Bl: 0-0 Vi: 0-0 Tstrap: 0-1 Ckp: 0-1
Best Rating: **75** 5/09 Hayd 5f good

Fair; effective at 5f and acts on good ground.

Strike The Deal (USA)

111(114) (110)**116**
4-y-o ch c Van Nistelrooy (USA)-Countess Gold (USA) (Mt. Livermore (USA))
J Noseda M Barber

Placings:15310224/5054305-441056110 (7305a)
2009: 5^{4}GF, 6^{4}GF, 6^{1}SD, 6^{0}GF, 6^{5}G, 6^{6}GF, 5^{1}GF, 5^{1}GF, 6^{0}F,

	Starts	1st	2nd	3rd	Win & Pl
Career Total (Turf)	21	3	2	2	216794
Career Total (AW)	3	2	0	0	42682

116 9/09 Newb 5f34y G-F £36900
113 9/09 Donc 5f G-F £23704
110 5/09 Ling 6f STD £9714
109 8/07 Gdwd 6f G-F £39746
76 6/07 Ling 6f STD £2817
Total win prize-money £112882

Going (Turf): Sf: 0-1 GS: 0-0 Gd: 0-6 **GF: 3-12** Fm: 0-1
Distance: **5f/6f: 5-16** 7f-8f: 0-7 9f-13f: 0-1 14f+: 0-0
Track : **LH: 2-4** RH: 0-0 **Tight: 2-2** Gall: 0-1
Aids: Bl: 0-1 **Vi: 3-10** Tstrap: 0-0 Ckp: 0-0
Best Rating: **116** 9/09 Newb 5f34y gd-fm

Group class; winner of the Group 2 Richmond Stakes at two and placed in the Mill Reef, the Prix Robert Papin and the Middle Park; won a Group 3 at Newbury in 2009; suited by 5f-6f; acts on fast ground; goes on Polytrack; has worn a visor and blinkers.

Strike The Tiger (USA)

101 **101**
2-y-o b/br g Tiger Ridge (USA)-R Lucky Strike (USA) (In Excess)
Wesley A Ward Wesley Ward, Mitch Dutko & Ray Sainz

Placings:110 (2995)
2009: 4^{1}SY, 5^{1}GF, 8^{0}SD,

	Starts	1st	2nd	3rd	Win & Pl
Career Total (Turf)	1	1	0	0	28385
Career Total (AW)	2	1	0	0	7917

101 6/09 Asct 5f G-F £28385
4/09 Chur 4f110y SLP £7916
Total win prize-money £36302

Going (Turf): Sf: 0-0 GS: 0-0 Gd: 0-0 **GF: 1-1** Fm: 0-0
Distance: **5f/6f: 1-1** 7f-8f: 0-0 9f-13f: 0-1 14f+: 0-0
Track : LH: 0-0 RH: 0-0 Tight: 0-0 Gall: 0-0
Aids: **Bl: 2-2** Vi: 0-0 Tstrap: 0-0 Ckp: 0-0
Best Rating: **101** 6/09 Asct 5f gd-fm

Very useful; trained in the US; won the 2009 Windsor Castle; effective over 5f; acts on fast ground.

Strike Up The Band

108(107) (103)**110**
6-y-o b g Cyrano De Bergerac-Green Supreme (Primo Dominie)
D Nicholls Barker Moser Nicholls Short

Placings:121221/033040321/0**003**030050/040002422102 4-**000**442630304 (7090)
2009: 6^{0}FT, 6^{0}FT, 5^{0}FT, 5^{4}SD, 5^{4}GF, 5^{2}GF, 5^{6}G, 5^{3}GF, 5^{0}GF, 5^{3}GS, 5^{0}G, 5^{4}SD,

	Starts	1st	2nd	3rd	Win & Pl
Career Total (Turf)	43	5	9	6	172423
Career Total (AW)	7	0	0	1	6101

106 8/08 Asct 5f (0-105)H GD £17278
110 10/06 Chan 5f110y SFT £17241
106 7/05 Gdwd 5f G-S £29000
96 5/05 Gdwd 5f G-F £14500
95 4/05 Pont 5f GD £5460
Total win prize-money £83479

Going (Turf): Sf: 1-4 GS: 1-8 **Gd: 2-13** GF: 1-16 Fm: 0-1
Distance: **5f/6f: 5-46** 7f-8f: 0-4 9f-13f: 0-0 14f+: 0-0
Track : **LH: 1-13** RH: 0-0 Tight: 0-7 Gall: 0-5
Aids: Bl: 0-0 Vi: 0-1 Tstrap: 0-0 Ckp: 0-0
Best Rating: **112** 3/07 Ling 5f stand

Smart; effective at 5f-6f; acts on most ground and on Polytrack; has worn a visor; likes to race prominently.

Strikemaster (IRE)

100(94) (54)**73**

3-y-o b g Xaar-Mas A Fuera (IRE) (Alzao (USA))

B Ellison (J W Hills 26/5) Dan Gilbert

Placings:00640340-3204312 (4470)

2009: 9^{3}SD, 12^{2}SF, 12^{0}SD, 14^{4}F, 12^{3}GF, 16^{1}G, 16^{2}HY,

	Starts	1st	2nd	3rd	Win & Pl
Career Total (Turf)	8	1	1	2	4296
Career Total (AW)	7	0	1	1	1248

69 7/09 Bevl 2m35y (0-65)H GD £2590

Total win prize-money £2590

Going (Turf): Sf: 0-3 GS: 0-1 **Gd: 1-2** GF: 0-1 Fm: 0-1
Distance: 5f/6f: 0-0 7f-8f: 0-3 9f-13f: 0-9 **14f+: 1-3**
Track : LH: 0-10 **RH: 1-3 Tight: 1-5** Gall: 0-1
Aids: Bl: 0-0 Vi: 0-0 Tstrap: 0-0 Ckp: 0-0
Best Rating: 73 7/09 Nott 2m9y heavy

Moderate; stays 2m; acts on fast ground and Polytrack.

Striker Torres (IRE)

95(107) (73)**80**

3-y-o ch g Danehill Dancer (IRE)-Silver Skates (IRE) (Slip Anchor)

B Smart R C Bond

Placings:4322-56050021 (7813)

2009: 7^{5}GF, 7^{6}GS, 8^{0}GF, 8^{5}GF, 10^{0}G, 7^{0}G, 7^{2}SD, 7^{1}SD,

	Starts	1st	2nd	3rd	Win & Pl
Career Total (Turf)	10	0	2	1	4056
Career Total (AW)	2	1	1	0	2752

73 12/09 Wolv 7f32y (0-68)H STD £2047

Total win prize-money £2047

Going (Turf): Sf: 0-1 GS: 0-1 Gd: 0-4 GF: 0-4 Fm: 0-0
Distance: 5f/6f: 0-2 **7f-8f: 1-8** 9f-13f: 0-2 14f+: 0-0
Track : LH: 1-4 RH: 0-1 **Tight: 1-3** Gall: 0-1
Aids: Bl: 0-0 **Vi: 1-2** Tstrap: 0-0 Ckp: 0-0
Best Rating: 80 10/08 Donc 7f good

Modest; effective over 7f; acts on fast and heavy ground and Polytrack; has worn a visor.

Striking Spirit

112 **106**

4-y-o b g Oasis Dream-Aspiring Diva (USA) (Distant View (USA))

D Nicholls N & Z Aboobaker & Bon Accord Racing

Placings:512/6306-1000100000 (6091)

2009: 6^{1}GF, 6^{0}GF, 6^{0}G, 6^{0}GF, 6^{1}GF, 6^{0}G, 6^{0}S, 6^{0}GF, 5^{0}GF, 6^{0}G,

	Starts	1st	2nd	3rd	Win & Pl
Career Total (Turf)	17	3	1	1	21835

106 7/09 York 6f (0-95)H G-F £7771
99 5/09 Asct 6f (0-95)H G-F £7771
77 9/07 Hayd 6f G-F £2590

Total win prize-money £18133

Going (Turf): Sf: 0-1 GS: 0-1 Gd: 0-8 **GF: 3-7** Fm: 0-0
Distance: 5f/6f: 3-16 7f-8f: 0-1 9f-13f: 0-0 14f+: 0-0
Track : LH: 0-1 RH: 0-0 Tight: 0-1 Gall: 0-0
Aids: Bl: 0-0 Vi: 0-0 Tstrap: 0-0 Ckp: 0-0
Best Rating: 106 7/09 York 6f gd-fm

Very useful; effective over 6f; best on good and faster ground; likes to race prominently.

Stringsofmyheart

84(108) (81)**82**

5-y-o b m Halling (USA)-Heart's Harmony (Blushing Groom (FR))

J J Quinn bettingjobs.com

Placings:0/**023151030**/211163334P0-03 (2322)

2009: 12^{0}SD, 12^{3}G,

	Starts	1st	2nd	3rd	Win & Pl
Career Total (Turf)	14	4	1	3	16233
Career Total (AW)	9	1	1	3	4827

82 6/08 Ling 1m2f (0-75)H GD £2331
72 5/08 Chep 1m4f23y (0-75)H SFT £3885
68 5/08 GrLe 1m2f (0-70)H STD £2590
63 6/07 Haml 1m3f16y GD £2590
74 4/07 Pont 1m4f8y (0-70)H G-F £3886

Total win prize-money £15284

Going (Turf): Sf: 1-3 GS: 0-2 **Gd: 2-5** GF: 1-4 Fm: 0-0
Distance: 5f/6f: 0-0 7f-8f: 0-1 **9f-13f: 5-17** 14f+: 0-5
Track : LH: 4-16 RH: 1-6 **Tight: 2-6** Gall: 1-5
Aids: Bl: 0-1 Vi: 0-0 Tstrap: 2-3 Ckp: 2-3
Best Rating: 82 7/08 Asct 1m4f gd-sft

Fair; in top form in the spring of 2008 completing a hat-trick in Class 5 handicaps; effective over 1m2f-1m6f; acts on most ground, including Polytrack.

Strong Storm (USA)

99(95) (71)**74**

3-y-o ch g Giant's Causeway (USA)-Sweeping Story (USA) (End Sweep (USA))

H J Collingridge (J Noseda 30/8) The Storm Again Syndicate

Placings:0-1503310 (7428)

2009: 8^{1}SD, 11^{5}GF, 10^{0}GF, 10^{3}GF, 9^{3}F, 10^{1}GF, **10^{0}SD**,

	Starts	1st	2nd	3rd	Win & Pl
Career Total (Turf)	6	1	0	2	3040
Career Total (AW)	2	1	0	0	2730

59 8/09 Yarm 1m2f21y G-F £2201
71 1/09 Ling 1m STD £2729

Total win prize-money £4932

Going (Turf): Sf: 0-0 GS: 0-0 Gd: 0-0 **GF: 1-5** Fm: 0-1
Distance: 5f/6f: 0-0 7f-8f: 1-2 9f-13f: 1-6 14f+: 0-0
Track : LH: 2-4 RH: 0-2 **Tight: 2-5** Gall: 0-0
Aids: Bl: 0-0 Vi: 0-0 Tstrap: 0-1 Ckp: 0-1
Best Rating: 74 4/09 Wind 1m3f135y gd-fm

Fair; stays 1m and acts on Polytrack.

Strong Vigilance (IRE)

85 **65**

2-y-o ch c Mr Greeley (USA)-Zabadani (Zafonic (USA))

P W Chapple-Hyam Lawrie Inman

Placings:4 (6991)

2009: 7^{4}G,

	Starts	1st	2nd	3rd	Win & Pl
Career Total (Turf)	1	0	0	0	337

Going (Turf): Sf: 0-0 GS: 0-0 Gd: 0-1 GF: 0-0 Fm: 0-0
Distance: 5f/6f: 0-0 7f-8f: 0-1 9f-13f: 0-0 14f+: 0-0
Track : LH: 0-0 RH: 0-0 Tight: 0-0 Gall: 0-0
Aids: Bl: 0-0 Vi: 0-0 Tstrap: 0-0 Ckp: 0-0
Best Rating: 65 10/09 Donc 7f good

Strongarm

91(65) **49**

3-y-o b g Refuse To Bend (IRE)-Surf The Net (Cape Cross (IRE))

A Bailey P T Tellwright

Placings:000-060 (3923)

2009: 11^{0}GF, 10^{6}GF, 12^{0}SD,

	Starts	1st	2nd	3rd	Win & Pl
Career Total (Turf)	5	0	0	0	
Career Total (AW)	1	0	0	0	

Going (Turf): Sf: 0-1 GS: 0-2 Gd: 0-0 GF: 0-2 Fm: 0-0
Distance: 5f/6f: 0-0 7f-8f: 0-2 9f-13f: 0-4 14f+: 0-0
Track : LH: 0-3 RH: 0-0 Tight: 0-2 Gall: 0-0
Aids: Bl: 0-2 Vi: 0-0 Tstrap: 0-0 Ckp: 0-0
Best Rating: 49 10/08 Nott 1m75y soft

Stroppi Poppi

(57) (37)**7**

5-y-o b m Mtoto-Capricious Lass (Corvaro (USA))

Norma Twomey D M & Mrs M A Newland

Placings:050/0-00 (0647)

2009: 12^{0}SD, 10^{0}SD,

	Starts	1st	2nd	3rd	Win & Pl
Career Total (Turf)	1	0	0	0	
Career Total (AW)	5	0	0	0	0

Going (Turf): Sf: 0-0 GS: 0-0 Gd: 0-1 GF: 0-0 Fm: 0-0
Distance: 5f/6f: 0-0 7f-8f: 0-0 9f-13f: 0-6 14f+: 0-0
Track : LH: 0-5 RH: 0-1 Tight: 0-5 Gall: 0-0
Aids: Bl: 0-1 Vi: 0-0 Tstrap: 0-0 Ckp: 0-0
Best Rating: 37 11/07 Ling 1m4f stand

Stubbs Art (IRE)

107(99) (84)**113**

4-y-o ch c Hawk Wing (USA)-Rich Dancer (Halling (USA))

M F De Kock Sheikh Rashid bin Humaid Al Nuaimi

Placings:053213/5336650-3006 (4543)

2009: 7^{3}G, 8^{0}FT, 7^{0}G, 8^{6}G,

	Starts	1st	2nd	3rd	Win & Pl
Career Total (Turf)	16	1	1	5	94462
Career Total (AW)	1	0	0	0	

82 9/07 NmkR 1m1f (0-85) G-F £6477

Total win prize-money £6477

Going (Turf): Sf: 0-0 GS: 0-3 Gd: 0-7 **GF: 1-5** Fm: 0-1
Distance: 5f/6f: 0-2 7f-8f: 0-10 **9f-13f: 1-5** 14f+: 0-0
Track : LH: 0-2 RH: 0-3 Tight: 0-0 Gall: 0-5
Aids: Bl: 0-3 Vi: 0-0 Tstrap: 0-0 Ckp: 0-0
Best Rating: 113 5/08 Curr 1m firm

Smart; formerly Group class; third in both the English and Irish 2000 Guineas in 2008 when trained by D. Elsworth; effective at 1m and acts on most ground; has worn blinkers.

Style Award

100(105) (71)**87**

4-y-o b f Acclamation-Elegant (IRE) (Marju (IRE))

W J H Ratcliffe Bolton Hall Partnership 1

Placings:314162244431/160445005450-**550**010060303 (7280)

2009: 5^{5}SD, 6^{5}SD, 5^{0}SD, 5^{0}F, 6^{1}GF, 6^{0}GF, 5^{0}GF, 8^{6}S, 6^{0}G, 5^{3}GF, 6^{0}GS, 5^{3}SD,

	Starts	1st	2nd	3rd	Win & Pl
Career Total (Turf)	30	4	2	3	23500

	Starts	1st	2nd	3rd	Win & Pl
Career Total (AW)	6	1	0	1	4454

71 5/09 Wind 6f (0-75)H G-F £2729
84 3/08 Ling 5f (0-85)H STD £4100
75 11/07 Muss 5f (0-85) GD £5181
70 7/07 Bevl 5f HVY £5181
65 6/07 Catt 5f G-F £2730
Total win prize-money £19925

Going (Turf): Sf: 1-6 GS: 0-2 Gd: 1-9 **GF: 2-11** Fm: 0-2
Distance: **5f/6f: 5-34** 7f-8f: 0-2 9f-13f: 0-0 14f+: 0-0
Track : **LH: 1-12** RH: 0-1 Tight: 1-9 Gall: 1-2
Aids: Bl: 0-0 Vi: 0-0 Tstrap: 1-7 Ckp: 1-7
Best Rating: **87** 5/08 York 5f gd-fm

Modest; effective at 5f-6f; acts on most ground.

Style Icon

93(83) (62)62
4-y-o ch g Mark Of Esteem (IRE)-Break Point (Reference Point)
Rae Guest Brian Cooper And Miss Elaine Reffo

Placings:0404-6056 (3261)
2009: 7^{6}G, 5^{0}GF, 6^{5}S, 5^{6}F,

	Starts	1st	2nd	3rd	Win & Pl
Career Total (Turf)	7	0	0	0	216
Career Total (AW)	1	0	0	0	289

Going (Turf): **Sf: 0-1 GS: 0-0 Gd: 0-3 GF: 0-2 Fm: 0-1**
Distance: 5f/6f: 0-2 7f-8f: 0-6 9f-13f: 0-0 14f+: 0-0
Track : LH: 0-3 RH: 0-0 Tight: 0-1 Gall: 0-2
Aids: Bl: 0-0 Vi: 0-0 Tstrap: 0-0 Ckp: 0-0
Best Rating: **62** 5/08 Ling 7f stand

Modest; stays 7f; acts on fast ground.

Stylish Mover

92(86) (44)45
4-y-o b g Auction House (USA)-Dam Certain (IRE) (Damister (USA))
R Ingram Peter J Burton

Placings:60040 (6255)
2009: 6^{6}SD, 7^{0}SD, 7^{0}G, 6^{4}GF, 7^{0}SD,

	Starts	1st	2nd	3rd	Win & Pl
Career Total (Turf)	2	0	0	0	149
Career Total (AW)	3	0	0	0	0

Going (Turf): **Sf: 0-0 GS: 0-0 Gd: 0-1 GF: 0-1 Fm: 0-0**
Distance: 5f/6f: 0-1 7f-8f: 0-4 9f-13f: 0-0 14f+: 0-0
Track : LH: 0-3 RH: 0-0 Tight: 0-3 Gall: 0-0
Aids: Bl: 0-0 Vi: 0-0 Tstrap: 0-0 Ckp: 0-0
Best Rating: **45** 9/09 Yarm 6f3y gd-fm

Suailce (IRE)

110 (78)102
4-y-o gr f Singspiel (IRE)-Katch Me Katie (Danehill (USA))
D K Weld H E The President Of Ireland

Placings:2/22212313-34460 (6467a)
2009: 14^{3}HY, 14^{4}G, 14^{4}Y, 14^{6}G, 10^{0}SD,

	Starts	1st	2nd	3rd	Win & Pl
Career Total (Turf)	11	2	3	3	78853
Career Total (AW)	3	0	2	0	2900

99 9/08 Curr 2m H YLD £38294
85 8/08 Gway 1m4f GD £9573
Total win prize-money £47868

Going (Turf): Sf: 0-2 GS: 0-0 **Gd: 1-3** GF: 0-2 Fm: 0-0
Distance: 5f/6f: 0-0 7f-8f: 0-1 9f-13f: 1-7 14f+: 1-6
Track : LH: 0-7 **RH: 2-7** Tight: 0-1 Gall: 0-0
Aids: **Bl: 1-7** Vi: 0-0 Tstrap: 0-0 Ckp: 0-0
Best Rating: **102** 6/09 Curr 1m6f yield

Very useful; effective over 1m4f-2m; acts on good and easy ground.

Suakin Dancer (IRE)

85(87) (58)59
3-y-o ch f Danehill Dancer (IRE)-Wedding Morn (IRE) (Sadler's Wells (USA))
H Morrison J Bernstein

Placings:0000-0006 (4240)
2009: 10^{0}GF, 8^{0}GF, 6^{0}GF, 7^{6}F,

	Starts	1st	2nd	3rd	Win & Pl
Career Total (Turf)	7	0	0	0	0
Career Total (AW)	1	0	0	0	

Going (Turf): **Sf: 0-0 GS: 0-1 Gd: 0-1 GF: 0-4 Fm: 0-1**
Distance: 5f/6f: 0-1 7f-8f: 0-6 9f-13f: 0-1 14f+: 0-0
Track : LH: 0-2 RH: 0-0 Tight: 0-2 Gall: 0-0
Aids: Bl: 0-0 Vi: 0-0 Tstrap: 0-0 Ckp: 0-0
Best Rating: **59** 8/08 Newb 6f8y gd-sft

Suba (USA)

107(101) (83)86
3-y-o b f Seeking The Gold (USA)-Zomaradah (Deploy)
L M Cumani Sheikh Mohammed Obaid Al Maktoum

Placings:302-1544 (6346)
2009: 8^{1}GF, 8^{5}GF, 9^{4}GF, 9^{4}SD,

	Starts	1st	2nd	3rd	Win & Pl
Career Total (Turf)	5	1	0	1	1252
Career Total (AW)	2	0	1	0	1592

Going (Turf): Sf: 0-0 GS: 0-1 Gd: 0-1 **GF: 1-3** Fm: 0-0
Distance: 5f/6f: 0-0 7f-8f: 0-4 **9f-13f: 1-3** 14f+: 0-0
Track : **LH: 1-3** RH: 0-1 Tight: 0-3 Gall: 0-0
Aids: Bl: 0-0 Vi: 0-0 Tstrap: 0-0 Ckp: 0-0
Best Rating: **86** 6/09 Nott 1m75y gd-fm

Useful; stays 1m; acts on fast and easy ground and on Polytrack.

Subasta

62
4-y-o b f Auction House (USA)-Travel Mystery (Godswalk (USA))
M Brittain Mel Brittain

Placings:0 (6766)
2009: 12^{0}GS,

	Starts	1st	2nd	3rd	Win & Pl
Career Total (Turf)	1	0	0	0	

Going (Turf): **Sf: 0-0 GS: 0-1 Gd: 0-0 GF: 0-0 Fm: 0-0**
Distance: 5f/6f: 0-0 7f-8f: 0-0 9f-13f: 0-1 14f+: 0-0
Track : LH: 0-1 RH: 0-0 Tight: 0-0 Gall: 0-1
Aids: Bl: 0-0 Vi: 0-0 Tstrap: 0-0 Ckp: 0-0

Subtefuge

96 80
2-y-o b f Observatory (USA)-Artifice (Green Desert (USA))
H R A Cecil Dr Catherine Wills

Placings:2510 (7013)
2009: 6^{2}GF, 6^{5}GF, 7^{1}GF, 7^{0}GS,

	Starts	1st	2nd	3rd	Win & Pl
Career Total (Turf)	4	1	1	0	5362

80 9/09 Wwck 7f26y G-F £4094
Total win prize-money £4094

Going (Turf): Sf: 0-0 GS: 0-1 Gd: 0-0 **GF: 1-3** Fm: 0-0
Distance: 5f/6f: 0-1 **7f-8f: 1-3** 9f-13f: 0-0 14f+: 0-0
Track : **LH: 1-1** RH: 0-0 Tight: 0-0 Gall: 0-0
Aids: Bl: 0-0 Vi: 0-0 Tstrap: 0-0 Ckp: 0-0
Best Rating: **80** 9/09 Wwck 7f26y gd-fm

Fair; stays 7f; acts on fast ground.

Suburbia (USA)

88 50
3-y-o b g Street Cry (IRE)-Green Lady (IRE) (Green Desert (USA))
M A Jarvis Sheikh Ahmed Al Maktoum

Placings:00 (6390)
2009: 7^{0}GF, 8^{0}GF,

	Starts	1st	2nd	3rd	Win & Pl
Career Total (Turf)	2	0	0	0	

Going (Turf): **Sf: 0-0 GS: 0-0 Gd: 0-0 GF: 0-2 Fm: 0-0**
Distance: 5f/6f: 0-0 7f-8f: 0-1 9f-13f: 0-1 14f+: 0-0
Track : LH: 0-1 RH: 0-0 Tight: 0-0 Gall: 0-0
Aids: Bl: 0-0 Vi: 0-0 Tstrap: 0-0 Ckp: 0-0
Best Rating: **50** 9/09 Nott 1m75y gd-fm

Such Optimism

102(93) (70)87
3-y-o b f Sakhee (USA)-Optimistic (Reprimand)
R M Beckett G C Myddelton

Placings:120-0063 (7841)
2009: 8^{0}S, 9^{0}G, 10^{6}G, 11^{3}SS,

	Starts	1st	2nd	3rd	Win & Pl
Career Total (Turf)	6	1	1	0	4311
Career Total (AW)	1	0	0	1	722

87 8/08 Sals 6f212y G-S £2914
Total win prize-money £2914

Going (Turf): Sf: 0-2 **GS: 1-1** Gd: 0-3 GF: 0-0 Fm: 0-0
Distance: 5f/6f: 0-0 **7f-8f: 1-4** 9f-13f: 0-3 14f+: 0-0
Track : LH: 0-2 RH: 0-1 Tight: 0-1 Gall: 0-0
Aids: Bl: 0-0 Vi: 0-0 Tstrap: 0-0 Ckp: 0-0
Best Rating: **87** 8/08 Sals 6f212y gd-sft

Useful, stays 1m; acts on good and easier ground.

Sudden Impact (IRE)

111(88) (59)96
4-y-o b/br f Modigliani (USA)-Suddenly (Puissance)
Paul Green Terry Cummins

Placings:300161600/022205600-3032114600 (6089)
2009: 8^{3}SD, 7^{0}GF, 5^{3}G, 5^{2}GF, 5^{1}S, 6^{1}G, 6^{4}GF, 7^{6}G, 5^{0}GS, 6^{0}G,

	Starts	1st	2nd	3rd	Win & Pl
Career Total (Turf)	26	4	4	2	127910
Career Total (AW)	2	0	0	1	703

95 7/09 Thsk 6f (0-85)H GD £5634
91 7/09 Hayd 5f (0-80)H SFT £5504
96 8/07 Curr 6f SFT £99324
85 7/07 Thsk 5f GD £5181
Total win prize-money £115645

Going (Turf): **Sf: 2-6** GS: 0-3 **Gd: 2-9** GF: 0-8 Fm: 0-0
Distance: **5f/6f: 4-23** 7f-8f: 0-5 9f-13f: 0-0 14f+: 0-0
Track : LH: 0-5 RH: 0-0 Tight: 0-1 Gall: 0-0
Aids: Bl: 0-0 Vi: 0-0 Tstrap: 0-0 Ckp: 0-0
Best Rating: **96** 7/08 Asct 6f gd-fm

Useful; effective over 5f-6f; acts on fast and easy ground; has worn an eyeshield.

Sudden Impulse

96(100) (76)78

8-y-o b m Silver Patriarch (IRE)-Sanshang (FR) (Astronef)
A D Brown S Nellis

Placings:60/000000/4263021240112200/03106140200/24 542600036104403-25505 **(2975)**
2009: 10^{2}G, 12^{5}GS, 10^{5}GS, 10^{0}G, 10^{5}GS,

	Starts	1st	2nd	3rd	Win & Pl
Career Total (Turf)	37	6	7	2	28499
Career Total (AW)	20	0	2	2	2490

73 8/08 Muss 1m4f (0-65)H GD £2914
72 6/07 Muss 1m4f (0-70)H G-S £3238
74 5/07 Newc 1m4f93y (0-70)H G-F £4210
62 8/06 Bevl 1m1f207y (0-60)H G-S £3238
57 8/06 Leic 1m1f218y (0-60)H G-S £3238
55 7/06 Muss 1m4f (0-55)H GD £2730
Total win prize-money £19571

Going (Turf): Sf: 0-4 **GS: 3-9** Gd: 2-12 GF: 1-10 Fm: 0-2
Distance: 5f/6f: 0-0 7f-8f: 0-3 **9f-13f: 6-53** 14f+: 0-1
Track : LH: 1-34 **RH: 5-22 Tight: 3-23** Gall: 1-8
Aids: Bl: 0-0 Vi: 0-0 Tstrap: 0-1 Ckp: 0-1
Best Rating: **78** 5/08 Newc 1m2f32y gd-fm

Modest; effective at around 1m2f-1m4f; acts on fast and easy ground; also goes on Polytrack.

Sue And Sue

60

2-y-o b f Needwood Blade-Bahamian Belle (Bahamian Bounty)
G Woodward Mr & Mrs Bloom

Placings:0 **(5934)**
2009: 5^{0}GF,

	Starts	1st	2nd	3rd	Win & Pl
Career Total (Turf)	1	0	0	0	

Going (Turf): **Sf: 0-0 GS: 0-0 Gd: 0-0 GF: 0-1 Fm: 0-0**
Distance: 5f/6f: 0-1 7f-8f: 0-0 9f-13f: 0-0 14f+: 0-0
Track : LH: 0-0 RH: 0-0 Tight: 0-0 Gall: 0-0
Aids: Bl: 0-0 Vi: 0-0 Tstrap: 0-0 Ckp: 0-0

Sue Princesse (IRE)

(88) (49)49

6-y-o ch m Alhaarth (IRE)-Princesse Sharpo (USA) (Trempolino (USA))
Ruaidhri Joseph Tierney Longford Syndicate

Placings:000/02252604433312040/60040 **(6625a)**
2009: 12^{6}SD, 12^{0}SD, 14^{0}GF, 14^{4}G, 14^{0}G,

	Starts	1st	2nd	3rd	Win & Pl
Career Total (Turf)	23	1	4	3	11937
Career Total (AW)	2	0	0	0	0

66 8/06 Tram 1m4f SFT £4288
Total win prize-money £4289

Going (Turf): **Sf: 1-4** GS: 0-0 Gd: 0-6 GF: 0-6 Fm: 0-3
Distance: 5f/6f: 0-2 7f-8f: 0-2 **9f-13f: 1-18** 14f+: 0-3
Track : LH: 0-4 **RH: 1-17** Tight: 0-0 Gall: 0-0
Aids: Bl: 0-2 Vi: 0-0 Tstrap: 1-5 Ckp: 1-5
Best Rating: **69** 9/06 Tral 1m4f good

Sufad

96(92) (53)81

4-y-o b g Alhaarth (IRE)-Alshakr (Bahri (USA))
T D McCarthy (G L Moore 23/1) Mark Hoaren

Placings:244/203160-000560 **(6566)**
2009: 10^{0}SD, 21^{0}G, 16^{0}SD, 12^{5}GF, 14^{6}GF, 12^{0}GS,

	Starts	1st	2nd	3rd	Win & Pl
Career Total (Turf)	13	1	2	1	10146
Career Total (AW)	2	0	0	0	

75 5/08 Tram 1m6f G-F £6097
Total win prize-money £6097

Going (Turf): Sf: 0-1 GS: 0-1 Gd: 0-2 **GF: 1-4** Fm: 0-1
Distance: 5f/6f: 0-0 7f-8f: 0-5 9f-13f: 0-6 **14f+: 1-4**
Track : LH: 0-6 **RH: 1-8** Tight: 0-5 Gall: 0-0
Aids: Bl: 0-2 Vi: 0-0 Tstrap: 0-0 Ckp: 0-0
Best Rating: **81** 4/08 Naas 1m yield

Useful; ex-Irish; stays 1m6f; acts on fast ground; has worn blinkers.

Sufficient Warning

(92) (48)

5-y-o b g Warningford-Efficacious (IRE) (Efisio)
R J Smith Mrs Maggie Brighton

Placings:0/000450632/3516160-0330000 **(7433)**
2009: 9^{0}G, 8^{3}SD, 10^{3}SD, 8^{0}SD, 8^{0}SD, 8^{0}SD, 8^{0}SD,

	Starts	1st	2nd	3rd	Win & Pl
Career Total (Turf)	4	0	0	0	0
Career Total (AW)	20	2	1	4	11746

8/08 Mija 1m165y H STD £3676
7/08 Mija 1m3f H STD £3676
Total win prize-money £7352

Going (Turf): **Sf: 0-1 GS: 0-0 Gd: 0-3 GF: 0-0 Fm: 0-0**
Distance: 5f/6f: 0-0 7f-8f: 0-7 **9f-13f: 2-17** 14f+: 0-0
Track : LH: 0-2 RH: 0-2 Tight: 0-2 Gall: 0-0
Aids: Bl: 0-3 Vi: 0-0 Tstrap: 0-0 Ckp: 0-0
Best Rating: **48** 11/09 Ling 1m stand

Suffolk Punch (IRE)

96(93) (63)82

2-y-o ch c Barathea (IRE)-Lamanka Lass (USA) (Woodman (USA))
A M Balding Marcus Evans

Placings:34105 **(5347)**
2009: 6^{3}GF, 5^{4}SD, 7^{1}GF, 7^{0}G, 7^{5}G,

	Starts	1st	2nd	3rd	Win & Pl
Career Total (Turf)	4	1	0	1	5951
Career Total (AW)	1	0	0	0	289

80 7/09 Epsm 7f G-F £5180
Total win prize-money £5181

Going (Turf): Sf: 0-0 GS: 0-0 Gd: 0-2 **GF: 1-2** Fm: 0-0
Distance: 5f/6f: 0-1 **7f-8f: 1-4** 9f-13f: 0-0 14f+: 0-0
Track : **LH: 1-3** RH: 0-1 **Tight: 1-2** Gall: 0-0
Aids: Bl: 0-0 Vi: 0-0 Tstrap: 0-0 Ckp: 0-0
Best Rating: **82** 8/09 Wwck 7f26y good

Useful; stays 7f and acts on fast ground.

Sugar Free (IRE)

107 99

3-y-o b f Oasis Dream-Much Faster (IRE) (Fasliyev (USA))
T Stack Rick Barnes

Placings:35150-241030 **(6427)**
2009: 5^{2}HY, 6^{4}GF, 5^{1}GF, 5^{0}G, 5^{3}HY, 5^{0}GF,

	Starts	1st	2nd	3rd	Win & Pl
Career Total (Turf)	11	2	1	2	49735

98 6/09 Ayr 5f G-F £22708
82 8/08 Tipp 5f SFT £8637
Total win prize-money £31346

Going (Turf): **Sf: 1-4** GS: 0-0 Gd: 0-1 **GF: 1-5** Fm: 0-1
Distance: **5f/6f: 2-10** 7f-8f: 0-1 9f-13f: 0-0 14f+: 0-0
Track : **LH: 1-3** RH: 0-0 Tight: 0-0 Gall: 0-0
Aids: Bl: 0-0 Vi: 0-0 Tstrap: 0-0 Ckp: 0-0
Best Rating: **99** 8/08 Curr 7f soft

Smart; Irish trained; Listed winner; effective over 5f-6f and acts on most ground but well suited by fast.

Sugar Ray (IRE)

108 107

5-y-o b g Danehill (USA)-Akuna Bay (USA) (Mr Prospector (USA))
Saeed Bin Suroor Godolphin

Placings:0/3123/13102-53440 **(4408)**
2009: 12^{5}GS, 12^{3}G, 12^{4}GF, 14^{4}GF, 14^{0}G,

	Starts	1st	2nd	3rd	Win & Pl
Career Total (Turf)	15	3	2	4	87530

106 6/08 Asct 1m4f (0-105)H G-F £37386
93 4/08 Bath 1m3f144y (0-85)H GD £5180
84 8/07 Wind 1m2f7y G-F £3886
Total win prize-money £46453

Going (Turf): Sf: 0-1 GS: 0-1 Gd: 1-6 **GF: 2-7** Fm: 0-0
Distance: 5f/6f: 0-0 7f-8f: 0-1 **9f-13f: 3-12** 14f+: 0-2
Track : LH: 1-6 **RH: 2-8 Tight: 2-3** Gall: 1-8
Aids: Bl: 0-0 Vi: 0-5 Tstrap: 0-0 Ckp: 0-0
Best Rating: **107** 6/09 Pont 1m4f8y gd-fm

Smart; effective at 1m4f; acts on fast and easy ground; has worn a tongue tie and visor; likes to race prominently.

Sugar State

64(78) (38)

4-y-o gr g M'Bebe-Sweet Patoopie (Indian Ridge)
J L Spearing Advantage Chemicals Holdings Ltd

Placings:0000 **(4388)**
2009: 9^{0}SD, 12^{0}SD, 9^{0}SD, 16^{0}G,

	Starts	1st	2nd	3rd	Win & Pl
Career Total (Turf)	1	0	0	0	
Career Total (AW)	3	0	0	0	

Going (Turf): **Sf: 0-0 GS: 0-0 Gd: 0-1 GF: 0-0 Fm: 0-0**
Distance: 5f/6f: 0-0 7f-8f: 0-0 9f-13f: 0-3 14f+: 0-1
Track : LH: 0-4 RH: 0-0 Tight: 0-4 Gall: 0-0
Aids: Bl: 0-0 Vi: 0-0 Tstrap: 0-0 Ckp: 0-0
Best Rating: **38** 2/09 Wolv 1m4f50y stand

Sugarbaby Princess (IRE)

78(73) (23)1

3-y-o gr f Verglas (IRE)-Alkifaf (USA) (Mtoto)
S W James S W James

Placings:0-0 (3205)
2009: 12^{0}G,

	Starts	1st	2nd	3rd	Win & Pl
Career Total (Turf)	1	0	0	0	
Career Total (AW)	1	0	0	0	

Going (Turf): **Sf: 0-0 GS: 0-0 Gd: 0-1 GF: 0-0 Fm: 0-0**
Distance: 5f/6f: 0-0 7f-8f: 0-1 9f-13f: 0-1 14f+: 0-0
Track : LH: 0-2 RH: 0-0 Tight: 0-1 Gall: 0-0
Aids: Bl: 0-0 Vi: 0-0 Tstrap: 0-0 Ckp: 0-0
Best Rating: **23** 10/08 Ling 7f stand

Suhailah

65(96) (63)
3-y-o ch f Sulamani (IRE)-Vrennan (Suave Dancer (USA))
M J Attwater Canisbay Bloodstock

Placings:0565506**00006** (7590)
2009: **10**^{0}SD, **12**^{5}SD, **12**^{6}SD, **12**^{5}SD, **12**^{5}SD, 11^{0}GF, 10^{6}GF, **12**^{0}SD, **10**^{0}SS, **12**^{0}SD, 12^{0}SD, **12**^{6}SD,

	Starts	1st	2nd	3rd	Win & Pl
Career Total (Turf)	2	0	0	0	0
Career Total (AW)	10	0	0	0	0

Going (Turf): **Sf: 0-0 GS: 0-0 Gd: 0-0 GF: 0-2 Fm: 0-0**
Distance: 5f/6f: 0-0 7f-8f: 0-0 9f-13f: 0-12 14f+: 0-0
Track : LH: 0-9 RH: 0-3 Tight: 0-9 Gall: 0-0
Aids: Bl: 0-0 Vi: 0-1 Tstrap: 0-4 Ckp: 0-4
Best Rating: **63** 3/09 Ling 1m4f stand

Moderate; stays 1m2f; acts on Polytrack; has worn cheek-pieces.

Suhayl Star (IRE)

96(104) (70)**64**
5-y-o b g Trans Island-Miss Odlum (IRE) (Mtoto)
P Burgoyne Mrs C Leigh-Turner

Placings:25040661200/**562**00003**00/060225240-2021416122050** (7627)
2009: **5**^{2}SD, **6**^{0}SD, **8**^{2}SD, **7**^{1}SD, **7**^{4}SD, 7^{1}SD, **7**^{6}SD, **6**^{1}SD, 6^{2}GF, 6^{2}SD, 6^{0}GF, **6**^{5}SD, 7^{0}SD,

	Starts	1st	2nd	3rd	Win & Pl
Career Total (Turf)	17	1	2	0	7354
Career Total (AW)	26	3	8	1	12127

70 4/09 Ling 6f (0-65)H STD £2306
65 4/09 Ling 7f (0-60)H STD £2047
60 3/09 Ling 7f (0-65)H STD £2047
67 8/06 Thsk 7f GD £3886
Total win prize-money £10287

Going (Turf): Sf: 0-1 GS: 0-1 **Gd: 1-6** GF: 0-7 Fm: 0-2
Distance: 5f/6f: 1-17 **7f-8f: 3-24** 9f-13f: 0-2 14f+: 0-0
Track : **LH: 4-25** RH: 0-10 **Tight: 4-21** Gall: 0-0
Aids: Bl: 0-0 Vi: 0-1 Tstrap: 0-1 Ckp: 0-1
Best Rating: **71** 8/06 Ches 7f2y good

Modest; effective over 6f-7f; acts on Polytrack; goes well at Lingfield.

Suitably Accoutred (IRE)

98(66) **54**
3-y-o b f Acclamation-Cliveden Gail (IRE) (Law Society (USA))
Mrs A Duffield Miss Helen Wynne

Placings:00-000510 (3561)
2009: 8^{0}GF, 11^{0}SD, 12^{0}GF, 14^{5}GF, 12^{1}GF, 12^{0}GF,

	Starts	1st	2nd	3rd	Win & Pl
Career Total (Turf)	7	1	0	0	1943
Career Total (AW)	1	0	0	0	

54 6/09 Haml 1m4f17y (0-65)H G-F £1942
Total win prize-money £1943

Going (Turf): Sf: 0-1 GS: 0-0 Gd: 0-0 **GF: 1-6** Fm: 0-0
Distance: 5f/6f: 0-0 7f-8f: 0-1 **9f-13f: 1-6** 14f+: 0-1
Track : LH: 0-3 **RH: 1-3 Tight: 1-3** Gall: 0-0
Aids: Bl: 0-0 Vi: 0-0 Tstrap: 0-0 Ckp: 0-0
Best Rating: **54** 6/09 Haml 1m4f17y gd-fm

Suited And Booted (IRE)

96 **81**
2-y-o ch c Tagula (IRE)-Carpet Lady (IRE) (Night Shift (USA))
R Hannon R Morecombe, D Anderson & S Leech

Placings:0424 (6061)
2009: 7^{0}G, 7^{4}G, 7^{2}G, 6^{4}GF,

	Starts	1st	2nd	3rd	Win & Pl
Career Total (Turf)	4	0	1	0	2215

Going (Turf): **Sf: 0-0 GS: 0-0 Gd: 0-3 GF: 0-1 Fm: 0-0**
Distance: 5f/6f: 0-1 7f-8f: 0-3 9f-13f: 0-0 14f+: 0-0
Track : LH: 0-0 RH: 0-0 Tight: 0-0 Gall: 0-0
Aids: Bl: 0-0 Vi: 0-0 Tstrap: 0-0 Ckp: 0-0
Best Rating: **81** 8/09 NmkJ 7f good

Fair-looking juvenile.; stays 7f; acts on a sound surface.

Suits Me

110(112) (112)**103**
6-y-o ch g Bertolini (USA)-Fancier Bit (Lion Cavern (USA))
T P Tate D E Cook

Placings:11/**6**030350/**364**2631103511/40652303022**1111**
2-1200606**32** (7809)
2009: **10**^{1}SD, **10**^{2}SD, **10**^{0}SD, 8^{0}GF, 9^{6}GF, 9^{0}GS, 10^{6}G, **10**^{3}SD, **10**^{2}SD,

	Starts	1st	2nd	3rd	Win & Pl
Career Total (Turf)	34	7	4	6	59225
Career Total (AW)	13	4	3	2	70583

85 2/09 Ling 1m2f STD £17031
112 12/08 GrLe 1m2f (0-100)H STD £11215
106 11/08 Kemp 1m2f (0-100)H STD £11215
101 11/08 Ayr 1m (0-90)H HVY £9714
89 11/07 Ayr 1m1f20y (0-85)H HVY £6232
84 10/07 Donc 1m2f60y (0-80)H GD £6246
81 8/07 Ripn 1m1f170y (0-90)H G-F £9348
76 7/07 Ripn 1m1f170y (0-85)H HVY £6309
71 8/05 Newc 1m3y G-F £2611
67 8/05 Thsk 7f G-F £4192
Total win prize-money £84116

Going (Turf): **Sf: 3-9** GS: 0-5 Gd: 1-5 **GF: 3-14** Fm: 0-1
Distance: 5f/6f: 0-1 7f-8f: 2-6 **9f-13f: 9-40** 14f+: 0-0
Track : **LH: 7-32** RH: 3-9 **Tight: 5-15** Gall: 2-8
Aids: Bl: 0-0 Vi: 0-0 Tstrap: 0-0 Ckp: 0-0
Best Rating: **112** 2/09 Ling 1m2f stand

Smart; winner in Listed company; stays 1m2f; acts on any ground; goes on Polytrack; suited by forcing tactics.

Sula Dream

89(71) **45**
3-y-o ch g Sulamani (IRE)-Bonella (IRE) (Eagle Eyed (USA))
J Pearce The Wayfarers

Placings:0000 (6445)
2009: 9^{0}GS, 10^{0}GF, 11^{0}GF, 12^{0}SS,

	Starts	1st	2nd	3rd	Win & Pl
Career Total (Turf)	3	0	0	0	
Career Total (AW)	1	0	0	0	

Going (Turf): **Sf: 0-0 GS: 0-1 Gd: 0-0 GF: 0-2 Fm: 0-0**
Distance: 5f/6f: 0-0 7f-8f: 0-0 9f-13f: 0-4 14f+: 0-0
Track : LH: 0-2 RH: 0-2 Tight: 0-3 Gall: 0-0
Aids: Bl: 0-0 Vi: 0-0 Tstrap: 0-0 Ckp: 0-0
Best Rating: **45** 9/09 Leic 1m3f183y gd-fm

Sularno

99(99) (78)**63**
5-y-o ch g Medicean-Star Precision (Shavian)
J Pearce (H Morrison 19/5) Macniler Racing Partnership

Placings:0**01**/0**2000**/5**0110440-0002**3**000** (6862)
2009: **8**^{0}SD, **11**^{0}SD, **12**^{0}SD, 0^{2}G, **8**^{3}SD, **8**^{0}SD, 7^{0}GF, **8**^{0}SD,

	Starts	1st	2nd	3rd	Win & Pl
Career Total (Turf)	7	0	1	0	578
Career Total (AW)	17	3	1	1	9005

73 6/08 GrLe 1m (0-60)H STD £2266
78 6/08 Sthl 1m (0-60)H STD £1774
71 11/06 Sthl 7f STD £3562
Total win prize-money £7603

Going (Turf): **Sf: 0-1 GS: 0-2 Gd: 0-1 GF: 0-3 Fm: 0-0**
Distance: 5f/6f: 0-0 **7f-8f: 3-14** 9f-13f: 0-9 14f+: 0-1
Track : **LH: 3-18** RH: 0-4 Tight: 0-7 **Gall: 1-2**
Aids: Bl: 0-1 Vi: 0-1 Tstrap: 0-1 Ckp: 0-1
Best Rating: **78** 6/08 Sthl 1m stand

Modest; stays 1m; acts on most ground; goes on Fibresand.

Sullenberger (IRE)

94(102) (70)**61**
3-y-o ch g Namid-Bint Alhaarth (IRE) (Alhaarth (IRE))
J A Osborne J A Osborne

Placings:210004320 (7065)
2009: **8**^{2}SD, **8**^{1}SD, 8^{0}GF, 9^{0}G, **12**^{0}SD, **9**^{4}SD, **9**^{3}SD, **8**^{2}SD, **8**^{0}SD,

	Starts	1st	2nd	3rd	Win & Pl
Career Total (Turf)	2	0	0	0	
Career Total (AW)	7	1	2	1	4263

70 3/09 Wolv 1m141y STD £2217
Total win prize-money £2218

Going (Turf): **Sf: 0-0 GS: 0-0 Gd: 0-1 GF: 0-1 Fm: 0-0**
Distance: 5f/6f: 0-0 7f-8f: 0-1 **9f-13f: 1-8** 14f+: 0-0
Track : **LH: 1-6** RH: 0-3 **Tight: 1-8** Gall: 0-0
Aids: Bl: 0-0 Vi: 0-0 Tstrap: 0-1 Ckp: 0-1
Best Rating: **70** 3/09 Wolv 1m141y stand

Moderate; stays 1m; acts on Polytrack; should improve.

Sultan's Choice

92(92) (58)**60**
2-y-o b f Sulamani (IRE)-Royal Wish (Royal Applause)
P D Evans (J M P Eustace 11/6) Jim Ennis

Placings:4145 (5573)
2009: 7^{4}S, 7^{1}S, 7^{4}SD, 8^{5}SD,

	Starts	1st	2nd	3rd	Win & Pl
Career Total (Turf)	2	1	0	0	2192
Career Total (AW)	2	0	0	0	337

60 7/09 Catt 7f SFT £2047
Total win prize-money £2047

Going (Turf): **Sf: 1-2** GS: 0-0 Gd: 0-0 GF: 0-0 Fm: 0-0
Distance: 5f/6f: 0-0 **7f-8f: 1-4** 9f-13f: 0-0 14f+: 0-0
Track : **LH: 1-2** RH: 0-1 **Tight: 1-2** Gall: 0-0
Aids: Bl: 0-0 Vi: 0-0 Tstrap: 0-0 Ckp: 0-0
Best Rating: **60** 7/09 Catt 7f soft

Moderate; suited by 7f; acts on soft ground and on Polytrack.

Sultana (GER)

83 (8)20

7-y-o b m Law Society (USA)-Sweet Second (IRE) (Second Set (IRE))
J J Lambe (Mrs L C Jewell 25/6) D J McCormack

Placings:3/221500200/000 (3291)
2009: 7^{0}SD, 11^{0}Y, 13^{0}GF,

	Starts	1st	2nd	3rd	Win & Pl
Career Total (Turf)	9	1	2	1	4182
Career Total (AW)	4	0	1	0	638

6/05 Hasl 1m GD £1843
Total win prize-money £1844

Going (Turf): Sf: 0-2 GS: 0-1 **Gd: 1-4** GF: 0-1 Fm: 0-0
Distance: 5f/6f: 0-0 **7f-8f: 1-7** 9f-13f: 0-5 14f+: 0-1
Track : LH: 0-2 RH: 0-2 Tight: 0-1 Gall: 0-0
Aids: Bl: 0-0 Vi: 0-0 Tstrap: 0-0 Ckp: 0-0
Best Rating: **20** 6/09 Haml 1m5f9y gd-fm

Sultans Way (IRE)

91(94) (61)67

3-y-o b g Indian Ridge-Roses From Ridey (IRE) (Petorius)
P F I Cole H R H Sultan Ahmad Shah

Placings:6160-004640 (6339)
2009: 8^{0}GF, 8^{0}G, 7^{4}SD, 7^{6}GF, 7^{4}SD, 6^{0}GF,

	Starts	1st	2nd	3rd	Win & Pl
Career Total (Turf)	8	1	0	0	2590
Career Total (AW)	2	0	0	0	0

67 8/08 Catt 7f G-F £2590
Total win prize-money £2590

Going (Turf): Sf: 0-1 GS: 0-0 Gd: 0-1 **GF: 1-6** Fm: 0-0
Distance: 5f/6f: 0-0 **7f-8f: 1-8** 9f-13f: 0-2 14f+: 0-0
Track : **LH: 1-6** RH: 0-1 **Tight: 1-5** Gall: 0-1
Aids: Bl: 0-1 Vi: 0-0 Tstrap: 0-0 Ckp: 0-0
Best Rating: **67** 8/08 Catt 7f gd-fm

Modest; stays 7f; acts on a sound surface; has worn blinkers.

Sulution

(90) (74)

3-y-o b c Sulamani (IRE)-Streccia (Old Vic)
M Botti Dr Carlini Cozzi & Mrs Sally Doyle

Placings:2 (0548)
2009: 8^{2}SD,

	Starts	1st	2nd	3rd	Win & Pl
Career Total (Turf)	0	0	0	0	
Career Total (AW)	1	0	1	0	806

Going (Turf): **Sf: 0-0 GS: 0-0 Gd: 0-0 GF: 0-0 Fm: 0-0**
Distance: 5f/6f: 0-0 7f-8f: 0-1 9f-13f: 0-0 14f+: 0-0
Track : LH: 0-1 RH: 0-0 Tight: 0-1 Gall: 0-0
Aids: Bl: 0-0 Vi: 0-0 Tstrap: 0-0 Ckp: 0-0
Best Rating: **74** 2/09 Ling 1m stand

Fair debut over 1m on Polytrack.

Sulwaan (IRE)

101 85

2-y-o b g King's Best (USA)-Iktidar (Green Desert (USA))
M Johnston Hamdan Al Maktoum

Placings:411 (5970)
2009: 7^{4}GF, 8^{1}F, 8^{1}GF,

	Starts	1st	2nd	3rd	Win & Pl
Career Total (Turf)	3	2	0	0	8542

85 9/09 Yarm 1m3y (0-85) G-F £4415
73 8/09 Bevl 1m100y FRM £3885
Total win prize-money £8302

Going (Turf): Sf: 0-0 GS: 0-0 Gd: 0-0 **GF: 1-2 Fm: 1-1**
Distance: 5f/6f: 0-0 7f-8f: 0-1 **9f-13f: 2-2** 14f+: 0-0
Track : LH: 0-0 **RH: 1-1** Tight: 0-0 Gall: 0-0
Aids: Bl: 0-0 Vi: 0-0 Tstrap: 0-0 Ckp: 0-0
Best Rating: **85** 9/09 Yarm 1m3y gd-fm

Useful; stays 1m and acts on fast ground.

Sumani (FR)

100(101) (71)66

3-y-o b g Della Francesca (USA)-Sumatra (IRE) (Mukaddamah (USA))
S Dow T G Parker

Placings:60-4501322024 (6376)
2009: 7^{4}SD, 8^{5}SD, 9^{0}G, 10^{1}SD, 9^{3}G, 12^{2}GF, 12^{2}SD, 10^{0}G, 12^{2}GF, 12^{4}SD,

	Starts	1st	2nd	3rd	Win & Pl
Career Total (Turf)	6	0	2	1	2448
Career Total (AW)	6	1	1	0	3046

65 5/09 Ling 1m2f (0-60)H STD £2047
Total win prize-money £2047

Going (Turf): **Sf: 0-0 GS: 0-0 Gd: 0-4 GF: 0-2 Fm: 0-0**
Distance: 5f/6f: 0-0 7f-8f: 0-4 **9f-13f: 1-8** 14f+: 0-0
Track : **LH: 1-5** RH: 0-6 **Tight: 1-9** Gall: 0-0
Aids: Bl: 0-0 Vi: 0-0 Tstrap: 0-0 Ckp: 0-0
Best Rating: **71** 7/09 Ling 1m4f stand

Modest; best at around 1m2f; acts on Polytrack.

Sumay Buoy (IRE)

80 48

2-y-o b c Fasliyev (USA)-Mourir D'Aimer (USA) (Trempolino (USA))
Mrs J C McGregor William Allan

Placings:000 (6408)
2009: 6^{0}S, 6^{0}GS, 6^{0}GF,

	Starts	1st	2nd	3rd	Win & Pl
Career Total (Turf)	3	0	0	0	

Going (Turf): **Sf: 0-1 GS: 0-1 Gd: 0-0 GF: 0-1 Fm: 0-0**
Distance: 5f/6f: 0-3 7f-8f: 0-0 9f-13f: 0-0 14f+: 0-0
Track : LH: 0-0 RH: 0-0 Tight: 0-0 Gall: 0-0
Aids: Bl: 0-0 Vi: 0-0 Tstrap: 0-0 Ckp: 0-0
Best Rating: **48** 9/09 Ayr 6f gd-sft

Sumbe (USA)

89 73

3-y-o b/br g Giant's Causeway (USA)-Sumoto (Mtoto)
M P Tregoning Nurlan Bizakov

Placings:6-05 (1872)
2009: 10^{0}GF, 11^{5}GF,

	Starts	1st	2nd	3rd	Win & Pl
Career Total (Turf)	3	0	0	0	1749

Going (Turf): **Sf: 0-0 GS: 0-0 Gd: 0-1 GF: 0-2 Fm: 0-0**
Distance: 5f/6f: 0-0 7f-8f: 0-1 9f-13f: 0-2 14f+: 0-0
Track : LH: 0-1 RH: 0-0 Tight: 0-1 Gall: 0-0
Aids: Bl: 0-0 Vi: 0-0 Tstrap: 0-0 Ckp: 0-0
Best Rating: **73** 8/08 NmkJ 7f good

Summa Cum Laude

83(68) (3)48

2-y-o gr f With Approval (CAN)-Sulitelma (USA) (The Minstrel (CAN))
Mrs A Duffield Miss K Rausing

Placings:050000 (6343)
2009: 5^{0}GF, 5^{5}S, 5^{0}SD, 6^{0}GF, 5^{0}GF, 5^{0}SD,

	Starts	1st	2nd	3rd	Win & Pl
Career Total (Turf)	4	0	0	0	0
Career Total (AW)	2	0	0	0	

Going (Turf): **Sf: 0-1 GS: 0-0 Gd: 0-0 GF: 0-3 Fm: 0-0**
Distance: 5f/6f: 0-6 7f-8f: 0-0 9f-13f: 0-0 14f+: 0-0
Track : LH: 0-2 RH: 0-0 Tight: 0-2 Gall: 0-0
Aids: Bl: 0-0 Vi: 0-2 Tstrap: 0-0 Ckp: 0-0
Best Rating: **48** 7/09 Ripn 5f soft

Summer Affair (IRE)

(94) (59)

4-y-o b g Alhaarth (IRE)-Late Summer (USA) (Gone West (USA))
B I Case B I Case

Placings:4034 (7495)
2009: 12^{4}SD, 11^{0}SD, 9^{3}SD, 12^{4}SD,

	Starts	1st	2nd	3rd	Win & Pl
Career Total (Turf)	0	0	0	0	
Career Total (AW)	4	0	0	1	578

Going (Turf): **Sf: 0-0 GS: 0-0 Gd: 0-0 GF: 0-0 Fm: 0-0**
Distance: 5f/6f: 0-0 7f-8f: 0-0 9f-13f: 0-4 14f+: 0-0
Track : LH: 0-2 RH: 0-2 Tight: 0-2 Gall: 0-0
Aids: Bl: 0-0 Vi: 0-0 Tstrap: 0-0 Ckp: 0-0
Best Rating: **59** 10/09 Kemp 1m3f stand

Moderate; should stay further than 1m4f; acts on Polytrack; may do better.

Summer Bounty

92(102) (51)52

13-y-o b g Lugana Beach-Tender Moment (IRE) (Caerleon (USA))
F Jordan Tim Powell

Placings:035/1443602/06002000/040310100000/0311202003/64222450/01103205/200050040505/051400040030/050033515146/0400350056540-0445000 (6918)
2009: 13^{0}SD, 9^{4}SD, 9^{4}SD, 12^{5}GF, 17^{0}GS, 12^{0}GF, 12^{0}SD,

	Starts	1st	2nd	3rd	Win & Pl
Career Total (Turf)	76	7	8	9	40403
Career Total (AW)	36	3	1	1	8097

55 11/07 Kemp 1m3f (0-50)H STD £2047
51 10/07 Wolv 1m4f50y (0-45) STD £1706
69 4/06 Wwck 1m2f188y (0-60)H G-S £2730
81 5/04 Nott 1m1f213yE(0-70)H GD £3662

72 5/04 Wwck 1m22y E(0-70)H HVY £3737
64 5/02 Nott 1m1f213yF(0-60)H G-F £2975
59 5/02 Pont 1m4y F(0-60)H G-F £3444
53 7/01 Bath 1m3f144y F FRM £2359
58 7/01 Wwck 1m22y G(0-60)H G-F £2279
64 2/99 Ling 1m2f D STD £3021
Total win prize-money £27964

Going (Turf): Sf: 1-10GS: 1-11Gd: 1-19**GF: 3-32** Fm: 1-4
Distance: 5f/6f: 0-0 7f-8f: 0-3 **9f-13f: 10-104** 14f+: 0-5
Track : **LH: 9-82** RH: 1-27 **Tight: 3-51** Gall: 0-8
Aids: Bl: 0-1 Vi: 0-0 Tstrap: 0-0 Ckp: 0-0
Best Rating: 86 6/99 Gdwd 1m1f192y gd-fm

Moderate; stays 1m4f; acts on most ground.

Summer Capers (USA)

80(91) (62)61
4-y-o b f Mt. Livermore (USA)-Crown Capers (USA) (Chief's Crown (USA))
J Gallagher O Murphy

Placings:050205/6040040-06 (2184)
2009: 7^{0}GF, 6^{6}SD,

	Starts	1st	2nd	3rd	Win & Pl
Career Total (Turf)	9	0	0	0	633
Career Total (AW)	6	0	1	0	1414

Going (Turf): **Sf: 0-3 GS: 0-0 Gd: 0-1 GF: 0-2 Fm: 0-0**
Distance: 5f/6f: 0-10 7f-8f: 0-5 9f-13f: 0-0 14f+: 0-0
Track : LH: 0-4 RH: 0-5 Tight: 0-1 Gall: 0-0
Aids: Bl: 0-0 Vi: 0-0 Tstrap: 0-0 Ckp: 0-0
Best Rating: 68 11/07 Dund 1m stand

Summer Dancer (IRE)

107(96) (83)89
5-y-o br g Fasliyev (USA)-Summer Style (IRE) (Indian Ridge)
P T Midgley The Howarting's Partnership

Placings:0401/0216334345/2060050-06651144512300 (6278)
2009: 8^{0}F, 8^{6}G, 7^{6}GF, 7^{5}G, 7^{1}GF, 7^{1}GF, 7^{4}GF, 7^{4}GF, 7^{5}GF, 7^{1}G, 7^{2}GF, 7^{3}G, 6^{0}GF, 7^{0}GF,

	Starts	1st	2nd	3rd	Win & Pl
Career Total (Turf)	30	4	3	4	21683
Career Total (AW)	5	1	0	0	2740

83 8/09 Muss 7f30y (0-75)H GD £3885
80 6/09 Bevl 7f100y (0-70)H G-F £2914
77 6/09 Muss 7f30y (0-65)H G-F £2590
73 6/07 Newb 7f (0-75)H G-F £3562
70 12/06 Kemp 1m STD £2388
Total win prize-money £15341

Going (Turf): Sf: 0-4 GS: 0-3 Gd: 1-7 **GF: 3-15** Fm: 0-1
Distance: 5f/6f: 0-1 **7f-8f: 5-30** 9f-13f: 0-4 14f+: 0-0
Track : LH: 0-10 **RH: 4-9 Tight: 2-11** Gall: 0-1
Aids: Bl: 0-0 Vi: 0-0 Tstrap: 0-0 Ckp: 0-0
Best Rating: 89 8/09 Wwck 7f26y good

Fair; effective over 7f-1m; acts on fast and soft ground; also goes on Polytrack.

Summer Fete (IRE)

106 104
3-y-o gr f Pivotal-Tamarillo (Daylami (IRE))
B Smart H E Sheikh Rashid Bin Mohammed

Placings:141-0310 (5710a)
2009: 7^{0}GF, 7^{3}S, 7^{1}G, 8^{0}GS,

	Starts	1st	2nd	3rd	Win & Pl
Career Total (Turf)	7	3	0	1	63557

104 7/09 Gdwd 7f GD £36900
97 10/08 Newb 7f SFT £17031
85 8/08 Ripn 6f GD £4209
Total win prize-money £58141

Going (Turf): Sf: 1-3 GS: 0-1 **Gd: 2-2** GF: 0-1 Fm: 0-0
Distance: 5f/6f: 1-2 **7f-8f: 2-5** 9f-13f: 0-0 14f+: 0-0
Track : LH: 0-0 **RH: 1-1** Tight: 0-0 Gall: 0-0
Aids: Bl: 0-0 Vi: 0-0 Tstrap: 0-0 Ckp: 0-0
Best Rating: 104 7/09 Gdwd 7f good

Smart; Group 3 winner; effective over 6-7f; acts on good and softer ground.

Summer Gold (IRE)

109 87
5-y-o b m Barathea (IRE)-Eman's Joy (Lion Cavern (USA))
E J Alston J Stephenson

Placings:0/364/10140-4034210030 (6485)
2009: 10^{4}G, 8^{0}G, 8^{3}GF, 8^{4}F, 8^{2}S, 10^{1}G, 10^{0}G, 10^{0}GF, 10^{3}GF, 8^{0}GF,

	Starts	1st	2nd	3rd	Win & Pl
Career Total (Turf)	19	3	1	3	28363

87 7/09 York 1m2f88y (0-90)H GD £9714
84 7/08 Donc 1m (0-80)H GD £5459
81 5/08 Newc 1m2f32y (0-80)H G-F £4533
Total win prize-money £19706

Going (Turf): Sf: 0-2 GS: 0-0 **Gd: 2-6** GF: 1-7 Fm: 0-1
Distance: 5f/6f: 0-0 7f-8f: 1-8 **9f-13f: 2-11** 14f+: 0-0
Track : **LH: 2-10** RH: 0-3 Tight: 0-0 **Gall: 2-3**
Aids: Bl: 0-0 Vi: 0-0 Tstrap: 0-0 Ckp: 0-0
Best Rating: 87 7/09 York 1m2f88y good

Useful; effective at 1m-1m2f; acts on most ground.

Summer Lodge

106(106) (75)79
6-y-o b g Indian Lodge (IRE)-Summer Siren (FR) (Saint Cyrien (FR))
J A Glover (A J McCabe 25/6) Paul J Dixon

Placings:044/0532232333644/5544000/335130530-0242212154253 (7357)
2009: 12^{0}SD, 13^{2}SD, 16^{4}SD, 12^{2}GF, 11^{2}SD, 12^{1}GS, 13^{2}GF, 12^{1}GF, 12^{5}GF, 11^{4}S, 12^{2}GF, 12^{5}SD, 13^{3}SD,

	Starts	1st	2nd	3rd	Win & Pl
Career Total (Turf)	22	2	6	4	15746
Career Total (AW)	23	1	2	6	7607

76 7/09 Bevl 1m4f16y (0-70)H G-F £3238
69 6/09 Ripn 1m4f10y (0-75)H G-S £3238
69 10/08 Wolv 1m4f50y (0-70)H STD £3238
Total win prize-money £9714

Going (Turf): Sf: 0-5 **GS: 1-1** Gd: 0-8 **GF: 1-8** Fm: 0-0
Distance: 5f/6f: 0-1 7f-8f: 0-3 **9f-13f: 3-36** 14f+: 0-5
Track : LH: 1-30 **RH: 2-12 Tight: 3-22** Gall: 0-6
Aids: Bl: 0-14 Vi: 0-3 Tstrap: 2-7 Ckp: 2-7
Best Rating: 79 9/09 Newc 1m4f93y gd-fm

Fair; stays 1m4f; acts on fast ground and on Polytrack; winning hurdler.

Summer Rose

71(96) (56)22
4-y-o gr f Kyllachy-Roses Of Spring (Shareef Dancer (USA))
R M H Cowell Bottisham Heath Stud

Placings:00604251-5000 (7703)
2009: 5^{5}SD, 5^{0}G, 5^{0}SD, 6^{0}SD,

	Starts	1st	2nd	3rd	Win & Pl
Career Total (Turf)	4	0	0	0	0
Career Total (AW)	8	1	1	0	2580

56 12/08 Ling 5f (0-55)H STD £1706
Total win prize-money £1706

Going (Turf): **Sf: 0-0 GS: 0-0 Gd: 0-2 GF: 0-2 Fm: 0-0**
Distance: **5f/6f: 1-11** 7f-8f: 0-1 9f-13f: 0-0 14f+: 0-0
Track : **LH: 1-4** RH: 0-2 **Tight: 1-3** Gall: 0-2
Aids: **Bl: 1-4** Vi: 0-3 Tstrap: 0-4 Ckp: 0-4
Best Rating: 56 12/08 Ling 5f stand

Moderate; effective over 5f; acts on Fibresand and on Polytrack; won in blinkers.

Summer Soul (IRE)

105 77
7-y-o b g Danehill (USA)-Blend Of Pace (IRE) (Sadler's Wells (USA))
Miss Lucinda V Russell Bissett Racing

Placings:1266/20/01/3-133466 (7170)
2009: 16^{1}GS, 13^{3}G, 14^{3}GS, 17^{4}G, 16^{6}GS, 15^{6}S,

	Starts	1st	2nd	3rd	Win & Pl
Career Total (Turf)	15	3	2	3	20649

77 5/09 Newc 2m19y (0-70)H G-S £4144
78 8/07 Bell 1m6f GD £5135
70 7/05 Klny 1m6f FRM £5390
Total win prize-money £14672

Going (Turf): Sf: 0-1 **GS: 1-3 Gd: 1-4** GF: 0-6 **Fm: 1-1**
Distance: 5f/6f: 0-0 7f-8f: 0-0 9f-13f: 0-3 **14f+: 3-12**
Track : **LH: 3-8** RH: 0-7 Tight: 0-1 **Gall: 1-2**
Aids: Bl: 1-7 Vi: 0-1 Tstrap: 1-5 Ckp: 1-5
Best Rating: 87 7/05 Gway 1m4f gd-fm

Fair; stays 2m; acts on fast and easy ground; has worn blinkers and cheekpieces; winning hurdler.

Summer Winds

106(107) (82)88
4-y-o ch g Where Or When (IRE)-Jetbeeah (IRE) (Lomond (USA))
T G Mills John Humphreys

Placings:0/123265032-24101340 (5725)
2009: 10^{2}SD, 10^{4}SD, 10^{1}GF, 10^{0}GF, 10^{1}GS, 10^{3}GF, 9^{4}G, 9^{0}GF,

	Starts	1st	2nd	3rd	Win & Pl
Career Total (Turf)	10	2	1	2	13033
Career Total (AW)	8	1	3	1	8879

88 6/09 NmkJ 1m2f (0-80)H G-S £5607
83 5/09 NmkR 1m2f (0-75)H G-F £3885
72 3/08 Ling 1m2f STD £4731
Total win prize-money £14226

Going (Turf): Sf: 0-0 **GS: 1-1** Gd: 0-3 **GF: 1-6** Fm: 0-0
Distance: 5f/6f: 0-0 7f-8f: 0-1 **9f-13f: 3-17** 14f+: 0-0
Track : LH: 1-6 RH: 1-9 Tight: 1-8 Gall: 1-3
Aids: **Bl: 2-6** Vi: 0-0 Tstrap: 0-0 Ckp: 0-0
Best Rating: 88 6/09 NmkJ 1m2f gd-sft

Useful; stays 1m2f; acts on Polytrack.

Summer's Lease

85 86

4-y-o b f Pivotal-Finlaggan (Be My Chief (USA))

M L W Bell Mrs C R Philipson & Mrs H G Lascelles

Placings:130-00 **(1860)**

2009: 10^{0}G, 8^{0}GF,

	Starts	1st	2nd	3rd	Win & Pl
Career Total (Turf)	5	1	0	1	3960

82 8/08 Nott 1m75y GD £3238

Total win prize-money £3238

Going (Turf): Sf: 0-1 GS: 0-1 **Gd: 1-2** GF: 0-1 Fm: 0-0
Distance: 5f/6f: 0-0 7f-8f: 0-1 **9f-13f: 1-4** 14f+: 0-0
Track : **LH: 1-4** RH: 0-0 Tight: 0-0 Gall: 0-2
Aids: Bl: 0-0 Vi: 0-0 Tstrap: 0-0 Ckp: 0-0
Best Rating: **86** 10/08 Newb 1m2f6y gd-sft

Useful; effective over 1m-1m2f; acts on good and easy ground.

Summercove (IRE)

98(90) (67)67

4-y-o b f Cape Cross (IRE)-Reasonably Devout (CAN) (St Jovite (USA))

John Joseph Murphy Mrs John J Murphy

Placings:020/6000-06003306 **(6822)**

2009: 8^{0}S, 10^{6}SD, 6^{0}G, 7^{0}G, 8^{3}YS, 11^{3}G, 14^{0}YS, 14^{6}GF,

	Starts	1st	2nd	3rd	Win & Pl
Career Total (Turf)	11	0	0	2	819
Career Total (AW)	4	0	1	0	1795

Going (Turf): **Sf: 0-2 GS: 0-0 Gd: 0-3 GF: 0-2 Fm: 0-0**
Distance: 5f/6f: 0-1 7f-8f: 0-4 9f-13f: 0-8 14f+: 0-2
Track : LH: 0-5 RH: 0-6 Tight: 0-1 Gall: 0-2
Aids: Bl: 0-4 Vi: 0-0 Tstrap: 0-0 Ckp: 0-0
Best Rating: **72** 10/07 Dund 1m stand

Summerinthecity (IRE)

105 85

2-y-o ch c Indian Ridge-Miss Assertive (Zafonic (USA))

J Noseda Mrs Susan Roy

Placings:21 **(4000)**

2009: 6^{2}G, 6^{1}GS,

	Starts	1st	2nd	3rd	Win & Pl
Career Total (Turf)	2	1	1	0	5947

85 7/09 Donc 6f G-S £3885

Total win prize-money £3886

Going (Turf): Sf: 0-0 **GS: 1-1** Gd: 0-1 GF: 0-0 Fm: 0-0
Distance: **5f/6f: 1-2** 7f-8f: 0-0 9f-13f: 0-0 14f+: 0-0
Track : LH: 0-0 RH: 0-0 Tight: 0-0 Gall: 0-0
Aids: Bl: 0-0 Vi: 0-0 Tstrap: 0-0 Ckp: 0-0
Best Rating: **85** 7/09 Donc 6f gd-sft

Useful; effective over 6f; acts on easy ground.

Summers Target (USA)

95(82) (36)86

3-y-o ch g Mr Greeley (USA)-She's Enough (USA) (Exploit (USA))

R M H Cowell Keith Robinson & Ian Robinson

Placings:2230-5330500 **(5591)**

2009: 7^{5}GF, 6^{3}GF, 6^{3}GF, 6^{0}GF, 7^{5}GF, 7^{0}G, 7^{0}GS,

	Starts	1st	2nd	3rd	Win & Pl
Career Total (Turf)	10	0	2	3	5479
Career Total (AW)	1	0	0	0	

Going (Turf): **Sf: 0-0 GS: 0-1 Gd: 0-2 GF: 0-7 Fm: 0-0**
Distance: 5f/6f: 0-4 7f-8f: 0-7 9f-13f: 0-0 14f+: 0-0
Track : LH: 0-1 RH: 0-2 Tight: 0-1 Gall: 0-1
Aids: Bl: 0-0 Vi: 0-0 Tstrap: 0-1 Ckp: 0-1
Best Rating: **86** 7/08 Asct 7f gd-fm

Useful; effective over 6-7f; acts on fast ground.

Summon Up Theblood (IRE)

98(96) (65)97

4-y-o b g Red Ransom (USA)-Diddymu (IRE) (Revoque (IRE))

M R Channon Derek And Jean Clee

Placings:0436/61110000-0 **(1684)**

2009: 8^{0}GF,

	Starts	1st	2nd	3rd	Win & Pl
Career Total (Turf)	11	3	0	1	24768
Career Total (AW)	2	0	0	0	0

97	6/08	Ayr	1m	(0-100)H	G-F	£15577
89	5/08	Thsk	1m	(0-85)H	GD	£5180
80	4/08	Wind	1m67y	(0-75)H	G-F	£3070

Total win prize-money £23830

Going (Turf): Sf: 0-0 GS: 0-1 Gd: 1-3 **GF: 2-7** Fm: 0-0
Distance: 5f/6f: 0-0 **7f-8f: 2-9** 9f-13f: 1-4 14f+: 0-0
Track : **LH: 2-5** RH: 1-6 **Tight: 2-4** Gall: 0-1
Aids: Bl: 0-0 Vi: 0-0 Tstrap: 0-0 Ckp: 0-0
Best Rating: **97** 6/08 Ayr 1m gd-fm

Useful; effective at around 1m; acts on good and fast ground.

Sun Catcher (IRE)

99(110) (74)57

6-y-o b g Cape Cross (IRE)-Taalluf (USA) (Hansel (USA))

P G Murphy Mike Conway

Placings:0600100/06100640/2164240326056505/6020010 000000-50020 **(3983)**

2009: 6^{5}GF, 6^{0}G, 7^{0}GF, 7^{2}SD, 7^{0}SD,

	Starts	1st	2nd	3rd	Win & Pl
Career Total (Turf)	19	2	0	0	11282
Career Total (AW)	30	2	5	1	13535

74	5/08	Sthl	1m	(0-75)H	STD	£3238
85	1/07	Ling	6f	(0-75)H	STD	£2914
81	8/06	Epsm	6f	(0-80)H	GD	£6477
81	9/05	Folk	6f		G-F	£3454

Total win prize-money £16085

Going (Turf): Sf: 0-2 GS: 0-5 **Gd: 1-6 GF: 1-6** Fm: 0-0
Distance: **5f/6f: 3-14** 7f-8f: 1-31 9f-13f: 0-4 14f+: 0-0
Track : **LH: 3-21** RH: 0-16 **Tight: 2-15** Gall: 0-3
Aids: Bl: 0-8 Vi: 0-1 Tstrap: 1-11 Ckp: 1-11
Best Rating: **85** 5/07 Ling 1m stand

Modest; effective over 6f-1m; acts on a range of surfaces; has worn headgear.

Sunarise (IRE)

89(94) (80)63

2-y-o b f Galileo (IRE)-Sun Silk (USA) (Gone West (USA))

R Hannon Mrs J Wood

Placings:010 **(7187)**

2009: 7^{0}GF, 7^{1}SD, 8^{0}G,

	Starts	1st	2nd	3rd	Win & Pl
Career Total (Turf)	2	0	0	0	7840
Career Total (AW)	1	1	0	0	2388

80 10/09 Ling 7f STD £2388

Total win prize-money £2388

Going (Turf): **Sf: 0-0 GS: 0-0 Gd: 0-1 GF: 0-1 Fm: 0-0**
Distance: 5f/6f: 0-0 **7f-8f: 1-3** 9f-13f: 0-0 14f+: 0-0
Track : **LH: 1-1** RH: 0-0 **Tight: 1-1** Gall: 0-0
Aids: Bl: 0-0 Vi: 0-0 Tstrap: 0-0 Ckp: 0-0
Best Rating: **80** 10/09 Ling 7f stand

Fair; stays 7f and acts on Polytrack.

Sunceleb (IRE)

101 73

3-y-o ch f Peintre Celebre (USA)-Suntory (IRE) (Royal Applause)

H Morrison Stonethorn Stud Farms Limited

Placings:5341066 **(6742)**

2009: 8^{5}GF, 8^{3}F, 8^{4}GF, 7^{1}F, 8^{0}G, 9^{6}F, 11^{6}GS,

	Starts	1st	2nd	3rd	Win & Pl
Career Total (Turf)	7	1	0	1	4158

69 7/09 Brig 7f214y FRM £3532

Total win prize-money £3532

Going (Turf): Sf: 0-0 GS: 0-1 Gd: 0-1 GF: 0-2 **Fm: 1-3**
Distance: 5f/6f: 0-0 **7f-8f: 1-2** 9f-13f: 0-5 14f+: 0-0
Track : **LH: 1-4** RH: 0-1 Tight: 0-3 Gall: 0-0
Aids: Bl: 0-0 Vi: 0-0 Tstrap: 0-0 Ckp: 0-0
Best Rating: **73** 5/09 Nott 1m75y firm

Fair; stays 1m; acts on fast ground.

Sundae

110(81) (35)96

5-y-o b g Bahamian Bounty-Merry Rous (Rousillon (USA))

C F Wall Peter Gregory

Placings:6/211113/04000-06100 **(7454)**

2009: 6^{0}GS, 6^{6}GF, 6^{1}G, 6^{0}G, 6^{0}SD,

	Starts	1st	2nd	3rd	Win & Pl
Career Total (Turf)	15	5	1	1	31389
Career Total (AW)	2	0	0	0	0

94	7/09	Yarm	6f3y	(0-85)H	GD	£4792
99	7/07	Newc	6f	(0-90)H	GD	£9348
94	6/07	NmkJ	5f	(0-85)H	G-S	£5181
87	6/07	Sand	5f6y	(0-75)H	G-S	£4533
67	5/07	Nott	6f15y		GD	£2914

Total win prize-money £26771

Going (Turf): Sf: 0-2 GS: 2-4 **Gd: 3-5** GF: 0-4 Fm: 0-0
Distance: **5f/6f: 3-12** 7f-8f: 2-5 9f-13f: 0-0 14f+: 0-0
Track : LH: 0-1 RH: 0-1 Tight: 0-1 Gall: 0-0
Aids: Bl: 0-1 Vi: 0-0 Tstrap: 0-0 Ckp: 0-0
Best Rating: **99** 7/07 Newc 6f good

Useful; effective at 5f-6f and acts on most ground.

Sundream

87 64

2-y-o b f Desert Sun-I Have A Dream (SWE) (Mango Express)

Tom Dascombe Mayden Stud

Placings:050 **(6728)**

2009: 6^{0}GF, 7^{5}G, 8^{0}S,

	Starts	1st	2nd	3rd	Win & Pl
Career Total (Turf)	3	0	0	0	0

Going (Turf): Sf: 0-1 GS: 0-0 Gd: 0-1 GF: 0-1 Fm: 0-0
Distance: 5f/6f: 0-0 7f-8f: 0-3 9f-13f: 0-0 14f+: 0-0
Track : LH: 0-1 RH: 0-0 Tight: 0-0 Gall: 0-0
Aids: Bl: 0-0 Vi: 0-0 Tstrap: 0-0 Ckp: 0-0
Best Rating: 64 8/09 Wwck 7f26y good

Moderate form at 7f on a sound surface.

Sunley Smiles

61(91) (50)
4-y-o ch f Arkadian Hero (USA)-Sunley Scent (Wolfhound (USA))
P Howling Mrs J P Howling

Placings:0/5050-0 (1940)
2009: 7^0GF,

	Starts	1st	2nd	3rd	Win & Pl
Career Total (Turf)	1	0	0	0	
Career Total (AW)	5	0	0	0	0

Going (Turf): Sf: 0-0 GS: 0-0 Gd: 0-0 GF: 0-1 Fm: 0-0
Distance: 5f/6f: 0-2 7f-8f: 0-3 9f-13f: 0-1 14f+: 0-0
Track : LH: 0-4 RH: 0-1 Tight: 0-4 Gall: 0-0
Aids: Bl: 0-0 Vi: 0-0 Tstrap: 0-0 Ckp: 0-0
Best Rating: 50 3/08 Ling 7f stand

Sunley Sovereign

103 (61)64
5-y-o b g Josr Algarhoud (IRE)-Pharsical (Pharly (FR))
Mrs R A Carr David W Chapman

Placings:05306/3615000000/00016000-5100406400242262 (6161)
2009: 5^5G, 5^1GF, 5^0GF, 6^0GF, 6^4GF, 7^0G, 6^6G, 6^4G, 6^0GF, 7^0GF, 5^2GS, 5^4GS, 5^2HY, 5^2GF, 5^6GS, 5^2G,

	Starts	1st	2nd	3rd	Win & Pl
Career Total (Turf)	32	2	4	1	10172
Career Total (AW)	7	1	0	1	2569

56 5/09 Haml 5f4y (0-70)H G-F £4094
56 9/08 Haml 5f4y (0-65)H SFT £2590
56 3/07 Sthl 7f STD £2184
Total win prize-money £8868

Going (Turf): Sf: 1-8 GS: 0-4 Gd: 0-8 GF: 1-11 Fm: 0-1
Distance: 5f/6f: 2-27 7f-8f: 1-10 9f-13f: 0-2 14f+: 0-0
Track : LH: 1-9 RH: 0-3 Tight: 0-6 Gall: 0-2
Aids: Bl: 2-20 Vi: 0-0 Tstrap: 0-3 Ckp: 0-3
Best Rating: 65 7/06 Brig 6f209y firm

Moderate; effective over 5f-7f; acts on any ground; goes on Fibresand and Polytrack; has worn blinkers and cheek-pieces.

Sunley Spinalonga

(79) (37)
2-y-o ch f With Approval (CAN)-Sunley Scent (Wolfhound (USA))
D R C Elsworth Sunley, Heaney & Elsworth

Placings:0 (7772)
2009: 7^0SD,

	Starts	1st	2nd	3rd	Win & Pl
Career Total (Turf)	0	0	0	0	
Career Total (AW)	1	0	0	0	

Going (Turf): Sf: 0-0 GS: 0-0 Gd: 0-0 GF: 0-0 Fm: 0-0
Distance: 5f/6f: 0-0 7f-8f: 0-1 9f-13f: 0-0 14f+: 0-0
Track : LH: 0-1 RH: 0-0 Tight: 0-1 Gall: 0-0
Aids: Bl: 0-0 Vi: 0-0 Tstrap: 0-0 Ckp: 0-0
Best Rating: 37 12/09 Ling 7f stand

Sunnandaeg

95 85
2-y-o ch c Haafhd-Come Away With Me (IRE) (Machiavellian (USA))
I Semple A Gauley

Placings:3154 (7013)
2009: 7^3GS, 6^1GF, 6^5G, 7^4GS,

	Starts	1st	2nd	3rd	Win & Pl
Career Total (Turf)	4	1	0	1	5363

84 8/09 Ayr 6f G-F £4015
Total win prize-money £4015

Going (Turf): Sf: 0-0 GS: 0-2 Gd: 0-1 GF: 1-1 Fm: 0-0
Distance: 5f/6f: 1-2 7f-8f: 0-2 9f-13f: 0-0 14f+: 0-0
Track : LH: 0-0 RH: 0-0 Tight: 0-0 Gall: 0-0
Aids: Bl: 0-0 Vi: 0-0 Tstrap: 0-0 Ckp: 0-0
Best Rating: 85 10/09 Donc 7f gd-sft

Useful; suited by 6f and acts on most ground.

Sunny Future (IRE)

96(92) (76)78
3-y-o b g Masterful (USA)-Be Magic (Persian Bold)
M S Saunders M S Saunders

Placings:33200-0204430 (7065)
2009: 6^0GF, 8^2G, 8^0GF, 7^4S, 8^4GS, 8^3GS, 8^0SD,

	Starts	1st	2nd	3rd	Win & Pl
Career Total (Turf)	10	0	2	2	3564
Career Total (AW)	2	0	0	1	539

Going (Turf): Sf: 0-2 GS: 0-3 Gd: 0-1 GF: 0-4 Fm: 0-0
Distance: 5f/6f: 0-1 7f-8f: 0-7 9f-13f: 0-4 14f+: 0-0
Track : LH: 0-5 RH: 0-0 Tight: 0-5 Gall: 0-0
Aids: Bl: 0-0 Vi: 0-0 Tstrap: 0-0 Ckp: 0-0
Best Rating: 78 8/08 Sals 6f212y gd-sft

Modest; stays 1m; acts on most ground; also goes on Polytrack.

Sunny Spells

(103) (73)52
4-y-o b g Zamindar (USA)-Bright Spells (Salse (USA))
S C Williams W E Enticknap

Placings:5000421-00513 (7867)
2009: 8^0SD, 10^0SD, 12^5SD, 12^1SS, 14^3SS,

	Starts	1st	2nd	3rd	Win & Pl
Career Total (Turf)	5	0	0	0	221
Career Total (AW)	8	2	1	1	6190

73 12/09 Sthl 1m4f (0-60)H SS £2047
65 9/08 GrLe 1m6f (0-70)H STD £2590
Total win prize-money £4637

Going (Turf): Sf: 0-1 GS: 0-2 Gd: 0-2 GF: 0-0 Fm: 0-0
Distance: 5f/6f: 0-0 7f-8f: 0-4 9f-13f: 1-7 14f+: 1-2
Track : LH: 2-7 RH: 0-4 Tight: 0-3 Gall: 1-3
Aids: Bl: 0-0 Vi: 0-0 Tstrap: 0-0 Ckp: 0-0
Best Rating: 73 12/09 Sthl 1m4f std-slw

Modest; stays 1m6f and acts on Polytrack and on Fibresand.

Sunny Sprite

(79) (70)69
4-y-o b g Lujain (USA)-Dragon Star (Rudimentary (USA))
J M P Eustace T H Barma

Placings:24/5400-5 (0495)
2009: 7^5SD,

	Starts	1st	2nd	3rd	Win & Pl
Career Total (Turf)	4	0	0	0	385
Career Total (AW)	3	0	1	0	578

Going (Turf): Sf: 0-1 GS: 0-0 Gd: 0-0 GF: 0-3 Fm: 0-0
Distance: 5f/6f: 0-2 7f-8f: 0-4 9f-13f: 0-1 14f+: 0-0
Track : LH: 0-2 RH: 0-2 Tight: 0-2 Gall: 0-0
Aids: Bl: 0-0 Vi: 0-0 Tstrap: 0-0 Ckp: 0-0
Best Rating: 70 8/07 Ling 6f stand

Modest; stays 6f; acts on Polytrack.

Sunnyside Tom (IRE)

107(99) (84)92
5-y-o b g Danetime (IRE)-So Kind (Kind Of Hush)
R A Fahey The Sunnyside Racing Partnership

Placings:61/5560350020/411400000-6131201224 (6946)
2009: 7^6GS, 7^1GF, 8^3G, 7^1G, 7^2G, 8^0G, 9^1HY, 9^2G, 9^2GF, 8^4SD,

	Starts	1st	2nd	3rd	Win & Pl
Career Total (Turf)	30	6	4	2	39048
Career Total (AW)	1	0	0	0	433

84 8/09 Haml 1m1f36y HVY £5180
84 6/09 Carl 7f200y (0-80)H GD £6476
80 5/09 Carl 7f200y (0-80)H G-F £5180
81 6/08 Muss 1m (0-80)H G-F £6476
78 6/08 Muss 1m (0-80)H G-F £4673
77 8/06 Carl 5f G-F £2730
Total win prize-money £30717

Going (Turf): Sf: 1-3 GS: 0-4 Gd: 1-9 GF: 4-13 Fm: 0-1
Distance: 5f/6f: 1-7 7f-8f: 4-16 9f-13f: 1-8 14f+: 0-0
Track : LH: 0-7 RH: 6-15 Tight: 3-7 Gall: 1-2
Aids: Bl: 0-0 Vi: 0-2 Tstrap: 0-1 Ckp: 0-1
Best Rating: 92 7/09 Carl 7f200y good

Fair; stays 1m1f; acts on any ground; has worn various headgear.

Sunraider (IRE)

101 83
2-y-o b c Namid-Doctrine (Barathea (IRE))
B W Hills Ron Young & SW Group Logistics Ltd

Placings:310 (5795)
2009: 6^3G, 6^1GF, 6^0GF,

	Starts	1st	2nd	3rd	Win & Pl
Career Total (Turf)	3	1	0	1	13133

83 8/09 Wind 6f G-F £3561
Total win prize-money £3562

Going (Turf): Sf: 0-0 GS: 0-0 Gd: 0-1 GF: 1-2 Fm: 0-0
Distance: 5f/6f: 1-2 7f-8f: 0-1 9f-13f: 0-0 14f+: 0-0
Track : LH: 0-0 RH: 0-0 Tight: 0-0 Gall: 1-2
Aids: Bl: 0-0 Vi: 0-0 Tstrap: 0-0 Ckp: 0-0
Best Rating: 83 9/09 Donc 6f110y gd-fm

Useful; effective over 6f; acts on fast ground.

Sunrise Lyric (IRE)

(87) (63)
2-y-o b f Rock Of Gibraltar (IRE)-Dawn Air (USA) (Diesis)
P F I Cole Mrs Carmen Burrell

Placings:6 **(5752)**
2009: 7^{6}SD,

	Starts	1st	2nd	3rd	Win & Pl
Career Total (Turf)	0	0	0	0	
Career Total (AW)	1	0	0	0	0

Going (Turf): **Sf: 0-0 GS: 0-0 Gd: 0-0 GF: 0-0 Fm: 0-0**
Distance: 5f/6f: 0-0 7f-8f: 0-1 9f-13f: 0-0 14f+: 0-0
Track : LH: 0-1 RH: 0-0 Tight: 0-1 Gall: 0-0
Aids: Bl: 0-0 Vi: 0-0 Tstrap: 0-0 Ckp: 0-0
Best Rating: **63** 9/09 Ling 7f stand

Sunrise Safari (IRE)

108(100) (73)94
6-y-o b g Mozart (IRE)-Lady Scarlett (Woodman (USA))
R A Fahey Timeform Betfair Racing Club Ltd

Placings:32303364/310/014013414/0000030-02460351054060 **(7395)**
2009: 5^{0}GF, 6^{2}GF, 6^{4}GF, 7^{6}G, 6^{0}G, 6^{3}S, 7^{5}G, 6^{1}G, 6^{0}G, 6^{5}GF, 6^{4}GF, 6^{0}G, 6^{6}G, 6^{0}SD,

	Starts	1st	2nd	3rd	Win & Pl
Career Total (Turf)	39	5	2	8	62770
Career Total (AW)	2	0	0	0	
94	7/09	Pont	6f	(0-90)H	GD £9346
104	10/07	Donc	5f	(0-100)H	GD £12464
96	7/07	Newc	5f	(0-85)H	GD £6232
92	5/07	Ayr	5f	(0-90)H	G-S £7124
70	5/06	Haml	6f5y		G-F £3886

Total win prize-money £39054

Going (Turf): Sf: 0-4 GS: 1-2 **Gd: 3-15** GF: 1-17 Fm: 0-1
Distance: **5f/6f: 4-34** 7f-8f: 1-7 9f-13f: 0-0 14f+: 0-0
Track : **LH: 1-10** RH: 0-1 Tight: 0-4 Gall: 0-7
Aids: Bl: 0-0 **Vi: 5-26** Tstrap: 0-2 Ckp: 0-2
Best Rating: **106** 11/07 Donc 6f gd-fm

Useful; effective over 5f-6f; acts on most ground; usually wears a visor or cheekpieces.

Sunrise Shuffle

81 59
2-y-o b f Danehill Dancer (IRE)-Silky Dawn (IRE) (Night Shift (USA))
B W Hills D J Deer

Placings:0 **(7182)**
2009: 7^{0}G,

	Starts	1st	2nd	3rd	Win & Pl
Career Total (Turf)	1	0	0	0	

Going (Turf): **Sf: 0-0 GS: 0-0 Gd: 0-1 GF: 0-0 Fm: 0-0**
Distance: 5f/6f: 0-0 7f-8f: 0-1 9f-13f: 0-0 14f+: 0-0
Track : LH: 0-0 RH: 0-0 Tight: 0-0 Gall: 0-0
Aids: Bl: 0-0 Vi: 0-0 Tstrap: 0-0 Ckp: 0-0
Best Rating: **59** 10/09 NmkR 7f good

Sunset Boulevard (IRE)

80(102) (68)46
6-y-o b g Montjeu (IRE)-Lucy In The Sky (IRE) (Lycius (USA))
Miss Tor Sturgis Miss Tor Sturgis

Placings:656/1013/55-6102122020 **(3923)**
2009: 12^{6}SD, 12^{1}SD, 12^{0}SD, 12^{2}SD, 12^{1}SD, 12^{2}SD, 12^{2}SD, 10^{0}GF, 12^{2}SD, 12^{0}SD,

	Starts	1st	2nd	3rd	Win & Pl
Career Total (Turf)	4	0	0	1	578
Career Total (AW)	15	4	4	0	13026
67	3/09	Ling	1m4f		STD £2047
68	1/09	Ling	1m4f	(0-70)H	STD £2900
75	5/07	Ling	1m4f	(0-70)H	STD £3238
64	1/07	Ling	1m4f		STD £2169

Total win prize-money £10356

Going (Turf): **Sf: 0-2 GS: 0-0 Gd: 0-0 GF: 0-2 Fm: 0-0**
Distance: 5f/6f: 0-0 7f-8f: 0-0 **9f-13f: 4-19** 14f+: 0-0
Track : **LH: 4-15** RH: 0-4 **Tight: 4-15** Gall: 0-2
Aids: Bl: 0-0 Vi: 0-1 Tstrap: 0-0 Ckp: 0-0
Best Rating: **75** 5/07 Leic 1m3f183y gd-fm

Modest; stays 1m4f; acts on Polytrack.

Sunshine Always (IRE)

108(104) (87)89
3-y-o gr g Verglas (IRE)-Easy Sunshine (IRE) (Sadler's Wells (USA))
T D McCarthy (W J Haggas 2/9) Miss Maureen Stopher

Placings:1422413264464 **(7891)**
2009: 7^{1}SD, 7^{4}GF, 8^{2}S, 8^{2}G, 7^{4}HY, 8^{1}SD, 8^{3}SD, 7^{2}SD, 8^{6}SD, 7^{4}SD, 8^{4}SD, 7^{6}SD, 7^{4}SD,

	Starts	1st	2nd	3rd	Win & Pl
Career Total (Turf)	4	0	2	0	6640
Career Total (AW)	9	2	1	1	7940
85	9/09	Kemp	1m		STD £2047
78	5/09	Wolv	7f32y		STD £2729

Total win prize-money £4777

Going (Turf): **Sf: 0-2 GS: 0-0 Gd: 0-1 GF: 0-1 Fm: 0-0**
Distance: 5f/6f: 0-0 **7f-8f: 2-13** 9f-13f: 0-0 14f+: 0-0
Track : LH: 1-4 RH: 1-7 **Tight: 1-2** Gall: 0-1
Aids: Bl: 0-0 Vi: 0-0 Tstrap: 0-0 Ckp: 0-0
Best Rating: **89** 6/09 Newc 1m soft

Useful; stays 1m; acts on most ground on turf and on Polytrack.

Sunshine Buddy

(62) (6)
2-y-o b f Reel Buddy (USA)-Bullion (Sabrehill (USA))
J R Holt No Illusions Partnership

Placings:0 **(3979)**
2009: 7^{0}SD,

	Starts	1st	2nd	3rd	Win & Pl
Career Total (Turf)	0	0	0	0	
Career Total (AW)	1	0	0	0	

Going (Turf): **Sf: 0-0 GS: 0-0 Gd: 0-0 GF: 0-0 Fm: 0-0**
Distance: 5f/6f: 0-0 7f-8f: 0-1 9f-13f: 0-0 14f+: 0-0
Track : LH: 0-0 RH: 0-1 Tight: 0-0 Gall: 0-0
Aids: Bl: 0-0 Vi: 0-0 Tstrap: 0-0 Ckp: 0-0
Best Rating: **6** 7/09 Kemp 7f stand

Sunshine Ellie

(92) (44)51
3-y-o ch f Desert Sun-Lindoras Glory (USA) (Gone West (USA))
D Shaw Derek Shaw

Placings:0000-6006 **(7714)**
2009: 6^{6}SS, 7^{0}SD, 5^{0}SD, 5^{6}SD,

	Starts	1st	2nd	3rd	Win & Pl
Career Total (Turf)	2	0	0	0	
Career Total (AW)	6	0	0	0	0

Going (Turf): **Sf: 0-0 GS: 0-0 Gd: 0-1 GF: 0-1 Fm: 0-0**
Distance: 5f/6f: 0-3 7f-8f: 0-5 9f-13f: 0-0 14f+: 0-0
Track : LH: 0-5 RH: 0-2 Tight: 0-4 Gall: 0-0
Aids: Bl: 0-0 Vi: 0-0 Tstrap: 0-0 Ckp: 0-0
Best Rating: **51** 9/08 Gdwd 7f gd-fm

Suntrap

88 61
2-y-o ch g Desert Sun-Regal Gallery (IRE) (Royal Academy (USA))
W J Knight Mrs B Sumner

Placings:56 **(6199)**
2009: 7^{5}G, 7^{6}G,

	Starts	1st	2nd	3rd	Win & Pl
Career Total (Turf)	2	0	0	0	0

Going (Turf): **Sf: 0-0 GS: 0-0 Gd: 0-2 GF: 0-0 Fm: 0-0**
Distance: 5f/6f: 0-0 7f-8f: 0-2 9f-13f: 0-0 14f+: 0-0
Track : LH: 0-0 RH: 0-1 Tight: 0-0 Gall: 0-0
Aids: Bl: 0-0 Vi: 0-0 Tstrap: 0-0 Ckp: 0-0
Best Rating: **61** 9/09 Gdwd 7f good

Supaseus

111 112
6-y-o b g Spinning World (USA)-Supamova (USA) (Seattle Slew (USA))
H Morrison Ben & Sir Martyn Arbib

Placings:02/100150/1400/4310300-006510 **(6812)**
2009: 9^{0}FT, 8^{0}G, 10^{6}G, 10^{5}GF, 9^{1}GF, 9^{0}G,

	Starts	1st	2nd	3rd	Win & Pl
Career Total (Turf)	24	5	1	2	212660
Career Total (AW)	1	0	0	0	
109	10/09	NmkR	1m1f	H	G-F £99696
110	6/08	Asct	1m2f	(0-110)H	FRM £34062
102	5/07	NmkR	1m1f	H	G-F £31160
99	9/06	Asct	1m	(0-100)H	G-S £18696
78	5/06	NmkR	1m		GD £4857

Total win prize-money £188472

Going (Turf): Sf: 0-2 GS: 1-3 Gd: 1-5 **GF: 2-13** Fm: 1-1
Distance: 5f/6f: 0-0 7f-8f: 2-9 **9f-13f: 3-16** 14f+: 0-0
Track : LH: 0-8 **RH: 1-4** Tight: 0-1 **Gall: 1-5**
Aids: Bl: 0-0 Vi: 0-0 Tstrap: 0-0 Ckp: 0-0
Best Rating: **112** 7/08 York 1m2f88y gd-fm

Listed class; winner of 2009 Cambridgeshire; stays 1m2f; acts on most ground but well suited by fast; likes to race prominently.

Supaverdi (USA)

105(99) (73)89
4-y-o br f Green Desert (USA)-Supamova (USA) (Seattle Slew (USA))
H Morrison Ben & Sir Martyn Arbib

Placings:531-160611 **(5128)**
2009: 8^{1}GF, 8^{6}GF, 8^{0}GF, 10^{6}SD, 10^{1}HY, 10^{1}GF,

	Starts	1st	2nd	3rd	Win & Pl
Career Total (Turf)	6	3	0	0	10685
Career Total (AW)	3	1	0	1	3641

89 8/09 Nott 1m2f50y (0-80)H G-F £4857
84 7/09 Hayd 1m2f95y (0-75)H HVY £3238
81 4/09 Bath 1m5y (0-75)H G-F £2590
73 12/08 Wolv 1m141y STD £3238
Total win prize-money £13923

Going (Turf): Sf: 1-2 GS: 0-0 Gd: 0-0 **GF: 2-4** Fm: 0-0
Distance: 5f/6f: 0-0 7f-8f: 0-2 **9f-13f: 4-7** 14f+: 0-0
Track : **LH: 4-7** RH: 0-0 **Tight: 2-4** Gall: 0-0
Aids: Bl: 0-0 Vi: 0-0 Tstrap: 0-0 Ckp: 0-0
Best Rating: 89 8/09 Nott 1m2f50y gd-fm

Fair; effective at 1m; acts on fast ground and Polytrack.

Super Academy (USA)

98(95) (69)75
3-y-o ch f Royal Academy (USA)-Super Supreme (IND) (Zafonic (USA))
J A Osborne Ben Arbib & Partners

Placings:22100 (5902)
2009: 7²SD, 7²SD, 6¹GF, 7⁰SD, 5⁰F,

	Starts	1st	2nd	3rd	Win & Pl
Career Total (Turf)	2	1	0	0	3886
Career Total (AW)	3	0	2	0	1713

75 6/09 Sals 6f212y G-F £3885
Total win prize-money £3886

Going (Turf): Sf: 0-0 GS: 0-0 Gd: 0-0 **GF: 1-1** Fm: 0-1
Distance: 5f/6f: 0-1 **7f-8f: 1-4** 9f-13f: 0-0 14f+: 0-0
Track : LH: 0-3 RH: 0-1 Tight: 0-2 Gall: 0-1
Aids: Bl: 0-0 Vi: 0-0 Tstrap: 0-0 Ckp: 0-0
Best Rating: 75 6/09 Sals 6f212y gd-fm

Fair; stays 7f and acts on Polytrack.

Super Collider

95 77
2-y-o b g Montjeu (IRE)-Astorg (USA) (Lear Fan (USA))
M A Jarvis B E Nielsen

Placings:623 (6285)
2009: 7⁶G, 8²G, 8³GF,

	Starts	1st	2nd	3rd	Win & Pl
Career Total (Turf)	3	0	1	1	2168

Going (Turf): **Sf: 0-0 GS: 0-0 Gd: 0-2 GF: 0-1 Fm: 0-0**
Distance: 5f/6f: 0-0 7f-8f: 0-2 9f-13f: 0-1 14f+: 0-0
Track : LH: 0-2 RH: 0-0 Tight: 0-1 Gall: 0-0
Aids: Bl: 0-0 Vi: 0-0 Tstrap: 0-0 Ckp: 0-0
Best Rating: 77 8/09 Thsk 1m good

Fair form in maidens at up to 1m; acts on good ground.

Super Duplex

92(85) (62)65
2-y-o b c Footstepsinthesand-Penelope Tree (IRE) (Desert Prince (IRE))
P M Phelan Special Piping Materials Ltd

Placings:4336000 (6906)
2009: 5⁴SD, 6³GF, 6³G, 6⁶G, 5⁰SD, 6⁰GS, 6⁰G,

	Starts	1st	2nd	3rd	Win & Pl
Career Total (Turf)	5	0	0	2	915
Career Total (AW)	2	0	0	0	0

Going (Turf): **Sf: 0-0 GS: 0-1 Gd: 0-3 GF: 0-1 Fm: 0-0**
Distance: 5f/6f: 0-7 7f-8f: 0-0 9f-13f: 0-0 14f+: 0-0
Track : LH: 0-3 RH: 0-0 Tight: 0-3 Gall: 0-1

Aids: Bl: 0-0 Vi: 0-0 Tstrap: 0-0 Ckp: 0-0
Best Rating: 65 7/09 Epsm 6f good

Super Fourteen

101(100) (60)65
3-y-o b c Lucky Story (USA)-Beechnut (IRE) (Mujadil (USA))
Ray Fielder (R Hannon 30/9) Fred Camis

Placings:0043531-033003 (6370)
2009: 8⁰GF, 8³SD, 8³G, 8⁰G, 7⁰SD, 8³SD,

	Starts	1st	2nd	3rd	Win & Pl
Career Total (Turf)	10	1	0	3	4508
Career Total (AW)	3	0	0	2	591

61 9/08 Brig 6f209y G-F £2396
Total win prize-money £2396

Going (Turf): Sf: 0-1 GS: 0-1 Gd: 0-3 **GF: 1-5** Fm: 0-0
Distance: 5f/6f: 0-2 **7f-8f: 1-8** 9f-13f: 0-3 14f+: 0-0
Track : **LH: 1-3** RH: 0-5 Tight: 0-3 Gall: 0-1
Aids: Bl: 0-0 Vi: 0-0 Tstrap: 0-0 Ckp: 0-0
Best Rating: 65 9/08 Leic 7f9y soft

Modest; stays 7f; acts on fast and easy ground.

Super Frank (IRE)

103(111) (86)73
6-y-o b g Cape Cross (IRE)-Lady Joshua (IRE) (Royal Academy (USA))
J Akehurst A D Spence

Placings:065/140000001/111346404/4221000000050-531101160000 (6562)
2009: 7⁵SD, 7³SD, 7¹SD, 6¹SD, 6⁰SD, 6¹G, 6¹GF, 6⁶F, 6⁰GF, 6⁰GF, 6⁰GF, 7⁰GS,

	Starts	1st	2nd	3rd	Win & Pl
Career Total (Turf)	19	2	0	1	6466
Career Total (AW)	27	8	2	1	29642

71 4/09 Folk 6f (0-75)H G-F £3070
73 4/09 Folk 6f (0-60)H GD £2047
84 3/09 Ling 6f (0-75)H STD £2900
81 2/09 Ling 7f (0-70)H STD £2900
86 2/08 Kemp 7f (0-85)H STD £4210
87 2/07 Ling 7f (0-85)H STD £4857
80 1/07 Ling 7f (0-80)H STD £4674
75 1/07 Kemp 7f (0-60)H STD £2388
68 12/06 Ling 7f (0-58)H STD £1706
64 1/06 Ling 7f (0-60)H STD £2047
Total win prize-money £30803

Going (Turf): Sf: 0-1 GS: 0-3 **Gd: 1-3 GF: 1-11** Fm: 0-1
Distance: 5f/6f: 3-8 **7f-8f: 7-31** 9f-13f: 0-7 14f+: 0-0
Track : **LH: 6-22** RH: 2-11 **Tight: 6-20** Gall: 0-2
Aids: Bl: 1-3 Vi: 0-0 Tstrap: 4-9 Ckp: 4-9
Best Rating: 87 2/07 Ling 7f stand

Fair; effective over 7f and acts well on Polytrack; has worn cheekpieces; suited by forcing tactics.

Super King

82(81) (41)37
8-y-o b g Kingsinger (IRE)-Super Sisters (AUS) (Call Report (USA))
A D Brown Mrs Susan Johnson

Placings:02/00052300/006650003000/0-005000 (5423)
2009: 8⁰SD, 11⁰SD, 10⁵SD, 12⁰SD, 10⁰GF, 9⁰GF,

	Starts	1st	2nd	3rd	Win & Pl
Career Total (Turf)	21	0	2	1	2433
Career Total (AW)	10	0	0	1	421

Going (Turf): **Sf: 0-3 GS: 0-3 Gd: 0-7 GF: 0-8 Fm: 0-0**
Distance: 5f/6f: 0-0 7f-8f: 0-8 9f-13f: 0-23 14f+: 0-0
Track : LH: 0-22 RH: 0-8 Tight: 0-5 Gall: 0-8
Aids: Bl: 0-1 Vi: 0-1 Tstrap: 0-0 Ckp: 0-0
Best Rating: 67 8/04 Bevl 1m1f207y gd-sft

Super Sensation (GER)

(104) (53)
8-y-o ch g Platini (GER)-Studford Girl (Midyan (USA))
G L Moore The Sanderson Partnership

Placings:136/006332213020/45136040000/425/43 (0732)
2009: 12⁴SD, 16³SD,

	Starts	1st	2nd	3rd	Win & Pl
Career Total (Turf)	24	2	3	5	6495
Career Total (AW)	7	1	1	1	2302

5/06 Colo 1m1f55y H GD £2069
8/05 Neus 1m1f110y H STD £1418
4/04 Duin 1m1f GD £423
Total win prize-money £3910

Going (Turf): Sf: 0-8 GS: 0-0 **Gd: 2-15** GF: 0-0 Fm: 0-0
Distance: 5f/6f: 0-0 7f-8f: 0-3 **9f-13f: 3-27** 14f+: 0-1
Track : LH: 0-6 RH: 0-1 Tight: 0-5 Gall: 0-0
Aids: Bl: 0-5 Vi: 0-0 Tstrap: 0-0 Ckp: 0-0
Best Rating: 59 6/07 Ling 1m4f stand

Plating-class; stays 1m4f; handles Polytrack.

Super Sleuth (IRE)

112 110
3-y-o ch f Selkirk (USA)-Enemy Action (USA) (Forty Niner (USA))
B J Meehan Mrs Lucinda Freedman

Placings:0252-230 (2304a)
2009: 7²S, 8³GF, 8⁰HY,

	Starts	1st	2nd	3rd	Win & Pl
Career Total (Turf)	7	0	3	1	68228

Going (Turf): **Sf: 0-2 GS: 0-1 Gd: 0-2 GF: 0-2 Fm: 0-0**
Distance: 5f/6f: 0-0 7f-8f: 0-7 9f-13f: 0-0 14f+: 0-0
Track : LH: 0-0 RH: 0-1 Tight: 0-0 Gall: 0-1
Aids: Bl: 0-0 Vi: 0-0 Tstrap: 0-0 Ckp: 0-0
Best Rating: 110 4/09 Newb 7f soft

Smart; runner-up in the Fred Darling and third in the 1000 Guineas; effective over 7f-1m on good and soft ground.

Super Yellow

(92) (59)
2-y-o b c Exceed And Excel (AUS)-Almost Amber (USA) (Mt. Livermore (USA))
J A Osborne A Taylor & K Conlan

Placings:50 (7376)
2009: 5⁵SD, 7⁰SD,

	Starts	1st	2nd	3rd	Win & Pl
Career Total (Turf)	0	0	0	0	
Career Total (AW)	2	0	0	0	0

Going (Turf): **Sf: 0-0 GS: 0-0 Gd: 0-0 GF: 0-0 Fm: 0-0**
Distance: 5f/6f: 0-1 7f-8f: 0-1 9f-13f: 0-0 14f+: 0-0
Track : LH: 0-2 RH: 0-0 Tight: 0-2 Gall: 0-0

Aids: Bl: 0-0 Vi: 0-0 Tstrap: 0-0 Ckp: 0-0
Best Rating: 59 10/09 Wolv 5f216y stand

Supera (IRE)

88(86) (43)43
3-y-o ch f Spartacus (IRE)-Lauretta Blue (IRE) (Bluebird (USA))
M H Tompkins Raceworld

Placings:00-040 (4177)
2009: 8^{0}GF, 7^{4}GF, 10^{0}GS,

	Starts	1st	2nd	3rd	Win & Pl
Career Total (Turf)	4	0	0	0	192
Career Total (AW)	1	0	0	0	

Going (Turf): Sf: 0-0 GS: 0-1 Gd: 0-1 GF: 0-2 Fm: 0-0
Distance: 5f/6f: 0-1 7f-8f: 0-3 9f-13f: 0-1 14f+: 0-0
Track : LH: 0-2 RH: 0-1 Tight: 0-1 Gall: 0-1
Aids: Bl: 0-0 Vi: 0-0 Tstrap: 0-0 Ckp: 0-0
Best Rating: 43 7/09 Bevl 7f100y gd-fm

Supercast (IRE)

106(106) (83)82
6-y-o b g Alhaarth (IRE)-Al Euro (FR) (Mujtahid (USA))
N J Vaughan (F Sheridan 13/9) Mrs Lynn Vaughan

Placings:3124000/0040403500453/0025606000/22130441 1033613-0235441004054 (7848)
2009: 9^{0}SD, 9^{2}SD, 10^{3}SD, 9^{5}SD, 10^{4}G, 10^{4}S, 9^{1}GF, 10^{0}G, 9^{0}GF, 9^{4}SD, 9^{0}G, 10^{5}SD, 9^{4}SD,

	Starts	1st	2nd	3rd	Win & Pl
Career Total (Turf)	32	4	1	4	27073
Career Total (AW)	26	2	4	4	11817

82 6/09 Gdwd 1m1f192y (0-75)H G-F £3885
82 11/08 Wolv 1m1f103y (0-85)H STD £5180
79 7/08 Haml 1m1f36y (0-75)H GD £3885
75 6/08 Ayr 1m2f (0-75)H G-F £4533
68 2/08 Wolv 1m141y (0-60)H STD £1774
78 6/05 Carl 5f G-F £4095
Total win prize-money £23356

Going (Turf): Sf: 0-3 GS: 0-4 Gd: 1-13 GF: 3-12 Fm: 0-0
Distance: 5f/6f: 1-24 7f-8f: 0-8 9f-13f: 5-26 14f+: 0-0
Track : LH: 3-29 RH: 3-14 Tight: 4-25 Gall: 1-7
Aids: Bl: 0-4 Vi: 0-0 Tstrap: 0-2 Ckp: 0-2
Best Rating: 87 7/05 Vich 5f gd-sft

Fair; stays 1m2f; acts on fast ground; goes on Polytrack.

Superduper

104(95) (46)88
4-y-o b f Erhaab (USA)-I'm Magic (First Trump)
R Hannon David & Jennifer Sieff & Bloomsbury Stud

Placings:03540/32151240-26003 (4982)
2009: 6^{2}GS, 6^{6}GF, 6^{0}GF, 5^{0}G, 6^{3}SD,

	Starts	1st	2nd	3rd	Win & Pl
Career Total (Turf)	17	2	3	2	15499
Career Total (AW)	1	0	0	1	302

85 7/08 Wind 6f (0-85)H G-F £5828
82 6/08 Chep 6f16y (0-70)H G-F £2590
Total win prize-money £8418

Going (Turf): Sf: 0-3 GS: 0-2 Gd: 0-2 GF: 2-10 Fm: 0-0
Distance: 5f/6f: 1-15 7f-8f: 1-3 9f-13f: 0-0 14f+: 0-0
Track : LH: 0-1 RH: 0-1 Tight: 0-0 Gall: 1-5
Aids: Bl: 0-0 Vi: 0-0 Tstrap: 0-0 Ckp: 0-0
Best Rating: 88 4/09 Wind 6f gd-sft

Useful; effective over 6f-7f; acts on fast and soft ground.

Superhoops

63(36) 31
2-y-o b g Hunting Lion (IRE)-Colonial Lady (Dansili)
H S Howe Mrs Jayne Thompson

Placings:000 (5868)
2009: 8^{0}SD, 8^{0}GF, 8^{0}G,

	Starts	1st	2nd	3rd	Win & Pl
Career Total (Turf)	2	0	0	0	
Career Total (AW)	1	0	0	0	

Going (Turf): Sf: 0-0 GS: 0-0 Gd: 0-1 GF: 0-1 Fm: 0-0
Distance: 5f/6f: 0-0 7f-8f: 0-2 9f-13f: 0-1 14f+: 0-0
Track : LH: 0-2 RH: 0-1 Tight: 0-2 Gall: 0-1
Aids: Bl: 0-0 Vi: 0-0 Tstrap: 0-0 Ckp: 0-0
Best Rating: 31 8/09 Wind 1m67y gd-fm

Superior Duchess

94(89) (44)57
4-y-o b f Superior Premium-Downclose Duchess (King's Signet (USA))
Jane Chapple-Hyam Mrs Jane Chapple-Hyam

Placings:5350-66400 (7652)
2009: 8^{6}GF, 7^{6}G, 8^{4}G, 12^{0}SD, 8^{0}SD,

	Starts	1st	2nd	3rd	Win & Pl
Career Total (Turf)	5	0	0	1	403
Career Total (AW)	4	0	0	0	0

Going (Turf): Sf: 0-1 GS: 0-1 Gd: 0-2 GF: 0-1 Fm: 0-0
Distance: 5f/6f: 0-0 7f-8f: 0-4 9f-13f: 0-5 14f+: 0-0
Track : LH: 0-4 RH: 0-2 Tight: 0-3 Gall: 0-0
Aids: Bl: 0-0 Vi: 0-0 Tstrap: 0-0 Ckp: 0-0
Best Rating: 57 9/08 Wwck 1m22y soft

Superior Edge

82 54
2-y-o b f Exceed And Excel (AUS)-Beveled Edge (Beveled (USA))
B Palling Christopher J Mason

Placings:05 (5380)
2009: 6^{0}GF, 5^{5}G,

	Starts	1st	2nd	3rd	Win & Pl
Career Total (Turf)	2	0	0	0	0

Going (Turf): Sf: 0-0 GS: 0-0 Gd: 0-1 GF: 0-1 Fm: 0-0
Distance: 5f/6f: 0-1 7f-8f: 0-1 9f-13f: 0-0 14f+: 0-0
Track : LH: 0-1 RH: 0-0 Tight: 0-0 Gall: 0-1
Aids: Bl: 0-0 Vi: 0-0 Tstrap: 0-0 Ckp: 0-0
Best Rating: 54 8/09 Bath 5f11y good

Modest form in sprint maidens.

Superior Service

37
2-y-o b f Superior Premium-Dolly Bevan (Another Realm)
C C Bealby C C Bealby

Placings:0 (4100)
2009: 5^{0}S,

	Starts	1st	2nd	3rd	Win & Pl
Career Total (Turf)	1	0	0	0	

Going (Turf): Sf: 0-1 GS: 0-0 Gd: 0-0 GF: 0-0 Fm: 0-0
Distance: 5f/6f: 0-1 7f-8f: 0-0 9f-13f: 0-0 14f+: 0-0
Track : LH: 0-0 RH: 0-0 Tight: 0-0 Gall: 0-0
Aids: Bl: 0-0 Vi: 0-0 Tstrap: 0-0 Ckp: 0-0

Supermassive Muse (IRE)

103(101) (90)93
4-y-o br g Captain Rio-Cautionary (IRE) (Warning)
E S McMahon Nick Hughes

Placings:021065/32044166l232-60000540 (6459)
2009: 5^{6}GF, 5^{0}G, 5^{0}G, 5^{0}GF, 6^{0}GF, 5^{5}GF, 5^{4}GF, 5^{0}SD,

	Starts	1st	2nd	3rd	Win & Pl
Career Total (Turf)	24	3	4	1	20931
Career Total (AW)	2	0	0	1	770

90 8/08 Ches 5f16y (0-85)H G-F £5504
80 7/08 Hayd 5f (0-80)H HVY £5504
75 6/07 Bath 5f11y G-S £2072
Total win prize-money £13083

Going (Turf): Sf: 1-3 GS: 1-6 Gd: 0-5 GF: 1-10 Fm: 0-0
Distance: 5f/6f: 3-25 7f-8f: 0-1 9f-13f: 0-0 14f+: 0-0
Track : LH: 2-10 RH: 0-0 Tight: 1-8 Gall: 1-2
Aids: Bl: 0-1 Vi: 0-0 Tstrap: 2-16 Ckp: 2-16
Best Rating: 93 10/08 Catt 5f gd-sft

Useful; effective at 5f and handles most ground; has worn a tongue tie and cheekpieces.

Supernoverre (IRE)

103(103) (73)78
3-y-o b g Noverre (USA)-Caviare (Cadeaux Genereux)
P Howling (Mrs A J Perrett 24/2) Paul Terry

Placings:045540412-4541311650506356 (7214)
2009: 10^{4}SD, 10^{5}SD, 11^{4}SD, 10^{1}SD, 8^{3}SD, 12^{1}SD, 11^{1}GF, 12^{6}GS, 10^{5}G, 14^{0}G, 10^{5}SD, 12^{0}SD, 12^{6}SD, 12^{3}SD, 16^{5}SD, 13^{6}SD,

	Starts	1st	2nd	3rd	Win & Pl
Career Total (Turf)	10	1	0	0	3276
Career Total (AW)	15	3	1	2	8851

78 4/09 Catt 1m3f214y (0-75)H G-F £2590
73 3/09 Kemp 1m4f (0-75)H STD £2590
67 2/09 Ling 1m2f STD £2047
71 11/08 Kemp 1m2f STD £2047
Total win prize-money £9274

Going (Turf): Sf: 0-0 GS: 0-2 Gd: 0-3 GF: 1-5 Fm: 0-0
Distance: 5f/6f: 0-0 7f-8f: 0-4 9f-13f: 4-18 14f+: 0-3
Track : LH: 2-9 RH: 2-12 Tight: 2-10 Gall: 0-2
Aids: Bl: 0-1 Vi: 0-0 Tstrap: 1-2 Ckp: 1-2
Best Rating: 78 4/09 Catt 1m3f214y gd-fm

Fair; effective over 1m-1m4f; acts on fast ground and on Polytrack; has worn cheekpieces.

Superstitious Me (IRE)

98(105) (57)57
3-y-o b f Desert Prince (IRE)-Royal Rival (IRE) (Marju (IRE))
B Palling Tredodridge Associates

Placings:03400-0240000 (7417)
2009: 10^{0}GS, 8^{2}SD, 7^{4}GF, 8^{0}F, 7^{0}G, 8^{0}SD, 8^{0}SD,

	Starts	1st	2nd	3rd	Win & Pl
Career Total (Turf)	6	0	0	1	818
Career Total (AW)	6	0	1	0	893

Going (Turf): Sf: 0-0 GS: 0-1 Gd: 0-2 GF: 0-2 Fm: 0-1

Distance: 5f/6f: 0-3 7f-8f: 0-3 9f-13f: 0-6 14f+: 0-0
Track : LH: 0-8 RH: 0-1 Tight: 0-6 Gall: 0-0
Aids: Bl: 0-0 Vi: 0-0 Tstrap: 0-0 Ckp: 0-0
Best Rating: **57** 6/09 Leic 7f9y gd-fm

Moderate; effective over 1m; acts on fast ground and on Polytrack.

Supplementary (IRE)

(91) (52)
7-y-o b m Rudimentary (USA)-Will She What (IRE) (Lafontaine (USA))
M J Coombe J Coombe

Placings:0000 **(7666)**
2009: 9^{0}SD, 11^{0}SD, 12^{0}SD, 10^{0}SD,

	Starts	1st	2nd	3rd	Win & Pl
Career Total (Turf)	0	0	0	0	
Career Total (AW)	4	0	0	0	

Going (Turf): **Sf: 0-0 GS: 0-0 Gd: 0-0 GF: 0-0 Fm: 0-0**
Distance: 5f/6f: 0-0 7f-8f: 0-0 9f-13f: 0-4 14f+: 0-0
Track : LH: 0-3 RH: 0-1 Tight: 0-3 Gall: 0-0
Aids: Bl: 0-0 Vi: 0-0 Tstrap: 0-0 Ckp: 0-0
Best Rating: **52** 11/09 Ling 1m4f stand

Support Fund (IRE)

101(102) (73)81
5-y-o ch m Intikhab (USA)-Almost A Lady (IRE) (Entitled)
Eve Johnson Houghton Foxtrot Racing Helping Heroes

Placings:33/20041020615/32130305060130-03442160**352366** **(7664)**
2009: 7^{0}GF, 7^{3}GF, 8^{4}G, 6^{4}GF, 7^{2}GF, 7^{1}G, 7^{6}G, 7^{0}GF, 7^{3}SD, 7^{5}SD, 8^{2}G, 8^{3}SD, 8^{6}SD, 8^{6}SD,

	Starts	1st	2nd	3rd	Win & Pl
Career Total (Turf)	33	5	5	7	26562
Career Total (AW)	8	0	0	2	770

79 7/09 Epsm 7f (0-80)H GD £5180
77 10/08 Bath 1m5y (0-70)H GD £3238
81 5/08 Wwck 7f26y (0-70)H G-S £3238
69 10/07 Brig 6f209y (0-70)H G-S £3238
64 7/07 Brig 5f213y GD £2072
Total win prize-money £16969

Going (Turf): Sf: 0-1 GS: 2-4 **Gd: 3-15** GF: 0-13 Fm: 0-0
Distance: 5f/6f: 1-9 **7f-8f: 3-25** 9f-13f: 1-7 14f+: 0-0
Track : **LH: 5-26** RH: 0-7 **Tight: 2-12** Gall: 0-1
Aids: Bl: 0-0 Vi: 0-0 Tstrap: 0-0 Ckp: 0-0
Best Rating: **81** 5/08 Wwck 7f26y gd-sft

Fair; effective at around 6f-1m; acts on good ground.

Supreme Glimpse

3-y-o b f Piccolo-Running Glimpse (IRE) (Runnett)
Mrs N Smith Team Supreme

Placings:00 **(1838)**
2009: 5^{0}GF, 7^{0}GF,

	Starts	1st	2nd	3rd	Win & Pl
Career Total (Turf)	2	0	0	0	

Going (Turf): **Sf: 0-0 GS: 0-0 Gd: 0-0 GF: 0-2 Fm: 0-0**
Distance: 5f/6f: 0-1 7f-8f: 0-1 9f-13f: 0-0 14f+: 0-0
Track : LH: 0-1 RH: 0-0 Tight: 0-0 Gall: 0-1
Aids: Bl: 0-0 Vi: 0-0 Tstrap: 0-0 Ckp: 0-0

Supreme Speedster

93(96) (62)59
5-y-o br g Superior Premium-Effervescent (Efisio)
A G Newcombe W I Bloomfield

Placings:100/0450000-0500200060 **(5788)**
2009: 5^{0}SD, 6^{5}SD, 6^{0}GF, 6^{0}GF, 5^{2}GF, 5^{0}F, 5^{0}G, 5^{0}G, 6^{6}GS, 6^{0}G,

	Starts	1st	2nd	3rd	Win & Pl
Career Total (Turf)	14	1	1	0	5760
Career Total (AW)	6	0	0	0	0

79 5/06 Bevl 5f G-S £5181
Total win prize-money £5182

Going (Turf): Sf: 0-0 **GS: 1-2** Gd: 0-7 GF: 0-4 Fm: 0-1
Distance: **5f/6f: 1-16** 7f-8f: 0-4 9f-13f: 0-0 14f+: 0-0
Track : LH: 0-7 RH: 0-0 Tight: 0-1 Gall: 0-1
Aids: Bl: 0-0 Vi: 0-0 Tstrap: 0-0 Ckp: 0-0
Best Rating: **79** 5/06 Bevl 5f gd-sft

Moderate; effective over 6f; acts on fast and easy ground.

Supsonic

73(106) (79)70
6-y-o br g Marju (IRE)-Nicely (IRE) (Bustino)
R Le Gal (R J Price 3/7) W Gavan

Placings:0/0501/2131000001220
2009: 12^{2}SD, 14^{1}SD, 12^{3}SD, 16^{1}SD, 16^{0}GS, 14^{0}G, 15^{0}GS, 12^{0}SD, 12^{0}SD, 12^{1}G, 15^{2}G, 15^{2}S, 15^{0}VS,

	Starts	1st	2nd	3rd	Win & Pl
Career Total (Turf)	12	2	2	0	23039
Career Total (AW)	6	2	1	1	6168

63 9/09 Chan 1m4f GD £8738
79 3/09 Sthl 2m (0-70)H STD £2729
71 3/09 Sthl 1m6f STD £2047
75 8/06 Deau 1m7f SFT £6552
Total win prize-money £20067

Going (Turf): **Sf: 1-4** GS: 0-4 **Gd: 1-3** GF: 0-0 Fm: 0-0
Distance: 5f/6f: 0-0 7f-8f: 0-1 9f-13f: 1-8 **14f+: 3-9**
Track : LH: 2-7 RH: 2-7 Tight: 0-0 Gall: 0-1
Aids: Bl: 0-0 Vi: 0-0 Tstrap: 0-0 Ckp: 0-0
Best Rating: **79** 3/09 Sthl 2m stand

Modest; ex-French; winning hurdler; stays 2m; acts on Fibresand.

Suranam

84(92) (77)66
2-y-o ch g Tobougg (IRE)-Miss Grimm (USA) (Irish River (FR))
W J Haggas Lok Ho Ting

Placings:6203 **(7582)**
2009: 5^{6}GF, 5^{2}SF, 7^{0}SD, 5^{3}SF,

	Starts	1st	2nd	3rd	Win & Pl
Career Total (Turf)	1	0	0	0	0
Career Total (AW)	3	0	1	1	1187

Going (Turf): **Sf: 0-0 GS: 0-0 Gd: 0-0 GF: 0-1 Fm: 0-0**
Distance: 5f/6f: 0-3 7f-8f: 0-1 9f-13f: 0-0 14f+: 0-0
Track : LH: 0-4 RH: 0-0 Tight: 0-3 Gall: 0-0
Aids: Bl: 0-0 Vi: 0-0 Tstrap: 0-0 Ckp: 0-0
Best Rating: **77** 10/09 Wolv 5f216y std-fst

Fair; effective at 5-6f; acts on Polytrack.

Sure Fire (GER)

(90) (68)
4-y-o b g Monsun (GER)-Suivez (FR) (Fioravanti (USA))
B J Curley Curley Leisure

Placings:63 **(7725)**
2009: 12^{6}SD, 12^{3}SD,

	Starts	1st	2nd	3rd	Win & Pl
Career Total (Turf)	0	0	0	0	
Career Total (AW)	2	0	0	1	504

Going (Turf): **Sf: 0-0 GS: 0-0 Gd: 0-0 GF: 0-0 Fm: 0-0**
Distance: 5f/6f: 0-0 7f-8f: 0-0 9f-13f: 0-2 14f+: 0-0
Track : LH: 0-2 RH: 0-0 Tight: 0-1 Gall: 0-0
Aids: Bl: 0-0 Vi: 0-0 Tstrap: 0-0 Ckp: 0-0
Best Rating: **68** 12/09 Sthl 1m4f stand

Modest brother to German Group2 winner; promise on both starts on the Flat; should stay 1m4f.

Surprise Party

103 85
3-y-o b f Red Ransom (USA)-Surprise Visitor (IRE) (Be My Guest (USA))
C F Wall The Leap Year Partnership

Placings:4350-552111 **(4956)**
2009: 8^{5}GF, 8^{5}GF, 8^{2}S, 8^{1}GS, 8^{1}G, 8^{1}G,

	Starts	1st	2nd	3rd	Win & Pl
Career Total (Turf)	10	3	1	1	12168

85 8/09 Sand 1m14y (0-80)H GD £4857
82 8/09 Yarm 1m3y (0-75)H GD £2978
72 7/09 Yarm 1m3y (0-70)H G-S £2849
Total win prize-money £10685

Going (Turf): Sf: 0-2 GS: 1-3 **Gd: 2-2** GF: 0-3 Fm: 0-0
Distance: 5f/6f: 0-0 7f-8f: 0-5 **9f-13f: 3-5** 14f+: 0-0
Track : LH: 0-1 **RH: 1-2** Tight: 0-0 Gall: 0-0
Aids: Bl: 0-0 Vi: 0-0 Tstrap: 0-0 Ckp: 0-0
Best Rating: **85** 8/09 Sand 1m14y good

Fair; stays 1m and acts on good and softer ground.

Surprise Pension (IRE)

103(98) (56)66
5-y-o b g Fruits Of Love (USA)-Sheryl Lynn (Miller's Mate)
J J Quinn Roberts Green Whittall-Williams Savidge

Placings:000/166/0142-60013 **(3421)**
2009: 9^{6}SD, 12^{0}G, 10^{0}GF, 9^{1}GF, 9^{3}G,

	Starts	1st	2nd	3rd	Win & Pl
Career Total (Turf)	14	3	1	1	9181
Career Total (AW)	1	0	0	0	0

63 5/09 Leic 1m1f218y (0-70)H G-F £3238
63 9/08 Haml 1m3f16y (0-65)H SFT £2590
56 6/07 Haml 1m65y (0-60)H GD £2266
Total win prize-money £8095

Going (Turf): **Sf: 1-4** GS: 0-1 **Gd: 1-6 GF: 1-3** Fm: 0-0
Distance: 5f/6f: 0-2 7f-8f: 0-2 **9f-13f: 3-11** 14f+: 0-0
Track : LH: 0-6 **RH: 3-6 Tight: 2-7** Gall: 0-1
Aids: Bl: 0-0 Vi: 0-0 Tstrap: 0-0 Ckp: 0-0
Best Rating: **66** 10/08 Catt 1m3f214y gd-sft

Moderate; stays 1m4f; acts on fast and easy ground.

Suruor (IRE)

110(99) (79)101
3-y-o b g Intikhab (USA)-Kismah (Machiavellian (USA))

D M Simcock Dr Marwan Koukash

Placings:521003-2110210 (5874)
2009: 7²SD, 7¹GF, 8¹GF, 8⁰GF, 7²GF, 7¹GS, 7⁰GF,

	Starts	1st	2nd	3rd	Win & Pl
Career Total (Turf)	12	4	2	1	54912
Career Total (AW)	1	0	1	0	964

101	7/09	Gdwd	7f	(0-105)H	G-S	£24924
91	5/09	NmkR	1m	(0-90)H	G-F	£9066
84	5/09	Wwck	7f26y	(0-80)H	G-F	£5828
70	7/08	Ayr	6f		GD	£3238

Total win prize-money £43056

Going (Turf): Sf: 0-0 GS: 1-2 Gd: 1-3 **GF: 2-6** Fm: 0-1
Distance: 5f/6f: 1-1 **7f-8f: 3-12** 9f-13f: 0-0 14f+: 0-0
Track : LH: 1-4 RH: 1-4 Tight: 0-3 Gall: 0-0
Aids: Bl: 0-0 Vi: 0-0 Tstrap: 0-0 Ckp: 0-0
Best Rating: 101 7/09 Gdwd 7f gd-sft

Very useful; effective over 6f-1m; acts on fast and easy ground and on Polytrack.

Surwaki (USA)

(102) (67)79
7-y-o b g Miswaki (USA)-Quinella (Generous (IRE))
R M H Cowell T W Morley

Placings:320/P/0230B4100/0650201054/25600203-13 (0471)
2009: 8¹SD, 7³SD,

	Starts	1st	2nd	3rd	Win & Pl
Career Total (Turf)	23	2	4	2	18849
Career Total (AW)	10	1	1	2	3188

67	1/09	Ling	1m		STD	£1978
68	7/07	Wwck	1m22y		SFT	£3238
84	8/06	Leic	1m60y	(0-75)H	GD	£4533

Total win prize-money £9752

Going (Turf): **Sf: 1-2** GS: 0-5 **Gd: 1-7** GF: 0-8 Fm: 0-1
Distance: 5f/6f: 0-0 7f-8f: 1-25 **9f-13f: 2-8** 14f+: 0-0
Track : **LH: 2-13** RH: 1-9 **Tight: 1-9** Gall: 0-1
Aids: Bl: 0-0 Vi: 0-0 Tstrap: 0-2 Ckp: 0-2
Best Rating: 84 8/06 Leic 1m60y good

Moderate gelding; stays 1m; acts on most ground and Polytrack.

Sushitan (GER)

89(103) (72)66
4-y-o ch g Lomitas-Subia (GER) (Konigsstuhl (GER))
G L Moore Andrew Bradmore

Placings:26-6355 (6258)
2009: 9⁶G, 12³SD, 13⁵G, 13⁵SD,

	Starts	1st	2nd	3rd	Win & Pl
Career Total (Turf)	4	0	1	0	882
Career Total (AW)	2	0	0	1	591

Going (Turf): **Sf: 0-1 GS: 0-0 Gd: 0-3 GF: 0-0 Fm: 0-0**
Distance: 5f/6f: 0-0 7f-8f: 0-0 9f-13f: 0-4 14f+: 0-2
Track : LH: 0-3 RH: 0-1 Tight: 0-4 Gall: 0-0
Aids: Bl: 0-0 Vi: 0-0 Tstrap: 0-0 Ckp: 0-0
Best Rating: 72 9/09 Wolv 1m5f194y stand

Modest; stays 1m6f; acts on Polytrack.

Sussex Dancer (IRE)

89(90) (70)52
3-y-o ch f Danehill Dancer (IRE)-Wadud (Nashwan (USA))
J A Osborne Ben Arbib & Partners

Placings:3033-005 (3661)
2009: 8⁰SD, 7⁰SD, 9⁵F,

	Starts	1st	2nd	3rd	Win & Pl
Career Total (Turf)	2	0	0	0	118
Career Total (AW)	5	0	0	3	1517

Going (Turf): **Sf: 0-1 GS: 0-0 Gd: 0-0 GF: 0-0 Fm: 0-1**
Distance: 5f/6f: 0-0 7f-8f: 0-4 9f-13f: 0-3 14f+: 0-0
Track : LH: 0-4 RH: 0-2 Tight: 0-2 Gall: 0-0
Aids: Bl: 0-0 Vi: 0-0 Tstrap: 0-0 Ckp: 0-0
Best Rating: 70 11/08 Wolv 1m141y stand

Fair; stays 1m and acts on Polytrack.

Susurrayshaan

93(86) (49)52
3-y-o b g Dilshaan-Magic Mistral (Thowra (FR))
Mrs G S Rees Maggie and Eric Hemming

Placings:000065-4504000**50** (5885)
2009: 10⁴GF, 9⁵GF, 14⁰GF, 10⁴GF, 12⁰GF, 10⁰GS, 10⁰GF, 8⁵SD, 16⁰SD,

	Starts	1st	2nd	3rd	Win & Pl
Career Total (Turf)	11	0	0	0	241
Career Total (AW)	4	0	0	0	0

Going (Turf): **Sf: 0-1 GS: 0-3 Gd: 0-0 GF: 0-7 Fm: 0-0**
Distance: 5f/6f: 0-1 7f-8f: 0-3 9f-13f: 0-9 14f+: 0-2
Track : LH: 0-12 RH: 0-2 Tight: 0-4 Gall: 0-1
Aids: Bl: 0-0 Vi: 0-2 Tstrap: 0-9 Ckp: 0-9
Best Rating: 52 6/09 Hayd 1m2f95y gd-fm

Sutton Veny (IRE)

101(105) (75)70
3-y-o b f Acclamation-Carabine (USA) (Dehere (USA))
J R Gask The Sutton Veny Syndicate

Placings:04100201 (7739)
2009: 6⁰GF, 6⁴G, 6¹G, 5⁰GF, 5⁰GF, 5²SD, 5⁰SD, 6¹SD,

	Starts	1st	2nd	3rd	Win & Pl
Career Total (Turf)	5	1	0	0	2970
Career Total (AW)	3	1	1	0	3230

75	12/09	Kemp	6f	(0-70)H	STD	£2266
70	8/09	Ling	6f		GD	£2729

Total win prize-money £4997

Going (Turf): Sf: 0-0 GS: 0-0 **Gd: 1-2** GF: 0-3 Fm: 0-0
Distance: **5f/6f: 2-8** 7f-8f: 0-0 9f-13f: 0-0 14f+: 0-0
Track : LH: 0-2 **RH: 1-1** Tight: 0-2 Gall: 0-1
Aids: Bl: 0-0 Vi: 0-0 Tstrap: 0-0 Ckp: 0-0
Best Rating: 75 12/09 Kemp 6f stand

Modest sprinter; acts on fast ground and Polytrack.

Suzhou

88 53
2-y-o b f Tiger Hill (IRE)-Tora Bora (Grand Lodge (USA))
Tom Dascombe Lady Carolyn Warren

Placings:0 (7288)
2009: 6⁰S,

	Starts	1st	2nd	3rd	Win & Pl
Career Total (Turf)	1	0	0	0	

Going (Turf): **Sf: 0-1 GS: 0-0 Gd: 0-0 GF: 0-0 Fm: 0-0**
Distance: 5f/6f: 0-1 7f-8f: 0-0 9f-13f: 0-0 14f+: 0-0
Track : LH: 0-0 RH: 0-0 Tight: 0-0 Gall: 0-0
Aids: Bl: 0-0 Vi: 0-0 Tstrap: 0-0 Ckp: 0-0
Best Rating: 53 11/09 Donc 6f soft

Suzi Spends (IRE)

103(108) (86)86
4-y-o b m Royal Applause-Clever Clogs (Nashwan (USA))
H J Collingridge Greenstead Hall Racing Ltd

Placings:3204310/00341203121-53045305 (7775)
2009: 8⁵GF, 10³GS, 10⁰G, 9⁴HY, 9⁵SD, 8³SD, 10⁰SD, 10⁵SD,

	Starts	1st	2nd	3rd	Win & Pl
Career Total (Turf)	13	1	0	3	7143
Career Total (AW)	13	3	3	3	21143

86	11/08	Ling	1m2f	(0-90)H	STD	£9066
82	10/08	GrLe	1m2f	(0-75)H	STD	£3238
76	8/08	GrLe	1m	(0-75)H	STD	£2590
72	10/07	Wind	1m67y	(0-75)	SFT	£2817

Total win prize-money £17711

Going (Turf): **Sf: 1-3** GS: 0-2 Gd: 0-3 GF: 0-4 Fm: 0-1
Distance: 5f/6f: 0-2 7f-8f: 1-7 **9f-13f: 3-17** 14f+: 0-0
Track : **LH: 3-15** RH: 1-7 Tight: 2-6 Gall: 2-8
Aids: Bl: 0-0 Vi: 0-0 Tstrap: 0-0 Ckp: 0-0
Best Rating: 86 6/09 Donc 1m2f60y gd-sft

Useful; stays 1m2f; acts on most ground and on Polytrack.

Suzi's A Smartlady (IRE)

97(84) (57)63
2-y-o b f Rakti-Shesasmartlady (IRE) (Dolphin Street (FR))
M Johnston Greenstead Hall Racing Ltd

Placings:03400 (6844)
2009: 6⁰SD, 6³GF, 6⁴GF, 7⁰GF, 7⁰G,

	Starts	1st	2nd	3rd	Win & Pl
Career Total (Turf)	4	0	0	1	891
Career Total (AW)	1	0	0	0	

Going (Turf): **Sf: 0-0 GS: 0-0 Gd: 0-1 GF: 0-3 Fm: 0-0**
Distance: 5f/6f: 0-3 7f-8f: 0-2 9f-13f: 0-0 14f+: 0-0
Track : LH: 0-2 RH: 0-0 Tight: 0-2 Gall: 0-0
Aids: Bl: 0-0 Vi: 0-0 Tstrap: 0-0 Ckp: 0-0
Best Rating: 63 7/09 Rdcr 6f gd-fm

Moderate; best at 6f on fast ground.

Suzi's Challenger

76 39
2-y-o b f Tobougg (IRE)-La Tiziana (Rudimentary (USA))
H J Collingridge Greenstead Hall Racing Ltd

Placings:000 (7061)
2009: 8⁰GF, 8⁰GF, 5⁰GF,

	Starts	1st	2nd	3rd	Win & Pl
Career Total (Turf)	3	0	0	0	

Going (Turf): **Sf: 0-0 GS: 0-0 Gd: 0-0 GF: 0-3 Fm: 0-0**
Distance: 5f/6f: 0-1 7f-8f: 0-0 9f-13f: 0-2 14f+: 0-0
Track : LH: 0-1 RH: 0-1 Tight: 0-0 Gall: 0-0
Aids: Bl: 0-0 Vi: 0-0 Tstrap: 0-0 Ckp: 0-0
Best Rating: 39 10/09 Leic 5f218y gd-fm

Suzi's Dancer

(96) (57)

3-y-o b f Groom Dancer (USA)-La Tiziana (Rudimentary (USA))

H J Collingridge Greenstead Hall Racing Ltd

Placings:0543 (7686)

2009: 7^{0}SD, 8^{5}SD, 7^{4}SD, 6^{3}SD,

	Starts	1st	2nd	3rd	Win & Pl
Career Total (Turf)	0	0	0	0	
Career Total (AW)	4	0	0	1	578

Going (Turf): Sf: 0-0 GS: 0-0 Gd: 0-0 GF: 0-0 Fm: 0-0
Distance: 5f/6f: 0-1 7f-8f: 0-2 9f-13f: 0-1 14f+: 0-0
Track : LH: 0-1 RH: 0-3 Tight: 0-1 Gall: 0-0
Aids: Bl: 0-0 Vi: 0-0 Tstrap: 0-0 Ckp: 0-0
Best Rating: 57 12/09 Kemp 6f stand

Moderate; stays 7f; acts on Polytrack.

Suzi's Decision

108 107

4-y-o gr f Act One-Funny Girl (IRE) (Darshaan)

P W D'Arcy Greenstead Hall Racing Ltd

Placings:431/2101131-1 (2482)

2009: 11^{1}G,

	Starts	1st	2nd	3rd	Win & Pl
Career Total (Turf)	11	6	1	2	80069
107	5/09	Hayd	1m3f200y	GD	£34062
102	8/08	Newb	1m4f5y	GD	£24978
94	7/08	Leic	1m1f218y (0-80)H	G-F	£6854
82	6/08	Newb	1m2f6y (0-85)H	G-F	£4533
85	5/08	Pont	1m2f6y (0-70)H	G-F	£3238
66	9/07	Leic	5f218y	FRM	£3238

Total win prize-money £76905

Going (Turf): Sf: 0-1 GS: 0-0 Gd: 2-2 **GF: 3-7** Fm: 1-1
Distance: 5f/6f: 1-1 7f-8f: 0-3 **9f-13f: 5-7** 14f+: 0-0
Track : **LH: 4-5** RH: 1-2 Tight: 0-1 **Gall: 2-3**
Aids: Bl: 0-0 Vi: 0-0 Tstrap: 0-0 Ckp: 0-0
Best Rating: 107 5/09 Hayd 1m3f200y good

Smart; Listed winner in 2008; effective over 1m2f-1m4f; acts on fast ground.

Suzie Quw

101(84) (46)80

3-y-o ch f Bahamian Bounty-Bonkers (Efisio)

A P Jarvis (K R Burke 25/7) Aricabeau Racing Limited

Placings:6125-010000 (6879)

2009: 6^{0}G, 6^{1}HY, 6^{0}GS, 7^{0}G, 6^{0}G, 6^{0}SD,

	Starts	1st	2nd	3rd	Win & Pl
Career Total (Turf)	9	2	1	0	11747
Career Total (AW)	1	0	0	0	
80	5/09	Hayd	6f (0-80)H	HVY	£5504
77	7/08	Haml	5f4y	GD	£2388

Total win prize-money £7893

Going (Turf): **Sf: 1-4** GS: 0-1 **Gd: 1-4** GF: 0-0 Fm: 0-0
Distance: **5f/6f: 2-9** 7f-8f: 0-1 9f-13f: 0-0 14f+: 0-0
Track : LH: 0-2 RH: 0-1 Tight: 0-0 Gall: 0-1
Aids: Bl: 0-0 Vi: 0-0 Tstrap: 0-0 Ckp: 0-0
Best Rating: 80 5/09 Hayd 6f heavy

Fair; effective at around 6f; acts on testing ground.

Suzy Alexander

55

2-y-o b f Red Ransom (USA)-Fiveofive (IRE) (Fairy King (USA))

G G Margarson Mrs T A Foreman

Placings:0 (5478)

2009: 6^{0}GF,

	Starts	1st	2nd	3rd	Win & Pl
Career Total (Turf)	1	0	0	0	

Going (Turf): Sf: 0-0 GS: 0-0 Gd: 0-0 GF: 0-1 Fm: 0-0
Distance: 5f/6f: 0-0 7f-8f: 0-1 9f-13f: 0-0 14f+: 0-0
Track : LH: 0-0 RH: 0-0 Tight: 0-0 Gall: 0-0
Aids: Bl: 0-0 Vi: 0-0 Tstrap: 0-0 Ckp: 0-0

Suzybee

(78) (29)

2-y-o b f Bahamian Bounty-Greenfly (Green Desert (USA))

M R Hoad Terry Locke

Placings:00 (7825)

2009: 8^{0}SD, 8^{0}SD,

	Starts	1st	2nd	3rd	Win & Pl
Career Total (Turf)	0	0	0	0	
Career Total (AW)	2	0	0	0	

Going (Turf): Sf: 0-0 GS: 0-0 Gd: 0-0 GF: 0-0 Fm: 0-0
Distance: 5f/6f: 0-0 7f-8f: 0-2 9f-13f: 0-0 14f+: 0-0
Track : LH: 0-0 RH: 0-2 Tight: 0-0 Gall: 0-0
Aids: Bl: 0-0 Vi: 0-0 Tstrap: 0-0 Ckp: 0-0
Best Rating: 29 12/09 Kemp 1m stand

Suzys Dream (IRE)

65(50) 6

2-y-o gr f Arakan (USA)-Blue Velvet (Formidable (USA))

P T Midgley Anthony D Copley

Placings:000 (2800)

2009: 6^{0}GS, 5^{0}SD, 5^{0}F,

	Starts	1st	2nd	3rd	Win & Pl
Career Total (Turf)	2	0	0	0	
Career Total (AW)	1	0	0	0	

Going (Turf): Sf: 0-0 GS: 0-1 Gd: 0-0 GF: 0-0 Fm: 0-1
Distance: 5f/6f: 0-3 7f-8f: 0-0 9f-13f: 0-0 14f+: 0-0
Track : LH: 0-0 RH: 0-0 Tight: 0-0 Gall: 0-0
Aids: Bl: 0-0 Vi: 0-0 Tstrap: 0-0 Ckp: 0-0
Best Rating: 6 5/09 Ripn 6f gd-sft

Svindal (IRE)

93(96) (67)60

3-y-o ch g Tomba-Princess Sadie (Shavian)

K A Ryan Mrs P Good

Placings:400325222-2100 (3274)

2009: 10^{2}SD, 9^{1}SD, 8^{0}GS, 8^{0}SD,

	Starts	1st	2nd	3rd	Win & Pl
Career Total (Turf)	5	0	0	1	462
Career Total (AW)	8	1	5	0	5752
67	1/09	Wolv	1m1f103y (0-70)H	STD	£2729

Total win prize-money £2730

Going (Turf): Sf: 0-2 GS: 0-1 Gd: 0-2 GF: 0-0 Fm: 0-0
Distance: 5f/6f: 0-1 7f-8f: 0-10 **9f-13f: 1-2** 14f+: 0-0
Track : **LH: 1-8** RH: 0-2 **Tight: 1-5** Gall: 0-1
Aids: **Bl: 1-9** Vi: 0-0 Tstrap: 0-1 Ckp: 0-1
Best Rating: 67 1/09 Wolv 1m1f103y stand

Modest; stays 1m2f; acts on soft ground; goes on sand; has worn blinkers.

Swain's Quest (USA)

(60)

2-y-o b f Swain (IRE)-Questonia (Rainbow Quest (USA))

Eve Johnson Houghton Stuart McPhee & Mike Webley

Placings:0 (7816)

2009: 8^{0}SD,

	Starts	1st	2nd	3rd	Win & Pl
Career Total (Turf)	0	0	0	0	
Career Total (AW)	1	0	0	0	

Going (Turf): Sf: 0-0 GS: 0-0 Gd: 0-0 GF: 0-0 Fm: 0-0
Distance: 5f/6f: 0-0 7f-8f: 0-0 9f-13f: 0-1 14f+: 0-0
Track : LH: 0-1 RH: 0-0 Tight: 0-1 Gall: 0-0
Aids: Bl: 0-0 Vi: 0-0 Tstrap: 0-0 Ckp: 0-0

Swallow Senora (IRE)

(89) (34)37

7-y-o b m Entrepreneur-Sangra (USA) (El Gran Senor (USA))

M C Chapman Peter W Tomlinson

Placings:0/4P0036/00000450/0405/56000-00 (0981)

2009: 7^{0}SS, 9^{0}SD,

	Starts	1st	2nd	3rd	Win & Pl
Career Total (Turf)	15	0	0	0	512
Career Total (AW)	11	0	0	1	409

Going (Turf): Sf: 0-1 GS: 0-3 Gd: 0-4 GF: 0-6 Fm: 0-1
Distance: 5f/6f: 0-15 7f-8f: 0-9 9f-13f: 0-2 14f+: 0-0
Track : LH: 0-14 RH: 0-1 Tight: 0-5 Gall: 0-0
Aids: Bl: 0-5 Vi: 0-0 Tstrap: 0-0 Ckp: 0-0
Best Rating: 54 10/04 NmkR 7f gd-sft

Swan Wings

98 89

2-y-o b f Bahamian Bounty-Star Tulip (Night Shift (USA))

A M Balding Nicholas Jones

Placings:210040 (5822)

2009: 5^{2}G, 5^{1}GF, 6^{0}G, 6^{0}G, 5^{4}GF, 5^{0}GF,

	Starts	1st	2nd	3rd	Win & Pl
Career Total (Turf)	6	1	1	0	7848
79	6/09	Sals	5f	G-F	£4695

Total win prize-money £4695

Going (Turf): Sf: 0-0 GS: 0-0 Gd: 0-3 **GF: 1-3** Fm: 0-0
Distance: **5f/6f: 1-6** 7f-8f: 0-0 9f-13f: 0-0 14f+: 0-0
Track : LH: 0-0 RH: 0-0 Tight: 0-0 Gall: 0-0
Aids: Bl: 0-0 Vi: 0-0 Tstrap: 0-0 Ckp: 0-0
Best Rating: 89 8/09 Newb 5f34y gd-fm

Useful; effective over 5f; goes well on fast ground.

Swans A Swimming (IRE)

96(90) (58)60

3-y-o b c Mujadil (USA)-Danestar (Danehill (USA))

Mme L Braem (J A Osborne 14/5) Ecurie Avant Garde

Placings:2430

2009: 6^{2}SD, 5^{4}SD, 6^{3}F, 7^{0}GS,

	Starts	1st	2nd	3rd	Win & Pl
Career Total (Turf)	2	0	0	1	482
Career Total (AW)	2	0	1	0	1099

Going (Turf): Sf: 0-0 GS: 0-1 Gd: 0-0 GF: 0-0 Fm: 0-1
Distance: 5f/6f: 0-2 7f-8f: 0-2 9f-13f: 0-0 14f+: 0-0
Track : LH: 0-2 RH: 0-1 Tight: 0-2 Gall: 0-0
Aids: Bl: 0-0 Vi: 0-0 Tstrap: 0-0 Ckp: 0-0
Best Rating: 60 5/09 Sals 6f212y firm

Modest; stays 7f; acts on fast ground and Polytrack.

Swansea Jack

88 **48**

2-y-o ch g Singspiel (IRE)-Welsh Diva (Selkirk (USA))
S C Williams K J Mercer

Placings:00 **(6922)**
2009: 6^{0}GS, 6^{0}GF,

	Starts	1st	2nd	3rd	Win & Pl
Career Total (Turf)	2	0	0	0	

Going (Turf): Sf: 0-0 GS: 0-1 Gd: 0-0 GF: 0-1 Fm: 0-0
Distance: 5f/6f: 0-1 7f-8f: 0-1 9f-13f: 0-0 14f+: 0-0
Track : LH: 0-0 RH: 0-0 Tight: 0-0 Gall: 0-1
Aids: Bl: 0-0 Vi: 0-0 Tstrap: 0-0 Ckp: 0-0
Best Rating: 48 10/09 Yarm 6f3y gd-fm

Sweet Applause (IRE)

96(102) (76)**82**

3-y-o b f Acclamation-Nice Spice (IRE) (Common Grounds)
A P Jarvis A B Parr

Placings:0502000404420-53052044 **(7411)**
2009: 5^{5}SD, 5^{3}SD, 5^{0}GS, 6^{5}GF, 5^{2}F, 5^{0}GS, 5^{4}SD, 5^{4}SD,

	Starts	1st	2nd	3rd	Win & Pl
Career Total (Turf)	11	0	2	0	1445
Career Total (AW)	10	0	1	1	3168

Going (Turf): Sf: 0-2 GS: 0-3 Gd: 0-1 GF: 0-4 Fm: 0-1
Distance: 5f/6f: 0-19 7f-8f: 0-2 9f-13f: 0-0 14f+: 0-0
Track : LH: 0-7 RH: 0-4 Tight: 0-4 Gall: 0-3
Aids: Bl: 0-0 Vi: 0-0 Tstrap: 0-0 Ckp: 0-0
Best Rating: 82 6/08 Asct 5f gd-fm

Fair; suited by 5f; acts on easy ground; goes on Polytrack.

Sweet Avon

(87) (56)

2-y-o gr f Avonbridge-Sweet Whisper (Petong)
Matthew Salaman Brig C K Price

Placings:0 **(7585)**
2009: 6^{0}SD,

	Starts	1st	2nd	3rd	Win & Pl
Career Total (Turf)	0	0	0	0	
Career Total (AW)	1	0	0	0	

Going (Turf): Sf: 0-0 GS: 0-0 Gd: 0-0 GF: 0-0 Fm: 0-0
Distance: 5f/6f: 0-1 7f-8f: 0-0 9f-13f: 0-0 14f+: 0-0
Track : LH: 0-0 RH: 0-1 Tight: 0-0 Gall: 0-0
Aids: Bl: 0-0 Vi: 0-0 Tstrap: 0-0 Ckp: 0-0
Best Rating: 56 11/09 Kemp 6f stand

Sweet Baby Jane (IRE)

79 **48**

2-y-o b f Royal Applause-Nebulae (IRE) (Unfuwain (USA))
R A Fahey John M Troy

Placings:6000 **(6923)**
2009: 5^{6}GF, 5^{0}GF, 6^{0}G, 8^{0}GF,

	Starts	1st	2nd	3rd	Win & Pl
Career Total (Turf)	4	0	0	0	0

Going (Turf): Sf: 0-0 GS: 0-0 Gd: 0-1 GF: 0-3 Fm: 0-0
Distance: 5f/6f: 0-3 7f-8f: 0-0 9f-13f: 0-1 14f+: 0-0
Track : LH: 0-1 RH: 0-0 Tight: 0-0 Gall: 0-0
Aids: Bl: 0-0 Vi: 0-0 Tstrap: 0-0 Ckp: 0-0
Best Rating: 48 6/09 Thsk 6f good

Sweet Caroline (IRE)

(66) (22)

2-y-o b f Motivator-Figlette (Darshaan)
B W Hills Mr & Mrs Christopher Wright

Placings:0 **(7396)**
2009: 7^{0}SD,

	Starts	1st	2nd	3rd	Win & Pl
Career Total (Turf)	0	0	0	0	
Career Total (AW)	1	0	0	0	

Going (Turf): Sf: 0-0 GS: 0-0 Gd: 0-0 GF: 0-0 Fm: 0-0
Distance: 5f/6f: 0-0 7f-8f: 0-1 9f-13f: 0-0 14f+: 0-0
Track : LH: 0-1 RH: 0-0 Tight: 0-1 Gall: 0-0
Aids: Bl: 0-0 Vi: 0-0 Tstrap: 0-0 Ckp: 0-0
Best Rating: 22 11/09 Wolv 7f32y stand

Sweet Child O'Mine

(101) (74)

2-y-o b f Singspiel (IRE)-Vendors Mistake (IRE) (Danehill (USA))
R C Guest EERC

Placings:13 **(7844)**
2009: 8^{1}SD, 8^{3}SD,

	Starts	1st	2nd	3rd	Win & Pl
Career Total (Turf)	0	0	0	0	
Career Total (AW)	2	1	0	1	4463

69 12/09 Sthl 1m STD £3885
Total win prize-money £3886

Going (Turf): Sf: 0-0 GS: 0-0 Gd: 0-0 GF: 0-0 Fm: 0-0
Distance: 5f/6f: 0-0 **7f-8f: 1-1** 9f-13f: 0-1 14f+: 0-0
Track : **LH: 1-2** RH: 0-0 Tight: 0-1 Gall: 0-0
Aids: Bl: 0-0 Vi: 0-0 Tstrap: 0-0 Ckp: 0-0
Best Rating: 74 12/09 Wolv 1m141y stand

Modest; stays 1m and acts on Fibresand.

Sweet Clementine (IRE)

81(83) (52)**55**

2-y-o b f Shamardal (USA)-Heavenly Whisper (IRE) (Halling (USA))
W J Knight D G Hardisty Bloodstock

Placings:00 **(7135)**
2009: 6^{0}S, 7^{0}SD,

	Starts	1st	2nd	3rd	Win & Pl
Career Total (Turf)	1	0	0	0	
Career Total (AW)	1	0	0	0	

Going (Turf): Sf: 0-1 GS: 0-0 Gd: 0-0 GF: 0-0 Fm: 0-0
Distance: 5f/6f: 0-0 7f-8f: 0-2 9f-13f: 0-0 14f+: 0-0
Track : LH: 0-1 RH: 0-0 Tight: 0-1 Gall: 0-0
Aids: Bl: 0-0 Vi: 0-0 Tstrap: 0-0 Ckp: 0-0
Best Rating: 55 10/09 Sals 6f212y soft

Sweet Gale (IRE)

103(102) (82)**79**

5-y-o b m Soviet Star (USA)-Lady Moranbon (USA) (Trempolino (USA))
Mike Murphy Ms L M Bartlett

Placings:0311/00000-3002112453625450 **(6726)**
2009: 7^{3}SD, 7^{0}SD, 7^{0}SD, 7^{2}SD, 7^{1}SD, 5^{1}GF, 7^{2}SD, 6^{4}GF, 7^{5}GF, 6^{3}GF, 6^{6}G, 6^{2}G, 7^{5}SD, 6^{4}GF, 7^{5}SD, 7^{0}SD,

	Starts	1st	2nd	3rd	Win & Pl
Career Total (Turf)	11	2	1	1	9172
Career Total (AW)	14	2	2	2	8385

77	6/09	Leic	5f218y	(0-70)H	G-F	£3238
73	6/09	Kemp	7f	(0-65)H	STD	£2047
81	6/07	Ling	7f	(0-75)H	G-F	£2914
82	5/07	Sthl	7f		STD	£3238

Total win prize-money £11439

Going (Turf): Sf: 0-0 GS: 0-0 Gd: 0-4 **GF: 2-7** Fm: 0-0
Distance: 5f/6f: 1-6 **7f-8f: 3-18** 9f-13f: 0-1 14f+: 0-0
Track : LH: 1-8 RH: 1-8 Tight: 0-5 Gall: 0-1
Aids: Bl: 0-0 Vi: 0-0 Tstrap: 0-0 Ckp: 0-0
Best Rating: 82 6/09 Kemp 7f stand

Fair; effective at 7f; acts on fast ground and on sand; has worn tongue tie.

Sweet Hollow

103(108) (79)**83**

3-y-o b f Beat Hollow-Three Piece (Jaazeiro (USA))
C G Cox The City & Provincial Partnership

Placings:4-220015163 **(6936)**
2009: 12^{2}GF, 12^{2}GF, 12^{0}G, 11^{0}GS, 11^{1}SD, 11^{5}SD, 12^{1}GF, 12^{6}GF, 11^{3}G,

	Starts	1st	2nd	3rd	Win & Pl
Career Total (Turf)	8	1	2	1	8450
Career Total (AW)	2	1	0	0	4727

83	9/09	Newb	1m4f5y	(0-85)H	G-F	£4857
77	8/09	Kemp	1m3f	(0-80)H	STD	£4727

Total win prize-money £9584

Going (Turf): Sf: 0-0 GS: 0-1 Gd: 0-3 **GF: 1-4** Fm: 0-0
Distance: 5f/6f: 0-0 7f-8f: 0-1 **9f-13f: 2-9** 14f+: 0-0
Track : LH: 1-6 RH: 1-4 Tight: 0-2 **Gall: 1-4**
Aids: **Bl: 2-5** Vi: 0-0 Tstrap: 0-0 Ckp: 0-0
Best Rating: 83 10/09 Bath 1m3f144y good

Fair; stays 1m4f; acts on fast ground; goes on Polytrack; has worn blinkers.

Sweet Kiss (USA)

92(99) (66)**71**

4-y-o gr f Yes It's True (USA)-Always Freezing (USA) (Robyn Dancer (USA))
M J Attwater Ms K J Austin

Placings:305/004366500-000304000 (7770)
2009: 7^{0}SD, 8^{0}GF, 6^{0}GF, 6^{3}SD, 6^{0}G, 6^{4}SD, 6^{0}SD, 6^{0}SD, 6^{0}SD,

	Starts	1st	2nd	3rd	Win & Pl
Career Total (Turf)	11	0	0	2	1984
Career Total (AW)	10	0	0	1	302

Going (Turf): Sf: 0-0 GS: 0-0 Gd: 0-1 GF: 0-10 Fm: 0-0
Distance: 5f/6f: 0-10 7f-8f: 0-11 9f-13f: 0-0 14f+: 0-0
Track : LH: 0-4 RH: 0-7 Tight: 0-3 Gall: 0-1
Aids: Bl: 0-2 Vi: 0-1 Tstrap: 0-1 Ckp: 0-1
Best Rating: 81 7/07 NmkJ 6f gd-fm

Modest; effective at 6f; acts on fast ground.

Sweet Lightning

113(109) (93)97
4-y-o b g Fantastic Light (USA)-Sweetness Herself (Unfuwain (USA))
W R Muir A J De V Patrick & M J Caddy

Placings:2104133446-266203 (6106)
2009: 11^{2}SD, 10^{6}G, 10^{6}GF, 9^{2}G, 10^{0}G, 10^{3}GF,

	Starts	1st	2nd	3rd	Win & Pl
Career Total (Turf)	10	1	1	3	26642
Career Total (AW)	6	1	2	0	12226
93 6/08 Ches	1m4f66y (0-85)H			GD	£5180
76 4/08 Kemp	1m3f			STD	£2590

Total win prize-money £7771

Going (Turf): Sf: 0-0 GS: 0-1 Gd: 1-5 GF: 0-4 Fm: 0-0
Distance: 5f/6f: 0-0 7f-8f: 0-0 9f-13f: 2-15 14f+: 0-1
Track : LH: 1-9 RH: 1-7 Tight: 1-4 Gall: 0-5
Aids: Bl: 0-0 Vi: 0-0 Tstrap: 0-0 Ckp: 0-0
Best Rating: 97 9/09 Newb 1m2f6y gd-fm

Useful; effective at 1m2f-1m6f; acts on good ground; also goes on Polytrack.

Sweet Lilly

102 (74)106
5-y-o b m Tobougg (IRE)-Maristax (Reprimand)
M R Channon Jaber Abdullah

Placings:03311141/020546153/403250152050-3650 (6003)
2009: 10^{3}G, 9^{6}GF, 10^{5}G, 10^{0}GF,

	Starts	1st	2nd	3rd	Win & Pl
Career Total (Turf)	32	6	3	4	138192
Career Total (AW)	1	0	0	1	578
106 7/08 York	1m2f88y			G-F	£22708
98 9/07 Sand	1m14y			G-F	£14762
101 10/06 Pont	1m4y			G-S	£22712
80 8/06 Sals	1m			GD	£3562
76 8/06 Yarm	7f3y			G-F	£2331
68 7/06 Yarm	7f3y			FRM	£2331

Total win prize-money £68409

Going (Turf): Sf: 0-4 GS: 1-4 Gd: 1-11 GF: 3-12 Fm: 1-1
Distance: 5f/6f: 0-0 7f-8f: 3-12 9f-13f: 3-21 14f+: 0-0
Track : LH: 2-15 RH: 1-10 Tight: 0-6 Gall: 1-8
Aids: Bl: 0-0 Vi: 0-0 Tstrap: 0-0 Ckp: 0-0
Best Rating: 113 8/07 Gdwd 1m1f192y gd-fm

Smart; Listed winner and Group placed; stays 1m2f; acts on most ground; not straightforward.

Sweet Mirasol (IRE)

91(67) (17)64
2-y-o b f Celtic Swing-Sallwa (IRE) (Entrepreneur)
K A Ryan Mrs Margaret Forsyth

Placings:6356000 (6901)
2009: 6^{6}HY, 6^{3}GF, 6^{5}GS, 6^{6}SD, 6^{0}GF, 5^{0}GF, 8^{0}GF,

	Starts	1st	2nd	3rd	Win & Pl
Career Total (Turf)	6	0	0	1	337
Career Total (AW)	1	0	0	0	0

Going (Turf): Sf: 0-1 GS: 0-1 Gd: 0-0 GF: 0-4 Fm: 0-0
Distance: 5f/6f: 0-5 7f-8f: 0-1 9f-13f: 0-1 14f+: 0-0
Track : LH: 0-2 RH: 0-0 Tight: 0-0 Gall: 0-0
Aids: Bl: 0-0 Vi: 0-0 Tstrap: 0-1 Ckp: 0-1
Best Rating: 64 6/09 Haml 6f5y gd-fm

Modest; stays 6f; best effort on fast ground.

Sweet Pilgrim

84(92) (40)49
2-y-o b f Talkin Man (CAN)-Faraway Moon (Distant Relative)
M D I Usher Mr & Mrs Richard Hames And Friends

Placings:00 (7365)
2009: 6^{0}G, 5^{0}SD,

	Starts	1st	2nd	3rd	Win & Pl
Career Total (Turf)	1	0	0	0	
Career Total (AW)	1	0	0	0	

Going (Turf): Sf: 0-0 GS: 0-0 Gd: 0-1 GF: 0-0 Fm: 0-0
Distance: 5f/6f: 0-1 7f-8f: 0-1 9f-13f: 0-0 14f+: 0-0
Track : LH: 0-1 RH: 0-0 Tight: 0-1 Gall: 0-0
Aids: Bl: 0-0 Vi: 0-0 Tstrap: 0-0 Ckp: 0-0
Best Rating: 49 10/09 Newb 6f110y good

Sweet Possession (USA)

96(87) (62)72
3-y-o b f Belong To Me (USA)-Bingo Meeting (USA) (General Meeting (USA))
A P Jarvis Geoffrey Bishop

Placings:0300-403364 (4940)
2009: 7^{4}SD, 8^{0}GF, 6^{3}GF, 7^{3}GF, 6^{6}GF, 7^{4}GF,

	Starts	1st	2nd	3rd	Win & Pl
Career Total (Turf)	9	0	0	3	2167
Career Total (AW)	1	0	0	0	192

Going (Turf): Sf: 0-0 GS: 0-1 Gd: 0-1 GF: 0-7 Fm: 0-0
Distance: 5f/6f: 0-2 7f-8f: 0-7 9f-13f: 0-1 14f+: 0-0
Track : LH: 0-1 RH: 0-1 Tight: 0-0 Gall: 0-0
Aids: Bl: 0-0 Vi: 0-0 Tstrap: 0-0 Ckp: 0-0
Best Rating: 72 7/08 Asct 6f gd-fm

Modest; stays 7f and acts on fast ground.

Sweet Request

86(97) (55)53
5-y-o ch m Best Of The Bests (IRE)-Sweet Revival (Claude Monet (USA))
Dr J R J Naylor Mrs S P Elphick

Placings:6/00250242325/0000-600 (3798)
2009: 12^{6}SD, 12^{0}SD, 12^{0}GF,

	Starts	1st	2nd	3rd	Win & Pl
Career Total (Turf)	14	0	3	1	3535
Career Total (AW)	5	0	1	0	756

Going (Turf): Sf: 0-1 GS: 0-0 Gd: 0-5 GF: 0-7 Fm: 0-1
Distance: 5f/6f: 0-0 7f-8f: 0-3 9f-13f: 0-15 14f+: 0-1
Track : LH: 0-14 RH: 0-4 Tight: 0-9 Gall: 0-1
Aids: Bl: 0-1 Vi: 0-0 Tstrap: 0-1 Ckp: 0-1
Best Rating: 71 8/07 Chep 1m2f36y gd-fm

Sweet Secret

96 68
2-y-o ch f Singspiel (IRE)-Ballymore Celebre (IRE) (Peintre Celebre (USA))
R Hannon Carmel Stud

Placings:05 (7029)
2009: 6^{0}G, 8^{5}S,

	Starts	1st	2nd	3rd	Win & Pl
Career Total (Turf)	2	0	0	0	0

Going (Turf): Sf: 0-1 GS: 0-0 Gd: 0-1 GF: 0-0 Fm: 0-0
Distance: 5f/6f: 0-0 7f-8f: 0-2 9f-13f: 0-0 14f+: 0-0
Track : LH: 0-0 RH: 0-0 Tight: 0-0 Gall: 0-0
Aids: Bl: 0-0 Vi: 0-0 Tstrap: 0-0 Ckp: 0-0
Best Rating: 68 10/09 Newb 1m soft

Sweet Sixteen (IRE)

(91) (61)89
4-y-o b f Sadler's Wells (USA)-User Friendly (Slip Anchor)
J R Jenkins Fhad Al Harthi

Placings:50000-5 (0876)
2009: 10^{5}SD,

	Starts	1st	2nd	3rd	Win & Pl
Career Total (Turf)	5	0	0	0	
Career Total (AW)	1	0	0	0	0

Going (Turf): Sf: 0-2 GS: 0-0 Gd: 0-2 GF: 0-0 Fm: 0-0
Distance: 5f/6f: 0-0 7f-8f: 0-0 9f-13f: 0-5 14f+: 0-1
Track : LH: 0-2 RH: 0-4 Tight: 0-0 Gall: 0-0
Aids: Bl: 0-0 Vi: 0-0 Tstrap: 0-0 Ckp: 0-0
Best Rating: 89 8/08 Cork 1m4f gd-yld

Sweet Sonnet (USA)

99 97
2-y-o ch f Seeking The Gold (USA)-Minister's Melody (USA) (Deputy Minister (CAN))
Saeed Bin Suroor Godolphin

Placings:102 (5606)
2009: 6^{1}GF, 6^{0}GF, 6^{2}S,

	Starts	1st	2nd	3rd	Win & Pl
Career Total (Turf)	3	1	1	0	14245
76 5/09 York	6f		G-F	£6605	

Total win prize-money £6606

Going (Turf): Sf: 0-1 GS: 0-0 Gd: 0-0 GF: 1-2 Fm: 0-0
Distance: 5f/6f: 1-3 7f-8f: 0-0 9f-13f: 0-0 14f+: 0-0
Track : LH: 0-0 RH: 0-0 Tight: 0-0 Gall: 0-0
Aids: Bl: 0-0 Vi: 0-0 Tstrap: 0-0 Ckp: 0-0
Best Rating: 97 9/09 Sals 6f soft

Very useful; effective at 6f; handles quick and soft ground.

Sweet Virginia (USA)

(89) (50)27
3-y-o b/hr f Arch (USA)-Hey Hey Sunny (USA) (Known Fact (USA))

K R Burke Mrs Elaine M Burke

Placings:06006-0365 (1106)
2009: 8^{0}SD, 8^{3}SD, 10^{6}SD, 8^{5}SD,

	Starts	1st	2nd	3rd	Win & Pl
Career Total (Turf)	3	0	0	0	0
Career Total (AW)	6	0	0	1	279

Going (Turf): Sf: 0-0 GS: 0-1 Gd: 0-1 GF: 0-1 Fm: 0-0
Distance: 5f/6f: 0-2 7f-8f: 0-4 9f-13f: 0-3 14f+: 0-0
Track : LH: 0-6 RH: 0-1 Tight: 0-4 Gall: 0-1
Aids: Bl: 0-1 Vi: 0-0 Tstrap: 0-0 Ckp: 0-0
Best Rating: 50 2/09 Ling 1m stand

Plating-class; stays 1m; acts on Polytrack.

Sweet World

(105) (64)**69**
5-y-o b g Agnes World (USA)-Douce Maison (IRE) (Fools Holme (USA))
B J Llewellyn B J Llewellyn

Placings:400303/1210134003164/46623004056120-0 (0500)
2009: 10^{0}SD,

	Starts	1st	2nd	3rd	Win & Pl
Career Total (Turf)	13	2	1	1	11063
Career Total (AW)	21	3	2	4	10500

61 8/08 Rdcr 1m2f G-S £2047
69 9/07 Ayr 1m2f G-S £6477
64 3/07 Kemp 1m2f STD £2047
63 2/07 Ling 1m STD £2184
64 1/07 Wolv 1m141y STD £2730
Total win prize-money £15486

Going (Turf): Sf: 0-2 **GS: 2-2** Gd: 0-5 GF: 0-3 Fm: 0-1
Distance: 5f/6f: 0-1 7f-8f: 1-11 **9f-13f: 4-22** 14f+: 0-0
Track : **LH: 4-20** RH: 1-11 **Tight: 3-18** Gall: 0-0
Aids: Bl: 0-0 Vi: 0-1 Tstrap: 0-2 Ckp: 0-2
Best Rating: 69 9/07 Ayr 1m2f gd-sft

Moderate; stays 1m2f; acts on soft ground; also goes on Polytrack.

Sweetheart

113 (73)**83**
5-y-o b m Sinndar (IRE)-Love And Adventure (USA) (Halling (USA))
Jamie Poulton R W Huggins

Placings:64/1053506320/0-1142140 (6851)
2009: 16^{1}G, 16^{1}GF, 16^{4}GF, 16^{2}G, 21^{1}G, 16^{4}GF, 18^{0}G,

	Starts	1st	2nd	3rd	Win & Pl
Career Total (Turf)	16	3	2	1	43965
Career Total (AW)	4	1	0	1	2748

83 7/09 Gdwd 2m5f (0-95)H GD £31155
76 6/09 Folk 2m93y (0-70)H G-F £2729
72 5/09 Gdwd 2m (0-80)H GD £4857
73 1/07 Wolv 1m1f103y SS £2266
Total win prize-money £41009

Going (Turf): Sf: 0-0 GS: 0-6 **Gd: 2-5** GF: 1-5 Fm: 0-0
Distance: 5f/6f: 0-0 7f-8f: 0-1 9f-13f: 1-6 **14f+: 3-13**
Track : LH: 1-6 **RH: 3-13 Tight: 4-10** Gall: 0-4
Aids: Bl: 0-0 Vi: 0-0 Tstrap: 0-0 Ckp: 0-0
Best Rating: 83 7/09 Gdwd 2m5f good

Useful; stays 2m5f; acts on most ground and on Polytrack.

Swift Chap

106(100) (76)**92**
3-y-o b g Diktat-Regent's Folly (IRE) (Touching Wood (USA))
B R Millman M A Swift and A J Chapman

Placings:61510-0053001120 (7189)
2009: 8^{0}SD, 8^{0}S, 8^{5}G, 10^{3}G, 10^{0}F, 10^{0}GF, 8^{1}GF, 8^{1}G, 8^{2}GF, 7^{0}G,

	Starts	1st	2nd	3rd	Win & Pl
Career Total (Turf)	14	4	1	1	21835
Career Total (AW)	1	0	0	0	

85 10/09 Newb 1m7y (0-75)H GD £2590
78 10/09 Gdwd 1m (0-75)H G-F £3238
82 8/08 Sand 7f16y (0-85) GD £6476
68 7/08 Wwck 7f26y GD £6476
Total win prize-money £18780

Going (Turf): Sf: 0-1 GS: 0-0 **Gd: 3-7** GF: 1-5 Fm: 0-1
Distance: 5f/6f: 0-1 **7f-8f: 3-8** 9f-13f: 1-6 14f+: 0-0
Track : LH: 2-4 RH: 2-8 Tight: 0-1 **Gall: 1-2**
Aids: Bl: 0-0 Vi: 0-0 Tstrap: 0-0 Ckp: 0-0
Best Rating: 92 10/09 Leic 1m60y gd-fm

Fair; stays 1m; acts on good, fast ground.

Swift Gift

109(107) (89)**103**
4-y-o b g Cadeaux Genereux-Got To Go (Shareef Dancer (USA))
B J Meehan Social and Affordable Racing Partnership

Placings:341/3425**4**65-1010 (6270)
2009: 7^{1}GF, 7^{0}GF, 7^{1}GF, 7^{0}G,

	Starts	1st	2nd	3rd	Win & Pl
Career Total (Turf)	11	2	1	2	69603
Career Total (AW)	3	1	0	0	2327

100 8/09 Newb 7f (0-95)H G-F £8723
101 5/09 Asct 7f H G-F £52963
85 11/07 Wolv 7f32y STD £2047
Total win prize-money £63735

Going (Turf): Sf: 0-0 GS: 0-0 Gd: 0-4 **GF: 2-7** Fm: 0-0
Distance: 5f/6f: 0-0 **7f-8f: 3-14** 9f-13f: 0-0 14f+: 0-0
Track : **LH: 1-5** RH: 0-2 **Tight: 1-3** Gall: 0-2
Aids: Bl: 0-0 Vi: 0-0 Tstrap: 0-0 Ckp: 0-0
Best Rating: 103 9/09 Asct 7f good

Useful; effective over 7f; acts on Polytrack and fast ground.

Swift Return

93(92) (75)**73**
2-y-o b g Fantastic Light (USA)-Swift Dispersal (Shareef Dancer (USA))
S C Williams D A Shekells

Placings:5230 (7096)
2009: 6^{5}GF, 7^{2}GS, 8^{3}SD, 7^{0}G,

	Starts	1st	2nd	3rd	Win & Pl
Career Total (Turf)	3	0	1	0	1060
Career Total (AW)	1	0	0	1	302

Going (Turf): Sf: 0-0 GS: 0-1 Gd: 0-1 GF: 0-1 Fm: 0-0
Distance: 5f/6f: 0-1 7f-8f: 0-3 9f-13f: 0-0 14f+: 0-0
Track : LH: 0-0 RH: 0-1 Tight: 0-0 Gall: 0-1
Aids: Bl: 0-0 Vi: 0-0 Tstrap: 0-0 Ckp: 0-0
Best Rating: 75 9/09 Kemp 1m stand

Fair; stays 7f and acts on easy ground.

Swift Sailing (USA)

91 (48)**64**
8-y-o b g Storm Cat (USA)-Saytarra (USA) (Seeking The Gold (USA))
Patrick Allen His N Hers Syndicate

Placings:015/00024/0030**5**306/605/0202R1035R50/26050 000-55404 (4874)
2009: 14^{5}HY, 14^{5}Y, 12^{4}GF, 10^{0}Y, 12^{4}G,

	Starts	1st	2nd	3rd	Win & Pl
Career Total (Turf)	40	2	4	3	18823
Career Total (AW)	4	0	0	0	

65 8/07 Tram 1m4f (50-70)H G-Y £5135
73 7/03 Sals 6f D GD £5193
Total win prize-money £10330

Going (Turf): Sf: 0-3 GS: 0-1 **Gd: 1-10** GF: 0-14 Fm: 0-2
Distance: 5f/6f: 1-2 7f-8f: 0-15 9f-13f: 1-20 14f+: 0-7
Track : LH: 0-17 **RH: 1-18** Tight: 0-1 Gall: 0-3
Aids: Bl: 0-3 Vi: 0-0 Tstrap: 0-3 Ckp: 0-3
Best Rating: 76 9/05 Cork 1m100y gd-fm

Swilly Ferry (USA)

103(91) (79)**96**
2-y-o b c Wiseman's Ferry (USA)-Keepers Hill (IRE) (Danehill (USA))
B W Hills John C Grant

Placings:3310334100 (6677)
2009: 5^{3}GF, 5^{3}GF, 6^{1}SD, 6^{0}G, 6^{3}G, 6^{3}GF, 6^{4}GF, 6^{1}GF, 7^{0}GF, 6^{0}G,

	Starts	1st	2nd	3rd	Win & Pl
Career Total (Turf)	9	1	0	4	204104
Career Total (AW)	1	1	0	0	2388

96 9/09 Donc 6f110y G-F £183517
79 6/09 Ling 6f STD £2388
Total win prize-money £185905

Going (Turf): Sf: 0-0 GS: 0-0 Gd: 0-3 **GF: 1-6** Fm: 0-0
Distance: 5f/6f: 1-8 7f-8f: 1-2 9f-13f: 0-0 14f+: 0-0
Track : **LH: 1-2** RH: 0-0 **Tight: 1-2** Gall: 0-0
Aids: Bl: 0-0 Vi: 0-0 Tstrap: 0-0 Ckp: 0-0
Best Rating: 96 9/09 Donc 6f110y gd-fm

Very useful; effective at around 6f; won a valuable sales race at Doncaster in September; acts on fast ground and on Polytrack.

Swinbrook (USA)

103(106) (82)**82**
8-y-o ch g Stravinsky (USA)-Dance Diane (USA) (Affirmed (USA))
R A Harris (R A Fahey 27/7) Mrs Ruth M Serrell

Placings:52/002100/00**6**231/41006404**4**/564036**6**6**50**/21423 644**2**0**4-011**02**3**1316**11**305**20000** (7679)
2009: 6^{0}SS, **6**^{1}SD, **6**^{1}SD, 6^{0}GF, **6**^{2}SD, 5^{3}F, **6**^{1}SD, 6^{3}G, 6^{1}G, 6^{6}GS, 6^{1}SD, 5^{1}G, 5^{3}GF, 5^{0}GF, 5^{5}F, **5**^{2}SD, **5**^{0}SD, **6**^{0}SD, **6**^{0}SD, **6**^{0}SD,

	Starts	1st	2nd	3rd	Win & Pl
Career Total (Turf)	44	5	5	6	37980
Career Total (AW)	19	5	3	0	18036

81 8/09 Bath 5f161y GD £1942
71 7/09 Sthl 6f STD £2047
81 6/09 Pont 6f (0-70)H GD £3238
76 5/09 Ling 6f STD £2047
82 3/09 Sthl 6f (0-85)H STD £4857
72 3/09 Sthl 6f STD £2047
83 4/08 Sthl 6f (0-85)H STD £4209
95 4/06 Leic 5f218y (0-85)H GD £6232
87 10/05 Nott 6f15y (0-75)H SFT £3692
67 6/04 Folk 5f D G-F £3770
Total win prize-money £34083

Going (Turf): Sf: 1-5 GS: 0-7 **Gd: 3-12** GF: 1-18 Fm: 0-2
Distance: **5f/6f: 9-51** 7f-8f: 1-12 9f-13f: 0-0 14f+: 0-0
Track : **LH: 7-26** RH: 0-0 Tight: 1-11 Gall: 1-4
Aids: Bl: 0-2 **Vi: 8-45** Tstrap: 0-1 Ckp: 0-1
Best Rating: 96 7/06 Wind 6f gd-fm

Fair; effective over 5f-6f; acts on most ground on turf; goes on Fibresand; has worn cheekpieces and a visor.

Swindler (IRE)

90 92

3-y-o b g Sinndar (IRE)-Imitation (Darshaan)

A M Balding Mr & Mrs P McMahon & Mr & Mrs R Gorell

Placings:2-0 (4405)

2009: 12^{0}G,

	Starts	1st	2nd	3rd	Win & Pl
Career Total (Turf)	2	0	1	0	2891

Going (Turf): **Sf: 0-1 GS: 0-0 Gd: 0-1 GF: 0-0 Fm: 0-0**
Distance: 5f/6f: 0-0 7f-8f: 0-1 9f-13f: 0-1 14f+: 0-0
Track : LH: 0-0 RH: 0-1 Tight: 0-1 Gall: 0-0
Aids: Bl: 0-0 Vi: 0-0 Tstrap: 0-0 Ckp: 0-0
Best Rating: **92** 7/09 Gdwd 1m4f good

Runner-up on debut in 2008; effective at around 7f; handles soft ground.

Swing It Ruby (IRE)

90(85) (48)48

3-y-o br f Celtic Swing-Golconda (IRE) (Lahib (USA))

Mrs D J Sanderson R J Budge

Placings:060-000 (3450)

2009: 12^{0}GF, 12^{0}SD, 10^{0}GF,

	Starts	1st	2nd	3rd	Win & Pl
Career Total (Turf)	4	0	0	0	
Career Total (AW)	2	0	0	0	0

Going (Turf): **Sf: 0-1 GS: 0-0 Gd: 0-1 GF: 0-2 Fm: 0-0**
Distance: 5f/6f: 0-1 7f-8f: 0-2 9f-13f: 0-3 14f+: 0-0
Track : LH: 0-3 RH: 0-1 Tight: 0-2 Gall: 0-0
Aids: Bl: 0-0 Vi: 0-0 Tstrap: 0-0 Ckp: 0-0
Best Rating: **48** 9/08 Wolv 5f216y stand

Swingkeel (IRE)

110(107) (96)104

4-y-o ch g Singspiel (IRE)-Anniversary (Salse (USA))

J L Dunlop Mrs M E Slade

Placings:043031644-2213130 (6851)

2009: 16^{2}S, 16^{2}GF, **16**^{1}SD, 21^{3}G, 16^{1}GF, 16^{3}GF, 18^{0}G,

	Starts	1st	2nd	3rd	Win & Pl
Career Total (Turf)	14	2	2	4	33953
Career Total (AW)	2	1	0	0	7704

104 8/09 York 2m88y (0-95)H G-F £16190
96 7/09 Kemp 2m (0-90)H STD £7352
86 7/08 Ling 2m (0-75)H G-F £2590
Total win prize-money £26133

Going (Turf): Sf: 0-2 GS: 0-1 Gd: 0-6 **GF: 2-5** Fm: 0-0
Distance: 5f/6f: 0-0 7f-8f: 0-0 9f-13f: 0-3 **14f+: 3-13**
Track : **LH: 2-5** RH: 1-10 Tight: 1-4 Gall: 1-5
Aids: Bl: 0-0 Vi: 0-0 Tstrap: 0-0 Ckp: 0-0
Best Rating: **104** 8/09 York 2m88y gd-fm

Very useful; stays 2m; acts on most ground.

Swirl Tango

72(65)

3-y-o b f Lujain (USA)-Tangolania (FR) (Ashkalani (IRE))

F Jordan Tony Cocum

Placings:00 (6794)

2009: 8^{0}SD, 10^{0}S,

	Starts	1st	2nd	3rd	Win & Pl
Career Total (Turf)	1	0	0	0	
Career Total (AW)	1	0	0	0	

Going (Turf): **Sf: 0-1 GS: 0-0 Gd: 0-0 GF: 0-0 Fm: 0-0**
Distance: 5f/6f: 0-0 7f-8f: 0-1 9f-13f: 0-1 14f+: 0-0
Track : LH: 0-1 RH: 0-1 Tight: 0-0 Gall: 0-0
Aids: Bl: 0-0 Vi: 0-0 Tstrap: 0-0 Ckp: 0-0

Swish Dish (CAN)

79 55

2-y-o b/br f El Corredor (USA)-Amelia Saratoga (JPN) (Dehere (USA))

R Hannon Mrs J Wood

Placings:00 (7183)

2009: 6^{0}G, 7^{0}G,

	Starts	1st	2nd	3rd	Win & Pl
Career Total (Turf)	2	0	0	0	

Going (Turf): **Sf: 0-0 GS: 0-0 Gd: 0-2 GF: 0-0 Fm: 0-0**
Distance: 5f/6f: 0-0 7f-8f: 0-2 9f-13f: 0-0 14f+: 0-0
Track : LH: 0-0 RH: 0-0 Tight: 0-0 Gall: 0-0
Aids: Bl: 0-0 Vi: 0-0 Tstrap: 0-0 Ckp: 0-0
Best Rating: **55** 10/09 NmkR 7f good

Swiss Act

(107) (95)89

5-y-o ch g Act One-Dancing Mirage (IRE) (Machiavellian (USA))

M Johnston Markus Graff

Placings:431/100/**50602166** (1555a)

2009: 8^{5}SD, 8^{0}SD, 4^{6}FZ, 10^{0}FZ, 12^{2}SF, 12^{1}SD, 11^{6}SD, 11^{6}G,

	Starts	1st	2nd	3rd	Win & Pl
Career Total (Turf)	8	2	0	1	15177
Career Total (AW)	6	1	1	0	8623

95 3/09 Sthl 1m4f (0-85)H STD £5322
89 5/07 Ches 1m4f66y (0-95)H G-F £10039
81 9/06 Haml 1m65y G-S £3886
Total win prize-money £19248

Going (Turf): Sf: 0-1 **GS: 1-1** Gd: 0-3 **GF: 1-2** Fm: 0-0
Distance: 5f/6f: 0-0 7f-8f: 0-3 **9f-13f: 3-10** 14f+: 0-0
Track : **LH: 2-6** RH: 1-5 **Tight: 2-6** Gall: 0-1
Aids: Bl: 0-0 Vi: 0-0 Tstrap: 0-0 Ckp: 0-0
Best Rating: **95** 3/09 Sthl 1m4f stand

Very useful; stays 1m4f and acts on most ground and Fibresand.

Swiss Art (IRE)

93(109) (78)61

3-y-o b g One Cool Cat (USA)-Alpine Park (IRE) (Barathea (IRE))

R Hollinshead (Mrs R A Carr 4/12) The Cartmel Syndicate

Placings:20465-35311605151210434001055 (7858)

2009: 6^{3}SS, 7^{5}SD, 7^{3}SD, 8^{1}SD, 8^{1}SD, 7^{6}SD, 10^{0}GF, 6^{5}F, 7^{1}SD, 5^{5}SD, 8^{1}SD, 6^{2}SD, 8^{1}SD, 8^{0}G, 7^{4}SD, 8^{3}S, 8^{4}SD, 8^{0}SD, 8^{0}SD, 8^{1}SD, 8^{0}SD, 8^{5}SD,

	Starts	1st	2nd	3rd	Win & Pl
Career Total (Turf)	4	0	0	1	636
Career Total (AW)	24	6	2	2	17074

71 11/09 Sthl 1m STD £2047
78 7/09 Sthl 1m (0-70)H STD £3238
65 7/09 Sthl 1m STD £2729
78 6/09 Sthl 7f STD £2047
70 3/09 Sthl 1m STD £2047
63 3/09 Sthl 1m STD £2047
Total win prize-money £14156

Going (Turf): **Sf: 0-1 GS: 0-0 Gd: 0-1 GF: 0-1 Fm: 0-1**
Distance: 5f/6f: 0-4 **7f-8f: 6-21** 9f-13f: 0-3 14f+: 0-0
Track : **LH: 6-23** RH: 0-4 Tight: 0-8 Gall: 0-1
Aids: **Bl: 1-3** Vi: 0-0 Tstrap: 0-3 Ckp: 0-3
Best Rating: **78** 7/09 Sthl 1m stand

Fair; effective over 6f-1m; goes well on Fibresand; has worn blinkers and cheepieces.

Swiss Cross

99 86

2-y-o b c Cape Cross (IRE)-Swiss Lake (USA) (Indian Ridge)

G A Butler A D Spence

Placings:5316 (7013)

2009: 6^{5}G, 5^{3}GF, 7^{1}GF, 7^{6}GS,

	Starts	1st	2nd	3rd	Win & Pl
Career Total (Turf)	4	1	0	1	7246

86 10/09 NmkR 7f G-F £6476
Total win prize-money £6476

Going (Turf): Sf: 0-0 GS: 0-1 Gd: 0-1 **GF: 1-2** Fm: 0-0
Distance: 5f/6f: 0-1 **7f-8f: 1-3** 9f-13f: 0-0 14f+: 0-0
Track : LH: 0-0 RH: 0-0 Tight: 0-0 Gall: 0-0
Aids: Bl: 0-0 Vi: 0-0 Tstrap: 0-0 Ckp: 0-0
Best Rating: **86** 10/09 NmkR 7f gd-fm

Useful stays 7f; acts on fast ground.

Swiss Diva

110(105) (94)106

3-y-o br f Pivotal-Swiss Lake (USA) (Indian Ridge)

D R C Elsworth Lordship Stud

Placings:03221-313142 (5434)

2009: 6^{3}GF, 6^{1}SD, 6^{3}GF, 6^{1}G, 6^{4}G, 6^{2}GF,

	Starts	1st	2nd	3rd	Win & Pl
Career Total (Turf)	9	1	3	3	83654
Career Total (AW)	2	2	0	0	11333

104 6/09 York 6f (0-105)H GD £64760
94 5/09 Ling 6f (0-90)H STD £7771
82 11/08 Ling 6f STD £3561
Total win prize-money £76093

Going (Turf): Sf: 0-0 GS: 0-2 **Gd: 1-3** GF: 0-4 Fm: 0-0
Distance: **5f/6f: 3-11** 7f-8f: 0-0 9f-13f: 0-0 14f+: 0-0
Track : **LH: 2-2** RH: 0-0 **Tight: 2-2** Gall: 0-0
Aids: Bl: 0-0 Vi: 0-0 Tstrap: 0-0 Ckp: 0-0
Best Rating: **106** 8/09 NmkJ 6f gd-fm

Smart; Listed placed; stays 6f and acts on most ground, but best with cut; also goes on Polytrack.

Swiss Franc

(112) (105)107

4-y-o br g Mr Greeley (USA)-Swiss Lake (USA) (Indian Ridge)

D R C Elsworth Lordship Stud

Placings:312233/3630-24 (0633)

2009: 5^{2}SD, 6^{4}SD,

	Starts	1st	2nd	3rd	Win & Pl
Career Total (Turf)	8	1	2	4	49776

Career Total (AW) 4 0 1 1 9925
87 5/07 NmkR 5f G-S £4533
Total win prize-money £4534

Going (Turf): Sf: 0-0 GS: 1-2 Gd: 0-3 GF: 0-3 Fm: 0-0
Distance: 5f/6f: 1-11 7f-8f: 0-1 9f-13f: 0-0 14f+: 0-0
Track : LH: 0-3 RH: 0-1 Tight: 0-3 Gall: 0-1
Aids: Bl: 0-0 Vi: 0-0 Tstrap: 0-1 Ckp: 0-1
Best Rating: 107 7/07 NmkJ 6f gd-fm

Smart; runner-up in the 2007 Coventry Stakes; effective over 5f-6f; acts on most ground on turf; goes on Polytrack; has worn cheekpieces.

Swiss Lake Sweetie (USA)

(83) (49)62
3-y-o ch f Action This Day (USA)-Almost Blue (USA) (Mr Greeley (USA))
George Baker Jerry Jamgotchian

Placings:564-0 (0019)
2009: 5[0]SD,

	Starts	1st	2nd	3rd	Win & Pl
Career Total (Turf)	2	0	0	0	0
Career Total (AW)	2	0	0	0	0

Going (Turf): Sf: 0-1 GS: 0-0 Gd: 0-1 GF: 0-0 Fm: 0-0
Distance: 5f/6f: 0-4 7f-8f: 0-0 9f-13f: 0-0 14f+: 0-0
Track : LH: 0-2 RH: 0-0 Tight: 0-2 Gall: 0-0
Aids: Bl: 0-0 Vi: 0-0 Tstrap: 0-0 Ckp: 0-0
Best Rating: 62 8/08 Catt 5f good

Moderate; stays 6f; acts on Polytrack.

Swop (IRE)

109(108) (91)108
6-y-o b g Shinko Forest (IRE)-Changing Partners (Rainbow Quest (USA))
L M Cumani Mrs Angie Silver

Placings:1/21233-0410600 (6480)
2009: 8[0]G, 8[4]GF, 7[1]G, 8[0]GF, 7[6]GF, 8[0]GF, 9[0]GF,

	Starts	1st	2nd	3rd	Win & Pl
Career Total (Turf)	11	2	1	2	87046
Career Total (AW)	2	1	1	0	4166

108 2/09 Ndas 7f110y (95-110)H GD £50000
96 6/08 Donc 1m (0-85)H G-F £4533
87 10/07 Ling 7f STD £2817
Total win prize-money £57350

Going (Turf): Sf: 0-0 GS: 0-0 Gd: 1-4 GF: 1-7 Fm: 0-0
Distance: 5f/6f: 0-0 7f-8f: 3-10 9f-13f: 0-3 14f+: 0-0
Track : LH: 2-5 RH: 0-3 Tight: 1-1 Gall: 1-4
Aids: Bl: 0-0 Vi: 0-0 Tstrap: 0-0 Ckp: 0-0
Best Rating: 108 2/09 Ndas 7f110y good

Smart; effective over 7f-1m2f; acts on good and fast ground; also goes on Polytrack.

Swords

61(105) (71)56
7-y-o b g Vettori (IRE)-Pomorie (IRE) (Be My Guest (USA))
R E Peacock R E Peacock

Placings:0050/0003332/0262151403/00630/04011211005 24-400350540125 (7635)
2009: 14[4]SS, 13[0]SD, 12[0]GS, 14[3]SD, 13[5]SF, 12[0]SD, 16[5]SD, 12[4]SD, 13[0]SD, 12[1]SD, 12[2]SD, 14[5]SD,

	Starts	1st	2nd	3rd	Win & Pl
Career Total (Turf)	10	0	0	0	262
Career Total (AW)	41	7	6	6	24150

61 11/09 Sthl 1m4f (0-55)H STD £2047
69 8/08 Wolv 1m4f50y (0-70)H STD £3238
71 8/08 Wolv 1m5f194y (0-65)H STD £2729
62 7/08 Sthl 1m4f (0-65)H STD £1978
59 7/08 Wolv 2m119y (0-65)H STD £2388
66 9/06 Kemp 1m4f (0-65)H STD £3238
64 8/06 Wolv 2m119y (0-55)H STD £2730
Total win prize-money £18351

Going (Turf): Sf: 0-1 GS: 0-3 Gd: 0-4 GF: 0-2 Fm: 0-0
Distance: 5f/6f: 0-0 7f-8f: 0-5 9f-13f: 4-26 14f+: 3-20
Track : LH: 6-42 RH: 1-5 Tight: 4-25 Gall: 0-1
Aids: Bl: 0-0 Vi: 0-0 Tstrap: 0-0 Ckp: 0-0
Best Rating: 73 10/04 Leic 1m1f218y good

Moderate; effective over 1m4f-2m; acts on sand.

Swordsman (GER)

104 (81)76
7-y-o b g Acatenango (GER)-Saiga (Windwurf (GER))
C Gordon Mrs Kate Digweed

Placings:414304/350041/540056/5213000 (6692)
2009: 16[5]GF, 16[2]GF, 16[1]GF, 16[3]GS, 21[0]G, 16[0]G, 16[0]GS,

	Starts	1st	2nd	3rd	Win & Pl
Career Total (Turf)	22	3	1	3	30653
Career Total (AW)	3	0	0	0	4648

76 7/09 Ling 2m (0-75)H G-F £2729
11/06 Mchl 1m3f165y GD £4137
5/05 Belm 1m2f FRM £13750
Total win prize-money £20618

Going (Turf): Sf: 0-1 GS: 0-4 Gd: 1-10 GF: 1-4 Fm: 1-4
Distance: 5f/6f: 0-0 7f-8f: 0-0 9f-13f: 2-12 14f+: 1-13
Track : LH: 1-6 RH: 0-9 Tight: 1-7 Gall: 0-2
Aids: Bl: 0-5 Vi: 0-0 Tstrap: 0-0 Ckp: 0-0
Best Rating: 99 9/05 Belm 1m3f firm

Modest; stays 2m; handles good ground and faster; has worn a tongue tie.

Sybil's Surprise

79 19
4-y-o b f Puissance-Fervent Fan (IRE) (Soviet Lad (USA))
J Mackie Major W R Paton-Smith

Placings:00 (5549)
2009: 8[0]GF, 9[0]G,

	Starts	1st	2nd	3rd	Win & Pl
Career Total (Turf)	2	0	0	0	

Going (Turf): Sf: 0-0 GS: 0-0 Gd: 0-1 GF: 0-1 Fm: 0-0
Distance: 5f/6f: 0-0 7f-8f: 0-0 9f-13f: 0-2 14f+: 0-0
Track : LH: 0-1 RH: 0-1 Tight: 0-1 Gall: 0-0
Aids: Bl: 0-0 Vi: 0-0 Tstrap: 0-0 Ckp: 0-0
Best Rating: 19 7/09 Nott 1m75y gd-fm

Sydney Bridge

87 60
2-y-o b g Danbird (AUS)-Miss Prim (Case Law)
I Semple Mrs J Penman

Placings:65000 (6983)
2009: 5[6]G, 6[5]G, 6[0]GS, 7[0]GF, 6[0]G,

	Starts	1st	2nd	3rd	Win & Pl
Career Total (Turf)	5	0	0	0	0

Going (Turf): Sf: 0-0 GS: 0-1 Gd: 0-3 GF: 0-1 Fm: 0-0
Distance: 5f/6f: 0-4 7f-8f: 0-1 9f-13f: 0-0 14f+: 0-0
Track : LH: 0-0 RH: 0-1 Tight: 0-0 Gall: 0-1
Aids: Bl: 0-0 Vi: 0-0 Tstrap: 0-3 Ckp: 0-3
Best Rating: 60 9/09 Ayr 6f gd-sft

Sydney Cove (IRE)

93(73) (35)47
3-y-o b g Cape Cross (IRE)-First Fleet (USA) (Woodman (USA))
R Allan Big Teri Racing

Placings:000-00366000 (5331)
2009: 9[0]G, 8[0]GS, 11[3]GF, 12[6]GF, 11[6]G, 9[0]G, 10[0]GF, 10[0]S,

	Starts	1st	2nd	3rd	Win & Pl
Career Total (Turf)	10	0	0	1	353
Career Total (AW)	1	0	0	0	

Going (Turf): Sf: 0-1 GS: 0-2 Gd: 0-4 GF: 0-3 Fm: 0-0
Distance: 5f/6f: 0-0 7f-8f: 0-2 9f-13f: 0-9 14f+: 0-0
Track : LH: 0-3 RH: 0-6 Tight: 0-4 Gall: 0-1
Aids: Bl: 0-0 Vi: 0-0 Tstrap: 0-0 Ckp: 0-0
Best Rating: 47 10/08 Nott 1m75y gd-sft

Sydneysider

84(95) (63)67
4-y-o b g Averti (IRE)-Cajole (IRE) (Barathea (IRE))
Eve Johnson Houghton Mrs C J Hue Williams

Placings:034-0550 (7610)
2009: 6[0]G, 8[5]SD, 7[5]SD, 7[0]SD,

	Starts	1st	2nd	3rd	Win & Pl
Career Total (Turf)	4	0	0	1	1155
Career Total (AW)	3	0	0	0	0

Going (Turf): Sf: 0-1 GS: 0-0 Gd: 0-1 GF: 0-2 Fm: 0-0
Distance: 5f/6f: 0-2 7f-8f: 0-5 9f-13f: 0-0 14f+: 0-0
Track : LH: 0-1 RH: 0-3 Tight: 0-0 Gall: 0-0
Aids: Bl: 0-0 Vi: 0-0 Tstrap: 0-0 Ckp: 0-0
Best Rating: 67 7/08 Sals 6f gd-fm

Modest; effective at 6f; acts on most ground.

Synonymy

78(103) (66)62
6-y-o b g Sinndar (IRE)-Peony (Lion Cavern (USA))
M Blanshard Messrs Chambers Mitchell & Bickers-Price

Placings:000/3306003442162/4441305063003120200/503 10165046006500-0 (2760)
2009: 16[0]GF,

	Starts	1st	2nd	3rd	Win & Pl
Career Total (Turf)	27	2	2	3	11152
Career Total (AW)	26	3	2	4	11261

61 5/08 Wwck 1m6f213y (0-75)H G-F £3561
66 4/08 Wolv 2m119y (0-65)H STD £2047
58 8/07 Sals 1m6f21y (0-70)H G-F £3238
75 3/07 Wolv 2m119y (0-65)H SF £2388
68 10/06 Wolv 2m119y (0-75)H STD £3238
Total win prize-money £14476

Going (Turf): Sf: 0-4 GS: 0-5 Gd: 0-9 GF: 2-9 Fm: 0-0
Distance: 5f/6f: 0-0 7f-8f: 0-2 9f-13f: 0-8 14f+: 5-43
Track : LH: 4-35 RH: 1-17 Tight: 4-30 Gall: 0-1
Aids: Bl: 4-33 Vi: 0-0 Tstrap: 0-0 Ckp: 0-0
Best Rating: 75 3/07 Kemp 2m stand

Moderate; suited by 1m6f-2m; acts on a sound surface and Polytrack; has worn blinkers.

Syrian

95 **94**

2-y-o b g Hawk Wing (USA)-Lady Lahar (Fraam)
M L W Bell Highclere Thoroughbred Racing (Donoghue)

Placings:153 **(6011)**
2009: 7^{1}G, 8^{5}S, 8^{3}GS,

	Starts	1st	2nd	3rd	Win & Pl
Career Total (Turf)	**3**	**1**	**0**	**1**	**4399**
83 7/09 Yarm 7f3y			GD		£2590

Total win prize-money £2590

Going (Turf): Sf: 0-1 GS: 0-1 **Gd: 1-1** GF: 0-0 Fm: 0-0
Distance: 5f/6f: 0-0 **7f-8f: 1-2** 9f-13f: 0-1 14f+: 0-0
Track : LH: 0-2 RH: 0-0 Tight: 0-0 Gall: 0-0
Aids: Bl: 0-0 Vi: 0-0 Tstrap: 0-0 Ckp: 0-0
Best Rating: 94 9/09 Hayd 1m30y soft

Useful alf-brother to three winners out of a Group 3 winner; ready debut winner over 7f on easy ground.

Syrinx (IRE)

(94) (70)**73**

3-y-o b f One Cool Cat (USA)-Latest Chapter (IRE) (Ahonoora)
J Noseda Michael Tabor

Placings:534-1 **(0154)**
2009: 7^{1}SD,

	Starts	1st	2nd	3rd	Win & Pl
Career Total (Turf)	**1**	**0**	**0**	**1**	**674**
Career Total (AW)	**3**	**1**	**0**	**0**	**2879**
70 1/09 Kemp 7f			STD		£2590

Total win prize-money £2590

Going (Turf): Sf: 0-0 GS: 0-0 Gd: 0-1 GF: 0-0 Fm: 0-0
Distance: 5f/6f: 0-1 **7f-8f: 1-3** 9f-13f: 0-0 14f+: 0-0
Track : LH: 0-1 **RH: 1-2** Tight: 0-1 Gall: 0-0
Aids: Bl: 0-0 Vi: 0-0 Tstrap: 0-0 Ckp: 0-0
Best Rating: 73 8/08 NmkJ 7f good

Fair; stays 7f; acts on Polytrack.

Syvilla

105 **95**

4-y-o b f Nayef (USA)-Dance Steppe (Rambo Dancer (CAN))
Rae Guest T J Cooper

Placings:5/022216-40026405 **(7291)**
2009: 10^{4}G, 11^{0}G, 10^{0}GS, 10^{2}GF, 12^{6}G, 9^{4}GF, 9^{0}GF, 10^{5}S,

	Starts	1st	2nd	3rd	Win & Pl
Career Total (Turf)	**15**	**1**	**4**	**0**	**17765**
80 9/08 Bath 1m3f144y			SFT		£2719

Total win prize-money £2720

Going (Turf): Sf: 1-3 GS: 0-2 Gd: 0-6 GF: 0-3 Fm: 0-0
Distance: 5f/6f: 0-0 7f-8f: 0-1 **9f-13f: 1-14** 14f+: 0-0
Track : **LH: 1-9** RH: 0-5 **Tight: 1-5** Gall: 0-3
Aids: Bl: 0-0 Vi: 0-0 Tstrap: 0-0 Ckp: 0-0
Best Rating: 95 10/08 Deau 1m4f110y v soft

Very useful; Listed placed; stays 1m3f; acts on most ground.

Szaba

(98) (51)**28**

4-y-o ch f Tipsy Creek (USA)-Compton Alice (Compton Place)
J Akehurst Mrs Pam Akhurst

Placings:6504000-0006 **(0598)**

2009: 6^{0}SD, 8^{0}SD, 6^{0}SD, 8^{6}SD,

	Starts	1st	2nd	3rd	Win & Pl
Career Total (Turf)	**2**	**0**	**0**	**0**	
Career Total (AW)	**9**	**0**	**0**	**0**	**0**

Going (Turf): Sf: 0-0 GS: 0-1 Gd: 0-1 GF: 0-0 Fm: 0-0
Distance: 5f/6f: 0-6 7f-8f: 0-5 9f-13f: 0-0 14f+: 0-0
Track : LH: 0-6 RH: 0-3 Tight: 0-6 Gall: 0-0
Aids: Bl: 0-1 Vi: 0-0 Tstrap: 0-1 Ckp: 0-1
Best Rating: 51 2/08 Ling 5f stand

Ta Aleem

71

3-y-o ch f Galileo (IRE)-Tadris (USA) (Red Ransom (USA))
M P Tregoning Hamdan Al Maktoum

Placings:5 **(5151)**
2009: 9^{5}GF,

	Starts	1st	2nd	3rd	Win & Pl
Career Total (Turf)	**1**	**0**	**0**	**0**	**0**

Going (Turf): Sf: 0-0 GS: 0-0 Gd: 0-0 GF: 0-1 Fm: 0-0
Distance: 5f/6f: 0-0 7f-8f: 0-0 9f-13f: 0-1 14f+: 0-0
Track : LH: 0-0 RH: 0-1 Tight: 0-1 Gall: 0-0
Aids: Bl: 0-0 Vi: 0-0 Tstrap: 0-0 Ckp: 0-0

Taajub (IRE)

109 **109**

2-y-o b c Exceed And Excel (AUS)-Purple Tiger (IRE) (Rainbow Quest (USA))
W J Haggas Hamdan Al Maktoum

Placings:21222 **(6660)**
2009: 6^{2}G, 6^{1}G, 6^{2}GF, 6^{2}GF, 5^{2}GS,

	Starts	1st	2nd	3rd	Win & Pl
Career Total (Turf)	**5**	**1**	**4**	**0**	**124125**
89 7/09 NmkJ 6f			GD		£5180

Total win prize-money £5181

Going (Turf): Sf: 0-0 GS: 0-1 **Gd: 1-2** GF: 0-2 Fm: 0-0
Distance: **5f/6f: 1-4** 7f-8f: 0-1 9f-13f: 0-0 14f+: 0-0
Track : LH: 0-0 RH: 0-0 Tight: 0-0 Gall: 0-0
Aids: Bl: 0-0 Vi: 0-0 Tstrap: 0-0 Ckp: 0-0
Best Rating: 109 8/09 York 6f gd-fm

Smart; Group placed; effective over 5f-6f; acts on fast and easy ground.

Taameer

100 **108**

3-y-o b c Beat Hollow-Vayavaig (Damister (USA))
M P Tregoning Hamdan Al Maktoum

Placings:12-5 **(1485)**
2009: 10^{5}G,

	Starts	1st	2nd	3rd	Win & Pl
Career Total (Turf)	**3**	**1**	**1**	**0**	**23724**
96 9/08 Newb 1m			GD		£11215

Total win prize-money £11216

Going (Turf): Sf: 0-0 GS: 0-1 **Gd: 1-2** GF: 0-0 Fm: 0-0
Distance: 5f/6f: 0-0 **7f-8f: 1-2** 9f-13f: 0-1 14f+: 0-0
Track : LH: 0-0 RH: 0-2 Tight: 0-0 Gall: 0-1
Aids: Bl: 0-0 Vi: 0-0 Tstrap: 0-0 Ckp: 0-0
Best Rating: 108 10/08 Asct 1m gd-sft

Overcame inexperience to win Haynes, Hanson & Clark first time out in 2008; lightly raced since; effective over 1m; acts on good ground.

Taarab

95 **84**

3-y-o ch g Refuse To Bend (IRE)-Tanzania (USA) (Darshaan)
Saeed Bin Suroor Godolphin

Placings:2-25 **(2090)**
2009: 10^{2}GS, 12^{5}G,

	Starts	1st	2nd	3rd	Win & Pl
Career Total (Turf)	**3**	**0**	**2**	**0**	**1966**

Going (Turf): Sf: 0-1 GS: 0-1 Gd: 0-1 GF: 0-0 Fm: 0-0
Distance: 5f/6f: 0-0 7f-8f: 0-0 9f-13f: 0-3 14f+: 0-0
Track : LH: 0-2 RH: 0-0 Tight: 0-1 Gall: 0-1
Aids: Bl: 0-0 Vi: 0-0 Tstrap: 0-0 Ckp: 0-0
Best Rating: 84 10/08 Yarm 1m3y soft

Taaresh (IRE)

(85) (40)**80**

4-y-o b c Sakhee (USA)-Tanaghum (Darshaan)
K A Morgan P Doughty

Placings:210-60 **(7823)**
2009: 13^{6}SD, 10^{0}SD,

	Starts	1st	2nd	3rd	Win & Pl
Career Total (Turf)	**3**	**1**	**1**	**0**	**4070**
Career Total (AW)	**2**	**0**	**0**	**0**	**0**
69 8/08 Ripn 1m			G-S		£2914

Total win prize-money £2914

Going (Turf): Sf: 0-1 **GS: 1-1** Gd: 0-0 GF: 0-1 Fm: 0-0
Distance: 5f/6f: 0-0 **7f-8f: 1-1** 9f-13f: 0-4 14f+: 0-0
Track : LH: 0-1 **RH: 1-4 Tight: 1-2** Gall: 0-0
Aids: Bl: 0-0 Vi: 0-0 Tstrap: 0-0 Ckp: 0-0
Best Rating: 80 7/08 Sand 1m14y gd-fm

Fair; effective over 1m; acts on fast and easy ground.

Tabaahi (IRE)

(93) (52)**62**

4-y-o ch g Alhaarth (IRE)-Lovelyst (IRE) (Machiavellian (USA))
Gordon Elliott (D K Weld 31/8) Rathgar Dandies Syndicate

Placings:000-00300650 **(7732)**
2009: 5^{0}S, 10^{0}GY, 10^{3}HY, 10^{0}GF, 10^{0}S, 9^{6}SD, 9^{5}SD, 12^{0}SD,

	Starts	1st	2nd	3rd	Win & Pl
Career Total (Turf)	**7**	**0**	**0**	**1**	**517**
Career Total (AW)	**4**	**0**	**0**	**0**	**0**

Going (Turf): Sf: 0-4 GS: 0-0 Gd: 0-0 GF: 0-1 Fm: 0-1
Distance: 5f/6f: 0-3 7f-8f: 0-0 9f-13f: 0-8 14f+: 0-0
Track : LH: 0-7 RH: 0-4 Tight: 0-3 Gall: 0-0
Aids: Bl: 0-4 Vi: 0-0 Tstrap: 0-0 Ckp: 0-0
Best Rating: 62 6/08 Navn 1m2f firm

Tabaran (FR)

86(90) (58)**19**

6-y-o ch g Polish Precedent (USA)-Tabariya (IRE) (Doyoun)
Mrs A M Thorpe (L A Dace 11/6) Mrs A M Thorpe

Placings:00/0/500 **(2429)**
2009: 12^{5}SD, 16^{0}SD, 16^{0}G,

	Starts	1st	2nd	3rd	Win & Pl
Career Total (Turf)	**4**	**0**	**0**	**0**	**0**
Career Total (AW)	**2**	**0**	**0**	**0**	**0**

Going (Turf): **Sf: 0-2 GS: 0-0 Gd: 0-2 GF: 0-0 Fm: 0-0**
Distance: 5f/6f: 0-0 7f-8f: 0-2 9f-13f: 0-2 14f+: 0-2
Track : LH: 0-1 RH: 0-3 Tight: 0-1 Gall: 0-0
Aids: Bl: 0-1 Vi: 0-0 Tstrap: 0-0 Ckp: 0-0
Best Rating: **58** 4/09 Kemp 1m4f stand

Tabaret

105(103) (99)**100**

6-y-o ch g Bertolini (USA)-Luanshya (First Trump)
R M Whitaker T L Adams

Placings:231013/0F0/06020400405/0604012000640-06230040400 **(7414)**
2009: 6^{0}GF, 5^{6}G, 5^{2}G, 6^{3}GF, 6^{0}G, 5^{0}GF, 5^{4}GS, 5^{0}SD, 5^{4}GF, 5^{0}SD, 5^{0}SD,

	Starts	1st	2nd	3rd	Win & Pl
Career Total (Turf)	**38**	**3**	**4**	**3**	**59068**
Career Total (AW)	**6**	**0**	**0**	**0**	**1868**

96 6/08 Rdcr 6f (0-95)H FRM £6799
100 8/05 York 5f GD £18000
91 7/05 Bevl 5f GD £4998
Total win prize-money £29799

Going (Turf): Sf: 0-1 GS: 0-4 **Gd: 2-13** GF: 0-17 Fm: 1-3
Distance: **5f/6f: 3-44** 7f-8f: 0-0 9f-13f: 0-0 14f+: 0-0
Track : LH: 0-6 RH: 0-0 Tight: 0-2 Gall: 0-3
Aids: Bl: 0-0 Vi: 0-0 Tstrap: 1-10 Ckp: 1-10
Best Rating: **101** 5/07 NmkR 5f gd-fm

Useful; seems best at 5f; acts on good or faster ground and on Polytrack; has worn cheekpieces.

Tabassum (IRE)

108 **108**

2-y-o b f Nayef (USA)-Tomoohat (USA) (Danzig (USA))
Sir Michael Stoute Hamdan Al Maktoum

Placings:113 **(6852)**
2009: 7^{1}G, 7^{1}GF, 7^{3}G,

	Starts	1st	2nd	3rd	Win & Pl
Career Total (Turf)	**3**	**2**	**0**	**1**	**41858**

108 10/09 NmkR 7f G-F £28385
80 8/09 NmkJ 7f GD £4857
Total win prize-money £33242

Going (Turf): Sf: 0-0 GS: 0-0 **Gd: 1-2 GF: 1-1** Fm: 0-0
Distance: 5f/6f: 0-0 **7f-8f: 2-3** 9f-13f: 0-0 14f+: 0-0
Track : LH: 0-0 RH: 0-0 Tight: 0-0 Gall: 0-0
Aids: Bl: 0-0 Vi: 0-0 Tstrap: 0-0 Ckp: 0-0
Best Rating: **108** 10/09 NmkR 7f gd-fm

Very useful; effective over 7f; acts on good and fast ground.

Taboor (IRE)

99(101) (61)**58**

11-y-o b g Mujadil (USA)-Christoph's Girl (Efisio)
R M H Cowell T W Morley

Placings:24331002/00002346435042401/4350041000/0005005020601V2052400/000001136200 4/43233021160400/6246505000403/3544100001030404-2436300 **(7100)**
2009: 5^{2}SD, 5^{4}SD, 5^{3}SD, 5^{6}SD, 5^{3}S, 5^{0}GS, 5^{0}G,

	Starts	1st	2nd	3rd	Win & Pl
Career Total (Turf)	**65**	**8**	**6**	**6**	**42713**
Career Total (AW)	**54**	**2**	**6**	**8**	**11394**

58 7/08 Yarm 5f43y (0-60)H G-F £2047
61 3/08 Wolv 5f20y (0-55)H STD £2047
73 6/06 Yarm 5f43y (0-75)H GD £3886
65 5/06 Haml 5f4y (0-70)H GD £3886
62 8/05 NmkJ 5f (0-75)H G-S £4149
59 8/05 Catt 5f (0-55)H G-F £3067
62 8/04 Brig 5f59y D(0-80)H FRM £6662
66 5/03 Carl 5f F(0-60) G-F £3513
73 7/01 Leic 5f2y F GD £2450
Total win prize-money £31710

Going (Turf): Sf: 0-7 GS: 1-17 **Gd: 3-15 GF: 3-22** Fm: 1-4
Distance: **5f/6f: 10-117** 7f-8f: 0-2 9f-13f: 0-0 14f+: 0-0
Track : **LH: 3-62** RH: 1-7 **Tight: 2-39** Gall: 1-8
Aids: **Bl: 3-49** Vi: 0-0 Tstrap: 1-5 Ckp: 1-5
Best Rating: **78** 1/03 Ling 5f stand

Moderate; best over a stiff 5f; acts on most ground; also goes on Polytrack.

Taborcillo

87 **66**

2-y-o b g Lucky Story (USA)-Trust In Paula (USA) (Arazi (USA))
T D Barron Tim D Barron

Placings:200 **(5977)**
2009: 5^{2}GS, 5^{0}GS, 5^{0}GF,

	Starts	1st	2nd	3rd	Win & Pl
Career Total (Turf)	**3**	**0**	**1**	**0**	**1638**

Going (Turf): **Sf: 0-0 GS: 0-2 Gd: 0-0 GF: 0-1 Fm: 0-0**
Distance: 5f/6f: 0-3 7f-8f: 0-0 9f-13f: 0-0 14f+: 0-0
Track : LH: 0-0 RH: 0-0 Tight: 0-0 Gall: 0-0
Aids: Bl: 0-0 Vi: 0-0 Tstrap: 0-0 Ckp: 0-0
Best Rating: **66** 8/09 Thsk 5f gd-sft

Tabulate

88(105) (66)**43**

6-y-o b m Dansili-Let Alone (Warning)
P Howling Richard Berenson

Placings:0/555300224/30001430000 6000/4310062656613204656-6545440 **(4667)**
2009: 10^{6}SD, 10^{5}SD, 10^{4}SD, 11^{5}SD, 8^{4}SF, 11^{4}GF, 8^{0}G,

	Starts	1st	2nd	3rd	Win & Pl
Career Total (Turf)	**7**	**0**	**0**	**0**	**241**
Career Total (AW)	**44**	**3**	**4**	**5**	**10320**

63 7/08 Ling 1m2f STD £1978
53 2/08 Kemp 1m2f (0-45) STD £1365
66 5/07 Sthl 1m (0-60)H STD £2388
Total win prize-money £5733

Going (Turf): **Sf: 0-2 GS: 0-1 Gd: 0-3 GF: 0-1 Fm: 0-0**
Distance: 5f/6f: 0-1 7f-8f: 1-12 **9f-13f: 2-38** 14f+: 0-0
Track : **LH: 2-35** RH: 1-12 **Tight: 1-26** Gall: 0-2
Aids: Bl: 0-0 Vi: 0-0 Tstrap: 0-0 Ckp: 0-0
Best Rating: **66** 8/08 Ling 1m2f stand

Moderate; effective over 1m-1m4f; acts on Polytrack.

Tactful (IRE)

96(105) (93)**89**

4-y-o b f Intikhab (USA)-Crozon (Peintre Celebre (USA))
R M Beckett Mrs David Aykroyd

Placings:110-4400 **(6876)**
2009: 8^{4}SD, 10^{4}GS, 9^{0}S, 8^{0}SD,

	Starts	1st	2nd	3rd	Win & Pl
Career Total (Turf)	**2**	**0**	**0**	**0**	**1203**
Career Total (AW)	**5**	**2**	**0**	**0**	**11214**

89 10/08 GrLe 1m (0-85)H STD £5180
71 9/08 GrLe 1m STD £3885
Total win prize-money £9067

Going (Turf): **Sf: 0-1 GS: 0-1 Gd: 0-0 GF: 0-0 Fm: 0-0**
Distance: 5f/6f: 0-0 **7f-8f: 2-4** 9f-13f: 0-3 14f+: 0-0
Track : **LH: 2-4** RH: 0-2 Tight: 0-0 **Gall: 2-3**
Aids: Bl: 0-0 Vi: 0-0 Tstrap: 0-0 Ckp: 0-0
Best Rating: **93** 4/09 Kemp 1m stand

Useful; stays 1m and acts on Polytrack.

Tactic

112 **106**

3-y-o b c Sadler's Wells (USA)-Tanaghum (Darshaan)
J L Dunlop Hamdan Al Maktoum

Placings:43-21442454 **(7059)**
2009: 11^{2}GS, 12^{1}GF, 11^{4}HY, 16^{4}GF, 13^{2}G, 12^{4}G, 14^{5}S, 11^{4}GF,

	Starts	1st	2nd	3rd	Win & Pl
Career Total (Turf)	**10**	**1**	**2**	**1**	**29479**

89 5/09 Gdwd 1m4f G-F £3238
Total win prize-money £3238

Going (Turf): Sf: 0-2 GS: 0-2 Gd: 0-3 **GF: 1-3** Fm: 0-0
Distance: 5f/6f: 0-0 7f-8f: 0-2 **9f-13f: 1-6** 14f+: 0-2
Track : LH: 0-2 **RH: 1-6 Tight: 1-3** Gall: 0-3
Aids: Bl: 0-0 Vi: 0-0 Tstrap: 0-0 Ckp: 0-0
Best Rating: **106** 7/09 Gdwd 1m4f good

Very useful; Group 3 placed; stays 1m4f plus; acts on fast and easy ground.

Tactician

92 **82**

2-y-o b c Motivator-Tempting Prospect (Shirley Heights)
M L W Bell The Queen

Placings:24 **(6617)**
2009: 8^{2}GF, 8^{4}G,

	Starts	1st	2nd	3rd	Win & Pl
Career Total (Turf)	**2**	**0**	**1**	**0**	**2384**

Going (Turf): **Sf: 0-0 GS: 0-0 Gd: 0-1 GF: 0-1 Fm: 0-0**
Distance: 5f/6f: 0-0 7f-8f: 0-2 9f-13f: 0-0 14f+: 0-0
Track : LH: 0-0 RH: 0-0 Tight: 0-0 Gall: 0-0
Aids: Bl: 0-0 Vi: 0-0 Tstrap: 0-0 Ckp: 0-0
Best Rating: **82** 9/09 Donc 1m gd-fm

Runner-up in useful 1m maiden on fast ground on debut.

Tadalavil

91(96) (76)**81**

4-y-o gr g Clodovil (IRE)-Blandish (USA) (Wild Again (USA))
Miss L A Perratt Ayrshire Racing

Placings:2315053045/50043502103 3203-00003 **(4311)**
2009: 5^{0}GF, 5^{0}GF, 5^{0}GF, 6^{0}G, 5^{3}GS,

	Starts	1st	2nd	3rd	Win & Pl
Career Total (Turf)	**28**	**2**	**3**	**7**	**19090**
Career Total (AW)	**2**	**0**	**0**	**0**	**245**

77 8/08 Sand 5f6y (0-75)H G-S £4533
80 8/07 Ripn 6f GD £3886
Total win prize-money £8419

Going (Turf): Sf: 0-5 **GS: 1-4 Gd: 1-6** GF: 0-13 Fm: 0-0
Distance: **5f/6f: 2-23** 7f-8f: 0-7 9f-13f: 0-0 14f+: 0-0
Track : LH: 0-3 RH: 0-2 Tight: 0-1 Gall: 0-2
Aids: Bl: 0-0 Vi: 0-0 Tstrap: 0-0 Ckp: 0-0
Best Rating: **85** 11/07 NmkR 6f good

Fair; effective over 5f-6f; acts on most ground.

Tadhkeer

79 **45**

2-y-o ch g Refuse To Bend (IRE)-Shuruk (Cadeaux Genereux)

W J Haggas Hamdan Al Maktoum

Placings:50 **(6842)**
2009: 6^{5}GF, 7^{0}G,

	Starts	1st	2nd	3rd	Win & Pl
Career Total (Turf)	2	0	0	0	0

Going (Turf): **Sf: 0-0 GS: 0-0 Gd: 0-1 GF: 0-1 Fm: 0-0**
Distance: 5f/6f: 0-1 7f-8f: 0-1 9f-13f: 0-0 14f+: 0-0
Track : LH: 0-2 RH: 0-0 Tight: 0-1 Gall: 0-0
Aids: Bl: 0-0 Vi: 0-0 Tstrap: 0-0 Ckp: 0-0
Best Rating: **45** 10/09 Wwck 6f gd-fm

Tadlil

96(100) (58)**58**
7-y-o b g Pivotal-Pretty Poppy (Song)
J M Bradley E A Hayward

Placings:056/400010131/000000040524026-02355300040023 **(7869)**
2009: 6^{0}SS, 6^{2}SD, 5^{3}SD, 5^{5}SD, 7^{5}SD, 5^{3}F, 6^{0}GF, 5^{0}GF, 6^{0}GS, 6^{4}GS, 6^{0}SD, 6^{0}SD, 6^{2}SD, 6^{3}SS,

	Starts	1st	2nd	3rd	Win & Pl
Career Total (Turf)	24	3	0	2	11408
Career Total (AW)	17	0	4	2	2928

78	8/06	Rdcr	6f	(0-75)H	G-F	£3238
77	8/06	Hayd	6f	(0-70)H	G-F	£3238
66	7/06	Ripn	6f	(0-70)H	GD	£3886

Total win prize-money £10364

Going (Turf): Sf: 0-2 GS: 0-4 Gd: 1-7 **GF: 2-10** Fm: 0-1
Distance: **5f/6f: 3-30** 7f-8f: 0-11 9f-13f: 0-0 14f+: 0-0
Track : LH: 0-14 RH: 0-6 Tight: 0-5 Gall: 0-5
Aids: Bl: 0-2 Vi: 0-21 Tstrap: 0-0 Ckp: 0-0
Best Rating: **78** 8/06 Rdcr 6f gd-fm

Moderate; effective at 6f; acts on sand.

Tae Kwon Do (USA)

101(96) (61)**60**
3-y-o b g Thunder Gulch (USA)-Judy's Magic (USA) (Wavering Monarch (USA))
Miss J A Camacho Lee Bolingbroke Racing 1

Placings:0445000-5333240060 **(5952)**
2009: 8^{5}SD, 9^{3}SF, 9^{3}SD, 11^{3}SD, 12^{2}GF, 14^{4}GF, 12^{0}GF, 14^{0}GF, 11^{6}GS, 14^{0}GF,

	Starts	1st	2nd	3rd	Win & Pl
Career Total (Turf)	9	0	1	0	771
Career Total (AW)	8	0	0	3	1186

Going (Turf): **Sf: 0-1 GS: 0-1 Gd: 0-0 GF: 0-7 Fm: 0-0**
Distance: 5f/6f: 0-0 7f-8f: 0-6 9f-13f: 0-8 14f+: 0-3
Track : LH: 0-12 RH: 0-3 Tight: 0-11 Gall: 0-0
Aids: Bl: 0-0 Vi: 0-0 Tstrap: 0-1 Ckp: 0-1
Best Rating: **61** 7/08 Ling 7f stand

Moderate; stays 1m4f; acts on fast ground; handles Polytrack.

Taeping (IRE)

81(85) (52)**56**
2-y-o b c Invincible Spirit (IRE)-Simil (USA) (Apalachee (USA))
R Hollinshead John L Marriott

Placings:04036006 **(7793)**
2009: 6^{0}GF, 6^{4}GF, 6^{0}G, 6^{3}SD, 7^{6}SF, 5^{0}SD, 5^{0}SD, 5^{6}SS,

	Starts	1st	2nd	3rd	Win & Pl
Career Total (Turf)	3	0	0	0	313
Career Total (AW)	5	0	0	1	302

Going (Turf): **Sf: 0-0 GS: 0-0 Gd: 0-1 GF: 0-2 Fm: 0-0**
Distance: 5f/6f: 0-7 7f-8f: 0-1 9f-13f: 0-0 14f+: 0-0
Track : LH: 0-4 RH: 0-0 Tight: 0-2 Gall: 0-0
Aids: Bl: 0-0 Vi: 0-0 Tstrap: 0-1 Ckp: 0-1
Best Rating: **56** 10/09 Wwck 6f gd-fm

Moderate; effective over 6f; acts on Fibresand.

Tafaool (IRE)

106(91) (64)**83**
3-y-o b f Green Desert (USA)-Sundus (USA) (Sadler's Wells (USA))
M P Tregoning Hamdan Al Maktoum

Placings:0-33 **(7126)**
2009: 8^{3}GF, 8^{3}G,

	Starts	1st	2nd	3rd	Win & Pl
Career Total (Turf)	2	0	0	2	1252
Career Total (AW)	1	0	0	0	

Going (Turf): **Sf: 0-0 GS: 0-0 Gd: 0-1 GF: 0-1 Fm: 0-0**
Distance: 5f/6f: 0-0 7f-8f: 0-2 9f-13f: 0-1 14f+: 0-0
Track : LH: 0-2 RH: 0-0 Tight: 0-1 Gall: 0-0
Aids: Bl: 0-0 Vi: 0-0 Tstrap: 0-0 Ckp: 0-0
Best Rating: **83** 8/09 NmkJ 1m gd-fm

Useful; stays 1m and acts on fast ground.

Tafawut

81 **44**
2-y-o b f Nayef (USA)-Rohita (IRE) (Waajib)
B W Hills Hamdan Al Maktoum

Placings:0 **(5398)**
2009: 7^{0}G,

	Starts	1st	2nd	3rd	Win & Pl
Career Total (Turf)	1	0	0	0	

Going (Turf): **Sf: 0-0 GS: 0-0 Gd: 0-1 GF: 0-0 Fm: 0-0**
Distance: 5f/6f: 0-0 7f-8f: 0-1 9f-13f: 0-0 14f+: 0-0
Track : LH: 0-0 RH: 0-0 Tight: 0-0 Gall: 0-0
Aids: Bl: 0-0 Vi: 0-0 Tstrap: 0-0 Ckp: 0-0
Best Rating: **44** 8/09 NmkJ 7f good

Tag Team (IRE)

72(104) (61)**43**
8-y-o ch g Tagula (IRE)-Okay Baby (IRE) (Treasure Kay)
John A Harris Cleartherm Glass Sealed Units Ltd

Placings:0/1130513200203/6661603320000523641/642000216020/00064315023231/26050600-0560304002642 **(7869)**
2009: 6^{0}SS, 5^{5}SD, 6^{6}SD, 6^{0}SS, 5^{3}SD, 6^{0}SD, 6^{4}SD, 6^{0}GF, 5^{0}SD, 5^{2}SD, 6^{6}SD, 6^{4}SS, 6^{2}SS,

	Starts	1st	2nd	3rd	Win & Pl
Career Total (Turf)	19	1	0	4	6906
Career Total (AW)	61	7	12	6	36566

73	1/08	Sthl	6f	(0-75)H	STD	£2593
67	8/07	Wolv	5f216y	(0-60)H	STD	£2388
72	10/06	Wolv	5f216y	(0-65)H	SF	£3412
74	12/05	Sthl	5f		STD	£2852
74	2/05	Ling	5f		STD	£2919
78	5/04	Bath	5f161y	E(0-75)H	FRM	£4299
81	2/04	Ling	6f	E(0-70)H	STD	£3444
61	2/04	Ling	5f	D	STD	£3721

Total win prize-money £25633

Going (Turf): Sf: 0-1 GS: 0-3 Gd: 0-4 GF: 0-10 **Fm: 1-1**
Distance: **5f/6f: 8-78** 7f-8f: 0-2 9f-13f: 0-0 14f+: 0-0
Track : **LH: 7-52** RH: 0-1 **Tight: 5-33** Gall: 1-2
Aids: Bl: 0-4 Vi: 0-7 Tstrap: 0-5 Ckp: 0-5
Best Rating: **87** 2/05 Ling 5f stand

Moderate sprinter; stays 6f; acts on fast ground and sand; has worn cheekpieces; suited by forcing tactics.

Tagalura (IRE)

(63)
3-y-o b g Tagula (IRE)-Allurah (IRE) (Goldmark (USA))
P T Midgley Sunpak Potatoes

Placings:0-0 **(0621)**
2009: 11^{0}SD,

	Starts	1st	2nd	3rd	Win & Pl
Career Total (Turf)	1	0	0	0	
Career Total (AW)	1	0	0	0	

Going (Turf): **Sf: 0-0 GS: 0-0 Gd: 0-1 GF: 0-0 Fm: 0-0**
Distance: 5f/6f: 0-1 7f-8f: 0-0 9f-13f: 0-1 14f+: 0-0
Track : LH: 0-1 RH: 0-0 Tight: 0-0 Gall: 0-0
Aids: Bl: 0-0 Vi: 0-0 Tstrap: 0-0 Ckp: 0-0
Best Rating:

Tagseed (IRE)

96 **72**
3-y-o b c Elusive City (USA)-Allegorica (IRE) (Alzao (USA))
W J Haggas Hamdan Al Maktoum

Placings:3 **(1840)**
2009: 6^{3}GF,

	Starts	1st	2nd	3rd	Win & Pl
Career Total (Turf)	1	0	0	1	385

Going (Turf): **Sf: 0-0 GS: 0-0 Gd: 0-0 GF: 0-1 Fm: 0-0**
Distance: 5f/6f: 0-0 7f-8f: 0-1 9f-13f: 0-0 14f+: 0-0
Track : LH: 0-0 RH: 0-0 Tight: 0-0 Gall: 0-0
Aids: Bl: 0-0 Vi: 0-0 Tstrap: 0-0 Ckp: 0-0
Best Rating: **72** 5/09 Nott 6f15y gd-fm

Half-brother to a couple of winners at up to a mile; promise on debut at 6f on fast ground.

Tagula Breeze (IRE)

103 **82**
3-y-o b g Tagula (IRE)-Pearl Egg (IRE) (Mukaddamah (USA))
I W McInnes Terence Elsey

Placings:0413400-5434060010 **(5421)**
2009: 6^{5}GF, 6^{4}GF, 6^{3}GF, 5^{4}GF, 6^{0}G, 6^{6}G, 5^{0}G, 5^{0}G, 5^{1}G, 5^{0}GF,

	Starts	1st	2nd	3rd	Win & Pl
Career Total (Turf)	17	2	0	2	10675

77	8/09	Thsk	5f	(0-70)H	GD	£4274
76	6/08	Rdcr	6f		G-F	£2331

Total win prize-money £6605

Going (Turf): Sf: 0-1 GS: 0-1 **Gd: 1-7 GF: 1-8** Fm: 0-0
Distance: **5f/6f: 2-16** 7f-8f: 0-1 9f-13f: 0-0 14f+: 0-0
Track : LH: 0-1 RH: 0-0 Tight: 0-0 Gall: 0-0
Aids: Bl: 0-1 Vi: 0-0 Tstrap: 0-2 Ckp: 0-2
Best Rating: **82** 6/09 Ripn 6f gd-fm

Fair; stays 6f; acts on fast ground.

Tagula Minx (IRE)

(84) (51)**20**

3-y-o b f Tagula (IRE)-Persian Fantasia (Alzao (USA))

J Pearce M M Foulger

Placings:06-000 **(7818)**

2009: 9^{0}SD, 7^{0}SD, 9^{0}SD,

	Starts	1st	2nd	3rd	Win & Pl
Career Total (Turf)	1	0	0	0	
Career Total (AW)	4	0	0	0	0

Going (Turf): **Sf: 0-0 GS: 0-1 Gd: 0-0 GF: 0-0 Fm: 0-0**
Distance: 5f/6f: 0-0 7f-8f: 0-2 9f-13f: 0-3 14f+: 0-0
Track : LH: 0-2 RH: 0-2 Tight: 0-2 Gall: 0-0
Aids: Bl: 0-0 Vi: 0-0 Tstrap: 0-0 Ckp: 0-0
Best Rating: **51** 11/08 Kemp 1m stand

Tagula Night (IRE)

104(99) (90)**84**

3-y-o ch g Tagula (IRE)-Carpet Lady (IRE) (Night Shift (USA))

W R Swinburn Hodgson, Hufford, Moss & Papworth

Placings:002-1105 **(6631)**

2009: 6^{1}GF, 6^{1}SD, 6^{0}GF, 6^{5}SS,

	Starts	1st	2nd	3rd	Win & Pl
Career Total (Turf)	3	1	0	0	2730
Career Total (AW)	4	1	1	0	6241

90 8/09 Ling 6f (0-80)H STD £5180
84 8/09 Wind 6f (0-75)H G-F £2729
Total win prize-money £7911

Going (Turf): Sf: 0-0 GS: 0-0 Gd: 0-1 **GF: 1-2** Fm: 0-0
Distance: **5f/6f: 2-7** 7f-8f: 0-0 9f-13f: 0-0 14f+: 0-0
Track : **LH: 1-3** RH: 0-1 Tight: 1-2 Gall: 1-3
Aids: Bl: 0-0 **Vi: 2-5** Tstrap: 0-0 Ckp: 0-0
Best Rating: **90** 8/09 Ling 6f stand

Useful; suited by 6f; acts on Polytrack; has worn a visor and a tongue tie.

Tagula Pearl (IRE)

78(66) **43**

2-y-o b f Tagula (IRE)-Pearl Egg (IRE) (Mukaddamah (USA))

I W McInnes T Elsey, S A Elsey, R Mustill

Placings:0400000 **(7713)**

2009: 5^{0}GF, 5^{4}GF, 6^{0}G, 5^{0}GF, 6^{0}G, 7^{0}SD, 5^{0}SD,

	Starts	1st	2nd	3rd	Win & Pl
Career Total (Turf)	5	0	0	0	289
Career Total (AW)	2	0	0	0	

Going (Turf): **Sf: 0-0 GS: 0-0 Gd: 0-2 GF: 0-3 Fm: 0-0**
Distance: 5f/6f: 0-6 7f-8f: 0-1 9f-13f: 0-0 14f+: 0-0
Track : LH: 0-2 RH: 0-0 Tight: 0-2 Gall: 0-0
Aids: Bl: 0-1 Vi: 0-0 Tstrap: 0-1 Ckp: 0-1
Best Rating: **43** 5/09 York 6f good

Tagula Sands (IRE)

(89) (42)

5-y-o b g Tagula (IRE)-Pomme Pomme (USA) (Dayjur (USA))

J C Fox Salisbury Racing Club

Placings:0000/000660-000 **(0245)**

2009: 8^{0}SD, 6^{0}SD, 6^{0}SD,

	Starts	1st	2nd	3rd	Win & Pl
Career Total (Turf)	2	0	0	0	0
Career Total (AW)	11	0	0	0	0

Going (Turf): **Sf: 0-0 GS: 0-0 Gd: 0-1 GF: 0-1 Fm: 0-0**
Distance: 5f/6f: 0-3 7f-8f: 0-9 9f-13f: 0-1 14f+: 0-0
Track : LH: 0-4 RH: 0-7 Tight: 0-3 Gall: 0-1
Aids: Bl: 0-0 Vi: 0-0 Tstrap: 0-2 Ckp: 0-2
Best Rating: **42** 11/07 Kemp 1m stand

Taguna (IRE)

85 **14**

3-y-o ch f Tagula (IRE)-Tahlil (Cadeaux Genereux)

M Brittain Mel Brittain

Placings:00 **(5621)**

2009: 6^{0}GF, 7^{0}S,

	Starts	1st	2nd	3rd	Win & Pl
Career Total (Turf)	2	0	0	0	

Going (Turf): **Sf: 0-1 GS: 0-0 Gd: 0-0 GF: 0-1 Fm: 0-0**
Distance: 5f/6f: 0-1 7f-8f: 0-1 9f-13f: 0-0 14f+: 0-0
Track : LH: 0-1 RH: 0-0 Tight: 0-1 Gall: 0-0
Aids: Bl: 0-0 Vi: 0-0 Tstrap: 0-0 Ckp: 0-0
Best Rating: **14** 8/09 Ripn 6f gd-fm

Tahayab (ITY)

84 **57**

3-y-o b f Nayef (USA)-Zaffrani (IRE) (Danehill (USA))

M Johnston Hamdan Al Maktoum

Placings:60 **(3093)**

2009: 7^{6}GF, 7^{0}G,

	Starts	1st	2nd	3rd	Win & Pl
Career Total (Turf)	2	0	0	0	0

Going (Turf): **Sf: 0-0 GS: 0-0 Gd: 0-1 GF: 0-1 Fm: 0-0**
Distance: 5f/6f: 0-0 7f-8f: 0-2 9f-13f: 0-0 14f+: 0-0
Track : LH: 0-1 RH: 0-1 Tight: 0-0 Gall: 0-0
Aids: Bl: 0-0 Vi: 0-0 Tstrap: 0-0 Ckp: 0-0
Best Rating: **57** 5/09 Bevl 7f100y gd-fm

Tahfeez (IRE)

85(93) (59)**50**

3-y-o b f Alhaarth (IRE)-Ghazal (USA) (Gone West (USA))

I Semple Bob W Smith

Placings:06-05 **(4013)**

2009: 8^{0}GF, 8^{5}GF,

	Starts	1st	2nd	3rd	Win & Pl
Career Total (Turf)	2	0	0	0	0
Career Total (AW)	2	0	0	0	0

Going (Turf): **Sf: 0-0 GS: 0-0 Gd: 0-0 GF: 0-2 Fm: 0-0**
Distance: 5f/6f: 0-1 7f-8f: 0-1 9f-13f: 0-2 14f+: 0-0
Track : LH: 0-2 RH: 0-2 Tight: 0-1 Gall: 0-1
Aids: Bl: 0-0 Vi: 0-0 Tstrap: 0-1 Ckp: 0-1
Best Rating: **59** 11/08 GrLe 6f stand

Tahkeem

101(64) (16)**72**

3-y-o b f Green Desert (USA)-Katayeb (IRE) (Machiavellian (USA))

M P Tregoning Hamdan Al Maktoum

Placings:0-10 **(6420)**

2009: 9^{1}GF, 11^{0}GF,

	Starts	1st	2nd	3rd	Win & Pl
Career Total (Turf)	2	1	0	0	3238
Career Total (AW)	1	0	0	0	

72 9/09 Gdwd 1m1f192y G-F £3238
Total win prize-money £3238

Going (Turf): Sf: 0-0 GS: 0-0 Gd: 0-0 **GF: 1-2** Fm: 0-0
Distance: 5f/6f: 0-0 7f-8f: 0-1 **9f-13f: 1-2** 14f+: 0-0
Track : LH: 0-0 **RH: 1-3 Tight: 1-2** Gall: 0-0
Aids: Bl: 0-0 Vi: 0-0 Tstrap: 1-2 Ckp: 1-2
Best Rating: **72** 9/09 Gdwd 1m1f192y gd-fm

Fair sort; stays 1m2f; has worn cheekpieces.

Tahseen

93 **67**

2-y-o b c Haafhd-Merayaat (IRE) (Darshaan)

M P Tregoning Hamdan Al Maktoum

Placings:54 **(6962)**

2009: 8^{5}GF, 6^{4}G,

	Starts	1st	2nd	3rd	Win & Pl
Career Total (Turf)	2	0	0	0	702

Going (Turf): **Sf: 0-0 GS: 0-0 Gd: 0-1 GF: 0-1 Fm: 0-0**
Distance: 5f/6f: 0-0 7f-8f: 0-2 9f-13f: 0-0 14f+: 0-0
Track : LH: 0-1 RH: 0-0 Tight: 0-0 Gall: 0-0
Aids: Bl: 0-0 Vi: 0-0 Tstrap: 0-0 Ckp: 0-0
Best Rating: **67** 10/09 Brig 6f209y good

Tai Hang (IRE)

71 **17**

2-y-o br f Celtic Swing-Victoria Peek (IRE) (Cape Cross (IRE))

A P Jarvis Ambrose Turnbull

Placings:00 **(6096)**

2009: 6^{0}G, 5^{0}GF,

	Starts	1st	2nd	3rd	Win & Pl
Career Total (Turf)	2	0	0	0	

Going (Turf): **Sf: 0-0 GS: 0-0 Gd: 0-1 GF: 0-1 Fm: 0-0**
Distance: 5f/6f: 0-2 7f-8f: 0-0 9f-13f: 0-0 14f+: 0-0
Track : LH: 0-1 RH: 0-0 Tight: 0-1 Gall: 0-0
Aids: Bl: 0-0 Vi: 0-0 Tstrap: 0-0 Ckp: 0-0
Best Rating: **17** 7/09 Asct 6f good

Taikoo

102(107) (92)**88**

4-y-o b g Dr Fong (USA)-So True (So Blessed)

H Morrison Miss B Swire

Placings:04/120015541-4220 **(2932)**

2009: 14^{4}SD, 11^{2}SD, 12^{2}G, 12^{0}G,

	Starts	1st	2nd	3rd	Win & Pl
Career Total (Turf)	7	1	1	0	9313
Career Total (AW)	8	2	2	0	9030

92 12/08 Sthl 1m4f (0-75)H STD £2729
81 9/08 Gdwd 1m4f (0-85)H SFT £7771
77 1/08 Sthl 1m SS £2457
Total win prize-money £12958

Going (Turf): **Sf: 1-1** GS: 0-0 Gd: 0-5 GF: 0-1 Fm: 0-0
Distance: 5f/6f: 0-0 7f-8f: 1-2 **9f-13f: 2-11** 14f+: 0-2
Track : **LH: 2-12** RH: 1-2 **Tight: 1-2** Gall: 0-3
Aids: Bl: 0-0 Vi: 0-0 Tstrap: 0-1 Ckp: 0-1
Best Rating: 92 12/08 Sthl 1m4f stand

Useful; effective at 1m4f and acts on good ground and Fibresand.

Taine (IRE)

91 (70)44

4-y-o b c Invincible Spirit (IRE)-Farjah (IRE) (Charnwood Forest (IRE))
J R Gask Horses First Racing Limited

Placings:3/0 **(5717)**
2009: 5^{0}G,

	Starts	1st	2nd	3rd	Win & Pl
Career Total (Turf)	1	0	0	0	
Career Total (AW)	1	0	0	1	438

Going (Turf): **Sf: 0-0 GS: 0-0 Gd: 0-1 GF: 0-0 Fm: 0-0**
Distance: 5f/6f: 0-2 7f-8f: 0-0 9f-13f: 0-0 14f+: 0-0
Track : LH: 0-2 RH: 0-0 Tight: 0-1 Gall: 0-1
Aids: Bl: 0-0 Vi: 0-0 Tstrap: 0-0 Ckp: 0-0
Best Rating: 70 12/07 Wolv 5f20y stand

Tajaaweed (USA)

112 115

4-y-o br c Dynaformer (USA)-Uforia (USA) (Zilzal (USA))
Sir Michael Stoute Hamdan Al Maktoum

Placings:10/105-00 **(3139)**
2009: 10^{0}G, 12^{0}GF,

	Starts	1st	2nd	3rd	Win & Pl
Career Total (Turf)	7	2	0	0	42181

115 5/08 Ches 1m2f75y GD £36900
86 10/07 Nott 1m54y G-S £2590
Total win prize-money £39492

Going (Turf): Sf: 0-0 **GS: 1-1 Gd: 1-4** GF: 0-2 Fm: 0-0
Distance: 5f/6f: 0-0 7f-8f: 0-1 **9f-13f: 2-6** 14f+: 0-0
Track : **LH: 2-4** RH: 0-2 **Tight: 1-2** Gall: 0-2
Aids: Bl: 0-0 Vi: 0-0 Tstrap: 0-0 Ckp: 0-0
Best Rating: 115 5/08 Ches 1m2f75y good

Group class; winner of the Group 3 Dee Stakes in 2008 but did not stay in the Derby; stays 1m2f; acts on good and softer ground.

Tajneed (IRE)

106(102) (94)103

6-y-o b g Alhaarth (IRE)-Indian Express (Indian Ridge)
D Nicholls Alex Nicholls Robert Gilmartin Finola Devaney

Placings:24101/23200000/31012-5005000 **(6282)**
2009: 5^{5}SD, 6^{0}S, 6^{0}G, 6^{5}G, 7^{0}Y, 6^{0}GS, 6^{0}G, 6^{0}GF,

	Starts	1st	2nd	3rd	Win & Pl
Career Total (Turf)	25	4	4	2	119061
Career Total (AW)	1	0	0	0	419

103 8/08 Ripn 6f (0-105)H G-S £37386
98 4/08 Ripn 6f (0-85)H G-S £4209
96 10/06 Curr 6f H HVY £28060
66 8/06 Gway 1m100y GD £8339
Total win prize-money £77995

Going (Turf): Sf: 1-5 **GS: 2-4** Gd: 1-9 GF: 0-2 Fm: 0-0
Distance: **5f/6f: 3-17** 7f-8f: 0-7 9f-13f: 1-2 14f+: 0-0
Track : LH: 0-2 **RH: 1-6** Tight: 0-0 Gall: 0-1
Aids: **Bl: 1-10** Vi: 0-0 Tstrap: 0-0 Ckp: 0-0

Best Rating: 103 8/08 Ripn 6f gd-sft

Useful; ex-Irish; best over 6f; acts on soft ground; has worn blinkers and a tongue tie; likes to race prominently.

Takaamul

95(102) (59)62

6-y-o ch g Almutawakel-Mafaatin (IRE) (Royal Academy (USA))
K A Morgan K A Morgan

Placings:356/00/000**202/1000-4025**20161 **(4665)**
2009: 8^{4}SD, 7^{0}SD, 6^{2}SD, 7^{5}SD, 8^{2}GF, 8^{0}SD, 7^{1}G, 7^{6}GF, 7^{1}G,

	Starts	1st	2nd	3rd	Win & Pl
Career Total (Turf)	12	2	1	1	7135
Career Total (AW)	12	1	3	0	4021

62 8/09 Yarm 7f3y (0-70)H GD £2849
58 6/09 Yarm 7f3y (0-60)H GD £2320
59 1/08 Kemp 1m (0-55)H STD £2047
Total win prize-money £7217

Going (Turf): Sf: 0-2 GS: 0-0 **Gd: 2-6** GF: 0-4 Fm: 0-0
Distance: 5f/6f: 0-4 **7f-8f: 3-18** 9f-13f: 0-2 14f+: 0-0
Track : LH: 0-12 **RH: 1-3** Tight: 0-8 Gall: 0-1
Aids: Bl: 0-0 Vi: 0-0 Tstrap: 0-1 Ckp: 0-1
Best Rating: 73 8/05 Curr 7f good

Moderate; effective over 7f-1m; acts on fast ground; goes on Polytrack.

Takaatuf (IRE)

109 91

3-y-o b g Dubai Destination (USA)-Karlaka (IRE) (Barathea (IRE))
M Johnston Hamdan Al Maktoum

Placings:051-31400000 **(6100)**
2009: 9^{3}GF, 10^{1}GF, 10^{4}GF, 12^{0}GF, 10^{0}G, 9^{0}G, 10^{0}GF, 11^{0}GF,

	Starts	1st	2nd	3rd	Win & Pl
Career Total (Turf)	11	2	0	1	19738

91 5/09 NmkR 1m2f (0-100)H G-F £12462
81 9/08 Pont 1m4y G-F £5180
Total win prize-money £17643

Going (Turf): Sf: 0-1 GS: 0-0 Gd: 0-3 **GF: 2-7** Fm: 0-0
Distance: 5f/6f: 0-1 7f-8f: 0-0 **9f-13f: 2-10** 14f+: 0-0
Track : **LH: 1-3** RH: 0-5 Tight: 0-3 Gall: 0-2
Aids: Bl: 0-0 Vi: 0-0 Tstrap: 0-0 Ckp: 0-0
Best Rating: 91 5/09 NmkR 1m2f gd-fm

Useful; stays 1m2f and acts on fast ground; likes to race prominently.

Takafu (USA)

106 (68)79

7-y-o b g Lemon Drop Kid (USA)-Proper Protocol (USA) (Deputy Minister (CAN))
W S Kittow Midd Shire Racing

Placings:50130/000521463**0/51621650/400** **(4988)**
2009: 16^{4}G, 14^{0}G, 13^{0}GF,

	Starts	1st	2nd	3rd	Win & Pl
Career Total (Turf)	25	4	2	2	29052
Career Total (AW)	1	0	0	0	

88 7/07 Sand 1m6f (0-85)H GD £6477
86 5/07 Wwck 1m6f213y (0-75)H G-S £3886
85 7/06 Wwck 1m6f213y (0-80)H G-F £6477
80 7/05 Pont 1m2f6y G-F £6240
Total win prize-money £23080

Going (Turf): Sf: 0-4 GS: 1-3 Gd: 1-10 **GF: 2-7** Fm: 0-1
Distance: 5f/6f: 0-0 7f-8f: 0-1 9f-13f: 1-8 **14f+: 3-17**
Track : **LH: 3-11** RH: 1-14 Tight: 0-9 Gall: 0-5

Aids: Bl: 0-0 Vi: 0-0 Tstrap: 0-0 Ckp: 0-0
Best Rating: 88 7/07 Sand 1m6f good

Fair; effective at up to 2m; acts on most ground.

Take It Easee (IRE)

103 (33)80

4-y-o b f Noverre (USA)-Fairy Lore (IRE) (Fairy King (USA))
Mrs Prunella Dobbs David M Fitzgerald

Placings:003544-502005031 **(7247)**
2009: 10^{5}GF, 10^{0}SD, 9^{2}HY, 9^{0}S, 8^{0}G, 7^{5}HY, 7^{0}G, 8^{3}Y, 10^{1}S,

	Starts	1st	2nd	3rd	Win & Pl
Career Total (Turf)	14	1	1	2	6028
Career Total (AW)	1	0	0	0	

80 11/09 Nott 1m2f50y (0-75)H SFT £2914
Total win prize-money £2914

Going (Turf): **Sf: 1-4** GS: 0-2 Gd: 0-3 GF: 0-4 Fm: 0-0
Distance: 5f/6f: 0-3 7f-8f: 0-6 **9f-13f: 1-6** 14f+: 0-0
Track : **LH: 1-9** RH: 0-3 Tight: 0-1 Gall: 0-0
Aids: Bl: 0-0 Vi: 0-0 Tstrap: 0-0 Ckp: 0-0
Best Rating: 80 11/09 Nott 1m2f50y soft

Modest; stays 1m2f; acts on fast and soft ground.

Take It There

(101) (47)47

7-y-o ch m Cadeaux Genereux-Feel Free (IRE) (Generous (IRE))
A J Lidderdale Entertainments Committee

Placings:00/065/**000010/0/30-0** **(6208)**
2009: 10^{0}SD,

	Starts	1st	2nd	3rd	Win & Pl
Career Total (Turf)	6	0	0	0	0
Career Total (AW)	9	1	0	1	2172

61 11/06 Sthl 1m (0-60)H STD £1977
Total win prize-money £1978

Going (Turf): **Sf: 0-1 GS: 0-0 Gd: 0-2 GF: 0-2 Fm: 0-1**
Distance: 5f/6f: 0-1 **7f-8f: 1-9** 9f-13f: 0-5 14f+: 0-0
Track : **LH: 1-9** RH: 0-3 Tight: 0-7 Gall: 0-1
Aids: Bl: 0-0 Vi: 0-0 Tstrap: 0-0 Ckp: 0-0
Best Rating: 66 9/05 Bath 1m5y firm

Moderate; stays 1m; acts on both All-Weather surfaces.

Take It To The Max

98 95

2-y-o b c Bahamian Bounty-Up And About (Barathea (IRE))
G M Moore Mrs Phillipa Davies

Placings:00321041 **(7184)**
2009: 5^{0}GF, 5^{0}GF, 6^{3}S, 6^{2}GF, 6^{1}GS, 7^{0}GF, 8^{4}S, 10^{1}G,

	Starts	1st	2nd	3rd	Win & Pl
Career Total (Turf)	8	2	1	1	17662

95 10/09 NmkR 1m2f GD £8723
81 7/09 Pont 6f G-S £5180
Total win prize-money £13904

Going (Turf): Sf: 0-2 **GS: 1-1 Gd: 1-1** GF: 0-4 Fm: 0-0
Distance: 5f/6f: 1-5 7f-8f: 0-1 9f-13f: 1-2 14f+: 0-0
Track : **LH: 1-3** RH: 0-0 Tight: 0-0 Gall: 0-1
Aids: Bl: 0-0 Vi: 0-0 Tstrap: 0-0 Ckp: 0-0
Best Rating: 95 10/09 NmkR 1m2f good

Fair; Bahamian Bounty half-sister to a UAE Oaks winner

and several other middle-distance winners; stays 6f; acts on fast and easy ground.

Take Me There

(108) (82)

6-y-o b g Cape Cross (IRE)-Mill Path (Mill Reef (USA))

Kevin O'Sullivan (John Berry 29/4) Leave Me There Syndicate

Placings:1-23 **(0325)**

2009: 12^{2}SD, 14^{3}SD,

	Starts	1st	2nd	3rd	Win & Pl
Career Total (Turf)	0	0	0	0	
Career Total (AW)	3	1	1	1	5042

71 12/08 Sthl 1m3f STD £2729

Total win prize-money £2730

Going (Turf): Sf: 0-0 GS: 0-0 Gd: 0-0 GF: 0-0 Fm: 0-0
Distance: 5f/6f: 0-0 7f-8f: 0-0 **9f-13f: 1-2** 14f+: 0-1
Track : **LH: 1-3** RH: 0-0 Tight: 0-0 Gall: 0-0
Aids: Bl: 0-0 Vi: 0-0 Tstrap: 0-0 Ckp: 0-0
Best Rating: 82 1/09 Sthl 1m4f stand

Fair; stays 1m4f and acts on Fibresand.

Take My Hand

91(88) (56)56

2-y-o ch f Imperial Dancer-Royal Logic (Royal Applause)

M R Channon Miss Bridget Coyle

Placings:06036 **(6590)**

2009: 5^{0}GF, 7^{6}GF, 7^{0}GF, 5^{3}SD, 6^{6}GS,

	Starts	1st	2nd	3rd	Win & Pl
Career Total (Turf)	4	0	0	0	0
Career Total (AW)	1	0	0	1	353

Going (Turf): Sf: 0-0 GS: 0-1 Gd: 0-0 GF: 0-3 Fm: 0-0
Distance: 5f/6f: 0-2 7f-8f: 0-3 9f-13f: 0-0 14f+: 0-0
Track : LH: 0-1 RH: 0-0 Tight: 0-1 Gall: 0-0
Aids: Bl: 0-0 Vi: 0-0 Tstrap: 0-0 Ckp: 0-0
Best Rating: 56 9/09 Wolv 5f216y stand

Take Ten

103 94

2-y-o b c Bahamian Bounty-See You Later (Emarati (USA))

M Johnston Sheikh Hamdan Bin Mohammed Al Maktoum

Placings:5211523 **(6478)**

2009: 5^{5}G, 5^{2}F, 5^{1}G, 6^{1}GF, 6^{5}GF, 6^{2}GF, 7^{3}GF,

	Starts	1st	2nd	3rd	Win & Pl
Career Total (Turf)	7	2	2	1	174165

90 8/09 Wwck 6f (0-85) G-F £5180
70 8/09 Thsk 5f GD £4274

Total win prize-money £9455

Going (Turf): Sf: 0-0 GS: 0-0 **Gd: 1-2 GF: 1-4** Fm: 0-1
Distance: **5f/6f: 2-5** 7f-8f: 0-2 9f-13f: 0-0 14f+: 0-0
Track : **LH: 1-2** RH: 0-0 Tight: 0-0 Gall: 0-1
Aids: Bl: 0-0 Vi: 0-0 Tstrap: 0-0 Ckp: 0-0
Best Rating: 94 10/09 NmkR 7f gd-fm

Very useful 210,000gns half-brother to amongst others the useful sprinter Aahayson; stays 6f; acts on good and fast ground.

Take That

78(66) 25

4-y-o b g Kasakov-Baby Be (Bold Arrangement)

S P Griffiths Thomas Grant

Placings:00-0000 **(7219)**

2009: 5^{0}GF, 5^{0}HY, 5^{0}GF, 5^{0}S,

	Starts	1st	2nd	3rd	Win & Pl
Career Total (Turf)	5	0	0	0	
Career Total (AW)	1	0	0	0	

Going (Turf): Sf: 0-2 GS: 0-1 Gd: 0-0 GF: 0-2 Fm: 0-0
Distance: 5f/6f: 0-5 7f-8f: 0-1 9f-13f: 0-0 14f+: 0-0
Track : LH: 0-2 RH: 0-0 Tight: 0-2 Gall: 0-0
Aids: Bl: 0-0 Vi: 0-0 Tstrap: 0-1 Ckp: 0-1
Best Rating: 25 4/09 Catt 5f212y gd-fm

Take The Hint

109 107

3-y-o b f Montjeu (IRE)-Insinuate (USA) (Mr Prospector (USA))

Mme C Head-Maarek (J H M Gosden 28/10) K Abdulla

Placings:01-16654 **(7347a)**

2009: 10^{1}GF, 12^{6}GF, 11^{6}GF, 10^{5}VS, 10^{4}VS,

	Starts	1st	2nd	3rd	Win & Pl
Career Total (Turf)	7	2	0	0	46753

106 5/09 NmkR 1m2f G-F £28385
86 10/08 Yarm 1m3y G-S £3532

Total win prize-money £31917

Going (Turf): Sf: 0-0 **GS: 1-1** Gd: 0-0 **GF: 1-4** Fm: 0-0
Distance: 5f/6f: 0-0 7f-8f: 0-1 **9f-13f: 2-6** 14f+: 0-0
Track : LH: 0-2 RH: 0-2 Tight: 0-0 Gall: 0-1
Aids: Bl: 0-0 Vi: 0-0 Tstrap: 0-0 Ckp: 0-0
Best Rating: 107 10/09 StCl 1m2f110y v soft

Smart; Listed winner; effective over 1m2f and acts on fast and easy ground.

Take The Micky

89(93) (69)69

3-y-o b g Beat Hollow-Ailincala (IRE) (Pursuit Of Love)

C F Wall (W J Knight 3/6) Botham, Dale, Nunns & Shopland

Placings:001-0000 **(7769)**

2009: 8^{0}SD, 8^{0}GF, 8^{0}SD, 8^{0}SD,

	Starts	1st	2nd	3rd	Win & Pl
Career Total (Turf)	3	0	0	0	
Career Total (AW)	4	1	0	0	1943

69 10/08 Ling 7f STD £1942

Total win prize-money £1943

Going (Turf): Sf: 0-0 GS: 0-0 Gd: 0-2 GF: 0-1 Fm: 0-0
Distance: 5f/6f: 0-0 **7f-8f: 1-7** 9f-13f: 0-0 14f+: 0-0
Track : **LH: 1-1** RH: 0-4 **Tight: 1-1** Gall: 0-0
Aids: Bl: 0-0 Vi: 0-0 Tstrap: 0-0 Ckp: 0-0
Best Rating: 69 4/09 Kemp 1m stand

Fair; stays 7f and acts on Polytrack.

Takeover Bid (USA)

(102) (84)70

3-y-o b g Empire Maker (USA)-Seba (Alzao (USA))

Niall O'Callaghan (M Johnston 30/3) Kilmichael Racing Syndicate

Placings:3610-16120006 **(7532a)**

2009: 6^{1}SS, 5^{6}SD, 6^{1}SD, 7^{2}SD, 8^{0}S, 8^{0}GY, 7^{0}SD, 10^{6}SD,

	Starts	1st	2nd	3rd	Win & Pl
Career Total (Turf)	4	0	0	1	722
Career Total (AW)	8	3	1	0	11817

84 3/09 Sthl 6f (0-85)H STD £4727
82 1/09 Sthl 6f (0-75)H SS £2729
73 11/08 Wolv 7f32y STD £2914

Total win prize-money £10371

Going (Turf): Sf: 0-1 GS: 0-1 Gd: 0-1 GF: 0-0 Fm: 0-0
Distance: **5f/6f: 2-3** 7f-8f: 1-6 9f-13f: 0-3 14f+: 0-0
Track : **LH: 3-10** RH: 0-1 **Tight: 1-4** Gall: 0-0
Aids: Bl: 0-2 Vi: 0-0 Tstrap: 0-0 Ckp: 0-0
Best Rating: 84 3/09 Ling 7f stand

Fair; effective over 6f-7f and acts on sand.

Takeover Target (AUS)

110 121

10-y-o b g Celtic Swing-Shady Stream (AUS) (Archregent (CAN))

Joe Janiak J & B Janiak

Placings:1111111/43024011/13113021/5214211/2312411-1100 **(3819)**

2009: 6^{1}GS, 6^{1}S, 6^{0}G, 6^{0}GF,

	Starts	1st	2nd	3rd	Win & Pl
Career Total (Turf)	41	21	6	4	2590934

120 5/09 Morp 6f H SFT £92888
121 4/09 Rand 6f G-S £146650
112 12/08 Asco 7f GD £35793
115 11/08 Asco 6f GD £107930
117 5/08 Kran 6f GD £201742
122 12/07 Rand 6f G-S £26209
12/07 Rand 6f G-S £26210
123 5/07 Doom 6f165y GD £170403
125 10/06 Naka 6f FRM £486039
124 6/06 Asct 5f G-F £113560
121 3/06 Flem 6f H GD £258547
115 2/06 Flem 5f GD £129274
12/05 Doom 6f165y GD £52694
12/05 Doom 6f GD £52694
115 10/04 Flem 6f GD £137395
7/04 Graf 6f GD £34685
6/04 Gsfd 6f GD £27731
6/04 Rose 6f GD £13655
5/04 Kens 7f GD £5462
5/04 Wagg 6f GD £3277
4/04 Quen 6f GD £1912

Total win prize-money £2124751

Going (Turf): Sf: 1-5 GS: 3-5 **Gd: 15-23** GF: 1-7 Fm: 1-1
Distance: **5f/6f: 17-33** 7f-8f: 4-8 9f-13f: 0-0 14f+: 0-0
Track : **LH: 3-5** RH: 1-1 Tight: 0-0 Gall: 0-0
Aids: Bl: 0-0 Vi: 0-0 Tstrap: 0-1 Ckp: 0-1
Best Rating: 125 10/06 Naka 6f firm

High-class; multiple winner at Group level in Australia; winner of the King's Stand Stakes in 2006 and runner-up in 2008; runner-up in Golden Jubilee Stakes in 2007; most effective over 5f-6f though has won over 7f; acts on good and faster ground; has worn cheekpieces.

Takitwo

99(103) (65)65

6-y-o b g Delta Dancer-Tiama (IRE) (Last Tycoon)

P D Cundell Miss M C Fraser

Placings:000/10011400/**45135135030030**/**00305362030-165255630000** **(6719)**

2009: 7^{1}SD, 7^{6}SD, 7^{5}SD, 8^{2}SD, 8^{5}SD, 8^{6}SD, 7^{6}SD, 6^{3}GF, 8^{0}SD, 8^{0}SD, 7^{0}SD, 8^{0}SD,

	Starts	1st	2nd	3rd	Win & Pl
Career Total (Turf)	22	4	0	5	16073
Career Total (AW)	26	2	2	3	7182

62 1/09 Kemp 7f (0-54)H STD £2047
69 6/07 Brig 6f209y (0-75)H G-F £2775

72 3/07 Kemp 7f (0-70)H STD £2817
74 8/06 Folk 7f (0-70)H G-F £3886
71 7/06 Folk 7f (0-60)H G-F £2730
64 6/06 Sals 6f212y (0-60)H GD £3238
Total win prize-money £17495

Going (Turf): Sf: 0-2 GS: 0-2 Gd: 1-8 **GF: 3-9** Fm: 0-1
Distance: 5f/6f: 0-1 **7f-8f: 6-46** 9f-13f: 0-1 14f+: 0-0
Track : LH: 1-10 **RH: 2-21** Tight: 0-7 Gall: 0-1
Aids: Bl: 0-2 **Vi: 1-6** Tstrap: 0-0 Ckp: 0-0
Best Rating: 74 8/06 Folk 7f gd-fm

Moderate; effective at around 7f; acts on fast ground; goes on Polytrack; has worn a visor.

Takizada (IRE)

91(85) (38)**80**
4-y-o b f Sendawar (IRE)-Takarouna (USA) (Green Dancer (USA))
J R Gask The Takizada Syndicate

Placings:2/23005-040 (5227)
2009: 8^{0}SD, 10^{4}HY, 12^{0}SF,

	Starts	1st	2nd	3rd	Win & Pl
Career Total (Turf)	7	0	2	1	12123
Career Total (AW)	2	0	0	0	

Going (Turf): Sf: 0-1 GS: 0-2 Gd: 0-3 GF: 0-0 Fm: 0-0
Distance: 5f/6f: 0-0 7f-8f: 0-2 9f-13f: 0-7 14f+: 0-0
Track : LH: 0-3 RH: 0-2 Tight: 0-2 Gall: 0-0
Aids: Bl: 0-0 Vi: 0-0 Tstrap: 0-0 Ckp: 0-0
Best Rating: 80 6/08 MsnL 1m good

Moderate; stays 1m2f; acts on soft ground.

Talamahana

93(96) (49)**48**
4-y-o b f Kyllachy-Bahawir Pour (USA) (Green Dancer (USA))
A B Haynes Mrs A De Weck & P De Weck

Placings:50000**0044/041313500**000**00**-400603P5330**002** (7592)
2009: 5^{4}GF, 6^{0}GF, 6^{0}GF, 5^{6}G, 5^{0}GF, 5^{3}G, 5^{P}GS, 5^{5}G, 5^{3}F, 5^{3}G, 5^{0}F, 6^{0}SD, 7^{0}SD, 7^{2}SD,

	Starts	1st	2nd	3rd	Win & Pl
Career Total (Turf)	19	0	0	3	912
Career Total (AW)	18	2	1	2	5131

60 2/08 Kemp 6f (0-55)H STD £2047
55 1/08 Wolv 7f32y (0-55)H STD £2047
Total win prize-money £4096

Going (Turf): Sf: 0-1 GS: 0-2 Gd: 0-5 GF: 0-9 Fm: 0-2
Distance: 5f/6f: 1-18 7f-8f: 1-18 9f-13f: 0-1 14f+: 0-0
Track : LH: 1-20 RH: 1-5 **Tight: 1-11** Gall: 0-8
Aids: **Bl: 2-11** Vi: 0-11 Tstrap: 0-2 Ckp: 0-2
Best Rating: 63 3/08 Ling 7f stand

Moderate; effective at around 6f-7f; acts on Polytrack; has worn a visor.

Talayeb

96(87) (44)**76**
4-y-o b/br g Nayef (USA)-Paper Chase (FR) (Machiavellian (USA))
M P Tregoning Hamdan Al Maktoum

Placings:044/40023-30 (4822)
2009: 8^{3}GF, 10^{0}GF,

	Starts	1st	2nd	3rd	Win & Pl
Career Total (Turf)	9	0	1	2	4614
Career Total (AW)	1	0	0	0	192

Going (Turf): Sf: 0-0 GS: 0-1 Gd: 0-2 GF: 0-6 Fm: 0-0
Distance: 5f/6f: 0-0 7f-8f: 0-5 9f-13f: 0-5 14f+: 0-0
Track : LH: 0-2 RH: 0-4 Tight: 0-4 Gall: 0-0
Aids: Bl: 0-1 Vi: 0-0 Tstrap: 0-1 Ckp: 0-1
Best Rating: 81 9/07 Newb 1m gd-fm

Fair; effective at around 1m; acts on fast ground; has worn cheekpieces/blinkers.

Talenti (IRE)

(88) (75)**96**
6-y-o b g Sadler's Wells (USA)-Sumoto (Mtoto)
Miss E C Lavelle Fraser Miller Racing

Placings:15/30-**0** (1007)
2009: 16^{0}SD,

	Starts	1st	2nd	3rd	Win & Pl
Career Total (Turf)	4	1	0	1	7595
Career Total (AW)	1	0	0	0	

85 5/06 Naas 1m2f Y-S £6195
Total win prize-money £6195

Going (Turf): Sf: 0-1 GS: 0-1 Gd: 0-1 GF: 0-0 Fm: 0-0
Distance: 5f/6f: 0-0 7f-8f: 0-0 **9f-13f: 1-2** 14f+: 0-3
Track : **LH: 1-2** RH: 0-3 Tight: 0-0 Gall: 0-1
Aids: Bl: 0-0 Vi: 0-0 Tstrap: 0-0 Ckp: 0-0
Best Rating: 96 4/08 Nott 1m6f15y gd-sft

Very useful; ex-Irish; missed the 2007 Flat season; suited by 1m2f and soft ground.

Taliesin

52 **14**
2-y-o br g Passing Glance-Silver Bird (IRE) (Vision (USA))
Mrs A M Thorpe Cwmbach Racing

Placings:000 (6331)
2009: 5^{0}G, 8^{0}GF, 10^{0}F,

	Starts	1st	2nd	3rd	Win & Pl
Career Total (Turf)	3	0	0	0	

Going (Turf): Sf: 0-0 GS: 0-0 Gd: 0-1 GF: 0-1 Fm: 0-1
Distance: 5f/6f: 0-1 7f-8f: 0-1 9f-13f: 0-1 14f+: 0-0
Track : LH: 0-2 RH: 0-0 Tight: 0-1 Gall: 0-1
Aids: Bl: 0-0 Vi: 0-0 Tstrap: 0-0 Ckp: 0-0
Best Rating: 14 9/09 Ffos 1m gd-fm

Talimos (IRE)

108 **80**
3-y-o b g Lomitas-Silvertone (FR) (Highest Honor (FR))
D E Pipe (R M Beckett 10/7) A E Frost

Placings:24106 (3827)
2009: 12^{2}GF, 11^{4}G, 11^{1}G, 16^{0}GF, 14^{6}G,

	Starts	1st	2nd	3rd	Win & Pl
Career Total (Turf)	5	1	1	0	4563

79 6/09 Brig 1m3f196y GD £3406
Total win prize-money £3406

Going (Turf): Sf: 0-0 GS: 0-0 **Gd: 1-3** GF: 0-2 Fm: 0-0
Distance: 5f/6f: 0-0 7f-8f: 0-0 **9f-13f: 1-3** 14f+: 0-2
Track : **LH: 1-3** RH: 0-2 Tight: 0-2 Gall: 0-2
Aids: Bl: 0-1 Vi: 0-0 Tstrap: 0-0 Ckp: 0-0
Best Rating: 80 6/09 Asct 2m gd-fm

Fair; stays 1m4f; acts on good/fast ground.

Talk Of Saafend (IRE)

102(99) (78)**83**
4-y-o b f Barathea (IRE)-Sopran Marida (IRE) (Darshaan)
P Monteith Dennis J Coppola

Placings:0**560**23201/20006124**1**113-00066652B63 (4896)
2009: 8^{0}GF, 7^{0}GF, 8^{0}GF, 9^{6}GS, 8^{6}G, 9^{6}G, 9^{5}GF, 9^{2}GF, 10^{B}GF, 9^{6}S, 8^{3}GS,

	Starts	1st	2nd	3rd	Win & Pl
Career Total (Turf)	28	4	5	3	50752
Career Total (AW)	4	1	0	0	2047

79 9/08 Haml 1m1f36y SFT £5180
65 9/08 Yarm 1m3y GD £3154
78 9/08 Kemp 1m STD £2047
76 7/08 Sals 1m G-F £3238
80 10/07 NmkR 7f G-F £18696
Total win prize-money £32316

Going (Turf): Sf: 1-4 GS: 0-4 Gd: 1-4 **GF: 2-15** Fm: 0-1
Distance: 5f/6f: 0-3 **7f-8f: 3-18** 9f-13f: 2-11 14f+: 0-0
Track : LH: 0-5 **RH: 2-15 Tight: 1-11** Gall: 0-2
Aids: Bl: 0-0 Vi: 0-0 Tstrap: 0-0 Ckp: 0-0
Best Rating: 83 9/08 Muss 1m good

Useful; stays 1m; acts on most ground and on Polytrack.

Talking Hands

91(99) (90)**100**
3-y-o b g Mujahid (USA)-With Distinction (Zafonic (USA))
S Kirk Deauville Daze Partnership

Placings:0211154536-000 (6106)
2009: 9^{0}SD, 7^{0}GF, 10^{0}GF,

	Starts	1st	2nd	3rd	Win & Pl
Career Total (Turf)	9	2	0	0	35054
Career Total (AW)	4	1	1	1	8438

96 7/08 Asct 7f G-F £17031
89 7/08 Asct 6f G-S £6476
79 6/08 Wolv 7f32y STD £3626
Total win prize-money £27134

Going (Turf): Sf: 0-1 **GS: 1-3** Gd: 0-2 **GF: 1-3** Fm: 0-0
Distance: 5f/6f: 1-3 **7f-8f: 2-8** 9f-13f: 0-2 14f+: 0-0
Track : **LH: 1-4** RH: 0-4 **Tight: 1-2** Gall: 0-3
Aids: Bl: 0-0 Vi: 0-0 Tstrap: 0-0 Ckp: 0-0
Best Rating: 100 8/08 Sand 7f16y good

Smart; Listed winner; effective from 6f-1m; acts on most surfaces, including Polytrack.

Tallawalla (IRE)

89 **67**
2-y-o b f Oratorio (IRE)-Edetana (USA) (Diesis)
M R Channon The Mystery Partnership

Placings:060 (5741)
2009: 7^{0}G, 7^{6}GF, 8^{0}GF,

	Starts	1st	2nd	3rd	Win & Pl
Career Total (Turf)	3	0	0	0	0

Going (Turf): Sf: 0-0 GS: 0-0 Gd: 0-1 GF: 0-2 Fm: 0-0
Distance: 5f/6f: 0-0 7f-8f: 0-3 9f-13f: 0-0 14f+: 0-0
Track : LH: 0-0 RH: 0-1 Tight: 0-0 Gall: 0-0
Aids: Bl: 0-0 Vi: 0-0 Tstrap: 0-0 Ckp: 0-0
Best Rating: 67 8/09 Folk 7f gd-fm

Tallest Peak (USA)

(102) (63)
4-y-o b g Giant's Causeway (USA)-Hum Along (USA) (Fappiano (USA))
M G Quinlan The Chicken On A Chain Partnership

Placings:00060330-0016 **(7802)**
2009: 8^0SD, 9^0SD, 7^1SD, 8^6SD,

	Starts	1st	2nd	3rd	Win & Pl
Career Total (Turf)	0	0	0	0	
Career Total (AW)	12	1	0	2	2297

63 12/09 Wolv 7f32y (0-50)H STD £1706
Total win prize-money £1706

Going (Turf): **Sf: 0-0 GS: 0-0 Gd: 0-0 GF: 0-0 Fm: 0-0**
Distance: 5f/6f: 0-0 **7f-8f: 1-7** 9f-13f: 0-5 14f+: 0-0
Track : **LH: 1-10** RH: 0-2 **Tight: 1-8** Gall: 0-1
Aids: **Bl: 1-2** Vi: 0-0 Tstrap: 0-0 Ckp: 0-0
Best Rating: **63** 12/09 Wolv 7f32y stand

Moderate; stays 1m; acts on Polytrack; has worn blinkers.

Tallulah Mai

(84) (59)
2-y-o b f Kayf Tara-Al Awaalah (Mukaddamah (USA))
Matthew Salaman M Salaman

Placings:0 **(7622)**
2009: 8^0SD,

	Starts	1st	2nd	3rd	Win & Pl
Career Total (Turf)	0	0	0	0	
Career Total (AW)	1	0	0	0	

Going (Turf): **Sf: 0-0 GS: 0-0 Gd: 0-0 GF: 0-0 Fm: 0-0**
Distance: 5f/6f: 0-0 7f-8f: 0-1 9f-13f: 0-0 14f+: 0-0
Track : LH: 0-1 RH: 0-0 Tight: 0-1 Gall: 0-0
Aids: Bl: 0-0 Vi: 0-0 Tstrap: 0-0 Ckp: 0-0
Best Rating: **59** 12/09 Ling 1m stand

Tallulah Sunrise

82(95) (58)24
4-y-o b f Auction House (USA)-Tallulah Belle (Crowning Honors (CAN))
M D I Usher Saxon House Racing

Placings:05433/3-006000000 **(5063)**
2009: 6^0SD, 7^0SD, 10^6SD, 10^0SD, 8^0SD, 8^0SD, 10^0GF, 7^0GS, 8^0GF,

	Starts	1st	2nd	3rd	Win & Pl
Career Total (Turf)	4	0	0	0	
Career Total (AW)	11	0	0	3	1277

Going (Turf): **Sf: 0-0 GS: 0-1 Gd: 0-0 GF: 0-3 Fm: 0-0**
Distance: 5f/6f: 0-4 7f-8f: 0-7 9f-13f: 0-4 14f+: 0-0
Track : LH: 0-10 RH: 0-3 Tight: 0-8 Gall: 0-2
Aids: Bl: 0-0 Vi: 0-0 Tstrap: 0-0 Ckp: 0-0
Best Rating: **69** 12/07 Ling 7f stand

Tallulah's Secret

80 23
3-y-o b f Bertolini (USA)-Ascend (IRE) (Glint Of Gold)
J Gallagher Woodmere Racing

Placings:000-6 **(1046)**
2009: 7^6G,

	Starts	1st	2nd	3rd	Win & Pl
Career Total (Turf)	4	0	0	0	0

Going (Turf): **Sf: 0-0 GS: 0-1 Gd: 0-1 GF: 0-2 Fm: 0-0**
Distance: 5f/6f: 0-2 7f-8f: 0-2 9f-13f: 0-0 14f+: 0-0
Track : LH: 0-1 RH: 0-0 Tight: 0-0 Gall: 0-0
Aids: Bl: 0-0 Vi: 0-0 Tstrap: 0-0 Ckp: 0-0
Best Rating: **23** 3/09 Folk 7f good

Talon (IRE)

83(92) (48)59
4-y-o ch g Indian Ridge-Brief Lullaby (IRE) (Brief Truce (USA))
G A Swinbank S S Anderson

Placings:0000/653651000-0 **(2389)**
2009: 6^0G,

	Starts	1st	2nd	3rd	Win & Pl
Career Total (Turf)	12	1	0	1	4223
Career Total (AW)	2	0	0	0	

59 8/08 Muss 1m (0-70)H GD £3885
Total win prize-money £3886

Going (Turf): Sf: 0-3 GS: 0-3 **Gd: 1-3** GF: 0-3 Fm: 0-0
Distance: 5f/6f: 0-1 **7f-8f: 1-9** 9f-13f: 0-4 14f+: 0-0
Track : LH: 0-5 **RH: 1-5 Tight: 1-4** Gall: 0-2
Aids: Bl: 0-1 Vi: 0-0 Tstrap: 1-4 Ckp: 1-4
Best Rating: **59** 8/08 Muss 1m good

Moderate; stays 1m and acts on fast ground; has worn blinkers/visor/tongue tie.

Talsarnau (IRE)

(87) (53)35
3-y-o b g Kheleyf (USA)-Ezilana (IRE) (Shardari)
W M Brisbourne W M Clare

Placings:000-500 **(0196)**
2009: 8^5SD, 9^0SD, 8^0SD,

	Starts	1st	2nd	3rd	Win & Pl
Career Total (Turf)	3	0	0	0	
Career Total (AW)	3	0	0	0	0

Going (Turf): **Sf: 0-0 GS: 0-0 Gd: 0-2 GF: 0-0 Fm: 0-1**
Distance: 5f/6f: 0-1 7f-8f: 0-2 9f-13f: 0-3 14f+: 0-0
Track : LH: 0-5 RH: 0-0 Tight: 0-5 Gall: 0-0
Aids: Bl: 0-0 Vi: 0-0 Tstrap: 0-0 Ckp: 0-0
Best Rating: **53** 1/09 Wolv 1m141y stand

Talulah Bells

(69) (14)42
3-y-o br f Superior Premium-Hullo Mary Doll (Lidhame)
A W Carroll A W Carroll

Placings:654464-5 **(0005)**
2009: 8^5SS,

	Starts	1st	2nd	3rd	Win & Pl
Career Total (Turf)	5	0	0	0	180
Career Total (AW)	2	0	0	0	0

Going (Turf): **Sf: 0-2 GS: 0-1 Gd: 0-1 GF: 0-1 Fm: 0-0**
Distance: 5f/6f: 0-5 7f-8f: 0-2 9f-13f: 0-0 14f+: 0-0
Track : LH: 0-4 RH: 0-0 Tight: 0-1 Gall: 0-1
Aids: Bl: 0-1 Vi: 0-0 Tstrap: 0-0 Ckp: 0-0
Best Rating: **42** 4/08 Wwck 5f soft

Tamaathul

102 84
2-y-o gr c Tiger Hill (IRE)-Tahrir (IRE) (Linamix (FR))
B W Hills Hamdan Al Maktoum

Placings:21 **(6990)**
2009: 8^2G, 7^1G,

	Starts	1st	2nd	3rd	Win & Pl
Career Total (Turf)	2	1	1	0	5978

84 10/09 Donc 7f GD £4533
Total win prize-money £4533

Going (Turf): Sf: 0-0 GS: 0-0 **Gd: 1-2** GF: 0-0 Fm: 0-0
Distance: 5f/6f: 0-0 **7f-8f: 1-2** 9f-13f: 0-0 14f+: 0-0
Track : LH: 0-0 RH: 0-0 Tight: 0-0 Gall: 0-0
Aids: Bl: 0-0 Vi: 0-0 Tstrap: 0-0 Ckp: 0-0
Best Rating: **84** 10/09 Donc 7f good

Useful first foal of a useful dual 7f winner; stays 1m; acts on good/easy ground

Tamagin (USA)

113(113) (109)114
6-y-o b g Stravinsky (USA)-Luia (USA) (Forty Niner (USA))
J Pearce (K A Ryan 27/6) Killarney Glen

Placings:6056040/510251215461030442 0/1122211/25003000-5230152012024120 **(6661)**
2009: 6^5SD, 7^2SD, 5^3SD, 6^0GF, 6^1GF, 6^5G, 6^2SD, 6^0GF, 6^1GF, 6^2G, 6^0S, 6^2GF, 6^4GF, 6^1GF, 6^2GF, 6^0GS,

	Starts	1st	2nd	3rd	Win & Pl
Career Total (Turf)	32	6	5	1	144166
Career Total (AW)	25	5	7	2	42868

113 9/09 Gdwd 6f G-F £22708
111 6/09 Wind 6f (0-105)H G-F £28039
106 4/09 Newc 6f (0-105)H G-F £11656
106 11/07 Ling 6f (0-95)H STD £7790
102 10/07 Donc 6f (0-100)H GD £15544
91 8/07 NmkJ 6f (0-85)H G-F £5181
87 7/07 Rdcr 6f (0-85)H G-S £6477
86 5/06 Ling 7f (0-80)H STD £5505
86 4/06 Ling 1m (0-75)H STD £3238
73 3/06 Ling 1m (0-70)H STD £3238
54 2/06 Ling 7f STD £2914
Total win prize-money £112297

Going (Turf): Sf: 0-3 GS: 1-5 Gd: 1-10 **GF: 4-12** Fm: 0-2
Distance: **5f/6f: 7-33** 7f-8f: 4-23 9f-13f: 0-1 14f+: 0-0
Track : **LH: 5-25** RH: 0-4 **Tight: 5-22** Gall: 1-2
Aids: Bl: 0-1 Vi: 0-0 Tstrap: 5-30 Ckp: 5-30
Best Rating: **114** 8/09 Ripn 6f gd-fm

Smart; Listed winner; effective over 6f-1m; acts on most ground and on Polytrack; has worn cheekpieces and blinkers; very much suited by forcing tactics.

Tamanaco (IRE)

88 74
2-y-o b g Catcher In The Rye (IRE)-Right After Moyne (IRE) (Imperial Ballet (IRE))
T D Walford Pedro Rosas

Placings:301 **(4067)**
2009: 6^3GS, 6^0GF, 6^1S,

	Starts	1st	2nd	3rd	Win & Pl
Career Total (Turf)	3	1	0	1	5111

74 7/09 Pont 6f SFT £4533
Total win prize-money £4533

Going (Turf): **Sf: 1-1** GS: 0-1 Gd: 0-0 GF: 0-1 Fm: 0-0
Distance: **5f/6f: 1-3** 7f-8f: 0-0 9f-13f: 0-0 14f+: 0-0
Track : **LH: 1-1** RH: 0-0 Tight: 0-0 Gall: 0-0
Aids: Bl: 0-0 Vi: 0-0 Tstrap: 0-0 Ckp: 0-0
Best Rating: **74** 7/09 Pont 6f soft

First foal of a half-sister to winners at 1m-1m4f; promise on debut over 6f on easy ground.

Tamarah

91 73

3-y-o b f Beat Hollow-Valagalore (Generous (IRE))

Miss D Mountain Al-Abdulmalik Hassan

Placings:0020-00 (4720)

2009: 9^{0}GS, 8^{0}G,

	Starts	1st	2nd	3rd	Win & Pl
Career Total (Turf)	6	0	1	0	1416

Going (Turf): Sf: 0-0 GS: 0-1 Gd: 0-3 GF: 0-2 Fm: 0-0
Distance: 5f/6f: 0-2 7f-8f: 0-2 9f-13f: 0-2 14f+: 0-0
Track : LH: 0-2 RH: 0-0 Tight: 0-1 Gall: 0-0
Aids: Bl: 0-0 Vi: 0-0 Tstrap: 0-0 Ckp: 0-0
Best Rating: 73 9/08 Yarm 7f3y good

Tamarind (IRE)

107 105

3-y-o b f Sadler's Wells (USA)-Sharata (IRE) (Darshaan)

A P O'Brien Mrs John Magnier & Mrs David Nagle

Placings:45115 (5201)

2009: 9^{4}HY, 10^{5}GY, 12^{1}YS, 12^{1}S, 12^{5}GF,

	Starts	1st	2nd	3rd	Win & Pl
Career Total (Turf)	5	2	0	0	72854

105	8/09	Cork	1m4f		SFT	£56873
75	7/09	Tipp	1m4f		Y-S	£7044

Total win prize-money £63918

Going (Turf): Sf: 1-2 GS: 0-0 Gd: 0-0 GF: 0-1 Fm: 0-0
Distance: 5f/6f: 0-0 7f-8f: 0-0 9f-13f: 2-5 14f+: 0-0
Track : LH: 1-3 RH: 1-2 Tight: 0-0 Gall: 0-1
Aids: Bl: 0-0 Vi: 0-0 Tstrap: 0-0 Ckp: 0-0
Best Rating: 105 8/09 Cork 1m4f soft

Smart; Group 3 winner in 2009; stays 1m4f; acts on soft ground.

Tamarind Hill (IRE)

80(97) (66)42

2-y-o b g Shamardal (USA)-Amandian (IRE) (Indian Ridge)

A J McCabe (C R Egerton 19/12) A C Timms

Placings:066042303 (7850)

2009: 6^{0}GF, 7^{5}SS, 7^{6}SD, 7^{0}SD, 7^{4}SD, 6^{2}SD, 5^{3}SD, 6^{0}SD, 5^{3}SS,

	Starts	1st	2nd	3rd	Win & Pl
Career Total (Turf)	1	0	0	0	
Career Total (AW)	8	0	1	2	1240

Going (Turf): Sf: 0-0 GS: 0-0 Gd: 0-0 GF: 0-1 Fm: 0-0
Distance: 5f/6f: 0-4 7f-8f: 0-5 9f-13f: 0-0 14f+: 0-0
Track : LH: 0-6 RH: 0-1 Tight: 0-6 Gall: 0-0
Aids: Bl: 0-4 Vi: 0-0 Tstrap: 0-1 Ckp: 0-1
Best Rating: 66 11/09 Ling 7f stand

Modest; stays 6f; acts on Polytrack; has worn blinkers.

Tamasou (IRE)

106(103) (83)83

4-y-o b g Tamarisk (IRE)-Soubresaut (IRE) (Danehill (USA))

A J McCabe (Garry Moss 31/7) Brooklands Racing

Placings:2423/4465412440-243012201025 (7759)

2009: 8^{2}G, 8^{4}G, 10^{3}GF, 8^{0}HY, 7^{1}SD, 7^{2}SD, 8^{2}SF, 7^{0}SS, 7^{1}S, 7^{0}S, 8^{2}SD, 8^{5}SD,

	Starts	1st	2nd	3rd	Win & Pl
Career Total (Turf)	16	2	3	1	12056
Career Total (AW)	10	1	4	1	7011

83	11/09	Catt	7f	(0-80)H	SFT	£5180
78	9/09	Kemp	7f	(0-65)H	STD	£2047
68	7/08	Muss	1m	(0-65)H	GD	£2590

Total win prize-money £9818

Going (Turf): Sf: 1-6 GS: 0-1 Gd: 1-7 GF: 0-2 Fm: 0-0
Distance: 5f/6f: 0-1 7f-8f: 3-14 9f-13f: 0-11 14f+: 0-0
Track : LH: 1-14 RH: 2-7 Tight: 2-9 Gall: 0-1
Aids: Bl: 0-0 Vi: 0-0 Tstrap: 0-0 Ckp: 0-0
Best Rating: 83 12/09 Wolv 1m141y stand

Fair; effective over 7f-1m; acts on easy ground; goes on Polytrack.

Tamimi's History

106(102) (89)92

5-y-o b g Kalanisi (IRE)-Polish Pink (IRE) (Polish Precedent (USA))

P D Evans Jim Ennis

Placings:324/231215/00-004 (1519)

2009: 9^{0}SD, 11^{0}SD, 16^{4}GF,

	Starts	1st	2nd	3rd	Win & Pl
Career Total (Turf)	12	2	3	2	21801
Career Total (AW)	2	0	0	0	

101	6/07	Leop	1m2f	(60-90)H	SFT	£7003
96	5/07	Rosc	1m4f		GD	£4668

Total win prize-money £11672

Going (Turf): Sf: 1-3 GS: 0-1 Gd: 1-4 GF: 0-2 Fm: 0-0
Distance: 5f/6f: 0-0 7f-8f: 0-5 9f-13f: 2-8 14f+: 0-1
Track : LH: 1-5 RH: 1-6 Tight: 0-2 Gall: 0-2
Aids: Bl: 0-0 Vi: 0-0 Tstrap: 0-0 Ckp: 0-0
Best Rating: 105 8/07 Gway 1m4f good

Useful; winner over hurdles; effective at up to 1m4f; acts on good and soft ground.

Taminas Desert

(91) (54)

4-y-o b f Green Desert (USA)-Tamise (USA) (Time For A Change (USA))

M Botti Mrs R J Jacobs

Placings:6-P (0678)

2009: 9^{P}SF,

	Starts	1st	2nd	3rd	Win & Pl
Career Total (Turf)	0	0	0	0	
Career Total (AW)	2	0	0	0	0

Going (Turf): Sf: 0-0 GS: 0-0 Gd: 0-0 GF: 0-0 Fm: 0-0
Distance: 5f/6f: 0-0 7f-8f: 0-0 9f-13f: 0-2 14f+: 0-0
Track : LH: 0-1 RH: 0-1 Tight: 0-1 Gall: 0-0
Aids: Bl: 0-0 Vi: 0-0 Tstrap: 0-0 Ckp: 0-0
Best Rating: 54 6/08 Kemp 1m2f stand

Tamino (IRE)

79(104) (62)67

6-y-o b g Mozart (IRE)-Stop Out (Rudimentary (USA))

P Howling Paul Howling

Placings:000/0361220/5043101320/060604005263-03600003162 (7880)

2009: 6^{0}SD, 6^{3}SD, 7^{6}SD, 5^{0}SD, 6^{0}GF, 7^{0}GF, 7^{0}SD, 8^{3}SD, 6^{1}SD, 8^{6}SD, 7^{2}SD,

	Starts	1st	2nd	3rd	Win & Pl
Career Total (Turf)	24	3	3	3	15069
Career Total (AW)	19	1	2	3	3519

58	12/09	Ling	6f	(0-55)H	STD	£1637
77	8/07	Newb	6f8y	(0-75)H	GD	£3238
71	7/07	Sals	6f	(0-75)H	G-F	£3123
66	8/06	Sand	5f6y	(0-75)H	G-F	£3238

Total win prize-money £11239

Going (Turf): Sf: 0-0 GS: 0-6 Gd: 1-7 GF: 2-11 Fm: 0-0
Distance: 5f/6f: 3-27 7f-8f: 1-15 9f-13f: 0-1 14f+: 0-0
Track : LH: 1-14 RH: 0-8 Tight: 1-8 Gall: 0-7
Aids: Bl: 0-0 Vi: 0-0 Tstrap: 0-0 Ckp: 0-0
Best Rating: 80 10/07 Brig 5f213y good

Moderate; just about stays 1m, also effective at shorter; acts on Polytrack.

Tammela

(89) (56)

2-y-o b f Beat Hollow-On The Wing (Pivotal)

A P Jarvis Grant & Bowman Limited

Placings:00 (6607)

2009: 8^{0}SD, 8^{0}SD,

	Starts	1st	2nd	3rd	Win & Pl
Career Total (Turf)	0	0	0	0	
Career Total (AW)	2	0	0	0	

Going (Turf): Sf: 0-0 GS: 0-0 Gd: 0-0 GF: 0-0 Fm: 0-0
Distance: 5f/6f: 0-0 7f-8f: 0-2 9f-13f: 0-0 14f+: 0-0
Track : LH: 0-0 RH: 0-2 Tight: 0-0 Gall: 0-0
Aids: Bl: 0-0 Vi: 0-0 Tstrap: 0-0 Ckp: 0-0
Best Rating: 56 10/09 Kemp 1m stand

Tampa Boy (IRE)

(98) (70)

7-y-o b g Montjeu (IRE)-Tirolean Dance (IRE) (Tirol)

M F Harris M Harris

Placings:56-446 (0333)

2009: 12^{4}SS, 16^{4}SD, 16^{6}SD,

	Starts	1st	2nd	3rd	Win & Pl
Career Total (Turf)	0	0	0	0	
Career Total (AW)	5	0	0	0	0

Going (Turf): Sf: 0-0 GS: 0-0 Gd: 0-0 GF: 0-0 Fm: 0-0
Distance: 5f/6f: 0-0 7f-8f: 0-0 9f-13f: 0-3 14f+: 0-2
Track : LH: 0-5 RH: 0-0 Tight: 0-3 Gall: 0-0
Aids: Bl: 0-1 Vi: 0-0 Tstrap: 0-0 Ckp: 0-0
Best Rating: 70 1/09 Wolv 2m119y stand

Tamtara

88(87) (61)64

2-y-o b f Red Ransom (USA)-Tamalain (USA) (Royal Academy (USA))

Mrs A J Perrett Mr & Mrs R Scott

Placings:066 (6781)

2009: 7^{0}GF, 8^{6}GF, 7^{6}SS,

	Starts	1st	2nd	3rd	Win & Pl
Career Total (Turf)	2	0	0	0	0
Career Total (AW)	1	0	0	0	0

Going (Turf): Sf: 0-0 GS: 0-0 Gd: 0-0 GF: 0-2 Fm: 0-0
Distance: 5f/6f: 0-0 7f-8f: 0-3 9f-13f: 0-0 14f+: 0-0
Track : LH: 0-1 RH: 0-1 Tight: 0-1 Gall: 0-0
Aids: Bl: 0-0 Vi: 0-0 Tstrap: 0-0 Ckp: 0-0
Best Rating: 64 9/09 Gdwd 1m gd-fm

Tan Bonita (USA)

87(93) (40)34

4-y-o b/br f More Than Ready (USA)-Time For Hennessy (USA) (Hennessy (USA))

R J Smith Pedro Rosas

Placings:310033/100364-300000 (7689)

2009: 5^{3}G, 6^{0}SD, 5^{0}F, 5^{0}GF, 6^{0}SD, 5^{0}SD,

	Starts	1st	2nd	3rd	Win & Pl
Career Total (Turf)	9	1	0	3	5361
Career Total (AW)	9	1	0	2	6185

3/08 Mija 6f110y STD £5147
73 5/07 Catt 5f FRM £2730

Total win prize-money £7877

Going (Turf): Sf: 0-1 GS: 0-0 Gd: 0-4 GF: 0-2 Fm: 1-2
Distance: 5f/6f: 1-15 7f-8f: 1-3 9f-13f: 0-0 14f+: 0-0
Track : LH: 0-3 RH: 0-1 Tight: 0-2 Gall: 0-2
Aids: Bl: 0-0 Vi: 0-0 Tstrap: 0-0 Ckp: 0-0
Best Rating: 73 5/07 Catt 5f firm

Moderate sprinter; Spanish-trained; suited by 5f and fast ground; suited by forcing tactics; has worn a tongue tie.

Tanfidh

102 94

3-y-o b f Marju (IRE)-Wijdan (USA) (Mr Prospector (USA))

M P Tregoning Hamdan Al Maktoum

Placings:02116 (6996)

2009: 8^{0}G, 11^{2}GF, 10^{1}F, 9^{1}G, 10^{6}GS,

	Starts	1st	2nd	3rd	Win & Pl
Career Total (Turf)	5	2	1	0	7763

94 10/09 Leic 1m1f218y (0-75)H GD £2914
79 9/09 Bath 1m2f46y FRM £3885

Total win prize-money £6800

Going (Turf): Sf: 0-0 GS: 0-1 Gd: 1-2 GF: 0-1 Fm: 1-1
Distance: 5f/6f: 0-0 7f-8f: 0-1 9f-13f: 2-4 14f+: 0-0
Track : LH: 1-2 RH: 1-3 Tight: 1-2 Gall: 0-1
Aids: Bl: 0-0 Vi: 0-0 Tstrap: 0-0 Ckp: 0-0
Best Rating: 94 10/09 Leic 1m1f218y good

Fair; effective at 1m2f-1m4f; acts on fast ground.

Tanforan

104(106) (70)71

7-y-o b g Mujahid (USA)-Florentynna Bay (Aragon)

B P J Baugh F Gillespie

Placings:03/355002103010100/64602202000000005200/505000061225/20530066430152634-000260115242566 (6217)

2009: 9^{0}SD, 8^{0}G, 8^{0}G, 8^{2}GF, 8^{6}GF, 8^{0}GS, 8^{1}GF, 8^{1}G, 8^{5}GF, 8^{2}S, 8^{4}HY, 8^{2}G, 9^{5}S, 8^{6}G, 8^{6}GF,

	Starts	1st	2nd	3rd	Win & Pl
Career Total (Turf)	51	6	7	3	36719
Career Total (AW)	29	1	5	3	9259

70 7/09 Nott 1m75y (0-70)H GD £2590
65 6/09 Wwck 1m22y (0-70)H G-F £2498
65 8/08 Hayd 1m30y (0-70)H G-S £3238
67 11/07 Wolv 7f32y (0-68)H STD £2968
81 7/05 Ches 7f122y (0-90)H GD £9787
77 7/05 Catt 7f (0-75)H GD £3554
71 5/05 Thsk 1m (0-75)H GD £4202

Total win prize-money £28838

Going (Turf): Sf: 0-8 GS: 1-8 Gd: 4-19 GF: 1-15 Fm: 0-1
Distance: 5f/6f: 0-8 7f-8f: 4-49 9f-13f: 3-23 14f+: 0-0
Track : LH: 7-50 RH: 0-16 Tight: 4-41 Gall: 0-2
Aids: Bl: 0-9 Vi: 0-0 Tstrap: 0-6 Ckp: 0-6
Best Rating: 87 5/06 Wind 6f gd-sft

Modest; effective at around 6f-1m; acts best on good ground; also goes on Polytrack.

Tangerine Trees

103(100) (73)79

4-y-o b g Mind Games-Easy To Imagine (USA) (Cozzene (USA))

B Smart Tangerine Trees Partnership

Placings:026300631534-3211100330 (7506)

2009: 5^{3}GF, 5^{2}GF, 6^{1}GF, 6^{1}GF, 6^{1}G, 6^{0}GF, 5^{0}GF, 7^{3}G, 7^{3}SD, 6^{0}SD,

	Starts	1st	2nd	3rd	Win & Pl
Career Total (Turf)	16	3	2	4	13637
Career Total (AW)	6	1	0	2	4274

79 7/09 Haml 6f5y (0-75)H GD £4533
72 6/09 Haml 6f5y (0-65)H G-F £2388
71 6/09 Haml 6f5y (0-70)H G-F £3238
65 10/08 Wolv 5f216y SF £3070

Total win prize-money £13230

Going (Turf): Sf: 0-1 GS: 0-2 Gd: 1-5 GF: 2-7 Fm: 0-1
Distance: 5f/6f: 1-17 7f-8f: 3-5 9f-13f: 0-0 14f+: 0-0
Track : LH: 1-8 RH: 0-1 Tight: 1-6 Gall: 0-0
Aids: Bl: 0-1 Vi: 0-3 Tstrap: 0-1 Ckp: 0-1
Best Rating: 79 7/09 Haml 6f5y good

Modest; effective at 5f-6f; acts on fast going and Polytrack.

Tango Step (IRE)

88(88) (40)45

9-y-o b g Sesaro (USA)-Leitrim Lodge (IRE) (Classic Music (USA))

D Carroll (Bernard Lawlor 7/6) Mrs Moira Behan

Placings:000000/002040600/0030000221/1631312446400/204304000365200/4000065/0060-0000005 (7723)

2009: 5^{0}SD, 5^{0}S, 7^{0}GF, 7^{0}SS, 5^{0}S, 5^{0}SD, 8^{5}SD,

	Starts	1st	2nd	3rd	Win & Pl
Career Total (Turf)	57	3	5	5	23114
Career Total (AW)	14	1	1	0	3191

63 7/05 Baln 6f (36-60)H G-F £4165
53 6/05 Bell 5f (36-60)H GD £4410
56 4/05 Navn 5f (36-60)H SH £4410
48 12/04 Ling 7f (0-45) STD £1568

Total win prize-money £14556

Going (Turf): Sf: 0-14 GS: 0-0 Gd: 1-12 GF: 1-10 Fm: 0-6
Distance: 5f/6f: 3-40 7f-8f: 1-25 9f-13f: 0-6 14f+: 0-0
Track : LH: 3-39 RH: 1-9 Tight: 1-8 Gall: 0-0
Aids: Bl: 0-4 Vi: 0-0 Tstrap: 0-13 Ckp: 0-13
Best Rating: 72 9/06 List 6f heavy

Moderate; best at about 1m; acts on Polytrack; has worn headgear.

Tanley

97(102) (60)59

4-y-o gr g Compton Admiral-Schatzi (Chilibang)

J F Coupland J F Coupland

Placings:45202040/0240060342103300-20003006 (7815)

2009: 5^{2}GF, 5^{0}SD, 5^{0}S, 5^{0}S, 5^{3}SD, 5^{0}SD, 5^{0}SD, 5^{6}SD,

	Starts	1st	2nd	3rd	Win & Pl
Career Total (Turf)	20	0	4	2	3698
Career Total (AW)	12	1	1	2	3841

57 10/08 GrLe 5f (0-50)H STD £2266

Total win prize-money £2267

Going (Turf): Sf: 0-4 GS: 0-4 Gd: 0-3 GF: 0-9 Fm: 0-0
Distance: 5f/6f: 1-31 7f-8f: 0-1 9f-13f: 0-0 14f+: 0-0
Track : LH: 1-11 RH: 0-2 Tight: 0-5 Gall: 1-2
Aids: Bl: 0-1 Vi: 0-0 Tstrap: 1-17 Ckp: 1-17
Best Rating: 62 10/07 Catt 5f212y good

Moderate; effective over 5f-6f; acts on most ground and on sand; has worn blinkers.

Tanoura (IRE)

108 109

3-y-o b f Dalakhani (IRE)-Takarouna (USA) (Green Dancer (USA))

John M Oxx H H Aga Khan

Placings:13-62133 (6504a)

2009: 9^{6}HY, 12^{2}G, 12^{1}GF, 14^{3}G, 12^{3}GS,

	Starts	1st	2nd	3rd	Win & Pl
Career Total (Turf)	7	2	1	3	65668

109 8/09 York 1m4f G-F £23704
81 8/08 Leop 7f HVY £9573

Total win prize-money £33278

Going (Turf): Sf: 1-2 GS: 0-1 Gd: 0-2 GF: 1-1 Fm: 0-0
Distance: 5f/6f: 0-0 7f-8f: 1-2 9f-13f: 1-4 14f+: 0-1
Track : LH: 2-3 RH: 0-4 Tight: 0-0 Gall: 1-3
Aids: Bl: 0-0 Vi: 0-0 Tstrap: 0-0 Ckp: 0-0
Best Rating: 109 10/09 Lonc 1m4f110y gd-sft

Smart; Irish trained; Listed winner; effective over 1m4f; acts on fast and heavy ground.

Tanto Faz (IRE)

109(100) (88)91

4-y-o b g Rock Of Gibraltar (IRE)-Sharakawa (IRE) (Darshaan)

J J Quinn (W J Haggas 12/10) Tanto Faz Partnership

Placings:21355-030030 (6724)

2009: 8^{0}GS, 8^{3}GF, 8^{0}G, 8^{0}SD, 12^{3}GF, 12^{0}SD,

	Starts	1st	2nd	3rd	Win & Pl
Career Total (Turf)	8	1	1	3	8864
Career Total (AW)	3	0	0	0	419

89 7/08 Hayd 1m30y GD £2752

Total win prize-money £2752

Going (Turf): Sf: 0-0 GS: 0-2 Gd: 1-3 GF: 0-3 Fm: 0-0
Distance: 5f/6f: 0-0 7f-8f: 0-2 9f-13f: 1-9 14f+: 0-0
Track : LH: 1-5 RH: 0-5 Tight: 0-2 Gall: 0-3
Aids: Bl: 0-0 Vi: 0-0 Tstrap: 0-0 Ckp: 0-0
Best Rating: 91 5/09 Ripn 1m gd-sft

Useful half-brother to four winners at distances from 7f to 1m4f; effective over 1m; acts on good ground.

Tanto Quanto (IRE)

86(92) (75)70

2-y-o b c Le Vie Dei Colori-Fear Not (IRE) (Alzao (USA))

W R Muir Mrs J M Muir

Placings:62106 (6491)

2009: 6^{6}G, 7^{2}G, 8^{1}SD, 8^{0}G, 8^{6}SD,

	Starts	1st	2nd	3rd	Win & Pl
Career Total (Turf)	3	0	1	0	578
Career Total (AW)	2	1	0	0	4209

75 8/09 Sthl 1m STD £4209

Total win prize-money £4209

Going (Turf): Sf: 0-0 GS: 0-0 Gd: 0-3 GF: 0-0 Fm: 0-0
Distance: 5f/6f: 0-1 7f-8f: 1-3 9f-13f: 0-1 14f+: 0-0
Track : LH: 1-3 RH: 0-0 Tight: 0-1 Gall: 0-0
Aids: Bl: 1-4 Vi: 0-0 Tstrap: 0-0 Ckp: 0-0
Best Rating: 75 8/09 Sthl 1m stand

Fair; stays 1m and acts on Fibresand; has worn blinkers.

Tantris (IRE)

(95) (68)**65**

4-y-o b g High Chaparral (IRE)-Emerald Cut (Rainbow Quest (USA))

Peter McCreery (J A Osborne 16/4) Mrs P D McCreery

Placings:5/500206-50 **(1314)**

2009: 12^{5}SD, 9^{0}SD,

	Starts	1st	2nd	3rd	Win & Pl
Career Total (Turf)	5	0	1	0	812
Career Total (AW)	4	0	0	0	0

Going (Turf): **Sf: 0-0 GS: 0-1 Gd: 0-1 GF: 0-3 Fm: 0-0**
Distance: 5f/6f: 0-1 7f-8f: 0-2 9f-13f: 0-6 14f+: 0-0
Track : LH: 0-5 RH: 0-3 Tight: 0-5 Gall: 0-1
Aids: Bl: 0-0 Vi: 0-0 Tstrap: 0-0 Ckp: 0-0
Best Rating: **68** 4/08 Wolv 7f32y stand

Tantsor (FR)

52(58)

2-y-o ch g Brier Creek (USA)-Norova (FR) (Hawker's News (IRE))

P T Midgley The French Bred Syndicate

Placings:000 **(7266)**

2009: 8^{0}F, 8^{0}GS, 8^{0}SD,

	Starts	1st	2nd	3rd	Win & Pl
Career Total (Turf)	2	0	0	0	
Career Total (AW)	1	0	0	0	

Going (Turf): **Sf: 0-0 GS: 0-1 Gd: 0-0 GF: 0-0 Fm: 0-1**
Distance: 5f/6f: 0-0 7f-8f: 0-2 9f-13f: 0-1 14f+: 0-0
Track : LH: 0-2 RH: 0-1 Tight: 0-0 Gall: 0-1
Aids: Bl: 0-0 Vi: 0-0 Tstrap: 0-0 Ckp: 0-0

Tap Dance Way (IRE)

(83) (50)

2-y-o b f Azamour (IRE)-Dance Lively (USA) (Kingmambo (USA))

P R Chamings Mrs Alexandra J Chandris

Placings:0 **(6164)**

2009: 7^{0}SD,

	Starts	1st	2nd	3rd	Win & Pl
Career Total (Turf)	0	0	0	0	
Career Total (AW)	1	0	0	0	

Going (Turf): **Sf: 0-0 GS: 0-0 Gd: 0-0 GF: 0-0 Fm: 0-0**
Distance: 5f/6f: 0-0 7f-8f: 0-1 9f-13f: 0-0 14f+: 0-0
Track : LH: 0-0 RH: 0-1 Tight: 0-0 Gall: 0-0
Aids: Bl: 0-0 Vi: 0-0 Tstrap: 0-0 Ckp: 0-0
Best Rating: **50** 9/09 Kemp 7f stand

Tapas Lad (IRE)

74(100) (62)**57**

4-y-o b c Modigliani (USA)-Missish (Mummy's Pet)

G J Smith Graham Smith

Placings:00063333305/3154644602531000056026-00000 **(2333)**

2009: 9^{0}SD, 9^{0}SD, 8^{0}SD, 9^{0}SD, 9^{0}GF,

	Starts	1st	2nd	3rd	Win & Pl
Career Total (Turf)	10	0	0	2	688
Career Total (AW)	29	2	2	5	6392

58	5/08	GrLe	1m2f	(0-55)	STD	£1774
61	1/08	Wolv	1m141y		STD	£1774

Total win prize-money £3549

Going (Turf): **Sf: 0-3 GS: 0-3 Gd: 0-2 GF: 0-2 Fm: 0-0**
Distance: 5f/6f: 0-2 7f-8f: 0-13 **9f-13f: 2-24** 14f+: 0-0
Track : **LH: 2-29** RH: 0-5 Tight: 1-19 Gall: 1-5
Aids: Bl: 0-1 **Vi: 2-31** Tstrap: 0-0 Ckp: 0-0
Best Rating: **62** 1/08 Wolv 1m1f103y stand

Moderate; stays 1m2f; acts on easy ground and sand; has worn a visor.

Taper Jean Girl (IRE)

(92) (65)

2-y-o b f Elusive City (USA)-Ruacana Falls (USA) (Storm Bird (CAN))

Mrs R A Carr (M Botti 17/11) Michael Hill

Placings:40041046 **(7756)**

2009: 7^{4}SD, 8^{0}SD, 7^{0}SD, 7^{4}SD, 7^{1}SD, 7^{0}SD, 8^{4}SD, 7^{6}SD,

	Starts	1st	2nd	3rd	Win & Pl
Career Total (Turf)	0	0	0	0	
Career Total (AW)	8	1	0	0	2480

55	11/09	Sthl	7f	STD	£2047

Total win prize-money £2047

Going (Turf): **Sf: 0-0 GS: 0-0 Gd: 0-0 GF: 0-0 Fm: 0-0**
Distance: 5f/6f: 0-0 **7f-8f: 1-8** 9f-13f: 0-0 14f+: 0-0
Track : **LH: 1-6** RH: 0-2 Tight: 0-2 Gall: 0-0
Aids: Bl: 0-0 Vi: 0-0 Tstrap: 0-0 Ckp: 0-0
Best Rating: **65** 9/09 Kemp 7f stand

Modest; effective over 7f; acts on Fibresand.

Tapis Wizard

100 **76**

3-y-o b g Alhaarth (IRE)-Just Call Me (NZ) (Blues Traveller (IRE))

M W Easterby Bamford Trading & U C Developments

Placings:53640-053032 **(4280)**

2009: 8^{0}GS, 8^{5}GS, 12^{3}S, 12^{0}GS, 10^{3}GS, 12^{2}G,

	Starts	1st	2nd	3rd	Win & Pl
Career Total (Turf)	11	0	1	3	4399

Going (Turf): **Sf: 0-3 GS: 0-5 Gd: 0-1 GF: 0-2 Fm: 0-0**
Distance: 5f/6f: 0-2 7f-8f: 0-4 9f-13f: 0-5 14f+: 0-0
Track : LH: 0-6 RH: 0-1 Tight: 0-3 Gall: 0-3
Aids: Bl: 0-0 Vi: 0-0 Tstrap: 0-0 Ckp: 0-0
Best Rating: **76** 7/08 York 6f heavy

Modest; effective at 1m4f; acts on fast and easy ground.

Tappanappa (IRE)

69 **14**

2-y-o b c High Chaparral (IRE)-Itsibitsi (IRE) (Brief Truce (USA))

A M Balding McMahon/Gorell/Pausewang

Placings:0 **(7029)**

2009: 8^{0}S,

	Starts	1st	2nd	3rd	Win & Pl
Career Total (Turf)	1	0	0	0	

Going (Turf): **Sf: 0-1 GS: 0-0 Gd: 0-0 GF: 0-0 Fm: 0-0**
Distance: 5f/6f: 0-0 7f-8f: 0-1 9f-13f: 0-0 14f+: 0-0
Track : LH: 0-0 RH: 0-0 Tight: 0-0 Gall: 0-0
Aids: Bl: 0-0 Vi: 0-0 Tstrap: 0-0 Ckp: 0-0
Best Rating: **14** 10/09 Newb 1m soft

Taqdeyr

108(109) (105)**106**

4-y-o ch g Dubai Destination (USA)-Pastorale (Nureyev (USA))

M A Jarvis Richie Baines & Stephen Dartnell

Placings:521-11526013 **(6487)**

2009: 7^{1}SD, 7^{1}SD, 7^{5}GF, 6^{2}GF, 7^{6}G, 7^{0}G, 7^{1}G, 7^{3}GF,

	Starts	1st	2nd	3rd	Win & Pl
Career Total (Turf)	8	1	2	1	19270
Career Total (AW)	3	3	0	0	14810

103	8/09	Wwck	7f26y		GD	£7771
103	4/09	Kemp	7f	(0-95)H	STD	£7352
105	4/09	Kemp	7f	(0-85)H	STD	£4727
88	11/08	Sthl	7f		STD	£2729

Total win prize-money £22581

Going (Turf): Sf: 0-1 GS: 0-0 **Gd: 1-4** GF: 0-3 Fm: 0-0
Distance: 5f/6f: 0-2 **7f-8f: 4-8** 9f-13f: 0-1 14f+: 0-0
Track : LH: 2-4 RH: 2-2 Tight: 0-0 Gall: 0-1
Aids: Bl: 0-0 Vi: 0-0 Tstrap: 0-0 Ckp: 0-0
Best Rating: **106** 7/09 Hayd 6f gd-fm

Very useful; stays 7f; acts on good/fast ground and on sand.

Taqleed (IRE)

80 **42**

2-y-o b/br c Shamardal (USA)-Thakafaat (IRE) (Unfuwain (USA))

J H M Gosden Hamdan Al Maktoum

Placings:0 **(6617)**

2009: 8^{0}G,

	Starts	1st	2nd	3rd	Win & Pl
Career Total (Turf)	1	0	0	0	

Going (Turf): **Sf: 0-0 GS: 0-0 Gd: 0-1 GF: 0-0 Fm: 0-0**
Distance: 5f/6f: 0-0 7f-8f: 0-1 9f-13f: 0-0 14f+: 0-0
Track : LH: 0-0 RH: 0-0 Tight: 0-0 Gall: 0-0
Aids: Bl: 0-0 Vi: 0-0 Tstrap: 0-0 Ckp: 0-0
Best Rating: **42** 10/09 Newb 1m good

Tar (IRE)

18(93) (55)**79**

5-y-o b g Danzig (USA)-Royal Show (IRE) (Sadler's Wells (USA))

John A Harris (Francis Ennis 24/4) Mrs A E Harris

Placings:045040300/030000 **(7499)**

2009: 10^{0}S, 11^{3}SD, 8^{0}SD, 9^{0}SD, 12^{0}SD, 8^{0}SD,

	Starts	1st	2nd	3rd	Win & Pl
Career Total (Turf)	10	0	0	1	1564
Career Total (AW)	5	0	0	1	385

Going (Turf): **Sf: 0-4 GS: 0-0 Gd: 0-1 GF: 0-3 Fm: 0-0**
Distance: 5f/6f: 0-0 7f-8f: 0-6 9f-13f: 0-9 14f+: 0-0
Track : LH: 0-11 RH: 0-2 Tight: 0-1 Gall: 0-0
Aids: Bl: 0-5 Vi: 0-5 Tstrap: 0-0 Ckp: 0-0
Best Rating: **79** 6/07 Leop 1m1f good

Tara's Garden

93(84) (41)**61**

4-y-o b f Dr Fong (USA)-Tremiere (FR) (Anabaa (USA))

M Blanshard T Wellman & Partners

Placings:00/2404060-00000 (4376)
2009: 8^{0}GF, 10^{0}G, 12^{0}GF, 8^{0}GF, 8^{0}SD,

	Starts	1st	2nd	3rd	Win & Pl
Career Total (Turf)	11	0	1	0	1069
Career Total (AW)	3	0	0	0	

Going (Turf): Sf: 0-4 GS: 0-2 Gd: 0-1 GF: 0-4 Fm: 0-0
Distance: 5f/6f: 0-0 7f-8f: 0-3 9f-13f: 0-11 14f+: 0-0
Track : LH: 0-6 RH: 0-3 Tight: 0-4 Gall: 0-0
Aids: Bl: 0-2 Vi: 0-0 Tstrap: 0-0 Ckp: 0-0
Best Rating: 61 7/08 Ling 1m1f soft

Taran Tregarth

(71) (42)34
5-y-o b m Tobougg (IRE)-Little Change (Grundy)
W M Brisbourne Stephen Jones

Placings:006000**2000**/50**500**/6 (0240)
2009: 12^{6}SD,

	Starts	1st	2nd	3rd	Win & Pl
Career Total (Turf)	6	0	0	0	0
Career Total (AW)	10	0	1	0	806

Going (Turf): Sf: 0-1 GS: 0-1 Gd: 0-1 GF: 0-3 Fm: 0-0
Distance: 5f/6f: 0-2 7f-8f: 0-4 9f-13f: 0-9 14f+: 0-1
Track : LH: 0-15 RH: 0-0 Tight: 0-11 Gall: 0-0
Aids: Bl: 0-4 Vi: 0-0 Tstrap: 0-1 Ckp: 0-1
Best Rating: 42 10/07 Wolv 1m4f50y stand

Tarawa Atoll

83(98) (57)48
3-y-o b f Imperial Dancer-Musical Capers (Piccolo)
Miss Sheena West (M R Channon 31/5) The Stewkley Shindiggers & Janet Menzies

Placings:024453640-3500 (2515)
2009: 8^{3}SD, 7^{5}SD, 8^{0}SD, 8^{0}F,

	Starts	1st	2nd	3rd	Win & Pl
Career Total (Turf)	5	0	1	1	790
Career Total (AW)	8	0	0	1	545

Going (Turf): Sf: 0-1 GS: 0-1 Gd: 0-2 GF: 0-0 Fm: 0-1
Distance: 5f/6f: 0-3 7f-8f: 0-6 9f-13f: 0-4 14f+: 0-0
Track : LH: 0-11 RH: 0-1 Tight: 0-6 Gall: 0-3
Aids: Bl: 0-0 Vi: 0-0 Tstrap: 0-0 Ckp: 0-0
Best Rating: 57 11/08 GrLe 1m stand

Targs (IRE)

72 17
3-y-o b c Elusive City (USA)-Cannikin (IRE) (Lahib (USA))
Peter Grayson Haldane Racing

Placings:00 (4425)
2009: 7^{0}GS, 7^{0}S,

	Starts	1st	2nd	3rd	Win & Pl
Career Total (Turf)	2	0	0	0	

Going (Turf): Sf: 0-1 GS: 0-1 Gd: 0-0 GF: 0-0 Fm: 0-0
Distance: 5f/6f: 0-0 7f-8f: 0-2 9f-13f: 0-0 14f+: 0-0
Track : LH: 0-1 RH: 0-0 Tight: 0-1 Gall: 0-0
Aids: Bl: 0-0 Vi: 0-0 Tstrap: 0-0 Ckp: 0-0
Best Rating: 17 7/09 Catt 7f gd-sft

Tariq

106 119
5-y-o ch h Kyllachy-Tatora (Selkirk (USA))
P W Chapple-Hyam Saleh Al Homaizi & Imad Al Sagar

Placings:13/501115/305-6060 (6848)
2009: 8^{6}S, 7^{0}G, 7^{6}GF, 7^{0}G,

	Starts	1st	2nd	3rd	Win & Pl
Career Total (Turf)	15	4	0	2	190205

118	7/07	Gdwd	7f	GD	£85170
117	6/07	Asct	7f	G-F	£36907
109	5/07	NmkR	7f	G-F	£15330
92	5/06	NmkR	6f	SFT	£4533

Total win prize-money £141942

Going (Turf): Sf: 1-3 GS: 0-0 Gd: 1-5 **GF: 2-7** Fm: 0-0
Distance: 5f/6f: 1-2 **7f-8f: 3-13** 9f-13f: 0-0 14f+: 0-0
Track : LH: 0-1 **RH: 1-3** Tight: 0-0 Gall: 0-0
Aids: Bl: 0-0 Vi: 0-0 Tstrap: 0-0 Ckp: 0-0
Best Rating: 119 5/08 Newb 1m good

Group class; won Group 3 Jersey Stakes at Ascot at three, also the Group 2 Lennox Stakes; effective over 6f-7f but seems to get a mile; acts best on fast ground but handles soft.

Tarita (IRE)

99 74
2-y-o ch f Bahamian Bounty-Zonic (Zafonic (USA))
R Hannon De La Warr Racing

Placings:4410 (5797)
2009: 6^{4}GF, 5^{4}GF, 5^{1}G, 6^{0}GF,

	Starts	1st	2nd	3rd	Win & Pl
Career Total (Turf)	4	1	0	0	5788

74	8/09	Bevl	5f	GD	£5018

Total win prize-money £5019

Going (Turf): Sf: 0-0 GS: 0-0 **Gd: 1-1** GF: 0-3 Fm: 0-0
Distance: **5f/6f: 1-3** 7f-8f: 0-1 9f-13f: 0-0 14f+: 0-0
Track : LH: 0-0 RH: 0-0 Tight: 0-0 Gall: 0-0
Aids: Bl: 0-0 Vi: 0-0 Tstrap: 0-0 Ckp: 0-0
Best Rating: 74 8/09 Bevl 5f good

Fair; effective at 5-6f; acts on fast ground.

Tarkamara (IRE)

(102) (58)61
5-y-o ch m Medicean-Tarakana (USA) (Shahrastani (USA))
P F I Cole A H Robinson

Placings:240/0**222**50/000**13**-**324** (0211)
2009: 9^{3}SD, 8^{2}SD, 8^{4}SD,

	Starts	1st	2nd	3rd	Win & Pl
Career Total (Turf)	8	0	2	0	2533
Career Total (AW)	9	1	3	2	5721

51	12/08	Ling	1m	(0-45)	STD	£2183

Total win prize-money £2184

Going (Turf): Sf: 0-0 GS: 0-0 Gd: 0-4 GF: 0-3 Fm: 0-1
Distance: 5f/6f: 0-8 **7f-8f: 1-7** 9f-13f: 0-2 14f+: 0-0
Track : **LH: 1-7** RH: 0-4 **Tight: 1-4** Gall: 0-2
Aids: Bl: 0-1 Vi: 0-0 Tstrap: 0-0 Ckp: 0-0
Best Rating: 78 4/06 NmkR 5f gd-fm

Moderate; effective over 6f and stays 1m2f; acts on Polytrack; has worn a tongue tie.

Tarqua (IRE)

86 44
3-y-o b f King Charlemagne (USA)-Shining Creek (CAN) (Bering)

R Hannon Lord Carnarvon

Placings:00000 (4223)
2009: 6^{0}GF, 6^{0}GF, 8^{0}GF, 9^{0}GF, 5^{0}G,

	Starts	1st	2nd	3rd	Win & Pl
Career Total (Turf)	5	0	0	0	

Going (Turf): Sf: 0-0 GS: 0-0 Gd: 0-1 GF: 0-4 Fm: 0-0
Distance: 5f/6f: 0-1 7f-8f: 0-3 9f-13f: 0-1 14f+: 0-0
Track : LH: 0-2 RH: 0-0 Tight: 0-1 Gall: 0-1
Aids: Bl: 0-0 Vi: 0-0 Tstrap: 0-0 Ckp: 0-0
Best Rating: 44 6/09 Sals 6f212y gd-fm

Tarraad

47(51)
3-y-o b g Selkirk (USA)-Mingora (USA) (Mtoto)
M Botti Enrico Massi

Placings:00 (1286)
2009: 10^{0}G, 12^{0}SD,

	Starts	1st	2nd	3rd	Win & Pl
Career Total (Turf)	1	0	0	0	
Career Total (AW)	1	0	0	0	

Going (Turf): Sf: 0-0 GS: 0-0 Gd: 0-1 GF: 0-0 Fm: 0-0
Distance: 5f/6f: 0-0 7f-8f: 0-0 9f-13f: 0-2 14f+: 0-0
Track : LH: 0-1 RH: 0-1 Tight: 0-0 Gall: 0-1
Aids: Bl: 0-0 Vi: 0-0 Tstrap: 0-0 Ckp: 0-0

Tarrants Way

83(82) (51)51
2-y-o b c Auction House (USA)-Thicket (Wolfhound (USA))
Jennie Candlish P and Mrs G A Clarke

Placings:0430000 (5935)
2009: 6^{0}S, 5^{4}SD, 5^{3}G, 5^{0}S, 5^{0}G, 5^{0}G, 7^{0}GF,

	Starts	1st	2nd	3rd	Win & Pl
Career Total (Turf)	6	0	0	1	482
Career Total (AW)	1	0	0	0	0

Going (Turf): Sf: 0-2 GS: 0-0 Gd: 0-3 GF: 0-1 Fm: 0-0
Distance: 5f/6f: 0-6 7f-8f: 0-1 9f-13f: 0-0 14f+: 0-0
Track : LH: 0-1 RH: 0-1 Tight: 0-0 Gall: 0-1
Aids: Bl: 0-0 Vi: 0-0 Tstrap: 0-1 Ckp: 0-1
Best Rating: 51 6/09 Carl 5f good

Modest; suited by 5f and fast ground.

Tarruji (IRE)

86(85) (70)60
3-y-o gr g Verglas (IRE)-Polish Affair (IRE) (Polish Patriot (USA))
P Monfort (Mme G Rarick 1/8) F Sabban

Placings:040-05053305
2009: 5^{0}SD, 5^{5}G, 5^{0}SD, 7^{5}SD, 9^{3}SD, 9^{3}SD, 9^{0}G, 9^{5}SD,

	Starts	1st	2nd	3rd	Win & Pl
Career Total (Turf)	4	0	0	0	536
Career Total (AW)	7	0	0	2	8009

Going (Turf): Sf: 0-0 GS: 0-1 Gd: 0-3 GF: 0-0 Fm: 0-0
Distance: 5f/6f: 0-4 7f-8f: 0-3 9f-13f: 0-4 14f+: 0-0
Track : LH: 0-3 RH: 0-2 Tight: 0-2 Gall: 0-0
Aids: Bl: 0-1 Vi: 0-0 Tstrap: 0-0 Ckp: 0-0
Best Rating: 70 10/09 Deau 1m1f110y stand

Tartan Bearer (IRE)

116 125

4-y-o ch c Spectrum (IRE)-Highland Gift (IRE) (Generous (IRE))

Sir Michael Stoute Ballymacoll Stud

Placings:2/1123-122 (4298)

2009: 10^{1}G, 10^{2}GF, 12^{2}G,

	Starts	1st	2nd	3rd	Win & Pl
Career Total (Turf)	**8**	**3**	**4**	**1**	**843787**

120	4/09	Sand	1m2f7y	GD	£36900
119	5/08	York	1m2f88y	G-F	£85155
73	4/08	Leic	1m1f218y	G-S	£2590

Total win prize-money £124646

Going (Turf): Sf: 0-0 **GS: 1-1 Gd: 1-4 GF: 1-2** Fm: 0-0
Distance: 5f/6f: 0-0 7f-8f: 0-1 **9f-13f: 3-7** 14f+: 0-0
Track : LH: 1-2 **RH: 2-5** Tight: 0-1 **Gall: 1-3**
Aids: Bl: 0-0 Vi: 0-0 Tstrap: 0-0 Ckp: 0-0
Best Rating: **125** 7/09 Asct 1m4f good

Group class; winner of the Group 2 Dante Stakes and runner-up in the Derby in 2008; finished second in the 2009 King George; effective from 1m2f-1m4f; handles most ground.

Tartan Gigha (IRE)

110(108) (96)99

4-y-o b g Green Desert (USA)-High Standard (Kris)

M Johnston Mrs I Bird

Placings:00321604-12620120100040202 (6480)

2009: 7^{1}SD, 8^{2}SD, 7^{6}GF, 8^{2}SD, 8^{0}G, 8^{1}GF, 8^{2}GF, 8^{0}GS, 8^{1}G, 7^{0}GF, 8^{0}GF, 8^{0}G, 8^{4}GS, 7^{0}GF, 8^{2}SD, 8^{0}GF, 9^{2}GF,

	Starts	1st	2nd	3rd	Win & Pl
Career Total (Turf)	**19**	**3**	**3**	**0**	**61014**
Career Total (AW)	**6**	**1**	**3**	**1**	**14935**

97	6/09	Epsm	1m114y	(0-105)H	GD	£18693
94	5/09	Bevl	1m100y	(0-85)H	G-F	£4759
88	3/09	Kemp	7f	(0-85)H	STD	£4727
82	7/08	Carl	6f192y		FRM	£2590

Total win prize-money £30770

Going (Turf): Sf: 0-1 GS: 0-4 **Gd: 1-4 GF: 1-9 Fm: 1-1**
Distance: 5f/6f: 0-0 7f-8f: 2-18 9f-13f: 2-7 14f+: 0-0
Track : LH: 1-8 **RH: 3-11 Tight: 1-6** Gall: 0-4
Aids: Bl: 0-0 Vi: 0-0 Tstrap: 0-0 Ckp: 0-0
Best Rating: **99** 10/09 NmkR 1m1f gd-fm

Useful; effective over 7f-1m; acts on good and faster ground and on Polytrack.

Tartan Gunna

105(105) (84)96

3-y-o b g Anabaa (USA)-Embraced (Pursuit Of Love)

M Johnston Mrs I Bird

Placings:022-113125505154 (6665)

2009: 7^{1}SD, 8^{1}SD, 7^{3}SD, 7^{1}GF, 7^{2}GF, 7^{5}GF, 7^{5}G, 8^{0}GF, 8^{5}SD, 9^{1}GF, 8^{5}GF, 10^{4}GS,

	Starts	1st	2nd	3rd	Win & Pl
Career Total (Turf)	**9**	**2**	**1**	**0**	**24878**
Career Total (AW)	**6**	**2**	**2**	**1**	**10249**

95	9/09	Gdwd	1m1f	(0-100)H	G-F	£11215
93	4/09	Bevl	7f100y	(0-90)H	G-F	£7641
84	2/09	Ling	1m	(0-85)H	STD	£4857
78	1/09	Wolv	7f32y		STD	£2729

Total win prize-money £26445

Going (Turf): Sf: 0-1 GS: 0-1 Gd: 0-1 **GF: 2-6** Fm: 0-0
Distance: 5f/6f: 0-0 **7f-8f: 3-13** 9f-13f: 1-2 14f+: 0-0
Track : LH: 2-10 RH: 2-3 **Tight: 3-6** Gall: 0-3
Aids: Bl: 0-0 Vi: 0-0 Tstrap: 0-0 Ckp: 0-0
Best Rating: **96** 9/09 Asct 1m gd-fm

Useful; effective over 7f-1m1f; acts on fast ground; goes on sand; likes to race prominently.

Tartan Trip

96(94) (77)80

2-y-o b g Selkirk (USA)-Marajuana (Robellino (USA))

A M Balding Kingsclere Racing CLub

Placings:443 (6943)

2009: 6^{4}G, 7^{4}GF, 7^{3}SD,

	Starts	1st	2nd	3rd	Win & Pl
Career Total (Turf)	**2**	**0**	**0**	**0**	**996**
Career Total (AW)	**1**	**0**	**0**	**1**	**578**

Going (Turf): **Sf: 0-0 GS: 0-0 Gd: 0-1 GF: 0-1 Fm: 0-0**
Distance: 5f/6f: 0-1 7f-8f: 0-2 9f-13f: 0-0 14f+: 0-0
Track : LH: 0-0 RH: 0-1 Tight: 0-0 Gall: 0-0
Aids: Bl: 0-0 Vi: 0-0 Tstrap: 0-0 Ckp: 0-0
Best Rating: **80** 10/09 NmkR 7f gd-fm

Tartan Turban (IRE)

(90) (51)65

3-y-o b c Invincible Spirit (IRE)-Tappen Zee (Sandhurst Prince)

R Hannon R Hannon

Placings:0100400-00 (0231)

2009: 5^{0}SD, 8^{0}SD,

	Starts	1st	2nd	3rd	Win & Pl
Career Total (Turf)	**4**	**1**	**0**	**0**	**2730**
Career Total (AW)	**5**	**0**	**0**	**0**	**0**

65	7/08	Wind	6f	GD	£2729

Total win prize-money £2730

Going (Turf): Sf: 0-1 GS: 0-1 **Gd: 1-2** GF: 0-0 Fm: 0-0
Distance: **5f/6f: 1-7** 7f-8f: 0-2 9f-13f: 0-0 14f+: 0-0
Track : LH: 0-5 RH: 0-1 Tight: 0-4 **Gall: 1-1**
Aids: Bl: 0-0 Vi: 0-0 Tstrap: 0-0 Ckp: 0-0
Best Rating: **65** 7/08 Wind 6f good

Fair half-brother to Paco Boy; effective at 6f; acts on good ground.

Tartatartufata

105(105) (70)72

7-y-o b m Tagula (IRE)-It's So Easy (Shaadi (USA))

J G Given Peter Swann

Placings:0400200/3312211160560/000631120/3450001 3231/10500435030006-03225052030003 (7852)

2009: 5^{0}SS, 5^{3}HY, 5^{2}F, 5^{2}G, 5^{5}GF, 5^{0}HY, 5^{5}SD, 6^{2}S, 5^{0}S, 5^{3}S, 5^{0}SD, 5^{0}SD, 5^{0}SD, 5^{3}SS,

	Starts	1st	2nd	3rd	Win & Pl
Career Total (Turf)	**31**	**2**	**5**	**4**	**18635**
Career Total (AW)	**38**	**7**	**3**	**7**	**42147**

89	1/08	Sthl	5f	(0-85)H	STD	£4210
91	1/08	Sthl	5f	(0-100)H	STD	£10525
81	11/07	Wolv	5f20y	(0-70)H	STD	£2968
83	11/06	Wolv	5f20y	(0-65)H	STD	£2730
77	11/06	Wolv	5f20y	(0-75)H	SF	£3238
81	6/05	Ayr	5f	(0-85)H	G-S	£6713
79	6/05	Wolv	5f20y	(0-70)H	STD	£5486
65	4/05	Catt	5f	(0-60)H	SFT	£2909
66	3/05	Sthl	5f	(0-70)H	STD	£3396

Total win prize-money £42177

Going (Turf): **Sf: 1-10 GS: 1-9** Gd: 0-9 GF: 0-2 Fm: 0-1
Distance: **5f/6f: 9-69** 7f-8f: 0-0 9f-13f: 0-0 14f+: 0-0
Track : **LH: 4-21** RH: 0-1 **Tight: 4-19** Gall: 0-3
Aids: Bl: 0-1 **Vi: 9-58** Tstrap: 0-0 Ckp: 0-0
Best Rating: **91** 2/08 Ling 5f stand

Modest formerly useful; suited by 5f but stays 6f; acts on sand; handles soft turf; wears a visor; suited by forcing tactics.

Tartufo Dolce (IRE)

70(98) (71)57

2-y-o b f Key Of Luck (USA)-Corn Futures (Nomination)

J G Given Danethorpe Racing Partnership

Placings:44515 (7636)

2009: 5^{4}GF, 5^{4}SD, 5^{5}SF, 5^{1}SD, 5^{5}SD,

	Starts	1st	2nd	3rd	Win & Pl
Career Total (Turf)	**1**	**0**	**0**	**0**	**192**
Career Total (AW)	**4**	**1**	**0**	**0**	**4126**

71	11/09	Wolv	5f20y	STD	£3885

Total win prize-money £3886

Going (Turf): **Sf: 0-0 GS: 0-0 Gd: 0-0 GF: 0-1 Fm: 0-0**
Distance: **5f/6f: 1-5** 7f-8f: 0-0 9f-13f: 0-0 14f+: 0-0
Track : **LH: 1-3** RH: 0-0 **Tight: 1-3** Gall: 0-0
Aids: Bl: 0-0 Vi: 0-0 Tstrap: 0-0 Ckp: 0-0
Best Rating: **71** 11/09 Wolv 5f20y stand

Fair; effective over 5f; acts on Polytrack.

Tarus (IRE)

94 (12)52

5-y-o ch m Tagula (IRE)-Wasaif (IRE) (Lomond (USA))

A Berry Alan Berry

Placings:0/400640-000546000 (6410)

2009: 6^{0}GF, 5^{0}GF, 6^{0}GF, 5^{0}GF, 6^{5}GF, 5^{4}GF, 5^{6}GS, 5^{0}GF, 5^{0}GS, 5^{0}GF,

	Starts	1st	2nd	3rd	Win & Pl
Career Total (Turf)	**16**	**0**	**0**	**0**	**1075**
Career Total (AW)	**1**	**0**	**0**	**0**	

Going (Turf): **Sf: 0-1 GS: 0-2 Gd: 0-0 GF: 0-9 Fm: 0-1**
Distance: 5f/6f: 0-11 7f-8f: 0-6 9f-13f: 0-0 14f+: 0-0
Track : LH: 0-5 RH: 0-1 Tight: 0-1 Gall: 0-0
Aids: Bl: 0-0 Vi: 0-0 Tstrap: 0-0 Ckp: 0-0
Best Rating: **52** 7/08 Naas 6f yield

Tarzan (IRE)

107 86

3-y-o ch g Spinning World (USA)-Run To Jane (IRE) (Doyoun)

M Johnston Highclere Thoroughbred Racing(Persimmon)

Placings:534-42120045460 (6680)

2009: 9^{4}GF, 8^{2}GF, 9^{1}F, 8^{2}GF, 10^{0}G, 8^{0}GF, 8^{4}G, 8^{5}GF, 8^{4}GF, 8^{6}GF, 10^{0}G,

	Starts	1st	2nd	3rd	Win & Pl
Career Total (Turf)	**14**	**1**	**2**	**1**	**6123**

79	5/09	Rdcr	1m1f	(0-75)H	FRM	£2590

Total win prize-money £2590

Going (Turf): Sf: 0-0 GS: 0-1 Gd: 0-3 GF: 0-9 **Fm: 1-1**
Distance: 5f/6f: 0-0 7f-8f: 0-6 **9f-13f: 1-8** 14f+: 0-0
Track : **LH: 1-5** RH: 0-4 **Tight: 1-4** Gall: 0-1
Aids: Bl: 0-2 Vi: 0-0 Tstrap: 0-0 Ckp: 0-0
Best Rating: **86** 5/09 Newc 1m3y gd-fm

Fair; effective at 1m-1m2f and acts on fast ground; likes to race prominently.

Tasheba

100(107) (91)**91**

4-y-o ch g Dubai Destination (USA)-Tatanka (IRE) (Lear Fan (USA))

N J Henderson Terry Benson

Placings:001/423113-4 **(3143)**

2009: 21^{4}GF,

	Starts	1st	2nd	3rd	Win & Pl
Career Total (Turf)	9	2	1	2	12686
Career Total (AW)	1	1	0	0	2590

88	7/08	Wwck	1m6f213y (0-75)H	G-F	£3885
91	6/08	GrLe	1m6f (0-75)H	STD	£2590
73	10/07	Yarm	7f3y	G-S	£3238

Total win prize-money £9715

Going (Turf): Sf: 0-2 **GS: 1-2** Gd: 0-3 **GF: 1-2** Fm: 0-0
Distance: 5f/6f: 0-0 7f-8f: 1-2 9f-13f: 0-3 **14f+: 2-5**
Track : **LH: 2-6** RH: 0-2 Tight: 0-0 **Gall: 1-3**
Aids: Bl: 0-0 Vi: 0-0 Tstrap: 0-0 Ckp: 0-0
Best Rating: **91** 8/08 Nott 1m6f15y soft

Useful; stays 1m7f; acts on most ground and on Polytrack; winning hurdler.

Tashkandi (IRE)

(100) (69)**84**

9-y-o gr g Polish Precedent (USA)-Tashiriya (IRE) (Kenmare (FR))

Mrs S J Humphrey Mrs S J Humphrey

Placings:4/1132/06/010/**6-00** **(0528)**

2009: 12^{0}SD, 12^{0}SD,

	Starts	1st	2nd	3rd	Win & Pl
Career Total (Turf)	9	3	1	1	44569
Career Total (AW)	4	0	0	0	0

84	6/06	Chep	1m2f36y (0-75)H	G-S	£3368
110	5/03	Chan	1m	G-S	£13312
	5/03	Lonc	1m110y	G-S	£7143

Total win prize-money £23823

Going (Turf): Sf: 0-1 **GS: 3-4** Gd: 0-1 GF: 0-3 Fm: 0-0
Distance: 5f/6f: 0-0 7f-8f: 1-3 **9f-13f: 2-9** 14f+: 0-1
Track : LH: 1-6 RH: 1-5 Tight: 0-3 Gall: 0-1
Aids: Bl: 0-2 Vi: 0-0 Tstrap: 0-0 Ckp: 0-0
Best Rating: **113** 7/03 Deau 1m gd-sft

Useful performer; previously trained in France; best at around ten furlongs on easy ground.

Tashzara (IRE)

97 **85**

2-y-o ch f Intikhab (USA)-Sun Shower (IRE) (Indian Ridge)

Christopher Phillips E Joseph Logan

Placings:326 **(7187)**

2009: 7^{3}GF, 8^{2}GY, 8^{6}G,

	Starts	1st	2nd	3rd	Win & Pl
Career Total (Turf)	3	0	1	1	3562

Going (Turf): **Sf: 0-0 GS: 0-0 Gd: 0-1 GF: 0-1 Fm: 0-0**
Distance: 5f/6f: 0-0 7f-8f: 0-3 9f-13f: 0-0 14f+: 0-0
Track : LH: 0-1 RH: 0-1 Tight: 0-0 Gall: 0-0
Aids: Bl: 0-0 Vi: 0-0 Tstrap: 0-0 Ckp: 0-0
Best Rating: **85** 10/09 Navn 1m gd-yld

Useful half-sister to dual 7f-1m winner Mull Of Killough; effective over 1m; acts on easy ground.

Tasmeem (IRE)

100 **83**

2-y-o gr c Acclamation-Park Approach (IRE) (Indian Ridge)

B W Hills Hamdan Al Maktoum

Placings:5210 **(5658)**

2009: 6^{5}HY, 6^{2}G, 6^{1}GF, 6^{0}GS,

	Starts	1st	2nd	3rd	Win & Pl
Career Total (Turf)	4	1	1	0	5331

83	8/09	Ripn	6f	G-F	£3885

Total win prize-money £3886

Going (Turf): Sf: 0-1 GS: 0-1 Gd: 0-1 **GF: 1-1** Fm: 0-0
Distance: **5f/6f: 1-2** 7f-8f: 0-2 9f-13f: 0-0 14f+: 0-0
Track : LH: 0-0 RH: 0-0 Tight: 0-0 Gall: 0-0
Aids: Bl: 0-0 Vi: 0-0 Tstrap: 0-0 Ckp: 0-0
Best Rating: **83** 8/09 Ripn 6f gd-fm

Useful 135,000gns purchase; related to plenty of winners; stays 6f; acts on a sound surface.

Tastahil (IRE)

114(109) (94)**114**

5-y-o ch g Singspiel (IRE)-Luana (Shaadi (USA))

B W Hills Hamdan Al Maktoum

Placings:616/0/223203-131320 **(7293)**

2009: 12^{1}G, 12^{3}S, 13^{1}S, 16^{3}G, 12^{2}S, 12^{0}S,

	Starts	1st	2nd	3rd	Win & Pl
Career Total (Turf)	14	2	4	3	86764
Career Total (AW)	2	1	0	1	5654

114	5/09	Newb	1m5f61y	SFT	£22708
110	3/09	Donc	1m4f	GD	£12952
76	9/06	Kemp	1m	STD	£4533

Total win prize-money £40194

Going (Turf): **Sf: 1-7** GS: 0-1 **Gd: 1-4** GF: 0-2 Fm: 0-0
Distance: 5f/6f: 0-0 7f-8f: 1-4 9f-13f: 1-10 14f+: 1-2
Track : **LH: 2-8** RH: 1-4 Tight: 0-0 **Gall: 2-9**
Aids: Bl: 0-0 Vi: 0-0 Tstrap: 0-0 Ckp: 0-0
Best Rating: **114** 5/09 Newb 1m5f61y soft

Group class; effective at 1m4f-2m; acts on most ground and on Polytrack.

Taste Of Honey (IRE)

88(97) (60)**39**

3-y-o b f Deportivo-Long Tall Sally (IRE) (Danehill Dancer (IRE))

D W P Arbuthnot Noel Cronin

Placings:00-5100000 **(3741)**

2009: 7^{5}SD, 7^{1}SD, 6^{0}F, 5^{0}GF, 7^{0}SD, 8^{0}SD, 9^{0}GF,

	Starts	1st	2nd	3rd	Win & Pl
Career Total (Turf)	4	0	0	0	
Career Total (AW)	5	1	0	0	2047

55	4/09	Ling	7f	STD	£2047

Total win prize-money £2047

Going (Turf): **Sf: 0-0 GS: 0-0 Gd: 0-0 GF: 0-3 Fm: 0-1**
Distance: 5f/6f: 0-3 **7f-8f: 1-5** 9f-13f: 0-1 14f+: 0-0
Track : **LH: 1-4** RH: 0-3 **Tight: 1-2** Gall: 0-2
Aids: Bl: 0-0 Vi: 0-0 Tstrap: 0-0 Ckp: 0-0
Best Rating: **60** 4/09 Kemp 7f stand

Modest; stays 7f and acts on Polytrack.

Taste The Victory (USA)

101 **76**

2-y-o b g Victory Gallop (CAN)-Tastetheteardrops (USA) (What Luck (USA))

G A Swinbank Mrs T Blackett

Placings:22 **(7116)**

2009: 7^{2}G, 8^{2}GS,

	Starts	1st	2nd	3rd	Win & Pl
Career Total (Turf)	2	0	2	0	3334

Going (Turf): **Sf: 0-0 GS: 0-1 Gd: 0-1 GF: 0-0 Fm: 0-0**
Distance: 5f/6f: 0-0 7f-8f: 0-2 9f-13f: 0-0 14f+: 0-0
Track : LH: 0-1 RH: 0-1 Tight: 0-1 Gall: 0-1
Aids: Bl: 0-0 Vi: 0-0 Tstrap: 0-0 Ckp: 0-0
Best Rating: **76** 10/09 York 7f good

Taste The Wine (IRE)

105(101) (67)**74**

3-y-o gr g Verglas (IRE)-Azia (IRE) (Desert Story (IRE))

J S Moore Jimmy & Susie Wenman

Placings:00000-040110505604242 **(7831)**

2009: 8^{0}GF, 10^{4}GS, **11^{0}SD**, 12^{1}GF, 14^{1}GF, 14^{0}S, 14^{5}GF, 12^{0}G, 14^{5}G, 13^{6}G, 12^{0}GF, 14^{4}GF, **12^{2}SD**, **12^{4}SD**, 12^{2}SD,

	Starts	1st	2nd	3rd	Win & Pl
Career Total (Turf)	16	2	0	0	4857
Career Total (AW)	4	0	2	0	806

74	6/09	Nott	1m6f15y (0-70)H	G-F	£2590
64	5/09	Chep	1m4f23y (0-60)H	G-F	£2266

Total win prize-money £4857

Going (Turf): Sf: 0-1 GS: 0-2 Gd: 0-5 **GF: 2-8** Fm: 0-0
Distance: 5f/6f: 0-0 7f-8f: 0-4 9f-13f: 1-10 14f+: 1-6
Track : **LH: 2-12** RH: 0-4 Tight: 0-6 Gall: 0-1
Aids: Bl: 0-0 Vi: 0-0 Tstrap: 0-0 Ckp: 0-0
Best Rating: **74** 6/09 Nott 1m6f15y gd-fm

Modest; effective over 1m4f-1m6f; acts on fast ground; goes on Polytrack.

Tatawor (IRE)

66(90) (71)**25**

2-y-o b g Kheleyf (USA)-Romea (Muhtarram (USA))

M P Tregoning Hamdan Al Maktoum

Placings:03 **(4537)**

2009: 6^{0}G, 5^{3}SD,

	Starts	1st	2nd	3rd	Win & Pl
Career Total (Turf)	1	0	0	0	
Career Total (AW)	1	0	0	1	496

Going (Turf): **Sf: 0-0 GS: 0-0 Gd: 0-1 GF: 0-0 Fm: 0-0**
Distance: 5f/6f: 0-2 7f-8f: 0-0 9f-13f: 0-0 14f+: 0-0
Track : LH: 0-1 RH: 0-0 Tight: 0-1 Gall: 0-0
Aids: Bl: 0-0 Vi: 0-0 Tstrap: 0-0 Ckp: 0-0
Best Rating: **71** 8/09 Ling 5f stand

Tatiana Romanova (USA)

102(93) (61)**74**

2-y-o ch f Mr Greeley (USA)-Bank On Her (USA) (Rahy (USA))

R A Fahey Martin M Dempsey

Placings:241 (7114)
2009: 6^{2}G, 6^{4}SD, 7^{1}GS,

	Starts	1st	2nd	3rd	Win & Pl
Career Total (Turf)	2	1	1	0	5042
Career Total (AW)	1	0	0	0	337

74 10/09 Muss 7f30y G-S £3885
Total win prize-money £3886

Going (Turf): Sf: 0-0 **GS: 1-1** Gd: 0-1 GF: 0-0 Fm: 0-0
Distance: 5f/6f: 0-1 **7f-8f: 1-2** 9f-13f: 0-0 14f+: 0-0
Track : LH: 0-0 **RH: 1-2 Tight: 1-1** Gall: 0-0
Aids: Bl: 0-0 Vi: 0-0 Tstrap: 0-0 Ckp: 0-0
Best Rating: **74** 10/09 Muss 7f30y gd-sft

Fair filly; effective at 7f; goes well on easy ground.

Tattercoats (FR)

85(80) (44)**24**
3-y-o b f Whywhywhy (USA)-Driscilla (USA) (Stately Don (USA))
M Botti D J Erwin & Templeton Stud

Placings:050-0 (5905)
2009: 8^{0}F,

	Starts	1st	2nd	3rd	Win & Pl
Career Total (Turf)	1	0	0	0	
Career Total (AW)	3	0	0	0	0

Going (Turf): **Sf: 0-0 GS: 0-0 Gd: 0-0 GF: 0-0 Fm: 0-1**
Distance: 5f/6f: 0-1 7f-8f: 0-2 9f-13f: 0-1 14f+: 0-0
Track : LH: 0-3 RH: 0-1 Tight: 0-2 Gall: 0-1
Aids: Bl: 0-0 Vi: 0-0 Tstrap: 0-0 Ckp: 0-0
Best Rating: **44** 12/08 GrLe 1m stand

Taurus Twins

103(100) (64)**82**
3-y-o b g Deportivo-Intellibet One (Compton Place)
R J Price G E Amey

Placings:0460-60210012152025210 (7395)
2009: 5^{6}SD, 6^{0}SD, 5^{2}SD, 5^{1}SD, 5^{0}SD, 5^{6}GF, 5^{1}GF, 6^{2}F, 6^{1}GF, 5^{5}G, 5^{2}GS, 6^{0}G, 5^{2}GS, 5^{5}G, 5^{2}GF, 5^{1}G, 6^{0}SD,

	Starts	1st	2nd	3rd	Win & Pl
Career Total (Turf)	14	3	4	0	12456
Career Total (AW)	7	1	1	0	2818

80 10/09 Nott 5f13y (0-75)H GD £2266
72 5/09 Nott 6f15y (0-70)H G-F £2590
69 5/09 Muss 5f (0-65)H G-F £2266
62 3/09 Sthl 5f (0-65)H STD £2047
Total win prize-money £9171

Going (Turf): Sf: 0-0 GS: 0-2 Gd: 1-6 **GF: 2-5** Fm: 0-1
Distance: **5f/6f: 3-20** 7f-8f: 1-1 9f-13f: 0-0 14f+: 0-0
Track : LH: 0-5 RH: 0-1 Tight: 0-2 Gall: 0-1
Aids: **Bl: 3-12** Vi: 0-0 Tstrap: 0-0 Ckp: 0-0
Best Rating: **82** 10/09 Pont 5f gd-fm

Fair; effective at 5f-6f; acts on fast ground but prefers give underfoot; goes on Fibresand and Polytrack.

Tawaabb

105 **99**
2-y-o ch c Kyllachy-Penmayne (Inchinor)
M R Channon Sheikh Ahmed Al Maktoum

Placings:213055 (6660)
2009: 5^{2}GF, 5^{1}G, 5^{3}GF, 6^{0}G, 5^{5}GS, 5^{5}GS,

	Starts	1st	2nd	3rd	Win & Pl
Career Total (Turf)	6	1	1	1	17080

87 5/09 Leic 5f2y GD £4857
Total win prize-money £4857

Going (Turf): Sf: 0-0 GS: 0-2 **Gd: 1-2** GF: 0-2 Fm: 0-0
Distance: **5f/6f: 1-6** 7f-8f: 0-0 9f-13f: 0-0 14f+: 0-0
Track : LH: 0-0 RH: 0-0 Tight: 0-0 Gall: 0-1
Aids: Bl: 0-0 Vi: 0-0 Tstrap: 0-0 Ckp: 0-0
Best Rating: **99** 10/09 Asct 5f gd-sft

Very useful; Group 2 placed stays 5f and should stay 6f; acts on good/fast ground.

Tax Dodger (IRE)

62(87) (26)**55**
3-y-o b g Catcher In The Rye (IRE)-Stonor Lady (USA) (French Deputy (USA))
Liam McAteer Gary Whearty

Placings:6050-0000 (7416)
2009: 10^{0}GY, 11^{0}YS, 8^{0}S, 8^{0}SD,

	Starts	1st	2nd	3rd	Win & Pl
Career Total (Turf)	7	0	0	0	0
Career Total (AW)	1	0	0	0	

Going (Turf): **Sf: 0-3 GS: 0-2 Gd: 0-0 GF: 0-0 Fm: 0-0**
Distance: 5f/6f: 0-0 7f-8f: 0-5 9f-13f: 0-3 14f+: 0-0
Track : LH: 0-3 RH: 0-2 Tight: 0-1 Gall: 0-1
Aids: Bl: 0-0 Vi: 0-0 Tstrap: 0-1 Ckp: 0-1
Best Rating: **55** 5/09 Clon 1m2f gd-yld

Tax Free (IRE)

115 (89)**117**
7-y-o b g Tagula (IRE)-Grandel (Owington)
D Nicholls Ian Hewitson

Placings:13111/33054113/4011102313/522411-131040 (6522a)
2009: 6^{1}GF, 6^{3}GF, 5^{1}G, 5^{0}GF, 5^{4}GF, 5^{0}G,

	Starts	1st	2nd	3rd	Win & Pl
Career Total (Turf)	33	14	3	7	480354
Career Total (AW)	2	0	0	0	5102

117 5/09 Chan 5f GD £71942
111 4/09 NmkR 6f G-F £25546
117 6/08 Curr 5f G-Y £47794
114 6/08 Naas 5f G-F £28720
113 9/07 Lonc 5f GD £27027
116 6/07 Naas 5f G-Y £21993
111 5/07 NmkR 5f G-F £28390
112 4/07 Thsk 6f FRM £7478
115 9/06 Gdwd 6f GD £17034
109 9/06 Leic 5f2y G-F £6232
107 8/05 York 6f (0-105)H GD £56306
95 7/05 NmkJ 6f (0-105)H GD £34800
94 6/05 Donc 7f (0-85)H G-F £10238
87 4/05 Thsk 7f G-S £5746
Total win prize-money £389249

Going (Turf): Sf: 0-1 GS: 1-4 **Gd: 5-9 GF: 5-14** Fm: 1-1
Distance: **5f/6f: 12-32** 7f-8f: 2-3 9f-13f: 0-0 14f+: 0-0
Track : **LH: 3-7** RH: 0-0 **Tight: 1-2** Gall: 0-2
Aids: Bl: 0-0 Vi: 0-0 Tstrap: 0-0 Ckp: 0-0
Best Rating: **117** 5/09 Chan 5f good

Group-class; winner in Group 2 company and Listed winner; effective from 5f-7f; acts on any ground; likes to race prominently.

Taxman (IRE)

(101) (60)**77**
7-y-o ch g Singspiel (IRE)-Love Of Silver (USA) (Arctic Tern (USA))
A G Newcombe A G Newcombe

Placings:04/030533662123/1023201215455350/000502-24 (0449)
2009: 16^{2}SD, 13^{4}SD,

	Starts	1st	2nd	3rd	Win & Pl
Career Total (Turf)	16	2	2	3	10962
Career Total (AW)	22	2	5	3	15325

75 7/06 Wolv 1m5f194y (0-85)H STD £6477
75 5/06 Yarm 1m3f101y (0-65)H GD £3108
69 2/06 Ling 1m4f (0-70)H STD £3238
68 9/05 Newc 2m19y (0-70)H G-F £3556
Total win prize-money £16381

Going (Turf): Sf: 0-2 GS: 0-1 **Gd: 1-4 GF: 1-9** Fm: 0-0
Distance: 5f/6f: 0-0 7f-8f: 0-1 9f-13f: 2-13 14f+: 2-24
Track : **LH: 4-28** RH: 0-9 **Tight: 3-24** Gall: 1-5
Aids: Bl: 0-0 Vi: 0-0 Tstrap: 3-30 Ckp: 3-30
Best Rating: **77** 11/06 Wolv 1m5f194y stand

Moderate; effective at up to 2m; acts on fast ground; goes on Polytrack; wears cheekpieces; consistent.

Tayacoba (CAN)

91 **57**
2-y-o b/br g Smart Strike (CAN)-Bienandanza (USA) (Bien Bien (USA))
J H M Gosden H R H Princess Haya Of Jordan

Placings:6 (6930)
2009: 8^{6}G,

	Starts	1st	2nd	3rd	Win & Pl
Career Total (Turf)	1	0	0	0	0

Going (Turf): **Sf: 0-0 GS: 0-0 Gd: 0-1 GF: 0-0 Fm: 0-0**
Distance: 5f/6f: 0-0 7f-8f: 0-0 9f-13f: 0-1 14f+: 0-0
Track : LH: 0-1 RH: 0-0 Tight: 0-1 Gall: 0-0
Aids: Bl: 0-0 Vi: 0-0 Tstrap: 0-0 Ckp: 0-0
Best Rating: **57** 10/09 Bath 1m5y good

Tayman (IRE)

(93) (43)**66**
7-y-o b/br g Sinndar (IRE)-Sweet Emotion (IRE) (Bering)
N A Twiston-Davies (Carl Llewellyn 28/6) John Goodman

Placings:40/6030105/4/54-0 (7005)
2009: 16^{0}SD,

	Starts	1st	2nd	3rd	Win & Pl
Career Total (Turf)	9	1	0	1	4483
Career Total (AW)	4	0	0	0	0

70 8/06 Folk 1m4f (0-70)H G-S £3238
Total win prize-money £3239

Going (Turf): Sf: 0-0 **GS: 1-3** Gd: 0-1 GF: 0-5 Fm: 0-0
Distance: 5f/6f: 0-0 7f-8f: 0-0 **9f-13f: 1-10** 14f+: 0-3
Track : LH: 0-7 **RH: 1-6 Tight: 1-6** Gall: 0-1
Aids: Bl: 0-1 Vi: 0-0 Tstrap: 0-1 Ckp: 0-1
Best Rating: **70** 8/06 Folk 1m4f gd-sft

Moderate; acts on good to soft and Polytrack; stays 15f and acts on most ground; has worn a visor.

Tazbar (IRE)

68 **73**
7-y-o b g Tiraaz (USA)-Candy Bar (IRE) (Montelimar (USA))
K G Reveley The Supreme Partnership

Placings:60-0 (7221)
2009: 11^{0}S,

	Starts	1st	2nd	3rd	Win & Pl
Career Total (Turf)	3	0	0	0	176

Going (Turf):	Sf: 0-2 GS: 0-0 Gd: 0-1 GF: 0-0 Fm: 0-0
Distance:	5f/6f: 0-0 7f-8f: 0-0 9f-13f: 0-2 14f+: 0-1
Track :	LH: 0-3 RH: 0-0 Tight: 0-2 Gall: 0-0
Aids:	Bl: 0-0 Vi: 0-0 Tstrap: 0-0 Ckp: 0-0
Best Rating:	**73** 10/08 Pont 2m1f216y good

Tazeez (USA)

116 **117**

5-y-o b/br g Silver Hawk (USA)-Soiree Russe (USA) (Nureyev (USA))

J H M Gosden Hamdan Al Maktoum

Placings:22/1031401-1056 **(4329)**

2009: 9^{1}GF, 9^{0}S, 10^{5}GF, 10^{6}G,

	Starts	1st	2nd	3rd	Win & Pl
Career Total (Turf)	**13**	**4**	**2**	**1**	**174008**

117	4/09	NmkR	1m1f		G-F	£36900
115	10/08	NmkR	1m1f	H	G-F	£99696
109	8/08	NmkJ	1m2f	(0-100)H	G-S	£12952
97	5/08	Yarm	1m3y		GD	£2914

Total win prize-money £152463

Going (Turf):	Sf: 0-1 GS: 1-2 Gd: 1-4 **GF: 2-6** Fm: 0-0
Distance:	5f/6f: 0-0 7f-8f: 0-0 **9f-13f: 4-13** 14f+: 0-0
Track :	LH: 0-4 **RH: 1-5** Tight: 0-0 **Gall: 1-5**
Aids:	Bl: 0-0 Vi: 0-0 Tstrap: 0-0 Ckp: 0-0
Best Rating:	**117** 4/09 NmkR 1m1f gd-fm

Group-class; winner of the 2008 Cambridgeshire and Group 3 Earl Of Sefton Stakes in 2009; effective over 1m-1m2f and acts on most ground; likes to race prominently.

Teachers Choice (IRE)

100 (65)**76**

6-y-o b g Fruits Of Love (USA)-Son Chou (Cyrano De Bergerac)

Adrian McGuinness Equine Business Syndicate

Placings:600/1220020/00304032240/050010000-00004020000 **(6863a)**

2009: 7^{0}SH, 7^{0}Y, 7^{0}Y, 6^{0}Y, 6^{4}G, 5^{0}Y, 6^{2}SD, 6^{0}S, 7^{0}GF, 7^{0}GF, 6^{0}GY,

	Starts	1st	2nd	3rd	Win & Pl
Career Total (Turf)	**38**	**2**	**5**	**2**	**20002**
Career Total (AW)	**3**	**0**	**1**	**0**	**1407**

76	9/08	Gowr	7f	(55-80)H	GD	£6351
62	5/06	Baln	6f	(40-60)H	GD	£3812

Total win prize-money £10163

Going (Turf):	Sf: 0-8 GS: 0-0 **Gd: 2-11** GF: 0-6 Fm: 0-3
Distance:	5f/6f: 1-17 7f-8f: 1-23 9f-13f: 0-1 14f+: 0-0
Track :	LH: 0-13 **RH: 2-10** Tight: 0-0 Gall: 0-0
Aids:	Bl: 0-1 Vi: 0-0 Tstrap: 0-2 Ckp: 0-2
Best Rating:	**83** 10/07 Curr 6f yield

Fair sprinter but stays 7f; handles good ground.

Tealing

48(96) (67)

2-y-o ch g Ishiguru (USA)-Renaissance Lady (IRE) (Imp Society (USA))

R C Guest (T D Barron 24/11) Future Racing (Notts) Limited

Placings:04121 **(7791)**

2009: 6^{0}GF, 7^{4}SD, 7^{1}SD, 8^{2}SD, 7^{1}SS,

	Starts	1st	2nd	3rd	Win & Pl
Career Total (Turf)	**1**	**0**	**0**	**0**	
Career Total (AW)	**4**	**2**	**1**	**0**	**4699**

67	12/09	Sthl	7f	(0-65)	SS	£2047
63	11/09	Sthl	7f		STD	£2047

Total win prize-money £4094

Going (Turf):	**Sf: 0-0 GS: 0-0 Gd: 0-0 GF: 0-1 Fm: 0-0**
Distance:	5f/6f: 0-1 **7f-8f: 2-4** 9f-13f: 0-0 14f+: 0-0
Track :	**LH: 2-5** RH: 0-0 Tight: 0-0 Gall: 0-0
Aids:	Bl: 0-0 Vi: 0-0 Tstrap: 0-0 Ckp: 0-0
Best Rating:	**67** 12/09 Sthl 7f std-slw

Modest; stays 7f; handles Fibresand.

Teasing

91(106) (82)**73**

5-y-o b m Lujain (USA)-Movieland (USA) (Nureyev (USA))

J Pearce D Leech

Placings:00132/46003122210/5642123030554425-2431140434533F **(2499)**

2009: 10^{2}SD, 10^{4}SD, 8^{3}SD, 8^{1}SD, 8^{1}SD, 8^{4}SD, 9^{0}SD, 8^{4}SD, 8^{3}GF, 9^{4}G, 10^{5}GF, 11^{3}GF, 12^{3}SD, 12^{F}GF,

	Starts	1st	2nd	3rd	Win & Pl
Career Total (Turf)	**11**	**0**	**0**	**2**	**2080**
Career Total (AW)	**35**	**6**	**8**	**6**	**29719**

82	1/09	Wolv	1m141y	(0-85)H	STD	£5180
73	1/09	Wolv	1m141y		STD	£2047
77	3/08	Wolv	7f32y		STD	£2590
86	12/07	Wolv	7f32y	(0-75)H	STD	£2968
78	10/07	Ling	7f	(0-75)H	STD	£3562
75	11/06	Wolv	5f216y		STD	£3562

Total win prize-money £19912

Going (Turf):	**Sf: 0-0 GS: 0-2 Gd: 0-1 GF: 0-8 Fm: 0-0**
Distance:	5f/6f: 1-6 **7f-8f: 3-26** 9f-13f: 2-14 14f+: 0-0
Track :	**LH: 6-33** RH: 0-6 **Tight: 6-29** Gall: 0-3
Aids:	Bl: 0-0 **Vi: 2-16** Tstrap: 1-8 Ckp: 1-8
Best Rating:	**86** 12/07 Wolv 7f32y stand

Fair; effective at around 1m-1m2f; acts on Polytrack; usually held up; has worn cheekpieces and a visor.

Tecktal (FR)

98(100) (58)**57**

6-y-o ch m Pivotal-Wenge (USA) (Housebuster (USA))

P M Phelan Ermyn Lodge Stud

Placings:000/00/0-51446523 **(4449)**

2009: 12^{5}SD, 11^{1}SD, 11^{4}SD, 12^{4}SD, 12^{6}SD, 10^{5}G, 12^{2}GF, 12^{3}G,

	Starts	1st	2nd	3rd	Win & Pl
Career Total (Turf)	**7**	**0**	**1**	**1**	**1445**
Career Total (AW)	**7**	**1**	**0**	**0**	**2192**

54	2/09	Kemp	1m3f	(0-52)H	STD	£2047

Total win prize-money £2047

Going (Turf):	**Sf: 0-0 GS: 0-1 Gd: 0-3 GF: 0-2 Fm: 0-1**
Distance:	5f/6f: 0-2 7f-8f: 0-1 **9f-13f: 1-11** 14f+: 0-0
Track :	LH: 0-6 **RH: 1-6** Tight: 0-5 Gall: 0-1
Aids:	Bl: 0-0 Vi: 0-0 Tstrap: 0-0 Ckp: 0-0
Best Rating:	**62** 12/06 Kemp 1m2f stand

Moderate; stays 1m3f; acts on Polytrack and fast turf.

Ted Spread

98 **93**

2-y-o b c Beat Hollow-Highbrook (USA) (Alphabatim (USA))

M H Tompkins False Nose 'N Glasses Partnership

Placings:013 **(7184)**

2009: 7^{0}G, 9^{1}GS, 10^{3}G,

	Starts	1st	2nd	3rd	Win & Pl
Career Total (Turf)	**3**	**1**	**0**	**1**	**6487**

78	10/09	Gdwd	1m1f	G-S	£5180

Total win prize-money £5181

Going (Turf):	Sf: 0-0 **GS: 1-1** Gd: 0-2 GF: 0-0 Fm: 0-0
Distance:	5f/6f: 0-0 7f-8f: 0-1 **9f-13f: 1-2** 14f+: 0-0
Track :	LH: 0-0 **RH: 1-1 Tight: 1-1** Gall: 0-0
Aids:	Bl: 0-0 Vi: 0-0 Tstrap: 0-0 Ckp: 0-0
Best Rating:	**93** 10/09 NmkR 1m2f good

Teddy West (IRE)

86(93) (45)**55**

3-y-o b g Trans Island-Duckmore Bay (IRE) (Titus Livius (FR))

Patrick Morris Mrs Pamela MacDonald

Placings:00-0566 **(1691)**

2009: 11^{0}SD, 9^{5}SD, 9^{6}GF, 8^{6}G,

	Starts	1st	2nd	3rd	Win & Pl
Career Total (Turf)	**4**	**0**	**0**	**0**	**0**
Career Total (AW)	**2**	**0**	**0**	**0**	**0**

Going (Turf):	**Sf: 0-1 GS: 0-1 Gd: 0-1 GF: 0-1 Fm: 0-0**
Distance:	5f/6f: 0-0 7f-8f: 0-1 9f-13f: 0-5 14f+: 0-0
Track :	LH: 0-3 RH: 0-3 Tight: 0-4 Gall: 0-0
Aids:	Bl: 0-1 Vi: 0-1 Tstrap: 0-0 Ckp: 0-0
Best Rating:	**55** 10/08 Nott 1m75y heavy

Teeky

107(106) (82)**85**

3-y-o b f Daylami (IRE)-Las Flores (IRE) (Sadler's Wells (USA))

J H M Gosden George Strawbridge

Placings:55-2012510 **(7569a)**

2009: 10^{2}GF, 10^{0}G, 12^{1}G, 11^{2}SD, 16^{5}SD, 12^{1}G, 12^{0}VS,

	Starts	1st	2nd	3rd	Win & Pl
Career Total (Turf)	**7**	**2**	**1**	**0**	**13380**
Career Total (AW)	**2**	**0**	**1**	**0**	**1407**

85	10/09	NmkR	1m4f	(0-90)H	GD	£8723
83	7/09	NmkJ	1m4f	(0-70)H	GD	£3885

Total win prize-money £12609

Going (Turf):	Sf: 0-0 GS: 0-0 **Gd: 2-4** GF: 0-2 Fm: 0-0
Distance:	5f/6f: 0-0 7f-8f: 0-2 **9f-13f: 2-6** 14f+: 0-1
Track :	LH: 0-3 **RH: 2-4** Tight: 0-1 **Gall: 2-3**
Aids:	Bl: 0-0 Vi: 0-0 Tstrap: 0-0 Ckp: 0-0
Best Rating:	**85** 10/09 NmkR 1m4f good

Fair; stays 1m4f; acts on good and fast ground and Polytrack.

Teen Ager (FR)

93(102) (69)**65**

5-y-o b g Invincible Spirit (IRE)-Tarwiya (IRE) (Dominion)

P Burgoyne L Tomlin

Placings:6/314002060/065604560-04010560354126 **(3104)**

2009: 6^{0}SD, 5^{4}SD, 5^{0}SD, 5^{1}SD, 5^{0}SD, 5^{5}SD, 5^{6}SD, 6^{0}SD, 6^{3}SD, 6^{5}GF, 7^{4}SD, 8^{1}SD, 8^{2}SD, 8^{6}G,

	Starts	1st	2nd	3rd	Win & Pl
Career Total (Turf)	**10**	**0**	**0**	**0**	**0**
Career Total (AW)	**23**	**3**	**2**	**2**	**10635**

67	5/09	Ling	1m	(0-65)H	STD	£2047
65	2/09	Ling	5f	(0-65)H	STD	£1878
77	4/07	Ling	7f		STD	£2730

Total win prize-money £6655

Going (Turf):	**Sf: 0-0 GS: 0-1 Gd: 0-4 GF: 0-5 Fm: 0-0**
Distance:	5f/6f: 1-18 **7f-8f: 2-15** 9f-13f: 0-0 14f+: 0-0
Track :	**LH: 3-23** RH: 0-4 **Tight: 3-20** Gall: 0-1
Aids:	Bl: 0-0 Vi: 0-0 Tstrap: 0-0 Ckp: 0-0

Best Rating: 80 8/07 Ling 6f stand

Moderate gelding who often pulls hard; effective over 5f-7f; acts on Polytrack.

Teeraha (IRE)

75(86) (40)12
2-y-o b f Arakan (USA)-Lovely Me (IRE) (Vision (USA))
D Shaw W I Bloomfield

Placings:000600 (6590)
2009: 6⁰GF, 5⁰GS, 7⁰SD, 5⁶SD, 5⁰GF, 6⁰GS,

	Starts	1st	2nd	3rd	Win & Pl
Career Total (Turf)	4	0	0	0	
Career Total (AW)	2	0	0	0	0

Going (Turf): Sf: 0-0 GS: 0-2 Gd: 0-0 GF: 0-2 Fm: 0-0
Distance: 5f/6f: 0-3 7f-8f: 0-3 9f-13f: 0-0 14f+: 0-0
Track : LH: 0-2 RH: 0-0 Tight: 0-2 Gall: 0-0
Aids: Bl: 0-0 Vi: 0-0 Tstrap: 0-0 Ckp: 0-0
Best Rating: 40 9/09 Wolv 5f216y stand

Teia Tephi

89(77) (11)43
3-y-o ch f Elnadim (USA)-Tatora (Selkirk (USA))
P W Chapple-Hyam A Black

Placings:00 (5373)
2009: 6⁰G, 6⁰SD,

	Starts	1st	2nd	3rd	Win & Pl
Career Total (Turf)	1	0	0	0	
Career Total (AW)	1	0	0	0	

Going (Turf): Sf: 0-0 GS: 0-0 Gd: 0-1 GF: 0-0 Fm: 0-0
Distance: 5f/6f: 0-1 7f-8f: 0-1 9f-13f: 0-0 14f+: 0-0
Track : LH: 0-1 RH: 0-0 Tight: 0-0 Gall: 0-0
Aids: Bl: 0-0 Vi: 0-0 Tstrap: 0-0 Ckp: 0-0
Best Rating: 43 8/09 Yarm 6f3y good

Tejime

(99) (75)
3-y-o b g Royal Applause-Pizzicato (Statoblest)
J H M Gosden H R H Princess Haya Of Jordan

Placings:230 (7853)
2009: 7²SD, 7³SD, 6⁰SS,

	Starts	1st	2nd	3rd	Win & Pl
Career Total (Turf)	0	0	0	0	
Career Total (AW)	3	0	1	1	1108

Going (Turf): Sf: 0-0 GS: 0-0 Gd: 0-0 GF: 0-0 Fm: 0-0
Distance: 5f/6f: 0-1 7f-8f: 0-2 9f-13f: 0-0 14f+: 0-0
Track : LH: 0-3 RH: 0-0 Tight: 0-2 Gall: 0-0
Aids: Bl: 0-0 Vi: 0-0 Tstrap: 0-0 Ckp: 0-0
Best Rating: 75 11/09 Wolv 7f32y stand

Modest; stays 7f; acts on Polytrack.

Tell Halaf

91 64
2-y-o b c Oasis Dream-Topkamp (Pennekamp (USA))
M L W Bell Baron F C Oppenheim

Placings:06 (7288)
2009: 6⁰G, 6⁶S,

	Starts	1st	2nd	3rd	Win & Pl
Career Total (Turf)	2	0	0	0	0

Going (Turf): Sf: 0-1 GS: 0-0 Gd: 0-1 GF: 0-0 Fm: 0-0
Distance: 5f/6f: 0-2 7f-8f: 0-0 9f-13f: 0-0 14f+: 0-0
Track : LH: 0-0 RH: 0-0 Tight: 0-0 Gall: 0-0
Aids: Bl: 0-0 Vi: 0-0 Tstrap: 0-0 Ckp: 0-0
Best Rating: 64 11/09 Donc 6f soft

Tell Me A Story

94 69
2-y-o ch f Lucky Story (USA)-Cantina (Tina's Pet)
M Brittain Northgate Grey

Placings:210 (6983)
2009: 5²S, 5¹GF, 6⁰G,

	Starts	1st	2nd	3rd	Win & Pl
Career Total (Turf)	3	1	1	0	4456

69 7/09 Bevl 5f G-F £2914
Total win prize-money £2914

Going (Turf): Sf: 0-1 GS: 0-0 Gd: 0-1 GF: 1-1 Fm: 0-0
Distance: 5f/6f: 1-3 7f-8f: 0-0 9f-13f: 0-0 14f+: 0-0
Track : LH: 0-0 RH: 0-0 Tight: 0-0 Gall: 0-0
Aids: Bl: 0-0 Vi: 0-0 Tstrap: 0-0 Ckp: 0-0
Best Rating: 69 7/09 Bevl 5f gd-fm

Moderst; effective at 5f on fast ground.

Telling Stories (IRE)

(96) (55)35
3-y-o b f Lucky Story (USA)-Yes Virginia (USA) (Roanoke (USA))
B D Leavy Barry Leavy

Placings:040004-46 (1441)
2009: 12⁴SD, 11⁶SD,

	Starts	1st	2nd	3rd	Win & Pl
Career Total (Turf)	1	0	0	0	
Career Total (AW)	7	0	0	0	241

Going (Turf): Sf: 0-0 GS: 0-1 Gd: 0-0 GF: 0-0 Fm: 0-0
Distance: 5f/6f: 0-0 7f-8f: 0-3 9f-13f: 0-5 14f+: 0-0
Track : LH: 0-8 RH: 0-0 Tight: 0-5 Gall: 0-0
Aids: Bl: 0-0 Vi: 0-0 Tstrap: 0-0 Ckp: 0-0
Best Rating: 55 11/08 Sthl 1m stand

Moderate form to date.

Temperence Hall (USA)

93(98) (69)66
3-y-o ch g Graeme Hall (USA)-Sue's Temper (USA) (Temperence Hill (USA))
J R Best Kent Bloodstock

Placings:403030-000032023 (5581)
2009: 7⁰GF, 9⁰GF, 7⁰G, 8⁰GF, 6³SD, 6²SD, 6⁰G, 7²SD, 7³SD,

	Starts	1st	2nd	3rd	Win & Pl
Career Total (Turf)	7	0	0	1	327
Career Total (AW)	8	0	2	3	5510

Going (Turf): Sf: 0-0 GS: 0-0 Gd: 0-2 GF: 0-5 Fm: 0-0
Distance: 5f/6f: 0-5 7f-8f: 0-8 9f-13f: 0-2 14f+: 0-0
Track : LH: 0-6 RH: 0-3 Tight: 0-8 Gall: 0-0
Aids: Bl: 0-1 Vi: 0-5 Tstrap: 0-0 Ckp: 0-0
Best Rating: 69 8/08 Ling 7f stand

Moderate; effective over 6f-7f; acts on fast ground and on Polytrack; has worn a visor.

Templar Knight

92 (55)70
3-y-o b g Montjeu (IRE)-Vas Y Carla (USA) (Gone West (USA))
Gordon Elliott (Sir Michael Stoute 20/7) Sean F Gallagher

Placings:0400 (7532a)
2009: 9⁰G, 10⁴GF, 9⁰YS, 10⁰SD,

	Starts	1st	2nd	3rd	Win & Pl
Career Total (Turf)	3	0	0	0	0
Career Total (AW)	1	0	0	0	

Going (Turf): Sf: 0-0 GS: 0-0 Gd: 0-1 GF: 0-1 Fm: 0-0
Distance: 5f/6f: 0-0 7f-8f: 0-0 9f-13f: 0-4 14f+: 0-0
Track : LH: 0-1 RH: 0-3 Tight: 0-2 Gall: 0-0
Aids: Bl: 0-0 Vi: 0-0 Tstrap: 0-0 Ckp: 0-0
Best Rating: 70 7/09 Wind 1m2f7y gd-fm

Temple Fair (USA)

84(80) (48)55
2-y-o b g Tiger Hill (IRE)-Forty Marchanta (ARG) (Roar (USA))
M Johnston Sheikh Hamdan Bin Mohammed Al Maktoum

Placings:040 (6931)
2009: 7⁰SD, 8⁴GF, 8⁰G,

	Starts	1st	2nd	3rd	Win & Pl
Career Total (Turf)	2	0	0	0	378
Career Total (AW)	1	0	0	0	

Going (Turf): Sf: 0-0 GS: 0-0 Gd: 0-1 GF: 0-1 Fm: 0-0
Distance: 5f/6f: 0-0 7f-8f: 0-1 9f-13f: 0-2 14f+: 0-0
Track : LH: 0-2 RH: 0-0 Tight: 0-2 Gall: 0-0
Aids: Bl: 0-0 Vi: 0-0 Tstrap: 0-0 Ckp: 0-0
Best Rating: 55 9/09 Yarm 1m3y gd-fm

Temple Queen

88(92) (65)49
2-y-o ch f Sulamani (IRE)-Indiana Blues (Indian Ridge)
S Kirk J C Smith

Placings:5460 (6905)
2009: 8⁵SD, 8⁴SD, 7⁶SD, 6⁰G,

	Starts	1st	2nd	3rd	Win & Pl
Career Total (Turf)	1	0	0	0	
Career Total (AW)	3	0	0	0	0

Going (Turf): Sf: 0-0 GS: 0-0 Gd: 0-1 GF: 0-0 Fm: 0-0
Distance: 5f/6f: 0-1 7f-8f: 0-3 9f-13f: 0-0 14f+: 0-0
Track : LH: 0-1 RH: 0-2 Tight: 0-1 Gall: 0-1
Aids: Bl: 0-0 Vi: 0-0 Tstrap: 0-0 Ckp: 0-0
Best Rating: 65 9/09 Kemp 1m stand

Templet (USA)

93(81) (31)44
9-y-o b g Souvenir Copy (USA)-Two Step Trudy (USA) (Capote (USA))
T T Clement Miss E Johnston

Placings:4/23453002140422254/344000006604U0/46054425/6/0000-000 (3552)
2009: 12⁰SD, 10⁰G, 11⁰GF,

	Starts	1st	2nd	3rd	Win & Pl
Career Total (Turf)	30	1	2	2	10813

Career Total (AW) 18 0 4 1 7451
73 8/04 Haml 1m1f36y D G-S £5551
Total win prize-money £5551

Going (Turf): Sf: 0-5 GS: 1-3 Gd: 0-11 GF: 0-10 Fm: 0-1
Distance: 5f/6f: 0-0 7f-8f: 0-7 9f-13f: 1-37 14f+: 0-4
Track : LH: 0-33 RH: 1-15 Tight: 1-29 Gall: 0-4
Aids: Bl: 1-30 Vi: 0-9 Tstrap: 0-2 Ckp: 0-2
Best Rating: 81 2/05 Wolv 1m141y stand

Templetuohy Max (IRE)

103(105) (72)79
4-y-o b g Orpen (USA)-Eladawn (IRE) (Ela-Mana-Mou)
J D Bethell Craig Monty

Placings:P/000030324216-12041400444 (6490)
2009: 9^{1}SD, 9^{2}SD, 9^{0}SD, 10^{4}F, 9^{1}GF, 8^{4}GF, 10^{0}GF, 10^{0}GF, 9^{4}G, 8^{4}GF, 10^{4}GF,

	Starts	1st	2nd	3rd	Win & Pl
Career Total (Turf)	15	1	0	1	3859
Career Total (AW)	9	2	3	1	8022

79 5/09 Rdcr 1m1f (0-70)H G-F £2590
71 1/09 Wolv 1m1f103y (0-65)H STD £2388
65 12/08 Wolv 1m1f103y STD £2388
Total win prize-money £7366

Going (Turf): Sf: 0-1 GS: 0-1 Gd: 0-1 GF: 1-11 Fm: 0-1
Distance: 5f/6f: 0-1 7f-8f: 0-4 9f-13f: 3-19 14f+: 0-0
Track : LH: 3-16 RH: 0-4 Tight: 3-16 Gall: 0-1
Aids: Bl: 0-0 Vi: 3-19 Tstrap: 0-0 Ckp: 0-0
Best Rating: 79 6/09 Donc 1m gd-fm

Modest; stays 1m4f but effective over shorter; acts on fast ground and on Polytrack; has worn a visor.

Ten Day Wonder

87 52
4-y-o gr f Daylami (IRE)-Tenable (Polish Precedent (USA))
R W Price Future Electrical Services Ltd

Placings:0 (4145)
2009: 10^{0}GF,

	Starts	1st	2nd	3rd	Win & Pl
Career Total (Turf)	1	0	0	0	

Going (Turf): Sf: 0-0 GS: 0-0 Gd: 0-0 GF: 0-1 Fm: 0-0
Distance: 5f/6f: 0-0 7f-8f: 0-0 9f-13f: 0-1 14f+: 0-0
Track : LH: 0-0 RH: 0-1 Tight: 0-1 Gall: 0-0
Aids: Bl: 0-0 Vi: 0-0 Tstrap: 0-0 Ckp: 0-0
Best Rating: 52 7/09 Wind 1m2f7y gd-fm

Ten Down

101(105) (77)73
4-y-o b g Royal Applause-Upstream (Prince Sabo)
M Quinn A G MacLennan

Placings:22154000611/12110000300005-010521400003006 (7807)
2009: 5^{0}SD, 5^{1}SD, 5^{0}SD, 5^{5}SD, 5^{2}SD, 5^{1}SD, 5^{4}G, 5^{0}F, 5^{0}GF, 5^{0}SD, 5^{0}GF, 5^{3}F, 5^{0}GF, 5^{0}SD, 5^{0}SD, 5^{6}SD,

	Starts	1st	2nd	3rd	Win & Pl
Career Total (Turf)	18	1	2	2	8812
Career Total (AW)	23	7	2	0	22275

77 3/09 Ling 5f (0-75)H STD £2900
70 1/09 Ling 5f (0-65)H STD £1706
85 4/08 Wolv 5f20y (0-85)H STD £4209
80 3/08 Wolv 5f20y STD £2730
79 1/08 Kemp 5f STD £2047
79 12/07 Ling 5f (0-85) STD £4210
73 11/07 Wolv 5f20y STD £2388
81 5/07 Wind 5f10y GD £3886
Total win prize-money £24078

Going (Turf): Sf: 0-0 GS: 0-0 Gd: 1-5 GF: 0-10 Fm: 0-3
Distance: 5f/6f: 8-41 7f-8f: 0-0 9f-13f: 0-0 14f+: 0-0
Track : LH: 6-21 RH: 1-5 Tight: 6-17 Gall: 1-6
Aids: Bl: 0-2 Vi: 0-0 Tstrap: 0-0 Ckp: 0-0
Best Rating: 85 4/08 Wolv 5f20y stand

Modest; effective over 5f; acts on fast ground; also goes on Polytrack; has worn blinkers; likes to race prominently.

Ten Pole Tudor

88(99) (66)78
4-y-o b g Royal Applause-Amaniy (USA) (Dayjur (USA))
R A Harris Mrs Jan Adams

Placings:602255114/0U3504600300-62046024200466001001422 (7858)
2009: 9^{6}SD, 7^{2}SD, 7^{0}SD, 8^{4}SD, 8^{6}SD, 7^{0}SD, 8^{2}SD, 9^{4}G, 9^{2}SD, 8^{0}SD, 6^{0}GF, 8^{4}SD, 7^{6}GF, 7^{6}SD, 8^{0}SD, 8^{0}SD, 8^{1}SF, 9^{0}SD, 9^{0}SD, 8^{1}SD, 8^{4}SD, 9^{2}SD,

	Starts	1st	2nd	3rd	Win & Pl
Career Total (Turf)	15	0	2	2	3693
Career Total (AW)	29	4	5	0	15165

62 12/09 Sthl 1m STD £2047
60 11/09 Wolv 1m141y SF £2388
79 11/07 Wolv 7f32y (0-85) STD £4210
74 11/07 Wolv 7f32y STD £2968
Total win prize-money £11614

Going (Turf): Sf: 0-0 GS: 0-2 Gd: 0-4 GF: 0-8 Fm: 0-1
Distance: 5f/6f: 0-0 7f-8f: 3-30 9f-13f: 1-14 14f+: 0-0
Track : LH: 4-33 RH: 0-4 Tight: 3-22 Gall: 0-0
Aids: Bl: 0-2 Vi: 0-0 Tstrap: 2-17 Ckp: 2-17
Best Rating: 79 11/07 Wolv 7f32y stand

Modest; effective at up to 1m2f; acts on good ground; goes on Fibresand and Polytrack; has worn cheekpieces.

Ten Spot (IRE)

(103) (64)21
4-y-o b f Intikhab (USA)-Allergy (Alzao (USA))
Stef Liddiard Mrs Felicity Ashfield

Placings:610050004/31P00000-3603 (0517)
2009: 9^{3}SD, 9^{6}SD, 16^{0}SD, 12^{3}SD,

	Starts	1st	2nd	3rd	Win & Pl
Career Total (Turf)	4	0	0	0	0
Career Total (AW)	17	2	0	3	4846

64 2/08 Sthl 1m (0-60)H STD £1911
57 9/07 Wolv 7f32y STD £2047
Total win prize-money £3959

Going (Turf): Sf: 0-1 GS: 0-2 Gd: 0-0 GF: 0-0 Fm: 0-1
Distance: 5f/6f: 0-0 7f-8f: 2-12 9f-13f: 0-8 14f+: 0-1
Track : LH: 2-15 RH: 0-6 Tight: 1-10 Gall: 0-0
Aids: Bl: 1-3 Vi: 1-10 Tstrap: 0-1 Ckp: 0-1
Best Rating: 64 2/08 Sthl 1m stand

Moderate; effective at around 1m; acts on Polytrack and Fibresand; has worn a tongue tie.

Ten To The Dozen

(95) (55)66
6-y-o b g Royal Applause-Almost Amber (USA) (Mt. Livermore (USA))
S T Mason The Mason Racing Partnership I

Placings:2/0400000/0600614326010/0100422026030 0-3 (0210)
2009: 8^{3}SD,

	Starts	1st	2nd	3rd	Win & Pl
Career Total (Turf)	25	3	5	1	13542
Career Total (AW)	11	0	0	2	706

63 7/08 Wwck 1m22y GD £3412
62 10/07 Leic 7f9y G-S £3238
59 8/07 Brig 6f209y G-S £1943
Total win prize-money £8594

Going (Turf): Sf: 0-1 GS: 2-7 Gd: 1-8 GF: 0-8 Fm: 0-1
Distance: 5f/6f: 0-2 7f-8f: 2-27 9f-13f: 1-7 14f+: 0-0
Track : LH: 2-25 RH: 0-5 Tight: 0-6 Gall: 0-0
Aids: Bl: 0-4 Vi: 0-0 Tstrap: 0-0 Ckp: 0-0
Best Rating: 69 8/05 Sals 6f gd-sft

Moderate; effective at around 7f-1m; acts on most ground; has worn blinkers.

Tenacestream (CAN)

(99) (79)
2-y-o b c Grand Slam (USA)-Heart Lake (CAN) (Unbridled (USA))
J R Best Kent Bloodstock

Placings:14 (7878)
2009: 6^{1}SD, 6^{4}SD,

	Starts	1st	2nd	3rd	Win & Pl
Career Total (Turf)	0	0	0	0	
Career Total (AW)	2	1	0	0	3527

79 11/09 Ling 6f STD £3238
Total win prize-money £3238

Going (Turf): Sf: 0-0 GS: 0-0 Gd: 0-0 GF: 0-0 Fm: 0-0
Distance: 5f/6f: 1-2 7f-8f: 0-0 9f-13f: 0-0 14f+: 0-0
Track : LH: 1-2 RH: 0-0 Tight: 1-2 Gall: 0-0
Aids: Bl: 0-0 Vi: 0-0 Tstrap: 0-0 Ckp: 0-0
Best Rating: 79 11/09 Ling 6f stand

Useful; suited by 6f and acts on Polytrack.

Tenacious

(80) (13)
5-y-o b m Pivotal-Invincible (Slip Anchor)
F Sheridan Scuderia A4/5

Placings:60300204/4-0 (0976)
2009: 5^{0}SD,

	Starts	1st	2nd	3rd	Win & Pl
Career Total (Turf)	9	0	1	1	2377
Career Total (AW)	1	0	0	0	

Going (Turf): Sf: 0-1 GS: 0-1 Gd: 0-7 GF: 0-0 Fm: 0-0
Distance: 5f/6f: 0-4 7f-8f: 0-4 9f-13f: 0-2 14f+: 0-0
Track : LH: 0-0 RH: 0-0 Tight: 0-0 Gall: 0-0
Aids: Bl: 0-0 Vi: 0-0 Tstrap: 0-0 Ckp: 0-0
Best Rating: 13 3/09 Sthl 5f stand

Tenancy (IRE)

99(103) (61)57
5-y-o b g Rock Of Gibraltar (IRE)-Brush Strokes (Cadeaux Genereux)
S A Harris (R C Guest 22/5) S A Harris

Placings:3044/645033000003/400210400222000000U101-0002050045 (7869)
2009: 5^{0}SD, 5^{0}G, 5^{0}SD, 5^{2}HY, 5^{0}G, 5^{5}G, 5^{0}S, 6^{0}SD, 5^{4}SD, 6^{5}SS,

	Starts	1st	2nd	3rd	Win & Pl
Career Total (Turf)	19	1	1	3	4714

	Starts	1st	2nd	3rd	Win & Pl
Career Total (AW)	28	2	4	1	7146

61 11/08 Sthl 6f (0-50)H STD £1706
57 11/08 Muss 5f (0-65)H SFT £2186
53 1/08 Sthl 6f (0-50)H STD £2047
Total win prize-money £5940

Going (Turf): **Sf: 1-5** GS: 0-2 Gd: 0-8 GF: 0-3 Fm: 0-1
Distance: **5f/6f: 3-35** 7f-8f: 0-9 9f-13f: 0-3 14f+: 0-0
Track : **LH: 2-22** RH: 0-4 Tight: 0-7 Gall: 0-2
Aids: Bl: 0-2 Vi: 0-0 Tstrap: 1-16 Ckp: 1-16
Best Rating: **69** 5/07 Ling 7f good

Moderate; effective over 5f-6f; acts on soft ground; goes on sand.

Tender Charm (USA)

94(88) (58)**61**
3-y-o b/br g Malibu Moon (USA)-Tender Years (CAN) (Regal Classic (CAN))
R M Beckett R Roberts

Placings:36000 **(4322)**
2009: 6^{3}SD, 6^{6}GF, 6^{0}GF, 8^{0}SD, 8^{0}GF,

	Starts	1st	2nd	3rd	Win & Pl
Career Total (Turf)	3	0	0	0	0
Career Total (AW)	2	0	0	1	403

Going (Turf): **Sf: 0-0 GS: 0-0 Gd: 0-0 GF: 0-3 Fm: 0-0**
Distance: 5f/6f: 0-2 7f-8f: 0-3 9f-13f: 0-0 14f+: 0-0
Track : LH: 0-1 RH: 0-1 Tight: 0-1 Gall: 0-0
Aids: Bl: 0-0 Vi: 0-1 Tstrap: 0-0 Ckp: 0-0
Best Rating: **61** 5/09 Sals 6f gd-fm

Tender Moments

105(84) (40)**60**
5-y-o br m Tomba-Cherish Me (Polar Falcon (USA))
B Smart Mrs Patricia Brown

Placings:130/0/0052-0032600 **(6845)**
2009: 10^{0}GS, 8^{0}SD, 9^{3}G, 12^{2}GF, 12^{6}G, 13^{0}S, 13^{0}G,

	Starts	1st	2nd	3rd	Win & Pl
Career Total (Turf)	14	1	2	2	6931
Career Total (AW)	1	0	0	0	

73 5/06 Hayd 6f HVY £3886
Total win prize-money £3886

Going (Turf): **Sf: 1-3** GS: 0-5 Gd: 0-3 GF: 0-3 Fm: 0-0
Distance: **5f/6f: 1-2** 7f-8f: 0-4 9f-13f: 0-7 14f+: 0-2
Track : LH: 0-6 RH: 0-6 Tight: 0-6 Gall: 0-1
Aids: Bl: 0-0 Vi: 0-0 Tstrap: 0-0 Ckp: 0-0
Best Rating: **77** 7/06 Hayd 6f gd-fm

Moderate; stays 1m2f, acts on soft ground.

Tender Process (IRE)

(103) (74)**65**
6-y-o b g Monashee Mountain (USA)-Appledorn (Doulab (USA))
J R Boyle (R A Fahey 5/2) M Khan X2

Placings:6521401/3000/05036041555-431100 **(1438)**
2009: 7^{4}SS, 6^{3}SD, 7^{1}SD, 6^{1}SD, 6^{0}SD, 7^{0}SD,

	Starts	1st	2nd	3rd	Win & Pl
Career Total (Turf)	15	2	1	1	11808
Career Total (AW)	13	3	0	2	7695

72 2/09 Sthl 6f STD £2047
74 1/09 Wolv 7f32y (0-65)H STD £2388
71 11/08 Wolv 7f32y (0-62)H STD £2729
84 10/06 Ayr 5f (0-70)H HVY £3238
77 8/06 Thsk 5f (0-85)H G-S £6477
Total win prize-money £16881

Going (Turf): **Sf: 1-5 GS: 1-4** Gd: 0-3 GF: 0-3 Fm: 0-0
Distance: **5f/6f: 3-20** 7f-8f: 2-8 9f-13f: 0-0 14f+: 0-0
Track : **LH: 3-14** RH: 0-1 **Tight: 2-4** Gall: 0-1
Aids: Bl: 1-8 **Vi: 2-7** Tstrap: 0-0 Ckp: 0-0
Best Rating: **84** 10/06 Ayr 5f heavy

Modest; stays 7f; acts on soft ground and on sand; has worn blinkers and a visor.

Tenement (IRE)

(101) (56)**53**
5-y-o b g Mull Of Kintyre (USA)-Afifah (Nashwan (USA))
Jamie Poulton Chris Steward

Placings:002400/4600400046-550 **(0186)**
2009: 10^{5}SD, 10^{5}SD, 10^{0}SD,

	Starts	1st	2nd	3rd	Win & Pl
Career Total (Turf)	4	0	0	0	212
Career Total (AW)	15	0	1	0	818

Going (Turf): **Sf: 0-0 GS: 0-0 Gd: 0-2 GF: 0-2 Fm: 0-0**
Distance: 5f/6f: 0-0 7f-8f: 0-5 9f-13f: 0-13 14f+: 0-1
Track : LH: 0-17 RH: 0-1 Tight: 0-14 Gall: 0-1
Aids: Bl: 0-0 Vi: 0-0 Tstrap: 0-1 Ckp: 0-1
Best Rating: **57** 1/07 Ling 1m stand

Tenessee

92 **76**
2-y-o b c Nayef (USA)-Shukran (Hamas (IRE))
C G Cox Ms Liza Judd

Placings:3 **(6620)**
2009: 8^{3}G,

	Starts	1st	2nd	3rd	Win & Pl
Career Total (Turf)	1	0	0	1	722

Going (Turf): **Sf: 0-0 GS: 0-0 Gd: 0-1 GF: 0-0 Fm: 0-0**
Distance: 5f/6f: 0-0 7f-8f: 0-1 9f-13f: 0-0 14f+: 0-0
Track : LH: 0-0 RH: 0-0 Tight: 0-0 Gall: 0-0
Aids: Bl: 0-0 Vi: 0-0 Tstrap: 0-0 Ckp: 0-0
Best Rating: **76** 10/09 Newb 1m good

Fair half-brother to dual 7f winner Hazytoo; promise on debut over 1m on good ground.

Tenga Venga

65(84) (54)**34**
2-y-o ch g Beat Hollow-Fanny's Fancy (Groom Dancer (USA))
P S McEntee Eventmaker Racehorses

Placings:000440 **(7865)**
2009: 6^{0}GF, 8^{0}SD, 6^{0}SD, 7^{4}SD, 7^{4}SD, 8^{0}SS,

	Starts	1st	2nd	3rd	Win & Pl
Career Total (Turf)	1	0	0	0	
Career Total (AW)	5	0	0	0	0

Going (Turf): **Sf: 0-0 GS: 0-0 Gd: 0-0 GF: 0-1 Fm: 0-0**
Distance: 5f/6f: 0-2 7f-8f: 0-4 9f-13f: 0-0 14f+: 0-0
Track : LH: 0-4 RH: 0-1 Tight: 0-0 Gall: 0-0
Aids: Bl: 0-0 Vi: 0-0 Tstrap: 0-2 Ckp: 0-2
Best Rating: **54** 12/09 Sthl 7f stand

Plating-class form at 6f-1m on various surfaces.

Tenjack King

89(104) (80)**61**
4-y-o b g Kyllachy-Rash (Pursuit Of Love)
Joss Saville Ownaracehorse.co.uk (Lowbeck)

Placings:333/321-000 **(7867)**
2009: 8^{0}GS, 8^{0}GF, 14^{0}SS,

	Starts	1st	2nd	3rd	Win & Pl
Career Total (Turf)	3	0	0	1	433
Career Total (AW)	6	1	1	3	4687

80 3/08 Kemp 1m (0-75)H STD £2590
Total win prize-money £2591

Going (Turf): **Sf: 0-0 GS: 0-1 Gd: 0-0 GF: 0-2 Fm: 0-0**
Distance: 5f/6f: 0-0 **7f-8f: 1-3** 9f-13f: 0-5 14f+: 0-1
Track : LH: 0-5 **RH: 1-3** Tight: 0-3 Gall: 0-1
Aids: Bl: 0-0 Vi: 0-0 Tstrap: 0-0 Ckp: 0-0
Best Rating: **80** 3/08 Kemp 1m stand

Fair; effective at around 1m; acts on fast ground; also goes on Polytrack.

Tentears

77(99) (78)**22**
3-y-o b f Cadeaux Genereux-Garmoucheh (USA) (Silver Hawk (USA))
H R A Cecil Malih L Al Basti

Placings:003 **(5193)**
2009: 8^{0}GF, 8^{0}GF, 7^{3}SD,

	Starts	1st	2nd	3rd	Win & Pl
Career Total (Turf)	2	0	0	0	
Career Total (AW)	1	0	0	1	530

Going (Turf): **Sf: 0-0 GS: 0-0 Gd: 0-0 GF: 0-2 Fm: 0-0**
Distance: 5f/6f: 0-0 7f-8f: 0-3 9f-13f: 0-0 14f+: 0-0
Track : LH: 0-1 RH: 0-1 Tight: 0-1 Gall: 0-0
Aids: Bl: 0-0 Vi: 0-0 Tstrap: 0-0 Ckp: 0-0
Best Rating: **78** 8/09 Ling 7f stand

Fair; stays 1m and acts on Polytrack.

Tepmokea (IRE)

108(99) (71)**84**
3-y-o ch c Noverre (USA)-Eroica (GER) (Highest Honor (FR))
R A Fahey (K R Burke 13/6) Keep Racing

Placings:4200001-22205 **(5419)**
2009: 10^{2}G, 12^{2}S, 10^{2}G, 10^{0}G, 9^{5}GF,

	Starts	1st	2nd	3rd	Win & Pl
Career Total (Turf)	11	0	4	0	15240
Career Total (AW)	1	1	0	0	5459

71 10/08 Wolv 1m141y (0-80) STD £5459
Total win prize-money £5459

Going (Turf): **Sf: 0-3 GS: 0-1 Gd: 0-4 GF: 0-3 Fm: 0-0**
Distance: 5f/6f: 0-2 7f-8f: 0-3 **9f-13f: 1-7** 14f+: 0-0
Track : **LH: 1-6** RH: 0-3 **Tight: 1-2** Gall: 0-3
Aids: Bl: 0-0 Vi: 0-0 Tstrap: 0-0 Ckp: 0-0
Best Rating: **84** 6/09 Epsm 1m2f18y good

Useful; effective at 1m2f-1m4f; acts on good ground and on Polytrack; likes to race prominently.

Terenzium (IRE)

102 (52)**59**
7-y-o br g Cape Cross (IRE)-Tatanka (ITY) (Luge)
Micky Hammond O'Sunburn Partnership

Placings:0/00000400/315260/03005040/0-6362010 **(6899)**

2009: 14^{6}GF, 16^{3}GF, 16^{6}G, 16^{2}S, 14^{0}GF, 13^{1}HY, 17^{0}GF,

	Starts	1st	2nd	3rd	Win & Pl
Career Total (Turf)	26	1	1	2	4074
Career Total (AW)	6	1	1	1	4023

59 8/09 Haml 1m5f9y (0-65)H HVY £2307
58 5/06 Kemp 1m (0-45) STD £2388
Total win prize-money £4697

Going (Turf): **Sf: 1-3** GS: 0-1 Gd: 0-8 GF: 0-11 Fm: 0-3
Distance: 5f/6f: 0-1 7f-8f: 1-11 9f-13f: 0-13 14f+: 1-7
Track : LH: 0-16 **RH: 2-13 Tight: 1-14** Gall: 0-1
Aids: Bl: 0-0 Vi: 0-3 Tstrap: 1-12 Ckp: 1-12
Best Rating: **63** 6/05 Nott 1m54y good

Moderate; stays 2m; acts on Polytrack and any surface on turf; has worn cheekpieces.

Terminate (GER)

101(106) (63)**66**
7-y-o ch g Acatenango (GER)-Taghareed (USA) (Shadeed (USA))
A Berry (Ian Williams 10/8) T Blane

Placings:005000/112002020230/00001000/0563140/31422 140006053-220213215234060 **(7113)**
2009: 12^{2}SD, 13^{2}SD, 13^{0}SD, 11^{2}GF, 11^{1}F, 11^{3}G, 13^{2}GF, 12^{1}SD, 10^{5}G, 12^{2}SD, 11^{3}S, 14^{4}G, 13^{0}GF, 10^{6}GF, 9^{0}GS,

	Starts	1st	2nd	3rd	Win & Pl
Career Total (Turf)	39	4	4	3	16601
Career Total (AW)	22	4	6	3	17041

57 6/09 Ling 1m4f STD £2047
60 5/09 Bath 1m3f144y (0-65)H FRM £2072
66 5/08 Bath 1m3f144y (0-65)H G-F £1942
64 3/08 Wolv 1m4f50y (0-60)H STD £2047
59 10/07 Wwck 1m2f188y (0-60)H G-F £1977
67 7/06 Bevl 1m1f207y (0-75)H G-F £3562
70 1/05 Ling 1m2f (0-70)H STD £3441
65 1/05 Ling 1m2f (0-70)H STD £3417
Total win prize-money £20509

Going (Turf): Sf: 0-4 GS: 0-5 Gd: 0-11 **GF: 3-18** Fm: 1-1
Distance: 5f/6f: 0-0 7f-8f: 0-5 **9f-13f: 8-52** 14f+: 0-4
Track : **LH: 7-45** RH: 1-11 **Tight: 6-41** Gall: 0-6
Aids: **Bl: 1-5** Vi: 0-0 Tstrap: 0-2 Ckp: 0-2
Best Rating: **79** 8/05 NmkJ 1m2f good

Modest; stays 1m4f; acts on fast ground and on Polytrack; has worn a tongue tie and cheekpieces.

Terracotta Warrior

91(91) (47)**47**
3-y-o ch g Dubai Destination (USA)-Tamesis (IRE) (Fasliyev (USA))
J Jay K Snell

Placings:40000-0060 **(4196)**
2009: 11^{0}SD, 8^{0}SD, 9^{6}G, 8^{0}GS,

	Starts	1st	2nd	3rd	Win & Pl
Career Total (Turf)	4	0	0	0	0
Career Total (AW)	5	0	0	0	0

Going (Turf): **Sf: 0-0 GS: 0-1 Gd: 0-2 GF: 0-1 Fm: 0-0**
Distance: 5f/6f: 0-2 7f-8f: 0-4 9f-13f: 0-3 14f+: 0-0
Track : LH: 0-5 RH: 0-2 Tight: 0-1 Gall: 0-1
Aids: Bl: 0-1 Vi: 0-0 Tstrap: 0-0 Ckp: 0-0
Best Rating: **47** 7/08 NmkJ 7f gd-fm

Terrasini (FR)

107 **59**
4-y-o gr g Linamix (FR)-Trazando (Forzando)
J Howard Johnson Andrea & Graham Wylie

Placings:60/400-4 **(1399)**
2009: 21^{4}F,

	Starts	1st	2nd	3rd	Win & Pl
Career Total (Turf)	6	0	0	0	505

Going (Turf): **Sf: 0-1 GS: 0-1 Gd: 0-1 GF: 0-2 Fm: 0-1**
Distance: 5f/6f: 0-1 7f-8f: 0-1 9f-13f: 0-2 14f+: 0-2
Track : LH: 0-3 RH: 0-3 Tight: 0-3 Gall: 0-1
Aids: Bl: 0-0 Vi: 0-0 Tstrap: 0-0 Ckp: 0-0
Best Rating: **59** 7/08 Bevl 2m35y gd-fm

Moderate; stays 2m5f; acts on fast ground.

Terrymene Prince

86(86) (11)**31**
3-y-o b g Bollin Terry-Princess Ismene (Sri Pekan (USA))
L A Mullaney K Humphries & Sons Roofing Contractors

Placings:060000 **(3711)**
2009: 12^{0}GF, 9^{6}GS, 10^{0}G, 12^{0}GF, 9^{0}G, 8^{0}SD,

	Starts	1st	2nd	3rd	Win & Pl
Career Total (Turf)	5	0	0	0	0
Career Total (AW)	1	0	0	0	

Going (Turf): **Sf: 0-0 GS: 0-1 Gd: 0-2 GF: 0-2 Fm: 0-0**
Distance: 5f/6f: 0-0 7f-8f: 0-1 9f-13f: 0-5 14f+: 0-0
Track : LH: 0-3 RH: 0-3 Tight: 0-4 Gall: 0-1
Aids: Bl: 0-0 Vi: 0-3 Tstrap: 0-0 Ckp: 0-0
Best Rating: **31** 7/09 Ripn 1m1f170y good

Tertiary (USA)

99(83) (48)**71**
2-y-o b c Singspiel (IRE)-Allez Les Trois (USA) (Riverman (USA))
Saeed Bin Suroor Godolphin

Placings:15 **(7267)**
2009: 7^{1}G, 8^{5}SD,

	Starts	1st	2nd	3rd	Win & Pl
Career Total (Turf)	1	1	0	0	5452
Career Total (AW)	1	0	0	0	0

71 10/09 Brig 7f214y GD £5452
Total win prize-money £5452

Going (Turf): Sf: 0-0 GS: 0-0 **Gd: 1-1** GF: 0-0 Fm: 0-0
Distance: 5f/6f: 0-0 **7f-8f: 1-2** 9f-13f: 0-0 14f+: 0-0
Track : **LH: 1-2** RH: 0-0 Tight: 0-0 Gall: 0-0
Aids: Bl: 0-0 Vi: 0-0 Tstrap: 0-0 Ckp: 0-0
Best Rating: **71** 10/09 Brig 7f214y good

Fair; stays 1m; acts on good ground.

Tesserae

99(99) (46)**57**
3-y-o b f Reset (AUS)-Moxby (Efisio)
A B Haynes WCR V - The Conkwell Connection

Placings:563324054 **(7670)**
2009: 11^{5}G, 10^{6}GS, 11^{3}G, 11^{3}F, 12^{2}G, 12^{4}GF, 11^{0}G, 12^{5}SD, 12^{4}SD,

	Starts	1st	2nd	3rd	Win & Pl
Career Total (Turf)	7	0	1	2	1685
Career Total (AW)	2	0	0	0	0

Going (Turf): **Sf: 0-0 GS: 0-1 Gd: 0-4 GF: 0-1 Fm: 0-1**
Distance: 5f/6f: 0-0 7f-8f: 0-0 9f-13f: 0-9 14f+: 0-0
Track : LH: 0-7 RH: 0-2 Tight: 0-4 Gall: 0-0
Aids: Bl: 0-0 Vi: 0-1 Tstrap: 0-0 Ckp: 0-0
Best Rating: **57** 6/09 Brig 1m3f196y good

Moderate; stays 1m4f; acts on good ground.

Tessie Bear

(78) (47)
4-y-o b f Red Ransom (USA)-Macaerleon (IRE) (Caerleon (USA))
E J Creighton B Little G McGrath G Hodson

Placings:004/0 **(1442)**
2009: 12^{0}SD,

	Starts	1st	2nd	3rd	Win & Pl
Career Total (Turf)	0	0	0	0	
Career Total (AW)	4	0	0	0	289

Going (Turf): **Sf: 0-0 GS: 0-0 Gd: 0-0 GF: 0-0 Fm: 0-0**
Distance: 5f/6f: 0-0 7f-8f: 0-3 9f-13f: 0-1 14f+: 0-0
Track : LH: 0-4 RH: 0-0 Tight: 0-3 Gall: 0-0
Aids: Bl: 0-0 Vi: 0-0 Tstrap: 0-0 Ckp: 0-0
Best Rating: **47** 11/07 Ling 1m stand

Tesslam

97(102) (70)**80**
2-y-o ch g Singspiel (IRE)-Rowaasi (Green Desert (USA))
M A Jarvis Sheikh Ahmed Al Maktoum

Placings:024 **(7209)**
2009: 7^{0}GS, 7^{2}GF, 7^{4}SD,

	Starts	1st	2nd	3rd	Win & Pl
Career Total (Turf)	2	0	1	0	1542
Career Total (AW)	1	0	0	0	241

Going (Turf): **Sf: 0-0 GS: 0-1 Gd: 0-0 GF: 0-1 Fm: 0-0**
Distance: 5f/6f: 0-0 7f-8f: 0-3 9f-13f: 0-0 14f+: 0-0
Track : LH: 0-1 RH: 0-0 Tight: 0-1 Gall: 0-0
Aids: Bl: 0-0 Vi: 0-0 Tstrap: 0-0 Ckp: 0-0
Best Rating: **80** 10/09 Rdcr 7f gd-fm

Fair; stays 7f; acts on fast ground.

Tevez

102(97) (63)**67**
4-y-o b g Sakhee (USA)-Sosumi (Be My Chief (USA))
D Donovan (Miss Amy Weaver 20/1) River Racing

Placings:0536/120060-630402036 **(5329)**
2009: 8^{6}SD, 9^{3}G, 10^{0}GS, 12^{4}SD, 9^{0}GF, 7^{2}GF, 8^{0}G, 10^{3}GF, 8^{6}SD,

	Starts	1st	2nd	3rd	Win & Pl
Career Total (Turf)	8	0	1	2	2871
Career Total (AW)	11	1	1	1	4148

69 1/08 Sthl 1m STD £2457
Total win prize-money £2457

Going (Turf): **Sf: 0-0 GS: 0-1 Gd: 0-3 GF: 0-4 Fm: 0-0**
Distance: 5f/6f: 0-1 **7f-8f: 1-8** 9f-13f: 0-10 14f+: 0-0
Track : **LH: 1-14** RH: 0-2 Tight: 0-7 Gall: 0-3
Aids: **Bl: 1-4** Vi: 0-2 Tstrap: 0-1 Ckp: 0-1
Best Rating: **78** 1/08 Wolv 1m141y stand

Modest; stays 1m; acts on fast ground and on sand.

Tewin Wood

99(100) (74)**72**
2-y-o ch g Zaha (CAN)-Green Run (USA) (Green Dancer (USA))

A Bailey (M D Squance 14/8) The Perle d'Or Partnership

Placings:043160 (7654)
2009: 7^{0}G, 7^{4}G, 6^{3}GF, 7^{1}SD, 7^{6}SD, 7^{0}SD,

	Starts	1st	2nd	3rd	Win & Pl
Career Total (Turf)	3	0	0	1	566
Career Total (AW)	3	1	0	0	4533

74 11/09 Wolv 7f32y (0-80) STD £4533
Total win prize-money £4533

Going (Turf): Sf: 0-0 GS: 0-0 Gd: 0-2 GF: 0-1 Fm: 0-0
Distance: 5f/6f: 0-0 7f-8f: 1-6 9f-13f: 0-0 14f+: 0-0
Track : LH: 1-4 RH: 0-0 Tight: 1-3 Gall: 0-1
Aids: Bl: 0-0 Vi: 0-0 Tstrap: 0-0 Ckp: 0-0
Best Rating: 74 11/09 Wolv 7f32y stand

Fair; stays 7f; acts on fast ground and on Polytrack.

Texan Star (IRE)

91 80
2-y-o b c Galileo (IRE)-Guignol (IRE) (Anita's Prince)
J H M Gosden Magnolia Racing LLC

Placings:20 (4524)
2009: 7^{2}S, 7^{0}S,

	Starts	1st	2nd	3rd	Win & Pl
Career Total (Turf)	2	0	1	0	1927

Going (Turf): Sf: 0-2 GS: 0-0 Gd: 0-0 GF: 0-0 Fm: 0-0
Distance: 5f/6f: 0-0 7f-8f: 0-2 9f-13f: 0-0 14f+: 0-0
Track : LH: 0-0 RH: 0-1 Tight: 0-0 Gall: 0-0
Aids: Bl: 0-0 Vi: 0-0 Tstrap: 0-0 Ckp: 0-0
Best Rating: 80 7/09 Newb 7f soft

Runner-up on debut; effective over 7f; acts on soft ground.

Texas Queen

94(98) (76)69
2-y-o b f Shamardal (USA)-Min Asl Wafi (IRE) (Octagonal (NZ))
M R Channon M Channon

Placings:6423033 (7843)
2009: 6^{0}GF, 7^{4}G, 7^{2}SD, 5^{3}GF, 7^{0}GF, 5^{3}SD, 5^{3}SD,

	Starts	1st	2nd	3rd	Win & Pl
Career Total (Turf)	4	0	0	1	939
Career Total (AW)	3	0	1	2	2216

Going (Turf): Sf: 0-0 GS: 0-0 Gd: 0-1 GF: 0-3 Fm: 0-0
Distance: 5f/6f: 0-3 7f-8f: 0-4 9f-13f: 0-0 14f+: 0-0
Track : LH: 0-4 RH: 0-0 Tight: 0-4 Gall: 0-0
Aids: Bl: 0-0 Vi: 0-0 Tstrap: 0-0 Ckp: 0-0
Best Rating: 76 9/09 Ling 7f stand

Fair; stays 7f and acts on Polytrack.

Thaahira (USA)

95 67
2-y-o b f Dynaformer (USA)-Mehthaaf (USA) (Nureyev (USA))
M A Jarvis Hamdan Al Maktoum

Placings:5 (6729)
2009: 6^{5}S,

	Starts	1st	2nd	3rd	Win & Pl
Career Total (Turf)	1	0	0	0	0

Going (Turf): Sf: 0-1 GS: 0-0 Gd: 0-0 GF: 0-0 Fm: 0-0
Distance: 5f/6f: 0-0 7f-8f: 0-1 9f-13f: 0-0 14f+: 0-0
Track : LH: 0-0 RH: 0-0 Tight: 0-0 Gall: 0-0
Aids: Bl: 0-0 Vi: 0-0 Tstrap: 0-0 Ckp: 0-0
Best Rating: 67 10/09 Sals 6f212y soft

Thabaat

(98) (62)87
5-y-o ch g Pivotal-Maraatib (IRE) (Green Desert (USA))
J M Bradley E A Hayward

Placings:22/10020/0000300646235-46500 (0793)
2009: 7^{4}SD, 7^{6}SD, 7^{5}SD, 7^{0}SD, 7^{0}SD,

	Starts	1st	2nd	3rd	Win & Pl
Career Total (Turf)	14	1	3	1	9487
Career Total (AW)	11	0	1	1	957

80 4/07 Folk 7f GD £2914
Total win prize-money £2915

Going (Turf): Sf: 0-3 GS: 0-3 Gd: 1-6 GF: 0-2 Fm: 0-0
Distance: 5f/6f: 0-5 7f-8f: 1-20 9f-13f: 0-0 14f+: 0-0
Track : LH: 0-10 RH: 0-7 Tight: 0-5 Gall: 0-2
Aids: Bl: 0-14 Vi: 0-0 Tstrap: 0-0 Ckp: 0-0
Best Rating: 87 9/07 Ches 7f2y good

Moderate; effective at around 7f; acts on good and good to soft; has worn blinkers.

Thabit (USA)

(93) (74)
3-y-o ch c Mr Greeley (USA)-Matsue (USA) (Lure (USA))
M A Jarvis Hamdan Al Maktoum

Placings:5 (1730)
2009: 8^{5}SD,

	Starts	1st	2nd	3rd	Win & Pl
Career Total (Turf)	0	0	0	0	
Career Total (AW)	1	0	0	0	0

Going (Turf): Sf: 0-0 GS: 0-0 Gd: 0-0 GF: 0-0 Fm: 0-0
Distance: 5f/6f: 0-0 7f-8f: 0-1 9f-13f: 0-0 14f+: 0-0
Track : LH: 0-0 RH: 0-1 Tight: 0-0 Gall: 0-0
Aids: Bl: 0-0 Vi: 0-0 Tstrap: 0-0 Ckp: 0-0
Best Rating: 74 5/09 Kemp 1m stand

Thaliwarru

87(81) (46)61
2-y-o b g Barathea (IRE)-Autumn Pearl (Orpen (USA))
J R Gask (G G Margarson 14/8) Tony Bloom

Placings:06020 (6609)
2009: 5^{0}GF, 6^{6}GF, 7^{0}G, 7^{2}GF, 7^{0}SD,

	Starts	1st	2nd	3rd	Win & Pl
Career Total (Turf)	4	0	1	0	605
Career Total (AW)	1	0	0	0	

Going (Turf): Sf: 0-0 GS: 0-0 Gd: 0-1 GF: 0-3 Fm: 0-0
Distance: 5f/6f: 0-2 7f-8f: 0-3 9f-13f: 0-0 14f+: 0-0
Track : LH: 0-1 RH: 0-1 Tight: 0-1 Gall: 0-2
Aids: Bl: 0-0 Vi: 0-0 Tstrap: 0-0 Ckp: 0-0
Best Rating: 61 6/09 Wind 6f gd-fm

Modest; stays 7f and acts on fast ground.

That Boy Ronaldo

(89) (47)55
3-y-o b f Pyrus (USA)-Red Millennium (IRE) (Tagula (IRE))
A Berry Alan Berry

Placings:666605060006250-40 (0363)
2009: 7^{4}SD, 8^{0}SD,

	Starts	1st	2nd	3rd	Win & Pl
Career Total (Turf)	9	0	0	0	0
Career Total (AW)	8	0	1	0	605

Going (Turf): Sf: 0-3 GS: 0-2 Gd: 0-1 GF: 0-3 Fm: 0-0
Distance: 5f/6f: 0-12 7f-8f: 0-5 9f-13f: 0-0 14f+: 0-0
Track : LH: 0-11 RH: 0-0 Tight: 0-3 Gall: 0-1
Aids: Bl: 0-0 Vi: 0-0 Tstrap: 0-0 Ckp: 0-0
Best Rating: 55 8/08 Hayd 6f gd-sft

That'll Do Nicely (IRE)

100(102) (70)73
6-y-o b g Bahhare (USA)-Return Again (IRE) (Top Ville)
N G Richards J D Flood

Placings:562-03131344000 (6385)
2009: 8^{0}SD, 9^{3}SD, 11^{1}SD, 12^{3}GF, 14^{1}G, 14^{3}GF, 14^{4}GF, 14^{4}G, 13^{0}G, 12^{0}S, 12^{0}GF,

	Starts	1st	2nd	3rd	Win & Pl
Career Total (Turf)	8	1	0	2	5781
Career Total (AW)	6	1	1	1	3001

70 5/09 Muss 1m6f (0-70)H GD £3885
70 3/09 Sthl 1m3f (0-60)H STD £1942
Total win prize-money £5829

Going (Turf): Sf: 0-1 GS: 0-0 Gd: 1-3 GF: 0-4 Fm: 0-0
Distance: 5f/6f: 0-0 7f-8f: 0-0 9f-13f: 1-9 14f+: 1-5
Track : LH: 1-9 RH: 1-5 Tight: 1-11 Gall: 0-2
Aids: Bl: 0-0 Vi: 0-0 Tstrap: 0-0 Ckp: 0-0
Best Rating: 73 5/09 Muss 1m6f gd-fm

Modest; stays 1m6f; acts on Polytrack and Fibresand and fast ground.

That'lldonowthen (IRE)

87(80) (33)54
2-y-o ch c Chineur (FR)-Credit Crunch (IRE) (Caerleon (USA))
J S Moore Roger Ambrose & Richard Moore

Placings:0056656 (5613)
2009: 6^{0}GS, 6^{0}G, 5^{5}GF, 6^{6}G, 5^{6}G, 5^{5}G, 7^{6}SD,

	Starts	1st	2nd	3rd	Win & Pl
Career Total (Turf)	6	0	0	0	0
Career Total (AW)	1	0	0	0	0

Going (Turf): Sf: 0-0 GS: 0-1 Gd: 0-4 GF: 0-1 Fm: 0-0
Distance: 5f/6f: 0-5 7f-8f: 0-2 9f-13f: 0-0 14f+: 0-0
Track : LH: 0-2 RH: 0-0 Tight: 0-1 Gall: 0-2
Aids: Bl: 0-0 Vi: 0-0 Tstrap: 0-2 Ckp: 0-2
Best Rating: 54 7/09 Yarm 6f3y good

Plating-class; best effort over 5f on fast ground.

That's My Style

85 52
2-y-o gr f Dalakhani (IRE)-Pearl Dance (USA) (Nureyev (USA))
J H M Gosden George Strawbridge

Placings:0 (6992)
2009: 8^{0}GS,

	Starts	1st	2nd	3rd	Win & Pl
Career Total (Turf)	1	0	0	0	

Going (Turf): Sf: 0-0 GS: 0-1 Gd: 0-0 GF: 0-0 Fm: 0-0
Distance: 5f/6f: 0-0 7f-8f: 0-1 9f-13f: 0-0 14f+: 0-0
Track : LH: 0-1 RH: 0-0 Tight: 0-0 Gall: 0-1
Aids: Bl: 0-0 Vi: 0-0 Tstrap: 0-0 Ckp: 0-0
Best Rating: 52 10/09 Donc 1m gd-sft

That's Showbiz

(63) (56)
2-y-o sk g I Was Framed (USA)-Angelic Dancer (Komaite (USA))
W J Knight Mrs Mette Campbell-Andenaes

Placings:0 (7663)
2009: 8^{0}SD,

	Starts	1st	2nd	3rd	Win & Pl
Career Total (Turf)	0	0	0	0	
Career Total (AW)	1	0	0	0	

Going (Turf): Sf: 0-0 GS: 0-0 Gd: 0-0 GF: 0-0 Fm: 0-0
Distance: 5f/6f: 0-0 7f-8f: 0-1 9f-13f: 0-0 14f+: 0-0
Track : LH: 0-1 RH: 0-0 Tight: 0-1 Gall: 0-0
Aids: Bl: 0-0 Vi: 0-0 Tstrap: 0-0 Ckp: 0-0
Best Rating: 56 12/09 Ling 1m stand

Thatlittlecolt

(80) (35)
2-y-o ch g Ishiguru (USA)-Bhima (Polar Falcon (USA))
D H Brown Jarvis Jepson & Cupitt Hughes

Placings:006 (7868)
2009: 5^{0}SD, 6^{0}SD, 7^{6}SS,

	Starts	1st	2nd	3rd	Win & Pl
Career Total (Turf)	0	0	0	0	
Career Total (AW)	3	0	0	0	0

Going (Turf): Sf: 0-0 GS: 0-0 Gd: 0-0 GF: 0-0 Fm: 0-0
Distance: 5f/6f: 0-2 7f-8f: 0-1 9f-13f: 0-0 14f+: 0-0
Track : LH: 0-1 RH: 0-1 Tight: 0-0 Gall: 0-0
Aids: Bl: 0-0 Vi: 0-0 Tstrap: 0-1 Ckp: 0-1
Best Rating: 35 11/09 Sthl 5f stand

Thaumatology (USA)

(86) (57)
3-y-o ch f Distorted Humor (USA)-Crystal Ballet (USA) (Royal Academy (USA))
S Parr Frontier Racing Group

Placings:0660-6400 (0808)
2009: 5^{6}SD, 7^{4}SD, 5^{0}SD, 8^{0}SD,

	Starts	1st	2nd	3rd	Win & Pl
Career Total (Turf)	0	0	0	0	
Career Total (AW)	8	0	0	0	74

Going (Turf): Sf: 0-0 GS: 0-0 Gd: 0-0 GF: 0-0 Fm: 0-0
Distance: 5f/6f: 0-2 7f-8f: 0-5 9f-13f: 0-1 14f+: 0-0
Track : LH: 0-6 RH: 0-1 Tight: 0-3 Gall: 0-1
Aids: Bl: 0-0 Vi: 0-0 Tstrap: 0-1 Ckp: 0-1
Best Rating: 57 11/08 GrLe 1m stand

The Bear

104(92) (56)78
6-y-o ch g Rambling Bear-Precious Girl (Precious Metal)
Miss L A Perratt (D A Nolan 28/5) Cincinnati Club

Placings:14401/6/000/001423030300-000036110400 (7171)
2009: 5^{0}SD, 5^{0}GF, 6^{0}G, 6^{0}G, 5^{3}G, 5^{6}G, 5^{1}GS, 5^{1}HY, 5^{0}GS, 5^{4}G, 6^{0}GF, 7^{0}S,

	Starts	1st	2nd	3rd	Win & Pl
Career Total (Turf)	30	5	1	4	27416
Career Total (AW)	3	0	0	0	

69	8/09	Haml	5f4y	(0-60)H	HVY	£2266
66	8/09	Haml	5f4y	(0-75)H	G-S	£3238
76	5/08	Haml	6f5y	(0-70)H	G-S	£2590
92	7/05	Ayr	6f		GD	£8141
65	4/05	Newc	5f		SFT	£4046

Total win prize-money £20282

Going (Turf): Sf: 2-8 GS: 2-4 Gd: 1-9 GF: 0-7 Fm: 0-2
Distance: 5f/6f: 4-28 7f-8f: 1-5 9f-13f: 0-0 14f+: 0-0
Track : LH: 0-2 RH: 0-1 Tight: 0-0 Gall: 0-0
Aids: Bl: 0-0 Vi: 0-1 Tstrap: 0-0 Ckp: 0-0
Best Rating: 93 7/05 NmkJ 6f gd-sft

Modest; stays 6f and best on good or softer ground; can race prominently.

The Beat Is On

(89) (26)11
3-y-o b f Beat All (USA)-Lady Ezzabella (Ezzoud (IRE))
A W Carroll G Fry & R D Willis

Placings:000-00 (6918)
2009: 12^{0}SD, 12^{0}SD,

	Starts	1st	2nd	3rd	Win & Pl
Career Total (Turf)	3	0	0	0	
Career Total (AW)	2	0	0	0	

Going (Turf): Sf: 0-0 GS: 0-0 Gd: 0-1 GF: 0-2 Fm: 0-0
Distance: 5f/6f: 0-1 7f-8f: 0-2 9f-13f: 0-2 14f+: 0-0
Track : LH: 0-1 RH: 0-1 Tight: 0-1 Gall: 0-1
Aids: Bl: 0-0 Vi: 0-0 Tstrap: 0-0 Ckp: 0-0
Best Rating: 26 9/09 Kemp 1m4f stand

The Betchworth Kid

112 (83)107
4-y-o b g Tobougg (IRE)-Runelia (Runnett)
A King (M L W Bell 27/9) W H Ponsonby

Placings:5153443/0233031132-233503015 (6306)
2009: 14^{2}GF, 13^{3}S, 13^{3}S, 14^{5}G, 16^{0}S, 16^{3}G, 14^{0}GF, 14^{1}S, 16^{5}GF,

	Starts	1st	2nd	3rd	Win & Pl
Career Total (Turf)	25	4	3	9	114616
Career Total (AW)	1	0	0	0	481

104	9/09	Sals	1m6f21y	SFT	£12462
103	9/08	Donc	1m6f132y (0-110)H	SFT	£32380
94	8/08	Nott	1m6f15y (0-90)H	SFT	£7771
79	7/07	Brig	6f209y	G-F	£2590

Total win prize-money £55204

Going (Turf): Sf: 3-9 GS: 0-0 Gd: 0-4 GF: 1-12 Fm: 0-0
Distance: 5f/6f: 0-0 7f-8f: 1-6 9f-13f: 0-8 14f+: 3-12
Track : LH: 3-13 RH: 1-8 Tight: 1-5 Gall: 1-9
Aids: Bl: 0-0 Vi: 0-1 Tstrap: 0-0 Ckp: 0-0
Best Rating: 107 11/08 Donc 1m4f soft

Smart; Group placed; stays 1m6f; acts on most ground, but seems best on soft; usually held up.

The Blue Dog (IRE)

63(80) (42)32
2-y-o b f High Chaparral (IRE)-Jules (IRE) (Danehill (USA))
George Baker Mrs V P Baker & Partners

Placings:04066 (7816)
2009: 8^{0}G, 7^{4}SD, 7^{0}SD, 7^{6}SD, 8^{6}SD,

	Starts	1st	2nd	3rd	Win & Pl
Career Total (Turf)	1	0	0	0	
Career Total (AW)	4	0	0	0	289

Going (Turf): Sf: 0-0 GS: 0-0 Gd: 0-1 GF: 0-0 Fm: 0-0
Distance: 5f/6f: 0-0 7f-8f: 0-3 9f-13f: 0-2 14f+: 0-0
Track : LH: 0-4 RH: 0-1 Tight: 0-3 Gall: 0-0
Aids: Bl: 0-0 Vi: 0-0 Tstrap: 0-0 Ckp: 0-0
Best Rating: 42 11/09 Wolv 7f32y stand

The Boat Shed (IRE)

75(93) (50)38
3-y-o b g Barathea (IRE)-Silver Hut (USA) (Silver Hawk (USA))
B W Duke Brendan W Duke Racing

Placings:050 (2074)
2009: 11^{0}GS, 11^{5}SD, 10^{0}S,

	Starts	1st	2nd	3rd	Win & Pl
Career Total (Turf)	2	0	0	0	
Career Total (AW)	1	0	0	0	0

Going (Turf): Sf: 0-1 GS: 0-1 Gd: 0-0 GF: 0-0 Fm: 0-0
Distance: 5f/6f: 0-0 7f-8f: 0-0 9f-13f: 0-3 14f+: 0-0
Track : LH: 0-3 RH: 0-0 Tight: 0-0 Gall: 0-2
Aids: Bl: 0-0 Vi: 0-0 Tstrap: 0-0 Ckp: 0-0
Best Rating: 50 5/09 Sthl 1m3f stand

The Buck (IRE)

80 52
6-y-o ch g Quws-Erin Anam Cara (IRE) (Exit To Nowhere (USA))
John Joseph Murphy Mid-Cork Tarmacadam Limited

Placings:03020/0/032/603-40 (4462)
2009: 16^{4}GF, 13^{0}G,

	Starts	1st	2nd	3rd	Win & Pl
Career Total (Turf)	14	0	2	3	4316

Going (Turf): Sf: 0-1 GS: 0-0 Gd: 0-4 GF: 0-6 Fm: 0-1
Distance: 5f/6f: 0-1 7f-8f: 0-3 9f-13f: 0-3 14f+: 0-7
Track : LH: 0-3 RH: 0-9 Tight: 0-2 Gall: 0-0
Aids: Bl: 0-0 Vi: 0-0 Tstrap: 0-0 Ckp: 0-0
Best Rating: 62 8/07 Wxfd 2m gd-fm

The Bully Wee

91(96) (62)62
3-y-o b c Bishop Of Cashel-Red Barons Lady (IRE) (Electric)
J Jay Mrs V P Caplan

Placings:5-300000 (3741)
2009: 8^{3}SD, 10^{0}GF, 11^{0}SD, 8^{0}GF, 9^{0}GF, 9^{0}GF,

	Starts	1st	2nd	3rd	Win & Pl
Career Total (Turf)	5	0	0	0	0

Career Total (AW)	2	0	0	1	385

Going (Turf): **Sf: 0-1 GS: 0-0 Gd: 0-0 GF: 0-4 Fm: 0-0**
Distance: 5f/6f: 0-0 7f-8f: 0-3 9f-13f: 0-4 14f+: 0-0
Track : LH: 0-3 RH: 0-2 Tight: 0-3 Gall: 0-0
Aids: Bl: 0-0 Vi: 0-0 Tstrap: 0-0 Ckp: 0-0
Best Rating: **62** 4/09 NmkR 1m2f gd-fm

The Canny Dove (USA)

26(86) (33)**34**
3-y-o b g Monashee Mountain (USA)-Who's Sorry Now (USA) (Ogygian (USA))
T D Barron Dovebrace Ltd Air-Conditioning-Projects

Placings:5006-**00660** **(3031)**
2009: 8^{0}SD, 8^{0}SD, 8^{6}SD, 5^{6}SD, 6^{0}G,

	Starts	1st	2nd	3rd	Win & Pl
Career Total (Turf)	5	0	0	0	0
Career Total (AW)	4	0	0	0	0

Going (Turf): **Sf: 0-0 GS: 0-0 Gd: 0-2 GF: 0-3 Fm: 0-0**
Distance: 5f/6f: 0-4 7f-8f: 0-5 9f-13f: 0-0 14f+: 0-0
Track : LH: 0-4 RH: 0-0 Tight: 0-1 Gall: 0-0
Aids: Bl: 0-1 Vi: 0-0 Tstrap: 0-0 Ckp: 0-0
Best Rating: **34** 7/08 Thsk 6f gd-fm

The Caped Crusader (IRE)

85 **60**
2-y-o b g Cape Cross (IRE)-Phariseek (IRE) (Rainbow Quest (USA))
T P Tate Mrs Sylvia Clegg and Louise Worthington

Placings:0650 **(4396)**
2009: 6^{0}GF, 7^{6}GF, 7^{5}G, 7^{0}GF,

	Starts	1st	2nd	3rd	Win & Pl
Career Total (Turf)	4	0	0	0	0

Going (Turf): **Sf: 0-0 GS: 0-0 Gd: 0-1 GF: 0-3 Fm: 0-0**
Distance: 5f/6f: 0-1 7f-8f: 0-3 9f-13f: 0-0 14f+: 0-0
Track : LH: 0-1 RH: 0-1 Tight: 0-0 Gall: 0-1
Aids: Bl: 0-0 Vi: 0-0 Tstrap: 0-0 Ckp: 0-0
Best Rating: **60** 7/09 York 7f good

The Cardinal's Hat (FR)

84(82) (57)**66**
2-y-o b c High Yield (USA)-Rince Deas (IRE) (Alzao (USA))
P Winkworth Looks A Bright Prospect Racing

Placings:3000 **(6211)**
2009: 5^{3}F, 6^{0}G, 8^{0}SD, 8^{0}SD,

	Starts	1st	2nd	3rd	Win & Pl
Career Total (Turf)	2	0	0	1	578
Career Total (AW)	2	0	0	0	

Going (Turf): **Sf: 0-0 GS: 0-0 Gd: 0-1 GF: 0-0 Fm: 0-1**
Distance: 5f/6f: 0-1 7f-8f: 0-3 9f-13f: 0-0 14f+: 0-0
Track : LH: 0-2 RH: 0-1 Tight: 0-1 Gall: 0-1
Aids: Bl: 0-0 Vi: 0-0 Tstrap: 0-0 Ckp: 0-0
Best Rating: **66** 5/09 Bath 5f11y firm

The Carlton Cannes

(109) (98)**90**
5-y-o b h Grand Lodge (USA)-Miss Riviera Golf (Hernando (FR))
M L W Bell J L C Pearce

Placings:66/1/1232-5 **(1117)**
2009: 12^{5}SD,

	Starts	1st	2nd	3rd	Win & Pl
Career Total (Turf)	3	0	0	1	770
Career Total (AW)	5	2	2	0	8900

87	3/08	Kemp	1m4f	(0-75)H	STD	£2590
74	12/07	Ling	1m2f		STD	£2817

Total win prize-money £5408

Going (Turf): **Sf: 0-1 GS: 0-1 Gd: 0-1 GF: 0-0 Fm: 0-0**
Distance: 5f/6f: 0-0 7f-8f: 0-2 **9f-13f: 2-5** 14f+: 0-1
Track : LH: 1-3 RH: 1-3 **Tight: 1-2** Gall: 0-1
Aids: Bl: 0-0 Vi: 0-0 Tstrap: 0-0 Ckp: 0-0
Best Rating: **98** 10/08 Kemp 1m4f stand

Useful; stays 1m4f; acts on Polytrack.

The Cayterers

108(105) (96)**96**
7-y-o b g Cayman Kai (IRE)-Silky Smooth (IRE) (Thatching)
A W Carroll R D Willis and M C Watts

Placings:04/511011/26000460/0001021-46351114602 **(7574)**
2009: 7^{4}SD, 7^{6}SD, 8^{3}GF, 8^{5}GF, 8^{1}GF, 8^{1}GF, 10^{1}G, 10^{4}G, 8^{6}GF, 9^{0}GF, 10^{2}SD,

	Starts	1st	2nd	3rd	Win & Pl
Career Total (Turf)	28	7	1	1	35134
Career Total (AW)	6	2	2	0	12297

96	7/09	Wind	1m2f7y	(0-85)H	GD	£5180
93	6/09	Wind	1m67y	(0-90)H	G-F	£7771
85	6/09	Wind	1m67y	(0-75)H	G-F	£3070
80	12/08	Ling	7f	(0-70)H	STD	£3885
73	9/08	GrLe	6f	(0-70)H	STD	£3885
78	9/06	Brig	5f213y	(0-70)H	G-F	£3238
72	9/06	Bath	5f161y	(0-75)H	G-F	£4533
68	8/06	Leic	5f218y	(0-70)H	GD	£3886
66	7/06	Leic	7f9y	(0-60)H	G-F	£3238

Total win prize-money £38693

Going (Turf): Sf: 0-1 GS: 0-0 Gd: 2-12 **GF: 5-15** Fm: 0-0
Distance: **5f/6f: 4-15** 7f-8f: 2-10 9f-13f: 3-9 14f+: 0-0
Track : **LH: 4-11** RH: 3-8 **Tight: 4-9** Gall: 2-7
Aids: Bl: 0-1 Vi: 0-0 Tstrap: 0-4 Ckp: 0-4
Best Rating: **96** 11/09 Ling 1m2f stand

Useful; effective over 5f-1m; acts on fast ground and Polytrack; has worn cheekpieces.

The Cheka (IRE)

100 **106**
3-y-o b c Xaar-Velled Beauty (USA) (Royal Academy (USA))
Eve Johnson Houghton Anthony Pye-Jeary And Mel Smith

Placings:12-1 **(4052)**
2009: 7^{1}S,

	Starts	1st	2nd	3rd	Win & Pl
Career Total (Turf)	3	2	1	0	24713

106	7/09	Newb	7f	SFT	£7477
100	7/08	Asct	7f	G-S	£6476

Total win prize-money £13953

Going (Turf): **Sf: 1-1 GS: 1-1** Gd: 0-1 GF: 0-0 Fm: 0-0
Distance: 5f/6f: 0-0 **7f-8f: 2-3** 9f-13f: 0-0 14f+: 0-0
Track : LH: 0-0 RH: 0-1 Tight: 0-0 Gall: 0-0
Aids: Bl: 0-0 Vi: 0-0 Tstrap: 0-0 Ckp: 0-0
Best Rating: **106** 7/09 Newb 7f soft

Smart; effective at 7f; acts on easy ground.

The Chip Chopman (IRE)

(76) (25)**53**
7-y-o b g Sri Pekan (USA)-Firstrusseofsummer (USA) (Summer Squall (USA))
R A Harris (Sabrina J Harty 18/10) Ridge House Stables Ltd

Placings:00040/6503330/00/011130/00000-3000 **(7578)**
2009: 12^{3}G, 14^{0}G, 14^{0}YS, 13^{0}SF,

	Starts	1st	2nd	3rd	Win & Pl
Career Total (Turf)	27	3	0	5	16499
Career Total (AW)	2	0	0	0	

73	6/07	Slig	1m4f	(42-60)H	Y-S	£4435
67	6/07	Limk	1m4f	(42-60)H	Y-S	£4435
63	6/07	Baln	2m	(42-60)H	G-Y	£4202

Total win prize-money £13072

Going (Turf): **Sf: 0-3 GS: 0-0 Gd: 0-10 GF: 0-3 Fm: 0-2**
Distance: 5f/6f: 0-0 7f-8f: 0-5 **9f-13f: 2-14** 14f+: 1-10
Track : LH: 0-8 **RH: 3-19** Tight: 0-2 Gall: 0-0
Aids: Bl: 0-0 Vi: 0-0 Tstrap: 0-1 Ckp: 0-1
Best Rating: **73** 8/07 Gway 1m4f gd-yld

The City Kid (IRE)

79(102) (68)**25**
6-y-o b m Danetime (IRE)-Unfortunate (Komaite (USA))
G D Blake (Miss Gay Kelleway 2/1) Luke McGarrigle

Placings:5003602**116**/3065**002461**/422U0120603453121 2/425644502-56005366 **(7877)**
2009: 7^{5}SS, 5^{6}SD, 7^{0}GS, 7^{0}SF, 7^{5}SD, 7^{3}SF, 7^{6}SD, 7^{6}SD,

	Starts	1st	2nd	3rd	Win & Pl
Career Total (Turf)	14	0	1	2	1988
Career Total (AW)	41	6	8	3	23322

66	10/07	Wolv	7f32y	(0-60)H	STD	£2047
65	9/07	Wolv	7f32y	(0-55)H	STD	£2388
62	3/07	Wolv	1m1f103y		STD	£3238
55	12/06	Wolv	1m141y		STD	£2590
65	12/05	Sthl	6f		STD	£5337
75	11/05	Sthl	6f		STD	£1423

Total win prize-money £17027

Going (Turf): **Sf: 0-4 GS: 0-3 Gd: 0-4 GF: 0-3 Fm: 0-0**
Distance: 5f/6f: 2-13 7f-8f: 2-24 9f-13f: 2-18 14f+: 0-0
Track : **LH: 6-45** RH: 0-1 **Tight: 4-29** Gall: 0-0
Aids: Bl: 2-12 Vi: 2-12 Tstrap: 0-4 Ckp: 0-4
Best Rating: **75** 11/05 Sthl 6f stand

Moderate; formerly useful; effective from 7f-1m1f; acts on a sound surface and on sand.

The Coach

(80) (37)
3-y-o ch g Central Park (IRE)-E Minor (IRE) (Blushing Flame (USA))
T Wall Derek & Mrs Marie Dean

Placings:P000 **(7557)**
2009: 8^{P}SD, 8^{0}SF, 8^{0}SD, 13^{0}SD,

	Starts	1st	2nd	3rd	Win & Pl
Career Total (Turf)	0	0	0	0	
Career Total (AW)	4	0	0	0	

Going (Turf): Sf: 0-0 GS: 0-0 Gd: 0-0 GF: 0-0 Fm: 0-0
Distance: 5f/6f: 0-0 7f-8f: 0-0 9f-13f: 0-3 14f+: 0-1
Track : LH: 0-4 RH: 0-0 Tight: 0-4 Gall: 0-0
Aids: Bl: 0-0 Vi: 0-0 Tstrap: 0-0 Ckp: 0-0
Best Rating: 37 8/09 Wolv 1m141y std-fst

The Composer

103(95) (60)61

7-y-o b g Royal Applause-Superspring (Superlative)
M Blanshard A D Jones

Placings:41/6500050/001630406/0065600/104244-0044030 (6692)
2009: 16^{0}SD, 11^{0}G, 16^{4}G, 14^{4}G, 16^{0}GF, 17^{3}F, 16^{0}GS,

	Starts	1st	2nd	3rd	Win & Pl
Career Total (Turf)	33	3	0	2	15418
Career Total (AW)	5	0	1	0	605

60	7/08	Sals	1m4f	(0-60)H	G-F	£2914
78	5/06	Hayd	1m2f120y	(0-75)H	HVY	£3238
81	9/04	Sals	1m		G-S	£5804

Total win prize-money £11958

Going (Turf): Sf: 1-6 GS: 1-9 Gd: 0-9 GF: 1-8 Fm: 0-1
Distance: 5f/6f: 0-0 7f-8f: 1-2 9f-13f: 2-23 14f+: 0-13
Track : LH: 1-19 RH: 1-17 Tight: 1-15 Gall: 0-4
Aids: Bl: 0-0 Vi: 0-0 Tstrap: 0-0 Ckp: 0-0
Best Rating: 82 4/05 Sand 1m14y gd-sft

Moderate; stays 2m; acts with give and on fast ground, and on Polytrack.

The Confessor

90 72

2-y-o b c Piccolo-Twilight Mistress (Bin Ajwaad (IRE))
H Candy Six Too Many

Placings:033 (6896)
2009: 6^{0}GF, 6^{3}GS, 6^{3}GF,

	Starts	1st	2nd	3rd	Win & Pl
Career Total (Turf)	3	0	0	2	963

Going (Turf): Sf: 0-0 GS: 0-1 Gd: 0-0 GF: 0-2 Fm: 0-0
Distance: 5f/6f: 0-2 7f-8f: 0-1 9f-13f: 0-0 14f+: 0-0
Track : LH: 0-1 RH: 0-0 Tight: 0-0 Gall: 0-0
Aids: Bl: 0-0 Vi: 0-0 Tstrap: 0-0 Ckp: 0-0
Best Rating: 72 10/09 Gdwd 6f gd-sft

Fair; stays 6f; acts on easy ground.

The Cuckoo

82(96) (73)38

3-y-o b g Invincible Spirit (IRE)-Aravonian (Night Shift (USA))
M Quinn M Quinn

Placings:304105-5420000 (7241)
2009: 5^{5}SD, 5^{4}SD, 5^{2}SD, 5^{0}GF, 6^{0}SD, 5^{0}GF, 5^{0}S,

	Starts	1st	2nd	3rd	Win & Pl
Career Total (Turf)	3	0	0	0	
Career Total (AW)	10	1	1	1	4365

73	9/08	Sthl	5f	(0-70)	STD	£2797

Total win prize-money £2798

Going (Turf): Sf: 0-1 GS: 0-0 Gd: 0-0 GF: 0-2 Fm: 0-0
Distance: 5f/6f: 1-13 7f-8f: 0-0 9f-13f: 0-0 14f+: 0-0
Track : LH: 0-6 RH: 0-1 Tight: 0-4 Gall: 0-2
Aids: Bl: 0-0 Vi: 0-0 Tstrap: 0-0 Ckp: 0-0
Best Rating: 73 9/08 Sthl 5f stand

Fair; effective over 5f; acts on Fibresand.

The Desert Saint

97(92) (71)69

3-y-o b g Dubai Destination (USA)-Maria Theresa (Primo Dominie)
A M Balding A Taylor & J C Smith

Placings:20-4000 (3982)
2009: 6^{4}GF, 7^{0}S, 7^{0}GF, 7^{0}SD,

	Starts	1st	2nd	3rd	Win & Pl
Career Total (Turf)	4	0	0	0	289
Career Total (AW)	2	0	1	0	1445

Going (Turf): Sf: 0-1 GS: 0-0 Gd: 0-1 GF: 0-2 Fm: 0-0
Distance: 5f/6f: 0-3 7f-8f: 0-3 9f-13f: 0-0 14f+: 0-0
Track : LH: 0-1 RH: 0-2 Tight: 0-0 Gall: 0-0
Aids: Bl: 0-0 Vi: 0-1 Tstrap: 0-0 Ckp: 0-0
Best Rating: 71 5/08 Kemp 5f stand

The Dial House

83(104) (77)75

3-y-o b g Tagula (IRE)-Marliana (IRE) (Mtoto)
J A Osborne J Palmer-Brown

Placings:22164-50035304 (7776)
2009: 9^{5}SD, 8^{0}G, 10^{0}GF, 10^{3}SD, 10^{5}SD, 12^{3}SD, 10^{0}SD, 10^{4}SD,

	Starts	1st	2nd	3rd	Win & Pl
Career Total (Turf)	4	1	0	0	3784
Career Total (AW)	9	0	2	2	2361

75	6/08	Brig	5f213y	G-F	£3302

Total win prize-money £3303

Going (Turf): Sf: 0-0 GS: 0-0 Gd: 0-1 GF: 1-3 Fm: 0-0
Distance: 5f/6f: 1-3 7f-8f: 0-2 9f-13f: 0-8 14f+: 0-0
Track : LH: 1-4 RH: 0-8 Tight: 0-3 Gall: 0-1
Aids: Bl: 0-0 Vi: 0-0 Tstrap: 0-0 Ckp: 0-0
Best Rating: 77 9/09 Kemp 1m2f stand

Modest; effective at around 1m2f-1m4f; acts well on Polytrack; has worn a tongue tie.

The Ducking Stool

72(73) (18)43

2-y-o ch f Where Or When (IRE)-Dance Sequel (Selkirk (USA))
H J Collingridge Tapas Partnership

Placings:000 (6874)
2009: 7^{0}GF, 6^{0}G, 7^{0}SD,

	Starts	1st	2nd	3rd	Win & Pl
Career Total (Turf)	2	0	0	0	
Career Total (AW)	1	0	0	0	

Going (Turf): Sf: 0-0 GS: 0-0 Gd: 0-1 GF: 0-1 Fm: 0-0
Distance: 5f/6f: 0-1 7f-8f: 0-2 9f-13f: 0-0 14f+: 0-0
Track : LH: 0-1 RH: 0-0 Tight: 0-0 Gall: 0-0
Aids: Bl: 0-0 Vi: 0-0 Tstrap: 0-0 Ckp: 0-0
Best Rating: 43 7/09 NmkJ 6f good

The Fifth Member (IRE)

106(109) (96)96

5-y-o b g Bishop Of Cashel-Palace Soy (IRE) (Tagula (IRE))
J R Boyle Chris Simpson, Miss Elizabeth Ross

Placings:540/02012010/043113241-440032020 (7560)
2009: 8^{4}GF, 8^{4}SD, 8^{0}G, 8^{0}G, 8^{3}GS, 10^{2}G, 10^{0}S, 8^{2}SD, 8^{0}SD,

	Starts	1st	2nd	3rd	Win & Pl
Career Total (Turf)	19	3	4	3	24961
Career Total (AW)	10	2	1	0	15689

96	10/08	Gdwd	1m	(0-85)H	G-S	£5180
87	7/08	Kemp	1m	(0-80)H	STD	£4727
85	7/08	Kemp	1m	(0-80)H	STD	£4727
89	10/07	Folk	7f	(0-75)H	HVY	£2914
78	8/07	Ling	7f140y	(0-65)H	G-F	£2047

Total win prize-money £19598

Going (Turf): Sf: 1-3 GS: 1-5 Gd: 0-6 GF: 1-5 Fm: 0-0
Distance: 5f/6f: 0-0 7f-8f: 5-19 9f-13f: 0-10 14f+: 0-0
Track : LH: 0-8 RH: 3-14 Tight: 0-7 Gall: 0-2
Aids: Bl: 0-0 Vi: 0-0 Tstrap: 0-0 Ckp: 0-0
Best Rating: 96 11/09 Wolv 1m141y stand

Useful; stays 1m; acts on most ground and on Polytrack.

The Fonz

99(94) (74)83

3-y-o b g Oasis Dream-Crystal Cavern (USA) (Be My Guest (USA))
Sir Michael Stoute Anthony & David de Rothschild

Placings:34-1342 (4299)
2009: 8^{1}GF, 10^{3}GF, 10^{4}GF, 12^{2}G,

	Starts	1st	2nd	3rd	Win & Pl
Career Total (Turf)	5	1	1	2	6708
Career Total (AW)	1	0	0	0	265

79	4/09	Bevl	1m100y	G-F	£2590

Total win prize-money £2590

Going (Turf): Sf: 0-0 GS: 0-0 Gd: 0-1 GF: 1-4 Fm: 0-0
Distance: 5f/6f: 0-1 7f-8f: 0-1 9f-13f: 1-4 14f+: 0-0
Track : LH: 0-1 RH: 1-4 Tight: 0-2 Gall: 0-1
Aids: Bl: 0-0 Vi: 0-0 Tstrap: 0-0 Ckp: 0-0
Best Rating: 83 7/09 Asct 1m4f good

Useful; stays 1m4f; acts on good ground.

The Frying Pan (IRE)

72(70) (30)27

2-y-o ch f Barathea (IRE)-Hello Mary (IRE) (Dolphin Street (FR))
Dr J D Scargill Nigel Shaw

Placings:600000 (7706)
2009: 7^{6}SD, 7^{0}G, 7^{0}G, 8^{0}GS, 7^{0}SD, 8^{0}SD,

	Starts	1st	2nd	3rd	Win & Pl
Career Total (Turf)	3	0	0	0	
Career Total (AW)	3	0	0	0	0

Going (Turf): Sf: 0-0 GS: 0-1 Gd: 0-2 GF: 0-0 Fm: 0-0
Distance: 5f/6f: 0-0 7f-8f: 0-5 9f-13f: 0-1 14f+: 0-0
Track : LH: 0-2 RH: 0-2 Tight: 0-1 Gall: 0-0
Aids: Bl: 0-4 Vi: 0-0 Tstrap: 0-0 Ckp: 0-0
Best Rating: 30 6/09 Kemp 7f stand

The Galloping Shoe

105(104) (83)84

4-y-o b g Observatory (USA)-My Way (IRE) (Marju (IRE))
A C Whillans (J Noseda 22/10) G Brown & W Orr

Placings:1-24004036344 (7287)

2009: 8^{2}G, 8^{4}SD, 8^{0}HY, 6^{0}GF, 7^{4}G, 6^{0}GS, 6^{3}GF, 7^{6}GF, 6^{3}GS, 5^{4}G, 7^{4}S,

	Starts	1st	2nd	3rd	Win & Pl
Career Total (Turf)	11	1	1	2	7804
Career Total (AW)	1	0	0	0	361

80 4/08 Brig 7f214y G-S £2914

Total win prize-money £2914

Going (Turf): Sf: 0-2 **GS: 1-3** Gd: 0-3 GF: 0-3 Fm: 0-0
Distance: 5f/6f: 0-5 **7f-8f: 1-5** 9f-13f: 0-2 14f+: 0-0
Track : **LH: 1-4** RH: 0-1 Tight: 0-2 Gall: 0-2
Aids: Bl: 0-0 Vi: 0-0 Tstrap: 0-0 Ckp: 0-0
Best Rating: **84** 4/09 Wind 1m67y good

Fair; effective over 1m; acts on easy ground and on Polytrack.

The Game

(113) (98)**86**

4-y-o b g Compton Place-Emanant (Emarati (USA))
Tom Dascombe M Khan X2

Placings:51506013/32300610211-4 (0204)
2009: 6^{4}SD,

	Starts	1st	2nd	3rd	Win & Pl
Career Total (Turf)	8	2	0	0	11657
Career Total (AW)	12	3	2	3	26390

97 12/08 GrLe 5f (0-100)H STD £11656
98 12/08 Ling 6f (0-80)H STD £5180
86 7/08 NmkJ 6f (0-90)H G-F £9066
81 12/07 Ling 6f (0-85) STD £4210
73 7/07 Catt 5f212y G-S £2590

Total win prize-money £32705

Going (Turf): Sf: 0-0 **GS: 1-1** Gd: 0-3 **GF: 1-4** Fm: 0-0
Distance: **5f/6f: 5-18** 7f-8f: 0-2 9f-13f: 0-0 14f+: 0-0
Track : **LH: 4-16** RH: 0-1 **Tight: 3-13** Gall: 1-3
Aids: Bl: 0-0 Vi: 0-0 Tstrap: 0-0 Ckp: 0-0
Best Rating: **98** 12/08 Ling 6f stand

Very useful; effective over 5f-6f; acted on most ground and on Polytrack. (DEAD)

The Geester

(104) (67)**51**

5-y-o b g Rambling Bear-Cledeschamps (Doc Marten)
Stef Liddiard (S R Bowring 18/5) Mrs Anne & Fred Cowley

Placings:05053502/0030535002/2641325006140-21260 (7807)

2009: 5^{2}SD, 5^{1}SD, 5^{2}SD, 5^{6}SD, 5^{0}SD,

	Starts	1st	2nd	3rd	Win & Pl
Career Total (Turf)	9	0	0	0	0
Career Total (AW)	28	3	6	4	11598

65 1/09 Sthl 5f (0-65)H STD £2047
65 11/08 Sthl 5f (0-55)H STD £2047
63 3/08 Sthl 6f (0-50)H STD £1911

Total win prize-money £6005

Going (Turf): Sf: 0-1 GS: 0-1 Gd: 0-5 GF: 0-2 Fm: 0-0
Distance: **5f/6f: 3-29** 7f-8f: 0-7 9f-13f: 0-1 14f+: 0-0
Track : **LH: 1-16** RH: 0-2 Tight: 0-9 Gall: 0-1
Aids: **Bl: 3-32** Vi: 0-0 Tstrap: 0-2 Ckp: 0-2
Best Rating: **67** 2/09 Wolv 5f20y stand

Moderate; effective over 5f-6f and acts on sand; has worn blinkers.

The Gillie

90 **56**

2-y-o b g Pivotal-Red Tiara (USA) (Mr Prospector (USA))
R A Fahey George Murray

Placings:6 (7289)
2009: 6^{6}S,

	Starts	1st	2nd	3rd	Win & Pl
Career Total (Turf)	1	0	0	0	0

Going (Turf): **Sf: 0-1 GS: 0-0 Gd: 0-0 GF: 0-0 Fm: 0-0**
Distance: 5f/6f: 0-1 7f-8f: 0-0 9f-13f: 0-0 14f+: 0-0
Track : LH: 0-0 RH: 0-0 Tight: 0-0 Gall: 0-0
Aids: Bl: 0-0 Vi: 0-0 Tstrap: 0-0 Ckp: 0-0
Best Rating: **56** 11/09 Donc 6f soft

The Graig

92(101) (60)**58**

5-y-o b g Josr Algarhoud (IRE)-Souadah (USA) (General Holme (USA))
J R Holt J R Holt

Placings:606/**5000**6/**5000**45**5**00-**2103**5**1**60000 (7755)
2009: 8^{2}SD, 8^{1}SD, 10^{0}SD, 8^{3}SD, 8^{5}SD, 9^{1}SD, 10^{6}GF, 9^{0}GF, 8^{0}SD, 8^{0}SD, 8^{0}SD,

	Starts	1st	2nd	3rd	Win & Pl
Career Total (Turf)	10	0	0	0	0
Career Total (AW)	18	2	1	1	4724

60 3/09 Wolv 1m1f103y (0-55)H STD £1942
59 1/09 Kemp 1m (0-50)H STD £1706

Total win prize-money £3649

Going (Turf): **Sf: 0-1 GS: 0-1 Gd: 0-1 GF: 0-6 Fm: 0-1**
Distance: 5f/6f: 0-3 7f-8f: 1-8 9f-13f: 1-17 14f+: 0-0
Track : LH: 1-17 RH: 1-7 **Tight: 1-9** Gall: 0-1
Aids: Bl: 0-1 Vi: 0-0 Tstrap: 0-0 Ckp: 0-0
Best Rating: **60** 3/09 Wolv 1m1f103y stand

Moderate; effective at around 1m; acts on Polytrack.

The Great Husk (IRE)

88(79) (26)**49**

2-y-o b g Alamshar (IRE)-Stardance (USA) (Rahy (USA))
J S Moore M Fulcher & J S Moore

Placings:0046 (7683)
2009: 7^{0}GF, 7^{0}GS, 7^{4}GF, 10^{6}SD,

	Starts	1st	2nd	3rd	Win & Pl
Career Total (Turf)	3	0	0	0	144
Career Total (AW)	1	0	0	0	0

Going (Turf): **Sf: 0-0 GS: 0-1 Gd: 0-0 GF: 0-2 Fm: 0-0**
Distance: 5f/6f: 0-0 7f-8f: 0-3 9f-13f: 0-1 14f+: 0-0
Track : LH: 0-0 RH: 0-1 Tight: 0-0 Gall: 0-0
Aids: Bl: 0-0 Vi: 0-0 Tstrap: 0-0 Ckp: 0-0
Best Rating: **49** 8/09 NmkJ 7f gd-sft

The Grey One (IRE)

96(103) (74)**66**

6-y-o gr g Dansili-Marie Dora (FR) (Kendor (FR))
J M Bradley R Miles

Placings:6560/0320050220/**3521**540221645426**0300**/000 000444**3**3030**011252**-0600000**6**200**243**55351353245 (7823)
2009: 10^{0}SD, 7^{6}GF, 6^{0}GF, 8^{0}G, 8^{0}GF, 10^{0}G, 8^{0}G, 8^{6}SD, 8^{2}SF, 8^{0}SD, 8^{0}G, 9^{2}SD, 8^{4}SF, 8^{3}SD, 8^{5}SD, 9^{5}SD, 8^{3}SD, 8^{5}SD, 9^{1}SD, 8^{3}SD, 8^{5}SD, 10^{3}SD,

	Starts	1st	2nd	3rd	Win & Pl
Career Total (Turf)	48	1	6	4	11773
Career Total (AW)	32	4	6	6	14960

69 10/09 Wolv 1m1f103y (0-60)H STD £2217
65 10/08 Wolv 1m141y (0-52)H STD £2388
62 10/08 Kemp 1m (0-50)H STD £1706
70 6/07 Wwck 1m22y (0-70)H G-S £3562
66 4/07 Sthl 1m (0-55)H STD £2590

Total win prize-money £12465

Going (Turf): Sf: 0-10 **GS: 1-4** Gd: 0-16 GF: 0-16 Fm: 0-2
Distance: 5f/6f: 0-7 7f-8f: 2-26 **9f-13f: 3-47** 14f+: 0-0
Track : **LH: 4-45** RH: 1-19 **Tight: 2-22** Gall: 0-3
Aids: Bl: 0-2 Vi: 0-0 Tstrap: 5-73 Ckp: 5-73
Best Rating: **74** 12/09 Wolv 1m1f103y stand

Moderate; effective at around 1m-1m4f; acts on most ground on turf; goes on sand; has worn cheekpieces.

The Hague

99(94) (68)**69**

3-y-o b c Xaar-Cox Orange (USA) (Trempolino (USA))
J H M Gosden H R H Princess Haya Of Jordan

Placings:00-3452 (3099)
2009: 6^{3}SD, 8^{4}SD, 8^{5}G, 9^{2}G,

	Starts	1st	2nd	3rd	Win & Pl
Career Total (Turf)	4	0	1	0	1156
Career Total (AW)	2	0	0	1	895

Going (Turf): **Sf: 0-0 GS: 0-0 Gd: 0-2 GF: 0-2 Fm: 0-0**
Distance: 5f/6f: 0-3 7f-8f: 0-1 9f-13f: 0-2 14f+: 0-0
Track : LH: 0-1 RH: 0-2 Tight: 0-1 Gall: 0-1
Aids: Bl: 0-0 Vi: 0-0 Tstrap: 0-0 Ckp: 0-0
Best Rating: **69** 6/09 Gdwd 1m1f192y good

Modest; stays 1m2f; acts on good ground.

The Happy Hammer (IRE)

99(98) (64)**64**

3-y-o b g Acclamation-Emma's Star (ITY) (Darshaan)
E V Stanford (M D Squance 24/4) D D C One

Placings:60-6401005330 (7479)
2009: 7^{6}SD, 8^{4}SD, 7^{0}S, 8^{1}G, 8^{0}GF, 8^{0}SD, 8^{5}SD, 7^{3}SD, 7^{3}SD, 7^{0}SD,

	Starts	1st	2nd	3rd	Win & Pl
Career Total (Turf)	5	1	0	0	4857
Career Total (AW)	7	0	0	2	945

64 7/09 Sand 1m14y (0-80)H GD £4857

Total win prize-money £4857

Going (Turf): Sf: 0-1 GS: 0-0 **Gd: 1-3** GF: 0-1 Fm: 0-0
Distance: 5f/6f: 0-0 7f-8f: 0-10 **9f-13f: 1-2** 14f+: 0-0
Track : LH: 0-3 **RH: 1-5** Tight: 0-3 Gall: 0-0
Aids: Bl: 0-0 Vi: 0-0 Tstrap: 0-0 Ckp: 0-0
Best Rating: **64** 10/09 Wolv 7f32y stand

Modest half-brother to winning sprinters Genki and Hazelrigg; stays 1m; acts on a sound surface and Polytrack.

The Hermitage (IRE)

90 **84**

2-y-o b f Kheleyf (USA)-Russian Countess (USA) (Nureyev (USA))
M Johnston Sheikh Hamdan Bin Mohammed Al Maktoum

Placings:21200 (6486)
2009: 5^{2}GF, 5^{1}GF, 5^{2}GF, 5^{0}GF, 6^{0}GF,

	Starts	1st	2nd	3rd	Win & Pl
Career Total (Turf)	5	1	2	0	10920

84 5/09 NmkR 5f G-F £3885
Total win prize-money £3886

Going (Turf): Sf: 0-0 GS: 0-0 Gd: 0-0 **GF: 1-5** Fm: 0-0
Distance: **5f/6f: 1-5** 7f-8f: 0-0 9f-13f: 0-0 14f+: 0-0
Track : LH: 0-0 RH: 0-0 Tight: 0-0 Gall: 0-0
Aids: Bl: 0-0 Vi: 0-0 Tstrap: 0-0 Ckp: 0-0
Best Rating: **84** 5/09 Bevl 5f gd-fm

Useful; Listed placed; suited by 5f and acts on fast ground.

The History Man (IRE)

102(96) (63)**72**
6-y-o b g Titus Livius (FR)-Handsome Anna (IRE) (Bigstone (IRE))
B D Leavy (M Mullineaux 16/7) D E Simpson & R Farrington-Kirkham

Placings:223310001/040250020503/**0**000131515000/**6**002 001400000-**2**3300030**2**35414 **(7086)**
2009: 5²SD, 5³F, 5³GF, 6⁰GF, 5⁰GF, 5⁰GS, 5³G, 5⁰SD, 6²G, 5³SD, 5⁵SD, 6⁴GS, 5¹G, 5⁴S,

	Starts	1st	2nd	3rd	Win & Pl
Career Total (Turf)	**54**	**7**	**6**	**7**	**40677**
Career Total (AW)	**7**	**0**	**1**	**1**	**961**

64	10/09	Bath	5f161y	(0-58)H	GD	£1878
72	8/08	Thsk	6f	(0-70)H	G-S	£4338
76	8/07	Pont	5f	(0-75)H	FRM	£4533
73	7/07	Bevl	5f	(0-65)H	HVY	£2914
69	7/07	Ayr	5f	(0-65)H	GD	£2637
76	10/05	Ayr	6f	(0-75)	HVY	£4221
69	7/05	York	5f		G-F	£7117

Total win prize-money £27643

Going (Turf): **Sf: 2-13** GS: 1-10**Gd: 2-13**GF: 1-15 Fm: 1-3
Distance: **5f/6f: 7-56** 7f-8f: 0-5 9f-13f: 0-0 14f+: 0-0
Track : **LH: 2-11** RH: 0-2 Tight: 0-7 **Gall: 1-2**
Aids: **Bl: 5-48** Vi: 0-0 Tstrap: 1-2 Ckp: 1-2
Best Rating: **77** 7/06 York 6f gd-fm

Moderate; effective over 5f-6f; acts on most ground on turf; often wears headgear.

The Human League

95 **84**
2-y-o b g Tobougg (IRE)-Noble Desert (FR) (Green Desert (USA))
M R Channon Findlay & Bloom

Placings:3160 **(4488)**
2009: 6³GF, 6¹S, 6⁶G, 7⁰G,

	Starts	1st	2nd	3rd	Win & Pl
Career Total (Turf)	**4**	**1**	**0**	**1**	**7001**

84 6/09 Newc 6f SFT £6231
Total win prize-money £6231

Going (Turf): **Sf: 1-1** GS: 0-0 Gd: 0-2 GF: 0-1 Fm: 0-0
Distance: **5f/6f: 1-3** 7f-8f: 0-1 9f-13f: 0-0 14f+: 0-0
Track : LH: 0-0 RH: 0-1 Tight: 0-0 Gall: 0-0
Aids: Bl: 0-0 Vi: 0-0 Tstrap: 0-0 Ckp: 0-0
Best Rating: **84** 7/09 Gdwd 7f good

Useful; effective over 6f; suited by easy ground.

The Jailer

90(101) (64)**67**
6-y-o b m Mujahid (USA)-Once Removed (Distant Relative)
J G M O'Shea N G H Ayliffe

Placings:0600/**5**2362433**6**/54241**5**1**5**02/02243312645000-00006 **(3948)**
2009: 7⁰SD, 6⁰SD, 6⁰GF, 7⁰GF, 6⁶GF,

	Starts	1st	2nd	3rd	Win & Pl
Career Total (Turf)	**22**	**2**	**2**	**1**	**5640**
Career Total (AW)	**20**	**1**	**5**	**4**	**5788**

67	5/08	Brig	6f209y		G-F	£1683
59	10/07	Kemp	7f	(0-52)H	STD	£2047
53	9/07	Bath	1m5y		FRM	£1943

Total win prize-money £5675

Going (Turf): Sf: 0-1 GS: 0-3 Gd: 0-5 **GF: 1-10 Fm: 1-3**
Distance: 5f/6f: 0-4 **7f-8f: 2-26** 9f-13f: 1-12 14f+: 0-0
Track : **LH: 2-23** RH: 1-14 **Tight: 1-16** Gall: 0-1
Aids: Bl: 0-0 Vi: 0-2 Tstrap: 2-20 Ckp: 2-20
Best Rating: **67** 5/08 Brig 6f209y gd-sft

Modest; effective over 7f-1m; acts on quick and easy ground; also goes on Polytrack; has worn headgear.

The Jobber (IRE)

105(105) (93)**92**
8-y-o b g Foxhound (USA)-Clairification (IRE) (Shernazar)
M Blanshard Mrs Rosemary Wilkerson & Partners

Placings:021/4062205/101300**44**0/**01**0006601101/456462 00/600065015202-005412304020500 **(6972)**
2009: 5⁰SD, 5⁰G, 5⁵HY, 5⁴SD, 5¹GF, 5²G, 5³G, 5⁰GF, 5⁴G, 5⁰GF, 5²G, 5⁰GF, 5⁵SD, 5⁰G, 5⁰SD,

	Starts	1st	2nd	3rd	Win & Pl
Career Total (Turf)	**56**	**8**	**6**	**2**	**80518**
Career Total (AW)	**10**	**1**	**2**	**0**	**12204**

92	6/09	Sals	5f	(0-85)H	G-F	£4857
89	9/08	Yarm	5f43y	(0-85)H	GD	£5046
107	9/06	Leic	5f2y	(0-95)H	G-F	£7790
103	8/06	Hayd	5f	(0-100)H	G-F	£16192
98	8/06	Newb	5f34y	(0-85)H	G-F	£5505
93	5/06	Ling	5f	(0-85)H	STD	£6477
89	7/05	Newb	5f34y	(0-85)H	G-S	£6860
90	7/05	Sand	5f6y	(0-95)H	GD	£9776
67	9/03	Hayd	6f	D	SFT	£3188

Total win prize-money £65694

Going (Turf): Sf: 1-6 GS: 1-8 Gd: 2-15 **GF: 4-27** Fm: 0-0
Distance: **5f/6f: 9-64** 7f-8f: 0-2 9f-13f: 0-0 14f+: 0-0
Track : **LH: 1-11** RH: 0-1 **Tight: 1-11** Gall: 0-3
Aids: Bl: 0-0 Vi: 0-0 Tstrap: 0-0 Ckp: 0-0
Best Rating: **107** 9/06 Leic 5f2y gd-fm

Useful; best at 5f-6f; acts on most ground and on Polytrack.

The Jostler

91(101) (84)**91**
4-y-o b f Dansili-The Jotter (Night Shift (USA))
Mrs L Wadham (B W Hills 21/1) Mr And Mrs A E Pakenham

Placings:0010/0203210005-000 **(3537)**
2009: 8⁰SD, 7⁰G, 7⁰GF,

	Starts	1st	2nd	3rd	Win & Pl
Career Total (Turf)	**14**	**2**	**2**	**1**	**17004**
Career Total (AW)	**3**	**0**	**0**	**0**	**282**

91	8/08	NmkJ	7f	(0-95)H	GD	£9066
75	9/07	Gdwd	6f		G-F	£3886

Total win prize-money £12952

Going (Turf): Sf: 0-1 GS: 0-3 **Gd: 1-4 GF: 1-6** Fm: 0-0
Distance: 5f/6f: 1-2 7f-8f: 1-15 9f-13f: 0-0 14f+: 0-0
Track : LH: 0-3 RH: 0-3 Tight: 0-1 Gall: 0-1
Aids: Bl: 0-0 Vi: 0-0 Tstrap: 0-0 Ckp: 0-0
Best Rating: **91** 8/08 NmkJ 7f good

Useful; effective over 6f-7f; acts on good and faster ground and on Polytrack.

The Kyllachy Kid

103(106) (93)**89**
3-y-o b g Kyllachy-All Business (Entrepreneur)
S Gollings (T P Tate 6/7) P J Martin

Placings:5533213-30260015 **(7558)**
2009: 6³GF, 6⁰G, 6²GS, 6⁶G, 6⁰SD, 7⁰S, 7¹SD, 7⁵SD,

	Starts	1st	2nd	3rd	Win & Pl
Career Total (Turf)	**12**	**1**	**2**	**4**	**10667**
Career Total (AW)	**3**	**1**	**0**	**0**	**5463**

93	11/09	Wolv	7f32y	(0-85)H	STD	£5180
80	10/08	Ayr	6f		HVY	£2914

Total win prize-money £8095

Going (Turf): **Sf: 1-3** GS: 0-3 Gd: 0-2 GF: 0-4 Fm: 0-0
Distance: 5f/6f: 1-7 7f-8f: 1-8 9f-13f: 0-0 14f+: 0-0
Track : **LH: 1-7** RH: 0-3 **Tight: 1-6** Gall: 0-0
Aids: Bl: 0-0 Vi: 0-0 Tstrap: 0-0 Ckp: 0-0
Best Rating: **93** 11/09 Wolv 7f32y stand

Useful; effective over 6f-7f; acts on most ground.

The Last Alzao (IRE)

103(104) (70)**76**
3-y-o b f Alzao (USA)-Balakera (FR) (Lashkari)
R A Fahey G Devlin

Placings:06001110 **(5009)**
2009: 5⁰SF, 6⁶SD, 6⁰F, 8⁰GS, 10¹G, 12¹SD, 9¹GF, 10⁰G,

	Starts	1st	2nd	3rd	Win & Pl
Career Total (Turf)	**5**	**2**	**0**	**0**	**3921**
Career Total (AW)	**3**	**1**	**0**	**0**	**3238**

76	7/09	Bevl	1m1f207y	(0-65)H	G-F	£1873
70	7/09	Wolv	1m4f50y	(0-75)H	STD	£3238
58	6/09	Rdcr	1m2f	(0-55)H	GD	£2047

Total win prize-money £7159

Going (Turf): Sf: 0-0 GS: 0-1 **Gd: 1-2 GF: 1-1** Fm: 0-1
Distance: 5f/6f: 0-3 7f-8f: 0-0 **9f-13f: 3-5** 14f+: 0-0
Track : **LH: 2-6** RH: 1-1 **Tight: 2-3** Gall: 0-0
Aids: Bl: 0-0 Vi: 0-0 Tstrap: 0-0 Ckp: 0-0
Best Rating: **76** 7/09 Bevl 1m1f207y gd-fm

Modest; stays 1m4f; acts on good ground and on Polytrack; likely to progress further.

The Last Bottle (IRE)

(99) (64)**65**
4-y-o ch g Hawk Wing (USA)-Mesmerist (USA) (Green Desert (USA))
W M Brisbourne Shropshire Wolves

Placings:56602/0026543332-0 **(7648)**
2009: 12⁰SD,

	Starts	1st	2nd	3rd	Win & Pl
Career Total (Turf)	**9**	**0**	**0**	**1**	**1069**
Career Total (AW)	**7**	**0**	**3**	**2**	**3497**

Going (Turf): **Sf: 0-0 GS: 0-2 Gd: 0-2 GF: 0-5 Fm: 0-0**
Distance: 5f/6f: 0-2 7f-8f: 0-6 9f-13f: 0-7 14f+: 0-1
Track : LH: 0-11 RH: 0-2 Tight: 0-9 Gall: 0-0
Aids: Bl: 0-0 Vi: 0-0 Tstrap: 0-0 Ckp: 0-0
Best Rating: **66** 6/08 Wolv 1m141y stand

Modest; just about stays 1m4f; acts on Polytrack.

The Last Don (IRE)

96(105) (95)81
3-y-o b c Redback-Banco Solo (Distant Relative)
D R Lanigan P Brosnan

Placings:60012111 **(6121)**
2009: 8^6G, 8^0SD, 8^0SD, 12^1SD, 14^2SD, 12^1G, 16^1SD, 13^1SD,

	Starts	1st	2nd	3rd	Win & Pl
Career Total (Turf)	2	1	0	0	3886
Career Total (AW)	6	3	1	0	14046

95	9/09	Wolv	1m5f194y	(0-85)H	STD	£6308
93	9/09	Kemp	2m	(0-80)H	STD	£4727
81	8/09	NmkJ	1m4f	(0-70)H	GD	£3885
74	7/09	Kemp	1m4f	(0-65)H	STD	£2047

Total win prize-money £16968

Going (Turf): Sf: 0-0 GS: 0-0 **Gd: 1-2** GF: 0-0 Fm: 0-0
Distance: 5f/6f: 0-0 7f-8f: 0-2 9f-13f: 2-3 14f+: 2-3
Track : LH: 1-4 **RH: 3-3** Tight: 1-3 Gall: 1-1
Aids: Bl: 0-0 Vi: 0-0 Tstrap: 0-0 Ckp: 0-0
Best Rating: 95 9/09 Wolv 1m5f194y stand

Useful; stays 1m6f; acts on Polytrack and on Fibresand and good ground on turf.

The Little Master (IRE)

(100) (59)53
5-y-o b/br g Tendulkar (USA)-Minatina (IRE) (Ela-Mana-Mou)
D R C Elsworth D R C Elsworth

Placings:504302-0 **(0193)**
2009: 10^0SD,

	Starts	1st	2nd	3rd	Win & Pl
Career Total (Turf)	3	0	0	0	168
Career Total (AW)	4	0	1	1	907

Going (Turf): Sf: 0-1 GS: 0-0 Gd: 0-1 GF: 0-1 Fm: 0-0
Distance: 5f/6f: 0-0 7f-8f: 0-0 9f-13f: 0-7 14f+: 0-0
Track : LH: 0-2 RH: 0-5 Tight: 0-2 Gall: 0-2
Aids: Bl: 0-0 Vi: 0-0 Tstrap: 0-0 Ckp: 0-0
Best Rating: 59 11/08 Kemp 1m3f stand

Moderate; stays 1m4f; acts on Polytrack.

The London Gang

(99) (60)43
6-y-o b g Mind Games-Nom Francais (First Trump)
S Wynne Miss Gillian Milner

Placings:2624510464505/**036000042**001605**300151/3504 46000000/000200-00601000** **(3467)**
2009: 8^0SD, 8^0SD, 9^6SD, 7^0SD, 7^1SD, 8^0SD, 7^0SD, 7^0SD,

	Starts	1st	2nd	3rd	Win & Pl
Career Total (Turf)	24	2	2	1	13730
Career Total (AW)	36	3	2	2	8435

60	3/09	Wolv	7f32y		STD	£1706
64	12/06	Wolv	7f32y		STD	£2730
63	12/06	Wolv	5f216y		SS	£2388
67	7/06	Ayr	6f	(0-60)H	FRM	£3238
72	7/05	Ling	6f		GD	£3552

Total win prize-money £13616

Going (Turf): Sf: 0-3 GS: 0-4 **Gd: 1-8** GF: 0-8 **Fm: 1-1**
Distance: 5f/6f: 3-24 7f-8f: 2-23 9f-13f: 0-13 14f+: 0-0
Track : LH: 3-35 RH: 0-5 **Tight: 3-28** Gall: 0-2
Aids: Bl: 1-16 **Vi: 4-28** Tstrap: 0-2 Ckp: 0-2
Best Rating: 72 7/05 Ches 6f18y good

Moderate; effective at around 7f; acts on most ground on turf; goes on Polytrack; has worn blinkers.

The Lord

98(95) (63)74
9-y-o b g Averti (IRE)-Lady Longmead (Crimson Beau)
W G M Turner Mrs M S Teversham

Placings:13101025/0206000/306065/**500**113520000**530/ 10400110060/50040/0000-63600** **(2130)**
2009: 5^6SD, 5^3SD, 5^6G, 6^0SD, 6^0SD,

	Starts	1st	2nd	3rd	Win & Pl
Career Total (Turf)	45	7	3	3	99162
Career Total (AW)	18	1	0	2	9422

108	5/06	Gdwd	5f		SFT	£17034
108	5/06	Gdwd	5f	(0-100)H	G-S	£11217
92	1/06	Sthl	5f	(0-85)H	STD	£6477
96	4/05	Kemp	5f	(0-85)H	G-S	£6964
94	3/05	Muss	5f	(0-100)H	G-S	£13291
101	7/02	Ches	5f16y	D	GD	£6955
93	5/02	Ches	5f16y	B	G-F	£8810
87	3/02	Donc	5f	C	SFT	£7085

Total win prize-money £77835

Going (Turf): Sf: 2-13**GS: 3-5** Gd: 1-15 GF: 1-12 Fm: 0-0
Distance: 5f/6f: 8-62 7f-8f: 0-1 9f-13f: 0-0 14f+: 0-0
Track : LH: 2-18 RH: 0-1 **Tight: 2-16** Gall: 0-1
Aids: Bl: 0-0 Vi: 0-1 Tstrap: 0-1 Ckp: 0-1
Best Rating: 108 5/06 Gdwd 5f soft

Useful; effective over 5f-6f; acts on any ground, but possibly best suited by some give; has worn a visor and cheekpieces in the past.

The Love Guru

76(93) (62)40
2-y-o b g Ishiguru (USA)-Beauty (IRE) (Alzao (USA))
J R Boyle M Khan X2

Placings:000512 **(7849)**
2009: 8^0SD, 8^0S, 7^0SD, 7^5SD, 6^1SD, 6^2SS,

	Starts	1st	2nd	3rd	Win & Pl
Career Total (Turf)	1	0	0	0	
Career Total (AW)	5	1	1	0	2853

59	12/09	Sthl	6f	(0-60)	STD	£2047

Total win prize-money £2047

Going (Turf): Sf: 0-1 GS: 0-0 Gd: 0-0 GF: 0-0 Fm: 0-0
Distance: 5f/6f: 1-2 7f-8f: 0-3 9f-13f: 0-1 14f+: 0-0
Track : LH: 1-5 RH: 0-1 Tight: 0-1 Gall: 0-0
Aids: Bl: 1-4 Vi: 0-0 Tstrap: 0-0 Ckp: 0-0
Best Rating: 62 12/09 Sthl 6f std-slw

Moderate; effective over 6f-7f; acts on Polytrack and Fibresand; has worn blinkers.

The Magic Blanket (IRE)

84(102) (71)44
4-y-o b g Bahamian Bounty-Zietunzeen (IRE) (Zieten (USA))
Stef Liddiard David Gilbert

Placings:0305443/1000500-110005 **(7689)**
2009: 5^1SD, 5^1SD, 5^0F, 5^0SD, 5^0GF, 5^5SD,

	Starts	1st	2nd	3rd	Win & Pl
Career Total (Turf)	10	0	0	1	498
Career Total (AW)	10	3	0	1	6376

71	3/09	Ling	5f	(0-65)H	STD	£2047
63	1/09	Ling	5f	(0-52)H	STD	£1978
60	3/08	Kemp	5f		STD	£2047

Total win prize-money £6074

Going (Turf): Sf: 0-0 GS: 0-2 Gd: 0-2 GF: 0-4 Fm: 0-2
Distance: 5f/6f: 3-20 7f-8f: 0-0 9f-13f: 0-0 14f+: 0-0
Track : LH: 2-8 RH: 1-6 **Tight: 2-4** Gall: 0-4
Aids: Bl: 0-0 Vi: 0-0 Tstrap: 0-0 Ckp: 0-0
Best Rating: 71 3/09 Ling 5f stand

Modest; effective over 5-6f; acts on Polytrack.

The Magic Of Rio

93(98) (86)88
3-y-o b f Captain Rio-Good Health (Magic Ring (IRE))
Peter Grayson Haldane Racing & D L Rhodes

Placings:5332101**162413-P550000** **(7136)**
2009: 5^PSD, 6^5GF, 5^5SD, 5^0SD, 6^0SS, 5^0SD, 5^0SD,

	Starts	1st	2nd	3rd	Win & Pl
Career Total (Turf)	8	2	2	1	8458
Career Total (AW)	12	2	0	2	6896

64	12/08	Sthl	6f		STD	£2047
86	8/08	GrLe	5f	(0-85)	STD	£3885
79	8/08	Brig	5f59y		GD	£2964
77	7/08	Nott	5f13y		FRM	£2914

Total win prize-money £11812

Going (Turf): Sf: 0-0 GS: 0-1 **Gd: 1-3** GF: 0-3 **Fm: 1-1**
Distance: 5f/6f: 4-20 7f-8f: 0-0 9f-13f: 0-0 14f+: 0-0
Track : LH: 3-10 RH: 0-3 Tight: 0-5 **Gall: 1-4**
Aids: Bl: 0-2 Vi: 0-0 Tstrap: 0-0 Ckp: 0-0
Best Rating: 88 10/08 Wind 5f10y gd-sft

Useful; effective over 5f-6f; acts on good and fast ground; goes on Fibresand.

The Midshipmaid

83(67) (6)51
2-y-o b f Zafeen (FR)-Ebba (Elmaamul (USA))
Lucinda Featherstone K F Ridley

Placings:05600 **(5526)**
2009: 6^0G, 5^5GF, 6^6G, 5^0SD, 5^0G,

	Starts	1st	2nd	3rd	Win & Pl
Career Total (Turf)	4	0	0	0	0
Career Total (AW)	1	0	0	0	

Going (Turf): Sf: 0-0 GS: 0-0 Gd: 0-3 GF: 0-1 Fm: 0-0
Distance: 5f/6f: 0-5 7f-8f: 0-0 9f-13f: 0-0 14f+: 0-0
Track : LH: 0-1 RH: 0-1 Tight: 0-0 Gall: 0-0
Aids: Bl: 0-0 Vi: 0-0 Tstrap: 0-0 Ckp: 0-0
Best Rating: 51 6/09 Donc 6f good

The Mighty Atom (USA)

88 (76)54
2-y-o ch f Sky Mesa (USA)-Nurse Cleo (USA) (Rahy (USA))
P J Prendergast Thistle Bloodstock Limited

Placings:050 **(6743a)**
2009: 5^0SD, 5^5G, 7^0S,

	Starts	1st	2nd	3rd	Win & Pl
Career Total (Turf)	2	0	0	0	0
Career Total (AW)	1	0	0	0	

Going (Turf): Sf: 0-1 GS: 0-0 Gd: 0-1 GF: 0-0 Fm: 0-0
Distance: 5f/6f: 0-2 7f-8f: 0-1 9f-13f: 0-0 14f+: 0-0
Track : LH: 0-1 RH: 0-0 Tight: 0-0 Gall: 0-0

Aids: Bl: 0-1 Vi: 0-0 Tstrap: 0-0 Ckp: 0-0
Best Rating: 76 8/09 Dund 5f stand

The Mighty Mod (USA)

79 **54**

2-y-o b g Gone West (USA)-Michelle's Monarch (USA) (Wavering Monarch (USA))
M Johnston A D Spence

Placings:0000 (6901)
2009: 7⁰GF, 8⁰GF, 8⁰G, 8⁰GF,

	Starts	1st	2nd	3rd	Win & Pl
Career Total (Turf)	4	0	0	0	

Going (Turf): Sf: 0-0 GS: 0-0 Gd: 0-1 GF: 0-3 Fm: 0-0
Distance: 5f/6f: 0-0 7f-8f: 0-3 9f-13f: 0-1 14f+: 0-0
Track: LH: 0-2 RH: 0-0 Tight: 0-0 Gall: 0-1
Aids: Bl: 0-0 Vi: 0-0 Tstrap: 0-0 Ckp: 0-0
Best Rating: 54 9/09 Ffos 1m gd-fm

The Miniver Rose (IRE)

111 **106**

3-y-o b f High Chaparral (IRE)-Bloemfontain (IRE) (Cape Cross (IRE))
R Hannon Mrs J Wood

Placings:013-442510 (7047a)
2009: 10⁴GF, 10⁴GF, 10²G, 12⁵G, 14¹G, 15⁰S,

	Starts	1st	2nd	3rd	Win & Pl
Career Total (Turf)	9	2	1	1	182190
106 9/09 Donc 1m6f132y				GD	£56770
78 9/08 Donc 1m				SFT	£6152

Total win prize-money £62922

Going (Turf): Sf: 1-3 GS: 0-0 **Gd: 1-3** GF: 0-3 Fm: 0-0
Distance: 5f/6f: 0-0 7f-8f: 1-3 9f-13f: 0-4 14f+: 1-2
Track: **LH: 1-3** RH: 0-1 Tight: 0-1 **Gall: 1-2**
Aids: Bl: 0-0 Vi: 0-0 Tstrap: 0-0 Ckp: 0-0
Best Rating: 106 9/09 Donc 1m6f132y good

Smart; fifth in the Oaks and won the Group 2 Park Hill Stakes at Doncaster in September; effective over 1m2f-1m6f; acts on fast and soft ground.

The Mouse Carroll (IRE)

90(98) (64)**70**

5-y-o b g Barathea (IRE)-Grecian Glory (IRE) (Zafonic (USA))
B R Johnson (D M Leigh 20/11) David Lawlor

Placings:0300200500 (7830)
2009: 10⁰HY, 7³S, 10⁰Y, 7⁰SH, 7²SD, 7⁰GF, 8⁰SD, 6⁵GY, 6⁰SD, 7⁰SD,

	Starts	1st	2nd	3rd	Win & Pl
Career Total (Turf)	6	0	0	1	586
Career Total (AW)	4	0	1	0	1172

Going (Turf): Sf: 0-2 GS: 0-0 Gd: 0-0 GF: 0-1 Fm: 0-0
Distance: 5f/6f: 0-2 7f-8f: 0-6 9f-13f: 0-2 14f+: 0-0
Track: LH: 0-3 RH: 0-4 Tight: 0-0 Gall: 0-0
Aids: Bl: 0-2 Vi: 0-0 Tstrap: 0-0 Ckp: 0-0
Best Rating: 70 7/09 Fair 7f soft

Modest; effective at 7f; acts on soft ground.

The Mumbo

86(99) (66)**49**

3-y-o b f Bahamian Bounty-Mandolin (IRE) (Sabrehill (USA))
W Jarvis Willie W Robertson

Placings:0-10546 (7456)
2009: 8¹SD, 8⁰GF, 7⁵SS, 8⁴SD, 8⁶SD,

	Starts	1st	2nd	3rd	Win & Pl
Career Total (Turf)	1	0	0	0	
Career Total (AW)	5	1	0	0	2730
66 1/09 Ling 1m				STD	£2729

Total win prize-money £2730

Going (Turf): **Sf: 0-0 GS: 0-0 Gd: 0-0 GF: 0-1 Fm: 0-0**
Distance: 5f/6f: 0-1 **7f-8f: 1-4** 9f-13f: 0-1 14f+: 0-0
Track: **LH: 1-3** RH: 0-3 **Tight: 1-4** Gall: 0-0
Aids: Bl: 0-3 Vi: 0-0 Tstrap: 0-0 Ckp: 0-0
Best Rating: 66 1/09 Ling 1m stand

Modest; effective over 1m; acts on Polytrack; has worn blinkers.

The Name Is Frank

101(97) (59)**64**

4-y-o b g Lujain (USA)-Zaragossa (Paris House)
Mark Gillard Don Hazzard

Placings:003610/0000640-0020230322123**6620** (7835)
2009: 5⁰G, 6⁰GF, 5²GF, 5⁰G, 5²G, 5³GF, 6⁰GF, 6³GS, 5²GF, 5²GF, 5¹GF, 5²G, 6³SD, 6⁶SD, 5⁶SD, 6²SD, 6⁰SD,

	Starts	1st	2nd	3rd	Win & Pl
Career Total (Turf)	25	2	5	3	11531
Career Total (AW)	5	0	1	1	484
62 10/09 Catt 5f	(0-55)H			G-F	£2307
71 7/07 Sals 6f				SFT	£4210

Total win prize-money £6518

Going (Turf): **Sf: 1-2** GS: 0-3 Gd: 0-10 **GF: 1-10** Fm: 0-0
Distance: **5f/6f: 2-24** 7f-8f: 0-4 9f-13f: 0-2 14f+: 0-0
Track: LH: 0-8 RH: 0-3 Tight: 0-4 Gall: 0-4
Aids: Bl: 0-0 Vi: 0-0 Tstrap: 0-0 Ckp: 0-0
Best Rating: 71 7/07 Sals 6f soft

Moderate sprinter; handles quick ground and Polytrack; has worn a tongue tie.

The Nifty Fox

107(100) (80)**93**

5-y-o b g Foxhound (USA)-Nifty Alice (First Trump)
T D Easterby Roy Peebles

Placings:465360524613/64101306006054/562301500200-063145125410 (7015)
2009: 5⁰GS, 5⁶GF, 5³GF, 5¹S, 5⁴GF, 5⁵GS, 5¹S, 5²S, 5⁵G, 5⁴SD, 5¹G, 5⁰GS,

	Starts	1st	2nd	3rd	Win & Pl
Career Total (Turf)	49	7	4	5	58010
Career Total (AW)	1	0	0	0	722
93 10/09 Catt 5f	(0-95)H			GD	£9714
89 8/09 Muss 5f	(0-95)H			SFT	£9346
88 7/09 Catt 5f	(0-85)H			SFT	£5180
87 6/08 Haml 5f4y	(0-80)H			GD	£6476
83 6/07 Ayr 5f	(0-85)H			GD	£5829
79 5/07 Rdcr 5f	(0-85)H			GD	£4728
73 10/06 Catt 5f				GD	£3238

Total win prize-money £44514

Going (Turf): Sf: 2-8 GS: 0-7 **Gd: 5-19** GF: 0-14 Fm: 0-1
Distance: **5f/6f: 7-49** 7f-8f: 0-1 9f-13f: 0-0 14f+: 0-0
Track: LH: 0-6 RH: 0-2 Tight: 0-4 Gall: 0-2

Aids: Bl: 0-5 Vi: 0-1 Tstrap: 0-0 Ckp: 0-0
Best Rating: 93 10/09 Catt 5f good

Useful; effective at 5f-6f and acts on most ground; has worn blinkers and a visor; likes to race prominently.

The Only Boss (IRE)

100 **90**

2-y-o ch c Exceed And Excel (AUS)-Aljafliyah (Halling (USA))
W J Haggas Mohammed Jaber

Placings:511 (6841)
2009: 7⁵GF, 6¹GF, 5¹G,

	Starts	1st	2nd	3rd	Win & Pl
Career Total (Turf)	3	2	0	0	9449
90 10/09 Catt 5f				GD	£4209
74 9/09 Newc 6f				G-F	£5051

Total win prize-money £9260

Going (Turf): Sf: 0-0 GS: 0-0 **Gd: 1-1 GF: 1-2** Fm: 0-0
Distance: **5f/6f: 2-2** 7f-8f: 0-1 9f-13f: 0-0 14f+: 0-0
Track: LH: 0-0 RH: 0-0 Tight: 0-0 Gall: 0-0
Aids: Bl: 0-0 Vi: 0-0 Tstrap: 0-0 Ckp: 0-0
Best Rating: 90 10/09 Catt 5f good

Fair; suited by 6f and fast ground.

The Osteopath (IRE)

109 **98**

6-y-o ch g Danehill Dancer (IRE)-Miss Margate (IRE) (Don't Forget Me)
M Dods Kevin Kirkup

Placings:34655/3165000/30661533350/1100020042-00110000 (7294)
2009: 8⁰GF, 8⁰GF, 7¹GS, 8¹GF, 8⁰G, 8⁰G, 7⁰G, 7⁰S,

	Starts	1st	2nd	3rd	Win & Pl
Career Total (Turf)	41	6	2	6	55343
98 6/09 Newc 1m3y	(0-100)H			G-F	£12462
98 5/09 Newc 7f	(0-90)H			G-S	£7443
88 4/08 Leic 7f9y	(0-85)H			SFT	£4209
88 3/08 Rdcr 1m	(0-85)H			G-S	£4210
79 6/07 Wwck 7f26y	(0-80)H			SFT	£4857
79 6/06 Ayr 7f50y	(0-85)H			GD	£7772

Total win prize-money £40954

Going (Turf): **Sf: 2-13 GS: 2-6** Gd: 1-16 GF: 1-6 Fm: 0-0
Distance: 5f/6f: 0-3 **7f-8f: 5-29** 9f-13f: 1-9 14f+: 0-0
Track: **LH: 2-21** RH: 0-2 Tight: 0-9 Gall: 0-1
Aids: Bl: 0-3 Vi: 0-0 Tstrap: 2-13 Ckp: 2-13
Best Rating: 98 6/09 Newc 1m3y gd-fm

Very useful; effective over 7f-1m; acts on most ground; has worn blinkers or cheekpieces.

The Power Of Phil

(94) (47)

5-y-o b g Komaite (USA)-Starboard Tack (FR) (Saddlers' Hall (IRE))
Tom Dascombe Alan Solomon

Placings:0/0600024/03030-554 (0323)
2009: 8⁵SD, 8⁵SD, 8⁴SD,

	Starts	1st	2nd	3rd	Win & Pl
Career Total (Turf)	1	0	0	0	
Career Total (AW)	15	0	1	2	1008

Going (Turf): Sf: 0-0 GS: 0-0 Gd: 0-0 GF: 0-0 Fm: 0-1
Distance: 5f/6f: 0-5 7f-8f: 0-4 9f-13f: 0-7 14f+: 0-0
Track : LH: 0-12 RH: 0-4 Tight: 0-8 Gall: 0-2
Aids: Bl: 0-0 Vi: 0-1 Tstrap: 0-0 Ckp: 0-0
Best Rating: 47 3/08 Wolv 1m141y stand

Plating class; stays 1m, acts on Polytrack.

The Quiet Genius

96(88) (36)**63**

3-y-o b g Daylami (IRE)-Shallat (IRE) (Pennekamp (USA))
Jedd O'Keeffe A Walker

Placings:0650503**0** **(6432)**
2009: 6^{0}GF, 9^{6}GF, 10^{5}GS, 12^{0}GF, 10^{5}G, 14^{0}G, 12^{3}GS, **16**^{0}SD,

	Starts	1st	2nd	3rd	Win & Pl
Career Total (Turf)	**7**	**0**	**0**	**1**	**376**
Career Total (AW)	**1**	**0**	**0**	**0**	

Going (Turf): Sf: 0-0 GS: 0-2 Gd: 0-2 GF: 0-3 Fm: 0-0
Distance: 5f/6f: 0-1 7f-8f: 0-0 9f-13f: 0-5 14f+: 0-2
Track : LH: 0-6 RH: 0-1 Tight: 0-2 Gall: 0-3
Aids: Bl: 0-0 Vi: 0-0 Tstrap: 0-0 Ckp: 0-0
Best Rating: 63 5/09 Newc 1m2f32y gd-sft

The Rectifier (USA)

94 **79**

2-y-o b/br c Langfuhr (CAN)-Western Vision (USA) (Gone West (USA))
Stef Liddiard Mrs Anne Cowley

Placings:042 **(6616)**
2009: 7^{0}GF, 7^{4}GF, 6^{2}G,

	Starts	1st	2nd	3rd	Win & Pl
Career Total (Turf)	**3**	**0**	**1**	**0**	**1830**

Going (Turf): Sf: 0-0 GS: 0-0 Gd: 0-1 GF: 0-2 Fm: 0-0
Distance: 5f/6f: 0-0 7f-8f: 0-3 9f-13f: 0-0 14f+: 0-0
Track : LH: 0-0 RH: 0-0 Tight: 0-0 Gall: 0-0
Aids: Bl: 0-0 Vi: 0-0 Tstrap: 0-0 Ckp: 0-0
Best Rating: 79 10/09 Newb 6f110y good

Fair; stays 6f plus; acts on a sound surface.

The Salwick Flyer (IRE)

41(107) (64)**64**

6-y-o b g Tagula (IRE)-Shimla (IRE) (Rudimentary (USA))
I Semple The Irish Mafia

Placings:0500/4**6**3052010040/0603**1**6304**0**1/21**4**4023660 0-0 **(3021)**
2009: 6^{0}G,

	Starts	1st	2nd	3rd	Win & Pl
Career Total (Turf)	**28**	**2**	**2**	**4**	**10813**
Career Total (AW)	**11**	**2**	**1**	**0**	**4346**

64	1/08	Wolv	1m141y	(0-55)H	STD	£1774
57	12/07	Sthl	7f	(0-53)H	SS	£2047
57	8/07	Haml	6f5y	(0-65)H	G-S	£2266
55	9/06	Catt	5f212y		G-S	£3886

Total win prize-money £9976

Going (Turf): Sf: 0-5 **GS: 2-12** Gd: 0-5 GF: 0-4 Fm: 0-2
Distance: 5f/6f: 1-21 **7f-8f: 2-16** 9f-13f: 1-2 14f+: 0-0
Track : **LH: 3-19** RH: 0-4 **Tight: 2-16** Gall: 0-0
Aids: Bl: 0-0 Vi: 0-0 Tstrap: 0-1 Ckp: 0-1
Best Rating: 64 7/08 Carl 6f192y firm

Moderate sprinter; stays 7f; acts on soft ground and both All-Weather surfaces.

The Saucy Snipe

97(95) (64)**59**

3-y-o b f Josr Algarhoud (IRE)-The Dark Eider (Superlative)
D C O'Brien (P Winkworth 2/10) C Attrell, A Achilleous & D O'Brien

Placings:66**4**0**05**-0051**5**4**5**0 **(6446)**
2009: 9^{0}G, 9^{0}GF, 11^{5}GF, 11^{1}GF, 11^{5}GF, **16**^{4}SD, **16**^{5}SD, **12**^{0}SS,

	Starts	1st	2nd	3rd	Win & Pl
Career Total (Turf)	**8**	**1**	**0**	**0**	**2123**
Career Total (AW)	**6**	**0**	**0**	**0**	**192**

56	7/09	Wind	1m3f135y	G-F	£1978

Total win prize-money £1979

Going (Turf): Sf: 0-0 GS: 0-0 Gd: 0-1 **GF: 1-7** Fm: 0-0
Distance: 5f/6f: 0-5 7f-8f: 0-1 **9f-13f: 1-6** 14f+: 0-2
Track : LH: 0-4 RH: 0-6 **Tight: 1-6** Gall: 0-2
Aids: Bl: 0-0 Vi: 0-0 Tstrap: 0-0 Ckp: 0-0
Best Rating: 64 10/08 Ling 1m stand

Moderate; effective at around 1m3f; acts on fast ground.

The Scorching Wind (IRE)

99(109) (97)**78**

3-y-o b c Fasliyev (USA)-Rose Of Mooncoin (IRE) (Brief Truce (USA))
S C Williams Chris Watkins And David N Reynolds

Placings:00-0021621**1200** **(7827)**
2009: 7^{0}G, 6^{0}GF, 6^{2}G, 6^{1}G, 7^{6}S, 7^{2}G, **8**^{1}SD, **7**^{1}SD, **8**^{2}SD, 8^{0}G, 8^{0}SD,

	Starts	1st	2nd	3rd	Win & Pl
Career Total (Turf)	**9**	**1**	**2**	**0**	**4738**
Career Total (AW)	**4**	**2**	**1**	**0**	**10226**

97	9/09	Kemp	7f	(0-85)H	STD	£4727
85	9/09	Kemp	1m	(0-80)H	STD	£4727
69	6/09	Donc	6f	(0-70)H	GD	£3238

Total win prize-money £12692

Going (Turf): Sf: 0-2 GS: 0-0 **Gd: 1-6** GF: 0-1 Fm: 0-0
Distance: 5f/6f: 1-2 **7f-8f: 2-11** 9f-13f: 0-0 14f+: 0-0
Track : LH: 0-0 **RH: 2-4** Tight: 0-0 Gall: 0-0
Aids: Bl: 0-0 Vi: 0-0 Tstrap: 0-0 Ckp: 0-0
Best Rating: 97 9/09 Kemp 7f stand

Fair; effective over 6f-1m; acts on good ground and on Polytrack; has worn a tongue tie.

The Shuffler

90(84) (64)**60**

2-y-o b g Reset (AUS)-Lucky Dice (Perugino (USA))
G L Moore Heart Of The South Racing

Placings:04565400 **(6589)**
2009: 5^{0}GF, 5^{4}GF, 6^{5}SD, 6^{6}GF, 5^{5}GF, 6^{4}S, 5^{0}SD, 6^{0}GS,

	Starts	1st	2nd	3rd	Win & Pl
Career Total (Turf)	**6**	**0**	**0**	**0**	**1311**
Career Total (AW)	**2**	**0**	**0**	**0**	**0**

Going (Turf): Sf: 0-1 GS: 0-1 Gd: 0-0 GF: 0-4 Fm: 0-0
Distance: 5f/6f: 0-7 7f-8f: 0-1 9f-13f: 0-0 14f+: 0-0
Track : LH: 0-2 RH: 0-0 Tight: 0-2 Gall: 0-1
Aids: Bl: 0-0 Vi: 0-0 Tstrap: 0-0 Ckp: 0-0
Best Rating: 64 6/09 Ling 6f stand

The Slider

(93) (48)**15**

5-y-o b m Erhaab (USA)-Cottage Maid (Inchinor)
Mrs L C Jewell R I B Young and Mrs F J Meekins

Placings:4142/35000054/0500000-00 **(2708)**
2009: 10^{0}SD, 12^{0}SD,

	Starts	1st	2nd	3rd	Win & Pl
Career Total (Turf)	**4**	**1**	**0**	**0**	**3731**
Career Total (AW)	**17**	**0**	**1**	**1**	**1008**

51	7/06	Bevl	7f100y	FRM	£3562

Total win prize-money £3562

Going (Turf): Sf: 0-0 GS: 0-0 Gd: 0-1 GF: 0-1 **Fm: 1-2**
Distance: 5f/6f: 0-0 **7f-8f: 1-8** 9f-13f: 0-12 14f+: 0-1
Track : LH: 0-11 **RH: 1-9** Tight: 0-9 Gall: 0-1
Aids: Bl: 0-0 Vi: 0-2 Tstrap: 0-8 Ckp: 0-8
Best Rating: 54 7/06 Wolv 7f32y stand

The Snatcher (IRE)

89(104) (96)**96**

6-y-o b h Indian Danehill (IRE)-Saninka (IRE) (Doyoun)
R Hannon Mrs R Ablett

Placings:22121400152/63361530/0**5**60000**3**06**503**/15225 02420-**0300060** **(7054)**
2009: 8^{0}SD, **8**^{3}SD, 8^{0}G, 7^{0}G, **8**^{0}SD, **7**^{6}SD, **8**^{0}SD,

	Starts	1st	2nd	3rd	Win & Pl
Career Total (Turf)	**38**	**5**	**7**	**3**	**61483**
Career Total (AW)	**11**	**0**	**1**	**3**	**5740**

94	4/08	Bath	1m5y	(0-85)H	GD	£5180
95	7/06	Sand	7f16y	(0-95)H	G-F	£8724
88	9/05	NmkR	6f	(0-85)	GD	£5616
88	6/05	Wind	6f		GD	£4251
83	5/05	Ripn	5f		SFT	£4795

Total win prize-money £28569

Going (Turf): Sf: 1-9 GS: 0-9 **Gd: 3-11** GF: 1-9 Fm: 0-0
Distance: **5f/6f: 3-12** 7f-8f: 1-32 9f-13f: 1-5 14f+: 0-0
Track : LH: 1-10 RH: 1-19 Tight: 1-6 Gall: 1-5
Aids: Bl: 0-0 Vi: 0-1 Tstrap: 0-0 Ckp: 0-0
Best Rating: 96 9/08 Ayr 1m heavy

Useful; effective at around 7f-1m; acts on most ground and on Polytrack; likes to race prominently.

The Spicer

65(82) (58)

4-y-o b g Lujain (USA)-Spicey (Mizoram (USA))
F Sheridan Frank Sheridan

Placings:00000 **(3632)**
2009: 7^{0}SD, 8^{0}SD, 6^{0}G, 8^{0}SD, 6^{0}G,

	Starts	1st	2nd	3rd	Win & Pl
Career Total (Turf)	**2**	**0**	**0**	**0**	
Career Total (AW)	**3**	**0**	**0**	**0**	

Going (Turf): Sf: 0-0 GS: 0-0 Gd: 0-2 GF: 0-0 Fm: 0-0
Distance: 5f/6f: 0-1 7f-8f: 0-3 9f-13f: 0-1 14f+: 0-0
Track : LH: 0-2 RH: 0-1 Tight: 0-2 Gall: 0-0
Aids: Bl: 0-1 Vi: 0-0 Tstrap: 0-0 Ckp: 0-0
Best Rating: 58 4/09 Kemp 7f stand

The Staffy (IRE)

87(97) (62)**35**

4-y-o b g Redback-Lady Charlotte (Night Shift (USA))
Tom Dascombe (N J Vaughan 15/6) MO, SP, NB, CM

Placings:5-26000P (6831)
2009: 9^{2}SD, 9^{6}SD, 8^{0}GF, 10^{0}GS, 7^{0}SF, 9^{P}SF,

	Starts	1st	2nd	3rd	Win & Pl
Career Total (Turf)	2	0	0	0	
Career Total (AW)	5	0	1	0	806

Going (Turf): Sf: 0-0 GS: 0-1 Gd: 0-0 GF: 0-1 Fm: 0-0
Distance: 5f/6f: 0-0 7f-8f: 0-2 9f-13f: 0-5 14f+: 0-0
Track : LH: 0-5 RH: 0-1 Tight: 0-4 Gall: 0-0
Aids: Bl: 0-0 Vi: 0-1 Tstrap: 0-0 Ckp: 0-0
Best Rating: 62 2/09 Wolv 1m1f103y stand

Modest; effective over 1m1f; acts on Polytrack.

The Starboard Bow

92(94) (86)86
2-y-o b c Observatory (USA)-Overboard (IRE) (Rainbow Quest (USA))
S Kirk C Wright & The Hon Mrs J M Corbett

Placings:10200 (6805)
2009: 7^{1}G, 8^{0}G, 8^{2}SD, 7^{0}GF, 8^{0}SD,

	Starts	1st	2nd	3rd	Win & Pl
Career Total (Turf)	3	1	0	0	2590
Career Total (AW)	2	0	1	0	1008

78	8/09	Yarm	7f3y	GD	£2590

Total win prize-money £2590

Going (Turf): Sf: 0-0 GS: 0-0 Gd: 1-2 GF: 0-1 Fm: 0-0
Distance: 5f/6f: 0-0 7f-8f: 1-3 9f-13f: 0-2 14f+: 0-0
Track : LH: 0-2 RH: 0-0 Tight: 0-2 Gall: 0-0
Aids: Bl: 0-0 Vi: 0-0 Tstrap: 0-0 Ckp: 0-0
Best Rating: 86 9/09 Wolv 1m141y stand

Useful; debut winner at Yarmouth over 7f in August; acts on good ground and Polytrack.

The Strig

80(94) (69)47
2-y-o b g Mujahid (USA)-Pretty Kool (Inchinor)
S C Williams Brian Piper & David Cobill

Placings:053 (7571)
2009: 5^{0}GF, 5^{5}SD, 6^{3}SD,

	Starts	1st	2nd	3rd	Win & Pl
Career Total (Turf)	1	0	0	0	
Career Total (AW)	2	0	0	1	482

Going (Turf): Sf: 0-0 GS: 0-0 Gd: 0-0 GF: 0-1 Fm: 0-0
Distance: 5f/6f: 0-3 7f-8f: 0-0 9f-13f: 0-0 14f+: 0-0
Track : LH: 0-1 RH: 0-1 Tight: 0-1 Gall: 0-0
Aids: Bl: 0-0 Vi: 0-0 Tstrap: 0-0 Ckp: 0-0
Best Rating: 69 11/09 Ling 6f stand

Fair; stays 6f and acts on Polytrack.

The Tatling (IRE)

105(108) (92)88
12-y-o b/br g Perugino (USA)-Aunty Eileen (Ahonoora)
J M Bradley J M Bradley

Placings:364121262/0300/020/006001052102013/222436 1312655340/234103221320/05003222165/0540066466060 /3150400505000/00450603165415-41053632432424311523305302 (7872)
2009: 5^{4}SS, 5^{1}SD, 5^{0}SD, 5^{5}SD, 5^{3}SD, 5^{6}GF, 5^{3}GF, 6^{2}GF, 6^{4}GF, 6^{3}GF, 5^{2}F, 5^{4}F, 5^{2}G, 5^{4}G, 5^{3}GF, 5^{1}G, 5^{1}G, 5^{5}G, 5^{2}GF, 5^{3}GF, 5^{3}F, 5^{0}GF, 5^{5}GS, 5^{0}SD, 5^{5}SD,

	Starts	1st	2nd	3rd	Win & Pl
Career Total (Turf)	124	14	21	17	664926
Career Total (AW)	14	2	1	2	12860

86	8/09	Newb	5f34y	(0-85)H	GD	£4857
78	7/09	Bath	5f11y		GD	£2072
92	2/09	Sthl	5f	(0-85)H	STD	£4857
92	12/08	Sthl	5f	(0-85)H	STD	£4857
88	10/08	Brig	5f213y	(0-80)H	G-S	£5929
105	5/07	Muss	5f		G-F	£12464
116	9/05	Newb	5f34y		G-F	£29000
119	9/04	Newb	5f34y		GD	£29000
119	6/04	Asct	5f	A	G-F	£81200
111	7/03	Gdwd	5f	A	GD	£29000
116	7/03	Sand	5f6y	A	GD	£18560
107	10/02	York	6f	B(0-105)H	G-F	£25496
96	8/02	Sand	5f6y	B(0-100)H	G-F	£11838
90	7/02	Catt	5f	F	G-F	£2933
83	8/99	Brig	5f59y	E	SFT	£2749
92	7/99	Yarm	5f43y	D	G-F	£3557

Total win prize-money £268372

Going (Turf): Sf: 1-10 GS: 1-18 Gd: 5-29 GF: 7-60 Fm: 0-5
Distance: 5f/6f: 16-133 7f-8f: 0-5 9f-13f: 0-0 14f+: 0-0
Track : LH: 3-17 RH: 0-3 Tight: 0-7 Gall: 1-9
Aids: Bl: 0-0 Vi: 0-0 Tstrap: 0-0 Ckp: 0-0
Best Rating: 119 10/04 Lonc 5f good

Useful; formerly Group class; winner of the Group 2 King's Stand Stakes in 2004; effective over 5f-6f; acts on good ground or faster and on Fibresand; likes to come late off a strong pace.

The Thrifty Bear

(85) (17)16
6-y-o ch g Rambling Bear-Prudent Pet (Distant Relative)
C W Fairhurst Mrs C A Arnold

Placings:410/00000400/00000000/0000-0 (0535)
2009: 5^{0}SD,

	Starts	1st	2nd	3rd	Win & Pl
Career Total (Turf)	23	1	0	0	7111
Career Total (AW)	2	0	0	0	

69	8/05	Thsk	6f	G-F	£6500

Total win prize-money £6500

Going (Turf): Sf: 0-3 GS: 0-4 Gd: 0-5 GF: 1-10 Fm: 0-1
Distance: 5f/6f: 1-20 7f-8f: 0-4 9f-13f: 0-1 14f+: 0-0
Track : LH: 0-3 RH: 0-5 Tight: 0-6 Gall: 0-1
Aids: Bl: 0-7 Vi: 0-0 Tstrap: 0-1 Ckp: 0-1
Best Rating: 69 8/05 Thsk 6f gd-fm

The Two G's

75(88) (56)31
2-y-o b f Mark Of Esteem (IRE)-Intellibet One (Compton Place)
P D Evans G E Amey

Placings:00505056 (7757)
2009: 5^{0}GF, 5^{0}GF, 5^{5}SD, 6^{0}SD, 5^{5}SD, 5^{0}SD, 6^{5}SD, 6^{6}SD,

	Starts	1st	2nd	3rd	Win & Pl
Career Total (Turf)	2	0	0	0	
Career Total (AW)	6	0	0	0	0

Going (Turf): Sf: 0-0 GS: 0-0 Gd: 0-0 GF: 0-2 Fm: 0-0
Distance: 5f/6f: 0-8 7f-8f: 0-0 9f-13f: 0-0 14f+: 0-0
Track : LH: 0-4 RH: 0-2 Tight: 0-1 Gall: 0-0
Aids: Bl: 0-0 Vi: 0-0 Tstrap: 0-1 Ckp: 0-1
Best Rating: 56 9/09 Kemp 5f stand

The Wee Chief (IRE)

91(100) (69)64
3-y-o ch g King Charlemagne (USA)-La Belle Clare (IRE) (Paris House)
J C Fox Rick Kavanagh & Johnny Lonergan

Placings:410 (7738)
2009: 6^{4}GF, 6^{1}SD, 6^{0}SD,

	Starts	1st	2nd	3rd	Win & Pl
Career Total (Turf)	1	0	0	0	289
Career Total (AW)	2	1	0	0	2047

69	11/09	Kemp	6f	STD	£2047

Total win prize-money £2047

Going (Turf): Sf: 0-0 GS: 0-0 Gd: 0-0 GF: 0-1 Fm: 0-0
Distance: 5f/6f: 1-3 7f-8f: 0-0 9f-13f: 0-0 14f+: 0-0
Track : LH: 0-0 RH: 1-2 Tight: 0-0 Gall: 0-0
Aids: Bl: 0-0 Vi: 0-0 Tstrap: 0-0 Ckp: 0-0
Best Rating: 69 11/09 Kemp 6f stand

Modest; stays 6f; acts on fast ground and on Polytrack; may do better.

The Which Doctor

107(109) (91)93
4-y-o b g Medicean-Oomph (Shareef Dancer (USA))
J Noseda G C Stevens

Placings:21/30031551-043506105 (7035)
2009: 8^{0}GF, 8^{4}SD, 8^{3}G, 10^{5}G, 10^{0}GF, 10^{6}G, 10^{1}GF, 9^{0}GF, 10^{5}S,

	Starts	1st	2nd	3rd	Win & Pl
Career Total (Turf)	15	2	1	3	18827
Career Total (AW)	4	2	0	0	11340

93	9/09	Newb	1m2f6y	(0-85)H	G-F	£4857
91	10/08	Ling	1m	(0-95)H	STD	£8100
89	7/08	Sand	1m14y	(0-80)H	G-F	£7123
76	10/07	Ling	7f		STD	£2590

Total win prize-money £22672

Going (Turf): Sf: 0-1 GS: 0-1 Gd: 0-5 GF: 2-8 Fm: 0-0
Distance: 5f/6f: 0-0 7f-8f: 2-7 9f-13f: 2-12 14f+: 0-0
Track : LH: 3-7 RH: 1-9 Tight: 2-7 Gall: 1-2
Aids: Bl: 0-0 Vi: 0-0 Tstrap: 0-0 Ckp: 0-0
Best Rating: 93 9/09 Newb 1m2f6y gd-fm

Useful; stays 1m2f; acts on a sound surface; handles Polytrack.

The Wily Woodcock

63(98) (64)36
5-y-o b g Mark Of Esteem (IRE)-Lonely Shore (Blakeney)
T Wall (G L Moore 23/3) Miss R E Price

Placings:00/4040/2400030634-600000 (7500)
2009: 8^{6}SD, 8^{0}F, 7^{0}SD, 9^{0}SD, 7^{0}SD, 8^{0}SD,

	Starts	1st	2nd	3rd	Win & Pl
Career Total (Turf)	7	0	0	0	337
Career Total (AW)	15	0	1	2	1878

Going (Turf): Sf: 0-2 GS: 0-0 Gd: 0-2 GF: 0-2 Fm: 0-1
Distance: 5f/6f: 0-0 7f-8f: 0-10 9f-13f: 0-12 14f+: 0-0
Track : LH: 0-15 RH: 0-6 Tight: 0-11 Gall: 0-3
Aids: Bl: 0-1 Vi: 0-0 Tstrap: 0-2 Ckp: 0-2
Best Rating: 71 5/08 GrLe 1m stand

The Winged Assasin (USA)

101(96) (68)**74**

3-y-o b g Fusaichi Pegasus (USA)-Gran Dama (USA) (Rahy (USA))

J Akehurst Bill Hinge & John Searchfield

Placings:00-25150060R (6547)

2009: 6^{2}SD, 8^{5}SD, 6^{1}GF, 8^{5}G, 8^{0}G, 8^{0}GF, 7^{6}GF, 9^{0}GF, 8^{R}G,

	Starts	1st	2nd	3rd	Win & Pl
Career Total (Turf)	9	1	0	0	3071
Career Total (AW)	2	0	1	0	806

74 4/09 Folk 6f (0-75)H G-F £3070

Total win prize-money £3071

Going (Turf): Sf: 0-1 GS: 0-0 Gd: 0-3 **GF: 1-4** Fm: 0-0
Distance: **5f/6f: 1-2** 7f-8f: 0-4 9f-13f: 0-5 14f+: 0-0
Track : LH: 0-5 RH: 0-5 Tight: 0-6 Gall: 0-0
Aids: Bl: 0-0 Vi: 0-0 Tstrap: 0-0 Ckp: 0-0
Best Rating: **74** 4/09 Folk 6f gd-fm

Fair; effective over 6f; acts on good ground and on Polytrack.

Theatre Street (IRE)

100(95) (73)**80**

3-y-o b f Invincible Spirit (IRE)-Markova (IRE) (Marju (IRE))

S Dow (J Noseda 14/4) Mark McAllister

Placings:2-213016 (5805)

2009: 5^{2}SD, 5^{1}SD, 6^{3}SD, 5^{0}G, 6^{1}G, 6^{6}GF,

	Starts	1st	2nd	3rd	Win & Pl
Career Total (Turf)	3	1	0	0	3238
Career Total (AW)	4	1	2	1	5064

80 8/09 Epsm 6f (0-75)H GD £3238
73 1/09 Ling 5f STD £2729

Total win prize-money £5968

Going (Turf): Sf: 0-0 GS: 0-0 **Gd: 1-2** GF: 0-1 Fm: 0-0
Distance: **5f/6f: 2-7** 7f-8f: 0-0 9f-13f: 0-0 14f+: 0-0
Track : **LH: 2-6** RH: 0-0 **Tight: 2-6** Gall: 0-0
Aids: Bl: 0-0 Vi: 0-0 Tstrap: 0-0 Ckp: 0-0
Best Rating: **80** 8/09 Epsm 6f good

Fair; effective over 5f-6f; acts on Polytrack.

Thebes

109(111) (97)**101**

4-y-o ch g Cadeaux Genereux-See You Later (Emarati (USA))

M Johnston Sheikh Hamdan Bin Mohammed Al Maktoum

Placings:2111000154300**0**-1400232451000000406 (7227)

2009: 5^{1}SD, 7^{4}SD, 6^{0}GF, 7^{0}SD, 6^{2}F, 6^{3}GF, 6^{2}GF, 6^{4}GF, 6^{5}S, 6^{1}GF, 6^{0}G, 7^{0}G, 6^{0}S, 6^{0}GF, 6^{0}GS, 6^{0}G, 7^{4}GF, 7^{0}G, 6^{6}SD,

	Starts	1st	2nd	3rd	Win & Pl
Career Total (Turf)	24	2	2	2	56792
Career Total (AW)	9	4	1	0	22165

101 7/09 Chep 6f16y (0-100)H G-F £12616
95 3/09 Wolv 5f216y (0-100)H STD £11215
94 8/08 NmkJ 6f (0-105)H GD £18693
91 3/08 Kemp 6f (0-85)H STD £4210
93 3/08 Wolv 7f32y (0-70)H STD £2457
86 2/08 Sthl 6f SS £2457

Total win prize-money £51649

Going (Turf): Sf: 0-3 GS: 0-3 **Gd: 1-5 GF: 1-11** Fm: 0-1
Distance: **5f/6f: 4-20** 7f-8f: 2-13 9f-13f: 0-0 14f+: 0-0
Track : **LH: 3-9** RH: 1-3 **Tight: 2-5** Gall: 0-0
Aids: Bl: 0-0 Vi: 0-0 Tstrap: 0-0 Ckp: 0-0
Best Rating: **101** 7/09 Chep 6f16y gd-fm

Useful; has won over 7f, but seems best suited by shorter; acts on good ground and on sand; likes to race prominently.

Thefillyfromepsom

79(95) (55)**19**

3-y-o b f Royal Academy (USA)-For Love (USA) (Sultry Song (USA))

P M Phelan Timesquare Ltd

Placings:50-00000 (4643)

2009: 7^{0}SD, 10^{0}SD, 7^{0}GF, 7^{0}GF, 5^{0}GF,

	Starts	1st	2nd	3rd	Win & Pl
Career Total (Turf)	3	0	0	0	
Career Total (AW)	4	0	0	0	0

Going (Turf): **Sf: 0-0 GS: 0-0 Gd: 0-0 GF: 0-3 Fm: 0-0**
Distance: 5f/6f: 0-1 7f-8f: 0-4 9f-13f: 0-2 14f+: 0-0
Track : LH: 0-3 RH: 0-2 Tight: 0-2 Gall: 0-0
Aids: Bl: 0-0 Vi: 0-1 Tstrap: 0-0 Ckp: 0-0
Best Rating: **55** 3/09 Ling 7f stand

Theflyingscottie

73(87) (55)**57**

7-y-o gr g Paris House-Miss Flossa (FR) (Big John (FR))

D Shaw Roger Milward

Placings:00/00/3623515402040/5-0 (2294)

2009: 12^{0}GF,

	Starts	1st	2nd	3rd	Win & Pl
Career Total (Turf)	10	1	0	1	2651
Career Total (AW)	9	0	2	1	1654

57 7/07 Thsk 2m (0-60)H SFT £2218

Total win prize-money £2218

Going (Turf): **Sf: 1-2** GS: 0-0 Gd: 0-2 GF: 0-5 Fm: 0-1
Distance: 5f/6f: 0-2 7f-8f: 0-1 9f-13f: 0-5 **14f+: 1-11**
Track : **LH: 1-14** RH: 0-3 **Tight: 1-11** Gall: 0-3
Aids: Bl: 0-0 **Vi: 1-10** Tstrap: 0-0 Ckp: 0-0
Best Rating: **57** 7/07 Thsk 2m soft

Moderate; stays 2m; wears a visor; acts on Polytrack and soft ground.

Thegirlsgonewild (USA)

91(87) (52)**47**

3-y-o b/br f Gone West (USA)-Coconut Girl (USA) (Cryptoclearance (USA))

H J L Dunlop H E Sheikh Sultan Bin Khalifa Al Nahyan

Placings:0-060 (2709)

2009: 8^{0}SD, 10^{6}S, 10^{0}SD,

	Starts	1st	2nd	3rd	Win & Pl
Career Total (Turf)	1	0	0	0	0
Career Total (AW)	3	0	0	0	

Going (Turf): **Sf: 0-1 GS: 0-0 Gd: 0-0 GF: 0-0 Fm: 0-0**
Distance: 5f/6f: 0-1 7f-8f: 0-1 9f-13f: 0-2 14f+: 0-0
Track : LH: 0-2 RH: 0-2 Tight: 0-1 Gall: 0-0
Aids: Bl: 0-0 Vi: 0-0 Tstrap: 0-0 Ckp: 0-0
Best Rating: **52** 10/08 Kemp 6f stand

Theladyinquestion

97 **78**

2-y-o b f Dubawi (IRE)-Whazzat (Daylami (IRE))

A M Balding D H Caslon & Mildmay Racing

Placings:510 (6241)

2009: 6^{5}GF, 6^{1}G, 6^{0}G,

	Starts	1st	2nd	3rd	Win & Pl
Career Total (Turf)	3	1	0	0	3238

78 8/09 Sals 6f GD £3238

Total win prize-money £3238

Going (Turf): Sf: 0-0 GS: 0-0 **Gd: 1-2** GF: 0-1 Fm: 0-0
Distance: **5f/6f: 1-1** 7f-8f: 0-2 9f-13f: 0-0 14f+: 0-0
Track : LH: 0-0 RH: 0-0 Tight: 0-0 Gall: 0-0
Aids: Bl: 0-0 Vi: 0-0 Tstrap: 0-0 Ckp: 0-0
Best Rating: **78** 8/09 Sals 6f good

Fair; effective over 6f; acts on good ground.

Theladyisatramp

83(85) (57)**40**

2-y-o b f Bahamian Bounty-Affair Of State (IRE) (Tate Gallery (USA))

M L W Bell Stephen Crown & Maurice Manasseh

Placings:000 (6774)

2009: 6^{0}GF, 7^{0}SD, 6^{0}SD,

	Starts	1st	2nd	3rd	Win & Pl
Career Total (Turf)	1	0	0	0	
Career Total (AW)	2	0	0	0	

Going (Turf): **Sf: 0-0 GS: 0-0 Gd: 0-0 GF: 0-1 Fm: 0-0**
Distance: 5f/6f: 0-2 7f-8f: 0-1 9f-13f: 0-0 14f+: 0-0
Track : LH: 0-0 RH: 0-2 Tight: 0-0 Gall: 0-1
Aids: Bl: 0-0 Vi: 0-0 Tstrap: 0-0 Ckp: 0-0
Best Rating: **57** 9/09 Kemp 7f stand

Themanforacrisis (IRE)

88 **61**

2-y-o b c Oratorio (IRE)-Sister Golden Hair (IRE) (Glint Of Gold)

R M Beckett Broadway Racing

Placings:5006 (6391)

2009: 6^{5}S, 6^{0}GF, 7^{0}G, 10^{6}GF,

	Starts	1st	2nd	3rd	Win & Pl
Career Total (Turf)	4	0	0	0	0

Going (Turf): **Sf: 0-1 GS: 0-0 Gd: 0-1 GF: 0-2 Fm: 0-0**
Distance: 5f/6f: 0-0 7f-8f: 0-3 9f-13f: 0-1 14f+: 0-0
Track : LH: 0-2 RH: 0-0 Tight: 0-0 Gall: 0-0
Aids: Bl: 0-0 Vi: 0-0 Tstrap: 0-0 Ckp: 0-0
Best Rating: **61** 7/09 Sals 6f212y soft

Theme Catcher (IRE)

90(67) **63**

4-y-o b g Red Ransom (USA)-Canouan (IRE) (Sadler's Wells (USA))

G Brown F J Harty

Placings:50/00-60 (5683)

2009: 12^{6}GF, 8^{0}SD,

	Starts	1st	2nd	3rd	Win & Pl
Career Total (Turf)	5	0	0	0	0

	Starts	1st	2nd	3rd	Win & Pl
Career Total (AW)	1	0	0	0	

Going (Turf): Sf: 0-1 GS: 0-0 Gd: 0-0 GF: 0-2 Fm: 0-0
Distance: 5f/6f: 0-0 7f-8f: 0-2 9f-13f: 0-4 14f+: 0-0
Track : LH: 0-3 RH: 0-2 Tight: 0-2 Gall: 0-0
Aids: Bl: 0-0 Vi: 0-1 Tstrap: 0-0 Ckp: 0-0
Best Rating: 69 10/07 Curr 7f soft

Theocritus (USA)

106 (89)90

4-y-o b g Theatrical-Candace In Aspen (USA) (Woodman (USA))
D M Simcock Dr Marwan Koukash

Placings:6122243-06112401123 (5963)
2009: 10^{0}G, 11^{6}GF, 9^{1}GF, 9^{1}G, 8^{2}GF, 10^{4}GF, 10^{0}G, 9^{1}F, 10^{1}GF, 9^{2}GF, 10^{3}G,

	Starts	1st	2nd	3rd	Win & Pl
Career Total (Turf)	17	5	5	1	26286
Career Total (AW)	1	0	0	1	1472

73 8/09 Yarm 1m2f21y G-F £2072
79 8/09 Brig 1m1f209y (0-70)H FRM £3038
64 6/09 Brig 1m1f209y GD £1942
68 5/09 Brig 1m1f209y G-F £1942
83 5/08 Leop 1m2f GD £7621
Total win prize-money £16618

Going (Turf): Sf: 0-0 GS: 0-0 Gd: 2-7 GF: 2-6 Fm: 1-1
Distance: 5f/6f: 0-0 7f-8f: 0-2 9f-13f: 5-16 14f+: 0-0
Track : LH: 5-14 RH: 0-3 Tight: 1-7 Gall: 0-0
Aids: Bl: 0-3 Vi: 0-0 Tstrap: 0-0 Ckp: 0-0
Best Rating: 90 7/08 Klny 1m3f good

Fair; ex-Irish; stays 1m2f; acts on good and faster ground; has worn blinkers.

Theola (IRE)

107(91) (51)85

3-y-o bl f Kalanisi (IRE)-Third Dimension (FR) (Suave Dancer (USA))
M H Tompkins E Buddle

Placings:0-6332211 (6676)
2009: 12^{6}GF, 12^{3}GF, 14^{3}HY, 14^{2}GF, 16^{2}G, 17^{1}GF, 18^{1}G,

	Starts	1st	2nd	3rd	Win & Pl
Career Total (Turf)	7	2	2	2	13616
Career Total (AW)	1	0	0	0	

85 10/09 York 2m2f (0-85)H GD £7641
80 9/09 Pont 2m1f22y (0-75)H G-F £3238
Total win prize-money £10880

Going (Turf): Sf: 0-1 GS: 0-0 Gd: 1-2 GF: 1-4 Fm: 0-0
Distance: 5f/6f: 0-0 7f-8f: 0-0 9f-13f: 0-3 14f+: 2-5
Track : LH: 2-7 RH: 0-1 Tight: 0-2 Gall: 1-2
Aids: Bl: 0-0 Vi: 0-0 Tstrap: 0-0 Ckp: 0-0
Best Rating: 85 10/09 York 2m2f good

Useful; stays 2m1f; acts on fast and on heavy ground.

Theologist (IRE)

102 76

3-y-o b c Galileo (IRE)-Medina (IRE) (Pennekamp (USA))
Mrs A J Perrett A D Spence

Placings:00-346523233 (6935)
2009: 7^{3}GF, 9^{4}GF, 11^{6}G, 12^{5}G, 14^{2}G, 16^{3}G, 14^{2}GF, 14^{3}GF, 17^{3}G,

	Starts	1st	2nd	3rd	Win & Pl
Career Total (Turf)	11	0	2	4	3790

Going (Turf): Sf: 0-0 GS: 0-0 Gd: 0-5 GF: 0-6 Fm: 0-0
Distance: 5f/6f: 0-0 7f-8f: 0-3 9f-13f: 0-3 14f+: 0-5
Track : LH: 0-2 RH: 0-6 Tight: 0-6 Gall: 0-1
Aids: Bl: 0-0 Vi: 0-2 Tstrap: 0-0 Ckp: 0-0
Best Rating: 76 9/09 Sals 1m6f21y gd-fm

Modest; stays 1m6f-plus; acts on fast ground.

Theology

95 77

2-y-o b c Galileo (IRE)-Biographie (Mtoto)
J Noseda Highclere Thoroughbred Racing Touchstone

Placings:30 (6810)
2009: 8^{3}GF, 8^{0}G,

	Starts	1st	2nd	3rd	Win & Pl
Career Total (Turf)	2	0	0	1	770

Going (Turf): Sf: 0-0 GS: 0-0 Gd: 0-1 GF: 0-1 Fm: 0-0
Distance: 5f/6f: 0-0 7f-8f: 0-2 9f-13f: 0-0 14f+: 0-0
Track : LH: 0-0 RH: 0-0 Tight: 0-0 Gall: 0-0
Aids: Bl: 0-0 Vi: 0-0 Tstrap: 0-0 Ckp: 0-0
Best Rating: 77 10/09 NmkR 1m gd-fm

Useful; stays 1m and acts on fast ground.

Theonebox (USA)

102(105) (84)80

4-y-o ch g Johannesburg (USA)-Khalifa Of Kushog (USA) (Air Forbes Won (USA))
N P Moore (N J Vaughan 30/6) Mrs Ruth M Serrell

Placings:0/02001-6603000 (7759)
2009: 8^{6}SD, 9^{6}SD, 7^{0}GF, 8^{3}G, 9^{0}GF, 10^{0}SD, 8^{0}SD,

	Starts	1st	2nd	3rd	Win & Pl
Career Total (Turf)	8	0	1	1	2158
Career Total (AW)	5	1	0	0	3886

84 12/08 Wolv 1m141y (0-75)H STD £3885
Total win prize-money £3886

Going (Turf): Sf: 0-1 GS: 0-1 Gd: 0-2 GF: 0-4 Fm: 0-0
Distance: 5f/6f: 0-1 7f-8f: 0-3 9f-13f: 1-9 14f+: 0-0
Track : LH: 1-10 RH: 0-2 Tight: 1-6 Gall: 0-2
Aids: Bl: 0-0 Vi: 0-0 Tstrap: 0-0 Ckp: 0-0
Best Rating: 84 12/08 Wolv 1m141y stand

There We Go (IRE)

81 34

3-y-o b g Pyrus (USA)-Ghayaat (USA) (Lyphard (USA))
G A Swinbank B Valentine

Placings:604 (4531)
2009: 7^{6}GS, 9^{0}G, 6^{4}S,

	Starts	1st	2nd	3rd	Win & Pl
Career Total (Turf)	3	0	0	0	192

Going (Turf): Sf: 0-1 GS: 0-1 Gd: 0-1 GF: 0-0 Fm: 0-0
Distance: 5f/6f: 0-0 7f-8f: 0-2 9f-13f: 0-1 14f+: 0-0
Track : LH: 0-1 RH: 0-1 Tight: 0-1 Gall: 0-0
Aids: Bl: 0-0 Vi: 0-0 Tstrap: 0-0 Ckp: 0-0
Best Rating: 34 7/09 Carl 1m1f61y good

Thereafter (USA)

(90) (71)

2-y-o ch f Lion Heart (USA)-Alvernia (USA) (Alydar (USA))
R Charlton K Abdulla

Placings:30 (6164)
2009: 6^{3}SD, 7^{0}SD,

	Starts	1st	2nd	3rd	Win & Pl
Career Total (Turf)	0	0	0	0	
Career Total (AW)	2	0	0	1	770

Going (Turf): Sf: 0-0 GS: 0-0 Gd: 0-0 GF: 0-0 Fm: 0-0
Distance: 5f/6f: 0-1 7f-8f: 0-1 9f-13f: 0-0 14f+: 0-0
Track : LH: 0-0 RH: 0-2 Tight: 0-0 Gall: 0-0
Aids: Bl: 0-0 Vi: 0-0 Tstrap: 0-0 Ckp: 0-0
Best Rating: 71 9/09 Kemp 6f stand

Modest; should be suited by 7f; acts on Polytrack.

Thescottishsoldier

76 25

2-y-o ch g Observatory (USA)-Twenty Seven (IRE) (Efisio)
A G Foster R Colvin

Placings:000 (7116)
2009: 7^{0}GS, 6^{0}GF, 8^{0}GS,

	Starts	1st	2nd	3rd	Win & Pl
Career Total (Turf)	3	0	0	0	

Going (Turf): Sf: 0-0 GS: 0-2 Gd: 0-0 GF: 0-1 Fm: 0-0
Distance: 5f/6f: 0-1 7f-8f: 0-2 9f-13f: 0-0 14f+: 0-0
Track : LH: 0-0 RH: 0-1 Tight: 0-1 Gall: 0-0
Aids: Bl: 0-0 Vi: 0-0 Tstrap: 0-0 Ckp: 0-0
Best Rating: 25 10/09 Ayr 6f gd-fm

Theta Wave (USA)

102(95) (62)68

3-y-o ch g Buckhar (USA)-Let's Dance (USA) (Thorn Dance (USA))
J R Gask For Sale

Placings:0-43001000 (6252)
2009: 6^{4}SD, 5^{3}SD, 5^{0}SD, 6^{0}GF, 5^{1}G, 6^{0}GF, 5^{0}G, 5^{0}SD,

	Starts	1st	2nd	3rd	Win & Pl
Career Total (Turf)	4	1	0	0	2590
Career Total (AW)	5	0	0	1	596

68 8/09 Ripn 5f (0-65)H GD £2590
Total win prize-money £2590

Going (Turf): Sf: 0-0 GS: 0-0 Gd: 1-2 GF: 0-2 Fm: 0-0
Distance: 5f/6f: 1-8 7f-8f: 0-1 9f-13f: 0-0 14f+: 0-0
Track : LH: 0-6 RH: 0-0 Tight: 0-4 Gall: 0-2
Aids: Bl: 0-0 Vi: 0-0 Tstrap: 0-2 Ckp: 0-2
Best Rating: 68 8/09 Ripn 5f good

Modest; effective over 5f-6f; acts on Polytrack.

Thetearsthaticry (IRE)

96(90) (39)44

5-y-o b g King Charlemagne (USA)-Zeddaana (FR) (Arctic Tern (USA))
A E Jones N F Glynn

Placings:0/006-06 (2912)
2009: 8^{0}SD, 10^{6}F,

	Starts	1st	2nd	3rd	Win & Pl
Career Total (Turf)	5	0	0	0	0
Career Total (AW)	1	0	0	0	

Going (Turf): Sf: 0-0 GS: 0-0 Gd: 0-1 GF: 0-2 Fm: 0-1
Distance: 5f/6f: 0-0 7f-8f: 0-1 9f-13f: 0-5 14f+: 0-0
Track : LH: 0-2 RH: 0-4 Tight: 0-2 Gall: 0-0

Aids: Bl: 0-0 Vi: 0-0 Tstrap: 0-0 Ckp: 0-0
Best Rating: **44** 7/08 Baln 1m4f good

Thewaytosanjose (IRE)

(93) (57)**38**
3-y-o b f Fasliyev (USA)-Soltura (IRE) (Sadler's Wells (USA))
Patrick J Flynn (S Kirk 12/3) Mrs Paul Shanahan

Placings:00010-155000 **(6867a)**
2009: 8^{1}SD, 9^{5}SD, 8^{5}SD, 8^{0}SD, 10^{0}HY, 8^{0}G,

	Starts	1st	2nd	3rd	Win & Pl
Career Total (Turf)	4	0	0	0	
Career Total (AW)	7	2	0	0	4094

56 1/09 Wolv 1m141y (0-60)H STD £2047
57 12/08 Sthl 1m (0-65) STD £2047
Total win prize-money £4094

Going (Turf): **Sf: 0-1 GS: 0-0 Gd: 0-2 GF: 0-1 Fm: 0-0**
Distance: 5f/6f: 0-0 7f-8f: 1-6 9f-13f: 1-5 14f+: 0-0
Track : **LH: 2-5** RH: 0-4 **Tight: 1-3** Gall: 0-1
Aids: Bl: 0-0 Vi: 0-0 Tstrap: 0-0 Ckp: 0-0
Best Rating: **57** 12/08 Sthl 1m stand

Moderate; effective over 1m and acts on Polytrack.

Thewinnatakesitall

84(91) (58)**58**
2-y-o ch f King's Best (USA)-Powder Puff (IRE) (Sadler's Wells (USA))
H J Evans Malcolm O'Hair

Placings:004000205 **(7778)**
2009: 5^{0}SD, 6^{0}GF, 7^{4}HY, 8^{0}SD, 6^{0}GS, 7^{0}GF, 5^{2}SD, 5^{0}SD, 5^{5}SD,

	Starts	1st	2nd	3rd	Win & Pl
Career Total (Turf)	4	0	0	0	385
Career Total (AW)	5	0	1	0	605

Going (Turf): **Sf: 0-1 GS: 0-1 Gd: 0-0 GF: 0-2 Fm: 0-0**
Distance: 5f/6f: 0-4 7f-8f: 0-5 9f-13f: 0-0 14f+: 0-0
Track : LH: 0-2 RH: 0-1 Tight: 0-2 Gall: 0-0
Aids: Bl: 0-0 Vi: 0-0 Tstrap: 0-3 Ckp: 0-3
Best Rating: **58** 11/09 Sthl 5f stand

Moderate; effective over 5f; acts on Fibresand.

They All Laughed

101(110) (79)**78**
6-y-o ch g Zafonic (USA)-Royal Future (IRE) (Royal Academy (USA))
Mrs Marjorie Fife (P W Hiatt 23/6) Green Lane

Placings:0000/60005510405565/0465052221312150 3/31 1603503200-024332313550315053354 **(7842)**
2009: 14^{0}SS, 13^{2}SD, 12^{4}SD, 13^{3}SD, 16^{3}SD, 14^{2}SD, 14^{3}SD, 12^{1}SD, 13^{0}GF, 12^{5}SD, 14^{5}GF, 14^{0}S, 12^{3}GF, 12^{1}GF, 11^{5}HY, 12^{0}GS, 13^{5}GF, 15^{3}G, 14^{3}SD, 12^{5}SD, 14^{4}SS,

	Starts	1st	2nd	3rd	Win & Pl
Career Total (Turf)	35	3	2	5	14151
Career Total (AW)	33	5	5	7	20498

63 6/09 Bevl 1m4f16y G-F £2331
79 3/09 Sthl 1m4f (0-75)H STD £2729
82 3/08 Sthl 1m6f (0-75)H STD £2457
79 2/08 Sthl 1m4f (0-70)H SS £2593
70 7/07 Brig 1m3f196y (0-70)H G-S £2849
70 5/07 NmkR 1m4f (0-70)H G-S £3747
73 4/07 Sthl 1m4f (0-60)H STD £3071
62 6/06 Wolv 1m141y (0-60)H STD £2730
Total win prize-money £22511

Going (Turf): Sf: 0-3 **GS: 2-8** Gd: 0-8 GF: 1-15 Fm: 0-1
Distance: 5f/6f: 0-2 7f-8f: 0-10 **9f-13f: 7-29** 14f+: 1-27
Track : **LH: 6-48** RH: 2-15 **Tight: 2-23** Gall: 1-5
Aids: **Bl: 1-6** Vi: 0-0 Tstrap: 0-6 Ckp: 0-6
Best Rating: **82** 3/08 Sthl 1m6f stand

Moderate; effective at around 1m4f-1m6f; acts on fast and easy ground and on sand; has worn blinkers and cheek-pieces.

Theymistim

91 **80**
2-y-o b g Kyllachy-Dance Sequence (USA) (Mr Prospector (USA))
Mrs L Stubbs Ian Blakey

Placings:1 **(4889)**
2009: 5^{1}G,

	Starts	1st	2nd	3rd	Win & Pl
Career Total (Turf)	1	1	0	0	3562

80 8/09 Bevl 5f GD £3561
Total win prize-money £3562

Going (Turf): Sf: 0-0 GS: 0-0 **Gd: 1-1** GF: 0-0 Fm: 0-0
Distance: **5f/6f: 1-1** 7f-8f: 0-0 9f-13f: 0-0 14f+: 0-0
Track : LH: 0-0 RH: 0-0 Tight: 0-0 Gall: 0-0
Aids: Bl: 0-0 Vi: 0-0 Tstrap: 0-0 Ckp: 0-0
Best Rating: **80** 8/09 Bevl 5f good

Fair; effective at 5f on good ground.

Thief

80 **64**
3-y-o b c Falbrav (IRE)-Eurolink Raindance (IRE) (Alzao (USA))
L M Cumani Antoniades Family

Placings:00-5 **(2338)**
2009: 8^{5}GF,

	Starts	1st	2nd	3rd	Win & Pl
Career Total (Turf)	3	0	0	0	0

Going (Turf): **Sf: 0-0 GS: 0-1 Gd: 0-1 GF: 0-1 Fm: 0-0**
Distance: 5f/6f: 0-0 7f-8f: 0-1 9f-13f: 0-2 14f+: 0-0
Track : LH: 0-1 RH: 0-1 Tight: 0-1 Gall: 0-0
Aids: Bl: 0-0 Vi: 0-0 Tstrap: 0-0 Ckp: 0-0
Best Rating: **64** 8/08 NmkJ 1m good

Best effort over 1m on fast ground.

Thief Of Time (IRE)

103(103) (92)**90**
3-y-o b g Clodovil (IRE)-Cape Flattery (IRE) (Cape Cross (IRE))
P W Chapple-Hyam Michael Daffey & Robert Markwick

Placings:212205402 **(6944)**
2009: 7^{2}SD, 8^{1}SD, 9^{2}GF, 8^{2}G, 8^{0}HY, 9^{5}G, 7^{4}G, 8^{0}GF, 7^{2}SD,

	Starts	1st	2nd	3rd	Win & Pl
Career Total (Turf)	6	0	2	0	7508
Career Total (AW)	3	1	2	0	4907

75 1/09 Ling 1m STD £2729
Total win prize-money £2730

Going (Turf): **Sf: 0-1 GS: 0-0 Gd: 0-3 GF: 0-2 Fm: 0-0**
Distance: 5f/6f: 0-0 **7f-8f: 1-5** 9f-13f: 0-4 14f+: 0-0
Track : **LH: 1-2** RH: 0-6 **Tight: 1-1** Gall: 0-0
Aids: Bl: 0-0 Vi: 0-0 Tstrap: 0-0 Ckp: 0-0
Best Rating: **92** 10/09 Kemp 7f stand

Useful; stays 1m2f; acts on fast ground; goes on Polytrack.

Thin Red Line (IRE)

105(99) (92)**93**
3-y-o b c Red Ransom (USA)-Albaiyda (IRE) (Brief Truce (USA))
E A L Dunlop Byculla Thoroughbreds

Placings:6001-4012001 **(6724)**
2009: 9^{4}SD, 8^{0}GF, 10^{1}G, 11^{2}GF, 11^{0}G, 10^{0}GF, 12^{1}SD,

	Starts	1st	2nd	3rd	Win & Pl
Career Total (Turf)	6	1	1	0	10962
Career Total (AW)	5	2	0	0	7842

92 10/09 Kemp 1m4f (0-85)H STD £4727
90 6/09 Pont 1m2f6y (0-85)H GD £5180
80 12/08 Ling 1m (0-75) STD £2729
Total win prize-money £12638

Going (Turf): Sf: 0-0 GS: 0-0 **Gd: 1-3** GF: 0-3 Fm: 0-0
Distance: 5f/6f: 0-1 7f-8f: 1-3 **9f-13f: 2-7** 14f+: 0-0
Track : **LH: 2-7** RH: 1-3 **Tight: 1-4** Gall: 0-2
Aids: Bl: 0-0 Vi: 0-0 Tstrap: 0-0 Ckp: 0-0
Best Rating: **93** 7/09 Hayd 1m3f200y gd-fm

Useful; effective over 1m2f-1m4f; acts on good ground; goes on Polytrack.

Think Its All Over (USA)

94 **75**
2-y-o b c Tiznow (USA)-A P Petal (USA) (A.P. Indy (USA))
T P Tate Mrs Fitri Hay

Placings:41 **(6136)**
2009: 7^{4}GF, 8^{1}G,

	Starts	1st	2nd	3rd	Win & Pl
Career Total (Turf)	2	1	0	0	4222

75 9/09 Haml 1m65y GD £3885
Total win prize-money £3886

Going (Turf): Sf: 0-0 GS: 0-0 **Gd: 1-1** GF: 0-1 Fm: 0-0
Distance: 5f/6f: 0-0 7f-8f: 0-1 **9f-13f: 1-1** 14f+: 0-0
Track : LH: 0-0 **RH: 1-1 Tight: 1-1** Gall: 0-0
Aids: Bl: 0-0 Vi: 0-0 Tstrap: 0-0 Ckp: 0-0
Best Rating: **75** 9/09 Haml 1m65y good

Fair; stays 1m; acts on good ground.

Thinking

94(86) (47)**62**
2-y-o b g Makbul-Concentration (IRE) (Mind Games)
T D Easterby Habton Farms

Placings:005003 **(7242)**
2009: 6^{0}GF, 6^{0}S, 5^{5}GF, 5^{0}SD, 6^{0}G, 5^{3}S,

	Starts	1st	2nd	3rd	Win & Pl
Career Total (Turf)	5	0	0	1	482
Career Total (AW)	1	0	0	0	

Going (Turf): **Sf: 0-2 GS: 0-0 Gd: 0-1 GF: 0-2 Fm: 0-0**
Distance: 5f/6f: 0 6 7f-8f: 0-0 9f-13f: 0-0 14f+: 0-0
Track : LH: 0-0 RH: 0-0 Tight: 0-0 Gall: 0-0
Aids: Bl: 0-1 Vi: 0-0 Tstrap: 0-0 Ckp: 0-0
Best Rating: **62** 9/09 Bevl 5f gd-fm

Moderate; effective over 5f; acts on soft ground; has worn blinkers.

Thirtyfourthstreet (IRE)

81(95) (51)**36**

4-y-o gr f Beat Hollow-Peacock Alley (IRE) (Salse (USA))
W R Muir Mr & Mrs G Middlebrook

Placings:000-63006 **(1430)**
2009: 9^{6}SF, 12^{3}SD, 12^{0}SD, 12^{0}GF, 12^{6}SD,

	Starts	1st	2nd	3rd	Win & Pl
Career Total (Turf)	3	0	0	0	
Career Total (AW)	5	0	0	1	403

Going (Turf): Sf: 0-0 GS: 0-0 Gd: 0-0 GF: 0-3 Fm: 0-0
Distance: 5f/6f: 0-0 7f-8f: 0-0 9f-13f: 0-8 14f+: 0-0
Track : LH: 0-4 RH: 0-4 Tight: 0-6 Gall: 0-0
Aids: Bl: 0-2 Vi: 0-0 Tstrap: 0-0 Ckp: 0-0
Best Rating: 51 3/09 Wolv 1m4f50y stand

This Ones For Eddy

105(106) (77)**76**

4-y-o b g Kyllachy-Skirt Around (Deploy)
J Balding (S Parr 4/7) Willie McKay

Placings:4650032040646124-24361031234020000604320 **(7192)**
2009: 5^{2}SD, 6^{4}SD, 6^{3}SD, 6^{6}SD, 7^{1}SD, 12^{0}G, 8^{3}GF, 8^{1}F, 8^{2}G, 8^{3}G, 7^{4}G, 7^{0}GF, 8^{2}GF, 7^{0}GF, 8^{0}GF, 8^{0}G, 9^{0}G, 7^{6}GF, 7^{0}SD, 8^{4}GF, 7^{3}G, 6^{2}G, 7^{0}SD,

	Starts	1st	2nd	3rd	Win & Pl
Career Total (Turf)	26	1	4	4	8070
Career Total (AW)	13	2	2	1	6543

76 4/09 Pont 1m4y (0-75)H FRM £3238
76 3/09 Sthl 7f (0-70)H STD £2590
77 12/08 Sthl 6f (0-60)H STD £1706
Total win prize-money £7534

Going (Turf): Sf: 0-1 GS: 0-1 Gd: 0-11 GF: 0-12 Fm: 1-1
Distance: 5f/6f: 1-13 7f-8f: 1-17 9f-13f: 1-9 14f+: 0-0
Track : LH: 3-22 RH: 0-8 Tight: 0-12 Gall: 0-2
Aids: Bl: 0-1 Vi: 0-0 Tstrap: 0-1 Ckp: 0-1
Best Rating: 77 12/08 Sthl 6f stand

Modest; effective over 6f-1m; acts on fast ground; goes on sand.

This Ones For Pat (USA)

85(102) (68)**41**

4-y-o b/br g Proud Citizen (USA)-Lace Curtain Irish (USA) (Cryptoclearance (USA))
S Parr Willie McKay

Placings:0060001410-2000 **(1591)**
2009: 5^{2}SD, 6^{0}GF, 7^{0}SD, 5^{0}GS,

	Starts	1st	2nd	3rd	Win & Pl
Career Total (Turf)	3	0	0	0	
Career Total (AW)	11	2	1	0	4017

67 12/08 Sthl 5f (0-60)H STD £1706
62 12/08 Sthl 5f (0-55)H SS £1706
Total win prize-money £3412

Going (Turf): Sf: 0-0 GS: 0-1 Gd: 0-1 GF: 0-1 Fm: 0-0
Distance: 5f/6f: 2-10 7f-8f: 0-3 9f-13f: 0-1 14f+: 0-0
Track : LH: 0-6 RH: 0-3 Tight: 0-3 Gall: 0-0
Aids: Bl: 0-1 Vi: 0-0 Tstrap: 1-2 Ckp: 1-2
Best Rating: 68 3/09 Sthl 5f stand

Moderate; effective over 5f and acts on Fibresand.

Thistimesforgood (IRE)

(75) (48)**56**

6-y-o ch g Rossini (USA)-Midsummer Night (IRE) (Fairy King (USA))
Paul Stafford Sean F Gallagher

Placings:0010/5/0600042060-03260 **(7632)**
2009: 7^{0}G, 9^{3}Y, 7^{2}HY, 10^{6}SD, 9^{0}SD,

	Starts	1st	2nd	3rd	Win & Pl
Career Total (Turf)	15	0	2	1	3022
Career Total (AW)	5	1	0	0	2591

60 11/06 Wolv 7f32y SF £2590
Total win prize-money £2591

Going (Turf): Sf: 0-3 GS: 0-0 Gd: 0-3 GF: 0-3 Fm: 0-1
Distance: 5f/6f: 0-3 7f-8f: 1-12 9f-13f: 0-5 14f+: 0-0
Track : LH: 1-14 RH: 0-5 Tight: 1-4 Gall: 0-0
Aids: Bl: 0-2 Vi: 0-0 Tstrap: 0-6 Ckp: 0-6
Best Rating: 60 11/06 Wolv 7f32y std-fst

Moderate Irish-trained gelding; stays at least 7f; handles Polytrack.

Thistle

(88) (49)**55**

8-y-o ch g Selkirk (USA)-Ardisia (USA) (Affirmed (USA))
George Baker Lady Forwood & Partners

Placings:02221/5446/5560/05/60 **(5377)**
2009: 8^{6}SD, 11^{0}SD,

	Starts	1st	2nd	3rd	Win & Pl
Career Total (Turf)	15	1	3	0	9277
Career Total (AW)	2	0	0	0	0

70 10/04 Wind 1m67y GD £4147
Total win prize-money £4147

Going (Turf): Sf: 0-0 GS: 0-2 Gd: 1-3 GF: 0-9 Fm: 0-1
Distance: 5f/6f: 0-0 7f-8f: 0-7 9f-13f: 1-10 14f+: 0-0
Track : LH: 0-8 RH: 1-7 Tight: 1-7 Gall: 0-1
Aids: Bl: 0-0 Vi: 0-0 Tstrap: 0-1 Ckp: 0-1
Best Rating: 77 6/05 Rdcr 1m gd-fm

Thistlestar (USA)

86(92) (65)**60**

2-y-o b/br f Lion Heart (USA)-Katiba (USA) (Gulch (USA))
R A Fahey Mrs H Steel

Placings:355 **(7800)**
2009: 7^{3}G, 6^{5}SD, 7^{5}SD,

	Starts	1st	2nd	3rd	Win & Pl
Career Total (Turf)	1	0	0	1	722
Career Total (AW)	2	0	0	0	0

Going (Turf): Sf: 0-0 GS: 0-0 Gd: 0-1 GF: 0-0 Fm: 0-0
Distance: 5f/6f: 0-1 7f-8f: 0-2 9f-13f: 0-0 14f+: 0-0
Track : LH: 0-2 RH: 0-1 Tight: 0-1 Gall: 0-0
Aids: Bl: 0-0 Vi: 0-0 Tstrap: 0-0 Ckp: 0-0
Best Rating: 65 11/09 Kemp 6f stand

Modest; stays 7f; acts on Polytrack.

Thomas Baines (USA)

85(95) (74)**76**

2-y-o b g Johannesburg (USA)-Foofaraw (USA) (Cherokee Run (USA))
M L W Bell R A Green

Placings:3035613 **(6071)**
2009: 5^{3}G, 5^{0}GF, 5^{3}GF, 5^{5}GF, 6^{6}GF, 7^{1}SD, 7^{3}SD,

	Starts	1st	2nd	3rd	Win & Pl
Career Total (Turf)	5	0	0	2	942
Career Total (AW)	2	1	0	1	5576

70 9/09 Wolv 7f32y (0-80) STD £5046
Total win prize-money £5046

Going (Turf): Sf: 0-0 GS: 0-0 Gd: 0-1 GF: 0-4 Fm: 0-0
Distance: 5f/6f: 0-4 7f-8f: 1-3 9f-13f: 0-0 14f+: 0-0
Track : LH: 1-2 RH: 0-0 Tight: 1-2 Gall: 0-2
Aids: Bl: 0-0 Vi: 0-0 Tstrap: 0-0 Ckp: 0-0
Best Rating: 76 4/09 Wind 5f10y gd-fm

Fair; stays 6f; acts on fast ground and on Polytrack.

Thompsons Walls (IRE)

90(92) (59)**74**

4-y-o b g Trans Island-Nordic Living (IRE) (Nordico (USA))
D Nicholls (S T Mason 30/4) Middleham Park Racing Xi

Placings:4120U4/16-0060 **(1955)**
2009: 9^{0}SD, 8^{0}GF, 6^{6}GF, 8^{0}GF,

	Starts	1st	2nd	3rd	Win & Pl
Career Total (Turf)	9	2	1	0	5385
Career Total (AW)	3	0	0	0	0

74 5/08 Haml 1m65y G-S £1942
79 8/07 Newc 6f G-F £2266
Total win prize-money £4210

Going (Turf): Sf: 0-1 GS: 1-2 Gd: 0-0 GF: 1-6 Fm: 0-0
Distance: 5f/6f: 1-3 7f-8f: 0-4 9f-13f: 1-5 14f+: 0-0
Track : LH: 0-5 RH: 1-3 Tight: 1-4 Gall: 0-0
Aids: Bl: 0-2 Vi: 0-0 Tstrap: 0-0 Ckp: 0-0
Best Rating: 79 8/07 Rdcr 7f gd-fm

Fair; stays 1m; acts on fast and easy ground.

Thoosa

74(86) (42)**14**

3-y-o ch f Best Of The Bests (IRE)-Natural Grace (Zamindar (USA))
P S McEntee Robert J Gough

Placings:0436000 **(2862)**
2009: 5^{0}SD, 5^{4}SD, 6^{3}SD, 5^{6}SD, 6^{0}G, 6^{0}GF, 6^{0}S,

	Starts	1st	2nd	3rd	Win & Pl
Career Total (Turf)	3	0	0	0	
Career Total (AW)	4	0	0	1	403

Going (Turf): Sf: 0-1 GS: 0-0 Gd: 0-1 GF: 0-1 Fm: 0-0
Distance: 5f/6f: 0-5 7f-8f: 0-2 9f-13f: 0-0 14f+: 0-0
Track : LH: 0-3 RH: 0-0 Tight: 0-3 Gall: 0-0
Aids: Bl: 0-0 Vi: 0-1 Tstrap: 0-0 Ckp: 0-0
Best Rating: 42 2/09 Ling 6f stand

Thornaby Green

(101) (59)**67**

8-y-o b g Whittingham (IRE)-Dona Filipa (Precocious)
T D Barron K J Alderson

Placings:5415600/441054020/44000560000666464516/34 0423100002034104/024136215600435/00622020200532-3000 **(0368)**
2009: 8^{3}SS, 8^{0}SD, 11^{0}SD, 12^{0}SD,

	Starts	1st	2nd	3rd	Win & Pl
Career Total (Turf)	68	5	9	2	31241
Career Total (AW)	19	2	1	5	5244

67 8/07 Newc 1m2f32y (0-70)H GD £3785
61 6/07 Newc 1m2f32y (0-70)H HVY £3562
59 11/06 Wolv 1m1f103y (0-45) STD £1535
52 7/06 Newc 1m2f32y (0-55)H FRM £2388
52 11/05 Sthl 1m (0-45) SS £1429
67 7/04 Haml 6f5y E(0-70)H G-F £4436
63 5/03 Muss 5f E G-F £5369
Total win prize-money £22507

Going (Turf): Sf: 1-13GS: 0-7 Gd: 1-14 **GF: 2-28** Fm: 1-6
Distance: 5f/6f: 1-15 7f-8f: 2-29 **9f-13f: 4-43** 14f+: 0-0
Track : **LH: 5-59** RH: 0-13 Tight: 1-33 **Gall: 3-13**
Aids: Bl: 0-1 **Vi: 1-6** Tstrap: 0-1 Ckp: 0-1
Best Rating: **67** 8/07 Newc 1m2f32y good

Moderate; stays 1m2f; acts on fast and heavy ground; also goes on sand.

Thornton George

82 **40**
4-y-o b g Piccolo-Princess Emily (IRE) (Dolphin Street (FR))
T J Fitzgerald Ms Denise S Doyle

Placings:00 (3120)
2009: 12^{0}GS, 10^{0}GF,

	Starts	1st	2nd	3rd	Win & Pl
Career Total (Turf)	2	0	0	0	

Going (Turf): **Sf: 0-0 GS: 0-1 Gd: 0-0 GF: 0-1 Fm: 0-0**
Distance: 5f/6f: 0-0 7f-8f: 0-0 9f-13f: 0-2 14f+: 0-0
Track : LH: 0-2 RH: 0-0 Tight: 0-1 Gall: 0-1
Aids: Bl: 0-1 Vi: 0-0 Tstrap: 0-0 Ckp: 0-0
Best Rating: **40** 6/09 Rdcr 1m2f gd-fm

Thorny Mandate

104(107) (64)**63**
7-y-o b g Diktat-Rosa Canina (Bustino)
W M Brisbourne R C Naylor

Placings:00/03051236/0100440/004160513340000/65261 03464225-461644305260000 (6280)
2009: 12^{4}SD, 12^{6}SD, 13^{1}SD, 16^{6}SD, 14^{4}GF, 13^{4}SD, 13^{3}GF, 12^{0}GF, 13^{5}GF, 12^{2}GF, 12^{6}GF, 12^{0}GF, 14^{0}G, 12^{0}SD, 13^{0}SD, 13^{0}GF,

	Starts	1st	2nd	3rd	Win & Pl
Career Total (Turf)	39	2	3	6	16791
Career Total (AW)	22	4	2	0	10818

64 3/09 Wolv 1m5f194y (0-60)H STD £1942
63 6/08 Ches 1m4f66y (0-70)H G-F £3435
68 7/07 Wolv 1m4f50y (0-65)H STD £2388
66 6/07 Wolv 1m4f50y (0-60)H STD £2388
67 5/06 Pont 1m2f6y (0-70)H G-F £4533
62 7/05 Ling 1m2f (0-55)H STD £2682
Total win prize-money £17372

Going (Turf): Sf: 0-2 GS: 0-4 Gd: 0-10 **GF: 2-23** Fm: 0-0
Distance: 5f/6f: 0-0 7f-8f: 0-2 **9f-13f: 5-48** 14f+: 1-11
Track : **LH: 6-49** RH: 0-9 **Tight: 5-43** Gall: 0-4
Aids: Bl: 0-0 Vi: 0-0 Tstrap: 0-0 Ckp: 0-0
Best Rating: **69** 8/07 Muss 1m5f gd-fm

Moderate; effective from 1m2f-1m5f; acts on easy ground; goes on Polytrack.

Thoughtful (IRE)

84(84) (56)**42**
2-y-o b f Acclamation-Truly Generous (IRE) (Generous (IRE))
J W Hills J W Hills

Placings:50 (6241)
2009: 6^{5}SD, 6^{0}G,

	Starts	1st	2nd	3rd	Win & Pl
Career Total (Turf)	1	0	0	0	
Career Total (AW)	1	0	0	0	0

Going (Turf): **Sf: 0-0 GS: 0-0 Gd: 0-1 GF: 0-0 Fm: 0-0**
Distance: 5f/6f: 0-1 7f-8f: 0-1 9f-13f: 0-0 14f+: 0-0
Track : LH: 0-0 RH: 0-1 Tight: 0-0 Gall: 0-0
Aids: Bl: 0-0 Vi: 0-0 Tstrap: 0-0 Ckp: 0-0
Best Rating: **56** 9/09 Kemp 6f stand

Moderate; acts on Polytrack.

Thoughtsofstardom

102(106) (81)**71**
6-y-o b g Mind Games-Alustar (Emarati (USA))
P S McEntee Eventmaker Racehorses

Placings:014U001405/125460435005653300006/016233 06212006230/5063321244003312206505525001211-5665400660560035350003410521614 (7838)
2009: 5^{5}SD, 5^{6}SD, 6^{6}SD, 6^{5}SD, 6^{4}SD, 5^{0}SD, 5^{0}SF, 5^{6}GF, 5^{6}G, 5^{0}F, 5^{5}F, 5^{6}GF, 6^{0}G, 5^{0}GF, 5^{3}G, 5^{5}GF, 5^{3}GF, 5^{5}GF, 5^{0}F, 5^{0}S, 5^{0}G, 5^{3}SD, 5^{4}SD, 5^{1}GF,

	Starts	1st	2nd	3rd	Win & Pl
Career Total (Turf)	48	4	3	7	16206
Career Total (AW)	62	9	9	6	28875

67 12/09 Ling 5f (0-70)H STD £2388
67 12/09 Sthl 5f (0-55)H STD £1706
56 9/09 Folk 5f (0-60)H G-F £2047
81 12/08 Ling 5f (0-70)H STD £2729
69 12/08 Ling 5f (0-60)H STD £2388
67 12/08 Ling 5f (0-60)H STD £2047
68 6/08 Folk 5f (0-60)H G-F £2047
67 2/08 Kemp 5f (0-55)H STD £1943
57 6/07 Haml 5f4y GD £2266
57 1/07 Wolv 5f20y (0-50)H SS £1706
58 1/06 Wolv 5f20y STD £2388
67 10/05 Wolv 5f20y STD £2625
64 7/05 Leic 5f2y G-F £2919
Total win prize-money £29202

Going (Turf): Sf: 0-2 GS: 0-3 Gd: 1-13 **GF: 3-22** Fm: 0-8
Distance: **5f/6f: 13-105** 7f-8f: 0-5 9f-13f: 0-0 14f+: 0-0
Track : **LH: 7-62** RH: 1-10 **Tight: 7-44** Gall: 0-3
Aids: **Bl: 3-22** Vi: 0-5 Tstrap: 0-7 Ckp: 0-7
Best Rating: **81** 12/08 Ling 5f stand

Modest; effective at 5f-6f; acts on a sound surface; goes on Fibresand and Polytrack; has worn an eyeshield and blinkers.

Thousand Miles (IRE)

101 **88**
3-y-o br c Danehill Dancer (IRE)-Mille Miglia (IRE) (Caerleon (USA))
P W Chapple-Hyam J C Fretwell

Placings:52-1553500 (6731)
2009: 8^{1}G, 8^{5}S, 8^{5}GF, 7^{3}GF, 7^{5}G, 8^{0}G, 6^{0}S,

	Starts	1st	2nd	3rd	Win & Pl
Career Total (Turf)	9	1	1	1	9270

84 4/09 Yarm 1m3y GD £3469
Total win prize-money £3469

Going (Turf): Sf: 0-3 GS: 0-0 **Gd: 1-4** GF: 0-2 Fm: 0-0
Distance: 5f/6f: 0-0 7f-8f: 0-7 **9f-13f: 1-2** 14f+: 0-0
Track : LH: 0-2 RH: 0-2 Tight: 0-0 Gall: 0-0
Aids: Bl: 0-0 Vi: 0-0 Tstrap: 0-0 Ckp: 0-0
Best Rating: **88** 7/09 NmkJ 1m gd-fm

Useful; stays 1m; acts on good and soft ground.

Thousandkissesdeep (IRE)

89 **77**
2-y-o b f Night Shift (USA)-Interim Payment (USA) (Red Ransom (USA))
J H M Gosden Lady Bamford & Alice Bamford

Placings:02 (6920)
2009: 8^{0}G, 8^{2}GF,

	Starts	1st	2nd	3rd	Win & Pl
Career Total (Turf)	2	0	1	0	1227

Going (Turf): **Sf: 0-0 GS: 0-0 Gd: 0-1 GF: 0-1 Fm: 0-0**
Distance: 5f/6f: 0-0 7f-8f: 0-0 9f-13f: 0-2 14f+: 0-0
Track : LH: 0-0 RH: 0-0 Tight: 0-0 Gall: 0-0
Aids: Bl: 0-0 Vi: 0-0 Tstrap: 0-0 Ckp: 0-0
Best Rating: **77** 10/09 Yarm 1m3y gd-fm

Three Boars

63(111) (67)**17**
7-y-o ch g Most Welcome-Precious Poppy (Polish Precedent (USA))
S Gollings P Whinham

Placings:000/00052164/2005045033112/1130600122/106 100050-0206 (7760)
2009: 14^{0}SD, 16^{2}SD, 16^{0}G, 16^{6}SD,

	Starts	1st	2nd	3rd	Win & Pl
Career Total (Turf)	19	1	1	1	4434
Career Total (AW)	28	7	5	2	20471

76 3/08 Sthl 2m (0-75)H STD £2593
74 1/08 Sthl 1m4f (0-70)H STD £2457
79 12/07 Sthl 1m6f (0-75)H STD £2968
78 3/07 Sthl 1m6f (0-65)H STD £2266
71 3/07 Sthl 1m4f (0-75)H STD £3071
61 11/06 Wolv 1m5f194y (0-45) STD £1365
55 11/06 Kemp 1m3f (0-45) STD £1295
59 7/05 Yarm 1m2f21y FRM £2520
Total win prize-money £18538

Going (Turf): Sf: 0-0 GS: 0-3 Gd: 0-5 GF: 0-8 **Fm: 1-3**
Distance: 5f/6f: 0-0 7f-8f: 0-2 9f-13f: 4-23 14f+: 4-22
Track : **LH: 7-35** RH: 1-10 **Tight: 2-20** Gall: 0-2
Aids: **Bl: 8-40** Vi: 0-0 Tstrap: 0-0 Ckp: 0-0
Best Rating: **79** 12/07 Sthl 1m6f stand

Moderate; effective from 1m4f-2m; acts on fast ground and Polytrack, but goes very well on Fibresand; usually travels well.

Three Ducks

98(93) (74)**74**
3-y-o b f Diktat-Three Terns (USA) (Arctic Tern (USA))
L M Cumani Mrs James Wigan

Placings:431-002 (3551)
2009: 8^{0}F, 9^{0}G, 9^{2}GF,

	Starts	1st	2nd	3rd	Win & Pl
Career Total (Turf)	4	0	1	0	192
Career Total (AW)	2	1	0	1	3120

74 12/08 GrLe 1m STD £2590
Total win prize-money £2590

Going (Turf): **Sf: 0-0 GS: 0-1 Gd: 0-1 GF: 0-1 Fm: 0-1**
Distance: 5f/6f: 0-1 **7f-8f: 1-2** 9f-13f: 0-3 14f+: 0-0
Track : **LH: 1-3** RH: 0-2 Tight: 0-2 **Gall: 1-1**
Aids: Bl: 0-0 Vi: 0-0 Tstrap: 0-0 Ckp: 0-0
Best Rating: **74** 7/09 Yarm 1m1f gd-fm

Fair; stays 1m; acts on Polytrack.

Three Gold Leaves

77(87) (52)29

4-y-o ch g Zaha (CAN)-Tab's Gift (Bijou D'Inde)

D W Thompson R N Pennell

Placings:0/00-500 (2532)

2009: 10^{5}GF, 10^{0}GS, 7^{0}GF,

	Starts	1st	2nd	3rd	Win & Pl
Career Total (Turf)	5	0	0	0	0
Career Total (AW)	1	0	0	0	

Going (Turf): Sf: 0-0 GS: 0-2 Gd: 0-1 GF: 0-2 Fm: 0-0
Distance: 5f/6f: 0-0 7f-8f: 0-2 9f-13f: 0-4 14f+: 0-0
Track : LH: 0-4 RH: 0-1 Tight: 0-0 Gall: 0-4
Aids: Bl: 0-0 Vi: 0-0 Tstrap: 0-0 Ckp: 0-0
Best Rating: 52 5/08 GrLe 1m2f stand

Three Good Friends (IRE)

77(90) (69)29

2-y-o b f Orpen (USA)-Eastern Blue (IRE) (Be My Guest (USA))

P T Midgley Anthony D Copley

Placings:01 (2741)

2009: 5^{0}G, 5^{1}SD,

	Starts	1st	2nd	3rd	Win & Pl
Career Total (Turf)	1	0	0	0	
Career Total (AW)	1	1	0	0	2730
69 6/09 Sthl 5f			STD	£2729	

Total win prize-money £2730

Going (Turf): Sf: 0-0 GS: 0-0 Gd: 0-1 GF: 0-0 Fm: 0-0
Distance: 5f/6f: 1-2 7f-8f: 0-0 9f-13f: 0-0 14f+: 0-0
Track : LH: 0-0 RH: 0-0 Tight: 0-0 Gall: 0-0
Aids: Bl: 0-0 Vi: 0-0 Tstrap: 0-0 Ckp: 0-0
Best Rating: 69 6/09 Sthl 5f stand

Modest; effective at 5f on Fibresand.

Three Moons (IRE)

108(89) (73)103

3-y-o b f Montjeu (IRE)-Three Owls (IRE) (Warning)

H J L Dunlop Mrs Ben Goldsmith

Placings:22220-12 (1701)

2009: 9^{1}GF, 10^{2}GF,

	Starts	1st	2nd	3rd	Win & Pl
Career Total (Turf)	6	1	4	0	18885
Career Total (AW)	1	0	1	0	1349
76 4/09 Folk 1m1f149y			G-F	£2729	

Total win prize-money £2730

Going (Turf): Sf: 0-0 GS: 0-1 Gd: 0-2 GF: 1-3 Fm: 0-0
Distance: 5f/6f: 0-0 7f-8f: 0-4 9f-13f: 1-3 14f+: 0-0
Track : LH: 0-0 RH: 1-3 Tight: 1-1 Gall: 0-0
Aids: Bl: 0-0 Vi: 0-0 Tstrap: 0-0 Ckp: 0-0
Best Rating: 103 5/09 NmkR 1m2f gd-fm

Very useful; Listed placed; stays 1m2f; acts on fast ground and on Polytrack.

Three Sons

77(66) (16)30

2-y-o b g Reset (AUS)-Zuloago (USA) (Stravinsky (USA))

I W McInnes Ivy House Racing

Placings:0000 (4138)

2009: 5^{0}F, 5^{0}SD, 6^{0}S, 5^{0}G,

	Starts	1st	2nd	3rd	Win & Pl
Career Total (Turf)	3	0	0	0	
Career Total (AW)	1	0	0	0	

Going (Turf): Sf: 0-1 GS: 0-0 Gd: 0-1 GF: 0-0 Fm: 0-1
Distance: 5f/6f: 0-4 7f-8f: 0-0 9f-13f: 0-0 14f+: 0-0
Track : LH: 0-1 RH: 0-0 Tight: 0-1 Gall: 0-0
Aids: Bl: 0-4 Vi: 0-0 Tstrap: 0-0 Ckp: 0-0
Best Rating: 30 6/09 Bevl 5f firm

Three Strings (USA)

(107) (70)63

6-y-o b g Stravinsky (USA)-Just Cause (Law Society (USA))

P D Niven Michael Paley

Placings:06000/504310205/30603145410-613 (4373)

2009: 12^{6}SS, 11^{1}SD, 12^{3}SD,

	Starts	1st	2nd	3rd	Win & Pl
Career Total (Turf)	22	2	1	3	8787
Career Total (AW)	6	2	0	1	4670
70 4/09 Sthl 1m3f (0-60)H			STD	£2320	
64 11/08 Sthl 1m4f (0-65)H			STD	£2047	
63 8/08 Haml 1m3f16y (0-65)H			G-S	£2388	
60 7/06 Muss 1m1f (0-65)H			GD	£3412	

Total win prize-money £10168

Going (Turf): Sf: 0-2 GS: 1-5 Gd: 1-9 GF: 0-4 Fm: 0-2
Distance: 5f/6f: 0-2 7f-8f: 0-6 9f-13f: 4-19 14f+: 0-1
Track : LH: 2-17 RH: 2-8 Tight: 2-9 Gall: 0-0
Aids: Bl: 0-0 Vi: 0-0 Tstrap: 4-19 Ckp: 4-19
Best Rating: 70 7/09 Sthl 1m4f stand

Modest; stays 1m4f; acts on fast and soft ground and Fibresand.

Three Thieves (UAE)

(100) (47)55

6-y-o ch g Jade Robbery (USA)-Melisendra (FR) (Highest Honor (FR))

Jim Best Bill Wallace

Placings:621/000555/02121250360/0000000-66 (7688)

2009: 12^{6}SD, 12^{6}SD,

	Starts	1st	2nd	3rd	Win & Pl
Career Total (Turf)	6	1	1	0	7357
Career Total (AW)	23	2	3	1	8077
76 3/07 Wolv 1m5f194y (0-70)H			STD	£2307	
69 2/07 Wolv 1m4f50y (0-70)H			SS	£2717	
77 10/05 Muss 1m1f			GD	£5447	

Total win prize-money £10472

Going (Turf): Sf: 0-0 GS: 0-0 Gd: 1-3 GF: 0-2 Fm: 0-1
Distance: 5f/6f: 0-0 7f-8f: 0-1 9f-13f: 2-22 14f+: 1-6
Track : LH: 2-21 RH: 1-7 Tight: 3-22 Gall: 0-0
Aids: Bl: 0-0 Vi: 0-1 Tstrap: 0-0 Ckp: 0-0
Best Rating: 80 10/05 Pont 1m2f6y good

Moderate; stays 1m5f; acts well on Polytrack.

Three Times

69(72) (24)32

2-y-o ch f Bahamian Bounty-Triple Joy (Most Welcome)

D R Lanigan Saif Ali & Saeed H Altayer

Placings:60 (7183)

2009: 7^{6}SD, 7^{0}G,

	Starts	1st	2nd	3rd	Win & Pl
Career Total (Turf)	1	0	0	0	
Career Total (AW)	1	0	0	0	0

Going (Turf): Sf: 0-0 GS: 0-0 Gd: 0-1 GF: 0-0 Fm: 0-0
Distance: 5f/6f: 0-0 7f-8f: 0-2 9f-13f: 0-0 14f+: 0-0
Track : LH: 0-1 RH: 0-0 Tight: 0-0 Gall: 0-0
Aids: Bl: 0-0 Vi: 0-0 Tstrap: 0-0 Ckp: 0-0
Best Rating: 32 10/09 NmkR 7f good

Three's A Crowd

85(85) (55)53

2-y-o b f Royal Applause-Thracian (Green Desert (USA))

D R C Elsworth C J Harper

Placings:6400 (6775)

2009: 6^{6}GF, 5^{4}SD, 7^{0}GF, 6^{0}SD,

	Starts	1st	2nd	3rd	Win & Pl
Career Total (Turf)	2	0	0	0	0
Career Total (AW)	2	0	0	0	265

Going (Turf): Sf: 0-0 GS: 0-0 Gd: 0-0 GF: 0-2 Fm: 0-0
Distance: 5f/6f: 0-3 7f-8f: 0-1 9f-13f: 0-0 14f+: 0-0
Track : LH: 0-1 RH: 0-1 Tight: 0-1 Gall: 0-0
Aids: Bl: 0-0 Vi: 0-0 Tstrap: 0-0 Ckp: 0-0
Best Rating: 55 6/09 Ling 5f stand

Threestepstoheaven

95 74

3-y-o b g Haafhd-Bella Bianca (IRE) (Barathea (IRE))

B W Hills John C Grant & Phil Cunningham

Placings:0202-500 (3695)

2009: 10^{5}GS, 10^{0}GS, 10^{0}G,

	Starts	1st	2nd	3rd	Win & Pl
Career Total (Turf)	7	0	2	0	2996

Going (Turf): Sf: 0-1 GS: 0-2 Gd: 0-3 GF: 0-1 Fm: 0-0
Distance: 5f/6f: 0-1 7f-8f: 0-3 9f-13f: 0-3 14f+: 0-0
Track : LH: 0-1 RH: 0-2 Tight: 0-3 Gall: 0-0
Aids: Bl: 0-0 Vi: 0-0 Tstrap: 0-0 Ckp: 0-0
Best Rating: 74 10/08 Rdcr 7f good

Fair maiden form to date; stays 7f; acts on fast ground.

Thrill

102(93) (72)81

2-y-o ch f Pivotal-Irresistible (Cadeaux Genereux)

J H M Gosden Cheveley Park Stud

Placings:310 (7187)

2009: 7^{3}SD, 6^{1}S, 8^{0}G,

	Starts	1st	2nd	3rd	Win & Pl
Career Total (Turf)	2	1	0	0	2914
Career Total (AW)	1	0	0	1	698
81 10/09 Sals 6f212y			SFT	£2914	

Total win prize-money £2914

Going (Turf): Sf: 1-1 GS: 0-0 Gd: 0-1 GF: 0-0 Fm: 0-0
Distance: 5f/6f: 0-0 7f-8f: 1-3 9f-13f: 0-0 14f+: 0-0
Track : LH: 0-0 RH: 0-1 Tight: 0-0 Gall: 0-0
Aids: Bl: 0-0 Vi: 0-0 Tstrap: 0-0 Ckp: 0-0
Best Rating: 81 10/09 Sals 6f212y soft

Useful; gets 7f, should stay 1m; acts on soft ground and Polytrack.

Through The Forest (USA)

85(101) (58)52

3-y-o b/br f Forestry (USA)-Lakefront (USA) (Deputy Minister (CAN))

W R Swinburn Mrs Doreen M Swinburn

Placings:000431 **(7794)**

2009: 8^0G, 8^0GF, 10^0G, 10^4SD, 11^3SD, 11^1SS,

	Starts	1st	2nd	3rd	Win & Pl
Career Total (Turf)	3	0	0	0	
Career Total (AW)	3	1	0	1	3032

56 12/09 Sthl 1m3f (0-70)H SS £2729

Total win prize-money £2730

Going (Turf): **Sf: 0-0 GS: 0-0 Gd: 0-2 GF: 0-1 Fm: 0-0**
Distance: 5f/6f: 0-0 7f-8f: 0-0 **9f-13f: 1-6** 14f+: 0-0
Track : **LH: 1-1** RH: 0-5 Tight: 0-2 Gall: 0-0
Aids: Bl: 0-0 Vi: 0-0 Tstrap: 0-2 Ckp: 0-2
Best Rating: **58** 9/09 Kemp 1m3f stand

Moderate; stays 1m3f; acts on Fibresand.

Throw The Dice

71 (29)24

7-y-o b g Lujain (USA)-Euridice (IRE) (Woodman (USA))

A Berry Alan Berry

Placings:214/620060/0000063260030 0/00224400450165 43504/0000-00 **(3657)**

2009: 5^0GF, 5^0G,

	Starts	1st	2nd	3rd	Win & Pl
Career Total (Turf)	47	2	5	3	18253
Career Total (AW)	1	0	0	0	

60 9/07 Haml 5f4y (0-65)H G-F £2590
77 8/04 Hayd 6f E GD £3601

Total win prize-money £6192

Going (Turf): Sf: 0-7 GS: 0-10 **Gd: 1-9 GF: 1-18** Fm: 0-3
Distance: **5f/6f: 2-39** 7f-8f: 0-9 9f-13f: 0-0 14f+: 0-0
Track : LH: 0-6 RH: 0-3 Tight: 0-2 Gall: 0-4
Aids: Bl: 0-0 **Vi: 1-19** Tstrap: 0-9 Ckp: 0-9
Best Rating: **87** 5/05 Nott 6f15y gd-fm

Thrust Control (IRE)

85 74

2-y-o ch g Fath (USA)-Anazah (USA) (Diesis)

M R Channon Mrs T Burns

Placings:1 **(6544)**

2009: 7^1GF,

	Starts	1st	2nd	3rd	Win & Pl
Career Total (Turf)	1	1	0	0	3238

74 10/09 Wwck 7f26y G-F £3238

Total win prize-money £3238

Going (Turf): Sf: 0-0 GS: 0-0 Gd: 0-0 **GF: 1-1** Fm: 0-0
Distance: 5f/6f: 0-0 **7f-8f: 1-1** 9f-13f: 0-0 14f+: 0-0
Track : **LH: 1-1** RH: 0-0 Tight: 0-0 Gall: 0-0
Aids: Bl: 0-0 Vi: 0-0 Tstrap: 0-0 Ckp: 0-0
Best Rating: **74** 10/09 Wwck 7f26y gd-fm

Fair; stays 7f; acts on fast ground.

Thumberlina

93(85) (40)48

3-y-o b f Choisir (AUS)-Capstick (JPN) (Machiavellian (USA))

Mrs C A Dunnett The College Girls

Placings:00-0000405050000000 **(6335)**

2009: 6^0SD, 6^0SD, 5^0SD, 5^0SD, 5^4GF, 5^0GF, 5^5GF, 5^0G, 5^5F, 5^0S, 6^0G, 5^0GS, 5^0SD, 5^0GF, 5^0GF, 5^0GF,

	Starts	1st	2nd	3rd	Win & Pl
Career Total (Turf)	12	0	0	0	192
Career Total (AW)	6	0	0	0	

Going (Turf): **Sf: 0-1 GS: 0-1 Gd: 0-3 GF: 0-6 Fm: 0-1**
Distance: 5f/6f: 0-16 7f-8f: 0-2 9f-13f: 0-0 14f+: 0-0
Track : LH: 0-8 RH: 0-1 Tight: 0-5 Gall: 0-0
Aids: Bl: 0-2 Vi: 0-7 Tstrap: 0-3 Ckp: 0-3
Best Rating: **48** 4/09 Nott 5f13y gd-fm

Thunder Bay

98(100) (64)76

4-y-o b g Hunting Lion (IRE)-Floral Spark (Forzando)

R A Fahey Northumbria Leisure Ltd & B Morton

Placings:1215035102250/04006200-001003005003022500 **(7645)**

2009: 5^0GF, 6^0G, 5^1GF, 5^0G, 5^0GF, 5^3GF, 5^0GF, 5^0G, 6^5GF, 5^0GF, 6^0GF, 5^3GF, 5^0GF, 6^2SD, 5^2SD, 5^5SD, 5^0SD, 5^0SD,

	Starts	1st	2nd	3rd	Win & Pl
Career Total (Turf)	30	3	3	3	21372
Career Total (AW)	9	1	3	0	4303

65 5/09 Muss 5f (0-65)H G-F £2266
84 8/07 Sand 5f6y G-F £5181
74 4/07 Thsk 5f G-F £5181
60 4/07 Ling 5f STD £2388

Total win prize-money £15020

Going (Turf): Sf: 0-0 GS: 0-5 Gd: 0-8 **GF: 3-17** Fm: 0-0
Distance: **5f/6f: 4-36** 7f-8f: 0-3 9f-13f: 0-0 14f+: 0-0
Track : **LH: 1-11** RH: 0-2 **Tight: 1-11** Gall: 0-2
Aids: Bl: 0-1 Vi: 0-3 Tstrap: 0-3 Ckp: 0-3
Best Rating: **87** 9/07 Ches 5f16y good

Moderate; suited by 5f-6f; acts on fast ground; goes on Polytrack.

Thunder Gorge (USA)

102(97) (74)78

4-y-o b g Thunder Gulch (USA)-Renaissance Fair (USA) (Theatrical)

Mouse Hamilton-Fairley Bramshill Racing

Placings:040206/5062235130-501036000 **(6568)**

2009: 8^5SD, 8^0GF, 8^1GF, 8^0CS, 8^3GF, 9^6S, 8^0F, 8^0GF, 7^0GF,

	Starts	1st	2nd	3rd	Win & Pl
Career Total (Turf)	23	2	3	3	15959
Career Total (AW)	2	0	0	0	117

78 5/09 NmkR 1m (0-75)H G-F £3885
76 9/08 Gdwd 1m (0-80)H SFT £4857

Total win prize-money £8743

Going (Turf): **Sf: 1-3** GS: 0-4 Gd: 0-3 **GF: 1-12** Fm: 0-1
Distance: 5f/6f: 0-3 **7f-8f: 2-14** 9f-13f: 0-8 14f+: 0-0
Track : LH: 0-4 **RH: 1-10** Tight: 0-3 Gall: 0-3
Aids: Bl: 0-0 Vi: 0-0 Tstrap: 0-0 Ckp: 0-0
Best Rating: **78** 7/09 Sand 1m14y gd-fm

Fair; effective at around 1m; acts on fast and soft ground.

Thunder Rock (IRE)

96 75

7-y-o b g King's Best (USA)-Park Express (Ahonoora)

Jonjo O'Neill Mrs Gay Smith

Placings:313/350645/5 **(4793)**

2009: 16^5G,

	Starts	1st	2nd	3rd	Win & Pl
Career Total (Turf)	10	1	0	3	14236

79 6/05 Yarm 1m3f101y GD £3451

Total win prize-money £3452

Going (Turf): Sf: 0-0 GS: 0-3 **Gd: 1-3** GF: 0-4 Fm: 0-0
Distance: 5f/6f: 0-0 7f-8f: 0-0 **9f-13f: 1-9** 14f+: 0-1
Track : **LH: 1-4** RH: 0-5 **Tight: 1-1** Gall: 0-6
Aids: Bl: 0-0 Vi: 0-0 Tstrap: 0-1 Ckp: 0-1
Best Rating: **97** 6/06 Asct 1m4f gd-fm

Useful; stays 1m 3f; acts on good and faster ground.

Thunderball

104(106) (86)84

3-y-o ch g Haafhd-Trustthunder (Selkirk (USA))

J A Glover (A J McCabe 26/6) Paul J Dixon & Brian Morton

Placings:03231250-0320320244 **(7360)**

2009: 10^0G, 7^3GF, 7^2GF, 7^0GS, 7^3F, 7^2GF, 8^0GF, 8^2SD, 10^4SD, 9^4SD,

	Starts	1st	2nd	3rd	Win & Pl
Career Total (Turf)	13	0	4	4	12503
Career Total (AW)	5	1	1	0	7608

77 8/08 GrLe 1m STD £4533

Total win prize-money £4533

Going (Turf): **Sf: 0-2 GS: 0-1 Gd: 0-4 GF: 0-5 Fm: 0-1**
Distance: 5f/6f: 0-1 **7f-8f: 1-13** 9f-13f: 0-4 14f+: 0-0
Track : **LH: 1-8** RH: 0-3 Tight: 0-2 **Gall: 1-4**
Aids: Bl: 0-2 Vi: 0-1 Tstrap: 0-2 Ckp: 0-2
Best Rating: **86** 10/09 Kemp 1m stand

Fair; effective over 7f-1m; acts on fast ground; has worn cheekpieces/blinkers and a visor.

Thundering Home

(95) (72)

2-y-o gr c Storming Home-Citrine Spirit (IRE) (Soviet Star (USA))

E A L Dunlop Salem Suhail

Placings:031 **(7865)**

2009: 8^0SD, 8^3SD, 8^1SS,

	Starts	1st	2nd	3rd	Win & Pl
Career Total (Turf)	0	0	0	0	
Career Total (AW)	3	1	0	1	2883

72 12/09 Sthl 1m SS £2590

Total win prize-money £2590

Going (Turf): **Sf: 0-0 GS: 0-0 Gd: 0-0 GF: 0-0 Fm: 0-0**
Distance: 5f/6f: 0-0 **7f-8f: 1-3** 9f-13f: 0-0 14f+: 0-0
Track : **LH: 1-3** RH: 0-0 Tight: 0-2 Gall: 0-0
Aids: Bl: 0-0 Vi: 0-0 Tstrap: 0-0 Ckp: 0-0
Best Rating: **72** 12/09 Sthl 1m std-slw

Modest; stays 1m and acts on both AW surfaces.

Thunderonthemount

55

4-y-o ch g Zaha (CAN)-Vrennan (Suave Dancer (USA))

M J Attwater Canisbay Bloodstock

Placings:0 **(3791)**

2009: 12^0GF,

	Starts	1st	2nd	3rd	Win & Pl
Career Total (Turf)	1	0	0	0	

Going (Turf): Sf: 0-0 GS: 0-0 Gd: 0-0 GF: 0-1 Fm: 0-0
Distance: 5f/6f: 0-0 7f-8f: 0-0 9f-13f: 0-1 14f+: 0-0
Track : LH: 0-1 RH: 0-0 Tight: 0-0 Gall: 0-0
Aids: Bl: 0-0 Vi: 0-0 Tstrap: 0-0 Ckp: 0-0

Thunderous Mood (USA)

97(111) (81)102

3-y-o b/br c Storm Cat (USA)-Warm Mood (USA) (Alydar (USA))

P F I Cole Mrs Fitri Hay

Placings:310022-00040054 (7613)

2009: 5^{0}G, 7^{0}GF, 6^{0}G, 5^{4}F, 6^{0}G, 7^{0}G, 6^{5}SD, 6^{4}SD,

	Starts	1st	2nd	3rd	Win & Pl
Career Total (Turf)	12	1	2	1	22176
Career Total (AW)	2	0	0	0	351

82 5/08 York 5f GD £7123

Total win prize-money £7124

Going (Turf): Sf: 0-0 GS: 0-1 **Gd: 1-8** GF: 0-2 Fm: 0-1
Distance: **5f/6f: 1-12** 7f-8f: 0-2 9f-13f: 0-0 14f+: 0-0
Track : LH: 0-1 RH: 0-2 Tight: 0-0 Gall: 0-1
Aids: Bl: 0-4 Vi: 0-0 Tstrap: 0-0 Ckp: 0-0
Best Rating: **102** 9/08 Chan 5f110y good

Useful; effective at 5f; handles good ground.

Thunderstruck

98(105) (83)74

4-y-o b g Bertolini (USA)-Trustthunder (Selkirk (USA))

J A Glover (A J McCabe 10/6) Paul J Dixon

Placings:541/550056430-000042211243 (7823)

2009: 9^{0}G, 8^{0}G, 9^{0}GF, 11^{0}GS, 9^{4}GF, 10^{2}GF, **9^{2}SD**, **10^{1}SD**, 8^{1}SD, 10^{2}SD, 9^{4}SD, **10^{3}SD**,

	Starts	1st	2nd	3rd	Win & Pl
Career Total (Turf)	17	1	1	0	4205
Career Total (AW)	7	2	2	2	6946

73 11/09 Wolv 1m141y (0-60)H STD £2388
71 11/09 Kemp 1m2f (0-65)H STD £2047
81 9/07 Bevl 7f100y G-F £2590

Total win prize-money £7026

Going (Turf): Sf: 0-2 GS: 0-5 Gd: 0-3 **GF: 1-7** Fm: 0-0
Distance: 5f/6f: 0-0 7f-8f: 1-4 **9f-13f: 2-20** 14f+: 0-0
Track : LH: 1-12 **RH: 2-11 Tight: 1-8** Gall: 0-2
Aids: Bl: 0-5 Vi: 0-0 Tstrap: 2-7 Ckp: 2-7
Best Rating: **83** 11/09 Kemp 1m2f stand

Fair; stays 1m2f; acts on Polytrack; has worn cheekpieces.

Thunderwing (IRE)

97(90) (39)65

7-y-o b/br g Indian Danehill (IRE)-Scandisk (IRE) (Kenmare (FR))

James Moffatt David And Nicky Robinson

Placings:31115/20000042/000060360/256040562/4036-030 (2044)

2009: 13^{0}SD, 15^{3}GF, 16^{0}GS,

	Starts	1st	2nd	3rd	Win & Pl
Career Total (Turf)	32	3	3	4	22928
Career Total (AW)	6	0	1	0	645

93 9/04 Ayr 1m G-S £5408
90 8/04 Newc 1m3y F HVY £2933
80 8/04 Thsk 7f E G-S £3750

Total win prize-money £12092

Going (Turf): Sf: 1-8 **GS: 2-11** Gd: 0-6 GF: 0-6 Fm: 0-1
Distance: 5f/6f: 0-1 **7f-8f: 2-13** 9f-13f: 1-20 14f+: 0-4
Track : **LH: 2-27** RH: 0-7 **Tight: 1-15** Gall: 0-4
Aids: Bl: 0-0 Vi: 0-2 Tstrap: 0-3 Ckp: 0-3
Best Rating: **93** 9/04 Ayr 1m gd-sft

Moderate; stays 1m2f; handles most ground.

Thurston (IRE)

(96) (66)

3-y-o ch g Barathea (IRE)-Campiglia (IRE) (Fairy King (USA))

D J S Ffrench Davis Thirstin Partnership

Placings:002-60000 (6442)

2009: 7^{6}SD, 7^{0}SD, 7^{0}SD, 7^{0}SD, 7^{0}SS,

	Starts	1st	2nd	3rd	Win & Pl
Career Total (Turf)	1	0	0	0	
Career Total (AW)	7	0	1	0	806

Going (Turf): **Sf: 0-0 GS: 0-1 Gd: 0-0 GF: 0-0 Fm: 0-0**
Distance: 5f/6f: 0-1 7f-8f: 0-7 9f-13f: 0-0 14f+: 0-0
Track : LH: 0-7 RH: 0-0 Tight: 0-3 Gall: 0-0
Aids: Bl: 0-3 Vi: 0-0 Tstrap: 0-0 Ckp: 0-0
Best Rating: **66** 12/08 Sthl 7f std-slw

Modest; effective over 7f; acts on Fibresand.

Tia Juana (IRE)

94(87) (65)60

2-y-o b f Shamardal (USA)-Tiavanita (USA) (J O Tobin (USA))

Saeed Bin Suroor Godolphin

Placings:444 (5969)

2009: 6^{4}SD, 5^{4}G, 6^{4}GF,

	Starts	1st	2nd	3rd	Win & Pl
Career Total (Turf)	2	0	0	0	642
Career Total (AW)	1	0	0	0	0

Going (Turf): **Sf: 0-0 GS: 0-0 Gd: 0-1 GF: 0-1 Fm: 0-0**
Distance: 5f/6f: 0-2 7f-8f: 0-1 9f-13f: 0-0 14f+: 0-0
Track : LH: 0-2 RH: 0-0 Tight: 0-1 Gall: 0-1
Aids: Bl: 0-0 Vi: 0-0 Tstrap: 0-0 Ckp: 0-0
Best Rating: **65** 8/09 Ling 6f stand

Modest half-sister to Island Sands; modest ability in maidens on turf and Polytrack.

Ticket To Freedom (NZ)

91 65

7-y-o bl g Cape Cross (IRE)-Macrowave (NZ) (Crested Wave (USA))

J J Quinn Exors Of The Late Lady Anne Bentinck

Placings:00/510/3 (2944)

2009: 14^{3}GF,

	Starts	1st	2nd	3rd	Win & Pl
Career Total (Turf)	6	1	0	1	1772

3/06 Wang 1m2f GD £1240

Total win prize-money £1240

Going (Turf): Sf: 0-1 GS: 0-1 **Gd: 1-3** GF: 0-1 Fm: 0-0
Distance: 5f/6f: 0-1 7f-8f: 0-2 **9f-13f: 1-2** 14f+: 0-1
Track : LH: 0-1 RH: 0-0 Tight: 0-0 Gall: 0-1
Aids: Bl: 0-0 Vi: 0-0 Tstrap: 0-0 Ckp: 0-0
Best Rating: **65** 6/09 Donc 1m6f132y gd-fm

Ticket To Paradise

72 16

2-y-o b c Singspiel (IRE)-Dream Ticket (USA) (Danzig (USA))

D R Lanigan Saeed H Altayer

Placings:0 (7243)

2009: 8^{0}S,

	Starts	1st	2nd	3rd	Win & Pl
Career Total (Turf)	1	0	0	0	

Going (Turf): **Sf: 0-1 GS: 0-0 Gd: 0-0 GF: 0-0 Fm: 0-0**
Distance: 5f/6f: 0-0 7f-8f: 0-0 9f-13f: 0-1 14f+: 0-0
Track : LH: 0-1 RH: 0-0 Tight: 0-0 Gall: 0-0
Aids: Bl: 0-0 Vi: 0-0 Tstrap: 0-0 Ckp: 0-0
Best Rating: **16** 11/09 Nott 1m75y soft

Tidal Force (USA)

98(93) (61)76

3-y-o ch g High Yield (USA)-Shady Waters (CAN) (Rahy (USA))

A J McCabe (P F I Cole 29/7) Tariq Al Nisf

Placings:010-0305000 (7627)

2009: 8^{0}SD, 7^{3}GF, 7^{0}GF, 8^{5}GS, 6^{0}GF, 7^{0}S, 7^{0}SD,

	Starts	1st	2nd	3rd	Win & Pl
Career Total (Turf)	8	1	0	1	5111
Career Total (AW)	2	0	0	0	

76 7/08 NmkJ 6f G-F £4533

Total win prize-money £4533

Going (Turf): Sf: 0-1 GS: 0-1 Gd: 0-2 **GF: 1-4** Fm: 0-0
Distance: **5f/6f: 1-2** 7f-8f: 0-8 9f-13f: 0-0 14f+: 0-0
Track : LH: 0-1 RH: 0-2 Tight: 0-1 Gall: 0-1
Aids: Bl: 0-4 Vi: 0-0 Tstrap: 0-0 Ckp: 0-0
Best Rating: **76** 7/08 NmkJ 6f gd-fm

Fair; effective over 6f; acts on fast ground.

Tiddliwinks

94(103) (89)57

3-y-o b g Piccolo-Card Games (First Trump)

K A Ryan Guy Reed

Placings:4410021 (7692)

2009: 8^{4}SF, 7^{4}GF, **7^{1}SD**, 7^{0}G, 7^{0}S, 8^{2}SD, **7^{1}SD**,

	Starts	1st	2nd	3rd	Win & Pl
Career Total (Turf)	3	0	0	0	289
Career Total (AW)	4	2	1	0	8141

89 12/09 Ling 7f (0-85)H STD £4981
78 9/09 Wolv 7f32y STD £2388

Total win prize-money £7370

Going (Turf): **Sf: 0-1 GS: 0-0 Gd: 0-1 GF: 0-1 Fm: 0-0**
Distance: 5f/6f: 0-0 **7f-8f: 2-6** 9f-13f: 0-1 14f+: 0-0
Track : **LH: 2-5** RH: 0-0 **Tight: 2-4** Gall: 0-0
Aids: Bl: 0-0 Vi: 0-0 Tstrap: 0-0 Ckp: 0-0
Best Rating: **89** 12/09 Ling 7f stand

Useful; stays 7f; acts on Polytrack.

Tiegs (IRE)

(95) (52)47

7-y-o ch m Desert Prince (IRE)-Helianthus (Groom Dancer (USA))

P W Hiatt The Fox Inn Partnership

Placings:0/034000/40140/1030404024 4/1000-00 (0300)
2009: 11^{0}SD, 14^{0}SD,

	Starts	1st	2nd	3rd	Win & Pl
Career Total (Turf)	10	0	1	1	2170
Career Total (AW)	19	3	0	1	6260

52 1/08 Kemp 1m4f (0-45) STD £1365
49 1/07 Sthl 1m4f STD £2184
52 3/06 Sthl 1m4f (0-55)H STD £2388
Total win prize-money £5938

Going (Turf): Sf: 0-1 GS: 0-2 Gd: 0-3 GF: 0-4 Fm: 0-0
Distance: 5f/6f: 0-0 7f-8f: 0-1 9f-13f: 3-24 14f+: 0-4
Track : LH: 2-20 RH: 1-8 Tight: 0-8 Gall: 0-0
Aids: Bl: 0-0 Vi: 0-0 Tstrap: 0-2 Ckp: 0-2
Best Rating: 56 8/05 Ling 1m6f soft

Plating-class mare; stays 1m4f and acts on sand; suited by forcing tactics.

Tifernati

87(91) (86)94
5-y-o b g Dansili-Pain Perdu (IRE) (Waajib)
G L Moore The Gingerbread Men

Placings:6/15550444113/331443-0 (1458)
2009: 12^{0}G,

	Starts	1st	2nd	3rd	Win & Pl
Career Total (Turf)	17	3	0	3	44342
Career Total (AW)	2	1	0	1	5483

94 6/08 Haml 1m4f17y (0-90)H G-F £21808
85 8/07 Newb 1m4f5y (0-80)H GD £12492
72 8/07 NmkJ 1m4f (0-70)H G-F £3886
73 3/07 Kemp 6f STD £4728
Total win prize-money £42915

Going (Turf): Sf: 0-4 GS: 0-2 Gd: 1-4 GF: 2-7 Fm: 0-0
Distance: 5f/6f: 1-2 7f-8f: 0-4 9f-13f: 3-12 14f+: 0-1
Track : LH: 1-9 RH: 3-6 Tight: 1-5 Gall: 2-7
Aids: Bl: 0-1 Vi: 0-0 Tstrap: 0-1 Ckp: 0-1
Best Rating: 94 6/08 Haml 1m4f17y gd-fm

Useful; effective over 1m4f; acts on good and faster ground.

Tiffany Lady

(94) (44)
3-y-o ch f Generous (IRE)-Art Deco Lady (Master Willie)
M D I Usher Mrs Jill Pellett

Placings:0-0506000 (7666)
2009: 9^{0}SD, 7^{5}SD, 8^{0}SD, 9^{6}SD, 12^{0}SS, 12^{0}SD, 10^{0}SD,

	Starts	1st	2nd	3rd	Win & Pl
Career Total (Turf)	0	0	0	0	
Career Total (AW)	8	0	0	0	0

Going (Turf): Sf: 0-0 GS: 0-0 Gd: 0-0 GF: 0-0 Fm: 0-0
Distance: 5f/6f: 0-0 7f-8f: 0-3 9f-13f: 0-5 14f+: 0-0
Track : LH: 0-7 RH: 0-1 Tight: 0-6 Gall: 0-0
Aids: Bl: 0-0 Vi: 0-0 Tstrap: 0-0 Ckp: 0-0
Best Rating: 44 1/09 Wolv 7f32y stand

Tiger Breeze (USA)

89 55
3-y-o b g Roar Of The Tiger (USA)-M. S. Gripsholm (USA) (Goldwater (USA))
Miss Jo Crowley Mrs Liz Nelson

Placings:06 (4303)
2009: 6^{0}GF, 7^{6}G,

	Starts	1st	2nd	3rd	Win & Pl
Career Total (Turf)	2	0	0	0	0

Going (Turf): Sf: 0-0 GS: 0-0 Gd: 0-1 GF: 0-1 Fm: 0-0
Distance: 5f/6f: 0-0 7f-8f: 0-2 9f-13f: 0-0 14f+: 0-0
Track : LH: 0-0 RH: 0-0 Tight: 0-0 Gall: 0-0
Aids: Bl: 0-0 Vi: 0-0 Tstrap: 0-0 Ckp: 0-0
Best Rating: 55 6/09 Sals 6f212y gd-fm

Tiger Court

73 41
2-y-o b f Tiger Hill (IRE)-Cruinn A Bhord (Inchinor)
E A L Dunlop Lord Derby

Placings:0 (7182)
2009: 7^{0}G,

	Starts	1st	2nd	3rd	Win & Pl
Career Total (Turf)	1	0	0	0	

Going (Turf): Sf: 0-0 GS: 0-0 Gd: 0-1 GF: 0-0 Fm: 0-0
Distance: 5f/6f: 0-0 7f-8f: 0-1 9f-13f: 0-0 14f+: 0-0
Track : LH: 0-0 RH: 0-0 Tight: 0-0 Gall: 0-0
Aids: Bl: 0-0 Vi: 0-0 Tstrap: 0-0 Ckp: 0-0
Best Rating: 41 10/09 NmkR 7f good

Tiger Dream

102(102) (79)88
4-y-o b g Oasis Dream-Grey Way (USA) (Cozzene (USA))
K A Ryan Mrs Angie Bailey & Mrs T Marnane

Placings:222/1060400-002225200003251502 (7523)
2009: 7^{0}GF, 8^{0}GF, 7^{2}SD, 7^{2}GS, 8^{2}HY, 10^{5}G, 8^{2}G, 7^{0}G, 7^{0}G, 8^{0}GF, 8^{0}GS, 8^{3}GS, 8^{2}GF, 7^{5}GF, 8^{1}GF, 9^{5}SD, 10^{0}G, 8^{2}SD,

	Starts	1st	2nd	3rd	Win & Pl
Career Total (Turf)	24	2	7	1	19905
Career Total (AW)	4	0	2	0	2213

78 9/09 Hayd 1m30y (0-80)H G-F £5504
71 5/08 Thsk 1m G-F £3885
Total win prize-money £9391

Going (Turf): Sf: 0-2 GS: 0-4 Gd: 0-8 GF: 2-10 Fm: 0-0
Distance: 5f/6f: 0-0 7f-8f: 1-17 9f-13f: 1-11 14f+: 0-0
Track : LH: 2-13 RH: 0-7 Tight: 1-5 Gall: 0-5
Aids: Bl: 0-1 Vi: 0-0 Tstrap: 1-12 Ckp: 1-12
Best Rating: 88 5/08 Hayd 1m30y gd-fm

Fair; effective over 7f-1m2f; acts on fast and soft ground and Polytrack; has worn cheekpieces.

Tiger Flash

101(92) (69)77
3-y-o b c Dansili-Miss Penton (Primo Dominie)
W J Haggas M S Bloodstock Ltd

Placings:5-33023324 (6758)
2009: 8^{3}G, 9^{3}GF, 10^{0}G, 10^{2}G, 10^{3}GF, 12^{3}SD, 10^{2}G, 11^{4}G,

	Starts	1st	2nd	3rd	Win & Pl
Career Total (Turf)	8	0	2	3	2928
Career Total (AW)	1	0	0	1	530

Going (Turf): Sf: 0-1 GS: 0-0 Gd: 0-5 GF: 0-2 Fm: 0-0
Distance: 5f/6f: 0-0 7f-8f: 0-1 9f-13f: 0-8 14f+: 0-0
Track : LH: 0-3 RH: 0-4 Tight: 0-4 Gall: 0-0
Aids: Bl: 0-1 Vi: 0-0 Tstrap: 0-0 Ckp: 0-0
Best Rating: 77 4/09 Yarm 1m3y good

Modest; stays 1m2f; acts on good ground.

Tiger Girl

71 27
2-y-o b f Tiger Hill (IRE)-Girl Of My Dreams (IRE) (Marju (IRE))
R Charlton A Parker (London)

Placings:0 (4792)
2009: 7^{0}G,

	Starts	1st	2nd	3rd	Win & Pl
Career Total (Turf)	1	0	0	0	

Going (Turf): Sf: 0-0 GS: 0-0 Gd: 0-1 GF: 0-0 Fm: 0-0
Distance: 5f/6f: 0-0 7f-8f: 0-1 9f-13f: 0-0 14f+: 0-0
Track : LH: 0-0 RH: 0-0 Tight: 0-0 Gall: 0-0
Aids: Bl: 0-0 Vi: 0-0 Tstrap: 0-0 Ckp: 0-0
Best Rating: 27 8/09 NmkJ 7f good

Tiger Hawk (USA)

85(91) (63)45
2-y-o b c Tale Of The Cat (USA)-Aura Of Glory (CAN) (Halo (USA))
P D Evans (K M Prendergast 10/9) Freddie Ingram

Placings:06300100410 (7791)
2009: 7^{0}G, 7^{6}G, 7^{3}G, 7^{0}G, 7^{0}SD, 8^{1}SD, 10^{0}SD, 8^{0}SD, 8^{4}SD, 8^{1}SD, 7^{0}SS,

	Starts	1st	2nd	3rd	Win & Pl
Career Total (Turf)	4	0	0	1	289
Career Total (AW)	7	2	0	0	3990

63 12/09 Sthl 1m STD £1942
60 11/09 Sthl 1m STD £2047
Total win prize-money £3990

Going (Turf): Sf: 0-0 GS: 0-0 Gd: 0-4 GF: 0-0 Fm: 0-0
Distance: 5f/6f: 0-0 7f-8f: 2-8 9f-13f: 0-3 14f+: 0-0
Track : LH: 2-7 RH: 0-1 Tight: 0-4 Gall: 0-0
Aids: Bl: 2-9 Vi: 0-0 Tstrap: 0-0 Ckp: 0-0
Best Rating: 63 12/09 Sthl 1m stand

Plating-class; stays 1m; acts on Fibresand; has worn blinkers.

Tiger Reigns

109 97
3-y-o b g Tiger Hill (IRE)-Showery (Rainbow Quest (USA))
M Dods Joe Buzzeo

Placings:33-11421114 (6094)
2009: 5^{1}GF, 8^{1}GS, 10^{4}GF, 8^{2}GF, 8^{1}S, 8^{1}GS, 8^{1}S, 8^{4}G,

	Starts	1st	2nd	3rd	Win & Pl
Career Total (Turf)	10	5	1	2	34583

97 9/09 Thsk 1m (0-95)H SFT £8159
94 8/09 Hayd 1m30y (0-95)H G-S £8095
91 6/09 Newc 1m (0-85)H SFT £4984
80 5/09 Newc 1m (0-70)H G-S £2978
58 4/09 Catt 5f212y G-F £2266
Total win prize-money £26486

Going (Turf): Sf: 2-3 GS: 2-3 Gd: 0-1 GF: 1-3 Fm: 0-0
Distance: 5f/6f: 1-1 7f-8f: 3-7 9f-13f: 1-2 14f+: 0-0
Track : LH: 5-8 RH: 0-0 Tight: 2-3 Gall: 2-2
Aids: Bl: 0-0 Vi: 0-0 Tstrap: 0-0 Ckp: 0-0
Best Rating: 97 9/09 Ayr 1m good

Useful; stays 1m; acts on most ground but well suited by soft.

Tiger Star

(100) (78)

2-y-o b g Tiger Hill (IRE)-Rosy Outlook (USA) (Trempolino (USA))

J M P Eustace J C Smith

Placings:02 (7763)

2009: 7^{0}SD, 8^{2}SD,

	Starts	1st	2nd	3rd	Win & Pl
Career Total (Turf)	0	0	0	0	
Career Total (AW)	2	0	1	0	1156

Going (Turf): Sf: 0-0 GS: 0-0 Gd: 0-0 GF: 0-0 Fm: 0-0
Distance: 5f/6f: 0-0 7f-8f: 0-2 9f-13f: 0-0 14f+: 0-0
Track : LH: 0-0 RH: 0-2 Tight: 0-0 Gall: 0-0
Aids: Bl: 0-1 Vi: 0-0 Tstrap: 0-0 Ckp: 0-0
Best Rating: 78 12/09 Kemp 1m stand

Fair; stays 1m; acts on Polytrack.

Tiger Tee (IRE)

(97) (53)**51**

4-y-o b g Spectrum (IRE)-Frill (Henbit (USA))

John A Quinn Thomas C Farrell

Placings:00000/000-1 (4862)

2009: 16^{1}SD,

	Starts	1st	2nd	3rd	Win & Pl
Career Total (Turf)	7	0	0	0	
Career Total (AW)	2	1	0	0	2388

53 8/09 Wolv 2m119y (0-65)H STD £2388
Total win prize-money £2388

Going (Turf): Sf: 0-1 GS: 0-0 Gd: 0-3 GF: 0-1 Fm: 0-1
Distance: 5f/6f: 0-3 7f-8f: 0-2 9f-13f: 0-3 **14f+: 1-1**
Track : **LH: 1-6** RH: 0-1 **Tight: 1-1** Gall: 0-0
Aids: Bl: 0-0 Vi: 0-0 Tstrap: 0-0 Ckp: 0-0
Best Rating: 63 6/07 Leop 6f good

Moderate; stays 2m and acts on Polytrack.

Tiger Trail (GER)

94(84) (51)**65**

5-y-o b g Tagula (IRE)-Tweed Mill (Selkirk (USA))

Mrs N Smith Mrs C A Remington

Placings:00/030460-004024 (6422)

2009: 5^{0}GF, 6^{0}GF, 6^{4}GF, 5^{0}GF, 5^{2}G, 5^{4}GF,

	Starts	1st	2nd	3rd	Win & Pl
Career Total (Turf)	12	0	1	1	2272
Career Total (AW)	2	0	0	0	0

Going (Turf): Sf: 0-0 GS: 0-2 Gd: 0-4 GF: 0-6 Fm: 0-0
Distance: 5f/6f: 0-10 7f-8f: 0-3 9f-13f: 0-1 14f+: 0-0
Track : LH: 0-3 RH: 0-1 Tight: 0-2 Gall: 0-1
Aids: Bl: 0-0 Vi: 0-0 Tstrap: 0-1 Ckp: 0-1
Best Rating: 65 6/08 Folk 6f gd-sft

Modesrate colt; stays 6f; acts on good.

Tiger's Rocket (IRE)

(97) (71)**66**

4-y-o b c Monashee Mountain (USA)-Brown Foam (Horage)

S Gollings Phil Dukes

Placings:00006304551/41231455-3000 (0514)

2009: 8^{3}SD, 8^{0}SD, 12^{0}SD, 8^{0}SD,

	Starts	1st	2nd	3rd	Win & Pl
Career Total (Turf)	8	1	0	0	2111
Career Total (AW)	15	2	1	3	7382

66 4/08 Folk 7f SFT £1774
71 1/08 Wolv 1m1f103y STD £2590
67 12/07 Wolv 7f32y (0-65) STD £2730
Total win prize-money £7095

Going (Turf): Sf: 1-3 GS: 0-2 Gd: 0-1 GF: 0-2 Fm: 0-0
Distance: 5f/6f: 0-4 **7f-8f: 2-13** 9f-13f: 1-6 14f+: 0-0
Track : **LH: 2-11** RH: 0-6 **Tight: 2-5** Gall: 0-1
Aids: Bl: 0-2 Vi: 0-2 Tstrap: 0-0 Ckp: 0-0
Best Rating: 71 1/08 Wolv 1m1f103y stand

Modest; effective at around 1m-1m1f; acts on Polytrack.

Tigerbythetale (IRE)

(100) (55)

4-y-o b g Tiger Hill (IRE)-Goldkatze (GER) (Czaravich (USA))

D R C Elsworth D R C Elsworth

Placings:5 (0171)

2009: 10^{5}SD,

	Starts	1st	2nd	3rd	Win & Pl
Career Total (Turf)	0	0	0	0	
Career Total (AW)	1	0	0	0	0

Going (Turf): Sf: 0-0 GS: 0-0 Gd: 0-0 GF: 0-0 Fm: 0-0
Distance: 5f/6f: 0-0 7f-8f: 0-0 9f-13f: 0-1 14f+: 0-0
Track : LH: 0-1 RH: 0-0 Tight: 0-0 Gall: 0-1
Aids: Bl: 0-0 Vi: 0-0 Tstrap: 0-0 Ckp: 0-0
Best Rating: 55 1/09 GrLe 1m2f stand

Tightrope (IRE)

97(92) (58)**47**

3-y-o b g Refuse To Bend (IRE)-Sisal (IRE) (Danehill (USA))

T D McCarthy Cavendish Star Racing

Placings:00000-504630500055550 (7774)

2009: 8^{5}SD, 7^{0}SD, 6^{4}SD, 6^{6}SD, 5^{3}GF, 5^{0}GF, 5^{5}F, 5^{0}G, 6^{0}GF, 5^{0}F, 5^{5}GF, 5^{5}F, 5^{5}GF, 5^{5}SD, 6^{0}SD,

	Starts	1st	2nd	3rd	Win & Pl
Career Total (Turf)	12	0	0	1	430
Career Total (AW)	8	0	0	0	0

Going (Turf): Sf: 0-1 GS: 0-1 Gd: 0-2 GF: 0-5 Fm: 0-3
Distance: 5f/6f: 0-15 7f-8f: 0-5 9f-13f: 0-0 14f+: 0-0
Track : LH: 0-12 RH: 0-2 Tight: 0-6 Gall: 0-1
Aids: Bl: 0-6 Vi: 0-0 Tstrap: 0-0 Ckp: 0-0
Best Rating: 58 3/09 Ling 1m stand

Tignello (IRE)

103(95) (68)**63**

4-y-o b g Kendor (FR)-La Genereuse (Generous (IRE))

G L Moore Mrs Mette Campbell-Andenaes

Placings:0662-03335600 (5905)

2009: 9^{0}GF, 8^{3}GS, 8^{3}GF, 8^{3}SD, 8^{5}GF, 8^{6}GF, 7^{0}GS, 8^{0}F,

	Starts	1st	2nd	3rd	Win & Pl
Career Total (Turf)	8	0	0	2	886
Career Total (AW)	4	0	1	1	907

Going (Turf): Sf: 0-0 GS: 0-2 Gd: 0-0 GF: 0-5 Fm: 0-1
Distance: 5f/6f: 0-0 7f-8f: 0-5 9f-13f: 0-7 14f+: 0-0
Track : LH: 0-4 RH: 0-6 Tight: 0-5 Gall: 0-0
Aids: Bl: 0-0 Vi: 0-0 Tstrap: 0-0 Ckp: 0-0
Best Rating: 68 10/08 Kemp 7f stand

Modest; effective over 7f; acts on Polytrack.

Tikka Masala (IRE)

100(91) (65)**73**

3-y-o b f One Cool Cat (USA)-Raysiza (IRE) (Alzao (USA))

Tom Dascombe A Black

Placings:54-2016000 (7028)

2009: 7^{2}SD, 7^{0}SD, 7^{1}GF, 8^{6}F, 8^{0}GF, 7^{0}GF, 6^{0}SD,

	Starts	1st	2nd	3rd	Win & Pl
Career Total (Turf)	5	1	0	0	3238
Career Total (AW)	4	0	1	0	771

73 6/09 Leic 7f9y (0-70)H G-F £3238
Total win prize-money £3238

Going (Turf): Sf: 0-0 GS: 0-1 Gd: 0-0 **GF: 1-3** Fm: 0-1
Distance: 5f/6f: 0-3 **7f-8f: 1-4** 9f-13f: 0-2 14f+: 0-0
Track : LH: 0-4 RH: 0-3 Tight: 0-5 Gall: 0-0
Aids: Bl: 0-0 Vi: 0-1 Tstrap: 0-0 Ckp: 0-0
Best Rating: 73 6/09 Leic 7f9y gd-fm

Fair, stays 7f; acts on Polytrack and fast turf; has worn tongue tie.

Tilapia (IRE)

(110) (69)**77**

5-y-o ch g Daggers Drawn (USA)-Mrs Fisher (IRE) (Salmon Leap (USA))

Miss Gay Kelleway Bill Hinge

Placings:420/10113/331560600000-0 (3721)

2009: 12^{0}SD,

	Starts	1st	2nd	3rd	Win & Pl
Career Total (Turf)	3	0	0	0	
Career Total (AW)	18	4	1	3	18291

92 2/08 Kemp 1m3f (0-85)H STD £4210
88 5/07 Sthl 1m (0-75)H STD £3071
80 5/07 Sthl 1m (0-80)H STD £5181
70 1/07 Ling 1m (0-65)H STD £2388
Total win prize-money £14852

Going (Turf): Sf: 0-0 GS: 0-2 Gd: 0-1 GF: 0-0 Fm: 0-0
Distance: 5f/6f: 0-3 **7f-8f: 3-9** 9f-13f: 1-9 14f+: 0-0
Track : **LH: 3-15** RH: 1-6 **Tight: 1-8** Gall: 0-4
Aids: Bl: 0-1 Vi: 0-1 Tstrap: 0-0 Ckp: 0-0
Best Rating: 92 3/08 Ling 1m4f stand

Useful; stays 1m3f and acts well on sand; has worn blinkers and a visor; likes to race prominently.

Tilerium's Dream (IRE)

92 **54**

3-y-o b g Tillerman-Thai Princess (IRE) (Hamas (IRE))

K A Ryan Hokey Cokey Partnership (2)

Placings:0-054000 (5972)

2009: 8^{0}GF, 7^{5}GF, 8^{4}F, 6^{0}GS, 8^{0}GF, 7^{0}GF,

	Starts	1st	2nd	3rd	Win & Pl
Career Total (Turf)	7	0	0	0	0

Going (Turf): Sf: 0-1 GS: 0-1 Gd: 0-0 GF: 0-4 Fm: 0-1
Distance: 5f/6f: 0-2 7f-8f: 0-5 9f-13f: 0-0 14f+: 0-0
Track : LH: 0-0 RH: 0-1 Tight: 0-1 Gall: 0-0
Aids: Bl: 0-0 Vi: 0-0 Tstrap: 0-2 Ckp: 0-2
Best Rating: 54 4/09 Rdcr 7f gd-fm

Tillers Satisfied (IRE)

88(98) (63)**62**

3-y-o b f Tillerman-Lady Of Pleasure (IRE) (Marju (IRE))

R Hollinshead Dean Wootton

Placings:36641016-420003 **(3225)**

2009: 7^{4}SD, 5^{2}SD, 6^{0}GF, 5^{0}SD, 6^{0}GS, 5^{3}SD,

	Starts	1st	2nd	3rd	Win & Pl
Career Total (Turf)	**6**	**0**	**0**	**1**	**1011**
Career Total (AW)	**8**	**2**	**1**	**1**	**5473**

63 12/08 Wolv 5f216y STD £2388
60 10/08 Wolv 5f20y STD £2047
Total win prize-money £4435

Going (Turf): **Sf: 0-1 GS: 0-1 Gd: 0-0 GF: 0-3 Fm: 0-1**
Distance: **5f/6f: 2-11** 7f-8f: 0-3 9f-13f: 0-0 14f+: 0-0
Track : **LH: 2-13** RH: 0-0 **Tight: 2-8** Gall: 0-2
Aids: Bl: 0-0 Vi: 0-0 Tstrap: 0-1 Ckp: 0-1
Best Rating: **63** 12/08 Wolv 5f216y stand

Moderate; effective over 5f-6f; acts on Polytrack.

Tillietudlem (FR)

101(83) (35)**49**

3-y-o gr g Kutub (IRE)-Queenhood (FR) (Linamix (FR))

J S Goldie Mr & Mrs C J Smith

Placings:60-063363 **(5442)**

2009: 9^{0}SD, 11^{6}GF, 12^{3}GF, 11^{3}G, 11^{6}GS, 14^{3}GF,

	Starts	1st	2nd	3rd	Win & Pl
Career Total (Turf)	**6**	**0**	**0**	**3**	**963**
Career Total (AW)	**2**	**0**	**0**	**0**	

Going (Turf): **Sf: 0-1 GS: 0-1 Gd: 0-1 GF: 0-3 Fm: 0-0**
Distance: 5f/6f: 0-0 7f-8f: 0-2 9f-13f: 0-5 14f+: 0-1
Track : LH: 0-3 RH: 0-5 Tight: 0-8 Gall: 0-0
Aids: Bl: 0-0 Vi: 0-0 Tstrap: 0-0 Ckp: 0-0
Best Rating: **49** 6/09 Haml 1m4f17y gd-fm

Very moderate; stays 1m3f and acts on good ground.

Tilly Shilling (IRE)

82(93) (50)**47**

5-y-o b m Montjeu (IRE)-Antiguan Jane (Shirley Heights)

Tim Vaughan (Norma Twomey 18/5) Mrs L M Edwards

Placings:50/400 **(2127)**

2009: 12^{4}SD, 12^{0}SD, 17^{0}GS,

	Starts	1st	2nd	3rd	Win & Pl
Career Total (Turf)	**3**	**0**	**0**	**0**	**0**
Career Total (AW)	**2**	**0**	**0**	**0**	**0**

Going (Turf): **Sf: 0-0 GS: 0-1 Gd: 0-1 GF: 0-1 Fm: 0-0**
Distance: 5f/6f: 0-0 7f-8f: 0-0 9f-13f: 0-4 14f+: 0-1
Track : LH: 0-4 RH: 0-1 Tight: 0-5 Gall: 0-0
Aids: Bl: 0-0 Vi: 0-0 Tstrap: 0-0 Ckp: 0-0
Best Rating: **52** 8/07 Bath 1m3f144y good

Tillys Tale

97 **81**

2-y-o ch f Lucky Story (USA)-Otylia (Wolfhound (USA))

P T Midgley Mrs M Hills

Placings:5410230252 **(5552)**

2009: 5^{5}GF, 5^{4}GF, 5^{1}G, 5^{0}GF, 5^{2}GF, 5^{3}GF, 5^{0}GF, 5^{2}GS, 5^{5}G, 5^{2}GS,

	Starts	1st	2nd	3rd	Win & Pl
Career Total (Turf)	**10**	**1**	**3**	**1**	**11936**

73 5/09 Thsk 5f GD £5569
Total win prize-money £5569

Going (Turf): Sf: 0-0 GS: 0-2 **Gd: 1-2** GF: 0-6 Fm: 0-0
Distance: **5f/6f: 1-10** 7f-8f: 0-0 9f-13f: 0-0 14f+: 0-0
Track : LH: 0-1 RH: 0-0 Tight: 0-1 Gall: 0-0
Aids: Bl: 0-0 Vi: 0-0 Tstrap: 0-0 Ckp: 0-0
Best Rating: **81** 9/09 Ripn 5f gd-sft

Fair; stays 5f; acts on most ground.

Tilos Gem (IRE)

97(101) (82)**81**

3-y-o ch c Trans Island-Alpine Flair (IRE) (Tirol)

M Johnston Grant Mercer

Placings:036-210303320 **(7373)**

2009: 8^{2}SD, 8^{1}F, 8^{0}G, 8^{3}G, 9^{0}G, 12^{3}GF, 12^{3}GF, 12^{2}SD, 12^{0}SD,

	Starts	1st	2nd	3rd	Win & Pl
Career Total (Turf)	**9**	**1**	**0**	**4**	**5477**
Career Total (AW)	**3**	**0**	**2**	**0**	**1678**

69 6/09 Bath 1m5y FRM £2266
Total win prize-money £2267

Going (Turf): Sf: 0-1 GS: 0-0 Gd: 0-4 GF: 0-3 **Fm: 1-1**
Distance: 5f/6f: 0-0 7f-8f: 0-1 **9f-13f: 1-11** 14f+: 0-0
Track : **LH: 1-7** RH: 0-2 **Tight: 1-5** Gall: 0-1
Aids: Bl: 0-0 Vi: 0-0 Tstrap: 0-0 Ckp: 0-0
Best Rating: **82** 10/09 Kemp 1m4f stand

Fair; stays 1m4f; handles quick ground; goes on Polytrack.

Tilsworth Glenboy

(80) (62)

2-y-o b c Doyen (IRE)-Chara (Deploy)

J R Jenkins M Ng

Placings:05 **(7538)**

2009: 7^{0}SD, 7^{5}SD,

	Starts	1st	2nd	3rd	Win & Pl
Career Total (Turf)	**0**	**0**	**0**	**0**	
Career Total (AW)	**2**	**0**	**0**	**0**	**0**

Going (Turf): **Sf: 0-0 GS: 0-0 Gd: 0-0 GF: 0-0 Fm: 0-0**
Distance: 5f/6f: 0-0 7f-8f: 0-2 9f-13f: 0-0 14f+: 0-0
Track : LH: 0-0 RH: 0-2 Tight: 0-0 Gall: 0-0
Aids: Bl: 0-0 Vi: 0-0 Tstrap: 0-0 Ckp: 0-0
Best Rating: **62** 11/09 Kemp 7f stand

Tilt

108(112) (94)**99**

7-y-o b g Daylami (IRE)-Tromond (Lomond (USA))

B Ellison The Seasiders

Placings:0/15434/5133036/430330344/2300062-003360RR5 **(7465)**

2009: 12^{0}G, 18^{0}GF, 12^{3}GS, 16^{3}G, 16^{6}S, 18^{0}G, 14^{R}SD, 12^{R}S, 12^{5}SD,

	Starts	1st	2nd	3rd	Win & Pl
Career Total (Turf)	**34**	**2**	**1**	**11**	**69806**
Career Total (AW)	**4**	**0**	**1**	**0**	**4558**

89 5/06 Haml 1m5f9y (0-80)H GD £8096
75 4/05 Bevl 1m100y SFT £4212
Total win prize-money £12308

Going (Turf): **Sf: 1-7** GS: 0-8 **Gd: 1-14** GF: 0-5 Fm: 0-0
Distance: 5f/6f: 0-0 7f-8f: 0-0 9f-13f: 1-13 14f+: 1-25
Track : LH: 0-23 **RH: 2-15 Tight: 1-16** Gall: 0-11
Aids: Bl: 0-1 Vi: 0-0 Tstrap: 0-13 Ckp: 0-13
Best Rating: **99** 5/09 Hayd 2m45y good

Useful; effective over 1m4f-2m2f; acts on most ground and on Polytrack; has worn cheekpieces.

Timbaa (USA)

97(91) (50)**51**

3-y-o b g Anabaa (USA)-Timber Ice (USA) (Woodman (USA))

Rae Guest Rae Guest & Derek J Willis

Placings:000-4036 **(3740)**

2009: 12^{4}SD, 12^{0}SD, 9^{3}F, 10^{6}GF,

	Starts	1st	2nd	3rd	Win & Pl
Career Total (Turf)	**4**	**0**	**0**	**1**	**289**
Career Total (AW)	**3**	**0**	**0**	**0**	**0**

Going (Turf): **Sf: 0-0 GS: 0-1 Gd: 0-1 GF: 0-1 Fm: 0-1**
Distance: 5f/6f: 0-0 7f-8f: 0-3 9f-13f: 0-4 14f+: 0-0
Track : LH: 0-4 RH: 0-1 Tight: 0-3 Gall: 0-0
Aids: Bl: 0-0 Vi: 0-0 Tstrap: 0-0 Ckp: 0-0
Best Rating: **51** 10/08 NmkR 7f gd-sft

Moderate; stays 1m4f; acts on Polytrack.

Timber Treasure (USA)

99(101) (64)**85**

5-y-o b/br g Forest Wildcat (USA)-Lady Ilsley (USA) (Trempolino (USA))

Paul Green Gary Williams

Placings:6/05235/**0**462315010-00006143030065 **(7275)**

2009: 7^{0}GF, 5^{0}GF, 5^{0}GF, 6^{0}GF, 6^{6}F, 6^{1}G, 6^{4}G, 5^{3}GS, 7^{0}G, 8^{3}S, 10^{0}GF, 8^{0}GF, 5^{6}SD, 7^{5}SD,

	Starts	1st	2nd	3rd	Win & Pl
Career Total (Turf)	**24**	**3**	**2**	**4**	**13637**
Career Total (AW)	**6**	**0**	**0**	**0**	**0**

76 7/09 Carl 6f192y (0-75)H GD £3238
85 7/08 Bevl 5f (0-75)H G-F £3238
83 6/08 Hayd 6f (0-75)H G-F £2590
Total win prize-money £9066

Going (Turf): Sf: 0-2 GS: 0-1 Gd: 1-5 **GF: 2-15** Fm: 0-1
Distance: **5f/6f: 2-14** 7f-8f: 1-10 9f-13f: 0-6 14f+: 0-0
Track : LH: 0-12 **RH: 1-4** Tight: 0-10 Gall: 0-0
Aids: **Bl: 2-16** Vi: 0-3 Tstrap: 0-0 Ckp: 0-0
Best Rating: **85** 7/08 Bevl 5f gd-fm

Fair; effective over 6f and acts on fast ground; has worn blinkers.

Time 'N' Talent

102 (85)**81**

3-y-o b c Act One-Turn Of A Century (Halling (USA))

James Leavy Tomas Singleton

Placings:0-14003 **(7382a)**

2009: 8^{1}G, 7^{4}Y, 9^{0}GF, 9^{0}GF, 10^{3}SD,

	Starts	1st	2nd	3rd	Win & Pl
Career Total (Turf)	**5**	**1**	**0**	**0**	**7798**
Career Total (AW)	**1**	**0**	**0**	**1**	**931**

70 5/09 Klny 1m100y GD £7379
Total win prize-money £7380

Going (Turf): Sf: 0-0 GS: 0-0 **Gd: 1-2** GF: 0-2 Fm: 0-0
Distance: 5f/6f: 0-0 7f-8f: 0-2 **9f-13f: 1-4** 14f+: 0-0
Track : **LH: 1-2** RH: 0-2 Tight: 0-1 Gall: 0-0

Aids: Bl: 0-0 Vi: 0-0 Tstrap: 0-0 Ckp: 0-0
Best Rating: 85 11/09 Dund 1m2f150y stand

Time Book (IRE)

100(105) (77)79
3-y-o b c Galileo (IRE)-Pocket Book (IRE) (Reference Point)
J H M Gosden George Strawbridge

Placings:0351 (7504)
2009: 11^{0}GS, 10^{3}S, 11^{5}S, 12^{1}SD,

	Starts	1st	2nd	3rd	Win & Pl
Career Total (Turf)	3	0	0	1	482
Career Total (AW)	1	1	0	0	2730

77 11/09 Sthl 1m4f STD £2729
Total win prize-money £2730

Going (Turf): Sf: 0-2 GS: 0-1 Gd: 0-0 GF: 0-0 Fm: 0-0
Distance: 5f/6f: 0-0 7f-8f: 0-0 9f-13f: 1-4 14f+: 0-0
Track : LH: 1-4 RH: 0-0 Tight: 0-1 Gall: 0-1
Aids: Bl: 0-0 Vi: 0-0 Tstrap: 0-0 Ckp: 0-0
Best Rating: 79 10/09 Nott 1m2f50y soft

Useful; stays 1m4f; handles Fibresand.

Time For Old Time

84(95) (59)59
3-y-o b f Olden Times-Pink Supreme (Night Shift (USA))
I A Wood C S Tateson

Placings:412-00000 (7592)
2009: 6^{0}GF, 5^{0}G, 6^{0}GF, 7^{0}SD, 7^{0}SD,

	Starts	1st	2nd	3rd	Win & Pl
Career Total (Turf)	5	1	0	0	2072
Career Total (AW)	3	0	1	0	867

59 7/08 Brig 5f213y FRM £2072
Total win prize-money £2072

Going (Turf): Sf: 0-0 GS: 0-0 Gd: 0-1 GF: 0-3 Fm: 1-1
Distance: 5f/6f: 1-5 7f-8f: 0-3 9f-13f: 0-0 14f+: 0-0
Track : LH: 1-2 RH: 0-2 Tight: 0-1 Gall: 0-1
Aids: Bl: 0-0 Vi: 0-0 Tstrap: 0-1 Ckp: 0-1
Best Rating: 59 7/08 Wolv 5f216y stand

Modest; effective over 6f; acts on fast ground; also goes on Polytrack.

Time Loup

82(88) (43)56
3-y-o b g Loup Sauvage (USA)-Bird Of Time (IRE) (Persian Bold)
S R Bowring S R Bowring

Placings:501000500-5560 (2581)
2009: 6^{5}SD, 5^{5}GF, 5^{6}GF, 5^{0}SD,

	Starts	1st	2nd	3rd	Win & Pl
Career Total (Turf)	7	1	0	0	1943
Career Total (AW)	6	0	0	0	0

56 7/08 Leic 5f2y GD £1942
Total win prize-money £1943

Going (Turf): Sf: 0-3 GS: 0-0 Gd: 1-1 GF: 0-3 Fm: 0-0
Distance: 5f/6f: 1-11 7f-8f: 0-2 9f-13f: 0-0 14f+: 0-0
Track : LH: 0-5 RH: 0-0 Tight: 0-1 Gall: 0-1
Aids: Bl: 0-2 Vi: 0-0 Tstrap: 0-0 Ckp: 0-0
Best Rating: 56 7/08 Leic 5f2y good

Moderate; effective at 5f on good ground.

Time Machine (UAE)

102 (67)80
3-y-o ch g Halling (USA)-Tempting Fate (IRE) (Persian Bold)
Robert Alan Hennessy (J H M Gosden 19/6) W Hennessy

Placings:242166 (6297a)
2009: 10^{2}G, 12^{4}GF, 9^{2}GF, 10^{1}GF, 10^{6}SD, 9^{6}GF,

	Starts	1st	2nd	3rd	Win & Pl
Career Total (Turf)	5	1	2	0	6998
Career Total (AW)	1	0	0	0	

80 6/09 NmkJ 1m2f G-F £5180
Total win prize-money £5181

Going (Turf): Sf: 0-0 GS: 0-0 Gd: 0-1 GF: 1-4 Fm: 0-0
Distance: 5f/6f: 0-0 7f-8f: 0-0 9f-13f: 1-6 14f+: 0-0
Track : LH: 0-2 RH: 1-4 Tight: 0-3 Gall: 1-1
Aids: Bl: 0-0 Vi: 0-0 Tstrap: 0-0 Ckp: 0-0
Best Rating: 80 9/09 Gowr 1m1f100y gd-fm

Fair; effective over 1m2f; acts on fast ground.

Time Medicean

102(95) (62)85
3-y-o gr g Medicean-Ribbons And Bows (IRE) (Dr Devious (IRE))
M R Channon Jaber Abdullah

Placings:3-6123405 (5523)
2009: 7^{6}SD, 6^{1}F, 5^{2}G, 7^{3}G, 6^{4}GS, 6^{0}GF, 6^{5}G,

	Starts	1st	2nd	3rd	Win & Pl
Career Total (Turf)	7	1	1	2	7788
Career Total (AW)	1	0	0	0	0

76 4/09 Pont 6f FRM £3238
Total win prize-money £3238

Going (Turf): Sf: 0-1 GS: 0-1 Gd: 0-3 GF: 0-1 Fm: 1-1
Distance: 5f/6f: 1-4 7f-8f: 0-4 9f-13f: 0-0 14f+: 0-0
Track : LH: 1-3 RH: 0-1 Tight: 0-1 Gall: 0-0
Aids: Bl: 0-0 Vi: 0-0 Tstrap: 0-0 Ckp: 0-0
Best Rating: 85 6/09 Epsm 7f good

Useful; effective over 6f-7f; acts on fast ground.

Time To Play

75(92) (62)65
4-y-o b g Best Of The Bests (IRE)-Primavera (Anshan)
T T Clement Mrs K W Sneath

Placings:44635-006 (7687)
2009: 8^{0}SD, 7^{0}GF, 12^{6}SD,

	Starts	1st	2nd	3rd	Win & Pl
Career Total (Turf)	2	0	0	0	0
Career Total (AW)	6	0	0	1	1155

Going (Turf): Sf: 0-0 GS: 0-1 Gd: 0-0 GF: 0-1 Fm: 0-0
Distance: 5f/6f: 0-0 7f-8f: 0-3 9f-13f: 0-5 14f+: 0-0
Track : LH: 0-5 RH: 0-2 Tight: 0-0 Gall: 0-3
Aids: Bl: 0-0 Vi: 0-0 Tstrap: 0-0 Ckp: 0-0
Best Rating: 65 10/08 Nott 1m2f50y gd-sft

Moderate; stays 1m2f; acts on Polytrack.

Time To Regret

94(101) (69)63
9-y-o b g Presidium-Scoffera (Scottish Reel)
I W McInnes I D Woolfitt

Placings:06/060024235/6240100025164/000004460241/2 6300600/111300050056054114006/330004012004300-050342440 (4313)
2009: 8^{0}SD, 8^{5}SD, 8^{0}GF, 9^{3}SD, 8^{4}GF, 8^{2}G, 8^{4}SD, 8^{4}SD, 8^{0}GS,

	Starts	1st	2nd	3rd	Win & Pl
Career Total (Turf)	58	4	7	2	22989
Career Total (AW)	31	5	1	5	11532

63 8/08 Thsk 1m (0-65)H SFT £2978
63 11/07 Wolv 1m141y (0-52)H STD £2047
63 10/07 Wolv 1m141y (0-55)H STD £2047
66 1/07 Wolv 1m141y (0-55)H STD £2388
64 1/07 Kemp 1m (0-45) STD £1365
56 1/07 Kemp 1m (0-45) STD £1365
58 11/05 Nott 1m54y (0-55)H HVY £2683
63 10/04 Rdcr 1m1f (0-55)H G-S £3961
57 7/04 Pont 1m4y E(0-70)H G-F £4377
Total win prize-money £23218

Going (Turf): Sf: 2-9 GS: 1-7 Gd: 0-11 GF: 1-29 Fm: 0-2
Distance: 5f/6f: 0-3 7f-8f: 3-39 9f-13f: 6-47 14f+: 0-0
Track : LH: 7-55 RH: 2-26 Tight: 5-38 Gall: 0-0
Aids: Bl: 0-0 Vi: 0-0 Tstrap: 6-46 Ckp: 6-46
Best Rating: 69 8/08 Wolv 1m141y stand

Moderate; effective at around 1m; acts on most ground on turf; goes on Fibresand and Polytrack; has worn cheek-pieces.

Timeless Dream

104(102) (74)71
3-y-o b f Oasis Dream-Simply Times (USA) (Dodge (USA))
P W Chapple-Hyam Allan Belshaw

Placings:020-021066 (6824)
2009: 7^{0}SD, 6^{2}GF, 6^{1}SD, 5^{0}SD, 5^{6}GF, 7^{6}GF,

	Starts	1st	2nd	3rd	Win & Pl
Career Total (Turf)	5	0	2	0	1928
Career Total (AW)	4	1	0	0	3238

74 9/09 Ling 6f (0-70)H STD £3238
Total win prize-money £3238

Going (Turf): Sf: 0-0 GS: 0-0 Gd: 0-2 GF: 0-3 Fm: 0-0
Distance: 5f/6f: 1-5 7f-8f: 0-4 9f-13f: 0-0 14f+: 0-0
Track : LH: 1-3 RH: 0-1 Tight: 1-2 Gall: 0-1
Aids: Bl: 0-0 Vi: 0-0 Tstrap: 0-0 Ckp: 0-0
Best Rating: 74 9/09 Ling 6f stand

Fair; acts on good; stays 6f.

Timeless Elegance (IRE)

86 52
2-y-o b f Invincible Spirit (IRE)-Tidy Wager (IRE) (Catrail (USA))
J Howard Johnson Transcend Bloodstock LLP

Placings:043 (6378)
2009: 7^{0}G, 5^{4}S, 6^{3}GF,

	Starts	1st	2nd	3rd	Win & Pl
Career Total (Turf)	3	0	0	1	566

Going (Turf): Sf: 0-1 GS: 0-0 Gd: 0-1 GF: 0-1 Fm: 0-0
Distance: 5f/6f: 0-2 7f-8f: 0-1 9f-13f: 0-0 14f+: 0-0
Track : LH: 0-1 RH: 0-0 Tight: 0-1 Gall: 0-0
Aids: Bl: 0-0 Vi: 0-0 Tstrap: 0-0 Ckp: 0-0
Best Rating: 52 9/09 Newc 6f gd-fm

Moderate; stays 6f; acts on fast ground.

Timelord (IRE)

94(90) (59)67
2-y-o ch g Chineur (FR)-My Gray (FR) (Danehill (USA))

S Kirk R Gander

Placings:03403020005 **(6963)**
2009: 5^{0}G, 6^{3}GF, 6^{4}GF, 6^{0}G, 6^{3}GF, 6^{0}GF, 7^{2}GS, 8^{0}G, 7^{0}SD, 7^{0}SD, 6^{5}G,

	Starts	1st	2nd	3rd	Win & Pl
Career Total (Turf)	9	0	1	2	2741
Career Total (AW)	2	0	0	0	

Going (Turf): Sf: 0-0 GS: 0-1 Gd: 0-4 GF: 0-4 Fm: 0-0
Distance: 5f/6f: 0-6 7f-8f: 0-4 9f-13f: 0-1 14f+: 0-0
Track : LH: 0-4 RH: 0-2 Tight: 0-2 Gall: 0-1
Aids: Bl: 0-0 Vi: 0-0 Tstrap: 0-0 Ckp: 0-0
Best Rating: 67 9/09 Epsm 7f gd-sft

Modest; stays 7f and acts on most ground.

Timely Jazz (IRE)

102(96) (84)**97**
2-y-o b c Noverre (USA)-Ricadonna (Kris)
B J Meehan Joe L Allbritton

Placings:0221400 **(6849)**
2009: 7^{0}G, 7^{2}G, 7^{2}G, 7^{1}SD, 7^{4}GF, 8^{0}G, 7^{0}G,

	Starts	1st	2nd	3rd	Win & Pl
Career Total (Turf)	6	0	2	0	6043
Career Total (AW)	1	1	0	0	3886
84 8/09 Wolv 7f32y		STD	£3885		

Total win prize-money £3886

Going (Turf): Sf: 0-0 GS: 0-0 Gd: 0-5 GF: 0-1 Fm: 0-0
Distance: 5f/6f: 0-0 **7f-8f: 1-7** 9f-13f: 0-0 14f+: 0-0
Track : **LH: 1-1** RH: 0-2 **Tight: 1-1** Gall: 0-1
Aids: Bl: 0-0 Vi: 0-0 Tstrap: 0-0 Ckp: 0-0
Best Rating: 97 9/09 Gdwd 7f gd-fm

Very useful; effective at 7f; acts on good ground and on Polytrack.

Timepiece

104(101) (80)**101**
2-y-o b f Zamindar (USA)-Clepsydra (Sadler's Wells (USA))
H R A Cecil K Abdulla

Placings:211 **(7187)**
2009: 8^{2}GF, 8^{1}SS, 8^{1}G,

	Starts	1st	2nd	3rd	Win & Pl
Career Total (Turf)	2	1	1	0	18573
Career Total (AW)	1	1	0	0	3886
101 10/09 NmkR 1m		GD	£17031		
80 10/09 Ling 1m		SS	£3885		

Total win prize-money £20917

Going (Turf): Sf: 0-0 GS: 0-0 **Gd: 1-1** GF: 0-1 Fm: 0-0
Distance: 5f/6f: 0-0 **7f-8f: 2-3** 9f-13f: 0-0 14f+: 0-0
Track : **LH: 1-1** RH: 0-0 **Tight: 1-1** Gall: 0-0
Aids: Bl: 0-0 Vi: 0-0 Tstrap: 0-0 Ckp: 0-0
Best Rating: 101 10/09 NmkR 1m good

Useful; stays 1m; acts on fast ground and Polytrack.

Times Ahead (USA)

85 **62**
2-y-o b c Proud Citizen (USA)-Nanas Cozy Account (USA) (Langfuhr (CAN))
P W Chapple-Hyam Times Of Wigan

Placings:0 **(4756)**
2009: 7^{0}GS,

	Starts	1st	2nd	3rd	Win & Pl
Career Total (Turf)	1	0	0	0	

Going (Turf): Sf: 0-0 GS: 0-1 Gd: 0-0 GF: 0-0 Fm: 0-0
Distance: 5f/6f: 0-0 7f-8f: 0-1 9f-13f: 0-0 14f+: 0-0
Track : LH: 0-0 RH: 0-0 Tight: 0-0 Gall: 0-0
Aids: Bl: 0-0 Vi: 0-0 Tstrap: 0-0 Ckp: 0-0
Best Rating: 62 8/09 NmkJ 7f gd-sft

Times Up

108 **98**
3-y-o b g Olden Times-Princess Genista (Ile De Bourbon (USA))
J L Dunlop Mrs I H Stewart-Brown & M J Meacock

Placings:2-23315130 **(6734)**
2009: 10^{2}GF, 11^{3}GF, 10^{3}GF, 12^{1}GS, 12^{5}S, 12^{1}GF, 14^{3}G, 14^{0}S,

	Starts	1st	2nd	3rd	Win & Pl
Career Total (Turf)	9	2	2	3	14667
95 8/09 NmkJ 1m4f (0-85)H		G-F	£5180		
89 7/09 Pont 1m4f8y		G-S	£3238		

Total win prize-money £8419

Going (Turf): Sf: 0-2 **GS: 1-1** Gd: 0-2 **GF: 1-4** Fm: 0-0
Distance: 5f/6f: 0-0 7f-8f: 0-1 **9f-13f: 2-6** 14f+: 0-2
Track : LH: 1-3 RH: 1-5 Tight: 0-2 **Gall: 1-4**
Aids: Bl: 0-0 Vi: 0-0 Tstrap: 0-0 Ckp: 0-0
Best Rating: 98 9/09 Ffos 1m6f good

Very useful; stays 1m6f; acts on good and faster ground.

Timeteam (IRE)

100(100) (87)**88**
3-y-o b g Danetime (IRE)-Ceannanas (IRE) (Magical Wonder (USA))
A Bailey (S Kirk 8/7) A Bailey

Placings:622314562**114**-0200004 **(7692)**
2009: 7^{0}GS, 6^{2}GF, 6^{0}GF, 7^{0}G, 6^{0}GF, 6^{0}G, 7^{4}SD,

	Starts	1st	2nd	3rd	Win & Pl
Career Total (Turf)	14	1	3	1	17699
Career Total (AW)	5	2	1	0	8601
87 10/08 Ling 6f		STD	£3885		
82 10/08 GrLe 6f		STD	£3238		
76 8/08 Bath 5f161y		GD	£3885		

Total win prize-money £11010

Going (Turf): Sf: 0-2 GS: 0-2 **Gd: 1-4** GF: 0-6 Fm: 0-0
Distance: **5f/6f: 3-14** 7f-8f: 0-5 9f-13f: 0-0 14f+: 0-0
Track : **LH: 3-8** RH: 0-0 Tight: 1-4 **Gall: 2-5**
Aids: Bl: 0-0 Vi: 0-0 Tstrap: 0-0 Ckp: 0-0
Best Rating: 88 5/09 Sals 6f gd-fm

Useful; suited by 5f-6f; acts on most ground and on Polytrack.

Timetowynagain

59
2-y-o ch g Reset (AUS)-Ideal Figure (Zafonic (USA))
C W Fairhurst Mrs Shirley France

Placings:00 **(6763)**
2009: 6^{0}GF, 8^{0}GS,

	Starts	1st	2nd	3rd	Win & Pl
Career Total (Turf)	2	0	0	0	

Going (Turf): Sf: 0-0 GS: 0-1 Gd: 0-0 GF: 0-1 Fm: 0-0
Distance: 5f/6f: 0-1 7f-8f: 0-1 9f-13f: 0-0 14f+: 0-0
Track : LH: 0-1 RH: 0-0 Tight: 0-0 Gall: 0-1
Aids: Bl: 0-0 Vi: 0-0 Tstrap: 0-0 Ckp: 0-0

Timocracy

92 **81**
4-y-o br g Cape Cross (IRE)-Tithcar (Cadeaux Genereux)
T D Walford Ms J Loylert

Placings:0/5012235-13030 **(5334)**
2009: 10^{1}G, 12^{3}GF, 12^{0}S, 9^{3}S, 10^{0}S,

	Starts	1st	2nd	3rd	Win & Pl
Career Total (Turf)	13	2	2	3	11339
81 4/09 Pont 1m2f6y (0-75)H		GD	£3238		
77 9/08 Brig 1m1f209y (0-65)H		SFT	£2072		

Total win prize-money £5310

Going (Turf): Sf: 1-6 GS: 0-4 **Gd: 1-1** GF: 0-2 Fm: 0-0
Distance: 5f/6f: 0-0 7f-8f: 0-3 **9f-13f: 2-10** 14f+: 0-0
Track : **LH: 2-8** RH: 0-4 Tight: 0-4 Gall: 0-2
Aids: Bl: 0-0 Vi: 0-0 Tstrap: 0-0 Ckp: 0-0
Best Rating: 81 4/09 Pont 1m2f6y good

Fair; effective over 1m2f-1m4f; acts on good and soft ground.

Tin Cha Woody (USA)

(99) (81)**63**
4-y-o b/br g Johannesburg (USA)-I'm Beguiled Again (USA) (Wild Again (USA))
Daniel Mark Loughnane Leo Cox

Placings:512/005-00030 **(7752)**
2009: 7^{0}SD, 8^{0}SD, 6^{0}SD, 7^{3}SD, 9^{0}SD,

	Starts	1st	2nd	3rd	Win & Pl
Career Total (Turf)	1	0	0	0	
Career Total (AW)	10	1	1	1	9028
86 11/07 Dund 6f		STD	£5836		

Total win prize-money £5836

Going (Turf): Sf: 0-1 GS: 0-0 Gd: 0-0 GF: 0-0 Fm: 0-0
Distance: **5f/6f: 1-3** 7f-8f: 0-6 9f-13f: 0-2 14f+: 0-0
Track : LH: 0-7 RH: 0-1 Tight: 0-3 Gall: 0-1
Aids: Bl: 0-0 Vi: 0-0 Tstrap: 0-0 Ckp: 0-0
Best Rating: 86 12/07 Dund 7f stand

Modest; effective over 7f; acts on Polytrack.

Tina's Best (IRE)

92 (64)**79**
4-y-o b f King's Best (USA)-Phantom Waters (Pharly (FR))
E J Alston Con Harrington

Placings:50503405/3206124400-0300 **(6755)**
2009: 7^{0}GF, 8^{3}GF, 7^{0}GF, 7^{0}G,

	Starts	1st	2nd	3rd	Win & Pl
Career Total (Turf)	21	1	2	3	11822
Career Total (AW)	1	0	0	0	0
79 6/08 Ling 7f140y (0-75)H		G-F	£2331		

Total win prize-money £2331

Going (Turf): Sf: 0-1 GS: 0-5 Gd: 0-4 **GF: 1-9** Fm: 0-2
Distance: 5f/6f: 0-6 **7f-8f: 1-15** 9f-13f: 0-1 14f+: 0-0
Track : LH: 0-5 RH: 0-2 Tight: 0-3 Gall: 0-2
Aids: Bl: 0-0 Vi: 0-0 Tstrap: 0-0 Ckp: 0-0
Best Rating: 79 6/08 Brig 6f209y firm

Modest; effective at 7f-1m; acts on fast and easy ground.

Tinaar (USA)

99(111) (95)**78**
3-y-o b f Giant's Causeway (USA)-Seattle Tac (USA) (Seattle Slew (USA))
G A Butler Fawzi Abdulla Nass

Placings:641132 (7066)
2009: 10^{6}G, 8^{4}GF, 10^{1}G, 11^{1}SD, 12^{3}SD, 12^{2}SD,

	Starts	1st	2nd	3rd	Win & Pl
Career Total (Turf)	3	1	0	0	3259
Career Total (AW)	3	1	1	1	7370

86 9/09 Kemp 1m3f (0-85)H STD £4727
78 8/09 Wind 1m2f7y GD £2729
Total win prize-money £7457

Going (Turf): Sf: 0-0 GS: 0-0 **Gd: 1-2** GF: 0-1 Fm: 0-0
Distance: 5f/6f: 0-0 7f-8f: 0-1 **9f-13f: 2-5** 14f+: 0-0
Track : LH: 0-1 **RH: 2-4 Tight: 1-2** Gall: 0-1
Aids: Bl: 0-0 Vi: 0-0 Tstrap: 0-0 Ckp: 0-0
Best Rating: 95 10/09 Ling 1m4f stand

Useful; stays 1m4f; acts on good ground and Polytrack.

Ting Ting (USA)

86(78) (37)53
2-y-o b f Empire Maker (USA)-My Sweet Heart (USA) (You And I (USA))
T P Tate Mrs Fitri Hay

Placings:330 (6672)
2009: 8^{3}F, 9^{3}GF, 8^{0}SD,

	Starts	1st	2nd	3rd	Win & Pl
Career Total (Turf)	2	0	0	2	1107
Career Total (AW)	1	0	0	0	

Going (Turf): Sf: 0-0 GS: 0-0 Gd: 0-0 GF: 0-1 Fm: 0-1
Distance: 5f/6f: 0-0 7f-8f: 0-0 9f-13f: 0-3 14f+: 0-0
Track : LH: 0-2 RH: 0-1 Tight: 0-2 Gall: 0-0
Aids: Bl: 0-0 Vi: 0-0 Tstrap: 0-0 Ckp: 0-0
Best Rating: 53 9/09 Rdcr 1m1f gd-fm

Moderate; stays 1m and acts on fast ground.

Tinkerbelle (IRE)

95(99) (64)56
3-y-o br f Marju (IRE)-Pershaan (IRE) (Darshaan)
J L Dunlop Windflower Overseas Holdings Inc

Placings:000-42330415 (6807)
2009: 10^{4}SD, 12^{2}GF, 14^{3}S, 12^{3}SD, 12^{0}GF, 12^{4}SD, 12^{1}SS, 12^{5}SD,

	Starts	1st	2nd	3rd	Win & Pl
Career Total (Turf)	6	0	1	1	1079
Career Total (AW)	5	1	0	1	1995

64 10/09 Ling 1m4f (0-60)H SS £1706
Total win prize-money £1706

Going (Turf): Sf: 0-2 GS: 0-0 Gd: 0-0 GF: 0-4 Fm: 0-0
Distance: 5f/6f: 0-0 7f-8f: 0-2 **9f-13f: 1-8** 14f+: 0-1
Track : LH: 1-6 RH: 0-3 **Tight: 1-5** Gall: 0-0
Aids: Bl: 0-0 Vi: 0-0 Tstrap: 1-2 Ckp: 1-2
Best Rating: 64 10/09 Ling 1m4f std-slw

Moderate; stays 1m6f and acts on most ground and Polytrack; has worn cheekpieces.

Tinshu (IRE)

103(108) (90)83
3-y-o ch f Fantastic Light (USA)-Ring Of Esteem (Mark Of Esteem (IRE))
D Haydn Jones Llewelyn, Runeckles

Placings:05-125401202255116 (7489)
2009: 9^{1}SD, 10^{2}SD, 10^{5}SD, 10^{4}G, 12^{0}SD, 10^{1}GF, 9^{2}GF, 9^{0}GF, 8^{2}G, 8^{2}GF, 8^{5}GS, 10^{5}GS, 10^{1}SD, 10^{1}SD, 10^{6}SD,

	Starts	1st	2nd	3rd	Win & Pl
Career Total (Turf)	8	1	3	0	8080
Career Total (AW)	9	3	1	0	17084

90 11/09 Ling 1m2f (0-90)H STD £7641
86 11/09 Kemp 1m2f (0-85)H STD £4727
77 5/09 Wind 1m2f7y (0-75)H G-F £3070
71 1/09 Wolv 1m1f103y STD £2729
Total win prize-money £18170

Going (Turf): Sf: 0-0 GS: 0-2 Gd: 0-2 **GF: 1-4** Fm: 0-0
Distance: 5f/6f: 0-0 7f-8f: 0-1 **9f-13f: 4-16** 14f+: 0-0
Track : LH: 2-8 RH: 2-9 **Tight: 3-11** Gall: 0-1
Aids: Bl: 0-0 Vi: 0-0 Tstrap: 0-0 Ckp: 0-0
Best Rating: 90 11/09 Ling 1m2f stand

Useful; stays 1m2f; acts on fast ground and on Polytrack.

Tip Top Style

74 (54)29
6-y-o b g Tipsy Creek (USA)-Eliza Jane (Mistertopogigo (IRE))
A Crook Lucky Catch Partnership

Placings:66000062/40/0 (2264)
2009: 11^{0}G,

	Starts	1st	2nd	3rd	Win & Pl
Career Total (Turf)	3	0	0	0	
Career Total (AW)	8	0	1	0	523

Going (Turf): Sf: 0-0 GS: 0-1 Gd: 0-2 GF: 0-0 Fm: 0-0
Distance: 5f/6f: 0-0 7f-8f: 0-7 9f-13f: 0-4 14f+: 0-0
Track : LH: 0-10 RH: 0-1 Tight: 0-3 Gall: 0-0
Aids: Bl: 0-0 Vi: 0-0 Tstrap: 0-5 Ckp: 0-5
Best Rating: 54 12/06 Sthl 1m stand

Tipperary Boutique (IRE)

96 75
2-y-o b f Danehill Dancer (IRE)-Moselle (Mtoto)
B W Hills Noel O'Callaghan

Placings:51 (7167)
2009: 7^{5}G, 7^{1}S,

	Starts	1st	2nd	3rd	Win & Pl
Career Total (Turf)	2	1	0	0	3886

75 10/09 Ayr 7f50y SFT £3885
Total win prize-money £3886

Going (Turf): Sf: 1-1 GS: 0-0 Gd: 0-1 GF: 0-0 Fm: 0-0
Distance: 5f/6f: 0-0 **7f-8f: 1-2** 9f-13f: 0-0 14f+: 0-0
Track : LH: 1-1 RH: 0-0 Tight: 0-0 Gall: 0-0
Aids: Bl: 0-0 Vi: 0-0 Tstrap: 0-0 Ckp: 0-0
Best Rating: 75 10/09 Ayr 7f50y soft

90,000 euros filly with a middle-distance pedigree; stays 7f; acts on good and soft ground.

Tiradito (USA)

86(86) (57)72
2-y-o b/br c Tale Of The Cat (USA)-Saratoga Sugar (USA) (Gone West (USA))
M Botti El Catorce

Placings:2530 (7824)
2009: 5^{2}GF, 5^{5}F, 6^{3}GF, 7^{0}SD,

	Starts	1st	2nd	3rd	Win & Pl
Career Total (Turf)	3	0	1	1	1850
Career Total (AW)	1	0	0	0	

Going (Turf): Sf: 0-0 GS: 0-0 Gd: 0-0 GF: 0-2 Fm: 0-1
Distance: 5f/6f: 0-3 7f-8f: 0-1 9f-13f: 0-0 14f+: 0-0
Track : LH: 0-0 RH: 0-1 Tight: 0-0 Gall: 0-0

Aids: Bl: 0-0 Vi: 0-0 Tstrap: 0-0 Ckp: 0-0
Best Rating: 72 5/09 NmkR 6f gd-fm

Fair; stays 6f; acts on fast ground.

Tisifone

91(75) (11)59
3-y-o b f American Post-Mary Rose (ITY) (Royal Academy (USA))
C G Cox H E Sheikh Sultan Bin Khalifa Al Nahyan

Placings:4000 (5103)
2009: 8^{4}GF, 10^{0}GF, 9^{0}G, 9^{0}SD,

	Starts	1st	2nd	3rd	Win & Pl
Career Total (Turf)	3	0	0	0	216
Career Total (AW)	1	0	0	0	

Going (Turf): Sf: 0-0 GS: 0-0 Gd: 0-1 GF: 0-2 Fm: 0-0
Distance: 5f/6f: 0-0 7f-8f: 0-0 9f-13f: 0-4 14f+: 0-0
Track : LH: 0-3 RH: 0-1 Tight: 0-3 Gall: 0-0
Aids: Bl: 0-0 Vi: 0-0 Tstrap: 0-0 Ckp: 0-0
Best Rating: 59 5/09 Wwck 1m22y gd-fm

Tislaam (IRE)

90 77
2-y-o gr c With Approval (CAN)-Lady Angola (USA) (Lord At War (ARG))
M R Channon Jaber Abdullah

Placings:035250 (6009)
2009: 6^{0}G, 6^{3}G, 6^{5}GF, 6^{2}GF, 6^{5}GF, 6^{0}GS,

	Starts	1st	2nd	3rd	Win & Pl
Career Total (Turf)	6	0	1	1	1734

Going (Turf): Sf: 0-0 GS: 0-1 Gd: 0-2 GF: 0-3 Fm: 0-0
Distance: 5f/6f: 0-5 7f-8f: 0-1 9f-13f: 0-0 14f+: 0-0
Track : LH: 0-0 RH: 0-0 Tight: 0-0 Gall: 0-0
Aids: Bl: 0-0 Vi: 0-1 Tstrap: 0-0 Ckp: 0-0
Best Rating: 77 7/09 Sals 6f gd-fm

Fair; stays 6f; acts on fast ground.

Tislimeen

88 66
2-y-o b f Alhaarth (IRE)-Torgau (IRE) (Zieten (USA))
M R Channon Jaber Abdullah

Placings:50 (7033)
2009: 6^{5}S, 7^{0}S,

	Starts	1st	2nd	3rd	Win & Pl
Career Total (Turf)	2	0	0	0	0

Going (Turf): Sf: 0-2 GS: 0-0 Gd: 0-0 GF: 0-0 Fm: 0-0
Distance: 5f/6f: 0-0 7f-8f: 0-2 9f-13f: 0-0 14f+: 0-0
Track : LH: 0-0 RH: 0-0 Tight: 0-0 Gall: 0-0
Aids: Bl: 0-0 Vi: 0-0 Tstrap: 0-0 Ckp: 0-0
Best Rating: 66 9/09 Sals 6f212y soft

Modest half-sister to a 7f winner out of the Cherry Hinton winner Torgau; stays 7f.

Titan Triumph

64(115) (101)72
5-y-o b g Zamindar (USA)-Triple Green (Green Desert (USA))
W J Knight Canisbay Bloodstock

Placings:04/330130**133**/5040**34001111**-21006 (1640)

2009: 8^{2}SD, 8^{1}SD, 8^{0}GF, 8^{0}SD, 7^{6}SD,

	Starts	1st	2nd	3rd	Win & Pl
Career Total (Turf)	11	1	0	2	5164
Career Total (AW)	17	6	1	4	36355

101	2/09	Ling	1m	(0-100)H	STD	£11527
91	12/08	Ling	1m	(0-85)H	STD	£4727
83	12/08	Ling	1m	(0-80)H	STD	£4727
78	11/08	Ling	1m	(0-75)H	STD	£2388
79	10/08	GrLe	1m	(0-75)H	STD	£2914
88	11/07	Ling	7f	(0-75)H	STD	£2914
79	8/07	Gdwd	7f	(0-70)H	GD	£3238

Total win prize-money £32437

Going (Turf): Sf: 0-2 GS: 0-1 **Gd: 1-3** GF: 0-5 Fm: 0-0
Distance: 5f/6f: 0-4 **7f-8f: 7-24** 9f-13f: 0-0 14f+: 0-0
Track : **LH: 6-12** RH: 1-10 **Tight: 5-11** Gall: 1-2
Aids: Bl: 0-0 Vi: 0-0 Tstrap: 0-0 Ckp: 0-0
Best Rating: **101** 2/09 Ling 1m stand

Very useful; stays 1m; acts on most ground and on Polytrack; often wears a tongue tie; usually held up; has a fine record at Lingfield.

Titfer (IRE)

(95) (57)**65**

4-y-o ch g Fath (USA)-Fur Hat (Habitat)
G A Ham (Mrs C J Ikin 30/7) G A Ham

Placings:0500**030**/60150000-0 (0116)

2009: 11^{0}SD,

	Starts	1st	2nd	3rd	Win & Pl
Career Total (Turf)	11	1	0	0	2047
Career Total (AW)	5	0	0	1	302

56	6/08	Wwck	1m22y	(0-65)H	FRM	£2047

Total win prize-money £2047

Going (Turf): Sf: 0-3 GS: 0-2 Gd: 0-2 GF: 0-2 **Fm: 1-2**
Distance: 5f/6f: 0-2 7f-8f: 0-4 **9f-13f: 1-10** 14f+: 0-0
Track : **LH: 1-7** RH: 0-5 Tight: 0-1 Gall: 0-3
Aids: Bl: 0-0 Vi: 0-0 Tstrap: 0-0 Ckp: 0-0
Best Rating: **65** 6/07 NmkJ 7f gd-sft

Titinius (IRE)

95 **68**

9-y-o ch g Titus Livius (FR)-Maiyria (IRE) (Shernazar)
Micky Hammond Paul & Anne Sellars

Placings:43/102/030460/3543564265**0**/0005342042/5200 0-403440 (3450)

2009: 12^{4}GF, 9^{0}GF, 11^{3}GF, 11^{4}G, 9^{4}GF, 10^{0}GF,

	Starts	1st	2nd	3rd	Win & Pl
Career Total (Turf)	43	1	5	6	18403

75	5/03	Nott	6f15y	E	G-F	£4030

Total win prize-money £4030

Going (Turf): Sf: 0-3 GS: 0-5 Gd: 0-8 **GF: 1-24** Fm: 0-3
Distance: 5f/6f: 0-10 **7f-8f: 1-18** 9f-13f: 0-15 14f+: 0-0
Track : LH: 0-23 RH: 0-8 Tight: 0-16 Gall: 0-2
Aids: Bl: 0-0 Vi: 0-1 Tstrap: 0-6 Ckp: 0-6
Best Rating: **83** 6/03 NmkJ 6f gd-fm

Modest performer; suited by 7f but stays 1m1f; acts on fast ground.

Tito (IRE)

59(91) (41)**69**

4-y-o b g Diktat-T G's Girl (Selkirk (USA))
B N Pollock (Paul Mason 18/5) Mrs Sally Pearson

Placings:02/2640-00 (5465)

2009: 5^{0}SD, 7^{0}GF,

	Starts	1st	2nd	3rd	Win & Pl
Career Total (Turf)	7	0	2	0	1927
Career Total (AW)	1	0	0	0	

Going (Turf): **Sf: 0-2 GS: 0-2 Gd: 0-2 GF: 0-1 Fm: 0-0**
Distance: 5f/6f: 0-5 7f-8f: 0-3 9f-13f: 0-0 14f+: 0-0
Track : LH: 0-2 RH: 0-1 Tight: 0-1 Gall: 0-1
Aids: Bl: 0-0 Vi: 0-0 Tstrap: 0-0 Ckp: 0-0
Best Rating: **69** 9/08 Rdcr 6f gd-sft

Modest; suited by 6f and good or softer ground.

Titoli Di Coda (IRE)

81(81) (27)**43**

2-y-o ch f Bertolini (USA)-Mystic Tempo (USA) (El Gran Senor (USA))
L M Cumani Scuderia Archi Romani

Placings:0000 (6938)

2009: 5^{0}GF, 5^{0}G, 6^{0}GF, 5^{0}SD,

	Starts	1st	2nd	3rd	Win & Pl
Career Total (Turf)	3	0	0	0	
Career Total (AW)	1	0	0	0	

Going (Turf): **Sf: 0-0 GS: 0-0 Gd: 0-1 GF: 0-2 Fm: 0-0**
Distance: 5f/6f: 0-4 7f-8f: 0-0 9f-13f: 0-0 14f+: 0-0
Track : LH: 0-0 RH: 0-1 Tight: 0-0 Gall: 0-0
Aids: Bl: 0-0 Vi: 0-0 Tstrap: 0-0 Ckp: 0-0
Best Rating: **43** 7/09 Ling 5f good

Titus Andronicus (IRE)

104 **92**

3-y-o b g Danetime (IRE)-Scarlet Empress (Second Empire (IRE))
K A Ryan John Browne & Paddy McGinty

Placings:53233451-152230200 (5203)

2009: 5^{1}GF, 5^{5}GS, 5^{2}G, 5^{2}GF, 5^{3}GF, 5^{0}GF, 5^{2}GS, 5^{0}G, 5^{0}GF,

	Starts	1st	2nd	3rd	Win & Pl
Career Total (Turf)	17	2	4	4	15930

87	4/09	Muss	5f	(0-75)H	G-F	£3885
78	10/08	Catt	5f		GD	£2266

Total win prize-money £6153

Going (Turf): Sf: 0-3 GS: 0-2 **Gd: 1-4 GF: 1-8** Fm: 0-0
Distance: **5f/6f: 2-17** 7f-8f: 0-0 9f-13f: 0-0 14f+: 0-0
Track : LH: 0-5 RH: 0-0 Tight: 0-4 Gall: 0-0
Aids: Bl: 0-0 Vi: 0-0 Tstrap: 0-0 Ckp: 0-0
Best Rating: **92** 7/09 Catt 5f gd-sft

Useful; suited by 5f; acts on good/fast ground.

Titus Gent

95(105) (75)**69**

4-y-o ch g Tumbleweed Ridge-Genteel (IRE) (Titus Livius (FR))
R A Harris (J Ryan 10/10) Alan & Adam Darlow, A Darlow Productions

Placings:2000-05045000215631320**26** (7673)

2009: 8^{0}SD, 7^{5}SD, 8^{0}SD, 7^{4}SD, 5^{5}SD, 6^{0}SD, 6^{0}G, 6^{0}F, 6^{2}SD, 6^{1}GS, 6^{5}GF, 6^{6}GF, **5^{3}SD**, **5^{1}SD**, 5^{3}SD, 6^{2}SD, 5^{0}SD, 6^{2}SD, 5^{6}SD,

	Starts	1st	2nd	3rd	Win & Pl
Career Total (Turf)	5	1	0	0	2873
Career Total (AW)	18	1	4	2	5977

75	10/09	Wolv	5f216y		STD	£2047
69	8/09	Thsk	6f	(0-55)H	G-S	£2873

Total win prize-money £4920

Going (Turf): Sf: 0-0 **GS: 1-1** Gd: 0-1 GF: 0-2 Fm: 0-1
Distance: **5f/6f: 2-15** 7f-8f: 0-8 9f-13f: 0-0 14f+: 0-0
Track : **LH: 1-16** RH: 0-3 **Tight: 1-14** Gall: 0-0
Aids: Bl: 0-0 Vi: 0-0 Tstrap: 0-1 Ckp: 0-1
Best Rating: **75** 10/09 Wolv 5f216y stand

Modest; stays 6f; acts on Polytrack.

Tivers Song (USA)

100(96) (57)**53**

5-y-o gr g Buddha (USA)-Rousing (USA) (Alydar (USA))
John A Harris Robert Dixon

Placings:0630/64004/00322523340 (7594)

2009: 12^{0}SS, 12^{0}SD, 10^{3}GF, 9^{2}GF, 10^{2}GF, 9^{5}GF, 9^{2}GF, 10^{3}GF, 12^{3}SD, 13^{4}SD, 13^{0}SD,

	Starts	1st	2nd	3rd	Win & Pl
Career Total (Turf)	10	0	3	2	2693
Career Total (AW)	10	0	0	2	1241

Going (Turf): **Sf: 0-1 GS: 0-0 Gd: 0-0 GF: 0-9 Fm: 0-0**
Distance: 5f/6f: 0-0 7f-8f: 0-2 9f-13f: 0-13 14f+: 0-5
Track : LH: 0-13 RH: 0-6 Tight: 0-9 Gall: 0-1
Aids: Bl: 0-9 Vi: 0-1 Tstrap: 0-1 Ckp: 0-1
Best Rating: **69** 11/06 Wolv 1m141y stand

Moderate; has worn cheekpieces/tongue tie; acts on Polytrack; has worn various headgear.

To Be Or Not To Be

102(104) (73)**81**

4-y-o b f Tobougg (IRE)-Lady Mayor (Kris)
John Berry W Thomas

Placings:6/6411-2**41**004046 (7032)

2009: 7^{2}SD, 7^{4}SD, 7^{1}GF, 7^{0}G, 6^{0}G, 7^{4}G, 7^{0}SD, 8^{4}GF, 7^{6}S,

	Starts	1st	2nd	3rd	Win & Pl
Career Total (Turf)	6	1	0	0	3927
Career Total (AW)	8	2	1	0	6481

81	5/09	Yarm	7f3y	(0-75)H	G-F	£2719
73	12/08	Wolv	7f32y	(0-75)H	SF	£3238
73	11/08	Kemp	7f	(0-65)H	STD	£2047

Total win prize-money £8005

Going (Turf): Sf: 0-1 GS: 0-0 Gd: 0-3 **GF: 1-2** Fm: 0-0
Distance: 5f/6f: 0-0 **7f-8f: 3-13** 9f-13f: 0-1 14f+: 0-0
Track : LH: 1-7 RH: 1-4 **Tight: 1-6** Gall: 0-1
Aids: Bl: 0-0 Vi: 0-0 Tstrap: 0-0 Ckp: 0-0
Best Rating: **81** 5/09 Yarm 7f3y gd-fm

Modest; effective over 7f-1m; acts on Polytrack and fast ground.

To Bubbles

(101) (68)**39**

4-y-o b f Tobougg (IRE)-Effervescent (Efisio)
A G Newcombe A G Newcombe

Placings:0/6621000-06300 (0979)

2009: 7^{0}SS, 7^{6}SD, 8^{3}SD, 8^{0}SD, 8^{0}SD,

	Starts	1st	2nd	3rd	Win & Pl
Career Total (Turf)	3	0	0	0	
Career Total (AW)	10	1	1	1	4092

67	7/08	Sthl	6f		STD	£2729

Total win prize-money £2730

Going (Turf): **Sf: 0-2 GS: 0-1 Gd: 0-0 GF: 0-0 Fm: 0-0**
Distance: **5f/6f: 1-3** 7f-8f: 0-9 9f-13f: 0-1 14f+: 0-0

Track : **LH: 1-10** RH: 0-0 Tight: 0-2 Gall: 0-0
Aids: Bl: 0-0 Vi: 0-0 Tstrap: 0-0 Ckp: 0-0
Best Rating: 68 5/08 Sthl 7f stand

Tobago Bay

102(92) (49)66
4-y-o b g Tobougg (IRE)-Perfect Dream (Emperor Jones (USA))
Miss Sheena West Heart Of The South Racing

Placings:050**006**/**043**023-253 (4703)
2009: 15^{2}G, 17^{5}F, 15^{3}GF,

	Starts	1st	2nd	3rd	Win & Pl
Career Total (Turf)	9	0	2	2	2805
Career Total (AW)	6	0	0	1	435

Going (Turf): Sf: 0-0 GS: 0-2 Gd: 0-2 GF: 0-4 Fm: 0-1
Distance: 5f/6f: 0-1 7f-8f: 0-5 9f-13f: 0-4 14f+: 0-5
Track : LH: 0-6 RH: 0-6 Tight: 0-7 Gall: 0-0
Aids: Bl: 0-8 Vi: 0-1 Tstrap: 0-0 Ckp: 0-0
Best Rating: 66 4/09 Folk 1m7f92y good

Modest; stays 2m; acts on a sound surface.

Tobago Reef

95(90) (56)46
5-y-o b g Tobougg (IRE)-Silly Mid-On (Midyan (USA))
C W Moore C W Moore

Placings:30560**32211**/**3500**30/5-6000 (4710)
2009: 8^{6}SF, 7^{0}GF, 7^{0}GF, 10^{0}GS,

	Starts	1st	2nd	3rd	Win & Pl
Career Total (Turf)	8	0	0	1	770
Career Total (AW)	13	2	2	3	9676
75 12/06 Wolv	7f32y	(0-75)		STD	£3886
73 12/06 Wolv	7f32y	(0-65)		SS	£3238

Total win prize-money £7125

Going (Turf): Sf: 0-0 GS: 0-1 Gd: 0-2 GF: 0-5 Fm: 0-0
Distance: 5f/6f: 0-3 **7f-8f: 2-14** 9f-13f: 0-4 14f+: 0-0
Track : **LH: 2-16** RH: 0-2 **Tight: 2-16** Gall: 0-1
Aids: Bl: 0-1 Vi: 0-1 Tstrap: 2-14 Ckp: 2-14
Best Rating: 75 12/06 Wolv 7f32y stand

Toballa

94(95) (47)51
4-y-o b f Tobougg (IRE)-Ball Gown (Jalmood (USA))
P Leech Prima Racing Partnership

Placings:6/0045000-60600500 (7727)
2009: 9^{6}GF, 8^{0}G, 10^{6}G, 10^{0}GF, 8^{0}GF, 8^{5}SD, 7^{0}SD, 7^{0}SD,

	Starts	1st	2nd	3rd	Win & Pl
Career Total (Turf)	10	0	0	0	192
Career Total (AW)	6	0	0	0	0

Going (Turf): Sf: 0-1 GS: 0-2 Gd: 0-3 GF: 0-4 Fm: 0-0
Distance: 5f/6f: 0-0 7f-8f: 0-7 9f-13f: 0-9 14f+: 0-0
Track : LH: 0-10 RH: 0-3 Tight: 0-5 Gall: 0-3
Aids: Bl: 0-0 Vi: 0-0 Tstrap: 0-2 Ckp: 0-2
Best Rating: 51 5/09 Yarm 1m3y good

Tobar Suil Lady (IRE)

95(99) (69)61
4-y-o b f Statue Of Liberty (USA)-Stellarette (IRE) (Lycius (USA))
D M Christie (J L Spearing 14/1) Eye Opener Syndicate

Placings:3216/600**4015**-00000060**2** (7543a)
2009: 8^{0}SD, 7^{0}G, 7^{0}HY, 8^{0}S, 8^{0}SD, 7^{0}S, 7^{6}S, 5^{0}Y, 7^{2}SD,

	Starts	1st	2nd	3rd	Win & Pl
Career Total (Turf)	12	0	1	1	1416
Career Total (AW)	8	2	1	0	5189
69 11/08 Kemp	7f	(0-65)H		STD	£1706
70 10/07 Wolv	5f216y			STD	£2388

Total win prize-money £4095

Going (Turf): Sf: 0-5 GS: 0-0 Gd: 0-3 GF: 0-2 Fm: 0-1
Distance: 5f/6f: 1-8 7f-8f: 1-12 9f-13f: 0-0 14f+: 0-0
Track : LH: 1-8 RH: 1-6 **Tight: 1-3** Gall: 0-1
Aids: Bl: 0-1 Vi: 0-0 Tstrap: 0-1 Ckp: 0-1
Best Rating: 71 9/07 Rdcr 6f firm

Modest; stays 7f; acts on fast ground and Polytrack.

Toberogan (IRE)

90(63) (17)58
8-y-o b g Docksider (USA)-Beltisaal (FR) (Belmez (USA))
W A Murphy John A Murphy

Placings:040550/60000540300/1025024030/00000/00033006/6001000-01000 (6411)
2009: 8^{0}SD, 8^{1}HY, 7^{0}HY, 10^{0}G, 8^{0}GF,

	Starts	1st	2nd	3rd	Win & Pl
Career Total (Turf)	48	3	2	4	20113
Career Total (AW)	4	0	0	0	0
55 8/09 Bell	1m	(47-65)H		HVY	£5031
58 8/08 Bell	1m	(45-60)H		G-Y	£4826
60 3/05 Cork	6f	(36-60)H		SFT	£3920

Total win prize-money £13780

Going (Turf): Sf: 2-15 GS: 0-2 Gd: 0-8 GF: 0-8 Fm: 0-3
Distance: 5f/6f: 1-31 **7f-8f: 2-20** 9f-13f: 0-1 14f+: 0-0
Track : **LH: 2-20** RH: 0-2 Tight: 0-1 Gall: 0-1
Aids: Bl: 0-0 Vi: 0-0 Tstrap: 0-0 Ckp: 0-0
Best Rating: 67 10/05 Cork 6f yld-sft

Modest Irish-trained sprinter; stays 1m; acts on heavy ground.

Toboggan Lady

100 (46)70
5-y-o b m Tobougg (IRE)-Northbend (Shirley Heights)
Mrs A Duffield T P McMahon and D McMahon

Placings:06/0021120**21**/24600-66 (2262)
2009: 16^{6}GF, 16^{6}G,

	Starts	1st	2nd	3rd	Win & Pl
Career Total (Turf)	16	3	4	0	12917
Career Total (AW)	2	0	0	0	0
66 10/07 Pont	2m1f216y	(0-75)H		GD	£3886
56 7/07 Catt	1m3f214y	(0-70)H		GD	£3238
53 7/07 Haml	1m4f17y	(0-65)H		SFT	£2266

Total win prize-money £9392

Going (Turf): Sf: 1-1 GS: 0-4 **Gd: 2-6** GF: 0-4 Fm: 0-1
Distance: 5f/6f: 0-0 7f-8f: 0-1 **9f-13f: 2-6** 14f+: 1-11
Track : **LH: 2-14** RH: 1-4 **Tight: 2-10** Gall: 0-2
Aids: Bl: 0-0 Vi: 0-0 Tstrap: 0-1 Ckp: 0-1
Best Rating: 70 4/08 Catt 1m7f177y gd-sft

Modest but improving performer; stays 2m; acts on fast and in soft ground.

Tobond (IRE)

94(100) (96)86
3-y-o b g Tobougg (IRE)-Rajmata (IRE) (Prince Sabo)
M Botti Giuliano Manfredini

Placings:01321-6606 (2855)
2009: 7^{6}SD, 6^{6}GF, 7^{0}GF, 8^{6}G,

	Starts	1st	2nd	3rd	Win & Pl
Career Total (Turf)	3	0	0	0	0
Career Total (AW)	6	2	1	1	11851
90 11/08 Wolv	7f32y	(0-85)		STD	£5180
79 10/08 Kemp	7f			STD	£3885

Total win prize-money £9067

Going (Turf): Sf: 0-0 GS: 0-0 Gd: 0-1 GF: 0-2 Fm: 0-0
Distance: 5f/6f: 0-1 **7f-8f: 2-7** 9f-13f: 0-1 14f+: 0-0
Track : LH: 1-6 RH: 1-2 **Tight: 1-2** Gall: 0-3
Aids: Bl: 0-0 Vi: 0-0 Tstrap: 0-0 Ckp: 0-0
Best Rating: 96 3/09 Ling 7f stand

Very useful; effective over 7f-1m and acts on Polytrack.

Tobouggie On Down

84 55
2-y-o ch f Tobougg (IRE)-Park Ave Princess (IRE) (Titus Livius (FR))
J A Glover Sexy Six Partnership

Placings:6 (5949)
2009: 6^{6}GF,

	Starts	1st	2nd	3rd	Win & Pl
Career Total (Turf)	1	0	0	0	0

Going (Turf): Sf: 0-0 GS: 0-0 Gd: 0-0 GF: 0-1 Fm: 0-0
Distance: 5f/6f: 0-1 7f-8f: 0-0 9f-13f: 0-0 14f+: 0-0
Track : LH: 0-0 RH: 0-0 Tight: 0-0 Gall: 0-0
Aids: Bl: 0-0 Vi: 0-0 Tstrap: 0-0 Ckp: 0-0
Best Rating: 55 9/09 Rdcr 6f gd-fm

Tobrata

94(98) (64)64
3-y-o ch g Tobougg (IRE)-Sabrata (IRE) (Zino)
M Brittain Mel Brittain

Placings:552233 (7753)
2009: 7^{5}G, 8^{5}G, 8^{2}SD, 7^{2}SD, 8^{3}SD, 8^{3}SD,

	Starts	1st	2nd	3rd	Win & Pl
Career Total (Turf)	2	0	0	0	0
Career Total (AW)	4	0	2	2	3124

Going (Turf): Sf: 0-0 GS: 0-0 Gd: 0-2 GF: 0-0 Fm: 0-0
Distance: 5f/6f: 0-0 7f-8f: 0-4 9f-13f: 0-2 14f+: 0-0
Track : LH: 0-5 RH: 0-1 Tight: 0-4 Gall: 0-0
Aids: Bl: 0-0 Vi: 0-0 Tstrap: 0-0 Ckp: 0-0
Best Rating: 64 12/09 Wolv 1m141y stand

Modest; stays 1m; acts on Fibresand and Polytrack.

Toby Tyler

97(99) (74)70
3-y-o b g Best Of The Bests (IRE)-Pain Perdu (IRE) (Waajib)
P T Midgley Anthony D Copley

Placings:134060-105406 (4660)
2009: 7^{1}SD, 8^{0}GF, 7^{5}SD, 7^{4}GF, 7^{0}G, 8^{6}G,

	Starts	1st	2nd	3rd	Win & Pl
Career Total (Turf)	10	1	0	1	6448
Career Total (AW)	2	1	0	0	3071
74 3/09 Sthl	7f	(0-75)H		STD	£3070
68 4/08 Pont	5f			SFT	£4857

Total win prize-money £7928

Going (Turf): **Sf: 1-2** GS: 0-2 Gd: 0-2 GF: 0-4 Fm: 0-0
Distance: 5f/6f: 1-4 7f-8f: 1-6 9f-13f: 0-2 14f+: 0-0
Track: **LH: 2-5** RH: 0-0 Tight: 0-0 Gall: 0-0
Aids: Bl: 0-0 Vi: 0-0 Tstrap: 0-0 Ckp: 0-0
Best Rating: 74 3/09 Sthl 7f stand

Fair; effective over 7f; acts on soft ground and on Fibresand.

Today's The Day

96(98) (73)69
3-y-o b f Alhaarth (IRE)-Dayville (USA) (Dayjur (USA))
M A Jarvis T G & Mrs M E Holdcroft

Placings:0325203233-452 **(1618)**
2009: 6^{4}GF, 5^{5}GF, 6^{2}GF,

	Starts	1st	2nd	3rd	Win & Pl
Career Total (Turf)	6	0	2	0	2183
Career Total (AW)	7	0	2	4	3433

Going (Turf): **Sf: 0-0 GS: 0-2 Gd: 0-1 GF: 0-3 Fm: 0-0**
Distance: 5f/6f: 0-9 7f-8f: 0-4 9f-13f: 0-0 14f+: 0-0
Track: LH: 0-6 RH: 0-3 Tight: 0-2 Gall: 0-1
Aids: Bl: 0-6 Vi: 0-0 Tstrap: 0-3 Ckp: 0-3
Best Rating: 73 7/08 Kemp 6f stand

Fair; effective over 6f-7f; acts on easy ground; has worn blinkers and cheekpieces.

Todber

101(103) (78)71
4-y-o b f Cape Cross (IRE)-Dominica (Alhaarth (IRE))
M P Tregoning Major & Mrs R B Kennard And Partner

Placings:00/060011-45140 **(7518)**
2009: 5^{4}GF, 5^{5}SS, 6^{1}SD, 5^{4}SD, 6^{0}SD,

	Starts	1st	2nd	3rd	Win & Pl
Career Total (Turf)	4	1	0	0	2590
Career Total (AW)	9	2	0	0	4638

78 10/09 Kemp 6f (0-70)H STD £2590
68 9/08 Muss 5f (0-65)H GD £2590
65 9/08 Kemp 5f (0-60)H STD £2047
Total win prize-money £7227

Going (Turf): Sf: 0-0 GS: 0-1 **Gd: 1-1** GF: 0-2 Fm: 0-0
Distance: **5f/6f: 3-10** 7f-8f: 0-3 9f-13f: 0-0 14f+: 0-0
Track: LH: 0-6 **RH: 2-4** Tight: 0-5 Gall: 0-1
Aids: Bl: 0-0 **Vi: 3-7** Tstrap: 0-0 Ckp: 0-0
Best Rating: 78 10/09 Kemp 6f stand

Fair; effective over 5f-6f; acts on Polytrack and good ground on turf; has worn a visor.

Toga Tiger (IRE)

96(97) (87)82
2-y-o b g Antonius Pius (USA)-Minerwa (GER) (Protektor (GER))
M R Channon Ridgeway Downs Racing

Placings:32251310506 **(6993)**
2009: 5^{3}G, 5^{2}F, 6^{2}GF, 6^{5}G, 7^{1}GF, 7^{3}GF, 7^{1}SD, 8^{0}G, 8^{5}GF, 7^{0}GS, 8^{6}GS,

	Starts	1st	2nd	3rd	Win & Pl
Career Total (Turf)	10	1	2	2	5572
Career Total (AW)	1	1	0	0	2590

87 7/09 Kemp 7f STD £2590
82 6/09 Ling 7f G-F £2729
Total win prize-money £5320

Going (Turf): Sf: 0-0 GS: 0-2 Gd: 0-3 **GF: 1-4** Fm: 0-1
Distance: 5f/6f: 0-4 **7f-8f: 2-7** 9f-13f: 0-0 14f+: 0-0
Track: LH: 0-4 **RH: 1-2** Tight: 0-0 Gall: 0-3
Aids: Bl: 0-0 Vi: 0-0 Tstrap: 0-0 Ckp: 0-0
Best Rating: 87 7/09 Kemp 7f stand

Useful; effective at 5-7f; acts on fast ground.

Togiak (IRE)

100(94) (81)98
2-y-o b c Azamour (IRE)-Hawksbill Special (IRE) (Taufan (USA))
E A L Dunlop Mrs Susan Roy

Placings:4125 **(6664)**
2009: 7^{4}GS, 8^{1}SD, 8^{2}GF, 8^{5}GS,

	Starts	1st	2nd	3rd	Win & Pl
Career Total (Turf)	3	0	1	0	3051
Career Total (AW)	1	1	0	0	3562

81 8/09 Kemp 1m STD £3561
Total win prize-money £3562

Going (Turf): **Sf: 0-0 GS: 0-2 Gd: 0-0 GF: 0-1 Fm: 0-0**
Distance: 5f/6f: 0-0 **7f-8f: 1-3** 9f-13f: 0-1 14f+: 0-0
Track: LH: 0-0 **RH: 1-2** Tight: 0-0 Gall: 0-1
Aids: Bl: 0-0 Vi: 0-0 Tstrap: 0-0 Ckp: 0-0
Best Rating: 98 10/09 Asct 1m gd-sft

Very useful; stays 1m; acts on Polytrack and easy ground on turf.

Toledo Gold (IRE)

98 79
3-y-o ch g Needwood Blade-Eman's Joy (Lion Cavern (USA))
Mrs S J Smith (E J Alston 3/10) J Stephenson

Placings:0130-230000 **(6485)**
2009: 7^{2}GF, 7^{3}GF, 6^{0}G, 8^{0}GS, 8^{0}GF, 8^{0}GF,

	Starts	1st	2nd	3rd	Win & Pl
Career Total (Turf)	10	1	1	2	5220

70 7/08 Rdcr 6f G-F £2763
Total win prize-money £2764

Going (Turf): Sf: 0-1 GS: 0-2 Gd: 0-1 **GF: 1-6** Fm: 0-0
Distance: **5f/6f: 1-4** 7f-8f: 0-5 9f-13f: 0-1 14f+: 0-0
Track: LH: 0-2 RH: 0-0 Tight: 0-1 Gall: 0-0
Aids: Bl: 0-0 Vi: 0-0 Tstrap: 0-0 Ckp: 0-0
Best Rating: 79 6/09 Newc 7f gd-fm

Fair; stays 7f and acts on fast ground.

Toll Road

(96) (51)
3-y-o b f Dubai Destination (USA)-Endorsement (Warning)
E A L Dunlop Cliveden Stud

Placings:5-6 **(0115)**
2009: 8^{6}SD,

	Starts	1st	2nd	3rd	Win & Pl
Career Total (Turf)	0	0	0	0	
Career Total (AW)	2	0	0	0	0

Going (Turf): **Sf: 0-0 GS: 0-0 Gd: 0-0 GF: 0-0 Fm: 0-0**
Distance: 5f/6f: 0-0 7f-8f: 0-2 9f-13f: 0-0 14f+: 0-0
Track: LH: 0-1 RH: 0-1 Tight: 0-0 Gall: 0-1
Aids: Bl: 0-0 Vi: 0-0 Tstrap: 0-0 Ckp: 0-0
Best Rating: 51 12/08 GrLe 1m stand

Tom Folan

95(86) (54)70
2-y-o b f Namid-My Golly (Mozart (IRE))
H J Collingridge Tapas Partnership

Placings:2335106 **(4868)**
2009: 5^{2}G, 5^{3}GF, 5^{3}GF, 5^{5}GF, 5^{1}S, 6^{0}G, 5^{6}SD,

	Starts	1st	2nd	3rd	Win & Pl
Career Total (Turf)	6	1	1	2	3404
Career Total (AW)	1	0	0	0	0

Going (Turf): **Sf: 1-1** GS: 0-0 Gd: 0-2 GF: 0-3 Fm: 0-0
Distance: **5f/6f: 1-7** 7f-8f: 0-0 9f-13f: 0-0 14f+: 0-0
Track: LH: 0-2 RH: 0-0 Tight: 0-2 Gall: 0-0
Aids: Bl: 0-0 Vi: 0-0 Tstrap: 1-3 Ckp: 1-3
Best Rating: 70 7/09 Hayd 5f soft

Fair; effective over 5f; suited by soft ground.

Tom Tower (IRE)

107 77
5-y-o b g Cape Cross (IRE)-La Belle Katherine (USA) (Lyphard (USA))
A C Whillans Play Fair Partnership

Placings:051300/56/00000-131032 **(5673)**
2009: 8^{1}G, 7^{3}G, 8^{1}S, 8^{0}HY, 8^{3}S, 8^{2}S,

	Starts	1st	2nd	3rd	Win & Pl
Career Total (Turf)	19	3	1	3	14064

73 7/09 Hayd 1m30y (0-75)H SFT £3238
68 6/09 Ayr 1m (0-70)H GD £3885
71 5/06 Chep 5f16y SFT £3368
Total win prize-money £10492

Going (Turf): **Sf: 2-7** GS: 0-2 Gd: 1-8 GF: 0-2 Fm: 0-0
Distance: 5f/6f: 1-7 7f-8f: 1-10 9f-13f: 1-2 14f+: 0-0
Track: **LH: 2-11** RH: 0-1 Tight: 0-2 Gall: 0-2
Aids: Bl: 0-0 Vi: 0-0 Tstrap: 0-0 Ckp: 0-0
Best Rating: 77 9/09 Thsk 1m soft

Moderate; stays 1m; acts on good and soft ground; has worn a tongue tie.

Tom Wade (IRE)

(90) (64)
2-y-o b g Rakti-Plutonia (Sadler's Wells (USA))
M A Jarvis Highclere Thoroughbred Racing (VC2)

Placings:500 **(7199)**
2009: 8^{5}SD, 8^{0}SD, 8^{0}SD,

	Starts	1st	2nd	3rd	Win & Pl
Career Total (Turf)	0	0	0	0	
Career Total (AW)	3	0	0	0	0

Going (Turf): **Sf: 0-0 GS: 0-0 Gd: 0-0 GF: 0-0 Fm: 0-0**
Distance: 5f/6f: 0-0 7f-8f: 0-3 9f-13f: 0-0 14f+: 0-0
Track: LH: 0-1 RH: 0-2 Tight: 0-1 Gall: 0-0
Aids: Bl: 0-0 Vi: 0-0 Tstrap: 0-0 Ckp: 0-0
Best Rating: 64 9/09 Kemp 1m stand

Tomatin

86(92) (70)80
2-y-o b c Kyllachy-Lowrianna (IRE) (Cyrano De Bergerac)
P W Chapple-Hyam P W Chapple-Hyam

Placings:40 **(7016)**
2009: 5^{4}SD, 6^{0}GS,

	Starts	1st	2nd	3rd	Win & Pl
Career Total (Turf)	1	0	0	0	
Career Total (AW)	1	0	0	0	265

Going (Turf): **Sf: 0-0 GS: 0-1 Gd: 0-0 GF: 0-0 Fm: 0-0**
Distance: 5f/6f: 0-2 7f-8f: 0-0 9f-13f: 0-0 14f+: 0-0

Track : LH: 0-1 RH: 0-0 Tight: 0-1 Gall: 0-0
Aids: Bl: 0-0 Vi: 0-0 Tstrap: 0-0 Ckp: 0-0
Best Rating: 80 10/09 Donc 6f gd-sft

Fair; acts on easy ground and Polytrack; stays 6f.

Tombi (USA)

110 **112**

5-y-o b g Johannesburg (USA)-Tune In To The Cat (USA) (Tunerup (USA))
J Howard Johnson Transcend Bloodstock LLP

Placings:3450/12414/10226-466060 **(6487)**
2009: 7^{4}GF, 6^{6}GF, 6^{6}G, 7^{0}GF, 6^{6}G, 7^{0}GF,

	Starts	1st	2nd	3rd	Win & Pl
Career Total (Turf)	**20**	**3**	**3**	**1**	**48894**

108	5/08	York	6f	(0-100)H	G-F	£12952
95	8/07	Ripn	6f	(0-85)H	G-F	£5362
85	5/07	Nott	6f15y		G-F	£2914

Total win prize-money £21230

Going (Turf): Sf: 0-0 GS: 0-2 Gd: 0-8 **GF: 3-10** Fm: 0-0
Distance: **5f/6f: 2-12** 7f-8f: 1-8 9f-13f: 0-0 14f+: 0-0
Track : LH: 0-4 RH: 0-1 Tight: 0-1 Gall: 0-2
Aids: Bl: 0-0 Vi: 0-0 Tstrap: 0-0 Ckp: 0-0
Best Rating: 112 9/09 Ayr 6f good

Smart; stays 7f, but best over 6f; acts on fast ground; has worn a tongue tie.

Tombov (FR)

83 **74**

3-y-o b/br g Laveron-Zamsara (FR) (Zino)
A King Mr And Mrs J D Cotton

Placings:01-06 **(4687)**
2009: 10^{0}G, 11^{6}G,

	Starts	1st	2nd	3rd	Win & Pl
Career Total (Turf)	**4**	**1**	**0**	**0**	**2590**

74	8/08	Folk	7f	G-S	£2590

Total win prize-money £2590

Going (Turf): Sf: 0-1 **GS: 1-1** Gd: 0-2 GF: 0-0 Fm: 0-0
Distance: 5f/6f: 0-0 **7f-8f: 1-1** 9f-13f: 0-3 14f+: 0-0
Track : LH: 0-3 RH: 0-0 Tight: 0-1 Gall: 0-0
Aids: Bl: 0-0 Vi: 0-0 Tstrap: 0-0 Ckp: 0-0
Best Rating: 74 8/08 Folk 7f gd-sft

Fair; stays 7f; acts on easy ground.

Tominator

99 **98**

2-y-o gr g Generous (IRE)-Jucinda (Midyan (USA))
R Hollinshead Mrs Susy Haslehurst

Placings:521612 **(6898)**
2009: 7^{5}GS, 7^{2}G, 7^{1}G, 7^{6}GS, 7^{1}GF, 8^{2}GF,

	Starts	1st	2nd	3rd	Win & Pl
Career Total (Turf)	**6**	**2**	**2**	**0**	**18626**

86	9/09	Catt	7f	(0-85)H	G-F	£4533
79	8/09	Bevl	7f100y		GD	£5018

Total win prize-money £9552

Going (Turf): Sf: 0-0 GS: 0-2 **Gd: 1-2 GF: 1-2** Fm: 0-0
Distance: 5f/6f: 0-0 **7f-8f: 2-5** 9f-13f: 0-1 14f+: 0-0
Track : LH: 1-5 RH: 1-1 **Tight: 1-2** Gall: 0-1
Aids: Bl: 0-0 Vi: 0-0 Tstrap: 0-0 Ckp: 0-0
Best Rating: 98 10/09 Pont 1m4y gd-fm

Fair; effective over 7f; acts on good/easy ground.

Tomintoul Singer (IRE)

103 **98**

2-y-o ch f Johannesburg (USA)-Shivaree (Rahy (USA))
H R A Cecil Angus Dundee Distillers plc

Placings:2213 **(7147)**
2009: 5^{2}GF, 6^{2}G, 5^{1}GF, 6^{3}G,

	Starts	1st	2nd	3rd	Win & Pl
Career Total (Turf)	**4**	**1**	**2**	**1**	**9009**

77	7/09	Folk	5f	G-F	£3561

Total win prize-money £3562

Going (Turf): Sf: 0-0 GS: 0-0 Gd: 0-2 **GF: 1-2** Fm: 0-0
Distance: **5f/6f: 1-3** 7f-8f: 0-1 9f-13f: 0-0 14f+: 0-0
Track : LH: 0-0 RH: 0-0 Tight: 0-0 Gall: 0-0
Aids: Bl: 0-0 Vi: 0-0 Tstrap: 0-0 Ckp: 0-0
Best Rating: 98 10/09 NmkR 6f good

Fair; stays 6f; acts on good and faster ground.

Tomintoul Star

94 **61**

3-y-o gr f Dansili-Lixian (Linamix (FR))
H R A Cecil Angus Dundee Distillers plc

Placings:05-066 **(5286)**
2009: 10^{0}G, 12^{6}G, 12^{6}GF,

	Starts	1st	2nd	3rd	Win & Pl
Career Total (Turf)	**5**	**0**	**0**	**0**	**132**

Going (Turf): **Sf: 0-0 GS: 0-0 Gd: 0-4 GF: 0-1 Fm: 0-0**
Distance: 5f/6f: 0-0 7f-8f: 0-1 9f-13f: 0-4 14f+: 0-0
Track : LH: 0-1 RH: 0-3 Tight: 0-1 Gall: 0-1
Aids: Bl: 0-0 Vi: 0-0 Tstrap: 0-0 Ckp: 0-0
Best Rating: 61 8/09 NmkJ 1m4f good

Modest maiden form to date.

Tommy Tobougg

92 (43)**52**

5-y-o ch g Tobougg (IRE)-Celebrate (IRE) (Generous (IRE))
Miss Lucinda V Russell Totally Scottish Partnership

Placings:5/0016060/3050 **(3105)**
2009: 10^{3}GF, 9^{0}G, 11^{5}GF, 7^{0}GF,

	Starts	1st	2nd	3rd	Win & Pl
Career Total (Turf)	**11**	**1**	**0**	**1**	**2610**
Career Total (AW)	**1**	**0**	**0**	**0**	

54	7/07	Muss	7f30y	GD	£2266

Total win prize-money £2267

Going (Turf): Sf: 0-0 GS: 0-1 **Gd: 1-6** GF: 0-4 Fm: 0-0
Distance: 5f/6f: 0-0 **7f-8f: 1-6** 9f-13f: 0-6 14f+: 0-0
Track : LH: 0-4 **RH: 1-7 Tight: 1-7** Gall: 0-1
Aids: Bl: 0-0 Vi: 0-0 Tstrap: 0-0 Ckp: 0-0
Best Rating: 61 4/07 Hayd 1m3f200y good

Moderate; effective over 1m2f; acts on fast ground.

Tomodachi (IRE)

100 **78**

2-y-o b f Arakan (USA)-Ivory Bride (Domynsky)
M Botti Joseph Barton

Placings:2 **(6921)**
2009: 8^{2}GF,

	Starts	1st	2nd	3rd	Win & Pl
Career Total (Turf)	**1**	**0**	**1**	**0**	**1227**

Going (Turf): **Sf: 0-0 GS: 0-0 Gd: 0-0 GF: 0-1 Fm: 0-0**
Distance: 5f/6f: 0-0 7f-8f: 0-0 9f-13f: 0-1 14f+: 0-0
Track : LH: 0-0 RH: 0-0 Tight: 0-0 Gall: 0-0
Aids: Bl: 0-0 Vi: 0-0 Tstrap: 0-0 Ckp: 0-0
Best Rating: 78 10/09 Yarm 1m3y gd-fm

Promising debut over 1m on fast ground.

Toms Laughter

100(107) (92)**102**

5-y-o ch g Mamalik (USA)-Time Clash (Timeless Times (USA))
R A Harris Mrs D J Hughes

Placings:450020153365/4111511622014035-060530000 **(7862)**
2009: 5^{0}GF, 5^{6}G, 5^{0}GF, 5^{5}G, 5^{3}SD, 6^{0}SD, 5^{0}SD, 5^{0}SD, 5^{0}SD,

	Starts	1st	2nd	3rd	Win & Pl
Career Total (Turf)	**21**	**4**	**2**	**3**	**65773**
Career Total (AW)	**16**	**3**	**1**	**1**	**8196**

102	7/08	Asct	5f	H	G-F	£43617
93	6/08	Folk	6f	(0-75)H	G-S	£3238
86	5/08	Leic	5f218y	(0-75)H	G-F	£3238
78	3/08	Kemp	6f	(0-65)H	STD	£2047
74	3/08	Kemp	5f	(0-65)H	STD	£2047
68	2/08	Wolv	5f216y	(0-60)H	STD	£2047
67	6/07	Chep	6f16y	(0-70)H	SFT	£2914

Total win prize-money £59152

Going (Turf): Sf: 1-4 GS: 1-2 Gd: 0-5 **GF: 2-10** Fm: 0-0
Distance: **5f/6f: 6-26** 7f-8f: 1-11 9f-13f: 0-0 14f+: 0-0
Track : LH: 1-14 **RH: 2-3 Tight: 1-10** Gall: 0-0
Aids: Bl: 1-14 Vi: 0-0 Tstrap: 4-8 Ckp: 4-8
Best Rating: 102 9/08 Newb 5f34y good

Useful; suited by 5f-6f; acts on most ground; also goes on Polytrack; often wears cheekpieces/blinkers.

Tongalooma

87(97) (56)**36**

3-y-o ch f Shinko Forest (IRE)-Schatzi (Chilibang)
James Moffatt Mrs Jennie Moffatt

Placings:0410 **(7595)**
2009: 7^{0}GF, 5^{4}SD, 5^{1}SD, 5^{0}SD,

	Starts	1st	2nd	3rd	Win & Pl
Career Total (Turf)	**1**	**0**	**0**	**0**	
Career Total (AW)	**3**	**1**	**0**	**0**	**2730**

56	10/09	Wolv	5f20y	STD	£2729

Total win prize-money £2730

Going (Turf): **Sf: 0-0 GS: 0-0 Gd: 0-0 GF: 0-1 Fm: 0-0**
Distance: **5f/6f: 1-3** 7f-8f: 0-1 9f-13f: 0-0 14f+: 0-0
Track : **LH: 1-3** RH: 0-0 **Tight: 1-3** Gall: 0-0
Aids: Bl: 0-0 Vi: 0-0 Tstrap: 0-0 Ckp: 0-0
Best Rating: 56 10/09 Wolv 5f20y stand

Moderate; suited by 5f and Polytrack.

Tony The Tap

107(103) (95)**95**

8-y-o b g Most Welcome-Laleston (Junius (USA))
W R Muir K J Mercer & Mrs S Mercer

Placings:4/122252100520/6245523026/605500/52406633 65210/0063540110-650120 **(5860)**
2009: 5^{6}G, 5^{5}GF, 5^{0}GF, 5^{1}G, 5^{2}GF, 5^{0}GF,

	Starts	1st	2nd	3rd	Win & Pl
Career Total (Turf)	**46**	**3**	**10**	**3**	**65758**
Career Total (AW)	**12**	**3**	**1**	**1**	**14555**

93	8/09	Chep	5f16y	(0-90)H	GD	£7771
95	10/08	Wolv	5f20y	(0-85)H	STD	£5180
91	9/08	Leic	5f2y	(0-85)H	GD	£4857

87 11/07 Wolv 5f216y (0-75)H STD £2968
86 7/04 Epsm 6f D(0-80)H G-F £8190
65 2/04 Ling 5f D STD £3997
Total win prize-money £32966

Going (Turf): Sf: 0-1 GS: 0-5 **Gd: 2-13** GF: 1-25 Fm: 0-2
Distance: **5f/6f: 6-52** 7f-8f: 0-6 9f-13f: 0-0 14f+: 0-0
Track : **LH: 4-17** RH: 0-0 **Tight: 4-15** Gall: 0-3
Aids: **Bl: 1-3** Vi: 0-3 Tstrap: 0-0 Ckp: 0-0
Best Rating: 95 8/09 Sand 5f6y gd-fm

Very useful; effective over 5f-6f; acts on most ground and on Polytrack; has worn blinkers and a visor.

Too Grand

(101) (62)**53**
4-y-o ch f Zaha (CAN)-Gold Linnet (Nashwan (USA))
J J Bridger J J Bridger

Placings:0550**65**1020**40**/**54**6252000**55**20000-1500**44** **(0945)**
2009: 7[1]SD, 8[5]SD, 8[0]SD, 7[0]SD, 8[4]SD, 7[4]SD,

	Starts	1st	2nd	3rd	Win & Pl
Career Total (Turf)	8	0	0	0	0
Career Total (AW)	26	2	4	0	6667

61 1/09 Kemp 7f (0-50)H STD £2047
61 10/07 Kemp 5f (0-60) STD £2047
Total win prize-money £4095

Going (Turf): **Sf: 0-2 GS: 0-0 Gd: 0-1 GF: 0-3 Fm: 0-2**
Distance: 5f/6f: 1-9 7f-8f: 1-22 9f-13f: 0-3 14f+: 0-0
Track : LH: 0-14 **RH: 2-16** Tight: 0-12 Gall: 0-2
Aids: Bl: 0-0 **Vi: 2-15** Tstrap: 0-0 Ckp: 0-0
Best Rating: 62 9/08 Kemp 1m stand

Moderate; effective at 7f-1m; seems best on Polytrack, but handles fast ground; has worn a visor.

Too Much Trouble

105 **102**
3-y-o b g Barathea (IRE)-Tentpole (USA) (Rainbow Quest (USA))
M R Channon Jaber Abdullah

Placings:1-1645604 **(6114)**
2009: 11[1]GF, 12[6]GF, 10[4]GF, 13[5]G, 12[6]G, 14[0]GF, 10[4]GF,

	Starts	1st	2nd	3rd	Win & Pl
Career Total (Turf)	8	2	0	0	19576

102 4/09 Catt 1m3f214y G-F £7352
82 8/08 Sand 1m14y G-S £5180
Total win prize-money £12534

Going (Turf): Sf: 0-0 **GS: 1-1** Gd: 0-2 **GF: 1-5** Fm: 0-0
Distance: 5f/6f: 0-0 7f-8f: 0-0 **9f-13f: 2-7** 14f+: 0-1
Track : LH: 1-3 RH: 1-4 **Tight: 1-3** Gall: 0-3
Aids: Bl: 0-0 Vi: 0-0 Tstrap: 0-0 Ckp: 0-0
Best Rating: 102 6/09 Asct 1m2f gd-fm

Very useful; stays 1m4f; acts on most ground.

Too Putra (IRE)

(84) (73)
2-y-o b c Oratorio (IRE)-Urgent Liaison (IRE) (High Estate)
R Charlton H R H Sultan Ahmad Shah

Placings:1 **(7538)**
2009: 7[1]SD,

	Starts	1st	2nd	3rd	Win & Pl
Career Total (Turf)	0	0	0	0	
Career Total (AW)	1	1	0	0	3238

73 11/09 Kemp 7f STD £3238
Total win prize-money £3238

Going (Turf): **Sf: 0-0 GS: 0-0 Gd: 0-0 GF: 0-0 Fm: 0-0**
Distance: 5f/6f: 0-0 **7f-8f: 1-1** 9f-13f: 0-0 14f+: 0-0
Track : LH: 0-0 **RH: 1-1** Tight: 0-0 Gall: 0-0
Aids: Bl: 0-0 Vi: 0-0 Tstrap: 0-0 Ckp: 0-0
Best Rating: 73 11/09 Kemp 7f stand

Fair; stays 7f; acts on Polytrack; sure to improve.

Too Tall

100(99) (73)**72**
3-y-o b c Medicean-Embark (Soviet Star (USA))
Tim Vaughan (J R Boyle 18/11) M Khan X2

Placings:244-05523332 **(7426)**
2009: 8[0]GF, 7[5]G, 5[5]GS, 6[2]F, 9[3]SD, 12[3]SF, 10[3]G, 10[2]SD,

	Starts	1st	2nd	3rd	Win & Pl
Career Total (Turf)	8	0	2	1	4146
Career Total (AW)	3	0	1	2	1664

Going (Turf): **Sf: 0-0 GS: 0-2 Gd: 0-3 GF: 0-2 Fm: 0-1**
Distance: 5f/6f: 0-1 7f-8f: 0-5 9f-13f: 0-5 14f+: 0-0
Track : LH: 0-5 RH: 0-2 Tight: 0-3 Gall: 0-0
Aids: Bl: 0-2 Vi: 0-0 Tstrap: 0-0 Ckp: 0-0
Best Rating: 73 10/09 Wolv 1m4f50y std-fst

Modest; stays 1m2f; acts on fast and easy ground and on Polytrack; has worn blinkers.

Toolentidhaar (USA)

97(96) (72)**72**
5-y-o b m Swain (IRE)-Rababah (USA) (Woodman (USA))
Andrew Turnell Griffiths Gifts Limited

Placings:323000 **(5780)**
2009: 8[3]GF, 8[2]SD, 10[3]GF, 8[0]GF, 8[0]GF, 8[0]SD,

	Starts	1st	2nd	3rd	Win & Pl
Career Total (Turf)	4	0	0	2	1059
Career Total (AW)	2	0	1	0	1445

Going (Turf): **Sf: 0-0 GS: 0-0 Gd: 0-0 GF: 0-4 Fm: 0-0**
Distance: 5f/6f: 0-0 7f-8f: 0-3 9f-13f: 0-3 14f+: 0-0
Track : LH: 0-1 RH: 0-5 Tight: 0-3 Gall: 0-0
Aids: Bl: 0-0 Vi: 0-0 Tstrap: 0-0 Ckp: 0-0
Best Rating: 72 7/09 Epsm 1m2f18y gd-fm

Fair; stays 1m and acts on Polytrack.

Top Bid

101(102) (59)**69**
5-y-o b g Auction House (USA)-Trump Street (First Trump)
T D Easterby John & Marilyn Williams

Placings:4145/50623000/0000**41**0-620142400U604 **(7122)**
2009: 5[6]GF, 5[2]GF, 5[0]G, 5[1]G, 5[4]G, 6[2]G, 5[4]HY, 5[0]GF, 6[0]S, 6[U]GF, 6[6]G, 6[0]G, 5[4]G,

	Starts	1st	2nd	3rd	Win & Pl
Career Total (Turf)	30	3	3	1	17386
Career Total (AW)	2	0	0	0	192

66 7/09 Hayd 5f (0-75)H GD £3238
68 11/08 Nott 5f13y (0-55)H HVY £2047
84 5/06 Leic 5f2y G-S £4533
Total win prize-money £9819

Going (Turf): **Sf: 1-5 GS: 1-3 Gd: 1-16** GF: 0-6 Fm: 0-0
Distance: **5f/6f: 3-29** 7f-8f: 0-3 9f-13f: 0-0 14f+: 0-0
Track : LH: 0-4 RH: 0-0 Tight: 0-2 Gall: 0-1
Aids: **Bl: 2-19** Vi: 0-0 Tstrap: 0-0 Ckp: 0-0
Best Rating: 84 4/07 Ripn 6f gd-fm

Moderate; effective at around 5f-6f; acts on fast and soft ground; often blinkered.

Top Flight Splash

89(96) (54)**49**
3-y-o b f Bertolini (USA)-Making Waves (IRE) (Danehill (USA))
Mrs G S Rees P Bamford

Placings:000**104**-4**22**003600 **(7727)**
2009: 7[4]GF, 6[2]SD, 7[2]SD, 6[0]GS, 7[0]G, 7[3]SD, 7[6]SD, 5[0]SD, 7[0]SD,

	Starts	1st	2nd	3rd	Win & Pl
Career Total (Turf)	5	0	0	0	0
Career Total (AW)	10	1	2	1	3559

54 11/08 Sthl 6f (0-65) STD £2047
Total win prize-money £2047

Going (Turf): **Sf: 0-1 GS: 0-2 Gd: 0-1 GF: 0-1 Fm: 0-0**
Distance: **5f/6f: 1-8** 7f-8f: 0-7 9f-13f: 0-0 14f+: 0-0
Track : **LH: 1-13** RH: 0-1 Tight: 0-5 Gall: 0-0
Aids: Bl: 0-0 Vi: 0-8 Tstrap: 0-1 Ckp: 0-1
Best Rating: 54 5/09 Sthl 6f stand

Moderate; suited by 6f; acts on Fibresand.

Top Jaro (FR)

(96) (52)**77**
6-y-o b g Marathon (USA)-Shahmy (USA) (Lear Fan (USA))
Mrs R A Carr David W Chapman

Placings:10/202061/**0004**205013413036/25511**00-66000** **(0567)**
2009: 8[6]SD, 8[6]SD, 14[0]SD, 11[0]SD, 12[0]SD,

	Starts	1st	2nd	3rd	Win & Pl
Career Total (Turf)	25	6	4	3	31185
Career Total (AW)	12	0	0	0	0

66 9/08 Muss 1m1f GD £5180
66 9/08 Rdcr 1m2f G-S £2047
68 8/07 Rdcr 1m GD £2047
62 6/07 Carl 7f200y GD £2047
82 10/06 Ayr 1m1f20y (0-85)H HVY £6232
68 9/05 Ripn 1m GD £4416
Total win prize-money £21972

Going (Turf): Sf: 1-8 GS: 1-5 **Gd: 4-8** GF: 0-2 Fm: 0-2
Distance: 5f/6f: 0-0 7f-8f: 3-12 9f-13f: 3-23 14f+: 0-2
Track : LH: 2-24 **RH: 3-9 Tight: 3-14** Gall: 0-1
Aids: Bl: 0-5 Vi: 0-0 Tstrap: 0-0 Ckp: 0-0
Best Rating: 82 10/06 Ayr 1m1f20y heavy

Modest; stays 1m2f and acts on most types of ground.

Top Man Dan (IRE)

96 **59**
4-y-o b g Danetime (IRE)-Aphra Benn (IRE) (In The Wings)
T D Walford T W Heseltine

Placings:5/000240530-60 **(2975)**
2009: 12[6]GS, 10[0]GS,

	Starts	1st	2nd	3rd	Win & Pl
Career Total (Turf)	12	0	1	1	1123

Going (Turf): **Sf: 0-2 GS: 0-5 Gd: 0-3 GF: 0-1 Fm: 0-1**
Distance: 5f/6f: 0-0 7f-8f: 0-3 9f-13f: 0-9 14f+: 0-0
Track : LH: 0-9 RH: 0-3 Tight: 0-4 Gall: 0-3

Aids: Bl: 0-0 Vi: 0-1 Tstrap: 0-0 Ckp: 0-0
Best Rating: 64 10/07 York 1m gd-sft

Moderate; effective over 1m; acts on good ground.

Top Rocker

84 25

5-y-o b g Rock City-Top Hand (First Trump)
E W Tuer E Tuer

Placings:056035/0 (4848)
2009: 16^{0}G,

	Starts	1st	2nd	3rd	Win & Pl
Career Total (Turf)	7	0	0	1	482

Going (Turf): **Sf: 0-0 GS: 0-1 Gd: 0-3 GF: 0-3 Fm: 0-0**
Distance: 5f/6f: 0-0 7f-8f: 0-0 9f-13f: 0-6 14f+: 0-1
Track : LH: 0-5 RH: 0-2 Tight: 0-6 Gall: 0-1
Aids: Bl: 0-0 Vi: 0-0 Tstrap: 0-0 Ckp: 0-0
Best Rating: 51 7/07 Catt 1m3f214y good

Top Seed (IRE)

91(103) (68)72

8-y-o b g Cadeaux Genereux-Midnight Heights (Persian Heights)
M S Tuck (Ian Williams 29/3) J & D Syndicate

Placings:2314530362**4**/2403200PP**6**/60**5**605566000/5110 0420000**4**20056/000/6013120-6020006 (6806)
2009: 9^{6}SD, 12^{0}SD, 10^{2}G, 10^{0}GS, 8^{0}GS, 12^{0}SD, 9^{6}SD,

	Starts	1st	2nd	3rd	Win & Pl
Career Total (Turf)	52	4	7	5	113321
Career Total (AW)	16	1	1	0	4303
68 6/08 Kemp 1m3f (0-60)H				STD	£2047
68 4/08 Bath 1m2f46y (0-55)H				GD	£2719
90 5/06 Gdwd 1m3f (0-80)H				GD	£6800
85 4/06 Bath 1m3f144y (0-85)H				GD	£7886
86 7/03 Bevl 7f100y D				G-F	£4719

Total win prize-money £24173

Going (Turf): Sf: 0-5 GS: 0-9 **Gd: 3-14** GF: 1-19 Fm: 0-4
Distance: 5f/6f: 0-0 7f-8f: 1-9 **9f-13f: 4-54** 14f+: 0-5
Track : LH: 2-40 **RH: 3-22 Tight: 3-26** Gall: 0-23
Aids: Bl: 0-0 Vi: 0-1 Tstrap: 0-0 Ckp: 0-0
Best Rating: 112 5/04 York 1m2f88y gd-sft

Modest; seems best at around 1m2f-1m4f; acts on fast ground, but possibly better with cut.

Top Spin (IRE)

96 85

2-y-o b/br c Cape Cross (IRE)-Beguine (USA) (Green Dancer (USA))
John Joseph Murphy Mrs John J Murphy

Placings:0300 (6898)
2009: 7^{0}S, 7^{3}GF, 8^{0}G, 8^{0}GF,

	Starts	1st	2nd	3rd	Win & Pl
Career Total (Turf)	4	0	0	1	722

Going (Turf): **Sf: 0-1 GS: 0-0 Gd: 0-1 GF: 0-2 Fm: 0-0**
Distance: 5f/6f: 0-0 7f-8f: 0-3 9f-13f: 0-1 14f+: 0-0
Track : LH: 0-1 RH: 0-1 Tight: 0-0 Gall: 0-1
Aids: Bl: 0-0 Vi: 0-0 Tstrap: 0-0 Ckp: 0-0
Best Rating: 85 9/09 Curr 1m good

Top Ticket (IRE)

95(90) (69)82

4-y-o ch g Alhaarth (IRE)-Tathkara (USA) (Alydar (USA))
D E Pipe Lancer Scott Ltd

Placings:33/21360200-05 (5217)
2009: 10^{0}G, 14^{5}G,

	Starts	1st	2nd	3rd	Win & Pl
Career Total (Turf)	11	1	1	3	5986
Career Total (AW)	1	0	1	0	771
79 4/08 Bath 1m2f46y				G-S	£2460

Total win prize-money £2461

Going (Turf): Sf: 0-1 **GS: 1-5** Gd: 0-3 GF: 0-2 Fm: 0-0
Distance: 5f/6f: 0-0 7f-8f: 0-0 **9f-13f: 1-11** 14f+: 0-1
Track : **LH: 1-5** RH: 0-5 **Tight: 1-7** Gall: 0-1
Aids: Bl: 0-0 Vi: 0-0 Tstrap: 0-1 Ckp: 0-1
Best Rating: 82 5/08 Gdwd 1m3f gd-fm

Useful; stays 1m3f; acts on good to firm and good to soft.

Top Tiger

83(101) (67)65

5-y-o b g Mtoto-Topatori (IRE) (Topanoora)
D W Barker (M H Tompkins 28/1) Chris Tremewan

Placings:4/53105/054200-02660 (1058)
2009: 12^{0}SD, 12^{2}SD, 12^{6}SD, 14^{6}SD, 15^{0}GF,

	Starts	1st	2nd	3rd	Win & Pl
Career Total (Turf)	7	0	0	1	1107
Career Total (AW)	10	1	2	0	3357
66 10/07 Kemp 1m4f				STD	£2047

Total win prize-money £2048

Going (Turf): **Sf: 0-1 GS: 0-2 Gd: 0-3 GF: 0-1 Fm: 0-0**
Distance: 5f/6f: 0-0 7f-8f: 0-1 **9f-13f: 1-10** 14f+: 0-6
Track : LH: 0-15 **RH: 1-2** Tight: 0-4 Gall: 0-5
Aids: Bl: 0-1 Vi: 0-0 Tstrap: 0-0 Ckp: 0-0
Best Rating: 73 10/06 York 1m soft

Moderate; stays 1m6f; acts on Fibresand and Polytrack.

Top Tigress

(87) (63)

2-y-o b f Tiger Hill (IRE)-Top Romance (IRE) (Entrepreneur)
Sir Michael Stoute Mrs Denis Haynes

Placings:4 (7276)
2009: 7^{4}SD,

	Starts	1st	2nd	3rd	Win & Pl
Career Total (Turf)	0	0	0	0	
Career Total (AW)	1	0	0	0	241

Going (Turf): **Sf: 0-0 GS: 0-0 Gd: 0-0 GF: 0-0 Fm: 0-0**
Distance: 5f/6f: 0-0 7f-8f: 0-1 9f-13f: 0-0 14f+: 0-0
Track : LH: 0-1 RH: 0-0 Tight: 0-1 Gall: 0-0
Aids: Bl: 0-0 Vi: 0-0 Tstrap: 0-0 Ckp: 0-0
Best Rating: 63 11/09 Wolv 7f32y stand

Top Tinker

86(86) (51)41

3-y-o b g Vettori (IRE)-Topatori (IRE) (Topanoora)
M H Tompkins Chris Tremewan

Placings:000-0060 (3157)
2009: 10^{0}SD, 14^{0}GF, 12^{6}SD, 12^{0}SD,

	Starts	1st	2nd	3rd	Win & Pl
Career Total (Turf)	3	0	0	0	
Career Total (AW)	4	0	0	0	0

Going (Turf): **Sf: 0-0 GS: 0-0 Gd: 0-2 GF: 0-1 Fm: 0-0**
Distance: 5f/6f: 0-0 7f-8f: 0-3 9f-13f: 0-3 14f+: 0-1
Track : LH: 0-4 RH: 0-1 Tight: 0-3 Gall: 0-0
Aids: Bl: 0-1 Vi: 0-0 Tstrap: 0-0 Ckp: 0-0
Best Rating: 51 11/08 Ling 1m stand

Top Town Girl

98(95) (73)85

3-y-o b f Efisio-Halland Park Girl (IRE) (Primo Dominie)
R M Beckett Landmark Racing Limited

Placings:0103-00444404 (6739)
2009: 6^{0}SD, 6^{0}G, 5^{4}G, 6^{4}SD, 6^{4}G, 6^{4}G, 6^{0}SD, 6^{4}GS,

	Starts	1st	2nd	3rd	Win & Pl
Career Total (Turf)	9	1	0	1	5955
Career Total (AW)	3	0	0	0	351
80 9/08 Sand 5f6y				SFT	£3885

Total win prize-money £3886

Going (Turf): **Sf: 1-2** GS: 0-3 Gd: 0-4 GF: 0-0 Fm: 0-0
Distance: **5f/6f: 1-10** 7f-8f: 0-2 9f-13f: 0-0 14f+: 0-0
Track : LH: 0-0 RH: 0-3 Tight: 0-0 Gall: 0-3
Aids: Bl: 0-0 Vi: 0-0 Tstrap: 0-2 Ckp: 0-2
Best Rating: 85 10/08 Newb 6f8y gd-sft

Useful; effective over 5f-6f; acts on soft ground.

Top Tribute

97(57) 66

4-y-o b g Acclamation-Mary Hinge (Dowsing (USA))
T P Tate T P Tate

Placings:20026-0025 (6217)
2009: 7^{0}F, 7^{0}SD, 8^{2}GF, 8^{5}GF,

	Starts	1st	2nd	3rd	Win & Pl
Career Total (Turf)	8	0	3	0	2409
Career Total (AW)	1	0	0	0	

Going (Turf): **Sf: 0-2 GS: 0-2 Gd: 0-1 GF: 0-2 Fm: 0-1**
Distance: 5f/6f: 0-0 7f-8f: 0-7 9f-13f: 0-2 14f+: 0-0
Track : LH: 0-4 RH: 0-1 Tight: 0-2 Gall: 0-0
Aids: Bl: 0-0 Vi: 0-0 Tstrap: 0-0 Ckp: 0-0
Best Rating: 66 10/08 Rdcr 7f good

Modest; bred to be a sprinter but stays 1m; acts on soft ground.

Topcroft

87(105) (75)49

3-y-o b g Mujahid (USA)-Starminda (Zamindar (USA))
D Shaw (Mrs C A Dunnett 30/9) Mrs V Franklin & Partners

Placings:0-05505111 (7784)
2009: 8^{0}SD, 8^{5}GF, 8^{5}SD, 7^{0}G, 8^{5}SD, 8^{1}SD, 6^{1}SD, 8^{1}SD,

	Starts	1st	2nd	3rd	Win & Pl
Career Total (Turf)	3	0	0	0	0
Career Total (AW)	6	3	0	0	6142
74 12/09 Sthl 1m (0-60)H				STD	£2047
75 12/09 Kemp 6f (0-50)H				STD	£2047
69 12/09 Kemp 1m (0-50)H				STD	£2047

Total win prize-money £6141

Going (Turf): **Sf: 0-0 GS: 0-0 Gd: 0-2 GF: 0-1 Fm: 0-0**
Distance: 5f/6f: 1-1 **7f-8f: 2-6** 9f-13f: 0-2 14f+: 0-0
Track : LH: 1-3 **RH: 2-3** Tight: 0-2 Gall: 0-0
Aids: Bl: 0-0 **Vi: 3-3** Tstrap: 0-0 Ckp: 0-0
Best Rating: 75 12/09 Kemp 6f stand

Fair; effective over 6f-1m; acts on sand; has worn a visor; gets on well with Lee Topliss.

Topflightrebellion

(90) (52)43

4-y-o b f Mark Of Esteem (IRE)-Jamarj (Tyrnavos)

Mrs G S Rees P Bamford

Placings:03/300665-40 **(1568)**

2009: 8^{4}SD, 11^{0}SD,

	Starts	1st	2nd	3rd	Win & Pl
Career Total (Turf)	4	0	0	0	0
Career Total (AW)	6	0	0	2	706

Going (Turf): **Sf: 0-1 GS: 0-1 Gd: 0-1 GF: 0-1 Fm: 0-0**
Distance: 5f/6f: 0-2 7f-8f: 0-3 9f-13f: 0-5 14f+: 0-0
Track : LH: 0-8 RH: 0-2 Tight: 0-3 Gall: 0-0
Aids: Bl: 0-0 Vi: 0-0 Tstrap: 0-2 Ckp: 0-2
Best Rating: **56** 1/08 Sthl 7f stand

Topolski (IRE)

102 91

3-y-o b g Peintre Celebre (USA)-Witching Hour (IRE) (Alzao (USA))

M Johnston Kennet Valley Thoroughbreds V

Placings:004-1102500 **(5170)**

2009: 9^{1}GF, 10^{1}GF, 10^{0}GF, 12^{2}F, 12^{5}GF, 12^{0}G, 12^{0}GF,

	Starts	1st	2nd	3rd	Win & Pl
Career Total (Turf)	10	2	1	0	8195

86 4/09 Rdcr 1m2f (0-75)H G-F £2590
82 4/09 Bevl 1m1f207y (0-70)H G-F £2590
Total win prize-money £5180

Going (Turf): Sf: 0-2 GS: 0-1 Gd: 0-1 **GF: 2-5** Fm: 0-1
Distance: 5f/6f: 0-1 7f-8f: 0-2 **9f-13f: 2-7** 14f+: 0-0
Track : LH: 1-4 RH: 1-4 **Tight: 1-3** Gall: 0-3
Aids: Bl: 0-0 Vi: 0-0 Tstrap: 0-0 Ckp: 0-0
Best Rating: **91** 6/09 Asct 1m4f gd-fm

Useful; stays 1m4f; acts on fast ground.

Tora Petcha (IRE)

92(70) (44)48

6-y-o b g Bahhare (USA)-Magdalene (FR) (College Chapel)

B D Leavy (R Hollinshead 4/1) N Heath

Placings:6100000/440500/0-0 **(4742)**

2009: 14^{0}G,

	Starts	1st	2nd	3rd	Win & Pl
Career Total (Turf)	13	1	0	0	8570
Career Total (AW)	2	0	0	0	

79 7/05 York 6f G-F £7312
Total win prize-money £7313

Going (Turf): Sf: 0-1 GS: 0-0 Gd: 0-8 **GF: 1-4** Fm: 0-0
Distance: **5f/6f: 1-6** 7f-8f: 0-4 9f-13f: 0-4 14f+: 0-1
Track : LH: 0-6 RH: 0-2 Tight: 0-2 Gall: 0-0
Aids: Bl: 0-0 Vi: 0-0 Tstrap: 0-0 Ckp: 0-0
Best Rating: **82** 9/05 NmkR 6f good

Torch Of Freedom (IRE)

88(104) (80)76

4-y-o b g Statue Of Liberty (USA)-Danse Royale (IRE) (Caerleon (USA))

Sir Mark Prescott J Fishpool - Osborne House

Placings:412/3-40601505 **(5108)**

2009: 8^{4}SD, 8^{0}SD, 8^{6}SD, 10^{0}SD, 10^{1}SD, 9^{5}SD, 10^{0}G, 10^{5}GF,

	Starts	1st	2nd	3rd	Win & Pl
Career Total (Turf)	4	0	0	1	941
Career Total (AW)	8	2	1	0	6321

78 3/09 Kemp 1m2f STD £1942
76 11/07 Kemp 6f STD £3141
Total win prize-money £5084

Going (Turf): **Sf: 0-0 GS: 0-0 Gd: 0-1 GF: 0-3 Fm: 0-0**
Distance: 5f/6f: 1-1 7f-8f: 0-5 9f-13f: 1-6 14f+: 0-0
Track : LH: 0-7 **RH: 2-4** Tight: 0-5 Gall: 0-0
Aids: Bl: 0-0 Vi: 0-0 Tstrap: 0-0 Ckp: 0-0
Best Rating: **80** 1/09 Ling 1m stand

Fair; stays 1m2f; acts on fast ground and Polytrack.

Torina (IRE)

(94) (61)63

4-y-o ch f Golan (IRE)-Tordasia (IRE) (Dr Devious (IRE))

M J Grassick M C Grassick/Mrs M J Grassick/J Crowley

Placings:00002410-23240203 **(7732)**

2009: 11^{2}Y, 14^{3}Y, 14^{2}G, 14^{4}G, 16^{0}YS, 14^{2}YS, 14^{0}G, 12^{3}SD,

	Starts	1st	2nd	3rd	Win & Pl
Career Total (Turf)	13	1	4	1	10008
Career Total (AW)	3	0	0	1	302

53 9/08 Baln 1m6f (45-60)H YLD £4318
Total win prize-money £4319

Going (Turf): **Sf: 0-0 GS: 0-0 Gd: 0-4 GF: 0-0 Fm: 0-0**
Distance: 5f/6f: 0-0 7f-8f: 0-2 9f-13f: 0-7 **14f+: 1-7**
Track : LH: 0-5 **RH: 1-9** Tight: 0-1 Gall: 0-0
Aids: Bl: 0-1 Vi: 0-0 Tstrap: 0-0 Ckp: 0-0
Best Rating: **63** 9/09 Baln 1m6f yld-sft

Tornadodancer (IRE)

108 (86)92

6-y-o b g Princely Heir (IRE)-Purty Dancer (IRE) (Foxhound (USA))

T G McCourt John P McGovern

Placings:0550360/0054200000/62220116405-00034062520010 **(7566a)**

2009: 6^{0}S, 5^{0}SD, 5^{0}S, 5^{3}GF, 6^{4}GY, 5^{0}HY, 5^{6}S, 5^{2}S, 5^{5}SD, 6^{2}G, 6^{0}SD, 6^{0}SD, 6^{1}SD, 6^{0}SD,

	Starts	1st	2nd	3rd	Win & Pl
Career Total (Turf)	31	1	5	2	32038
Career Total (AW)	12	2	1	0	18640

79 11/09 Dund 6f STD £7044
84 8/08 Tipp 5f SFT £10052
72 8/08 Dund 5f STD £10530
Total win prize-money £27627

Going (Turf): **Sf: 1-12** GS: 0-0 Gd: 0-6 GF: 0-5 Fm: 0-2
Distance: **5f/6f: 3-36** 7f-8f: 0-7 9f-13f: 0-0 14f+: 0-0
Track : **LH: 3-26** RH: 0-5 Tight: 0-1 Gall: 0-0
Aids: **Bl: 1-10** Vi: 0-1 Tstrap: 0-0 Ckp: 0-0
Best Rating: **92** 8/09 Muss 5f soft

Useful; suited by 5f; acts on most ground and on Polytrack; has worn blinkers and a visor.

Torquemada (IRE)

56(103) (60)61

8-y-o ch g Desert Sun-Gaelic's Fantasy (IRE) (Statoblest)

M J Attwater Canisbay Bloodstock

Placings:60/30003001532/25405042/36301042100/30301 00200/606P3004002-533000050 **(7517)**

2009: 7^{5}SD, 7^{3}SD, 7^{3}SD, 7^{0}SD, 6^{0}SD, 7^{0}GF, 7^{0}GF, 7^{5}SD, 7^{0}SD,

	Starts	1st	2nd	3rd	Win & Pl
Career Total (Turf)	37	4	3	3	19708
Career Total (AW)	25	0	3	7	5850

71 9/07 Leic 7f9y (0-70)H G-F £3238
71 9/06 Leic 7f9y (0-70)H G-F £3238
69 6/06 Ling 7f (0-65)H G-F £3071
69 9/04 Leic 7f9y (0-70)H G-F £3842
Total win prize-money £13392

Going (Turf): Sf: 0-1 GS: 0-8 Gd: 0-7 **GF: 4-18** Fm: 0-3
Distance: 5f/6f: 0-11 **7f-8f: 4-49** 9f-13f: 0-2 14f+: 0-0
Track : LH: 0-23 RH: 0-10 Tight: 0-18 Gall: 0-3
Aids: Bl: 0-0 Vi: 0-0 Tstrap: 0-8 Ckp: 0-8
Best Rating: **78** 10/07 Ling 1m stand

Moderate; effective over 7f-1m; suited by fast ground; also goes on sand; has worn a tongue tie and cheekpieces.

Torran Sound

(83) (45)

2-y-o b g Tobougg (IRE)-Velvet Waters (Unfuwain (USA))

J M P Eustace The MacDougall Two

Placings:00 **(7571)**

2009: 6^{0}SD, 6^{0}SD,

	Starts	1st	2nd	3rd	Win & Pl
Career Total (Turf)	0	0	0	0	
Career Total (AW)	2	0	0	0	

Going (Turf): **Sf: 0-0 GS: 0-0 Gd: 0-0 GF: 0-0 Fm: 0-0**
Distance: 5f/6f: 0-2 7f-8f: 0-0 9f-13f: 0-0 14f+: 0-0
Track : LH: 0-1 RH: 0-1 Tight: 0-1 Gall: 0-0
Aids: Bl: 0-0 Vi: 0-0 Tstrap: 0-0 Ckp: 0-0
Best Rating: **45** 11/09 Kemp 6f stand

Torrens (IRE)

95(102) (64)66

7-y-o b g Royal Anthem (USA)-Azure Lake (USA) (Lac Ouimet (USA))

P D Evans Diamond Racing Ltd

Placings:4100305/00411301050/04552060/64531261066 3045252/50260225244-300 **(1936)**

2009: 10^{3}G, 10^{0}GF, 13^{0}SD,

	Starts	1st	2nd	3rd	Win & Pl
Career Total (Turf)	44	6	3	5	46109
Career Total (AW)	14	0	5	0	5635

83 6/07 Ches 1m2f75y (0-85)H GD £5505
77 4/07 Pont 1m2f6y (0-70)H G-F £3886
88 8/05 Ches 1m2f75y (0-90)H G-F £9170
83 7/05 Ches 1m2f75y (0-85)H G-F £7007
76 7/05 Ripn 1m4f10y (0-80)H GD £6099
70 8/04 Chep 1m14y D SFT £3542
Total win prize-money £35212

Going (Turf): Sf: 1-9 GS: 0-5 Gd: 2-15 **GF: 3-15** Fm: 0-0
Distance: 5f/6f: 0-0 7f-8f: 0-5 **9f-13f: 6-52** 14f+: 0-1
Track : **LH: 4-40** RH: 1-13 **Tight: 4-32** Gall: 0-8
Aids: Bl: 0-0 Vi: 0-0 Tstrap: 0-0 Ckp: 0-0
Best Rating: **88** 8/05 Ches 1m2f75y gd-fm

Moderate; effective at around 1m2f-1m4f; acts on most ground and on Polytrack; has worn a tongue tie.

Torres Del Paine

(95) (66)

2-y-o b c Compton Place-Noble Story (Last Tycoon)

J C Fox The Fairy Story Partnership

Placings:042 (7736)
2009: 6^{0}SD, 6^{4}SD, 6^{2}SD,

	Starts	1st	2nd	3rd	Win & Pl
Career Total (Turf)	0	0	0	0	
Career Total (AW)	3	0	1	0	1204

Going (Turf): **Sf: 0-0 GS: 0-0 Gd: 0-0 GF: 0-0 Fm: 0-0**
Distance: 5f/6f: 0-3 7f-8f: 0-0 9f-13f: 0-0 14f+: 0-0
Track : LH: 0-2 RH: 0-1 Tight: 0-2 Gall: 0-0
Aids: Bl: 0-0 Vi: 0-0 Tstrap: 0-0 Ckp: 0-0
Best Rating: **66** 12/09 Kemp 6f stand

Modest; effective at 6f on Polytrack.

Toshi (USA)

100 (57)**60**
7-y-o b g Kingmambo (USA)-Majestic Role (FR) (Theatrical)
J S Goldie E Nisbet & Miss L McFadzean

Placings:00/2221020300**6**/2300040**6**/01055/0-0513 **(4462)**
2009: 12^{0}G, 9^{5}GF, 12^{1}GF, 13^{3}G,

	Starts	1st	2nd	3rd	Win & Pl
Career Total (Turf)	27	3	5	3	23442
Career Total (AW)	4	0	0	0	0
60 6/09 Ches 1m4f66y (0-70)H				G-F	£3903
71 5/07 Muss 1m4f (0-75)H				G-F	£3238
86 6/05 Haml 1m1f36y				G-S	£3526

Total win prize-money £10669

Going (Turf): Sf: 0-1 GS: 1-5 Gd: 0-8 **GF: 2-11** Fm: 0-2
Distance: 5f/6f: 0-1 7f-8f: 0-2 **9f-13f: 3-25** 14f+: 0-3
Track : LH: 1-15 **RH: 2-14 Tight: 3-21** Gall: 0-4
Aids: Bl: 0-0 Vi: 0-1 Tstrap: 0-2 Ckp: 0-2
Best Rating: **88** 6/06 Haml 1m65y gd-fm

Fair gelding; stays ten furlongs; acts on fast and easy ground; has worn cheekpieces; difficult to win with.

Tot Hill

70(71) **29**
6-y-o b m Syrtos-Galava (CAN) (Graustark)
C N Kellett Mrs J Breeden

Placings:R0000-0 **(3631)**
2009: 10^{0}G,

	Starts	1st	2nd	3rd	Win & Pl
Career Total (Turf)	4	0	0	0	
Career Total (AW)	2	0	0	0	

Going (Turf): **Sf: 0-1 GS: 0-0 Gd: 0-1 GF: 0-2 Fm: 0-0**
Distance: 5f/6f: 0-1 7f-8f: 0-1 9f-13f: 0-4 14f+: 0-0
Track : LH: 0-4 RH: 0-2 Tight: 0-2 Gall: 0-0
Aids: Bl: 0-0 Vi: 0-0 Tstrap: 0-0 Ckp: 0-0
Best Rating: **29** 8/08 Ches 7f122y soft

Total Command

101 **85**
2-y-o b c Sadler's Wells (USA)-Wince (Selkirk (USA))
Sir Michael Stoute K Abdulla

Placings:62 **(7029)**
2009: 7^{6}GF, 8^{2}S,

	Starts	1st	2nd	3rd	Win & Pl
Career Total (Turf)	2	0	1	0	1445

Going (Turf): **Sf: 0-1 GS: 0-0 Gd: 0-0 GF: 0-1 Fm: 0-0**
Distance: 5f/6f: 0-0 7f-8f: 0-2 9f-13f: 0-0 14f+: 0-0
Track : LH: 0-0 RH: 0-0 Tight: 0-0 Gall: 0-0
Aids: Bl: 0-0 Vi: 0-0 Tstrap: 0-0 Ckp: 0-0
Best Rating: **85** 10/09 Newb 1m soft

Useful; stays 1m; acts on soft ground.

Total Gallery (IRE)

115 **121**
3-y-o br c Namid-Diary (IRE) (Green Desert (USA))
J S Moore Coleman Bloodstock Limited

Placings:261521-150012216 **(7745a)**
2009: 6^{1}GF, 5^{5}HY, 7^{0}GF, 5^{0}G, 6^{1}G, 5^{2}G, 5^{2}GF, 5^{1}G, 6^{6}G,

	Starts	1st	2nd	3rd	Win & Pl
Career Total (Turf)	15	5	4	0	406269
121 10/09 Lonc 5f				GD	£138689
110 7/09 NmkJ 6f (0-105)H				GD	£62310
106 4/09 Asct 6f				G-F	£22708
101 10/08 Rdcr 6f				GD	£113540
96 7/08 Bevl 5f				GD	£4047

Total win prize-money £341294

Going (Turf): Sf: 0-2 GS: 0-0 **Gd: 4-8** GF: 1-5 Fm: 0-0
Distance: **5f/6f: 5-14** 7f-8f: 0-1 9f-13f: 0-0 14f+: 0-0
Track : LH: 0-0 RH: 0-0 Tight: 0-0 Gall: 0-0
Aids: Bl: 0-0 Vi: 0-0 Tstrap: 0-0 Ckp: 0-0
Best Rating: **121** 10/09 Lonc 5f good

Group class; winner of the Group 1 Prix de l'Abbaye; effective over 5f-6f; acts on most ground on turf.

Total Impact

106(101) (82)**95**
6-y-o ch g Pivotal-Rise 'n Shine (Night Shift (USA))
R A Fahey The Wakey Exiles

Placings:05/**2**1154405**0**/**0040000**/412233100005-1040001324231 **(7852)**
2009: 5^{1}GF, 5^{0}G, 5^{4}G, 5^{0}S, 5^{0}GS, 5^{0}GF, 5^{1}GF, 5^{3}GF, 5^{2}GF, 5^{4}F, 6^{2}SD, 6^{3}SS, 5^{1}SS,

	Starts	1st	2nd	3rd	Win & Pl
Career Total (Turf)	26	4	3	3	44019
Career Total (AW)	17	3	2	1	22180
79 12/09 Sthl 5f				SS	£2047
93 9/09 Donc 5f (0-85)H				G-F	£6152
94 5/09 Rdcr 5f (0-85)H				G-F	£4857
95 7/08 Gdwd 5f (0-90)H				G-F	£12952
87 5/08 Donc 5f (0-75)H				GD	£3238
91 4/06 Kemp 5f (0-105)H				STD	£11217
74 3/06 Wolv 5f216y				STD	£3886

Total win prize-money £44350

Going (Turf): Sf: 0-4 GS: 0-3 Gd: 1-5 **GF: 3-12** Fm: 0-2
Distance: **5f/6f: 7-41** 7f-8f: 0-2 9f-13f: 0-0 14f+: 0-0
Track : LH: 1-17 RH: 1-3 **Tight: 1-12** Gall: 0-2
Aids: Bl: 0-2 Vi: 0-0 Tstrap: 0-0 Ckp: 0-0
Best Rating: **95** 7/08 Gdwd 5f gd-fm

Useful; effective at 5f-6f; acts on good and faster ground; goes on Polytrack and Fibresand; has worn blinkers.

Totalitarian

99(94) (68)**69**
3-y-o ch g Pivotal-Shalimar (IRE) (Indian Ridge)
S A Callaghan Joseph Barton

Placings:335 **(6430)**
2009: 7^{3}SD, 7^{3}GF, 7^{5}SD,

	Starts	1st	2nd	3rd	Win & Pl
Career Total (Turf)	1	0	0	1	409
Career Total (AW)	2	0	0	1	385

Going (Turf): **Sf: 0-0 GS: 0-0 Gd: 0-0 GF: 0-1 Fm: 0-0**
Distance: 5f/6f: 0-0 7f-8f: 0-3 9f-13f: 0-0 14f+: 0-0
Track : LH: 0-1 RH: 0-1 Tight: 0-1 Gall: 0-0
Aids: Bl: 0-0 Vi: 0-0 Tstrap: 0-0 Ckp: 0-0
Best Rating: **69** 9/09 Rdcr 7f gd-fm

Modest; stays 7f and should stay 1m; acts on Polytrack; sure to improve.

Totally Devoted (USA)

106 **98**
3-y-o b/br f Seeking The Gold (USA)-Crystal Crossing (IRE) (Royal Academy (USA))
A P O'Brien Michael Tabor

Placings:300024143055 **(6884a)**
2009: 8^{3}Y, 8^{0}G, 8^{0}HY, 12^{0}GF, 8^{2}Y, 8^{4}GY, 8^{1}GY, 8^{4}GY, 7^{3}HY, 7^{0}GF, 7^{5}GF, 8^{5}GY,

	Starts	1st	2nd	3rd	Win & Pl
Career Total (Turf)	12	1	1	2	21480
83 8/09 Klny 1m100y				G-Y	£6037

Total win prize-money £6038

Going (Turf): **Sf: 0-2 GS: 0-0 Gd: 0-1 GF: 0-3 Fm: 0-0**
Distance: 5f/6f: 0-0 7f-8f: 0-10 **9f-13f: 1-2** 14f+: 0-0
Track : **LH: 1-8** RH: 0-3 Tight: 0-0 Gall: 0-3
Aids: Bl: 0-0 Vi: 0-0 Tstrap: 0-0 Ckp: 0-0
Best Rating: **98** 9/09 Leop 1m gd-yld

Useful; stays 1m; acts on good and easy ground.

Totally Focussed (IRE)

(107) (87)**55**
4-y-o gr/ro g Trans Island-Premier Place (USA) (Out Of Place (USA))
S Dow The St Cloud Partnership

Placings:055/**22021350634-246530** **(7883)**
2009: 7^{2}SD, 8^{4}SD, 7^{6}SD, 8^{5}SD, 7^{3}SD, 8^{0}SD,

	Starts	1st	2nd	3rd	Win & Pl
Career Total (Turf)	5	0	0	0	0
Career Total (AW)	15	1	4	3	13354
87 6/08 Kemp 1m (0-80)H				STD	£4209

Total win prize-money £4209

Going (Turf): **Sf: 0-1 GS: 0-1 Gd: 0-2 GF: 0-1 Fm: 0-0**
Distance: 5f/6f: 0-2 **7f-8f: 1-17** 9f-13f: 0-1 14f+: 0-0
Track : LH: 0-6 **RH: 1-9** Tight: 0-5 Gall: 0-1
Aids: Bl: 0-0 Vi: 0-0 Tstrap: 0-0 Ckp: 0-0
Best Rating: **87** 6/08 Kemp 1m stand

Fair; stays 1m; acts on Polytrack.

Totally Invincible (IRE)

96 **84**
2-y-o b f Invincible Spirit (IRE)-Sebastene (IRE) (Machiavellian (USA))
E S McMahon Premspace Ltd

Placings:04110 **(4407)**
2009: 5^{0}GF, 5^{4}GS, 5^{1}GF, 5^{1}GF, 5^{0}G,

	Starts	1st	2nd	3rd	Win & Pl
Career Total (Turf)	5	2	0	0	13952
84 7/09 Ches 5f16y				G-F	£9777
80 7/09 Catt 5f				G-F	£3885

Total win prize-money £13663

Going (Turf): Sf: 0-0 GS: 0-1 Gd: 0-1 **GF: 2-3** Fm: 0-0

Distance: **5f/6f: 2-5** 7f-8f: 0-0 9f-13f: 0-0 14f+: 0-0
Track : **LH: 1-2** RH: 0-0 **Tight: 1-1** Gall: 0-0
Aids: Bl: 0-0 Vi: 0-0 Tstrap: 0-0 Ckp: 0-0
Best Rating: **84** 7/09 Ches 5f16y gd-fm

Useful; well suited by 5f; acts on fast ground.

Totally Ours

(102) (76)
2-y-o b/br f Singspiel (IRE)-Totally Yours (IRE) (Desert Sun)
W R Muir Foursome Thoroughbreds

Placings:01 **(7177)**
2009: 6^{0}SD, 7^{1}SD,

	Starts	1st	2nd	3rd	Win & Pl
Career Total (Turf)	0	0	0	0	
Career Total (AW)	2	1	0	0	2590

76 10/09 Kemp 7f STD £2590
Total win prize-money £2590

Going (Turf): **Sf: 0-0 GS: 0-0 Gd: 0-0 GF: 0-0 Fm: 0-0**
Distance: 5f/6f: 0-1 **7f-8f: 1-1** 9f-13f: 0-0 14f+: 0-0
Track : LH: 0-0 **RH: 1-2** Tight: 0-0 Gall: 0-0
Aids: Bl: 0-0 Vi: 0-0 Tstrap: 0-0 Ckp: 0-0
Best Rating: **76** 10/09 Kemp 7f stand

Fair; stays 7f; acts on Polytrack.

Toto Skyllachy

108(100) (84)**89**
4-y-o b g Kyllachy-Little Tramp (Trempolino (USA))
S Gollings (T P Tate 18/7) P J Martin

Placings:R41/2650-01053405 **(7617)**
2009: 8^{0}GF, 8^{1}GS, 8^{0}G, 8^{5}HY, 7^{3}SD, 7^{4}S, 7^{0}S, 7^{5}SD,

	Starts	1st	2nd	3rd	Win & Pl
Career Total (Turf)	13	2	1	0	18853
Career Total (AW)	2	0	0	1	891

89 5/09 Ripn 1m (0-100)H G-S £11354
81 7/07 Wwck 7f26y SFT £4857
Total win prize-money £16212

Going (Turf): **Sf: 1-5 GS: 1-3** Gd: 0-2 GF: 0-3 Fm: 0-0
Distance: 5f/6f: 0-2 **7f-8f: 2-8** 9f-13f: 0-5 14f+: 0-0
Track : LH: 1-8 RH: 1-5 **Tight: 1-4** Gall: 0-2
Aids: Bl: 0-0 Vi: 0-0 Tstrap: 0-0 Ckp: 0-0
Best Rating: **89** 5/09 Ripn 1m gd-sft

Useful; effective over 7f-1m and acts well on soft ground.

Tottie

104(87) (55)**95**
3-y-o b f Fantastic Light (USA)-Katy Nowaitee (Komaite (USA))
Mrs A J Perrett J H Richmond-Watson

Placings:0415-305546 **(4715)**
2009: 11^{3}GF, 12^{0}G, 10^{5}GF, 10^{5}G, 9^{4}G, 10^{6}GS,

	Starts	1st	2nd	3rd	Win & Pl
Career Total (Turf)	9	1	0	1	11936
Career Total (AW)	1	0	0	0	

87 10/08 Brig 7f214y GD £3469
Total win prize-money £3469

Going (Turf): Sf: 0-0 GS: 0-3 **Gd: 1-4** GF: 0-2 Fm: 0-0
Distance: 5f/6f: 0-0 **7f-8f: 1-3** 9f-13f: 0-7 14f+: 0-0
Track : **LH: 1-6** RH: 0-3 Tight: 0-3 Gall: 0-2
Aids: Bl: 0-2 Vi: 0-0 Tstrap: 0-1 Ckp: 0-1
Best Rating: **95** 11/08 NmkR 1m gd-sft

Very useful; stays 1m3f; acts on good and easy ground.

Touch Of Style (IRE)

89(102) (63)**70**
5-y-o b g Desert Style (IRE)-No Hard Feelings (IRE) (Alzao (USA))
T D McCarthy (J R Boyle 25/2) Inside Track Racing Club

Placings:40/502016002/3002450000-56035000 **(6770)**
2009: 10^{5}SD, 12^{6}SD, 11^{0}SD, 10^{3}SD, 10^{5}SD, 10^{0}G, 10^{0}GF, 12^{0}SD,

	Starts	1st	2nd	3rd	Win & Pl
Career Total (Turf)	9	0	1	0	1733
Career Total (AW)	20	1	2	2	5605

81 9/07 Kemp 1m (0-75)H STD £2817
Total win prize-money £2817

Going (Turf): **Sf: 0-2 GS: 0-0 Gd: 0-4 GF: 0-3 Fm: 0-0**
Distance: 5f/6f: 0-0 **7f-8f: 1-9** 9f-13f: 0-19 14f+: 0-1
Track : LH: 0-14 **RH: 1-12** Tight: 0-9 Gall: 0-3
Aids: Bl: 0-0 Vi: 0-3 Tstrap: 0-8 Ckp: 0-8
Best Rating: **81** 9/07 Kemp 1m stand

Moderate; effective at around 1m2f; acts on fast ground and Polytrack.

Touch Tone

88 **67**
2-y-o b f Selkirk (USA)-Payphone (Anabaa (USA))
B W Hills K Abdulla

Placings:65 **(5397)**
2009: 7^{6}GS, 7^{5}GF,

	Starts	1st	2nd	3rd	Win & Pl
Career Total (Turf)	2	0	0	0	0

Going (Turf): **Sf: 0-0 GS: 0-1 Gd: 0-0 GF: 0-1 Fm: 0-0**
Distance: 5f/6f: 0-0 7f-8f: 0-2 9f-13f: 0-0 14f+: 0-0
Track : LH: 0-0 RH: 0-0 Tight: 0-0 Gall: 0-0
Aids: Bl: 0-0 Vi: 0-0 Tstrap: 0-0 Ckp: 0-0
Best Rating: **67** 8/09 NmkJ 7f gd-fm

Touching (IRE)

88(97) (78)**92**
3-y-o b f Kheleyf (USA)-Feminine Touch (IRE) (Sadler's Wells (USA))
R Hannon T Hely-Hutchinson & Lord Donoughmore

Placings:31336-0006 **(7181)**
2009: 7^{0}S, 8^{0}SD, 8^{0}GF, 7^{6}SD,

	Starts	1st	2nd	3rd	Win & Pl
Career Total (Turf)	6	0	0	3	5522
Career Total (AW)	3	1	0	0	3886

78 7/08 Kemp 6f STD £3885
Total win prize-money £3886

Going (Turf): **Sf: 0-1 GS: 0-0 Gd: 0-1 GF: 0-4 Fm: 0-0**
Distance: **5f/6f: 1-2** 7f-8f: 0-6 9f-13f: 0-1 14f+: 0-0
Track : LH: 0-0 **RH: 1-6** Tight: 0-0 Gall: 0-1
Aids: Bl: 0-0 Vi: 0-0 Tstrap: 0-0 Ckp: 0-0
Best Rating: **92** 10/08 NmkR 7f gd-fm

Very useful; Listed placed; effective over 6f-7f; acts on good/fast ground and on Polytrack.

Toufan Express

109 (75)**87**
7-y-o ch g Fraam-Clan Scotia (Clantime)
Adrian McGuinness Our Lads Syndicate

Placings:5300/101/66/401-2003233343300110 **(6678)**
2009: 8^{2}SD, 8^{0}SD, 9^{0}G, 8^{3}GF, 8^{2}G, 8^{3}GF, 9^{3}Y, 8^{3}S, 7^{4}SH, 9^{3}S, 8^{3}G, 9^{0}GY, 8^{0}S, 7^{1}Y, 6^{1}G, 6^{0}G,

	Starts	1st	2nd	3rd	Win & Pl
Career Total (Turf)	26	5	1	7	74990
Career Total (AW)	2	0	1	0	4172

87 9/09 Curr 6f H GD £33498
82 9/09 List 7f (60-100)H YLD £15168
70 10/08 Gowr 1m (50-70)H HVY £5080
79 6/06 Leop 1m1f (40-70)H G-F £5242
78 4/06 Gowr 1m1f100y (40-70)H GD £5242
Total win prize-money £64232

Going (Turf): Sf: 1-4 GS: 0-0 **Gd: 2-7** GF: 1-6 Fm: 0-1
Distance: 5f/6f: 1-2 7f-8f: 2-13 9f-13f: 2-13 14f+: 0-0
Track : LH: 2-13 RH: 2-11 Tight: 0-0 Gall: 0-1
Aids: Bl: 0-1 Vi: 0-0 Tstrap: 0-0 Ckp: 0-0
Best Rating: **87** 10/09 York 6f good

Useful; suited by 6f-7f; acts on good and softer ground.

Tough Regime (IRE)

53(86) (63)**21**
2-y-o ch f Trans Island-Lady Naryana (IRE) (Val Royal (FR))
Niall Moran Thirty Something Syndicate

Placings:000404 **(7816)**
2009: 6^{0}S, 7^{0}YS, 7^{0}S, 7^{4}SD, 9^{0}SD, 8^{4}SD,

	Starts	1st	2nd	3rd	Win & Pl
Career Total (Turf)	3	0	0	0	
Career Total (AW)	3	0	0	0	730

Going (Turf): **Sf: 0-2 GS: 0-0 Gd: 0-0 GF: 0-0 Fm: 0-0**
Distance: 5f/6f: 0-1 7f-8f: 0-3 9f-13f: 0-2 14f+: 0-0
Track : LH: 0-4 RH: 0-2 Tight: 0-2 Gall: 0-0
Aids: Bl: 0-0 Vi: 0-0 Tstrap: 0-0 Ckp: 0-0
Best Rating: **63** 11/09 Dund 7f stand

Moderate; effective over 7f; acts on Polytrack.

Toujours Souriante

108 **76**
3-y-o b f Lucky Story (USA)-Tous Les Jours (USA) (Dayjur (USA))
Miss Tracy Waggott (M Johnston 14/8) On The Way Up

Placings:0033010 **(4988)**
2009: 7^{0}GF, 8^{0}GF, 8^{3}GF, 9^{3}GF, 12^{0}G, 13^{1}G, 13^{0}GF,

	Starts	1st	2nd	3rd	Win & Pl
Career Total (Turf)	7	1	0	2	6647

76 7/09 Haml 1m5f9y (0-85)H GD £5828
Total win prize-money £5828

Going (Turf): Sf: 0-0 GS: 0-0 **Gd: 1-2** GF: 0-5 Fm: 0-0
Distance: 5f/6f: 0-0 7f-8f: 0-1 9f-13f: 0-4 **14f+: 1-2**
Track : LH: 0-3 **RH: 1-4 Tight: 1-3** Gall: 0-1
Aids: Bl: 0-0 Vi: 0-0 Tstrap: 0-0 Ckp: 0-0
Best Rating: **76** 7/09 Haml 1m5f9y good

Modest; stays 1m5f; acts on good and faster ground.

Tour D'Amour (IRE)

91(105) (54)**55**
6-y-o b m Fruits Of Love (USA)-Touraneena (Robellino (USA))
R Craggs Ray Craggs

Placings:0305043100064602 01/13323323050 0/264240020255/555503-4401 (3545)
2009: 8^{4}SD, 10^{4}GS, 9^{0}GF, 10^{1}F,

	Starts	1st	2nd	3rd	Win & Pl
Career Total (Turf)	32	2	4	6	17511
Career Total (AW)	20	2	3	2	8622

55	7/09	Rdcr	1m2f	(0-70)H	FRM	£3238
59	3/06	Sthl	7f		STD	£2388
64	12/05	Sthl	7f		STD	£2518
63	7/05	Wwck	7f26y		G-F	£3393

Total win prize-money £11538

Going (Turf): Sf: 0-3 GS: 0-4 Gd: 0-11 **GF: 1-11 Fm: 1-3**
Distance: 5f/6f: 0-6 **7f-8f: 3-33** 9f-13f: 1-13 14f+: 0-0
Track : **LH: 4-33** RH: 0-5 **Tight: 1-15** Gall: 0-4
Aids: Bl: 0-8 Vi: 0-0 Tstrap: 1-1 Ckp: 1-1
Best Rating: 71 6/06 Thsk 1m gd-fm

Moderate; stays 1m; acts on fast and soft ground; has worn cheekpieces.

Tourist

95(107) (88)**80**
4-y-o b g Oasis Dream-West Devon (USA) (Gone West (USA))
D Shaw M Shirley

Placings:03/410-43235026305050 2101334 (7866)
2009: 8^{4}SD, 8^{3}SD, 9^{2}SD, 9^{3}SD, 8^{5}SD, 10^{0}G, 8^{2}SD, 8^{6}SD, 8^{3}SD, 7^{0}SD, 7^{5}GF, 8^{0}SD, 8^{5}GF, 9^{0}SD, 8^{2}SD, 7^{1}SD, 7^{0}SD, 5^{1}SD, 7^{3}SD, 7^{3}SD, 5^{4}SS,

	Starts	1st	2nd	3rd	Win & Pl
Career Total (Turf)	8	1	0	1	3151
Career Total (AW)	18	2	3	5	16939

88	11/09	Wolv	5f216y	(0-75)H	STD	£3238
84	10/09	Wolv	7f32y	(0-70)H	STD	£3238
80	6/08	Nott	1m75y		G-F	£2428

Total win prize-money £8904

Going (Turf): Sf: 0-1 GS: 0-0 Gd: 0-3 **GF: 1-4** Fm: 0-0
Distance: 5f/6f: 1-2 7f-8f: 1-12 9f-13f: 1-12 14f+: 0-0
Track : **LH: 3-17** RH: 0-6 **Tight: 2-13** Gall: 0-2
Aids: Bl: 0-0 Vi: 0-0 Tstrap: 0-0 Ckp: 0-0
Best Rating: 88 11/09 Wolv 5f216y stand

Useful; effective at 6f-1m; acts on fast ground; goes on Polytrack.

Tournedos (IRE)

105(95) (75)**105**
7-y-o b g Rossini (USA)-Don't Care (IRE) (Nordico (USA))
D Nicholls Mike Browne

Placings:12201032526/0000105440/0510540/000400600410/010-0400000040 (6670)
2009: 5^{0}SD, 5^{4}GF, 5^{0}G, 5^{0}GF, 5^{0}G, 5^{0}GF, 5^{0}GF, 6^{0}G, 5^{4}GF, 5^{0}SD,

	Starts	1st	2nd	3rd	Win & Pl
Career Total (Turf)	50	6	4	1	155760
Career Total (AW)	4	0	0	0	

105	5/08	York	5f	(0-100)H	G-F	£16513
97	9/07	Curr	5f	(60-100)H	YLD	£11436
103	7/06	Ches	5f16y		G-F	£15898
108	7/05	Ches	5f16y		G-F	£17400
102	7/04	Gdwd	5f	A	GD	£23200
92	4/04	Newb	5f34y	D	GD	£5694

Total win prize-money £90142

Going (Turf): Sf: 0-5 GS: 0-3 Gd: 2-23 **GF: 3-15** Fm: 0-1
Distance: **5f/6f: 6-52** 7f-8f: 0-2 9f-13f: 0-0 14f+: 0-0
Track : **LH: 2-14** RH: 0-1 **Tight: 2-9** Gall: 0-3
Aids: Bl: 0-0 Vi: 0-0 Tstrap: 0-2 Ckp: 0-2
Best Rating: 108 7/06 Curr 5f gd-fm

Very useful; stays 6f, but best at 5f; handles most types of ground; has been tried in cheekpieces.

Tous Les Deux

(107) (87)**70**
6-y-o b g Efisio-Caerosa (Caerleon (USA))
G L Moore A Grinter

Placings:2150/3205650002231454/0614630500306432300 5455/000010103102-0112326 (1283)
2009: 7^{0}SD, 8^{1}SD, 8^{1}SD, 7^{2}SD, 8^{3}SD, 8^{2}SD, 8^{6}SD,

	Starts	1st	2nd	3rd	Win & Pl
Career Total (Turf)	15	1	1	1	6543
Career Total (AW)	47	7	7	7	36480

83	2/09	Kemp	1m	(0-85)H	STD	£4857
80	2/09	Ling	1m	(0-75)H	STD	£2729
77	11/08	Kemp	1m	(0-65)H	STD	£2047
71	10/08	Kemp	6f	(0-60)H	STD	£2047
66	8/08	Wolv	1m141y	(0-55)H	STD	£2729
77	1/07	Ling	1m2f	(0-70)H	STD	£2914
76	11/06	Wolv	1m1f103y	(0-70)H	STD	£3886
76	5/05	Wind	5f10y		G-F	£4888

Total win prize-money £26100

Going (Turf): Sf: 0-3 GS: 0-2 Gd: 0-5 **GF: 1-5** Fm: 0-0
Distance: 5f/6f: 2-22 7f-8f: 3-15 9f-13f: 3-25 14f+: 0-0
Track : **LH: 4-41** RH: 3-11 **Tight: 4-39** Gall: 1-4
Aids: Bl: 0-0 Vi: 0-0 Tstrap: 0-0 Ckp: 0-0
Best Rating: 87 3/09 Wolv 7f32y stand

Fair; stays 1m2f but effective over 6f; acts well on Polytrack.

Towanda (USA)

88(91) (53)**60**
3-y-o b f Dynaformer (USA)-Desert Gold (USA) (Seeking The Gold (USA))
J H M Gosden H R H Princess Haya Of Jordan

Placings:64 (1430)
2009: 9^{6}GF, 12^{4}SD,

	Starts	1st	2nd	3rd	Win & Pl
Career Total (Turf)	1	0	0	0	0
Career Total (AW)	1	0	0	0	192

Going (Turf): **Sf: 0-0 GS: 0-0 Gd: 0-0 GF: 0-1 Fm: 0-0**
Distance: 5f/6f: 0-0 7f-8f: 0-0 9f-13f: 0-2 14f+: 0-0
Track : LH: 0-0 RH: 0-2 Tight: 0-1 Gall: 0-0
Aids: Bl: 0-0 Vi: 0-0 Tstrap: 0-0 Ckp: 0-0
Best Rating: 60 4/09 Folk 1m1f149y gd-fm

Towbaat

85 **69**
2-y-o b f Halling (USA)-Nasmatt (Danehill (USA))
M A Jarvis Sheikh Ahmed Al Maktoum

Placings:0 (6920)
2009: 8^{0}GF,

	Starts	1st	2nd	3rd	Win & Pl
Career Total (Turf)	1	0	0	0	

Going (Turf): **Sf: 0-0 GS: 0-0 Gd: 0-0 GF: 0-1 Fm: 0-0**
Distance: 5f/6f: 0-0 7f-8f: 0-0 9f-13f: 0-1 14f+: 0-0
Track : LH: 0-0 RH: 0-0 Tight: 0-0 Gall: 0-0
Aids: Bl: 0-0 Vi: 0-0 Tstrap: 0-0 Ckp: 0-0
Best Rating: 69 10/09 Yarm 1m3y gd-fm

Town And Gown

95(95) (73)**56**
4-y-o br f Oasis Dream-Degree (Warning)
J S Goldie The Vital Sparks

Placings:00243/30345060-000002544 (6160)
2009: 5^{0}GF, 5^{0}G, 5^{0}G, 5^{0}GF, 6^{0}GF, 5^{2}GS, 5^{5}G, 5^{4}GS, 5^{4}G,

	Starts	1st	2nd	3rd	Win & Pl
Career Total (Turf)	14	0	1	1	1849
Career Total (AW)	8	0	1	2	1567

Going (Turf): **Sf: 0-0 GS: 0-3 Gd: 0-5 GF: 0-6 Fm: 0-0**
Distance: 5f/6f: 0-21 7f-8f: 0-1 9f-13f: 0-0 14f+: 0-0
Track : LH: 0-7 RH: 0-1 Tight: 0-5 Gall: 0-1
Aids: Bl: 0-0 Vi: 0-0 Tstrap: 0-1 Ckp: 0-1
Best Rating: 73 10/07 Ling 6f stand

Modest; effective from 5f-6f; acts on fast ground and Polytrack.

Town House

95(102) (53)**57**
7-y-o gr m Paris House-Avondale Girl (IRE) (Case Law)
B P J Baugh J H Chrimes

Placings:50210000/0000040/350060560/263000000/4325610666-00005630050 (7100)
2009: 5^{0}SD, 5^{0}SF, 5^{0}HY, 5^{0}GF, 5^{5}G, 5^{6}GS, 5^{3}GS, 5^{0}G, 5^{0}GF, 5^{5}GF, 5^{0}G,

	Starts	1st	2nd	3rd	Win & Pl
Career Total (Turf)	33	2	1	1	7169
Career Total (AW)	21	0	2	3	1824

57	6/08	Leic	5f2y	(0-70)H	G-F	£2498
66	5/04	Nott	5f13y	H	G-F	£1655

Total win prize-money £4154

Going (Turf): Sf: 0-4 GS: 0-4 Gd: 0-10 **GF: 2-14** Fm: 0-1
Distance: **5f/6f: 2-54** 7f-8f: 0-0 9f-13f: 0-0 14f+: 0-0
Track : LH: 0-24 RH: 0-0 Tight: 0-21 Gall: 0-1
Aids: Bl: 0-0 Vi: 0-0 Tstrap: 0-0 Ckp: 0-0
Best Rating: 68 5/04 Ches 5f16y soft

Moderate; effective over 5f-6f; acts on fast and soft ground; handles Polytrack.

Towneley Arms (IRE)

76 **46**
2-y-o b c Pyrus (USA)-Grangeclare Lily (UAE) (Green Desert (USA))
G A Harker John J Maguire

Placings:0 (4396)
2009: 7^{0}GF,

	Starts	1st	2nd	3rd	Win & Pl
Career Total (Turf)	1	0	0	0	

Going (Turf): **Sf: 0-0 GS: 0-0 Gd: 0-0 GF: 0-1 Fm: 0-0**
Distance: 5f/6f: 0-0 7f-8f: 0-1 9f-13f: 0-0 14f+: 0-0
Track : LH: 0-0 RH: 0-1 Tight: 0-0 Gall: 0-0
Aids: Bl: 0-0 Vi: 0-0 Tstrap: 0-0 Ckp: 0-0
Best Rating: 46 7/09 Bevl 7f100y gd-fm

Towthorpe

94 **65**
3-y-o ch g Tobougg (IRE)-Snow Shoes (Sri Pekan (USA))
M Brittain Mel Brittain

Placings:34000 (5954)
2009: 7^{3}GF, 8^{4}GF, 9^{0}GF, 8^{0}S, 7^{0}GF,

	Starts	1st	2nd	3rd	Win & Pl
Career Total (Turf)	5	0	0	1	746

Going (Turf): Sf: 0-1 GS: 0-0 Gd: 0-0 GF: 0-4 Fm: 0-0
Distance: 5f/6f: 0-0 7f-8f: 0-3 9f-13f: 0-2 14f+: 0-0
Track : LH: 0-2 RH: 0-1 Tight: 0-2 Gall: 0-0
Aids: Bl: 0-0 Vi: 0-0 Tstrap: 0-0 Ckp: 0-0
Best Rating: 65 8/09 Pont 1m4y gd-fm

Towy Boy (IRE)

101(99) (71)70

4-y-o b g King Charlemagne (USA)-Solar Flare (IRE) (Danehill (USA))
I A Wood C R Lambourne

Placings:3050200/3002622250-000600424U235463 **(6880)**
2009: 6^{0}SD, 6^{0}SD, 6^{0}G, 5^{6}SD, 5^{0}GS, 6^{0}G, 6^{4}GF, 6^{2}GF, 6^{4}SD, 5^{U}S, 6^{2}SD, 5^{3}GF, 5^{5}G, 5^{4}SD, 5^{6}GF, 7^{3}SD,

	Starts	1st	2nd	3rd	Win & Pl
Career Total (Turf)	17	0	4	2	4455
Career Total (AW)	16	0	3	2	3011

Going (Turf): Sf: 0-2 GS: 0-3 Gd: 0-5 GF: 0-6 Fm: 0-1
Distance: 5f/6f: 0-24 7f-8f: 0-9 9f-13f: 0-0 14f+: 0-0
Track : LH: 0-19 RH: 0-4 Tight: 0-10 Gall: 0-7
Aids: Bl: 0-1 Vi: 0-10 Tstrap: 0-0 Ckp: 0-0
Best Rating: 71 9/08 GrLe 6f stand

Moderate; effective over 6f-7f; acts on good ground; goes on Polytrack; has worn a visor and a tongue tie.

Towy Valley

92(103) (75)67

4-y-o b f Bertolini (USA)-Ulysses Daughter (IRE) (College Chapel)
C G Cox The Godparents

Placings:02-413245 **(1412)**
2009: 6^{4}SD, 5^{1}SD, 5^{3}SD, 5^{2}SD, 5^{4}GF, 5^{5}SD,

	Starts	1st	2nd	3rd	Win & Pl
Career Total (Turf)	2	0	0	0	192
Career Total (AW)	6	1	2	1	6689

71 1/09 Kemp 5f STD £4727
Total win prize-money £4727

Going (Turf): Sf: 0-0 GS: 0-1 Gd: 0-0 GF: 0-1 Fm: 0-0
Distance: 5f/6f: 1-8 7f-8f: 0-0 9f-13f: 0-0 14f+: 0-0
Track : LH: 0-3 RH: 1-4 Tight: 0-2 Gall: 0-2
Aids: Bl: 0-0 Vi: 0-0 Tstrap: 0-0 Ckp: 0-0
Best Rating: 75 3/09 Wolv 5f20y stand

Modest; effective over 6f; acts on Polytrack.

Toy Razor (IRE)

78 41

2-y-o b c Refuse To Bend (IRE)-Child Prodigy (IRE) (Ballad Rock)
H Candy Tony Bloom

Placings:0 **(6451)**
2009: 7^{0}GF,

	Starts	1st	2nd	3rd	Win & Pl
Career Total (Turf)	1	0	0	0	

Going (Turf): Sf: 0-0 GS: 0-0 Gd: 0-0 GF: 0-1 Fm: 0-0
Distance: 5f/6f: 0-0 7f-8f: 0-1 9f-13f: 0-0 14f+: 0-0
Track : LH: 0-0 RH: 0-0 Tight: 0-0 Gall: 0-0
Aids: Bl: 0-0 Vi: 0-0 Tstrap: 0-0 Ckp: 0-0
Best Rating: 41 10/09 NmkR 7f gd-fm

Toy Top (USA)

103 (14)69

6-y-o gr/ro m Tactical Cat (USA)-I'll Flutter By (USA) (Concorde's Tune (USA))
M Dods D Vic Roper

Placings:60000530/22134311240500/00000403426110040/0035010000-0012260400 **(6220)**
2009: 5^{0}F, 5^{0}GS, 5^{1}F, 5^{2}GF, 5^{2}G, 5^{6}G, 5^{0}GF, 5^{4}G, 5^{0}GF, 5^{0}GF,

	Starts	1st	2nd	3rd	Win & Pl
Career Total (Turf)	58	7	6	5	39903
Career Total (AW)	1	0	0	0	

61	6/09	Thsk	5f	(0-75)H	FRM	£4274
69	6/08	Thsk	5f	(0-65)H	FRM	£2729
67	8/07	Catt	5f	(0-65)H	G-F	£2730
71	8/07	Thsk	5f	(0-70)H	G-F	£3886
84	7/06	Wwck	5f	(0-80)H	GD	£6477
75	6/06	Newc	5f	(0-75)H	G-F	£4857
68	4/06	Catt	5f	(0-60)H	FRM	£3412

Total win prize-money £28368

Going (Turf): Sf: 0-3 GS: 0-8 Gd: 1-16 GF: 3-23 Fm: 3-8
Distance: 5f/6f: 7-58 7f-8f: 0-1 9f-13f: 0-0 14f+: 0-0
Track : LH: 1-5 RH: 0-2 Tight: 0-5 Gall: 0-1
Aids: Bl: 7-55 Vi: 0-0 Tstrap: 0-0 Ckp: 0-0
Best Rating: 87 7/06 Hayd 5f gd-fm

Modest; best over 5f and acts on most ground; has worn blinkers.

Trachonitis (IRE)

96(108) (76)86

5-y-o b g Dansili-Hasina (IRE) (King's Theatre (IRE))
J R Jenkins Mr & Mrs C Schwick

Placings:23334/44106/0621213500-0306514501 **(7851)**
2009: 11^{0}GS, 13^{0}GF, 13^{0}GF, 12^{6}GF, 14^{5}G, 12^{1}GF, 12^{4}G, 13^{5}SS, 12^{0}SD, 11^{1}SS,

	Starts	1st	2nd	3rd	Win & Pl
Career Total (Turf)	21	3	1	5	24235
Career Total (AW)	9	2	2	0	7339

76	12/09	Sthl	1m3f	(0-75)H	SS	£2729
76	9/09	Gdwd	1m4f	(0-85)H	G-F	£5180
86	5/08	NmkR	1m6f	(0-85)H	FRM	£5180
82	2/08	Kemp	2m	(0-70)H	STD	£2590
71	7/07	Wxfd	1m5f		YLD	£4668

Total win prize-money £20352

Going (Turf): Sf: 0-1 GS: 0-1 Gd: 0-5 GF: 1-7 Fm: 1-2
Distance: 5f/6f: 0-0 7f-8f: 0-5 9f-13f: 3-17 14f+: 2-8
Track : LH: 1-14 RH: 4-15 Tight: 1-10 Gall: 1-5
Aids: Bl: 0-0 Vi: 0-0 Tstrap: 0-0 Ckp: 0-0
Best Rating: 86 5/08 NmkR 1m6f firm

Modest; ex-Irish; stays 2m but effective at shorter; acts on most ground and on sand.

Trade Centre

102(105) (77)79

4-y-o b g Dubai Destination (USA)-Khubza (Green Desert (USA))
George Baker (W R Muir 9/12) Sir Alex Ferguson

Placings:21430000130314 **(7845)**
2009: 5^{2}SD, 6^{1}SD, 6^{4}SD, 6^{3}G, 7^{0}GF, 7^{0}GS, 7^{0}SF, 7^{0}SD, 7^{1}SD, 7^{3}SS, 8^{0}SD, 7^{3}SD, 7^{1}SD, 7^{4}SD,

	Starts	1st	2nd	3rd	Win & Pl
Career Total (Turf)	3	0	0	1	403
Career Total (AW)	11	3	1	2	9582

72	12/09	Ling	7f		STD	£1978
77	9/09	Kemp	7f	(0-70)H	STD	£2590
68	3/09	Ling	6f		STD	£2590

Total win prize-money £7159

Going (Turf): Sf: 0-0 GS: 0-1 Gd: 0-1 GF: 0-1 Fm: 0-0
Distance: 5f/6f: 1-4 7f-8f: 2-10 9f-13f: 0-0 14f+: 0-0
Track : LH: 2-10 RH: 1-2 Tight: 2-9 Gall: 0-1
Aids: Bl: 0-0 Vi: 0-0 Tstrap: 0-0 Ckp: 0-0
Best Rating: 79 4/09 Wind 6f good

Fair; effective over 6f-7f; acts on Polytrack.

Trade Fairle

57(60) (4)

2-y-o ch c Trade Fair-Lady Le Quesne (IRE) (Alhaarth (IRE))
P R Webber Shully Liebermann

Placings:600 **(4219)**
2009: 5^{6}GF, 6^{0}SD, 5^{0}G,

	Starts	1st	2nd	3rd	Win & Pl
Career Total (Turf)	2	0	0	0	0
Career Total (AW)	1	0	0	0	

Going (Turf): Sf: 0-0 GS: 0-0 Gd: 0-1 GF: 0-1 Fm: 0-0
Distance: 5f/6f: 0-3 7f-8f: 0-0 9f-13f: 0-0 14f+: 0-0
Track : LH: 0-2 RH: 0-0 Tight: 0-1 Gall: 0-1
Aids: Bl: 0-0 Vi: 0-1 Tstrap: 0-0 Ckp: 0-0
Best Rating: 4 7/09 Ling 6f stand

Trade Name (IRE)

92(78) (44)62

2-y-o b f Trade Fair-Red Rabbit (Suave Dancer (USA))
H Candy Henry Candy

Placings:045 **(7061)**
2009: 7^{0}SD, 6^{4}GS, 5^{5}GF,

	Starts	1st	2nd	3rd	Win & Pl
Career Total (Turf)	2	0	0	0	0
Career Total (AW)	1	0	0	0	

Going (Turf): Sf: 0-0 GS: 0-1 Gd: 0-0 GF: 0-1 Fm: 0-0
Distance: 5f/6f: 0-2 7f-8f: 0-1 9f-13f: 0-0 14f+: 0-0
Track : LH: 0-1 RH: 0-0 Tight: 0-1 Gall: 0-0
Aids: Bl: 0-1 Vi: 0-0 Tstrap: 0-0 Ckp: 0-0
Best Rating: 62 10/09 Leic 5f218y gd-fm

Modest; stays 6f; acts on fast ground.

Trade Price (GR)

95(86) (30)50

3-y-o b g Kyllachy-Snowdrift (Desert Prince (IRE))
I Semple (J A Osborne 30/4) A Gauley

Placings:5040305050 **(6415)**
2009: 5^{5}SD, 5^{0}GF, 6^{4}GF, 5^{0}GF, 7^{3}GF, 6^{0}S, 5^{5}GF, 8^{0}S, 9^{5}G, 7^{0}GF,

	Starts	1st	2nd	3rd	Win & Pl
Career Total (Turf)	9	0	0	1	337
Career Total (AW)	1	0	0	0	0

Going (Turf): Sf: 0-2 GS: 0-0 Gd: 0-1 GF: 0-6 Fm: 0-0
Distance: 5f/6f: 0-4 7f-8f: 0-5 9f-13f: 0-1 14f+: 0-0
Track : LH: 0-2 RH: 0-3 Tight: 0-4 Gall: 0-0
Aids: Bl: 0-2 Vi: 0-1 Tstrap: 0-2 Ckp: 0-2
Best Rating: 50 6/09 Muss 7f30y gd-fm

Moderate; stays at least 7f; acts on fast ground; has worn various headgear.

Trade Secret

94 71

2-y-o b c Trade Fair-Kastaway (Distant Relative)

M Brittain Mel Brittain

Placings:424256 (6646)

2009: 5^{4}GF, 5^{2}GF, 6^{4}G, 5^{2}GS, 5^{5}GF, 6^{6}G,

	Starts	1st	2nd	3rd	Win & Pl
Career Total (Turf)	6	0	2	0	4979

Going (Turf): Sf: 0-0 GS: 0-1 Gd: 0-2 GF: 0-3 Fm: 0-0
Distance: 5f/6f: 0-6 7f-8f: 0-0 9f-13f: 0-0 14f+: 0-0
Track : LH: 0-0 RH: 0-0 Tight: 0-0 Gall: 0-0
Aids: Bl: 0-0 Vi: 0-0 Tstrap: 0-0 Ckp: 0-0
Best Rating: 71 6/09 York 5f gd-sft

Cheaply-bought half-brother to a 5f winner out of a multiple winning juvenile and related to several winning two-year-olds; fair form; acts on fast and easy ground.

Trading Nation (USA)

97(72) 74

3-y-o b g Tiznow (USA)-Nidd (USA) (Known Fact (USA))

P W Hiatt (R Charlton 11/6) Mark Goodall

Placings:5-2000 (7627)

2009: 6^{2}GF, 6^{0}GF, 7^{0}GF, 7^{0}SD,

	Starts	1st	2nd	3rd	Win & Pl
Career Total (Turf)	4	0	1	0	771
Career Total (AW)	1	0	0	0	

Going (Turf): Sf: 0-0 GS: 0-0 Gd: 0-0 GF: 0-4 Fm: 0-0
Distance: 5f/6f: 0-1 7f-8f: 0-4 9f-13f: 0-0 14f+: 0-0
Track : LH: 0-1 RH: 0-0 Tight: 0-1 Gall: 0-0
Aids: Bl: 0-0 Vi: 0-0 Tstrap: 0-0 Ckp: 0-0
Best Rating: 74 5/09 Nott 6f15y gd-fm

Fair; stays 6f; acts on fast ground.

Trafalgar Bay (IRE)

104 98

6-y-o b g Fruits Of Love (USA)-Chatsworth Bay (IRE) (Fairy King (USA))

K R Burke Mogeely Stud & Mrs Maura Gittins

Placings:21641/31506650/52000/05-515P (2927)

2009: 7^{5}GF, 8^{1}GF, 7^{5}GF, 7^{P}G,

	Starts	1st	2nd	3rd	Win & Pl
Career Total (Turf)	24	4	2	1	37106
98	4/09	Asct	1m	(0-85)H	G-F £7123
100	5/06	Asct	6f	(0-95)H	G-F £9715
90	10/05	Newb	6f8y	(0-85)	G-S £7072
78	8/05	Folk	7f		GD £3100

Total win prize-money £27013

Going (Turf): Sf: 0-4 GS: 1-6 Gd: 1-4 GF: 2-9 Fm: 0-1
Distance: 5f/6f: 1-8 7f-8f: 3-16 9f-13f: 0-0 14f+: 0-0
Track : LH: 0-3 RH: 0-1 Tight: 0-1 Gall: 0-1
Aids: Bl: 0-0 Vi: 0-0 Tstrap: 0-0 Ckp: 0-0
Best Rating: 100 5/07 NmkR 6f gd-sft

Very useful; effective over 6f-1m; acts on most ground; usually held up.

Trafalgar Square

94(110) (89)73

7-y-o b g King's Best (USA)-Pat Or Else (Alzao (USA))

M J Attwater Canisbay Bloodstock

Placings:0/5660314130/6561000/100/30060066**4006215-113000000020065** (7603)

2009: 7^{1}SD, 7^{1}SD, 7^{3}SD, 8^{0}GF, 7^{0}G, 7^{0}SD, 8^{0}SD, 8^{0}G, 9^{0}GF, 8^{0}SD, 7^{0}SD, 7^{2}SS, 8^{0}G, 7^{0}SD, 7^{6}SD, 8^{5}SD,

	Starts	1st	2nd	3rd	Win & Pl
Career Total (Turf)	34	4	0	3	35380
Career Total (AW)	18	3	2	1	15288
89	1/09	Ling	7f	(0-85)H	STD £4857
86	1/09	Ling	7f	(0-75)H	STD £2900
80	12/08	Ling	1m	(0-75)H	STD £2729
96	5/07	NmkR	7f	(0-95)H	GD £9067
92	5/06	Gdwd	1m	(0-85)H	SFT £7124
80	9/05	Rdcr	7f	(0-75)	G-F £5876
81	7/05	Yarm	7f3y	(0-70)H	G-S £4147

Total win prize-money £36704

Going (Turf): Sf: 1-5 GS: 1-5 Gd: 1-11 GF: 1-12 Fm: 0-1
Distance: 5f/6f: 0-0 7f-8f: 7-43 9f-13f: 0-9 14f+: 0-0
Track : LH: 3-10 RH: 1-25 Tight: 3-15 Gall: 0-2
Aids: Bl: 0-0 Vi: 0-0 Tstrap: 0-3 Ckp: 0-3
Best Rating: 96 5/07 NmkR 7f good

Fair; stays 1m; acts on most ground and on Polytrack.

Traffic Guard (USA)

110(97) (89)121

5-y-o b h More Than Ready (USA)-Street Scene (IRE) (Zafonic (USA))

P F I Cole (H J Brown 26/2) Mrs Fitri Hay

Placings:110/**2260**4120/540320225-66634120 (6890a)

2009: 8^{6}GF, 8^{6}G, 9^{6}FT, 10^{3}GS, 10^{4}G, 11^{1}GF, 12^{2}GF, 12^{0}GS,

	Starts	1st	2nd	3rd	Win & Pl
Career Total (Turf)	24	4	5	2	277963
Career Total (AW)	4	0	2	0	51410
114	8/09	Wind	1m3f135y		G-F £22708
105	7/07	NmkJ	1m		G-F £12464
97	9/06	NmkR	6f		G-F £7124
87	7/06	Newb	6f8y		GD £6477

Total win prize-money £48774

Going (Turf): Sf: 0-0 GS: 0-3 Gd: 1-11 GF: 3-9 Fm: 0-0
Distance: 5f/6f: 1-1 7f-8f: 2-11 9f-13f: 1-16 14f+: 0-0
Track : LH: 0-15 RH: 0-5 Tight: 1-3 Gall: 0-12
Aids: Bl: 0-0 Vi: 0-0 Tstrap: 1-7 Ckp: 1-7
Best Rating: 121 9/08 Leop 1m2f yield

Listed class; placed in Group company; stays 1m4f; acts on fast and easy ground and on sand; has worn cheekpieces.

Trailblazing

93 86

2-y-o b c Green Desert (USA)-Pioneer Bride (USA) (Gone West (USA))

M Johnston Sheikh Hamdan Bin Mohammed Al Maktoum

Placings:62103 (6471)

2009: 6^{6}GF, 5^{2}G, 6^{1}G, 6^{0}GF, 7^{3}GF,

	Starts	1st	2nd	3rd	Win & Pl
Career Total (Turf)	5	1	1	1	10237
82	7/09	Asct	6f	GD	£7771

Total win prize-money £7771

Going (Turf): Sf: 0-0 GS: 0-0 Gd: 1-2 GF: 0-3 Fm: 0-0
Distance: 5f/6f: 1-3 7f-8f: 0-2 9f-13f: 0-0 14f+: 0-0
Track : LH: 0-1 RH: 0-1 Tight: 0-1 Gall: 0-0
Aids: Bl: 0-0 Vi: 0-0 Tstrap: 0-0 Ckp: 0-0
Best Rating: 86 10/09 Epsm 7f gd-fm

Useful; suited by 6f but stays 7f; acts on fast ground.

Tranos (USA)

78 (65)10

6-y-o b g Bahri (USA)-Balancoire (USA) (Diesis)

Micky Hammond Joe Buzzeo

Placings:04600603/060/6 (3035)

2009: 12^{6}GS,

	Starts	1st	2nd	3rd	Win & Pl
Career Total (Turf)	10	0	0	1	698
Career Total (AW)	2	0	0	0	0

Going (Turf): Sf: 0-1 GS: 0-2 Gd: 0-4 GF: 0-3 Fm: 0-0
Distance: 5f/6f: 0-0 7f-8f: 0-2 9f-13f: 0-10 14f+: 0-0
Track : LH: 0-7 RH: 0-3 Tight: 0-3 Gall: 0-4
Aids: Bl: 0-0 Vi: 0-2 Tstrap: 0-0 Ckp: 0-0
Best Rating: 65 8/06 Kemp 1m2f stand

Moderate; effective at around 1m2f; acts on fast ground.

Tranquil Tiger

111(113) (112)117

5-y-o ch h Selkirk (USA)-Serene View (USA) (Distant View (USA))

H R A Cecil K Abdulla

Placings:6/21510014/041212515-130311 (7809)

2009: 9^{1}GF, 10^{3}G, 10^{0}G, 10^{3}G, 10^{1}SD, 10^{1}SD,

	Starts	1st	2nd	3rd	Win & Pl
Career Total (Turf)	22	7	3	2	119447
Career Total (AW)	2	2	0	0	45416
112	12/09	Ling	1m2f		STD £22708
108	11/09	Ling	1m2f		STD £22708
115	5/09	Gdwd	1m1f192y		G-F £22708
106	6/08	Pont	1m4f8y		G-F £16824
117	5/08	Newb	1m5f61y		GD £17031
113	9/07	Sals	1m6f21y		G-F £9971
107	7/07	NmkJ	1m5f		G-F £17034
87	5/07	NmkR	1m2f		G-F £5181

Total win prize-money £134166

Going (Turf): Sf: 0-2 GS: 0-0 Gd: 1-9 GF: 6-10 Fm: 0-1
Distance: 5f/6f: 0-0 7f-8f: 0-1 9f-13f: 7-18 14f+: 2-5
Track : LH: 4-9 RH: 4-12 Tight: 5-9 Gall: 2-9
Aids: Bl: 4-9 Vi: 0-0 Tstrap: 0-0 Ckp: 0-0
Best Rating: 117 9/08 Gdwd 1m1f192y gd-fm

Smart; multiple winner at Listed level; effective at 1m2f-1m6f; acts on good and faster ground; goes on Polytrack; has worn blinkers.

Trans Siberian

104(110) (92)92

5-y-o b g Soviet Star (USA)-Dina Line (USA) (Diesis)

P F I Cole C Shiacolas

Placings:01/2214226566-552040 (6795)

2009: 8^{5}G, 10^{5}S, 10^{2}GF, 10^{0}SD, 10^{4}GF, 10^{0}S,

	Starts	1st	2nd	3rd	Win & Pl
Career Total (Turf)	14	1	4	0	13436
Career Total (AW)	4	1	1	0	4531
87	5/08	Wind	1m2f7y (0-85)H		GD £5180
78	6/07	Wolv	1m141y		STD £2266

Total win prize-money £7448

Going (Turf): Sf: 0-3 GS: 0-3 Gd: 1-4 GF: 0-4 Fm: 0-0
Distance: 5f/6f: 0-0 7f-8f: 0-1 9f-13f: 2-17 14f+: 0-0
Track : LH: 1-6 RH: 1-12 Tight: 2-7 Gall: 0-5
Aids: Bl: 0-0 Vi: 0-0 Tstrap: 0-1 Ckp: 0-1
Best Rating: 92 5/09 Wind 1m2f7y gd-fm

Useful; effective over 1m-1m2f; acts on good and easier ground and on Polytrack; has worn cheekpieces.

Trans Sonic

81(105) (73)67

6-y-o ch g Trans Island-Sankaty Light (USA) (Summer Squall (USA))

J Hetherton (A J Lockwood 7/6) Mrs Lynne Lumley

Placings:020006/**211**006**0**00**4646**/02600/4500010010**45**-2355002 **(7855)**

2009: 12^{2}SS, 11^{3}SD, 12^{5}SD, 11^{5}SD, 7^{0}GF, 8^{0}SD, 8^{2}SS,

	Starts	1st	2nd	3rd	Win & Pl
Career Total (Turf)	26	2	2	0	7772
Career Total (AW)	17	2	3	1	14852

67	9/08	Catt	7f	(0-60)H	G-S	£2388
65	8/08	Rdcr	1m	(0-60)H	G-S	£2388
83	4/06	Kemp	1m	(0-80)H	STD	£7790
78	2/06	Ling	7f		STD	£3886

Total win prize-money £16452

Going (Turf): Sf: 0-2 **GS: 2-10** Gd: 0-6 GF: 0-8 Fm: 0-0
Distance: 5f/6f: 0-7 **7f-8f: 4-19** 9f-13f: 0-17 14f+: 0-0
Track : **LH: 2-19** RH: 1-14 **Tight: 2-8** Gall: 0-2
Aids: Bl: 1-5 Vi: 1-12 Tstrap: 0-0 Ckp: 0-0
Best Rating: 86 6/05 Gdwd 6f gd-sft

Moderate; stays 1m; acts on easy ground and on Polytrack and Fibresand; has worn blinkers.

Transcend

83(105) (100)103

5-y-o ch g Beat Hollow-Pleasuring (Good Times (ITY))

J H M Gosden H R H Princess Haya Of Jordan

Placings:04/23106201/143-0 **(3116)**

2009: 7^{0}GF,

	Starts	1st	2nd	3rd	Win & Pl
Career Total (Turf)	12	3	2	2	25138
Career Total (AW)	2	0	0	0	934

103	4/08	Thsk	7f	(0-90)H	GD	£7771
96	10/07	Brig	5f213y	(0-85)H	GD	£6309
84	5/07	NmkR	7f		G-S	£5181

Total win prize-money £19262

Going (Turf): Sf: 0-2 GS: 1-5 **Gd: 2-3** GF: 0-2 Fm: 0-0
Distance: 5f/6f: 1-2 **7f-8f: 2-11** 9f-13f: 0-1 14f+: 0-0
Track : **LH: 2-4** RH: 0-2 **Tight: 1-2** Gall: 0-0
Aids: Bl: 0-1 Vi: 0-0 Tstrap: 1-3 Ckp: 1-3
Best Rating: 103 4/08 Thsk 7f good

Very useful; effective over 6f-1m; acts on fast and easy ground, and on Polytrack; has worn cheekpieces and blinkers.

Transcentral

70(94) (54)69

3-y-o ch f Kheleyf (USA)-Khafayif (USA) (Swain (IRE))

T Wall (W M Brisbourne 13/7) Miss R E Price

Placings:4344616045-0044000 **(5326)**

2009: 5^{0}SD, 6^{0}F, 5^{4}SD, 5^{4}SD, 5^{0}SD, 5^{0}SF, 6^{0}SD,

	Starts	1st	2nd	3rd	Win & Pl
Career Total (Turf)	8	1	0	1	6646
Career Total (AW)	9	0	0	0	216

69	7/08	Ches	6f18y	G-S	£5828

Total win prize-money £5828

Going (Turf): Sf: 0-1 **GS: 1-4** Gd: 0-1 GF: 0-1 Fm: 0-1
Distance: 5f/6f: 0-16 **7f-8f: 1-1** 9f-13f: 0-0 14f+: 0-0
Track : **LH: 1-14** RH: 0-0 **Tight: 1-9** Gall: 0-1
Aids: Bl: 0-0 Vi: 0-0 Tstrap: 0-0 Ckp: 0-0
Best Rating: 69 7/08 Ches 6f18y gd-sft

Transfer

97(103) (89)76

4-y-o br g Trans Island-Sankaty Light (USA) (Summer Squall (USA))

A M Balding D H Back

Placings:34/15000-405 **(6547)**

2009: 7^{4}SD, 7^{0}SD, 8^{5}G,

	Starts	1st	2nd	3rd	Win & Pl
Career Total (Turf)	4	0	0	0	329
Career Total (AW)	6	1	0	1	3543

89	6/08	Ling	7f	STD	£2388

Total win prize-money £2388

Going (Turf): Sf: 0-0 GS: 0-0 Gd: 0-3 GF: 0-1 Fm: 0-0
Distance: 5f/6f: 0-0 **7f-8f: 1-9** 9f-13f: 0-1 14f+: 0-0
Track : **LH: 1-3** RH: 0-6 **Tight: 1-4** Gall: 0-0
Aids: Bl: 0-0 Vi: 0-0 Tstrap: 0-0 Ckp: 0-0
Best Rating: 89 6/08 Ling 7f stand

Fair; stays 7f and acts on Polytrack.

Transfered (IRE)

97(100) (47)55

3-y-o b f Trans Island-Second Omen (Rainbow Quest (USA))

Lucinda Featherstone J Roundtree

Placings:003500-200600 **(7557)**

2009: 14^{2}G, 14^{0}G, 16^{0}GS, 12^{6}SD, 13^{0}SD, 13^{0}SD,

	Starts	1st	2nd	3rd	Win & Pl
Career Total (Turf)	5	0	1	1	867
Career Total (AW)	7	0	0	0	0

Going (Turf): Sf: 0-1 GS: 0-1 Gd: 0-2 GF: 0-1 Fm: 0-0
Distance: 5f/6f: 0-1 7f-8f: 0-4 9f-13f: 0-2 14f+: 0-5
Track : LH: 0-7 RH: 0-2 Tight: 0-2 Gall: 0-2
Aids: Bl: 0-0 Vi: 0-0 Tstrap: 0-0 Ckp: 0-0
Best Rating: 55 8/09 Nott 1m6f15y good

Moderate; stays 1m6f; acts on good ground.

Transfixed (IRE)

100(100) (78)79

2-y-o b f Trans Island-Rectify (IRE) (Mujadil (USA))

P D Evans Mrs I M Folkes

Placings:12313213233012020501245**15362** **(7878)**

2009: 5^{1}GF, 5^{2}GF, 5^{3}GF, 6^{1}GS, 6^{3}G, 6^{2}F, 6^{1}GF, 5^{3}GF, 6^{2}G, 5^{3}G, 6^{3}G, 6^{0}GF, 7^{1}GF, 7^{2}GF, 7^{0}GF, 7^{2}GF, 6^{0}G, 5^{5}GF, 6^{0}G, 7^{1}G, 6^{2}G, 7^{4}S, 7^{5}SD, 7^{1}SD, 6^{5}SD, 5^{3}SD,

	Starts	1st	2nd	3rd	Win & Pl
Career Total (Turf)	22	5	6	5	31995
Career Total (AW)	6	1	1	1	9660

74	11/09	Ling	7f		STD	£7641
77	10/09	Catt	7f	(0-85)	GD	£4533
70	8/09	Epsm	7f		G-F	£5180
68	7/09	Ches	6f18y		G-F	£5828
58	5/09	Ripn	6f		G-S	£2590
54	4/09	Wwck	5f		G-F	£2047

Total win prize-money £27821

Going (Turf): Sf: 0-1 GS: 1-1 Gd: 1-8 **GF: 3-11** Fm: 0-1
Distance: 5f/6f: 2-14 **7f-8f: 4-14** 9f-13f: 0-0 14f+: 0-0
Track : **LH: 5-17** RH: 0-0 **Tight: 4-14** Gall: 0-2
Aids: Bl: 0-0 Vi: 0-0 Tstrap: 0-0 Ckp: 0-0
Best Rating: 79 10/09 Brig 6f209y good

Fair; stays 7f; acts on Polytrack; tough and reliable.

Transformer (IRE)

93(102) (64)57

3-y-o b g Trans Island-Lady At War (Warning)

W J Knight Miss S Bowles

Placings:00-40463**2**4012 **(6705)**

2009: 8^{4}SD, 8^{0}GF, 9^{4}G, 9^{6}GF, 10^{3}G, 10^{2}SD, 11^{4}SD, 12^{0}SD, 10^{1}SS, 10^{2}SS,

	Starts	1st	2nd	3rd	Win & Pl
Career Total (Turf)	4	0	0	1	767
Career Total (AW)	8	1	2	0	2889

62	10/09	Ling	1m2f	(0-65)H	SS	£1706

Total win prize-money £1706

Going (Turf): Sf: 0-0 GS: 0-0 Gd: 0-2 GF: 0-2 Fm: 0-0
Distance: 5f/6f: 0-0 7f-8f: 0-3 **9f-13f: 1-9** 14f+: 0-0
Track : **LH: 1-8** RH: 0-4 **Tight: 1-7** Gall: 0-2
Aids: Bl: 0-0 Vi: 0-1 Tstrap: 1-2 Ckp: 1-2
Best Rating: 64 10/09 Ling 1m2f std-slw

Modest; stays 1m3f; acts on fast ground; goes on Polytrack; has worn cheekpieces.

Transmission (IRE)

99(105) (73)70

4-y-o b g Galileo (IRE)-Individual (USA) (Gulch (USA))

B Smart M Barber

Placings:632350/50525**634**-**122**000200024 **(7855)**

2009: 8^{1}SS, 8^{2}SS, 8^{2}SD, 8^{0}SD, 10^{0}GF, 10^{0}GF, 8^{2}G, 9^{0}G, 8^{0}SD, 8^{0}SD, 8^{2}SD, 8^{4}SS,

	Starts	1st	2nd	3rd	Win & Pl
Career Total (Turf)	15	0	3	2	4532
Career Total (AW)	11	1	3	1	4365

73	1/09	Sthl	1m	SS	£2047

Total win prize-money £2047

Going (Turf): Sf: 0-5 GS: 0-2 Gd: 0-3 GF: 0-5 Fm: 0-0
Distance: 5f/6f: 0-1 **7f-8f: 1-14** 9f-13f: 0-11 14f+: 0-0
Track : **LH: 1-18** RH: 0-3 Tight: 0-5 Gall: 0-3
Aids: Bl: 0-0 Vi: 0-1 Tstrap: 0-0 Ckp: 0-0
Best Rating: 77 7/07 York 7f soft

Modest; effective over 1m-1m2f; acts on soft ground and on sand.

Transmit (IRE)

77 44

2-y-o ch g Trans Island-Apple Brandy (USA) (Cox's Ridge (USA))

T D Easterby A Arton

Placings:60 **(5408)**

2009: 6^{6}G, 8^{0}G,

	Starts	1st	2nd	3rd	Win & Pl
Career Total (Turf)	2	0	0	0	0

Going (Turf): Sf: 0-0 GS: 0-0 Gd: 0-2 GF: 0-0 Fm: 0-0
Distance: 5f/6f: 0-1 7f-8f: 0-1 9f-13f: 0-0 14f+: 0-0
Track : LH: 0-2 RH: 0-0 Tight: 0-1 Gall: 0-0
Aids: Bl: 0-0 Vi: 0-0 Tstrap: 0-0 Ckp: 0-0
Best Rating: 44 8/09 Pont 6f good

Transporter (IRE)

87 39

3-y-o b g Trans Island-Ascoli (Skyliner)

T D Easterby D F Sills

Placings:000-40 (4142)
2009: 12⁴GS, 16⁰G,

	Starts	1st	2nd	3rd	Win & Pl
Career Total (Turf)	5	0	0	0	241

Going (Turf): Sf: 0-2 GS: 0-1 Gd: 0-2 GF: 0-0 Fm: 0-0
Distance: 5f/6f: 0-0 7f-8f: 0-3 9f-13f: 0-1 14f+: 0-1
Track : LH: 0-1 RH: 0-2 Tight: 0-1 Gall: 0-0
Aids: Bl: 0-0 Vi: 0-0 Tstrap: 0-0 Ckp: 0-0
Best Rating: 39 7/09 Pont 1m4f8y gd-sft

Transvaal Sky

99(94) (81)87
2-y-o b/br f Avonbridge-Glider (IRE) (Silver Kite (USA))
Tom Dascombe Findlay & Bloom

Placings:6145 (6481)
2009: 6⁶S, 6¹SD, 6⁴GF, 7⁵GF,

	Starts	1st	2nd	3rd	Win & Pl
Career Total (Turf)	3	0	0	0	1516
Career Total (AW)	1	1	0	0	2730

81 8/09 Ling 6f STD £2729
Total win prize-money £2730

Going (Turf): Sf: 0-1 GS: 0-0 Gd: 0-0 GF: 0-2 Fm: 0-0
Distance: 5f/6f: 1-2 7f-8f: 0-2 9f-13f: 0-0 14f+: 0-0
Track : LH: 1-1 RH: 0-0 Tight: 1-1 Gall: 0-0
Aids: Bl: 0-0 Vi: 0-0 Tstrap: 0-0 Ckp: 0-0
Best Rating: 87 10/09 NmkR 7f gd-fm

Useful; stays 7f; acts on Polytrack and fast turf.

Transvestite (IRE)

(98) (79)84
7-y-o b g Trans Island-Christoph's Girl (Efisio)
Miss Tor Sturgis Delamere Racing

Placings:54360301/2454451600/45300314253245/005551 5400/610000-1 (0330)
2009: 12¹SD,

	Starts	1st	2nd	3rd	Win & Pl
Career Total (Turf)	39	3	2	4	28479
Career Total (AW)	10	3	1	1	18784

79 1/09 Wolv 1m4f50y (0-85)H STD £4727
78 5/08 Brig 1m3f196y (0-75)H G-S £2525
84 7/07 Kemp 1m3f (0-80)H STD £4728
87 7/06 Sand 1m2f7y (0-75)H G-F £3238
78 8/05 Gdwd 1m (0-80)H GD £6802
75 11/04 Wolv 7f32y (0-75) STD £4124
Total win prize-money £26146

Going (Turf): Sf: 0-3 GS: 1-6 Gd: 1-17 GF: 1-11 Fm: 0-2
Distance: 5f/6f: 0-4 7f-8f: 2-7 9f-13f: 4-38 14f+: 0-0
Track : LH: 3-29 RH: 3-12 Tight: 2-21 Gall: 0-7
Aids: Bl: 0-0 Vi: 3-13 Tstrap: 0-0 Ckp: 0-0
Best Rating: 93 10/06 Ling 1m4f stand

Fair; stays 1m 4f; acts on fast and easy ground; also goes on Polytrack.

Traphalgar (IRE)

106(105) (83)88
4-y-o br g Cape Cross (IRE)-Conquestadora (Hernando (FR))
P D Evans (Ollie Pears 4/12) J L Guillambert

Placings:00111/30020-0621003112230 (7848)
2009: 8⁰GF, 8⁶G, 10²G, 9¹GF, 10⁰G, 10⁰GS, 9³GF, 9¹GF, 10¹GF, 12²SD, 10²SD, 10³SD, 9⁰SD,

	Starts	1st	2nd	3rd	Win & Pl
Career Total (Turf)	15	3	2	1	13324
Career Total (AW)	8	3	2	2	24944

66 10/09 Rdcr 1m2f G-F £3238
69 9/09 Leic 1m1f218y G-F £1942
86 6/09 Bevl 1m1f207y (0-80)H G-F £4727
91 12/07 Deau 7f110y STD £11149
80 11/07 Ling 1m (0-85) STD £4533
74 11/07 Ling 7f STD £4210
Total win prize-money £29801

Going (Turf): Sf: 0-0 GS: 0-4 Gd: 0-3 GF: 3-7 Fm: 0-0
Distance: 5f/6f: 0-1 7f-8f: 3-8 9f-13f: 3-14 14f+: 0-0
Track : LH: 3-10 RH: 2-8 Tight: 3-10 Gall: 0-1
Aids: Bl: 0-0 Vi: 0-0 Tstrap: 0-0 Ckp: 0-0
Best Rating: 93 4/08 Ling 1m stand

Fair; effective at around 1m2f-1m4f; acts on fast ground; goes on Polytrack; likes to race prominently.

Travellers Kingdom (IRE)

81 45
2-y-o b f Xaar-Mermaid Melody (Machiavellian (USA))
P D Evans R Piff

Placings:0 (1404)
2009: 5⁰GF,

	Starts	1st	2nd	3rd	Win & Pl
Career Total (Turf)	1	0	0	0	

Going (Turf): Sf: 0-0 GS: 0-0 Gd: 0-0 GF: 0-1 Fm: 0-0
Distance: 5f/6f: 0-1 7f-8f: 0-0 9f-13f: 0-0 14f+: 0-0
Track : LH: 0-0 RH: 0-0 Tight: 0-0 Gall: 0-1
Aids: Bl: 0-0 Vi: 0-0 Tstrap: 0-0 Ckp: 0-0
Best Rating: 45 4/09 Wind 5f10y gd-fm

Treadingtheboards

(50)
2-y-o b f Haafhd-Rada's Daughter (Robellino (USA))
Mouse Hamilton-Fairley Anric Racing

Placings:0 (6372)
2009: 7⁰SD,

	Starts	1st	2nd	3rd	Win & Pl
Career Total (Turf)	0	0	0	0	
Career Total (AW)	1	0	0	0	

Going (Turf): Sf: 0-0 GS: 0-0 Gd: 0-0 GF: 0-0 Fm: 0-0
Distance: 5f/6f: 0-0 7f-8f: 0-1 9f-13f: 0-0 14f+: 0-0
Track : LH: 0-0 RH: 0-1 Tight: 0-0 Gall: 0-0
Aids: Bl: 0-0 Vi: 0-0 Tstrap: 0-0 Ckp: 0-0

Treadwell (IRE)

101(99) (90)93
2-y-o b c Footstepsinthesand-Lady Wells (IRE) (Sadler's Wells (USA))
J A Osborne Mrs F Walwyn & A Taylor

Placings:152515 (7063)
2009: 5¹GF, 6⁵GF, 7²GF, 7⁵GS, 6¹SD, 6⁵SD,

	Starts	1st	2nd	3rd	Win & Pl
Career Total (Turf)	4	1	1	0	9450
Career Total (AW)	2	1	0	0	2590

90 10/09 Kemp 6f STD £2590
81 6/09 Sand 5f6y G-F £3238
Total win prize-money £5828

Going (Turf): Sf: 0-0 GS: 0-1 Gd: 0-0 GF: 1-3 Fm: 0-0
Distance: 5f/6f: 2-4 7f-8f: 0-2 9f-13f: 0-0 14f+: 0-0
Track : LH: 0-1 RH: 1-2 Tight: 0-1 Gall: 0-0
Aids: Bl: 0-0 Vi: 0-0 Tstrap: 0-0 Ckp: 0-0
Best Rating: 93 6/09 Asct 6f gd-fm

Very useful; won on debut over 5f but stays 7f; acts on fast ground and on Polytrack.

Treasure Islands (IRE)

(91) (56)52
4-y-o b f Trans Island-Gold Prospector (IRE) (Spectrum (IRE))
S W Hall Mrs J C Howard

Placings:06/4000-0 (0670)
2009: 11⁰SD,

	Starts	1st	2nd	3rd	Win & Pl
Career Total (Turf)	2	0	0	0	
Career Total (AW)	5	0	0	0	137

Going (Turf): Sf: 0-0 GS: 0-2 Gd: 0-0 GF: 0-0 Fm: 0-0
Distance: 5f/6f: 0-0 7f-8f: 0-3 9f-13f: 0-4 14f+: 0-0
Track : LH: 0-4 RH: 0-2 Tight: 0-2 Gall: 0-0
Aids: Bl: 0-0 Vi: 0-0 Tstrap: 0-0 Ckp: 0-0
Best Rating: 56 1/08 Ling 1m stand

Treasure Town

79(97) (79)73
2-y-o b c King's Best (USA)-Shinko Hermes (IRE) (Sadler's Wells (USA))
Saeed Bin Suroor Godolphin

Placings:31 (7064)
2009: 8³G, 8¹SD,

	Starts	1st	2nd	3rd	Win & Pl
Career Total (Turf)	1	0	0	1	770
Career Total (AW)	1	1	0	0	2730

79 10/09 Ling 1m STD £2729
Total win prize-money £2730

Going (Turf): Sf: 0-0 GS: 0-0 Gd: 0-1 GF: 0-0 Fm: 0-0
Distance: 5f/6f: 0-0 7f-8f: 1-1 9f-13f: 0-1 14f+: 0-0
Track : LH: 1-1 RH: 0-1 Tight: 1-1 Gall: 0-0
Aids: Bl: 0-0 Vi: 0-0 Tstrap: 0-0 Ckp: 0-0
Best Rating: 79 10/09 Ling 1m stand

Fair; stays 1m; acts on Polytrack; handles good ground.

Treasure Way

86 62
2-y-o ch f Galileo (IRE)-Gold Mark (Mark Of Esteem (IRE))
P R Chamings Mrs Alexandra J Chandris

Placings:0 (5741)
2009: 8⁰GF,

	Starts	1st	2nd	3rd	Win & Pl
Career Total (Turf)	1	0	0	0	

Going (Turf): Sf: 0-0 GS: 0-0 Gd: 0-0 GF: 0-1 Fm: 0-0
Distance: 5f/6f: 0-0 7f-8f: 0-1 9f-13f: 0-0 14f+: 0-0
Track : LH: 0-0 RH: 0-1 Tight: 0-0 Gall: 0-0
Aids: Bl: 0-0 Vi: 0-0 Tstrap: 0-0 Ckp: 0-0
Best Rating: 62 9/09 Gdwd 1m gd-fm

Treasury Bond

81 42

2-y-o ch g Monsieur Bond (IRE)-Rainbow Treasure (IRE) (Rainbow Quest (USA))

P T Midgley Frank & Annette Brady

Placings:0044 **(3958)**

2009: 6^{0}G, 6^{0}GS, 7^{4}GF, 7^{4}S,

	Starts	1st	2nd	3rd	Win & Pl
Career Total (Turf)	4	0	0	0	289

Going (Turf): **Sf: 0-1 GS: 0-1 Gd: 0-1 GF: 0-1 Fm: 0-0**
Distance: 5f/6f: 0-2 7f-8f: 0-2 9f-13f: 0-0 14f+: 0-0
Track : LH: 0-0 RH: 0-0 Tight: 0-0 Gall: 0-0
Aids: Bl: 0-0 Vi: 0-0 Tstrap: 0-0 Ckp: 0-0
Best Rating: **42** 6/09 Rdcr 7f gd-fm

Treble Jig (USA)

98 85

2-y-o b c Gone West (USA)-Light Jig (Danehill (USA))

Sir Michael Stoute K Abdulla

Placings:01 **(5401)**

2009: 7^{0}GS, 7^{1}G,

	Starts	1st	2nd	3rd	Win & Pl
Career Total (Turf)	2	1	0	0	4857

85 8/09 NmkJ 7f GD £4857

Total win prize-money £4857

Going (Turf): Sf: 0-0 GS: 0-1 **Gd: 1-1** GF: 0-0 Fm: 0-0
Distance: 5f/6f: 0-0 **7f-8f: 1-2** 9f-13f: 0-0 14f+: 0-0
Track : LH: 0-0 RH: 0-0 Tight: 0-0 Gall: 0-0
Aids: Bl: 0-0 Vi: 0-0 Tstrap: 0-0 Ckp: 0-0
Best Rating: **85** 8/09 NmkJ 7f good

Useful; stays 7f; acts on good ground.

Treeko (IRE)

87 (28)35

4-y-o b g Alhaarth (IRE)-Allegheny River (USA) (Lear Fan (USA))

P A Kirby Emma Burdon & The Topspec Racing Club

Placings:6500/0-0 **(5438)**

2009: 10^{0}GF,

	Starts	1st	2nd	3rd	Win & Pl
Career Total (Turf)	5	0	0	0	
Career Total (AW)	1	0	0	0	

Going (Turf): **Sf: 0-0 GS: 0-0 Gd: 0-1 GF: 0-2 Fm: 0-1**
Distance: 5f/6f: 0-0 7f-8f: 0-5 9f-13f: 0-1 14f+: 0-0
Track : LH: 0-4 RH: 0-1 Tight: 0-1 Gall: 0-0
Aids: Bl: 0-0 Vi: 0-0 Tstrap: 0-4 Ckp: 0-4
Best Rating: **72** 9/07 Leop 7f gd-fm

Trees Of Green (USA)

(101) (49)26

5-y-o b/br g Elusive Quality (USA)-Grazia (Sharpo)

M Wigham Allan Darke

Placings:224206/**0000000-0** **(0760)**

2009: 8^{0}SF,

	Starts	1st	2nd	3rd	Win & Pl
Career Total (Turf)	7	0	3	0	3637
Career Total (AW)	7	0	0	0	

Going (Turf): **Sf: 0-1 GS: 0-2 Gd: 0-2 GF: 0-2 Fm: 0-0**
Distance: 5f/6f: 0-7 7f-8f: 0-6 9f-13f: 0-1 14f+: 0-0
Track : LH: 0-9 RH: 0-2 Tight: 0-6 Gall: 0-2
Aids: Bl: 0-1 Vi: 0-1 Tstrap: 0-0 Ckp: 0-0
Best Rating: **78** 9/07 Newc 1m gd-fm

Treetops Hotel (IRE)

87(89) (7)52

10-y-o ch g Grand Lodge (USA)-Rousinette (Rousillon (USA))

L R James L R James Limited

Placings:532613/655/**000000000**/**2**0002420**044**/**05000**0015 33106/**6166**4302011**145**/**6**00552**14**115303/**6660**300-0000000000 **(7733)**

2009: 13^{0}SD, 12^{0}G, 11^{0}GF, 10^{0}GF, 10^{0}GF, 14^{0}GF, 15^{0}GS, 10^{0}GF, 10^{0}GF, 12^{0}SD,

	Starts	1st	2nd	3rd	Win & Pl
Career Total (Turf)	49	4	5	5	21018
Career Total (AW)	37	5	1	3	13793

66	9/07	Kemp	1m4f	(0-60)H	STD	£2047
56	8/07	Ling	1m1f		G-F	£2047
55	6/07	Ling	1m4f		STD	£2047
68	10/06	Ling	2m	(0-65)H	STD	£2730
67	9/06	Ling	1m4f	(0-60)H	STD	£2730
57	2/06	Ling	1m2f	(0-52)H	STD	£2047
59	10/05	Brig	1m1f209y	(0-45)	GD	£1519
55	8/05	Brig	7f214y	(0-70)H	FRM	£3450
83	9/01	Gdwd	6f	D	G-S	£4098

Total win prize-money £22720

Going (Turf): Sf: 0-2 **GS: 1-7 Gd: 1-7 GF: 1-30 Fm: 1-3**
Distance: 5f/6f: 1-10 7f-8f: 1-20 **9f-13f: 6-48** 14f+: 1-8
Track : **LH: 7-54** RH: 1-14 **Tight: 5-45** Gall: 0-5
Aids: Bl: 0-1 Vi: 0-2 Tstrap: 0-10 Ckp: 0-10
Best Rating: **86** 2/03 Ling 1m stand

Modest; effective over 1m4f-2m; acts on fast ground; also goes on Polytrack.

Tregony Bridge

74(84) (47)21

2-y-o b g Avonbridge-Serotina (IRE) (Mtoto)

M Blanshard J Gale, M Holland & Partner

Placings:000 **(7177)**

2009: 8^{0}GS, 7^{0}SD, 7^{0}SD,

	Starts	1st	2nd	3rd	Win & Pl
Career Total (Turf)	1	0	0	0	
Career Total (AW)	2	0	0	0	

Going (Turf): **Sf: 0-0 GS: 0-1 Gd: 0-0 GF: 0-0 Fm: 0-0**
Distance: 5f/6f: 0-0 7f-8f: 0-2 9f-13f: 0-1 14f+: 0-0
Track : LH: 0-1 RH: 0-1 Tight: 0-1 Gall: 0-0
Aids: Bl: 0-0 Vi: 0-0 Tstrap: 0-0 Ckp: 0-0
Best Rating: **47** 10/09 Ling 7f stand

Trelawny Wells

70 25

2-y-o b g Pastoral Pursuits-Kythia (IRE) (Kahyasi)

M R Channon Box 41

Placings:300 **(3500)**

2009: 5^{3}G, 6^{0}G, 6^{0}GF,

	Starts	1st	2nd	3rd	Win & Pl
Career Total (Turf)	3	0	0	1	530

Going (Turf): **Sf: 0-0 GS: 0-0 Gd: 0-2 GF: 0-1 Fm: 0-0**
Distance: 5f/6f: 0-2 7f-8f: 0-1 9f-13f: 0-0 14f+: 0-0
Track : LH: 0-1 RH: 0-0 Tight: 0-0 Gall: 0-1
Aids: Bl: 0-0 Vi: 0-0 Tstrap: 0-0 Ckp: 0-0
Best Rating: **25** 5/09 Bath 5f11y good

Trempari

95(90) (37)54

6-y-o ch g Trempolino (USA)-Ariadne (GER) (Kings Lake (USA))

Mike Murphy M Murphy

Placings:0406041000 **(7608)**

2009: 12^{0}SD, 12^{4}G, 11^{0}GF, 17^{6}G, 16^{0}G, 18^{4}G, 16^{1}GF, 17^{0}GF, 16^{0}GS, 16^{0}SD,

	Starts	1st	2nd	3rd	Win & Pl
Career Total (Turf)	8	1	0	0	2216
Career Total (AW)	2	0	0	0	

53 9/09 Ling 2m (0-65)H G-F £2047

Total win prize-money £2047

Going (Turf): Sf: 0-0 GS: 0-1 Gd: 0-4 **GF: 1-3** Fm: 0-0
Distance: 5f/6f: 0-0 7f-8f: 0-0 9f-13f: 0-3 **14f+: 1-7**
Track : **LH: 1-6** RH: 0-4 **Tight: 1-6** Gall: 0-1
Aids: **Bl: 1-4** Vi: 0-0 Tstrap: 0-0 Ckp: 0-0
Best Rating: **54** 4/09 Folk 1m4f good

Moderate; stays 2m; acts on good/fast ground; has worn blinkers.

Tres Amigos

88(97) (75)59

2-y-o ch g Exceed And Excel (AUS)-Canterloupe (IRE) (Wolfhound (USA))

D Nicholls Dab Hand Racing

Placings:651 **(6874)**

2009: 7^{6}G, 7^{5}GF, 7^{1}SD,

	Starts	1st	2nd	3rd	Win & Pl
Career Total (Turf)	2	0	0	0	0
Career Total (AW)	1	1	0	0	3886

75 10/09 Sthl 7f STD £3885

Total win prize-money £3886

Going (Turf): **Sf: 0-0 GS: 0-0 Gd: 0-1 GF: 0-1 Fm: 0-0**
Distance: 5f/6f: 0-0 **7f-8f: 1-3** 9f-13f: 0-0 14f+: 0-0
Track : **LH: 1-2** RH: 0-0 Tight: 0-0 Gall: 0-0
Aids: Bl: 0-0 Vi: 0-0 Tstrap: 0-0 Ckp: 0-0
Best Rating: **75** 10/09 Sthl 7f stand

Fair; effective over 7f; acts on Fibresand.

Tres Chic (FR)

85 57

3-y-o gr f Kaldounevees (FR)-Chic Emilie (FR) (Policeman (FR))

S Curran The Chicanery Partnership

Placings:0-00 **(1752)**

2009: 10^{0}GS, 8^{0}GF,

	Starts	1st	2nd	3rd	Win & Pl
Career Total (Turf)	3	0	0	0	

Going (Turf): **Sf: 0-0 GS: 0-2 Gd: 0-0 GF: 0-1 Fm: 0-0**
Distance: 5f/6f: 0-0 7f-8f: 0-0 9f-13f: 0-3 14f+: 0-0
Track : LH: 0-2 RH: 0-1 Tight: 0-1 Gall: 0-1
Aids: Bl: 0-0 Vi: 0-0 Tstrap: 0-0 Ckp: 0-0
Best Rating: **57** 4/09 Newb 1m2f6y gd-sft

Tres Coronas (IRE)

100(100) (83)77

2-y-o b g Key Of Luck (USA)-Almansa (IRE) (Dr Devious (IRE))

T D Barron J Cringan & D Pryde

Placings:312204031 (7267)

2009: 5^{3}GF, 5^{1}GS, 6^{2}GS, 7^{2}GF, 7^{0}G, 8^{4}GF, 8^{0}G, 8^{3}GF, 8^{1}SD,

	Starts	1st	2nd	3rd	Win & Pl
Career Total (Turf)	8	1	2	2	9910
Career Total (AW)	1	1	0	0	6152

83 11/09 Sthl 1m (0-85) STD £6152
69 5/09 Newc 5f G-S £3238
Total win prize-money £9390

Going (Turf): Sf: 0-0 **GS: 1-2** Gd: 0-2 GF: 0-4 Fm: 0-0
Distance: 5f/6f: 1-3 7f-8f: 1-4 9f-13f: 0-2 14f+: 0-0
Track : **LH: 1-3** RH: 0-1 Tight: 0-0 Gall: 0-0
Aids: **Bl: 1-1** Vi: 0-0 Tstrap: 0-0 Ckp: 0-0
Best Rating: 83 11/09 Sthl 1m stand

Fair; stays 1m; acts on fast and easy ground, and on Fibresand.

Tres Froide (FR)

94(89) (73)67

4-y-o ch f Bering-Charmgoer (USA) (Nureyev (USA))

N Tinkler Leeds Plywood And Doors Ltd

Placings:63/34061-00600010 (7127)

2009: 12^{0}GF, 10^{0}G, 8^{6}GF, 8^{0}HY, 8^{0}SD, 12^{0}GS, 10^{1}GF, 10^{0}G,

	Starts	1st	2nd	3rd	Win & Pl
Career Total (Turf)	12	2	0	2	15830
Career Total (AW)	3	0	0	0	2500

67 10/09 Rdcr 1m2f (0-60)H G-F £1648
11/08 Cros 1m1f HVY £6985
Total win prize-money £8633

Going (Turf): **Sf: 1-4** GS: 0-1 Gd: 0-3 **GF: 1-3** Fm: 0-0
Distance: 5f/6f: 0-0 7f-8f: 0-4 **9f-13f: 2-11** 14f+: 0-0
Track : **LH: 1-10** RH: 0-2 **Tight: 1-1** Gall: 0-4
Aids: Bl: 0-0 Vi: 0-0 Tstrap: 0-0 Ckp: 0-0
Best Rating: 73 8/08 Deau 1m4f stand

Moderate; best at around 1m3f; acts on most types of ground.

Trevian

(94) (60)54

8-y-o ch g Atraf-Ascend (IRE) (Glint Of Gold)

Tim Vaughan Folly Road Racing Partners (1996)

Placings:056/01665006/0600002102060/054314000150/6 6534346104600 4/03656-P (5246)

2009: 13^{P}F,

	Starts	1st	2nd	3rd	Win & Pl
Career Total (Turf)	38	3	2	4	13792
Career Total (AW)	19	2	0	0	5310

60 8/07 Ling 1m2f (0-55)H STD £2047
59 9/06 Brig 7f214y (0-60)H G-F £2730
61 6/06 Ripn 1m (0-65)H G-F £2590
59 8/05 Chep 1m14y (0-70)H GD £4601
68 1/04 Ling 1m E(0-75)H STD £3262
Total win prize-money £15232

Going (Turf): Sf: 0-2 GS: 0-2 Gd: 1-5 **GF: 2-25** Fm: 0-4
Distance: 5f/6f: 0-5 **7f-8f: 3-24** 9f-13f: 2-26 14f+: 0-2
Track : **LH: 3-34** RH: 1-9 **Tight: 3-26** Gall: 0-1
Aids: Bl: 0-1 Vi: 0-1 Tstrap: 0-0 Ckp: 0-0
Best Rating: 68 1/04 Ling 1m stand

Trewarthenick

89(84) (59)55

2-y-o br g Cape Cross (IRE)-Play With Fire (FR) (Priolo (USA))

A M Balding Marcus Evans

Placings:66 (5312)

2009: 6^{6}G, 8^{6}SD,

	Starts	1st	2nd	3rd	Win & Pl
Career Total (Turf)	1	0	0	0	0
Career Total (AW)	1	0	0	0	0

Going (Turf): **Sf: 0-0 GS: 0-0 Gd: 0-1 GF: 0-0 Fm: 0-0**
Distance: 5f/6f: 0-0 7f-8f: 0-2 9f-13f: 0-0 14f+: 0-0
Track : LH: 0-0 RH: 0-1 Tight: 0-0 Gall: 0-0
Aids: Bl: 0-0 Vi: 0-0 Tstrap: 0-0 Ckp: 0-0
Best Rating: 59 8/09 Kemp 1m stand

Moderate half-brother to decent sprinters Coconut Penang and Milbag; ran green on debut over 6f on good.

Tri Chara (IRE)

92(106) (73)48

5-y-o ch g Grand Slam (USA)-Lamzena (IRE) (Fairy King (USA))

R Hollinshead The Tri Chara Partnership

Placings:60025023/10000304120-14564405062040 (7680)

2009: 7^{1}SD, 7^{4}SD, 7^{5}SD, 7^{6}SD, 7^{4}SD, 6^{4}SD, 7^{0}G, 7^{5}SD, 6^{0}G, 6^{6}SD, 5^{2}SD, 7^{0}SD, 7^{4}SD, 6^{0}SD,

	Starts	1st	2nd	3rd	Win & Pl
Career Total (Turf)	11	0	1	0	1349
Career Total (AW)	22	3	3	2	10098

73 1/09 Sthl 7f (0-75)H STD £2729
68 12/08 Sthl 7f (0-55)H STD £1706
67 1/08 Wolv 7f32y STD £2457
Total win prize-money £6893

Going (Turf): **Sf: 0-2 GS: 0-1 Gd: 0-4 GF: 0-4 Fm: 0-0**
Distance: 5f/6f: 0-6 **7f-8f: 3-17** 9f-13f: 0-10 14f+: 0-0
Track : **LH: 3-28** RH: 0-3 **Tight: 1-18** Gall: 0-0
Aids: Bl: 0-0 Vi: 0-2 Tstrap: 2-20 Ckp: 2-20
Best Rating: 73 1/09 Sthl 7f stand

Moderate; effective over 6f-1m; acts on Fibresand and Polytrack; has worn cheekpieces.

Tribal Myth (IRE)

86 57

2-y-o b g Johannesburg (USA)-Shadow Play (USA) (Theatrical)

K A Ryan Mr & Mrs K Hughes and Dr J Gozzard

Placings:0660 (5595)

2009: 6^{0}GF, 7^{6}GS, 7^{6}G, 7^{0}GF,

	Starts	1st	2nd	3rd	Win & Pl
Career Total (Turf)	4	0	0	0	0

Going (Turf): **Sf: 0-0 GS: 0-1 Gd: 0-1 GF: 0-2 Fm: 0-0**
Distance: 5f/6f: 0-1 7f-8f: 0-3 9f-13f: 0-0 14f+: 0-0
Track : LH: 0-1 RH: 0-0 Tight: 0-1 Gall: 0-0
Aids: Bl: 0-0 Vi: 0-0 Tstrap: 0-0 Ckp: 0-0
Best Rating: 57 7/09 Leic 7f9y gd-sft

Tribal Rule

91(84) (38)70

3-y-o gr c Daylami (IRE)-Native Justice (USA) (Alleged (USA))

Mrs A J Perrett K Abdulla

Placings:660 (6287)

2009: 10^{6}GF, 9^{6}GF, 10^{0}SD,

	Starts	1st	2nd	3rd	Win & Pl
Career Total (Turf)	2	0	0	0	0
Career Total (AW)	1	0	0	0	

Going (Turf): **Sf: 0-0 GS: 0-0 Gd: 0-0 GF: 0-2 Fm: 0-0**
Distance: 5f/6f: 0-0 7f-8f: 0-0 9f-13f: 0-3 14f+: 0-0
Track : LH: 0-0 RH: 0-3 Tight: 0-2 Gall: 0-0
Aids: Bl: 0-0 Vi: 0-0 Tstrap: 0-0 Ckp: 0-0
Best Rating: 70 5/09 Wind 1m2f7y gd-fm

Tribe

102(99) (73)72

7-y-o b g Danehill (USA)-Leo Girl (USA) (Seattle Slew (USA))

P R Webber Iain Russell Watters

Placings:053/0554/1000/50046-263 (3986)

2009: 16^{2}GF, 16^{6}GF, 16^{3}GF,

	Starts	1st	2nd	3rd	Win & Pl
Career Total (Turf)	18	1	1	2	6419
Career Total (AW)	1	0	0	0	0

83 4/07 Pont 2m1f216y (0-75)H GD £3886
Total win prize-money £3886

Going (Turf): Sf: 0-0 GS: 0-3 **Gd: 1-6** GF: 0-8 Fm: 0-1
Distance: 5f/6f: 0-0 7f-8f: 0-2 9f-13f: 0-4 **14f+: 1-13**
Track : **LH: 1-12** RH: 0-6 Tight: 0-4 Gall: 0-7
Aids: Bl: 0-0 Vi: 0-0 Tstrap: 0-0 Ckp: 0-0
Best Rating: 83 4/07 Pont 2m1f216y good

Modest; stays 2m2f; acts on fast and easy ground.

Trick Or Two

61(98) (68)

3-y-o gr g Desert Style (IRE)-Vax Star (Petong)

Mrs R A Carr David W Chapman

Placings:0051-4450 (1232)

2009: 5^{4}SD, 6^{4}SD, 5^{5}SD, 5^{0}GF,

	Starts	1st	2nd	3rd	Win & Pl
Career Total (Turf)	1	0	0	0	
Career Total (AW)	7	1	0	0	1979

68 12/08 Sthl 5f STD £1978
Total win prize-money £1979

Going (Turf): **Sf: 0-0 GS: 0-0 Gd: 0-0 GF: 0-1 Fm: 0-0**
Distance: **5f/6f: 1-7** 7f-8f: 0-1 9f-13f: 0-0 14f+: 0-0
Track : LH: 0-6 RH: 0-0 Tight: 0-5 Gall: 0-0
Aids: Bl: 0-1 Vi: 0-0 Tstrap: 0-0 Ckp: 0-0
Best Rating: 68 12/08 Sthl 5f stand

Modest; suited by 5f and Fibresand.

Tricky Situation

95 76

3-y-o b f Mark Of Esteem (IRE)-Trick Of Ace (USA) (Clever Trick (USA))

J G Given Peter Onslow & Ian Henderson

Placings:2-33 (2843)

2009: 8^{3}GS, 10^{3}GF,

	Starts	1st	2nd	3rd	Win & Pl
Career Total (Turf)	3	0	1	2	2023

Going (Turf): **Sf: 0-1 GS: 0-1 Gd: 0-0 GF: 0-1 Fm: 0-0**
Distance: 5f/6f: 0-0 7f-8f: 0-0 9f-13f: 0-3 14f+: 0-0

Track : LH: 0-3 RH: 0-0 Tight: 0-0 Gall: 0-0
Aids: Bl: 0-0 Vi: 0-0 Tstrap: 0-0 Ckp: 0-0
Best Rating: 76 10/08 Nott 1m75y soft

Placed in maidens; effective over 1m; should get further; acts on soft ground.

Tricky Trev (USA)

94(93) (62)52
3-y-o ch g Toccet (USA)-Lady Houston (USA) (Houston (USA))
S Curran L M Power

Placings:650056-6003300 (7572)
2009: 7^{6}SD, 8^{0}F, 5^{0}GF, 5^{3}F, 5^{3}GF, 5^{0}GF, 6^{0}SD,

	Starts	1st	2nd	3rd	Win & Pl
Career Total (Turf)	7	0	0	2	347
Career Total (AW)	6	0	0	0	0

Going (Turf): Sf: 0-0 GS: 0-1 Gd: 0-1 GF: 0-3 Fm: 0-2
Distance: 5f/6f: 0-10 7f-8f: 0-2 9f-13f: 0-1 14f+: 0-0
Track : LH: 0-11 RH: 0-0 Tight: 0-6 Gall: 0-1
Aids: Bl: 0-2 Vi: 0-0 Tstrap: 0-0 Ckp: 0-0
Best Rating: 62 8/08 Ling 6f stand

Moderate; stays 7f and acts on fast ground; has worn a tongue tie.

Tried And True (FR)

91(98) (62)66
4-y-o b f Marju (IRE)-Test The Rest (USA) (Take Me Out (USA))
H R A Cecil H E Sheikh Sultan Bin Khalifa Al Nahyan

Placings:0/633-405 (2537)
2009: 9^{4}GF, 10^{0}SD, 9^{5}GF,

	Starts	1st	2nd	3rd	Win & Pl
Career Total (Turf)	6	0	0	2	1829
Career Total (AW)	1	0	0	0	

Going (Turf): Sf: 0-1 GS: 0-0 Gd: 0-3 GF: 0-2 Fm: 0-0
Distance: 5f/6f: 0-0 7f-8f: 0-0 9f-13f: 0-7 14f+: 0-0
Track : LH: 0-1 RH: 0-2 Tight: 0-1 Gall: 0-0
Aids: Bl: 0-1 Vi: 0-0 Tstrap: 0-0 Ckp: 0-0
Best Rating: 66 4/09 Leic 1m1f218y gd-fm

Modest; stays 1m2f; acts on fast ground.

Trifti

(104) (79)51
8-y-o b g Vettori (IRE)-Time For Tea (IRE) (Imperial Frontier (USA))
Miss Jo Crowley Mrs Liz Nelson

Placings:4000420010/60011050601301/20620200605540 0025/434460404364225/1P30526-315P56 (7823)
2009: 10^{3}SD, 10^{1}SD, 10^{5}SD, 9^{P}GF, 10^{6}SD, 10^{6}SD,

	Starts	1st	2nd	3rd	Win & Pl
Career Total (Turf)	15	0	1	1	1641
Career Total (AW)	55	7	7	4	40803

79	3/09	Ling	1m2f	(0-75)H	STD	£2900
74	3/08	Ling	1m2f	(0-70)H	STD	£2590
86	11/05	Wolv	1m1f103y	(0-85)H	SF	£5741
83	10/05	Wolv	1m141y	(0-75)H	STD	£3464
78	3/05	Wolv	7f32y	(0-70)H	STD	£3435
75	2/05	Ling	7f		STD	£2898
62	11/04	Wolv	1m141y		STD	£3464

Total win prize-money £24495

Going (Turf): Sf: 0-0 GS: 0-1 Gd: 0-5 GF: 0-7 Fm: 0-2
Distance: 5f/6f: 0-2 7f-8f: 2-25 9f-13f: 5-41 14f+: 0-2
Track : LH: 7-57 RH: 0-8 Tight: 7-53 Gall: 0-1
Aids: Bl: 0-3 Vi: 0-0 Tstrap: 0-0 Ckp: 0-0
Best Rating: 93 1/06 Wolv 1m141y stand

Fair; stays 1m2f; acts on fast ground, but seems best on Polytrack; has worn blinkers.

Trimlestown (IRE)

(105) (76)83
6-y-o b g Orpen (USA)-Courtier (Saddlers' Hall (IRE))
P D Evans P D Evans

Placings:03/50313211/0005200/0003052105016-6060350 (7762)
2009: 5^{6}SD, 5^{0}SD, 7^{6}SD, 7^{0}SD, 5^{3}SD, 7^{5}SD, 7^{0}SD,

	Starts	1st	2nd	3rd	Win & Pl
Career Total (Turf)	21	3	3	3	22639
Career Total (AW)	16	2	0	2	6185

76	12/08	Wolv	5f216y	(0-75)H	STD	£3238
74	10/08	Ling	7f		STD	£1978
89	10/06	NmkR	7f	(0-85)H	SFT	£5505
84	9/06	Newb	7f	(0-80)H	GD	£6477
71	7/06	Ling	7f		G-F	£3238

Total win prize-money £20438

Going (Turf): Sf: 1-4 GS: 0-5 Gd: 1-5 GF: 1-7 Fm: 0-0
Distance: 5f/6f: 1-7 7f-8f: 4-29 9f-13f: 0-1 14f+: 0-0
Track : LH: 2-18 RH: 0-4 Tight: 2-16 Gall: 0-1
Aids: Bl: 0-1 Vi: 0-2 Tstrap: 2-12 Ckp: 2-12
Best Rating: 89 10/06 NmkR 7f soft

Modest; effective over 6f-7f; acts on most ground on turf; also goes on Polytrack; has worn various headgear.

Trincot (FR)

115 119
4-y-o b c Peintre Celebre (USA)-Royal Lights (FR) (Royal Academy (USA))
Saeed Bin Suroor (P Demercastel 5/4) Godolphin

Placings:544223/11106310-01203 (4364a)
2009: 10^{0}HY, 10^{1}G, 10^{2}GF, 10^{0}GF, 10^{3}G,

	Starts	1st	2nd	3rd	Win & Pl
Career Total (Turf)	19	5	3	3	276822

119	4/09	Lonc	1m2f	GD	£71942
114	10/08	Lonc	1m1f165y	GD	£54485
101	5/08	Chan	1m1f	GD	£29412
98	4/08	StCl	1m	HVY	£12500
	3/08	Comp	1m	HVY	£10661

Total win prize-money £179001

Going (Turf): Sf: 2-7 GS: 0-2 Gd: 3-8 GF: 0-2 Fm: 0-0
Distance: 5f/6f: 0-2 7f-8f: 2-6 9f-13f: 3-11 14f+: 0-0
Track : LH: 1-3 RH: 3-11 Tight: 0-0 Gall: 0-1
Aids: Bl: 0-0 Vi: 0-0 Tstrap: 0-2 Ckp: 0-2
Best Rating: 119 4/09 Lonc 1m2f good

Group-class; ex-French; Group 2 winner; effective at 1m2f; acts on good and fast ground; has worn cheekpieces.

Trinculo (IRE)

(97) (67)71
12-y-o b g Anita's Prince-Fandangerina (USA) (Grey Dawn II)
R A Harris Peter A Price

Placings:31354/0034040003/3052321020/00066004000/0 0006632000160/000U250060005100/401114103/5001201 00-0064400 (2134)
2009: 5^{0}SD, 6^{0}SD, 5^{6}SF, 5^{4}SD, 6^{4}SD, 5^{0}SD, 6^{0}SD,

	Starts	1st	2nd	3rd	Win & Pl
Career Total (Turf)	93	13	7	8	484729
Career Total (AW)	43	3	4	4	20215

71	5/08	Wwck	6f	(0-65)H	G-F	£1942
67	4/08	Wolv	5f216y	(0-60)H	STD	£1977
66	12/07	Sthl	6f	(0-57)H	STD	£2047
67	9/07	Chep	7f16y	(0-60)H	G-F	£2590
78	10/06	Catt	5f		SFT	£2730
79	8/06	Catt	5f		SFT	£2730
96	5/06	York	5f	(0-100)H	SFT	£16516
93	4/06	Bevl	5f	(0-95)H	G-S	£9067
93	9/05	Ches	5f16y	(0-85)H	SFT	£7494
93	7/05	Bevl	5f	(0-90)H	GD	£12649
93	6/05	Sand	5f6y		G-F	£3425
80	6/05	Newc	5f		GD	£2632
91	11/04	Catt	5f		SFT	£3024
99	11/03	Sthl	5f	C(0-95)H	STD	£6905
	9/01	ShTn	6f	H	YLD	£97686
77	8/99	Leic	5f218y	F	G-F	£2931

Total win prize-money £176353

Going (Turf): Sf: 5-13GS: 1-15Gd: 2-24GF: 4-33 Fm: 0-1
Distance: 5f/6f: 15-1227f-8f: 1-13 9f-13f 0-1 14f+: 0-0
Track : LH: 4-39 RH: 0-5 Tight: 2-24 Gall: 0-6
Aids: Bl: 5-49 Vi: 0-0 Tstrap: 1-20 Ckp: 1-20
Best Rating: 108 9/00 Asct 6f soft

Modest front-running sprint handicapper; stays 7f but mainly campaigned over shorter distances; handles most types of ground and both All-Weather surfaces; has worn headgear.

Trinder

95 75
2-y-o b c Pastoral Pursuits-Quiz Show (Primo Dominie)
R A Fahey Mrs Janis Macpherson

Placings:262400 (6556)
2009: 5^{2}GF, 6^{6}G, 5^{2}GF, 6^{4}G, 6^{0}GF, 5^{0}G,

	Starts	1st	2nd	3rd	Win & Pl
Career Total (Turf)	6	0	2	0	3963

Going (Turf): Sf: 0-0 GS: 0-0 Gd: 0-3 GF: 0-3 Fm: 0-0
Distance: 5f/6f: 0-6 7f-8f: 0-0 9f-13f: 0-0 14f+: 0-0
Track : LH: 0-0 RH: 0-0 Tight: 0-0 Gall: 0-0
Aids: Bl: 0-0 Vi: 0-0 Tstrap: 0-0 Ckp: 0-0
Best Rating: 75 7/09 Bevl 5f gd-fm

Modest; suited by 5f and fast ground.

Trip Switch

93(99) (69)58
3-y-o b g Reset (AUS)-Caribbean Star (Soviet Star (USA))
G Prodromou (W R Muir 25/9) George Prodromou

Placings:214600000 (7890)
2009: 6^{2}SD, 6^{1}SD, 5^{4}SD, 7^{6}GF, 6^{0}SD, 7^{0}GF, 6^{0}SD, 5^{0}SD, 6^{0}SD,

	Starts	1st	2nd	3rd	Win & Pl
Career Total (Turf)	2	0	0	0	0
Career Total (AW)	7	1	1	0	3877

69	3/09	Ling	6f	STD	£3070

Total win prize-money £3071

Going (Turf): Sf: 0-0 GS: 0-0 Gd: 0-0 GF: 0-2 Fm: 0-0
Distance: 5f/6f: 1-7 7f-8f: 0-2 9f-13f: 0-0 14f+: 0-0
Track : LH: 1-6 RH: 0-2 Tight: 1-5 Gall: 0-0
Aids: Bl: 0-3 Vi: 0-0 Tstrap: 0-0 Ckp: 0-0
Best Rating: 69 3/09 Ling 6f stand

Modest; effective over 6f; acts on Polytrack.

Trip The Light

105(113) (92)89

4-y-o b g Fantastic Light (USA)-Jumaireyah (Fairy King (USA))

R A Fahey The Matthewman One Partnership

Placings:050/054131155-01651212435124 (7465)

2009: 12^{0}G, 11^{1}GF, 14^{6}G, 12^{5}GF, 12^{1}GF, 14^{2}F, 11^{1}G, 11^{2}GF, 14^{4}G, 13^{3}SD, 14^{5}GS, 12^{1}G, 14^{2}SD, 12^{4}SD,

	Starts	1st	2nd	3rd	Win & Pl
Career Total (Turf)	20	7	2	1	28849
Career Total (AW)	6	0	1	1	4580

89	10/09	York	1m4f	(0-85)H	GD	£6476
84	8/09	Hayd	1m3f200y	(0-75)H	GD	£3238
75	6/09	Thsk	1m4f	(0-80)H	G-F	£5569
77	4/09	Catt	1m3f214y	(0-70)H	G-F	£2914
72	8/08	Rdcr	1m6f19y	(0-60)H	GD	£2266
65	7/08	Bevl	1m4f16y	(0-70)H	G-F	£2914
56	5/08	Rdcr	1m6f19y	(0-65)H	G-F	£2047

Total win prize-money £25425

Going (Turf): Sf: 0-2 GS: 0-1 Gd: 3-7 **GF: 4-9** Fm: 0-1
Distance: 5f/6f: 0-2 7f-8f: 0-1 **9f-13f: 5-13** 14f+: 2-10
Track : **LH: 6-22** RH: 1-4 **Tight: 5-13** Gall: 1-6
Aids: Bl: 0-0 **Vi: 6-16** Tstrap: 0-0 Ckp: 0-0
Best Rating: **92** 11/09 Wolv 1m4f50y stand

Useful; stays 1m6f; handles most ground; has worn a visor.

Tripbiyah (USA)

93(96) (61)64

3-y-o b g Trippi (USA)-Jathibiyah (USA) (Nureyev (USA))

G A Swinbank D & A Bell & K & A Sutton

Placings:5345 (6637)

2009: 8^{5}G, 8^{3}GF, 5^{4}GS, 7^{5}SD,

	Starts	1st	2nd	3rd	Win & Pl
Career Total (Turf)	3	0	0	1	958
Career Total (AW)	1	0	0	0	0

Going (Turf): **Sf: 0-0 GS: 0-1 Gd: 0-1 GF: 0-1 Fm: 0-0**
Distance: 5f/6f: 0-1 7f-8f: 0-1 9f-13f: 0-2 14f+: 0-0
Track : LH: 0-3 RH: 0-0 Tight: 0-1 Gall: 0-0
Aids: Bl: 0-0 Vi: 0-0 Tstrap: 0-0 Ckp: 0-0
Best Rating: **64** 7/09 Pont 1m4y good

Fair-looking sort; best effort at 1m on good/fast ground.

Tripitaka

(104) (84)

3-y-o b g Sulamani (IRE)-Memo (Groom Dancer (USA))

M A Jarvis The Tripitaka Partnership

Placings:101 (7612)

2009: 11^{1}SD, 12^{0}SD, 12^{1}SD,

	Starts	1st	2nd	3rd	Win & Pl
Career Total (Turf)	0	0	0	0	
Career Total (AW)	3	2	0	0	7318

84	12/09	Kemp	1m4f	(0-85)H	STD	£4727
82	4/09	Kemp	1m3f		STD	£2590

Total win prize-money £7317

Going (Turf): **Sf: 0-0 GS: 0-0 Gd: 0-0 GF: 0-0 Fm: 0-0**
Distance: 5f/6f: 0-0 7f-8f: 0-0 **9f-13f: 2-3** 14f+: 0-0
Track : LH: 0-0 **RH: 2-3** Tight: 0-0 Gall: 0-0
Aids: Bl: 0-0 Vi: 0-0 Tstrap: 0-0 Ckp: 0-0
Best Rating: **84** 12/09 Kemp 1m4f stand

Useful; stays 1m4f; acts on Polytrack.

Triple Aspect (IRE)

112 116

3-y-o b c Danetime (IRE)-Wicken Wonder (IRE) (Distant Relative)

W J Haggas Tony Bloom

Placings:111-21242 (6661)

2009: 6^{2}G, 5^{1}G, 5^{2}G, 5^{4}GF, 6^{2}GS,

	Starts	1st	2nd	3rd	Win & Pl
Career Total (Turf)	8	4	3	0	102232

116	6/09	Sand	5f6y	GD	£22708
105	9/08	Chan	5f110y	GD	£29412
101	8/08	Bath	5f161y	GD	£4857
92	7/08	Sand	5f6y	G-F	£5180

Total win prize-money £62158

Going (Turf): Sf: 0-0 GS: 0-1 **Gd: 3-5** GF: 1-2 Fm: 0-0
Distance: **5f/6f: 4-7** 7f-8f: 0-1 9f-13f: 0-0 14f+: 0-0
Track : **LH: 1-1** RH: 0-0 Tight: 0-0 **Gall: 1-1**
Aids: Bl: 0-0 Vi: 0-0 Tstrap: 0-0 Ckp: 0-0
Best Rating: **116** 6/09 Sand 5f6y good

Group class; winner in Group 3 company in France as a juvenile; Listed winner in 2009; effective over 5f-6f; acts on good and faster ground.

Triple Axel (IRE)

(101) (65)54

5-y-o b m Danehill Dancer (IRE)-Across The Ice (USA) (General Holme (USA))

J Noseda Mrs Paul Shanahan

Placings:05050/400524231-33 (0297)

2009: 7^{3}SD, 7^{3}SD,

	Starts	1st	2nd	3rd	Win & Pl
Career Total (Turf)	11	0	1	0	1757
Career Total (AW)	5	1	1	3	5064

64	12/08	Sthl	6f	STD	£2729

Total win prize-money £2730

Going (Turf): **Sf: 0-1 GS: 0-0 Gd: 0-2 GF: 0-1 Fm: 0-1**
Distance: **5f/6f: 1-8** 7f-8f: 0-8 9f-13f: 0-0 14f+: 0-0
Track : **LH: 1-11** RH: 0-3 Tight: 0-1 Gall: 0-0
Aids: Bl: 0-0 Vi: 0-0 Tstrap: 0-2 Ckp: 0-2
Best Rating: **65** 1/09 Wolv 7f32y stand

Modest; suited by 6f; acts on Fibresand.

Triple Cee (IRE)

102(99) (62)71

3-y-o b f Cape Cross (IRE)-Karri Valley (USA) (Storm Bird (CAN))

M R Channon Nigel Bunter

Placings:3006-4606360324560 (7857)

2009: 10^{4}SD, 10^{6}G, 8^{0}G, 9^{6}GF, 10^{3}G, 10^{6}G, 13^{0}G, 10^{3}GF, 9^{2}GF, 10^{4}SS, 10^{5}SD, 10^{6}SD, 9^{0}SD,

	Starts	1st	2nd	3rd	Win & Pl
Career Total (Turf)	12	0	1	3	2909
Career Total (AW)	5	0	0	0	337

Going (Turf): **Sf: 0-1 GS: 0-0 Gd: 0-6 GF: 0-5 Fm: 0-0**
Distance: 5f/6f: 0-0 7f-8f: 0-3 9f-13f: 0-13 14f+: 0-1
Track : LH: 0-10 RH: 0-3 Tight: 0-6 Gall: 0-1
Aids: Bl: 0-0 Vi: 0-0 Tstrap: 0-0 Ckp: 0-0
Best Rating: **71** 6/08 Newb 7f gd-fm

Modest; stays 1m2f and acts on good ground.

Triple Dream

104(95) (68)86

4-y-o ch g Vision Of Night-Triple Joy (Most Welcome)

J M Bradley J M Bradley

Placings:00400-6052052541211230 (6666)

2009: 7^{6}G, 7^{0}SD, 6^{5}GF, 5^{2}GF, 6^{0}GF, 5^{5}GF, 5^{2}GF, 5^{5}S, 5^{4}GF, 5^{1}GF, 6^{2}G, 5^{1}S, 5^{1}GF, 6^{2}GF, 5^{3}GF, 5^{0}GS,

	Starts	1st	2nd	3rd	Win & Pl
Career Total (Turf)	17	3	4	1	13013
Career Total (AW)	4	0	0	0	192

86	9/09	Rdcr	5f	(0-70)H	G-F	£2590
76	9/09	Sals	5f	(0-70)H	SFT	£3238
70	8/09	Bath	5f161y	(0-75)H	G-F	£2849

Total win prize-money £8677

Going (Turf): Sf: 1-2 GS: 0-1 Gd: 0-3 **GF: 2-10** Fm: 0-1
Distance: **5f/6f: 3-13** 7f-8f: 0-7 9f-13f: 0-1 14f+: 0-0
Track : **LH: 1-6** RH: 0-1 Tight: 0-1 **Gall: 1-5**
Aids: Bl: 0-0 Vi: 0-0 Tstrap: 3-14 Ckp: 3-14
Best Rating: **86** 9/09 Rdcr 5f gd-fm

Fair; effective at 5f-6f; acts on most ground and on Polytrack; has worn cheekpieces.

Trireme (IRE)

78 53

5-y-o b g Fantastic Light (USA)-Dreamboat (USA) (Mr Prospector (USA))

K A Morgan J D M Stables

Placings:60500-00 (4220)

2009: 10^{0}SD, 10^{0}G,

	Starts	1st	2nd	3rd	Win & Pl
Career Total (Turf)	6	0	0	0	0
Career Total (AW)	1	0	0	0	

Going (Turf): **Sf: 0-2 GS: 0-0 Gd: 0-2 GF: 0-2 Fm: 0-0**
Distance: 5f/6f: 0-0 7f-8f: 0-0 9f-13f: 0-7 14f+: 0-0
Track : LH: 0-5 RH: 0-1 Tight: 0-3 Gall: 0-0
Aids: Bl: 0-0 Vi: 0-0 Tstrap: 0-0 Ckp: 0-0
Best Rating: **53** 6/08 Nott 1m75y gd-fm

Triskaidekaphobia

90(106) (55)44

6-y-o b g Bertolini (USA)-Seren Teg (Timeless Times (USA))

Miss J R Tooth Raymond Tooth And Steve Gilbey

Placings:5516100451/0050000000/04631300002530011/61053400353-000000001 (7657)

2009: 5^{0}SD, 5^{0}SD, 5^{0}SF, 5^{0}SD, 5^{0}SD, 5^{0}G, 5^{0}F, 5^{0}SD, 5^{1}SD,

	Starts	1st	2nd	3rd	Win & Pl
Career Total (Turf)	23	3	0	0	26161
Career Total (AW)	34	5	1	6	13942

55	12/09	Ling	5f	(0-60)H	STD	£2047
71	1/08	Wolv	5f20y	(0-65)H	STD	£2388
66	12/07	Wolv	5f20y	(0-55)H	STD	£2047
63	12/07	Wolv	5f20y	(0-65)H	STD	£1706
63	3/07	Wolv	5f20y	(0-58)H	STD	£2730
91	10/05	Muss	5f	(0-95)	GD	£11020
92	7/05	York	5f		GD	£8502
80	6/05	Thsk	5f		G-F	£5538

Total win prize-money £35980

Going (Turf): Sf: 0-0 GS: 0-1 **Gd: 2-9** GF: 1-12 Fm: 0-1
Distance: **5f/6f: 8-56** 7f-8f: 0-1 9f-13f: 0-0 14f+: 0-0
Track : **LH: 5-35** RH: 0-4 **Tight: 5-30** Gall: 0-4
Aids: Bl: 0-6 Vi: 0-1 Tstrap: 0-0 Ckp: 0-0
Best Rating: **92** 7/05 York 5f good

Moderate; suited by 5f; acts on a sound surface; also goes on Polytrack; likes to dominate.

Triumphant Welcome

91(95) (63)**68**

4-y-o b g Piccolo-Shoof (USA) (Dayjur (USA))

H J Evans Mrs J Evans

Placings:310000-0030000 **(7869)**

2009: 5^{0}SD, 5^{0}GF, 6^{3}SD, 5^{0}SD, 5^{0}G, 6^{0}SD, 6^{0}SS,

	Starts	1st	2nd	3rd	Win & Pl
Career Total (Turf)	6	1	0	0	3238
Career Total (AW)	7	0	0	2	706

68 8/08 Gdwd 6f G-S £3238

Total win prize-money £3238

Going (Turf): Sf: 0-1 **GS: 1-1** Gd: 0-3 GF: 0-1 Fm: 0-0
Distance: **5f/6f: 1-13** 7f-8f: 0-0 9f-13f: 0-0 14f+: 0-0
Track : LH: 0-9 RH: 0-0 Tight: 0-5 Gall: 0-2
Aids: Bl: 0-1 Vi: 0-0 Tstrap: 0-0 Ckp: 0-0
Best Rating: **68** 8/08 Gdwd 6f gd-sft

Moderate; effective over 6f; acts on easy ground.

Trivia (IRE)

96(102) (81)**44**

5-y-o br m Marju (IRE)-Lehua (IRE) (Linamix (FR))

J J Bridger (Ms J S Doyle 13/4) W Wood

Placings:0310210/0040040003000-66000650 **(4051)**

2009: 7^{6}SD, 6^{6}SD, 6^{0}GF, 6^{0}F, 8^{0}GF, 7^{6}GF, 5^{5}GF, 5^{0}S,

	Starts	1st	2nd	3rd	Win & Pl
Career Total (Turf)	13	1	1	1	6426
Career Total (AW)	15	1	0	1	3637

81 10/07 Wolv 1m141y (0-75)H STD £2968
73 6/07 Bevl 7f100y G-F £3886

Total win prize-money £6855

Going (Turf): Sf: 0-1 GS: 0-0 Gd: 0-4 **GF: 1-7** Fm: 0-1
Distance: 5f/6f: 0-4 7f-8f: 1-21 9f-13f: 1-3 14f+: 0-0
Track : LH: 1-9 RH: 1-9 **Tight: 1-8** Gall: 0-0
Aids: Bl: 0-0 Vi: 0-0 Tstrap: 0-0 Ckp: 0-0
Best Rating: **81** 10/07 Wolv 1m141y stand

Modest; suited by 1m; acts on a sound surface and Polytrack.

Troopingthecolour

101(102) (86)**86**

3-y-o b c Nayef (USA)-Hyperspectra (Rainbow Quest (USA))

J H M Gosden H R H Princess Haya Of Jordan

Placings:22221 **(7550)**

2009: 10^{2}G, 10^{2}S, 10^{2}S, 10^{2}SD, 10^{1}SD,

	Starts	1st	2nd	3rd	Win & Pl
Career Total (Turf)	3	0	3	0	2891
Career Total (AW)	2	1	1	0	3536

86 11/09 Ling 1m2f STD £2729

Total win prize-money £2730

Going (Turf): **Sf: 0-2 GS: 0-0 Gd: 0-1 GF: 0-0 Fm: 0-0**
Distance: 5f/6f: 0-0 7f-8f: 0-0 **9f-13f: 1-5** 14f+: 0-0
Track : **LH: 1-4** RH: 0-1 **Tight: 1-2** Gall: 0-1
Aids: Bl: 0-0 Vi: 0-0 Tstrap: 0-0 Ckp: 0-0
Best Rating: **86** 11/09 Ling 1m2f stand

Useful; stays 1m2f; acts on fast and easy ground; goes on Polytrack.

Tropical Bachelor (IRE)

101(86) (52)**72**

3-y-o b g Bachelor Duke (USA)-Tropical Coral (IRE) (Pennekamp (USA))

T J Pitt (D W P Arbuthnot 24/1) M & A McBride,M Brennan & J Kilbride

Placings:0-53530250220 **(6845)**

2009: 10^{5}GF, 7^{3}GF, 12^{5}S, 12^{3}GF, 12^{0}G, 14^{2}GF, 14^{5}G, 17^{0}GF, 13^{2}GF, 12^{2}GF, 13^{0}G,

	Starts	1st	2nd	3rd	Win & Pl
Career Total (Turf)	11	0	3	2	3206
Career Total (AW)	1	0	0	0	

Going (Turf): **Sf: 0-1 GS: 0-0 Gd: 0-3 GF: 0-7 Fm: 0-0**
Distance: 5f/6f: 0-0 7f-8f: 0-2 9f-13f: 0-5 14f+: 0-5
Track : LH: 0-9 RH: 0-3 Tight: 0-7 Gall: 0-1
Aids: Bl: 0-3 Vi: 0-0 Tstrap: 0-1 Ckp: 0-1
Best Rating: **72** 5/09 Bevl 1m4f16y gd-fm

Modest; effective over 1m6f; acts on fast ground.

Tropical Blue

97(100) (79)**77**

3-y-o b g Fath (USA)-Tropical Zone (Machiavellian (USA))

Jennie Candlish P and Mrs G A Clarke

Placings:63262-236403 **(7785)**

2009: 10^{2}HY, 10^{3}GF, 14^{6}GF, 9^{4}S, 10^{0}GF, 13^{3}SD,

	Starts	1st	2nd	3rd	Win & Pl
Career Total (Turf)	10	0	3	2	4465
Career Total (AW)	1	0	0	1	482

Going (Turf): **Sf: 0-2 GS: 0-1 Gd: 0-1 GF: 0-6 Fm: 0-0**
Distance: 5f/6f: 0-1 7f-8f: 0-4 9f-13f: 0-4 14f+: 0-2
Track : LH: 0-7 RH: 0-1 Tight: 0-5 Gall: 0-0
Aids: Bl: 0-0 Vi: 0-2 Tstrap: 0-0 Ckp: 0-0
Best Rating: **79** 12/09 Wolv 1m5f194y stand

Fair; stays 1m6f; acts on fast and easy ground.

Tropical Duke (IRE)

97(86) (62)**65**

3-y-o ch g Bachelor Duke (USA)-Tropical Dance (USA) (Thorn Dance (USA))

R E Barr (D W P Arbuthnot 8/5) Brian Morton

Placings:0-400001313 **(6818)**

2009: 10^{4}SD, 10^{0}SD, 11^{0}GF, 14^{0}F, 9^{0}G, 8^{1}GF, 8^{3}GF, 9^{1}GF, 10^{3}GF,

	Starts	1st	2nd	3rd	Win & Pl
Career Total (Turf)	7	2	0	2	4764
Career Total (AW)	3	0	0	0	0

65 9/09 Bevl 1m1f207y (0-60)H G-F £2186
55 8/09 Rdcr 1m (0-60)H G-F £2047

Total win prize-money £4233

Going (Turf): Sf: 0-0 GS: 0-0 Gd: 0-1 **GF: 2-5** Fm: 0-1
Distance: 5f/6f: 0-0 7f-8f: 1-2 9f-13f: 1-7 14f+: 0-1
Track : LH: 0-4 **RH: 1-4** Tight: 0-4 Gall: 0-0
Aids: Bl: 0-0 Vi: 0-0 Tstrap: 0-0 Ckp: 0-0
Best Rating: **65** 9/09 Bevl 1m1f207y gd-fm

Moderate; effective at 1m-1m4f; acts on fast ground and Polytrack.

Tropical Paradise (IRE)

108(107) (92)**104**

3-y-o gr f Verglas (IRE)-Ladylishandra (IRE) (Mujadil (USA))

P Winkworth S Lovelace & R Muddle

Placings:32161-4210 **(6272)**

2009: 7^{4}S, 6^{2}G, 6^{1}S, 7^{0}GF,

	Starts	1st	2nd	3rd	Win & Pl
Career Total (Turf)	8	2	2	1	30811
Career Total (AW)	1	1	0	0	6670

104 9/09 Sals 6f212y (0-100)H SFT £18693
92 10/08 Kemp 6f (0-90) STD £6670
85 8/08 Wind 6f G-S £3885

Total win prize-money £29249

Going (Turf): **Sf: 1-3 GS: 1-2** Gd: 0-1 GF: 0-2 Fm: 0-0
Distance: **5f/6f: 2-5** 7f-8f: 1-4 9f-13f: 0-0 14f+: 0-0
Track : LH: 0-0 **RH: 1-1** Tight: 0-0 **Gall: 1-1**
Aids: Bl: 0-0 Vi: 0-0 Tstrap: 0-0 Ckp: 0-0
Best Rating: **104** 9/09 Sals 6f212y soft

Very useful; stays 7f; acts on most ground and on Polytrack.

Tropical Strait (IRE)

106(107) (102)**106**

6-y-o b g Intikhab (USA)-Tropical Dance (USA) (Thorn Dance (USA))

D W P Arbuthnot Francis Ward and Anthony Ward

Placings:422114/2012013-4 **(2075)**

2009: 13^{4}S,

	Starts	1st	2nd	3rd	Win & Pl
Career Total (Turf)	8	2	2	0	88271
Career Total (AW)	6	2	2	1	15987

106 11/08 Donc 1m4f H SFT £52963
101 8/08 Newb 1m5f61y (0-90)H G-S £7771
91 10/07 Wolv 1m4f50y (0-85)H STD £5181
91 9/07 Kemp 1m4f STD £4728

Total win prize-money £70645

Going (Turf): **Sf: 1-3 GS: 1-3** Gd: 0-1 GF: 0-1 Fm: 0-0
Distance: 5f/6f: 0-0 7f-8f: 0-0 **9f-13f: 3-9** 14f+: 1-5
Track : **LH: 3-8** RH: 1-6 Tight: 1-4 **Gall: 2-6**
Aids: Bl: 0-0 Vi: 0-0 Tstrap: 0-0 Ckp: 0-0
Best Rating: **106** 5/09 Newb 1m5f61y soft

Very useful; November Handicap winner in 2008; stays 1m6f; acts on good and soft ground and on Polytrack.

Tropical Tradition (IRE)

(103) (67)

4-y-o ch g Traditionally (USA)-Tropical Coral (IRE) (Pennekamp (USA))

D W P Arbuthnot George Ward

Placings:06613-30 **(0202)**

2009: 11^{3}SD, 12^{0}SD,

	Starts	1st	2nd	3rd	Win & Pl
Career Total (Turf)	0	0	0	0	
Career Total (AW)	7	1	0	2	2836

65 11/08 Kemp 1m3f (0-55) STD £2047

Total win prize-money £2047

Going (Turf): **Sf: 0-0 GS: 0-0 Gd: 0-0 GF: 0-0 Fm: 0-0**
Distance: 5f/6f: 0-0 7f-8f: 0-2 **9f-13f: 1-5** 14f+: 0-0
Track : LH: 0-5 **RH: 1-2** Tight: 0-4 Gall: 0-1

Aids: Bl: 0-0 Vi: 0-0 Tstrap: 0-0 Ckp: 0-0
Best Rating: **67** 12/08 Ling 1m4f stand

Modest; stays 1m4f; acts on Polytrack.

Tropical Treat

101 **85**

2-y-o b f Bahamian Bounty-Notjustaprettyface (USA) (Red Ransom (USA))
R M Beckett J C Smith

Placings:10 **(7016)**
2009: 5^{1}G, 6^{0}GS,

	Starts	1st	2nd	3rd	Win & Pl
Career Total (Turf)	**2**	**1**	**0**	**0**	**4695**

80 7/09 Wind 5f10y GD £4695
Total win prize-money £4695

Going (Turf): Sf: 0-0 GS: 0-1 **Gd: 1-1** GF: 0-0 Fm: 0-0
Distance: **5f/6f: 1-2** 7f-8f: 0-0 9f-13f: 0-0 14f+: 0-0
Track : LH: 0-0 RH: 0-0 Tight: 0-0 **Gall: 1-1**
Aids: Bl: 0-0 Vi: 0-0 Tstrap: 0-0 Ckp: 0-0
Best Rating: **85** 10/09 Donc 6f gd-sft

Useful; suited by 5f and good ground.

Trouble Mountain (USA)

103(83) (26)**68**

12-y-o br g Mt. Livermore (USA)-Trouble Free (USA) (Nodouble (USA))
M W Easterby Mrs Jean Turpin

Placings:1132/650006/0000000104020/56255031620006/012050030005440**23**/**3**3352440214235/6020043000005/03122136451245/50006433442/4601000306-006140626**0** **(7093)**
2009: 9^{0}GF, 10^{0}GS, 10^{6}G, 10^{1}GF, 10^{4}G, 10^{0}GF, 10^{6}GF, 10^{2}GS, 10^{6}GF, **11^{0}**SD,

	Starts	1st	2nd	3rd	Win & Pl
Career Total (Turf)	**122**	**11**	**14**	**12**	**116810**
Career Total (AW)	**5**	**0**	**1**	**2**	**1517**

59 6/09 Rdcr 1m2f (0-70)H G-F £2590
68 6/08 Newc 1m2f32y (0-70)H G-S £3238
77 9/06 Rdcr 1m2f (0-75)H GD £5181
78 6/06 Hayd 1m2f120y (0-85)H G-F £6477
73 5/06 Nott 1m1f213y (0-60)H SFT £3238
75 8/04 Hayd 1m2f120yD(0-80)H HVY £5687
78 4/03 Bevl 1m1f207yD(0-85)H FRM £5573
78 8/02 Donc 1m2f60yD(0-85)H SFT £19500
78 9/01 York 1m2f85yE(0-70)H G-F £6838
96 7/99 Donc 7f C G-F £6360
97 7/99 Hayd 6f D FRM £3663
Total win prize-money £68351

Going (Turf): Sf: 3-22GS: 1-25 Gd: 1-30**GF: 4-39** Fm: 2-6
Distance: 5f/6f: 1-2 7f-8f: 1-14 **9f-13f: 9-110** 14f+: 0-1
Track : **LH: 8-94** RH: 1-20 Tight: 2-30 **Gall: 3-35**
Aids: Bl: 0-9 Vi: 0-0 Tstrap: 0-0 Ckp: 0-0
Best Rating: **103** 9/99 Newb 6f8y gd-fm

Modest; stays 1m4f; acts on any ground; has worn blinkers and a tongue tie.

Troubletimestwo (FR)

95(92) (60)**58**

3-y-o gr g Linamix (FR)-Time Of Trouble (FR) (Warning)
A W Carroll (H J L Dunlop 7/5) Mill House Racing Syndicate

Placings:60-450 **(1811)**
2009: 9^{4}SD, 12^{5}GF, 10^{0}GF,

	Starts	1st	2nd	3rd	Win & Pl
Career Total (Turf)	**4**	**0**	**0**	**0**	**0**
Career Total (AW)	**1**	**0**	**0**	**0**	**216**

Going (Turf): **Sf: 0-1 GS: 0-0 Gd: 0-1 GF: 0-2 Fm: 0-0**
Distance: 5f/6f: 0-0 7f-8f: 0-2 9f-13f: 0-3 14f+: 0-0
Track : LH: 0-1 RH: 0-2 Tight: 0-3 Gall: 0-0
Aids: Bl: 0-0 Vi: 0-0 Tstrap: 0-0 Ckp: 0-0
Best Rating: **60** 3/09 Wolv 1m1f103y stand

Trovare (USA)

89 **61**

2-y-o b c Smart Strike (CAN)-Abita (USA) (Dynaformer (USA))
Mrs A J Perrett John Connolly

Placings:000 **(7146)**
2009: 7^{0}GF, 8^{0}G, 7^{0}G,

	Starts	1st	2nd	3rd	Win & Pl
Career Total (Turf)	**3**	**0**	**0**	**0**	

Going (Turf): **Sf: 0-0 GS: 0-0 Gd: 0-2 GF: 0-1 Fm: 0-0**
Distance: 5f/6f: 0-0 7f-8f: 0-3 9f-13f: 0-0 14f+: 0-0
Track : LH: 0-0 RH: 0-0 Tight: 0-0 Gall: 0-0
Aids: Bl: 0-0 Vi: 0-0 Tstrap: 0-0 Ckp: 0-0
Best Rating: **61** 10/09 NmkR 7f good

Truckers Delight (IRE)

105 (64)**84**

8-y-o b g Darazari (IRE)-Windmill Star (IRE) (Orchestra)
John Joseph Hanlon Mrs A F Mee

Placings:623-2100 **(6851)**
2009: 16^{2}GF, 16^{1}GY, 16^{0}S, 18^{0}G,

	Starts	1st	2nd	3rd	Win & Pl
Career Total (Turf)	**6**	**1**	**2**	**0**	**27410**
Career Total (AW)	**1**	**0**	**0**	**1**	**626**

84 6/09 Curr 2m (60-100)H G-Y £22121
Total win prize-money £22121

Going (Turf): **Sf: 0-1 GS: 0-0 Gd: 0-2 GF: 0-1 Fm: 0-0**
Distance: 5f/6f: 0-0 7f-8f: 0-0 9f-13f: 0-1 **14f+: 1-6**
Track : LH: 0-3 **RH: 1-4** Tight: 0-0 Gall: 0-1
Aids: Bl: 0-0 Vi: 0-0 Tstrap: 0-0 Ckp: 0-0
Best Rating: **84** 6/09 Curr 2m gd-yld

Useful; effective over 2m; acts on fast and easy ground.

True Britannia

91(96) (64)**55**

3-y-o b f Lujain (USA)-Surf Bird (Shareef Dancer (USA))
N B King (A M Hales 19/5) N Catterwell C Flinton R Swinfen B Williams

Placings:30**00010613-1613**0633 **(2169)**
2009: 10^{1}SD, **10^{6}**SD, **10^{1}**SD, **10^{3}**SD, **10^{0}**SD, 10^{6}G, 6^{3}F, 8^{3}GF,

	Starts	1st	2nd	3rd	Win & Pl
Career Total (Turf)	**5**	**0**	**0**	**3**	**1107**
Career Total (AW)	**13**	**4**	**0**	**2**	**9457**

64 2/09 Ling 1m2f (0-65)H STD £2047
59 1/09 Ling 1m2f (0-75)H STD £2900
57 12/08 Kemp 7f STD £2047
54 11/08 Kemp 1m (0-60) STD £1706
Total win prize-money £8700

Going (Turf): **Sf: 0-0 GS: 0-0 Gd: 0-2 GF: 0-2 Fm: 0-1**
Distance: 5f/6f: 0-5 7f-8f: 2-5 9f-13f: 2-8 14f+: 0-0
Track : LH: 2-8 RH: 2-7 **Tight: 2-7** Gall: 0-0
Aids: Bl: 0-0 **Vi: 3-8** Tstrap: 0-0 Ckp: 0-0
Best Rating: **64** 2/09 Ling 1m2f stand

Modest; stays 1m2f and acts on Polytrack; has worn a visor.

True Decision

94(101) (69)**62**

3-y-o b g Reset (AUS)-True Precision (Presidium)
S Kirk Dr B Matalon & T R Lock

Placings:0-**21**00**500554503** **(7426)**
2009: **6^{2}**SD, 7^{1}SD, **6^{0}**SD, 5^{0}G, 6^{5}F, **8^{0}**SD, 7^{0}SD, **8^{5}**SD, **6^{5}**SD, 7^{4}SD, **10^{5}**SD, **8^{0}**SD, **10^{3}**SD,

	Starts	1st	2nd	3rd	Win & Pl
Career Total (Turf)	**2**	**0**	**0**	**0**	**0**
Career Total (AW)	**12**	**1**	**1**	**1**	**3004**

68 3/09 Sthl 7f STD £2047
Total win prize-money £2047

Going (Turf): **Sf: 0-0 GS: 0-0 Gd: 0-1 GF: 0-0 Fm: 0-1**
Distance: 5f/6f: 0-6 **7f-8f: 1-5** 9f-13f: 0-3 14f+: 0-0
Track : **LH: 1-9** RH: 0-4 Tight: 0-6 Gall: 0-1
Aids: Bl: 0-0 Vi: 0-0 Tstrap: 0-0 Ckp: 0-0
Best Rating: **69** 3/09 Ling 6f stand

Modest; suited by 6f-7f; acts on Fibresand and Polytrack.

True Loves Kiss

91 **66**

2-y-o ch f Tobougg (IRE)-Bob's Princess (Bob's Return (IRE))
J A Glover (A J McCabe 26/5) Kennerley, Lane & Lennon

Placings:600 **(5669)**
2009: 5^{6}GS, 6^{0}GF, 7^{0}S,

	Starts	1st	2nd	3rd	Win & Pl
Career Total (Turf)	**3**	**0**	**0**	**0**	**0**

Going (Turf): **Sf: 0-1 GS: 0-1 Gd: 0-0 GF: 0-1 Fm: 0-0**
Distance: 5f/6f: 0-2 7f-8f: 0-1 9f-13f: 0-0 14f+: 0-0
Track : LH: 0-1 RH: 0-0 Tight: 0-1 Gall: 0-0
Aids: Bl: 0-0 Vi: 0-0 Tstrap: 0-0 Ckp: 0-0
Best Rating: **66** 5/09 Rdcr 6f gd-fm

True Red (IRE)

91(94) (57)**64**

2-y-o ch f Redback-Red Trance (IRE) (Soviet Star (USA))
Mrs N S Evans (B R Millman 21/8) Mrs Helen Llewelyn

Placings:025542**2**5230**52006** **(7778)**
2009: **5^{0}**SD, 5^{2}GF, 5^{5}GF, 5^{5}GF, 6^{4}G, 5^{2}G, **5^{2}**SD, 5^{5}G, 5^{2}G, 5^{3}GF, 5^{0}GF, **5^{5}**SD, **5^{2}**SD, **5^{0}**SD, **5^{0}**SD, **5^{6}**SD,

	Starts	1st	2nd	3rd	Win & Pl
Career Total (Turf)	**9**	**0**	**3**	**1**	**2794**
Career Total (AW)	**7**	**0**	**2**	**0**	**1209**

Going (Turf): **Sf: 0-0 GS: 0-0 Gd: 0-4 GF: 0-5 Fm: 0-0**
Distance: 5f/6f: 0-15 7f-8f: 0-1 9f-13f: 0-0 14f+: 0-0
Track : LH: 0-7 RH: 0-2 Tight: 0-3 Gall: 0-3
Aids: Bl: 0-0 Vi: 0-0 Tstrap: 0-0 Ckp: 0-0
Best Rating: **64** 4/09 Bath 5f11y gd-fm

Moderate; suited by 5f; acts on good ground; goes on Fibresand.

True To Form (IRE)

(84) (44)

2-y-o b g Rock Of Gibraltar (IRE)-Truly Yours (IRE) (Barathea (IRE))

Sir Mark Prescott G Moore - Osborne House

Placings:0000 (7177)

2009: 6^{0}SD, 5^{0}SD, 5^{0}SD, 7^{0}SD,

	Starts	1st	2nd	3rd	Win & Pl
Career Total (Turf)	0	0	0	0	
Career Total (AW)	4	0	0	0	

Going (Turf): **Sf: 0-0 GS: 0-0 Gd: 0-0 GF: 0-0 Fm: 0-0**
Distance: 5f/6f: 0-3 7f-8f: 0-1 9f-13f: 0-0 14f+: 0-0
Track : LH: 0-3 RH: 0-1 Tight: 0-2 Gall: 0-0
Aids: Bl: 0-0 Vi: 0-0 Tstrap: 0-0 Ckp: 0-0
Best Rating: **44** 10/09 Wolv 5f216y stand

Trueblue Wizard (IRE)

(100) (74)

3-y-o ch g Bachelor Duke (USA)-Truly Bewitched (USA) (Affirmed (USA))

W R Muir M J Caddy

Placings:1-44660 (6977)

2009: 7^{4}SD, 8^{4}SD, 10^{6}SD, 8^{6}SS, 8^{0}SD,

	Starts	1st	2nd	3rd	Win & Pl
Career Total (Turf)	0	0	0	0	
Career Total (AW)	6	1	0	0	3648

74 12/08 Sthl 7f STD £3070
Total win prize-money £3071

Going (Turf): **Sf: 0-0 GS: 0-0 Gd: 0-0 GF: 0-0 Fm: 0-0**
Distance: 5f/6f: 0-0 **7f-8f: 1-5** 9f-13f: 0-1 14f+: 0-0
Track : **LH: 1-4** RH: 0-2 Tight: 0-2 Gall: 0-0
Aids: Bl: 0-3 Vi: 0-0 Tstrap: 0-0 Ckp: 0-0
Best Rating: **74** 12/08 Sthl 7f stand

Fair; stays 7f; acts on Fibresand.

Truism

109 93

3-y-o b g Daylami (IRE)-Real Trust (USA) (Danzig (USA))

Mrs A J Perrett K Abdulla

Placings:61-5222 (6535)

2009: 7^{5}GS, 8^{2}GF, 8^{2}GF, 8^{2}GF,

	Starts	1st	2nd	3rd	Win & Pl
Career Total (Turf)	6	1	3	0	7298

82 10/08 Gdwd 7f G-F £3238
Total win prize-money £3238

Going (Turf): Sf: 0-0 GS: 0-2 Gd: 0-0 **GF: 1-4** Fm: 0-0
Distance: 5f/6f: 0-0 **7f-8f: 1-4** 9f-13f: 0-2 14f+: 0-0
Track : LH: 0-1 **RH: 1-3** Tight: 0-1 Gall: 0-0
Aids: Bl: 0-0 Vi: 0-0 Tstrap: 0-0 Ckp: 0-0
Best Rating: **93** 9/09 Gdwd 1m gd-fm

Useful; effective over 7f; acts on fast and easy ground.

Truly Asia (IRE)

100 82

3-y-o b g Acclamation-Tasha's Dream (USA) (Woodman (USA))

R Charlton H R H Sultan Ahmad Shah

Placings:4322231 (6937)

2009: 7^{4}GS, 8^{3}GF, 7^{2}G, 8^{2}G, 9^{2}GF, 8^{3}GF, 8^{1}G,

	Starts	1st	2nd	3rd	Win & Pl
Career Total (Turf)	7	1	3	2	8197

82 10/09 Bath 1m5y (0-75)H GD £2590
Total win prize-money £2590

Going (Turf): Sf: 0-0 GS: 0-1 **Gd: 1-3** GF: 0-3 Fm: 0-0
Distance: 5f/6f: 0-0 7f-8f: 0-3 **9f-13f: 1-4** 14f+: 0-0
Track : **LH: 1-2** RH: 0-3 **Tight: 1-4** Gall: 0-0
Aids: Bl: 0-0 Vi: 0-0 Tstrap: 0-0 Ckp: 0-0
Best Rating: **82** 10/09 Bath 1m5y good

Fair; stays 1m; acts on good and easy ground.

Truly Divine

80(98) (62)64

4-y-o b g Invincible Spirit (IRE)-Shabarana (FR) (Nishapour (FR))

C A Dwyer S B Components (international) Ltd

Placings:05340-400000 (7880)

2009: 6^{4}SD, 7^{0}G, 6^{0}SD, 8^{0}SD, 6^{0}SD, 7^{0}SD,

	Starts	1st	2nd	3rd	Win & Pl
Career Total (Turf)	5	0	0	1	753
Career Total (AW)	6	0	0	0	0

Going (Turf): **Sf: 0-0 GS: 0-2 Gd: 0-2 GF: 0-1 Fm: 0-0**
Distance: 5f/6f: 0-4 7f-8f: 0-7 9f-13f: 0-0 14f+: 0-0
Track : LH: 0-5 RH: 0-1 Tight: 0-4 Gall: 0-0
Aids: Bl: 0-0 Vi: 0-1 Tstrap: 0-1 Ckp: 0-1
Best Rating: **64** 9/08 Haml 6f5y gd-sft

Truly Magic

94(66) (5)60

2-y-o ch f Traditionally (USA)-Truly Bewitched (USA) (Affirmed (USA))

H J L Dunlop The Ex Pats

Placings:0006140 (6895)

2009: 6^{0}SD, 7^{0}GF, 5^{0}G, 5^{6}G, 7^{1}GF, 7^{4}CF, 8^{0}CF,

	Starts	1st	2nd	3rd	Win & Pl
Career Total (Turf)	6	1	0	0	4402
Career Total (AW)	1	0	0	0	

60 9/09 Leic 7f9y (0-70) G-F £4209
Total win prize-money £4209

Going (Turf): Sf: 0-0 GS: 0-0 Gd: 0-2 **GF: 1-4** Fm: 0-0
Distance: 5f/6f: 0-3 **7f-8f: 1-3** 9f-13f: 0-1 14f+: 0-0
Track : LH: 0-5 RH: 0-1 Tight: 0-0 Gall: 0-2
Aids: Bl: 0-0 Vi: 0-0 Tstrap: 0-0 Ckp: 0-0
Best Rating: **60** 9/09 Wwck 7f26y gd-fm

Modest; effective over 7f; acts on fast ground.

Trumpet Lily

109(91) (66)91

4-y-o b f Acclamation-Periwinkle (FR) (Perrault)

J G Portman Mrs J Edwards-Heathcote

Placings:640/4022100-130650340 (7132)

2009: 8^{1}GF, 8^{3}GF, 8^{0}G, 8^{6}G, 8^{5}G, 9^{0}G, 8^{3}GF, 10^{4}GF, 8^{0}SD,

	Starts	1st	2nd	3rd	Win & Pl
Career Total (Turf)	17	2	2	2	18811
Career Total (AW)	2	0	0	0	313

91 4/09 Wind 1m67y (0-85)H G-F £5180
86 8/08 NmkJ 1m (0-80)H SFT £5828
Total win prize-money £11009

Going (Turf): **Sf: 1-2** GS: 0-2 Gd: 0-8 **GF: 1-5** Fm: 0-0
Distance: 5f/6f: 0-0 7f-8f: 1-9 9f-13f: 1-10 14f+: 0-0
Track : LH: 0-4 **RH: 1-8 Tight: 1-6** Gall: 0-2
Aids: Bl: 0-0 Vi: 0-0 Tstrap: 0-0 Ckp: 0-0
Best Rating: **91** 4/09 Wind 1m67y gd-fm

Useful; stays 1m; acts on good and soft ground.

Trumpstoo (USA)

97 72

3-y-o b g Perfect Soul (IRE)-Cozzy Love (USA) (Cozzene (USA))

R A Fahey Mrs Suzanne Hart

Placings:51-0053065 (6384)

2009: 8^{0}GF, 10^{0}GF, 8^{5}G, 8^{3}G, 8^{0}S, 10^{6}GF, 16^{5}GF,

	Starts	1st	2nd	3rd	Win & Pl
Career Total (Turf)	9	1	0	1	4301

72 10/08 Newc 7f HVY £3723
Total win prize-money £3724

Going (Turf): **Sf: 1-3** GS: 0-0 Gd: 0-2 GF: 0-4 Fm: 0-0
Distance: 5f/6f: 0-0 **7f-8f: 1-4** 9f-13f: 0-4 14f+: 0-1
Track : LH: 0-4 RH: 0-4 Tight: 0-3 Gall: 0-2
Aids: Bl: 0-0 Vi: 0-0 Tstrap: 0-0 Ckp: 0-0
Best Rating: **72** 10/08 Newc 7f heavy

Fair; stays 1m; acts on good and softer ground.

Trusted Venture (USA)

(95) (59)14

3-y-o b g Trust N Luck (USA)-Afleet Canadian (CAN) (Bucksplasher (USA))

J R Best New Venture Racing

Placings:0601-64000 (6998)

2009: 7^{6}SD, 7^{4}SD, 8^{0}SD, 8^{0}SD, 9^{0}SD,

	Starts	1st	2nd	3rd	Win & Pl
Career Total (Turf)	1	0	0	0	
Career Total (AW)	8	1	0	0	2639

59 12/08 GrLe 1m (0-60) STD £2638
Total win prize-money £2639

Going (Turf): **Sf: 0-0 GS: 0-0 Gd: 0-0 GF: 0-1 Fm: 0-0**
Distance: 5f/6f: 0-2 **7f-8f: 1-6** 9f-13f: 0-1 14f+: 0-0
Track : **LH: 1-4** RH: 0-5 Tight: 0-3 **Gall: 1-1**
Aids: Bl: 0-0 Vi: 0-0 Tstrap: 0-0 Ckp: 0-0
Best Rating: **59** 12/08 GrLe 1m stand

Modest; stays 1m; acts on Polytrack; should improve.

Tryst

107(97) (87)98

4-y-o gr g Highest Honor (FR)-Courting (Pursuit Of Love)

Sir Michael Stoute Cheveley Park Stud

Placings:2-1230 (6480)

2009: 7^{1}SD, 7^{2}GF, 10^{3}G, 9^{0}GF,

	Starts	1st	2nd	3rd	Win & Pl
Career Total (Turf)	4	0	2	1	6160
Career Total (AW)	1	1	0	0	3562

87 5/09 Ling 7f STD £3561
Total win prize-money £3562

Going (Turf): **Sf: 0-0 GS: 0-0 Gd: 0-2 GF: 0-2 Fm: 0-0**
Distance: 5f/6f: 0-0 **7f-8f: 1-3** 9f-13f: 0-2 14f+: 0-0
Track : **LH: 1-1** RH: 0-1 **Tight: 1-1** Gall: 0-1
Aids: Bl: 0-0 Vi: 0-0 Tstrap: 0-0 Ckp: 0-0
Best Rating: **98** 5/09 NmkR 7f gd-fm

Very useful; effective at 7f-1m2f; acts on good and faster ground; goes on Polytrack.

Tsar Bomba (USA)

89 66

2-y-o b/br g Red Bullet (USA)-Larry's Blackhoney (USA) (Hennessy (USA))

T D Barron Miss N J Barron

Placings:5 (2339)

2009: 5^{5}GF,

	Starts	1st	2nd	3rd	Win & Pl
Career Total (Turf)	1	0	0	0	0

Going (Turf): Sf: 0-0 GS: 0-0 Gd: 0-0 GF: 0-1 Fm: 0-0
Distance: 5f/6f: 0-1 7f-8f: 0-0 9f-13f: 0-0 14f+: 0-0
Track : LH: 0-0 RH: 0-0 Tight: 0-0 Gall: 0-0
Aids: Bl: 0-0 Vi: 0-0 Tstrap: 0-0 Ckp: 0-0
Best Rating: 66 5/09 Rdcr 5f gd-fm

Tubby Littlejohns (IRE)

92 57

5-y-o ch h Desert Sun-Brookhouse Lady (IRE) (Polish Patriot (USA))

B J Llewellyn B J Llewellyn

Placings:25 (5061)

2009: 15^{2}G, 11^{5}GF,

	Starts	1st	2nd	3rd	Win & Pl
Career Total (Turf)	2	0	1	0	605

Going (Turf): Sf: 0-0 GS: 0-0 Gd: 0-1 GF: 0-1 Fm: 0-0
Distance: 5f/6f: 0-0 7f-8f: 0-0 9f-13f: 0-1 14f+: 0-1
Track : LH: 0-2 RH: 0-0 Tight: 0-2 Gall: 0-0
Aids: Bl: 0-0 Vi: 0-0 Tstrap: 0-0 Ckp: 0-0
Best Rating: 57 8/09 Bath 1m3f144y gd-fm

Moderate; stays 1m3f plus; acts on fast ground.

Tucker's Law

86(91) (67)70

2-y-o b g Country Reel (USA)-Silvereine (FR) (Bering)

B R Millman Mrs J Laws

Placings:02565466521 (7210)

2009: 5^{0}G, 5^{2}GF, 6^{5}GF, 5^{6}GF, 6^{5}HY, 6^{4}SD, 6^{6}SD, 5^{6}SD, 5^{5}SF, 6^{2}SD, 7^{1}SD,

	Starts	1st	2nd	3rd	Win & Pl
Career Total (Turf)	5	0	1	0	1397
Career Total (AW)	6	1	1	0	3282

57 11/09 Wolv 7f32y STD £2388
Total win prize-money £2388

Going (Turf): Sf: 0-1 GS: 0-0 Gd: 0-1 GF: 0-3 Fm: 0-0
Distance: 5f/6f: 0-9 7f-8f: 1-2 9f-13f: 0-0 14f+: 0-0
Track : LH: 1-4 RH: 0-4 Tight: 1-2 Gall: 0-1
Aids: Bl: 0-0 Vi: 0-0 Tstrap: 0-0 Ckp: 0-0
Best Rating: 70 5/09 Sals 5f gd-fm

Modest; stays 7f; acts on fast ground; goes on Polytrack.

Tudor Key (IRE)

104(101) (94)91

3-y-o br g Key Of Luck (USA)-Anne Boleyn (Rainbow Quest (USA))

Mrs A J Perrett Coombelands Racing Syndicate

Placings:4451-550100063 (6474)

2009: 10^{5}GF, 10^{5}GF, 8^{0}GF, 8^{1}SD, 8^{0}G, 8^{0}SD, 8^{0}GF, 8^{6}GF, 8^{3}GF,

	Starts	1st	2nd	3rd	Win & Pl
Career Total (Turf)	11	1	0	1	9955
Career Total (AW)	2	1	0	0	8743

94 7/09 Ling 1m (0-90) STD £8742
88 9/08 NmkR 1m G-F £5180
Total win prize-money £13924

Going (Turf): Sf: 0-0 GS: 0-1 Gd: 0-2 GF: 1-8 Fm: 0-0
Distance: 5f/6f: 0-0 7f-8f: 2-9 9f-13f: 0-4 14f+: 0-0
Track : LH: 1-2 RH: 0-2 Tight: 1-2 Gall: 0-0
Aids: Bl: 0-0 Vi: 0-0 Tstrap: 0-0 Ckp: 0-0
Best Rating: 94 7/09 Ling 1m stand

Useful; stays 1m; acts on fast ground; goes on Polytrack.

Tudor Prince (IRE)

100(105) (76)82

5-y-o b/br g Cape Cross (IRE)-Savona (IRE) (Cyrano De Bergerac)

A W Carroll Allan Jones

Placings:03022216/0535061/06003000502-10344002010 (7496)

2009: 6^{1}SD, 6^{0}HY, 6^{3}GF, 6^{4}GF, 6^{4}SD, 6^{0}G, 6^{0}G, 5^{2}SD, 6^{0}GS, 7^{1}SD, 5^{0}SD,

	Starts	1st	2nd	3rd	Win & Pl
Career Total (Turf)	29	2	2	4	19179
Career Total (AW)	8	2	3	0	6837

76 10/09 Kemp 7f (0-65)H STD £1619
74 4/09 Kemp 6f (0-70)H STD £2590
82 10/07 Yarm 6f3y (0-75)H G-S £2914
91 8/06 NmkJ 6f SFT £4533
Total win prize-money £11658

Going (Turf): Sf: 1-12 GS: 1-4 Gd: 0-7 GF: 0-6 Fm: 0-0
Distance: 5f/6f: 2-26 7f-8f: 2-11 9f-13f: 0-0 14f+: 0-0
Track : LH: 0-8 RH: 2-6 Tight: 0-6 Gall: 0-2
Aids: Bl: 0-1 Vi: 0-1 Tstrap: 0-0 Ckp: 0-0
Best Rating: 91 8/06 NmkJ 6f soft

Modest; effective over 6f-7f; acts on most ground and Polytrack; has worn a visor.

Tudor Princess

90 52

2-y-o b f King's Best (USA)-Santorini (USA) (Spinning World (USA))

W R Muir Usk Valley Stud

Placings:00 (6563)

2009: 6^{0}GF, 6^{0}GS,

	Starts	1st	2nd	3rd	Win & Pl
Career Total (Turf)	2	0	0	0	

Going (Turf): Sf: 0-0 GS: 0-1 Gd: 0-0 GF: 0-1 Fm: 0-0
Distance: 5f/6f: 0-1 7f-8f: 0-1 9f-13f: 0-0 14f+: 0-0
Track : LH: 0-0 RH: 0-0 Tight: 0-0 Gall: 0-0
Aids: Bl: 0-0 Vi: 0-0 Tstrap: 0-0 Ckp: 0-0
Best Rating: 52 9/09 Yarm 6f3y gd-fm

Tufton

102(103) (83)82

6-y-o b g King's Best (USA)-Mythical Magic (Green Desert (USA))

R A Fahey G Brogan

Placings:12/0244062204/31156-25311004 (7118)

2009: 10^{2}G, 10^{5}GS, 10^{3}GF, 11^{1}GF, 10^{1}GF, 9^{0}G, 10^{0}GS, 12^{4}GS,

	Starts	1st	2nd	3rd	Win & Pl
Career Total (Turf)	18	5	4	1	21561
Career Total (AW)	7	0	1	1	1561

76 7/09 Rdcr 1m2f G-F £2047
67 7/09 Haml 1m3f16y G-F £2388
71 7/08 Rdcr 1m2f GD £2388
82 5/08 Hayd 1m2f120y (0-75)H G-F £2590
80 8/05 Wind 6f G-F £5801
Total win prize-money £15214

Going (Turf): Sf: 0-2 GS: 0-3 Gd: 1-6 GF: 4-6 Fm: 0-1
Distance: 5f/6f: 1-1 7f-8f: 0-3 9f-13f: 4-21 14f+: 0-0
Track : LH: 3-14 RH: 1-8 Tight: 3-8 Gall: 1-5
Aids: Bl: 0-0 Vi: 0-0 Tstrap: 0-0 Ckp: 0-0
Best Rating: 94 4/07 Pont 1m4y good

Fair; stays 1m3f; acts on fast ground; goes on Polytrack; has worn a tongue-tie.

Tukitinyasok (IRE)

94(91) (63)84

2-y-o b g Fath (USA)-Mevlana (IRE) (Red Sunset)

R F Fisher Des Johnston

Placings:313403 (7717)

2009: 7^{3}GF, 7^{1}G, 7^{3}S, 6^{4}G, 7^{0}GF, 8^{3}SD,

	Starts	1st	2nd	3rd	Win & Pl
Career Total (Turf)	5	1	0	2	4804
Career Total (AW)	1	0	0	1	1322

80 7/09 Ayr 7f50y GD £2914
Total win prize-money £2914

Going (Turf): Sf: 0-1 GS: 0-0 Gd: 1-2 GF: 0-2 Fm: 0-0
Distance: 5f/6f: 0-0 7f-8f: 1-5 9f-13f: 0-1 14f+: 0-0
Track : LH: 1-3 RH: 0-0 Tight: 0-2 Gall: 0-0
Aids: Bl: 0-0 Vi: 0-0 Tstrap: 0-0 Ckp: 0-0
Best Rating: 84 7/09 Newb 7f soft

Useful; stays 7f on a sound surface.

Tulip Explosion

76(89) (45)42

2-y-o b f Exceed And Excel (AUS)-Comme Ca (Cyrano De Bergerac)

D Shaw Phil Middleton & Tuesday Rhodes

Placings:00030 (5776)

2009: 5^{0}G, 5^{0}SD, 5^{0}G, 5^{3}SF, 5^{0}SD,

	Starts	1st	2nd	3rd	Win & Pl
Career Total (Turf)	2	0	0	0	
Career Total (AW)	3	0	0	1	403

Going (Turf): Sf: 0-0 GS: 0-0 Gd: 0-2 GF: 0-0 Fm: 0-0
Distance: 5f/6f: 0-5 7f-8f: 0-0 9f-13f: 0-0 14f+: 0-0
Track : LH: 0-1 RH: 0-1 Tight: 0-1 Gall: 0-0
Aids: Bl: 0-0 Vi: 0-0 Tstrap: 0-0 Ckp: 0-0
Best Rating: 45 8/09 Wolv 5f20y std-fst

Tumblecloud (IRE)

(77) (45)43

4-y-o b f Mujadil (USA)-Sudden Interest (FR) (Highest Honor (FR))

W A Murphy John A Murphy

Placings:0/0050-00 (7379a)

2009: 9^{0}SF, 7^{0}SD,

	Starts	1st	2nd	3rd	Win & Pl
Career Total (Turf)	2	0	0	0	

Career Total (AW) 5 0 0 0

Going (Turf): Sf: 0-0 GS: 0-0 Gd: 0-1 GF: 0-0 Fm: 0-0
Distance: 5f/6f: 0-0 7f-8f: 0-4 9f-13f: 0-3 14f+: 0-0
Track: LH: 0-5 RH: 0-1 Tight: 0-1 Gall: 0-0
Aids: Bl: 0-2 Vi: 0-0 Tstrap: 0-0 Ckp: 0-0
Best Rating: 45 8/08 Dund 7f stand

Tumbled Again

33(76) (24)
2-y-o br g Tumbleweed Ridge-Amber Brown (Thowra (FR))
M E Rimmer Winning Circle Partnership

Placings:00 (7199)
2009: 6^{0}G, 8^{0}SD,

	Starts	1st	2nd	3rd	Win & Pl
Career Total (Turf)	1	0	0	0	
Career Total (AW)	1	0	0	0	

Going (Turf): Sf: 0-0 GS: 0-0 Gd: 0-1 GF: 0-0 Fm: 0-0
Distance: 5f/6f: 0-1 7f-8f: 0-1 9f-13f: 0-0 14f+: 0-0
Track: LH: 0-1 RH: 0-0 Tight: 0-1 Gall: 0-0
Aids: Bl: 0-0 Vi: 0-0 Tstrap: 0-0 Ckp: 0-0
Best Rating: 24 11/09 Ling 1m stand

Tumbleweed Di

73 (47)47
5-y-o ro m Tumbleweed Ridge-Peggotty (Capricorn Line)
John A Harris Derby House Racing

Placings:406605/060640-0 (5982)
2009: 8^{0}GF,

	Starts	1st	2nd	3rd	Win & Pl
Career Total (Turf)	9	0	0	0	366
Career Total (AW)	4	0	0	0	0

Going (Turf): Sf: 0-0 GS: 0-0 Gd: 0-0 GF: 0-8 Fm: 0-1
Distance: 5f/6f: 0-11 7f-8f: 0-1 9f-13f: 0-1 14f+: 0-0
Track: LH: 0-2 RH: 0-3 Tight: 0-2 Gall: 0-0
Aids: Bl: 0-0 Vi: 0-0 Tstrap: 0-1 Ckp: 0-1
Best Rating: 50 5/08 Rdcr 6f gd-fm

Tump Mac

79(59) 61
5-y-o ch g Compton Admiral-Petite Elite (Anfield)
N Bycroft N Bycroft

Placings:560000-000000 (6488)
2009: 6^{0}GF, 7^{0}GF, 10^{0}S, 7^{0}GF, 7^{0}GF, 10^{0}GF,

	Starts	1st	2nd	3rd	Win & Pl
Career Total (Turf)	11	0	0	0	0
Career Total (AW)	1	0	0	0	

Going (Turf): Sf: 0-1 GS: 0-0 Gd: 0-3 GF: 0-7 Fm: 0-0
Distance: 5f/6f: 0-4 7f-8f: 0-5 9f-13f: 0-3 14f+: 0-0
Track: LH: 0-5 RH: 0-1 Tight: 0-2 Gall: 0-0
Aids: Bl: 0-0 Vi: 0-0 Tstrap: 0-0 Ckp: 0-0
Best Rating: 61 6/08 Donc 6f good

Tunder Bool (IRE)

(83) (22)
4-y-o b g Intikhab (USA)-Tirolean Dance (IRE) (Tirol)
F Sheridan (P Giannotti 6/1) Frank Sheridan

Placings:050/520620230510043000022-00 (0537)
2009: 11^{0}S, 9^{0}SD,

	Starts	1st	2nd	3rd	Win & Pl
Career Total (Turf)	24	1	5	2	7779
Career Total (AW)	1	0	0	0	

5/08 Casc 1m1f H HVY £2205
Total win prize-money £2206

Going (Turf): Sf: 1-12 GS: 0-0 Gd: 0-11 GF: 0-0 Fm: 0-0
Distance: 5f/6f: 0-0 7f-8f: 0-4 9f-13f: 1-21 14f+: 0-0
Track: LH: 0-1 RH: 0-0 Tight: 0-1 Gall: 0-0
Aids: Bl: 0-4 Vi: 0-0 Tstrap: 0-0 Ckp: 0-0
Best Rating: 22 2/09 Wolv 1m1f103y stand

Tune Up The Band

(83) (22)60
5-y-o b g Bandmaster (USA)-Name That Tune (Fayruz)
R J Hodges Beckington Racing

Placings:3/2-0 (0475)
2009: 5^{0}SD,

	Starts	1st	2nd	3rd	Win & Pl
Career Total (Turf)	2	0	1	1	1031
Career Total (AW)	1	0	0	0	

Going (Turf): Sf: 0-0 GS: 0-1 Gd: 0-0 GF: 0-1 Fm: 0-0
Distance: 5f/6f: 0-3 7f-8f: 0-0 9f-13f: 0-0 14f+: 0-0
Track: LH: 0-3 RH: 0-0 Tight: 0-1 Gall: 0-2
Aids: Bl: 0-0 Vi: 0-0 Tstrap: 0-0 Ckp: 0-0
Best Rating: 66 4/06 Bath 5f11y gd-sft

Tungsten Strike (USA)

106 113
8-y-o ch g Smart Strike (CAN)-Bathilde (IRE) (Generous (IRE))
Mrs A J Perrett John Connolly

Placings:400/0113210/020102/210300/150610/4032140-540060 (6273)
2009: 16^{5}GF, 16^{4}G, 16^{0}G, 16^{0}GS, 14^{6}G, 16^{0}GF,

	Starts	1st	2nd	3rd	Win & Pl
Career Total (Turf)	41	8	5	3	287315

110 8/08 Gdwd 1m6f G-S £28385
116 8/07 Gdwd 1m6f GD £17034
113 5/07 Asct 2m G-F £28390
114 5/06 Sand 2m78y SFT £51102
107 9/05 Sals 1m6f15y G-F £9193
110 9/04 NmkR 1m6f GD £17400
89 7/04 Ling 2m E(0-75)H GD £4251
81 7/04 Kemp 1m6f92yD(0-80)H G-F £8092
Total win prize-money £163848

Going (Turf): Sf: 1-3 GS: 1-7 Gd: 3-15 GF: 3-16 Fm: 0-0
Distance: 5f/6f: 0-0 7f-8f: 0-3 9f-13f: 0-3 14f+: 8-35
Track: LH: 1-8 RH: 7-31 Tight: 4-13 Gall: 2-19
Aids: Bl: 0-0 Vi: 0-2 Tstrap: 1-6 Ckp: 1-6
Best Rating: 116 8/07 Gdwd 1m6f good

Very useful; winner of the Group 2 Henry II Stakes back in 2006; stays 2m, but effective at shorter; effective on most ground; has worn cheekpieces and a visor; likes to race prominently.

Tuning Fork

(98) (53)4
9-y-o b g Alzao (USA)-Tuning (Rainbow Quest (USA))
M J Attwater Canisbay Bloodstock

Placings:126650/0000030000/000000000/2205000/03/62 3066006040-000 (3269)
2009: 7^{0}SD, 11^{0}SD, 8^{0}SD,

	Starts	1st	2nd	3rd	Win & Pl
Career Total (Turf)	32	1	3	1	51987
Career Total (AW)	17	0	1	2	994

83 5/03 Hayd 1m2f120y D SFT £5726
Total win prize-money £5727

Going (Turf): Sf: 1-3 GS: 0-3 Gd: 0-9 GF: 0-15 Fm: 0-2
Distance: 5f/6f: 0-1 7f-8f: 0-22 9f-13f: 1-25 14f+: 0-1
Track: LH: 1-19 RH: 0-21 Tight: 0-16 Gall: 0-6
Aids: Bl: 0-0 Vi: 0-1 Tstrap: 0-2 Ckp: 0-2
Best Rating: 111 5/03 York 1m2f88y gd-fm

Moderate performer; formerly Group class and was runner-up in the 2003 Dante, stays 1m2f, but better at shorter; acts on most types of ground; has worn a visor, cheek-pieces, eyeshield and tongue tie; suited by forcing tactics.

Tuppenny Piece

71(96) (59)16
3-y-o ch f Sakhee (USA)-Tuppenny (Salse (USA))
W R Swinburn Mrs Doreen M Swinburn

Placings:00-40440 (7214)
2009: 11^{4}SD, 11^{0}G, 11^{4}SD, 12^{4}SD, 13^{0}SD,

	Starts	1st	2nd	3rd	Win & Pl
Career Total (Turf)	1	0	0	0	
Career Total (AW)	6	0	0	0	192

Going (Turf): Sf: 0-0 GS: 0-0 Gd: 0-1 GF: 0-0 Fm: 0-0
Distance: 5f/6f: 0-0 7f-8f: 0-2 9f-13f: 0-4 14f+: 0-1
Track: LH: 0-3 RH: 0-4 Tight: 0-3 Gall: 0-0
Aids: Bl: 0-0 Vi: 0-0 Tstrap: 0-1 Ckp: 0-1
Best Rating: 59 9/09 Kemp 1m4f stand

Turbo Shandy

84(91) (43)47
6-y-o b g Piccolo-Carn Maire (Northern Prospect (USA))
D Burchell (M G Rimell 25/5) The Beefeaters

Placings:0660 (7495)
2009: 6^{0}GF, 5^{6}GS, 8^{6}F, 12^{0}SD,

	Starts	1st	2nd	3rd	Win & Pl
Career Total (Turf)	3	0	0	0	140
Career Total (AW)	1	0	0	0	

Going (Turf): Sf: 0-0 GS: 0-1 Gd: 0-0 GF: 0-1 Fm: 0-1
Distance: 5f/6f: 0-2 7f-8f: 0-0 9f-13f: 0-2 14f+: 0-0
Track: LH: 0-2 RH: 0-0 Tight: 0-2 Gall: 0-0
Aids: Bl: 0-0 Vi: 0-0 Tstrap: 0-0 Ckp: 0-0
Best Rating: 47 7/09 Sals 6f gd-fm

Turf Time

68(90) (46)
2-y-o b g Zafeen (FR)-Next Time (IRE) (Danetime (IRE))
J A Glover (A J McCabe 17/6) Sexy Six Partnership

Placings:500002 (7778)
2009: 5^{5}SD, 5^{0}G, 5^{0}SD, 5^{0}GF, 5^{0}GF, 5^{2}SD,

	Starts	1st	2nd	3rd	Win & Pl
Career Total (Turf)	3	0	0	0	
Career Total (AW)	3	0	1	0	605

Going (Turf): Sf: 0-0 GS: 0-0 Gd: 0-1 GF: 0-2 Fm: 0-0

Distance: 5f/6f: 0-6 7f-8f: 0-0 9f-13f: 0-0 14f+: 0-0
Track : LH: 0-1 RH: 0-0 Tight: 0-1 Gall: 0-0
Aids: Bl: 0-0 Vi: 0-0 Tstrap: 0-1 Ckp: 0-1
Best Rating: 46 12/09 Sthl 5f stand

Moderate; suited by 5f and acts on Fibresand.

Turf Trivia

91 **64**
2-y-o gr g Alhaarth (IRE)-Exclusive Approval (USA) (With Approval (CAN))
G M Moore Mrs Phillipa Davies

Placings:4530 **(6793)**
2009: 6^{4}S, 7^{5}GF, 7^{3}GS, 8^{0}S,

	Starts	1st	2nd	3rd	Win & Pl
Career Total (Turf)	4	0	0	1	842

Going (Turf): Sf: 0-2 GS: 0-1 Gd: 0-0 GF: 0-1 Fm: 0-0
Distance: 5f/6f: 0-1 7f-8f: 0-2 9f-13f: 0-1 14f+: 0-0
Track : LH: 0-1 RH: 0-0 Tight: 0-0 Gall: 0-0
Aids: Bl: 0-0 Vi: 0-0 Tstrap: 0-0 Ckp: 0-0
Best Rating: 64 6/09 Donc 7f gd-fm

Modwstr; stays 7f; acts on fast ground.

Turfwolke (GER)

95(93) (51)**65**
4-y-o b f Medicean-Turfaue (GER) (Big Shuffle (USA))
Mrs H S Main Wetumpka Racing

Placings:6240-400600 **(7614)**
2009: 7^{4}GF, 7^{0}SD, 8^{0}GF, 7^{6}GS, **10^{0}SD**, 7^{0}SD,

	Starts	1st	2nd	3rd	Win & Pl
Career Total (Turf)	7	0	1	0	1830
Career Total (AW)	3	0	0	0	

Going (Turf): Sf: 0-0 GS: 0-2 Gd: 0-2 GF: 0-3 Fm: 0-0
Distance: 5f/6f: 0-0 7f-8f: 0-6 9f-13f: 0-4 14f+: 0-0
Track : LH: 0-5 RH: 0-3 Tight: 0-3 Gall: 0-0
Aids: Bl: 0-0 Vi: 0-0 Tstrap: 0-0 Ckp: 0-0
Best Rating: 65 5/09 Wwck 7f26y gd-fm

Modest; suited by 1m and fast ground.

Turjuman (USA)

103(78) (10)**73**
4-y-o ch g Swain (IRE)-Hachiyah (IRE) (Generous (IRE))
W J Musson I Johnson & John D Jacques

Placings:6/346264000-411355 **(6473)**
2009: 10^{4}GS, 11^{1}GF, 11^{1}G, 12^{3}GF, 12^{5}GF, 12^{5}GF,

	Starts	1st	2nd	3rd	Win & Pl
Career Total (Turf)	15	2	1	2	18448
Career Total (AW)	1	0	0	0	

67	7/09	Wind	1m3f135y	(0-80)H	GD	£5375
67	6/09	Wind	1m3f135y	(0-70)H	G-F	£2729

Total win prize-money £8105

Going (Turf): Sf: 0-4 GS: 0-2 **Gd: 1-4 GF: 1-4** Fm: 0-0
Distance: 5f/6f: 0-0 7f-8f: 0-1 **9f-13f: 2-15** 14f+: 0-0
Track : LH: 0-6 RH: 0-6 **Tight: 2-7** Gall: 0-2
Aids: Bl: 0-0 Vi: 0-0 Tstrap: 0-0 Ckp: 0-0
Best Rating: 80 3/08 StCl 1m2f110y heavy

Modest; stays 1m3f; acts on good and faster ground.

Turkish Lokum

97(96) (63)**64**
3-y-o b f Bertolini (USA)-Malabarista (FR) (Assert)
J M P Eustace Yildirim Gelgin

Placings:040-0035330 **(7052)**
2009: 7^{0}SD, 5^{0}G, 7^{3}G, 8^{5}GS, **5^{3}SD**, 7^{3}SF, 7^{0}SD,

	Starts	1st	2nd	3rd	Win & Pl
Career Total (Turf)	6	0	0	1	644
Career Total (AW)	4	0	0	2	756

Going (Turf): Sf: 0-1 GS: 0-1 Gd: 0-2 GF: 0-2 Fm: 0-0
Distance: 5f/6f: 0-5 7f-8f: 0-4 9f-13f: 0-1 14f+: 0-0
Track : LH: 0-4 RH: 0-1 Tight: 0-3 Gall: 0-1
Aids: Bl: 0-0 Vi: 0-0 Tstrap: 0-0 Ckp: 0-0
Best Rating: 64 6/09 Wwck 7f26y good

Fair; effective over 6f; acts on soft ground.

Turkish Sultan (IRE)

86(102) (57)**55**
6-y-o b g Anabaa (USA)-Odalisque (IRE) (Machiavellian (USA))
J M Bradley Miss Diane Hill

Placings:220/22530/05543003200/106000402264033-00653043000530 **(7718)**
2009: 9^{0}SD, 10^{0}SD, 8^{6}SD, 10^{5}SD, 9^{3}SD, 11^{0}SD, 8^{4}SD, 8^{3}SD, 10^{0}GF, 8^{0}SD, 8^{0}SD, 9^{5}SD, 8^{3}SD, 9^{0}SD,

	Starts	1st	2nd	3rd	Win & Pl
Career Total (Turf)	26	1	5	3	8859
Career Total (AW)	22	0	2	5	2721

55	4/08	Bath	1m5y	(0-55)	GD	£1942

Total win prize-money £1943

Going (Turf): Sf: 0-8 GS: 0-2 **Gd: 1-6** GF: 0-8 Fm: 0-2
Distance: 5f/6f: 0-6 7f-8f: 0-23 **9f-13f: 1-19** 14f+: 0-0
Track : **LH: 1-26** RH: 0-10 **Tight: 1-17** Gall: 0-1
Aids: Bl: 0-1 Vi: 0-3 Tstrap: 1-34 Ckp: 1-34
Best Rating: 72 8/05 Thsk 7f gd-fm

Moderate; effective over 7f-1m; acts on fast and heavy ground; has worn cheekpieces.

Turn Me On (IRE)

107(101) (85)**88**
6-y-o b g Tagula (IRE)-Jacobina (Magic Ring (IRE))
T D Walford David Dickson

Placings:33/0435/02210000246/136223143-11020502600 **(7083)**
2009: 7^{1}F, 7^{1}GF, 7^{0}G, 7^{2}GF, 7^{0}G, 7^{5}G, 7^{0}GS, 8^{2}GF, **9^{6}SD**, 7^{0}G, 7^{0}S,

	Starts	1st	2nd	3rd	Win & Pl
Career Total (Turf)	30	4	6	5	24715
Career Total (AW)	7	1	1	1	3386

85	5/09	Catt	7f	(0-80)H	G-F	£4727
84	4/09	Thsk	7f	(0-75)H	FRM	£4274
80	8/08	Catt	5f212y	(0-75)H	GD	£2590
73	5/08	Catt	7f	(0-75)H	G-F	£2729
70	6/07	Wolv	1m141y	(0-60)H	SF	£2307

Total win prize-money £16629

Going (Turf): Sf: 0-1 GS: 0-4 Gd: 1-10 **GF: 2-13** Fm: 1-2
Distance: 5f/6f: 1-8 **7f-8f: 3-23** 9f-13f: 1-6 14f+: 0-0
Track : **LH: 5-26** RH: 0-5 **Tight: 5-21** Gall: 0-3
Aids: Bl: 0-1 Vi: 0-0 Tstrap: 0-0 Ckp: 0-0
Best Rating: 88 9/09 Pont 1m4y gd-fm

Useful; effective at 6f-1m; acts on most ground; has worn a tongue-tie.

Turn On The Style

(109) (109)**107**
7-y-o ch g Pivotal-Elegant Rose (Noalto)
J Balding The Haydock Badgeholders

Placings:00210621/14220/660/1115024023125/14050011-2460 **(7488)**
2009: 6^{2}SD, 5^{4}SD, 5^{6}SD, 6^{0}SD,

	Starts	1st	2nd	3rd	Win & Pl
Career Total (Turf)	19	3	4	0	61498
Career Total (AW)	22	7	4	1	60986

109	12/08	Ling	6f	(0-100)H	STD	£11656
107	12/08	Sthl	5f	(0-95)H	STD	£7771
107	2/08	Ndas	6f	(95-110)H	GD	£36180
105	12/07	Ling	6f	(0-95)H	STD	£6855
99	2/07	Ling	5f	(0-100)H	STD	£11217
98	1/07	Ling	5f	(0-75)H	STD	£3238
93	1/07	Sthl	6f	(0-85)H	STD	£4857
83	5/05	Hayd	6f	(0-85)H	SFT	£7373
75	12/04	Wolv	5f20y	(0-75)	STD	£3425
67	10/04	Catt	5f		GD	£3415

Total win prize-money £95995

Going (Turf): Sf: 1-3 GS: 0-3 **Gd: 2-9** GF: 0-4 Fm: 0-0
Distance: **5f/6f: 10-41** 7f-8f: 0-0 9f-13f: 0-0 14f+: 0-0
Track : **LH: 7-21** RH: 0-1 **Tight: 5-17** Gall: 1-4
Aids: **Bl: 9-36** Vi: 0-0 Tstrap: 0-0 Ckp: 0-0
Best Rating: 109 12/08 Ling 6f stand

Smart; effective over 5f-6f; acts on any ground and on sand; has worn blinkers.

Turn To Dreams

73(98) (58)**51**
3-y-o b f Auction House (USA)-Seren Teg (Timeless Times (USA))
P D Evans Mrs I M Folkes

Placings:0043256040204400-24542346252506005 **(7818)**
2009: 8^{2}SD, 8^{4}SD, 8^{5}SD, 8^{4}SD, 8^{2}SD, 8^{3}SD, 9^{4}SD, 8^{6}SD, 9^{2}SD, 8^{5}SD, 9^{2}SD, 9^{5}SF, 8^{0}SD, 8^{6}SD, 10^{0}G, 8^{0}SD, 9^{5}SD,

	Starts	1st	2nd	3rd	Win & Pl
Career Total (Turf)	7	0	1	1	1314
Career Total (AW)	25	0	5	1	3916

Going (Turf): Sf: 0-1 GS: 0-1 Gd: 0-2 GF: 0-3 Fm: 0-0
Distance: 5f/6f: 0-13 7f-8f: 0-6 9f-13f: 0-13 14f+: 0-0
Track : LH: 0-23 RH: 0-4 Tight: 0-18 Gall: 0-6
Aids: Bl: 0-0 Vi: 0-7 Tstrap: 0-0 Ckp: 0-0
Best Rating: 58 2/09 Wolv 1m1f103y stand

Moderate; effective at 1m-1m1f; acts on fast ground; goes on Polytrack.

Turner's Touch

89(104) (60)**73**
7-y-o ch g Compton Place-Chairmans Daughter (Unfuwain (USA))
G L Moore G L Moore

Placings:53625406031/3116140012/46031205330434423/01322030000360-334200645005 **(7658)**
2009: 12^{3}SD, 12^{3}SD, 12^{4}SD, 12^{2}SD, 12^{0}SD, 12^{0}SD, 12^{6}SD, 11^{4}GF, 11^{5}GF, 11^{0}G, 12^{0}SD, 12^{5}SD,

	Starts	1st	2nd	3rd	Win & Pl
Career Total (Turf)	16	0	1	3	3265
Career Total (AW)	48	7	6	10	26009

70	3/08	Ling	1m4f		STD	£1774
77	3/07	Ling	1m4f	(0-70)H	STD	£2914
76	12/06	Kemp	1m4f	(0-65)H	STD	£2388

69 4/06 Kemp 1m4f (0-65)H STD £3238
68 3/06 Ling 1m2f (0-60)H STD £2388
60 2/06 Ling 1m2f (0-60)H STD £2047
61 12/05 Ling 1m2f (0-45) STD £1460
Total win prize-money £16216

Going (Turf): **Sf: 0-0 GS: 0-2 Gd: 0-6 GF: 0-7 Fm: 0-1**
Distance: 5f/6f: 0-0 7f-8f: 0-4 **9f-13f: 7-59** 14f+: 0-1
Track : **LH: 5-40** RH: 2-21 **Tight: 5-36** Gall: 0-2
Aids: **Bl: 6-49** Vi: 0-2 Tstrap: 1-3 Ckp: 1-3
Best Rating: 79 1/07 Ling 1m4f stand

Moderate; stays 1m4f; acts on fast ground and on Polytrack; often wears eyeshield/blinkers; does not always put it all in.

Turning Circle

(92) (49)
3-y-o b c Spinning World (USA)-Willow Dale (IRE) (Danehill (USA))
M Brittain Mel Brittain

Placings:0 **(7671)**
2009: 8^{0}SD,

	Starts	1st	2nd	3rd	Win & Pl
Career Total (Turf)	0	0	0	0	
Career Total (AW)	1	0	0	0	

Going (Turf): **Sf: 0-0 GS: 0-0 Gd: 0-0 GF: 0-0 Fm: 0-0**
Distance: 5f/6f: 0-0 7f-8f: 0-0 9f-13f: 0-1 14f+: 0-0
Track : LH: 0-1 RH: 0-0 Tight: 0-1 Gall: 0-0
Aids: Bl: 0-0 Vi: 0-0 Tstrap: 0-0 Ckp: 0-0
Best Rating: 49 12/09 Wolv 1m141y stand

Turning Top (IRE)

101(89) (59)**86**
3-y-o b f Pivotal-Pietra Dura (Cadeaux Genereux)
S A Callaghan Michael Tabor

Placings:0-36102310 **(5607)**
2009: 8^{3}G, 8^{6}SD, 7^{1}GF, 8^{0}G, 7^{2}G, 5^{3}F, 8^{1}GF, 6^{0}S,

	Starts	1st	2nd	3rd	Win & Pl
Career Total (Turf)	7	2	1	2	7455
Career Total (AW)	2	0	0	0	0

86 8/09 Wind 1m67y (0-75)H G-F £2729
70 6/09 Wwck 7f26y G-F £2914
Total win prize-money £5644

Going (Turf): Sf: 0-1 GS: 0-0 Gd: 0-3 **GF: 2-2** Fm: 0-1
Distance: 5f/6f: 0-1 7f-8f: 1-6 9f-13f: 1-2 14f+: 0-0
Track : LH: 1-5 RH: 1-1 **Tight: 1-4** Gall: 0-0
Aids: Bl: 0-0 Vi: 0-0 Tstrap: 0-0 Ckp: 0-0
Best Rating: 86 8/09 Wind 1m67y gd-fm

Fair; effective over 7f-1m; acts on fast ground.

Turnkey

102 **100**
7-y-o br g Pivotal-Persian Air (Persian Bold)
D Nicholls Middleham Park Racing Xxiii

Placings:21540/162503/302/0005201620000/61400-06153110 **(6050)**
2009: 6^{0}GF, 6^{6}GF, 6^{1}GS, 5^{5}S, 5^{3}G, 6^{1}GF, 5^{1}GS, 6^{0}G,

	Starts	1st	2nd	3rd	Win & Pl
Career Total (Turf)	41	7	5	3	80425

85 8/09 Carl 5f193y G-S £2590
80 8/09 Ayr 6f G-F £2590
83 6/09 Ripn 6f G-S £3238
100 4/08 Pont 6f (0-100)H G-S £11215
101 7/07 Pont 6f (0-90)H GD £9348
99 4/05 Leic 5f218y SFT £6113
98 5/04 Kemp 5f D HVY £5388
Total win prize-money £40484

Going (Turf): Sf: 2-10 **GS: 3-11**Gd: 1-10 GF: 1-7 Fm: 0-0
Distance: **5f/6f: 7-33** 7f-8f: 0-8 9f-13f: 0-0 14f+: 0-0
Track : **LH: 2-7** RH: 1-5 Tight: 0-2 Gall: 0-0
Aids: Bl: 0-3 Vi: 0-1 Tstrap: 0-0 Ckp: 0-0
Best Rating: 106 11/05 Leop 7f sft-hvy

Useful; effective over 6f-7f; acts on most ground; usually held up.

Tuscan Gold

83(85) (63)**49**
2-y-o ch c Medicean-Louella (USA) (El Gran Senor (USA))
Sir Mark Prescott The Green Door Partnership

Placings:006 **(6912)**
2009: 6^{0}GF, 7^{0}SD, 7^{6}SD,

	Starts	1st	2nd	3rd	Win & Pl
Career Total (Turf)	1	0	0	0	
Career Total (AW)	2	0	0	0	0

Going (Turf): **Sf: 0-0 GS: 0-0 Gd: 0-0 GF: 0-1 Fm: 0-0**
Distance: 5f/6f: 0-1 7f-8f: 0-2 9f-13f: 0-0 14f+: 0-0
Track : LH: 0-1 RH: 0-1 Tight: 0-1 Gall: 0-0
Aids: Bl: 0-0 Vi: 0-0 Tstrap: 0-0 Ckp: 0-0
Best Rating: 63 9/09 Kemp 7f stand

Tuscan King

78(99) (68)**35**
2-y-o ch g Medicean-Castaway Queen (IRE) (Selkirk (USA))
P Howling (W R Muir 21/11) J L Guillambert

Placings:563133 **(7788)**
2009: 7^{5}G, 7^{6}SD, 8^{3}SD, 8^{1}SD, 9^{3}SD, 8^{3}SD,

	Starts	1st	2nd	3rd	Win & Pl
Career Total (Turf)	1	0	0	0	0
Career Total (AW)	5	1	0	3	4000

68 11/09 Wolv 1m141y STD £2729
Total win prize-money £2730

Going (Turf): **Sf: 0-0 GS: 0-0 Gd: 0-1 GF: 0-0 Fm: 0-0**
Distance: 5f/6f: 0-0 7f-8f: 0-3 **9f-13f: 1-3** 14f+: 0-0
Track : **LH: 1-5** RH: 0-0 **Tight: 1-5** Gall: 0-0
Aids: **Bl: 1-4** Vi: 0-0 Tstrap: 0-0 Ckp: 0-0
Best Rating: 68 11/09 Wolv 1m141y stand

Moderate; effective over 1m; acts on Polytrack; has worn blinkers.

Tusculum (IRE)

89(92) (53)**38**
6-y-o b g Sadler's Wells (USA)-Turbaine (USA) (Trempolino (USA))
B J Curley (A P Stringer 4/2) Curley Leisure

Placings:31/415/00/0000-10 **(1767)**
2009: 12^{1}SD, 15^{0}GF,

	Starts	1st	2nd	3rd	Win & Pl
Career Total (Turf)	12	2	0	1	45241
Career Total (AW)	1	1	0	0	1365

53 2/09 Kemp 1m4f (0-45) STD £1364
111 8/06 Curr 1m6f G-F £24693
83 10/05 Navn 1m SH £5880
Total win prize-money £31939

Going (Turf): Sf: 0-2 GS: 0-0 Gd: 0-5 **GF: 1-4** Fm: 0-0
Distance: 5f/6f: 0-0 7f-8f: 1-2 9f-13f: 1-3 14f+: 1-8
Track : LH: 1-6 **RH: 2-7** Tight: 0-2 Gall: 0-3
Aids: Bl: 0-1 Vi: 0-0 Tstrap: 0-1 Ckp: 0-1
Best Rating: 113 9/06 York 1m5f197y good

Modest formerly smart colt but now moderate; stays 14f; acts on most ground.

Tut (IRE)

94 **73**
2-y-o b f Intikhab (USA)-Radiant Energy (IRE) (Spectrum (IRE))
A P Jarvis (K R Burke 1/7) Hubert John Strecker

Placings:310 **(6088)**
2009: 5^{3}GF, 7^{1}S, 8^{0}G,

	Starts	1st	2nd	3rd	Win & Pl
Career Total (Turf)	3	1	0	1	5888

73 8/09 Ayr 7f50y SFT £5310
Total win prize-money £5310

Going (Turf): **Sf: 1-1** GS: 0-0 Gd: 0-1 GF: 0-1 Fm: 0-0
Distance: 5f/6f: 0-1 **7f-8f: 1-2** 9f-13f: 0-0 14f+: 0-0
Track : **LH: 1-2** RH: 0-0 Tight: 0-0 Gall: 0-0
Aids: Bl: 0-0 Vi: 0 0 Tstrap: 0-0 Ckp: 0-0
Best Rating: 73 8/09 Ayr 7f50y soft

Fair; effective over 7f; acts on soft ground.

Tutor (IRE)

(100) (72)**66**
5-y-o ch g Dr Fong (USA)-Glandore (IRE) (Persian Bold)
Mrs A M Thorpe Formula One Racing

Placings:15600/30 **(0631)**
2009: 16^{3}SD, 13^{0}SD,

	Starts	1st	2nd	3rd	Win & Pl
Career Total (Turf)	3	0	0	0	0
Career Total (AW)	4	1	0	1	3300

77 2/07 Wolv 1m141y STD £2914
Total win prize-money £2915

Going (Turf): **Sf: 0-1 GS: 0-0 Gd: 0-2 GF: 0-0 Fm: 0-0**
Distance: 5f/6f: 0-0 7f-8f: 0-0 **9f-13f: 1-6** 14f+: 0-1
Track : **LH: 1-4** RH: 0-3 **Tight: 1-3** Gall: 0-0
Aids: Bl: 0-3 Vi: 0-0 Tstrap: 0-1 Ckp: 0-1
Best Rating: 77 4/07 Wolv 1m141y stand

Tuxedo

97(104) (77)**75**
4-y-o ch g Cadeaux Genereux-Serengeti Bride (USA) (Lion Cavern (USA))
P W Hiatt Phil Kelly

Placings:000011-01350624130442 **(7327)**
2009: 8^{0}SD, 7^{1}SD, 7^{3}SD, 7^{5}SD, 7^{0}GF, 7^{6}GF, 7^{2}G, 8^{4}GF, 7^{1}GS, 7^{3}G, 7^{0}GF, 7^{4}SD, 7^{4}SD, 7^{2}SD,

	Starts	1st	2nd	3rd	Win & Pl
Career Total (Turf)	9	1	1	1	4436
Career Total (AW)	11	3	1	1	8594

75 7/09 Yarm 7f3y (0-75)H G-S £2719
74 2/09 Kemp 7f (0-65)H STD £2047
67 12/08 Kemp 7f (0-70)H STD £2914
60 12/08 Kemp 7f (0-55) STD £2047
Total win prize-money £9728

Going (Turf): Sf: 0-0 **GS: 1-1** Gd: 0-3 GF: 0-5 Fm: 0-0
Distance: 5f/6f: 0-0 **7f-8f: 4-16** 9f-13f: 0-4 14f+: 0-0
Track : LH: 0-7 **RH: 3-9** Tight: 0-5 Gall: 0-1
Aids: Bl: 0-0 Vi: 0-0 Tstrap: 0-0 Ckp: 0 0
Best Rating: 77 11/09 Kemp 7f stand

Fair; effective at 7f; acts on good ground ground and on Polytrack.

Tuxsumdoin

(77) (7)

5-y-o ch m Zaha (CAN)-Roisin Clover (Faustus (USA))

J R Weymes Ray Burton

Placings:6 (0001)

2009: 11^{6}SS,

	Starts	1st	2nd	3rd	Win & Pl
Career Total (Turf)	0	0	0	0	
Career Total (AW)	1	0	0	0	0

Going (Turf): **Sf: 0-0 GS: 0-0 Gd: 0-0 GF: 0-0 Fm: 0-0**
Distance: 5f/6f: 0-0 7f-8f: 0-0 9f-13f: 0-1 14f+: 0-0
Track : LH: 0-1 RH: 0-0 Tight: 0-0 Gall: 0-0
Aids: Bl: 0-0 Vi: 0-0 Tstrap: 0-0 Ckp: 0-0
Best Rating: **7** 1/09 Sthl 1m3f std-slw

Twenty Score

82(99) (65)34

3-y-o ch f Lear Spear (USA)-Milladella (FR) (Nureyev (USA))

Miss J R Tooth Raymond Tooth

Placings:25-05006 (2681)

2009: 7^{0}SD, 6^{5}SD, 5^{0}F, 7^{0}G, 9^{6}SD,

	Starts	1st	2nd	3rd	Win & Pl
Career Total (Turf)	2	0	0	0	
Career Total (AW)	5	0	1	0	1542

Going (Turf): **Sf: 0-0 GS: 0-0 Gd: 0-1 GF: 0-0 Fm: 0-1**
Distance: 5f/6f: 0-3 7f-8f: 0-3 9f-13f: 0-1 14f+: 0-0
Track : LH: 0-6 RH: 0-0 Tight: 0-4 Gall: 0-2
Aids: Bl: 0-0 Vi: 0-0 Tstrap: 0-1 Ckp: 0-1
Best Rating: **65** 12/08 GrLe 6f stand

Modest; stays 6f and acts on Polytrack.

Twice Over

119 (125)123

4-y-o b c Observatory (USA)-Double Crossed (Caerleon (USA))

H R A Cecil K Abdulla

Placings:11/133102-33401113 (7311a)

2009: 9^{3}GF, 8^{3}S, 10^{4}GF, 10^{0}G, 10^{1}G, 9^{1}G, 10^{1}G, 10^{3}FT,

	Starts	1st	2nd	3rd	Win & Pl
Career Total (Turf)	15	7	1	4	657050
Career Total (AW)	1	0	0	1	381944

123 10/09 NmkR 1m2f GD £213739
119 9/09 Gdwd 1m1f192y GD £22708
119 9/09 Donc 1m2f60y GD £15577
114 7/08 MsnL 1m2f GD £167647
121 4/08 NmkR 1m GD £28385
98 11/07 NmkR 1m2f GD £9348
93 10/07 NmkR 1m GD £6477
Total win prize-money £463882

Going (Turf): Sf: 0-1 GS: 0-0 **Gd: 7-10** GF: 0-4 Fm: 0-0
Distance: 5f/6f: 0-0 7f-8f: 2-4 **9f-13f: 5-12** 14f+: 0-0
Track : LH: 1-3 RH: 1-5 Tight: 1-1 Gall: 1-4
Aids: Bl: 0-0 Vi: 0-0 Tstrap: 0-0 Ckp: 0-0
Best Rating: **125** 11/09 SnAt 1m2f fast

High class; winner of the Champion Stakes in 2009 and third in the Breeders' Cup Classic; effective at 1m-1m2f; acts on good and faster ground; goes on synthetics.

Twilight Dawn

100 72

5-y-o ch m Muhtarram (USA)-Indigo Dawn (Rainbow Quest (USA))

L Lungo Len Lungo Racing Limited

Placings:50/1500-43 (2445)

2009: 9^{4}GF, 14^{3}GS,

	Starts	1st	2nd	3rd	Win & Pl
Career Total (Turf)	8	1	0	1	3588

72 4/08 Newc 1m3y G-S £2914
Total win prize-money £2914

Going (Turf): Sf: 0-2 **GS: 1-3** Gd: 0-2 GF: 0-1 Fm: 0-0
Distance: 5f/6f: 0-0 7f-8f: 0-0 **9f-13f: 1-7** 14f+: 0-1
Track : LH: 0-6 RH: 0-1 Tight: 0-0 Gall: 0-1
Aids: Bl: 0-0 Vi: 0-0 Tstrap: 0-0 Ckp: 0-0
Best Rating: **72** 4/08 Newc 1m3y gd-sft

Modest; stays 1m6f; acts in soft ground.

Twilight Memory (USA)

78 48

2-y-o ch f Smart Strike (CAN)-Southern Swing (USA) (Dixieland Band (USA))

B J Meehan Mrs B V Sangster

Placings:05 (6389)

2009: 6^{0}S, 8^{5}GF,

	Starts	1st	2nd	3rd	Win & Pl
Career Total (Turf)	2	0	0	0	0

Going (Turf): **Sf: 0-1 GS: 0-0 Gd: 0-0 GF: 0-1 Fm: 0-0**
Distance: 5f/6f: 0-0 7f-8f: 0-1 9f-13f: 0-1 14f+: 0-0
Track : LH: 0-1 RH: 0-0 Tight: 0-0 Gall: 0-0
Aids: Bl: 0-0 Vi: 0-0 Tstrap: 0-0 Ckp: 0-0
Best Rating: **48** 9/09 Nott 1m75y gd-fm

Twilight Star (IRE)

101(107) (84)89

5-y-o b g Green Desert (USA)-Heavenly Whisper (IRE) (Halling (USA))

R A Teal G M Harris

Placings:41/504610600540-16023603 (6336)

2009: 8^{1}G, 8^{6}GF, 7^{0}SD, 8^{2}G, 7^{3}GF, 7^{6}GF, 8^{0}G, 6^{3}GF,

	Starts	1st	2nd	3rd	Win & Pl
Career Total (Turf)	14	3	1	2	21754
Career Total (AW)	8	0	0	0	921

84 4/09 Sand 1m14y (0-80)H GD £7123
89 6/08 Sand 1m14y (0-90)H G-S £6799
78 7/07 Pont 1m4y G-S £4533
Total win prize-money £18458

Going (Turf): Sf: 0-1 **GS: 2-4** Gd: 1-3 GF: 0-6 Fm: 0-0
Distance: 5f/6f: 0-0 7f-8f: 0-13 **9f-13f: 3-9** 14f+: 0-0
Track : LH: 1-12 **RH: 2-7** Tight: 0-10 Gall: 0-1
Aids: Bl: 0-1 Vi: 0-0 Tstrap: 0-0 Ckp: 0-0
Best Rating: **89** 6/08 Sand 1m14y gd-sft

Fair; stays 1m and acts on good and easy ground; has worn a tongue tie.

Twilight Tear

74 45

2-y-o ch f Rock Of Gibraltar (IRE)-Clara Bow (IRE) (Sadler's Wells (USA))

M L W Bell Lady Bamford

Placings:0 (6920)

2009: 8^{0}GF,

	Starts	1st	2nd	3rd	Win & Pl
Career Total (Turf)	1	0	0	0	

Going (Turf): **Sf: 0-0 GS: 0-0 Gd: 0-0 GF: 0-1 Fm: 0-0**
Distance: 5f/6f: 0-0 7f-8f: 0-0 9f-13f: 0-1 14f+: 0-0
Track : LH: 0-0 RH: 0-0 Tight: 0-0 Gall: 0-0
Aids: Bl: 0-0 Vi: 0-0 Tstrap: 0-0 Ckp: 0-0
Best Rating: **45** 10/09 Yarm 1m3y gd-fm

Twill (IRE)

(102) (67)83

6-y-o ch g Barathea (IRE)-Khafaya (Unfuwain (USA))

D Burchell T G Williams

Placings:001/400200140/50/0-40 (3721)

2009: 12^{4}SD, 12^{0}SD,

	Starts	1st	2nd	3rd	Win & Pl
Career Total (Turf)	11	1	1	0	9339
Career Total (AW)	6	1	0	0	4301

83 9/06 Gdwd 2m (0-85)H GD £5505
80 11/05 Sthl 1m SS £4012
Total win prize-money £9518

Going (Turf): Sf: 0-3 GS: 0-3 **Gd: 1-3** GF: 0-2 Fm: 0-0
Distance: 5f/6f: 0-0 7f-8f: 1-2 9f-13f: 0-6 14f+: 1-9
Track : LH: 1-10 RH: 1-7 **Tight: 1-7** Gall: 0-3
Aids: Bl: 0-1 Vi: 0-1 Tstrap: 0-0 Ckp: 0-0
Best Rating: **83** 9/06 Gdwd 2m good

Twinned (IRE)

(102) (59)45

6-y-o ch g Soviet Star (USA)-Identical (IRE) (Machiavellian (USA))

Mike Murphy Ms L M Bartlett

Placings:3230250030/16400456610400/6500320/2423600 4-0 (0173)

2009: 5^{0}SD,

	Starts	1st	2nd	3rd	Win & Pl
Career Total (Turf)	12	0	2	2	3774
Career Total (AW)	28	2	3	3	8191

58 11/06 Wolv 5f20y SF £2730
63 4/06 Wolv 5f20y STD £2388
Total win prize-money £5119

Going (Turf): **Sf: 0-0 GS: 0-2 Gd: 0-3 GF: 0-5 Fm: 0-2**
Distance: **5f/6f: 2-39** 7f-8f: 0-0 9f-13f: 0-1 14f+: 0-0
Track : **LH: 2-25** RH: 0-5 **Tight: 2-20** Gall: 0-5
Aids: Bl: 0-2 Vi: 0-0 Tstrap: 2-16 Ckp: 2-16
Best Rating: **66** 3/05 Kemp 5f gd-sft

Moderate; suited by 5f; acts on good ground; also goes on Polytrack.

Twist Again (IRE)

102(99) (56)77

3-y-o b f Sakhee (USA)-Dance Clear (IRE) (Marju (IRE))

P Howling Liam Sheridan

Placings:0500331161 (6384)

2009: 8^{0}SD, 10^{5}GF, 10^{0}GF, 12^{0}SD, 11^{3}GS, 11^{3}G, 14^{1}G, 14^{1}GF, 14^{6}GF, 16^{1}GF,

	Starts	1st	2nd	3rd	Win & Pl
Career Total (Turf)	8	3	0	2	7805
Career Total (AW)	2	0	0	0	

77 9/09 Newc 2m19y (0-70)H G-F £2978

71 8/09 Rdcr 1m6f19y (0-65)H G-F £2266
67 8/09 Nott 1m6f15y (0-60)H GD £1942
Total win prize-money £7189

Going (Turf): Sf: 0-0 GS: 0-1 Gd: 1-2 **GF: 2-5** Fm: 0-0
Distance: 5f/6f: 0-0 7f-8f: 0-1 9f-13f: 0-5 **14f+: 3-4**
Track : **LH: 3-8** RH: 0-1 Tight: 1-6 Gall: 1-1
Aids: Bl: 0-0 Vi: 0-0 Tstrap: 0-0 Ckp: 0-0
Best Rating: **77** 9/09 Newc 2m19y gd-fm

Modest; stays 2m and acts on most ground.

Twist Bookie (IRE)

(93) (64)**63**
9-y-o br g Perugino (USA)-Twist Scarlett (GER) (Lagunas)
S Lycett Frank Dronzek

Placings:60405/10002632026012/00313020032/0000/003 31/32/520-0 **(1153)**
2009: 8^{0}SD,

	Starts	1st	2nd	3rd	Win & Pl
Career Total (Turf)	34	3	6	4	16555
Career Total (AW)	11	1	2	3	5755

57 12/06 Wolv 1m4f50y (0-55)H STD £3071
5/04 Duss 1m H SFT £4225
11/03 Mulh 1m H HVY £1901
3/03 Mulh 1m HVY £1972
Total win prize-money £11169

Going (Turf): **Sf: 3-15** GS: 0-0 Gd: 0-16 GF: 0-3 Fm: 0-0
Distance: 5f/6f: 0-1 **7f-8f: 3-28** 9f-13f: 1-13 14f+: 0-3
Track : LH: 1-12 RH: 1-3 **Tight: 1-8** Gall: 0-1
Aids: Bl: 0-0 Vi: 0-0 Tstrap: 0-0 Ckp: 0-0
Best Rating: **64** 12/07 Wolv 1m4f50y stand

Modest ex-German performer; won 1m4f Class 6 handicap at Wolverhampton December 2006; stays 1m6f; acts on good or softer and Polytrack.

Twisted

99 **76**
3-y-o ch c Selkirk (USA)-Winding (USA) (Irish River (FR))
J H M Gosden P G Goulandris

Placings:5-340 **(2943)**
2009: 10^{3}S, 10^{4}GF, 12^{0}GF,

	Starts	1st	2nd	3rd	Win & Pl
Career Total (Turf)	4	0	0	1	1204

Going (Turf): **Sf: 0-1 GS: 0-0 Gd: 0-0 GF: 0-3 Fm: 0-0**
Distance: 5f/6f: 0-0 7f-8f: 0-1 9f-13f: 0-3 14f+: 0-0
Track : LH: 0-2 RH: 0-1 Tight: 0-0 Gall: 0-2
Aids: Bl: 0-0 Vi: 0-0 Tstrap: 0-0 Ckp: 0-0
Best Rating: **76** 5/09 Newb 1m2f6y soft

Useful; stays 1m2f; acts on good ground.

Two Kisses (IRE)

93(94) (65)**66**
2-y-o b f Spartacus (IRE)-Flight Sequence (Polar Falcon (USA))
B G Powell Brian McNamee & Jeff Mould

Placings:565305**0**61 **(7799)**
2009: 5^{5}GF, 6^{6}GF, 6^{5}GF, 5^{3}F, 7^{0}G, 5^{5}G, 8^{0}SD, 7^{6}SD, 5^{1}SD,

	Starts	1st	2nd	3rd	Win & Pl
Career Total (Turf)	6	0	0	1	530
Career Total (AW)	3	1	0	0	2730

65 12/09 Wolv 5f216y STD £2729
Total win prize-money £2730

Going (Turf): **Sf: 0-0 GS: 0-0 Gd: 0-2 GF: 0-3 Fm: 0-1**
Distance: **5f/6f: 1-6** 7f-8f: 0-3 9f-13f: 0-0 14f+: 0-0
Track : **LH: 1-5** RH: 0-1 **Tight: 1-2** Gall: 0-2
Aids: Bl: 0-0 Vi: 0-0 Tstrap: 0-0 Ckp: 0-0
Best Rating: **66** 6/09 Bath 5f161y firm

Modest; effective over 6f; acts on fast ground and on Polytrack.

Two Together (USA)

87(82) (52)**48**
3-y-o b c Theatrical-Miasma (USA) (Lear Fan (USA))
D R Lanigan Saif Ali & Saeed H Altayer

Placings:00 **(6974)**
2009: 10^{0}S, 11^{0}SD,

	Starts	1st	2nd	3rd	Win & Pl
Career Total (Turf)	1	0	0	0	
Career Total (AW)	1	0	0	0	

Going (Turf): **Sf: 0-1 GS: 0-0 Gd: 0-0 GF: 0-0 Fm: 0-0**
Distance: 5f/6f: 0-0 7f-8f: 0-0 9f-13f: 0-2 14f+: 0-0
Track : LH: 0-1 RH: 0-1 Tight: 0-0 Gall: 0-0
Aids: Bl: 0-0 Vi: 0-0 Tstrap: 0-0 Ckp: 0-0
Best Rating: **52** 10/09 Kemp 1m3f stand

Two Tone

80 **28**
3-y-o b/br g Diktat-Fireburst (Spectrum (IRE))
G Woodward Mr & Mrs Bloom

Placings:060 **(4354)**
2009: 8^{0}GF, 8^{6}F, 8^{0}G,

	Starts	1st	2nd	3rd	Win & Pl
Career Total (Turf)	3	0	0	0	0

Going (Turf): **Sf: 0-0 GS: 0-0 Gd: 0-1 GF: 0-1 Fm: 0-1**
Distance: 5f/6f: 0-0 7f-8f: 0-1 9f-13f: 0-2 14f+: 0-0
Track : LH: 0-2 RH: 0-0 Tight: 0-0 Gall: 0-0
Aids: Bl: 0-0 Vi: 0-0 Tstrap: 0-0 Ckp: 0-0
Best Rating: **28** 7/09 Hayd 1m30y firm

Two Turtle Doves (IRE)

98(90) (38)**60**
3-y-o b f Night Shift (USA)-Purple Rain (IRE) (Celtic Swing)
M Mullineaux J P Turner

Placings:00666202455 **(7082)**
2009: 7^{0}GF, 6^{0}G, 8^{6}G, 5^{6}SD, 7^{6}GF, 5^{2}G, 6^{0}G, 6^{2}S, 6^{4}G, 7^{5}GF, 5^{5}S,

	Starts	1st	2nd	3rd	Win & Pl
Career Total (Turf)	10	0	2	0	1550
Career Total (AW)	1	0	0	0	0

Going (Turf): **Sf: 0-2 GS: 0-0 Gd: 0-5 GF: 0-3 Fm: 0-0**
Distance: 5f/6f: 0-4 7f-8f: 0-7 9f-13f: 0-0 14f+: 0-0
Track : LH: 0-5 RH: 0-2 Tight: 0-3 Gall: 0-1
Aids: Bl: 0-0 Vi: 0-0 Tstrap: 0-0 Ckp: 0-0
Best Rating: **60** 8/09 Haml 6f5y soft

Moderate; stays 6f; acts on good ground.

Twoellies

77(83) (37)**15**
2-y-o ch f Trade Fair-Fancier Bit (Lion Cavern (USA))
Ollie Pears P Wilkinson

Placings:000 **(7788)**
2009: 5^{0}GF, 6^{0}GF, 8^{0}SD,

	Starts	1st	2nd	3rd	Win & Pl
Career Total (Turf)	2	0	0	0	
Career Total (AW)	1	0	0	0	

Going (Turf): **Sf: 0-0 GS: 0-0 Gd: 0-0 GF: 0-2 Fm: 0-0**
Distance: 5f/6f: 0-2 7f-8f: 0-0 9f-13f: 0-1 14f+: 0-0
Track : LH: 0-1 RH: 0-0 Tight: 0-1 Gall: 0-0
Aids: Bl: 0-0 Vi: 0-0 Tstrap: 0-0 Ckp: 0-0
Best Rating: **37** 12/09 Wolv 1m141y stand

Twos And Eights (IRE)

(82) (53)**19**
3-y-o b/br g Kyllachy-Docklands Grace (USA) (Honour And Glory (USA))
Paul Mason Seven Plus Seven

Placings:0400-0 **(0831)**
2009: 5^{0}SD,

	Starts	1st	2nd	3rd	Win & Pl
Career Total (Turf)	2	0	0	0	
Career Total (AW)	3	0	0	0	216

Going (Turf): **Sf: 0-0 GS: 0-1 Gd: 0-0 GF: 0-1 Fm: 0-0**
Distance: 5f/6f: 0-4 7f-8f: 0-1 9f-13f: 0-0 14f+: 0-0
Track : LH: 0-2 RH: 0-1 Tight: 0-1 Gall: 0-2
Aids: Bl: 0-1 Vi: 0-0 Tstrap: 0-0 Ckp: 0-0
Best Rating: **53** 4/08 GrLe 5f stand

Twosheetstothewind

104(98) (68)**76**
5-y-o ch m Bahamian Bounty-Flag (Selkirk (USA))
M Dods P Taylor

Placings:3153250/**4062**05000-42016412 **(4136)**
2009: 5^{4}GF, 5^{2}GS, 5^{0}GF, 5^{1}GF, 5^{6}GF, 5^{4}G, 5^{1}GF, 5^{2}G,

	Starts	1st	2nd	3rd	Win & Pl
Career Total (Turf)	18	3	4	2	13785
Career Total (AW)	6	0	0	0	0

76 7/09 Ayr 5f (0-65)H G-F £2388
69 6/09 Thsk 5f (0-65)H G-F £3139
59 5/07 Muss 5f GD £2817
Total win prize-money £8344

Going (Turf): Sf: 0-1 GS: 0-6 Gd: 1-5 **GF: 2-6** Fm: 0-0
Distance: **5f/6f: 3-23** 7f-8f: 0-1 9f-13f: 0-0 14f+: 0-0
Track : LH: 0-5 RH: 0-3 Tight: 0-3 Gall: 0-4
Aids: Bl: 0-0 Vi: 0-0 Tstrap: 1-3 Ckp: 1-3
Best Rating: **76** 7/09 Ayr 5f gd-fm

Moderate; suited by 5f; acts on most ground and Polytrack.

Tycoon's Buddy

(77) (29)
4-y-o ch g Reel Buddy (USA)-Tycoon's Last (Nalchik (USA))
S Wynne L R Owen

Placings:0000-00 **(0255)**
2009: 7^{0}SD, 8^{0}SD,

	Starts	1st	2nd	3rd	Win & Pl
Career Total (Turf)	2	0	0	0	
Career Total (AW)	4	0	0	0	

Going (Turf): Sf: 0-1 GS: 0-0 Gd: 0-0 GF: 0-1 Fm: 0-0
Distance: 5f/6f: 0-1 7f-8f: 0-3 9f-13f: 0-2 14f+: 0-0
Track : LH: 0-5 RH: 0-0 Tight: 0-3 Gall: 0-1
Aids: Bl: 0-0 Vi: 0-0 Tstrap: 0-0 Ckp: 0-0
Best Rating: 29 7/08 Wolv 1m141y stand

Tyfos

105(98) (74)83
4-y-o b g Bertolini (USA)-Warminghamsharpish (Nalchik (USA))
W M Brisbourne J Tomlinson/G Williams

Placings:0010/424006-4161343 (5247)
2009: 6[4]G, 6[1]S, 6[6]GF, 6[1]G, 6[3]G, 6[4]G, 5[3]GF,

	Starts	1st	2nd	3rd	Win & Pl
Career Total (Turf)	14	2	1	2	12407
Career Total (AW)	3	1	0	0	2969
82 7/09 Epsm	6f	(0-80)H		GD	£5180
80 6/09 Yarm	6f3y	(0-70)H		SFT	£2719
74 11/07 Wolv	5f216y			STD	£2968

Total win prize-money £10870

Going (Turf): Sf: 1-2 GS: 0-1 Gd: 1-5 GF: 0-6 Fm: 0-0
Distance: 5f/6f: 2-11 7f-8f: 1-6 9f-13f: 0-0 14f+: 0-0
Track : LH: 2-7 RH: 0-0 Tight: 2-6 Gall: 0-0
Aids: Bl: 0-0 Vi: 0-0 Tstrap: 0-0 Ckp: 0-0
Best Rating: 83 7/09 Ayr 6f good

Fair; effective over 6f-7f; acts on most ground and on Polytrack.

Typical Female

60(69) (22)
2-y-o b f Pursuit Of Love-Angel Maid (Forzando)
A B Haynes Gary B Watts

Placings:00U0 (7669)
2009: 7[0]SD, 7[0]G, 9[U]SD, 8[0]SD,

	Starts	1st	2nd	3rd	Win & Pl
Career Total (Turf)	1	0	0	0	
Career Total (AW)	3	0	0	0	

Going (Turf): Sf: 0-0 GS: 0-0 Gd: 0-1 GF: 0-0 Fm: 0-0
Distance: 5f/6f: 0-0 7f-8f: 0-2 9f-13f: 0-2 14f+: 0-0
Track : LH: 0-2 RH: 0-1 Tight: 0-2 Gall: 0-0
Aids: Bl: 0-0 Vi: 0-0 Tstrap: 0-0 Ckp: 0-0
Best Rating: 22 8/09 Kemp 7f stand

Tyrana (GER)

102(99) (64)57
6-y-o ch m Acatenango (GER)-Tascalina (GER) (Big Shuffle (USA))
Ian Williams (G F Bridgwater 26/6) T Bhoot

Placings:1421/453032/0000-40501 (7766)
2009: 12[4]SD, 10[0]GF, 10[5]G, 8[0]SD, 11[1]SD,

	Starts	1st	2nd	3rd	Win & Pl
Career Total (Turf)	12	2	2	2	7223
Career Total (AW)	7	1	0	0	1706
64 12/09 Kemp	1m3f	(0-60)H		STD	£1706
9/06 Kref	1m2f55y	H		SFT	£1827
7/06 BDob	1m1f110y			GD	£1793

Total win prize-money £5327

Going (Turf): Sf: 1-3 GS: 0-0 Gd: 1-8 GF: 0-1 Fm: 0-0
Distance: 5f/6f: 0-0 7f-8f: 0-4 9f-13f: 3-15 14f+: 0-0
Track : LH: 0-5 RH: 1-5 Tight: 0-2 Gall: 0-0
Aids: Bl: 0-0 Vi: 0-0 Tstrap: 0-0 Ckp: 0-0
Best Rating: 64 12/09 Kemp 1m3f stand

Moderate; ex-German; stays 1m4f; handles Fibresand.

Tyrannosaurus Rex (IRE)

106(111) (73)86
5-y-o b g Bold Fact (USA)-Dungeon Princess (IRE) (Danehill (USA))
D Shaw Market Avenue Racing Club Ltd

Placings:630620/60020104050-016612112000 (5247)
2009: 6[0]SD, 5[1]SD, 5[6]SD, 5[6]SD, 5[1]SD, 5[2]SD, 5[1]F, 5[1]GF, 5[2]G, 5[0]G, 5[0]G, 5[0]GF,

	Starts	1st	2nd	3rd	Win & Pl
Career Total (Turf)	12	3	2	0	14197
Career Total (AW)	17	2	2	1	7153
84 6/09 Ches	5f16y	(0-85)H		G-F	£5180
75 5/09 Nott	5f13y	(0-70)H		FRM	£3885
70 3/09 Wolv	5f20y	(0-60)H		STD	£2217
68 2/09 Wolv	5f20y	(0-65)H		STD	£2047
66 8/08 Nott	5f13y	(0-55)H		GD	£2047

Total win prize-money £15379

Going (Turf): Sf: 0-0 GS: 0-2 Gd: 1-6 GF: 1-3 Fm: 1-1
Distance: 5f/6f: 5-23 7f-8f: 0-6 9f-13f: 0-0 14f+: 0-0
Track : LH: 3-13 RH: 0-4 Tight: 3-11 Gall: 0-1
Aids: Bl: 0-0 Vi: 1-10 Tstrap: 0-0 Ckp: 0-0
Best Rating: 86 7/09 Hayd 5f good

Fair; effective over 5f-7f; acts on Polytrack and fast turf.

Tyrrells Wood (IRE)

111(110) (88)98
4-y-o b g Sinndar (IRE)-Diner De Lune (IRE) (Be My Guest (USA))
T G Mills Dr Marwan Koukash

Placings:0455/01052-2122 (4417)
2009: 13[2]SD, 17[1]G, 21[2]GF, 21[2]G,

	Starts	1st	2nd	3rd	Win & Pl
Career Total (Turf)	10	2	2	0	26890
Career Total (AW)	3	0	2	0	1627
91 6/09 Pont	2m1f22y	(0-80)H		GD	£5180
79 7/08 Brig	1m3f196y	(0-75)H		G-F	£2712

Total win prize-money £7893

Going (Turf): Sf: 0-0 GS: 0-2 Gd: 1-5 GF: 1-3 Fm: 0-0
Distance: 5f/6f: 0-0 7f-8f: 0-1 9f-13f: 1-6 14f+: 1-6
Track : LH: 2-5 RH: 0-8 Tight: 0-3 Gall: 0-2
Aids: Bl: 0-0 Vi: 0-0 Tstrap: 0-0 Ckp: 0-0
Best Rating: 98 7/09 Gdwd 2m5f good

Very useful; stays 2m2f; acts on fast ground and Polytrack.

Tyzack (IRE)

(110) (75)58
8-y-o b g Fasliyev (USA)-Rabea (USA) (Devil's Bag (USA))
Stef Liddiard Mrs S J Roberts

Placings:25240/50000/1/111102400/00606014000/05-26 (0618)
2009: 7[2]SD, 8[6]SD,

	Starts	1st	2nd	3rd	Win & Pl
Career Total (Turf)	22	2	3	0	13592
Career Total (AW)	13	4	1	0	12043
81 9/07 Sals	1m	(0-70)H		G-F	£3238
89 4/06 Sthl	1m	(0-75)H		STD	£3238
84 4/06 Sthl	7f	(0-70)H		STD	£3562
77 3/06 Sthl	7f	(0-65)H		STD	£2388
67 3/06 Sthl	7f	(0-60)H		STD	£2047
60 9/05 Yarm	7f3y	(0-55)H		G-F	£3803

Total win prize-money £18281

Going (Turf): Sf: 0-3 GS: 0-2 Gd: 0-3 GF: 2-11 Fm: 0-3
Distance: 5f/6f: 0-1 7f-8f: 6-27 9f-13f: 0-7 14f+: 0-0
Track : LH: 4-23 RH: 0-2 Tight: 0-4 Gall: 0-1
Aids: Bl: 0-0 Vi: 0-0 Tstrap: 0-0 Ckp: 0-0
Best Rating: 89 6/06 Hayd 1m30y gd-fm

Fair; stays 1m; acts on fast ground and on Fibresand.

Uace Mac

93 70
5-y-o b m Compton Place-Umbrian Gold (IRE) (Perugino (USA))
N Bycroft N Bycroft

Placings:0/30F/0036100-000300 (5150)
2009: 6[0]GS, 7[0]GF, 6[0]G, 6[3]G, 6[0]GF, 5[0]GS,

	Starts	1st	2nd	3rd	Win & Pl
Career Total (Turf)	17	1	0	3	4728
70 8/08 Rdcr	7f			GD	£2590

Total win prize-money £2590

Going (Turf): Sf: 0-1 GS: 0-4 Gd: 1-7 GF: 0-5 Fm: 0-0
Distance: 5f/6f: 0-13 7f-8f: 1-4 9f-13f: 0-0 14f+: 0-0
Track : LH: 0-2 RH: 0-2 Tight: 0-0 Gall: 0-2
Aids: Bl: 0-0 Vi: 0-0 Tstrap: 0-0 Ckp: 0-0
Best Rating: 70 8/08 Rdcr 7f good

Moderate; stays 7f and acts on good ground.

Ubenkor (IRE)

100 (31)73
4-y-o b g Diktat-Lucky Dancer (FR) (Groom Dancer (USA))
B Smart Prime Equestrian

Placings:0/02321640-04 (2257)
2009: 7[0]GS, 7[4]G,

	Starts	1st	2nd	3rd	Win & Pl
Career Total (Turf)	10	1	2	1	5119
Career Total (AW)	1	0	0	0	
73 8/08 Catt	7f	(0-65)H		G-F	£2388

Total win prize-money £2388

Going (Turf): Sf: 0-2 GS: 0-4 Gd: 0-2 GF: 1-2 Fm: 0-0
Distance: 5f/6f: 0-3 7f-8f: 1-8 9f-13f: 0-0 14f+: 0-0
Track : LH: 1-4 RH: 0-2 Tight: 1-3 Gall: 0-0
Aids: Bl: 0-0 Vi: 0-0 Tstrap: 0-0 Ckp: 0-0
Best Rating: 73 8/08 Bevl 7f100y soft

Fair; effective up to 7f; handles most ground.

Ubiquitous

99(52) 56
4-y-o b f Erhaab (USA)-Lady Isabell (Rambo Dancer (CAN))
S Dow T Staplehurst

Placings:0000000-05222 (5152)
2009: 9[0]F, 9[5]G, 11[2]GF, 11[2]G, 12[2]GF,

	Starts	1st	2nd	3rd	Win & Pl
Career Total (Turf)	12	0	3	0	2620
Career Total (AW)	1	0	0	0	

Going (Turf): Sf: 0-0 GS: 0-1 Gd: 0-2 GF: 0-8 Fm: 0-1
Distance: 5f/6f: 0-0 7f-8f: 0-1 9f-13f: 0-12 14f+: 0-0
Track : LH: 0-6 RH: 0-5 Tight: 0-9 Gall: 0-0
Aids: Bl: 0-0 Vi: 0-0 Tstrap: 0-0 Ckp: 0-0
Best Rating: 56 8/09 Folk 1m4f gd-fm

Moderate; stays 1m4f and acts on fast ground.

Udabaa (IRE)

(89) (71)

2-y-o b/br c Alhaarth (IRE)-Addaya (IRE) (Persian Bold)

M P Tregoning Hamdan Al Maktoum

Placings:3 **(5312)**

2009: 8^{3}SD,

	Starts	1st	2nd	3rd	Win & Pl
Career Total (Turf)	0	0	0	0	
Career Total (AW)	1	0	0	1	530

Going (Turf): Sf: 0-0 GS: 0-0 Gd: 0-0 GF: 0-0 Fm: 0-0
Distance: 5f/6f: 0-0 7f-8f: 0-1 9f-13f: 0-0 14f+: 0-0
Track : LH: 0-0 RH: 0-1 Tight: 0-0 Gall: 0-0
Aids: Bl: 0-0 Vi: 0-0 Tstrap: 0-0 Ckp: 0-0
Best Rating: 71 8/09 Kemp 1m stand

Fair; stays 1m; acts on Polytrack.

Uddy Mac

99 61

2-y-o ch f Reel Buddy (USA)-Befriend (USA) (Allied Forces (USA))

N Bycroft N Bycroft

Placings:5004054 **(5980)**

2009: 5^{5}G, 6^{0}GF, 7^{0}G, 6^{4}GF, 6^{0}GF, 7^{5}GS, 7^{4}GF,

	Starts	1st	2nd	3rd	Win & Pl
Career Total (Turf)	7	0	0	0	818

Going (Turf): Sf: 0-0 GS: 0-1 Gd: 0-2 GF: 0-4 Fm: 0-0
Distance: 5f/6f: 0-4 7f-8f: 0-3 9f-13f: 0-0 14f+: 0-0
Track : LH: 0-1 RH: 0-1 Tight: 0-0 Gall: 0-1
Aids: Bl: 0-1 Vi: 0-0 Tstrap: 0-0 Ckp: 0-0
Best Rating: 61 9/09 Bevl 7f100y gd-fm

Ugenius

91(103) (74)56

5-y-o b g Killer Instinct-I'm Sophic (IRE) (Shalford (IRE))

Mrs C A Dunnett Mrs Christine Dunnett

Placings:400/5660/100032630022213-040040003321642101 **(7065)**

2009: 7^{0}SD, 8^{4}SD, 7^{0}SD, 8^{0}SD, 7^{4}G, 8^{0}SD, 8^{0}GF, 7^{0}G, 8^{3}SD, 8^{3}SD, 8^{2}SD, 7^{1}SD, 7^{6}SD, 8^{4}SD, 7^{2}SD, 7^{1}SD, 7^{0}SD, 8^{1}SD,

	Starts	1st	2nd	3rd	Win & Pl
Career Total (Turf)	6	0	0	1	452
Career Total (AW)	34	5	6	4	16550

74 10/09 Ling 1m (0-70)H STD £3070
71 9/09 Wolv 7f32y (0-65)H STD £2388
69 7/09 Sthl 7f (0-65)H STD £2047
69 12/08 Sthl 7f (0-60)H STD £2047
53 3/08 Sthl 7f (0-52)H STD £1911
Total win prize-money £11464

Going (Turf): Sf: 0-0 GS: 0-1 Gd: 0-4 GF: 0-1 Fm: 0-0
Distance: 5f/6f: 0-3 **7f-8f: 5-30** 9f-13f: 0-7 14f+: 0-0
Track : **LH: 5-27** RH: 0-9 **Tight: 2-13** Gall: 0-0
Aids: Bl: 0-0 Vi: 0-0 Tstrap: 0-0 Ckp: 0-0
Best Rating: 74 10/09 Ling 1m stand

Moderate; stays 1m; acts on good ground; goes on sand.

Ugly Betty

64(79) (16)25

4-y-o b f Where Or When (IRE)-Dancing Steps (Zafonic (USA))

Bruce Hellier J W Barrett

Placings:00/0600-000 **(6766)**

2009: 9^{0}SD, 10^{0}GF, 12^{0}GS,

	Starts	1st	2nd	3rd	Win & Pl
Career Total (Turf)	7	0	0	0	0
Career Total (AW)	2	0	0	0	

Going (Turf): Sf: 0-1 GS: 0-3 Gd: 0-1 GF: 0-2 Fm: 0-0
Distance: 5f/6f: 0-2 7f-8f: 0-3 9f-13f: 0-4 14f+: 0-0
Track : LH: 0-7 RH: 0-0 Tight: 0-1 Gall: 0-2
Aids: Bl: 0-0 Vi: 0-0 Tstrap: 0-0 Ckp: 0-0
Best Rating: 25 8/08 Ayr 7f50y gd-sft

Uhuru Peak

93(64) (51)61

8-y-o ch g Bal Harbour-Catherines Well (Junius (USA))

M W Easterby Peter Easterby

Placings:30500320603/0011020/30000415244O/0004530 05/5201200-0000 **(4932)**

2009: 8^{0}G, 8^{0}GF, 7^{0}G, 8^{0}G,

	Starts	1st	2nd	3rd	Win & Pl
Career Total (Turf)	38	4	4	4	18006
Career Total (AW)	12	0	1	1	1119

59 8/08 Bevl 1m100y (0-65)H SFT £2186
62 8/06 Carl 7f200y (0-70)H G-F £3123
62 6/05 Wwck 1m22y (0-55)H G-F £3161
56 5/05 Rdcr 6f (0-60)H FRM £2790
Total win prize-money £11260

Going (Turf): Sf: 1-4 GS: 0-3 Gd: 0-10 **GF: 2-17** Fm: 1-4
Distance: 5f/6f: 1-8 7f-8f: 1-22 **9f-13f: 2-20** 14f+: 0-0
Track : LH: 1-22 **RH: 2-14** Tight: 0-12 Gall: 0-0
Aids: **Bl: 4-30** Vi: 0-0 Tstrap: 0-0 Ckp: 0-0
Best Rating: 62 8/06 Carl 7f200y gd-fm

Moderate; effective over 6f-1m; acts on fast ground and Polytrack; has worn blinkers/tongue tie.

Uig

98(96) (68)72

8-y-o ch m Bien Bien (USA)-Madam Zando (Forzando)

H S Howe B P Jones

Placings:003204202/030541314240/050600/6215601200 0/26122600000-45505530030 **(6770)**

2009: 10^{4}F, 9^{5}GF, 10^{5}GF, 9^{0}GF, 10^{5}GF, 10^{5}G, 11^{3}GF, 12^{0}G, 11^{0}GS, 10^{3}G, 12^{0}SD,

	Starts	1st	2nd	3rd	Win & Pl
Career Total (Turf)	48	4	7	5	41173
Career Total (AW)	12	1	2	0	4450

68 5/08 Ling 1m2f (0-70)H STD £2590
73 8/07 Sand 1m1f (0-75)H GD £5181
68 5/07 Chep 1m2f36y (0-75)H GD £3886
76 7/05 Ling 1m2f (0-90)H G-F £9418
73 6/05 Chep 1m2f36y (0-75)H SFT £3775
Total win prize-money £24853

Going (Turf): Sf: 1-7 GS: 0-7 **Gd: 2-16** GF: 1-17 Fm: 0-1
Distance: 5f/6f: 0-0 7f-8f: 0-1 **9f-13f: 5-59** 14f+: 0-0
Track : **LH: 4-34** RH: 1-24 **Tight: 2-35** Gall: 0-5
Aids: Bl: 0-0 Vi: 0-0 Tstrap: 0-0 Ckp: 0-0
Best Rating: 77 8/04 Wind 1m67y gd-sft

Modest handicapper; stays 1m2f; acts on most ground and Polytrack; very much suited by forcing tactics.

Ullalujah

80 39

7-y-o b m Josr Algarhoud (IRE)-Ulla Laing (Mummy's Pet)

L Wells Paul Zetter

Placings:6 **(1427)**

2009: 12^{6}G,

	Starts	1st	2nd	3rd	Win & Pl
Career Total (Turf)	1	0	0	0	0

Going (Turf): Sf: 0-0 GS: 0-0 Gd: 0-1 GF: 0-0 Fm: 0-0
Distance: 5f/6f: 0-0 7f-8f: 0-0 9f-13f: 0-1 14f+: 0-0
Track : LH: 0-0 RH: 0-1 Tight: 0-1 Gall: 0-0
Aids: Bl: 0-0 Vi: 0-0 Tstrap: 0-0 Ckp: 0-0
Best Rating: 39 4/09 Folk 1m4f good

Ultimate

97(106) (94)80

3-y-o b c Anabaa (USA)-Nirvana (Marju (IRE))

B Ellison (H Morrison 21/10) Dan Gilbert

Placings:063-15401 **(6946)**

2009: 8^{1}SD, 9^{5}GF, 11^{4}GS, 10^{0}G, 8^{1}SD,

	Starts	1st	2nd	3rd	Win & Pl
Career Total (Turf)	4	0	0	0	385
Career Total (AW)	4	2	0	1	9136

94 10/09 Sthl 1m (0-85)H STD £5828
69 1/09 Sthl 1m STD £2729
Total win prize-money £8558

Going (Turf): Sf: 0-0 GS: 0-2 Gd: 0-1 GF: 0-1 Fm: 0-0
Distance: 5f/6f: 0-0 **7f-8f: 2-4** 9f-13f: 0-4 14f+: 0-0
Track : **LH: 2-6** RH: 0-1 Tight: 0-2 Gall: 0-2
Aids: Bl: 0-0 Vi: 0-0 Tstrap: 0-0 Ckp: 0-0
Best Rating: 94 10/09 Sthl 1m stand

Fair sort; effective at a mile; handles Polytrack.

Ultimate Respect (USA)

91(98) (72)59

3-y-o b c Elusive Quality (USA)-Zelanda (IRE) (Night Shift (USA))

M Johnston Sheikh Hamdan Bin Mohammed Al Maktoum

Placings:0646300 **(6462)**

2009: 8^{0}GF, 8^{6}SD, 6^{4}S, 6^{6}G, 8^{3}SD, 7^{0}GF, 8^{0}SD,

	Starts	1st	2nd	3rd	Win & Pl
Career Total (Turf)	4	0	0	0	0
Career Total (AW)	3	0	0	1	626

Going (Turf): Sf: 0-1 GS: 0-0 Gd: 0-1 GF: 0-2 Fm: 0-0
Distance: 5f/6f: 0-1 7f-8f: 0-3 9f-13f: 0-3 14f+: 0-0
Track : LH: 0-3 RH: 0-3 Tight: 0-3 Gall: 0-0
Aids: Bl: 0-1 Vi: 0-0 Tstrap: 0-0 Ckp: 0-0
Best Rating: 72 9/09 Wolv 1m141y stand

Modest; stays 1m and acts on Polytrack.

Ultravox (USA)

96 77

2-y-o b c Lemon Drop Kid (USA)-Lynnwood Chase (USA) (Horse Chestnut (SAF))

B J Meehan Mrs Carmen Burrell & Jonathan Harvey

Placings:53 **(4908)**

2009: 7^{5}S, 7^{3}G,

	Starts	1st	2nd	3rd	Win & Pl
Career Total (Turf)	2	0	0	1	482

Going (Turf): Sf: 0-1 GS: 0-0 Gd: 0-1 GF: 0-0 Fm: 0-0
Distance: 5f/6f: 0-0 7f-8f: 0-2 9f-13f: 0-0 14f+: 0-0
Track : LH: 0-0 RH: 0-1 Tight: 0-0 Gall: 0-0

Aids: Bl: 0-0 Vi: 0-0 Tstrap: 0-0 Ckp: 0-0
Best Rating: 77 8/09 Sand 7f16y good

Fair; stays 7f; acts on good and soft ground.

Ulysees (IRE)

95 (52)56
10-y-o b g Turtle Island (IRE)-Tamasriya (IRE) (Doyoun)
I Semple Johnny Higgins

Placings:50633/004103/0500006**600**/1031050040050/104 554**600**/4141166465344500/000005/0000026U3-520200 (7174)
2009: 11^{5}GS, 8^{2}S, 8^{0}GS, 11^{2}G, 9^{0}GS, 9^{0}S,

	Starts	1st	2nd	3rd	Win & Pl
Career Total (Turf)	74	7	3	6	43674
Career Total (AW)	6	0	0	0	0

67	6/06	Haml	1m65y		G-F	£3238
65	6/06	Muss	1m		G-F	£3238
73	5/06	Haml	1m1f36y	(0-70)H	G-F	£3886
75	4/05	Haml	6f5y	(0-70)H	G-S	£3711
77	6/04	Ayr	6f	D(0-80)H	GD	£5638
79	4/04	Haml	6f5y	E(0-75)H	GD	£3867
81	7/02	Gway	7f		SFT	£6984

Total win prize-money £30568

Going (Turf): Sf: 1-21GS: 1-13 Gd: 2-18**GF: 3-16** Fm: 0-1
Distance: 5f/6f: 1-17 **7f-8f: 4-32** 9f-13f: 2-31 14f+: 0-0
Track : LH: 0-23 **RH: 3-23 Tight: 3-28** Gall: 0-2
Aids: Bl: 0-0 Vi: 0-1 Tstrap: 0-3 Ckp: 0-3
Best Rating: 89 9/02 Gway 7f soft

Very moderate; stays 1m1f; acts on good or softer ground; goes well fresh; has worn a visor and cheekpieces.

Ulzana (IRE)

(95) (69)
3-y-o b g High Chaparral (IRE)-Maritsa (IRE) (Danehill (USA))
Sir Mark Prescott Rectory Racing

Placings:3 (5840)
2009: 8^{3}SD,

	Starts	1st	2nd	3rd	Win & Pl
Career Total (Turf)	0	0	0	0	
Career Total (AW)	1	0	0	1	403

Going (Turf): Sf: 0-0 GS: 0-0 Gd: 0-0 GF: 0-0 Fm: 0-0
Distance: 5f/6f: 0-0 7f-8f: 0-0 9f-13f: 0-1 14f+: 0-0
Track : LH: 0-1 RH: 0-0 Tight: 0-1 Gall: 0-0
Aids: Bl: 0-0 Vi: 0-0 Tstrap: 0-0 Ckp: 0-0
Best Rating: 69 9/09 Wolv 1m141y stand

Modest; stays 1m; acts on Polytrack; sure to improve.

Umpa Loompa (IRE)

(93) (32)14
5-y-o ch g Indian Lodge (IRE)-Bold Fashion (FR) (Nashwan (USA))
B J McMath Chocolate Factory

Placings:0005/0**0**403106/**066**000-6 (4982)
2009: 6^{6}SD,

	Starts	1st	2nd	3rd	Win & Pl
Career Total (Turf)	14	1	0	1	4932
Career Total (AW)	5	0	0	0	0

65	10/07	Newc	6f	(0-70)H	G-S	£4210

Total win prize-money £4210

Going (Turf): Sf: 0-0 **GS: 1-2** Gd: 0-8 GF: 0-3 Fm: 0-1

Distance: **5f/6f: 1-13** 7f-8f: 0-6 9f-13f: 0-0 14f+: 0-0
Track : LH: 0-6 RH: 0-2 Tight: 0-3 Gall: 0-1
Aids: Bl: 0-1 **Vi: 1-13** Tstrap: 0-0 Ckp: 0-0
Best Rating: 65 10/07 Newc 6f gd-sft

Umverti

100 77
4-y-o b f Averti (IRE)-Umbrian Gold (IRE) (Perugino (USA))
N Bycroft Mrs C M Whatley

Placings:005/01000-531621100 (5671)
2009: 9^{5}GF, 8^{3}GF, 10^{1}G, 9^{6}F, 9^{2}GF, 9^{1}GF, 12^{1}S, 10^{0}G, 12^{0}S,

	Starts	1st	2nd	3rd	Win & Pl
Career Total (Turf)	17	4	1	1	14438

77	7/09	Pont	1m4f8y	(0-75)H	SFT	£3238
70	7/09	Bevl	1m1f207y	(0-75)H	G-F	£3561
67	5/09	Pont	1m2f6y	(0-70)H	GD	£3238
59	6/08	Carl	6f192y	(0-70)H	G-F	£2590

Total win prize-money £12628

Going (Turf): Sf: 1-2 GS: 0-1 Gd: 1-7 **GF: 2-6** Fm: 0-1
Distance: 5f/6f: 0-1 7f-8f: 1-7 **9f-13f: 3-9** 14f+: 0-0
Track : LH: 2-5 RH: 2-7 Tight: 0-2 Gall: 0-0
Aids: Bl: 0-0 Vi: 0-0 Tstrap: 0-1 Ckp: 0-1
Best Rating: 77 7/09 Pont 1m4f8y soft

Fair; stays 1m4f and acts on fast ground.

Una Pelota (IRE)

100 80
3-y-o b c Refuse To Bend (IRE)-Sombreffe (Polish Precedent (USA))
N J Vaughan Money Never Sleeps Racing

Placings:534 (2229)
2009: 8^{5}GF, 10^{3}GF, 8^{4}HY,

	Starts	1st	2nd	3rd	Win & Pl
Career Total (Turf)	3	0	0	1	1300

Going (Turf): Sf: 0-1 GS: 0-0 Gd: 0-0 GF: 0-2 Fm: 0-0
Distance: 5f/6f: 0-0 7f-8f: 0-0 9f-13f: 0-3 14f+: 0-0
Track : LH: 0-3 RH: 0-0 Tight: 0-1 Gall: 0-0
Aids: Bl: 0-0 Vi: 0-0 Tstrap: 0-0 Ckp: 0-0
Best Rating: 80 5/09 Ches 1m2f75y gd-fm

Useful; stays 1m2f; acts on fast ground.

Unawatuna

106 64
4-y-o b f Golden Snake (USA)-Laylee (Deploy)
Mrs K Walton Trainers House Enterprises Ltd

Placings:000023-240011 (6767)
2009: 16^{2}GF, 17^{4}G, 16^{0}GS, 17^{0}GF, 16^{1}GS, 16^{1}GS,

	Starts	1st	2nd	3rd	Win & Pl
Career Total (Turf)	12	2	2	1	8074

64	10/09	Newc	2m19y	(0-75)H	G-S	£2978
59	9/09	Ripn	2m	(0-65)H	G-S	£2590

Total win prize-money £5569

Going (Turf): Sf: 0-1 **GS: 2-5** Gd: 0-3 GF: 0-3 Fm: 0-0
Distance: 5f/6f: 0-0 7f-8f: 0-0 9f-13f: 0-3 **14f+: 2-9**
Track : LH: 1-8 RH: 1-4 Tight: 1-5 Gall: 1-4
Aids: Bl: 0-0 Vi: 0-0 Tstrap: 0-0 Ckp: 0-0
Best Rating: 64 10/09 Newc 2m19y gd-sft

Moderate; effective over 2m; acts on fast and easy ground.

Unbelievable Jeff

96(89) (37)51
3-y-o b g Oasis Dream-Sunshine N'Showers (Spectrum (IRE))
J Balding (S Parr 26/6) Willie McKay

Placings:0002245 (6140)
2009: 6^{0}SD, 8^{0}SD, 5^{0}SD, 5^{2}GF, 5^{2}GF, 6^{4}G, 6^{5}G,

	Starts	1st	2nd	3rd	Win & Pl
Career Total (Turf)	4	0	2	0	1539
Career Total (AW)	3	0	0	0	

Going (Turf): Sf: 0-0 GS: 0-0 Gd: 0-2 GF: 0-2 Fm: 0-0
Distance: 5f/6f: 0-5 7f-8f: 0-2 9f-13f: 0-0 14f+: 0-0
Track : LH: 0-3 RH: 0-0 Tight: 0-1 Gall: 0-0
Aids: Bl: 0-0 Vi: 0-0 Tstrap: 0-0 Ckp: 0-0
Best Rating: 51 6/09 Rdcr 5f gd-fm

Moderate; best at 5f but stays 6f; acts on fast ground.

Unbreak My Heart (IRE)

107 98
4-y-o ch g Bahamian Bounty-Golden Heart (Salse (USA))
R A Fahey J C Parsons & J J Gilmartin

Placings:0311/2002003-1560000 (6093)
2009: 8^{1}GF, 10^{5}G, 10^{6}GF, 10^{0}GF, 9^{0}G, 10^{0}GS, 10^{0}G,

	Starts	1st	2nd	3rd	Win & Pl
Career Total (Turf)	18	3	2	2	25390

98	4/09	Pont	1m4y	(0-95)H	G-F	£7477
88	10/07	Gdwd	7f	(0-85)	SFT	£5505
81	10/07	Wind	6f		G-S	£2817

Total win prize-money £15799

Going (Turf): **Sf: 1-4 GS: 1-3** Gd: 0-6 **GF: 1-5** Fm: 0-0
Distance: 5f/6f: 1-3 7f-8f: 1-3 9f-13f: 1-12 14f+: 0-0
Track : LH: 1-9 RH: 1-4 Tight: 0-3 **Gall: 1-2**
Aids: Bl: 0-0 Vi: 0-0 Tstrap: 0-0 Ckp: 0-0
Best Rating: 98 4/09 Pont 1m4y gd-fm

Very useful; stays 1m; acts on fast and soft ground.

Uncle Bertie

97(101) (69)72
4-y-o b g Bertolini (USA)-Resourceful (IRE) (Entrepreneur)
Tim Vaughan (Tom Dascombe 2/10) Owen Promotions Limited

Placings:010040 (6460)
2009: 9^{0}SD, 9^{1}SD, 10^{0}G, 10^{0}S, 9^{4}GF, 9^{0}SD,

	Starts	1st	2nd	3rd	Win & Pl
Career Total (Turf)	3	0	0	0	192
Career Total (AW)	3	1	0	0	2590

69	3/09	Wolv	1m1f103y	STD	£2590

Total win prize-money £2590

Going (Turf): Sf: 0-1 GS: 0-0 Gd: 0-1 GF: 0-1 Fm: 0-0
Distance: 5f/6f: 0-0 7f-8f: 0-0 **9f-13f: 1-6** 14f+: 0-0
Track : **LH: 1-6** RH: 0-0 **Tight: 1-4** Gall: 0-0
Aids: Bl: 0-0 Vi: 0-0 Tstrap: 0-0 Ckp: 0-0
Best Rating: 72 4/09 Pont 1m2f6y good

Modest; stays 9f; acts on Polytrack.

Uncle Brit

74(104) (71)12
3-y-o b c Efisio-Tarneem (USA) (Zilzal (USA))

Sir Mark Prescott P J D Pottinger

Placings:0000414040 (5806)
2009: 6^{0}SD, 6^{0}SD, 6^{0}SD, 7^{0}SD, 7^{4}SD, 8^{1}SD, 8^{4}SD, 10^{0}G, 8^{4}SD, 8^{0}SD,

	Starts	1st	2nd	3rd	Win & Pl
Career Total (Turf)	1	0	0	0	
Career Total (AW)	9	1	0	0	3913

71 7/09 Sthl 1m (0-70)H STD £3432
Total win prize-money £3432

Going (Turf): Sf: 0-0 GS: 0-0 Gd: 0-1 GF: 0-0 Fm: 0-0
Distance: 5f/6f: 0-3 **7f-8f: 1-6** 9f-13f: 0-1 14f+: 0-0
Track : **LH: 1-9** RH: 0-1 Tight: 0-5 Gall: 0-0
Aids: Bl: 0-1 Vi: 0-0 Tstrap: 0-0 Ckp: 0-0
Best Rating: 71 7/09 Sthl 1m stand

Modest brother to the smart 7f-1m2f winner Enforcer; stays 1m; acts on Fibresand.

Uncle Fred

105(105) (91)86
4-y-o b g Royal Applause-Karla June (Unfuwain (USA))
P R Chamings P R Chamings M A Kirby

Placings:536 212010 (7233)
2009: 8^{2}SD, 8^{1}GF, 8^{2}SD, 7^{0}GF, 10^{1}SD, 10^{0}SD,

	Starts	1st	2nd	3rd	Win & Pl
Career Total (Turf)	3	1	0	0	5505
Career Total (AW)	6	1	2	1	7483

91 10/09 Kemp 1m2f (0-80)H STD £4727
86 5/09 Newb 1m (0-80)H G-F £5504
Total win prize-money £10232

Going (Turf): Sf: 0-0 GS: 0-1 Gd: 0-0 **GF: 1-2** Fm: 0-0
Distance: 5f/6f: 0-0 7f-8f: 1-7 9f-13f: 1-2 14f+: 0-0
Track : LH: 0-3 **RH: 1-4** Tight: 0-2 Gall: 0-0
Aids: Bl: 0-0 Vi: 0-0 Tstrap: 0-0 Ckp: 0-0
Best Rating: 91 10/09 Kemp 1m2f stand

Useful; effective over 7f-1m2f; acts on fast ground and on Polytrack.

Uncle Keef (IRE)

86(85) (60)44
3-y-o b g Sadler's Wells (USA)-Love For Ever (IRE) (Darshaan)
M P Tregoning R A H Evans

Placings:000 (6974)
2009: 10^{0}GF, 10^{0}S, 11^{0}SD,

	Starts	1st	2nd	3rd	Win & Pl
Career Total (Turf)	2	0	0	0	
Career Total (AW)	1	0	0	0	

Going (Turf): Sf: 0-1 GS: 0-0 Gd: 0-0 GF: 0-1 Fm: 0-0
Distance: 5f/6f: 0-0 7f-8f: 0-0 9f-13f: 0-3 14f+: 0-0
Track : LH: 0-2 RH: 0-1 Tight: 0-1 Gall: 0-0
Aids: Bl: 0-0 Vi: 0-0 Tstrap: 0-0 Ckp: 0-0
Best Rating: 60 10/09 Kemp 1m3f stand

Unconsoled

91(97) (48)63
3-y-o b f Ishiguru (USA)-Chantilly (FR) (Sanglamore (USA))
J Hetherton R Fell & K Everitt

Placings:50000-40606040 (7678)
2009: 7^{4}GS, 7^{0}GF, 7^{6}GS, 6^{0}GF, 5^{6}GF, 8^{0}GF, 7^{4}SD, 7^{0}SD,

	Starts	1st	2nd	3rd	Win & Pl
Career Total (Turf)	10	0	0	0	0
Career Total (AW)	3	0	0	0	0

Going (Turf): Sf: 0-1 GS: 0-2 Gd: 0-0 GF: 0-6 Fm: 0-1
Distance: 5f/6f: 0-5 7f-8f: 0-7 9f-13f: 0-1 14f+: 0-0
Track : LH: 0-7 RH: 0-2 Tight: 0-2 Gall: 0-0
Aids: Bl: 0-2 Vi: 0-0 Tstrap: 0-0 Ckp: 0-0
Best Rating: 63 6/08 Navn 5f182y firm

Undaunted Affair (IRE)

98 (79)92
3-y-o ch f Spartacus (IRE)-Party Bag (Cadeaux Genereux)
K A Ryan L M Rutherford

Placings:313-500000 (7297a)
2009: 7^{5}GF, 8^{0}G, 6^{0}S, 6^{0}G, 7^{0}S, 7^{0}SD,

	Starts	1st	2nd	3rd	Win & Pl
Career Total (Turf)	8	1	0	2	11074
Career Total (AW)	1	0	0	0	

88 5/08 Hayd 6f G-F £3853
Total win prize-money £3853

Going (Turf): Sf: 0-2 GS: 0-0 Gd: 0-3 **GF: 1-3** Fm: 0-0
Distance: **5f/6f: 1-5** 7f-8f: 0-4 9f-13f: 0-0 14f+: 0-0
Track : LH: 0-3 RH: 0-0 Tight: 0-0 Gall: 0-0
Aids: Bl: 0-0 Vi: 0-0 Tstrap: 0-0 Ckp: 0-0
Best Rating: 92 3/09 Leop 7f gd-fm

Very useful; Group 3 placed; effective at 6f; acts on a fast surface.

Under Fire (IRE)

80(105) (66)66
6-y-o b g Lear Spear (USA)-Kahyasi Moll (IRE) (Brief Truce (USA))
A W Carroll Marita Bayley and Trevor Turner

Placings:050/000400441105 0/420500000102/242113660 404533322200-00002 (7767)
2009: 8^{0}SD, 8^{0}SD, 7^{0}G, 7^{0}SD, 11^{2}SD,

	Starts	1st	2nd	3rd	Win & Pl
Career Total (Turf)	22	2	2	3	9013
Career Total (AW)	32	3	6	1	10028

69 2/08 Kemp 1m (0-60)H STD £2047
62 2/08 Kemp 1m (0-55)H STD £2047
55 11/07 Kemp 1m (0-52)H STD £2047
59 10/06 Brig 7f214y (0-58)H G-S £2914
53 8/06 Bath 1m5y (0-65)H G-F £2849
Total win prize-money £11909

Going (Turf): Sf: 0-1 **GS: 1-5** Gd: 0-6 **GF: 1-8** Fm: 0-2
Distance: 5f/6f: 0-0 **7f-8f: 4-25** 9f-13f: 1-29 14f+: 0-0
Track : LH: 2-30 **RH: 3-22 Tight: 1-16** Gall: 0-1
Aids: Bl: 0-0 Vi: 0-0 Tstrap: 0-0 Ckp: 0-0
Best Rating: 70 2/08 Kemp 1m stand

Moderate; effective over 1m; acts on fast and easy ground; also goes on Polytrack.

Under Review (IRE)

104(98) (73)70
3-y-o b g Danetime (IRE)-Coloma (JPN) (Forty Niner (USA))
T D Barron (S A Callaghan 25/4) J Browne

Placings:215050446 (7355)
2009: 5^{2}SD, 5^{1}SD, 6^{5}SD, 5^{0}GF, 5^{5}GF, 5^{0}GF, 5^{4}GF, 5^{4}G, 5^{6}SD,

	Starts	1st	2nd	3rd	Win & Pl
Career Total (Turf)	5	0	0	0	457
Career Total (AW)	4	1	1	0	3536

73 2/09 Sthl 5f STD £2729
Total win prize-money £2730

Going (Turf): Sf: 0-0 GS: 0-0 Gd: 0-1 GF: 0-4 Fm: 0-0
Distance: **5f/6f: 1-9** 7f-8f: 0-0 9f-13f: 0-0 14f+: 0-0
Track : LH: 0-2 RH: 0-0 Tight: 0-2 Gall: 0-0
Aids: Bl: 0-1 Vi: 0-0 Tstrap: 0-0 Ckp: 0-0
Best Rating: 73 2/09 Sthl 5f stand

Fair; suited by 5f; acts on sand and fast ground.

Under Warranty (ITY)

(101) (75)
5-y-o ch g Della Scala (IRE)-Serengate (GER) (Highest Honor (FR))
F Sheridan A Zanoboni

Placings:0/003/06162164012-241 (0352)
2009: 5^{2}SD, 5^{4}SD, 5^{1}SD,

	Starts	1st	2nd	3rd	Win & Pl
Career Total (Turf)	12	3	1	1	10338
Career Total (AW)	6	1	2	0	4387

75 1/09 Wolv 5f216y (0-60)H STD £2047
7/08 Agno 5f GD £1838
3/08 Capa 6f H SFT £2941
2/08 Agno 5f H SFT £3860
Total win prize-money £10686

Going (Turf): Sf: 2-5 GS: 0-0 Gd: 1-7 GF: 0-0 Fm: 0-0
Distance: **5f/6f: 4-15** 7f-8f: 0-3 9f-13f: 0-0 14f+: 0-0
Track : **LH: 1-3** RH: 0-0 **Tight: 1-3** Gall: 0-0
Aids: Bl: 0-0 Vi: 0-0 Tstrap: 0-1 Ckp: 0-1
Best Rating: 75 1/09 Wolv 5f216y stand

Modest; multiple winner in Italy; effective at 6f; goes on Polytrack.

Underworld Dandy

93(94) (65)63
2-y-o gr g Fraam-Eastern Lyric (Petong)
P D Evans (Tom Dascombe 25/5) David Mort

Placings:51600415503545 (7669)
2009: 5^{5}GF, 6^{1}G, 6^{6}GF, 7^{0}S, 6^{0}GF, 7^{4}SD, 8^{1}SD, 8^{5}SD, 8^{5}SD, 6^{0}G, 9^{3}SD, 8^{5}SD, 10^{4}SD, 8^{5}SD,

	Starts	1st	2nd	3rd	Win & Pl
Career Total (Turf)	6	1	0	0	2047
Career Total (AW)	8	1	0	1	2400

65 9/09 Kemp 1m (0-65) STD £2047
60 5/09 Chep 6f16y GD £2047
Total win prize-money £4094

Going (Turf): Sf: 0-1 GS: 0-0 **Gd: 1-2** GF: 0-3 Fm: 0-0
Distance: 5f/6f: 0-1 **7f-8f: 2-8** 9f-13f: 0-5 14f+: 0-0
Track : LH: 0-7 **RH: 1-3** Tight: 0-6 Gall: 0-1
Aids: Bl: 0-0 Vi: 0-2 Tstrap: 0-1 Ckp: 0-1
Best Rating: 65 9/09 Kemp 1m stand

Modest; effective at 6f-1m; acts on good ground and Polytrack; has worn cheekpieces.

Union Island (IRE)

109(95) (68)89
3-y-o b g Rock Of Gibraltar (IRE)-Daftiyna (IRE) (Darshaan)
K A Ryan Clipper Logistics

Placings:2232-12020500 (6209)

2009: 9^{1}GF, 10^{2}GF, 10^{0}G, 10^{2}G, 10^{0}G, 9^{5}GF, 10^{0}GF, 10^{0}SD,

	Starts	1st	2nd	3rd	Win & Pl
Career Total (Turf)	11	1	5	1	13233
Career Total (AW)	1	0	0	0	

69 4/09 Muss 1m1f G-F £2590

Total win prize-money £2590

Going (Turf): Sf: 0-2 GS: 0-1 Gd: 0-3 **GF: 1-5** Fm: 0-0
Distance: 5f/6f: 0-0 7f-8f: 0-1 **9f-13f: 1-11** 14f+: 0-0
Track : LH: 0-7 **RH: 1-4 Tight: 1-3** Gall: 0-3
Aids: Bl: 0-0 Vi: 0-1 Tstrap: 0-0 Ckp: 0-0
Best Rating: 89 6/09 York 1m2f88y good

Useful; stays 1m2f; acts on most ground.

Union Jack Jackson (IRE)

101(91) (43)**52**

7-y-o b g Daggers Drawn (USA)-Beechwood Quest (IRE) (River Falls)
John A Harris Mrs A E Harris

Placings:4006441232/**5**000000/**0006221510300003/050112 154520/0000030600**0-0005100 **(6674)**

2009: 6^{0}GS, 5^{0}GF, 5^{0}GF, 8^{5}G, 7^{1}G, 8^{0}GF, 7^{0}SD,

	Starts	1st	2nd	3rd	Win & Pl
Career Total (Turf)	21	1	1	1	4902
Career Total (AW)	41	6	5	3	19155

52 8/09 Bevl 7f100y GD £2590
65 5/07 Sthl 6f (0-55)H STD £3241
61 4/07 Ling 6f (0-50)H STD £2388
55 3/07 Wolv 7f32y (0-50)H STD £1535
58 5/06 Sthl 6f (0-45) STD £1706
52 4/06 Sthl 6f (0-45) STD £1467
66 12/04 Wolv 1m141y (0-65) STD £2590

Total win prize-money £15520

Going (Turf): Sf: 0-2 GS: 0-3 **Gd: 1-9** GF: 0-7 Fm: 0-0
Distance: **5f/6f: 4-28** 7f-8f: 2-22 9f-13f: 1-12 14f+: 0-0
Track : **LH: 6-43** RH: 1-1 **Tight: 3-16** Gall: 0-0
Aids: **Bl: 5-31** Vi: 1-4 Tstrap: 0-4 Ckp: 0-4
Best Rating: 76 12/04 Sthl 1m stand

Moderate; effective at around 6f; acts on Fibresand and Polytrack.

Uniquely Poised (USA)

99(101) (92)**84**

3-y-o b/br g More Than Ready (USA)-No Other Like You (USA) (Cozzene (USA))
J H M Gosden Malih L Al Basti

Placings:01000 **(6633)**

2009: 10^{0}GF, 8^{1}SD, 8^{0}S, 8^{0}GF, 8^{0}SS,

	Starts	1st	2nd	3rd	Win & Pl
Career Total (Turf)	3	0	0	0	
Career Total (AW)	2	1	0	0	4404

92 5/09 Kemp 1m STD £4403

Total win prize-money £4404

Going (Turf): **Sf: 0-1 GS: 0-0 Gd: 0-0 GF: 0-2 Fm: 0-0**
Distance: 5f/6f: 0-0 **7f-8f: 1-4** 9f-13f: 0-1 14f+: 0-0
Track : LH: 0-1 **RH: 1-1** Tight: 0-1 Gall: 0-0
Aids: Bl: 0-0 Vi: 0-0 Tstrap: 0-1 Ckp: 0-1
Best Rating: 92 5/09 Kemp 1m stand

Very useful; stays 1m and acts on Polytrack.

United Nations

(106) (81)**80**

8-y-o ch g Halling (USA)-Congress(IRE) (Dancing Brave (USA))
N Wilson Feenan & Tobin

Placings:1340/000060/**3522160/2400014605/04001-1133626** **(7723)**

2009: 8^{1}SS, 8^{1}SD, 8^{3}SD, 8^{3}SD, 12^{6}SD, 8^{2}SD, 8^{6}SD,

	Starts	1st	2nd	3rd	Win & Pl
Career Total (Turf)	20	2	2	1	16440
Career Total (AW)	19	4	2	3	15303

81 1/09 Sthl 1m (0-70)H STD £2729
76 1/09 Sthl 1m (0-70)H SS £2729
74 12/08 Sthl 1m (0-60)H STD £2047
76 8/07 Bevl 1m100y G-F £2914
79 9/06 Wolv 1m141y (0-75)H STD £3238
92 4/04 NmkR 1m D GD £6955

Total win prize-money £20616

Going (Turf): Sf: 0-2 GS: 0-4 **Gd: 1-5 GF: 1-9** Fm: 0-0
Distance: 5f/6f: 0-0 **7f-8f: 4-16** 9f-13f: 2-23 14f+: 0-0
Track : **LH: 4-30** RH: 1-5 **Tight: 1-16** Gall: 0-4
Aids: **Bl: 3-8** Vi: 0-2 Tstrap: 0-1 Ckp: 0-1
Best Rating: 93 9/04 Muss 1m good

Fair; effective at around 1m; acts on easy ground; goes on sand; has worn blinkers.

Universal Circus

103(95) (74)**80**

2-y-o b f Imperial Dancer-Wansdyke Lass (Josr Algarhoud (IRE))
M R Channon Steve Fisher

Placings:04316346 **(6805)**

2009: 7^{0}GF, 7^{4}GF, 7^{3}G, 7^{1}G, 8^{6}S, 7^{3}GF, 7^{4}GF, 8^{6}SD,

	Starts	1st	2nd	3rd	Win & Pl
Career Total (Turf)	7	1	0	2	7509
Career Total (AW)	1	0	0	0	0

76 7/09 Epsm 7f GD £4533

Total win prize-money £4533

Going (Turf): Sf: 0-1 GS: 0-0 **Gd: 1-2** GF: 0-4 Fm: 0-0
Distance: 5f/6f: 0-0 **7f-8f: 1-6** 9f-13f: 0-2 14f+: 0-0
Track : **LH: 1-4** RH: 0-0 **Tight: 1-3** Gall: 0-0
Aids: Bl: 0-0 Vi: 0-0 Tstrap: 0-0 Ckp: 0-0
Best Rating: 80 10/09 Epsm 7f gd-fm

Fair filly; stays 7f and acts on easy ground.

Universal Pride

71 **33**

2-y-o b f Danbird (AUS)-Frisson (Slip Anchor)
J Gallagher Universal Racing

Placings:00 **(6544)**

2009: 6^{0}GF, 7^{0}GF,

	Starts	1st	2nd	3rd	Win & Pl
Career Total (Turf)	2	0	0	0	

Going (Turf): **Sf: 0-0 GS: 0-0 Gd: 0-0 GF: 0-2 Fm: 0-0**
Distance: 5f/6f: 0-1 7f-8f: 0-1 9f-13f: 0-0 14f+: 0-0
Track : LH: 0-2 RH: 0-0 Tight: 0-1 Gall: 0-0
Aids: Bl: 0-0 Vi: 0-0 Tstrap: 0-0 Ckp: 0-0
Best Rating: 33 10/09 Wwck 7f26y gd-fm

Unleashed (IRE)

108(103) (94)**107**

4-y-o br g Storming Home-Uriah (GER) (Acatenango (GER))
H R A Cecil Ennismore Racing II

Placings:5/1104-00435030 **(6662)**

2009: 12^{0}S, 13^{0}S, 12^{4}GF, 12^{3}GF, 12^{5}G, 13^{0}GF, 12^{3}GF, 12^{0}GS,

	Starts	1st	2nd	3rd	Win & Pl
Career Total (Turf)	11	0	0	2	12976
Career Total (AW)	2	2	0	0	6152

94 6/08 Kemp 1m4f (0-85)H STD £4209
73 5/08 GrLe 1m2f STD £1942

Total win prize-money £6152

Going (Turf): **Sf: 0-3 GS: 0-2 Gd: 0-1 GF: 0-4 Fm: 0-1**
Distance: 5f/6f: 0-0 7f-8f: 0-0 **9f-13f: 2-10** 14f+: 0-3
Track : LH: 1-5 RH: 1-8 Tight: 0-3 **Gall: 1-7**
Aids: Bl: 0-2 Vi: 0-0 Tstrap: 0-0 Ckp: 0-0
Best Rating: 107 6/09 Pont 1m4f8y gd-fm

Smart; stays 1m4f; acts on Polytrack and soft ground.

Unnefer (FR)

112 **114**

4-y-o b c Danehill Dancer (IRE)-Mimalia (USA) (Silver Hawk (USA))
P Bary (H R A Cecil 15/8) Niarchos Family

Placings:01222/12103-21002

2009: 8^{2}GF, 10^{1}GF, 8^{0}G, 10^{0}G, 10^{2}S,

	Starts	1st	2nd	3rd	Win & Pl
Career Total (Turf)	15	4	6	1	85405

114 5/09 Ling 1m2f G-F £12462
107 5/08 NmkR 1m2f FRM £17031
109 4/08 Newb 1m2f6y G-S £6854
81 6/07 NmkJ 7f G-S £4533

Total win prize-money £40881

Going (Turf): Sf: 0-1 **GS: 2-2** Gd: 0-5 GF: 1-6 Fm: 1-1
Distance: 5f/6f: 0-1 7f-8f: 1-5 **9f-13f: 3-9** 14f+: 0-0
Track : **LH: 2-5** RH: 0-4 Tight: 1-3 Gall: 1-3
Aids: Bl: 0-0 Vi: 0-0 Tstrap: 0-0 Ckp: 0-0
Best Rating: 114 5/09 Ling 1m2f gd-fm

Group class; winner in Listed company and runner-up in the 2008 Dee Stakes; stays 1m2f; acts on fast and easy ground.

Unshakable (IRE)

101 (96)**99**

10-y-o b g Eagle Eyed (USA)-Pepper And Salt (IRE) (Double Schwartz)
Bob Jones Unshakable Partnership

Placings:52/11023/0620000/0013054500/00214/0630060/ 213660/201000-0000 **(6594)**

2009: 8^{0}G, 7^{0}G, 10^{0}GF, 10^{0}GS,

	Starts	1st	2nd	3rd	Win & Pl
Career Total (Turf)	50	6	5	4	208565
Career Total (AW)	2	0	1	0	3677

99 8/08 NmkJ 1m2f (0-95)H G-F £9066
97 6/07 Epsm 1m114y (0-105)H G-S £21812
98 7/05 Gdwd 1m H G-S £87000
96 4/04 Sand 1m14y C(0-95)H G-S £12586
99 8/02 Sand 1m14y C(0-95)H G-F £11407
79 4/02 Hayd 7f30y D G-F £4212

Total win prize-money £146084

Going (Turf): Sf: 0-7 **GS: 3-13** Gd: 0-13 **GF: 3-17** Fm: 0-0
Distance: 5f/6f: 0-0 7f-8f: 2-31 **9f-13f: 4-21** 14f+: 0-0
Track : LH: 2-12 **RH: 4-21** Tight: 1-3 Gall: 1-10
Aids: Bl: 0-0 Vi: 0-0 Tstrap: 0-0 Ckp: 0-0
Best Rating: 106 7/03 Newb 1m gd-fm

Useful; stays 1m2f; acts on most ground; also goes on Polytrack.

Unshakable Will (IRE)

98 79

2-y-o b g Refuse To Bend (IRE)-Miss Devious (IRE) (Dr Devious (IRE))

B Smart Richard Page

Placings:52120 **(7013)**

2009: 6^{5}GF, 7^{2}GF, 7^{1}G, 7^{2}G, 7^{0}GS,

	Starts	1st	2nd	3rd	Win & Pl
Career Total (Turf)	5	1	2	0	7937

77 9/09 Ayr 7f50y GD £4857

Total win prize-money £4857

Going (Turf): Sf: 0-0 GS: 0-1 **Gd: 1-2** GF: 0-2 Fm: 0-0
Distance: 5f/6f: 0-0 **7f-8f: 1-5** 9f-13f: 0-0 14f+: 0-0
Track : **LH: 1-2** RH: 0-0 Tight: 0-1 Gall: 0-0
Aids: Bl: 0-0 Vi: 0-0 Tstrap: 0-0 Ckp: 0-0
Best Rating: **79** 10/09 Catt 7f good

Fair; effective over 7f; acts on good and fast ground.

Until The Man (IRE)

95(99) (59)61

2-y-o b c Tillerman-Canoe Cove (IRE) (Grand Lodge (USA))

R Ingram S. G. M.

Placings:0005232 **(7886)**

2009: 6^{0}GF, 7^{0}G, 7^{0}G, 6^{5}GS, 8^{2}GF, 8^{3}SD, 7^{2}SD,

	Starts	1st	2nd	3rd	Win & Pl
Career Total (Turf)	5	0	1	0	1156
Career Total (AW)	2	0	1	1	773

Going (Turf): **Sf: 0-0 GS: 0-1 Gd: 0-2 GF: 0-2 Fm: 0-0**
Distance: 5f/6f: 0-1 7f-8f: 0-5 9f-13f: 0-1 14f+: 0-0
Track : LH: 0-2 RH: 0-2 Tight: 0-2 Gall: 0-0
Aids: Bl: 0-0 Vi: 0-0 Tstrap: 0-4 Ckp: 0-4
Best Rating: **61** 10/09 Yarm 1m3y gd-fm

Modest; stays 1m; acts on fast and on easy ground and Polytrack; has worn cheekpieces.

Until When (USA)

94 (70)73

5-y-o b g Grand Slam (USA)-Chez Cherie (Wolfhound (USA))

B Smart B Smart

Placings:04344/45/0204-3 **(1096)**

2009: 5^{3}GF,

	Starts	1st	2nd	3rd	Win & Pl
Career Total (Turf)	11	0	1	2	2857
Career Total (AW)	1	0	0	0	337

Going (Turf): **Sf: 0-1 GS: 0-1 Gd: 0-4 GF: 0-4 Fm: 0-1**
Distance: 5f/6f: 0-5 7f-8f: 0-6 9f-13f: 0-1 14f+: 0-0
Track : LH: 0-1 RH: 0-3 Tight: 0-3 Gall: 0-0
Aids: Bl: 0-0 Vi: 0-4 Tstrap: 0-0 Ckp: 0-0
Best Rating: **73** 7/08 Ayr 5f good

Modest sprinter; acts on good ground; has worn a visor.

Up At Last

77 54

2-y-o b f Cape Cross (IRE)-Upend (Main Reef)

W J Haggas P D Player

Placings:0 **(6920)**

2009: 8^{0}GF,

	Starts	1st	2nd	3rd	Win & Pl
Career Total (Turf)	1	0	0	0	

Going (Turf): **Sf: 0-0 GS: 0-0 Gd: 0-0 GF: 0-1 Fm: 0-0**
Distance: 5f/6f: 0-0 7f-8f: 0-0 9f-13f: 0-1 14f+: 0-0
Track : LH: 0-0 RH: 0-0 Tight: 0-0 Gall: 0-0
Aids: Bl: 0-0 Vi: 0-0 Tstrap: 0-0 Ckp: 0-0
Best Rating: **54** 10/09 Yarm 1m3y gd-fm

Up In Arms (IRE)

100(97) (73)66

5-y-o b g Daggers Drawn (USA)-Queenliness (Exit To Nowhere (USA))

P Winkworth P Winkworth

Placings:002400/020005015212/0-046U46 **(1980)**

2009: 12^{0}SD, 16^{4}SD, 16^{6}SD, 12^{U}GF, 15^{4}G, 11^{6}F,

	Starts	1st	2nd	3rd	Win & Pl
Career Total (Turf)	19	1	3	0	8278
Career Total (AW)	6	1	1	0	2924

70 11/07 Kemp 2m (0-65)H STD £2047
65 8/07 Newb 1m2f6y GD £4857

Total win prize-money £6906

Going (Turf): Sf: 0-0 GS: 0-5 **Gd: 1-5** GF: 0-8 Fm: 0-1
Distance: 5f/6f: 0-1 7f-8f: 0-5 9f-13f: 1-13 14f+: 1-6
Track : LH: 1-11 RH: 1-6 Tight: 0-13 **Gall: 1-2**
Aids: Bl: 0-2 Vi: 0-0 Tstrap: 0-0 Ckp: 0-0
Best Rating: **73** 12/07 Wolv 2m119y stand

Modest; stays 2m; acts on good and softer ground and on Polytrack.

Uphold

88 58

2-y-o b c Oasis Dream-Allegro Viva (USA) (Distant View (USA))

B W Hills K Abdulla

Placings:0 **(7146)**

2009: 7^{0}G,

	Starts	1st	2nd	3rd	Win & Pl
Career Total (Turf)	1	0	0	0	

Going (Turf): **Sf: 0-0 GS: 0-0 Gd: 0-1 GF: 0-0 Fm: 0-0**
Distance: 5f/6f: 0-0 7f-8f: 0-1 9f-13f: 0-0 14f+: 0-0
Track : LH: 0-0 RH: 0-0 Tight: 0-0 Gall: 0-0
Aids: Bl: 0-0 Vi: 0-0 Tstrap: 0-0 Ckp: 0-0
Best Rating: **58** 10/09 NmkR 7f good

Upper Key

76 30

3-y-o b g Exceed And Excel (AUS)-Ard Na Sighe (IRE) (Kenmare (FR))

K A Ryan Joy And Valentine Feerick

Placings:00 **(2234)**

2009: 8^{0}GF, 6^{0}GS,

	Starts	1st	2nd	3rd	Win & Pl
Career Total (Turf)	2	0	0	0	

Going (Turf): **Sf: 0-0 GS: 0-1 Gd: 0-0 GF: 0-1 Fm: 0-0**
Distance: 5f/6f: 0-1 7f-8f: 0-1 9f-13f: 0-0 14f+: 0-0
Track : LH: 0-1 RH: 0-0 Tight: 0-1 Gall: 0-0
Aids: Bl: 0-0 Vi: 0-0 Tstrap: 0-0 Ckp: 0-0
Best Rating: **30** 5/09 Thsk 1m gd-fm

Upstairs

82(104) (67)59

5-y-o ch g Sugarfoot-Laena (Roman Warrior)

Paul Henderson (D R C Elsworth 24/1) Paul Henderson

Placings:0/50545051-546000 **(3421)**

2009: 8^{5}SD, 6^{4}SD, 8^{6}SD, 6^{0}F, 6^{0}GF, 9^{0}G,

	Starts	1st	2nd	3rd	Win & Pl
Career Total (Turf)	6	0	0	0	0
Career Total (AW)	9	1	0	0	2047

67 12/08 Ling 7f (0-55)H STD £2047

Total win prize-money £2047

Going (Turf): **Sf: 0-0 GS: 0-1 Gd: 0-2 GF: 0-2 Fm: 0-1**
Distance: 5f/6f: 0-4 **7f-8f: 1-9** 9f-13f: 0-2 14f+: 0-0
Track : **LH: 1-8** RH: 0-2 **Tight: 1-7** Gall: 0-2
Aids: Bl: 0-0 Vi: 0-0 Tstrap: 0-0 Ckp: 0-0
Best Rating: **67** 12/08 Ling 7f stand

Moderate; stays 7f and acts on Polytrack.

Upton Seas

100(89) (60)78

3-y-o b f Josr Algarhoud (IRE)-Crystal Seas (Zamindar (USA))

M W Easterby Stephen Curtis & Eric Brook

Placings:660-11515064 **(7020)**

2009: 9^{1}GF, 12^{1}G, 9^{5}G, 9^{1}G, 12^{5}GF, 10^{0}G, 11^{6}SD, 10^{4}GS,

	Starts	1st	2nd	3rd	Win & Pl
Career Total (Turf)	9	3	0	0	10852
Career Total (AW)	2	0	0	0	0

78 8/09 Ripn 1m1f170y (0-70)H GD £2914
67 7/09 Thsk 1m4f (0-70)H GD £4338
60 7/09 Bevl 1m1f207y (0-70)H G-F £3238

Total win prize-money £10491

Going (Turf): Sf: 0-1 GS: 0-1 **Gd: 2-5** GF: 1-2 Fm: 0-0
Distance: 5f/6f: 0-0 7f-8f: 0-2 **9f-13f: 3-9** 14f+: 0-0
Track : LH: 1-7 **RH: 2-4 Tight: 2-3** Gall: 0-2
Aids: Bl: 0-0 Vi: 0-0 Tstrap: 0-0 Ckp: 0-0
Best Rating: **78** 8/09 Ripn 1m1f170y good

Modest; effective at 1m4f; acts on fast and easy ground.

Uptown Lad (IRE)

96 46

10-y-o b g Definite Article-Shoka (FR) (Kaldoun (FR))

R Johnson Robert Johnson

Placings:004/0405/003006 **(6899)**

2009: 16^{0}G, 16^{0}GF, 17^{3}G, 16^{0}GS, 16^{0}GS, 17^{6}GF,

	Starts	1st	2nd	3rd	Win & Pl
Career Total (Turf)	11	0	0	1	302
Career Total (AW)	2	0	0	0	0

Going (Turf): **Sf: 0-2 GS: 0-3 Gd: 0-3 GF: 0-2 Fm: 0-1**
Distance: 5f/6f: 0-3 7f-8f: 0-1 9f-13f: 0-3 14f+: 0-6
Track : LH: 0-8 RH: 0-3 Tight: 0-2 Gall: 0-5
Aids: Bl: 0-0 Vi: 0-1 Tstrap: 0-0 Ckp: 0-0
Best Rating: **50** 9/02 Rdcr 1m2f firm

Urban Bounty

4-y-o ch f Bahamian Bounty-Bathe In Light (USA) (Sunshine Forever (USA))

M J McGrath A Morris

Placings:0 **(2633)**
2009: 10^{0}GF,

	Starts	1st	2nd	3rd	Win & Pl
Career Total (Turf)	1	0	0	0	

Going (Turf): **Sf: 0-0 GS: 0-0 Gd: 0-0 GF: 0-1 Fm: 0-0**
Distance: 5f/6f: 0-0 7f-8f: 0-0 9f-13f: 0-1 14f+: 0-0
Track : LH: 0-1 RH: 0-0 Tight: 0-1 Gall: 0-0
Aids: Bl: 0-0 Vi: 0-0 Tstrap: 0-0 Ckp: 0-0

Urban Clubber

89 **70**
2-y-o b g Dubai Destination (USA)-Surprise Visitor (IRE) (Be My Guest (USA))
J Howard Johnson Transcend Bloodstock LLP

Placings:6546 **(4190)**
2009: 6^{6}G, 6^{5}G, 5^{4}GF, 7^{6}S,

	Starts	1st	2nd	3rd	Win & Pl
Career Total (Turf)	4	0	0	0	350

Going (Turf): **Sf: 0-1 GS: 0-0 Gd: 0-2 GF: 0-1 Fm: 0-0**
Distance: 5f/6f: 0-3 7f-8f: 0-1 9f-13f: 0-0 14f+: 0-0
Track : LH: 0-2 RH: 0-1 Tight: 0-1 Gall: 0-0
Aids: Bl: 0-0 Vi: 0-0 Tstrap: 0-0 Ckp: 0-0
Best Rating: **70** 5/09 Pont 6f good

Urban Poet (USA)

106 **109**
3-y-o b/br c Dynaformer (USA)-Preach (USA) (Mr Prospector (USA))
Saeed Bin Suroor (M Johnston 28/7) Godolphin

Placings:136610 **(6854)**
2009: 11^{1}GF, 12^{3}G, 14^{6}G, 12^{6}GF, 17^{1}GF, 16^{0}G,

	Starts	1st	2nd	3rd	Win & Pl
Career Total (Turf)	6	2	0	1	20016

100 10/09 Pont 2m1f216y G-F £9346
97 7/09 Haml 1m3f16y G-F £2590
Total win prize-money £11937

Going (Turf): Sf: 0-0 GS: 0-0 Gd: 0-3 **GF: 2-3** Fm: 0-0
Distance: 5f/6f: 0-0 7f-8f: 0-0 9f-13f: 1-3 14f+: 1-3
Track : LH: 1-2 RH: 1-4 **Tight: 1-4** Gall: 0-1
Aids: Bl: 0-0 Vi: 0-0 Tstrap: 0-0 Ckp: 0-0
Best Rating: **109** 7/09 Gdwd 1m4f good

Smart; stays 1m4f and acts on good/fast ground.

Urban Space

99(82) (53)**71**
3-y-o ch g Sulamani (IRE)-Rasmalai (Sadler's Wells (USA))
D Burchell (B G Powell 17/8) Jason Tucker

Placings:005-661350214025 **(6116)**
2009: 12^{6}SD, 11^{6}SD, 10^{1}GF, 12^{3}G, 11^{5}GF, 11^{0}GF, 11^{2}G, 11^{1}GF, 12^{4}GF, 13^{0}G, 11^{2}GF, 12^{5}GF,

	Starts	1st	2nd	3rd	Win & Pl
Career Total (Turf)	13	2	2	1	7371
Career Total (AW)	2	0	0	0	0

71 6/09 Wind 1m3f135y (0-75)H G-F £3070
66 4/09 Nott 1m2f50y (0-60)H G-F £2047
Total win prize-money £5118

Going (Turf): Sf: 0-0 GS: 0-0 Gd: 0-5 **GF: 2-8** Fm: 0-0
Distance: 5f/6f: 0-0 7f-8f: 0-1 **9f-13f: 2-14** 14f+: 0-0
Track : **LH: 1-6** RH: 0-4 **Tight: 1-5** Gall: 0-3
Aids: Bl: 0-0 Vi: 0-0 Tstrap: 0-0 Ckp: 0-0
Best Rating: **71** 6/09 Wind 1m3f135y gd-fm

Fair; stays 1m4f; acts on fast ground.

Urban Tiger (GER)

(73) (23)**87**
6-y-o b g Marju (IRE)-Ukraine Venture (Slip Anchor)
Tim Vaughan J H Frost

Placings:334240/603131/0/0 **(6724)**
2009: 12^{0}SD,

	Starts	1st	2nd	3rd	Win & Pl
Career Total (Turf)	13	2	1	4	30040
Career Total (AW)	1	0	0	0	

87 8/06 Wind 1m2f7y (0-85)H G-F £16192
83 6/06 Sand 1m2f7y (0-75)H G-F £4533
Total win prize-money £20727

Going (Turf): Sf: 0-0 GS: 0-1 Gd: 0-3 **GF: 2-9** Fm: 0-0
Distance: 5f/6f: 0-1 7f-8f: 0-5 **9f-13f: 2-8** 14f+: 0-0
Track : LH: 0-1 **RH: 2-8 Tight: 1-5** Gall: 0-0
Aids: Bl: 0-0 Vi: 0-0 Tstrap: 0-0 Ckp: 0-0
Best Rating: **87** 8/06 Wind 1m2f7y gd-fm

Urban Warrior

(103) (74)**75**
5-y-o b g Zilzal (USA)-Perfect Poppy (Shareef Dancer (USA))
Ian Williams B W Bedford

Placings:222154404060306/5431636650/235622560-06 **(0836)**
2009: 9^{0}SD, 12^{6}SD,

	Starts	1st	2nd	3rd	Win & Pl
Career Total (Turf)	24	2	2	2	11807
Career Total (AW)	12	0	4	2	4386

75 4/07 Hayd 1m2f120y (0-75)H GD £3238
71 4/06 Folk 5f G-S £2730
Total win prize-money £5969

Going (Turf): Sf: 0-1 **GS: 1-6 Gd: 1-11** GF: 0-6 Fm: 0-0
Distance: 5f/6f: 1-8 7f-8f: 0-8 9f-13f: 1-16 14f+: 0-4
Track : **LH: 1-17** RH: 0-11 Tight: 0-16 Gall: 0-0
Aids: Bl: 0-0 Vi: 0-3 Tstrap: 0-0 Ckp: 0-0
Best Rating: **75** 5/07 Wind 1m3f135y gd-sft

Modest; stays 1m6f; acts on Fibresand and Polytrack; also goes on easy turf.

Ursis (FR)

103(93) (62)**80**
8-y-o b g Trempolino (USA)-Bold Virgin (USA) (Sadler's Wells (USA))
S Gollings P J Martin

Placings:23122/211535/0/6/45002-220 **(3510)**
2009: 14^{2}S, 14^{2}GS, 16^{0}SD,

	Starts	1st	2nd	3rd	Win & Pl
Career Total (Turf)	19	3	7	2	44704
Career Total (AW)	2	0	0	0	

5/04 Nant 1m4f G-S £10563
4/04 Nant 1m4f SFT £7394
9/03 Chol 1m1f110y VS £3571
Total win prize-money £21528

Going (Turf): **Sf: 1-3 GS: 1-5** Gd: 0-10 GF: 0-0 Fm: 0-0
Distance: 5f/6f: 0-0 7f-8f: 0-2 **9f-13f: 3-14** 14f+: 0-5
Track : LH: 0-5 RH: 0-5 Tight: 0-2 Gall: 0-2
Aids: Bl: 0-1 Vi: 0-0 Tstrap: 0-0 Ckp: 0-0
Best Rating: **96** 9/04 Chan 1m4f good

Fair ex-French gelding; stays 1m6f; acts on soft and easy ground; winning hurdler.

Ursula (IRE)

105(102) (86)**85**
3-y-o b f Namid-Fritta Mista (IRE) (Linamix (FR))
R M Beckett (K R Burke 25/7) Tweenhills Racing XIV

Placings:41-3514350 **(7478)**
2009: 7^{3}S, 7^{5}G, 6^{1}G, 6^{4}GS, 7^{3}SD, 7^{5}SD, 6^{0}SD,

	Starts	1st	2nd	3rd	Win & Pl
Career Total (Turf)	6	2	0	1	10362
Career Total (AW)	3	0	0	1	755

85 7/09 Donc 6f (0-80)H GD £4857
75 9/08 Hayd 5f HVY £3885
Total win prize-money £8743

Going (Turf): **Sf: 1-3** GS: 0-1 **Gd: 1-2** GF: 0-0 Fm: 0-0
Distance: **5f/6f: 2-5** 7f-8f: 0-4 9f-13f: 0-0 14f+: 0-0
Track : LH: 0-3 RH: 0-2 Tight: 0-2 Gall: 0-0
Aids: Bl: 0-0 Vi: 0-0 Tstrap: 0-0 Ckp: 0-0
Best Rating: **86** 10/09 Wolv 7f32y stand

Useful; effective over 5f-7f; acts on soft/heavy ground.

Ursus

103(94) (52)**63**
4-y-o ch g Rambling Bear-Adar Jane (Ardar)
C R Wilson David Bartlett

Placings:0/00011404040-3640602000 **(7709)**
2009: 5^{3}GS, 5^{6}GF, 5^{4}S, 6^{0}GF, 5^{6}GF, 6^{0}GS, 5^{2}GF, 5^{0}S, 5^{0}SD, 5^{0}SD,

	Starts	1st	2nd	3rd	Win & Pl
Career Total (Turf)	20	2	1	1	8172
Career Total (AW)	2	0	0	0	

63 6/08 Newc 6f (0-75)H SFT £4209
54 6/08 Rdcr 5f (0-60)H G-F £2047
Total win prize-money £6256

Going (Turf): **Sf: 1-6** GS: 0-5 Gd: 0-3 **GF: 1-6** Fm: 0-0
Distance: **5f/6f: 2-20** 7f-8f: 0-1 9f-13f: 0-1 14f+: 0-0
Track : LH: 0-2 RH: 0-1 Tight: 0-2 Gall: 0-0
Aids: Bl: 0-1 Vi: 0-0 Tstrap: 0-5 Ckp: 0-5
Best Rating: **63** 6/08 Newc 6f soft

Moderate; effective over 5f-6f; handles most ground; has worn cheekpieces.

Usetheforce (IRE)

69(94) (53)**35**
4-y-o ch g Black Minnaloushe (USA)-Polynesian Goddess (IRE) (Salmon Leap (USA))
M Quinn M Quinn

Placings:0/00000-060 **(2420)**
2009: 7^{0}SD, 12^{6}SD, 10^{0}G,

	Starts	1st	2nd	3rd	Win & Pl
Career Total (Turf)	2	0	0	0	
Career Total (AW)	7	0	0	0	0

Going (Turf): **Sf: 0-0 GS: 0-0 Gd: 0-2 GF: 0-0 Fm: 0-0**
Distance: 5f/6f: 0-2 7f-8f: 0-5 9f-13f: 0-2 14f+: 0-0
Track : LH: 0-7 RH: 0-1 Tight: 0-6 Gall: 0-1
Aids: Bl: 0-0 Vi: 0-1 Tstrap: 0-0 Ckp: 0-0
Best Rating: **53** 1/08 Kemp 7f stand

Usquaebach

57(90) (53)

2-y-o b f Trade Fair-Mashmoum (Lycius (USA))

S Curran (H J Collingridge 29/5) Dave Clayton

Placings:00360300 **(6970)**

2009: 5^{0}GF, 5^{0}GF, 5^{3}SD, 6^{6}GF, 6^{0}GS, 5^{3}SD, 6^{0}SD, 5^{0}SD,

	Starts	1st	2nd	3rd	Win & Pl
Career Total (Turf)	4	0	0	0	0
Career Total (AW)	4	0	0	2	806

Going (Turf): **Sf: 0-0 GS: 0-1 Gd: 0-0 GF: 0-3 Fm: 0-0**
Distance: 5f/6f: 0-7 7f-8f: 0-1 9f-13f: 0-0 14f+: 0-0
Track : LH: 0-1 RH: 0-1 Tight: 0-0 Gall: 0-0
Aids: Bl: 0-3 Vi: 0-3 Tstrap: 0-0 Ckp: 0-0
Best Rating: **53** 8/09 Sthl 5f stand

Moderate; suited by 5f and Fibresand.

Usual Suspects

(83) (38)**46**

3-y-o b f Royal Applause-Soft Breeze (Zafonic (USA))

Peter Grayson Boys In Blue

Placings:00460-0 **(0273)**

2009: 5^{0}SD,

	Starts	1st	2nd	3rd	Win & Pl
Career Total (Turf)	3	0	0	0	283
Career Total (AW)	3	0	0	0	

Going (Turf): **Sf: 0-0 GS: 0-0 Gd: 0-1 GF: 0-2 Fm: 0-0**
Distance: 5f/6f: 0-5 7f-8f: 0-1 9f-13f: 0-0 14f+: 0-0
Track : LH: 0-3 RH: 0-1 Tight: 0-3 Gall: 0-0
Aids: Bl: 0-0 Vi: 0-0 Tstrap: 0-0 Ckp: 0-0
Best Rating: **46** 7/08 Yarm 5f43y gd-fm

Utmost Respect

115 **121**

5-y-o b g Danetime (IRE)-Utmost (IRE) (Most Welcome)

R A Fahey The Rumpole Partnership

Placings:11/0310/10414361-11 **(2287a)**

2009: 6^{1}GF, 6^{1}HY,

	Starts	1st	2nd	3rd	Win & Pl
Career Total (Turf)	16	8	0	2	241345

121	5/09	Curr	6f		HVY	£45752
118	5/09	York	6f		G-F	£60545
110	11/08	MsnL	6f		HVY	£29412
116	6/08	Newc	6f		SFT	£28385
114	4/08	Thsk	6f		GD	£7477
113	9/07	Ayr	6f	H	SFT	£21812
97	9/06	Ayr	6f	(0-85)	G-S	£6477
79	9/06	Hayd	5f		HVY	£3886

Total win prize-money £203746

Going (Turf): **Sf: 5-7** GS: 1-2 Gd: 1-4 GF: 1-3 Fm: 0-0
Distance: **5f/6f: 8-13** 7f-8f: 0-3 9f-13f: 0-0 14f+: 0-0
Track : LH: 0-0 RH: 0-2 Tight: 0-0 Gall: 0-0
Aids: Bl: 0-0 Vi: 0-0 Tstrap: 0-0 Ckp: 0-0
Best Rating: **121** 5/09 Curr 6f heavy

Group class; winner in Group 3 and Group 2 company; placed at Group 1 level, best at 6f; acted on fast ground, but even better on soft. (DEAD)

Uvinza

108(106) (83)**101**

3-y-o ch f Bertolini (USA)-Baddi Heights (FR) (Shirley Heights)

W J Knight Mrs Alison Ruggles

Placings:251-4333050 **(7131)**

2009: 8^{4}GF, 10^{3}G, 12^{3}GF, 12^{3}G, 12^{0}GF, 12^{5}G, 13^{0}SD,

	Starts	1st	2nd	3rd	Win & Pl
Career Total (Turf)	8	0	1	3	28625
Career Total (AW)	2	1	0	0	2267

69 10/08 Ling 1m STD £2266

Total win prize-money £2267

Going (Turf): **Sf: 0-1 GS: 0-0 Gd: 0-4 GF: 0-3 Fm: 0-0**
Distance: 5f/6f: 0-0 **7f-8f: 1-4** 9f-13f: 0-6 14f+: 0-0
Track : **LH: 1-4** RH: 0-4 **Tight: 1-2** Gall: 0-6
Aids: Bl: 0-0 Vi: 0-0 Tstrap: 0-0 Ckp: 0-0
Best Rating: **101** 6/09 Asct 1m4f gd-fm

Smart; Group 2 placed; stays 1m4f; acts on most ground.

Vadition (IRE)

85(69) (13)**43**

2-y-o b f Halling (USA)-Retail Therapy (IRE) (Bahhare (USA))

J J Bridger Bravado Racing

Placings:0000000 **(7390)**

2009: 5^{0}F, 5^{0}SD, 7^{0}GF, 8^{0}G, 9^{0}G, 8^{0}GS, 8^{0}SD,

	Starts	1st	2nd	3rd	Win & Pl
Career Total (Turf)	5	0	0	0	
Career Total (AW)	2	0	0	0	

Going (Turf): **Sf: 0-0 GS: 0-1 Gd: 0-2 GF: 0-1 Fm: 0-1**
Distance: 5f/6f: 0-2 7f-8f: 0-3 9f-13f: 0-2 14f+: 0-0
Track : LH: 0-1 RH: 0-3 Tight: 0-3 Gall: 0-0
Aids: Bl: 0-0 Vi: 0-0 Tstrap: 0-0 Ckp: 0-0
Best Rating: **43** 6/09 Newb 7f gd-fm

Vaduz

84(69) (20)**53**

2-y-o b f Imperial Dancer-Summer Shades (Green Desert (USA))

M R Channon Capital

Placings:03400 **(3719)**

2009: 5^{0}GF, 5^{3}GF, 5^{4}F, 6^{0}GF, 5^{0}SD,

	Starts	1st	2nd	3rd	Win & Pl
Career Total (Turf)	4	0	0	1	620
Career Total (AW)	1	0	0	0	

Going (Turf): **Sf: 0-0 GS: 0-0 Gd: 0-0 GF: 0-3 Fm: 0-1**
Distance: 5f/6f: 0-4 7f-8f: 0-1 9f-13f: 0-0 14f+: 0-0
Track : LH: 0-3 RH: 0-0 Tight: 0-1 Gall: 0-1
Aids: Bl: 0-0 Vi: 0-0 Tstrap: 0-0 Ckp: 0-0
Best Rating: **53** 4/09 Bath 5f11y gd-fm

Vain Boteli (GER)

67(63) **3**

3-y-o b g Bertolini (USA)-Vanity Fair (Nashwan (USA))

R Ford (P Schiergen 27/6) D W Watson

Placings:122100 **(7272)**

2009: 8^{1}G, 8^{2}S, 8^{2}G, 8^{1}G, 8^{0}GF, 12^{0}SD,

	Starts	1st	2nd	3rd	Win & Pl
Career Total (Turf)	5	2	2	0	9951
Career Total (AW)	1	0	0	0	

6/09	Hamb	1m	GD	£4854
4/09	Brem	1m	GD	£2912

Total win prize-money £7767

Going (Turf): Sf: 0-1 GS: 0-0 **Gd: 2-3** GF: 0-1 Fm: 0-0
Distance: 5f/6f: 0-0 **7f-8f: 2-3** 9f-13f: 0-3 14f+: 0-0
Track : LH: 0-1 RH: 0-1 Tight: 0-0 Gall: 0-0
Aids: Bl: 0-0 Vi: 0-0 Tstrap: 0-0 Ckp: 0-0
Best Rating: **3** 9/09 Leic 1m60y gd-fm

Vainglory (USA)

107(107) (94)**96**

5-y-o ch h Swain (IRE)-Infinite Spirit (USA) (Maria's Mon (USA))

D M Simcock DXB Bloodstock Ltd

Placings:313034103/40323605004-4631235645 **(6876)**

2009: 8^{4}SD, 10^{6}GF, 8^{3}G, 8^{1}GF, 8^{2}GF, 10^{3}G, 10^{5}G, 8^{6}SD, 8^{4}GF, 8^{5}SD,

	Starts	1st	2nd	3rd	Win & Pl
Career Total (Turf)	17	2	1	6	22303
Career Total (AW)	13	1	1	2	15484

91	6/09	Leic	1m60y (0-85)H	G-F	£6308
93	11/07	Wolv	1m1f103y (0-95)H	STD	£7124
84	6/07	Yarm	6f3y	SFT	£2849

Total win prize-money £16283

Going (Turf): **Sf: 1-5** GS: 0-1 Gd: 0-4 **GF: 1-7** Fm: 0-0
Distance: 5f/6f: 0-1 7f-8f: 1-16 **9f-13f: 2-13** 14f+: 0-0
Track : LH: 1-16 RH: 1-10 **Tight: 1-8** Gall: 0-7
Aids: Bl: 0-0 Vi: 0-0 Tstrap: 0-0 Ckp: 0-0
Best Rating: **96** 6/08 Epsm 1m114y good

Useful; effective at 1m-1m2f; acts on most ground; goes on Polytrack.

Val C

97(85) (55)**67**

2-y-o b f Dubawi (IRE)-Valjarv (IRE) (Bluebird (USA))

N P Littmoden Franconson Partners

Placings:03345305 **(5950)**

2009: 5^{0}GF, 5^{3}GS, 5^{3}GF, 5^{4}GF, 5^{5}SD, 5^{3}GF, 6^{0}G, 5^{5}GF,

	Starts	1st	2nd	3rd	Win & Pl
Career Total (Turf)	7	0	0	3	2167
Career Total (AW)	1	0	0	0	0

Going (Turf): **Sf: 0-0 GS: 0-1 Gd: 0-1 GF: 0-5 Fm: 0-0**
Distance: 5f/6f: 0-8 7f-8f: 0-0 9f-13f: 0-0 14f+: 0-0
Track : LH: 0-2 RH: 0-0 Tight: 0-1 Gall: 0-0
Aids: Bl: 0-0 Vi: 0-0 Tstrap: 0-0 Ckp: 0-0
Best Rating: **67** 6/09 Wwck 5f gd-sft

Modest; effective over 5f; acts on fast and easy ground.

Val's Princess

57(58)

2-y-o b f Trade Fair-Eleonora D'Arborea (Prince Sabo)

J R Jenkins Rowley

Placings:00 **(2414)**

2009: 5^{0}SD, 6^{0}G,

	Starts	1st	2nd	3rd	Win & Pl
Career Total (Turf)	1	0	0	0	
Career Total (AW)	1	0	0	0	

Going (Turf): **Sf: 0-0 GS: 0-0 Gd: 0-1 GF: 0-0 Fm: 0-0**
Distance: 5f/6f: 0-1 7f-8f: 0-1 9f-13f: 0-0 14f+: 0-0
Track : LH: 0-0 RH: 0-0 Tight: 0-0 Gall: 0-0
Aids: Bl: 0-0 Vi: 0-0 Tstrap: 0-0 Ckp: 0-0

Valantino Oyster (IRE)

78 41

2-y-o b/br g Pearl Of Love (IRE)-Mishor (Slip Anchor)
J Howard Johnson J Howard Johnson

Placings:500 (2940)
2009: 5^{5}GS, 6^{0}GS, 6^{0}GF,

	Starts	1st	2nd	3rd	Win & Pl
Career Total (Turf)	3	0	0	0	0

Going (Turf): Sf: 0-0 GS: 0-2 Gd: 0-0 GF: 0-1 Fm: 0-0
Distance: 5f/6f: 0-3 7f-8f: 0-0 9f-13f: 0-0 14f+: 0-0
Track : LH: 0-0 RH: 0-0 Tight: 0-0 Gall: 0-0
Aids: Bl: 0-0 Vi: 0-0 Tstrap: 0-0 Ckp: 0-0
Best Rating: 41 5/09 Haml 5f4y gd-sft

Valatrix (IRE)

101(102) (85)83

4-y-o b f Acclamation-Dramatic Entry (IRE) (Persian Bold)
C F Wall Mrs Valerie Gordon

Placings:0/13220-2554000 (6630)
2009: 5^{2}SD, 6^{5}SD, 6^{5}GF, 7^{4}GF, 6^{0}G, 7^{0}G, 7^{0}SS,

	Starts	1st	2nd	3rd	Win & Pl
Career Total (Turf)	8	1	1	0	4699
Career Total (AW)	5	0	2	1	3083
76 5/08 Yarm 6f3y			G-F	£2266	

Total win prize-money £2267

Going (Turf): Sf: 0-1 GS: 0-1 Gd: 0-3 GF: 1-3 Fm: 0-0
Distance: 5f/6f: 0-8 7f-8f: 1-5 9f-13f: 0-0 14f+: 0-0
Track : LH: 0-6 RH: 0-1 Tight: 0-4 Gall: 0-1
Aids: Bl: 0-0 Vi: 0-0 Tstrap: 0-0 Ckp: 0-0
Best Rating: 85 4/09 Wolv 5f216y stand

Fair; effective at 6f; acts on fast ground; also goes on Polytrack.

Valdan (IRE)

105(106) (71)81

5-y-o b g Val Royal (FR)-Danedrop (IRE) (Danehill (USA))
M A Barnes (P D Evans 6/8) D Maloney

Placings:4102/00006000/0050326463561050024216-16452006 (6855)
2009: 12^{1}GF, 11^{6}GF, 12^{4}GF, 12^{5}GF, 12^{2}GF, 21^{0}G, 11^{0}F, 12^{6}SD,

	Starts	1st	2nd	3rd	Win & Pl
Career Total (Turf)	28	2	3	2	20746
Career Total (AW)	14	2	2	0	6861
80 5/09 Thsk 1m4f	(0-80)H		G-F	£5569	
71 12/08 Ling 1m4f	(0-75)H		STD	£2729	
63 9/08 GrLe 1m2f	(0-55)		STD	£2729	
76 7/06 York 6f			G-F	£6541	

Total win prize-money £17571

Going (Turf): Sf: 0-0 GS: 0-3 Gd: 0-9 GF: 2-15 Fm: 0-1
Distance: 5f/6f: 1-4 7f-8f: 0-11 9f-13f: 3-26 14f+: 0-1
Track : LH: 3-21 RH: 0-13 Tight: 2-14 Gall: 1-4
Aids: Bl: 0-0 Vi: 0-0 Tstrap: 0-0 Ckp: 0-0
Best Rating: 92 9/06 Sthl 6f gd-fm

Fair; effective at around 1m4f; acts on fast ground and on Polytrack.

Valdemar

92(96) (54)50

3-y-o ch g Tobougg (IRE)-Stealthy Times (Timeless Times (USA))
A D Brown John Wills

Placings:0004060-0260104553 (2964)
2009: 5^{0}SD, 5^{2}SD, 5^{6}SD, 5^{0}SD, 6^{1}SD, 5^{0}SD, 7^{4}GF, 7^{5}GF, 7^{5}SD, 5^{3}GF,

	Starts	1st	2nd	3rd	Win & Pl
Career Total (Turf)	5	0	0	1	302
Career Total (AW)	12	1	1	0	2652
50 2/09 Kemp 6f	(0-55)H		STD	£2047	

Total win prize-money £2047

Going (Turf): Sf: 0-1 GS: 0-0 Gd: 0-1 GF: 0-3 Fm: 0-0
Distance: 5f/6f: 1-13 7f-8f: 0-4 9f-13f: 0-0 14f+: 0-0
Track : LH: 0-9 RH: 1-4 Tight: 0-6 Gall: 0-0
Aids: Bl: 0-1 Vi: 0-3 Tstrap: 1-8 Ckp: 1-8
Best Rating: 54 9/08 Sthl 6f stand

Moderate; suited by 6f and acts on Polytrack; has worn cheekpieces.

Vale Of York (IRE)

107 (116)116

2-y-o b c Invincible Spirit (IRE)-Red Vale (IRE) (Halling (USA))
Saeed Bin Suroor Godolphin

Placings:151321 (7307a)
2009: 7^{1}G, 7^{5}GF, 7^{1}GF, 8^{3}G, 8^{2}S, 8^{1}FT,

	Starts	1st	2nd	3rd	Win & Pl
Career Total (Turf)	5	2	1	1	131523
Career Total (AW)	1	1	0	0	750000
116 11/09 SnAt 1m110y			FST	£750000	
101 9/09 Gdwd 7f			G-F	£17031	
91 7/09 York 7f			GD	£5180	

Total win prize-money £772212

Going (Turf): Sf: 0-1 GS: 0-0 Gd: 1-2 GF: 1-2 Fm: 0-0
Distance: 5f/6f: 0-0 7f-8f: 2-5 9f-13f: 1-1 14f+: 0-0
Track : LH: 2-3 RH: 1-3 Tight: 0-0 Gall: 1-3
Aids: Bl: 0-0 Vi: 0-0 Tstrap: 0-0 Ckp: 0-0
Best Rating: 116 11/09 SnAt 1m110y fast

Group class; surprise winner of the 2009 Breeders' Cup Juvenile; stays 1m; handles fast and soft ground; goes on synthetics.

Valentine Bay

49(74) (18)42

3-y-o b f Reel Buddy (USA)-Bullion (Sabrehill (USA))
M Mullineaux R Rayner

Placings:060000-0000 (7270)
2009: 6^{0}GF, 5^{0}SD, 8^{0}SD, 6^{0}SD,

	Starts	1st	2nd	3rd	Win & Pl
Career Total (Turf)	5	0	0	0	0
Career Total (AW)	5	0	0	0	

Going (Turf): Sf: 0-3 GS: 0-0 Gd: 0-1 GF: 0-1 Fm: 0-0
Distance: 5f/6f: 0-7 7f-8f: 0-3 9f-13f: 0-0 14f+: 0-0
Track : LH: 0-6 RH: 0-0 Tight: 0-3 Gall: 0-0
Aids: Bl: 0-4 Vi: 0-0 Tstrap: 0-1 Ckp: 0-1
Best Rating: 42 10/08 Rdcr 6f good

Valentine Blue

(97) (50)50

4-y-o ch g Tobougg (IRE)-Blue Topaz (IRE) (Bluebird (USA))
A B Haynes WCR V - The Conkwell Connection

Placings:00P0/00430-245 (0918)
2009: 12^{2}SD, 12^{4}SD, 11^{5}SD,

	Starts	1st	2nd	3rd	Win & Pl
Career Total (Turf)	7	0	0	1	530
Career Total (AW)	5	0	1	0	806

Going (Turf): Sf: 0-3 GS: 0-2 Gd: 0-0 GF: 0-2 Fm: 0-0
Distance: 5f/6f: 0-1 7f-8f: 0-3 9f-13f: 0-8 14f+: 0-0
Track : LH: 0-7 RH: 0-4 Tight: 0-3 Gall: 0-1
Aids: Bl: 0-0 Vi: 0-0 Tstrap: 0-5 Ckp: 0-5
Best Rating: 56 9/07 Gdwd 7f gd-sft

Plating-class; stays 1m4f; acts on Polytrack.

Valentino Rossi (BRZ)

86 82

7-y-o b g New Colony (USA)-Great Sola (BRZ) (Duke Of Marmalade (USA))
A G Foster Joshua Snellings

Placings:02531/32/24210-000 (3390)
2009: 14^{0}GF, 20^{0}GF, 16^{0}S,

	Starts	1st	2nd	3rd	Win & Pl
Career Total (Turf)	8	2	0	0	5269
Career Total (AW)	7	0	4	2	2139
5/08 Cida 2m			FRM	£4031	
12/06 Cida 1m2f			GD	£1179	

Total win prize-money £5210

Going (Turf): Sf: 0-2 GS: 0-1 Gd: 1-2 GF: 0-2 Fm: 1-1
Distance: 5f/6f: 0-0 7f-8f: 0-4 9f-13f: 1-6 14f+: 1-5
Track : LH: 0-2 RH: 0-2 Tight: 0-1 Gall: 0-3
Aids: Bl: 0-1 Vi: 0-0 Tstrap: 0-0 Ckp: 0-0
Best Rating: 82 5/09 York 1m6f gd-fm

Very useful; former Listed winner in Brazil; stays 2m; acts on good and faster ground; handles dirt.

Valentino Swing (IRE)

79(102) (69)73

6-y-o ch g Titus Livius (FR)-Farmers Swing (IRE) (River Falls)
Miss T Spearing D J Oseman

Placings:011461/040205030451040/2/06230003600020-4405003012 (7890)
2009: 7^{4}SD, 5^{4}SD, 7^{0}SD, 7^{5}SD, 6^{0}G, 7^{0}SD, 6^{3}SD, 7^{0}SD, 6^{1}SD, 6^{2}SD,

	Starts	1st	2nd	3rd	Win & Pl
Career Total (Turf)	25	4	3	2	19128
Career Total (AW)	21	1	2	2	3701
64 12/09 Kemp 6f	(0-55)H		STD	£1706	
74 10/06 Wwck 7f26y	(0-70)H		SFT	£3238	
74 9/05 Nott 6f15y	(0-75)		GD	£3796	
66 7/05 Ling 6f			G-F	£4342	
51 6/05 Yarm 6f3y			FRM	£2569	

Total win prize-money £15652

Going (Turf): Sf: 1-3 GS: 0-5 Gd: 1-7 GF: 1-9 Fm: 1-1
Distance: 5f/6f: 2-11 7f-8f: 3-34 9f-13f: 0-1 14f+: 0-0
Track : LH: 1-18 RH: 1-7 Tight: 0-14 Gall: 0-4
Aids: Bl: 0-5 Vi: 0-1 Tstrap: 0-5 Ckp: 0-5
Best Rating: 74 11/06 Wolv 7f32y std-fst

Moderate; effective at around 6f-7f; acts on soft ground; goes on Polytrack.

Valery Borzov (IRE)

114(108) (94)111

5-y-o b g Iron Mask (USA)-Fay's Song (IRE) (Fayruz)
D Nicholls D Kilburn/I Hewitson/D Nicholls

Placings:1/100302/02112050120-00415 0600 (6091)
2009: 6^{0}G, 6^{0}GF, 6^{4}GF, 6^{1}S, 6^{5}SD, 6^{0}G, 6^{6}S, 6^{0}GF, 6^{0}G,

	Starts	1st	2nd	3rd	Win & Pl
Career Total (Turf)	24	5	3	1	58534
Career Total (AW)	3	1	1	0	5558

111	5/09	York	6f	(0-105)H	SFT	£11527
107	8/08	Hayd	6f	(0-95)H	HVY	£12952
98	5/08	Thsk	6f	(0-90)H	GD	£7771
94	4/08	Kemp	6f	(0-80)H	STD	£4209
88	4/07	Muss	5f	(0-75)H	G-F	£3238
72	10/06	Catt	5f212y		SFT	£3412

Total win prize-money £43111

Going (Turf): **Sf: 3-9** GS: 0-1 Gd: 1-6 GF: 1-8 Fm: 0-0
Distance: **5f/6f: 6-24** 7f-8f: 0-3 9f-13f: 0-0 14f+: 0-0
Track : LH: 1-4 RH: 1-2 **Tight: 1-2** Gall: 0-2
Aids: Bl: 0-0 **Vi: 3-13** Tstrap: 0-0 Ckp: 0-0
Best Rating: **111** 5/09 York 6f soft

Smart; effective at 5f-6f; acts on any ground on turf; goes on Polytrack; has worn a visor; likes to race prominently.

Valfurva (IRE)

94(99) (64)55

3-y-o b f Celtic Swing-Kiriyaki (USA) (Secretariat (USA))
L M Cumani Scuderia Archi Romani

Placings:50605 (6437)
2009: 8^{5}SD, 9^{0}GS, 7^{6}SD, 8^{0}SD, 7^{5}SD,

	Starts	1st	2nd	3rd	Win & Pl
Career Total (Turf)	1	0	0	0	
Career Total (AW)	4	0	0	0	0

Going (Turf): **Sf: 0-0 GS: 0-1 Gd: 0-0 GF: 0-0 Fm: 0-0**
Distance: 5f/6f: 0-0 7f-8f: 0-4 9f-13f: 0-1 14f+: 0-0
Track : LH: 0-2 RH: 0-3 Tight: 0-2 Gall: 0-0
Aids: Bl: 0-0 Vi: 0-0 Tstrap: 0-0 Ckp: 0-0
Best Rating: **64** 10/09 Wolv 7f32y stand

Valiant Knight (FR)

95 79

2-y-o ch c Night Shift (USA)-Pilgrim Of Grace (FR) (Bering)
R Hannon Mrs Sue Brendish

Placings:03200 (6199)
2009: 7^{0}G, 8^{3}GF, 7^{2}GF, 7^{0}G, 7^{0}G,

	Starts	1st	2nd	3rd	Win & Pl
Career Total (Turf)	5	0	1	1	2023

Going (Turf): **Sf: 0-0 GS: 0-0 Gd: 0-3 GF: 0-2 Fm: 0-0**
Distance: 5f/6f: 0-0 7f-8f: 0-4 9f-13f: 0-1 14f+: 0-0
Track : LH: 0-1 RH: 0-3 Tight: 0-1 Gall: 0-0
Aids: Bl: 0-0 Vi: 0-0 Tstrap: 0-0 Ckp: 0-0
Best Rating: **79** 8/09 Sand 7f16y gd-fm

Fair; stays 7f; acts on fast ground.

Valiant Romeo

96 (15)56

9-y-o b g Primo Dominie-Desert Lynx (IRE) (Green Desert (USA))
R Bastiman Mrs P Bastiman

Placings:3144506324110/0000000/522405203330/01452 21600/000000/666502655/660300-05400 (3445)
2009: 7^{0}F, 5^{5}F, 5^{4}GF, 5^{0}GF, 5^{0}GF,

	Starts	1st	2nd	3rd	Win & Pl
Career Total (Turf)	63	5	7	6	33473
Career Total (AW)	5	0	0	0	

63	8/05	Folk	5f	(0-55)H	G-F	£3075
61	5/05	Muss	5f	(0-45)	G-F	£1589
89	10/02	NmkR	5f	C(0-95)	G-F	£7637
83	9/02	Chep	5f16y	E(0-75)	G-F	£3409
78	4/02	Brig	5f59y	D	FRM	£2835

Total win prize-money £18547

Going (Turf): Sf: 0-4 GS: 0-10Gd: 0-12 **GF: 4-32** Fm: 1-5
Distance: **5f/6f: 5-64** 7f-8f: 0-4 9f-13f: 0-0 14f+: 0-0
Track : **LH: 1-9** RH: 0-1 Tight: 0-5 Gall: 0-0
Aids: Bl: 0-1 **Vi: 3-28** Tstrap: 1-10 Ckp: 1-10
Best Rating: **89** 10/02 NmkR 5f gd-fm

Moderate sprint handicapper; acts well on a sound surface; has worn blinkers/visor.

Valid Point (IRE)

100(103) (75)87

3-y-o b g Val Royal (FR)-Ricadonna (Kris)
Sir Mark Prescott W E Sturt - Osborne House

Placings:0000-664111115 (6360)
2009: 6^{6}SD, 7^{6}SD, 7^{4}F, 10^{1}S, 9^{1}F, 9^{1}SD, 11^{1}G, 10^{1}GF, 12^{5}SD,

	Starts	1st	2nd	3rd	Win & Pl
Career Total (Turf)	7	4	0	0	11809
Career Total (AW)	6	1	0	0	2047

87	9/09	Pont	1m2f6y	(0-75)H	G-F	£3238
80	9/09	Haml	1m3f16y	(0-70)H	GD	£3238
75	9/09	Wolv	1m1f103y	(0-55)H	STD	£2047
59	8/09	Bevl	1m1f207y	(0-60)H	FRM	£2752
67	8/09	Ayr	1m2f	(0-65)H	SFT	£2388

Total win prize-money £13663

Going (Turf): **Sf: 1-1** GS: 0-1 **Gd: 1-2 GF: 1-1 Fm: 1-2**
Distance: 5f/6f: 0-4 7f-8f: 0-3 **9f-13f: 5-6** 14f+: 0-0
Track : **LH: 3-8** RH: 2-4 **Tight: 2-4** Gall: 0-1
Aids: Bl: 0-0 Vi: 0-0 Tstrap: 0-0 Ckp: 0-0
Best Rating: **87** 9/09 Pont 1m2f6y gd-fm

Useful; effective over 1m2f; acts on most ground on turf; goes on Polytrack.

Valid Reason

(96) (77)

2-y-o b c Observatory (USA)-Real Trust (USA) (Danzig (USA))
Mrs A J Perrett K Abdulla

Placings:31 (7764)
2009: 8^{3}SD, 8^{1}SD,

	Starts	1st	2nd	3rd	Win & Pl
Career Total (Turf)	0	0	0	0	
Career Total (AW)	2	1	0	1	4415

77	12/09	Kemp	1m	STD	£3885

Total win prize-money £3886

Going (Turf): **Sf: 0-0 GS: 0-0 Gd: 0-0 GF: 0-0 Fm: 0-0**
Distance: 5f/6f: 0-0 **7f-8f: 1-2** 9f-13f: 0-0 14f+: 0-0
Track : LH: 0-1 **RH: 1-1** Tight: 0-1 Gall: 0-0
Aids: Bl: 0-0 Vi: 0-0 Tstrap: 0-0 Ckp: 0-0
Best Rating: **77** 12/09 Kemp 1m stand

Fair; stays 1m; acts on Polytrack; should improve.

Valkov

89(92) (64)60

2-y-o b f Val Royal (FR)-Petrikov (IRE) (In The Wings)
Tom Dascombe Mayden Stud

Placings:06403 (7513)
2009: 5^{0}SF, 6^{6}GF, 7^{4}G, 7^{0}GF, 7^{3}SD,

	Starts	1st	2nd	3rd	Win & Pl
Career Total (Turf)	3	0	0	0	265
Career Total (AW)	2	0	0	1	252

Going (Turf): **Sf: 0-0 GS: 0-0 Gd: 0-1 GF: 0-2 Fm: 0-0**
Distance: 5f/6f: 0-1 7f-8f: 0-4 9f-13f: 0-0 14f+: 0-0
Track : LH: 0-2 RH: 0-1 Tight: 0-1 Gall: 0-0
Aids: Bl: 0-0 Vi: 0-0 Tstrap: 0-0 Ckp: 0-0
Best Rating: **64** 11/09 Kemp 7f stand

Moderate; stays 7f; acts on good ground and Polytrack.

Valkyrie (IRE)

95(97) (57)53

3-y-o b f Danehill Dancer (IRE)-Ridotto (Salse (USA))
N P Littmoden D & C Bloodstock 2

Placings:06-60563043334 (7324)
2009: 7^{6}SD, 10^{0}SD, 8^{6}SD, 11^{6}SD, 10^{3}GF, 12^{0}SD, 10^{4}G, 11^{3}SD, 12^{0}SS, 16^{3}SD, 12^{4}SD,

	Starts	1st	2nd	3rd	Win & Pl
Career Total (Turf)	3	0	0	1	472
Career Total (AW)	10	0	0	3	863

Going (Turf): **Sf: 0-0 GS: 0-0 Gd: 0-1 GF: 0-2 Fm: 0-0**
Distance: 5f/6f: 0-1 7f-8f: 0-3 9f-13f: 0-8 14f+: 0-1
Track : LH: 0-9 RH: 0-3 Tight: 0-6 Gall: 0-0
Aids: Bl: 0-1 Vi: 0-0 Tstrap: 0-3 Ckp: 0-3
Best Rating: **57** 9/08 Wolv 7f32y std-fst

Moderate; stays 2m; acts on fast ground and on Fibresand and Polytrack.

Valmari (IRE)

105(107) (80)91

6-y-o b m Kalanisi (IRE)-Penza (Soviet Star (USA))
C E Brittain Emmanouil Zografakis

Placings:6213/60141231/4443562/0336020-0041045 (6113)
2009: 12^{0}G, 16^{0}SD, 11^{4}GF, 12^{1}G, 16^{0}GF, 14^{4}GF, 12^{5}GF,

	Starts	1st	2nd	3rd	Win & Pl
Career Total (Turf)	6	1	0	0	6351
Career Total (AW)	27	4	4	5	74058

90	6/09	Donc	1m4f	(0-85)H	GD	£4857
	12/06	Mkpl	1m1f		STD	£18124
	10/06	Mkpl	1m1f		STD	£18124
	6/06	Mkpl	6f		STD	£7048
	11/05	Mkpl	6f		STD	£6730

Total win prize-money £54884

Going (Turf): Sf: 0-0 GS: 0-0 **Gd: 1-2** GF: 0-4 Fm: 0-0
Distance: 5f/6f: 2-6 7f-8f: 0-3 **9f-13f: 3-19** 14f+: 0-5
Track : **LH: 1-6** RH: 0-1 Tight: 0-3 **Gall: 1-4**
Aids: **Bl: 1-5** Vi: 0-0 Tstrap: 0-0 Ckp: 0-0
Best Rating: **91** 9/09 Yarm 1m6f17y gd-fm

Useful; ex Greek trained; stays 1m4f; acts on good ground and sand.

Valmina

78(101) (74)42

2-y-o b c Val Royal (FR)-Minnina (IRE) (In The Wings)

Tom Dascombe Mayden Stud

Placings:002122 **(7707)**
2009: 7⁰GF, 6⁰GS, 5²SD, 5¹SD, 6²SD, 6²SD,

	Starts	1st	2nd	3rd	Win & Pl
Career Total (Turf)	2	0	0	0	
Career Total (AW)	4	1	3	0	6067

73 11/09 Wolv 5f20y (0-75) STD £3238
Total win prize-money £3238

Going (Turf): Sf: 0-0 GS: 0-1 Gd: 0-0 GF: 0-1 Fm: 0-0
Distance: 5f/6f: 1-5 7f-8f: 0-1 9f-13f: 0-0 14f+: 0-0
Track : LH: 1-4 RH: 0-0 Tight: 1-3 Gall: 0-1
Aids: Bl: 0-0 Vi: 0-0 Tstrap: 0-0 Ckp: 0-0
Best Rating: 74 12/09 Ling 6f stand

Fair sprinter; handles Polytrack and Fibresand; has worn a tongue tie.

Valvigneres (IRE)

60(104) (76)71
4-y-o gr g Dalakhani (IRE)-Albacora (IRE) (Fairy King (USA))
E A L Dunlop Miltil Consortium

Placings:03/04-333 **(4670)**
2009: 12³SD, 13³SD, 14³G,

	Starts	1st	2nd	3rd	Win & Pl
Career Total (Turf)	3	0	0	1	635
Career Total (AW)	4	0	0	3	1478

Going (Turf): Sf: 0-1 GS: 0-1 Gd: 0-1 GF: 0-0 Fm: 0-0
Distance: 5f/6f: 0-0 7f-8f: 0-1 9f-13f: 0-5 14f+: 0-1
Track : LH: 0-4 RH: 0-3 Tight: 0-6 Gall: 0-0
Aids: Bl: 0-0 Vi: 0-0 Tstrap: 0-0 Ckp: 0-0
Best Rating: 76 5/09 Ling 1m5f stand

Fair; stays 1m5f; acts on Polytrack.

Vamos (IRE)

96(103) (65)61
3-y-o b g Royal Applause-Feather Boa (IRE) (Sri Pekan (USA))
J R Gask Horses First Racing Limited

Placings:6-3230542355142 **(7417)**
2009: 5³SD, 6²SD, 5³G, 6⁰F, 6⁵SD, 6⁴GF, 6²S, 7³SD, 7⁵SD, 7⁵SS, 8¹SD, 8⁴SD, 8²SD,

	Starts	1st	2nd	3rd	Win & Pl
Career Total (Turf)	4	0	1	1	1421
Career Total (AW)	10	1	2	2	4634

65 10/09 Wolv 1m141y (0-65)H STD £2388
Total win prize-money £2388

Going (Turf): Sf: 0-1 GS: 0-0 Gd: 0-1 GF: 0-1 Fm: 0-1
Distance: 5f/6f: 0-7 7f-8f: 0-4 9f-13f: 1-3 14f+: 0-0
Track : LH: 1-11 RH: 0-1 Tight: 1-8 Gall: 0-2
Aids: Bl: 0-2 Vi: 0-0 Tstrap: 0-0 Ckp: 0-0
Best Rating: 65 11/09 Wolv 1m141y stand

Modest; stays 1m; acts on soft ground; goes on Polytrack; has worn blinkers.

Van Bossed (CAN)

102(99) (88)101
4-y-o ch g Van Nistelrooy (USA)-Embossed (CAN) (Silver Deputy (CAN))
D Nicholls Mike & Maureen Browne

Placings:4301/02113002-000000000 **(5697)**
2009: 5⁰G, 6⁰GF, 6⁰G, 6⁰GF, 6⁰S, 5⁰GF, 6⁰G, 5⁰G, 7⁰GS,

	Starts	1st	2nd	3rd	Win & Pl
Career Total (Turf)	19	3	1	2	21854
Career Total (AW)	2	0	1	0	1349

100 4/08 Ripn 6f (0-95)H GD £9346
91 4/08 Ripn 6f (0-85)H G-S £4209
84 8/07 Catt 5f G-F £2730
Total win prize-money £16286

Going (Turf): Sf: 0-2 GS: 1-3 Gd: 1-8 GF: 1-6 Fm: 0-0
Distance: 5f/6f: 3-18 7f-8f: 0-3 9f-13f: 0-0 14f+: 0-0
Track : LH: 0-3 RH: 0-2 Tight: 0-2 Gall: 0-1
Aids: Bl: 0-0 Vi: 0-0 Tstrap: 0-0 Ckp: 0-0
Best Rating: 101 9/08 Asct 6f good

Useful; stays 6f; acts on most ground and on Polytrack; has worn a tongue tie.

Vanadium

97(101) (66)71
7-y-o b g Dansili-Musianica (Music Boy)
A J Lidderdale (G L Moore 7/10) Kachina Racing

Placings:13105520/0001450364/000001460/31000544020-2546620053204050 **(7592)**
2009: 7²SD, 8⁵G, 6⁴GF, 7⁶SD, 6⁶G, 7²G, 6⁰S, 7⁰GF, 7⁵SD, 8³SD, 7²SD, 5⁰G, 7⁴SD, 6⁰S, 8⁵SD, 7⁰SD,

	Starts	1st	2nd	3rd	Win & Pl
Career Total (Turf)	34	4	2	2	26850
Career Total (AW)	20	1	3	2	5288

71 5/08 Sals 6f212y (0-70)H GD £3238
70 10/07 Wolv 7f32y (0-60)H STD £2047
81 8/06 Newc 6f (0-80)H G-S £7478
83 5/05 Sand 7f16y (0-80)H GD £7046
71 5/05 Nott 6f15y GD £3601
Total win prize-money £23411

Going (Turf): Sf: 0-6 GS: 1-6 Gd: 3-11 GF: 0-11 Fm: 0-0
Distance: 5f/6f: 1-17 7f-8f: 4-33 9f-13f: 0-4 14f+: 0-0
Track : LH: 1-20 RH: 1-10 Tight: 1-14 Gall: 0-4
Aids: Bl: 0-0 Vi: 0-0 Tstrap: 0-6 Ckp: 0-6
Best Rating: 89 9/05 Hayd 6f gd-sft

Moderate; effective at 6f-1m; acts on most ground and on Polytrack; has worn cheekpieces/tongue tie.

Vanatina (IRE)

(98) (53)46
5-y-o b m Tagula (IRE)-Final Trick (Primo Dominie)
W M Brisbourne Black Diamond Racing

Placings:0003/60/6040000544450-5510000 **(1781)**
2009: 6⁵SS, 7⁵SD, 7¹SD, 6⁰SD, 7⁰SD, 7⁰SD, 6⁰SD,

	Starts	1st	2nd	3rd	Win & Pl
Career Total (Turf)	10	0	0	1	794
Career Total (AW)	16	1	0	0	1365

51 1/09 Sthl 7f (0-45) STD £1364
Total win prize-money £1365

Going (Turf): Sf: 0-2 GS: 0-3 Gd: 0-4 GF: 0-1 Fm: 0-0
Distance: 5f/6f: 0-10 7f-8f: 1-12 9f-13f: 0-4 14f+: 0-0
Track : LH: 1-21 RH: 0-1 Tight: 0-10 Gall: 0-0
Aids: Bl: 0-0 Vi: 0-0 Tstrap: 0-0 Ckp: 0-0
Best Rating: 53 11/08 Sthl 1m stand

Very moderate; stays 1m; acts on Polytrack and Fibresand.

Vanilla Bally (ISR)

90(71) (3)40
4-y-o ch f Supreme Commander (FR)-Rozalyn Bally (ISR) (Verardi)
George Baker James, Dean & Partners

Placings:11/12311-000 **(4938)**
2009: 8⁰SD, 10⁰G, 8⁰G,

	Starts	1st	2nd	3rd	Win & Pl
Career Total (Turf)	2	0	0	0	
Career Total (AW)	8	5	1	1	

Going (Turf): Sf: 0-0 GS: 0-0 Gd: 0-2 GF: 0-0 Fm: 0-0
Distance: 5f/6f: 0-0 7f-8f: 4-6 9f-13f: 0-3 14f+: 0-0
Track : LH: 0-2 RH: 0-0 Tight: 0-2 Gall: 0-0
Aids: Bl: 0-0 Vi: 0-0 Tstrap: 0-0 Ckp: 0-0
Best Rating: 40 7/09 Yarm 1m2f21y good

Vanilla Loan (IRE)

(88) (62)
2-y-o b f Invincible Spirit (IRE)-Alexander Anapolis (IRE) (Spectrum (IRE))
M Botti Noel O'Callaghan

Placings:003 **(6947)**
2009: 7⁰SD, 7⁰SD, 7³SD,

	Starts	1st	2nd	3rd	Win & Pl
Career Total (Turf)	0	0	0	0	
Career Total (AW)	3	0	0	1	578

Going (Turf): Sf: 0-0 GS: 0-0 Gd: 0-0 GF: 0-0 Fm: 0-0
Distance: 5f/6f: 0-0 7f-8f: 0-3 9f-13f: 0-0 14f+: 0-0
Track : LH: 0-2 RH: 0-1 Tight: 0-1 Gall: 0-0
Aids: Bl: 0-0 Vi: 0-0 Tstrap: 0-0 Ckp: 0-0
Best Rating: 62 10/09 Sthl 7f stand

Vanilla Rum

96 74
2-y-o b g Reset (AUS)-Snoozy (Cadeaux Genereux)
H Candy Six Too Many

Placings:64 **(7058)**
2009: 6⁶S, 5⁴GF,

	Starts	1st	2nd	3rd	Win & Pl
Career Total (Turf)	2	0	0	0	385

Going (Turf): Sf: 0-1 GS: 0-0 Gd: 0-0 GF: 0-1 Fm: 0-0
Distance: 5f/6f: 0-1 7f-8f: 0-1 9f-13f: 0-0 14f+: 0-0
Track : LH: 0-0 RH: 0-0 Tight: 0-0 Gall: 0-0
Aids: Bl: 0-0 Vi: 0-0 Tstrap: 0-0 Ckp: 0-0
Best Rating: 74 10/09 Leic 5f218y gd-fm

Vanishing Grey (IRE)

98 85
2-y-o gr f Verglas (IRE)-Native Force (IRE) (Indian Ridge)
B J Meehan Andrew Rosen

Placings:4631000 **(6660)**
2009: 5⁴GF, 6⁶G, 6³G, 5¹G, 5⁰G, 6⁰GF, 5⁰GS,

	Starts	1st	2nd	3rd	Win & Pl
Career Total (Turf)	7	1	0	1	4732

74 8/09 Bath 5f11y GD £3561
Total win prize-money £3562

Going (Turf): Sf: 0-0 GS: 0-1 Gd: 1-4 GF: 0-2 Fm: 0-0
Distance: 5f/6f: 1-6 7f-8f: 0-1 9f-13f: 0-0 14f+: 0-0
Track : LH: 1-1 RH: 0-0 Tight: 0-0 Gall: 1-1
Aids: Bl: 0-1 Vi: 0-0 Tstrap: 0-0 Ckp: 0-0

Best Rating: **85** 6/09 NmkJ 6f good

Useful; effective over 5f; acts on good ground.

Vanquisher (IRE)

(105) (56)**71**

5-y-o br g Xaar-Naziriya (FR) (Darshaan)

Ian Williams Dr Marwan Koukash

Placings:552/**22**450421/4454060044-**2220** **(0449)**

2009: 11^{2}SD, 16^{2}SD, 16^{2}SD, 13^{0}SD,

	Starts	1st	2nd	3rd	Win & Pl
Career Total (Turf)	14	1	2	0	8140
Career Total (AW)	11	0	5	0	3519

71 9/07 NmkR 1m4f G-F £4533

Total win prize-money £4534

Going (Turf): Sf: 0-3 GS: 0-1 Gd: 0-4 **GF: 1-6** Fm: 0-0
Distance: 5f/6f: 0-0 7f-8f: 0-3 **9f-13f: 1-14** 14f+: 0-8
Track : LH: 0-18 **RH: 1-5** Tight: 0-12 **Gall: 1-3**
Aids: Bl: 0-1 Vi: 0-2 Tstrap: 1-6 Ckp: 1-6
Best Rating: **79** 6/07 Gdwd 1m1f192y gd-fm

Moderate; stays 1m4f; acts on most ground; has worn cheekpieces, tongue tie and a visor.

Vaporetto (IRE)

(90) (55)**51**

7-y-o gr m Soviet Star (USA)-Tarikhana (Mouktar)

P J Rothwell P J Rothwell

Placings:000/0300/5304/04141050 **(7443a)**

2009: 12^{0}GY, 10^{4}GF, 9^{1}GF, 8^{4}G, 8^{1}SD, 9^{0}Y, 9^{5}SD, 8^{0}SD,

	Starts	1st	2nd	3rd	Win & Pl
Career Total (Turf)	16	1	0	2	7076
Career Total (AW)	3	1	0	0	5032

55 7/09 Dund 1m (47-65)H STD £5031
51 6/09 Baln 1m1f (47-65)H G-F £5366

Total win prize-money £10399

Going (Turf): Sf: 0-0 GS: 0-0 Gd: 0-3 **GF: 1-6** Fm: 0-0
Distance: 5f/6f: 0-0 7f-8f: 1-6 9f-13f: 1-12 14f+: 0-1
Track : LH: 1-8 RH: 1-9 Tight: 0-1 Gall: 0-0
Aids: Bl: 0-0 Vi: 0-0 Tstrap: 2-8 Ckp: 2-8
Best Rating: **55** 7/09 Dund 1m stand

Varachi

93 **66**

2-y-o b g Kyllachy-Miss Rimex (IRE) (Ezzoud (IRE))

E A L Dunlop V I Araci

Placings:065 **(6962)**

2009: 8^{0}GF, 8^{6}GS, 6^{5}G,

	Starts	1st	2nd	3rd	Win & Pl
Career Total (Turf)	3	0	0	0	141

Going (Turf): **Sf: 0-0 GS: 0-1 Gd: 0-1 GF: 0-1 Fm: 0-0**
Distance: 5f/6f: 0-0 7f-8f: 0-2 9f-13f: 0-1 14f+: 0-0
Track : LH: 0-2 RH: 0-0 Tight: 0-0 Gall: 0-0
Aids: Bl: 0-0 Vi: 0-0 Tstrap: 0-0 Ckp: 0-0
Best Rating: **66** 10/09 Brig 6f209y good

Varah

(35)

3-y-o b g Tobougg (IRE)-Relativity (IRE) (Distant Relative)

R A Harris P Nurcombe

Placings:0 **(6673)**

2009: 9^{0}SD,

	Starts	1st	2nd	3rd	Win & Pl
Career Total (Turf)	0	0	0	0	
Career Total (AW)	1	0	0	0	

Going (Turf): **Sf: 0-0 GS: 0-0 Gd: 0-0 GF: 0-0 Fm: 0-0**
Distance: 5f/6f: 0-0 7f-8f: 0-0 9f-13f: 0-1 14f+: 0-0
Track : LH: 0-1 RH: 0-0 Tight: 0-1 Gall: 0-0
Aids: Bl: 0-0 Vi: 0-0 Tstrap: 0-0 Ckp: 0-0

Vaultage (USA)

80(89) (68)**57**

2-y-o ch f El Corredor (USA)-Ten Carats (USA) (Capote (USA))

E A L Dunlop St Albans Bloodstock LLP

Placings:02 **(7430)**

2009: 7^{0}G, 7^{2}SD,

	Starts	1st	2nd	3rd	Win & Pl
Career Total (Turf)	1	0	0	0	
Career Total (AW)	1	0	1	0	1253

Going (Turf): **Sf: 0-0 GS: 0-0 Gd: 0-1 GF: 0-0 Fm: 0-0**
Distance: 5f/6f: 0-0 7f-8f: 0-2 9f-13f: 0-0 14f+: 0-0
Track : LH: 0-0 RH: 0-1 Tight: 0-0 Gall: 0-0
Aids: Bl: 0-0 Vi: 0-0 Tstrap: 0-0 Ckp: 0-0
Best Rating: **68** 11/09 Kemp 7f stand

Modest; stays 7f; acts on Polytrack.

Vegas Baby (IRE)

92(100) (81)**81**

3-y-o ch f Kheleyf (USA)-Gift Of Spring (USA) (Gilded Time (USA))

J A Osborne William Durkan

Placings:5521**444**-3554106 **(2759)**

2009: 6^{3}SD, 6^{5}SD, 7^{5}SD, 5^{4}F, 6^{1}G, 5^{0}GF, 6^{6}GF,

	Starts	1st	2nd	3rd	Win & Pl
Career Total (Turf)	9	2	1	0	11549
Career Total (AW)	5	0	0	1	1578

61 5/09 Wind 6f GD £2729
79 6/08 Navn 5f FRM £6351

Total win prize-money £9081

Going (Turf): Sf: 0-0 GS: 0-0 **Gd: 1-1** GF: 0-3 **Fm: 1-3**
Distance: **5f/6f: 2-13** 7f-8f: 0-1 9f-13f: 0-0 14f+: 0-0
Track : **LH: 1-8** RH: 0-1 Tight: 0-3 **Gall: 1-2**
Aids: **Bl: 1-4** Vi: 0-0 Tstrap: 0-0 Ckp: 0-0
Best Rating: **81** 2/09 Ling 6f stand

Vegas Palace (IRE)

89(102) (83)**73**

2-y-o ch f Captain Rio-Verify (IRE) (Polish Precedent (USA))

Tom Dascombe The Brian & Bcn Partnership

Placings:321 **(7351)**

2009: 6^{3}S, 7^{2}SD, 7^{1}SD,

	Starts	1st	2nd	3rd	Win & Pl
Career Total (Turf)	1	0	0	1	433
Career Total (AW)	2	1	1	0	4363

83 11/09 Sthl 7f STD £3207

Total win prize-money £3207

Going (Turf): **Sf: 0-1 GS: 0-0 Gd: 0-0 GF: 0-0 Fm: 0-0**
Distance: 5f/6f: 0-0 **7f-8f: 1-3** 9f-13f: 0-0 14f+: 0-0
Track : **LH: 1-2** RH: 0-0 Tight: 0-0 Gall: 0-0
Aids: Bl: 0-0 Vi: 0-0 Tstrap: 0-0 Ckp: 0-0
Best Rating: **83** 11/09 Sthl 7f stand

Useful; stays 7f and acts on Fibresand.

Veiled

102(104) (85)**89**

3-y-o b f Sadler's Wells (USA)-Evasive Quality (FR) (Highest Honor (FR))

J Pearce (Sir Mark Prescott 25/9) Pump & Plant Services Ltd

Placings:0000-313114 **(6258)**

2009: 14^{3}SD, 14^{1}GF, 16^{3}SD, 14^{1}GF, 16^{1}GF, 13^{4}SD,

	Starts	1st	2nd	3rd	Win & Pl
Career Total (Turf)	3	3	0	0	8710
Career Total (AW)	7	0	0	2	1822

89 9/09 Yarm 2m (0-70)H G-F £3238
83 9/09 Rdcr 1m6f19y (0-70)H G-F £2752
76 8/09 Yarm 1m6f17y (0-70)H G-F £2719

Total win prize-money £8710

Going (Turf): Sf: 0-0 GS: 0-0 Gd: 0-0 **GF: 3-3** Fm: 0-0
Distance: 5f/6f: 0-0 7f-8f: 0-4 9f-13f: 0-0 **14f+: 3-6**
Track : **LH: 3-9** RH: 0-1 **Tight: 3-5** Gall: 0-2
Aids: Bl: 0-0 Vi: 0-0 Tstrap: 0-0 Ckp: 0-0
Best Rating: **89** 9/09 Yarm 2m gd-fm

Useful; stays 2m; acts on Fibresand and quick ground; likely to improve.

Veiled Applause

105(99) (75)**92**

6-y-o b g Royal Applause-Scarlet Veil (Tyrnavos)

J J Quinn Far 2 Many Sues

Placings:000/521**444**/2221522100/26150502-0646365605134 **(7014)**

2009: 8^{0}SD, 13^{6}SD, 10^{4}G, 8^{6}GF, 10^{3}G, 9^{6}GF, 9^{5}GS, 8^{6}G, 8^{0}GF, 8^{5}G, 10^{1}G, 9^{3}G, 10^{4}GS,

	Starts	1st	2nd	3rd	Win & Pl
Career Total (Turf)	34	4	8	2	32613
Career Total (AW)	6	1	0	0	5339

85 10/09 York 1m2f88y (0-85)H GD £5180
89 5/08 Ripn 1m1f170y (0-85)H G-F £4857
85 9/07 Wolv 1m1f103y (0-85)H STD £4857
79 6/07 Wind 1m67y (0-75)H G-S £3238
73 8/06 Chep 1m14y (0-70)H GD £5505

Total win prize-money £23640

Going (Turf): Sf: 0-1 GS: 1-6 **Gd: 2-14** GF: 1-12 Fm: 0-1
Distance: 5f/6f: 0-3 7f-8f: 0-6 **9f-13f: 5-30** 14f+: 0-1
Track : LH: 2-20 RH: 2-14 **Tight: 3-13** Gall: 1-10
Aids: Bl: 0-0 Vi: 0-0 Tstrap: 0-0 Ckp: 0-0
Best Rating: **92** 8/08 Ripn 1m1f170y gd-sft

Fair; placed over hurdles; effective at around 1m-1m2f; acts on most surfaces.

Vella

86(80) (43)**50**

3-y-o b f Mtoto-Villella (Sadler's Wells (USA))

H J L Dunlop Mrs John Moore

Placings:0-6000 **(3303)**

2009: 10^{6}G, 9^{0}F, 12^{0}GF, 12^{0}SD,

	Starts	1st	2nd	3rd	Win & Pl
Career Total (Turf)	3	0	0	0	0
Career Total (AW)	2	0	0	0	

Going (Turf): **Sf: 0-0 GS: 0-0 Gd: 0-1 GF: 0-1 Fm: 0-1**

Distance: 5f/6f: 0-0 7f-8f: 0-1 9f-13f: 0-4 14f+: 0-0
Track : LH: 0-2 RH: 0-3 Tight: 0-2 Gall: 0-0
Aids: Bl: 0-1 Vi: 0-0 Tstrap: 0-0 Ckp: 0-0
Best Rating: 50 4/09 Bath 1m2f46y good

Velle Est Valere

55

2-y-o b f Reset (AUS)-Bond Solitaire (Atraf)
C J Teague Miss K Watson

Placings:0 (7289)
2009: 6^0S,

	Starts	1st	2nd	3rd	Win & Pl
Career Total (Turf)	1	0	0	0	

Going (Turf): Sf: 0-1 GS: 0-0 Gd: 0-0 GF: 0-0 Fm: 0-0
Distance: 5f/6f: 0-1 7f-8f: 0-0 9f-13f: 0-0 14f+: 0-0
Track : LH: 0-0 RH: 0-0 Tight: 0-0 Gall: 0-0
Aids: Bl: 0-0 Vi: 0-0 Tstrap: 0-0 Ckp: 0-0

Velvet Band

97(90) (72)**75**

2-y-o gr f Verglas (IRE)-Applaud (USA) (Rahy (USA))
P F I Cole Denford Stud

Placings:32610004 (6774)
2009: 6^3G, 5^2GF, 5^6GS, 5^1F, 6^0G, 5^0G, 7^0GF, 6^4SD,

	Starts	1st	2nd	3rd	Win & Pl
Career Total (Turf)	7	1	1	1	5471
Career Total (AW)	1	0	0	0	0

75 7/09 Brig 5f213y FRM £3784
Total win prize-money £3785

Going (Turf): Sf: 0-0 GS: 0-1 Gd: 0-3 GF: 0-2 **Fm: 1-1**
Distance: **5f/6f: 1-7** 7f-8f: 0-1 9f-13f: 0-0 14f+: 0-0
Track : **LH: 1-3** RH: 0-1 Tight: 0-0 Gall: 0-0
Aids: Bl: 0-0 Vi: 0-0 Tstrap: 0-0 Ckp: 0-0
Best Rating: 75 7/09 Brig 5f213y firm

Fair; stays 6f; acts on good ground.

Velvet Nayef

81 **28**

3-y-o b f Nayef (USA)-Laughing Girl (USA) (Woodman (USA))
J Pearce The Ace Partnership

Placings:0 (4270)
2009: 12^0G,

	Starts	1st	2nd	3rd	Win & Pl
Career Total (Turf)	1	0	0	0	

Going (Turf): Sf: 0-0 GS: 0-0 Gd: 0-1 GF: 0-0 Fm: 0-0
Distance: 5f/6f: 0-0 7f-8f: 0-0 9f-13f: 0-1 14f+: 0-0
Track : LH: 0-0 RH: 0-1 Tight: 0-0 Gall: 0-1
Aids: Bl: 0-0 Vi: 0-0 Tstrap: 0-0 Ckp: 0-0
Best Rating: 28 7/09 NmkJ 1m4f good

Venetian Lady

83(90) (58)**41**

3-y-o b f Tobougg (IRE)-Perfect Partner (Be My Chief (USA))
Mrs A Duffield Stewart Dalziel

Placings:00040-050000 (6255)
2009: 7^0GF, 7^5SD, 6^0GF, 6^0S, 6^0G, 7^0SD,

	Starts	1st	2nd	3rd	Win & Pl
Career Total (Turf)	7	0	0	0	
Career Total (AW)	4	0	0	0	289

Going (Turf): Sf: 0-2 GS: 0-0 Gd: 0-3 GF: 0-2 Fm: 0-0
Distance: 5f/6f: 0-7 7f-8f: 0-3 9f-13f: 0-1 14f+: 0-0
Track : LH: 0-5 RH: 0-2 Tight: 0-4 Gall: 0-0
Aids: Bl: 0-1 Vi: 0-0 Tstrap: 0-1 Ckp: 0-1
Best Rating: 58 10/08 Wolv 5f216y stand

Plating-class; best effort on Polytrack; stays 6f.

Veni Vedi Veci (IRE)

85(71) (26)**57**

2-y-o b f Antonius Pius (USA)-Consultant Stylist (IRE) (Desert Style (IRE))
A M Balding Favourites Racing VIII

Placings:00 (6620)
2009: 8^0SD, 8^0G,

	Starts	1st	2nd	3rd	Win & Pl
Career Total (Turf)	1	0	0	0	
Career Total (AW)	1	0	0	0	

Going (Turf): Sf: 0-0 GS: 0-0 Gd: 0-1 GF: 0-0 Fm: 0-0
Distance: 5f/6f: 0-0 7f-8f: 0-2 9f-13f: 0-0 14f+: 0-0
Track : LH: 0-0 RH: 0-1 Tight: 0-0 Gall: 0-0
Aids: Bl: 0-0 Vi: 0-0 Tstrap: 0-0 Ckp: 0-0
Best Rating: 57 10/09 Newb 1m good

Venir Rouge

95(102) (72)**76**

5-y-o ch g Dancing Spree (USA)-Al Awaalah (Mukaddamah (USA))
Matthew Salaman (M Salaman 10/7) A A Byrne

Placings:00004002/0201255052/0350050-516546 (7847)
2009: 10^5GF, 11^1GF, 13^6GF, 12^5SD, 11^4SD, 12^6SD,

	Starts	1st	2nd	3rd	Win & Pl
Career Total (Turf)	24	2	2	1	9050
Career Total (AW)	7	0	2	0	1669

76 6/09 Newb 1m3f5y (0-70)H G-F £2590
80 8/07 Newb 1m2f6y (0-70)H G-F £3435
Total win prize-money £6025

Going (Turf): Sf: 0-2 GS: 0-5 Gd: 0-5 **GF: 2-11** Fm: 0-1
Distance: 5f/6f: 0-1 7f-8f: 0-8 **9f-13f: 2-20** 14f+: 0-2
Track : **LH: 2-15** RH: 0-8 Tight: 0-10 **Gall: 2-7**
Aids: Bl: 0-1 Vi: 0-0 Tstrap: 0-0 Ckp: 0-0
Best Rating: 81 9/07 Gdwd 1m4f gd-fm

Modest; effective over middle distances; acts on fast ground and Polytrack; has been tried in blinkers.

Ventura Cove (IRE)

96 **77**

2-y-o ch g Bahamian Bounty-Baby Bunting (Wolfhound (USA))
R A Fahey Keith Denham

Placings:225 (2260)
2009: 5^2G, 5^2GF, 5^5G,

	Starts	1st	2nd	3rd	Win & Pl
Career Total (Turf)	3	0	2	0	4589

Going (Turf): Sf: 0-0 GS: 0-0 Gd: 0-2 GF: 0-1 Fm: 0-0
Distance: 5f/6f: 0-3 7f-8f: 0-0 9f-13f: 0-0 14f+: 0-0
Track : LH: 0-0 RH: 0-0 Tight: 0-0 Gall: 0-0
Aids: Bl: 0-0 Vi: 0-0 Tstrap: 0-0 Ckp: 0-0
Best Rating: 77 5/09 York 5f gd-fm

Fair; effective over 5f; acts on fast ground.

Venture Capitalist

99(91) (63)**69**

3-y-o b c Diktat-Ventura Highway (Machiavellian (USA))
B Ellison (L M Cumani 18/8) Brian Ellison & Kristian Strangeway

Placings:003-02020300 (7863)
2009: 8^0GS, 9^2GF, 11^0S, 9^2F, 11^0GS, 11^3F, 12^0SD, 8^0SD,

	Starts	1st	2nd	3rd	Win & Pl
Career Total (Turf)	8	0	2	1	2014
Career Total (AW)	3	0	0	1	433

Going (Turf): Sf: 0-1 GS: 0-3 Gd: 0-0 GF: 0-2 Fm: 0-2
Distance: 5f/6f: 0-0 7f-8f: 0-3 9f-13f: 0-8 14f+: 0-0
Track : LH: 0-8 RH: 0-2 Tight: 0-5 Gall: 0-0
Aids: Bl: 0-0 Vi: 0-0 Tstrap: 0-0 Ckp: 0-0
Best Rating: 69 7/09 Brig 1m1f209y firm

Modest; stays 1m2f; acts on fast ground; goes on Polytrack.

Venture Girl (IRE)

88(89) (54)**53**

2-y-o ch f Footstepsinthesand-Bold Assumption (Observatory (USA))
T D Easterby Peter C Bourke

Placings:66540 (6169)
2009: 6^6GS, 6^6GF, 6^5S, 5^4SD, 5^0GF,

	Starts	1st	2nd	3rd	Win & Pl
Career Total (Turf)	4	0	0	0	0
Career Total (AW)	1	0	0	0	0

Going (Turf): Sf: 0-1 GS: 0-1 Gd: 0-0 GF: 0-2 Fm: 0-0
Distance: 5f/6f: 0-5 7f-8f: 0-0 9f-13f: 0-0 14f+: 0-0
Track : LH: 0-0 RH: 0-0 Tight: 0-0 Gall: 0-0
Aids: Bl: 0-0 Vi: 0-0 Tstrap: 0-0 Ckp: 0-0
Best Rating: 54 8/09 Sthl 5f stand

Venutius

98(100) (78)**74**

2-y-o b g Doyen (IRE)-Boadicea's Chariot (Commanche Run)
E S McMahon Mrs Fiona Williams

Placings:33214 (7003)
2009: 7^3G, 8^3GS, 8^2SD, 8^1SD, 8^4SD,

	Starts	1st	2nd	3rd	Win & Pl
Career Total (Turf)	2	0	0	2	722
Career Total (AW)	3	1	1	0	3909

78 10/09 Wolv 1m141y STD £2729
Total win prize-money £2730

Going (Turf): Sf: 0-0 GS: 0-1 Gd: 0-1 GF: 0-0 Fm: 0-0
Distance: 5f/6f: 0-0 7f-8f: 0-1 **9f-13f: 1-4** 14f+: 0-0
Track : **LH: 1-3** RH: 0-0 **Tight: 1-3** Gall: 0-0
Aids: Bl: 0-0 Vi: 0-0 Tstrap: 0-0 Ckp: 0-0
Best Rating: 78 10/09 Wolv 1m141y stand

Fair; stays 1m; acts on good ground and on Polytrack.

Veracity

104 (73)116

5-y-o ch h Lomitas-Vituisa (Bering)

Saeed Bin Suroor Godolphin

Placings:0/211225/5113-213P (3048)

2009: 13^{2}GF, 16^{1}GF, 14^{3}GS, 20^{P}GF,

	Starts	1st	2nd	3rd	Win & Pl
Career Total (Turf)	14	4	4	2	239026
Career Total (AW)	1	1	0	0	2969

116 2/09 Ndas 2m G-F £72916
112 10/08 NmkR 2m GD £36900
102 10/08 Pont 2m1f216y GD £9346
88 5/07 NmkR 1m4f (0-100)H GD £12954
73 4/07 Wolv 1m4f50y STD £2968

Total win prize-money £135088

Going (Turf): Sf: 0-1 GS: 0-4 **Gd: 3-5** GF: 1-4 Fm: 0-0
Distance: 5f/6f: 0-0 7f-8f: 0-0 9f-13f: 2-5 **14f+: 3-10**
Track : LH: 2-6 RH: 2-7 Tight: 1-4 **Gall: 2-6**
Aids: Bl: 0-0 Vi: 0-0 Tstrap: 0-0 Ckp: 0-0
Best Rating: **116** 2/09 Ndas 2m gd-fm

Group class; winner of the 2008 Jockey Club Cup; runner-up in the 2007 Queen's Vase and Goodwood Cup and third in the Prix Royal-Oak; successful in Dubai in 2009; stayed 2m; acted on good ground and Polytrack. (DEAD)

Verdant

79(99) (80)70

2-y-o b c Singspiel (IRE)-Orford Ness (Selkirk (USA))

Sir Michael Stoute K Abdulla

Placings:21 (6627)

2009: 7^{2}GF, 7^{1}SS,

	Starts	1st	2nd	3rd	Win & Pl
Career Total (Turf)	1	0	1	0	1542
Career Total (AW)	1	1	0	0	3562

80 10/09 Ling 7f SS £3561

Total win prize-money £3562

Going (Turf): **Sf: 0-0 GS: 0-0 Gd: 0-0 GF: 0-1 Fm: 0-0**
Distance: 5f/6f: 0-0 **7f-8f: 1-2** 9f-13f: 0-0 14f+: 0-0
Track : **LH: 1-1** RH: 0-0 **Tight: 1-1** Gall: 0-0
Aids: Bl: 0-0 Vi: 0-0 Tstrap: 0-0 Ckp: 0-0
Best Rating: **80** 10/09 Ling 7f std-slw

Fair; stays 7f; acts on Polytrack.

Verinco

100(90) (67)78

3-y-o b g Bahamian Bounty-Dark Eyed Lady (IRE) (Exhibitioner)

B Smart B Smart

Placings:42U263626-3434030 (7762)

2009: 5^{3}S, 5^{4}GS, 6^{3}GF, 6^{4}G, 5^{0}G, 6^{3}SD, 7^{0}SD,

	Starts	1st	2nd	3rd	Win & Pl
Career Total (Turf)	13	0	3	3	6147
Career Total (AW)	3	0	0	1	454

Going (Turf): **Sf: 0-2 GS: 0-1 Gd: 0-6 GF: 0-4 Fm: 0-0**
Distance: 5f/6f: 0-11 7f-8f: 0-5 9f-13f: 0-0 14f+: 0-0
Track : LH: 0-7 RH: 0-0 Tight: 0-2 Gall: 0-0
Aids: Bl: 0-3 Vi: 0-0 Tstrap: 0-6 Ckp: 0-6
Best Rating: **78** 6/08 Haml 6f5y good

Modest; effective at 6f; acts on fast ground and on Fibresand; has worn blinkers and cheekpieces.

Verity Lane (USA)

(97) (79)

2-y-o b f Yes It's True (USA)-Easy Pass (USA) (Easy Goer (USA))

R M H Cowell Yvonne Jacques Julia Morley Mr & Mrs R Foulkes

Placings:304 (7277)

2009: 8^{3}SD, 8^{0}SS, 8^{4}SD,

	Starts	1st	2nd	3rd	Win & Pl
Career Total (Turf)	0	0	0	0	
Career Total (AW)	3	0	0	1	504

Going (Turf): **Sf: 0-0 GS: 0-0 Gd: 0-0 GF: 0-0 Fm: 0-0**
Distance: 5f/6f: 0-0 7f-8f: 0-1 9f-13f: 0-2 14f+: 0-0
Track : LH: 0-3 RH: 0-0 Tight: 0-3 Gall: 0-0
Aids: Bl: 0-0 Vi: 0-0 Tstrap: 0-0 Ckp: 0-0
Best Rating: **79** 9/09 Wolv 1m141y stand

Fair; stays 1m; acts on Polytrack.

Verona Lad

80 55

2-y-o gr c Needwood Blade-Silver Spell (Aragon)

Jennie Candlish P and Mrs G A Clarke

Placings:6000 (5938)

2009: 7^{6}GS, 5^{0}S, 7^{0}G, 7^{0}GF,

	Starts	1st	2nd	3rd	Win & Pl
Career Total (Turf)	4	0	0	0	0

Going (Turf): **Sf: 0-1 GS: 0-1 Gd: 0-1 GF: 0-1 Fm: 0-0**
Distance: 5f/6f: 0-1 7f-8f: 0-3 9f-13f: 0-0 14f+: 0-0
Track : LH: 0-2 RH: 0-0 Tight: 0-1 Gall: 0-0
Aids: Bl: 0-0 Vi: 0-0 Tstrap: 0-0 Ckp: 0-0
Best Rating: **55** 7/09 Hayd 7f30y gd-sft

Veronicas Boy

99 70

3-y-o br c Diktat-Thamud (IRE) (Lahib (USA))

G M Moore J Stevenson

Placings:216626504-4444440 (5011)

2009: 10^{4}GF, 9^{4}GF, 8^{4}G, 8^{4}S, 9^{4}G, 12^{4}G, 14^{0}G,

	Starts	1st	2nd	3rd	Win & Pl
Career Total (Turf)	16	1	2	0	7706

70 5/08 Haml 5f4y G-S £3238

Total win prize-money £3238

Going (Turf): Sf: 0-2 **GS: 1-5** Gd: 0-5 GF: 0-4 Fm: 0-0
Distance: **5f/6f: 1-5** 7f-8f: 0-5 9f-13f: 0-5 14f+: 0-1
Track : LH: 0-5 RH: 0-4 Tight: 0-4 Gall: 0-0
Aids: Bl: 0-0 Vi: 0-0 Tstrap: 0-1 Ckp: 0-1
Best Rating: **70** 7/08 Haml 6f5y good

Modest; effective at 6f but stays 1m; acts on soft ground.

Veronicas Way

(87) (38)40

4-y-o b f High Estate-Mimining (Tower Walk)

G J Smith A C Birkle

Placings:04100/60006600-005 (0536)

2009: 8^{0}SD, 8^{0}SD, 8^{5}SD,

	Starts	1st	2nd	3rd	Win & Pl
Career Total (Turf)	11	1	0	0	4175
Career Total (AW)	5	0	0	0	0

61 9/07 Thsk 7f G-F £3886

Total win prize-money £3886

Going (Turf): Sf: 0-1 GS: 0-3 Gd: 0-3 **GF: 1-4** Fm: 0-0
Distance: 5f/6f: 0-3 **7f-8f: 1-10** 9f-13f: 0-3 14f+: 0-0
Track : **LH: 1-9** RH: 0-3 **Tight: 1-5** Gall: 0-2
Aids: Bl: 0-0 Vi: 0-3 Tstrap: 0-1 Ckp: 0-1
Best Rating: **61** 9/07 Thsk 7f gd-fm

Modest filly; stays 7f; acts on good and fast ground.

Veroon (IRE)

102(105) (82)78

3-y-o b g Noverre (USA)-Waroonga (IRE) (Brief Truce (USA))

J G Given Danethorpe Racing Partnership

Placings:5306-2146621421205 (7233)

2009: 8^{2}F, 8^{1}GF, 8^{4}G, 10^{6}G, 11^{6}GS, 10^{2}G, 9^{1}G, 9^{4}GF, **9**^{2}SD, 10^{1}GF, **10**^{2}SD, 10^{0}G, **10**^{5}SD,

	Starts	1st	2nd	3rd	Win & Pl
Career Total (Turf)	14	3	2	1	18204
Career Total (AW)	3	0	2	0	2213

78 9/09 Ches 1m2f75y (0-75)H G-F £4047
71 8/09 Bevl 1m1f207y (0-70)H GD £3238
70 6/09 Ripn 1m G-F £3238

Total win prize-money £10523

Going (Turf): Sf: 0-1 GS: 0-1 Gd: 1-6 **GF: 2-5** Fm: 0-1
Distance: 5f/6f: 0-4 7f-8f: 1-1 **9f-13f: 2-12** 14f+: 0-0
Track : LH: 1-9 **RH: 2-5 Tight: 2-6** Gall: 0-1
Aids: Bl: 0-2 Vi: 0-0 Tstrap: 2-8 Ckp: 2-8
Best Rating: **82** 9/09 Kemp 1m2f stand

Fair; effective over 1m-1m2f; acts on fast ground and on Polytrack; has worn blinkers and cheekpieces.

Versaki (IRE)

94(94) (61)93

3-y-o gr g Verglas (IRE)-Mythie (FR) (Octagonal (NZ))

Ian Williams (D Nicholls 4/5) Dr Marwan Koukash

Placings:1043500-0000003366 (7105)

2009: 7^{0}FT, 6^{0}G, **6**^{0}SD, 7^{0}GF, 7^{0}G, **7**^{0}SD, 7^{3}GF, 7^{3}GF, **8**^{6}SD, 7^{6}SD,

	Starts	1st	2nd	3rd	Win & Pl
Career Total (Turf)	12	1	0	3	6345
Career Total (AW)	5	0	0	0	0

85 5/08 Gdwd 6f SFT £4371

Total win prize-money £4371

Going (Turf): **Sf: 1-1** GS: 0-2 Gd: 0-4 GF. 0-5 Fm: 0-0
Distance: **5f/6f: 1-4** 7f-8f: 0-13 9f-13f: 0-0 14f+: 0-0
Track : LH: 0-6 RH: 0-2 Tight: 0-1 Gall: 0-2
Aids: Bl: 0-1 Vi: 0-0 Tstrap: 0-0 Ckp: 0-0
Best Rating: **93** 8/08 Newb 6f8y gd-sft

Useful; effective at 6f; handles easy ground.

Vert Chapeau

(85) (60)

2-y-o ch f Sakhee (USA)-Green Bonnet (IRE) (Green Desert (USA))

E F Vaughan Saeed Manana

Placings:00 (6722)

2009: 7^{0}SD, 6^{0}SD,

	Starts	1st	2nd	3rd	Win & Pl
Career Total (Turf)	0	0	0	0	
Career Total (AW)	2	0	0	0	

Going (Turf): **Sf: 0-0 GS: 0-0 Gd: 0-0 GF: 0-0 Fm: 0-0**

Distance: 5f/6f: 0-1 7f-8f: 0-1 9f-13f: 0-0 14f+: 0-0
Track : LH: 0-0 RH: 0-2 Tight: 0-0 Gall: 0-0
Aids: Bl: 0-0 Vi: 0-0 Tstrap: 0-0 Ckp: 0-0
Best Rating: **60** 9/09 Kemp 7f stand

Vertigo On Course (IRE)

101(94) (56)**68**

4-y-o b f Anabaa (USA)-Due South (Darshaan)
R A Fahey G Devlin

Placings:00024425-133 (7113)
2009: 7^{1}GF, 8^{3}SD, 9^{3}GS,

	Starts	1st	2nd	3rd	Win & Pl
Career Total (Turf)	8	1	1	1	4429
Career Total (AW)	3	0	1	1	1630

66 9/09 Yarm 7f3y (0-60)H G-F £2007
Total win prize-money £2008

Going (Turf): Sf: 0-4 GS: 0-1 Gd: 0-0 **GF: 1-1** Fm: 0-0
Distance: 5f/6f: 0-0 **7f-8f: 1-6** 9f-13f: 0-5 14f+: 0-0
Track : LH: 0-5 RH: 0-5 Tight: 0-2 Gall: 0-0
Aids: Bl: 0-0 Vi: 0-0 Tstrap: 0-0 Ckp: 0-0
Best Rating: **68** 10/09 Muss 1m1f gd-sft

Moderate; ex-Irish; suited by 7f and fast ground; acts on Polytrack.

Vertueux (FR)

72(82) (36)**60**

4-y-o gr g Verglas (IRE)-Shahrazad (FR) (Bering)
A W Carroll John Rutter

Placings:102-000 (7124)
2009: 14^{0}GF, 16^{0}SD, 16^{0}G,

	Starts	1st	2nd	3rd	Win & Pl
Career Total (Turf)	5	1	1	0	6250
Career Total (AW)	1	0	0	0	

4/08 Lisi 1m5f GD £2573
Total win prize-money £2574

Going (Turf): Sf: 0-1 GS: 0-0 **Gd: 1-3** GF: 0-1 Fm: 0-0
Distance: 5f/6f: 0-0 7f-8f: 0-0 **9f-13f: 1-2** 14f+: 0-4
Track : LH: 0-3 RH: 0-1 Tight: 0-1 Gall: 0-0
Aids: Bl: 0-0 Vi: 0-0 Tstrap: 0-1 Ckp: 0-1
Best Rating: **60** 6/08 Lonc 1m7f good

Very Distinguished

94(93) (62)**67**

3-y-o b f Diktat-Dignify (IRE) (Rainbow Quest (USA))
S Kirk (M G Quinlan 21/7) Barry Payne & Tommy Cummins

Placings:0205056-00000603200 (7856)
2009: 8^{0}GF, 9^{0}G, 11^{0}GF, 9^{0}G, 11^{0}GS, 8^{6}SD, 9^{0}SD, 8^{3}SD, 12^{2}SD, 12^{0}SD, 9^{0}SD,

	Starts	1st	2nd	3rd	Win & Pl
Career Total (Turf)	12	0	1	0	1428
Career Total (AW)	6	0	1	1	907

Going (Turf): **Sf: 0-2 GS: 0-4 Gd: 0-2 GF: 0-4 Fm: 0-0**
Distance: 5f/6f: 0-0 7f-8f: 0-6 9f-13f: 0-12 14f+: 0-0
Track : LH: 0-7 RH: 0-6 Tight: 0-6 Gall: 0-0
Aids: Bl: 0-0 Vi: 0-0 Tstrap: 0-0 Ckp: 0-0
Best Rating: **67** 11/08 NmkR 1m2f gd-sft

Moderate; stays 1m4f; acts on soft ground and Polytrack.

Very Good Day (FR)

91 **73**

2-y-o b c Sinndar (IRE)-Picture Princess (Sadler's Wells (USA))
M R Channon Jaber Abdullah

Placings:2 (4953)
2009: 8^{2}G,

	Starts	1st	2nd	3rd	Win & Pl
Career Total (Turf)	1	0	1	0	1542

Going (Turf): **Sf: 0-0 GS: 0-0 Gd: 0-1 GF: 0-0 Fm: 0-0**
Distance: 5f/6f: 0-0 7f-8f: 0-0 9f-13f: 0-1 14f+: 0-0
Track : LH: 0-0 RH: 0-1 Tight: 0-0 Gall: 0-0
Aids: Bl: 0-0 Vi: 0-0 Tstrap: 0-0 Ckp: 0-0
Best Rating: **73** 8/09 Sand 1m14y good

Fair; stays 1m and acts on good ground.

Very Well Red

103(103) (63)**75**

6-y-o b m First Trump-Little Scarlett (Mazilier (USA))
P W Hiatt Phil Kelly

Placings:04652111504001560540/600010300005064240-035201140014623006OU0 (7784)
2009: 8^{0}SS, 8^{3}SD, 8^{5}SD, 8^{2}SD, 8^{0}SD, 8^{1}SD, 8^{1}SD, 8^{4}SD, 8^{0}G, 8^{0}G, 8^{1}F, 8^{4}GF, 8^{6}GF, 8^{2}HY, 8^{3}GF, 8^{0}GF, 8^{0}S, 8^{6}GF, 8^{0}GF, 8^{U}SD, 8^{0}SD,

	Starts	1st	2nd	3rd	Win & Pl
Career Total (Turf)	28	5	1	2	17975
Career Total (AW)	30	3	3	1	8076

74 6/09 Bath 1m5y (0-70)H FRM £2719
63 3/09 Ling 1m (0-60)H STD £2047
59 3/09 Sthl 1m (0-55) STD £1706
72 7/08 Nott 1m75y (0-75)H G-F £3238
74 10/07 Bath 1m5y (0-75)H GD £3238
74 5/07 Bevl 1m100y (0-70)H G-F £3562
69 5/07 Nott 1m54y (0-60)H SFT £2914
57 5/07 Wolv 1m141y (0-50)H SF £2266
Total win prize-money £21694

Going (Turf): Sf: 1-5 GS: 0-4 Gd: 1-8 **GF: 2-10** Fm: 1-1
Distance: 5f/6f: 0-0 7f-8f: 2-27 **9f-13f: 6-31** 14f+: 0-0
Track : **LH: 7-44** RH: 1-13 **Tight: 4-26** Gall: 0-1
Aids: Bl: 0-6 Vi: 0-0 Tstrap: 0-0 Ckp: 0-0
Best Rating: **75** 8/09 Leic 1m60y heavy

Modest; stays 1m; acts on fast ground and on sand.

Vested Interest

93(73) (18)**76**

2-y-o ch g Footstepsinthesand-Ingozi (Warning)
George Baker Mrs Susan Roy

Placings:01 (3547)
2009: 5^{0}SD, 6^{1}GF,

	Starts	1st	2nd	3rd	Win & Pl
Career Total (Turf)	1	1	0	0	1943
Career Total (AW)	1	0	0	0	

76 7/09 Yarm 6f3y G-F £1942
Total win prize-money £1943

Going (Turf): Sf: 0-0 GS: 0-0 Gd: 0-0 **GF: 1-1** Fm: 0-0
Distance: 5f/6f: 0-1 **7f-8f: 1-1** 9f-13f: 0-0 14f+: 0-0
Track : LH: 0-0 RH: 0-0 Tight: 0-0 Gall: 0-0
Aids: Bl: 0-0 Vi: 0-0 Tstrap: 0-0 Ckp: 0-0
Best Rating: **76** 7/09 Yarm 6f3y gd-fm

Fair; effective at 6f on fast ground.

Vhujon (IRE)

106(108) (90)**94**

4-y-o b g Mujadil (USA)-Livius Lady (IRE) (Titus Livius (FR))
P D Evans Nick Shutts

Placings:1001004P6200/105520000015000000-444015220044000050022 (7875)
2009: 6^{4}SD, 6^{4}GF, 6^{4}GF, 5^{0}GF, 6^{1}GF, 5^{5}G, 6^{2}GF, 6^{2}GF, 6^{0}GF, 5^{0}GS, 6^{4}G, 6^{4}GF, 6^{0}GF, 6^{0}G, 6^{0}GF, 6^{0}G, 7^{5}GF, 6^{0}GF, 6^{0}SD, 6^{2}SD, 6^{2}SD,

	Starts	1st	2nd	3rd	Win & Pl
Career Total (Turf)	37	3	4	0	73018
Career Total (AW)	13	2	2	0	17998

94 5/09 Sals 6f (0-85)H G-F £4857
90 9/08 Kemp 6f (0-85)H STD £4727
96 3/08 Kemp 6f (0-105)H STD £9971
86 7/07 Sals 6f G-F £4210
89 4/07 Bath 5f11y FRM £2914
Total win prize-money £26680

Going (Turf): Sf: 0-3 GS: 0-3 Gd: 0-10 **GF: 2-20** Fm: 1-1
Distance: **5f/6f: 5-43** 7f-8f: 0-7 9f-13f: 0-0 14f+: 0-0
Track : LH: 1-8 **RH: 2-7** Tight: 0-4 **Gall: 1-5**
Aids: Bl: 0-0 Vi: 0-1 Tstrap: 0-0 Ckp: 0-0
Best Rating: **96** 3/08 Kemp 6f stand

Fair; effective over 5f-6f; acts on fast ground; goes on Polytrack; has worn a tongue tie; can start slowly.

Via Aurelia (IRE)

90 **60**

2-y-o b f Antonius Pius (USA)-Goldthroat (IRE) (Zafonic (USA))
J R Fanshawe The Hons W G & A G Vestey

Placings:440 (7061)
2009: 6^{4}GF, 6^{4}GF, 5^{0}GF,

	Starts	1st	2nd	3rd	Win & Pl
Career Total (Turf)	3	0	0	0	481

Going (Turf): **Sf: 0-0 GS: 0-0 Gd: 0-0 GF: 0-3 Fm: 0-0**
Distance: 5f/6f: 0-2 7f-8f: 0-1 9f-13f: 0-0 14f+: 0-0
Track : LH: 0-0 RH: 0-0 Tight: 0-0 Gall: 0-0
Aids: Bl: 0-0 Vi: 0-0 Tstrap: 0-0 Ckp: 0-0
Best Rating: **60** 8/09 Yarm 6f3y gd-fm

Modest; stays 6f; acts on fast ground.

Via Mia

89(101) (73)**62**

3-y-o b f Namid-Coming Home (Vettori (IRE))
George Baker (P F I Cole 14/5) Stuart McCallum

Placings:310-063236 (7615)
2009: 5^{0}GF, 5^{6}SD, 7^{3}SD, 8^{2}SD, 10^{3}SD, 8^{6}SD,

	Starts	1st	2nd	3rd	Win & Pl
Career Total (Turf)	3	0	0	1	337
Career Total (AW)	6	1	1	2	4381

73 9/08 Wolv 5f216y STD £2729
Total win prize-money £2730

Going (Turf): **Sf: 0-0 GS: 0-2 Gd: 0-0 GF: 0-1 Fm: 0-0**
Distance: **5f/6f: 1-4** 7f-8f: 0-2 9f-13f: 0-3 14f+: 0-0
Track : **LH: 1-7** RH: 0-1 **Tight: 1-6** Gall: 0-1
Aids: Bl: 0-0 Vi: 0-0 Tstrap: 0-0 Ckp: 0-0
Best Rating: **73** 10/09 Wolv 1m141y stand

Modest; stays 1m; acts on Polytrack.

Viable

89 (63)**49**

7-y-o b g Vettori (IRE)-Danseuse Davis (FR) (Glow (USA))

Mrs P Sly Thorney Racing Club

Placings:0/3052000/**0**300420/**40**6515**25**/30-0 **(2420)**

2009: 10^0G,

	Starts	1st	2nd	3rd	Win & Pl
Career Total (Turf)	**21**	**1**	**2**	**3**	**6222**
Career Total (AW)	**5**	**0**	**1**	**0**	**822**

64 8/07 Yarm 1m3y (0-65)H G-F £1943

Total win prize-money £1943

Going (Turf): Sf: 0-2 GS: 0-5 Gd: 0-3 **GF: 1-11** Fm: 0-0
Distance: 5f/6f: 0-0 7f-8f: 0-5 **9f-13f: 1-21** 14f+: 0-0
Track : LH: 0-12 RH: 0-12 Tight: 0-7 Gall: 0-0
Aids: Bl: 0-0 Vi: 0-0 Tstrap: 0-0 Ckp: 0-0
Best Rating: 71 6/05 Leic 1m1f218y gd-fm

Moderate; effective over 1m-1m2f; acts on fast ground.

Vicious Warrior

103(92) (72)**80**

10-y-o b g Elmaamul (USA)-Ling Lane (Slip Anchor)

R M Whitaker James Marshall & Mrs Susan Marshall

Placings:4503/0432215043135U/40002004020/20530223 06133/00403206004036/10432536100/503100003130/066 044240305-003 **(3034)**

2009: 10^0S, 12^0GF, 9^3GS,

	Starts	1st	2nd	3rd	Win & Pl
Career Total (Turf)	**79**	**6**	**10**	**14**	**113567**
Career Total (AW)	**15**	**1**	**0**	**3**	**8203**

91 10/07 Ayr 1m1f20y (0-85)H SFT £5181
91 7/07 York 1m (0-90)H HVY £9715
92 9/06 Ayr 1m (0-100)H G-S £15580
87 5/06 Ayr 1m (0-75)H GD £5505
81 11/04 Ling 1m (0-77)H STD £3435
95 9/02 Donc 1m2f60yC(0-95)H G-F £19987
89 6/02 Ripn 1m2f D(0-85)H G-S £5564

Total win prize-money £64970

Going (Turf): Sf: 2-14 GS: 2-8 Gd: 1-22 GF: 1-33 Fm: 0-2
Distance: 5f/6f: 0-0 **7f-8f: 4-45** 9f-13f: 3-49 14f+: 0-0
Track : LH: 6-53 RH: 1-29 Tight: 2-30 Gall: 2-21
Aids: Bl: 0-0 Vi: 0-0 Tstrap: 0-0 Ckp: 0-0
Best Rating: 95 9/02 Donc 1m2f60y gd-fm

Fair; suited by 1m-1m2f; acts on most types of ground, including Polytrack.

Victoire De Lyphar (IRE)

98 **82**

2-y-o b g Bertolini (USA)-Victory Peak (Shirley Heights)

P C Haslam Middleham Park Racing Xviii

Placings:612026 **(6035)**

2009: 6^6GS, 6^1GF, 7^2G, 7^0GF, 7^2GS, 7^6GF,

	Starts	1st	2nd	3rd	Win & Pl
Career Total (Turf)	**6**	**1**	**2**	**0**	**8256**

81 6/09 Donc 6f G-F £4209

Total win prize-money £4209

Going (Turf): Sf: 0-0 GS: 0-2 Gd: 0-1 **GF: 1-3** Fm: 0-0
Distance: 5f/6f: 1-2 7f-8f: 0-4 9f-13f: 0-0 14f+: 0-0
Track : LH: 0-1 RH: 0-0 Tight: 0-0 Gall: 0-1
Aids: Bl: 0-1 Vi: 0-1 Tstrap: 0-0 Ckp: 0-0
Best Rating: 82 9/09 York 7f gd-sft

Fair; effective over 6f-7f; acts on fast ground; should improve further.

Victoria Montoya

110(104) (78)**101**

4-y-o br f High Chaparral (IRE)-Spurned (USA) (Robellino (USA))

A M Balding Kingsclere Racing CLub

Placings:233131055-122320 **(5796)**

2009: 14^1GF, 14^2G, 16^2G, 14^3G, 14^2G, 14^0G,

	Starts	1st	2nd	3rd	Win & Pl
Career Total (Turf)	**12**	**3**	**3**	**3**	**66580**
Career Total (AW)	**3**	**0**	**1**	**1**	**1530**

92 5/09 NmkR 1m6f (0-105)H G-F £24924
84 7/08 Sand 1m6f (0-95)H G-F £9714
80 6/08 Gdwd 1m6f (0-75)H GD £3238

Total win prize-money £37876

Going (Turf): Sf: 0-1 GS: 0-1 Gd: 1-7 **GF: 2-3** Fm: 0-0
Distance: 5f/6f: 0-0 7f-8f: 0-0 9f-13f: 0-4 **14f+: 3-11**
Track : LH: 0-3 **RH: 3-12** Tight: 1-4 Gall: 1-6
Aids: Bl: 0-0 Vi: 0-0 Tstrap: 1-4 Ckp: 1-4
Best Rating: 101 8/09 Gdwd 1m6f good

Very useful; Group and Listed placed; stays 2m; acts on fast and easy ground and on Polytrack; has worn cheek-pieces.

Victoria Sponge (IRE)

104(104) (86)**94**

3-y-o b f Marju (IRE)-Trill (Highest Honor (FR))

R Hannon Simon Leech

Placings:2531-3021146351 **(6731)**

2009: 8^3SD, 7^0GF, 8^2GF, 7^1G, 7^1GF, 6^4GF, 7^6G, 6^3SD, 6^5GF, 6^1S,

	Starts	1st	2nd	3rd	Win & Pl
Career Total (Turf)	**11**	**3**	**2**	**1**	**17096**
Career Total (AW)	**3**	**1**	**0**	**2**	**3996**

94 10/09 Sals 6f212y (0-85)H SFT £4857
91 7/09 Epsm 7f (0-85)H G-F £4857
87 6/09 Gdwd 7f (0-85)H GD £5180
75 10/08 Kemp 6f (0-75) STD £2590

Total win prize-money £17485

Going (Turf): Sf: 1-2 GS: 0-0 **Gd: 1-2 GF: 1-7** Fm: 0-0
Distance: 5f/6f: 1-7 **7f-8f: 3-7** 9f-13f: 0-0 14f+: 0-0
Track : LH: 1-3 **RH: 2-4 Tight: 1-1** Gall: 0-1
Aids: Bl: 0-0 Vi: 0-0 Tstrap: 0-0 Ckp: 0-0
Best Rating: 94 10/09 Sals 6f212y soft

Useful; stays 7f and acts on fast ground.

Victorian Art (IRE)

98(95) (60)**72**

2-y-o b f Chineur (FR)-Alexander Nitelady (IRE) (Night Shift (USA))

M A Magnusson Matthew Green & East Wind Racing

Placings:35025 **(3006)**

2009: 5^3SD, 5^5SD, 6^0GF, 5^2F, 5^5G,

	Starts	1st	2nd	3rd	Win & Pl
Career Total (Turf)	**3**	**0**	**1**	**0**	**617**
Career Total (AW)	**2**	**0**	**0**	**1**	**403**

Going (Turf): Sf: 0-0 GS: 0-0 Gd: 0-1 GF: 0-1 Fm: 0-1
Distance: 5f/6f: 0-5 7f-8f: 0-0 9f-13f: 0-0 14f+: 0-0
Track : LH: 0-3 RH: 0-0 Tight: 0-2 Gall: 0-1
Aids: Bl: 0-0 Vi: 0-2 Tstrap: 0-0 Ckp: 0-0
Best Rating: 72 6/09 Bath 5f11y firm

Modest; effective at 5f; acts on Polytrack and fast turf.

Victorian Bounty

95(95) (71)**97**

4-y-o b g Bahamian Bounty-Baby Bunting (Wolfhound (USA))

Stef Liddiard David Gilbert

Placings:41**2**22150/40162000-0060 **(2946)**

2009: 6^0SD, 6^0G, 5^6GF, 5^0GF,

	Starts	1st	2nd	3rd	Win & Pl
Career Total (Turf)	**16**	**3**	**2**	**0**	**43896**
Career Total (AW)	**4**	**0**	**2**	**0**	**2023**

91 5/08 Sals 6f (0-100)H GD £12462
82 8/07 Catt 5f212y GD £5181
75 6/07 Muss 5f GD £3886

Total win prize-money £21530

Going (Turf): Sf: 0-1 GS: 0-1 **Gd: 3-7** GF: 0-6 Fm: 0-1
Distance: 5f/6f: 3-19 7f-8f: 0-1 9f-13f: 0-0 14f+: 0-0
Track : LH: 1-6 RH: 0-1 **Tight: 1-4** Gall: 0-1
Aids: Bl: 0-1 Vi: 0-2 Tstrap: 0-0 Ckp: 0-0
Best Rating: 97 6/08 York 6f good

Very useful; effective over 5f-6f; acts on a sound surface; also goes on Polytrack.

Victorian Tycoon (IRE)

100(95) (66)**68**

3-y-o b c Choisir (AUS)-New Tycoon (IRE) (Last Tycoon)

E J O'Neill Victory Racing

Placings:050252-2404026230 **(7037a)**

2009: 8^2GF, 9^4GF, 8^0G, 8^4SD, 7^0SD, 12^2SD, 12^6G, 13^2VS, 15^3VS, 12^0VS,

	Starts	1st	2nd	3rd	Win & Pl
Career Total (Turf)	**10**	**0**	**2**	**1**	**6028**
Career Total (AW)	**6**	**0**	**3**	**0**	**5776**

Going (Turf): Sf: 0-2 GS: 0-0 Gd: 0-2 GF: 0-3 Fm: 0-0
Distance: 5f/6f: 0-1 7f-8f: 0-5 9f-13f: 0-8 14f+: 0-2
Track : LH: 0-7 RH: 0-4 Tight: 0-3 Gall: 0-1
Aids: Bl: 0-3 Vi: 0-0 Tstrap: 0-0 Ckp: 0-0
Best Rating: 68 4/09 Nott 1m75y gd-fm

Modest; stays 1m; acts on Polytrack.

Victory Ide Say (IRE)

(94) (67)

2-y-o ch g Fath (USA)-Ide Say (IRE) (Grand Lodge (USA))

P W Chapple-Hyam P W Chapple-Hyam

Placings:3 **(7736)**

2009: 6^3SD,

	Starts	1st	2nd	3rd	Win & Pl
Career Total (Turf)	**0**	**0**	**0**	**0**	
Career Total (AW)	**1**	**0**	**0**	**1**	**482**

Going (Turf): Sf: 0-0 GS: 0-0 Gd: 0-0 GF: 0-0 Fm: 0-0
Distance: 5f/6f: 0-1 7f-8f: 0-0 9f-13f: 0-0 14f+: 0-0
Track : LH: 0-0 RH: 0-1 Tight: 0-0 Gall: 0-0
Aids: Bl: 0-0 Vi: 0-0 Tstrap: 0-0 Ckp: 0-0
Best Rating: 67 12/09 Kemp 6f stand

Victory Quest (IRE)

106(100) (79)**70**

9-y-o b g Victory Note (USA)-Marade (USA) (Dahar (USA))

Mrs S Lamyman Mrs S Lamyman

Placings:000125212/00114/0603605/0510026402113005 032112/305425002143631-301355550 (7867)
2009: 14^{3}SS, 14^{0}SD, 14^{1}SD, 14^{3}SD, 14^{5}SD, 21^{5}F, 14^{5}SD, 16^{5}SD, 14^{0}SS,

	Starts	1st	2nd	3rd	Win & Pl
Career Total (Turf)	13	1	1	0	6532
Career Total (AW)	54	11	8	8	43233

79	2/09	Sthl	1m6f	(0-75)H	STD	£2729
76	12/08	Sthl	2m	(0-75)H	STD	£2729
73	10/08	Sthl	1m6f	(0-65)H	STD	£2388
75	12/07	Sthl	2m	(0-75)H	SS	£2968
65	12/07	Sthl	1m6f	(0-75)H	SS	£2968
73	2/07	Sthl	2m	(0-65)H	SLW	£2388
69	1/07	Sthl	2m	(0-75)H	STD	£2914
71	2/06	Sthl	2m	(0-65)H	STD	£2388
86	2/04	Sthl	2m	D(0-85)H	SS	£4026
80	2/04	Sthl	1m6f	D(0-80)H	STD	£4046
74	12/03	Sthl	1m6f	E(0-75)H	STD	£2044
65	6/03	Gdwd	1m6f	E(0-75)H	G-F	£4329

Total win prize-money £35925

Going (Turf): Sf: 0-1 GS: 0-2 Gd: 0-4 **GF: 1-5** Fm: 0-1
Distance: 5f/6f: 0-0 7f-8f: 0-1 9f-13f: 0-11 **14f+: 12-55**
Track : **LH: 11-63** RH: 1-4 **Tight: 1-12** Gall: 0-2
Aids: Bl: 0-0 **Vi: 12-64** Tstrap: 0-0 Ckp: 0-0
Best Rating: **86** 2/04 Sthl 2m std-slw

Modest; stays 2m; suited by Fibresand; has worn a visor.

Victory Spirit

92(100) (55)**45**
5-y-o b g Invincible Spirit (IRE)-Tanouma (USA) (Miswaki (USA))
D A Nolan (I Semple 23/1) Robert Reid

Placings:40210/00000/024-0004000 (3657)
2009: 9^{0}SD, 8^{0}SD, 7^{0}SD, 6^{4}GF, 9^{0}GF, 7^{0}GF, 5^{0}G,

	Starts	1st	2nd	3rd	Win & Pl
Career Total (Turf)	13	1	1	0	5715
Career Total (AW)	7	0	1	0	705

70	9/06	Folk	6f	G-F	£4210

Total win prize-money £4210

Going (Turf): Sf: 0-1 GS: 0-2 Gd: 0-2 **GF: 1-8** Fm: 0-0
Distance: **5f/6f: 1-9** 7f-8f: 0-7 9f-13f: 0-4 14f+: 0-0
Track : LH: 0-9 RH: 0-2 Tight: 0-10 Gall: 0-0
Aids: Bl: 0-4 Vi: 0-0 Tstrap: 0-2 Ckp: 0-2
Best Rating: **71** 7/06 NmkJ 6f gd-fm

Vien (IRE)

(98) (49)**50**
3-y-o br c Captain Rio-Fairy Free (Rousillon (USA))
R Hannon Louis Stalder

Placings:00050-060 (0296)
2009: 8^{0}SD, 9^{6}SD, 8^{0}SD,

	Starts	1st	2nd	3rd	Win & Pl
Career Total (Turf)	3	0	0	0	
Career Total (AW)	5	0	0	0	0

Going (Turf): **Sf: 0-2 GS: 0-0 Gd: 0-0 GF: 0-1 Fm: 0-0**
Distance: 5f/6f: 0-1 7f-8f: 0-3 9f-13f: 0-4 14f+: 0-0
Track : LH: 0-5 RH: 0-1 Tight: 0-5 Gall: 0-0
Aids: Bl: 0-0 Vi: 0-0 Tstrap: 0-0 Ckp: 0-0
Best Rating: **50** 8/08 Gdwd 1m soft

View From The Top

(89) (60)**50**
5-y-o b g Mujahid (USA)-Aethra (USA) (Trempolino (USA))
Patrick Allen Michael Gavigan/Vincent Duff

Placings:4000/020041026/0500661-605000 (5683)
2009: 10^{6}SD, 7^{0}SD, 10^{5}GF, 10^{0}GF, 9^{0}SD, 8^{0}SD,

	Starts	1st	2nd	3rd	Win & Pl
Career Total (Turf)	12	0	1	0	1209
Career Total (AW)	14	2	1	0	7636

60	11/08	Dund	1m2f150y	(45-60)H	STD	£4572
66	8/07	Wolv	1m1f103y		STD	£2388

Total win prize-money £6962

Going (Turf): **Sf: 0-1 GS: 0-1 Gd: 0-4 GF: 0-5 Fm: 0-1**
Distance: 5f/6f: 0-0 7f-8f: 0-7 **9f-13f: 2-19** 14f+: 0-0
Track : **LH: 2-17** RH: 0-7 **Tight: 1-9** Gall: 0-0
Aids: Bl: 0-1 Vi: 0-0 Tstrap: 1-7 Ckp: 1-7
Best Rating: **71** 6/07 Wolv 1m141y stand

Modest; effective over 1m4f; acts on good ground; also goes on Polytrack.

Viewforth

46(92) (41)**35**
11-y-o b g Emarati (USA)-Miriam (Forzando)
S T Mason (M Wigham 28/1) C Handley & J Cleeve

Placings:4300/303150604600/0000111540/000222051125 4600/4400000430000003/20221264040/00023133300246 5540/0003405331100/00000-50 (1259)
2009: 6^{5}SD, 6^{0}G,

	Starts	1st	2nd	3rd	Win & Pl
Career Total (Turf)	97	10	9	12	72874
Career Total (AW)	11	0	1	0	744

63	9/07	Bevl	5f	(0-50)H	G-F	£2266
63	9/07	Ling	6f	(0-50)H	G-F	£2730
63	7/06	Haml	6f5y	(0-70)H	G-F	£3886
74	6/05	Haml	5f4y	(0-70)H	GD	£4352
89	8/03	Bevl	5f	E(0-75)H	G-F	£10725
81	8/03	Hayd	6f	C(0-90)H	G-F	£10088
70	6/02	Haml	6f5y	E(0-75)H	SFT	£4426
71	6/02	Haml	5f4y	E	HVY	£3024
66	6/02	Haml	5f4y	F(0-60)H	HVY	£4078
55	6/01	Muss	5f	D	G-F	£3432

Total win prize-money £49010

Going (Turf): Sf: 3-19 GS: 0-22Gd: 1-26**GF: 6-29** Fm: 0-1
Distance: **5f/6f: 8-85** 7f-8f: 2-23 9f-13f: 0-0 14f+: 0-0
Track : LH: 0-11 RH: 0-6 Tight: 0-7 Gall: 0-4
Aids: **Bl: 9-79** Vi: 0-2 Tstrap: 0-1 Ckp: 0-1
Best Rating: **91** 9/03 Hayd 5f gd-sft

Plater, effective at 5f and 6f; acts on most types of ground; regularly blinkered.

Vigorosa (IRE)

81(91) (46)**28**
3-y-o b f Red Ransom (USA)-Hejraan Two (IRE) (Green Desert (USA))
P Howling The Circle Bloodstock I Limited

Placings:00000560 (7666)
2009: 8^{0}SD, 7^{0}GF, 7^{0}GF, 12^{0}SD, 9^{0}SF, 9^{5}SD, 10^{6}SD, 10^{0}SD,

	Starts	1st	2nd	3rd	Win & Pl
Career Total (Turf)	2	0	0	0	
Career Total (AW)	6	0	0	0	0

Going (Turf): **Sf: 0-0 GS: 0-0 Gd: 0-0 GF: 0-2 Fm: 0-0**
Distance: 5f/6f: 0-0 7f-8f: 0-3 9f-13f: 0-5 14f+: 0-0
Track : LH: 0-4 RH: 0-2 Tight: 0-4 Gall: 0-0
Aids: Bl: 0-0 Vi: 0-0 Tstrap: 0-2 Ckp: 0-2
Best Rating: **46** 11/09 Ling 1m2f stand

Viking Awake (IRE)

99(78) (46)**68**
3-y-o b g Almutawakel-Norwegian Queen (IRE) (Affirmed (USA))
J W Unett P Fetherston-Godley

Placings:5540-066400 (6175)
2009: 7^{0}GF, 8^{6}GF, 5^{6}GF, 6^{4}GF, 7^{0}G, 7^{0}GF,

	Starts	1st	2nd	3rd	Win & Pl
Career Total (Turf)	9	0	0	0	649
Career Total (AW)	1	0	0	0	

Going (Turf): **Sf: 0-1 GS: 0-1 Gd: 0-1 GF: 0-6 Fm: 0-0**
Distance: 5f/6f: 0-2 7f-8f: 0-6 9f-13f: 0-2 14f+: 0-0
Track : LH: 0-4 RH: 0-2 Tight: 0-2 Gall: 0-0
Aids: Bl: 0-0 Vi: 0-0 Tstrap: 0-0 Ckp: 0-0
Best Rating: **68** 8/08 Hayd 1m30y soft

Viking Dancer

97 **80**
2-y-o b c Danehill Dancer (IRE)-Blue Siren (Bluebird (USA))
A M Balding J C Smith

Placings:0524 (6364)
2009: 6^{0}G, 7^{5}GF, 7^{2}G, 7^{4}GF,

	Starts	1st	2nd	3rd	Win & Pl
Career Total (Turf)	4	0	1	0	1324

Going (Turf): **Sf: 0-0 GS: 0-0 Gd: 0-2 GF: 0-2 Fm: 0-0**
Distance: 5f/6f: 0-1 7f-8f: 0-3 9f-13f: 0-0 14f+: 0-0
Track : LH: 0-1 RH: 0-1 Tight: 0-0 Gall: 0-0
Aids: Bl: 0-0 Vi: 0-0 Tstrap: 0-0 Ckp: 0-0
Best Rating: **80** 9/09 Chep 7f16y good

Fair; stays 7f; acts on a sound surface.

Viking Spirit

104(108) (107)**105**
7-y-o b g Mind Games-Dane Dancing (IRE) (Danehill (USA))
W R Swinburn The Masterminds

Placings:022110/23300/50322/4010200/010400-63020460 (7227)
2009: 6^{6}GF, 6^{3}GF, 6^{0}G, 6^{2}G, 6^{0}GF, 6^{4}SD, 6^{6}GS, 6^{0}SD,

	Starts	1st	2nd	3rd	Win & Pl
Career Total (Turf)	28	4	4	3	62959
Career Total (AW)	9	0	3	1	14066

105	5/08	Gdwd	6f	(0-100)H	SFT	£12462
108	7/07	Chep	6f16y	(0-100)H	SFT	£12464
96	9/04	Nott	6f15y	(0-75)	G-S	£4403
87	9/04	Wwck	6f21y	(0-85)H	G-F	£6162

Total win prize-money £35492

Going (Turf): **Sf: 2-2** GS: 1-8 Gd: 0-9 GF: 1-9 Fm: 0-0
Distance: 5f/6f: 1-29 **7f-8f: 3-8** 9f-13f: 0-0 14f+: 0-0
Track : **LH: 1-6** RH: 0-5 Tight: 0-3 Gall: 0-4
Aids: Bl: 0-0 Vi: 0-1 Tstrap: 0-2 Ckp: 0-2
Best Rating: **108** 7/07 Chep 6f16y soft

Very useful; suited by 6f-7f; acts on most ground and on Polytrack; has worn a visor, cheekpieces and tongue tie.

Villaruz (IRE)

95(99) (65)**54**
3-y-o b g Fayruz-Villaminta (IRE) (Grand Lodge (USA))
J W Unett (D Flood 29/6) S Lau

Placings:0-302204100 (7815)
2009: 5^{3}SD, 5^{0}SD, 5^{2}SD, 7^{2}SF, 7^{0}SD, 5^{4}F, 5^{1}SD, 5^{0}SD, 5^{0}SD,

	Starts	1st	2nd	3rd	Win & Pl
Career Total (Turf)	2	0	0	0	144
Career Total (AW)	8	1	2	1	3950

65 4/09 Wolv 5f20y (0-65)H STD £2388
Total win prize-money £2388

Going (Turf): Sf: 0-1 GS: 0-0 Gd: 0-0 GF: 0-0 Fm: 0-1
Distance: 5f/6f: 1-8 7f-8f: 0-2 9f-13f: 0-0 14f+: 0-0
Track : LH: 1-9 RH: 0-0 Tight: 1-8 Gall: 0-0
Aids: Bl: 1-2 Vi: 0-0 Tstrap: 0-0 Ckp: 0-0
Best Rating: 65 4/09 Wolv 5f20y stand

Moderate; effective over 5f-6f; acts on Polytrack.

Vilnius

97(95) (59)**61**
2-y-o b f Imperial Dancer-Aces Dancing (GER) (Big Shuffle (USA))
M R Channon P Trant

Placings:41223562440503211OO (7884)
2009: 5^{4}GF, 5^{1}GF, 5^{2}F, 5^{2}GS, 5^{3}GF, 5^{5}S, 5^{6}G, 5^{2}GF, 5^{4}SD, 5^{4}GF, 5^{0}GF, 5^{5}SD, 5^{0}GF, 5^{3}GF, 5^{2}SD, 5^{1}S, 5^{1}SD, 5^{0}SD, 7^{0}SD,

	Starts	1st	2nd	3rd	Win & Pl
Career Total (Turf)	13	2	3	2	11341
Career Total (AW)	6	1	1	0	4078

59 11/09 Wolv 5f20y (0-60) STD £2729
56 11/09 Nott 5f13y (0-70) SFT £3238
61 4/09 Catt 5f G-F £2047
Total win prize-money £8015

Going (Turf): Sf: 1-2 GS: 0-1 Gd: 0-1 GF: 1-8 Fm: 0-1
Distance: 5f/6f: 3-18 7f-8f: 0-1 9f-13f: 0-0 14f+: 0-0
Track : LH: 1-7 RH: 0-1 Tight: 1-5 Gall: 0-1
Aids: Bl: 0-0 Vi: 0-0 Tstrap: 0-0 Ckp: 0-0
Best Rating: 61 4/09 Catt 5f gd-fm

Moderate; effective over 5f; acts on fast and easy ground; goes on Polytrack.

Vimiero (USA)

94 **85**
2-y-o b/br c Dynaformer (USA)-Merrymaker (ARG) (Rainbow Corner)
W R Swinburn P W Harris

Placings:43 (6663)
2009: 7^{4}GF, 7^{3}GS,

	Starts	1st	2nd	3rd	Win & Pl
Career Total (Turf)	2	0	0	1	1644

Going (Turf): Sf: 0-0 GS: 0-1 Gd: 0-0 GF: 0-1 Fm: 0-0
Distance: 5f/6f: 0-0 7f-8f: 0-2 9f-13f: 0-0 14f+: 0-0
Track : LH: 0-0 RH: 0-0 Tight: 0-0 Gall: 0-0
Aids: Bl: 0-0 Vi: 0-0 Tstrap: 0-0 Ckp: 0-0
Best Rating: 85 10/09 Asct 7f gd-sft

Useful; stays 7f; acts on easy ground.

Vin De Rose

89(73) (37)**35**
3-y-o b g Tipsy Creek (USA)-Rosewings (In The Wings)
John A Harris Miss Vivian Pratt

Placings:0-0000000 (6170)
2009: 8^{0}G, 8^{0}SD, 10^{0}G, 11^{0}G, 10^{0}GF, 8^{0}SD, 7^{0}GF,

	Starts	1st	2nd	3rd	Win & Pl
Career Total (Turf)	6	0	0	0	
Career Total (AW)	2	0	0	0	

Going (Turf): Sf: 0-1 GS: 0-0 Gd: 0-3 GF: 0-2 Fm: 0-0
Distance: 5f/6f: 0-0 7f-8f: 0-1 9f-13f: 0-7 14f+: 0-0
Track : LH: 0-5 RH: 0-0 Tight: 0-5 Gall: 0-0
Aids: Bl: 0-0 Vi: 0-0 Tstrap: 0-0 Ckp: 0-0
Best Rating: 37 6/09 Wolv 1m141y stand

Vinces

101(103) (71)**71**
5-y-o gr g Lomitas-Vadinaxa (FR) (Linamix (FR))
T D McCarthy Eastwell Manor Racing Ltd

Placings:23/1005320020-601615345052200 (7777)
2009: 13^{6}SD, 13^{0}SD, 10^{1}SD, 10^{6}SD, 10^{1}SD, 9^{5}GF, 9^{3}GF, 10^{4}GF, 10^{5}G, 10^{0}GS, 10^{5}F, 12^{2}GS, 10^{2}SD, 10^{0}SD, 12^{0}SD,

	Starts	1st	2nd	3rd	Win & Pl
Career Total (Turf)	14	1	2	2	5842
Career Total (AW)	13	2	3	1	7029

71 4/09 Ling 1m2f (0-65)H STD £2047
68 3/09 Ling 1m2f (0-70)H STD £2590
71 5/08 Ling 1m2f G-F £3238
Total win prize-money £7875

Going (Turf): Sf: 0-3 GS: 0-3 Gd: 0-1 GF: 1-6 Fm: 0-1
Distance: 5f/6f: 0-0 7f-8f: 0-0 9f-13f: 3-24 14f+: 0-3
Track : LH: 3-16 RH: 0-9 Tight: 3-18 Gall: 0-4
Aids: Bl: 0-0 Vi: 0-0 Tstrap: 0-0 Ckp: 0-0
Best Rating: 71 11/09 Ling 1m2f stand

Modest; effective from 1m2f-1m6f; acts on most ground and on Polytrack.

Vinorine (FR)

(96) (49)**34**
5-y-o b m Majorien-Vin Sur Vin (FR) (Saint Estephe (FR))
R P Burns Philip McGee

Placings:016/5010201655/0-000 (3181a)
2009: 9^{0}SD, 11^{0}Y, 12^{0}GF,

	Starts	1st	2nd	3rd	Win & Pl
Career Total (Turf)	16	3	1	0	12752
Career Total (AW)	1	0	0	0	

9/07 Crao 1m3f G-S £4391
6/07 Lrsy 1m4f GD £2364
9/06 Vire 1m1f GD £2413
Total win prize-money £9171

Going (Turf): Sf: 0-2 GS: 1-7 Gd: 2-3 GF: 0-1 Fm: 0-0
Distance: 5f/6f: 0-1 7f-8f: 0-1 9f-13f: 3-14 14f+: 0-1
Track : LH: 0-1 RH: 0-2 Tight: 0-1 Gall: 0-0
Aids: Bl: 0-0 Vi: 0-0 Tstrap: 0-1 Ckp: 0-1
Best Rating: 62 11/07 Pari 1m5f soft

Vintage (IRE)

(112) (87)**66**
5-y-o b g Danetime (IRE)-Katherine Gorge (USA) (Hansel (USA))
J Akehurst Taylor And Sheldon Partners

Placings:0/000015/1005222152-40 (7832)
2009: 6^{4}SD, 6^{0}SD,

	Starts	1st	2nd	3rd	Win & Pl
Career Total (Turf)	4	0	0	0	
Career Total (AW)	15	3	4	0	16204

85 8/08 Ling 6f (0-80)H STD £4727
72 4/08 Kemp 6f (0-70)H STD £2590
68 10/07 Wolv 5f216y (0-55) STD £2047
Total win prize-money £9365

Going (Turf): Sf: 0-0 GS: 0-2 Gd: 0-1 GF: 0-1 Fm: 0-0
Distance: 5f/6f: 3-15 7f-8f: 0-4 9f-13f: 0-0 14f+: 0-0
Track : LH: 2-9 RH: 1-6 Tight: 2-8 Gall: 0-1
Aids: Bl: 0-0 Vi: 0-0 Tstrap: 0-0 Ckp: 0-0
Best Rating: 87 10/08 Ling 6f stand

Fair; seems best over 6f; acts on Polytrack; has worn a tongue tie.

Viola Rosa (IRE)

81(80) (42)**32**
4-y-o b f Fraam-Bleu Cerise (Sadler's Wells (USA))
J G Given Danethorpe Racing Partnership

Placings:00060/000 (4550)
2009: 10^{0}G, 10^{0}GF, 7^{0}GS,

	Starts	1st	2nd	3rd	Win & Pl
Career Total (Turf)	5	0	0	0	
Career Total (AW)	3	0	0	0	0

Going (Turf): Sf: 0-0 GS: 0-2 Gd: 0-1 GF: 0-2 Fm: 0-0
Distance: 5f/6f: 0-0 7f-8f: 0-6 9f-13f: 0-2 14f+: 0-0
Track : LH: 0-5 RH: 0-2 Tight: 0-3 Gall: 0-2
Aids: Bl: 0-0 Vi: 0-0 Tstrap: 0-0 Ckp: 0-0
Best Rating: 42 12/07 Kemp 7f stand

Violent Velocity (IRE)

105 (71)**85**
6-y-o b g Namid-Lear's Crown (USA) (Lear Fan (USA))
J J Quinn Mrs S Quinn

Placings:54/100000/46203110453422600/032224431244444000-00015332110200 (7220)
2009: 7^{0}GF, 8^{0}F, 8^{0}GF, 7^{1}G, 7^{5}G, 7^{3}GF, 7^{3}G, 7^{2}G, 7^{1}GF, 7^{1}GF, 7^{0}G, 7^{2}GS, 7^{0}GF, 7^{0}S,

	Starts	1st	2nd	3rd	Win & Pl
Career Total (Turf)	49	6	8	6	38287
Career Total (AW)	7	1	1	0	4009

81 8/09 Epsm 7f (0-75)H G-F £3885
78 8/09 Newc 7f (0-75)H G-F £2901
74 6/09 NmkJ 7f (0-70)H GD £3885
83 7/08 Thsk 7f (0-75)H G-F £4274
72 5/07 Muss 7f30y (0-65)H G-F £2590
71 4/07 Catt 5f212y (0-65)H G-F £2730
79 2/06 Wolv 7f32y SF £3238
Total win prize-money £23508

Going (Turf): Sf: 0-6 GS: 0-8 Gd: 1-15 GF: 5-18 Fm: 0-2
Distance: 5f/6f: 1-10 7f-8f: 6-43 9f-13f: 0-3 14f+: 0-0
Track : LH: 4-36 RH: 1-7 Tight: 5-31 Gall: 0-4
Aids: Bl: 0-0 Vi: 0-2 Tstrap: 0-0 Ckp: 0-0
Best Rating: 85 7/08 York 1m heavy

Fair; stays 1m; acts on fast and easy ground; also goes on Polytrack.

Viper

71(97) (89)**95**
7-y-o b g Polar Prince (IRE)-Maradata (IRE) (Shardari)
R Hollinshead Geoff Lloyd

Placings:11-0025 (7701)
2009: 16^{0}G, 18^{0}G, 16^{2}SD, 16^{5}SD,

	Starts	1st	2nd	3rd	Win & Pl
Career Total (Turf)	4	2	0	0	12304

Career Total (AW) 2 0 1 0 1407
95 10/08 NmkR 2m (0-90)H G-S £9066
86 10/08 Gdwd 1m6f G-F £3238
Total win prize-money £12304

Going (Turf): Sf: 0-0 **GS: 1-1** Gd: 0-2 **GF: 1-1** Fm: 0-0
Distance: 5f/6f: 0-0 7f-8f: 0-0 9f-13f: 0-0 **14f+: 2-6**
Track : LH: 0-0 **RH: 2-6** Tight: 1-1 Gall: 1-2
Aids: Bl: 0-0 Vi: 0-0 Tstrap: 0-0 Ckp: 0-0
Best Rating: 95 10/08 NmkR 2m gd-sft

Useful; stays 2m; acts on easy ground; handles Polytrack.

Virginia Hall

92(98) (75)104
2-y-o b f Medicean-Odette (Pursuit Of Love)
Sir Mark Prescott C G Rowles Nicholson

Placings:02121226 (5825)
2009: 5[0]GS, **5[2]SD**, 5[1]GF, 5[2]GF, 6[1]SD, 6[2]S, 7[2]G, 8[6]GF,

	Starts	1st	2nd	3rd	Win & Pl
Career Total (Turf)	6	1	3	0	31565
Career Total (AW)	2	1	1	0	5154

75 7/09 Sthl 6f STD £4094
80 6/09 Wind 5f10y G-F £2729
Total win prize-money £6824

Going (Turf): Sf: 0-1 GS: 0-1 Gd: 0-1 **GF: 1-3** Fm: 0-0
Distance: **5f/6f: 2-6** 7f-8f: 0-2 9f-13f: 0-0 14f+: 0-0
Track : **LH: 1-3** RH: 0-1 Tight: 0-1 **Gall: 1-1**
Aids: Bl: 0-0 Vi: 0-0 Tstrap: 0-0 Ckp: 0-0
Best Rating: 104 8/09 Deau 7f good

Fair; effective over 6-7f; acts on fast ground, on Polytrack and on Fibresand.

Virtual

114 119
4-y-o b c Pivotal-Virtuous (Exit To Nowhere (USA))
J H M Gosden Cheveley Park Stud

Placings:22/130111-316330 (6850)
2009: 8[3]G, 8[1]S, 10[6]GF, 8[3]G, 8[3]GS, 10[0]G,

	Starts	1st	2nd	3rd	Win & Pl
Career Total (Turf)	14	5	2	4	336879

119 5/09 Newb 1m SFT £141925
117 11/08 NmkR 1m G-S £22708
102 10/08 MsnL 1m1f SFT £20221
103 9/08 Donc 1m (0-110)H SFT £12952
92 4/08 NmkR 7f GD £5180
Total win prize-money £202987

Going (Turf): **Sf: 3-4** GS: 1-2 Gd: 1-5 GF: 0-3 Fm: 0-0
Distance: 5f/6f: 0-0 **7f-8f: 4-9** 9f-13f: 1-5 14f+: 0-0
Track : LH: 0-0 **RH: 1-5** Tight: 0-0 Gall: 0-1
Aids: Bl: 0-0 Vi: 0-0 Tstrap: 0-0 Ckp: 0-0
Best Rating: 119 5/09 Newb 1m soft

High class; progressed to just land Lockinge Stakes in 2009; stays 1m1f; acts on most ground, but ideally suited by give.

Virtuality (USA)

91(72) (16)60
4-y-o b/br f Elusive Quality (USA)-Hold To Ransom (USA) (Red Ransom (USA))
B Smart Crossfields Racing

Placings:60250-5000 (4432)
2009: 6[5]F, 6[0]G, 6[0]SD, 7[0]GF,

	Starts	1st	2nd	3rd	Win & Pl
Career Total (Turf)	8	0	1	0	964
Career Total (AW)	1	0	0	0	

Going (Turf): Sf: 0-0 GS: 0-2 Gd: 0-3 GF: 0-2 Fm: 0-1
Distance: 5f/6f: 0-3 7f-8f: 0-6 9f-13f: 0-0 14f+: 0-0
Track : LH: 0-4 RH: 0-0 Tight: 0-2 Gall: 0-0
Aids: Bl: 0-0 Vi: 0-0 Tstrap: 0-0 Ckp: 0-0
Best Rating: 60 6/08 Donc 6f good

Viscaya (IRE)

(84) (26)57
4-y-o b f Xaar-Fearfully Grand (Grand Lodge (USA))
N J Vaughan A Black

Placings:0650/20-0 (0215)
2009: 8[0]SD,

	Starts	1st	2nd	3rd	Win & Pl
Career Total (Turf)	6	0	1	0	907
Career Total (AW)	1	0	0	0	

Going (Turf): Sf: 0-0 GS: 0-1 Gd: 0-2 GF: 0-2 Fm: 0-1
Distance: 5f/6f: 0-4 7f-8f: 0-1 9f-13f: 0-2 14f+: 0-0
Track : LH: 0-3 RH: 0-1 Tight: 0-4 Gall: 0-0
Aids: Bl: 0-0 Vi: 0-0 Tstrap: 0-2 Ckp: 0-2
Best Rating: 57 9/07 Hayd 6f gd-fm

Viscount Nelson (USA)

104 112
2-y-o b c Giant's Causeway (USA)-Imagine (IRE) (Sadler's Wells (USA))
A P O'Brien Mrs John Magnier & Mrs David Nagle

Placings:31120 (7304a)
2009: 7[3]S, 8[1]Y, 7[1]S, 7[2]GF, 8[0]F,

	Starts	1st	2nd	3rd	Win & Pl
Career Total (Turf)	5	2	1	1	67614

98 8/09 Tipp 7f100y SFT £33182
83 7/09 Leop 1m YLD £11740
Total win prize-money £44922

Going (Turf): **Sf: 1-2** GS: 0-0 Gd: 0-0 GF: 0-1 Fm: 0-1
Distance: 5f/6f: 0-0 **7f-8f: 2-5** 9f-13f: 0-0 14f+: 0-0
Track : **LH: 2-3** RH: 0-0 Tight: 0-0 Gall: 0-0
Aids: Bl: 0-0 Vi: 0-0 Tstrap: 0-0 Ckp: 0-0
Best Rating: 112 9/09 Donc 7f gd-fm

Listed winner; half-brother to high-class but ill-fated 7f 2yo winner Horatio Nelson, smart middle-distance performer Red Rock Canyon and 7f Group 2 winner Kitty Matcham; dam won Oaks and Irsh 1000 Guineas; effective over 1m; acts on softish ground.

Viscount Rossini

(96) (50)50
7-y-o b/br g Rossini (USA)-Spain (Polar Falcon (USA))
S Gollings L M Baker

Placings:0405/05460005/050463660-5 (0169)
2009: 13[5]SD,

	Starts	1st	2nd	3rd	Win & Pl
Career Total (Turf)	9	0	0	0	192
Career Total (AW)	13	0	0	1	608

Going (Turf): Sf: 0-0 GS: 0-1 Gd: 0-3 GF: 0-3 Fm: 0-2
Distance: 5f/6f: 0-0 7f-8f: 0-0 9f-13f: 0-18 14f+: 0-4
Track : LH: 0-21 RH: 0-0 Tight: 0-12 Gall: 0-1
Aids: Bl: 0-3 Vi: 0-1 Tstrap: 0-1 Ckp: 0-1
Best Rating: 50 7/08 Nott 1m2f50y gd-sft

Vision D'Etat (FR)

117 124
4-y-o b c Chichicastenango (FR)-Uberaba (FR) (Garde Royale)
E Libaud Jacques Detre

Placings:11/11115-311201 (7747a)
2009: 10[3]G, 10[1]G, 10[1]GF, 12[2]G, 12[0]G, 10[1]G,

	Starts	1st	2nd	3rd	Win & Pl
Career Total (Turf)	13	9	1	1	2305700

124 12/09 ShTn 1m2f GD £1023339
124 6/09 Asct 1m2f G-F £255465
121 4/09 Lonc 1m2f110y GD £166427
117 9/08 Lonc 1m4f G-S £54485
122 6/08 Chan 1m2f110y SFT £630221
109 4/08 Chan 1m2f VS £20221
101 3/08 StCl 1m2f HLD £12500
93 11/07 Fntb 1m1f VS £11486
9/07 Sabl 1m1f165y GD £6418
Total win prize-money £2180563

Going (Turf): Sf: 1-1 GS: 1-2 **Gd: 3-6** GF: 1-1 Fm: 0-0
Distance: 5f/6f: 0-0 7f-8f: 0-0 **9f-13f: 9-13** 14f+: 0-0
Track : LH: 1-1 **RH: 6-10** Tight: 0-0 **Gall: 1-1**
Aids: Bl: 0-0 Vi: 0-0 Tstrap: 0-0 Ckp: 0-0
Best Rating: 124 12/09 ShTn 1m2f good

High-class; won Prix du Jockey Club in 2008 and Prix Ganay, Prince of Wales's Stakes and Hong Kong Cup in 2009; effective at 1m2f-1m4f; acts on most ground.

Visions Of Johanna (USA)

101(107) (88)87
4-y-o b g Johannesburg (USA)-Belle Turquoise (FR) (Tel Quel (FR))
R A Fahey Dr Marwan Koukash

Placings:22145-522000 (5409)
2009: 8[5]S, 11[2]GF, 10[2]S, 9[0]S, 8[0]GF, 7[0]G,

	Starts	1st	2nd	3rd	Win & Pl
Career Total (Turf)	7	1	2	0	5655
Career Total (AW)	4	0	2	0	2394

82 7/08 Sand 1m14y G-F £3885
Total win prize-money £3886

Going (Turf): Sf: 0-3 GS: 0-0 Gd: 0-1 **GF: 1-3** Fm: 0-0
Distance: 5f/6f: 0-0 7f-8f: 0-6 **9f-13f: 1-5** 14f+: 0-0
Track : LH: 0-5 **RH: 1-6** Tight: 0-6 Gall: 0-0
Aids: Bl: 0-0 Vi: 0-0 Tstrap: 0-2 Ckp: 0-2
Best Rating: 88 12/08 Ling 1m stand

Useful; stays 1m3f; acts on fast ground; also goes on Polytrack.

Visite Royale (USA)

101(88) (66)79
3-y-o b f Danehill Dancer (IRE)-Fantasy Royale (USA) (Pleasant Colony (USA))
Sir Michael Stoute Mrs Elizabeth Moran

Placings:4-2421 (4347)
2009: 7[2]G, 8[4]GF, 9[2]G, 9[1]G,

	Starts	1st	2nd	3rd	Win & Pl
Career Total (Turf)	4	1	2	0	5865
Career Total (AW)	1	0	0	0	313

73 7/09 Carl 1m1f61y GD £2590
Total win prize-money £2590

Going (Turf): Sf: 0-0 GS: 0-0 **Gd: 1-3** GF: 0-1 Fm: 0-0
Distance: 5f/6f: 0-0 7f-8f: 0-3 **9f-13f: 1-2** 14f+: 0-0
Track : LH: 0-0 **RH: 1-5** Tight: 0-0 Gall: 0-0
Aids: Bl: 0-0 Vi: 0-0 Tstrap: 0-0 Ckp: 0-0
Best Rating: 79 7/09 Leic 1m1f218y good

Fair; stays 1m2f and acts on good and fast ground.

Visterre (IRE)

84 **83**

3-y-o ch f Noverre (USA)-Twiggy's Sister (IRE) (Flying Spur (AUS))
B Smart Prime Equestrian

Placings:4011315-00 **(3096)**
2009: 5^{0}GS, 6^{0}G,

	Starts	1st	2nd	3rd	Win & Pl
Career Total (Turf)	**9**	**3**	**0**	**1**	**14639**

83 10/08 Muss 5f (0-85) G-S £6476
80 7/08 Muss 5f G-F £3885
66 6/08 Muss 5f G-F £3238
Total win prize-money £13600

Going (Turf): Sf: 0-3 GS: 1-2 Gd: 0-1 **GF: 2-3** Fm: 0-0
Distance: **5f/6f: 3-9** 7f-8f: 0-0 9f-13f: 0-0 14f+: 0-0
Track : LH: 0-0 RH: 0-2 Tight: 0-0 Gall: 0-1
Aids: Bl: 0-0 Vi: 0-0 Tstrap: 0-0 Ckp: 0-0
Best Rating: 83 10/08 Muss 5f gd-sft

Useful; effective over 5f-6f; acts on quick and soft ground.

Vita Mia

102(97) (52)**68**

3-y-o b f Central Park (IRE)-Ma Vie (Salse (USA))
P D Evans Lady Lonsdale & Mickley Stud

Placings:00-04004516211640335 **(6784)**
2009: 9^{0}GF, 9^{4}F, **11**^{0}SD, 8^{0}GF, 8^{4}GF, 10^{5}GF, 11^{1}GF, 14^{6}S, 9^{2}F, 12^{1}GF, 10^{1}G, 11^{6}GF, 13^{4}G, 10^{0}GF, 13^{3}GF, 9^{3}GF, **10**^{5}SS,

	Starts	1st	2nd	3rd	Win & Pl
Career Total (Turf)	**16**	**3**	**1**	**2**	**12725**
Career Total (AW)	**3**	**0**	**0**	**0**	**0**

68 8/09 Ches 1m2f75y (0-75)H GD £4435
58 7/09 Folk 1m4f (0-70)H G-F £3070
59 6/09 Leic 1m3f183y (0-70)H G-F £2590
Total win prize-money £10097

Going (Turf): Sf: 0-1 GS: 0-0 Gd: 1-3 **GF: 2-10** Fm: 0-2
Distance: 5f/6f: 0-0 7f-8f: 0-1 **9f-13f: 3-15** 14f+: 0-3
Track : LH: 1-13 **RH: 2-4 Tight: 2-12** Gall: 0-0
Aids: Bl: 0-0 Vi: 0-0 Tstrap: 0-0 Ckp: 0-0
Best Rating: 68 8/09 Ches 1m2f75y good

Modest; effective over 1m2f-1m5f; acts on good ground.

Vito Volterra (IRE)

93(97) (69)**73**

2-y-o b c Antonius Pius (USA)-River Abouali (Bluebird (USA))
A B Haynes (J R Best 16/10) Ms J Loylert

Placings:061131 **(7661)**
2009: 6^{0}G, 7^{6}SS, 7^{1}GF, 7^{1}G, 7^{3}SD, **6**^{1}SD,

	Starts	1st	2nd	3rd	Win & Pl
Career Total (Turf)	**3**	**2**	**0**	**0**	**3990**
Career Total (AW)	**3**	**1**	**0**	**1**	**2382**

69 12/09 Ling 6f STD £1978
66 10/09 Yarm 7f3y GD £1942
73 10/09 Rdcr 7f G-F £2047
Total win prize-money £5969

Going (Turf): Sf: 0-0 GS: 0-0 **Gd: 1-2 GF: 1-1** Fm: 0-0
Distance: 5f/6f: 1-2 **7f-8f: 2-4** 9f-13f: 0-0 14f+: 0-0
Track : **LH: 1-3** RH: 0-0 **Tight: 1-3** Gall: 0-1
Aids: Bl: 0-0 Vi: 0-0 Tstrap: 0-0 Ckp: 0-0
Best Rating: 73 10/09 Rdcr 7f gd-fm

Fair; stays 7f; acts on fast ground and on Polytrack.

Vitoria (IRE)

104(92) (79)**102**

3-y-o b f Exceed And Excel (AUS)-Karayb (IRE) (Last Tycoon)
B Smart H E Sheikh Rashid Bin Mohammed

Placings:212-00262132 **(6814)**
2009: 10^{0}GF, 8^{0}GF, 7^{2}G, 8^{6}GF, 7^{2}GF, 6^{1}G, 6^{3}GF, 6^{2}G,

	Starts	1st	2nd	3rd	Win & Pl
Career Total (Turf)	**10**	**2**	**4**	**1**	**212882**
Career Total (AW)	**1**	**0**	**1**	**0**	**1445**

102 9/09 Haml 6f5y (0-95)H GD £11009
81 7/08 Thsk 7f G-F £5569
Total win prize-money £16578

Going (Turf): Sf: 0-0 GS: 0-0 **Gd: 1-3 GF: 1-7** Fm: 0-0
Distance: 5f/6f: 0-2 **7f-8f: 2-8** 9f-13f: 0-1 14f+: 0-0
Track : **LH: 1-2** RH: 0-2 **Tight: 1-1** Gall: 0-2
Aids: Bl: 0-0 Vi: 0-0 Tstrap: 0-0 Ckp: 0-0
Best Rating: 102 10/09 NmkR 6f good

Very useful; effective over 6f-7f; acts on fast ground; goes on Polytrack.

Vittachi

83(89) (48)**46**

2-y-o b g Bertolini (USA)-Miss Lorilaw (FR) (Homme De Loi (IRE))
J D Bethell Clarendon Thoroughbred Racing

Placings:056504 **(7788)**
2009: 7^{0}G, 7^{5}GF, 7^{6}GF, 8^{5}GF, 8^{0}SD, 8^{4}SD,

	Starts	1st	2nd	3rd	Win & Pl
Career Total (Turf)	**4**	**0**	**0**	**0**	**233**
Career Total (AW)	**2**	**0**	**0**	**0**	**0**

Going (Turf): **Sf: 0-0 GS: 0-0 Gd: 0-1 GF: 0-3 Fm: 0-0**
Distance: 5f/6f: 0-0 7f-8f: 0-4 9f-13f: 0-2 14f+: 0-0
Track : LH: 0-4 RH: 0-1 Tight: 0-2 Gall: 0-0
Aids: Bl: 0-2 Vi: 0-0 Tstrap: 0-2 Ckp: 0-2
Best Rating: 48 12/09 Wolv 1m141y stand

Vitznau (IRE)

111(109) (109)**105**

5-y-o b h Val Royal (FR)-Neat Dish (CAN) (Stalwart (USA))
R Hannon Louis Stalder

Placings:403641/221162442/01540465-24050605405 **(6732)**
2009: 7^{2}SD, 6^{4}GF, 7^{0}G, 8^{5}G, 7^{0}G, 7^{6}GF, 8^{0}G, **8**^{5}SD, 7^{4}GF, 7^{0}G, 8^{5}S,

	Starts	1st	2nd	3rd	Win & Pl
Career Total (Turf)	**27**	**3**	**2**	**1**	**57167**
Career Total (AW)	**7**	**1**	**3**	**0**	**22534**

108 4/08 Kemp 7f (0-100)H STD £9969
92 6/07 Ches 7f2y (0-90)H SFT £9463
90 6/07 Epsm 7f (0-100)H G-S £18696
73 10/06 Wind 6f G-S £3886
Total win prize-money £42016

Going (Turf): Sf: 1-4 **GS: 2-5** Gd: 0-9 GF: 0-9 Fm: 0-0
Distance: 5f/6f: 1-9 **7f-8f: 3-23** 9f-13f: 0-2 14f+: 0-0
Track : **LH: 2-8** RH: 1-9 **Tight: 2-7** Gall: 1-3
Aids: Bl: 0-0 Vi: 0-0 Tstrap: 0-0 Ckp: 0-0
Best Rating: 109 3/09 Wolv 7f32y stand

Smart; Listed placed; effective over 6f-1m; acts on most ground and on Polytrack.

Viva Averti

85 **35**

4-y-o b g Averti (IRE)-Julia Domna (Dominion)
R M Beckett (Christian Wroe 3/5) Christian Wroe

Placings:0P **(3460)**
2009: 6^{0}GF, 6^{P}GF,

	Starts	1st	2nd	3rd	Win & Pl
Career Total (Turf)	**2**	**0**	**0**	**0**	

Going (Turf): **Sf: 0-0 GS: 0-0 Gd: 0-0 GF: 0-2 Fm: 0-0**
Distance: 5f/6f: 0-2 7f-8f: 0-0 9f-13f: 0-0 14f+: 0-0
Track : LH: 0-0 RH: 0-0 Tight: 0-0 Gall: 0-1
Aids: Bl: 0-0 Vi: 0-0 Tstrap: 0-0 Ckp: 0-0
Best Rating: 35 5/09 Sals 6f gd-fm

Viva La Vida

93(83) (36)**66**

3-y-o ch f Medicean-Moonlight (IRE) (Night Shift (USA))
J Ryan (Jane Chapple-Hyam 29/5) Dallas Racing

Placings:0650000 **(5806)**
2009: 7^{0}SD, 7^{6}GF, 7^{5}GF, 9^{0}G, 8^{0}G, 8^{0}S, **8**^{0}SD,

	Starts	1st	2nd	3rd	Win & Pl
Career Total (Turf)	**5**	**0**	**0**	**0**	**0**
Career Total (AW)	**2**	**0**	**0**	**0**	

Going (Turf): **Sf: 0-1 GS: 0-0 Gd: 0-2 GF: 0-2 Fm: 0-0**
Distance: 5f/6f: 0-0 7f-8f: 0-5 9f-13f: 0-2 14f+: 0-0
Track : LH: 0-2 RH: 0-3 Tight: 0-4 Gall: 0-0
Aids: Bl: 0-0 Vi: 0-1 Tstrap: 0-0 Ckp: 0-0
Best Rating: 66 5/09 Ches 7f2y gd-fm

Speedily-bred; promise in maidens at up to 7f; acts on fast ground.

Viva Ronaldo (IRE)

97(99) (92)**99**

3-y-o b g Xaar-Papaha (FR) (Green Desert (USA))
R A Fahey Aykroyd And Sons Ltd

Placings:2214160-540060 **(5432)**
2009: **8**^{5}SD, 7^{4}GF, 8^{0}HY, 8^{0}GF, 7^{6}HY, 7^{0}GF,

	Starts	1st	2nd	3rd	Win & Pl
Career Total (Turf)	**12**	**2**	**2**	**0**	**34304**
Career Total (AW)	**1**	**0**	**0**	**0**	**1076**

99 8/08 Ches 6f18y G-F £9777
84 6/08 York 5f G-F £6929
Total win prize-money £16706

Going (Turf): Sf: 0-3 GS: 0-1 Gd: 0-2 **GF: 2-6** Fm: 0-0
Distance: 5f/6f: 1-5 7f-8f: 1-7 9f-13f: 0-1 14f+: 0-0
Track : **LH: 1-4** RH: 0-1 **Tight: 1-3** Gall: 0-0
Aids: Bl: 0-0 Vi: 0-0 Tstrap: 0-0 Ckp: 0-0
Best Rating: 99 8/08 Ches 6f18y gd-fm

Very useful; effective over 5f-7f; acts on fast ground.

Viva Vettori

107(109) (95)**93**

5-y-o ch h Vettori (IRE)-Cruinn A Bhord (Inchinor)

D R C Elsworth Mike Watson

Placings:351/160-25203 (3282)
2009: 8^{2}SD, 10^{5}SD, 9^{2}GF, 8^{0}GF, 8^{3}GF,

	Starts	1st	2nd	3rd	Win & Pl
Career Total (Turf)	6	0	1	2	11684
Career Total (AW)	5	2	1	0	14476

95 5/08 Kemp 1m (0-90)H STD £9346
82 9/07 Kemp 1m2f STD £2817
Total win prize-money £12164

Going (Turf): **Sf: 0-1 GS: 0-1 Gd: 0-0 GF: 0-4 Fm: 0-0**
Distance: 5f/6f: 0-0 7f-8f: 1-6 9f-13f: 1-5 14f+: 0-0
Track : LH: 0-0 **RH: 2-6** Tight: 0-0 Gall: 0-0
Aids: Bl: 0-0 Vi: 0-0 Tstrap: 0-0 Ckp: 0-0
Best Rating: **95** 5/08 Kemp 1m stand

Useful; effective at 1m-1m2f; acts on fast ground and on Polytrack; suited by forcing tactics; can take a hold.

Viva Volta

106 (83)**79**
6-y-o b g Superior Premium-La Volta (Komaite (USA))
A C Whillans Mrs L Irving

Placings:31000/1635230/064120615640/056006-221 (6765)
2009: 7^{2}GF, 7^{2}GF, 6^{1}G,

	Starts	1st	2nd	3rd	Win & Pl
Career Total (Turf)	31	5	4	3	25035
Career Total (AW)	2	0	0	0	351

79 10/09 Newc 6f (0-75)H GD £2525
84 8/07 Newc 7f (0-75)H G-F £4100
81 6/07 Newc 7f (0-70)H GD £3562
72 4/06 Bevl 7f100y (0-70)H G-S £3562
68 8/05 Carl 5f G-F £3474
Total win prize-money £17225

Going (Turf): Sf: 0-4 GS: 1-4 **Gd: 2-9 GF: 2-13** Fm: 0-1
Distance: 5f/6f: 2-9 **7f-8f: 3-23** 9f-13f: 0-1 14f+: 0-0
Track : LH: 0-10 **RH: 2-6** Tight: 0-10 **Gall: 1-3**
Aids: **Bl: 2-12** Vi: 1-1 Tstrap: 0-0 Ckp: 0-0
Best Rating: **84** 8/07 Newc 7f gd-fm

Fair; effective over 6f-1m; acts on fast ground and easy ground; has worn blinkers.

Vivachi (IRE)

100(101) (70)**78**
3-y-o b f Red Ransom (USA)-Charita (IRE) (Lycius (USA))
R M Beckett Trevor Stewart & Anthony Stroud

Placings:042166 (6740)
2009: 10^{0}SD, 9^{4}G, 10^{2}GF, 9^{1}HY, 11^{6}SD, 10^{6}GS,

	Starts	1st	2nd	3rd	Win & Pl
Career Total (Turf)	4	1	1	0	4980
Career Total (AW)	2	0	0	0	0

78 8/09 Leic 1m1f218y (0-70)H HVY £3885
Total win prize-money £3886

Going (Turf): **Sf: 1-1** GS: 0-1 Gd: 0-1 GF: 0-1 Fm: 0-0
Distance: 5f/6f: 0-0 7f-8f: 0-0 **9f-13f: 1-6** 14f+: 0-0
Track : LH: 0-1 **RH: 1-5** Tight: 0-4 Gall: 0-0
Aids: Bl: 0-0 Vi: 0-0 Tstrap: 0-0 Ckp: 0-0
Best Rating: **78** 8/09 Leic 1m1f218y heavy

Fair; effective over 1m2f; acts on any ground.

Viviani (IRE)

93 **67**
2-y-o ch g Galileo (IRE)-Bintalreef (USA) (Diesis)
Mrs A J Perrett John Connolly

Placings:0605 (6965)
2009: 7^{0}GF, 8^{6}GF, 9^{0}GS, 7^{5}G,

	Starts	1st	2nd	3rd	Win & Pl
Career Total (Turf)	4	0	0	0	204

Going (Turf): **Sf: 0-0 GS: 0-1 Gd: 0-1 GF: 0-2 Fm: 0-0**
Distance: 5f/6f: 0-0 7f-8f: 0-3 9f-13f: 0-1 14f+: 0-0
Track : LH: 0-1 RH: 0-1 Tight: 0-1 Gall: 0-0
Aids: Bl: 0-1 Vi: 0-0 Tstrap: 0-0 Ckp: 0-0
Best Rating: **67** 9/09 Sals 1m gd-fm

Vocabulary

(75) (31)
2-y-o br f Observatory (USA)-Zathonia (Zafonic (USA))
B W Hills K Abdulla

Placings:0 (7326)
2009: 7^{0}SD,

	Starts	1st	2nd	3rd	Win & Pl
Career Total (Turf)	0	0	0	0	
Career Total (AW)	1	0	0	0	

Going (Turf): **Sf: 0-0 GS: 0-0 Gd: 0-0 GF: 0-0 Fm: 0-0**
Distance: 5f/6f: 0-0 7f-8f: 0-1 9f-13f: 0-0 14f+: 0-0
Track : LH: 0-0 RH: 0-1 Tight: 0-0 Gall: 0-0
Aids: Bl: 0-0 Vi: 0-0 Tstrap: 0-0 Ckp: 0-0
Best Rating: **31** 11/09 Kemp 7f stand

Vocalised (USA)

108 **109**
3-y-o b c Vindication (USA)-Serena's Tune (USA) (Mr Prospector (USA))
J S Bolger Mrs J S Bolger

Placings:41-111055 (5921a)
2009: 7^{1}Y, 7^{1}S, 7^{1}HY, 8^{0}G, 6^{5}SH, 6^{5}S,

	Starts	1st	2nd	3rd	Win & Pl
Career Total (Turf)	8	4	0	0	129095

109 5/09 Curr 7f HVY £53723
108 4/09 Newb 7f SFT £36900
102 4/09 Curr 7f YLD £28441
80 9/08 Leop 7f YLD £9573
Total win prize-money £128640

Going (Turf): **Sf: 2-3** GS: 0-0 Gd: 0-1 GF: 0-0 Fm: 0-0
Distance: 5f/6f: 0-2 **7f-8f: 4-6** 9f-13f: 0-0 14f+: 0-0
Track : **LH: 1-2** RH: 0-0 Tight: 0-0 Gall: 0-0
Aids: Bl: 0-0 Vi: 0-0 Tstrap: 0-0 Ckp: 0-0
Best Rating: **109** 5/09 Curr 7f heavy

Smart; Listed winner; stays 7f; acts on easy ground; has worn a tongue tie.

Vodka Shot (USA)

(92) (50)
3-y-o b/br f Holy Bull (USA)-Absoluta (IRE) (Royal Academy (USA))
M L W Bell Christopher Wright

Placings:0500-00 (0296)
2009: 8^{0}SD, 8^{0}SD,

	Starts	1st	2nd	3rd	Win & Pl
Career Total (Turf)	0	0	0	0	
Career Total (AW)	6	0	0	0	0

Going (Turf): **Sf: 0-0 GS: 0-0 Gd: 0-0 GF: 0-0 Fm: 0-0**
Distance: 5f/6f: 0-0 7f-8f: 0-3 9f-13f: 0-3 14f+: 0-0
Track : LH: 0-5 RH: 0-1 Tight: 0-4 Gall: 0-0
Aids: Bl: 0-0 Vi: 0-0 Tstrap: 0-0 Ckp: 0-0
Best Rating: **50** 11/08 Wolv 1m141y stand

Vogarth

86(102) (69)**57**
5-y-o ch g Arkadian Hero (USA)-Skara Brae (Inchinor)
M C Chapman (B R Millman 4/1) Mrs M Chapman

Placings:034530/000403022100-14260 (7813)
2009: 7^{1}SS, 8^{4}SD, 8^{2}SD, 7^{6}GF, 7^{0}SD,

	Starts	1st	2nd	3rd	Win & Pl
Career Total (Turf)	13	0	0	3	1879
Career Total (AW)	10	2	3	0	6245

69 1/09 Sthl 7f SS £2047
64 11/08 Sthl 1m (0-60)H STD £1648
Total win prize-money £3695

Going (Turf): **Sf: 0-3 GS: 0-2 Gd: 0-1 GF: 0-6 Fm: 0-1**
Distance: 5f/6f: 0-8 **7f-8f: 2-15** 9f-13f: 0-0 14f+: 0-0
Track : **LH: 2-11** RH: 0-1 Tight: 0-1 Gall: 0-6
Aids: Bl: 0-3 **Vi: 1-2** Tstrap: 0-0 Ckp: 0-0
Best Rating: **69** 1/09 Sthl 7f std-slw

Moderate; effective at around 7f-1m; acts on easy ground and on Fibresand.

Volatilis (IRE)

84(84) (56)**63**
2-y-o b c Antonius Pius (USA)-Fire Flower (Sri Pekan (USA))
J W Hills P Abberley

Placings:065350 (5589)
2009: 6^{0}G, 6^{6}G, 6^{5}GF, 5^{3}GF, 7^{5}SD, 7^{0}GS,

	Starts	1st	2nd	3rd	Win & Pl
Career Total (Turf)	5	0	0	1	415
Career Total (AW)	1	0	0	0	0

Going (Turf): **Sf: 0-0 GS: 0-1 Gd: 0-2 GF: 0-2 Fm: 0-0**
Distance: 5f/6f: 0-3 7f-8f: 0-3 9f-13f: 0-0 14f+: 0-0
Track : LH: 0-2 RH: 0-1 Tight: 0-1 Gall: 0-0
Aids: Bl: 0-0 Vi: 0-0 Tstrap: 0-0 Ckp: 0-0
Best Rating: **63** 6/09 Sals 6f gd-fm

Volito

99(101) (67)**70**
3-y-o ch c Bertolini (USA)-Vax Rapide (Sharpo)
Jonjo O'Neill Mrs Liz Brazier

Placings:345041000 (4783)
2009: 7^{3}SD, 6^{4}SD, 5^{5}SD, 5^{0}G, 6^{4}F, 6^{1}GF, 6^{0}G, 6^{0}G, 6^{0}GF,

	Starts	1st	2nd	3rd	Win & Pl
Career Total (Turf)	6	1	0	0	2590
Career Total (AW)	3	0	0	1	403

70 6/09 Nott 6f15y (0-70)H G-F £2590
Total win prize-money £2590

Going (Turf): Sf: 0-0 GS: 0-0 Gd: 0-3 **GF: 1-2** Fm: 0-1
Distance: 5f/6f: 0-6 **7f-8f: 1-3** 9f-13f: 0-0 14f+: 0-0
Track : LH: 0-5 RH: 0-0 Tight: 0-3 Gall: 0-1
Aids: Bl: 0-0 Vi: 0-0 Tstrap: 0-0 Ckp: 0-0
Best Rating: **70** 6/09 Nott 6f15y gd-fm

Fair; stays 6f; acts on fast ground.

Volochkova (USA)

98(101) (79)**80**
3-y-o b f War Chant (USA)-Ballerina Princess (USA) (Mr Prospector (USA))

J R Fanshawe Mrs C C Regalado-Gonzalez

Placings:52-6105140 (4799)
2009: 8^{6}G, 7^{1}SD, 7^{0}GS, 6^{5}GF, 7^{1}SF, 7^{4}G, 8^{0}G,

	Starts	1st	2nd	3rd	Win & Pl
Career Total (Turf)	5	0	0	0	1203
Career Total (AW)	4	2	1	0	8087

79 7/09 Wolv 7f32y (0-75)H SF £3885
75 4/09 Ling 7f (0-70)H STD £3238
Total win prize-money £7124

Going (Turf): **Sf: 0-0 GS: 0-1 Gd: 0-3 GF: 0-1 Fm: 0-0**
Distance: 5f/6f: 0-0 **7f-8f: 2-8** 9f-13f: 0-1 14f+: 0-0
Track : **LH: 2-4** RH: 0-0 **Tight: 2-4** Gall: 0-0
Aids: Bl: 0-0 Vi: 0-0 Tstrap: 0-0 Ckp: 0-0
Best Rating: **80** 7/09 NmkJ 7f good

Fair; stays 7f; acts on Polytrack; has worn a tongue tie.

Von Jawlensky (IRE)

107 **106**
3-y-o b c Montjeu (IRE)-Zivania (IRE) (Shernazar)
A P O'Brien Michael Tabor

Placings:03-126010 (6710a)
2009: 10^{1}S, 12^{2}HY, 14^{6}Y, 14^{0}GF, 12^{1}Y, 12^{0}S,

	Starts	1st	2nd	3rd	Win & Pl
Career Total (Turf)	8	2	1	1	30782

106 9/09 List 1m4f YLD £12956
94 6/09 Curr 1m2f SFT £9056
Total win prize-money £22014

Going (Turf): **Sf: 1-4** GS: 0-0 Gd: 0-1 GF: 0-1 Fm: 0-0
Distance: 5f/6f: 0-0 7f-8f: 0-2 **9f-13f: 2-4** 14f+: 0-2
Track : LH: 1-3 RH: 1-5 Tight: 0-0 Gall: 0-1
Aids: Bl: 0-0 Vi: 0-0 Tstrap: 0-0 Ckp: 0-0
Best Rating: **106** 9/09 List 1m4f yield

Smart; effective over 1m4f; acts on soft ground.

Voortrekker

94(87) (71)**73**
3-y-o b g Imperial Dancer-Sweet Wilhelmina (Indian Ridge)
D J Coakley Chris Van Hoorn

Placings:321000 (6908)
2009: 8^{3}GF, 8^{2}F, 8^{1}SD, 10^{0}G, 9^{0}GF, 8^{0}G,

	Starts	1st	2nd	3rd	Win & Pl
Career Total (Turf)	5	0	1	1	1078
Career Total (AW)	1	1	0	0	3071

71 6/09 Wolv 1m141y STD £3070
Total win prize-money £3071

Going (Turf): **Sf: 0-0 GS: 0-0 Gd: 0-2 GF: 0-2 Fm: 0-1**
Distance: 5f/6f: 0-0 7f-8f: 0-0 **9f-13f: 1-6** 14f+: 0-0
Track : **LH: 1-3** RH: 0-3 **Tight: 1-6** Gall: 0-0
Aids: Bl: 0-0 Vi: 0-0 Tstrap: 0-0 Ckp: 0-0
Best Rating: **73** 5/09 Wind 1m67y gd-fm

Fair; stays 1m; acts on firm ground and Polytrack.

Vumbura (IRE)

83 **47**
2-y-o b g Alhaarth (IRE)-Mathaayl (USA) (Shadeed (USA))
W J Knight Mr and Mrs Mark Tracey

Placings:00 (7146)
2009: 7^{0}G, 7^{0}G,

	Starts	1st	2nd	3rd	Win & Pl
Career Total (Turf)	2	0	0	0	

Going (Turf): **Sf: 0-0 GS: 0-0 Gd: 0-2 GF: 0-0 Fm: 0-0**
Distance: 5f/6f: 0-0 7f-8f: 0-2 9f-13f: 0-0 14f+: 0-0
Track : LH: 0-0 RH: 0-0 Tight: 0-0 Gall: 0-0
Aids: Bl: 0-0 Vi: 0-0 Tstrap: 0-0 Ckp: 0-0
Best Rating: **47** 10/09 NmkR 7f good

Waabel

85 **58**
2-y-o b/br c Green Desert (USA)-Najah (IRE) (Nashwan (USA))
M A Jarvis Hamdan Al Maktoum

Placings:6 (4093)
2009: 6^{6}G,

	Starts	1st	2nd	3rd	Win & Pl
Career Total (Turf)	1	0	0	0	0

Going (Turf): **Sf: 0-0 GS: 0-0 Gd: 0-1 GF: 0-0 Fm: 0-0**
Distance: 5f/6f: 0-1 7f-8f: 0-0 9f-13f: 0-0 14f+: 0-0
Track : LH: 0-0 RH: 0-0 Tight: 0-0 Gall: 0-0
Aids: Bl: 0-0 Vi: 0-0 Tstrap: 0-0 Ckp: 0-0
Best Rating: **58** 7/09 NmkJ 6f good

Some promise on debut over 6f on good.

Waahej

95(100) (67)**66**
3-y-o b g Haafhd-Madam Ninette (Mark Of Esteem (IRE))
P W Hiatt (J L Dunlop 26/6) P W Hiatt

Placings:565-0503**6123036** (7752)
2009: 8^{0}GF, 8^{5}GS, 7^{0}GF, 8^{3}GF, 8^{6}SD, 9^{1}SD, 10^{2}SS, 11^{3}SD, 8^{0}SD, 9^{3}SD, 9^{6}SD,

	Starts	1st	2nd	3rd	Win & Pl
Career Total (Turf)	7	0	0	1	433
Career Total (AW)	7	1	1	2	5355

67 9/09 Wolv 1m1f103y (0-75)H STD £3885
Total win prize-money £3886

Going (Turf): **Sf: 0-0 GS: 0-2 Gd: 0-2 GF: 0-3 Fm: 0-0**
Distance: 5f/6f: 0-1 7f-8f: 0-7 **9f-13f: 1-6** 14f+: 0-0
Track : **LH: 1-8** RH: 0-1 **Tight: 1-4** Gall: 0-0
Aids: Bl: 0-0 Vi: 0-0 Tstrap: 0-0 Ckp: 0-0
Best Rating: **67** 12/09 Wolv 1m1f103y stand

Modest; stays 1m1f; acts on fast ground and on Polytrack.

Waarid

(83) (50)**66**
4-y-o b g Alhaarth (IRE)-Nibbs Point (IRE) (Sure Blade (USA))
G L Moore The Bad Boys

Placings:0650-6 (0300)
2009: 14^{6}SD,

	Starts	1st	2nd	3rd	Win & Pl
Career Total (Turf)	4	0	0	0	0
Career Total (AW)	1	0	0	0	0

Going (Turf): **Sf: 0-0 GS: 0-1 Gd: 0-2 GF: 0-1 Fm: 0-0**
Distance: 5f/6f: 0-0 7f-8f: 0-0 9f-13f: 0-4 14f+: 0-1
Track : LH: 0-2 RH: 0-3 Tight: 0-1 Gall: 0-0
Aids: Bl: 0-2 Vi: 0-0 Tstrap: 0-1 Ckp: 0-1
Best Rating: **66** 6/08 Leic 1m3f183y good

Wabbraan (USA)

93(109) (78)**59**
4-y-o b g Aldebaran (USA)-Madame Modjeska (USA) (Danzig (USA))

M Hill Martin Hill

Placings:060/0F032-1613000546 (7785)
2009: 12^{1}SD, 16^{6}SD, 12^{1}SD, 16^{3}SD, 16^{0}S, 12^{0}GS, 14^{0}G, 12^{5}SD, 16^{4}SD, 13^{6}SD,

	Starts	1st	2nd	3rd	Win & Pl
Career Total (Turf)	7	0	0	1	308
Career Total (AW)	11	2	1	1	6873

77 3/09 Sthl 1m4f (0-75)H STD £3070
65 2/09 Sthl 1m4f STD £2047
Total win prize-money £5118

Going (Turf): **Sf: 0-1 GS: 0-3 Gd: 0-2 GF: 0-1 Fm: 0-0**
Distance: 5f/6f: 0-0 7f-8f: 0-4 **9f-13f: 2-8** 14f+: 0-6
Track : **LH: 2-13** RH: 0-3 Tight: 0-6 Gall: 0-3
Aids: Bl: 0-1 Vi: 0-1 Tstrap: 0-0 Ckp: 0-0
Best Rating: **78** 4/09 Kemp 2m stand

Modest; stays 1m4f; acts on good ground and on Fibresand and Polytrack.

Wabi Sabi (IRE)

90(91) (63)**60**
3-y-o b f Xaar-Taroudannt (IRE) (Danehill (USA))
N Tinkler Killoran Civil Engineering Ltd

Placings:4360-05055 (3054)
2009: 7^{0}GF, 8^{5}G, 8^{0}G, 7^{5}GF, 9^{5}GF,

	Starts	1st	2nd	3rd	Win & Pl
Career Total (Turf)	8	0	0	0	529
Career Total (AW)	1	0	0	1	482

Going (Turf): **Sf: 0-0 GS: 0-1 Gd: 0-3 GF: 0-4 Fm: 0-0**
Distance: 5f/6f: 0-1 7f-8f: 0-5 9f-13f: 0-3 14f+: 0-0
Track : LH: 0-4 RH: 0-1 Tight: 0-2 Gall: 0-0
Aids: Bl: 0-0 Vi: 0-0 Tstrap: 0-1 Ckp: 0-1
Best Rating: **63** 9/08 Ling 7f stand

Wacato King (IRE)

(94) (48)
3-y-o br g King Charlemagne (USA)-Daralaka (IRE) (The Minstrel (CAN))
R A Farrant Eagle, Farrant, Fitzgerald, Sawers

Placings:0-000 (7755)
2009: 7^{0}SD, 7^{0}SD, 8^{0}SD,

	Starts	1st	2nd	3rd	Win & Pl
Career Total (Turf)	0	0	0	0	
Career Total (AW)	4	0	0	0	

Going (Turf): **Sf: 0-0 GS: 0-0 Gd: 0-0 GF: 0-0 Fm: 0-0**
Distance: 5f/6f: 0-1 7f-8f: 0-2 9f-13f: 0-1 14f+: 0-0
Track : LH: 0-4 RH: 0-0 Tight: 0-3 Gall: 0-0
Aids: Bl: 0-0 Vi: 0-0 Tstrap: 0-0 Ckp: 0-0
Best Rating: **48** 12/09 Wolv 1m141y stand

Wadaat

101(105) (73)**107**
3-y-o b f Diktat-Shining Vale (USA) (Twilight Agenda (USA))
C E Brittain Saeed Manana

Placings:32102030 (4094)
2009: 8^{3}SD, 10^{2}SD, 8^{1}G, 11^{0}GF, 11^{2}GF, 12^{0}G, 8^{3}G, 12^{0}G,

	Starts	1st	2nd	3rd	Win & Pl
Career Total (Turf)	6	1	1	1	94278
Career Total (AW)	2	0	1	1	1509

75	4/09	Yarm	1m3y	GD	£4533

Total win prize-money £4533

Going (Turf): Sf: 0-0 GS: 0-0 **Gd: 1-4** GF: 0-2 Fm: 0-0
Distance: 5f/6f: 0-0 7f-8f: 0-1 **9f-13f: 1-7** 14f+: 0-0
Track : LH: 0-3 RH: 0-4 Tight: 0-3 Gall: 0-1
Aids: Bl: 0-0 Vi: 0-0 Tstrap: 0-0 Ckp: 0-0
Best Rating: 107 5/09 Siro 1m3f gd-fm

Smart; close second in 2009 Italian Oaks; stays 1m3f; acts on good ground and on Polytrack.

Wadnaan

(89) (73)
2-y-o ch c Shamardal (USA)-Australian Dreams (Magic Ring (IRE))
M Johnston Sheikh Hamdan Bin Mohammed Al Maktoum

Placings:3 **(5371)**
2009: 8^{3}SD,

	Starts	1st	2nd	3rd	Win & Pl
Career Total (Turf)	0	0	0	0	
Career Total (AW)	1	0	0	1	626

Going (Turf): Sf: 0-0 GS: 0-0 Gd: 0-0 GF: 0-0 Fm: 0-0
Distance: 5f/6f: 0-0 7f-8f: 0-1 9f-13f: 0-0 14f+: 0-0
Track : LH: 0-1 RH: 0-0 Tight: 0-0 Gall: 0-0
Aids: Bl: 0-0 Vi: 0-0 Tstrap: 0-0 Ckp: 0-0
Best Rating: 73 8/09 Sthl 1m stand

Fair; stays 1m and acts on Fibresand.

Waffle (IRE)

107 **107**
3-y-o ch g Kheleyf (USA)-Saphire (College Chapel)
J Noseda Mrs Susan Roy

Placings:10522-5203 **(7015)**
2009: 5^{5}G, 5^{2}GF, 6^{0}GS, 5^{3}GS,

	Starts	1st	2nd	3rd	Win & Pl
Career Total (Turf)	9	1	3	1	22144

81	4/08	Leic	5f2y	G-S	£2590

Total win prize-money £2590

Going (Turf): Sf: 0-1 **GS: 1-4** Gd: 0-2 GF: 0-2 Fm: 0-0
Distance: **5f/6f: 1-9** 7f-8f: 0-0 9f-13f: 0-0 14f+: 0-0
Track : LH: 0-0 RH: 0-0 Tight: 0-0 Gall: 0-0
Aids: Bl: 0-0 Vi: 0-0 Tstrap: 0-0 Ckp: 0-0
Best Rating: 107 10/08 Asct 5f gd-sft

Smart; placed in Group company; effective at 5f and acts on most ground.

Wahan (USA)

89(97) (58)**44**
3-y-o b g Theatrical-Abrade (USA) (Mr Prospector (USA))
C E Brittain Saeed Manana

Placings:00-006200405 **(3985)**
2009: 7^{0}SD, 8^{0}SD, 12^{6}SD, 12^{2}SD, 11^{0}SD, 10^{0}GF, 10^{4}SD, 9^{0}G, 10^{5}GF,

	Starts	1st	2nd	3rd	Win & Pl
Career Total (Turf)	4	0	0	0	0
Career Total (AW)	7	0	1	0	605

Going (Turf): Sf: 0-0 GS: 0-0 Gd: 0-1 GF: 0-3 Fm: 0-0
Distance: 5f/6f: 0-0 7f-8f: 0-4 9f-13f: 0-7 14f+: 0-0
Track : LH: 0-7 RH: 0-3 Tight: 0-4 Gall: 0-0
Aids: Bl: 0-0 Vi: 0-0 Tstrap: 0-0 Ckp: 0-0
Best Rating: 58 4/09 Kemp 1m4f stand

Moderate; probably stays 1m4f; handles Polytrack.

Wahoo Sam (USA)

88(98) (68)**73**
9-y-o ch g Sandpit (BRZ)-Good Reputation (USA) (Gran Zar (MEX))
P D Evans Mrs I M Folkes

Placings:511/**U**0000/00311012010/050014100/**150**030200400/**1316**0036**6**40100005**0**/0100310**334**0**0005-200**10 **(1883)**
2009: 10^{2}SD, 8^{0}SD, 9^{0}SD, 8^{1}GF, 8^{0}F,

	Starts	1st	2nd	3rd	Win & Pl
Career Total (Turf)	52	10	2	4	52258
Career Total (AW)	26	5	1	3	19992

	5/09	Lanc	1m	H	G-F	£1700
73	6/08	Bath	1m5y	(0-70)H	FRM	£3561
68	5/08	Nott	1m75y	(0-60)H	GD	£2266
72	8/07	Muss	1m	(0-65)H	GD	£2590
78	1/07	Sthl	1m	(0-75)H	STD	£3071
78	1/07	Wolv	7f32y		STD	£2388
83	1/06	Wolv	7f32y	(0-85)H	STD	£5505
80	8/05	Ripn	1m1f170y	(0-90)H	G-F	£7699
77	6/05	Haml	1m65y	(0-70)	G-F	£3542
83	12/04	Sthl	1m	(0-77)H	STD	£3367
78	7/04	Haml	1m1f36yE	(0-75)H	G-F	£4907
72	7/04	Haml	1m1f36yE	(0-75)H	GD	£4176
68	6/04	Haml	1m1f36yE	(0-75)H	G-S	£3948
83	7/02	Thsk	7f	C	G-F	£7973
78	7/02	Sthl	6f	F	STD	£2779

Total win prize-money £59479

Going (Turf): Sf: 0-4 GS: 1-8 Gd: 3-18 **GF: 5-18** Fm: 1-4
Distance: 5f/6f: 1-3 7f-8f: 7-38 9f-13f: 7-37 14f+: 0-0
Track : **LH: 8-45** RH: 6-26 **Tight: 10-41** Gall: 0-5
Aids: Bl: 0-2 Vi: 0-0 Tstrap: 3-15 Ckp: 3-15
Best Rating: 83 1/06 Wolv 7f32y stand

Moderate; effective at around 1m; acts on fast ground; goes well on sand.

Wait For The Light

85(101) (76)**32**
5-y-o b g Fantastic Light (USA)-Lady In Waiting (Kylian (USA))
Mrs S Leech J O'Brien & M A Gray

Placings:61/4035**0**/0**320-265**0 **(4988)**
2009: 12^{2}SD, 12^{6}SD, 16^{5}SD, 13^{0}GF,

	Starts	1st	2nd	3rd	Win & Pl
Career Total (Turf)	7	0	0	1	1507
Career Total (AW)	8	1	2	1	4435

77	10/06	Wolv	7f32y	SF	£2590

Total win prize-money £2591

Going (Turf): Sf: 0-0 GS: 0-2 Gd: 0-2 GF: 0-2 Fm: 0-1
Distance: 5f/6f: 0-0 **7f-8f: 1-1** 9f-13f: 0-11 14f+: 0-3
Track : **LH: 1-5** RH: 0-8 **Tight: 1-7** Gall: 0-1
Aids: Bl: 0-1 Vi: 0-0 Tstrap: 0-3 Ckp: 0-3
Best Rating: 84 5/07 Wind 1m3f135y good

Fair; stays 1m4f; acts on good ground; goes on Polytrack.

Wajaha (IRE)

89(107) (99)**71**
3-y-o ch f Haafhd-Amanah (USA) (Mr Prospector (USA))
J H M Gosden Hamdan Al Maktoum

Placings:41-1000 **(6229)**
2009: 8^{1}SD, 7^{0}GF, 8^{0}GF, 8^{0}SD,

	Starts	1st	2nd	3rd	Win & Pl
Career Total (Turf)	3	0	0	0	457
Career Total (AW)	3	2	0	0	11009

99	4/09	Kemp	1m	(0-85)H	STD	£5180
81	10/08	GrLe	1m		STD	£5828

Total win prize-money £11009

Going (Turf): Sf: 0-0 GS: 0-0 Gd: 0-0 GF: 0-3 Fm: 0-0
Distance: 5f/6f: 0-0 **7f-8f: 2-6** 9f-13f: 0-0 14f+: 0-0
Track : LH: 1-1 RH: 1-2 Tight: 0-0 **Gall: 1-1**
Aids: Bl: 0-0 Vi: 0-0 Tstrap: 0-0 Ckp: 0-0
Best Rating: 99 4/09 Kemp 1m stand

Useful; stays 1m; acts on fast ground; goes on Polytrack.

Wajanaat

(90) (70)
2-y-o b f Sakhee (USA)-Tadris (USA) (Red Ransom (USA))
M P Tregoning Hamdan Al Maktoum

Placings:4 **(5643)**
2009: 8^{4}SD,

	Starts	1st	2nd	3rd	Win & Pl
Career Total (Turf)	0	0	0	0	
Career Total (AW)	1	0	0	0	0

Going (Turf): Sf: 0-0 GS: 0-0 Gd: 0-0 GF: 0-0 Fm: 0-0
Distance: 5f/6f: 0-0 7f-8f: 0-1 9f-13f: 0-0 14f+: 0-0
Track : LH: 0-1 RH: 0-0 Tight: 0-1 Gall: 0-0
Aids: Bl: 0-0 Vi: 0-0 Tstrap: 0-0 Ckp: 0-0
Best Rating: 70 9/09 Ling 1m stand

Fair debut over 1m on Polytrack.

Wake Me Now (IRE)

100(92) (69)**77**
3-y-o b f Almutawakel-Shiyra (Darshaan)
Gary Stevens (R M Beckett 11/6) Roberts & Pawle

Placings:232-51 **(2858)**
2009: 10^{5}GS, 10^{1}G,

	Starts	1st	2nd	3rd	Win & Pl
Career Total (Turf)	3	1	1	0	3265
Career Total (AW)	2	0	1	1	1844

77	6/09	Nott	1m2f50y	(0-75)H	GD	£2590

Total win prize-money £2590

Going (Turf): Sf: 0-0 GS: 0-2 **Gd: 1-1** GF: 0-0 Fm: 0-0
Distance: 5f/6f: 0-1 7f-8f: 0-2 **9f-13f: 1-2** 14f+: 0-0
Track : **LH: 1-4** RH: 0-1 Tight: 0-1 Gall: 0-2
Aids: Bl: 0-0 Vi: 0-0 Tstrap: 0-0 Ckp: 0-0
Best Rating: 77 6/09 Nott 1m2f50y good

Fair; stays 1m and acts on Polytrack.

Wake Up Call

97(105) (78)**73**
3-y-o b f Noverre (USA)-Up And About (Barathea (IRE))
C F Wall J G Lambton

Placings:2213 **(7519)**
2009: 8^{2}GF, 7^{2}GF, 6^{1}SD, 6^{3}SD,

	Starts	1st	2nd	3rd	Win & Pl
Career Total (Turf)	2	0	2	0	2348
Career Total (AW)	2	1	0	1	2943

76	10/09	Kemp	6f	STD	£2590

Total win prize-money £2590

Going (Turf): Sf: 0-0 GS: 0-0 Gd: 0-0 GF: 0-2 Fm: 0-0
Distance: **5f/6f: 1-2** 7f-8f: 0-2 9f-13f: 0-0 14f+: 0-0
Track : LH: 0-1 **RH: 1-1** Tight: 0-1 Gall: 0-0
Aids: Bl: 0-0 Vi: 0-0 Tstrap: 0-0 Ckp: 0-0

Best Rating: 78 11/09 Ling 6f stand

Fair; effective from 6f-1m and acts on fast ground and on Polytrack.

Wakita (IRE)

(102) (62)49

6-y-o b m Bold Fact (USA)-Pleasant Outlook (USA) (El Gran Senor (USA))

Aidan Anthony Howard Mrs Nuala Howard

Placings:05030/03025143-3460 (7444a)

2009: 8^{3}SD, 7^{4}SD, 8^{6}SD, 8^{0}SD,

	Starts	1st	2nd	3rd	Win & Pl
Career Total (Turf)	8	0	0	2	1309
Career Total (AW)	9	1	1	2	4626

56 10/08 Wolv 1m141y (0-52)H STD £2388

Total win prize-money £2388

Going (Turf): Sf: 0-2 GS: 0-0 Gd: 0-0 GF: 0-3 Fm: 0-1
Distance: 5f/6f: 0-0 7f-8f: 0-12 9f-13f: 1-5 14f+: 0-0
Track : LH: 1-12 RH: 0-3 Tight: 1-4 Gall: 0-0
Aids: Bl: 0-0 Vi: 0-0 Tstrap: 0-0 Ckp: 0-0
Best Rating: 64 8/06 Bell 1m firm

Moderate; effective over 1m; acts on Polytrack.

Walcot Square (IRE)

94 71

2-y-o b g Marju (IRE)-Lyrical Dance (USA) (Lear Fan (USA))

R Charlton De La Warr Racing

Placings:662 (5564)

2009: 7^{6}S, 7^{6}GF, 6^{2}F,

	Starts	1st	2nd	3rd	Win & Pl
Career Total (Turf)	3	0	1	0	1133

Going (Turf): Sf: 0-1 GS: 0-0 Gd: 0-0 GF: 0-1 Fm: 0-1
Distance: 5f/6f: 0-0 7f-8f: 0-3 9f-13f: 0-0 14f+: 0-0
Track : LH: 0-1 RH: 0-0 Tight: 0-0 Gall: 0-0
Aids: Bl: 0-0 Vi: 0-0 Tstrap: 0-0 Ckp: 0-0
Best Rating: 71 9/09 Brig 6f209y firm

Fair; stays 7f on fast ground.

Waldorf (IRE)

98(100) (66)60

4-y-o b c Sadler's Wells (USA)-Durrah Green (Green Desert (USA))

W R Muir Mr & Mrs G Middlebrook

Placings:0-461200504 (3768)

2009: 8^{4}SD, 12^{6}SD, 8^{1}SF, 8^{2}SD, 10^{0}SD, 12^{0}SD, 8^{5}G, 7^{0}SD, 12^{4}G,

	Starts	1st	2nd	3rd	Win & Pl
Career Total (Turf)	2	0	0	0	385
Career Total (AW)	8	1	1	0	2652

64 2/09 Wolv 1m141y (0-58)H SF £2047

Total win prize-money £2047

Going (Turf): Sf: 0-0 GS: 0-0 Gd: 0-2 GF: 0-0 Fm: 0-0
Distance: 5f/6f: 0-0 7f-8f: 0-2 9f-13f: 1-8 14f+: 0-0
Track : LH: 1-9 RH: 0-1 Tight: 1-7 Gall: 0-1
Aids: Bl: 0-0 Vi: 0-0 Tstrap: 0-0 Ckp: 0-0
Best Rating: 66 3/09 Wolv 1m141y stand

Moderate; effective over 1m; acts on Polytrack.

Waldvogel (IRE)

104(106) (102)106

5-y-o ch g Polish Precedent (USA)-Wurftaube (GER) (Acatenango (GER))

L M Cumani Craig Bennett

Placings:41/0410133/632240-6000623 (7789)

2009: 12^{6}G, 14^{0}G, 14^{0}GF, 14^{0}GF, 12^{6}GF, 10^{2}SD, 9^{3}SD,

	Starts	1st	2nd	3rd	Win & Pl
Career Total (Turf)	20	3	2	3	40138
Career Total (AW)	2	0	1	1	5001

7/07 Mulh 1m6f165y SFT £4729
89 6/07 Brem 1m2f110y GD £8108
9/06 Frnk 1m GD £2068

Total win prize-money £14907

Going (Turf): Sf: 1-7 GS: 0-0 Gd: 2-10 GF: 0-3 Fm: 0-0
Distance: 5f/6f: 0-0 7f-8f: 1-2 9f-13f: 1-9 14f+: 1-11
Track : LH: 0-5 RH: 1-11 Tight: 0-2 Gall: 0-4
Aids: Bl: 0-2 Vi: 0-0 Tstrap: 0-0 Ckp: 0-0
Best Rating: 106 5/08 Badn 2m good

Very useful; ex-German; placed in Group and Listed company; effective from 1m2f-2m; acts on good ground; has worn blinkers.

Walk On Water

101 94

2-y-o ch f Exceed And Excel (AUS)-The Cat's Whiskers (NZ) (Tale Of The Cat (USA))

H R A Cecil Bloomsbury Stud

Placings:116 (5606)

2009: 6^{1}G, 6^{1}GF, 6^{6}S,

	Starts	1st	2nd	3rd	Win & Pl
Career Total (Turf)	3	2	0	0	20219

94 8/09 Ches 6f18y G-F £12616
83 7/09 Asct 6f GD £7123

Total win prize-money £19740

Going (Turf): Sf: 0-1 GS: 0-0 Gd: 1-1 GF: 1-1 Fm: 0-0
Distance: 5f/6f: 1-2 7f-8f: 1-1 9f-13f: 0-0 14f+: 0-0
Track : LH: 1-1 RH: 0-0 Tight: 1-1 Gall: 0-0
Aids: Bl: 0-0 Vi: 0-0 Tstrap: 0-0 Ckp: 0-0
Best Rating: 94 8/09 Ches 6f18y gd-fm

Very useful; made winning debut at 6f on fast ground.

Walking Talking

98(103) (99)101

5-y-o b g Rainbow Quest (USA)-Wooden Doll (USA) (Woodman (USA))

H R A Cecil K Abdulla

Placings:2/013/33-50 (2055)

2009: 12^{5}S, 12^{0}GS,

	Starts	1st	2nd	3rd	Win & Pl
Career Total (Turf)	7	1	1	2	13463
Career Total (AW)	1	0	0	1	1120

88 6/07 Sand 1m2f7y GD £3886

Total win prize-money £3886

Going (Turf): Sf: 0-3 GS: 0-1 Gd: 1-1 GF: 0-2 Fm: 0-0
Distance: 5f/6f: 0-0 7f-8f: 0-2 9f-13f: 1-6 14f+: 0-0
Track : LH: 0-3 RH: 1-3 Tight: 0-0 Gall: 0-4
Aids: Bl: 0-0 Vi: 0-0 Tstrap: 0-0 Ckp: 0-0
Best Rating: 101 4/09 Newb 1m4f5y soft

Very useful; stays 1m4f; acts on most types of ground and Polytrack.

Walkingonthemoon

99 95

2-y-o ch c Footstepsinthesand-Bendis (GER) (Danehill (USA))

Tom Dascombe The Tipperary Partners

Placings:15224300 (7016)

2009: 5^{1}GS, 5^{5}GF, 6^{2}G, 6^{2}G, 6^{4}S, 7^{3}G, 6^{0}GF, 6^{0}GS,

	Starts	1st	2nd	3rd	Win & Pl
Career Total (Turf)	8	1	2	1	24301

83 4/09 Newb 5f34y G-S £5180

Total win prize-money £5181

Going (Turf): Sf: 0-1 GS: 1-2 Gd: 0-3 GF: 0-2 Fm: 0-0
Distance: 5f/6f: 1-6 7f-8f: 0-2 9f-13f: 0-0 14f+: 0-0
Track : LH: 0-2 RH: 0-1 Tight: 0-1 Gall: 0-0
Aids: Bl: 0-0 Vi: 0-0 Tstrap: 0-0 Ckp: 0-0
Best Rating: 95 6/09 Epsm 6f good

Very useful; stays 7f; acts on good and easy ground.

Wallgate

76 29

2-y-o b f Namid-Lay A Whisper (Night Shift (USA))

Miss J A Camacho Miss Julie Camacho

Placings:600 (4800)

2009: 5^{6}GS, 6^{0}GF, 6^{0}GF,

	Starts	1st	2nd	3rd	Win & Pl
Career Total (Turf)	3	0	0	0	0

Going (Turf): Sf: 0-0 GS: 0-1 Gd: 0-0 GF: 0-2 Fm: 0-0
Distance: 5f/6f: 0-3 7f-8f: 0-0 9f-13f: 0-0 14f+: 0-0
Track : LH: 0-0 RH: 0-0 Tight: 0-0 Gall: 0-0
Aids: Bl: 0-0 Vi: 0-0 Tstrap: 0-0 Ckp: 0-0
Best Rating: 29 5/09 Rdcr 6f gd-fm

Walls Way

81(80) (33)31

5-y-o ch g Karinga Bay-Wilming (Komaite (USA))

A W Carroll J M Wall & R D Willis

Placings:00 (6225)

2009: 10^{0}GF, 12^{0}SD,

	Starts	1st	2nd	3rd	Win & Pl
Career Total (Turf)	1	0	0	0	
Career Total (AW)	1	0	0	0	

Going (Turf): Sf: 0-0 GS: 0-0 Gd: 0-0 GF: 0-1 Fm: 0-0
Distance: 5f/6f: 0-0 7f-8f: 0-0 9f-13f: 0-2 14f+: 0-0
Track : LH: 0-0 RH: 0-2 Tight: 0-1 Gall: 0-0
Aids: Bl: 0-0 Vi: 0-0 Tstrap: 0-0 Ckp: 0-0
Best Rating: 33 9/09 Kemp 1m4f stand

Walnut Rise

85 34

2-y-o b f Mujahid (USA)-Seasonal Blossom (IRE) (Fairy King (USA))

M H Tompkins Miss Clare Hollest

Placings:00000 (7098)

2009: 6^{0}GF, 7^{0}G, 7^{0}GS, 7^{0}G, 7^{0}G,

	Starts	1st	2nd	3rd	Win & Pl
Career Total (Turf)	5	0	0	0	

Going (Turf): Sf: 0-0 GS: 0-1 Gd: 0-3 GF: 0-1 Fm: 0-0
Distance: 5f/6f: 0-1 7f-8f: 0-4 9f-13f: 0-0 14f+: 0-0

Track : LH: 0-1 RH: 0-0 Tight: 0-0 Gall: 0-0
Aids: Bl: 0-0 Vi: 0-0 Tstrap: 0-0 Ckp: 0-0
Best Rating: 34 10/09 Yarm 7f3y good

Walragnek

89(96) (59)**54**

5-y-o gr g Mind Games-Eastern Lyric (Petong)
J G M O'Shea L G Racing

Placings:552240550060-00000 **(5345)**
2009: 5^{0}GF, 5^{0}GF, 6^{0}GF, 5^{0}GF, 5^{0}G,

	Starts	1st	2nd	3rd	Win & Pl
Career Total (Turf)	10	0	0	0	144
Career Total (AW)	7	0	2	0	1737

Going (Turf): Sf: 0-0 GS: 0-0 Gd: 0-3 GF: 0-7 Fm: 0-0
Distance: 5f/6f: 0-15 7f-8f: 0-2 9f-13f: 0-0 14f+: 0-0
Track : LH: 0-9 RH: 0-2 Tight: 0-3 Gall: 0-1
Aids: Bl: 0-1 Vi: 0-2 Tstrap: 0-0 Ckp: 0-0
Best Rating: 59 4/08 Kemp 5f stand

Moderate sprinter; acts on both All-Weather surfaces.

Waltz Around (IRE)

88 **73**

2-y-o b f Bertolini (USA)-Mellow Jazz (Lycius (USA))
C E Brittain Saif Ali

Placings:1305 **(5992)**
2009: 5^{1}S, 6^{3}GS, 7^{0}GF, 5^{5}S,

	Starts	1st	2nd	3rd	Win & Pl
Career Total (Turf)	4	1	0	1	4140

70 7/09 Leic 5f218y SFT £3561
Total win prize-money £3562

Going (Turf): Sf: 1-2 GS: 0-1 Gd: 0-0 GF: 0-1 Fm: 0-0
Distance: **5f/6f: 1-2** 7f-8f: 0-2 9f-13f: 0-0 14f+: 0-0
Track : LH: 0-0 RH: 0-0 Tight: 0-0 Gall: 0-0
Aids: Bl: 0-0 Vi: 0-0 Tstrap: 0-0 Ckp: 0-0
Best Rating: 73 8/09 Nott 6f15y gd-sft

Fair; speedily-bred; stays 6f; acts on soft ground.

Waltzalong (IRE)

87 **54**

3-y-o b f Carnival Dancer-Flawless (Warning)
T D Easterby Habton Farms

Placings:004000 **(4819)**
2009: 9^{0}GS, 10^{0}GF, 11^{4}G, 10^{0}F, 16^{0}G, 8^{0}GF,

	Starts	1st	2nd	3rd	Win & Pl
Career Total (Turf)	6	0	0	0	241

Going (Turf): Sf: 0-0 GS: 0-1 Gd: 0-2 GF: 0-2 Fm: 0-1
Distance: 5f/6f: 0-0 7f-8f: 0-1 9f-13f: 0-4 14f+: 0-1
Track : LH: 0-3 RH: 0-2 Tight: 0-4 Gall: 0-1
Aids: Bl: 0-0 Vi: 0-0 Tstrap: 0-0 Ckp: 0-0
Best Rating: 54 6/09 Catt 1m3f214y good

Waltzing Buddy

87(70) (21)**46**

3-y-o ch f Reel Buddy (USA)-Waltzing Star (IRE) (Danehill (USA))
P T Midgley L Mason

Placings:0-00005 **(2624)**
2009: 7^{0}GF, 6^{0}GF, 6^{0}SD, 5^{0}GF, 6^{5}GF,

	Starts	1st	2nd	3rd	Win & Pl
Career Total (Turf)	5	0	0	0	0
Career Total (AW)	1	0	0	0	

Going (Turf): Sf: 0-0 GS: 0-0 Gd: 0-1 GF: 0-4 Fm: 0-0
Distance: 5f/6f: 0-4 7f-8f: 0-2 9f-13f: 0-0 14f+: 0-0
Track : LH: 0-2 RH: 0-0 Tight: 0-0 Gall: 0-0
Aids: Bl: 0-0 Vi: 0-0 Tstrap: 0-0 Ckp: 0-0
Best Rating: 46 4/09 Pont 6f gd-fm

Walvis Bay (IRE)

99 **82**

2-y-o gr g Footstepsinthesand-Limpopo (Green Desert (USA))
T P Tate Mrs Sylvia Clegg and Louise Worthington

Placings:2516 **(7290)**
2009: 5^{2}GS, 6^{5}GS, 6^{1}G, 6^{6}S,

	Starts	1st	2nd	3rd	Win & Pl
Career Total (Turf)	4	1	1	0	8629

81 10/09 York 6f GD £6605
Total win prize-money £6606

Going (Turf): Sf: 0-1 GS: 0-2 **Gd: 1-1** GF: 0-0 Fm: 0-0
Distance: **5f/6f: 1-4** 7f-8f: 0-0 9f-13f: 0-0 14f+: 0-0
Track : LH: 0-0 RH: 0-0 Tight: 0-0 Gall: 0-0
Aids: Bl: 0-0 Vi: 0-0 Tstrap: 0-0 Ckp: 0-0
Best Rating: 82 11/09 Donc 6f soft

Useful; effective over 5f; acts on good and easy ground.

Wanchai Whisper

89(106) (66)**57**

2-y-o b f Bahamian Bounty-Tiger Waltz (Pivotal)
P D Evans (W J Haggas 21/8) M&R Refurbishments Ltd

Placings:5610001030211 **(7871)**
2009: 6^{5}G, 7^{6}G, 5^{1}SF, 5^{0}F, 5^{0}SD, 5^{0}SF, 5^{1}SD, 5^{0}SD, 6^{3}SD, 5^{0}SD, 5^{2}SD, 5^{1}SD, 5^{1}SD,

	Starts	1st	2nd	3rd	Win & Pl
Career Total (Turf)	3	0	0	0	0
Career Total (AW)	10	4	1	1	10488

12/09 Kemp 5f (0-75) STD £2590
58 12/09 Kemp 5f STD £2047
62 10/09 Kemp 5f STD £2047
66 8/09 Wolv 5f20y SF £2729
Total win prize-money £9414

Going (Turf): Sf: 0-0 GS: 0-0 Gd: 0-2 GF: 0-0 Fm: 0-1
Distance: **5f/6f: 4-11** 7f-8f: 0-2 9f-13f: 0-0 14f+: 0-0
Track : LH: 1-7 **RH: 3-4 Tight: 1-6** Gall: 0-1
Aids: Bl: 0-0 Vi: 0-0 Tstrap: 0-0 Ckp: 0-0
Best Rating: 66 8/09 Wolv 5f20y std-fst

Modest; effective over 5f; acts on Polytrack.

Wandering Minstral

89 **45**

6-y-o br g Accordion-Vagrancy (Dancing Brave (USA))
H J L Dunlop The See You Then Partnership

Placings:60 **(3531)**
2009: 10^{6}GF, 8^{0}F,

	Starts	1st	2nd	3rd	Win & Pl
Career Total (Turf)	2	0	0	0	0

Going (Turf): Sf: 0-0 GS: 0-0 Gd: 0-0 GF: 0-1 Fm: 0-1
Distance: 5f/6f: 0-0 7f-8f: 0-0 9f-13f: 0-2 14f+: 0-0
Track : LH: 0-2 RH: 0-0 Tight: 0-0 Gall: 0-0
Aids: Bl: 0-0 Vi: 0-0 Tstrap: 0-0 Ckp: 0-0
Best Rating: 45 6/09 Hayd 1m2f95y gd-fm

Wannabe King

109 **108**

3-y-o b c King's Best (USA)-Wannabe Grand (IRE) (Danehill (USA))
D R Lanigan Saif Ali & Saeed H Altayer

Placings:51-264421110 **(6480)**
2009: 7^{2}GS, 8^{6}GF, 7^{4}HY, 7^{4}S, 8^{2}GF, 8^{1}GF, 8^{1}GF, 8^{1}G, 9^{0}GF,

	Starts	1st	2nd	3rd	Win & Pl
Career Total (Turf)	11	4	2	0	31075

108 8/09 Ripn 1m (0-100)H GD £12462
99 8/09 Epsm 1m114y (0-85)H G-F £5180
97 8/09 Wind 1m67y (0-85)H G-F £4857
80 7/08 Yarm 7f3y G-F £3784
Total win prize-money £26285

Going (Turf): Sf: 0-2 GS: 0-1 Gd: 1-1 **GF: 3-7** Fm: 0-0
Distance: 5f/6f: 0-1 7f-8f: 2-6 9f-13f: 2-4 14f+: 0-0
Track : LH: 1-2 **RH: 2-3 Tight: 3-4** Gall: 0-0
Aids: Bl: 0-0 Vi: 0-0 Tstrap: 3-4 Ckp: 3-4
Best Rating: 108 8/09 Ripn 1m good

Very useful; stays 1m and acts on most ground; has worn cheekpieces.

Wannabee (IRE)

67(81) (41)**15**

2-y-o ch f Bahamian Bounty-Lyric Dances (FR) (Sendawar (IRE))
J J Bridger J J Bridger

Placings:000 **(7585)**
2009: 6^{0}SD, 6^{0}GS, 6^{0}SD,

	Starts	1st	2nd	3rd	Win & Pl
Career Total (Turf)	1	0	0	0	
Career Total (AW)	2	0	0	0	

Going (Turf): Sf: 0-0 GS: 0-1 Gd: 0-0 GF: 0-0 Fm: 0-0
Distance: 5f/6f: 0-3 7f-8f: 0-0 9f-13f: 0-0 14f+: 0-0
Track : LH: 0-0 RH: 0-2 Tight: 0-0 Gall: 0-0
Aids: Bl: 0-0 Vi: 0-0 Tstrap: 0-0 Ckp: 0-0
Best Rating: 41 11/09 Kemp 6f stand

Wannarock (IRE)

99(75) (17)**65**

4-y-o b/br g Rock Of Gibraltar (IRE)-Propensity (Habitat)
M C Chapman Dr A Shubsachs

Placings:653/050-60665430503 **(6037)**
2009: 11^{6}GF, 10^{0}GF, 12^{6}GF, 18^{6}G, 11^{5}G, 12^{4}GS, 16^{3}GF, 9^{0}GF, 16^{5}G, 16^{0}GS, 16^{3}GF,

	Starts	1st	2nd	3rd	Win & Pl
Career Total (Turf)	16	0	0	3	2080
Career Total (AW)	1	0	0	0	

Going (Turf): Sf: 0-1 GS: 0-2 Gd: 0-6 GF: 0-7 Fm: 0-0
Distance: 5f/6f: 0-1 7f-8f: 0-2 9f-13f: 0-9 14f+: 0-5
Track : LH: 0-8 RH: 0-7 Tight: 0-9 Gall: 0-2
Aids: Bl: 0-0 Vi: 0-0 Tstrap: 0-0 Ckp: 0-0
Best Rating: 72 11/07 Nott 1m54y gd-fm

Moderate; probably stays 2m; acts on good ground.

War And Peace (IRE)

102(101) (79)77

5-y-o b g Danehill (USA)-Pipalong (IRE) (Pips Pride)

Jane Chapple-Hyam Jane Chapple-Hyam & Hon Andrew Peacock

Placings:0332/22003-222350056 (7679)

2009: 5^{2}SD, 5^{2}SD, 5^{2}SD, 6^{3}GF, 6^{5}GF, 6^{0}GF, 7^{0}SD, 5^{5}SD, 6^{6}SD,

	Starts	1st	2nd	3rd	Win & Pl
Career Total (Turf)	10	0	3	3	4812
Career Total (AW)	8	0	3	1	3369

Going (Turf): Sf: 0-0 GS: 0-2 Gd: 0-3 GF: 0-5 Fm: 0-0
Distance: 5f/6f: 0-12 7f-8f: 0-5 9f-13f: 0-1 14f+: 0-0
Track : LH: 0-7 RH: 0-5 Tight: 0-4 Gall: 0-3
Aids: Bl: 0-0 Vi: 0-0 Tstrap: 0-0 Ckp: 0-0
Best Rating: 79 1/09 Wolv 5f216y stand

Modest; effective over 6f-7f; acts on good and easy ground and on Polytrack.

War Artist (AUS)

113(109) (116)120

6-y-o b g Orpen (USA)-Royal Solitaire (AUS) (Brocco (USA))

J M P Eustace R Plersch

Placings:1/12131/26223-441130 (7745a)

2009: 6^{4}S, 6^{4}S, 6^{1}G, 5^{1}G, 5^{3}G, 6^{0}G,

	Starts	1st	2nd	3rd	Win & Pl
Career Total (Turf)	16	6	3	3	287157
Career Total (AW)	1	0	1	0	5595

119	9/09	Lonc	5f		GD	£38835
116	8/09	Badn	6f		GD	£38835
	7/07	Clai	6f		GD	£18115
	4/07	Scot	6f	H	GD	£3170
	3/07	Grey	5f		GD	£2717
	11/06	Grey	6f		GD	£3274

Total win prize-money £104948

Going (Turf): Sf: 0-3 GS: 0-0 Gd: 6-11 GF: 0-2 Fm: 0-0
Distance: 5f/6f: 6-14 7f-8f: 0-3 9f-13f: 0-0 14f+: 0-0
Track : LH: 1-2 RH: 0-0 Tight: 0-1 Gall: 0-0
Aids: Bl: 0-0 Vi: 0-0 Tstrap: 0-0 Ckp: 0-0
Best Rating: 120 6/08 Asct 6f gd-fm

Group class; placed three times at Group 1 level in Europe; Grade 1 winner in South Africa in 2008; effective at 5f-7f; acts on good and softer ground and on Polytrack.

War Native (IRE)

100(96) (96)94

3-y-o b c Cape Cross (IRE)-Walkamia (FR) (Linamix (FR))

J Noseda Ballygallon Stud Limited

Placings:110-03 (1664)

2009: 7^{0}S, 7^{3}G,

	Starts	1st	2nd	3rd	Win & Pl
Career Total (Turf)	4	1	0	1	6300
Career Total (AW)	1	1	0	0	4416

96	8/08	Ling	7f	STD	£4415
87	8/08	NmkJ	6f	G-F	£5180

Total win prize-money £9597

Going (Turf): Sf: 0-2 GS: 0-0 Gd: 0-1 GF: 1-1 Fm: 0-0
Distance: 5f/6f: 1-1 7f-8f: 1-4 9f-13f: 0-0 14f+: 0-0
Track : LH: 1-1 RH: 0-0 Tight: 1-1 Gall: 0-0
Aids: Bl: 0-0 Vi: 0-0 Tstrap: 0-0 Ckp: 0-0
Best Rating: 96 8/08 Ling 7f stand

Useful; dam was a high-class triple 1m-1m2f winner at in France; stays 7f; acts on fast ground and Polytrack.

War Of The Roses (IRE)

(109) (91)54

6-y-o b g Singspiel (IRE)-Calvia Rose (Sharpo)

R Brotherton P S J Croft

Placings:0/0011000620011/12226001226-0160 (1215)

2009: 12^{0}SD, 12^{1}SD, 12^{6}SD, 16^{0}SD,

	Starts	1st	2nd	3rd	Win & Pl
Career Total (Turf)	4	0	0	0	
Career Total (AW)	25	7	6	0	23139

90	2/09	Ling	1m4f	(0-85)H	STD	£4727
83	9/08	Ling	1m4f	(0-75)H	STD	£2590
74	1/08	Ling	1m5f	(0-70)H	STD	£2331
73	12/07	Ling	1m5f	(0-65)H	STD	£1943
58	11/07	Ling	1m4f	(0-52)H	STD	£2047
59	3/07	Kemp	1m2f	(0-45)	STD	£1365
55	3/07	Kemp	1m	(0-45)	STD	£1365

Total win prize-money £16370

Going (Turf): Sf: 0-0 GS: 0-2 Gd: 0-1 GF: 0-1 Fm: 0-0
Distance: 5f/6f: 0-1 7f-8f: 1-3 9f-13f: 6-22 14f+: 0-3
Track : LH: 5-22 RH: 2-7 Tight: 5-19 Gall: 0-3
Aids: Bl: 0-0 Vi: 0-0 Tstrap: 0-0 Ckp: 0-0
Best Rating: 91 10/08 Ling 1m4f stand

Useful; stays 1m5f and acts on Polytrack.

War Party

104 87

5-y-o b g Fantastic Light (USA)-War Game (FR) (Caerleon (USA))

Dr R D P Newland J A Provan,C E Stedman,Prof D E Newland

Placings:244212/63134000-6500 (3587)

2009: 12^{6}GF, 12^{5}G, 12^{0}G, 14^{0}G,

	Starts	1st	2nd	3rd	Win & Pl
Career Total (Turf)	18	2	3	2	53829

85	6/08	Lonc	1m4f	H	GD	£17279
	10/07	Nanc	1m1f110y		SFT	£6418

Total win prize-money £23698

Going (Turf): Sf: 1-6 GS: 0-6 Gd: 1-4 GF: 0-1 Fm: 0-0
Distance: 5f/6f: 0-0 7f-8f: 0-0 9f-13f: 2-16 14f+: 0-2
Track : LH: 0-5 RH: 1-10 Tight: 0-1 Gall: 0-2
Aids: Bl: 0-0 Vi: 0-0 Tstrap: 0-0 Ckp: 0-0
Best Rating: 87 6/09 Epsm 1m4f10y good

Useful; ex-French; best at around 1m4f; acts on good and soft ground.

War Wolf

75 36

2-y-o br g Lucky Story (USA)-Bollin Janet (Sheikh Albadou)

T D Easterby C H Stevens

Placings:04000 (6821)

2009: 6^{0}GS, 6^{4}GF, 5^{0}G, 6^{0}GF, 8^{0}GF,

	Starts	1st	2nd	3rd	Win & Pl
Career Total (Turf)	5	0	0	0	192

Going (Turf): Sf: 0-0 GS: 0-1 Gd: 0-1 GF: 0-3 Fm: 0-0
Distance: 5f/6f: 0-4 7f-8f: 0-1 9f-13f: 0-0 14f+: 0-0
Track : LH: 0-0 RH: 0-0 Tight: 0-0 Gall: 0-0
Aids: Bl: 0-0 Vi: 0-0 Tstrap: 0-0 Ckp: 0-0
Best Rating: 36 8/09 Ripn 6f gd-fm

Warling (IRE)

80 56

2-y-o gr f Montjeu (IRE)-Walkamia (FR) (Linamix (FR))

J Noseda Ballygallon Stud Limited

Placings:0 (7183)

2009: 7^{0}G,

	Starts	1st	2nd	3rd	Win & Pl
Career Total (Turf)	1	0	0	0	

Going (Turf): Sf: 0-0 GS: 0-0 Gd: 0-1 GF: 0-0 Fm: 0-0
Distance: 5f/6f: 0-0 7f-8f: 0-1 9f-13f: 0-0 14f+: 0-0
Track : LH: 0-0 RH: 0-0 Tight: 0-0 Gall: 0-0
Aids: Bl: 0-0 Vi: 0-0 Tstrap: 0-0 Ckp: 0-0
Best Rating: 56 10/09 NmkR 7f good

Warne's Way (IRE)

89 71

6-y-o ch g Spinning World (USA)-Kafayef (USA) (Secreto (USA))

B G Powell Nigel Stafford

Placings:0000/1 (7036)

2009: 12^{1}S,

	Starts	1st	2nd	3rd	Win & Pl
Career Total (Turf)	4	1	0	0	3123
Career Total (AW)	1	0	0	0	

71	10/09	Newb	1m4f5y	(0-75)H	SFT	£3123

Total win prize-money £3123

Going (Turf): Sf: 1-1 GS: 0-0 Gd: 0-2 GF: 0-1 Fm: 0-0
Distance: 5f/6f: 0-0 7f-8f: 0-1 9f-13f: 1-4 14f+: 0-0
Track : LH: 1-2 RH: 0-3 Tight: 0-2 Gall: 1-2
Aids: Bl: 0-0 Vi: 0-0 Tstrap: 0-0 Ckp: 0-0
Best Rating: 71 10/09 Newb 1m4f5y soft

Fair; better known as a hurdler; stays 1m4f; acts on soft ground.

Warners Bay (IRE)

87 (38)49

4-y-o b g Iron Mask (USA)-Romangoddess (IRE) (Rhoman Rule (USA))

R Bastiman Robin Bastiman

Placings:300/00-000000 (6005)

2009: 6^{0}GF, 6^{0}GF, 7^{0}GS, 6^{0}GS, 6^{0}GF, 7^{0}GF,

	Starts	1st	2nd	3rd	Win & Pl
Career Total (Turf)	10	0	0	1	578
Career Total (AW)	1	0	0	0	

Going (Turf): Sf: 0-0 GS: 0-2 Gd: 0-2 GF: 0-6 Fm: 0-0
Distance: 5f/6f: 0-7 7f-8f: 0-4 9f-13f: 0-0 14f+: 0-0
Track : LH: 0-4 RH: 0-1 Tight: 0-3 Gall: 0-0
Aids: Bl: 0-0 Vi: 0-0 Tstrap: 0-0 Ckp: 0-0
Best Rating: 60 10/07 Pont 6f good

Warning Song (USA)

97(95) (77)77

2-y-o b/br c Successful Appeal (USA)-Tia Lea (USA) (Songandaprayer (USA))

Mrs A J Perrett G Harwood

Placings:433523 (7325)

2009: 5^4F, 5^3GF, 5^3GF, 6^5GS, 7^2SD, 7^3SD,

	Starts	1st	2nd	3rd	Win & Pl
Career Total (Turf)	4	0	0	2	1540
Career Total (AW)	2	0	1	1	1493

Going (Turf): Sf: 0-0 GS: 0-1 Gd: 0-0 GF: 0-2 Fm: 0-1
Distance: 5f/6f: 0-4 7f-8f: 0-2 9f-13f: 0-0 14f+: 0-0
Track : LH: 0-0 RH: 0-2 Tight: 0-0 Gall: 0-0
Aids: Bl: 0-0 Vi: 0-0 Tstrap: 0-0 Ckp: 0-0
Best Rating: 77 10/09 Kemp 7f stand

Fair; $75,000 first foal from a sprinting family in USA; stays 7f; handles fast ground and Polytrack.

Warpedsenseofhumor (FR)

99 79

3-y-o ch c Distorted Humor (USA)-Eden (USA) (Holy Bull (USA))
H R A Cecil H E Sheikh Sultan Bin Khalifa Al Nahyan

Placings:15 (4827)

2009: 9^1F, 10^5G,

	Starts	1st	2nd	3rd	Win & Pl
Career Total (Turf)	2	1	0	0	2590
76 4/09 Rdcr 1m1f			FRM	£2590	

Total win prize-money £2590

Going (Turf): Sf: 0-0 GS: 0-0 Gd: 0-1 GF: 0-0 **Fm: 1-1**
Distance: 5f/6f: 0-0 7f-8f: 0-0 **9f-13f: 1-2** 14f+: 0-0
Track : **LH: 1-1** RH: 0-1 **Tight: 1-2** Gall: 0-0
Aids: Bl: 0-0 Vi: 0-0 Tstrap: 0-0 Ckp: 0-0
Best Rating: 79 8/09 Wind 1m2f7y good

American-bred; winner on debut over 1m1f on fast ground.

Warrants Attention (IRE)

98(81) (27)58

3-y-o b g Fruits Of Love (USA)-Irish Lover (USA) (Irish River (FR))
A M Balding Roger Parry

Placings:056060 (5775)

2009: 10^0G, 12^5G, 12^6GF, 14^0G, 12^6G, 10^0SD,

	Starts	1st	2nd	3rd	Win & Pl
Career Total (Turf)	5	0	0	0	0
Career Total (AW)	1	0	0	0	

Going (Turf): Sf: 0-0 GS: 0-0 Gd: 0-4 GF: 0-1 Fm: 0-0
Distance: 5f/6f: 0-0 7f-8f: 0-0 9f-13f: 0-5 14f+: 0-1
Track : LH: 0-3 RH: 0-3 Tight: 0-0 Gall: 0-0
Aids: Bl: 0-0 Vi: 0-0 Tstrap: 0-0 Ckp: 0-0
Best Rating: 58 7/09 Wwck 1m4f134y gd-fm

Warren Bank

(89) (57)

4-y-o b g Nayef (USA)-Neptunalia (Slip Anchor)
Mrs Mary Hambro Mrs Richard Hambro

Placings:0/200 (7766)

2009: 9^2SD, 12^0SD, 11^0SD,

	Starts	1st	2nd	3rd	Win & Pl
Career Total (Turf)	0	0	0	0	
Career Total (AW)	4	0	1	0	771

Going (Turf): Sf: 0-0 GS: 0-0 Gd: 0-0 GF: 0-0 Fm: 0-0
Distance: 5f/6f: 0-0 7f-8f: 0-1 9f-13f: 0-3 14f+: 0-0
Track : LH: 0-2 RH: 0-2 Tight: 0-1 Gall: 0-0
Aids: Bl: 0-0 Vi: 0-0 Tstrap: 0-0 Ckp: 0-0
Best Rating: 57 11/09 Wolv 1m1f103y stand

Warringah

109 (62)114

4-y-o b g Galileo (IRE)-Threefold (USA) (Gulch (USA))
Chris Waller (Sir Michael Stoute 29/8) G G Syndicate

Placings:6/24120-0122520 (7215a)

2009: 12^0GS, 11^1GF, 14^2GF, 12^2G, 14^5GF, 11^2GF, 16^0GS,

	Starts	1st	2nd	3rd	Win & Pl
Career Total (Turf)	12	2	5	0	55075
Career Total (AW)	1	0	0	0	0
108 6/09 Wind 1m3f135y (0-100)H				G-F	£11656
100 6/08 Newb 1m4f5y (0-75)H				G-S	£2590

Total win prize-money £14247

Going (Turf): Sf: 0-1 **GS: 1-4** Gd: 0-2 **GF: 1-5** Fm: 0-0
Distance: 5f/6f: 0-0 7f-8f: 0-1 **9f-13f: 2-8** 14f+: 0-4
Track : **LH: 1-8** RH: 0-3 Tight: 1-6 Gall: 1-5
Aids: Bl: 0-0 Vi: 0-0 Tstrap: 0-0 Ckp: 0-0
Best Rating: 114 7/09 Gdwd 1m4f good

Smart; Group placed; effective over 1m4f-1m6f; acts on fast and easy ground; likes to race prominently.

Warrior Conquest

97(102) (73)65

4-y-o b g Alhaarth (IRE)-Eilean Shona (Suave Dancer (USA))
W J Knight Mrs B Sumner

Placings:6-03620304 (6400)

2009: 12^0GF, 11^3G, 12^6GF, 16^2SD, 16^0G, 16^3SD, 16^0SD, 14^4GF,

	Starts	1st	2nd	3rd	Win & Pl
Career Total (Turf)	5	0	0	1	644
Career Total (AW)	4	0	1	1	1474

Going (Turf): Sf: 0-0 GS: 0-0 Gd: 0-2 GF: 0-3 Fm: 0-0
Distance: 5f/6f: 0-0 7f-8f: 0-0 9f-13f: 0-4 14f+: 0-5
Track : LH: 0-2 RH: 0-7 Tight: 0-5 Gall: 0-0
Aids: Bl: 0-0 Vi: 0-1 Tstrap: 0-0 Ckp: 0-0
Best Rating: 73 7/09 Kemp 2m stand

Modest; stays 2m; acts on Polytrack and fast ground.

Warrior Nation (FR)

56(77) (73)73

3-y-o br g Statue Of Liberty (USA)-Tadawul (USA) (Diesis)
A J Chamberlain (G M Lyons 8/7) P F Bartlett

Placings:3540606-2000000 (7732)

2009: 10^2SD, 10^0SD, 10^0GY, 11^0GS, 8^0SD, 8^0SD, 12^0SD,

	Starts	1st	2nd	3rd	Win & Pl
Career Total (Turf)	8	0	0	1	1271
Career Total (AW)	6	0	1	0	1407

Going (Turf): Sf: 0-1 GS: 0-1 Gd: 0-0 GF: 0-2 Fm: 0-1
Distance: 5f/6f: 0-3 7f-8f: 0-6 9f-13f: 0-5 14f+: 0-0
Track : LH: 0-9 RH: 0-3 Tight: 0-3 Gall: 0-0
Aids: Bl: 0-3 Vi: 0-0 Tstrap: 0-1 Ckp: 0-1
Best Rating: 73 4/09 Dund 1m2f150y stand

Warrior One

92 83

3-y-o gr g Act One-River Cara (USA) (Irish River (FR))
J Howard Johnson Mrs B Halman & J H Johnson

Placings:514-05 (2767)

2009: 10^0GF, 10^5G,

	Starts	1st	2nd	3rd	Win & Pl
Career Total (Turf)	5	1	0	0	6143
83 8/08 Haml 1m65y			SFT	£5180	

Total win prize-money £5181

Going (Turf): Sf: 1-2 GS: 0-0 Gd: 0-1 GF: 0-2 Fm: 0-0
Distance: 5f/6f: 0-0 7f-8f: 0-2 **9f-13f: 1-3** 14f+: 0-0
Track : LH: 0-2 **RH: 1-1 Tight: 1-1** Gall: 0-1
Aids: Bl: 0-0 Vi: 0-0 Tstrap: 0-0 Ckp: 0-0
Best Rating: 83 9/08 Donc 1m soft

Useful son of Act One; effective over 1m; acts on soft ground.

Warsaw Pact (IRE)

79 (93)47

6-y-o b g Polish Precedent (USA)-Always Friendly (High Line)
P J Hobbs Mrs Diana L Whateley

Placings:550/12111224/0 (1790)

2009: 18^0GF,

	Starts	1st	2nd	3rd	Win & Pl
Career Total (Turf)	5	1	1	0	6343
Career Total (AW)	7	3	2	0	19859
93 7/06 Wolv 1m4f50y (0-80)H				STD	£6477
87 7/06 Ling 1m4f (0-85)H				STD	£6477
88 7/06 Wolv 1m4f50y (0-75)H				STD	£3238
74 5/06 Leic 1m3f183y (0-75)H				G-S	£4416

Total win prize-money £20609

Going (Turf): Sf: 0-1 **GS: 1-2** Gd: 0-0 GF: 0-2 Fm: 0-0
Distance: 5f/6f: 0-1 7f-8f: 0-1 **9f-13f: 4-7** 14f+: 0-3
Track : **LH: 3-8** RH: 1-3 **Tight: 3-8** Gall: 0-1
Aids: Bl: 0-0 Vi: 0-0 Tstrap: 0-0 Ckp: 0-0
Best Rating: 93 8/06 Wolv 1m5f194y std-fst

Useful; effective over 1m4f, but stays further; acts on most ground and on Polytrack; likes to race prominently; winning hurdler.

Wasan

107(111) (111)104

4-y-o ch c Pivotal-Solaia (USA) (Miswaki (USA))
E A L Dunlop Hamdan Al Maktoum

Placings:1/13101-01222 (6644)

2009: 8^0G, 10^1SD, 12^2G, 10^2SD, 10^2G,

	Starts	1st	2nd	3rd	Win & Pl
Career Total (Turf)	8	3	2	1	39061
Career Total (AW)	3	2	1	0	14410
111 5/09 Ling 1m2f				STD	£8742
104 9/08 Donc 1m2f60y (0-110)H				SFT	£12952
104 6/08 Hayd 1m30y (0-90)H				GD	£9714
93 4/08 Nott 1m75y (0-75)H				G-S	£2914
70 11/07 Ling 7f				STD	£3465

Total win prize-money £37788

Going (Turf): Sf: 1-1 GS: 1-2 Gd: 1-4 GF: 0-1 Fm: 0-0
Distance: 5f/6f: 0-0 7f-8f: 1-3 **9f-13f: 4-8** 14f+: 0-0
Track : **LH: 5-8** RH: 0-3 **Tight: 2-3** Gall: 1-5
Aids: Bl: 0-1 Vi: 0-0 Tstrap: 0-0 Ckp: 0-0
Best Rating: 111 5/09 Ling 1m2f stand

Smart; stays 1m4f; acts on soft ground; goes on Polytrack; has worn blinkers.

Waseet

107 109

2-y-o ch c Selkirk (USA)-Najayeb (USA) (Silver Hawk (USA))
J L Dunlop Hamdan Al Maktoum

Placings:312 (6268)
2009: 7^{3}G, 8^{1}G, 8^{2}G,

	Starts	1st	2nd	3rd	Win & Pl
Career Total (Turf)	3	1	1	1	38623

88 8/09 Sand 1m14y GD £5180
Total win prize-money £5181

Going (Turf): Sf: 0-0 GS: 0-0 **Gd: 1-3** GF: 0-0 Fm: 0-0
Distance: 5f/6f: 0-0 7f-8f: 0-2 **9f-13f: 1-1** 14f+: 0-0
Track : LH: 0-0 **RH: 1-2** Tight: 0-0 Gall: 0-1
Aids: Bl: 0-0 Vi: 0-0 Tstrap: 0-0 Ckp: 0-0
Best Rating: **109** 9/09 Asct 1m good

Smart; runner-up in the Royal Lodge Stakes; stays 1m and acts on good ground.

Washington Irving (IRE)

101 114

4-y-o b g Montjeu (IRE)-Shouk (Shirley Heights)
J Howard Johnson Andrea & Graham Wylie

Placings:4/2250261-4P (3048)
2009: 14^{4}GS, 20^{P}GF,

	Starts	1st	2nd	3rd	Win & Pl
Career Total (Turf)	10	1	3	0	88869

86 10/08 Navn 1m2f SH £6097
Total win prize-money £6097

Going (Turf): **Sf: 0-3 GS: 0-1 Gd: 0-2 GF: 0-1 Fm: 0-0**
Distance: 5f/6f: 0-0 7f-8f: 0-1 **9f-13f: 1-6** 14f+: 0-3
Track : **LH: 1-7** RH: 0-2 Tight: 0-1 Gall: 0-3
Aids: Bl: 0-0 Vi: 0-0 Tstrap: 0-0 Ckp: 0-0
Best Rating: **114** 6/08 Epsm 1m4f10y good

Smart; runner-up in the Group 2 Derrinstown Derby Trial and fifth in the Derby in 2008; stays 1m4f and acts on good and softer ground.

Wasmi (IRE)

86(97) (79)48

2-y-o b f Exceed And Excel (AUS)-Trim (IRE) (Ela-Mana-Mou)
C E Brittain Saeed Manana

Placings:04144110 (6643)
2009: 6^{0}GF, 5^{4}G, 7^{1}SD, 6^{4}G, 7^{4}SD, 6^{1}SD, 6^{1}SD, 6^{0}G,

	Starts	1st	2nd	3rd	Win & Pl
Career Total (Turf)	4	0	0	0	443
Career Total (AW)	4	3	0	0	8611

79 9/09 Kemp 6f (0-70) STD £2590
66 9/09 Kemp 6f (0-70) STD £2266
68 7/09 Wolv 7f32y STD £3561
Total win prize-money £8419

Going (Turf): **Sf: 0-0 GS: 0-0 Gd: 0-3 GF: 0-1 Fm: 0-0**
Distance: **5f/6f: 2-5** 7f-8f: 1-3 9f-13f: 0-0 14f+: 0-0
Track : LH: 1-1 **RH: 2-3 Tight: 1-1** Gall: 0-0
Aids: Bl: 0-0 Vi: 0-0 Tstrap: 0-0 Ckp: 0-0
Best Rating: **79** 9/09 Kemp 6f stand

Fair; stays 7f; best effort on Polytrack.

Wasp (AUS)

100(113) (94)86

7-y-o b/br g Octagonal (NZ)-Establishment (AUS) (Star Watch (AUS))
W Jarvis Dr J Walker

Placings:1/11300/300040000/610-1540550 (3525)
2009: 8^{1}SD, 8^{5}SD, 8^{4}SD, 8^{0}GF, 10^{5}GF, 7^{5}G, 8^{0}GF,

	Starts	1st	2nd	3rd	Win & Pl
Career Total (Turf)	21	3	0	2	70410
Career Total (AW)	4	2	0	0	14694

94 1/09 Wolv 1m141y (0-95)H STD £7352
92 10/08 Wolv 7f32y (0-85)H SF £6476
3/06 Wrkf 1m GD £23824
2/06 Rand 7f GD £23824
9/05 Kemb 7f G-S £5224
Total win prize-money £66703

Going (Turf): Sf: 0-1 GS: 1-2 **Gd: 2-8** GF: 0-9 Fm: 0-1
Distance: 5f/6f: 0-1 **7f-8f: 4-20** 9f-13f: 1-4 14f+: 0-0
Track : **LH: 2-6** RH: 0-3 **Tight: 2-6** Gall: 0-0
Aids: Bl: 0-3 Vi: 0-0 Tstrap: 0-0 Ckp: 0-0
Best Rating: **107** 1/07 ShTn 1m gd-fm

Useful; ex-Hong Kong trained; effective at 7f-1m; acts on fast ground; goes on Polytrack.

Watch Amigo (IRE)

(102) (74)

3-y-o b g Royal Applause-Miss Red Ink (USA) (Red Ransom (USA))
W R Swinburn Ian Harris & Tim Halpin

Placings:21 (7730)
2009: 7^{2}SD, 7^{1}SD,

	Starts	1st	2nd	3rd	Win & Pl
Career Total (Turf)	0	0	0	0	
Career Total (AW)	2	1	1	0	3435

74 12/09 Wolv 7f32y STD £2729
Total win prize-money £2730

Going (Turf): **Sf: 0-0 GS: 0-0 Gd: 0-0 GF: 0-0 Fm: 0-0**
Distance: 5f/6f: 0-0 **7f-8f: 1-2** 9f-13f: 0-0 14f+: 0-0
Track : **LH: 1-2** RH: 0-0 **Tight: 1-2** Gall: 0-0
Aids: Bl: 0-0 Vi: 0-0 Tstrap: 0-0 Ckp: 0-0
Best Rating: **74** 12/09 Wolv 7f32y stand

Moderate; stays 7f and acts on Polytrack.

Watch Chain (IRE)

94(92) (54)70

2-y-o b c Traditionally (USA)-Dangle (IRE) (Desert Style (IRE))
M H Tompkins Miss Clare Hollest

Placings:566413606 (7268)
2009: 5^{5}GF, 6^{6}GS, 6^{6}G, 5^{4}GF, 5^{1}SD, 6^{3}F, 5^{6}GF, 6^{0}GF, 5^{6}SD,

	Starts	1st	2nd	3rd	Win & Pl
Career Total (Turf)	7	0	0	1	842
Career Total (AW)	2	1	0	0	2730

54 8/09 Sthl 5f (0-65) STD £2729
Total win prize-money £2730

Going (Turf): **Sf: 0-0 GS: 0-1 Gd: 0-1 GF: 0-4 Fm: 0-1**
Distance: **5f/6f: 1-9** 7f-8f: 0-0 9f-13f: 0-0 14f+: 0-0
Track : LH: 0-1 RH: 0-0 Tight: 0-0 Gall: 0-0
Aids: Bl: 0-0 Vi: 0-0 Tstrap: 0-0 Ckp: 0-0
Best Rating: **70** 9/09 Folk 6f firm

Moderate; suited by 5f and Fibresand.

Watch Out

(102) (46)45

5-y-o b g Observatory (USA)-Ballet Fame (USA) (Quest For Fame)
D Burchell (G A Ham 5/9) The Beefeaters

Placings:U200/4066/23-6 (7154)
2009: 16^{6}SD,

	Starts	1st	2nd	3rd	Win & Pl
Career Total (Turf)	8	0	1	0	1301
Career Total (AW)	3	0	1	1	605

Going (Turf): **Sf: 0-4 GS: 0-0 Gd: 0-1 GF: 0-3 Fm: 0-0**
Distance: 5f/6f: 0-1 7f-8f: 0-2 9f-13f: 0-4 14f+: 0-4
Track : LH: 0-6 RH: 0-4 Tight: 0-9 Gall: 0-0
Aids: Bl: 0-2 Vi: 0-0 Tstrap: 0-0 Ckp: 0-0
Best Rating: **47** 2/08 Wolv 2m119y stand

Plating class; stays a 1m4f; acts on fast ground and Polytrack; has worn a tongue tie.

Watch The Master

69(86) (60)4

3-y-o b g Passing Glance-Fine Arts (Cadeaux Genereux)
B I Case Neil Hulley

Placings:50-000 (5328)
2009: 12^{0}G, 10^{0}SD, 11^{0}SD,

	Starts	1st	2nd	3rd	Win & Pl
Career Total (Turf)	1	0	0	0	
Career Total (AW)	4	0	0	0	0

Going (Turf): **Sf: 0-0 GS: 0-0 Gd: 0-1 GF: 0-0 Fm: 0-0**
Distance: 5f/6f: 0-0 7f-8f: 0-2 9f-13f: 0-3 14f+: 0-0
Track : LH: 0-4 RH: 0-1 Tight: 0-2 Gall: 0-1
Aids: Bl: 0-0 Vi: 0-1 Tstrap: 0-0 Ckp: 0-0
Best Rating: **60** 11/08 Wolv 7f32y stand

Watchmaker

73(108) (73)62

6-y-o b g Bering-Watchkeeper (IRE) (Rudimentary (USA))
Miss Tor Sturgis Miss Ann Sturgis

Placings:0/52150506220/1633000-2140 (2039)
2009: 9^{2}SD, 9^{1}SD, 10^{4}SD, 10^{0}GS,

	Starts	1st	2nd	3rd	Win & Pl
Career Total (Turf)	4	0	0	0	
Career Total (AW)	19	3	4	2	10920

73 4/09 Wolv 1m1f103y STD £2047
71 1/08 Kemp 1m2f (0-65)H STD £2047
72 2/07 Ling 1m2f (0-70)H STD £3071
Total win prize-money £7166

Going (Turf): **Sf: 0-1 GS: 0-1 Gd: 0-1 GF: 0-1 Fm: 0-0**
Distance: 5f/6f: 0-0 7f-8f: 0-0 **9f-13f: 3-22** 14f+: 0-1
Track : **LH: 2-14** RH: 1-9 **Tight: 2-12** Gall: 0-2
Aids: Bl: 0-0 Vi: 0-0 Tstrap: 0-0 Ckp: 0-0
Best Rating: **73** 4/09 Wolv 1m1f103y stand

Modest; stays 1m4f but effective over shorter; acts on Polytrack.

Watchoverme

92(87) (30)58

3-y-o ch f Haafhd-Bryony Brind (IRE) (Kris)
J R Fanshawe Mrs Denis Haynes

Placings:05066 (5483)
2009: 10^{0}GF, 12^{5}GS, 12^{0}SD, 10^{6}GF, 14^{6}GF,

	Starts	1st	2nd	3rd	Win & Pl
Career Total (Turf)	4	0	0	0	0
Career Total (AW)	1	0	0	0	

Going (Turf): Sf: 0-0 GS: 0-1 Gd: 0-0 GF: 0-3 Fm: 0-0
Distance: 5f/6f: 0-0 7f-8f: 0-0 9f-13f: 0-4 14f+: 0-1
Track : LH: 0-4 RH: 0-1 Tight: 0-4 Gall: 0-0
Aids: Bl: 0-0 Vi: 0-2 Tstrap: 0-0 Ckp: 0-0
Best Rating: 58 8/09 Yarm 1m2f21y gd-fm

Water Biscuit

98 **83**

2-y-o b f Bertolini (USA)-Waterfall One (Nashwan (USA))
B J Meehan Lady Rothschild

Placings:221600 (6844)
2009: 6^{2}GS, 6^{2}GF, 7^{1}GS, 7^{6}G, 6^{0}GF, 7^{0}G,

	Starts	1st	2nd	3rd	Win & Pl
Career Total (Turf)	6	1	2	0	18059
79 7/09 Gdwd 7f			G-S	£12952	

Total win prize-money £12952

Going (Turf): Sf: 0-0 **GS: 1-2** Gd: 0-2 GF: 0-2 Fm: 0-0
Distance: 5f/6f: 0-2 **7f-8f: 1-4** 9f-13f: 0-0 14f+: 0-0
Track : LH: 0-1 **RH: 1-2** Tight: 0-1 Gall: 0-0
Aids: Bl: 0-0 Vi: 0-0 Tstrap: 0-0 Ckp: 0-0
Best Rating: 83 7/09 NmkJ 6f gd-fm

Useful; effective over 6f-7f; acts on fast and easy ground.

Water Gipsy

88 **55**

2-y-o b/br f Piccolo-Creek Dancer (Josr Algarhoud (IRE))
G L Moore Mrs A E V Wadman

Placings:0 (6061)
2009: 6^{0}GF,

	Starts	1st	2nd	3rd	Win & Pl
Career Total (Turf)	1	0	0	0	

Going (Turf): Sf: 0-0 GS: 0-0 Gd: 0-0 GF: 0-1 Fm: 0-0
Distance: 5f/6f: 0-1 7f-8f: 0-0 9f-13f: 0-0 14f+: 0-0
Track : LH: 0-0 RH: 0-0 Tight: 0-0 Gall: 0-0
Aids: Bl: 0-0 Vi: 0-0 Tstrap: 0-0 Ckp: 0-0
Best Rating: 55 9/09 NmkR 6f gd-fm

Water Hen (IRE)

95(78) (60)**65**

3-y-o b f Diktat-Waterfall One (Nashwan (USA))
R Charlton Lady Rothschild

Placings:600-50 (3279)
2009: 11^{5}GF, 9^{0}GF,

	Starts	1st	2nd	3rd	Win & Pl
Career Total (Turf)	4	0	0	0	0
Career Total (AW)	1	0	0	0	

Going (Turf): Sf: 0-0 GS: 0-1 Gd: 0-1 GF: 0-2 Fm: 0-0
Distance: 5f/6f: 0-0 7f-8f: 0-3 9f-13f: 0-2 14f+: 0-0
Track : LH: 0-1 RH: 0-2 Tight: 0-2 Gall: 0-0
Aids: Bl: 0-0 Vi: 0-0 Tstrap: 0-0 Ckp: 0-0
Best Rating: 65 8/08 Newb 7f gd-sft

Watergate (IRE)

108(96) (79)**89**

3-y-o gr g Verglas (IRE)-Moy Water (IRE) (Tirol)
Sir Mark Prescott Charles C Walker-Osborne House III

Placings:44164-400302 (6594)
2009: 8^{4}G, 10^{0}GF, 9^{0}GF, 9^{3}GF, 8^{0}SD, 10^{2}GS,

	Starts	1st	2nd	3rd	Win & Pl
Career Total (Turf)	9	1	1	1	7824
Career Total (AW)	2	0	0	0	289
84 7/08 Catt 7f			G-F	£3691	

Total win prize-money £3691

Going (Turf): Sf: 0-0 GS: 0-1 Gd: 0-3 **GF: 1-5** Fm: 0-0
Distance: 5f/6f: 0-2 **7f-8f: 1-5** 9f-13f: 0-4 14f+: 0-0
Track : **LH: 1-4** RH: 0-3 **Tight: 1-4** Gall: 0-0
Aids: Bl: 0-0 Vi: 0-0 Tstrap: 0-0 Ckp: 0-0
Best Rating: 89 7/09 NmkJ 1m good

Useful; effective over 1m-1m2f; acts on fast ground; goes on Polytrack; likes to race prominently.

Waterloo Corner

97(98) (65)**58**

7-y-o b g Cayman Kai (IRE)-Rasin Luck (Primitive Rising (USA))
R Craggs Ray Craggs

Placings:062/42233/6630/6500033602143/3640-54300 (4944)
2009: 10^{5}G, 14^{4}GF, 16^{3}G, 10^{0}GF, 10^{0}GF,

	Starts	1st	2nd	3rd	Win & Pl
Career Total (Turf)	19	0	1	5	3162
Career Total (AW)	15	1	3	3	5274
61 11/07 Wolv 1m1f103y (0-58)H			STD	£1706	

Total win prize-money £1706

Going (Turf): **Sf: 0-1 GS: 0-2 Gd: 0-8 GF: 0-6 Fm: 0-2**
Distance: 5f/6f: 0-0 7f-8f: 0-7 **9f-13f: 1-25** 14f+: 0-2
Track : **LH: 1-30** RH: 0-3 **Tight: 1-19** Gall: 0-2
Aids: Bl: 0-3 Vi: 0-3 Tstrap: 0-2 Ckp: 0-2
Best Rating: 71 6/06 Rdcr 1m3f firm

Moderate; stays 1m3f; acts on Polytrack and Fibresand and fast turf.

Waterloo Dock

(100) (68)**50**

4-y-o b g Hunting Lion (IRE)-Scenic Air (Hadeer)
M Quinn M J Quinn

Placings:055/220003-41200 (7691)
2009: 8^{4}SD, 6^{1}SD, 6^{2}SD, 6^{0}SD, 7^{0}SD,

	Starts	1st	2nd	3rd	Win & Pl
Career Total (Turf)	3	0	0	0	0
Career Total (AW)	11	1	3	1	4745
65 2/09 Ling 6f			STD	£2729	

Total win prize-money £2730

Going (Turf): Sf: 0-0 GS: 0-0 Gd: 0-0 GF: 0-3 Fm: 0-0
Distance: **5f/6f: 1-4** 7f-8f: 0-10 9f-13f: 0-0 14f+: 0-0
Track : **LH: 1-10** RH: 0-2 **Tight: 1-9** Gall: 0-1
Aids: Bl: 0-0 Vi: 0-0 Tstrap: 0-0 Ckp: 0-0
Best Rating: 68 4/09 Ling 6f stand

Modest; suited by 6f; acts on Polytrack.

Waterside (IRE)

105(103) (91)**69**

10-y-o ch g Lake Coniston (IRE)-Classic Ring (IRE) (Auction Ring (USA))
S Curran L M Power

Placings:43220/21000010/0002631404/003031124603100/1043553030134435142/5000410411215100/52123610006223530460/1103-00510505252 (5179)
2009: 8^{0}SD, 10^{0}SD, 11^{5}SD, 8^{1}SD, 9^{0}SD, 8^{5}SD, 10^{0}GF, 12^{5}SD, 10^{2}GF, 9^{5}SD, 8^{2}G,

	Starts	1st	2nd	3rd	Win & Pl
Career Total (Turf)	58	9	9	10	96161
Career Total (AW)	50	10	4	4	82309
71 4/09 Wolv 1m141y				STD	£2047
77 1/08 Kemp 1m2f				STD	£1774
80 1/08 Kemp 7f				STD	£2047
108 3/07 Kemp 7f	(0-100)H			STD	£9971
102 1/07 Sthl 6f				STD	£11334
96 8/06 Sand 7f16y	(0-90)H			G-F	£8096
90 6/06 Gdwd 1m	(0-85)H			G-F	£6800
89 6/06 Gdwd 7f	(0-85)H			G-F	£6800
93 5/06 Kemp 1m	(0-90)H			STD	£11217
90 3/06 Sthl 1m	(0-85)H			STD	£6477
88 11/05 Ling 1m	(0-85)H			STD	£5742
86 6/05 Epsm 1m114y				G-F	£4134
86 1/05 Ling 7f	(0-85)H			STD	£6773
91 8/04 Gdwd 7f	D(0-75)			G-S	£5642
83 6/04 Sand 7f16y	C(0-100)H			G-F	£12325
76 6/04 Folk 7f	E(0-70)			G-F	£3493
76 10/03 Wind 6f	E(0-75)H			G-F	£2182
84 11/02 Ling 7f	E(0-75)H			STD	£3503
78 5/02 Wind 6f	D			SFT	£4758

Total win prize-money £115125

Going (Turf): Sf: 1-4 GS: 1-11 Gd: 0-15 **GF: 7-28** Fm: 0-0
Distance: 5f/6f: 3-20**7f-8f: 13-71** 9f-13f: 3-17 14f+: 0-0
Track : LH: 7-59 **RH: 9-29 Tight: 5-44** Gall: 2-11
Aids: Bl: 0-0 Vi: 0-0 Tstrap: 0-0 Ckp: 0-0
Best Rating: 108 3/07 Kemp 7f stand

Useful on turf/smart on the All-Weather; effective from 6f-1m; acts on most ground; tough and reliable, a credit to his trainer.

Watson's Bay

104(108) (73)**74**

4-y-o b c Royal Applause-Multaka (USA) (Gone West (USA))
P Howling (Miss Tor Sturgis 25/5) Paul Terry

Placings:0456646-154303433342333460230 (6244)
2009: 8^{1}SD, 8^{5}SD, 9^{4}SD, 9^{3}SD, 10^{0}SD, 10^{3}SD, 9^{4}GF, 11^{3}GF, 12^{3}SD, 11^{3}GF, 13^{4}GF, 12^{2}GF, 12^{3}G, 12^{3}G, 12^{3}GF, 12^{4}G, 11^{6}F, 10^{0}GF, 12^{2}SF, 11^{3}GF, 12^{0}G,

	Starts	1st	2nd	3rd	Win & Pl
Career Total (Turf)	16	0	1	6	5593
Career Total (AW)	12	1	1	3	5261
73 1/09 Wolv 1m141y				STD	£2729

Total win prize-money £2730

Going (Turf): **Sf: 0-0 GS: 0-0 Gd: 0-5 GF: 0-8 Fm: 0-1**
Distance: 5f/6f: 0-0 7f-8f: 0-7 **9f-13f: 1-21** 14f+: 0-0
Track : **LH: 1-16** RH: 0-10 **Tight: 1-15** Gall: 0-4
Aids: Bl: 0-0 Vi: 0-0 Tstrap: 0-0 Ckp: 0-0
Best Rating: 74 7/09 Epsm 1m4f10y good

Modest; stays 1m5f; acts on Polytrack; handles fast turf.

Waveband

100(98) (73)**86**

2-y-o ch f Exceed And Excel (AUS)-Licence To Thrill (Wolfhound (USA))
M Johnston Sheikh Hamdan Bin Mohammed Al Maktoum

Placings:43233103 (6477)
2009: 5^{4}GF, 5^{3}GF, 6^{2}GF, 5^{3}GF, 6^{3}GF, 5^{1}SD, 6^{0}GF, 7^{3}GF,

	Starts	1st	2nd	3rd	Win & Pl
Career Total (Turf)	7	0	1	4	84701

	Starts	1st	2nd	3rd	Win & Pl
Career Total (AW)	1	1	0	0	3886

73 9/09 Wolv 5f20y STD £3885
Total win prize-money £3886

Going (Turf): Sf: 0-0 GS: 0-0 Gd: 0-0 GF: 0-7 Fm: 0-0
Distance: 5f/6f: 1-7 7f-8f: 0-1 9f-13f: 0-0 14f+: 0-0
Track : LH: 1-2 RH: 0-0 Tight: 1-2 Gall: 0-0
Aids: Bl: 0-0 Vi: 0-0 Tstrap: 0-0 Ckp: 0-0
Best Rating: 86 10/09 NmkR 7f gd-fm

Fair; suited by 5f-7f; acts on fast ground or Polytrack.

Wavertree Bounty

83 **53**
2-y-o b f Pastoral Pursuits-Grecian Halo (USA) (Southern Halo (USA))
C F Wall Wavertree Racing Partnership F

Placings:060 **(7095)**
2009: 7^{0}C, 8^{6}S, 8^{0}G,

	Starts	1st	2nd	3rd	Win & Pl
Career Total (Turf)	3	0	0	0	0

Going (Turf): Sf: 0-1 GS: 0-0 Gd: 0-2 GF: 0-0 Fm: 0-0
Distance: 5f/6f: 0-0 7f-8f: 0-2 9f-13f: 0-1 14f+: 0-0
Track : LH: 0-0 RH: 0-0 Tight: 0-0 Gall: 0-0
Aids: Bl: 0-0 Vi: 0-0 Tstrap: 0-0 Ckp: 0-0
Best Rating: 53 10/09 Sals 1m soft

Wavertree Princess (IRE)

86(90) (72)**67**
4-y-o gr f Invincible Spirit (IRE)-Blushing Queen (IRE) (Desert King (IRE))
C F Wall Wavertree Racing Partnership D

Placings:6625615/4600500-0000 **(7241)**
2009: 5^{0}GS, 5^{0}G, 5^{0}G, 5^{0}S,

	Starts	1st	2nd	3rd	Win & Pl
Career Total (Turf)	12	0	1	0	1156
Career Total (AW)	6	1	0	0	3251

72 11/07 Ling 5f STD £2914
Total win prize-money £2915

Going (Turf): Sf: 0-1 GS: 0-2 Gd: 0-3 GF: 0-6 Fm: 0-0
Distance: 5f/6f: 1-17 7f-8f: 0-1 9f-13f: 0-0 14f+: 0-0
Track : LH: 1-6 RH: 0-1 Tight: 1-4 Gall: 0-2
Aids: Bl: 0-0 Vi: 0-0 Tstrap: 0-0 Ckp: 0-0
Best Rating: 74 11/07 Donc 6f gd-fm

Fair; effective over 5f; acts on fast ground; also goes on Polytrack.

Wavertree Warrior (IRE)

100(106) (90)**60**
7-y-o br g Indian Lodge (IRE)-Karamana (Habitat)
N P Littmoden Wavertree Racing Partnership C

Placings:032030/3155152205/0343012161020424/01005062004504633 4/000404003-42340040600 **(5791)**
2009: 8^{4}SD, 8^{2}SD, 8^{3}SD, 8^{4}SD, 10^{0}SD, 8^{0}SD, 8^{4}GF, 8^{0}GS, 8^{6}G, 7^{0}GS, 8^{0}G,

	Starts	1st	2nd	3rd	Win & Pl
Career Total (Turf)	39	4	6	3	51997
Career Total (AW)	31	2	2	6	29659

96 2/07 Ling 7f (0-100)H STD £11217
95 6/06 Sand 7f16y (0-100)H G-F £12464
93 5/06 Gdwd 7f (0-80)H G-S £7124
86 4/06 Wind 1m67y (0-85)H GD £6477
83 7/05 Ling 1m (0-80)H STD £6987
75 5/05 Bath 1m5y G-F £3367
Total win prize-money £47639

Going (Turf): Sf: 0-5 GS: 1-14 Gd: 1-11 GF: 2-7 Fm: 0-1
Distance: 5f/6f: 0-1 7f-8f: 4-51 9f-13f: 2-18 14f+: 0-0
Track : LH: 3-41 RH: 3-17 Tight: 4-39 Gall: 0-4
Aids: Bl: 0-25 Vi: 0-1 Tstrap: 0-1 Ckp: 0-1
Best Rating: 96 2/07 Ling 7f stand

Fair; effective over 7f-1m; acts on most ground; also goes on Polytrack; needs a strong pace to be seen at his best; has worn blinkers.

Waziri (IRE)

94 **35**
8-y-o b g Mtoto-Euphorie (GER) (Feenpark (GER))
M Hill The Holdsworth Family

Placings:464/1003000/00600/50 **(4992)**
2009: 12^{5}GF, 9^{0}GF,

	Starts	1st	2nd	3rd	Win & Pl
Career Total (Turf)	13	1	0	1	6290
Career Total (AW)	4	0	0	0	0

76 6/04 Gdwd 1m1f192yD(0-80)H G-F £5655
Total win prize-money £5655

Going (Turf): Sf: 0-1 GS: 0-1 Gd: 0-6 GF: 1-5 Fm: 0-0
Distance: 5f/6f: 0-0 7f-8f: 0-3 9f-13f: 1-13 14f+: 0-1
Track : LH: 0-11 RH: 1-5 Tight: 1-11 Gall: 0-3
Aids: Bl: 0-0 Vi: 0-1 Tstrap: 0-0 Ckp: 0-0
Best Rating: 76 8/04 Newb 1m1f gd-sft

We Have A Dream

107(102) (78)**92**
4-y-o b/br g Oasis Dream-Final Shot (Dalsaan)
W R Muir The Dreaming Squires

Placings:000132011/6125116006000-0025031221102 **(6994)**
2009: 6^{0}GF, 6^{0}GF, 6^{2}GF, 6^{5}GF, 5^{0}GF, 6^{3}G, 6^{1}G, 6^{2}SD, 6^{2}GS, 6^{1}G, 6^{1}GS, 6^{0}GS, 6^{2}G,

	Starts	1st	2nd	3rd	Win & Pl
Career Total (Turf)	29	8	4	2	42904
Career Total (AW)	6	1	2	0	4803

92 10/09 Folk 6f (0-80)H G-S £5180
89 9/09 Gdwd 6f (0-80)H GD £4857
78 7/09 Ayr 6f (0-80)H GD £6476
81 6/08 Folk 6f (0-85)H G-F £4533
83 5/08 Leic 5f218y (0-80)H G-F £4209
83 4/08 Folk 6f (0-75)H G-S £2331
69 10/07 Nott 6f15y (0-75) SFT £3238
66 9/07 Kemp 6f (0-65) STD £2047
59 7/07 Ling 6f SFT £3238
Total win prize-money £36113

Going (Turf): Sf: 2-6 GS: 2-4 Gd: 2-7 GF: 2-12 Fm: 0-0
Distance: 5f/6f: 8-30 7f-8f: 1-5 9f-13f: 0-0 14f+: 0-0
Track : LH: 0-6 RH: 1-2 Tight: 0-4 Gall: 0-7
Aids: Bl: 0-1 Vi: 0-0 Tstrap: 0-0 Ckp: 0-0
Best Rating: 92 10/09 Folk 6f gd-sft

Useful; effective over 6f; acts on most ground and on Polytrack; suited by forcing tactics.

We'll Come

109 **113**
5-y-o b g Elnadim (USA)-Off The Blocks (Salse (USA))
M A Jarvis Stephen Dartnell

Placings:202/21333/40236304-010100 **(6448)**
2009: 7^{0}GF, 8^{1}GF, 8^{0}G, 8^{1}GS, 8^{0}GF, 8^{0}GF,

	Starts	1st	2nd	3rd	Win & Pl
Career Total (Turf)	22	3	4	5	77120

113 8/09 Asct 1m (0-100)H G-S £17230
106 6/09 Sals 1m (0-100)H G-F £11215
94 5/07 Yarm 1m3y GD £2914
Total win prize-money £31362

Going (Turf): Sf: 0-5 GS: 1-2 Gd: 1-6 GF: 1-9 Fm: 0-0
Distance: 5f/6f: 0-2 7f-8f: 2-17 9f-13f: 1-3 14f+: 0-0
Track : LH: 0-3 RH: 1-3 Tight: 0-0 Gall: 1-2
Aids: Bl: 2-9 Vi: 0-0 Tstrap: 0-4 Ckp: 0-4
Best Rating: 113 8/09 Asct 1m gd-sft

Very useful; effective over 7f-1m; acts on most ground; has worn blinkers and cheekpieces.

We'll Deal Again

95(91) (64)**70**
2-y-o b c Gentleman's Deal (IRE)-Emma Amour (Emarati (USA))
M W Easterby K Wreglesworth

Placings:20303523 **(7168)**
2009: 6^{2}GS, 7^{0}G, 6^{3}G, 6^{0}GF, 7^{3}GS, 8^{5}GF, 6^{2}SD, 7^{3}S,

	Starts	1st	2nd	3rd	Win & Pl
Career Total (Turf)	7	0	1	3	3227
Career Total (AW)	1	0	1	0	746

Going (Turf): Sf: 0-1 GS: 0-2 Gd: 0-2 GF: 0-2 Fm: 0-0
Distance: 5f/6f: 0-4 7f-8f: 0-3 9f-13f: 0-1 14f+: 0-0
Track : LH: 0-5 RH: 0-0 Tight: 0-0 Gall: 0-2
Aids: Bl: 0-0 Vi: 0-0 Tstrap: 0-0 Ckp: 0-0
Best Rating: 70 5/09 Ripn 6f gd-sft

Modest; effective over 7f; acts on easy ground.

We're Delighted

102 (55)**75**
4-y-o b g Tobougg (IRE)-Samadilla (IRE) (Mujadil (USA))
N B King (T D Walford 27/9) B M V Williams & N J Catterwell

Placings:35503/10060520-3506405 **(4941)**
2009: 8^{3}GF, 7^{5}GS, 7^{0}G, 9^{6}GF, 9^{4}GF, 10^{0}G, 8^{5}GF,

	Starts	1st	2nd	3rd	Win & Pl
Career Total (Turf)	19	1	1	3	6446
Career Total (AW)	1	0	0	0	

72 5/08 Newc 7f (0-75)H G-F £3238
Total win prize-money £3238

Going (Turf): Sf: 0-3 GS: 0-3 Gd: 0-6 GF: 1-7 Fm: 0-0
Distance: 5f/6f: 0-2 7f-8f: 1-9 9f-13f: 0-9 14f+: 0-0
Track : LH: 0-8 RH: 0-4 Tight: 0-4 Gall: 0-0
Aids: Bl: 0-0 Vi: 0-0 Tstrap: 0-0 Ckp: 0-0
Best Rating: 75 4/09 Newc 1m3y gd-fm

Fair; stays 1m; best on fast ground.

Weald Park (USA)

107(101) (97)**101**
3-y-o ch g Cozzene (USA)-Promptly (IRE) (Lead On Time (USA))
R Hannon The Heffer Syndicate

Placings:212020-5000006 **(7393)**
2009: 9^{5}SD, 10^{0}GF, 10^{0}S, 8^{0}G, 10^{0}G, 8^{0}GS, 10^{6}SD,

	Starts	1st	2nd	3rd	Win & Pl
Career Total (Turf)	11	1	3	0	39985
Career Total (AW)	2	0	0	0	2075

84 6/08 NmkJ 7f FRM £5180
Total win prize-money £5181

Going (Turf): Sf: 0-1 GS: 0-2 Gd: 0-4 GF: 0-2 **Fm: 1-2**
Distance: 5f/6f: 0-1 **7f-8f: 1-7** 9f-13f: 0-5 14f+: 0-0
Track : LH: 0-2 RH: 0-3 Tight: 0-1 Gall: 0-2
Aids: Bl: 0-0 Vi: 0-1 Tstrap: 0-0 Ckp: 0-0
Best Rating: 101 7/08 NmkJ 7f good

Very useful; Group 2 placed; effective at 7f; act on fast and easy ground.

Webbow (IRE)

110 (69)**101**
7-y-o b g Dr Devious (IRE)-Ower (IRE) (Lomond (USA))
N Tinkler Wentdale Limited

Placings:21305/21411/4320-230244035 (7294)
2009: 8^{2}GF, 8^{3}GS, 7^{0}GF, 8^{2}GF, 8^{4}G, 8^{4}GF, 8^{0}GF, 7^{3}G, 7^{5}S,

	Starts	1st	2nd	3rd	Win & Pl
Career Total (Turf)	21	3	4	4	55861
Career Total (AW)	2	1	1	0	3256

95 8/07 Donc 1m (0-95)H G-F £12285
88 8/07 Thsk 1m (0-90)H G-F £7772
90 6/07 Carl 7f200y H G-S £5181
69 3/06 Sthl 7f STD £2388
Total win prize-money £27628

Going (Turf): Sf: 0-5 GS: 1-3 Gd: 0-3 **GF: 2-10** Fm: 0-0
Distance: 5f/6f: 0-0 **7f-8f: 4-18** 9f-13f: 0-5 14f+: 0-0
Track : **LH: 3-12** RH: 1-5 Tight: 1-6 Gall: 1-5
Aids: Bl: 0-0 Vi: 0-0 Tstrap: 0-0 Ckp: 0-0
Best Rating: 101 7/09 York 1m gd-fm

Very useful; effective at around 1m; acts on most types of ground; goes on sand.

Wedding Dream

65(101) (56)
2-y-o b f Oasis Dream-Gretna (Groom Dancer (USA))
K A Ryan J H Henderson

Placings:000551 (7722)
2009: 5^{0}GF, 5^{0}SD, 6^{0}GF, 7^{5}SD, 7^{5}SD, 8^{1}SD,

	Starts	1st	2nd	3rd	Win & Pl
Career Total (Turf)	2	0	0	0	
Career Total (AW)	4	1	0	0	2047

56 12/09 Sthl 1m (0-65) STD £2047
Total win prize-money £2047

Going (Turf): Sf: 0-0 GS: 0-0 Gd: 0-0 GF: 0-2 Fm: 0-0
Distance: 5f/6f: 0-3 **7f-8f: 1-3** 9f-13f: 0-0 14f+: 0-0
Track : **LH: 1-3** RH: 0-0 Tight: 0-0 Gall: 0-0
Aids: Bl: 0-1 Vi: 0-0 Tstrap: 0-1 Ckp: 0-1
Best Rating: 56 12/09 Sthl 1m stand

Moderate; stays 1m; handles Fibresand; has worn head-gear.

Wedding List

87(102) (83)**58**
3-y-o ch f Pivotal-Confetti (Groom Dancer (USA))
W J Haggas Cheveley Park Stud

Placings:021-0 (2821)
2009: 6^{0}GF,

	Starts	1st	2nd	3rd	Win & Pl
Career Total (Turf)	2	0	0	0	
Career Total (AW)	2	1	1	0	6144

83 11/08 GrLe 6f STD £5180
Total win prize-money £5181

Going (Turf): Sf: 0-0 GS: 0-0 Gd: 0-1 GF: 0-1 Fm: 0-0
Distance: **5f/6f: 1-3** 7f-8f: 0-1 9f-13f: 0-0 14f+: 0-0
Track : **LH: 1-2** RH: 0-0 Tight: 0-0 **Gall: 1-2**
Aids: Bl: 0-0 Vi: 0-0 Tstrap: 0-0 Ckp: 0-0
Best Rating: 83 11/08 GrLe 6f stand

Useful; effective over 6f and acts on Polytrack.

Wednesdays Boy (IRE)

85(99) (54)**61**
6-y-o b g Alhaarth (IRE)-Sheen Falls (IRE) (Prince Rupert (FR))
P D Niven Michael Paley

Placings:0500064/2203416/65500511544-000045 (7174)
2009: 8^{0}G, 8^{0}GS, 8^{0}G, 7^{0}G, 9^{4}SD, 9^{5}S,

	Starts	1st	2nd	3rd	Win & Pl
Career Total (Turf)	25	3	1	1	10244
Career Total (AW)	6	0	1	0	1087

61 8/08 Ayr 1m (0-60)H SFT £2590
58 8/08 Ayr 1m (0-65)H G-S £2729
61 8/06 Ayr 1m2f (0-60)H G-S £3238
Total win prize-money £8559

Going (Turf): Sf: 1-8 **GS: 2-6** Gd: 0-9 GF: 0-1 Fm: 0-1
Distance: 5f/6f: 0-6 **7f-8f: 2-9** 9f-13f: 1-16 14f+: 0-0
Track : **LH: 3-19** RH: 0-9 Tight: 0-10 Gall: 0-1
Aids: Bl: 0-1 Vi: 0-0 Tstrap: 3-17 Ckp: 3-17
Best Rating: 61 10/08 Ayr 1m heavy

Moderate; stays 1m2f; acts on easy ground.

Wee Bizzom

84(90) (50)**44**
3-y-o b f Makbul-Lone Pine (Sesaro (USA))
A Berry Alan Berry

Placings:0564650664-524060600 (3651)
2009: 6^{5}SS, 5^{2}SD, 5^{4}SD, 5^{0}SD, 5^{6}GF, 5^{0}GF, 7^{6}GF, 7^{0}GF, 6^{0}G,

	Starts	1st	2nd	3rd	Win & Pl
Career Total (Turf)	11	0	0	0	289
Career Total (AW)	8	0	1	0	797

Going (Turf): Sf: 0-2 GS: 0-0 Gd: 0-3 GF: 0-5 Fm: 0-1
Distance: 5f/6f: 0-17 7f-8f: 0-2 9f-13f: 0-0 14f+: 0-0
Track : LH: 0-6 RH: 0-3 Tight: 0-7 Gall: 0-1
Aids: Bl: 0-1 Vi: 0-0 Tstrap: 0-0 Ckp: 0-0
Best Rating: 50 1/09 Sthl 5f stand

Moderate; effective over 5f; acts on Fibresand.

Wee Bobbie

87(80) (33)**36**
2-y-o b f Acclamation-Bobbie Dee (Blakeney)
Mrs P N Dutfield Mrs Nerys Dutfield

Placings:00 (6911)
2009: 5^{0}G, 7^{0}SD,

	Starts	1st	2nd	3rd	Win & Pl
Career Total (Turf)	1	0	0	0	
Career Total (AW)	1	0	0	0	

Going (Turf): Sf: 0-0 GS: 0-0 Gd: 0-1 GF: 0-0 Fm: 0-0
Distance: 5f/6f: 0-1 7f-8f: 0-1 9f-13f: 0-0 14f+: 0-0
Track : LH: 0-2 RH: 0-0 Tight: 0-1 Gall: 0-1
Aids: Bl: 0-0 Vi: 0-0 Tstrap: 0-0 Ckp: 0-0
Best Rating: 36 9/09 Bath 5f11y good

Wee Buns

51(99) (69)**59**
4-y-o b g Piccolo-Gigetta (IRE) (Brief Truce (USA))
P Burgoyne Mrs C Leigh-Turner

Placings:054103443/5131230300-0000 (1152)
2009: 6^{0}SD, 7^{0}SD, 5^{0}SD, 6^{0}G,

	Starts	1st	2nd	3rd	Win & Pl
Career Total (Turf)	3	0	0	0	154
Career Total (AW)	20	3	1	5	8310

68 2/08 Kemp 6f (0-65)H STD £2047
59 2/08 Kemp 6f STD £2047
65 9/07 Wolv 5f216y (0-65) STD £2047
Total win prize-money £6144

Going (Turf): Sf: 0-0 GS: 0-0 Gd: 0-3 GF: 0-0 Fm: 0-0
Distance: **5f/6f: 3-14** 7f-8f: 0-9 9f-13f: 0-0 14f+: 0-0
Track : LH: 1-16 **RH: 2-5 Tight: 1-14** Gall: 0-3
Aids: Bl: 0-2 Vi: 0-0 Tstrap: 0-0 Ckp: 0-0
Best Rating: 69 3/08 Ling 7f stand

Modest; effective over 6f-7f; acts on Polytrack.

Wee Charlie Castle (IRE)

103(103) (71)**82**
6-y-o b g Sinndar (IRE)-Seasonal Blossom (IRE) (Fairy King (USA))
I Semple Mrs Francesca Mitchell

Placings:63024023200052/25525105015/03300544553/2 22012210265-23141053 (6986)
2009: 11^{2}GF, 10^{3}GF, 14^{1}G, 14^{4}S, 12^{1}F, 12^{0}GF, 14^{5}GF, 10^{3}G,

	Starts	1st	2nd	3rd	Win & Pl
Career Total (Turf)	32	4	8	4	27186
Career Total (AW)	25	2	5	3	10388

82 8/09 Bevl 1m4f16y (0-75)H FRM £3885
81 7/09 Muss 1m6f (0-75)H GD £3885
72 7/08 Sand 1m2f7y (0-75)H G-F £3238
67 6/08 Yarm 1m2f21y (0-60)H G-F £2137
71 11/06 Kemp 1m4f (0-65)H STD £2388
66 8/06 Kemp 1m2f (0-65)H STD £3238
Total win prize-money £18775

Going (Turf): Sf: 0-1 GS: 0-3 Gd: 1-8 **GF: 2-18** Fm: 1-2
Distance: 5f/6f: 0-3 7f-8f: 0-13 **9f-13f: 5-38** 14f+: 1-3
Track : LH: 1-23 **RH: 5-21 Tight: 3-19** Gall: 0-2
Aids: Bl: 0-4 Vi: 0-6 Tstrap: 0-0 Ckp: 0-0
Best Rating: 82 8/09 Bevl 1m4f16y firm

Fair; effective at up to 1m4f; acts on fast ground and on Polytrack; has worn a visor.

Wee Giant (USA)

94(97) (77)**60**
3-y-o ch g Giant's Causeway (USA)-Christmas In Aiken (USA) (Affirmed (USA))
K A Ryan Errigal Racing

Placings:01-0006 (7141)
2009: 10^{0}GF, 10^{0}G, 10^{0}GS, 8^{6}SD,

	Starts	1st	2nd	3rd	Win & Pl
Career Total (Turf)	4	0	0	0	
Career Total (AW)	2	1	0	0	2914

77 11/08 Wolv 7f32y STD £2914
Total win prize-money £2914

Going (Turf): Sf: 0-0 GS: 0-2 Gd: 0-1 GF: 0-1 Fm: 0-0
Distance: 5f/6f: 0-0 **7f-8f: 1-1** 9f-13f: 0-5 14f+: 0-0

Track : LH: 1-6 RH: 0-0 Tight: 1-3 Gall: 0-2
Aids: Bl: 0-0 Vi: 0-0 Tstrap: 0-0 Ckp: 0-0
Best Rating: 77 11/08 Wolv 7f32y stand

Fair; effective over 7f; acts on Polytrack.

Wee Sonny (IRE)

97(100) (78)75
3-y-o b g Refuse To Bend (IRE)-Coup De Coeur (IRE) (Kahyasi)
Liam Lennon (Noel T Chance 20/9) M R J Houston

Placings:63-03443 (4562)
2009: 11^0GS, 9^3GF, 9^4GF, 11^4G, 10^3G,

	Starts	1st	2nd	3rd	Win & Pl
Career Total (Turf)	5	0	0	2	2017
Career Total (AW)	2	0	0	1	435

Going (Turf): Sf: 0-0 GS: 0-1 Gd: 0-2 GF: 0-2 Fm: 0-0
Distance: 5f/6f: 0-0 7f-8f: 0-2 9f-13f: 0-5 14f+: 0-0
Track : LH: 0-4 RH: 0-2 Tight: 0-4 Gall: 0-2
Aids: Bl: 0-0 Vi: 0-0 Tstrap: 0-0 Ckp: 0-0
Best Rating: 78 12/08 Ling 1m stand

Modest; effective over 1m; acts on Polytrack.

Wee Ziggy

(90) (31)45
6-y-o b g Ziggy's Dancer (USA)-Midnight Arrow (Robellino (USA))
M Mullineaux Miss Gill Quincey

Placings:000/0000P00/6 (7608)
2009: 16^6SD,

	Starts	1st	2nd	3rd	Win & Pl
Career Total (Turf)	8	0	0	0	
Career Total (AW)	3	0	0	0	0

Going (Turf): Sf: 0-1 GS: 0-2 Gd: 0-2 GF: 0-1 Fm: 0-2
Distance: 5f/6f: 0-1 7f-8f: 0-4 9f-13f: 0-4 14f+: 0-2
Track : LH: 0-7 RH: 0-3 Tight: 0-8 Gall: 0-0
Aids: Bl: 0-1 Vi: 0-0 Tstrap: 0-1 Ckp: 0-1
Best Rating: 45 8/07 Hayd 1m6f gd-fm

Weekend Away (IRE)

92(95) (63)55
3-y-o b g Invincible Spirit (IRE)-March Star (IRE) (Mac's Imp (USA))
S Kirk Patrick Wilmott

Placings:0500000 (7275)
2009: 8^0G, 6^5GF, 8^0SD, 8^0G, 5^0SD, 5^0SD, 7^0SD,

	Starts	1st	2nd	3rd	Win & Pl
Career Total (Turf)	3	0	0	0	0
Career Total (AW)	4	0	0	0	

Going (Turf): Sf: 0-0 GS: 0-0 Gd: 0-2 GF: 0-1 Fm: 0-0
Distance: 5f/6f: 0-2 7f-8f: 0-3 9f-13f: 0-2 14f+: 0-0
Track : LH: 0-3 RH: 0-1 Tight: 0-3 Gall: 0-0
Aids: Bl: 0-0 Vi: 0-0 Tstrap: 0-0 Ckp: 0-0
Best Rating: 63 8/09 Kemp 1m stand

Weekend Millionair (IRE)

95 68
2-y-o ch g Arakan (USA)-Almi Ad (USA) (Silver Hawk (USA))
P D Evans Bathwick Gold Partnership

Placings:334 (6214)
2009: 6^3S, 7^3S, 7^4GF,

	Starts	1st	2nd	3rd	Win & Pl
Career Total (Turf)	3	0	0	2	1483

Going (Turf): Sf: 0-2 GS: 0-0 Gd: 0-0 GF: 0-1 Fm: 0-0
Distance: 5f/6f: 0-0 7f-8f: 0-3 9f-13f: 0-0 14f+: 0-0
Track : LH: 0-1 RH: 0-0 Tight: 0-0 Gall: 0-0
Aids: Bl: 0-0 Vi: 0-0 Tstrap: 0-0 Ckp: 0-0
Best Rating: 68 9/09 Rdcr 7f gd-fm

Modest; stays 7f; handles most ground.

Weeping Willow (IRE)

80 41
2-y-o b f Kheleyf (USA)-Bezant (IRE) (Zamindar (USA))
J H M Gosden H R H Princess Haya Of Jordan

Placings:0 (4603)
2009: 6^0GF,

	Starts	1st	2nd	3rd	Win & Pl
Career Total (Turf)	1	0	0	0	

Going (Turf): Sf: 0-0 GS: 0-0 Gd: 0-0 GF: 0-1 Fm: 0-0
Distance: 5f/6f: 0-1 7f-8f: 0-0 9f-13f: 0-0 14f+: 0-0
Track : LH: 0-0 RH: 0-0 Tight: 0-0 Gall: 0-1
Aids: Bl: 0-0 Vi: 0-0 Tstrap: 0-0 Ckp: 0-0
Best Rating: 41 8/09 Wind 6f gd-fm

Weet A Surprise

102(107) (79)69
4-y-o b f Bertolini (USA)-Ticcatoo (IRE) (Dolphin Street (FR))
J W Unett (R Hollinshead 19/3) J E Price

Placings:61055351011 1/562600400-654153332154631 (7273)
2009: 5^6SD, 6^5SD, 5^4HY, 5^1SD, 5^5GF, 5^3G, 5^3G, 5^3HY, 5^2G, 5^1SD, 5^5SD, 5^4GF, 5^6SD, 7^3SD, 5^1SD,

	Starts	1st	2nd	3rd	Win & Pl
Career Total (Turf)	17	1	2	3	7842
Career Total (AW)	19	7	0	2	18984

77	11/09	Wolv	5f216y	(0-70)H	STD	£3238
79	9/09	Wolv	5f216y	(0-65)H	STD	£2729
71	6/09	Wolv	5f20y	(0-55)H	STD	£2729
76	12/07	Sthl	5f	(0-75)	STD	£2047
73	12/07	Sthl	5f	(0-75)	STD	£2047
71	11/07	Wolv	5f20y	(0-75)	STD	£2968
67	10/07	Wolv	5f20y	(0-65)	STD	£2388
63	6/07	Wwck	5f		G-S	£3238

Total win prize-money £21391

Going (Turf): Sf: 0-5 **GS: 1-2** Gd: 0-4 GF: 0-6 Fm: 0-0
Distance: **5f/6f: 8-35** 7f-8f: 0-1 9f-13f: 0-0 14f+: 0-0
Track : **LH: 6-20** RH: 0-1 **Tight: 5-14** Gall: 0-2
Aids: Bl: 0-0 **Vi: 3-13** Tstrap: 0-0 Ckp: 0-0
Best Rating: 79 9/09 Wolv 5f216y stand

Modest; effective over 5f-6f; acts on easy ground; also goes on sand; has worn a visor.

Weet In Nerja

83(94) (55)26
3-y-o b g Captain Rio-Persian Fortune (Forzando)
J W Unett (R Hollinshead 24/4) J E Price

Placings:64300-2553054000 (7609)
2009: 5^2SD, 5^5SD, 5^5SD, 5^3SD, 5^0SD, 7^5SF, 5^4SD, 7^0SD, 8^0G, 8^0SD,

	Starts	1st	2nd	3rd	Win & Pl
Career Total (Turf)	2	0	0	0	
Career Total (AW)	13	0	1	2	1485

Going (Turf): Sf: 0-1 GS: 0-0 Gd: 0-1 GF: 0-0 Fm: 0-0
Distance: 5f/6f: 0-10 7f-8f: 0-5 9f-13f: 0-0 14f+: 0-0
Track : LH: 0-12 RH: 0-1 Tight: 0-11 Gall: 0-0
Aids: Bl: 0-0 Vi: 0-1 Tstrap: 0-8 Ckp: 0-8
Best Rating: 55 1/09 Wolv 5f216y stand

Moderate; suited by 6f and Polytrack.

Weetentherty

82 51
2-y-o b c Bertolini (USA)-Binaa (IRE) (Marju (IRE))
J S Goldie C & B Racing Club

Placings:0005 (4035)
2009: 5^0G, 5^0GF, 6^0G, 6^5G,

	Starts	1st	2nd	3rd	Win & Pl
Career Total (Turf)	4	0	0	0	0

Going (Turf): Sf: 0-0 GS: 0-0 Gd: 0-3 GF: 0-1 Fm: 0-0
Distance: 5f/6f: 0-3 7f-8f: 0-1 9f-13f: 0-0 14f+: 0-0
Track : LH: 0-0 RH: 0-0 Tight: 0-0 Gall: 0-0
Aids: Bl: 0-0 Vi: 0-2 Tstrap: 0-0 Ckp: 0-0
Best Rating: 51 5/09 Ayr 6f good

Weetfromthechaff

64(98) (62)3
4-y-o gr g Weet-A-Minute (IRE)-Weet Ees Girl (IRE) (Common Grounds)
M A Barnes (R Hollinshead 23/2) J M Carlyle

Placings:005044/44452400-050440 (1562)
2009: 5^0SD, 7^5SD, 9^0SD, 5^4SD, 5^4SD, 12^0GF,

	Starts	1st	2nd	3rd	Win & Pl
Career Total (Turf)	5	0	0	0	176
Career Total (AW)	15	0	1	0	773

Going (Turf): Sf: 0-1 GS: 0-0 Gd: 0-1 GF: 0-2 Fm: 0-1
Distance: 5f/6f: 0-11 7f-8f: 0-7 9f-13f: 0-2 14f+: 0-0
Track : LH: 0-15 RH: 0-1 Tight: 0-13 Gall: 0-1
Aids: Bl: 0-0 Vi: 0-6 Tstrap: 0-5 Ckp: 0-5
Best Rating: 62 2/09 Wolv 5f216y stand

Moderate; effective over 6f-7f; acts on Polytrack.

Weimarland (IRE)

(86) (55)
2-y-o b c Elusive City (USA)-Night Spirit (IRE) (Night Shift (USA))
J A Osborne H R H Prince of Saxe-Weimar

Placings:6650 (7698)
2009: 6^6SD, 6^6SD, 5^5SF, 5^0SD,

	Starts	1st	2nd	3rd	Win & Pl
Career Total (Turf)	0	0	0	0	
Career Total (AW)	4	0	0	0	0

Going (Turf): Sf: 0-0 GS: 0-0 Gd: 0-0 GF: 0-0 Fm: 0-0
Distance: 5f/6f: 0-4 7f-8f: 0-0 9f-13f: 0-0 14f+: 0-0
Track : LH: 0-2 RH: 0-2 Tight: 0-1 Gall: 0-0
Aids: Bl: 0-0 Vi: 0-0 Tstrap: 0-0 Ckp: 0-0
Best Rating: 55 11/09 Wolv 5f20y std-fst

Moderate; effective at 5-6f; acts on Polytrack.

Welcome Applause (IRE)

78(89) (57)**57**

3-y-o b f Acclamation-Waseyla (IRE) (Sri Pekan (USA))

M G Quinlan R O Simpson

Placings:0666000-040 **(3862)**

2009: 10^{0}GF, 9^{4}GF, 8^{0}GF,

	Starts	1st	2nd	3rd	Win & Pl
Career Total (Turf)	7	0	0	0	144
Career Total (AW)	3	0	0	0	0

Going (Turf): **Sf: 0-1 GS: 0-1 Gd: 0-1 GF: 0-4 Fm: 0-0**
Distance: 5f/6f: 0-1 7f-8f: 0-6 9f-13f: 0-3 14f+: 0-0
Track : LH: 0-3 RH: 0-4 Tight: 0-2 Gall: 0-0
Aids: Bl: 0-1 Vi: 0-0 Tstrap: 0-0 Ckp: 0-0
Best Rating: **57** 8/08 Ling 7f stand

Welcome Approach

94(107) (64)**54**

6-y-o b g Most Welcome-Lucky Thing (Green Desert (USA))

J R Weymes T A Scothern

Placings:0123053000/4126262600/062503355423223350/0000004055**1565140-50006362611** **(7815)**

2009: 5^{5}SD, 5^{0}SD, 5^{0}GF, 5^{0}GF, 5^{6}G, 7^{3}GF, 5^{6}SD, 5^{2}SD, 5^{6}SD, 5^{1}SD, 5^{1}SD,

	Starts	1st	2nd	3rd	Win & Pl
Career Total (Turf)	51	2	8	8	28388
Career Total (AW)	15	4	1	0	11074

64	12/09	Wolv	5f216y	(0-63)H	STD	£1706
60	11/09	Wolv	5f216y	(0-65)H	STD	£2047
64	10/08	Wolv	5f216y	(0-70)H	STD	£3885
61	8/08	Wolv	5f216y	(0-50)H	STD	£2729
73	5/06	Muss	5f	(0-70)H	G-F	£3886
65	7/05	Muss	5f		G-F	£4381

Total win prize-money £18636

Going (Turf): Sf: 0-2 GS: 0-2 Gd: 0-16 **GF: 2-28** Fm: 0-3
Distance: **5f/6f: 6-63** 7f-8f: 0-3 9f-13f: 0-0 14f+: 0-0
Track : **LH: 4-24** RH: 0-7 **Tight: 4-15** Gall: 0-4
Aids: Bl: 0-3 Vi: 0-0 Tstrap: 0-0 Ckp: 0-0
Best Rating: **76** 8/07 Muss 5f gd-fm

Moderate; effective over 5f-6f; acts on fast ground and Polytrack.

Welcome Bounty

51

2-y-o ch c Bahamian Bounty-Welcome Home (Most Welcome)

D R Lanigan Saif Ali & Saeed H Altayer

Placings:0 **(7243)**

2009: 8^{0}S,

	Starts	1st	2nd	3rd	Win & Pl
Career Total (Turf)	1	0	0	0	

Going (Turf): **Sf: 0-1 GS: 0-0 Gd: 0-0 GF: 0-0 Fm: 0-0**
Distance: 5f/6f: 0-0 7f-8f: 0-0 9f-13f: 0-1 14f+: 0-0
Track : LH: 0-1 RH: 0-0 Tight: 0-0 Gall: 0-0
Aids: Bl: 0-0 Vi: 0-0 Tstrap: 0-0 Ckp: 0-0

Welcome Cat (USA)

(91) (67)**73**

5-y-o b g Tale Of The Cat (USA)-Mangano (USA) (Quiet American (USA))

A D Brown R G Fell

Placings:6644/0505**042615230030**/6000-00 **(0805)**

2009: 14^{0}SD, 11^{0}SD,

	Starts	1st	2nd	3rd	Win & Pl
Career Total (Turf)	13	1	1	0	11726
Career Total (AW)	13	0	1	2	8185

73	8/07	Deau	1m7f		VS	£6757

Total win prize-money £6757

Going (Turf): **Sf: 0-1 GS: 0-3 Gd: 0-4 GF: 0-2 Fm: 0-0**
Distance: 5f/6f: 0-0 7f-8f: 0-2 9f-13f: 0-19 **14f+: 1-5**
Track : LH: 0-10 **RH: 1-5** Tight: 0-4 Gall: 0-1
Aids: Bl: 0-3 Vi: 0-0 Tstrap: 0-1 Ckp: 0-1
Best Rating: **75** 8/07 Deau 1m4f stand

Welcome Releaf

(98) (63)**64**

6-y-o ch g Most Welcome-Mint Leaf (IRE) (Sri Pekan (USA))

P Leech Miss C Elbrow

Placings:06/025005026/40513166000600-060 **(0601)**

2009: 7^{0}SD, 11^{6}SD, 12^{0}SD,

	Starts	1st	2nd	3rd	Win & Pl
Career Total (Turf)	7	0	0	1	337
Career Total (AW)	21	2	2	0	7005

63	4/08	Sthl	7f	(0-60)H	STD	£1774
61	4/08	Sthl	6f		STD	£3399

Total win prize-money £5174

Going (Turf): **Sf: 0-0 GS: 0-1 Gd: 0-4 GF: 0-1 Fm: 0-1**
Distance: 5f/6f: 1-7 7f-8f: 1-14 9f-13f: 0-7 14f+: 0-0
Track : **LH: 2-19** RH: 0-4 Tight: 0-8 Gall: 0-1
Aids: Bl: 0-1 Vi: 0-4 Tstrap: 0-2 Ckp: 0-2
Best Rating: **64** 4/08 Yarm 6f3y good

Moderate; effective at around 6f-1m; acts on Fibresand and Polytrack.

Weliketobouggie

69(84) (54)**36**

2-y-o b c Tobougg (IRE)-Country Spirit (Sayf El Arab (USA))

J S Moore Wall To Wall Partnership

Placings:06 **(4201)**

2009: 6^{0}G, 7^{6}SD,

	Starts	1st	2nd	3rd	Win & Pl
Career Total (Turf)	1	0	0	0	
Career Total (AW)	1	0	0	0	0

Going (Turf): **Sf: 0-0 GS: 0-0 Gd: 0-1 GF: 0-0 Fm: 0-0**
Distance: 5f/6f: 0-1 7f-8f: 0-1 9f-13f: 0-0 14f+: 0-0
Track : LH: 0-1 RH: 0-0 Tight: 0-1 Gall: 0-0
Aids: Bl: 0-0 Vi: 0-0 Tstrap: 0-0 Ckp: 0-0
Best Rating: **54** 7/09 Ling 7f stand

Well Of Echoes

96(97) (53)**59**

3-y-o b f Diktat-Seeker (Rainbow Quest (USA))

A J McCabe (J A Glover 21/10) M Shirley

Placings:6000-3**0000**04050**30** **(7880)**

2009: 8^{3}GF, 10^{0}GF, 8^{0}SF, 7^{0}SD, 8^{0}GF, 5^{0}SD, 7^{4}G, 5^{0}SD, 7^{5}SD, 8^{0}SD, 7^{3}SD, 7^{0}SD,

	Starts	1st	2nd	3rd	Win & Pl
Career Total (Turf)	8	0	0	1	770
Career Total (AW)	8	0	0	1	252

Going (Turf): **Sf: 0-0 GS: 0-2 Gd: 0-3 GF: 0-3 Fm: 0-0**
Distance: 5f/6f: 0-4 7f-8f: 0-9 9f-13f: 0-3 14f+: 0-0
Track : LH: 0-9 RH: 0-2 Tight: 0-5 Gall: 0-2
Aids: Bl: 0-2 Vi: 0-0 Tstrap: 0-2 Ckp: 0-2
Best Rating: **59** 7/08 Donc 7f good

Moderate; stays 1m; acts on fast ground.

Wellesley

91(91) (63)**58**

3-y-o b g Bertolini (USA)-Markova's Dance (Mark Of Esteem (IRE))

W R Swinburn P W Harris

Placings:65-044600 **(6183)**

2009: 7^{0}GF, 8^{4}GF, 8^{4}S, 10^{6}GF, 9^{0}SD, 9^{0}GF,

	Starts	1st	2nd	3rd	Win & Pl
Career Total (Turf)	5	0	0	0	154
Career Total (AW)	3	0	0	0	0

Going (Turf): **Sf: 0-1 GS: 0-0 Gd: 0-0 GF: 0-4 Fm: 0-0**
Distance: 5f/6f: 0-0 7f-8f: 0-3 9f-13f: 0-5 14f+: 0-0
Track : LH: 0-5 RH: 0-2 Tight: 0-5 Gall: 0-0
Aids: Bl: 0-0 Vi: 0-0 Tstrap: 0-1 Ckp: 0-1
Best Rating: **63** 12/08 Ling 7f stand

Wellington Fair

101 **80**

2-y-o br g Trade Fair-Milly's Lass (Mind Games)

C G Cox Ken Lock Racing

Placings:5U513 **(6550)**

2009: 6^{5}GF, 5^{U}G, 5^{5}G, 5^{1}GF, 5^{3}G,

	Starts	1st	2nd	3rd	Win & Pl
Career Total (Turf)	5	1	0	1	5951

80	9/09	Sand	5f6y	G-F	£5180

Total win prize-money £5181

Going (Turf): Sf: 0-0 GS: 0-0 Gd: 0-3 **GF: 1-2** Fm: 0-0
Distance: **5f/6f: 1-5** 7f-8f: 0-0 9f-13f: 0-0 14f+: 0-0
Track : LH: 0-0 RH: 0-0 Tight: 0-0 Gall: 0-2
Aids: Bl: 0-2 **Vi: 1-1** Tstrap: 0-0 Ckp: 0-0
Best Rating: **80** 9/09 Sand 5f6y gd-fm

Useful; effective at 5f but stays 6f; acts on fast ground; has worn blinkers and a visor.

Wellington Square

105(104) (89)**89**

4-y-o b g Millkom-Tempestosa (Northern Tempest (USA))

H Morrison Roger Barby & Sir T Cassel

Placings:3300115-0130053 **(6830)**

2009: 12^{0}GF, 7^{1}G, 7^{3}GF, 8^{0}G, 7^{0}G, 8^{5}GS, 8^{3}SF,

	Starts	1st	2nd	3rd	Win & Pl
Career Total (Turf)	9	1	0	3	6560
Career Total (AW)	5	2	0	1	8212

89	6/09	Gdwd	7f	(0-80)H	GD	£4857
86	12/08	Ling	1m2f	(0-80)H	STD	£4727
76	11/08	Kemp	1m		STD	£2729

Total win prize-money £12314

Going (Turf): Sf: 0-0 GS: 0-2 **Gd: 1-4** GF: 0-3 Fm: 0-0
Distance: 5f/6f: 0-0 **7f-8f: 2-6** 9f-13f: 1-8 14f+: 0-0
Track : LH: 1-7 **RH: 2-7 Tight: 1-5** Gall: 0-4
Aids: Bl: 0-0 Vi: 0-0 Tstrap: 0-0 Ckp: 0-0
Best Rating: **89** 10/09 Wolv 1m141y std-fst

Useful; effective from 7f-1m2f; acts on fast ground and on Polytrack.

Wellmarked (IRE)

(101) (86)
2-y-o b g Choisir (AUS)-Radiance (IRE) (Thatching)
John A Quinn Charles McGrath

Placings:211 (7846)
2009: 5^{2}SD, 5^{1}SD, 7^{1}SD,

	Starts	1st	2nd	3rd	Win & Pl
Career Total (Turf)	0	0	0	0	
Career Total (AW)	3	2	1	0	9520

86	12/09	Wolv	7f32y	(0-85)	STD	£5677
76	12/09	Wolv	5f216y		STD	£2590

Total win prize-money £8267

Going (Turf): **Sf: 0-0 GS: 0-0 Gd: 0-0 GF: 0-0 Fm: 0-0**
Distance: 5f/6f: 1-2 7f-8f: 1-1 9f-13f: 0-0 14f+: 0-0
Track : **LH: 2-3** RH: 0-0 **Tight: 2-3** Gall: 0-0
Aids: Bl: 0-0 Vi: 0-0 Tstrap: 0-0 Ckp: 0-0
Best Rating: **86** 12/09 Wolv 7f32y stand

Fair; stays 7f and acts on Polytrack; has worn a tongue tie.

Wells Lyrical (IRE)

110 **100**
4-y-o b c Sadler's Wells (USA)-Lyrical (Shirley Heights)
B Smart M Barber

Placings:56/2333111-22360 (6851)
2009: 16^{2}GF, 16^{2}S, 16^{3}G, 13^{6}GF, 18^{0}G,

	Starts	1st	2nd	3rd	Win & Pl
Career Total (Turf)	14	3	3	4	60524

94	10/08	Donc	1m6f132y	(0-85)H	GD	£6476
85	9/08	Muss	1m6f	(0-80)H	GD	£5828
80	7/08	Haml	1m3f16y		GD	£3238

Total win prize-money £15542

Going (Turf): Sf: 0-1 GS: 0-1 **Gd: 3-8** GF: 0-4 Fm: 0-0
Distance: 5f/6f: 0-0 7f-8f: 0-1 9f-13f: 1-6 **14f+: 2-7**
Track : LH: 1-7 **RH: 2-7 Tight: 2-7** Gall: 1-3
Aids: Bl: 0-0 Vi: 0-0 Tstrap: 0-0 Ckp: 0-0
Best Rating: **100** 7/09 Sand 2m78y good

Very useful; runner-up in the 2009 Northumberland Plate; stays 2m; acts on good and easier ground.

Welsh Anthem

96(95) (61)**71**
3-y-o b f Singspiel (IRE)-Khubza (Green Desert (USA))
W R Muir Usk Valley Stud

Placings:4-360520 (4498)
2009: 8^{3}GF, 8^{6}G, 8^{0}GF, 8^{5}SD, 10^{2}G, 12^{0}G,

	Starts	1st	2nd	3rd	Win & Pl
Career Total (Turf)	6	0	1	1	1477
Career Total (AW)	1	0	0	0	0

Going (Turf): **Sf: 0-1 GS: 0-0 Gd: 0-3 GF: 0-2 Fm: 0-0**
Distance: 5f/6f: 0-0 7f-8f: 0-3 9f-13f: 0-4 14f+: 0-0
Track : LH: 0-2 RH: 0-4 Tight: 0-2 Gall: 0-1
Aids: Bl: 0-3 Vi: 0-0 Tstrap: 0-0 Ckp: 0-0
Best Rating: **71** 7/09 Bath 1m2f46y good

Modest; stays 1m2f and acts on good ground; has worn blinkers.

Welsh Artist

(86) (67)
2-y-o b g Sakhee (USA)-Gwen John (USA) (Peintre Celebre (USA))
Mrs A J Perrett K J Mercer

Placings:063 (7538)
2009: 6^{0}SD, 7^{6}SD, 7^{3}SD,

	Starts	1st	2nd	3rd	Win & Pl
Career Total (Turf)	0	0	0	0	
Career Total (AW)	3	0	0	1	482

Going (Turf): **Sf: 0-0 GS: 0-0 Gd: 0-0 GF: 0-0 Fm: 0-0**
Distance: 5f/6f: 0-1 7f-8f: 0-2 9f-13f: 0-0 14f+: 0-0
Track : LH: 0-0 RH: 0-3 Tight: 0-0 Gall: 0-0
Aids: Bl: 0-0 Vi: 0-0 Tstrap: 0-0 Ckp: 0-0
Best Rating: **67** 11/09 Kemp 7f stand

Modest; stays 7f; acts on Polytrack.

Welsh Emperor (IRE)

100 (89)**111**
10-y-o b g Emperor Jones (USA)-Simply Times (USA) (Dodge (USA))
T P Tate Mrs Sylvia Clegg

Placings:3322130201/36026510251/0342426/14652010/0136012/101020/0342621/20441624525-6010P (7019)
2009: 7^{6}G, 7^{0}G, 7^{1}S, 7^{0}GS, 7^{2}GS,

	Starts	1st	2nd	3rd	Win & Pl
Career Total (Turf)	71	13	15	7	369778
Career Total (AW)	1	0	0	0	

106	7/09	Hayd	7f30y		SFT	£9714
108	7/08	Hayd	7f30y		HVY	£11333
104	10/07	Leic	7f9y		G-S	£5678
115	8/06	Newb	7f		G-S	£51102
114	4/06	Thsk	6f		GD	£11217
116	10/05	NmkR	6f		G-S	£29000
112	5/05	Hayd	7f30y		SFT	£16240
111	9/04	Haml	6f5y		SFT	£12174
107	4/04	Thsk	6f	C	SFT	£8363
101	11/02	MsnL	6f		HVY	£12577
101	8/02	Hayd	6f	C(0-85)	HVY	£8645
94	10/01	Catt	5f	D	SFT	£3818
71	7/01	Haml	6f5y	E	G-S	£3220

Total win prize-money £183084

Going (Turf): **Sf: 8-27**GS: 4-17 Gd: 1-22 GF: 0-1 Fm: 0-2
Distance: 5f/6f: 6-31 **7f-8f: 7-40** 9f-13f: 0-1 14f+: 0-0
Track : **LH: 3-19** RH: 0-9 Tight: 0-8 Gall: 0-3
Aids: **Bl: 7-46** Vi: 0-0 Tstrap: 0-0 Ckp: 0-0
Best Rating: **117** 9/06 Lonc 7f good

Smart; winner in Listed, Group 3 and Group 2 company, also been placed at Group 1 level; effective over 6f-1m; relishes soft ground; has worn blinkers; very tough and a credit to connections.

Welsh Legacy (IRE)

79(87) (43)**41**
2-y-o b g Saffron Walden (FR)-Silver Harbour (USA) (Silver Hawk (USA))
B W Duke Brendan W Duke Racing

Placings:00050 (7055)
2009: 6^{0}G, 6^{0}GF, 6^{0}GF, 7^{5}SD, 7^{0}GF,

	Starts	1st	2nd	3rd	Win & Pl
Career Total (Turf)	4	0	0	0	
Career Total (AW)	1	0	0	0	0

Going (Turf): **Sf: 0-0 GS: 0-0 Gd: 0-1 GF: 0-3 Fm: 0-0**
Distance: 5f/6f: 0-2 7f-8f: 0-3 9f-13f: 0-0 14f+: 0-0
Track : LH: 0-1 RH: 0-0 Tight: 0-0 Gall: 0-1
Aids: Bl: 0-0 Vi: 0-0 Tstrap: 0-0 Ckp: 0-0
Best Rating: **43** 7/09 Sthl 7f stand

Welsh Opera

101(102) (70)**64**
4-y-o b f Noverre (USA)-Welsh Diva (Selkirk (USA))
S C Williams Paul W Stevens

Placings:034/05620023022-362104100513330 (6926)
2009: 6^{3}SD, 5^{6}SD, 5^{2}SD, 5^{1}SD, 5^{0}SD, 5^{4}SD, 5^{1}SD, 5^{0}S, 6^{0}G, 5^{5}G, 6^{1}GF, 5^{3}GF, 5^{3}GF, 5^{3}SD, 6^{0}GF,

	Starts	1st	2nd	3rd	Win & Pl
Career Total (Turf)	10	1	0	2	2628
Career Total (AW)	19	2	5	4	11000

64	9/09	Yarm	6f3y	(0-60)H	G-F	£2007
70	3/09	Wolv	5f20y	(0-75)H	STD	£3885
65	2/09	Kemp	5f	(0-60)H	STD	£2266

Total win prize-money £8161

Going (Turf): Sf: 0-3 GS: 0-0 Gd: 0-2 **GF: 1-5** Fm: 0-0
Distance: **5f/6f: 2-17** 7f-8f: 1-9 9f-13f: 0-3 14f+: 0-0
Track : LH: 1-14 RH: 1-7 **Tight: 1-11** Gall: 0-4
Aids: Bl: 0-0 **Vi: 2-8** Tstrap: 0-0 Ckp: 0-0
Best Rating: **70** 3/09 Wolv 5f20y stand

Moderate; effective over 6f-1m; acts on fast ground and Polytrack; has worn a tongue tie and visor.

Welsh Passion

71(61) **10**
3-y-o b f Marju (IRE)-Focosa (ITY) (In The Wings)
D Haydn Jones Five To Follow

Placings:000-00 (5789)
2009: 8^{0}GF, 7^{0}G,

	Starts	1st	2nd	3rd	Win & Pl
Career Total (Turf)	4	0	0	0	
Career Total (AW)	1	0	0	0	

Going (Turf): **Sf: 0-1 GS: 0-0 Gd: 0-1 GF: 0-2 Fm: 0-0**
Distance: 5f/6f: 0-0 7f-8f: 0-3 9f-13f: 0-2 14f+: 0-0
Track : LH: 0-3 RH: 0-1 Tight: 0-3 Gall: 0-0
Aids: Bl: 0-1 Vi: 0-0 Tstrap: 0-0 Ckp: 0-0
Best Rating: **10** 8/09 Wind 1m67y gd-fm

Wessex (USA)

(103) (93)**88**
9-y-o ch g Gone West (USA)-Satin Velvet (USA) (El Gran Senor (USA))
R Curtis Nigel Shields

Placings:010/0600500031/1123220000141/52210625/030020/02030-060 (2576)
2009: 8^{0}SD, 6^{6}SD, 7^{0}SD,

	Starts	1st	2nd	3rd	Win & Pl
Career Total (Turf)	14	1	1	0	10022
Career Total (AW)	34	6	7	4	56261

100	2/06	Sthl	6f	(0-100)H	STD	£12954
94	12/05	Wolv	7f32y	(0-85)H	STD	£5787
84	11/05	Sthl	6f	(0-75)H	STD	£4037

77 2/05 Wolv 7f32y (0-70)H STD £3386
79 2/05 Sthl 1m (0-70)H STD £3378
74 12/04 Sthl 7f STD £2639
88 6/03 York 7f205y D G-F £7085
Total win prize-money £39269

Going (Turf): Sf: 0-0 GS: 0-2 Gd: 0-4 **GF: 1-7** Fm: 0-1
Distance: 5f/6f: 2-10 **7f-8f: 5-32** 9f-13f: 0-6 14f+: 0-0
Track : **LH: 7-39** RH: 0-6 **Tight: 2-18** Gall: 1-2
Aids: Bl: 0-0 Vi: 0-3 Tstrap: 0-0 Ckp: 0-0
Best Rating: 100 2/06 Sthl 6f stand

Useful; effective over 6f-1m; acts well on Fibresand and Polytrack; has worn a visor and a tongue tie; rarely seen on turf in recent seasons.

West End Lad

104(104) (74)**79**
6-y-o b g Tomba-Cliburnel News (IRE) (Horage)
S R Bowring K Nicholls

Placings:0500002/03210520140135323-**104**00161660660**4** (7783)
2009: 8^{1}SD, 8^{0}SD, 8^{4}SD, 8^{0}SD, 8^{0}SD, 8^{1}G, 8^{6}G, 8^{1}GF, 8^{6}HY, 8^{6}GF, 7^{0}GF, 7^{6}GF, 8^{6}GF, 7^{0}GF, 8^{4}SD,

	Starts	1st	2nd	3rd	Win & Pl
Career Total (Turf)	21	4	1	2	12036
Career Total (AW)	18	2	3	2	6442

79 7/09 Nott 1m75y (0-70)H G-F £2590
74 5/09 Nott 1m75y (0-65)H GD £2047
74 1/09 Sthl 1m (0-65)H STD £2047
71 8/08 Bevl 7f100y SFT £2590
68 7/08 Nott 1m75y (0-70)H G-S £3238
61 3/08 Sthl 1m (0-55) STD £1774
Total win prize-money £14287

Going (Turf): Sf: 1-6 GS: 1-3 Gd: 1-4 GF: 1-8 Fm: 0-0
Distance: 5f/6f: 0-0 7f-8f: 3-21 9f-13f: 3-17 14f+: 0-1
Track : **LH: 5-30** RH: 1-6 Tight: 0-7 Gall: 0-0
Aids: **Bl: 6-28** Vi: 0-0 Tstrap: 0-6 Ckp: 0-6
Best Rating: 79 7/09 Nott 1m75y gd-fm

Modest; effective from 1m-1m4f; acts on most ground and on Fibresand; has worn blinkers.

West Kirk

98(92) (62)**70**
3-y-o b g Alhaarth (IRE)-Naughty Crown (USA) (Chief's Crown (USA))
W Jarvis Dr J Walker

Placings:5540 (7803)
2009: 7^{5}SD, 8^{5}GF, 8^{4}SD, 9^{0}SD,

	Starts	1st	2nd	3rd	Win & Pl
Career Total (Turf)	1	0	0	0	0
Career Total (AW)	3	0	0	0	192

Going (Turf): Sf: 0-0 GS: 0-0 Gd: 0-0 GF: 0-1 Fm: 0-0
Distance: 5f/6f: 0-0 7f-8f: 0-2 9f-13f: 0-2 14f+: 0-0
Track : LH: 0-2 RH: 0-1 Tight: 0-2 Gall: 0-0
Aids: Bl: 0-0 Vi: 0-0 Tstrap: 0-0 Ckp: 0-0
Best Rating: 70 10/09 Yarm 1m3y gd-fm

West Leake (IRE)

97(102) (68)**66**
3-y-o b g Acclamation-Kilshanny (Groom Dancer (USA))
B W Hills Henry Barton

Placings:0620263-613000 (4061)
2009: 8^{6}GF, 6^{1}SD, 6^{3}GF, 6^{0}G, 6^{0}GF, 6^{0}S,

	Starts	1st	2nd	3rd	Win & Pl
Career Total (Turf)	9	0	0	1	385
Career Total (AW)	4	1	2	1	7904

68 4/09 Sthl 6f (0-80)H STD £5180
Total win prize-money £5181

Going (Turf): Sf: 0-3 GS: 0-1 Gd: 0-2 GF: 0-3 Fm: 0-0
Distance: **5f/6f: 1-6** 7f-8f: 0-6 9f-13f: 0-1 14f+: 0-0
Track : **LH: 1-4** RH: 0-0 Tight: 0-1 Gall: 0-3
Aids: Bl: 0-1 Vi: 0-0 Tstrap: 0-0 Ckp: 0-0
Best Rating: 68 4/09 Sthl 6f stand

Modest; effective over 5f-6f; acts on easy ground and on sand.

West Leake Star (IRE)

97(92) (63)**73**
2-y-o b c Antonius Pius (USA)-Red Beach (IRE) (Turtle Island (IRE))
B W Hills Henry Barton

Placings:002405 (6737)
2009: 6^{0}G, 5^{0}G, 5^{2}S, **5^{4}SD**, 6^{0}SD, 6^{5}GS,

	Starts	1st	2nd	3rd	Win & Pl
Career Total (Turf)	4	0	1	0	1445
Career Total (AW)	2	0	0	0	313

Going (Turf): Sf: 0-1 GS: 0-1 Gd: 0-2 GF: 0-0 Fm: 0-0
Distance: 5f/6f: 0-5 7f-8f: 0-1 9f-13f: 0-0 14f+: 0-0
Track : LH: 0-3 RH: 0-0 Tight: 0-1 Gall: 0-2
Aids: Bl: 0-0 Vi: 0-0 Tstrap: 0-0 Ckp: 0-0
Best Rating: 73 7/09 Leic 5f218y soft

Fair; stays 6f and acts on soft ground.

West With The Wind (USA)

103(92) (69)**74**
3-y-o b f Gone West (USA)-Opera Aida (IRE) (Sadler's Wells (USA))
P W Chapple-Hyam Miss K Rausing

Placings:030-524120 (6257)
2009: 7^{5}SD, 8^{2}G, 7^{4}G, 8^{1}GF, 8^{2}GF, 9^{0}SD,

	Starts	1st	2nd	3rd	Win & Pl
Career Total (Turf)	6	1	2	1	5790
Career Total (AW)	3	0	0	0	0

70 8/09 Newc 1m3y (0-70) G-F £3154
Total win prize-money £3154

Going (Turf): Sf: 0-1 GS: 0-0 Gd: 0-3 **GF: 1-2** Fm: 0-0
Distance: 5f/6f: 0-0 7f-8f: 0-5 **9f-13f: 1-4** 14f+: 0-0
Track : LH: 0-3 RH: 0-1 Tight: 0-4 Gall: 0-0
Aids: Bl: 0-0 Vi: 0-0 Tstrap: 0-0 Ckp: 0-0
Best Rating: 74 8/09 Wind 1m67y gd-fm

Modest; effective at around 1m.

West With The Wind

91(106) (81)**88**
4-y-o b g Fasliyev (USA)-Midnight Angel (GER) (Acatenango (GER))
Evan Williams (T P Tate 23/9) Mrs Janet Davies

Placings:02/2563021-0600 (6218)
2009: 11^{0}GF, 12^{6}S, 10^{0}GF, 10^{0}GF,

	Starts	1st	2nd	3rd	Win & Pl
Career Total (Turf)	12	0	3	1	4436
Career Total (AW)	1	1	0	0	2730

81 11/08 Sthl 1m4f STD £2729
Total win prize-money £2730

Going (Turf): Sf: 0-2 GS: 0-0 Gd: 0-2 GF: 0-8 Fm: 0-0
Distance: 5f/6f: 0-0 7f-8f: 0-1 **9f-13f: 1-11** 14f+: 0-1
Track : **LH: 1-8** RH: 0-3 Tight: 0-4 Gall: 0-4
Aids: Bl: 0-1 Vi: 0-0 Tstrap: 0-0 Ckp: 0-0
Best Rating: 88 6/08 Muss 1m4f gd-fm

Fair; stays 1m4f; acts on fast ground; goes on Polytrack.

Wester Lodge (IRE)

90(104) (62)**58**
7-y-o ch g Fraam-Reamzafonic (Grand Lodge (USA))
J M P Eustace Mrs James Eustace

Placings:020/03140/53406205**000/5-352665006332** (7154)
2009: 12^{3}SD, 8^{5}SD, 13^{2}SD, 10^{6}G, 8^{6}SD, 13^{5}SD, 10^{0}GF, 12^{0}GS, 11^{6}GF, 16^{3}SD, 16^{3}SD, 16^{2}SD,

	Starts	1st	2nd	3rd	Win & Pl
Career Total (Turf)	19	1	2	2	10114
Career Total (AW)	13	0	2	3	2630

76 7/05 Bath 1m3f144y (0-75)H GD £4239
Total win prize-money £4239

Going (Turf): Sf: 0-1 GS: 0-2 **Gd: 1-5** GF: 0-9 Fm: 0-2
Distance: 5f/6f: 0-0 7f-8f: 0-3 **9f-13f: 1-21** 14f+: 0-8
Track : **LH: 1-22** RH: 0-5 **Tight: 1-19** Gall: 0-3
Aids: Bl: 0-3 Vi: 0-1 Tstrap: 0-1 Ckp: 0-1
Best Rating: 76 6/06 Ches 1m2f75y good

Moderate; effective over 1m4f-2m; acts on good and fast ground; goes on Polytrack.

Wester Ross (IRE)

97 **71**
5-y-o b g Fruits Of Love (USA)-Diabaig (Precocious)
J M P Eustace Peter Hillman

Placings:4/6160/004364353-454 (6622)
2009: 9^{4}F, 14^{5}GF, 16^{4}G,

	Starts	1st	2nd	3rd	Win & Pl
Career Total (Turf)	17	1	0	3	5679

71 5/07 Wind 1m2f7y G-S £3238
Total win prize-money £3239

Going (Turf): Sf: 0-2 **GS: 1-5** Gd: 0-4 GF: 0-5 Fm: 0-1
Distance: 5f/6f: 0-0 7f-8f: 0-1 **9f-13f: 1-11** 14f+: 0-5
Track : LH: 0-4 **RH: 1-12 Tight: 1-9** Gall: 0-2
Aids: Bl: 0-1 Vi: 0-0 Tstrap: 0-0 Ckp: 0-0
Best Rating: 75 6/07 NmkJ 1m4f gd-sft

Modest; stays 1m6f; acts on fast and easy ground.

Western Art (USA)

96(84) (24)**55**
4-y-o b/br g Hennessy (USA)-Madam West (USA) (Gone West (USA))
Miss Gay Kelleway (M W Easterby 16/9) Miss Gay Kelleway

Placings:21/0-00000300 (7802)
2009: 7^{0}SD, 6^{0}SD, 7^{0}SD, 7^{0}SD, 6^{0}GS, 8^{3}GF, 7^{0}S, 8^{0}SD,

	Starts	1st	2nd	3rd	Win & Pl
Career Total (Turf)	6	1	1	1	13448
Career Total (AW)	5	0	0	0	

99 7/07 Sand 5f6y SFT £12207
Total win prize-money £12208

Going (Turf): Sf: 1-2 GS: 0-1 Gd: 0-0 GF: 0-2 Fm: 0-1
Distance: 5f/6f: 1-4 7f-8f: 0-5 9f-13f: 0-2 14f+: 0-0
Track : LH: 0-6 RH: 0-1 Tight: 0-3 Gall: 0-0
Aids: Bl: 0-0 Vi: 0-0 Tstrap: 0-0 Ckp: 0-0
Best Rating: 99 7/07 Sand 5f6y soft

Very useful; Listed winner; effective at 5f and handles most ground.

Western Pearl

(88) (64)
2-y-o b f High Chaparral (IRE)-Pulau Pinang (IRE) (Dolphin Street (FR))
W J Knight Mrs N Welby

Placings:5 (7451)
2009: 8^5SD,

	Starts	1st	2nd	3rd	Win & Pl
Career Total (Turf)	0	0	0	0	
Career Total (AW)	1	0	0	0	0

Going (Turf): Sf: 0-0 GS: 0-0 Gd: 0-0 GF: 0-0 Fm: 0-0
Distance: 5f/6f: 0-0 7f-8f: 0-1 9f-13f: 0-0 14f+: 0-0
Track : LH: 0-0 RH: 0-1 Tight: 0-0 Gall: 0-0
Aids: Bl: 0-0 Vi: 0-0 Tstrap: 0-0 Ckp: 0-0
Best Rating: 64 11/09 Kemp 1m stand

Western Roots

103(104) (72)73
8-y-o ch g Dr Fong (USA)-Chrysalis (Soviet Star (USA))
P Butler (A M Balding 5/5) Miss M Bryant

Placings:140/240061550002002O/322226030055113/353 50000066361364/4603310400604V50/440056141213130 0-213000000 (7776)
2009: 10^2SD, 9^1G, 10^3GF, 10^0GF, 9^0GF, 9^0F, 8^0G, 9^0SD, 10^0SD,

	Starts	1st	2nd	3rd	Win & Pl
Career Total (Turf)	29	4	1	4	14373
Career Total (AW)	63	7	8	8	43334

73	4/09	Brig	1m1f209y		GD	£1942
73	8/08	Newb	1m2f6y	(0-70)H	GD	£2498
63	6/08	Sals	1m1f198y	(0-70)H	G-F	£3238
74	5/08	GrLe	1m2f		STD	£2266
64	4/08	Kemp	1m2f	(0-55)H	STD	£2266
70	6/07	Wolv	1m1f103y	(0-70)H	STD	£2914
69	11/06	Wolv	1m141y	(0-65)H	STD	£2266
70	12/05	Wolv	1m1f103y	(0-75)H	STD	£3032
67	11/05	Wolv	1m1f103y	(0-58)H	STD	£2574
74	6/04	Leic	1m9y	F	GD	£3367
74	3/03	Ling	5f	B	STD	£15196

Total win prize-money £41565

Going (Turf): Sf: 0-3 GS: 0-4 Gd: 3-6 GF: 1-15 Fm: 0-1
Distance: 5f/6f: 1-2 7f-8f: 0-18 9f-13f: 10-72 14f+: 0-0
Track : LH: 8-74 RH: 3-14 Tight: 6-63 Gall: 2-4
Aids: Bl: 0-0 Vi: 0-1 Tstrap: 2-16 Ckp: 2-16
Best Rating: 81 1/04 Ling 7f stand

Fair; effective over 1m-1m2f; acts on good ground; also goes on Polytrack; has worn cheekpieces.

Westlin' Winds (IRE)

92(95) (71)69
3-y-o b c Montjeu (IRE)-Uliana (USA) (Darshaan)
C R Egerton AAlinsonJAlinsonLord DaresburyWVestey

Placings:6544 (6027)
2009: 8^6SD, 10^5GF, 11^4GF, 13^4SD,

	Starts	1st	2nd	3rd	Win & Pl
Career Total (Turf)	2	0	0	0	202
Career Total (AW)	2	0	0	0	216

Going (Turf): Sf: 0-0 GS: 0-0 Gd: 0-0 GF: 0-2 Fm: 0-0
Distance: 5f/6f: 0-0 7f-8f: 0-1 9f-13f: 0-2 14f+: 0-1
Track : LH: 0-3 RH: 0-1 Tight: 0-4 Gall: 0-0
Aids: Bl: 0-0 Vi: 0-0 Tstrap: 0-0 Ckp: 0-0
Best Rating: 71 9/09 Wolv 1m5f194y stand

Westport

91(103) (81)81
6-y-o b g Xaar-Connemara (IRE) (Mujadil (USA))
R Bastiman Mrs P Bastiman

Placings:4142105602/55601234/2404220056-004600 (7499)
2009: 5^0GF, 5^0G, 5^4GS, 7^6GF, 9^0GS, 8^0SD,

	Starts	1st	2nd	3rd	Win & Pl
Career Total (Turf)	21	1	4	0	10868
Career Total (AW)	13	2	2	1	13481

82	6/07	Wolv	5f216y	(0-85)H	STD	£5829
80	5/06	Rdcr	6f	(0-70)H	G-F	£3238
71	2/06	Sthl	1m		STD	£3238

Total win prize-money £12307

Going (Turf): Sf: 0-1 GS: 0-8 Gd: 0-7 GF: 1-5 Fm: 0-0
Distance: 5f/6f: 2-22 7f-8f: 1-11 9f-13f: 0-1 14f+: 0-0
Track : LH: 2-14 RH: 0-4 Tight: 1-10 Gall: 0-0
Aids: Bl: 0-0 Vi: 0-0 Tstrap: 0-3 Ckp: 0-3
Best Rating: 85 10/07 Pont 5f good

Fair; suited by 6f; acts on a sound surface and on sand.

Weststern (GER)

90(99) (75)66
6-y-o b g Dashing Blade-Westafrika (GER) (Aspros (GER))
G L Moore Partners In Crime

Placings:5/01232/11221260/00 (6204)
2009: 12^0SD, 12^0G,

	Starts	1st	2nd	3rd	Win & Pl
Career Total (Turf)	15	4	5	1	22165
Career Total (AW)	1	0	0	0	

7/07	Aabe	1m2f	H	GD	£8108
5/07	Colo	1m	H	GD	£2702
4/07	Colo	1m	H	SFT	£2702

Total win prize-money £15307

Going (Turf): Sf: 1-5 GS: 0-0 Gd: 2-8 GF: 0-0 Fm: 0-0
Distance: 5f/6f: 0-0 7f-8f: 3-6 9f-13f: 1-10 14f+: 0-0
Track : LH: 0-1 RH: 0-1 Tight: 0-2 Gall: 0-0
Aids: Bl: 0-0 Vi: 0-0 Tstrap: 0-0 Ckp: 0-0
Best Rating: 75 2/09 Ling 1m4f stand

Westwood

105(102) (77)77
4-y-o ch g Captain Rio-Consignia (IRE) (Definite Article)
D Haydn Jones Merry Llewelyn And Runeckles

Placings:023010/0000030022-100000 (7828)
2009: 6^1GS, 6^0HY, 5^0G, 6^0G, 5^0SD, 6^0SD,

	Starts	1st	2nd	3rd	Win & Pl
Career Total (Turf)	16	2	1	2	12460
Career Total (AW)	6	0	2	0	1310

77	4/09	Wind	6f	(0-80)H	G-S	£4857
89	9/07	Hayd	6f	(0-85)	SFT	£4857

Total win prize-money £9715

Going (Turf): Sf: 1-4 GS: 1-3 Gd: 0-5 GF: 0-3 Fm: 0-1
Distance: 5f/6f: 2-19 7f-8f: 0-3 9f-13f: 0-0 14f+: 0-0
Track : LH: 0-6 RH: 0-2 Tight: 0-2 Gall: 1-6
Aids: Bl: 0-0 Vi: 0-0 Tstrap: 0-0 Ckp: 0-0
Best Rating: 89 9/07 Hayd 6f soft

Modest; effective over 6f; suited by soft ground and Fibresand.

Westwood Dawn

(102) (61)
4-y-o gr g Clodovil (IRE)-Ivory Dawn (Batshoof)
D Shaw Godfrey Horsford

Placings:000004/5054025320-5222452 (7510)
2009: 5^5SD, 5^2SD, 5^2SD, 5^2SD, 7^4SD, 5^5SD, 5^2SD,

	Starts	1st	2nd	3rd	Win & Pl
Career Total (Turf)	3	0	0	0	
Career Total (AW)	20	0	6	1	4689

Going (Turf): Sf: 0-0 GS: 0-1 Gd: 0-0 GF: 0-1 Fm: 0-1
Distance: 5f/6f: 0-18 7f-8f: 0-5 9f-13f: 0-0 14f+: 0-0
Track : LH: 0-13 RH: 0-3 Tight: 0-8 Gall: 0-5
Aids: Bl: 0-0 Vi: 0-14 Tstrap: 0-1 Ckp: 0-1
Best Rating: 61 10/09 Wolv 5f20y stand

Moderate; suited by 5f-6f; acts on Polytrack; has worn a visor, tongue tie and cheekpieces.

Wet Feet

74 49
2-y-o br g Footstepsinthesand-Swoon (Night Shift (USA))
P R Chamings P R Chamings M A Kirby

Placings:0 (4900)
2009: 6^0GF,

	Starts	1st	2nd	3rd	Win & Pl
Career Total (Turf)	1	0	0	0	

Going (Turf): Sf: 0-0 GS: 0-0 Gd: 0-0 GF: 0-1 Fm: 0-0
Distance: 5f/6f: 0-1 7f-8f: 0-0 9f-13f: 0-0 14f+: 0-0
Track : LH: 0-0 RH: 0-0 Tight: 0-0 Gall: 0-0
Aids: Bl: 0-0 Vi: 0-0 Tstrap: 0-0 Ckp: 0-0
Best Rating: 49 8/09 Sals 6f gd-fm

Weybridge Light

101(104) (76)67
4-y-o b g Fantastic Light (USA)-Nuryana (Nureyev (USA))
Eoin Griffin Mrs Martina Griffin

Placings:0002211124-00630 (7701)
2009: 16^0GY, 14^0YS, 16^6SD, 13^3SD, 16^0SD,

	Starts	1st	2nd	3rd	Win & Pl
Career Total (Turf)	6	1	1	0	5325
Career Total (AW)	9	2	2	1	9650

71	12/08	GrLe	1m5f66y	(0-70)H	STD	£3238
61	11/08	GrLe	1m6f	(0-75)H	STD	£3238
57	10/08	Tram	1m4f	(45-60)H	Y-S	£4318

Total win prize-money £10795

Going (Turf): Sf: 0-1 GS: 0-0 Gd: 0-1 GF: 0-0 Fm: 0-0
Distance: 5f/6f: 0-0 7f-8f: 0-1 9f-13f: 1-5 14f+: 2-9
Track : LH: 2-9 RH: 1-6 Tight: 0-2 Gall: 2-4
Aids: Bl: 3-10 Vi: 0-1 Tstrap: 0-0 Ckp: 0-0
Best Rating: 76 12/08 GrLe 1m6f stand

Modest; stays 1m6f; acts on easy ground; goes on Polytrack; has worn blinkers.

Whaston (IRE)

103(93) (58)58
4-y-o b g Hawk Wing (USA)-Sharafanya (IRE) (Zafonic (USA))

J D Bethell Clarendon Thoroughbred Racing

Placings:000/2260061040-002656150 (5513)
2009: 8^{0}SD, 8^{0}F, 9^{2}GF, 9^{6}GF, 9^{5}GF, 8^{6}G, 10^{1}GF, 10^{5}GF, 8^{0}GF,

	Starts	1st	2nd	3rd	Win & Pl
Career Total (Turf)	14	2	1	0	6729
Career Total (AW)	8	0	2	0	1454

58 7/09 Ayr 1m2f (0-70)H G-F £2914
58 7/08 Ayr 1m (0-65)H GD £3043
Total win prize-money £5958

Going (Turf): Sf: 0-0 GS: 0-0 **Gd: 1-3 GF: 1-10** Fm: 0-1
Distance: 5f/6f: 0-0 7f-8f: 1-9 9f-13f: 1-13 14f+: 0-0
Track : **LH: 2-15** RH: 0-4 Tight: 0-11 Gall: 0-2
Aids: Bl: 0-0 **Vi: 2-13** Tstrap: 0-0 Ckp: 0-0
Best Rating: 58 7/09 Ayr 1m2f gd-fm

Moderate; effective over 7f-1m; acts on good ground and on Polytrack; has worn a visor.

What A Day

97 67
3-y-o b g Daylami (IRE)-Sensation (Soviet Star (USA))
J J Quinn Mrs J Bletsoe and Mrs E Bletsoe

Placings:0025-5000020 (5470)
2009: 8^{5}F, 8^{0}F, 8^{0}GF, 12^{0}GF, 10^{0}GS, 9^{2}G, 9^{0}F,

	Starts	1st	2nd	3rd	Win & Pl
Career Total (Turf)	11	0	2	0	1734

Going (Turf): **Sf: 0-4 GS: 0-1 Gd: 0-1 GF: 0-2 Fm: 0-3**
Distance: 5f/6f: 0-0 7f-8f: 0-4 9f-13f: 0-7 14f+: 0-0
Track : LH: 0-6 RH: 0-4 Tight: 0-1 Gall: 0-1
Aids: Bl: 0-0 Vi: 0-0 Tstrap: 0-1 Ckp: 0-1
Best Rating: 67 9/08 Bevl 7f100y soft

Modest half-brother to Systematic; modest form at up to 1m; acts on soft.

What A Fella

102(71) 60
3-y-o b g Lujain (USA)-Fred's Dream (Cadeaux Genereux)
Mrs A Duffield Trevor Wilson

Placings:2534600-453301302040 (6161)
2009: 6^{4}GF, 7^{5}GF, 6^{3}F, 5^{3}GF, 5^{0}GF, 5^{1}GF, 5^{3}G, 5^{0}G, 5^{2}GF, 5^{0}SD, 5^{4}GF, 5^{0}G,

	Starts	1st	2nd	3rd	Win & Pl
Career Total (Turf)	17	1	2	4	5270
Career Total (AW)	2	0	0	0	

51 7/09 Haml 5f4y G-F £2388
Total win prize-money £2388

Going (Turf): Sf: 0-2 GS: 0-1 Gd: 0-6 **GF: 1-7** Fm: 0-1
Distance: **5f/6f: 1-18** 7f-8f: 0-1 9f-13f: 0-0 14f+: 0-0
Track : LH: 0-1 RH: 0-3 Tight: 0-2 Gall: 0-2
Aids: Bl: 0-1 Vi: 0-0 Tstrap: 1-7 Ckp: 1-7
Best Rating: 60 7/08 Ayr 6f good

Moderate; effective over 5f; acts on fast ground.

What Do You Know

96(104) (76)87
6-y-o b g Compton Place-How Do I Know (Petong)
A M Hales Gary P Martin

Placings:14/0460055/623322321505010/45031100006-502 (2224)
2009: 5^{5}G, 8^{0}SD, 5^{2}GF,

	Starts	1st	2nd	3rd	Win & Pl
Career Total (Turf)	18	2	2	1	9984
Career Total (AW)	20	3	3	3	13760

87 5/08 NmkR 5f (0-80)H G-S £4857
82 4/08 Brig 5f59y (0-70)H GD £2460
82 8/07 Kemp 5f (0-70)H STD £3238
79 6/07 Kemp 5f (0-70)H STD £2914
72 10/05 Wolv 5f216y STD £3438
Total win prize-money £16911

Going (Turf): Sf: 0-1 **GS: 1-5 Gd: 1-7** GF: 0-3 Fm: 0-2
Distance: **5f/6f: 5-30** 7f-8f: 0-8 9f-13f: 0-0 14f+: 0-0
Track : LH: 2-20 RH: 2-8 **Tight: 1-14** Gall: 0-2
Aids: Bl: 1-7 **Vi: 2-6** Tstrap: 0-2 Ckp: 0-2
Best Rating: 87 5/08 NmkR 5f gd-sft

Useful; effective over 5f-7f; acts on good ground; also goes on Polytrack; has worn blinkers/visor.

What Katie Did (IRE)

104(105) (78)74
4-y-o b g Invincible Spirit (IRE)-Chatterberry (Aragon)
J M Bradley Mr & Mrs M B Carver

Placings:606121006112/160050356344-130111400 (2911)
2009: 6^{1}SD, 5^{3}SD, 6^{0}SD, 6^{1}SD, 6^{1}SD, 6^{1}G, 5^{4}G, 5^{0}F, 5^{0}F,

	Starts	1st	2nd	3rd	Win & Pl
Career Total (Turf)	11	1	0	0	3114
Career Total (AW)	22	8	2	3	25363

74 4/09 Wind 6f (0-75)H GD £2729
76 3/09 Kemp 6f (0-65)H STD £2047
77 3/09 Kemp 6f (0-70)H STD £2590
68 1/09 Kemp 6f (0-60)H STD £1706
78 3/08 Ling 6f (0-75)H STD £2590
73 10/07 Wolv 7f32y STD £2388
68 10/07 Wolv 5f216y STD £2047
73 8/07 Wolv 5f216y STD £4533
65 8/07 Kemp 6f STD £3886
Total win prize-money £24521

Going (Turf): Sf: 0-0 GS: 0-2 **Gd: 1-3** GF: 0-3 Fm: 0-3
Distance: **5f/6f: 8-27** 7f-8f: 1-6 9f-13f: 0-0 14f+: 0-0
Track : LH: 4-16 RH: 4-9 **Tight: 4-13** Gall: 1-4
Aids: Bl: 0-1 Vi: 0-0 Tstrap: 4-15 Ckp: 4-15
Best Rating: 78 3/08 Ling 6f stand

Fair; effective over 6f-7f; acts on Polytrack.

What's Up Doc (IRE)

100(106) (82)79
8-y-o b g Dr Massini (IRE)-Surprise Treat (IRE) (Shalford (IRE))
Mrs Lawney Hill M B Clarke

Placings:533/160/1/0/0402001/603015-034111 (4450)
2009: 10^{0}SD, 8^{3}SD, 8^{4}SD, 9^{1}SD, 9^{1}GF, 10^{1}G,

	Starts	1st	2nd	3rd	Win & Pl
Career Total (Turf)	19	4	1	3	24201
Career Total (AW)	8	3	0	1	11145

79 7/09 Epsm 1m2f18y GD £3238
76 6/09 Brig 1m1f209y G-F £1942
62 4/09 Wolv 1m1f103y STD £1942
69 9/08 Ling 1m2f STD £2590
82 11/07 Dund 1m (50-80)H STD £6069
84 6/05 Leop 1m (60-100)H G-F £11542
82 5/04 Newc 1m2f32y E G-F £3526
Total win prize-money £30853

Going (Turf): Sf: 0-5 GS: 0-0 Gd: 1-4 **GF: 3-3** Fm: 0-2
Distance: 5f/6f: 0-0 7f-8f: 2-12 **9f-13f: 5-15** 14f+: 0-0
Track : **LH: 6-12** RH: 0-10 **Tight: 3-5** Gall: 1-5
Aids: Bl: 0-0 Vi: 0-0 Tstrap: 1-4 Ckp: 1-4
Best Rating: 84 6/05 Leop 1m gd-fm

Fair; effective over 1m-1m2f; acts on fast ground, but may be best with cut; goes well on Polytrack.

Whatagoodcatch (IRE)

92(90) (47)72
3-y-o b f Bachelor Duke (USA)-Truly Generous (IRE) (Generous (IRE))
R Hannon (John M Oxx 20/6) Byerley Thoroughbred Racing

Placings:0340 (4648)
2009: 8^{0}G, 10^{3}GF, 10^{4}GF, 8^{0}SD,

	Starts	1st	2nd	3rd	Win & Pl
Career Total (Turf)	3	0	0	1	1176
Career Total (AW)	1	0	0	0	

Going (Turf): **Sf: 0-0 GS: 0-0 Gd: 0-1 GF: 0-2 Fm: 0-0**
Distance: 5f/6f: 0-0 7f-8f: 0-2 9f-13f: 0-2 14f+: 0-0
Track : LH: 0-2 RH: 0-2 Tight: 0-0 Gall: 0-0
Aids: Bl: 0-0 Vi: 0-0 Tstrap: 0-0 Ckp: 0-0
Best Rating: 72 6/09 Navn 1m2f gd-fm

Fair; stays 1m2f; acts on fast ground.

Whatami

(99) (68)56
3-y-o br/gr f Daylami (IRE)-Wosaita (Generous (IRE))
E A L Dunlop Geoffrey Bishop

Placings:6-63 (2922)
2009: 10^{6}SD, 12^{3}SD,

	Starts	1st	2nd	3rd	Win & Pl
Career Total (Turf)	1	0	0	0	0
Career Total (AW)	2	0	0	1	403

Going (Turf): **Sf: 0-0 GS: 0-1 Gd: 0-0 GF: 0-0 Fm: 0-0**
Distance: 5f/6f: 0-0 7f-8f: 0-0 9f-13f: 0-3 14f+: 0-0
Track : LH: 0-3 RH: 0-0 Tight: 0-2 Gall: 0-0
Aids: Bl: 0-0 Vi: 0-0 Tstrap: 0-0 Ckp: 0-0
Best Rating: 68 6/09 Ling 1m4f stand

Whatyouwoodwishfor (USA)

96(101) (76)76
3-y-o ch g Forestry (USA)-Wishful Splendor (USA) (Smart Strike (CAN))
R A Fahey Mel Roberts & Ms Nicola Meese 1

Placings:500215-405000 (7813)
2009: 6^{4}GF, 7^{0}GS, 6^{5}GF, 6^{0}G, 6^{0}G, 7^{0}SD,

	Starts	1st	2nd	3rd	Win & Pl
Career Total (Turf)	9	0	1	0	1541
Career Total (AW)	3	1	0	0	7789

76 11/08 GrLe 6f STD £7788
Total win prize-money £7789

Going (Turf): **Sf: 0-0 GS: 0-1 Gd: 0-5 GF: 0-3 Fm: 0-0**
Distance: **5f/6f: 1-9** 7f-8f: 0-3 9f-13f: 0-0 14f+: 0-0
Track : **LH: 1-6** RH: 0-0 Tight: 0-2 **Gall: 1-1**
Aids: Bl: 0-0 Vi: 0-0 Tstrap: 0-0 Ckp: 0-0
Best Rating: 76 4/09 Donc 6f gd-fm

Fair; effective over 6f; acts on Polytrack; has refused to enter the stalls.

Whaxaar (IRE)

(102) (63)**68**

5-y-o b g Xaar-Sheriyna (FR) (Darshaan)

R Ingram G F Chesneaux

Placings:006/55042/610531300643-20 (7873)

2009: 16^{2}SD, 16^{0}SD,

	Starts	1st	2nd	3rd	Win & Pl
Career Total (Turf)	5	0	0	2	819
Career Total (AW)	17	2	2	1	6035

68 4/08 GrLe 2m (0-55)H STD £1942

53 1/08 Ling 1m4f STD £2331

Total win prize-money £4275

Going (Turf): Sf: 0-2 GS: 0-0 Gd: 0-2 GF: 0-0 Fm: 0-1

Distance: 5f/6f: 0-0 7f-8f: 0-5 9f-13f: 1-7 14f+: 1-10

Track : **LH: 2-10** RH: 0-11 Tight: 1-7 Gall: 1-2

Aids: Bl: 0-0 Vi: 0-0 Tstrap: 0-0 Ckp: 0-0

Best Rating: 68 5/08 Gdwd 2m soft

Moderate; stays 2m and acts on Polytrack.

Whelkeen Rock (IRE)

60 **18**

2-y-o b c Xaar-Mizillablack (IRE) (Eagle Eyed (USA))

K A Ryan Mrs Ger O'Driscoll

Placings:0P (2449)

2009: 6^{0}S, 5^{P}GF,

	Starts	1st	2nd	3rd	Win & Pl
Career Total (Turf)	2	0	0	0	

Going (Turf): Sf: 0-1 GS: 0-0 Gd: 0-0 GF: 0-1 Fm: 0-0

Distance: 5f/6f: 0-2 7f-8f: 0-0 9f-13f: 0-0 14f+: 0-0

Track : LH: 0-0 RH: 0-0 Tight: 0-0 Gall: 0-0

Aids: Bl: 0-0 Vi: 0-0 Tstrap: 0-0 Ckp: 0-0

Best Rating: 18 5/09 Hayd 6f soft

When Doves Cry

98(86) (49)**63**

3-y-o b f Grandera (IRE)-Deeply (IRE) (Darshaan)

B W Hills Phil Cunningham

Placings:640-0306 (3693)

2009: 11^{0}GS, 8^{3}GF, 8^{0}G, 8^{6}G,

	Starts	1st	2nd	3rd	Win & Pl
Career Total (Turf)	6	0	0	1	692
Career Total (AW)	1	0	0	0	

Going (Turf): Sf: 0-0 GS: 0-1 Gd: 0-3 GF: 0-2 Fm: 0-0

Distance: 5f/6f: 0-1 7f-8f: 0-2 9f-13f: 0-4 14f+: 0-0

Track : LH: 0-1 RH: 0-2 Tight: 0-3 Gall: 0-1

Aids: Bl: 0-0 Vi: 0-0 Tstrap: 0-0 Ckp: 0-0

Best Rating: 63 6/09 Wind 1m67y gd-fm

Whenever

94 **89**

5-y-o ch g Medicean-Alessandra (Generous (IRE))

R T Phillips Mr & Mrs W J Williams

Placings:311/25400-0603 (6400)

2009: 14^{0}G, 16^{6}G, 16^{0}GS, 14^{3}GF,

	Starts	1st	2nd	3rd	Win & Pl
Career Total (Turf)	12	2	1	2	15034

85 10/07 Donc 1m6f132y (0-85)H GD £6477

79 10/07 Gdwd 1m6f SFT £4210

Total win prize-money £10687

Going (Turf): Sf: 1-1 GS: 0-3 **Gd: 1-6** GF: 0-2 Fm: 0-0

Distance: 5f/6f: 0-0 7f-8f: 0-0 9f-13f: 0-1 **14f+: 2-11**

Track : LH: 1-2 RH: 1-10 Tight: 1-3 Gall: 1-7

Aids: Bl: 0-1 Vi: 0-0 Tstrap: 0-0 Ckp: 0-0

Best Rating: 89 7/08 Asct 2m gd-sft

Fair; stays 2m and acts on most ground; usually held up.

Where To Now

(88) (28)**29**

4-y-o b f Where Or When (IRE)-Starminda (Zamindar (USA))

Mrs C A Dunnett A S Machin

Placings:00/06-00 (0765)

2009: 8^{0}SD, 8^{0}SD,

	Starts	1st	2nd	3rd	Win & Pl
Career Total (Turf)	3	0	0	0	0
Career Total (AW)	3	0	0	0	

Going (Turf): Sf: 0-1 GS: 0-1 Gd: 0-0 GF: 0-1 Fm: 0-0

Distance: 5f/6f: 0-0 7f-8f: 0-2 9f-13f: 0-4 14f+: 0-0

Track : LH: 0-3 RH: 0-1 Tight: 0-2 Gall: 0-1

Aids: Bl: 0-0 Vi: 0-2 Tstrap: 0-0 Ckp: 0-0

Best Rating: 29 10/07 Yarm 1m3y soft

Where You Will

(92) (42)**55**

3-y-o ch f Where Or When (IRE)-Red Duchess (Halling (USA))

S W Hall The Welhers Partnership

Placings:40-05 (0520)

2009: 8^{0}SD, 8^{5}SD,

	Starts	1st	2nd	3rd	Win & Pl
Career Total (Turf)	1	0	0	0	231
Career Total (AW)	3	0	0	0	0

Going (Turf): Sf: 0-0 GS: 0-1 Gd: 0-0 GF: 0-0 Fm: 0-0

Distance: 5f/6f: 0-0 7f-8f: 0-3 9f-13f: 0-1 14f+: 0-0

Track : LH: 0-4 RH: 0-0 Tight: 0-2 Gall: 0-0

Aids: Bl: 0-0 Vi: 0-0 Tstrap: 0-0 Ckp: 0-0

Best Rating: 55 10/08 Brig 6f209y gd-sft

Where's Charlie

89 **47**

3-y-o br g Where Or When (IRE)-Kennedys Prima (Primo Dominie)

P Leech Middleton Stud

Placings:6 (5435)

2009: 8^{6}GF,

	Starts	1st	2nd	3rd	Win & Pl
Career Total (Turf)	1	0	0	0	0

Going (Turf): Sf: 0-0 GS: 0-0 Gd: 0-0 GF: 0-1 Fm: 0-0

Distance: 5f/6f: 0-0 7f-8f: 0-1 9f-13f: 0-0 14f+: 0-0

Track : LH: 0-0 RH: 0-0 Tight: 0-0 Gall: 0-0

Aids: Bl: 0-0 Vi: 0-0 Tstrap: 0-0 Ckp: 0-0

Best Rating: 47 8/09 NmkJ 1m gd-fm

Where's Dids

(84) (22)**42**

4-y-o b f Piccolo-Who Goes There (Wolfhound (USA))

P D Evans W A Harrison-Allan

Placings:60004-00 (0104)

2009: 6^{0}SD, 7^{0}SD,

	Starts	1st	2nd	3rd	Win & Pl
Career Total (Turf)	5	0	0	0	144
Career Total (AW)	2	0	0	0	

Going (Turf): Sf: 0-1 GS: 0-0 Gd: 0-1 GF: 0-3 Fm: 0-0

Distance: 5f/6f: 0-4 7f-8f: 0-3 9f-13f: 0-0 14f+: 0-0

Track : LH: 0-1 RH: 0-1 Tight: 0-1 Gall: 0-0

Aids: Bl: 0-0 Vi: 0-0 Tstrap: 0-1 Ckp: 0-1

Best Rating: 42 5/08 Sals 6f gd-fm

Where's Killoran

84(93) (46)**27**

4-y-o b f Iron Mask (USA)-Calypso Lady (IRE) (Priolo (USA))

E J Alston Paul Bolton

Placings:0505/30-4405 (1476)

2009: 7^{4}SD, 8^{4}SD, 7^{0}F, 7^{5}SD,

	Starts	1st	2nd	3rd	Win & Pl
Career Total (Turf)	1	0	0	0	
Career Total (AW)	9	0	0	1	373

Going (Turf): Sf: 0-0 GS: 0-0 Gd: 0-0 GF: 0-0 Fm: 0-1

Distance: 5f/6f: 0-5 7f-8f: 0-4 9f-13f: 0-1 14f+: 0-0

Track : LH: 0-8 RH: 0-1 Tight: 0-6 Gall: 0-0

Aids: Bl: 0-0 Vi: 0-0 Tstrap: 0-0 Ckp: 0-0

Best Rating: 46 4/09 Wolv 1m141y stand

Where's Reiley (USA)

104(96) (66)**68**

3-y-o b/br g Doneraile Court (USA)-Plateau (USA) (Seeking The Gold (USA))

T D Barron Dovebrace Ltd Air-Conditioning-Projects

Placings:20-33515243400 (7815)

2009: 5^{3}SD, 5^{3}SD, 5^{5}GF, 6^{1}GS, 6^{5}GF, 6^{2}GF, 7^{4}G, 6^{3}G, 6^{4}S, 6^{0}GF, 5^{0}SD,

	Starts	1st	2nd	3rd	Win & Pl
Career Total (Turf)	10	1	2	1	6076
Career Total (AW)	3	0	0	2	788

67 5/09 Newc 6f (0-70)H G-S £2849

Total win prize-money £2849

Going (Turf): Sf: 0-1 **GS: 1-2** Gd: 0-2 GF: 0-5 Fm: 0-0

Distance: **5f/6f: 1-10** 7f-8f: 0-3 9f-13f: 0-0 14f+: 0-0

Track : LH: 0-2 RH: 0-1 Tight: 0-3 Gall: 0-0

Aids: Bl: 0-2 Vi: 0-0 Tstrap: 0-0 Ckp: 0-0

Best Rating: 68 5/09 Rdcr 6f gd-fm

Modest; effective at around 5f-6f; acts on easy ground and on Polytrack.

Where's Susie

102(105) (65)**68**

4-y-o ch f Where Or When (IRE)-Linda's Schoolgirl (IRE) (Grand Lodge (USA))

M Madgwick Recycled Products Limited

Placings:06/440000-1421336 (7695)

2009: 13^{1}GS, 11^{4}F, 14^{2}GF, 11^{1}GF, 12^{3}GF, 16^{3}SD, 12^{6}SD,

	Starts	1st	2nd	3rd	Win & Pl
Career Total (Turf)	10	2	1	1	7934
Career Total (AW)	5	0	0	1	385

66 7/09 Ling 1m3f106y (0-70)H G-F £3070
67 5/09 Bath 1m5f22y (0-70)H G-S £2719
Total win prize-money £5791

Going (Turf): Sf: 0-1 **GS: 1-3** Gd: 0-2 **GF: 1-3** Fm: 0-1
Distance: 5f/6f: 0-0 7f-8f: 0-3 9f-13f: 1-9 14f+: 1-3
Track : **LH: 2-6** RH: 0-9 **Tight: 2-11** Gall: 0-0
Aids: Bl: 0-0 Vi: 0-0 Tstrap: 0-1 Ckp: 0-1
Best Rating: 68 8/09 Sals 1m4f gd-fm

Modest; stays 1m5f and acts on most ground; winning hurdler; has worn cheekpieces.

Where's The Soap (FR)

95 (85)**86**
2-y-o b/br f Country Reel (USA)-Sister Celestine (Bishop Of Cashel)
C Boutin (Tom Dascombe 25/9) G Pariente

Placings:54**14**50350**0**
2009: 5^{5}GF, 6^{4}GF, **6**^{1}SD, **6**^{4}SD, 7^{5}G, 6^{0}G, 8^{3}S, 7^{5}GS, 6^{0}VS, 7^{0}SD,

	Starts	1st	2nd	3rd	Win & Pl
Career Total (Turf)	**7**	**0**	**0**	**1**	**9656**
Career Total (AW)	**3**	**1**	**0**	**0**	**17379**

76 8/09 Deau 6f110y STD £14078
Total win prize-money £14078

Going (Turf): Sf: 0-1 GS: 0-1 Gd: 0-2 GF: 0-2 Fm: 0-0
Distance: 5f/6f: 0-3 **7f-8f: 1-7** 9f-13f: 0-0 14f+: 0-0
Track : LH: 0-1 RH: 0-3 Tight: 0-1 Gall: 0-0
Aids: Bl: 0-0 Vi: 0-0 Tstrap: 0-1 Ckp: 0-1
Best Rating: 86 10/09 Lonc 7f gd-sft

Modest; stays 6f plus; acts on Polytrack and handles fast turf.

Wheresmeneckstrap (IRE)

(73) (3)**37**
4-y-o b g Tel Quel (FR)-St Clair (Distant Relative)
T G McCourt Sean Foran/B Battersby/Mrs P McCourt

Placings:00 **(7790)**
2009: 8^{0}GY, 12^{0}SD,

	Starts	1st	2nd	3rd	Win & Pl
Career Total (Turf)	**1**	**0**	**0**	**0**	
Career Total (AW)	**1**	**0**	**0**	**0**	

Going (Turf): Sf: 0-0 GS: 0-0 Gd: 0-0 GF: 0-0 Fm: 0-0
Distance: 5f/6f: 0-0 7f-8f: 0-1 9f-13f: 0-1 14f+: 0-0
Track : LH: 0-2 RH: 0-0 Tight: 0-1 Gall: 0-0
Aids: Bl: 0-0 Vi: 0-0 Tstrap: 0-0 Ckp: 0-0
Best Rating: 37 9/09 List 1m gd-yld

Whiepa Snappa (IRE)

94(86) (61)**65**
2-y-o b g Whipper (USA)-Boudica (IRE) (Alhaarth (IRE))
P M Phelan G D C

Placings:5653333 **(6735)**
2009: 7^{5}GF, 7^{6}G, 7^{5}G, 8^{3}G, 8^{3}SD, 10^{3}GF, 8^{3}GS,

	Starts	1st	2nd	3rd	Win & Pl
Career Total (Turf)	**6**	**0**	**0**	**3**	**1220**
Career Total (AW)	**1**	**0**	**0**	**1**	**302**

Going (Turf): Sf: 0-0 GS: 0-1 Gd: 0-3 GF: 0-2 Fm: 0-0

Distance: 5f/6f: 0-0 7f-8f: 0-5 9f-13f: 0-2 14f+: 0-0
Track : LH: 0-3 RH: 0-2 Tight: 0-3 Gall: 0-0
Aids: Bl: 0-0 Vi: 0-0 Tstrap: 0-0 Ckp: 0-0
Best Rating: 65 7/09 Epsm 7f good

Modest; stays 1m; acts on good ground and on Polytrack.

Whinhill House

84(94) (49)**72**
9-y-o ch g Paris House-Darussalam (Tina's Pet)
T T Clement Miss E Johnston

Placings:300**065/031**0630/00030**3031/11015**02101120010000/**000**50002505030000/**0110**431006414/036421410-6000060 **(3283)**
2009: **5**^{6}SD, 5^{0}GF, **6**^{0}SD, **5**^{0}SD, 6^{0}GF, 6^{6}G, 6^{0}GF,

	Starts	1st	2nd	3rd	Win & Pl
Career Total (Turf)	**61**	**8**	**4**	**5**	**41490**
Career Total (AW)	**26**	**7**	**0**	**4**	**23367**

72 7/08 Catt 5f G-F £2217
72 6/08 Muss 5f G-F £2266
66 7/07 Thsk 5f (0-75)H GD £3886
69 5/07 Muss 5f G-F £1943
64 4/07 Sthl 6f STD £2184
69 4/07 Sthl 5f (0-60)H STD £2388
96 7/05 Ayr 5f (0-95)H G-F £8363
91 5/05 Carl 5f (0-80)H FRM £6795
85 5/05 Carl 5f (0-60)H G-F £3046
76 5/05 Catt 5f (0-60)H G-S £2969
79 2/05 Sthl 5f (0-85)H STD £6753
72 1/05 Wolv 5f216y (0-55)H STD £2949
65 1/05 Ling 6f (0-55)H STD £2963
67 12/04 Sthl 5f (0-45) STD £1470
56 2/03 Sthl 5f E(0-75)H STD £3334
Total win prize-money £53535

Going (Turf): Sf: 0-1 GS: 1-10 Gd: 1-18 **GF: 5-24** Fm: 1-8
Distance: **5f/6f: 15-82** 7f-8f: 0-5 9f-13f: 0-0 14f+: 0-0
Track : **LH: 3-22** RH: 2-5 Tight: 2-12 Gall: 2-4
Aids: Bl: 0-1 **Vi: 6-23** Tstrap: 5-35 Ckp: 5-35
Best Rating: 96 7/05 Ayr 5f gd-fm

Modest; effective over 5f-6f; acts on Fibresand and Polytrack; has worn visors.

Whip Up (IRE)

53
2-y-o b g Whipper (USA)-Fizz Up (Alzao (USA))
J G Portman Berkeley Racing

Placings:000 **(2319)**
2009: 5^{0}G, 5^{0}GF, 6^{0}G,

	Starts	1st	2nd	3rd	Win & Pl
Career Total (Turf)	**3**	**0**	**0**	**0**	

Going (Turf): Sf: 0-0 GS: 0-0 Gd: 0-2 GF: 0-1 Fm: 0-0
Distance: 5f/6f: 0-2 7f-8f: 0-1 9f-13f: 0-0 14f+: 0-0
Track : LH: 0-2 RH: 0-0 Tight: 0-0 Gall: 0-2
Aids: Bl: 0-1 Vi: 0-0 Tstrap: 0-0 Ckp: 0-0

Whipma Whopma Gate (IRE)

102(97) (59)**57**
4-y-o b f Rossini (USA)-The Gibson Girl (IRE) (Norwich)
D Carroll John Seed & Mrs Angela Seed

Placings:5000-02B20640103 **(6999)**
2009: 8^{0}G, 8^{2}G, 10^{B}GF, 10^{2}S, 9^{0}GF, 10^{6}GF, 12^{4}S, 9^{0}G, 8^{1}GS, 10^{0}GF, 8^{3}SD,

	Starts	1st	2nd	3rd	Win & Pl
Career Total (Turf)	**14**	**1**	**2**	**0**	**4062**
Career Total (AW)	**1**	**0**	**0**	**1**	**353**

52 9/09 Newc 1m G-S £1942
Total win prize-money £1943

Going (Turf): Sf: 0-3 **GS: 1-1** Gd: 0-4 GF: 0-6 Fm: 0-0
Distance: 5f/6f: 0-0 **7f-8f: 1-3** 9f-13f: 0-12 14f+: 0-0
Track : **LH: 1-9** RH: 0-6 Tight: 0-6 **Gall: 1-2**
Aids: **Bl: 1-4** Vi: 0-0 Tstrap: 0-0 Ckp: 0-0
Best Rating: 59 10/09 Wolv 1m141y stand

Moderate; stays 1m; acts on good and easy ground; has worn blinkers.

Whipper's Delight (IRE)

73(84) (55)**33**
2-y-o b f Whipper (USA)-Darling Smile (IRE) (Darshaan)
D Donovan M B Clarke

Placings:000 **(7130)**
2009: 6^{0}GF, 5^{0}SF, 7^{0}SD,

	Starts	1st	2nd	3rd	Win & Pl
Career Total (Turf)	**1**	**0**	**0**	**0**	
Career Total (AW)	**2**	**0**	**0**	**0**	

Going (Turf): Sf: 0-0 GS: 0-0 Gd: 0-0 GF: 0-1 Fm: 0-0
Distance: 5f/6f: 0-1 7f-8f: 0-2 9f-13f: 0-0 14f+: 0-0
Track : LH: 0-2 RH: 0-0 Tight: 0-2 Gall: 0-0
Aids: Bl: 0-0 Vi: 0-0 Tstrap: 0-0 Ckp: 0-0
Best Rating: 55 10/09 Wolv 5f216y std-fst

Whippers Love (IRE)

106(96) (67)**83**
2-y-o b c Whipper (USA)-Danadoo (FR) (Septieme Ciel (USA))
M Johnston Crone Stud Farms Ltd

Placings:0004**2**31140 **(6993)**
2009: 5^{0}GF, 5^{0}GF, 6^{0}G, 6^{4}GF, **7**^{2}SD, 7^{3}S, 7^{1}G, 8^{1}G, 8^{4}GF, 8^{0}GS,

	Starts	1st	2nd	3rd	Win & Pl
Career Total (Turf)	**9**	**2**	**0**	**1**	**10151**
Career Total (AW)	**1**	**0**	**1**	**0**	**771**

83 8/09 NmkJ 1m GD £5180
78 8/09 Bevl 7f100y (0-75) GD £3238
Total win prize-money £8419

Going (Turf): Sf: 0-1 GS: 0-1 **Gd: 2-3** GF: 0-4 Fm: 0-0
Distance: 5f/6f: 0-4 **7f-8f: 2-6** 9f-13f: 0-0 14f+: 0-0
Track : LH: 0-2 **RH: 1-2** Tight: 0-1 Gall: 0-1
Aids: Bl: 0-0 Vi: 0-0 Tstrap: 0-0 Ckp: 0-0
Best Rating: 83 8/09 NmkJ 1m good

Useful; effective over 1m; acts on good and soft ground, and on Polytrack.

Whipperway (IRE)

92(93) (56)**72**
2-y-o b f Whipper (USA)-Prince's Passion (Brief Truce (USA))
M R Channon Jon and Julia Aisbitt

Placings:030402**561** **(7482)**
2009: 6^{0}GF, 7^{3}GS, 7^{0}F, 7^{4}G, 8^{0}GS, 7^{2}G, **7**^{5}SD, **7**^{6}SD, **8**^{1}SD,

	Starts	1st	2nd	3rd	Win & Pl
Career Total (Turf)	**6**	**0**	**1**	**1**	**2769**
Career Total (AW)	**3**	**1**	**0**	**0**	**1979**

56 11/09 Ling 1m STD £1978
Total win prize-money £1979

Going (Turf): Sf: 0-0 GS: 0-2 Gd: 0-2 GF: 0-1 Fm: 0-1
Distance: 5f/6f: 0-1 7f-8f: 1-7 9f-13f: 0-1 14f+: 0-0
Track : LH: 1-3 RH: 0-3 Tight: 1-4 Gall: 0-1
Aids: Bl: 0-0 Vi: 1-1 Tstrap: 0-0 Ckp: 0-0
Best Rating: 72 7/09 Gdwd 7f gd-sft

Moderate; effective over 1m; acts on Polytrack; worn a visor with success.

Whirlijig (IRE)

97 68

4-y-o ch f Spinning World (USA)-Dariyba (IRE) (Kahyasi)
G A Swinbank Mrs T Blackett

Placings:32303 (5549)
2009: 9^{3}G, 10^{2}GF, 10^{3}GS, 12^{0}G, 9^{3}G,

	Starts	1st	2nd	3rd	Win & Pl
Career Total (Turf)	5	0	1	3	2761

Going (Turf): Sf: 0-0 GS: 0-1 Gd: 0-3 GF: 0-1 Fm: 0-0
Distance: 5f/6f: 0-0 7f-8f: 0-0 9f-13f: 0-5 14f+: 0-0
Track : LH: 0-3 RH: 0-2 Tight: 0-2 Gall: 0-2
Aids: Bl: 0-0 Vi: 0-0 Tstrap: 0-0 Ckp: 0-0
Best Rating: 68 7/09 Pont 1m2f6y gd-sft

Modest; stays 1m2f and acts on fast ground.

Whirly Dancer

98(97) (72)75

2-y-o b f Danehill Dancer (IRE)-Whirly Bird (Nashwan (USA))
H R A Cecil Woodcote Stud Ltd

Placings:02232 (6844)
2009: 6^{0}GF, 7^{2}GF, 7^{2}GF, 7^{3}SD, 7^{2}G,

	Starts	1st	2nd	3rd	Win & Pl
Career Total (Turf)	4	0	3	0	3999
Career Total (AW)	1	0	0	1	530

Going (Turf): Sf: 0-0 GS: 0-0 Gd: 0-1 GF: 0-3 Fm: 0-0
Distance: 5f/6f: 0-0 7f-8f: 0-5 9f-13f: 0-0 14f+: 0-0
Track : LH: 0-2 RH: 0-2 Tight: 0-2 Gall: 0-0
Aids: Bl: 0-0 Vi: 0-0 Tstrap: 0-0 Ckp: 0-0
Best Rating: 75 10/09 Catt 7f good

Fair; stays 7f; acts on a sound surface and Polytrack.

Whiskey Creek

102(109) (89)83

4-y-o ch g Tipsy Creek (USA)-Judiam (Primo Dominie)
C A Dwyer Mrs L Wheeler

Placings:400063/0536215-511112224000450 (2938)
2009: 6^{5}SD, 6^{1}SD, 5^{1}SD, 5^{1}SD, 5^{1}SD, 5^{2}SD, 5^{2}SD, 5^{2}SD, 5^{4}SD, 5^{0}GF, 5^{0}G, 5^{0}GF, 5^{4}GF, 5^{5}SD, 6^{0}G,

	Starts	1st	2nd	3rd	Win & Pl
Career Total (Turf)	12	0	0	0	594
Career Total (AW)	16	5	4	2	18065

84	2/09	Sthl	5f	(0-75)H	STD	£2729
79	1/09	Ling	5f	(0-62)H	STD	£2047
77	1/09	Sthl	5f	(0-60)H	STD	£2729
65	1/09	Ling	6f	(0-58)H	STD	£1978
63	12/08	Kemp	6f	(0-55)	STD	£2047

Total win prize-money £11533

Going (Turf): Sf: 0-0 GS: 0-2 Gd: 0-3 GF: 0-7 Fm: 0-0
Distance: 5f/6f: 5-27 7f-8f: 0-1 9f-13f: 0-0 14f+: 0-0
Track : LH: 2-10 RH: 1-6 Tight: 2-7 Gall: 0-3
Aids: Bl: 5-15 Vi: 0-3 Tstrap: 0-0 Ckp: 0-0
Best Rating: 89 2/09 Ling 5f stand

Fair; effective over 5f-6f; acts on sand; has worn blinkers.

Whiskey Junction

103(104) (94)88

5-y-o b g Bold Edge-Victoria Mill (Free State)
M Quinn Steven Astaire

Placings:32040/2/51111005-05566011520 (6666)
2009: 6^{0}SD, 5^{5}G, 5^{5}GF, 6^{6}GF, 6^{6}SD, 5^{0}SD, 5^{1}GF, 6^{1}SD, 6^{5}SD, 5^{2}GF, 5^{0}GS,

	Starts	1st	2nd	3rd	Win & Pl
Career Total (Turf)	12	3	1	0	13971
Career Total (AW)	13	3	2	1	14407

83	8/09	Kemp	6f		STD	£2047
84	7/09	Bath	5f161y	(0-80)H	G-F	£6308
94	7/08	Ling	6f	(0-85)H	STD	£5046
86	6/08	Kemp	6f	(0-80)H	STD	£4209
88	6/08	Bath	5f161y	(0-85)H	GD	£4209
75	5/08	Bath	5f11y		G-F	£1942

Total win prize-money £23762

Going (Turf): Sf: 0-1 GS: 0-1 Gd: 1-4 GF: 2-6 Fm: 0-0
Distance: 5f/6f: 6-25 7f-8f: 0-0 9f-13f: 0-0 14f+: 0-0
Track : LH: 4-14 RH: 2-6 Tight: 1-7 Gall: 3-7
Aids: Bl: 0-0 Vi: 0-0 Tstrap: 0-1 Ckp: 0-1
Best Rating: 94 7/08 Ling 6f stand

Useful; effective over 5f-6f; acts on a sound surface and on Polytrack; suited by forcing tactics; has worn cheekpieces.

Whisky Galore

102 74

3-y-o ch c Kyllachy-Owdbetts (IRE) (High Estate)
C G Cox Mr And Mrs P Hargreaves & A D Spence

Placings:663-050205 (6742)
2009: 8^{0}GF, 9^{5}GF, 10^{0}G, 11^{2}GS, 16^{0}G, 11^{5}GS,

	Starts	1st	2nd	3rd	Win & Pl
Career Total (Turf)	9	0	1	1	1263

Going (Turf): Sf: 0-0 GS: 0-4 Gd: 0-3 GF: 0-2 Fm: 0-0
Distance: 5f/6f: 0-0 7f-8f: 0-2 9f-13f: 0-6 14f+: 0-1
Track : LH: 0-2 RH: 0-4 Tight: 0-4 Gall: 0-0
Aids: Bl: 0-0 Vi: 0-2 Tstrap: 0-0 Ckp: 0-0
Best Rating: 74 8/09 Ling 1m3f106y gd-sft

Fair; stays 1m3f plus; acts on easy ground; has worn a visor.

Whisky Jack

87(95) (70)70

3-y-o b g Bahamian Bounty-Dress Design (IRE) (Brief Truce (USA))
W R Muir B & Q Partnership

Placings:20003324-040100 (7000)
2009: 5^{0}SD, 8^{4}SD, 7^{0}G, 7^{1}SD, 7^{0}SD, 7^{0}SD,

	Starts	1st	2nd	3rd	Win & Pl
Career Total (Turf)	7	0	1	2	3202
Career Total (AW)	7	1	1	0	2645

70	9/09	Ling	7f	(0-65)H	STD	£1706

Total win prize-money £1706

Going (Turf): Sf: 0-4 GS: 0-0 Gd: 0-1 GF: 0-2 Fm: 0-0
Distance: 5f/6f: 0-7 7f-8f: 1-6 9f-13f: 0-1 14f+: 0-0
Track : LH: 1-7 RH: 0-1 Tight: 1-6 Gall: 0-2
Aids: Bl: 1-8 Vi: 0-0 Tstrap: 0-0 Ckp: 0-0
Best Rating: 70 9/09 Ling 7f stand

Fair; effective over 6f; acts on most ground and on Polytrack; has worn blinkers.

Whisper Softly (IRE)

89 41

3-y-o b f Tagula (IRE)-Whisper Dawn (IRE) (Fasliyev (USA))
T D Walford B Selective Partnership

Placings:00050 (3938)
2009: 6^{0}GS, 5^{0}GS, 6^{0}G, 5^{5}GF, 5^{0}GF,

	Starts	1st	2nd	3rd	Win & Pl
Career Total (Turf)	5	0	0	0	0

Going (Turf): Sf: 0-0 GS: 0-2 Gd: 0-1 GF: 0-2 Fm: 0-0
Distance: 5f/6f: 0-5 7f-8f: 0-0 9f-13f: 0-0 14f+: 0-0
Track : LH: 0-0 RH: 0-0 Tight: 0-0 Gall: 0-0
Aids: Bl: 0-0 Vi: 0-0 Tstrap: 0-0 Ckp: 0-0
Best Rating: 41 5/09 Donc 6f gd-sft

Whispered Dreams (GER)

97 (75)99

4-y-o ch f Platini (GER)-Waconda (GER) (Pursuit Of Love)
Mario Hofer Judy Rumbold

Placings:1/11142253
2009: 6^{1}S, 7^{1}S, 7^{1}G, 8^{4}S, 8^{2}G, 8^{2}G, 8^{5}GF, 7^{3}G,

	Starts	1st	2nd	3rd	Win & Pl
Career Total (Turf)	8	3	2	1	30105
Career Total (AW)	1	1	0	0	3465

	5/09	Badn	7f	GD	£4854
	5/09	Colo	7f	SFT	£2330
	4/09	Kref	6f	SFT	£3398
75	10/07	Ling	7f	STD	£3465

Total win prize-money £14047

Going (Turf): Sf: 2-3 GS: 0-0 Gd: 1-4 GF: 0-1 Fm: 0-0
Distance: 5f/6f: 1-1 7f-8f: 3-7 9f-13f: 0-1 14f+: 0-0
Track : LH: 1-3 RH: 0-2 Tight: 1-2 Gall: 0-0
Aids: Bl: 0-0 Vi: 0-0 Tstrap: 0-0 Ckp: 0-0
Best Rating: 99 8/09 Duss 7f good

Useful; stays 7f and acts on Polytrack.

Whispered Lands (IRE)

83(90) (38)43

3-y-o b f Elusive City (USA)-Happy Talk (IRE) (Hamas (IRE))
J R Boyle The Paddock Space Partnership 2

Placings:0000P (6289)
2009: 7^{0}SD, 10^{0}GF, 10^{0}GF, 8^{0}SD, 10^{P}SD,

	Starts	1st	2nd	3rd	Win & Pl
Career Total (Turf)	2	0	0	0	
Career Total (AW)	3	0	0	0	

Going (Turf): Sf: 0-0 GS: 0-0 Gd: 0-0 GF: 0-2 Fm: 0-0
Distance: 5f/6f: 0-0 7f-8f: 0-2 9f-13f: 0-3 14f+: 0-0
Track : LH: 0-1 RH: 0-4 Tight: 0-3 Gall: 0-0
Aids: Bl: 0-0 Vi: 0-0 Tstrap: 0-0 Ckp: 0-0
Best Rating: 43 7/09 Wind 1m2f7y gd-fm

Whispered Times (USA)

92(80) (41)**77**

2-y-o b/br g More Than Ready (USA)-Lightning Show (USA) (Storm Cat (USA))

P C Haslam Blue Lion Racing VIII

Placings:4105000 **(7419)**

2009: 5^{4}GS, 6^{1}GF, 6^{0}F, 6^{5}GS, 7^{0}GF, 5^{0}S, 7^{0}SD,

	Starts	1st	2nd	3rd	Win & Pl
Career Total (Turf)	6	1	0	0	2831
Career Total (AW)	1	0	0	0	

77 6/09 Haml 6f5y G-F £2590

Total win prize-money £2590

Going (Turf): Sf: 0-1 GS: 0-2 Gd: 0-0 **GF: 1-2** Fm: 0-1
Distance: 5f/6f: 0-3 **7f-8f: 1-4** 9f-13f: 0-0 14f+: 0-0
Track : LH: 0-1 RH: 0-0 Tight: 0-0 Gall: 0-0
Aids: Bl: 0-1 Vi: 0-0 Tstrap: 0-1 Ckp: 0-1
Best Rating: 77 6/09 Haml 6f5y gd-fm

Fair; stays 6f; acts on fast ground; has worn blinkers.

Whispered Wish

81 **41**

3-y-o b f Rainbow Quest (USA)-Cyclone Connie (Dr Devious (IRE))

W J Haggas Mrs Charles Cyzer

Placings:0 **(1269)**

2009: 8^{0}G,

	Starts	1st	2nd	3rd	Win & Pl
Career Total (Turf)	1	0	0	0	

Going (Turf): Sf: 0-0 GS: 0-0 Gd: 0-1 GF: 0-0 Fm: 0-0
Distance: 5f/6f: 0-0 7f-8f: 0-0 9f-13f: 0-1 14f+: 0-0
Track : LH: 0-0 RH: 0-0 Tight: 0-0 Gall: 0-0
Aids: Bl: 0-0 Vi: 0-0 Tstrap: 0-0 Ckp: 0-0
Best Rating: 41 4/09 Yarm 1m3y good

Whispering Gallery

107 **114**

3-y-o b g Daylami (IRE)-Echoes In Eternity (IRE) (Spinning World (USA))

M Johnston Sheikh Hamdan Bin Mohammed Al Maktoum

Placings:1411 **(5170)**

2009: 9^{1}G, 12^{4}G, 10^{1}G, 12^{1}GF,

	Starts	1st	2nd	3rd	Win & Pl
Career Total (Turf)	4	3	0	0	35625

114 8/09 York 1m4f (0-100)H G-F £19428
106 8/09 NmkJ 1m2f (0-100)H GD £12952
95 6/09 Haml 1m1f36y GD £2388

Total win prize-money £34768

Going (Turf): Sf: 0-0 GS: 0-0 **Gd: 2-3** GF: 1-1 Fm: 0-0
Distance: 5f/6f: 0-0 7f-8f: 0-0 **9f-13f: 3-4** 14f+: 0-0
Track : LH: 1-2 **RH: 2-2** Tight: 1-1 **Gall: 2-3**
Aids: Bl: 0-0 Vi: 0-0 Tstrap: 0-0 Ckp: 0-0
Best Rating: 114 8/09 York 1m4f gd-fm

Smart stays 1m4f; acts on good/fast ground.

Whispering Spirit (IRE)

106(90) (58)**64**

3-y-o b f Catcher In The Rye (IRE)-Celtic Guest (IRE) (Be My Guest (USA))

Mrs A Duffield Middleham Park Racing XLII

Placings:2340-41001 **(5621)**

2009: 8^{4}GS, 7^{1}GS, 7^{0}SD, 8^{0}G, 7^{1}S,

	Starts	1st	2nd	3rd	Win & Pl
Career Total (Turf)	7	2	1	1	6154
Career Total (AW)	2	0	0	0	0

56 9/09 Catt 7f SFT £2388
59 7/09 Catt 7f G-S £2388

Total win prize-money £4776

Going (Turf): Sf: 1-1 GS: 1-3 Gd: 0-3 GF: 0-0 Fm: 0-0
Distance: 5f/6f: 0-3 **7f-8f: 2-5** 9f-13f: 0-1 14f+: 0-0
Track : **LH: 2-6** RH: 0-1 **Tight: 2-4** Gall: 0-1
Aids: Bl: 0-0 **Vi: 1-1** Tstrap: 0-0 Ckp: 0-0
Best Rating: 64 8/08 Ripn 5f gd-sft

Modest; effective over 5f; acts on good and easy ground.

Whistle Blower

101(100) (69)**67**

2-y-o b c Exceed And Excel (AUS)-Song Of Hope (Chief Singer)

J H M Gosden H R H Princess Haya Of Jordan

Placings:04013 **(7363)**

2009: 7^{0}GS, 8^{4}GS, 8^{0}GF, 6^{1}G, 7^{3}SD,

	Starts	1st	2nd	3rd	Win & Pl
Career Total (Turf)	4	1	0	0	4169
Career Total (AW)	1	0	0	1	385

67 10/09 Brig 6f209y (0-75) GD £3784

Total win prize-money £3784

Going (Turf): Sf: 0-0 GS: 0-2 **Gd: 1-1** GF: 0-1 Fm: 0-0
Distance: 5f/6f: 0-0 **7f-8f: 1-4** 9f-13f: 0-1 14f+: 0-0
Track : **LH: 1-3** RH: 0-0 Tight: 0-2 Gall: 0-0
Aids: Bl: 0-1 Vi: 0-0 Tstrap: 0-0 Ckp: 0-0
Best Rating: 69 11/09 Ling 7f stand

Fair; stays 7f; acts on good ground and on Polytrack; has worn blinkers.

Whistledownwind

104(107) (106)**106**

4-y-o b g Danehill Dancer (IRE)-Mountain Ash (Dominion)

J Noseda Mrs Susan Roy

Placings:01/240003-4200 **(1352)**

2009: 8^{4}SD, 8^{2}SD, 8^{0}GF, 8^{0}S,

	Starts	1st	2nd	3rd	Win & Pl
Career Total (Turf)	9	1	1	0	17879
Career Total (AW)	3	0	1	1	5222

88 10/07 Newb 1m SFT £6153

Total win prize-money £6153

Going (Turf): Sf: 1-3 GS: 0-1 Gd: 0-3 GF: 0-2 Fm: 0-0
Distance: 5f/6f: 0-0 **7f-8f: 1-8** 9f-13f: 0-3 14f+: 0-1
Track : LH: 0-4 RH: 0-3 Tight: 0-4 Gall: 0-2
Aids: Bl: 0-0 Vi: 0-2 Tstrap: 0-0 Ckp: 0-0
Best Rating: 106 12/08 Ling 7f stand

Very useful; stays 1m2f but effective at 1m; acts on good and soft ground and Polytrack.

Whistleinthewind (IRE)

96(100) (81)**75**

2-y-o b g Oratorio (IRE)-Lady Scarlett (Woodman (USA))

G L Moore R A Green

Placings:231 **(7522)**

2009: 8^{2}G, 8^{3}SD, 8^{1}SD,

	Starts	1st	2nd	3rd	Win & Pl
Career Total (Turf)	1	0	1	0	674
Career Total (AW)	2	1	0	1	4066

81 11/09 Ling 1m STD £3561

Total win prize-money £3562

Going (Turf): Sf: 0-0 GS: 0-0 Gd: 0-1 GF: 0-0 Fm: 0-0
Distance: 5f/6f: 0-0 **7f-8f: 1-2** 9f-13f: 0-1 14f+: 0-0
Track : **LH: 1-3** RH: 0-0 **Tight: 1-3** Gall: 0-0
Aids: Bl: 0-0 Vi: 0-0 Tstrap: 0-0 Ckp: 0-0
Best Rating: 81 11/09 Ling 1m stand

Fair; effective over 1m; acts on Polytrack.

Whistleupthewind

(95) (53)**60**

6-y-o b m Piccolo-The Frog Queen (Bin Ajwaad (IRE))

J M P Eustace Mrs James Eustace

Placings:00/00042110522**2050/33006**03040310/000-6 **(0087)**

2009: 6^{6}SD,

	Starts	1st	2nd	3rd	Win & Pl
Career Total (Turf)	19	3	2	2	11604
Career Total (AW)	14	0	1	2	1568

60 9/07 Folk 7f (0-65)H G-F £2590
63 7/06 Ling 7f (0-75)H G-F £3238
55 6/06 Yarm 1m3y (0-65)H G-F £2590

Total win prize-money £8421

Going (Turf): Sf: 0-4 GS: 0-2 Gd: 0-3 **GF: 3-8** Fm: 0-2
Distance: 5f/6f: 0-11 **7f-8f: 2-16** 9f-13f: 1-6 14f+: 0-0
Track : LH: 0-17 RH: 0-2 Tight: 0-14 Gall: 0-1
Aids: **Bl: 2-20** Vi: 0-0 Tstrap: 0-2 Ckp: 0-2
Best Rating: 63 8/06 Ling 7f stand

Moderate; effective at around 7f-1m; acts on fast and soft ground; also goes on Polytrack.

Whistling Wind

52

2-y-o b g Needwood Blade-Empire Of The Sun (Second Empire (IRE))

Paul Green Paddy Mason

Placings:00 **(3572)**

2009: 5^{0}GF, 6^{0}G,

	Starts	1st	2nd	3rd	Win & Pl
Career Total (Turf)	2	0	0	0	

Going (Turf): Sf: 0-0 GS: 0-0 Gd: 0-1 GF: 0-1 Fm: 0-0
Distance: 5f/6f: 0-2 7f-8f: 0-0 9f-13f: 0-0 14f+: 0-0
Track : LH: 0-1 RH: 0-0 Tight: 0-1 Gall: 0-0
Aids: Bl: 0-0 Vi: 0-0 Tstrap: 0-0 Ckp: 0-0

Whiston Pat

(93) (45)

4-y-o ch g Lomitas-Fille De Bucheron (USA) (Woodman (USA))

S R Bowring Clark Industrial Services Partnership

Placings:0-65 **(0178)**

2009: 12^{6}SS, 12^{5}SD,

	Starts	1st	2nd	3rd	Win & Pl
Career Total (Turf)	0	0	0	0	
Career Total (AW)	3	0	0	0	0

Going (Turf): Sf: 0-0 GS: 0-0 Gd: 0-0 GF: 0-0 Fm: 0-0
Distance: 5f/6f: 0-0 7f-8f: 0-1 9f-13f: 0-2 14f+: 0-0
Track : LH: 0-3 RH: 0-0 Tight: 0-0 Gall: 0-0

Aids: Bl: 0-0 Vi: 0-0 Tstrap: 0-0 Ckp: 0-0
Best Rating: 45 1/09 Sthl 1m4f stand

Whitbarrow (IRE)

(106) (78)90
10-y-o b g Royal Abjar (USA)-Danccini (IRE) (Dancing Dissident (USA))
B R Millman Mrs H Brain

Placings:01110100**4**/16630000/**056**/5001000000000**5**400 32**605**/00500506**634**/**60200**0620023600**56**/**01111415001**5 **0/0462555230-33523520431** **(7762)**
2009: 6^{3}SS, 7^{3}SD, 7^{5}SD, 6^{2}SD, 7^{3}SD, 7^{5}SD, 7^{2}SS, 7^{0}SD, 7^{4}SD, 5^{3}SD, 7^{1}SD,

	Starts	1st	2nd	3rd	Win & Pl
Career Total (Turf)	**64**	**7**	**3**	**3**	**122669**
Career Total (AW)	**40**	**6**	**5**	**6**	**27622**

73	12/09	Sthl	7f	(0-65)H	STD	£2047
80	10/07	Wolv	5f216y		STD	£2047
90	7/07	Carl	5f193y	(0-80)H	G-F	£6477
87	5/07	Sthl	6f	(0-80)H	STD	£6477
85	5/07	Sthl	6f	(0-70)H	STD	£3886
73	5/07	Wolv	5f216y	(0-55)H	SF	£2266
76	4/07	Sthl	6f		STD	£2184
101	5/04	Gdwd	5f	B(0-110)H	G-F	£12093
111	5/02	Hayd	6f	A(0-110)H	G-S	£17400
105	8/01	Gdwd	5f	A	G-F	£27000
103	6/01	Epsm	6f	A	G-F	£23200
92	5/01	Wind	5f10y	B	GD	£7624
97	5/01	Ling	5f	D	G-S	£3607

Total win prize-money £116311

Going (Turf): Sf: 0-9 GS: 2-11 Gd: 1-19 **GF: 4-23** Fm: 0-2
Distance: **5f/6f: 12-85** 7f-8f: 1-19 9f-13f: 0-0 14f+: 0-0
Track : **LH: 7-44** RH: 1-5 **Tight: 3-22** Gall: 1-6
Aids: **Bl: 8-46** Vi: 0-4 Tstrap: 0-5 Ckp: 0-5
Best Rating: **111** 5/02 Hayd 6f gd-sft

Modest; seems best at 6f but stays 7f; acts on fast ground; goes on sand; has worn blinkers.

Whitby (IRE)

(88) (51)
2-y-o br f Dubawi (IRE)-Hymenee (USA) (Chief's Crown (USA))
M W Easterby M W Easterby

Placings:453 **(7705)**
2009: 8^{4}SD, 8^{5}SD, 7^{3}SD,

	Starts	1st	2nd	3rd	Win & Pl
Career Total (Turf)	0	0	0	0	
Career Total (AW)	3	0	0	1	747

Going (Turf): **Sf: 0-0 GS: 0-0 Gd: 0-0 GF: 0-0 Fm: 0-0**
Distance: 5f/6f: 0-0 7f-8f: 0-3 9f-13f: 0-0 14f+: 0-0
Track : LH: 0-3 RH: 0-0 Tight: 0-0 Gall: 0-0
Aids: Bl: 0-0 Vi: 0-0 Tstrap: 0-0 Ckp: 0-0
Best Rating: **51** 11/09 Sthl 1m stand

Modest; stays 7f; acts on Fibresand.

Whitcombe Minister (USA)

96(106) (98)98
4-y-o b c Deputy Minister (CAN)-Pronghorn (USA) (Gulch (USA))
M Halford (M Botti 30/5) Khaled A Rahim

Placings:41/205400050-300000 **(6301a)**
2009: 8^{3}SD, 11^{0}SD, 10^{0}SD, 10^{0}SD, 9^{0}GY, 8^{0}GF,

	Starts	1st	2nd	3rd	Win & Pl
Career Total (Turf)	**10**	**0**	**0**	**0**	**3512**
Career Total (AW)	**7**	**1**	**1**	**1**	**12300**

78	12/07	Ling	7f	STD	£2817

Total win prize-money £2817

Going (Turf): **Sf: 0-1 GS: 0-2 Gd: 0-4 GF: 0-2 Fm: 0-0**
Distance: 5f/6f: 0-0 **7f-8f: 1-6** 9f-13f: 0-11 14f+: 0-0
Track : **LH: 1-7** RH: 0-8 **Tight: 1-3** Gall: 0-5
Aids: Bl: 0-3 Vi: 0-0 Tstrap: 0-0 Ckp: 0-0
Best Rating: **98** 3/09 Wolv 1m141y stand

Very useful; stays 1m1f; acts on easy ground and on Polytrack; has worn blinkers.

Whitcombe Spirit

98(92) (65)62
4-y-o b g Diktat-L'Evangile (Danehill (USA))
Jamie Poulton Telscombe Racing

Placings:004/34-6434236 **(6692)**
2009: 15^{6}G, 16^{4}G, 16^{3}G, 16^{4}GF, 16^{2}GS, 16^{3}G, 16^{6}GS,

	Starts	1st	2nd	3rd	Win & Pl
Career Total (Turf)	**8**	**0**	**1**	**2**	**1753**
Career Total (AW)	**4**	**0**	**0**	**1**	**383**

Going (Turf): **Sf: 0-0 GS: 0-3 Gd: 0-4 GF: 0-1 Fm: 0-0**
Distance: 5f/6f: 0-0 7f-8f: 0-2 9f-13f: 0-3 14f+: 0-7
Track : LH: 0-7 RH: 0-4 Tight: 0-4 Gall: 0-2
Aids: Bl: 0-0 Vi: 0-0 Tstrap: 0-0 Ckp: 0-0
Best Rating: **65** 12/07 Kemp 1m2f stand

Modest; stays 2m; acts on Fibresand and good ground on turf.

White Daffodil (IRE)

96 70
2-y-o b f Footstepsinthesand-Sparky's Song (Electric)
R Hannon Knockainey Stud

Placings:4210440 **(6169)**
2009: 5^{4}GF, 5^{2}G, 5^{1}GF, 5^{0}GF, 5^{4}GF, 6^{4}GF, 5^{0}GF,

	Starts	1st	2nd	3rd	Win & Pl
Career Total (Turf)	**7**	**1**	**1**	**0**	**6316**

68	6/09	Nott	5f13y	G-F	£3885

Total win prize-money £3886

Going (Turf): Sf: 0-0 GS: 0-0 Gd: 0-1 **GF: 1-6** Fm: 0-0
Distance: **5f/6f: 1-7** 7f-8f: 0-0 9f-13f: 0-0 14f+: 0-0
Track : LH: 0-1 RH: 0-0 Tight: 0-0 Gall: 0-2
Aids: Bl: 0-0 Vi: 0-0 Tstrap: 0-0 Ckp: 0-0
Best Rating: **70** 5/09 Wind 5f10y good

Fair; suited by 5f and fast ground.

White Dart

94(100) (79)73
2-y-o b c Rakti-Feather Boa (IRE) (Sri Pekan (USA))
M R Channon Leon Crouch

Placings:006221 **(6373)**
2009: 6^{0}S, 7^{0}G, 7^{6}G, 7^{2}GF, 8^{2}SD, 8^{1}SD,

	Starts	1st	2nd	3rd	Win & Pl
Career Total (Turf)	**4**	**0**	**1**	**0**	**1253**
Career Total (AW)	**2**	**1**	**1**	**0**	**4490**

79	9/09	Kemp	1m	(0-85)	STD	£3885

Total win prize-money £3886

Going (Turf): **Sf: 0-1 GS: 0-0 Gd: 0-2 GF: 0-1 Fm: 0-0**
Distance: 5f/6f: 0-0 **7f-8f: 1-6** 9f-13f: 0-0 14f+: 0-0
Track : LH: 0-0 **RH: 1-2** Tight: 0-0 Gall: 0-0
Aids: Bl: 0-0 Vi: 0-0 Tstrap: 0-0 Ckp: 0-0
Best Rating: **79** 9/09 Kemp 1m stand

Modest; effective over 7f; acts on fast ground.

White Deer (USA)

105(100) (83)86
5-y-o b g Stravinsky (USA)-Brookshield Baby (IRE) (Sadler's Wells (USA))
G A Harker (D Nicholls 2/5) Ian Bellamy

Placings:4213/361202500/00600255**536**-6240130001000 **(7492)**
2009: 7^{6}SD, 7^{2}F, 8^{4}SD, 10^{0}G, 7^{1}GF, 8^{3}G, 7^{0}G, 7^{0}GF, 7^{0}GF, 8^{1}GF, 8^{0}GF, 7^{0}G, 8^{0}SD,

	Starts	1st	2nd	3rd	Win & Pl
Career Total (Turf)	**32**	**4**	**5**	**3**	**36546**
Career Total (AW)	**5**	**0**	**0**	**1**	**482**

86	9/09	Rdcr	1m		G-F	£5180
86	6/09	Thsk	7f	(0-75)H	G-F	£4274
94	6/07	Thsk	7f	(0-85)H	G-F	£5181
80	8/06	Epsm	7f		GD	£4533

Total win prize-money £19171

Going (Turf): Sf: 0-4 GS: 0-5 Gd: 1-10 **GF: 3-12** Fm: 0-1
Distance: 5f/6f: 0-1 **7f-8f: 4-30** 9f-13f: 0-6 14f+: 0-0
Track : **LH: 3-23** RH: 0-7 **Tight: 3-14** Gall: 0-5
Aids: Bl: 0-7 Vi: 1-5 Tstrap: 1-4 Ckp: 1-4
Best Rating: **101** 8/07 Gdwd 7f good

Useful; best over 7f-1m; acts on most ground and Polytrack; has worn blinkers/visor/cheekpieces.

White Devil

99 75
2-y-o ch g Zafeen (FR)-Costa Balena (CHI) (Great Regent (CAN))
A M Balding Robert Hanson & Partners

Placings:0342 **(5801)**
2009: 7^{0}G, 7^{3}G, 7^{4}G, 7^{2}GF,

	Starts	1st	2nd	3rd	Win & Pl
Career Total (Turf)	**4**	**0**	**1**	**1**	**2553**

Going (Turf): **Sf: 0-0 GS: 0-0 Gd: 0-3 GF: 0-1 Fm: 0-0**
Distance: 5f/6f: 0-0 7f-8f: 0-4 9f-13f: 0-0 14f+: 0-0
Track : LH: 0-1 RH: 0-3 Tight: 0-1 Gall: 0-0
Aids: Bl: 0-0 Vi: 0-0 Tstrap: 0-0 Ckp: 0-0
Best Rating: **75** 9/09 Epsm 7f gd-fm

Fair; stays 7f; acts on fast ground.

White Ledger (IRE)

93(97) (47)50
10-y-o ch g Ali-Royal (IRE)-Boranwood (IRE) (Exhibitioner)
R E Peacock R E Peacock

Placings:06636/2023321500610/00000/00311062/0/0000 05/00/02020500-00200 **(7815)**
2009: 7^{0}GF, 8^{0}G, 5^{2}GS, 6^{0}SD, 5^{0}SD,

	Starts	1st	2nd	3rd	Win & Pl
Career Total (Turf)	**25**	**3**	**2**	**2**	**16395**
Career Total (AW)	**28**	**1**	**5**	**2**	**7646**

62	8/04	Sand	5f6y	E(0-75)H	SFT	£5642
55	8/04	Catt	5f	F	SFT	£3031
74	9/02	Sand	5f6y	D(0-85)H	G-F	£5278
71	6/02	Wolv	5f	E(0-70)H	STD	£3360

Total win prize-money £17311

Going (Turf): **Sf: 2-4** GS: 0-5 Gd: 0-4 GF: 1-11 Fm: 0-1
Distance: **5f/6f: 4-47** 7f-8f: 0-5 9f-13f: 0-1 14f+: 0-0
Track : **LH: 1-33** RH: 0-1 **Tight: 1-23** Gall: 0-1
Aids: Bl: 0-1 **Vi: 3-14** Tstrap: 0-5 Ckp: 0-5
Best Rating: **74** 9/02 Sand 5f6y gd-fm

Moderate sprint handicapper; stays 7f but better over shorter; acts on fast, soft ground and both All-Weather surfaces.

White Moss (IRE)

85(93) (50)67

5-y-o b m Peintre Celebre (USA)-Saint Ann (USA) (Geiger Counter (USA))

Jim Best Bill Wallace

Placings:0300320340/21-050 **(1318)**

2009: 12^{0}SD, 11^{5}G, 10^{0}SD,

	Starts	1st	2nd	3rd	Win & Pl
Career Total (Turf)	12	1	2	3	5722
Career Total (AW)	3	0	0	0	

67	8/08	Bevl	1m1f207y	(0-65)H	SFT	£2201

Total win prize-money £2202

Going (Turf): **Sf: 1-1** GS: 0-2 Gd: 0-6 GF: 0-3 Fm: 0-0
Distance: 5f/6f: 0-0 7f-8f: 0-2 **9f-13f: 1-13** 14f+: 0-0
Track : LH: 0-9 **RH: 1-5** Tight: 0-5 Gall: 0-3
Aids: Bl: 0-0 Vi: 0-0 Tstrap: 0-0 Ckp: 0-0
Best Rating: **67** 8/08 Bevl 1m1f207y soft

Moderate; stays 1m4f and acts on most ground.

White Shift (IRE)

104(100) (87)88

3-y-o b f Night Shift (USA)-Ivy Queen (IRE) (Green Desert (USA))

P Howling (P D Evans 13/5) Paul Terry

Placings:131002600-44055112210604256**0000** **(7738)**

2009: 5^{4}SD, 5^{4}SD, 6^{0}GF, 5^{5}F, 5^{5}GF, 5^{1}F, 6^{1}GF, 6^{2}GF, 6^{2}GF, 6^{1}GS, 5^{0}GF, 6^{6}GS, 6^{0}G, 6^{4}GF, 5^{2}F, 5^{5}F, 6^{6}GS, 6^{0}SD, 6^{0}SD, 5^{0}SD, 6^{0}SD,

	Starts	1st	2nd	3rd	Win & Pl
Career Total (Turf)	22	4	4	1	40574
Career Total (AW)	8	1	0	0	3294

84	6/09	Ripn	6f	(0-95)H	G-S	£8831
78	5/09	NmkR	6f	(0-85)H	G-F	£5828
76	5/09	Bath	5f161y		FRM	£1942
88	5/08	Wind	5f10y		G-F	£11354
74	4/08	GrLe	5f		STD	£2914

Total win prize-money £30870

Going (Turf): Sf: 0-0 GS: 1-3 Gd: 0-3 **GF: 2-12** Fm: 1-4
Distance: **5f/6f: 5-30** 7f-8f: 0-0 9f-13f: 0-0 14f+: 0-0
Track : **LH: 2-9** RH: 0-3 Tight: 0-5 **Gall: 3-6**
Aids: Bl: 0-0 Vi: 0-0 Tstrap: 0-0 Ckp: 0-0
Best Rating: **88** 6/08 Wind 5f10y gd-fm

Useful; effective over 5f-6f; acts on fast ground; goes on Polytrack.

Whitechapel

69 34

2-y-o b g Oasis Dream-Barathiki (Barathea (IRE))

W R Muir Mr & Mrs Middlebrook/Mr & Mrs Nicholson

Placings:0 **(4323)**

2009: 6^{0}GF,

	Starts	1st	2nd	3rd	Win & Pl
Career Total (Turf)	1	0	0	0	

Going (Turf): **Sf: 0-0 GS: 0-0 Gd: 0-0 GF: 0-1 Fm: 0-0**
Distance: 5f/6f: 0-1 7f-8f: 0-0 9f-13f: 0-0 14f+: 0-0
Track : LH: 0-0 RH: 0-0 Tight: 0-0 Gall: 0-0
Aids: Bl: 0-0 Vi: 0-0 Tstrap: 0-0 Ckp: 0-0
Best Rating: **34** 7/09 Sals 6f gd-fm

Whiteoak Lady (IRE)

99(89) (50)76

4-y-o ch f Medecis-French Toast (IRE) (Last Tycoon)

J L Spearing Leonard Kinsella

Placings:416/65331430-000010 **(6596)**

2009: 6^{0}G, 6^{0}GF, 6^{0}SD, 5^{0}S, 6^{1}G, 6^{0}GS,

	Starts	1st	2nd	3rd	Win & Pl
Career Total (Turf)	16	3	0	3	12341
Career Total (AW)	1	0	0	0	

72	8/09	Thsk	6f		GD	£4274
76	8/08	Hayd	6f	(0-70)H	SFT	£3238
68	7/07	Chep	6f16y		HVY	£2849

Total win prize-money £10362

Going (Turf): **Sf: 2-8** GS: 0-2 Gd: 1-5 GF: 0-1 Fm: 0-0
Distance: **5f/6f: 2-8** 7f-8f: 1-9 9f-13f: 0-0 14f+: 0-0
Track : LH: 0-3 RH: 0-0 Tight: 0-1 Gall: 0-2
Aids: **Bl: 1-2** Vi: 0-0 Tstrap: 0-0 Ckp: 0-0
Best Rating: **76** 8/08 Yarm 6f3y soft

Fair; suited by 6f; acts on good and soft ground; has worn blinkers.

Whiterocks

93(84) (34)51

3-y-o ch g Imperial Dancer-Thailand (Lycius (USA))

M R Channon R Bastian

Placings:500500 **(5775)**

2009: 7^{5}F, 10^{0}GF, 11^{0}G, 12^{5}G, 16^{0}G, 10^{0}SD,

	Starts	1st	2nd	3rd	Win & Pl
Career Total (Turf)	5	0	0	0	132
Career Total (AW)	1	0	0	0	

Going (Turf): **Sf: 0-0 GS: 0-0 Gd: 0-3 GF: 0-1 Fm: 0-1**
Distance: 5f/6f: 0-0 7f-8f: 0-1 9f-13f: 0-4 14f+: 0-1
Track : LH: 0-3 RH: 0-3 Tight: 0-3 Gall: 0-0
Aids: Bl: 0-0 Vi: 0-0 Tstrap: 0-0 Ckp: 0-0
Best Rating: **51** 8/09 Chep 1m4f23y good

Whitley Bay (USA)

(35)

2-y-o b c Lion Heart (USA)-Sea Witch (USA) (Sea Hero (USA))

J R Best John Foulger

Placings:0 **(7376)**

2009: 7^{0}SD,

	Starts	1st	2nd	3rd	Win & Pl
Career Total (Turf)	0	0	0	0	
Career Total (AW)	1	0	0	0	

Going (Turf): **Sf: 0-0 GS: 0-0 Gd: 0-0 GF: 0-0 Fm: 0-0**
Distance: 5f/6f: 0-0 7f-8f: 0-1 9f-13f: 0-0 14f+: 0-0
Track : LH: 0-1 RH: 0-0 Tight: 0-1 Gall: 0-0
Aids: Bl: 0-0 Vi: 0-0 Tstrap: 0-0 Ckp: 0-0

Who Art Thou (USA)

51

3-y-o b/br g More Than Ready (USA)-Silk Sails (USA) (Ocean Crest (USA))

D R Gandolfo Mrs D McCabe

Placings:0640-0 **(5872)**

2009: 10^{0}G,

	Starts	1st	2nd	3rd	Win & Pl
Career Total (Turf)	5	0	0	0	289

Going (Turf): **Sf: 0-1 GS: 0-0 Gd: 0-3 GF: 0-1 Fm: 0-0**
Distance: 5f/6f: 0-2 7f-8f: 0-1 9f-13f: 0-2 14f+: 0-0
Track : LH: 0-1 RH: 0-0 Tight: 0-0 Gall: 0-1
Aids: Bl: 0-0 Vi: 0-0 Tstrap: 0-0 Ckp: 0-0
Best Rating: **51** 7/08 Hayd 6f heavy

Who's Shirl

102 74

3-y-o b f Shinko Forest (IRE)-Shirl (Shirley Heights)

C W Fairhurst Mrs Shirley France

Placings:060-223022150 **(6309)**

2009: 6^{2}F, 6^{2}GF, 5^{3}GF, 7^{0}GF, 6^{2}GF, 6^{2}GF, 6^{1}GF, 6^{5}GF, 7^{0}GF,

	Starts	1st	2nd	3rd	Win & Pl
Career Total (Turf)	12	1	4	1	5982

74	8/09	Newc	6f	(0-65)H	G-F	£2590

Total win prize-money £2590

Going (Turf): Sf: 0-0 GS: 0-2 Gd: 0-1 **GF: 1-8** Fm: 0-1
Distance: **5f/6f: 1-7** 7f-8f: 0-4 9f-13f: 0-1 14f+: 0-0
Track : LH: 0-1 RH: 0-2 Tight: 0-1 Gall: 0-0
Aids: Bl: 0-0 Vi: 0-0 Tstrap: 0-0 Ckp: 0-0
Best Rating: **74** 9/09 Rdcr 6f gd-fm

Moderate; effective over 6f; acts on fast ground.

Who's Winning (IRE)

100(98) (63)64

8-y-o ch g Docksider (USA)-Quintellina (Robellino (USA))

B G Powell Miss Anna Bucknall

Placings:15640436/00602121**102/022**010640404000/**0020** 06606413542036**0433/**4351145240002266**0500**/0015401 000002430-6563465431223 **(6587)**

2009: 6^{6}G, 5^{5}GF, 5^{6}GS, 6^{3}GF, 6^{4}G, 5^{6}F, 5^{5}F, 6^{4}F, 5^{3}F, 6^{1}G, 6^{2}SD, 5^{2}GF, 7^{3}SD,

	Starts	1st	2nd	3rd	Win & Pl
Career Total (Turf)	82	11	7	6	71348
Career Total (AW)	24	0	6	4	11933

59	9/09	Chep	6f16y		GD	£1942
64	8/08	Brig	5f213y		GD	£1942
64	6/08	Folk	6f		G-F	£2047
83	5/07	Gdwd	6f	(0-80)H	GD	£6477
81	5/07	Folk	6f	(0-75)H	G-F	£2914
75	7/06	Brig	5f213y	(0-75)H	FRM	£3886
90	5/05	NmkR	6f	(0-95)H	GD	£9765
87	9/04	Kemp	6f	(0-85)H	G-F	£8420
80	9/04	Gdwd	5f	(0-70)H	G-F	£3495
72	8/04	Brig	5f213y	D(0-80)H	FRM	£6656
68	4/03	Folk	5f	D	G-F	£4043

Total win prize-money £51592

Going (Turf): Sf: 0-1GS: 0-12Gd: 4-20 **GF: 5-35** Fm: 2-14
Distance: **5f/6f: 10-87** 7f-8f: 1-19 9f-13f: 0-0 14f+: 0-0
Track : **LH: 3-48** RH: 0-8 Tight: 0-18 Gall: 0-14
Aids: Bl: 0-2 Vi: 0-1 Tstrap: 0-1 Ckp: 0-1
Best Rating: **91** 8/05 NmkJ 6f good

Moderate; effective at around 6f; acts on fast ground; also goes on Polytrack; has worn a tongue tie.

Whodunit (UAE)

(103) (63)47

5-y-o b g Mark Of Esteem (IRE)-Mystery Play (IRE) (Sadler's Wells (USA))

P W Hiatt Exors of the Late John Hedges

Placings:050020005/66010-0100 (7876)

2009: 9⁰SD, 8¹SD, 8⁰SF, 7⁰SD,

	Starts	1st	2nd	3rd	Win & Pl
Career Total (Turf)	**5**	**0**	**1**	**0**	**848**
Career Total (AW)	**13**	**2**	**0**	**0**	**3753**

63 2/09 Kemp 1m (0-50)H STD £2047
56 12/08 Ling 1m2f (0-52)H STD £1706
Total win prize-money £3753

Going (Turf): **Sf: 0-1 GS: 0-1 Gd: 0-1 GF: 0-2 Fm: 0-0**
Distance: 5f/6f: 0-0 7f-8f: 1-4 9f-13f: 1-14 14f+: 0-0
Track : LH: 1-11 RH: 1-6 **Tight: 1-9** Gall: 0-0
Aids: **Bl: 2-7** Vi: 0-0 Tstrap: 0-0 Ckp: 0-0
Best Rating: **63** 2/09 Kemp 1m stand

Moderate; effective over 1m-1m4f; acts on an easy surface; goes on Polytrack; has worn blinkers.

Whooshka (USA)

99 80

3-y-o b f Smart Strike (CAN)-Bushra (USA) (Danzig (USA))

P W Chapple-Hyam C G P Wyatt

Placings:1400 (6996)

2009: 10¹GF, 9⁴G, 11⁰GS, 10⁰GS,

	Starts	1st	2nd	3rd	Win & Pl
Career Total (Turf)	**4**	**1**	**0**	**0**	**4399**

72 6/09 Newb 1m2f6y G-F £3885
Total win prize-money £3886

Going (Turf): Sf: 0-0 GS: 0-2 Gd: 0-1 **GF: 1-1** Fm: 0-0
Distance: 5f/6f: 0-0 7f-8f: 0-0 **9f-13f: 1-4** 14f+: 0-0
Track : **LH: 1-3** RH: 0-1 Tight: 0-0 **Gall: 1-2**
Aids: Bl: 0-0 Vi: 0-0 Tstrap: 0-0 Ckp: 0-0
Best Rating: **80** 7/09 Leic 1m1f218y good

Fair filly; made winning debut over 1m2f on fast ground.

Whotsit (IRE)

101(100) (57)66

3-y-o ch g Choisir (AUS)-Charming Victoria (IRE) (Mujadil (USA))

Miss Amy Weaver Miss A Weaver

Placings:001255066221206 (6052)

2009: 7⁰SD, 8⁰SD, 8¹SD, 8²SD, 8⁵SD, 8⁵SD, 8⁰GF, 8⁶GF, 8⁶GF, 8²G, 8²G, 7¹GS, 7²GF, 9⁰GF, 8⁶G,

	Starts	1st	2nd	3rd	Win & Pl
Career Total (Turf)	**9**	**1**	**3**	**0**	**4138**
Career Total (AW)	**6**	**1**	**1**	**0**	**2632**

66 8/09 Ling 7f140y (0-65)H G-S £2047
57 2/09 Ling 1m STD £2047
Total win prize-money £4094

Going (Turf): Sf: 0-0 **GS: 1-1** Gd: 0-3 GF: 0-5 Fm: 0-0
Distance: 5f/6f: 0-0 **7f-8f: 2-9** 9f-13f: 0-6 14f+: 0-0
Track : **LH: 1-8** RH: 0-1 **Tight: 1-7** Gall: 0-0
Aids: **Bl: 2-13** Vi: 0-0 Tstrap: 0-0 Ckp: 0-0
Best Rating: **66** 8/09 Ling 7f140y gd-fm

Modest; stays 1m; acts on Polytrack and good ground on turf; has worn blinkers.

Whozart (IRE)

98(100) (62)62

6-y-o b g Mozart (IRE)-Hertford Castle (Reference Point)

A Dickman Alan Harrison

Placings:00/031260030/023030330422015-266554050 (3002)

2009: 5²SD, 6⁶SS, 5⁶SD, 6⁵SD, 5⁵SD, 5⁴G, 5⁰GF, 6⁵GF, 5⁰GF,

	Starts	1st	2nd	3rd	Win & Pl
Career Total (Turf)	**25**	**2**	**3**	**5**	**8145**
Career Total (AW)	**10**	**0**	**2**	**1**	**1390**

62 10/08 Catt 5f (0-55)H GD £2307
52 5/07 Rdcr 6f (0-60)H GD £1977
Total win prize-money £4286

Going (Turf): Sf: 0-3 GS: 0-3 **Gd: 2-9** GF: 0-9 Fm: 0-1
Distance: **5f/6f: 2-32** 7f-8f: 0-3 9f-13f: 0-0 14f+: 0-0
Track : LH: 0-9 RH: 0-1 Tight: 0-4 Gall: 0-1
Aids: Bl: 0-1 Vi: 0-0 Tstrap: 0-1 Ckp: 0-1
Best Rating: **63** 11/07 Catt 5f gd-fm

Moderate, effective over 5f-6f and acts on most ground.

Whozthecat (IRE)

101 80

2-y-o b c One Cool Cat (USA)-Intaglia (GER) (Lomitas)

D Carroll Ninerus

Placings:516 (5038)

2009: 5⁵G, 5¹F, 6⁶GF,

	Starts	1st	2nd	3rd	Win & Pl
Career Total (Turf)	**3**	**1**	**0**	**0**	**2047**

80 5/09 Rdcr 5f FRM £2047
Total win prize-money £2047

Going (Turf): Sf: 0-0 GS: 0-0 Gd: 0-1 GF: 0-1 **Fm: 1-1**
Distance: **5f/6f: 1-3** 7f-8f: 0-0 9f-13f: 0-0 14f+: 0-0
Track : LH: 0-0 RH: 0-0 Tight: 0-0 Gall: 0-0
Aids: Bl: 0-0 Vi: 0-0 Tstrap: 0-0 Ckp: 0-0
Best Rating: **80** 5/09 Rdcr 5f firm

Why Nee Amy

101(100) (65)59

3-y-o ch f Tipsy Creek (USA)-Ashleen (Chilibang)

T Keddy (Miss Gay Kelleway 7/7) B Neaves

Placings:6024-4352321000015321 (7426)

2009: 7⁴SD, 8³SD, 7⁵SD, 8²SD, 10³SD, 8²G, 8¹GF, 10⁰GF, 8⁰S, 9⁰G, 8⁰G, 8¹GF, 9⁵SD, 8³GF, 8²SD, 10¹SD,

	Starts	1st	2nd	3rd	Win & Pl
Career Total (Turf)	**9**	**2**	**1**	**1**	**4735**
Career Total (AW)	**11**	**1**	**3**	**2**	**5123**

62 11/09 Kemp 1m2f STD £2047
59 9/09 Bevl 1m100y (0-55) G-F £1876
55 5/09 Yarm 1m3y G-F £1942
Total win prize-money £5867

Going (Turf): Sf: 0-1 GS: 0-0 Gd: 0-3 **GF: 2-5** Fm: 0-0
Distance: 5f/6f: 0-1 7f-8f: 0-8 **9f-13f: 3-11** 14f+: 0-0
Track : LH: 0-12 **RH: 2-3** Tight: 0-10 Gall: 0-0
Aids: Bl: 0-0 Vi: 0-1 Tstrap: 1-5 Ckp: 1-5
Best Rating: **65** 11/08 Wolv 7f32y stand

Moderate; effective over 1m-1m2f; acts on good ground; goes on Polytrack, has worn cheekpieces.

Wi Dud

109 109

5-y-o b g Elnadim (USA)-Hopesay (Warning)

K A Ryan J Duddy,L Duddy,P McBride,Mrs J Ryan

Placings:12212/502450/350403020-34330020050 (7015)

2009: 6³F, 5⁴S, 5³G, 5³HY, 5⁰GF, 5⁰GF, 5²GS, 5⁰GF, 6⁰G, 6⁵G, 5⁰GS,

	Starts	1st	2nd	3rd	Win & Pl
Career Total (Turf)	**31**	**2**	**6**	**5**	**190253**

112 9/06 York 5f GD £39746
91 6/06 York 5f G-F £7124
Total win prize-money £46871

Going (Turf): Sf: 0-5 GS: 0-8 **Gd: 1-10 GF: 1-7** Fm: 0-1
Distance: **5f/6f: 2-30** 7f-8f: 0-1 9f-13f: 0-0 14f+: 0-0
Track : LH: 0-1 RH: 0-0 Tight: 0-0 Gall: 0-0
Aids: Bl: 0-9 Vi: 0-0 Tstrap: 0-1 Ckp: 0-1
Best Rating: **115** 9/06 NmkR 6f soft

Very useful; winner of the Group 2 Flying Childers at York in 2006 and also runner-up in the Group 1 Middle Park Stakes; effective over 5f-6f; acts on most ground; has worn blinkers.

Wibbadune (IRE)

95(110) (82)80

5-y-o ch m Daggers Drawn (USA)-Becada (GER) (Cadeaux Genereux)

D Shaw Simon Mapletoft Racing I

Placings:005043222/0215/045152111264000216-50605000020 (4886)

2009: 5⁵SD, 5⁰SD, 5⁶SD, 5⁰GF, 5⁵GF, 5⁰GF, 5⁰G, 5⁰GF, 5⁰S, 5²S, 5⁰GS,

	Starts	1st	2nd	3rd	Win & Pl
Career Total (Turf)	**16**	**3**	**2**	**0**	**9765**
Career Total (AW)	**26**	**3**	**6**	**1**	**12625**

82 10/08 Ling 5f (0-75)H STD £2590
79 6/08 Ling 5f (0-70)H G-F £2456
70 5/08 Ling 5f (0-70)H G-S £2331
63 5/08 Yarm 5f43y (0-65)H G-F £1942
58 3/08 Ling 5f (0-52)H STD £1876
50 12/07 Kemp 5f STD £2047
Total win prize-money £13246

Going (Turf): Sf: 0-4 GS: 1-3 Gd: 0-3 **GF: 2-6** Fm: 0-0
Distance: **5f/6f: 6-42** 7f-8f: 0-0 9f-13f: 0-0 14f+: 0-0
Track : **LH: 2-20** RH: 1-4 **Tight: 2-18** Gall: 0-2
Aids: Bl: 0-2 Vi: 0-1 Tstrap: 0-0 Ckp: 0-0
Best Rating: **82** 10/08 Ling 5f stand

Fair; best over 5f; acts on most ground and on Polytrack, has worn a visor and blinkers.

Wicked Daze (IRE)

106(114) (92)96

6-y-o ch g Generous (IRE)-Thrilling Day (Groom Dancer (USA))

K A Ryan (Ian Williams 27/6) Dr Marwan Koukash

Placings:026/2221/1211000-6045220243 (7701)

2009: 16⁶SD, 16⁰GF, 14⁴GF, 15⁵GF, 16²GF, 11²GF, 16⁰G, 16²SD, 13⁴SD, 16³SD,

	Starts	1st	2nd	3rd	Win & Pl
Career Total (Turf)	**14**	**1**	**4**	**0**	**19477**
Career Total (AW)	**10**	**3**	**4**	**1**	**17525**

96 7/08 Asct 2m (0-100)H G-F £12952
95 2/08 Ling 2m (0-85)H STD £4100
89 1/08 Ling 1m4f (0-85)H STD £4100
65 1/08 Sthl 1m3f STD £1911
Total win prize-money £23065

Going (Turf): Sf: 0-1 GS: 0-1 Gd: 0-4 **GF: 1-8** Fm: 0-0
Distance: 5f/6f: 0-1 7f-8f: 0-2 9f-13f: 2-9 14f+: 2-12
Track : **LH: 3-13** RH: 1-9 **Tight: 2-10** Gall: 1-9
Aids: Bl: 0-0 Vi: 0-3 Tstrap: 0-1 Ckp: 0-1

Best Rating: **96** 7/08 Asct 2m gd-fm

Useful; stays 2m; acts on good and faster ground; goes on sand; has worn a visor and a tongue tie.

Wicked Wilma (IRE)

102(93) (44)**67**

5-y-o b m Tagula (IRE)-Wicked (Common Grounds)
A Berry Mrs Thelma White

Placings:3331/6040266040610232**0**-2235565631020 **(7119)**
2009: 5^{2}GF, 5^{2}GF, 5^{3}G, 5^{5}GF, 5^{5}G, 5^{6}G, 5^{5}G, 5^{6}GS, 5^{3}G, 5^{1}G, 5^{0}GS, 5^{2}GF, 5^{0}GS,

	Starts	1st	2nd	3rd	Win & Pl
Career Total (Turf)	**33**	**3**	**6**	**6**	**17674**
Career Total (AW)	**1**	**0**	**0**	**0**	

67 9/09 Muss 5f (0-70)H GD £3238
63 9/08 Bevl 5f (0-50)H HVY £2104
59 8/06 Muss 5f GD £4210
Total win prize-money £9553

Going (Turf): Sf: 1-5 GS: 0-7 **Gd: 2-10** GF: 0-11 Fm: 0-0
Distance: **5f/6f: 3-34** 7f-8f: 0-0 9f-13f: 0-0 14f+: 0-0
Track : LH: 0-1 RH: 0-3 Tight: 0-1 Gall: 0-3
Aids: Bl: 0-0 Vi: 0-0 Tstrap: 0-0 Ckp: 0-0
Best Rating: **67** 9/09 Muss 5f good

Moderate; suited by 5f; acts on good and softer ground.

Wickedly Fast (USA)

(82) (49)

3-y-o b f Gulch (USA)-Need More Business (IRE) (Alzao (USA))
George Baker Jerry Jamgotchian

Placings:30-00 **(0594)**
2009: 7^{0}SD, 7^{0}SD,

	Starts	1st	2nd	3rd	Win & Pl
Career Total (Turf)	0	0	0	0	
Career Total (AW)	4	0	0	1	302

Going (Turf): **Sf: 0-0 GS: 0-0 Gd: 0-0 GF: 0-0 Fm: 0-0**
Distance: 5f/6f: 0-0 7f-8f: 0-4 9f-13f: 0-0 14f+: 0-0
Track : LH: 0-4 RH: 0-0 Tight: 0-4 Gall: 0-0
Aids: Bl: 0-0 Vi: 0-0 Tstrap: 0-0 Ckp: 0-0
Best Rating: **49** 10/08 Wolv 7f32y std-fst

Wicklewood

94(97) (49)**45**

3-y-o b g Mujahid (USA)-Pinini (Pivotal)
Mrs C A Dunnett Christine Dunnett Racing

Placings:P0-**50**060**45**00**4**060**040** **(7787)**
2009: 6^{5}SD, 6^{0}SD, 7^{0}GF, 7^{6}GF, 5^{0}GF, 8^{4}SD, 6^{5}SD, 6^{0}G, 6^{0}G, 7^{4}GF, 6^{0}SD, 7^{6}GF, 11^{0}GF, 8^{0}SD, 7^{4}SD, 7^{0}SD,

	Starts	1st	2nd	3rd	Win & Pl
Career Total (Turf)	**9**	**0**	**0**	**0**	**212**
Career Total (AW)	**9**	**0**	**0**	**0**	**192**

Going (Turf): **Sf: 0-0 GS: 0-1 Gd: 0-2 GF: 0-6 Fm: 0-0**
Distance: 5f/6f: 0-7 7f-8f: 0-10 9f-13f: 0-1 14f+: 0-0
Track : LH: 0-9 RH: 0-2 Tight: 0-5 Gall: 0-1
Aids: Bl: 0-2 Vi: 0-6 Tstrap: 0-1 Ckp: 0-1
Best Rating: **49** 12/09 Kemp 7f stand

Plating-class; stays 7f; acts on Fibresand; has worn a visor.

Wicksy Creek

88(91) (55)**41**

4-y-o b g Tipsy Creek (USA)-Bridal White (Robellino (USA))
G C Bravery Martin Marris

Placings:42/**00500-200000505000** **(5509)**
2009: 5^{2}SD, 5^{0}SD, 5^{0}GF, 5^{0}SD, 5^{0}G, 6^{0}GF, 6^{5}SD, 5^{0}GS, 10^{5}G, 11^{0}GF, 6^{0}GF, 12^{0}G,

	Starts	1st	2nd	3rd	Win & Pl
Career Total (Turf)	**11**	**0**	**1**	**0**	**722**
Career Total (AW)	**8**	**0**	**1**	**0**	**806**

Going (Turf): **Sf: 0-1 GS: 0-1 Gd: 0-3 GF: 0-6 Fm: 0-0**
Distance: 5f/6f: 0-11 7f-8f: 0-5 9f-13f: 0-3 14f+: 0-0
Track : LH: 0-7 RH: 0-1 Tight: 0-7 Gall: 0-2
Aids: Bl: 0-1 Vi: 0-0 Tstrap: 0-1 Ckp: 0-1
Best Rating: **55** 2/09 Ling 5f stand

Wide Ranging

(87) (57)

2-y-o gr c With Approval (CAN)-Widescreen (USA) (Distant View (USA))
R Charlton K Abdulla

Placings:0 **(6607)**
2009: 8^{0}SD,

	Starts	1st	2nd	3rd	Win & Pl
Career Total (Turf)	**0**	**0**	**0**	**0**	
Career Total (AW)	**1**	**0**	**0**	**0**	

Going (Turf): **Sf: 0-0 GS: 0-0 Gd: 0-0 GF: 0-0 Fm: 0-0**
Distance: 5f/6f: 0-0 7f-8f: 0-1 9f-13f: 0-0 14f+: 0-0
Track : LH: 0-0 RH: 0-1 Tight: 0-0 Gall: 0-0
Aids: Bl: 0-0 Vi: 0-0 Tstrap: 0-0 Ckp: 0-0
Best Rating: **57** 10/09 Kemp 1m stand

Widezain (IRE)

90 **64**

2-y-o b c Chineur (FR)-Silk Fan (IRE) (Unfuwain (USA))
M R Channon Jaber Abdullah

Placings:6 **(6066)**
2009: 8^{6}GF,

	Starts	1st	2nd	3rd	Win & Pl
Career Total (Turf)	**1**	**0**	**0**	**0**	**0**

Going (Turf): **Sf: 0-0 GS: 0-0 Gd: 0-0 GF: 0-1 Fm: 0-0**
Distance: 5f/6f: 0-0 7f-8f: 0-1 9f-13f: 0-0 14f+: 0-0
Track : LH: 0-0 RH: 0-0 Tight: 0-0 Gall: 0-0
Aids: Bl: 0-0 Vi: 0-0 Tstrap: 0-0 Ckp: 0-0
Best Rating: **64** 9/09 NmkR 1m gd-fm

Wigan Lane

91(91) (63)**68**

2-y-o b f Kheleyf (USA)-Nesting (Thatching)
P Howling (R A Fahey 21/8) Paul Terry

Placings:63100**43050** **(7389)**
2009: 6^{6}GF, 5^{3}GF, 6^{1}G, 6^{0}GF, 6^{0}GF, 5^{4}SF, 6^{3}SD, 5^{0}SD, 6^{5}SD, 7^{0}SD,

	Starts	1st	2nd	3rd	Win & Pl
Career Total (Turf)	**5**	**1**	**0**	**1**	**4380**
Career Total (AW)	**5**	**0**	**0**	**1**	**337**

68 6/09 Donc 6f GD £3561
Total win prize-money £3562

Wiggy Smith

Going (Turf): Sf: 0-0 GS: 0-0 **Gd: 1-1** GF: 0-4 Fm: 0-0
Distance: **5f/6f: 1-9** 7f-8f: 0-1 9f-13f: 0-0 14f+: 0-0
Track : LH: 0-4 RH: 0-2 Tight: 0-4 Gall: 0-0
Aids: Bl: 0-0 Vi: 0-0 Tstrap: 0-0 Ckp: 0-0
Best Rating: **68** 6/09 Donc 6f good

Moderate; stays 6f; acts on fast ground and on Polytrack.

Wiggy Smith

107 (84)**86**

10-y-o ch g Master Willie-Monsoon (Royal Palace)
H Candy Mrs George Tricks

Placings:03**6**22615/41/5012/044**4**/06/301-30343 **(5028)**
2009: 10^{3}GS, 10^{0}G, 10^{3}GS, 10^{4}GF, 12^{3}GF,

	Starts	1st	2nd	3rd	Win & Pl
Career Total (Turf)	**26**	**4**	**3**	**5**	**34330**
Career Total (AW)	**2**	**0**	**0**	**0**	**983**

81 10/08 Leic 1m1f218y (0-75)H GD £3238
90 8/04 Epsm 1m2f18yC(0-90)H GD £10426
86 7/03 Newb 1m3f5yD(0-85)H G-F £5798
72 10/02 Wind 1m67y D G-S £3682
Total win prize-money £23144

Going (Turf): Sf: 0-4 GS: 1-6 **Gd: 2-9** GF: 1-7 Fm: 0-0
Distance: 5f/6f: 0-0 7f-8f: 0-1 **9f-13f: 4-27** 14f+: 0-0
Track : LH: 2-14 RH: 2-13 **Tight: 2-9** Gall: 1-7
Aids: Bl: 0-0 Vi: 0-0 Tstrap: 0-0 Ckp: 0-0
Best Rating: **92** 9/05 Ling 1m2f stand

Fair; stays 1m4f; acts on most types of ground.

Wightgold

98(93) (47)**52**

3-y-o ch f Golden Snake (USA)-Main Brand (Main Reef)
H J L Dunlop Mrs J S Ignarski

Placings:00-60**4**0342 **(6935)**
2009: 6^{6}G, 8^{0}GF, 10^{4}SD, 10^{0}SD, 12^{3}GF, 15^{4}GF, 17^{2}G,

	Starts	1st	2nd	3rd	Win & Pl
Career Total (Turf)	**6**	**0**	**1**	**1**	**1252**
Career Total (AW)	**3**	**0**	**0**	**0**	**144**

Going (Turf): **Sf: 0-0 GS: 0-1 Gd: 0-2 GF: 0-3 Fm: 0-0**
Distance: 5f/6f: 0-2 7f-8f: 0-1 9f-13f: 0-4 14f+: 0-2
Track : LH: 0-4 RH: 0-3 Tight: 0-6 Gall: 0-0
Aids: Bl: 0-0 Vi: 0-0 Tstrap: 0-0 Ckp: 0-0
Best Rating: **52** 10/09 Bath 2m1f34y good

Moderate; stays 2m; acts on good ground; goes on Polytrack.

Wigmore Hall (IRE)

99 **90**

2-y-o b g High Chaparral (IRE)-Love And Laughter (IRE) (Theatrical)
M L W Bell M B Hawtin

Placings:015 **(6663)**
2009: 7^{0}G, 8^{1}GF, 7^{5}GS,

	Starts	1st	2nd	3rd	Win & Pl
Career Total (Turf)	**3**	**1**	**0**	**0**	**4200**

90 9/09 NmkR 1m G-F £3885
Total win prize-money £3886

Going (Turf): Sf: 0-0 GS: 0-1 Gd: 0-1 **GF: 1-1** Fm: 0-0
Distance: 5f/6f: 0-0 **7f-8f: 1-3** 9f-13f: 0-0 14f+: 0-0
Track : LH: 0-0 RH: 0-0 Tight: 0-0 Gall: 0-0
Aids: Bl: 0-0 Vi: 0-0 Tstrap: 0-0 Ckp: 0-0
Best Rating: **90** 9/09 NmkR 1m gd-fm

Useful; stays 1m; acts on fast ground.

Wigram's Turn (USA)

96(108) (96)**87**

4-y-o ch g Hussonet (USA)-Stacey's Relic (USA) (Houston (USA))

A M Balding David Brownlow

Placings:130/225655-250310 (7431)

2009: 7^{2}SD, 7^{5}SD, 7^{0}GF, 7^{3}SD, 7^{1}SD, 7^{0}SD,

	Starts	1st	2nd	3rd	Win & Pl
Career Total (Turf)	7	1	0	1	4613
Career Total (AW)	8	1	3	1	10309

94	9/09	Kemp	7f	(0-85)H	STD	£4727
80	5/07	Rdcr	5f		G-F	£2817

Total win prize-money £7544

Going (Turf): Sf: 0-0 GS: 0-2 Gd: 0-1 **GF: 1-4** Fm: 0-0
Distance: 5f/6f: 1-4 7f-8f: 1-11 9f-13f: 0-0 14f+: 0-0
Track : LH: 0-1 **RH: 1-9** Tight: 0-0 Gall: 0-1
Aids: Bl: 0-0 Vi: 0-4 Tstrap: 0-0 Ckp: 0-0
Best Rating: 96 4/09 Kemp 7f stand

Useful; stays 7f; acts on fast ground and Polytrack.

Wigwam Willie (IRE)

105 **96**

7-y-o b g Indian Rocket-Sweet Nature (IRE) (Classic Secret (USA))

K A Ryan Neil & Anne Dawson Partnership

Placings:4520/20210/50546104/0104010/4300313043-0621400 (6094)

2009: 8^{0}GF, 8^{6}GF, 9^{2}GS, 9^{1}GS, 8^{4}SH, 8^{0}HY, 8^{0}G,

	Starts	1st	2nd	3rd	Win & Pl
Career Total (Turf)	41	6	4	4	59730

92	6/09	Ripn	1m1f170y	(0-85)H	G-S	£5180
86	6/08	Ripn	1m1f170y	(0-85)H	CD	£4857
92	9/07	Ayr	1m	(0-85)H	SFT	£6477
88	6/07	Newc	1m3y	(0-85)H	HVY	£6232
88	9/06	Ayr	1m	(0-85)H	G-S	£6477
88	10/05	Donc	7f	(0-85)H	HVY	£7085

Total win prize-money £36309

Going (Turf): Sf: 3-11 GS: 2-7 Gd: 1-16 GF: 0-6 Fm: 0-0
Distance: 5f/6f: 0-4 7f-8f: 3-22 9f-13f: 3-15 14f+: 0-0
Track : LH: 2-14 RH: 2-12 **Tight: 2-8** Gall: 0-2
Aids: Bl: 0-1 Vi: 0-0 Tstrap: 5-29 Ckp: 5-29
Best Rating: 96 5/09 Ripn 1m1f170y gd-sft

Useful; effective up to 1m2f; acts on most ground but suited by soft ground; wears cheekpieces; has been tongue tied.

Wijikura (IRE)

89 **62**

2-y-o ch c Zafeen (FR)-Azolia (IRE) (Alzao (USA))

J J Quinn Mrs S Quinn

Placings:556460 (6215)

2009: 5^{5}GF, 5^{5}G, 6^{6}GF, 5^{4}G, 6^{6}G, 8^{0}GF,

	Starts	1st	2nd	3rd	Win & Pl
Career Total (Turf)	6	0	0	0	265

Going (Turf): Sf: 0-0 GS: 0-0 Gd: 0-3 GF: 0-3 Fm: 0-0
Distance: 5f/6f: 0-5 7f-8f: 0-1 9f-13f: 0-0 14f+: 0-0
Track : LH: 0-1 RH: 0-0 Tight: 0-0 Gall: 0-0
Aids: Bl: 0-0 Vi: 0-1 Tstrap: 0-0 Ckp: 0-0

Best Rating: 62 7/09 Pont 5f good

Modest; should stay 6f; acts on fast ground; sure to improve and win a race.

Wikaala (USA)

101(100) (79)**80**

4-y-o ch g Diesis-Roseate Tern (Blakeney)

Gordon Elliott Sean F Gallagher

Placings:0/31640202-066631 (7544a)

2009: 12^{0}Y, 7^{6}SD, 9^{6}G, 9^{6}SD, 12^{3}SD, 12^{1}SD,

	Starts	1st	2nd	3rd	Win & Pl
Career Total (Turf)	6	1	0	0	3046
Career Total (AW)	9	1	2	2	8317

79	11/09	Dund	1m4f	(47-70)H	STD	£4696
76	6/08	Bevl	1m100y		G-F	£2331

Total win prize-money £7027

Going (Turf): Sf: 0-1 GS: 0-0 Gd: 0-1 **GF: 1-3** Fm: 0-0
Distance: 5f/6f: 0-0 7f-8f: 0-6 **9f-13f: 2-9** 14f+: 0-0
Track : LH: 1-9 RH: 1-5 Tight: 0-6 Gall: 0-2
Aids: Bl: 1-4 Vi: 0-1 Tstrap: 0-0 Ckp: 0-0
Best Rating: 80 8/08 Gdwd 1m1f soft

Fair; stays an extended 1m; acts on fast ground; also goes on Polytrack; has worn blinkers.

Wilbury Star (IRE)

101(99) (78)**80**

3-y-o br g Trans Island-Gold Blended (IRE) (Goldmark (USA))

N J Henderson (R Hannon 1/10) John Tobin, Ian Higginson & Fergus Carey

Placings:3210625-062532601323 (6421)

2009: 10^{0}SD, 9^{6}GF, 8^{2}G, 8^{5}GF, 8^{3}SD, 9^{2}GF, 8^{6}SD, 8^{0}GF, 9^{1}GF, 10^{3}F, 10^{2}GF, 8^{3}GF,

	Starts	1st	2nd	3rd	Win & Pl
Career Total (Turf)	15	2	5	3	14200
Career Total (AW)	4	0	0	1	703

78	8/09	Sals	1m1f198y	(0-70)H	G-F	£3238
76	7/08	Leic	7f9y		G-F	£3885

Total win prize-money £7124

Going (Turf): Sf: 0-0 GS: 0-2 Gd: 0-1 **GF: 2-10** Fm: 0-2
Distance: 5f/6f: 0-0 7f-8f: 1-9 9f-13f: 1-10 14f+: 0-0
Track : LH: 0-8 **RH: 1-7 Tight: 1-9** Gall: 0-1
Aids: Bl: 1-4 Vi: 0-0 Tstrap: 0-0 Ckp: 0-0
Best Rating: 80 10/08 Bath 1m5y gd-sft

Fair; effective at 7f-1m2f; acts on fast ground.

Wild By Nature

87(65) **40**

4-y-o b f Tipsy Creek (USA)-Kinraddie (Wuzo (USA))

P Leech Miss C Elbrow

Placings:P-0000 (3241)

2009: 11^{0}SD, 8^{0}GF, 8^{0}G, 7^{0}GF,

	Starts	1st	2nd	3rd	Win & Pl
Career Total (Turf)	3	0	0	0	
Career Total (AW)	2	0	0	0	

Going (Turf): Sf: 0-0 GS: 0-0 Gd: 0-1 GF: 0-2 Fm: 0-0
Distance: 5f/6f: 0-0 7f-8f: 0-1 9f-13f: 0-4 14f+: 0-0
Track : LH: 0-2 RH: 0-1 Tight: 0-0 Gall: 0-1
Aids: Bl: 0-0 Vi: 0-0 Tstrap: 0-0 Ckp: 0-0
Best Rating: 40 5/09 Yarm 1m3y gd-fm

Wild Cat Card (USA)

(91) (56)

3-y-o b/br f Mr Greeley (USA)-Wildcat Victory (USA) (Forest Wildcat (USA))

D M Simcock Dr Ali Ridha

Placings:4 (0729)

2009: 6^{4}SD,

	Starts	1st	2nd	3rd	Win & Pl
Career Total (Turf)	0	0	0	0	
Career Total (AW)	1	0	0	0	192

Going (Turf): Sf: 0-0 GS: 0-0 Gd: 0-0 GF: 0-0 Fm: 0-0
Distance: 5f/6f: 0-1 7f-8f: 0-0 9f-13f: 0-0 14f+: 0-0
Track : LH: 0-1 RH: 0-0 Tight: 0-1 Gall: 0-0
Aids: Bl: 0-0 Vi: 0-0 Tstrap: 0-0 Ckp: 0-0
Best Rating: 56 3/09 Ling 6f stand

Wild Desert (FR)

(102) (85)**92**

4-y-o b/br g Desert Prince (IRE)-Sallivera (IRE) (Sillery (USA))

Ian Williams Jim White & Stephen Dunn

Placings:0100-53 (0549)

2009: 12^{5}SD, 12^{3}SD,

	Starts	1st	2nd	3rd	Win & Pl
Career Total (Turf)	4	1	0	0	4044
Career Total (AW)	2	0	0	1	703

6/08	Drtl	1m3f	GD	£4044

Total win prize-money £4044

Going (Turf): Sf: 0-0 GS: 0-0 **Gd: 1-4** GF: 0-0 Fm: 0-0
Distance: 5f/6f: 0-0 7f-8f: 0-0 **9f-13f: 1-6** 14f+: 0-0
Track : LH: 0-3 RH: 0-2 Tight: 0-2 Gall: 0-2
Aids: Bl: 0-0 Vi: 0-0 Tstrap: 0-0 Ckp: 0-0
Best Rating: 92 8/08 NmkJ 1m2f good

Wild Fell Hall (IRE)

90(94) (80)**77**

6-y-o ch g Grand Lodge (USA)-Genoa (Zafonic (USA))

J Hetherton Akv Cladding Fabrications Ltd

Placings:60/0/03211/00054050-000 (4972)

2009: 12^{0}G, 12^{0}G, 11^{0}GF,

	Starts	1st	2nd	3rd	Win & Pl
Career Total (Turf)	14	1	1	1	5406
Career Total (AW)	5	1	0	0	4728

87	6/07	Kemp	1m4f	(0-85)H	STD	£4728
81	6/07	Sals	1m4f	(0-75)H	G-F	£3238

Total win prize-money £7967

Going (Turf): Sf: 0-2 GS: 0-1 Gd: 0-4 **GF: 1-7** Fm: 0-0
Distance: 5f/6f: 0-0 7f-8f: 0-2 **9f-13f: 2-15** 14f+: 0-2
Track : LH: 0-8 **RH: 2-10 Tight: 1-8** Gall: 0-3
Aids: Bl: 0-2 Vi: 0-0 Tstrap: 0-3 Ckp: 0-3
Best Rating: 87 6/07 Kemp 1m4f stand

Wild Heather

(87) (42)

2-y-o b f Bertolini (USA)-Heather Mix (Linamix (FR))

J R Holt J R Holt

Placings:05060 (7843)

2009: 6^{0}SD, 5^{5}SD, 5^{0}SD, 5^{6}SD, 5^{0}SD,

	Starts	1st	2nd	3rd	Win & Pl
Career Total (Turf)	0	0	0	0	
Career Total (AW)	5	0	0	0	0

Going (Turf): Sf: 0-0 GS: 0-0 Gd: 0-0 GF: 0-0 Fm: 0-0
Distance: 5f/6f: 0-5 7f-8f: 0-0 9f-13f: 0-0 14f+: 0-0
Track : LH: 0-3 RH: 0-2 Tight: 0-3 Gall: 0-0
Aids: Bl: 0-0 Vi: 0-0 Tstrap: 0-0 Ckp: 0-0
Best Rating: 42 12/09 Wolv 5f216y stand

Wild Lyph

(60) (17)
3-y-o b g Loup Sauvage (USA)-A Lyph (USA) (Lypheor)
N P Mulholland Larkinglass Ltd

Placings:00 **(1176)**
2009: 12^{0}SD, 7^{0}G,

	Starts	1st	2nd	3rd	Win & Pl
Career Total (Turf)	1	0	0	0	
Career Total (AW)	1	0	0	0	

Going (Turf): Sf: 0-0 GS: 0-0 Gd: 0-1 GF: 0-0 Fm: 0-0
Distance: 5f/6f: 0-0 7f-8f: 0-1 9f-13f: 0-1 14f+: 0-0
Track : LH: 0-2 RH: 0-0 Tight: 0-1 Gall: 0-0
Aids: Bl: 0-0 Vi: 0-0 Tstrap: 0-0 Ckp: 0-0
Best Rating: 17 3/09 Ling 1m4f stand

Wild Rhubarb

105 86
4-y-o ch f Hernando (FR)-Diamant Noir (Sir Harry Lewis (USA))
Jonjo O'Neill (C G Cox 28/6) D J Burke

Placings:23-21633 **(3380)**
2009: 12^{2}G, 14^{1}GF, 16^{6}G, 14^{3}G, 14^{3}GF,

	Starts	1st	2nd	3rd	Win & Pl
Career Total (Turf)	7	1	2	3	7216

85 5/09 Wwck 1m6f213y (0-75)H G-F £3238
Total win prize-money £3238

Going (Turf): Sf: 0-1 GS: 0-0 Gd: 0-4 **GF: 1-2** Fm: 0-0
Distance: 5f/6f: 0-0 7f-8f: 0-0 9f-13f: 0-2 **14f+: 1-5**
Track : **LH: 1-5** RH: 0-2 Tight: 0-2 Gall: 0-1
Aids: Bl: 0-0 Vi: 0-0 Tstrap: 0-0 Ckp: 0-0
Best Rating: 86 6/09 Sand 1m6f good

Useful; stays at least 1m6f; acts on most ground.

Wild Rockette

99(94) (72)72
2-y-o b f Rock Of Gibraltar (IRE)-Wild Floridian (IRE) (Indian Ridge)
B J Meehan Mrs M D Stewart

Placings:04024 **(7434)**
2009: 6^{0}GF, 6^{4}S, 7^{0}SD, 8^{2}GS, 8^{4}SD,

	Starts	1st	2nd	3rd	Win & Pl
Career Total (Turf)	3	0	1	0	1162
Career Total (AW)	2	0	0	0	289

Going (Turf): Sf: 0-1 GS: 0-1 Gd: 0-0 GF: 0-1 Fm: 0-0
Distance: 5f/6f: 0-0 7f-8f: 0-4 9f-13f: 0-1 14f+: 0-0
Track : LH: 0-1 RH: 0-2 Tight: 0-2 Gall: 0-0
Aids: Bl: 0-0 Vi: 0-0 Tstrap: 0-0 Ckp: 0-0
Best Rating: 72 11/09 Ling 1m stand

Fair; stays 1m; acts on Polytrack.

Wild Rose

88(98) (82)60
2-y-o gr f Doyen (IRE)-Makhsusah (IRE) (Darshaan)
M L W Bell Saif Ali & Saeed H Altayer

Placings:5110 **(7187)**
2009: 8^{5}G, 8^{1}SD, 8^{1}SD, 8^{0}G,

	Starts	1st	2nd	3rd	Win & Pl
Career Total (Turf)	2	0	0	0	0
Career Total (AW)	2	2	0	0	7094

82 10/09 Wolv 1m141y (0-85) STD £5046
74 9/09 Kemp 1m STD £2047
Total win prize-money £7093

Going (Turf): Sf: 0-0 GS: 0-0 Gd: 0-2 GF: 0-0 Fm: 0-0
Distance: 5f/6f: 0-0 7f-8f: 1-2 9f-13f: 1-2 14f+: 0-0
Track : LH: 1-1 RH: 1-1 **Tight: 1-1** Gall: 0-0
Aids: Bl: 0 0 Vi: 0-0 Tstrap: 0-0 Ckp: 0-0
Best Rating: 82 10/09 Wolv 1m141y stand

Useful; stays 1m; acts on Polytrack.

Wildcat Wizard (USA)

98 99
3-y-o b g Forest Wildcat (USA)-Tip the Scale (USA) (Valiant Nature (USA))
P F I Cole A D Spence

Placings:11435-0360 **(6482)**
2009: 7^{0}GF, 7^{3}GF, 7^{6}GF, 7^{0}GF,

	Starts	1st	2nd	3rd	Win & Pl
Career Total (Turf)	9	2	0	2	23580

89 6/08 Donc 7f GD £6476
80 6/08 York 6f GD £6929
Total win prize-money £13405

Going (Turf): Sf: 0-0 GS: 0-0 **Gd: 2-4** GF: 0-5 Fm: 0-0
Distance: 5f/6f: 1-2 7f-8f: 1-7 9f-13f: 0-0 14f+: 0-0
Track : LH: 0-0 RH: 0-1 Tight: 0-0 Gall: 0-0
Aids: Bl: 0-0 Vi: 0-0 Tstrap: 0-0 Ckp: 0-0
Best Rating: 99 5/09 NmkR 7f gd-fm

Smart; effective at 6f-7f; acts on good and fast ground.

Wilfred Pickles (IRE)

97 79
3-y-o ch g Cadeaux Genereux-Living Daylights (IRE) (Night Shift (USA))
Mrs A J Perrett Mrs Valda Burke & Mrs Amanda Perrett

Placings:032-2623424 **(6823)**
2009: 8^{2}GF, 10^{6}GF, 8^{2}GF, 8^{3}F, 8^{4}GF, 7^{2}GF, 6^{4}GF,

	Starts	1st	2nd	3rd	Win & Pl
Career Total (Turf)	10	0	4	2	6464

Going (Turf): Sf: 0-1 GS: 0-0 Gd: 0-2 GF: 0-6 Fm: 0-1
Distance: 5f/6f: 0-1 7f-8f: 0-6 9f-13f: 0-3 14f+: 0-0
Track : LH: 0-2 RH: 0-3 Tight: 0-1 Gall: 0-0
Aids: Bl: 0-0 Vi: 0-0 Tstrap: 0-1 Ckp: 0-1
Best Rating: 79 9/09 Newb 7f gd-fm

Fair; effective over 7f-1m; acts on good and fast ground.

Will Exell (IRE)

(71) (10)
6-y-o b m Exit To Nowhere (USA)-Woodhouse Bay (IRE) (Zaffaran (USA))
M J Scudamore Mrs J J Fenn & W J Fenn

Placings:0 **(0678)**
2009: 9^{0}SF,

	Starts	1st	2nd	3rd	Win & Pl
Career Total (Turf)	0	0	0	0	
Career Total (AW)	1	0	0	0	

Going (Turf): Sf: 0-0 GS: 0-0 Gd: 0-0 GF: 0-0 Fm: 0-0
Distance: 5f/6f: 0-0 7f-8f: 0-0 9f-13f: 0-1 14f+: 0-0
Track : LH: 0-1 RH: 0-0 Tight: 0-1 Gall: 0-0
Aids: Bl: 0-0 Vi: 0-0 Tstrap: 0-0 Ckp: 0-0
Best Rating: 10 2/09 Wolv 1m1f103y std-fst

Will He Wish

102(108) (89)82
13-y-o b g Winning Gallery-More To Life (Northern Tempest (USA))
S Gollings Mrs D Dukes

Placings:00110153451261/0056000000136200/0032530100041/315065000646/4251600050 13/3152303662-22250625 **(5003)**
2009: 11^{2}SD, 9^{2}SD, 8^{2}GF, 9^{5}GF, 8^{0}G, 8^{6}G, 8^{2}G, 8^{5}G,

	Starts	1st	2nd	3rd	Win & Pl
Career Total (Turf)	56	9	5	4	78635
Career Total (AW)	27	3	5	5	23688

89 1/08 Wolv 1m141y (0-85)H STD £4533
85 10/07 Wolv 7f32y (0-75)H STD £2914
87 6/07 Hayd 1m30y (0-90)H G-F £9715
96 5/06 Muss 7f30y (0-90)H FRM £8101
94 12/05 Wolv 5f216y (0-85)H STD £5571
94 8/05 Sand 7f16y (0-90)H G-F £8816
96 7/04 Yarm 7f3y D(0-85)H GD £5798
97 10/03 Leic 7f9y C FRM £6572
91 9/03 Donc 7f C(0-95)H GD £7358
83 7/03 Kemp 7f E(0-70)H G-F £3818
80 7/03 Yarm 6f3y E(0-70)H G-F £3870
66 6/03 Rdcr 6f D FRM £3672
Total win prize-money £70746

Going (Turf): Sf: 0-1 GS: 0-7 Gd: 2-14 **GF: 4-29** Fm: 3-5
Distance: 5f/6f: 2-8 **7f-8f: 8-58** 9f-13f: 2-17 14f+: 0-0
Track : **LH: 4-31** RH: 3-23 **Tight: 4-24** Gall: 1-4
Aids: **Bl: 8-43** Vi: 0-5 Tstrap: 0-0 Ckp: 0-0
Best Rating: 97 7/06 Ches 7f2y gd-fm

Fair; effective over 7f-1m2f; suited by a sound surface; also goes on Polytrack; has worn blinkers.

Willent

86 35
3-y-o b g Lend A Hand-Lapu-Lapu (Prince Sabo)
Miss J A Camacho Jamie Spence

Placings:0000 **(5145)**
2009: 9^{0}GS, 8^{0}GS, 6^{0}GS, 5^{0}GS,

	Starts	1st	2nd	3rd	Win & Pl
Career Total (Turf)	4	0	0	0	

Going (Turf): Sf: 0-0 GS: 0-4 Gd: 0-0 GF: 0-0 Fm: 0-0
Distance: 5f/6f: 0-2 7f-8f: 0-0 9f-13f: 0-2 14f+: 0-0
Track : LH: 0-1 RH: 0-2 Tight: 0-1 Gall: 0-0
Aids: Bl: 0-0 Vi: 0-0 Tstrap: 0-0 Ckp: 0-0
Best Rating: 35 6/09 Ripn 6f gd-sft

William Arnold

95 63
2-y-o ch g Rambling Bear-Dancing Shirl (Dancing Spree (USA))

C W Fairhurst Mrs C A Arnold

Placings:00523000 **(6557)**
2009: 5^0GF, 5^0G, 7^5GF, 7^2G, 7^3G, 7^0GF, 7^0GF, 7^0G,

	Starts	1st	2nd	3rd	Win & Pl
Career Total (Turf)	8	0	1	1	1445

Going (Turf): Sf: 0-0 GS: 0-0 Gd: 0-4 GF: 0-4 Fm: 0-0
Distance: 5f/6f: 0-2 7f-8f: 0-6 9f-13f: 0-0 14f+: 0-0
Track : LH: 0-4 RH: 0-1 Tight: 0-4 Gall: 0-0
Aids: Bl: 0-0 Vi: 0-0 Tstrap: 0-0 Ckp: 0-0
Best Rating: 63 8/09 Catt 7f good

Modest; best around 7f on a sound surface.

William Blake

108(111) (93)93
4-y-o b g Rainbow Quest (USA)-Land Of Dreams (Cadeaux Genereux)
M Johnston Sheikh Hamdan Bin Mohammed Al Maktoum

Placings:11100325604O-436244033260 **(7035)**
2009: 10^4G, 10^3GF, 12^6GF, 10^2G, 9^4G, 12^4GS, 10^0GF, 10^3GF, 11^3SD, 10^2GF, 12^6G, 10^0S,

	Starts	1st	2nd	3rd	Win & Pl
Career Total (Turf)	19	1	3	3	27625
Career Total (AW)	5	2	0	1	8219

92 4/08 Bevl 1m1f207y (0-80)H G-S £4533
78 3/08 Ling 1m2f (0-85)H STD £4100
79 2/08 Sthl 1m STD £2457
Total win prize-money £11091

Going (Turf): Sf: 0-3 GS: 1-3 Gd: 0-5 GF: 0-8 Fm: 0-0
Distance: 5f/6f: 0-0 7f-8f: 1-1 9f-13f: 2-23 14f+: 0-0
Track : LH: 2-10 RH: 1-14 Tight: 1-4 Gall: 0-11
Aids: Bl: 0-0 Vi: 0-0 Tstrap: 0-0 Ckp: 0-0
Best Rating: 93 10/08 Kemp 1m4f stand

Useful; effective at 1m2f-1m4f; acts on most ground and on Polytrack; likes to race prominently.

William Hogarth

(75)85
4-y-o b g High Chaparral (IRE)-Mountain Holly (Shirley Heights)
W K Goldsworthy ROL Plant Hire Ltd

Placings:64/30106-0 **(5909)**
2009: 12^0GF,

	Starts	1st	2nd	3rd	Win & Pl
Career Total (Turf)	6	0	0	1	1809
Career Total (AW)	2	1	0	0	6097

75 9/08 Dund 1m4f STD £6097
Total win prize-money £6097

Going (Turf): Sf: 0-0 GS: 0-0 Gd: 0-2 GF: 0-2 Fm: 0-0
Distance: 5f/6f: 0-0 7f-8f: 0-2 9f-13f: 1-5 14f+: 0-1
Track : LH: 1-4 RH: 0-3 Tight: 0-0 Gall: 0-1
Aids: Bl: 0-0 Vi: 0-0 Tstrap: 0-0 Ckp: 0-0
Best Rating: 85 4/08 Leop 1m2f gd-yld

William Morgan (IRE)

99 76
2-y-o ch g Arakan (USA)-Dry Lightning (Shareef Dancer (USA))
R A Fahey P D Smith Holdings Ltd

Placings:4362110 **(5795)**
2009: 5^4G, 5^3G, 6^6GF, 7^2GF, 7^1GF, 7^1GS, 6^0GF,

	Starts	1st	2nd	3rd	Win & Pl
Career Total (Turf)	7	2	1	1	10264

76 9/09 York 7f (0-85) G-S £5828
75 9/09 Rdcr 7f (0-75) G-F £2590
Total win prize-money £8418

Going (Turf): Sf: 0-0 GS: 1-1 Gd: 0-2 GF: 1-4 Fm: 0-0
Distance: 5f/6f: 0-3 7f-8f: 2-4 9f-13f: 0-0 14f+: 0-0
Track : LH: 1-1 RH: 0-2 Tight: 0-0 Gall: 1-1
Aids: Bl: 0-0 Vi: 0-0 Tstrap: 0-0 Ckp: 0-0
Best Rating: 76 9/09 York 7f gd-sft

Fair; effective over 7f; acts on fast and easy ground.

William Van Gogh

98 80
2-y-o b c Dansili-Flower Girl (Pharly (FR))
J H M Gosden W J Gredley

Placings:25 **(6810)**
2009: 8^2GF, 8^5G,

	Starts	1st	2nd	3rd	Win & Pl
Career Total (Turf)	2	0	1	0	1542

Going (Turf): Sf: 0-0 GS: 0-0 Gd: 0-1 GF: 0-1 Fm: 0-0
Distance: 5f/6f: 0-0 7f-8f: 0-2 9f-13f: 0-0 14f+: 0-0
Track : LH: 0-0 RH: 0-0 Tight: 0-0 Gall: 0-0
Aids: Bl: 0-0 Vi: 0-0 Tstrap: 0-0 Ckp: 0-0
Best Rating: 80 10/09 NmkR 1m gd-fm

Useful; stays 1m and acts on fast ground.

William's Way

102(105) (74)82
7-y-o b g Fraam-Silk Daisy (Barathea (IRE))
I A Wood Neardown Stables

Placings:035162504O022/11003040/00600000430-051412550 **(1966)**
2009: 12^0SD, 10^5SD, 12^1SD, 13^4SD, 13^1SD, 14^2SD, 10^5G, 11^5GS, 13^0SD,

	Starts	1st	2nd	3rd	Win & Pl
Career Total (Turf)	16	1	1	1	4948
Career Total (AW)	25	4	3	2	16145

72 3/09 Wolv 1m5f194y (0-70)H STD £2307
70 1/09 Ling 1m4f (0-70)H STD £2472
89 5/07 Wolv 1m1f103y (0-75)H STD £3238
81 4/07 Sthl 1m3f (0-75)H STD £3238
73 7/06 Wind 1m2f7y (0-75)H G-F £3238
Total win prize-money £14497

Going (Turf): Sf: 0-1 GS: 0-7 Gd: 0-4 GF: 1-4 Fm: 0-0
Distance: 5f/6f: 0-0 7f-8f: 0-1 9f-13f: 4-37 14f+: 1-3
Track : LH: 4-27 RH: 1-12 Tight: 4-24 Gall: 0-4
Aids: Bl: 0-0 Vi: 0-0 Tstrap: 0-0 Ckp: 0-0
Best Rating: 89 6/07 NmkJ 1m2f gd-sft

Modest; effective over 1m2f-1m6f; acts on most ground on turf; goes on sand.

Williamtown Lad (IRE)

(39)
8-y-o b g Anshan-Hazy River (Over The River (FR))
J R Boyle Bluefriar Construction Ltd

Placings:0 **(4205)**
2009: 12^0SD,

	Starts	1st	2nd	3rd	Win & Pl
Career Total (Turf)	0	0	0	0	
Career Total (AW)	1	0	0	0	

Going (Turf): Sf: 0-0 GS: 0-0 Gd: 0-0 GF: 0-0 Fm: 0-0
Distance: 5f/6f: 0-0 7f-8f: 0-0 9f-13f: 0-1 14f+: 0-0
Track : LH: 0-1 RH: 0-0 Tight: 0-1 Gall: 0-0
Aids: Bl: 0-0 Vi: 0-0 Tstrap: 0-0 Ckp: 0-0

Willie Ever

(106) (76)56
5-y-o b g Agnes World (USA)-Miss Meltemi (IRE) (Miswaki Tern (USA))
I W McInnes M Shirley

Placings:006/4221110-000R **(0868)**
2009: 7^0SD, 8^0SD, 8^0SD, 7^RSD,

	Starts	1st	2nd	3rd	Win & Pl
Career Total (Turf)	3	0	1	0	608
Career Total (AW)	11	3	1	0	8619

76 7/08 Wolv 1m141y (0-75)H STD £3238
71 7/08 Wolv 7f32y (0-65)H STD £2388
72 6/08 Wolv 1m141y (0-60)H STD £2388
Total win prize-money £8014

Going (Turf): Sf: 0-0 GS: 0-0 Gd: 0-2 GF: 0-1 Fm: 0-0
Distance: 5f/6f: 0-1 7f-8f: 1-5 9f-13f: 2-8 14f+: 0-0
Track : LH: 3-11 RH: 0-1 Tight: 3-12 Gall: 0-0
Aids: Bl: 0-1 Vi: 0-1 Tstrap: 0-0 Ckp: 0-0
Best Rating: 76 7/08 Wolv 1m141y stand

Modest; effective over 7f-1m; acts on fast ground; also goes on Polytrack.

Willing Foe (USA)

(92) (63)
2-y-o b/br c Dynaformer (USA)-Thunder Kitten (USA) (Storm Cat (USA))
Saeed Bin Suroor Godolphin

Placings:6 **(7400)**
2009: 9^6SD,

	Starts	1st	2nd	3rd	Win & Pl
Career Total (Turf)	0	0	0	0	
Career Total (AW)	1	0	0	0	0

Going (Turf): Sf: 0-0 GS: 0-0 Gd: 0-0 GF: 0-0 Fm: 0-0
Distance: 5f/6f: 0-0 7f-8f: 0-0 9f-13f: 0-1 14f+: 0-0
Track : LH: 0-1 RH: 0-0 Tight: 0-1 Gall: 0-0
Aids: Bl: 0-0 Vi: 0-0 Tstrap: 0-0 Ckp: 0-0
Best Rating: 63 11/09 Wolv 1m1f103y stand

Willkandoo (USA)

(105) (86)78
4-y-o b/br g Unbridled's Song (USA)-Shannkara (IRE) (Akarad (FR))
D M Simcock Dr Marwan Koukash

Placings:0/06311561331533-6023 **(0730)**
2009: 7^6SD, 7^0SD, 8^2SD, 8^3SD,

	Starts	1st	2nd	3rd	Win & Pl
Career Total (Turf)	9	3	0	2	11062
Career Total (AW)	10	1	1	4	9385

84 10/08 Dund 1m (60-80)H STD £6351
78 8/08 Catt 7f (0-80)H GD £4857
71 6/08 Leic 1m60y (0-75)H G-F £3238
76 6/08 Haml 1m65y (0-60)H G-F £1942
Total win prize-money £16389

Going (Turf): Sf: 0-0 GS: 0-1 Gd: 1-3 GF: 2-5 Fm: 0-0

Distance: 5f/6f: 0-0 7f-8f: 2-10 9f-13f: 2-9 14f+: 0-0
Track : LH: 2-13 RH: 2-5 **Tight: 2-13** Gall: 0-1
Aids: Bl: 0-0 Vi: 0-0 Tstrap: 1-4 Ckp: 1-4
Best Rating: 86 12/08 Wolv 7f32y stand

Progressive at modest level; effective at 7f-1m2f; best on fast ground; has worn cheekpieces.

Willow Dancer (IRE)

101(106) (88)**95**
5-y-o ch g Danehill Dancer (IRE)-Willowbridge (IRE) (Entrepreneur)
W R Swinburn Mrs G Godfrey & Mrs A Horner

Placings:566350/031221201-0006 **(6633)**
2009: 8^{0}GF, 8^{0}G, 8^{0}G, 8^{6}33,

	Starts	1st	2nd	3rd	Win & Pl
Career Total (Turf)	**14**	**3**	**2**	**1**	**20511**
Career Total (AW)	**5**	**0**	**1**	**1**	**1874**

95 10/08 NmkR 1m (0-95)H G-F £9346
89 7/08 Sand 1m14y (0-80)H G-F £5180
76 6/08 Bath 1m5y (0-70)H GD £2914
Total win prize-money £17442

Going (Turf): Sf: 0-1 GS: 0-2 Gd: 1-3 **GF: 2-8** Fm: 0-0
Distance: 5f/6f: 0-0 7f-8f: 1-5 **9f-13f: 2-14** 14f+: 0-0
Track : LH: 1-8 RH: 1-10 **Tight: 1-8** Gall: 0-0
Aids: Bl: 0-0 Vi: 0-0 Tstrap: 3-11 Ckp: 3-11
Best Rating: 95 10/08 NmkR 1m gd-fm

Very useful; effective at around 1m-1m1f; acts on good to firm and good to soft ground; has worn cheekpieces.

Willow Mist

58
2-y-o b f Gentleman's Deal (IRE)-Baymist (Mind Games)
M W Easterby Mrs E Wright

Placings:0 **(2896)**
2009: 6^{0}GS,

	Starts	1st	2nd	3rd	Win & Pl
Career Total (Turf)	**1**	**0**	**0**	**0**	

Going (Turf): Sf: 0-0 GS: 0-1 Gd: 0-0 GF: 0-0 Fm: 0-0
Distance: 5f/6f: 0-1 7f-8f: 0-0 9f-13f: 0-0 14f+: 0-0
Track : LH: 0-0 RH: 0-0 Tight: 0-0 Gall: 0-0
Aids: Bl: 0-0 Vi: 0-0 Tstrap: 0-0 Ckp: 0-0

Willridge

73(81) (38)**72**
4-y-o ch g Tumbleweed Ridge-Minnina (IRE) (In The Wings)
J M Bradley E A Hayward

Placings:0310-0000 **(5019)**
2009: 6^{0}GF, 7^{0}GF, 7^{0}SD, 7^{0}GF,

	Starts	1st	2nd	3rd	Win & Pl
Career Total (Turf)	**6**	**1**	**0**	**1**	**4463**
Career Total (AW)	**2**	**0**	**0**	**0**	

72 8/08 Sals 6f212y G-S £3885
Total win prize-money £3886

Going (Turf): Sf: 0-0 **GS: 1-2** Gd: 0-0 GF: 0-4 Fm: 0-0
Distance: 5f/6f: 0-2 **7f-8f: 1-4** 9f-13f: 0-2 14f+: 0-0
Track : LH: 0-3 RH: 0-0 Tight: 0-3 Gall: 0-0
Aids: Bl: 0-0 Vi: 0-0 Tstrap: 0-1 Ckp: 0-1
Best Rating: 72 8/08 Sals 6f212y gd-sft

Fair; stays 7f; acts on most ground; has worn cheekpieces and a tongue tie.

Willyn (IRE)

102 (48)**60**
4-y-o b f Lujain (USA)-Lamasat (USA) (Silver Hawk (USA))
J S Goldie Caledonia Racing

Placings:6440021020300/5445422260-34302000 **(5944)**
2009: 9^{3}G, 8^{4}GF, 10^{3}G, 9^{0}G, 10^{2}GF, 8^{0}GF, 10^{0}GF, 9^{0}G,

	Starts	1st	2nd	3rd	Win & Pl
Career Total (Turf)	**30**	**1**	**5**	**3**	**11425**
Career Total (AW)	**1**	**0**	**1**	**0**	**605**

60 8/07 Thsk 7f G-F £3886
Total win prize-money £3886

Going (Turf): Sf: 0-5 GS: 0-1 Gd: 0-13 **GF: 1-11** Fm: 0-0
Distance: 5f/6f: 0-6 **7f-8f: 1-16** 9f-13f: 0-9 14f+: 0-0
Track : **LH: 1-14** RH: 0-10 **Tight: 1-15** Gall: 0-0
Aids: Bl: 0-0 Vi: 0-1 Tstrap: 0-7 Ckp: 0-7
Best Rating: 63 9/07 Rdcr 7f gd-fm

Moderate filly; stays 1m; handles Polytrack and most ground on turf; has worn cheekpieces.

Wilmington

93(62) (69)**59**
5-y-o ch g Compton Place-Bahawir Pour (USA) (Green Dancer (USA))
Mrs J C McGregor Off And Running

Placings:0020635/365050/0306-06003000 **(5947)**
2009: 8^{0}SD, 9^{6}GF, 9^{0}G, 7^{0}GF, 8^{3}G, 8^{0}GF, 9^{0}G, 12^{0}G,

	Starts	1st	2nd	3rd	Win & Pl
Career Total (Turf)	**17**	**0**	**1**	**3**	**1300**
Career Total (AW)	**8**	**0**	**0**	**1**	**433**

Going (Turf): Sf: 0-0 GS: 0-4 Gd: 0-5 GF: 0-8 Fm: 0-0
Distance: 5f/6f: 0-5 7f-8f: 0-13 9f-13f: 0-7 14f+: 0-0
Track : LH: 0-14 RH: 0-8 Tight: 0-13 Gall: 0-2
Aids: Bl: 0-4 Vi: 0-0 Tstrap: 0-1 Ckp: 0-1
Best Rating: 72 8/06 Wind 6f gd-fm

Modest maiden; stays 1m and acts on most ground.

Wiltshire (IRE)

102(104) (65)**62**
7-y-o br g Spectrum (IRE)-Mary Magdalene (Night Shift (USA))
P T Midgley David Mann

Placings:000010300/1U10005405/00443202003040/1201533006/65130362660-02300342542622 **(4372)**
2009: 6^{0}SD, 5^{2}SD, 6^{3}SD, 5^{0}SD, 5^{0}SD, 6^{3}SD, 6^{4}SD, 6^{2}SD, 7^{5}F, 6^{4}F, 6^{2}SD, 6^{6}GF, 5^{2}GF, 6^{2}SD,

	Starts	1st	2nd	3rd	Win & Pl
Career Total (Turf)	**30**	**2**	**3**	**3**	**8152**
Career Total (AW)	**38**	**4**	**6**	**6**	**16233**

65 2/08 Kemp 6f (0-52)H STD £2047
59 4/07 Sthl 7f G-F £2184
59 2/07 Kemp 6f (0-50)H STD £2047
65 2/05 Ling 1m (0-70)H STD £3476
60 1/05 Wolv 7f32y (0-55)H STD £2907
58 9/04 Brig 5f59y FRM £2583
Total win prize-money £15247

Going (Turf): Sf: 0-0 GS: 0-2 Gd: 0-7 **GF: 1-14 Fm: 1-7**
Distance: 5f/6f: 3-28 **7f-8f: 3-29** 9f-13f: 0-11 14f+: 0-0
Track : **LH: 4-38** RH: 2-18 **Tight: 3-33** Gall: 0-0
Aids: **Bl: 2-12** Vi: 1-26 Tstrap: 0-2 Ckp: 0-2
Best Rating: 65 2/08 Kemp 6f stand

Moderate; effective over 6f-1m; acts on fast ground; goes on sand; has worn a visor.

Wind Flow

(105) (81)**58**
5-y-o b g Dr Fong (USA)-Spring (Sadler's Wells (USA))
C A Dwyer Super Six Partnership

Placings:06/632/12444131500140016 1-123014522400003220 **(7066)**
2009: 16^{1}SD, 13^{2}SD, 13^{3}SD, 13^{0}SD, 12^{1}SD, 13^{4}SD, 12^{5}SD, 12^{2}SD, 12^{2}SD, 12^{4}SD, 12^{0}SD, 11^{0}SD, 11^{0}SD, 12^{0}SF, 12^{3}SD, 12^{2}SF, 12^{2}SS, 12^{0}SF, 12^{0}SD,

	Starts	1st	2nd	3rd	Win & Pl
Career Total (Turf)	**2**	**0**	**0**	**0**	**0**
Career Total (AW)	**40**	**8**	**7**	**4**	**32610**

78 2/09 Wolv 1m4f50y (0-100)H STD £7352
66 1/09 Ling 2m STD £2047
59 12/08 Ling 1m4f STD £1978
58 11/08 Ling 1m4f STD £1978
73 9/08 Kemp 1m4f STD £2047
78 5/08 GrLe 1m6f (0-70)H STD £2590
71 4/08 Wolv 1m5f194y (0-75)H STD £2590
64 1/08 Kemp 1m3f (0-60)H STD £2047
Total win prize-money £22633

Going (Turf): Sf: 0-0 GS: 0-0 Gd: 0-1 GF: 0-0 Fm: 0-1
Distance: 5f/6f: 0-0 7f-8f: 0-3 **9f-13f: 5-33** 14f+: 3-6
Track : **LH: 6-26** RH: 2-15 **Tight: 5-23** Gall: 1-3
Aids: **Bl: 6-19** Vi: 0-10 Tstrap: 0-1 Ckp: 0-1
Best Rating: 81 5/09 Wolv 1m4f50y stand

Fair; effective at 1m4f-2m; acts on Polytrack; has worn blinkers; front-runner; consistent.

Wind Shuffle (GER)

104 **85**
6-y-o b g Big Shuffle (USA)-Wiesensturmerin (GER) (Lagunas)
J S Goldie Mrs S Bruce & Mrs L Mackay

Placings:5/24/0030/033431141131442-33200 **(4102)**
2009: 8^{3}GF, 9^{3}G, 9^{2}GS, 7^{0}GF, 9^{0}S,

	Starts	1st	2nd	3rd	Win & Pl
Career Total (Turf)	**27**	**5**	**3**	**7**	**32387**

84 9/08 Ayr 1m2f (0-75)H HVY £4860
80 8/08 Haml 1m1f36y (0-75)H GD £3238
77 7/08 Haml 1m1f36y (0-70)H G-S £3238
73 7/08 Carl 7f200y (0-80)H GD £5180
71 6/08 Carl 7f200y (0-80)H SFT £5180
Total win prize-money £21698

Going (Turf): Sf: 2-8 GS: 1-7 **Gd: 2-5** GF: 0-7 Fm: 0-0
Distance: 5f/6f: 0-1 7f-8f: 2-17 **9f-13f: 3-9** 14f+: 0-0
Track : LH: 1-8 **RH: 4-17 Tight: 2-13** Gall: 0-0
Aids: Bl: 0-0 Vi: 0-0 Tstrap: 0-0 Ckp: 0-0
Best Rating: 85 5/09 Haml 1m1f36y gd-sft

Fair; effective at around 7f-1m2f; acts on any ground.

Wind Star

105 **91**
6-y-o ch g Piccolo-Starfleet (Inchinor)
G A Swinbank B Harker, R Hall & Dr C Emmerson

Placings:64221103/3020306050/0032551-41164 **(3374)**
2009: 9^{4}G, 10^{1}GS, 9^{1}GF, 10^{6}GF, 10^{4}GF,

	Starts	1st	2nd	3rd	Win & Pl
Career Total (Turf)	**30**	**5**	**4**	**4**	**42367**

91 5/09 Bevl 1m1f207y (0-85)H G-F £4727
86 5/09 Newc 1m2f32y (0-80)H G-S £4727
85 9/08 Muss 1m1f SFT £2590
94 8/06 Haml 1m1f36y (0-75)H G-F £3886

79 7/06 Ayr 1m (0-75)H G-F £3886
Total win prize-money £19816

Going (Turf): Sf: 1-2 GS: 1-3 Gd: 0-7 **GF: 3-18** Fm: 0-0
Distance: 5f/6f: 0-0 7f-8f: 1-6 **9f-13f: 4-23** 14f+: 0-1
Track : LH: 2-16 **RH: 3-13 Tight: 2-14** Gall: 1-7
Aids: Bl: 0-1 Vi: 0-0 Tstrap: 0-0 Ckp: 0-0
Best Rating: 94 7/07 NmkJ 1m2f gd-fm

Fair; effective at around 1m1f-1m4f; acts on most ground.

Windjammer

93(99) (63)**73**
5-y-o b g Kyllachy-Absolve (USA) (Diesis)
L A Mullaney L A Mullaney

Placings:660/31102242000/0060104065064003-00200 (7241)
2009: 5⁰GF, 5⁰GS, 5²GS, 5⁰GF, 5⁰S,

	Starts	1st	2nd	3rd	Win & Pl
Career Total (Turf)	34	3	4	1	15308
Career Total (AW)	2	0	0	1	353

73 6/08 Catt 5f (0-70)H G-S £2590
74 5/07 Muss 5f (0-70)H G-F £3238
73 4/07 Catt 5f (0-60)H G-F £2730
Total win prize-money £8559

Going (Turf): Sf: 0-6 GS: 1-7 Gd: 0-9 **GF: 2-12** Fm: 0-0
Distance: **5f/6f: 3-36** 7f-8f: 0-0 9f-13f: 0-0 14f+: 0-0
Track : LH: 0-2 RH: 0-1 Tight: 0-2 Gall: 0-1
Aids: **Bl: 1-11** Vi: 0-2 Tstrap: 0-0 Ckp: 0-0
Best Rating: 76 6/07 Hayd 5f gd-fm

Moderate; effective over 5f; acts on fast and soft ground; goes on Polytrack; has worn blinkers.

Windpfeil (IRE)

97(95) (57)**64**
3-y-o bl g Indian Ridge-Flying Kiss (IRE) (Sadler's Wells (USA))
S C Burrough (J H M Gosden 12/10) Mrs Deborah Potter

Placings:050-305001 (6742)
2009: 11³S, 12⁰SD, 11⁵GS, 14⁰G, 16⁰SD, 11¹GS,

	Starts	1st	2nd	3rd	Win & Pl
Career Total (Turf)	4	1	0	1	3038
Career Total (AW)	5	0	0	0	0

64 10/09 Wind 1m3f135y (0-70)H G-S £2729
Total win prize-money £2730

Going (Turf): Sf: 0-1 **GS: 1-2** Gd: 0-1 GF: 0-0 Fm: 0-0
Distance: 5f/6f: 0-0 7f-8f: 0-2 **9f-13f: 1-5** 14f+: 0-2
Track : LH: 0-5 RH: 0-3 **Tight: 1-4** Gall: 0-1
Aids: **Bl: 1-3** Vi: 0-0 Tstrap: 0-1 Ckp: 0-1
Best Rating: 64 10/09 Wind 1m3f135y gd-sft

Modest; stays 1m3f and acts on soft ground.

Wine 'n Dine

93(113) (96)**76**
4-y-o b g Rainbow Quest (USA)-Seasonal Splendour (IRE) (Prince Rupert (FR))
B J Llewellyn (G L Moore 30/5) Alex James

Placings:4/0221-1320200 (2475)
2009: 16¹SD, 12³SD, 12²SD, 16⁰SD, 16²SD, 14⁰GF, 12⁰G,

	Starts	1st	2nd	3rd	Win & Pl
Career Total (Turf)	4	0	0	0	433
Career Total (AW)	8	2	4	1	18430

91 1/09 Kemp 2m (0-85)H STD £4727
83 12/08 Kemp 1m4f (0-85)H STD £5180
Total win prize-money £9908

Going (Turf): Sf: 0-1 GS: 0-0 Gd: 0-2 GF: 0-1 Fm: 0-0
Distance: 5f/6f: 0-0 7f-8f: 0-1 9f-13f: 1-7 14f+: 1-4
Track : LH: 0-4 **RH: 2-7** Tight: 0-6 Gall: 0-1
Aids: Bl: 0-0 Vi: 0-0 Tstrap: 0-0 Ckp: 0-0
Best Rating: 96 4/09 Ling 2m stand

Useful; effective over 1m4f-2m; acts on Polytrack.

Wing Collar

63 **101**
8-y-o b g In The Wings-Riyoom (USA) (Vaguely Noble)
T D Easterby Mr And Mrs J D Cotton

Placings:4440/033204312/0302161/230/215/36040-0 (1519)
2009: 16⁰GF,

	Starts	1st	2nd	3rd	Win & Pl
Career Total (Turf)	32	4	5	6	68332

103 7/07 York 1m6f (0-110)H HVY £19873
89 8/05 York 1m5f197y (0-85)H G-F £7520
87 7/05 York 1m5f197y (0-85)H G-F £7325
74 9/04 Bevl 1m4f16y (0-70)H G-F £5635
Total win prize-money £40356

Going (Turf): Sf: 1-7 GS: 0-4 Gd: 0-5 **GF: 3-16** Fm: 0-0
Distance: 5f/6f: 0-0 7f-8f: 0-3 9f-13f: 1-11 **14f+: 3-18**
Track : **LH: 3-18** RH: 1-14 Tight: 1-15 **Gall: 3-10**
Aids: Bl: 0-0 Vi: 0-0 Tstrap: 3-12 Ckp: 3-12
Best Rating: 103 7/07 York 1m6f heavy

Very useful; stays 2m; acts on any going; often wears cheekpieces.

Wing Diva (IRE)

67(100) (62)**55**
4-y-o b f Hawk Wing (USA)-Sasimoto (USA) (Saratoga Six (USA))
B Smart M Barber

Placings:42-46232 (7728)
2009: 11⁴SD, 10⁶S, 11²SD, 12³SD, 8²SD,

	Starts	1st	2nd	3rd	Win & Pl
Career Total (Turf)	2	0	0	0	241
Career Total (AW)	5	0	3	1	2856

Going (Turf): Sf: 0-2 GS: 0-0 Gd: 0-0 GF: 0-0 Fm: 0-0
Distance: 5f/6f: 0-0 7f-8f: 0-1 9f-13f: 0-6 14f+: 0-0
Track : LH: 0-7 RH: 0-0 Tight: 0-0 Gall: 0-0
Aids: Bl: 0-0 Vi: 0-0 Tstrap: 0-0 Ckp: 0-0
Best Rating: 62 10/09 Sthl 1m3f stand

Moderate; stays 1m3f; acts on Fibresand.

Wing Forward (IRE)

72 **26**
2-y-o b f Hawk Wing (USA)-Stroppy (IRE) (Xaar)
A Berry Alan Berry

Placings:660 (5512)
2009: 5⁶GS, 6⁶GF, 7⁰GF,

	Starts	1st	2nd	3rd	Win & Pl
Career Total (Turf)	3	0	0	0	0

Going (Turf): Sf: 0-0 GS: 0-1 Gd: 0-0 GF: 0-2 Fm: 0-0
Distance: 5f/6f: 0-2 7f-8f: 0-1 9f-13f: 0-0 14f+: 0-0
Track : LH: 0-0 RH: 0-0 Tight: 0-0 Gall: 0-0
Aids: Bl: 0-0 Vi: 0-0 Tstrap: 0-0 Ckp: 0-0
Best Rating: 26 8/09 Ayr 6f gd-fm

Wing N Prayer (IRE)

80 **43**
2-y-o b f Xaar-Jazmeer (Sabrehill (USA))
A Berry William Burns

Placings:400 (6408)
2009: 7⁴GF, 7⁰GS, 6⁰GF,

	Starts	1st	2nd	3rd	Win & Pl
Career Total (Turf)	3	0	0	0	168

Going (Turf): Sf: 0-0 GS: 0-1 Gd: 0-0 GF: 0-2 Fm: 0-0
Distance: 5f/6f: 0-1 7f-8f: 0-2 9f-13f: 0-0 14f+: 0-0
Track : LH: 0-0 RH: 0-2 Tight: 0-2 Gall: 0-0
Aids: Bl: 0-0 Vi: 0-0 Tstrap: 0-0 Ckp: 0-0
Best Rating: 43 6/09 Muss 7f30y gd-fm

Wing Of Faith

88(92) (58)**60**
2-y-o ch c Kirkwall-Angel Wing (Barathea (IRE))
S Kirk J C Smith

Placings:066402045 (6970)
2009: 6⁰G, 5⁶GF, 7⁶GF, 5⁴GS, 8⁰G, 6²SD, 6⁰GS, 6⁴SD, 5⁵SD,

	Starts	1st	2nd	3rd	Win & Pl
Career Total (Turf)	6	0	0	0	289
Career Total (AW)	3	0	1	0	674

Going (Turf): Sf: 0-0 GS: 0-2 Gd: 0-2 GF: 0-2 Fm: 0-0
Distance: 5f/6f: 0-7 7f-8f: 0-2 9f-13f: 0-0 14f+: 0-0
Track : LH: 0-1 RH: 0-3 Tight: 0-0 Gall: 0-1
Aids: Bl: 0-0 Vi: 0-0 Tstrap: 0-0 Ckp: 0-0
Best Rating: 60 7/09 Wwck 7f26y gd-fm

Moderate; stays 6f; acts on Polytrack.

Wing Play (IRE)

111(106) (94)**87**
4-y-o b g Hawk Wing (USA)-Toy Show (IRE) (Danehill (USA))
H Morrison Watching Brief

Placings:051/0340001226-600122103513 (7574)
2009: 7⁶SD, 7⁰GF, 8⁰F, 10¹SD, 10²GF, 10²G, 10¹GS, 9⁰GS, 10³GF, 10⁵GS, 9¹SD, 10³SD,

	Starts	1st	2nd	3rd	Win & Pl
Career Total (Turf)	14	1	2	2	8601
Career Total (AW)	11	4	2	1	21371

94 10/09 Wolv 1m1f103y (0-90)H STD £7569
85 8/09 Sand 1m2f7y (0-80)H G-S £4857
75 6/09 Ling 1m2f (0-70)H STD £3238
72 10/08 GrLe 1m (0-75)H STD £2914
76 11/07 Wolv 1m141y STD £3465
Total win prize-money £22044

Going (Turf): Sf: 0-0 **GS: 1-4** Gd: 0-3 GF: 0-6 Fm: 0-1
Distance: 5f/6f: 0-0 7f-8f: 1-5 **9f-13f: 4-20** 14f+: 0-0
Track : **LH: 4-18** RH: 1-6 **Tight: 3-14** Gall: 1-2
Aids: Bl: 0-1 Vi: 0-0 Tstrap: 4-14 Ckp: 4-14
Best Rating: 94 11/09 Ling 1m2f stand

Useful; best at around 1m2f; acts on fast and easy ground and Polytrack; usually wears cheekpieces or blinkers.

Wing Stealth (IRE)

(68) (64)**70**
4-y-o br f Hawk Wing (USA)-Starlight Smile (USA) (Green Dancer (USA))

M G Quinlan Mrs J Quinlan

Placings:530/00200-0 **(0011)**
2009: 12^{0}SS,

	Starts	1st	2nd	3rd	Win & Pl
Career Total (Turf)	7	0	1	1	1999
Career Total (AW)	2	0	0	0	

Going (Turf): **Sf: 0-0 GS: 0-0 Gd: 0-5 GF: 0-1 Fm: 0-1**
Distance: 5f/6f: 0-0 7f-8f: 0-3 9f-13f: 0-6 14f+: 0-0
Track : LH: 0-4 RH: 0-3 Tight: 0-0 Gall: 0-0
Aids: Bl: 0-5 Vi: 0-0 Tstrap: 0-0 Ckp: 0-0
Best Rating: **70** 7/08 Leop 1m4f good

Winged (IRE)

71(87) (61)48
2-y-o b f Hawk Wing (USA)-Aurelia (Rainbow Quest (USA))
B W Hills Cavendish Investing Ltd

Placings:04 **(4646)**
2009: 7^{0}S, 7^{4}SD,

	Starts	1st	2nd	3rd	Win & Pl
Career Total (Turf)	1	0	0	0	
Career Total (AW)	1	0	0	0	192

Going (Turf): **Sf: 0-1 GS: 0-0 Gd: 0-0 GF: 0-0 Fm: 0-0**
Distance: 5f/6f: 0-0 7f-8f: 0-2 9f-13f: 0-0 14f+: 0-0
Track : LH: 0-0 RH: 0-1 Tight: 0-0 Gall: 0-0
Aids: Bl: 0-0 Vi: 0-0 Tstrap: 0-0 Ckp: 0-0
Best Rating: **61** 8/09 Kemp 7f stand

Winged Arrow (IRE)

(98) (68)78
7-y-o b g In The Wings-Lightstorm (IRE) (Darshaan)
Jonjo O'Neill John P McManus

Placings:03012/0034/50/00400-30 **(0459)**
2009: 16^{3}SD, 16^{0}SD,

	Starts	1st	2nd	3rd	Win & Pl
Career Total (Turf)	16	1	1	2	14051
Career Total (AW)	2	0	0	1	252

83 5/05 Limk 1m3f SFT £8821
Total win prize-money £8821

Going (Turf): **Sf: 1-8** GS: 0-0 Gd: 0-3 GF: 0-0 Fm: 0-0
Distance: 5f/6f: 0-0 7f-8f: 0-1 **9f-13f: 1-13** 14f+: 0-4
Track : LH: 0-4 RH: 0-11 Tight: 0-1 Gall: 0-1
Aids: Bl: 0-0 Vi: 0-0 Tstrap: 0-0 Ckp: 0-0
Best Rating: **88** 10/05 Navn 1m1f good

Winged D'Argent (IRE)

101 87
8-y-o b/br g In The Wings-Petite-D-Argent (Noalto)
B J Llewellyn Terry Warner

Placings:15112/3143500/0502030003/00061064/26100-400 **(4092)**
2009: 16^{4}S, 18^{0}G, 16^{0}GS,

	Starts	1st	2nd	3rd	Win & Pl
Career Total (Turf)	38	6	3	4	108442

85 6/08 Newc 2m19y (0-80)H G-S £5361
78 7/07 Nott 1m6f15y (0-80)H SFT £6477
109 4/05 Nott 1m6f15y SFT £16240
97 10/04 Donc 1m6f132y (0-92)H SFT £7178
89 10/04 Ayr 1m5f13y (0-85)H G-S £8199
71 4/04 Pont 1m2f6yE SFT £4075
Total win prize-money £47533

Going (Turf): **Sf: 4-15** GS: 2-10 Gd: 0-6 GF: 0-7 Fm: 0-0
Distance: 5f/6f: 0-0 7f-8f: 0-0 9f-13f: 1-2 **14f+: 5-36**
Track : **LH: 6-25** RH: 0-13 Tight: 0-7 **Gall: 2-15**
Aids: **Bl: 2-18** Vi: 0-1 Tstrap: 0-2 Ckp: 0-2
Best Rating: **114** 6/05 York 2m4f gd-fm

Useful; stays 2m4f, but effective over shorter; suited by cut in the ground; has worn blinkers, cheekpieces and a visor.

Winged Farasi

94(100) (58)37
5-y-o b h Desert Style (IRE)-Clara Vale (IRE) (In The Wings)
Miss J E Foster The Smash Block Partnership

Placings:53/3430210406**0342/202500340-4000** **(1276)**
2009: 8^{4}SD, 8^{0}SD, 8^{0}SD, 8^{0}GF,

	Starts	1st	2nd	3rd	Win & Pl
Career Total (Turf)	10	1	1	1	4613
Career Total (AW)	19	0	3	4	3464

66 6/07 Sals 1m (0-65)H G-F £3238
Total win prize-money £3239

Going (Turf): Sf: 0-0 GS: 0-3 Gd: 0-3 **GF: 1-4** Fm: 0-0
Distance: 5f/6f: 0-1 **7f-8f: 1-16** 9f-13f: 0-12 14f+: 0-0
Track : LH: 0-18 RH: 0-7 Tight: 0-11 Gall: 0-0
Aids: Bl: 0-1 Vi: 0-0 Tstrap: 0-7 Ckp: 0-7
Best Rating: **69** 3/07 Wolv 1m141y stand

Moderate; stays at least 1m; acts on fast and easy ground; also goes on Polytrack; has worn headgear.

Winged Harriet (IRE)

99 80
3-y-o b/br f Hawk Wing (USA)-Hawala (IRE) (Warning)
W J Haggas Exors of the Late F C T Wilson

Placings:24-41 **(2268)**
2009: 7^{4}GF, 5^{1}G,

	Starts	1st	2nd	3rd	Win & Pl
Career Total (Turf)	4	1	1	0	3930

58 5/09 Catt 5f212y GD £2388
Total win prize-money £2388

Going (Turf): Sf: 0-0 GS: 0-0 **Gd: 1-1** GF: 0-3 Fm: 0-0
Distance: **5f/6f: 1-2** 7f-8f: 0-2 9f-13f: 0-0 14f+: 0-0
Track : **LH: 1-1** RH: 0-0 **Tight: 1-1** Gall: 0-0
Aids: Bl: 0-0 Vi: 0-0 Tstrap: 0-0 Ckp: 0-0
Best Rating: **80** 10/08 NmkR 7f gd-fm

Fair; effective over 6f; acts on good ground.

Wings Of Kintyre (IRE)

51
5-y-o b m Mull Of Kintyre (USA)-Tiger Wings (IRE) (Thatching)
A Berry Mrs Candice Reilly

Placings:0 **(5731)**
2009: 8^{0}GS,

	Starts	1st	2nd	3rd	Win & Pl
Career Total (Turf)	1	0	0	0	

Going (Turf): **Sf: 0-0 GS: 0-1 Gd: 0-0 GF: 0-0 Fm: 0-0**
Distance: 5f/6f: 0-0 7f-8f: 0-1 9f-13f: 0-0 14f+: 0-0
Track : LH: 0-1 RH: 0-0 Tight: 0-0 Gall: 0-1
Aids: Bl: 0-0 Vi: 0-0 Tstrap: 0-0 Ckp: 0-0

Winifred Jo

(86) (46)
2-y-o ch f Bahamian Bounty-Coming Home (Vettori (IRE))
J R Gask F Lisewski

Placings:60 **(6722)**
2009: 5^{6}SD, 6^{0}SD,

	Starts	1st	2nd	3rd	Win & Pl
Career Total (Turf)	0	0	0	0	
Career Total (AW)	2	0	0	0	0

Going (Turf): **Sf: 0-0 GS: 0-0 Gd: 0-0 GF: 0-0 Fm: 0-0**
Distance: 5f/6f: 0-2 7f-8f: 0-0 9f-13f: 0-0 14f+: 0-0
Track : LH. 0-0 RH. 0-2 Tight. 0-0 Gall. 0-0
Aids: Bl: 0-0 Vi: 0-0 Tstrap: 0-0 Ckp: 0-0
Best Rating: **46** 9/09 Kemp 5f stand

Winker Watson

104 116
4-y-o ch c Piccolo-Bonica (Rousillon (USA))
P W Chapple-Hyam The Comic Strip Heroes

Placings:111/0405-400 **(3398)**
2009: 7^{4}GF, 8^{0}S, 7^{0}G,

	Starts	1st	2nd	3rd	Win & Pl
Career Total (Turf)	10	3	0	0	109852

116 7/07 NmkJ 6f G-F £39746
107 6/07 Asct 5f G-F £39746
90 4/07 Newb 5f34y G-F £6477
Total win prize-money £85969

Going (Turf): Sf: 0-1 GS: 0-0 Gd: 0-3 **GF: 3-6** Fm: 0-0
Distance: **5f/6f: 3-4** 7f-8f: 0-6 9f-13f: 0-0 14f+: 0-0
Track : LH: 0-1 RH: 0-3 Tight: 0-0 Gall: 0-1
Aids: Bl: 0-1 Vi: 0-0 Tstrap: 0-0 Ckp: 0-0
Best Rating: **116** 7/08 Gdwd 1m gd-fm

Smart; winner of the Norfolk Stakes and July Stakes at two; stays 1m; acts on fast ground.

Winning Show

(100) (60)70
5-y-o b g Muhtarram (USA)-Rose Show (Belmez (USA))
C Gordon Roger Alwen

Placings:3660500/2250640-301 **(7767)**
2009: 12^{3}SD, 12^{0}SD, 11^{1}SD,

	Starts	1st	2nd	3rd	Win & Pl
Career Total (Turf)	9	0	1	0	963
Career Total (AW)	8	1	1	2	3121

60 12/09 Kemp 1m3f (0-60)H STD £1706
Total win prize-money £1706

Going (Turf): **Sf: 0-0 GS: 0-1 Gd: 0-3 GF: 0-3 Fm: 0-2**
Distance: 5f/6f: 0-3 7f-8f: 0-6 **9f-13f: 1-8** 14f+: 0-0
Track : LH: 0-10 **RH: 1-4** Tight: 0-5 Gall: 0-4
Aids: Bl: 0-0 Vi: 0-0 Tstrap: 0-0 Ckp: 0-0
Best Rating: **70** 7/07 NmkJ 7f good

Moderate; effective over 1m; acts on easy ground; also goes on Polytrack.

Winrob

96(79) (37)57
3-y-o b g Exceed And Excel (AUS)-High Standard (Kris)
Patrick Morris Rob Lloyd Racing Limited

Placings:06004210 (4588)

2009: 7^{0}GF, 7^{6}GF, 7^{0}SD, 10^{0}GF, 9^{4}F, 8^{2}GF, 8^{1}G, 7^{0}G,

	Starts	1st	2nd	3rd	Win & Pl
Career Total (Turf)	7	1	1	0	3798
Career Total (AW)	1	0	0	0	

57 7/09 Thsk 1m (0-65)H GD £2978

Total win prize-money £2979

Going (Turf): Sf: 0-0 GS: 0-0 **Gd: 1-2** GF: 0-4 Fm: 0-1
Distance: 5f/6f: 0-0 **7f-8f: 1-5** 9f-13f: 0-3 14f+: 0-0
Track : **LH: 1-4** RH: 0-3 **Tight: 1-5** Gall: 0-0
Aids: Bl: 0-0 Vi: 0-0 Tstrap: 0-0 Ckp: 0-0
Best Rating: **57** 7/09 Thsk 1m good

Moderate; stays 1m and acts on fast and easy ground.

Winston's Lad

76(80) (43)**31**

2-y-o gr g Act One-Hernani (FR) (Ezzoud (IRE))
P Howling Miss Mary Rose Woodham

Placings:000 (5839)

2009: 6^{0}G, 6^{0}GF, 8^{0}SD,

	Starts	1st	2nd	3rd	Win & Pl
Career Total (Turf)	2	0	0	0	
Career Total (AW)	1	0	0	0	

Going (Turf): Sf: 0-0 GS: 0-0 Gd: 0-1 GF: 0-1 Fm: 0-0
Distance: 5f/6f: 0-1 7f-8f: 0-1 9f-13f: 0-1 14f+: 0-0
Track : LH: 0-1 RH: 0-0 Tight: 0-1 Gall: 0-1
Aids: Bl: 0-0 Vi: 0-0 Tstrap: 0-0 Ckp: 0-0
Best Rating: **43** 9/09 Wolv 1m141y stand

Winter Fever (SAF)

(101) (87)**82**

5-y-o ch g Western Winter (USA)-Fashion Fever (SAF) (Model Man (SAF))
J M P Eustace (A Manuel 27/2) R Plersch

Placings:413/5231-4000 (7827)

2009: 8^{4}G, 7^{0}GS, 8^{0}SD, 8^{0}SD,

	Starts	1st	2nd	3rd	Win & Pl
Career Total (Turf)	9	2	1	2	13865
Career Total (AW)	2	0	0	0	

6/08 Clai 1m1f110y GD £5744
10/07 Clai 6f SFT £2717

Total win prize-money £8462

Going (Turf): Sf: 1-2 GS: 0-1 **Gd: 1-6** GF: 0-0 Fm: 0-0
Distance: 5f/6f: 1-2 7f-8f: 0-8 9f-13f: 1-1 14f+: 0-0
Track : LH: 0-0 RH: 0-1 Tight: 0-0 Gall: 0-0
Aids: Bl: 0-0 Vi: 0-0 Tstrap: 0-0 Ckp: 0-0
Best Rating: **87** 12/09 Kemp 1m stand

Winterbourne

83(94) (44)**44**

3-y-o gr/ro f Cadeaux Genereux-Snowing (Tate Gallery (USA))
M Blanshard Mrs C J Ward

Placings:060-4000 (7651)

2009: 5^{4}SD, 6^{0}G, 5^{0}SD, 5^{0}SD,

	Starts	1st	2nd	3rd	Win & Pl
Career Total (Turf)	4	0	0	0	0
Career Total (AW)	3	0	0	0	0

Going (Turf): Sf: 0-1 GS: 0-1 Gd: 0-1 GF: 0-1 Fm: 0-0
Distance: 5f/6f: 0-7 7f-8f: 0-0 9f-13f: 0-0 14f+: 0-0
Track : LH: 0-4 RH: 0-0 Tight: 0-3 Gall: 0-0
Aids: Bl: 0-0 Vi: 0-0 Tstrap: 0-0 Ckp: 0-0
Best Rating: **44** 12/09 Ling 5f stand

Winterbrook King

103(99) (59)**64**

3-y-o br g Gleaming (IRE)-Alice Holt (Free State)
J R Best Fielden Racing

Placings:00020-0006211 (4703)

2009: 9^{0}GF, 10^{0}SD, 11^{0}F, 12^{6}SD, 12^{2}GF, 16^{1}HY, 15^{1}GF,

	Starts	1st	2nd	3rd	Win & Pl
Career Total (Turf)	6	2	1	0	5792
Career Total (AW)	6	0	1	0	504

58 8/09 Folk 1m7f92y (0-70)H G-F £3070
64 7/09 Nott 2m9y (0-60)H HVY £2047

Total win prize-money £5118

Going (Turf): Sf: 1-2 GS: 0-0 Gd: 0-0 **GF: 1-3** Fm: 0-1
Distance: 5f/6f: 0-0 7f-8f: 0-4 9f-13f: 0-6 **14f+: 2-2**
Track : LH: 1-5 RH: 1-6 **Tight: 1-6** Gall: 0-1
Aids: Bl: 0-0 Vi: 0-0 Tstrap: 0-0 Ckp: 0-0
Best Rating: **64** 7/09 Nott 2m9y heavy

Moderate; stays 1m and acts on Polytrack.

Wintercast

107(107) (93)**97**

4-y-o ch g Spinning World (USA)-Bright Hope (IRE) (Danehill (USA))
W R Swinburn P W Harris

Placings:1/3522005 (7375)

2009: 8^{3}SD, 8^{5}G, 10^{2}G, 10^{2}G, 10^{0}GS, 10^{0}S, 8^{5}SD,

	Starts	1st	2nd	3rd	Win & Pl
Career Total (Turf)	6	1	2	0	9034
Career Total (AW)	2	0	0	1	1520

85 11/07 Nott 1m54y G-F £2590

Total win prize-money £2591

Going (Turf): Sf: 0-1 GS: 0-1 Gd: 0-3 **GF: 1-1** Fm: 0-0
Distance: 5f/6f: 0-0 7f-8f: 0-1 **9f-13f: 1-7** 14f+: 0-0
Track : **LH: 1-3** RH: 0-5 Tight: 0-1 Gall: 0-3
Aids: Bl: 0-0 Vi: 0-0 Tstrap: 0-0 Ckp: 0-0
Best Rating: **97** 6/09 NmkJ 1m2f good

Useful half-brother to multiple winner Birkside; stays 1m2f; handles quick ground.

Winterfell

89(96) (56)**57**

3-y-o b f Haafhd-It Girl (Robellino (USA))
C F Wall Ms Aida Fustoq

Placings:0-004633 (6771)

2009: 8^{0}GF, 9^{0}GS, 6^{4}G, 8^{6}G, 7^{3}SD, 8^{3}SD,

	Starts	1st	2nd	3rd	Win & Pl
Career Total (Turf)	5	0	0	0	173
Career Total (AW)	2	0	0	2	655

Going (Turf): Sf: 0-0 GS: 0-1 Gd: 0-2 GF: 0-2 Fm: 0-0
Distance: 5f/6f: 0-0 7f-8f: 0-4 9f-13f: 0-3 14f+: 0-0
Track : LH: 0-1 RH: 0-3 Tight: 0-3 Gall: 0-0
Aids: Bl: 0-0 Vi: 0-0 Tstrap: 0-0 Ckp: 0-0
Best Rating: **57** 4/09 Wind 1m67y gd-fm

Moderate; stays 1m; acts on fast ground.

Wisdom's Kiss

(105) (82)**69**

5-y-o b g Ocean Of Wisdom (USA)-April Magic (Magic Ring (IRE))
J D Bethell Hornblower Racing

Placings:0/0400200/2125011010420-5 (0017)

2009: 8^{5}SD,

	Starts	1st	2nd	3rd	Win & Pl
Career Total (Turf)	8	0	1	0	1182
Career Total (AW)	14	4	3	0	11518

82 8/08 Wolv 7f32y (0-70)H STD £2729
77 5/08 GrLe 1m (0-65)H STD £1942
73 5/08 Wolv 1m141y (0-55) STD £2047
59 2/08 Wolv 1m141y (0-60)H STD £2047

Total win prize-money £8768

Going (Turf): Sf: 0-1 GS: 0-2 Gd: 0-0 GF: 0-4 Fm: 0-1
Distance: 5f/6f: 0-0 7f-8f: 2-12 9f-13f: 2-10 14f+: 0-0
Track : **LH: 4-14** RH: 0-8 **Tight: 3-14** Gall: 1-1
Aids: **Bl: 3-11** Vi: 0-0 Tstrap: 1-5 Ckp: 1-5
Best Rating: **82** 10/08 Wolv 1m141y stand

Fair; stays 1m; acts on fast and soft ground; goes on Polytrack; has worn blinkers.

Wise Dennis

107(69) (15)**101**

7-y-o b g Polar Falcon (USA)-Bowden Rose (Dashing Blade)
A P Jarvis Allen B Pope

Placings:0033312/6106050/004040/11240602/311000-55400000 (6876)

2009: 8^{5}GF, 8^{5}GF, 10^{4}GF, 8^{0}GF, 10^{0}G, 8^{0}GF, 10^{0}GS, 8^{0}SD,

	Starts	1st	2nd	3rd	Win & Pl
Career Total (Turf)	38	5	2	3	237939
Career Total (AW)	4	1	1	1	17367

112 2/08 Ndas 1m GD £60301
113 2/08 Ndas 1m194y (100-112)H GD £52763
113 5/07 Asct 7f H G-S £52972
103 4/07 Sthl 7f (0-100)H STD £11217
108 5/05 York 7f (0-110)H SFT £17400
95 9/04 Asct 7f G-F £12644

Total win prize-money £207300

Going (Turf): Sf: 1-4 GS: 1-9 **Gd: 2-10** GF: 1-15 Fm: 0-0
Distance: 5f/6f: 0-1 **7f-8f: 5-29** 9f-13f: 1-12 14f+: 0-0
Track : **LH: 4-23** RH: 0-4 Tight: 0-2 **Gall: 3-15**
Aids: Bl: 0-0 Vi: 0-2 Tstrap: 0-0 Ckp: 0-0
Best Rating: **113** 2/08 Ndas 1m194y good

Smart; winner of 2007 Victoria Cup; successful in Listed company in Dubai in 2008; effective over 7f-1m; acts on most ground, including sand; usually held up.

Wise Melody

103(105) (90)**97**

4-y-o b f Zamindar (USA)-Swellegant (Midyan (USA))
W J Haggas I A Southcott

Placings:41/0421032-52 (2102)

2009: 6^{5}GF, 6^{2}GS,

	Starts	1st	2nd	3rd	Win & Pl
Career Total (Turf)	8	1	2	1	16559
Career Total (AW)	3	1	1	0	4287

89 6/08 Ripn 6f (0-95)H G-F £7885
80 12/07 Wolv 5f216y STD £2047

Total win prize-money £9933

Going (Turf): Sf: 0-0 GS: 0-2 Gd: 0-3 **GF: 1-3** Fm: 0-0
Distance: **5f/6f: 2-10** 7f-8f: 0-1 9f-13f: 0-0 14f+: 0-0
Track : **LH: 1-2** RH: 0-1 **Tight: 1-1** Gall: 0-2

Aids: Bl: 0-0 Vi: 0-0 Tstrap: 0-0 Ckp: 0-0
Best Rating: **97** 5/09 Ripn 6f gd-sft

Useful; effective at 6f; acts on fast ground and Polytrack.

Wise Princess

63(62)
3-y-o ch f Riverwise (USA)-Princess Penny (King's Signet (USA))
W G M Turner Mrs A F Horsington

Placings:00 **(2808)**
2009: 10^{0}SD, 9^{0}G,

	Starts	1st	2nd	3rd	Win & Pl
Career Total (Turf)	1	0	0	0	
Career Total (AW)	1	0	0	0	

Going (Turf): **Sf: 0-0 GS: 0-0 Gd: 0-1 GF: 0-0 Fm: 0-0**
Distance: 5f/6f: 0-0 7f-8f: 0-0 9f-13f: 0-2 14f+: 0-0
Track : LH: 0-2 RH: 0-0 Tight: 0-1 Gall: 0-0
Aids: Bl: 0-0 Vi: 0-0 Tstrap: 0-0 Ckp: 0-0

Wisecraic

97 84
2-y-o ch c Kheleyf (USA)-Belle Genius (USA) (Beau Genius (CAN))
Tom Dascombe L Mann, S Briddon, N Attenborough

Placings:140 **(6105)**
2009: 5^{1}G, 6^{4}S, 6^{0}GF,

	Starts	1st	2nd	3rd	Win & Pl
Career Total (Turf)	3	1	0	0	22818
80	7/09	Bath	5f161y	GD	£3885

Total win prize-money £3886

Going (Turf): Sf: 0-1 GS: 0-0 **Gd: 1-1** GF: 0-1 Fm: 0-0
Distance: **5f/6f: 1-2** 7f-8f: 0-1 9f-13f: 0-0 14f+: 0-0
Track : **LH: 1-1** RH: 0-1 Tight: 0-0 **Gall: 1-1**
Aids: Bl: 0-0 Vi: 0-0 Tstrap: 0-0 Ckp: 0-0
Best Rating: **84** 9/09 Newb 6f8y gd-fm

Useful 14,000euros colt; winning debut over an extended 5f on good ground; also handles soft.

Wiseman's Diamond (USA)

102(96) (68)73
4-y-o b f Wiseman's Ferry (USA)-Aswhatilldois (IRE) (Blues Traveller (IRE))
P T Midgley D I Perry

Placings:452121/34235050-0000332221101 **(6023)**
2009: 7^{0}SD, 7^{0}GF, 7^{0}G, 7^{0}GF, 7^{3}GF, 7^{3}GF, 8^{2}F, 8^{2}GF, 8^{2}GF, 8^{1}GF, 8^{1}G, 8^{0}GF, 8^{1}GF,

	Starts	1st	2nd	3rd	Win & Pl
Career Total (Turf)	18	4	4	3	13727
Career Total (AW)	9	1	2	1	3806

73	9/09	Pont	1m4y	(0-70)H	G-F	£3238
70	8/09	Bevl	1m100y	(0-65)H	GD	£2186
70	8/09	Newc	1m3y	(0-60)H	G-F	£2072
68	12/07	Wolv	1m141y	(0-65)	STD	£1706
62	10/07	Leic	7f9y	(0-65)	G-S	£2590

Total win prize-money £11793

Going (Turf): Sf: 0-1 GS: 1-3 Gd: 1-2 **GF: 2-11** Fm: 0-1
Distance: 5f/6f: 0-5 7f-8f: 1-14 **9f-13f: 4-8** 14f+: 0-0
Track : **LH: 2-15** RH: 1-6 **Tight: 1-9** Gall: 0-1
Aids: Bl: 0-0 Vi: 0-0 Tstrap: 1-4 Ckp: 1-4
Best Rating: **73** 9/09 Pont 1m4y gd-fm

Modest; effective over 1m; acts on most ground, also Polytrack; has worn cheekpieces.

Wishbone (IRE)

96 78
2-y-o b f Danehill Dancer (IRE)-Intricate Design (Zafonic (USA))
M G Quinlan G Morrin

Placings:631 **(6378)**
2009: 6^{6}GF, 6^{3}GF, 6^{1}GF,

	Starts	1st	2nd	3rd	Win & Pl
Career Total (Turf)	3	1	0	1	4427
78	9/09	Newc	6f	G-F	£3784

Total win prize-money £3785

Going (Turf): Sf: 0-0 GS: 0-0 Gd: 0-0 **GF: 1-3** Fm: 0-0
Distance: **5f/6f: 1-1** 7f-8f: 0-2 9f-13f: 0-0 14f+: 0-0
Track : LH: 0-0 RH: 0-0 Tight: 0-0 Gall: 0-0
Aids: Bl: 0-0 Vi: 0-0 Tstrap: 0-0 Ckp: 0-0
Best Rating: **78** 9/09 Newc 6f gd-fm

Fair; stays 6f and acts on fast ground.

Wishformore (IRE)

(94) (58)
2-y-o b f Chevalier (IRE)-Terra Nova (Polar Falcon (USA))
J S Moore The Moore The Merrier

Placings:2 **(7463)**
2009: 7^{2}SD,

	Starts	1st	2nd	3rd	Win & Pl
Career Total (Turf)	0	0	0	0	
Career Total (AW)	1	0	1	0	806

Going (Turf): **Sf: 0-0 GS: 0-0 Gd: 0-0 GF: 0-0 Fm: 0-0**
Distance: 5f/6f: 0-0 7f-8f: 0-1 9f-13f: 0-0 14f+: 0-0
Track : LH: 0-1 RH: 0-0 Tight: 0-1 Gall: 0-0
Aids: Bl: 0-0 Vi: 0-0 Tstrap: 0-0 Ckp: 0-0
Best Rating: **58** 11/09 Wolv 7f32y stand

Modest; effective over 7f; acts on Polytrack.

Witch Of The Wave (IRE)

64(100) (57)
3-y-o ch f Dr Fong (USA)-Clipper (Salse (USA))
Miss J S Davis W K Syndicate

Placings:00-540 **(1747)**
2009: 8^{5}SD, 12^{4}SF, 12^{0}GF,

	Starts	1st	2nd	3rd	Win & Pl
Career Total (Turf)	1	0	0	0	
Career Total (AW)	4	0	0	0	0

Going (Turf): **Sf: 0-0 GS: 0-0 Gd: 0-0 GF: 0-1 Fm: 0-0**
Distance: 5f/6f: 0-0 7f-8f: 0-3 9f-13f: 0-2 14f+: 0-0
Track : LH: 0-3 RH: 0-2 Tight: 0-2 Gall: 0-0
Aids: Bl: 0-0 Vi: 0-1 Tstrap: 0-0 Ckp: 0-0
Best Rating: **57** 1/09 Kemp 1m stand

Moderate; effective over 1m4f; acts on Polytrack.

Witchry

99(90) (50)71
7-y-o gr g Green Desert (USA)-Indian Skimmer (USA) (Storm Bird (CAN))
A G Newcombe Nigel Hardy

Placings:4310/005054/04631002325 5/565/014451400-20300 **(7275)**
2009: 5^{2}S, 6^{0}GF, 7^{3}GF, 5^{0}SD, 7^{0}SD,

	Starts	1st	2nd	3rd	Win & Pl
Career Total (Turf)	29	4	2	4	20913
Career Total (AW)	10	0	1	0	1285

71	9/08	Bath	5f161y	(0-75)H	SFT	£2914
69	5/08	Chep	6f16y	(0-65)H	SFT	£2331
78	7/06	Folk	5f	(0-70)H	G-F	£3886
87	7/04	Pont	5f	D	G-F	£5577

Total win prize-money £14708

Going (Turf): **Sf: 2-7** GS: 0-4 Gd: 0-5 **GF: 2-11** Fm: 0-2
Distance: **5f/6f: 3-35** 7f-8f: 1-4 9f-13f: 0-0 14f+: 0-0
Track : **LH: 2-15** RH: 0-1 Tight: 0-6 **Gall: 1-6**
Aids: Bl: 0-0 Vi: 0-0 Tstrap: 0-0 Ckp: 0-0
Best Rating: **87** 7/04 Pont 5f gd-fm

Modest sprinter; effective over 6f; acts on good to firm and soft ground.

Without A Prayer (IRE)

109(114) (116)114
4-y-o ch c Intikhab (USA)-Prayer (IRE) (Rainbow Quest (USA))
R M Beckett McDonagh Murphy And Nixon

Placings:213/01501-032541661 **(7588)**
2009: 8^{0}FT, 10^{3}G, 10^{2}GF, 10^{5}SD, 8^{4}G, 8^{1}GF, 8^{6}GF, 8^{6}GF, 8^{1}SD,

	Starts	1st	2nd	3rd	Win & Pl
Career Total (Turf)	11	2	1	2	66320
Career Total (AW)	6	3	1	0	47690

116	11/09	Kemp	1m	STD	£22708
114	6/09	Wind	1m67y	G-F	£22708
108	12/08	Deau	1m1f110y	STD	£19118
105	5/08	NmkR	1m	G-F	£6799
78	7/07	Ling	7f	STD	£2266

Total win prize-money £73601

Going (Turf): Sf: 0-1 GS: 0-1 Gd: 0-3 **GF: 2-6** Fm: 0-0
Distance: 5f/6f: 0-0 **7f-8f: 3-9** 9f-13f: 2-8 14f+: 0-0
Track : LH: 1-8 **RH: 2-4 Tight: 2-5** Gall: 0-6
Aids: Bl: 0-0 Vi: 0-0 Tstrap: 0-0 Ckp: 0-0
Best Rating: **116** 11/09 Kemp 1m stand

Smart; Listed winner and Group placed; just about stays 1m2f but better at around 1m; acts on good and faster ground and on Polytrack.

Without Prejudice (USA)

106(102) (87)94
4-y-o ch g Johannesburg (USA)-Awesome Strike (USA) (Theatrical)
J Noseda C Fox & J Wright

Placings:321010-0030141006 **(6815)**
2009: 7^{0}GF, 7^{0}S, 7^{3}G, 7^{0}G, 7^{1}G, 7^{4}GF, 7^{1}GS, 7^{0}G, 7^{0}SS, 7^{6}G,

	Starts	1st	2nd	3rd	Win & Pl
Career Total (Turf)	13	3	1	2	16248
Career Total (AW)	3	1	0	0	2590

94	9/09	York	7f	(0-80)H	G-S	£5828
88	7/09	NmkJ	7f	(0-85)H	GD	£5180
85	10/08	Kemp	7f	(0-75)H	STD	£2590
62	8/08	Ling	6f		G-F	£2590

Total win prize-money £16189

Going (Turf): Sf: 0-1 **GS: 1-1 Gd: 1-6 GF: 1-5** Fm: 0-0
Distance: 5f/6f: 1-3 **7f-8f: 3-13** 9f-13f: 0-0 14f+: 0-0
Track : LH: 1-4 RH: 1-1 Tight: 0-2 **Gall: 1-2**

Aids: Bl: 0-0 **Vi: 2-6** Tstrap: 0-0 Ckp: 0-0
Best Rating: 94 9/09 York 7f gd-sft

Useful; effective at 6f-7f; acts on fast and easy ground; goes on Polytrack; has worn a visor.

Wivny (USA)

87(76) (7)**41**
4-y-o b f Yonaguska (USA)-Mostly Sassy (USA) (Green Dancer (USA))
H J Evans B Preece

Placings:000-00000 **(5717)**
2009: 8^{0}G, 8^{0}SD, 7^{0}GF, 5^{0}GS, 5^{0}G,

	Starts	1st	2nd	3rd	Win & Pl
Career Total (Turf)	7	0	0	0	
Career Total (AW)	1	0	0	0	

Going (Turf): Sf: 0-0 GS: 0-1 Gd: 0-3 GF: 0-3 Fm: 0-0
Distance: 5f/6f: 0-2 7f-8f: 0-3 9f-13f: 0-3 14f+: 0-0
Track : LH: 0-3 RH: 0-2 Tight: 0-1 Gall: 0-1
Aids: Bl: 0-1 Vi: 0-0 Tstrap: 0-0 Ckp: 0-0
Best Rating: 42 5/08 Newb 7f good

Wizard Looking

98(96) (69)**59**
8-y-o b g Wizard King-High Stepping (IRE) (Taufan (USA))
P T Midgley T H Heckingbottom

Placings:60526/600600/02112030/000/100121545-062640 **(3223)**
2009: 12^{0}SD, 12^{6}SD, 12^{2}SD, 11^{6}G, 12^{4}GS, 12^{0}SD,

	Starts	1st	2nd	3rd	Win & Pl
Career Total (Turf)	24	3	3	1	11934
Career Total (AW)	13	2	2	0	5435

59 6/08 Folk 1m4f (0-60)H G-F £2047
69 5/08 Wolv 1m4f50y (0-55)H STD £2307
62 2/08 Ling 1m4f (0-52)H STD £1813
68 6/05 Yarm 1m3f101y (0-55)H GD £3026
58 6/05 Nott 1m1f213y (0-55)H G-F £3101
Total win prize-money £12296

Going (Turf): Sf: 0-0 GS: 0-1 Gd: 1-8 **GF: 2-14** Fm: 0-1
Distance: 5f/6f: 0-1 7f-8f: 0-10 **9f-13f: 5-23** 14f+: 0-3
Track : **LH: 4-25** RH: 1-8 **Tight: 4-16** Gall: 0-2
Aids: Bl: 0-1 Vi: 0-0 Tstrap: 0-1 Ckp: 0-1
Best Rating: 69 5/08 Wolv 1m4f50y stand

Modest; effective at around 1m4f; acts on fast ground; also goes on Polytrack.

Wizard Of Us

93(99) (53)**43**
9-y-o b g Wizard King-Sian's Girl (Mystiko (USA))
M Mullineaux P Currey

Placings:05005/0/10205/00/202003/105-060 **(5732)**
2009: 7^{0}G, 13^{8}S, 12^{0}GS,

	Starts	1st	2nd	3rd	Win & Pl
Career Total (Turf)	19	1	3	1	5991
Career Total (AW)	6	1	0	0	1295

52 1/08 Wolv 1m4f50y (0-45) STD £1295
63 10/04 Ayr 7f50y (0-70)H G-S £3606
Total win prize-money £4902

Going (Turf): Sf: 0-5 **GS: 1-2** Gd: 0-7 GF: 0-5 Fm: 0-0
Distance: 5f/6f: 0-4 7f-8f: 1-5 9f-13f: 1-13 14f+: 0-3
Track : **LH: 2-20** RH: 0-3 **Tight: 1-6** Gall: 0-2
Aids: Bl: 0-0 Vi: 0-0 Tstrap: 0-0 Ckp: 0-0
Best Rating: 66 11/04 Nott 1m54y heavy

Wizzy Izzy (IRE)

(65) **30**
4-y-o gr/ro f Shinko Forest (IRE)-Strelitzia (IRE) (Bluebird (USA))
N Wilson A Rhodes N C Wilson

Placings:0600/00 **(0227)**
2009: 8^{0}SD, 6^{0}SD,

	Starts	1st	2nd	3rd	Win & Pl
Career Total (Turf)	4	0	0	0	0
Career Total (AW)	2	0	0	0	

Going (Turf): Sf: 0-1 GS: 0-1 Gd: 0-1 GF: 0-1 Fm: 0-0
Distance: 5f/6f: 0-5 7f-8f: 0-0 9f-13f: 0-1 14f+: 0-0
Track : LH: 0-2 RH: 0-0 Tight: 0-1 Gall: 0-0
Aids: Bl: 0-1 Vi: 0-0 Tstrap: 0-0 Ckp: 0-0
Best Rating: 30 7/07 Thsk 5f good

Wogan's Sister

97(97) (65)**72**
4-y-o b f Lahib (USA)-Dublivia (Midyan (USA))
D R C Elsworth Ten Green Bottles Racing

Placings:000/10051130-50 **(2246)**
2009: 10^{5}GF, 10^{0}G,

	Starts	1st	2nd	3rd	Win & Pl
Career Total (Turf)	7	2	0	1	4497
Career Total (AW)	6	1	0	0	1775

72 8/08 Yarm 1m1f (0-65)H SFT £1942
61 8/08 Yarm 1m2f21y GD £2072
57 3/08 Wolv 1m141y (0-60)H STD £1774
Total win prize-money £5790

Going (Turf): Sf: 1-1 GS: 0-1 **Gd: 1-2** GF: 0-3 Fm: 0-0
Distance: 5f/6f: 0-0 7f-8f: 0-4 **9f-13f: 3-9** 14f+: 0-0
Track : **LH: 3-9** RH: 0-3 **Tight: 3-8** Gall: 0-2
Aids: Bl: 0-0 Vi: 0-0 Tstrap: 0-0 Ckp: 0-0
Best Rating: 72 8/08 Yarm 1m1f soft

Modest; stays 1m2f; acts on good ground; also goes on Polytrack.

Woldgate

87(84) (58)**53**
2-y-o b g Monsieur Bond (IRE)-Chicago Bond (USA) (Real Quiet (USA))
G R Oldroyd R C Bond

Placings:000 **(6679)**
2009: 5^{0}GF, 5^{0}SF, 7^{0}G,

	Starts	1st	2nd	3rd	Win & Pl
Career Total (Turf)	2	0	0	0	
Career Total (AW)	1	0	0	0	

Going (Turf): Sf: 0-0 GS: 0-0 Gd: 0-1 GF: 0-1 Fm: 0-0
Distance: 5f/6f: 0-2 7f-8f: 0-1 9f-13f: 0-0 14f+: 0-0
Track : LH: 0-2 RH: 0-0 Tight: 0-1 Gall: 0-1
Aids: Bl: 0-0 Vi: 0-0 Tstrap: 0-0 Ckp: 0-0
Best Rating: 58 10/09 Wolv 5f216y std-fst

Wolverton (IRE)

69(84) (38)**24**
3-y-o ch g Alhaarth (IRE)-Debbie's Next (USA) (Arctic Tern (USA))
N P Littmoden K R Parker

Placings:0-006 **(4175)**
2009: 10^{0}SD, 10^{0}GF, 14^{6}SD,

	Starts	1st	2nd	3rd	Win & Pl
Career Total (Turf)	2	0	0	0	
Career Total (AW)	2	0	0	0	0

Going (Turf): Sf: 0-0 GS: 0-1 Gd: 0-0 GF: 0-1 Fm: 0-0
Distance: 5f/6f: 0-0 7f-8f: 0-0 9f-13f: 0-3 14f+: 0-1
Track : LH: 0-2 RH: 0-2 Tight: 0-2 Gall: 0-1
Aids: Bl: 0-0 Vi: 0-0 Tstrap: 0-0 Ckp: 0-0
Best Rating: 38 5/09 Ling 1m2f stand

Womaniser (IRE)

98(98) (58)**58**
5-y-o br g Rock Of Gibraltar (IRE)-Top Table (Shirley Heights)
T Keddy Mrs H Keddy

Placings:00/006-5400600 **(7662)**
2009: 8^{5}G, 8^{4}SD, 9^{0}SD, 9^{0}SD, 7^{6}SD, 8^{0}SD, 7^{0}SD,

	Starts	1st	2nd	3rd	Win & Pl
Career Total (Turf)	1	0	0	0	0
Career Total (AW)	11	0	0	0	0

Going (Turf): Sf: 0-0 GS: 0-0 Gd: 0-1 GF: 0-0 Fm: 0-0
Distance: 5f/6f: 0-1 7f-8f: 0-5 9f-13f: 0-6 14f+: 0-0
Track : LH: 0-8 RH: 0-4 Tight: 0-7 Gall: 0-1
Aids: Bl: 0-3 Vi: 0-0 Tstrap: 0-1 Ckp: 0-1
Best Rating: 58 12/09 Ling 7f stand

Very moderate; stays 1m; acts on Polytrack; has worn cheekpieces and blinkers.

Wood Fair

88 **62**
2-y-o b f Trade Fair-To The Woods (IRE) (Woodborough (USA))
A P Jarvis (K R Burke 21/6) The Wood Fair Partnership

Placings:0600 **(6215)**
2009: 6^{0}GF, 6^{6}G, 6^{0}GF, 8^{0}GF,

	Starts	1st	2nd	3rd	Win & Pl
Career Total (Turf)	4	0	0	0	0

Going (Turf): Sf: 0-0 GS: 0-0 Gd: 0-1 GF: 0-3 Fm: 0-0
Distance: 5f/6f: 0-3 7f-8f: 0-1 9f-13f: 0-0 14f+: 0-0
Track : LH: 0-2 RH: 0-0 Tight: 0-0 Gall: 0-0
Aids: Bl: 0-0 Vi: 0-0 Tstrap: 0-0 Ckp: 0-0
Best Rating: 62 6/09 Pont 6f good

Wood Fairy

102(101) (61)**69**
3-y-o b f Haafhd-Woodbeck (Terimon)
R A Fahey B H Farr

Placings:1005044 **(7665)**
2009: 7^{1}G, 8^{0}GS, 8^{0}GF, 10^{5}GF, 8^{0}G, 10^{4}SD, 12^{4}SD,

	Starts	1st	2nd	3rd	Win & Pl
Career Total (Turf)	5	1	0	0	3950
Career Total (AW)	2	0	0	0	192

69 7/09 Thsk 7f GD £3950
Total win prize-money £3950

Going (Turf): Sf: 0-0 GS: 0-1 **Gd: 1-2** GF: 0-2 Fm: 0-0
Distance: 5f/6f: 0-0 **7f-8f: 1-3** 9f-13f: 0-4 14f+: 0-0
Track : **LH: 1-4** RH: 0-2 **Tight: 1-4** Gall: 0-1
Aids: Bl: 0-0 Vi: 0-0 Tstrap: 0-0 Ckp: 0-0
Best Rating: 69 9/09 Rdcr 1m2f gd-fm

Fair; half-sister to Franklins Gardens and Polar Ben; winner on debut over 7f on easy ground.

Woodcote (IRE)

92(111) (86)83

7-y-o b g Monashee Mountain (USA)-Tootle (Main Reef)

Peter Grayson (P R Chamings 25/2) Jasper Partnership

Placings:13/5002000/0362204501/0000003/3004004361 456**60604-021326400000000** **(7709)**

2009: 5^{0}SD, 5^{2}SD, 5^{1}SD, 5^{3}SD, 5^{2}SD, 5^{6}SD, 5^{4}SD, 5^{0}G, 5^{0}GF, 5^{0}SD, 5^{0}SD, 5^{0}SD, 5^{0}SD, 5^{0}SD, 5^{0}SD,

	Starts	1st	2nd	3rd	Win & Pl
Career Total (Turf)	**39**	**2**	**3**	**4**	**51245**
Career Total (AW)	**21**	**2**	**2**	**2**	**8404**

77	2/09	Ling	5f		STD	£2047
86	8/08	Kemp	5f	(0-75)H	STD	£2590
102	10/06	Asct	5f	(0-105)H	G-S	£12464
83	8/04	Wind	5f10y	D	G-S	£4966

Total win prize-money £22067

Going (Turf): Sf: 0-3 **GS: 2-8** Gd: 0-11 GF: 0-17 Fm: 0-0
Distance: **5f/6f: 4-58** 7f-8f: 0-2 9f-13f: 0-0 14f+: 0-0
Track : LH: 1-16 RH: 1-6 Tight: 1-13 Gall: 1-5
Aids: Bl: 0-7 **Vi: 2-20** Tstrap: 1-17 Ckp: 1-17
Best Rating: **102** 10/06 Asct 5f gd-sft

Fair; effective over 5f-6f; acts on most ground; has worn a visor and a tongue tie.

Woodcote Place

106(105) (92)95

6-y-o b g Lujain (USA)-Giant Nipper (Nashwan (USA))

P R Chamings The Foxford House Partnership

Placings:24/6022061102/0305460/02500322-021220 **(4409)**

2009: 7^{0}SD, 7^{2}SD, 7^{1}GF, 7^{2}SD, 7^{2}G, 8^{0}G,

	Starts	1st	2nd	3rd	Win & Pl
Career Total (Turf)	**25**	**3**	**5**	**2**	**26587**
Career Total (AW)	**8**	**0**	**5**	**0**	**6224**

89	5/09	Gdwd	7f	(0-80)H	G-F	£4857
93	9/06	Gdwd	7f	(0-85)H	GD	£5505
86	8/06	Wwck	7f26y		GD	£3238

Total win prize-money £13601

Going (Turf): Sf: 0-2 GS: 0-3 **Gd: 2-10** GF: 1-10 Fm: 0-0
Distance: 5f/6f: 0-1 **7f-8f: 3-28** 9f-13f: 0-4 14f+: 0-0
Track : LH: 1-6 **RH: 2-18** Tight: 0-7 Gall: 0-0
Aids: Bl: 0-0 Vi: 0-0 Tstrap: 0-0 Ckp: 0-0
Best Rating: **95** 7/09 Leic 7f9y good

Useful; effective over 7f-1m; suited by a sound surface or Polytrack; usually held up.

Wooden King (IRE)

99(104) (59)58

4-y-o b g Danetime (IRE)-Olympic Rock (IRE) (Ballad Rock)

M S Saunders (P D Evans 29/5) Hitchcock & King

Placings:60006/000000055P**60031-00**20060 **(5065)**

2009: 8^{0}SD, 7^{0}SD, 6^{2}GF, 8^{0}GF, 6^{0}S, 6^{6}GF, 5^{0}GF,

	Starts	1st	2nd	3rd	Win & Pl
Career Total (Turf)	**19**	**0**	**1**	**0**	**1181**
Career Total (AW)	**8**	**1**	**0**	**1**	**1706**

59	12/08	Ling	7f	(0-52)H	STD	£1706

Total win prize-money £1706

Going (Turf): **Sf: 0-3 GS: 0-4 Gd: 0-5 GF: 0-7 Fm: 0-0**
Distance: 5f/6f: 0-6 **7f-8f: 1-19** 9f-13f: 0-2 14f+: 0-0
Track : **LH: 1-7** RH: 0-7 **Tight: 1-5** Gall: 0-1
Aids: Bl: 0-0 Vi: 0-2 Tstrap: 0-1 Ckp: 0-1
Best Rating: **59** 12/08 Ling 7f stand

Moderate sort; effective at 7f; handles Polytrack.

Woodenitbenice

(79) (34)

2-y-o gr f Needwood Blade-Nightingale (Night Shift (USA))

D Shaw Derek Shaw

Placings:00000 **(7722)**

2009: 5^{0}SD, 7^{0}SD, 5^{0}SD, 7^{0}SD, 8^{0}SD,

	Starts	1st	2nd	3rd	Win & Pl
Career Total (Turf)	**0**	**0**	**0**	**0**	
Career Total (AW)	**5**	**0**	**0**	**0**	

Going (Turf): **Sf: 0-0 GS: 0-0 Gd: 0-0 GF: 0-0 Fm: 0-0**
Distance: 5f/6f: 0-2 7f-8f: 0-3 9f-13f: 0-0 14f+: 0-0
Track : LH: 0-5 RH: 0-0 Tight: 0-4 Gall: 0-0
Aids: Bl: 0-0 Vi: 0-0 Tstrap: 0-0 Ckp: 0-0
Best Rating: **34** 8/09 Wolv 7f32y stand

Woodface

80 37

2-y-o ch c Avonbridge-Amazed (Clantime)

B J Meehan Clipper Logistics

Placings:0000 **(4915)**

2009: 6^{0}GF, 6^{0}G, 6^{0}G, 7^{0}G,

	Starts	1st	2nd	3rd	Win & Pl
Career Total (Turf)	**4**	**0**	**0**	**0**	

Going (Turf): **Sf: 0-0 GS: 0-0 Gd: 0-3 GF: 0-1 Fm: 0-0**
Distance: 5f/6f: 0-3 7f-8f: 0-1 9f-13f: 0-0 14f+: 0-0
Track : LH: 0-0 RH: 0-0 Tight: 0-0 Gall: 0-2
Aids: Bl: 0-1 Vi: 0-0 Tstrap: 0-0 Ckp: 0-0
Best Rating: **37** 7/09 Wind 6f good

Woodford Belle (USA)

89 72

2-y-o b/br f Arch (USA)-Tis Me (USA) (Notebook (USA))

B J Meehan Catesby W Clay

Placings:44 **(6762)**

2009: 8^{4}GF, 8^{4}GS,

	Starts	1st	2nd	3rd	Win & Pl
Career Total (Turf)	**2**	**0**	**0**	**0**	**673**

Going (Turf): **Sf: 0-0 GS: 0-1 Gd: 0-0 GF: 0-1 Fm: 0-0**
Distance: 5f/6f: 0-0 7f-8f: 0-2 9f-13f: 0-0 14f+: 0-0
Track : LH: 0-1 RH: 0-0 Tight: 0-0 Gall: 0-1
Aids: Bl: 0-0 Vi: 0-0 Tstrap: 0-0 Ckp: 0-0
Best Rating: **72** 9/09 NmkR 1m gd-fm

Woodhouse Mill (IRE)

76 35

2-y-o b f Oratorio (IRE)-Wurfklinge (GER) (Acatenango (GER))

N Tinkler Philip J Grundy

Placings:000000 **(5981)**

2009: 6^{0}G, 6^{0}G, 6^{0}S, 6^{0}GF, 7^{0}GF, 7^{0}GF,

	Starts	1st	2nd	3rd	Win & Pl
Career Total (Turf)	**6**	**0**	**0**	**0**	

Going (Turf): **Sf: 0-1 GS: 0-0 Gd: 0-2 GF: 0-3 Fm: 0-0**
Distance: 5f/6f: 0-4 7f-8f: 0-2 9f-13f: 0-0 14f+: 0-0
Track : LH: 0-0 RH: 0-1 Tight: 0-0 Gall: 0-0
Aids: Bl: 0-0 Vi: 0-1 Tstrap: 0-0 Ckp: 0-0
Best Rating: **35** 8/09 Ripn 6f gd-fm

Woodland Violet

(90) (44)

3-y-o b f Reset (AUS)-Be My Tinker (Be My Chief (USA))

I A Wood C S Tateson

Placings:0-0506 **(7660)**

2009: 8^{0}SD, 8^{5}SD, 8^{0}SD, 10^{6}SD,

	Starts	1st	2nd	3rd	Win & Pl
Career Total (Turf)	**0**	**0**	**0**	**0**	
Career Total (AW)	**5**	**0**	**0**	**0**	**0**

Going (Turf): **Sf: 0-0 GS: 0-0 Gd: 0-0 GF: 0-0 Fm: 0-0**
Distance: 5f/6f: 0-0 7f-8f: 0-4 9f-13f: 0-1 14f+: 0-0
Track : LH: 0-3 RH: 0-2 Tight: 0-3 Gall: 0-0
Aids: Bl: 0-0 Vi: 0-0 Tstrap: 0-0 Ckp: 0-0
Best Rating: **44** 12/09 Ling 1m2f stand

Woodlark Island (IRE)

108(103) (81)76

3-y-o b g Tagula (IRE)-Be My Lover (Pursuit Of Love)

D E Pipe (M P Tregoning 7/10) Eminence Grise Partnership

Placings:04-242155 **(6583)**

2009: 7^{2}SD, 8^{4}SD, 10^{2}GF, 8^{1}SD, 8^{5}G, 10^{5}SD,

	Starts	1st	2nd	3rd	Win & Pl
Career Total (Turf)	**3**	**0**	**1**	**0**	**1445**
Career Total (AW)	**5**	**1**	**1**	**0**	**3741**

81	9/09	Ling	1m	STD	£2729

Total win prize-money £2730

Going (Turf): **Sf: 0-1 GS: 0-0 Gd: 0-1 GF: 0-1 Fm: 0-0**
Distance: 5f/6f: 0-0 **7f-8f: 1-5** 9f-13f: 0-3 14f+: 0-0
Track : **LH: 1-4** RH: 0-2 **Tight: 1-2** Gall: 0-2
Aids: Bl: 0-0 Vi: 0-1 Tstrap: 0-1 Ckp: 0-1
Best Rating: **81** 9/09 Ling 1m stand

Fair; stays 1m2f; acts on fast ground and on Polytrack; has worn a visor.

Woodsley House (IRE)

102 (61)76

7-y-o b g Orpen (USA)-Flame And Shadow (IRE) (Turtle Island (IRE))

A G Foster Mrs V L Davis

Placings:2225/0020/001**00**/006011160-060130056540650 **(7113)**

2009: 6^{0}F, 6^{6}G, 6^{0}GS, 7^{1}GF, 7^{3}G, 7^{0}GF, 6^{0}G, 7^{5}G, 7^{6}GF, 8^{5}S, 8^{4}S, 9^{0}G, 8^{6}GF, 7^{5}G, 9^{0}GS,

	Starts	1st	2nd	3rd	Win & Pl
Career Total (Turf)	**35**	**5**	**4**	**1**	**27779**
Career Total (AW)	**2**	**0**	**0**	**0**	

75	5/09	Muss	7f30y	(0-70)H	G-F	£3885
76	9/08	Rdcr	6f	(0-75)H	G-S	£2590
76	8/08	Ayr	6f	(0-70)H	SFT	£2914
67	8/08	Rdcr	6f	(0-60)H	G-S	£2388
74	8/06	Gdwd	6f		GD	£5505

Total win prize-money £17283

Going (Turf): Sf: 1-6 **GS: 2-10** Gd: 1-10 GF: 1-8 Fm: 0-1
Distance: **5f/6f: 4-10** 7f-8f: 1-23 9f-13f: 0-4 14f+: 0-0
Track : LH: 0-9 **RH: 1-8 Tight: 1-9** Gall: 0-2
Aids: Bl: 0-0 Vi: 0-0 Tstrap: 0-5 Ckp: 0-5
Best Rating: **86** 10/04 Newb 7f soft

Modest; effective over 6f-1m; acts on most ground; has worn cheekpieces.

Woody Valentine (USA)

85 **44**

8-y-o ch g Woodman (USA)-Mudslinger (USA) (El Gran Senor (USA))
Mrs E Slack (Mrs Dianne Sayer 1/4) A Slack

Placings:321400/421661200524/00000-0 **(1058)**
2009: 15^{0}GF,

	Starts	1st	2nd	3rd	Win & Pl
Career Total (Turf)	**24**	**3**	**4**	**1**	**30498**

84 7/04 Epsm 1m2f18y D(0-80) G-F £5330
89 4/04 Pont 1m2f6yD(0-85)H HVY £9349
74 9/03 Haml 1m65y D G-F £5073
Total win prize-money £19753

Going (Turf): Sf: 1-5 GS: 0-0 Gd: 0-7 **GF: 2-12** Fm: 0-0
Distance: 5f/6f: 0-0 7f-8f: 0-7 **9f-13f: 3-16** 14f+: 0-1
Track : **LH: 2-13** RH: 1-10 **Tight: 2-12** Gall: 0-3
Aids: Bl: 0-0 Vi: 0-0 Tstrap: 0-2 Ckp: 0-2
Best Rating: **89** 4/04 Pont 1m2f6y heavy

Woody Waller

98 **75**

4-y-o ch g Lomitas-Reamzafonic (Grand Lodge (USA))
J Howard Johnson W M G Black & Mrs S Johnson

Placings:214-50 **(6053)**
2009: 12^{5}GF, 17^{0}G,

	Starts	1st	2nd	3rd	Win & Pl
Career Total (Turf)	**5**	**1**	**1**	**0**	**4131**

75 7/08 Catt 1m5f175y GD £2590
Total win prize-money £2590

Going (Turf): Sf: 0-0 GS: 0-1 **Gd: 1-3** GF: 0-1 Fm: 0-0
Distance: 5f/6f: 0-0 7f-8f: 0-0 9f-13f: 0-3 **14f+: 1-2**
Track : **LH: 1-4** RH: 0-1 **Tight: 1-4** Gall: 0-0
Aids: Bl: 0-0 Vi: 0-0 Tstrap: 0-0 Ckp: 0-0
Best Rating: **75** 7/08 Catt 1m5f175y good

Fair; lightly raced; stays 1m5f plus; acts on good ground.

Woolfall Sovereign (IRE)

(95) (63)

3-y-o b c Noverre (USA)-Mandragore (USA) (Slew O'Gold (USA))
G G Margarson Woolfall Manor Stud

Placings:1 **(7753)**
2009: 8^{1}SD,

	Starts	1st	2nd	3rd	Win & Pl
Career Total (Turf)	**0**	**0**	**0**	**0**	
Career Total (AW)	**1**	**1**	**0**	**0**	**2730**

63 12/09 Wolv 1m141y STD £2729
Total win prize-money £2730

Going (Turf): **Sf: 0-0 GS: 0-0 Gd: 0-0 GF: 0-0 Fm: 0-0**
Distance: 5f/6f: 0-0 7f-8f: 0-0 **9f-13f: 1-1** 14f+: 0-0
Track : **LH: 1-1** RH: 0-0 **Tight: 1-1** Gall: 0-0
Aids: Bl: 0-0 Vi: 0-0 Tstrap: 0-0 Ckp: 0-0
Best Rating: **63** 12/09 Wolv 1m141y stand

Winner on debut; effective over 1m; acts on Polytrack.

Woolfall Treasure

110 **94**

4-y-o gr g Daylami (IRE)-Treasure Trove (USA) (The Minstrel (CAN))
G L Moore Findlay & Bloom

Placings:60205/2312002-164220 **(6851)**
2009: 14^{1}GF, 20^{6}GF, 21^{4}G, 17^{2}F, 16^{2}GF, 18^{0}G,

	Starts	1st	2nd	3rd	Win & Pl
Career Total (Turf)	**18**	**2**	**6**	**1**	**34816**

94 5/09 Sals 1m6f21y (0-105)H G-F £11215
76 5/08 Newc 1m2f32y G-F £3885
Total win prize-money £15102

Going (Turf): Sf: 0-1 GS: 0-1 Gd: 0-6 **GF: 2-9** Fm: 0-1
Distance: 5f/6f: 0-0 7f-8f: 0-5 9f-13f: 1-6 14f+: 1-7
Track : LH: 1-3 RH: 1-9 Tight: 1-5 Gall: 1-6
Aids: Bl: 0-2 Vi: 0-0 Tstrap: 0-1 Ckp: 0-1
Best Rating: **94** 5/09 Sals 1m6f21y gd-fm

Useful; stays 2m1f and acts on good and faster ground; has worn various headgear; likes to race prominently; winning hurdler.

Woolston Ferry (IRE)

89(101) (80)**77**

3-y-o b g Fath (USA)-Cathy Garcia (IRE) (Be My Guest (USA))
David Pinder (M R Channon 13/3) Ms L Burns

Placings:23351505**213**-4116006**5050** **(7432)**
2009: 5^{4}SD, 7^{1}SD, 7^{1}SD, 8^{6}SD, 8^{0}SD, 7^{0}GF, 7^{6}SD, 8^{5}SD, 7^{0}SD, 7^{5}SD, 7^{0}SD,

	Starts	1st	2nd	3rd	Win & Pl
Career Total (Turf)	**8**	**0**	**1**	**2**	**2235**
Career Total (AW)	**14**	**4**	**1**	**1**	**11406**

77 3/09 Ling 7f STD £2047
74 1/09 Ling 7f STD £2047
80 11/08 Wolv 7f32y STD £3070
76 8/08 Ling 7f (0-75) STD £2590
Total win prize-money £9755

Going (Turf): **Sf: 0-1 GS: 0-1 Gd: 0-4 GF: 0-2 Fm: 0-0**
Distance: 5f/6f: 0-6 **7f-8f: 4-15** 9f-13f: 0-1 14f+: 0-0
Track : **LH: 4-12** RH: 0-4 **Tight: 4-11** Gall: 0-1
Aids: Bl: 0-0 Vi: 0-0 Tstrap: 0-0 Ckp: 0-0
Best Rating: **80** 1/09 Wolv 5f216y stand

Fair; effective over 6f-7f; acts on Polytrack.

Woqoodd

91(92) (54)**63**

5-y-o b g Royal Applause-Intervene (Zafonic (USA))
D Shaw George Houghton

Placings:034/0010**406**/400306052-0600 **(3465)**
2009: 5^{0}SD, 6^{6}GS, 5^{0}GF, 5^{0}SD,

	Starts	1st	2nd	3rd	Win & Pl
Career Total (Turf)	**15**	**1**	**0**	**2**	**4921**
Career Total (AW)	**8**	**0**	**1**	**0**	**504**

72 8/07 Pont 6f (0-75)H FRM £3886
Total win prize-money £3886

Going (Turf): Sf: 0-1 GS: 0-2 Gd: 0-5 GF: 0-6 **Fm: 1-1**
Distance: **5f/6f: 1-22** 7f-8f: 0-1 9f-13f: 0-0 14f+: 0-0
Track : **LH: 1-9** RH: 0-1 Tight: 0-6 Gall: 0-1
Aids: Bl: 0-2 Vi: 0-4 Tstrap: 0-0 Ckp: 0-0
Best Rating: **72** 8/07 Pont 6f firm

Moderate; effective at 6f; acts on fast ground and Polytrack; has worn blinkers.

Workforce

101 **93**

2-y-o b c King's Best (USA)-Soviet Moon (IRE) (Sadler's Wells (USA))
Sir Michael Stoute K Abdulla

Placings:1 **(6199)**
2009: 7^{1}G,

	Starts	1st	2nd	3rd	Win & Pl
Career Total (Turf)	**1**	**1**	**0**	**0**	**3562**

93 9/09 Gdwd 7f GD £3561
Total win prize-money £3562

Going (Turf): Sf: 0-0 GS: 0-0 **Gd: 1-1** GF: 0-0 Fm: 0-0
Distance: 5f/6f: 0-0 **7f-8f: 1-1** 9f-13f: 0-0 14f+: 0-0
Track : LH: 0-0 **RH: 1-1** Tight: 0-0 Gall: 0-0
Aids: Bl: 0-0 Vi: 0-0 Tstrap: 0-0 Ckp: 0-0
Best Rating: **93** 9/09 Gdwd 7f good

Useful; stays 7f; acts on good ground.

World Of Choice (USA)

96(102) (66)**57**

4-y-o b g Distorted Humor (USA)-Palace Weekend (USA) (Seattle Dancer (USA))
M W Easterby Mrs Jean Turpin

Placings:03/**005**-5115005 **(5732)**
2009: 7^{5}SD, 11^{1}SD, 12^{1}SD, 12^{5}SD, 12^{0}SD, 11^{0}G, 12^{5}GS,

	Starts	1st	2nd	3rd	Win & Pl
Career Total (Turf)	**4**	**0**	**0**	**1**	**337**
Career Total (AW)	**8**	**2**	**0**	**0**	**4037**

66 5/09 Sthl 1m4f (0-65)H STD £2388
62 2/09 Sthl 1m3f (0-52)H STD £1648
Total win prize-money £4036

Going (Turf): **Sf: 0-0 GS: 0-1 Gd: 0-3 GF: 0-0 Fm: 0-0**
Distance: 5f/6f: 0-0 7f-8f: 0-4 **9f-13f: 2-8** 14f+: 0-0
Track : **LH: 2-10** RH: 0-2 Tight: 0-2 Gall: 0-1
Aids: **Bl: 2-6** Vi: 0-0 Tstrap: 0-0 Ckp: 0-0
Best Rating: **66** 5/09 Sthl 1m4f stand

Moderate; ex-Godolphin; stays 1m3f and acts on Fibresand; has worn blinkers.

World Time

91(90) (57)**76**

4-y-o ch g Dalakhani (IRE)-Time Ahead (Spectrum (IRE))
Tim Vaughan Notalottery

Placings:4000165-5 **(5936)**
2009: 9^{5}GF,

	Starts	1st	2nd	3rd	Win & Pl
Career Total (Turf)	**7**	**1**	**0**	**0**	**2135**
Career Total (AW)	**1**	**0**	**0**	**0**	

76 6/08 Yarm 1m3f101y (0-65)H G-F £1942
Total win prize-money £1943

Going (Turf): Sf: 0-2 GS: 0-2 Gd: 0-0 **GF: 1-3** Fm: 0-0
Distance: 5f/6f: 0-0 7f-8f: 0-0 **9f-13f: 1-8** 14f+: 0-0
Track : **LH: 1-3** RH: 0-4 **Tight: 1-4** Gall: 0-0
Aids: Bl: 0-1 Vi: 0-1 Tstrap: 0-0 Ckp: 0-0
Best Rating: **76** 6/08 Yarm 1m3f101y gd-fm

Fair; stays 1m4f; acts on fast ground has worn blinkers.

Worth A King's

102(110) (93)**91**

3-y-o b g Red Ransom (USA)-Top Romance (IRE) (Entrepreneur)

D McCain Jnr (Sir Michael Stoute 9/10) David A Price

Placings:030U1-4043**4112** **(6636)**

2009: 10^{4}G, 12^{0}GF, 12^{4}S, 12^{3}G, **11^{4}SD**, 13^{1}SD, 12^{1}GF, 13^{2}SD,

	Starts	1st	2nd	3rd	Win & Pl
Career Total (Turf)	7	1	0	1	7848
Career Total (AW)	6	2	1	1	9335

91 10/09 Epsm 1m4f10y (0-80)H G-F £6476
82 9/09 Wolv 1m5f194y (0-75)H STD £2914
72 10/08 GrLe 1m (0-85) STD £3885
Total win prize-money £13276

Going (Turf): Sf: 0-1 GS: 0-0 Gd: 0-3 **GF: 1-2** Fm: 0-1
Distance: 5f/6f: 0-0 7f-8f: 1-4 9f-13f: 1-7 14f+: 1-2
Track : **LH: 3-8** RH: 0-3 **Tight: 2-4** Gall: 1-5
Aids: Bl: 0-0 **Vi: 2-4** Tstrap: 0-0 Ckp: 0-0
Best Rating: 93 10/09 Wolv 1m5f194y stand

Useful; effective at 1m4f; acts on good/fast ground and Polytrack; has worn a visor.

Wotashirtfull (IRE)

104(105) (89)**89**

4-y-o ch g Namid-Madrina (Waajib)

J R Boyle (K A Ryan 15/1) M Khan X2

Placings:33223/21130342-**132132220016** **(5592)**

2009: 5^{1}SD, 5^{3}SD, 6^{2}SD, 6^{1}SD, 6^{3}SD, 6^{2}SD, 5^{2}G, 5^{2}G, 5^{0}GF, 5^{0}G, 5^{1}SD, 6^{6}GS,

	Starts	1st	2nd	3rd	Win & Pl
Career Total (Turf)	17	2	5	5	18177
Career Total (AW)	8	3	3	2	23117

89 8/09 Ling 5f (0-85)H STD £6476
86 2/09 Ling 6f (0-85)H STD £4857
86 1/09 GrLe 5f (0-85)H STD £5180
85 6/08 Ripn 5f (0-75)H SFT £2914
79 6/08 Newc 5f (0-75)H G-S £3238
Total win prize-money £22666

Going (Turf): Sf: 1-4 GS: 1-3 Gd: 0-5 GF: 0-5 Fm: 0-0
Distance: 5f/6f: 5-25 7f-8f: 0-0 9f-13f: 0-0 14f+: 0-0
Track : LH: 3-11 RH: 0-0 **Tight: 2-3** Gall: 1-3
Aids: Bl: 0-0 Vi: 0-3 Tstrap: 5-15 Ckp: 5-15
Best Rating: 89 8/09 Ling 5f stand

Useful; effective over 5f-6f; acts on a most ground and on sand; has worn cheekpieces and a visor.

Wotasparkler

100(31) **66**

3-y-o b f Pyrus (USA)-Colourflash (IRE) (College Chapel)

W S Kittow Miss E J Tanner

Placings:0620135050 **(5582)**

2009: 7^{0}GS, 6^{6}GF, 5^{2}G, 6^{0}G, 6^{1}G, 5^{3}G, 6^{5}G, 6^{0}GF, 8^{5}G, 7^{0}SD,

	Starts	1st	2nd	3rd	Win & Pl
Career Total (Turf)	9	1	1	1	4263
Career Total (AW)	1	0	0	0	

61 6/09 Wwck 6f GD £2914
Total win prize-money £2914

Going (Turf): Sf: 0-0 GS: 0-1 **Gd: 1-6** GF: 0-2 Fm: 0-0
Distance: 5f/6f: 1-7 7f-8f: 0-3 9f-13f: 0-0 14f+: 0-0
Track : LH: 1-2 RH: 0-0 Tight: 0-1 Gall: 0-1
Aids: Bl: 0-0 Vi: 0-1 Tstrap: 0-0 Ckp: 0-0
Best Rating: 66 5/09 Leic 5f218y good

Modest; stays 6f; acts on a sound surface.

Wotatomboy

92(96) (63)**68**

3-y-o ch f Captain Rio-Keen Melody (USA) (Sharpen Up)

R M Whitaker Mrs Jill Willows

Placings:024051-04600006 **(7417)**

2009: 7^{0}GF, 5^{4}GF, 6^{6}G, 5^{0}SD, 8^{0}GF, 7^{0}GF, 7^{0}SD, 8^{6}SD,

	Starts	1st	2nd	3rd	Win & Pl
Career Total (Turf)	10	0	1	0	1384
Career Total (AW)	4	1	0	0	3071

63 10/08 Sthl 6f STD £3070
Total win prize-money £3071

Going (Turf): Sf: 0-1 GS: 0-1 Gd: 0-2 GF: 0-5 Fm: 0-1
Distance: 5f/6f: 1-9 7f-8f: 0-3 9f-13f: 0-2 14f+: 0-0
Track : LH: 1-6 RH: 0-3 Tight: 0-3 Gall: 0-1
Aids: Bl: 0-0 Vi: 0-0 Tstrap: 0-0 Ckp: 0-0
Best Rating: 68 7/08 Carl 5f firm

Modest; stays 6f; handles fast ground and acts on Fibresand.

Wotavadun (IRE)

(70) (33)**22**

6-y-o ch g King Of Kings (IRE)-Blush With Love (USA) (Mt. Livermore (USA))

D Flood Barrie Kirby

Placings:000/0606066/0/0-00 **(0291)**

2009: 6^{0}SD, 7^{0}SD,

	Starts	1st	2nd	3rd	Win & Pl
Career Total (Turf)	4	0	0	0	0
Career Total (AW)	10	0	0	0	0

Going (Turf): Sf: 0-0 GS: 0-0 Gd: 0-2 GF: 0-1 Fm: 0-1
Distance: 5f/6f: 0-12 7f-8f: 0-2 9f-13f: 0-0 14f+: 0-0
Track : LH: 0-10 RH: 0-1 Tight: 0-9 Gall: 0-0
Aids: Bl: 0-9 Vi: 0-0 Tstrap: 0-0 Ckp: 0-0
Best Rating: 37 1/06 Wolv 5f216y stand

Wotchalike (IRE)

95(100) (65)**60**

7-y-o ch g Spectrum (IRE)-Juno Madonna (IRE) (Sadler's Wells (USA))

Miss S Johnstone (Mrs C Ferguson 6/4) Miss S Johnstone

Placings:5022165/2333000300**U006**/060**4665/06/**2432-550 **(4848)**

2009: 16^{5}G, 16^{5}GF, 16^{0}G,

	Starts	1st	2nd	3rd	Win & Pl
Career Total (Turf)	20	1	3	2	10067
Career Total (AW)	17	0	2	3	7185

77 10/04 Bath 1m5y SFT £4537
Total win prize-money £4537

Going (Turf): Sf: 1-4 GS: 0-5 Gd: 0-6 GF: 0-5 Fm: 0-0
Distance: 5f/6f: 0-1 7f-8f: 0-5 **9f-13f: 1-19** 14f+: 0-12
Track : LH: 1-23 RH: 0-8 **Tight: 1-18** Gall: 0-5
Aids: Bl: 0-0 Vi: 0-7 Tstrap: 0-8 Ckp: 0-8
Best Rating: 83 10/04 NmkR 1m2f gd-sft

Modest; stays 2m; acts on most ground and Polytrack.

Woteva

100(98) (67)**71**

3-y-o b f Kyllachy-Happy Omen (Warning)

T P Tate (B Ellison 22/5) M Laverack

Placings:26050601365-0000**0500** **(7650)**

2009: 12^{0}GF, 8^{0}SD, 8^{0}G, 8^{0}GS, 7^{0}G, 8^{5}S, **10^{0}SD**, 8^{0}SD,

	Starts	1st	2nd	3rd	Win & Pl
Career Total (Turf)	15	1	1	1	5147
Career Total (AW)	4	0	0	0	0

71 9/08 Bevl 7f100y (0-65) HVY £1942
Total win prize-money £1943

Going (Turf): Sf: 1-4 GS: 0-4 Gd: 0-3 GF: 0-4 Fm: 0-0
Distance: 5f/6f: 0-4 **7f-8f: 1-7** 9f-13f: 0-8 14f+: 0-0
Track : LH: 0-8 **RH: 1-4** Tight: 0-6 Gall: 0-0
Aids: Bl: 0-0 Vi: 0-0 Tstrap: 1-8 Ckp: 1-8
Best Rating: 74 4/08 Bevl 5f gd-sft

Fair; effective over 1m; acts on easy ground.

Would I Lie To You

75(71) (10)**16**

5-y-o b g Bahamian Bounty-Pallas Athene (Jupiter Island)

J R Jenkins Miss Clare Hobson

Placings:000 **(1941)**

2009: 8^{0}SD, 7^{0}SD, 8^{0}GF,

	Starts	1st	2nd	3rd	Win & Pl
Career Total (Turf)	1	0	0	0	
Career Total (AW)	2	0	0	0	

Going (Turf): Sf: 0-0 GS: 0-0 Gd: 0-0 GF: 0-1 Fm: 0-0
Distance: 5f/6f: 0-0 7f-8f: 0-2 9f-13f: 0-1 14f+: 0-0
Track : LH: 0-1 RH: 0-1 Tight: 0-1 Gall: 0-0
Aids: Bl: 0-0 Vi: 0-0 Tstrap: 0-0 Ckp: 0-0
Best Rating: 16 5/09 Yarm 1m3y gd-fm

Wovoka (IRE)

105 (81)**86**

6-y-o b g Mujadil (USA)-Common Cause (Polish Patriot (USA))

K A Ryan (D W Barker 11/7) Dales Homes Ltd

Placings:136025122243510**1/4005**3006/002004210600/04 60030202600020-110165400601560 **(6924)**

2009: 8^{1}GF, 8^{1}F, 8^{0}GF, 8^{1}GS, 8^{6}GF, 8^{5}G, 8^{4}GF, 8^{0}GF, 7^{0}GS, 9^{6}GF, 8^{0}S, 8^{1}GF, 9^{5}GF, 10^{6}GF, 8^{0}GF,

	Starts	1st	2nd	3rd	Win & Pl
Career Total (Turf)	63	9	9	4	101319
Career Total (AW)	4	0	0	0	1058

75 8/09 Newc 1m3y G-F £2266
86 5/09 Donc 1m (0-85)H G-S £4857
80 4/09 Rdcr 1m (0-85)H FRM £4857
81 4/09 Newc 1m3y (0-80)H G-F £4604
89 7/07 Asct 1m (0-85)H G-S £6477
99 11/05 Leop 1m1f SH £23085
94 10/05 Newb 7f (0-85) G-S £5733
85 8/05 Rdcr 6f G-F £11066
75 3/05 Muss 5f GD £3425
Total win prize-money £66373

Going (Turf): Sf: 0-11**GS: 3-13** Gd: 1-15**GF: 3-22** Fm: 1-1
Distance: 5f/6f: 2-9 **7f-8f: 4-32** 9f-13f: 3-26 14f+: 0-0
Track : LH: 2-27 RH: 0-9 Tight: 0-12 **Gall: 1-12**
Aids: Bl: 0-0 **Vi: 1-2** Tstrap: 0-0 Ckp: 0-0
Best Rating: 99 5/06 NmkR 1m gd-fm

Fair; stays 1m1f; acts on most ground on turf; has worn a visor.

Wray Castle (IRE)

(91) (71)

4-y-o b g Desert Prince (IRE)-Blushing Gleam (Caerleon (USA))

C Heard (Ian Williams 27/2) Mrs K Heard

Placings:25 **(0704)**

2009: 12^{2}SD, 12^{5}SD,

	Starts	1st	2nd	3rd	Win & Pl
Career Total (Turf)	0	0	0	0	
Career Total (AW)	2	0	1	0	806

Going (Turf): Sf: 0-0 GS: 0-0 Gd: 0-0 GF: 0-0 Fm: 0-0
Distance: 5f/6f: 0-0 7f-8f: 0-0 9f-13f: 0-2 14f+: 0-0
Track : LH: 0-2 RH: 0-0 Tight: 0-2 Gall: 0-0
Aids: Bl: 0-0 Vi: 0-0 Tstrap: 0-0 Ckp: 0-0
Best Rating: 71 2/09 Wolv 1m4f50y stand

Modest; effective over 1m4f; acts on Polytrack.

Wrecker's Moon (IRE)

61(66) (12)

4-y-o b f Shinko Forest (IRE)-Coast Is Clear (IRE) (Rainbow Quest (USA))

T J Etherington Miss Z C Willis

Placings:000-0 **(2789)**

2009: 8^{0}G,

	Starts	1st	2nd	3rd	Win & Pl
Career Total (Turf)	2	0	0	0	
Career Total (AW)	2	0	0	0	

Going (Turf): Sf: 0-0 GS: 0-0 Gd: 0-1 GF: 0-1 Fm: 0-0
Distance: 5f/6f: 0-0 7f-8f: 0-3 9f-13f: 0-1 14f+: 0-0
Track : LH: 0-2 RH: 0-1 Tight: 0-1 Gall: 0-1
Aids: Bl: 0-0 Vi: 0-0 Tstrap: 0-0 Ckp: 0-0
Best Rating: 12 8/08 GrLe 1m stand

Wreningham

94(105) (69)61

4-y-o br g Diktat-Slave To The Rythm (IRE) (Hamas (IRE))

P Leech (M D Squance 16/9) Mervyn Ayers

Placings:404205264/0022621100-0506506 **(7397)**

2009: 5^{0}GF, 5^{5}GS, 5^{0}G, 6^{6}SD, 5^{5}SD, 5^{0}SD, 5^{6}SD,

	Starts	1st	2nd	3rd	Win & Pl
Career Total (Turf)	7	0	0	0	154
Career Total (AW)	19	2	5	0	9718

69	10/08	GrLe	5f	(0-70)H	STD	£3238
64	9/08	GrLe	5f		STD	£2590

Total win prize-money £5828

Going (Turf): Sf: 0-0 GS: 0-1 Gd: 0-4 GF: 0-2 Fm: 0-0
Distance: **5f/6f: 2-24** 7f-8f: 0-2 9f-13f: 0-0 14f+: 0-0
Track : **LH: 2-15** RH: 0-5 Tight: 0-8 **Gall: 2-6**
Aids: Bl: 0-1 Vi: 0-0 Tstrap: 0-0 Ckp: 0-0
Best Rating: 69 10/08 GrLe 5f stand

Modest; effective over 5f-6f; acts on good ground and Polytrack.

Wrens Hope

91 44

3-y-o ch f Shinko Forest (IRE)-Star Dancer (Groom Dancer (USA))

N Bycroft Mrs J W Pennington P Cozens

Placings:004-6040 **(4596)**

2009: 5^{6}F, 6^{0}GS, 5^{4}GF, 5^{0}G,

	Starts	1st	2nd	3rd	Win & Pl
Career Total (Turf)	7	0	0	0	289

Going (Turf): Sf: 0-2 GS: 0-2 Gd: 0-1 GF: 0-1 Fm: 0-1
Distance: 5f/6f: 0-7 7f-8f: 0-0 9f-13f: 0-0 14f+: 0-0
Track : LH: 0-1 RH: 0-0 Tight: 0-1 Gall: 0-0
Aids: Bl: 0-0 Vi: 0-0 Tstrap: 0-0 Ckp: 0-0
Best Rating: 44 9/08 Bevl 5f soft

Moderate; effective at 5f; handles fast ground.

Wriggle (IRE)

92(85) (62)75

2-y-o b g Refuse To Bend (IRE)-Isana (JPN) (Sunday Silence (USA))

W J Haggas Findlay & Bloom

Placings:366 **(6493)**

2009: 7^{3}GF, 7^{6}SD, 5^{6}SF,

	Starts	1st	2nd	3rd	Win & Pl
Career Total (Turf)	1	0	0	1	506
Career Total (AW)	2	0	0	0	0

Going (Turf): Sf: 0-0 GS: 0-0 Gd: 0-0 GF: 0-1 Fm: 0-0
Distance: 5f/6f: 0-1 7f-8f: 0-2 9f-13f: 0-0 14f+: 0-0
Track : LH: 0-3 RH: 0-0 Tight: 0-2 Gall: 0-0
Aids: Bl: 0-0 Vi: 0-0 Tstrap: 0-1 Ckp: 0-1
Best Rating: 75 7/09 Wwck 7f26y gd-fm

Wrighty Almighty (IRE)

98(103) (76)76

7-y-o b g Danehill Dancer (IRE)-Persian Empress (IRE) (Persian Bold)

P R Chamings The Boccy Hall Evans Tyrrell Partnership

Placings:11450/00044000/02205212135 01/21230020364 2060-4003045 **(2807)**

2009: 8^{4}SD, 10^{0}SD, 8^{0}SD, 7^{3}F, 6^{0}GF, 6^{4}GS, 7^{5}G,

	Starts	1st	2nd	3rd	Win & Pl
Career Total (Turf)	27	4	6	2	23357
Career Total (AW)	21	2	2	2	7035

72	1/08	Kemp	1m	(0-75)H	STD	£2590
70	12/07	Ling	1m	(0-60)H	STD	£2137
70	9/07	Chep	1m14y	(0-65)H	G-F	£2590
64	8/07	Brig	7f214y	(0-60)H	FRM	£1943
85	6/05	NmkJ	6f	(0-85)H	GD	£6812
76	6/05	Donc	6f		G-F	£4251

Total win prize-money £20325

Going (Turf): Sf: 0-0 GS: 0-4 Gd: 1-8 **GF: 2-11** Fm: 1-4
Distance: 5f/6f: 2-6 **7f-8f: 3-33** 9f-13f: 1-9 14f+: 0-0
Track : **LH: 2-23** RH: 1-12 **Tight: 1-12** Gall: 0-1
Aids: Bl: 0-1 Vi: 0-0 Tstrap: 0-4 Ckp: 0-4
Best Rating: 85 6/05 NmkJ 6f good

Modest; stays 1m; acts on a sound surface; goes on Polytrack.

Writ (IRE)

(92) (52)60

7-y-o ch g Indian Lodge (IRE)-Carnelly (IRE) (Priolo (USA))

I Semple Clarke Boon

Placings:0020010/041230611451/3101060/000-0 **(0289)**

2009: 7^{0}SD,

	Starts	1st	2nd	3rd	Win & Pl
Career Total (Turf)	7	0	0	0	0
Career Total (AW)	23	7	2	2	26509

82	3/07	Ling	1m		STD	£2184
82	1/07	Wolv	7f32y	(0-85)H	STD	£4857
78	12/06	Wolv	7f32y	(0-75)H	STD	£3238
80	10/06	Wolv	1m141y	(0-70)H	STD	£3886
74	10/06	Wolv	1m141y	(0-65)H	SF	£2730
68	6/06	Ling	1m	(0-65)H	STD	£3238
57	8/05	Wolv	7f32y		STD	£3031

Total win prize-money £23167

Going (Turf): Sf: 0-2 GS: 0-1 Gd: 0-1 GF: 0-3 Fm: 0-0
Distance: 5f/6f: 0-0 **7f-8f: 5-17** 9f-13f: 2-13 14f+: 0-0
Track : **LH: 7-26** RH: 0-3 **Tight: 7-27** Gall: 0-0
Aids: Bl: 0-0 Vi: 0-0 Tstrap: 0-0 Ckp: 0-0
Best Rating: 82 3/07 Ling 1m stand

Fair; effective over 7f-1m; acts on Polytrack.

Wulfrida (IRE)

99 76

2-y-o b f King's Best (USA)-Panna (Polish Precedent (USA))

J R Fanshawe Lord Halifax

Placings:04 **(6921)**

2009: 8^{0}GF, 8^{4}GF,

	Starts	1st	2nd	3rd	Win & Pl
Career Total (Turf)	2	0	0	0	307

Going (Turf): Sf: 0-0 GS: 0-0 Gd: 0-0 GF: 0-2 Fm: 0-0
Distance: 5f/6f: 0-0 7f-8f: 0-1 9f-13f: 0-1 14f+: 0-0
Track : LH: 0-0 RH: 0-0 Tight: 0-0 Gall: 0-0
Aids: Bl: 0-0 Vi: 0-0 Tstrap: 0-0 Ckp: 0-0
Best Rating: 76 10/09 Yarm 1m3y gd-fm

Wulimaster (USA)

94(98) (59)59

6-y-o br g Silver Hawk (USA)-Kamaina (USA) (Mr Prospector (USA))

Miss Paula Hearn (D W Barker 15/7) Miss Paula Hearn

Placings:5/32/5320405006030544/5015662003420 0-045446 **(3974)**

2009: 15^{0}GF, 14^{4}GF, 13^{5}GF, 13^{4}GF, 13^{4}GF, 11^{6}GS,

	Starts	1st	2nd	3rd	Win & Pl
Career Total (Turf)	34	1	3	3	6638
Career Total (AW)	5	0	1	1	1159

59	5/08	Bevl	1m4f16y	(0-55)	GD	£1774

Total win prize-money £1774

Going (Turf): Sf: 0-2 GS: 0-8 **Gd: 1-12** GF: 0-12 Fm: 0-0
Distance: 5f/6f: 0-0 7f-8f: 0-2 **9f-13f: 1-26** 14f+: 0-11
Track : LH: 0-26 **RH: 1-12 Tight: 1-25** Gall: 0-1
Aids: Bl: 0-0 Vi: 0-3 Tstrap: 0-1 Ckp: 0-1
Best Rating: 76 4/07 Pont 1m4f8y good

Moderate; stays 1m4f; acts on a sound surface; also goes on Polytrack; has worn cheekpieces.

Wunder Strike (USA)

103(105) (67)64

3-y-o b g Smart Strike (CAN)-Bishop's Mate (USA) (Lyphard (USA))

J R Boyle Mrs B Powell B Walsh P Hughes C Murphy

Placings:005-**1**42**1**2600000**3111** (7742)
2009: 8^{1}SD, 8^{4}SD, 8^{2}GF, 8^{1}GF, 8^{2}GS, 8^{6}GF, 8^{0}GF, 8^{0}GF, 8^{0}G, 6^{0}G, 7^{0}G, 8^{3}SD, 8^{1}SD, 8^{1}SD, 8^{1}SD,

	Starts	1st	2nd	3rd	Win & Pl
Career Total (Turf)	11	1	2	0	4138
Career Total (AW)	7	4	0	1	7824

66	12/09	Kemp	1m	(0-70)H	STD	£2590
67	12/09	Ling	1m	(0-62)H	STD	£1978
60	11/09	Ling	1m	(0-55)H	STD	£1637
64	4/09	Leic	1m60y	(0-70)H	G-F	£2590
57	3/09	Kemp	1m	(0-45)	STD	£1364

Total win prize-money £10162

Going (Turf): Sf: 0-1 GS: 0-1 Gd: 0-4 **GF: 1-5** Fm: 0-0
Distance: 5f/6f: 0-4 **7f-8f: 4-7** 9f-13f: 1-7 14f+: 0-0
Track : LH: 2-9 **RH: 3-7 Tight: 2-9** Gall: 0-1
Aids: Bl: 0-0 Vi: 0-0 Tstrap: 4-10 Ckp: 4-10
Best Rating: 67 12/09 Ling 1m stand

Modest; effective over 1m; acts on fast ground; goes on Polytrack; has worn cheekpieces.

Wusuul

89(95) (60)68

4-y-o br f Kyllachy-Cartuccia (IRE) (Doyoun)
R A Harris Mrs Ruth M Serrell

Placings:4/30050-035400 (1535)
2009: 9^{0}SD, 9^{3}SF, 8^{5}SD, 8^{4}SD, 7^{0}SD, 6^{0}GF,

	Starts	1st	2nd	3rd	Win & Pl
Career Total (Turf)	7	0	0	1	996
Career Total (AW)	5	0	0	1	754

Going (Turf): Sf: 0-1 GS: 0-0 Gd: 0-1 GF: 0-5 Fm: 0-0
Distance: 5f/6f: 0-0 7f-8f: 0-7 9f-13f: 0-5 14f+: 0-0
Track : LH: 0-7 RH: 0-3 Tight: 0-4 Gall: 0-1
Aids: Bl: 0-5 Vi: 0-0 Tstrap: 0-0 Ckp: 0-0
Best Rating: 69 9/07 Bevl 7f100y gd-fm

Fair; probably effective at a mile.

Wyatt Earp (IRE)

104(99) (91)93

8-y-o b g Piccolo-Tribal Lady (Absalom)
P Salmon Los Bandidos Racing

Placings:046/0100023/02310400660125/4211050/601600 04330/600601604031000-362550065 (5516)
2009: 6^{3}G, 6^{6}G, 5^{2}G, 5^{5}GF, 6^{5}GF, 6^{0}GF, 6^{0}G, 6^{6}GF, 6^{5}GF,

	Starts	1st	2nd	3rd	Win & Pl
Career Total (Turf)	61	8	4	5	115091
Career Total (AW)	5	0	1	1	2728

93	9/08	Ches	6f18y	(0-85)H	G-F	£6476
88	7/08	Rdcr	6f	(0-85)H	GD	£4857
100	5/07	York	6f	(0-100)H	GD	£12954
98	7/06	York	6f	(0-105)H	G-F	£31160
93	7/06	York	6f	(0-95)H	G-F	£9715
90	11/05	Catt	7f	(0-80)H	SFT	£7114
87	6/05	Rdcr	6f	(0-100)H	G-F	£14001
78	5/04	Newb	6f8y	D(0-85)H	GD	£6188

Total win prize-money £92466

Going (Turf): Sf: 1-5 GS: 0-8 Gd: 3-22 **GF: 4-24** Fm: 0-1
Distance: 5f/6f: 5-54 7f-8f: 3-12 9f-13f: 0-0 14f+: 0-0
Track : LH: 2-16 RH: 0-2 **Tight: 2-11** Gall: 0-1
Aids: Bl: 2-13 Vi: 0-0 Tstrap: 0-0 Ckp: 0-0
Best Rating: 100 5/07 York 6f good

Useful; effective over 5f-7f and acts on any ground; has worn blinkers.

Wyeth

(105) (75)67

5-y-o ch g Grand Lodge (USA)-Bordighera (USA) (Alysheba (USA))
G L Moore D R Hunnisett

Placings:6/00/25065**1**5**1**-**1** (0668)
2009: 16^{1}SD,

	Starts	1st	2nd	3rd	Win & Pl
Career Total (Turf)	9	1	1	0	3201
Career Total (AW)	3	2	0	0	4812

75	2/09	Ling	2m	(0-75)H	STD	£2900
70	12/08	Ling	2m	(0-60)H	STD	£1911
64	9/08	Bath	1m5f22y	(0-70)H	SFT	£2623

Total win prize-money £7435

Going (Turf): Sf: 1-3 GS: 0-2 Gd: 0-1 GF: 0-3 Fm: 0-0
Distance: 5f/6f: 0-0 7f-8f: 0-0 9f-13f: 0-8 **14f+: 3-4**
Track : LH: 3-8 RH: 0-3 **Tight: 3-7** Gall: 0-0
Aids: Bl: 1-2 Vi: 0-0 Tstrap: 2-3 Ckp: 2-3
Best Rating: 75 2/09 Ling 2m stand

Modest; brother to top-class middle-distance older horse Grandera, and half-brother to top-class George Washington; stays 2m; acts on Polytrack.

Wymering File (IRE)

100(88) (90)83

4-y-o b f Medecis-Ensenada (IRE) (Sri Pekan (USA))
M J Grassick (Petros Petroutsios 12/8) Costas N Georgiou

Placings:11/2112212**1**-**111**006040 (7382a)
2009: 5^{1}SD, 12^{1}SD, 9^{1}SD, 9^{0}GF, 8^{0}SD, 10^{6}SD, 10^{0}SD, 10^{4}SD, 10^{0}SD,

	Starts	1st	2nd	3rd	Win & Pl
Career Total (Turf)	1	0	0	0	
Career Total (AW)	18	9	4	0	65503

6/09	Mkpl	1m1f		STD	£20412
3/09	Nico	1m4f55y		STD	£11971
1/09	Nico	5f	H	STD	£3723
11/08	Nico	1m3f55y		STD	£9067
9/08	Nico	5f	H	STD	£2819
5/08	Nico	1m		STD	£7351
3/08	Nico	7f110y		STD	£2514
11/07	Nico	6f		STD	£1357
10/07	Nico	5f		STD	£1278

Total win prize-money £60492

Going (Turf): Sf: 0-0 GS: 0-0 Gd: 0-0 GF: 0-1 Fm: 0-0
Distance: 5f/6f: 4-7 7f-8f: 2-3 9f-13f: 3-9 14f+: 0-0
Track : LH: 0-5 RH: 0-1 Tight: 0-2 Gall: 0-0
Aids: Bl: 0-0 Vi: 0-0 Tstrap: 0-0 Ckp: 0-0
Best Rating: 90 11/09 Dund 1m2f150y stand

Useful; formerly the top filly in Cyprus; acts on an artifical surface; effective from 5f to 1m4f.

Wyn Dixie (IRE)

77 18

10-y-o b g Great Commotion (USA)-Duchess Affair (IRE) (Digamist (USA))
B Storey Lifes Good Lads

Placings:6 (4874)
2009: 12^{6}G,

	Starts	1st	2nd	3rd	Win & Pl
Career Total (Turf)	1	0	0	0	0

Going (Turf): Sf: 0-0 GS: 0-0 Gd: 0-1 GF: 0-0 Fm: 0-0
Distance: 5f/6f: 0-0 7f-8f: 0-0 9f-13f: 0-1 14f+: 0-0
Track : LH: 0-0 RH: 0-1 Tight: 0-1 Gall: 0-0
Aids: Bl: 0-0 Vi: 0-0 Tstrap: 0-0 Ckp: 0-0
Best Rating: 18 8/09 Muss 1m4f100y good

Wynberg (IRE)

(103) (73)66

4-y-o b g Danetime (IRE)-Jayzdoll (IRE) (Stravinsky (USA))
Stef Liddiard John Cast & Bill Hinge

Placings:0000**5**0/03**1**1**1**425436600-600 (0661)
2009: 5^{6}SD, 5^{0}SD, 7^{0}SD,

	Starts	1st	2nd	3rd	Win & Pl
Career Total (Turf)	8	0	1	0	1170
Career Total (AW)	15	3	0	2	4953

62	1/08	Kemp	6f	(0-60)H	STD	£1774
56	1/08	Kemp	5f	(0-55)H	STD	£2047

Total win prize-money £3823

Going (Turf): Sf: 0-0 GS: 0-2 Gd: 0-2 GF: 0-4 Fm: 0-0
Distance: 5f/6f: 3-21 7f-8f: 0-2 9f-13f: 0-0 14f+: 0-0
Track : LH: 1-12 **RH: 2-6 Tight: 1-6** Gall: 0-2
Aids: Bl: 0-1 Vi: 0-0 Tstrap: 0-1 Ckp: 0-1
Best Rating: 73 2/08 Ling 6f stand

Modest; stays 6f and acts on Polytrack.

Xaara Star (IRE)

88 56

2-y-o b f Xaar-Bint Kaldoun (IRE) (Kaldoun (FR))
Eve Johnson Houghton Betfair Club ROA

Placings:0604300 (4689)
2009: 5^{0}GF, 6^{6}GF, 6^{0}GF, 5^{4}GF, 5^{3}G, 6^{0}G, 5^{0}G,

	Starts	1st	2nd	3rd	Win & Pl
Career Total (Turf)	7	0	0	1	567

Going (Turf): Sf: 0-0 GS: 0-0 Gd: 0-3 GF: 0-4 Fm: 0-0
Distance: 5f/6f: 0-6 7f-8f: 0-1 9f-13f: 0-0 14f+: 0-0
Track : LH: 0-2 RH: 0-0 Tight: 0-0 Gall: 0-2
Aids: Bl: 0-2 Vi: 0-0 Tstrap: 0-0 Ckp: 0-0
Best Rating: 56 6/09 Sals 6f gd-fm

Plating-class; stays 6f; acts ona sound surface; has worn blinkers.

Xandra (IRE)

35(93) (52)44

4-y-o b f Xaar-Talah (Danehill (USA))
W M Brisbourne Jones & Brisbourne

Placings:03600-000 (1745)
2009: 9^{0}SD, 7^{0}SD, 8^{0}GF,

	Starts	1st	2nd	3rd	Win & Pl
Career Total (Turf)	3	0	0	0	
Career Total (AW)	5	0	0	1	385

Going (Turf): Sf: 0-1 GS: 0-0 Gd: 0-1 GF: 0-1 Fm: 0-0
Distance: 5f/6f: 0-2 7f-8f: 0-4 9f-13f: 0-2 14f+: 0-0
Track : LH: 0-6 RH: 0-0 Tight: 0-2 Gall: 0-3
Aids: Bl: 0-0 Vi: 0-0 Tstrap: 0-0 Ckp: 0-0
Best Rating: 52 10/08 GrLe 1m stand

Xilerator (IRE)

92 73

2-y-o b g Arakan (USA)-Grandel (Owington)
D Nicholls Ian Hewitson

Placings:2 (7167)
2009: 7²S,

	Starts	1st	2nd	3rd	Win & Pl
Career Total (Turf)	1	0	1	0	1156

Going (Turf): Sf: 0-1 GS: 0-0 Gd: 0-0 GF: 0-0 Fm: 0-0
Distance: 5f/6f: 0-0 7f-8f: 0-1 9f-13f: 0-0 14f+: 0-0
Track : LH: 0-1 RH: 0-0 Tight: 0-0 Gall: 0-0
Aids: Bl: 0-0 Vi: 0-0 Tstrap: 0-0 Ckp: 0-0
Best Rating: 73 10/09 Ayr 7f50y soft

Fair debut over 7f on soft ground.

Xpres Maite

101(112) (93)84
6-y-o b g Komaite (USA)-Antonias Melody (Rambo Dancer (CAN))
S R Bowring Charterhouse Holdings Plc

Placings:655115406/4603350466/25110511123000600040-5121042000150563526020 (7759)
2009: 7⁵SS, 6¹SS, 6²SD, 6¹SD, 5⁰SD, 7⁴SD, 6²SD, 7⁰GF, 8⁰G, 7⁰GF, 7¹GF, 8⁵G, 7⁰G, 7⁵SF, 5⁶S, 5³SD, 5⁵SD, 8²SD, 7⁶SD, 8⁰SD, 8²SD, 8⁰SD,

	Starts	1st	2nd	3rd	Win & Pl
Career Total (Turf)	22	2	0	3	7535
Career Total (AW)	38	8	6	1	44785

75	5/09	Yarm	7f3y	(0-70)H	G-F	£2719
92	2/09	Sthl	6f	(0-95)H	STD	£7771
93	1/09	Sthl	6f	(0-85)H	SS	£4857
96	4/08	Wolv	7f32y	(0-75)H	STD	£2590
87	4/08	Sthl	1m	(0-75)H	STD	£2456
74	4/08	Sthl	7f	(0-70)H	GD	£2456
78	1/08	Wolv	7f32y	(0-75)H	STD	£2457
77	1/08	Wolv	7f32y	(0-65)H	STD	£2047
76	7/06	Sthl	6f	(0-70)H	STD	£3886
73	7/06	Wolv	5f216y	(0-65)H	STD	£2730

Total win prize-money £33973

Going (Turf): Sf: 0-3 GS: 0-2 **Gd: 1-7 GF: 1-9** Fm: 0-1
Distance: 5f/6f: 4-19 **7f-8f: 6-32** 9f-13f: 0-9 14f+: 0-0
Track : **LH: 9-42** RH: 0-4 **Tight: 5-16** Gall: 0-3
Aids: Bl: 3-23 **Vi: 5-20** Tstrap: 0-1 Ckp: 0-1
Best Rating: 96 4/08 Wolv 7f32y stand

Useful; suited by 7f-1m and acts on sand; has worn blinkers and a visor.

Xtension (IRE)

111 117
2-y-o br c Xaar-Great Joy (IRE) (Grand Lodge (USA))
C G Cox Brighthelm Racing

Placings:1213 (6849)
2009: 6¹G, 6²GF, 7¹G, 7³G,

	Starts	1st	2nd	3rd	Win & Pl
Career Total (Turf)	4	2	1	1	104353

110	7/09	Gdwd	7f	GD	£45416
82	5/09	Gdwd	6f	GD	£3238

Total win prize-money £48654

Going (Turf): Sf: 0-0 GS: 0-0 **Gd: 2-3** GF: 0-1 Fm: 0-0
Distance: 5f/6f: 1-2 7f-8f: 1-2 9f-13f: 0-0 14f+: 0-0
Track : LH: 0-0 **RH: 1-1** Tight: 0-0 Gall: 0-0
Aids: Bl: 0-0 Vi: 0-0 Tstrap: 0-0 Ckp: 0-0
Best Rating: 117 10/09 NmkR 7f good

Very useful; runner-up in the 2009 Coventry Stakes; won the Group 2 Vintage Stakes and third in the Dewhurst; effective over 6-7f; acts on fast ground.

Xtra Special

94(87) (46)70
3-y-o b f Xaar-Misleading Lady (Warning)
Sir Michael Stoute J M Greetham

Placings:45 (5987)
2009: 10⁴GF, 12⁵SD,

	Starts	1st	2nd	3rd	Win & Pl
Career Total (Turf)	1	0	0	0	385
Career Total (AW)	1	0	0	0	0

Going (Turf): Sf: 0-0 GS: 0-0 Gd: 0-0 GF: 0-1 Fm: 0-0
Distance: 5f/6f: 0-0 7f-8f: 0-0 9f-13f: 0-2 14f+: 0-0
Track : LH: 0-0 RH: 0-1 Tight: 0-0 Gall: 0-0
Aids: Bl: 0-0 Vi: 0-0 Tstrap: 0-0 Ckp: 0-0
Best Rating: 70 5/09 NmkR 1m2f gd-fm

Xtra Torrential (USA)

(96) (77)100
7-y-o b g Torrential (USA)-Offering (USA) (Majestic Light (USA))
D M Simcock The Wight Wons

Placings:14/003/60000/1/00-666 (1316)
2009: 8⁶SD, 7⁶SD, 8⁶SD,

	Starts	1st	2nd	3rd	Win & Pl
Career Total (Turf)	5	1	0	1	13804
Career Total (AW)	11	1	0	0	11218

97	1/07	Wolv	1m141y	SS	£11217
76	9/04	York	7f205y	GD	£9542

Total win prize-money £20760

Going (Turf): Sf: 0-2 GS: 0-1 **Gd: 1-2** GF: 0-0 Fm: 0-0
Distance: 5f/6f: 0-0 7f-8f: 1-11 9f-13f: 1-5 14f+: 0-0
Track : **LH: 2-11** RH: 0-2 Tight: 1-8 Gall: 1-4
Aids: Bl: 0-0 Vi: 0-0 Tstrap: 0-0 Ckp: 0-0
Best Rating: 100 4/06 Leic 7f9y good

Very useful; stays 1m; acts on good ground and on Polytrack.

Xtravaganza (IRE)

76(68) (59)68
4-y-o b f Xaar-Royal Jubilee (IRE) (King's Theatre (IRE))
Jamie Snowden Mrs P De W Johnson

Placings:560050/2051502-0 (5631)
2009: 8⁰GS,

	Starts	1st	2nd	3rd	Win & Pl
Career Total (Turf)	10	1	2	0	4062
Career Total (AW)	4	0	0	0	0

68	7/08	Folk	1m1f149y	(0-70)H	SFT	£2590

Total win prize-money £2590

Going (Turf): **Sf: 1-3** GS: 0-2 Gd: 0-4 GF: 0-1 Fm: 0-0
Distance: 5f/6f: 0-3 7f-8f: 0-4 **9f-13f: 1-7** 14f+: 0-0
Track : LH: 0-4 **RH: 1-5 Tight: 1-2** Gall: 0-4
Aids: Bl: 0-0 Vi: 0-0 Tstrap: 0-0 Ckp: 0-0
Best Rating: 68 10/08 Folk 1m4f soft

Modest; effective at around 1m2f; acts on soft ground; also goes on Polytrack.

Xtreme (IRE)

86(87) (54)51
2-y-o b g Xaar-Emerald Storm (USA) (Diesis)
A Bailey Bridgewater Equine Ltd

Placings:00 (7120)
2009: 8⁰SD, 8⁰GF,

	Starts	1st	2nd	3rd	Win & Pl
Career Total (Turf)	1	0	0	0	
Career Total (AW)	1	0	0	0	

Going (Turf): Sf: 0-0 GS: 0-0 Gd: 0-0 GF: 0-1 Fm: 0-0
Distance: 5f/6f: 0-0 7f-8f: 0-0 9f-13f: 0-2 14f+: 0-0
Track : LH: 0-2 RH: 0-0 Tight: 0-1 Gall: 0-0
Aids: Bl: 0-1 Vi: 0-0 Tstrap: 0-0 Ckp: 0-0
Best Rating: 54 10/09 Wolv 1m141y stand

Ya Boy Sir (IRE)

91(86) (51)59
2-y-o ch c Alhaarth (IRE)-Champs Elysees (USA) (Distant Relative)
N Wilson (I Semple 13/11) David M Roan

Placings:4653602 (7757)
2009: 6⁴GF, 5⁶G, 7⁵GS, 7³G, 6⁶G, 5⁰SD, 6²SD,

	Starts	1st	2nd	3rd	Win & Pl
Career Total (Turf)	5	0	0	1	626
Career Total (AW)	2	0	1	0	605

Going (Turf): Sf: 0-0 GS: 0-1 Gd: 0-3 GF: 0-1 Fm: 0-0
Distance: 5f/6f: 0-4 7f-8f: 0-3 9f-13f: 0-0 14f+: 0-0
Track : LH: 0-2 RH: 0-3 Tight: 0-3 Gall: 0-0
Aids: Bl: 0-0 Vi: 0-0 Tstrap: 0-0 Ckp: 0-0
Best Rating: 59 6/09 Haml 6f5y gd-fm

Moderate; stays 7f and acts on good ground.

Yaa Wayl (IRE)

104 90
2-y-o b g Whipper (USA)-Lidanna (Nicholas (USA))
M A Jarvis Sheikh Ahmed Al Maktoum

Placings:41242 (7013)
2009: 6⁴G, 5¹G, 6²GS, 6⁴GF, 7²GS,

	Starts	1st	2nd	3rd	Win & Pl
Career Total (Turf)	5	1	2	0	12070

81	7/09	Thsk	5f	GD	£4274

Total win prize-money £4274

Going (Turf): Sf: 0-0 GS: 0-2 **Gd: 1-2** GF: 0-1 Fm: 0-0
Distance: **5f/6f: 1-4** 7f-8f: 0-1 9f-13f: 0-0 14f+: 0-0
Track : LH: 0-1 RH: 0-0 Tight: 0-0 Gall: 0-1
Aids: Bl: 0-1 Vi: 0-0 Tstrap: 0-0 Ckp: 0-0
Best Rating: 90 10/09 Donc 7f gd-sft

Useful; stays 7f and acts on most ground; has worn blinkers and a tongue tie.

Yab Adee

(97) (67)58
5-y-o b g Mark Of Esteem (IRE)-Kotdiji (Mtoto)
M P Tregoning M P N Tregoning

Placings:33530/60001-0 (6342)
2009: 12⁰SD,

	Starts	1st	2nd	3rd	Win & Pl
Career Total (Turf)	2	0	0	0	
Career Total (AW)	9	1	0	3	3156

67	11/08	Kemp	1m4f	STD	£2047

Total win prize-money £2047

Going (Turf): Sf: 0-0 GS: 0-1 Gd: 0-0 GF: 0-1 Fm: 0-0
Distance: 5f/6f: 0-0 7f-8f: 0-0 **9f-13f: 1-10** 14f+: 0-1

Track : LH: 0-7 **RH: 1-4** Tight: 0-7 Gall: 0-0
Aids: Bl: 0-0 Vi: 0-0 Tstrap: 0-0 Ckp: 0-0
Best Rating: **67** 11/08 Kemp 1m4f stand

Moderate; stays 1m4f; acts on Polytrack.

Yabtree (IRE)

94(73) (33)**64**
2-y-o b c Clodovil (IRE)-Lorientaise (IRE) (Xaar)
R Charlton James D Wolfensohn

Placings:350 (7326)
2009: 7^{3}G, 8^{5}G, 7^{0}SD,

	Starts	1st	2nd	3rd	Win & Pl
Career Total (Turf)	2	0	0	1	530
Career Total (AW)	1	0	0	0	

Going (Turf): **Sf: 0-0 GS: 0-0 Gd: 0-2 GF: 0-0 Fm: 0-0**
Distance: 5f/6f: 0-0 7f-8f: 0-2 9f-13f: 0-1 14f+: 0-0
Track : LH: 0-1 RH: 0-1 Tight: 0-1 Gall: 0-0
Aids: Bl: 0-0 Vi: 0-0 Tstrap: 0-0 Ckp: 0-0
Best Rating: **64** 9/09 Chep 7f16y good

Modest; stays 7f; acts on good ground.

Yahrab (IRE)

110(109) (114)**109**
4-y-o gr g Dalakhani (IRE)-Loire Valley (IRE) (Sadler's Wells (USA))
Saeed Bin Suroor (M bin Shafya 22/3) Godolphin

Placings:21363/0550111-0020200 (2327)
2009: 10^{0}G, 8^{0}GF, 10^{2}GF, 12^{0}GF, 11^{2}GF, 10^{0}GF, 9^{0}GF,

	Starts	1st	2nd	3rd	Win & Pl
Career Total (Turf)	15	1	3	2	49014
Career Total (AW)	4	3	0	0	41695

114 11/08 Ling 1m2f STD £22708
113 11/08 GrLe 1m2f STD £7771
106 9/08 GrLe 1m2f (0-100)H STD £11215
88 8/07 Newb 7f G-F £5181
Total win prize-money £46877

Going (Turf): Sf: 0-1 GS: 0-1 Gd: 0-3 **GF: 1-10** Fm: 0-0
Distance: 5f/6f: 0-0 7f-8f: 1-7 **9f-13f: 3-12** 14f+: 0-0
Track : **LH: 3-11** RH: 0-3 Tight: 1-4 **Gall: 2-10**
Aids: Bl: 0-0 Vi: 0-0 Tstrap: 0-0 Ckp: 0-0
Best Rating: **114** 11/08 Ling 1m2f stand

Listed class; winner in Listed company and Group placed; stays 1m2f; acts on fast ground; also goes on Polytrack.

Yahwudhee (FR)

74(87) (34)**79**
4-y-o b g Zamindar (USA)-Lady Marshall (FR) (Octagonal (NZ))
M W Easterby (N Wilson 22/7) M W Easterby

Placings:410-60000 (5883)
2009: 5^{6}SD, 6^{0}SD, 6^{0}G, 5^{0}S, 7^{0}SD,

	Starts	1st	2nd	3rd	Win & Pl
Career Total (Turf)	5	1	0	0	3023
Career Total (AW)	3	0	0	0	0

77 5/08 Leic 7f9y G-F £2590
Total win prize-money £2590

Going (Turf): Sf: 0-2 GS: 0-0 Gd: 0-2 **GF: 1-1** Fm: 0-0
Distance: 5f/6f: 0-5 **7f-8f: 1-3** 9f-13f: 0-0 14f+: 0-0
Track : LH: 0-2 RH: 0-0 Tight: 0-1 Gall: 0-0
Aids: Bl: 0-0 Vi: 0-0 Tstrap: 0-0 Ckp: 0-0
Best Rating: **79** 5/08 Newb 7f good

Useful; effective over 7f; acts on fast ground.

Yakama (IRE)

98(97) (62)**61**
4-y-o b g Indian Danehill (IRE)-Working Progress (IRE) (Marju (IRE))
Mrs C A Dunnett Mark Riley

Placings:400/34304403200336424-0006250 (7716)
2009: 8^{0}SD, 10^{0}G, 7^{0}GF, 8^{6}GF, 7^{2}F, 8^{5}G, 7^{0}SD,

	Starts	1st	2nd	3rd	Win & Pl
Career Total (Turf)	18	0	2	5	3676
Career Total (AW)	9	0	1	0	605

Going (Turf): **Sf: 0-2 GS: 0-5 Gd: 0-5 GF: 0-4 Fm: 0-2**
Distance: 5f/6f: 0-0 7f-8f: 0-14 9f-13f: 0-13 14f+: 0-0
Track : LH: 0-17 RH: 0-4 Tight: 0-9 Gall: 0-1
Aids: Bl: 0-12 Vi: 0-1 Tstrap: 0-3 Ckp: 0-3
Best Rating: **62** 12/08 Ling 1m stand

Moderate; effective over 1m-1m2f; acts on fast and soft ground; has worn blinkers/cheekpieces.

Yaldas Girl (USA)

(89) (39)**48**
3-y-o gr/ro f Unbridled's Song (USA)-Marina De Chavon (USA) (Exploit (USA))
J R Best D Gorton

Placings:000-00600 (7324)
2009: 8^{0}SD, 7^{0}SD, 9^{6}SF, 16^{0}SD, 12^{0}SD,

	Starts	1st	2nd	3rd	Win & Pl
Career Total (Turf)	3	0	0	0	
Career Total (AW)	5	0	0	0	0

Going (Turf): **Sf: 0-0 GS: 0-1 Gd: 0-2 GF: 0-0 Fm: 0-0**
Distance: 5f/6f: 0-2 7f-8f: 0-3 9f-13f: 0-2 14f+: 0-1
Track : LH: 0-4 RH: 0-1 Tight: 0-4 Gall: 0-1
Aids: Bl: 0-0 Vi: 0-0 Tstrap: 0-0 Ckp: 0-0
Best Rating: **48** 8/08 Wind 6f gd-sft

Yamal (IRE)

110(106) (108)**115**
4-y-o b g Green Desert (USA)-Pioneer Bride (USA) (Gone West (USA))
Saeed Bin Suroor Godolphin

Placings:1551211310-21213 (2476)
2009: 7^{2}GF, 8^{1}FT, 7^{2}G, 8^{1}G, 8^{3}G,

	Starts	1st	2nd	3rd	Win & Pl
Career Total (Turf)	12	5	3	2	79465
Career Total (AW)	3	2	0	0	48165

115 5/09 York 1m (0-110)H GD £23704
108 2/09 Ndas 1m (90-105)H FST £45833
102 7/08 Gdwd 1m (0-90)H GD £12952
95 7/08 Bath 1m5y (0-80)H GD £6572
95 7/08 Ches 7f122y (0-80)H G-S £5828
85 6/08 Thsk 7f (0-75)H FRM £3885
75 3/08 Ling 6f STD £2331
Total win prize-money £101108

Going (Turf): Sf: 0-1 GS: 1-2 **Gd: 3-6** GF: 0-2 Fm: 1-1
Distance: 5f/6f: 1-1 **7f-8f: 5-12** 9f-13f: 1-2 14f+: 0-0
Track : **LH: 6-10** RH: 1-3 **Tight: 4-5** Gall: 2-4
Aids: Bl: 0-0 Vi: 0-0 Tstrap: 0-0 Ckp: 0-0
Best Rating: **115** 5/09 York 1m good

Smart; effective over 6f-1m; acts on fast and easy ground; also goes on dirt and Polytrack.

Yanbu (USA)

85(61) **45**
4-y-o b f Swain (IRE)-Dufoof (USA) (Kingmambo (USA))
R W Price Future Electrical Services Ltd

Placings:00 (3951)
2009: 8^{0}G, 12^{0}SD,

	Starts	1st	2nd	3rd	Win & Pl
Career Total (Turf)	1	0	0	0	
Career Total (AW)	1	0	0	0	

Going (Turf): **Sf: 0-0 GS: 0-0 Gd: 0-1 GF: 0-0 Fm: 0-0**
Distance: 5f/6f: 0-0 7f-8f: 0-0 9f-13f: 0-2 14f+: 0-0
Track : LH: 0-1 RH: 0-0 Tight: 0-0 Gall: 0-0
Aids: Bl: 0-0 Vi: 0-0 Tstrap: 0-0 Ckp: 0-0
Best Rating: **45** 5/09 Yarm 1m3y good

Yankee Bright (USA)

87 **69**
2-y-o b f Elusive Quality (USA)-Sharp Minister (CAN) (Deputy Minister (CAN))
J G Given Brighton Farm Ltd

Placings:530 (7187)
2009: 8^{5}GF, 8^{3}GS, 8^{0}G,

	Starts	1st	2nd	3rd	Win & Pl
Career Total (Turf)	3	0	0	1	578

Going (Turf): **Sf: 0-0 GS: 0-1 Gd: 0-1 GF: 0-1 Fm: 0-0**
Distance: 5f/6f: 0-0 7f-8f: 0-2 9f-13f: 0-1 14f+: 0-0
Track : LH: 0-2 RH: 0-0 Tight: 0-0 Gall: 0-1
Aids: Bl: 0-0 Vi: 0-0 Tstrap: 0-0 Ckp: 0-0
Best Rating: **69** 9/09 Hayd 1m30y gd-fm

Modest; effective over 1m; acts on easy ground.

Yankee Doodle

113 **115**
3-y-o gr c Dalakhani (IRE)-Bella Lambada (Lammtarra (USA))
A P O'Brien Derrick Smith

Placings:0-221232 (4033a)
2009: 10^{2}GY, 10^{2}G, 11^{1}YS, 16^{2}GF, 14^{3}Y, 14^{2}Y,

	Starts	1st	2nd	3rd	Win & Pl
Career Total (Turf)	7	1	4	1	39789

84 5/09 Wxfd 1m3f160y Y-S £6037
Total win prize-money £6038

Going (Turf): **Sf: 0-0 GS: 0-0 Gd: 0-1 GF: 0-1 Fm: 0-0**
Distance: 5f/6f: 0-0 7f-8f: 0-1 **9f-13f: 1-3** 14f+: 0-3
Track : LH: 0-4 RH: 0-2 Tight: 0-0 Gall: 0-1
Aids: Bl: 0-0 Vi: 0-0 Tstrap: 0-0 Ckp: 0-0
Best Rating: **115** 6/09 Curr 1m6f yield

Very useful; stays 2m; acts on most ground.

Yankee Storm

(102) (78)**62**
4-y-o b g Yankee Gentleman (USA)-Yes Virginia (USA) (Roanoke (USA))
H J Collingridge (M Quinn 3/9) Greenstead Hall Racing Ltd

Placings:5004221/156102350500-0532362030 (7738)
2009: 7^{0}SD, 6^{5}SD, 6^{3}SD, 6^{2}SD, 5^{3}SD, 5^{6}SD, 7^{2}SD, 7^{0}SD, 6^{3}SD, 6^{0}SD,

	Starts	1st	2nd	3rd	Win & Pl
Career Total (Turf)	5	0	0	0	0
Career Total (AW)	24	3	5	4	14208

77	5/08	GrLe	5f	(0-75)H	STD	£2590
73	1/08	Sthl	6f	(0-65)H	STD	£1911
67	12/07	Sthl	6f	(0-65)	SS	£2047

Total win prize-money £6549

Going (Turf): Sf: 0-0 GS: 0-0 Gd: 0-0 GF: 0-5 Fm: 0-0
Distance: **5f/6f: 3-19** 7f-8f: 0-8 9f-13f: 0-2 14f+: 0-0
Track : **LH: 3-20** RH: 0-4 Tight: 0-9 **Gall: 1-6**
Aids: Bl: 0-0 Vi: 0-0 Tstrap: 0-2 Ckp: 0-2
Best Rating: 78 6/08 GrLe 6f stand

Modest; effective over 6f-7f; acts on Polytrack and Fibresand.

Yanza

91(100) (68)70
3-y-o b f Bahamian Bounty-Locharia (Wolfhound (USA))
J R Gask Horses First Racing Limited

Placings:423-100004223000 (7852)
2009: 5^{1}SD, 5^{0}GF, 6^{0}GF, 6^{0}SD, 6^{0}SD, 5^{4}SD, 5^{2}SD, 5^{2}SD, 6^{3}SD, 5^{0}SD, 5^{0}SD, 5^{0}SS,

	Starts	1st	2nd	3rd	Win & Pl
Career Total (Turf)	5	0	1	1	1565
Career Total (AW)	10	1	2	1	4001
67 4/09 Kemp 5f			STD		£2590

Total win prize-money £2590

Going (Turf): Sf: 0-1 GS: 0-2 Gd: 0-0 GF: 0-2 Fm: 0-0
Distance: **5f/6f: 1-14** 7f-8f: 0-1 9f-13f: 0-0 14f+: 0-0
Track : LH: 0-10 **RH: 1-2** Tight: 0-7 Gall: 0-3
Aids: Bl: 0-6 Vi: 0-0 Tstrap: 0-0 Ckp: 0-0
Best Rating: 70 8/08 Bath 5f11y gd-sft

Modest; effective over 5f; acts on soft ground and on Polytrack; has worn blinkers.

Yarra River

96 79
2-y-o b/br g Dr Fong (USA)-River Cara (USA) (Irish River (FR))
A M Balding David Brownlow

Placings:23220 (6478)
2009: 6^{2}GF, 7^{3}G, 7^{2}S, 7^{2}GF, 7^{0}GF,

	Starts	1st	2nd	3rd	Win & Pl
Career Total (Turf)	5	0	3	1	6136

Going (Turf): Sf: 0-1 GS: 0-0 Gd: 0-1 GF: 0-3 Fm: 0-0
Distance: 5f/6f: 0-1 7f-8f: 0-4 9f-13f: 0-0 14f+: 0-0
Track : LH: 0-1 RH: 0-1 Tight: 0-1 Gall: 0-1
Aids: Bl: 0-0 Vi: 0-0 Tstrap: 0-0 Ckp: 0-0
Best Rating: 79 8/09 Gdwd 7f soft

Useful; effective over 7f; acts on fast and soft ground.

Yashkur

86(84) (31)51
3-y-o ch f Needwood Blade-Silent Tribute (IRE) (Lion Cavern (USA))
C E Brittain Saeed Manana

Placings:660000 (6223)
2009: 10^{6}GF, 6^{6}GF, 9^{0}GS, 8^{0}GF, 8^{0}SD, 8^{0}SD,

	Starts	1st	2nd	3rd	Win & Pl
Career Total (Turf)	4	0	0	0	0
Career Total (AW)	2	0	0	0	

Going (Turf): Sf: 0-0 GS: 0-1 Gd: 0-0 GF: 0-3 Fm: 0-0
Distance: 5f/6f: 0-0 7f-8f: 0-4 9f-13f: 0-2 14f+: 0-0
Track : LH: 0-3 RH: 0-1 Tight: 0-2 Gall: 0-1
Aids: Bl: 0-0 Vi: 0-0 Tstrap: 0-0 Ckp: 0-0
Best Rating: 51 5/09 Newc 1m2f32y gd-fm

Yawary

96(91) (57)64
2-y-o b f Medicean-Sociable (Danehill (USA))
C E Brittain Saeed Manana

Placings:04205466 (5934)
2009: 6^{0}GF, 6^{4}G, 5^{2}GF, 6^{0}G, 7^{5}GS, 5^{4}SD, 8^{6}SD, 5^{6}GF,

	Starts	1st	2nd	3rd	Win & Pl
Career Total (Turf)	6	0	1	0	1250
Career Total (AW)	2	0	0	0	289

Going (Turf): Sf: 0-0 GS: 0-1 Gd: 0-2 GF: 0-3 Fm: 0-0
Distance: 5f/6f: 0-5 7f-8f: 0-3 9f-13f: 0-0 14f+: 0-0
Track : LH: 0-2 RH: 0-1 Tight: 0-1 Gall: 0-0
Aids: Bl: 0-0 Vi: 0-0 Tstrap: 0-0 Ckp: 0-0
Best Rating: 64 6/09 Brig 5f213y gd-fm

Modest; effective over 5f-7f; acts on fast ground.

Yeadon

90(93) (71)76
2-y-o b c Fraam-Harryana (Efisio)
R A Fahey A Rhodes Haulage And P Timmins

Placings:3224444426 (7805)
2009: 6^{3}GS, 5^{2}GF, 5^{2}SD, 6^{4}GF, 5^{4}SD, 5^{4}GF, 5^{4}SF, 5^{4}SD, 6^{2}SD, 6^{6}SD,

	Starts	1st	2nd	3rd	Win & Pl
Career Total (Turf)	4	0	1	1	2128
Career Total (AW)	6	0	2	0	2251

Going (Turf): Sf: 0-0 GS: 0-1 Gd: 0-0 GF: 0-3 Fm: 0-0
Distance: 5f/6f: 0-10 7f-8f: 0-0 9f-13f: 0-0 14f+: 0-0
Track : LH: 0-5 RH: 0-1 Tight: 0-4 Gall: 0-1
Aids: Bl: 0-1 Vi: 0-0 Tstrap: 0-0 Ckp: 0-0
Best Rating: 76 6/09 Carl 5f gd-fm

Modest; effective over 5f-6f; acts on easy ground and on Fibresand and Polytrack.

Yeah

73(84) (43)54
2-y-o b g Gentleman's Deal (IRE)-Snugfit Dubarry (Ali-Royal (IRE))
Patrick Morris Chester Racing Club Ltd

Placings:46400 (6610)
2009: 5^{4}G, 6^{6}G, 6^{4}G, 5^{0}SD, 6^{0}SD,

	Starts	1st	2nd	3rd	Win & Pl
Career Total (Turf)	3	0	0	0	722
Career Total (AW)	2	0	0	0	

Going (Turf): Sf: 0-0 GS: 0-0 Gd: 0-3 GF: 0-0 Fm: 0-0
Distance: 5f/6f: 0-4 7f-8f: 0-1 9f-13f: 0-0 14f+: 0-0
Track : LH: 0-0 RH: 0-1 Tight: 0-0 Gall: 0-0
Aids: Bl: 0-0 Vi: 0-0 Tstrap: 0-0 Ckp: 0-0
Best Rating: 54 7/09 Ffos 6f good

Moderate; will stay 6f; acts on a sound surface.

Yeats (IRE)

115 126
8-y-o b h Sadler's Wells (USA)-Lyndonville (IRE) (Top Ville)
A P O'Brien Mrs John Magnier & Mrs David Nagle

Placings:1/11/21046/1120/11113/11151-6103 (6527a)
2009: 13^{6}S, 20^{1}GF, 14^{0}S, 20^{3}G,

	Starts	1st	2nd	3rd	Win & Pl
Career Total (Turf)	26	15	2	2	1317179

125	6/09	Asct	2m4f	G-F	£141925
117	10/08	Lonc	1m7f110y	G-S	£105037
126	7/08	Gdwd	2m	G-F	£56770
124	6/08	Asct	2m4f	G-F	£141925
113	4/08	Navn	1m5f	G-Y	£23933
122	9/07	Curr	1m6f	G-F	£115945
122	6/07	Asct	2m4f	G-F	£127755
122	5/07	Leop	1m6f	G-F	£28591
124	4/07	Navn	1m5f	FRM	£21993
126	8/06	Gdwd	2m	G-F	£56780
122	6/06	Asct	2m4f	G-F	£136953
124	6/05	Epsm	1m4f10y	GD	£145000
111	5/04	Leop	1m2f	G-Y	£60563
117	4/04	Leop	1m2f	SFT	£34063
94	9/03	Curr	1m	G-F	£8441

Total win prize-money £1205677

Going (Turf): Sf: 1-4 GS: 1-3 Gd: 1-6 **GF: 9-9** Fm: 1-1
Distance: 5f/6f: 0-0 7f-8f: 1-1 9f-13f: 5-9 **14f+: 9-16**
Track : LH: 6-10 **RH: 9-16** Tight: 3-3 **Gall: 5-5**
Aids: Bl: 0-0 Vi: 0-0 Tstrap: 0-0 Ckp: 0-0
Best Rating: 126 7/08 Gdwd 2m gd-fm

Top-class stayer; winner of the 2005 Coronation Cup; four-time Ascot Gold Cup winner 2006-2009; won the Goodwood Cup in 2006 and 2008, the Irish St Leger in 2007 and Prix Royal-Oak in 2008; effective from 1m4f-2m4f; acts on most ground.

Yellow Printer

101(101) (76)77
3-y-o b g Royal Applause-Robsart (IRE) (Robellino (USA))
F J Brennan (Tom Dascombe 9/6) Seasons Holidays

Placings:521-0334230603 (7456)
2009: 8^{0}SD, 8^{3}GF, 8^{3}F, 8^{4}GF, 6^{2}GF, 8^{3}GF, 8^{0}G, 8^{6}SS, 8^{0}SD, 8^{3}SD,

	Starts	1st	2nd	3rd	Win & Pl
Career Total (Turf)	7	0	1	3	3491
Career Total (AW)	6	1	1	1	3982
76 12/08 Ling 7f			STD		£2729

Total win prize-money £2730

Going (Turf): Sf: 0-0 GS: 0-1 Gd: 0-1 GF: 0-4 Fm: 0-1
Distance: 5f/6f: 0-1 **7f-8f: 1-8** 9f-13f: 0-4 14f+: 0-0
Track : **LH: 1-6** RH: 0-4 **Tight: 1-4** Gall: 0-1
Aids: Bl: 0-0 Vi: 0-1 Tstrap: 0-0 Ckp: 0-0
Best Rating: 77 5/09 Wwck 1m22y firm

Fair; effective over 7f-1m; acts on fast ground; goes on Polytrack; has worn a visor.

Yellow Ridge (IRE)

(81) (32)48
6-y-o ch g On The Ridge (IRE)-Jonathan's Rose (IRE) (Law Society (USA))
Luke Comer Luke Comer

Placings:0044100000/0000005/560-00 (6917)
2009: 16^{0}SD, 12^{0}SD,

	Starts	1st	2nd	3rd	Win & Pl
Career Total (Turf)	18	1	0	0	9842
Career Total (AW)	4	0	0	0	
69 8/06 Gway 7f			G-Y		£8979

Total win prize-money £8979

Going (Turf): Sf: 0-2 GS: 0-0 Gd: 0-2 GF: 0-8 Fm: 0-2

Distance:	5f/6f: 0-0 **7f-8f: 1-9** 9f-13f: 0-11 14f+: 0-2
Track :	LH: 0-10 **RH: 1-11** Tight: 0-4 Gall: 0-0
Aids:	Bl: 0-2 Vi: 0-0 Tstrap: 0-0 Ckp: 0-0
Best Rating:	**82** 4/07 Curr 1m2f gd-fm

Yellow River (USA)

87(89) (44)**68**

3-y-o ch f Johannesburg (USA)-Ascension (IRE) (Night Shift (USA))

E J Creighton (S A Callaghan 8/1) Travel Spot LLP

Placings:33400-**2005**00000 **(6340)**

2009: 7^{2}SD, 6^{0}SD, 7^{0}SD, 8^{5}SD, 6^{0}G, 7^{0}S, 5^{0}G, 6^{0}G, 5^{0}GF,

	Starts	1st	2nd	3rd	Win & Pl
Career Total (Turf)	9	0	0	2	3860
Career Total (AW)	5	0	1	0	605

Going (Turf):	**Sf: 0-1 GS: 0-3 Gd: 0-4 GF: 0-1 Fm: 0-0**
Distance:	5f/6f: 0-5 7f-8f: 0-9 9f-13f: 0-0 14f+: 0-0
Track :	LH: 0-7 RH: 0-0 Tight: 0-2 Gall: 0-1
Aids:	Bl: 0-1 Vi: 0-0 Tstrap: 0-0 Ckp: 0-0
Best Rating:	**68** 8/08 Buch 7f gd-sft

Modest; ex-French; effective at around 7f; acts on easy ground.

Yellowstone (IRE)

104 **116**

5-y-o b h Rock Of Gibraltar (IRE)-Love And Affection (USA) (Exclusive Era (USA))

P F I Cole Mrs Fitri Hay

Placings:103/5020341260/005130-640402 **(7038a)**

2009: 13^{6}S, 14^{4}GF, 12^{0}GF, 12^{4}G, 12^{0}GS, 14^{2}VS,

	Starts	1st	2nd	3rd	Win & Pl
Career Total (Turf)	25	3	3	3	197519
116 7/08 York 1m6f	(0-110)H			HVY	£24978
108 7/07 Gdwd 1m4f				GD	£28390
70 7/06 Cork 1m				FRM	£8979

Total win prize-money £62348

Going (Turf):	**Sf: 1-2** GS: 0-6 **Gd: 1-6** GF: 0-7 **Fm: 1-2**
Distance:	5f/6f: 0-0 7f-8f: 1-5 9f-13f: 1-14 14f+: 1-6
Track :	LH: 1-11 **RH: 2-11** Tight: 1-2 Gall: 1-12
Aids:	Bl: 0-1 Vi: 0-0 Tstrap: 1-7 Ckp: 1-7
Best Rating:	**118** 7/07 Sand 1m2f7y gd-sft

Very useful; winner of the Group 3 Gordon Stakes in 2007 for Aidan O'Brien and regularly placed in top company; stays 1m6f, but effective at shorter; acts on most ground; has worn blinkers and cheekpieces.

Yeoman Of England (IRE)

91(87) (64)**64**

3-y-o b g Pyrus (USA)-Regal Lustre (Averti (IRE))

C F Wall Hintlesham Thoroughbreds

Placings:04403-0000405 **(6919)**

2009: 7^{0}GF, 7^{0}G, 6^{0}GS, 8^{0}G, 10^{4}GF, 9^{0}GF, 11^{5}GF,

	Starts	1st	2nd	3rd	Win & Pl
Career Total (Turf)	11	0	0	0	313
Career Total (AW)	1	0	0	1	404

Going (Turf):	**Sf: 0-2 GS: 0-2 Gd: 0-3 GF: 0-4 Fm: 0-0**
Distance:	5f/6f: 0-0 7f-8f: 0-7 9f-13f: 0-5 14f+: 0-0
Track :	LH: 0-6 RH: 0-3 Tight: 0-5 Gall: 0-0
Aids:	Bl: 0-1 Vi: 0-0 Tstrap: 0-0 Ckp: 0-0
Best Rating:	**64** 10/08 Wolv 7f32y stand

Modest; effective over 1m; acts on soft ground and on Polytrack.

Yer Woman (IRE)

94(101) (89)**81**

2-y-o b f Kyllachy-Genny Lim (IRE) (Barathea (IRE))

R Hannon Exors Of The Late Mrs R McArdle

Placings:2101041 **(7536)**

2009: 5^{2}GF, 5^{1}G, 6^{0}G, 5^{1}GF, 6^{0}GF, 6^{4}GF, 6^{1}SD,

	Starts	1st	2nd	3rd	Win & Pl
Career Total (Turf)	6	2	1	0	8534
Career Total (AW)	1	1	0	0	3886
89 11/09 Kemp 6f	(0-90)			STD	£3885
81 7/09 Sand 5f6y				GF	£3238
74 5/09 Wind 5f10y				GD	£3885

Total win prize-money £11010

Going (Turf):	Sf: 0-0 GS: 0-0 **Gd: 1-2 GF: 1-4** Fm: 0-0
Distance:	**5f/6f: 3-6** 7f-8f: 0-1 9f-13f: 0-0 14f+: 0-0
Track :	LH: 0-2 **RH: 1-1** Tight: 0-0 **Gall: 1-2**
Aids:	Bl: 0-0 Vi: 0-0 Tstrap: 0-0 Ckp: 0-0
Best Rating:	**89** 11/09 Kemp 6f stand

Useful; effective over 5f-6f; acts on fast ground and on Polytrack.

Yes Chef

92 **62**

2-y-o ch c Best Of The Bests (IRE)-Lady Chef (Double Trigger (IRE))

J Gallagher Coombeshead Racing

Placings:04 **(6990)**

2009: 8^{0}G, 7^{4}G,

	Starts	1st	2nd	3rd	Win & Pl
Career Total (Turf)	2	0	0	0	337

Going (Turf):	**Sf: 0-0 GS: 0-0 Gd: 0-2 GF: 0-0 Fm: 0-0**
Distance:	5f/6f: 0-0 7f-8f: 0-1 9f-13f: 0-1 14f+: 0-0
Track :	LH: 0-0 RH: 0-1 Tight: 0-0 Gall: 0-0
Aids:	Bl: 0-0 Vi: 0-0 Tstrap: 0-0 Ckp: 0-0
Best Rating:	**62** 10/09 Donc 7f good

Yes Maggie (IRE)

71 **42**

2-y-o b f Vindication (USA)-Westerly Gale (USA) (Gone West (USA))

M R Channon Liam Mulryan

Placings:0 **(6108)**

2009: 7^{0}GF,

	Starts	1st	2nd	3rd	Win & Pl
Career Total (Turf)	1	0	0	0	

Going (Turf):	**Sf: 0-0 GS: 0-0 Gd: 0-0 GF: 0-1 Fm: 0-0**
Distance:	5f/6f: 0-0 7f-8f: 0-1 9f-13f: 0-0 14f+: 0-0
Track :	LH: 0-0 RH: 0-0 Tight: 0-0 Gall: 0-0
Aids:	Bl: 0-0 Vi: 0-0 Tstrap: 0-0 Ckp: 0-0
Best Rating:	**42** 9/09 Newb 7f gd-fm

Yes Mr President (IRE)

109(96) (82)**106**

4-y-o b g Montjeu (IRE)-Royals Special (IRE) (Caerleon (USA))

M Johnston T J Monaghan

Placings:5/410403-412042310 **(6851)**

2009: 12^{4}GS, 14^{1}G, 11^{2}GF, 11^{0}GF, 14^{4}G, 16^{2}GS, 12^{3}GF, 14^{1}S, 18^{0}G,

	Starts	1st	2nd	3rd	Win & Pl
Career Total (Turf)	13	2	2	2	77939
Career Total (AW)	3	1	0	0	2457
106 9/09 Hayd 1m6f	(0-105)H			SFT	£48570
93 6/09 Gdwd 1m6f	(0-100)H			GD	£11215
82 2/08 Wolv 1m1f103y				STD	£2457

Total win prize-money £62243

Going (Turf):	**Sf: 1-1** GS: 0-2 **Gd: 1-4** GF: 0-6 Fm: 0-0
Distance:	5f/6f: 0-0 7f-8f: 0-2 9f-13f: 1-9 **14f+: 2-5**
Track :	**LH: 2-8** RH: 1-8 **Tight: 2-5** Gall: 0-6
Aids:	Bl: 0-2 Vi: 0-0 Tstrap: 0-0 Ckp: 0-0
Best Rating:	**106** 9/09 Hayd 1m6f soft

Very useful; stays 1m6f; acts on most ground; goes on Polytrack; has worn blinkers.

Yes One (IRE)

(106) (78)**87**

5-y-o ch g Peintre Celebre (USA)-Copious (IRE) (Generous (IRE))

K A Ryan Mrs J Ryan

Placings:00521406**6**/132214-06554 **(1409)**

2009: 7^{0}SS, 8^{6}SD, 7^{5}SD, 8^{5}SD, 9^{4}SD,

	Starts	1st	2nd	3rd	Win & Pl
Career Total (Turf)	8	2	2	0	11608
Career Total (AW)	12	1	1	1	3780
87 5/08 Thsk 7f	(0-85)H			GD	£5180
78 2/08 Wolv 1m141y	(0-75)H			STD	£2590
74 6/07 Ches 1m2f75y	(0-70)H			GD	£3562

Total win prize-money £11334

Going (Turf):	Sf: 0-1 GS: 0-3 **Gd: 2-2** GF: 0-2 Fm: 0-0
Distance:	5f/6f: 0-0 7f-8f: 1-7 **9f-13f: 2-13** 14f+: 0-0
Track :	**LH: 3-14** RH: 0-6 **Tight: 3-13** Gall: 0-1
Aids:	Bl: 0-0 Vi: 0-0 Tstrap: 0-0 Ckp: 0-0
Best Rating:	**87** 5/08 Thsk 7f good

Fair; stays 1m2f but fully effective over much shorter; acts on fast ground and Polytrack.

Yes Please

88(95) (42)**56**

4-y-o b g Efisio-Shall We Dance (Rambo Dancer (CAN))

K A Ryan Guy Reed

Placings:00300 **(5842)**

2009: 6^{0}SD, 7^{0}G, 6^{3}S, 7^{0}S, 7^{0}SD,

	Starts	1st	2nd	3rd	Win & Pl
Career Total (Turf)	3	0	0	1	403
Career Total (AW)	2	0	0	0	

Going (Turf):	**Sf: 0-2 GS: 0-0 Gd: 0-1 GF: 0-0 Fm: 0-0**
Distance:	5f/6f: 0-1 7f-8f: 0-4 9f-13f: 0-0 14f+: 0-0
Track :	LH: 0-4 RH: 0-0 Tight: 0-2 Gall: 0-0
Aids:	Bl: 0-0 Vi: 0-1 Tstrap: 0-0 Ckp: 0-0
Best Rating:	**56** 8/09 Haml 6f5y soft

Yes She Can Can

72(86) (34)

3-y-o ch f Monsieur Bond (IRE)-Antonia's Folly (Music Boy)

Peter Grayson Peter Grayson Racing Clubs Limited

Placings:000-04000 **(1064)**

2009: 5^{0}SD, 5^{4}SD, 5^{0}SD, 5^{0}SD, 5^{0}GF,

	Starts	1st	2nd	3rd	Win & Pl
Career Total (Turf)	1	0	0	0	
Career Total (AW)	7	0	0	0	0

Going (Turf): Sf: 0-0 GS: 0-0 Gd: 0-0 GF: 0-1 Fm: 0-0
Distance: 5f/6f: 0-8 7f-8f: 0-0 9f-13f: 0-0 14f+: 0-0
Track : LH: 0-5 RH: 0-1 Tight: 0-5 Gall: 0-0
Aids: Bl: 0-2 Vi: 0-0 Tstrap: 0-0 Ckp: 0-0
Best Rating: 34 11/08 Wolv 5f20y stand

Yesnabay (USA)

97 86

2-y-o b/br g Grand Slam (USA)-Speedy Sonata (USA) (Stravinsky (USA))
Larry Rivelli (G A Swinbank 20/7) Richard Ravin

Placings:310
2009: 5^3GF, 6^1G, 8^0F,

	Starts	1st	2nd	3rd	Win & Pl
Career Total (Turf)	3	1	0	1	5648
86 7/09 Ayr 6f			GD	£5018	

Total win prize-money £5019

Going (Turf): Sf: 0-0 GS: 0-0 **Gd: 1-1** GF: 0-1 Fm: 0-1
Distance: **5f/6f: 1-2** 7f-8f: 0-1 9f-13f: 0-0 14f+: 0-0
Track : LH: 0-1 RH: 0-0 Tight: 0-0 Gall: 0-0
Aids: Bl: 0-0 Vi: 0-0 Tstrap: 0-0 Ckp: 0-0
Best Rating: 86 7/09 Ayr 6f good

Useful' stays 6f; acts on good ground.

Yirga

102(87) (76)87

3-y-o b c Cape Cross (IRE)-Auratum (USA) (Carson City (USA))
Saeed Bin Suroor Godolphin

Placings:23-31120 (4794)
2009: 8^3HY, 8^1G, 8^1G, 9^2GF, 10^0G,

	Starts	1st	2nd	3rd	Win & Pl
Career Total (Turf)	6	2	2	1	13828
Career Total (AW)	1	0	0	1	626
87 6/09 Thsk 1m (0-85)H				GD	£5569
86 6/09 Sand 1m14y (0-85)H				GD	£5180

Total win prize-money £10750

Going (Turf): Sf: 0-2 GS: 0-0 **Gd: 2-3** GF: 0-1 Fm: 0-0
Distance: 5f/6f: 0-0 7f-8f: 1-3 9f-13f: 1-4 14f+: 0-0
Track : LH: 1-2 RH: 1-4 **Tight: 1-2** Gall: 0-1
Aids: Bl: 0-0 Vi: 0-0 Tstrap: 0-0 Ckp: 0-0
Best Rating: 87 6/09 Thsk 1m good

Useful; suited by 1m-1m2f; acts on good and softer ground and on Polytrack; has worn a tongue tie.

Ykikamoocow

96 68

3-y-o b f Cape Town (IRE)-Pigeon (Casteddu)
G A Harker Mrs Eve Sweetman & Paul Benson

Placings:14053-10503 (6984)
2009: 7^1G, 7^0G, 8^5G, 7^0GF, 7^3G,

	Starts	1st	2nd	3rd	Win & Pl
Career Total (Turf)	10	2	0	2	5949
68 6/09 Catt 7f (0-75)H				GD	£2914
66 4/08 Catt 5f				G-S	£2047

Total win prize-money £4961

Going (Turf): Sf: 0-0 **GS: 1-2 Gd: 1-7** GF: 0-1 Fm: 0-0
Distance: 5f/6f: 1-4 7f-8f: 1-6 9f-13f: 0-0 14f+: 0-0
Track : **LH: 1-5** RH: 0-0 **Tight: 1-3** Gall: 0-0
Aids: Bl: 0-0 Vi: 0-0 Tstrap: 0-0 Ckp: 0-0
Best Rating: 68 6/09 Catt 7f good

Fair; stays 7f and handles easy ground.

Ymir

98(99) (65)58

3-y-o b c Zaha (CAN)-Anastasia Venture (Lion Cavern (USA))
M J Attwater Canisbay Bloodstock

Placings:465-0003300200246 (7693)
2009: 8^0SD, 8^0G, 7^0G, 8^3G, 7^3GF, 8^0GS, 8^0SD, 7^2SD, 8^0SD, 7^0SD, 8^7SD, 8^4SD, 8^6SD,

	Starts	1st	2nd	3rd	Win & Pl
Career Total (Turf)	5	0	0	2	915
Career Total (AW)	11	0	2	0	1477

Going (Turf): **Sf: 0-0 GS: 0-1 Gd: 0-3 GF: 0-1 Fm: 0-0**
Distance: 5f/6f: 0-0 7f-8f: 0-15 9f-13f: 0-1 14f+: 0-0
Track : LH: 0-6 RH: 0-9 Tight: 0-5 Gall: 0-0
Aids: Bl: 0-0 Vi: 0-0 Tstrap: 0-6 Ckp: 0-6
Best Rating: 65 12/08 Ling 1m stand

Moderate; effective over 1m; acts on Polytrack.

Yogaroo (USA)

70 (90)59

2-y-o ch g Bring The Heat (USA)-Harper N Abbey (USA) (Outflanker (USA))
Wesley A Ward Brewer Racing Stable And Wesley A Ward

Placings:2100 (3046)
2009: 2^2FT, 4^1FT, 5^0GF, 6^0FT,

	Starts	1st	2nd	3rd	Win & Pl
Career Total (Turf)	1	0	0	0	
Career Total (AW)	3	1	1	0	24292
90 4/09 Keen 4f110y			FST	£18944	

Total win prize-money £18944

Going (Turf): **Sf: 0-0 GS: 0-0 Gd: 0-0 GF: 0-1 Fm: 0-0**
Distance: 5f/6f: 0-2 7f-8f: 0-0 9f-13f: 0-0 14f+: 0-0
Track : LH: 0-0 RH: 0-0 Tight: 0-0 Gall: 0-0
Aids: **Bl: 1-4** Vi: 0-0 Tstrap: 0-0 Ckp: 0-0
Best Rating: 90 4/09 Keen 4f110y fast

Yonder

105(92) (45)72

5-y-o br m And Beyond (IRE)-Dominance (Dominion)
H Morrison The Champagne Elite Partnership

Placings:03-43011000 (5802)
2009: 12^4SF, 17^3GF, 21^0F, 12^1GF, 14^1GF, 16^0GF, 12^0GF, 12^0GF,

	Starts	1st	2nd	3rd	Win & Pl
Career Total (Turf)	9	2	0	2	7319
Career Total (AW)	1	0	0	0	0
72 6/09 Ling 1m6f (0-70)H				G-F	£3238
67 6/09 Sals 1m4f (0-75)H				G-F	£3238

Total win prize-money £6476

Going (Turf): Sf: 0-0 GS: 0-0 Gd: 0-1 **GF: 2-7** Fm: 0-1
Distance: 5f/6f: 0-0 7f-8f: 0-0 9f-13f: 1-6 14f+: 1-4
Track : LH: 1-6 RH: 1-4 **Tight: 2-7** Gall: 0-1
Aids: Bl: 0-2 Vi: 0-0 Tstrap: 0-0 Ckp: 0-0
Best Rating: 72 6/09 Ling 1m6f gd-fm

Modest; bumper winner; stays 1m6f; acts on fast ground.

Yorgunnabelucky (USA)

103 89

3-y-o b c Giant's Causeway (USA)-Helsinki (Machiavellian (USA))
M Johnston Mrs S J Brookhouse

Placings:20-1000555 (6535)
2009: 10^1GF, 10^0S, 10^0GF, 9^0GF, 8^5GF, 8^5GF, 8^5GF,

	Starts	1st	2nd	3rd	Win & Pl
Career Total (Turf)	9	1	1	0	3890
89 6/09 Rdcr 1m2f			G-F	£2590	

Total win prize-money £2590

Going (Turf): Sf: 0-2 GS: 0-0 Gd: 0-0 **GF: 1-7** Fm: 0-0
Distance: 5f/6f: 0-0 7f-8f: 0-2 **9f-13f: 1-7** 14f+: 0-0
Track : **LH: 1-5** RH: 0-3 **Tight: 1-1** Gall: 0-3
Aids: Bl: 0-1 Vi: 0-0 Tstrap: 0-0 Ckp: 0-0
Best Rating: 89 6/09 Rdcr 1m2f gd-fm

Useful; stays 1m2f and acts on fast ground; has worn blinkers.

York Cliff

90(98) (62)61

11-y-o b g Marju (IRE)-Azm (Unfuwain (USA))
W M Brisbourne Mark Brisbourne

Placings:3/14/20200/**054500004510**/**2430404206**4**332230**/**46543104514222553**3134260/**44**1420240003**450**/404351 020334**206-0406**3000 (7670)
2009: 16^0SS, 12^4SD, 11^0SD, 12^6SD, 16^3S, 12^0G, 12^0GF, 12^0SD,

	Starts	1st	2nd	3rd	Win & Pl
Career Total (Turf)	45	3	6	6	28065
Career Total (AW)	54	4	8	8	20020
51 7/08 Wolv 1m4f50y (0-60)				STD	£2047
64 5/07 Ayr 1m7f (0-60)H				G-S	£2590
59 6/06 Ayr 1m5f13y (0-70)H				GD	£3238
58 3/06 Sthl 1m4f (0-45)				STD	£1876
54 2/06 Wolv 1m4f50y				STD	£2388
69 12/04 Wolv 1m141y (0-62)H				STD	£2983
86 4/01 Newb 1m D				G-S	£4615

Total win prize-money £19741

Going (Turf): Sf: 0-9 **GS: 2-9** Gd: 1-14 GF: 0-13 Fm: 0-0
Distance: 5f/6f: 0-0 7f-8f: 1-6 **9f-13f: 4-61** 14f+: 2-32
Track : **LH: 6-82** RH: 0-13 **Tight: 3-72** Gall: 0-2
Aids: Bl: 0-0 Vi: 0-1 Tstrap: 0-2 Ckp: 0-2
Best Rating: 88 8/03 Sand 1m14y soft

Moderate; effective at around 1m4f-1m6f; acts on easy ground; also goes on sand; has worn cheekpieces and a visor.

York Key Bar

92(87) (53)70

3-y-o b g Presidium-Onemoretime (Timeless Times (USA))
B Ellison York Chambers Racing

Placings:3234-0346530 (3999)
2009: 7^0GF, 5^3SD, 5^4GF, 6^6GS, 5^5SD, 5^3GS, 5^0GS,

	Starts	1st	2nd	3rd	Win & Pl
Career Total (Turf)	8	0	1	3	3371
Career Total (AW)	3	0	0	1	302

Going (Turf): **Sf: 0-2 GS: 0-4 Gd: 0-0 GF: 0-2 Fm: 0-0**
Distance: 5f/6f: 0-10 7f-8f: 0-1 9f-13f: 0-0 14f+: 0-0
Track : LH: 0-3 RH: 0-0 Tight: 0-2 Gall: 0-0
Aids: Bl: 0-0 Vi: 0-0 Tstrap: 0-0 Ckp: 0-0
Best Rating: 70 10/08 Catt 5f gd-sft

Modest; effective over 5f; acts on soft ground.

Yorke's Folly (USA)

98 (38)54

8-y-o b m Stravinsky (USA)-Tommelise (USA) (Dayjur (USA))

C W Fairhurst Mrs A M Leggett

Placings:50/0000350/360442300/40265202/005040/60060 0-26 (5041)

2009: 5^{2}GF, 5^{6}GF,

	Starts	1st	2nd	3rd	Win & Pl
Career Total (Turf)	38	0	5	3	8140
Career Total (AW)	2	0	0	0	

Going (Turf): **Sf: 0-1 GS: 0-4 Gd: 0-8 GF: 0-23 Fm: 0-2**
Distance: 5f/6f: 0-37 7f-8f: 0-3 9f-13f: 0 0 14f+: 0-0
Track : LH: 0-4 RH: 0-2 Tight: 0-1 Gall: 0-1
Aids: Bl: 0-20 Vi: 0-10 Tstrap: 0-0 Ckp: 0-0
Best Rating: **54** 8/09 Muss 5f gd-fm

Yorkshire Blue

103 (43)73

10-y-o b g Atraf-Something Blue (Petong)

J S Goldie John Murphy

Placings:010600/0104600000/001105100/6451261430050 0/00021121350041/02005045641050/0500634520204603045-0651626 (6989)

2009: 6^{0}GF, 6^{6}GF, 7^{5}GF, 6^{1}GF, 6^{6}GF, 6^{2}GF, 6^{6}G,

	Starts	1st	2nd	3rd	Win & Pl
Career Total (Turf)	87	12	7	4	74555
Career Total (AW)	6	1	0	0	3388

62	9/09	Rdcr	6f	(0-70)H	G-F	£2752
76	9/07	Haml	6f5y		G-F	£2388
89	10/06	Ayr	6f	(0-80)H	HVY	£6232
81	7/06	Ayr	6f	(0-70)H	GD	£4210
76	6/06	Haml	6f5y	(0-65)H	G-F	£2730
71	6/06	Haml	6f5y	(0-75)H	G-S	£4533
70	8/05	Hayd	6f	(0-70)H	G-F	£3637
66	7/05	Donc	7f	(0-75)H	GD	£4425
66	8/04	Rdcr	7f	D(0-80)H	FRM	£7260
63	6/04	Donc	7f	D(0-80)H	G-F	£5671
56	5/04	Ayr	7f50y	D(0-80)H	G-F	£5525
63	5/03	Rdcr	7f	F	G-F	£3640
68	7/02	Wolv	6f	D	STD	£3388

Total win prize-money £56394

Going (Turf): Sf: 1-12 S: 1-11 Gd: 2-21 **GF: 7-40** Fm: 1-3
Distance: 5f/6f: 5-35 **7f-8f: 8-55** 9f-13f: 0-3 14f+: 0-0
Track : **LH: 2-22** RH: 0-6 **Tight: 1-12** Gall: 0-2
Aids: Bl: 0-2 Vi: 0-0 Tstrap: 1-6 Ckp: 1-6
Best Rating: **89** 10/06 Ayr 6f heavy

Moderate; effective at up to 7f; acts on most ground on turf; goes on Fibresand; has worn cheekpieces.

Yorksters Girl (IRE)

94 93

3-y-o ch f Bachelor Duke (USA)-Isadora Duncan (IRE) (Sadler's Wells (USA))

M G Quinlan B P York

Placings:20313-00 (3641)

2009: 7^{0}S, 8^{0}G,

	Starts	1st	2nd	3rd	Win & Pl
Career Total (Turf)	7	1	1	2	8078
87	10/08 Newc	7f		HVY	£2315

Total win prize-money £2315

Going (Turf): **Sf: 1-4** GS: 0-1 Gd: 0-1 GF: 0-1 Fm: 0-0
Distance: 5f/6f: 0-0 **7f-8f: 1-6** 9f-13f: 0-1 14f+: 0-0
Track : LH: 0-0 RH: 0-1 Tight: 0-0 Gall: 0-0
Aids: Bl: 0-0 Vi: 0-0 Tstrap: 0-0 Ckp: 0-0
Best Rating: **93** 10/08 Newb 7f soft

Very useful; Listed placed; stays 7f and acts on most ground.

Yorksters Prince (IRE)

85(88) (59)44

2-y-o b g Beat Hollow-Odalisque (IRE) (Machiavellian (USA))

M G Quinlan Wexford Racing

Placings:04 (7844)

2009: 8^{0}G, 8^{4}SD,

	Starts	1st	2nd	3rd	Win & Pl
Career Total (Turf)	1	0	0	0	
Career Total (AW)	1	0	0	0	289

Going (Turf): **Sf: 0-0 GS: 0-0 Gd: 0-1 GF: 0-0 Fm: 0-0**
Distance: 5f/6f: 0-0 7f-8f: 0-1 9f-13f: 0-1 14f+: 0-0
Track : LH: 0-1 RH: 0-0 Tight: 0-1 Gall: 0-0
Aids: Bl: 0-0 Vi: 0-0 Tstrap: 0-0 Ckp: 0-0
Best Rating: **59** 12/09 Wolv 1m141y stand

Yossi (IRE)

96 83

5-y-o b g Montjeu (IRE)-Raindancing (IRE) (Tirol)

Jim Best Mr & Mrs Frank Golding & Michael Hills

Placings:234/2622413045/0202-200 (5802)

2009: 12^{2}G, 12^{0}G, 12^{0}GF,

	Starts	1st	2nd	3rd	Win & Pl
Career Total (Turf)	20	1	7	2	16568
64	8/07 Catt	1m3f214y		GD	£3238

Total win prize-money £3239

Going (Turf): Sf: 0-4 GS: 0-7 **Gd: 1-7** GF: 0-2 Fm: 0-0
Distance: 5f/6f: 0-0 7f-8f: 0-0 **9f-13f: 1-16** 14f+: 0-4
Track : **LH: 1-18** RH: 0-2 **Tight: 1-8** Gall: 0-3
Aids: Bl: 0-6 Vi: 0-1 Tstrap: 0-0 Ckp: 0-0
Best Rating: **83** 7/09 Epsm 1m4f10y good

Fair; stays 1m6f; acts on good or softer ground; likes to be held up; has worn blinkers.

You Avin A Laugh

78(97) (61)33

3-y-o ch g Bertolini (USA)-High Stepping (IRE) (Taufan (USA))

C A Dwyer Mrs J A Chapman & Mrs Shelley Dwyer

Placings:0-60345203040 (3464)

2009: 6^{6}SD, 5^{0}SD, 5^{3}SD, 5^{4}SD, 5^{5}SD, 5^{2}SD, 5^{0}GF, 5^{3}SD, 5^{0}G, 5^{4}SD, 5^{0}SD,

	Starts	1st	2nd	3rd	Win & Pl
Career Total (Turf)	3	0	0	0	
Career Total (AW)	9	0	1	2	1527

Going (Turf): **Sf: 0-0 GS: 0-0 Gd: 0-1 GF: 0-2 Fm: 0-0**
Distance: 5f/6f: 0-12 7f-8f: 0-0 9f-13f: 0-0 14f+: 0-0
Track : LH: 0-8 RH: 0-0 Tight: 0-8 Gall: 0-0
Aids: Bl: 0-1 Vi: 0-0 Tstrap: 0-0 Ckp: 0-0
Best Rating: **61** 4/09 Wolv 5f20y stand

Modest; effective at 5f on Polytrack; has worn blinkers.

You Say I Say (USA)

103 66

3-y-o b/br f Unbridled's Song (USA)-Insight (FR) (Sadler's Wells (USA))

Sir Michael Stoute Niarchos Family

Placings:0-6 (2006)

2009: 9^{6}F,

	Starts	1st	2nd	3rd	Win & Pl
Career Total (Turf)	2	0	0	0	0

Going (Turf): **Sf: 0-0 GS: 0-1 Gd: 0-0 GF: 0-0 Fm: 0-1**
Distance: 5f/6f: 0-0 7f-8f: 0-1 9f-13f: 0-1 14f+: 0-0
Track : LH: 0-0 RH: 0-1 Tight: 0-1 Gall: 0-0
Aids: Bl: 0-0 Vi: 0-0 Tstrap: 0-0 Ckp: 0-0
Best Rating: **66** 5/09 Sals 1m1f198y firm

You'll Be Mine (USA)

105 105

2-y-o b f Kingmambo (USA)-Quarter Moon (IRE) (Sadler's Wells (USA))

A P O'Brien Mrs R Henry & Mrs John Magnier

Placings:413 (6269)

2009: 7^{4}G, 7^{1}GY, 8^{3}G,

	Starts	1st	2nd	3rd	Win & Pl
Career Total (Turf)	3	1	0	1	36595
84	9/09 Leop	7f		G-Y	£12419

Total win prize-money £12420

Going (Turf): **Sf: 0-0 GS: 0-0 Gd: 0-2 GF: 0-0 Fm: 0-0**
Distance: 5f/6f: 0-0 **7f-8f: 1-3** 9f-13f: 0-0 14f+: 0-0
Track : **LH: 1-2** RH: 0-1 Tight: 0-0 Gall: 0-1
Aids: Bl: 0-0 Vi: 0-0 Tstrap: 0-0 Ckp: 0-0
Best Rating: **105** 9/09 Asct 1m good

Smart filly; stays 1m; acts on good and easy ground.

You'relikemefrank

69(98) (50)

3-y-o ch g Bahamian Bounty-Proudfoot (IRE) (Shareef Dancer (USA))

J Balding Kate Barrett, Paul & David Clarkson

Placings:000-63346263 (6206)

2009: 5^{6}SD, 5^{3}SD, 5^{3}SD, 5^{4}SD, 5^{6}S, 5^{2}SD, 5^{6}SD, 5^{3}SD,

	Starts	1st	2nd	3rd	Win & Pl
Career Total (Turf)	2	0	0	0	0
Career Total (AW)	9	0	1	3	2002

Going (Turf): **Sf: 0-2 GS: 0-0 Gd: 0-0 GF: 0-0 Fm: 0-0**
Distance: 5f/6f: 0-11 7f-8f: 0-0 9f-13f: 0-0 14f+: 0-0
Track : LH: 0-6 RH: 0-1 Tight: 0-6 Gall: 0-0
Aids: Bl: 0-1 Vi: 0-0 Tstrap: 0-7 Ckp: 0-7
Best Rating: **50** 9/09 Kemp 5f stand

Plater; effective over 5f; acts on Polytrack.

You've Been Mowed

101(97) (68)68

3-y-o ch f Ishiguru (USA)-Sandblaster (Most Welcome)

R J Price Mrs K Oseman

Placings:50235330-306031215606010 (6778)

2009: 5^{3}SD, 5^{0}SD, 5^{6}G, 5^{0}F, 5^{3}GF, 7^{1}SD, 8^{2}F, 8^{1}G, 8^{5}G, 8^{6}G, 7^{0}SD, 7^{6}G, 7^{0}SD, 7^{1}GF, 8^{0}SS,

	Starts	1st	2nd	3rd	Win & Pl
Career Total (Turf)	**15**	**2**	**2**	**2**	**8973**
Career Total (AW)	**8**	**1**	**0**	**3**	**3327**

67 9/09 Brig 7f214y (0-70)H G-F £3027
63 6/09 Chep 1m14y (0-70)H GD £2914
60 6/09 Sthl 7f (0-55)H STD £2047
Total win prize-money £7989

Going (Turf): Sf: 0-0 GS: 0-0 **Gd: 1-6 GF: 1-6** Fm: 0-3
Distance: 5f/6f: 0-13 **7f-8f: 2-6** 9f-13f: 1-4 14f+: 0-0
Track : **LH: 2-14** RH: 0-0 Tight: 0-7 Gall: 0-5
Aids: Bl: 0-0 Vi: 0-0 Tstrap: 0-0 Ckp: 0-0
Best Rating: 68 9/08 Ling 6f stand

Moderate; stays 7f; acts on fast ground and on sand.

Youcanalwaysdream (IRE)

83(107) (80)**27**
2-y-o b f Exceed And Excel (AUS)-Al Shadeedah (USA) (Nureyev (USA))
K A Ryan Mrs T Marnane

Placings:00221 (7582)
2009: 5^{0}G, 5^{0}SD, 5^{2}SD, 5^{2}SD, 5^{1}SF,

	Starts	1st	2nd	3rd	Win & Pl
Career Total (Turf)	**1**	**0**	**0**	**0**	
Career Total (AW)	**4**	**1**	**2**	**0**	**5454**

80 11/09 Wolv 5f20y SF £3238
Total win prize-money £3238

Going (Turf): Sf: 0-0 GS: 0-0 Gd: 0-1 GF: 0-0 Fm: 0-0
Distance: **5f/6f: 1-5** 7f-8f: 0-0 9f-13f: 0-0 14f+: 0-0
Track : **LH: 1-5** RH: 0-0 **Tight: 1-4** Gall: 0-1
Aids: Bl: 0-0 Vi: 0-0 Tstrap: 0-0 Ckp: 0-0
Best Rating: 80 11/09 Wolv 5f20y std-fst

Fair; suited by 5f and Polytrack.

Youm Jamil (USA)

96 **76**
2-y-o gr/ro c Mizzen Mast (USA)-Millie's Choice (IRE) (Taufan (USA))
B J Meehan Jaber Abdullah

Placings:22 (7146)
2009: 8^{2}GF, 7^{2}G,

	Starts	1st	2nd	3rd	Win & Pl
Career Total (Turf)	2	0	2	0	2939

Going (Turf): Sf: 0-0 GS: 0-0 Gd: 0-1 GF: 0-1 Fm: 0-0
Distance: 5f/6f: 0-0 7f-8f: 0-2 9f-13f: 0-0 14f+: 0-0
Track : LH: 0-0 RH: 0-0 Tight: 0-0 Gall: 0-0
Aids: Bl: 0-0 Vi: 0-0 Tstrap: 0-0 Ckp: 0-0
Best Rating: 76 10/09 NmkR 7f good

Fair; stays 1macts on good/fast ground.

Youmzain (IRE)

117 **128**
6-y-o b h Sinndar (IRE)-Sadima (IRE) (Sadler's Wells (USA))
M R Channon Jaber Abdullah

Placings:031/1301121/335242/52132-423320 (7744a)
2009: 12^{4}G, 12^{2}G, 12^{3}S, 12^{3}S, 12^{2}G, 12^{0}G,

	Starts	1st	2nd	3rd	Win & Pl
Career Total (Turf)	**27**	**6**	**7**	**7**	**3193567**

127 6/08 StCl 1m4f G-S £168059
118 9/06 Colo 1m4f GD £68966
119 8/06 York 1m4f G-S £76653
113 7/06 NmkJ 1m5f G-F £15898
101 4/06 Catt 1m3f214y FRM £6232
87 8/05 Gdwd 1m GD £3620
Total win prize-money £339429

Going (Turf): Sf: 0-2 **GS: 2-7 Gd: 2-11** GF: 1-5 Fm: 1-1
Distance: 5f/6f: 0-0 7f-8f: 1-2 **9f-13f: 5-25** 14f+: 0-0
Track : LH: 3-14 RH: 3-12 Tight: 1-3 **Gall: 2-9**
Aids: Bl: 0-0 Vi: 0-2 Tstrap: 0-0 Ckp: 0-0
Best Rating: 128 10/08 Lonc 1m4f gd-sft

High class; winner in Group 1 company on the continent; runner-up in the 2007 King George and three times runner-up in the Arc (2007, 2008 and 2009). Also runner-up in the Coronation Cup in both 2008 and 2009; stays 1m5f; acts on most ground; has worn a visor; likes to be held up.

Young Americans (IRE)

84(98) (65)**64**
3-y-o b f Nayef (USA)-Life At Night (IRE) (Night Shift (USA))
S Botti (M Botti 19/8) Effevi Snc

Placings:10000
2009: 7^{1}G, 8^{0}G, 10^{0}G, 11^{0}SD, 11^{0}GS,

	Starts	1st	2nd	3rd	Win & Pl
Career Total (Turf)	**4**	**1**	**0**	**0**	**8738**
Career Total (AW)	**1**	**0**	**0**	**0**	

3/09 Siro 7f110y GD £8738
Total win prize-money £8738

Going (Turf): Sf: 0-0 GS: 0-1 **Gd: 1-3** GF: 0-0 Fm: 0-0
Distance: 5f/6f: 0-0 **7f-8f: 1-1** 9f-13f: 0-4 14f+: 0-0
Track : LH: 0-1 RH: 0-2 Tight: 0-0 Gall: 0-1
Aids: Bl: 0-0 Vi: 0-0 Tstrap: 0-0 Ckp: 0-0
Best Rating: 65 8/09 Kemp 1m3f stand

Young Bertie

(103) (70)**77**
6-y-o ch g Bertolini (USA)-Urania (Most Welcome)
H Morrison M T Bevan

Placings:0500/342321530/00442321116/4300051-00 (0505)
2009: 8^{0}SD, 8^{0}SD,

	Starts	1st	2nd	3rd	Win & Pl
Career Total (Turf)	**22**	**3**	**3**	**4**	**13861**
Career Total (AW)	**11**	**2**	**1**	**1**	**7915**

70 12/08 Ling 1m (0-70)H STD £3070
77 10/07 Wind 1m67y (0-70)H GD £2817
78 10/07 Brig 7f214y (0-70)H G-S £2914
72 9/07 Pont 1m4y (0-65)H FRM £3238
73 8/06 Ling 7f (0-65)H STD £3238
Total win prize-money £15281

Going (Turf): Sf: 0-1 **GS: 1-4 Gd: 1-7** GF: 0-9 **Fm: 1-1**
Distance: 5f/6f: 0-10 **7f-8f: 3-17** 9f-13f: 2-6 14f+: 0-0
Track : **LH: 4-14** RH: 1-6 **Tight: 3-11** Gall: 0-3
Aids: Bl: 0-0 **Vi: 5-20** Tstrap: 0-5 Ckp: 0-5
Best Rating: 78 10/07 Brig 7f214y gd-sft

Fair; effective over 6f-1m; acts on fast and easy ground; also goes on Polytrack; usually wears a visor; has worn cheekpieces.

Young Dottie

100(109) (79)**70**
3-y-o b f Desert Sun-Auntie Dot Com (Tagula (IRE))
P M Phelan Tony Smith

Placings:342021-043650041 (7664)
2009: 8^{0}G, 7^{4}GF, 7^{3}GF, 7^{6}GF, 8^{5}GF, 10^{0}SD, 8^{0}GF, 10^{4}G, 8^{1}SD,

	Starts	1st	2nd	3rd	Win & Pl
Career Total (Turf)	**11**	**0**	**1**	**2**	**2975**
Career Total (AW)	**4**	**2**	**1**	**0**	**5347**

79 12/09 Ling 1m (0-75)H STD £2729
75 10/08 Ling 7f STD £1942
Total win prize-money £4673

Going (Turf): Sf: 0-0 GS: 0-1 Gd: 0-2 GF: 0-8 Fm: 0-0
Distance: 5f/6f: 0-3 **7f-8f: 2-8** 9f-13f: 0-4 14f+: 0-0
Track : **LH: 2-5** RH: 0-4 **Tight: 2-7** Gall: 0-2
Aids: Bl: 0-0 Vi: 0-0 Tstrap: 0-0 Ckp: 0-0
Best Rating: 79 12/09 Ling 1m stand

Fair; stays 1m; acts on fast ground and on Polytrack.

Young Firth

82(69) (23)**52**
2-y-o b g Lucky Story (USA)-Le Petit Diable (IRE) (Trans Island)
J R Norton Jaffa Racing Syndicate

Placings:0660 (6639)
2009: 7^{0}SD, 7^{6}GS, 8^{6}GS, 8^{0}SD,

	Starts	1st	2nd	3rd	Win & Pl
Career Total (Turf)	**2**	**0**	**0**	**0**	**0**
Career Total (AW)	**2**	**0**	**0**	**0**	

Going (Turf): Sf: 0-0 GS: 0-2 Gd: 0-0 GF: 0-0 Fm: 0-0
Distance: 5f/6f: 0-0 7f-8f: 0-2 9f-13f: 0-2 14f+: 0-0
Track : LH: 0-3 RH: 0-0 Tight: 0-2 Gall: 0-0
Aids: Bl: 0-0 Vi: 0-0 Tstrap: 0-0 Ckp: 0-0
Best Rating: 52 7/09 Newc 7f gd-sft

Young George

72(79) (38)**10**
2-y-o b g Danroad (AUS)-Bo' Babbity (Strong Gale)
C W Fairhurst North Cheshire Trading & Storage Ltd

Placings:00 (7556)
2009: 5^{0}G, 5^{0}SD,

	Starts	1st	2nd	3rd	Win & Pl
Career Total (Turf)	**1**	**0**	**0**	**0**	
Career Total (AW)	**1**	**0**	**0**	**0**	

Going (Turf): Sf: 0-0 GS: 0-0 Gd: 0-1 GF: 0-0 Fm: 0-0
Distance: 5f/6f: 0-2 7f-8f: 0-0 9f-13f: 0-0 14f+: 0-0
Track : LH: 0-1 RH: 0-0 Tight: 0-1 Gall: 0-0
Aids: Bl. 0-0 Vi. 0-0 Tstrap: 0-0 Ckp: 0-0
Best Rating: 38 11/09 Wolv 5f216y stand

Young Gladiator (IRE)

107(98) (69)**65**
4-y-o b g Spartacus (IRE)-Savona (IRE) (Cyrano De Bergerac)
Miss J A Camacho
Barrett,Hope,Postill,Adamson,Wainwright

Placings:3321330050-01061062 (7348)
2009: 7^{0}SD, 7^{1}G, 7^{0}SD, 5^{6}G, 7^{1}GS, 7^{0}GF, 7^{6}G, 7^{2}SD,

	Starts	1st	2nd	3rd	Win & Pl
Career Total (Turf)	**9**	**2**	**0**	**2**	**6312**
Career Total (AW)	**9**	**1**	**2**	**2**	**4957**

65 7/09 Newc 7f G-S £2072

62 6/09 Newc 7f (0-70)H GD £3238
64 4/08 Sthl 6f STD £3002
Total win prize-money £8313

Going (Turf): Sf: 0-0 GS: 1-3 Gd: 1-4 GF: 0-2 Fm: 0-0
Distance: 5f/6f: 1-5 7f-8f: 2-13 9f-13f: 0-0 14f+: 0-0
Track : LH: 1-10 RH: 0-2 Tight: 0-3 Gall: 0-0
Aids: Bl: 2-7 Vi: 0-1 Tstrap: 0-1 Ckp: 0-1
Best Rating: 69 11/09 Sthl 7f stand

Modest; stays 7f and acts on sand; has worn blinkers.

Young Ivanhoe

92(96) (54)50
4-y-o b g Oasis Dream-Cybinka (Selkirk (USA))
C A Dwyer S B Components (international) Ltd

Placings:032/1000004004060-40460460 (2456)
2009: 5^{4}SD, 5^{0}SD, 6^{4}SD, 6^{6}SD, 6^{0}SD, 6^{4}F, 5^{6}GF, 6^{0}GF,

	Starts	1st	2nd	3rd	Win & Pl
Career Total (Turf)	9	0	0	0	577
Career Total (AW)	15	1	1	1	3201

68 2/08 Ling 6f STD £2331
Total win prize-money £2332

Going (Turf): Sf: 0-0 GS: 0-1 Gd: 0-3 GF: 0-4 Fm: 0-1
Distance: 5f/6f: 1-18 7f-8f: 0-6 9f-13f: 0-0 14f+: 0-0
Track : LH: 1-16 RH: 0-2 Tight: 1-8 Gall: 0-3
Aids: Bl: 0-4 Vi: 0-3 Tstrap: 0-0 Ckp: 0-0
Best Rating: 70 11/07 Wolv 5f216y stand

Plating class; stays 7f; acts on a sound surface; has worn a tongue tie and an eyeshield.

Young Mick

105(101) (91)111
7-y-o br g King's Theatre (IRE)-Just Warning (Warning)
G G Margarson M F Kentish

Placings:0340/45000430/0111221112346161131/0025/00 0422502010-02610043405 (7237)
2009: 12^{0}SD, 12^{2}GF, 13^{6}GF, 12^{1}G, 12^{0}GF, 12^{0}G, 16^{4}GF, 14^{3}GF, 12^{4}GF, 12^{0}GS, 12^{5}SD,

	Starts	1st	2nd	3rd	Win & Pl
Career Total (Turf)	39	7	5	3	308695
Career Total (AW)	19	5	3	2	22938

106 2/09 Ndas 1m4f (95-110)H GD £62500
102 10/08 Leic 1m3f183y G-S £7569
116 9/06 Asct 1m4f G-S £28390
110 8/06 Asct 1m4f (0-100)H G-F £19696
102 7/06 Asct 1m4f (0-105)H GD £46740
98 6/06 Asct 1m4f (0-105)H G-F £34276
92 3/06 Yarm 1m3f101y (0-90)H FRM £11217
80 3/06 Kemp 1m4f (0-75)H STD £3238
76 3/06 Wolv 1m4f50y (0-70)H STD £3238
66 1/06 Wolv 1m1f103y (0-55)H STD £2388
67 1/06 Ling 1m2f (0-65)H STD £2047
60 1/06 Wolv 1m1f103y STD £1365
Total win prize-money £222670

Going (Turf): Sf: 0-2 GS: 2-9 Gd: 2-9 GF: 2-18 Fm: 1-1
Distance: 5f/6f: 0-0 7f-8f: 0-4 9f-13f: 12-48 14f+: 0-6
Track : LH: 6-25 RH: 6-28 Tight: 5-15 Gall: 5-23
Aids: Bl: 0-4 Vi: 12-44 Tstrap: 0-0 Ckp: 0-0
Best Rating: 116 9/06 Asct 1m4f gd-sft

Very useful; winner in Group 3 company; stays 1m6f, but best at shorter; acts on most ground and on Polytrack; has worn blinkers, but usually wears a visor.

Young Ollie

38 14
4-y-o ch f Piccolo-Miss Michelle (Jalmood (USA))
E A Wheeler E A Wheeler

Placings:000-0 (1420)
2009: 8^{0}GF,

	Starts	1st	2nd	3rd	Win & Pl
Career Total (Turf)	4	0	0	0	

Going (Turf): Sf: 0-1 GS: 0-0 Gd: 0-0 GF: 0-3 Fm: 0-0
Distance: 5f/6f: 0-0 7f-8f: 0-0 9f-13f: 0-4 14f+: 0-0
Track : LH: 0-1 RH: 0-2 Tight: 0-3 Gall: 0-0
Aids: Bl: 0-0 Vi: 0-0 Tstrap: 0-0 Ckp: 0-0
Best Rating: 14 5/08 Wind 1m67y gd-fm

Young Pretender (FR)

106 112
4-y-o b c Oasis Dream-Silent Heir (AUS) (Sunday Silence (USA))
Saeed Bin Suroor Godolphin

Placings:115/53-524 (7245)
2009: 8^{5}GF, 7^{2}GS, 8^{4}S,

	Starts	1st	2nd	3rd	Win & Pl
Career Total (Turf)	8	2	1	1	56336

112 9/07 Lonc 7f GD £27027
91 8/07 NmkJ 6f GD £6477
Total win prize-money £33504

Going (Turf): Sf: 0-1 GS: 0-2 Gd: 2-3 GF: 0-2 Fm: 0-0
Distance: 5f/6f: 1-1 7f-8f: 1-4 9f-13f: 0-3 14f+: 0-0
Track : LH: 0-3 RH: 1-2 Tight: 0-1 Gall: 0-1
Aids: Bl: 0-0 Vi: 0-0 Tstrap: 0-0 Ckp: 0-0
Best Rating: 112 10/09 NmkR 1m gd-fm

Smart; winner in Group 3 company at two; stays 1m; acts on good ground.

Young Simon

95(89) (55)77
2-y-o ch c Piccolo-Fragrant Cloud (Zilzal (USA))
G G Margarson M F Kentish

Placings:0205 (7234)
2009: 6^{0}GF, 6^{2}GF, 5^{0}G, 6^{5}SD,

	Starts	1st	2nd	3rd	Win & Pl
Career Total (Turf)	3	0	1	0	771
Career Total (AW)	1	0	0	0	0

Going (Turf): Sf: 0-0 GS: 0-0 Gd: 0-1 GF: 0-2 Fm: 0-0
Distance: 5f/6f: 0-3 7f-8f: 0-1 9f-13f: 0-0 14f+: 0-0
Track : LH: 0-0 RH: 0-1 Tight: 0-0 Gall: 0-2
Aids: Bl: 0-0 Vi: 0-0 Tstrap: 0-0 Ckp: 0-0
Best Rating: 77 8/09 Yarm 6f3y gd-fm

Modest; stays 6f; acts on fast ground.

Young Star Gazer

91 68
3-y-o ch g Observatory (USA)-Ash Glade (Nashwan (USA))
D E Pipe (H R A Cecil 14/7) Pkd Partnership

Placings:0363 (3960)
2009: 8^{0}GF, 8^{3}GF, 10^{6}GF, 9^{3}S,

	Starts	1st	2nd	3rd	Win & Pl
Career Total (Turf)	4	0	0	2	886

Going (Turf): Sf: 0-1 GS: 0-0 Gd: 0-0 GF: 0-3 Fm: 0-0
Distance: 5f/6f: 0-0 7f-8f: 0-0 9f-13f: 0-4 14f+: 0-0
Track : LH: 0-2 RH: 0-2 Tight: 0-3 Gall: 0-0
Aids: Bl: 0-0 Vi: 0-0 Tstrap: 0-0 Ckp: 0-0
Best Rating: 68 5/09 Leic 1m60y gd-fm

Modest; stays 1m; acts on soft and fast ground.

Your Golf Travel

90(92) (48)40
4-y-o b f Bertolini (USA)-Scottish Spice (Selkirk (USA))
M Wigham Your Golf Travel Ltd

Placings:000400-2000 (3004)
2009: 8^{2}SD, 7^{0}F, 10^{0}G, 10^{0}G,

	Starts	1st	2nd	3rd	Win & Pl
Career Total (Turf)	9	0	0	0	168
Career Total (AW)	2	0	1	0	605

Going (Turf): Sf: 0-1 GS: 0-1 Gd: 0-4 GF: 0-2 Fm: 0-1
Distance: 5f/6f: 0-1 7f-8f: 0-8 9f-13f: 0-2 14f+: 0-0
Track : LH: 0-4 RH: 0-4 Tight: 0-4 Gall: 0-0
Aids: Bl: 0-1 Vi: 0-0 Tstrap: 0-0 Ckp: 0-0
Best Rating: 48 1/09 Kemp 1m stand

Moderate; stays a mile; handles Polytrack.

Your Lad

(82) (51)
2-y-o b c Dubawi (IRE)-Krisalya (Kris)
C F Wall Des Thurlby

Placings:0 (7764)
2009: 8^{0}SD,

	Starts	1st	2nd	3rd	Win & Pl
Career Total (Turf)	0	0	0	0	
Career Total (AW)	1	0	0	0	

Going (Turf): Sf: 0-0 GS: 0-0 Gd: 0-0 GF: 0-0 Fm: 0-0
Distance: 5f/6f: 0-0 7f-8f: 0-1 9f-13f: 0-0 14f+: 0-0
Track : LH: 0-0 RH: 0-1 Tight: 0-0 Gall: 0-0
Aids: Bl: 0-0 Vi: 0-0 Tstrap: 0-0 Ckp: 0-0
Best Rating: 51 12/09 Kemp 1m stand

Your Old Pal

110 107
3-y-o ch c Rock Of Gibraltar (IRE)-Questabelle (Rainbow Quest (USA))
J Noseda Raffles Racing

Placings:1-5142 (3087)
2009: 10^{5}GS, 10^{1}GF, 10^{4}GF, 12^{2}GF,

	Starts	1st	2nd	3rd	Win & Pl
Career Total (Turf)	5	2	1	0	71551

107 5/09 NmkR 1m2f G-F £28385
95 10/08 Newb 1m SFT £5504
Total win prize-money £33890

Going (Turf): Sf: 1-1 GS: 0-1 Gd: 0-0 GF: 1-3 Fm: 0-0
Distance: 5f/6f: 0-0 7f-8f: 1-1 9f-13f: 1-4 14f+: 0-0
Track : LH: 0-1 RH: 0-1 Tight: 0-0 Gall: 0-2
Aids: Bl: 0-0 Vi: 0-0 Tstrap: 0-0 Ckp: 0-0
Best Rating: 107 6/09 Asct 1m4f gd-fm

Smart; winner in Listed company and placed at Group 2 level; stays 1m4f and acts on most ground.

Your True Love (IRE)

82 36
3-y-o b f Pyrus (USA)-Columbine (IRE) (Pivotal)

A Berry E Nisbet

Placings:060 (2157)

2009: 5^{0}GF, 6^{0}GS, 5^{0}GF,

	Starts	1st	2nd	3rd	Win & Pl
Career Total (Turf)	3	0	0	0	0

Going (Turf): Sf: 0-0 GS: 0-1 Gd: 0-0 GF: 0-2 Fm: 0-0

Distance: 5f/6f: 0-2 7f-8f: 0-1 9f-13f: 0-0 14f+: 0-0

Track : LH: 0-1 RH: 0-0 Tight: 0-1 Gall: 0-0

Aids: Bl: 0-0 Vi: 0-0 Tstrap: 0-0 Ckp: 0-0

Best Rating: 36 4/09 Catt 5f212y gd-fm

Yourgolftravel Com

71 13

4-y-o b g Fasliyev (USA)-Hiddnah (USA) (Affirmed (USA))

M Wigham Your Golf Travel Ltd

Placings:0 (2862)

2009: 6^{0}S,

	Starts	1st	2nd	3rd	Win & Pl
Career Total (Turf)	1	0	0	0	

Going (Turf): Sf: 0-1 GS: 0-0 Gd: 0-0 GF: 0-0 Fm: 0-0

Distance: 5f/6f: 0-0 7f-8f: 0-1 9f-13f: 0-0 14f+: 0-0

Track : LH: 0-0 RH: 0-0 Tight: 0-0 Gall: 0-0

Aids: Bl: 0-0 Vi: 0-0 Tstrap: 0-0 Ckp: 0-0

Best Rating: 13 6/09 Yarm 6f3y soft

Ytartfawn (IRE)

81 36

2-y-o ch c Chineur (FR)-Lady Montekin (Montekin)

P T Midgley I Hodgson

Placings:65056 (3626)

2009: 5^{6}GF, 5^{5}GF, 5^{0}G, 6^{5}G, 5^{6}G,

	Starts	1st	2nd	3rd	Win & Pl
Career Total (Turf)	5	0	0	0	0

Going (Turf): Sf: 0-0 GS: 0-0 Gd: 0-3 GF: 0-2 Fm: 0-0

Distance: 5f/6f: 0-5 7f-8f: 0-0 9f-13f: 0-0 14f+: 0-0

Track : LH: 0-0 RH: 0-0 Tight: 0-0 Gall: 0-0

Aids: Bl: 0-1 Vi: 0-0 Tstrap: 0-0 Ckp: 0-0

Best Rating: 36 6/09 Rdcr 6f good

Yughanni

98(80) (45)53

3-y-o b f Oasis Dream-Bedazzling (IRE) (Darshaan)

C E Brittain Saeed Manana

Placings:0-000306 (3476)

2009: 7^{0}SD, 6^{0}SD, 7^{0}GF, 7^{3}GF, 5^{0}GF, 6^{6}F,

	Starts	1st	2nd	3rd	Win & Pl
Career Total (Turf)	5	0	0	1	482
Career Total (AW)	2	0	0	0	

Going (Turf): Sf: 0-0 GS: 0-0 Gd: 0-1 GF: 0-3 Fm: 0-1

Distance: 5f/6f: 0-2 7f-8f: 0-5 9f-13f: 0-0 14f+: 0-0

Track : LH: 0-2 RH: 0-1 Tight: 0-1 Gall: 0-0

Aids: Bl: 0-0 Vi: 0-0 Tstrap: 0-0 Ckp: 0-0

Best Rating: 53 6/09 Leic 7f9y gd-fm

Yungaburra (IRE)

99(108) (92)71

5-y-o b g Fath (USA)-Nordic Living (IRE) (Nordico (USA))

J Balding (S Parr 25/2) Willie McKay

Placings:05311131/000032000**036/02005**0003600010305 3513063-346560 (4355)

2009: 5^{3}SD, 5^{4}SD, 5^{6}SD, 5^{5}GF, 5^{6}GF, 5^{0}G,

	Starts	1st	2nd	3rd	Win & Pl
Career Total (Turf)	25	0	1	3	4155
Career Total (AW)	26	6	1	7	29925

89	11/08	Wolv	5f20y	(0-80)H	STD	£5677
81	9/08	Wolv	5f216y	(0-75)H	STD	£2729
95	12/06	Wolv	5f20y	(0-85)	STD	£4533
86	11/06	Wolv	5f20y		STD	£3886
86	11/06	Wolv	5f20y	(0-85)	SF	£3886
72	11/06	Wolv	5f20y	(0-65)	SF	£2388

Total win prize-money £23102

Going (Turf): Sf: 0-3 GS: 0-2 Gd: 0-12 GF: 0-8 Fm: 0-0

Distance: 5f/6f: 6-50 7f-8f: 0-1 9f-13f: 0-0 14f+: 0-0

Track : LH: 6-23 RH: 0-4 **Tight: 6-19** Gall: 0-2

Aids: Bl: 1-11 Vi: 0-0 Tstrap: 0-4 Ckp: 0-4

Best Rating: 95 9/07 Donc 5f gd-fm

Useful; stays 6f and acts well on Polytrack; has worn blinkers and a tongue tie.

Yurituni

103 83

2-y-o b f Bahamian Bounty-Vax Star (Petong)

Eve Johnson Houghton Mrs M Findlay

Placings:44012120 (6660)

2009: 5^{4}GF, 5^{4}GF, 6^{0}GF, 6^{1}GF, 6^{2}GF, 5^{1}F, 5^{2}GF, 5^{0}GS,

	Starts	1st	2nd	3rd	Win & Pl
Career Total (Turf)	8	2	2	0	31469

83	9/09	Bath	5f161y	(0-85)H	FRM	£4415
75	8/09	York	6f	H	G-F	£16190

Total win prize-money £20606

Going (Turf): Sf: 0-0 GS: 0-1 Gd: 0-0 **GF: 1-6 Fm: 1-1**

Distance: 5f/6f: 2-7 7f-8f: 0-1 9f-13f: 0-0 14f+: 0-0

Track : LH: 1-2 RH: 0-0 Tight: 0-1 **Gall: 1-3**

Aids: Bl: 0-0 Vi: 0-0 Tstrap: 0-0 Ckp: 0-0

Best Rating: 83 9/09 Bath 5f161y firm

Useful; effective over 5f-6f; acts on quick ground.

Yvonne Evelyn (USA)

94(102) (67)60

4-y-o gr/ro f Cozzene (USA)-One Great Lady (USA) (Fappiano (USA))

J R Gask Horses First Racing Limited

Placings:0063-60350 (6584)

2009: 10^{6}GF, 12^{0}S, 10^{3}SD, 11^{5}GS, 12^{0}SD,

	Starts	1st	2nd	3rd	Win & Pl
Career Total (Turf)	3	0	0	0	0
Career Total (AW)	6	0	0	2	880

Going (Turf): Sf: 0-1 GS: 0-1 Gd: 0-0 GF: 0-1 Fm: 0-0

Distance: 5f/6f: 0-0 7f-8f: 0-1 9f-13f: 0-8 14f+: 0-0

Track : LH: 0-5 RH: 0-4 Tight: 0-7 Gall: 0-0

Aids: Bl: 0-0 Vi: 0-0 Tstrap: 0-0 Ckp: 0-0

Best Rating: 67 12/08 Kemp 1m2f stand

Modest; effective over 1m2f; acts on Polytrack.

Za Za

92 57

3-y-o br f Barathea (IRE)-Madiyla (Darshaan)

H R A Cecil Bloomsbury Stud

Placings:0-30 (4270)

2009: 10^{3}GF, 12^{0}G,

	Starts	1st	2nd	3rd	Win & Pl
Career Total (Turf)	3	0	0	1	722

Going (Turf): Sf: 0-0 GS: 0-1 Gd: 0-1 GF: 0-1 Fm: 0-0

Distance: 5f/6f: 0-0 7f-8f: 0-0 9f-13f: 0-3 14f+: 0-0

Track : LH: 0-2 RH: 0-1 Tight: 0-0 Gall: 0-2

Aids: Bl: 0-0 Vi: 0-0 Tstrap: 0-0 Ckp: 0-0

Best Rating: 57 6/09 Donc 1m2f60y gd-fm

Modest; stays 1m2f and acts on fast ground.

Za Za Zoom (IRE)

95 97

2-y-o b f Le Vie Dei Colori-Emma's Star (ITY) (Darshaan)

B W Hills Simon Brooke & Steve Smith

Placings:512 (7033)

2009: 6^{5}GF, 6^{1}GS, 7^{2}S,

	Starts	1st	2nd	3rd	Win & Pl
Career Total (Turf)	3	1	1	0	10342

75	10/09	Wind	6f	G-S	£3885

Total win prize-money £3886

Going (Turf): Sf: 0-1 **GS: 1-1** Gd: 0-0 GF: 0-1 Fm: 0-0

Distance: 5f/6f: 1-1 7f-8f: 0-2 9f-13f: 0-0 14f+: 0-0

Track : LH: 0-0 RH: 0-0 Tight: 0-0 **Gall: 1-1**

Aids: Bl: 0-0 Vi: 0-0 Tstrap: 0-0 Ckp: 0-0

Best Rating: 97 10/09 Newb 7f soft

Fair half-sister to several winners at up to 1m including Genki; stays 6f; acts on fast and easy ground.

Zaahid (IRE)

106 107

5-y-o ch h Sakhee (USA)-Murjana (IRE) (Pleasant Colony (USA))

B W Hills Hamdan Al Maktoum

Placings:0/1126013/431000-200 (1861)

2009: 8^{2}GF, 8^{0}S, 7^{0}GF,

	Starts	1st	2nd	3rd	Win & Pl
Career Total (Turf)	17	4	2	2	107088

107	5/08	Asct	7f	H	G-F	£52963
99	9/07	Hayd	1m30y	(0-90)H	SFT	£9348
88	6/07	Sand	7f16y	(0-85)H	GD	£6477
77	5/07	Newb	7f		G-S	£5829

Total win prize-money £74618

Going (Turf): Sf: 1-3 GS: 1-3 Gd: 1-4 GF: 1-7 Fm: 0-0

Distance: 5f/6f: 0-0 **7f-8f: 3-16** 9f-13f: 1-1 14f+: 0-0

Track : LH: 1-3 RH: 1-1 Tight: 0-0 Gall: 0-2

Aids: Bl: 0-0 Vi: 0-0 Tstrap: 0-0 Ckp: 0-0

Best Rating: 107 5/08 Asct 7f gd-fm

Very useful; winner of the 2008 Victoria Cup; effective over 7f-1m; acts on any ground.

Zaahy (USA)

82(100) (90)69

2-y-o ch c More Than Ready (USA)-Sangam (USA) (Majestic Light (USA))

P W Chapple-Hyam M Al-Qatami & K M Al-Mudhaf

Placings:41 (5580)
2009: 7^{4}G, 7^{1}SD,

	Starts	1st	2nd	3rd	Win & Pl
Career Total (Turf)	1	0	0	0	481
Career Total (AW)	1	1	0	0	3238

90 9/09 Ling 7f STD £3238
Total win prize-money £3238

Going (Turf): **Sf: 0-0 GS: 0-0 Gd: 0-1 GF: 0-0 Fm: 0-0**
Distance: 5f/6f: 0-0 **7f-8f: 1-2** 9f-13f: 0-0 14f+: 0-0
Track : **LH: 1-1** RH: 0-0 **Tight: 1-1** Gall: 0-0
Aids: Bl: 0-0 Vi: 0-0 Tstrap: 0-0 Ckp: 0-0
Best Rating: **90** 9/09 Ling 7f stand

Useful; stays 7f; handles Polytrack.

Zaaqya

105 **91**
3-y-o b f Nayef (USA)-Classical Dancer (Dr Fong (USA))
J L Dunlop Hamdan Al Maktoum

Placings:61615-063133036 **(7148)**
2009: 10^{0}GF, 9^{6}F, 9^{3}GF, 12^{1}GF, 12^{3}S, 13^{3}GF, 12^{0}GF, 12^{3}G, 12^{6}G,

	Starts	1st	2nd	3rd	Win & Pl
Career Total (Turf)	14	3	0	4	20475

86 7/09 Newb 1m4f5y (0-85)H G-F £4857
76 9/08 Pont 1m4y (0-85) G-F £4533
75 7/08 Donc 7f GD £5459
Total win prize-money £14849

Going (Turf): Sf: 0-1 GS: 0-0 Gd: 1-5 **GF: 2-7** Fm: 0-1
Distance: 5f/6f: 0-0 7f-8f: 1-4 **9f-13f: 2-9** 14f+: 0-1
Track : **LH: 2-6** RH: 0-4 Tight: 0-4 **Gall: 1-5**
Aids: Bl: 0-0 Vi: 0-0 Tstrap: 0-0 Ckp: 0-0
Best Rating: **91** 8/09 Newb 1m5f61y gd-fm

Fair; stays 1m4f; acts on good and faster ground.

Zabeel House

64(98) (69)**19**
6-y-o b g Anabaa (USA)-Divine Quest (Kris)
John A Harris Mr Vijay Kara

Placings:21035/5643000**346**/000**650013**/045000-062040 **(1276)**
2009: 9^{0}SD, 8^{6}SD, 8^{2}SD, 10^{0}SD, 8^{4}SD, 8^{0}GF,

	Starts	1st	2nd	3rd	Win & Pl
Career Total (Turf)	15	1	1	2	8652
Career Total (AW)	21	1	1	2	3871

65 12/07 Wolv 1m141y (0-55) STD £2047
86 6/05 Ripn 6f G-F £4886
Total win prize-money £6935

Going (Turf): Sf: 0-1 GS: 0-2 Gd: 0-3 **GF: 1-9** Fm: 0-0
Distance: 5f/6f: 1-3 7f-8f: 0-19 9f-13f: 1-14 14f+: 0-0
Track : **LH: 1-18** RH: 0-11 **Tight: 1-16** Gall: 0-0
Aids: Bl: 0-0 Vi: 0-1 Tstrap: 1-14 Ckp: 1-14
Best Rating: **87** 9/05 NmkR 1m good

Modest; effective over 1m; acts on fast ground and Polytrack; has worn cheekpieces.

Zabeel Tower

102(81) (10)**79**
6-y-o b g Anabaa (USA)-Bint Kaldoun (IRE) (Kaldoun (FR))
R Allan Anthony White

Placings:40042340/51600/0013503453**300**/115211341430 65-0356452640500 **(7403)**
2009: 7^{0}GF, 7^{3}GF, 7^{5}G, 7^{6}GF, 8^{4}GF, 6^{5}G, 7^{2}G, 8^{6}GF, 7^{4}G, 9^{0}S, 7^{5}GF, 7^{0}G, 8^{0}SD,

	Starts	1st	2nd	3rd	Win & Pl
Career Total (Turf)	49	7	3	7	30194
Career Total (AW)	4	0	0	1	302

79 8/08 Muss 7f30y (0-75)H SFT £3885
74 6/08 Ches 7f122y (0-70)H GD £3561
71 6/08 Muss 7f30y (0-65)H G-F £2590
63 5/08 Muss 7f30y (0-60)H G-F £2266
59 5/08 Thsk 7f (0-55)H G-F £2590
56 6/07 Ayr 1m1f20y (0-55)H GD £2590
59 4/06 Ripn 1m1f170y GD £3238
Total win prize-money £20725

Going (Turf): Sf: 1-6 GS: 0-6 **Gd: 3-17 GF: 3-18** Fm: 0-2
Distance: 5f/6f: 0-2 **7f-8f: 5-31** 9f-13f: 2-19 14f+: 0-1
Track : LH: 3-19 **RH: 4-24 Tight: 6-33** Gall: 0-0
Aids: Bl: 0-0 Vi: 0-4 Tstrap: 5-24 Ckp: 5-24
Best Rating: **79** 9/08 Muss 7f30y good

Modest; effective over 7f-1m 2f; acts on a sound surface; has worn cheekpieces.

Zabellah

(45)
4-y-o ch f Zaha (CAN)-Polar Refrain (Polar Falcon (USA))
J Balding Brandsby Racing

Placings:5 **(0323)**
2009: 8^{5}SD,

	Starts	1st	2nd	3rd	Win & Pl
Career Total (Turf)	0	0	0	0	
Career Total (AW)	1	0	0	0	0

Going (Turf): **Sf: 0-0 GS: 0-0 Gd: 0-0 GF: 0-0 Fm: 0-0**
Distance: 5f/6f: 0-0 7f-8f: 0-1 9f-13f: 0-0 14f+: 0-0
Track : LH: 0-1 RH: 0-0 Tight: 0-0 Gall: 0-0
Aids: Bl: 0-0 Vi: 0-0 Tstrap: 0-0 Ckp: 0-0

Zabougg

93 **52**
4-y-o b g Tobougg (IRE)-Double Fault (IRE) (Zieten (USA))
D W Barker Mrs Judy Allen

Placings:540/0065600600-000 **(1556)**
2009: 15^{0}GF, 16^{0}F, 10^{0}GF,

	Starts	1st	2nd	3rd	Win & Pl
Career Total (Turf)	16	0	0	0	209

Going (Turf): **Sf: 0-1 GS: 0-3 Gd: 0-5 GF: 0-6 Fm: 0-1**
Distance: 5f/6f: 0-2 7f-8f: 0-6 9f-13f: 0-6 14f+: 0-2
Track : LH: 0-10 RH: 0-2 Tight: 0-8 Gall: 0-1
Aids: Bl: 0-0 Vi: 0-1 Tstrap: 0-3 Ckp: 0-3
Best Rating: **66** 7/07 Rdcr 7f gd-sft

Modest; effective over 6f; acts on good ground.

Zach's Harmoney (USA)

(97) (63)**69**
5-y-o ch g Diesis-Cool Ashlee (USA) (Mister Baileys)
Miss M E Rowland Sarnian Racing

Placings:42006/05662206400-0 **(0105)**
2009: 9^{0}SD,

	Starts	1st	2nd	3rd	Win & Pl
Career Total (Turf)	9	0	2	0	1686
Career Total (AW)	8	0	1	0	1147

Going (Turf): **Sf: 0-1 GS: 0-2 Gd: 0-2 GF: 0-4 Fm: 0-0**
Distance: 5f/6f: 0-0 7f-8f: 0-5 9f-13f: 0-12 14f+: 0-0
Track : LH: 0-11 RH: 0-4 Tight: 0-8 Gall: 0-0
Aids: Bl: 0-0 Vi: 0-0 Tstrap: 0-1 Ckp: 0-1
Best Rating: **69** 7/08 Pont 1m2f6y gd-fm

Modest sort; stays 1m2f; handles quick ground.

Zachary Boy (IRE)

80(94) (63)**46**
2-y-o b c Orpen (USA)-Shun (Selkirk (USA))
B G Powell B G Powell

Placings:0002 **(7319)**
2009: 6^{0}GF, 5^{0}GF, 7^{0}GS, 7^{2}SD,

	Starts	1st	2nd	3rd	Win & Pl
Career Total (Turf)	3	0	0	0	
Career Total (AW)	1	0	1	0	806

Going (Turf): **Sf: 0-0 GS: 0-1 Gd: 0-0 GF: 0-2 Fm: 0-0**
Distance: 5f/6f: 0-2 7f-8f: 0-2 9f-13f: 0-0 14f+: 0-0
Track : LH: 0-1 RH: 0-0 Tight: 0-1 Gall: 0-0
Aids: Bl: 0-0 Vi: 0-0 Tstrap: 0-0 Ckp: 0-0
Best Rating: **63** 11/09 Wolv 7f32y stand

Moderate; stays 7f and acts on Polytrack.

Zacinto

111 **125**
3-y-o b c Dansili-Ithaca (USA) (Distant View (USA))
Sir Michael Stoute K Abdulla

Placings:12-1120 **(7308a)**
2009: 8^{1}S, 8^{1}G, 8^{2}GF, 8^{0}F,

	Starts	1st	2nd	3rd	Win & Pl
Career Total (Turf)	6	3	2	0	177624

116 8/09 Gdwd 1m GD £67442
107 8/09 Gdwd 1m SFT £28385
95 7/08 Sand 7f16y G-F £6476
Total win prize-money £102304

Going (Turf): **Sf: 1-2** GS: 0-0 **Gd: 1-1 GF: 1-2** Fm: 0-1
Distance: 5f/6f: 0-0 **7f-8f: 3-6** 9f-13f: 0-0 14f+: 0-0
Track : LH: 0-1 **RH: 3-4** Tight: 0-0 Gall: 0-1
Aids: Bl: 0-0 Vi: 0-0 Tstrap: 0-0 Ckp: 0-0
Best Rating: **125** 9/09 Asct 1m gd-fm

Group class; Listed winner; runner-up in the Group 1 Queen Elizabeth II Stakes; effective at 7f-1m; acts on most ground.

Zaffaan

64(97) (88)**84**
3-y-o ch g Efisio-Danceabout (Shareef Dancer (USA))
E A L Dunlop Hamdan Al Maktoum

Placings:01420-00 **(2270)**
2009: 8^{0}G, 7^{0}HY,

	Starts	1st	2nd	3rd	Win & Pl
Career Total (Turf)	6	1	0	0	8445
Career Total (AW)	1	0	1	0	1156

84 7/08 Asct 6f G-S £7771
Total win prize-money £7771

Going (Turf): Sf: 0-2 **GS: 1-1** Gd: 0-1 GF: 0-2 Fm: 0-0
Distance: **5f/6f: 1-4** 7f-8f: 0-2 9f-13f: 0-1 14f+: 0-0
Track : LH: 0-2 RH: 0-1 Tight: 0-0 Gall: 0-1
Aids: Bl: 0-0 Vi: 0-0 Tstrap: 0-0 Ckp: 0-0
Best Rating: **88** 8/08 GrLe 6f stand

Very useful; effective at 6f; acts on easy ground and on Polytrack.

Zaffature

91(90) (59)58

2-y-o b f Zafeen (FR)-Alice Blackthorn (Forzando)
M Botti Giuliano Manfredini

Placings:454222 (7120)
2009: 7^{4}SD, 7^{5}SD, 7^{4}G, 7^{2}SD, 7^{2}SD, 8^{2}GF,

	Starts	1st	2nd	3rd	Win & Pl
Career Total (Turf)	2	0	1	0	749
Career Total (AW)	4	0	2	0	2034

Going (Turf): Sf: 0-0 GS: 0-0 Gd: 0-1 GF: 0-1 Fm: 0-0
Distance: 5f/6f: 0-0 7f-8f: 0-5 9f-13f: 0-1 14f+: 0-0
Track : LH: 0-4 RH: 0-1 Tight: 0-3 Gall: 0-0
Aids: Bl: 0-1 Vi: 0-0 Tstrap: 0-0 Ckp: 0-0
Best Rating: 59 7/09 Kemp 7f stand

Moderate; stays 1m; acts on good ground; goes on Polytrack.

Zaffeu

(103) (66)65

8-y-o ch g Zafonic (USA)-Leaping Flame (USA) (Trempolino (USA))
A G Juckes Whispering Winds

Placings:06624510600002500/6140134440530634/23322203155/4250065/141110-24200 (1936)
2009: 16^{2}SS, 14^{4}SD, 14^{2}SD, 16^{0}SD, 13^{0}SD,

	Starts	1st	2nd	3rd	Win & Pl
Career Total (Turf)	15	1	2	0	6918
Career Total (AW)	47	7	7	6	22110

69	3/08	Sthl	1m6f	(0-65)H	STD	£1774
62	3/08	Sthl	1m6f		STD	£1774
59	2/08	Wolv	2m119y	(0-60)H	STD	£1774
66	1/08	Sthl	1m4f	(0-50)H	STD	£1774
55	11/06	Wolv	1m5f194y		STD	£2730
57	2/05	Ling	1m4f	(0-55)H	STD	£2952
59	1/05	Wolv	1m4f50y	(0-55)H	STD	£2598
71	6/04	Bath	1m3f144y	E(0-70)	FRM	£4251

Total win prize-money £19632

Going (Turf): Sf: 0-2 GS: 0-2 Gd: 0-4 GF: 0-5 Fm: 1-2
Distance: 5f/6f: 0-0 7f-8f: 0-0 9f-13f: 4-38 14f+: 4-24
Track : LH: 8-61 RH: 0-1 Tight: 5-46 Gall: 0-1
Aids: Bl: 0-2 Vi: 0-0 Tstrap: 0-0 Ckp: 0-0
Best Rating: 73 4/04 Pont 1m4f8y heavy

Modest; stays 2m; acts on fast ground; goes on sand.

Zafranagar (IRE)

72 74

4-y-o b g Cape Cross (IRE)-Zafaraniya (IRE) (Doyoun)
A W Carroll Paul Downing

Placings:22/223-0 (7221)
2009: 11^{0}S,

	Starts	1st	2nd	3rd	Win & Pl
Career Total (Turf)	6	0	4	1	18086

Going (Turf): Sf: 0-2 GS: 0-1 Gd: 0-2 GF: 0-0 Fm: 0-0
Distance: 5f/6f: 0-1 7f-8f: 0-2 9f-13f: 0-3 14f+: 0-0
Track : LH: 0-1 RH: 0-2 Tight: 0-1 Gall: 0-0
Aids: Bl: 0-0 Vi: 0-0 Tstrap: 0-0 Ckp: 0-0
Best Rating: 85 7/07 Chan 7f good

Zaftil (IRE)

92(74) (2)35

3-y-o br f Tillerman-Zafine (Zafonic (USA))
H S Howe Horses Away Racing Club

Placings:0000-05000 (3209)
2009: 8^{0}SD, 6^{5}GF, 5^{0}F, 6^{0}GF, 8^{0}G,

	Starts	1st	2nd	3rd	Win & Pl
Career Total (Turf)	8	0	0	0	0
Career Total (AW)	1	0	0	0	

Going (Turf): Sf: 0-0 GS: 0-1 Gd: 0-2 GF: 0-2 Fm: 0-3
Distance: 5f/6f: 0-4 7f-8f: 0-4 9f-13f: 0-1 14f+: 0-0
Track : LH: 0-4 RH: 0-1 Tight: 0-0 Gall: 0-4
Aids: Bl: 0-0 Vi: 0-0 Tstrap: 0-0 Ckp: 0-0
Best Rating: 35 5/09 Chep 6f16y gd-fm

Zagarock

87 52

2-y-o b f Rock Of Gibraltar (IRE)-Zagaleta (Sri Pekan (USA))
B Palling Flying Eight Partnership

Placings:005 (6931)
2009: 8^{0}GF, 8^{0}G, 8^{5}G,

	Starts	1st	2nd	3rd	Win & Pl
Career Total (Turf)	3	0	0	0	0

Going (Turf): Sf: 0-0 GS: 0-0 Gd: 0-2 GF: 0-1 Fm: 0-0
Distance: 5f/6f: 0-0 7f-8f: 0-1 9f-13f: 0-2 14f+: 0-0
Track : LH: 0-1 RH: 0-1 Tight: 0-1 Gall: 0-0
Aids: Bl: 0-0 Vi: 0-0 Tstrap: 0-0 Ckp: 0-0
Best Rating: 52 10/09 Bath 1m5y good

Zaham (USA)

107(105) (98)116

5-y-o ch g Silver Hawk (USA)-Guerre Et Paix (USA) (Soviet Star (USA))
M Johnston Hamdan Al Maktoum

Placings:2113111322/02-646 (3190)
2009: 12^{6}GF, 10^{4}SD, 12^{6}GF,

	Starts	1st	2nd	3rd	Win & Pl
Career Total (Turf)	10	3	3	2	158251
Career Total (AW)	5	2	1	0	14167

112	6/07	Asct	1m2f		G-F	£31229
103	6/07	Epsm	1m2f18y	(0-105)H	GD	£46740
94	5/07	Newb	1m2f6y	(0-105)H	G-S	£38638
91	4/07	Kemp	1m	(0-90)H	STD	£8724
74	3/07	Ling	1m		STD	£3886

Total win prize-money £129218

Going (Turf): Sf: 0-1 GS: 1-2 Gd: 1-2 GF: 1-5 Fm: 0-0
Distance: 5f/6f: 0-0 7f-8f: 2-3 9f-13f: 3-12 14f+: 0-0
Track : LH: 3-9 RH: 2-6 Tight: 2-6 Gall: 2-5
Aids: Bl: 0-1 Vi: 0-0 Tstrap: 0-0 Ckp: 0-0
Best Rating: 116 4/08 Newb 1m4f5y soft

Group class; winner in Listed company; Group placed; effective over 1m2f-1m4f; acts on good and softer ground; also goes on Polytrack; suited by forcing tactics.

Zahoo (IRE)

93 75

2-y-o b f Nayef (USA)-Tanaghum (Darshaan)
J L Dunlop Hamdan Al Maktoum

Placings:531 (6284)
2009: 7^{5}G, 8^{3}GF, 8^{1}GF,

	Starts	1st	2nd	3rd	Win & Pl
Career Total (Turf)	3	1	0	1	4415

74	9/09	Hayd	1m30y	G-F	£3885

Total win prize-money £3886

Going (Turf): Sf: 0-0 GS: 0-0 Gd: 0-1 GF: 1-2 Fm: 0-0
Distance: 5f/6f: 0-0 7f-8f: 0-2 9f-13f: 1-1 14f+: 0-0
Track : LH: 1-1 RH: 0-1 Tight: 0-0 Gall: 0-0
Aids: Bl: 0-0 Vi: 0-0 Tstrap: 0-0 Ckp: 0-0
Best Rating: 75 8/09 NmkJ 7f good

Fair; effective over 1m; acts on fast ground.

Zaif (IRE)

97(98) (68)82

6-y-o b g Almutawakel-Colourful (FR) (Gay Mecene (USA))
D J S Ffrench Davis Miss R Wakeford

Placings:02/0416520/0016026556/534560-005000010 (7490)
2009: 10^{0}GF, 10^{0}G, 11^{5}SD, 12^{0}GF, 12^{0}G, 10^{0}SD, 12^{0}SD, 11^{1}G, 12^{0}SD,

	Starts	1st	2nd	3rd	Win & Pl
Career Total (Turf)	30	3	3	1	28083
Career Total (AW)	4	0	0	0	0

65	10/09	Brig	1m3f196y	(0-55)H	GD	£2590
87	6/07	Bevl	1m1f207y	(0-80)H	G-F	£5181
88	7/06	NmkJ	1m2f		G-F	£7772

Total win prize-money £15544

Going (Turf): Sf: 0-5 GS: 0-6 Gd: 1-7 GF: 2-11 Fm: 0-1
Distance: 5f/6f: 0-0 7f-8f: 0-4 9f-13f: 3-30 14f+: 0-0
Track : LH: 1-7 RH: 2-22 Tight: 0-8 Gall: 1-14
Aids: Bl: 0-1 Vi: 0-0 Tstrap: 1-2 Ckp: 1-2
Best Rating: 94 9/06 Asct 1m2f soft

Fair; stays 1m2f and acts on most ground; has worn cheekpieces; usually held up.

Zain (IRE)

89(79) (22)48

5-y-o b g Alhaarth (IRE)-Karenaragon (Aragon)
J G Given Mrs G A Jennings

Placings:04050/60215023/0066-0000 (7581)
2009: 10^{0}G, 8^{0}G, 8^{0}GS, 8^{0}SF,

	Starts	1st	2nd	3rd	Win & Pl
Career Total (Turf)	16	1	2	1	6766
Career Total (AW)	5	0	0	0	0

51	8/07	Ayr	1m2f	(0-65)H	G-F	£3238

Total win prize-money £3239

Going (Turf): Sf: 0-2 GS: 0-7 Gd: 0-4 GF: 1-3 Fm: 0-0
Distance: 5f/6f: 0-3 7f-8f: 0-3 9f-13f: 1-15 14f+: 0-0
Track : LH: 1-14 RH: 0-5 Tight: 0-8 Gall: 0-1
Aids: Bl: 0-0 Vi: 0-0 Tstrap: 0-0 Ckp: 0-0
Best Rating: 66 8/07 Pont 1m4y gd-sft

Modest performer; stays 1m2f; acts on easy and on fast ground.

Zalkani (IRE)

(109) (66)47

9-y-o ch g Cadeaux Genereux-Zallaka (IRE) (Shardari)
J Pearce Mrs Lisa Matthews

Placings:600/3300050040020114/1023250024020032365 60/3601304210111440P21206/06103640225560/504011061-545424015365006 (6918)
2009: 12^{5}SD, 10^{4}SD, 13^{5}SD, 13^{4}SD, 13^{2}SD, 12^{4}SD, 13^{0}SD, 12^{1}SD, 12^{5}SD, 13^{3}SF, 12^{6}SD, 12^{5}SD, 12^{0}SD, 13^{0}SS, 12^{6}SD,

	Starts	1st	2nd	3rd	Win & Pl
Career Total (Turf)	17	0	2	0	1586
Career Total (AW)	83	14	10	9	52930

66	4/09	Wolv	1m4f50y	(0-65)H	STD	£2388
65	12/08	Ling	1m5f	(0-60)H	STD	£2047
59	9/08	Wolv	1m4f50y	(0-60)H	STD	£2388

61	9/08	Wolv	1m4f50y	(0-50)H	STD	£2388
66	3/07	Ling	1m4f		STD	£2184
64	11/06	Ling	1m4f	(0-70)H	STD	£3123
64	6/06	Wolv	1m4f50y		STD	£3238
57	6/06	Wolv	1m4f50y		STD	£3412
66	5/06	Wolv	1m4f50y		STD	£2730
70	4/06	Ling	1m2f		STD	£2388
81	2/06	Ling	1m2f	(0-75)H	STD	£3238
80	1/05	Ling	1m2f	(0-70)H	STD	£3485
73	12/04	Ling	1m2f	(0-62)H	STD	£2955
57	12/04	Ling	1m2f		STD	£1575

Total win prize-money £37544

Going (Turf): Sf: 0-1 GS: 0-3 Gd: 0-4 GF: 0-7 Fm: 0-2
Distance: 5f/6f: 0-0 7f-8f: 0-6 9f-13f: 14-85 14f+: 0-9
Track : LH: 14-89 RH: 0-9 Tight: 14-83 Gall: 0-2
Aids: Bl: 0-0 Vi: 0-0 Tstrap: 0-0 Ckp: 0-0
Best Rating: 81 2/06 Ling 1m2f stand

Modest; effective at around 1m4f; acts on Polytrack.

Zambuka (FR)

77 45
2-y-o gr f Zieten (USA)-Mercalle (FR) (Kaldoun (FR))
R Curtis Ms M J Hughes

Placings:00 (1866)
2009: 5^0GF, 6^0G,

	Starts	1st	2nd	3rd	Win & Pl
Career Total (Turf)	2	0	0	0	

Going (Turf): Sf: 0-0 GS: 0-0 Gd: 0-1 GF: 0-1 Fm: 0-0
Distance: 5f/6f: 0-2 7f-8f: 0-0 9f-13f: 0-0 14f+: 0-0
Track : LH: 0-0 RH: 0-0 Tight: 0-0 Gall: 0-0
Aids: Bl: 0-0 Vi: 0-0 Tstrap: 0-0 Ckp: 0-0
Best Rating: 45 4/09 NmkR 5f gd-fm

Zando's Pearl

(27)
2-y-o b f Forzando-Siouxtabul (Makbul)
C J Price John & David Heymans & Ron Squires

Placings:0 (7556)
2009: 5^0SD,

	Starts	1st	2nd	3rd	Win & Pl
Career Total (Turf)	0	0	0	0	
Career Total (AW)	1	0	0	0	

Going (Turf): Sf: 0-0 GS: 0-0 Gd: 0-0 GF: 0-0 Fm: 0-0
Distance: 5f/6f: 0-1 7f-8f: 0-0 9f-13f: 0-0 14f+: 0-0
Track : LH: 0-1 RH: 0-0 Tight: 0-1 Gall: 0-0
Aids: Bl: 0-0 Vi: 0-0 Tstrap: 0-0 Ckp: 0-0

Zaplamation (IRE)

100(88) (40)63
4-y-o b g Acclamation-Zapatista (Rainbow Quest (USA))
J J Quinn (D W Barker 29/6) Andrew Turton & David Barker

Placings:0040050/5634603330-4012221 (6817)
2009: 10^4GF, 10^0GF, 8^1GS, 8^2GF, 8^2GS, 8^2GF, 10^1GF,

	Starts	1st	2nd	3rd	Win & Pl
Career Total (Turf)	23	2	3	4	7261
Career Total (AW)	1	0	0	0	0

63	10/09	Rdcr	1m2f	(0-60)H	G-F	£1648
57	7/09	Newc	1m3y	(0-60)H	G-S	£2072

Total win prize-money £3720

Going (Turf): Sf: 0-3 GS: 1-4 Gd: 0-5 GF: 1-11 Fm: 0-0
Distance: 5f/6f: 0-5 7f-8f: 0-5 9f-13f: 2-14 14f+: 0-0
Track : LH: 1-12 RH: 0-6 Tight: 1-7 Gall: 0-2
Aids: Bl: 0-0 Vi: 0-0 Tstrap: 0-0 Ckp: 0-0
Best Rating: 63 10/09 Rdcr 1m2f gd-fm

Moderate; stays 1m2f; acts on fast and easy ground.

Zarilan (IRE)

(79) (51)67
4-y-o b g Namid-Zarlana (IRE) (Darshaan)
Evan Williams Peter Conway

Placings:330-3 (0488)
2009: 8^3SS,

	Starts	1st	2nd	3rd	Win & Pl
Career Total (Turf)	3	0	0	2	1566
Career Total (AW)	1	0	0	1	403

Going (Turf): Sf: 0-1 GS: 0-0 Gd: 0-1 GF: 0-0 Fm: 0-0
Distance: 5f/6f: 0-0 7f-8f: 0-3 9f-13f: 0-1 14f+: 0-0
Track : LH: 0-2 RH: 0-2 Tight: 0-0 Gall: 0-1
Aids: Bl: 0-0 Vi: 0-0 Tstrap: 0-0 Ckp: 0-0
Best Rating: 67 6/08 Curr 1m yield

Zarinski (IRE)

102 (79)90
3-y-o b g Dalakhani (IRE)-Zarafsha (IRE) (Alzao (USA))
N J Henderson (Jim Best 1/8) C Duggan,B Gilligan,A Carr & W Hawkes

Placings:6426-140 (4520)
2009: 12^1SD, 12^4GF, 11^0G,

	Starts	1st	2nd	3rd	Win & Pl
Career Total (Turf)	4	0	0	0	2848
Career Total (AW)	3	1	1	0	9155

77	4/09	Dund	1m4f	STD	£7379

Total win prize-money £7380

Going (Turf): Sf: 0-0 GS: 0-0 Gd: 0-2 GF: 0-1 Fm: 0-0
Distance: 5f/6f: 0-0 7f-8f: 0-4 9f-13f: 1-3 14f+: 0-0
Track : LH: 1-4 RH: 0-3 Tight: 0-1 Gall: 0-1
Aids: Bl: 0-0 Vi: 0-0 Tstrap: 0-1 Ckp: 0-1
Best Rating: 90 6/09 Asct 1m4f gd-fm

Useful; stays 1m4f; acts on fast ground and Polytrack; has worn cheekpieces.

Zars Gold (IRE)

91(97) (67)67
4-y-o b f Xaar-Affirmed Crown (USA) (Affirmed (USA))
J Gallagher O Murphy

Placings:4/40423406-50400 (2185)
2009: 6^5SD, 7^0SD, 7^4GF, 6^0GF, 7^0SD,

	Starts	1st	2nd	3rd	Win & Pl
Career Total (Turf)	10	0	1	1	3407
Career Total (AW)	4	0	0	0	377

Going (Turf): Sf: 0-2 GS: 0-0 Gd: 0-1 GF: 0-4 Fm: 0-1
Distance: 5f/6f: 0-4 7f-8f: 0-10 9f-13f: 0-0 14f+: 0-0
Track : LH: 0-6 RH: 0-5 Tight: 0-1 Gall: 0-0
Aids: Bl: 0-1 Vi: 0-0 Tstrap: 0-1 Ckp: 0-1
Best Rating: 71 10/07 Leop 7f gd-fm

Modest; stays 7f; acts on fast and on heavy ground and Polytrack.

Zaskia (IRE)

86(84) (46)44
2-y-o ch f Tomba-Flamenco Dancer (Mark Of Esteem (IRE))
K A Ryan Mrs P Good

Placings:50405030 (7089)
2009: 5^5SD, 5^0GF, 6^4F, 6^0G, 5^5SD, 5^0SD, 5^3G, 6^0SD,

	Starts	1st	2nd	3rd	Win & Pl
Career Total (Turf)	4	0	0	1	620
Career Total (AW)	4	0	0	0	0

Going (Turf): Sf: 0-0 GS: 0-0 Gd: 0-2 GF: 0-1 Fm: 0-1
Distance: 5f/6f: 0-8 7f-8f: 0-0 9f-13f: 0-0 14f+: 0-0
Track : LH: 0-3 RH: 0-0 Tight: 0-2 Gall: 0-0
Aids: Bl: 0-1 Vi: 0-0 Tstrap: 0-0 Ckp: 0-0
Best Rating: 46 7/09 Sthl 5f stand

Zazous

81(100) (64)51
8-y-o b g Zafonic (USA)-Confidentiality (USA) (Lyphard (USA))
J J Bridger J J Bridger

Placings:03/63000/00250303100363/01612202020144003 1/66040440152500/4005330000060010-0 (1710)
2009: 6^0GF,

	Starts	1st	2nd	3rd	Win & Pl
Career Total (Turf)	28	2	3	3	12119
Career Total (AW)	42	5	3	6	12863

55	10/08	Kemp	1m	(0-50)H	STD	£1706
63	5/07	Sals	6f212y	(0-65)H	G-F	£3123
67	11/06	Ling	6f	(0-57)H	STD	£2590
65	8/06	Newb	6f8y	(0-70)H	GD	£3238
58	2/06	Ling	6f	(0-45)	STD	£1365
55	2/06	Ling	6f	(0-45)	STD	£1365
54	11/05	Ling	5f	(0-45)	STD	£1416

Total win prize-money £14805

Going (Turf): Sf: 0-3 GS: 0-5 Gd: 1-8 GF: 1-11 Fm: 0-1
Distance: 5f/6f: 4-29 7f-8f: 3-39 9f-13f: 0-2 14f+: 0-0
Track : LH: 4-35 RH: 1-14 Tight: 4-31 Gall: 0-1
Aids: Bl: 0-0 Vi: 0-0 Tstrap: 0-0 Ckp: 0-0
Best Rating: 67 3/07 Ling 7f stand

Moderate; effective at around 6f-1m; acts on Polytrack.

Zazy's Gift

62 7
2-y-o b f Pastoral Pursuits-Tintac (Intikhab (USA))
George Baker Mrs K R Smith-Maxwell

Placings:00 (6965)
2009: 7^0GF, 7^0G,

	Starts	1st	2nd	3rd	Win & Pl
Career Total (Turf)	2	0	0	0	

Going (Turf): Sf: 0-0 GS: 0-0 Gd: 0-1 GF: 0-1 Fm: 0-0
Distance: 5f/6f: 0-0 7f-8f: 0-2 9f-13f: 0-0 14f+: 0-0
Track : LH: 0-2 RH: 0-0 Tight: 0-0 Gall: 0-0
Aids: Bl: 0-0 Vi: 0-0 Tstrap: 0-0 Ckp: 0-0
Best Rating: 7 9/09 Wwck 7f26y gd-fm

Ze Finale

60
2-y-o b f Zafeen (FR)-Dominelle (Domynsky)
T D Easterby Mrs Sue Tindall

Placings:00 (1624)
2009: 5^{0}F, 5^{0}GF,

	Starts	1st	2nd	3rd	Win & Pl
Career Total (Turf)	2	0	0	0	

Going (Turf): **Sf: 0-0 GS: 0-0 Gd: 0-0 GF: 0-1 Fm: 0-1**
Distance: 5f/6f: 0-2 7f-8f: 0-0 9f-13f: 0-0 14f+: 0-0
Track : LH: 0-1 RH: 0-0 Tight: 0-0 Gall: 0-0
Aids: Bl: 0-0 Vi: 0-0 Tstrap: 0-0 Ckp: 0-0

Zebrano

104(92) (77)**83**
3-y-o br g Storming Home-Ambience Lady (Batshoof)
Miss E C Lavelle Caloona Racing

Placings:032322-05021030 (7395)
2009: 10^{0}GF, 8^{5}SD, 7^{0}GF, 6^{2}F, 7^{1}S, 7^{0}GF, 5^{3}G, 6^{0}SD,

	Starts	1st	2nd	3rd	Win & Pl
Career Total (Turf)	10	1	4	1	8152
Career Total (AW)	4	0	0	2	794

83 7/09 Chep 7f16y (0-75)H SFT £3238
Total win prize-money £3238

Going (Turf): **Sf: 1-2** GS: 0-0 Gd: 0-1 GF: 0-6 Fm: 0-1
Distance: 5f/6f: 0-4 **7f-8f: 1-9** 9f-13f: 0-1 14f+: 0-0
Track : LH: 0-5 RH: 0-3 Tight: 0-4 Gall: 0-0
Aids: Bl: 0-0 Vi: 0-0 Tstrap: 0-0 Ckp: 0-0
Best Rating: 83 10/09 Brig 5f213y good

Fair; effective at 7f; acts on fast ground and on Polytrack.

Zeffirelli

92(105) (62)**59**
4-y-o ch g Tomba-Risky Valentine (Risk Me (FR))
M Quinn A G MacLennan

Placings:3224033140-4506526 (7796)
2009: 7^{4}SD, 7^{5}G, 8^{0}GF, 7^{6}GF, 7^{5}HY, 7^{2}SD, 7^{6}SS,

	Starts	1st	2nd	3rd	Win & Pl
Career Total (Turf)	8	1	1	1	3526
Career Total (AW)	9	0	2	2	1794

59 9/08 Yarm 7f3y GD £1942
Total win prize-money £1943

Going (Turf): Sf: 0-2 GS: 0-1 **Gd: 1-3** GF: 0-2 Fm: 0-0
Distance: 5f/6f: 0-0 **7f-8f: 1-14** 9f-13f: 0-3 14f+: 0-0
Track : LH: 0-9 RH: 0-0 Tight: 0-3 Gall: 0-0
Aids: Bl: 0-0 Vi: 0-0 Tstrap: 0-0 Ckp: 0-0
Best Rating: 62 12/09 Sthl 7f stand

Moderate; probably stays 1m; acts on good and soft ground and Fibresand.

Zefooha (FR)

101 (68)**68**
5-y-o ch m Lomitas-Bezzaaf (Machiavellian (USA))
T D Walford Mrs A T Preston

Placings:41/000352/0051122405 (6385)
2009: 12^{0}G, 16^{0}F, 14^{5}G, 14^{1}GF, 14^{1}GF, 14^{2}F, 14^{2}G, 14^{4}GF, 11^{0}GS, 12^{5}GF,

	Starts	1st	2nd	3rd	Win & Pl
Career Total (Turf)	17	3	2	1	12025
Career Total (AW)	1	0	1	0	907

66 6/09 Carl 1m6f32y (0-70)H G-F £2914
64 5/09 Rdcr 1m6f19y (0-65)H G-F £1942
71 7/06 Folk 7f G-F £4533
Total win prize-money £9391

Going (Turf): Sf: 0-0 GS: 0-1 Gd: 0-4 **GF: 3-8** Fm: 0-4
Distance: 5f/6f: 0-0 7f-8f: 1-3 9f-13f: 0-6 **14f+: 2-9**
Track : LH: 1-10 RH: 1-5 **Tight: 1-11** Gall: 0-2
Aids: Bl: 0-0 Vi: 0-0 Tstrap: 0-1 Ckp: 0-1
Best Rating: 71 7/06 Folk 7f gd-fm

Moderate; stays 1m6f; acts on fast ground; also goes on Polytrack.

Zegna (IRE)

(103) (78)**78**
3-y-o gr g Clodovil (IRE)-Vade Retro (IRE) (Desert Sun)
B Smart Clipper Logistics

Placings:523-210 (7875)
2009: 5^{2}SD, 6^{1}SD, 6^{0}SD,

	Starts	1st	2nd	3rd	Win & Pl
Career Total (Turf)	3	0	1	1	1266
Career Total (AW)	3	1	1	0	3396

78 12/09 Kemp 6f STD £2590
Total win prize-money £2590

Going (Turf): **Sf: 0-1 GS: 0-2 Gd: 0-0 GF: 0-0 Fm: 0-0**
Distance: **5f/6f: 1-6** 7f-8f: 0-0 9f-13f: 0-0 14f+: 0-0
Track : LH: 0-3 **RH: 1-2** Tight: 0-2 Gall: 0-0
Aids: Bl: 0-0 Vi: 0-0 Tstrap: 0-0 Ckp: 0-0
Best Rating: 78 12/09 Kemp 6f stand

Fair; effective over 6f; acts on easy ground; goes on Polytrack.

Zeitoper

106 **102**
2-y-o b c Singspiel (IRE)-Kazzia (GER) (Zinaad)
Saeed Bin Suroor Godolphin

Placings:111 (6889a)
2009: 8^{1}GS, 8^{1}GF, 9^{1}GS,

	Starts	1st	2nd	3rd	Win & Pl
Career Total (Turf)	3	3	0	0	51493

102 10/09 Lonc 1m1f G-S £38835
98 10/09 Epsm 1m114y G-F £7477
80 9/09 Sand 1m14y G-S £5180
Total win prize-money £51493

Going (Turf): Sf: 0-0 **GS: 2-2** Gd: 0-0 GF: 1-1 Fm: 0-0
Distance: 5f/6f: 0-0 7f-8f: 0-0 **9f-13f: 3-3** 14f+: 0-0
Track : LH: 1-1 **RH: 2-2 Tight: 1-1** Gall: 0-0
Aids: Bl: 0-0 Vi: 0-0 Tstrap: 0-0 Ckp: 0-0
Best Rating: 102 10/09 Lonc 1m1f gd-sft

Smart brother to Dubai Sheema Classic winner Eastern Anthem; out of a mare who won the 1000 Guineas and Oaks; promising colt; made winning debut over 1m on easy ground and following up on fast.

Zeloca (IRE)

52(59)
2-y-o ch f Refuse To Bend (IRE)-Lily's Girl (IRE) (Hamas (IRE))
Mrs L C Jewell Valence Racing

Placings:000 (6122)
2009: 6^{0}G, 8^{0}SD, 7^{0}SD,

	Starts	1st	2nd	3rd	Win & Pl
Career Total (Turf)	1	0	0	0	
Career Total (AW)	2	0	0	0	

Going (Turf): **Sf: 0-0 GS: 0-0 Gd: 0-1 GF: 0-0 Fm: 0-0**
Distance: 5f/6f: 0-1 7f-8f: 0-2 9f-13f: 0-0 14f+: 0-0
Track : LH: 0-2 RH: 0-0 Tight: 0-2 Gall: 0-1
Aids: Bl: 0-0 Vi: 0-0 Tstrap: 0-0 Ckp: 0-0

Zelos Diktator

97(78) (38)**63**
3-y-o br g Diktat-Chanterelle (IRE) (Indian Ridge)
Rae Guest (J G Given 1/8) Tremousser Partnership

Placings:00-606061 (6766)
2009: 8^{6}SD, 10^{0}GF, 8^{6}GS, 10^{0}S, 12^{6}GF, 12^{1}GS,

	Starts	1st	2nd	3rd	Win & Pl
Career Total (Turf)	7	1	0	0	2590
Career Total (AW)	1	0	0	0	0

63 10/09 Newc 1m4f93y G-S £2590
Total win prize-money £2590

Going (Turf): Sf: 0-1 **GS: 1-3** Gd: 0-1 GF: 0-2 Fm: 0-0
Distance: 5f/6f: 0-1 7f-8f: 0-0 **9f-13f: 1-7** 14f+: 0-0
Track : **LH: 1-7** RH: 0-1 Tight: 0-2 **Gall: 1-3**
Aids: Bl: 0-0 Vi: 0-1 Tstrap: 1-2 Ckp: 1-2
Best Rating: 63 10/09 Newc 1m4f93y gd-sft

Modest; stays 1m4f; acts on easy ground; has worn various headgear.

Zelos Dream (IRE)

88(95) (60)**64**
2-y-o ch f Redback-Endless Peace (IRE) (Russian Revival (USA))
R A Harris (Rae Guest 22/10) Ridge House Stables Ltd

Placings:45224103336 (7713)
2009: 5^{4}SD, 6^{5}G, 5^{2}G, 5^{2}G, 5^{4}GF, 5^{1}GF, 6^{0}SD, 5^{3}SD, 6^{3}SD, 6^{3}SD, 5^{6}SD,

	Starts	1st	2nd	3rd	Win & Pl
Career Total (Turf)	5	1	2	0	4300
Career Total (AW)	6	0	0	3	897

64 9/09 Bevl 5f (0-65) G-F £2729
Total win prize-money £2730

Going (Turf): Sf: 0-0 GS: 0-0 Gd: 0-3 **GF: 1-2** Fm: 0-0
Distance: **5f/6f: 1-11** 7f-8f: 0-0 9f-13f: 0-0 14f+: 0-0
Track : LH: 0-5 RH: 0-2 Tight: 0-2 Gall: 0-2
Aids: Bl: 0-0 Vi: 0-0 Tstrap: 0-0 Ckp: 0-0
Best Rating: 64 9/09 Bevl 5f gd-fm

Moderate; effective over 5f; acts on good ground; goes on Fibresand and Polytrack.

Zelos Girl (IRE)

97(89) (50)**72**
3-y-o ch f Exceed And Excel (AUS)-Sedna (FR) (Bering)
J G Given (Rae Guest 19/8) Beadle, Davies & Jennings

Placings:310-06460403 (6308)
2009: 5^{0}GF, 5^{6}G, 5^{4}GF, 5^{6}G, 6^{0}GF, 5^{4}S, 5^{0}SD, 5^{3}GF,

	Starts	1st	2nd	3rd	Win & Pl
Career Total (Turf)	9	1	0	2	3674
Career Total (AW)	2	0	0	0	

72 8/08 Carl 5f GD £2590
Total win prize-money £2590

Going (Turf): Sf: 0-1 GS: 0-0 **Gd: 1-4** GF: 0-4 Fm: 0-0
Distance: **5f/6f: 1-11** 7f-8f: 0-0 9f-13f: 0-0 14f+: 0-0
Track : LH: 0-3 **RH: 1-1** Tight: 0-1 **Gall: 1-4**
Aids: Bl: 0-0 Vi: 0-0 Tstrap: 0-0 Ckp: 0-0
Best Rating: 72 8/08 Carl 5f good

Modest; effective over 5f; acts on good ground.

Zelos Spirit

77 **23**
2-y-o b f Tiger Hill (IRE)-Good Mood (USA) (Devil's Bag

(USA))
Rae Guest Beadle, Davies & Jennings

Placings:0 (6796)
2009: 6⁰S,

	Starts	1st	2nd	3rd	Win & Pl
Career Total (Turf)	1	0	0	0	

Going (Turf): Sf: 0-1 GS: 0-0 Gd: 0-0 GF: 0-0 Fm: 0-0
Distance: 5f/6f: 0-0 7f-8f: 0-1 9f-13f: 0-0 14f+: 0-0
Track : LH: 0-0 RH: 0-0 Tight: 0-0 Gall: 0-0
Aids: Bl: 0-0 Vi: 0-0 Tstrap: 0-0 Ckp: 0-0
Best Rating: 23 10/09 Nott 6f15y soft

Zemario (IRE)

99 **75**
3-y-o b g Dalakhani (IRE)-Noushkey (Polish Precedent (USA))
M A Jarvis Sheikh Ahmed Al Maktoum

Placings:1 (5322)
2009: 10¹GF,

	Starts	1st	2nd	3rd	Win & Pl
Career Total (Turf)	1	1	0	0	2730
75 8/09 Wind 1m2f7y		G-F	£2729		

Total win prize-money £2730

Going (Turf): Sf: 0-0 GS: 0-0 Gd: 0-0 GF: 1-1 Fm: 0-0
Distance: 5f/6f: 0-0 7f-8f: 0-0 9f-13f: 1-1 14f+: 0-0
Track : LH: 0-0 RH: 1-1 Tight: 1-1 Gall: 0-0
Aids: Bl: 0-0 Vi: 0-0 Tstrap: 0-0 Ckp: 0-0
Best Rating: 75 8/09 Wind 1m2f7y gd-fm

Winner on debut; effective over 1m2f; acts on fast ground.

Zenarinda

90 **64**
2-y-o b f Zamindar (USA)-Tenpence (Bob Back (USA))
M H Tompkins Dullingham Park

Placings:44 (7099)
2009: 6⁴G, 8⁴G,

	Starts	1st	2nd	3rd	Win & Pl
Career Total (Turf)	2	0	0	0	596

Going (Turf): Sf: 0-0 GS: 0-0 Gd: 0-2 GF: 0-0 Fm: 0-0
Distance: 5f/6f: 0-1 7f-8f: 0-0 9f-13f: 0-1 14f+: 0-0
Track : LH: 0-0 RH: 0-0 Tight: 0-0 Gall: 0-0
Aids: Bl: 0-0 Vi: 0-0 Tstrap: 0-0 Ckp: 0-0
Best Rating: 64 10/09 Yarm 1m3y good

Zennerman (IRE)

93(96) (50)**72**
6-y-o b g Observatory (USA)-Precocious Miss (USA) (Diesis)
W M Brisbourne Shropshire Wolves

Placings:0142103050/6243043650/54016030626/0456250341-0001600 (6024)
2009: 7⁰GF, 9⁰G, 8⁰G, 8¹GF, 8⁶SF, 8⁰SD, 7⁰SD,

	Starts	1st	2nd	3rd	Win & Pl
Career Total (Turf)	35	4	3	5	23299
Career Total (AW)	13	1	1	0	4167
66 8/09 Nott 1m75y (0-75)H			SFT	£2914	
72 8/08 Ches 7f122y (0-65)H			SFT	£2729	
79 7/07 Wolv 7f32y (0-75)H			STD	£3562	
83 7/05 Wwck 7f26y			SFT	£3770	
76 5/05 Hayd 5f			G-F	£3848	

Total win prize-money £16824

Going (Turf): Sf: 2-5 GS: 0-4 Gd: 0-7 GF: 2-19 Fm: 0-0
Distance: 5f/6f: 1-3 7f-8f: 3-36 9f-13f: 1-9 14f+: 0-0
Track : LH: 4-28 RH: 0-13 Tight: 2-25 Gall: 0-2
Aids: Bl: 2-11 Vi: 1-5 Tstrap: 0-6 Ckp: 0-6
Best Rating: 85 6/06 Muss 1m gd-fm

Modest; effective over 7f-1m; acts on most ground; also goes on Polytrack; has worn a visor.

Zepnove (IRE)

79(89) (62)**47**
3-y-o b f Noverre (USA)-Royal Zephyr (USA) (Royal Academy (USA))
N B King (M Wigham 30/6) Stephen Lower Insurance Services Ltd

Placings:1000-0004 (2487)
2009: 8⁰GS, 9⁰GF, 8⁰GF, 12⁴SD,

	Starts	1st	2nd	3rd	Win & Pl
Career Total (Turf)	5	0	0	0	
Career Total (AW)	3	1	0	0	7621
62 5/08 Dund 7f			STD	£7621	

Total win prize-money £7621

Going (Turf): Sf: 0-0 GS: 0-1 Gd: 0-1 GF: 0-2 Fm: 0-0
Distance: 5f/6f: 0-0 7f-8f: 1-4 9f-13f: 0-4 14f+: 0-0
Track : LH: 1-3 RH: 0-4 Tight: 0-2 Gall: 0-0
Aids: Bl: 0-3 Vi: 0-0 Tstrap: 0-0 Ckp: 0-0
Best Rating: 62 5/08 Dund 7f stand

Zero Cool (USA)

(106) (83)**82**
5-y-o br g Forestry (USA)-Fabulous (USA) (Seeking The Gold (USA))
G L Moore Dedman Properties

Placings:62130/60430360323-42436 (1604)
2009: 10⁴SD, 10²SD, 8⁴SD, 10³SD, 10⁶SD,

	Starts	1st	2nd	3rd	Win & Pl
Career Total (Turf)	8	1	0	2	5497
Career Total (AW)	13	0	3	4	4121
86 10/07 Wind 1m67y			G-S	£2817	

Total win prize-money £2817

Going (Turf): Sf: 0-4 GS: 1-3 Gd: 0-0 GF: 0-1 Fm: 0-0
Distance: 5f/6f: 0-0 7f-8f: 0-6 9f-13f: 1-15 14f+: 0-0
Track : LH: 0-12 RH: 1-8 Tight: 1-15 Gall: 0-1
Aids: Bl: 0-0 Vi: 0-0 Tstrap: 0-3 Ckp: 0-3
Best Rating: 87 10/07 Wind 1m2f7y soft

Fair; effective over 1m-1m2f; acts on easy ground; goes on Polytrack.

Zero Money (IRE)

99(96) (75)**79**
3-y-o ch g Bachelor Duke (USA)-Dawn Chorus (IRE) (Mukaddamah (USA))
R Charlton Ms Gillian Khosla

Placings:3-1355 (6976)
2009: 5¹G, 7³GF, 7⁵GS, 7⁵SD,

	Starts	1st	2nd	3rd	Win & Pl
Career Total (Turf)	4	1	0	2	3963
Career Total (AW)	1	0	0	0	0
79 5/09 Leic 5f218y			GD	£2590	

Total win prize-money £2590

Going (Turf): Sf: 0-0 GS: 0-2 Gd: 1-1 GF: 0-1 Fm: 0-0
Distance: 5f/6f: 1-2 7f-8f: 0-3 9f-13f: 0-0 14f+: 0-0
Track : LH: 0-0 RH: 0-1 Tight: 0-0 Gall: 0-0
Aids: Bl: 0-0 Vi: 0-0 Tstrap: 0-0 Ckp: 0-0
Best Rating: 79 9/09 Newb 7f gd-fm

Fair; stays 6f and should stay 7f; acts on a sound surface; should improve.

Zero Seven

73 **35**
2-y-o b c Halling (USA)-Tempting Fate (IRE) (Persian Bold)
C E Brittain Mohammed Al Shafar

Placings:00 (2358)
2009: 5⁰GF, 5⁰GF,

	Starts	1st	2nd	3rd	Win & Pl
Career Total (Turf)	2	0	0	0	

Going (Turf): Sf: 0-0 GS: 0-0 Gd: 0-0 GF: 0-2 Fm: 0-0
Distance: 5f/6f: 0-2 7f-8f: 0-0 9f-13f: 0-0 14f+: 0-0
Track : LH: 0-0 RH: 0-0 Tight: 0-0 Gall: 0-0
Aids: Bl: 0-0 Vi: 0-0 Tstrap: 0-0 Ckp: 0-0
Best Rating: 35 5/09 Leic 5f218y gd-fm

Zerzura

(99)
3-y-o b g Oasis Dream-River Fantasy (USA) (Irish River (FR))
H R A Cecil Robert Brown & Partners

Placings:5 (7882)
2009: 10⁵SD,

	Starts	1st	2nd	3rd	Win & Pl
Career Total (Turf)	0	0	0	0	
Career Total (AW)	1	0	0	0	0

Going (Turf): Sf: 0-0 GS: 0-0 Gd: 0-0 GF: 0-0 Fm: 0-0
Distance: 5f/6f: 0-0 7f-8f: 0-0 9f-13f: 0-1 14f+: 0-0
Track : LH: 0-1 RH: 0-0 Tight: 0-1 Gall: 0-0
Aids: Bl: 0-0 Vi: 0-0 Tstrap: 0-0 Ckp: 0-0
Best Rating:

Half-brother to Frenchmans Bay.

Zeyadah (IRE)

(96) (67)**42**
3-y-o b f Red Ransom (USA)-Beraysim (Lion Cavern (USA))
M A Jarvis Sheikh Ahmed Al Maktoum

Placings:0-520 (4085)
2009: 8⁵SD, 10²SD, 10⁰SD,

	Starts	1st	2nd	3rd	Win & Pl
Career Total (Turf)	1	0	0	0	
Career Total (AW)	3	0	1	0	771

Going (Turf): Sf: 0-1 GS: 0-0 Gd: 0-0 GF: 0-0 Fm: 0-0
Distance: 5f/6f: 0-1 7f-8f: 0-1 9f-13f: 0-2 14f+: 0-0
Track : LH: 0-1 RH: 0-2 Tight: 0-1 Gall: 0-0
Aids: Bl: 0-0 Vi: 0-0 Tstrap: 0-0 Ckp: 0-0
Best Rating: 67 6/09 Kemp 1m2f stand

Modest; stays 1m2f; acts on Polytrack.

Zeydnaa (IRE)

(40)**56**
9-y-o b g Bahhare (USA)-Hadawah (USA) (Riverman (USA))
C R Wilson Mrs J Wilson (durham)

Placings:003534610/306000/0/0 **(2344)**
2009: 14^{0}GF,

	Starts	1st	2nd	3rd	Win & Pl
Career Total (Turf)	16	1	0	3	4519
Career Total (AW)	1	0	0	0	

54 10/05 Catt 1m7f177y (0-55)H G-F £2980
Total win prize-money £2981

Going (Turf): Sf: 0-0 GS: 0-1 Gd: 0-3 **GF: 1-9** Fm: 0-3
Distance: 5f/6f: 0-0 7f-8f: 0-1 9f-13f: 0-4 **14f+: 1-12**
Track : **LH: 1-15** RH: 0-2 **Tight: 1-16** Gall: 0-1
Aids: Bl: 0-0 Vi: 0-0 Tstrap: 0-0 Ckp: 0-0
Best Rating: **56** 6/06 Haml 1m5f9y gd-fm

Zhukhov (IRE)

103 (81)**81**
6-y-o ch g Allied Forces (USA)-Karameg (IRE) (Danehill (USA))
T G McCourt Barry Doyle

Placings:04306/0000305251000/404401142300/0030552534135-0040002200100053 0 **(7530a)**
2009: 6^{0}YS, 5^{0}Y, 5^{4}S, 7^{0}YS, 6^{0}HY, 7^{0}G, 8^{2}Y, 6^{2}S, 8^{0}HY, 5^{0}SH, 6^{1}S, 6^{0}G, 8^{0}SD, 5^{0}Y, 7^{5}S, 7^{3}SD, 8^{0}SD,

	Starts	1st	2nd	3rd	Win & Pl
Career Total (Turf)	55	5	5	6	68830
Career Total (AW)	5	0	0	1	1944

81	9/09	List	6f60y	(50-80)H	SFT	£8721
78	9/08	Curr	5f	H	SH	£28720
79	7/07	Fair	6f	(60-90)H	HVY	£7003
70	7/07	Bell	5f	(42-60)H	Y-S	£4435
65	8/06	Cork	5f	(40-70)H	G-F	£4765

Total win prize-money £53646

Going (Turf): **Sf: 2-12** GS: 0-0 Gd: 0-12 GF: 1-5 Fm: 0-7
Distance: **5f/6f: 4-36** 7f-8f: 1-22 9f-13f: 0-2 14f+: 0-0
Track : **LH: 2-24** RH: 1-19 Tight: 0-0 Gall: 0-0
Aids: Bl: 0-0 Vi: 0-0 Tstrap: 0-0 Ckp: 0-0
Best Rating: **81** 11/09 Dund 7f stand

Zidane

108 (94)**113**
7-y-o b g Danzero (AUS)-Juliet Bravo (Glow (USA))
J R Fanshawe Jan and Peter Hopper

Placings:21/0212104/4101400/15020020-03015000 (7294)
2009: 6^{0}GF, 6^{3}G, 6^{0}GF, 6^{1}S, 6^{5}GF, 6^{0}G, 6^{0}G, 7^{0}S,

	Starts	1st	2nd	3rd	Win & Pl
Career Total (Turf)	31	7	5	1	152337
Career Total (AW)	1	0	0	0	887

105	8/09	Donc	6f		SFT	£7477
113	4/08	NmkR	6f		GD	£17031
110	8/07	Gdwd	6f	H	G-F	£62320
107	5/07	Asct	6f	(0-95)H	SFT	£9067
95	6/06	NmkJ	6f	(0-80)H	G-F	£6477
86	5/06	Thsk	6f	(0-75)H	GD	£5505
70	10/05	Rdcr	6f		G-F	£3883

Total win prize-money £111762

Going (Turf): Sf: 2-5 GS: 0-3 Gd: 2-12 **GF: 3-11** Fm: 0-0
Distance: **5f/6f: 7-28** 7f-8f: 0-4 9f-13f: 0-0 14f+: 0-0
Track : LH: 0-1 RH: 0-0 Tight: 0-1 Gall: 0-1
Aids: Bl: 0-0 Vi: 0-0 Tstrap: 0-0 Ckp: 0-0
Best Rating: **113** 6/08 Newc 6f soft

Smart; winner of the 2007 Stewards' Cup and in Listed company in 2008; effective over 6f; acts on most ground; has worn a tongue tie; usually held up.

Ziggy Lee

98(104) (80)**82**
3-y-o b g Lujain (USA)-Mary O'Grady (USA) (Swain (IRE))
S C Williams Rothmere Racing Limited

Placings:30-60121 **(2219)**
2009: 7^{6}SD, 7^{0}SD, 5^{1}SD, 5^{2}GF, 5^{1}GF,

	Starts	1st	2nd	3rd	Win & Pl
Career Total (Turf)	4	1	1	1	5228
Career Total (AW)	3	1	0	0	2914

82	5/09	Brig	5f59y	(0-75)H	G-F	£3532
80	4/09	Wolv	5f20y	(0-70)H	STD	£2914

Total win prize-money £6446

Going (Turf): Sf: 0-0 GS: 0-1 Gd: 0-0 **GF: 1-2** Fm: 0-1
Distance: **5f/6f: 2-5** 7f-8f: 0-2 9f-13f: 0-0 14f+: 0-0
Track : **LH: 2-4** RH: 0-1 **Tight: 1-1** Gall: 0-1
Aids: Bl: 0-0 Vi: 0-0 Tstrap: 0-0 Ckp: 0-0
Best Rating: **82** 5/09 Brig 5f59y gd-fm

Fair; effective over 5f; acts on fast ground and on Polytrack.

Zim Ho

67(96) (67)
3-y-o b c Zilzal (USA)-Robanna (Robellino (USA))
J Akehurst Green Pastures Farm

Placings:461-000000 **(6777)**
2009: 7^{0}GF, 7^{0}SD, 7^{0}G, 7^{0}SD, 7^{0}SD, 6^{0}SD,

	Starts	1st	2nd	3rd	Win & Pl
Career Total (Turf)	2	0	0	0	
Career Total (AW)	7	1	0	0	2533

63 12/08 Ling 7f STD £2388
Total win prize-money £2388

Going (Turf): **Sf: 0-0 GS: 0-0 Gd: 0-1 GF: 0-1 Fm: 0-0**
Distance: 5f/6f: 0-1 **7f-8f: 1-8** 9f-13f: 0-0 14f+: 0-0
Track : **LH: 1-4** RH: 0-3 **Tight: 1-4** Gall: 0-0
Aids: Bl: 0-0 Vi: 0-1 Tstrap: 0-0 Ckp: 0-0
Best Rating: **67** 11/08 Kemp 7f stand

Fair; stays 7f and acts on Polytrack.

Zinjbar (USA)

93(88) (62)**72**
2-y-o b f Dynaformer (USA)-Renowned Cat (USA) (Storm Cat (USA))
C E Brittain Saeed Manana

Placings:033454 **(6063)**
2009: 5^{0}GF, 5^{3}GF, 6^{3}GF, 7^{4}SD, 6^{5}SD, 7^{4}GF,

	Starts	1st	2nd	3rd	Win & Pl
Career Total (Turf)	4	0	0	2	1925
Career Total (AW)	2	0	0	0	192

Going (Turf): **Sf: 0-0 GS: 0-0 Gd: 0-0 GF: 0-4 Fm: 0-0**
Distance: 5f/6f: 0-3 7f-8f: 0-3 9f-13f: 0-0 14f+: 0-0
Track : LH: 0-0 RH: 0-2 Tight: 0-0 Gall: 0-1
Aids: Bl: 0-0 Vi: 0-0 Tstrap: 0-0 Ckp: 0-0
Best Rating: **72** 7/09 Newb 6f8y gd-fm

Modest; $350,000 first foal from a good American family; stays 6f; acts on fast ground.

Zip Lock (IRE)

82 **31**
3-y-o b g Invincible Spirit (IRE)-Buckle (IRE) (Common Grounds)
J Noseda The Searchers

Placings:0 **(1703)**
2009: 6^{0}GF,

	Starts	1st	2nd	3rd	Win & Pl
Career Total (Turf)	1	0	0	0	

Going (Turf): **Sf: 0-0 GS: 0-0 Gd: 0-0 GF: 0-1 Fm: 0-0**
Distance: 5f/6f: 0-1 7f-8f: 0-0 9f-13f: 0-0 14f+: 0-0
Track : LH: 0-0 RH: 0-0 Tight: 0-0 Gall: 0-0
Aids: Bl: 0-0 Vi: 0-0 Tstrap: 0-0 Ckp: 0-0
Best Rating: **31** 5/09 Sals 6f gd-fm

Zizou (IRE)

(84) (27)**56**
6-y-o b g Fantastic Light (USA)-Search Committee (USA) (Roberto (USA))
S Curran Ian Hutchins

Placings:020600200/30000506040033000/00/0 **(7766)**
2009: 11^{0}SD,

	Starts	1st	2nd	3rd	Win & Pl
Career Total (Turf)	18	0	2	1	3367
Career Total (AW)	11	0	0	2	834

Going (Turf): **Sf: 0-2 GS: 0-2 Gd: 0-3 GF: 0-7 Fm: 0-4**
Distance: 5f/6f: 0-1 7f-8f: 0-9 9f-13f: 0-18 14f+: 0-1
Track : LH: 0-13 RH: 0-11 Tight: 0-18 Gall: 0-0
Aids: Bl: 0-0 Vi: 0-1 Tstrap: 0-1 Ckp: 0-1
Best Rating: **68** 7/05 Sand 7f16y good

Zomerlust

106 **98**
7-y-o b g Josr Algarhoud (IRE)-Passiflora (Night Shift (USA))
J J Quinn Dawson And Quinn

Placings:3124423/024100046/0100000620/650222016000/000010055000-0045151600 **(7060)**
2009: 7^{0}GF, 7^{0}GF, 7^{4}G, 7^{5}GF, 7^{1}GF, 7^{5}GF, 7^{1}S, 7^{6}G, 7^{0}G, 8^{0}GF,

	Starts	1st	2nd	3rd	Win & Pl
Career Total (Turf)	60	7	7	2	114037

94	8/09	Ayr	7f50y	(0-85)H	SFT	£6476
89	7/09	York	7f	(0-80)H	G-F	£6476
98	7/08	York	6f	(0-95)H	HVY	£10361
103	7/07	York	6f	(0-105)H	HVY	£31160
104	4/06	Pont	6f	(0-90)H	GD	£11217
95	6/05	Ripn	6f	(0-95)H	G-S	£8374
69	8/04	Ripn	6f	E	SFT	£5023

Total win prize-money £79089

Going (Turf): **Sf: 4-16**GS: 1-9 Gd: 1-16 GF: 1-18 Fm: 0-1
Distance: **5f/6f: 5-33** 7f-8f: 2-26 9f-13f: 0-1 14f+: 0-0
Track : **LH: 3-15** RH: 0-1 Tight: 0-7 **Gall: 1-1**
Aids: Bl: 0-1 **Vi: 3-11** Tstrap: 0-1 Ckp: 0-1
Best Rating: **104** 4/06 Pont 6f good

Useful; effective over 6f-7f; acts on most ground; has worn cheekpieces and a visor.

Zonic Boom (FR)

79 (56)**2**
9-y-o b/br g Zafonic (USA)-Rosi Zambotti (IRE) (Law Society (USA))
Heather Dalton C Fletcher

Placings:00/530306/00015140354/00/00100/0 **(5483)**
2009: 14^{0}GF,

	Starts	1st	2nd	3rd	Win & Pl
Career Total (Turf)	21	2	0	3	8824
Career Total (AW)	6	1	0	0	2389

56 7/07 Wolv 2m119y (0-65)H STD £2388
67 6/05 Gdwd 1m1f (0-70)H GD £3705
61 5/05 Nott 1m54y (0-60)H G-F £2721
Total win prize-money £8816

Going (Turf): Sf: 0-1 GS: 0-2 **Gd: 1-6 GF: 1-11** Fm: 0-1
Distance: 5f/6f: 0-0 7f-8f: 0-1 **9f-13f: 2-21** 14f+: 1-5
Track : **LH: 2-19** RH: 1-8 **Tight: 2-13** Gall: 0-2
Aids: Bl: 0-1 Vi: 0-0 Tstrap: 1-5 Ckp: 1-5
Best Rating: 69 4/04 Wind 1m67y good

Zouk

99 **70**
3-y-o ch g Zilzal (USA)-Annette Vallon (IRE) (Efisio)
W R Swinburn P W Harris

Placings:45053 **(5503)**
2009: 8^{4}GF, 8^{5}GF, 8^{0}G, 8^{5}GS, 8^{3}G,

	Starts	1st	2nd	3rd	Win & Pl
Career Total (Turf)	5	0	0	1	915

Going (Turf): Sf: 0-0 GS: 0-1 Gd: 0-2 GF: 0-2 Fm: 0-0
Distance: 5f/6f: 0-0 7f-8f: 0-2 9f-13f: 0-3 14f+: 0-0
Track : LH: 0-1 RH: 0-3 Tight: 0-2 Gall: 0-0
Aids: Bl: 0-0 Vi: 0-0 Tstrap: 0-0 Ckp: 0-0
Best Rating: 70 8/09 Chep 1m14y good

Fair; stays 1m; acts on good ground.

Zowington

105 (29)**91**
7-y-o gr g Zafonic (USA)-Carmela Owen (Owington)
S C Williams O Pointing

Placings:0416201**0**/1600030**0**/0440/61040056-00321106220000 **(7189)**
2009: 5^{0}G, 6^{0}GS, 5^{3}GF, 6^{2}GF, 5^{1}GF, 6^{1}GF, 5^{0}GF, 6^{6}GS, 6^{2}GS, 6^{2}GF, 7^{0}GF, 7^{0}GF, 5^{0}GS, 7^{0}G,

	Starts	1st	2nd	3rd	Win & Pl
Career Total (Turf)	39	5	4	2	54926
Career Total (AW)	3	1	0	0	3471

87 6/09 Folk 6f (0-85)H G-F £14247
83 6/09 Leic 5f218y (0-75)H G-F £3238
91 5/08 Ling 5f (0-85)H G-F £4100
94 4/06 Epsm 5f (0-95)H G-F £9348
95 10/05 Newb 6f8y (0-100)H SFT £11804
85 7/05 Wolv 5f216y STD £3471
Total win prize-money £46208

Going (Turf): Sf: 1-6 GS: 0-11 Gd: 0-7 **GF: 4-15** Fm: 0-0
Distance: **5f/6f: 5-37** 7f-8f: 1-5 9f-13f: 0-0 14f+: 0-0
Track : **LH: 1-3** RH: 0-1 **Tight: 1-2** Gall: 0-5
Aids: Bl: 0-1 **Vi: 2-11** Tstrap: 0-0 Ckp: 0-0
Best Rating: 96 9/06 Hayd 6f good

Useful; effective over 5f-6f; acts on most ground and Polytrack; has worn a visor.

Zubova

95(99) (73)**75**
2-y-o b f Dubawi (IRE)-Jalousie (IRE) (Barathea (IRE))
M J Attwater (R Hannon 19/12) J M Duggan & T P Duggan

Placings:24332222 **(7864)**
2009: 6^{2}S, 6^{4}G, 6^{3}GF, 5^{3}SD, 6^{2}SD, 7^{2}SD, 6^{2}SD, 6^{2}SS,

	Starts	1st	2nd	3rd	Win & Pl
Career Total (Turf)	3	0	1	1	3284
Career Total (AW)	5	0	4	1	3577

Going (Turf): Sf: 0-1 GS: 0-0 Gd: 0-1 GF: 0-1 Fm: 0-0
Distance: 5f/6f: 0-6 7f-8f: 0-2 9f-13f: 0-0 14f+: 0-0
Track : LH: 0-4 RH: 0-1 Tight: 0-3 Gall: 0-1
Aids: Bl: 0-0 Vi: 0-0 Tstrap: 0-0 Ckp: 0-0
Best Rating: 75 7/09 Newb 6f8y soft

Fair; effective over 6f-7f; acts on soft ground; goes on Polytrack.

Zulu Chief (USA)

87 (95)**106**
4-y-o b g Fusaichi Pegasus (USA)-La Lorgnette (CAN) (Val De L'Orne (FR))
M F De Kock Sheikh Mohammed Bin Khalifa Al Maktoum

Placings:31340-5 **(5995)**
2009: 8^{5}GS,

	Starts	1st	2nd	3rd	Win & Pl
Career Total (Turf)	5	1	0	2	17482
Career Total (AW)	1	0	0	0	

106 7/08 Naas 1m2f YLD £5588
Total win prize-money £5589

Going (Turf): Sf: 0-2 GS: 0-1 Gd: 0-1 GF: 0-0 Fm: 0-0
Distance: 5f/6f: 0-0 7f-8f: 0-2 **9f-13f: 1-4** 14f+: 0-0
Track : **LH: 1-3** RH: 0-2 Tight: 0-0 Gall: 0-1
Aids: Bl: 0-0 Vi: 0-0 Tstrap: 0-0 Ckp: 0-0
Best Rating: 106 7/08 Naas 1m2f yield

Very useful half-brother to Hawk Wing; stays 1m2f ; acts on easy ground.

Zulu Moon

(94) (71)**56**
3-y-o b g Passing Glance-Mory Kante (USA) (Icecapade (USA))
A M Balding M E Wates

Placings:64-4 **(1963)**
2009: 8^{4}SD,

	Starts	1st	2nd	3rd	Win & Pl
Career Total (Turf)	1	0	0	0	0
Career Total (AW)	2	0	0	0	192

Going (Turf): Sf: 0-0 GS: 0-1 Gd: 0-0 GF: 0-0 Fm: 0-0
Distance: 5f/6f: 0-0 7f-8f: 0-3 9f-13f: 0-0 14f+: 0-0
Track : LH: 0-2 RH: 0-0 Tight: 0-2 Gall: 0-0
Aids: Bl: 0-0 Vi: 0-0 Tstrap: 0-0 Ckp: 0-0
Best Rating: 71 5/09 Ling 1m stand

Zuwaar

108(103) (78)**77**
4-y-o b g Nayef (USA)-Raheefa (USA) (Riverman (USA))
Ian Williams Dr Marwan Koukash

Placings:0**6**10400**22011-150**1302253524**334** **(7760)**
2009: **16**^{1}SD, **16**^{5}SD, **16**^{0}SF, 14^{1}GF, 14^{3}F, 14^{0}S, 14^{2}GF, 15^{2}GF, 16^{5}G, 15^{3}GF, 14^{5}G, 17^{2}GF, 13^{4}GF, **13**^{3}SF, **16**^{3}SD, **16**^{4}SD,

	Starts	1st	2nd	3rd	Win & Pl
Career Total (Turf)	16	2	3	2	14493
Career Total (AW)	12	3	2	2	9710

75 4/09 Hayd 1m6f (0-80)H G-F £5504
78 1/09 Kemp 2m (0-70)H STD £2590
73 12/08 Wolv 2m119y (0-70)H STD £3154
69 12/08 Wolv 2m119y (0-65)H STD £2388
76 7/08 Brig 1m1f209y FRM £2775
Total win prize-money £16413

Going (Turf): Sf: 0-1 GS: 0-2 Gd: 0-4 **GF: 1-7 Fm: 1-2**
Distance: 5f/6f: 0-0 7f-8f: 0-1 9f-13f: 1-6 **14f+: 4-21**
Track : **LH: 4-23** RH: 1-3 **Tight: 2-13** Gall: 0-3
Aids: Bl: 0-0 Vi: 0-1 Tstrap: 1-13 Ckp: 1-13
Best Rating: 78 1/09 Kemp 2m stand

Modest; stays 2m; acts on fast ground; goes on Polytrack; has worn cheekpieces and a tongue tie.

Zuzu (IRE)

94 **93**
3-y-o b f Acclamation-Green Life (Green Desert (USA))
M A Jarvis Stephen Dartnell

Placings:3110-4000 **(5654)**
2009: 6^{4}HY, 6^{0}GF, 5^{0}S, 5^{0}GS,

	Starts	1st	2nd	3rd	Win & Pl
Career Total (Turf)	8	2	0	1	13935

93 8/08 Ripn 6f G-S £6938
84 7/08 Nott 6f15y GD £3885
Total win prize-money £10825

Going (Turf): Sf: 0-2 **GS: 1-2 Gd: 1-3** GF: 0-1 Fm: 0-0
Distance: 5f/6f: 1-7 7f-8f: 1-1 9f-13f: 0-0 14f+: 0-0
Track : LH: 0-0 RH: 0-0 Tight: 0-0 Gall: 0-0
Aids: Bl: 0-0 Vi: 0-0 Tstrap: 0-1 Ckp: 0-1
Best Rating: 93 8/08 Ripn 6f gd-sft

Very useful sprinter; effective at 6f; handles good and easy ground.

LEADING FLAT JOCKEYS 2009

(28 March–7 November 2009)

NAME	WIN-RIDES (%)	2nd	3rd	4th	WIN £	TOTAL £	+/- £
Ryan Moore	179–874 20%	140	112	90	£3,097,314	£4,871,255	-157.64
Richard Hughes	144–768 19%	98	92	70	£1,375,507	£2,245,151	+35.38
Jamie Spencer	130–695 19%	110	82	65	£1,070,055	£1,755,946	-111.48
Chris Catlin	121–1261 10%	134	110	125	£507,409	£821,303	-338.29
N Callan	119–881 14%	124	84	91	£1,004,765	£1,539,774	-176.33
Paul Hanagan	119–999 12%	115	128	120	£720,817	£1,188,089	-115.10
Robert Winston	119–906 13%	104	111	93	£495,995	£827,668	-181.58
Jim Crowley	117–1042 11%	109	121	84	£562,128	£1,023,547	-119.00
T P Queally	108–821 13%	93	99	94	£1,472,779	£2,080,319	-35.99
Joe Fanning	108–696 16%	91	72	71	£641,856	£1,111,537	+8.64
Seb Sanders	106–790 13%	77	91	95	£1,063,529	£1,387,967	-69.28
Phillip Makin	106–737 14%	70	78	82	£513,047	£713,545	-143.64
L Dettori	103–429 24%	57	47	45	£1,401,355	£2,267,057	-21.22
R Hills	98–424 23%	70	49	33	£1,986,100	£2,814,792	+26.29
Eddie Ahern	98–689 14%	92	80	79	£872,254	£1,278,942	-77.68
Ted Durcan	94–617 15%	73	73	53	£927,636	£1,321,893	-75.90
Steve Drowne	91–875 10%	82	91	90	£541,011	£877,853	-56.53
Tom Eaves	85–983 9%	91	106	89	£341,264	£696,122	-396.20
Greg Fairley	85–575 15%	67	65	54	£483,192	£685,553	-122.00
Dane O'Neill	83–802 10%	83	88	88	£417,627	£701,953	-134.78
Martin Dwyer	82–764 11%	87	78	83	£561,933	£1,158,276	-117.03
Adam Kirby	82–718 11%	89	82	88	£371,428	£720,863	-105.10
Jimmy Quinn	81–1016 8%	116	121	107	£296,181	£550,356	-298.20
Grah'm Gibbons	80–701 11%	83	65	77	£314,968	£550,506	-10.59
Shane Kelly	77–761 10%	69	101	88	£364,058	£595,998	-260.44
David Probert	77–672 11%	60	71	77	£291,608	£476,633	-0.83
Darryll Holland	74–553 13%	60	52	62	£351,571	£613,672	-91.41
Jimmy Fortune	73–586 12%	70	73	63	£1,336,859	£2,380,045	-106.35
L P Keniry	73–788 9%	69	72	84	£344,042	£507,149	-158.46
Frederik Tylicki	71–495 14%	84	53	44	£392,346	£582,499	-24.85
S De Sousa	68–507 13%	58	45	49	£328,739	£475,209	+70.60
Luke Morris	68–788 9%	61	105	78	£244,199	£387,045	-210.27
William Buick	66–543 12%	57	60	50	£669,705	£977,813	-55.48
Rich. Kingscote	66–536 12%	58	60	56	£287,443	£469,522	-97.04
Fergus Sweeney	64–703 9%	71	71	100	£253,874	£410,392	-269.27
George Baker	63–609 10%	72	66	84	£460,338	£676,008	-211.26
Tony Hamilton	63–613 10%	59	67	56	£280,516	£428,464	-134.78
Pat Cosgrave	61–577 11%	57	44	58	£273,190	£424,271	-95.90
S Donohoe	59–642 9%	64	60	60	£224,005	£427,503	-190.12
Hayley Turner	57–527 11%	71	62	62	£246,499	£472,356	-107.23
Michael Hills	56–386 15%	51	40	39	£628,816	£1,025,908	-110.63
Francis Norton	55–523 11%	54	51	57	£356,600	£555,567	+111.36
Tony Culhane	53–608 9%	70	68	59	£295,885	£501,465	-157.50
Alan Munro	51–592 9%	71	51	61	£307,807	£753,497	-198.61
K Fallon	50–292 17%	37	36	24	£343,696	£556,827	-10.34
T P O'Shea	49–454 11%	38	53	35	£377,915	£568,213	-149.44

LEADING FLAT TRAINERS 2009

(28 March–7 November 2009)

NAME	WINS-RUNS	2nd	3rd	4th	WIN £	TOTAL £	£1 STKE
Sir M Stoute	99–429 23%	81	57	42	£2,077,609	£3,421,892	-64.76
A P O'Brien	12–78 15%	14	10	6	£1,593,835	£2,984,713	+32.53
M Johnston	214–1214 18%	163	137	128	£1,740,023	£2,833,484	-130.50
R Hannon	188–1365 14%	162	156	152	£1,751,642	£2,812,241	-187.61
S Bin Suroor	148–530 28%	82	72	44	£1,743,062	£2,758,262	+17.67
J H M Gosden	88–514 17%	79	65	55	£1,447,841	£2,308,709	-95.55
B W Hills	87–565 15%	73	70	53	£1,357,837	£1,949,046	-52.61
R A Fahey	164–108415%	137	142	123	£1,121,010	£1,651,517	+44.22
John M Oxx	5–12 42%	0	2	1	£1,599,639	£1,634,280	+7.57
H R A Cecil	62–322 19%	54	47	36	£930,851	£1,388,360	+8.00
W J Haggas	69–345 20%	50	49	39	£793,312	£1,319,411	-52.39
M R Channon	108–1110 10%	134	144	123	£655,057	£1,258,045	-418.19
B J Meehan	61–503 12%	59	58	60	£623,844	£1,227,797	-33.91
M L W Bell	47–369 13%	43	42	49	£793,607	£1,180,870	-97.13
D Nicholls	84–685 12%	74	65	68	£742,938	£1,167,733	-10.59
J Noseda	61–332 18%	47	53	46	£710,380	£1,157,282	-63.89
R M Beckett	56–389 14%	43	46	46	£839,644	£1,054,241	+73.94
K A Ryan	96–858 11%	121	78	80	£603,356	£1,022,124	-304.68
M A Jarvis	71–376 19%	60	37	44	£634,768	£939,952	-42.84
C E Brittain	44–361 12%	36	33	44	£592,748	£888,175	+14.96
C G Cox	51–350 15%	45	44	33	£568,679	£863,588	+68.95
A M Balding	67–496 14%	61	54	51	£458,009	£780,823	-40.77
J L Dunlop	50–366 14%	57	51	32	£445,644	£766,705	-107.86
L M Cumani	48–317 15%	50	30	34	£484,661	£704,993	-79.46
T D Easterby	54–628 9%	50	80	74	£423,562	£691,719	-229.88
P D Evans	109–920 12%	97	94	107	£427,832	£647,218	-32.39
P Ch'pple-Hyam	35–245 14%	29	21	24	£298,228	£591,693	+16.26
H Morrison	56–431 13%	49	42	55	£391,741	£571,221	+71.13
B Smart	49–470 10%	57	66	51	£287,974	£542,754	-154.73
D M Simcock	42–346 12%	53	35	48	£347,667	£537,980	-79.77
M P Tregoning	30–180 17%	18	23	16	£375,329	£522,133	-38.03
E A L Dunlop	40–408 10%	51	53	41	£289,490	£499,781	-115.08
J R Fanshawe	24–192 13%	21	17	23	£306,666	£490,942	+0.25
P F I Cole	37–404 9%	43	38	47	£204,133	£486,673	-147.07
T D Barron	50–346 14%	39	32	35	£373,503	£481,279	+18.57
K R Burke	38–292 13%	35	39	31	£222,029	£468,431	-28.16
J S Goldie	35–400 9%	38	47	43	£219,096	£423,529	-82.00
Tom Dascombe	56–419 13%	53	42	46	£255,262	£419,056	-109.08
G L Moore	49–532 9%	56	53	63	£248,164	£414,782	-265.63

LEADING FLAT OWNERS 2009

(28 March–7 November 2009)

NAME	WINS-RUNS	2nd	3rd	4th	WIN £	TOTAL £
Hamdan Al Maktoum	134–678 20%	96	86	57	£2,218,058	£3,149,091
Godolphin	148–530 28%	82	72	44	£1,743,062	£2,758,262
K Abdulla	73–310 24%	42	41	29	£1,440,729	£2,074,047
Christopher Tsui	4–4 100%	0	0	0	£1,575,935	£1,575,935
Sh. Hamdan Bin Moham'd	101–500 20%	71	62	46	£750,128	£1,368,028
Ballymacoll Stud	10–47 21%	10	2	7	£703,377	£1,210,417
Smith, Mrs Magnier, Tabor	4–30 13%	7	4	0	£346,834	£989,064
Tabor, Smith, Mrs Magnier	3–19 16%	3	2	2	£653,259	£924,981
Cheveley Park Stud	48–251 19%	50	41	20	£482,764	£896,333
Saeed Manana	35–307 11%	27	32	36	£436,989	£681,782
Mrs Magnier, Tabor, Smith	2–22 9%	3	3	3	£312,235	£632,697
Princess Haya Of Jordan	32–181 18%	29	21	23	£299,297	£619,026
Mrs M E Slade	5–21 24%	6	4	1	£573,985	£597,453
Dr Marwan Koukash	44–336 13%	51	38	37	£333,619	£554,850
Sh. Ahmed Al Maktoum	20–155 13%	20	22	22	£366,751	£476,933
The Searchers	6–15 40%	3	1	1	£254,167	£384,242
Findlay & Bloom	26–197 13%	19	29	26	£247,369	£376,217
Jaber Abdullah	23–132 17%	25	17	15	£215,799	£371,240
Lady Bamford	5–15 33%	1	3	2	£249,028	£361,080
Patrick J Fahey	4–14 29%	0	3	1	£225,163	£334,307
Mrs J Wood	16–109 15%	9	8	15	£157,510	£328,914
J C Smith	19–169 11%	11	15	29	£197,485	£327,151
Dab Hand Racing	10–38 26%	9	5	2	£246,272	£325,637
Calvera Partnership No 2	2–13 15%	1	0	5	£224,242	£324,298
R A Green	7–57 12%	6	11	3	£305,615	£319,144
The Queen	20–100 20%	10	15	16	£199,612	£318,949
Mrs P Good	6–37 16%	5	4	2	£113,866	£304,804
Saeed Suhail	12–62 19%	9	13	6	£201,752	£284,464
Jacques Detre	1–1 100%	0	0	0	£255,465	£255,465
Mrs Fitri Hay	10–129 8%	15	8	19	£100,697	£254,148
Lawrie Inman	2–10 20%	1	2	2	£89,764	£253,034
A D Spence	18–164 11%	26	22	15	£133,164	£247,329
Golding Kirtland Callaghan	0–6 —	2	1	0	£0	£238,380
George Strawbridge	10–42 24%	7	5	4	£97,777	£235,734
Windflower Overseas Inc	9–71 13%	13	8	9	£148,271	£235,336
Mr & Mrs R Scott	6–44 14%	9	5	7	£159,224	£234,347
John C Grant	4–23 17%	1	6	2	£197,702	£221,966
J Edgar & W Donaldson	2–6 33%	1	1	1	£158,956	£199,306
V Hubbard & I Higginson	6–9 67%	0	2	0	£173,026	£196,512
Normandie Stud Ltd	12–61 20%	8	9	8	£109,924	£196,229
D A West	7–34 21%	6	3	4	£167,474	£190,534
Lord Lloyd-Webber	1–2 50%	1	0	0	£175,987	£189,975
Coleman Bloodstock Ltd	3–21 14%	3	5	0	£97,480	£187,202

WINNERS OF PRINCIPAL RACES

CLASSICS

2000 GUINEAS
2009 Sea The Stars
2008 Henrythenavigator
2007 Cockney Rebel
2006 George Washington
2005 Footstepsinthesand
2004 Haafhd
2003 Refuse To Bend
2002 Rock Of Gibraltar
2001 Golan
2000 King's Best

1000 GUINEAS
2009 Ghanaati
2008 Natagora
2007 Finsceal Beo
2006 Speciosa
2005 Virginia Waters
2004 Attraction
2003 Russian Rhythm
2002 Kazzia
2001 Ameerat
2000 Lahan

DERBY
2009 Sea The Stars
2008 New Approach
2007 Authorized
2006 Sir Percy
2005 Motivator
2004 North Light
2003 Kris Kin
2002 High Chaparral
2001 Galileo
2000 Sinndar

OAKS
2009 Sariska
2008 Look Here
2007 Light Shift
2006 Alexandrova
2005 Eswarah
2004 Ouija Board
2003 Casual Look
2002 Kazzia
2001 Imagine
2000 Love Divine

ST LEGER
2009 Mastery
2008 Conduit
2007 Lucarno
2006 Sixties Icon (York)
2005 Scorpion
2004 Rule Of Law
2003 Brian Boru
2002 Bollin Eric
2001 Milan
2000 Millenary

GROUP 1 RACES

LOCKINGE STAKES
2009 Virtual
2008 Creachadoir
2007 Red Evie
2006 Peeress
2005 Rakti
2004 Russian Rhythm
2003 Hawk Wing
2002 Keltos
2001 Medicean
2000 Aljabr

CORONATION CUP
2009 Ask
2008 Soldier Of Fortune
2007 Scorpion
2006 Shirocco
2005 Yeats
2004 Warrsan
2003 Warrsan
2002 Boreal
2001 Mutafaweq
2000 Daliapour

QUEEN ANNE STAKES
2009 Paco Boy
2008 Haradasun
2007 Ramonti
2006 Ad Valorem
2005 Valixir (run at York)
2004 Refuse To Bend
2003 Dubai Destination
2002 No Excuse Needed
2001 Medicean
2000 Kalanisi

KING'S STAND STAKES
2009 Scenic Blast
2008 Equiano
2007 Miss Andretti
2006 Takeover Target
2005 Chineur (run at York)
2004 The Tatling
2003 Choisir
2002 Dominica
2001 Cassandra Go
2000 Nuclear Debate

ST JAMES'S PALACE STAKES
2009 Mastercraftsman
2008 Henrythenavigator
2007 Excellent Art
2006 Araafa
2005 Shamardal (York)
2004 Azamour
2003 Zafeen
2002 Rock Of Gibraltar
2001 Black Minnaloushe
2000 Giant's Causeway

PRINCE OF WALES'S STAKES
2009 Vision D'Etat
2008 Duke Of Marmalade
2007 Manduro
2006 Ouija Board
2005 Azamour (run at York)
2004 Rakti
2003 Nayef
2002 Grandera
2001 Fantastic Light
2000 Dubai Millennium

GOLD CUP
2009 Yeats
2008 Yeats
2007 Yeats
2006 Yeats
2005 Westerner (York)
2004 Papineau
2003 Mr Dinos
2002 Royal Rebel
2001 Royal Rebel
2000 Kayf Tara

CORONATION STAKES
2009 Ghanaati
2008 Lush Lashes
2007 Indian Ink
2006 Nannina
2005 Maids Causeway (York)
2004 Attraction
2003 Russian Rhythm
2002 Sophisticat
2001 Banks Hill
2000 Crimplene

GOLDEN JUBILEE STAKES
2009 Art Connoisseur
2008 Kingsgate Native
2007 Soldier's Tale
2006 Les Arcs
2005 Cape Of Good Hope (run at York)
2004 Fayr Jag
2003 Choisir
2002 Malhub
2001 Harmonic Way
2000 Superior Premium

CORAL-ECLIPSE STAKES
2009 Sea The Stars
2008 Mount Nelson
2007 Notnowcato
2006 David Junior
2005 Oratorio
2004 Refuse To Bend
2003 Falbrav
2002 Hawk Wing
2001 Medicean
2000 Giant's Causeway

FALMOUTH STAKES
2009 Goldikova
2008 Nahoodh
2007 Simply Perfect
2006 Rajeem
2005 Soviet Song
2004 Soviet Song
2003 Macadamia
2002 Tashawak
2001 Proudwings
2000 Alshakr

JULY CUP
2009 Fleeting Spirit
2008 Marchand D'Or
2007 Sakhee's Secret
2006 Les Arcs
2005 Pastoral Pursuits
2004 Frizzante
2003 Oasis Dream
2002 Continent
2001 Mozart
2000 Agnes World

KING GEORGE VI & QUEEN ELIZABETH DIAMOND STAKES
2009 Conduit
2008 Duke Of Marmalade
2007 Dylan Thomas
2006 Hurricane Run

2005 Azamour (Newbury)
2004 Doyen
2003 Alamshar
2002 Golan
2001 Galileo
2000 Montjeu

SUSSEX STAKES
2009 Rip Van Winkle
2008 Henrythenavigator
2007 Ramonti
2006 Court Masterpiece
2005 Proclamation
2004 Soviet Song
2003 Reel Buddy
2002 Rock Of Gibraltar
2001 Noverre
2000 Giant's Causeway

NASSAU STAKES
2009 Midday
2008 Halfway To Heaven
2007 Peeping Fawn
2006 Ouija Board
2005 Alexander Goldrun
2004 Favourable Terms
2003 Russian Rhythm
2002 Islington
2001 Lailani
2000 Crimplene

JUDDMONTE INTERNATIONAL
2009 Sea The Stars
2008 Duke of Marmalade (run at Newmarket)
2007 Authorized
2006 Notnowcato
2005 Electrocutionist
2004 Sulamani
2003 Falbrav
2002 Nayef
2001 Sakhee
2000 Giant's Causeway

YORKSHIRE OAKS
2009 Dar Re Mi
2008 Lush Lashes (Newmkt)
2007 Peeping Fawn
2006 Alexandrova
2005 Punctilious
2004 Quiff
2003 Islington
2002 Islington
2001 Super Tassa
2000 Petrushka

NUNTHORPE STAKES
2009 Borderlescott
2008 Borderlescott (Newmarket)
2007 Kingsgate Native
2006 Reverence
2005 La Cucaracha
2004 Bahamian Pirate
2003 Oasis Dream
2002 Kyllachy
2001 Mozart
2000 Nuclear Debate

STANLEYBET SPRINT CUP
2009 Regal Parade
2008 African Rose (Doncaster)
2007 Red Clubs
2006 Reverence
2005 Goodricke
2004 Tante Rose
2003 Somnus
2002 Invincible Spirit
2001 Nuclear Debate
2000 Pipalong

QUEEN ELIZABETH II STAKES
2009 Rip Van Winkle
2008 Raven's Pass
2007 Ramonti
2006 George Washington
2005 Starcraft (Newmarket)
2004 Rakti
2003 Falbrav
2002 Where Or When
2001 Summoner
2000 Observatory

SUN CHARIOT STAKES
2009 Sahpresa
2008 Halfway To Heaven
2007 Majestic Roi
2006 Spinning Queen
2005 Peeress
2004 Attraction
2003 Echoes In Eternity
2002 Dress To Thrill
2001 Independence
2000 Danceabout

CHAMPION STAKES
2009 Twice Over
2008 New Approach
2007 Literato
2006 Pride
2005 David Junior
2004 Haafhd
2003 Rakti
2002 Storming Home
2001 Nayef
2000 Kalanisi

GROUP 2 RACES

BETFRED.COM MILE
2009 Paco Boy
2008 Major Cadeaux
2007 Jeremy
2006 Rob Roy
2005 Hurricane Alan
2004 Hurricane Alan
2003 Desert Deer
2002 Swallow Flight
2001 Nicobar
2000 Indian Lodge

JOCKEY CLUB STAKES
2009 Bronze Cannon
2008 Getaway
2007 Sixties Icon
2006 Shirocco
2005Alkaased
2004 Gamut
2003 Warrsan
2002 Marienbard
2001 Millenary
2000 Blueprint

DUKE OF YORK STAKES
2009 Utmost Respect
2008 Assertive
2007 Amadeus Wolf
2006 Steenberg
2005 The Kiddykid
2004 Monsieur Bond
2003 Twilight Blues
2002 Invincible Spirit
2001 Pipalong
2000 Lend A Hand

DANTE STAKES
2009 Black Bear Island
2008 Tartan Bearer
2007 Authorized
2006 Septimus
2005 Motivator
2004 North Light
2003 Magistretti
2002 Moon Ballad
2001 Dilshaan
2000 Sakhee

YORKSHIRE CUP
2009 Ask
2008 Geordieland
2007 Sergeant Cecil
2006 Percussionist
2005 Franklins Gardens
2004 Millenary
2003 Mamool
2002 Zindabad
2001 Marienbard
2000 Kayf Tara

TEMPLE STAKES
(Haydock since 2008)
2009 Look Busy
2008 Fleeting Spirit
2007 Sierra Vista
2006 Reverence
2005 Celtic Mill
2004 Night Prospector (Epsom)
2003 Airwave
2002 Kyllachy
2001 Cassandra Go
2000 Perryston View

HENRY II STAKES
2009 Geordieland
2008 Finalmente
2007 Allegretto
2006 Tungsten Strike
2005 Fight Your Corner
2004 Papineau
2003 Mr Dinos
2002 Akbar
2001 Solo Mio
2000 Persian Punch

RIBBLESDALE STAKES
2009 Flying Cloud
2008 Michita
2007 Silkwood
2006 Mont Etoile
2005 Thakafaat (York)
2004 Punctilious
2003 Spanish Sun
2002 Irresistible Jewel
2001 Sahara Slew
2000 Miletrian

WINDSOR FOREST STAKES
2009 Spacious
2008 Sabana Perdida

2007 Nannina
2006 Soviet Song
2005 Peeress (York)
2004 Favourable Terms

KING EDWARD VII STAKES
2009 Father Time
2008 Campanologist
2007 Boscabel
2006 Papal Bull
2005 Plea Bargain (York)
2004 Five Dynasties
2003 High Accolade
2002 Balakheri
2001 Storming Home
2000 Subtle Power

HARDWICKE STAKES
2009 Bronze Cannon
2008 MacArthur
2007 Maraahel
2006 Maraahel
2005 Bandari (run at York)
2004 Doyen
2003 Indian Creek
2002 Zindabad
2001 Sandmason
2000 Fruits of Love

PRINCESS OF WALES'S STAKES
2009 Doctor Fremantle
2008 Lucarno
2007 Papal Bull
2006 Soapy Danger
2005 Gamut
2004 Bandari
2003 Millenary
2002 Millenary
2001 Mutamam
2000 Little Rock

LANCASHIRE OAKS
2009 Barshiba
2008 Anna Pavlova
2007 Turbo Linn (Newmarket)
2006 Allegretto
2005 Playful Act
2004 Pongee
2003 Place Rouge
2002 Mellow Park
2001 Sacred Song
2000 Ela Athena

BETFAIR CUP
2009 Finjaan
2008 Paco Boy
2007 Tariq
2006 Iffraaj
2005 Court Masterpiece
2004 Byron
2003 Nayyir
2002 Nayyir
2001 Observatory

GOODWOOD CUP
2009 Schiaparelli
2008 Yeats
2007 Allegretto
2006 Yeats
2005 Distinction
2004 Darasim
2003 Persian Punch
2002 Jardines Lookout
2001 Persian Punch
2000 Royal Rebel

HUNGERFORD STAKES
2009 Balthazaar's Gift
2008 Paco Boy
2007 Red Evie
2006 Welsh Emperor
2005 Sleeping Indian
2004 Chic
2003 With Reason
2002 Reel Buddy
2001 Atavus
2000 Arkadian Hero

LONSDALE CUP
2009 Askar Tau
2008 Abandoned
2007 Septimus
2006 Sergeant Cecil
2005 Millenary
2004 First Charter
2003 Bollin Eric
2002 Boreas
2001 Persian Punch
2000 Royal Rebel

GREAT VOLTIGEUR STAKES
2009 Monitor Closely
2008 Centennial (Goodwood)
2007 Lucarno
2006 Youmzain
2005 Hard Top
2004 Rule Of Law
2003 Powerscourt
2002 Bandari
2001 Milan
2000 Air Marshall

CELEBRATION MILE
2009 Zacinto
2008 Raven's Pass
2007 Echelon
2006 Caradak
2005 Chic
2004 Chic
2003 Priors Lodge
2002 Tillerman
2001 No Excuse Needed
2000 Medicean

PARK STAKES
2009 Duff
2008 Arabian Gleam
2007 Arabian Gleam
2006 Iffraaj (York)
2005 Iffraaj
2004 Pastoral Pursuits
2003 Polar Ben
2002 Duck Row
2001 Tough Speed
2000 Distant Music

DONCASTER CUP
2009 Askar Tau
2008 Honolulu
2007 Septimus
2006 Sergeant Cecil (York)
2005 Millenary
2004 Millenary
2003 Persian Punch
2002 Boreas
2001 Alleluia
2000 Enzeli

PARK HILL STAKES
2009 The Miniver Rose
2008 Allegretto
2007 Hi Calypso
2006 Rising Cross (York)
2005 Sweet Stream
2004 Echoes In Eternity
2003 Discreet Brief
2002 Alexander Three D
2001 Ranin
2000 Miletrian

DIADEM STAKES
2009 Sayif
2008 King's Apostle
2007 Haatef
2006 Red Clubs
2005 Baron's Pit
(Newmarket)
2004 Pivotal Point
2003 Acclamation
2002 Crystal Castle
2001 Nice One Clare
2000 Sampower Star

CHALLENGE STAKES
2009 Arabian Gleam
2008 Stimulation
2007 Miss Lucifer
2006 Sleeping Indian
2005 Le Vie Dei Colori
2004 Firebreak
2003 Just James
2002 Nayyir
2001 Munir
2000 Last Resort

TOP TWO-YEAR-OLD RACES

COVENTRY STAKES
2009 Canford Cliffs
2008 Art Connoisseur
2007 Henrythenavigator
2006 Hellvelyn
2005 Red Clubs (York)
2004 Iceman
2003 Three Valleys
2002 Statue Of Liberty
2001 Landseer
2000 CD Europe

QUEEN MARY STAKES
2009 Jealous Again
2008 Langs Lash
2007 Elletelle
2006 Gilded
2005 Flashy Wings (run at York)
2004 Damson
2003 Attraction
2002 Romantic Liaison
2001 Queen's Logic
2000 Romantic Myth

JULY STAKES
2009 Arcano
2008 Classic Blade
2007 Winker Watson
2006 Strategic Prince
2005 Ivan Denisovich
2004 Captain Hurricane
2003 Nevisian Lad
2002 Mister Links
2001 Meshaheer

2000 Noverre

CHERRY HINTON STAKES

2009 Misheer
2008 Please Sing
2007 You'resothrilling
2006 Sander Camillo
2005 Donna Blini
2004 Jewel In The Sand
2003 Attraction
2002 Spinola
2001 Silent Honour
2000 Dora Carrington

VEUVE CLIQUOT VINTAGE STAKES

2009 Xtension
2008 Orizaba
2007 Rio De La Plata
2006 Strategic Prince
2005 Sir Percy
2004 Shamardal
2003 Lucky Story
2002 Dublin
2001 Naheef
2000 No Excuse Needed

RICHMOND STAKES

2009 Dick Turpin
2008 Prolific
2007 Strike The Deal
2006 Hamoody
2005 Always Hopeful
2004 Montgomery's Arch
2003 Carrizo Creek
2002 Elusive City
2001 Mister Cosmi
2000 Endless Summer

LOWTHER STAKES

2009 Lady Of The Desert
2008 Infamous Angel (Newmarket)
2007 Nahoodh
2006 Silk Blossom
2005 Flashy Wings
2004 Soar
2003 Carry On Katie
2002 Russian Rhythm
2001 Queen's Logic
2000 Enthused

GIMCRACK STAKES

2009 Showcasing
2008 Shaweel (Newbury)
2007 Sir Gerry
2006 Conquest
2005 Amadeus Wolf
2004 Tony James
2003 Balmont
2002 Country Reel
2001 Rock of Gibraltar
2000 Bannister

CHAMPAGNE STAKES

2009 Poet's Voice
2008 Westphalia
2007 McCartney
2006 Vital Equine (York)
2005 Close To You
2004 Etlaala
2003 Lucky Story
2002 Almushahar
2001 Dubai Destination
2000 Noverre

MAY HILL STAKES

2009 Pollenator
2008 Rainbow View
2007 Spacious
2006 Simply Perfect (York)
2005 Nasheej
2004 Playful Air
2003 Kinnaird
2002 Summitville
2001 Half Glance
2000 Karasta

FLYING CHILDERS STAKES

2009 Sand Vixen
2008 Madame Trop Vite
2007 Fleeting Spirit
2006 Wi Dud (York)
2005 Godfrey Street
2004 Chateau Istana
2003 Howick Falls
2002 Wunders Dream
2001 Saddad
2000 Superstar Leo

MILL REEF STAKES

2009 Awzaan
2008 Lord Shanakill
2007 Dark Angel
2006 Excellent Art
2005 Cool Creek
2004 Galeota
2003 Byron
2002 Zafeen
2001 Firebreak
2000 Bouncing Bowdler

ROYAL LODGE STAKES

2009 Joshua Tree
2008 Jukebox Jury
2007 City Leader
2006 Admiralofthefleet
2005 Leo (Newmarket)
2004 Perfectperformance
2003 Snow Ridge
2002 Al Jadeed
2001 Mutinyonthebounty
2000 Atlantis Prince

MEON VALLEY STUD FILLIES' MILE

2009 Hibaayeb
2008 Rainbow View
2007 Listen
2006 Simply Perfect
2005 Nannina (Newmarket)
2004 Playful Act
2003 Red Bloom
2002 Soviet Song
2001 Gossamer
2000 Crystal Music

CHEVELEY PARK STAKES

2009 Special Duty
2008 Serious Attitude
2007 Natagora
2006 Indian Ink
2005 Donna Blini
2004 Magical Romance
2003 Carry On Katie
2002 Airwave
2001 Queen's Logic
2000 Regal Rose

MIDDLE PARK STAKES

2009 Awzaan
2008 Bushranger
2007 Dark Angel
2006 Dutch Art
2005 Amadeus Wolf
2004 Ad Valorem
2003 Three Valleys
2002 Oasis Dream
2001 Johannesburg
2000 Minardi

DEWHURST STAKES

2009 Beethoven
2008 Intense Focus
2007 New Approach
2006 Teofilo
2005 Sir Percy
2004 Shamardal
2003 Milk It Mick
2002 Tout Seul
2001 Rock of Gibraltar
2000 Tobougg

ROCKFEL STAKES

2009 Music Show
2008 Lahaleeb
2007 Kitty Matcham
2006 Finsceal Beo
2005 Speciosa
2004 Maids Causeway
2003 Cairns
2002 Luvah Girl
2001 Distant Valley
2000 Sayedah

RACING POST TROPHY

2009 St Nicholas Abbey
2008 Crowded House
2007 Ibn Khaldun
2006 Authorized (Newbury)
2005 Palace Episode
2004 Motivator
2003 American Post
2002 Brian Boru
2001 High Chaparral
2000 Dilshaan

MAJOR HANDICAPS

LINCOLN HANDICAP

2009 Expresso Star
2008 Smokey Oakey
2007 Very Wise (Newcastle)
2006 Blythe Knight (Redcar)
2005 Stream Of Gold
2004 Babodana
2003 Pablo
2002 Zucchero
2001 Nimello
2000 John Ferneley

ROYAL HUNT CUP

2009 Forgotten Voice
2008 Mr Aviator
2007 Royal Oath
2006 Cesare
2005 New Seeker (York)
2004 Mine
2003 Macadamia

2002 Norton
2001 Surprise Encounter
2000 Caribbean Monarch

WOKINGHAM HANDICAP
2009 High Standing
2008 Big Timer
2007 Dark Missile
2006 Baltic King
2005 Iffraaj (York)
2004 Lafi
2003 Fayr Jag/Ratio (d/h)
2002 Capricho
2001 Nice One Clare
2000 Harmonic Way

NORTHUMBERLAND PLATE
2009 Som Tala
2008 Arc Bleu
2007 Juniper Girl
2006 Toldo
2005 Sergeant Cecil
2004 Mirjan
2003 Unleash
2002 Bangalore
2001 Archduke Ferdinand
2000 Bay Of Islands

JOHN SMITH'S CUP
2009 Sirvino
2008 Flying Clarets
2007 Charlie Tokyo
2006 Fairmile
2005 Mullins Bay
2004 Arcalis
2003 Far Lane
2002 Vintage Premium
2001 Foreign Affairs
2000 Sobriety

STEWARDS' CUP
2009 Genki
2008 Conquest
2007 Zidane
2006 Borderlescott
2005 Gift Horse
2004 Pivotal Point
2003 Patavellian
2002 Bond Boy
2001 Guinea Hunter
2000 Tayseer

EBOR HANDICAP
2009 Sesenta
2008 All The Good (run at Newbury as Newburgh Handicap)
2007 Purple Moon
2006 Mudawin
2005 Sergeant Cecil
2004 Mephisto
2003 Saint Alebe
2002 Hugs Dancer
2001 Mediterranean
2000 Give The Slip

AYR GOLD CUP
2009 Jimmy Styles
2008 Regal Parade
2007 Advanced
2006 Fonthill Road
2005 Presto Shinko
2004 Funfair Wane
2003 Quito
2002 Funfair Wane
2001 Continent
2000 Bahamian Pirate

CAMBRIDGESHIRE HANDICAP
2009 Supaseus
2008 Tazeez
2007 Pipedreamer
2006 Formal Decree
2005 Blue Monday
2004 Spanish Don
2003 Chivalry
2002 Beauchamp Pilot
2001 I Cried For You
2000 Katy Nowaitee

CESAREWITCH HANDICAP
2009 Darley Sun
2008 Caracciola
2007 Leg Spinner
2006 Detroit City
2005 Sergeant Cecil
2004 Contact Dancer
2003 Landing Light
2002 Miss Fara
2001 Distant Prospect
2000 Heros Fatal

RACEFORM MEDIAN TIMES FOR 2009

ASCOT
5f 1m 0.5
5f 110y 1m 07.5
6f 1m 14.4
6f 110y 1m 21.8
7f 1m 28.0
1m Str 1m 40.6
1m Rnd 1m 40.7
1m 2f....................2m 7.0
1m 4f 2m 32.5
2m....................3m 29.0
2m 4f 4m 21.0
2m 5f 194y 4m 56.5

AYR
5f 1m 0.1
6f 1m 13.6
7f 50y 1m 33.4
1m....................1m 43.8
1m 1f 20y 1m 58.4
1m 2f....................2m 12.0
1m 5f 13y....................2m 54.0
1m 7f....................3m 20.4
2m 1f 105y....................4m 0.5

BATH
5f 11y 1m 2.5
5f 161y 1m 11.2
1m 5y 1m 40.8
1m 2f 46y 2m 11.0
1m 3f 144y 2m 30.6
1m 5f 22y 2m 52.0
2m 1f 34y 3m 51.9

BEVERLEY
5f 1m 3.5
7f 100y 1m 33.8
1m 100y....................1m 47.6
1m 1f 207y....................2m 7.0
1m 4f 16y 2m 40.9
2m 35y....................3m 39.8

BRIGHTON
5f 59y 1m 2.3
5f 213y 1m 10.2
6f 209y 1m 23.1
7f 214y 1m 36.0
1m 1f 209y....................2m 3.6
1m 3f 196y....................2m 32.7

CARLISLE
5f 1m 0.8
5f 193y 1m 13.7
6f 192y 1m 27.1
7f 200y 1m 40.0
1m 1f 61y 1m 57.6
1m 3f 107y....................2m 23.1
1m 6f 32y 3m 7.5
2m 1f 52y 3m 53.0

CATTERICK
5f 59.8s
5f 212y 1m 13.6
7f 1m 27.0
1m 3f 214y 2m 38.9
1m 5f 175y....................3m 3.6
1m 7f 177y 3m 32.0

CHEPSTOW
5f 16y 59.3s
6f 16y 1m 12.0
7f 16y 1m 23.2
1m 14y 1m 36.2
1m 2f 36y 2m 10.6
1m 4f 23y 2m 39.0
2m 49y 3m 38.9
2m 2f....................4m 3.6

CHESTER
5f 16y 1m 1.0
6f 18y....................1m 13.8
7f 2y.................... 1m
26.5
7f 122y 1m 33.8
1m 2f 75y 2m 12.2
1m 3f 79y 2m 26.6
1m 4f 66y 2m 39.9
1m 5f 89y 2m 53.2
1m 7f 195y....................3m 28.0
2m 2f 147y 4m 4.8

DONCASTER
5f 1m 0.5
5f 140y 1m 8.5
6f 1m 13.6
6f 110y 1m 19.9
7f 1m 26.3
1m Str 1m 39.3
1m Rnd 1m 39.7
1m 2f 60y 2m 11.2
1m 4f 2m 35.1
1m 6f 132y....................3m 6.7
2m 110y....................3m 40.4
2m 2f....................3m 58.2

EPSOM
5f 55.7s
6f 1m 9.4
7f 1m 23.3
1m 114y....................1m 46.1
1m 2f 18y 2m 9.7
1m 4f 10y 2m 38.9

FOLKESTONE
5f 1m
6f 1m 12.7
7f 1m 27.3
1m 1f 149y 2m 4.9
1m 4f 2m 40.9
1m 7f 92y 3m 29.7
2m 93y 3m 37.2

GOODWOOD
5f 58.4s
6f 1m 12.2
7f 1m 27.4
1m....................1m 39.9
1m 1f....................1m 56.3
1m 1f 192y....................2m 8.0
1m 3f....................2m 28.3
1m 4f 2m 38.4
1m 6f....................3m 3.6
2m....................3m 29.0
2m 5f....................4m 33.1

HAMILTON
5f 4y....................1m
6f 5y....................1m 12.2
1m 65y....................1m 48.4
1m 1f 36y 1m 59.7
1m 3f 16y 2m 25.6
1m 4f 17y 2m 38.6
1m 5f 9y 2m 53.9

HAYDOCK
5f (inner) 1m 1.1
5f (outer) 1m 0.5
6f (inner) 1m 14.5
6f (outer) 1m 14.0
7f 30y....................1m 30.2
1m 30y 1m 43.8
1m 2f 95y 2m 13.0
1m 3f 200y 2m 33.2
1m 6f....................3m 4.3
2m 45y 3m 36.0

KEMPTON A-W
5f 1m 0.5
6f 1m 13.1
7f 1m 26.0
1m....................1m 39.8
1m 1f....................1m 55.8
1m 2f....................2m 8.0
1m 3f....................2m 21.9
1m 4f 2m 34.5
2m....................3m 30.1

LEICESTER
5f 2y....................1m
5f 218y 1m 13.0
7f 9y....................1m 26.2
1m 60y 1m 45.1
1m 1f 218y....................2m 7.9
1m 3f 183y....................2m 33.9

LINGFIELD TURF
5f 58.2s
6f 1m 11.2
7f 1m 23.3
7f 140y 1m 32.3
1m 1f....................1m 56.6
1m 2f....................2m 10.5
1m 3f 106y....................2m 31.5
1m 6f....................3m 10.0
2m....................3m 34.8

LINGFIELD A-W
5f 58.8s
6f 1m 11.9
7f 1m 24.8
1m.. ....1m 38.2
1m 2f....................2m 6.6
1m 4f 2m 33.0
1m 5f 2m 46.0
2m....................3m 25.7

MUSSELBURGH
5f 1m 0.4
7f 30y 1m 30.3
1m....................1m 41.2
1m 1f....................1m 54.7
1m 4f 2m 39.7
1m 4f 100y 2m 42.0
1m 5f....................2m 52.0
1m 6f....................3m 5.3
2m....................3m 36.1

NEWBURY
5f 34y....................1m 1.4
6f 8y....................1m 13.0
6f 110y 1m 19.3
7f 1m 25.7
1m....................1m 39.7
1m 1f....................1m 55.5
1m 2f 6y....................2m 8.8
1m 3f 5y 2m 21.2
1m 4f 5y 2m 35.5
1m 5f 61y 2m 52.0
2m....................3m 32.0

NEWCASTLE
5f 1m 0.7
6f 1m 15.2
7f 1m 28.7
1m Rnd 1m 45.3
1m 3y Str 1m 43.2
1m 1f 9y 1m 58.1
1m 2f 32y 2m 11.9
1m 4f 93y 2m 45.6
1m 6f 97y 3m 11.3
2m 19y 3m 36.2

NEWMARKET ROWLEY MILE
5f 59.1s
6f 1m 12.2
7f 1m 25.4
1m....................1m 38.6
1m 1f....................1m 51.7
1m 2f....................2m 5.8
1m 4f 2m 33.5
1m 6f....................2m 58.5
2m....................3m 30.8
2m 2f....................3m 54.8

NEWMARKET JULY
5f 59.1s
6f 1m 12.5
7f 1m 25.7
1m....................1m 40.0
1m 2f....................2m 5.5
1m 4f 2m 32.9
1m5f....................2m 44.0
1m 6f 175y....................3m 11.3
2m 24y 3m 27.0

NOTTINGHAM
Due to reconfiguration of the track there is currently insufficient data to calculate median times.

PONTEFRACT
5f 1m 3.3
6f 1m 16.9
1m 4y 1m 45.9
1m 2f 6y 2m 13.7
1m 4f 8y....................2m 40.8
2m 1f 22y 3m 50.0
2m 1f 216y....................4m 3.9
2m 5f 122y....................5m 8.8

REDCAR
5f 58.6s
6f 1m 11.8
7f 1m 24.5
1m....................1m 38.0
1m 1f....................1m 53.0
1m 2f....................2m 7.1
1m 3f....................2m 21.7
1m 6f 19y 3m 4.7
2m 4y 3m 31.4

RIPON
5f 1m 0.7
6f 1m 13.0
1m....................1m 41.4
1m 1f....................1m 54.7
1m 1f 170y....................2m 5.4
1m 4f 10y 2m 36.7
2m....................3m 31.8

SALISBURY
5f 1m 0.8
6f 1m 14.8
6f 212y 1m 29.0
1m....................1m 43.5
1m 1f 198y....................2m 9.9
1m 4f 2m 38.0
1m 6f 21y 3m 7.4

SANDOWN
5f 6y....................1m 1.6
7f 16y 1m 29.5
1m 14y 1m 43.3
1m 1f....................1m 56.3
1m 2f 7y 2m 10.5
1m 6f....................3m 6.6
2m 78y 3m 38.7

SOUTHWELL TURF
6f 1m 15.8
7f 1m 29.4
1m 2f....................2m 13.1
1m 3f....................2m 27.8
1m 4f 2m 41.7
2m....................3m 38.6

SOUTHWELL A-W
5f 59.7s
6f 1m 16.5
7f 1m 30.3
1m....................1m 43.7
1m 3f....................2m 28.0
1m 4f 2m 41.0

1m 6f....................3m 8.3
2m....................3m 45.5

THIRSK
5f 59.6s
6f 1m 12.7
7f 1m 27.2
1m....................1m 40.1
1m 4f 2m 36.2
2m....................3m 32.8

WARWICK
5f 59.6s
5f 110y 1m 5.9
6f 1m 11.8
7f 26y 1m 24.6
1m 22y....................1m 41.0
1m 2f 188y 2m 21.1
1m 4f 134y 2m 44.6
1m 6f 213y....................3m 19.0
2m 39y 3m 33.8

WINDSOR
5f 10y 1m 0.3
6f 1m 13.0
1m 67y 1m 44.7
1m 2f 7y 2m 8.7
1m 3f 135y....................2m 29.5

WOLVERHAMPTON A-W
5f 20y 1m 2.3
5f 216y 1m 15.0
7f 32y 1m 29.6
1m 141y....................1m 50.5
1m 1f 103y....................2m 1.7
1m 4f 50y....................2m 41.1
1m 5f 194y 3m 6.0
2m 119y....................3m 41.8

YARMOUTH
5f 43y....................1m 2.2
6f 3y....................1m 14.4
7f 3y....................1m 26.6
1m 3y....................1m 40.6
1m 2f 21y 2m 10.5
1m 3f 101y....................2m 28.7
1m 6f 17y 3m 7.6
2m....................3m 34.6

YORK
5f 59.3s
5f 89y....................1m 4.3
6f 1m 11.9
7f 1m 25.3
1m....................1m 38.8
1m 208y 1m 52.0
1m 2f 88y 2m 12.5
1m 4f 2m 33.2
1m 6f....................3m 0.2
2m 88y....................3m 34.5
2m 2f....................3m 58.4

HIGHEST RACEFORM SPEED FIGURES 2009

Best time performances achieved between 1st January - 31st December 2009

THREE YEAR-OLDS AND UPWARDS – TURF

A

Acquisition 113 (14f,Hay,S,Sep 5)
Acrostic 114 (8f,Yor,GF,Aug 20)
Adjaliya 110 (12f,Leo,GY,Sep 5)
Adlerflug 116 ($10\frac{1}{2}$f,Lon,G,Apr 26)
Advanced 111 (6f,Rip,GF,Aug 15)
African Rose 111 (5f,Cha,G,May 31)
Again 110 (8f,Cur,HY,May 24)
Age Of Aquarius 115 (12f,Lon,GS,Jly 14)
Aizavoski 116 (15f,Lon,GS,Oct 3)
Akbabend 110 (12f,Cat,GF,Aug 14)
Akmal 112 (14f,Nmk,GF,Oct 1)
Al Muheer 112 (7f,Asc,G,Jly 25)
Alanbrooke 111 (18f,Nmk,GF,Sep 19)
Alandi 116 (20f,Lon,G,Oct 4)
Alazeyab 115 (8f,Yor,GF,Aug 20)
Albaqaa 110 ($10\frac{1}{2}$f,Yor,GF,Jly 11)
Alexandros 112 (9f,Nad,G,Mar 28)
All The Aces 111 (13f,Nby,S,May 16)
Allied Powers 110 (12f,Ham,G,May 15)
Allybar 111 (10f,Dea,G,Aug 16)
Almiqdaad 115 (10f,Nby,GF,Sep 19)
Alpen Glen 111 ($10\frac{1}{2}$f,Chs,GF,Jun 26)
Alpine Rose 116 (12f,Sai,S,Jun 28)
Alwaary 115 (12f,Asc,G,Jly 25)
Amico Mio 111 (15f,Lon,GS,Sep 6)
Amour Propre 114 (5f,Yor,GF,Aug 21)
Antinori 110 (10f,Nby,GF,Sep 19)
Aqlaam 119 (8f,Dea,G,Aug 16)
Arabian Gleam 111 (7f,Nmk,G,Oct 17)
Arch Rebel 113 (10f,Ayr,G,Sep 19)
Armure 112 (20f,Lon,G,Oct 4)
Aromatic 110 (10f,Sal,F,May 14)
Art Connoisseur 110 (6f,Asc,GF,Jun 20)
Arthur's Edge 110 (6f,Don,S,Nov 7)
As De Trebol 113 (7f,Lon,G,May 30)
Ashram 112 (7f,Nby,GF,Sep 18)
Ask 116 (12f,Asc,G,Jly 25)
Askar Tau 113 (20f,Lon,G,Oct 4)
Aspectoflove 111 (8f,Leo,G,Aug 13)
Asset 114 (6f,Asc,GF,Jun 20)
Axiom 110 (7f,Asc,G,Sep 26)

B

Baila Me 114 (10f,Ayr,G,Sep 19)
Balcarce Nov 112 (7f,Yor,GF,Aug 21)
Balius 115 (9f,Nad,GF,Mar 5)
Balthazaar's Gift 110 (7f,Chs,GF,Jly 11)
Bankable 112 (10f,Wdr,GF,Aug 29)
Barney McGrew 110 ($5\frac{1}{2}$f,Yor,GF,Aug 18)
Barshiba 115 (10f,Nmk,G,Oct 17)
Bassel 110 ($15\frac{1}{2}$f,Lon,G,Sep 13)
Beach Bunny 113 (8f,Cur,HY,May 23)
Beacon Lodge 113 (8f,Cha,GS,Jun 14)
Becqu Adoree 112 (12f,Lon,G,Sep 13)
Beheshtam 114 (12f,Lon,G,Oct 4)
Benbaun 116 (5f,Yor,GF,Aug 21)
Bernie The Bolt 113 (18f,Nmk,GF,Sep 19)
Biarritz 112 ($7\frac{1}{2}$f,Nad,G,Jan 22)
Black Bear Island 113 ($10\frac{1}{2}$f,Yor,G,May 14)
Black Mambazo 114 (5f,Cha,G,May 31)
Blek 111 ($15\frac{1}{2}$f,Sai,HY,Nov 14)
Blue Cayenne 111 (6f,Msn,HO,Nov 3)
Blue Ksar 110 (9f,Nad,GF,Mar 5)
Bluefields 110 ($15\frac{1}{2}$f,Lon,G,Sep 13)
Board Meeting 112 (12f,Lon,G,Sep 13)
Bon Grain 112 (10f,Lon,GS,Oct 3)
Bonnie Charlie 110 (6f,Asc,GS,Oct 10)
Borderlescott 117 (5f,Yor,GF,Aug 21)
Boulavogue 111 (16f,Leo,HY,Nov 5)
Brave Prospector 111 (6f,Asc,GS,Oct 10)
Brett Vale 110 (10f,San,G,Aug 12)
Bronze Cannon 116 (12f,Asc,GF,Jun 20)
Buccellati 112 (12f,Lon,G,Sep 13)
Byword 111 (10f,Dea,G,Aug 16)

C

Callow Lake 112 (16f,Leo,GY,Aug 6)
Calming Influence 116 ($7\frac{1}{2}$f,Nad,G,Jan 22)
Calvados Blues 110 (8f,Cha,G,Jly 5)
Campanologist 115 (12f,Asc,GF,Jun 20)
Candy Gift 117 (15f,Dea,G,Aug 23)
Caracciola 110 (16f,Goo,G,Jly 30)
Cassique Lady 110 (11f,War,GS,Jun 15)
Casual Conquest 115 (10f,Cur,SH,Aug 16)
Cat Junior 110 (7f,Goo,GF,Aug 30)
Cavalryman 117 (12f,Lon,G,Oct 4)
Celebrissime 118 (9f,Lon,S,May 17)
Cesare 112 (8f,Asc,GF,Jun 16)
Changing The Guard 110 ($10\frac{1}{2}$f,Yor,G,Jun 13)
Charm School 113 (10f,Nby,GF,Sep 19)
Chasing Stars 112 (7f,Lon,G,May 30)
Checklow 110 ($10\frac{1}{2}$f,Yor,GF,May 13)
Chiberta King 112 (12f,Nmk,GF,May 16)
Chief Editor 111 (5f,Nby,GS,Apr 17)
Chinchon 110 (10f,Lon,GS,Sep 6)
Chinese White 112 (10f,Cur,S,Sep 12)
Chock A Block 110 (12f,Nmk,GF,Oct 2)
Cill Rialaig 112 (10f,Nby,GF,Sep 19)
Cima De Triomphe 114 ($10\frac{1}{2}$f,Lon,G,Apr 26)
Cirrus Des Aigles 115 (12f,Lon,GS,Oct 18)
City Leader 116 (10f,Nmk,G,Oct 17)
Claremont 113 (11f,Lon,G,May 4)
Class Is Class 113 (10f,Nby,GF,Sep 19)
Classic Vintage 111 (12f,Goo,G,Jly 29)
Clerk's Choice 112 ($10\frac{1}{2}$f,Chs,GF,Aug 21)
Clowance 114 (14f,Cur,S,Sep 12)
Clowance House 110 (12f,Nmk,GF,May 16)
Colleoni 111 (16f,Leo,HY,Nov 5)
Conduit 118 (12f,Asc,G,Jly 25)
Confront 115 (7f,Yor,GF,Aug 21)
Cool Strike 112 (12f,Nmk,GF,Jly 10)
Court Canibal 110 (10f,Lon,G,Apr 5)
Croisultan 110 (6f,Cur,SH,Aug 16)
Crossharbour 114 (12f,Lon,G,Sep 13)
Cruel Sea 112 (12f,Leo,GY,Sep 5)
Crystal Capella 110 (10f,Lon,G,Oct 4)
Cuis Ghaire 113 (8f,Nmk,GF,May 3)
Curtain Call 114 (9f,Lon,S,May 17)
Cutlass Bay 111 (10f,Sai,HY,May 12)

D

Dandy Man 110 (5f,Yor,GF,Aug 21)
Dane Blue 110 (8f,Cur,HY,May 23)
Dansant 113 (12f,Asc,GF,Jun 20)
Danse Grecque 111 (10f,Dea,G,Aug 23)
Dar Re Mi 116 (12f,Lon,G,Oct 4)
Daring Man 118 (6f,Cur,HY,Jly 26)
Darley Sun 112 (18f,Nmk,G,Oct 17)
Dazinski 111 (16f,Chs,GF,Aug 22)
Deauville Vision 111 (8f,Cur,HY,May 23)
Debussy 111 (12f,Chs,GF,May 7)
Deem 110 (8f,Nad,G,Feb 5)
Delegator 114 (8f,Nmk,GF,May 2)
Demolition 110 (10f,Ayr,GS,Sep 17)
Deposer 110 ($8\frac{1}{2}$f,Eps,G,Jun 5)
Desert Sea 111 ($16\frac{1}{2}$f,San,G,Jly 4)
Designated Decoy 110 (8f,Cur,S,Mar 22)
Diana's Choice 112 (6f,Nad,GF,Feb 6)
Diyakalanie 111 (10f,Lon,G,Apr 5)
Dohasa 111 (6f,Nad,GF,Feb 26)
Donnas Palm 112 (16f,Leo,HY,Nov 5)
Dream Eater 115 (7f,Yor,GF,Aug 21)
Dream Lodge 112 (10f,Ayr,G,Sep 19)
Drill Sergeant 111 (12f,Don,G,Mar 29)
Drumfire 111 (10f,San,G,May 28)
Drunken Sailor 114 (10f,Nby,GF,Sep 19)
Duncan 111 (12f,Asc,GF,May 9)
Dunkerque 113 ($6\frac{1}{2}$f,Dea,GS,Aug 9)

E

Ebadiyan 111 (16f,Cur,Y,Apr 5)
Edge Closer 110 (6f,Wdr,GF,Jun 1)
Elusive Wave 112 (8f,Dea,S,Aug 2)
Elyaadi 110 (12f,Leo,GY,Sep 5)
Embsay Crag 113 ($10\frac{1}{2}$f,Chs,GF,Aug 21)
Emily Blake 114 (8f,Cur,HY,May 23)
Enroller 111 (12f,Asc,GF,Jun 20)
Equiano 110 (6f,Nmk,GF,Apr 16)
Estrela Brage 111 (8f,Cur,S,Mar 22)
Ethics Girl 110 (9f,San,G,Aug 13)
Eva's Request 111 (8f,Goo,G,May 2)
Evasive 111 (8f,Nmk,GF,May 2)
Exceptional Art 112 (5f,Bev,GF,Aug 29)

F

Falcon Rock 113 (12f,Don,GF,Sep 12)
Fame And Glory 123 (10f,Leo,GY,Sep 5)
Famous Name 116 (8f,Cur,GY,Jun 28)
Fastnet Storm 112 ($10\frac{1}{2}$f,Chs,GF,Aug 21)
Fateh Field 117 ($7\frac{1}{2}$f,Nad,GS,Jan 15)
Father Time 113 (12f,Asc,GF,Jun 19)
Fergus McIver 111 (10f,Leo,GY,Apr 19)
Fiery Lad 110 (9f,Leo,G,Jun 18)
Final Approach 110 (16f,Leo,HY,Nov 5)
Finjaan 110 (7f,Goo,G,Jly 28)
Firebet 110 (8f,Ayr,GF,Jun 20)
Fiulin 111 (14f,Not,GF,Apr 8)
Fleeting Spirit 116 (6f,Nmk,GF,Jly 10)
Forgotten Voice 110 (8f,Goo,G,Jly 29)
Freemantle 113 (12f,Lon,GS,Jly 14)
Fuisse 111 ($10\frac{1}{2}$f,Cha,G,Jun 7)
Fullandby 111 (6f,Don,S,Nov 7)
Fully Funded 110 (12f,Lon,GS,Apr 12)
Furmigadelagiusta 111 (12f,Pon,GF,Jun 21)
Furnace 111 (8f,Nad,GF,Feb 26)

G

Gan Amhras 113 (8f,Nmk,GF,May 2)
Geordieland 119 ($16\frac{1}{2}$f,San,G,May 28)
Georgebernardshaw 111 (7f,Cur,S,Jly 11)
Getaway 112 (12f,Lon,G,Oct 4)
Ghanaati 115 (8f,Nmk,GF,May 3)
Girouette 113 (6f,Cur,SH,Aug 16)
Gitano Hernando 110 (10f,Don,G,Mar 29)
Gladiatorus 119 ($7\frac{1}{2}$f,Nad,G,Jan 22)
Glass Harmonium 111 ($10\frac{1}{2}$f,Yor,G,May 14)
Glow Star 110 ($7\frac{1}{2}$f,Nad,G,Feb 5)
Golden Sword 114 (12f,Chs,GF,May 7)
Goldikova 125 (8f,Dea,G,Aug 16)
Goliaths Boy 112 ($10\frac{1}{2}$f,Chs,GF,Aug 21)
Good Again 110 (8f,Pon,GF,Oct 5)
Grand Ducal 113 (10f,Leo,GY,Sep 5)
Grantley Adams 111 ($7\frac{1}{2}$f,Nad,G,Feb 5)
Grey Soldier 111 (8f,Dea,G,Aug 16)
Gris De Gris 121 (9f,Lon,S,May 17)
Guest Ville 112 (11f,Lon,G,May 4)

H

Halicarnassus 110 (10f,Goo,GF,May 25)
Hallie's Comet 112 (7f,Cur,Y,Jun 27)
Handsome Maestro 110 (8f,Dea,G,Aug 30)
Harrison George 110 (6f,Yor,S,May 15)
Hatta Fort 111 (6f,Nad,GF,Feb 26)

Hattan 110 (10f,Nad,G,Feb 12)
Hawridge King 110 (16f,Chs,GF,Aug 22)
Headford View 113 (7f,Cur,Y,Jun 27)
Heart Shaped 112 (8f,Nmk,GF,May 3)
Heaven Sent 112 (8f,Leo,GY,Sep 5)
Hidden Brief 110 (11½f,Chs,GF,May 6)
High Heeled 111 (12f,Eps,G,Jun 5)
High Standing 115 (6f,Asc,GF,Jun 20)
Holberg 115 (16f,Asc,GF,Jun 19)
Hollo Ladies 110 (16f,Cur,Y,Apr 5)
Huntdown 112 (7f,Yor,GF,Aug 21)
Hunting Tower 110 (8f,Nad,G,Feb 19)

I

Ialysos 113 (5f,San,G,Jly 4)
Icelandic 111 (6f,Cur,SH,Aug 16)
Ideal World 114 (12f,Sai,S,Jun 28)
Illustrious Blue 111 (12f,Asc,GF,Jun 20)
Imbongi 113 (9f,Nad,GF,Mar 5)
Imposing 110 (10f,Nmk,GF,Apr 16)
Incanto Dream 113 (15½f,Lon,G,Sep 13)
Indian Days 110 (10f,San,G,May 28)
Indiana Gal 110 (8f,Cur,GY,Jun 28)
Inestimable 111 (12½f,Dea,G,Aug 30)
Instant Recall 111 (6f,Nad,GF,Feb 6)
Intrepid Jack 110 (6f,Wdr,GF,Jun 1)
Investissement 112 (15f,Lon,GS,Sep 6)
Invincible Force 121 (6f,Cur,HY,Jly 26)
Inxile 113 (5f,Lon,G,May 10)
Irian 113 (8f,Cha,G,Jly 5)
Irish Heartbeat 113 (6f,Cur,HY,Jly 26)

J

J J The Jet Plane 116 (6f,Wdr,GF,Jun 1)
Jay Peg 113 (9f,Nad,GF,Mar 5)
Jimmy Styles 110 (6f,Asc,GF,May 9)
Judd Street 111 (6f,Sal,GF,Jun 14)
Judge 'n Jury 110 (5f,Cur,HY,Aug 30)
Jukebox Jury 115 (12½f,Dea,G,Aug 30)
Jumbajukiba 111 (6f,Cur,HY,May 23)

K

Kachgai 111 (8f,Dea,G,Aug 30)
Kaolak 110 (9f,Goo,GF,Aug 30)
Kargali 111 (8f,Leo,GY,Apr 19)
Kasbah Bliss 115 (20f,Lon,G,Oct 4)
Kayf Aramis 110 (18f,Yor,G,May 14)
Kenchop 110 (7f,Lon,G,May 30)
Khateeb 111 (8f,Pon,G,Jly 26)
King Jock 115 (7½f,Nad,G,Feb 5)
King's Apostle 117 (6½f,Dea,GS,Aug 9)
Kingdom Of Fife 112 (10½f,Yor,GF,Jly 11)
Kingsgate Native 113 (5f,Goo,G,Jly 30)
Kirklees 113 (10f,Nad,G,Feb 12)
Kite Wood 111 (10½f,Yor,G,May 14)
Knot In Wood 111 (6f,Don,GF,Mar 28)
Kudu Country 110 (14f,Hay,S,Sep 5)

L

La Boum 115 (12f,Lon,G,Oct 4)
Laa Rayb 111 (8f,Goo,G,Jly 31)
Lady Marian 113 (10f,Dea,G,Aug 23)
Le Havre 113 (10½f,Cha,G,Jun 7)
Les Fazzani 113 (12f,Leo,GY,Sep 5)
Lesson In Humility 116 (6½f,Dea,GS,Aug 9)
Libano 111 (7f,Leo,HY,Nov 5)
Libel Law 111 (10½f,Hay,G,Aug 8)
Little White Lie 112 (7½f,Nad,G,Feb 5)
Loch Long 110 (15f,Lon,GS,Oct 3)
Look Busy 110 (5f,Hay,HY,May 23)
Look Here 110 (12f,Asc,G,Jly 25)
Lord Admiral 113 (10f,Leo,YS,Jly 23)
Lord Shanakill 114 (8f,Cha,G,Jly 5)
Los Cristianos 117 (15f,Lon,GS,Oct 3)
Loup Breton 116 (10½f,Lon,G,Apr 26)
Luisant 114 (6f,Cur,HY,Jly 26)

M

Mac Gille Eoin 112 (6f,Goo,GF,Sep 12)
Mac Love 112 (8½f,Eps,G,Jun 5)
Mad About You 113 (7f,Cur,Y,Apr 5)
Mad Rush 111 (12f,Goo,GF,Jun 5)
Magadan 115 (12f,Lon,G,Oct 4)
Main Aim 114 (6f,Nmk,GF,Jly 10)
Makt 111 (12f,Lon,GS,Oct 18)
Manifest 110 (14f,Nmk,GF,Oct 1)
Manighar 118 (15f,Lon,GS,Oct 3)
Manyriverstocross 111 (14f,Goo,G,Jly 28)
Mariol 116 (6½f,Dea,GS,Aug 9)
Markab 112 (6f,Rip,GF,Aug 15)
Masta Plasta 111 (5f,San,G,Jly 4)
Mastercraftsman 122 (10½f,Yor,GF,Aug 18)
Masterofthehorse 112 (12f,Chs,GF,May 7)
Mastery 113 (12f,Lon,GS,Jly 14)
Matsunosuke 110 (5f,San,G,Jly 4)
Mawatheeq 118 (10f,Nmk,G,Oct 17)
Mick's Dancer 112 (10½f,Chs,GF,Jly 11)
Midday 112 (12f,Eps,G,Jun 5)
Mischief Making 110 (16f,Asc,GF,Apr 29)
Mojave Moon 118 (15f,Dea,G,Aug 23)
Monitor Closely 112 (10f,Nmk,GF,Apr 15)
Mood Music 111 (5f,Lon,G,May 10)
Moonquake 111 (10½f,Yor,GF,May 13)
Mountain Coral 110 (6f,Cur,GY,Jun 28)
Mourayan 113 (12f,Cur,GY,Jun 28)
Mourilyan 118 (16f,Goo,G,Jly 30)
Mujood 110 (8f,Goo,G,May 30)
Mullein 111 (6f,Asc,GF,Sep 27)
Mundybash 112 (10f,Lon,GS,Oct 3)
Munsef 111 (12f,Hay,GF,Jly 4)

N

Naaqoos 110 (8f,Lon,G,May 10)
Nanton 112 (10f,Ayr,G,Sep 19)
Nehaam 113 (10f,Nmk,GF,Apr 15)
Never On Sunday 122 (9f,Lon,S,May 17)
Night Crescendo 111 (12f,Don,GF,Sep 12)
Noble Storm 110 (5f,Bev,GF,Aug 29)
Norwegian Dancer 112 (10½f,Chs,GF,Aug 21)

O

Oiseau De Feu 113 (8f,Cha,G,Jly 5)
Omokoroa 111 (14f,Hay,S,Sep 5)
Only Green 111 (7f,Lon,G,Jun 22)
Opinion Poll 111 (12f,Asc,GS,Oct 10)
Ordnance Row 112 (7f,Goo,GF,Aug 30)
Orion Star 112 (20f,Lon,G,Oct 4)
Otterstown Lady 113 (16f,Leo,GY,Aug 6)
Ottomax 111 (7f,Lon,G,May 30)
Ouqba 110 (7f,Asc,GF,Jun 17)

P

Paco Boy 115 (8f,Goo,G,Jly 29)
Palace Moon 111 (6f,Nmk,GF,Aug 29)
Parfum Des Dieux 112 (7f,Lon,G,May 30)
Patkai 116 (16½f,San,G,May 28)
Penny's Gift 111 (8f,Nmk,GF,May 3)
Perfect Polly 112 (6f,Cur,SH,Aug 16)
Perfect Stride 111 (10f,Asc,GF,Jun 19)
Perfect Truth 114 (11½f,Chs,GF,May 6)
Perpetually 111 (10f,Nmk,GF,Apr 16)
Petrovsky 111 (12f,Nmk,GF,May 16)
Phillipina 113 (11½f,Chs,GF,May 6)
Pipedreamer 117 (10f,Nmk,G,Oct 17)
Plum Pudding 110 (7f,War,GF,Apr 13)
Plumania 112 (12f,Lon,G,Sep 13)
Poet 112 (10f,Leo,GY,Sep 5)
Pointilliste 113 (15½f,Lon,G,Sep 13)
Pointing North 111 (7f,Yor,GF,Aug 21)
Pollen 112 (8f,Cur,S,Mar 22)
Popmurphy 110 (16f,Asc,GF,Jun 19)
Pouvoir Absolu 114 (12½f,Dea,G,Aug 30)
Precision Break 114 (12f,Don,GF,Sep 12)
Premio Loco 111 (8f,Goo,G,May 30)
Present Alchemy 111 (5f,Bev,GF,Aug 29)
Press The Button 111 (10f,Nby,GF,Sep 19)
Presvis 114 (9f,Nad,G,Mar 28)
Prime Defender 115 (6f,Don,GF,Mar 28)
Prince Siegfried 117 (10f,Ayr,G,Sep 19)
Princess Taylor 110 (12f,Nmk,G,Jly 18)
Profound Beauty 113 (14f,Cur,Y,Jun 27)
Prospect Wells 110 (10f,Lon,G,Apr 5)
Proviso 116 (9f,Lon,S,May 17)
Pure Poetry 110 (8f,Goo,G,May 30)
Pusey Street Lady 114 (6f,Don,GF,Mar 28)

Q

Quinmaster 110 (8f,Leo,GF,Jun 4)

R

Racinger 113 (8f,Dea,G,Aug 30)
Ragheed 111 (7½f,Nad,GF,Jan 29)
Rainbow View 114 (8f,Leo,GY,Sep 5)
Raise Your Heart 111 (10f,Leo,Y,Oct 26)
Rayeni 111 (6f,Cur,S,Oct 11)
Red Merlin 112 (12f,Hay,GF,Jly 4)
Red Rock Canyon 113 (10½f,Lon,G,Apr 26)
Regal Parade 115 (6f,Hay,GS,Sep 5)
Rekaab 110 (16f,Leo,GY,Aug 6)
Reverence 112 (5f,Cur,HY,Aug 30)
Riggins 111 (8f,Goo,G,May 30)
Rip Van Winkle 121 (10f,San,G,Jly 4)
Rite Of Passage 116 (16f,Leo,HY,Nov 5)
River Captain 110 (10f,Eps,G,Jun 6)
Roaring Forte 117 (8f,Yor,GF,Aug 20)
Rock And Roll Kid 110 (8f,Cur,S,Mar 22)
Rock Of Rochelle 110 (6f,Asc,GF,Jun 20)
Rockhampton 111 (10f,Nmk,GF,Apr 15)
Roker Park 111 (5f,Bev,GF,Aug 29)
Roman Empress 112 (12f,Yor,GF,Aug 20)
Rose Hip 110 (8f,Leo,G,Aug 13)
Roses For The Lady 113 (12f,Cur,HY,Jly 12)
Royal Confidence 114 (7f,Yor,GF,Aug 21)
Royal Executioner 110 (8f,Hay,G,Jun 20)
Royal Rock 113 (6f,Asc,GS,Oct 10)
Runaway 118 (9f,Lon,S,May 17)
Russian Sage 113 (9f,Nad,GF,Mar 5)

S

Sahpresa 114 (8f,Nmk,GF,Oct 3)
Salut L'Africain 112 (6f,Msn,HO,Nov 3)
Salute Him 110 (10f,Asc,GF,Jun 19)
Sam Sharp 111 (10½f,Chs,GF,Aug 21)
San Sicharia 110 (7f,Lin,GF,May 9)
Sans Frontieres 112 (10½f,Yor,G,May 14)
Saptapadi 110 (12f,Chs,GF,May 7)
Sariska 117 (10f,Nmk,G,Oct 17)
Sayif 115 (6½f,Dea,GS,Aug 9)
Scenic Blast 115 (5f,Asc,GF,Jun 16)
Schiaparelli 120 (15f,Dea,G,Aug 23)
Scuffle 110 (8f,Yor,GF,Aug 20)
Sea The Stars 125 (10f,Leo,GY,Sep 5)
Secret Society 114 (7f,Yor,GF,Aug 21)
Seeking The Buck 110 (10½f,Yor,GF,Jly 11)
Seihali 112 (7½f,Nad,GS,Jan 15)
Serious Attitude 113 (6f,Yor,G,Jly 10)
Serva Jugum 111 (10f,Wdr,GF,Aug 29)
Set Sail 110 (8f,Lon,GS,Apr 12)
Sevenna 110 (14f,Goo,G,Jly 30)
Shahwardi 110 (12f,Lon,GS,Oct 18)
Shalanaya 114 (10f,Lon,G,Oct 4)
Shamwari Lodge 111 (8f,Yor,GF,Aug 19)
She's Our Mark 114 (10f,Leo,YS,Jly 23)
Sherman McCoy 111 (14f,Hay,S,Sep 5)
Shreyas 113 (8f,Leo,GF,Jun 4)
Sight Unseen 110 (12f,Chs,GF,May 7)
Silver Frost 113 (8f,Lon,GS,Apr 12)
Silver Mist 119 (7½f,Nad,GS,Jan 15)
Sirvino 115 (10½f,Yor,GF,Jly 11)
Smooth Operator 113 (7f,Lon,G,Jun 22)
Snaefell 113 (6f,Cur,S,Sep 13)
Snoqualmie Girl 111 (12f,Chs,GF,Sep 12)
Soberania 112 (12f,Lon,G,Sep 13)
Sohraab 111 (5f,Bev,GF,Aug 29)
Spacious 111 (8f,Nmk,G,Jly 8)

Spanish Moon 117 (12f,Sai,S,Jun 28)
Sporting Gesture 110 (12f,Pon,G,Jly 26)
Sri Putra 112 (10f,Dea,G,Aug 16)
Stacelita 115 (12f,Lon,G,Oct 4)
Starla Dancer 111 (10½f,Yor,G,Oct 10)
Starlish 114 (10f,Lon,GS,Oct 3)
Stately Home 110 (16f,Asc,GF,Jun 19)
Staying On 113 (8f,Don,GF,Apr 18)
Steele Tango 112 (9f,Nmk,GF,Apr 16)
Stern Opinion 112 (5f,Lon,G,Sep 13)
Stoic 111 (8f,Nmk,GF,Aug 29)
Stotsfold 114 (10f,Lon,GS,Oct 3)
Strategic News 110 (9f,Nad,GF,Mar 5)
Strawberrydaiquiri 110 (8f,Asc,G,Jly 24)
Strike The Deal 111 (5f,Don,GF,Sep 9)
Striking Spirit 112 (6f,Asc,GF,May 9)
Suailce 110 (14f,Cur,Y,Jun 27)
Sudden Impact 111 (6f,Thi,G,Jly 31)
Suits Me 110 (10f,Lon,GS,Oct 3)
Summit Surge 117 (7½f,Nad,G,Feb 5)
Sundae 110 (6f,Yar,G,Jly 27)
Supaseus 111 (9f,Nmk,GF,Oct 3)
Super Sleuth 112 (8f,Nmk,GF,May 3)
Suruor 110 (7f,Asc,GF,Jly 11)
Sweet Hearth 112 (7f,Lon,GS,Oct 3)
Sweet Lightning 113 (10f,Nby,GF,Sep 19)
Sweetheart 113 (21f,Goo,G,Jly 29)
Swingkeel 110 (21f,Goo,G,Jly 29)
Swiss Diva 110 (6f,Yor,G,Jun 13)

T

Tactic 112 (16f,Asc,GF,Jun 19)
Tajaaweed 112 (10½f,Lon,G,Apr 26)
Takeover Target 110 (6f,Nmk,GF,Jly 10)
Tamagin 113 (6f,Goo,GF,Sep 12)
Tangaspeed 114 (12f,Lon,G,Oct 4)
Taralga 110 (12f,Leo,GY,Sep 5)
Tartan Bearer 116 (12f,Asc,G,Jly 25)
Tartan Gigha 110 (8½f,Eps,G,Jun 5)
Tastahil 114 (16½f,San,G,May 28)
Tax Free 115 (5f,Cha,G,May 31)
Tazeez 116 (9f,Nmk,GF,Apr 16)
Telluride 113 (11f,Lon,G,May 4)
The Betchworth Kid 112 (16f,Goo,G,Jly 30)
The Bogberry 114 (10½f,Lon,G,Apr 26)
The Miniver Rose 111 (10f,Nmk,GF,Apr 15)
Thewayyouare 115 (10½f,Lon,G,Apr 26)
Third Set 111 (9f,Nad,GS,Jan 15)
Three Bodies 111 (10f,Dea,G,Aug 16)
Three Rocks 113 (7f,Cur,S,Jly 11)
Tis Mighty 110 (7f,Cur,Y,Jun 27)
Tiza 113 (6½f,Dea,GS,Aug 9)
Tombi 110 (7f,Yor,GF,Aug 21)
Total Gallery 115 (5f,Lon,G,Oct 4)
Traffic Guard 110 (10½f,Hay,G,Aug 8)
Trajano 111 (7f,Lon,G,May 30)
Tranquil Tiger 111 (10f,Goo,GF,May 25)
Tres Rapide 110 (12f,Lon,G,Sep 13)
Tres Rock Danon 110 (15½f,Sai,HY,Nov 14)
Trincot 115 (10f,Lon,G,Apr 5)
Triple Aspect 112 (5f,San,G,Jly 4)
Trois Rois 110 (10f,Lon,GS,Sep 6)
Twice Over 119 (10f,Nmk,G,Oct 17)
Tyrrells Wood 111 (21f,Goo,G,Jly 29)

U

Unnefer 112 (8f,Don,GF,Apr 18)
Utmost Respect 115 (6f,Cur,HY,May 23)

V

Valedictum 111 (9f,Nad,GF,Mar 5)
Valery Borzov 114 (6f,Yor,S,May 15)
Varenar 115 (6½f,Dea,GS,Aug 9)
Vesuve 111 (10f,Dea,G,Aug 16)
Victoria Montoya 110 (16½f,San,G,Jly 4)
Virtual 114 (8f,Dea,G,Aug 16)
Vision D'Etat 117 (10½f,Lon,G,Apr 26)
Vitznau 111 (6f,Don,GF,Mar 28)
Vodka 113 (9f,Nad,GF,Mar 5)

W

Wajir 115 (15f,Lon,GS,Sep 6)
War Artist 113 (5f,Lon,G,Sep 13)
Webbow 110 (8f,Yor,GF,Aug 20)
Wells Lyrical 110 (16½f,San,G,Jly 4)
Westphalia 112 (8f,Lon,GS,Apr 12)
Wing Express 111 (12½f,Dea,G,Aug 30)
Wing Play 111 (10½f,Chs,GF,Jly 11)
Winkle 111 (15½f,Lon,G,Sep 13)
Woolfall Treasure 110 (21f,Goo,G,Jly 29)
World Heritage 110 (10f,Lon,G,Sep 19)
Worldly Wise 111 (8f,Cur,S,Sep 13)

Y

Yahrab 110 (10f,Nad,GF,Feb 26)
Yamal 110 (8f,Goo,G,May 30)
Yankee Doodle 113 (16f,Asc,GF,Jun 19)
Yeats 115 (20f,Lon,G,Oct 4)
Youmzain 117 (12f,Lon,G,Oct 4)
Your Old Pal 110 (12f,Asc,GF,Jun 19)

Z

Zacinto 111 (8f,Asc,GF,Sep 26)
Zarinava 112 (16f,Cur,Y,Apr 5)
Zorija Rose 110 (7f,Cur,Y,Jun 27)

THREE YEAR-OLDS AND UPWARDS – SAND

A

Abbondanza 118 (8f,Lin,SD,Mar 1)
Ace Of Hearts 116 (10f,Lin,SD,Feb 7)
Aeroplane 110 (7f,Lin,SD,Mar 21)
Agilete 112 (9½f,Wol,SD,Feb 16)
Ahlawy 110 (9½f,Wol,SD,Jan 19)
Al Gillani 113 (6f,Kem,SD,Mar 25)
Al Muheer 113 (10f,Lin,SD,Feb 7)
All The Aces 111 (12f,Kem,SD,Sep 5)
Almaty Express 112 (5f,Wol,SD,Mar 26)
Ancien Regime 110 (6f,Lin,SD,Aug 20)
Ancient Lights 112 (10f,Lin,SD,May 1)
Arganil 111 (5f,Lin,SD,Mar 21)
Art Man 112 (10f,Lin,SD,Jan 10)
Artistic License 110 (6f,Wol,SD,Feb 27)
Asiatic Boy 115 (10f,Nad,FT,Mar 5)
Autumn Blades 112 (7f,Sth,SD,Mar 11)

B

Baila Me 116 (13f,Lin,SD,Oct 29)
Bassinet 110 (12f,Lin,SD,Mar 1)
Baylini 116 (10f,Lin,SD,Feb 7)
Bazergan 114 (8f,Lin,SD,Mar 1)
Bell Island 111 (13f,Lin,SD,Feb 21)
Big City Man 117 (6f,Nad,FT,Mar 28)
Billy Red 112 (6f,Grl,SD,Jan 15)
Bonus 110 (8f,Kem,SD,Feb 8)
Born Tobouggie 111 (8f,Kem,SD,Apr 11)
Brave Tin Soldier 110 (8f,Nad,FT,Mar 28)
Brief Look 110 (11f,Sth,SD,Aug 10)
Bronze Cannon 110 (10f,Lin,SD,Mar 21)
Broomielaw 111 (12f,Wol,SD,Nov 20)
Bugaku 110 (11f,Kem,SD,Sep 4)

C

Calzaghe 111 (13f,Lin,SD,Apr 19)
Cape Express 111 (12f,Wol,SD,Jan 7)
Capricorn Run 112 (7f,Lin,SD,May 1)
Caprio 111 (7f,Sth,SD,Mar 11)
Carte Diamond 113 (16f,Lin,SD,Apr 19)
Ceremonial Jade 111 (6f,Lin,SD,Feb 21)
Charm School 112 (11f,Kem,SD,Sep 4)
Chjimes 117 (5f,Lin,SD,Mar 4)
Cloudy Start 114 (8f,Kem,SD,Jun 25)
Colonel Sherman 110 (10f,Lin,SD,Jan 9)
Contest 111 (6f,Lin,SD,Jan 10)
Copperbeech 110 (10f,Kem,SD,Sep 26)

D

Daddy's Gift 113 (6f,Kem,SD,Dec 2)
Dance The Star 113 (12f,Wol,SD,Nov 20)
Davids Mark 111 (6f,Kem,SD,Feb 8)
Dayia 111 (14f,Wol,SD,Oct 9)
Desert Party 116 (7f,Nad,FT,Jan 22)
Dijeerr 110 (8f,Nad,FT,Feb 19)
Dirar 116 (12f,Wol,SD,Dec 11)
Dishdasha 112 (12f,Kem,SD,Feb 11)
Distinctive Image 110 (12f,Sth,SD,Aug 10)
Don Renato 111 (8f,Nad,FT,Mar 28)
Doric Lady 110 (6f,Lin,SD,Nov 14)
Doubtful Sound 113 (6f,Lin,SD,Jan 17)
Dubai Dynamo 110 (8f,Kem,SD,Apr 21)
Duff 115 (6f,Lin,SD,Feb 21)
Dvinsky 110 (6f,Kem,SD,Dec 2)

E

Ebraam 113 (6f,Wol,SD,Feb 27)
Elna Bright 110 (7f,Lin,SD,Nov 21)
Emerald Wilderness 112 (11f,Kem,SD,Feb 18)
Eseej 111 (11f,Sth,SD,Oct 18)
Evident Pride 110 (12f,Lin,SD,Jan 3)

F

Fairmile 110 (12f,Wol,SD,Nov 20)
Fathsta 112 (6f,Kem,SD,Dec 2)
Flame Of Gibraltar 110 (13f,Lin,SD,Oct 29)
Flipando 117 (8f,Lin,SD,Mar 1)
Flowing Cape 111 (6f,Wol,SD,Feb 17)
Formation 117 (10f,Lin,SD,Feb 7)
Fortuni 113 (12f,Lin,SD,May 1)
Fromsong 113 (5f,Lin,SD,Mar 4)
Fullandby 110 (6f,Kem,SD,Nov 3)

G

Gandalf 112 (16f,Kem,SD,Sep 4)
Gayego 113 (6f,Nad,FT,Mar 5)
Giganticus 110 (7f,Lin,SD,Mar 21)
Gilt Edge Girl 110 (5f,Wol,SD,Nov 16)
Gitano Hernando 112 (9f,Wol,SD,Sep 17)
Global City 111 (6f,Lin,SD,Nov 14)
Gloria De Campeao 111 (9f,Nad,FT,Feb 26)
Grand Passion 111 (11f,Kem,SD,Feb 18)
Green Manalishi 110 (5f,Lin,SD,Nov 1)
Greylami 110 (11f,Kem,SD,Feb 18)

H

Happy Boy 113 (10f,Nad,FT,Mar 5)
Harry Up 112 (5f,Wol,SD,Jan 22)
Heliodor 112 (10f,Kem,SD,Sep 26)
Highland Glen 112 (12f,Kem,SD,Sep 21)
Himalya 110 (6f,Lin,SD,Nov 21)
Honour Devil 113 (8f,Nad,FT,Mar 5)

I

Imprimis Tagula 110 (7f,Sth,SD,Dec 22)
Indian Blessing 115 (6f,Nad,FT,Mar 28)
Internationaldebut 113 (8f,Lin,SD,Feb 14)
Ivory Silk 110 (6f,Kem,SD,Dec 2)

J

Jaconet 114 (6f,Lin,SD,Nov 21)
Jadalee 111 (16f,Kem,SD,Sep 4)
Jessica Wigmo 111 (6f,Kem,SD,Feb 9)
John Terry 113 (10f,Lin,SD,Jan 10)

K

Keenes Day 115 (16f,Lin,SD,Apr 19)
Kings Maiden 111 (14f,Wol,SD,May 11)
Kirklees 112 (12f,Kem,SD,Sep 5)

L

Lady Jane Digby 116 (10f,Lin,SD,Jan 10)
Laterly 113 (12f,Wol,SD,Nov 20)
Laurel Creek 113 (12f,Wol,SD,Feb 14)
Les Fazzani 112 (12f,Kem,SD,Nov 29)

Little Edward 110 (6f,Lin,SD,Jan 17)
Little Pete 111 (6f,Kem,SD,Dec 2)
Luscivious 111 (6f,Sth,SD,Jly 14)

M

Majuro 113 (8f,Lin,SD,Feb 14)
Matsunosuke 116 (6f,Lin,SD,Feb 21)
Merchant Of Dubai 114 (12f,Wol,SD,Nov 20)
Merlin's Dancer 112 (5f,Lin,SD,Mar 4)
Methaaly 110 (6f,Wol,SD,Feb 17)
Mia's Boy 110 (9f,Wol,SD,Sep 17)
Middle Of Nowhere 111 (12f,Sth,SD,Feb 10)
Mister New York 114 (12f,Wol,SD,Dec 11)
Monetary Fund 110 (11f,Sth,SD,Aug 10)
Mooakada 111 (12f,Kem,SD,Nov 29)
Morbick 110 (12f,Wol,SD,Feb 14)
Muktasb 110 (6f,Kem,SD,Feb 8)
Murcar 110 (14f,Wol,SD,Sep 11)
Mutamared 111 (6f,Wol,SD,Feb 27)
Mutheeb 111 (6f,Lin,SD,May 27)
My Indy 113 (8f,Nad,SD,Jan 15)

N

Nemo Spirit 112 (16f,Lin,SD,Apr 19)
Nightjar 111 (7f,Sth,SD,Jan 20)
Nota Bene 111 (6f,Lin,SD,May 27)

O

Obe Royal 111 (7f,Sth,SD,Feb 12)
Old Romney 110 (10f,Lin,SD,Jan 28)
Opus Maximus 113 (8f,Lin,SD,Mar 1)
Orchard Supreme 111 (8f,Lin,SD,Feb 14)
Orpsie Boy 112 (6f,Lin,SD,Feb 21)
Ottoman Empire 112 (11f,Sth,SD,Aug 10)

P

Pachattack 110 (12f,Kem,SD,Nov 29)
Paktolos 110 (12f,Wol,SD,Nov 20)
Pelham Crescent 110 (9½f,Wol,SD,Feb 16)
Philario 111 (8f,Kem,SD,Feb 8)
Philatelist 115 (10f,Lin,SD,Feb 7)
Premio Loco 113 (8f,Kem,SD,Feb 8)
Prince Charlemagne 110 (13f,Lin,SD,Apr 19)
Princess Taylor 111 (13f,Lin,SD,Oct 29)

Q

Qadar 114 (5f,Lin,SD,Mar 4)

R

Ray Of Joy 111 (6f,Kem,SD,Apr 1)
Re Barolo 111 (8f,Kem,SD,Nov 29)
Red Somerset 113 (8f,Lin,SD,Mar 1)
Redding Colliery 111 (7f,Nad,FT,Jan 22)
Regal Ransom 115 (7f,Nad,FT,Jan 22)
Riguez Dancer 111 (14f,Wol,SD,Jan 19)
River Kirov 112 (6f,Kem,SD,Jan 3)
Rosika 113 (13f,Lin,SD,Oct 29)
Royal Envoy 112 (6f,Kem,SD,Feb 8)

S

Safari Sunup 113 (10f,Lin,SD,May 1)
Saloon 110 (14f,Wol,SD,May 11)
Saphira's Fire 111 (12f,Kem,SD,Nov 29)
Scintillo 112 (10f,Lin,SD,Mar 21)
Seek The Fair Land 112 (7f,Kem,SD,Dec 13)
Sehoy 110 (12f,Lin,SD,May 1)
Set The Trend 110 (8f,Kem,SD,Jun 25)
Settigano 110 (10f,Lin,SD,Dec 19)
Sevenna 112 (16f,Lin,SD,Apr 19)
Sgt Schultz 114 (10f,Lin,SD,Jan 10)
Shakalaka 110 (10f,Lin,SD,Dec 30)
Smarten Die 110 (6f,Lin,SD,Feb 21)
Snaafy 116 (8f,Nad,FT,Mar 5)
Son Of The Cat 110 (6f,Lin,SD,Nov 14)
Southandwest 112 (8f,Lin,SD,Mar 1)
Spectait 111 (9½f,Wol,SD,Jan 7)
Stand Guard 110 (9f,Wol,SD,Nov 13)
Star Choice 111 (12f,Wol,SD,Feb 14)
Star Crowned 112 (6f,Nad,FT,Jan 22)
Storyland 111 (13f,Lin,SD,Oct 29)
Strike The Deal 114 (6f,Lin,SD,May 27)
Suits Me 112 (10f,Lin,SD,Dec 19)
Summer Doldrums 110 (8f,Nad,FT,Mar 28)
Swiss Franc 112 (6f,Lin,SD,Feb 21)

T

Tamagin 113 (6f,Lin,SD,May 27)
Thebes 111 (7f,Lin,SD,Mar 21)
They All Laughed 110 (14f,Wol,SD,Jan 19)
Thunderous Mood 111 (6f,Kem,SD,Dec 2)
Tilt 112 (12f,Wol,SD,Nov 20)
Tinaar 111 (12f,Kem,SD,Sep 21)
Titan Triumph 115 (8f,Lin,SD,Feb 14)
Tiz Now Tiz Then 110 (8f,Nad,FT,Mar 28)
Trafalgar Square 110 (7f,Lin,SD,Jan 16)
Tranquil Tiger 113 (10f,Lin,SD,Dec 19)
Trip The Light 113 (12f,Wol,SD,Nov 20)
Two Step Salsa 115 (8f,Nad,FT,Mar 28)
Tyrannosaurus Rex 111 (5f,Wol,SD,Feb 6)
Tyrrells Wood 110 (13f,Lin,SD,Feb 21)
Tyzack 110 (7f,Sth,SD,Feb 12)

W

Wasan 111 (10f,Kem,SD,Sep 26)
Wasp 113 (8f,Lin,SD,Mar 1)
Well Armed 121 (10f,Nad,FT,Mar 28)
Wibbadune 110 (5f,Lin,SD,Mar 4)
William Blake 111 (11f,Kem,SD,Sep 4)
Wine 'n Dine 113 (16f,Lin,SD,Apr 19)
Without A Prayer 114 (8f,Kem,SD,Nov 29)
Woodcote 111 (5f,Lin,SD,Feb 10)
Worth A King'S 110 (14f,Wol,SD,Oct 9)

X

Xpres Maite 112 (6f,Sth,SS,Jan 6)

TWO YEAR-OLDS – TURF

A

Above Limits 109 (5f,Don,GF,Sep 9)
Absolute Music 106 (7f,Msn,HO,Nov 3)
Admire The View 105 (7f,Thi,G,Jly 24)
Alfred Nobel 105 (7f,Leo,G,May 28)
Ameer 106 (8f,Nby,GF,Sep 18)
American Nizzy 106 (8f,Lon,G,Oct 4)
Arasin 105 (8f,Lon,G,Sep 19)
Arcano 112 (6f,Nmk,G,Jly 9)
Atasari 109 (7f,Nmk,G,Oct 17)
Awzaan 109 (6f,Nmk,GF,Oct 2)
Azizi 105 (8f,Don,GF,Sep 12)
Azmeel 105 (7f,Nby,GF,Aug 15)

B

Baahama 105 (8f,Lon,G,Oct 4)
Beethoven 112 (7f,Nmk,G,Oct 17)
Behkabad 106 (8f,Lon,G,Sep 19)
Blue Maiden 105 (7f,Nmk,G,Aug 8)
Bossy Kitty 106 (6f,Yor,G,Oct 9)
Bould Mover 108 (5f,Don,GF,Sep 11)
Buzzword 109 (7f,Lon,G,Oct 4)

C

Cabaret 108 (7f,Leo,Y,Jly 16)
Canford Cliffs 113 (6f,Asc,GF,Jun 16)
Carnaby Street 105 (7f,Nby,S,Oct 24)

D

Dick Turpin 107 (7f,Lon,G,Oct 4)
Dolled Up 107 (6f,Dea,G,Aug 23)

E

Elusive Pimpernel 111 (7f,Yor,GF,Aug 18)
Emerald Commander 110(7f,Yor,GF,Aug 18)
Ercolini 106 (7f,Msn,HO,Nov 3)
Exotic Beauty 105 (6f,Rip,GF,Aug 15)

F

Fencing Master 111 (7f,Nmk,G,Oct 17)
Free Judgement 106 (7f,Leo,Y,Oct 26)

G

Green Dandy 108 (8f,Lon,G,Oct 4)

H

Hibaayeb 108 (8f,Asc,G,Sep 26)
Hot Prospect 107 (8f,San,GF,Sep 11)

I

Iver Bridge Lad 109 (5f,Asc,GS,Oct 10)

J

Jealous Again 107 (5f,Asc,GF,Jun 17)
Jeannie Galloway 106 (6f,Yor,G,Oct 9)
Joanna 109 (8f,Lon,G,Oct 4)
Joshua Tree 109 (8f,Asc,G,Sep 26)

L

Lady Darshaan 107 (8f,Asc,G,Sep 26)
Lady Of The Desert 108 (6f,Yor,GF,Aug 20)
Lady Springbank 105 (7f,Cur,G,Sep 27)
Layali Al Andalus 105 (8f,Ncs,GF,Aug 31)
Layla's Hero 110 (6f,Hay,GS,Sep 5)
Lillie Langtry 105 (7f,Nmk,GF,Oct 3)
Lixirova 109 (7f,Msn,HO,Nov 3)
Long Lashes 107 (7f,Nmk,G,Aug 8)
Lope De Vega 108 (7f,Lon,G,Oct 4)
Lucky Like 109 (6f,Red,GF,Oct 3)

M

Marie De Medici 107 (7f,Lei,GF,Oct 6)
Mikhail Glinka 107 (10f,Sai,HY,Nov 14)
Misheer 105 (6f,Nmk,G,Jly 8)
Mister Manannan 108 (5f,Don,GF,Sep 11)
Monsieur Chevalier 110 (5f,Lon,G,Oct 4)
Morana 105 (8f,San,GF,Sep 11)
Multames 105 (8f,Nby,S,Oct 24)
Music Show 110 (7f,Nmk,G,Oct 17)

N

Nebula Storm 106 (7f,Leo,HY,Nov 5)

O

Olvia 106 (8f,Lon,G,Oct 4)
On Verra 110 (8f,Lon,G,Oct 4)
Orpen Grey 111 (6f,Nmk,G,Jly 9)
Our Jonathan 110 (5f,Asc,GS,Oct 10)

P

Party Doctor 108 (7f,Yor,GF,Aug 18)
Passion For Gold 112 (10f,Sai,HY,Nov 14)
Pleasant Day 106 (7f,Asc,GF,Sep 27)
Poet's Voice 110 (7f,Yor,GF,Aug 18)
Pounced 110 (7f,Lon,G,Oct 4)
Private Story 105 (8f,Nby,GF,Sep 18)

R

Radiohead 114 (5f,Yor,GF,Aug 21)
Red Jazz 107 (6f,Nmk,G,Jly 9)
Rezwaan 105 (8f,Nmk,G,Aug 28)
Rosanara 112 (8f,Lon,G,Oct 4)
Rose Blossom 106 (5f,Don,GF,Sep 11)

S

Sand Vixen 110 (5f,Don,GF,Sep 11)
Sent From Heaven 105 (8f,Asc,G,Sep 26)
Shamandar 105 (5f,Nby,GS,Jly 18)
Showcasing 107 (6f,Nmk,GF,Oct 2)
Silver Grecian 105 (7f,Nmk,G,Oct 17)
Sir Parky 105 (7f,Nmk,GF,Oct 1)

Siyouni 112 (7f,Lon,G,Oct 4)
Special Duty 108 (6f,Nmk,GF,Oct 2)
Steinbeck 111 (7f,Nmk,G,Oct 17)
Summerinthecity 105 (6f,Don,GS,Jly 16)

T

Taajub 109 (5f,Asc,GS,Oct 10)
Tabassum 108 (7f,Nmk,G,Oct 17)
Tawaabb 105 (5f,Asc,GS,Oct 10)

V

Vale Of York 107 (8f,Asc,G,Sep 26)

W

Waseet 107 (8f,Asc,G,Sep 26)
Wedding March 109 (8f,Lon,G,Oct 4)
Whippers Love 106 (8f,Nmk,G,Aug 28)
Wonderfilly 105 (7f,Msn,HO,Nov 3)

X

Xtension 111 (7f,Nmk,G,Oct 17)

TWO-YEAR-OLDS – SAND

Avonvalley 105 (5f,Wol,SD,May 11)

Diamond Laura 106 (5f,Wol,SD,May 11)

Elspeth's Boy 107 (7f,Wol,SD,Nov 2)

Memorandum 108 (5f,Lin,SD,Nov 13)
Mirabella 105 (7f,Lin,SD,Nov 13)
Music Maestro 105 (7f,Wol,SD,Nov 2)

Nafura 106 (9f,Wol,SD,Nov 12)

Sakile 107 (5f,Lin,SD,Nov 13)

Wanchai Whisper 106 (5f,Kem,SD,Dec 30)

Youcanalwaysdream 107 (5f,Lin,SD,Nov 13)